Abbreviations Used in this D
Abréviations utilisées dans ce

mythology	*Myth*	mythologie
noun	*n*	nom
shipping	*Naut*	nautisme
term used in Northern England	*NEng*	terme utilisé dans le nord de l'Angleterre
feminine noun	*nf*	nom féminin
feminine plural noun	*nfpl*	nom féminin pluriel
masculine noun	*nm*	nom masculin
masculine and feminine noun	*nmf*	nom masculin et féminin
masculine plural noun	*nmpl*	nom masculin pluriel
plural noun	*npl*	nom pluriel
proper noun	*npr*	nom propre
nuclear	*Nucl*	nucléaire
New Zealand English	*NZ*	anglais de Nouvelle-Zélande
obstetrics	*Obst*	obstétrique
officially recommended term	*Offic*	recommandation officielle
onomatopoeia	*onomat*	onomatopée
optics	*Opt*	optique
computing	*Ordinat*	informatique
birds	*Orn*	oiseaux
parliament	*Parl*	parlement
pejorative	*Pej, Péj*	péjoratif
petroleum industry	*Petr, Pétr*	industrie pétrolière
pharmacy	*Pharm*	pharmacie
philosophy	*Phil*	philosophie
photography	*Phot*	photographie
physics	*Phys*	physique
physiology	*Physiol*	physiologie
plural	*pl*	pluriel
politics	*Pol*	politique
past participle	*pp*	participe passé
predeterminer	*predet*	prédéterminant
prefix	*pref, préf*	préfixe
preposition	*prep, prép*	préposition
proper noun	*pr n*	nom propre
pronoun	*pron*	pronom
proverb	*Prov*	proverbe
psychology, psychiatry	*Psy*	psychologie, psychiatrie
past tense	*pt*	prétérit
something	*qch*	quelque chose
somebody	*qn*	quelqu'un
registered trademark	®	marque déposée
radio	*Rad*	radio
rail	*Rail*	chemins de fer
religion	*Rel*	religion
South African En		
somebody	*sb*	quelqu'un
school	*Sch, Scol*	scolaire
Scottish English	*Scot*	anglais d'Écosse
term used in Southern England	*SEng*	terme utilisé dans le sud de l'Angleterre
singular	*sing*	singulier
formal	*Sout*	soutenu
specialist term	*Spec, Spéc*	vocabulaire de spécialité
Stock Exchange	*St Exch*	Bourse
something	*sth*	quelque chose
suffixe	*suff*	suffixe
superlative	*superl*	superlatif
technology	*Tech*	technologie
telecommunications	*Tel, Tél*	télécommunications
textiles	*Tex*	textile
theatre	*Theat, Théât*	théâtre
transport	*Transp*	transports
television	*TV*	télévision
typography, printing	*Typ*	typographie, imprimerie
European Union	*UE*	Union européenne
university	*Univ*	université
verb	*v*	verbe
intransitive verb	*vi*	verbe intransitif
reflexive verb	*vpr*	verbe pronominal
transitive verb	*vt*	verbe transitif
transitive verb used with a preposition [eg **parvenir à** (to reach); ils sont **parvenus à** un accord (they reached an agreement)]	*vt ind*	verbe transitif indirect [par exemple: **parvenir à**; ils sont **parvenus à** un accord]
inseparable transitive verb [phrasal verb where the verb and the adverb or preposition cannot be separated, eg **look after**; he **looked after** the children]	*vt insep*	verbe transitif à particule inséparable [par exemple: **look after** (s'occuper de); he **looked after** the children (il s'occupait des enfants)]
separable transitive verb [phrasal verb where the adverb and preposition can be separated, eg **send back**; she **sent** the present **back** *or* she **sent back** the present]	*vt sep*	verbe transitif à particule séparable [par exemple: **send** back (rendre); she **sent** the present **back** *ou* she **sent** back the present (elle a rendu le cadeau)]
veterinary medicine	*Vet, Vét*	médecine vétérinaire
vulgar	*Vulg*	vulgaire
zoology	*Zool*	zoologie

HARRAP'S
shorter

ANGLAIS-FRANÇAIS
FRANÇAIS-ANGLAIS

HARRAP

HARRAP est une marque des éditions Chambers Harrap Publishers Ltd
7 Hopetoun Crescent, Edinburgh, EH7 4AY
Grande-Bretagne

Chambers Harrap est une société du groupe Hachette UK
Harrap® est une marque déposée de Chambers Harrap Publishers Ltd

Neuvième édition

ISBN 978 0245 50837 0

10 9 8 7 6 5 4 3 2 1

Dépôt légal : décembre 2008

www.harrap.com

Maquette réalisée par Chambers Harrap Publishers Ltd, Edinburgh
Composé en Cheltenham and Frutiger par Sharon McTeir
Imprimé et relié en par La Tipografica Varese SPA, Italie

Chambers French Dictionary

Chambers

CHAMBERS
An imprint of Chambers Harrap Publishers Ltd
7 Hopetoun Crescent, Edinburgh, EH7 4AY

Chambers Harrap is an Hachette UK company

This 9th edition published by Chambers Harrap Publishers Ltd 2009

A CIP catalogue record for this book is available from the British Library.

ISBN 978 0550 10499 1

10 9 8 7 6 5 4 3 2 1

www.chambers.co.uk

Designed by Chambers Harrap Publishers Ltd, Edinburgh
Typeset in Cheltenham and Frutiger by Sharon McTeir
Printed and bound in Italy by La Tipografica Varese SPA

Contributors to 9th edition/Ont participé à la 9e édition

Project editor/Directrice de projet

Anna Stevenson

with/avec

Nadia Cornuau
Stuart Fortey
Pauline Gaberel
Alex Hepworth
Susan Howarth
Laurence Larroche
Val McNulty
Kate Nicholson
Georges Pilard
Christian Salzédo

Illustrations

Glen McBeth

Prepress/Prépresse

Nicolas Echallier

Publishing manager/Direction éditoriale

Anna Stevenson

Contents/Table des matières

Preface

The aim of any dictionary publisher should be to bring together all the tools of the trade to present an accurate snapshot of language as it is really used. Chambers has done just that, combining editorial and lexicographical expertise with the use of our own corpus – a vast database, updated daily, containing real language in the form of many millions of English and French words extracted electronically from sources such as books and newspapers.

The world is in a permanent state of flux, with new issues, concerns and events continually emerging, and our language is correspondingly expanding in response to this changing world. We have taken care to ensure that this book contains the most up-to-date items of English and French, providing the user with all the vocabulary necessary to read and write about the contemporary world. Environmental issues currently preoccupy much of the English- and French-speaking worlds, with buzzwords such as **carbon footprint** and **food miles** now an established part of the lexicon and thus taking their place in this dictionary. The world of IT and computer technology, and in particular online interaction, also continues to shape the language, with new terms coming into existence almost every week. Some that have lasted the course and have made their way into this book include **blogosphere**, **instant messaging** and **social networking**. Finally, there is always space in the dictionary for the more light-hearted side of language, and with slang and colloquial language evolving perhaps faster than any other area, all the more reason to include such humorous terms as **man flu**, **muffin top** and **wardrobe malfunction**.

We have taken care to ensure that the *Chambers French Dictionary* is more than a reference tool for encoding and decoding the language; the book also benefits from extensive supplementary material, created specially to meet the needs of advanced learners. The first, "Living Language", is an indispensable guide to communication and self-expression; it includes many hundreds of sentences which may be used to describe a wide range of opinions and emotions and to communicate in situations such as interviews and telephone conversations. Next, as many readers may be intending to work in a French-speaking country, whether on a summer placement or on a more permanent basis, "World of Work" will provide all the information you need for success in your job hunt. Finally, as idioms are often something of a minefield for language learners, our full-colour, illustrated guide to 500 of the most common will both inform and entertain.

Préface

Au cours des trois années qui se sont écoulées depuis la dernière édition du *Harrap's Shorter* le monde a vécu de nouveaux bouleversements et a dû faire face à de nouveaux problèmes et à de nouveaux défis. Comme toujours la langue se fait le reflet vivant de ces changements.

L'environnement continue d'être un sujet de préoccupation majeur dans le monde entier ; il a donc beaucoup été question d'**empreinte écologique**, de **biodiesel** et de **préjudice écologique**, et ces termes ont bien évidemment trouvé leur place dans cette nouvelle édition de notre ouvrage. Par ailleurs, les monde de l'informatique et de l'Internet restent des sources intarissables de nouveaux mots et expressions. Les termes qui se sont fait une place dans la langue, du type **blogosphère**, **messagerie instantanée** et **télédéclaration** ont été inclus dans le *Shorter*. Enfin, nous ne négligeons jamais l'aspect ludique de la langue et c'est pourquoi l'argot et la langue familière sont comme toujours très bien représentés dans le *Shorter* avec l'inclusion de termes et expressions comme **pipolisation**, **se ringardiser** et **être à la ramasse**.

Mais le *Shorter* est beaucoup plus qu'un simple outil de décodage et d'encodage. Conformément à une tradition désormais bien établie il propose des suppléments pratiques pour répondre aux besoins des utilisateurs. Le premier de ces suppléments, intitulé "La Langue en action", est un guide de communication et d'expression qui comprend plusieurs centaines de phrases employées pour exprimer opinions et émotions et pour mieux communiquer. Enfin, pour ceux et celles qui envisagent d'aller travailler en pays anglophone, que ce soit pour un petit boulot ou sur le long terme, le supplément intitulé "Le Monde du travail" fournira toutes les informations nécessaires pour trouver l'emploi recherché.

Structure of entries/Structure des entrées

Headwords are presented in blue in this dictionary and appear in alphabetical order. Homographs are numbered.
Les entrées du dictionnaire apparaissent en bleu et sont classées par ordre alphabétique. Les homographes sont numérotés.

The different senses of a word are numbered.
Les différents sens des mots sont numérotés.

In instances where a term is given two translations, one technical and the other non-technical, the technical translation is placed second and preceded by the label *Spéc* on the French-English side of the dictionary and *Spec* on the English-French side. The technical translation has been given in addition to the neutral one where the word being translated can be used in both technical and non-technical contexts.
Dans le cas où un mot de la langue source comporte deux traductions, l'une de registre technique et l'autre qui s'utilise dans la langue de tous les jours, la traduction technique est placée en seconde position et précédée de l'abréviation* Spéc *du côté francais-anglais et* Spec *du côté anglais-francais. Une traduction technique est fournie en plus de la traduction habituelle lorsque le mot traduit s'utilise dans des contextes techniques et non techniques.

The grammatical classification of an entry is marked in blue small capital letters (ADJ, ADV, N, etc). All the abbreviated labels are included in the list of abbreviations on the inside front and back covers of the dictionary.
Les différentes catégories grammaticales sont indiquées en bleu et en petites capitales (ADJ, ADV, N, etc). La liste des abréviations des indicateurs de catégories grammaticales figure en début et en fin de dictionnaire.

Nuances of senses, or semantic splits required to show different translations for the same sense, are shown within the same sense category by using indicating material in brackets.
Les nuances et les distinctions sémantiques qui nécessitent des traductions différentes au sein d'une même catégorie sont signalées par des indicateurs de sens qui apparaissent entre parenthèses.

The full form of abbreviations and acronyms is systematically given after the headword for greater ease of use.
Pour une plus grande facilité d'utilisation la forme développée des abréviations et acronymes est donnée systématiquement à la suite du mot de tête.

When an abbreviation or acronym has a written form only, this is clearly indicated.
Les abréviations et acronymes qui n'apparaissent qu'à la forme écrite sont clairement indiqués.

A term will frequently have no exact translation equivalent in the other language. In such cases a cultural equivalent (preceded by the ≃ sign) with similar connotations in the target language may be given.
Il n'est pas rare qu'un terme ne dispose pas d'une traduction exacte dans l'autre langue. Dans ce cas on optera parfois pour un équivalent culturel aux connotations comparables (précédé du signe ≃).

cahier [kaje] **NM** 1 *Scol* notebook; **c. de maths/géographie** maths/geography copybook; **c. de brouillon** notebook *(for drafts)*, *Br* roughbook; **c. de correspondance** = notebook used by schoolteachers to write notes to pupils' parents, *Br* ≃ homework diary; **c. d'exercices** exercise book; **c. de textes** *(d'élève)* homework notebook; *(de professeur)* (work) record book; **c. de travaux pratiques** lab book
2 *(recueil) Compta* **c. des achats** purchase ledger; **c. des charges** *(de matériel)* specifications; *(dans un contrat)* terms and conditions; **c. de revendications** claims register
3 *(d'un journal)* section
4 *Typ* gathering
• **cahiers** **NMPL** **1** *Littérature (mémoires)* diary, memoirs **2** *Hist* **cahiers de doléances** book of grievances **3** *Journ* review, journal

calcul[2] [kalkyl] **NM** *Méd* stone, *Spéc* calculus; **c. biliaire** gall stone; **c. urinaire** *ou* **rénal** kidney stone

calculateur, -trice [kalkylatœr, -tris] **ADJ** *Péj* calculating, scheming
NM,F **1** *(qui compte)* **c'est un bon/mauvais c.** he's good/bad at figures *or* sums **2** *Péj (personne intéressée)* **un fin c.** a shrewd operator; **un ignoble c.** a scheming character
NM **1** *Vieilli Ordinat (ordinateur)* computer; **c. digital** *ou* **numérique** digital computer; **c. électronique** electronic computer **2** *Aut* **c. embarqué** on-board computer
• **calculatrice** **NF** *Math (machine)* calculator; **calculatrice de bureau** desktop calculator; **calculatrice imprimante** print-out calculator; **calculatrice de poche** pocket calculator

calendrier [kalɑ̃drije] **NM** **1** *(tableau, livret, système)* calendar; *Hist* **c. grégorien/républicain** Gregorian/Republican calendar; **c. perpétuel/à effeuiller** perpetual/tear-off calendar **2** *(emploi du temps)* timetable, schedule; *(plan ▸ de réunions)* schedule, calendar; *(▸ d'un festival)* calendar; *(▸ d'un voyage)* schedule; **j'ai un c. très chargé** I have a very busy schedule *or* timetable; **établir un c.** to draw up a timetable *or* schedule; **c. de campagne** campaign schedule; *Mktg* media schedule; *Bourse* **c. des émissions** calendar of issues; *Bourse* **c. de remboursement** repayment schedule; *Sport* **c. des rencontres** *Br* fixture list, *Am* match schedule

CAO [seao] **NF** *Ordinat (abrév* **conception assistée par ordinateur**) CAD

CAPES, Capes [kapes] **NM** *Univ (abrév* **certificat d'aptitude au professorat de l'enseignement du second degré**) = secondary school teaching qualification, *Br* ≃ PGCE

cc **1** *(abrév écrite* **cuillère à café**) tsp **2** *(abrév écrite* **charges comprises**) inclusive of maintenance costs

CCP [sesepe] **NM** *Banque (abrév* **compte chèque postal, compte courant postal**) = post office account, *Br* ≃ Giro account, *Am* ≃ Post Office checking account

chacal, -als [ʃakal] **NM 1** *Zool* jackal **2** *Péj (personne)* vulture, jackal

chat-huant [ʃaɥɑ̃] *(pl* **chats-huants***)* **NM** *Orn* brown owl

chauffe-assiettes [ʃofasjɛt] **NM INV** plate warmer

ciseau, -x [sizo] **NM 1** *Tech (outil)* chisel; **c. à froid** cold chisel **2** *Sport (prise de catch, de lutte)* scissors hold

• **ciseaux NMPL 1** *(outil)* **(une paire de) ciseaux** (a pair of) scissors; **(une paire de) grands ciseaux** (a pair of) shears; **donner un coup de ciseaux dans un tissu** to cut a piece of material with scissors; **donner des coups de ciseaux dans un texte** to make cuts in a text; **ciseaux à bouts ronds** blunt- *or* round-ended scissors; **ciseaux de couturière** dressmaking scissors; **ciseaux à denteler** pinking shears; **ciseaux à ongles** nail scissors **2** *Sport* **saut en ciseaux** scissor jump; **sauter en ciseaux** to do a scissor jump **3** *Gym* **faire des ciseaux** to do the scissors

cliquer [3] [klike] **VI** *Ordinat* to click **(sur on)**; **c. deux fois** to double-click; **c. avec le bouton gauche/droit de la souris** to left-click/right-click; **c. et glisser** to click and drag

> **CO-** — PREFIX
>
> The prefix **co-** is widely used in French to convey the idea of TOGETHERNESS or COMMUNITY OF INTERESTS. It is worth noting three relatively recent coinages or uses:
>
> • **cohabitation**: although not a recent word in itself, **la cohabitation** has come to refer to three episodes in French political life, between 1986 and 2002, when a Prime Minister from one side of the political spectrum has had to share power with a president from the other side (see cultural box at the entry **cohabitation**)
>
> • **covoiturage**: this word was given particular prominence in 1995, when a national public transport strike forced commuters to resort to car-pooling
>
> • **cododo**: this is the colloquial equivalent of *sommeil partagé* (from the baby talk word *dodo*, meaning "sleep"), a practice where parents share a bed, or at least a bedroom, with their offspring

cohabitation [kɔabitasjɔ̃] **NF 1** *(vie commune)* cohabitation, cohabiting, living together **2** *Pol* = coexistence of an elected head of state and an opposition parliamentary majority

> **LA COHABITATION**
>
> Originally, this term refers to the period (1986–1988) during which the socialist President (François Mitterrand) had a right-wing Prime Minister (Jacques Chirac), following the victory of the RPR in the legislative elections and Mitterrand's decision not to resign as President. It has since been used to refer to the similar situation which arose following the 1993 elections (with Édouard Balladur as Prime Minister) and also after the 1997 elections (with the left-wing government of Lionel Jospin co-ruling with the President Jacques Chirac).

Coton-Tige® [kɔtɔ̃tiʒ] *(pl* **Cotons-Tiges***)* **NM** *Br* cotton bud, *Am* Q-tip®

cru[2], -e[1] [kry] **ADJ 1** *(non cuit ▸ denrée)* raw, uncooked; *(▸ céramique)* unfired
2 *(non pasteurisé ▸ beurre, lait)* unpasteurized
3 *(sans préparation ▸ soie)* raw; *(▸ minerai)* crude; *(▸ bois)* untreated
4 *(aveuglant ▸ couleur)* crude, harsh, glaring; *(▸ éclairage)* harsh, blinding, glaring
5 *(net)* blunt, uncompromising; **c'est la vérité toute crue** it's the pure, unadorned truth
6 *(osé)* coarse, crude
7 *Belg, Can & Suisse (temps, bâtiment)* damp and cold

Structure of entries/Structure des entrées

When a French noun has an irregular plural, this is shown immediately after the headword.
Du côté francais-anglais, le pluriel irrégulier des noms est indiqué juste après l'intitulé de l'entrée.

The plural of hyphenated French nouns is always given, unless the noun does not change its form in the plural, in which case it is marked *inv*.
Le pluriel des noms composés avec trait d'union est donné systématiquement. Pour les noms invariables la mention inv figure juste après l'abréviation qui indique la catégorie grammaticale.

Pronunciation information has been given using the International Phonetic Alphabet (IPA).
La prononciation des entrées est donnée en alphabet phonétique international (API).

Prepositions that commonly collocate with a particular term are given in brackets immediately after the translation.
Les prépositions les plus couramment employées avec un terme donné figurent entre parenthèses juste après la traduction.

A number in square brackets is given after each verb. This number has a corresponding conjugation model in the list of French conjugations in the supplement in the middle of the book.
Du côté francais–anglais un numéro entre crochets apparaît après chaque verbe et renvoit à un tableau de conjugaisons situé dans le supplément en milieu de l'ouvrage.

More than one hundred notes on common prefixes and suffixes provide the user with useful information on word-building.
Plus de cent encadrés sur des préfixes et suffixes courants renseignent l'utilisateur sur la formation des mots.

The dictionary contains about two hundred notes on cultural topics, providing extra information in addition to the translation.
Le dictionnaire contient environ deux cents encadrés intégrés au texte qui portent sur des points de culture, de société, de politique ou d'histoire. Ils donnent un complément d'information lorsqu'une traduction ou une glose ne suffisent pas.

When a French term has different translations in British and American English, the American variant translation is clearly indicated.
Lorsqu'un terme francais se traduit différemment en anglais britannique et en anglais américain, la traduction américaine est clairement indiquée.

Numerous Canadian, Swiss and Belgian terms are given with the labels *Can, Suisse* and *Belg* respectively.
***Les nombreux canadianismes, helvétismes et belgicismes sont indiqués par les étiquettes* Can, Suisse *et* Belg.**

Compounds of two or more words have been presented under the entry for the first word of the compound. They appear in alphabetical order in a block at the end of the entry. The block is introduced by the symbol ▸▸
Les noms composés de deux éléments ou plus apparaissent dans l'article consacré au premier élément du mot composé. Ils sont présentés à la fin de l'article et sont classés par ordre alphabétique. La section des mots composés est signalée par le symbole ▸▸

A term will frequently have no exact translation equivalent in the other language. In such cases an explanation (preceded by the = sign) may be given.
Il n'est pas rare qu'un terme ne dispose pas d'une traduction exacte dans l'autre langue. Dans ce cas on optera parfois pour une explication (précédée du signe =).

The register of all words and phrases in the source language is clearly indicated. Register labels are used to indicate the level of language – whether formal (*Formal/Sout*), informal (*Fam*), very informal (*very Fam/très Fam*) or vulgar (*Vulg*) – and also to indicate usage, showing whether a word is, for example, pejorative, ironic or euphemistic (*Pej/Péj, Ironic/Ironique* and *Euph*).
Le registre de toutes les expressions et tous les mots donnés en langue source est clairement indiqué. Des indicateurs de registre sont donnés pour préciser le niveau de langue, qu'il soit soutenu* (Formal/Sout)*, familier* (Fam)*, très familier* (very Fam/très Fam)*, ou vulgaire* (Vulg)*. Les nuances sont également indiquées lorsqu'un terme est employé en tant qu'euphémisme ou de façon péjorative ou ironique* (Euph, Pej/Péj *et* Ironic/Ironique)*.

American variant spellings are cross-referred to the corresponding entry in British English.
Les mots orthographiés à l'américaine sont renvoyés à l'entrée britannique correspondante.

American spelling variants are clearly shown at headword level.
Les variantes orthographiques américaines sont clairement indiquées au niveau du libellé de l'entrée.

Menus appear at the beginning of many long entries. The aim of these menus is twofold: (i) to summarize the main translations of an entry; (ii) to make use of the knowledge the user already has to help them find the sense they are looking for more quickly.
Des"menus" apparaissent en tête des articles longs pour faciliter la recherche de l'utilisateur. L'utilité de ces menus est double: 1/ ils présentent en résumé les traductions d'un terme suivant ses différentes acceptions 2/ ils permettent au lecteur de repérer facilement le sens qu'il recherche.

The dicionary features a vast number of specialized items of vocabulary. A full list of the abbreviated field labels used to mark these terms is to be found on the inside front and back covers of the book.
Le dictionnaire comporte un très grand nombre de termes techniques. La liste complète des abréviations des domaines de spécialité utilisés dans le dictionnaire figure en début et en fin d'ouvrage.

Register labels can occur in various combinations. For example, a word can be either archaic or literary, old fashioned or humorous.
Un terme peut comporter plusieurs indicateurs de registre. À titre d'exemple, un mot archaïque peut également être utilisé pour ses accents littéraires, et l'on peut choisir d'employer un terme vieilli et familier de façon à produire un effet humoristique.

cabbage ['kæbɪdʒ] **N 1** *(vegetable)* chou *m* **2** *Br Fam (brain-damaged person)* légume *m*; *Pej (dull person)* larve *f*; **I'd rather die than be a c. for the rest of my life** plutôt mourir que vivre comme un légume jusqu'à la fin de mes jours **3** *Am Fam (money)* fric *m*, blé *m*, oseille *f*
▸▸ ***cabbage lettuce*** laitue *f* pommée; ***cabbage patch*** carré *m* de salade; ***cabbage rose*** rose *f* centfeuilles; ***cabbage white*** *(butterfly)* piéride *f* du chou

cabin ['kæbɪn] **N 1** *(hut)* cabane *f*, hutte *f*
2 *Naut* cabine *f*
3 *Aviat* cabine *f*; **the first class c.** la cabine de première classe
4 *Br Rail (signal box)* cabine *f* d'aiguillage
5 *Br (of lorry, train)* cabine *f*
▸▸ *Aviat* ***cabin attendant*** *(male)* steward *m*; *(female)* hôtesse *f* de l'air; *Naut* ***cabin boy*** mousse *m*; *Naut* ***cabin class*** deuxième classe *f*; *Aviat* ***cabin crew*** personnel *m* de cabine; *Naut* ***cabin cruiser*** cruiser *m*, yacht *m* de croisière; ***cabin fever*** = dépression ou mauvaise humeur dues à de longues périodes d'isolement; *Aviat* ***cabin staff*** personnel *m* de cabine; ***cabin trunk*** malle-cabine *f*

cahoots [kə'hu:ts] **NPL** *Fam (idiom)* **to be in c. (with sb)** être de mèche (avec qn)

caliber *Am* = **calibre**

calibre, *Am* **caliber** ['kælɪbə(r)] **N 1** *(of gun, tube)* calibre *m* **2** *(quality)* qualité *f*; **their work is of the highest c.** ils font un travail de grande qualité; **the two applicants are not of the same c.** les deux candidats ne sont pas du même calibre *ou* n'ont pas la même envergure

CALL [kɔ:l]

VI
- appeler **1, 2, 6**
- passer **4**
- pousser un cri **3**
- s'arrêter **5**

VT
- appeler **1, 2, 4, 7**
- annoncer **6, 10**
- réveiller **3**
- juger **9**

N
- appel **1–3**
- demande **6, 8, 10**
- annonce **10**
- visite **4**
- jugement **9**

calliper, *Am* **caliper** ['kælɪpə(r)] **N 1** *Math* **a pair of c. compasses** *or* **callipers** un compas **2** *Med* **c. (splint)** attelle-étrier *f* **3** *Tech (for brake)* étrier *m*

campfire ['kæmp,faɪə(r)] **N** feu *m* de camp

camphor ['kæmfə(r)] **N** *Chem* camphre *m*
▸▸ ***camphor oil*** essence *f* de camphre; ***camphor tree*** camphrier *m*

camphorated ['kæmfəreɪtɪd] **ADJ** *Chem* camphré

camping ['kæmpɪŋ] **N** camping *m*; **to go c.** faire du camping, camper
COMP *(equipment)* de camping
▸▸ ***camping gas*** butane *m*; ***camping ground, camping grounds*** *(private)* camp *m*; *(commercial)* terrain *m* de camping, camping *m*; *(clearing)* emplacement *m* de camping, endroit *m* où camper; ***camping holiday*** vacances *fpl* (en) camping; ***camping site*** *(private)* camp *m*; *(commercial)* terrain *m* de camping, camping *m*; *(clearing)* emplacement *m* de camping, endroit *m* où camper; ***camping stool*** pliant *m*; ***camping stove*** camping-gaz *m*

charger ['tʃɑ:dʒə(r)] **N 1** *Elec* chargeur *m* **2** *Arch or Literary (horse)* cheval *m* de bataille

cellphone ['selfəʊn] **N** téléphone *m* cellulaire; *Am (mobile phone)* (téléphone *m*) portable *m*, *Belg* GSM *m*, *Suisse* Natel® *m*, *Can* cellulaire *m*

chandelier [ˌʃændəˈlɪə(r)] **N** lustre *m* *(pour éclairer)*

Note that the French word **chandelier** is a false friend and is never a translation for the English word **chandelier**. Its most common meaning is **candlestick** or **candelabra**.

cheer [tʃɪə(r)] **N 1** *(cry)* hourra *m*, bravo *m*; **I heard a c. go up** j'ai entendu des acclamations; **three cheers for the winner!** un ban *ou* hourra pour le gagnant!; **three cheers!** hourra! **2** *Fam* **cheers!** *(toast)* (à votre) santé!; *Br (at parting)* salut!, ciao!; *Br (thanks)* merci! **3** *Literary (good spirits)* bonne humeur *f*, gaieté *f*; **words of good c.** paroles *fpl* d'encouragement; **be of good c.!** prenez courage!

VT 1 *(make cheerful ▸ person)* remonter le moral à, réconforter **2** *(encourage by shouts)* acclamer

VI pousser des acclamations *ou* des hourras

▸**cheer on** **VT SEP** encourager (par des acclamations); **his supporters cheered him on to victory** les acclamations de ses supporters l'ont encouragé jusqu'à la victoire

▸**cheer up** **VT SEP 1** *(person)* remonter le moral à, réconforter **2** *(house, room)* égayer

VI *(become more cheerful)* s'égayer, se dérider; **c. up!** courage!; **the weather's cheered up** le temps s'est arrangé

chook [tʃuːk] **N** *Austr Fam* *(chicken)* poulet *m*

churchman ['tʃɜːtʃmən] *(pl* **churchmen** [-mən]) **N** *(clergyman)* ecclésiastique *m*; *(churchgoer)* pratiquant *m*

cling [klɪŋ] *(pt & pp* **clung** [klʌŋ]) **VI 1** *(hold on tightly)* s'accrocher, se cramponner; **they clung to one another** ils se sont enlacés, ils se sont cramponnés l'un à l'autre; *Fig* **to c. to a hope/to a belief/to the past** se raccrocher à un espoir/à une croyance/au passé; **she clings to her children even though they are now grown up** elle s'accroche à ses enfants bien qu'ils soient maintenant adultes **2** *(stick)* adhérer, coller; **a dress that clings to the body** une robe très près du corps *ou* très ajustée **3** *(smell)* persister

colleen ['kɒliːn, kɒ'liːn] **N** *Ir* jeune fille *f*; *(Irish girl)* jeune Irlandaise *f*

confidant [ˌkɒnfɪˈdænt] **N** confident *m*

Attention: ne pas confondre avec l'adjectif anglais **confident**.

consume [kənˈsjuːm] **VT 1** *(eat or drink)* consommer **2** *(use up ▸ energy, fuel)* consommer; *(▸ time)* dépenser **3** *(burn up ▸ of fire, flames)* consumer; **the city was consumed by fire** la ville a brûlé; *Fig* **to be consumed with desire/love** brûler de désir/d'amour; *Fig* **to be consumed with grief** être miné par le chagrin; *Fig* **to be consumed with hatred/jealousy** être dévoré par la haine/la jalousie

When translating **to consume**, note that the French verbs **consommer** and **consumer** are not interchangeable. **Consommer** always refers to consumer activity, while **consumer** is used to describe the process of being eaten up or destroyed, especially by fire.

Belgian, Canadian and Swiss variant translations are shown as appropriate.
Des traductions en francais de Belgique, du Canada et de Suisse sont fournies lorsque nécessaire.

The dictionary contains hundreds of usage notes to facilitate translation, including a large number which warn the user about the pitfalls presented by false friends.
Le dictionnaire propose des centaines de notes d'aide à la traduction dont une large proportion renseignent l'utilisateur sur les difficultés de traduction présentées par les faux amis.

Phrasal verbs are listed alphabetically after the main entry and are clearly indicated by a blue triangle.
Les verbes à particule sont classés alphabétiquement à la suite de l'entrée principale et sont facilement repérables grâce à un triangle bleu.

Terms in Australian English are clearly indicated.
Les termes d'anglais d'Australie sont clairement indiqués.

English irregular plurals are given after the headword.
Les pluriels irréguliers anglais apparaissent à la suite du mot de tête.

Irregular forms of English verbs are given after the headword.
La forme irrégulière des verbes anglais est donnée après le mot de tête.

In examples ,when the word in question corresponds to the exact form of the headword, only the initial letter of the word is given.
Dans les exemples, seule l'initiale du mot traité apparaît quand il correspond à la forme du mot de tête.

Terms in Irish English are clearly indicated.
Les termes d'anglais d'Irlande sont clairement indiqués.

Words which are often confused are clearly marked.
Les termes susceptibles d'être confondus sont clairement indiqués.

Numerous usage notes warn the user against common translation errors.
De nombreuses notes d'usage mettent en garde contre des fautes de traduction communément commises.

Prononciation de l'anglais

Pour indiquer la prononciation anglaise, nous avons utilisé dans ce dictionnaire les symboles de l'API (Alphabet phonétique international). Pour chaque son anglais, vous trouverez dans le tableau ci-dessous des exemples de mots anglais, suivis de mots français présentant un son similaire.Une explication est donnée lorsqu'il n'y a pas d'équivalent en français.

Caractère API	Exemple en anglais	Exemple en français
Consonnes		
[b]	babble	bébé
[d]	dig	dent
[dʒ]	giant, jig	jean
[f]	fit, physics	face
[g]	grey, big	gag
[h]	happy	h aspiré : à quelques rares exceptions près, il est toujours prononcé en anglais
[j]	yellow	yaourt
[k]	clay, kick	car
[l]	lip, pill	lilas
[m]	mummy	maman
[n]	nip, pin	né
[ŋ]	sing	parking
[p]	pip	papa
[r]	rig, write	Pas d'équivalent français : se prononce en plaçant le bout de la langue au milieu du palais
[(r)]		Seulement prononcé en cas de liaison avec la voyelle qui suit comme dans : far away; the car is blue
[s]	sick, science	silence
[ʃ]	ship, nation	chèvre
[t]	tip, butt	tartine
[tʃ]	chip, batch	atchoum
[θ]	thick	Son proche du [s] français, il se prononce en plaçant le bout de la langue entre les dents du haut et celles du bas
[ð]	this, with	Son proche du [z] français, il se prononce en plaçant le bout de la langue entre les dents du haut et celles du bas
[v]	vague, give	vie
[w]	wit, why	whisky
[z]	zip, physics	rose
[ʒ]	pleasure	je
[χ]	loch	Existe seulement dans certains mots écossais. Pas d'équivalent français : se prononce du fond de la gorge, comme Bach en allemand ou la 'jotà' espagnole.
Voyelles		
[æ]	rag	natte
[ɑː]	large, half	pâte
[e]	set	[e] moins ouvert que le [ɛ] français
[ɜː]	curtain, were	heure
[ə]	utter, about	cheval

Caractère API	Exemple en anglais	Exemple en français
[ɪ]	big, women	[i] bref, à mi-chemin entre les sons [ɛ] et [i] français (plus proche de 'net' que de 'vite')
[iː]	leak, wee	[i] plus long que le [i] français
[ɒ]	lock	bonne – mais plus ouvert et prononcé au fond du palais
[ɔː]	wall, cork	baume – mais plus ouvert et prononcé au fond du palais
[ʊ]	put, look	Son à mi-chemin entre un [u] bref et un [ɔ]
[uː]	moon	Son [u] prolongé
[ʌ]	cup	À mi-chemin entre un [a] et un [ɛ]
Diphtongues : Elles sont rares en français et sont la combinaison de deux sons.		
[aɪ]	why, high, lie	**aïe**
[aʊ]	how	miaou, aoûtat – mais se prononce comme un seul son
[eə]	bear, share, where	**flair**
[eɪ]	day, make, main	**merveille**
[əʊ]	show, go	Combinaison d'un [o] et d'un [u]
[ɪə]	here, gear	Combinaison d'un [i] long suivi d'un [ɛ] bref
[ɔɪ]	boy, soil	langue d'oïl
[ʊə]	sure	Combinaison d'un son [u] suivi d'un [ɛ] bref

French pronunciation

French pronunciation is shown in this dictionary using the symbols of the IPA (International Phonetic Alphabet). In the table below, examples of French words using these sounds are given, followed by English words which have a similar sound. Where there is no equivalent in English, an explanation is given.

IPA symbol	French example	English example
Consonants		
[b]	bébé	but
[d]	donner	door
[f]	forêt	fire
[g]	gare	get
[ʒ]	jour	pleasure
[k]	carte	kitten
[l]	lire	lonely
[m]	maman	mat
[n]	ni	now
[ŋ]	parking	singing
[ɲ]	campagne	canyon
[p]	patte	pat
[r]	rare	Like an English [r] but pronounced at the back of the throat
[s]	soir	sit
[ʃ]	chose	sham
[t]	table	tap
[v]	valeur	value
[z]	zéro	zero
Vowels		
[a]	chat	cat
[ɑ]	âge	gasp
[e]	été	bay
[ɛ]	père	bed
[ə]	le	amend
[ø]	deux	Does not exist in English: [e] pronounced with the lips rounded
[œ]	seul	curtain
[i]	vite	bee – not quite as long as the English [iː]
[ɔ]	donner	cot – slightly more open than the English [ɒ]
[o]	chaud	daughter – but higher than its English equivalent
[u]	tout	you – but shorter than its English equivalent
[y]	voiture	Does not exist in English: [i] with lips rounded
[ɑ̃]	enfant	Nasal sound pronounced lower and further back in the mouth than [ɔ̃]
[ɛ̃]	vin	Nasal sound: [a] sound pronounced letting air pass through the nose
[ɔ̃]	bonjour	Nasal sound: closed [o] sound pronounced letting air pass through the nose
[œ̃]	un	Nasal sound: like [ɛ̃] but with lips more rounded

IPA symbol	French example	English example
Semi-vowels		
[w]	v**oi**r	**w**eek
[j]	**y**o**y**o, pai**ll**e	**y**ard
[ɥ]	n**ui**t	Does not exist in English: the vowel [y] elided with the following vowel

English – French

Anglais – Français

a

A[1], **a**[1] [eɪ] **N 1** *(letter)* A, a *m inv*; **two a's** deux a; **A for Andrew** A comme Anatole; **6A Bothwell Street** 6 bis Bothwell Street; **I'm not going because a) I've no money and b) I've no time** je n'y vais pas parce que primo je n'ai pas d'argent et secundo je n'ai pas le temps; *Br* **the A5** *(road)* la RN 5; **from A to Z** de A à Z; **from A to B** de A à B; **the car's old, but it gets me from A to B** c'est une vieille voiture mais elle me permet de me déplacer; **the roads are so crowded that it takes forever to get from A to B** les routes sont si encombrées que le moindre trajet prend une éternité; **from point A to point B** d'un point A à un point B **2** *Sch* **to get an A** avoir une très bonne note, avoir entre 16 et 20; *Am Sch & Univ* **he got straight A's** *(top marks)* il a eu de très bonnes notes partout **3** *Mus* la *m inv*; **in A flat** en la bémol

ADJ *Mus (string)* de la

►► *Br* ***A road*** route *f* nationale

A[2] *Elec* (*written abbr* **ampere**) A

a[2] [ə, *stressed* eɪ]

> a devient **an** [ən, *accentué* æn] devant voyelle ou h muet

INDEF ART 1 *(before countable nouns)* un (une); **a book** un livre; **a car** une voiture; **a hotel** [əˌhəʊ'tel], *Old-fashioned* **an hotel** [ənˌəʊ'tel] un hôtel; **an hour** [ən'aʊə(r)] une heure; **a unit** [ə'juːnɪt] une unité; **an uncle** [ən'ʌŋkəl] un oncle; **an MP** [ənem'piː] un député; **a man and (a) woman** un homme et une femme; **a cup and saucer** une tasse et sa soucoupe; **a wife and mother** *(same person)* une épouse et mère; **I can't see a thing** je ne vois rien; **he has a broken leg** il a une jambe cassée; **would you like a coffee?** voulez-vous un café?; **an expensive German wine** un vin allemand cher

2 *(before professions, nationalities)* **she's a doctor** elle est médecin; **he is an Englishman/a father** il est anglais/père

3 *(before numbers)* **a thousand dollars** mille dollars; **a dozen eggs** une douzaine d'œufs; **a third/fifth** un tiers/cinquième; **a twentieth of a second** un vingtième de seconde; **an hour and a half** une heure et demie

4 *(per)* **£2 a dozen/a hundred grammes** deux livres la douzaine/les cent grammes; **50 euros a head** 50 euros par tête; **three times a year** trois fois par an; **50 kilometres an hour** 50 kilomètres à l'heure

5 *(before terms of quantity, amount)* **a few weeks/months** quelques semaines/mois; **a lot of money** beaucoup d'argent; **a great many visitors** de très nombreux visiteurs; **have a little more wine** reprenez donc un peu de vin; **he raised a number of interesting points** il a soulevé un certain nombre de questions intéressantes

6 *(before periods of time)* un (une); **I'm going for a week/month/year** je pars (pour) une semaine/un mois/un an; **we talked for a while** nous avons parlé un moment

7 *(before days, months, festivals)* un (une); **the meeting was on a Tuesday** la réunion a eu lieu un mardi; **it was an exceptionally cold March** ce fut un mois de mars particulièrement froid; **we had an unforgettable Christmas** nous avons passé un Noël inoubliable

8 *(before nouns in apposition)* **Caen, a large town in Normandy** Caen, ville importante de Normandie; **40 years a sailor and he still gets seasick!** il a beau être marin depuis 40 ans, il lui arrive toujours d'avoir le mal de mer

9 *(in generalizations)* **a triangle has three sides** le triangle a trois côtés; **a computer is a useful machine** les ordinateurs sont des machines bien utiles

10 *(before uncountable nouns)* **a wide knowledge of the subject** une connaissance approfondie du sujet; **he felt a joy he could not conceal** il éprouvait une joie qu'il ne pouvait dissimuler

11 *(before verbal nouns)* **there's been a general falling off in sales** il y a eu une chute des ventes

12 *(taking definite article in French)* **to have a red nose** avoir le nez rouge; **I have a sore throat/back/knee** j'ai mal à la gorge/au dos/au genou; **to have a taste for sth** avoir le goût de qch

13 *(before personal names)* **a Miss Jones was asking for you** une certaine Miss Jones vous a demandé; **he's been described as a new James Dean** on le donne pour le nouveau James Dean

14 *(before names of artists)* **it's a genuine Matisse** c'est un Matisse authentique; **there's a new Stephen King/Spielberg out next month** il y a un nouveau Stephen King/Spielberg qui sort le mois prochain

15 *(after half, rather, such, what)* **half a glass of wine** un demi-verre de vin; **she's rather an interesting person** c'est quelqu'un d'assez intéressant; **you're such an idiot!** tu es tellement bête!; **what a lovely dress!** quelle jolie robe!

16 *(after as, how, too + adj)* **that's too big a slice for me** cette tranche est trop grosse pour moi; **how big a bit do you want?** combien en veux-tu?; **she's as nice a girl as you could wish to meet** c'est la fille la plus gentille du monde

A-1 [ˌeɪ'wʌn] **ADJ 1** *(first-class, perfect)* **everything's A-1** tout est parfait **2** *(in health)* **to be A-1** être en pleine santé *ou* forme **3** *Naut* en excellent état

A3 [ˌeɪ'θriː] *Typ* **N** *(paper size)* format *m* A3

ADJ A3 paper papier *m* (format) A3

A4 [ˌeɪ'fɔː(r)] *Typ* **N** *(paper size)* format *m* A4

ADJ A4 paper papier *m* (format) A4

AA[1] [ˌeɪ'eɪ] **ADJ** *Mil* (*abbr* **anti-aircraft**) DCA *f*; **AA fire/guns** tir *m*/canons *mpl* de DCA

N 1 *Aut* (*abbr* **Automobile Association**) = automobile club britannique et compagnie d'assurances, qui garantit le dépannage de ses adhérents et propose des services touristiques et juridiques, ACF *m*, TCF *m*

2 (*abbr* **Alcoholics Anonymous**) AA *mpl*; **an AA meeting** une réunion des alcooliques anonymes

3 *Mktg* (*abbr* **Advertising Association**) = organisme britannique dont le rôle est de veiller à la qualité des publicités et de défendre les intérêts des annonceurs et des agences de publicité

4 *Am Univ* (*abbr* **Associate in Arts**) *(person)* = titulaire d'un diplôme universitaire américain de lettres; *(qualification)* diplôme *m* universitaire américain de lettres

AA[2] [ˌdʌbəl'eɪ] **N** *Banking & St Exch* (notation *f*) AA *f*

AAA[1] **N 1** [ˌθriː'eɪz] *Formerly Sport* (*abbr* **Amateur Athletics Association**) = ancien nom de la fédération britannique d'athlétisme (remplacé en octobre 1991 par la "British Athletics Federation") **2** [ˌeɪeɪ'eɪ, ˌtrɪpəl'eɪ] *Aut* (*abbr* **American Automobile Association**) = automobile club américain, ACF *m*, TCF *m*

AAA[2] [ˌtrɪpəl'eɪ] **N** *Banking & St Exch* (notation *f*) AAA *f*

Aachen ['ɑːkən] **N** Aix-la-Chapelle

AAI [ˌeɪeɪ'aɪ] **N** *Br TV* (*abbr* **Audience Appreciation Index**) = indice de mesure de satisfaction du public

A & E [eɪən'diː] **N** *Br Med* (*abbr* **accident and emergency**) service *m* des urgences, urgences *fpl*

AAU [ˌeɪeɪ'juː] **N** *Am Sport* (*abbr* **Amateur Athletic Union**) = organisme chargé de superviser les manifestations sportives, en particulier dans les universités

AB[1] [ˌeɪ'biː] **N 1** *Am Univ* (*abbr* **Artium Baccalaureus**) *(person)* = titulaire d'une licence de lettres; *(qualification)* licence *f* de lettres **2** *Br Naut* (*abbr* **able-bodied seaman**) matelot *m* de deuxième classe

AB[2] (*written abbr* **Alberta**) Alberta *f*

ABA ['eɪbiː'eɪ] **N 1** *Boxing* (*abbr* **Amateur Boxing Association**) Association *f* de boxe amateur **2** *Law* (*abbr* **American Bar Association**) = association d'avocats américains qui sert de centre d'information et de formation continue à ses membres

aback [ə'bæk] **ADV to be taken a.** être pris au dépourvu, être interloqué; *Naut* être pris bout au vent; **I was quite taken a. by what he said** j'étais très surpris par ce qu'il m'a dit

abacus ['æbəkəs] (*pl* **abacuses** *or* **abaci** [-saɪ]) **N** boulier *m*

abaft [ə'bɑːft] *Naut* **ADV** à l'arrière

PREP en arrière de

abalone [ˌæbə'ləʊnɪ] **N** *Ich* oreille-de-mer *f*, ormeau *m*

abandon [ə'bændən] **VT 1** *(leave* ► *person, object)* abandonner; *(*► *post, place)* déserter, quitter; *Naut* **to a. ship** abandonner *ou* quitter le navire; **we had to a. the car in the snow** nous avons dû abandonner la voiture dans la neige; **they were abandoned to their fate** on les abandonna à leur sort; *Fig* **to a. oneself to despair** se laisser aller *ou* s'abandonner au désespoir **2** *(give up* ► *search)* abandonner, renoncer à; *(*► *studies, struggle)* renoncer à; *(*► *idea, cause)* laisser tomber; *Comput (file, routine)* abandonner; **we abandoned the struggle** nous avons renoncé à lutter; *Sport* **to a. play** *(temporarily)* interrompre la partie; *(permanently)* annuler la partie; **the match was abandoned because of bad weather** on a interrompu le match en raison du mauvais temps; **to a. all hope (of doing sth)** abandonner tout espoir (de faire qch) **3** *Ins (for insurance)* **they abandoned the car to the insurance company** ils ont cédé la voiture à la compagnie d'assurances

N 1 *(neglect)* abandon *m*; **in a state of a.** laissé à l'abandon **2** *(lack of inhibition)* désinvolture *f*, laisser-aller *m*; **they leapt about with wild** *or* **gay a.** ils sautaient de joie sans aucune retenue

abandoned [ə'bændənd] **ADJ 1** *(person)* abandonné, délaissé; *(house, car, settlement)* abandonné; **the building had an a. look** le bâtiment avait l'air abandonné **2** *Old-fashioned (dissolute*

▸ *behaviour, person)* débauché; (▸ *life)* de débauche

abandonment [əˈbændənmənt] **N** abandon *m*

abase [əˈbeɪs] **VT** *Literary* **to a. oneself** s'humilier, s'abaisser

abasement [əˈbeɪsmənt] **N** *Literary* humiliation *f*

abashed [əˈbæʃt] **ADJ** penaud; **to be** *or* **to feel a. (at sth)** avoir honte (de qch)

abate [əˈbeɪt] **VI** *(storm, fear, anger)* s'apaiser; *(pain)* se calmer; *(flood)* baisser; *(noise)* s'atténuer

abatement [əˈbeɪtmənt] **N** *(of storm, fear, anger)* apaisement *m*; *(of pain, of noise)* atténuation *f*; *(of flood)* abaissement *m*

> Note that the French word **abattement** is a false friend and is never a translation for the English word **abatement**. Its most common meaning is **despondency**.

abattoir [ˈæbətwɑː(r)] **N** abattoirs *mpl*

abbess [ˈæbes] **N** *Rel* abbesse *f*

abbey [ˈæbɪ] **N** *Rel* abbaye *f*; **Westminster A.** l'abbaye de Westminster
COMP *(grounds)* de l'abbaye

abbot [ˈæbət] **N** *Rel* abbé *m (dans un monastère)*

abbreviate [əˈbriːvɪeɪt] **VT** *(text, title)* abréger; **"for example" is abbreviated to "eg"** "par exemple" est abrégé en "p. ex."

abbreviation [əˌbriːvɪˈeɪʃən] **N** *(of expression, title, word)* abréviation *f*; **"Dr" is the a. for "doctor"** "Dr" est l'abréviation de "docteur"

ABC[1] [ˈeɪbiːˈsiː], *Am* **ABCs** [eɪbiːˈsiz] **N 1** *(rudiments)* rudiments *mpl*, b.a.-ba *m*; **the A. of woodwork** le b.a.-ba de la menuiserie **2** *Ling (alphabet)* alphabet *m*; **it's as easy as A.** c'est simple comme bonjour

ABC[2] **N 1** *TV* (*abbr* **American Broadcasting Company**) = chaîne de télévision américaine **2** *TV* (*abbr* **Australian Broadcasting Corporation**) = chaîne de télévision australienne

abdicate [ˈæbdɪkeɪt] **VT 1** *Pol (of monarch)* **to a. the throne** abdiquer **2** *Law (right)* renoncer à; *(responsibility)* abandonner
VI abdiquer

abdication [ˌæbdɪˈkeɪʃən] **N 1** *Pol (of throne)* abdication *f* **2** *Law (of right)* renonciation *f*; *(of responsibility)* abandon *m*

abdomen [ˈæbdəmən] **N** *Anat* abdomen *m*

abdominal [æbˈdɒmɪnəl] **ADJ** *Anat* abdominal
▸▸ ***abdominal muscles*** abdominaux *mpl*

abdominoplasty [æbˈdɒmɪnəʊˌplæstɪ] **N** *Med* abdominoplastie *f*

abduct [æbˈdʌkt] **VT** *Law* enlever, kidnapper

abduction [æbˈdʌkʃən] **N** *Law* rapt *m*, enlèvement *m*

abductor [əbˈdʌktə(r)] **N 1** *Law (of person)* ravisseur(euse) *m,f* **2** *Anat* (muscle *m*) abducteur *m*

abeam [əˈbiːm] **ADV** *Naut & Aviat* par le travers

abed [əˈbed] **ADV** *Literary* dans son lit, au lit

aberrant [æˈberənt] **ADJ** *(gen) & Biol* aberrant

aberration [ˌæbəˈreɪʃən] **N 1** *(action, idea)* aberration *f*; **a mental a.** une aberration mentale; **it's an a.** c'est aberrant; **in a moment of a.** dans un moment de folie **2** *Astron, Biol & Opt* aberration *f*

abet [əˈbet] *(pt & pp* **abetted**, *cont* **abetting)** **VT** *(aid)* aider; *(encourage)* encourager; *Law* **to a. sb in a crime** aider qn à commettre un crime

abetting [əˈbetɪŋ] **N** *Law* **aiding and a.** complicité *f*

abeyance [əˈbeɪəns] **N** *Formal* **1** *(disuse)* désuétude *f*; **to fall into a.** tomber en dé-suétude; **the law is in temporary a.** la loi a momentanément cessé d'être appliquée; *Law* **estate in a.** succession *f* vacante **2** *(suspense)* suspens *m*; **the question was left in a.** la question a été laissée en suspens;

abhor [əbˈhɔː(r)] *(pt & pp* **abhorred**, *cont* **abhorring)** **VT** *Formal* détester, avoir en horreur; **nature abhors a vacuum** la nature a horreur du vide

abhorrence [əbˈhɒrəns] **N** *Formal* aversion *f*, horreur *f*; **to have an a. of sth, to hold sth in a.** avoir horreur de qch *ou* une aversion pour qch, avoir qch en horreur

abhorrent [əbˈhɒrənt] **ADJ** *Formal (detestable* ▸ *practice, attitude)* odieux, exécrable; **I find their attitude a., their attitude is a. to me** je trouve leur attitude détestable

abide [əˈbaɪd] *(pt & pp* **abode** [əˈbəʊd] *or* **abided)**
VT *(tolerate)* supporter; **she can't a. him** elle ne peut pas le souffrir *ou* supporter; **I can't a. people smoking in restaurants** je ne peux pas supporter les gens qui fument au restaurant; **if there's one thing I can't a., it's hypocrisy** s'il y a quelque chose que je ne supporte pas, c'est l'hypocrisie;
VI *Literary* **1** *(live)* demeurer, habiter; *Rel* **a. with me** restez avec moi **2** *(endure)* continuer, durer

▸**abide by VT INSEP** *Law (decision, law)* se conformer à, respecter; *(promise)* tenir; *(result)* supporter, assumer; **I a. by my decision/what I said** je maintiens ma décision/ce que j'ai dit

abiding [əˈbaɪdɪŋ] **ADJ** constant, permanent; *(impression)* durable; **an a. sense of gratitude** un sentiment de gratitude éternelle; **my a. memory of him is his generosity** je garde de lui le souvenir de quelqu'un de très généreux;

ability [əˈbɪlətɪ] *(pl* **abilities)** **N 1** *(mental or physical)* capacité *f*, capacités *fpl*, aptitude *f*; **he has great a.** il a beaucoup de capacités, il est très capable; **to lack a.** manquer de capacités; **children at different levels of a./of different abilities** des enfants de niveaux intellectuels différents/aux compétences diverses; **I'll do it to the best of my a.** je le ferai du mieux que je peux, je ferai de mon mieux **2** *(special talent)* capacités *fpl*, aptitude *f*; *(artistic or musical)* dons *mpl*, capacités *fpl*; **her acting a.** *or* **abilities remained unrecognized** ses talents d'actrice sont restés méconnus

abject [ˈæbdʒekt] **ADJ 1** *(despicable* ▸ *person, deed)* abject, vil **2** *(servile* ▸ *apology, flattery)* servile **3** *(miserable)* misérable; **they live in a. poverty** ils vivent dans une misère noire

abjectly [ˈæbdʒektlɪ] **ADV 1** *(despicably* ▸ *act, refuse)* de manière abjecte **2** *(in a servile manner)* avec servilité, servilement **3** *(miserably)* misérablement

abjure [əbˈdʒʊə(r)] **VT** *Formal (belief, faith)* renier; *(religion)* abjurer; *(right)* renoncer à;

ablative [ˈæblətɪv] **N** *Gram* ablatif *m*
▸▸ ***ablative absolute*** ablatif *m* absolu; ***the ablative case*** l'ablatif *m*

ablaze [əˈbleɪz] **ADJ 1** *(on fire)* en flammes; **the factory was already a. when the firemen arrived** l'usine était déjà en flammes lorsque les pompiers sont arrivés **2** *(luminous)* **a. with light** brillant de lumière; **the offices were a. with light** toutes les lumières brillaient dans les bureaux **3** *(face)* brillant; *(eyes)* enflammé, pétillant; **her eyes were a. with anger** ses yeux étaient enflammés de colère
ADV to set sth a. embraser qch

able [ˈeɪbəl] *(compar* **abler**, *superl* **ablest)** **ADJ 1** *(capable)* **to be a. to do sth** *(know how)* savoir faire qch, être capable de faire qch; *(be physically capable)* pouvoir faire qch; *(succeed)* réussir à faire qch; **I won't be a. to come** je ne pourrai pas venir; **I wasn't a. to see** je ne voyais pas; **she wasn't a. to explain** elle était incapable d'expliquer; **I haven't been a. to find out very much** je n'ai pas pu savoir grand-chose; **I'm not a. to tell you** je ne suis pas en mesure de vous le dire; **she's better** *or* **more a. to explain than I am** elle est mieux à même de vous expliquer que moi **2** *(competent)* capable; **an a. piece of work** un travail compétent *ou* bien fait **3** *(talented)* talentueux, de talent
▸▸ *Naut* ***able seaman*** matelot *m* breveté

> **SUFFIXE**
>
> **-ABLE, -ABILITY, -IBLE, -IBILITY**
>
> • Le suffixe **-able** or **-ible**, ajouté à la racine d'un verbe, crée un adjectif qui indique la double notion de passivation et de POSSIBILITÉ. Les adjectifs de ce type sont très nombreux en anglais et se traduisent le plus souvent (mais pas systématiquement) par un adjectif formé sur le même modèle en français:
>
> **doable** faisable; **believable** croyable; **divisible** divisible; **digestible** digeste; **collectable** ou **collectible** prisé par les collectionneurs.
>
> Parfois la racine n'est pas celle d'un verbe anglais mais celle d'un terme d'origine latine:
>
> **edible** comestible; **possible** possible; **tenable** défendable.
>
> On peut créer une infinité d'adjectifs plus ou moins familiers en ajoutant **-able** (mais pas **-ible**) à presque n'importe quel verbe, y compris les verbes à particule:
>
> **a shoutable slogan** un slogan que l'on peut scander; **a runnable distance** une distance que l'on peut parcourir en courant; **a stick-on-able label** une étiquette que l'on peut coller.
>
> L'adjectif **unputdownable** est particulièrement intéressant: il est formé à partir du verbe **to put down** (poser) et s'emploie pour parler d'un livre tellement passionnant que le lecteur ne peut se résoudre à le poser.
>
> • Le suffixe **-able** sert également à former à partir de noms des adjectifs indiquant une QUALITÉ. La traduction de ces adjectifs varie selon les cas:
>
> **comfortable** confortable; **reasonable** raisonnable; **knowledgeable** bien informé; **fashionable** à la mode.
>
> • On peut également créer des noms à partir d'une racine verbale en ajoutant **-ability** ou **-ibility**:
>
> **accessibility** accessibilité; **reversibility** réversibilité; **marketability** possibilité de commercialisation; **suitability** caractère convenable; **washability** fait d'être lavable.
>
> Tous ces noms véhiculent la notion de possibilité. (Pour véhiculer la notion de qualité, les noms sont le plus souvent construits avec le suffixe **-ness**: **reasonableness** caractère raisonnable.)
>
> Il est possible de créer de nombreux noms plus ou moins familiers grâce au suffixe **-ability**:
>
> **the danceability of a song** le caractère dansable d'une chanson; **the unputdownability of a book** le caractère passionnant d'un livre.

able-bodied **ADJ** robuste, solide; **every a. person helped in the search** toute personne en état de le faire a participé aux recherches
▸▸ *Naut* ***able-bodied seaman*** matelot *m* breveté

ablutions [əˈbluːʃənz] **NPL 1** *Rel* ablution *f* **2** *Hum (washing)* **to do** *or* **to perform one's a.** faire ses ablutions **3** *Fam Mil slang (building)* lavabos *mpl*

ably [ˈeɪblɪ] **ADV** d'une façon compétente; **she performed a. in the 100 metres** elle s'est bien comportée dans le 100 mètres; **a. assisted by** efficacement assisté par

abnegation [ˌæbnɪˈgeɪʃən] **N** *Formal Law* abnégation *f*

abnormal [æbˈnɔːməl] **ADJ** anormal
▸▸ *Psy* ***abnormal psychology*** psychopathologie *f*

abnormality [ˌæbnɔːˈmælətɪ] *(pl* **abnormalities)** **N 1** *(abnormal state, condition etc)* anormalité *f*, caractère *m* anormal **2** *(abnormal feature) & Med & Biol* anomalie *f*; *(physical deformity)* malformation *f*;

abnormally [æbˈnɔːməlɪ] **ADV** anormalement; **he was a. shy** il était d'une timidité maladive

abo [ˈæbəʊ] *(pl* **abos)** **N** *Austr Fam* = terme injurieux désignant un aborigène

aboard [əˈbɔːd] **ADV** à bord; **to go a.** monter à bord; **to take sth a.** embarquer qch; **all a.!** *Naut* tout le monde à bord!; *Rail* en voiture!; **welcome a.!** *(onto ship, aeroplane)* bienvenue à bord!; *Fig (onto team)* bienvenue dans l'équipe!
PREP *(ship, aeroplane)* à bord de; *(train, bus)* dans; **a. ship** à bord du bateau

abode [əˈbəʊd] *pt & pp of* **abide**
N *Formal or Literary* demeure *f*; **welcome to my humble a.** bienvenu dans mon petit chez-moi; *Law* **place of a.** domicile *m*; **of no fixed a.** sans domicile fixe; *Law* **right of a.** droit *m* de séjour

abolish [əˈbɒlɪʃ] **VT** *(privilege, slavery, custom)* abolir; *(right)* supprimer; *(law)* supprimer, abroger

abolition [ˌæbəˈlɪʃən] **N** *(of privilege, slavery, custom)* abolition *f*; *(of right)* suppression *f*; *(of law)* suppression *f*, abrogation *f*

A-bomb **N** *Mil* bombe *f* A

abominable [əˈbɒmɪnəbəl] **ADJ 1** *(very bad)* abominable, lamentable, affreux **2** *(odious)* abominable, odieux

▸▸ ***the abominable snowman*** l'abominable homme *m* des neiges

abominably [əˈbɒmɪnəblɪ] **ADV 1** *(very badly)* abominablement, lamentablement, affreusement **2** *(as intensifier)* extrêmement, abominablement; **it's a. difficult** c'est abominablement difficile **3** *(odiously)* abominablement, odieusement

abominate [əˈbɒmɪneɪt] **VT** *Formal* détester, exécrer

abomination [əˌbɒmɪˈneɪʃən] **N 1** *Formal (loathing)* abomination *f*; **we hold such behaviour in a.** ce genre de comportement nous fait horreur *ou* nous horrifie **2** *Formal (detestable act)* abomination *f*, acte *m* abominable **3** *(awful thing)* abomination *f*, chose *f* abominable; **the building is an a.** l'immeuble est une abomination

aboriginal [ˌæbəˈrɪdʒənəl] **ADJ 1** *(culture, legend)* aborigène, des aborigènes **2** *Bot & Zool* aborigène

• **Aboriginal** **ADJ** aborigène, des aborigènes **N** *(person)* aborigène *mf* (d'Australie)

aborigine [ˌæbəˈrɪdʒənɪ] **N** *(original inhabitant)* aborigène *mf*

ADJ aborigène, des aborigènes

• **Aborigine** **N 1** *(person)* aborigène *mf* (d'Australie) **2** *(language)* langue *f* aborigène

• **aborigines** **NPL** *Bot & Zool* flore *f* et faune *f* aborigènes

abort [əˈbɔːt] **N 1** *(of mission, spacecraft)* interruption *f* **2** *Comput (of program)* suspension *f* d'exécution, abandon *m*

VT 1 *(mission, flight)* interrompre, mettre un terme à; *(plan)* faire échouer **2** *Med (woman)* avorter; **the foetus was aborted** la grossesse a été interrompue **3** *Comput (program)* suspendre l'exécution de, abandonner

VI 1 *(mission, plans)* avorter, échouer; *Aviat (flight)* avorter; **the controller gave the order to a.** l'aiguilleur du ciel a donné l'ordre d'abandonner *ou* de suspendre le vol **2** *Med (woman)* avorter; *(foetus)* ne pas tenir

abortion [əˈbɔːʃən] **N 1** *Med* avortement *m*, interruption *f* (volontaire) de grossesse; **to have an a.** se faire avorter; **to perform an a.** faire un avortement; **a. on demand** avortement *m* libre **2** *(of plans, mission)* avortement *m* **3** *very Fam (person, animal)* avorton *m*, monstre *m*

▸▸ ***abortion clinic*** clinique *f* d'avortement; ***abortion law*** loi *f* sur l'avortement; ***abortion pill*** pilule *f* abortive

abortionist [əˈbɔːʃənɪst] **N 1** *Med (practitioner)* avorteur(euse) *m,f* **2** *Law (advocate)* partisan *m* de l'avortement (légal)

abortive [əˈbɔːtɪv] **ADJ** *(plan, mission)* avorté, manqué; *(attempt)* manqué

abound [əˈbaʊnd] **VI** *(fish, resources)* abonder; *(explanations, ideas)* abonder, foisonner; **to a. in** *or* **with sth** abonder en qch, regorger de qch; **the area abounds in** *or* **with natural resources** la région abonde en *ou* regorge de ressources naturelles

ABOUT [əˈbaʊt]

PREP	
• à propos de **1**	• au sujet de **1**
• concernant **1**	• partout **4**
• autour de **5**	
ADV	
• environ **1**	• à peu près **1**
• dans les parages **2**	• par ici **2**
• sur le point de **5**	

PREP 1 *(concerning, on the subject of)* à propos de, au sujet de, concernant; **she's had a letter a. the loan** elle a reçu une lettre concernant le prêt; **I'm worried a. her** je suis inquiet à son sujet; **what are they talking a.?** de quoi parlent-ils?; **what are you talking a.? of course I remembered!** qu'est-ce que tu racontes? bien sûr que j'y ai pensé!; **I don't know a. you, but I fancy a drink** toi, je ne sais pas, mais moi je boirais bien un verre; **I'm not happy a. her going** ça ne me plaît pas qu'elle y aille; **there's no doubt a. it** cela ne fait aucun doute, il n'y a aucun doute là-dessus; **now, a. your request for a salary increase...** bon, en ce qui concerne votre demande d'augmentation...; **OK, what's this all a.?** bon, qu'est-ce qui se passe?; **what's the book a.?** c'est un livre sur quoi?; **it's a book a. the life of Mozart** c'est un livre sur la vie de Mozart; **I don't know what all the fuss is a.** je ne vois pas pourquoi tout le monde se met dans cet état; **what do you want to see me a.?** vous voulez me voir à quel sujet?; **that's what life's all a.** c'est ça la vie; **he asked us a. the war** il nous a posé des questions sur la guerre; **you should do something a. your headaches** vous devriez faire quelque chose pour vos maux de tête; **I can't do anything a. it** je n'y peux rien; **what do YOU know a. it?** qu'est-ce que vous en savez, vous?; **I don't know much a. Egyptian art** je ne m'y connais pas beaucoup en art égyptien; **I didn't know a. your accident** je ne savais pas que vous aviez eu un accident; **tell me a. your holidays** parle-moi de tes vacances; **I was thinking a. my mother** je pensais à ma mère; **I warned them a. the political situation** je les ai mis en garde en ce qui concerne la situation politique; **how** *or* **what a. a game of bridge/going to Paris?** si on faisait un bridge/allait à Paris?

2 *(in the character of)* **there's something strange about her** il y a quelque chose de bizarre chez elle **what I don't like a. the house is all the stairs** ce qui me déplaît dans cette maison, ce sont tous les escaliers; **she found something amusing a. the situation** elle a trouvé que la situation avait quelque chose d'amusant

3 *(busy with)* **while I'm a. it** pendant que j'y suis; **be quick a. it!** faites vite!, dépêchez-vous!

4 *(all over)* partout; **there were clothes lying all a. the room** il y avait des vêtements qui traînaient partout; **you mustn't leave money lying a. the house** il ne faut pas laisser de l'argent traîner dans la maison; **the children were running a. the garden** les enfants couraient dans le jardin

5 *(surrounding)* autour de; **the people a. us** les gens auprès de nous, les gens qui nous entourent; **it's good to have a few new faces a. the place** c'est bien de voir de nouvelles têtes par ici; **there is a high wall a. the castle** un rempart entoure le château

6 *Formal (on)* **to have sth a. one's person** avoir qch sur soi; **he had a dangerous weapon a. his person** il portait une arme dangereuse

ADV 1 *(more or less)* environ, à peu près; **a. a year** environ *ou* à peu près un an; **a. £50** 50 livres environ; **a. five o'clock** vers cinq heures; **she's a. my age** elle a à peu près mon âge; **that looks a. right** ça a l'air d'être à peu près ça; **he's a. as tall as you** il est à peu près de ta taille; **you've got a. as much intelligence as a two-year-old!** tu es à peu près aussi futé qu'un gamin de deux ans!; **I've just a. finished** j'ai presque fini; **I've had just a. enough!** j'en ai vraiment assez!; **it's a. time** il serait *ou* est temps; **it's a. time you started** il serait grand temps que vous vous y mettiez; **that's a. it for now** c'est à peu près tout pour l'instant

2 *(somewhere near)* dans les parages, par ici; **is there anyone a.?** il y a quelqu'un?; **is Jack a.?** est-ce que Jack est là?; **there was no one a. when I left the building** il n'y avait personne dans les parages quand j'ai quitté l'immeuble; **my keys must be a. somewhere** mes clés doivent être quelque part par ici; **there weren't many people a.** il n'y avait pas grand monde

3 *(in all directions, places)* **there's a lot of flu a.** il y a beaucoup de grippe en ce moment; **watch out, there are pickpockets a.** méfie-toi, il y a beaucoup de pickpockets qui traînent; **there are some terrible rumours going a.** il court des rumeurs terribles; **to run a.** courir dans tous les sens; **to follow sb a.** suivre qn partout; **don't leave your money lying a.** ne laissez pas traîner votre argent; **they've been sitting a. all day** ils ont passé toute la journée assis à ne rien faire; **she was waving her arms a.** elle agitait les bras dans tous les sens

4 *(in opposite direction)* **to turn a.** se retourner; **the other way a.** en sens inverse, dans le sens contraire

5 *(expressing imminent action)* **to be a. to do sth** être sur le point de faire qch; **what were you a. to say?** qu'est-ce que vous alliez dire?; **I was just a. to leave** j'allais partir, j'étais sur le point de partir

6 *(expressing reluctance)* **I'm not a. to answer that kind of question** je ne suis pas prêt à répondre à ce genre de question; **he's not a. to change his ways just because of that** il n'y a pas de risque qu'il change ses manières de faire rien que pour ça

about-turn, *Am* **about-face** **EXCLAM** *Mil (to right)* demi-tour...droite!; *(to left)* demi-tour...gauche!

VI 1 *Mil* faire un demi-tour **2** *(change opinion)* faire volte-face

N 1 *Mil* demi-tour *m*; **to do an a.** faire un demi-tour **2** *(change of opinion)* volte-face *f inv*; **to do an a.** faire volte-face

ABOVE [əˈbʌv]

PREP	
• au-dessus de **1, 2, 6**	• plus que **3**
• au-delà de **4**	• par-dessus **7**
ADJ	
• ci-dessus	
ADV	
• au-dessus **1**	• en haut **3**
• plus haut **4**	• là-haut **5**
• ci-dessus **4**	

PREP 1 *(in a higher place or position than)* au-dessus de; **a. our heads** au-dessus de nos têtes; **in the sky a. us** dans le ciel au-dessus de nous; **smoke rose a. the town** de la fumée s'élevait au-dessus de la ville; **a. the equator** au-dessus de l'équateur; **a. ground** en surface; **a. sea level** au-dessus du niveau de la mer; **the water reached a. their knees** l'eau leur montait jusqu'au-dessus des genoux; **skirts are a. the knee this year** les jupes se portent au-dessus du genou cette année; **they live a. the shop** ils habitent au-dessus du magasin; **a village on the river a. Oxford** un village (situé) en amont d'Oxford;

2 *(greater in degree or quantity than)* au-dessus de; **a. 40 kilos** au-dessus de 40 kilos; **a. $100** plus de 100 dollars; **it's a. my price limit** c'est au-dessus du prix *ou* ça dépasse le prix que je me suis fixé; **his temperature is a. normal** sa température est supérieure à *ou* au-dessus de la normale; **the temperature didn't rise a. 10°C** la température n'a pas dépassé 10°C; **a. average** au-dessus de la moyenne

3 *(in preference to)* plus que; **he values friendship a. success** il accorde plus d'importance à l'amitié qu'à la réussite; **he respected her a. all others** il la respectait entre toutes

4 *(beyond)* au-delà de; **the discussion was all rather a. me** la discussion me dépassait complètement

5 *(morally or intellectually superior to)* **she's a. that sort of thing** elle est au-dessus de ça; **a. suspicion/reproach** au-dessus de tout soupçon/reproche; **he's not a. cheating** il irait jusqu'à tricher; **I'm not a. asking for favours** je ne répugne pas à demander des faveurs; **she's not a. telling the occasional lie** il lui arrive de mentir de temps en temps **to get a. oneself** ne pas se prendre pour n'importe qui

6 *(superior in rank, quality to)* au-dessus de; **to marry a. one's station** se marier au-dessus de son rang; **she's ranked a. the other athletes** elle se classe devant les autres athlètes

7 *(in volume, sound)* par-dessus; **it's difficult to make oneself heard a. all this noise** il est difficile de se faire entendre avec tout ce bruit; **a scream rose a. the noise of the engines** un cri se fit entendre par-dessus le bruit des moteurs

ADJ *Formal* ci-dessus; *Admin* précité; **the a. facts** les faits cités plus haut; **the names on the a. list** les noms qui figurent sur la liste ci-dessus

ADV 1 *(in a higher place or position)* au-dessus; **the stars a.** le ciel constellé; **the people in the flat a.** les voisins du dessus; **to fall from a.** tomber d'en haut; **two lines a.** deux lignes plus haut

2 *(greater in degree or quantity)* **aged 20 and a.** âgé de 20 ans et plus; **£5 and a.** 5 livres ou plus

3 *(a higher rank or authority)* en haut; **we've had**

orders from a. nous avons reçu des ordres d'en haut

4 *(in book, document)* ci-dessus, plus haut; **the paragraph a.** le paragraphe ci-dessus; **as a.** comme ci-dessus

N *Formal* **the a.** *(fact, item)* ce qui se trouve ci-dessus; *(person)* le (la) susnommé(e); *(persons)* les susnommé(e)s; **the a. is a quotation from 'Hamlet'** le passage ci-dessus est une citation de 'Hamlet'

• **above all** ADV avant tout, surtout

above-board ADJ 1 *(person)* honnête, régulier 2 *(action, behaviour)* franc (franche), honnête

ADV 1 *(openly)* ouvertement, au grand jour 2 *(honestly)* honnêtement, de façon régulière 3 *(frankly)* franchement, cartes sur table

aboveground [ˌəbʌvˈgraʊnd] ADJ en surface

above-mentioned [-ˈmenʃənd] *(pl* **inv***)* *Formal* ADJ cité plus haut, susmentionné; *Admin* précité

N **the a.** *(person)* le (la) susmentionné(e)

above-the-line N *Mktg* publicité *f* média

ADJ *Acct (expenses)* au-dessus de la ligne

►► *Acct* ***above-the-line accounts*** comptes *mpl* de résultats courants; *Mktg* ***above-the-line advertising*** publicité *f* média; ***above-the-line costs*** *Acct* dépenses *fpl* au-dessus de la ligne; *Mktg* coûts *mpl* média; ***above-the-line expenditure*** *Acct* dépenses *fpl* de création; *Mktg* dépenses *fpl* média

abracadabra [ˌæbrəkəˈdæbrə] EXCLAM abracadabra!

abrasion [əˈbreɪʒən] N 1 *Tech (on surface)* abrasion *f* 2 *Med (on skin)* éraflure *f*, écorchure *f* 3 *Geol* abrasion *f*

abrasive [əˈbreɪsɪv] ADJ 1 *Tech (surface, substance)* abrasif 2 *(character)* rêche; *(criticism, wit)* corrosif; *(person, voice)* caustique

N *Tech* abrasif *m*

abreast [əˈbrest] ADV *(march, ride)* côte à côte, de front; **the children were cycling three a.** les enfants faisaient du vélo à trois de front; *Naut* **(in) line a.** en ligne de front

• **abreast of** PREP 1 *(alongside)* à la hauteur de, au même niveau que; *Naut* **their ship came** *or* **drew a. of ours** leur navire est arrivé à la hauteur du nôtre 2 *(in touch with)* **to be a. of sth** être au courant de qch; **to keep a. of recent research** rester informé *ou* au courant des recherches récentes; **she likes to keep a. of current affairs/the latest fashions** elle aime se tenir au courant de l'actualité/de la dernière mode

abridge [əˈbrɪdʒ] VT *(book)* abréger; *(article, play, speech)* écourter, abréger

abridged [əˈbrɪdʒd] ADJ abrégé

abridgment, abridgement [əˈbrɪdʒmənt] N 1 *(result)* résumé *m*, abrégé *m* 2 *(action)* abrègement *m*

abroad [əˈbrɔːd] ADV 1 *(overseas)* à l'étranger; **to go a.** aller à l'étranger; **to live/to study a.** vivre/faire ses études à l'étranger 2 *(over wide area)* au loin; *(in all directions)* de tous côtés, partout; **there are rumours a. about possible redundancies** le bruit court qu'il va y avoir des licenciements; **the news got a.** la nouvelle s'est répandue 3 *Literary (out of doors)* (au) dehors; **to venture a.** sortir (de la maison)

abrogate [ˈæbrəgeɪt] VT *Law* abroger, abolir

abrogation [ˌæbrəˈgeɪʃən] N *Law* abrogation *f*

abrupt [əˈbrʌpt] ADJ 1 *(sudden* ► *change, drop, movement)* brusque, soudain; *(*► *laugh, question)* brusque; *(*► *departure)* brusque, précipité, brutal; **the evening came to an a. end** la soirée s'acheva brusquement; **there was an a. change in the weather** le temps a changé brutalement

2 *(behaviour, person* ► *on one occasion)* brusque; *(*► *character trait)* bourru, abrupt

3 *(style)* haché, décousu

4 *(slope)* abrupt, raide

abruptly [əˈbrʌptlɪ] ADV 1 *(change, drop, move)* brusquement, tout à coup; *(ask, laugh, interrupt)* abruptement; *(depart)* brusquement, précipitamment 2 *(behave, speak)* avec brusquerie, brusquement 3 *(fall, rise)* en pente raide, à pic

abruptness [əˈbrʌptnɪs] N 1 *(of change, drop, movement)* soudaineté *f*; *(of departure)* précipitation *f*

2 *(of behaviour, person)* brusquerie *f*, rudesse *f*

3 *(of style)* décousu *m*

4 *(of slope)* raideur *f*

ABS [ˈeɪbiːˈes] N *Aut (abbr* **Anti-lock Braking System***)* ABS *m*

abs [æbz] NPL *Fam (abdominal muscles)* abdos *mpl*

abscess [ˈæbsɪs, ˈæbses] N *Med* abcès *m*

abscond [əbˈskɒnd] VI *Formal Law* soustraire à la justice; **to a. from prison** s'échapper de prison, s'évader; *Hum* **he absconded with our money** il s'est enfui avec notre argent

absconder [əbˈskɒndə(r)] N *Formal Law (gen)* fugitif(ive) *m,f*; *(from prison)* évadé(e) *m,f*

absconding [əbˈskɒndɪŋ] N *Formal Law (gen)* fuite *f*; *(from prison)* évasion *f*

► **abseil down** VI *Sport* descendre en rappel

abseiling [ˈæbseɪlɪŋ] N *Sport* (descente *f* en) rappel *m*

absence [ˈæbsəns] N 1 *(state of being away)* absence *f*; **in** *or* **during my a.** pendant mon absence; **in the a. of the manager** en l'absence du directeur; *Prov* **a. makes the heart grow fonder** l'éloignement renforce l'affection

2 *(instance of being away)* absence *f*; **unexcused absences from school** absences *fpl* injustifiées

3 *(lack)* absence *f*; **in the a. of adequate information** en l'absence d'informations satisfaisantes, faute de renseignements

4 *Law* non-comparution *f*, défaut *m*; **he was tried in his a.** il fut jugé par contumace

absent ADJ [ˈæbsənt] 1 *(not present)* absent; **he was a. from the meeting** il n'a pas participé à la réunion; *Mil* **to be** *or* **to go a. without leave** être absent sans permission, être porté manquant; **to a. friends!** *(toast)* à tous nos amis absents! 2 *(lacking)* absent; **all signs of warmth were a. from her voice** il n'y avait aucune chaleur dans sa voix 3 *(inattentive* ► *person)* distrait; *(*► *manner)* absent, distrait

VT [æbˈsent] **to a. oneself (from sth)** *(leave)* s'absenter (de qch); *(not attend)* être absent (à qch)

absentee [ˌæbsənˈtiː] N *(someone not present)* absent(e) *m,f*; *(habitually)* absentéiste *mf*

ADJ absentéiste

►► *Law* ***absentee landlord*** propriétaire *m* absentéiste

absenteeism [ˌæbsənˈtiːɪzəm] N absentéisme *m*

absently [ˈæbsəntlɪ] ADV distraitement

absent-minded [-ˈmaɪndɪd] ADJ *(person)* distrait; *(manner)* absent, distrait; *Fam* **he's the perfect example of an a. professor** c'est un vrai professeur Tournesol

absent-mindedly [-ˈmaɪndɪdlɪ] ADV distraitement, d'un air distrait; **she a. left it on the train** elle l'a laissé dans le train par distraction

absent-mindedness [-ˈmaɪndɪdnɪs] N distraction *f*, absence *f*

absinth, absinthe [ˈæbsɪnθ] N absinthe *f*

absolute [ˈæbsəluːt] ADJ 1 *(as intensifier)* absolu, total; **what a. nonsense!** quelles bêtises, vraiment!; **he's an a. idiot** c'est un parfait crétin *ou* imbécile; **the whole thing is an a. mess** c'est un véritable gâchis *ou* un vrai fatras

2 *(entire* ► *secrecy, truth)* absolu

3 *Pol (unlimited* ► *power)* absolu, souverain; *(*► *ruler, monarch)* absolu

4 *(definite, unconditional* ► *decision, refusal)* absolu, formel; *(*► *fact)* indiscutable; *(* ► *proof)* formel, irréfutable

5 *(independent, not relative)* absolu; **in a. terms** en valeurs absolues

6 *Law (court order, decree)* définitif; **the decree was made a.** le décret a été prononcé

N *Phil* **the a.** l'absolu *m*

►► *Pol* ***absolute majority*** majorité *f* absolue; *Am Mus* ***absolute pitch*** oreille *f* absolue; *Law & Pol* ***absolute veto*** véto *m* absolu *ou* formel; *Phys* ***absolute zero*** zéro *m* absolu

absolutely [ˈæbsəluːtlɪ] ADV 1 *(as intensifier)* vraiment; **she's a. adorable!** elle est vraiment adorable! 2 *(in expressing opinions)* absolument; **I a. agree** je suis tout à fait d'accord; **I a. refuse** je refuse catégoriquement; **but he's an excellent teacher – oh, a.!** mais c'est un excellent professeur – oh, absolument *ou* mais certainement!; **do you agree? – a. not!** êtes-vous d'accord? – absolument pas! 3 *(deny, refuse)* absolument, formellement; **I a. insist that you attend the meeting** je tiens absolument à ce que vous soyez présent à la réunion; **it is a. forbidden** c'est absolument *ou* formellement interdit

absolution [ˌæbsəˈluːʃən] N absolution *f*; **to grant sb a.** promettre à qn l'absolution

absolutism [ˈæbsəluːtɪzəm] N *Pol* absolutisme *m*

absolve [əbˈzɒlv] VT 1 *(from blame, sin etc)* absoudre (**from** *or* **of** de); *(from obligation)* décharger, délier (**from** *or* **of** de); **to a. sb from** *or* **of all blame** décharger qn de toute responsabilité 2 *Law* acquitter (**of** de)

absorb [əbˈsɔːb] VT 1 *also Fig (changes, cost, light, liquid, heat)* absorber; *(surplus)* absorber, résorber; *(idea, information)* absorber, assimiler; *(loss)* essuyer; **black absorbs heat** le noir absorbe la chaleur; **the project absorbed all my time** ce projet a pris tout mon temps; **it's too much to a. all in one day** cela en fait trop à absorber pour une seule journée

2 *(shock, sound)* amortir

3 *Com (incorporate* ► *company)* absorber, incorporer; *(*► *group, people)* absorber, assimiler; *Fin (*► *debts)* absorber; **the newcomers were quickly absorbed into the community** les nouveaux venus ont été rapidement intégrés *ou* assimilés à la communauté

4 *(usu passive) (engross)* absorber; **to be/become absorbed in sth** être absorbé par/s'absorber dans qch; **she was absorbed in what she was doing** elle était absorbée par ce qu'elle faisait; **the task completely absorbed our attention** ce travail a complètement accaparé notre attention

absorbency [əbˈsɔːbənsɪ] N *(gen)* pouvoir *m* absorbant; *Chem & Phys* absorptivité *f*

absorbent [əbˈsɔːbənt] N absorbant *m*

ADJ absorbant

absorbing [əbˈsɔːbɪŋ] ADJ *(activity, book)* fascinant, passionnant; *(work)* absorbant, passionnant

absorption [əbˈsɔːpʃən] N 1 *(of light, liquid, heat)* absorption *f*; *(of surplus)* résorption *f*

2 *(of shock, sound)* amortissement *m*

3 *Com (of company)* absorption *f*, incorporation *f*; *(of group, people)* absorption *f*, assimilation *f*

4 *(fascination)* passion *f*, fascination *f*; *(concentration)* concentration *f* (d'esprit); **her a. in the book was so great that…** elle était tellement absorbée dans son livre que…

abstain [əbˈsteɪn] VI 1 *(refrain)* s'abstenir; **to a. from sth/doing sth** s'abstenir de qch/faire qch; **to a. from alcohol** s'abstenir de boire de l'alcool 2 *Pol & Admin (not vote)* s'abstenir

abstainer [əbˈsteɪnə(r)] N 1 *(teetotaller)* abstinent(e) *m,f*; **to be a total a.** ne pas boire d'alcool; **he's become a total a.** il a complètement arrêté de boire 2 *Pol & Admin (person not voting)* abstentionniste *mf*

abstemious [æbˈstiːmɪəs] ADJ *(person)* sobre, abstinent; *(diet, meal)* frugal

abstemiously [əbˈstiːmɪəslɪ] ADV sobrement; *(eat)* frugalement

abstemiousness [æbˈstiːmɪəsnɪs] N *(of person)* sobriété *f*, frugalité *f*; *(of diet, meal)* frugalité *f*

abstention [əbˈstenʃən] N 1 *(from action)* abstention *f*; *(from drink, food)* abstinence *f*; **their a. from making any comment** le fait qu'ils se soient abstenus de tout commentaire 2 *Pol & Admin (in vote)* abstention *f*

abstinence [ˈæbstɪnəns] N abstinence *f* (**from** de); *Rel* **day of a.** jour *m* d'abstinence

abstract ADJ [ˈæbstrækt] 1 *(number, noun, art)* abstrait 2 *(obscure)* abstrait, abstrus

N [ˈæbstrækt] 1 *(idea, term)* abstrait *m*; **in the a.** dans l'abstrait 2 *(summary)* résumé *m*, abrégé *m* 3 *Art (work of art)* œuvre *f* abstraite

VT [æbˈstrækt] 1 *Formal (remove)* extraire (**from** de)

2 *Euph or Hum (steal)* soustraire, dérober

3 *Phil (regard theoretically)* abstraire

4 *(summarize)* résumer, abréger

►► *Art* ***abstract artist*** artiste *m* abstrait, abstrait *m*

abstracted [æb'stræktɪd] ADJ *(preoccupied)* préoccupé, absorbé; *(absent-minded)* distrait

abstractedly [æb'stræktɪdlɪ] ADV distraitement, d'un air distrait

abstraction [æb'strækʃən] N **1** *(concept)* idée *f* abstraite, abstraction *f*

2 *Phil* abstraction *f*

3 *Formal (act of removing)* extraction *f*

4 *(preoccupation)* préoccupation *f*; *(absent-mindedness)* distraction *f*; **she wore her customary look of a.** elle avait son air distrait habituel

abstractly ['æbstræktlɪ] ADV abstraitement

abstruse [æb'stru:s] ADJ abstrus

abstruseness [æb'stru:snɪs] N caractère *m* abstrus

absurd [əb'sɜ:d] ADJ *(unreasonable)* absurde, insensé; *(ludicrous)* absurde, ridicule; **don't be a.!** ne sois pas ridicule!; **the idea is utterly a.** c'est une idée complètement ridicule *ou* idiote; **I feel/I look a. in this get-up** je me sens/j'ai l'air ridicule dans cet accoutrement

N *Phil* **the a.** l'absurde *m*

absurdity [əb'sɜ:dɪtɪ] (*pl* **absurdities**) N absurdité *f*; **the a. of paying people not to work** l'absurdité consistant à payer des gens à ne pas travailler

absurdly [əb'sɜ:dlɪ] ADV *(behave, dress)* d'une manière insensée, d'une façon absurde; *(as intensifier)* ridiculement; **rather a. I seem to have forgotten your name** c'est absurde mais je crois bien que j'ai oublié votre nom; **it was a. complicated** c'était d'une complexité absurde

ABTA ['æbtə] N (*abbr* **Association of British Travel Agents**) = association des agences de voyage britanniques

abundance [ə'bʌndəns] N **1** *(plenty)* abondance *f*, profusion *f*; **there was food in a.** il y avait à manger à profusion; **she has an a. of talent** elle est bourrée de talent **2** *Biol (of species etc)* abondance *f*

abundant [ə'bʌndənt] ADJ *(plentiful)* abondant (**in** en); **there's an a. supply of food** il y a des provisions (de nourriture) en quantité; **there is a. evidence that he's guilty** il y a de nombreuses preuves qui démontrent qu'il est coupable

abundantly [ə'bʌndəntlɪ] ADV **1** *(profusely)* abondamment; *(eat, serve)* abondamment, copieusement; *(grow)* à foison **2** *(as intensifier)* extrêmement; **it became a. clear that...** il devint tout à fait clair que...; **she made it a. clear that I was not welcome** elle me fit comprendre très clairement que j'étais indésirable

abuse N [ə'bju:s] **1** *(misuse)* abus *m* (**of** de); *Law* **a. of authority** abus *m* d'autorité *ou* de pouvoir; *Parl* **a. of privilege** abus *m* de droit; **a. of trust** abus de confiance **2** *(UNCOUNT) (insults)* injures *fpl*, insultes *fpl*; **to heap** *or* **to shower a. on sb** accabler qn d'injures **3** *(UNCOUNT) (cruel treatment)* mauvais traitements *mpl*

VT [ə'bju:z] **1** *(authority, position, someone's trust, patience)* abuser de; **a much abused word** un mot employé abusivement **2** *(insult)* injurier, insulter **3** *(treat cruelly)* maltraiter, malmener; *(sexually)* faire subir des sévices à

> Note that the French verb **abuser** never means **to insult**.

abuser [ə'bju:zə(r)] N abuseur(euse) *m,f*

abusive [ə'bju:sɪv] ADJ **1** *(language)* offensant, grossier; *(person)* grossier; *(phone call)* obscène; **to be a. to sb** être grossier envers qn **2** *(behaviour, treatment)* brutal; **an a. father** un père abuseur

abusively [ə'bju:sɪvlɪ] ADV **1** *(speak)* grossièrement **2** *(behave, treat)* brutalement

abutment [ə'bʌtmənt], **abuttal** [ə'bʌtəl] N **1** *(point of junction)* jointure *f*, point *m* de jonction **2** *Archit & Constr (support)* contrefort *m*; *(on bridge)* butée *f*, culée *f*; *(of arch)* piédroit *m*

abut on, abut against [ə'bʌt] (*pt & pp* **abutted**, *cont* **abutting**) VT INSEP **1** *Formal (adjoin)* être adjacent *ou* contigu à **2** *Archit & Constr* s'appuyer contre, buter contre

abysmal [ə'bɪzməl] ADJ **1** *(immeasurable)* infini, abyssal; **a. ignorance** une ignorance crasse **2** *(very bad)* épouvantable, exécrable

abysmally [ə'bɪzməlɪ] ADV atrocement; *(fail)* lamentablement; **a. ignorant** d'une ignorance profonde; **the area is a. lacking in good restaurants** le quartier est absolument dépourvu de bons restaurants

abyss [ə'bɪs] N *Geol Fig* abîme *m*, gouffre *m*; *(in sea)* abysse *m*

abyssal [ə'bɪsəl] ADJ *Geol* abyssal

Abyssinia [,æbɪ'sɪnɪə] N *Geog & Hist* Abyssinie *f*; **in A.** en Abyssinie

Abyssinian [,æbɪ'sɪnɪən] N **1** *(person)* Abyssinien(enne) *m,f* **2** *(language)* abyssinien *m*

ADJ abyssinien, abyssin

►► *Hist* **the Abyssinian Empire** l'empire *m* d'Éthiopie

AC [,eɪ'si:] N **1** *Elec* (*abbr* **alternating current**) courant *m* alternatif **2** *Tech* (*abbr* **air conditioning**) climatisation *f*

.ac ['dɒtei'si:, 'dɒt'æk] *Comput* (*abbr* **academic**) = abréviation désignant les universités et les sites éducatifs dans les adresses électroniques britanniques

a/c *Br Banking & Fin* (*written abbr* **account**) c

acacia [ə'keɪʃə] N *Bot* acacia *m*; **false a.** faux acacia *m*

academia [,ækə'di:mɪə] N *Univ* le milieu universitaire

academic [,ækə'demɪk] ADJ **1** *Sch & Univ (related to formal study* ► *of school)* scolaire; (► *of university)* universitaire; **we aim for a. excellence** notre objectif est l'excellence de notre enseignement; **her a. achievements are impressive** elle a fait de brillantes études; **the first a. study of...** la première étude faite par un universitaire de...

2 *(intellectual* ► *standard, style, work)* intellectuel; (► *person)* studieux, intellectuel; (► *subjects)* d'enseignement général

3 *Phil (theoretical)* théorique, spéculatif; *(not practical)* sans intérêt pratique, théorique; **their speculations were purely a.** leurs spéculations étaient purement théoriques; **out of a. interest** par simple curiosité; **whether he comes or not is all a.** qu'il vienne ou pas, cela n'a pas d'importance

4 *(conventional)* académique; *Art* **an a. painter** un peintre académique

N *Univ (university teacher)* universitaire *mf*; *(intellectual)* intellectuel(elle) *m,f*

►► **academic year** année *f* universitaire

academically [,ækə'demɪkəlɪ] ADV *(advanced, competent, talented)* sur le plan intellectuel; *(sound)* intellectuellement; **to be a. qualified** posséder les diplômes requis; **to be a. gifted** être doué intellectuellement; **she's not very a. inclined** elle n'est pas très douée pour les études; **the school doesn't have a tremendous reputation a.** l'école n'est pas fabuleusement cotée pour la qualité de son enseignement

academician [ə,kædə'mɪʃən] N *Univ* académicien(enne) *m,f*

academicism [,ækə'demɪsɪzəm], **academism** [ə'kædəmɪzəm] N *esp Pej Art* académisme *m*

academy [ə'kædəmɪ] (*pl* **academies**) N **1** *(society)* académie *f*, société *f* **2** *(school) Scot* lycée *m*; *Eng & Am (private)* collège *m* privé; **an a. of music** un conservatoire de musique; **riding a.** académie *f* d'équitation **3** *Cin* **the A. (of Motion Picture Arts and Sciences)** l'Académie *f* des arts et des sciences cinématographiques *(association américaine de professionnels du cinéma, répartis selon leur métier)*

►► *Cin* **Academy Award** oscar *m*

acai berry [æsæ'i:-] N baie *f* d'acai *ou* d'açaï

acanthus [ə'kænθəs] (*pl* **acanthuses** *or* **acanthi** [-θaɪ]) N **1** *Bot* acanthe *f* **2** *Archit* (feuille *f* d')acanthe *f*

a cappella [,ɑ:kə'pelə] *Mus* ADJ a cappella; **a. singing** chant *m* a cappella

ADV a cappella

Acapulco [,ækə'pʊlkəʊ] N Acapulco

acardiac [,eɪ'kɑ:dɪæk] ADJ *Med* acardiaque

ACAS ['eɪkæs] N *Ind* (*abbr* **Advisory, Conciliation and Arbitration Service**) = organisme britannique de conciliation et d'arbitrage des conflits du travail, conseil *m* de prud'hommes

accede [æk'si:d] VI *Formal* **1** *(agree)* agréer, accepter; **to a. to sth** *(demand, request)* donner suite *ou* accéder à qch; *(plan, suggestion)* accepter *ou* agréer qch **2 to a. to sth** *(attain)* accéder à qch; **to a. to the throne** monter sur le trône; **to a. to office** entrer en fonction **3** *Law* **to a. to a treaty** adhérer à un traité

accelerant [ək'selərənt] N *Chem* accélérateur *m*; **tanning a.** accélérateur *m* de bronzage

accelerate [ək'seləreɪt] VT *(pace, process, rhythm)* accélérer; *(decline, event)* précipiter, accélérer; *(work)* activer

VI **1** *(move faster)* s'accélérer **2** *Aut (driver)* accélérer

accelerated [ək'seləreɪtɪd] ADJ *(pace, process, rhythm)* accéléré

►► *Sch & Univ* **accelerated classes** cours *mpl ou* niveaux *mpl* accélérés; *Phys* **accelerated motion** accéléré *m*

acceleration [ək,selə'reɪʃən] N accélération *f*; **the car has good a.** cette voiture a une bonne accélération

►► *Fin* **acceleration clause** clause *f* accélératrice; *Fin* **acceleration premium** prime *f* de rendement; *Econ* **acceleration principle** principe *m* d'accélération

accelerator [ək'seləreɪtə(r)] N **1** *Aut (in vehicle)* accélérateur *m*; **to step on the a.** appuyer sur l'accélérateur, accélérer **2** *Phys & Comput* accélérateur *m*

►► *Comput* **accelerator board, accelerator card** carte *f* accélératrice; *Aut* **accelerator pedal** pédale *f* d'accélérateur; *Econ* **accelerator principle** principe *m* d'accélération

accent N ['æksent] **1** *Ling (way of speaking)* accent *m*; **she has** *or* **she speaks with a Spanish/Liverpool a.** elle a l'accent espagnol/de Liverpool; **she speaks French with/without an a.** elle parle français avec un/sans accent; **he has a strange a.** il a un drôle d'accent

2 *Gram & Mus (stress)* accent *m*; **the a. is on the final syllable** l'accent est sur la dernière syllabe

3 *Fig (emphasis)* accent *m*; **the a. here is on team work** ici on met l'accent sur le travail d'équipe; **fashion with the a. on youth** mode qui met l'accent sur la jeunesse

4 *Gram (written mark)* accent *m*

5 *(contrasting detail)* accent *m*; **the room is painted white with green accents** la pièce est peinte en blanc avec des touches de vert

VT [æk'sent] *(syllable etc)* accentuer

accented ['æksentɪd] ADJ *Gram* accentué

►► **accented character** caractère *m* accentué

accentuate [æk'sentjʊeɪt] VT **1** *(word)* accentuer, mettre l'accent sur **2** *(feature, importance)* souligner, accentuer; *(contrast)* accuser; **to a. the need for sth** accentuer la nécessité de qch; **the thin dress only accentuated her frailness** la robe légère ne faisait qu'accentuer *ou* que souligner son air fragile

accentuated [æk'sentjʊeɪtɪd] ADJ accentué; *(limp, stutter)* fortement marqué; *Mus* **the offbeat is a.** le temps faible est accentué

accentuation [æk,sentjʊ'eɪʃən] N accentuation *f*

accept [ək'sept] VT **1** *(take when offered* ► *apology, gift, invitation)* accepter; (► *advice, suggestion)* accepter, écouter; **please a. my apologies** je vous prie de bien vouloir accepter mes excuses; **the machine only accepts coins** la machine n'accepte que les pièces

2 *(believe as right, true)* accepter, admettre; **I can't a. what he says** je ne peux accepter *ou* admettre ce qu'il dit; **I refuse to a. that he's guilty** je me refuse à le croire coupable, je refuse de croire qu'il soit coupable; **it is generally accepted that...** il est généralement reconnu que...; **while we a. that this may be more expensive...** tout en admettant que ceci puisse être plus cher...

3 *(face up to* ► *danger)* faire face à, affronter; (► *challenge)* accepter, relever; (► *one's fate)* se résigner à; **she hasn't really accepted his death** elle n'a pas vraiment accepté sa mort; **you have to a. the inevitable** il vous faut accepter l'inévitable

4 *(take on* ► *blame, responsibility)* accepter, prendre; (► *job, task)* se charger de, accepter; **to a. responsibility for sth** prendre *ou* accepter la responsabilité de qch; **to a. no responsibility** décliner toute responsabilité

5 *(admit ▸ to job, school)* accepter, prendre; *(▸ to club, university)* accepter, admettre; **they accepted her into the club** ils l'ont admise au club; **she's been accepted** *Br* **at** *or Am* **to Harvard** elle a été admise à Harvard

6 *Com (goods)* prendre livraison de; *Fin (bill of exchange)* accepter

VI accepter; **they offered me a contract and I accepted** ils m'ont proposé un contrat que j'ai accepté

acceptability [ək͵septə'bɪlɪtɪ] **N** acceptabilité *f*, admissibilité *f*

acceptable [ək'septəbəl] **ADJ 1** *(satisfactory)* acceptable, convenable; *(tolerable)* acceptable, admissible; **her behaviour just isn't socially a.** son attitude est tout simplement intolérable en société; **they found her work a.** ils ont trouvé son travail convenable; **are these conditions a. to you?** ces conditions vous conviennent-elles? **2** *(welcome)* bienvenu, opportun; **flowers always make an a. gift** les fleurs sont toujours une bonne idée de cadeau *ou* font toujours plaisir; **your cheque was most a.** votre chèque était fort apprécié

▸▸ *Comput* ***Acceptable Use Policy*** = code de conduite défini par un fournisseur d'accès à l'internet

acceptance [ək'septəns] **N 1** *(of gift, invitation, apology)* acceptation *f*

2 *(assent ▸ to proposal, suggestion)* consentement *m*; **his a. of his fate** sa résignation devant son sort

3 *(to club, school, university, group)* admission *f*; *Univ* **she's got two provisional acceptances** *(for university)* elle a été provisoirement admise dans deux universités

4 *(approval, favour)* approbation *f*, réception *f* favorable; **his suggestion met with everyone's a.** tout le monde approuva sa suggestion; **the idea is gaining a.** l'idée fait son chemin

5 *(belief)* **there is general a. now that smoking causes cancer** il est généralement reconnu maintenant que le tabac provoque le cancer

6 *Com (of goods)* réception *f*; *Fin (of bill of exchange)* acceptation *f*; *(document)* effet *m* accepté, effet *m* à payer; *Fin* **to present a bill for a.** présenter un effet *ou* une traite à l'acceptation

▸▸ *Br Old-fashioned Banking* ***acceptance bank*** banque *f* d'acceptation; ***acceptance speech*** discours *m* de réception; *Comput & Tech* ***acceptance test, acceptance trial*** test *m* d'acceptabilité

acceptation [͵æksep'teɪʃən] **N** *Ling (of term, word)* acception *f*, signification *f*; **in the full a. of the word** dans toute l'acception du mot

accepting house [ək'septɪŋ-] **N** *Br Old-fashioned Banking* maison *f* d'acceptation, banque *f* d'acceptation

acceptor [ək'septə(r)] **N** *Chem & Fin* accepteur *m*

access ['ækses] **N 1** *(means of entry)* entrée *f*, ouverture *f*; *(means of approach)* accès *m*, abord *m*; *Law* droit *m* de passage; **there is easy a. to the beach** on accède facilement à la plage; **the kitchen gives a. to the garage** la cuisine donne accès au garage; **how did the thieves gain a.?** comment les voleurs se sont-ils introduits?; **a. only** *(sign)* sauf riverains (et livreurs)

2 *(right to contact, use)* accès *m*; **to have a. to sb/sth** avoir accès auprès de qn/à qch; **I have a. to confidential files** j'ai accès à des dossiers confidentiels; **he has direct a. to the minister** il a ses entrées auprès du ministre; *Br Law* **the father has a. to the children at weekends** le père a droit de visite le week-end pour voir ses enfants

3 *Br Literary (bout ▸ of illness)* accès *m*, attaque *f*; *(▸ of fever, anger)* accès *m*

4 *Comput* accès *m*; **to have a. to a file** avoir accès à un fichier; **up to 56K a.** accès *m* jusqu'à 56K; **a. denied** *(DOS message)* accès refusé

COMP *Transp (port, route)* d'accès

VT accéder à

▸▸ *Comput* ***access authorization code*** code *m* d'autorisation d'accès; *Econ* ***access barrier*** barrière *f* d'accès; *TV* ***access broadcasting*** télévision *f* ouverte; *TV* ***access channel*** canal *m* d'accès; *Comput* ***access code*** code *m* d'accès; *Comput* ***access level*** *(in network)* niveau *m* d'accès; *Comput* ***access number*** *(to ISP)* numéro *m* d'accès; *Comput* ***access point*** *(for wireless Internet connection)* borne *f* d'accès; *Comput* ***access privileges*** droits *mpl* d'accès; *Comput* ***access provider*** fournisseur *m* d'accès; ***access ramp*** bretelle *f* d'accès; *Br Law* ***access rights*** *(of divorced parent to child)* droits *mpl* de visite; ***access road*** *(gen)* route *f* d'accès; *(to motorway)* bretelle *f* d'accès *ou* de raccordement; *Comput* ***access speed*** vitesse *f* d'accès; *TV* ***access television*** télévision *f* ouverte; *Comput* ***access time*** temps *m* d'accès

accessary [ək'sesərɪ] *(pl* **accessaries)** *Law* **N** = **accessory N 2**

accessibility [ək͵sesə'bɪlətɪ] **N** accessibilité *f*

accessible [ək'sesəbəl] **ADJ 1** *(place)* accessible, d'accès facile; *(person)* d'un abord facile; **the teacher's very a.** ce professeur est facile à aborder *ou* est d'un abord facile **2** *(available)* accessible; **computers are now a. to everyone** maintenant les ordinateurs sont accessibles à tous **3** *(easily understandable ▸ novel, style)* à la portée de tous, accessible

accession [æk'seʃən] **N 1** *(to office, position, power)* accession *f* (**to** à); *(to fortune)* accession *f*, entrée *f* en possession; **Queen Victoria's a. (to the throne)** l'accession *f* au trône *ou* l'avènement *m* de la reine Victoria

2 *(addition to collection)* nouvelle acquisition *f*

3 *(increase)* augmentation *f*, accroissement *m*

4 *Law (consent)* assentiment *m*, accord *m*; *(of treaty)* adhésion *f*

VT enregistrer

▸▸ *EU* ***accession country*** pays *m* en phase d'adhésion; ***accession number*** *(of book)* numéro *m* de catalogue

accessory [ək'sesərɪ] *(pl* **accessories) N 1** *(usu pl) (supplementary article)* accessoire *m*; **car accessories** accessoires *mpl* automobiles; **a suit with matching accessories** un ensemble avec (ses) accessoires coordonnés **2** *Law* complice *mf* (**to** de); **an a. after/before the fact** un complice par assistance/par instigation

ADJ 1 *(supplementary)* accessoire (**to** à) **2** *Law* complice

▸▸ *Phot* ***accessory shoe*** fiche *f* pour accessoires

accident ['æksɪdənt] **N 1** *(mishap)* accident *m*, malheur *m*; *(unforeseen event)* événement *m* fortuit, accident *m*; **to have an a.** avoir un accident; **her son had a car a.** son fils a eu un accident de voiture; **their last child was an a.** leur dernier enfant est un accident; **accidents in the home** accidents *mpl* domestiques; **it was an a. waiting to happen** c'est un accident qui devait arriver; *Prov* **accidents will happen** on ne peut pas parer à tout **2** *(chance)* hasard *m*, chance *f*; **it was purely by a. that we met** nous nous sommes rencontrés tout à fait par accident; **any success we had was more by a. than by design** notre réussite a été plus accidentelle qu'autre chose; **it's no a. that she made the film here** ce n'est pas par hasard si elle a tourné le film ici **3** *Law* cas *m* fortuit

COMP *(figures, rate)* des accidents

▸▸ *Br Med* ***accident and emergency (unit)*** *(in hospital)* service *m* des urgences, urgences *fpl*; *Ins* ***accident insurance*** assurance *f* (contre les) accidents; ***accident prevention*** la prévention des accidents; ***accident victim*** victime *f* d'un/de l'accident

accidental [͵æksɪ'dentəl] **ADJ 1** *(occurring by chance ▸ death, poisoning)* accidentel; *(▸ meeting)* fortuit **2** *Formal (nonessential)* accessoire, extrinsèque **3** *Phil & Mus* accidentel

N *Mus* accident *m*

▸▸ *Law* ***accidental death*** mort *f* accidentelle; *Law* ***accidental homicide*** homicide *m* involontaire *ou* par imprudence

accidentally [͵æksɪ'dentəlɪ] **ADV** *(break, drop)* accidentellement; *(meet)* par hasard; **she a. tore the page** elle a déchiré la page sans le vouloir; *Hum* **he did it a. on purpose** il l'a fait "exprès sans le vouloir"

accident-prone ADJ to be a. être prédisposé aux accidents

acclaim [ə'kleɪm] **VT 1** *(praise)* acclamer, faire l'éloge de; *(applaud)* acclamer, applaudir; **her acclaimed portrayal of Cleopatra** sa représentation acclamée de Cléopâtre **2** *(proclaim)* proclamer; **Charlemagne was acclaimed emperor** Charlemagne fut acclamé *ou* proclamé empereur

N *(UNCOUNT)* acclamation *f*, acclamations *fpl*; **his play met with great critical a.** sa pièce a été très applaudie par la critique; **the a. of his peers** la reconnaissance de ses pairs

acclamation [͵ækləˈmeɪʃən] **N** *(UNCOUNT)* acclamation *f*, acclamations *fpl*; **to be elected by a.** être plébiscité;

acclimate ['æklɪmeɪt] *Am* = **acclimatize**

acclimation [͵æklɪ'meɪʃən] *Am* = **acclimatization**

acclimatization, -isation [ə͵klaɪmətaɪ'zeɪʃən] **N** *(to climate)* acclimatation *f*; *(to conditions, customs)* accoutumance *f*, acclimatement *m*

acclimatize, -ise [ə'klaɪmətaɪz] **VT** *(animal, plant)* acclimater; **to a. oneself to sth, to become acclimatized to sth** *(climate)* s'habituer à qch, s'accoutumer à qch; *(conditions, customs)* s'acclimater à qch, s'habituer à qch, s'accoutumer à qch

VI to a. to sth *(climate)* s'habituer à qch, s'accoutumer à qch; *(conditions, customs)* s'acclimater à qch, s'habituer à qch, s'accoutumer à qch

accolade ['ækəleɪd] **N 1** *(praise)* acclamation *f*, acclamations *fpl*; *(approval)* marque *f* d'approbation; *(honour)* honneur *m*; **the prize is the highest a. a writer can receive** ce prix est le plus grand honneur qu'un écrivain puisse recevoir

accommodate [ə'kɒmədeɪt] **VT 1** *(provide lodging for)* loger; *(provide with something needed)* équiper, pourvoir; *(provide with loan)* prêter de l'argent à; **can you a. me until my cheque comes through?** pouvez-vous me prêter de l'argent en attendant que je reçoive mon chèque?

2 *(have room for ▸ of car)* contenir; *(▸ of house, room)* contenir, recevoir; **the restaurant can a. 150 people** le restaurant peut recevoir 150 personnes; **the apartment accommodates up to six people** dans l'appartement, on peut loger jusqu'à six (personnes)

3 *(oblige)* répondre aux besoins de; **we will try to a. you** nous essaierons de vous satisfaire; **to do sth to a. sb** faire qch pour arranger qn; **the bill is designed to a. special interest groups** cette loi vise à prendre en compte les besoins de groupes d'intérêts particuliers

4 *(adapt)* accommoder, adapter; **to a. oneself to sth** s'adapter à qch

VI to a. to sth s'accommoder *ou* s'habituer à qch

> Note that the French verb **accommoder** is a false friend and is rarely a translation for the English verb **to accommodate**.

accommodating [ə'kɒmədeɪtɪŋ] **ADJ** *(willing to help)* obligeant; *(easy to please)* accommodant, complaisant

accommodation [ə͵kɒmə'deɪʃən] **N 1** *(UNCOUNT) (lodging)* logement *m*; *(lodging and services)* prestations *fpl*; **to look for a.** *(flat to rent)* chercher un logement; *(hotel room)* chercher une chambre (d'hôtel); **the hotel has no a. available** l'hôtel est complet; **furnished a.** chambre *f* meublée, (logement *m*) meublé *m*; **the high cost of rented a.** le prix élevé des locations; *Admin* **office a.** bureaux *mpl* à louer; **sleeping a.** chambres *fpl*

2 *Law (settlement of disagreement)* accord *m*, accommodement *m*; *(compromise)* compromis *m*; **to come to an a.** arriver à un compromis; *Fin (with one's creditors)* parvenir à un arrangement

3 *Anat & Psy* accommodation *f*

4 *Com & Fin (loan)* prêt *m* de complaisance

• **accommodations NPL** *Am* **1** *(lodging, food and services)* hébergement *m* **2** *Naut & Rail (on boat, train)* place *f*

▸▸ *Br* ***accommodation address*** adresse *f (utilisée uniquement pour la correspondance)*; ***accommodation agency*** agence *f* de logement; ***accommodation allowance*** indemnité *f* de logement; *Fin* ***accommodation bill*** traite *f ou* effet *m* de complaisance; ***accommodation bureau*** agence *f* de logement; *Naut* ***accommodation ladder*** échelle *f* de coupée; *Transp* ***accommodation road*** route *f* de desserte

accompaniment [ə'kʌmpənɪmənt] **N 1** *(gen)* accompagnement *m*; **he entered to the a. of wild applause** il entra sous un tonnerre d'applaudissements **2** *Culin* accompagnement *m*, garniture *f* **3** *Mus* accompagnement *m* (**on** à); **guitar/piano**

accompaniment accompagnement *m* à la guitare/au piano

accompanist [əˈkʌmpənɪst] **N** *Mus* accompagnateur(trice) *m,f*

accompany [əˈkʌmpənɪ] (*pt & pp* **accompanied**) **VT 1** *(escort)* accompagner, escorter; **she was accompanied by her brother** elle était accompagnée de son frère; **she accompanied me to the door** elle m'a raccompagné jusqu'à la porte
2 *(supplement)* accompagner; **she accompanied her advice with a warning** ses conseils s'accompagnaient d'une mise en garde; **her photos a. the text** ses photos accompagnent le texte; **the hot weather is often accompanied by afternoon thunderstorms** la chaleur s'accompagne souvent d'orages dans l'après-midi
3 *Culin* accompagner, garnir
4 *Mus* accompagner (**on** à); **he accompanies her on the piano** il l'accompagne au piano

accompanying [əˈkʌmpənɪɪŋ] **ADJ the a. documents** les documents ci-joints; **children will not be allowed in without an a. adult** l'entrée est interdite aux enfants non accompagnés; **an a. letter** une lettre d'accompagnement

accomplice [əˈkʌmplɪs] **N** *(gen) & Law* complice *mf*; **to be an a. to** *or* **in sth** être complice de qch

accomplish [əˈkʌmplɪʃ] **VT 1** *(manage to do ▸ task, work)* accomplir, exécuter; *(▸ desire, dream)* réaliser; *(▸ distance, trip)* effectuer; **the talks accomplished nothing** les pourparlers n'ont pas abouti; **to a. one's object** atteindre son but **2** *(finish successfully)* venir à bout de, mener à bonne fin

accomplished [əˈkʌmplɪʃt] **ADJ 1** *(cook, singer)* accompli, doué; *(performance)* accompli **2** *(successfully completed)* accompli; **an a. fact** un fait accompli

accomplishment [əˈkʌmplɪʃmənt] **N 1** *(skill)* talent *m*; **one of her many accomplishments** un de ses nombreux talents **2** *(feat)* exploit *m*, œuvre *f* (accomplie); **that's quite an a.** c'est un véritable exploit, c'est une véritable prouesse **3** *(completion ▸ of task, trip)* accomplissement *m*; *(▸ of ambition)* réalisation *f*

accord [əˈkɔːd] **N 1** *(consent)* accord *m*, consentement *m*; **to be in a. with sb** être d'accord avec qn; **I'm in complete a. with you** je suis totalement d'accord avec vous
2 *(conformity)* accord *m*, conformité *f*; **to be in a. with sth** être en accord *ou* en conformité avec qch
3 *(harmony)* accord *m*, harmonie *f*
4 *Law & Pol (agreement)* accord *m*; *(treaty)* traité *m*
VT *(permission, significance, status)* accorder; *(welcome)* réserver; **to a. sb permission** accorder une autorisation *ou* une permission à qn;
VI s'accorder, concorder; **what he said did not a. with our instructions** ce qu'il a dit n'était pas conforme à nos instructions
• **of one's own accord ADV to do sth of one's own a.** faire qch de son plein gré; **the table seemed to be moving of its own a.** la table avait l'air de bouger toute seule
• **with one accord ADV** d'un commun accord

accordance [əˈkɔːdəns] **N 1** *(conformity)* accord *m*, conformité *f* **2** *Formal (granting)* octroi *m*
• **in accordance with PREP** conformément à; *Law* **in a. with the law** aux termes de *ou* conformément à la loi; **her statement is not in a. with company policy** sa déclaration n'est pas dans la ligne de l'entreprise

according [əˈkɔːdɪŋ] **according as CONJ** *Formal* selon que, suivant que; **a. as they pass or fail the exam** suivant *ou* selon qu'ils ont réussi ou échoué à l'examen
• **according to PREP 1** *(on the evidence of)* selon, d'après; **a. to John, it's too late** selon *ou* pour John, il est trop tard; **a. to what you say** d'après ce que vous dites; *Bible* **the Gospel a. to St Luke** l'Évangile selon saint Luc **2** *(in relation to)* **arranged a. to height** disposés par ordre de taille; **prices vary a. to how long the job will take** le prix varie selon le temps qu'il faut pour effectuer le travail **3** *(in accordance with)* suivant, conformément à; **a. to instructions** conformément aux *ou* suivant les instructions; **everything went a. to plan** tout s'est passé comme prévu

accordingly [əˈkɔːdɪŋlɪ] **ADV 1** *(appropriately)* en conséquence **2** *(consequently)* par conséquent; **a., I wrote to him** je lui ai donc écrit, par conséquent je lui ai écrit

accordion [əˈkɔːdɪən] **N** *Mus* accordéon *m*
▸▸ *Typ* ***accordion fold*** pliure *f* en accordéon; ***accordion player*** accordéoniste *mf*; *Sewing* ***accordion pleat*** pli *m* (en) accordéon

accordionist [əˈkɔːdɪənɪst] **N** *Mus* accordéoniste *mf*

accost [əˈkɒst] **VT** *Law (gen)* accoster, aborder; *(of prostitute)* racoler

account [əˈkaʊnt] **N 1** *(report)* récit *m*, compte rendu *m*; **to give an a. of sth** faire le récit de qch; **her a. differs from her husband's** sa version diffère de celle de son mari, son récit diffère de celui de son mari; **an interesting a. of his travels** un récit intéressant de ses voyages; **his latest book contains an amusing a. of how he learned to drive** son dernier livre relate de façon amusante la manière dont il a appris à conduire; **he gave his a. of the accident** il a donné sa version de l'accident; **by his own a. he had had too much to drink** à l'en croire, il avait trop bu
2 *(explanation)* compte rendu *m*, explication *f*; **to bring** *or* **to call sb to a. (for sth)** demander des comptes à qn (de qch); **to be brought to a.** devoir rendre des comptes; **you will be held to a. for all damages** il vous faudra rendre des comptes pour tous les dommages causés
3 *(consideration)* importance *f*, valeur *f*; **a town of little a.** une ville de peu d'importance *ou* insignifiante; **what you think is of no a. to me** ce que vous pensez ne m'intéresse pas; **to take sth into a., to take a. of sth** tenir compte de qch, prendre qch en compte; **he took little a. of her feelings** il ne tenait pas compte *ou* faisait peu de cas de ses sentiments; **taking everything into a.** tout bien calculé
4 *(advantage, profit)* profit *m*; **to put** *or* **to turn one's skills to good a.** tirer parti de ses compétences; **to turn sth to a.** tirer parti *ou* avantage de qch, mettre qch à profit
5 *Com (responsibility)* **to set up in business on one's own a.** s'établir à son compte; **I started working on my own a.** j'ai commencé à travailler à mon compte
6 *(rendition)* interprétation *f*, version *f*; **the pianist gave a sensitive a. of the concerto** le pianiste a donné du concerto une interprétation d'une grande sensibilité; **to give a good a. of oneself** bien se débrouiller; **she gave a good a. of herself in the interview** elle a réussi à bien se définir au cours de cette entrevue
7 *Com (with shop)* compte *m*; **we have an a. at the garage** nous avons un compte chez le garagiste; **put it on** *or* **charge it to my a.** mettez cela sur mon compte; **I'd like to settle my a.** je voudrais régler ma note; **cash or a.?** vous payez *ou* réglez comptant ou est-ce que vous avez un compte chez nous?; *Fig* **to settle** *or* **to square accounts with sb** régler ses comptes avec qn; **to a. rendered** suivant compte remis
8 *Banking* compte *m*; **to open/close an a.** ouvrir/fermer un compte; **to pay money into one's a.** verser de l'argent sur son compte; **to pay sb's salary directly into his/her a.** verser le salaire de qn par virement direct sur son compte; **to overdraw an a.** mettre un compte à découvert
9 *Fin, Com & Acct (of expenses)* état *m*, note *f*; *(of transactions)* exposé *m*; **as per** *or* **to a. rendered** *(on statement)* suivant compte *ou* relevé remis
10 *Com & Mktg (in advertising, marketing, PR)* budget *m*; **one of our major accounts** un de nos plus gros clients; **the agency secured the Brook a.** l'agence s'est assuré le budget Brook
11 *Comput (with Internet service provider)* abonnement *m* (**with** auprès de); **to set up an a. with sb** s'abonner auprès de qn
12 *St Exch* **the A.** la liquidation
VT *Formal (consider)* estimer, considérer; **to a. sb guilty** tenir qn pour coupable
• **accounts NPL** *Acct (of company)* comptabilité *f*; **to keep the accounts** tenir les livres *ou* les écritures *ou* la comptabilité; **to enter sth in the accounts** comptabiliser qch; **she does the accounts** *(for business)* elle fait *ou* tient la comptabilité; *(for the family)* elle tient les comptes
• **by all accounts ADV** au dire de tout le monde, d'après ce que tout le monde dit
• **on account ADV** *Com & Fin* à crédit; **we bought the car on a.** nous avons acheté la voiture à crédit; **payment on a.** paiement *m* à compte *ou* à crédit; **I paid £100 on a.** j'ai versé un acompte de 100 livres
• **on account of PREP** en raison de; *(in negative contexts)* à cause de; **on a. of the weather** à cause du temps; **don't leave on a. of me** *or* **on my a.** ne partez pas à cause de moi; **I did it on your a.** *(to help you)* je l'ai fait pour vous; **I did it on a. of you** *(reproaching)* je l'ai fait à cause de vous; **we didn't go on a. of there being a storm** nous n'y sommes pas allés à cause de la tempête
• **on no account ADV** en aucun cas, sous aucun prétexte; **on no a. do I want to talk to her** je ne veux lui parler en aucun cas *ou* sous aucun prétexte
▸▸ ***account balance*** *(status)* situation *f* de compte; *Acct (after audit)* reliquat *m* de compte; *Acct* ***account book*** livre *m* de comptes, registre *m* de comptabilité; ***account card*** *Fin (record of charges)* fiche *f* de compte *ou* de facture; *Com (for use in department store)* carte-clients *f*; ***account charges*** frais *mpl* de tenue de compte; ***accounts clerk*** employé(e) *m,f* aux écritures; ***account credit*** avoir *m* de compte; *St Exch* ***account day*** (jour *m* de) liquidation *f*, (jour *m* de) règlement *m*; ***accounts department*** (service *m* de la) comptabilité *f*; *Com & Mktg* ***account director*** *(in advertising, marketing, PR)* directeur(trice) *m,f* des comptes-clients; *Am* ***account executive*** agent *m* de change; ***account fee*** commission *f* de compte; *Com & Mktg* ***account handler*** *(in advertising, marketing, PR)* responsable *mf* des comptes-clients; ***account handling fee*** commission *f* de tenue de compte; ***account holder*** titulaire *mf*; ***account manager*** *Banking & Fin* chargé(e) *m,f* de compte; *Com & Mktg (in advertising, marketing, PR)* responsable *mf* de budget; ***account number*** numéro *m* de compte; *Acct* ***account payable*** compte *m* créditeur, dette *f* fournisseur; *Acct* ***accounts payable*** dettes *fpl* passives, dettes *fpl* fournisseurs; *Acct* ***accounts payable ledger*** livre *m* des créanciers; *Acct* ***account receivable*** compte *m* client, compte *m* débiteur; *Acct* ***accounts receivable*** dettes *fpl* actives, créances *fpl* (clients); *Acct* ***accounts receivable ledger*** livre *m* des débiteurs; ***account statement*** relevé *m ou* état *m ou* bordereau *m* de compte

▸**account for VT INSEP 1** *(explain)* expliquer, rendre compte de; **that accounts for his interest in baseball** voilà qui explique son intérêt pour le base-ball; **there's no accounting for his recent odd behaviour** il n'y a aucune explication à son comportement bizarre des derniers temps; **there's no accounting for taste** les goûts et les couleurs, ça ne se discute pas
2 *(answer for)* rendre compte de; **he has to a. for every penny he spends** il doit rendre compte de chaque centime d'euro qu'il dépense; **all the children are accounted for** aucun des enfants n'a été oublié; **two hostages have not yet been accounted for** deux otages n'ont toujours pas été retrouvés
3 *(represent)* représenter; **wine accounts for cinq percent of all exports** le vin représente five pour cent des exportations totales; **the North Sea accounts for a large proportion of our petroleum** la mer du Nord produit une grande partie de notre pétrole
4 *Formal (shoot, kill)* abattre, tuer; *(catch)* attraper

accountability [əˌkaʊntəˈbɪlɪtɪ] **N** responsabilité *f* (**to** envers); **the public wants more police a.** le public souhaite que la police réponde davantage de ses actes; **public a.** transparence *f*

accountable [əˈkaʊntəbəl] **ADJ** *(responsible)* responsable; **to be a. to sb for sth** être responsable de qch envers qn; **to hold sb a. (for sth)** tenir qn (pour) responsable (de qch); **she is not a. for her actions** elle n'est pas responsable de ses actes; **I'm a. to your mother for you** je suis responsable de toi devant ta mère; **I am a. to no one** je n'ai de comptes à rendre à personne; **they cannot be**

held a. for the accident on ne peut les tenir responsables de l'accident

accountancy [əˈkaʊntənsɪ] **N** *Br Acct (subject, work)* comptabilité *f*, expertise *f* comptable; *(profession)* profession *f* de comptable

▸▸ ***accountancy firm*** cabinet *m* d'expertise comptable *ou* d'expert-comptable

accountant [əˈkaʊntənt] **N** *Acct* comptable *mf*, agent *m* comptable

accounting [əˈkaʊntɪŋ] **N** *Acct* comptabilité *f*, expertise *f* comptable

▸▸ ***accounting clerk*** commis *m* aux écritures; ***accounting control*** contrôle *m* de la comptabilité; ***accounting day*** journée *f* comptable; ***accounting entry*** écriture *f* comptable; ***accounting entry form, accounting entry sheet*** bordereau *m* de saisie; ***accounting firm*** cabinet *m* d'expertise comptable *ou* d'expert-comptable; ***accounting method*** méthode *f* de comptabilité, procédé *m ou* mode *m* comptable; ***accounting period*** exercice *m* (financier), période *f* comptable; ***accounting policy*** politique *f* comptable; ***accounting procedure*** pratique *f* comptable; ***acccounting records*** états *mpl* comptables; *Comput* ***accounting software*** logiciel *m* de comptabilité; ***accounting system*** système *m ou* plan *m* comptable; ***accounting year*** exercice *m* (financier), année *f* comptable

accoutrements, *Am* **accouterments** [əˈkuːtrəmənts] **NPL** *(equipment)* attirail *m*; *Mil* équipement *m*

accredit [əˈkredɪt] **VT 1** *(credit)* attribuer; **she is accredited with having discovered radium** on lui attribue la découverte du radium **2** *(provide with credentials)* accréditer; **he's the ambassador accredited to Morocco** c'est l'ambassadeur accrédité au Maroc

accreditation [əˌkredɪˈteɪʃən] **N** accréditation *f*; **to seek a.** chercher à se faire accréditer *ou* reconnaître

accredited [əˈkredɪtɪd] **ADJ 1** *(idea, rumour)* admis, accepté **2** *(official, person)* accrédité, autorisé; **the a. representative to the United Nations** le représentant accrédité aux Nations unies; **a. schools** = établissements délivrant des diplômes reconnus par l'État

accretion [æˈkriːʃən] **N 1** *(growth* ▸ *in size)* accroissement *m*; *(*▸ *of dirt, wealth)* accroissement *m*, accumulation *f* **2** *(addition)* addition *f* **3** *Zool (adhesion)* accrétion *f*; *(deposit)* concrétion *f*

accrual [əˈkruːəl] **N 1** *Fin (of interest, debt, cost)* accumulation *f* **2** *Acct* **accruals** *(expenses)* charges *fpl* à payer; *(income)* produits *mpl* à recevoir

▸▸ *Acct* ***accrual accounting*** comptabilité *f* d'engagements; ***accruals concept*** principe *m* d'indépendance des exercices *ou* de rattachement à l'exercice; ***accrual rate*** taux *m* d'accumulation *ou* d'accroissement

accrue [əˈkruː] *Formal* **VI 1** *Fin (increase)* s'accroître, s'accumuler; *(interest)* s'accumuler, courir; **interest accrues (as) from the 5th of the month** les intérêts courent à partir du 5 du mois **2** *(benefit, gain)* **to a. to sb** revenir à qn

VT accumuler; *Fin (interest)* produire

▸▸ ***accrued benefits*** *(under pension scheme)* points *mpl* de retraite; *Acct* ***accrued charges*** effets *mpl* à payer; ***accrued dividends*** dividendes *mpl* accrus; *Acct* ***accrued expenses*** frais *mpl* cumulés *ou* accumulés; *Acct* ***accrued income*** recettes *fpl* échues, effets *mpl ou* produit *m* à recevoir; ***accrued interest*** intérêts *mpl* courus

accruing interest [əˈkruːɪŋ-] **N** *Fin* intérêts *mpl* à échoir

accumulate [əˈkjuːmjʊleɪt] **VT** accumuler; *(objects)* amonceler, entasser; *Phys & Elec (heat, electricity)* emmagasiner

VI s'accumuler

accumulated [əˈkjuːmjʊleɪtɪd] **ADJ** accumulé

▸▸ *Fin* ***accumulated depreciation*** amortissement *m* cumulé

accumulation [əˌkjuːmjʊˈleɪʃən] **N 1** *(process)* accumulation *f* **2** *(things collected* ▸ *objects)* amas *m*, tas *m*; *(*▸ *facts, evidence)* accumulation *f* **3** *Fin (of capital)* accroissement *m*; *(of interest)* accumulation *f*

accumulative [əˈkjuːmjʊlətɪv] **ADJ** cumulatif, qui s'accumule; *Fin* cumulatif

accumulator [əˈkjuːmjʊleɪtə(r)] **N 1** *Elec (battery)* accumulateur *m* **2** *Br Horseracing (bet)* = pari par report **3** *(person)* **he's an a. of useless gadgets** il accumule les gadgets inutiles

accuracy [ˈækjʊrəsɪ] **N** *(of description, report)* précision *f*, justesse *f*; *(of aim, instrument, weapon)* précision *f*; *(of figures, watch)* exactitude *f*; *(of estimate, prediction)* justesse *f*; *(of memory, translation)* fidélité *f*, exactitude *f*

accurate [ˈækjʊrət] **ADJ** *(description, report)* précis, juste; *(aim, instrument, weapon)* précis; *(figures, watch)* exact; *(estimate, prediction)* juste; *(memory, translation)* fidèle; **the report was a. in every detail** le compte rendu était fidèle jusque dans les moindres détails; **to be more a., there were 15 of them** pour être plus précis, ils étaient 15

accurately [ˈækjʊrətlɪ] **ADV** *(count, draw, aim)* avec précision; *(tell)* exactement; *(judge, estimate, predict)* avec justesse; *(remember, translate)* fidèlement

accurateness [ˈækjʊrətnɪs] **N** *(of description, report)* précision *f*, justesse *f*; *(of aim, instrument, weapon)* précision *f*; *(of figures, watch)* exactitude *f*; *(of estimate, prediction)* justesse *f*; *(of memory, translation)* fidélité *f*, exactitude *f*

accursed [əˈkɜːsɪd] **ADJ** *Literary* maudit

accusation [ˌækjuːˈzeɪʃən] **N 1** *(gen)* accusation *f*; **to make an a. (against sb)** porter une accusation (contre qn); **there was a note of a. in her voice** sa voix prenait des accents un tant soit peu accusateurs; **she had no answer to the a. that her fiscal policies had failed** elle n'avait rien à répondre aux accusations selon lesquelles sa politique fiscale avait échoué **2** *Law* accusation *f*, plainte *f*; **they brought an a. of theft against him** ils ont porté plainte contre lui pour vol

accusative [əˈkjuːzətɪv] *Gram*

N accusatif *m*; **in the a.** à l'accusatif

ADJ accusatif

accusatory [əˈkjuːzətərɪ] **ADJ** *Law* accusateur

accuse [əˈkjuːz] **VT** accuser; **to a. sb of sth/doing sth** accuser qn de qch/de faire qch; **he is** *or* **he stands accused of tax fraud** il est accusé de fraude fiscale; *Ironic* **no one could a. her of being punctual** on ne peut pas l'accuser d'être ponctuelle

accused [əˈkjuːzd] *(pl* **inv***)* **N** *Law* **the a.** l'accusé(e) *m,f*, l'inculpé(e) *m,f*

accuser [əˈkjuːzə(r)] **N** accusateur(trice) *m,f*

accusing [əˈkjuːzɪŋ] **ADJ** accusateur

accusingly [əˈkjuːzɪŋlɪ] **ADV** de façon accusatrice; *(look, stare)* d'un air *ou* d'un œil accusateur

accustom [əˈkʌstəm] **VT** habituer, accoutumer; **to a. sb to sth/to doing sth** habituer qn à qch/à faire qch; **to a. oneself to sth** s'habituer *ou* se faire *ou* s'accoutumer à qch; **she's gradually accustoming herself to her new way of life** elle s'habitue peu à peu à son nouveau style de vie

accustomed [əˈkʌstəmd] **ADJ 1** *(familiar)* habitué, accoutumé; **to get** *or* **to grow a. to sth** s'habituer *ou* s'accoutumer à qch; **they weren't a. to strangers/politeness** ils n'étaient pas habitués aux étrangers/à la politesse; **her eyes had got a. to the dark** ses yeux s'étaient accoutumés à l'obscurité; **she's not a. to being interrupted** elle n'a pas l'habitude qu'on l'interrompe **2** *(regular)* habituel, coutumier

AC/DC [ˌeɪsiːˈdiːsiː] **N** *Elec (abbr* **alternating current/direct current***)* CA/CC *m*

ADJ *Fam (bisexual)* **to be A.** marcher à voile et à vapeur

ace [eɪs] **N 1** *Cards* as *m*; **the a. of spades** l'as *m* de pique; *Fig* **to have an a. up one's sleeve, to have an a. in the hole** avoir un atout en réserve; **to come within an a. of doing sth** être à deux doigts de faire qch **2** *(expert)* as *m*; **flying a.** as de l'aviation **3** *Sport (in tennis)* ace *m*; **to serve an a.** servir un ace

ADJ *Fam* super, génial; **she's an a. skier, she's a. at skiing** c'est une skieuse formidable;

VT *Am Fam* **to a. an exam** réussir un examen les doigts dans le nez

ACE inhibitor [eɪs-] **N** inhibiteur *m* de l'enzyme de conversion de l'angiotensine

acerbic [əˈsɜːbɪk] **ADJ** *(taste)* âpre; *(person, tone)* acerbe

acerbity [əˈsɜːbətɪ] **N** *(of taste)* âpreté *f*; *(of person, tone)* aigreur *f*

acetate [ˈæsɪteɪt] **N** *Chem* acétate *m*

▸▸ *Typ* ***acetate foil*** feuille *f* d'acétate

acetic [əˈsiːtɪk] **ADJ** *Chem* acétique

▸▸ ***acetic acid*** acide *m* acétique

acetone [ˈæsɪtəʊn] **N** *Chem* acétone *f*

acetylene [əˈsetɪliːn] *Chem* **N** acétylène *m*

COMP *(burner, lamp, torch)* à acétylène; *(welding)* à l'acétylène

acetylsalicylic acid [ˈæsetaɪlˌsælɪˈsɪlɪk-] **N** *Chem* acide *m* acétylsalicylique

ACH [ˌeɪsiːˈeɪtʃ] **N** *Banking (abbr* **automated clearing house***)* chambre *f* de compensation automatisée

ache [eɪk] **VI 1** *(feel pain)* faire mal, être douloureux; **I a. all over** j'ai mal partout; **my head/tooth aches** j'ai mal à la tête/aux dents; *Fig* **her heart ached to see them so unhappy** elle souffrait de les voir si malheureux **2** *(feel desire)* avoir très envie; **she was aching for them to leave** elle mourait d'envie de les voir partir

N *(physical)* douleur *f*; *(emotional)* peine *f*; **a dull a.** une douleur sourde; **aches and pains** douleurs *fpl*, maux *mpl*

achieve [əˈtʃiːv] **VT** *(gen)* accomplir, faire; *(desire, dream, increase)* réaliser; *(level, objective)* arriver à, atteindre; *(independence, success)* obtenir; *(honour, notoriety)* acquérir; *(reputation)* se faire; **she achieved the impossible** elle a accompli l'impossible; **he'll never a. anything in life** il n'arrivera jamais à rien dans sa vie; **we really achieved something today** on a vraiment bien avancé aujourd'hui; **we achieved what we set out to do** nous avons rempli nos objectifs; **the demonstration achieved nothing** la manifestation n'a servi à rien; **the plan achieved its objectives** le plan a atteint ses objectifs; **this policy achieved very little** cette politique n'a pas donné de grands résultats; **what will that a.?** *(suggestion etc)* qu'est-ce que ça fera de plus?, pour en venir à quoi?

> Note that the French verb **achever** is a false friend and is never a translation for the English verb **to achieve**. Its most common meaning is **to complete**.

achievement [əˈtʃiːvmənt] **N 1** *(deed)* exploit *m*, réussite *f*; **convincing her to come was quite an a.** c'est un véritable exploit d'avoir réussi à la convaincre de venir; **a lasting a.** une réalisation durable **2** *(successful completion)* accomplissement *m*, réalisation *f*; **I felt a real sense of a.** j'ai vraiment eu le sentiment d'avoir accompli quelque chose

▸▸ *Sch* ***achievement tests*** tests *mpl* de niveau

> Note that the French word **achèvement** is a false friend and is never a translation for the English word **achievement**. It means **completion.**

achievement-orientated, *Am* **achievement-oriented ADJ to be a.** mettre l'accent sur la réussite

achiever [əˈtʃiːvə(r)] **N** fonceur(euse) *m,f*

Achilles [əˈkɪliːz] **PR N** *Myth* Achille

▸▸ *Myth* ***Achilles heel*** talon *m* d'Achille; *Fig* **gambling is his A. heel** le jeu est son point faible; *Anat* ***Achilles tendon*** tendon *m* d'Achille

aching [ˈeɪkɪŋ] **ADJ** douloureux, endolori; **oh, my a. head!** oh, ma pauvre tête!; **to have an a. heart** avoir une peine de cœur; **her death left an a. void in his life** sa mort a laissé un vide douloureux dans sa vie

achromatic [ˌækrəʊˈmætɪk] **ADJ** *Opt* achromatique

achromatous [əˈkrəʊmətəs], **achromous** [əˈkrəʊməs] **ADJ** *Phot* achrome

achy [ˈeɪkɪ] **ADJ** douloureux, endolori; **I feel a. all over** je suis tout courbaturé, j'ai mal partout; **I have an a. feeling in my joints** j'ai mal aux articulations

acid ['æsɪd] N **1** *Chem* acide *m* **2** *Fam (LSD)* acide *m*
ADJ **1** *(drink, taste)* acide **2** *(remark, tone, wit)* mordant, acide; *(person)* revêche, caustique **3** *Chem* acide
►► *Culin* **acid drop** bonbon *m* acidulé; *Mus* **acid house** house *f*; *Med* **acid indigestion** aigreurs *fpl* d'estomac; *Mus* **acid jazz** acid jazz *m*; *Ecol* **acid rain** pluies *fpl* acides; **acid test** épreuve *f* à la pierre de touche; *Fig* épreuve *f* décisive

acidic [ə'sɪdɪk] ADJ *Chem* acide

acidification [əˌsɪdɪfɪ'keɪʃən] N *Chem* acidification *f*

acidify [ə'sɪdɪfaɪ] *(pt & pp* **acidified***)* *Chem* VT acidifier
VI s'acidifier

acidity [ə'sɪdətɪ] N *Chem* acidité *f*; *Fig* aigreur *f*, acidité *f*

acidly ['æsɪdlɪ] ADV *Chem* aigrement; *Fig* d'un ton acide

acidophilus [ˌæsɪ'dɒfɪləs] N *Biol* Lactobacillus acidophilus *m*

acidosis [ˌæsɪ'dəʊsɪs] N *Med* acidose *f*

acidulous [ə'sɪdjʊləs] ADJ acidulé

ack-ack [ˌæk'æk] *Br Fam Mil slang Old-fashioned* N défense *f* contre avions⁻, DCA⁻*f*
COMP de DCA⁻, antiaérien⁻
►► **ack-ack fire** tir *m* de DCA⁻

acknowledge [ək'nɒlɪdʒ] VT **1** *(admit truth of)* reconnaître, admettre; *(defeat, mistake)* reconnaître, avouer; **we a. (the fact) that we were wrong** nous admettons notre erreur; **she acknowledged her guilt** elle a avoué *ou* reconnu sa culpabilité; **acknowledged as the** *or* **to be the best Chinese restaurant in the city** reconnu comme le meilleur restaurant chinois de la ville
2 *(show recognition of* ► *person)* **he didn't even a. my presence** il a fait comme si je n'étais pas là; **she acknowledged him with a nod** elle lui a adressé un signe de la tête; **he acknowledged her child (as his)** il a reconnu l'enfant (comme étant le sien)
3 *(confirm receipt of* ► *greeting, message)* répondre à; *Admin (*► *letter, package)* accuser réception de; **sign here to a. receipt** *(on form)* signez ici pour accuser réception
4 *(express gratitude for)* **he acknowledged the cheers of the crowd** il a salué en réponse aux applaudissements de la foule; **I'd like to a. the help given me by my family** j'aimerais remercier ma famille pour l'aide qu'elle m'a apportée
►► *Comput* **acknowledge character** *(in datacommunications)* caractère *m* d'accusé de réception

acknowledged [ək'nɒlɪdʒd] ADJ *(expert, authority)* reconnu

acknowledgment, acknowledgement [ək'nɒlɪdʒmənt] N **1** *(admission)* reconnaissance *f*; *(of mistake)* reconnaissance *f*, aveu *m*; **I waved/smiled at him, but received no a.** je lui ai fait signe/ai souri mais il ne m'a pas répondu; **in a. of your letter** en réponse à votre lettre; **he received a watch in a. of his work** il a reçu une montre en reconnaissance *ou* remerciement de son travail **2** *Admin & Fin (letter, receipt)* accusé *m* de réception; *(for payment)* quittance *f*, reçu *m*
• **acknowledgements** NPL *(in article, book)* remerciements *mpl*
►► *Admin* **acknowledgement of receipt** accusé *m* de réception

acme ['ækmɪ] N apogée *m*, point *m* culminant; **to reach the a. of one's desires** parvenir au comble de ses désirs

acne ['æknɪ] N *Med* acné *f*

acolyte ['ækəlaɪt] N *(gen) & Rel* acolyte *m*

ACORN ['eɪkɔːn] N *Mktg (abbr* **A Classification Of Residential Neighbourhoods***)* = classement des différents types de quartiers résidentiels existant en Grande-Bretagne en 54 catégories, utilisé par les entreprises pour mieux cibler leurs clients potentiels lors de campagnes commerciales

acorn ['eɪkɔːn] N *Bot* gland *m*

acoustic [ə'kuːstɪk] ADJ *(feature, phonetics, nerve)* acoustique
►► *Comput & Tel* **acoustic coupler** coupleur *m* acoustique; *Tech* **acoustic engineer** acousticien (enne) *m,f*; **acoustic feedback** effet *m* Larsen, rétroaction *f* acoustique, bouclage *m* acoustique; *Mus* **acoustic guitar** guitare *f* sèche; **acoustic hood** capot *m* antibruit; **acoustic screen** écran *m* acoustique; **acoustic signal** signal *m* acoustique; *Constr* **acoustic tile** carreau *m* acoustique

acoustically [ə'kuːstɪkəlɪ] ADV du point de vue de l'acoustique

acoustics [ə'kuːstɪks] N *(UNCOUNT) (subject)* acoustique *f*
NPL *(of room, theatre)* acoustique *f*; **to have bad/good a.** avoir une mauvaise/bonne acoustique

ACPO ['ækpəʊ] N *(abbr* **Association of Chief Police Officers***)* = syndicat d'officiers supérieurs de la police britannique

acquaint [ə'kweɪnt] VT **1** *(inform)* aviser, renseigner; **I'll a. you with the facts** je vais vous mettre au courant des faits; **let me a. you with the situation** laissez-moi vous mettre au fait de la situation; **a stay in the jungle had acquainted him with these dangers** un séjour dans la jungle l'avait familiarisé avec ces dangers **2** *(familiarize)* **to be acquainted with** *(person, place, subject)* connaître; *(fact, situation)* être au courant de; **to become** *or* **get acquainted** *(two people)* faire connaissance; **she is well acquainted with the mayor** elle connaît très bien le maire; **I got acquainted with him later** j'ai fait sa connaissance plus tard; **we were just getting acquainted** on venait juste de faire connaissance; **to become acquainted with the facts** prendre connaissance des faits; **I'm fully acquainted with the facts** je suis tout à fait au courant des faits

acquaintance [ə'kweɪntəns] N **1** *(person)* connaissance *f*, relation *f*; **he is an a. (of mine)** c'est quelqu'un que je connais; **he has a wide circle of acquaintances** il a des relations très étendues **2** *(knowledge)* connaissance *f*; **to make sb's a.** faire la connaissance de qn; **during our brief a.** pendant la courte période où nous avons été en contact; **on closer** *or* **further a. he seems quite intelligent** quand on le connaît un peu mieux, il semble assez intelligent; **to have a nodding** *or* **passing a. with sb/sth** connaître vaguement qn/qch

acquiesce [ˌækwɪ'es] VI acquiescer, consentir (**in** *or* **to** à); **she finally acquiesced** elle a finalement acquiescé; **he acquiesced in the terms we had drawn up** il a consenti aux conditions que nous avions établies

acquiescence [ˌækwɪ'esəns] N acquiescement *m*, consentement *m* (**in** *or* **to** à)

acquiescent [ˌækwɪ'esənt] ADJ consentant

acquire [ə'kwaɪə(r)] VT **1** *(advantage, experience, possession, success)* acquérir; *(reputation, friend)* se faire; **they have recently acquired the house next door** ils ont récemment acquis *ou* se sont récemment rendus acquéreurs de la maison d'à côté; **we seem to have acquired a cat** il semble qu'on ait hérité d'un chat
2 *(information, language)* apprendre; *(knowledge)* acquérir; **it took her years to a. fluency in German** ça lui a pris des années pour apprendre couramment l'allemand
3 *(habit)* prendre, contracter; **I've acquired a taste for champagne** j'ai pris goût au champagne
4 *Com & Fin (other company)* prendre le contrôle de, racheter; *(shares)* acheter; **to a. an interest in a company** prendre une participation dans une société

acquired [ə'kwaɪəd] ADJ acquis; **it's an a. taste** on finit par y prendre goût
►► *Biol* **acquired characteristic** caractère *m* acquis; *Med* **acquired immune deficiency syndrome** syndrome *m* immunodéficitaire acquis

acquirement [ə'kwaɪəmənt] N acquisition *f*

acquisition [ˌækwɪ'zɪʃən] N acquisition *f*; *Fin (of company)* acquisition *f*, prise *f* de contrôle; **she's the team's latest a.** elle est la dernière acquisition de l'équipe
►► *Acct* **acquisition accounting** = base de préparation des comptes consolidés où une société a pris le contrôle d'une autre; *Acct* **acquisition cost** coût *m* d'acquisition

acquisitive [ə'kwɪzɪtɪv] ADJ *(greedy)* avide; *(for money)* avide, âpre au gain, cupide

acquit [ə'kwɪt] *(pt & pp* **acquitted**, *cont* **acquitting***)* VT **1** *(release* ► *from duty, responsibility)* acquitter, décharger
2 *Law* acquitter, relaxer; **to a. sb of sth** acquitter qn de qch
3 *(perform)* **to a. oneself well/badly** bien/mal s'en sortir; **he acquitted himself well during the trial** il s'est bien conduit pendant le procès
4 *Fin (debt)* acquitter, s'acquitter de, régler

acquittal [ə'kwɪtəl] N **1** *(of duty, responsibility)* accomplissement *m* **2** *Law* acquittement *m* **3** *Fin (of debt)* acquittement *m*, décharge *f*, quittance *f*

acquittance [ə'kwɪtəns] N *Fin (of debt)* acquittement *m*, décharge *f*, quittance *f*

acre ['eɪkə(r)] N = 4047m², demi-hectare *m*; **acres of forest** des hectares *mpl* de forêts; *Fig* **they have acres of room** ils ont des kilomètres de place

acreage ['eɪkərɪdʒ] N aire *f*, superficie *f* *(en mesures agraires)*

acrid ['ækrɪd] ADJ **1** *(smell, taste, smoke)* âcre **2** *(language, remark)* acerbe, mordant

acrimonious [ˌækrɪ'məʊnɪəs] ADJ *(person, remark)* acrimonieux, hargneux; *(attack, dispute)* virulent; **the discussion was becoming a.** la discussion s'envenimait

acrimoniously [ˌækrɪ'məʊnɪəslɪ] ADV *(say)* avec acrimonie; **the meeting ended a.** la réunion s'est terminée dans l'amertume

acrimony ['ækrɪmənɪ] N acrimonie *f*, hargne *f*

acrobat ['ækrəbæt] N *Gym* acrobate *mf*

acrobatic [ˌækrə'bætɪk] ADJ *Gym* acrobatique

acrobatics [ˌækrə'bætɪks] NPL *Gym* acrobatie *f*; **to do** *or* **to perform a.** faire des acrobaties *ou* de l'acrobatie

acronym ['ækrənɪm] N *Gram* acronyme *m*

Acropolis [ə'krɒpəlɪs] N *Archit* Acropole *f*

across [ə'krɒs] PREP **1** *(from one side to the other of)* d'un côté à l'autre de; **she drew a line a. the page** elle a tiré un trait en travers de la page; **to walk a. sth** traverser qch; **she swam a. the lake** elle a traversé le lac à la nage; **I ran a. the street** j'ai traversé la rue en courant; **can you help me a. the road?** pouvez-vous m'aider à traverser la rue?; **she threw it a. the room** elle l'a jeté en travers de *ou* de l'autre côté de la pièce; **he lay a. the bed** il était couché *ou* allongé en travers du lit; **he's very broad a. the shoulders** il est très large d'épaules
2 *(on the other side of)* de l'autre côté de; **the house a. the street** la maison d'en face; **we live a. the street from them** nous habitons en face de chez eux; **there's a supermarket just a. the road from us/our house** il y a un supermarché juste en face/en face de notre maison; **just a. the border** de l'autre côté *ou* au-delà de la frontière; **he sat a. the table from me** il s'assit en face de moi; **she glanced a. the room at us** elle nous lança un regard de l'autre bout de la pièce
3 *(so as to cover)* **he leaned a. my desk** il s'est penché par-dessus mon bureau; **a smile spread a. her face** un sourire a éclairé son visage
4 *(so as to cross)* en travers de, à travers; **the study of literature a. cultures** l'étude de la littérature à travers différentes cultures; **the lines cut a. each other** les lignes se coupent
5 *(throughout)* **a. the political spectrum** dans l'ensemble de la classe politique
6 *(on)* **he hit me a. the face** il m'a frappé au visage
ADV **1** *(from one side to the other)* d'un côté à l'autre; **the room is three metres a.** la pièce fait trois mètres de large; **I helped him a.** je l'ai aidé à traverser **2** *(on or to the other side)* de l'autre côté; **he reached a. and picked the pen up** il a tendu le bras et a pris le stylo; **she walked a. to Mary** elle s'est dirigée vers Mary; **I looked a. at my mother** j'ai regardé ma mère **3** *(in crosswords)* horizontalement; **what's 23 a.?** *(clue)* quelle est la définition du 23 horizontal *ou* horizontalement?; *(solution)* quelle est la réponse du 23 horizontal *ou* horizontalement?
• **across from** PREP en face de; **the man sitting a. from me** l'homme qui est/était assis en face de moi
• **across the board** ADV systématiquement;

stock prices have fallen a. the board le prix des actions a baissé de façon systématique

across-the-board ADJ général, systématique; **an a. salary rise** une augmentation de salaire générale

acrostic [əˈkrɒstɪk] N acrostiche *m*

acrylic [əˈkrɪlɪk] *Chem & Tex* N *(fabric, paint)* acrylique *m*
ADJ acrylique; *(garment)* en acrylique

ACT [ækt]

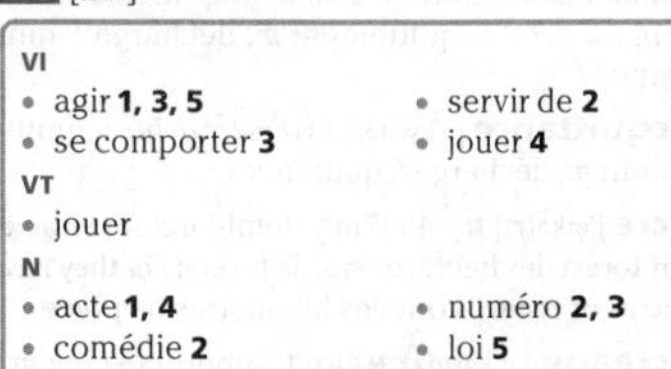

VI
- agir **1, 3, 5**
- servir de **2**
- se comporter **3**
- jouer **4**

VT
- jouer

N
- acte **1, 4**
- numéro **2, 3**
- comédie **2**
- loi **5**

VI **1** *(take action)* agir; **we must a. quickly to stop her** nous devons agir rapidement pour l'arrêter; **they acted for the best** ils ont agi pour le mieux; **to a. out of fear/greed/selfishness** agir sous l'emprise de la peur/par cupidité/par égoïsme; **she has a good lawyer acting for her** elle est représentée par un bon avocat; **to a. on behalf of sb, to a. on sb's behalf** agir au nom de qn
2 *(serve)* **to a. as** servir de, faire office de; **she acted as my interpreter** elle m'a servi d'interprète; **the trees a. as a windbreak** les arbres servent de barrière contre le vent; **to a. as a warning** servir d'avertissement; **the smell acts as a warning to other animals** les autres animaux sont avertis par l'odeur; **the engine acts as a brake** le moteur fait fonction de frein
3 *(behave)* agir, se comporter; **they acted very sensibly/responsibly** ils ont agi de façon très raisonnable/responsable; **they a. as if nothing had happened** ils se comportent *ou* ils font comme si rien ne s'était passé; **she just acts dumb** elle fait l'innocente; **to a. stupid/all innocent** faire l'idiot/l'innocent; **you acted like a fool** vous vous êtes conduit comme un imbécile
4 *Cin, Theat & TV (perform a part)* jouer; **he's been acting since he was a child** il joue depuis son enfance; **he can't a.** c'est un mauvais acteur; **I always wanted to a.** j'ai toujours voulu être acteur; **to a. in a film** tourner dans un film
5 *(produce an effect, work)* agir
VT *Cin, Theat & TV (part)* jouer, tenir; *(play)* jouer; **he's acting (the part of) King Lear** il joue le rôle du Roi Lear; *Fig* **he tries to a. the dutiful husband** il essaie de jouer les maris parfaits; **a. your age!** arrête de faire l'enfant!
N **1** *(action, deed)* acte *m*; **the a. of a criminal/madman** l'action *f* d'un criminel/fou; **to be caught in the a.** être pris sur le fait; **she was caught in the a. of taking the money** on l'a surprise en train de voler l'argent; **to get in on the a.** s'y mettre; **to be/to let sb in on the a.** être/mettre qn dans le coup
2 *(pretence)* comédie *f*, numéro *m*; **to put on an a.** jouer la comédie; **it's all an a.** tout ça c'est de la comédie; **I'm not fooled by your worried mother a.!** ton numéro de mère anxieuse ne prendra pas avec moi!
3 *(in circus, show)* numéro *m*; **a comedy a.** un numéro de comédie; *Fam Fig* **to get one's a. together** se reprendre◻; *Fam Fig* **to clean up one's a.** s'acheter une conduite, s'amender; *Am Fam* **to queer the a.** tout faire foirer
4 *Mus & Theat (part of play, opera)* acte *m*; **A. I, scene 1** Acte I, scène 1
5 *Law & Pol* loi *f*; **an a. of Congress/Parliament** une loi du Congrès/Parlement
▸▸ *Bible* ***the Acts of the Apostles*** les Actes *mpl* des Apôtres; *Rel* ***an act of faith*** un acte de foi; ***act of God*** *Rel* acte *m* divin; *Ins & Law* cas *m* de force majeure; *Mil* ***an act of war*** un acte de guerre

▸**act on** VT INSEP **1** *(advice, suggestion)* suivre; *(order)* exécuter; *(letter)* donner suite à; **she acted on the information we gave her** elle a suivi les *ou* s'est conformée aux indications que nous lui avons données; **acting on your instructions, we have closed your account** selon vos instructions, nous avons fermé votre compte **2** *Chem & Phys (chemical, drug)* agir sur; **acid acts on metal** l'acide agit sur le métal; **to a. on the brain/the bowels** exercer une action sur *ou* agir sur le cerveau/l'intestin

▸**act out** VT SEP *(fantasy)* réaliser; *(emotions)* extérioriser; *(event, story)* reconstituer; **local people a. out scenes from the town's history** les gens du coin jouent des scènes de l'histoire de leur ville

▸**act up** VI *Fam (person)* faire l'idiot, déconner; *(child)* faire des siennes; *(engine, machine)* déconner; **my knee/back is acting up again** mon genou/dos recommence à me faire souffrir

▸**act upon** = **act on**

ACTH [ˌeɪsiːtiːˈeɪtʃ] N *Biol (abbr* **adrenocorticotropic hormone***)* ACTH *f inv*

acting [ˈæktɪŋ] N *Cin, Theat & TV* **1** *(profession)* profession *f* d'acteur, profession *f* d'actrice; **I've done a bit of a.** *(theatre)* j'ai fait un peu de théâtre; *(cinema)* j'ai fait un peu de cinéma **2** *(performance)* interprétation *f*, jeu *m*; **the a. was superb** l'interprétation était superbe
COMP *Cin, Theat & TV (lessons, school)* de comédien
ADJ *(temporary)* intérimaire, par intérim

ACTION [ˈækʃən]

- action **1–3, 5, 6, 8–10**
- geste **2**
- activité **4**
- mécanique, mécanisme **8**
- combat **10**
- acte **2**
- effet **3**
- intrigue **6**
- procès **9**

N **1** *(process)* action *f*; **it's time for a.** il est temps d'agir, passons aux actes; **to go into a.** entrer en action; **to take a.** prendre des mesures; **a man of a.** un homme d'action; **we must take a. to stop them** nous devons agir pour les arrêter; **we want a. not words** nous voulons des actes non des paroles; **to put sth into a.** *(idea, policy)* mettre qch en pratique; *(plan)* mettre qch à exécution; *(machine)* mettre qch en marche; **she's an excellent dancer, you should see her in a.** c'est une excellente danseuse, vous devriez la voir en action; **out of a.** *(machine)* hors de service, hors d'usage; *(person)* hors de combat; *Br* **the car is out of a.** la voiture est en panne; **the storm put the telephone out of a.** le téléphone est en dérangement à cause de l'orage; **her accident will put her out of a. for four months** son accident va la mettre hors de combat pour quatre mois; **freedom of a.** liberté d'action
2 *(deed)* acte *m*, geste *m*, action *f*; **she defended her a. in dismissing him** elle a défendu son geste en le congédiant; **he's not responsible for his actions** il n'est pas responsable de ses actes; *Prov* **actions speak louder than words** les actes en disent plus long que les mots
3 *(of chemical, drug, force)* effet *m*, action *f*
4 *(activity, events)* activité *f*
5 *Fam (excitement)* action◻ *f*; **he wants to be where the a. is** il veut être au cœur de l'action; **they were looking for some a.** ils cherchaient un peu d'animation; **where's the a. around here?** où est-ce que ça bouge par ici?; **we want a piece of the a.** nous voulons notre part du gâteau
6 *(of book, film, play)* intrigue *f*, action *f*; **the a. takes place in a barber's shop** l'action se situe *ou* se passe chez un coiffeur
7 *(movement* ▸ *of person)* gestes *mpl*; *(*▸ *of animal)* allure *f*; *(*▸ *of heart)* fonctionnement *m*
8 *Tech (operating mechanism* ▸ *of clock)* mécanique *f*, mécanisme *m*; *(*▸ *of gun)* mécanisme *m*; *(*▸ *of piano)* action *f*, mécanique *f*; *(*▸ *of pump, lock)* jeu *m*
9 *Law* procès *m*, action *f* en justice; **to bring an a. against sb** intenter une action contre qn; **a. at law** action *f* en justice; *(trial)* procès *m*; **a. for libel** procès *m ou* plainte *f* en diffamation; **a. for damages** action *f* en dommages et intérêts; **a. for breach of contract** action *f* contractuelle
10 *Mil (fighting)* combat *m*, action *f*; **to go into a.** engager le combat; **to see a.** *(soldier)* combattre; **killed in a.** tué au combat; **ready for a.** prêt à combattre; **to send troops into a.** faire intervenir *ou* faire donner des troupes
EXCLAM *Cin* action!
COMP *Cin & Phot (photography)* d'action
VT *(idea, suggestion)* mettre en action *ou* en pratique; *(plan)* mettre à exécution
▸▸ *Cin* ***action movie*** film *m* d'action; *Art* ***action painting*** peinture *f* gestuelle; ***action plan*** plan *m* d'action; *Br TV* ***action replay*** = répétition immédiate d'une séquence; ***action stations*** *Mil* NPL postes *mpl* de combat EXCLAM à vos postes!

actionable [ˈækʃənəbəl] ADJ *Law (allegations, deed, person)* passible de poursuites; *(claim)* recevable

action-packed ADJ *(film, novel, match)* bourré d'action; *(day, holiday)* rempli d'activités, bien rempli

activate [ˈæktɪveɪt] VT **1** *(gen) & Chem & Tech* activer; *(mechanism, alarm)* déclencher **2** *Phys* rendre radioactif

activation [ˌæktɪˈveɪʃən] N activation *f*

active [ˈæktɪv] ADJ **1** *(lively* ▸ *person)* actif, dynamique; *(*▸ *imagination)* vif, actif; **to be still a.** *(elderly person)* être encore alerte *ou* actif
2 *(busy, involved* ▸ *person)* actif, énergique; *(*▸ *life, stock market)* actif; **to be a. in sth, to take an a. part in sth** prendre une part active à qch; **she's very a. in the party** elle est très active au sein du parti; **he was very a. in seeing that the measure was passed** il a contribué très activement à l'approbation de cette mesure; **to be politically a.** être engagé; **to be sexually a.** avoir une activité sexuelle; **how much of the population is in a. employment?** quel pourcentage de la population a un emploi?; *Mil* **he saw a.** *Br* **service** *or Am* **duty in the Far East** il a servi en Extrême-Orient; *Mil* **to be on the a. list** faire partie de l'armée active
3 *(keen* ▸ *encouragement, interest, dislike)* vif; **to take an a. dislike to sb** se prendre d'une vive aversion contre qn; **the proposal is under a. discussion** la proposition fait l'objet d'une vive discussion
4 *Banking (in operation* ▸ *account)* actif; *Law & Admin (*▸ *case, file)* en cours; *(*▸ *law, regulation)* en vigueur; *Geol (*▸ *volcano)* en activité
5 *Chem (chemical, ingredient)* actif
6 *Gram* actif
N *Gram (voice)* actif *m*, voix *f* active; *(verb)* verbe *m* actif; **a verb in the a.** un verbe à l'actif
▸▸ *Comput* ***active desktop*** bureau *m* actif; *Comput* ***active file*** fichier *m* actif; *Comput* ***active matrix screen*** écran *m* à matrice active; *Banking & Fin* ***active money*** monnaie *f* circulante; *Fin & Com* ***active partner*** *(in company)* associé(e) *m,f* gérant(e), commandité(e) *m,f*; *Comput* ***active program*** programme *m* en cours d'exécution; *Gram* ***the active voice*** la voix active, l'actif *m*; **in the a. voice** à l'actif; *Comput* ***active window*** fenêtre *f* active *ou* activée

actively [ˈæktɪvlɪ] ADV **1** *(involve, participate)* activement; **they were a. seeking peace** ils cherchaient activement à faire la paix **2** *(disagree, discourage)* vivement, activement; **to a. dislike sb** avoir une vive aversion pour qn

activist [ˈæktɪvɪst] N *Pol* militant(e) *m,f*, activiste *mf*; **anti-nuclear/peace activists** activistes *mfpl* antinucléaires/en faveur de la paix

activity [ækˈtɪvətɪ] *(pl* **activities***)* N **1** *(of brain, person)* activité *f*; *(of place, bank account)* mouvement *m*; **this week has seen a lot of a. on the Stock Market** la Bourse a été très active cette semaine; **economic/political a.** activité *f* économique/politique **2** *(occupation)* activité *f*; **activities** *(at holiday camp)* animation *f*; **leisure activities** activités *fpl* de loisir
▸▸ *Acct* ***activity accounting*** comptabilité *f* par centres de responsabilité; ***activity book*** livre-jeu *m*; ***activity break*** (courtes) vacances *fpl* actives; ***activity centre*** centre *m* aéré; ***activity chart*** graphique *m* des activités; *Br* ***activity holiday*** vacances *fpl* actives; *Econ* ***activity indicator*** indicateur *m* d'activité; *Econ* ***activity rate*** taux *m* d'activité; *Acct* ***activity ratio*** ratio *m ou* coefficent *m* d'activité, ratio *m* de gestion

actor [ˈæktə(r)] N *Cin, Theat & TV* acteur(trice) *m,f*, comédien(enne) *m,f*; **I'm a terrible a.** je suis un piètre comédien

actress [ˈæktrɪs] N actrice *f*, comédienne *f*; *Br Fam Hum* **he's got a huge one, as the a. said to the bishop** il en a une énorme, si j'ose dire

actual ['æktʃʊəl] ADJ **1** *(genuine)* réel, véritable; *(existing as a real fact)* concret(ète); **what were her a. words?** quels étaient ses mots exacts?; **to take an a. example** prendre un exemple concret; **the a. result was quite different** le résultat véritable était plutôt différent; **the a. cost was £1,000** le coût exact était de 1000 livres; **what's the a. cash value of the car?** quelle est la valeur réelle de la voiture? **2** *(emphatic use)* même; **the a. ceremony doesn't start until 10.30** la cérémonie même ne commence pas avant 10h30; **this is the a. house where she was born** voici en fait la maison où elle est née

• **actuals** NPL **1** *Acct & Fin (real figures)* chiffres *mpl* réels; **to compare budgeted amounts with actuals** comparer les prévisions budgétaires et les résultats obtenus **2** *St Exch* livraisons *fpl* physiques, marchandises *fpl* livrées au comptant

• **in actual fact** ADV en fait

►► *Law* ***actual bodily harm*** coups *mpl* et blessures *fpl*; *Acct & Fin* ***actual cost*** prix *m* de revient *ou* d'achat; *St Exch* ***actual quotations*** cours *mpl* effectifs; *Cin, Rad & TV* ***actual sound*** son *m* direct; ***actual value*** valeur *f* réelle

> Note that the French adjective **actuel** is a false friend and is never a translation for the English adjective **actual**. It means **current**.

actuality [ˌæktʃʊ'ælətɪ] (*pl* **actualities**) N réalité *f*; **in a.** en réalité; **the actualities of the situation** les conditions réelles de la situation

actually ['æktʃʊəlɪ] ADV **1** *(establishing a fact)* vraiment; **I haven't a. read the book** à vrai dire, je n'ai pas lu le livre; **what did he a. say?** qu'est-ce qu'il a dit vraiment?; **what a. happened?** que s'est-il passé au juste?; **what he a. means is...** ce qu'il veut vraiment dire, c'est...; **I didn't a. see it myself** en réalité, je ne l'ai pas vu de mes propres yeux; **the piano's just for decoration, no one a. plays it** le piano fait partie du décor, en fait personne n'en joue

2 *(emphatic use)* vraiment; **did you a. say that?** vous avez vraiment dit cela?; **he a. swore** il est (même) allé jusqu'à lâcher un juron; **she a. said good morning to me** à mon grand étonnement elle m'a dit bonjour; **he was a. on time for once** pour une fois il était à l'heure

3 *(contradicting or qualifying)* en fait; **she's a. older than she looks** en fait, elle est plus âgée qu'elle n'en a l'air; **I don't agree, a.** en fait, je ne suis pas d'accord; **he's not a very nice person, a.** il n'est pas très gentil à vrai dire; **a., yes, I do mind, very much!** à vrai dire, oui, ça m'ennuie beaucoup!; **I suppose you've never been there – I have, a.** je suppose que vous n'y êtes jamais allé – si, en fait

4 *(in requests, advice etc)* en fait; **a., you could set the table** en fait, tu pourrais mettre la table

> Note that the French adverb **actuellement** is a false friend and is never a translation for the English adverb **actually**. It means **at present**.

actuarial [ˌæktjʊ'eərɪəl] ADJ *Fin & Ins* actuariel

►► ***actuarial tables*** tables *fpl* de mortalité

actuary ['æktjʊərɪ] (*pl* **actuaries**) N *Fin & Ins* actuaire *mf*

actuate ['æktjʊeɪt] VT **1** *(machine, system)* mettre en marche, faire marcher **2** *Formal (person)* faire agir, inciter

actuation [ˌæktjʊ'eɪʃən] N *(of machine, system)* mise *f* en marche

actuator ['æktjʊeɪtə(r)] N *Tech* actionneur *m*

acuity [ə'kju:ətɪ] N *(of hearing, sight)* acuité *f*; *(of person, thought)* perspicacité *f*

acumen ['ækjʊmən] N perspicacité *f*, flair *m*

acupressure ['ækjʊpreʃə(r)] N *Med* digitopuncture *f*, acupressing *m*

acupuncture ['ækjʊpʌŋktʃə(r)] *Med* N acupuncture *f*, acuponcture *f*

COMP *(needle, treatment)* d'acupuncture, d'acuponcture

acupuncturist [ækjʊp'ʌŋktʃərɪst] N *Med* acupuncteur(trice) *m,f*, acuponcteur(trice) *m,f*

acute [ə'kju:t] ADJ **1** *(hearing, sense)* fin; *(sight)* pénétrant, perçant; **an a. sense of hearing** l'ouïe fine; **an a. sense of smell** l'odorat subtil *ou* développé

2 *(perceptive ► mind, person)* perspicace, pénétrant; (► *intelligence)* fin, vif; (► *analysis)* fin; **she has an a. awareness of their problems** elle a une perception pénétrante de leurs problèmes

3 *(severe ► pain)* aigu(ë), vif; (► *anxiety, distress)* vif; (► *shortage)* critique, grave; **to suffer a. embarrassment** être vivement embarrassé; **the problem was made more a.** le problème a été intensifié; **a. appendicitis** appendicite *f* aiguë

4 *Geom (angle)* aigu(ë)

5 *Ling (accent)* aigu(ë); **it's spelled with an "e" a.** ça s'écrit avec un "e" accent aigu

N *Gram* accent *m* aigu

►► *Med* ***acute care*** soins *mpl* médicaux de courte durée

acute-angled ADJ *Geom* à angle(s) aigu(s)

acutely [ə'kju:tlɪ] ADV **1** *(intensely ► be aware, feel)* vivement; (► *suffer)* intensément; **he felt the loss a.** il ressentit cette perte intensément; **we are a. aware** *or* **conscious of that** nous en sommes extrêmement conscients **2** *(extremely ► embarrassing, unhappy)* très, profondément **3** *(shrewdly)* avec perspicacité

acuteness [ə'kju:tnɪs] N **1** *(of hearing, sense)* finesse *f*

2 *(of mind, person)* perspicacité *f*, pénétration *f*; *(of analysis, observation)* finesse *f*

3 *(of anxiety, pain, distress)* violence *f*, intensité *f*; *(of illness)* violence *f*; *(of shortage)* sévérité *f*, gravité *f*

4 *Geom (of angle)* caractère *m* aigu

AD [ˌeɪ'di:] ADV *(abbr* **Anno Domini***)* apr. J.-C.; **in AD 3** en l'an 3 (après Jésus-Christ *ou* de notre ère)

N **1** *Cin & Theat (abbr* **art director***)* directeur(trice) *m,f* artistique **2** *(abbr* **antidepressant***)* **ADs** antidépresseurs *mpl*

ad [æd] N *Fam (for job, event, accommodation)* (petite) annonce *f*; *(for product, service)* pub *f*; **to put an ad in the newspaper** passer une annonce dans le journal; **an ad for toothpaste, a toothpaste ad** une pub pour du dentifrice; **while the ads are on** pendant la pub

►► ***ad agency*** agence *f* publicitaire; ***ad break*** coupure *f* publicitaire

adage ['ædɪdʒ] N *Ling* adage *m*

adagio [ə'dædʒɪəʊ] *Mus* N adagio *m*

ADJ adagio

ADV adagio

Adam ['ædəm] PR N *Bible* Adam; **I don't know him from A.** je ne le connais ni d'Ève ni d'Adam

►► *Br Fam Hum* ***Adam's ale*** flotte *f*, château-la-pompe *m*; *Anat* ***Adam's apple*** pomme *f* d'Adam

adam ['ædəm] N *Fam Drugs slang (ecstasy)* ecstasy *f*, exta *f*

adamant ['ædəmənt] ADJ résolu, inflexible; **he is a. on this point** sur ce point il ne transige pas; **she is a. that she saw him** elle affirme l'avoir vu et ne veut pas en démordre

adamantly ['ædəməntlɪ] ADV *(say, maintain)* de façon catégorique; *(refuse)* catégoriquement

adapt [ə'dæpt] VT **1** *(adjust)* adapter, ajuster **2** *(book, play)* adapter; **the play was adapted for television** la pièce a été adaptée pour la télévision; **adapted from Shakespeare** d'après Shakespeare; **to a. oneself to circumstances/new surroundings** s'adapter aux circonstances/à un nouvel environnement

VI s'adapter; **she adapted well to the change** elle s'est bien adaptée au changement; **it was a. or die** il fallait s'adapter à tout prix

adaptability [əˌdæptə'bɪlɪtɪ] N *(of person)* faculté *f* d'adaptation, adaptabilité *f*

adaptable [ə'dæptəbəl] ADJ **1** *(adjustable)* adaptable, ajustable (**to** à) **2** *(person)* souple, qui s'adapte facilement; *Bot & Zool (species)* qui s'adapte facilement

adaptation [ˌædæp'teɪʃən] N *(of person, animal, work)* adaptation *f*; **to make an a. of a play for radio** faire l'adaptation d'une pièce pour la radio

adapter [ə'dæptə(r)] N **1** *(plug)* transformateur *m*; *(with several sockets)* prise *f* multiple **2** *Tech (connecting pipes)* raccord *m* **3** *(person)* adaptateur(trice) *m,f*

►► *Comput* ***adapter card*** carte-adaptateur *f*

adaptive [ə'dæptɪv] ADJ *Biol (mechanism)* adaptif

adaptor = **adapter**

ADC [ˌeɪdi:'si:] N **1** *Mil (abbr* **aide-de-camp***)* aide *m* de camp **2** *Tech (abbr* **analogue-digital converter***)* CAN *m*

add [æd] VT **1** *(put together)* ajouter; **a. her name to the list** ajoute son nom à la liste; **they added ten percent for service** ils ont ajouté dix pour cent pour le service; **this book adds little to the debate** ce livre n'apporte pas grand-chose au débat; *Fig* **to a. fuel to the fire** jeter de l'huile sur le feu **2** *(say)* ajouter; **I have nothing to a.** je n'ai rien à ajouter **3** *Math (figures)* additionner; *(column of figures)* totaliser; **a. 4 and** *or* **to 9** additionnez 4 et 9; **a. these numbers together** additionnez ces nombres, faites l'addition de ces nombres

VI faire des additions

▸ **add on** VT SEP ajouter

▸ **add to** VT INSEP *(building)* faire une addition à, agrandir; *(difficulty, surprise etc)* augmenter, ajouter à; *(beauty)* rehausser; *(crisis)* accentuer; **inflation only added to our worries** l'inflation ne faisait qu'ajouter à nos soucis; **it will a. another £100 to the cost** cela augmentera le coût de 100 livres; **to a. to my misfortune** pour mettre le comble à mon malheur; **to a. to what we were saying yesterday...** pour compléter ce que nous disions hier...

▸ **add up** VT SEP *(find the sum of ► figures)* additionner; (► *bill, column of figures)* totaliser; **we added up the advantages and disadvantages** nous avons fait le total des avantages et des inconvénients; **when you a. it all up it was quite cheap** si on fait le total, c'était assez bon marché; **you've added this up wrong** tu t'es trompé dans l'addition

VI **1** *(give correct total)* se recouper; **these figures don't a. up** ces chiffres ne font pas le compte; **the bill doesn't a. up** la note n'est pas juste; *Fig* **it just doesn't a. up** il y a quelque chose qui cloche *ou* qui ne marche pas **2** *(calculate)* additionner; **that boy can't a. up** ce garçon ne sait pas additionner

▸ **add up to** VT INSEP **1** *(of figures)* s'élever à, se monter à; **it adds up to £22** cela s'élève à 22 livres **2** *Fig (of results, situation)* signifier, se résumer à; **it all adds up to our having to leave** autrement dit, nous devons partir; **what evidence we've got doesn't a. up to much really** les preuves dont nous disposons ne constituent pas vraiment grand-chose; **is that all you've done? it doesn't a. up to much** est-ce que c'est tout ce que tu as fait? ça ne fait pas beaucoup

add-back N *Acct* réintégration *f*

added ['ædɪd] ADJ **1** *(gen)* supplémentaire; **the tax is just an a. financial burden** l'impôt constitue simplement un fardeau financier supplémentaire **2** *(on food package)* **a. ingredients** autres ingrédients; **no a. sugar** sans ajout de sucre; **no a. preservatives** sans conservateurs

►► *Com, Mktg & Acct* ***added value*** valeur *f* ajoutée

addendum [ə'dendəm] (*pl* **addenda** [-də]) N addendum *m*, addenda *mpl*

adder ['ædə(r)] N **1** *Zool (snake)* vipère *f* **2** *(machine)* additionneur *m*

addict ['ædɪkt] N **1** *(to drugs)* intoxiqué(e) *m,f*, **(drug) a.** toxicomane *mf* **2** *Fig* fanatique *mf*, fana *mf*, mordu(e) *m,f*; **she's a film a.** c'est une fana *ou* mordue de cinéma; **I never miss an episode, I'm a complete a.** je ne rate jamais un épisode, je suis complètement accro

addiction [ə'dɪkʃən] N *(to drugs)* dépendance *f*, *Fig* penchant *m* fort, forte inclination *f*; **coffee at 4 o'clock had become something of an a. with her** elle ne pouvait plus se passer du café de 4 heures

addictive [ə'dɪktɪv] ADJ qui crée une dépendance; **chocolate is very a.** le chocolat, c'est une vraie drogue, on devient vite accro au chocolat; **it could become a.** on prend vite l'habitude; **to have an a. personality** avoir tendance à devenir dépendant

addictologist [ˌædɪk'tɒlədʒɪst] N addictologue *mf*

addictology [ædɪk'tɒlədʒɪ] N addictologie *f*

adding ['ædɪŋ] N addition *f*

►► ***adding machine*** calculatrice *f*, machine *f* à calculer; ***adding up*** addition *f*

Addis Ababa ['ædɪs'æbəbə] **N** Addis-Ababa, Addis-Abeba

addition [ə'dɪʃən] **N 1** *(gen) & Math* addition *f* **2** *(something or someone added)* addition *f*, ajout *m*; **a last-minute a. to the programme** un ajout de dernière minute au programme; **an important a. to our collection** une nouvelle pièce de choix à notre collection; **they're going to have an a. to the family** leur famille va s'agrandir; **she's a welcome new a. to our staff** nous sommes heureux de la compter au sein du personnel **3** *Am Constr (to house)* annexe *f*

• **in addition ADV** de plus, de surcroît

• **in addition to PREP** en plus de

additional [ə'dɪʃənəl] **ADJ** additionnel; *(supplementary)* supplémentaire; *Fin (investment, expenses)* supplémentaire; **a. information can be found on page 28** se référer à la page 28 pour des informations complémentaires; **this will require a. investment** cela nécessitera un investissement supplémentaire; **there is an a. charge on certain trains** il y a un supplément à payer pour certains trains; **for** *or* **at no a. charge** sans supplément

▸▸ *Law* ***additional clause*** avenant *m*; *Pol* ***additional member system*** = mode de scrutin en vigueur au pays de Galles et en Écosse selon lequel les électeurs votent deux fois: d'abord pour un candidat représentant leur circonscription locale puis au niveau régional, pour la liste d'un parti ou pour un candidat indépendant; *Fin* ***additional payment*** supplément *m*; ***additional postage*** surtaxe *f* postale; *Fin* ***additional voluntary contribution*** supplément *m* de cotisation retraite *(payé volontairement)*

additionally [ə'dɪʃənəlɪ] **ADV 1** *(further, more)* davantage, plus **2** *(moreover)* en outre, de plus

additive ['ædɪtɪv] **N** additif *m*

addled ['ædld] **ADJ 1** *(person)* aux idées confuses, brouillon; *(brain)* fumeux, brouillon; *(ideas)* confus **2** *Culin (egg)* pourri

add-on **N** *Comput* produit *m* supplémentaire, extension *f*

ADJ additionel

▸▸ *Comput* ***add-on board*** carte *f* d'extension; *Transp* ***add-on fare*** supplément *m*

address [ə'dres] **VT 1** *Admin (envelope, letter, package)* adresser, mettre l'adresse sur; **the letter is addressed to you** cette lettre vous est adressée; **it's incorrectly addressed** l'adresse est incorrecte

2 *(direct)* adresser; **a. all complaints to the manager** adressez vos doléances au directeur; **his remarks were addressed to you** ses remarques vous étaient adressées

3 *(speak to)* s'adresser à; *(write to)* écrire à; **she stood up and addressed the audience** elle s'est levée et a pris la parole devant l'assistance; **a judge should be addressed as "your honour"** on devrait s'adresser à un juge en disant "votre honneur"

4 *(deal with ▸ subject, theme)* traiter, examiner; *(▸ issue, problem)* aborder; **to a. oneself to a task** s'attaquer *ou* se mettre à une tâche

5 *(take position facing)* faire face à

6 *Comput* adresser, accéder à

7 *Golf (ball)* viser

N 1 *(of building, person, letter)* adresse *f*; **a Glasgow a.** une adresse à Glasgow; **what is your a.?** quelle est ton adresse?; **we've changed our a.** nous avons changé d'adresse; **have you notified him of any change of a.?** lui avez-vous fait part d'éventuels changements d'adresse?; **they left no (forwarding) a.** ils n'ont pas laissé d'adresse; **not known at this a.** *(on returned letter)* inconnu à cette adresse

2 *(speech)* discours *m*, allocution *f*

3 *Comput* adresse *f*

4 *(title)* **form of a.** titre *m*; **what's the correct form of a. for a bishop?** comment doit-on s'adresser à un évêque?

5 *Formal or Arch (skill)* habileté *f*, doigté *m*

6 *Arch (usu pl) (expression of affection)* **addresses** galanteries *fpl*; **to pay one's addresses to sb** faire la cour à qn

▸▸ *(gen) & Comput* ***address book*** carnet *m* d'adresses; *Comput* ***address bus*** bus *m* d'adresse; *Comput* ***address file*** fichier *m* d'adresses; ***address label*** étiquette *f* d'adresse

addressable [ə'dresəbəl] **ADJ** *Comput* adressable

▸▸ *Mktg* ***addressable audience*** audience *f* utile; *Mktg* ***addressable market*** marché *m* utile

addressee [ˌædre'siː] **N** destinataire *mf*

addressing [ə'dresɪŋ] **N** adressage *m*

▸▸ ***addressing machine*** machine *f* à adresser

adduce [ə'djuːs] **VT** *(explanation, proof, reason)* fournir, apporter; *(expert)* invoquer, citer

adduct [ə'dʌkt] **VT** *Anat (muscle)* déterminer l'adduction de

adduction [ə'dʌkʃən] **N** *Physiol* adduction *f*

adductor [ə'dʌktə(r)] **N** *Anat* adducteur *m*

adenoidal [ˌædɪ'nɔɪdəl] **ADJ** *Physiol* adénoïde

adenoids ['ædɪnɔɪdz] **NPL** *Anat* végétations *fpl* (adénoïdes)

adept **ADJ** [ə'dept] habile, adroit; **to be a. at doing sth** être adroit à faire qch

N ['ædept] expert *m* (**in** en)

adequacy ['ædɪkwəsɪ] **N 1** *(of amount, payment, sum)* fait *m* d'être suffisant **2** *(of person)* compétence *f*, compétences *fpl*, capacité *f*, capacités *fpl*; *(of description, expression)* justesse *f*; **they doubted her a. as a mother** ils doutaient de ses capacités de mère

adequate ['ædɪkwət] **ADJ 1** *(in amount, quantity)* suffisant, adéquat; **a. supplies** des réserves suffisantes; **to be given a. warning** être suffisamment averti; **to have adequate time to do sth** avoir suffisamment de temps pour faire qch; **the money we were given was more than a.** l'argent que l'on nous avait donné était plus que suffisant **2** *(appropriate)* adéquat, approprié; **he proved a. to the task** il s'est révélé être à la hauteur de la tâche; **this flat is hardly a. for a family of six** cet appartement ne convient guère à une famille de six personnes; **this one is quite a.** celui-ci fera très bien l'affaire **3** *(just satisfactory)* acceptable, satisfaisant

adequately ['ædɪkwətlɪ] **ADV 1** *(sufficiently)* suffisamment **2** *(satisfactorily)* convenablement

ADF [eɪdiː'ef] **N** *Comptr (abbr* **automatic document feeder**) dispositif *m* d'alimentation automatique

ADHD [ˌeɪdiːˌeɪtʃ'diː] **N** *Med (abbr* **attention deficit hyperactivity disorder**) Thada *m*

adhere [əd'hɪə(r)] **VI 1** *(stick)* coller, adhérer; **to a. to sth** coller à qch **2** *(remain loyal)* **to a. to** *(party, treaty)* adhérer à; *(rule)* observer; *(plan)* se conformer à; *(belief, idea)* adhérer à, souscrire à; **I don't a. to that philosophy at all** je n'adhère pas du tout à cette philosophie **3** *(join)* **to a. to a political party** adhérer à un parti politique

adherence [əd'hɪərəns] **N** *(to treaty, political party)* adhésion *f* (**to** à); *(to rule)* observation *f* (**to** de)

adherent [əd'hɪərənt] **N** *(to party)* adhérent(e) *m,f*, partisan(e) *m,f*; *(to agreement)* adhérent(e) *m,f*; *(to belief, religion)* adepte *mf*

adhesion [əd'hiːʒən] **N 1** *(stickiness)* adhérence *f* (**to** à) **2** *(of person)* adhésion *f* (**to** à)

adhesive [əd'hiːsɪv] **N** adhésif *m*

ADJ adhésif, collant; *(label)* gommé

▸▸ ***adhesive tape*** *(sticky tape)* ruban *m* adhésif, Scotch® *m*; *(sticking plaster)* sparadrap *m*

adhesiveness [əd'hiːsɪvnɪs] **N** adhérence *f*

ad hoc [ˌæd'hɒk] **ADJ** *(committee, market research)* ad hoc *(inv)*; *(decision, solution)* adapté aux circonstances, ponctuel; **the board meets on an a. basis** le conseil se réunit de façon ad hoc

ADV à l'improviste

ad hominem [ˌæd'hɒmɪnem] **ADJ** ad hominem

adieu [ə'djuː] *(pl* **adieus** *or* **adieux** [-'djuːz]) *Arch or Literary* **EXCLAM** adieu!

N adieu *m*; **I bid you a.** je vous fais mes adieux

ad infinitum [ˌædɪnfɪ'naɪtəm] **ADV** à l'infini; *Fam* **he went on talking a.** il parlait à n'en plus finir

adipose ['ædɪpəʊs] **ADJ** *Biol* adipeux

▸▸ *Anat* ***adipose tissue*** tissu *m* adipeux

adjacent [ə'dʒeɪsənt] **ADJ 1** *(sharing common boundary ▸ house, room)* contigu(ë), voisin; *(▸ building)* qui jouxte, mitoyen; *(▸ country, territory)* limitrophe; **their house is a. to the police station** leur maison jouxte le commissariat de police; **the two rooms are a.** les deux pièces sont contiguës **2** *(nearby ▸ street)* adjacent; *(▸ town)* proche, avoisinant **3** *Math* adjacent

adjectival [ˌædʒɪk'taɪvəl] **ADJ** *Gram* adjectif, adjectival

adjectivally [ˌædʒɪk'taɪvəlɪ] **ADV** *Gram* adjectivement; **present participle used a.** participe présent adjectivé

adjective ['ædʒɪktɪv] **N** *Gram* adjectif *m*

adjoin [ə'dʒɔɪn] **VT** *(house, land, room)* être contigu(ë) à, toucher à, attenir à; **they had rooms adjoining mine** leurs chambres étaient contiguës à la mienne; **Kansas adjoins Colorado** le Kansas est un état limitrophe du Colorado

VI être contigu(ë); **the two buildings a.** les deux bâtiments sont contigus

adjoining [ə'dʒɔɪnɪŋ] **ADJ** contigu(ë), attenant; *(state, country)* limitrophe; **the a. room** la pièce voisine *ou* à côté; **a. rooms** des pièces contiguës

adjourn [ə'dʒɜːn] **VT 1** *(break off)* suspendre; **the president adjourned the meeting** le président a levé la séance **2** *(defer)* ajourner, remettre, reporter; **let's a. this discussion until tomorrow** reportons cette discussion à demain; **the trial was adjourned until the next day** le procès fut ajourné au lendemain

VI 1 *(person, committee, court ▸ break off)* suspendre la séance; *(▸ end)* lever la séance **2** *(meeting etc ▸ be closed)* être levé; *(▸ be interrupted)* être suspendu **3** *(move elsewhere)* se retirer, passer; **shall we a. to the living room for coffee?** passerons-nous au salon pour prendre le café?

adjournment [ə'dʒɜːnmənt] **N** *(of discussion, meeting)* suspension *f*, ajournement *m*; *Law (of trial)* ajournement *m*; **to call for an a.** demander un ajournement; **to move the a.** demander la clôture

adjudge [ə'dʒʌdʒ] **VT** *Formal* **1** *(pronounce)* déclarer **2** *Law (judge)* prononcer, déclarer; *(award)* adjuger, accorder; **he was adjudged guilty of the murder** il a été déclaré coupable du meurtre; **the court adjudged damages in favour of the defendant** le tribunal a accordé des dommages et intérêts au défendeur

adjudicate [ə'dʒuːdɪkeɪt] **VI 1** *(give a decision)* se prononcer (**on** sur) **2** *Law (serve as judge)* arbitrer

VT *(claim, issue)* décider; *(competition)* juger; *Law* **to a. sb bankrupt** déclarer *ou* mettre qn en faillite

adjudication [əˌdʒuːdɪ'keɪʃən] **N** *(decision)* jugement *m*, décision *f*; *Law* arrêt *m*

▸▸ *Law* ***adjudication of bankruptcy*** déclaration *f* de faillite

adjudicator [ə'dʒuːdɪkeɪtə(r)] **N** *(of competition)* juge *m*, arbitre *m*; *Law (of dispute)* arbitre *m*

adjunct ['ædʒʌŋkt] **N 1** *(addition)* accessoire *m* **2** *(subordinate person)* adjoint(e) *m,f*, auxiliaire *mf* **3** *Gram* complément *m*

adjust [ə'dʒʌst] **VT 1** *(regulate ▸ heat, height, speed, pressure)* ajuster, régler; *(▸ knob, loudness)* ajuster; *(▸ brakes, machine, television)* régler, mettre au point; *(▸ clock, watch)* régler; *(▸ valve)* tarer; *Naut (▸ compass)* compenser, corriger; **to a. the controls of a device** mettre au point le réglage d'un appareil; **to a. the picture on a TV set** régler l'image d'un téléviseur; **the seat can be adjusted for height** la hauteur du siège est réglable

2 *(alter ▸ plan, programme)* ajuster, mettre au point; *(▸ length, size)* ajuster; *Com (▸ prices)* ajuster; *Fin (▸ figures, salaries)* rajuster, réajuster; *Acct (▸ accounts)* régulariser; *Fin* **the government has adjusted prices downwards/upwards** le gouvernement a relevé/baissé les prix; *Fin* **pensions have been adjusted upwards/downwards** les pensions ont été revues à la hausse/à la baisse *ou* ont été augmentées/diminuées; *Fin* **income adjusted for inflation** revenu réel compte tenu de l'inflation; *Fin* **figures adjusted for inflation** chiffres en monnaie constante

3 *(correct)* rectifier; **the figures have been seasonally adjusted** les chiffres sont les données corrigées des variations saisonnières

4 *(position of clothing, hat)* rajuster

5 *(adapt)* ajuster, adapter (**to** à); **to a. oneself to sth** s'adapter à qch

6 *Ins* **to a. a claim** régler *ou* répartir une demande d'indemnité; **to a. an average** répartir une avarie

VI 1 *(adapt)* s'adapter; **to a. to sth** s'adapter à qch **2** *(chair, machine)* se régler, s'ajuster; **the cover adjusts to fit all sizes** le couvercle se règle pour s'adapter à toutes les tailles

adjustable [ə'dʒʌstəbəl] **ADJ** *(chair, height, speed)* ajustable, réglable; *(shape, size)* ajustable, adaptable; *(hours, rate)* flexible; **the seat is a. for height** la hauteur du siège est réglable

▸▸ *Comput & Typ* ***adjustable line space*** interligne *f* réglable; *Tech Br* ***adjustable spanner***, *Am* ***adjustable wrench*** clé *f* à molette *ou* anglaise

adjustable-rate **ADJ** *Am (mortgage)* à taux variable

adjusted [ə'dʒʌstɪd] **ADJ** **well a.** équilibré; **badly a.** pas équilibré

▸▸ ***adjusted frequency*** *(in audio)* fréquence *f* réglée

adjuster [ə'dʒʌstə(r)] **N** *Tech (device)* appareil *m* de réglage; *Aut (on brake)* régleur *m*

▸▸ *Tech* ***adjuster nut*** écrou *m* de réglage; *Tech* ***adjuster screw*** vis *f* de réglage

adjusting [ə'dʒʌstɪŋ] **N** = **adjustment**

▸▸ *Acct* ***adjusting entry*** écriture *f* de régularisation; *Tech* ***adjusting screw*** vis *f* de réglage

adjustment [ə'dʒʌstmənt] **N 1** *(to heat, height, speed, pressure)* ajustement *m*, réglage *m*; *(to knob, loudness)* ajustement *m*; *(to brakes, machine, television)* réglage *m*, mise *f* au point; *(to clock, watch)* réglage *m*; **to make an a. to sth** régler qch, ajuster qch; **a slight a. improved the picture** une légère mise au point a amélioré l'image

2 *(to plan, programme)* ajustement *m*, mise *f* au point; *(to length, size)* ajustement *m*; *Fin (of figures, salaries)* rajustement *m*, réajustement *m*

3 *(correction)* rectification *f*; **no a. was made for seasonal variation** il n'y a pas eu de corrigé des variations saisonnières; **some adjustments had been made to the text** des modifications avaient été apportées au texte

4 *(adaptation* ▸ *of person)* adaptation *f*; **a period of a.** une période *ou* un temps d'adaptation

▸▸ *Acct* ***adjustment account*** compte *m* collectif; *Psy* ***adjustment disorder*** trouble *m* de l'adaptation

adjutant ['ædʒʊtənt] **N** *(assistant)* assistant(e) *m,f*, auxiliaire *mf*; *Mil* adjudant-major *m*

▸▸ *Orn* ***adjutant bird*** marabout *m*; ***adjutant general*** adjudant *m* général

ad-lib [,æd'lɪb] *(pt & pp* **ad-libbed**, *cont* **ad-libbing***)*

VT improviser

VI improviser

ADJ improvisé, impromptu

• **ad lib N** *(improvised performance)* improvisation *f*, improvisations *fpl*; *(witticism)* mot *m* d'esprit **ADV 1** *(without preparation)* à l'improviste; **to speak ad lib** improviser **2** *(without limit)* à volonté **3** *Mus* ad libitum

ad-libbing [,æd'lɪbɪŋ] **N** improvisation *f*

adman ['ædmæn] *(pl* **admen** [-men]*)* **N** *Fam* publicitaire□ *m*

admass ['ædmæs] *Br Mktg* **N** grand public *m*

COMP *(culture, society)* de grande consommation

admin ['ædmɪn] **N** *Fam Admin (abbr* **administration***)* *(work)* travail *m* administratif□; *(department)* administration□ *f*, **a. tasks** tâches *fpl* administratives; **are you (in) sales or a.?** vous êtes au service des ventes ou à l'administration?

administer [əd'mɪnɪstə(r)] **VT 1** *(manage* ▸ *business, institution)* diriger, administrer, gérer; *(*▸ *finances, fund)* gérer; *(*▸ *country, territory, public institution)* administrer; *(*▸ *estate)* régir **2** *Formal (dispense* ▸ *blow, medicine, punishment, test, last rites)* administrer; *Law (*▸ *law)* appliquer; **to a. justice** rendre la justice; *Law* **to a. an** *or* **the oath (to sb)** faire prêter serment (à qn)

administration [əd,mɪnɪ'streɪʃən] **N 1** *(process* ▸ *of business, institution)* direction *f*, administration *f*, gestion *f*; *(*▸ *of finances, fund)* gestion *f*; *(*▸ *of country, territory, public institution)* administration *f*; *(*▸ *of estate)* curatelle *f*

2 *Admin (administrative work)* travail *m* administratif; *(administrative department)* administration *f*

3 *(of help, justice, medicine, punishment)* administration *f*; *Law* **letters of a.** lettres *fpl* d'administration

4 *Law (of oath)* prestation *f*

5 *Com & Law (receivership)* **to go into a.** être placé sous contrôle judiciaire

• **Administration** **N** *Am Pol* **the A.** le gouvernement *m*; **the Bush A.** le gouvernement Bush

▸▸ *Acct* ***administration costs, administration expenses*** frais *mpl* d'administration, frais *mpl* de gestion; ***administration fee*** frais *mpl* de dossier

administrative [əd'mɪnɪstrətɪv] **ADJ** *Admin (work, skills)* administratif; *(error)* d'administration

▸▸ ***the administrative body*** le corps administratif; ***administrative costs*** frais *mpl* d'administration, frais *mpl* de gestion; *Br* ***the administrative grade*** *(in civil service)* les fonctionnaires *mpl* supérieurs; ***administrative headquarters*** siège *m* administratif; ***administrative staff*** personnel *m* administratif; ***administrative unit*** unité *f* administrative

administratively [əd'mɪnɪstrətɪvlɪ] **ADV** *Admin* administrativement

administrator [əd'mɪnɪstreɪtə(r)] **N 1** *(of business, institution)* directeur(trice) *m,f*, administrateur(trice) *m,f*; *(of area, public institution)* administrateur(trice) *m,f*; *(of estate)* curateur (trice) *m,f* **2** *Comput* administrateur *m*

admirable ['ædmərəbəl] **ADJ** admirable, excellent

admirably ['ædmərəblɪ] **ADV** admirablement; **she coped a.** elle s'en est tiré admirablement bien

admiral ['ædmərəl] **N 1** *Mil & Naut* amiral *m*; **a. of the fleet, fleet a.** amiral *m* de France **2** *Entom (butterfly)* vanesse *f*; **red a.** vulcain *m*

admiralty ['ædmərəltɪ] *(pl* **admiralties***)* **N** *Mil & Naut* amirauté *f*; *Br* **the A.** le ministère de la Marine; *Br* **First Lord of the A.** Ministre *m* de la Marine

▸▸ *Br* ***the Admiralty Board*** le ministère de la Marine; ***Admiralty Islands*** îles *fpl* de l'Amirauté

admiration [,ædmə'reɪʃən] **N 1** *(feeling)* admiration *f* (**for** pour); **to be full of a. for sb/sth** être plein d'admiration pour qn/qch, avoir une grande admiration pour qn/qch **2** *(person, thing)* **she was the a. of the entire class** elle faisait l'admiration de la classe entière

admire [əd'maɪə(r)] **VT** admirer; **he admired (her for) the way she dealt with the press** il admirait la façon dont elle savait s'y prendre avec la presse; **they a. him for sticking to his principles** ils l'admirent de s'en tenir à ses principes; **to a. oneself in the mirror** s'admirer dans le miroir; **you have to a. his persistence!** on ne peut qu'admirer sa persévérance!

admirer [əd'maɪərə(r)] **N 1** *(gen)* admirateur (trice) *m,f*; **I'm a great a. of people who speak their mind** j'admire énormément les gens qui disent ce qu'ils pensent **2** *Old-fashioned (suitor)* soupirant *m*; *Fam* **is that a letter from one of your admirers?** est-ce que c'est une lettre de l'un de tes admirateurs?

admiring [əd'maɪərɪŋ] **ADJ** admiratif

admiringly [əd'maɪərɪŋlɪ] **ADV** avec admiration

admissibility [əd,mɪsə'bɪlətɪ] **N** *(of behaviour, plan, argument)* admissibilité *f*; *Law (of appeal, testimony, claim, evidence)* recevabilité *f*

admissible [əd'mɪsəbəl] **ADJ** *(behaviour, plan, argument)* admissible; *(document)* valable; *Law (appeal, testimony, claim, evidence)* recevable

admission [əd'mɪʃən] **N 1** *(entry)* admission *f*, entrée *f*; *(to school)* admission *f*, accès *m*; *(to career)* accès *m*; **the a. of Poland to the EU** l'entrée de la Pologne dans l'Union européenne; **a. is free** l'entrée est gratuite; **no a. to minors** *(sign)* entrée interdite aux mineurs; **to gain a. to a club** être admis dans un club

2 *(fee)* droit *m* d'entrée; **a. £4.50** *(sign)* entrée £4.50

3 *(person admitted* ▸ *to theatre)* entrée *f*; *(*▸ *to school)* candidat(e) *m,f* accepté(e); *(*▸ *to club)* membre *m* accepté

4 *(statement)* déclaration *f*; *(confession)* aveu *m*; *(of allegation)* reconnaissance *f*; *(of crime)* confession *f*; **an a. of guilt** un aveu; **by** *or* **on one's own a.** de son propre aveu

5 *Tech (of steam, gas)* admission *f*, adduction *f*, entrée *f*; *(of water)* injection *f*

▸▸ *Sch & Univ* ***admissions office*** service *m* des inscriptions

admit [əd'mɪt] *(pt & pp* **admitted**, *cont* **admitting***)*

VT 1 *(concede)* admettre, reconnaître, avouer; **I a. I was wrong** je reconnais que j'ai eu tort; **I must a. it's more difficult than I thought** je dois admettre que c'est plus difficile que je ne pensais; **he admitted (that) he had failed** il a reconnu qu'il avait échoué; **she refused to a. defeat** elle a refusé de reconnaître sa défaite; **no one would a. doing it** personne ne voulait admettre l'avoir fait

2 *(confess)* avouer; **he admitted taking bribes** il a reconnu avoir accepté des pots-de-vin; **I had to a. to myself that...** j'ai dû m'avouer à moi-même que...

3 *(allow to enter* ▸ *person)* laisser entrer, faire entrer; *(*▸ *air, light)* laisser passer, laisser entrer; **a. two** *(on ticket)* valable pour deux personnes; **children not admitted** les enfants ne sont pas admis; **he was admitted to hospital** il a été hospitalisé

4 *Formal (allow)* admettre, permettre; **the facts a. no other explanation** d'après les faits, il n'y a pas d'autre explication possible

5 *Law (claim)* faire droit à; *(evidence)* admettre comme valable

▸ **admit of VT INSEP** *Br Formal* admettre, permettre; **her behaviour admits of no excuse** son attitude est inexcusable; **the text admits of only one interpretation** le texte n'admet *ou* ne permet qu'une seule interprétation

▸ **admit to VT INSEP** *(acknowledge)* admettre, reconnaître; *(confess)* avouer; **she did a. to a feeling of loss** elle a effectivement avoué ressentir un sentiment de perte

admittance [əd'mɪtəns] **N 1** *(permission to enter)* admission *f*, entrée *f*; **no a.** *(sign)* accès interdit au public; **to refuse sb a.** refuser de laisser entrer qn; **his supporters gained a. to the courtroom/to the president** ses supporters ont réussi à entrer dans le tribunal/à s'approcher du président **2** *Elec* admittance *f*

admittedly [əd'mɪtɪdlɪ] **ADV** de l'aveu général; **a., he's weak on economics, but he's an excellent manager** d'accord, l'économie n'est pas son point fort, mais il fait un excellent gestionnaire; **our members, although a. few in number, are very keen** nos membres, peu nombreux il faut le reconnaître, sont très enthousiastes; **they got there, two hours late a., but...** ils sont arrivés là-bas, avec deux heures de retard, j'en conviens, mais...

admixture [æd'mɪkstʃə(r)] **N 1** *Chem, Metal & Tech (mixture)* mélange *m* **2** *(ingredient)* ingrédient *m*; *Fig* **it's mainly comedy with an a. of satire** c'est principalement de la comédie avec un élément de satire

admonish [əd'mɒnɪʃ] **VT 1** *(rebuke)* réprimander, admonester; **he was admonished for not having acted more promptly** il a été réprimandé pour ne pas avoir agi plus rapidement **2** *(warn)* avertir, prévenir; *Law* admonester; **to a. sb against sth** mettre qn en garde contre qch

admonishing [,æd'mɒnɪʃɪŋ], **admonishment** [,æd'mɒnɪʃmənt], **admonition** [,ædmə'nɪʃən] **N 1** *(rebuke)* réprimande *f*, remontrance *f*, admonestation *f* **2** *(warning)* avertissement *m*; *Law* admonition *f*

ad nauseam [,æd'nɔːzɪæm] **ADV** jusqu'à la nausée; *Fig* à satiété; **she went on about her holiday a.** elle nous a raconté ses vacances à n'en plus finir

ado [ə'duː] **N** **without more** *or* **further a.** sans plus de cérémonie *ou* de manières

adobe [ə'dəʊbɪ] *Constr* **N** adobe *m*

COMP *(house, wall)* d'adobe

adolescence [,ædə'lesəns] **N** adolescence *f*

adolescent [,ædə'lesənt] **N** adolescent(e) *m,f*

ADJ *(boy, girl)* adolescent; *Pej (childish)* enfantin, puéril; **in his a. years** quand il était adolescent

Adonis [əˈdɒnɪs] PR N *Myth* Adonis; *Fig* **a young A.** un jeune Apollon

adopt [əˈdɒpt] VT **1** *(child)* adopter
2 *(choose ▸ plan, technique, guideline)* adopter, suivre, choisir; *(▸ country, name)* adopter, choisir; *(▸ measures, method)* adopter, instaurer; *(▸ career)* choisir, embrasser; *Pol (▸ candidate)* choisir; *Mktg (▸ product)* adopter; **he adopted the suggestion as his own** il a repris la proposition à son compte
3 *(assume ▸ position)* prendre; *(▸ accent, tone)* adopter, prendre
4 *Formal Admin (approve ▸ minutes, report)* approuver; *Pol (▸ bill, motion)* adopter

adopted [əˈdɒptɪd] ADJ *(child)* adopté; *(son, daughter)* adoptif; *(country)* d'adoption, adoptif

adoption [əˈdɒpʃən] N **1** *(of child, country, custom)* adoption *f*; **she's an American by a.** elle est américaine d'adoption; **they have two children of their own and another by a.** ils ont deux enfants à eux et un enfant adopté **2** *(of candidate, career, plan)* choix *m*; *(of measures, method)* instauration *f*; *Mktg (of product)* adoption *f* **3** *Formal Pol (of bill, motion)* adoption *f*
▸▸ ***adoption agency*** agence *f* d'adoption

adoptive [əˈdɒptɪv] ADJ *(child, parent)* adoptif; *(country)* d'adoption, adoptif

adorable [əˈdɔːrəbəl] ADJ adorable

adorably [əˈdɔːrəblɪ] ADV adorablement; **a. beautiful** beau à ravir

adoration [ˌædəˈreɪʃən] N adoration *f*

adore [əˈdɔː(r)] VT **1** *Rel* adorer **2** *Fam (like)* adorer□; **I a. walking in the rain** j'adore marcher sous la pluie

adorer [əˈdɔːrə(r)] N *Rel* adorateur(trice) *m,f*

adoring [əˈdɔːrɪŋ] ADJ *(look)* d'adoration; *(smile)* rempli d'adoration; *(mother)* dévoué; *(fans)* fervent; **a letter signed "your a. daughter"** une lettre signée "ta fille qui t'adore"

adoringly [əˈdɔːrɪŋlɪ] ADV avec adoration

adorn [əˈdɔːn] VT *Formal or Literary (decorate ▸ dress, hair)* orner, parer; *(▸ room, table)* orner; **she adorned herself with jewels** elle s'est parée de bijoux

adornment [əˈdɔːnmənt] N *Formal or Literary* **1** *(act, art)* décoration *f* **2** *(of dress, hair)* parure *f*; *(of room, table)* ornement *m*

ADP [ˌeɪdiːˈpiː] N **1** *Comput (abbr* **automatic data processing***)* traitement *m* automatique des données **2** *Chem (abbr* **adenosine diphosphate***)* ADP *f*

ADR [ˌeɪdiːˈɑː(r)] N **1** *Fin (abbr* **American Depositary Receipt***)* certificat *m* américain de dépôt **2** *Law (abbr* **alternative dispute resolution***)* règlement *m* extrajudiciaire des différends, règlement *m* amiable des différends

adrenal [əˈdriːnəl] *Anat* N surrénale *f*
ADJ surrénal
▸▸ ***adrenal gland*** surrénale *f*

adrenalin(e) [əˈdrenəlɪn] N *Chem & Physiol* adrénaline *f*; **it really gets the a. flowing** ça donne un bon coup d'adrénaline; **he runs on a.** il marche à l'adrénaline

Adriatic [ˌeɪdrɪˈætɪk] *Geog* N **the A.** la mer Adriatique, l'Adriatique *f*
ADJ **the A. Sea** la mer Adriatique, l'Adriatique *f*

adrift [əˈdrɪft] ADV **1 to run** *or* **go a.** *(boat)* aller à la dérive, dériver; **their boat had been cut a.** leur bateau avait été détaché; *Fig* **his parents turned him a.** ses parents l'ont laissé se débrouiller tout seul; *Fig* **to cut oneself a. from sb** rompre avec qn **2** *Br (undone)* **to come** *or* **to go a.** se détacher, se défaire; **our holiday plans seem to have gone a.** il semble que nos projets de vacances soient tombés à l'eau
ADJ *Naut (boat)* à la dérive; *Fig* abandonné; *Fig* **she was (all) a.** elle divaguait complètement

adroit [əˈdrɔɪt] ADJ adroit, habile

adroitly [əˈdrɔɪtlɪ] ADV adroitement, habilement

adroitness [əˈdrɔɪtnɪs] N adresse *f*

ADSL [ˌeɪdiːˌesˈel] N *Comput & Tel (abbr* **asymmetric digital subscriber line***)* ADSL *m*, *Can* LNPA *f*

adulation [ˌædjʊˈleɪʃən] N adulation *f*

adulatory [ˈædjʊˌleɪtərɪ] ADJ adulateur

adult [*Br* ˈædʌlt, *Am* əˈdʌlt] N adulte *mf*; **for adults only** *(sign)* interdit aux moins de 18 ans
ADJ **1** *(fully grown)* adulte **2** *(mature)* adulte; **she's very a. for her age** elle est très sérieuse *ou* elle a beaucoup de maturité pour son âge; **try and be a little more a. about this** essaie de faire preuve d'un peu plus de maturité **3** *(book, film, subject)* pour adultes
▸▸ *Euph* ***adult bookstore*** sex shop *m*; ***adult education*** enseignement *m* pour adultes; ***adult fare*** tarif *m* adulte

adulterate [əˈdʌltəreɪt] VT *(substance)* dénaturer; *(wine)* frelater; *(language)* corrompre; **they adulterated the wine with water** ils ont coupé le vin (avec de l'eau)

adulteration [əˌdʌltəˈreɪʃən] N *(of substance)* dénaturation *f*; *(of wine)* frelatage *m*; *(of language)* corruption *f*

adulterer [əˈdʌltərə(r)] N adultère *m (personne)*

adulteress [əˈdʌltərɪs] N adultère *f*

adulterous [əˈdʌltərəs] ADJ adultère

adulterously [əˈdʌltərəslɪ] ADV par adultère; *(live)* en état d'adultère; *(lust)* dans une passion adultère

adultery [əˈdʌltərɪ] N adultère *m (acte)*; **to commit a.** commettre l'adultère

adulthood [ˈædʌlthʊd] N âge *m* adulte; **to reach a.** devenir adulte, atteindre l'âge adulte

adults-only ADJ *(film)* classé X

adumbrate [ˈædʌmbreɪt] VT *Formal or Literary* **1** *(outline)* ébaucher, esquisser **2** *(foreshadow)* faire pressentir

ad valorem [ædvəˈlɔːrəm] ADJ *Fin (tax)* proportionnel, ad valorem

advance [ədˈvɑːns] VT **1** *(move forward ▸ clock, tape, film)* faire avancer; *(▸ time, event, chess piece)* avancer; **the date of the meeting was advanced by one week** la réunion a été avancée d'une semaine
2 *(further ▸ project, work)* avancer; *(▸ interest, cause)* promouvoir; *(▸ growth, development)* accélérer; **this discovery has advanced our research by months** cette découverte nous a fait gagner plusieurs mois de recherches
3 *(suggest ▸ idea, proposition)* avancer, mettre en avant; *(▸ opinion)* avancer, émettre; *(▸ explanation)* avancer
4 *Fin (money)* avancer, faire une avance de; **we advanced her £100 on her salary** nous lui avons avancé 100 livres sur son salaire; **sum advanced** avance *f*, acompte *m*
5 *Formal (increase)* augmenter, hausser
VI **1** *(go forward)* avancer, s'avancer; **to a. on** *or* **towards sth** avancer *ou* s'avancer vers qch; **the army advanced on Paris** l'armée avançait *ou* marchait sur Paris
2 *(make progress)* avancer, progresser, faire des progrès
3 *(time)* avancer, s'écouler; *(evening, winter)* avancer
4 *Formal Com & Fin (price, shares, rent)* augmenter (de prix), monter; **the shares advanced to their highest point in May** les actions ont atteint leur valeur la plus haute au mois de mai
5 *(be promoted)* avancer, obtenir de l'avancement; *Mil* monter en grade
N **1** *(forward movement)* avance *f*, marche *f* en avant; *Mil* avance *f*, progression *f*; **the enemy planned their a. on the city** l'ennemi a organisé son avance *ou* sa marche sur la ville; *Fig* **the a. of old age** le vieillissement
2 *(progress)* progrès *m*; **the great advances in medicine** les progrès importants dans le domaine de la médecine
3 *Fin (of funds)* avance *f*, acompte *m*; **he asked for an a. of £200 on his salary** il a demandé une avance de 200 livres sur son salaire
4 *Formal Com & Fin (in price, rent)* hausse *f*, augmentation *f*
5 *Com (increase at auction)* **any a.?** qui dit mieux?; **any a. on a hundred?** cent, qui dit mieux?
COMP *(prior)* préalable
• **advances** NPL avances *fpl*; **to make advances to** *or* **towards sb** faire des avances à qn
• **in advance** ADV *(beforehand ▸ pay, thank)* à l'avance, d'avance; *(▸ prepare, reserve, write, know)* à l'avance; **well in a.** largement à l'avance; **the agency asked for £50 in a.** l'agence a demandé 50 livres d'avance; **thanking you in a.** *(in letter)* en vous remerciant à l'avance, avec mes remerciements anticipés; **he sent the messenger on in a.** *(ahead)* il a envoyé le messager devant
• **in advance of** PREP avant; **they arrived in a. of their guests** ils sont arrivés en avance sur *ou* avant leurs invités
▸▸ *Fin* ***advance account*** compte *m* d'avances; ***advance booking*** réservation *f* à l'avance; **a. booking is advisable** il est recommandé de réserver à l'avance; ***advance booking office*** guichet *m* de location; ***advance check-in*** enregistrement *m* anticipé; ***advance copy*** *(of book)* exemplaire *m* de lancement; *(of speech)* texte *m* distribué à l'avance; *Fin* ***advance dividend*** dividende *m* anticipé; *Cin* ***advance funding*** préfinancement *m*; *Mil* ***advance guard*** avant-garde *f*; *Am Pol* ***advance man*** organisateur *m* de la publicité *(pour une campagne politique)*; ***advance notice*** préavis *m*, avertissement *m*; ***advance party*** *(gen)* groupe *m* de reconnaissance; *Mil* détachement *m* précurseur; *Fin* ***advance payment*** paiement *m* anticipé, paiement *m* par anticipation; ***advance publicity*** publicité *f* d'amorçage; *Press* ***advance story*** avant-papier *m*; ***advance warning*** avertissement *m*

advanced [ədˈvɑːnst] ADJ **1** *(course, education)* supérieur; *(child, country, pupil, ideas)* avancé; *(research, work)* poussé; *(equipment, technology)* avancé, de pointe; **the system is very a. technologically** le système est très en avance au niveau technologique; **he's a. for his age** il est avancé *ou* très en avance pour son âge; **a. mathematics** mathématiques *fpl* supérieures **2** *(afternoon, season)* avancé; **a woman of a. years, a woman a. in years** une femme d'un âge avancé; **the evening was already far a.** il était déjà tard dans la soirée **3** *(model, engine, reactor)* perfectionné; *(technique)* avancé
▸▸ *Nucl* ***advanced gas-cooled reactor*** réacteur *m* à gaz avancé; *Sch* ***Advanced level*** *(in England, Wales and Northern Ireland)* baccalauréat *m*; *Rail* ***advanced passenger train*** train *m* à grande vitesse, TGV *m*

advancement [ədˈvɑːnsmənt] N **1** *(promotion)* avancement *m*, promotion *f*; **there is little scope for a.** il y a peu de possibilités d'avancement **2** *(improvement)* progrès *m*, avancement *m*

advancing [ədˈvɑːnsɪŋ] ADJ qui approche, qui avance; **the a. army** l'armée en marche *ou* qui avance; **the a. tide** la marée qui monte

advantage [ədˈvɑːntɪdʒ] N **1** *(benefit)* avantage *m*; **her experience gives her an a. over the other candidates** son expérience lui donne un avantage sur les autres candidats; **they have an a. over us** *or* **the a. of us** ils ont un avantage sur nous; **the plan has the a. of being extremely cheap** le plan présente l'avantage d'être extrêmement bon marché; **it's to your a. to learn another language** c'est (dans) ton intérêt d'apprendre une autre langue; **that would be to their a.** cela leur serait avantageux, ils y auraient intérêt; **the recession/weather worked to their a.** la récession/le temps les a avantagés *ou* a travaillé pour eux; **to turn sth to a.** tirer parti de qch, mettre qch à profit; **she turned the situation to her a.** elle a tiré parti de la situation, elle a tourné la situation à son avantage; **to turn out to sb's a.** *(event)* tourner à l'avantage de qn, profiter à qn; **we took a. of the holiday weekend to do some gardening** nous avons profité du long week-end pour faire du jardinage; **to take a. of sb** *(make use of)* profiter de qn; *(exploit)* exploiter qn; *(abuse sexually)* abuser de qn; **they'll only take a.** *(of your generosity etc)* ils ne feront qu'en profiter; **that would be taking a.!** ce serait abuser!; **she uses her charm to great a.** elle sait user de son charme; **this lighting shows the pictures to their best a.** cet éclairage met les tableaux en valeur; *Br Formal* **you have the a. of me** à qui ai-je l'honneur? **2** *Sport (in tennis)* avantage *m*; **a. Federer** avantage Federer
VT avantager
▸▸ *Sport* ***advantage rule*** *(in football, rugby)* règle *f* de l'avantage; **to play the a. rule** laisser l'avantage, appliquer la règle de l'avantage

advantageous [ˌædvənˈteɪdʒəs] ADJ avantageux; **to be a. to sb** être avantageux pour qn, avantager qn

advantageously [ˌædvənˈteɪdʒəslɪ] ADV de façon avantageuse

advent ['ædvənt] **N** *(of spring, rainy season etc)* arrivée *f*; *(of era, computer age)* avènement *m*; *(of railways, the motor car, computerization)* introduction *f*

• **Advent N** *Rel* l'Avent *m*; **the Second A.** le second Avènement

▸▸ ***Advent calendar*** calendrier *m* de l'Avent; ***Advent Sunday*** le premier dimanche de l'Avent

Adventist ['ædvəntɪst] **N** *Rel* **(Seventh-day) A.** adventiste *mf* du septième jour

adventitious [ˌædven'tɪʃəs] **ADJ 1** *Formal (chance)* fortuit **2** *Phil* adventice

adventure [əd'ventʃə(r)] **N 1** *(experience)* aventure *f*; **to have an a.** avoir une aventure; **after many adventures** après bien des péripéties **2** *(excitement)* aventure *f*; **where's your sense of a.?** où est ton sens de l'aventure?; **to look for a.** chercher l'aventure

COMP *(film, novel)* d'aventures

▸▸ ***adventure holiday*** = vacances organisées avec des activités sportives; *Br* ***adventure playground*** = sorte d'aire de jeux

adventurer [əd'ventʃərə(r)] **N** aventurier(ère) *m,f*; *Pej* aventurier(ère) *m,f*, intrigant(e) *m,f*

adventuresome [əd'ventʃəsəm] **ADJ** *Am* aventureux, téméraire

adventuress [əd'ventʃərɪs] **N** aventurière *f*; *Pej* aventurière *f*, intrigante *f*

adventurous [əd'ventʃərəs] **ADJ** *(person, spirit)* aventureux, audacieux; *(life, project)* aventureux, hasardeux; **we had an a. trip** nous avons eu un voyage plein d'aventures; **be a., try the duck** sois un peu plus aventureux et essaie le canard

adventurously [əd'ventʃərəslɪ] **ADV** aventureusement, audacieusement

adventurousness [əd'ventʃərəsnɪs] **N** hardiesse *f*, audace *f*; *(liking adventure)* esprit *m* d'aventure

adverb ['ædvɜːb] **N** *Gram* adverbe *m*

adverbial [əd'vɜːbɪəl] **ADJ** *Gram* adverbial; **a. phrase** locution *f* adverbiale

adverbially [əd'vɜːbɪəlɪ] **ADV** *Gram* adverbialement

adversary ['ædvəsərɪ] *(pl* **adversaries***)* **N** adversaire *mf*

adverse ['ædvɜːs] **ADJ 1** *(comment, criticism, opinion)* défavorable, hostile; *(circumstances, report)* défavorable; *Fin (balance, budget)* déficitaire **2** *(effect)* opposé, contraire; *(wind)* contraire, debout; **the match was cancelled due to a. weather conditions** le match a été annulé à cause du mauvais temps; **the stock markets showed an a. reaction to the Chancellor's budget** les différentes places financières ont mal réagi au budget annoncé par le Chancelier de l'Échiquier

> Attention: ne pas confondre avec le mot anglais **averse**.

adversely ['ædvɜːslɪ] **ADV 1** *(affect)* **the harvest was a. affected by frost** la récolte a été très touchée par les gelées **2** *(comment)* **to comment a. on sth** faire des commentaires défavorables sur qch

adversity [əd'vɜːsətɪ] *(pl* **adversities***)* **N 1** *(distress)* adversité *f*; **in the face of a.** dans l'adversité **2** *(incident)* malheur *m*;

advert¹ ['ædvɜːt] **N** *Br Fam (for job, event, accommodation)* (petite) annonce *f*; *(for product)* pub *f*, *Can* annonce *f*; **you're a walking a. for Gucci** tu as l'air tout droit sorti d'une pub pour Gucci; **the adverts** *(on TV, in cinema)* la pub

advert² [əd'vɜːt] **VI** *Formal (refer)* se rapporter, se référer **(to** à**)**

advertise ['ædvətaɪz] **VT 1** *(publicize* ▸ *product, service)* faire de la publicité pour; **I heard his new record advertised on the radio** j'ai entendu la publicité pour son nouveau disque à la radio; **I saw it advertised in a magazine** j'ai vu une annonce là-dessus *ou* pour ça dans une revue; **as advertised on TV** vu à la télé **2** *(job)* mettre une (petite) annonce pour; *(event)* annoncer; **we advertised our house in the local paper** nous avons mis *ou* passé une annonce pour vendre notre maison dans le journal local **3** *(make known)* afficher; **you needn't a. the fact** vous n'avez pas besoin de le crier sur les toits; **you needn't a. your ignorance** ce n'est pas la peine d'étaler ton ignorance; **he didn't want to a. his presence** il ne voulait pas se faire remarquer

VI 1 *(to sell product, service)* faire de la publicité; **to a. in the press/on radio/on TV** faire de la publicité dans la presse/à la radio/à la télé; **it pays to a.** la publicité paie **2** *(place advertisement)* mettre une (petite) annonce **3** *(make a request)* chercher par voie d'annonce; **we advertised for a cook** nous avons mis *ou* fait paraître une annonce pour trouver une cuisinière

> Note that the French verb **avertir** is a false friend and is never a translation for the English verb **to advertise**. It means either **to inform** or **to warn**, according to the context.

advertised ['ædvətaɪzd] **ADJ the a. time of departure** *(of train, bus, plane)* l'heure *f* prévue pour le départ; *TV* **in a change to the a. programme** contrairement à ce qu'annonçait le programme

advertisement [*Br* əd'vɜːtɪsmənt, *Am* ˌædvər'taɪzmənt] **N 1** *(for product, service)* annonce *f* publicitaire, publicité *f*; *(on television)* spot *m* publicitaire; **an a. for toothpaste, a toothpaste a.** une publicité pour du dentifrice; **she made a cup of tea while the advertisements were on** elle est allée se faire une tasse de thé pendant la publicité **2** *(for job, event, accommodation)* (petite) annonce *f* **(for** pour**)**; *(on wall etc)* affiche *f*; **to put an a. in the paper** passer une annonce dans le journal; **I got the job through an a.** j'ai eu le poste grâce à une annonce **3** *Fig (example)* **this company is a good/poor a. for public ownership** la situation de cette société plaide/ne plaide pas en faveur de la nationalisation; **you're not a good a. for your school** vous ne faites pas honneur à votre école

> Note that the French word **avertissement** is a false friend and is never a translation for the English word **advertisement**. It means **warning**.

advertiser ['ædvətaɪzə(r)] **N** annonceur *m* (publicitaire)

advertising ['ædvətaɪzɪŋ] **N** *(UNCOUNT)* **1** *(promotion, advertisements)* publicité *f* **2** *(business)* publicité *f*; **he works in a.** il travaille dans la publicité

COMP *(budget, material)* publicitaire

▸▸ ***advertising agency*** agence *f* de publicité; ***advertising agent*** agent *m* de publicité; ***Advertising Association*** = organisme britannique dont le rôle est de veiller à la qualité des publicités et de défendre les intérêts des annonceurs et des agences de publicité; *Mktg* ***advertising awareness*** notoriété *f* publicitaire; *Comput* ***advertising banner*** *(on web page)* bandeau *f* publicitaire; ***advertising brochure*** plaquette *f* publicitaire; ***advertising campaign*** campagne *f* publicitaire *ou* de publicité; ***advertising concept*** idée *f* publicitaire; ***advertising consultant*** conseil *m* en publicité; ***advertising copy*** texte *m* publicitaire; ***advertising department*** service *m* de la publicité; ***advertising executive*** chef *m* de la publicité; ***advertising expenditure*** dépenses *fpl* publicitaires; ***advertising gimmick*** gadget *m* publicitaire; ***advertising insert*** encart *m* publicitaire; ***advertising jingle*** jingle *m*, *Offic* sonal *m*; ***advertising manager*** directeur (trice) *m,f* de la communication *ou* de la publicité; ***advertising medium*** média *m ou* support *m* publicitaire; ***advertising newspaper*** journal *m* d'annonces; ***advertising rates*** tarif *m* des insertions; ***advertising revenue*** recettes *fpl* publicitaires; ***advertising sales agency*** régie *f* publicitaire; ***advertising schedule*** programme *m* des annonces; ***advertising slot*** créneau *m* publicitaire; ***advertising space*** espace *m* publicitaire; ***advertising standards*** normes *fpl* publicitaires; *Br* ***Advertising Standards Authority*** Bureau *m* de vérification de la publicité; ***advertising strategy*** stratégie *f* publicitaire

advertorial [ˌædvə'tɔːrɪəl] **N** *Press* publireportage *m*

advice [əd'vaɪs] **N 1** *(UNCOUNT) (counsel)* conseil(s) *m(pl)* **(on** sur**)**; **a piece of a.** un conseil; **he asked his father's a., he asked his father for a.** il a demandé conseil à *ou* a consulté son père; **let me give you some a.** permettez que je vous donne un conseil *ou* que je vous conseille; **to take** *or* **follow sb's a.** suivre le conseil de qn; **when I want your a. I'll ask for it!** quand j'aurai besoin de tes conseils, je saurai te les demander!; **if you take my a. you'll not have anything to do with them** suis mon conseil, ne te mêle pas de leurs affaires; **my a. to you would be to write a letter of apology** je te conseille d'envoyer une lettre d'excuses; **I took** *or* **followed your a. and called him** suivant votre conseil, je l'ai appelé; **to take legal/medical a.** consulter un avocat/un médecin **2** *Admin (notification)* avis *m*; **a. of delivery/payment** avis *m* de livraison/de paiement; **as per a.** suivant avis

▸▸ *Press* ***advice column*** *(agony column)* courrier *m* du cœur; *(for practical advice)* rubrique *f* pratique; *Fin* ***advice note*** lettre *f* d'avis

> Attention à l'orthographe: ne pas confondre avec le verbe **to advise** et ses dérivés, qui prennent un **s** et non un **c**.

advisability [ədˌvaɪzə'bɪlətɪ] **N** opportunité *f*, bien-fondé *m*; **they discussed the a. of performing another operation** ils ont discuté de l'opportunité d'une nouvelle opération; **I question the a. of contacting the police** je doute qu'il soit opportun de faire appel à la police

advisable [əd'vaɪzəbəl] **ADJ** conseillé, recommandé; **it would be a. to lock the door** il serait prudent *ou* préférable que vous fermiez la porte à clé; **it is a. to book early** il est recommandé de réserver à l'avance; **it would perhaps be a. to warn them** peut-être conviendrait-il de les prévenir; **she thought it a. to call him** elle a cru bien faire en l'appelant; **if you consider** *or* **think it a.** si bon vous semble

advise [əd'vaɪz] **VT 1** *(give advice to)* conseiller, donner des conseils à; *(recommend)* recommander; **to a. sb to do sth** conseiller à qn de faire qch; **I strongly a. you to...** je vous recommande instamment de...; **customers are advised to book early** il est recommandé *ou* conseillé aux clients de réserver à l'avance; **what do you a. me to do?** que me conseillez-vous?; **we advised them to wait** nous leur avons conseillé d'attendre; **she advised caution** elle a recommandé la prudence; **I advised him against signing the contract** je lui ai conseillé de ne pas signer le contrat; **he advised them against taking legal action** il leur a déconseillé d'intenter une action en justice; **I would strongly a. against it** je le déconseille fortement; **you'd be well advised to take an umbrella** vous feriez bien de prendre un parapluie **2** *(act as counsel to)* conseiller **(on** en matière de**) 3** *Formal (inform)* aviser, informer; **we are pleased to a. you that...** nous avons le plaisir de vous informer que...; **keep me advised of your progress** tenez-moi au courant de vos progrès

> Attention à l'orthographe: ne pas confondre avec le nom **advice**, qui prend un **c** et non un **s**.

advisedly [əd'vaɪzɪdlɪ] **ADV** délibérément, en connaissance de cause

adviser, *Am* **advisor** [əd'vaɪzə(r)] **N** conseiller(ère) *m,f*

advising bank [əd'vaɪzɪŋ-] **N** *Banking* banque *f* notificatrice

advisor *Am* = **adviser**

advisory [əd'vaɪzərɪ] **ADJ** *(role, work)* consultatif, de conseil; **he's employed in an a. capacity** il est employé à titre consultatif

▸▸ *Pol* ***advisory committee*** comité *m* de restructuration; *Am* ***advisory service*** service *m* de renseignements

advocacy ['ædvəkəsɪ] **N** soutien *m* appuyé, plaidoyer *m*

advocate VT ['ædvəkeɪt] prôner, préconiser; **he advocates reducing** *or* **a reduction in defence spending** il préconise une réduction des dépenses militaires

N ['ædvəkət] **1** *(supporter)* défenseur *m*, avocat(e) *m,f*; **a strong a. of free enterprise** un fervent partisan de la libre entreprise; **they are advocates of**

civil rights ils défendent les droits civiques **2** *Scot Law (barrister)* avocat(e) *m,f* (plaidant(e))

adze, *Am* **adz** [ædz] **N** *Tech* herminette *f*

AEA [ˌeiːˈeɪ] **N** *Br Nucl & Ind (abbr* **Atomic Energy Authority***)* CEA *f*

Aegean [iːˈdʒiːən] *Geog* **N the A.** la mer Égée
ADJ égéen
▸▸ ***the Aegean Islands*** les îles *fpl* de la mer Égée; ***the Aegean Sea*** la mer Égée

aegis [ˈiːdʒɪs] **N** *Fig* égide *f*; **under the a. of** sous l'égide de

aegrotat [ˈiːgrəʊtæt] **N** *Br Univ* = équivalence d'un diplôme accordée à un bon étudiant qui était malade lors des examens

Aeneas [ɪˈniːəs] **PR N** *Myth* Énée

Aeneid [ɪˈniːɪd] **N** Énéide *f*

aeolian, *Am* **eolian** [iːˈəʊlɪən] **ADJ** *Agr, Geol & Met* éolien
▸▸ *Mus* ***aeolian harp*** harpe *f* éolienne

aeon, *Am* **eon** [ˈiːən] **N 1** *(age)* période *f* incommensurable; *Astron* milliard *m* d'années; *Fam* **aeons ago** il y a une éternité; **for aeons upon aeons** pendant des siècles *ou* des éternités **2** *Phil* éon *m*

AER [ˌeiːiːˈɑː(r)] **N** *Fin (abbr* **annual equivalent rate***)* taux *m* actuariel annuel

aerate [ˈeəreɪt] **VT 1** *(soil, water)* aérer **2** *Chem (mineral water, liquid)* gazéifier **3** *Physiol (blood)* oxygéner

aerated [ˈeəreɪtɪd] **ADJ 1** *Chem (soil, water)* aéré **2** *Chem (mineral water, liquid)* gazeux **3** *Br Fam (excited, upset)* **to be/get a. (about sth)** être énervé/s'énerver (à cause de qch)□

aeration [eəˈreɪʃən] **N 1** *Chem (of soil, water)* aération *f* **2** *(of mineral water, liquid)* gazéification *f* **3** *Physiol (of blood)* artérialisation *f*

aerial [ˈeərɪəl] **ADJ 1** *(in the air)* aérien **2** *Bot* aérien; *(orchid)* aéricole
N *Br (for TV, radio)* antenne *f*
▸▸ ***aerial assault course*** accrobranche® *m*; *Transp* ***aerial cable car*** téléphérique *m*; *Rad & TV* ***aerial curtain*** rideau *m* d'antennes; *Electron & TV* ***aerial engineer*** antenniste *mf*; ***aerial photograph*** photographie *f* aérienne; ***aerial railway*** téléphérique *m*; *Bot* ***aerial root*** racine *f* aérienne; *Cin* ***aerial shot*** prise *f* de vue aérienne; ***aerial walkway*** passerelle *f*; *Mil* ***aerial warfare*** combat *m* aérien

aerie [ˈeərɪ] **N** *Am* aire *f (d'aigle)*

aerobatics [ˌeərəʊˈbætɪks] **N** *(UNCOUNT)* acrobatie *f* aérienne, acrobaties *fpl* aériennes
▸▸ ***aerobatics display*** démonstration *f* aérienne

aerobics [eəˈrəʊbɪks] **N** *(UNCOUNT)* aérobic *m*; **to do a.** faire de l'aérobic; **are you going to a. tonight?** est-ce que tu vas au cours d'aérobic ce soir?
COMP *(class, teacher)* d'aérobic

aerodrome [ˈeərədrəʊm] **N** *Aviat* aérodrome *m*

aerodynamic [ˌeərəʊdaɪˈnæmɪk] **ADJ** *Phys* aérodynamique; **the car has a very a. shape** la voiture a une forme très aérodynamique
▸▸ ***aerodynamic drag*** résistance *f* de l'air; ***aerodynamic noise*** bruit *m* aérodynamique

aerodynamically [ˌeərəʊdaɪˈnæmɪklɪ] **ADV** *Phys* aérodynamiquement

aerodynamics [ˌeərəʊdaɪˈnæmɪks] **N** *(UNCOUNT) Phys* aérodynamique *f*

aero-engine [ˈeərəʊ-] **N** *Aviat* moteur *m* d'avion

aerofoil [ˈeərəʊfɔɪl] **N** *Aviat* surface *f* portante, plan *m* de sustentation

aerogel [ˈeərədʒel] **N** *Tech* aérogel *m*

aerogram [ˈeərəgræm] **N 1** *(letter)* aérogramme *m* **2** *(radiotelegram)* radiotélégramme *m*

aeromodeller, *Am* **aeromodeler** [ˈeərəʊˌmɒdələ(r)] **N** *Tech* aéromodéliste *mf*

aeromodelling, *Am* **aeromodeling** [ˈeərəʊˌmɒdəlɪŋ] **N** *Tech* aéromodélisme *m*

aeronaut [ˈeərənɔːt] **N** *Aviat* aéronaute *mf*

aeronautic [ˌeərəˈnɔːtɪk], **aeronautical** [ˌeərəˈnɔːtɪkəl] **ADJ** *Aviat & Phys* aéronautique

aeronautics [ˌeərəˈnɔːtɪks] **N** *(UNCOUNT) Aviat & Phys* aéronautique *f*

aerophobe [ˈeərəfəʊb] **N** aérophobe *mf*

aeroplane [ˈeərəpleɪn] **N** *Br* avion *m*

aerosol [ˈeərəsɒl] **N 1** *(suspension system)* aérosol *m* **2** *(container)* bombe *f*, aérosol *m*
COMP *(container)* aérosol; *(hairspray, paint)* en aérosol, en bombe
▸▸ ***aerosol spray*** atomiseur *m*

aerospace [ˈeərəʊˌspeɪs] *Aviat* **N** aérospatiale *f*
COMP *(industry, research)* aérospatial

aesthete, *Am* **esthete** [ˈiːsθiːt] **N** *Art & Phil* esthète *mf*

aesthetic, *Am* **esthetic** [iːsˈθetɪk] *Art & Phil* **ADJ** esthétique; **in a. terms** en termes d'esthétique
N esthétique *f*

aesthetically, *Am* **esthetically** [iːsˈθetɪkəlɪ] **ADV** *Art & Phil* esthétiquement

aestheticism, *Am* **estheticism** [iːsˈθetɪsɪzəm] **N** *Art & Phil* esthétisme *m*

aesthetics, *Am* **esthetics** [iːsˈθetɪks] **N** *(UNCOUNT) Art & Phil* esthétique *f*

aetiological, *Am* **etiological** [ˌiːtɪəˈlɒdʒɪkəl] **ADJ** *Med & Phil* étiologique

aetiology, *Am* **etiology** [ˌiːtɪˈɒlədʒɪ] *(pl* **aetiologies***)* **N** *Med & Phil* étiologie *f*

afar [əˈfɑː(r)] *Literary* **ADV** au loin, à (grande) distance
• **from afar ADV** de loin

AFC [ˌeɪefˈsiː] **N** *Rad (abbr* **automatic frequency control***)* correcteur *m* automatique de fréquence

afeared, afeard [əˈfɪəd] **ADJ** *Arch* effrayé, apeuré; **to be a. (of)** avoir peur (de)

A-feature N *Cin* film *m* projeté en exclusivité *(lors d'une séance où deux longs métrages sont projetés)*

affability [ˌæfəˈbɪlətɪ] **N** affabilité *f*, amabilité *f*

affable [ˈæfəbəl] **ADJ** *(person)* affable, aimable; *(conversation, interview)* chaleureux

affably [ˈæfəblɪ] **ADV** affablement, avec affabilité

affair [əˈfeə(r)] **N 1** *(event)* affaire *f*; **the meeting was a noisy a.** la réunion était bruyante; **the festival was a dull a.** le festival était dépourvu d'intérêt; **it was a sorry a.** c'était une histoire lamentable; **what kind of a. was it?** c'était comment?; **it was one of those black tie affairs** c'était une de ces soirées habillées; *Hist* **the Watergate a.** l'affaire *f* du Watergate
2 *(business, matter)* affaire *f*; **the a. in hand** l'affaire qui nous occupe
3 *(concern)* affaire *f*; **whether I go or not is my (own) a.** que j'y aille ou non ne regarde que moi; **it's no a. of his** ça ne le regarde *ou* ne le concerne pas, ça n'est pas son affaire
4 *(sexual)* liaison *f*, aventure *f*; **to have an a. with sb** avoir une liaison *ou* aventure avec qn
5 *Fam (thing)* truc *m*; **he was driving one of those sporty affairs** il conduisait une de ces voitures genre sport; **the cake's one of those fresh-cream affairs** c'est un de ces gâteaux à la crème fraîche; **the house is a three-storey a.** il s'agit d'une maison à trois étages
• **affairs NPL** *(business, matters)* affaires *fpl*; **he's looking after her financial affairs** il gère son argent; **I'm not interested in your private affairs** je ne m'intéresse pas à votre vie privée; **don't meddle in my affairs** ne vous mêlez pas de mes affaires, mêlez-vous de vos affaires; **to put one's affairs in order** mettre de l'ordre dans ses affaires; **given the current state of affairs** étant donné la situation actuelle, les choses étant ce qu'elles sont; *Ironic* **this is a fine state of affairs!** c'est du propre!; *Pol* **affairs of state** affaires *fpl* d'État

> Note that the French word **affaire** is never used to refer to a sexual relationship between two people.

affect¹ **VT** [əˈfekt] **1** *(have effect on ▸ person, life)* avoir un effet sur, affecter; *(influence ▸ decision, outcome)* influer sur, avoir une incidence sur; **how will these changes a. you?** en quoi serez-vous affecté *ou* concerné par ces changements?; **roads have been seriously affected by the flooding** les routes ont été fortement touchées par l'inondation; **these plants were badly affected by a late frost** ces plantes ont beaucoup souffert des gelées tardives; **the bad weather has affected sporting events this weekend** le mauvais temps a eu des répercussions sur les événements sportifs du week-end; **one of the factors that will a. the outcome of the next election** l'un des facteurs qui influera sur le résultat des prochaines élections
2 *(concern, involve)* toucher, concerner; **this new law affects everyone** cette nouvelle loi concerne *ou* touche tout le monde; **they are directly affected** ce sont eux les premiers intéressés, ils sont directement concernés
3 *(emotionally)* affecter, émouvoir, toucher; **he was deeply affected by her death** il a été très affecté *ou* touché par sa mort; **don't let it a. you** ne vous laissez pas abattre par cela
4 *(of illness, epidemic)* atteindre; *(of drug)* agir sur; **she has had a stroke, but her speech is not affected** elle a eu une attaque, mais les fonctions du langage ne sont pas atteintes; **a disease that affects the kidneys** une maladie qui affecte les reins
N [ˈæfekt] *Psy* affect *m*

affect² [əˈfekt] **VT 1** *Formal (pretend, feign ▸ indifference, surprise, interest)* affecter, feindre; *(▸ illness, pain)* feindre, simuler; **he affected a strong foreign accent** il affectait un fort accent étranger; **she affected not to see him** elle fit semblant de ne pas l'avoir vu **2** *Arch or Literary (be fond of)* affectionner, avoir un penchant pour

affectation [ˌæfekˈteɪʃən] **N 1** *(affectedness)* affectation *f*, manque *m* de naturel; **without a.** simple, sans manières **2** *(mannerism)* pose *f* **3** *(pretence)* semblant *m*, simulacre *m*; **with an a. of interest/boredom** en simulant l'intérêt/l'ennui

affected¹ [əˈfektɪd] **ADJ 1** *Med* atteint; **the lung is a.** le poumon est atteint *ou* touché; **apply to the a. part** appliquer sur la partie malade **2** *(emotionally)* ému, touché

affected² **ADJ 1** *Pej (person, behaviour)* affecté, maniéré; *(accent, dress, language)* affecté, recherché **2** *(pretended, fake)* simulé, feint

affectedly [əˈfektɪdlɪ] **ADV** *Pej* avec affectation, d'une manière affectée

affectedness [əˈfektɪdnɪs] **N** *(UNCOUNT) Pej* affectation *f*, manque *m* de naturel

affecting [əˈfektɪŋ] **ADJ** touchant, émouvant

affection [əˈfekʃən] **N 1** *(liking)* affection *f*, tendresse *f*; **to show sb a.** montrer de l'affection *ou* de la tendresse pour qn; **to feel a. for sb** avoir de l'affection *ou* de la tendresse pour qn; **a rare display of a.** une rare manifestation d'affection *ou* de tendresse; **she has (a) deep a. for him** elle a une profonde affection pour lui, elle l'aime profondément; **with much a.** *(in letter)* (bien) affectueusement; **he is held in great a.** il est très aimé **2** *(usu pl)* affection *f*; **to gain** *or* **to win (a place in) sb's affections** gagner l'affection *ou* le cœur de qn; **she transferred her affections to another man** elle a reporté son affection sur un autre homme; **this town has a special place in my affections** j'aime tout particulièrement cette ville **3** *Med* affection *f*, maladie *f*

affectionate [əˈfekʃənət] **ADJ** affectueux, tendre (**towards** avec *ou* envers); *Old-fashioned* **your a. niece** *(in letter)* votre nièce affectionnée

affectionately [əˈfekʃənətlɪ] **ADV** affectueusement; **yours a.** *(in letter)* (bien) affectueusement

affective [əˈfektɪv] **ADJ** *Ling & Psy* affectif

affidavit [ˌæfɪˈdeɪvɪt] **N** *Law* déclaration *f* écrite sous serment; **a sworn a.** une déclaration écrite sous serment

affiliate **VT** [əˈfɪlɪeɪt] affilier; **to a. oneself to** *or* **with** s'affilier à; **the local group decided not to a. itself to the national organization** la section locale a décidé de ne pas s'affilier au mouvement national
VI [əˈfɪlɪeɪt] **to a. to** *or* **with a society** s'affilier à une société
N [əˈfɪlɪət] *(person)* affilié(e) *m,f*; *(organization)* groupe *m* affilié; *Com (company)* société *f* affiliée, filiale *f*
COMP *(member, organization)* affilié

affiliation [əˌfɪlɪˈeɪʃən] **N 1** *Com (company)* affiliation *f*, société *f* affiliée, filiale *f* **2** *Law* attribution *f* de paternité **3** *(connection)* attache *f*; **his political affiliations** ses attaches *fpl* politiques
▸▸ *Law* ***affiliation order*** = injonction au père pu-

tatif de verser une pension pour l'entretien de son enfant

affinity [ə'fɪnətɪ] (*pl* **affinities**) **N 1** *(attraction)* affinité *f*, attraction *f*; **to have an a. with sb/sth** avoir des affinités avec qn/qch; **there is a strong a. between them** ils ont beaucoup de choses en commun *ou* d'affinités **2** *(connection, link)* lien *m*, affinité *f*; **the affinities between the English and German languages** la ressemblance *ou* la parenté entre l'anglais et l'allemand **3** *Biol* affinité *f*, parenté *f*; *Chem* affinité *f*

►► *Com & Fin* ***affinity card*** = carte de crédit résultant de la collaboration entre un organisme de crédit et une entreprise commerciale ou une association caritative

affirm [ə'fɜːm] **VT 1** *(state)* affirmer, soutenir; **she affirms that it's the truth** elle affirme *ou* soutient que c'est la vérité; **"I will be there," he affirmed** "j'y serai", assura-t-il

2 *(profess* ► *belief)* professer, proclamer; *(*► *intention)* proclamer

3 *(support* ► *person)* soutenir

4 *Law (verdict)* confirmer, homologuer

VI *Law* faire une affirmation *ou* déclaration solennelle

affirmation [ˌæfə'meɪʃən] **N 1** *(statement)* affirmation *f*, assertion *f* **2** *Law (of verdict)* confirmation *f*, homologation *f* **3** *Law (declaration)* déclaration *f ou* affirmation *f* solennelle

affirmative [ə'fɜːmətɪv] **N 1** *Gram* affirmatif *m*; **in the a.** à l'affirmatif, à la forme affirmative **2** *(in reply)* **the answer is in the a.** la réponse est affirmative; **to answer in the a.** répondre affirmativement *ou* par l'affirmative

ADJ affirmatif

EXCLAM affirmatif!

►► *Am* ***affirmative action*** *(UNCOUNT)* mesures *fpl* d'embauche anti-discriminatoires *(en faveur des minorités)*

affirmatively [ə'fɜːmətɪvlɪ] **ADV** affirmativement

affix **VT** [ə'fɪks] *(seal, signature)* apposer; *(stamp)* coller; *(poster)* afficher, poser

N ['æfɪks] *Ling* affixe *m*

afflict [ə'flɪkt] **VT** affecter; **to be afflicted with a disease** souffrir d'une maladie; **she was afflicted by acute feelings of guilt** elle était accablée d'un fort sentiment de culpabilité; *Ironic* **the family I'm afflicted with** la famille dont je suis affligé; *Fig* **the economic problems that a. the nation** les problèmes économiques qui accablent le pays

afflicted [ə'flɪktɪd] **ADJ** affligé; *(part, area* ► *by illness)* atteint

NPL the a. les affligés *mpl*; **don't mock the a.** ne te moque pas de moi/lui/*etc*

affliction [ə'flɪkʃən] **N 1** *(suffering)* affliction *f*; *(distress)* détresse *f*; **people in a.** les gens dans la détresse *ou* dans l'affliction **2** *(misfortune)* affliction *f*, souffrance *f*; **blindness is a terrible a.** la cécité est une grande infirmité

affluence ['æfluəns] **N** *(wealth)* richesse *f*; **to live in a.** vivre dans l'aisance; **in times of a.** en période de prospérité

affluent ['æfluənt] **ADJ** *(wealthy)* aisé, riche; **to be a.** vivre dans l'aisance; **the a. society** la société d'abondance

N *Geog* affluent *m*

affluently ['æfluəntlɪ] **ADV** *(live)* dans l'aisance

afford [ə'fɔːd] **VT 1** *(have enough money for)* **to be able to a. sth** avoir les moyens d'acheter qch; **I can't a. a holiday** je n'ai pas les moyens de prendre des vacances; **she couldn't a. to buy a car** elle n'avait pas les moyens d'acheter *ou* elle ne pouvait pas se permettre d'acheter une voiture; **can you a. it?** en avez-vous les moyens?, pouvez-vous vous le permettre?; **how much can you a.?** combien pouvez-vous mettre?, jusqu'à combien pouvez-vous aller?; **I can't a. £50!** je ne peux pas mettre 50 livres!; **give what you can a.** donnez selon vos possibilités; **it's more than we can a.** c'est au-dessus de nos moyens

2 *(have enough time, energy for)* **I can a. to wait** je peux attendre; **I'd love to come, but I can't a. the time** j'aimerais beaucoup venir mais je ne peux absolument pas me libérer

3 *(allow oneself)* se permettre; **I can't a. to take any risks** je ne peux pas me permettre de prendre des risques; **I can't a. not to** je n'ai pas vraiment le choix

4 *Literary or Formal (provide)* fournir, offrir; **to a. sb the opportunity to do sth** donner *ou* fournir à qn l'occasion de faire qch; **this affords me great pleasure** ceci me procure un grand plaisir; **the trees afforded very little shelter** les arbres ne fournissaient qu'un piètre abri

affordability [əˌfɔːdə'bɪlətɪ] **N measures to improve the a. of child care** des mesures destinées à rendre la garde d'enfants plus abordable; **the new model combines quality and a.** le nouveau modèle est à la fois de bonne qualité et abordable

affordable [ə'fɔːdəbəl] **ADJ** *(price, rent)* abordable; *(house, trip etc)* (d'un prix) abordable

afforest [æ'fɒrɪst] **VT** *Agr* boiser, reboiser

afforestation [æˌfɒrɪ'steɪʃən] **N** *Agr* boisement *m*

affray [ə'freɪ] **N** échauffourée *f*

affreightment [ə'freɪtmənt] **N** *Com* affrètement *m*

affront [ə'frʌnt] **N** affront *m*, insulte *f*

VT *(offend)* faire un affront à, insulter, offenser; *(embarrass)* gêner; **to be** *or* **to feel affronted** *(offended)* se sentir offensé; *(embarrassed)* se sentir gêné

Afghan ['æfgæn] **N 1** *(person)* Afghan(e) *m,f*

2 *(language)* afghan *m*

3 *(dog)* lévrier *m* afghan

4 *(coat)* afghan *m*

5 *Am (blanket)* couverture *f* en lainage

ADJ afghan

COMP *(embassy)* d'Afghanistan; *(history)* de l'Afghanistan; *(teacher)* d'afghan

►► ***Afghan hound*** lévrier *m* afghan

Afghanistan [æf'gænɪˌstæn] **N** *Geog* Afghanistan *m*

AFI [ˌeɪef'aɪ] **N** *Cin (abbr* **American Film Institute***)* American Film Institute *m (cinémathèque américaine dont le quartier général se trouve à Washington)*

aficionado [əˌfɪsjə'nɑːdəʊ] (*pl* **aficionados**) **N** aficionado *m*, amoureux(euse) *m,f*; **theatre aficionados, aficionados of the theatre** les aficionados du théâtre; **a tennis a.** un (une) mordu(e) de tennis

afield [ə'fɪld] **ADV to go far a.** aller loin; **people came from as far a. as Australia** les gens venaient même d'Australie; **they travelled further a. for their holidays this year** ils sont allés bien plus loin cette année pour leurs vacances

afire [ə'faɪə(r)] *Literary* **ADJ 1** *(burning)* en feu, en flammes **2** *Fig (with emotion)* enflammé (**with** de)

ADV to set sth a. mettre le feu à qch; *Fig* embraser qch

aflame [ə'fleɪm] *Literary* **ADJ 1** *(burning)* en flammes, en feu **2** *(emotionally)* enflammé; **to be a. with desire/anger** être enflammé de désir/colère **3** *(in colour)* **the sky was a. with colour** le ciel flamboyait de couleurs vives

ADV to set a. mettre le feu à; *Fig* exciter, enflammer; **he set her heart a.** il a fait battre son cœur

AFL-CIO [ˌeɪef'elˌsiːaɪ'əʊ] **N** *Admin & Ind (abbr* **American Federation of Labor and Congress of Industrial Organizations***)* = la plus grande confédération syndicale américaine

afloat [ə'fləʊt] **ADJ 1** *(swimmer)* qui surnage; *(boat)* à flot; *(cork, oil)* flottant; *Fig (business)* à flot **2** *(flooded)* inondé; **the kitchen was a.** la cuisine était inondée

ADV 1 *(floating)* à flot, sur l'eau; **we managed to get** *or* **to set the raft a.** nous avons réussi à mettre le radeau à flot; **to stay a.** *(swimmer)* garder la tête hors de l'eau, surnager; *(boat)* rester à flot; **to keep a.** rester à flot; **to keep sb/sth a.** maintenir qn/qch à flot; *Fig* **to get a business a.** *(from the start)* mettre une entreprise à flot; *(after financial difficulties)* renflouer une entreprise; **small businesses struggling to stay a.** des petites entreprises qui luttent pour se maintenir à flot **2** *(on boat)* **a holiday spent a.** *(on barge)* des vacances en péniche; *(at sea)* des vacances en mer

aflutter [ə'flʌtə(r)] **ADJ my heart was all a.** j'avais le cœur qui battait la chamade; **she set my heart a.** elle fit battre mon cœur

AFM [ˌeɪef'em] **N** *TV (abbr* **assistant floor manager***)* régisseur *m* de plateau adjoint

afoot [ə'fʊt] **ADV** *(in preparation)* **there's something a.** il se prépare *ou* il se trame quelque chose; **there is a scheme a. to build a new motorway** on a formé le projet *ou* on envisage de construire une nouvelle autoroute; **there was trouble a.** des ennuis se préparaient

afore [ə'fɔː(r)] *Arch* = **before**

aforementioned [əˈfɔːˌmenʃənd] *Formal* **ADJ** susmentionné, précité; **the a. persons** lesdites personnes

N the a. *(person)* le (la) susmentionné(e)

aforesaid [ə'fɔːsed] *Formal* **ADJ** susdit, précité

N the a. *(person)* le (la) susdit(e)

aforethought [ə'fɔːθɔːt] **ADJ** *Formal* prémédité

a fortiori [ˌɑːfɔːtɪ'ɔːrɪ] **ADV** a fortiori

afoul [ə'faʊl] **ADV** *Literary* **to run a. of sb** se mettre qn à dos, s'attirer le mécontentement de qn; **to run a. of the law** avoir des ennuis avec la police

afraid [ə'freɪd] **ADJ 1** *(frightened)* **to be a.** avoir peur; **don't be a.** n'ayez pas peur, ne craignez rien; **to make sb a.** faire peur à qn; **to be a. of sb/sth** avoir peur de qch/sth; **she is a. of the dark** elle a peur du noir; **there's nothing to be a. of** il n'y a rien à craindre; **she was a. (that) the dog would** *or* **might bite her** elle avait peur *ou* elle craignait que le chien (ne) la morde; **he is a. for his life** il craint pour sa vie **2** *(indicating reluctance, hesitation, worry)* **to be a. that…** avoir peur *ou* craindre que + *subjunctive*…; **he isn't a. of work** le travail ne lui fait pas peur; **don't be a. to speak** *or* **of speaking your mind** n'ayez pas peur de dire ce que vous pensez; **I'm a. (that) I'll say the wrong thing** je crains *ou* j'ai peur de ne pas dire ce qu'il faut; **that's (exactly) what I was a. of!** c'est bien ce que je craignais!; **he was a. to open his mouth** il n'osait pas dire un mot **3** *(indicating regret)* **I'm a. I won't be able to come** je regrette *ou* je suis désolé de ne pouvoir venir; **I'm a. I can't help you** je regrette *ou* je suis désolé, mais je ne peux pas vous aider; **I can't help you, I'm a.** je suis désolé, je crois que je ne peux rien faire pour vous; **I'm a. to say…** j'ai le regret de dire…; **I'm a. so** j'ai bien peur que oui, j'en ai bien peur; **I'm a. not** j'ai bien peur que non, j'en ai bien peur

afresh [ə'freʃ] **ADV** de nouveau; **to look at a problem a.** jeter un nouveau regard sur un problème; **we'll have to start a.** il va falloir recommencer *ou* reprendre à zéro

Africa ['æfrɪkə] **N** Afrique *f*; **in A.** en Afrique

African ['æfrɪkən] **N** Africain(e) *m,f*

ADJ africain

►► ***African American*** **N** Noir(e) *m,f* américain(e)

ADJ noir américain; *Zool* ***African elephant*** éléphant *m* d'Afrique; *Pol* ***African National Congress*** Congrès *m* national africain, ANC *m*; *Pol* ***African Union*** Union *f* africaine; *Bot* ***African violet*** saintpaulia *m*

Afrikaaner [ˌæfrɪ'kɑːnə(r)] **N** Afrikaner *mf*, Afrikaander *mf*

ADJ afrikaner, afrikaander

Afrikaans [ˌæfrɪ'kɑːns] **N** *(language)* afrikaans *m*

Afro ['æfrəʊ] (*pl* **Afros**) **N** coiffure *f* afro

ADJ *(hairstyle)* afro

Afro-American **N** Afro-Américain(e) *m,f*

ADJ afro-américain

aft [ɑːft] **ADV** *Naut & Aviat* à *ou* vers l'arrière; **to go a.** aller à *ou* vers l'arrière; **a. of the mast** sur l'arrière du mât; **to have the wind dead a.** avoir le vent en poupe

ADJ *Naut (deck)* arrière

AFTER ['ɑːftə(r)]

PREP
- après **1–7**
- d'après **8**
- derrière **5**

ADV
- ensuite

CONJ
- après que

PREP 1 *(in time ▸ gen)* après; *(▸ period)* après, au bout de; **a. a while** au bout d'un moment, après un moment; **a. breakfast** après le petit déjeuner; **a. dark** après la tombée de la nuit; **the day a. the battle** le lendemain de la bataille; **it is a. six o'clock already** il est déjà six heures passées *ou* plus de six heures; **shortly a. midday/three** peu après midi/trois heures; *Am* **it's twenty a. eight** il est huit heures vingt; **the day a. tomorrow** après-demain *m*

2 *(in space)* après; **the shopping centre is just a. the church** le centre commercial est juste après l'église; **there ought to be a comma a. "however"** il devrait y avoir une virgule après "however"

3 *(in series, priority etc)* après; **Rothman comes a. Richardson** Rothman vient après Richardson; **a. you** *(politely)* après vous (je vous en prie); **a. you with the paper** tu peux me passer le journal quand tu l'auras fini

4 *(following consecutively)* **day a. day** jour après jour; **time a. time** maintes (et maintes) fois; **(for) mile a. mile** sur des kilomètres et des kilomètres; **it's been one crisis a. another ever since she arrived** on va de crise en crise depuis son arrivée

5 *(behind)* après, derrière; **don't expect me to clean up a. you** ne croyez pas que je vais nettoyer derrière vous; **he locked up a. them** il a tout fermé après leur départ *ou* après qu'ils soient partis

6 *(in view of)* après; **a. what you told me** après ce que vous m'avez dit; **and a. all I've done for them!** et après tout ce que j'ai fait pour eux!

7 *(in spite of)* **a. all the trouble I took, no one came** après *ou* malgré tout le mal que je me suis donné, personne n'est venu

8 *(in the manner of)* **a. Rubens** d'après Rubens

9 *(in search of)* **to be a. sb/sth** chercher qn/qch; **she's a. you** *(angry with)* elle t'en veut; *(attracted to)* tu l'intéresses; **the police are a. him** la police est à ses trousses, il est recherché par la police; **he's a. her money** il en veut à son argent; *Fam* **what's he a.?** *(want)* qu'est-ce qu'il veut?❑; *(looking for)* qu'est-ce qu'il cherche?❑; *(intend)* qu'est-ce qu'il a derrière la tête?; *Fam* **I know what she's a.** je sais où elle veut en venir

10 *(as verb complement)* **to ask** *or* **to inquire a. sb** demander des nouvelles de qn; *Br* **to name a child a. sb** donner à un enfant le nom de qn; **to run a. sb** courir après qn

ADV après, ensuite; **the day a.** le lendemain, le jour suivant; **two days a.** deux jours après *ou* plus tard; **the week a.** la semaine d'après *ou* suivante; **for months a.** pendant des mois après; **soon/long a.** peu/longtemps après; **to follow (on) a.** suivre

CONJ *(when subject changes)* après que + *indicative ou Fam subjunctive*; *(when subject stays the same)* après + *infinitive*; **I arrived a. he had left** je suis arrivé après qu'il soit parti; **a. I had seen him I went out** après l'avoir vu, je suis sorti; **a. saying goodnight to the children** après avoir dit bonsoir aux enfants

ADJ 1 *(later)* **in a. life** *or* **years** plus tard dans la vie

2 *Naut (cabin, hold, mast)* arrière

• **afters NPL** *Br Fam Culin* dessert❑*m*; **what's for afters?** qu'est-ce qu'il y a pour le dessert *ou* comme dessert?; **there was ice cream for afters** il y avait de la glace en dessert *ou* pour le dessert

• **after all ADV 1** *(when all's said and done)* après tout; **a. all, she is very young** après tout, elle est très jeune; **it only costs £5 a. all** ça ne coûte que cinq livres après tout

2 *(against expectation)* après *ou* malgré tout; **so she was right a. all** alors elle avait raison en fait; **so you went to the party a. all?** alors, finalement, tu es allé à la soirée?

• **one after another, one after the other ADV** l'un après l'autre; **one a. another they got up and left the room** l'un après l'autre, ils se levèrent et quittèrent la pièce; **he made several mistakes one a. the other** il a fait plusieurs fautes d'affilée *ou* à la file

afterbirth ['ɑːftəbɜːθ] **N** *Obst* placenta *m*

afterburner ['ɑːftəbɜːnə(r)] **N** *Aviat* dispositif *m* de postcombustion; *Aut* catalyseur *m* de postcombustion

aftercare ['ɑːftəkeə(r)] **N 1** *Med (after treatment)* postcure *f*; *Obst (after giving birth)* soins *mpl* post-natals; *(after operation)* soins *mpl* post-opératoires; **good a. facilities** un bon suivi médical **2** *(of prisoner)* suivi *m (après la sortie de prison)*

afterdeck ['ɑːftədek] **N** *Naut* plage *f* arrière

after-dinner ADJ *(speaker, speech)* de fin de dîner *ou* banquet; **an a. drink** un digestif

aftereffect ['ɑːftərɪˌfekt] **N** *(usu pl) (of drug)* effet *m* secondaire; *Fig (of remark, event etc)* répercussion *f*, contrecoup *m*; **the aftereffects of war** les séquelles *fpl ou* les répercussions *fpl* de la guerre; **I'm still feeling the aftereffects of last night's drinking** je ne me suis toujours pas remis de ce que j'ai bu hier soir

afterglow ['ɑːftəgləʊ] **N 1** *(of sunset)* dernières lueurs *fpl*, derniers reflets *mpl*; *Fig (of pleasure)* sensation *f* de bien-être *(après coup)*; *Fig* **he was basking in the warm a. of his triumph** il savourait le sentiment de volupté dans lequel son triomphe l'avait laissé **2** *Comput (on screen)* rémanence *f*

after-hours ADJ *(after closing time)* qui suit la fermeture; *(after work)* qui suit le travail; *Br* **a. drinking** = verres servis après l'heure de fermeture légale des pubs; *Am* **an a. bar** un bar de nuit

• **after hours ADV** *(after closing time)* après la fermeture; *(after work)* après le travail

▸▸ *St Exch* ***after-hours dealing*** transactions *fpl* hors Bourse; *St Exch* ***after-hours market*** marché *m* hors Bourse; *St Exch* ***after-hours trading*** transactions *fpl* hors Bourse

afterimage ['ɑːftərˌɪmɪdʒ] **N** *Opt* image *f* récurrente *ou* consécutive; *TV* rémanence *f* à l'extinction

afterlife ['ɑːftəlaɪf] **N** *Rel* au-delà *m*, vie *f* après la mort; **we shall meet in the a.** nous nous retrouverons dans l'au-delà

aftermarket ['ɑːftəmɑːkɪt] **N** *St Exch* marché *m* secondaire

aftermath ['ɑːftəmæθ] **N 1** *(of event)* séquelles *fpl*, suites *fpl*; **the a. of war** *(after-effects)* les répercussions *fpl ou* le contrecoup de la guerre; **in the immediate a.** tout de suite après, dans la foulée **2** *Agr (second mowing or crop)* regain *m*

aftermost ['ɑːftəməʊst] **ADJ** *Naut* le plus en arrière, le plus à l'arrière

afternoon [ˌɑːftə'nuːn] **N** après-midi *m inv or f inv*; **this a.** cet après-midi; **every a.** tous les après-midi; **tomorrow/yesterday a.** demain/hier après-midi; **in the a.** *(in general)* l'après-midi; *(of particular day)* (dans) l'après-midi; **on Friday a.** *(in general)* le vendredi après-midi; *(of particular day)* vendredi après-midi; **in the early a.** tôt dans l'après-midi; **at two o'clock in the a.** à deux heures de l'après-midi; **on the a. of 16 May** (dans) l'après-midi du 16 mai; **on a summer a.** par un après-midi d'été; **good a.** *(hello)* bonjour; *(goodbye)* au revoir;

COMP *(class, train)* de l'après-midi; *(walk)* qui a lieu dans l'après-midi

• **afternoons ADV** *esp Am* (dans) l'après-midi

▸▸ *Cin & Theat* ***afternoon performance*** matinée *f*; ***afternoon tea*** = thé pris avec une légère collation dans le cours de l'après-midi

afterpains ['ɑːftəpeɪnz] **NPL** *Obst* tranchées *fpl* utérines

after-party N after *m*

after-sales ADJ *Mktg* après-vente *(inv)*

▸▸ ***after-sales department*** service *m* après-vente; ***after-sales marketing*** marketing *m* après-vente, MAV *m*; ***after-sales service*** service *m* après-vente

aftershave ['ɑːftəʃeɪv] **N** (lotion *f*) après-rasage *m*, (lotion *f*) after-shave *m*

▸▸ ***aftershave lotion*** (lotion *f*) après-rasage *m*, (lotion *f*) after-shave *m*

aftershock ['ɑːftəʃɒk] **N** *Geol* réplique *f* (d'un séisme)

aftersun ['ɑːftəsʌn] **N** crème *f* après-soleil

▸▸ ***aftersun cream*** crème *f* après-soleil

aftertaste ['ɑːftəteɪst] **N** *also Fig* arrière-goût *m*

after-tax ADJ *Fin (profits)* après impôts, net d'impôt; *(salary)* net d'impôt

afterthought ['ɑːftəθɔːt] **N** pensée *f* après coup; **I had an a.** j'ai pensé après coup; **I only mentioned it as an a.** j'en ai seulement parlé après coup, quand l'idée m'est venue; **the west wing was added as an a.** l'aile ouest a été ajoutée après coup

afterwards ['ɑːftəwədz], *Am* **afterward** ['æftərwərd] **ADV** après, ensuite; **a. they went home** ensuite *ou* après ils sont rentrés chez eux; **a long time a.** longtemps après; **soon** *or* **shortly a.** peu de temps après; **I only realized a.** je n'ai compris qu'après coup *ou* que plus tard

afterworld ['ɑːftəwɜːld] **N** *Rel* **the a.** l'au-delà *m*

Aga® ['ɑːgə] **N** = cuisinière en fonte à l'ancienne

AGAIN [ə'gen]

- encore (une fois) **1**
- re- + verbe **3**
- d'ailleurs **6**
- ne... plus **2**
- déjà **4**

ADV 1 *(once more)* encore une fois, de nouveau; **once a.** encore une fois, une fois de plus; **it's me a.!** c'est encore moi!, me revoici!; **you'll soon be well a.** vous serez bientôt remis; **(the) same a. please!** *(in bar)* remettez-nous ça *ou* la même chose s'il vous plaît!; **yet a.** encore une fois

2 *(with negative)* ne... plus; **I didn't see them a.** je ne les ai plus revus; **not a.!** encore?; **not you a.!** encore vous?; **never a.!** *(after bad experience)* plus jamais!; **a. and a., time and (time) a.** maintes et maintes fois, à maintes reprises; **she read the passage through over and over a.** elle a lu et relu le passage

3 *(with verbs)* **to begin a.** recommencer; **to come a.** revenir; **to do a.** refaire; **if I had to do it a.** si c'était à refaire; **don't do it a.!** ne recommencez pas!; **can you say it a.?** pouvez-vous répéter?; **don't make me have to tell you a.!** et que je n'aie pas à vous le répéter!

4 *(indicating forgetfulness)* déjà; **what's her name a.?** comment s'appelle-t-elle déjà?

5 *(in quantity)* **as much/many a.** encore autant; **half as much a.** encore la moitié de ça; **half as many pages a.** la moitié plus de pages; **it's as long/wide/far a. as that** ça fait encore la même longueur/largeur/distance que ça

6 *(furthermore)* d'ailleurs, qui plus est; **a., I am not sure that...** d'ailleurs je ne suis pas sûr que...

AGAINST [ə'genst]

PREP
- contre **1–3, 5–8, 10, 12**
- en prévision de **9**
- par rapport à **11**
- à l'encontre de **4**
- sur **10**
- en échange de **12**

ADV
- contre

PREP 1 *(indicating position)* contre; **he leant his bike (up) a. the wall** il appuya son vélo contre le mur; **she had her nose pressed a. the window** elle avait le nez écrasé au carreau; **put the chairs (back) a. the wall** remettez les chaises contre le mur

2 *(indicating impact)* contre; **I banged my knee a. the chair** je me suis cogné le genou contre la chaise; **the shutter was banging a. the window** le volet claquait contre la fenêtre

3 *(in the opposite direction to ▸ current, stream, grain)* contre

4 *(contrary to ▸ rules, principles)* à l'encontre de; **to go a. a trend** s'opposer à une *ou* aller à l'encontre d'une tendance; **it's a. the law** c'est illégal *ou* contraire à la loi; **it's a. the law to steal** le vol est interdit par la loi; **there's no law a. it** il n'y a pas de loi qui s'y oppose; **they sold the farm a. my advice/wishes** ils ont vendu la ferme sans tenir compte de mes conseils/de ce que je souhaitais

5 *(indicating opposition to ▸ person, proposal, government)* contre; **the fight a. inflation/crime** la lutte contre l'inflation/la criminalité; **to decide a. sth** décider de ne pas faire qch; **to vote a. sth** voter contre qch; **you're either for us or a. us** tu dois être avec nous ou contre nous; **she's a. telling him** elle trouve qu'on ne devrait pas le lui dire; **I advised her a. going** je lui ai déconseillé d'y aller; **what have you got a. him/the idea?** qu'est-ce que vous avez contre lui/l'idée?; **what have you got a. going?** pourquoi vous n'avez pas envie d'y aller?; **I've nothing a. it** je n'ai rien contre

6 *(unfavourable to)* contre; **conditions were a. them** les conditions leur étaient défavorables;

his appearance is a. him son physique ne joue pas en sa faveur

7 *(in competition with)* contre; *Ftbl* **United a. Everton** United contre Everton; **to run a. sb** *Sport* courir contre qn; *Pol* se présenter contre qn; **a race a. time** *or* **the clock** une course contre la montre

8 *(indicating defence, protection, precaution etc)* contre; **protected a. the cold** protégé contre le froid; **to be insured a. theft** être assuré contre le vol; **a. all risks** contre tous les risques

9 *Formal (in preparation for)* en vue de, en prévision de; **to save money a. one's retirement** faire des économies en prévision de *ou* pour la retraite

10 *(in contrast to)* contre, sur; **to stand a. the light** être à contre-jour; **the tall chimneys stood out a. the sky** les hautes cheminées se détachaient sur le ciel; **the red stood out a. the grey** le rouge contrastait avec le gris; *Fig* **these events took place a. a background of political violence** ces événements ont eu lieu dans un climat de violence politique

11 *(in comparison to, in relation to)* en comparaison de, par rapport à; **to check sth a. a list** vérifier qch d'après une liste; **they cost £10 here (as) a. only £7 at the supermarket** ils coûtent 10 livres ici contre *ou* au lieu de 7 livres au supermarché; *Fin* **the dollar rose/fell a. the yen** le dollar a augmenté/baissé par rapport au yen

12 *(in exchange for)* contre, en contrepartie de, en échange de; **to issue a ticket a. payment of...** remettre un ticket en contrepartie du paiement de...

ADV contre; **are you for or a.?** êtes-vous pour ou contre?; **the odds are 10 to 1 a.** *(gen)* il y a une chance sur dix; *(in horseracing)* la cote est à 10 contre 1

---

agape [ə'geɪp] ADJ bouche bée *(inv)*; **to stand a.** rester bouche bée

agar ['eɪgə(r)], **agar-agar** [ˌeɪgər'eɪgə(r)] N *Bot & Culin* agar-agar *m*, gélose *f*

agaric ['ægərɪk] N *Bot* agaric *m*

agate ['ægɪt] N *Miner* agate *f*

COMP *(brooch)* en agate

agave [ə'geɪvɪ] N *Bot* agave *m*

AGC [ˌeɪdʒiː'siː] N *Rad & Elec (abbr* **Automatic Gain Control***)* antifading *m*

AGE [eɪdʒ]

N
- âge **1, 3, 4**
- époque **4**
- vieillesse **3**
- éternité **5**

VI
- vieillir

VT
- vieillir

N **1** *(of person, animal, tree, building)* âge *m*; **what a. is he?** quel âge a-t-il?; **he is 25 years of a.** il est âgé de 25 ans; **at the a. of 25** à l'âge de 25 ans; **when I was your a.** quand j'avais votre âge; **she's the same a. as me** *or* **as I am** elle a le même âge que moi; **his wife is only half his a.** sa femme n'a que la moitié de son âge; **she's twice my a.** elle a le double de mon âge; **I have a son your a.** j'ai un fils de votre âge; **they're the same a.** ils sont du même âge, ils ont le même âge; **people of all ages** des gens de tout âge; **people over the a. of 50** les gens de plus de 50 ans; **he lived to a ripe old a.** il a vécu jusqu'à un bel âge *ou* très vieux; **she doesn't look her a.** elle ne fait pas son âge; **I'm beginning to feel my a.** je commence à me sentir vieux; **act** *or* **be your a.!** *(be reasonable)* sois raisonnable!; *(don't be silly)* ne sois pas stupide!; **he is at** *or* **of an a. when he should consider settling down** il est à un âge où il devrait penser à se ranger; **at your a. you should know** à ton âge, tu devrais savoir

2 *(adulthood) Law* **to be of a.** être majeur; **to come of a.** atteindre sa majorité, devenir majeur; *Law* **to be under a.** être mineur; *(not old enough to buy alcohol etc)* ne pas avoir l'âge

3 *(old age ▸ of person)* âge *m*, vieillesse *f*; *(▸ of wood, paper, wine)* âge *m*; **yellow** *or* **yellowed with a.** jauni par l'âge; **wisdom comes with a.** la sagesse vient avec l'âge; **a. has not been kind to her** elle est marquée par l'âge; **the house is falling to pieces with a.** la maison tombe de vieillesse *ou* de vétusté; **the car's beginning to show its a.** la voiture commence à donner des signes de vieillesse; **you're showing your a.!** *(remembering things like that)* tu es d'un autre âge!; *(you've lost touch)* tu te fais vieux!; *Hum* **a. before beauty!** *(when letting someone enter first)* c'est le privilège de l'âge!

4 *(period ▸ historical)* époque *f*, âge *m*; *Geol* âge *m*; **the a. we live in** notre siècle, le siècle où nous vivons; **in our a.** à notre époque; **in an earlier a. this wouldn't have been tolerated** il fut un temps où on n'aurait pas toléré cela; **in this a. of consumerism** en cette ère de consumérisme; **through the ages** à travers les âges

5 *(usu pl) (long time)* éternité *f*; **she was an a. getting dressed, it took her an a. to get dressed** elle a mis un temps fou à s'habiller; **I haven't seen you for** *or* **in ages!** cela fait une éternité que je ne vous ai (pas) vu!; **I've been waiting (for) ages** cela fait une éternité que j'attends; **it took him ages to do the work** il a mis très longtemps à faire le travail; **it's expensive, but it lasts for ages** c'est cher, mais ça dure très longtemps

VI vieillir, prendre de l'âge; **to a. ten years** vieillir de dix ans; **he had aged beyond recognition** il avait tellement vieilli qu'on ne le reconnaissait plus; **to a. well** *(person)* vieillir bien; *(wine, cheese)* s'améliorer en vieillissant

VT **1** *(person)* vieillir; **the years had aged him** il avait beaucoup vieilli; **illness has aged her** la maladie l'a vieillie

2 *(wine, cheese)* laisser vieillir *ou* mûrir; **aged in the wood** vieilli en fût

▸▸ ***age bracket*** tranche *f* d'âge; *Law* ***the age of consent*** = l'âge où les rapports sexuels sont autorisés; **they are below the a. of consent** ils tombent sous le coup de la loi sur la protection des mineurs; ***age group*** tranche *f* d'âge; **the 20 to 30 a. group** la tranche d'âge des 20 à 30 ans; ***age limit*** limite *f* d'âge; *Law* ***age of majority*** majorité *f*; *Hist* ***Age of Reason*** siècle *m* des lumières; ***age ring*** *(on tree)* cerne *m*

---

aged ADJ **1** [eɪdʒd] *(of the age of)* **a man a. 50** un homme (âgé) de 50 ans **2** ['eɪdʒɪd] *(old)* âgé, vieux (vieille); **my a. aunt** ma vieille tante

NPL ['eɪdʒɪd] **the a.** les personnes *fpl* âgées, les vieux *mpl*

▸▸ *Acct* ***aged debtors*** balance *f* âgée

ageing ['eɪdʒɪŋ] ADJ **1** *(person)* vieillissant, qui se fait vieux (vieille); *(society)* de vieux; *(machinery, car)* qui se fait vieux (vieille); **the a. process** le processus du vieillissement **2** *(clothes, hairstyle)* qui vieillit

N **1** *(of society, population)* vieillissement *m* **2** *(of wine, cheese)* vieillissement *m*

ageism ['eɪdʒɪzəm] N âgisme *m*

ageist ['eɪdʒɪst] N = personne qui fait preuve d'âgisme

ADJ *(action, policy)* qui relève de l'âgisme

ageless ['eɪdʒlɪs] ADJ *(person)* sans âge, qui n'a pas d'âge; *(work of art)* intemporel; *(beauty)* toujours jeune

agency ['eɪdʒənsɪ] *(pl* **agencies***)* N **1** *(for employment)* agence *f*, bureau *m*; *(for travel, accommodation)* agence *f* **2** *Admin* service *m*, bureau *m*; **international aid agencies** organisations *fpl* d'aide internationale; **a government a.** une agence gouvernementale **3** *(intermediary ▸ of person)* intermédiaire *m*, entremise *f*; *(▸ of fate)* jeu *m*; *(▸ of light, water)* action *f*; **through her a.** par son entremise, grâce à elle; **by the a. of direct sunlight** par l'action directe des rayons du soleil

▸▸ *Com* ***agency agreement*** accord *m* de représentation; ***agency copy*** dépêche *f* d'agence; ***agency fee*** frais *mpl* d'agence; *Banking* commission *f* de gestion; *Am* ***Agency for International Development*** = agence américaine pour le développement international; *Com* ***agency work*** travail *m* pour une agence

agenda [ə'dʒendə] N **1** *(for meeting)* ordre *m* du jour; *(for activities)* programme *m*; **what's on today's a.?, what's on the a. (for) today?** *(for meeting)* quel est l'ordre du jour?; *(for activities)* qu'est-ce qu'il y a au programme pour aujourd'hui?; *Fig* **drugs are back on the a.** la drogue revient à la une de l'actualité; **the problem of the homeless doesn't come very high on the government's a.** le problème des sans-abri ne figure pas parmi les priorités du gouvernement; *Fig* **it was top of the a.** c'était prioritaire; **to set the a.** mener le jeu **2** *(set of priorities)* **to have one's own a.** avoir son propre programme

▸▸ *EU* ***Agenda 2000*** Agenda *m* 2000; ***agenda setting*** = fait d'influencer la direction d'un débat

> Note that the French word **agenda** is a false friend and is never a translation for the English word **agenda**. It means **diary**.

agent ['eɪdʒənt] N **1** *Com* agent *m*, représentant (e) *m,f*; *(for travel, insurance)* agent *m*; *(for firm)* concessionnaire *mf*; *(for brand)* dépositaire *mf*; **he acted as my local a.** il agissait en tant qu'agent local; **the firm are sole agents for Pitkins** la société est agent exclusif de Pitkins; **where's the nearest Jaguar a.?** où est le concessionnaire Jaguar le plus proche?

2 *(for actor, sportsman, writer)* agent *m*

3 *(spy)* agent *m*; **(secret) a.** agent *m* secret

4 *(means)* agent *m*, moyen *m*; **by the working of some outside a.** par l'opération de quelque agent extérieur; **to be the a. of sth** être le moteur *ou* la cause de qch; **an a. of change** *(key person)* un acteur *m*; **her forceful nature turned out to be the a. of her downfall** son naturel énergique fut aussi la cause *ou* à l'origine de sa chute

5 *Chem & Ling* agent *m*

6 *Comput (software)* logiciel *m* client

▸▸ *Chem & Mil* ***Agent Orange*** agent *m* orange *(défoliant utilisé par les Américains pendant la guerre du Viêt-nam)*; ***agent provocateur*** (agent *m*) provocateur *m*

age-old ADJ séculaire, antique

agglomerate VT [ə'glɒməreɪt] agglomérer

VI [ə'glɒməreɪt] s'agglomérer

N [ə'glɒmərət] *Geol* agglomérat *m*

ADJ [ə'glɒmərət] aggloméré

agglomeration [əˌglɒmə'reɪʃən] N agglomération *f*

agglutinate VT [ə'gluːtɪneɪt] agglutiner

VI [ə'gluːtɪneɪt] s'agglutiner

ADJ [ə'gluːtɪnət] agglutiné

agglutination [əˌgluːtɪ'neɪʃən] N agglutination *f*

aggrandize, -ise [ə'grændaɪz] VT *Pej* agrandir; *(one's importance, role)* grossir, grandir

aggrandizement, -isement [ə'grændɪzmənt] N *Pej* agrandissement *m*; **personal a.** volonté *f* de se pousser en avant

aggravate ['ægrəveɪt] VT **1** *(worsen ▸ illness, conditions)* aggraver; *(▸ situation, problem)* aggraver, envenimer; *(▸ quarrel)* envenimer **2** *Fam (irritate ▸ person)* agacer ᵔ, exaspérer ᵔ

▸▸ *Law* ***aggravated assault*** coups *mpl* et blessures *fpl*

aggravating ['ægrəveɪtɪŋ] ADJ **1** *(worsening ▸ situation, illness, conditions)* aggravant **2** *Fam (irritating ▸ person, problem)* agaçant ᵔ, exaspérant ᵔ; **I've had a very a. day** j'ai passé une journée atroce

aggravation [ˌægrə'veɪʃən] N **1** *(of situation, crime, illness)* aggravation *f*; *(of wound, quarrel)* envenimement *m* **2** *Fam (irritation)* agacement ᵔ *m*, exaspération ᵔ *f*; **he does nothing but cause a.** il ne fait qu'embêter le monde; **I don't want to give** *or* **cause any more a.** je ne veux plus embêter qui que ce soit **3** *Fam (cause of irritation)* circonstance *f* agaçante *ou* exaspérante ᵔ

aggregate N ['ægrɪgət] **1** *(total)* ensemble *m*, total *m*; **in the a., on a.** dans l'ensemble, globalement; *Sport* **to win on a.** gagner au total des points ou des buts **2** *Constr & Geol* agrégat *m*

ADJ ['ægrɪgət] **1** *(total)* global, total; **for an a. period of three years** pendant trois ans en tout **2** *Bot & Geol* agrégé

VT ['ægrɪgeɪt] **1** *(bring together)* rassembler **2** *(add up to)* s'élever à, se monter à

▸▸ *Fin* ***aggregate amount*** montant *m* global; *Fin* ***aggregate expenditure*** dépenses *fpl* globales; *Fin* ***aggregate figure*** chiffre *m* global; *Com* ***aggregate output*** production *f* globale

aggregation [ægrɪ'geɪʃən] N **1** *Phys* agrégation *f*, agglomération *f* **2** *Miner* agrégat *m*

aggregator [ˈægrəgeɪtə(r)] **N** *Comput* aggrégateur *m*

aggression [əˈgreʃən] **N 1** *(attack)* agression *f* **2** *(aggressiveness)* agressivité *f*; **an act of a.** une agression;

aggressive [əˈgresɪv] **ADJ 1** *(gen) & Psy* agressif (**towards** envers) **2** *Mil (action, weapon)* offensif **3** *(businessperson)* combatif, dynamique; *(campaign)* énergique

aggressively [əˈgresɪvlɪ] **ADV 1** *(behave)* agressivement, avec agressivité; *(say)* d'un ton agressif; *(look at)* d'un air agressif **2** *(sell)* énergiquement, avec dynamisme; *(campaign)* avec dynamisme

aggressiveness [əˈgresɪvnɪs] **N 1** *(gen)* agressivité *f* **2** *(of businessperson)* combativité *f*; *(of campaign)* dynamisme *m*, fougue *f*

aggressor [əˈgresə(r)] **N** agresseur *m*

aggrieved [əˈgriːvd] **ADJ 1** *(gen)* contrarié (**at** *or* **about** par), mécontent (**at** *or* **about** de) **2** *Law* lésé; **the a. party** la partie lésée

aggro [ˈægrəʊ] **N** *Br Fam (UNCOUNT)* **1** *(violence, fighting)* grabuge *m*, bagarre *f*; **there was a bit of a. at the pub last night** il y a eu du grabuge *ou* ça a chauffé au pub hier soir **2** *(fuss, bother)* histoires *fpl*; **people don't complain because they don't want any a.** les gens ne se plaignent pas parce qu'ils ne veulent pas d'histoires; **my Mum's giving me so much a. at the moment** ma mère est toujours sur mon dos en ce moment

aghast [əˈgɑːst] **ADJ** *(astounded)* interloqué, pantois; *(horrified)* horrifié, atterré; **she was a. at the news** elle était atterrée par la nouvelle; **I stared at him a.** je l'ai regardé, atterré

agile [*Br* ˈædʒaɪl, *Am* ˈædʒəl] **ADJ 1** *(person, animal)* agile, leste **2** *(brain, mind)* vif

agilely [*Br* ˈædʒaɪllɪ, *Am* ˈædʒəllɪ] **ADV 1** *(move, jump)* agilement, avec agilité **2** *(argue, reason)* adroitement

agility [əˈdʒɪlətɪ] **N 1** *(physical)* agilité *f*, souplesse *f* **2** *(mental)* vivacité *f*

aging, agism *etc* = **ageing, ageism** *etc*

agio [ˈædʒɪəʊ] *(pl* **agios***)* **N** *Fin* **1** *(price)* agio *m*, prix *m* du change **2** *(business)* commerce *m* du change

agitate [ˈædʒɪteɪt] **VI to a. for/against sth** faire campagne en faveur de/contre qch; **they are agitating for better working conditions** ils réclament de meilleures conditions de travail

VT 1 *Chem (liquid)* agiter, remuer **2** *(emotionally)* agiter, troubler

agitated [ˈædʒɪteɪtɪd] **ADJ** agité, troublé; **to become** *or* **to get a.** se mettre dans tous ses états; **now don't get a.!** allons, ne t'agite pas comme ça!

agitatedly [ˈædʒɪteɪtɪdlɪ] **ADV** *(act)* de manière agitée; *(say)* avec agitation, d'une voix agitée

agitation [ˌædʒɪˈteɪʃən] **N 1** *(emotional)* agitation *f*, émoi *m*, trouble *m*; **to be in a state of a.** être dans tous ses états **2** *(unrest)* agitation *f*, troubles *mpl*; *Pol (campaign)* campagne *f* mouvementée; **there was a lot of a. in favour of nuclear disarmament** il y avait un fort mouvement de contestation pour réclamer le désarmement nucléaire **3** *(of sea)* agitation *f*

agitator [ˈædʒɪteɪtə(r)] **N 1** *(person)* agitateur (trice) *m,f* **2** *Tech (machine)* agitateur *m*

agitprop [ˈædʒɪtprɒp] *Pol* **N** agit-prop *f inv*

COMP *(art, theatre)* de l'agit-prop

aglitter [əˈglɪtə(r)] **ADJ** brillant; **her eyes were a. with mischief** ses yeux pétillaient de malice

aglow [əˈgləʊ] **ADJ** *(fire)* rougeoyant; *(sky)* embrasé; **to be a. with colour** briller de couleurs vives; *Fig* **his face was a. with excitement/health** son visage rayonnait d'émotion/de santé

AGM [ˌeɪdʒiːˈem] **N** *Br Admin* (*abbr* **annual general meeting**) AGA *f*

agnostic [ægˈnɒstɪk] *Rel* **N** agnostique *mf*

ADJ agnostique

agnosticism [ægˈnɒstɪsɪzəm] **N** *Rel* agnosticisme *m*

ago [əˈgəʊ] **ADV they moved here ten years a.** ils ont emménagé ici il y a dix ans; **how long a. did this happen?** cela c'est produit il y a combien de temps?, il y a combien de temps que cela s'est produit?; **that was years a.** ça fait des années de cela; **a little while a., a short time a.** tout à l'heure; **not so long a.** il n'y a pas si longtemps; **no longer a. than the last century** pas plus loin qu'au siècle dernier; **a long time a., long a.** il y a longtemps; **as long a. as 1900** en 1900 déjà, dès 1900

agog [əˈgɒg] **ADJ** en émoi (**about sth** à cause de qch); **everyone was a.** tout le monde était en émoi; **the children were all a. (with excitement)** les enfants étaient tout excités; **I was a. to discover what had happened** je brûlais d'impatience de savoir ce qui s'était passé; **the scandal set the whole town a.** le scandale a mis la ville entière en émoi

agonize, -ise [ˈægənaɪz] **VI 1** *(worry)* se tourmenter; **to a. over** *or* **about a decision** hésiter longuement avant de prendre une décision; **don't a. over it!** n'y passe pas trop de temps!; **to a. over how to do sth** se ronger les sangs *ou* se tracasser pour savoir comment faire qch **2** *Literary (suffer)* être au supplice *ou* au martyre

> Note that the French verb **agoniser** is a false friend and is never a translation for the English verb **to agonize**. It means **to be dying**.

agonized, -ised [ˈægənaɪzd] **ADJ** *(behaviour, reaction)* angoissé, d'angoisse; *(look)* angoissé, plein d'angoisse; *(cry)* déchirant; **with an a. expression (on her face)** le visage déchiré par l'angoisse

agonizing, -ising [ˈægənaɪzɪŋ] **ADJ** *(pain, worry, death)* atroce; *(sight)* navrant, angoissant; *(situation, silence, wait)* angoissant; *(decision, choice, dilemma)* pénible; **we had an a. half-hour** nous avons connu une demi-heure d'angoisse

N angoisse *f*; **why all this a. about something that can't be helped?** pourquoi se tourmenter à propos de quelque chose qu'on ne peut pas changer?

agonizingly, -isingly [ˈægənaɪzɪŋlɪ] **ADV** atrocement; **an a. difficult decision** une décision atrocement difficile

agony [ˈægənɪ] *(pl* **agonies***)* **N 1** *(physical* ► *pain)* douleur *f* atroce; (► *suffering)* souffrance *f* atroce, souffrances *fpl* atroces; **to be in a.** souffrir le martyre; **to cry out in a.** crier de douleur; **it was a. to stand up** je souffrais le martyre pour me lever; **death a.** agonie *f* (de la mort); *Fam* **it's a. walking in these shoes** c'est un véritable supplice de marcher avec ces chaussures **2** *(emotional, mental)* supplice *m*, angoisse *f*; **to be in an a. of doubt/remorse** être torturé par le doute/le remords; **it was a. just listening to him** le seul fait de l'écouter était un vrai supplice; *Fam* **to pile** *or* **put on the a.** forcer la dose

►► *Br* ***agony aunt*** = responsable du courrier du cœur; *Br* ***agony column*** courrier *m* du cœur

> Note that the French word **agonie** is a false friend. It means **death throes**.

agoraphobia [*Br* ˌægərəˈfəʊbɪə, *Am* əˌgɔːrəˈfəʊbɪə] **N** *Psy* agoraphobie *f*; **to have a.** souffrir d'agoraphobie

agoraphobic [ˌægərəˈfəʊbɪk] *Psy* **N** agoraphobe *mf*

ADJ agoraphobe

agrarian [əˈgreərɪən] *Agr* **N** agrarien(enne) *m,f*

ADJ agraire

agree [əˈgriː] **VT 1** *(share opinion)* **to a. that...** être d'accord avec le fait que...; **we all a. that he's innocent** nous sommes tous d'accord pour dire qu'il est innocent, nous sommes tous d'avis qu'il est innocent; **I don't a. that the police should be armed** je ne suis pas d'accord pour que la police soit armée

2 *(consent)* **to a. to do sth** accepter de *ou* consentir à faire qch

3 *(admit)* admettre, reconnaître; **they agreed that they had made a mistake** ils ont reconnu *ou* convenu qu'ils avaient fait une faute

4 *(reach agreement on)* convenir de; **to a. a date** convenir d'une date; **to a. a price** se mettre d'accord sur un prix; **to be agreed** *(date)* à convenir; *(price)* à débattre; **to a. to do sth** se mettre d'accord pour faire qch; **they agreed to share the cost** ils se sont mis d'accord pour partager les frais; **they agreed to take a taxi** ils ont décidé d'un commun accord de prendre un taxi; **we agreed to differ** nous sommes restés chacun sur notre position; **it was agreed that the money should be invested** il a été convenu que l'argent serait investi; **the budget has been agreed** le budget a été adopté; **as agreed** comme convenu; **unless otherwise agreed** sauf accord contraire

5 *(accept, approve* ► *statement, plan)* accepter; *Acct* **to a. the accounts** *or* **the books** faire accorder les livres; **the figures were agreed between the accountants** les chiffres ont été acceptés (d'un commun accord) par les experts-comptables

VI 1 *(share same opinion)* être d'accord (**about** sur); **I quite a.** je suis tout à fait d'accord (avec vous); **don't you a.?** n'êtes-vous pas d'accord?; **I think it's too expensive and Peter agrees** je pense que c'est trop cher et Peter est d'accord avec moi *ou* est du même avis; **to a. about sth** être d'accord sur qch; **I a. about going on a holiday** je suis d'accord pour partir en vacances; **to a. with sb** être d'accord avec *ou* être du même avis que qn; **I a. with you entirely** je suis entièrement d'accord avec vous; **they a. with me that it's a disgrace** ils trouvent comme moi que c'est une honte; **I couldn't a. (with you) more** je suis entièrement d'accord avec vous

2 *(assent)* consentir, donner son adhésion; **to a. to a proposal** donner son adhésion à *ou* accepter une proposition; **to a. to sb's request** consentir à la requête de qn; **her parents have agreed to her going abroad** ses parents ont consenti à ce qu'elle aille *ou* sont d'accord pour qu'elle aille à l'étranger

3 *(reach agreement)* se mettre d'accord (**about** sur); **the doctors couldn't a. about the best treatment** les médecins n'arrivaient pas à se mettre d'accord sur le traitement à suivre; **they agreed on Italy for the honeymoon** ils se sont mis d'accord sur l'Italie pour la lune de miel; **that was the price we agreed on** c'était le prix dont nous avions convenu *ou* sur lequel nous nous étions mis d'accord

4 *(correspond* ► *account, estimate, totals)* concorder; **your statement doesn't a. with hers** ta version *ou* ta déclaration ne correspond pas à la sienne, vos deux versions ne concordent pas

5 *Gram* s'accorder

►**agree with VT INSEP 1** *(be in favour of)* **I don't a. with censorship** je suis contre *ou* je n'admets pas la censure; **I don't a. with people smoking in public places** je ne suis pas d'accord pour que les gens fument dans les lieux publics **2** *(be suitable for)* **the climate here agrees with me** le climat d'ici me réussit *ou* me convient très bien; **rich food doesn't a. with me** la nourriture riche ne me réussit pas

agreeable [əˈgrɪəbəl] **ADJ 1** *(pleasant* ► *situation)* plaisant, agréable; (► *person)* agréable **2** *(willing)* consentant; **to be a. to sth** accepter qch, consentir à qch; **to be a. to doing sth** accepter de *ou* bien vouloir faire qch; **I am quite a. to his** *or* **him going** je veux bien *ou* je suis d'accord pour qu'il y aille; **if you are a.** si cela vous convient, si vous êtes d'accord **3** *(acceptable)* acceptable, satisfaisant; **I hope the terms are a. to you** j'espère que les conditions vous conviennent

agreeably [əˈgrɪəblɪ] **ADV** agréablement; **I was a. surprised** je fus agréablement surpris

agreed [əˈgriːd] **ADJ 1** *(in agreement)* d'accord; **is everyone a.?** est-ce que tout le monde est d'accord?; **it's a. that we leave on Friday** il est entendu *ou* convenu que nous partons vendredi **2** *(fixed* ► *time, place, price)* convenu; **as a.** comme convenu; **at the a. time** à l'heure convenue; **a. statement** *(in the media)* déclaration *f* commune

EXCLAM (c'est) d'accord *ou* entendu!

agreement [əˈgriːmənt] **N 1** *(gen)* accord *m*; **to be in a. (with sb/about sth)** être d'accord (avec qn/sur *ou* au sujet de qch); **we are both in a. on this point** nous sommes tous les deux d'accord *ou* du même avis à ce sujet; **to reach a.** parvenir à un accord; **by a. with the management** en accord avec la direction; **the proposal met with unanimous a.** la proposition a été reçue à l'unanimité; **there was a. on all sides that a change would be welcome** de toute part on convenait de l'opportunité d'un changement **2** *Com & Pol* accord *m*; **under the (terms of the) a.** selon les ter-

mes de l'accord; **to enter into** *or* **conclude an a. with sb** passer un accord *ou* un contrat avec qn; **an a. has been concluded between the two parties** un accord est intervenu entre les deux parties; **to have an a. with sb** avoir conclu *ou* passé un accord avec qn; **to hold sb to an a.** faire respecter un accord à qn; **to come to an a.** tomber d'accord, parvenir à un accord; **to break an a.** rompre un accord; *Law* **to sign a legal a. (to do sth)** s'engager (par) devant notaire (à faire qch)
3 *Gram* accord *m*

> Note that the French word **agrément** is a false friend. Its most common meaning is **pleasure**.

agribusiness [ˈægrɪˌbɪznɪs] **N** *(company)* agro-industrie *f*; *(sector)* agro-industries *fpl*

agrichemical [ˌægrɪˈkemɪkəl] **N** produit *m* agrochimique
ADJ agrochimique

agricultural [ˌægrɪˈkʌltʃərəl] **ADJ** *(produce, machinery, land, society)* agricole; *(expert)* agronome; **East Anglia is very a.** l'East Anglia est une région très agricole
►► ***agricultural college*** = école supérieure d'agriculture et d'agronomie; ***agricultural economy*** économie *f* du secteur agricole; ***agricultural engineer*** ingénieur *m* agronome; ***agricultural labourer*** ouvrier(ère) *m,f* agricole; ***agricultural show*** *(national)* salon *m* de l'agriculture; *(local)* foire *f* agricole; ***agricultural worker*** ouvrier(ère) *m,f* agricole

agriculturalist [ˌægrɪˈkʌltʃərəlɪst] **N** *(specialist)* agronome *mf*; *(farmer)* agriculteur(trice) *m,f*

agriculture [ˈægrɪˌkʌltʃə(r)] **N** agriculture *f*

agriculturist [ˌægrɪˈkʌltʃərɪst] **N** agriculteur (trice) *m,f*

agritourism [ˈægrɪˌtʊərɪzəm] **N** agrotourisme *m*, tourisme *m* agricole

agritourist [ˈægrɪˌtʊərɪst] **N** = personne qui pratique l'agrotourisme

agrochemical [ˌægrəʊˈkemɪkəl] **N** produit *m* agrochimique
ADJ agrochimique

agronomic [ˌægrəˈnɒmɪk], **agronomical** [ˌægrəˈnɒmɪkəl] **ADJ** agronomique

agronomist [əˈgrɒnəmɪst] **N** agronome *mf*

agronomy [əˈgrɒnəmɪ] **N** agronomie *f*

agroterrorism [ˌægrəʊˈterərɪzəm] **N** agroterrorisme *m*

aground [əˈgraʊnd] **ADJ** *(ship)* échoué; **to be a.** toucher le fond, être échoué
ADV to run *or* **to go a.** *(ship)* s'échouer; *Fig (policy, project etc)* échouer

ague [ˈeɪgjuː] **N** *Arch* **1** *Med (malarial fever)* fièvre *f* paludéenne **2** *Physiol (shivering)* frissons *mpl*

ah [ɑː] **EXCLAM** ah!; **ah, yes, now you come to mention it** euh, oui, maintenant que tu m'en parles

aha [ɑːˈhɑː] **EXCLAM** ah, ah!, tiens!

AHEAD [əˈhed]

> **ADV**
> • en avant, devant **1** • à venir, à l'avenir **2**
> • en avance, d'avance **3**

ADV 1 *(in space)* en avant, devant; **to send sb a.** envoyer qn en avant; **the road a.** la route devant nous/eux/*etc*; **there's a crossroads about half a mile a.** il y a un croisement à environ 800 mètres (d'ici); **go/drive on a. and I'll catch you up** vas-y *ou* pars en avant, je te rattraperai; **to push** *or* **press a. with a project** poursuivre un projet
2 *(in time)* **the years a.** les années à venir; **what lies a.?** qu'est-ce qui nous attend?; **to look a.** penser à l'avenir; **to plan a.** faire des projets; **you have to plan a. for a big wedding** il faut s'organiser à l'avance pour un grand mariage; **how far a. should one book?** combien de temps à l'avance faut-il retenir?; **we must think a.** nous devons prévoir
3 *(in competition, race)* en avance; **three lengths/five points a.** trois longueurs/cinq points d'avance; **to be a. on points** avoir des points d'avance; *Fig* **it's better to quit while you're a.** mieux vaut te retirer du jeu pendant que tu as l'avantage
4 *Naut* sur l'avant, en avant *(du navire)*; **the ship was right a.** le navire était droit devant; **to go a.** aller de l'avant
• **ahead of** **PREP 1** *(in front of)* devant; **there were ten people a. of us in the queue** il y avait dix personnes devant nous dans la queue
2 *(in time)* **he arrived ten minutes a. of me** il est arrivé dix minutes avant moi; **to finish a. of schedule** terminer plus tôt que prévu *ou* en avance; **the rest of the team are two months a. of us** les autres membres de l'équipe ont deux mois d'avance sur nous; **French time is one hour a. of British time** la France a une heure d'avance sur la Grande-Bretagne; **to arrive a. of time** arriver en avance *ou* avant l'heure; *Fig* **to be a. of one's time** être en avance sur son époque; **you've got your best years a. of you** vous avez vos meilleures années devant vous
3 *(in competition, race)* **he is five points a. of his nearest rival** il a cinq points d'avance sur son rival le plus proche, il devance son rival le plus proche de cinq points; **to be a. of one's competitors** devancer ses concurrents; *Sch* **he is a. of his class** il est en avance sur sa classe

ahem [əˈhem] **EXCLAM** hum!

> **-AHOLIC, -HOLIC, -OHOLIC** SUFFIXE
>
> • Ce suffixe aux connotations familières est construit sur le modèle du mot **alcoholic** (alcoolique) et indique l'ÉTAT DE DÉPENDANCE à l'égard de quelque chose. On l'ajoute à un verbe ou à un nom pour former un nouveau terme. Parmi les noms qui sont entrés dans la langue, citons:
> **a workaholic** un bourreau de travail; **a chocoholic** un(e) accro au chocolat; **he's a real shopaholic** c'est un fou du shopping.
> • Ce suffixe est très productif de néologismes du type **a bookaholic** un fou de lecture; **a game-aholic** un fou de jeux vidéo, etc. La forme suffixale **-aholic** est le plus souvent utilisée.
> • Bien que ce suffixe s'emploie généralement pour construire des noms, les mots ainsi formés s'emploient parfois comme adjectifs comme dans l'exemple suivant:
> **we live in a computerholic society** nous vivons dans une société obsédée par les ordinateurs.

ahoy [əˈhɔɪ] **EXCLAM** ohé!, holà!; **ship a.!** ohé du navire!

AI [ˈeɪˈaɪ] **N 1** *(abbr* **Amnesty International***)* Amnesty International **2** *Comput (abbr* **artificial intelligence***)* IA *f* **3** *Biol (abbr* **artificial insemination***)* insémination *f* artificielle
►► *Typ* ***AI sheet*** = descriptif d'un livre à paraître

AID [ˌeɪaɪˈdiː] **N 1** *Biol (abbr* **artificial insemination by donor***)* IAD *f* **2** *Am Admin & Econ (abbr* **Agency for International Development***)* = agence américaine pour le développement international

aid [eɪd] **N 1** *(help, assistance)* aide *f*; **with the a. of sb** avec l'aide de qn; **with the a. of sth** à l'aide de qch; **with the a. of half a dozen helpers** avec l'aide d'une demi-douzaine d'assistants; **I managed to open the tin with the a. of a screwdriver** à l'aide d'un tournevis, j'ai réussi à ouvrir la boîte; **to come to sb's a.** venir à l'aide de qn; **to go to sb's a.** se porter au secours de *ou* porter secours à qn
2 *Pol & Fin (to developing countries, for disaster relief)* aide *f*; **food a.** aide *f* alimentaire; **overseas a.** aide *f* au tiers-monde
3 *(helpful equipment)* aide *f*, support *m*; **teaching aids** supports *mpl ou* aides *fpl* pédagogiques; **visual aids** supports *mpl* visuels
4 *(assistant)* aide *mf*, assistant(e) *m,f*
5 *Sport (for climber)* piton *m*
VT 1 *(help ▸ person)* aider, venir en aide à; *(▸ financially)* aider, secourir; *(▸ digestion)* faciliter; **to a. sb with sth** aider qn pour qch; **they aided one another** ils se sont entraidés, ils se sont aidés les uns les autres
2 *(give support to ▸ region, industry)* aider, soutenir
3 *(encourage ▸ development, understanding, recovery)* contribuer à
4 *Law* **to a. and abet sb** être (le) complice de qn; *Fig* **aided and abetted by her sister** avec la complicité de sa sœur
• **in aid of** **PREP a collection in a. of the homeless** une collecte au profit des sans-abri; *Br Fam Fig* **what are the cakes in a. of?** les gâteaux sont en l'honneur de quoi?; *Fam* **what's all this noise in a. of?** qu'est-ce que c'est que tout ce bruit?
►► ***aid agency*** organisation *f* humanitaire; *Admin* ***aid organization*** organisme *m* d'aide; ***aid worker*** *(voluntary)* volontaire *mf*; *(paid)* employé(e) *m,f* d'une organisation humanitaire

AIDA [aɪˈiːdə] **N** *Mktg (abbr* **attention-interest-desire-action***)* AIDA *m*

aide [eɪd] **N** aide *mf*, assistant(e) *m,f*; *(to president etc)* conseiller(ère) *m,f*

aided [ˈeɪdɪd] **ADJ**
►► *Mktg* ***aided recall*** notoriété *f* assistée; *Br* ***aided school*** = école privée qui reçoit une aide de l'Etat mais garde un certain pouvoir de décision, notamment sur le contenu des cours d'instruction religieuse et le choix des enseignants

aide-de-camp [ˌeɪddəˈkɒŋ] *(pl* **aides-de-camp** [ˌeɪdz-]) **N** *Mil* aide *m* de camp

aide-mémoire [ˌeɪdmemˈwɑː(r)] *(pl* **aides-mémoire** [ˈeɪdz-]) **N** aide-mémoire *m inv*

aiding [ˈeɪdɪŋ] **N** *Law* **a. and abetting** complicité *f*

AIDS, Aids [eɪdz] *Med (abbr* **acquired immune deficiency syndrome***)* **N** sida *m*, SIDA *m*, Sida *m*
COMP *(clinic)* pour sidéens
►► ***Aids patient*** sidéen(enne) *m,f*; ***Aids sufferer*** sidéen(enne) *m,f*, malade *mf* atteint(e) du sida; ***the Aids virus*** le virus du sida

AIDS-related, Aids-related **ADJ** *Med* lié au sida
►► ***Aids-related complex*** ARC *m*; ***Aids-related virus*** ARV *m*

aikido [aɪˈkiːdəʊ] **N** *Sport* aïkido *m*

ail [eɪl] *Literary* **VT what ails you?** qu'avez-vous?, quelle mouche vous a piqué?
VI être souffrant

aileron [ˈeɪlərɒn] **N** *Aviat* aileron *m*

ailing [ˈeɪlɪŋ] **ADJ** *(person)* souffrant, en mauvaise santé; *(economy, industry)* malade; **the a. state of the economy/country** la mauvaise passe dans laquelle se trouve l'économie/le pays

ailment [ˈeɪlmənt] **N** mal *m*, affection *f*; **she has all kinds of ailments** elle souffre de toutes sortes de maux

AIM [ˌeɪaɪˈem] **N** *Br St Exch (abbr* **Alternative Investment Market***)* = marché hors-cote rattaché à la Bourse de Londres

aim [eɪm] **N 1** *(intention, purpose)* but *m*; **with the a. of** afin de, dans le but de; **she came to the meeting with the a. of causing trouble** elle est venue à la réunion dans le but de faire des histoires; **his a. is to get rich quickly** il a pour but *ou* il s'est donné comme but de s'enrichir rapidement; **her ultimate a. is to beat the world record** son but final est de battre le record du monde; **you need an a. in life** il faut un but dans la vie **2** *(with weapon)* **to take a. (at sb/sth)** viser (qn/qch); *Mil* **take a.!** en joue!; **to have a good a.** bien viser; **your a. isn't very good** vous ne visez pas très bien; **to miss one's a.** manquer la cible *ou* son but
VT 1 *(gun)* braquer; *(missile)* pointer; *(stone)* lancer; *(blow)* allonger, décocher; *(kick)* donner; **he aimed his gun at the man's head** il a braqué son pistolet sur la tête de l'homme; **he was aiming stones at the tree** il lançait des cailloux sur l'arbre; **the man aimed a kick at the dog** l'homme donna un coup de pied au chien **2** *Fig (criticism, product, programme)* destiner; **was that remark aimed at me?** est-ce que cette remarque m'était destinée?; **the programme is aimed at a teenage audience** l'émission est destinée à un public d'adolescents; **these measures are aimed at reducing unemployment** ces mesures visent une réduction du chômage
VI 1 *(take aim)* **to a. at sb/sth** viser qn/qch; **she aimed at** *or* **for the post, but missed** elle a visé le poteau, mais elle l'a manqué **2** *(have as goal)* **she's aiming to become a millionaire by the age of 30** son but, c'est d'être millionnaire à 30 ans; **we a. to arrive before midnight** nous avons l'intention *ou* nous nous sommes fixés d'arriver avant minuit; **he's aiming at quick promotion** il vise une promotion rapide; **to a. high** viser haut

aimless ['eɪmlɪs] **ADJ** *(person)* sans but, désœuvré; *(life)* sans but; *(occupation, task)* sans objet, futile

aimlessly ['eɪmlɪslɪ] **ADV** *(walk around)* sans but; *(stand around)* sans trop savoir quoi faire; **he wandered a. through the streets** il errait dans les rues

aimlessness ['eɪmlɪsnɪs] **N the a. of their existence** leur existence sans but

ain't [eɪnt] *Fam* **1** = **am not**
2 = **is not**
3 = **are not**
4 = **has not**
5 = **have not**

AIO [,eɪaɪ'əʊ] **N** *Mktg (abbr* **activities, interests and opinions***)* AIO
►► ***AIO research*** étude *f* AIO

air [eə(r)] **N 1** *(gen)* air *m*; **I need some (fresh) a.** j'ai besoin de prendre l'air; **I went out for a breath of (fresh) a.** je suis sorti prendre l'air; *Literary* **to take the a.** prendre le frais; **the divers came up for a.** les plongeurs sont remontés à la surface pour respirer; *Fig* **I need a change of a.** j'ai besoin de changer d'air; **to disappear** *or* **vanish into thin a.** se volatiliser, disparaître sans laisser de traces
2 *(sky)* air *m*, ciel *m*; **the smoke rose into the a.** la fumée s'éleva vers le ciel; **to throw sth up into the a.** lancer qch en l'air; **to fly through the a.** voler *ou* voltiger en l'air; **seen from the a., the fields looked like a chessboard** vus d'avion, les champs ressemblaient à un échiquier; **to take to the a.** *(bird)* s'envoler; *(plane)* décoller
3 *Aviat* **to travel by a.** voyager par avion
4 *Rad & TV* **to be on (the) a.** *(person)* être à *ou* avoir l'antenne; *(programme)* être à l'antenne; *(station)* émettre; **to go on the a.** *(person)* passer à l'antenne; *(programme)* passer à l'antenne, être diffusé; **you're on the a.** vous avez l'antenne; **to go off the a.** *(person)* rendre l'antenne; *(programme)* se terminer; *(station)* cesser d'émettre; **the station goes off the a. at midnight** les programmes finissent à minuit
5 *(manner, expression)* air *m*; **he has an a. about him** il en impose; **there is an a. of mystery about her** elle a un air mystérieux
6 *Mus* air *m*
COMP *Aviat & Mil (piracy, traffic, attack, defence)* aérien; *(traveller)* par avion; **to play a. guitar** = faire semblant de jouer de la guitare électrique
VT 1 *(ventilate* ► *room, bed)* aérer; *(dry* ► *linen)* faire sécher **2** *(express* ► *opinion, grievance)* exprimer, faire connaître; *(*► *suggestion, idea)* exprimer, avancer **3** *Am Rad & TV* diffuser
VI *Am Rad & TV* **the film airs next week** le film sera diffusé la semaine prochaine
• **airs NPL to put on** *or* **to give oneself airs** se donner de grands airs; *Br* **airs and graces** minauderies *fpl*
• **in the air ADV there's a rumour in the a. that they're going to sell** le bruit court qu'ils vont vendre; **there's something in the a.** il se trame quelque chose; **everything's up in the a.** *(uncertain)* rien n'a été décidé pour l'instant; **our holiday plans are still (up) in the a.** nos projets de vacances sont encore assez vagues
►► ***air ambulance*** avion *m* sanitaire; *Constr* ***air brick*** brique *f* creuse; ***air bubble*** *(in wallpaper, liquid)* bulle *f* d'air; *(in plastic, metal)* soufflure *f*; ***air cargo*** fret *m* aérien; *Br Mil* ***air commodore*** général *m* de brigade aérienne, *Can* brigadier-général *m*; ***air compressor*** compresseur *m* d'air; *Aviat* ***air corridor*** couloir *m* aérien; *Mil & Aviat* ***air cover*** couverture *f* aérienne; *Tech* ***air duct*** conduite *f* d'air, amenée *f* d'air; ***air filter*** filtre *m* à air; ***Air Force*** Armée *f* de l'air, Aviation *f*; *Chem* ***air freshener*** désodorisant *m (pour la maison)*; *Tech* ***air gauge*** micromètre *m* pneumatique; ***air hostess*** hôtesse *f* de l'air; *Aviat* ***air lane*** couloir *m* aérien *ou* de navigation aérienne; *Br Mil* ***air marshal*** général *m* de corps aérien, *Can & Belg* lieutenant-général *m*; ***air mattress*** matelas *m* pneumatique; *Aviat* ***air mile*** mille *m* marin; ***air miles*** = points que l'on peut accumuler lors de certains achats et qui permettent de bénéficier de réductions sur des billets d'avion; **to collect a. miles** accumuler des points; *Hist* **Air Ministry** Ministère *m* de l'Air; *Tech* ***air pistol*** pistolet *m* à air comprimé; ***air pocket*** *Met & Aviat (affecting plane)* trou *m* d'air; *Tech (in pipe)* poche *f* d'air; *Ecol* ***air pollution*** pollution *f* atmosphérique; *Mil & Aviat* ***air power*** puissance *f* aérienne; ***air quotes*** = guillemets mimés avec les mains en parlant; *Aviat* ***air rage*** rage *f* de l'air; *Mil* ***air raid*** attaque *f* aérienne, raid *m* aérien; *Tech* ***air rifle*** carabine *f* à air comprimé; *Aviat* ***air route*** route *f* aérienne; *Aviat* ***air service*** liaison *f* aérienne; ***air show*** *Com (exhibition)* salon *m* de l'aéronautique; *Aviat (display)* meeting *m* aérien; *Mil* ***air supremacy*** suprématie *f* aérienne; *Aviat* ***air taxi*** avion-taxi *m*; *Met* ***air temperature*** température *f* ambiante; *Aviat* ***air terminal*** aérogare *f*; *Aviat* ***air ticket*** billet *m* d'avion; *Aviat* ***air traffic*** circulation *f* aérienne, trafic *m* aérien; *Aviat* ***air transport*** transport *m* aérien *ou* par avion; *Aviat* ***air travel*** voyages *mpl* en avion; *Tech* ***air valve*** soupape *f (pour l'air)*; *Br Mil* ***air vice-marshal*** général *m* de division aérienne, *Can* major-général *m*, *Belg* général-major; *Com* ***air waybill*** lettre *f* de transport aérien, connaissement *m* aérien

airbag ['eəbæg] **N** *Aut* Air Bag® *m*

airborne ['eəbɔːn] **ADJ 1** *Aviat (plane)* en vol; *(balloon)* en l'air; **to become a.** *(plane)* décoller; **once we are a.** une fois que nous aurons décollé
2 *(particles, seeds)* en suspension dans l'air; *(disease)* présent dans l'air
3 *Mil (troops, division, regiment)* aéroporté
4 *Aviat (equipment, radar)* de bord
►► *Mil* ***airborne attack*** attaque *f* exécutée par des troupes aéroportées, assaut *m* vertical

airbrush ['eəbrʌʃ] *Art & Comput* **N** aérographe *m*
VT retoucher à l'aérographe
► **airbrush in VT SEP** *Art & Comput* ajouter à l'aérographe
► **airbrush out VT SEP** *Art & Comput* effacer à l'aérographe; *Fig* **to a. sb out of history** faire disparaître qn de l'histoire officielle

airbrushing ['eəbrʌʃɪŋ] **N** *Art & Comput* peinture *f ou* retouchage *m* à l'aérographe

Airbus® ['eəbʌs] **N** Airbus® *m*

aircon ['eəkɒn] **N** *(abbr* **air conditioning***)* clim *f*

air-conditioned ADJ climatisé

air-conditioning N climatisation *f*

air-cooled [-kuːld] **ADJ 1** *Aut & Tech (engine)* à refroidissement par air **2** *Am Tech (room)* climatisé

air-cooling N *Tech* refroidissement *m* par air

aircraft ['eəkrɑːft] *(pl* **inv***)* **N** *Aviat* avion *m*
►► *Naut & Mil* ***aircraft carrier*** porte-avions *m inv*; *Aviat* ***aircraft engineering*** ingénierie *f* aéronautique; ***aircraft factory*** usine *f* d'aviation; ***aircraft hangar*** hangar *m* à avions

aircraft(s)man ['eəkrɑːft(s)mən] *(pl* **aircraft(s) men** [-mən]*)* **N** *Br Mil* aviateur *m*, *Can* soldat *m*, *Belg* premier soldat *m*

aircraft(s)woman ['eəkrɑːft(s),wʊmən] *(pl* **aircraft(s)women** [-'wɪmɪn]*)* **N** *Br Mil* femme *f* soldat de deuxième classe *(dans l'armée de l'air)*

aircrew ['eəkruː] **N** *Aviat* équipage *m (d'avion)*

airdrome ['eədrəʊm] **N** *Am Aviat* aérodrome *m*

airdrop ['eədrɒp] *(pt & pp* **airdropped**, *cont* **airdropping***)* *Aviat* **N** parachutage *m*
VT parachuter

Airedale ['eədeɪl] **N** airedale *m*, airedale-terrier *m*
►► ***Airedale terrier*** airedale *m*, airedale-terrier *m*

airer ['eərə(r)] **N** *Br (for clothes)* séchoir *m*

airfield ['eəfiːld] **N** *Aviat* terrain *m* d'aviation, (petit) aérodrome *m*

airflow ['eəfləʊ] **N 1** *Tech* écoulement *m* d'air; **smooth/turbulent a.** écoulement *m* régulier/turbulent

airfoil ['eəfɔɪl] **N** *Am* surface *f* portante, plan *m* de sustentation

airframe ['eəfreɪm] **N** *Aviat* cellule *f* (d'avion)

airfreight ['eəfreɪt] *Aviat & Com* **N** *(cargo)* fret *m* aérien; *(transport)* transport *m* aérien; **to send sth by a.** expédier qch par voie aérienne *ou* par avion
VT expédier par fret aérien
►► *Aviat & Com* ***airfreight container*** conteneur-avion *m*

air/fuel mixture N *Aut* mélange *m* air/carburant

airhead ['eəhed] **N** *Fam* écervelé(e) *m,f*; *(woman)* évaporée *f*

airhole ['eəhəʊl] **N** *Tech* trou *m* d'aération

airily ['eərəlɪ] **ADV** avec désinvolture; *(to say)* d'un ton dégagé *ou* désinvolte

airiness ['eərɪnɪs] **N 1** *(of building, flat)* caractère *m* spacieux **2** *(of tone, manner)* désinvolture *f*

airing ['eərɪŋ] **N 1** *(of linen, room)* aération *f*; **the room needs an a.** la pièce a besoin d'être aérée; **give the clothes an a. outside** mets ces habits à l'air dehors **2** *Fig* **to give an idea an a.** agiter une idée, mettre une idée sur le tapis; **to give one's grievances/feelings an a.** exposer ses griefs/ses sentiments **3** *Am Rad & TV (of programme)* diffusion *f*, transmission *f*
►► ***airing cupboard*** = placard chauffé où l'on fait sécher le linge

air-kiss N to give sb an a. faire semblant de faire la bise à qn
VT = faire semblant de faire la bise à

airless ['eəlɪs] **ADJ 1** *(room)* qui manque d'air, qui sent le renfermé **2** *(weather)* lourd

airlessness ['eəlɪsnɪs] **N 1** *(of room)* manque *m* d'air *ou* d'aération **2** *Met (of weather)* lourdeur *f*

airlift ['eəlɪft] *Aviat* **N** pont *m* aérien
VT *(passengers, troops* ► *out)* évacuer par pont aérien; *(*► *in)* faire entrer par pont aérien; *(supplies, cargo)* acheminer par pont aérien

airline ['eəlaɪn] **N 1** *Aviat & Com (company)* compagnie *f* aérienne **2** *Naut & Tech (tube)* tuyau *m* d'air
►► *Aviat* ***airline club*** = programme de fidélisation de la clientèle d'une compagnie aérienne; *Aviat & Com* ***airline operator*** compagnie *f* aérienne; *Aviat* ***airline passenger*** passager(ère) *m,f* des compagnies aériennes; *Aviat* ***airline pilot*** pilote *m* de ligne

airliner ['eəlaɪnə(r)] **N** *Aviat* avion *m* de ligne

airlock ['eəlɒk] **N** *Tech* **1** *(in spacecraft, submarine)* sas *m* **2** *(in pipe)* poche *f ou* bulle *f* d'air

airmail ['eəmeɪl] *Aviat* **N** *(service)* poste *f* aérienne; *(letters etc)* courrier *m* par avion; **by a.** *(on envelope)* par avion
COMP *(parcel)* par avion
ADV par avion
VT expédier *ou* envoyer par avion
►► ***airmail letter*** *(letter sent by airmail)* lettre *f* par avion; *(bought at post office)* aérogramme *m*; ***airmail paper*** papier *m* avion; ***airmail sticker*** étiquette *f* par avion

airman ['eəmən] *(pl* **airmen** [-mən]*)* **N 1** *Aviat (gen)* aviateur *m* **2** *Am Mil* aviateur *m* de première classe, *Can* soldat *m*, *Belg* premier soldat *m*; **a. first class** caporal *m*

airpass ['eəpɑːs] **N** *Aviat* carte *f* d'abonnement de transport aérien

airplane ['eəpleɪn] **N** *Am* avion *m*

airplay ['eəpleɪ] **N** *Rad* **that record is getting a lot of a.** on entend souvent ce disque à la radio

airport ['eəpɔːt] **N** *Aviat* aéroport *m*
►► *Mktg* ***airport advertising*** publicité *f* dans les aéroports; ***airport apron*** aire *f* de stationnement (des avions); *Com* ***airport hotel*** hôtel *m* d'aéroport; *Fin* ***airport landing tax*** taxe *f* d'atterrissage; ***airport lounge*** hall *m* d'aéroport; *Com* ***airport shop*** boutique *f* d'aéroport; *Fin* ***airport tax*** taxe *f* d'aéroport; *Transp* ***airport taxi*** taxi *m* desservant l'aéroport; ***airport terminal*** aérogare *f*

airprox ['eəprɒks] **N** *Aviat* quasicollision *f* aérienne

airscrew ['eəskruː] **N** *Br Old-fashioned Aviat* hélice *f* (d'avion)

air-sea rescue N *Aviat* sauvetage *m* air-mer
►► ***air-sea rescue helicopter*** hélicoptère *m* de sauvetage en mer

airship ['eəʃɪp] **N** *Aviat* dirigeable *m*

airsick ['eəsɪk] **ADJ** *Aviat & Med* **to be** *or* **to get a.** avoir le mal de l'air

airsickness ['eə,sɪknɪs] **N** *Aviat & Med* mal *m* de l'air

airspace ['eəspeɪs] **N** *Aviat* espace *m* aérien

airspeed ['eəspiːd] **N** *Aviat* vitesse *f* relative

airstream ['eəstriːm] **N** *Met* courant *m* atmosphérique

airstrike ['eəstraɪk] N *Mil* raid *m* aérien, attaque *f* aérienne

airstrip ['eəstrɪp] N *Aviat* terrain *m ou* piste *f* d'atterrissage

airtight ['eətaɪt] ADJ hermétique, étanche (à l'air)

airtime ['eətaɪm] N *Rad & TV* **1** *(time allotted on programme)* **that record is getting a lot of a.** on entend souvent ce disque à la radio; **the subject didn't get much a.** on n'a pas consacré beaucoup de temps au sujet pendant l'émission **2** *(starting time)* heure *f* où commence l'émission; **five minutes to a.** on est à l'antenne dans cinq minutes **3** *Tel* communications *fpl*

►► *Tel* ***airtime provider*** fournisseur *m* de communications sans fil

air-to-air ADJ *Mil* air-air *(inv)*, avion-avion *(inv)*

air-to-ground ADJ *Mil* air-sol *(inv)*, air-terre *(inv)*

air-to-surface ADJ *Mil* air-sol *(inv)*

airwaves ['eəweɪvz] NPL *Phys & Rad* ondes *fpl* (hertziennes); **on the a.** sur les ondes, à la radio

airway ['eəweɪ] N **1** *Aviat (route)* voie *f* aérienne; *Com (company)* ligne *f* aérienne

2 *Med* voies *fpl* respiratoires

3 *Tech (shaft)* conduit *m* d'air

4 *Am Rad & TV* chaîne *f*

airwoman ['eə,wʊmən] *(pl* **airwomen** [-'wɪmɪn]*)* N **1** *(gen)* aviatrice *f* **2** *Mil* (femme *f*) auxiliaire *f (de l'armée de l'air)*

airworthiness ['eə,wɜːðɪnɪs] N *Aviat* tenue *f* en l'air, navigabilité *f*; **certificate of a.** certificat *m* de navigabilité

airworthy ['eə,wɜːðɪ] ADJ *Aviat* en état de navigation

airy ['eərɪ] *(compar* **airier**, *superl* **airiest***)* ADJ **1** *(room)* clair et spacieux **2** *Fig (casual* ► *manner)* insouciant, désinvolte; *(*► *ideas, plans, promises)* en l'air

airy-fairy ADJ *Br Fam (person, notion)* farfelu

aisle [aɪl] N **1** *Rel (in church)* bas-côté *m*, nef *f* latérale; **her father led her up the a.** c'est son père qui l'a menée à l'autel; *Fig* **to walk up the a.** se marier **2** *Com (in cinema, supermarket)* allée *f*; *Transp (on train, aeroplane)* couloir *m* (central)

►► *Mktg* ***aisle end display*** tête *f* de gondole; ***aisle seat*** *(in train, aeroplane)* siège *m* côté couloir

aitch [eɪtʃ] N H, h *m inv*; **to drop one's aitches** ne pas prononcer (correctement) les h

ajar [ə'dʒɑː(r)] ADJ *(door, window)* entrouvert, entrebâillé

ADV **the door stood a.** la porte était entrouverte; **to swing a.** s'entrouvrir, s'entrebâiller

aka [,eɪkeɪ'eɪ] ADV *(abbr* **also known as***)* alias

akimbo [ə'kɪmbəʊ] ADV **with arms a.** les mains *ou* poings sur les hanches

akin [ə'kɪn] ADJ **a. to** *(like)* qui ressemble à, qui tient de; *(related to)* apparenté à; **a feeling a. to fear** un sentiment voisin de la peur; **this is a. to treachery** cela s'apparente à de la traîtrise

alabaster [,ælə'bæstə(r)] N *Cer* albâtre *m*

COMP *Cer (figurine, vase etc)* en albâtre; *Fig (complexion, hands etc)* d'albâtre

à la carte [ælə'kɑːt] ADJ & ADV à la carte

alacrity [ə'lækrətɪ] N *Formal* empressement *m*; **he accepted with a.** il a accepté avec enthousiasme, il s'est empressé d'accepter

Aladdin [ə'lædɪn] PR N Aladin; **the shop is an A.'s cave** *(full of wonderful things)* cette boutique est une véritable caverne d'Ali Baba

alarm [ə'lɑːm] N **1** *(warning)* alarme *f*, alerte *f*; **to sound** *or* **to raise the a.** donner l'alarme *ou* l'alerte *ou* l'éveil; **false a.** fausse alerte

2 *Tech (for fire, burglary)* sonnette *f ou* sonnerie *f* d'alarme

3 *(anxiety)* inquiétude *f*, alarme *f*; **there is no cause for a.** il n'y a aucune raison de s'alarmer; **the government viewed events with increasing a.** le gouvernement s'est montré de plus en plus inquiet face à ces événements

4 *(clock)* réveil *m*, réveille-matin *m inv*; **he set the a. for eight o'clock** il a mis le réveil à sonner à huit heures *ou* pour huit heures

COMP d'alarme

VT **1** *(frighten, worry* ► *person)* alarmer, faire peur à; *(*► *animal)* effaroucher, faire peur à; **I don't want to a. you unduly** je ne veux pas vous alarmer sans raison; **to be alarmed at sth** s'alarmer *ou* s'effrayer de qch, être alarmé de qch; **don't be alarmed** ne vous effrayez pas **2** *(warn)* alerter

►► ***alarm bell*** sonnerie *f* d'alarme; *Fig* **to set (the) a. bells ringing** donner l'alerte; ***alarm call*** *(to wake sleeper)* réveil *m* téléphonique; ***alarm clock*** réveil *m*, réveille-matin *m inv*; ***alarm signal*** signal *m* d'alarme

alarming [ə'lɑːmɪŋ] ADJ alarmant

alarmingly [ə'lɑːmɪŋlɪ] ADV d'une manière alarmante; **the shots were coming a. close** les tirs se rapprochaient dangereusement; **to develop a. fast** se développer à une vitesse alarmante

alarmist [ə'lɑːmɪst] ADJ alarmiste

N alarmiste *mf*; **don't be such an a.** ne sois pas aussi alarmiste

alas [ə'læs] EXCLAM *Literary* hélas!

Alaska [ə'læskə] N l'Alaska *m*; **in A.** en Alaska

►► *Transp* ***the Alaska Highway*** la route de l'Alaska; ***the Alaska Range*** la chaîne de l'Alaska

alb [ælb] N *Rel* aube *f (d'un prêtre)*

Albania [æl'beɪnɪə] N Albanie *f*

Albanian [æl'beɪnɪən] N **1** *(person)* Albanais(e) *m,f* **2** *(language)* albanais *m*

ADJ albanais

COMP *(embassy)* d'Albanie; *(history)* de l'Albanie; *(teacher)* d'albanais

albatross ['ælbətrɒs] N **1** *Orn* albatros *m* **2** *Fig (handicap)* boulet *m*; **their past was an a. round their necks** ils traînaient leur passé comme un boulet; **this issue has become an a. around the government's neck** ce problème est devenu un gros handicap pour le gouvernement **3** *Golf* albatros *m*

albeit [,ɔːl'biːɪt] CONJ bien que, encore que, quoique; **an impressive, a. flawed work of art** une œuvre impressionnante bien qu'imparfaite *ou* quoiqu'imparfaite

albinism ['ælbɪnɪzəm] N *Med & Vet* albinisme *m*

albino [æl'biːnəʊ] *Med & Vet* N albinos *mf*

ADJ albinos *(inv)*

Albion ['ælbɪən] N *Literary* Albion *f*; **perfidious A.** la perfide Albion

album ['ælbəm] N *(book, LP)* album *m*

►► ***album cover*** *(of LP)* pochette *f* de disque

albumen ['ælbjʊmɪn] N **1** *Orn & Culin (egg white)* albumen *m*, blanc *m* de l'œuf **2** *Biol (in blood)* albumine *f*

albumin ['ælbjʊmɪn] N *Biol* albumine *f*; **a. deficiency** carence *f* en albumine

alchemist ['ælkəmɪst] N alchimiste *m*

alchemy ['ælkəmɪ] N alchimie *f*

alcohol ['ælkəhɒl] N alcool *m*; **to have an a. problem** être alcoolique

►► ***alcohol abuse*** abus *m* d'alcool; ***alcohol content*** teneur *f* en alcool; ***alcohol dependency*** alcoolodépendance *f*

alcohol-dependent ADJ alcoolodépendant

alcoholic [,ælkə'hɒlɪk] N alcoolique *mf*

ADJ *(drink)* alcoolisé; *(person)* alcoolique

►► ***Alcoholics Anonymous*** Alcooliques *mpl* anonymes, ligue *f* antialcoolique

alcoholism ['ælkəhɒlɪzəm] N alcoolisme *m*

alcopop ['ælkəʊpɒp] N alcopop *m*

alcove ['ælkəʊv] N *(in room)* alcôve *f*; *(in wall)* niche *f*; *(in garden)* tonnelle *f*; **dining a.** coin *m* des repas, coin *m* salle à manger

aldehyde ['ældɪhaɪd] N *Chem* aldéhyde *m*

alder ['ɔːldə(r)] N *Bot* aulne *m*, aune *m*

alderman ['ɔːldəmən] *(pl* **aldermen** [-mən]*)* N **1** *Br Formerly Am Admin (town councillor)* alderman *m*, conseiller *m* municipal; *Br (magistrate)* magistrat *m* **2** *Hist* échevin *m*

Alderney ['ɔːldənɪ] N Aurigny; *(cow)* vache *f* d'Aurigny

ale [eɪl] N **1** *(type of beer)* bière *f* anglaise, ale *f*; **pale/brown a.** = ale de couleur claire/foncée **2** *Br (beer)* bière *f*

Alec(k) ['ælɪk] N *Fam* **a smart A.** un(e) je-sais-tout; **who's the smart A. who forgot to switch it off?** quel est le malin qui a oublié de l'éteindre?

alehouse ['eɪlhaʊs, *pl* -haʊzɪz] N *Arch* taverne *f*

alert [ə'lɜːt] N alerte *f*; **to give the a.** donner l'alerte; **to be on the a.** *(gen)* être sur le qui-vive; *Mil* être en état d'alerte; **the sentries were told to be on the a. for an attack** les sentinelles avaient ordre de se tenir prêtes en cas d'attaque; **the navy has been put on full a.** l'alerte générale a été déclarée dans la marine; **they're always on the a. for interesting stories** ils sont toujours à l'affût d'histoires intéressantes

ADJ **1** *(vigilant)* vigilant, sur le qui-vive; **you should be a. to the possible dangers** soyez conscient des éventuels dangers **2** *(lively* ► *child, mind)* vif, éveillé

VT alerter, donner l'alerte à; **to a. sb to a danger** avertir qn d'un danger; **a noise alerted her to the presence of an intruder** un bruit l'avertit de la présence d'un intrus

►► *Comput* ***alert box*** message *m* d'alerte

alertness [ə'lɜːtnɪs] N **1** *(vigilance)* vigilance *f* **2** *(liveliness)* vivacité *f*, esprit *m* éveillé

A level N *(abbr* **Advanced level***) (in England, Wales and Northern Ireland)* **A levels, A. exams** baccalauréat *m*; **he teaches A. physics** il est professeur de physique en terminale; **he has an A. in maths** il a un diplôme de maths niveau bac; **to take one's A levels** passer son bac

A LEVEL

Cet examen, qui ouvre l'accès aux études supérieures en Angleterre, en Irlande du Nord et au pays de Galles, est beaucoup plus spécialisé que le baccalauréat français; il ne comprend que deux ou trois matières (exceptionnellement quatre). D'autre part, les mentions sont très importantes pour pouvoir choisir l'université où l'on souhaite faire ses études. En Écosse l'examen équivalent aux A-Levels s'appelle le "Higher" ou "Higher Grade".

Alexander [,ælɪg'zɑːndə(r)] PR N

►► ***Alexander the Great*** Alexandre le Grand; *Med* ***Alexander technique*** technique *f* Alexander *(visant à limiter les tensions exercées sur le corps en travaillant sur le maintien et les mouvements)*

Alexandria [,ælɪg'zɑːndrɪə] N *Geog* Alexandrie

alexandrine [,ælɪg'zændraɪn] *Literature* N alexandrin *m*

ADJ alexandrin

alfalfa [æl'fælfə] N *Bot* luzerne *f*

alfresco [æl'freskəʊ] ADJ en plein air

ADV en plein air

alga ['ælgə] *(pl* **algae** [-dʒiː]*)* N *Bot* algue *f*; **algae** algues *fpl*

algebra ['ældʒɪbrə] N algèbre *f*

algebraic [,ældʒɪ'breɪɪk] ADJ algébrique

Algeria [æl'dʒɪərɪə] N *Geog* Algérie *f*; **in A.** en Algérie

Algerian [æl'dʒɪərɪən] N Algérien(enne) *m,f*

ADJ algérien

COMP *(embassy)* d'Algérie; *(histoire)* de l'Algérie

Algiers [æl'dʒɪəz] N Alger

ALGOL, Algol ['ælgɒl] N *Comput (abbr* **algorithmic oriented language***)* ALGOL *m*

algorithm ['ælgərɪðəm] N *Math* algorithme *m*

algorithmic [,ælgə'rɪðmɪk] ADJ *Math* algorithmique

alias ['eɪlɪəs] ADV alias; **Burke, a. Brown** Burke, alias Brown

N **1** *(name)* nom *m* d'emprunt, faux nom *m*; *Literature (of author)* nom *m* de plume, pseudonyme *m* **2** *Comput (in e-mail, on desktop)* alias *m*

aliasing ['eɪlɪəsɪŋ] N *Comput* aliassage *m*, crénelage *m*

alibi ['ælɪbaɪ] N alibi *m*; *Fig* alibi *m*, excuse *f*; **to produce an a.** fournir un alibi; **to establish an a.** prouver *ou* établir son alibi

VT *Am Fam (person, action)* trouver des excuses à□

alien ['eɪljən] N **1** *Admin (foreigner)* étranger(ère) *m,f*; **illegal a.** clandestin(e) *m,f*, immigré(e) *m,f* clandestin(e) **2** *(in science fiction)* extraterrestre *mf,* alien *m*

ADJ 1 *(foreign ▸ customs, environment)* étranger **2** *(contrary)* **a. to sth** contraire *ou* opposé à qch; **violence is completely a. to his nature** il n'est pas du tout d'un naturel violent; **such practices are a. to their culture** de telles pratiques n'existent pas dans leur culture **3** *(from outer space)* extraterrestre; **a. abduction** enlèvement *m* par des extraterrestres; **a. life forms** d'autres formes *fpl* de vie

alienable ['eɪljənəbəl] **ADJ** *Law (property)* aliénable

alienate ['eɪljəneɪt] **VT 1** *(support, friends)* aliéner; **he has alienated all his former friends** il s'est aliéné tous ses anciens amis; **no government wishes to a. voters** aucun gouvernement ne souhaite s'aliéner les électeurs; **these young people feel alienated from society** ces jeunes gens se sentent en marge de la société **2** *Law & Psy* aliéner

alienation [,eɪljə'neɪʃən] **N 1** *(of support, friends)* fait *m* de décourager *ou* d'éloigner; **a sense of a.** un sentiment d'exclusion *ou* d'isolement **2** *Law & Psy* aliénation *f*

▸▸ *Theat* ***alienation effect*** distanciation *f*

alight [ə'laɪt] **VI** *(bird)* se poser; *(person ▸ from bus, train)* descendre; *(▸ from bike, horse)* descendre, mettre pied à terre

ADJ *(fire)* allumé; *(house)* en feu; *Fig* **his face was a. with happiness** son visage rayonnait de joie

ADV to set sth a. mettre le feu à qch; **to catch a.** prendre feu

align [ə'laɪn] **VT 1** *(place in line ▸ points, objects)* aligner, mettre en ligne; *(▸ paper in printer)* mettre bien droit

2 *Pol* aligner; **to a. oneself with sb** s'aligner sur qn

3 *Tech* aligner; *Aut* régler le parallélisme de

4 *Comput & Typ (characters, graphics)* aligner, cadrer

5 *Fin (currencies)* aligner (**on** sur)

VI 1 *(points, objects)* être aligné; *(persons, countries)* s'aligner; **to a. with sb** s'aligner sur qn **2** *(shafts)* coïncider

alignment [ə'laɪnmənt] **N 1** *(of points, objects)* alignement *m*; **to be in/out of a.** être/ne pas être dans l'alignement, être aligné/désaligné; **to bring sth into a. with the new regulations** aligner qch sur la nouvelle réglementation; **this is not in a. with current practice** ceci n'est pas conforme à ce qui se pratique actuellement

2 *Pol* alignement *m*

3 *Tech* alignement *m*; *Aut* parallélisme *m*; **the wheels are in/out of a.** le parallélisme des roues est bien/mal réglé; **steering a.** parallélisme *m* des roues avant

4 *(of railway)* tracé *m*

5 *Comput & Typ (of characters, graphics)* alignement *m,* cadrage *m*

6 *Fin (of currencies)* alignement *m*

alike [ə'laɪk] **ADJ** semblable; **the brothers are very a.** les deux frères se ressemblent beaucoup *ou* sont très semblables; **no two are a.** il n'y en a pas deux pareils; **you're all a.!** vous êtes tous les mêmes!; **two different words that sound a.** deux mots différents qui se ressemblent phonétiquement; **they look a.** ils se ressemblent; **they're very a. in the way they dress** leur façon de s'habiller se ressemble beaucoup

ADV *(act, speak, dress)* de la même façon *ou* manière; **we don't think a.** nous ne sommes pas d'accord, nous ne sommes pas du même avis; **she treats them all a.** elle les traite tous de la même manière; **this affects Peter and his brother a.** cela touche Peter aussi bien que son frère; **every day, summer and winter a.** tous les jours, été comme hiver

aliment ['ælɪmənt] **N** *Scot Law* pension *f* alimentaire

alimentary [,ælɪ'mentərɪ] **ADJ** alimentaire

▸▸ *Anat* ***alimentary canal*** tube *m* digestif

alimony ['ælɪmənɪ] **N** *Law* pension *f* alimentaire

▸▸ ***alimony suit*** demande *f* d'aliments

A-list **ADJ** *(star, celebrity, guest)* très en vue

N the A. les vedettes les plus en vue

alive [ə'laɪv] **ADJ 1** *(living)* vivant, en vie; **he is still a.** il est toujours vivant *ou* en vie; **while he was a.** de son vivant; **to be burnt a.** être brûlé vif; **to bury sb a.** enterrer qn vivant; **no one got out of the building a.** personne n'est sorti vivant de l'immeuble; **to keep a.** *(person)* maintenir en vie; *(hope)* garder; *(tradition)* préserver; **they kept her memory a.** ils sont restés fidèles à sa mémoire; **to stay a.** rester en vie, survivre; **he felt that he was the luckiest man a.** il se sentit l'homme le plus heureux du monde; **no man a. could endure such pain** personne au monde ne pourrait endurer de telles souffrances; **it's good to be a.** il fait bon vivre; **he's still a. and kicking** *(not dead)* il est toujours bien en vie; *(lively)* il est toujours d'attaque *ou* plein de vie; **to be a. and well** *(person)* être bien vivant; *(attitude, prejudice, custom)* être vivace; **Mr Evans was last seen a. on 21 June** c'est le 21 juin qu'on a vu M. Evans vivant pour la dernière fois; **the oldest man a.** l'homme le plus vieux au monde

2 *(lively, full of life)* plein de vie, vif, actif; **he came a. when someone mentioned food** il s'est réveillé quand quelqu'un a parlé de manger; **the town centre comes a. after lunchtime** le centre-ville s'anime après l'heure du déjeuner; *Fam* **look a.!** grouille-toi!, remue-toi!

3 *(alert, aware)* conscient, sensible; **to be a. to the dangers of sth** être conscient des *ou* sensible aux dangers de qch; **I am a. to the fact that...** je n'ignore pas que...

4 *(full, crowded)* **the evening air was a. with insects** il y avait des nuées d'insectes dans l'air ce soir-là; **the streets were a. with people** les rues fourmillaient *ou* grouillaient de monde

alkali ['ælkəlaɪ] **N** *Chem* alcali *m*

▸▸ ***alkali metal*** métal *m* alcalin

alkaline ['ælkəlaɪn] **ADJ** *Chem* alcalin

alkaloid ['ælkəlɔɪd] **N** *Chem* alcaloïde *m*

alkie, alky ['ælkɪ] *(pl* **alkies) N** *Fam* **1** *(abbr* **alcoholic)** alcolo *mf,* poivrot(e) *m,f* **2** *Am (abbr* **alcohol)** gnôle *f*

ALL [ɔːl] **ADJ 1** *(the whole of)* tout; **a. expenses will be reimbursed** tous les frais seront remboursés; **a. night** toute la nuit; **a. day and a. night** toute la journée et toute la nuit; **a. six of us want to go** nous voulons y aller tous/toutes les six; **to be a. things to a. men** être tout à tous

2 *(every one of)* tous (toutes); **a. kinds of people** toutes sortes de gens; **for children of a. ages** pour les enfants de tous les âges; *Sport* **the British a.-comers 100 m record** le record britannique de l'épreuve du 100 m ouverte à tous

3 *(the utmost)* **(with) a. my love** *(at end of letter)* bien affectueusement; **with a. speed** à toute vitesse; **in a. fairness (to sb)** pour être juste (avec qn)

PREDET 1 *(the whole of)* tout(e) *m,f*; **a. the butter** tout le beurre; **a. the beer** toute la bière; **a. my life** toute ma vie; **a. five women** les cinq femmes; **a. the way** *(of journey)* tout le long du chemin; *(of course of action)* jusqu'au bout; **is that a. the luggage you're taking?** c'est tout ce que vous emportez comme bagages?; **for a. his wealth** en dépit de *ou* malgré sa fortune; *Fam* **and a. that** et tout cela, et tout le reste; **of a. the stupid things to say/do!** de toutes les idioties possibles!; **of a. times to phone!** il/elle/*etc* a bien choisi son/*etc* heure pour téléphoner!; **you, of a. people, should know what I mean** toi au moins tu devrais savoir ce que je veux dire; **in a. honesty/sincerity** pour être honnête/sincère; **what's a. that noise?** qu'est-ce que c'est que tout ce bruit?; **a. that's nonsense** tout ça, c'est des bêtises; **for a. that they say he's a genius, I think...** ils ont beau dire que c'est un génie, moi, je pense...

2 *(with comparative adjectives)* **a. the better/worse (for me)** tant mieux/pis (pour moi); **you will be a. the better for it** vous vous en trouverez (d'autant) mieux; **a. the sooner** d'autant plus vite; **a. the harder** encore plus dur

PRON 1 *(everything)* tout; **I gave a. I had** j'ai donné tout ce que j'avais; **take it a.** prenez tout; **a. I want is to rest** tout ce que je veux c'est du repos; **that's a. I have to say** c'est tout ce que j'ai à dire; **a. will be well** tout ira bien; **will that be a.?** ce sera tout?; **I did a. I could** j'ai fait tout ce que j'ai pu; **it was a. I could do not to laugh** j'ai eu du mal à m'empêcher de rire; **it's a. his fault** c'est sa faute à lui; **for a. I know** autant que je sache; **for a. I care** pour (tout) ce que cela me fait; **you men are a. the same!** vous les hommes, vous êtes tous pareils *ou* tous les mêmes!; **a. or nothing** tout ou rien; **a. in good time** chaque chose en son temps; **when a. is said and done** en fin de compte, au bout du compte; **best/worst of a.,...** le mieux/pire, c'est que...; **most of a.** surtout, en particulier; *Prov* **a.'s well that ends well** tout est bien qui finit bien

2 *(everyone)* tous (toutes); **a. are agreed that...** tous sont d'accord que...; **a. of us** nous tous; **we a. love him** nous l'aimons tous; **we a. came** nous sommes tous venus; **good evening, a.!** bonsoir à tous!, bonsoir, tout le monde!; **don't a. speak at once!** ne parlez pas tous en même temps!; **they a. made the same mistake** ils ont tous fait la même erreur; **a. who knew her loved her** tous ceux qui la connaissaient l'aimaient; **a. together** tous à la fois, tous ensemble

3 *Sport* **the score is 5 a.** le score est de 5 partout; **30 a.** *(in tennis)* 30 partout, 30 à

4 *(as quantifier)* **a. of** tout; **a. of the butter/the cakes** tout le beurre, tous les gâteaux; **a. of London** Londres tout entier; **a. of it was sold** (le) tout a été vendu; **how much wine did they drink? – a. of it** combien de vin ont-ils bu? – tout ce qu'il y avait; **I want a. of it** je le veux en entier; **a. of you can come** vous pouvez tous venir; **listen, a. of you** écoutez-moi tous; **she knows a. of their names** elle connaît tous leurs noms; **he must be a. of 60** il doit avoir au moins 60 ans; **the book cost me a. of £10** le livre ne m'a coûté que 10 livres; *Hum* **it's a. of five minutes' walk away!** c'est au moins à cinq minutes à pied!

ADV *(as intensifier)* tout; **she was a. alone** elle était toute seule; **she was a. excited** elle était tout excitée; **she was a. dressed** *or* **she was dressed a. in black** elle était habillée tout en noir; **a. along the road** tout le long de la route; **a. around the edge** tout le long du bord; **I forgot a. about the meeting** j'ai complètement oublié qu'il y avait une réunion; **the soup went a. down my dress** la soupe s'est répandue partout sur ma robe; *Fam* **don't get your hands a. dirty** ne va pas te salir les mains!; *Fam* **the motor's a. rusty inside** le moteur est tout rouillé à l'intérieur; **a. at one go** (tout) d'un seul coup; **a. in one piece** *(furniture)* tout d'une pièce; *Fig (person)* sain et sauf; **I'm a. for it** moi, je suis tout à fait pour; **she's a. for giving children their freedom** elle est tout à fait convaincue qu'il faut donner aux enfants leur liberté; **my wife was a. for calling in a doctor** ma femme voulait à toute force *ou* à tout prix appeler un médecin; **he's not a. bad** il n'est pas entièrement mauvais; **that's a. to the good!** tout va pour le mieux!; *Fam* **it's a. up with him** il est fichu

N tout; **I would give my a. to be there** je donnerais tout ce que j'ai pour y être; **the team gave their a.** l'équipe a donné son maximum; **to stake one's a. on sth** tout miser sur qch

• **at all ADV** du tout; **do you know him at a.?** est-ce que vous le connaissez (un peu)?; **I didn't speak at a.** je n'ai pas parlé du tout; **I'm not at a. astonished** je n'en suis aucunement étonné; **he's not at a. patient** il n'est pas du tout patient; **not at a.** pas du tout, *Fam* du tout; *(when thanked)* je vous en prie; **nothing at a.** rien du tout; **if he comes at a.** s'il vient; **it seemed to worry him very little, if at a.** ça n'a pas eu l'air de l'inquiéter le moins du monde; **he comes rarely if at a.** il vient très rarement, voire jamais; **if you had any feelings at a.** si vous aviez le moindre sentiment; **if we had any money at a.** si nous avions le moindre argent *ou* ne serait-ce qu'un peu d'argent; **if you do any travelling at a., you'll know what I mean** si vous voyagez un tant soit peu, vous comprendrez ce que je veux dire; **if it is at a. cold** s'il fait un (tant soit) peu froid; **if it is at a. possible** si c'était possible; **why do it at a.?** pourquoi se donner la peine de le faire?

• **all along ADV** depuis le début; **that's what I've been saying a. along** c'est ce que je dis depuis le début

• **all at once ADV 1** *(suddenly)* tout d'un coup **2** *(all at the same time)* à la fois, en même temps

• **all but ADV** presque; **a. but finished** presque *ou* pratiquement fini; **I a. but missed it** j'ai bien failli le rater, c'est tout juste si je ne l'ai pas raté

• **all in** *Br* ADJ *Fam (exhausted)* **I'm a. in** je suis mort ADV *(everything included)* tout compris; **the rent is £250 a month a. in** le loyer est de 250 livres par mois tout compris
• **all in all** ADV tout compte fait
• **all out** ADV **to go a. out** y aller à fond; **to go a. out to do sth** se donner à fond pour faire qch
• **all over** ADJ *(finished)* fini; **that's a. over and done with now** tout ça c'est bien terminé maintenant; **it's a. over between them** tout est fini entre eux PREP partout; **there were toys scattered a. over the floor** il y avait des jouets éparpillés partout sur le sol; **you've got ink a. over you!** tu t'es mis de l'encre partout!; **a. over the world** dans le monde entier; **a. over Europe** dans toute l'Europe, partout en Europe; **it'll be a. over town tomorrow morning!** demain matin, toute la ville sera au courant!; *Fam* **a. over the place** *(everywhere)* partout[◻], dans tous les coins; *(very erratic, inaccurate)* pas au point[◻]; *Fam Fam* **the team was a. over the place** l'équipe a joué n'importe comment[◻]; *Fam* **he was a. over her** il ne l'a pas laissée tranquille un instant ADV *(everywhere)* partout; **painted green a. over** peint tout en vert; **it was like being a child a. over again** c'était comme retomber en enfance; *Fam* **that's him a. over!** ça c'est lui tout craché!
• **all round** ADV **taken a. round** tout bien considéré
• **all square** ADJ **1** *(financially)* **we're a. square now** nous ne sommes plus en compte maintenant
2 *Sport (level)* à égalité
• **all that** ADV **it isn't a. that difficult** *or* **as difficult as a. that** ce n'est pas si difficile que ça **you're not as ill as a. that** vous n'êtes pas aussi *ou* si malade que ça; **it's not a. that pleasant** ce n'est pas tellement agréable ADJ *Fam (excellent)* super, génial; **she thinks she's a. that** elle ne se prend pas pour n'importe qui
• **all the more** ADJ **a. the more reason for doing it again** raison de plus pour recommencer ADV encore plus; **it makes her a. the more interesting** ça la rend encore plus intéressante; **it's a. the more unfair since** *or* **as he promised not to put up the rent** c'est d'autant plus injuste qu'il a promis de ne pas augmenter le loyer
• **all the same** ADV *(nevertheless)* tout de même, quand même; **he paid up a. the same** il a payé quand même ADJ **it's a. the same to me** ça m'est complètement égal, peu m'importe; **if it's a. the same to you** si cela ne vous gêne pas
• **all told** ADV tout compris; **there were six of us a. told** nous étions six en tout
• **all too** ADV **a. too soon** bien trop vite; **the holidays went a. too quickly** les vacances ne sont passées que trop vite; **it's a. too easy to forget that** c'est tellement facile de l'oublier
►► ***the All Blacks*** les All Blacks *mpl (l'équipe nationale de rugby de la Nouvelle-Zélande)*; ***all clear*** N (signal *m* de) fin *f* d'alerte; **to sound the a. clear** sonner la fin de l'alerte; *Fig* **the tests came back negative and he's been given the a. clear** les résultats des tests sont revenus et tout est normal EXCLAM fin d'alerte!; ***All Fools' Day*** le premier avril; ***All Hallows*** Toussaint *f*; ***All Hallows' Eve*** la veille de la Toussaint; ***All Saints' Day*** (le jour de) la Toussaint; ***All Souls' Day*** le jour *ou* la fête des Morts

---

all-absorbing ADJ absorbant, passionnant; **of a. interest** fascinant

Allah ['æla] PR N *Rel* Allah

all-American ADJ cent pour cent américain; **the a. boy** le jeune américain type

all-around ADJ *Am* **1** *(versatile* ► *athlete, player)* complet(ète); *(*► *ability)* complet(ète), polyvalent; *(expert)* dans tous les domaines **2** *(comprehensive* ► *improvement)* général, sur toute la ligne

allay [ə'leɪ] VT *(fear)* apaiser; *(doubt, suspicion)* dissiper; *(pain, grief)* soulager, apaiser

all-conquering ADJ qui triomphe de tout

all-consuming ADJ *(passion, ambition)* dévorant

all-day ADJ qui dure toute la journée

allegation [,ælɪ'geɪʃən] N allégation *f*; **to make an a.** alléguer *ou* avancer quelque chose

allege [ə'ledʒ] VT alléguer, prétendre; **he alleges that he was beaten up** il prétend avoir été roué de coups; **it is alleged that…** on prétend que… + *indicative*; **the incident is alleged to have taken place the night before** l'incident aurait eu lieu *ou* on prétend que l'incident a eu lieu la veille au soir

alleged [ə'ledʒd] ADJ *(motive, incident, reason)* allégué, prétendu; *(thief)* présumé

allegedly [ə'ledʒɪdlɪ] ADV **they a. broke in and stole £300** ils seraient entrés par effraction et auraient volé 300 livres; **a. he's the greatest violinist since Paganini** on dit que c'est le plus grand violoniste depuis Paganini

allegiance [ə'li:dʒəns] N allégeance *f*; **political a.** allégeance *f* politique; **to swear a.** faire serment d'allégeance; **to switch a.** changer de bord; **to owe a. to sb** devoir fidélité et obéissance à qn

allegoric [,ælɪ'gɒrɪk], **allegorical** [,ælɪ'gɒrɪkəl] ADJ allégorique

allegorically [,ælɪ'gɒrɪkəlɪ] ADV sous forme d'allégorie, allégoriquement

allegory ['ælɪgərɪ] *(pl* **allegories)** N allégorie *f*

allegretto [,ælɪ'gretəʊ] *Mus* N allegretto *m* ADV allegretto

allegro [ə'legrəʊ] *Mus* N allegro *m* ADV allegro

alleluia [,ælɪ'lu:jə] EXCLAM *Rel* alléluia!

all-embracing ADJ *(study, survey)* exhaustif, complet(ète); *(term)* global; **a. knowledge** vaste érudition *f*

Allen key, *Am* **Allen wrench** ['ælən-] N *Tech* clé *f* Allen, clé *f* BTR

allergen ['ælədʒən] N *Med* allergène *m*

allergenic [ælə'dʒenɪk] ADJ *Med* allergisant

allergic [ə'lɜ:dʒɪk] ADJ *(reaction, person)* allergique; **I'm a. to cats** je suis allergique aux chats; *Hum* **he's a. to hard work** il est allergique au travail

allergy ['ælədʒɪ] *(pl* **allergies)** N allergie *f*

alleviate [ə'li:vɪeɪt] VT *(pain, suffering)* alléger, apaiser, soulager; *(problem, difficulties, poverty)* réduire; *(effect)* réduire, atténuer

alleviation [əli:vɪ'eɪʃən] N *(of pain, suffering)* apaisement *m*, soulagement *m*; *(of problem, difficulties)* amenuisement *m*; *(of poverty)* réduction *m*

all-expenses-paid ADJ tous frais payés

all-expense tour N voyage *m* à forfait

alley ['ælɪ] N **1** *(street)* ruelle *f*, passage *m*; *(in park, garden)* allée *f*; *Fig* **that's right up my a.** c'est tout à fait mon rayon; **I wouldn't like to meet him in a dark a.!** je n'aimerais pas le rencontrer au coin d'un bois!
2 *Am Sport (on tennis court)* couloir *m*
3 *Sport (for tenpin bowling, skittles)* bowling *m*, prise *f* de jeu
4 *(marble)* (grosse) bille *f*, calot *m*
►► ***alley cat*** chat *m* de gouttière

alleyway ['ælɪweɪ] N ruelle *f*, passage *m*

alliance [ə'laɪəns] N **1** *(agreement)* alliance *f*; **to enter into** *or* **to form an a. with sb** s'allier *ou* faire alliance avec qn; *Pol* **electoral a.** apparentement *m*, alliance *f* électorale **2** *(by marriage)* alliance *f*

allied ['ælaɪd] ADJ **1** *(force, nations)* allié **2** *(related* ► *subjects)* connexe, du même ordre; *Econ & Fin (*► *product, industry)* assimilé; *Biol* voisin **3** *(connected)* allié; **his natural talent, a. with his good looks, made him a star** son talent naturel allié à un physique agréable ont fait de lui une star
►► ***the Allied forces*** *(in World War II)* les forces *fpl* alliées; ***the Allied Powers*** les Puissances *fpl* alliées

alligator ['ælɪgeɪtə(r)] N alligator *m*
COMP *(bag, shoes)* en (peau d')alligator; *(skin)* d'alligator
►► *Cin* ***alligator clip*** pince *f* crocodile

all-important ADJ de la plus haute importance, d'une importance primordiale *ou* capitale; **she found the a. solution** elle a trouvé la solution essentielle; **it is a. that we get this contract** il est capital que nous obtenions ce contrat

all-in ADJ *Br (price, tariff)* net, tout compris, forfaitaire; *(insurance policy)* tous risques

all-inclusive ADJ *(price, tariff)* net, tout compris, forfaitaire
►► ***all-inclusive holiday*** forfait *m* vacances tout compris

alliteration [ə,lɪtə'reɪʃən] N *Ling* allitération *f*

alliterative [ə'lɪtərətɪv] ADJ *Ling* allitératif

all-new ADJ tout dernier; **the a. CD-ROM edition of the dictionary is proving very popular** la toute dernière édition de la version CD-ROM du dictionnaire connaît un grand succès; **the a. 2007 model** le tout dernier modèle 2007

all-night ADJ *(party, film)* qui dure toute la nuit; *(shop, restaurant)* de nuit, ouvert la nuit; **an a. sitting of Parliament** une session parlementaire de nuit
►► *Mil* ***all-night pass*** permission *f* de (la) nuit; *Cin* ***all-night showing*** = projection ininterrompue durant toute la nuit

all-nighter [-'naɪtə(r)] N *Am* **we pulled an a. for the physics exam** on a passé la nuit à réviser l'examen de physique; **it turned into another a.** finalement, ça a encore duré toute la nuit

allocate ['æləkeɪt] VT **1** *(assign* ► *resources, money, capital, duties)* affecter, attribuer (**to** à); *(*► *role, part)* attribuer (**to** à); *St Exch (*► *shares)* attribuer, allouer (**to** à); **funds allocated to research** des crédits affectés à la recherche; **allocated budget** enveloppe *f* budgétaire; **in the time allocated** dans le temps *ou* le délai imparti; **you'll need to a. your time carefully** il va falloir que tu répartisses ton temps avec précaution **2** *(share out)* répartir, distribuer **3** *Comput (memory)* attribuer

allocation [ælə'keɪʃən] N **1** *(assignment* ► *of resources, money, capital, duties)* affectation *f*, attribution *f*; *(*► *of role, part)* attribution *f*; *St Exch (*► *of shares)* attribution *f*, allocation *f*
2 *(sharing out)* répartition *f*
3 *(share* ► *of money)* part *f*; *(*► *of space)* portion *f*
4 *Comput (of memory)* attribution *f*

allograft ['æləʊ,grɑ:ft] N *Med* allogreffe *f*

allopathic [ælə'pæθɪk] ADJ *Med* allopathique

allopathy [ə'lɒpəθɪ] N *Med* allopathie *f*

all-or-none order N *St Exch* ordre *m* tout ou rien

allot [ə'lɒt] *(pt & pp* **allotted**, *cont* **allotting)** VT **1** *(assign* ► *money, duties, time)* allouer, assigner, attribuer (**to** à); *St Exch (*► *shares)* attribuer, allouer (**to** à); **in the allotted time** dans le délai *ou* temps imparti; **the farmers were allotted a few acres each** on a attribué aux fermiers quelques hectares chacun; **allotted budget** enveloppe *f* budgétaire **2** *(share out)* répartir, distribuer

allotment [ə'lɒtmənt] N **1** *(of money, duties, time)* allocation *f*, attribution *f*; *St Exch (of shares)* attribution *f*, allocation *f*; *St Exch* **letter of a.** (lettre *f* d')avis *m* d'attribution **2** *Br (land)* jardin *m* ouvrier
►► *St Exch* ***allotment letter*** (lettre *f* d')avis *m* d'attribution; *St Exch* ***allotment right*** droit *m* d'attribution

all-out ADJ *(strike, war)* total; *(effort)* maximum

all-over ADJ qui s'étend sur toute la surface; **an a. tan** un bronzage intégral

allow [ə'laʊ] VT **1** *(permit)* permettre, autoriser; **to a. sb to do sth** permettre à qn de faire qch, autoriser qn à faire qch; **he wasn't allowed to see her** il n'a pas été autorisé à la voir, il n'a pas eu le droit de la voir; **is he allowed sweets/help?** est-ce qu'il a le droit de manger des sucreries/de recevoir de l'aide?; **he was allowed a final cigarette** on lui a permis (de fumer) une dernière cigarette; **we weren't allowed in** on ne nous a pas permis d'entrer; **the dog is not allowed in the house** on ne laisse pas le chien entrer dans la maison, l'accès de la maison est interdit au chien; **smoking is not allowed** *(sign)* défense de fumer; **she allowed herself to be manipulated** elle s'est laissé manipuler; **he decided to a. events to take their course** il a décidé de laisser les événements suivre leur cours; **I won't a. such behaviour!** je ne tolérerai pas une telle conduite!; *Formal* **a. me to make a suggestion** permettez-moi de faire une suggestion; **if I may be allowed to make a point** si je peux me permettre (de faire) une remarque; **a. me!** vous permettez?

2 *(enable)* permettre; **the ramp allows people in wheelchairs to enter the building** la rampe permet l'accès de l'immeuble aux personnes en fauteuil roulant

3 *(grant ▸ money, time)* accorder, allouer; *(▸ opportunity)* donner; *(▸ claim)* admettre; **to a. sb a discount** faire un escompte *ou* une remise à qn; **three hours are allowed for the exam** trois heures sont accordées pour l'examen; **he is allowed £5 pocket money** on lui accorde *ou* donne cinq livres d'argent de poche; **she allowed herself a cream cake as a special treat** comme petit plaisir, elle s'est offert un gâteau à la crème; **how much time/money are we allowed?** de combien de temps/d'argent disposons-nous?; **the bank allows five percent interest on deposits** la banque alloue *ou* attribue cinq pour cent d'intérêt sur les dépôts

4 *(take into account)* prévoir, compter; **a. a week for delivery** il faut prévoir *ou* compter une semaine pour la livraison; **you need to a. a few extra inches for the hem** il faut laisser *ou* prévoir quelques centimètres de plus pour l'ourlet

5 *Literary (admit)* admettre, convenir

6 *Am Fam (maintain)* affirmer

▸ **allow for** VT INSEP **1** *(take into account)* tenir compte de; **allowing for the bad weather** compte tenu du mauvais temps; **we allowed for every possibility in our calculations** nous avons tenu compte de *ou* paré à toute éventualité dans nos calculs; **we must a. for the fact that she has been ill** il faut tenir compte du fait qu'elle a été malade **2** *(make allowance or provision for)* **remember to a. for the time difference** n'oublie pas de compter le décalage horaire; **we hadn't allowed for these extra costs** nous n'avions pas prévu ces frais supplémentaires; **after allowing for travel expenses** déduction faite des frais de voyage

▸ **allow of** VT INSEP *Formal* admettre, souffrir, autoriser; **the evidence allows of no other conclusion** les éléments dont nous disposons n'autorisent aucune autre conclusion

allowable [ə'lauəbəl] ADJ admissible, permis; *(claim)* recevable; *(expense)* déductible, remboursable; *Fin* **expenses a. against tax** dépenses *fpl* fiscalement déductibles

allowance [ə'lauəns] N **1** *Admin (grant)* allocation *f*; *Fin (for housing, travel, food)* indemnité *f*; *Law (alimony)* pension *f* alimentaire; *(for student ▸ from state)* bourse *f*; *(▸ from parents)* pension *f* alimentaire; *(pension)* pension *f*; *(income, salary)* revenu *m*, appointements *mpl*; **his parents give him a monthly a. of £100** ses parents lui versent une mensualité de 100 livres; **he gets a monthly a. of £300** il touche 300 livres par mois; **she makes an a. of £1,000 a year to her nephew** elle verse une rente *ou* une pension de 1000 livres par an à son neveu; **rent a.** allocation *f* (de) logement

2 *Fin (discount)* déduction *f*, concession *f*; *(for tax)* abattement *m*

3 *(entitlement)* **(free) baggage** *or* **luggage a.** *(on plane, coach etc)* bagages *mpl* en franchise; **there is an a. of one item of luggage per passenger** chaque passager a droit à un bagage; **what's the duty-free a.?** qu'est-ce qu'on a droit de ramener hors taxe?; *Sport* **time a.** concession *m* de temps

4 *Am (pocket money)* argent *m* de poche

5 *(idioms)* **to make allowances for sb** être indulgent avec qn; **to make a.** *or* **allowances for sth** tenir compte de qch, prendre qch en considération; **we must make a.** *or* **allowances for the children's age** il faut tenir compte de *ou* il ne faut pas oublier l'âge des enfants; **you have to make allowances for inflation** il faut faire la part de l'inflation; **some a. must be made for shrinkage** il faut tenir compte du rétrécissement

alloy N ['ælɔɪ] *Metal* alliage *m*

VT [ə'lɔɪ] **1** *Metal (metal)* allier, faire un alliage de **2** *Fig* dévaloriser, souiller

• **alloys** NPL ['ælɔɪz] *Aut* roues *fpl* en alliage léger

▸▸ *Metal* **alloy steel** acier *m* allié *ou* spécial; *Aut* **alloy wheels** roues *fpl ou* jantes *fpl* en alliage léger

alloyed [ə'lɔɪd] ADJ *Metal* allié (**with** à *ou* avec)

all-pervading, all-pervasive ADJ *(stench)* envahissant, qui se répand partout; *(fear, corruption, influence)* omniprésent

all-powerful ADJ tout-puissant

all-purpose ADJ *(gen)* qui répond à tous les besoins, passe-partout *(inv)*; *(tool, vehicle, room, building)* polyvalent; **a. cleaning fluid** détachant *m* tous usages

all right ADJ **1** *(adequate)* (assez) bien, pas mal; **the film was a.** le film n'était pas mal; **the money is a., but it could be better** le salaire est correct, mais ça pourrait être mieux

2 *(in good health)* en bonne santé; *(safe)* sain et sauf; **I hope they'll be a. on their own** j'espère qu'ils sauront se débrouiller tout seuls; **are you a.?** *(are you well?)* ça va?; *(did you hurt yourself?)* ça va?, vous ne vous êtes pas blessé?; *Ironic* tu ne te sens pas bien?; **he was quite ill, but he's a. now** il a été assez malade, mais ça va *ou* il est rétabli maintenant; **do you think the car will be a.?** tu crois que ça ira avec la voiture?

3 *(indicating agreement, approval)* **is it a. if they come too?** ça va s'ils viennent aussi?; **it's a.** *(no problem)* ça va; *(no matter)* ça ne fait rien, ce n'est pas grave; **I've come to see if everything is a.** je suis venu voir si tout va bien; **is everything a., Madam?** *(in shop, restaurant etc)* tout va bien, madame?; *Br* **it's a. by me** moi, ça me va; **it's a. for YOU to laugh!** tu peux rire, moi, ça ne m'amuse pas!

4 *(pleasant)* bien, agréable; *(nice-looking)* chouette; **the boss is a.** le patron est bien *ou* n'est pas trop mal; **she's a.** elle est pas mal

5 *(financially etc)* à l'aise, tranquille; **I'm a. until Monday** ça ira jusqu'à lundi; **are you a. for cash/cigarettes?** tu as assez de liquide/de cigarettes?

ADV **1** *(well, adequately)* bien; **they're doing a.** *(progressing well)* ça va (pour eux); *(succeeding in career, life)* ils se débrouillent bien; **everything went off a.** tout a bien marché **2** *(without doubt)* **it's rabies a.** c'est bien la rage; **he was listening a.** ça, pour écouter, il écoutait

EXCLAM *(indicating agreement, understanding)* entendu!, d'accord!; *(indicating approval)* c'est ça!, ça va!; *(indicating impatience)* ça va!, ça suffit!; *(indicating change or continuation of activity)* bon!; *Am (expressing great enthusiasm)* génial!; **a., a., I'm coming!** *(expressing irritation)* oui, oui, j'arrive!

all-risks insurance N assurance *f* tous risques

all-round, *Am* **all-around** ADJ **1** *(versatile ▸ athlete, player)* complet(ète); *(▸ ability)* complet (ète), polyvalent; *(expert)* dans tous les domaines **2** *(comprehensive ▸ improvement)* général, sur toute la ligne

all-rounder N *Br* **he's a good a.** *(gen)* il est doué dans tous les domaines, il est bon en tout; *Sport* c'est un sportif complet

all-seater stadium N = stade ayant uniquement des places assises

All-Share Index N *Br St Exch* = indice du 'Financial Times' et de l'Institut des actuaires britannique

allspice ['ɔ:lspaɪs] N *Bot & Culin* poivre *m* de la Jamaïque, toute-épice *m*

all-star ADJ *(show, performance)* avec beaucoup de vedettes, à vedettes; **with an a. cast** avec une distribution prestigieuse; *Sport* **an a. game** = un match dont les équipes réunissent les meilleurs joueurs professionnels

all-terrain ADJ *Aut* tout-terrain

all-time ADJ *(record)* absolu; **sales figures have reached an a. high/low** les chiffres de vente n'ont jamais été aussi bons/mauvais; **this film is one of the a. greats** ce film est l'un des meilleurs de tous les temps; **an a. best-seller** un best-seller jamais égalé

allude [ə'lu:d] VI **to a. to sb/sth** faire allusion à qn/qch; **I am not alluding to anybody in particular** je ne vise personne

allure [ə'ljuə(r)] N attrait *m*, charme *m*; **it holds no a. for me** ça ne m'attire pas du tout

VT attirer, séduire

> Note that the French word **allure** is a false friend. It means **pace, speed** or **appearance**, depending on the context.

alluring [ə'ljuərɪŋ] ADJ séduisant, attrayant

allusion [ə'lu:ʒən] N allusion *f*; **to make an a. to sth** faire allusion à qch

allusive [ə'lu:sɪv] ADJ allusif, qui contient une allusion/des allusions

alluvial [ə'lu:vɪəl] ADJ *Geol (ground)* alluvial; **a. deposits** alluvions *fpl*, dépôts *mpl* alluvionnaires

▸▸ ***alluvial plain*** plaine *f* alluviale

alluvium [ə'lu:vɪəm] *(pl* **alluviums** *or* **alluvia** [-vɪə]) N *Geol* alluvions *fpl*

all-weather ADJ *(surface)* de toute saison, tous temps

▸▸ *Sport* ***all-weather court*** *(for tennis)* (terrain *m* en) quick *m*; ***all-weather pitch*** terrain *m* tous temps

all-wheel drive N *Aut* quatre roues *fpl* motrices

ally *(pl* **allies)** N ['ælaɪ] allié(e) *m,f*; **to become allies** s'allier; **the two countries were allies** les deux pays étaient alliés

VT [ə'laɪ] allier, unir; **to a. oneself with sb** s'allier avec qn; **Italy was allied with Germany** l'Italie était alliée avec *ou* à l'Allemagne; **we must a. ourselves with other unions** nous devons nous allier à *ou* nous associer avec d'autres syndicats

• **Allies** NPL *Hist* **the Allies** les Alliés

Alma Mater, alma mater [ælmə'mɑ:tə(r)] N *Sch & Univ (institution)* = école ou université où l'on a fait ses études; *Am (anthem)* = hymne d'une école ou d'une université

almanac ['ɔ:lmənæk] N almanach *m*

almighty [ɔ:l'maɪtɪ] ADJ **1** *(omnipotent)* tout-puissant, omnipotent **2** *Fam (as intensifier ▸ row, racket)* formidable, sacré; **an a. din** un vacarme de tous les diables **3** *Rel* **A. God, God A.** Dieu Tout-Puissant

ADV *Am Fam* extrêmement, énormément

N *Rel* **the A.** le Tout-Puissant

almond ['ɑ:mənd] N **1** *(nut)* amande *f*; **sweet/bitter a.** amande *f* douce/amère; **ground almonds** amandes *fpl* pilées **2** *(tree)* amandier *m*

COMP *(icing, essence)* d'amandes; *(cake)* aux amandes

▸▸ ***almond eyes*** yeux *mpl* en amande; ***almond oil*** huile *f* d'amande; ***almond paste*** pâte *f* d'amande; ***almond tree*** amandier *m*

almoner ['ɑ:mənə(r)] N **1** *Hist* aumônier(ère) *m,f* **2** *Br Arch (social worker)* assistant(e) *m,f* social(e) *(dans un hôpital)*

almost ['ɔ:lməust] ADV presque; **a. all the people** presque tous les gens, la quasi-totalité des gens; **it's a. cooked/finished** c'est presque cuit/terminé; **I can a. reach it** j'arrive presque à l'atteindre; **I a. cried** j'ai failli pleurer; **I a. believed him** j'ai bien failli le croire, j'étais près de le croire; **we're a. there** nous sommes presque arrivés; **you're a. there** *(in answering question)* tu y es presque

alms [ɑ:mz] NPL *Hist* aumône *f*; **to give a. to sb** faire l'aumône *ou* la charité à qn

▸▸ *Hist* ***alms box*** tronc *m* (pour les pauvres)

almshouse ['ɑ:mz,haus, *pl* -hauzɪz] N *Br Hist* hospice *m (géré par des religieux ou par une association caritative)*

aloe ['æləu] N *Bot* aloès *m*; **bitter aloes** amer *m* d'aloès

▸▸ *Bot & Pharm* ***aloe vera*** aloe vera *m*

aloft [ə'lɒft] ADV **(up) a.** *(gen)* en haut, en l'air; *Aviat* en l'air; *Naut* dans la mâture

alone [ə'ləun] ADJ **1** *(on one's own)* seul; **to be a.** être seul; **I like being a.** j'aime la solitude *ou* être seul; **a. at last!** enfin seul(s)!; **I'm not a. in thinking that it's unfair** je ne suis pas le seul à penser que c'est injuste **2** *(lonely)* seul; **she felt very a.** elle se sentait très seule

ADV **1** *(on one's own)* seul; **he lives (all) a.** il vit (tout) seul; **she managed to open the box a.** elle a réussi à ouvrir la boîte toute seule; **I'd like to speak to you a.** je voudrais vous parler seul à seul; **to go it a.** faire cavalier seul **2** *(undisturbed)* **to leave** *or* **to let sb a.** laisser qn tranquille; **leave me a.** *(on my own)* laissez-moi seul; *(in peace)* laissez-moi tranquille, laissez-moi en paix; **to let** *or* **leave sth a.** *(not get involved)* ne pas se mêler de qch; **leave the bag a.!** laissez le sac tranquille!, ne touchez pas au sac!; **if I were you I would let well a.** si j'étais vous, je ne m'en mêlerais pas; **a subject better left a.** un sujet qu'il vaut mieux ne pas aborder **3** *(only)* seul; **she a. knows the truth** elle seule connaît la vérité; **time a. will tell** qui vivra verra; **with that charm which is his a.** avec ce charme qui lui est propre; **the frame a. is worth £50** le cadre seul vaut 50 livres

• **let alone** CONJ sans parler de; **he's never been to London, let a. Paris** il n'a jamais été à Londres, sans parler de Paris; **the soup wasn't even warm, let a. hot!** la soupe ne risquait pas d'être chaude, elle était à peine tiède!

along [ə'lɒŋ] PREP **1** *(the length of)* le long de; **we walked a. the road** nous avons marché le long de la route; **there were trees all a. the road** il y avait des arbres tout le long de la route, des arbres bordaient la route; **the railway runs a. the coast** la ligne de chemin de fer longe la côte; **to look a. the street/corridor** regarder dans la rue/le couloir **2** *(at or to a certain point in)* **could you move further a. the row** pourriez-vous vous déplacer vers le bout du rang?; **her office is a. here somewhere** son bureau est quelque part par ici; **the toilets are just a. the corridor** les toilettes sont juste un peu plus loin dans le couloir; **somewhere a. the way** en route, en chemin

ADV **1** *(in phrasal verbs)* **I was driving/strolling a. on a sunny afternoon, when...** je roulais/me baladais par un après-midi ensoleillé, quand...; **she was pulling a trolley a.** elle tirait *ou* traînait un chariot derrière elle; **just then a. came a policeman** c'est alors qu'un policier est arrivé; **bring a tent a. (with you)** apportez une tente; **can I bring a friend a.?** est-ce que je peux amener un ami? **2** *(indicating progress)* **how far a. is the project?** où en est le projet?; **things are going** *or* **coming a. nicely, thank you** les choses ne se présentent pas trop mal, merci **3** *(indicating imminent arrival)* **I'll be a. in a minute** j'arrive tout de suite; **she'll be a. later** elle viendra plus tard; **there'll be another bus a. shortly** un autre bus va passer bientôt

• **along with** PREP avec; **I put the coat away a. with the rest of my winter clothes** j'ai rangé le manteau avec mes autres vêtements d'hiver

alongside [əlɒŋ'saɪd] PREP **1** *(along)* le long de; **to come** *or* **to draw a. the quay** accoster le quai; **the railway runs a. the road** la ligne de chemin de fer longe la route **2** *(beside)* à côté de; **the car drew up a. me** la voiture s'est arrêtée à côté de moi **3** *(together with)* avec; **I worked a. her for two years** j'ai travaillé avec elle pendant deux ans; **if you look at it a. his earlier work** si vous le comparez à ses travaux plus anciens

ADV **1** *Naut* **to come a.** *(two ships)* naviguer à couple; *(at quayside)* accoster **2** *(gen* ▸ *at side)* **a police car pulled up a.** une voiture de police s'est arrêtée à côté

aloof [ə'lu:f] ADJ distant; **she is very a.** elle est très distante, elle est d'un abord difficile; **to keep** *or* **to remain a.** garder ses distances; **he keeps** *or* **remains a. from his colleagues** il ne se mêle guère à ses collègues

aloofness [ə'lu:fnɪs] N attitude *f* distante, réserve *f*

alopecia [ælə'pi:ʃə] N *(UNCOUNT) Med* alopécie *f*

aloud [ə'laʊd] ADV *(read)* à haute voix, à voix haute; *(think)* tout haut

alpaca [æl'pækə] N *Zool* alpaga *m*

COMP *(coat)* en alpaga, d'alpaga; *(wool)* d'alpaga

alpenhorn ['ælpənhɔ:n] N cor *m* des Alpes

alpha ['ælfə] N *(Greek letter)* alpha *m*; *Fig* **the a. and omega** l'alpha et l'oméga, le commencement et la fin

▸▸ *Zool* ***alpha male*** mâle *m* alpha; *Fig* **he's the a. male of the group** c'est lui qui domine le groupe; ***alpha order*** ordre *m* alphabétique; *Phys* ***alpha ray*** rayon *m* alpha; *Comput* ***alpha version*** version *f* alpha

alphabet ['ælfəbet] N alphabet *m*;

▸▸ ***alphabet soup*** *Culin* soupe *f* aux petites pâtes en forme de lettres; *Fig (speech, writing)* = charabia bourré de sigles et d'abréviations

alphabetical [,ælfə'betɪkəl] ADJ alphabétique; **in a. order** par ordre *ou* dans l'ordre alphabétique

alphabetically [,ælfə'betɪkəlɪ] ADV alphabétiquement, par ordre alphabétique

alphabetize, -ise ['ælfəbə,taɪz] VT classer par ordre alphabétique

alpha-hydroxy acid [,ælfəhaɪ'drɒksɪ-] N *Biol & Chem* alpha-hydroxy-acide *m*

alphanumeric [,ælfənju:'merɪk], **alphanumerical** [,ælfənju:'merɪkəl] ADJ alphanumérique

alphasort ['ælfə,sɔ:t] *Comput* N tri *m* alphabétique; **to do an a. on sth** trier qch par ordre alphabétique

VT trier par ordre alphabétique

alphatest ['ælfə,test] *Comput* N alpha-test *m*, essai *m* préliminaire

VT conduire les alpha-tests *ou* les essais préliminaires sur

alpine ['ælpaɪn] N *(plant* ▸ *at low altitude)* plante *f* alpestre; *(*▸ *at high altitude)* plante *f* alpine

ADJ **1** *Geog* des Alpes **2** *(climate, landscape)* alpestre; *(club, skiing, troops)* alpin

▸▸ ***alpine range*** chaîne *f* de montagnes alpine

alpinism ['ælpɪnɪzəm] N *Sport* alpinisme *m*

alpinist ['ælpɪnɪst] N *Sport* alpiniste *mf*

Alps [ælps] NPL **the A.** les Alpes *fpl*; **in the A.** dans les Alpes

Al Qaeda, Al Qaida [ælkæ'i:də, æl'kaɪdə] N Al-Qaida *m or f*

already [ɔ:l'redɪ] ADV déjà; **ten o'clock a.!** déjà dix heures!; *Am Fam* **enough, a.!** ça suffit comme ça!

alright [ɔ:l'raɪt] = **all right**

Alsatian [æl'seɪʃən] N **1** *(person)* Alsacien(enne) *m,f* **2** *(language)* alsacien *m* **3** *Br (dog)* berger *m* allemand

ADJ *(person)* d'Alsace, alsacien; *(wine)* d'Alsace

▸▸ *Br* ***Alsatian dog*** berger *m* allemand

also ['ɔ:lsəʊ] ADV **1** *(as well)* aussi, également; **she a. speaks Italian** elle parle aussi *ou* également l'italien; **the other two books are a. out of print** les deux autres livres sont aussi *ou* également épuisés; **he's lazy and a. stupid** il est paresseux et en plus il est bête **2** *(furthermore)* en outre, de plus, également; **a., it must be pointed out that...** en outre *ou* de plus, il faut signaler que..., il faut également signaler que...

also-ran N **1** *Sport (gen)* concurrent(e) *m,f* non classé(e); *Horseracing* cheval *m* non classé **2** *Fig (person)* perdant(e) *m,f*

alt [ɔ:lt] N *Comput (key)* touche *f* Alt

▸▸ ***alt key*** touche *f* Alt

altar ['ɔ:ltə(r)] N *Rel* autel *m*; *Fig* **to lead sb to the a.** conduire *ou* mener qn à l'autel; *Fig* **to be sacrificed on the a. of success** être sacrifié sur l'autel du succès

▸▸ ***altar boy*** enfant *m* de chœur; ***altar candle*** cierge *m*; ***altar cloth*** nappe *f* d'autel; ***altar rail*** balustrade *f (devant l'autel)*; **at the a. rail** devant l'autel

altarpiece ['ɔ:ltəpi:s] N *Rel* retable *m*

alter ['ɔ:ltə(r)] VT **1** *(change* ▸ *appearance, plan)* changer, modifier; *(*▸ *person)* changer; **this doesn't a. the fact that you should have known** cela ne change pas le fait que vous auriez dû être au courant; **this alters matters considerably** cela change vraiment tout; *Naut & Aviat* **to a. course** changer de cap *ou* de route

2 *Sewing (garment)* faire une retouche *ou* des retouches à, retoucher; **the dress needs to be altered at the neck** la robe a besoin d'être retouchée au col

3 *(falsify* ▸ *evidence, facts, figures, document)* falsifier, fausser

4 *Am Euph (castrate)* châtrer

VI changer, se modifier; **the town has altered a lot in the past few years** la ville a beaucoup changé ces dernières années; **her whole outlook has altered** elle a complètement changé d'horizon

alteration [ɔ:ltə'reɪʃən] N **1** *(changing)* changement *m*, modification *f*; *(touching up)* retouche *f* **2** *(change)* changement *m*, modification *f*; *(reorganization)* remaniement *m*; *(transformation)* transformation *f*; **to make an a. to sth** modifier qch, apporter une modification à qch; **subject to a.** *(programme, timetable etc)* susceptible de révisions, sauf modifications

3 *Sewing (of garment)* retouche *f*

4 *(falsification* ▸ *of evidence, facts, figures, document)* falsification *f*

5 *Constr* aménagement *m*, transformation *f*; **to have alterations done** faire faire des aménagements; **they've made major alterations to their house** ils ont fait des transformations importantes dans leur maison

altercation [,ɔ:ltə'keɪʃən] N *Formal* altercation *f*; **to have an a. with sb** se disputer *ou* avoir une altercation avec qn

alterglobalism [,ɔ:ltə'gləʊbəlɪzəm] N altermondialisme *m*

alterglobalist [,ɔ:ltə'gləʊbəlɪst] N altermondialiste *mf*

ADJ altermondialiste

alterglobalization, -isation [,ɔ:ltəgləʊbəlaɪ'zeɪʃən] N altermondialisation *f*

alternate ADJ [*Br* ɔ:l'tɜ:nət, *Am* 'ɔ:ltərnət] **1** *(by turns)* alterné; **a. spells of good and bad weather** des périodes alternées de beau et de mauvais temps

2 *(every other)* tous les deux; **on a. days** un jour sur deux, tous les deux jours **we visit her on a. weekends** nous lui rendons visite le week-end à tour de rôle

3 *Bot, Geom* alterne

4 *Am (alternative)* alternatif

VI ['ɔ:ltəneɪt] **1** *(happen by turns)* alterner; **wet days alternated with fine days** les jours pluvieux alternaient avec les beaux jours, les jours pluvieux et les beaux jours se succédaient

2 *(take turns)* se relayer; **two actors alternated in the leading role** deux acteurs jouaient le rôle principal en alternance *ou* à tour de rôle

3 *(vary)* alterner; **an economy that alternates between periods of growth and disastrous slumps** une économie où alternent la prospérité et le marasme le plus profond; **he alternates between depression and euphoria** il passe de la dépression à l'euphorie

4 *Elec* changer périodiquement de sens

VT ['ɔ:ltəneɪt] (faire) alterner, employer alternativement *ou* tour à tour; *Agr (crops)* alterner

N *Am* ['ɔ:ltərnət] remplaçant(e) *m,f*, suppléant(e) *m,f*

> Attention: ne pas confondre avec **alternative**.

alternately [ɔ:l'tɜ:nətlɪ] ADV alternativement, en alternance, tour à tour; **the film is a. comic and tragic** le film est tour à tour comique et tragique, le film est tantôt comique, tantôt tragique; **the meetings are held a. in Paris and Edinburgh** les réunions se tiennent en alternance à Paris et à Édimbourg; **they a. welcomed his help and saw it as an intrusion** tantôt ils appréciaient son aide, tantôt ils la ressentaient comme une intrusion

> Attention: ne pas confondre avec **alternatively**.

alternating ['ɔ:ltəneɪtɪŋ] ADJ **1** *(gen)* alternant, alterné **2** *Elec & Tech* alternatif **3** *Geom* alterné

▸▸ *Elec* ***alternating current*** courant *m* alternatif

alternation [,ɔ:ltə'neɪʃən] N alternance *f*

alternative [ɔ:l'tɜ:nətɪv] N *(choice)* solution *f*, choix *m*; **you have no other a.** vous n'avez pas d'autre solution *ou* choix; **he had no a. but to accept** il n'avait pas d'autre solution *ou* choix que d'accepter; **you leave me with no a.** vous ne me laissez pas le choix; **what's the a.?** quelle est l'autre solution?; **there are several alternatives** il y a plusieurs possibilités; **there are alternatives to nuclear power** le nucléaire n'est pas la seule solution possible; **the a. was starvation** c'était ça ou mourir de faim

ADJ **1** *(different, other* ▸ *solution, government)* autre, de rechange; **you'll have to find an a. solution** il faudra trouver une autre solution; **an a. proposal** une contre-proposition; **to make a. arrangements** s'arranger autrement; **an a. route** un itinéraire bis *ou* de délestage **2** *(not traditional* ▸

lifestyle) peu conventionnel, alternatif; *(▸ press, theatre)* parallèle, alternatif

▸▸ ***alternative comedy*** nouvelle comédie *f*; *Ecol* ***alternative energy*** énergies *fpl* de substitution; *Br St Exch* **Alternative Investment Market** = marché hors-cote rattaché à la Bourse de Londres; *Med* ***alternative medicine*** médecines *fpl* douces *ou* parallèles; ***the alternative society*** la société alternative; ***alternative technology*** technologies *fpl* douces; ***alternative tourism*** tourisme *m* vert

Attention: ne pas confondre avec **alternate**.

alternatively [ɔːlˈtɜːnətɪvlɪ] ADV **1** *(on the other hand)* sinon; **you could travel by train, or a. by bus** vous pourriez voyager en train ou bien en autobus **2** *(in a different way)* autrement; **I've been a. employed** j'étais occupé à autre chose

Attention: ne pas confondre avec **alternately**.

alternator [ˈɔːltəneɪtə(r)] N *Elec* alternateur *m*

although [ɔːlˈðəʊ] CONJ **1** *(despite the fact that)* bien que + *subjunctive*, quoique + *subjunctive*; **a. (he is) old, he is still active** bien qu'il soit vieux il est toujours actif; **a. I have never liked him, I do respect him** bien que *ou* quoique je ne l'aie jamais aimé je le respecte, je ne l'ai jamais aimé, néanmoins je le respecte; **a. not beautiful, she was attractive** sans être belle elle plaisait **2** *(but, however)* mais; **I don't think it will work, a. it's worth a try** je ne crois pas que ça va marcher, mais ça vaut la peine d'essayer

altimeter [ˈæltɪmiːtə(r)] N *Tech* altimètre *m*

altitude [ˈæltɪtjuːd] N altitude *f*; *(in mountains)* altitude *f*, hauteur *f*; **to fly at an a. of 8,000 metres** voler à une altitude de 8000 mètres; **at high a.** *or* **altitudes** en altitude, en hauteur; **at these altitudes** à cette altitude, à ces hauteurs

▸▸ *Tech* ***altitude recorder*** enregistreur *m* d'altitude; ***altitude sickness*** mal *m* d'altitude

alto [ˈæltəʊ] *(pl* **altos)** *Mus* N *(voice ▸ female)* contralto *m*; *(▸ male)* haute-contre *f*; *(instrument)* alto *m*

ADJ *(voice ▸ female)* de contralto; *(▸ male)* de haute-contre; *(instrument)* alto *(inv)*

▸▸ ***alto clef*** clé *f* d'ut; ***alto recorder*** flûte *f* alto; ***alto saxophone*** saxophone *m* alto

altocumulus [ˌæltəʊˈkjuːmjʊləs] N *Met* altocumulus *m*

altogether [ɔːltəˈgeðə(r)] ADV **1** *(entirely)* tout à fait, entièrement; **I don't a. agree with you** je ne suis pas tout à fait *ou* entièrement d'accord avec vous; **he isn't a. reliable** on ne peut pas toujours compter sur lui; **it's a. out of the question** il n'en est absolument pas question; **that's a different matter a.** c'est un tout autre problème; **I was not a. pleased** ça ne me faisait pas exactement plaisir **2** *(as a whole)* en tout; **I owe him £100 a.** je lui dois 100 livres en tout; **taken a.** à tout prendre **3** *(in general)* somme toute, tout compte fait; **a., it was an enjoyable evening** somme toute, c'était une soirée agréable

N *Br Fam Hum* **in the a.** tout nu ☐, à poil

altostratus [ˌæltəʊˈstrɑːtəs] N *Met* altostratus *m*

altruism [ˈæltruːɪzəm] N altruisme *m*

altruist [ˈæltrʊɪst] N altruiste *mf*

altruistic [ˌæltrʊˈɪstɪk] ADJ altruiste

ALU [ˌeɪelˈjuː] N *Comput (abbr* **arithmetic and logic unit)** unité *f* arithmétique et logique

alum[1] [ˈæləm] N *Chem & Miner* alun *m*

▸▸ *Phot* ***alum bath*** bain *m* aluné

alum[2] [əˈlʌm] N *Am Fam (alumnus) Sch* ancien (enne) élève *mf*; *Univ* ancien(enne) étudiant(e) *m,f*

alumina [əˈluːmɪnə] N *Chem* alumine *f*

aluminium [ˌæljʊˈmɪnɪəm], *Am* **aluminum** [əˈluːmɪnəm] N aluminium *m*

COMP *(utensil)* en aluminium; *(alloy, acetate)* d'aluminium

▸▸ ***aluminium foil*** papier *m* aluminium; *Chem* ***aluminium oxide*** alumine *f*

aluminize, -ise [əˈluːmɪnaɪz] VT **1** *Metal* combiner avec de l'aluminium **2** *(mirror)* aluminer **3** *Chem* aluminer; *(in dyeing)* aluner

▸▸ ***aluminized steel*** acier *m* à l'aluminium

aluminum [əˈluːmɪnəm] *Am* = **aluminium**

alumna [əˈlʌmnə] *(pl* **alumnae** [-niː]) N *Sch* ancienne élève *f*; *Univ* ancienne étudiante *f*

alumnus [əˈlʌmnəs] *(pl* **alumni** [-naɪ]) N *Sch* ancien élève *m*; *Univ* ancien étudiant *m*

alveolus [ælˈvɪələs] *(pl* **alveoli** [-laɪ]) N *Anat* **1** *(tooth socket)* alvéole *f* dentaire **2** *(air cell)* alvéole *f* pulmonaire

always [ˈɔːlweɪz] ADV toujours; **she a. comes on Mondays** elle vient toujours le lundi; **you can a. try phoning** vous pouvez toujours essayer de téléphoner; **she's a. complaining** elle est toujours en train de se plaindre; **I'll a. remember you!** je ne t'oublierai jamais!; **there's a. tomorrow** demain il fera jour

always-on ADJ *Comput (Internet connection)* permanent

alyssum [ˈælɪsəm] N *(UNCOUNT) Bot* alysse *f*

Alzheimer's (disease) [ˈælts‚haɪməz-] N *Med* maladie *f* d'Alzheimer

AM [ˌeɪˈem] N *Tel (abbr* **amplitude modulation)** AM

am [æm] *see* **be**

AMA [ˌeɪemˈeɪ] N **1** *Med (abbr* **American Medical Association)** = ordre américain des médecins **2** *Mktg (abbr* **American Marketing Association)** = institut américain de marketing

amalgam [əˈmælgəm] N *Chem, Med & Fig* amalgame *m*

amalgamate [əˈmælgə‚meɪt] VT **1** *Com (companies, businesses)* fusionner, unir **2** *(ideas, metals)* amalgamer; **their findings were amalgamated with ours to produce the final report** leurs conclusions et les nôtres ont été réunies pour constituer le rapport final

VI **1** *Com (companies, businesses)* fusionner **2** *(races)* se mélanger; *(ideas, metals)* s'amalgamer

amalgamation [ə‚mælgəˈmeɪʃən] N **1** *Com (of companies, businesses)* fusion *f* **2** *(of races)* mélange *m*; *(of ideas, metals)* amalgamation *f*

amaryllis [ˌæməˈrɪlɪs] N *Bot* amaryllis *f*

amass [əˈmæs] VT *(fortune, objects, information)* amasser, accumuler

amateur [ˈæmətə(r)] N *(gen) & Sport* amateur *m*; **he's a keen a.** c'est un amateur enthousiaste

ADJ *(sport, photographer, musician)* amateur; *(painting, psychology)* d'amateur; **a. championship** championnat *m* amateur; **he has an a. interest in psychology** il s'intéresse à la psychologie en amateur; *Pej* **they did a rather a. job** ils ont fait du travail d'amateur

▸▸ *Theat* ***amateur dramatics*** théâtre *m* amateur

amateurish [ˈæmətərɪʃ] ADJ *Pej* d'amateur

amateurishly [ˈæmətərɪʃlɪ] ADV *Pej* en amateur; *(presented, written)* avec amateurisme

amateurism [ˈæmətərɪzəm] N **1** *Sport* amateurisme *m* **2** *Pej (lack of professionalism)* amateurisme *m*, dilettantisme *m*

amatory [ˈæmətərɪ] ADJ *Literary (letter, verse, intentions, ambitions)* galant; *(feelings)* amoureux

amaze [əˈmeɪz] VT stupéfier, ébahir; **I was amazed at** *or* **by his intelligence** j'étais très impressionné par son intelligence, son intelligence m'a stupéfait *ou* ébahi; **you never cease to a. me!** tu m'étonneras toujours!; *Iron* **you a. me!** non, vraiment?; *Ironic* **go on, a. me!** vas-y, surprends-moi!

amazement [əˈmeɪzmənt] N stupéfaction *f*, stupeur *f*; **to our a.** à notre stupéfaction; **I watched in a.** j'ai regardé, complètement stupéfait

amazing [əˈmeɪzɪŋ] ADJ **1** *(astonishing)* stupéfiant, étonnant; **it's a. that no one was hurt** c'est étonnant que personne n'ait été blessé; **it's a. how fast they work** je ne reviens pas de la vitesse à laquelle ils travaillent; **that's a.!** je n'en reviens pas!; *Com* **a. offer** *(sign)* offre exceptionnelle **2** *(brilliant, very good)* extraordinaire, sensationnel

amazingly [əˈmeɪzɪŋlɪ] ADV incroyablement, extraordinairement; **he's a. patient** il est d'une patience extraordinaire *ou* étonnante; **he was a. good as Cyrano** il était absolument extraordinaire dans le rôle de Cyrano; **a. enough, she believed him** aussi étonnant que ça puisse paraître, elle l'a cru

Amazon [ˈæməzən] N **1** *(river)* **the (river) A.** l'Amazone *f* **2** *(region)* **the A.** l'Amazonie *f*; **in the A.** en Amazonie

PR N *Myth* Amazone *f*

• **amazon** N *Fig* **she's a bit of an a.** *(strong)* c'est une grande bonne femme; *(athletic)* c'est une vraie athlète; *(aggressive)* c'est une vraie virago

▸▸ *Geog* ***the Amazon Basin*** le bassin amazonien; *Orn* ***the Amazon rainforest*** la forêt (tropicale) amazonienne

Amazonian [ˌæməˈzəʊnɪən] ADJ amazonien

ambassador [æmˈbæsədə(r)] N *also Fig* ambassadeur(drice) *m,f*; **the Spanish a. to Morocco** l'ambassadeur d'Espagne au Maroc; **the a.'s wife** l'ambassadrice *f*

ambassadorial [æm‚bæsəˈdɔːrɪəl] ADJ d'ambassadeur

ambassadress [æmˈbæsədrɪs] N ambassadrice *f*

amber [ˈæmbə(r)] N *(colour, resin)* ambre *m*

COMP *(necklace, ring)* d'ambre

ADJ *(colour)* ambré; *Br* **the (traffic) lights turned a.** le feu est passé à l'orange

▸▸ *Br Fam Aut* ***amber gambler*** = automobiliste qui passe à l'orange; ***amber light*** feu *m* orange; *Br Fig* **to see the a. light** se raviser; *Br & Austr Fam Hum* ***amber nectar*** bière ☐*f*, mousse *f*

Amber Alert N *Am (abbr* **America's Missing: Broadcast Emergency Response)** = système d'alerte immédiate, par l'intermédaire des médias, déclenché en cas de disparition d'un enfant

ambergris [ˈæmbəgriːs] N *Chem* ambre *m* gris

ambidextrous [ˌæmbɪˈdekstrəs] ADJ ambidextre

ambience [ˈæmbɪəns] N ambiance *f*

ambient [ˈæmbɪənt] ADJ *(temperature, noise, light etc)* ambiant

N *Mus* ambient *m*

▸▸ ***ambient sound*** son *m* d'ambiance

ambiguity [ˌæmbɪˈgjuːətɪ] *(pl* **ambiguities)** N **1** *(uncertainty)* ambiguïté *f*, équivoque *f*; *(of expression, word)* ambiguïté *f*; **to avoid any a.** pour éviter tout malentendu **2** *(phrase)* expression *f* ambiguë

ambiguous [æmˈbɪgjʊəs] ADJ ambigu(uë), équivoque

ambiguously [æmˈbɪgjʊəslɪ] ADV de façon ambiguë *ou* équivoque

ambiguousness [æmˈbɪgjʊəsnɪs] N *(uncertainty)* ambiguïté *f*, équivoque *f*; *(of expression, word)* ambiguïté *f*

ambit [ˈæmbɪt] N *Formal (of regulation)* étendue *f*, portée *f*; *(of study)* champ *m*; *(of person)* compétences *fpl*, capacités *fpl*

ambition [æmˈbɪʃən] N ambition *f*; **her a. was to become a physicist** elle avait l'ambition *ou* son ambition était de devenir physicienne, elle ambitionnait de devenir physicienne; **he has political ambitions** il a des ambitions politiques; **to lack a.** manquer d'ambition; **my parents had great ambitions for me** mes parents avaient de grandes ambitions pour moi

ambitious [æmˈbɪʃəs] ADJ ambitieux; **to be a. to do sth** ambitionner de faire qch; **she's very a. for her children** elle a de grandes ambitions pour ses enfants; **an a. film** un film ambitieux; **our holidays were nothing more a. than a fortnight in Brighton** nos ambitions de vacances se sont bornées à aller passer quinze jours à Brighton

ambitiously [æmˈbɪʃəslɪ] ADV ambitieusement

ambitiousness [æmˈbɪʃəsnɪs] N *(of project, design)* caractère *m* ambitieux; *(of person)* ambition *f*

ambivalence [æmˈbɪvələns] N ambivalence *f*

ambivalent [æmˈbɪvələnt] ADJ ambivalent; **to be** *or* **to feel a. about sth** être *ou* se sentir indécis à propos de qch; **I have rather a. feelings about him** j'éprouve des sentiments partagés à son égard

amble [ˈæmbəl] VI *(person)* marcher *ou* aller d'un pas tranquille; *(horse)* aller l'amble; **he ambled through the park** il a traversé le parc d'un pas tranquille; **she whistled as she ambled along** elle flânait en sifflant; **he just ambles in at half-past**

ten il arrive à dix heures et demie les mains dans les poches *ou* en se baladant

N *(of person)* pas *m* tranquille; *(of horse)* amble *m*; **to walk at an a.** marcher sans se presser

ambrosia [æm'brəʊzɪə] **N** ambroisie *f*

ambrosial [æm'brəʊzɪəl] **ADJ** *Literary* ambrosiaque

ambulance ['æmbjʊləns] **N** ambulance *f*

▸▸ *Am Fam Pej* ***ambulance chaser*** = avocat qui ne s'occupe que d'affaires de demandes de dommages et intérêts pouvant rapporter gros; ***ambulance crew*** ambulanciers *mpl*; ***ambulance driver*** ambulancier(ère) *m,f*; ***ambulance man*** *(driver)* ambulancier *m*; *(nurse)* infirmier *m* d'ambulance; *(stretcher carrier)* brancardier *m*; ***ambulance ship*** navire *m* hôpital; ***ambulance train*** train *m* sanitaire; ***ambulance woman*** *(driver)* ambulancière *f*; *(nurse)* infirmière *f* d'ambulance; *(stretcher carrier)* brancardière *f*

ambulant ['æmbjʊlənt] **ADJ** ambulatoire

ambulatory ['æmbjʊlətərɪ] *(pl* **ambulatories***)* **N** *Archit & Rel* déambulatoire *m*

ADJ ambulatoire

▸▸ ***ambulatory medical care*** traitement *m* ambulatoire

ambush ['æmbʊʃ] **VT 1** *(lie in wait for)* tendre une embuscade à **2** *(attack)* attirer dans une embuscade; **they were ambushed** ils sont tombés dans une embuscade

N embuscade *f*, guet-apens *m*; **to lie in a.** se tenir en embuscade; *Fig* être à l'affût; **to lay** *or* **to set an a. for sb** tendre une embuscade à qn; **troops lying in a.** troupes embusquées; **the battalion was caught in an a.** le bataillon est tombé dans un guet-apens

ameba, amebic *Am* = **amoeba, amoebic**

ameliorate [ə'miːljə,reɪt] *Formal* **VT** améliorer

VI s'améliorer

amelioration [ə,miːljə'reɪʃən] **N** *Formal* amélioration *f*

amen [ɑː'men] *Rel* **N** amen *m inv*

EXCLAM amen!; *Fig* **a. to that!** bien dit!

amenable [ə'miːnəbəl] **ADJ 1** *(cooperative)* accommodant, souple; **to be a. to sth** être disposé à qch; **to be a. to reason** être raisonnable *ou* disposé à entendre raison; **the disease is a. to treatment** la maladie peut être traitée; **a. to kindness** sensible à la bonté **2** *Law (accountable)* responsable **3** *(able to be tested)* vérifiable; **this data is a. to analysis** c'est données sont susceptibles d'être vérifiées par analyse

amend [ə'mend] **VT 1** *(rectify* ▸ *mistake, text)* rectifier, corriger; *(*▸ *behaviour, habits)* réformer, *Formal* amender **2** *(change* ▸ *law, rule)* amender, modifier; *(*▸ *constitution)* amender

▸▸ *Fin* ***amended invoice*** facture *f* rectificative

amendment [ə'mendmənt] **N 1** *(correction)* rectification *f*, correction *f*; *(modification)* modification *f*, révision *f* **2** *(to bill, constitution)* amendement *m*; *(to contract)* avenant *m*; **an a. to the law** une révision de la loi; *Pol* **to move an a. (to sth)** proposer un amendement (à qch); **the third A.** *(to the American Constitution)* le troisième amendement

amends [ə'mendz] **NPL** réparation *f*, compensation *f*; **to make a.** faire amende honorable; **nothing could make a. for what they had done** rien ne pouvait réparer ce qu'ils avaient fait; **I'd like to make a. for my rudeness to you** j'aimerais réparer mon impolitesse envers vous

amenhorrhoea, *Am* **amenhorrhea** [əˈmenəˈrɪə] **N** *Med* aménorrhée *f*

amenity [ə'miːnətɪ] **N** *Formal (pleasantness)* charme *m*, agrément *m*

• **amenities NPL 1** *(features)* agréments *mpl*; *(facilities)* équipements *mpl*; **urban** *or* **public amenities** *(water, gas and electricity)* l'eau, le gaz et l'électricité; *(facilities)* équipements *mpl* collectifs; **close to all amenities** *(in advertisement for accommodation)* proximité tous commerces **2** *(social courtesy)* civilités *fpl*, politesses *fpl*

▸▸ *Br Med* ***amenity bed*** = dans un hôpital, catégorie de lits réservés aux malades qui paient pour avoir plus de confort et d'intimité

amenorrhoea, *Am* **amenorrhea** = **amenhorrhoea**

America [ə'merɪkə] **N 1** *(continent)* Amérique *f*; **North/South A.** Amérique *f* du Nord/Sud **2** *(United States)* les États-Unis *mpl* (d'Amérique)

• **Americas NPL the Americas** les Amériques *fpl*

▸▸ *Sport* ***America's Cup*** coupe *f* de l'America

American [ə'merɪkən] **N** Américain(e) *m,f*

ADJ américain

COMP *(embassy, history)* des États-Unis

▸▸ ***American Automobile Association*** = société de dépannage pour les automobilistes, Touring Club *m* de France; *Zool* ***American black bear*** baribal *m*, ours *m* noir; *Hist* ***the American Civil War*** la guerre de Sécession; *Tex* ***American cloth*** toile *f* cirée; ***the American Dream*** le rêve américain; ***American eagle*** aigle *m* d'Amérique; ***American English*** (anglais *m*) américain *m*; *Fin* ***American Express®*** American Express®; **to pay by A. Express®** payer par American Express®; ***American Express® card*** carte *f* American Express®; *Br* ***American football*** football *m* américain; ***American Indian*** Indien(enne) *m,f* d'Amérique, Amérindien(enne) *m,f*; *Sport* ***American League*** = l'une des deux ligues professionnelles de base-ball aux États-Unis; *Mus* ***American organ*** harmonium *m*; *Am* ***American plan*** *(in hotel)* pension *f* complète; *Hist* ***the American Revolution*** la Révolution américaine; ***the American Way*** le mode de vie américain

Americanism [ə'merɪkənɪzəm] **N** *Ling* américanisme *m*

Americanize, -ise [ə'merɪkə,naɪz] **VT** américaniser

American-style option N *St Exch* option *f* américaine

Amerind ['æmərɪnd], **Amerindian** [,æmə'rɪndɪən] **N** Indien(enne) *m,f* d'Amérique, Amérindien(enne) *m,f*

ADJ amérindien

amethyst ['æmɪθɪst] **N 1** *Miner (stone)* améthyste *f* **2** *(colour)* violet *m* d'améthyste

COMP *(necklace, ring)* d'améthyste

ADJ *(colour)* violet d'améthyste *(inv)*

Amex ['æmeks] **N 1** *St Exch (abbr* **American Stock Exchange***)* = deuxième place boursière des États-Unis **2** *Fin (abbr* **American Express®***)* American Express®

amiability [,eɪmɪə'bɪlətɪ] **N** amabilité *f*

amiable ['eɪmɪəbəl] **ADJ** aimable, gentil

> Attention: ne pas confondre avec **amicable**.

amiably ['eɪmɪəblɪ] **ADV** avec amabilité *ou* gentillesse, aimablement

amicability [,æmɪkə'bɪlɪtɪ] **N** nature *f ou* disposition *f* amicale; **the a. of his nature** sa nature amicale

amicable ['æmɪkəbəl] **ADJ** *(feeling, relationship)* amical, d'amitié; *(agreement, settlement, end)* à l'amiable

> Attention: ne pas confondre avec le terme anglais **amiable**.

amicably ['æmɪkəblɪ] **ADV** amicalement; *(part)* bons amis, en bons termes; **let's try and settle this a.** essayons de régler ce problème à l'amiable; **to live a. together** vivre en harmonie

AMICUS ['æmɪkəs] **N** = syndicat industriel britannique né de la fusion de l'AEEU et du MSF

amid [ə'mɪd] **PREP** au milieu de, parmi; **the news came a. revelations of corruption** la nouvelle survint en plein milieu *ou* au moment des révélations de corruption; **a. all the noise and confusion, she escaped** dans la confusion générale, elle s'est échappée

amide ['æmaɪd] **N** *Chem* amide *m*

amidships [ə'mɪdʃɪps] **ADJ & ADV** *Naut* au milieu *ou* par le milieu du navire

amidst [ə'mɪdst] = **amid**

amino acid [ə'miːnəʊ-] **N** *Chem* acide *m* aminé, aminoacide *m*

amiss [ə'mɪs] **ADV 1** *(incorrectly)* de travers, mal; **to take sth a.** mal prendre qch, prendre qch en mauvaise part; **don't take this criticism a.** ne prenez pas cette critique en mauvaise part **2** *(out of place)* **a little tact and diplomacy wouldn't go a.** un peu de tact et de diplomatie seraient les bienvenus *ou* ne feraient pas de mal; **a cup of coffee wouldn't come** *or* **go a.** une tasse de café serait la bienvenue

ADJ 1 *(wrong)* **something is a.** il y a quelque chose qui ne va pas *ou Fam* qui cloche **2** *(out of place)* déplacé; **have I said something a.?** ai-je dit quelque chose qu'il ne fallait pas?

amity ['æmətɪ] *(pl* **amities***)* **N** *Formal (friendship)* amitié *f*; *(good relations)* bonnes relations *fpl*, bons rapports *mpl*; **to live in a. with one's fellow man** vivre en paix *ou* en bonne intelligence avec ses semblables

ammeter ['æmɪtə(r)] **N** *Elec* ampèremètre *m*

ammo ['æməʊ] **N** *(UNCOUNT) Fam* munitions *fpl*

ammonia [ə'məʊnɪə] **N** *(gas)* ammoniac *m*; *(liquid)* ammoniaque *f*

ammoniac [ə'məʊnɪæk] **N** ammoniac *m*, gomme-ammoniaque *f*

ADJ *(substance)* ammoniacal; *(smell)* d'ammoniaque

ammonite ['æmənaɪt] **N 1** *Zool (mollusc)* ammonite *f* **2** *(explosive)* ammonal *m*

ammonium [ə'məʊnɪəm] **N** *Chem* ammonium *m*

▸▸ *Chem* ***ammonium carbonate*** carbonate *m* d'ammonium; ***ammonium sulphate*** sulfate *m* d'ammonium

ammunition [,æmjʊ'nɪʃən] **N** *(UNCOUNT) Mil* munitions *fpl*; **live a.** munitions *fpl* réelles *ou* pour tir réel; **round of a.** cartouche *f*; *Fig* **the letter could be used as a. against them** la lettre pourrait être utilisée contre eux

▸▸ *Mil* ***ammunition belt*** ceinturon *m*; *Mil* ***ammunition box*** coffre *m* à munitions; *Mil* ***ammunition dump*** dépôt *m* de munitions

amnesia [æm'niːzɪə] **N** *Med* amnésie *f*; **to have** *or* **suffer (from) a.** être atteint d'amnésie, être amnésique

amnesiac [æm'niːzɪæk], **amnesic** [æm'niːzɪk] *Med* **N** amnésique *mf*

ADJ amnésique

amnesty ['æmnəstɪ] *(pl* **amnesties***)* **N** amnistie *f*; **to declare an a.** déclarer une amnistie; **under an a.** en vertu d'une amnistie

VT amnistier

▸▸ ***Amnesty International*** Amnesty International

amniocentesis [,æmnɪəʊsen'tiːsɪs] *(pl* **amniocenteses** [-siːz]*)* **N** *Obst* amniocentèse *f*

amoeba, *Am* **ameba** [ə'miːbə] *(Br pl* **amoebae** [-biː] *or* **amoebas**, *Am pl* **amebae** [-biː] *or* **amebas***)* **N** *Biol* amibe *f*

amoebic, *Am* **amebic** [ə'miːbɪk] **ADJ** *Biol* amibien

▸▸ *Med* ***amoebic dysentery*** dysenterie *f* amibienne

amok [ə'mɒk] **ADV to run a.** être pris d'une crise de folie meurtrière *ou* furieuse; *Fig* devenir fou furieux, se déchaîner; **the football fans ran a.** les supporters de foot se sont déchaînés

among [ə'mʌŋ], **amongst** [ə'mʌŋst] **PREP 1** *(in the midst of)* au milieu de, parmi; **I moved a. the spectators** je circulais parmi les spectateurs; **she was lost a. the crowd** elle était perdue dans la foule; **it was found a. the rubble** on l'a trouvé parmi les gravats; **to be a. friends** être entre amis

2 *(forming part of)* parmi; **a. those who left was her brother** parmi ceux qui sont partis, il y avait son frère; **several members abstained, myself a. them** plusieurs membres se sont abstenus, dont moi; **it is a. her most important plays** c'est une de ses pièces les plus importantes; **a. other things** entre autres, entre autres choses

3 *(within a specified group)* parmi, entre; **it's a current expression a. teenagers** c'est une expression courante chez les jeunes; **we discussed it a. ourselves** nous en avons discuté entre nous; **I count her a. my friends** je la compte parmi *ou* au nombre de mes amis; **that cake won't go far a. twelve** ce gâteau ne donnera pas grand-chose, divisé entre douze personnes

4 *(to each of)* parmi, entre; **share the books a. you** partagez les livres entre vous, partagez-vous les livres

amoral [eɪˈmɒrəl] ADJ amoral

amorous [ˈæmərəs] ADJ *(person, couple)* amoureux; *(glance)* amoureux, ardent; *(letter)* d'amour; **a. advances** des avances *fpl*; **to be of an a. disposition** être romantique; **he became quite a.** il a commencé à me/lui/*etc* faire des avances

amorously [ˈæmərəslɪ] ADV amoureusement

amorphous [əˈmɔːfəs] ADJ *Biol & Chem* amorphe; *(shapeless)* amorphe; *Fig (personality)* amorphe, mou (molle); *(ideas)* informe, sans forme; *(plans)* vague

amortizable, -isable [əmɔːˈtaɪzəbəl] ADJ *Fin (debt)* amortissable

amortization, -isation [əmɔːtɪˈzeɪʃən] N *Fin (of debt)* amortissement *m*

amortize, -ise [əˈmɔːtaɪz] VT *Fin (debt)* amortir

amount [əˈmaʊnt] N **1** *(quantity)* quantité *f*; **in small/large amounts** en petites/grandes quantités; **great** *or* **large amounts of money** beaucoup d'argent; **a massive a. of time** énormément de temps; **no a. of talking can bring him back** on peut lui parler tant qu'on veut, ça ne le fera pas revenir; **I have a certain a. of respect for them** j'ai un certain respect pour eux; **any a. of** des quantités de, énormément de; **you'll have any a. of time for reading on holiday** tu auras tout ton temps pour lire pendant les vacances **2** *(sum, total)* montant *m*, total *m*; *(of money)* somme *f*; **do you have the exact a.?** avez-vous le compte (exact)?; **you're in credit to the a. of £100** vous avez un crédit de 100 livres; **please find enclosed a cheque to the a. of $100** veuillez trouver ci-joint un chèque (d'un montant) de 100 dollars; **a. due** *(on bill)* montant à régler; **no a. (of money) could make up for what I've lost** rien ne pourrait compenser ce que j'ai perdu; *Acct* **a. brought forward** montant *m* à reporter

▸ **amount to** VT INSEP **1** *(total)* se monter à, s'élever à; **he left debts amounting to over £1,800** il a laissé des dettes qui s'élèvent *ou* se montent à plus de 1800 livres; **profits last year amounted to several million dollars** les bénéfices pour l'année dernière se chiffrent à plusieurs millions de dollars; **after tax it doesn't a. to much** après impôts ça ne représente pas grand-chose; **he'll never a. to much** il ne fera jamais grand-chose **2** *(be equivalent to)* **it amounts to something not far short of stealing** c'est pratiquement du vol; **it amounts to the same thing** cela revient au même; **what his speech amounts to is an attack on democracy** en fait, avec ce discours, il attaque la démocratie

amour [əˈmʊə(r)] N *Literary or Hum* aventure *f* amoureuse, liaison *f*

A-movie N *Cin* film *m* projeté en exclusivité *(lors d'une séance où deux longs métrages sont projetés)*

amp [æmp] N **1** *Elec (abbr* **ampere***)* ampère *m*; **13-a. plug** fiche *f* de 13 ampères **2** *Fam (abbr* **amplifier***)* ampli *m*

ampere [ˈæmpeə(r)] N *Elec* ampère *m*

ampersand [ˈæmpəsænd] N esperluette *f*

amphetamine [æmˈfetəmiːn] N *Pharm* amphétamine *f*

▸▸ ***amphetamine addiction*** dépendance *f* aux amphétamines

amphibia [æmˈfɪbɪə] NPL *Zool* batraciens *mpl*, amphibiens *mpl*

amphibian [æmˈfɪbɪən] N **1** *Zool* amphibie *m*, amphibien *m* **2** *(plane)* avion *m* amphibie; *(car)* voiture *f* amphibie; *(tank)* char *m* amphibie
ADJ amphibie

amphibious [æmˈfɪbɪəs] ADJ *(animal, plane etc)* amphibie

amphitheatre, *Am* **amphitheater** [ˈæmfɪˌθɪətə(r)] N amphithéâtre *m*; **natural a.** cirque *m*

amphora [ˈæmfərə] *(pl* **amphorae** [-riː] *or* **amphoras***)* N *Antiq* amphore *f*

ample [ˈæmpəl] ADJ **1** *(large* ▸ *garment)* ample; *(*▸ *garden, lawn)* grand, vaste; *(*▸ *helping, stomach)* grand; **a woman of a. proportions** une femme forte **2** *(more than enough* ▸ *supplies)* bien *ou* largement assez de; *(*▸ *proof, reason)* solide; *(*▸ *fortune, means)* gros (grosse); **this will be a.** ceci sera amplement suffisant, ceci suffira amplement; **he was given a. opportunity to refuse** il a eu largement l'occasion de refuser; **we have a. reason to suspect foul play** nous avons de solides *ou* de bonnes raisons de soupçonner quelque chose de louche; **you'll have a. time to finish** vous aurez largement le temps de finir; **you'll be given a. warning** vous serez averti longtemps à l'avance

amplification [ˌæmplɪfɪˈkeɪʃən] N **1** *(of power, current, sound)* amplification *f* **2** *(further explanation)* explication *f*, développement *m*; **the facts require no a.** les faits ne demandent pas plus d'explications **3** *Opt (using lens)* grossissement *m*

amplifier [ˈæmplɪfaɪə(r)] N **1** *(for sound system)* amplificateur *m* **2** *Opt* (lentille *f*) amplificatrice *f*

amplify [ˈæmplɪfaɪ] VT **1** *(power, sound)* amplifier **2** *(facts, idea, speech)* développer

amplitude [ˈæmplɪtjuːd] N **1** *(breadth, scope* ▸ *of dimensions, resources)* ampleur *f*; *(*▸ *of operation)* envergure *f*; *Astron & Phys* amplitude *f* **2** *(expanse* ▸ *of sky, ocean)* étendue *f*

▸▸ ***amplitude modulation*** modulation *f* d'amplitude

amply [ˈæmplɪ] ADV amplement, largement; **a. proportioned** aux dimensions généreuses; **a. rewarded** largement récompensé; **as has been a. shown** comme il a été amplement démontré

ampoule, *Am* **ampule** [ˈæmpuːl] N ampoule *f* *(de médicament)*

amputate [ˈæmpjʊteɪt] VT amputer; **they had to a. her arm** ils ont dû l'amputer du bras; **her right arm was amputated** elle a été amputée du bras droit

amputation [ˌæmpjʊˈteɪʃən] N amputation *f*

amputee [ˌæmpjʊˈtiː] N amputé(e) *m,f*

Amtrak® [ˈæmtræk] N *Rail* = société nationale de chemins de fer aux États-Unis (pour le transport des voyageurs)

amuck [əˈmʌk] = **amok**

amulet [ˈæmjʊlɪt] N amulette *f*, fétiche *m*

amuse [əˈmjuːz] VT **1** *(occupy)* divertir, amuser, distraire; **he amused himself (by) building sandcastles** il s'est amusé à faire des châteaux de sable; **you'll have to a. yourself this afternoon** il va falloir trouver de quoi t'occuper cet après-midi **2** *(make laugh)* amuser, faire rire; **he amuses me** il me fait rire; **does the idea a. you?** l'idée vous amuse-t-elle?

amused [əˈmjuːzd] ADJ **1** *(occupied)* occupé, diverti; **to keep oneself a.** s'occuper, se distraire; **the game kept them a. for hours** le jeu les a occupé pendant des heures **2** *(delighted, entertained)* amusé; **they were greatly a. at** *or* **by the cat's behaviour** le comportement du chat les a bien fait rire; **I was a. to hear about his adventures** cela m'a amusé d'entendre parler de ses aventures; **she was not (at all) a.** elle n'a pas trouvé ça drôle (du tout); **an a. look/smile** un regard/sourire amusé; *Fam* **we are not a.** très drôle!

amusedly [əˈmjuːzɪdlɪ] ADV d'un air amusé

amusement [əˈmjuːzmənt] N **1** *(enjoyment)* amusement *m*, divertissement *m*; **she smiled in a.** elle a eu un sourire amusé; **I listened in a.** amusé, j'ai écouté; **we've arranged a party for your a.** nous avons prévu une soirée pour vous divertir *ou* vous distraire; **much to everyone's a.** au grand amusement de tous; **there was much a. at her untimely entrance** son entrée intempestive a fait rire tout le monde **2** *(pastime)* distraction *f*, amusement *m*; **there are few amusements in small towns** les petites villes offrent peu de distractions **3** *(at funfair)* attraction *f*; **to go on the amusements** monter sur les manèges

▸▸ ***amusement arcade*** salle *f* de jeux électroniques; ***amusement park*** parc *m* d'attractions

amusing [əˈmjuːzɪŋ] ADJ amusant, drôle

amusingly [əˈmjuːzɪŋlɪ] ADV d'une façon amusante

amylase [ˈæmɪleɪz] N *Biol & Chem* amylase *f*

an [ən, *stressed* æn] INDEF ART *see* a^2

ANA [ˌeɪenˈeɪ] N *Press (abbr* **American Newspaper Association***)* = syndicat américain de la presse écrite

> SUFFIXE
>
> **-ANA, -IANA**
>
> • Ce suffixe s'emploie pour désigner une COLLECTION D'OBJETS liés à une personne, une époque ou à un sujet particuliers. Par exemple le terme **Americana** s'emploie à propos d'objets ou de documents caractéristiques de l'héritage culturel américain. Citons également:
>
> **Victoriana** antiquités victoriennes, objets de l'époque victorienne; **cricketana** objets liés à l'histoire du cricket; **a collector of Churchilliana** un collectionneur de tout ce qui a trait à Churchill.
>
> • Quand on ajoute ce suffixe au nom d'un écrivain, le terme ainsi formé désigne essentiellement les écrits personnels de l'auteur (**a sale of Dickensiana** une vente d'écrits personnels de Dickens) ou bien des ouvrages à propos de cet auteur (**a section of the library is devoted to Dickensiana** une section de la bibliothèque est consacrée aux ouvrages sur Dickens).

anabaptist [ænəˈbæptɪst] *Rel & Hist* N anabaptiste *mf*
ADJ anabaptiste

anabolic [ˌænəˈbɒlɪk] ADJ *Chem* anabolisant

▸▸ *Pharm* ***anabolic steroid*** stéroïde *m* anabolisant

anachronism [əˈnækrənɪzəm] N anachronisme *m*; **to be an a.** faire figure d'anachronisme

anachronistic [əˌnækrəˈnɪstɪk] ADJ anachronique

anaconda [ænəˈkɒndə] N *Zool* anaconda *m*, eunecte *m*

anaemia, *Am* **anemia** [əˈniːmɪə] N *Med & Fig* anémie *f*; **to suffer from a.** être anémique

anaemic, *Am* **anemic** [əˈniːmɪk] ADJ **1** *Med & Fig* anémique; **to become a.** s'anémier **2** *(pale)* anémique, blême

anaesthesia, *Am* **anesthesia** [ˌænɪsˈθiːzɪə] N anesthésie *f*

anaesthetic, *Am* **anesthetic** [ˌænɪsˈθetɪk] N anesthésique *m*, anesthésiant *m*; **under a.** sous anesthésie; **to give sb an a.** anesthésier qn
ADJ anesthésique, anesthésiant

anaesthetist, *Am* **anesthetist** [əˈniːsθətɪst] N anesthésiste *mf*

anaesthetize, -ise, *Am* **anesthetize** [æˈniːsθətaɪz] VT anesthésier; *Fig* anesthésier, insensibiliser

anagram [ˈænəgræm] N anagramme *f*

anal [ˈeɪnəl] ADJ *Anat & Psy* anal; *Fam* **he's so a.** il est très maniaque

▸▸ ***anal intercourse, anal sex*** sodomie *f*

analeptic [ˌænəˈleptɪk] *Pharm* N analeptique *m*
ADJ analeptique

analgesia [ˌænælˈdʒiːzɪə] N *Physiol* analgésie *f*

analgesic [ˌænælˈdʒiːsɪk] *Pharm* N analgésique *m*
ADJ analgésique

analog *Am* = **analogue**

analogical [ænəˈlɒdʒɪk(ə)l] ADJ analogique

analogically [ˌænəˈlɒdʒɪkəlɪ] ADV analogiquement, par analogie; **a. speaking** analogiquement parlant

analogous [əˈnæləgəs] ADJ analogue; (**to** *or* **with** à)

analogously [əˈnæləgəslɪ] ADV d'une manière analogue

analogue, *Am* **analog** [ˈænəlɒg] N analogue *m*
COMP *(clock, watch, computer)* analogique

▸▸ ***analogue network*** réseau *m* analogique

analogy [əˈnælədʒɪ] *(pl* **analogies***)* N analogie *f*; **the author draws an a. between a fear of falling and the fear of death** l'auteur établit une analogie entre la peur de tomber et la peur de mourir; **by a. with sth** par analogie avec qch; **reasoning from a.** raisonnement par analogie

analyse, *Am* **analyze** [ˈænəlaɪz] VT **1** *(examine)* analyser, faire l'analyse de; *Gram (sentence)* analyser, faire l'analyse logique de **2** *Psy* psychanalyser

analysis [ə'næləsɪs] (*pl* **analyses** [-si:z]) **N 1** *(examination)* analyse *f*; *Gram (of sentence)* analyse *f* logique; **our a. is that…** notre analyse démontre que…; **to hold up under** *or* **to withstand a.** résister à l'analyse; **in the final** *or* **last** *or* **ultimate a.** *(ultimately)* en dernière analyse, en fin de compte **2** *Psy* psychanalyse *f*, analyse *f*; **to be in a.** être en analyse, suivre une analyse
▸▸ *Acct* ***analysis ledger*** journal *m* analytique

analyst ['ænəlɪst] **N 1** *(specialist)* analyste *mf* **2** *Psy* analyste *mf*, psychanalyste *mf*

analytic [ænə'lɪtɪk], **analytical** [ænə'lɪtɪkəl] **ADJ** analytique; **an a. mind** un esprit d'analyse

analyze ['ænəlaɪz] *Am* = **analyse**

analyzer ['ænəlaɪzə(r)] **N** *Comput* analyseur *m*

anamorphic [,ænə'mɔ:fɪk] **ADJ** *Bot & Opt* anamorphosique
▸▸ *Cin & TV* ***anamorphic format*** format *m* anamorphique; *Cin & TV* ***anamorphic lens*** objectif *m* anamorphoseur

anarchic [æ'nɑ:kɪk] **ADJ** anarchique

anarchist ['ænəkɪst] **N** anarchiste *mf*

anarchy ['ænəkɪ] **N** anarchie *f*

anastigmatic [,ænæstɪg'mætɪk] **ADJ** *Med* anastigmat, anastigmatique

anastomosis [ə,næstə'məʊsɪs] (*pl* **anastomoses** [-si:z]) **N** *Med* anastomose *f*

anathema [ə'næθəmə] **N 1** *Formal (detested thing)* abomination *f*; **such ideas are a. to the general public** le grand public a horreur de ces idées; **his books are a. to her** ses livres lui sont insupportables, elle a ses livres en abomination **2** *Rel & Fig* anathème *m*

anathematize, -ise [ə'næθəmətaɪz] **VT** *Rel* anathématiser, frapper d'anathème; *Fig* jeter l'anathème sur

anatomical [,ænə'tɒmɪkəl] **ADJ** anatomique; **a. specimen** pièce *f* d'anatomie, préparation *f* anatomique

anatomically [,ænə'tɒmɪkəlɪ] **ADV** anatomiquement; **a. correct** *(doll, model)* réaliste du point de vue anatomique

anatomist [ə'nætəmɪst] **N** anatomiste *mf*

anatomy [ə'nætəmɪ] **N 1** *(of animal, person)* anatomie *f*; *Fig (of situation, society)* structure *f* **2** *Biol (science)* anatomie *f*; *Fig (analysis)* analyse *f* **3** *Hum (body)* anatomie *f*; **every part of his a. hurt** il était plein de courbatures, il avait mal partout

ANC [,eɪen'si:] **N** *Pol (abbr* **African National Congress***)* ANC *m*

ancestor ['ænsestə(r)] **N** *(forefather) & Fig (of computer, system)* ancêtre *m*; **his ancestors** ses ancêtres *mpl*, *Literary* ses aïeux *mpl*
▸▸ ***ancestor worship*** culte *m* des ancêtres

ancestral [æn'sestrəl] **ADJ** ancestral
▸▸ ***ancestral home*** demeure *f* ancestrale

ancestress ['ænsestrɪs] **N** ancêtre *f*

ancestry ['ænsestrɪ] (*pl* **ancestries**) **N 1** *(lineage)* ascendance *f*; **both families were of French a.** les deux familles étaient d'ascendance française; **this custom is of more recent a.** cette coutume est d'apparition plus récente **2** *(ancestors)* ancêtres *mpl*, *Literary* aïeux *mpl*

anchor ['æŋkə(r)] **N 1** *Naut (for boat)* ancre *f*; **to lie** *or* **to ride at a.** être à l'ancre, être au mouillage; **to cast** *or* **to come to** *or* **to drop a.** jeter l'ancre, mouiller; **up** *or* **weigh a.!** levez l'ancre!
2 *(fastener)* attache *f*
3 *Fig (mainstay)* soutien *m*, point *m* d'ancrage; **religion is her a. in life** la religion est son soutien dans la vie; **many people need the a. of family life** beaucoup de gens ont besoin de la vie de famille comme point d'ancrage
4 *TV* présentateur(trice) *m,f*
5 *Sport* pilier *m*, pivot *m*
6 *(in mountaineering)* point *m* d'assurage
7 *Comput* ancre *f*
VI 1 *Naut (boat)* jeter l'ancre, mouiller **2** *(fasten)* s'ancrer, se fixer **3** *(settle)* se fixer, s'installer
VT 1 *Naut (boat)* ancrer **2** *(fasten)* ancrer, fixer; *Fig* **to be anchored to the spot** *(by indecision, terror)* être cloué sur place **3** *TV (programme)* présenter
▸▸ *Naut* ***anchor buoy*** bouée *f* de mouillage *ou* d'ancre; *Am* ***anchor store*** magasin-phare *m (d'un centre commercial)*

anchorage ['æŋkərɪdʒ] **N 1** *Naut (place)* mouillage *m*, ancrage *m*; *(fee)* droits *mpl* de mouillage *ou* d'ancrage **2** *(fastening)* ancrage *m*, attache *f* **3** *Fig (mainstay)* soutien *m*, point *m* d'ancrage

anchored ['æŋkəd] **ADJ** *Naut* ancré, mouillé, à l'ancre

anchoring ['æŋkərɪŋ] **N** *Naut* ancrage *m*, mouillage *m*

anchorite ['æŋkəraɪt] **N** ermite *m*, solitaire *m*; *Rel* anachorète *m*

anchorman ['æŋkəmæn] (*pl* **anchormen** [-men]) **N 1** *TV* présentateur *m* **2** *Sport* dernier partant *m*

anchorwoman ['æŋkə,wʊmən] (*pl* **anchorwomen** [-'wɪmɪn]) **N** *TV* présentatrice *f*

anchovy [*Br* 'æntʃəvɪ, *Am* 'æntʃəʊvɪ] (*pl* **inv** *or* **anchovies**) **N** *Ich & Culin* anchois *m*
▸▸ *Culin* ***anchovy butter*** beurre *m* d'anchois; *Culin* ***anchovy paste*** pâte *f* d'anchois

ancient ['eɪnʃənt] **ADJ 1** *(custom, ruins)* ancien; *(civilization, world)* antique; *(relic)* historique **2** *Hum (very old ▸ person)* très vieux (vieille); *(▸ thing)* antique, antédiluvien; **she drives an a. Volkswagen®** elle conduit une Volkswagen® qui a fait la guerre; **her husband's absolutely a.** son mari est vraiment très vieux
N *Hist* **the ancients** les anciens *mpl*
▸▸ ***ancient Greece*** la Grèce antique; *also Fig* ***ancient history*** histoire *f* ancienne; *Br* **their affair is a. history now** leur liaison est maintenant de l'histoire ancienne; *Br* ***ancient monument*** monument *m* historique *ou* classé; ***ancient Rome*** la Rome antique; ***ancient times*** les temps *mpl* anciens, l'antiquité *f*; ***the ancient world*** le monde antique

ancillary [æn'sɪlərɪ] (*pl* **ancillaries**) **N 1** *(helper)* auxiliaire *mf*; **hospital ancillaries** personnel *m* des services auxiliaires, agents *mpl* des hôpitaux **2** *(of firm)* filiale *f*
ADJ 1 *(supplementary)* auxiliaire **2** *(subsidiary ▸ reason)* subsidiaire; *(▸ advantage, cost)* accessoire
▸▸ *Law* ***ancillary rights*** droits *mpl* dérivés; ***ancillary staff*** *(gen)* personnel *m* auxiliaire; *(in hospital)* personnel *m* des services auxiliaires; *(in school)* personnel *m* auxiliaire, auxiliaires *mfpl*

AND [ænd] **N** *Comput*
▸▸ ***AND circuit*** circuit *m* ET; ***AND element*** élément *m* ET

and [ənd, ən, *stressed* ænd] **CONJ 1** *(in addition to)* et; **brother a. sister** frère et sœur; **get your hat a. coat** va chercher ton manteau et ton chapeau; **he went out without his shoes a. socks on** il est sorti sans mettre ses chaussures ni ses chaussettes; **he goes fishing winter a. summer (alike)** il va à la pêche en hiver comme en été; **you can't work for us A. work for our competitors** vous ne pouvez pas travailler ET pour nous ET pour nos concurrents; **there are champions a. (there are) great champions** il y a les champions et (il y a) les grands champions; **I got a letter from the bank – a.?** j'ai reçu une lettre de la banque – (et) alors?; **he speaks English, a. very well too** il parle anglais et même très bien
2 *(then)* **he opened the door a. went out** il a ouvert la porte et est sorti; **I fell a. cut my knee** je me suis ouvert le genou en tombant
3 *(with infinitive)* **go a. look for it** va le chercher; **try a. understand** essayez de comprendre
4 *(but)* mais; **I want to go a. he doesn't** je veux y aller, mais lui ne veut pas
5 *(in numbers)* **one hundred a. three** cent trois; **five pounds a. ten pence** cinq livres (et) dix (pence); **two hours a. ten minutes** deux heures dix (minutes); **three a. a half years** trois ans et demi; **four a. two thirds** quatre deux tiers
6 *(indicating continuity, repetition)* **he cried a. cried** il n'arrêtait pas de pleurer; **for hours a. hours** pendant des heures (et des heures); **over a. over again** maintes et maintes fois; **he goes on a. on about politics** quand il commence à parler politique il n'y a plus moyen de l'arrêter
7 *(with comparative adjectives)* **louder a. louder** de plus en plus fort
8 *(as intensifier)* **her room was nice a. sunny** sa chambre était bien ensoleillée; *Fam* **he's good a. mad** il est fou furieux
9 *(with implied conditional)* **one move a. you're dead** un geste et vous êtes mort
10 *(introducing questions)* et; **a. how's your family?** et comment va la famille?; **I went to New York – a. how did you like it?** je suis allé à New York – et alors, ça vous a plu?; **a. what if I AM going?** et si j'y allais?
11 *(introducing statement)* **a. now it's time for 'Kaleidoscope'** et maintenant, voici l'heure de 'Kaléidoscope'; **a. another thing…!** ah! autre chose *ou* j'oubliais…; **they started taking drugs, so I came home – a. a good thing too!** ils ont commencé à prendre de la drogue alors je suis rentré – tu as bien fait!
12 *(what's more)* **a. that's not all…** et ce n'est pas tout…
N I want no ifs, ands or buts je ne veux pas de discussion
• **and all ADV 1** *(and everything)* et tout (ce qui s'ensuit); **the whole lot went flying, plates, cups, teapot a. all** tout a volé, les assiettes, les tasses, la théière et tout **2** *Br Fam (as well)* aussi ▫; **you can wipe that grin off your face a. all** tu peux aussi arrêter de sourire comme ça
• **and so on (and so forth) ADV** et ainsi de suite

Andalusia [,ændə'lu:zɪə] **N** Andalousie *f*

andante [,æn'dæntɪ] *Mus* **N** andante *m*
ADV andante

andantino [,ændæn'ti:nəʊ] *Mus* **N** andantino *m*
ADV andantino

Andean ['ændi:ən] **ADJ** des Andes, andin

Andes ['ændi:z] **NPL** **the A.** les Andes *fpl*, la cordillère des Andes

andiron ['ændaɪən] **N** chenet *m*

Andorra [æn'dɔ:rə] **N** Andorre *f*; **the principality of A.** la principauté d'Andorre

Andorra-la-Vella [æn,dɔ:rəlæ'vellə] **N** Andorre-la-Vieille *f*

Andorran [æn'dɔ:rən] **N** Andorran(e) *m,f*
ADJ andorran
COMP *(embassy)* d'Andorre; *(history)* de l'Andorre

androgen ['ændrədʒən] **N** *Biol* androgène *m*

androgynous [æn'drɒdʒɪnəs] **ADJ** *Biol & Bot* androgyne

androgyny [æn'drɒdʒɪnɪ] **N** *Biol & Bot* androgynie *f*

anecdotal [ænek'dəʊtəl] **ADJ** anecdotique
▸▸ *Law* ***anecdotal evidence*** preuve *f ou* témoignage *m* anecdotique

anecdote ['ænɪkdəʊt] **N** anecdote *f*

anemia, anemic *Am* = **anaemia, anaemic**

anemometer [,ænɪ'mɒmɪtə(r)] **N** *Met* anémomètre *m*

anemone [ə'nemənɪ] **N** *Bot* anémone *f*

aneroid ['ænərɔɪd] **ADJ** anéroïde
▸▸ *Met* ***aneroid barometer*** baromètre *m* anéroïde

anesthesia, anesthetic *etc Am* = **anaesthesia, anaesthetic** *etc*

anesthesiologist [ænəsθi:zɪ'ɒlədʒɪst] **N** *Am Med* anesthésiste *mf*

aneurism ['ænjʊ,rɪzəm] **N** *Med* anévrisme *m*, anévrysme *m*

anew [ə'nju:] **ADV** *Literary* **1** *(again)* de nouveau, encore; **to begin a.** recommencer **2** *(in a new way)* à nouveau; **to create sth a.** créer qch à nouveau; **to start life a.** repartir à zéro

angel ['eɪndʒəl] **N 1** *Rel* ange *m*; **fallen a.** ange *m* déchu; **to go where angels fear to tread** s'aventurer en terrain dangereux
2 *(person)* ange *m*, amour *m*; **you a.!, you're an a.!** tu es un ange *ou* un amour!; **be an a. and fetch me a glass of water** sois gentil, va me chercher un verre d'eau
3 *Fam Fin (investor)* business angel *m*, investisseur *m* providentiel
4 *Fam Aviat* écho *m* radar non identifié ▫
5 *Culin* **angels on horseback** brochettes *fpl* d'huîtres à l'anglaise *(huîtres entourées d'une tranche de bacon et grillées)*
▸▸ *Culin* ***angel cake*** gâteau *m* de Savoie, *Can* gâteau *m* des anges; ***the Angel of Darkness*** l'ange *m* des ténèbres; *Fam Drugs slang* ***angel dust*** poudre

f d'ange; *Am Culin* **angel food cake** gâteau *m* de Savoie, *Can* gâteau *m* des anges

angelfish [ˈeɪndʒəlfɪʃ] (*pl* **inv** *or* **angelfishes**) **N** *Ich (aquarium fish)* scalaire *m*; *(shark)* ange *m*

angelic [ænˈdʒelɪk] **ADJ** angélique

angelica [ænˈdʒelɪkə] **N** *Bot & Culin* angélique *f*

angelically [ænˈdʒelɪkəlɪ] **ADV** comme un ange

angelus [ˈændʒələs] **N** *Rel (bell, prayer)* angélus *m*

anger [ˈæŋgə(r)] **N** colère *f*; **in a fit** *or* **a moment of a.** dans un accès *ou* un mouvement de colère; **he later regretted words spoken in a.** il regretta ensuite les paroles qu'il prononça sous le coup de la colère; **she spoke with barely suppressed a.** elle parla avec une colère à peine dissimulée *ou* en réprimant mal sa colère; **to move sb to a.** mettre qn en colère

VT mettre en colère, énerver; **he's easily angered** il se met facilement en colère, il s'emporte facilement; **he is angered by suggestions that he took bribes** cela le met en colère qu'on suggère qu'il ait pu accepter des pots-de-vin; **these remarks have angered Christians** ces commentaires ont provoqué la colère de la communauté chrétienne

▸▸ *Psy* ***anger management*** = thérapie pour aider les gens coléreux à mieux se maîtriser

angina [ænˈdʒaɪnə] **N** *(UNCOUNT) Med* angine *f* de poitrine

▸▸ ***angina pectoris*** angine *f* de poitrine

angiology [ˌændʒɪˈɒlədʒɪ] **N** *Med* angiologie *f*, angéiologie *f*

angioplasty [ˈændʒɪəˌplæstɪ] **N** *Med* angioplastie *f*

angiosperm [ˈændʒɪəʊspɜːm] **N** *Bot* angiosperme *m*

Angle [ˈæŋgəl] **N** *Hist* Angle *mf*

angle [ˈæŋgəl] **N 1** *(gen) & Geom* angle *m*; **at an a. of...** formant un angle de...; **the car hit us at an a.** la voiture nous a heurtés de biais; **she wore her hat at an a.** elle portait son chapeau penché; **cut at an a.** coupé en biseau; **the shop stands at an a. to the street** le magasin fait l'angle

2 *(corner)* angle *m*, coin *m*

3 *Fig (point of view)* point *m* de vue; *(aspect)* angle *m*; **seen from this a.** vu sous cet angle; **he examined the issue from all angles** il a étudié la question sous tous les angles; **from an economic a.** d'un point de vue économique; **what's your a. on the situation?** comment voyez-vous la situation?; **we need a new a.** il nous faut un éclairage *ou* un point de vue nouveau

VT 1 *(move)* orienter; **I angled the light towards the workbench** j'ai orienté *ou* dirigé la lumière sur l'établi

2 *Fig (slant)* présenter sous un certain angle; **the article was deliberately angled to provoke a certain response** l'article était rédigé de façon à provoquer une réaction bien précise; **it's angled towards the 16–18 age group** cela vise les 16–18 ans, c'est destiné aux 16–18 ans; **studies are angled towards exams** les études sont très axées sur les examens

3 *Sport* **to a. a shot** envoyer la balle en diagonale

VI 1 *(slant)* s'orienter; **the road angled (off) to the right** la route tournait à droite

2 *Fishing* pêcher à la ligne; **to go angling** aller à la pêche (à la ligne); *Fig* **to a. for sth** chercher (à avoir) qch; **he's always angling for an invitation/a job** il est toujours en train de chercher à se faire inviter/à se faire embaucher

▸▸ *Mil* ***angle of altitude*** angle *m* de hausse *ou* de tir positif; *Aviat* ***angle of attack*** angle *m* d'attaque; *Constr* ***angle bar*** cornière *f*, équerre *f*; *Constr* ***angle brace*** *(tool)* foret *m* à angle; *Typ* ***angle bracket*** crochet *m* en chevron; *Aviat & Mil* ***angle of climb*** angle *m* de montée; ***angle of elevation*** *Mil* angle *m* de hausse *ou* de tir positif; *Archit* angle *m* d'élévation; *Phys* ***angle of incidence*** angle *m* d'incidence; *Constr* ***angle iron*** cornière *f*, équerre *f*; *Constr* ***angle plate*** équerre *f*; *Cin & TV* ***angle shot*** cadrage *m* oblique; *Cin & TV* ***angle of shot*** angle *m* de prise de vue; *Mil* ***angle of sight*** angle *m* de mire *ou* de visée; *Cin & TV* ***angle of view*** angle *m* de prise de vue

angled [ˈæŋgəld] **ADJ** *(slanted* ▸ *report, account)* partial, tendancieux; *Sport* **a. shot** coup *m* en diagonale

Anglepoise® [ˈæŋgəlpɔɪz] **N A. (lamp)** lampe *f* d'architecte

angler [ˈæŋglə(r)] **N 1** *Fishing* pêcheur(euse) *m,f* (à la ligne) **2** *Ich* baudroie *f*, lotte *f* de mer

Anglican [ˈæŋglɪkən] **N** anglican(e) *m,f*

ADJ anglican

▸▸ ***the Anglican Church*** l'Église *f* anglicane; ***the Anglican Communion*** la communauté anglicane

Anglicanism [ˈæŋglɪkənɪzəm] **N** *Ling* anglicanisme *m*

anglicism [ˈæŋglɪsɪzəm] **N** *Ling* anglicisme *m*

Anglicist [ˈæŋglɪsɪst] **N** *Ling* angliciste *mf*

anglicization, -isation [ˌæŋglɪsaɪˈzeɪʃən] **N** *Ling* anglicisation *f*

anglicize, -ise [ˈæŋglɪsaɪz] **VT** *Ling* angliciser

angling [ˈæŋglɪŋ] **N** *Fishing* pêche *f* à la ligne

Anglo [ˈæŋgləʊ] (*pl* **Anglos**) **N 1** *Am* Américain(e) *m,f* blanc (blanche) **2** *Can* Canadien(enne) *m,f* anglophone

Anglo-American **N** Américain(e) *m,f* d'origine anglaise

ADJ anglo-américain

Anglo-Catholic **N** anglo-catholique *mf (anglican acceptant les préceptes de l'Église catholique sans pour autant se convertir)*

Anglo-French **ADJ** anglo-français, franco-anglais, franco-britannique

Anglo-Indian **N 1** *(person of mixed British and Indian descent)* métis(isse) *m,f* d'origine anglaise et indienne **2** *(English person living in India)* Anglais(e) *m,f* des Indes

ADJ anglo-indien

Anglo-Irish **NPL the A.** l'aristocratie *f* irlandaise d'origine anglaise

N *(language)* anglais *m* parlé en Irlande

ADJ anglo-irlandais

▸▸ *Pol* ***the Anglo-Irish Agreement*** = accord conclu en 1985 entre le Royaume-Uni et la république d'Irlande pour garantir la paix et la stabilité en Irlande du Nord

Anglophile [ˈæŋgləʊfaɪl] **N** anglophile *mf*

ADJ anglophile

anglophilia [ˌæŋgləʊˈfɪlɪə] **N** anglophilie *f*

Anglophobe [ˈæŋgləʊfəʊb] **N** anglophobe *mf*

ADJ anglophobe

anglophobia [ˌæŋgləʊˈfəʊbɪə] **N** anglophobie *f*

Anglophone [ˈæŋgləfəʊn] *Ling* **N** anglophone

ADJ anglophone

Anglo-Saxon **N 1** *(person)* Anglo-Saxon (onne) *m,f* **2** *(language)* anglo-saxon *m*

ADJ anglo-saxon

Angola [æŋˈgəʊlə] **N** Angola *m*; **in A.** en Angola

Angolan [æŋˈgəʊlən] **N** Angolais(e) *m,f*

ADJ angolais

COMP *(embassy)* d'Angola; *(history)* de l'Angola

angora [æŋˈgɔːrə] **N 1** *(animal)* angora *m* **2** *(cloth, yarn)* laine *f* angora, angora *m*

COMP *(coat, sweater)* en angora

ADJ *(animal)* angora *(inv)*

▸▸ ***angora cat*** chat *m* angora; ***angora goat*** chèvre *f* angora; ***angora rabbit*** lapin *m* angora

Angostura bitters® [ˌæŋgəˈstjʊərə-] **NPL** bitter *m* à base d'angustura

angrily [ˈæŋgrɪlɪ] **ADV** *(deny, speak)* avec colère *ou* emportement; *(leave, stand up)* en colère

angry [ˈæŋgrɪ] (*compar* **angrier**, *superl* **angriest**) **ADJ 1** *(person)* en colère, fâché; **to be a. at** *or* **with sb** être fâché *ou* en colère contre qn; **she's a. about** *or* **at not having been invited** elle est en colère parce qu'elle n'a pas été invitée; **they're a. at the price increase** ils sont très mécontents de l'augmentation des prix; **I'm a. with myself for having forgotten** je m'en veux d'avoir oublié; **to get a.** se mettre en colère, se fâcher; **to get a. with sb** se fâcher *ou* se mettre en colère contre qn; **her remarks made me a.** ses observations m'ont mis en colère

2 *(look, tone)* irrité, furieux; *(outburst, words)* violent; **in an a. voice** d'un ton irrité *ou* furieux; **he wrote her an a. letter** il lui a écrit une lettre dans laquelle il exprimait sa colère; **a. words were exchanged** il y eut un échange assez virulent

3 *Fig (sky)* menaçant; *(sea)* mauvais, démonté

4 *(inflamed)* enflammé, irrité; *(painful)* douloureux

▸▸ ***angry young man*** jeune rebelle *m*

> **ANGRY YOUNG MAN**
>
> "Angry young men" (les Jeunes Gens en colère) est le nom qui fut donné à un groupe de jeunes auteurs britanniques dans les années 50 parmi lesquels figuraient John Arden, Alan Sillitoe, Kingsley Amis et surtout John Osborne dont la pièce Look Back in Anger (La Paix du dimanche) met en scène Jimmy Porter, personnage qui est l'archétype du "angry young man". "Les Jeunes Gens en colère" exploraient le thème de l'aliénation sociale et s'insurgeaient contre les valeurs et le conformisme de la société anglaise de l'époque. Leur réalisme sans concessions et le fait qu'ils s'intéressaient aux milieux populaires tranchait radicalement avec ce qui se faisait à l'époque dans le monde des lettres. Aujourd'hui on utilise cette expression à propos de toute jeune personne exprimant des opinions radicales. Voir aussi **kitchen sink drama**.

angst [æŋst] **N** angoisse *f*

angstrom [ˈæŋstrəm] **N** *Phys* angström *m*, angstroem *m*

angsty [ˈæŋstɪ] **ADJ** *Fam* stressé

anguish [ˈæŋgwɪʃ] **N** *(mental, physical)* douleur *f* immense, tourment *m*; **to be in a.** être au supplice; **her indifference caused him great a.** son indifférence le faisait beaucoup souffrir

VT tourmenter, faire souffrir

anguished [ˈæŋgwɪʃt] **ADJ** plein de souffrance

angular [ˈæŋgjʊlə(r)] **ADJ 1** *(features, room)* anguleux; *(face, body)* anguleux, osseux **2** *(movement)* saccadé, haché **3** *(velocity, distance)* angulaire

anhydride [ænˈhaɪdraɪd] **N** *Chem* anhydride *m*

anhydrous [ænˈhaɪdrəs] **ADJ** *Chem* anhydre

aniline [ˈænɪliːn] **N** *Chem* aniline *f*

▸▸ ***aniline dye*** colorant *m* d'aniline

animal [ˈænɪməl] **N 1** *Zool* animal *m*; *(excluding humans)* animal *m*, bête *f*; **man is a social a.** l'homme est un animal sociable; **she's a political a.** elle a la politique dans le sang **2** *Pej (brute)* brute *f* **3** *(thing)* chose *f*; **French socialism is a very different a.** le socialisme à la française est complètement différent; **there's no such a.** ça n'existe pas

ADJ 1 *Zool (products, behaviour)* animal; **they wore clothes made of a. hides** ils se vêtaient de peaux de bêtes; **he specializes in a. photography** c'est un spécialiste de la photographie animalière **2** *(desire, needs)* animal, bestial; *(courage, instinct)* animal

▸▸ ***animal experimentation*** expérimentation *f* animale *ou* sur les animaux; ***animal husbandry*** élevage *m*; ***Animal Liberation Front*** = mouvement britannique militant pour la défense des droits des animaux; ***animal life*** faune *f*; ***animal lover*** ami(e) *m,f* des animaux *ou* des bêtes; ***animal magnetism*** *(charm)* magnétisme *m*, charme *m*; *Psy (form of hypnosis)* magnétisme *m* animal; ***animal painter*** animalier(ère) *m,f*; ***animal rights*** droits *mpl* des animaux

animalcule [ˌænɪˈmælkjuːl] **N** *Zool* animalcule *m*

animate **VT** [ˈænɪmeɪt] **1** *(give life to)* animer

2 *Fig (enliven* ▸ *face, look, party)* animer, égayer; *(*▸ *discussion)* animer, stimuler

3 *(move to action)* motiver, inciter

4 *Cin & TV* animer

ADJ [ˈænɪmət] vivant, animé; **to become a.** s'animer

animated [ˈænɪmeɪtɪd] **ADJ** animé; **to become a.** s'animer

▸▸ ***animated cartoon*** dessin *m* animé; ***animated film*** film *m* d'animation; *Comput* ***animated GIF*** (fichier *m*) GIF *m* animé

animatedly [ˈænɪmeɪtɪdlɪ] **ADV** *(behave, participate)* avec vivacité *ou* entrain; *(talk)* d'un ton animé, avec animation

animatic [ˌænɪˈmætɪk] **N** *(storyboard)* animatique *f*

animation [ænɪˈmeɪʃən] **N 1** *(of discussion, party)* animation *f*; *(of place, street)* activité *f*, animation *f*; *(of person)* vivacité *f*, entrain *m*; *(of face, look)* animation *f* **2** *Cin & TV* animation *f*

animator [ˈænɪmeɪtə(r)] **N** animateur(trice) *m,f*

animatronic [ˌænɪməˈtrɒnɪk] **ADJ** *(figure, character, puppet)* animé électroniquement
• **animatronics N** animatronique *f*

animism [ˈænɪmɪzəm] **N** *Phil & Rel* animisme *m*

animist [ˈænɪmɪst] *Phil & Rel* **N** animiste *mf*
ADJ animiste

animosity [ænɪˈmɒsətɪ] (*pl* **animosities**) **N** animosité *f*, antipathie *f*; **she felt great a. towards politicians** elle ressentait de l'animosité à l'égard des hommes politiques; **I sensed the a. between them** je sentais une certaine animosité entre eux

animus [ˈænɪməs] **N 1** *(hostility)* animosité *f*, antipathie *f* **2** *(motive)* animus *m* **3** *Psy* animus *m*

anion [ˈænaɪən] **N** *Phys* anion *m*

anise [ˈænɪs] **N** *Bot* anis *m*

aniseed [ˈænɪsiːd] *Bot & Culin* **N** graine *f* d'anis; **a.-flavoured** anisé
COMP *(cake, sweet)* à l'anis
►► ***aniseed ball*** bonbon *m* à l'anis

anisette [ænɪˈzet] **N** anisette *f*

ankle [ˈæŋkəl] **N** cheville *f*
►► ***ankle bone*** astragale *m*; ***ankle boot*** bottine *f*; ***ankle chain*** bracelet *m* de cheville; ***ankle joint*** articulation *f* du pied; ***ankle sock*** socquette *f*; ***ankle strap*** bride *f*; ***ankle support*** chevillière *f*

ankle-biter N *Fam (child)* gosse *mf*

anklet [ˈæŋklɪt] **N 1** *(chain)* bracelet *m* de cheville **2** *Am (ankle sock)* socquette *f*

ankylose [ˈæŋkɪləʊz] *Med* **VT** ankyloser
VI s'ankyloser

ankylosis [ˌæŋkɪˈləʊsɪs] **N** *Med* ankylose *f*

annalist [ˈænəlɪst] **N** annaliste *mf*

annals [ˈænəlz] **NPL** annales *fpl*

Anne [æn] **PR N A. of Austria** Anne d'Autriche

anneal [əˈniːl] **VT** *Tech (glass)* recuire; *(metal)* tremper, recuire

annealing [əˈniːlɪŋ] **N** *Tech (of glass)* recuit *m*, recuite *f*; *(of metal)* adoucissement *m*, recuit *m*, recuite *f*; **box** *or* **close a.** recuit *m* en vase clos
►► ***annealing furnace*** four *m* à recuire

annex N [ˈæneks] *Am (building, supplement to document)* annexe *f*
VT [æˈneks] annexer (**sth to sth** qch à qch)

annexation [ˌænekˈseɪʃən] **N** *(act)* annexion *f*; *(country)* pays *m* annexé; *(document)* document *m* annexe, annexe *f*

annexe, *Am* **annex** [ˈæneks] **N** *(building, supplement to document)* annexe *f*

annihilate [əˈnaɪəleɪt] **VT 1** *(destroy* ► *enemy, race)* anéantir; *(*► *argument)* démolir; *(*► *effort)* réduire à néant **2** *(defeat)* pulvériser, anéantir

annihilation [ənaɪəˈleɪʃən] **N 1** *(destruction* ► *of argument, enemy, effort)* anéantissement *m* **2** *(defeat)* défaite *f* (totale) **3** *Phys* annihilation *f*

anniversary [ænɪˈvɜːsərɪ] (*pl* **anniversaries**) **N** anniversaire *m (d'un événement)*, commémoration *f*
COMP *(celebration, dinner)* anniversaire, commémoratif

Anno Domini [ˌænəʊˈdɒmɪnaɪ] **ADV** *Formal* après Jésus-Christ

annotate [ˈænəteɪt] **VT** annoter

annotation [ˌænəˈteɪʃən] **N** *(action)* annotation *f*; *(note)* annotation *f*, note *f*

annotator [ˈænəteɪtə(r)] **N** annotateur(trice) *m,f*

announce [əˈnaʊns] **VT** annoncer; **to a. sth to sb** annoncer qch à qn; **we are pleased to a. the birth/marriage of our son** nous sommes heureux de vous faire part de la naissance/du mariage de notre fils; **a whistle announced the arrival of the train** un coup de sifflet annonça l'arrivée du train
VI *Am Pol* **to a. for the presidency** se déclarer candidat à la présidence

announcement [əˈnaʊnsmənt] **N** *(public statement)* annonce *f*; *Admin* avis *m*; *(notice of birth, marriage)* faire-part *m*; **here is a passenger a.** avis voyageurs; **this is a staff a.** appel de service

announcer [əˈnaʊnsə(r)] **N** *(gen)* annonceur (euse) *m,f*; *Rad & TV (newscaster)* journaliste *mf*; *(introducing programme)* speaker (speakerine) *m,f*, annonceur(euse) *m,f*

annoy [əˈnɔɪ] **VT 1** *(irritate)* ennuyer, agacer, embêter; **is this man annoying you?** cet homme vous ennuie-t-il *ou Formal* vous importune-t-il?; **he only did it to a. you** il l'a fait uniquement pour vous ennuyer *ou* contrarier **2** *(disturb* ► *noise, music)* déranger; **is the light/noise annoying you?** est-ce que la lumière/le bruit te dérange?

> Note that the French verb **ennuyer** often means **to bore**.

annoyance [əˈnɔɪəns] **N 1** *(displeasure)* contrariété *f*, mécontentement *m*; **with a look of a.** d'un air contrarié *ou* mécontent; **"no, I won't," she said with some a.** "non, je ne le ferai pas", déclara-t-elle d'un ton agacé; **to my great a.** à mon grand mécontentement *ou* déplaisir; **to cause a. to sb** contrarier qn **2** *(source of irritation)* ennui *m*, désagrément *m*

annoyed [əˈnɔɪd] **ADJ to be/to get a. with sb** être/se mettre en colère contre qn; **to be a. with oneself** s'en vouloir; **I felt really a. with him** j'étais vraiment en colère contre lui; **she was a. that he hadn't called** elle n'était pas contente qu'il n'ait pas appelé

annoying [əˈnɔɪɪŋ] **ADJ** *(bothersome)* gênant, ennuyeux; *(irritating)* énervant, agaçant, fâcheux; **the a. thing is…** ce qui est énervant dans l'histoire, c'est…; **how a.!** que c'est ennuyeux!

annoyingly [əˈnɔɪɪŋlɪ] **ADV** de manière gênante *ou* agaçante; **she was a. vague** elle était si vague que c'en était agaçant; **a., he was late** il était en retard, ce qui était ennuyeux

annual [ˈænjʊəl] **N 1** *(publication)* publication *f* annuelle; *Com (of association, firm)* annuaire *m*; *(for children)* album *m* annuel **2** *Bot* plante *f* annuelle
ADJ annuel; **what's your a. income?** combien gagnez-vous par an?
►► *Acct & Fin* ***annual accounts*** bilan *m* annuel, comptes *mpl* de clôture *ou* de fin d'exercice; ***annual budget*** budget *m* annuel; *Fin* ***annual contribution*** *(to pension scheme)* cotisation *f* annuelle; ***annual earnings*** *(of company)* recette(s) *f(pl)* annuelle(s); *(of person)* revenu *m* annuel; *Com* ***annual general meeting*** assemblée *f* générale (annuelle); ***annual income*** revenu *m* annuel; ***annual instalment*** annuité *f*; *Admin* ***annual leave*** congé *m* annuel; *Fin* ***annual percentage rate*** taux *m* effectif global; *Fin* ***annual report*** rapport *m* annuel de gestion; *Fin* ***annual returns*** déclarations *fpl* annuelles; *Fin* ***annual statement of results*** déclaration *f* annuelle de résultats; *Acct & Fin* ***annual turnover*** chiffre *m* d'affaires annuel

annually [ˈænjʊəlɪ] **ADV** *(in a year)* par an, annuellement; *(every year)* tous les ans

annuity [əˈnjuːɪtɪ] (*pl* **annuities**) **N** *Fin (regular income)* rente *f* (annuelle); **a. for life, life a.** viager *m*, rente *f* viagère; **to purchase an a.** placer de l'argent en viager; **to pay sb an a.** servir *ou* faire une rente à qn
►► ***annuity payment*** versement *m* d'annuité; *(investment)* viager *m*, rente *f* viagère

annul [əˈnʌl] (*pt & pp* **annulled**, *cont* **annulling**) **VT** *(law)* abroger, abolir; *(agreement)* annuler; *(contract)* résilier, annuler; *(marriage)* annuler; *(judgement)* casser, annuler

annular [ˈænjʊlə(r)] **ADJ** annulaire

annulment [əˈnʌlmənt] **N** *(of law)* abrogation *f*, abolition *f*; *(of agreement)* annulation *f*; *(of contract)* résiliation *f*, annulation *f*; *(of marriage)* annulation *f*; *(of judgement)* cassation *f*, annulation *f*; **decree of a.** décret *m* abolitif

Annunciation [əˌnʌnsɪˈeɪʃən] **N** *Rel* **the A.** l'Annonciation *f*

anode [ˈænəʊd] **N** *Chem & Elec* anode *f*

anodyne [ˈænədaɪn] **N** *Med* analgésique *m*, calmant *m*; *Fig* baume *m*
ADJ 1 *Med* analgésique, antalgique; *Fig* apaisant **2** *(inoffensive)* anodin

anoint [əˈnɔɪnt] **VT** *(in religious ceremony)* oindre, consacrer par l'onction; **to a. sb with oil** oindre qn d'huile; **they anointed him king** ils l'ont sacré roi

anointing [əˈnɔɪntɪŋ] **N** onction *f*; *(of ruler)* sacre *m*

anomalous [əˈnɒmələs] **ADJ** *(effect, growth, result)* anormal, irrégulier; *Gram* anormal

anomaly [əˈnɒməlɪ] (*pl* **anomalies**) **N** *(gen) & Astron* anomalie *f*

anon [əˈnɒn] **ADV** *Arch or Literary (soon)* bientôt, sous peu; *Hum* **see you a.** à bientôt; **more of this a.** je reviendrai sur cela

anonymity [ænəˈnɪmətɪ] **N 1** *(namelessness)* anonymat *m*; **to preserve one's a.** garder l'anonymat, préserver son anonymat **2** *(unexceptional quality)* banalité *f*

anonymization [əˌnɒnɪmaɪˈzeɪʃən] **N** anonymisation *f*

anonymize [əˈnɒnɪmaɪz] **VT** anonymiser

anonymous [əˈnɒnɪməs] **ADJ** anonyme; **an anonymous caller phoned the newspaper to say that…** la rédaction du journal a reçu un appel anonyme l'informant que…; **to remain anonymous** garder l'anonymat
►► *Mktg* ***anonymous buyer*** acheteur(euse) *m,f* anonyme; *Comput* ***anonymous FTP*** protocole *m* de transfert anonyme; *Comput* ***anonymous remailer*** service *m* de courrier électronique anonyme

anonymously [əˈnɒnɪməslɪ] **ADV** *(act, donate)* anonymement, en gardant l'anonymat; *(publish)* anonymement, sans nom d'auteur

anorak [ˈænəræk] **N 1** *(garment)* anorak *m* **2** *Br Fam Pej (person)* ringard(e) *m,f*

anorexia [ˌænəˈreksɪə] **N** anorexie *f*
►► ***anorexia nervosa*** anorexie *f* mentale

anorexic [ænəˈreksɪk] **N** anorexique *mf*
ADJ anorexique

another [əˈnʌðə(r)] **ADJ 1** *(additional)* un (une)… de plus, encore un (une); **have a. chocolate** prenez un autre *ou* reprenez un chocolat; **a. cup of tea?** vous reprendrez bien une tasse de thé?; **a. five miles** encore cinq miles; **can you wait a. ten minutes?** peux-tu attendre encore dix minutes?; **a. five minutes and we'd have missed the train** cinq minutes de plus et on ratait le train; **in a. three weeks** dans trois semaines; **without a. word** sans un mot de plus, sans ajouter un mot; **and for a. thing, he's ill** et de plus il est malade; **I don't want to see a. fish as long as I live** je ne veux plus voir un seul poisson de toute ma vie
2 *(second)* un (une) autre, un (une) second(e); **we're thinking of getting a. car** *(in addition to the one we have)* nous pensons acheter une deuxième voiture; **it could be a. Vietnam** ça pourrait être un second *ou* nouveau Viêt-nam; **he is a. Picasso** c'est le nouveau Picasso
3 *(different)* un (une) autre; **can't we do that a. time?** on ne peut pas remettre ça à plus tard *ou* à une autre fois?; **let's do it a. way** faisons-le autrement; **that's a. matter entirely!** ça, c'est une tout autre histoire!; **we're thinking of getting a. car** *(to replace the car we have)* nous pensons acheter une nouvelle voiture *ou* changer de voiture
PRON 1 *(a similar one)* un (une) autre, encore un (une); **a glass of milk and a. of water** un verre de lait et un verre d'eau; **she finished one cigarette and lit a.** elle finit une cigarette et en alluma une autre; **one way or a.** d'une façon ou d'une autre; **taking one thing with a., we just manage** l'un dans l'autre, on arrive à joindre les deux bouts; **what with one thing and a., I forgot** avec tout ça j'ai oublié
2 *(a different one)* **a. of the girls** une autre des filles; **bring a dessert of one sort or a.** apportez un dessert, (n'importe lequel); **science is one thing, art is a.** la science est une chose, l'art en est une autre
3 *(reciprocal)* **one a.** l'un l'autre; *(more than two people)* les uns les autres; **to help one a.** s'entraider; **love one a.** aimez-vous les uns les autres; **he and his wife adore one a.** lui et sa femme s'ado-

rent; **they give one a. presents** ils se donnent des cadeaux

4 *Arch or Literary (somebody else)* un (une) autre; **she loves a.** elle en aime un autre

Ansaphone® [ˈɑːnsəfəʊn] **N** *Tel* répondeur *m* (téléphonique)

ANSI [ˌeɪenˌesˈaɪ] **N** *Admin & Ind* (*abbr* **American National Standards Institute**) association *f* américaine de normalisation, AFNOR *f*

answer [ˈɑːnsə(r)] **VT 1** *(letter, person, telephone, advertisement)* répondre à; *(door)* aller *ou* venir ouvrir; **she answered with a shy grin** pour toute réponse elle a souri timidement; **I phoned earlier but nobody answered** j'ai téléphoné tout à l'heure mais ça ne répondait pas; **the maid answered the bell** la bonne a répondu au coup de sonnette; **to a. a prayer** exaucer une prière; **letters to be answered** courrier *m* en cours

2 *(respond correctly to)* **he could only a. two of the questions** il n'a su répondre qu'à deux des questions; **few of the students answered this question well** peu d'élèves ont bien traité cette question

3 *(fulfil)* répondre à, satisfaire; **the computer answers a number of requirements** l'ordinateur répond à plusieurs fonctions; **this should a. the purpose quite nicely** ceci fera très bien l'affaire; **it should a. the purposes of both students and translators** ce devrait être utile aux étudiants comme aux traducteurs

4 *(description)* répondre à, correspondre à; **a man answering this description was seen in the area** un homme répondant *ou* correspondant à ce signalement a été aperçu dans la région

5 *Law* **the defendant answered the charge** l'accusé a répondu à *ou* a réfuté l'accusation

6 *Naut* **to a. the helm** *(ship)* obéir à la barre

VI répondre, donner une réponse; **it's not answering** *(phone)* ça ne répond pas

N 1 *(reply ▸ to letter, person, request)* réponse *f*; *(▸ to criticism, objection)* réponse *f*, réplique *f*; **she made no a.** elle n'a pas répondu; **he couldn't think of an a.** il n'a rien trouvé à répondre; **in a. to her question he simply grinned** pour toute réponse à sa question, il a eu un large sourire; *Formal* **in a. to your letter** en réponse à votre lettre; **I rang the bell but there was no a.** j'ai sonné mais personne n'a répondu *ou* n'a ouvert; **I phoned but there was no a.** j'ai téléphoné mais ça ne répondait pas; **she won't take no for an a.** elle n'acceptera pas de refus; **he has an a. for everything** il a réponse à tout; **they had no a. to this** ils n'ont pas su quoi répondre; **there's no a. to that!** comment répondre à ça!; **it's the a. to the government's prayers** c'est exactement ce dont le gouvernement avait besoin; **he's the a. to our prayers** il est notre sauveur

2 *(solution)* solution *f*; *also Fig* **there's no easy a.** il n'y a pas de solution facile; **you think you know all the answers, don't you?** tu crois que tu sais tout, c'est ça?

3 *Sch & Univ (to exam question)* réponse *f*

4 *(equivalent)* **she's England's a. to Edith Piaf** elle est *ou* c'est l'Édith Piaf anglaise

▸▸ *Tel* ***answer mode*** mode *m* réponse; *Tel* ***answer tone*** tonalité *f* de réponse

▸answer back **VT SEP** répondre (avec insolence) à, répliquer à; **don't a. your father back!** ne réponds pas à ton père!

VI répondre (avec insolence)

▸answer for **VT INSEP 1** *(be responsible for)* répondre de, être responsable de; **this government has a lot to a. for** ce gouvernement a bien des comptes à rendre; **he/television has a lot to a. for** il/la télévision est à l'origine de bien des problèmes **2** *(vouch for)* garantir; **I can't a. for the quality of her work** je ne peux pas garantir la qualité de son travail

▸answer to **VT INSEP 1** *(respond to)* **the cat answers to (the name of) Mitzi** le chat répond au nom de Mitzi, le chat s'appelle Mitzi **2** *(correspond to)* répondre à, correspondre à; **to a. to a description** répondre à une description **3** *(be accountable to)* être responsable envers, rendre compte à; **you'll have me to a. to** *(if you do that)* c'est à moi que vous devrez rendre des comptes; **to a. to sb for sth** être responsable de qch envers qn

answerable [ˈɑːnsərəbəl] **ADJ 1** *(person)* responsable, comptable; **to be a. to sb for sth** être responsable de qch devant qn, être garant de qch envers qn; **he's a. only to the president** il ne relève que du président; **I'm a. to no one** je n'ai de comptes à rendre à personne **2** *(question)* susceptible de réponse, qui admet une réponse; *(accusation, argument)* réfutable

answerback [ˈɑːnsəbæk] **N** *Comput* réponse *f* en retour

answering [ˈɑːnsərɪŋ] **ADJ**

▸▸ *Tel* ***answering machine*** répondeur *m* (automatique *ou* téléphonique); *Tel* ***answering service*** *(manned)* permanence *f* téléphonique; *(unmanned)* répondeur *m* téléphonique

answerphone [ˈænsəfəʊn] **N** *Br* répondeur *m* (automatique *ou* téléphonique)

ant [ænt] **N** *Entom* fourmi *f*; *Fam* **to have ants in one's pants** avoir la bougeotte

▸▸ ***ant hill*** fourmilière *f*; *Entom* ***ant lion*** fourmilion *m*, fourmilion *m*

antacid [æntˈæsɪd] **N** (médicament *m*) alcalin *m*, antiacide *m*

ADJ alcalin, antiacide

antagonism [ænˈtæɡənɪzəm] **N** antagonisme *m*, hostilité *f*

antagonist [ænˈtæɡənɪst] **N** antagoniste *mf*, adversaire *mf*

antagonistic [ænˌtæɡəˈnɪstɪk] **ADJ** *(person)* opposé, hostile; *(feelings, ideas)* antagoniste, antagonique; **he's openly a. to the policy** il est ouvertement opposé *ou* hostile à la politique

antagonize, -ise [ænˈtæɡənaɪz] **VT** contrarier, mettre à dos; **we can't afford to a. the voters** nous ne pouvons pas nous permettre de nous aliéner les électeurs; **don't a. him!** ne te le mets pas à dos!

Antarctic [æntˈɑːktɪk] **N** *(ocean)* l'Antarctique *m*, l'océan *m* Antarctique; **in the A.** dans l'Antarctique

ADJ antarctique

▸▸ ***the Antarctic Circle*** le cercle polaire antarctique; ***the Antarctic Ocean*** l'Antarctique *m*, l'océan *m* Antarctique

Antarctica [æntˈɑːktɪkə] **N** l'Antarctique *f*, l'Antarctide *f*

ante [ˈæntɪ] **N 1** *Cards* mise *f*; **a £3 a.** une mise de 3 livres; *Fam* **to up the a.** *(in gambling)* augmenter la mise□; *Fig* placer la barre plus haut **2** *Fam (price)* part *f*

VI *Cards* faire une mise

▸ante up *Am Fam* **VT SEP** casquer

VI casquer

anteater [ˈæntˌiːtə(r)] **N** fourmilier *m*; **giant a.** grand fourmilier *m*; **lesser** *or* **collared a.** petit fourmilier *m*

antebellum [ˌæntɪˈbeləm] **ADJ** d'avant la guerre; *Am Hist* d'avant la guerre de Sécession

antecedence [ˌæntɪˈsiːdəns] **N 1** *(precedence)* antériorité *f* **2** *(priority)* priorité *f*

antecedent [ˌæntɪˈsiːdənt] **N** antécédent *m*

ADJ antérieur, précédent (**to** à)

• **antecedents** **NPL** *Formal (family)* ancêtres *mpl*; *(history)* passé *m*, antécédents *mpl*

antechamber [ˈæntɪˌtʃeɪmbə(r)] **N 1** *Archit* antichambre *f* **2** *Tech (in engine)* préchambre *f*

antedate [ˌæntɪˈdeɪt] **VT 1** *(precede in time)* précéder, dater d'avant **2** *(give earlier date to)* antidater **3** *(set an earlier date for)* avancer

antediluvian [ˌæntɪdɪˈluːvɪən] **ADJ** *Literary or Hum* antédiluvien

antelope [ˈæntɪləʊp] *(pl* **inv** *or* **antelopes)** **N** antilope *f*

ante meridian [ˌæntɪməˈrɪdɪən], **ante meridiem** [ˌæntɪməˈrɪdɪəm] **ADJ** *Formal* du matin

antenatal [ˌæntɪˈneɪtəl] *Br Obst* **ADJ** prénatal

N *Fam* consultation *f* prénatale□

▸▸ ***antenatal class*** = cours de préparation à l'accouchement; ***antenatal clinic*** service *m* de consultation prénatale

antenna [ænˈtenə] *(pl* **antennae** [-niː] *or* **antennas)** **N** antenne *f*

antepenultimate [æntɪpɪˈnʌltɪmət] **N** antépénultième *f*

ADJ antépénultième

anterior [ænˈtɪərɪə(r)] **ADJ** *Formal or Anat* antérieur (**to** à)

anteroom [ˈæntɪrʊm] **N** *Archit* antichambre *f*, vestibule *m*

anthem [ˈænθəm] **N** *(song)* chant *m*; *Rel* motet *m*; **national a.** hymne *m* national

anther [ˈænθə(r)] **N** *Bot* anthère *f*

anthologist [ænˈθɒlədʒɪst] **N** anthologiste *mf*

anthology [ænˈθɒlədʒɪ] *(pl* **anthologies)** **N** anthologie *f*

anthracite [ˈænθrəˌsaɪt] **N 1** *Miner* anthracite *m* **2** *(colour)* (gris *m*) anthracite *m inv*

ADJ *(colour)* (gris) anthracite *(inv)*

anthrax [ˈænθræks] **N** *Med & Vet (disease)* (maladie *f* du) charbon *m*; *(sore)* anthrax *m*

anthropoid [ˈænθrəpɔɪd] *Zool* **N** anthropoïde *m*

ADJ anthropoïde

anthropological [ˌænθrəpəˈlɒdʒɪkəl] **ADJ** anthropologique

anthropologist [ˌænθrəˈpɒlədʒɪst] **N** anthropologue *mf*

anthropology [ˌænθrəˈpɒlədʒɪ] **N** anthropologie *f*

anthropometry [ˌænθrəˈpɒmɪtrɪ] **N** anthropométrie *f*

anthropomorphic [ˌænθrəpəˈmɔːfɪk] **ADJ** anthropomorphique

anthropomorphism [ˌænθrəpəˈmɔːfɪzəm] **N** anthropomorphisme *m*

anthropomorphous [ˌænθrəpəˈmɔːfəs] **ADJ** anthropomorphe

anthropophagous [ˌænθrəˈpɒfəɡəs] **ADJ** anthropophage

anthropophagy [ˌænθrəˈpɒfədʒɪ] **N** anthropophagie *f*

anti- [ˈæntɪ] **PREF** anti-; **anti-American** antiaméricain

anti [ˈæntɪ] *Fam* **ADJ** **she's rather a.** elle est plutôt contre□; **he's a. everything** rien ne lui plaît;

N opposant(e)□ *m,f*

antiabortion [ˌæntɪəˈbɔːʃən] **ADJ** *(movement, campaigners)* anti-avortement

antiabortionist [ˌæntɪəˈbɔːʃənɪst] **N** adversaire *mf* de l'avortement

anti-ageing **ADJ** **a. cream/treatment** crème *f*/ traitement *m* antivieillissement

antiaircraft [ˌæntɪˈeəkrɑːft] **ADJ** *(system, weapon)* antiaérien

▸▸ ***antiaircraft defence*** défense *f* contre avions, DCA *f*

anti-aliasing **N** *Comput* anti-crénelage *m*, anti-aliassage *m*

antiapartheid [ˌæntɪəˈpɑːtaɪt] **ADJ** anti-apartheid

antibacterial [ˌæntɪbækˈtɪərɪəl] **ADJ** *Biol* antibactérien

antiballistic [ˌæntɪbəˈlɪstɪk] **ADJ** *Mil* antibalistique, antimissile

▸▸ *Mil* ***antiballistic missile*** engin *m ou* fusée *f* antimissile

antibiotic [ˌæntɪbaɪˈɒtɪk] **N** antibiotique *m*

ADJ antibiotique; **to be on antibiotics** être sous antibiotiques

antibody [ˈæntɪˌbɒdɪ] *(pl* **antibodies)** **N** *Biol* anticorps *m*

anti-burst lock **N** *Tech* serrure *f* renforcée

Antichrist [ˈæntɪˌkraɪst] **N** *Rel* **the A.** l'Antéchrist *m*

antichristian [ˌæntɪˈkrɪstʃən] **ADJ** *Rel* antichrétien

anticipate [ænˈtɪsɪˌpeɪt] **VT 1** *(think likely)* prévoir, s'attendre à; **they a. meeting some opposition, they a. that they will meet some opposition** ils s'attendent à rencontrer une certaine opposition; **we had anticipated a price increase** nous nous attendions à *ou* nous avions prévu une hausse des prix; **I didn't a. leaving so early** je ne m'attendais pas à ce qu'on parte si tôt; **we don't a. any objections** nous n'envisageons pas d'objections; **we do not a. any delays** aucun retard n'est prévu; **faster than anticipated** plus vite que prévu

2 *(be prepared for ▸ attack, decision, event)* anticiper, anticiper sur; *(▸ needs, wishes)* devancer, prévenir, aller au devant de; **we anticipated our competitors by launching our product first** nous avons devancé la concurrence en lançant notre produit les premiers

3 *(prefigure)* **her writing anticipated later developments in English fiction** son style annonçait *ou* préfigurait les développements futurs de la fiction anglaise

4 *(act on prematurely ▸ effect, success)* escompter; *Fin (▸ profit, salary)* anticiper sur

5 *(mention prematurely)* anticiper, anticiper sur; **don't a. the end of the story** n'anticipez pas la fin de l'histoire

VI anticiper

anticipation [æn,tɪsɪ'peɪʃən] **N 1** *(expectation)* attente *f*; **they raised their prices in a. of increased inflation** ils ont augmenté leurs prix en prévision d'une hausse de l'inflation **2** *Formal (readiness)* anticipation *f*; **in a. of your wishes, I've had the fire made up** pour aller au devant de *ou* pour devancer vos désirs, j'ai demandé qu'on fasse du feu; **thanking you in a.** *(in letter)* en vous remerciant d'avance, avec mes remerciements anticipés **3** *(eagerness)* impatience *f*, empressement *m*; **fans jostled at the gates in eager a.** les fans, ne tenant plus d'impatience, se bousculaient aux grilles d'entrée

anticipatory [æn,tɪsɪ'peɪtərɪ] **ADJ** d'anticipation
▸▸ *Com* ***anticipatory pricing*** fixation *f* des prix par anticipation

anticlerical [,æntɪ'klerɪkəl] *Pol & Rel* **N** anticlérical(e) *m,f*
ADJ anticlérical

anticlericalism [,æntɪ'klerɪkəlɪsəm] **N** *Pol & Rel* anticléricalisme *m*

anticlimax [,æntɪ'klaɪmæks] **N 1** *(disappointment)* déception *f*; **the opening ceremony was a bit of an a.** la cérémonie d'ouverture a été quelque peu décevante; **after all the waiting the news almost felt like an a.** après toute cette attente la nouvelle n'a pas produit tout l'effet escompté; **what an a.!** quelle douche froide! **2** *Literature* chute *f* dans le trivial

anticline ['æntɪklaɪn] **N** *Geol* anticlinal *m*

anticlockwise [,æntɪ'klɒkwaɪz] *Br* **ADV** dans le sens inverse *ou* contraire des aiguilles d'une montre
ADJ turn it in an a. direction tournez-le dans le sens inverse des aiguilles d'une montre

anticoagulant [,æntɪkəʊ'ægjʊlənt] *Pharm* **N** anticoagulant *m*
ADJ anticoagulant

anticolonialism [,æntɪkə'ləʊnɪəlɪzəm] **N** *Pol* anticolonialisme *m*

anticonstitutional [,æntɪ,kɒnstɪ'tju:ʃənəl] **ADJ** *Pol* anticonstitutionnel

anti-corrosion ADJ
▸▸ ***anti-corrosion guarantee*** garantie *f* anti-corrosion; *Tech* ***anti-corrosion primer*** apprêt *m* anticorrosion

antics ['æntɪks] **NPL** *(absurd behaviour)* cabrioles *fpl*, gambades *fpl*; *(jokes)* bouffonnerie *f*, pitrerie *f*; **I'm fed up with her silly a.** j'en ai assez de son cirque ridicule; **he's up to his (old) a. again** le voilà qui fait de nouveau des siennes

anticyclone [,æntɪ'saɪkləʊn] **N** *Met* anticyclone *m*

anti-dazzle ADJ *Br Aut* **a. headlights** phares *mpl* antiéblouissants

antidemocratic [,æntɪ,deməʊ'krætɪk] **ADJ** antidémocratique

antidepressant [,æntɪdə'presənt] **N** antidépresseur *m*
ADJ antidépresseur

antidote ['æntɪdəʊt] **N** *(gen) & Pharm* antidote *m*; **work is an a. to** *or* **for unhappiness** le travail est un antidote à *ou* contre la tristesse

anti-dumping ADJ *(laws, legislation)* anti-dumping *(inv)*

anti-Establishment ADJ *Pol* anticonformiste

antifascism [,æntɪ'fæʃɪzəm] **N** *Pol* antifascisme *m*

antifascist [,æntɪ'fæʃɪst] *Pol* **N** antifasciste *mf*
ADJ antifasciste

antifebrile [,æntɪ'fi:braɪl] *Pharm* **N** antipyrétique *m*, fébrifuge *m*
ADJ antipyrétique, fébrifuge

antifreeze ['æntɪfri:z] **N** antigel *m*

antifungal [,æntɪ'fʌŋgəl] **ADJ** antifongique
N antifongique *m*

antigen ['æntɪdʒən] **N** *Biol* antigène *m*

antiglare ['æntɪgleə(r)] **ADJ**
▸▸ *Comput* ***antiglare filter*** écran *m* antireflets; *Aut* ***antiglare headlights*** phares *mpl* antiéblouissants; ***antiglare mirror*** rétroviseur *m* jour/nuit; *Comput* ***antiglare screen*** écran *m* antireflets

antiglobalization, -isation [,æntɪ,gləʊbəlaɪ'zeɪʃən] *Pol* **N** antimondialisation *f*
ADJ d'antimondialisation

Antigua [æn'ti:gə] **N** Antigua; **A. and Barbuda** Antigua et Barbuda

antihero ['æntɪ,hɪərəʊ] *(pl* **antiheroes***)* **N** *Literature* antihéros *m*

antiheroine ['æntɪ,herəʊɪn] **N** *Literature* antihéroïne *f*

antihistamine [,æntɪ'hɪstəmɪn] **N** *Pharm* antihistaminique *m*

anti-icing N *Aut* antigel *m*; *Aviat* antigivrant *m*
ADJ antigivre *(inv)*

anti-imperialist *Pol* **N** anti-impérialiste *mf*
ADJ anti-impérialiste

anti-inflammatory *Pharm* **N** anti-inflammatoire *m*
ADJ anti-inflammatoire

anti-inflationary ADJ *Econ* anti-inflationniste

antiknock [,æntɪ'nɒk] **N** *Aut* antidétonant *m*

Antilles [æn'tɪli:z] **NPL** Antilles *fpl*; **the Greater/Lesser A.** les Grandes/Petites Antilles *fpl*

anti-lock ADJ *Aut*
▸▸ ***anti-lock brakes*** anti-blocage *m* des freins; ***anti-lock braking system*** système *m* anti-blocage des freins

antilog ['æntɪlɒg], **antilogarithm** [,æntɪ'lɒgərɪðəm] **N** *Math* antilogarithme *m*

antimacassar [,æntɪmə'kæsə(r)] **N** têtière *f*

antimalarial [,æntɪmə'leərɪəl] *Pharm* **N** antipaludique *m*, antipaludéen *m*
ADJ antipaludique, antipaludéen

antimatter ['æntɪ,mætə(r)] **N** *Phys* antimatière *f*

antimilitarism [,æntɪ'mɪlɪtərɪzəm] **N** *Pol* antimilitarisme *m*

antimissile [*Br* 'mɪsaɪl, *Am* ,æntɪ'mɪsɪl] *Mil* **N** missile *m* antimissile
ADJ antimissile *(inv)*

antimony ['æntɪmənɪ] **N** *Chem* antimoine *m*

antinazi [æntɪ'nɑ:tsɪ] *Pol* **N** antinazi, -e *m,f*
ADJ antinazi

antinuclear [,æntɪ'nju:klɪə(r)] **ADJ** antinucléaire

antiparticle ['æntɪ,pɑ:tɪkəl] **N** *Phys* antiparticule *f*

antipathetic [,æntɪpə'θetɪk] **ADJ** antipathique

antipathy [æn'tɪpəθɪ] **N** antipathie *f*; **to feel a. towards sb/sth** avoir *ou* éprouver de l'antipathie pour qn/qch

antipersonnel [,æntɪ,pɜ:sə'nel] **ADJ** *Euph* antipersonnel *(inv)*

antiperspirant [,æntɪ'pɜ:spərənt] **N** antiperspirant *m*
ADJ antiperspirant
▸▸ ***antiperspirant deodorant*** déodorant *m* antiperspirant

antiphon ['æntɪfən] **N** *Mus & Rel* antienne *f*

anti-piracy ADJ antipiratage *(inv)*

antipodean [æn,tɪpə'dɪən] **ADJ 1** *Geog* des antipodes **2** *Br (from Australia and/or New Zealand)* = d'Australie et/ou de Nouvelle-Zélande; *Hum* **our a. cousins** nos cousins d'Australie/de Nouvelle-Zélande

antipodes [æn'tɪpədi:z] **NPL** antipodes *mpl*
• **Antipodes NPL the A.** l'Australie *f* et la Nouvelle Zélande

anti-pollution ADJ anti-pollution

antiproton ['æntɪ,prəʊtɒn] **N** *Phys* antiproton *m*

antipyretic [,æntɪpaɪ'retɪk] *Pharm* **N** antipyrétique *m*, fébrifuge *m*
ADJ antipyrétique, fébrifuge

antiquarian [,æntɪ'kweərɪən] **N** *(collector)* collectionneur(euse) *m,f* d'antiquités; *(researcher)* archéologue *mf*; *(merchant)* antiquaire *mf*
ADJ *(collection, shop)* d'antiquités; *(bookseller, bookshop)* spécialisé dans les livres anciens

antiquary ['æntɪkwərɪ] *(pl* **antiquaries***)* **N** *(collector)* collectionneur(euse) *m,f* d'antiquités; *(researcher)* archéologue *mf*; *(merchant)* antiquaire *mf*

antiquated ['æntɪkweɪtɪd] **ADJ 1** *(outmoded ▸ machine, method)* vieillot, obsolète; *(▸ building, installation)* vétuste; *(▸ idea, manners)* vieillot, suranné; *(▸ person)* vieux jeu *(inv)*; **you have such a. ideas** tu es tellement vieux jeu **2** *(ancient)* très vieux (vieille)

antique [æn'ti:k] **ADJ 1** *(very old)* ancien; *Antiq (dating from Greek or Roman times)* antique; **an a. clock** une pendule ancienne *ou* d'époque **2** *Fam (outmoded ▸ machine, method)* vieillot□, obsolète□; *(▸ building, installation)* vétuste□
N *(piece of furniture)* meuble *m* ancien *ou* d'époque; *(vase)* vase *m* ancien *ou* d'époque; *(work of art)* objet *m* d'art ancien
COMP *(lover, shop)* d'antiquités
▸▸ ***antique dealer*** antiquaire *mf*

antiquity [æn'tɪkwətɪ] *(pl* **antiquities***)* **N** *Antiq* **1** *(ancient times)* l'Antiquité *f* **2** *(building, ruin)* monument *m* ancien, antiquité *f*; *(coin, statue)* objet *m* ancien; *(work of art)* objet *m* d'art ancien, antiquité *f* **3** *(oldness)* ancienneté *f*

anti-rabies ADJ antirabique

antiracism [,æntɪ'reɪsɪzəm] **N** antiracisme *m*

antiracist [,æntɪ'reɪsɪst] **ADJ** antiraciste

antiraid precautions [,æntɪ'reɪd-] **N** *Fin & St Exch* barrières *fpl* antiraid

anti-rejection ADJ *Med (drug)* antirejet *(inv)*

anti-roll bar N *Aut* barre *f* antiroulis

antirrhinum [,æntɪ'raɪnəm] **N** *Bot* muflier *m*, gueule-de-loup *f*

antirust [,æntɪ'rʌst] **ADJ** antirouille *(inv)*

anti-Semite N antisémite *mf*

anti-Semitic ADJ antisémite

anti-Semitism N antisémitisme *m*

antisepsis [,æntɪ'sepsɪs] **N** antisepsie *f*

antiseptic [,æntɪ'septɪk] **N** antiseptique *m*
ADJ antiseptique

antiserum [,æntɪ'sɪərəm] **N** antisérum *m*

antislavery [,æntɪ'sleɪvərɪ] **ADJ** *Pol* antiesclavagiste

antisocial [,æntɪ'səʊʃəl] **ADJ 1** *(behaviour, measure)* antisocial **2** *(unsociable)* sauvage; **don't be so a.** ne sois pas si sauvage; **I don't want to be a., but ...** *(I'd rather be alone)* désolé de faire bande à part, mais ...; *(I have to leave, you have to leave)* je m'en voudrais de gâcher l'ambiance, mais ...
▸▸ *Br* ***antisocial behaviour order*** = injonction contre une personne coupable de harcèlement ou de tout autre comportement antisocial à l'encontre d'une autre personne

antispasmodic [,æntɪspæz'mɒdɪk] *Pharm* **N** antispasmodique *m*
ADJ antispasmodique

antistatic [,æntɪ'stætɪk] **ADJ** antistatique

anti-submarine ADJ *Mil & Naut* anti-sous-marin

antitank [,æntɪ'tæŋk] **ADJ** *Mil* antichar

anti-terror ADJ antiterreur, antiterroriste

anti-terrorism ADJ antiterreur, antiterroriste
N antiterrorisme *m*

anti-terrorist ADJ antiterroriste

antitheft [,æntɪ'θeft] **ADJ** antivol; **an a. device** un antivol, un dispositif contre le vol *ou* antivol

antithesis [æn'tɪθɪsɪs] *(pl* **antitheses** [-si:z]*)* **N 1** *(exact opposite)* contraire *m*, opposé *m*, antithèse *m*; **he is the a. of a forceful young manager** c'est tout le contraire *ou* c'est l'antithèse du jeune cadre dynamique **2** *(contrast, opposition)* antithèse *f*, contraste *m*, opposition *f* **3** *Literature* antithèse *f*

antithetic [ˌæntɪˈθetɪk], **antithetical** [ˌæntɪˈθetɪkəl] ADJ antithétique

antitoxin [ˌæntɪˈtɒksɪn] N *Biol & Pharm* antitoxine *f*

antitrust [ˌæntɪˈtrʌst] ADJ *Am Law* antitrust *(inv)*; *Hist* **the Sherman A. Act** la loi antitrust Sherman
►► ***antitrust law*** loi *f* anti-trust

antitussive [ˌæntɪˈtʌsɪv] *Pharm* N antitussif *m*
ADJ antitussif

antivirus [ˈæntɪˌvaɪrəs] N *Comput* antivirus *m*
►► ***antivirus check*** vérification *f* antivirale; ***antivirus program*** programme *m* antivirus

antivivisectionist [ˌæntɪˌvɪvɪˈsekʃənɪst] N adversaire *mf* de la vivisection, antivivisection(n)iste *mf*

antler [ˈæntlə(r)] N *Zool* corne *f*; **the antlers** les bois *mpl*, la ramure

antonym [ˈæntənɪm] N *Ling* antonyme *m*

antsy [ˈæntsɪ] ADJ *Am Fam* agité❑, nerveux❑; **I'm feeling a.** j'ai la bougeotte

Antwerp [ˈæntwɜːp] N Anvers

anus [ˈeɪnəs] N anus *m*

anvil [ˈænvɪl] N enclume *f*

anxiety [æŋˈzaɪətɪ] *(pl* **anxieties***)* N **1** *(feeling of worry)* anxiété *f*, appréhension *f*; **rising interest rates have caused a.** la hausse des taux d'intérêt a suscité une vive anxiété; **to cause sb great a.** donner de grandes inquiétudes *ou* bien des soucis à qn; **there is no cause for a.** il n'y a pas de quoi s'inquiéter; **a source of deep a.** une source d'angoisse profonde; **to be in a state of high a.** être rempli d'angoisse
2 *(source of worry)* souci *m*; **her son is a great a. to her** son fils lui donne énormément de soucis *ou* l'inquiète énormément
3 *(intense eagerness)* désir *m* ardent; **in his a. to please her, he forgot everything else** il tenait tellement à lui faire plaisir qu'il en oubliait tout le reste
4 *Psy* anxiété *f*
►► ***Psy anxiety attack*** crise *f* d'angoisse

anxious [ˈæŋkʃəs] ADJ **1** *(worried)* inquiet(ète), anxieux; *(stronger)* angoissé; **she's a. about losing her job** elle a peur de perdre son travail; **an a. smile** un sourire anxieux *ou* inquiet; **she's a. for their safety** elle est inquiète *ou* elle craint pour leur sécurité; **she's a very a. person** c'est une anxieuse, elle est anxieuse; **a. friends and relatives waited for news** amis et parents attendaient des nouvelles dans l'angoisse
2 *(worrying)* inquiétant, angoissant; **these are a. times** nous vivons une sombre époque; **we had one or two a. moments** nous avons connu quelques moments d'anxiété *ou* d'inquiétude
3 *(eager)* anxieux, impatient; **they're a. to start** ils sont impatients *ou* pressés de commencer; **he was a. for them to go** il attendait impatiemment qu'ils partent *ou* leur départ; **he was very a. that we shouldn't be seen together** il tenait beaucoup à ce que l'on ne nous voie pas ensemble; **she's very a. to please** elle est très désireuse *ou* anxieuse de plaire
4 *Psy* anxieux

anxiously [ˈæŋkʃəslɪ] ADV **1** *(nervously)* avec inquiétude, anxieusement **2** *(eagerly)* impatiemment, avec impatience

ANY [ˈenɪ]

> ADJ
> • du, de la, des **1, 2** • aucun **3**
> • n'importe quel **4** • tout **5**
> ADV
> • ne... plus **2**
> PRON
> • ne... aucun **2** • n'importe lequel **3**
> • tout **4**

ADJ **1** *(some ► in questions)* **have you a. money?** avez-vous de l'argent?; **do they have a. others?** en ont-ils d'autres?; **have a. guests arrived?** des invités sont-ils arrivés?; **were you in a. danger?** étiez-vous en danger?; *Fam* **a. letters for me?** il y a du courrier pour moi?
2 *(some ► in conditional clauses)* **if there's a. cake left, can I have some?** s'il reste du gâteau, est-ce que je peux en avoir?; **if you have a. free time, call me** si vous avez un moment, appelez-moi; *Fam* **a. nonsense from you and you'll be out!** tu n'as qu'à bien te tenir, sinon, c'est la porte!
3 *(in negative phrases)* **he hasn't a. change/money/cigarettes** il n'a pas de monnaie/d'argent/de cigarettes; **you haven't a. reason to complain** vous n'avez aucune raison de vous plaindre; **without a. warning/fuss** sans le moindre avertissement/problème; **she's forbidden to do a. work** tout travail lui est interdit; **hardly** *or* **barely** *or* **scarcely a.** très peu de
4 *(no matter which)* n'importe quel (quelle); **ask a. woman** demandez à n'importe quelle femme; **choose a. colour you like** choisissez la couleur que vous voulez, choisissez n'importe quelle couleur; **I expect him a. moment now** je l'attends d'un instant à l'autre; **answer a. two of the questions in section C** répondez à deux des questions de la section C; **a. (old) cup will do** n'importe quelle tasse fera l'affaire; **she's not just a. (old) pianist!** ce n'est pas n'importe quelle pianiste!
5 *(all, every)* tout; **give me a. money you've got** donne-moi tout l'argent que tu as; **a. latecomers should report to the office** tous les retardataires doivent se présenter au bureau
6 *(unlimited)* **there are a. number of ways of winning** il y a mille façons de gagner; **she has a. amount** *or* **number of friends to help her** elle a (une) quantité d'amis qui peuvent l'aider
ADV **1** *(with comparative ► in questions, conditional statements)* **can you walk a. faster?** peux-tu marcher un peu plus vite?; **is she a. better today?** va-t-elle un peu mieux aujourd'hui?; **if the wind gets a. stronger, we shan't be able to set sail** si le vent se renforce, nous ne pourrons pas partir
2 *(with comparative ► in negative statements)* **he won't be a. (the) happier** il n'en sera pas plus heureux; **we can't go a. further** nous ne pouvons aller plus loin; **I don't see him a. longer** *or* **more** je ne le vois plus; **I don't like her a. more than you do** je ne l'aime pas plus que tu ne l'aimes; **I can't get this floor a. cleaner** je n'arrive pas à nettoyer le sol mieux que ça
3 *Fam (at all)* **you're not helping me a.** tu ne m'aides pas du tout❑; **has the situation improved a.?** la situation s'est-elle arrangée un tant soit peu?❑; **a. old how** n'importe comment❑
PRON **1** *(some, someone ► in questions, conditional statements)* **did you see a.?** en avez-vous vu?; **if a. of you wants them, do take them** si quelqu'un parmi vous *ou* si l'un d'entre vous les veut, il n'a qu'à les prendre; **few, if a., of his supporters remained loyal** aucun ou presque aucun de ses supporters ne lui est resté fidèle
2 *(even one ► in negative statements)* **he couldn't see a. of them** il ne voyait aucun d'entre eux; **there was hardly a. of it left** il n'en restait que très peu; **she's learned two foreign languages, I haven't learned a.** elle a étudié deux langues étrangères, je n'en ai étudié aucune; **I have absolutely no money and don't expect to get a.** je n'ai pas un sou et je ne m'attends pas à en avoir; *Fam* **he's not having a. (of it)** il ne marche pas
3 *(no matter which one)* n'importe lequel (laquelle); **which chocolate shall I have? – take a., they're all the same** quel chocolat est-ce que je vais prendre? – prends n'importe lequel, ils sont tous pareils
4 *(every one, all)* tout; **a. of the suspects would fit that description** cette description s'applique à tous les suspects

ANYBODY [ˈenɪˌbɒdɪ]

> • quelqu'un **1** • personne **2**
> • n'importe qui **3**

PRON **1** *(someone ► in questions, conditional statements)* quelqu'un; **has a. lost their glasses?** est-ce que quelqu'un a perdu ses lunettes?; **if a. asks, say I've gone abroad** si quelqu'un pose la question, dis que je suis à l'étranger; **(is) a. home?** il y a quelqu'un?; *Fam* **a. for more tea?** quelqu'un reveut du thé?❑; **she'll persuade them, if a. can** si quelqu'un peut les convaincre, c'est bien elle
2 *(someone ► in negative statements)* personne; **she's not accusing a.** elle n'accuse personne; **there was hardly a. there** il n'y avait presque personne; **she left without speaking to a.** elle est partie sans parler à personne
3 *(no matter who, everyone)* **a. who wants can join us** tous ceux qui veulent peuvent se joindre à nous; **invite a. you want** invitez qui vous voulez; **it could happen to a.** ça pourrait arriver à tout le monde *ou* n'importe qui; **I don't care what a. thinks** je me fiche de ce que pensent les gens; **she's cleverer than a. I know** c'est la personne la plus intelligente que je connaisse; **a. who saw the accident should come forward** ceux qui ont été témoins de l'accident sont priés de se faire connaître; **a. with any sense** *or* **in their right mind would have...** toute personne un peu sensée aurait...; **please, a. but him!** je t'en prie, pas lui!; **a. but him would have...** n'importe qui d'autre que lui *ou* tout autre que lui aurait...; **a. would think you'd just lost your best friend** on croirait que tu viens de perdre ton meilleur ami; **he's not just a., he's my brother!** ce n'est pas n'importe qui, c'est mon frère!; **it's a.'s guess!** qui sait?; *Hum* **a couple of gin and tonics and you're a.'s** deux ou trois gin-tonics et on fait tout ce qu'on veut de toi
4 *(important person)* quelqu'un d'important *ou* de connu; **a. who's a. will be there** tout le gratin sera là; **if you want to be a., you've got to work** si tu veux devenir quelqu'un tu dois travailler

anyhow [ˈenɪhaʊ] ADV **1** = **anyway 2** *(in any manner, by any means)* **you can do it a., but just get it done!** tu peux le faire n'importe comment, mais fais-le! **3** *Fam (haphazardly)* n'importe comment❑; **she threw her things down just a.** elle a jeté ses affaires en désordre par terre *ou* par terre n'importe comment

anyone [ˈenɪwʌn] = **anybody**

anyplace [ˈenɪpleɪs] *Am* = **anywhere**

ANYTHING [ˈenɪθɪŋ]

> • quelque chose **1, 2** • quoi que ce soit **2**
> • rien **3** • n'importe quoi **4**
> • tout **5**

PRON **1** *(something ► in questions)* quelque chose; **did you hear a.?** avez-vous entendu quelque chose?; **is there a. to eat?** est-ce qu'il y a quelque chose à manger?; **can't we do a.?** est-ce qu'il n'y a rien à faire?; **have you a. to write with?** avez-vous de quoi écrire?; **is there a. in** *or* **to what she says?** est-ce qu'il y a du vrai dans ce qu'elle dit?; **have you heard a. from them?** avez-vous eu de leurs nouvelles?; **will there be a. else, madam?** *(in shop)* désirez-vous autre chose, madame?, et avec cela, madame?; *Fam* **a. good on TV tonight?** est-ce qu'il y a quelque chose de bien à la télé ce soir?; *Fam* **a. the matter?** quelque chose ne va pas?; **have you a. smaller?** *(in different size)* est-ce que vous avez la taille en-dessous?; *(money)* vous n'avez pas plus petit?
2 *(in conditional statements)* **if a. should happen, take care of John for me** s'il m'arrivait quelque chose *ou* quoi que ce soit, occupez-vous de John
3 *(in negative statements)* rien; **I didn't say a.** je n'ai rien dit; **you can't believe a. he says** on ne peut rien croire de ce qu'il dit; **don't do a. stupid!** ne fais pas de bêtise!; **I don't know a. about computers** je ne m'y connais pas du tout *ou* je n'y connais rien en informatique; **there's hardly a. left** il ne reste presque rien; **without saying a.** sans rien dire; **she's not angry or a.** elle n'est pas fâchée ni rien; **do you want a book or a.?** voulez-vous un livre ou autre chose?
4 *(no matter what)* n'importe quoi; **just tell him a.** racontez-lui n'importe quoi; **a. you like** tout ce que vous voudrez; **I'd give a. to know the truth** je donnerais n'importe quoi pour savoir la vérité; **he won't read just a.** il ne lit pas n'importe quoi; **a. goes!** tout est permis!
5 *(all, everything)* tout; **her son eats a.** son fils mange de tout; **I like a. with chocolate in it** j'aime tout ce qui est au chocolat
6 *(in intensifying phrases)* **he isn't a. like his father** il ne ressemble pas du tout *ou* en rien à son père; **it doesn't taste a. like a tomato** ça n'a pas du tout le goût de tomate; **it isn't a. like as good as his last film** c'est loin d'être aussi bon que son dernier film; **I wouldn't miss it for a.** je ne le manquerais pour rien au monde; **it's as easy as a.** c'est facile comme tout; **to run like a.** courir comme un dératé; **he worked**

like a. il a travaillé comme un fou; **it rained like a.** il pleuvait des cordes

• **anything but** ADV tout sauf; **that music is a. but relaxing** cette musique est tout sauf reposante

anyway ['enɪweɪ], *Am* **anyways** ['enɪweɪz] ADV **1** *(in any case* ▸ *reinforcing)* de toute façon; **it's too late now a.** de toute façon, il est trop tard maintenant

2 *(summarizing, concluding)* en tout cas; **a., that's what I think** en tout cas, c'est mon avis *ou* ce que je pense; **a., I have to go** *(I'll be late)* bon, il faut que j'y aille; *(I don't have any choice)* enfin, il faut que j'y aille

3 *(nevertheless, notwithstanding)* quand même; **thanks a.** merci quand même; **we can invite them a.** on peut toujours *ou* quand même les inviter

4 *(returning to topic)* bref; **a., as I was saying...** bref, comme je disais...; **a., let's get back to what we were saying** enfin *ou* bon, revenons à ce que nous disions

ANYWHERE ['enɪweə(r)]

• quelque part **1**	• n'importe où **2**
• partout **3**	• nulle part **4**

ADV **1** *(in questions)* quelque part; **have you seen my keys a.?** avez-vous vu mes clés (quelque part)?; **are you going a. at Easter?** vous partez à Pâques?; **have you found a. to live?** avez-vous trouvé à vous loger?

2 *(in positive statements* ▸ *no matter where)* n'importe où; **just put it down a.** posez-le n'importe où; **sit a. you like** asseyez-vous où vous voulez; **a. you go it's the same story** où que vous alliez, c'est toujours pareil *ou* toujours la même chose; **I'd know her a.** je la reconnaîtrais entre mille

3 *(everywhere)* partout; **you can find that magazine a.** on trouve cette revue partout

4 *(in negative statements* ▸ *any place)* nulle part; **I can't find my keys a.** je ne trouve mes clés nulle part; **we're not getting a.** nous n'arrivons à rien, nous n'avançons pas; **look, this isn't getting us a.** écoute, tout ça ne nous mène à rien; **crying won't get you a.** pleurer ne te servira à rien; **he isn't a. near as quick as you are** il est loin d'être aussi rapide que toi;

PRON *(any place)* **do they need a. to stay?** ont-ils besoin d'un endroit où loger?; **they live miles from a.** ils habitent en pleine cambrousse

aob, AOB [ˌeɪəʊ'biː] N *Admin (abbr* **any other business***)* divers

A-OK [ˌeɪəʊ'keɪ] *Am Fam* ADJ excellent[□]; **everything's A.** tout baigne; **he's A.** c'est un type bien
ADV parfaitement[□]; **to go A.** se passer vachement bien

AOR [ˌeɪəʊ'ɑː(r)] N *(abbr* **adult-orientated rock***)* rock *m* FM, rock *m* mélodique

aorta [eɪ'ɔːtə] *(pl* **aortas** *or* **aortae** [-tiː]) N *Anat* aorte *f*

aortic [eɪ'ɔːtɪk] ADJ *Anat* aortique

AP ['eɪ'piː] N *(abbr* **Associated Press***)* AP *f*

apace [ə'peɪs] ADV *Literary* rapidement, vite

Apache [ə'pætʃɪ] *(pl* **inv** *or* **Apaches**) N **1** *(person)* Apache *mf* **2** *(language)* apache *m*
ADJ apache

apart [ə'pɑːt] ADV **1** *(separated* ▸ *in space)* **a couple of metres a.** à (une distance de) deux ou trois mètres l'un de l'autre; **the houses were about 10 kilometres a.** les maisons étaient à environ 10 kilomètres l'une de l'autre; **the lines must be 10 centimetres a.** les lignes doivent être espacées de 10 centimètres; **plant the seeds fairly far a.** plantez les graines assez loin les unes des autres; **cities as far a. as Johannesburg and Hong Kong** des villes aussi éloignées l'une de l'autre que Johannesburg et Hong Kong; **he stood with his legs wide a.** il se tenait (debout) les jambes bien écartées; **they can't bear to be a.** ils ne supportent pas d'être loin l'un de l'autre *ou* séparés; **they're living a.** *(because of circumstances)* ils n'habitent pas ensemble; *(because of divorce, break-up)* ils sont séparés, ils vivent séparément; **children born two years a.** des enfants nés à deux ans d'intervalle; *Fig* **we're miles a. when it comes to politics** nous avons des points de vue politiques très différents

2 *(in pieces)* en pièces, en morceaux; **to break a.** s'émietter; **to take a machine a.** démonter *ou* désassembler une machine

3 *(with verbs of motion)* **to push a.** éloigner (en poussant); **to grow a. from sb** s'éloigner de qn

4 *(isolated)* à l'écart; **she stood a. from the others** elle se tenait à l'écart des autres

5 *(aside)* à part; **joking a.** trêve de plaisanterie
ADJ *(after n) (distinct and special)* à part; **they regard it as a thing a.** ils considèrent que c'est quelque chose de complètement différent

• **apart from** PREP **1** *(except for)* à part; **a. from my salary, we have nothing** en dehors de *ou* à part mon salaire, nous n'avons rien; **it's fine, a. from a few minor mistakes** à part *ou* sauf quelques fautes sans importance, c'est très bien **2** *(as well as)* en plus de; **she has many interests a. from golf** elle s'intéresse à beaucoup de choses à part le *ou* en plus du golf; **a. from the fact that...** outre (le fait) que...

apartheid [ə'pɑːthaɪt] N apartheid *m*

apartment [ə'pɑːtmənt] N **1** *Am (flat)* appartement *m*, logement *m*; **a one-bedroom** *or* **one-bedroomed a.** un deux-pièces **2** *Br (usu pl) (room)* pièce *f*; *(bedroom)* chambre *f*; **state apartments** grands appartements *mpl*, salons *mpl* d'apparat; **the Royal apartments** la résidence royale
▸▸ *Am* ***apartment block, apartment building, apartment house*** immeuble *m (d'habitation)*, *Can* bloc-appartement *m*

apathetic [æpə'θetɪk] ADJ apathique, indifférent

apathetically [ˌæpə'θetɪkəlɪ] ADV avec apathie *ou* indifférence

apathy ['æpəθɪ] N apathie *f*, indifférence *f*; **an air of a.** un air apathique; **their a. about the issue** leur indifférence à l'égard de ce problème

ape [eɪp] N **1** *(monkey)* grand singe *m*, *Spec* anthropoïde *m* **2** *Pej (person)* brute *f* **3** *Fam* **to go a. (about sb/sth)** *(become angry)* piquer une crise (à propos de qn/qch); *(enthuse)* s'emballer (pour qn/qch)
VT *(imitate)* singer

apelike ['eɪplaɪk] ADJ *(face, appearance, creature)* simiesque; *(noises)* de singe

Apennines ['æpɪnaɪnz] NPL **the A.** l'Apennin *m*, les Apennins *mpl*

aperient [ə'pɪərɪənt] *Med & Pharm* N laxatif *m*
ADJ laxatif

aperitif [əperə'tiːf] N apéritif *m*

aperture ['æpəˌtjʊə(r)] N **1** *(opening)* ouverture *f*, orifice *m*; *(gap)* brèche *f*, trouée *f* **2** *Phot* ouverture *f* (du diaphragme)

apeshit ['eɪpʃɪt] ADV *very Fam* **to go a. (about sb/sth)** *(become angry)* piquer une crise (à propos de qn/qch); *(enthuse)* s'emballer (pour qn/qch)

APEX ['eɪpeks] N *Br (abbr* **advance purchase excursion***)* APEX *m (tarif préférentiel sujet à des restrictions de délai d'achat)*

apex ['eɪpeks] *(pl* **apexes** *or* **apices** [-ɪsiːz]) N *Geom (of triangle)* sommet *m*, apex *m*; *Fig* point *m* culminant, sommet *m*; *Br very Fam Hum* **to fall arse over a.** tomber cul par-dessus tête

aphasia [ə'feɪzɪə] N *Med* aphasie *f*

aphasic [ə'feɪzɪk] *Med* N aphasique *mf*
ADJ aphasique

aphid ['eɪfɪd] N *Entom* puceron *m*

aphis ['eɪfɪs] *(pl* **aphides** [-fɪdiːz]) N *Entom* aphididé *m*

aphorism ['æfərɪzəm] N *Ling* aphorisme *m*

aphoristic [æfə'rɪstɪk] ADJ *Ling* aphoristique

aphrodisiac [ˌæfrə'dɪzɪæk] N aphrodisiaque *m*
ADJ aphrodisiaque

API [ˌeɪpiː'aɪ] N *Press (abbr* **American Press Institute***)* = association de journalistes américains

apiarist ['eɪpɪərɪst] N *Entom* apiculteur(trice) *m,f*

apiary ['eɪpɪərɪ] *(pl* **apiaries**) N *Entom* rucher *m*

apiculture ['eɪpɪˌkʌltʃə(r)] N apiculture *f*

apiculturist [ˌeɪpɪ'kʌltʃərɪst] N apiculteur(trice) *m,f*

apiece [ə'piːs] ADV **1** *(for each item)* chacun(e), (la) pièce; **the plants are £3 a.** les plantes coûtent 3 livres (la) pièce *ou* chacune **2** *(for each person)* chacun(e), par personne; **we had two shirts a.** nous avions deux chemises chacun

aplenty [ə'plentɪ] ADV en abondance

aplomb [ə'plɒm] N assurance *f*, aplomb *m*; **with great a.** avec un aplomb formidable

apnoea, *Am* **apnea** [æp'nɪə] N *Med* apnée *f*

apocalypse [ə'pɒkəlɪps] N apocalypse *f*

• **Apocalypse** N *Bible* Apocalypse *f*; **the four horsemen of the A.** les quatre cavaliers *mpl* de l'Apocalypse

apocalyptic [əˌpɒkə'lɪptɪk] ADJ apocalyptique

Apocrypha [ə'pɒkrɪfə] NPL *Bible* **the A.** les apocryphes *mpl*

apocryphal [ə'pɒkrɪfəl] ADJ apocryphe; **the story's a.** je doute que l'histoire soit vraie

apogee ['æpədʒiː] N *Astron & Fig* apogée *m*; **to reach the a. of one's career** atteindre le sommet *ou* le point culminant de sa carrière

apolitical [ˌeɪpə'lɪtɪkəl] ADJ apolitique

Apollo [ə'pɒləʊ] PR N *Myth* Apollon

apologetic [əˌpɒlə'dʒetɪk] ADJ **1** *(person)* **she was very a. for being late** elle s'est excusée plusieurs fois d'être arrivée en retard; **he was most a.** il s'est confondu en excuses **2** *(letter, note)* d'excuse; *(look, smile)* contrit, désolé

apologetically [əˌpɒlə'dʒetɪkəlɪ] ADV *(say)* en s'excusant, pour s'excuser; *(smile)* d'un air désolé *ou* contrit

apologize, -ise [ə'pɒlədʒaɪz] VI s'excuser (**for sth** de qch); **to a. for doing sth** s'excuser d'avoir fait qch; **to a. to sb for sth** s'excuser de qch auprès de qn, faire *ou* présenter des *ou* ses excuses à qn pour qch; **I was wrong, I a.** j'ai eu tort, excusez-moi *ou* je m'excuse; **we a. for any inconvenience** veuillez nous excuser pour les désagréments occasionnés; **I had to a. for you** *or* **your behaviour** j'ai dû demander qu'on excuse ta conduite; **it's him you should be apologizing to** c'est à lui qu'il faut demander pardon, c'est auprès de lui que tu dois t'excuser; **there's no need to a.** vous n'avez pas à vous excuser; **I can't a. enough** je ne sais comment m'excuser

apology [ə'pɒlədʒɪ] *(pl* **apologies**) N **1** *(expression of regret)* excuses *fpl*; **to make/offer an a.** faire/présenter des excuses; **to make/send one's apologies** faire/envoyer ses excuses; **I owe him an a.** je lui dois des excuses; **will you accept this gift by way of an a.?** accepterez-vous ce cadeau avec mes excuses?; **we demand an a.** nous exigeons des excuses; **please accept my sincere a.** je vous présente mes plus sincères excuses; **the director sends his apologies** le directeur vous prie de l'excuser; **a letter of a.** une lettre d'excuses **2** *(defence)* apologie *f* **3** *Br Pej (poor example)* **he's a mere a. for a man** c'est un nul; **an a. for a dinner** un semblant de dîner

> Note that the French word **apologie** is a false friend. Its most common meaning is **eulogy**.

apoplectic [ˌæpə'plektɪk] ADJ apoplectique; **to be a. (with rage)** s'étrangler de rage; **she was a. when I told her** elle a failli avoir une attaque quand je le lui ai dit; **to have an a. fit** avoir *ou* faire une attaque d'apoplexie
N *Med* apoplectique *mf*

apoplexy ['æpəpleksɪ] N *Med* apoplexie *f*

apostasy [ə'pɒstəsɪ] *(pl* **apostasies**) N *Rel* apostasie *f*

apostate [ə'pɒsteɪt] *Rel* N apostat(e) *m,f*
ADJ apostat

apostatize, -ise [ə'pɒstətaɪz] VI *Rel* apostasier

apostle [ə'pɒsəl] N *Rel & Fig* apôtre *m*

apostolic [ˌæpəs'tɒlɪk], **apostolical** [æpəs'tɒlɪkəl] ADJ *Rel* apostolique

apostrophe [ə'pɒstrəfɪ] N *Gram* apostrophe *f*

apostrophize, -ise [ə'pɒstrəfaɪz] VT *Ling* apostropher

apothecary [ə'pɒθəkərɪ] *(pl* **apothecaries**) N *Formal or Arch* pharmacien(enne) *m,f*, *Arch* apothicaire *m*

apotheosis [əˌpɒθɪ'əʊsɪs] *(pl* **apotheoses** [-siːz]) N *Rel* apothéose *f*

app [æp] N *Fam Comput (abbr* **application**) application *f*

appal, *Am* **appall** [ə'pɔːl] (*pt & pp* **appalled,** *cont* **appalling**) VT *(scandalize)* choquer, scandaliser; *(horrify)* horrifier; **she was appalled at** *or* **by the very thought** l'idée même l'horrifiait; **I'm appalled!** c'est un scandale!

Appalachian [ˌæpə'leɪʃən] N **the Appalachians** *(mountains)* les (monts *mpl*) Appalaches *mpl*
ADJ appalachien

appalling [ə'pɔːlɪŋ] ADJ *(behaviour, conditions, smell)* épouvantable

appallingly [ə'pɔːlɪŋlɪ] ADV **1** *(badly)* épouvantablement *ou* effroyablement mal; **he speaks French quite a.** son français est épouvantable *ou* effroyable; **he's a. badly behaved** il est effroyablement mal élevé; **to treat sb a.** se conduire épouvantablement mal envers qn **2** *(as intensifier) (ugly, boring, rude)* effroyablement; **an a. bad film** un film effroyablement mauvais

apparatchik [ˌæpə'rætʃɪk] N *Pol* apparatchik *m*

apparatus [ˌæpə'reɪtəs] (*pl* **inv** *or* **apparatuses**) N **1** *(UNCOUNT) (equipment)* équipement *m*; *(set of instruments)* instruments *mpl*; **laboratory a.** appareils *mpl* de laboratoire; **a piece of a.** un appareil
2 *(UNCOUNT) (in gymnasium)* agrès *mpl*; **exercises on the a., a. work** exercices *mpl* aux agrès
3 *(machine)* appareil *m*; **breathing/heating a.** appareil *m* respiratoire/de chauffage
4 *Anat* appareil *m*; **the digestive a.** l'appareil *m* digestif
5 *(organization)* **the a. of government** la machine administrative, l'administration *f*

apparel [ə'pærəl] (*Br pt & pp* **apparelled,** *cont* **apparelling,** *Am pt & pp* **appareled,** *cont* **appareling**) N **1** *Literary or Arch (garb)* costume *m*, mise *f* **2** *Am (clothes)* habillement *m*, vêtements *mpl*
VT *Literary or Arch (dress)* vêtir, habiller; *(adorn)* orner

apparent [ə'pærənt] ADJ **1** *(obvious)* évident, apparent; **to make sth a.** indiquer qch clairement; **the tension between them had become a. to us all** nous sentions tous désormais la tension qui existait entre eux; **the truth became a. to her** la vérité lui apparut; **it was a. to me that…** pour moi il était évident que…; **for no a. reason** sans raison apparente **2** *(seeming)* apparent, supposé; **with a. ease** avec une facilité apparente; **I admire the a. ease with which she does the work** j'admire l'apparente facilité avec laquelle elle exécute le travail
▸▸ *Econ* ***apparent consumption*** consommation *f* apparente

apparently [ə'pærəntlɪ] ADV **1** *(seemingly)* apparemment, en apparence; **she was a. quite calm and collected** elle paraissait assez calme et sereine **2** *(according to rumour)* à ce qu'il paraît; **a., they had a huge row** il paraît qu'ils se sont violemment disputés; **is she leaving? – a. not** elle part? – on dirait que non

apparition [ˌæpə'rɪʃən] N apparition *f*

appeal [ə'piːl] N **1** *(request)* appel *m*; **she made an a. on behalf of the victims** elle a lancé un appel au profit des victimes; **we made an a. for money to help the refugees** nous avons fait un appel de fonds pour aider les réfugiés; **an a. for help** un appel au secours; *Com & Fin* **an a. for funds** un appel de fonds
2 *Law* appel *m*, pourvoi *m*; *Br* **to lodge an a.,** *Am* **to file an a.** interjeter appel, se pourvoir en appel; **on a.** en seconde instance; **notice of a.** intimation *f*; **right of a.** droit *m* d'appel; **with no right of a.** sans appel; **Court of A.** cour *f* d'appel
3 *(attraction)* attrait *m*, charme *m*; **to have great a.** *(thing)* être très attrayant; *(person)* avoir beaucoup de charme; **travelling has lost its a. for me** je n'aime plus voyager, les voyages ne m'intéressent plus; **the idea does have a certain a.** l'idée est bien séduisante; **their music has a wide a.** leur musique plaît à toutes sortes de gens
VI **1** *(make request)* faire un appel; *(publicly)* lancer un appel; *(plead)* supplier, implorer; **she appealed to me to be patient** elle m'a prié d'être patient; **they're appealing for help for the victims** ils lancent un appel au profit des victimes; *Com & Fin* **to a. for funds** faire un appel de fonds
2 to a. to sth *(invoke)* faire appel à qch; **she appealed to his sense of justice** elle a fait appel à son sens de la justice
3 *Law* interjeter appel, se pourvoir en appel; *Br* **to a. against a sentence** appeler d'un jugement, faire appel d'un jugement; *Br* **to a. against a decision** réclamer contre une décision, faire opposition à une décision; *Law* faire appel d'une décision
4 *(please)* plaire; **the programmes a. most to children** ces émissions plaisent particulièrement aux enfants; **the book appeals to the reader's imagination** ce livre parle à l'imagination du lecteur; **the idea appealed to me** l'idée m'a séduit; **it doesn't really a. to me** ça ne m'attire pas vraiment, ça ne me dit pas grand-chose
VT *Law (sentence)* appeler de, faire appel de; *(decision)* faire appel de
▸▸ *Law* ***appeal court*** cour *f* d'appel

> Note that the French verb **appeler** is a false friend. Its most common meaning is **to call.**

appealing [ə'piːlɪŋ] ADJ **1** *(attractive ▸ dress)* joli; *(▸ idea, plan)* séduisant, attrayant **2** *(likeable ▸ person)* sympathique, attachant **3** *(moving)* émouvant, attendrissant; *(imploring)* suppliant, implorant; **he had sad, a. eyes** il avait un regard triste et implorant

appealingly [ə'piːlɪŋlɪ] ADV **1** *(charmingly)* de façon attrayante **2** *(beseechingly ▸ look)* d'un air suppliant *ou* implorant; *(▸ say)* d'un ton suppliant

appear [ə'pɪə(r)] VI **1** *(come into view ▸ person, ghost, stars)* apparaître; **he suddenly appeared round the corner** il a soudain surgi au coin de la rue; **the sun appeared from behind a cloud** le soleil est sorti de derrière un nuage; **she appeared to him in a vision** elle lui est apparue dans une vision; **she only appears at meal times** elle n'apparaît qu'au moment des repas; **she finally appeared at about eight o'clock** elle est arrivée finalement vers vingt heures; **where did you a. from?** d'où est-ce que tu sors?; **to a. from nowhere** sortir de nulle part
2 *(come into being)* apparaître; *Com (new product)* apparaître, être mis sur le marché; *(book, newspaper)* paraître, sortir, être publié
3 *(feature)* paraître, figurer; **her name appears on the list** son nom figure sur la liste
4 *(be present officially)* se présenter, paraître; *Law (in court)* comparaître; **to a. before the court** *or* **the judge** comparaître devant le tribunal; **to fail to a.** faire défaut; **he appeared on a charge of murder** il a été jugé pour meurtre; **he appeared for the accused** *(defence counsel)* il a plaidé pour l'accusé
5 *(actor)* jouer; **she appeared as Antigone** elle a joué Antigone; **to a. in a play** jouer dans une pièce; **to a. on TV** passer à la télévision
6 *(seem)* paraître, sembler; **he appeared to hesitate** il paraissait *ou* semblait hésiter, il avait l'air d'hésiter; **she appeared nervous** elle avait l'air nerveux *ou* nerveuse; **to a. to be lost** avoir l'air d'être perdu; **how does the situation a. to you?** comment voyez-vous la situation?; **there appears to have been a mistake** il semble qu'il y ait eu erreur; **it appears not** il semble que non; **so it appears, so it would a.** c'est ce qu'il semble, on dirait bien; **it would a. that he was already known to the police** il semble qu'il était déjà connu des services de police
7 *(become apparent)* **it appeared later that he had killed his wife** il est ensuite apparu qu'il avait assassiné sa femme

appearance [ə'pɪərəns] N **1** *(act of appearing)* apparition *f*; **with the a. of fast-food restaurants** avec l'apparition *ou* l'arrivée des fast-foods; **she made a brief a. at the party** elle a fait une brève apparition à la fête; **the president made a personal a.** le président est apparu en personne; **to put in an a.** passer; *(as token gesture)* faire acte de présence
2 *(advent)* avènement *m*; *Com (of new product)* mise *f* sur le marché; *(of book, newspaper)* parution *f*
3 *Law (in court)* comparution *f*
4 *(performance)* **this was her first a. on the stage** c'était sa première apparition sur scène; **she's made a number of television appearances** elle est passée plusieurs fois à la télévision; **in order of a.** par ordre d'entrée en scène
5 *(outward aspect)* apparence *f*, aspect *m*; **from his a. one would say…** à son air *ou* son extérieur on dirait…; **to have a good a.** *(person)* présenter bien; **it has all the appearances of being a first-class show** si l'on en juge par les apparences, ce devrait être un spectacle de premier ordre; **to** *or* **by all appearances** selon toute apparence; **contrary to all appearances, against all appearances** contrairement à toute apparence; **appearances can be deceptive** les apparences sont parfois trompeuses; **don't judge by appearances** ne vous fiez pas aux apparences, il ne faut pas se fier aux apparences; **to keep up appearances** sauver les apparences; **for appearances' sake** pour la forme

appease [ə'piːz] VT **1** *(person)* apaiser, calmer **2** *(anger, hunger etc)* assouvir

appeasement [ə'piːzmənt], **appeasing** [ə'piːzɪŋ] N **1** *(of person)* apaisement *m*; *(of nation)* conciliation *f* (**of** avec); **a policy of a.** une politique de conciliation **2** *(of anger, hunger etc)* assouvissement *m*

appellant [ə'pelənt] *Law* N partie *f* appelante, appelant(e) *m,f*
ADJ appelant

appellate [ə'pelɪt] ADJ *Law (court, jurisdiction)* d'appel

appellation [ˌæpə'leɪʃən] N *Formal* appellation *f*

append [ə'pend] VT *Formal (document, note)* joindre (**to** à); *(signature)* apposer (**to** à); *Comput (to database)* ajouter (**to** à); **to a. a document to a file** annexer *ou* joindre un document à un dossier

appendage [ə'pendɪdʒ] N appendice *m*; **I will not be treated as a mere a. of my husband** je n'existe pas qu'en fonction de mon mari, j'existe aussi par moi-même

appendectomy [ˌæpen'dektəmɪ] (*pl* **appendectomies**), **appendicectomy** [əˌpendɪ'sektəmɪ] (*pl* **appendicectomies**) N appendicectomie *f*

appendicitis [əˌpendɪ'saɪtɪs] N *(UNCOUNT)* appendicite *f*; **have you had a.?** avez-vous eu l'appendicite?

appendix [ə'pendɪks] (*pl* **appendixes** *or* **appendices** [-siːz]) N **1** *Anat* appendice *m*; **to have one's a. out** se faire opérer de l'appendicite; **have you had your a. out?** est-ce que tu t'es fait opérer de l'appendicite? **2** *(to book)* appendice *m*; *(to report)* annexe *f*

appertain [ˌæpə'teɪn] VI *Formal* **1** *(belong)* **to a. to** appartenir à; **land appertaining to the Crown** des terres appartenant à la Couronne **2** *(relate)* **to a. to** relever de; **duties appertaining to his position** des devoirs qui incombent à ses fonctions

appetite ['æpɪtaɪt] N **1** *(for food)* appétit *m*; **she has a good a.** elle a bon appétit; **I've got no a.** je n'ai pas d'appétit; **I've lost my a.** j'ai perdu l'appétit; **don't have too many sweets, you'll spoil your a.** ne mange pas trop de bonbons, ça va te couper l'appétit; **to work up an a.** s'ouvrir l'appétit, se mettre en appétit **2** *Fig (for knowledge)* soif *f*; *(for travel)* goût *m*; *(for doing something)* envie *f*; **that whetted his a. for travel** cela a aiguisé son goût des voyages; **a. for revenge** soif *f* de vengeance; **she had an enormous a. for books** elle avait une immense soif de lecture, elle était avide de lecture; **to have little a. for a fight** être peu enclin à une querelle *ou* à se disputer; **sexual a.** appétit *m* sexuel
▸▸ ***appetite suppressant*** coupe-faim *m*

appetizer, -iser ['æpɪtaɪzə(r)] N *Culin (food)* hors-d'œuvre *m inv*, amuse-gueule *m*; *(drink)* apéritif *m*; *Fig* **that was just an a. for what was to come** ce n'était qu'un avant-goût de ce qui allait suivre

appetizing, -ising ['æpɪtaɪzɪŋ] ADJ *(food, smell)* appétissant, alléchant; *Fig* **he doesn't look very a.** il n'est pas ragoûtant

appetizingly, -isingly ['æpɪtaɪzɪŋlɪ] ADV d'une façon appétissante

applaud [ə'plɔːd] VT applaudir, approuver; **his efforts are to be applauded** il faut applaudir ses efforts
VI applaudir

applause [ə'plɔːz] N *(UNCOUNT)* applaudissements *mpl*, acclamations *fpl*; *Fig* approbation *f*,

his performance won enthusiastic a. from the audience son interprétation a été chaleureusement applaudie par le public; **to meet** *or* **to be greeted with a.** *(of performance, decision etc)* être applaudi

►► ***applause meter*** applaudimètre *m*

apple ['æpəl] **N** *(fruit)* pomme *f*; *(tree)* pommier *m*; *Fig Literary* **the a. of discord** la pomme de discorde; **he's a rotten a.** c'est un mauvais sujet; **the Big A.** = la ville de New York; **she's the a. of his eye** il tient à elle comme à la prunelle de ses yeux; *Prov* **an a. a day keeps the doctor away** = mangez une pomme par jour et vous resterez en bonne santé

►► ***apple blossom*** fleur *f* de pommier; *Am* ***apple core*** trognon *m* de pomme; ***apple corer*** vide-pommes *m inv*; ***apple juice*** jus *m* de pomme; ***apple orchard*** pommeraie *f*; ***apple pie*** *(covered)* tourte *f* aux pommes; *(open)* tarte *f* aux pommes; **as American as a. pie** typiquement américain; *Am* ***apple sauce*** compote *f* de pommes; *Culin* ***apple strudel*** strudel *m*; ***apple tree*** pommier *m*

applecart ['æpəlkɑːt] **N** *Fig* **to upset the a.** tout chambouler

applejack ['æpldʒæk] **N** eau-de-vie *f* de pommes

apple-pie **ADJ** *Fam* impeccable[□]; **in a. order** en ordre parfait

►► *Br* ***apple-pie bed*** lit *m* en portefeuille

applet ['æplət] **N** *Comput* appelette *f*, appliquette *f*, *Can* applet *m*

appliance [ə'plaɪəns] **N 1** *(device)* appareil *m*; *(small)* dispositif *m*, instrument *m*; **domestic** *or* **household appliances** appareils *mpl* électroménagers; **electrical appliances** appareils *mpl* électriques **2** *(fire engine)* autopompe *f*

applicable [ə'plɪkəbəl] **ADJ** applicable (**to** à); **not a.** *(on form)* sans rapport; **delete where not a.** *(on form)* rayer les mentions inutiles

applicant ['æplɪkənt] **N 1** *(for loan, funding, patent)* demandeur(euse) *m,f* (**for** de); *(for job)* candidat(e) *m,f* (**for** à), postulant(e) *m,f*; *St Exch (for shares)* souscripteur(trice) *m,f* (**for** de) **2** *Law* requérant(e) *m,f*

application [ˌæplɪ'keɪʃən] **N 1** *(use)* application *f*; **the practical applications of the research** les applications pratiques de la recherche

2 *(of lotion, paint)* application *f*; **for external a. only** *(on drugs packaging)* réservé à l'usage externe

3 *(request)* demande *f*; **a job a.** *(spontaneous)* une demande d'emploi; *(in answer to advertisement)* une candidature à un poste; **to submit an a.** faire une demande; **I submitted my a. for a scholarship** j'ai fait ma demande de bourse; **further** *or* **full details on a.** informations complètes sur demande; **we made an a. for citizenship** nous avons fait une demande de naturalisation

4 *St Exch* **a. for shares** demande *f* de titres en souscription, souscription *f* d'actions; **to make an a. for shares** souscrire (à) des actions

5 *(diligence)* application *f*, assiduité *f*; **this student lacks a.** cet étudiant manque d'assiduité, cet étudiant n'est pas très appliqué

6 *(relevance)* pertinence *f*

7 *Comput* application *f*

►► ***application form*** *(for grant, benefits)* formulaire *m* de demande; *(for membership)* demande *f* d'inscription; *(for job)* dossier *m* de candidature; *Univ* dossier *m* d'inscription; *St Exch (for shares)* bulletin *m* de souscription; *Comput* ***application program*** programme *m* d'application; *Comput* ***application software*** logiciel *m* d'application

> Note that the French word **application** is a false friend. It never means **request**.

applicator ['æplɪkeɪtə(r)] **N** applicateur *m*

applied [ə'plaɪd] **ADJ** *(maths)* appliqué; *(sciences)* expérimental

►► ***applied arts*** arts *mpl* décoratifs; ***applied psychology*** psychotechnique *f*

appliqué [æ'pliːkeɪ] **N** *(decoration)* application *f*; *(decorative work)* travail *m* d'application

VT coudre en application

apply [ə'plaɪ] *(pt & pp* **applied***)* **VT 1** *(use)* appliquer (**to** à), mettre en pratique *ou* en application; *(rule, law)* appliquer (**to** à); **we a. the same rule to all students** nous appliquons la même règle à *ou* pour tous les étudiants; **he would like to a. his experience in IT to industry** il voudrait utiliser ses compétences en informatique dans le domaine de l'industrie

2 *(pressure)* **to a. pressure to sth** exercer une pression *ou* appuyer sur qch; **she applied the brakes** elle a freiné; *Fig* **the bank applied pressure on him to repay his loan** la banque a fait pression sur lui pour qu'il rembourse son emprunt

3 *(paint, lotion etc)* appliquer, mettre (**to** sur); **a. antiseptic to the wound** désinfectez la plaie

4 *(devote)* **to a. one's mind to sth** s'appliquer à qch; **he must learn to a. himself** il faut qu'il apprenne à s'appliquer

VI 1 *(make an application)* s'adresser, avoir recours; **to a. to sb for sth** s'adresser *ou* recourir à qn pour obtenir qch; **a. within** *(sign)* s'adresser à l'intérieur *ou* ici; **to a. for a job** faire une demande d'emploi, poser sa candidature à un emploi, *Formal* solliciter *ou* postuler un emploi; **to a. for a loan** demander un prêt; **we applied for a patent** nous avons déposé une demande de brevet; **to a. in writing** écrire; **to a. in person** se présenter; *St Exch* **to a. for shares** souscrire (à) des actions **2** *(be relevant)* s'appliquer (**to** à); **and that applies to you too!** et ça s'applique aussi à toi!

appoint [ə'pɔɪnt] **VT 1** *(assign)* nommer, désigner; *(committee)* constituer, nommer; *(heir)* instituer; **she was appointed to the post of director** elle a été nommée directrice; **the members appointed him president** les adhérents l'ont nommé président **2** *(hire)* engager; **we have appointed a new cook** nous avons engagé un nouveau cuisinier **3** *(place, date, time)* fixer, désigner

appointed [ə'pɔɪntɪd] **ADJ 1** *(official)* nommé; *(agent)* attitré **2** *Formal (agreed* ► *place, date, time)* convenu, dit; **we met on the a. day** nous nous sommes rencontrés au jour dit *ou* convenu **3 a well a. house** une maison bien montée *ou* bien agencée

appointee [əˌpɔɪn'tiː] **N** candidat(e) *m,f* retenu(e)

appointment [ə'pɔɪntmənt] **N 1** *(meeting* ► *at doctor's etc)* rendez-vous *m*; *(*► *for business)* rendez-vous *m*, entrevue *f*; **I made an a. with the dentist** j'ai pris rendez-vous chez le dentiste; **I've made an a. with the doctor for you** je t'ai pris un rendez-vous chez le docteur; **they made an a. to have lunch together** ils se sont donné rendez-vous pour déjeuner; **she didn't keep our** *or* **the a.** elle n'est pas venue au rendez-vous; **I've got an a. with the doctor** j'ai rendez-vous chez le médecin; *(announcing arrival to receptionist)* j'ai rendez-vous avec le médecin; **to meet sb by a.** rencontrer qn sur rendez-vous; **by a. only** sur rendez-vous seulement; **have you got an a.?** avez-vous un rendez-vous?; *Admin* êtes-vous convoqué?

2 *(nomination)* nomination *f*, désignation *f*; *(office filled)* poste *m*; *(posting)* affectation *f*; **his a. to the office of Lord Chancellor** sa nomination au poste de grand chancelier; *Com* **by a. to Her Majesty the Queen** *(on packaging)* fournisseur de S. M. la Reine

3 appointments *(in newspaper)* offres *fpl* d'emploi

4 *Formal* **appointments** *(of house)* aménagement *m*

►► ***appointments diary*** carnet *m* de rendez-vous, agenda *m*

> Note that the French word **appointements** is a false friend and is never a translation for the English word **appointments**. It means **salary**.

apportion [ə'pɔːʃən] **VT** *(blame, praise)* répartir; *(costs, taxes, expenses, shares)* répartir, partager; *(rations)* allouer; *(funds)* affecter; *(property)* distribuer; **to a. sth to sb** assigner qch à qn

apportionment [ə'pɔːʃənmənt] **N** *(of blame, praise)* répartition *f*; *(of costs, taxes, expenses, shares)* répartition *f*, partage *m*; *(of rations)* allocation *f*; *(of funds)* affectation *f*; *(of property)* distribution *f*

apposite ['æpəzɪt] **ADJ** *(observation)* juste; *(action)* approprié (**to** à); **an a. remark** une remarque très à propos

apposition [ˌæpə'zɪʃən] **N** apposition *f*; *Gram* **a noun/phrase in a.** un nom/une expression en apposition

appraisal [ə'preɪzəl] **N** *(of standards, personnel, situation)* évaluation *f*; *Ins (of object)* estimation *f*, appréciation *f*; *(before auction)* prisée *f*; *Ins* **an official a.** *(of object)* une expertise; **performance a.** *(in company)* évaluation *f*

appraise [ə'preɪz] **VT** *(standards, personnel, situation)* évaluer; *Ins (object)* estimer, évaluer (la valeur de); *(importance, quality)* évaluer, apprécier; **to a. the value of sth** estimer *ou* apprécier la valeur de qch

appraisee [əˌpreɪ'ziː] **N** = personne soumise à une évaluation

appraiser [ə'preɪzə(r)] **N** évaluateur(trice) *m,f*

appreciable [ə'priːʃəbəl] **ADJ** *(difference, amount, distance)* appréciable, notable; *(change, improvement)* sensible

appreciably [ə'priːʃəblɪ] **ADV** *(differ)* appréciablement; *(change, improve)* sensiblement

appreciate [ə'priːʃɪeɪt] **VT 1** *(value)* apprécier; *(art)* apprécier, goûter; *(person)* apprécier (à sa juste valeur); **they a. good food** ils apprécient la bonne cuisine; **no one appreciates me** personne ne m'apprécie à ma juste valeur **2** *(be grateful for)* être reconnaissant de, être sensible à; **I a. your help** je vous suis reconnaissant de votre aide; **I would a. a prompt reply to this letter** je vous serais obligé de bien vouloir me répondre dans les plus brefs délais; **I a. it** j'en suis reconnaissant; *esp Am (thanks)* je vous en remercie; **I would a. it if you didn't smoke in the car** je vous serais reconnaissant *ou* je vous saurais gré de ne pas fumer dans la voiture; **thanks, I'd really a. that** ça me rendrait vraiment service **3** *(realize, understand)* se rendre compte de, être conscient de; **I fully a. (the fact) that...** je me rends bien compte que...; **I do a. your concern but...** votre sollicitude me touche beaucoup mais...; **I hadn't appreciated how difficult it is** je ne m'étais pas rendu compte que c'était aussi difficile

VI *(value, price)* augmenter; *(currency)* s'apprécier; *(goods, property, investment, shares)* prendre de la valeur

appreciation [əˌpriːʃɪ'eɪʃən] **N 1** *(thanks)* reconnaissance *f*, gratitude *f*; **let me show my a. for your help** laissez-moi vous témoigner ma reconnaissance *ou* ma gratitude pour l'aide que vous m'avez apportée; **as a sign of our a.** en témoignage de notre reconnaissance *ou* gratitude; **in a. of what you have done** en remerciement *ou* pour vous remercier de ce que vous avez fait; **the audience showed its a. of the performance by cheering** le public a acclamé le spectacle

2 *(understanding, awareness)* compréhension *f*; **he has a thorough a. of the situation** il comprend très bien la situation; **she has no a. of what is involved** elle ne se rend pas compte de ce que ça implique; **art a. course** cours *m* d'initiation à l'art; **literary a.** explication *f* de texte; **musical a.** appréciation *f* musicale; **a wine a. society** une société d'amateurs de vin

3 *Journ (review)* critique *f*; **to write an a. of a new play** faire la critique d'une nouvelle pièce

4 *(of value, price)* augmentation *f*; *(of currency)* appréciation *f*; *(of goods, property, investment, shares)* augmentation *f* de la valeur

appreciative [ə'priːʃɪətɪv] **ADJ 1** *(grateful)* reconnaissant; **I'm very a. of all you've done for me** je vous suis reconnaissant de tout ce que vous avez fait pour moi; **she's a very a. sort of person** c'est une personne qui sait faire preuve de reconnaissance *ou* de gratitude; **in a few a. words** avec quelques mots de reconnaissance

2 *(review, audience)* favorable; *(praising)* élogieux

3 *(showing liking)* **I gave him the present, but he wasn't very a.** je lui ai donné le cadeau, mais il ne l'a pas beaucoup aimé; **to be a. of music** apprécier la musique

4 *(showing understanding, awareness)* **to be a. of sth** comprendre l'importance de qch, être sensible à qch; **he was very a. of their problems** il s'est montré très sensible à leurs problèmes

appreciatively [əˈpriːʃɪətɪvlɪ] ADV **1** *(gratefully)* avec reconnaissance **2** *(showing understanding, praising ► review)* en termes élogieux, favorablement; *(► listen)* avec appréciation; **they clapped a.** ils applaudirent pour montrer leur enthousiasme; **she smiled a.** elle eut un sourire approbateur **3** *(showing liking)* **"excellent coffee," he said a.** "excellent, ce café", dit-il avec plaisir

apprehend [ˌæprɪˈhend] VT **1** *Law (arrest)* arrêter, appréhender **2** *Formal (understand)* comprendre, saisir **3** *Arch or Literary (fear, dread)* redouter, appréhender

apprehension [ˌæprɪˈhenʃən] N **1** *(fear)* inquiétude *f*, appréhension *f*; **there is no cause for a.** il n'y a pas de raison d'être inquiet **2** *Law (arrest)* arrestation *f* **3** *Formal (understanding)* compréhension *f*

apprehensive [ˌæprɪˈhensɪv] ADJ plein d'appréhension; **I'm feeling a bit a.** je me sens un peu nerveux; **he is a. about the interview** il appréhende l'entretien; **I am a. for your safety** je crains *ou* je suis inquiet pour votre sécurité

apprehensively [ˌæprɪˈhensɪvlɪ] ADV avec appréhension *ou* inquiétude

apprentice [əˈprentɪs] N apprenti(e) *m,f*; *(in arts and crafts)* élève *mf*

ADJ **an a. toolmaker/butcher** un apprenti outilleur/boucher; **an a. draughtsman** un élève dessinateur

VT **to a. sb to sb** placer *ou* mettre qn en apprentissage chez qn; **he is apprenticed to a sculptor** il suit une formation chez un sculpteur

apprenticeship [əˈprentɪʃɪp] N apprentissage *m*; **to serve one's a. (with sb)** faire son apprentissage (chez qn); *Fig* **to serve one's a.** faire ses débuts

apprise [əˈpraɪz] VT *Formal* **to a. sb of sth** apprendre qch à qn, prévenir *ou* informer qn de qch; **we were not apprised of his arrival** nous n'avons pas été informés de son arrivée

appro [ˈæprəʊ] N *Br Fam Com (abbr* **approval***)* **on a.** à *ou* sous condition□, à l'essai□

approach [əˈprəʊtʃ] VT **1** *(person)* s'approcher de; *(place)* approcher de; **as we approached Boston** comme nous approchions de Boston; **she is approaching fifty** elle approche de la cinquantaine; **speeds approaching the speed of light** des vitesses proches de celle de la lumière; **it was approaching Christmas** Noël approchait; **a feeling approaching hatred** un sentiment proche de la haine

2 *(consider)* aborder; **let's a. the problem from another angle** abordons le problème d'une autre façon; **that's not the way to a. it** ce n'est pas comme cela qu'il faut s'y prendre

3 *(speak to)* parler à; *(company, group, player)* pressentir, faire des propositions *ou* des ouvertures à; **to be easy/difficult to a.** être d'un abord facile/difficile; **I was approached by a man in the street** j'ai été abordé par un homme dans la rue; **I approached him about the job** je lui ai parlé du poste; **they approached him about doing a deal** ils sont entrés en contact avec lui pour conclure un marché

VI *(person, vehicle)* s'approcher; *(time, event)* approcher, être proche; **Christmas/spring is approaching** Noël/le printemps approche

N **1** *(of person, vehicle)* approche *f*, arrivée *f*; *(of spring)* approche *f*; *(of night)* tombée *f*; *(of death)* approche(s) *f(pl)*; **she heard his a.** elle l'a entendu venir; **the pilot began his a. to Heathrow** le pilote commença sa descente sur *ou* vers Heathrow

2 *(way of tackling)* méthode *f*; **another a. to the problem** une autre façon d'aborder le problème; **I don't like her a.** je n'aime pas sa façon de s'y prendre; **a new a. to dealing with unemployment** une nouvelle conception de la lutte contre le chômage, une nouvelle méthode de lutte contre le chômage; **let's try the direct a.** allons-y sans détours

3 *(proposal)* proposition *f*; **the shopkeeper made an a. to his suppliers** le commerçant a fait une proposition à ses fournisseurs

4 *(access)* voie *f* d'accès; **the approaches to the town** les voies d'accès de la ville; **the a. to the house/hotel** l'allée qui mène à la maison/à l'hôtel; **the a. to the summit** le chemin qui mène au sommet

5 *Formal (approximation)* **it's the nearest a. to an apology that they received** c'est ce qu'on leur a dit qui ressemblait le plus à des excuses

►► *Br Transp* ***approach road*** route *f* d'accès; *(to motorway)* voie *f* de raccordement, bretelle *f*; *Sport* ***approach shot*** *(in tennis)* coup *m* d'approche; *(in golf)* approche *f*

approachable [əˈprəʊtʃəbəl] ADJ *(place)* accessible; *(person)* d'un abord facile

approaching [əˈprəʊtʃɪŋ] ADJ *(event)* prochain, qui est proche; *(vehicle)* qui vient en sens inverse; *(storm)* qui arrive; **the a. war would have terrible consequences** la guerre qui approchait eut des conséquences terribles

approbation [ˌæprəˈbeɪʃən] N approbation *f*, consentement *m*; **a nod/smile of a.** un signe de tête/un sourire approbateur

appropriate ADJ [əˈprəʊprɪət] *(place, decision)* approprié; *(moment)* opportun; *(remark, word)* juste; *(name)* bien choisi; *(authority)* compétent; *(behaviour)* convenable; **the level of contribution a. for** *or* **to each country** la contribution appropriée à chaque pays; **music/remarks a. to the occasion** de la musique/des propos de circonstance; **it wouldn't be a. if she went** il ne serait pas convenable qu'elle y aille; **I am not the a. person to ask** ce n'est pas à moi qu'il faut poser la question

VT [əˈprəʊprɪeɪt] **1** *(take)* s'approprier, s'emparer de; *(keep for oneself)* s'attribuer, se réserver **2** *Fin (funds)* affecter (**to** *ou* **for** à); **£4,000 has been appropriated to upgrading the computers** 4000 livres ont été affectées à l'augmentation de mémoire des ordinateurs

appropriately [əˈprəʊprɪətlɪ] ADV *(behave)* convenablement; *(speak, react)* avec à-propos, pertinemment; *(decide)* à juste titre; **a. dressed** habillé comme il faut *ou* pour la circonstance

appropriateness [əˈprəʊprɪətnɪs] N *(of moment)* opportunité *f*; *(of remark, decision, word)* justesse *f*; *(of behaviour)* correction *f*, bienséance *f*

appropriation [əˌprəʊprɪˈeɪʃən] N **1** *(taking)* appropriation *f*, prise *f* de possession (**of** de) **2** *Fin (of funds)* affectation *f*; *(of payment)* imputation *f*; *Am Pol* crédit *m* budgétaire

approval [əˈpruːvəl] N **1** *(favourable opinion)* approbation *f*, accord *m*; **a gesture of a.** un signe approbateur; **the plan has your seal of a., then?** alors tu donnes ton approbation pour le projet?; **to submit sth for a. (by sb)** soumettre qch à l'approbation (de qn); **to meet with sb's a.** obtenir *ou* recevoir l'approbation de qn; **subject to a.** soumis à l'approbation **2** *Admin & Law (of document, treaty)* ratification *f*, homologation *f*; **for (your) a.** *(on document)* pour approbation **3** *Com* **on a.** à condition, à l'essai; **a book sent on a.** un livre envoyé à l'examen

• **approvals** NPL *Am Com (goods)* marchandises *fpl* envoyées à l'essai

►► ***approval rating*** *(of politician)* cote *f* de popularité; *Mktg (of product)* score *m* d'agrément

approve [əˈpruːv] VT *(plan, proposal etc)* approuver; *Admin & Law (document, treaty, decision)* ratifier, homologuer; **the plan must be approved by the committee** il faut que le projet reçoive l'approbation du comité; **approved by the government** agréé par l'État

VI être d'accord; **I told her what I had done and she seemed to a.** je lui ai dit ce que j'avais fait et elle a eu l'air de m'approuver; **I'm afraid I don't a.** je crains de ne pas être d'accord

► **approve of** VT INSEP approuver; *(person)* avoir une bonne opinion de; **I don't a. of his ideas** je n'approuve pas *ou* je désapprouve ses idées; **she doesn't a. of them smoking** ça ne lui plaît pas qu'ils fument; **she doesn't a. of her son's friends** les amis de son fils ne lui plaisent pas

approved [əˈpruːvd] ADJ **1** *(method, practice)* reconnu, admis **2** *(officially authorized)* agréé, autorisé

►► *Formerly* ***approved school*** = nom anciennement donné en Grande-Bretagne à un centre d'éducation surveillé (aujourd'hui appelé "community home")

approving [əˈpruːvɪŋ] ADJ approbateur, approbatif

approvingly [əˈpruːvɪŋlɪ] ADV *(look)* d'un air approbateur; *(say)* d'un ton approbateur; **to react a.** approuver

approx. *(written abbr* **approximately***)* approx., env.

approximate ADJ [əˈprɒksɪmət] **1** *(figure, date, calculation)* approximatif; **the a. distance to town is five miles** il y a à peu près cinq miles d'ici à la ville **2** *Biol & Phys* rapproché, proche, voisin

VI [əˈprɒksɪmeɪt] **to a. to sth** se rapprocher de qch; **to a. to the truth** se rapprocher de la vérité; **his answer approximated to a refusal** sa réponse était presque un refus

approximately [əˈprɒksɪmətlɪ] ADV à peu près, environ; **a pint is a. half a litre** une pinte correspond approximativement à un litre; **his income is a. £20,000** son revenu est d'environ 20000 livres

approximation [əˌprɒksɪˈmeɪʃən] N approximation *f*; **this figure is only an a.** ceci n'est qu'un chiffre approximatif; **his statement was no more than an a. of the truth** sa déclaration n'avait qu'un lointain rapport avec la réalité

appurtenance [əˈpɜːtɪnəns] N *(usu pl) Formal* accessoire *m*; **the property and its appurtenances** *(buildings, gardens etc)* la propriété et ses dépendances; *Law (legal rights and privileges)* la propriété et ses circonstances et dépendances

APR [ˌeɪpiːˈɑː(r)] N *Fin (abbr* **annual or annualized percentage rate***)* TEG *m*

Apr. *(written abbr* **April***)* avr.

après-ski [ˌæpreɪˈskiː] N = distractions après une séance de ski

> Note that the French word **après-ski** is a false friend and is never a translation for the English word **après-ski**. It means **snowboot**.

apricot [ˈeɪprɪkɒt] N **1** *(fruit)* abricot *m*; *(tree)* abricotier *m* **2** *(colour)* abricot *m inv*

COMP *(yoghurt, ice cream)* à l'abricot; *(jam)* d'abricots; *(tart)* aux abricots

ADJ *(colour)* abricot *(inv)*

►► ***apricot tree*** abricotier *m*

April [ˈeɪprəl] N avril *m*; *see also* **February**

►► ***April fool*** *(person)* = personne à qui l'on a fait un poisson d'avril; *(trick)* poisson *m* d'avril; **A. fool!** poisson d'avril!; ***April Fools' Day*** le premier avril; ***April showers*** giboulées *fpl* de mars

> **APRIL FOOLS' DAY**
>
> En Grande-Bretagne, le premier avril est l'occasion de farces en tous genres; en revanche, la tradition du poisson en papier n'existe pas.

a priori [ˌeɪpraɪˈɔːraɪ] ADJ a priori

apron [ˈeɪprən] N **1** *(clothing)* tablier *m*; **he's tied to his mother's a. strings** il est pendu aux jupes de sa mère **2** *Aviat* aire *f* de manœuvre *ou* de stationnement; *(for plane maintenance and repair)* tablier *m*, aire *f* en dur **3** *Theat* avant-scène *f*

►► *Theat* ***apron stage*** avant-scène *f*

apropos [ˌæprəˈpəʊ] ADJ opportun, à propos

ADV à propos, opportunément

• **apropos of** PREP à propos de; **...he said, a. of nothing** ...dit-il, de but en blanc

APS [ˌeɪpiːˈes] *(abbr* **advanced photo system***)* N APS *m inv*

►► ***APS camera*** appareil *m* photo APS

apse [æps] N **1** *Archit (in church)* abside *f* **2** *Astron* apside *f*

apt [æpt] ADJ **1** *(person)* **to be a. to do sth** avoir tendance à faire qch; **people are a. to believe the worst** les gens croient facilement le pire

2 *(things)* **to be a. to do sth** être susceptible de faire qch; **buttons are a. to get lost** les boutons se perdent facilement

3 *(suitable)* convenable, approprié; *(remark)* juste, qui convient; **it is very a. that it should end in this way** il est tout à fait approprié que cela se termine de cette manière

4 *(clever)* doué, intelligent

aptitude [ˈæptɪtjuːd] N aptitude *f*, disposition *f*; **to have an a. for sth** avoir une aptitude à *ou* une disposition pour qch; **he has an a. for languages** il a des dispositions *ou* un talent pour les langues; **a young musician who shows great a.** une jeune musicienne qui promet
▸▸ ***aptitude test*** test *m* d'aptitude

aptly [ˈæptlɪ] ADV à *ou* avec propos, avec justesse; **the dog, Spot, was a. named** le chien, Spot, portait *ou* méritait bien son nom; **as you so a. pointed out...** comme tu l'as si bien fait remarquer...

aptness [ˈæptnɪs] N **1** *(suitability)* à-propos *m*, justesse *f* **2** *(tendency)* tendance *f* **3** *(talent)* aptitude *f*, disposition *f*

aqualung [ˈækwəlʌŋ] N scaphandre *m* autonome

aquamarine [ˌækwəməˈriːn] N *Miner (stone)* aigue-marine *f*; *(colour)* bleu vert *m inv*
ADJ bleu vert *(inv)*

aquanaut [ˈækwənɔːt] N plongeur *m*, scaphandrier *m*

aquaplane [ˈækwəpleɪn] N *Sport* aquaplane *m*
VI **1** *Sport* faire de l'aquaplane **2** *Br (car)* partir en aquaplanage *ou* aquaplaning

aquaplaning [ˈækwəpleɪnɪŋ] N **1** *Sport* aquaplane *m* **2** *Br (of car)* aquaplanage *m*, aquaplaning *m*

aquarelle [ˌækwəˈrel] N *Art* aquarelle *f*

aquarium [əˈkweərɪəm] *(pl* **aquariums** *or* **aquaria** [-rɪə]) N aquarium *m*

Aquarius [əˈkweərɪəs] N *Astron & Astrol* le Verseau; **he's A., he's an A.** il est (du signe du) Verseau

aquarobics [ˌækwəˈrəʊbɪks] N aquagym *f*

aquatic [əˈkwætɪk] ADJ **1** *Biol* aquatique **2** *Sport (sport)* nautique
▸▸ *Orn* ***aquatic display*** numéro *m* aquatique

aquatics [əˈkwætɪks] NPL sports *mpl* nautiques

aquatint [ˈækwətɪnt] N *Art* aquatinte *f*

aqueduct [ˈækwɪdʌkt] N aqueduc *m*

aqueous [ˈækwɪəs, ˈeɪkwɪəs] ADJ *Chem* aqueux
▸▸ *Anat* ***aqueous humour*** humeur *f* aqueuse; *Chem* ***aqueous solution*** soluté *m*

aquilegia [ˌækwɪˈliːdʒɪə] N *Bot* ancolie *f*

aquiline [ˈækwɪlaɪn] ADJ *Orn* aquilin; *Anat (nose)* aquilin, en bec d'aigle

Arab [ˈærəb] N **1** *(person)* Arabe *mf* **2** *(horse)* cheval *m* arabe
ADJ arabe
▸▸ *Pol* ***the Arab League*** la Ligue arabe

> **ARAB**
>
> En anglais le mot "Arab" désigne l'ensemble des ressortissants des pays de culture arabe, et surtout de l'Arabie Saoudite. Il n'a pas le sens restreint de "Maghrébin" que l'on rencontre souvent en français: "the firm was bought by a wealthy Arab family".

arabesque [ˌærəˈbesk] N **1** *(usu pl) Art* arabesque *f* **2** *(in ballet)* arabesque *f*
ADJ *Art (decoration)* de style arabe

Arabia [əˈreɪbɪə] N Arabie *f*

Arabian [əˈreɪbɪən] N Arabe *mf*
ADJ arabe, d'Arabie
▸▸ ***the Arabian Gulf*** le golfe Arabique; ***the Arabian Nights*** les Mille et Une Nuits; ***the Arabian Peninsula*** la péninsule d'Arabie; ***the Arabian Sea*** la mer d'Arabie

Arabic [ˈærəbɪk] N *(language)* arabe *m*; **written A.** l'arabe *m* littéral
ADJ arabe
▸▸ *Math* ***Arabic numerals*** chiffres *mpl* arabes

Arabist [ˈærəbɪst] N *(scholar)* arabisant(e) *m,f*; *(politician)* pro-Arabe *mf*

arable [ˈærəbəl] ADJ *Agr* arable, cultivable; *(crops)* cultivable; *(farm)* agricole
▸▸ ***arable farmer*** cultivateur(trice) *m,f*; ***arable farming*** culture *f*

arachnid [əˈræknɪd] N *Zool* arachnide *m*; **the arachnids** les arachnides *mpl*

Aramaic [ˌærəˈmeɪɪk] N *Antiq & Ling* araméen *m*
ADJ araméen

arbiter [ˈɑːbɪtə(r)] N arbitre *m*, médiateur(trice) *m,f*, *Fig* **magazines act as arbiters of modern taste** les magazines se font les juges *ou* les arbitres des goûts de notre société

arbitrage [ˌɑːbɪˈtrɑːʒ] N *Fin & St Exch* arbitrage *m*

arbitrager, arbitrageur [ˈɑːbɪtrɑːʒə(r)] N *Fin & St Exch* arbitragiste *m*

arbitrarily [*Br* ˈɑːbɪtrərəlɪ, *Am* ˌɑːrbəˈtrerəlɪ] ADV arbitrairement

arbitrariness [ˈɑːbɪtrərɪnɪs] N *(of decision, choice)* nature *f* arbitraire

arbitrary [ˈɑːbɪtrərɪ] ADJ arbitraire

arbitrate [ˈɑːbɪtreɪt] VT arbitrer, juger
VI décider en qualité d'arbitre, arbitrer

arbitration [ˌɑːbɪˈtreɪʃən] N *(gen) & Ind* arbitrage *m*; **to go to a.** *(of union)* soumettre le différend à l'arbitrage; *(of dispute)* être soumis à l'arbitrage; **settlement by a.** règlement *m* par arbitrage
▸▸ ***arbitration award*** sentence *f* arbitrale; ***arbitration board*** commission *f* d'arbitrage; ***arbitration court*** instance *f* chargée d'arbitrer les conflits sociaux, tribunal *m* arbitral; ***arbitration clause*** clause *f* compromissoire; ***arbitration tribunal*** instance *f* chargée d'arbitrer les conflits sociaux, tribunal *m* arbitral

arbitrator [ˈɑːbɪtreɪtə(r)] N *(gen) & Ind* arbitre *m*

arbor [ˈɑːbə(r)] *Am* = **arbour**

arboreal [ɑːˈbɔːrɪəl] ADJ *Bot (relating to trees)* d'arbre(s); *(animal, technique)* arboricole

arboriculture [ˈɑːbərɪkʌltʃə(r)] N *Hort* arboriculture *f*

arbour, *Am* **arbor** [ˈɑːbə(r)] N *Bot & Hort* tonnelle *f*

arbutus [ɑːˈbjuːtəs] N *Bot & Hort* arbousier *m*

arc [ɑːk] N **1** *Geom (of circle)* arc *m*; **to describe an a.** décrire un arc; *Mil* **a. of fire** *(of cannon etc)* champ *m* de tir **2** *Elec* arc *m*
VI **1** *(gen)* décrire un arc; **the ball arced up into the air** la balle décrivit un arc de cercle dans les airs **2** *Elec* faire jaillir un arc électrique
▸▸ ***arc lamp, arc light*** *Elec* lampe *f* à arc; *Cin & TV* sunlight *m*

arcade [ɑːˈkeɪd] N **1** *Archit (set of arches)* arcade *f*, galerie *f* **2** *Com (for shopping)* galerie *f* marchande **3** *(amusement arcade)* salle *f* de jeux électroniques
▸▸ ***arcade game*** jeu *m* électronique

Arcadia [ɑːˈkeɪdɪə] N Arcadie *f*

Arcadian [ɑːˈkeɪdɪən] N Arcadien(enne) *m,f*
ADJ arcadien, d'Arcadie

arcane [ɑːˈkeɪn] ADJ mystérieux, ésotérique; *(knowledge, practice, ritual)* secret(ète)
N **the a.** le mystérieux

arch [ɑːtʃ] N **1** *Archit* arc *m*; *(in church)* arc *m*, voûte *f*; *Constr (of bridge, viaduct)* arche *f* **2** *Anat (of eyebrows)* courbe *f*; *(of foot)* cambrure *f*, voûte *f* plantaire; **to have fallen arches** avoir les pieds plats *ou Spec* un affaissement de la voûte plantaire
VT arquer, cambrer; **the cat arched its back** le chat fit le gros dos
VI former voûte, s'arquer
ADJ **1** *(leading)* grand, par excellence; **my a. rival** mon principal adversaire; **he is an a. traitor** c'est le traître par excellence **2** *(mischievous)* coquin, espiègle; *(look, smile, tone)* malin(igne), espiègle **3** *(supercilious* ▸ *voice, manner)* condescendant
▸▸ *Archit* ***arch stone*** claveau *m*, voussoir *m*

archaeological, *Am* **archeological** [ˌɑːkɪəˈlɒdʒɪkəl] ADJ archéologique

archaeologically, *Am* **archeologically** [ˌɑːkɪəˈlɒdʒɪkəlɪ] ADV archéologiquement

archaeologist, *Am* **archeologist** [ˌɑːkɪˈɒlədʒɪst] N archéologue *mf*

archaeology, *Am* **archeology** [ˌɑːkɪˈɒlədʒɪ] N archéologie *f*

archaic [ɑːˈkeɪɪk] ADJ archaïque

archaism [ˈɑːkeɪɪzəm] N *Ling* archaïsme *m*

archangel [ˈɑːkˌeɪndʒəl] N archange *m*; **the A. Gabriel** l'archange Gabriel, saint Gabriel archange

archbishop [ˌɑːtʃˈbɪʃəp] N *Rel* archevêque *m*; **a.'s palace** palais *m* archiépiscopal

archbishopric [ˌɑːtʃˈbɪʃəprɪk] N *Rel* archevêché *m*

archdeacon [ˌɑːtʃˈdiːkən] N *Rel* archidiacre *m*

archdiocese [ˌɑːtʃˈdaɪəsɪs] N *Rel* archidiocèse *m*

archduchess [ˌɑːtʃˈdʌtʃɪs] N archiduchesse *f*

archduchy [ˌɑːtʃˈdʌtʃɪ] *(pl* **archduchies**) N archiduché *m*

archduke [ˌɑːtʃˈdjuːk] N archiduc *m*

arched [ɑːtʃt] ADJ **1** *Archit (roof, window)* cintré **2** *Anat (back, foot)* cambré; *(eyebrows)* arqué

archeological, archeologically *etc Am* = **archaeological, archaeologically** *etc*

archer [ˈɑːtʃə(r)] N archer *m*; *Astron* **the A.** le Sagittaire

archery [ˈɑːtʃərɪ] N tir *m* à l'arc

archetypal [ˌɑːkɪˈtaɪpəl] ADJ **the a. English village** l'archétype *m* du village anglais

archetype [ˈɑːkɪtaɪp] N archétype *m*

archiepiscopal [ˌɑːkɪɪˈpɪskəpəl] ADJ *Rel* archiépiscopal

Archimedes [ˌɑːkɪˈmiːdiːz] PR N Archimède
▸▸ *Phys* ***Archimedes' principle*** le principe d'Archimède; *Tech* ***Archimedes' screw*** vis *f* d'Archimède

archipelago [ˌɑːkɪˈpelɪgəʊ] *(pl* **archipelagoes** *or* **archipelagos**) N *Geog* archipel *m*

architect [ˈɑːkɪtekt] N architecte *mf*; *Fig* artisan *m*, créateur(trice) *m,f*; **to be the a. of one's own downfall** être l'artisan de sa propre ruine

architectural [ˌɑːkɪˈtektʃərəl] ADJ architectural

architecturally [ˌɑːkɪˈtektʃərəlɪ] ADV au *ou* du point de vue architectural

architecture [ˈɑːkɪtektʃə(r)] N architecture *f*

architrave [ˈɑːkɪtreɪv] N *Archit* architrave *f*

archive [ˈɑːkaɪv] N *(usu pl)* **archives** archives *fpl*; **a national a. of photographs** des archives nationales de photographies
COMP *(photo)* d'archives
VT *(gen) & Comput* archiver
▸▸ *Comput* ***archive copy*** copie *f* archivée; *Comput* ***archive file*** fichier *m* d'archives; *TV* ***archive footage*** extraits *mpl* d'archives; ***archive material*** matériel *m* d'archives; *Comput* ***archive site*** site *m* FTP

archiving [ˈɑːkaɪvɪŋ] N *(gen) & Comput* archivage *m*

archivist [ˈɑːkɪvɪst] N archiviste *mf*

archly [ˈɑːtʃlɪ] ADV **1** *(mischievously)* d'un air espiègle *ou* malicieux; *(say)* d'un ton espiègle *ou* malicieux **2** *(condescendingly)* avec condescendance

archness [ˈɑːtʃnɪs] N **1** *(mischief)* espièglerie *f*, malice *f* **2** *(condescension)* condescendance *f*

archway [ˈɑːtʃweɪ] N porche *m*; *(long)* galerie *f*, arcades *fpl*

arctic [ˈɑːktɪk] ADJ **1** *Met* arctique **2** *Fam (very cold)* glacial
N *Am (overshoe)* couvre-chaussure *m*
• **Arctic** N **the A.** l'Arctique *m*; **an expedition to the A.** une expédition dans l'Arctique
▸▸ ***the Arctic Circle*** le cercle polaire arctique; *Zool* ***Arctic fox*** isatis *m*, renard *m* polaire; ***the Arctic Ocean*** l'(océan *m*) Arctique *m*

arc-weld VT *Tech* souder à l'arc

arc-welding N *Tech* soudure *f* à l'arc

ardent [ˈɑːdənt] ADJ *(desire, love)* passionné, ardent; **an a. admirer** un fervent admirateur

ardently [ˈɑːdəntlɪ] ADV ardemment, passionnément

ardour, *Am* **ardor** [ˈɑːdə(r)] N *(of passion, desire)* ardeur *f*; *(religious)* ferveur *f*

arduous [ˈɑːdjʊəs] ADJ ardu, difficile; *(work, task)* laborieux, pénible; *(path)* ardu, raide; *(hill)* raide, escarpé

arduously [ˈɑːdjʊəslɪ] ADV péniblement, laborieusement

arduousness [ˈɑːdjʊəsnɪs] N difficulté *f*

are[1] [ə(r), *stressed* ɑː(r)] *see* **be**

are[2] [ɑː(r)] N are *m*

area [ˈeərɪə] **N 1** *(surface size)* superficie *f*, aire *f*; **the garden is 500m² in a., the garden has** *or* **covers an a. of 500m²** le jardin a une superficie de 500m²

2 *(region)* territoire *m*, région *f*; *(of town)* zone *f*, quartier *m*; *(of lung, brain, diskette, surface)* zone *f*; **houses were searched over a wide a.** on a fouillé les maisons sur un large périmètre; **we're staying in the Boston a.** nous logeons dans la région de Boston; **in the whole a.** *(neighbourhood)* dans tout le quartier; *(political region)* dans toute la région; **a. of operations** branche *f* d'activité; **residential a.** *(in town)* quartier *m* résidentiel; **industrial/suburban a.** zone *f* industrielle/suburbaine; **cotton (growing)/mining a.** région *f* du coton/minière; **customs a.** territoire *m* douanier; *Fin* **currency a.** zone *f* monétaire; **the Greater London a.** l'agglomération *f* londonienne, le grand Londres; **a. of agreement** terrain *m* d'entente; **growth a.** secteur *m* de croissance; **prohibited** *or* **restricted a.** zone *f* prohibée; *Comput* **storage a.** zone *f* de mémoire; *Transp* **service a.** *(on motorway)* relais *m* d'autoroute; *Ecol* **a. of outstanding natural beauty** = zone naturelle protégée

3 *(part, section)* partie *f*; *(of room)* coin *m*; **living/eating a.** coin *m* salon/salle à manger; **a large kitchen a.** une grande cuisine; **play a.** *(in park)* aire *f* de jeu; **parking a.** parking *m*, aire *m ou Can* terrain *m* de stationnement; **smoking a.** espace *m* fumeurs

4 *(of study, investigation, experience)* domaine *m*, champ *m*; **a. of expertise** domaine *m* de compétence; **problem a.** domaine *m* problématique

COMP *(director, manager, office)* régional

►► *Mil* ***area bombing*** bombardement *m* sur zone; *Tel* ***area code*** indicatif *m* de zone; *Am* ***area rug*** tapis *m*, *Can* carpette *f*; *Mktg* ***area sample*** échantillon *m* par zone; *Mktg* ***area sampling*** échantillonnage *m* par zone

areaway [ˈeərɪəweɪ] **N** *Am* courette *f* en contrebas

areca [ˈærɪkə] **N** *Bot (tree)* aréquier *m*

►► ***areca nut*** noix *f* d'arec; ***areca tree*** aréquier *m*

arena [əˈriːnə] **N** arène *f*; *Fig (economic, international etc)* scène *f*; *Fig* **to enter the a.** entrer dans l'arène; *Fig* **the political a.** l'arène *f* politique

aren't [ɑːnt] **1 = are not 2 aren't I? = am I not?**

Argentina [ˌɑːdʒənˈtiːnə] **N** Argentine *f*

Argentine [ˈɑːdʒəntaɪn] **N 1** *Old-fashioned* **the A.** *(country)* l'Argentine *f* **2** *(person)* Argentin(e) *m,f*

ADJ argentin

Argentinian [ˌɑːdʒənˈtɪnɪən] **N** Argentin(e) *m,f*

ADJ argentin

COMP *(embassy)* d'Argentine; *(history)* de l'Argentine

argon [ˈɑːgɒn] **N** *Chem* argon *m*

Argonaut [ˈɑːgənɔːt] **N** *Myth* **the Argonauts** les Argonautes *mpl*

argot [ˈɑːgəʊ] **N** *Ling* argot *m*

arguable [ˈɑːgjʊəbəl] **ADJ 1** *(questionable)* discutable, contestable; **that's a.** c'est discutable; **it is a. whether it would have made any difference** on peut se demander si cela aurait changé quelque chose **2** *(plausible)* défendable; **it is a. that...** on peut soutenir que...

arguably [ˈɑːgjʊəblɪ] **ADV** possiblement; **the Beatles are a. the most popular group of all time** on pourrait dire *ou* on peut soutenir que les Beatles sont le groupe le plus populaire de tous les temps

argue [ˈɑːgjuː] **VT 1** *(debate)* discuter, débattre; **a well-argued case** une cause bien présentée *ou* défendue; **he argued the case for lower taxes** il a plaidé en faveur d'une baisse des impôts

2 *(persuade)* **he argued me into/out of staying** il m'a persuadé/dissuadé de rester

3 *(maintain)* soutenir, affirmer; **she argues that war is always pointless** elle affirme *ou* soutient que la guerre ne sert jamais à rien

4 *Formal (indicate)* indiquer

VI 1 *(quarrel)* se disputer; **to a. (with sb) about sth** se disputer (avec qn) au sujet de *ou* à propos de qch; **I'm not going to a. about it** *(I refuse to discuss it)* je ne veux pas en discuter; **let's not a.** ne nous disputons pas; **he's always arguing** c'est un argumentateur; **don't a.!** pas de discussion!

2 *(debate)* discuter; *(reason)* argumenter; **she argued for/against raising taxes** elle a soutenu qu'il fallait/ne fallait pas augmenter les impôts; **he argued from the historical aspect** ses arguments étaient de nature historique; **the facts a. for the evolutionary theory** les faits plaident en faveur de la théorie évolutionniste

3 *Law* témoigner; **everything argues in her favour** tout témoigne en sa faveur; **the evidence argues against him** les preuves sont contre lui

► **argue away VT SEP** *(make disappear)* nier l'importance de

► **argue out VT SEP** régler; **I left them to a. it out** je les ai laissés chercher une solution

arguing [ˈɑːgjuːɪŋ] **N that's enough a.** assez discuté; *Fam* **and no a.!** pas de discussion!

argument [ˈɑːgjʊmənt] **N 1** *(quarrel)* dispute *f*; **they had an a. about politics** ils se sont disputés à propos de politique; **to get into an a. (with/about)** se disputer (avec/à propos de); **to obey without a.** obéir sans discuter; *Hum* **he had an a. with a lamppost** il a rencontré un réverbère

2 *(debate)* discussion *f*, débat *m*; **for the sake of a.** à titre d'exemple; **it is open to a. whether...** on peut s'interroger pour savoir si...; **you should listen to both sides of the a.** vous devriez écouter les deux versions de l'histoire; **she got the better of the a.** elle l'a emporté dans la discussion

3 *(reasoning)* argument *m*; **I didn't follow his (line of) a.** je n'ai pas suivi son raisonnement; **there is a strong a. in favour of the proposal** il y a de bonnes raisons pour soutenir *ou* appuyer cette proposition

4 *Literature & Theat (of book, play)* argument *m*, sommaire *m*

argumentative [ˌɑːgjʊˈmentətɪv] **ADJ** *(person)* raisonneur, disposé à argumenter *ou* à disputailler; *(tone)* polémique, agressif; **don't be so a.** arrête de faire le raisonneur

Argy [ˈɑːdʒɪ] **N** *Br Fam* = terme injurieux désignant un Argentin

argy-bargy [ˌɑːdʒɪˈbɑːdʒɪ] **N** *(UNCOUNT) Fam* chamailleries *fpl*; **there was a bit of a. over who should do it** il y a eu des histoires pour savoir qui devait le faire

aria [ˈɑːrɪə] **N** *Mus* aria *f*

arid [ˈærɪd] **ADJ 1** *(dry)* aride **2** *Fig (of no interest)* aride, ingrat; *(fruitless)* stérile

aridity [əˈrɪdɪtɪ] **N** aridité *f*

Aries [ˈeəriːz] **N** *Astron & Astrol* le Bélier; **he's A.., he's an A.** il est (du signe du) Bélier

aright [əˈraɪt] **ADV** bien, correctement; **to set things a.** arranger les choses *ou* la situation

arise [əˈraɪz] *(pt* **arose** [-ˈrəʊz], *pp* **arisen** [-ˈrɪzən]) **VI 1** *(appear, happen)* survenir, se présenter; **if complications should a.** si des complications survenaient; **the question has not yet arisen** la question ne s'est pas encore posée; **if the need arises** en cas de besoin; **should the occasion arise** si l'occasion se présente **2** *(result)* résulter; **a problem that arises from this decision** un problème qui résulte *ou* découle de cette décision **3** *Literary (person)* se lever; *(sun)* se lever, paraître; *(storm)* se lever; **a., Sir John!** *(in knighthood ceremony)* relevez-vous, Sir John; **to a. from the dead** ressusciter (des morts)

aristocracy [ˌærɪˈstɒkrəsɪ] *(pl* **aristocracies**) **N** aristocratie *f*

aristocrat [*Br* ˈærɪstəkræt, *Am* əˈrɪstəkræt] **N** aristocrate *mf*

aristocratic [*Br* ˌærɪstəˈkrætɪk, *Am* əˌrɪstəˈkrætɪk] **ADJ** aristocratique

aristocratically [*Br* ˌærɪstəˈkrætɪkəlɪ, *Am* əˌrɪstəˈkrætɪkəlɪ] **ADV** aristocratiquement

Aristotelian [ˌærɪstɒˈtiːlɪən] *Phil* **N** aristotélicien(enne) *m,f*

ADJ aristotélicien

Aristotle [ˈærɪstɒtəl] **PR N** Aristote

arithmetic **N** [əˈrɪθmətɪk] *(calculations)* calcul *m*; *(subject)* arithmétique *f*; **my a. is absolutely appalling** je suis nul en calcul; **your a. is spot on** tes calculs tombent pile; **it's a simple question of a.** les chiffres parlent d'eux-mêmes

ADJ [ˌærɪθˈmetɪk] arithmétique

arithmetical [ˌærɪθˈmetɪkəl] **ADJ** arithmétique

arithmetically [ˌærɪθˈmetɪkəlɪ] **ADV** arithmétiquement

Ariz *(written abbr* **Arizona**) Arizona *m*

ark [ɑːk] **N** arche *f*; *Br Hum* **this machine must have come out of the a.** cet appareil doit remonter au déluge *ou* est vieux comme le monde; *Bible* **the A. of the Covenant** l'Arche *f* d'alliance

ARM [ˌeɪɑːrˈem] **N** *Am (abbr* **adjustable-rate mortgage**) prêt *m* immobilier à taux variable

arm [ɑːm] **N 1** *(part of the body)* bras *m*; **he carried a book under his a.** il portait un livre sous le bras; **to hold sb/sth in one's arms** tenir qn/qch dans ses bras; **to walk a. in a.** marcher bras dessus bras dessous; **give me your a.** donne-moi le *ou* ton bras; **she flung her arms around my neck** elle s'est jetée à mon cou; **he put his a. round her** il a passé son bras autour d'elle; **with arms folded** les bras croisés; *Fig* **to welcome sb/sth with open arms** accueillir qn/qch à bras ouverts; **within a.'s reach** à portée de la main; *Fig* **to keep sb at a.'s length** tenir qn à distance; **a list as long as your a.** une liste qui n'en finit pas *ou* interminable; **the long a. of the law** le bras de la justice; *Fam* **I'd give my right a. for that job** je donnerais cher *ou* n'importe quoi pour obtenir cet emploi

2 *(of clothing)* manche *f*

3 *Tech (of record player, machinery)* bras *m*; *(of chair)* bras *m*, accoudoir *m*; *(of spectacle frames)* branche *f*

4 *Geog (of sea)* bras *m*

5 *(section)* section *f*, branche *f*; **Sinn Fein is the political a. of the IRA** Sinn Fein est la section politique de l'IRA

VT 1 *(person, country)* armer; *Fig* **armed with an umbrella** muni *ou* armé d'un parapluie; *Fig* **to a. oneself with the facts/evidence** s'armer de faits/preuves **2** *Mil (missile)* munir d'une (tête d') ogive; *(bomb, fuse)* armer

VI s'armer, prendre les armes

►► *Fam* ***arm candy*** = personne qui joue un rôle purement décoratif au bras d'une autre personne; ***arm wrestling*** bras *m* de fer

armada [ɑːˈmɑːdə] **N** *Naut (fleet of warships)* armada *f*

• **Armada N** *Hist* **the (Spanish) A.** l'Invincible Armada *f*

armadillo [ˌɑːməˈdɪləʊ] *(pl* **armadillos**) **N** tatou *m*

Armageddon [ˌɑːməˈgedən] **N** *Bible* Apocalypse *f*; *Fig* apocalypse *f*

armament [ˈɑːməmənt] **N** *Mil* **1** *(weaponry)* armement *m*, matériel *m* de guerre **2** *(preparation for war)* armement *m* **3** *(fighting force)* force *f* de frappe

• **armaments NPL** armement *m*

armature [ˈɑːməˌtjʊə(r)] **N** *Tech (gen)* armature *f*; *(of magnet)* armature *f*; *Elec (of motor)* induit *m*; *Biol* carapace *f*

armband [ˈɑːmbænd] **N** brassard *m*; *(for swimming)* brassard *m*, flotteur *m*; **black a.** brassard *m* de deuil

armchair [ˈɑːmtʃeə(r)] **N** fauteuil *m*

COMP *(gardener, traveller)* en chambre

armed [ɑːmd] **ADJ 1** *(with weapons)* armé; **they were a. with knives** ils étaient armés de couteaux; *Fig* **he arrived a. with pages of statistics** il est arrivé armé *ou* muni de pages entières de statistiques; **a. to the teeth** armé jusqu'aux dents **2** *Mil (missile)* muni d'une (tête d')ogive; *(bomb, fuse)* armé

►► *Mil* ***armed conflict*** conflit *m* armé; *Mil* ***armed forces*** forces *fpl* armées; *Law* ***armed robbery*** vol *m ou* attaque *f* à main armée

Armenia [ɑːˈmiːnɪə] **N** Arménie *f*

Armenian [ɑːˈmiːnɪən] **N 1** *(person)* Arménien(enne) *m,f* **2** *(language)* arménien *m*

ADJ arménien

COMP *(embassy)* d'Arménie; *(history)* de l'Arménie; *(teacher)* d'arménien

armful [ˈɑːmfʊl] **N** brassée *f*; **in armfuls, by the a.** par pleines brassées, par brassées entières

armhole [ˈɑːmhəʊl] **N** emmanchure *f*

armistice [ˈɑːmɪstɪs] **N** *Mil* armistice *m*

►► ***Armistice Day*** l'Armistice *m*

armless [ˈɑːmlɪs] **ADJ** sans bras

armlet [ˈɑːmlɪt] N *(armband)* brassard *m*; *(bracelet)* bracelet *m*

armor, armored *etc Am* = **armour, armoured** *etc*

armorial [ɑːˈmɔːrɪəl] *Her* N armorial *m*
ADJ armorial
▸▸ ***armorial bearings*** armoiries *fpl*

armour, *Am* **armor** [ˈɑːmə(r)] N *(UNCOUNT)* **1** *Hist (of knight etc)* armure *f*; **suit of a.** armure *f* complète; **in full a.** armé de pied en cap
2 *Mil (of vehicle, tank etc)* blindage *m*; *(of ship)* cuirasse *f*, cuirassement *m*, blindage
3 *Mil (units, vehicles)* blindés *mpl*
4 *Zool (of animal)* carapace *f*
▸▸ *Mil* ***armour plate, armour plating*** blindage *m*; *(on ship)* cuirasse *f*

armoured, *Am* **armored** [ˈɑːməd] ADJ **1** *Mil* blindé **2** *(animal)* cuirassé, à carapace
▸▸ ***armoured car*** *Aut* voiture *f* blindée; *Mil* engin *m* blindé de reconnaissance; *Fin (for cash, gold etc)* fourgon *m* blindé; *Mil* ***armoured personnel carrier*** véhicule *m* blindé de transport de troupes

armourer, *Am* **armorer** [ˈɑːmərə(r)] N *Mil & Her* armurier *m*

armour-piercing, *Am* **armor-piercing** ADJ *Mil (mine, gun)* antichar; *(shell, bullet)* perforant

armour-plated, *Am* **armor-plated** ADJ *Mil* blindé

armour-plating, *Am* **armor-plating** N blindage *m*

armoury, *Am* **armory** [ˈɑːmərɪ] *(Br pl* **armouries,** *Am pl* **armories)** N *Mil* arsenal *m*, dépôt *m* d'armes; *Fig (resources)* arsenal *m*; *Am (arms factory)* armurerie *f*, fabrique *f* d'armes

armpit [ˈɑːmpɪt] N aisselle *f*

armrest [ˈɑːmrest] N accoudoir *m*

arms [ɑːmz] NPL **1** *Mil (weapons)* armes *fpl*; **to a.!** aux armes!; **to bear a.** porter les armes; **lay down your a.!** déposez vos armes!; **100,000 men under a.** 100 000 hommes sous les drapeaux; **to take up a. against sb/sth** s'insurger contre qn/qch; **the villagers are up in a. over the planned motorway** la proposition de construction d'une autoroute a provoqué une levée de boucliers parmi les villageois **2** *Her* armes *fpl*, armoiries *fpl*
▸▸ *Pol* ***arms control*** contrôle *m* des armements; *Mil* ***arms dealer*** armurier *m*; ***arms embargo*** embargo *m* sur les armes; *Pol* ***arms limitation*** limitation *f* des armements; *Pol* ***arms manufacturer*** fabricant *m* d'armes, armurier *m*; *Pol* ***arms race*** course *f* aux armements; ***the arms trade*** le commerce d'armes

arm's-length ADJ *(not intimate)* distant, froid; **they have an a. relationship** ils gardent leurs distances
▸▸ *Com* ***arm's-length price*** = prix fixé dans les conditions normales de la concurrence

army [ˈɑːmɪ] *(pl* **armies)** N **1** *Mil* armée *f* (de terre); **to go into** *or* **to join the a.** s'engager; **he was drafted into the a.** il a été appelé sous les drapeaux; **is he in the a.?** est-ce qu'il est militaire *ou* dans l'armée?; **an a. of occupation** une armée d'occupation **2** *Fig (multitude)* foule *f*, multitude *f*; *Entom (of ants)* armée *f*; **there was enough food for an a.** il y avait assez de nourriture pour un régiment; **an a. of tourists descends on the town every summer** une armée de touristes envahit la ville tous les étés
COMP *Mil (life, nurse, truck, uniform)* militaire; *(family)* de militaires
▸▸ *Entom* ***army ant*** fourmi *f* légionnaire; ***army barracks*** caserne *f*, baraquement *m* militaire; *Am* ***army corps*** corps *m* d'armée; *Br Mil* ***Army List*** annuaire *m* militaire *ou* des officiers de carrière *(de l'armée de terre)*; ***army officer*** officier *m* de l'armée de terre

arnica [ˈɑːnɪkə] N *Bot & Pharm* arnica *f*

A-road N *Br* route *f* nationale

aroma [əˈrəʊmə] N arôme *m*

aromatherapist [əˌrəʊməˈθerəpɪst] N aromathérapeute *mf*

aromatherapy [əˌrəʊməˈθerəpɪ] N aromathérapie *f*

aromatic [ˌærəˈmætɪk] N aromate *m*
ADJ *(herb, tea, smell)* aromatique
▸▸ *Chem* ***aromatic compound*** carbure *m* aromatique *ou* à noyau

AROUND [əˈraʊnd]

ADV	
• autour **1**	• pas loin **2**
• ici et là **4**	
PREP	
• autour de **1, 3**	• vers **3**

ADV **1** *(in all directions)* autour; **the fields all a.** les champs tout autour; **for five miles a.** sur *ou* dans un rayon de cinq miles; **people came from miles a.** les gens sont venus de partout *ou* de très loin
2 *(nearby)* pas loin; **stay** *or* **stick a.** reste dans les parages; **he's a. somewhere** il n'est pas loin, il est dans le coin; **will you be a. this afternoon?** tu seras là cet après-midi?; **see you a.!** à un de ces jours!
3 *(in existence)* **that firm has been a. for years** cette société existe depuis des années; **he's one of the most promising actors a. at the moment** c'est un des acteurs les plus prometteurs que l'on puisse voir en ce moment; **there wasn't much money a. in those days** les gens n'avaient pas beaucoup d'argent à l'époque
4 *(here and there)* ici et là; **to travel a.** voyager; **to wander a.** faire un tour; **I still see her a.** il m'arrive encore de la voir; **I don't know my way a. yet** je suis encore un peu perdu; *Fam* **he's been a.** *(has travelled widely)* il a pas mal roulé sa bosse; *(is experienced)* il n'est pas né d'hier
5 *(in circular motion)* **to turn a.** se retourner; **to spin** *or* **whirl** *or* **wheel a.** faire volte-face; **he was waving his arms a.** il gesticulait dans tous les sens
PREP **1** *(encircling)* autour de; **seated a. a table** assis autour d'une table; **the people a. us** les gens qui nous entourent *ou* autour de nous; **the area a. Berlin** les alentours *mpl ou* les environs *mpl* de Berlin; **the tree measures two metres a. the trunk** l'arbre mesure deux mètres de circonférence; *Fig* **find a way (to get) a. the problem** trouvez un moyen de contourner le problème; **my keys are somewhere a. here** mes clés sont quelque part par ici
2 *(within)* **they travelled a. Europe** ils ont voyagé à travers l'Europe; **we strolled a. town** nous nous sommes promenés en ville
3 *(approximately)* autour de; **a. midnight** autour de *ou* vers minuit; **a. five o'clock** vers cinq heures; **a. 1920** vers *ou* aux alentours de 1920; **he's a. your age** il a environ *ou* à peu près votre âge

arousal [əˈraʊzəl] N **1** *(stimulation)* excitation *f*, stimulation *f* **2** *(of interest, suspicion)* éveil *m*; *(of anger)* soulèvement *m*

arouse [əˈraʊz] VT **1** *(stimulate)* stimuler, provoquer; **the sound aroused their curiosity/suspicions** le bruit a éveillé leur curiosité/leurs soupçons; **his pleading aroused their contempt** ses implorations n'ont suscité que leur mépris; **sexually aroused** excité (sexuellement) **2** *(awaken)* réveiller, éveiller; **he aroused her from a deep sleep** il l'a tirée d'un profond sommeil

arpeggio [ɑːˈpedʒɪəʊ] N *Mus* arpège *m*

ARR [ˌeɪɑːˈrɑː(r)] N *Acct (abbr* **accounting rate of return)** taux *m* de rendement comptable

arr. *(written abbr* **arrives)** *(on timetable)* arrive

arrack [ˈærək] N arak *m*, arac *m*, arack *m*

arraign [əˈreɪn] VT *Law* traduire en justice; *Fig* accuser, mettre en cause

arraignment [əˈreɪnmənt] N *Law* **1** *(of person)* mise *f* en accusation *ou* en jugement **2** *(charges)* acte *m* d'accusation

arrange [əˈreɪndʒ] VT **1** *(put in order)* ranger, mettre en ordre; *(clothing, room)* arranger; *(flowers)* arranger, disposer; **the chairs were arranged in a circle** les chaises étaient disposées en cercle; **a. the books in alphabetical order** rangez les livres par ordre alphabétique
2 *(organize, plan)* organiser, arranger; *(date, time)* fixer; **I can a. a loan** je peux m'arranger pour obtenir un prêt; **it has been arranged for us to travel by train** il a été décidé *ou* convenu que nous voyagerions en train; **that can be arranged** cela peut s'arranger; **a. it amongst yourselves** arrangez cela entre vous, entendez-vous là-dessus; **the meeting is arranged for noon tomorrow** la réunion est prévue pour demain midi; **I've got nothing arranged** je n'ai rien de prévu; **here is the first instalment, as arranged** *(money)* voici le premier versement, comme convenu; **don't worry, I'll a. it** ne vous en faites pas, je vais m'en occuper; **everything is arranged** tout est déjà arrangé; **to a. one's affairs** mettre ses affaires en ordre; **to a. a marriage** arranger un mariage
3 *(dispute)* régler, arranger
4 *Mus & Theat* adapter; **he arranged the concerto for guitar** il a adapté le concerto pour la guitare
VI **to a. to do sth** *(make preparations)* s'arranger *ou* prendre ses dispositions pour faire qch; *(with somebody else)* convenir de faire qch; **I've arranged with the boss to leave early tomorrow** je me suis arrangé avec le patron pour partir de bonne heure demain; **we arranged to meet** nous avons prévu de nous rencontrer; **I think I'll a. to be out when he comes** je crois que je m'arrangerai pour être sorti quand il viendra; **he's arranged for the car to be repaired** il a fait le nécessaire pour faire réparer la voiture

arrangement [əˈreɪndʒmənt] N **1** *(usu pl) (plan)* disposition *f*, arrangement *m*; **an a. whereby you pay monthly** un arrangement selon lequel vous effectuez des paiements mensuels; **what are the sleeping arrangements?** où est-ce qu'on dort?; **I've made my own travel arrangements** j'ai déjà organisé mon voyage; **I've made all the arrangements** j'ai tout arrangé; **he made arrangements to leave work early** il s'est arrangé pour quitter son travail de bonne heure
2 *(understanding, agreement)* arrangement *m*; *Fin (with creditors)* accommodement *m*; **we can come to an** *or* **some a. on the price** pour le prix, nous pouvons nous arranger; **he came to an a. with the bank** il est parvenu à un accord avec la banque; **the a. was that I would call you when I arrived** on s'était mis d'accord pour que je t'appelle à mon arrivée; **a private a.** un accord à l'amiable
3 *(layout)* arrangement *m*, disposition *f*; *(of room)* aménagement *m*; *(of clothing, hair)* arrangement *m*
4 *Mus & Theat* adaptation *f*, arrangement *m*
• **by arrangement** ADV **price by a.** prix à débattre; **by prior a.** sur accord préalable; **viewing by a. with the owner** pour visiter, prenez rendez-vous avec *ou* contactez le propriétaire

arranger [əˈreɪndʒə(r)] N *Mus* arrangeur(euse) *m,f*

arrant [ˈærənt] ADJ fini, parfait; **don't talk such a. nonsense** comment est-ce que tu peux dire des bêtises pareilles?

array [əˈreɪ] N **1** *(collection)* ensemble *m* impressionnant, collection *f*; **a distinguished a. of people** une assemblée de gens distingués; **there was a fine a. of cakes in the window** il y avait une belle sélection de gâteaux en vitrine
2 *Law, Comput & Math* tableau *m*, matrice *f*; **an a. of data** un tableau de données
3 *(of solar panels, batteries etc)* série *f*
4 *Mil* rang *m*, ordre *m*; **in battle a.** en ordre de bataille; **in close a.** en rangs serrés
5 *(fine clothes)* parure *f*, atours *mpl*; *(ceremonial dress)* habit *m* d'apparat
VT **1** *(arrange)* disposer, étaler; *Mil (troops)* déployer, disposer **2** *Literary (adorn)* habiller, revêtir; **she was arrayed in silks** elle était vêtue de soie

arrears [əˈrɪəz] NPL *Fin* arriéré *m*; **your a. now amount to over £2,000** vos arriérés s'élèvent maintenant à plus de 2000 livres; **taxes in a.** arriéré *m* d'impôts; **to get into a.** s'arriérer; **we're six months in a. on the loan payments** nous devons six mois de traites; **to be paid a month in a.** être payé un mois après; **she's in a. with her correspondence** elle a du retard dans sa correspondance; **interest on a.** intérêts *mpl* moratoires; **a. of interest** intérêts *mpl* non payés; **a. of work** du travail en retard

arrest [əˈrest] N **1** *(detention)* arrestation *f*; **you're under a.!** vous êtes en état d'arrestation!; **he was put under a.** il a été arrêté; **several arrests were made** plusieurs personnes ont été arrêtées; **to make an a.** *(of police officer)* procéder à une arrestation; *Mil* **to be under a.** être aux arrêts;

open/close a. arrêts mpl simples/de rigueur 2 Formal (sudden stopping) arrêt m, suspension f
VT 1 (person) arrêter, appréhender; Scot (property, ship) saisir 2 Formal (growth, development ▸ halt) arrêter; (▸ slow down) entraver, retarder; in an effort to a. unemployment/inflation pour essayer d'enrayer le chômage/l'inflation; Med arrested development (physical) arrêt m de croissance; (mental) atrophie f de la personnalité; Law to a. judgment surseoir à un jugement, suspendre l'exécution d'un jugement 3 Formal (attention) attirer, retenir
▸▸ Law arrest warrant mandat m d'arrêt

arrester [ə'restə(r)] N Tech intercepteur m, séparateur m

arresting [ə'restɪŋ] ADJ 1 (spectacle, sight) saisissant, frappant 2 Jur the a. officer le policier qui a effectué/qui effectue l'arrestation

arrhythmia [ə'rɪðmɪə] N Med arythmie f

arrival [ə'raɪvəl] N 1 (of person, train, aeroplane etc) arrivée f; on or upon a. à l'arrivée; arrivals and departures les arrivées et les départs mpl
2 (newcomer) a new a. un nouveau venu (une nouvelle venue); (baby) un nouveau-né (une nouveau-née); (book) une dernière parution; late arrivals retardataires mpl
3 Com (of goods) arrivage m
4 (advent) avènement m; the a. of the motor car l'apparition f ou l'avènement m de l'automobile
▸▸ arrivals board tableau m des arrivées; arrivals lounge salon m des arrivées; arrival time heure f d'arrivée

arrive [ə'raɪv] VI 1 (person, train, aeroplane etc) arriver; I've just arrived j'arrive à l'instant; as soon as you a. dès votre arrivée, dès que vous arriverez; as soon as he arrived dès son arrivée; the first post arrives at eight o'clock le premier courrier est à huit heures; the baby arrived three weeks early le bébé est arrivé ou est né avec trois semaines d'avance; to a. on the scene survenir; to a. unexpectedly survenir, arriver à l'improviste; to a. at a decision arriver à ou en venir à ou aboutir à une décision; we arrived at a situation where or in which … nous en sommes arrivés à ou nous avons abouti à une situation dans laquelle … 2 Fam (achieve success) réussir, arriver; you know you've really arrived when… on sait qu'on a vraiment réussi le jour où…

arrogance ['ærəgəns] N arrogance f, morgue f

arrogant ['ærəgənt] ADJ arrogant, insolent

arrogantly ['ærəgəntlɪ] ADV de manière arrogante, avec arrogance

arrogate ['ærəgeɪt] VT Formal 1 (claim unjustly) revendiquer à tort, s'arroger; (victory) s'attribuer 2 (assign unjustly) attribuer injustement (to sb à qn)

arrow ['ærəʊ] N 1 (missile) flèche f; to loose or to shoot or to let fly an a. décocher une flèche; the ball flew as straight as an a. into the net la balle alla voler tout droit dans le filet; as swift as an a. vif comme l'éclair 2 (indicating direction ▸ on sign etc) flèche f; (▸ of surveyor) fiche f 3 Br Fam arrows (darts) fléchettes fpl
VT 1 (indicate ▸ on list) cocher; (▸ on road sign) flécher 2 (in editing) indiquer au moyen d'une flèche
▸▸ Comput arrow key touche f fléchée, touche f de direction; arrow slit (in building) arbalétrière f

arrowhead ['ærəʊhed] N 1 (of arrow) fer m, pointe f de flèche 2 Bot (plant) sagittaire f, flèche f d'eau

arrowroot ['ærəʊru:t] N (plant) marante f; Culin arrow-root m

arse [ɑ:s] Br Vulg N 1 (buttocks) cul m; move or shift your a. pousse ton cul; to get one's a. in(to) gear se remuer le cul; to be out on one's a. (get fired) se faire virer; my a.! mon cul!; kiss my a.! va te faire foutre!; get your a. over here! ramène ta fraise!, amène-toi!; it's my a. that's on the line ça risque de me retomber sur la gueule; he's been sitting on his a. all day il a rien foutu de la journée; he doesn't know his a. from his elbow il est complètement nul; she thinks the sun shines out of her a. elle se prend pas pour de la merde; he fell or went a. over tit or tip or apex il est tombé cul par-dessus tête 2 (person) crétin(e) m,f; to make an a. of oneself se ridiculiser
VT why don't you come with us? – I can't be arsed tu viens avec nous? – non, j'ai trop la flemme; he can't be arsed doing it himself il a pas envie de se faire chier à le faire lui-même
▸ arse about, arse around VI Br Vulg (act foolishly) faire le con, déconner; (waste time) glander, glandouiller

arsehole ['ɑ:shəʊl] N Br Vulg 1 (anus) trou m du cul; the a. of the universe (place) un coin paumé, un trou 2 Fig (stupid person) connard (connasse) m,f; (nasty person) salaud (salope) m,f; don't be such an a. ne sois pas si con

arseholed ['ɑ:shəʊld] ADJ Br Vulg (drunk) bourré comme un coing, complètement pété

arse-licker [-'lɪkə(r)] N Br Vulg lèche-cul m inv

arse-licking N Br Vulg too much a. goes on in this office! il y a un peu trop de lèche-culs dans ce bureau!

arsenal ['ɑ:sənəl] N Mil arsenal m

arsenic ['ɑ:snɪk] N Chem arsenic m
▸▸ arsenic poisoning empoisonnement m à l'arsenic

arsewipe ['ɑ:swaɪp] N Br Vulg (person) raclure f

arsey ['ɑ:si:] ADJ Br Vulg 1 (stupid) débile 2 (bad-tempered) de mauvais poil; she got really a. with me when I asked her for help elle a été super désagréable quand je lui ai demandé de m'aider

arson ['ɑ:sən] N Law incendie m criminel ou volontaire; to commit a. provoquer (volontairement) un incendie; to be charged with a. être accusé d'avoir provoqué un incendie; the police suspect a. la police suspecte un incendie criminel

arsonist ['ɑ:sənɪst] N Law incendiaire mf; (maniac) pyromane mf

art[1] [ɑ:t] N 1 (gen) art m; (school subject) dessin m; she studies a. elle est étudiante en art, elle fait des études d'art; a. for a.'s sake l'art pour l'art; a work of a. une œuvre d'art; arts and crafts artisanat m (d'art) 2 (skill) art m, habileté f; the a. of survival l'art m de survivre; the a. of war l'art m militaire, l'art m de la guerre; it's an a. in itself c'est tout un art; there's an a. to doing that c'est tout un art que de faire cela; she has got cooking down to a real or fine a. la cuisine chez elle, c'est du grand art 3 (cunning) ruse f, artifice m; (trick) artifice m, stratagème m
COMP (collection, critic) d'art; (teacher, class) de dessin
• arts NPL Univ lettres fpl; the arts les beaux-arts mpl; Univ Faculty of Arts (and Letters) faculté f des lettres (et sciences humaines)
▸▸ arts centre centre m culturel; art cinema cinéma m d'art et d'essai; the Arts Council (of Great Britain) = organisme public britannique de promotion des arts; art deco art m déco; art department service m création; Cin & TV art direction direction f artistique; art director directeur (trice) m,f artistique; art exhibition exposition f d'art; arts festival festival m culturel; art form moyen m d'expression artistique; painting is an a. form la peinture est un art; art gallery (museum) musée m d'art; (shop) galerie f d'art; Art nouveau Art m nouveau, modern style m; Typ art paper papier m couché classique; art school école f des Beaux-Arts; art student étudiant(e) m,f en art; Univ arts student étudiant(e) m,f de ou en lettres (et sciences humaines); Psy art therapy art-thérapie m

art[2] Arch or Bible = are

artefact = artifact

arterial [ɑ:'tɪərɪəl] ADJ Anat artériel
▸▸ Br Rail arterial line grande ligne f; Br arterial road route f ou voie f à grande circulation

arteriole [ɑ:'tɪərɪəʊl] N Anat artériole f

arteriosclerosis [ɑ:,tɪərɪəʊsklə'rəʊsɪs] N Med artériosclérose f

artery ['ɑ:tərɪ] (pl arteries) N 1 Anat artère f 2 Transp (road) artère f, route f ou voie f à grande circulation

artesian well [ɑ:'ti:zɪən-] N puits m artésien

artful ['ɑ:tfʊl] ADJ astucieux, habile; (crafty) rusé, malin(igne)
▸▸ artful dodger rusé(e) m,f (du nom d'un jeune voleur habile dans le roman de Dickens 'Oliver Twist')

artfully ['ɑ:tfʊlɪ] ADV (skilfully) habilement, avec finesse; (craftily) astucieusement, avec astuce

artfulness ['ɑ:tfʊlnɪs] N (skill) habileté f, finesse f; (cunning) astuce f, ruse f

arthouse ['ɑ:thaʊs, pl -haʊzɪz] N 1 (gallery) galerie f 2 (cinema) cinéma m d'art et d'essai
COMP Cin (director, producer) de films d'art et d'essai
▸▸ arthouse cinema cinéma m d'art et d'essai; arthouse film film m d'art et d'essai

arthritic [ɑ:'θrɪtɪk] Med N arthritique mf
ADJ arthritique; to have an a. hip avoir de l'arthrite à la hanche

arthritis [ɑ:'θraɪtɪs] N Med arthrite f

arthropod ['ɑ:θrəpɒd] N Entom & Zool arthropode m

arthrosis [ɑ:'θrəʊsɪs] N Med arthrose f

Arthurian [ɑ:'θjʊərɪən] ADJ Myth du roi Arthur

artic [ɑ:'tɪk] N Br Fam (abbr articulated lorry) semi-remorque m

artichoke ['ɑ:tɪtʃəʊk] N artichaut m
▸▸ artichoke hearts cœurs mpl d'artichauts

article ['ɑ:tɪkəl] N 1 (object) objet m; an a. of clothing un vêtement; articles of value des objets mpl de valeur; Fam it's the genuine a.! c'est du vrai de vrai!
2 Press (in press) article m
3 Law (clause, provision) article m; the articles of a contract les stipulations fpl d'un contrat; Br to do or to serve one's articles faire son apprentissage
4 Gram article m
5 Com article m, marchandise f
6 Comput (in newsgroups) article m
VT Br Com & Ind (to trade) mettre en apprentissage; (to profession) mettre en stage; to a. sb to a tradesman mettre qn en apprentissage chez un commerçant
▸▸ Law articles of apprenticeship contrat m d'apprentissage; Com articles of association statuts mpl (d'une société à responsabilité limitée); Rel article of faith article m de foi; Am Law articles of incorporation écriture f de constitution; Am Mil articles of war code m de justice militaire

articulate ADJ [ɑ:'tɪkjʊlət] 1 (writing, speech) clair, net; to be a. (person) s'exprimer facilement ou avec facilité; the child gave a very a. account l'enfant a fait un compte rendu très clair 2 (manner of speech) bien articulé, distinct 3 Anat & Bot articulé
VT [ɑ:'tɪkjʊleɪt] 1 (words, syllables) articuler; he doesn't a. his words il n'articule pas 2 Fig (wishes, thoughts) exprimer clairement 3 Anat & Bot articuler
VI [ɑ:'tɪkjʊleɪt] articuler

articulated [ɑ:'tɪkjʊleɪtɪd] ADJ
▸▸ articulated bus autobus m à soufflet; Br articulated lorry semi-remorque f

articulately [ɑ:'tɪkjʊlətlɪ] ADV Ling (speak) distinctement; (explain) clairement; as you so a. put it comme vous l'avez si bien exprimé

articulateness [ɑ:'tɪkjʊlətnɪs] N Ling 1 (of person) facilité f d'expression; (of writing, speech) clarté f 2 (manner of speech) articulation f nette, netteté f d'énonciation

articulation [ɑ:,tɪkjʊ'leɪʃən] N 1 Anat, Bot & Ling articulation f 2 Ling (of thought) expression f

artifact ['ɑ:tɪfækt] N objet m (fabriqué)

artifice ['ɑ:tɪfɪs] N 1 (trick) artifice m, ruse f, (scheme) stratagème m 2 (cleverness) art m, adresse f

artificial [,ɑ:tɪ'fɪʃəl] ADJ 1 (man-made) artificiel; Com synthétique, artificiel; a. flowers fleurs fpl artificielles 2 (affected ▸ person) factice, étudié; (sourire) forcé; she is very a. elle manque de naturel
▸▸ artificial fertilizer engrais m chimique; artificial flavouring parfum m artificiel ou synthétique; Astron artificial horizon horizon m artificiel; artificial insemination insémination f artificielle; Comput artificial intelligence intelligence f artificielle; Elec artificial light la lumière

artificielle; ***artificial limb*** prothèse *f*, membre *m* artificiel; *Med* ***artificial respiration*** respiration *f* artificielle; **to give sb a. respiration** faire la respiration artificielle à qn; ***artificial sweetener*** édulcorant *m* (de synthèse)

artificiality [ˌɑːtɪfɪʃɪ'ælətɪ] **N** manque *m* de naturel

artificially [ˌɑːtɪ'fɪʃəlɪ] **ADV** artificiellement; **the exchange rate is a. high at the moment** le taux de change est maintenu artificiellement à un niveau élevé

artillery [ɑː'tɪlərɪ] (*pl* **artilleries**) **N** *Mil* artillerie *f*
▸▸ ***artillery fire*** tir *m* d'artillerie; ***artillery regiment*** régiment *m* d'artillerie; ***artillery shell*** obus *m*

artilleryman [ɑː'tɪlərɪmən] (*pl* **artillerymen** [-mən]) **N** *Mil* artilleur *m*

artisan [ˌɑːtɪ'zæn] **N** artisan *m*

artist ['ɑːtɪst] **N** *(actor, painter, singer)* artiste *mf*; **he is an a.** *(painter)* il est artiste, il est peintre; *(footballer, athlete)* c'est un véritable artiste; **a.'s impression** vue *f* d'artiste

> Note that the French word **artiste** is not restricted to the contexts of painting or drawing and is used to describe someone who practises any kind of art.

artiste [ɑː'tiːst] **N** artiste *mf*

artistic [ɑː'tɪstɪk] **ADJ** artistique; *(design, product)* de bon goût, décoratif; *(style, temperament)* artiste; **she is an a. child** cette enfant a des dons artistiques; **she came from an a. family** elle venait d'une famille d'artistes; **I'm not at all a.** je n'ai aucune inclination artistique, je n'ai pas la fibre artistique
▸▸ *Cin & Theat* ***artistic director*** directeur(trice) *m,f* artistique

artistically [ɑː'tɪstɪkəlɪ] **ADV 1** *(tastefully)* avec art, artistiquement **2** *(from an artistic point of view)* d'un point de vue artistique

artistry ['ɑːtɪstrɪ] **N** art *m*, talent *m* artistique

artless ['ɑːtlɪs] **ADJ 1** *(natural)* naturel, ingénu; **with an a. smile** avec un sourire candide **2** *(naive)* naïf, ingénu **3** *(without skill)* grossier

artlessly ['ɑːtlɪslɪ] **ADV 1** *(naturally)* naturellement, sans artifice **2** *(naively)* naïvement, ingénument

artlessness ['ɑːtlɪsnɪs] **N 1** *(naturalness)* naturel *m*, simplicité *f* **2** *(naivety)* naïveté *f*, ingénuité *f*

artwork ['ɑːtwɜːk] **N 1** *(illustrations)* iconographie *f*, illustrations *fpl* **2** *Typ* documents *mpl*

arty ['ɑːtɪ] (*compar* **artier**, *superl* **artiest**) **ADJ** *Fam* **1** *(person, style, job, furniture)* artistique□; *(existence)* bohème□ **2** *Pej (person)* qui se veut artiste□; *(object, film, style)* prétentieux□; **he's an a. type** c'est le genre artiste; **the a. set** le milieu artiste

arty-crafty [-'krɑːftɪ] **ADJ** *Fam Pej (person)* qui se veut artiste *ou* bohème□; *(object, style)* bohème□, qui se veut artisanal□

arty-farty [-'fɑːtɪ], *Am* **artsy-fartsy** [ˌɑːtsɪˌfɑːtsɪ] **ADJ** *Fam Pej (person)* prétentieux□, poseur□; *(play, film)* prétentieux□

arugula [ə'ruːgələ] **N** *Am Bot & Culin* roquette *f*

arum ['eərəm] **N** *Bot* arum *m*
▸▸ ***arum lily*** calla *f*

arvo ['ɑːvəʊ] **N** *Austr Fam (afternoon)* après-midi□ *m or f*, aprème *m or f*

Aryan ['eərɪən] *Ling* **N** Aryen(enne) *m,f*
ADJ aryen

AS [əz, *stressed* æz]

> **CONJ**
> • alors que **1** • comme **2**
> • puisque **3** • que **5**
> **PREP**
> • en tant que, comme
> **ADV**
> • aussi

CONJ 1 *(while)* alors que; **the phone rang as I was coming in** le téléphone s'est mis à sonner alors que *ou* au moment où j'entrais; **I listened as she explained the plan to them** je l'ai écoutée leur expliquer le projet; **as he advanced, I retreated** (au fur et) à mesure qu'il avançait, je reculais; **take two aspirins as needed** prenez deux aspirines en cas de douleur

2 *(like)* comme, ainsi que; **A as in Abel** A comme Anatole; **as usual** comme d'habitude; **as shown by the unemployment rate** comme *ou* ainsi que le montre le taux de chômage; **as they say,...** comme on dit,...; **as often happens** comme il arrive souvent, ainsi qu'il arrive souvent; **as it is, we must...** les choses étant ainsi, il nous faut...; **she is a doctor, as is her sister** elle est médecin comme sa sœur; **why should I do as he says?** pourquoi devrais-je faire ce qu'il dit?; **do as you see fit** faites comme bon vous semble; **leave it as it is** laissez-le tel qu'il est *ou* tel quel; **to buy sth as is** acheter qch en l'état; *Mil* **as you were!** repos!

3 *(since)* puisque; **let her drive, as it's her car** laissez-la conduire, puisque c'est sa voiture; **as you're the one in charge, you'd better be there** étant donné que c'est vous le responsable, il faut que vous soyez là

4 *Formal (concessive use)* **old as I am, I can still keep up with them** malgré mon âge, j'arrive à les suivre; **try as they might, they couldn't persuade her** malgré tous leurs efforts, ils n'ont pu la convaincre

5 *(with "the same", "such")* **I had the same problems as you did** j'ai eu les mêmes problèmes que toi; **at the same time as last week** à la même heure que la semaine dernière; **such a problem as only an expert can solve** un problème que seul un expert peut résoudre

PREP en tant que, comme; **I advised him as his friend, not as his teacher** je l'ai conseillé en tant qu'ami, pas en tant que professeur; **to use sth as a flag** se servir de qch comme drapeau *ou* en guise de drapeau; **as her husband, he cannot testify** étant son mari, il ne peut pas témoigner; **he was dressed as a clown** il était habillé en clown; **as a student, he worked part-time** lorsqu'il était étudiant, il travaillait à mi-temps; **to act as interpreter** servir d'interprète; **with Vivien Leigh as Scarlett O'Hara** avec Vivien Leigh dans le rôle de Scarlett O'Hara

ADV *(in comparisons)* **it's twice as big** c'est deux fois plus grand; **it costs half as much again** ça coûte la moitié plus; **as... as** aussi... que; **he's as intelligent as his brother** il est aussi intelligent que son frère; **he isn't as talented as you (are)** il n'est pas aussi doué que vous; **as often as possible** aussi souvent que possible; **not as often as I would like** pas aussi souvent que je voudrais; **as white as a sheet** blanc comme un linge; **as recently as last week** pas plus tard que la semaine dernière; **they aren't as innocent as they look** ils ne sont pas aussi innocents qu'ils en ont l'air; **I worked as much for you as for me** j'ai travaillé autant pour toi que pour moi

• **as against PREP** contre; **he received 39 votes as against the 17 for his rival** il a obtenu 39 votes contre 17 pour son adversaire

• **as and when CONJ we'll buy new equipment as and when it's required** nous achèterons du nouveau matériel en temps voulu *ou* quand ce sera nécessaire **ADV** *Fam* en temps voulu□; **you'll be sent the money as and when** on vous enverra l'argent en temps voulu

• **as for PREP** quant à; **as for me, I don't intend to go** pour ma part *ou* quant à moi, je n'ai pas l'intention d'y aller; **as for your threats, they don't scare me in the least** pour ce qui est de *ou* quant à vos menaces, elles ne me font pas peur du tout

• **as from PREP** à partir de; **as from tomorrow** à partir de demain; **as from yesterday** depuis hier

• **as if CONJ** comme si; **he looks as if he's drunk** on dirait qu'il est soûl; **he carried on as if nothing had happened** il a continué comme si de rien n'était *ou* comme s'il ne s'était rien passé; **as if by chance** comme par hasard; **he moved as if to strike him** il a fait un mouvement comme pour le frapper; **it's not as if she were my sister** ce n'est quand même pas comme si c'était ma sœur; **as if it mattered!** comme si ça avait aucune importance!; *Hum* **as if!** tu parles!; **he said he would do it – as if!** il a dit qu'il le ferait – mon œil!

• **as it is ADV 1** *(in present circumstances)* les choses étant ce qu'elles sont; **she's hoping for promotion, but as it is there's little chance of that** elle espère obtenir une promotion, mais dans la situation actuelle *ou* les choses étant ce qu'elles sont, il est peu probable que cela arrive

2 *(already)* déjà; **you've got enough work as it is** vous avez déjà assez de travail, vous avez assez de travail comme ça

• **as it were ADV** pour ainsi dire

• **as of PREP** à partir de; **as of tomorrow** à partir de demain; **as of yesterday** depuis hier; **as of next week I'll be unemployed** je serai au chômage à partir de la semaine prochaine

• **as such ADV 1** *(properly speaking)* véritablement, à proprement parler; **it's not a contract as such, more a gentleman's agreement** ce n'est pas un véritable contrat *ou* pas un contrat à proprement parler *ou* pas véritablement un contrat, mais plutôt un accord entre hommes de parole

2 *(in itself)* même, en soi; **the place as such isn't great** l'endroit même *ou* en soi n'est pas terrible

3 *(in that capacity)* à ce titre, en tant que tel; **I'm his father and as such, I insist on knowing** je suis son père et à ce titre j'insiste pour qu'on me mette au courant

• **as though CONJ** comme si; **he looks as though he's drunk** on dirait qu'il est soûl; **he carried on as though nothing had happened** il a continué comme si de rien n'était *ou* comme s'il ne s'était rien passé

• **as to PREP** *(regarding)* **to question sb as to his/her motives** interroger qn sur ses motifs; **I'm still uncertain as to the nature of the problem** j'hésite encore sur la nature du problème; **as to that** quant à cela, pour cela

• **as well ADV 1** *(in addition)* en plus; *(also)* aussi; **I'd like one as well** j'en voudrais un aussi; **he bought the house and the land as well** il a acheté la maison et la propriété aussi; **and then the car broke down as well!** et par-dessus le marché la voiture est tombée en panne!

2 *(with modal verbs)* **you may as well tell me the truth** autant me dire *ou* tu ferais aussi bien de me dire la vérité; **now that we're here, we might as well stay** puisque nous sommes là, autant rester; **shall we go to the cinema? – we might as well** et si on allait au cinéma? – pourquoi pas?; **she was angry, as well she might be** elle était furieuse, et ça n'est pas surprenant; **perhaps I'd better leave – that might be as well** peut-être vaudrait-il mieux que je m'en aille – je crois que ça vaut mieux; **it would be as well not to break it** ce serait mieux si on pouvait éviter de le casser; **I decided not to write back – just as well really** j'ai décidé de ne pas répondre – c'est mieux comme ça; **it's just as well he missed his flight** c'est une bonne chose qu'il ait manqué l'avion

• **as well as CONJ** *(in addition to)* en plus de; **so she's a liar as well as a thief** alors comme ça, c'est une menteuse en plus d'être une voleuse; **Jim looks after the children as well as helping around the house** Jim s'occupe des enfants en plus de participer au ménage

• **as yet ADV** encore; **I don't have the answer as yet** je n'ai pas encore la réponse; **an as yet undisclosed sum** une somme qui n'a pas encore été révélée

ASA [ˌeɪes'eɪ] **N 1** *Br* (*abbr* **Advertising Standards Authority**) BVP *m*
2 (*abbr* **American Standards Association**) association *f* américaine de normalisation, AFNOR *f*
3 *Phot* (*abbr* **American Standards Association**) ASA *f*; **an A. 100 film, a 100 A. film** une pellicule 100 ASA
4 *Br* (*abbr* **Amateur Swimming Association**) fédération *f* de natation

asap [ˌeɪeseɪ'piː] **ADV** (*abbr* **as soon as possible**) aussitôt *ou* dès que possible; **we need to reply a.** il faut qu'on réponde dès que possible

asbestos [æs'bestəs] **N** amiante *f*, asbeste *f*
COMP *(board, cord)* d'amiante
▸▸ ***asbestos dust*** poudre *f* d'amiante; ***asbestos matting*** plaque *f* d'amiante

asbestosis [ˌæsbes'təʊsɪs] **N** *Med* asbestose *f*

ASBO, Asbo ['æsˌbəʊ] **N** *Br* (*abbr* **Antisocial Behaviour Order**) = injonction contre une personne coupable de harcèlement ou de tout autre comportement antisocial à l'encontre d'autres personnes

ASBO

ASBO (ou Asbo) est l'acronyme de "Antisocial Behaviour Order". Il s'agit d'un nouveau type de condamnation prononcée par des juges de proximité à la demande d'institutions locales (écoles, organismes HLM, municipalités...) et qui sanctionne des actes du type larcins, tapage nocturne, harcèlement ou vandalisme. Les injonctions sont adaptées au type de comportement antisocial manifesté par le délinquant, et prennent le plus souvent la forme d'interdictions de fréquenter tel ou tel lieu, de se trouver sur la voie publique après une certaine heure, d'écouter de la musique trop fort, de proférer des injures ou des menaces, etc. Les ASBO ne font pas l'unanimité chez les Britanniques; en effet, certains estiment que les municipalités ont tendance à en abuser et à ne pas toujours les utiliser à bon escient.

ascend [ə'send] VT *(stairs)* monter; *(ladder)* monter à; *(mountain)* gravir, faire l'ascension de; *(river)* remonter; *(throne)* monter sur

VI monter

ascendancy [ə'sendənsɪ] N ascendant *m*, empire *m*; **Japan has gained a. over its competitors in the electronics market** le Japon domine ses concurrents sur le marché de l'électronique

ascendant [ə'sendənt] ADJ dominant, puissant; *Astrol & Astron* ascendant

N *Astrol* ascendant *m*; **his star is in the a.** son étoile est à l'ascendant; *Fig* **his business is in the a.** ses affaires prospèrent

ascender [ə'sendə(r)] N **1** *Sport (in mountaineering)* ascendeur *m*, autobloqueur *m* **2** *Typ* hampe *f* montante

ascending [ə'sendɪŋ] ADJ **1** *(rising)* ascendant **2** *(increasing)* **in a. order** en ordre croissant **3** *Bot* montant

►► *Mus* ***ascending scale*** gamme *f* ascendante *ou* montante; ***ascending series*** progression *f* croissante; *Comput* ***ascending sort*** tri *m* en ordre croissant

ascension [ə'senʃən] N ascension *f*; **her a. to the throne** son élévation *f* sur le trône

• **Ascension** N **1** *Geog* île *f* de l'Ascension **2** *Rel* **the A.** l'Ascension *f*

►► *Rel* ***Ascension Day*** jour *m ou* fête *f* de l'Ascension; ***Ascension Island*** île *f* de l'Ascension

ascent [ə'sent] N **1** *(of mountain)* ascension *f*

2 *(incline)* montée *f*

3 *(in time)* retour *m*; **the line of a.** l'ascendance *f*

4 *(in rank)* montée *f*, avancement *m*

5 his a. to power son ascension jusqu'au pouvoir

Attention: ne pas confondre avec **assent**.

ascertain [,æsə'teɪn] VT *Formal (facts)* établir, déterminer; **the police ascertained their names and addresses** la police a vérifié leurs nom et adresse; **to a. that sth is the case** vérifier *ou* s'assurer que qch est vrai; **are we to a. from this that...?** devons-nous en déduire que...?; **he ascertained that it was safe to continue** il s'est assuré qu'on pouvait continuer sans danger

ascertainable [,æsə'teɪnəbəl] ADJ *Formal (information, fact)* qui peut être déterminé; *(truth)* vérifiable

ascertainment [,æsə'teɪnmənt] N *Formal (of information, fact)* détermination *f*; *(of truth)* vérification *f*

ascetic [ə'setɪk] *Rel & Fig* N ascète *mf*

ADJ ascétique

ascetically [ə'setɪkəlɪ] ADV *Rel (live)* comme un/une ascète

asceticism [ə'setɪsɪzəm] N *Rel* ascétisme *m*

ASCII ['æskɪ] N *Comput (abbr* **American Standard Code for Information Interchange**) ASCII *m*; **in A.** en ASCII

►► ***ASCII code*** code *m* ASCII

ascorbic acid [ə'skɔ:bɪk-] N *Chem* acide *m* ascorbique

ascribable [ə'skraɪbəbəl] ADJ attribuable (**to** à); *(fault, blame)* imputable (**to** à)

ascribe [ə'skraɪb] VT attribuer (**to** à); *(fault, blame)* imputer (**to** à); **this painting is sometimes ascribed to Millet** on attribue parfois ce tableau à Millet

ascription [ə'skrɪpʃən] N *Rel* attribution *f*; *(of fault, blame)* imputation *f*

asdic ['æzdɪk] N *Naut* asdic *m*

ASEAN [,eɪes,i:eɪ'en] N *(abbr* **Association of South-east Asian Nations**) ANASE *f*

asepsis [,eɪ'sepsɪs] N *Med* asepsie *f*

aseptic [,eɪ'septɪk] ADJ *Med* aseptique

asexual [,eɪ'sekʃʊəl] ADJ asexué; *Bot (flower)* neutre

►► *Biol* ***asexual reproduction*** reproduction *f* asexuée

ash [æʃ] N **1** *(from fire, cigarette)* cendre *f*; **he dropped a. on the carpet** il a laissé tomber sa cendre sur la moquette; **the fire reduced the house to ashes** l'incendie a réduit la maison en cendres; *Rel* **ashes to ashes, dust to dust** tu es poussière, et tu retourneras en poussière; **to rise from the ashes** renaître de ses cendres **2** *(colour)* cendré *m*, gris cendré *m (inv)* **3** *(tree, wood)* frêne *m*

• **Ashes** NPL *Sport (in cricket)* = trophée que les équipes anglaises et australiennes se disputent

►► ***ash bin*** *(for ashes)* cendrier *m*; *(for rubbish)* poubelle *f*, boîte *f* à ordures; *Rel* ***Ash Wednesday*** mercredi *m* des Cendres

THE ASHES

The Ashes (les cendres) est le nom d'une compétition de cricket qui se joue tous les deux ans entre l'Angleterre et l'Australie, ainsi que le nom du trophée que remporte l'équipe gagnante. Ce trophée est une urne qui contient les cendres d'une barre horizontale de guichet (d'où le nom "Ashes"). En 2005, l'Angleterre a gagné les Ashes pour la première fois depuis 1987; la victoire a été fêtée dans tout le pays et les joueurs ont acquis le statut de héros nationaux.

ashamed [ə'ʃeɪmd] ADJ confus, honteux; **to be a. (of oneself)** avoir honte; **to be a. of sb/sth** avoir honte de qn/qch; **to feel a.** être honteux *ou* confus; **he's a. of his behaviour/of having cried** il a honte de sa conduite/d'avoir pleuré; **I'm a. of you** j'ai honte de toi, tu me fais honte; **I'm a. to say that...** j'avoue à ma grande honte que...; **I'm not a. to admit it** je l'admets sans honte; **you ought to be a. of yourself** tu devrais avoir honte; **there is nothing to be a. of** il n'y a pas de quoi avoir honte

A-share N *St Exch* action *f* ordinaire sans droit de vote

ash-blond, ash-blonde N *(colour)* blond *m* cendré; **she's an a.** elle a les cheveux blond cendré

ADJ blond cendré *(inv)*

ashcan ['æʃkæn] N *Am* boîte *f* à ordures, poubelle *f*

ashen ['æʃən] ADJ *Literary (ash-coloured)* cendré, couleur de cendres; *(face)* blême, livide

ashen-faced ADJ *Literary* blême, livide

ashlar ['æʃlə(r)] N **1** *Miner (stone)* pierre *f* de taille **2** *Constr (facing)* parements *mpl*, revêtement *m*

ashore [ə'ʃɔ:(r)] ADV à terre; **he swam a.** il a nagé jusqu'à la rive; **debris from the wreck was washed a.** des morceaux de l'épave ont été rejetés sur la côte; *Naut* **to go a.** débarquer; *Naut* **the ship put the passengers a. at Plymouth** le navire a débarqué les passagers à Plymouth

ADJ à terre

ashpan ['æʃpæn] N *(for stove)* cendrier *m*

ashtanga [æʃ'tæŋgə] N **a. (yoga)** ashtanga yoga *m*, yoga *m* ashtanga

ashtray ['æʃtreɪ] N cendrier *m*

ashy ['æʃɪ] *(compar* **ashier**, *superl* **ashiest**) ADJ **1** *(ash-coloured)* cendré, couleur de cendre; *(pale)* blême, livide **2** *(covered with ashes)* couvert de cendres

Asia ['eɪʒə, 'eɪʃə] N Asie *f*

►► ***Asia Minor*** Asie *f* Mineure

Asian ['eɪʒən, 'eɪʃən] N Asiatique *mf*; *(Indian)* Indien(enne) *m,f*; *(Pakistani)* Pakistanais(e) *m,f*

ADJ asiatique; *(Indian)* indien; *(Pakistani)* pakistanais

►► ***Asian American***

N Américain(e) *m,f* d'origine asiatique

ADJ américain d'origine asiatique; *Fam* ***Asian babe*** Indienne *f*/Pakistanaise *f*/Orientale *f* super belle; ***Asian buffalo*** buffle *f* d'Asie, arni *m*; *Med* ***Asian flu*** grippe *f* asiatique; ***Asian pear*** *(fruit)* pomme-poire *f*, poire *f* asiatique, nashi *m*; *(tree)* nashi *m*

ASIAN

Pour les Britanniques, "Asian" désigne le plus souvent les habitants de l'Inde et des pays limitrophes: ainsi, l'expression "the Asian community in Birmingham" fait référence aux personnes d'origine indienne, pakistanaise et bangladaise qui habitent Birmingham.

Asiatic [,eɪʒɪ'ætɪk, ,eɪʃɪ'ætɪk] N Asiatique *mf*

ADJ asiatique

A-side N face *f* A *(d'un disque)*

aside [ə'saɪd] ADV de côté, à part; **she held a. the curtains** elle écarta les rideaux; **stand a.!** écartez-vous!; **I stepped a. to let her pass** je me suis écarté pour la laisser passer; **he took her a.** il l'a prise à part; **we've been putting money a. for the trip** nous avons mis de l'argent de côté pour le voyage; **would you put this dress a. for me?** pourriez-vous me mettre cette robe de côté *ou* me réserver cette robe?; **these problems a., we have been very successful** à part ces problèmes, ce fut un véritable succès; **(leaving) politics a., I think...** si on laisse de côté la politique, je pense...

N aparté *m*; **he said something to her in an a.** il lui a dit quelque chose en aparté; **(purely) as an a.** soit dit entre nous

• **aside from** PREP **1** *(except for)* sauf **2** *Am (as well as)* en plus de

asinine ['æsɪnaɪn] ADJ **1** *(person, behaviour)* stupide, sot (sotte) **2** *(like an ass)* asinien

ask [ɑ:sk] VT **1** *(for opinion, information)* **to a. sb sth** demander qch à qn; **I asked her the time** je lui ai demandé l'heure; **she asked him about his job** elle lui a posé des questions sur son travail; **may I a. you a question?** puis-je vous poser une question?; **if you a. me** si vous voulez mon avis; *Fam* **but how? I a. you!** mais comment? je vous le demande!; *Fam* **don't a. me!** est-ce que je sais, moi?; *Fam* **no one asked you!** on ne t'a rien demandé!

2 *(request)* demander, solliciter; **he asked them a favour** il leur a demandé un service; **to a. sb to do sth** demander à qn de faire qch; **I asked them to be quiet** je leur ai demandé de se taire; **a. him to wait/to come in** priez-le d'attendre/d'entrer; **that's asking a lot** c'est beaucoup demander; **to a. 600 euros for sth** demander 600 euros pour *ou* de qch; **what are you asking for it?** combien en voulez-vous *ou* demandez-vous?

3 *(invite)* inviter; **they asked her to join them** ils l'ont invitée à se joindre à eux; **he asked her to the pictures** il l'a invitée au cinéma; **she asked us up** elle nous a invités à monter

VI demander; **all you have to do is a.!** il n'y a qu'à demander!; **he was asking about the job** il s'informait *ou* se renseignait sur le poste; **I was only asking!** je ne faisais que demander!

►► *St Exch* ***ask price*** cours *m* offert, cours *m* vendeur

▸ **ask after** VT INSEP **she asked after you** elle a demandé de vos nouvelles; **I asked after her health** je me suis informé de sa santé

▸ **ask around** VI se renseigner; **I asked around about cheap flights** je me suis renseigné sur les vols pas chers

▸ **ask back** VT SEP *(invite again)* réinviter; *(for reciprocal visit)* inviter; **she asked us back for dinner** elle nous a rendu l'invitation à dîner

▸ **ask for** VT INSEP demander; **they asked for some water** ils ont demandé de l'eau; **to a. for sb** demander à voir qn; *(on the telephone)* demander à parler à qn; **you're asking for the moon** vous demandez la lune; **she asked for her book back** elle a demandé qu'on lui rende son livre; **you're just asking for trouble!** tu cherches des ennuis!; **he**

was asking for it! il l'a cherché!; **she left him – he was asking for it** elle l'a quitté – il l'a voulu, il l'a eu!

▸ **ask in** VT SEP inviter à entrer; **he asked us in for a drink** il nous a invités à (entrer) prendre un verre

▸ **ask out** VT SEP inviter à sortir; **they asked us out for dinner/to the theatre** ils nous ont invités au restaurant/au théâtre

▸ **ask round** VT SEP inviter (à venir); **we must a. him round soon** nous devrions l'inviter un de ces jours

askance [ə'skæns] ADV **1** *(with distrust)* **to look a. at sb/sth** regarder qn/qch avec méfiance; **he looked a. at her** il l'a regardée d'un air méfiant **2** *(disapprovingly)* **to look a. at sb** regarder qn de travers

askew [ə'skju:] ADV obliquement, de travers
ADJ *Am* **something's a. here** il y a quelque chose qui cloche

asking ['ɑ:skɪŋ] N **it's yours for the a.** il n'y a qu'à (le) demander; **it was theirs for the a.** ils n'ont eu qu'à demander
▸▸ ***asking price*** *Fin* prix *m* de départ, prix *m* demandé; *Am St Exch* cours *m* offert, cours *m* vendeur

aslant [ə'slɑ:nt] PREP en travers de
ADV de travers, de *ou* en biais

asleep [ə'sli:p] ADJ endormi; **to be a.** dormir; **to be fast** *or* **sound a.** dormir profondément *ou* à poings fermés; **to fall a.** s'endormir; **you're half a.** tu dors à moitié, tu es à moitié endormi; **he's a. on his feet** il dort debout

ASLEF ['æzlef] N *Rail* (*abbr* **Associated Society of Locomotive Engineers and Firemen**) = syndicat des cheminots en Grande-Bretagne

ASM [ˌeɪes'em] N **1** *Mil* (*abbr* **air-to-surface missile**) ASM *m* **2** *Theat* (*abbr* **assistant stage manager**) régisseur *m* général

as-new ADJ comme neuf

asocial [ˌeɪ'səʊʃəl] ADJ asocial

asp [æsp] N **1** *Zool* aspic *m* **2** *Arch Bot* tremble *m*

asparagus [ə'spærəgəs] N *(UNCOUNT)* asperges *fpl*; **a piece** *or* **spear of a.** une asperge
▸▸ ***asparagus fern*** asparagus *m*; ***asparagus soup*** soupe *f* aux asperges; ***asparagus tips*** pointes *fpl* d'asperges

aspect ['æspekt] N **1** *(of problem, subject)* aspect *m*, côté *m*; **we should examine all aspects of the problem** nous devrions étudier le problème sous tous ses aspects
2 *Literary (appearance)* air *m*, aspect *m*; **a young man of (a) serious a.** un jeune homme à la mine sérieuse
3 *(outlook)* orientation *f*, exposition *f*; **a house with a northern/southern a.** une maison exposée au nord/sud
4 *Astrol (of planets)* aspect *m*
5 *Gram* aspect *m*
▸▸ *Cin* ***aspect ratio*** rapport *m* hauteur/largeur, format *m* de l'image

aspen ['æspən] N *Bot* tremble *m*

Asperger's syndrome ['æsˌpɜ:gəz-] N *Med* syndrome *m* d'Asperger

asperity [æ'sperɪtɪ] (*pl* **asperities**) N *Formal* **1** *(of manner, voice)* aspérité *f* **2** *(of person)* rudesse *f* **3** *(of climate)* rigueur *f*

aspersions [ə'spɜ:ʃənz] NPL **to cast a. on sb** dénigrer qn; **he cast a. on her honour** il a porté atteinte à son honneur

asphalt ['æsfælt] *Constr* N asphalte *m*
COMP *(road, roof)* asphalté
VT asphalter
▸▸ ***asphalt jungle*** jungle *f* urbaine

asphalting ['æsfæltɪŋ] N *Constr* asphaltage *m*

asphyxia [əs'fɪksɪə] N *Med* asphyxie *f*

asphyxiate [əs'fɪksɪeɪt] *Med* VT asphyxier
VI s'asphyxier

asphyxiation [əsˌfɪksɪ'eɪʃən] N *Med* asphyxie *f*; **to die by** *or* **of a.** mourir d'asphyxie

aspic ['æspɪk] N *Culin* gelée *f*; **eggs in a.** œufs *mpl* en aspic; **salmon in a.** aspic *m* de saumon; *Fig* **preserved in a.** mis sous verre

aspidistra [ˌæspɪ'dɪstrə] N *Bot* aspidistra *m*

aspirant ['æspɪrənt] N candidat(e) *m,f*; **a. to the throne** prétendant *m* au trône
ADJ **a. journalists/diplomats** les gens qui aspirent à devenir journalistes/diplomates

aspirate *Ling* VT ['æspəreɪt] aspirer
ADJ ['æspərət] aspiré; **an a. h** un h aspiré
N ['æspərət] aspirée *f*

aspiration [ˌæspə'reɪʃən] N **1** *(ambition)* aspiration *f*; **young people with political aspirations** des jeunes qui ont des aspirations politiques; **to have aspirations to greater things/to become a doctor** aspirer à de grandes choses/à devenir médecin **2** *Ling* aspiration *f*

aspirational [ˌæspɪ'reɪʃənəl] ADJ *Mktg (product)* qui fait chic; *(consumer)* qui achète des produits de prestige; *(advertising)* qui joue sur le prestige d'un produit
▸▸ ***aspirational group*** groupe *m* de référence

aspirator ['æspəreɪtə(r)] N *Med & Tech* aspirateur *m*

aspire [ə'spaɪə(r)] VI **to a. to do sth** aspirer à *ou* ambitionner de faire qch; **to a. to fame** briguer la célébrité; **he aspires to political power** il aspire au pouvoir politique; **she aspires to** *or* **after higher things** elle vise plus haut, ses ambitions vont plus loin

aspirin ['æspərɪn] N aspirine *f*, *(tablet)* (comprimé *m* d')aspirine *f*

aspiring [ə'spaɪərɪŋ] ADJ *(artist etc)* en herbe; **to be an a. doctor/dancer** aspirer à devenir médecin/danseur

ass[1] [æs] N **1** *(donkey)* âne *m*; **she-a.** ânesse *f*; **a.'s milk** lait *m* d'ânesse **2** *Fam (idiot)* imbécile *mf*; **she's such an a.** elle est bête comme ses pieds; **to make an a. of oneself** se ridiculiser; *(make an exhibition of oneself)* se donner en spectacle; **don't be such an a.** ne fais pas l'imbécile **3** *Am very Fam (bottom)* cul *m*; **a kick in the a.** un coup de pied au cul; **to kick a.** être super; **kiss my a.!** va te faire foutre!; **you bet your a. I'll do it!** tu peux être sûr que je le ferai!; **get your a. out of here!** casse-toi!; **a piece of a.** *(sex)* une baise; *(woman)* une fille baisable

ass[2] *(written abbr* **assistant**) assistant(e) *m,f*

▸ **ass about, ass around** VI *Am Vulg* déconner

assail [ə'seɪl] VT attaquer, assaillir; *Fig* **he assailed her with questions** il l'a harcelée de questions; **assailed by doubt** assailli par le doute

assailant [ə'seɪlənt] N agresseur *m*, assaillant(e) *m,f*

assassin [ə'sæsɪn] N assassin *m*

assassinate [ə'sæsɪneɪt] VT assassiner

assassination [əˌsæsɪ'neɪʃən] N *Pol* assassinat *m*; **character a.** diffamation *f*
▸▸ ***assassination attempt*** attentat *m (contre quelqu'un)*

assault [ə'sɔ:lt] N **1** *(physical attack)* agression *f*; *Law* tentative *f* de voie de fait; *Law* **common a.** voie *f* de fait simple; *Law* **a. and battery** coups *mpl* et blessures *fpl* **2** *Mil* assaut *m*; **to lead an a.** se lancer à l'assaut; **they made** *or* **carried out an a. on the camp** ils sont montés à l'assaut du camp; *Fig* **the music is an a. on listeners' ears** cette musique est une agression pour les oreilles des auditeurs **3** *(attempt to overcome)* **their a. on K2** leur tentative d'ascension du K2; **the party launched an all-out a. on the opposition** le parti a lancé une offensive tous azimuts contre l'opposition
VT **1** *(attack ▸ person)* agresser, attaquer; *Law* se livrer à des voies de fait sur; *(sexually)* violenter; **to be assaulted** être victime d'une agression; *(sexually)* être victime d'un attentat à la pudeur **2** *Mil (town, position etc)* attaquer, assaillir, donner l'assaut à; *Fig (senses)* agresser
▸▸ *Mil* ***assault course*** parcours *m* du combattant; *Mil* ***assault craft*** engin *m* d'assaut; ***assault rifle*** fusil *m* d'assaut

assay [ə'seɪ] VT **1** *Metal (analyse ▸ metal)* essayer; *(▸gold, silver)* coupeller **2** *Arch (attempt)* essayer, tenter
N essai *m* (scientifique)
▸▸ ***assay office*** laboratoire *m* d'essais

assaying [ə'seɪɪŋ] N *Metal* analyse *f*, essai *m*

assemblage [ə'semblɪdʒ] N **1** *(collection)* collection *f*, groupe *m*; *(of people)* assemblée *f* **2** *(process)* montage *m*, assemblage *m*

assemble [ə'sembəl] VT **1** *(people)* rassembler, réunir; *(documents, evidence)* réunir; *(troops)* rassembler **2** *(put together)* monter, assembler; **factory assembled** monté en usine
VI se rassembler, se réunir

assembler [ə'semblə(r)] N *Comput* assembleur *m*

assembly [ə'semblɪ] (*pl* **assemblies**) N **1** *(meeting ▸ gen)* réunion *f*, assemblée *f*; **a place of a.** un lieu de réunion; **unlawful a.** attroupement *m*; **the right of a.** la liberté de réunion
2 *Pol* assemblée *f*; **National A.** l'Assemblée *f* nationale
3 *Br Sch* = réunion de tous les élèves de l'établissement
4 *Mil* rassemblement *m*
5 *(building ▸ process)* montage *m*, assemblage *m*; *(▸end product)* assemblage *m*; *Aut* **the engine a.** le bloc moteur
6 *Comput* assemblage *m*
▸▸ *Mil* ***assembly area*** zone *f* d'attente; *Br Sch* ***assembly hall*** = hall où les enfants se réunissent le matin avant d'entrer en classe; ***assembly instructions*** instructions *fpl* de montage *ou* d'assemblage; *Comput* ***assembly language*** langage *m* d'assemblage; ***assembly language program*** programme *m* en assembleur; *Ind* ***assembly line*** chaîne *f* de montage; **to work on an a. line** travailler à la chaîne; *Ind* ***assembly plant*** usine *f* de montage; ***assembly room*** *(gen)* salle *f* de réunion; *(at town hall)* salle *f* des fêtes; *(industrial)* atelier *m* de montage

assent [ə'sent] VI consentir, acquiescer; **they finally assented to the proposition** ils ont fini par donner leur assentiment à la proposition
N consentement *m*, assentiment *m*; **to give one's a. to sth** donner son assentiment à qch; **the royal a.** le consentement du souverain; **by common a.** du consentement de tous
▸▸ *EU* ***assent procedure*** procédure *f* de l'avis conforme

> Attention: ne pas confondre avec **ascent**.

assert [ə'sɜ:t] VT **1** *(proclaim)* affirmer, maintenir; *(innocence)* affirmer, protester de **2** *(defend)* défendre; *(lay claim to)* revendiquer; **we must a. our right to speak** nous devons faire valoir notre droit à la parole **3** *(impose)* **to a. oneself** se faire respecter, s'imposer; **I had to a. my authority** il a fallu que j'affirme mon autorité *ou* que je m'impose

assertion [ə'sɜ:ʃən] N **1** *(claim)* affirmation *f*, assertion *f* **2** *(of rights)* revendication *f*

assertive [ə'sɜ:tɪv] ADJ *(tone, person, manner etc)* assuré; **don't be too a.** ne te montre pas trop autoritaire; **he's not a. enough** il n'a pas assez d'autorité, il ne s'affirme pas assez

assertiveness [ə'sɜ:tɪvnɪs] N assurance *f*
▸▸ ***assertiveness training*** stage *m* d'affirmation de soi

assess [ə'ses] VT **1** *(judge ▸ effectiveness, performance)* évaluer; *(value)* estimer; **to a. the damage** évaluer les dégâts; **I had to a. the quality of their work** j'ai dû juger de la qualité de leur travail; **how do you a. the team's chances?** à votre avis, quelles sont les chances de l'équipe?, quelles chances accordez-vous à l'équipe?
2 *Fin (value)* fixer *ou* déterminer la valeur de; **to a. a property for taxation** évaluer *ou* calculer la valeur imposable d'une propriété; **the court assessed the damages at £2,000** la cour a fixé les dommages et intérêts à 2000 livres
3 *Fin (taxes)* évaluer
4 *Sch & Univ (of teacher, tutor ▸ knowledge, abilities)* évaluer; **students are continuously assessed** le niveau des étudiants est évalué par un contrôle continu
5 *Med & Psy (of doctor, social worker, psychologist)* évaluer

assessment [ə'sesmənt] N **1** *(judgement)* estimation *f*, évaluation *f*; **I don't accept his a. of our work** je ne suis pas d'accord avec son évaluation de notre travail; **what's your a. of the situation?** comment voyez-vous *ou* jugez-vous la situation?; **what is your a. of their chances?** à votre avis, quelles sont leurs chances?, quelles chances leur accordez-vous?
2 *Fin (valuation ▸ of amount due)* détermination

f, évaluation *f*; (▸ *of tax*) calcul *m* (de la valeur imposable); *Law (of damages)* évaluation *f*, estimation *f*

3 *Sch & Univ (by teacher, tutor)* contrôle *m* des connaissances; *(on report card)* appréciation *f* des professeurs; **methods of a.** méthodes *fpl* d'évaluation

4 *Med & Psy (by doctor, social worker, psychologist)* évaluation *f*

▸▸ *Br* ***assessment centre*** *Ind (for job candidates)* centre *f* d'évaluation des candidats; *Med (to assess needs of disabled children)* = service hospitalier dont le rôle est d'évaluer les besoins des enfants handicapés et de conseiller les parents

assessor [ə'sesə(r)] **N 1** *(for insurance)* expert *m* **2** *Law* (juge *m*) assesseur *m*

▸▸ *Am Fin* ***assessor of taxes*** inspecteur(trice) *m,f* des contributions directes

asset ['æset] **N** avantage *m*, atout *m*; **she's a great a. to our team** elle est un excellent atout pour notre équipe

• **assets** **NPL** *(possessions)* avoir *m*, capital *m*; *Acct, Fin & Law* actif *m*; *(personal)* patrimoine *m*; *(on liquidation after bankruptcy)* masse *f* active; **our total assets** tous nos biens; **total assets** total *m* de l'actif; **assets and liabilities** l'actif *m* et le passif

▸▸ *Fin* ***asset allocation*** répartition *f* des actifs; *Fin* ***asset management*** gestion *f* de biens, gestion *f* de capital; *(of individual's wealth)* gestion *f* de patrimoine; *Fin* ***asset turnover*** rotation *f* des capitaux

asset-stripper **N** *Fin* dépeceur *m* d'entreprise

asset-stripping [-'strɪpɪŋ] **N** *Fin* démembrement *m* d'entreprise

asseverate [ə'sevəreɪt] **VT** *Formal* déclarer; **he asseverated his innocence** il a juré de son innocence

asshole ['æshəʊl] **N** *Am Vulg* **1** *(anus)* trou *m* du cul **2** *Fig (stupid person)* connard (connasse) *m, f*; *(nasty person)* salaud (salope) *m,f*; **don't be such an a.!** ne sois pas si con!

assiduity [,æsɪ'djuːətɪ] **N** assiduité *f*, zèle *m*

assiduous [ə'sɪdjʊəs] **ADJ** assidu; **she was a. in her attention to detail** elle portait une attention assidue aux détails

assiduously [ə'sɪdjʊəslɪ] **ADV** assidûment

assign [ə'saɪn] **VT 1** *(allot)* assigner, attribuer (**to** à); *(funds)* affecter (**to** à); *(debts)* céder, transférer (**to** à); *St Exch (shares)* attribuer (**to** à); **the room was assigned to study groups** la salle fut affectée *ou* réservée aux groupes d'étude; **to a. a duty/task to sb** assigner une responsabilité/tâche à qn; **I assigned her the task of writing the report** je l'ai chargée de la rédaction du rapport; *Am* **assigned seating** *(in theatre)* places *fpl* numérotées

2 *(appoint)* nommer, désigner; **he's been assigned to Moscow** il a été affecté à Moscou

3 *(ascribe)* **to a. a reason for sth** donner la raison de qch; *Math* **we a. a value to X** nous attribuons *ou* assignons une valeur à X

4 *Law* céder, transférer

assignation [,æsɪg'neɪʃən] **N 1** *(meeting)* rendez-vous *m* clandestin; *Old-fashioned or Hum* **to have an a. with sb** avoir un rendez-vous secret avec qn **2** *(assignment)* attribution *f*; *(of money)* allocation *f*; *(of person)* affectation *f* **3** *Scot Law* cession *f*, transfert *m*

assignee [,æsaɪ'niː] **N** *Law* cessionnaire *mf*

assignment [ə'saɪnmənt] **N 1** *(task)* tâche *f*; *(official)* mission *f*; *Sch & Univ* devoir *m*; *Journ (of individual reporter)* reportage *m* assigné; **a dangerous a.** une tâche dangereuse; *Journ* **to be on a.** être en reportage

2 *(of duties, responsibilities)* allocation *f*; *(of person)* affectation *f*

3 *(of funds)* affectation *f*; *(of debts)* transfert *m*; *St Exch (of shares)* attribution *f*

4 *Law* cession *f*, transfert *m*; *(of patent)* cession *f*

▸▸ ***assignment of accounts receivable*** transfert *m* de créances; *Comput* ***assignment table*** table *f* d'affectation

assimilate [ə'sɪmɪleɪt] **VT 1** *(food, information)* assimiler **2** *(immigrants)* intégrer

VI 1 *(become absorbed)* s'assimiler, s'intégrer **2** *(immigrants)* s'intégrer; **foreigners find it difficult to a. into a new culture** les étrangers ont du mal à s'intégrer à une autre culture **3** *(become similar)* **to a. to** *or* **with sth** s'assimiler à qch

assimilation [ə,sɪmɪ'leɪʃən] **N** *(gen) & Ling* assimilation *f*

Assisi [ə'siːzɪ, ə'siːsɪ] **N** *Geog* Assise *f*

assist [ə'sɪst] **VT** *(help)* aider, assister; *(process)* faciliter; **he assisted her up/down the stairs** il l'a aidée à monter/descendre l'escalier; **to a. sb in doing sth** aider qn à faire qch; **a man is assisting police with their enquiries** la police est en train d'interroger un suspect

VI 1 *(help)* aider, prêter secours; **she assisted at the operation** elle a apporté son assistance pendant l'opération **2** *Arch (attend)* assister

N *Sport* = action qui permet à un coéquipier de marquer un point

▸▸ ***assisted living facility*** foyer-logement *m*; ***assisted suicide*** suicide *m* assisté

assistance [ə'sɪstəns] **N** aide *f*, secours *m*; **may I be of a. to you?** puis-je vous être utile?; **to come to sb's a.** venir au secours de qn; **with the a. of sb** avec l'aide de qn; **with the a. of sth** à l'aide de qch; **with the financial a. of the university** avec le concours financier de l'université

assistant [ə'sɪstənt] **N** assistant(e) *m,f*, aide *mf*; *Comput (program)* assistant *m*; **(shop) a.** vendeur(euse) *m,f*; **(foreign language) a.** *Sch* assistant(e) *m,f* (en langue étrangère); *Univ* lecteur (trice) *m,f* (en langue étrangère); **French a.** assistant(e) *m,f* de français; *Sch* **non-teaching a.** auxiliaire *mf*

COMP *(director, librarian, secretary)* adjoint

▸▸ ***assistant editor*** *TV* assistant monteur *m*; *Cin* monteur *m* adjoint; *Journ* rédacteur *m* en chef adjoint; *Law* ***assistant judge*** juge *mf* adjoint(e); *Com* ***assistant manager*** sous-directeur(trice) *m, f*, directeur(trice) *m,f* adjoint(e); *Br Am Univ* ***assistant professor*** maître-assistant *m*, *Can* professeur *m* adjoint; ***assistant referee*** *(in football)* juge *m* de touche; *Sch* ***assistant teacher*** *(primary)* instituteur(trice) *m,f*; *(secondary)* professeur *m* *(qui n'est pas responsable d'une section)*

assize [ə'saɪz] **N** réunion *f*; *Formerly Law* assises *fpl*; **court of assizes** cour *f* d'assises; **to be brought before the assizes** être traduit en cour d'assises

▸▸ *Formerly* ***assize court*** cour *f* d'assises

associate **VT** [ə'səʊʃɪeɪt] **1** *(mentally)* associer (**with sth** à qch; **with sb** avec qn) **I don't a. you with that kind of activity** je ne t'imagine pas dans ce genre d'activité; **I don't a. the two things** pour moi, les deux choses sont indépendantes **2** *(in partnership etc)* **to a. oneself (with sb)** s'associer (avec qn); **to be associated with sth** *(with project, research etc)* participer à qch; *(with company etc)* avoir des liens avec qch, travailler avec qch; **we are not associated in any way with that company** nous n'avons absolument rien à faire *ou* voir avec cette société; **the problems associated with nuclear power** les problèmes relatifs à l'énergie nucléaire; **that kind of behaviour is often associated with an unhappy childhood** ce type de comportement est souvent lié à une enfance malheureuse

VI [ə'səʊʃɪeɪt] **to a. with sb** fréquenter qn

N [ə'səʊʃɪət] **1** *(partner)* associé(e) *m,f*; *Law* complice *mf* **2** *(of club)* membre *m*, associé(e) *m,f*; *(of institution)* membre *m*

ADJ [ə'səʊʃɪət] associé, allié; **I'm only an a. member** je suis seulement membre associé

▸▸ *Com* ***associate company*** société *f* affiliée; *Cin* ***associate director*** assistant-réalisateur (assistante-réalisatrice) *m,f*; *Journ* ***associate editor*** rédacteur(trice) *m,f* associé(e); *Law* ***associate judge*** juge *m* assesseur; *Cin & TV* ***associate producer*** producteur(trice) *m,f* associé(e); *Am Univ* ***associate professor*** maître *m* de conférences, *Can* professeur *m* agrégé

associated [ə'səʊʃɪeɪtɪd] **ADJ** associé

▸▸ *Com* ***associated company*** société *f* affiliée; *Press* ***Associated Press*** Associated Press *f (agence de presse dont le siège est à New York)*

association [ə,səʊsɪ'eɪʃən] **N 1** *(grouping)* association *f*, société *f*; **the teachers have formed an a.** les enseignants ont constitué une association; *Com* **trade a.** association *f* professionnelle **2** *(involvement)* association *f*, fréquentation *f*; **through long a. with the medical profession** à force de fréquenter la profession médicale; **to do sth in a. with sb** faire qch en association avec qn; **this programme was made in a. with Belgian television** ce programme a été fait en collaboration avec la télévision belge; **I have no a. with that company** je n'ai pas de liens avec cette société **3** *(of ideas)* association *f*; **by a. of ideas** par association d'idées; **the name has unfortunate associations for her** ce nom lui évoque des pensées désagréables; **the associations of the name** ce qu'on associe à ce nom

▸▸ *Br Ftbl* ***association football*** football *m* association; ***Association of South East Asian Nations*** Association *f* des nations de l'Asie du Sud-Est; *Psy* ***association test*** test *m* d'association

associative [ə'səʊʃɪətɪv] **ADJ** *(gen) & Comput* associatif

assonance ['æsənəns] **N** *Ling* assonance *f*

assorted [ə'sɔːtɪd] **ADJ 1** *(various)* varié, divers; **in a. sizes** en différentes tailles; **an audience of a. academics and businessmen** un public très varié, composé d'universitaires et d'hommes d'affaires **2** *(matched)* assorti; **well-/ill-a.** bien/mal assorti

assortment [ə'sɔːtmənt] **N** assortiment *m*, collection *f*; *(of people)* mélange *m*; **there was a good a. of cakes** il y avait un grand choix *ou* une bonne sélection de gâteaux; **she certainly has an odd a. of friends!** ses amis forment un curieux mélange!

asst *(written abbr* **assistant***)* assistant(e) *m,f*

assuage [ə'sweɪdʒ] **VT** *(grief, pain)* soulager, apaiser; *(hunger, thirst)* assouvir; *(person)* apaiser, calmer

assume [ə'sjuːm] **VT 1** *(presume)* supposer, présumer; **we can't a. anything** nous ne pouvons présumer de rien; **if we a. there will be no problems,...** en supposant qu'il n'y aura aucun problème,...; **I a. that he will come** je présume qu'il viendra; **he was assumed to be rich** on le supposait riche; **in the absence of proof he must be assumed to be innocent** en l'absence de preuves, il doit être présumé innocent; **don't a. that people will like you because you are rich** ne crois pas que les gens t'aimeront parce que tu es riche; **let us a. that...** mettons *ou* supposons que...; **to a. the worst** mettre les choses au pis

2 *(take over* ▸ *responsibility)* prendre sur soi, assumer; (▸ *duty)* se charger de; (▸ *power, command)* prendre; (▸ *running of hotel, company etc)* prendre en main

3 *(adopt* ▸ *right, title etc)* s'attribuer, s'arroger, s'approprier; (▸ *name)* adopter, emprunter; *Law* **to a. ownership** faire acte de propriétaire

4 *(take on* ▸ *air, appearance, tone)* prendre, se donner; (▸ *shape, character)* affecter, revêtir; *(of problem* ▸ *importance)* prendre; **his voice assumed a tone of authority** sa voix prit un ton autoritaire

5 *(feign* ▸ *indifference)* feindre, simuler

> Note that the French verb **assumer** is a false friend. It never means **to suppose** or **to adopt**.

assumed [ə'sjuːmd] **ADJ** feint, faux (fausse); **with a. indifference** avec une indifférence feinte

▸▸ ***assumed name*** nom *m* d'emprunt; *(of author)* pseudonyme *m*; **he travels under an a. name** il se sert d'un nom d'emprunt pour voyager

assumption [ə'sʌmpʃən] **N 1** *(supposition)* supposition *f*, hypothèse *f*; **the assumptions on which society is based** les idées de base qui servent de fondement à la société; **on the a. that he agrees, we can go ahead** en supposant *ou* admettant qu'il soit d'accord, nous pouvons aller de l'avant; **we're working on the a. that what she says is true** nous partons du principe qu'elle dit la vérité **2** *(of power, responsibility etc)* prise *f*; **a. of office** entrée *f* en fonctions; *Law* **a. of risk** acceptation *f* des risques; **his a. of the role of chairman** *(after nomination)* son entrée en fonctions en tant que président; *(without consent)* le fait qu'il s'arroge la fonction de président **3** *(of attitude)* affectation *f*

• **Assumption** **N** *Rel* **the A.** l'Assomption *f*

▸▸ *Rel* ***Assumption Day*** jour *m* ou fête *f* de l'Assomption

assurance [əˈʃʊərəns] **N 1** *(assertion)* affirmation *f*, assurance *f*; *(pledge)* promesse *f*, assurance *f*; **I can give you an a. that...** je peux vous assurer *ou* vous affirmer que...; **she gave repeated assurances that she would not try to escape** elle a promis à plusieurs reprises qu'elle n'essaierait pas de s'enfuir; **he gave her a ring as an a. of his love** il lui a donné une bague comme gage de son amour **2** *(confidence)* assurance *f*, confiance *f* en soi; *(overconfidence)* arrogance *f*; **to lack a.** manquer de confiance en soi; **she said it with such a., I believed her** elle l'a dit avec une telle assurance que je l'ai crue; **they set out with absolute a. of their success** ils partirent, sûrs de leur réussite **3** *Br Ins (insurance)* assurance *f*; **life a.** assurance sur la vie *f*, assurance-vie *f*
▸▸ *Br* ***assurance company*** compagnie *f* d'assurances; *Br* ***assurance policy*** police *f* d'assurance

assure [əˈʃʊə(r)] **VT 1** *(affirm)* affirmer, assurer; **to a. sb of the truth of sth** assurer qn de la vérité de qch; **to a. sb of a fact** assurer *ou* affirmer un fait à qn; **he assures me that it is true** il me certifie que c'est vrai; **he assured me he was coming** il m'a assuré qu'il viendrait; **he will do it, I (can) a. you!** il le fera, je vous assure!; **she assured herself (of) a good pension** elle s'est assuré une bonne retraite **2** *(ensure* ▸ *peace, someone's happiness)* assurer **3** *Br (insure)* assurer

assured [əˈʃʊəd] **ADJ 1** *(certain)* assuré, certain; **they are a. of victory** ils sont certains de gagner; **she is a. a place in the finals** elle est certaine d'aller en finale; **you're a. of a warm welcome** on vous garantit un accueil chaleureux **2** *(self-confident)* assuré, sûr de soi; *(overconfident)* arrogant, effronté **3** *Br Ins (insured)* assuré
N assuré(e) *m,f*

assuredly [əˈʃʊərɪdlɪ] **ADV** assurément, sûrement, sans aucun doute; **when she returns, as she a. will, ...** quand elle reviendra, ce qui ne laisse aucun doute, ...

Assyria [əˈsɪrɪə] **N** Assyrie *f*

Assyrian [əˈsɪrɪən] **N** Assyrien(enne) *m,f*
ADJ assyrien

AST [ˌeɪesˈtiː] **N** *(abbr* **Atlantic Standard Time***)* = heure d'hiver des Provinces Maritimes du Canada et d'une partie des Caraïbes

aster [ˈæstə(r)] **N** *Bot & Biol* aster *m*

asterisk [ˈæstərɪsk] **N** astérisque *m*
VT marquer d'un astérisque

astern [əˈstɜːn] **ADV** *Naut* à *ou* sur l'arrière, en poupe; **to go a.** *(person)* aller à l'arrière *ou* en poupe; *(boat)* faire machine arrière, battre en arrière, culer; **full speed a.!** en arrière toutes!
ADJ à *ou* sur l'arrière

asteroid [ˈæstərɔɪd] **N** *Astron* astéroïde *m*
▸▸ ***asteroid belt*** ceinture *f* d'astéroïdes

asthma [ˈæsmə] **N** asthme *m*; **she has a.** elle est asthmatique
▸▸ ***asthma attack*** crise *f* d'asthme; ***asthma sufferer*** asthmatique *mf*

asthmatic [æsˈmætɪk] **N** asthmatique *mf*
ADJ asthmatique

astigmatic [ˌæstɪgˈmætɪk] **N** astigmate *mf*
ADJ astigmate

astigmatism [æˈstɪgmətɪzəm] **N** astigmatisme *m*

astir [əˈstɜː(r)] **ADJ** *Literary* **1** *(out of bed)* debout *(inv)*, levé **2** *(in motion)* animé

ASTMS [ˈæstiːmz, ˌeɪesˌtiːemˈes] **N** *(abbr* **Association of Scientific, Technical and Managerial Staffs***)* = ancien syndicat britannique des personnels scientifiques, techniques et administratifs

astonish [əˈstɒnɪʃ] **VT** *(surprise)* étonner; *(amaze)* stupéfier, ahurir; **you a. me** vous m'étonnez; **to be astonished at seeing sth** être étonné *ou* s'étonner de voir qch; **I was astonished at** *or* **by the price** j'ai été étonné du prix; **I am continually astonished by her audacity** son audace ne cesse de m'étonner; **I am astonished that...** cela m'étonne que... + *subjunctive*; **she had an astonished look on her face** elle avait l'air étonné(e) *ou* stupéfait(e)

astonishing [əˈstɒnɪʃɪŋ] **ADJ** *(surprising)* étonnant; *(amazing)* stupéfiant, ahurissant; **it's a. how he's changed** c'est stupéfiant comme il a changé; **with a. speed** à une vitesse incroyable *ou* étonnante

astonishingly [əˈstɒnɪʃɪŋlɪ] **ADV** incroyablement; **a., they both decided to leave** aussi étonnant que cela paraisse, ils ont tous les deux décidé de partir

astonishment [əˈstɒnɪʃmənt] **N** *(surprise)* étonnement *m*; *(amazement)* stupéfaction *f*, ahurissement *m*; **they stared in a.** ils avaient l'air stupéfait; **a look of a.** un regard stupéfait *ou* ahuri; **to our a.** à notre grand étonnement, à notre stupéfaction

astound [əˈstaʊnd] **VT** stupéfier, abasourdir; **we were astounded to hear the news** la nouvelle nous a stupéfaits; *Ironic* **you a. me!** comme c'est étonnant!

astounding [əˈstaʊndɪŋ] **ADJ** stupéfiant, ahurissant

astragal [ˈæstrəgæl] **N** *Archit* astragale *m*

Astrakhan [ˌæstrəˈkæn] **N** *Geog* Astrakan, Astrakhan
• **astrakhan N** *Tex* astrakan *m* **COMP** *(hat, jacket)* d'astrakan

astral [ˈæstrəl] **ADJ** *Astron* astral
▸▸ ***astral projection*** projection *f* astrale

astray [əˈstreɪ] **ADV 1** *(lost)* **to go a.** s'égarer, se perdre; **the letter went a.** la lettre s'est perdue; **my pen seems to have gone a.** j'ai égaré mon stylo **2** *(idioms)* **to go a.** *(morally)* se dévoyer, se détourner du droit chemin; **to lead sb a.** *(misinform)* mettre *ou* diriger qn sur une fausse piste; *(morally)* détourner qn du droit chemin

astride [əˈstraɪd] **PREP** à califourchon *ou* à cheval sur; **he sat a. the fence** il était assis à califourchon sur la barrière

astringence [əˈstrɪndʒəns], **astringency** [əˈstrɪndʒənsɪ] **N** astringence *f*

astringent [əˈstrɪndʒənt] **ADJ 1** *(remark)* acerbe, caustique; *(criticism)* dur, sévère **2** *(lotion)* astringent
N astringent *m*

astringently [əˈstrɪndʒəntlɪ] **ADV** *(say, remark)* d'un ton acerbe; **a. worded** virulent

astrologer [əˈstrɒlədʒə(r)] **N** astrologue *mf*

astrological [ˌæstrəˈlɒdʒɪkəl] **ADJ** astrologique

astrology [əˈstrɒlədʒɪ] **N** *Astrol* astrologie *f*

astronaut [ˈæstrənɔːt] **N** astronaute *mf*

astronautics [ˌæstrəˈnɔːtɪks] **N** *(UNCOUNT)* astronautique *f*

astronomer [əˈstrɒnəmə(r)] **N** astronome *mf*

astronomic [ˌæstrəˈnɒmɪk], **astronomical** [ˌæstrəˈnɒmɪkəl] **ADJ** *Astron (year, unit etc) & Fig (price)* astronomique; **an a. failure/disaster** un échec/désastre de proportions astronomiques

astronomically [ˌæstrəˈnɒmɪkəlɪ] **ADV** *Astron* astronomiquement; *Fig (increase)* de façon astronomique; **it's a. expensive** ça coûte les yeux de la tête

astronomy [əˈstrɒnəmɪ] **N** astronomie *f*

astrophysicist [ˌæstrəʊˈfɪzɪsɪst] **N** *Astron* astrophysicien(enne) *m,f*

astrophysics [ˌæstrəʊˈfɪzɪks] **N** *(UNCOUNT)* astrophysique *f*

Astroturf® [ˈæstrəʊˌtɜːf] **N** gazon *m* artificiel

astute [əˈstjuːt] **ADJ** *(person* ▸ *shrewd)* astucieux, fin, perspicace; *(*▸ *crafty)* malin(igne), rusé; *(investment, management)* astucieux; **how a. of you!** vous êtes malin!

astutely [əˈstjuːtlɪ] **ADV** astucieusement, avec finesse *ou* perspicacité

astuteness [əˈstjuːtnɪs] **N** finesse *f*, perspicacité *f*

asunder [əˈsʌndə(r)] **ADV** *Literary (to pieces)* **to tear sth a.** mettre qch en pièces; **the family had been torn a. by war** la famille avait été déchirée par la guerre; **to break a.** se casser en deux

asylee [ˌæsaɪˈliː] **N** demandeur(euse) *m,f* d'asile

asylum [əˈsaɪləm] **N 1** *(shelter)* (lieu *m* de) refuge *m*; *(in church etc)* asile *m* (inviolable); **to seek a.** chercher asile; **he was granted/refused a.** on lui a accordé/refusé l'asile; **the right to** *or* **of a.** le droit d'asile; **political a.** asile *m* politique **2** *(mental hospital)* asile *m* (d'aliénés)
▸▸ *Fam* ***asylum shopping, asylum surfing*** = pratique selon laquelle les demandeurs d'asile choisissent le pays offrant les conditions d'accueil les plus favorables

asylum-seeker N demandeur(euse) *m,f* d'asile

asymmetric [ˌeɪsɪˈmetrɪk] **ADJ** asymétrique

asymmetrical [ˌeɪsɪˈmetrɪkəl] **ADJ** asymétrique
▸▸ *Sport* ***asymmetrical bars*** barres *fpl* asymétriques

asymmetry [ˌeɪˈsɪmətrɪ] **N** asymétrie *f*

asymptomatic [eɪˌsɪmptəˈmætɪk] **ADJ** *Med* asymptomatique

asymptote [ˈæsɪmptəʊt] **N** *Geom* asymptote

asynchronous [ˌeɪˈsɪŋkrənəs] **ADJ** asynchrone
▸▸ *Comput* ***asynchronous transfer mode*** commutation *f* temporelle asynchrone

AT [ət, *stressed* æt]

• à **1, 2, 5**	• dans la direction de **3**
• en **7**	• arobase **9**

PREP 1 *(indicating point in space)* à; **at the door/the bus stop** à la porte/l'arrêt de bus; **at my house/the dentist's** chez moi/le dentiste; **I'm at the airport** je suis à l'aéroport; **she's at a wedding/a committee meeting** *(attending)* elle est à un mariage/en réunion avec le comité; **she was standing at the window** elle se tenait debout à la fenêtre; **turn left at the traffic lights/at the town hall** tournez à gauche au feu/à la mairie; *Rail* **change at Reading** prenez la correspondance à Reading; *Am* **where are you at with that report?** où en êtes-vous avec ce rapport?; *Fam* **this club is where it's at** ce club est très chic *ou* dans le vent; *Fam* **that's not where I'm at** c'est pas mon truc
2 *(indicating point in time)* à; **at noon/six o'clock** à midi/six heures; **at that time** *(period)* à cette époque, en ce temps-là; **at all times** tout le temps; **at the weekend** (pendant *ou* durant) le week-end; **I work at night** je travaille de nuit; **I like to work at night** j'aime travailler la nuit; **I'm busy at the moment** je suis occupé en ce moment; **at a time when...** à un moment où...; **he started working at 15** il a commencé à travailler à (l'âge de) 15 ans
3 *(indicating direction)* vers, dans la direction de; **look at this!** regarde ça!; **he shot at the rabbit** il a tiré sur le lapin; **to laugh at sb** se moquer de qn; **to swear at sb** jurer contre qn; **she grabbed at the purse** elle a essayé de s'emparer du portemonnaie; **don't shout at me!** ne me crie pas dessus!
4 *(indicating activity)* **my parents are at work** mes parents sont au travail; **he was at lunch** il était allé déjeuner; *Fam* **get me some coffee while you're at it** prenez-moi du café pendant que vous y êtes; *Fam* **she's at it again!** la voilà qui recommence!; *Fam* **keep at it!** continue!; *Fam* **don't let me catch you at it again!** que je ne t'y reprenne pas!
5 *(indicating level, rate, price)* à; **at 50 mph** à 80 km/h; **he drove at 50 mph** il faisait du 80 (à l'heure); **it's a bargain at £5** à 5 livres, c'est une bonne affaire; **we sell it at £1 a kilo** nous le vendons 1 livre le kilo; **the temperature stands at 30°** la température est de 30°; **the rise worked out at £1 an hour** l'augmentation correspondait à 1 livre de l'heure
6 *(state, condition)* **to be at war/peace** être en guerre/paix; **she's not at her best in the morning** le matin, elle n'est pas au mieux de sa forme; **at all events** en tout cas; **we'll leave it at that for today** nous en resterons là pour aujourd'hui; **the water level was at its highest/lowest** le niveau d'eau était au plus haut/au plus bas; **she's at her most/least effective in such situations** c'est là qu'elle est le plus/le moins efficace
7 *(as adjective complement)* en; **he's brilliant/hopeless at maths** il est excellent/nul en maths
8 *Fam (idiom)* **to be (on) at sb** harceler qn□; **his mother's always on at him to tidy his room** sa mère est toujours après lui *ou* le harcèle toujours pour qu'il range sa chambre
9 *Comput (in e-mail address)* arobase *f*, a *m* commercial; **"gwilson at transex, dot, co, dot, uk"** "gwilson, arobase, transex, point, co, point, uk"
• **at once ADV 1** *(immediately)* tout de suite, immédiatement
2 *(simultaneously)* en même temps; **they all came**

at once ils sont tous arrivés en même temps; **don't all talk at once** ne parlez pas tous en même temps

atavism ['ætəvɪzəm] **N** *Biol* atavisme *m*

atavistic [ˌætə'vɪstɪk] **ADJ** *Biol* atavique

ataxia [ə'tæksɪə] **N** *Med* ataxie *f*; **locomotor a.** ataxie *f* locomotrice progressive, tabes *m* dorsalis

atchoo [æ'tʃuː] *Am* = **atishoo**

ate [eɪt] *pt of* **eat**

atheism ['eɪθɪɪzəm] **N** *Rel* athéisme *m*

atheist ['eɪθɪɪst] *Rel* **N** athée *mf*
ADJ athée

atheistic [ˌeɪθɪ'ɪstɪk], **atheistical** [ˌeɪθɪ'ɪstɪkəl] **ADJ** athée

Athenian [ə'θiːnɪən] **N** Athénien(enne) *m,f*
ADJ athénien

Athens ['æθɪnz] **N** Athènes

athlete ['æθliːt] **N** *(gen)* sportif(ive) *m,f*; *(track and field competitor)* athlète *mf*
►► ***athlete's foot*** *(UNCOUNT)* mycose *f*; **to have a.'s foot** avoir une mycose

athletic [æθ'letɪk] **ADJ** *(sporty)* sportif; *(muscular)* athlétique; **she's very a.** elle est très sportive; **an a.-looking young man** un jeune homme athlétique; **I don't do anything very a.** je ne fais pas beaucoup de sport
►► *Sport* ***athletic support, athletic supporter*** *(underwear)* suspensoir *m*

athletically [æθ'letɪkəlɪ] **ADV** *(swim, ride, jump)* de façon sportive; **to be a. built** être athlétique, avoir un corps d'athlète

athletics [æθ'letɪks] **N** *(UNCOUNT)* athlétisme *m*
COMP *(club, meeting)* d'athlétisme; *(activity ► track and field)* athlétique; *(► other sport)* sportif
►► *Am* ***athletics coach*** entraîneur *m* (sportif)

at-home **N** = réception chez soi

> **-ATHON, -THON** — SUFFIXE
>
> • Dérivé du mot **marathon**, ce suffixe s'emploie de façon familière pour parler d'un événement de LONGUE DURÉE, et dans la plupart des cas un événement organisé pour collecter des fonds en faveur d'une bonne cause. Par exemple, un **swimathon** (de *to swim* nager) est un événement au cours duquel les participants doivent nager le plus longtemps possible en échange d'argent collecté auprès de parents, de voisins ou d'amis. De la même manière les écoliers qui participent à un **readathon** (de *to read* lire) doivent lire le plus longtemps ou le plus de livres possible et dans un **singathon** (de *to sing* chanter) il s'agit de chanter le plus longtemps possible.
> Le mot **telethon**, construit sur le même schéma, désigne une émission de télévision très longue organisée pour récolter des fonds pour une cause donnée.
> • Le mot américain **talkathon** désigne quant à lui un très long débat (au Congrès, par exemple) et n'a donc rien à voir avec quelque œuvre de bienfaisance que ce soit.

athwart [ə'θwɔːt] *Literary* **PREP 1** *(across the path of)* en travers de; *Naut* par le travers de **2** *(in opposition to)* contre, en opposition à
ADV en travers; *Naut* par le travers

atishoo [ə'tɪʃuː] **EXCLAM** *Br* atchoum!

Atlantic [ət'læntɪk] **N the A.** l'Atlantique *m*, l'océan *m* Atlantique
ADJ *(coast, community)* atlantique; *Met (wind)* de l'Atlantique
►► *Naut* ***Atlantic liner*** transatlantique *m*; ***the Atlantic Ocean*** l'Atlantique *m*, l'océan *m* Atlantique; ***the Atlantic Provinces*** *(in Canada)* les Provinces *fpl* atlantiques; ***Atlantic Standard Time*** = heure d'hiver des Provinces Maritimes du Canada et d'une partie des Caraïbes

Atlantis [ət'læntɪs] **PR N** *Myth* Atlantide *f*

Atlas ['ætləs] **PR N** *Myth* Atlas *m*
►► *Geog* ***the Atlas Mountains*** l'Atlas *m*

atlas ['ætləs] *(pl sense* **3 atlantes** [ət'læntiːz]) **N 1** *(book)* atlas *m* **2** *Anat* atlas *m* **3** *Archit* atlante *m*, télamon *m*

ATM [ˌeɪtiː'em] **N 1** *Am Banking (abbr* **automated teller machine, automatic teller machine**) DAB *m*, *Can* guichet *m* (bancaire) automatique, *Suisse* bancomat *m* **2** *Comput (abbr* **asynchronous transfer mode**) ATM *m*, commutation *f* temporelle asynchrone

atmosphere ['ætməˌsfɪə(r)] **N 1** *Geog & Phys* atmosphère; **the upper a.** la haute atmosphère **2** *(feeling, mood)* ambiance *f*, atmosphère *f*; **there was an a. of elation in the room** il régnait une joyeuse ambiance dans la pièce; **the place has no a.** l'endroit est impersonnel; **there's a really bad a. in the office just now** il y a une très mauvaise ambiance au bureau en ce moment

atmospheric [ˌætməs'ferɪk] **ADJ 1** *(pollution, pressure)* atmosphérique **2** *(lighting, music)* qui met dans l'ambiance; **the film was very a.** il y avait beaucoup d'atmosphère dans ce film

atmospherics [ˌætməs'ferɪks] **NPL** *Elec & Tel* parasites *mpl*

ATOL ['æˌtɒl] **N** *(abbr* **air travel organizer's licence**) licence *m* d'organisateur de voyages par avion

atoll ['ætɒl] **N** *Geog* atoll *m*

atom ['ætəm] **N 1** *Phys* atome *m* **2** *Fig* **there's not an a. of truth in what you say** il n'y a pas une once *ou* un brin de vérité dans ce que tu dis; **they haven't one a. of common sense** ils n'ont pas le moindre bon sens
►► ***atom bomb*** bombe *f* atomique

atomic [ə'tɒmɪk] **ADJ** *Phys & Nucl* atomique
►► ***atomic bomb*** bombe *f* atomique; *Tech* ***atomic clock*** horloge *f* atomique; ***atomic energy*** énergie *f* nucléaire *ou* atomique; ***Atomic Energy Authority*** = commissariat à l'énergie nucléaire en Grande-Bretagne; *Am* ***Atomic Energy Commission*** = commissariat à l'énergie nucléaire aux États-Unis et au Canada; ***atomic number*** nombre *m ou* numéro *m* atomique; ***atomic pile*** pile *f* atomique, réacteur *m* nucléaire; ***atomic power*** énergie *f* atomique, réacteur *m* nucléaire; ***atomic reactor*** réacteur *m* nucléaire; ***atomic warfare*** guerre *f* nucléaire *ou* atomique; ***atomic weight*** masse *f ou* poids *m* atomique

atomization, -isation [ˌætəmaɪ'zeɪʃən] **N** *Phys (of matter)* atomisation *f*; *Chem (of fuel)* atomisation *f*, pulvérisation *f*

atomize, -ise ['ætəmaɪz] **VT** *Phys (matter)* atomiser; *Chem (fuel)* atomiser, pulvériser; *Chem (in spray, liquid)* vaporiser

atomized, -ised ['ætəmaɪzd] **ADJ** *(life, society)* fragmenté

atomizer, -iser ['ætəmaɪzə(r)] **N** atomiseur *m*

atonal [eɪ'təʊnəl] **ADJ** *Mus* atonal

► **atone for** [ə'təʊn] **VT INSEP** *(sin, crime)* expier; *(mistake, behaviour)* racheter, réparer

atonement [ə'təʊnmənt] **N** *(of crime, sin)* expiation *f*; *(of mistake, behaviour)* réparation *f*; *Rel* **to make a. for one's sins** expier ses péchés; **in a. for a wrong** en réparation d'un tort; *Rel* **Day of A.** (fête *f* du) Grand Pardon *m*

atop [ə'tɒp] **PREP** *Literary* en haut de, sur; **sitting a. a suitcase** assis sur une valise

ATP [ˌeɪtiː'piː] **N 1** *Sport (abbr* **Association of Tennis Professionals**) ATP *f* **2** *Chem (abbr* **adenosine triphosphate**) ATP *m*

at-risk **ADJ an a. group** un groupe *ou* une population à risque

atrium ['eɪtrɪəm] *(pl* **atria** [-rɪə] *or* **atriums**) **N 1** *(court)* cour *f*; *Antiq* atrium *m* **2** *Anat* orifice *m* de l'oreillette

atrocious [ə'trəʊʃəs] **ADJ 1** *Fam (very bad ► pun, weather, journey)* atroce□, exécrable□; *(► clothes, design)* affreux□; *(► behaviour, manners)* ignoble□; *(► injuries)* atroce□; **his French is a.** son français est très mauvais; **his singing is a.** il chante atrocement *ou* affreusement mal **2** *(crime)* atroce; **an a. act** une atrocité

atrociously [ə'trəʊʃəslɪ] **ADV 1** *Fam (very badly)* exécrablement□; **a. bad** atroce□, exécrable□ **2** *(cruelly)* atrocement

atrociousness [ə'trəʊʃəsnɪs] **N 1** *Fam (of pun, weather)* caractère *m* exécrable□ *ou* atroce□ **2** *(of crime)* atrocité *f*

atrocity [ə'trɒsətɪ] *(pl* **atrocities**) **N 1** *(act)* atrocité *f* **2** *(of crime)* atrocité *f*

atrophied ['ætrəfɪd] **ADJ** *Med* atrophié

atrophy ['ætrəfɪ] *(pt & pp* **atrophied**) *Med* **N** atrophie *f*
VT atrophier
VI s'atrophier

at-sign **N** *Typ & Comput* arrobas *m*

attaboy ['ætəbɔɪ] **EXCLAM** *Fam* bravo!, vas-y mon petit!

attach [ə'tætʃ] **VT 1** *(connect ► handle, label)* attacher, fixer; *(► appendix, document)* joindre; **the attached letter** la lettre ci-jointe; **please find attached…** veuillez trouver ci-joint…
2 *(associate with)* **he attached himself to a group of walkers** il s'est joint à un groupe de randonneurs; **the kitten attached himself to her** *(followed her)* le chaton l'a adoptée
3 *(be part of)* **the research centre is attached to the science department** le centre de recherche dépend du *ou* est rattaché au département des sciences
4 *(attribute)* attacher, attribuer (**to** à); *(blame)* imputer (**to** à); **don't a. too much importance to this survey** n'accordez pas trop d'importance à cette enquête
5 *(place on temporary duty)* affecter; **an official attached to another department** un fonctionnaire détaché à un autre service; **to be attached to a unit** être affecté à une unité
6 *Law (person)* arrêter, appréhender; *(property, salary)* saisir
7 *Comput (file)* joindre (**to** à); **to a. a file to an e-mail** joindre un fichier à un e-mail
VI 1 to a. to *(fix on to)* s'accrocher à; *(appliance, shelves ► to wall)* se fixer à; *(rope, hook)* être relié à **2** *Formal (be attributed)* être attribué, être imputé; **no blame attaches to you for what happened** la responsabilité de ce qui s'est produit ne repose nullement sur vous

attaché [ə'tæʃeɪ] **N** *Pol* attaché(e) *m,f*
►► ***attaché case*** mallette *f*, attaché-case *m*

attached [ə'tætʃt] **ADJ** attaché; **he's very a. to his family** il est très attaché *ou* il tient beaucoup à sa famille; **she's (already) a.** elle a déjà quelqu'un dans sa vie; **I was very a. to that car** j'étais très attaché à cette voiture

attachment [ə'tætʃmənt] **N 1** *(fastening)* fixation *f*
2 *(accessory, part)* accessoire *m*
3 *Admin (document)* pièce *f* jointe; *Comput (to e-mail)* fichier *m* joint
4 *(affection)* attachement *m*, affection *f*; *(loyalty)* attachement *m*; **to form an a. to sb** s'attacher à qn, se prendre d'affection pour qn; **she has a strong a. to her grandfather** elle est très attachée à son grand-père
5 *Admin (temporary duty)* détachement *m*; **he's on a. to the hospital** il est en détachement à l'hôpital
6 *Law (of person)* arrestation *f*; *(of property)* saisie *f*

attack [ə'tæk] **VT 1** *(assault ► physically)* attaquer; *(► verbally)* attaquer, s'attaquer à; *Mil* attaquer, assaillir **2** *(tackle)* s'attaquer à; **a campaign to a. racism** une campagne pour combattre le racisme **3** *(of disease ► person, organ)* s'attaquer à, atteindre; *(of rust ► metal)* attaquer, s'attaquer à, ronger; *(of fear, doubts)* assaillir
VI attaquer
N 1 *(gen) & Sport* attaque *f*; *Mil* attaque *f*, assaut *m*; **attacks on old people are on the increase** les agressions contre les personnes âgées sont de plus en plus nombreuses; **to launch an a. on** *(enemy)* donner l'assaut à; *(crime)* lancer une opération contre; *(problem, policy)* s'attaquer à; **the a. on her life failed** l'attentat contre elle a échoué; **to go on the a.** passer à l'attaque; **the infantry was under a.** l'infanterie subissait un assaut *ou* était attaquée; **to come under a.** être en butte aux attaques; **she felt as though she were under a.** elle s'est sentie agressée; **a. is the best form of defence** l'attaque est la meilleure forme de défense **2** *(of illness)* crise *f*; **an a. of malaria/nerves** une crise de paludisme/de nerfs; **an a. of fever** un accès de fièvre; **to have an a. of giddiness/the shakes** être pris de vertiges/tremblements; **an a.**

of self-doubt une crise de doute **3** *Mus* attaque *f*
▸▸ ***attack dog*** chien *m* d'assaut

attacker [əˈtækə(r)] **N** *(gen)* agresseur *m*, attaquant(e) *m,f*; *Sport* attaquant *m*

attacking [əˈtækɪŋ] **ADJ** attaquant; *Sport (game, play)* d'attaque

attagirl [ˈætəgɜːl] **EXCLAM** *Fam* bravo!, vas-y ma petite!

attain [əˈteɪn] **VT 1** *(achieve* ▸ *ambition, hopes)* réaliser; *(*▸*objectives)* réaliser, atteindre; *(*▸ *happiness)* parvenir à; *(*▸ *independence)* accéder à; *(*▸*success)* obtenir; *(*▸ *knowledge)* acquérir **2** *(arrive at, reach)* atteindre, arriver à

attainable [əˈteɪnəbəl] **ADJ** *(ambition, level, objective, profits)* réalisable; *(position)* accessible; **a growth rate a. by industrialized countries** un taux de croissance à la portée des *ou* accessible aux pays industrialisés

attainment [əˈteɪnmənt] **N 1** *(of ambition, hopes, objectives)* réalisation *f*; *(of independence, success)* obtention *f*; *(of happiness)* conquête *f*; *(of knowledge)* acquisition *f* **2** *(accomplishment)* résultat *m* (obtenu); *(knowledge, skill)* connaissance *f*; **a man of considerable attainments** un homme qui a beaucoup d'instruction *ou* d'acquis; **her linguistic attainments** sa connaissance des langues

attempt [əˈtempt] **N 1** *(effort, try)* tentative *f*, essai *m*, effort *m*; **her feeble a. to justify herself** la piètre tentative qu'elle a faite pour se justifier; **an a. at a smile** l'esquisse *f* d'un sourire; **without (making) any a. at concealment** sans chercher à se cacher; **they made no a. to help** ils n'ont pas essayé d'aider; **a. to escape** tentative *f* d'évasion; **to make an a. at doing sth** *or* **to do sth** essayer *ou* tâcher de faire qch; **to make an a. on a record** *or* **to beat a record** essayer de battre un record; **to make an a. on Everest** tenter l'ascension de l'Everest; **first a.** coup *m* d'essai, première tentative *f*; **it wasn't bad for a first a.** ce n'était pas mal pour une première tentative *ou* un premier essai; **at the first a.** du premier coup; **I passed the test at my third a.** j'ai réussi l'examen la troisième fois; **to make another a.** renouveler ses tentatives, revenir à la charge; **to give up the a.** y renoncer; **he died in the a.** il est mort en essayant **2** *(attack)* attentat *m*; **a. on sb's life** tentative *f* d'assassinat; **to make an a. on sb's life** attenter à la vie de qn

VT 1 *(try)* tenter, essayer; *(undertake* ▸ *job, task)* entreprendre, s'attaquer à; **to a. to do sth** essayer *ou* tenter de faire qch, chercher à faire qch; **he attempted to cross the street, he attempted crossing the street** il a essayé de traverser la rue; **she plans to a. the record again in June** elle a l'intention de s'attaquer de nouveau au record en juin; **to a. the impossible** tenter l'impossible; **he has already attempted suicide once** il a déjà fait une tentative de suicide; **attempted murder/theft** tentative *f* d'assassinat/de vol **2** *(in mountaineering* ▸ *ascent, climb)* entreprendre; *(*▸ *mountain)* entreprendre l'escalade de

attend [əˈtend] **VT 1** *(go to* ▸ *conference, meeting)* assister à; *(*▸ *church, school)* aller à; *(*▸ *course)* suivre; **I attended a private school** j'ai fait mes études dans une école privée; **the concert was well attended** il y avait beaucoup de monde au concert **2** *(look after, care for)* servir, être au service de; **he was always attended by a manservant** un valet de chambre l'accompagnait partout; **a doctor attended the children** un médecin a soigné les enfants **3** *Formal (accompany)* accompagner; **serious consequences a. such an action** de telles actions entraînent de graves conséquences; **the mission was attended by great difficulties** la mission comportait de grandes difficultés

VI 1 *(be present)* être présent; **let us know if you are unable to a.** prévenez-nous si vous ne pouvez pas venir **2** *(pay attention)* faire *ou* prêter attention

▸ **attend to VT INSEP 1** *(deal with* ▸ *matter)* s'occuper de; *(*▸ *one's business)* vaquer à; *(*▸ *one's interests)* veiller à; *(*▸ *one's health, appearance)* soigner; *(*▸ *order)* exécuter; **I shall a. to it** je m'en occuperai, je m'en chargerai **2** *(customer)* s'occuper de; **are you being attended to?** est-ce qu'on s'occupe de vous? **3** *Formal (pay attention to)* faire *ou* prêter attention à; **a. to what I'm saying** écoutez attentivement ce que je dis

attendance [əˈtendəns] **N 1** *(presence* ▸ *at meeting)* présence *f*; **regular a.** assiduité *f*; **school a.** fréquentation *f* scolaire; **church attendances have fallen** le nombre de personnes qui vont à l'église a baissé; **his a. has been good/bad, he has a good/bad a. record** il a été/il n'a pas été assidu; **poor a.** manque *m* d'assiduité **2** *(people present)* assistance *f*; **there was a good a. at the meeting** il y avait une assistance nombreuse à la réunion; **there was a record a. at the final** la finale a attiré un nombre record de spectateurs; **the evening class had to be cancelled because of poor a.** le cours du soir a dû être annulé pour manque d'élèves **3 to be in a. on** *(doctor* ▸ *sick person)* donner des soins à; *(courtier* ▸ *king etc)* être de service auprès de; **with six bodyguards in a.** accompagné de six gardes du corps; **in close a.** à proximité

▸▸ *Br Fin & Med* ***attendance allowance*** = allocation pour les handicapés; *Br Law* ***attendance centre*** = maison de redressement où des délinquants assistent régulièrement à des réunions; ***attendance list*** *(for meetings)* liste *f* de présence; ***attendance register*** registre *m* de présence; ***attendance sheet*** *(for meetings)* feuille *f* de présence

attendant [əˈtendənt] **N 1** *(official)* surveillant(e) *m,f*; *(in public lavatory, cloakroom)* préposé(e) *m,f*; *(in museum, car park)* gardien(enne) *m,f*; *(in theatre)* ouvreuse *f*; **(petrol-)pump a.** pompiste *mf*; **swimming pool a.** maître *m* nageur **2** *(usu pl)* **attendants** *(of king etc)* gens *mpl*, suite *f*

ADJ *Formal (related)* **there are some disadvantages a. on working at home** le travail à domicile comporte certains inconvénients; **he talked about marriage and its a. problems** il parla du mariage et des problèmes qui l'accompagnent

attendee [əˌtenˈdiː] **N** *(at meeting, conference, seminar)* personne *f* présente

attending physician [əˈtendɪŋ-] **N** *Med* médecin *m* traitant

attention [əˈtenʃən] **N 1** *(concentration, thought)* attention *f*; **may I have your a. for a moment?** pourriez-vous m'accorder votre attention un instant?; **your a. please, ladies and gentlemen** mesdames et messieurs, votre attention s'il vous plaît; **you have my undivided a.** je suis tout à vous; **she knows how to hold an audience's a.** elle sait retenir l'attention d'un auditoire; **they were all a.** ils étaient (tout yeux et) tout oreilles *ou* tout ouïe; **to pay a. (to)** prêter attention (à); **I paid little a. to what she said** j'ai accordé peu d'attention à *ou* j'ai fait peu de cas de ce qu'elle a dit; **a. to detail** précision *f*, minutie *f*; **she switched her a. back to her book** elle est retournée à son livre

2 *(notice)* attention *f*; **he waved to attract** *or* **catch our a.** il a fait un geste de la main pour attirer notre attention; **to draw a. to oneself** se faire remarquer; **the news came to his a.** il a appris la nouvelle; **let me bring** *or* **direct** *or* **draw your a. to the matter of punctuality** permettez que j'attire votre attention sur le problème de la ponctualité; *Formal* **it has been brought to our a. that...** il a été porté à notre connaissance que...; **let us now turn our a. to the population problem** considérons maintenant le problème démographique; **the child doesn't get much a. at home** on ne s'occupe pas beaucoup de cet enfant chez lui; **he gets all the a.** il n'y en a que pour lui; **he just does it to get a.** il ne fait ça que pour se faire remarquer; **for the a. of Mr Smith** *(in letter)* à l'attention de M. Smith

3 *(care)* soins *mpl*, entretien *m*; **they need medical a.** ils ont besoin de soins médicaux; **the furnace requires constant a.** la chaudière demande un entretien régulier; **the bathroom looks as if it needs some a.** la salle de bains a besoin d'être un peu retapée

4 *Mil* garde-à-vous *m inv*; **to stand at/to come to a.** se tenir/se mettre au garde-à-vous

EXCLAM garde-à-vous!

• **attentions NPL** attentions *fpl*, égards *mpl*; **she felt irritated by his unwanted attentions** elle était agacée par les attentions dont il l'entourait

▸▸ *Med* ***attention deficit*** déficit *m* de l'attention, déficit *m* attentionnel; *Med* ***attention deficit disorder*** troubles *mpl* de l'attention; *Med* ***attention deficit hyperactivity disorder*** trouble *m* hyperactif avec déficit de l'attention; ***attention span*** capacité *f* de concentration; **a short/long a. span** une faible/bonne capacité de concentration; **his a. span is no longer than half an hour** il ne peut pas se concentrer pendant plus d'une demi-heure

attention-seeking N it's just a. il/elle/*etc* ne cherche qu'à attirer l'attention sur lui/elle/*etc*, il/elle/*etc* essaie juste de se/*etc* faire remarquer

ADJ her a. behaviour son besoin constant de se faire remarquer

attentive [əˈtentɪv] **ADJ 1** *(paying attention)* attentif; **a. to detail** méticuleux **2** *(considerate)* attentionné, prévenant; **to be a. to sb** être prévenant envers qn; **she was a. to our every need** elle était attentive à tous nos besoins

> When translating **attentive**, note that **attentif** and **attentionné** are not interchangeable. **Attentif** refers to someone who pays attention and **attentionné** to someone who is considerate.

attentively [əˈtentɪvlɪ] **ADV 1** *(paying attention)* attentivement, avec attention **2** *(with consideration)* avec beaucoup d'égards

attentiveness [əˈtentɪvnɪs] **N 1** *(concentration)* attention *f* **2** *(consideration)* égards *mpl*, prévenance *f*

attenuate VT [əˈtenjʊeɪt] **1** *(attack, remark)* atténuer, modérer; *(pain)* apaiser **2** *(form, line)* amincir, affiner **3** *(gas)* raréfier

VI [əˈtenjʊeɪt] s'atténuer, diminuer

ADJ [əˈtenjʊɪt] *Bot* atténué

attenuation [əˌtenjʊˈeɪʃən] **N 1** *(of attack, remark)* atténuation *f*, modération *f*; *(of pain)* atténuation *f*, apaisement *m* **2** *(of form, line)* amincissement *m*

attenuator [əˈtenjʊeɪtə(r)] **N** *Tech* atténuateur *m*

attest [əˈtest] *Formal* **VT 1** *(affirm)* attester, certifier; *(under oath)* affirmer sous serment; **the document attests the fact that...** le document atteste que...

2 *(be proof of)* démontrer, témoigner de

3 *(bear witness to)* témoigner; **to a. a signature** légaliser une signature

4 *(put oath to)* faire prêter serment à

VI témoigner, prêter serment; **she attested to the truth of the report** elle a témoigné de la véracité du rapport

▸▸ *Com* ***attested copy*** copie *f* certifiée conforme; *Agr* ***attested herd*** troupeau *m* ayant subi une tuberculination

attestation [ˌæteˈsteɪʃən] **N** *Law* **1** *(statement)* attestation *f*; *(in court)* attestation *f*, témoignage *m*

2 *(proof)* attestation *f*, preuve *f*

3 *(of signature)* légalisation *f*

4 *(taking of oath)* assermentation *f*, prestation *f* de serment

at-the-money option N *St Exch* option *f* au cours, option *f* à la monnaie

attic [ˈætɪk] **N** *(space)* grenier *m*; *(room)* mansarde *f*

▸▸ ***attic room*** mansarde *f*; ***attic window*** fenêtre *f* en mansarde; *(skylight)* lucarne *f*

Attica [ˈætɪkə] **N** *Antiq & Geog* Attique *f*

attire [əˈtaɪə(r)] *Formal* **N** *(UNCOUNT)* habits *mpl*, vêtements *mpl*; *(formal)* tenue *f*

VT vêtir, habiller, parer; **she attired herself in silk** elle se vêtit de soie

attitude [ˈætɪtjuːd] **N 1** *(way of thinking)* attitude *f*, disposition *f*; **what's your a. to abortion?** que pensez-vous de l'avortement?, quelle est votre attitude face à l'avortement?; **attitudes have changed** les mentalités ont changé; **she took the a. that...** elle est partie du principe que...; **an a. of mind** un état d'esprit; **he has a very positive a. of mind** il a une attitude extrêmement positive; **old-fashioned attitudes** des idées *fpl* démodées

2 *(behaviour, manner)* attitude *f*, manière *f*; **I don't like your a., young man** je n'aime pas vos manières, jeune homme; **well, if that's your a. you can go** eh bien, si c'est comme ça que tu le prends, tu peux t'en aller; **he's got an a. problem** il a des problèmes relationnels

3 *Formal (posture)* attitude *f*, position *f*; **to strike an a.** poser, prendre une pose affectée

4 *Fam (self-assurance, assertiveness)* assurance *f*; **he's got a.** il n'a pas froid aux yeux; **a car with a.** une voiture qui a du caractère

5 *Mktg (of consumer to product)* attitude *f*

▸▸ *Mktg* ***attitude research*** enquête *f* d'attitudes; *Mktg* ***attitude scale*** échelle *f* d'attitudes; *Mktg* ***attitude survey*** enquête *f* d'attitudes

attn (*written abbr* **for the attention of**) attn, à l'attention de

attorney [ə'tɜːnɪ] (*pl* **attorneys**) **N 1** *(representative)* mandataire *mf*, représentant(e) *m,f* **2** *Am (solicitor* ▸ *for documents, sales etc)* notaire *m*; (▸ *for court cases)* avocat(e) *m,f*; *(barrister)* avocat(e) *m,f*

▸▸ ***Attorney General*** *(in England, Wales and Northern Ireland)* = principal avocat de la couronne; *(in US)* ministre *m* de la Justice; *(in Canada)* procureur *m* général

attract [ə'trækt] **VT 1** *(draw, cause to come near)* attirer; **the proposal attracted a lot of attention/interest** la proposition a attiré l'attention/a éveillé l'intérêt de beaucoup de gens; **to a. criticism** s'attirer des critiques; **we hope to a. more young people to the church** nous espérons attirer davantage de jeunes à l'église **2** *(be attractive to)* attirer, séduire, plaire; **she's attracted to men with beards** elle est attirée par les barbus; **what really attracts me to him is his sense of humour** ce qui me plaît chez lui c'est son sens de l'humour; **what is it that attracts you about skiing?** qu'est-ce qui vous plaît *ou* séduit dans le ski?

VI s'attirer; **opposites a.** les contraires s'attirent

attraction [ə'trækʃən] **N 1** *Phys (pull)* attraction *f*; *Fig* attraction *f*, attirance *f*; **I don't understand your a. for** *or* **to her** je ne comprends pas ce qui te plaît chez *ou* en elle; **the idea holds no a. for me** cette idée ne me dit rien; **I can't** *or* **don't see the a. of it** je n'en vois pas l'intérêt **2** *(appeal* ▸ *of place, plan)* attrait *m*, fascination *f*; (▸ *of person)* charme *m*, charmes *mpl*; **it's the city's chief a.** c'est l'attrait principal de la ville; **the attractions of living in the country** les charmes de la vie à la campagne; **the main a. of our show** le clou *ou* la grande attraction de notre spectacle; **a tourist a.** un site touristique

attractive [ə'træktɪv] **ADJ 1** *(pretty* ▸ *person, smile)* séduisant; (▸ *dress, picture)* attrayant, beau (belle); **do you find him a.?** il te plaît?, tu le trouves séduisant? **2** *(interesting* ▸ *idea, price)* intéressant; (▸ *offer, opportunity)* intéressant, attrayant **3** *Phys (force)* attractif

attractively [ə'træktɪvlɪ] **ADV** de manière attrayante; **to dress a.** s'habiller de façon séduisante; **the meal was very a. presented** le repas était très agréablement présenté

attractiveness [ə'træktɪvnɪs] **N 1** *(of person, smile)* beauté *f*, charme *m*; *(of dress, picture)* beauté *f* **2** *(of idea, opportunity, price)* intérêt *m*, attrait *m* **3** *Phys* attraction *f*

attributable [ə'trɪbjutəbəl] **ADJ** attribuable, imputable, dû; **to be a. to sth** être attribuable *ou* imputable *ou* dû à qch

▸▸ *Acct* ***attributable profit*** bénéfices *mpl* nets

attribute VT [ə'trɪbjuːt] *(ascribe* ▸ *accident, failure)* attribuer, imputer; (▸ *invention, painting, quotation)* prêter, attribuer; (▸ *success)* attribuer; **to what do you a. your success?** à quoi attribuez-vous votre réussite?

N ['ætrɪbjuːt] **1** *(feature, quality)* attribut *m*; *(object)* attribut *m*, emblème *m* **2** *(in logic)* attribut *m* **3** *Ling* épithète *m*

attribution [,ætrɪ'bjuːʃən] **N** attribution *f*

attributive [ə'trɪbjutɪv] **N** *Ling* attribut *m*

ADJ 1 *(gen)* attributif **2** *Gram* épithète

attributively [ə'trɪbjutɪvlɪ] **ADV** *Ling* comme épithète

attrition [ə'trɪʃən] **N 1** *(wearing down)* usure *f* (par friction); *Mil* **war of a.** guerre *f* d'usure **2** *Econ & Ind* attrition *f*, départs *mpl* volontaires

attune [ə'tjuːn] **VT** accorder; **her ideas are closely attuned to his** ses idées sont en parfait accord avec les siennes; **to a. oneself** *or* **become attuned to sth** se faire à qch, s'accoutumer à qch

ATW [,eɪtiː'dʌbəljuː] **ADV** (*abbr* **around the world**) autour du monde

atypical [,eɪ'tɪpɪkəl] **ADJ** atypique; **this behaviour is a. of him** cela ne lui ressemble pas

aubergine ['əubəʒiːn] *Br* **N 1** *(vegetable)* aubergine *f* **2** *(colour)* violet *m* aubergine

ADJ aubergine *(inv)*

auburn ['ɔːbən] **N** (couleur *f*) auburn *m*

ADJ auburn *(inv)*

auction ['ɔːkʃən] **N** (vente *f* aux) enchères *fpl*; **sold at** *or* **by a.** vendu aux enchères; **to put sth up for a.** mettre qch en vente aux enchères; **they put the house up for a.** ils ont mis la maison en vente aux enchères

VT *(put up for auction)* mettre aux enchères; *(sell)* vendre aux enchères

▸▸ *Cards* ***auction bridge*** bridge *m* aux enchères; ***auction room*** salle *f* des ventes

▸ **auction off VT SEP** vendre aux enchères

auctioneer [,ɔːkjə'nɪə(r)] **N** commissaire-priseur *m*

audacious [ɔː'deɪʃəs] **ADJ 1** *(daring)* audacieux, intrépide **2** *(impudent)* effronté, impudent

audaciously [ɔː'deɪʃəslɪ] **ADV 1** *(daringly)* audacieusement, avec audace **2** *(impudently)* effrontément, impudemment

audaciousness [ɔː'deɪʃəsnɪs], **audacity** [ɔː'dæsətɪ] **N 1** *(daring)* audace *f*, intrépidité *f* **2** *(impudence)* effronterie *f*, impudence *f*

audibility [,ɔːdɪ'bɪlətɪ] **N** audibilité *f*

audible ['ɔːdəbəl] **ADJ** *(sound)* audible, perceptible; *(words)* intelligible, distinct; **the music was barely a.** on entendait à peine la musique

▸▸ *Phys* ***audible frequency*** fréquence *f* audible

audibly ['ɔːdəblɪ] **ADV** distinctement

audience ['ɔːdɪəns] **N 1** *(at film, match, play)* spectateurs *mpl*, public *m*; *(at concert, lecture)* auditoire *m*, public *m*; *(of author)* lecteurs *mpl*; *(of artist)* public *m*; **the a. gave him a standing ovation** le public s'est levé pour l'ovationner; **do we have any Americans in the a.?** y a-t-il des Américains dans la salle?; **was there a large a. at the play?** y avait-il beaucoup de monde au théâtre?; **his books reach a wide a.** ses livres sont lus par beaucoup de gens

2 *Rad* auditeurs *mpl*, audience *f*; *TV* téléspectateurs *mpl*, audience *f*

3 *Mktg (for product, advertisement)* audience *f*

4 *Formal (meeting)* audience *f*; **to grant sb an a.** accorder audience à qn

▸▸ *Br TV* ***Audience Appreciation Index*** = indice de mesure de satisfaction du public; *Mktg* ***audience exposure*** exposition *f* au public; *Rad & TV* ***audience figures*** indice *m* d'écoute; *Rad & TV* ***audience measurement*** mesure *f* d'audience; *Rad & TV* ***audience participation*** participation *f* de l'assistance (à ce qui se passe sur la scène); *Rad & TV* ***audience rating*** indice *m* d'écoute, taux *m* d'écoute; *Mktg* ***audience research*** études *fpl* d'audience; *Rad & TV* ***audience share*** part *f* d'audience; *Mktg* ***audience study*** étude *f* d'audience

> Note that the French word **audience** is rarely a translation for the English word **audience**.

audio ['ɔːdɪəu] **N** son *m*, acoustique *f*; **the a. has gone** il n'y a plus de son

▸▸ ***audio book*** livre *m* audio; ***audio cassette*** cassette *f* audio; ***audio equipment*** équipement *m* acoustique; *Phys* ***audio frequency*** audiofréquence *f*; ***audio guide*** audioguide *m*; ***audio library*** sonothèque *f*, phonothèque *f*; ***audio recording*** enregistrement *m* sonore; ***audio response*** réponse *f* acoustique; ***audio signal*** signal *m* audio, signal *m* son; ***audio sound recording*** enregistrement *m* son sonore; ***audio streaming*** audiostreaming *m*; ***audio system*** système *m* audio; ***audio tape*** bande *f* magnétique audio; ***audio tape recorder*** magnétophone *m* à bande

audiometer [,ɔːdɪ'ɒmɪtə(r)] **N** audiomètre *m*

audio-typing N audiotypie *f*

audio-typist N audiotypiste *mf*

audiovisual [,ɔːdɪəu'vɪʒuəl] **ADJ** audiovisuel

▸▸ ***audiovisual aids*** supports *mpl* audiovisuels; ***audiovisual equipment*** équipement *m* audiovisuel, matériel *m* audiovisuel

audit ['ɔːdɪt] **N** *Acct & Admin* vérification *f* des comptes, audit *m*

VT 1 *Acct (accounts)* vérifier, apurer, examiner **2** *Am Univ* **he audits several courses** il assiste à plusieurs cours en tant qu'auditeur libre

▸▸ *Admin* ***Audit office*** Cour *f* des Comptes; ***audit trail*** *Comput* protocole *m* de vérification *ou* de contrôle; *Fin* vérification *f* à rebours

auditing ['ɔːdɪtɪŋ] **N** *Acct* vérification *f* des comptes, audit *m*

audition [ɔː'dɪʃən] **N 1** *Theat* audition *f*; *Cin & TV* (séance *f* d')essai *m*; **to hold auditions** *Theat* organiser des auditions; *Cin & TV* organiser des essais; **to do an a.** *Theat* passer une audition; *Cin & TV* faire un essai **2** *(hearing)* ouïe *f*, audition *f*

VT *Theat* auditionner; *Cin & TV* faire faire un essai à

VI *Theat (director)* auditionner; *(actor)* passer une audition; *Cin & TV* faire un essai; **I auditioned for 'Woyzeck'** *Theat* j'ai passé une audition pour un rôle dans 'Woyzeck'; *Cin & TV* j'ai fait un essai pour un rôle dans 'Woyzeck'

auditor ['ɔːdɪtə(r)] **N 1** *Acct (of company)* audit *m*, auditeur(trice) *m,f*; *(officially appointed)* commissaire *m* aux comptes; *Admin (of public body)* vérificateur(trice) *m,f* des comptes, audit *m*, auditeur(trice) *m,f*; **firm of auditors** cabinet *m* d'audit, cabinet *m* comptable **2** *Formal (listener)* auditeur(trice) *m,f* **3** *Am Univ (student)* auditeur (trice) *m,f* libre

auditorium [,ɔːdɪ'tɔːrɪəm] (*pl* **auditoriums** *or* **auditoria** [-rɪə]) **N 1** *(of concert hall, theatre)* salle *f* **2** *(large meeting room)* amphithéâtre *m*

auditory ['ɔːdɪtərɪ] **ADJ** *Physiol* auditif

▸▸ ***auditory phonetics*** phonétique *f* auditive

AUEW [,eɪjuː,iː'dʌbəljuː] **N** *Formerly Ind* (*abbr* **Amalgamated Union of Engineering Workers**) = ancien syndicat britannique de l'industrie mécanique, aujourd'hui remplacée par l'AEEU

Aug. (*written abbr* **August**) août *m*

Augean [ɔː'dʒiːən] **ADJ** *Myth* **the A. Stables** les écuries *fpl* d'Augias

auger ['ɔːgə(r)] **N** *Carp (hand tool)* vrille *f*; *Tech* foreuse *f*

aught [ɔːt] *Arch or Literary* **PRON** ce que; **for a. I know** (pour) autant que je sache; **for a. I care** pour ce que cela me fait

augment [ɔːg'ment] **VT 1** *(increase)* augmenter, accroître; **her salary is augmented by** *or* **with gratuities** à son salaire s'ajoutent les pourboires **2** *Mus* augmenter

VI augmenter, s'accroître

augmentation [,ɔːgmen'teɪʃən] **N 1** *(increase)* augmentation *f*, accroissement *m* **2** *Mus* augmentation *f*

augur ['ɔːgə(r)] **VI it augurs ill/well** c'est de mauvais/bon augure; **it doesn't a. well for the future** cela ne présage *ou* n'annonce rien de bon

VT *(predict)* prédire, prévoir; *(be omen of)* présager; **it augurs no good** cela ne présage *ou* n'annonce rien de bon

N *(prophet)* augure *m*

augury ['ɔːgjʊrɪ] (*pl* **auguries**) **N 1** *(art)* art *m* augural; *(rite)* rite *m* augural **2** *(omen)* augure *m*, présage *m*; *(prediction)* prédiction *f*

August ['ɔːgəst] **N** août *m*; *see also* **February**

▸▸ ***August Bank Holiday*** = jour férié tombant le dernier lundi d'août en Angleterre et au pays de Galles, le premier lundi d'août en Écosse

august [ɔː'gʌst] **ADJ** *Literary (dignified)* auguste, vénérable; *(noble)* noble

Augustinian [,ɔːgə'stɪnɪən] *Rel* **N** *(follower)* augustinien *m*; *(monk)* augustin *m*

ADJ augustinien, de saint Augustin

Augustus [ɔː'gʌstəs] **PR N** Auguste

auk [ɔːk] **N** *Orn* alcidé *m*, alque *m*

auld [ɔːld] **ADJ** *Scot* vieux (vieille)

▸▸ *Mus* ***Auld Lang Syne*** = chanson sur l'air de "ce n'est qu'un au revoir" que l'on chante à minuit le soir du 31 décembre

aunt [ɑːnt] **N** tante *f*

▸▸ *Br* ***Aunt Sally*** *(at fairground)* jeu *m* de massacre; *Fig (person)* tête *f* de Turc

auntie, aunty ['ɑːntɪ] (*pl* **aunties**) *Br Fam* **N** tantine *f*, tata *f*, tatie *f*; **A. Susan** tante Susan

• **Auntie** N = surnom affectueux de la BBC, perçue comme une vieille tante détentrice des valeurs morales

AUP [ˌeɪjuːˈpiː] N *Comput* (*abbr* **Acceptable Use Policy**) = code de conduite défini par un fournisseur d'accès à l'Internet

au pair [ˌəʊˈpeə(r)] (*pl* **au pairs**) N (jeune fille *f*) au pair *f*; **she's working as an a.** elle travaille au pair, elle est (jeune fille) au pair
VI travailler au pair

aura [ˈɔːrə] (*pl* **auras** *or* **aurae** [-riː]) N **1** (*quality* ▸ *of person*) aura *f*, émanation *f*; (▸ *of place*) atmosphère *f*, ambiance *f*; **there's an a. of mystery about her** il y a quelque chose de mystérieux chez elle **2** (*surrounding body*) aura *f* **3** *Med* aura *f*

aural [ˈɔːrəl] ADJ **1** (*relating to hearing*) auditif, sonore **2** *Anat* (*relating to the ear*) auriculaire
▸▸ ***aural comprehension*** compréhension *f* orale; ***aural skills*** aptitudes *fpl* à la compréhension orale

> Attention: ne pas confondre avec l'adjectif anglais **oral**.

aureola [ɔːˈriːələ], **aureole** [ˈɔːriəʊl] N **1** *Art* (*of saint*) auréole *f* **2** *Astron* (*of sun*) auréole *f*

auricle [ˈɔːrɪkəl] N *Anat* **1** (*of ear*) auricule *f* **2** (*of heart*) oreillette *f*

auricular [ɔːˈrɪkjʊlə(r)] ADJ auriculaire

aurochs [ˈɔːrɒks] (*pl* **inv**) N *Zool* aurochs *m*

aurora [ɔːˈrɔːrə] (*pl* **auroras** *or* **aurorae** [-riː]) N *Astron* aurore *f*
• **Aurora** PR N *Myth* Aurore
▸▸ *Astron* ***aurora australis*** aurore *f* australe; *Astron* ***aurora borealis*** aurore *f* boréale

auscultate [ˈɔːskəlˌteɪt] VT *Med* ausculter

auscultation [ˌɔːskəlˈteɪʃən] N *Med* auscultation *f*

auspices [ˈɔːspɪsɪz] NPL auspices *mpl*; **under the a. of the UN** sous les auspices de l'ONU, sous l'égide de l'ONU

auspicious [ɔːˈspɪʃəs] ADJ (*event, start, occasion*) propice, favorable; (*sign*) de bon augure; **we made an a. start** nous avons pris un bon départ; **on this a. occasion** en ce jour mémorable

auspiciously [ɔːˈspɪʃəslɪ] ADV favorablement, sous d'heureux auspices; **the meeting began a.** la réunion a bien commencé

auspiciousness [ɔːˈspɪʃəsnɪs] N aspect *m* propice *ou* favorable

Aussie [ˈɒzɪ] *Fam* N Australien(enne)[□] *m,f*
ADJ australien[□]

austere [ɒˈstɪə(r)] ADJ **1** (*person*) austère, sévère; (*life*) austère, sobre, ascétique **2** (*design, interior*) austère, sobre

austerely [ɒˈstɪəlɪ] ADV **1** (*live*) austèrement, avec austérité, comme un ascète **2** (*dress, furnish*) austèrement, avec austérité, sobrement

austereness [ɒˈstɪənɪs], **austerity** [ɒˈsterətɪ] (*pl* **austerities**) N **1** (*simplicity*) austérité *f*, sobriété *f* **2** (*hardship*) austérité *f*; **a period of a.** une période d'austérité, des temps difficiles **3** (*usu pl*) (*practice*) austérité *f*, pratique *f* austère
▸▸ *Econ* ***austerity measures*** mesures *fpl* d'austérité

Australasia [ˌɒstrəˈleɪʒjə] N Australasie *f*

Australasian [ˌɒstrəˈleɪʒən] N natif(ive) *m,f* de l'Australasie
ADJ d'Australasie

Australia [ɒˈstreɪljə] N Australie *f*; **the Commonwealth of A.** l'Australie *f*
▸▸ ***Australia Day*** = premier lundi suivant le 26 janvier (commémorant l'arrivée des Britanniques en Australie en 1788)

Australian [ɒˈstreɪljən] N **1** (*person*) Australien(enne) *m,f* **2** *Ling* australien *m*
ADJ australien
COMP (*embassy*) d'Australie; (*history*) de l'Australie
▸▸ ***the Australian Alps*** les Alpes *fpl* australiennes; ***Australian Antarctic Territory*** Antarctique *f* australienne; *Sport* ***Australian Rules (football)*** football *m* australien

Austria [ˈɒstrɪə] N Autriche *f*

Austria-Hungary N *Hist* Autriche-Hongrie *f*

Austrian [ˈɒstrɪən] N Autrichien(enne) *m,f*
ADJ autrichien
COMP (*embassy*) d'Autriche; (*history*) de l'Autriche
▸▸ ***Austrian blind*** store *m* autrichien

Austro-Hungarian [ˈɒstrəʊ-] ADJ *Hist* austro-hongrois
▸▸ *Hist* ***the Austro-Hungarian Empire*** l'empire *m* d'Autriche-Hongrie

autarchy [ˈɔːtɑːkɪ] (*pl* **autarchies**) N *Pol* autocratie *f*

autarky [ˈɔːtɑːkɪ] (*pl* **autarkies**) N *Econ* **1** (*system*) autarcie *f* **2** (*country*) pays *m* en autarcie

auteur [ɔːˈtɜː(r)] N *Cin* auteur *m*

authentic [ɔːˈθentɪk] ADJ (*genuine*) authentique; (*accurate, reliable*) authentique, véridique; *Law* **each document being a.** chaque texte faisant foi

authentically [ɔːˈθentɪkəlɪ] ADV de façon authentique

authenticate [ɔːˈθentɪkeɪt] VT (*painting*) établir l'authenticité de; (*signature*) légaliser

authenticity [ˌɔːθenˈtɪsətɪ] N authenticité *f*

author [ˈɔːθə(r)] N **1** (*writer*) auteur *m*, écrivain *m*; **have you ever read this a.?** avez-vous déjà lu des livres de cet auteur? **2** (*of idea, plan*) auteur *m*; (*of painting, sculpture*) auteur *m*, créateur *m*; *Literary* **to be the a. of one's own misfortunes** être l'artisan de ses malheurs
VT être l'auteur de
▸▸ *Typ* ***author's correction*** correction *f* d'auteur

authoress [ˈɔːθərɪs] N **1** (*writer*) = femme auteur d'ouvrages s'adressant au grand public **2** (*of idea, plan*) auteur *m*; (*of painting, sculpture*) auteur *m*, créatrice *f*

authoritarian [ɔːˌθɒrɪˈteərɪən] N personne *f* autoritaire; **the boss is a strict a.** le patron est très autoritaire *ou* croit ferme à l'autorité
ADJ *Pol* autoritaire

> Attention: ne pas confondre avec **authoritative**.

authoritative [ɔːˈθɒrɪtətɪv] ADJ **1** (*article, report, person*) qui fait autorité; **I have it from an a. source that...** je tiens de source sûre que... **2** (*official*) autorisé, officiel

> Attention: ne pas confondre avec **authoritarian**.

authoritatively [ɔːˈθɒrɪtətɪvlɪ] ADV avec autorité

authority [ɔːˈθɒrətɪ] (*pl* **authorities**) N **1** (*power*) autorité *f*, pouvoir *m*; **who's in a. here?** qui est le responsable ici?; **in a position of a.** en position d'autorité; **to be in** *or* **have a. over sb** (*officially*) avoir autorité sur qn; (*have power*) avoir de l'ascendant sur qn; **he made his a. felt** il faisait sentir son autorité; *Pol* **those in a. in Haiti** ceux qui gouvernent en Haïti
2 (*forcefulness*) autorité *f*, assurance *f*; **his opinions carry a lot of a.** ses opinions font autorité; **her conviction gave a. to her argument** sa conviction a donné du poids à son raisonnement
3 (*permission*) autorisation *f*, droit *m*; **to give sb a. to do sth** autoriser qn à faire qch; **who gave him (the) a. to enter?** qui lui a donné l'autorisation d'entrer?, qui l'a autorisé à entrer?; **they had no a. to answer** ils n'étaient pas habilités à répondre; **I decided on my own a.** j'ai décidé de ma propre autorité *ou* de mon propre chef; **on whose a. did they search the house?** avec l'autorisation de qui ont-ils perquisitionné la maison?; **without a.** sans autorisation
4 (*usu pl*) (*people in command*) autorité *f*; *Pol* **the authorities** les autorités *fpl*, l'administration *f*; **the proper authorities** qui de droit, les autorités compétentes; **the education/housing a.** = les services chargés de l'éducation/du logement; **we'll go to the highest a. in the land** nous nous adresserons aux plus hautes instances du pays
5 (*expert*) autorité *f*, expert *m*; (*article, book*) autorité *f*; **he's an a. on China** c'est un grand spécialiste de la Chine
6 (*testimony*) **I have it on his a. that she was there** il m'a certifié qu'elle était présente; **we have it on good a. that...** nous tenons de source sûre *ou* de bonne source que...
7 (*permit*) autorisation *f*

authorization, -isation [ˌɔːθəraɪˈzeɪʃən] N (*act, permission*) autorisation *f*; (*official sanction*) pouvoir *m*, mandat *m*; **he has a. to leave the country** il est autorisé à quitter le pays; **you can't do anything without a. from the management** vous ne pouvez rien faire sans l'autorisation de la direction

authorize, -ise [ˈɔːθəraɪz] VT **1** (*empower*) autoriser; **she is authorized to act for her father** elle a pouvoir de représenter son père, elle est autorisée à représenter son père **2** (*sanction*) autoriser, sanctionner; *Fin* **to a. a loan** consentir un prêt; *Law* **to a. a drug for the market** homologuer un médicament

authorized, -ised [ˈɔːθəraɪzd] ADJ autorisé; *Fin & Law* **duly a. officer** représentant(e) *m,f* dûment habilité(e)
▸▸ *Com* ***authorized agent*** mandataire *mf*, agent *m* mandataire; *Fin* ***authorized capital*** capital *m* autorisé *ou* social *ou* nominal; *Com* ***authorized dealer*** distributeur *m* agréé; *Banking* ***authorized overdraft facility*** autorisation *f* de découvert; *Com* ***authorized representative*** mandataire *mf*, agent *m* mandataire; *St Exch* ***authorized share capital*** capital *m* autorisé; ***authorized signatory*** signataire *mf* autorisé(e) *ou* accrédité(e); *Bible* ***the Authorized Version*** = la version anglaise de la Bible de 1611, autorisée par le roi Jacques I d'Angleterre

authorship [ˈɔːθəʃɪp] N (*of book*) auteur *m*, paternité *f*; (*of invention*) paternité *f*; **a work of unknown a.** un ouvrage ou une œuvre anonyme; **they have established the a. of the book** ils ont identifié l'auteur du livre

autism [ˈɔːtɪzəm] N *Med* autisme *m*

autistic [ɔːˈtɪstɪk] ADJ *Med* autiste

auto [ˈɔːtəʊ] *Am* N voiture *f*, auto *f*
COMP d'auto, automobile
▸▸ ***auto accident*** accident *m* de voiture; *Ind* ***auto industry*** industrie *f* automobile; ***auto parts*** pièces *fpl* détachées (pour voiture)

auto- [ˈɔːtəʊ] PREF auto-

auto-addresser N *Comput* (*on laser printer*) adressage *m* automatique

auto-answer N *Comput* (*in datacomms*) réponse *f* automatique

auto-antigen N *Med* auto-antigène *m*

autobank [ˈɔːtəʊˌbæŋk] N distributeur *m* automatique de billets (de banque)

autobiographical [ˈɔːtəˌbaɪəˈɡræfɪkəl] ADJ autobiographique

autobiography [ˌɔːtəbaɪˈɒɡrəfɪ] (*pl* **autobiographies**) N autobiographie *f*

autocade [ˈɔːtəʊkeɪd] N *Am Aut* cortège *m* d'automobiles

autocorrect [ˌɔːtəʊkəˈrekt] VT *Comput* corriger automatiquement

autocracy [ɔːˈtɒkrəsɪ] (*pl* **autocracies**) N *Pol* autocratie *f*

autocrat [ˈɔːtəkræt] N *Pol* (*absolute ruler*) autocrate *m*; *Fig* despote *mf*

autocratic [ˌɔːtəˈkrætɪk] ADJ *Pol* (*government, policies*) autocratique; (*ruler*) absolu; *Fig* (*person*) despotique

autocratically [ˌɔːtəˈkrætɪkəlɪ] ADV *Pol* autocratiquement; *Fig* despotiquement

Autocue® [ˈɔːtəʊkjuː] N *Br TV* téléprompteur *m*

autodial [ˈɔːtəʊdaɪəl] N *Tel* numérotation *f* automatique; **a phone with a.** un poste à numérotation *f* automatique

autodialler [ˈɔːtəʊˌdaɪələ(r)] N *Tel* numéroteur *m* automatique

autodidact [ˌɔːtəʊˈdaɪdækt] N autodidacte *mf*

auto-dissolve N *TV & Cin* fondu *m* enchaîné automatique

autoerotic [ˌɔːtəʊɪˈrɒtɪk] ADJ autoérotique

autofocus [ˈɔːtəʊˌfəʊkəs] N *Phot* autofocus *m inv*; **camera with a.** appareil *m* autofocus
▸▸ ***autofocus camera*** appareil *m* autofocus

autogenous [ɔːˈtɒdʒənəs] ADJ *Med & Tech* autogène

autogiro [ˌɔːtəʊˈdʒaɪrəʊ] N *Aviat* autogire *m*

autograft [ˈɔːtəɡrɑːft] N *Med* autogreffe *f*

autograph ['ɔːtəgrɑːf] N autographe *m*
COMP *(letter)* autographe; *(album, collector)* d'autographes
VT *(book, picture, record)* dédicacer; *(letter, object)* signer
►► ***autograph hunter*** collectionneur(euse) *m,f* d'autographes

autogyro = **autogiro**

auto-ignition N auto-allumage *m*

autoload ['ɔːtəʊləʊd] VI *Comput* se charger automatiquement

automat ['ɔːtəmæt] N *(machine)* distributeur *m* automatique; *Am (room)* cafétéria *f* équipée de distributeurs automatiques

automatable [ˌɔːtə'meɪtəbəl] ADJ automatisable

automate ['ɔːtəmeɪt] VT automatiser

automated ['ɔːtəmeɪtɪd] ADJ automatisé
►► *Banking* ***automated clearing house*** chambre *f* de compensation automatisée; ***automated reservation*** réservation *f* télématique; *Am Banking* ***automated teller machine*** distributeur *m* automatique (de billets); ***automated ticket*** billet *m* informatisé; *Banking* ***automated withdrawal*** retrait *m* automatique

automatic [ˌɔːtə'mætɪk] ADJ *(machine)* automatique; *(answer, smile)* automatique, machinal
N **1** *(weapon)* automatique *m* **2** *Aut* voiture *f* à boîte *ou* à transmission automatique, automatique *f*; **a Volkswagen® a.** une Volkswagen® (à boîte *ou* à transmission) automatique
►► *Comput* ***automatic backup*** sauvegarde *f* automatique; *Comput* ***automatic data processing*** traitement *m* automatique des données; *Tel* ***automatic dialling*** composition *f* automatique de numéros; *Comput* ***automatic feed*** avance *f* automatique; *Rad & Elec* ***automatic frequency control*** correcteur *m* automatique de fréquence; *Rad & Elec* ***automatic gain control*** antifading *m*; *Typ* ***automatic line break*** coupure *f* automatique de fin de ligne; *Comput* ***automatic pagination*** séparation *f* automatique des pages; *Aviat* ***automatic pilot*** pilote *m* automatique; **on a. pilot** en pilotage automatique; *Fig* **to do sth on a. pilot** faire qch mécaniquement *ou* machinalement; ***automatic pistol*** pistolet *m* automatique, automatique *m*; ***automatic search*** *(on cassette player)* recherche *f* automatique (de séquences musicales); ***automatic teller machine*** distributeur *m* automatique (de billets); ***automatic ticket distributor*** distributeur *m* automatique de titres de transport; ***automatic ticket machine*** billetterie *f* automatique; *Banking* ***automatic transfer*** virement *m* automatique; *Aut* ***automatic transmission*** transmission *f* automatique; *Rad & Elec* ***automatic volume control*** antifading *m*

automatically [ˌɔːtə'mætɪkəlɪ] ADV automatiquement; *Fig* automatiquement, machinalement; **teachers are a. retired at the age of 65** les enseignants sont mis à la retraite d'office à l'âge de 65 ans; **I just a. assumed he was right** j'ai automatiquement supposé qu'il avait raison

automation [ˌɔːtə'meɪʃən] N *Tech (process of making automatic)* automatisation *f*; *(state of being automatic)* automation *f*; **factory** *or* **industrial a.** productique *f*

automatization, -isation [ˌɔːtəmətaɪ'zeɪʃən] N *Tech* automatisation *f*

automaton [ɔː'tɒmətən] *(pl* **automatons** *or* **automata** [-tə]) N *Tech* automate *m*

automobile ['ɔːtəməbiːl] N *Am* automobile *f*, voiture *f*
►► ***Automobile Association*** = société de dépannage pour les automobilistes, Touring Club *m* de France; ***automobile club*** club *m* automobile; ***the automobile industry*** l'industrie *f* automobile; ***automobile workers*** ouvriers *mpl* de l'industrie automobile

automotive [ˌɔːtə'məʊtɪv] ADJ *Tech (self-propelled)* automoteur
►► *Am* ***automotive engineering*** technique *f* automobile; *Am* ***automotive industry*** industrie *f* automobile

autonomous [ɔː'tɒnəməs] ADJ *Biol & Pol* autonome

autonomy [ɔː'tɒnəmɪ] *(pl* **autonomies)** N *Pol* **1** *(self-government)* autonomie *f* **2** *(country)* pays *m* autonome

autopilot [ˌɔːtəʊ'paɪlət] N *Aviat* pilote *m* automatique; **on a.** en pilotage automatique; *Fig* **I just went onto a.** j'ai poursuivi machinalement

autopsy ['ɔːtɒpsɪ] *(pl* **autopsies)** *Med* N autopsie *f*; **to carry out an a.** faire une autopsie; *Fig* faire une analyse
VT autopsier

auto-redial N *Tel* re-numérotation *f* automatique

auto-refresh N *Comput* autorafraîchissement *m*

autoreverse [ˌɔːtəʊrɪ'vɜːs] N *Tech* autoreverse *m*, inversion *f* automatique du sens de défilement

autosave ['ɔːtəʊˌseɪv] *Br Comput* N sauvegarde *f* automatique
VT sauvegarder automatiquement

autosome ['ɔːtəsəʊm] N *Biol* chromosome *m* somatique

autostart ['ɔːtəʊˌstɑːt] N *Comput* démarrage *m* automatique

autosuggestion [ˌɔːtəʊsə'dʒestʃən] N *Psy* autosuggestion *f*

autoswitch ['ɔːtəʊˌswɪtʃ] N *Comput* commutateur *m* automatique

autowinder ['ɔːtəʊˌwaɪndə(r)] N *Phot* avance *f* automatique du film

autumn ['ɔːtəm] N automne *m*; **in (the) a.** en automne; *Literary* **he was in the a. of his years** il était à l'automne de sa vie; **a. leaves** *(on tree)* feuilles *fpl* d'automne; *(dead)* feuilles *fpl* mortes
COMP *(colours, weather, evening)* d'automne, automnal

autumnal [ɔː'tʌmnəl] ADJ automnal, d'automne; **a. shades** teintes *fpl* automnales; **there was an a. feeling in the air, it was a.** il y avait de l'automne dans l'air
►► *Astron* ***autumnal equinox*** équinoxe *m* d'automne

auxiliary [ɔːg'zɪljərɪ] *(pl* **auxiliaries)** ADJ *(forces, workers, engine)* auxiliaire; *(heating, lighting)* d'appoint
N **1** *(assistant, subordinate)* auxiliaire *mf*; *Med* **nursing a.** infirmier(ère) *m,f* auxiliaire, aide-soignant(e) *m,f* **2** *Mil* **auxiliaries** auxiliaires *mpl* **3** *Gram* (verbe *m*) auxiliaire *m*
►► ***auxiliary power unit*** unité *f* auxiliaire d'alimentation; ***auxiliary staff*** *(gen)* le personnel auxiliaire, les auxiliaires *mpl*; *Br Sch* personnel *m* auxiliaire non enseignant; *Gram* ***auxiliary verb*** (verbe *m*) auxiliaire *m*

AV [ˌeɪ'viː] N *Br Bible (abbr* **Authorized Version)** = la version anglaise de la Bible de 1611, autorisée par le roi Jacques Ier d'Angleterre
ADJ *(abbr* **audiovisual)** audio-visuel

Av. *(written abbr* **avenue)** av

avail [ə'veɪl] N **to be of little a.** être peu utile *ou* peu avantageux; **his efforts were of no a.** ses efforts n'ont eu aucun effet; **to no a.** sans effet; **they argued with her to no a.** ils ont essayé en vain de la convaincre; **to little a.** sans grand effet; **we tried but it was to little a.** nous avons essayé mais cela n'a pas servi à grand-chose
VT **I availed myself of the opportunity to thank her** j'ai profité de l'occasion pour *ou* j'ai saisi cette occasion de la remercier
VI *Literary* servir; **nothing could a. against the storm** rien ne s'avéra efficace contre l'orage

availability [əˌveɪlə'bɪlətɪ] *(pl* **availabilities)** N **1** *(accessibility)* disponibilité *f*; *Com* **offer subject to a.** dans la limite des stocks disponibles; *(of tickets)* dans la limite des places disponibles; **the widespread a. of drugs** la facilité avec laquelle on peut se procurer de la drogue; **the a. of easy credit means that many people have got into serious debt** du fait qu'il est facile de se faire prêter de l'argent, beaucoup de gens se retrouvent couverts de dettes **2** *Am Pej Pol (of candidate)* = caractère inoffensif

available [ə'veɪləbəl] ADJ **1** *(accessible, to hand)* disponible; *(person ► for interview etc)* libre, disponible; **they made the data a. to us** ils ont mis les données à notre disposition; **they used the time a. to evacuate the area** ils ont utilisé le temps dont ils disposaient pour évacuer le secteur; **a. for work** disponible; **when are you a. to start work?** à partir de quand pouvez-vous commencer à travailler?; **we tried every a. means** nous avons essayé (par) tous les moyens possibles; *Com* **they're a. in three sizes** ils sont disponibles en trois tailles; *Com* **a. in all bookshops** en vente *ou* disponible chez tous les libraires; *Com* **also a. in white** existe également en blanc; **I'm catching the first a. flight** je prends le premier avion; *Com* **we regret that this offer is no longer a.** nous avons le regret de vous annoncer que cette offre n'est plus valable; **a. to download from our Web site** peut être téléchargé à partir de notre site web; **illegal drugs are readily a. in the town** on se procure facilement de la drogue dans cette ville; **legal aid should be a. to everyone** l'assistance juridique devrait être accessible à tous; **a. on CD-ROM/DVD** existe en CD-ROM/DVD; **a. for the Mac/PC** disponible pour Mac/PC **2** *(free)* libre, disponible; **the minister in charge was not a. for comment** le ministre responsable s'est refusé à toute déclaration; **were there any a. men at the party?** est-ce qu'il y avait des hommes disponibles *ou* libres à la soirée?
3 *Am Pej Pol (candidate)* sûr *(en raison de son caractère inoffensif)*
►► *Fin* ***available assets*** actif *m* disponible *ou* liquide; *Fin* ***available balance*** solde *m* disponible; *Fin* ***available capital*** capitaux *mpl* disponibles; *Fin* ***available cash flow*** cash-flow *m* disponible; *Fin* ***available funds*** fonds *mpl* liquides *ou* disponibles, disponibilités *fpl*; *Phot* ***available light*** lumière *f* naturelle; *Mktg* ***available market*** marché *m* effectif; *Comput* ***available memory*** mémoire *f* disponible

aval [æ'væl] N *Banking* aval *m* bancaire

avalanche ['ævəlɑːnʃ] N *also Fig* avalanche *f*
VI tomber en avalanche

avalize, -ise ['ævəlaɪz] VT *Banking* avaliser

avant-garde [ˌævɒŋ'gɑːd] N avant-garde *f*
ADJ d'avant-garde, avant-gardiste

avarice ['ævərɪs] N cupidité *f*

avaricious [ˌævə'rɪʃəs] ADJ cupide

avariciously [ˌævə'rɪʃəslɪ] ADV cupidement

avast [ə'vɑːst] EXCLAM *Old-fashioned Naut* tenez bon!, baste!

AVC [ˌeɪviː'siː] N *Fin (abbr* **additional voluntary contribution)** supplément *m* de cotisation retraite *(payé volontairement)*

Ave. *(written abbr* **avenue)** av

Ave (Maria) ['ɑːvɪ(mə'rɪə)] N *Rel* Ave *m* (Maria) *inv*

avenge [ə'vendʒ] VT venger; **he avenged his brother's death** il a vengé la mort de son frère; **he intends to a. himself on his enemy** il a l'intention de se venger de *ou* de prendre sa revanche sur son ennemi

avenger [ə'vendʒə(r)] N vengeur(eresse) *m,f*

avenging [ə'vendʒɪŋ] ADJ vengeur; **an a. angel** un ange exterminateur

avenue ['ævənjuː] N **1** *(public)* avenue *f*, boulevard *m*; *(private)* avenue *f*, allée *f (bordée d'arbres)*; *esp Am (wide street)* boulevard *m* **2** *Fig* possibilité *f*; **we must explore every a.** il faut explorer toutes les possibilités; **this opens up another a. of investigation** ceci ouvre une nouvelle voie de recherche; **an a. to fame/wealth** un moyen de parvenir à la gloire/fortune

aver [ə'vɜː(r)] *(pt & pp* **averred,** *cont* **averring)** VI *Literary* affirmer, déclarer; **everyone avers that he was present** au dire de chacun il était présent

average ['ævərɪdʒ] N **1** *(standard amount, quality)* moyenne *f*; **above/below a.** au-dessus/au-dessous de la moyenne; **on (an) a.** en moyenne; **we travelled an a. of 100 miles a day** nous avons fait une moyenne de 100 miles par jour *ou* 100 miles par jour en moyenne; **to spend an a. of £85 per week** dépenser en moyenne 85 livres par semaine; **the law of averages** la loi de la probabilité **2** *Math* moyenne *f*; **to work out the a.** établir la moyenne; **that gives an a. of six** ça fait une moyenne de six
3 *Ins & Naut (in marine insurance)* avarie(s) *f(pl)*

4 *St Exch* indice *m*
ADJ moyen; **of a. intelligence/height** d'intelligence/de taille moyenne; **the food is better than a.** la nourriture est au-dessus de la moyenne; **in an a. week** dans une semaine ordinaire; **how was your day? – a.** comment s'est passée ta journée? – moyen; *Fam* **a very a. singer** un chanteur de qualité très moyenne
VT 1 *Math* établir *ou* faire la moyenne de **2** *(perform typical number of)* atteindre la moyenne de; **household spending averages £80 per week** les dépenses des ménages sont de *ou* atteignent les 80 livres par semaine en moyenne; **to a. eight hours' work a day** travailler en moyenne huit heures par jour; **we a. 20 letters a day** nous recevons en moyenne 20 lettres par jour; **he averaged 100 km/h** il a fait du 100 km/h de moyenne
►► *Ins* ***average adjuster*** dispacheur *m*, expert-répartiteur *m*; *Ins* ***average adjustment*** dispache *f*; *Fin* ***average revenue*** produit *m* moyen; *Am Fin* ***average tax rate*** taux *m* d'imposition effectif *ou* moyen; *Fin* ***average yield*** rendement *m* moyen
►**average out VI profits a.e out at 10 percent** les bénéfices s'élèvent en moyenne à 10 pour cent; **factory production averages out at 120 cars a day** l'usine produit en moyenne 120 voitures par jour; **what does it a. out at?** ça fait combien en moyenne?
VT SEP faire la moyenne de

averse [ə'vɜːs] **ADJ to be a. to sth** *(to task, job)* répugner à qch; *(to criticism, change)* détester qch; **to be a. to doing sth** répugner à faire qch; **she's not a. to the occasional glass of wine** elle boit volontiers un verre de vin de temps à autre; **he's not a. to making money out of the crisis** ça ne le gêne pas de profiter de la crise pour se faire de l'argent

> Attention: ne pas confondre avec le mot anglais **adverse**.

aversion [ə'vɜːʃən] **N 1** *(dislike)* aversion *f*; **to have an a. to sth** avoir une aversion pour *ou* contre qch; **she has an a. to smoking** elle a horreur du tabac; **I have an a. to his brother** je ne supporte pas son frère, son frère m'est insupportable **2** *(object of dislike)* objet *m* d'aversion; *Br* **my pet a. is housework** ma bête noire *ou* ce que je déteste le plus, c'est le ménage
►► *Psy* ***aversion therapy*** thérapie *f* d'aversion

avert [ə'vɜːt] **VT 1** *(prevent)* prévenir, éviter **2** *(turn aside* ► *eyes, one's gaze, thoughts)* détourner; *(*► *blow)* détourner, parer; *(*► *suspicion)* écarter

avian flu ['eɪvɪən-] **N** grippe *f* aviaire

aviary ['eɪvjərɪ] *(pl* **aviaries)** **N** *Orn* volière *f*

aviation [ˌeɪvɪ'eɪʃən] **N** aviation *f*
COMP *(design)* d'aviation
►► ***aviation fuel*** kérosène *m*; ***aviation history*** histoire *f* de l'aviation; ***the aviation industry*** l'aéronautique *f*

aviator ['eɪvɪeɪtə(r)] *Aviat* **N** *Old-fashioned* aviateur(trice) *m,f*, pilote *m*
►► ***aviator sunglasses*** lunettes *fpl* de soleil sport

aviculture ['eɪvɪˌkʌltʃə(r)] **N** *Orn* aviculture *f*

avid ['ævɪd] **ADJ** avide; **a. for revenge** avide de revanche; **a. to learn** avide d'apprendre; **a. reader** lecteur(trice) *m,f* passionné(e)

avidity [ə'vɪdətɪ] **N** avidité *f*

avidly ['ævɪdlɪ] **ADV** avidement, avec avidité

avionics [ˌeɪvɪ'ɒnɪks] *Aviat & Tech* **N** *(UNCOUNT)* *(science)* avionique *f*
NPL *(instruments)* avionique *f*

avocado [ˌævə'kɑːdəʊ] *(pl* **avocados** *or* **avocadoes)** **N** *(fruit)* avocat *m*; *(tree)* avocatier *m*
►► ***avocado pear*** avocat *m*

Avogadro's number [ˌævəʊ'gædrəʊz-] **N** *Chem* nombre *m* d'Avogadro

avoid [ə'vɔɪd] **VT** *(object, person)* éviter; *(danger, task, punishment)* éviter, échapper à; *(blow)* esquiver; **she avoided my eyes** elle évita mon regard; **we can't a. inviting them** nous ne pouvons pas faire autrement que de les inviter; **you've been avoiding me** tu m'évites; **they couldn't a. hitting the car** ils n'ont pas pu éviter la voiture; **a. giving them too much information** évitez de leur donner trop d'informations; **don't a. the issue** n'essaie pas d'éviter *ou* d'éluder la question; **to a. sb/sth like the plague** fuir qn comme la peste/éviter qch à tout prix; *Fin* **to a. (paying) taxes** *(legally)* se soustraire à l'impôt; *(illegally)* frauder le fisc

avoidable [ə'vɔɪdəbəl] **ADJ** évitable
►► *Fin* ***avoidable costs*** coûts *mpl* évitables

avoidance [ə'vɔɪdəns] **N a. of work** le soin que l'on met à éviter le travail; **a. of duty** manquements *mpl* au devoir; *Fin* **a. of payment** non-paiement *m*; *Fin* **tax a.** évasion *f* fiscale

avoirdupois [ˌævədə'pɔɪz] **N 1** *(system)* avoirdupoids *m* **2** *Am (of person)* embonpoint *m*
COMP *(ounce, pound)* = conforme aux poids et mesures officiellement établis
►► ***avoirdupois ounce*** = 28,35g, once *f*; ***avoirdupois weight*** avoirdupoids *m*

avow [ə'vaʊ] **VT** *Formal (state)* affirmer, déclarer; *(admit)* admettre, reconnaître, confesser; **to a. oneself beaten** s'avouer vaincu; **he openly avowed himself a communist** il a ouvertement reconnu qu'il était communiste

avowal [ə'vaʊəl] **N** *Formal* aveu *m*

avowed [ə'vaʊd] **ADJ** *(enemy)* déclaré; *(aim, purpose)* avoué; **she's an a. Marxist** c'est une marxiste convaincue; **an a. homosexual** un homosexuel qui se revendique comme tel

avowedly [ə'vaʊɪdlɪ] **ADV** de son propre aveu

avuncular [ə'vʌŋkjʊlə(r)] **ADJ** avunculaire

AWACS ['eɪwæks] **N** *Aviat & Mil (abbr* **airborne warning and control system)** AWACS *m*

await [ə'weɪt] **VT 1** *(wait for)* attendre; **a long-awaited holiday** des vacances *fpl* qui se sont fait attendre; **awaiting your instructions** *(in letter, memo)* dans l'attente de vos instructions; **soldiers awaiting discharge** soldats *mpl* en instance de libération; **mail awaiting delivery** courrier *m* en souffrance; **awaiting collection** *(parcel, mail)* en souffrance; *Law* **she's awaiting trial** elle est en instance de procès **2** *(be in store for)* attendre, être réservé à; **a warm welcome awaited them** un accueil chaleureux leur fut réservé; **who knows what awaits us** qui sait ce qui nous attend *ou* est réservé

awake [ə'weɪk] *(pt* **awoke** [ə'wəʊk], *pp* **awoken** [ə'wəʊkən]) **ADJ 1** *(not sleeping)* éveillé, réveillé; **to be a.** être réveillé, ne pas dormir; **are you still a.?** tu ne dors pas encore?, tu n'es pas encore endormi?; **the noise kept me a.** le bruit m'a empêché de dormir; **I lay a. all night** je n'ai pas fermé l'œil de la nuit; **to stay a.** rester éveillé; **he was wide a.** il était bien éveillé **2** *(aware)* attentif, vigilant; **we're all a. to the dangers of our situation** nous sommes tous conscients des dangers de notre situation
VI 1 *(emerge from sleep)* se réveiller, s'éveiller; **I awoke from a deep sleep** je suis sorti d'un sommeil profond; **to a. from** *(trance, unconsciousness)* sortir de; **I awoke to the sound of birds singing** à mon réveil j'ai entendu chanter les oiseaux **2** *(become aware)* **to a. to** *(danger, fact etc)* se rendre compte de, prendre conscience de; *(possibility)* prendre conscience de; **he finally awoke from his illusions** il est enfin revenu de ses illusions
VT 1 *(person)* réveiller, éveiller **2** *Fig (curiosity, suspicions)* éveiller; *(memories)* réveiller, faire renaître; *(hope)* éveiller, faire naître; **to a. sb to sth** faire prendre conscience de qch à qn

awaken [ə'weɪkən] **VT** éveiller
VI s'éveiller

awakening [ə'weɪknɪŋ] **N 1** *also Fig (arousal)* réveil *m*; **it was a rude a.** c'était un réveil brutal *ou* pénible **2** *(beginning)* début *m*, commencement *m*
ADJ naissant

award [ə'wɔːd] **N 1** *(prize)* prix *m*; *(medal)* médaille *f*; *Mil* distinction *f* honorifique; *Sch* récompense *f*; **to make an a.** décerner un prix; *Sch* décerner une récompense; **to be given an a.** recevoir un prix; *Sch* recevoir une récompense; **the annual awards ceremony** la cérémonie annuelle de remise des prix; **he received an a. for bravery** il a reçu une médaille en reconnaissance de son courage
2 *Sch & Univ (scholarship)* bourse *f*
3 *Law (damages)* dommages-intérêts *mpl* accordés par le juge; *(decision)* décision *f*, sentence *f* (arbitrale); *Com (of contract)* adjudication *f*
4 *Austr & NZ Fin (minimum wage)* salaire *m* minimum interprofessionnel de croissance, SMIC *m*
VT 1 *(mark)* accorder; *(prize)* décerner; *Sch & Univ (scholarship)* attribuer, allouer; *Law (damages)* accorder; *Com (contract)* adjuger; *(pay increase, grant)* accorder; **she was awarded first prize** on lui a décerné le premier prix **2** *Sport (penalty, free kick)* accorder

award-winning **ADJ** *(person)* qui a reçu un prix; *(film, book)* primé; **he gave an a. performance in...** il a reçu un prix pour son rôle dans...

aware [ə'weə(r)] **ADJ 1** *(cognizant, conscious)* conscient; *(informed)* au courant, informé; **to be a. of sth** être conscient de qch; **I am quite a. of his feelings** je connais *ou* je n'ignore pas ses sentiments; **he's well a. of the risks** il est tout à fait conscient des risques; **I wasn't a. of his presence** je ne m'étais pas aperçu qu'il était là; **to become a. of sth** se rendre compte *ou* prendre conscience de qch; **she made us a. of the problem** elle nous a fait prendre conscience du problème; **as far as I am a.** autant que je sache; **not that I am a. of** pas que je sache; **without being a. of it** sans s'en rendre compte; **politically a.** politisé; **socially a.** au courant des problèmes sociaux **2** *(sensitive)* sensible

awareness [ə'weənɪs] **N** *(gen)* conscience *f*; **he has little a. of the situation** il n'a guère conscience de la situation; **a heightened a. of colour** une conscience plus aiguë des couleurs; **political a.** politisation *f*
►► *Mktg* ***awareness rating*** taux *m* de notoriété; *Mktg* ***awareness study*** étude *f* de notoriété

awash [ə'wɒʃ] **ADJ 1** *also Fig (flooded)* inondé; **a. with oil** inondé de pétrole; *Fig* **to be a. with money** *(sector, organization)* crouler sous l'argent **2** *Naut (submarine etc)* à fleur d'eau, qui affleure; **rocks a. at high tide** roches couvertes d'eau à marée haute

AWAY [ə'weɪ] **ADV 1** *(indicating movement)* **he got into his car and drove a.** il est monté dans sa voiture et il est parti; **to go a.** partir, s'en aller; **to look a.** détourner son regard; **to run/fly a.** s'enfuir/s'envoler; **they moved a. from the door** ils se sont éloignés de la porte; **they're a.!** *(at start of race)* ils sont partis; *Fam* **well a.** *(progressing)* bien en train; *(drunk)* soûl
2 *(indicating distance, position)* **the village is 10 miles a.** le village est à 10 miles; **it's less than five minutes' walk a.** c'est à moins de cinq minutes à pied; **the church was set a. from the road** l'église était située en retrait par rapport à la route; **a. in the distance** au loin, dans le lointain; **a. over there beyond the mountains** là-bas, bien loin audelà des montagnes
3 *(in time)* **it's two weeks a.** c'est dans deux semaines; **the holidays are only three weeks a.** les vacances sont dans trois semaines seulement; **a. back in the 20s** il y a bien longtemps, dans les années 20; **a. back in 1970** il y a longtemps déjà, en 1970
4 *(absent)* absent; **he feeds the cat whenever we're a.** il donne à manger au chat quand nous ne sommes pas là *ou* quand nous sommes absents; **the boss is a. on business this week** le patron est en déplacement cette semaine; **they're a. on holiday/in Madrid** ils sont (partis) en vacances/à Madrid
5 *(indicating disappearance, decline)* **the water had boiled a.** l'eau s'était évaporée (à force de bouillir); **we danced the night a.** nous avons passé toute la nuit à danser; **to fade** *or* **to die a.** *(sound)* s'éteindre; *(protests)* se taire; **government support gradually fell a.** le soutien de l'État a disparu petit à petit
6 *(continuously)* **to work a.** travailler beaucoup; **she's working a. on her novel** elle travaille d'arrache-pied à son roman; **he was singing a. to himself** il fredonnait
7 *Sport* **the team is (playing) a. this Saturday** l'équipe joue à l'extérieur *ou* en déplacement samedi
8 *Formal (idioms)* **a. with** assez de; **a. with petty**

restrictions! assez de restrictions mesquines; *esp Arch* **a. with him!** emmenez-le!; *Fam* **a. with you!** *(don't be silly)* arrête tes bêtises!

• **away from** PREP *(indicating precise distance)* à...de; *(not at, not in)* loin de; **two metres a. from us** à deux mètres de nous; **somewhere well a. from the city** quelque part très loin de la ville; **when we're a. from home** quand nous partons, quand nous ne sommes pas chez nous

▸▸ *Sport* ***away game*** match *m* à l'extérieur; ***away goal*** = but marqué lors d'un match à l'extérieur; **they won on a. goals** ils ont gagné grâce aux buts qu'ils ont marqués lors de matchs joués à l'extérieur; ***away match*** match *m* à l'extérieur; ***away strip*** = tenue portée par l'équipe qui joue à l'extérieur lorsque l'équipe qui joue à domicile a une tenue similaire; ***the away team*** l'équipe *f* qui joue à l'extérieur, les visiteurs *mpl*

AWB [ˌeɪdʌbəlju:'bi:] N *Com (abbr* **air waybill**) LTA *f*

awe [ɔ:] N admiration *f* mêlée de respect; **to be** *or* **to stand in a. of sb/sth** être impressionné par qn/qch; **he stared at her in a.** il la regardait, plein d'admiration

VT impressionner; **the children were awed by the cathedral/the tone of her voice** les enfants ont été terriblement impressionnés par la cathédrale/le ton de sa voix; **the music awed them into silence** impressionnés par la musique, ils se sont tus

aweigh [ə'weɪ] ADV *Naut* **with anchor a.** l'ancre dérapée; **anchors a.!** levez l'ancre!

awe-inspiring ADJ *(impressive)* impressionnant, imposant; *(amazing)* stupéfiant; *(frightening)* terrifiant

awesome ['ɔ:səm] ADJ **1** *(impressive)* impressionnant, imposant; *(amazing)* stupéfiant; *(frightening)* terrifiant **2** *esp Am Fam (great)* génial

awe-struck ADJ *(intimidated)* intimidé, impressionné; *(amazed)* stupéfait; *(frightened)* frappé de terreur

awful ['ɔ:fʊl] ADJ **1** *(bad)* affreux, atroce; **he was simply a. to her** il a été absolument infecte *ou* horrible avec elle; **I feel a.** je me sens très mal; **she looks a.** *(ill)* elle a l'air malade; *(badly dressed)* elle est affreusement mal habillée; **how a. for you!** ça a dû être vraiment terrible (pour vous)!; **what an a. bore!** *(person)* ce qu'il/elle peut être assommant(e)!; *(task)* quelle corvée!; **you're a.!** tu es impossible!; **what a. weather!** quel temps affreux *ou* de chien!; **she's an a. woman** c'est quelqu'un d'épouvantable **2** *(horrific* ▸ *crime, news)* épouvantable, effroyable **3** *(as intensifier)* **I have an a. lot of work** j'ai énormément de travail; **they took an a. risk** ils ont pris un risque énorme *ou* considérable; **he's an a. fool** il est bien bête

ADV *Fam (very)* très▫, terriblement; **I'm a. glad to see you** je suis rudement content de vous voir; **an a. long time** terriblement longtemps

awfully ['ɔ:flɪ] ADV *(very)* très, terriblement; **a. funny/nice** extrêmement drôle/gentil; **he's an a. good writer** il écrit merveilleusement bien; **I'm a. sorry** je suis vraiment *ou* sincèrement désolé; **thanks a.** merci infiniment *ou* mille fois; *Fam Hum* **a. a.** = maniérisme utilisé pour décrire les manières et l'accent de la haute bourgeoisie britannique

awfulness ['ɔ:fʊlnɪs] N **1** *(of behaviour, treatment)* atrocité *f* **2** *(of accident, crime)* horreur *f*

awhile [ə'waɪl] ADV *Literary* (pendant) un instant *ou* un moment; **not yet a.** pas encore, pas de sitôt; **wait a.** attendez un peu

awkward ['ɔ:kwəd] ADJ **1** *(clumsy* ▸ *person)* maladroit, gauche; *(*▸ *gesture)* maladroit, peu élégant; *(*▸ *style)* lourd, gauche; **he's a. with his hands** il n'est pas très habile de ses mains; **the a. age** l'âge ingrat

2 *(embarrassed* ▸ *person)* gêné, ennuyé; *(*▸ *silence)* gêné, embarrassé; **she felt a. about going** cela la gênait d'y aller; **it would be a. if he met her** cela serait fâcheux *ou* gênant s'il la rencontrait

3 *(difficult* ▸ *problem, situation)* délicat, fâcheux; *(*▸ *task)* délicat; *(*▸ *question)* gênant, embarrassant; *(*▸ *person)* peu commode, difficile; **you've come at an a. time** vous êtes arrivé au mauvais moment; **an a. moment** un moment inopportun; **I'm sorry to be a.** *(but that doesn't suit me)* je suis désolé d'être peu accommodant; **they could make things a. for her** ils pourraient lui mettre des bâtons dans les roues; *Fam* **he's an a. customer** il n'est pas commode; **it's a. to use** ça n'est pas facile à utiliser; **the switch is in an a. place** l'interrupteur est situé à un endroit peu accessible; **their house is a. to get to** leur maison est d'un accès difficile

4 *(uncooperative)* peu coopératif; **he's just being a.** il essaie seulement de compliquer les choses

awkwardly ['ɔ:kwədlɪ] ADV **1** *(clumsily* ▸ *dance, move)* maladroitement, peu élégamment; *(*▸ *handle, speak)* maladroitement, gauchement; **an a. phrased sentence** une phrase lourde *ou* mal formulée; **to put sth a.** dire qch d'une façon maladroite **2** *(with embarrassment* ▸ *behave)* d'une façon gênée *ou* embarrassée; *(*▸ *reply, speak)* d'un ton embarrassé *ou* gêné, avec gêne; **she grinned a.** elle a souri d'un air gêné **3** *(inconveniently)* **the lever is a. placed** le levier est mal placé; **their house is a. situated** leur maison est mal située

awkwardness ['ɔ:kwədnɪs] N **1** *(clumsiness* ▸ *of movement, person)* maladresse *f*, gaucherie *f*; *(*▸ *of style)* lourdeur *f*, inélégance *f* **2** *(unease)* embarras *m*, gêne *f*; **the a. of the situation** le côté gênant *ou* embarrassant de la situation

awl [ɔ:l] N alène *f*, poinçon *m*

awn [ɔ:n] N *Bot* barbe *f*

awning ['ɔ:nɪŋ] N **1** *(over window)* store *m*; *(on shop display)* banne *f*, store *m*; *(at door of hotel, theatre etc)* marquise *f*, auvent *m*; *Naut* taud *m*, taude *f* **2** *(tent)* auvent *m*

AWOL ['eɪwɒl] ADJ *(abbr* **absent without leave**) *Mil* **to be/to go A.** être absent/s'absenter sans permission; *Fig Hum* **to go A.** *(person)* disparaître de la circulation; *(object)* disparaître

awry [ə'raɪ] ADJ de travers, de guingois

ADV de travers; **to go a.** *(of plans etc)* mal tourner, aller de travers

axe, *Am* **ax** [æks] *(pl* **axes**) N **1** *(tool)* hache *f*; **to have an a. to grind** *(ulterior motive)* prêcher pour sa paroisse, être intéressé; *(complaint)* avoir un compte à régler; *Fam* **to get the a.** *(person)* être viré; *(programme, plan etc)* être annulé *ou* supprimé▫ **2** *Fam (guitar)* gratte *f*, râpe *f*

VT **1** *(wood)* couper, hacher **2** *Fig (person)* virer; *(project)* annuler, abandonner; *(job, position)* supprimer; **to a. public expenditure** faire des coupes claires dans les dépenses publiques

▸▸ ***axe murderer*** = assassin qui tue ses victimes à coups de hache

axial ['æksɪəl] ADJ axial

axil ['æksɪl] N *Bot* aisselle *f*

axiom ['æksɪəm] N *Math* axiome *m*

axiomatic [ˌæksɪə'mætɪk] ADJ **1** *Math* axiomatique **2** *(self-evident)* évident

axis ['æksɪs] N *(pl* **axes** [-i:z]) axe *m*

• **Axis** N *Hist* **the A.** l'Axe *m*

axle ['æksəl] N *(gen)* axe *m*; *Aut* essieu *m*; **front/rear a.** essieu *m* avant/arrière

aye ADV [eɪ] *Arch or Scot & NEng* toujours

EXCLAM [aɪ] *Arch or Scot & NEng* oui; *Naut* **a., a. sir!** oui, mon commandant!

N [aɪ] oui *m inv*; **twenty-five ayes and three noes** vingt-cinq oui et trois non, vingt-cinq pour et trois contre; **the ayes have it** les oui l'emportent

▸▸ *Br Parl* ***Aye Lobby*** = salle où se réunissent les partisans d'une motion à la Chambre des communes; ***aye vote*** vote *m* favorable

ayurveda [ˌɑ:jʊ'veɪdə] N *Med* ayurvéda *m*

ayurvedic [ˌɑ:jʊ'veɪdɪk] ADJ *Med* ayurvédique

azalea [ə'zeɪljə] N *Bot* azalée *f*

Azerbaijan [ˌæzəbaɪ'dʒɑ:n] N Azerbaïdjan *m*

Azerbaijani [ˌæzəbaɪ'dʒɑ:nɪ] N **1** *(person)* Azerbaïdjanais(e) *m,f*, Azéri(e) *m,f* **2** *(language)* azéri

ADJ azerbaïdjanais, azéri

COMP *(embassy)* d'Azerbaïdjan; *(history)* de l'Azerbaïdjan; *(teacher)* d'azéri

AZERTY keyboard [eɪ'zɜ:tɪ-] N *Comput* clavier *m* AZERTY

azimuth ['æzɪməθ] N *Astron & Geog* azimut *m*

Azores [ə'zɔ:z] NPL **the A.** les Açores *fpl*

AZT [ˌeɪzed'ti:] N *Med (abbr* **azidothymidine**) AZT *f*

Aztec ['æztek] N Aztèque *mf*

ADJ aztèque

azure ['æʒʊər] *Literary* N azur *m*

ADJ azuré, d'azur

B, b[1] [biː] **N 1** *(letter)* B, b *m inv*; **two b's** deux b; **6B Napoleon Avenue** 6ter, Napoleon Avenue; *Br* **the B792** *(road)* la départementale 792 **2** *Sch* **to get a B** avoir une bonne note, avoir 14 ou 15 sur 20 **3** *Mus* si *m inv*; **in B flat** en si bémol

▸▸ *Physiol* ***B cell*** lymphocyte *m* B; *Br* ***B road*** route *f* secondaire

b[2] **1** *(written abbr* **billion***)* milliard *m* **2** *(written abbr* **born***)* né

B2B [ˌbiːtuːˈbiː] **ADJ** *(abbr* **business to business***)* B2B

B2C [ˌbiːtuːˈsiː] **ADJ** *(abbr* **business to consumer***)* B2C

BA [ˌbiːˈeɪ] **N** *Univ (abbr* **Bachelor of Arts***)* *(person)* = titulaire d'une licence de lettres; *(qualification)* licence *f* de lettres; **to have a BA in history** avoir une licence en histoire; **John Smith, BA** John Smith, licencié ès lettres/droit/*etc*

baa [bɑː] **N** bêlement *m*; **b.!** bêê!

VI bêler

baa-lamb **N** *(in children's language)* petit agneau *m*

baba [ˈbɑːbɑː] **N** *Culin* **(rum) b.** baba *m* (au rhum)

babble [ˈbæbəl] **VI 1** *(baby)* gazouiller, babiller; *(person* ▸ *nervously)* bredouiller, bafouiller; *(*▸ *foolishly)* jacasser **2** *(stream)* murmurer

VT bredouiller, bafouiller

N 1 *(of voices)* rumeur *f*, brouhaha *m*; *(of baby)* babillage *m*, babil *m*; **she could hear the b. of conversation** elle entendait le bruit des conversations **2** *(of stream)* murmure *m*, babil *m*

▸**babble away, babble on VI 1** *(baby)* gazouiller, babiller; *(person)* jacasser; **to b. on about sth** parler de qch de façon incessante **2** *(stream)* murmurer

babbler [ˈbæblə(r)] **N** *(gen) & Orn* bavard(e) *m,f*

babbling [ˈbæblɪŋ] **N 1** *(of voices)* rumeur *f*; *(of baby)* babillage *m*, babil *m*; *(of stream)* gazouillement *m*, babil *m* **2** *(chatter)* bavardage *m*

ADJ babillard; **I felt like a b. idiot** j'avais l'impression que je racontais n'importe quoi

babe [beɪb] **N 1** *(baby)* bébé *m*; **b. in arms** enfant *m* au berceau; *Fig* **she's a b. in arms** elle est comme l'enfant qui vient de naître **2** *Fam (attractive person)* canon *m* **3** *Fam (term of endearment)* chéri(e) *m,f*; **hey b.!** salut ma belle!

ADJ *Fam* **his car's a real b. magnet** sa voiture attire les filles comme des mouches

babel [ˈbeɪbəl] **N** *(of voices)* brouhaha *m*

• **Babel N** *Bible* **the tower of B.** la tour de Babel

baboon [bəˈbuːn] **N** babouin *m*

baby [ˈbeɪbɪ] *(pl* **babies,** *pt & pp* **babied***)* **N 1** *(infant)* bébé *m*; **we've known her since she was a b.** nous l'avons connue toute petite *ou* bébé; **he's the b. of the family** il est le plus jeune *ou* le benjamin de la famille; **don't be such a b.!** ne fais pas l'enfant!; **they left him holding the b.** il l'ont laissé tomber et il a fallu qu'il se débrouille tout seul; **to throw the b. out with the bathwater** jeter le bébé avec l'eau du bain, pécher par excès de zèle

2 *Am Fam (young woman)* belle gosse *f*, minette *f* **3** *Am Fam (term of endearment)* chéri(e) *m,f*; **hey b.!** salut ma belle!

4 *Fam (pet project)* **the new library is the mayor's b.** la nouvelle bibliothèque est un projet qui tient particulièrement à cœur au maire

5 *Am Fam (person)* personne[□] *f*; **he's one tough b.** c'est un coriace *ou* un dur à cuire

6 *Am Fam (machine)* merveille *f*; **this b. drives like a dream** cette voiture est une pure merveille à conduire

VT dorloter, cajoler

ADJ *(animal)* bébé, petit; **b. cat** chaton *m*, petit chat *m*; **b. elephant** éléphanteau *m*, bébé *m* éléphant; **b. brother/sister** petit frère *m*/petite sœur *f*; **b. girl** petite fille *f*; **b. carrots/aubergines** carottes *fpl*/aubergines *fpl* naines

▸▸ ***baby batterer*** bourreau *m* d'enfants; ***baby battering*** = violences commises sur un bébé; *Fam* ***the baby blues*** *(post-natal depression)* le baby blues; ***baby boom*** baby boom *m*; ***baby boomer*** enfant *mf* du baby boom; *Br* ***baby's bottle,*** *Am* ***baby bottle*** biberon *m*; *Bot* ***baby's breath*** gypsophile *f*, brouillard *m*; *Br* ***Baby buggy®*** *(pushchair)* poussette *f*; *Am* ***baby buggy, baby carriage*** voiture *f* d'enfant, landau *m*; ***baby carrier*** porte-bébé *m inv*, Kangourou® *m*; ***baby care*** soins *mpl* pour bébés; ***baby clothes*** layette *f*; ***baby doll*** poupée *f*; ***baby face*** visage *m* de bébé; ***baby fat*** rondeurs *fpl (chez l'enfant)*; ***baby food*** aliments *mpl* pour bébés; *Mus* ***baby grand*** (piano *m*) demi-queue *m*; ***baby milk*** lait *m* maternisé *ou* pour nourrissons; ***baby monitor*** babyphone *m*; ***baby scales*** pèse-bébé *m*; *Aut* ***baby seat*** siège *m* auto pour bébé, siège *m* enfant; ***baby sling*** porte-bébé *m inv*, Kangourou® *m*; ***baby talk*** langage *m* enfantin *ou* de bébé; ***baby tooth*** dent *f* de lait

Babycham® [ˈbeɪbɪʃæm] **N** = boisson pétillante légèrement alcoolisée

baby-changing area N *(in shop, shopping centre, airport)* coin-bébé *m*; *(on motorway)* relais-bébé *m*

baby-doll ADJ b. pyjamas, b. nightdress baby-doll *m*

baby-face, baby-faced ADJ au visage poupin

Baby-gro® [ˈbeɪbɪgrəʊ] **N** *Br* grenouillère *f*

babyhood [ˈbeɪbɪhʊd] **N** petite *ou* première enfance *f*

babyish [ˈbeɪbɪɪʃ] **ADJ** *Pej (features, voice)* puéril, enfantin; *(behaviour)* puéril, enfantin, infantile

baby-listening ADJ

▸▸ ***baby-listening microphone*** babyphone *m*; ***baby-listening service*** service *m* de surveillance à distance des bébés, service *m* babyphone

Babylon [ˈbæbɪlɒn] **N** Babylone

Babylonia [ˌbæbɪˈləʊnjə] **N** Babylonie *f*

Babylonian [ˌbæbɪˈləʊnjən] **N 1** *(person)* Babylonien(enne) *m,f* **2** *(language)* babylonien *m*

ADJ babylonien

baby-minder N nourrice *f*

babymoon [ˈbeɪbɪˌmuːn] **N** = dernières vacances à deux pour les couples qui attendent un enfant

babyproof [ˈbeɪbɪˌpruf] **VT** *(house, room)* sécuriser *(pour éviter qu'un bébé ne se blesse)*

baby-sit VT garder; **she used to b. me** elle me gardait quand j'étais enfant

VI garder des enfants, faire du baby-sitting; **she baby-sits for them** elle garde leur(s) enfant(s)

baby-sitter N baby-sitter *mf*, *Can* gardien (enne) *m,f* d'enfants

baby-sitting N garde *f* d'enfants, baby-sitting *m*

baby-walker N *Br* trotteur *m*

baccalaureate [ˌbækəˈlɔːrɪət] **N 1** *Univ* licence *f* **2** *Sch* baccalauréat *m* international

baccarat [ˈbækərɑː] **N** *Cards* baccara *m*

bacchanal [ˈbækənəl] **N** *(reveller)* noceur(euse) *m,f*; *(party)* bacchanale *f*

ADJ bachique

bacchanalia [ˌbækəˈneɪlɪə] **NPL** *Myth (rite)* bacchanales *fpl*; *(party)* bacchanale *f*

bacchanalian [ˌbækəˈneɪlɪən] **ADJ** *(gen) & Myth* bachique

baccy [ˈbækɪ] **N** *Br Fam* tabac[□] *m*

bachelor [ˈbætʃələ(r)] **N 1** *(man)* célibataire *m*; **a confirmed b.** un célibataire endurci **2** *Univ* licencié(e) *m,f*

ADJ *(brother, uncle)* célibataire; *(life)* de célibataire

▸▸ ***Bachelor of Arts*** *(person)* = titulaire d'une licence de lettres; *(qualification)* licence *f* de lettres; ***bachelor's degree*** licence *f*; ***Bachelor of Education*** *(person)* = titulaire d'une licence d'enseignement; *(qualification)* licence *f* d'enseignement; ***bachelor flat*** garçonnière *f*; ***bachelor girl*** célibataire *f*; ***bachelor pad*** garçonnière *f*; *Am* ***bachelor party*** enterrement *m* de vie de garçon; *Am* **to have a b. party** enterrer sa vie de garçon; ***Bachelor of Science*** *(person)* = titulaire d'une licence de sciences; *(qualification)* licence *f* de sciences; *Am* ***Bachelor of Surgery*** *(person)* = titulaire d'un diplôme sanctionnant trois années d'études de médecine; *(qualification)* = diplôme sanctionnant trois années d'études de médecine

bachelordom [ˈbætʃələdəm] **N** *(gen)* célibat *m*; *(of men)* vie *f* de garçon

bachelorette [ˌbætʃələˈret] *Am* **N** célibataire *f*

▸▸ ***bachelorette party*** enterrement *m* de vie de jeune fille

bachelorhood [ˈbætʃələhʊd] = **bachelordom**

bacillar [ˈbæsɪlə(r)], **bacillary** [bəˈsɪlərɪ] **ADJ** *Biol & Med (disease)* bacillaire; *(shape)* bacilliforme

bacillus [bəˈsɪləs] *(pl* **bacilli** [-laɪ]*)* **N** *Biol & Med* bacille *m*

BACK [bæk]

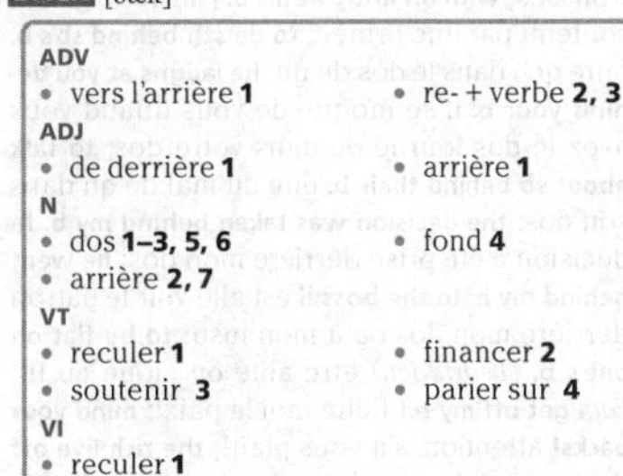

ADV
• vers l'arrière **1**
• re- + verbe **2, 3**

ADJ
• de derrière **1**
• arrière **1**

N
• dos **1–3, 5, 6**
• arrière **2, 7**
• fond **4**

VT
• reculer **1**
• soutenir **3**
• financer **2**
• parier sur **4**

VI
• reculer **1**

ADV 1 *(towards the rear)* vers l'arrière, en arrière; **he stepped b.** il a reculé d'un pas, il a fait un pas en arrière; **I pushed b. my chair** j'ai reculé ma chaise; **she tied her hair b.** elle a attaché ses cheveux; **he glanced b.** il a regardé derrière lui; **house set** *or* **standing b. from the road** maison écartée du chemin *ou* en retrait

2 *(into or in previous place)* **to come b.** revenir; **to go b.** *(return)* retourner; **to go** *or* **to turn b.** *(retrace footsteps)* rebrousser chemin; **we went b. home** nous sommes rentrés (à la maison); **my head-ache's b.** j'ai de nouveau mal à la tête, mon mal de tête a recommencé; **they'll be b. on Monday** ils rentrent *ou* ils seront de retour lundi; **I'll be right b.** je reviens tout de suite; **I'll be b.** *(threat)* vous me reverrez; **we expect him b. tomorrow** il doit rentrer demain; **as soon as you get b.** dès votre retour; **is he b. at work?** a-t-il repris le travail?; **he's just b. from Moscow** il arrive *ou* rentre de Moscou; **we went to town and b.** nous avons fait un saut en ville; **he went to his aunt's and b.** il a fait l'aller et retour chez sa tante; **the trip to Madrid and b. takes three hours** il faut trois heures pour aller à Madrid et revenir; **meanwhile, b. in Washington** entre-temps, à Washington; **b. home, there's no school on Saturdays** chez moi *ou* nous, il n'y a pas d'école le samedi

3 *(indicating return to previous state)* **she wants her children b.** elle veut qu'on lui rende ses enfants; **he went b. to sleep** il s'est rendormi; **business soon got b. to normal** les affaires ont vite repris leur cours normal; **miniskirts are coming b. (in fashion)** les minijupes reviennent à la mode

4 *(earlier)* **six pages b.** six pages plus haut; **b. in the 17th century** au 17ème siècle; **as far b. as I can remember** d'aussi loin que je m'en souvienne; **b. in November** déjà au mois de novembre; *Fam* **ten years b.** il y a dix ans□

5 *(in reply, in return)* **you should ask for your money b.** vous devriez demander un remboursement *ou* qu'on vous rembourse; **I hit him b.** je lui ai rendu son coup; **if you kick me I'll kick you b.** si tu me donnes un coup de pied, je te le rendrai; **she smiled b. at him** elle lui a répondu par un sourire; **to write b.** répondre (par écrit); **to get one's own b. (on sb)** prendre sa revanche (sur qn); **that's her way of getting b. at you** c'est sa façon de prendre sa revanche sur toi

ADJ 1 *(rear ▸ door, garden)* de derrière; *(▸ wheel)* arrière *(inv)*; **the b. legs of a horse** les pattes *fpl* arrière d'un cheval; **b. entrance** entrée *f* située à l'arrière; **to put sth on the b. burner** remettre qch à plus tard

2 *(overdue)* arriéré

3 *Ling (vowel)* postérieur

N 1 *(part of body)* dos *m*; **b. pain** mal *m* de dos; **to have a b. problem** avoir des problèmes de dos; **she carried her baby on her b.** elle portait son bébé sur son dos; **I fell flat on my b.** je suis tombé à la renverse *ou* sur le dos; **we lay on our backs** nous étions allongés sur le dos; **my b. aches** j'ai mal au dos; **the cat arched its b.** le chat a fait le gros dos; **I only saw them from the b.** je ne les ai vus que de dos; **she sat with her b. to the window** elle était assise le dos tourné à la fenêtre; **sitting with one's b. to the light** assis à contre-jour; **he was sitting with his b. to the wall** il était assis, dos au mur; *Fig* **to have one's b. to the wall** être au pied du mur; **to turn one's b. on sb** tourner le dos à qn; *Fig* abandonner qn; **when my b. was turned** quand j'avais le dos tourné; **you had your b. to me** tu me tournais le dos; **they have the police at their backs** *(in support)* ils ont la police avec eux; *(in pursuit)* ils ont la police à leurs trousses; **with an army at his b.** *(supporting him)* soutenu par une armée; **to do sth behind sb's b.** faire qch dans le dos de qn; **he laughs at you behind your b.** il se moque de vous quand vous avez le dos tourné *ou* dans votre dos; **to talk about sb behind their b.** dire du mal de qn dans son dos; **the decision was taken behind my b.** la décision a été prise derrière mon dos; **he went behind my b. to the boss** il est allé voir le patron derrière mon dos *ou* à mon insu; **to be flat on one's b.** *(bedridden)* être alité *ou* cloué au lit; *Fam* **get off my b.!** fiche-moi la paix!; **mind your backs!** attention, s'il vous plaît!; **the rich live off the backs of the poor** les riches vivent sur le dos des pauvres; **to put sb's b. up** énerver qn; **to put one's b. into sth** mettre toute son énergie dans qch; *Fam* **that's it, put your b. into it!** allez, un peu de nerf!; **to put one's b. out** se faire mal au dos; **I'll be glad to see the b. of her** je serai content de la voir partir *ou* d'être débarrassé d'elle

2 *(part opposite the front ▸ gen)* dos *m*, derrière *m*; *(▸ of coat, shirt, door)* dos *m*; *(▸ of vehicle, building, head)* arrière *m*; *(▸ of train)* queue *f*; *(▸ of book)* fin *f*; **to sit** *Br* **in the b.** *or Am* **in back** *(of car)* monter à l'arrière; **to sit at the b.** *(of bus)* s'asseoir à l'arrière; **the carriage at the b. of the train** la voiture en queue de *ou* du train; **at the b. of the book** à la fin du livre; **the garden is out** *or* **round the b.** le jardin se trouve derrière la maison; **the dress fastens at the b.** *or Am* **in b.** la robe s'agrafe dans le dos; **there was an advert on the b. of the bus** il y avait une publicité à l'arrière du bus; *Fam* **she's got a face like the b. of a bus** elle est moche comme un pou

3 *(other side ▸ of hand, spoon, envelope)* dos *m*; *(▸ of carpet, coin, medal)* revers *m*; *(▸ of fabric)* envers *m*; *(▸ of page)* verso *m*; *Fin (▸ of cheque)* dos *m*, verso *m*; **I know this town like the b. of my hand** je connais cette ville comme ma poche; *Fam* **you'll feel the b. of my hand in a minute!** tu vas en prendre une!

4 *(farthest from the front ▸ of cupboard, room, stage)* fond *m*; **b. of the mouth** arrière-bouche *f*; **b. of the throat** arrière-gorge *f*; **we'd like a table at the** *or* **in the very b.** nous voudrions une table tout au fond; *Fam* **in the b. of beyond** en pleine brousse, au diable vauvert; **it was always there at the b. of his mind that...** l'idée ne le quittait pas que...; **I've had it** *or* **it's been at the b. of my mind for ages** j'y pense depuis longtemps, ça fait longtemps que ça me travaille

5 *(binding)* dos *m*

6 *(of chair)* dos *m*, dossier *m*

7 *Sport* arrière *m*; **(full) b.** arrière *m*; **right/left b.** arrière *m* droit/gauche

VT 1 *(move backwards ▸ bicycle, car)* reculer; *(▸ horse)* faire reculer; *(▸ train)* refouler; **I backed the car into the garage** j'ai mis la voiture dans le garage en marche arrière; **she backed him into the next room** elle l'a fait reculer dans la pièce d'à côté

2 *Com (support financially ▸ company, venture)* financer, commanditer; *Fin (▸ loan)* garantir; *Fin* **to b. a bill** avaliser *ou* endosser un effet

3 *(encourage ▸ efforts, person, venture)* encourager, appuyer, soutenir; *Pol (▸ candidate, bill)* soutenir; **we backed her in her fight against racism** nous l'avons soutenue dans sa lutte contre le racisme

4 *(bet on)* parier sur, miser sur; *Sport* **to b. a winner** *(horse, team)* parier *ou* miser sur un gagnant; *Fin & Com (company, stock)* bien placer son argent; *Fig* jouer la bonne carte; *Fig* **to b. the wrong horse** parier *ou* miser sur le mauvais cheval

5 *Tex (strengthen, provide backing for ▸ curtain, material)* doubler; *(▸ picture, paper)* renforcer

6 *Mus (accompany)* accompagner

7 *Naut (sail)* masquer

VI 1 *(go in reverse ▸ car, train)* faire marche arrière; *(▸ horse, person)* reculer; **the car backed into the driveway** la voiture est entrée en marche arrière dans l'allée; **I backed into my neighbour's car** je suis rentré dans la voiture de mon voisin en reculant; **I backed into a corner** je me suis retiré dans un coin

2 *(wind)* tourner en sens inverse des aiguilles d'une montre

• **back and forth** ADV **to go b. and forth** *(person)* faire des allées et venues; *(machine, piston)* faire un mouvement de va-et-vient; **his eyes darted b. and forth** il regardait de droite à gauche

• **back to front** ADV devant derrière, à l'envers; **you've got your jumper on b. to front** tu as mis ton pull devant derrière

• **in back of** PREP *Am* derrière

▸▸ *Rad* **back announcement** = informations sur une émission qui vient d'être diffusée; *Tech* **back boiler** = ballon d'eau chaude situé derrière un foyer; *Press* **back copy** vieux numéro *m*; *Austr & NZ* **back country** campagne *f*, arrière-pays *m inv*; **back door** *(of building)* porte *f* de derrière; *Fin* financement *m* déguisé; *Fig* **to get in through** *or* **by the b. door** être pistonné; **back end** *(of car, bus)* arrière *m*; *(of train)* queue *f*; **the b. end of the year** l'arrière-saison *f*; *Ling* **back formation** dérivation *f* régressive; *Am* **back haul** = trajet de retour d'un camion; *Fin* **back interest** arrérages *mpl*, intérêts *mpl* arriérés; *Press* **back issue** vieux numéro *m*; *Cin & TV* **back light** décrochage *m*; *Cin* **back lot** plateau *m* extérieur *(d'un studio)*; *Typ* **back matter** annexes *fpl* en fin d'ouvrage; *Press* **back number** vieux numéro *m*; *Banking* **back office** back-office *m*; **back office staff** personnel *m* de back-office; *Com* **back orders** commandes *fpl* en souffrance; **back page** dernière page *f*; *Ftbl* **back pass** passe *f* en retrait; **back passage** *Anat* rectum *m*; *(alley)* ruelle *f*; **back pay** rappel *m* de salaire; *Cin & Theat* **back projection** rétroprojection *f*; **back rent** arriéré *m* de loyer; **back road** petite route *f*; **back room** *(in house)* pièce *f* de derrière; *(in shop)* arrière-boutique *f*; *(for research)* laboratoire *m* de recherche secret; **the b. room is the quietest** la pièce qui donne sur l'arrière est la plus calme; **back seat** siège *m* arrière; *Fig* **to take a b. seat** *(job, project)* passer au second plan; *(person)* s'effacer; **back shift** *(people)* = équipe du soir; **to work** *or* **be on the b. shift** être (de l'équipe) du soir; *Ling* **back slang** verlan *m*; **back straight** ligne *f* (droite) d'en face; **back street** petite rue *f*; **I grew up in the b. streets of Chicago** j'ai été élevé dans les mauvais quartiers de Chicago; *Horseracing* **back stretch** *(on race course)* ligne *f* d'en face; *Am Fam* **back talk** impertinence□ *f*, insolence□ *f*; *Fin* **back taxes** arriéré *m* d'impôts

▸ **back away** VI **1** *(car)* faire marche arrière **2** *(person)* (se) reculer; **she backed away from him** elle a reculé devant lui; *Fig* **they have backed away from making a decision** ils se sont abstenus de prendre une décision

▸ **back down** VI *(accept defeat ▸ in argument)* admettre qu'on est dans son tort; *(▸ in conflict)* faire marche arrière; **he finally backed down on the issue of membership** il a fini par céder sur la question de l'adhésion

▸ **back off** VI **1** *(withdraw)* reculer; *Fam Fig* **b. off, will you!** fiche-moi la paix!, lâche-moi les baskets! **2** *Am (accept defeat ▸ in argument)* admettre qu'on est dans son tort; *(▸ in conflict)* faire marche arrière

▸ **back onto** VT INSEP *(have back facing towards)* donner sur (à l'arrière); **the house backs onto the river** l'arrière de la maison donne sur la rivière

▸ **back out** VI **1** *(car)* sortir en marche arrière; *(person)* sortir à reculons **2** *Fig (withdraw)* se dérober, tirer son épingle du jeu; **don't b. out now!** ne faites pas marche arrière maintenant!; **they backed out of the deal** ils se sont retirés de l'affaire; **he's trying to b. out (of it)** il voudrait se dédire

▸ **back up** VI **1** *(car)* faire marche arrière **2** *(drain)* se boucher; *(water)* refouler **3** *Comput* sauvegarder

VT SEP 1 *(car, horse)* faire reculer; *(train)* refouler **2** *(support ▸ claim, story)* appuyer, soutenir; *(▸ person)* soutenir, épauler, seconder; **to b. sb up in an argument** donner raison à qn; **her story is backed up by eye witnesses** sa version des faits est confirmée par des témoins oculaires; **he backed this up with a few facts** il a étayé ça avec quelques faits

3 *Comput (data, file)* sauvegarder

4 *(accumulate)* **traffic is backed up for 5 miles** il y a un embouteillage sur 8 km

backache ['bækeɪk] N mal *m* de dos; **to have b.** avoir mal au dos

backbench ['bækbentʃ] *Parl* N = banc des membres du Parlement britannique sans fonction ministérielle; **discontent on the backbenches** mécontentement parmi les députés sans fonction ministérielle

▸▸ **backbench rebellion** rébellion *f* des députés de base

backbencher [ˌbæk'bentʃə(r)] N *Parl* = parlementaire sans fonction ministérielle, *Can* simple député(e) *m,f*, député(e) *m,f* d'arrière-banc

> **BACKBENCHER**
>
> Les "backbenchers" sont assis aux derniers rangs de la Chambre des communes, tandis que les rangs de devant sont réservés aux ministres et aux membres du "shadow cabinet" (voir aussi l'encadré sur **shadow cabinet**).

backbite ['bækbaɪt] VT *(person)* médire de VI médire

backbiting ['bæk,baɪtɪŋ] N médisance *f*

backboard ['bækbɔːd] N *Med & Tech (board)* planche *f*, panneau *m*; *Sport (in basketball)* panneau *m*

backbone ['bækbəʊn] N 1 *Anat* colonne *f* vertébrale; *Zool* épine *f* dorsale

2 *(of country, organization)* pivot *m*; **tourism is the b. of the economy** le tourisme est le pivot de l'économie; **she is the b. of the movement** elle est le moteur du mouvement

3 *Fig (strength of character)* fermeté *f*, caractère *m*; **he has no b.** il n'a rien dans le ventre

4 *Comput (of network)* épine *f* dorsale, réseau *m* d'interconnexion

backbreaking ['bæk,breɪkɪŋ] ADJ éreintant; **b. work** un travail à vous casser les reins

backburn ['bækbɜːn] *Austr* N *(to control forest fire)* contre-feu *m*

VI allumer un contre-feu

backchat ['bæktʃæt] N *Br Fam* impertinence[□] *f*, insolence[□] *f*; **and I want none of your b.** et je ne veux pas de discussions

backcloth ['bækklɒθ] N *Theat* toile *f* de fond; *Fig* toile *f* de fond, fond *m*

backcomb ['bækkəʊm] VT *(hair)* crêper

backdate [,bæk'deɪt] VT *(cheque, document)* antidater; **the pay rise is backdated to March** l'augmentation de salaire a un effet rétroactif à compter de mars

backdrop ['bækdrɒp] N 1 *Theat* toile *f* de fond; *(with perspective)* découverte *f* 2 *Fig (background)* toile *f* de fond, arrière-plan *m*; **against a b. of continuing violence** avec, comme arrière-plan *ou* toile de fond, un climat de violence permanente

-backed [bækt] SUFF 1 *(chair)* à dos, à dossier; **a high-b. chair** une chaise à dos *ou* dossier haut; **silk-b.** à dos *ou* dossier en soie; **a broad-b. man** un homme qui a le dos large 2 *(supported by)* **US-b. rebels** des rebelles soutenus par les États-Unis

back-end load N *Am St Exch* frais *mpl* de sortie

backer ['bækə(r)] N 1 *(supporter)* partisan(e) *m,f*; *(financial supporter)* commanditaire *mf*, bailleur (eresse) *m,f* de fonds; *Fin (of bill)* donneur *m* d'aval, avaliseur *m*; **we need a b.** il nous faut un mécène 2 *Sport (punter)* parieur(euse) *m,f*

backfill ['bækfɪl] *Constr* N *(of trench)* remplissage *m*

VT *(trench)* remplir

backfire [,bæk'faɪə(r)] VI 1 *(car)* pétarader 2 *(plan)* avoir l'effet inverse; **to b. on sb** se retourner contre qn

N 1 *(noise)* pétarade *f*; *(explosion)* retour *m* de flamme 2 *(controlled fire)* contre-feu *m*

backgammon ['bæk,gæmən] N backgammon *m*; **to play b.** jouer au backgammon

▸▸ **backgammon board** damier *m* de backgammon

background ['bækgraʊnd] N 1 *(scene, view)* fond *m*, arrière-plan *m*; *(sound)* fond *m* sonore; *Theat* fond *m*; **yellow flowers on a green b.** des fleurs jaunes sur fond vert; **in the b.** dans le fond, à l'arrière-plan; **music was playing in the b.** il y avait de la musique en bruit de fond; **there was a lot of noise in the b.** il y avait beaucoup de bruit de fond; *Fig* **his wife remains very much in the b.** sa femme est très effacée *ou* reste à l'écart

2 *(of person ▸ history)* antécédents *mpl*; *(▸ family)* milieu *m* socioculturel; *(▸ experience)* formation *f*, acquis *m*; *(▸ education)* formation *f*, bagage *m*; **people from a working-class b.** gens *mpl* de milieu ouvrier; **she has a good b. in history** elle a une bonne formation en histoire; **what is the candidate's b.?** *(social)* à quel milieu social appartient le candidat?; *(professional)* quelle est la formation du candidat?

3 *(of event, situation)* contexte *m*, climat *m*; **the economic b. to the crisis** les raisons économiques de la crise; **the talks are taking place against a b. of political tension** les débats ont lieu dans un climat de tension politique; **the report looks at the b. to the unrest** le rapport examine l'historique de l'agitation

4 *Comput* arrière-plan *m*; **the program works in the b.** le programme est exécuté en arrière-plan

ADJ 1 *(unobtrusive ▸ noise)* de fond; **b. colour** couleur *f* de fond 2 *(facts, material)* de base, de fond; **b. information** éléments *mpl* de référence *ou* de base; **I need a bit more b. information** j'ai besoin de plus de données

▸▸ *Comput* **background job** tâche *f* de fond; **background light** éclairage *m* d'ambiance; *Comput* **background (mode) printing** impression *f* en arrière-plan; **background music** musique *f* d'ambiance *ou* de fond; *Cin & Theat* fond *m* sonore; *Comput* **background processing** traitement *m* de données en tâches de fond; *Phys* **background radiation** rayonnement *m* naturel; **background reading** lectures *fpl* complémentaires; *Comput* **background task** tâche *f* d'arrière-plan

backhand ['bækhænd] N 1 *Sport* revers *m*; **her b. is weak** son revers manque de puissance; **keep serving to his b.** continue de servir sur son revers 2 *(writing)* écriture *f* renversée *ou* penchée à gauche

ADJ *Sport (stroke)* en revers; *(volley)* de revers

ADV en revers

backhanded ['bækhændɪd] ADJ 1 *(blow, slap)* donné avec le revers de la main 2 *(compliment, remark)* équivoque

▸▸ *Sport* **backhanded stroke** revers *m*

backhander ['bæk,hændə(r)] N 1 *(blow, stroke)* coup *m* du revers de la main; *Sport* revers *m* 2 *(comment)* remarque *f* équivoque 3 *Br Fam (bribe)* pot-de-vin *m*, dessous-de-table *m inv*

backing ['bækɪŋ] N 1 *(support)* soutien *m*, appui *m*; *(financial support)* financement *m*; **to give financial b. to sth** financer qch

2 *(material)* renfort *m*

3 *Mus (accompaniment)* accompagnement *m*

4 *Horseracing (bets)* paris *mpl*

▸▸ *Br Mus* **backing group** = musiciens qui accompagnent un chanteur; **backing track** piste *f* de fond; **backing vocalist** choriste *mf*; **backing vocals** chœurs *mpl*

backlash ['bæklæʃ] N retour *m* de manivelle; **a b. of violence** une réaction de violence

backless ['bæklɪs] ADJ *(dress, top)* dos nu *(inv)*

backlighting ['bæklaɪtɪŋ] N *Cin & TV* éclairage *m* en contre-jour

backlit ['bæklɪt] ADJ *Comput (screen)* rétroéclairé

backlog ['bæklɒg] N accumulation *f*, arriéré *m*; **to have a b. of correspondence/work** avoir du retard dans son courrier/travail, avoir du courrier/travail en retard; *Com* **a b. of orders** des commandes inexécutées *ou* en souffrance

backpack ['bækpæk] N sac *m* à dos

VI voyager sac au dos

backpacker ['bækpækə(r)] N routard(e) *m,f*

backpacking ['bækpækɪŋ] N **to go b.** voyager sac au dos; **b. is very popular with students** les étudiants aiment beaucoup voyager sac au dos

backpedal [,bæk'pedəl] *(Br pt & pp* **backpedalled**, *cont* **backpedalling**, *Am pt & pp* **backpedaled**, *cont* **backpedaling**) VI 1 *(on bicycle)* rétropédaler 2 *Fig (change mind)* faire marche arrière; **to b. on a promise** revenir sur une promesse

backpedalling, *Am* **backpedaling** ['bæk,pedəlɪŋ] N *(on bicycle)* rétropédalage *m*; *Fig* marche *f* arrière

back-pressure N *Tech* contre-pression *f*

back-scratcher N *(implement)* gratte-dos *m inv*

back-scratching N *Fig* échange *m* de faveurs

back-seat ADJ

▸▸ *Pej* **back-seat driver** *(in car)* = personne qui donne toujours des conseils au conducteur; *(interfering person)* donneur(euse) *m,f* de leçons; **back-seat passenger** passager *m* arrière

backsheesh, backshish [,bæk'ʃiːʃ] N *Fam* bakchich *m*

backside ['bæksaɪd] N *Fam* derrière *m*, fesses[□] *fpl*; **he just sits around on his b. all day** il reste assis toute la journée à ne rien faire

backsight ['bæksaɪt] N *(on rifle)* cran *m* de mire *ou* de hausse; *(in surveying)* rétrovisée *f*

backslash ['bækslæʃ] N barre *f* oblique inversée

backslide [,bæk'slaɪd] *(pt* **backslid** [-'slɪd], *pp* **backslid** [-'slɪd] *or* **backslidden** [-'slɪdən]) VI retomber, récidiver

backsliding ['bæk,slaɪdɪŋ] N récidive *f*; **no b.!** pas question de récidiver!

backspace ['bækspeɪs] *Comput & Typ* N espacement *m ou* retour *m* arrière

VT rappeler

VI faire un retour arrière

▸▸ **backspace key** touche *f* retour arrière

backstage [,bæk'steɪdʒ] N *Theat & Fig* coulisse *f*, coulisses *fpl*

ADV *Theat* dans la coulisse *ou* les coulisses, derrière la scène; *Fig* en coulisse, en secret; **to go b.** aller dans les coulisses

ADJ *Fig* secret(ète), furtif

backstairs [,bæk'steəz] NPL *(for servants)* escalier *m* de service; *(secret)* escalier *m* secret *ou* dérobé

ADJ *(secret)* secret(ète); *(unfair)* déloyal

▸▸ **backstairs gossip** commérages *mpl (des domestiques)*

backstitch ['bækstɪtʃ] *Sewing* N point *m* arrière

VT coudre en point arrière

VI coudre en point arrière

backstreet ['bækstriːt] ADJ *(secret)* secret(ète), furtif; *(underhand)* louche

▸▸ **backstreet abortion** avortement *m* clandestin; **backstreet abortionist** faiseuse *f* d'anges, *Pej* avorteur(euse) *m,f*

backstroke ['bækstrəʊk] N *Swimming* dos *m* crawlé, *Can* nage *f* sur le dos; **to do (the) b.** nager le dos crawlé, *Can* nager sur le dos

back-to-back ADJ *also Fig* dos à dos

ADV *also Fig* dos à dos; **they're showing the two films b.** ils passent les deux films l'un après l'autre; **to play two games b.** jouer deux parties l'une à la suite de l'autre

N *(houses)* **back-to-backs** = rangée de maisons construites dos à dos, typique des régions industrielles du nord de l'Angleterre

▸▸ *Fin* **back-to-back credit** crédit *m* dos-à-dos

backtrack ['bæktræk] VI revenir sur ses pas, rebrousser chemin; *Fig* faire marche arrière; **he's already backtracking from** *or* **on his agreement** il est déjà en train de revenir sur son accord

backup ['bækʌp] N 1 *(support)* soutien *m*, appui *m*; **to ask for b.** *(police)* demander des renforts

2 *(reserve)* réserve *f*; *(substitute)* remplaçant(e) *m,f*

3 *Comput* sauvegarde *f*; **to do the b.** faire la sauvegarde

4 *Am Mus* = musiciens qui accompagnent un chanteur

5 *Am (traffic jam)* embouteillage *m*

ADJ *(plan)* de secours; *(supplies)* supplémentaire, de réserve

▸▸ *Comput* **backup copy** copie *f* de sauvegarde; *Comput* **backup device** unité *f* de sauvegarde; *Comput* **backup disk** sauvegarde *f*; *Comput* **backup file** fichier *m* de sauvegarde; *Am Aut* **backup light** phare *m* de recul; *Comput* **backup storage** mémoire *f* auxiliaire; *Comput* **backup system** *(for doing the backup)* système *m* de sauvegarde; *(auxiliary system)* système *m* de secours; **backup team** *(which provides support)* équipe *f* de soutien; *(which acts as replacement)* équipe *f* de remplacement; *Mil* **backup troops** renforts *mpl*

backward ['bækwəd] ADJ 1 *(directed towards the rear)* en arrière, rétrograde; **without a b. look** sans jeter un regard en arrière; **b. and forward motion** mouvement *m* de va-et-vient 2 *(late in development ▸ country, society, child)* arriéré; **the b. state of the country** le retard dont souffre le pays 3 *(reluctant)* hésitant, peu disposé; **he's not b. about giving his opinion** il n'hésite pas à donner son avis; *Hum* **she's not b. at coming forward** elle n'hésite pas à se mettre en avant

ADV = **backwards**

▸▸ *Econ* **backward integration** intégration *f* en amont; *Econ* **backward pricing** rajustement *m* des prix; *Comput* **backward search** recherche *f* arrière

backwardation [,bækwə'deɪʃən] N *Fin & St Exch* déport *m*

backward-compatible ADJ *Comput* compatible avec les versions antérieures

backwardness ['bækwədnɪs] N 1 *(in development ▸ of country)* sous-développement *m*; *(▸ of person)* retard *m* mental, arriération *f*; *(▸ of econ-*

omy) retard *m* **2** *(reluctance)* hésitation *f*, lenteur *f*

backwards [ˈbækwədz] **ADV 1** *(towards the rear)* en arrière; *also Fig* **a step b.** un pas en arrière; **I fell b.** je suis tombé en arrière *ou* à la renverse
2 *(towards the past)* en arrière, vers le passé; **looking b. in time** en remontant dans le temps
3 *(with the back foremost)* **to walk b.** marcher à reculons; **you've got your sweater on b.** tu as mis ton pull à l'envers *ou* devant derrière
4 *(in reverse)* à l'envers; **now say it b.** dis-le à l'envers maintenant
5 *(thoroughly)* à fond, sur le bout des doigts; **she knows her subject b.** elle connaît son sujet sur le bout des doigts
• **backwards and forwards ADV to go b. and forwards** *(person)* aller et venir; *(machine, piston)* faire un mouvement de va-et-vient; *(pendulum)* osciller; **we walked b. and forwards along the beach** nous avons marché de long en large sur la plage; **she goes b. and forwards between London and Paris** elle fait la navette entre Londres et Paris

backwash [ˈbækwɒʃ] **N** remous *mpl*; *Naut (of ship)* sillage *m*, remous *mpl*; *(of waves)* ressac *m*; *Fig* **he was caught up in the b. of the scandal** il s'est retrouvé pris dans les contrecoups du scandale

backwater [ˈbæk,wɔːtə(r)] **N** *(of river)* bras *m* mort; *Fig (remote spot)* coin *m* tranquille; *Pej* coin *m* perdu; **a cultural b.** un désert culturel

backwoods [ˈbækwʊdz] **NPL** *(forest)* région *f* forestière *(peu peuplée)*; *Fig (remote spot)* coin *m* tranquille; *Pej* coin *m* perdu; **to live in the b.** habiter un trou perdu *ou* un bled
ADJ *(remote)* isolé; *(backward)* peu avancé

backwoodsman [ˈbækwʊdzmən] *(pl* **backwoodsmen** [-mən]**) N** *(who lives in forest)* habitant *m* de la forêt; *Pej (uncouth person)* rustre *m*, rustaud *m*

baclava = **baklava**

bacon [ˈbeɪkən] **N** lard *m* (maigre), bacon *m*; **a slice** *or* **rasher of b.** une tranche de lard; **b. and eggs** œufs *mpl* au bacon *ou* au lard; **b. sandwich** sandwich *m* au bacon; *Fig* **to save sb's b.** sauver la peau de qn; *Fam* **to bring home the b.** *(be the breadwinner)* faire bouillir la marmite; *(succeed)* décrocher la timbale *ou* le gros lot
►► ***bacon slicer*** coupe-jambon *m inv*

BACS [bæks] **N** *Banking (abbr* **Bankers' Automated Clearing Services**) système *m* électronique de compensation de chèques; **to pay by B.** payer par virement électronique

bacteria [bækˈtɪərɪə] **NPL** *Biol & Med* bactéries *fpl*

bacterial [bækˈtɪərɪəl] **ADJ** *Biol & Med* bactérien
►► *Biol* ***bacterial culture*** culture *f* microbienne

bacteriological [bæk,tɪərɪəˈlɒdʒɪkəl] **ADJ** *Biol* bactériologique
►► *Biol & Mil* ***bacteriological warfare*** guerre *f* bactériologique

bacteriologist [bæk,tɪərɪˈɒlədʒɪst] **N** *Biol* bactériologiste *mf*

bacteriology [bæk,tɪərɪˈɒlədʒɪ] **N** *Biol* bactériologie *f*

bacterium [bækˈtɪərɪəm] *(pl* **bacteria** [-rɪə]**) N** *Biol & Med* bactérie *f*

Bactrian camel [ˈbæktrɪən-] **N** chameau *m* de Bactriane

BAD [bæd]

ADJ	
• mauvais **1, 2, 4, 5, 7, 8**	• grave **3**
• malade **6**	• pourri **8**
N	
• mauvais	

(compar **worse** [wɜːs], *superl* **worst** [wɜːst])
ADJ 1 *(unpleasant* ► *breath, news, terms, weather)* mauvais; *(*► *smell, taste)* mauvais, désagréable; **that's too b.!** *(regrettable)* c'est *ou* quel dommage!; *(hard luck)* tant pis pour toi!; **it's too b. he had to leave** quel dommage qu'il ait été obligé de partir; **I have a b. feeling about this** j'ai le pressentiment que ça va mal tourner; **he's/she's not b.-looking** il/elle n'est pas mal; **he's in a b. mood** *or* **b. temper** il est de mauvaise humeur; **she has a b. temper** elle a un sale caractère, elle a un caractère de chien *ou* de cochon; **I'm on b. terms with her** nous sommes en mauvais termes; **to come to a b. end** mal finir; **it's a b. business** *(unpleasant)* c'est une sale affaire; *(unhappy)* c'est une triste affaire; **things went from b. to worse** les choses se sont gâtées *ou* sont allées de mal en pis
2 *(unfavourable* ► *effect, result)* mauvais, malheureux; *(*► *omen, report)* mauvais, défavorable; *(*► *opinion)* mauvais *(before n)*; **that looks b.** *(augurs ill)* c'est mauvais signe; **things look b.** la situation n'est pas brillante; **is this a b. time to ask for leave?** peut-être n'est-ce pas le moment de demander des congés?; **am I phoning at a b. time?** je vous dérange?; **please don't say anything b. about him** ne dis pas de mal de lui, s'il te plaît; **he's in a b. way** *(ill, unhappy)* il va mal, il est en piteux état; *(in trouble)* il est dans de sales draps
3 *(severe* ► *accident, mistake)* grave; *(*► *pain)* violent, aigu(e); *(*► *headache)* violent; *(*► *climate, winter)* rude, dur; **I have a b. cold** j'ai un gros rhume; **she has a b. case of flu** elle a une mauvaise grippe; **is the pain b.?** est-ce que cela fait très mal?; **that looks b.** *(injury, accident)* ça a l'air grave
4 *(evil, wicked* ► *person)* méchant, mauvais; *(*► *behaviour, habit)* mauvais, odieux; **to call sb b. names** traiter qn de tous les noms, injurier qn; **you've been a b. girl!** tu as fait la vilaine *ou* la méchante!; **b. boy!** vilain!; **b. language** gros mots *mpl*, grossièretés *fpl*
5 *(harmful)* mauvais, néfaste; **smoking is b. for your health** le tabac est mauvais pour la santé; **eating all these sweets is b. for him** c'est mauvais pour lui *ou* ça ne lui vaut rien de manger autant de sucreries; **to be** *or* **have a b. influence on sb** avoir une mauvaise influence sur qn
6 *(unhealthy* ► *leg, arm, person)* malade; *(*► *tooth)* carié; **to have b. teeth** avoir de mauvaises dents; **to have a b. back** avoir des problèmes de dos; **your grandmother is b. today** ta grand-mère ne va pas *ou* ne se sent pas bien aujourd'hui; **how are you? – not so b.** comment allez-vous? – on fait aller *ou* pas trop mal; *Fam* **he was taken b. at the office** il a eu un malaise au bureau; **to have a b. heart** être cardiaque, avoir le cœur malade
7 *(poor* ► *light, work)* mauvais, de mauvaise qualité; *(*► *actor, pay, performance, road)* mauvais; **he's got b. eyesight** il n'a pas de bons yeux; **that's not b. for a beginner** ce n'est pas mal pour un débutant; *Br Fam* **your painting isn't half b.** ton tableau n'est pas mal du tout□; **the salary isn't b.** le salaire est convenable; **it was a b. buy** ce n'était pas un bon investissement; **he speaks rather b. Spanish** il parle plutôt mal espagnol *ou* un espagnol plutôt mauvais; **it would be b. form** *or* **manners to refuse** ce serait impoli de refuser; **that looks b.** *(in eyes of other people)* c'est mal vu; **I've always been b. at maths** je n'ai jamais été doué pour les maths, j'ai toujours été mauvais en maths; **he's b. at keeping a secret** il ne sait pas garder un secret; **she's b. about paying bills on time** elle ne paie jamais ses factures à temps; *Fam* **he's always turning up like a b. penny** on n'arrive jamais à se débarrasser de lui; *Fam* **I'm having a b. hair day** *(my hair's a mess)* je n'arrive pas à me coiffer aujourd'hui□; *(I'm having a bad day)* aujourd'hui c'est un jour sans, c'est pas mon jour; **b. light stopped play** *(at cricket match)* la partie a été remise à cause d'un manque de lumière
8 *(food)* mauvais, pourri; **to go b.** *(milk)* tourner; *(meat)* pourrir, se gâter; **a b. apple** une pomme pourrie; *Fig* une brebis galeuse; *Fig* **one b. apple spoils the barrel** il ne faut qu'une brebis galeuse pour gâter un troupeau
9 *(unhappy, uncomfortable)* **I feel b. about leaving you alone** cela m'ennuie de te laisser tout seul; **he felt b. about the way he'd treated her** il s'en voulait de l'avoir traitée comme ça; **I feel b. about firing him but I'll have to** cela m'embête d'avoir à le renvoyer, mais il faudra bien que je le fasse
10 *Fam (very good)* terrible; **man, you're looking b.!** mon vieux, tu as l'air en super forme!
N mauvais *m*; **you have to take the b. with the good** il faut prendre les choses comme elles viennent, bonnes ou mauvaises; **he's gone to the b.** il a mal tourné; *Fin* **he is £5,000 to the b.** *(overdrawn)* il a un découvert de 5000 livres; *(after a deal)* il a perdu 5000 livres; *Fam* **she got in b. with her boss** elle n'a pas la cote avec son patron; *Fam* **my b.!** c'est ma faute!
ADV *Fam* **he wants it b.** il en meurt d'envie; **she's got it b. for him** elle l'a dans la peau; *Am* **he was beaten b.** il s'est fait méchamment tabasser
►► *Banking* ***bad cheque*** chèque *m* sans provision; *Comput* ***bad command*** commande *f* erronée; *Fin* ***bad debt*** créance *f* irrécouvrable *ou* douteuse; ***bad debt provision*** provision *f* pour créances douteuses; ***bad debtor*** créance *f* irrécouvrable *ou* douteuse; ***bad faith*** mauvaise foi *f*; *Comput* ***bad file name*** nom *m* de fichier erroné; *Comput* ***bad sector*** secteur *m* endommagé

bada bing [,bædəˈbɪŋ] **EXCLAM** *Am Fam* et voilà!

badass [ˈbædæs] *Am very Fam* **N** *(person)* dur(e) *m,f* (à cuire)
ADJ 1 *(intimidating, tough)* **to be b.** être un dur à cuire **2** *(excellent)* super, génial; **her new sneakers are so b.** ils sont super, ses nouveaux tennis

baddie, baddy [ˈbædɪ] **N** *Br Fam* méchant□ *m*; **he's the b.** c'est lui le méchant

bade [bæd, beɪd] *pt of* **bid**

badge [bædʒ] **N 1** *(gen)* insigne *m*; *(metal, plastic)* badge *m*; *(fabric)* écusson *m*; *(on lapel)* pin's *m inv*; *(of scout)* badge *m*; *Mil* insigne *m* **2** *Fig* signe *m*, marque *f*
►► ***badge of office*** insigne *m* de fonction

badger [ˈbædʒə(r)] **N** blaireau *m*
VT harceler, persécuter; **stop badgering your mother with questions** arrête de harceler ta mère de questions; **she badgered us into going** elle nous a harcelés jusqu'à ce que nous y allions
►► ***badger baiting*** = chasse au blaireau avec des chiens; ***badger sett*** terrier *m* de blaireau

badinage [ˈbædɪ,nɑːʒ] **N** *Literary* badinage *m*

badly [ˈbædlɪ] *(compar* **worse** [wɜːs], *superl* **worst** [wɜːst]) **ADV 1** *(poorly)* mal; **b. made/organized** mal fait/organisé; **b. lit** mal éclairé; **things aren't going too b.** ça ne va pas trop mal; **the candidate did** *or* **came off b. in the exams** le candidat ne s'en est pas bien sorti aux examens; **his business is doing b.** ses affaires marchent *ou* vont mal, il fait de mauvaises affaires; **I feel b. about it** *(sorry)* je le regrette beaucoup; *(embarrassed)* cela me gêne beaucoup; **don't think b. of him for what he did** ne lui en voulez pas de ce qu'il a fait; **she took the news b.** elle a mal pris la nouvelle; **to be b. off** *(financially)* être dans la gêne; **we're b. off for supplies** nous manquons de provisions
2 *(behave* ► *improperly)* mal; *(*► *cruelly)* méchamment, avec cruauté
3 *(severely* ► *burn, damage)* gravement, sérieusement; *(*► *hurt)* gravement, grièvement; **the town was b. affected by the storm** la ville a été sérieusement touchée par l'orage; **she had been b. beaten** elle avait reçu des coups violents; **the army was b. defeated** l'armée a subi une sévère défaite; **b. wounded** gravement *ou* grièvement blessé
4 *(very much)* énormément; **he b. needs** *or* **he's b. in need of a holiday** il a grand *ou* sérieusement besoin de (prendre des) vacances; **we b. want to see her** nous avons très envie de la voir

bad-mannered ADJ mal élevé

bad-minded [-ˈmaɪndɪd] **ADJ** *Fam* méchant□

badminton [ˈbædmɪntən] **N** *Sport* badminton *m*
►► ***badminton racket*** raquette *f* de badminton

badmouth [ˈbædmaʊθ] **VT** *esp Am Fam* débiner

badness [ˈbædnɪs] **N 1** *(wickedness)* méchanceté *f*, *(cruelty)* cruauté *f* **2** *(inferior quality)* mauvaise qualité *f*, mauvais état *m*

bad-tempered ADJ *(person)* grincheux; *(reply)* désagréable; **to be b.** *(temporarily)* être de mauvaise humeur; *(permanently)* avoir mauvais caractère

baffle [ˈbæfəl] **VT 1** *(puzzle)* déconcerter, dérouter; **the police admit they are baffled** la police reconnaît qu'elle est perplexe; **I'm baffled as to why she said that** je ne comprends vraiment pas pourquoi elle a dit ça **2** *(frustrate* ► *effort, plans)* faire échouer, déjouer; *(*► *expectations, hopes)* décevoir, tromper
N *Tech (deflector)* déflecteur *m*; *(acoustic)* baffle *m*, écran *m*

▸▸ *Tech* ***baffle board, baffle plate*** *(deflector)* déflecteur *m*; *(acoustic)* baffle *m*, écran *m*

baffling ['bæflɪŋ] **ADJ** *(behaviour)* déconcertant, déroutant; *(mystery, puzzle)* inexplicable; **a b. problem** un casse-tête

BAFTA ['bæftə] **N** *Cin & TV* *(abbr* **British Academy of Film and Television Awards***)* **B. (award)** = prix récompensant les meilleurs films et émissions de télévision en Grande-Bretagne

> **BAFTA**
>
> Le BAFTA est une récompense attribuée aux professionnels du cinéma et de la télévision qui se sont distingués pendant l'année. C'est en quelque sorte l'équivalent britannique des César français. Il existe deux cérémonies, l'une pour les professionnels du cinéma (qui a lieu en février), l'autre pour les gens de télévision (au mois d'avril).

bag [bæg] *(pt & pp* **bagged**, *cont* **bagging***)* **N 1** *(container)* sac *m*; **paper/plastic b.** sac *m* en papier/en plastique; **a b. of sweets/groceries** un sac de bonbons/d'épicerie; *Am Fam* **he was left holding the b.** tout lui est retombé dessus; *Fam* **her promotion is in the b.** son avancement, c'est dans la poche *ou* dans le sac *ou* du tout cuit; *Fam* **to pull sth out of the b.** sortir qch du chapeau; *Fam* **the whole b. of tricks** tout le tralala; *esp Am Fam Old-fashioned* **that's not my b.** *(I'm not good at it)* ce n'est pas mon fort; *(I'm not interested in it)* ce n'est pas mon truc

2 *(handbag)* sac *m* (à main); *(suitcase)* valise *f*; **bags** valises *fpl*, bagages *mpl*; **to pack one's bags** faire ses bagages; *Fig* **it's time to pack our bags** c'est le moment de plier bagage; *Fam* **they threw her out b. and baggage** ils l'ont mise à la porte avec toutes ses affaires

3 *(of cloth, skin)* poche *f*; **to have bags under one's eyes** avoir des poches sous les yeux; *Fam* **b. of bones** sac *m ou* tas *m* d'os

4 *Hunt* prise *f*; **did you get a good b.?** avez-vous fait bonne chasse?

5 *Fam Pej (woman)* **old b.** vieille peau *f*, vieille bique *f*; **you stupid b.!** espèce d'idiote!

6 *Fam Drugs slang (quantity of drugs)* dose▫ *f (en sachet ou dans un papier plié)*

VT 1 *(books, groceries)* mettre dans un sac; *(apples, sweets)* ensacher; *Am (supermarket purchases)* emballer **2** *Fam (seize)* mettre le grappin sur, s'emparer de▫; *(steal)* piquer, faucher; **he bagged the best seat for himself** il s'est réservé la meilleure place **3** *Hunt* tuer

VI goder, faire des poches; **his trousers b. at the knees** ses pantalons font des poches aux genoux

• **bags** *Fam* **NPL** *Br* **1** *(trousers)* pantalon▫ *m*, fute *m* **2** *(lots)* **there are bags of things to do** il y a plein de choses à faire; **we have bags of time** nous avons tout notre temps; **they've bags of money** ils sont pleins aux as **EXCLAM** *Br* **bags I go!** c'est à moi!▫; **bags I get the biggest one!** le plus gros est pour moi!▫

▸▸ *Fam* ***bag lady*** clocharde *f*

bagatelle [ˌbægə'tel] **N 1** *(trinket)* bagatelle *f*, babiole *f*; **a mere b.** une simple bagatelle **2** *(board game)* (sorte *f* de) flipper *m*; *(billiards)* billard *m* anglais **3** *Mus* bagatelle *f*

bagel ['beɪgəl] **N** *Culin* petit pain *m* en couronne, *Can* bagel *m*

baggage ['bægɪdʒ] **N 1** *(luggage)* valises *fpl*, bagages *mpl*; **one piece of b.** un bagage

2 *Fig* **to have a lot of (emotional) b.** avoir accumulé les échecs sentimentaux; **the party has jettisoned its traditional ideological b.** le parti s'est débarrassé de son idéologie traditionnelle

3 *Mil* équipement *m* (portatif)

4 *Fam Old-fashioned (cheeky girl)* coquine *f*; *(prostitute)* prostituée▫ *f*, traînée *f*

▸▸ *Am* ***baggage car*** fourgon *m (d'un train)*; ***baggage check*** *(inspection)* contrôle *m* des bagages; *Am (ticket)* ticket *m* d'enregistrement; *Am* ***baggage checkroom*** consigne *f*; ***baggage handler*** bagagiste *m*; ***baggage reclaim*** livraison *f* des bagages; *Am* ***baggage room*** consigne *f*; *Am* ***baggage tag*** bulletin *m* de consigne

Baggie® ['bægɪ] **N** *Am* = petit sachet hermétique en plastique

baggy ['bægɪ] *(compar* **baggier**, *superl* **baggiest***)* **ADJ** *(clothing ▸ too big)* trop ample *ou* grand; *(▸ loose-fitting)* ample, baggy; **b. trousers** un pantalon bouffant

Baghdad [bæg'dæd] **N** Bagdad

bagpipes ['bægpaɪps] **NPL** cornemuse *f*

bah [bɑː] **EXCLAM** bah!

Bahamas [bə'hɑːməz] **NPL** Bahamas *fpl*

Bahrain [bɑː'reɪn] **N** Bahreïn *m*, Bahrayn *m*

Bahraini [bɑː'reɪnɪ] **N** Bahreïni(e) *m,f*

ADJ bahreïni

bail [beɪl] **N 1** *Law (money)* caution *f*; *(guarantor)* caution *f*, répondant(e) *m,f*; *(release)* mise *f* en liberté provisoire sous caution; **on b.** sous caution; **the judge granted/refused b.** le juge a accordé/refusé la mise en liberté provisoire sous caution; **she was released on £2,000 b.** elle a été mise en liberté provisoire après avoir payé une caution de 2 000 livres; **to stand** *or* **to go b. for sb** se porter garant de qn; **the prisoner jumped** *or* **forfeited b.** le prisonnier s'est soustrait à la justice *(à la faveur d'une mise en liberté provisoire)* **2** *Sport (in cricket)* barre *f* horizontale *(du guichet)*, taquet *m*

VT 1 *Law (of guarantor)* payer la caution pour, se porter garant de; *(of judge)* mettre en liberté provisoire sous caution **2** *(water)* vider

▸▸ *Law* ***bail bond*** cautionnement *m*

▸ **bail on VT INSEP** *Fam (let down)* faire faux bond à; **he only asked me out because Nina bailed on him** il m'a demandé de sortir avec lui seulement parce que Nina lui a fait faux bond

▸ **bail out VT SEP 1** *Law (of guarantor)* payer la caution pour, se porter garant de; *(of judge)* mettre en liberté provisoire sous caution **2** *(help)* tirer *ou* sortir d'affaire; **his parents usually b. him out** la plupart du temps, ses parents le tirent d'affaire *ou* le renflouent **3** *Naut (boat)* écoper; *(cellar, water)* vider

VI *Aviat (parachute)* sauter en parachute *(d'un avion en perdition)*

bailer ['beɪlə(r)] **N** *Naut (bucket)* écope *f*

bailiff ['beɪlɪf] **N 1** *Law Br* huissier *m* de justice; *Am* huissier *m* audiencier **2** *Br Admin (on estate, farm)* régisseur *m*, intendant *m*; **water b.** garde-pêche *m*

bailiwick ['beɪlɪwɪk] **N 1** *Law* juridiction *f*, circonscription *f* **2** *Fig (interest)* domaine *m*; *Fig* **it's not my b.** *(field, area of expertise)* ce n'est pas mon domaine

bairn [beən] **N** *Scot* enfant *mf*

bait [beɪt] **N** appât *m*, amorce *f*; *Fig* appât *m*, leurre *m*; *also Fig* **to rise to** *or* **swallow** *or* **take the b.** mordre (à l'hameçon)

VT 1 *(hook, trap)* amorcer; *(line)* mettre l'appât à **2** *(tease)* harceler, tourmenter

3 *Hunt (badger, bear)* lâcher les chiens sur

4 *(entice)* tenter

baiting ['beɪtɪŋ] **N 1** *(of hook, trap, line)* amorçage *m* **2** *(teasing)* harcèlement *m* **3** *Hunt (of badger, bear)* = fait de lâcher les chiens sur la proie

baize [beɪz] **N** *Tex (fabric)* feutre *m*; *Sport (on billiard table)* tapis *m* de billard; **green b. door** = porte recouverte de feutre vert qui sépare l'office du reste de la maison dans une demeure bourgeoise

bake [beɪk] **VT 1** *(cook in oven)* faire cuire au four; **she's baking a cake for me** elle me fait un gâteau **2** *(dry, harden)* cuire; **the land was baked dry** la terre était desséchée

VI 1 *(person ▸ make bread)* faire du pain; *(▸ make cakes)* faire de la pâtisserie **2** *(cake, pottery)* cuire (au four); **the ground was baking in the sun** le sol se desséchait au soleil **3** *Fam (be hot)* **it's baking in here!** il fait une de ces chaleurs ici!; **I'm baking!** j'étouffe!, je crève de chaleur!

N 1 *(batch of food)* fournée *f*

2 *Br (baked dish)* gratin *m*; **pasta/vegetable b.** gratin *m* de pâtes/de légumes

3 *Br (biscuit)* = sorte de biscuit

4 *Am (party)* = fête où l'on sert un repas cuit au four

baked [beɪkt] **ADJ**

▸▸ *Culin* ***baked Alaska*** omelette *f* norvégienne; ***baked beans*** *Br (in tomato sauce)* haricots *mpl* blancs à la sauce tomate; *Am (dish)* haricots *mpl* au lard, *Can* fèves *fpl* au lard; ***baked potato*** pomme *f* de terre en robe de chambre *ou* en robe des champs

bake-off **N** *Am* concours *m* de gâteaux; *Fam (between companies)* = rivalité entre deux entreprises pour l'obtention d'un contrat

baker ['beɪkə(r)] **N** boulanger(ère) *m,f*; **I'm going to the b.'s (shop)** je vais à la boulangerie

▸▸ ***a baker's dozen*** treize à la douzaine

bakery ['beɪkərɪ] *(pl* **bakeries***)* **N** boulangerie *f*

Bakewell tart ['beɪkwel-] **N** *Br* = fond de tarte fourré au biscuit de Savoie, à la confiture et à la pâte d'amandes

baking ['beɪkɪŋ] **N 1** *(process)* cuisson *f* (au four); **I'll do some b. tomorrow** *(make cakes)* demain, je ferai de la pâtisserie; *(make bread)* demain, je ferai du pain **2** *(batch ▸ of food)* fournée *f*; *(▸ of bricks etc)* cuite *f*

ADJ *(hot ▸ pavement, sun)* brûlant; *(▸ day, weather)* torride

ADV **a b. hot afternoon** un après-midi torride

▸▸ ***baking beans*** = haricots de céramique dont on garnit les fonds de tarte pour les faire précuire; ***baking dish*** plat *m* allant au four; ***baking potatoes*** pommes *fpl* de terre à cuire au four; ***baking powder*** levure *f* (chimique); ***baking sheet*** plaque *f* (de four), tôle *f*; ***baking soda*** bicarbonate *m* de soude; ***baking tin*** moule *m* à gâteau; ***baking tray*** plaque *f* de four

baklava ['bɑːkləvɑː] **N** *Culin* baklava *m*

baksheesh [ˌbæk'ʃiːʃ] **N** *Fam Old-fashioned* bakchich *m*

Balaclava [ˌbælə'klɑːvə] **N** *Geog* Balaklava

balaclava (helmet) [bælə'klɑːvə-] **N** passe-montagne *m*

balalaika [ˌbælə'laɪkə] **N** *Mus* balalaïka *f*

BALANCE ['bæləns]

> **N**
> • équilibre **1, 2** • balance **3, 6**
> • contrepoids **4** • solde, reste **5**
>
> **VT**
> • mettre en équilibre **1** • faire contrepoids à **2**
> • peser **3**
> • équilibrer, balancer **4** • solder **5**
>
> **VI**
> être en équilibre **1** • s'équilibrer **2, 3**

N 1 *(of person ▸ physical)* équilibre *m*, aplomb *m*; *(▸ mental)* calme *m*, équilibre *m*; **she tried to keep her b.** elle a essayé de garder l'équilibre *ou* son équilibre; **I lost my b.** j'ai perdu l'équilibre *ou* mon équilibre; **off b.** *(physically, mentally)* déséquilibré; **he threw me off b.** il m'a fait perdre l'équilibre; *Fig* il m'a décontenancé; *Fig* **to catch sb off b.** prendre qn au dépourvu

2 *(of situation)* équilibre *m*; *Art (of painting, sculpture)* harmonie *f*; **she tried to strike a b. between the practical and the idealistic** elle a essayé de trouver un juste milieu entre la réalité et l'idéal; **the b. of nature** l'équilibre *m* naturel; **budgetary/economic b.** équilibre *m* budgétaire/économique

3 *(scales)* balance *f*; **to hang in the b.** être en jeu; **everything is still (hanging) in the b.** rien n'est encore certain; **his remark tipped the b. in his favour** sa remarque a fait pencher la balance en sa faveur

4 *(weight, force)* poids *m*, contrepoids *m*; **the b. of evidence is against him** la plupart des preuves lui sont défavorables; **she acts as a b. to his impulsiveness** elle sert de contrepoids à *ou* elle contrebalance son impulsivité

5 *(remainder)* solde *m*, reste *m*; *Com & Fin* solde *m*; *Acct* balance *f*, bilan *m*; **b. in hand** solde *m* en caisse; **b. carried forward** solde *m* à reporter; *(on balance sheet)* report *m* à nouveau; **b. brought forward** solde *m* reporté; *(on balance sheet)* report *m*; **b. due** solde *m* débiteur *ou* dû; **I'd like to pay the b. of my account** j'aimerais solder mon compte

6 *(on hi-fi, amplifier)* balance *f*

VT 1 *(put in stable position)* mettre en équilibre; *(hold in stable position)* tenir en équilibre; **she balanced the book on her head** elle a mis *ou* posé le livre en équilibre sur sa tête; *Aut* **to b. the wheels** équilibrer les roues

2 *(act as counterbalance, offset)* faire contrepoids à, contrebalancer; **we have to b. the right to privacy against the public's right to know** nous devons trouver le juste milieu entre le respect de la vie privée et le droit du public à être informé

3 *(weigh)* peser; *Fig* mettre en balance, comparer; **you have to b. its usefulness against the actual cost** vous devez mettre en balance *ou* comparer son utilité et le coût réel; **to b. the advantages against the disadvantages** peser le pour et le contre

4 *Math & Fin (equation, finances)* équilibrer, balancer; **to b. the budget** équilibrer le budget; **to b. the books** dresser *ou* établir le bilan, arrêter les comptes

5 *Fin (settle, pay)* régler, solder; *(debt)* compenser; **to b. an account** solder un compte

VI 1 *(remain in stable position)* se maintenir en équilibre; *(be in stable position)* être en équilibre; **to b. on one foot** se tenir en équilibre sur un pied; **she was balanced precariously at the top of a ladder** elle était en équilibre instable en haut de l'échelle

2 *(act as counterbalance)* **the weights b.** les poids s'équilibrent

3 *Acct & Fin (budget, finances)* s'équilibrer, balancer; **I can't get the accounts to b.** je n'arrive pas à équilibrer les comptes

• **on balance ADV** à tout prendre, tout bien considéré

►► ***balance beam*** *(in gymnastics)* poutre *f*; *Fin* ***balance book*** livre *m* d'inventaire; *Econ* ***balance of payments*** balance *f* des paiements; *Econ* ***balance of payments deficit*** déficit *m* de la balance des paiements, déficit *m* extérieur; *Pol* ***balance of power*** *(in government)* balance *f ou* équilibre *m* des pouvoirs; *(between states)* balance *f ou* équilibre *m* des forces; *Pol* **he holds the b. of power** il peut faire pencher la balance, tout dépend de lui; *Acct* ***balance sheet*** bilan *m*; **off the b. sheet** hors de bilan; *Acct* ***balance sheet item*** poste *m* de bilan; *Pol* ***balance of terror*** équilibre *m* de la terreur; *Econ* ***balance of trade*** balance *f* commerciale; *Econ* ***balance of trade surplus*** excédent *m* de la balance commerciale; *Tech* ***balance weight*** contrepoids *m*; *Tech* ***balance wheel*** balancier *m*

▸ **balance out VI the advantages and disadvantages b. out** les avantages contrebalancent *ou* compensent les inconvénients; **they b. each other out** *(because of their respective skills)* ils se complètent bien; *Fin* **the debits and credits should b. out** les débits et les crédits devraient s'équilibrer

> Note that the French word **balance** is a false friend. Its most common meaning is **scales**.

balanced ['bælənst] **ADJ 1** *(diet, scales, person)* équilibré; **to be well b.** *(person)* être équilibré; **a (well-)b. diet** un régime (alimentaire) équilibré **2** *(in strength, value)* égal; *Fin (budget)* équilibré; **the two teams were pretty well b.** les deux équipes étaient de force à peu près égale **3** *(programme, report)* impartial, objectif; **a b. view** une vue impartiale *ou* objective

balancer shaft ['bælənsə-] **N** *Aut* arbre *m* d'équilibrage

balancing ['bælənsɪŋ] **N 1** *(physical effort)* stabilisation *f* **2** *Acct* **b. of accounts** solde *m ou* alignement *m ou* arrêté *m* des comptes **3** *(of two things)* ajustement *m*; *(of something by something)* compensation *f*

►► ***balancing act*** numéro *m* d'équilibriste; *Fig* **it was a real b. act keeping everyone happy** ça n'a pas été une mince affaire de contenter tout le monde

balcony ['bælkənɪ] *(pl* **balconies***)* **N 1** *(of apartment, house)* balcon *m* **2** *Theat* deuxième balcon *m*

►► ***balcony bra*** balconnet *m*

bald [bɔːld] **ADJ 1** *(having no hair)* chauve; **he's going b.** il devient chauve, il se dégarnit; **his b. head** son crâne chauve; **a b. patch** *or* **spot** *(on person)* une tonsure; *(on animal)* un endroit sans poils; **he's got a b. patch** *or* **spot** il a le sommet du crâne chauve, il a une tonsure; *Fam* **as b. as a coot** chauve comme un œuf *ou* comme une boule de billard **2** *(carpet)* usé, pelé; *(mountain top)* pelé; *(tyre)* lisse **3** *(unadorned* ▸ *facts)* brutal; **the b. truth** la pure vérité, la vérité toute nue; **a b. statement of the facts** une simple exposition des faits

►► *Orn* ***bald eagle*** pygargue *m* à tête blanche

balderdash ['bɔːldədæʃ] *Old-fashioned* **EXCLAM** balivernes!, fadaises!

N *(UNCOUNT)* fadaises *fpl*; **the book is utter b.** le livre est un ramassis de fadaises

bald-headed ADJ chauve; **a b. man** un chauve

balding ['bɔːldɪŋ] **ADJ** à la calvitie naissante

baldly ['bɔːldlɪ] **ADV** brutalement; **to put it b.** pour parler franchement

baldness ['bɔːldnɪs] **N 1** *(of person)* calvitie *f*; *(of animal)* absence *f* de poils; **premature b.** calvitie *f* précoce **2** *(of mountain top)* nudité *f*; *(of carpet, tyre)* usure *f* **3** *(of facts)* brutalité *f*

bale [beɪl] **N** *(of cloth, hay)* balle *f*

VT 1 *(hay)* mettre en balles; *(cotton, merchandise)* emballer, empaqueter **2** *Br (water)* vider

▸ **bale out VT SEP** *Naut (boat)* écoper; *(cellar, water)* vider

VI *Aviat (parachute)* sauter en parachute *(d'un avion en perdition)*

Balearic [ˌbælɪ'ærɪk] **ADJ the B. Islands** les Baléares *fpl*

• **Balearics NPL the Balearics** les Baléares *fpl*

baleen ['beɪliːn] **N** *Zool (of whale)* fanon *m* de baleine

baleful ['beɪlfʊl] **ADJ 1** *(glance, presence)* menaçant; *(influence)* néfaste; **he looked at us with a b. eye** il nous a regardés d'un sale œil, il nous a jeté un regard mauvais **2** *(gloomy)* lugubre

balefully ['beɪlfʊlɪ] **ADV 1** *(menacingly* ▸ *look)* d'un sale œil; *(*▸ *say)* d'un ton menaçant **2** *(gloomily)* d'une façon lugubre

baler ['beɪlə(r)] **N** *Agr* ramasseuse-presse *f*

►► ***baler twine*** ficelle *f* agricole

Bali ['bɑːlɪ] **N** Bali

Balinese [ˌbɑːlɪ'niːz] *(pl* **inv***)* **N 1** *(person)* Balinais (e) *m,f* **2** *(language)* balinais *m*

ADJ balinais, de Bali

baling ['beɪlɪŋ] **N** *(of hay)* mise *f* en balles; *(of cotton, merchandise)* mise *f* en balles, empaquetage *m*

►► *Agr* ***baling machine*** botteleuse *f*

balk [bɔːk] **N 1** *Constr (beam)* bille *f*; *(of roof)* solive *f* **2** *Sport (in baseball)* feinte *f* irrégulière d'un lanceur **3** *(in snooker)* = espace entre la bande et la ligne

VT 1 *(thwart)* contrecarrer, contrarier **2** *(avoid)* éviter

VI the horse balked at the fence le cheval a refusé la barrière; **she balked at the idea of executing him** elle a reculé à l'idée de le faire exécuter; **he balked at the expense** il a rechigné à la dépense

►► ***balk line*** *(in snooker)* ligne *f* de départ; *(in croquet)* position *f* de départ

Balkan ['bɔːlkən] **ADJ** balkanique

►► ***the Balkan Mountains*** les monts *mpl* Balkans, la Stara Planina; ***the Balkan Peninsula*** la péninsule balkanique, les Balkans *mpl*; ***Balkan States*** États *mpl* balkaniques, Balkans *mpl*

Balkanization, balkanization, -isation [ˌbɔːlkənaɪ'zeɪʃən] **N** *Pol* balkanisation *f*

Balkanize, balkanize, -ise ['bɔːlkənaɪz] **VT** *Pol* balkaniser

Balkans ['bɔːlkənz] **NPL** Balkans *mpl*

ball [bɔːl] **N 1** *(sphere)* boule *f*; *(of wool)* pelote *f*; **he rolled up the sweater into a b.** il a roulé le pullover en boule; **the hedgehog was curled up in a b.** le hérisson était roulé en boule; *Fig* **to be a b. of fire** déborder d'énergie

2 *Sport (small)* balle *f*; *(large* ▸ *for playing football, rugby, basketball)* ballon *m*; *(in snooker)* bille *f*, boule *f*; *(in croquet)* boule *f*; *(in golf, tennis)* balle *f*; **to kick the b. about** *(play football)* s'amuser avec le ballon; **to knock the b. about** *(in tennis)* faire des balles; **the children were playing b.** les enfants jouaient au ballon

3 *Sport (shot* ▸ *in golf, tennis)* coup *m*; *(*▸ *in hockey)* tir *m*; *(*▸ *in cricket)* lancer *m*; *Ftbl* passe *f*; *Ftbl* **a long b.** une passe longue, une balle en profondeur; **it was a good b.** c'était bien joué

4 *(of foot)* avant-pied *m*; *(of thumb)* partie *f* charnue; **to be standing on the balls of one's feet** se tenir sur la pointe des pieds

5 *(dance)* bal *m*; **to have** *or* **to hold** *or* **to organize a b.** donner un bal; *Fam Fig* **I'm having a b.** je me marre comme un fou, je m'éclate

6 *(idioms)* **the b. is in his court now** c'est à lui de jouer maintenant, la balle est dans son camp; **to be on the b.** *(knowledgeable)* connaître son affaire; *(alert)* être sur le qui-vive; **he's well over 80 but he's still on the b.** il a plus de 80 ans mais il a toute sa tête; *Br* **to have the b. at one's feet** avoir la partie belle; **to keep the b. rolling** *(maintain interest)* maintenir l'intérêt; *(maintain activity)* assurer la continuité; *(maintain conversation)* soutenir la conversation; **to start** *or* **to set the b. rolling** *(in conversation)* lancer la conversation; *Com (in deal)* faire démarrer l'affaire; **to play b.** *Sport* jouer au ballon; *Am (baseball)* jouer au base-ball; *Fig* coopérer, jouer le jeu; *Am Fig* **that's the way the b. bounces!** c'est la vie!

VI 1 *(wool)* boulocher **2** *Am Vulg (have sex)* baiser

VT 1 *(fists)* serrer; *Am* **to b. sth up** rouler qch en boule **2** *Am Vulg (have sex with)* baiser

• **balls** *Vulg* **NPL 1** *(testicles)* couilles *fpl*; *Fig* **they've got you by the balls** t'es bien baisé; **balls to him!** qu'il aille se faire foutre! **2** *(courage)* **to have balls** avoir des couilles, en avoir; **that type of thing takes balls** il faut avoir des couilles pour faire ce genre de truc **3** *(rubbish)* conneries *fpl*; **what a load of balls!** c'est des conneries, tout ça!

EXCLAM quelles conneries!

►► *Tech* ***ball bearing*** *(ball)* bille *f* de roulement; *(bearing)* roulement *m* à billes; *Sport* ***ball boy*** ramasseur *m* de balles; ***ball game*** *(with small ball)* jeu *m* de balle; *(with large ball)* jeu *m* de ballon; *(baseball)* match *m* de base-ball; *Fam Fig* **it's a whole new b. game, it's a different b. game altogether** c'est une toute autre histoire; *Sport* ***ball girl*** ramasseuse *f* de balles; ***ball gown*** robe *f* de bal; *Anat* ***ball joint*** joint *m* à rotule; *Met* ***ball lightning*** éclair *m* en boule; ***ball park*** *(stadium)* stade *m* de base-ball; *Fam Fig* **his guess was in the right b. park** il avait plutôt bien deviné[□]; *Tech* ***ball peen hammer*** marteau *m* à panne ronde *ou* sphérique; *Tech* ***ball valve*** robinet *m* à tournant sphérique

> When translating **ball**, note that **balle** and **ballon** are not interchangeable.

ballad ['bæləd] **N** *Mus (song* ▸ *narrative)* ballade *f*; *(*▸ *popular, sentimental)* romance *f*; *(musical piece)* ballade *f*

ballast ['bæləst] **N** *(UNCOUNT)* **1** *Aviat & Naut (in balloon, ship)* lest *m*; **to drop b.** jeter du lest **2** *Constr (in road)* pierraille *f*; *Rail* ballast *m*

VT 1 *Aviat & Naut (balloon, ship)* lester **2** *Constr (road)* empierrer, caillouter; *Rail (railway)* ballaster

►► *Naut* ***ballast tank*** *(of submarine)* ballast *m*

ballerina [ˌbælə'riːnə] **N** ballerine *f (danseuse)*

ballet ['bæleɪ] **N** *Mus & Theat* ballet *m*; **I'm going to the b. this evening** je vais voir un ballet *ou* un spectacle de danse classique ce soir

►► *Mus & Theat* ***ballet dancer*** danseur(euse) *m,f* de ballet; ***ballet dancing*** danse *f* classique; *Mus & Theat* ***ballet dress*** robe *f* de ballet; *(skirt)* tutu *m*; ***ballet lesson*** cours *m* de danse classique; ***ballet shoe*** chausson *m* de danse

ballistic [bə'lɪstɪk] **ADJ** *Phys* balistique; *Fam Fig* **to go b.** *(get angry)* piquer une crise

►► *Mil* ***ballistic missile*** missile *m* balistique

ballistics [bə'lɪstɪks] **N** *(UNCOUNT)* *Phys* balistique *f*

balloon [bə'luːn] **N 1** *(toy)* ballon *m*

2 *(for carrying people or weather instruments)* ballon *m*, aérostat *m*; **(hot air) b.** montgolfière *f*; **to go up in a b.** monter en ballon; *Fam Fig* **when the b. goes up** quand ça démarre

3 *(in comic strip)* bulle *f*

4 *(brandy glass)* (verre *m*) ballon *m*

VI 1 *(billow* ▸ *sail, trousers)* **to b. (out)** gonfler **2** *Fig (grow dramatically)* augmenter démesurément; **unemployment has ballooned in recent months** le chômage a considérablement augmenté ces derniers mois

VT *Br Sport (ball)* projeter très haut en l'air

▸▸ ***balloon glass*** verre *m* ballon; *Naut* ***balloon sail*** foc *m* d'avant; ***balloon sleeve*** manche *f* ballon; *Aut* ***balloon tyre*** pneu *m* ballon

ballooning [bəˈluːnɪŋ] **N to go b.** *(regularly)* pratiquer la montgolfière; *(on one occasion)* faire un tour en montgolfière *ou* en ballon

balloonist [bəˈluːnɪst] **N** aéronaute *mf*

ballot [ˈbælət] *(pt & pp* **ballotted,** *cont* **ballotting)** **N 1** *(secret vote)* scrutin *m*; **to vote by b.** voter à bulletin secret; **in the second b.** au deuxième tour de scrutin; **to take a b.** procéder à un scrutin *ou* à un vote **2** *(voting paper)* bulletin *m* de vote; **to cast one's b. for sb** voter pour qn **3** *St Exch (when shares are oversubscribed)* allocation *f* d'actions par tirage au sort

VT sonder au moyen d'un vote; **union members will be ballotted on Tuesday** les membres du syndicat décideront par voie de scrutin mardi

VI *(vote)* voter par (voie de) scrutin; **to b. for/against sb** voter pour/contre qn

▸▸ ***ballot box*** *(for ballot papers)* urne *f*; *Fig* système *m* électoral *ou* démocratique; *Am* ***ballot box stuffing*** fraude *f* électorale; *Am* ***ballot initiative*** référendum *m*; ***ballot paper*** bulletin *m* de vote; ***ballot rigging*** fraude *f* électorale

balloting [ˈbælətɪŋ] **N** *(voting)* scrutin *m*

ball-park figure **N** *Fam* **a b.** un chiffre approximatif□

ballplayer [ˈbɔːlˌpleɪə(r)] **N** *Am Sport (basketball)* joueur(euse) *m,f* de basket; *(football)* joueur (euse) *m,f* de football américain; *(baseball)* joueur(euse) *m,f* de base-ball

ballpoint [ˈbɔːlpɔɪnt] **N** stylo *m* (à) bille, Bic® *m*

▸▸ ***ballpoint pen*** stylo *m* (à) bille, Bic® *m*

ballroom [ˈbɔːlrʊm] **N** salle *f* de bal

▸▸ ***ballroom dancing*** danse *f* de salon

balls-up, *Am* **ball-up** **N** *very Fam* bordel *m*; **to make a b. of sth** merder qch, *Can* faire de la merde de qch; **the trip was a complete b.** l'excursion a complètement foiré

▸**balls up** [bɔːlz] **VT SEP** *Br very Fam* foutre la merde dans; **he completely ballsed up the job** il a complètement salopé le boulot; **we're really ballsed up now** on est dans la merde jusqu'au cou

ballsy [ˈbɔːlzɪ] **ADJ** *Am very Fam* culotté, couillu

▸**ball-up** *Am* = **balls-up**

ball-up *Am* = **balls-up**

bally [ˈbælɪ] **ADJ** *Br Fam Old-fashioned* sacré; **you b. fool!** espèce de crétin!

ballyhoo [ˌbælɪˈhuː] *Fam* **N** *(commotion)* tapage *m*; *(publicity)* battage *m*, **what's all the b. about?** pourquoi tout ce remue-ménage?

VT *esp Am Mktg (book, show)* faire du battage (publicitaire) pour promouvoir□

balm [bɑːm] **N 1** *Pharm & Fig* baume *m* **2** *Bot* mélisse *f* officinale

balminess [ˈbɑːmɪnɪs] **N** *(mildness)* **the b. of the evening air** l'air embaumé du soir

Balmoral [bælˈmɒrəl] **N** = château situé dans le nord-est de l'Écosse et appartenant à la famille royale britannique

balmy [ˈbɑːmɪ] **ADJ 1** *(weather)* doux (douce) **2** *(scented)* embaumé, parfumé

balneotherapy [ˌbælnɪəʊˈθerəpɪ] **N** *Med* balnéothérapie *f*

baloney [bəˈləʊnɪ] *esp Am* **N 1** *(UNCOUNT) Fam (nonsense)* idioties *fpl*, balivernes *fpl*; **b., you don't know what you're talking about!** n'importe quoi, tu ne sais pas de quoi tu parles! **2** *Culin* = saucisse à base de bœuf, veau et porc, mangée froide

balsa [ˈbɔːlsə] **N** balsa *m*

balsam [ˈbɔːlsəm] **N 1** *Pharm (balm)* baume *m* **2** *Bot (plant)* balsamine *f*

▸▸ *Bot* ***balsam fir*** sapin *m* baumier

balsamic vinegar [ˌbɔːlˈsæmɪk-] **N** *Culin* vinaigre *m* balsamique

balti [ˈbɔːltɪ] **N** *Culin* **1** *(container)* = récipient métallique utilisé dans la cuisine indienne **2** *(food)* = plat épicé préparé dans un "balti"

Baltic [ˈbɔːltɪk] **N the B.** la Baltique

ADJ *(port, coast)* de la Baltique

▸▸ ***the Baltic Sea*** la mer Baltique; ***the Baltic States*** les pays *mpl* baltes

baluster [ˈbæləstə(r)] **N** balustre *m*; **the balusters** la rampe *(d'un escalier)*

balustrade [ˌbæləsˈtreɪd] **N** balustrade *f*

bamboo [bæmˈbuː] **N** bambou *m*

COMP *(screen, table)* de *ou* en bambou; *(forest)* de bambou

▸▸ ***Bamboo Curtain*** rideau *m* de bambou; ***bamboo shoots*** pousses *fpl* de bambou

bamboozle [bæmˈbuːzəl] **VT** *Fam* **1** *(cheat)* avoir, embobiner; **they were bamboozled into signing the contract** on les a embobinés pour qu'ils signent le contrat **2** *(confuse)* déboussoler; **the game had him completely bamboozled** le jeu l'avait complètement déboussolé

ban [bæn] *(pt & pp* **banned,** *cont* **banning)** **N 1** *(prohibition)* interdiction *f*, interdit *m*; **to put** *or* **impose a b. on sth** interdire qch; **to lift the b. on sth** lever l'interdiction qui porte sur qch; **they've put a b. on smoking in the office** ils ont interdit de fumer dans le bureau; **the nuclear test b.** l'interdiction des essais nucléaires **2** *Com (embargo)* embargo *m*; *(sanction)* sanctions *fpl* économiques

VT interdire; **he was banned from going into town** on lui a interdit d'aller en ville; **they are banned from the club** on leur a interdit l'accès à la boîte de nuit; **he was banned from driving for a year** il a eu une suspension de permis de conduire d'un an

banal [bəˈnɑːl] **ADJ** banal

banality [bəˈnælətɪ] **N** banalité *f*

banana [bəˈnɑːnə] **N** *(fruit)* banane *f*; *(tree)* bananier *m*

COMP *(milk shake, ice-cream)* à la banane

• **bananas ADJ** *Fam* maboul, dingue; **to go bananas** *(crazy)* devenir dingue; *(angry)* piquer une crise

▸▸ *Can Fam* ***banana belt*** région *f* chaude□; ***banana boat*** bananier *m (bateau)*; ***banana plantation*** bananeraie *f*; *Fam* ***banana republic*** république *f* bananière; ***banana skin*** peau *f* de banane; *Fig* **he slipped on a b. skin** il a fait une gaffe; *Culin* ***banana split*** banana split *m*; ***banana tree*** bananier *m*

bancassurance [ˈbæŋkəʃʊərəns] **N** *Banking* bancassurance *f*

band [bænd] **N 1** *Mus (musicians* ▸ *folk, rock, jazz)* groupe *m*; *(*▸ *brass, military)* fanfare *f*; **to be** *or* **to play in a b.** faire partie d'un groupe

2 *(group)* bande *f*, troupe *f*; **a b. of dedicated reformers** une bande de réformateurs convaincus

3 *(strip* ▸ *of cloth, metal)* bande *f*; *(*▸ *on hat)* ruban *m*; *(*▸ *of leather)* lanière *f*

4 *(stripe* ▸ *of colour)* bande *f*; *(*▸ *of sunlight)* rai *m*; *(*▸ *small)* bandelette *f*

5 *(as binding* ▸ *around wheel)* bandage *m*; *(*▸ *around books)* sangle *f*; *(*▸ *on cigar)* bague *f*; *(*▸ *on barrel)* cercle *m*

6 *Tech (drive belt)* courroie *f* de transmission

7 *Rad (range of frequency)* bande *f*; *Opt (in spectrum)* bande *f*; *Comput* bande *f* magnétique

8 *Br (range* ▸ *in age, price)* tranche *f*; **people in this age b.** les gens dans *ou* de cette tranche d'âge

9 *(ring)* anneau *m*; **wedding b.** alliance *f*

▸▸ *Tech* ***band saw*** scie *f* à ruban; *Phys* ***band spectrum*** spectre *m* de bandes

▸**band together** **VI** *(unite)* se grouper, se liguer; *(gang together)* former une bande

bandage [ˈbændɪdʒ] **N 1** *(strip of cloth)* bande *f*, bandage *m*; **he wrapped the b. around her hand** il a enroulé le bandage autour de sa main **2** *Med (prepared dressing)* pansement *m*

VT *Med (head, limb)* bander; *(wound)* mettre un bandage sur; *(with prepared dressing)* panser

▸**bandage up** **VT SEP** *Med (head, limb)* bander; *(wound)* mettre un bandage sur; *(with prepared dressing)* panser

bandaging [ˈbændɪdʒɪŋ] **N 1** *(strips of cloth)* bandes *fpl*, bandages *mpl* **2** *Med (prepared dressings)* pansements *mpl* **3** *Med (action)* bandage *m*

Band-Aid® [ˈbændeɪd] **N** *Am Med* sparadrap *m*; *Fig* **a B. solution/measure** une solution/une mesure provisoire *ou* en attendant

▸▸ *Fam* **Band-Aid baby** = enfant qu'un couple décide d'avoir dans l'espoir de se réconcilier ou de se rapprocher

bandana, bandanna [bænˈdænə] **N** bandana *m*

B & B, b and b [ˌbiːənˈbiː] **N** *esp Br (abbr* **bed and breakfast)** chambre *f* et petit déjeuner, chambre *f* d'hôte

bandbox [ˈbændbɒks] **N** *(gen)* boîte *f* cylindrique; *(for hats)* carton *m* à chapeaux

banded [ˈbændɪd] **ADJ** *(striped)* rayé; **a red wall b. with yellow** un mur rouge rayé de jaune

▸▸ *Com* ***banded pack*** lot *m*

bandit [ˈbændɪt] **N** *also Fig* bandit *m*

banditry [ˈbændɪtrɪ] **N** banditisme *m*

bandmaster [ˈbændˌmɑːstə(r)] **N** *Mus* chef *m* d'orchestre

bandoleer, bandolier [ˌbændəˈlɪə(r)] **N** *Mil* cartouchière *f*

bandsman [ˈbændzmən] *(pl* **bandsmen** [-mən]) **N** *Mus* membre *m* d'un orchestre; *Mil* membre *m* d'une fanfare

bandstand [ˈbændstænd] **N** *Mus* kiosque *m* à musique

bandwagon [ˈbændwægən] **N to jump** *or* **to climb on the b.** prendre le train en marche, *Pej* suivre le mouvement

bandwidth [ˈbændwɪdθ] **N 1** *Comput & Rad* largeur *f* de bande **2** *(in acoustics)* bande *f* passante

bandy [ˈbændɪ] *(pt & pp* **bandied,** *compar* **bandier,** *superl* **bandiest)** **VT 1** *(blows)* échanger **2** *(ideas, witticisms, insults)* échanger; **don't b. words with me** ne discute pas

ADJ *(person)* aux jambes arquées; *(leg* ▸ *of animal, person)* arqué

▸**bandy about, bandy around** **VT SEP** *(expression, story)* faire circuler; **his name is often bandied about** on parle souvent de lui; **this is just one of the explanations being bandied around** c'est une des nombreuses explications qui circulent

bandy-legged **ADJ to be b.** avoir les jambes arquées

bane [beɪn] **N** *(scourge, trial)* fléau *m*; **it's/he's the b. of my life** ça/il m'empoisonne la vie; **the tax has become the b. of local government** l'impôt est devenu la bête noire des collectivités locales

baneful [ˈbeɪnfʊl] **ADJ** *Literary* funeste; *(influence)* néfaste

banefully [ˈbeɪnfʊlɪ] **ADV** *Literary* funestement

bang [bæŋ] **N 1** *(loud noise* ▸ *explosion)* détonation *f*; *(*▸ *clatter)* fracas *m*; *(*▸ *slam)* claquement *m*; *(*▸ *supersonic)* bang *m*; **to shut the door with a b.** claquer la porte; **there was a big b.** il y a eu une forte détonation *ou* une explosion; *Fam* **to go** *Br* **over** *or Am* **out with a b., to go with a b.** avoir un succès fou; *Fam* **the show went (off) with a b.** le spectacle a eu un succès fou; *Am Fam* **I got a b. out of it** ça m'a fait marrer

2 *(bump)* coup *m* violent; **he got a nasty b. on the head** il s'est cogné la tête assez violemment

ADV 1 to go b. *(explode)* éclater; *Fam* **b. go my chances of winning!** envolées, mes chances de gagner!; *Fam* **b. goes another £10!** et pan, encore 10 livres de parties!

2 *Br (exactly)* **b. in the middle** au beau milieu, en plein milieu; **the missile was b. on target** le missile a atteint sa cible en plein dans le mille; **b. on time** pile à l'heure; **I walked b. into him** je suis tombé en plein sur lui; **his** *Br* **flat** *or Am* **apartment is b. in the middle of town** son appartement est en plein centre-ville

EXCLAM *(of gun)* pan!; *(of blow, slam)* vlan!; *(of explosion)* boum!

VT 1 *(hit* ▸ *table, window)* frapper violemment; **he banged his fist on the table** il a frappé la table du poing; **I banged my head on the ceiling** je me suis cogné la tête contre le *ou* au plafond; *Fig* **we're banging our heads against a brick wall** nous perdons notre temps, nous nous dépensons en pure perte

2 *(slam* ▸ *door, window)* claquer; **she banged the door shut** elle a claqué la porte

3 *Vulg (have sex with)* baiser

VI 1 *(slam)* claquer; **the door banged shut** la porte s'est refermée en claquant; **to b. at** *or* **on the door**

frapper à la porte à grands coups; **to b. on the table with one's fist** taper du poing sur la table
2 *(detonate ▸ gun)* détoner
3 *Vulg (have sex)* baiser
• **bangs** NPL *Am* frange *f*; **to have bangs** porter une frange
▸**bang about, bang around** *Fam* VT SEP *(books, crockery)* cogner les uns contre les autres⌑; *(person)* tabasser, cogner⌑
VI faire du bruit⌑, faire du pétard
▸**bang away** VI **1** *(detonate ▸ guns)* tonner **2** *(keep firing ▸ soldier)* tirer sans arrêt; *(keep hammering ▸ workmen)* faire du vacarme; *Fig (keep working)* continuer à travailler; **he was banging away on his typewriter** il tapait sans arrêt sur sa machine à écrire
▸**bang down** VT SEP *(books)* jeter violemment; *(dish)* poser brutalement; **he banged the receiver down** il a raccroché brutalement; **she banged down the lid** elle a violemment rabattu le couvercle
▸**bang into** VT INSEP *(collide with)* se cogner contre, heurter
▸**bang on** VI *Br Fam (talk at length)* rabâcher; **he's always banging on about it** il n'arrête pas de bassiner tout le monde avec ça
▸**bang out** VT SEP *Fam (tune)* jouer fort et mal⌑
▸**bang up** VT SEP *Br Fam (prisoner)* boucler; **to get banged up** être mis en taule *ou* à l'ombre

banger ['bæŋə(r)] N *Br Fam* **1** *(sausage)* saucisse⌑ *f*; **bangers and mash** saucisses-purée *(considéré comme un plat typiquement britannique)* **2** *(car)* tacot *m*, vieille guimbarde *f* **3** *(firework)* pétard⌑ *m*

Bangladesh [ˌbæŋglə'deʃ] N Bangladesh *m*

Bangladeshi [ˌbæŋglə'deʃɪ] N Bangladais(e) *m,f*, Bangladeshi *mf*
ADJ bangladais, bangladeshi

bangle ['bæŋgəl] N bracelet *m*

bang-up ADJ *Br Fam* super, génial

banish ['bænɪʃ] VT *(person)* bannir, exiler; *(thought)* bannir, chasser; **he was banished from Rome** il a été banni de Rome

banishment ['bænɪʃmənt] N *(of person)* exil *m*, bannissement *m*; **after his b. from the party** après son exclusion du parti

banister ['bænɪstə(r)] N rampe *f (d'escalier)*; **to slide down the banisters** glisser le long de la rampe d'escalier

banjax ['bændʒæks] VT *Ir & Scot Fam (break)* bousiller

banjo ['bændʒəʊ] *(Br pl* **banjoes**, *Am pl* **banjos**) N banjo *m*

banjoist ['bændʒəʊɪst] N joueur(euse) *m,f* de banjo, banjoiste *mf*

bank [bæŋk] N **1** *(building, institution)* banque *f*; **she has £10,000 in the b.** elle a 10 000 livres à la banque; **the B. of England/France** la Banque d'Angleterre/de France; **the b. of issue** la banque d'émission
2 *Cards* banque *f (de celui qui tient le jeu)*; *(in casino)* = argent qui appartient à la maison de jeu; **to break the b.** faire sauter la banque; *Fig* **it won't break the b.** ça ne va pas me/nous/*etc* ruiner
3 *(reserve ▸ of blood, sperm, data)* banque *f*
4 *(of lake, river)* bord *m*, rive *f*; *(above water)* berge *f*; *(of canal)* bord *m*, berge *f*; **we ran along the b.** nous avons couru le long de la berge; **the river has overflowed its banks** le fleuve est sorti de son lit; **the banks of Lake Como** les rives du lac de Côme; **the Left B.** *(in Paris)* la rive gauche
5 *(embankment, mound ▸ of earth, snow)* talus *m*; *Rail (▸ on railway)* remblai *m*; *(hill)* pente *f*; **he ran up the b. on to the road** il a grimpé la pente en courant jusqu'à la route
6 *(ridge ▸ on racetrack, road)* bord *m* relevé; *Transp (▸ by road)* talus *m*; *Geol (▸ of sand)* banc *m*; *(▸ by sea)* digue *f*
7 *Horseriding* banquette *f* irlandaise
8 *Bot & Hort (mass ▸ of flowers, shrubs)* massif *m*; *(▸ of cloud)* couche *f*, amoncellement *m*; *Mining (▸ of coal)* amoncellement *m*; *(▸ of fog)* banc *m*, couche *f*; *(▸ of sand)* banc *m*; **banks of flowers** des multitudes de fleurs
9 *Aviat* virage *m* incliné *ou* sur l'aile
10 *Tech (row ▸ of levers, switches)* rangée *f*; *Cin (of projectors)* rampe *f*; *(of speakers, transformers etc)* groupe *m*, batterie *f*
VT **1** *(enclose ▸ railway, road)* relever *(dans un virage)*; *(▸ river)* endiguer
2 *(heap up ▸ earth, stone)* amonceler; *(▸ fire)* couvrir; **to be banked** *(of clouds, snow)* être amoncelé
3 *Aviat* **to b. an aeroplane** faire faire à un avion un virage sur l'aile
4 *Fin (cheque, money)* mettre *ou* déposer à la banque
VI **1** *(have bank account)* **he banks with the National B.** il a un compte à la National Bank; **where do you b.?, who do you b. with?** à quelle banque êtes-vous *ou* avez-vous votre compte?, quelle est votre banque? **2** *(road)* être incliné; *Aviat (tip)* s'incliner sur l'aile; *(turn)* virer (sur l'aile)
▸▸ ***bank acceptance*** acceptation *f* de banque; ***bank account*** compte *m* bancaire; **to open/close a b. account** ouvrir/fermer un compte bancaire; ***bank advice*** avis *m* de la banque; ***bank balance*** solde *m* bancaire; ***bank base rate*** taux *m* de base bancaire; ***bank bill*** effet *m (tiré par une banque sur une autre)*; ***bank book*** livret *m* de caisse d'épargne, carnet *m* de banque; ***bank borrowings*** emprunts *mpl* bancaires, concours *m* bancaire; ***bank branch code*** code *m* guichet; ***bank buying rate*** taux *m* de change à l'achat; ***bank card*** carte *f* (d'identité) bancaire; ***bank charges*** frais *mpl* bancaires *ou* de banque; ***bank cheque*** chèque *m* bancaire; ***bank clerk*** employé(e) *m,f* de banque; ***bank credit*** avoir *m* en banque, crédit *m* bancaire; ***bank debts*** dettes *fpl* bancaires; ***bank details*** relevé *m* d'identité bancaire, RIB *m*; ***bank discount*** escompte *m* de banque, escompte *m* en dehors; ***bank discount rate*** escompte *m* officiel; ***bank draft*** traite *f* bancaire; ***bank guarantee*** garantie *f* bancaire, caution *f* de banque; ***bank holiday*** *(in UK)* jour *m* férié; *(in US)* jour *m* de fermeture des banques; ***bank holiday Monday*** lundi *m* férié *(jour de clôture des banques)*; ***bank interest*** intérêt *m* bancaire; ***bank lending*** concours *m* bancaire; ***bank loan*** *(money lent)* prêt *m* bancaire; *(money borrowed)* emprunt *m* bancaire; **to take out a b. loan** obtenir un prêt bancaire; **to pay off a b. loan** rembourser un emprunt bancaire; ***bank manager*** *(head of bank)* directeur(trice) *m,f* de banque; **my** *or* **the b. manager** *(head of bank)* le directeur de l'agence où j'ai mon compte; *(in charge of account)* le responsable de mon compte; *Hum* **I'll have to speak to my b. manager** il faudra que j'en parle à mon banquier; ***bank money*** monnaie *f* de banque, monnaie *f* scripturale; ***Bank of Mum and Dad*** = les parents, envisagés par leurs enfants comme prêteurs de dernier recours; **he knows he can always turn to the B. of Mum and Dad** il sait qu'il peut toujours demander de l'argent à ses parents; ***bank notification*** avis *m* de la banque; ***bank overdraft*** découvert *m* bancaire; ***bank rate*** taux *m* d'escompte *ou* de l'escompte, taux *m* bancaire; ***bank reconciliation*** rapprochement *m* bancaire; ***bank reserves*** réserves *fpl* bancaires; ***bank robber*** cambrioleur(euse) *m,f* de banque; ***bank selling rate*** taux *m* de change à la vente; *St Exch* ***bank shares*** valeurs *fpl* bancaires; ***bank sort code*** code *m* guichet; ***bank statement*** relevé *m* de compte; ***bank teller*** guichetier (ère) *m,f*; ***bank transactions*** transactions *fpl* bancaires; ***bank transfer*** virement *m* bancaire; ***bank treasurer*** trésorier(ère) *m,f* de banque
▸**bank on** VT INSEP *(count on)* compter sur; **I'm banking on it** je compte là-dessus
▸**bank up** VT SEP **1** *Constr (road)* relever *(dans un virage)*; *(river)* endiguer **2** *(fire)* couvrir; *(earth)* amonceler
VI *(cloud)* s'amonceler

bankable ['bæŋkəbəl] ADJ *Fin* bancable, escomptable; *Fig* **to be b.** être une valeur sûre

banker ['bæŋkə(r)] N **1** *Fin & Banking* banquier *m* **2** *Horseracing (in betting)* banquier *m*; **to be b.** *(in game)* tenir la banque
▸▸ *Banking* ***banker's acceptance*** acceptation *f* bancaire; *Comput* ***Bankers' Automated Clearing System*** = système électronique de compensation de chèques; ***banker's card*** carte *f* d'identité bancaire; ***banker's cheque*** traite *f* bancaire; ***banker's draft*** traite *f* bancaire; *Br* ***banker's order*** ordre *m* de virement bancaire

banking ['bæŋkɪŋ] N *(UNCOUNT)* **1** *(profession)* profession *f* de banquier, la banque; *(activity)* opérations *fpl* bancaires, activité *f* bancaire; **she's in b.** elle travaille dans la banque; **international b.** opérations *fpl* bancaires internationales **2** *Geog (embankment ▸ on river)* berge *f*; *Horseracing & Sport (▸ on racetrack)* bords *mpl* relevés **3** *Aviat* virage *m* sur l'aile
▸▸ *Am* ***banking account*** compte *m* en banque, compte *m* bancaire; ***banking controls*** contrôle *m* bancaire; ***banking hours*** heures *fpl* d'ouverture des banques; ***banking house*** maison *f* de banque, établissement *m* bancaire; ***banking services*** services *mpl* bancaires; ***banking system*** système *m* bancaire

banknote ['bæŋknəʊt] N billet *m* de banque

bankroll ['bæŋkrəʊl] *Am Fam* N fonds⌑ *mpl*, finances⌑ *fpl*
VT *(deal, project)* financer⌑

bankrupt ['bæŋkrʌpt] *Law*
N failli(e) *m,f*
ADJ *(insolvent)* failli; *Fig (person)* ruiné; **to go b.** faire faillite; **to be b.** être en faillite; **to adjudicate** *or* **declare sb b.** déclarer qn en faillite; **the firm was declared b.** la firme a été déclarée *ou* mise en faillite; *Fig* **morally b.** sans moralité
VT *(company, person)* mettre en faillite; *Fig (person)* ruiner

bankruptcy ['bæŋkrʌptsɪ] N *Law* faillite *f*; *Fig (destitution)* ruine *f*; **to present** *or* **file one's petition for b.** déposer son bilan; *Fig* **moral b.** ruine *f* morale
▸▸ *Br Law* ***bankruptcy court*** tribunal *m* de commerce; ***bankruptcy proceedings*** procédure *f* de faillite

banned [bænd] ADJ interdit

banner ['bænə(r)] N **1** *(flag)* étendard *m*; *(placard)* bannière *f*; *Fig* **to march/to campaign under sb's b.** se ranger/faire campagne sous la bannière de qn **2** *Comput & Mktg (for advertising on Internet)* bandeau *m*, bannière *f* publicitaire
ADJ *Am (year, season)* excellent
▸▸ *Comput* ***banner advertisement*** bandeau *m* publicitaire, bannière *f* publicitaire; *Press* ***banner headline*** gros titre *m*, manchette *f*; **in b. headlines** en gros titres

banning ['bænɪŋ] N interdiction *f*

bannister = **banister**

banns [bænz] NPL bans *mpl*; **to publish the b. (of marriage)** publier les bans (de mariage)

banoffee pie, banoffi pie [bən'ɒfɪ-] N *Culin* = gâteau à la banane et au caramel

banquet ['bæŋkwɪt] N *(formal dinner)* banquet *m*; *(big meal)* festin *m*
VT *(dignitary)* offrir un banquet à; *(treat lavishly)* offrir un festin à
VI *(dine formally)* faire un banquet; *(dine lavishly)* faire un festin

banqueting ['bæŋkwɪtɪŋ] N
▸▸ ***banqueting hall*** salle *f* de banquet; ***banqueting manager*** responsable *mf* des banquets; ***banqueting room*** salle *f* de banquet

banquette [bæŋ'ket] N **1** *(seat)* banquette *f* **2** *Constr (footbridge)* berme *f*

banshee ['bænʃiː] N *Myth* = fée de la mythologie irlandaise dont les cris présagent la mort; **the child was wailing like a b.** l'enfant hurlait comme un putois

bantam ['bæntəm] N *(hen)* poule *f* naine; *(cock)* coq *m* nain

bantamweight ['bæntəmweɪt] *Boxing* N *(boxer)* poids coq *m inv*
ADJ *(boxer)* poids coq *(inv)*

banter ['bæntə(r)] N *(UNCOUNT)* badinage *m*, plaisanterie *f*
VI badiner; **to b. with sb** badiner avec qn

bantering ['bæntərɪŋ] ADJ *Br (tone)* de plaisanterie, badin

Bantu [ˌbæn'tuː] *(pl* **inv** *or* **Bantus**) N **1** *(person)* Bantou(e) *m,f* **2** *(language)* bantou *m*
ADJ bantou

banyan ['bænɪən] N *Bot* banian *m*

BAOR [ˌbiːeɪəʊ'ɑː(r)] **N** *Mil (abbr* **British Army of the Rhine**) = forces britanniques en Allemagne

bap [bæp] **N** *Br* **1** *(roll)* = pain rond que l'on utilise pour faire un sandwich **2** *(usu pl) very Fam (breast)* **baps** nichons *mpl*, roberts *mpl*

baptism ['bæptɪzəm] **N** *Rel* baptême *m*; *Fig* **b. of fire** baptême *m* du feu

baptismal [bæp'tɪzməl] **ADJ** *Rel* baptismal, de baptême

►► ***baptismal font*** fonts *mpl* baptismaux; ***baptismal name*** nom *m* de baptême

Baptist ['bæptɪst] **N** *Rel* baptiste *mf*

►► ***the Baptist Church*** l'église *f* baptiste

baptistery, baptistry ['bæptɪstrɪ] *(pl* **baptisteries** *or* **baptisteries**) **N** *Rel* baptistère *m*; *(font in Baptist church)* fonts *mpl* baptismaux

baptize, -ise ['bæptaɪz, *Br* bæp'taɪz] **VT** *Rel & Fig* baptiser

BAR [bɑː(r)]

N
- bar **1, 13**
- barre **3, 6, 9, 12, 14**
- interdiction **4**
- obstacle **5**

VT
- munir de barreaux **1**
- barrer **2**
- exclure **3**

PREP
- sauf

(pt & pp **barred**, *cont* **barring**)

N 1 *(pub)* bar *m*, café *m*; *(in hotel, club)* bar *m*; *(in station)* café *m*, bar *m*; *(counter)* bar *m*; **we sat at the b. all night drinking** on est restés à boire au bar toute la nuit

2 *(small shop* ► *for coffee, tea)* buvette *f*; (► *for sandwiches)* snack *m*

3 *(long piece of metal)* barre *f*; *(on grating, cage, window)* barreau *m*; *(on door)* bâcle *f*; *Elec (element)* barre *f*; **an iron b.** une barre de fer; **to be behind (prison) bars** être sous les verrous *ou* derrière les barreaux; **they put him behind bars** ils l'ont mis sous les verrous

4 *(ban)* interdiction *f*; **there is a b. on bringing drink into the club** il est interdit d'introduire de l'alcool au sein du club; **there is no b. on foreign athletes** les athlètes étrangers sont autorisés à participer aux compétitions

5 *(obstacle)* empêchement *m*, obstacle *m*; *(in river, harbour)* barre *f* (de sable), traverse *f*; **to be a b. to sth** faire obstacle à qch

6 *(bank* ► *in lake, river)* banc *m*; *Am Geol (alluvial deposit)* barre *f*

7 *(slab* ► *of chocolate)* tablette *f*; (► *of gold)* lingot *m*; **a b. of soap** une savonnette, un pain de savon

8 *(stripe)* raie *f*; *(of sunlight)* rayon *m*

9 *Law (in court)* barre *f*; **the prisoner at the b.** l'accusé(e) *m,f*

10 *Mus* mesure *f*; **the opening/closing bars** les premières/dernières mesures

11 *Mil Br* barrette *f (portée sur le ruban d'une médaille)*; *Am* galon *m*

12 *Her* burelle *f*; *(dividing shield)* barre *f*

13 *Tech (unit of pressure)* bar *m*

14 *Comput (menu bar)* barre *f*

VT 1 *(put bars on* ► *window)* munir de barreaux; **b. the door** mettez la barre *ou* la bâcle à la porte; *Fig* **they barred the door against intruders** ils ont barré la porte aux intrus

2 *(obstruct)* barrer; **he barred her way** *or* **her path** il lui barra le passage

3 *(ban* ► *person)* exclure; (► *activity)* interdire; **members of the sect were barred from entering the country** l'entrée du pays était interdite aux membres de la secte; **he was barred from the club** il a été exclu du club

4 *(stripe)* rayer

PREP excepté, sauf; **b. accidents** sauf accident, sauf imprévu; **b. none** sans exception; **b. one** sauf un (une); **it's all over b. the shouting** les jeux sont faits

• **Bar N** *Law* **the B.** *(in UK)* le barreau; *(in US)* les avocats *mpl*; *Br* **to call sb to the B.**, *Am* **to admit sb to the B.** inscrire qn au barreau; **she was** *Br* **called** *or Am* **admitted to the B.** elle s'est inscrite au barreau

►► *Br* ***bar billiards*** = version du jeu de billard, couramment pratiquée dans les pubs, billard *m* russe; ***bar chart*** histogramme *m*; ***bar code*** code–barres *m*; ***bar code reader*** lecteur *m* de code–barres; *Eng Law* ***Bar Council*** = conseil de l'ordre des avocats; ***bar diagram*** histogramme *m*; *Am Law* ***Bar exam*** = examen obligatoire avant de pouvoir exercer en tant qu'avocat; ***bar food*** = repas simples servis dans les pubs; ***bar game*** = jeu pratiqué dans un pub; ***bar girl*** *Am (hostess)* entraîneuse *f* de bar; *Br (barmaid)* serveuse *f* (de bar); ***bar graph*** histogramme *m*; ***bar prices*** prix *mpl* des consommations; ***bar snack*** = repas simple pris dans un pub; ***bar staff*** personnel *m* de bar; ***bar stool*** tabouret *m* de bar; ***bar tariff*** liste *f* des prix des consommations

> When translating **bar**, note that **barre** and **barreau** are not interchangeable.

barb [bɑːb] **N 1** *(on fishhook)* barbillon *m*; *(on barbed wire)* barbe *f*, pointe *f*; *(on arrow)* barbelure *f*; *Orn (on feather)* barbe *f* **2** *(dig, gibe)* trait *m*, pointe *f*; **that was a cruel b.** c'était un trait cruel

Barbados [*Br* bɑː'beɪdɒs, *Am* bar'beɪdəʊz] **N** Barbade *f*

barbarian [bɑː'beərɪən] **N** *(boor, savage)* barbare *mf*

barbaric [bɑː'bærɪk] **ADJ** *also Fig* barbare

barbarism ['bɑːbərɪzəm] **N 1** *(state)* barbarie *f* **2** *(in language)* barbarisme *m*

barbarity [bɑː'bærətɪ] **N 1** *(brutality)* barbarie *f*, inhumanité *f* **2** *(atrocity)* atrocité *f*, acte *m* de barbarie; **the barbarities committed by the enemy** les atrocités commises par l'ennemi

barbarize, -ise ['bɑːbəraɪz] **VT to b. sb** faire de qn un monstre; *Ling* **to b. the language** estropier la langue

barbarous ['bɑːbərəs] **ADJ** *(language, manners, tribe)* barbare

barbarously ['bɑːbərəslɪ] **ADV** *(brutally)* cruellement, inhumainement; *(primitively)* d'une façon barbare

Barbary ['bɑːbərɪ] **N** *Geog* Barbarie *f*, États *mpl* barbaresques

►► ***Barbary ape*** singe *m* de Barbarie, magot *m*; ***the Barbary coast*** les côtes *fpl* de Barbarie; ***Barbary States*** États *mpl* barbaresques

barbecue ['bɑːbɪkjuː] *(pt & pp* **barbecued**, *cont* **barbecuing**) **N** *(grill, meal, party)* barbecue *m*; **to have a b.** faire un barbecue

VT *(steak)* griller au charbon de bois; *(pig, sheep)* rôtir tout entier

►► ***barbecue sauce*** sauce *f* barbecue

barbed [bɑːbd] **ADJ** *(arrow, hook)* barbelé; *(comment)* acéré, caustique

►► *Br* ***barbed wire*** (fil *m* de fer) barbelé *m*; *Br* ***barbed wire fence*** barbelés *mpl*

barbel ['bɑːbəl] **N** *Ich (fish)* barbeau *m*; *(smaller)* barbillon *m*; *(spine on fish)* barbillon *m*

barbell ['bɑːbel] **N** barre *f* à disques

barber ['bɑːbə(r)] **N** coiffeur *m* (pour hommes), *Can* barbier *m*; **to go to the b.'s** aller chez le coiffeur (pour hommes)

►► ***barber's pole*** enseigne *f* de coiffeur

barbershop ['bɑːbəʃɒp] **N** *Am* salon *m* de coiffure (pour hommes)

ADJ *(songs)* = chanté en harmonie étroite

►► ***barbershop quartet*** = quatuor d'hommes chantant en harmonie étroite

barbican ['bɑːbɪkən] **N** *Archit* barbacane *f*

barbie ['bɑːbɪ] **N** *Br & Austr Fam (barbecue)* barbecue[Q] *m*, barbeuk *m*; **to have a b.** se faire un barbeuk

Barbie doll® ['bɑːbiː-] **N** (poupée *f*) Barbie® *f*; *Fam Fig* **all his girlfriends have been real Barbie dolls** toutes ses petites amies ressemblent à des poupées Barbie®

barbital ['bɑːbɪtəl] **N** *Am Pharm* barbital *m*, véronal *m*

barbitone ['bɑːbɪtəʊn] **N** *Br Pharm* barbital *m*, véronal *m*

barbiturate [bɑː'bɪtjʊrət] **N** *Pharm* barbiturique *m*

►► *Med* ***barbiturate poisoning*** barbiturisme *m*

barbituric [ˌbɑːbɪ'tjʊrɪk] **ADJ** *Pharm* barbiturique

Barbour® jacket ['bɑːbə-] **N** *Br* = veste en toile cirée à col de velours souvent associée à un style de vie BCBG en Grande-Bretagne

barbwire ['bɑːbˌwaɪə(r)] **N** *Am* (fil *m* de fer) barbelé *m*

►► ***barbwire fence*** barbelés *mpl*

barcarole, barcarolle [ˌbɑːkə'rəʊl] **N** *Mus* barcarolle *f*

Barcelona [ˌbɑːsɪ'ləʊnə] **N** Barcelone

bard [bɑːd] **N** *(Celtic)* barde *m*; *(Greek)* aède *m*; *Literary (poet)* poète *m*; **the B. of Avon** = surnom donné à William Shakespeare, originaire de Stratford-upon-Avon

bardic ['bɑːdɪk] **ADJ** *(poetry, privileges)* du barde, des bardes

bardolatry [bɑː'dɒlətrɪ] **N** *Hum Pej* = admiration sans bornes pour Shakespeare et ses œuvres

Bardot ['bɑːdəʊ] **ADJ B. jumper** pull *m* à col Bardot; **B. neckline** col *m* Bardot

bare [beə(r)] *(compar* **barer**, *superl* **barest**) **ADJ 1** *(naked* ► *body, feet)* nu; **they were b. to the waist** ils étaient nus jusqu'à la taille; **in one's b. feet** pieds nus; **he killed a tiger with his b. hands** il a tué un tigre à mains nues; *Boxing* **to fight with b. hands** boxer à main nue

2 *(unadorned, uncovered)* nu; *Elec (wire)* dénudé; **we had to sleep on b. floorboards** nous avons dû coucher à même le plancher; **his head was b.** il était nu-tête; **b. wood** bois *m* naturel; **the tree was b. of leaves** l'arbre était dépouillé *ou* dénudé; **the lawn was just a b. patch of grass** la pelouse consistait en un maigre carré d'herbe; **a wall of b. rock** une paroi de roche nue; **to lay b. one's heart** mettre son cœur à nu; **to lay b. a plot** révéler *ou* dévoiler un complot

3 *(empty)* vide; **the cupboard was b.** le garde-manger était vide; **the room was b. of furniture/pictures** la pièce ne comportait aucun meuble/tableau

4 *(basic, plain)* simple, dépouillé; **I just told him the barest details** je lui ai donné le minimum de détails; **the b. facts** les faits *mpl* bruts; *Fig* **the b. bones of the story** le squelette de l'histoire

5 *(absolute)* absolu, strict; **the house was stripped to the b. essentials** la maison ne contenait que le strict nécessaire; **the b. necessities of life** le minimum vital; **the b. minimum** le strict minimum

6 *(meagre)* **a b. 20 percent of the population is literate** à peine 20 pour cent de la population est alphabétisée; **he earned a b. £200** il a gagné tout juste 200 livres; **they won by a b. majority** ils ont gagné de justesse; **they manage to scrape a b. living from the land** ils arrivent tout juste à vivoter en travaillant la terre

VT 1 *(part of body)* découvrir; *(teeth)* montrer; **to b. one's head** se découvrir la tête; **to b. one's soul** mettre son âme à nu **2** *(unsheath* ► *dagger, sword)* dégainer, tirer du fourreau; *Elec* (► *wire)* dénuder

bareback ['beəbæk] **ADJ** *Horseriding (rider)* qui monte à cru

ADV *Horseriding* **to ride b.** monter à cru; *very Fam Hum (have unprotected sex)* faire l'amour sans préservatif[Q]

bare-chested ADJ torse nu

barefaced ['beəfeɪst] **ADJ** *(liar)* effronté, éhonté; *(lie)* impudent, éhonté

barefoot ['beəfʊt] **ADJ** aux pieds nus

ADV nu-pieds, (les) pieds nus; **to go b.** marcher pieds nus

►► *Med* ***barefoot doctor*** médecin *m* aux pieds nus

barefooted [ˌbeə'fʊtɪd] **ADJ** aux pieds nus

ADV nu-pieds, (les) pieds nus; **to go b.** marcher pieds nus

bare-handed ADJ aux mains nues

ADV *(fight)* à mains nues

bareheaded [ˌbeə'hedɪd] **ADJ** nu-tête *(inv)*

ADV nu-tête, (la) tête nue

barelegged [ˌbeə'legd] **ADJ** aux jambes nues; **it was a warm day so he was b.** il était en short parce qu'il faisait chaud

ADV nu-jambes, (les) jambes nues; **she goes out b. even in winter** même en hiver elle ne porte pas de collant

barely ['beəlɪ] ADV **1** *(only just)* à peine, tout juste; **there was b. enough to go around** il y en avait à peine assez pour tout le monde; **I had b. arrived when I heard the news** j'étais à peine arrivé que j'ai entendu la nouvelle; **he can b. read and write** c'est tout juste s'il sait lire et écrire **2** *(sparsely)* très peu; *(poorly)* pauvrement

bareness ['beənɪs] N **1** *(nakedness ▸ of person)* nudité *f* **2** *(sparseness ▸ of style)* dépouillement *m*, *Pej* sécheresse *f*; *(▸ of furnishings)* pauvreté *f*; *(▸ of room)* dénuement *m* **3** *(simplicity)* dépouillement *m*

barf [bɑːf] VI *Fam* dégueuler

▸▸ ***barf bag*** sac *m* pour vomir$^{\square}$

barfly ['bɑːflaɪ] N *Am Fam* pilier *m* de bistrot

bargain ['bɑːgɪn] N **1** *(deal)* marché *m*, affaire *f*; **a good/bad b.** une bonne/mauvaise affaire; **to strike** *or* **to make a b. with sb** conclure un marché avec qn; **to drive a hard b.** marchander d'une façon acharnée; **you keep your end of the b. and I'll keep mine** vous respectez vos engagements et je respecterai les miens **2** *(good buy)* occasion *f*; **it's a real b.!** c'est une bonne affaire!, c'est une occasion!; **to go b. hunting** faire les soldes; *(in second-hand shops)* chiner

VI **1** *(haggle)* marchander; **she bargained with me over the price of the shoes** elle a marchandé avec moi au sujet du prix des chaussures **2** *(negotiate)* négocier; **the unions are bargaining with management for an eight percent pay rise** les syndicats négocient une hausse de salaire de huit pour cent avec la direction

• **into the bargain** ADV par-dessus le marché; **I was tired, hungry and had a headache into the b.** j'étais fatigué, j'avais faim et en plus j'avais mal à la tête

▸▸ ***bargain basement*** *(in shop)* = dans certains grands magasins, sous-sol où sont regroupés les articles en solde et autres bonnes affaires; ***bargain break*** séjour *m* discompté; ***bargain counter*** rayon *m* des soldes; ***bargain offer*** promotion *f*, offre *f* exceptionnelle; ***bargain price*** prix *m* avantageux; ***bargain sale*** soldes *mpl* exceptionnels; ***bargain store*** magasin *m* bon marché

▸ **bargain away** VT SEP *(rights, reputation)* brader; *(freedom)* sacrifier

▸ **bargain for** VT INSEP *(anticipate)* s'attendre à; **I hadn't bargained for this** je ne m'étais pas attendu à ça; **they got more than they bargained for** ils ne s'attendaient pas à un coup pareil; **things happened more quickly than he had bargained for** les choses sont allées plus vite qu'il n'avait pensé

▸ **bargain on** VT INSEP *(depend on)* compter sur; **I'm bargaining on it** je compte là-dessus; **I hadn't bargained on this happening!** je ne m'attendais pas à cela!

bargaining ['bɑːgɪnɪŋ] N *(haggling)* marchandage *m*; *(negotiating)* négociations *fpl*; **we are in a strong b. position** nous sommes en position de force pour négocier; **they have considerable b. power** ils ont beaucoup de poids dans les négociations

▸▸ ***bargaining chip***, *Br* ***bargaining counter*** monnaie *f* d'échange; **to use sb/sth as a b. chip** utiliser qn/qch comme monnaie d'échange; *Ind* ***bargaining table*** table *f* des négociations

barge [bɑːdʒ] N *Naut* **1** *(on canal)* chaland *m*; *(larger ▸ on river)* péniche *f*; **to live on a b.** vivre sur une péniche **2** *(ceremonial boat)* barque *f*; **the queen's b.** la barque de cérémonie de la reine; **the admiral's b.** la vedette de l'amiral

VI **they b. about as if they owned the place** ils vont et viennent comme si l'endroit leur appartenait; **he barged into the room** il fit irruption dans la pièce; **she barged past me** elle m'a bousculé en passant

VT *Sport (goalkeeper, player)* écarter d'un coup d'épaule; **to b. sb out of the way** écarter qn d'un geste brusque; **to b. one's way into a room** faire irruption dans une pièce

▸ **barge in** VI *(enter)* faire irruption; *(interrupt)* intervenir mal à propos; **I'm sorry for barging in like this** excusez-moi de faire ainsi irruption; **he keeps barging in on our conversation** il n'arrête pas de nous interrompre dans notre conversation

▸ **barge into** VT INSEP **1** *(bump into ▸ person)* rentrer dans; *(▸ piece of furniture)* rentrer dans, se cogner contre **2** *(enter abruptly ▸ room)* faire irruption dans

▸ **barge through** VT INSEP **to b. through a door** passer une porte en trombe; **to b. through a crowd** foncer à travers la foule

VT SEP **to b. one's way through the crowd** foncer à travers la foule; **just b. your way through** force le passage

bargee [bɑːˈdʒiː], *Am* **bargeman** ['bɑːdʒmən] *(pl* **bargemen** [-mən]) N *Naut* batelier *m*, marinier *m*

bargepole ['bɑːdʒpəʊl] N *Naut* gaffe *f*; *Br* **I wouldn't touch it with a b.** *(disgusting object)* je n'y toucherais pas avec des pincettes; *(risky affair, deal)* je ne m'en mêlerais pour rien au monde

barhop ['bɑːhɒp] VI *Am Fam* faire les bars

baritone ['bærɪtəʊn] *Mus* N *(singer, voice)* baryton *m*

ADJ *(part, voice)* de baryton

barium ['beərɪəm] N *Chem* baryum *m*

▸▸ *Med* ***barium enema*** lavement *m* baryté; *Med* ***barium meal*** bouillie *f* barytée

bark [bɑːk] N **1** *(of dog)* aboiement *m*; *(of fox)* glapissement *m*; *Fig (cough)* toux *f* sèche; **to give** *or* **to let out a b.** *(dog)* aboyer, pousser un aboiement; *(fox)* pousser un glapissement; **his b. is worse than his bite** il crie beaucoup mais il n'est pas méchant **2** *(of tree)* écorce *f*; **to strip** *or* **to take the b. off a tree** écorcer un arbre **3** *Am* = **barque**

VI *(dog)* aboyer; *(fox)* glapir; *Fig (cough)* tousser; *(speak harshly)* crier, aboyer; *(sell)* vendre à la criée; **the dog barked at the postman** le chien a aboyé après le facteur; *Fig* **to be barking up the wrong tree** faire fausse route

VT **1** *(order)* aboyer **2** *(tree)* écorcer; *(skin)* écorcher; **to b. one's shins** s'écorcher les jambes

▸ **bark out** VT SEP *(order)* aboyer

barkeep ['bɑːkiːp], **barkeeper** ['bɑːˌkiːpə(r)] N *Am Fam* barman$^{\square}$ *m*

barker ['bɑːkə(r)] N *(in fairground)* bonimenteur *m*

barking ['bɑːkɪŋ] N *(UNCOUNT) (of dog)* aboiements *mpl*; *(of fox)* glapissements *mpl*

ADJ **1** *(dog)* aboyeur; *(fox)* glapissant **2** *Br Fam* **b. (mad)** complètement cinglé

barley ['bɑːlɪ] N **1** *(crop, grain)* orge *f* **2** *(in cooking, distilling)* orge *m*; *(in soup)* orge *m* perlé; *(for whisky)* orge *m* mondé

▸▸ *Culin* ***barley sugar*** sucre *m* d'orge; *Br* ***barley water*** = sirop à base d'orge généralement parfumé au citron ou à l'orange; *Br* ***barley wine*** = bière très forte en alcool

barleycorn ['bɑːlɪkɔːn] N **1** *(grain)* grain *m* d'orge **2** *(barley)* orge *f*

barm [bɑːm] N levure *f* (de bière)

barmaid ['bɑːmeɪd] N barmaid *f*, serveuse *f (au bar)*

barman ['bɑːmən] *(pl* **barmen** [-mən]) N barman *m*, serveur *m (au bar)*

barminess ['bɑːmɪnɪs] N *Br Fam* folie$^{\square}$ *f*

barmy ['bɑːmɪ] *(compar* **barmier**, *superl* **barmiest**) ADJ *Br Fam* maboul, dingue

barn [bɑːn] N **1** *(for hay)* grange *f*; *(for horses)* écurie *f*; *(for cows)* étable *f*; *Fig* **their house is a great b. of a place** leur maison est une énorme bâtisse; *Fig* **it's as big as a b. door** c'est gros comme une maison; **he couldn't hit a b. door** *(he's a poor shot)* c'est un mauvais tireur **2** *Am (for railroad trucks)* dépôt *m*

▸▸ ***barn dance*** = bal de campagne où l'on danse des quadrilles; *Orn* ***barn owl*** (chouette *f*) effraie *f*, chouette *f* des clochers

barnacle ['bɑːnəkəl] N bernache *f*, bernacle *f (crustacé)*

▸▸ *Orn* ***barnacle goose*** bernache *f* (nonnette)

barnet N *Br Fam (rhyming slang* **Barnet fair** = **hair**) tifs *mpl*

barney ['bɑːnɪ] N *Br Fam* engueulade *f*; **to have a b.** avoir une engueulade *ou* une prise de bec

barnstorm ['bɑːnˌstɔːm] VI **1** *Sport* faire une tournée à la campagne; *Theat* jouer sur les tréteaux **2** *Am Pol* = faire une tournée électorale (dans les circonscriptions rurales)

barnstormer ['bɑːnˌstɔːmə(r)] N **1** *Theat (actor)* comédien(enne) *m,f* ambulant(e); *Gym (acrobat)* acrobate *mf* ambulant(e) **2** *Am Pol* orateur (trice) *m,f* électoral(e)

barnstorming ['bɑːnˌstɔːmɪŋ] N **1** *Theat* théâtre *m* ambulant **2** *Am Pol* tournée *f ou* campagne *f* électorale

ADJ *(speech, performance)* plein de brio

barnyard ['bɑːnjɑːd] N cour *f* de ferme

ADJ *(animals)* de basse-cour; *Fig (humour)* rustre

barometer [bəˈrɒmɪtə(r)] N *Met* baromètre *m*; **the b. is showing fair** le baromètre est au beau; *Fig* **the poll is a clear b. of public reaction** le sondage est un parfait baromètre des réactions du public

barometric [ˌbærəˈmetrɪk] ADJ *Met* barométrique

▸▸ ***barometric pressure*** pression *f* atmosphérique

baron ['bærən] N **1** *(noble)* baron *m* **2** *(magnate)* magnat *m*; **a press b.** un magnat de la presse **3** *Culin* **a b. of beef** un double aloyau de bœuf

baroness ['bærənɪs] N baronne *f*

baronet ['bærənɪt] N baronnet *m*

baronetcy ['bærənɪtsɪ] N *(title)* titre *m* de baronnet; *(position)* rang *m* de baronnet

baronial [bəˈrəʊnɪəl] ADJ de baron

▸▸ ***baronial hall*** demeure *f* seigneuriale

barony ['bærənɪ] N baronnie *f (terre)*

baroque [bəˈrɒk] *Art, Archit & Mus* N baroque *m*

ADJ baroque

barque, *Am* **bark** [bɑːk] N **1** *Literary* barque *f* **2** *Naut (with three masts)* trois-mâts *m inv*; *(with four masts)* quatre-mâts *m inv*

barrack ['bærək] VT **1** *Mil (soldiers)* caserner **2** *Br (heckle)* chahuter **3** *Austr Fam (support ▸ team)* supporter$^{\square}$; *(shout encouragement at ▸ player, team)* encourager$^{\square}$

• **barracks** N *Mil* caserne *f*; **infantry barracks** quartier *m* d'infanterie; **in barracks** à la caserne; **to be confined to barracks** être consigné; *Fig* **the school is a great barracks of a place** l'école est une espèce d'énorme bâtisse du genre caserne

▸▸ *Mil* ***barrack square*** cour *f* de caserne

> Note that the French word **baraque** is a false friend. Its most common meaning is **shack**.

barracking ['bærəkɪŋ] N *Br* chahut *m*; **he got** *or* **they gave him a terrible b.** on l'a chahuté violemment

barrack-room ADJ *Br (humour, joke)* de caserne; **b. language** langage *m* de corps de garde *ou* de caserne

barracuda [ˌbærəˈkuːdə] N *Ich* barracuda *m*

barrage ['bærɑːʒ] N **1** *Mil* tir *m* de barrage **2** *Fig (of punches, questions)* pluie *f*, déluge *m*; *(of insults, words)* déluge *m*, flot *m* **3** *Constr (dam)* barrage *m*

VT **to b. sb with sth** *(questions, insults etc)* assaillir qn de qch

▸▸ *Mil* ***barrage balloon*** ballon *m* de barrage

barred [bɑːd] ADJ *(locked ▸ door)* barré; *(with bars on ▸ window)* à barreaux

barrel ['bærəl] *(Br pt & pp* **barrelled**, *cont* **barrelling**, *Am pt & pp* **barreled**, *cont* **barreling**) N **1** *(cask, unit of capacity ▸ of wine)* tonneau *m*, fût *m*; *(▸ of cider)* fût *m*; *(▸ of beer)* tonneau *m*; *Petr (▸ of oil, tar)* baril *m*; *(▸ of fish)* caque *f*; **they have a production capacity of 2 million barrels a day** leur capacité de production est de 2 millions de barils par jour; *Fam* **to have sb over a b.** tenir qn à sa merci$^{\square}$ **2** *Tech (hollow cylinder ▸ of gun, key)* canon *m*; *(▸ of clock, lock)* barillet *m*; *(▸ of pen)* corps *m*; *(of capstan, winch)* fusée *f*, mèche *f*, tambour *m*; *Mil (of artillery piece)* tube *m*; *Fam* **to give sb both barrels** passer un savon à qn **3** *Fam (lot)* **it wasn't a b. of laughs** *(interview, project)* ça n'a pas été une partie de plaisir; *(film, show)* ce n'était pas très rigolo; **he's a b. of fun** il est vraiment marrant; *Am* **it was more fun than a b. of monkeys** c'était marrant comme tout

VT *(beer)* mettre en tonneau; *Petr (oil)* mettre en baril

VI *Am Fam* **to b. (along)** foncer, aller à toute pompe

►► *Mus* ***barrel organ*** orgue *m* de Barbarie; *Aviat* ***barrel roll*** tonneau *m* en spirale; *Archit* ***barrel vault*** voûte *f* en berceau

barren ['bærən] **ADJ 1** *(land* ► *infertile)* stérile, improductif; *(*► *bare)* désertique; *(*► *dry)* aride **2** *Literary (sterile* ► *woman)* stérile **3** *(dull* ► *film, play)* aride; *(*► *discussion)* stérile; *(*► *writing)* aride, sec (sèche)

N lande *f*; **the pine barrens of Frankonia** les landes de la Franconie

barrenness ['bærənnɪs] **N 1** *(of land* ► *infertility)* stérilité *f*; *(*► *bareness)* désolation *f*; *(*► *dryness)* aridité *f* **2** *Literary (sterility* ► *of woman)* stérilité *f* **3** *(dullness* ► *of film, play, writing)* aridité *f*; *(*► *of discussion)* stérilité *f*

barrette [bə'ret] **N** *Am* barrette *f (pour cheveux)*

barricade ['bærɪˌkeɪd] **N** *Naut & Constr* barricade *f*

VT *(door, street)* barricader; **they barricaded themselves in** ils se sont barricadés

► **barricade off VT SEP** *(street)* barrer

barrier ['bærɪə(r)] **N 1** *(fence, gate)* barrière *f*; *(at railway station)* portillon *m* **2** *(obstacle)* obstacle *m*; **lack of investment is a b. to economic growth** le manque d'investissement est un obstacle à la croissance économique; **the language b.** le barrage *ou* la barrière de la langue

►► ***barrier cream*** crème *f* protectrice; ***barrier ice*** banquise *f*; ***barrier method*** méthode *f* de contraception locale; ***barrier reef*** barrière *f* de corail

barring ['bɑːrɪŋ] **PREP** excepté, sauf; **b. rain the concert will take place tomorrow** à moins qu'il ne pleuve, le concert aura lieu demain; **b. accidents** sauf accident, sauf imprévu

barrister ['bærɪstə(r)], **barrister-at-law N** *Br Law* avocat(e) *m,f*

barrow ['bærəʊ] **N 1** *(wheelbarrow)* brouette *f*; *(fruitseller's)* voiture *f* des quatre saisons; *(for luggage)* diable *m*; *Mining* wagonnet *m*; **I wheeled** *or* **carried the bricks in a b.** j'ai brouetté les briques **2** *(burial mound)* tumulus *m*

►► *Br* ***barrow boy*** marchand *m* ambulant

bartender ['bɑːtendə(r)] **N** *Am (man)* barman *m*, serveur *m (au bar)*; *(woman)* barmaid *f*, serveuse *f (au bar)*

barter ['bɑːtə(r)] *Com* **N** *(UNCOUNT)* échange *m*, troc *m*; **a system of b.** une économie de troc

VT échanger, troquer; **they bartered animals for cloth** ils ont échangé des animaux contre du tissu

VI *(exchange)* faire un échange *ou* un troc; *(haggle)* marchander

►► *Com* ***barter economy*** économie *f* de troc; ***barter society*** société *f* vivant du troc; ***barter system*** économie *f* de troc

basal ['beɪsəl] **ADJ 1** *Physiol* basal **2** *(fundamental)* fondamental

basalt ['bæsɔːlt] **N** *Geol* basalte *m*

►► ***basalt column*** colonne *f* basaltique

basaltic [bə'sɔːltɪk] **ADJ** *Geol* basaltique

bascule ['bæskjuːl] **N** *Tech* bascule *f*

►► *Constr* ***bascule bridge*** pont *m* à bascule

base [beɪs] *(compar* **baser**, *superl* **basest)** **N 1** *(bottom* ► *gen)* partie *f* inférieure, base *f*; *(*► *of tree, column)* pied *m*; *(*► *of bowl, glass)* fond *m*; *(*► *of triangle)* base *f*; **the bud grows at the b. of the branch** le bourgeon pousse à la base de la branche

2 *(support, stand* ► *of statue, pillar)* socle *m*

3 *(of food, paint)* base *f*; **the stock forms the b. of your sauce** le fond constitue la base de votre sauce

4 *(basis* ► *of knowledge)* base *f*; *(*► *of experience)* réserve *f*

5 *Econ & Pol* base *f*; **an industrial b.** une zone industrielle

6 *(centre of activities)* point *m* de départ; *Mil* base *f*; **the explorers returned to b.** les explorateurs sont retournés au camp de base; **the visitors made central London their b.** les visiteurs ont pris le centre de Londres comme point de départ; **Glasgow is a good b. from which to explore the Highlands** Glasgow est un bon point d'attache pour rayonner dans les Highlands; *Com* **the company's b.** le siège de la société

7 *Chem, Comput, Geom & Math* base *f*

8 *Sport (in baseball and rounders)* base *f*; *Am Fam Fig* **he's way off b.** il est complètement à côté de la plaque; **first b.** *(in baseball)* première base *f*; *Fig* **to get to first b.** réussir la première étape; *Fam Fig* **I couldn't get past first b. with her** elle m'a laissé l'embrasser, mais pas plus; **I just thought I'd touch b.** je voulais juste garder le contact

VT 1 *(found* ► *opinion, project)* baser, fonder; **the project is based on cooperation from all regions** le projet est fondé sur la coopération de toutes les régions; **the film is based on a true story/on a short story by Herman Melville** le film est tiré d'une histoire vraie/d'une nouvelle de Herman Melville

2 *(locate)* baser; **where are you based?** où êtes-vous installé?; **the job is based in Tokyo** le poste est basé à Tokyo

ADJ *(motive, thoughts, conduct)* bas, indigne; *(origins)* bas; *(ingratitude)* flagrant; *(coinage)* faux (fausse)

►► *Am Tech* ***base burner*** = poêle où le charbon alimente le feu automatiquement; *Mil* ***base camp*** camp *m* de base; ***base coat*** *(of paint)* première couche *f*; *Fin* ***base date*** date *f* de base; ***base hit*** *(in baseball)* = coup permettant au batteur d'atteindre la première base; *Sport* ***base jumping*** = saut en chute libre à partir d'un pont, d'une falaise ou d'une montagne, avec parachute plié que l'on ouvre le plus tard possible; *Fin & Banking* ***base lending rate*** = taux de base du crédit bancaire; *Com & Elec* ***base load*** charge *f* minimum; *Metal* ***base metal*** métal *m* vil; *Am* ***base pay*** salaire *m* de base; *Banking* ***base rate*** taux *m* de base (bancaire) *(utilisé par les banques pour déterminer leur taux de prêt)*; *Am* ***base salary*** salaire *m* de base; *Rad & Tel* ***base station*** station *f* de base; *Banking* ***base year*** année *f* de référence

baseball ['beɪsbɔːl] **N** *Sport* base-ball *m*

►► ***baseball cap*** casquette *f* de base-ball; ***baseball game*** match *m* de base-ball; ***baseball glove, baseball mitt*** gant *m* de base-ball

baseboard ['beɪsbɔːd] **N** *Am Constr* plinthe *f*

Basel ['bɑːzəl] **N** Bâle *f*

baseless ['beɪslɪs] **ADJ** *(gossip)* sans fondement; *(suspicion)* injustifié; *(fear, superstition)* déraisonnable

baseline ['beɪslaɪn] **N 1** *Sport (in baseball)* ligne *f* des bases; *(in tennis)* ligne *f* de fond

2 *(in surveying)* base *f*; *(in diagram)* ligne *f* zéro; *Art* ligne *f* de fuite

3 *(standard)* point *m* de comparaison

4 *Comput (in desktop publishing)* ligne *f* de base

►► *Fin* ***baseline costs*** coûts *mpl* de base; *Sport* ***baseline player*** joueur(euse) *m,f* de fond de court; *Com* ***baseline sales*** ventes *fpl* de base

basely ['beɪslɪ] **ADV** bassement, vilement

basement ['beɪsmənt] **N** sous-sol *m*; **in the b.** au sous-sol

ADJ *(kitchen, bedroom)* en sous-sol

►► ***basement flat*** (appartement *m* en) sous-sol *m*

baseness ['beɪsnɪs] **N** *(of motives, thoughts, conduct, origins)* bassesse *f*

bash [bæʃ] *Fam* **N 1** *(blow)* coup❑ *m*; *(with fist)* coup *m* de poing❑; **he gave me a b. on the nose** il m'a donné un coup de poing sur le nez

2 *(dent* ► *in wood)* entaille❑ *f*; *(*► *in metal)* bosse❑ *f*, bosselure❑ *f*; **my car door got a b.** la porte de ma voiture a été cabossée

3 *Br (party)* fête❑ *f*; **we're having a bit of a b.** nous organisons une petite fête

4 *Br (attempt)* **to have a b. at doing sth** essayer de faire qch❑; **I'm willing to give it a b.** je vais essayer un coup

VT 1 *(person, one's head)* frapper❑, cogner❑; **she bashed him on the head** elle l'a assommé **2** *(dent* ► *wooden box, table)* entailler❑; *(*► *car)* cabosser❑, bosseler❑ **3** *Fig (criticize)* critiquer❑; *Fig* **it's part of their campaign to b. the unions** leur campagne a en partie pour but d'enfoncer les syndicats

► **bash about, bash around VT SEP** *Fam* **1** *(hit* ► *person)* flanquer des coups à; *(punch)* flanquer des coups de poing à **2** *(ill-treat* ► *person)* maltraiter❑, rudoyer❑; *(*► *car)* mettre à rude épreuve❑; **the package has been bashed about** *or* **around** le paquet a souffert

► **bash down VT SEP** *Fam (door)* enfoncer❑

► **bash in VT SEP** *Fam (door)* enfoncer❑; *(car, hat)* cabosser❑

► **bash on VI** *Br Fam (with journey, task)* continuer (tant bien que mal)❑

► **bash up VT SEP** *Fam (car)* bousiller; *(person)* tabasser

bashful ['bæʃfʊl] **ADJ** *(shy)* timide; *(modest)* pudique

bashfully ['bæʃfʊlɪ] **ADV** *(shyly)* timidement; *(modestly)* avec pudeur

bashfulness ['bæʃfʊlnɪs] **N** *(shyness)* timidité *f*; *(modesty)* pudeur *f*

bashing ['bæʃɪŋ] **N** *Fam* raclée *f*, peignée *f*; **to take** *or* **get a b.** prendre une raclée *ou* une peignée

BASIC ['beɪsɪk] **N** *Comput (abbr* **beginner's all-purpose symbolic instruction code)** basic *m*

basic ['beɪsɪk] **ADJ 1** *(fundamental* ► *problem, theme)* fondamental; *(*► *aim, belief)* principal; **these things are b. to a good marriage** ces choses sont fondamentales *ou* vitales pour un mariage heureux

2 *(elementary* ► *rule, skill)* élémentaire; *(*► *knowledge, vocabulary)* de base; **b. English** anglais *m* de base; **my French is a bit b.** mon français est plutôt rudimentaire; **I've got the b. idea** je vois de quoi il s'agit en gros; *Math* **the four b. operations** les quatre opérations *fpl* fondamentales

3 *(essential)* essentiel; **b. foodstuffs** denrées *fpl* de base; **the b. necessities of life** les besoins *mpl* vitaux; **b. precautions** précautions *fpl* élémentaires *ou* essentielles

4 *(primitive* ► *furniture, accommodation, skills)* rudimentaire; **their** *Br* **flat** *or Am* **apartment is really b.** leur appartement est très rudimentaire

5 *(as a starting point* ► *hours)* de base; **this is the b. model of the car** voici la voiture dans son modèle de base

6 *Chem* basique

• **basics NPL the basics** l'essentiel *m*; **let's get down to basics** venons-en à l'essentiel; **I learned the basics of computing** j'ai acquis les notions de base en informatique; **to get back to basics** *(important things in life)* retourner aux choses essentielles

►► *Econ* ***basic commodity*** denrée *f* de base; *Mktg* ***basic consumer goods*** denrées *fpl* de consommation courante; *Ins* ***basic cover*** assurance *f* de garantie de base; *Econ* ***basic industry*** industrie *f* de base; *Fin* ***basic pay*** salaire *m* de base; *Econ* ***basic population*** population *f* mère; *Br Fin* ***basic rate*** taux *m* de base (bancaire); **most people are b. rate taxpayers** la plupart des gens sont imposés au taux de base; *Br Fin* ***basic rate tax*** impôt *m* forfaitaire; *Br Fin* ***basic salary*** salaire *m* de base, traitement *m* de base; ***basic slag*** scorie *f* de déphosphoration; *Fin* ***basic wage*** salaire *m* de base

basically ['beɪsɪkəlɪ] **ADV** au fond; **they are both b. the same** au fond, ils sont tous les deux identiques; **b. I agree with you** dans l'ensemble *ou* en gros je suis d'accord avec vous; **she's b. a shy person, she's b. shy** c'est une personne foncièrement timide; **b., she doesn't know what to think** dans le fond, elle ne sait pas quoi penser

basil [*Br* 'bæzəl, *Am* 'beɪzəl] **N** *Bot & Culin* basilic *m*

basilica [bə'zɪlɪkə] **N** *Archit & Rel* basilique *f*

basilisk ['bæzɪlɪsk] **N** *Her, Myth & Zool* basilic *m*

basin ['beɪsən] **N 1** *Culin* bol *m*; *(for cream)* jatte *f*

2 *(for washing)* cuvette *f*, bassine *f*; *(plumbed in)* lavabo *m*

3 *Geog (of river)* bassin *m*; *(of valley)* cuvette *f*; **the Paris B.** le Bassin parisien

4 *(for fountain)* vasque *f*, coupe *f*; *(in harbour)* bassin *m*

►► ***basin cut*** *(haircut)* coupe *f* au bol

basinful ['beɪsənfʊl] **N** *(of milk)* bol *m*; *(of cream)* jatte *f*; *(of water)* pleine cuvette *f*; *Fam* **to have had a b. (of sb/sth)** en avoir ras le bol (de qn/qch)

basing point pricing ['beɪsɪŋ-] **N** *Econ* = tarification des frais de transport à partir d'un point de base unique

basis ['beɪsɪs] (*pl* **bases** [-si:z]) **N 1** *(foundation)* base *f*; **he can't survive on that b.** il ne peut pas survivre dans ces conditions-là; **on the b. of what I was told** d'après ce qu'on m'a dit; *Fin* **the b. for assessing income tax** l'assiette *f* de l'impôt sur le revenu **2** *(reason)* raison *f*; *(grounds)* motif *m*; **he did it on the b. that he'd nothing to lose** il l'a fait en partant du principe qu'il n'avait rien à perdre; **there was no rational b. for his decision** sa décision n'avait aucun fondement rationnel **3** *(system, scheme)* **on a worldwide b.** à l'échelle mondiale; **employed on a part-time b.** employé à mi-temps; **paid on a weekly b.** payé à la semaine; **the centre is organized on a voluntary b.** le centre fonctionne sur la base du bénévolat; **I will be taking part on an unofficial b.** je participerai à titre non officiel

bask [bɑ:sk] **VI 1** *(lie)* **to b. in the sun** lézarder **2** *(revel)* se réjouir, se délecter; **he basked in all the unexpected publicity** il se réjouissait de toute cette publicité imprévue

basket ['bɑ:skɪt] **N 1** *(container ▸ gen)* corbeille *f*; *(▸ for shopping, carrying)* panier *m*; *(▸ for wastepaper)* corbeille *f* à papier; *(▸ for linen)* panier *m* à linge; *(▸ for baby)* couffin *m*; *(▸ on donkey)* panier *m*; *(▸ on someone's back)* hotte *f*

2 *(quantity)* panier *m*; **a b. of apples** un panier de pommes

3 *(group)* assortiment *m*; *Fin* **a b. of European currencies** un panier de devises européennes

4 *Sport (in basketball ▸ net, point)* panier *m*; **to score a b.** marquer un panier

▸▸ *Fam* ***basket case*** *(nervous wreck)* paquet *m* de nerfs; *(mad person)* cinglé(e) *m,f*, barjo *mf*; *Am (invalid)* grand(e) invalide *mf*; ***basket chair*** chaise *f* en osier; *Fin* ***basket clause*** clause *f* fourre-tout; ***basket maker*** vannier *m*; ***basket making*** vannerie *f*; *Tex* ***basket weave*** armure *f* nattée

basketball ['bɑ:skɪtbɔ:l] **N** *Sport* basket-ball *m*, basket *m*

▸▸ ***basketball game*** match *m* de basket; ***basketball player*** basketteur(euse) *m,f*

basketful ['bɑ:skɪtfʊl] **N** plein panier *m*

basketry ['bɑ:skɪtrɪ] **N** vannerie *f*

basking shark ['bɑ:skɪŋ-] **N** *Ich* requin *m* pèlerin, pèlerin *m*

Basle [bɑ:l] **N** Bâle *f*

basmati rice [bæs'mætɪ-] **N** riz *m* basmati

Basque [bɑ:sk] **N 1** *(person)* Basque *mf* **2** *(language)* basque *m*

ADJ basque

▸▸ ***the Basque Country*** le Pays basque

basque [bɑ:sk] **N** corsage *m* très ajusté; *(bodice)* guêpière *f*; *(of jacket)* basque *f*

bas-relief [ˌbæsrɪ'li:f] **N** *Art & Archit* bas-relief *m*

bass[1] [beɪs] *Mus* **N 1** *(part, singer)* basse *f*; **to sing b.** chanter dans les basses **2** *(bass guitar)* basse *f*; *(double bass)* contrebasse *f* **3** *(on stereo)* basses *fpl*, graves *mpl*; *(knob)* bouton *m* de réglage des graves

ADJ *(note, pitch)* grave, bas; **a part for a b. voice** une partie pour voix de basse

▸▸ ***bass clarinet*** clarinette *f* basse; *Mus* ***bass clef*** clef *f* de fa; ***bass drum*** grosse caisse *f*; ***bass guitar*** guitare *f* basse; *Mus* ***bass viol*** viole *f* de gambe

bass[2] [bæs] **N** *Ich (freshwater fish)* perche *f*; *(sea fish)* bar *m*, loup *m*

bass[3] [bæs] **N** *Tex (material)* tille *f*, filasse *f*

basset ['bæsɪt] **N** basset *m (chien)*

▸▸ ***basset hound*** basset *m (chien)*

bassinet [ˌbæsɪ'net] **N 1** *(cradle ▸ wickerwork)* moïse *m*; *(▸ wooden)* berceau *m* **2** *(pram)* voiture *f* d'enfant

bassist ['beɪsɪst] **N** *Mus* bassiste *mf* de basse

bassoon [bə'su:n] **N** basson *m*

bassoonist [bə'su:nɪst] **N** basson *m*, bassoniste *mf*

basso-profondo, basso-profundo ['bæsəʊprə'fʌndəʊ] **N** *Mus* basse *f* profonde

bast [bæst] **N** *Tex (material)* tille *f*, filasse *f*

bastard ['bɑ:stəd] **N 1** *Literary or Pej (child)* bâtard (e) *m,f*

2 *very Fam Pej (nasty person)* salaud (salope) *m, f*; **some b. traffic warden gave me a parking ticket** une salope de contractuelle m'a collé un papillon

3 *very Fam (derisively)* **poor b.!** le pauvre!; **he's a stupid b.!** c'est un pauvre con!

4 *very Fam (affectionately)* **you lucky b.!** sacré veinard!; **how are you, you old b.?** comment ça va, enfoiré?

5 *very Fam (difficult case, job)* truc *m* chiant; **it's a b. of a book to translate** ce livre est vachement dur à traduire; **this job's a real b.** ce boulot est une vraie vacherie

ADJ 1 *Literary or Pej (child)* bâtard **2** *Ling (language)* corrompu

bastardize, -ise ['bɑ:stədaɪz] **VT** *Ling (language, style)* abâtardir

bastardy ['bɑ:stədɪ] **N** *Literary or Pej* bâtardise *f*

baste [beɪst] **VT 1** *Culin* arroser **2** *Sewing* bâtir, faufiler **3** *(beat)* rouer de coups, rosser

baster ['beɪstə(r)] **N** *Culin* pompe *f* à jus

basting ['beɪstɪŋ] **N 1** *Culin* arrosage *m* **2** *Sewing* bâtissage *m* **3** *(beating)* raclée *f*, correction *f*

bastion ['bæstɪən] **N** *also Fig* bastion *m*; **the last b. of Stalinism** le dernier bastion du stalinisme

bat [bæt] *(pt & pp* **batted**, *cont* **batting) N 1** *Sport (in baseball, cricket)* batte *f*; *(in table tennis)* raquette *f*; *Am Fam* **right off the b.** sur-le-champ▫; *Br Fam* **to do sth off one's own b.** faire qch de sa propre initiative▫

2 *(shot, blow)* coup *m*

3 *(animal)* chauve-souris *f*; *Fam Pej* **she's an old b.** c'est une vieille bique *ou* chouette; *Fam* **to have bats in the** *or* **one's belfry** avoir une araignée au plafond; *Fam* **to run/to drive like a b. out of hell** courir/conduire comme si l'on avait le diable à ses trousses

4 *Am very Fam (spree)* fête▫ *f*, bringue *f*; **to go off on a b.** aller faire la bringue

VI *Sport (baseball player, cricketer ▸ play)* manier la batte; *(▸ take one's turn at playing)* être à la batte; **he batted for Pakistan** il était à la batte pour l'équipe pakistanaise; **to go in to b.** aller à la batte; *Am Fam Fig* **to go to b. for sb** intervenir en faveur de qn▫; *Fam* **to b. for the other side** *(of gay man)* en être, être pédé; *(of gay woman)* être gouine; *Fam* **to b. for both sides** *(of bisexual)* marcher à voile et à vapeur

VT 1 *(hit)* donner un coup à **2** *(blink)* **she batted her eyelids at him** elle battit des paupières en le regardant; *Fig* **he didn't b. an eyelid** il n'a pas sourcillé *ou* bronché; *Fig* **she did it without batting an eyelid** elle l'a fait sans broncher

batch [bætʃ] **N** *(of letters)* paquet *m*, liasse *f*; *(of people)* groupe *m*; *(of refugees)* convoi *m*; *(of bread)* fournée *f*; *(of recruits)* contingent *m*; *Com* lot *m*; **in batches of 20** *(people)* par groupes de 20; *(files etc)* par lots de 20

VT grouper

▸▸ *Comput* ***batch capture*** numérisation *f* en lots; *Comput* ***batch command*** commande *f* séquentielle; *Comput* ***batch file*** fichier *m* de commandes; *Comput* ***batch processing*** traitement *m* par lots; *Ind* ***batch production*** production *f* par lots

bated ['beɪtɪd] **ADJ we waited with b. breath** nous avons attendu en retenant notre souffle

bath [bɑ:θ] (*pl* **baths** [bɑ:ðz], *pt & pp* **bathed**) **N 1** *(wash)* bain *m*; *(tub)* baignoire *f*, *Can* bain *m*; **to give sb a b.** donner un bain à qn; **to** *Br* **have** *or Am* **take a b.** prendre un bain; **she's in the b.** elle prend son bain, elle est dans son bain; **to run** *or Formal* **to draw a b.** se faire couler un bain; **a room with b.** *(in hotel)* une chambre avec salle de bains **2** *Chem (for chemicals, dye)* bain *m*; *Phot* cuvette *f*

VT *(baby, person)* baigner, donner un bain à

VI *Br* prendre un bain

• **baths NPL** *Br Old-fashioned (swimming pool)* piscine *f*; *(public baths)* bains-douches *mpl*; *(at spa)* thermes *mpl*

▸▸ *Culin* ***bath bun*** = petit pain rond aux raisins secs souvent servi chaud et beurré; *Am* ***bath cap*** bonnet *m* de bain; ***bath chair*** fauteuil *m* roulant; *Br* ***bath cube*** cube *m* de sels de bain; ***bath mat*** tapis *m* de bain; ***bath oil*** huile *f* de bain; ***bath pearls*** perles *fpl* de bain; ***bath rail*** barre *f* de soutien; ***bath salts*** sels *mpl* de bain; ***bath sheet*** drap *m* de bain; ***bath towel*** serviette *f* de bain

bathe [beɪð] *(pt & pp* **bathed**) **VI 1** *Br Old-fashioned (swim)* se baigner; **we bathed in the sea/the river** nous avons pris un bain de mer/dans la rivière **2** *Am (bath)* prendre un bain

VT 1 *(wound)* laver; *(eyes, feet)* baigner; **he bathed his eyes** il s'est baigné les yeux **2** *(covered)* **I was bathed in sweat** j'étais en nage, je ruisselais de sueur; **the hills were bathed in light** les collines étaient éclairées d'une lumière douce; **her face was bathed in tears** son visage était baigné de larmes **3** *Am (bath)* baigner, donner un bain à

N *Br Old-fashioned* bain *m (dans la mer, dans une rivière)*; **to have a b.** se baigner; **we went for a b.** nous sommes allés nous baigner

bather ['beɪðə(r)] **N** *(swimmer)* baigneur(euse) *m,f*

• **bathers NPL** *Austr Fam (costume)* maillot *m* de bain▫

bathing ['beɪðɪŋ] **N** *(UNCOUNT)* **1** *Br (swimming)* baignade *f*; **the water isn't warm enough for b.** l'eau n'est pas assez chaude pour se baigner **2** *(washing ▸ of wound)* lavage *m*

▸▸ ***bathing beauty*** belle *f* baigneuse; ***bathing cap*** bonnet *m* de bain; ***bathing costume*** maillot *m* de bain; ***bathing hut*** cabine *f* de bains; ***bathing machine*** cabine *f* de bains roulante; ***bathing suit*** maillot *m* de bain; *Br* ***bathing trunks*** maillot *m* de bain

bathos ['beɪθɒs] **N** *(UNCOUNT) Literature* chute *f* du sublime au ridicule

bathrobe ['bɑ:θrəʊb] **N 1** *(for bathroom, swimming pool)* peignoir *m* de bain **2** *Am (dressing gown)* robe *f* de chambre

bathroom ['bɑ:θrʊm] **N** salle *f* de bains; *Euph* **to use** *or* **to go to the b.** aller aux toilettes

COMP *(cabinet, mirror)* de salle de bains

▸▸ ***bathroom scales*** pèse-personne *m*; ***bathroom suite*** salle *f* de bains *(mobilier)*

bathtime ['bɑ:θtaɪm] **N** l'heure *f* du bain

bathtub ['bɑ:θtʌb] **N** baignoire *f*, *Can* bain *m*

batik [bə'ti:k] *Tex* **N** *(cloth, technique)* batik *m*

COMP *(scarf, skirt)* en batik

batman ['bætmən] (*pl* **batmen** [-mən]) **N** *Br Mil* ordonnance *m or f*

baton ['bætən] **N 1** *Mus (conductor's)* baguette *f*; **under the b. of** sous la baguette *ou* la direction de **2** *(policeman's ▸ in traffic)* bâton *m*; *(▸ in riots)* matraque *f* **3** *Sport* témoin *m*; *Fig* **to pass the b. to sb** donner le relais à qn

▸▸ ***baton charge*** charge *f* à la matraque; ***baton gun*** fusil *m* à balles en plastique; ***baton microphone*** microphone *m* tenu à la main; ***baton round*** balle *f* en plastique

bats [bæts] **ADJ** *Fam* timbré, cinglé

batsman ['bætsmən] (*pl* **batsmen** [-mən]) **N** *Sport* batteur *m*

battalion [bə'tæljən] **N** *Mil & Fig* bataillon *m*

batten ['bætən] **N** *Carp & Constr (board)* latte *f*, lambourde *f*; *(in roof)* volige *f*; *(in floor)* latte *f*, lame *f* de parquet; *Naut* latte *f* de voile; *Theat* herse *f*

VT *Carp & Constr* latter; *(floor)* planchéier; *(roof)* voliger

▸ **batten down VT SEP to b. down the hatches** fermer les écoutilles, condamner les panneaux; *Fig* dresser ses batteries

▸ **batten on, batten upon VT INSEP** *Br* **she immediately battened on me for help** elle s'est immédiatement accrochée à moi comme une sangsue pour que je l'aide

batter ['bætə(r)] **VT 1** *(beat ▸ person)* battre, maltraiter **2** *(hammer ▸ door, wall)* frapper sur **3** *(buffet)* **the ship was battered by the waves** le vaisseau était battu par les vagues; *Fig* **he felt battered by the experience** il se sentait ravagé par l'expérience

VI *(hammer)* **to b. at** *or* **on the door** frapper à la porte à coups redoublés; **the waves battered against the coast** les vagues s'abattaient le long de la côte

N 1 *Culin* pâte *f* à crêpes; **fried in b.** frit dans la pâte **2** *Sport (in baseball)* batteur *m*

▸**batter down** VT SEP *Agr (vegetation)* fouler; *(wall)* démolir; *(tree)* abattre

▸**batter in** VT SEP *(skull)* défoncer; *(door)* enfoncer; *Carp (nail)* enfoncer à grands coups

battered ['bætəd] ADJ **1** *(building)* délabré; *(car, hat)* cabossé, bosselé; *(briefcase, suitcase)* cabossé; *(face* ▸ *beaten)* meurtri; *(*▸ *ravaged)* buriné; **a b. child** un(e) enfant martyr(e) *ou* battu (e); **a refuge for b. wives** un refuge pour femmes battues **2** *Culin (fried in batter)* frit dans la pâte; **b. cod** cabillaud *m* frit dans la pâte

battering ['bætərɪŋ] N **1** *(beating)* **he got a bad b.** on l'a rossé sévèrement **2** *(hammering)* **the building took a b. in the war** le bâtiment a été durement éprouvé pendant la guerre; **his confidence took a b.** sa confiance en soi en a pris un coup; **the team took a bad b.** l'équipe a été battue à plate(s) couture(s)

▸▸ ***battering ram*** bélier *m*

battery ['bætərɪ] *(pl* **batteries***)* N **1** *(in clock, radio)* pile *f*; *(in car)* batterie *f*, accumulateurs *mpl*; **batteries not included** *(on packaging, in catalogue)* livré sans piles

2 *Mil (of guns, missiles)* batterie *f*

3 *(barrage)* tir *m* de barrage; **a b. of insults** une pluie d'insultes; **a b. of criticism** un feu roulant de critiques

4 *Law see* **assault**

5 *Agr* batterie *f*

▸▸ *Elec* ***battery charger*** chargeur *m*; *Agr* ***battery farming*** élevage *m* intensif *ou* en batterie; *Agr* ***battery hen*** poule *f* de batterie; *Elec* ***battery pack*** boîtier *m* d'alimentation par pile

batting ['bætɪŋ] N *Sport* maniement *m* de la batte; **he has a high b. average** il a un score élevé à la batte

battle ['bætəl] N **1** *(fight)* bataille *f*; *Fig* lutte *f*; **he was killed in b.** il a été tué au combat; **to do** *or* **to give** *or* **to join b.** livrer bataille; **to do b. with sb** livrer bataille à qn; **in b. order** en bataille; **a b. between the two companies** une lutte entre les deux entreprises; **a b. for control of the government** un combat pour obtenir le contrôle du gouvernement; **the b. between** *or* **of the sexes** la lutte des sexes; **a b. of wits** une joute d'esprit **2** *(struggle)* lutte *f*; **the b. against poverty** la lutte contre la pauvreté; **to do b. for** lutter pour; **to do b. against** *or* **with** lutter contre; **we're fighting the same b.** nous nous battons pour la même cause; **don't fight his battles for him** ne te bats pas à sa place; **it's half the b.** la partie est presque gagnée

COMP *Mil (dress)* de combat

VI se battre, lutter; **she battled to save his life** elle s'est battue pour lui sauver la vie; **he's battling against the system** il se bat contre le système

VT *Am Mil* combattre

▸▸ *Hist* ***the Battle of Britain*** la bataille d'Angleterre; *Hist* ***the Battle of the Bulge*** la bataille des Ardennes; *Hum* ***the battle of the bulge*** la lutte contre les kilos; *Naut & Mil* ***battle cruiser*** croiseur *m* cuirassé; *Mil* ***battle cry*** cri *m* de guerre; ***battle fatigue*** psychose *f* traumatique; *Hist* ***the Battle of Hastings*** la bataille de Hastings; ***battle royal*** *(fight)* bagarre *f*; *(argument)* querelle *f*; *Mil* ***battle zone*** zone *f* de bataille *ou* d'engagement

battleaxe, *Am* **battleax** ['bætəlæks] N **1** *Hist & Mil (weapon)* hache *f* d'armes **2** *Fam Pej (woman)* virago *f*, mégère *f*

battlebus ['bætəl,bʌs] N = autobus transportant les candidats en tournée électorale ainsi que leur entourage

battledore ['bætəldɔ:(r)] N *Sport (racket)* raquette *f*; **b. (and shuttlecock)** *(game)* jeu *m* de volant

battledress ['bætəldres] N *Mil* tenue *f* de combat

battlefield ['bætəlfi:ld], **battleground** ['bætəlgraʊnd] N *Mil & Fig* champ *m* de bataille

battle-hardened ADJ *Mil* aguerri

battlement ['bætəlmənt] N *(crenellation)* créneau *m*

• **battlements** NPL *(wall)* remparts *mpl*

battle-scarred ADJ *Mil (army, landscape)* marqué par les combats; *(person)* marqué par la vie; *Hum (car, table)* abîmé

battleship ['bætəl,ʃɪp] N *Naut & Mil* cuirassé *m*

batty ['bætɪ] *(compar* **battier,** *superl* **battiest***)* ADJ *Fam (crazy)* cinglé, dingue; *(eccentric)* farfelu

batwing sleeve ['bætwɪŋ-] N manche *f* chauve-souris

bauble ['bɔ:bəl] N *(trinket)* babiole *f*, colifichet *m*; *(for Christmas tree)* boule *f* de Noël

baud [bɔ:d] N *Comput & Elec* baud *m*

▸▸ ***baud rate*** débit *m* en bauds

baulk = **balk**

bauxite ['bɔ:ksaɪt] N *Miner* bauxite *f*

Bavaria [bə'veərɪə] N Bavière *f*

Bavarian [bə'veərɪən] N Bavarois(e) *m,f*

ADJ bavarois

▸▸ *Culin* ***Bavarian cream*** bavaroise *f*

bawdiness ['bɔ:dɪnɪs] N paillardise *f*

bawdy ['bɔ:dɪ] ADJ paillard

▸▸ *Arch* ***bawdy house*** maison *f* close

bawl [bɔ:l] VI **1** *(yell)* brailler; **to b. at sb** crier après qn **2** *Fam (weep)* brailler

VT **1** *(yell)* brailler, hurler **2** *Fam (weep)* brailler; **the baby was bawling his head off** le bébé braillait à pleins poumons

▸**bawl out** VT SEP **1** *(yell)* brailler, hurler **2** *Fam (reprimand)* passer un savon à; **she really bawled him out** elle lui a passé un bon savon **3** *Fam (weep)* **the child was bawling his eyes out** l'enfant braillait à pleins poumons

bawling ['bɔ:lɪŋ] N **1** *(yelling)* hurlements *mpl*, braillements *mpl* **2** *Fam (weeping)* braillement (s) *m(pl)*; **stop that b.** arrête de brailler

▸▸ *Fam* ***bawling out*** *(reprimand)* engueulade *f*; **to give sb a b. out** engueuler qn; **to get a b. out** se faire engueuler

bay [beɪ] N **1** *Geog* baie *f*; *(smaller)* anse *f*

2 *Archit* travée *f*; *(recess)* renfoncement *m*, niche *f*; *(window)* fenêtre *f* en saillie

3 *Br (in bus station, car park)* aire *f* de stationnement; *Rail* voie *f* d'arrêt

4 *Bot & Culin* laurier *m*; **sweet b.** laurier *m* commun, laurier *m* des poètes

5 *Hunt & Fig* **to be at b.** être aux abois; *Hunt* **to bring an animal to b.** acculer un animal; **to keep** *or* **hold at b.** *Mil (the enemy)* tenir en échec; *(assailant)* tenir en respect; *(creditors, persistent caller etc)* tenir à distance; **to keep boredom/hunger at b.** tromper l'ennui/la faim; **I'm managing to keep my cold at b.** jusqu'ici j'ai réussi à combattre le rhume

6 *Zool (horse)* cheval *m* bai

7 *Comput (for disk drive)* baie *f*

8 *(compartment* ▸ *in plane, ship)* soute *f*

VI *(bark)* aboyer, donner de la voix; **to b. at the moon** hurler *ou* aboyer à la lune; *Fig* **to b. for sb's blood** réclamer la tête de qn

ADJ *(colour)* bai

▸▸ ***the Bay of Bengal*** le golfe du Bengale; ***the Bay of Biscay*** le golfe de Gascogne; *Bot & Culin* ***bay laurel*** laurier *m* commun, laurier *m* des poètes; *Bot & Culin* ***bay leaf*** feuille *f* de laurier; *Hist* ***the Bay of Pigs*** la baie des Cochons; *Bot* ***bay tree*** laurier *m*; ***bay window*** *Archit* fenêtre *f* en saillie; *Am Fam (stomach)* gros bide *m*

baying ['beɪɪŋ] N *(UNCOUNT) (barking)* aboiement *m*

bayonet ['beɪənɪt] *(pt & pp* **bayoneted** *or* **bayonetted,** *cont* **bayoneting** *or* **bayonetting***)* *Mil* N baïonnette *f*; **with fixed bayonets** baïonnette au canon; **at b. point** à la pointe de la baïonnette

VT passer à la baïonnette

▸▸ *Mil* ***bayonet charge*** charge *f* à la baïonnette; *Tech* ***bayonet joint*** joint *m* à baïonnette; *Tech* ***bayonet socket*** douille *f* à baïonnette

bayou ['baɪu:] N *Am Geog* bayou *m*, marécages *mpl*

bazaar [bə'zɑ:(r)] N *(in East)* bazar *m*; *(sale for charity)* vente *f* de charité; *(shop)* bazar *m*

bazooka [bə'zu:kə] N *Mil* bazooka *m*

BBC [,bi:bi:'si:] N *(abbr* **British Broadcasting Corporation***)* **the B.** la BBC *(office national britannique de radiodiffusion)*; **BBC1** = chaîne généraliste de la BBC; **BBC2** = chaîne à vocation culturelle de la BBC

▸▸ ***BBC World Service*** = émissions radiophoniques de la BBC diffusées dans le monde entier

> **BBC**
>
> Les deux chaînes de télévision principales de la BBC sont BBC1 (divertissements, dramatiques, informations nationales et régionales) et BBC2 (émissions éducatives, dramatiques et comédies moins grand public que BBC1). Ce sont des chaînes hertziennes accessibles à tous, mais la BBC propose également des chaînes de télévision numérique spécialisées. La BBC est financée avec l'argent de la redevance télévision – obligatoire pour tout foyer possédant un téléviseur – et ne diffuse pas de messages publicitaires.

BBFC [,bi:bi:ef'si:] N *Cin (abbr* **British Board of Film Classification***)* = organisme britannique délivrant les visas de sortie pour les films

BBQ [,bi:bi:'kju:] N *(abbr* **barbecue***)* barbecue *m*

BBS [,bi:bi:'es] N *Comput (abbr* **bulletin board system***)* serveur *m* télématique, *Can* babillard *m*

BC[1] [,bi:'si:] *(abbr* **before Christ***)* av. J.C.; **in the year 25 BC** en l'an 25 avant Jésus-Christ

BC[2] *(written abbr* **British Columbia***)* Colombie-Britannique *f*

BCE [,bi:si:'i:] N *(abbr* **Board of Customs and Excise***)* = douane britannique

BCG® [,bi:si:'dʒi:] N *Med (abbr* **bacille Calmette-Guérin***)* BCG® *m*

▸▸ ***BCG® vaccination*** vaccin *m* BCG®

BE [,bi:'i:] N *(abbr* **Bank of England***)* Banque *f* d'Angleterre

BE [bi:]

VI	
• être **1–3, 6, 8, 9, 13, 15, 16**	• avoir **3, 5**
• mesurer **7**	• aller **4, 15**
• il y a **11**	• coûter **10**
• faire **14, 17**	• voici, voilà **12**
	• venir **15**
V AUX	
• être **2, 11, 12**	• dans les question tags **10**
• avoir **12**	

(pres 1st sing **am** [əm, *stressed* æm], *pres 2nd sing* **are** [ə, *stressed* ɑ:(r)], *pres 3rd sing* **is** [ɪz], *pres pl* **are** [ə, *stressed* ɑ:(r)], *pt 1st sing* **was** [wəz, *stressed* wɒz], *pt 2nd sing* **were** [wə, *stressed* wɜ:(r)], *pt 3rd sing* **was** [wəz, *stressed* wɒz], *pt pl* **were** [wə, *stressed* wɜ:(r)], *pp* **been** [bi:n], *cont* **being** ['bi:ɪŋ])

> À l'oral et dans un style familier à l'écrit, le verbe **be** peut être contracté: **I am** devient **I'm, he/she/it is** deviennent **he's/she's/it's** et **you/we/they are** deviennent **you're/we're/they're.** Les formes négatives **is not/are not/was not** et **were not** se contractent respectivement en **isn't/aren't/wasn't** et **weren't.**

VI **1** *(exist, live)* être, exister; **I think, therefore I am** je pense, donc je suis; **to be or not to be** être ou ne pas être; **God is** Dieu existe; **the greatest scientist that ever was** le plus grand savant qui ait jamais existé *ou* de tous les temps; **there are no such things as ghosts** les fantômes n'existent pas; **she's a genius if ever there was one** c'est *ou* voilà un génie si jamais il en fut; **as happy as can be** heureux comme un roi; **that may be, but...** cela se peut, mais..., peut-être, mais...

2 *(used to identify, describe)* être; **she is my sister** c'est ma sœur; **I'm Elaine** je suis *ou* je m'appelle Elaine; **she's a doctor/engineer** elle est médecin/ingénieur; **the glasses were crystal** les verres étaient en cristal; **he is American** il est américain, c'est un Américain; **be careful!** soyez prudent!; **to be frank...** pour être franc..., franchement...; **being the boy's mother, I have a right to know** étant la mère de l'enfant, j'ai le droit de savoir; **the situation being what** *or* **as it is...** la situation étant ce qu'elle est...; **the problem is knowing** *or* **is to know when to stop** le problème, c'est de savoir quand s'arrêter; **the rule is: when in doubt, don't do it** la règle c'est: dans le doute abstienstoi; **seeing is believing** voir, c'est croire; **just be yourself** soyez vous-même, soyez naturel; **you be Batman and I'll be Robin** *(children playing)* on dirait que tu es Batman et moi je suis Robin

3 *(indicating temporary state or condition)* **he was angry/tired** il était fâché/fatigué; **I am hungry/ thirsty/afraid** j'ai faim/soif/peur; **my feet/hands are frozen** j'ai les pieds gelés/mains gelées

4 *(indicating health)* aller, se porter; **how are you?** comment allez-vous?, comment ça va?; **I am fine** ça va; **he is not well** il est malade, il ne va pas bien

5 *(indicating age)* avoir; **how old are you?** quel âge avez-vous?; **I'm twelve (years old)** j'ai douze ans; **you'll see when you're 50** tu verras quand tu auras 50 ans

6 *(indicating location)* être; **the hotel is next to the river** l'hôtel se trouve *ou* est près de la rivière; **be there at nine o'clock** soyez-y à neuf heures; **where was I?** où étais-je?; *Fig (in book, speech)* où en étais-je?

7 *(indicating measurement)* **the table is one metre long** la table fait un mètre de long; **how tall is he?** combien mesure-t-il?; **he is two metres tall** il mesure *ou* fait deux mètres; **the school is two kilometres from here** l'école est à deux kilomètres d'ici

8 *(indicating time, date)* être; **it's five o'clock** il est cinq heures; **yesterday was Monday** hier on était *ou* c'était lundi; **today is Tuesday** nous sommes *ou* c'est mardi aujourd'hui; **what date is it today?** le combien sommes-nous aujourd'hui?; **it's the 16th of December** nous sommes *ou* c'est le 16 décembre

9 *(happen, occur)* être, avoir lieu; **the concert is on Saturday night** le concert est *ou* a lieu samedi soir; **when is your birthday?** quand est *ou* c'est quand ton anniversaire?; **the spring holidays are in March this year** les vacances de printemps tombent en mars cette année; **how is it that you arrived so quickly?** comment se fait-il que vous soyez arrivé si vite?

10 *(indicating cost)* coûter; **how much is this table?** combien coûte *ou* vaut cette table?; **it is expensive** ça coûte *ou* c'est cher; **the phone bill is £75** la facture de téléphone est de 75 livres

11 *(with "there")* **there is, there are** il y a, *Literary* il est; **there is** *or* **has been no snow** il n'y a pas de neige; **there are six of them** ils sont *ou* il y en a six; **what is there to do?** qu'est-ce qu'il y a à faire?; **there will be swimming** on nagera; **there is nothing funny about it** il n'y a rien d'amusant làdedans, ce n'est pas drôle

12 *(calling attention to)* **this is my friend John** voici mon ami John; **here are the reports you wanted** voici les rapports que vous vouliez; **there is our car** voilà notre voiture; **there are the others** voilà les autres; **here I am** me voici; **there you are!** *(I've found you)* ah, te voilà!; *(take this)* tiens, voilà!; **now there's an idea!** voilà une bonne idée!

13 *(with "it")* **who is it? – it's us!** qui est-ce? – c'est nous!; **it was your mother who decided** c'est ta mère qui a décidé

14 *(indicating weather)* faire; **it is cold/hot/grey** il fait froid/chaud/gris; **it is windy** il y a du vent

15 *(go)* aller, être; *(come)* être, venir; **she's been to visit her mother** elle a été *ou* est allée rendre visite à sa mère; **I have never been to China** je ne suis jamais allé *ou* je n'ai jamais été en Chine; **have you been home since Christmas?** est-ce que tu es rentré (chez toi) depuis Noël?; **has the plumber been?** le plombier est-il (déjà) passé?; **wait for us, we'll be there in ten minutes** attendsnous, nous serons là dans dix minutes; **he was into/out of the house in a flash** il est entré dans/ sorti de la maison en coup de vent; **I know, I've been there** je sais, j'y suis allé; *Fig* je sais, j'ai connu ça; **she is from Egypt** elle vient d'Égypte; **your brother has been and gone** votre frère est venu et reparti; **someone had been there in her absence** quelqu'un est venu pendant son absence; *Br Fam* **he's only been and wrecked the car!** il est allé casser la voiture!

16 *(indicating hypothesis, supposition)* **if I were you** si j'étais vous *ou* à votre place; **if we were younger** si nous étions plus jeunes; *Formal* **were it not for my sister** sans ma sœur

17 *(in calculations)* faire; **1 and 1 are 2** 1 et 1 font 2; **what is 5 less 3?** combien fait 5 moins 3?

V AUX 1 *(forming continuous tenses)* **he is having breakfast** il prend *ou* il est en train de prendre son petit déjeuner; **they are always giggling** ils sont toujours en train de glousser; **where are you going?** où allez-vous?; **I have just been thinking about you** je pensais justement à toi; **we've been waiting hours for you** ça fait des heures que nous t'attendons; **when will she be leaving?** quand est-ce qu'elle part *ou* va-t-elle partir?; **what are you going to do about it?** qu'est-ce que vous allez *ou* comptez faire?; **why aren't you working? – but I AM working!** pourquoi ne travaillez-vous pas? – mais je travaille!

2 *(forming passive voice)* **she is known as a good negotiator** elle est connue pour ses talents de négociatrice; **the car was found** la voiture a été retrouvée; **plans are being made** on fait des projets; **smoking is not permitted** il est interdit *ou* défendu de fumer; **socks are sold by the pair** les chaussettes se vendent par deux; **it is said/ thought/assumed that...** on dit/pense/suppose que...; **not to be confused with** à ne pas confondre avec

3 *(with infinitive ▸ indicating future event)* **the next meeting is to take place on Wednesday** la prochaine réunion aura lieu mercredi; **he's to be the new headmaster** c'est lui qui sera le nouveau directeur; **she was to become a famous pianist** elle allait devenir une pianiste renommée; **we were never to see him again** nous ne devions jamais le revoir

4 *(with infinitive ▸ indicating expected event)* **they were to have been married in June** ils devaient se marier en juin

5 *(with infinitive ▸ indicating obligation)* **I'm to be home by ten o'clock** il faut que je rentre avant dix heures; **you are not to speak to strangers** il ne faut pas parler aux inconnus

6 *(with infinitive ▸ expressing opinion)* **you are to be congratulated** on doit vous féliciter; **they are to be pitied** ils sont à plaindre

7 *(with infinitive ▸ requesting information)* **are we then to assume that taxes will decrease?** faut-il *ou* doit-on en conclure que les impôts vont diminuer?; **what am I to say to them?** qu'est-ce que je vais leur dire?

8 *(with passive infinitive ▸ indicating possibility)* **bargains are to be found even in the West End** on peut faire de bonnes affaires même dans le West End; **she was not to be dissuaded** rien ne devait *ou* il fut impossible de lui faire changer d'avis

9 *Formal (with infinitive ▸ indicating hypothesis)* **if he were** *or* **were he to die** s'il venait à mourir, à supposer qu'il meure

10 *(in question tags)* **he's always causing trouble, isn't he? – yes, he is** il est toujours en train de créer des problèmes, n'est-ce pas? – oui, toujours; **you're back, are you?** vous êtes revenu alors?; **you're not leaving already, are you?** vous ne partez pas déjà, j'espère?

11 *(in ellipsis)* **is she satisfied? – she is** est-elle satisfaite? – oui(, elle l'est); **you're angry – no I'm not – oh yes you are!** tu es fâché – non – mais si!; **it's a touching scene – not for me, it isn't** c'est une scène émouvante – je ne trouve pas *ou* pas pour moi; **I was pleased to see him but the children weren't** (moi,) j'étais content de le voir mais pas les enfants

12 *(forming perfect tenses)* **we're finished** nous avons terminé; *Rel* **Christ is risen** (le) Christ est ressuscité; **when I looked again, they were gone** quand j'ai regardé de nouveau, ils étaient partis

13 *(as suffix)* **the husband-to-be** le futur mari; **the father-to-be** le futur père

• **be that as it may** ADV quoi qu'il en soit

beach [biːtʃ] N *(seaside)* plage *f*; *(shore ▸ sand, shingle)* grève *f*; *(at lake)* rivage *m*

COMP de plage

VT *Naut (boat)* échouer; **beached whale** baleine *f* échouée

▸▸ ***beach ball*** ballon *m* de plage; ***beach buggy*** buggy *m*; *Fam* ***beach bum*** = jeune qui passe son temps à la plage; *Am Fam* ***beach bunny*** petite pépée *f (qui passe son temps à la plage)*; ***beach hut*** cabine *f* (de bains *ou* de plage); ***beach soccer*** football *m* de plage, beach soccer *m*; ***beach towel*** drap *m* de plage; ***beach umbrella*** parasol *m*; *Sport* ***beach volleyball*** beach-volley *m*

beachcomber ['biːtʃ,kəʊmə(r)] N *(collector)* = personne qui ramasse des objets sur les plages; *(wave)* vague *f* déferlante

beachhead ['biːtʃhed] N *Mil* tête *f* de pont; **to establish** *or* **to secure a b.** mettre en place une tête de pont sur la plage

beacon ['biːkən] N **1** *(warning signal)* phare *m*, signal *m* lumineux; *(lantern)* fanal *m*; *(marking channel, runway)* balise *f*; *Fig* phare *m*; **a b. of hope** une source d'espoir **2** *(bonfire on hill)* feu *m* d'alarme

▸▸ ***beacon light*** balise *f*

bead [biːd] N **1** *(of glass, wood)* perle *f*; *Rel (for rosary)* grain *m*; **b. necklace** collier *m* de perles (artificielles); **where are my beads?** où est mon collier?; *Rel* **to tell one's beads** égrener *ou* dire son chapelet **2** *(drop ▸ of sweat)* goutte *f*; *(▸ of water, dew)* perle *f*; *(bubble)* bulle *f*; **beads of sweat stood out on her forehead** la sueur perlait sur son front **3** *Tech (on gun)* guidon *m*; *Br* **to draw a b. on sb** viser qn

VT **1** *(decorate)* décorer de perles **2** *Archit & Carp* appliquer une baguette sur

VI *(form drops)* perler

▸▸ ***bead curtain*** rideau *m* de perles

beaded ['biːdɪd] ADJ *(decorated)* couvert *ou* orné de perles; **a b. evening bag** un sac (à main) de soirée brodé de perles

beading ['biːdɪŋ] N **1** *Archit* astragale *m*; *(in carpentry)* baguette *f* **2** *Sewing (trim)* garniture *f* de perles; *(over cloth)* broderie *f* perlée

beadle ['biːdəl] N **1** *Rel* bedeau *m* **2** *Br Univ* appariteur *m*

beady ['biːdɪ] *(compar* **beadier**, *superl* **beadiest**) ADJ *(eyes, gaze)* perçant; *Br Fam* **I've got my b. eye on you** je t'ai à l'œil

beagle ['biːgəl] N beagle *m*

beagling ['biːglɪŋ] N *Hunt* **to go b.** aller à la chasse avec des beagles

beak [biːk] N **1** *(of bird, tortoise, jug, vase etc)* bec *m* **2** *Fam (nose)* blair *m*, tarin *m*; *(hooked)* nez *m* crochu ▫ **3** *Br Fam (judge)* juge ▫ *m*; *(headmaster)* dirlo *m*

beaked [biːkt] ADJ *(nose)* crochu

beaker ['biːkə(r)] N gobelet *m*; *Chem* vase *m* à bec

be-all and end-all N *Fam (aim)* but *m* suprême ▫, fin *f* des fins ▫; **it's not the b. if it doesn't work** ce n'est pas la fin du monde si ça ne marche pas

beam [biːm] N **1** *Carp & Constr (bar of wood ▸ in house)* poutre *f*; *(▸ big)* madrier *m*; *(▸ small)* poutrelle *f*; *(▸ in gymnastics)* poutre *f*

2 *Naut (cross member)* barrot *m*; *(breadth)* largeur *f*; **on the port b.** à bâbord; **on the starboard b.** à tribord

3 *Tech (of scales)* fléau *m*; *(of engine)* balancier *m*; *(of loom)* ensouple *f*, rouleau *m*; *Agr (of plough)* age *m*

4 *(ray ▸ of sunlight)* rayon *m*; *(▸ of searchlight, headlamp)* faisceau *m* lumineux; *Phys* faisceau *m*; **to be off (the) b.** *Aviat* ne pas être dans le chenal de radioguidage; *Br Fam Fig* dérailler

5 *(smile)* sourire *m* radieux

6 *Aut* **the headlights were on full b.** la voiture était en pleins phares; *Am* **high beams** phares *mpl*; **he flicked on his high beams** il a mis ses phares

VI **1** *(smile)* faire un grand sourire; **their faces were beaming with pleasure** leurs visages étaient rayonnants de plaisir; **he beamed when he saw us** il eut un sourire radieux en nous apercevant **2** *(shine ▸ sun)* briller, darder ses rayons

VT **1** *Rad & TV (message)* transmettre par émission dirigée; **the pictures were beamed all over the world** les images ont été diffusées dans le monde entier **2** *(smile)* **she beamed her thanks** elle a fait un grand sourire en guise de remerciement

▸▸ *Rad & TV Br* **beam aerial**, *Am* **beam antenna** antenne *f* directive; *Tech* **beam balance** balance *f* à fléau; *Geom* **beam compass** compas *m* à verge

beam-ends NPL *Naut* **on her b.** couché sur le flanc; *Br Fam* **to be on one's b.** tirer le diable par la queue

beaming ['biːmɪŋ] ADJ radieux, resplendissant

bean [biːn] N **1** *Bot & Culin* haricot *m*

2 *(of coffee)* grain *m*; *(of cocoa)* graine *f*, fève *f*

3 *Am Fam (head)* caboche *f*, pomme *f*; *(brains)* cervelle ▫ *f*

4 *Fam (idioms)* **to be full of beans** péter le feu; **I haven't got a b.** je n'ai pas un rond; *Br Old-fashioned or Hum* **hello, old b.!** salut, mon vieux!; **that car isn't worth a b.** cette voiture-là ne vaut rien;

Am **he doesn't know beans about it** il n'y connaît rien

VT *Am Fam* **to b. sb** frapper qn (sur la tête)

►► *Culin* **bean curd** pâte *f* de soja

beanbag ['bi:nbæg] **N** *(in game)* balle *f* lestée; *(seat)* sacco *m*

bean-counter N *Am Fam* petit(e) comptable *mf*

beanery ['bi:nərɪ] *(pl* **beaneries) N** *Am Fam* gargote *f*

beanfeast ['bi:nfi:st] **N** *Br Fam* gueuleton *m*

beanie ['bi:nɪ] **N b. (hat)** bonnet *m*

beano ['bi:nəʊ] **N** *Br Fam (meal)* gueuleton *m*; *(spree)* bombe *f*; **to have** *or* **to go on a b.** faire la bombe

beanpole ['bi:npəʊl] **N** *Agr* rame *f*; *Fig (person)* (grande) perche *f*

beanstalk ['bi:nstɔ:k] **N** *Bot* tige *f* de haricot

BEAR [beə(r)]

VT
- porter **1, 6, 8, 9**
- supporter **2–5**
- donner naissance à **7**

VI
- diriger **1**

N
- ours **1, 2, 4**

(pt **bore** [bɔ:(r)], *pp* **borne** [bɔ:n])

VT 1 *(carry ► goods, burden)* porter; *(► gift, message)* apporter; *(► sound)* porter, transporter; **a convoy of lorries bore the refugees away** *or* **off** un convoi de camions emmena les réfugiés; **they arrived bearing fruit** ils sont arrivés, chargés de fruits; *Naut* **the wind bore the ship west** le vent poussait le navire vers l'ouest; **to be borne along by the crowd/current** être emporté par la foule/le courant

2 *(sustain ► weight)* supporter; **the ice couldn't b. his weight** la glace ne pouvait pas supporter son poids; *Fig* **the system can only b. a certain amount of pressure** le système ne peut supporter qu'une certaine pression

3 *(endure)* tolérer, supporter; **she can't b. the sight of blood** elle ne supporte pas la vue du sang; **I can't b. to see you go** je ne supporte pas que tu t'en ailles; **I can't b. that man** je ne supporte pas cet homme; **I can't b. the suspense** ce suspense est insupportable; **she bore the pain with great fortitude** elle a supporté la douleur avec beaucoup de courage

4 *(accept ► responsibility, blame)* assumer; *(► costs)* supporter

5 *(allow ► examination)* soutenir, supporter; **his theory doesn't really b. close analysis** sa théorie ne supporte pas une analyse approfondie; **his language does not b. repeating** il a été si grossier que je n'ose même pas répéter ce qu'il a dit; **his work bears comparison with Hemingway and Steinbeck** son œuvre soutient la comparaison avec Hemingway et Steinbeck; **it doesn't b. thinking about** je n'ose pas *ou* je préfère ne pas y penser

6 *(show ► mark, name, sign etc)* porter; **I still b. the scars** j'en porte encore les cicatrices; **the murder bore all the marks of a mafia killing** le meurtre avait tout d'un crime mafieux; **he bears no resemblance to his father** il ne ressemble pas du tout à son père; **his account bears no relation to the truth** sa version n'a rien à voir avec ce qui s'est vraiment passé; **to b. witness to sth** *(person)* attester qch; *(thing, quality)* témoigner de qch

7 *(give birth to)* donner naissance à; **she bore him two sons** elle lui donna deux fils

8 *(produce)* porter, produire; **the cherry tree bears beautiful blossom in spring** le cerisier donne de belles fleurs au printemps; *Fig* **all my efforts have borne fruit** mes efforts ont porté leurs fruits; *Fin* **his investment bore 8 percent interest** ses investissements lui ont rapporté 8 pour cent d'intérêt

9 *(feel)* porter, avoir en soi; **I b. you no ill will** je ne t'en veux pas; **to b. a grudge against sb** en vouloir *ou* garder rancune à qn

10 *(behave)* **he bore himself like a man** il s'est comporté en homme; **she bore herself with dignity** elle est restée très digne

11 *St Exch (market, prices, shares)* chercher à faire baisser

VI 1 *(move)* diriger; **b. to your left** prenez sur la gauche *ou* à gauche; **we bore due west** nous fîmes route vers l'ouest; *Am* **b. left ahead** *(sign)* tournez à gauche, filez à gauche

2 *(tree ► fruit)* produire, donner; *(► flower)* fleurir

3 *St Exch* spéculer à la baisse

4 *(idioms)* **to bring pressure to b. on sb** faire pression sur qn; **to bring one's mind to b. on sth** s'appliquer à qch

N 1 *Zool (animal)* ours(e) *m,f*; *Br Fam* **he's like a b. with a sore head** il est d'une humeur massacrante

2 *Pej (person)* ours *m*; **he's a big b. of a man** *(physically)* c'est un grand costaud

3 *St Exch (person)* baissier(ère) *m,f*, spéculateur (trice) *m,f* à la baisse; **to go a b.** spéculer *ou* jouer à la baisse

4 *(toy)* ours *m* (en peluche)

►► *St Exch* ***bear closing*** arbitrage *m* à la baisse; ***bear cub*** ourson *m*; ***bear garden*** *Hist* fosse *f* aux ours; *Fig* pétaudière *f*; *Fam St Exch* ***bear hug*** = communiqué d'information annonçant une OPA immédiate; **to give sb a b. hug** *(embrace)* serrer qn très fort dans ses bras; *St Exch* ***bear market*** marché *m* à la baisse *ou* baissier; *Zool* ***bear pit*** fosse *f* aux ours; *St Exch* ***bear speculation*** spéculation *f* à la baisse; ***bear tracks*** empreintes *fpl* d'ours; *St Exch* ***bear trading*** spéculation *f* à la baisse

►**bear down VI 1** *(approach)* **to b. down on** *or* **upon** *(ship)* venir sur; *(person)* foncer sur; **a lorry was bearing down on me** un camion fonçait sur moi **2** *(press)* appuyer; *Obst (in childbirth)* pousser

►**bear on VT INSEP** *(be relevant to)* se rapporter à, être relatif à; *(concern)* intéresser, concerner

►**bear out VT SEP** *Br* confirmer, corroborer; **to b. sb out, to b. out what sb says** corroborer ce que qn dit; **the results don't b. out the hypothesis** les résultats ne confirment pas l'hypothèse; **he will b. me out on this matter** il sera d'accord avec moi sur ce sujet

►**bear up VI** *Br* tenir le coup, garder le moral; **she's bearing up under the pressure** elle ne se laisse pas décourager par le stress

►**bear upon = bear on**

►**bear with VT INSEP** *(be patient with)* supporter patiemment; **if you'll just b. with me a minute** je vous demande un peu de patience; **if you'll b. with me I'll explain** si vous patientez un instant, je vais vous expliquer

bearable ['beərəbəl] **ADJ** supportable, tolérable

bearably ['beərəblɪ] **ADV** d'une façon supportable; **it was hot but b. so** il faisait chaud mais c'était supportable

bearbaiting ['beəˌbeɪtɪŋ] **N** combat *m* d'ours et de chiens

beard [bɪəd] **N 1** *(on person)* barbe *f*; *(goatee)* barbiche *f*; **to have a b.** avoir la barbe; **a man with a b.** un (homme) barbu; **to grow a b.** se laisser pousser la barbe; **he wears a full b.** il porte la barbe; **a two-day b.** une barbe de deux jours **2** *(on goat)* barbiche *f*; *Ich (on fish, oyster, mussel)* barbe *f*; *Bot (on plant)* arête *f*, barbe *f*

VT *Literary (confront)* affronter, braver; **to b. the lion in his den** aller braver le lion dans sa tanière

►► ***beard trimmer*** tondeuse *f* à barbe

bearded ['bɪədɪd] **ADJ** barbu

►► ***bearded lady*** femme *f* à barbe; *Orn* ***bearded tit*** mésange *f* à moustaches

beardless ['bɪədlɪs] **ADJ** imberbe, sans barbe; *Literary* **a b. youth** un jeunet

bearer ['beərə(r)] **N 1** *(of news, letter)* porteur (euse) *m,f*; *(of load, coffin)* battue porteur(euse) *m,f*; *(servant)* serviteur *m*; **I hate to be the b. of bad tidings** j'ai horreur d'annoncer les mauvaises nouvelles **2** *(of cheque, title)* porteur(euse) *m,f*; *(of passport)* titulaire *mf*; *Banking* **cheque made payable to b.** chèque *m* (payable) au porteur

►► *Fin* ***bearer bill*** effet *m ou* billet *m* au porteur; *St Exch* ***bearer bond*** titre *m ou* obligation *f* au porteur; *Banking* ***bearer cheque*** chèque *m* au porteur; *Fin* ***bearer paper*** papier *m* au porteur; *St Exch* ***bearer share*** action *f* au porteur

bearing ['beərɪŋ] **N 1** *(relevance)* rapport *m*, relation *f*; **his comments have some** *or* **a b. on the present situation** ses remarques ont un certain rapport avec la situation actuelle; **the event had no b. on the outcome of the war** l'événement n'eut aucune incidence sur l'issue de la guerre

2 *(deportment)* maintien *m*, port *m*; **her queenly b.** son port de reine

3 *(endurance)* **it's beyond** *or* **past all b.** c'est absolument insupportable

4 *(direction)* position *f*; *Constr (in surveying)* gisement *m*, azimut *m*; *Naut & Aviat* relèvement *m*, position *f*; **to take a (compass) b. (on sth)** relever la position (de qch) au compas; *Naut* **to take a ship's b.** faire le point; **to get** *or* **to find one's bearings** *Naut* retrouver sa direction *ou* sa route; *Fig* se repérer, s'orienter; **to lose one's bearings** *Naut* perdre sa direction *ou* sa route; *Fig* perdre le nord

5 *Tech* palier *m*

-bearing ['beərɪŋ] **SUFF rain-b. clouds** des nuages *mpl* chargés de pluie; **fruit-b. trees** des arbres *mpl* fructifères; **interest-b. capital** capital *m* qui rapporte; **oxygen-b. water** de l'eau *f* riche en oxygène

bearish ['beərɪʃ] **ADJ 1** *Pej (person)* bourru **2** *St Exch (market, trend)* à la baisse, baissier; **to be b.** *(person)* spéculer *ou* jouer à la baisse

bearskin ['beəskɪn] **N 1** *Tex (piece of fur)* peau *f* d'ours **2** *Mil (hat)* bonnet *m* à poils

beast [bi:st] **N 1** *(animal)* bête *f*, animal *m*; **the king of the beasts** le roi des animaux; *Bible* **the B.** l'Antéchrist *m*, la bête de l'Apocalypse; **b. of burden** bête *f* de somme; **b. of prey** bête *f* de proie

2 *(savage nature)* **the b. in man** la bête en l'homme

3 *(person ► unpleasant)* chameau *m*; *(► cruel)* brute *f*; **you b.!** vous êtes dégoûtant!

4 *Fam (unpleasant thing)* **a b. of a job** un sale boulot; **I've had a b. of a day** j'ai eu une journée affreuse

beastliness ['bi:stlɪnɪs] **N** *(of person)* méchanceté *f*; *(of act)* bestialité *f*; *(of language)* obscénité *f*

beastly ['bi:stlɪ] *Br Fam* **ADJ** *(person, behaviour)* vache; *(food)* infect; **he's a b. child** c'est un enfant intenable; **he was b. to her** il a été vache avec elle; **a b. job** *(task)* un sale boulot; **what b. weather!** quel sale temps!

ADV vachement; **it's b. cold!** il fait vachement froid!

BEAT [bi:t] *(pt* **beat**, *pp* **beaten** ['bi:tən]) **VT 1** *(hit ► dog, person)* frapper, battre; *(► carpet, metal)* battre; *Culin (eggs)* battre, fouetter; **to b. sb with a stick** donner des coups de bâton à qn; **to b. sth flat** aplatir qch *(en tapant dessus)*; **to b. sb black and blue** battre qn comme plâtre; *Literary* **she b. her breast** elle se frappa la poitrine; *Am Vulg* **to b. one's meat** *(masturbate)* se branler

2 *Mus* **to b. time** battre la mesure; **she b. time to the music with her foot** elle marquait le rythme de la musique avec son pied; **to b. a drum** battre du tambour

3 *(move ► wing)* battre; **the bird was beating its wings** l'oiseau battait des ailes

4 *(defeat ► at game, sport)* battre, vaincre; **she b. him at poker** elle l'a battu au poker; **Liverpool were beaten** Liverpool a perdu; **to b. the world record** battre le record mondial; *Fig* **b. the rush hour, travel early** évitez l'heure de pointe, voyagez plus tôt; **to b. the system** tirer son épingle du jeu en magouillant; *Am Fam* **to b. the rap** échapper à la tôle; **we've got to b. racism** il faut en finir avec le racisme; **if you can't b. them, join them** mieux vaut s'allier aux gens que l'on ne peut pas vaincre; *Fam* **to b. sb hollow** *or Br* **hands down, to b. the pants off sb** battre qn à plate couture; *Fam* **the problem has me beaten** le problème me dépasse complètement; *Fam* **(it) beats me** cela me dépasse; *Fam* **it beats me** *or* **what beats me is how he gets away with it** je ne comprends pas *ou* ça me dépasse qu'il s'en tire à chaque fois; *Fam* **he b. me to it** *(arrived, telephoned before me etc)* il m'a devancé

5 *(outdo)* **you can't b. the Chinese for inventiveness** on ne peut pas trouver plus inventifs que les Chinois; **nothing beats a cup of**

tea rien ne vaut une tasse de thé; **b. that!** voyons si tu peux faire mieux!; *Fig* pas mal, hein?; *Fam* **that beats the lot!, that takes some beating!** ça, c'est le bouquet!; *Fam* **can you b. it!** tu as déjà vu ça, toi!

6 *(path)* se frayer; **to b. a way through the undergrowth** se frayer un chemin à travers la végétation; *Fig* **the new doctor soon had people beating a path to his door** très vite, les gens se pressèrent chez le nouveau docteur

7 *Mil (retreat)* **to b. the retreat** battre la retraite; *Fig* **they b. a hasty retreat when they saw the police arrive** ils ont décampé en vitesse quand ils ont vu arriver la police

8 *Hunt* **to b. the woods/the moors** battre les bois/ les landes

9 *Fam (idioms)* **to b. it,** *Am* **to b. feet** *(go away)* se tirer, se barrer; **b. it!** dégage!

VI 1 *(rain)* battre; *(sun)* taper; *(wind)* souffler en rafales; **to b. on** *or* **at the door** cogner à la porte; **the waves b. against the sea wall** les vagues venaient battre la digue; **the rain was beating against the roof** la pluie battait contre le toit; **he doesn't b.** *Br* **about** *or Am* **around the bush** il n'y va pas par quatre chemins; **so, not to b.** *Br* **about** *or Am* **around the bush, I've lost my job** enfin bref, j'ai perdu mon emploi

2 *(heart, pulse, wing)* battre; **his heart was beating with terror** son cœur palpitait de terreur; **I heard the drums beating** j'entendis le roulement des tambours

3 *Naut* **to b. to windward** louvoyer au plus près

N 1 *(of heart, pulse, wing)* battement *m*, pulsation *f*; *Mus (of drums)* battement *m Mil* **to march to the b. of the drum** marcher au son du tambour

2 *Mus (time)* temps *m*; *(in jazz and pop)* rythme *m*; **a strong/weak b.** un temps fort/faible; **a funky b.** un rythme funky

3 *(of policeman)* ronde *f*, secteur *m*; *Mil (of sentry)* ronde *f*; **we need more policemen on the b.** il faudrait qu'il y ait plus de policiers à faire des rondes; **he saw the robbery when he was on his b.** il a été témoin du vol pendant qu'il effectuait sa ronde; *Fam Fig* **it's off my b. altogether** cela ne relève pas de ma compétence□, ce n'est pas de mon ressort□

4 *Hunt* battue *f*

5 *Fam (beatnik)* beatnik□ *mf*

ADJ 1 *Fam (exhausted)* crevé, vidé

2 *Fam (defeated)* **you've got me b.** *(defeated)* je m'avoue vaincu; *(unable to answer)* je sèche; **this crossword's got me b.** je sèche sur ces mots croisés

3 *Fam* beatnik□; **a b. poet** un poète beatnik

▸▸ ***the Beat generation*** = mouvement littéraire et culturel américain des années 50–60 dont les adeptes (les "beatniks") refusaient les conventions de la société moderne

▸ **beat back VT SEP** *Mil (enemy, flames)* repousser

▸ **beat down VT SEP 1** *(grass)* **the wind had beaten the grass down** le vent avait couché les herbes; **the horses had beaten down the crops** les chevaux avaient foulé les récoltes **2** *Br Com (seller)* faire baisser; **I b. him down to £20** je lui ai fait baisser son prix à 20 livres

VI *(sun)* taper; *(rain)* tomber à verse *ou* à torrents; **the rain was beating down on the tin roof** la pluie s'abattait sur le toit en tôle

▸ **beat in VT SEP** *(door)* défoncer; **I'll b. his head in!** je lui défoncerai le crâne!

▸ **beat off VT SEP** *Mil (enemy, attack)* repousser

VI *Vulg (masturbate)* se branler

▸ **beat out VT SEP 1** *(flames)* étouffer

2 *(metal)* étaler au marteau; *Fam Fig* **to b. one's brains out** se creuser la cervelle; *Fam* **to b. sb's brains out** défoncer le crâne à qn

3 *Mus (rhythm)* marquer; **she b. the rhythm out on a drum** elle marquait le rythme *ou* elle battait la mesure sur un tambour

4 *Am Sport (opponent)* battre

▸ **beat up VT SEP 1** *Fam (person)* tabasser, passer à tabac; *Fig* **everyone makes mistakes, don't b. yourself up about it** tout le monde peut se tromper, ne t'en fais pas **2** *Culin (egg white)* faire monter; *(cream, egg)* fouetter, battre

▸ **beat up on VT INSEP** *esp Am Fam (hit)* battre, tabasser; **stop beating up on yourself** arrête de culpabiliser

beatbox ['bi:tbɒks] **N** boîte *f* à rythme(s)

VI = imiter avec sa bouche les sons produits par une boîte à rythme

beat-'em-up N *Fam (video game)* jeu *m* vidéo violent

beaten ['bi:tən] *pp of* **beat**

ADJ 1 *(gold)* battu, martelé; *(earth, path)* battu; *Culin (eggs, cream)* battu, fouetté; *Fig* **off the b. track** dans un endroit reculé, à l'écart **2** *(defeated)* vaincu, battu **3** *(exhausted)* éreinté, épuisé

beater ['bi:tə(r)] **N 1** *Culin (manual)* fouet *m*; *(electric)* batteur *m*

2 *(for carpet)* tapette *f*

3 *Hunt* rabatteur *m*

4 *Am Fam (old car)* vieille guimbarde *f*

beatific [ˌbi:ə'tɪfɪk] **ADJ** *Rel* béat; **a b. smile** un sourire béat

beatifically [ˌbi:ə'tɪfɪkəlɪ] **ADV** *Rel* avec béatitude

beatification [bi:ˌætɪfɪ'keɪʃən] **N** *Rel* béatification *f*

beatify [bi:'ætɪfaɪ] **VT** *Rel* béatifier

beating ['bi:tɪŋ] **ADJ** *(heart)* battant, palpitant; *(rain)* battant

N 1 *(thrashing)* correction *f*; **to give sb a b.** donner une correction à qn; **to get a b.** recevoir une correction

2 *(defeat)* défaite *f*; **to take** *or* **get a b.** se faire battre à plate couture

3 *(of wings, heart)* battement *m*

4 *Fam (outdoing)* **it takes some** *or* **a lot of b.** c'est difficile de faire mieux

5 *(UNCOUNT) Tech (of metal)* batte *f*; *Mus (of drums)* battement *m*, roulement *m*; *Tex (of carpet)* battage *m*

6 *Hunt* battue *f* de beauté;

▸▸ *Fam* ***beating up*** passage *m* à tabac, raclée *f*

beatitude [bi:'ætɪˌtju:d] *Rel* **N** béatitude *f*

• **Beatitudes NPL the Beatitudes** les béatitudes *fpl*

beatnik ['bi:tnɪk] **N** beatnik *mf*

beat-up ADJ *Fam (car)* bousillé, déglingué; *Am (person)* amoché

beau [bəʊ] *(pl* **beaux** [bəʊz]) **N** *(dandy)* dandy *m*; *(suitor)* galant *m*

beaut [bju:t] *Fam* **N that's a b.** c'est super, c'est génial; **(what a) b.!** super!

ADJ *Austr* super, génial

beautician [ˌbju:'tɪʃən] **N** esthéticien(enne) *m,f*; *Cin, TV & Theat (make-up artist)* visagiste *mf*

beautiful ['bju:tɪful] **ADJ 1** *(attractive* ▸ *person, dress)* beau (belle); **a b. woman** une belle femme; **what a b. photo/song!** quelle belle photo/chanson!; **the b. game** *(soccer)* le beau jeu; **the b. people** *(famous)* les gens *mpl* riches et célèbres; *Am (hippies)* les hippies *mpl* **2** *(splendid* ▸ *weather, meal)* magnifique, superbe; **what a b. shot!** bien joué!, joli!

EXCLAM *Fam* magnifique!

beautifully ['bju:təfəlɪ] **ADV 1** *(sing, dress)* admirablement, à la perfection **2** *(splendidly)* **it was a b. played shot** c'était bien joué, c'était une belle balle; **that will do b.** cela convient parfaitement **3** *(as intensifier* ▸ *peaceful, warm)* merveilleusement

beautify ['bju:tɪfaɪ] *(pt & pp* **beautified**) **VT** embellir, orner; **to b. oneself** se faire une beauté

beauty ['bju:tɪ] *(pl* **beauties**) **N 1** *(loveliness)* beauté *f*; **a thing of b.** un objet d'une rare beauté; *Prov* **b. is in the eye of the beholder** ce qu'on aime est toujours beau; *Prov* **b. is only skin-deep** la beauté n'est pas tout; *Hum* **I need my b. sleep** j'ai besoin de mon compte de sommeil pour être frais le matin

2 *(beautiful person)* beauté *f*; **she's a/she's no b.** c'est une/ce n'est pas une beauté; **the beauties of nature** les merveilles *fpl* de la nature

3 *Fam (excellent thing)* merveille□ *f*; **this new bike's a real b.** cette nouvelle bicyclette est une vraie merveille; *Fam* **that black eye is a real b.** quel beau coquard!

4 *(attraction)* **the b. of the system is its simplicity** ce qui est bien dans ce système, c'est sa simplicité; **that's the b. of it** c'est ça qui est formidable

COMP *(cream, product, treatment)* de beauté

EXCLAM *Br Fam* **(you) b.!** super!

▸▸ ***beauty competition, beauty contest*** concours *m* de beauté; *Br* ***beauty parlour,*** *Am* ***beauty parlor*** institut *m* de beauté; ***beauty queen*** reine *f* de beauté; ***beauty salon*** institut *m* de beauté; *Am* ***beauty shop*** institut *m* de beauté; ***beauty specialist*** esthéticien(enne) *m,f*; ***beauty spot*** *(on skin)* grain *m* de beauté; *(artificial)* mouche *f*; *(scenic place)* site *m* touristique; ***beauty therapist*** esthéticien(enne) *m,f*

beaver ['bi:və(r)] **N 1** *(animal, fur)* castor *m*; *Fam* **to work like a b.** travailler d'arrache-pied **2** *Vulg (female genitals)* chatte *f*

COMP *(coat, hat)* de castor

▸ **beaver away VI** *Br Fam* **to b. away (at sth)** travailler d'arrache-pied (à qch)

became [bɪ'keɪm] *pt of* **become**

because [bɪ'kɒz] **CONJ** parce que; **he came b. it was his duty** il est venu parce que c'était son devoir; **if she won it was b. she deserved to** si elle a gagné, c'est qu'elle le méritait; **it was all the more difficult b. he was sick** c'était d'autant plus difficile qu'il était malade; **just b. you're my sister, it doesn't mean you can boss me about** ce n'est pas parce que tu es ma sœur que tu peux me donner des ordres; **why? – (just) b.** pourquoi? – parce que; **why can't I go? – b. you can't!** pourquoi est-ce que je ne peux pas y aller? – parce que (c'est comme ça)!

• **because of PREP** à cause de; **we couldn't move b. of the snow** nous étions bloqués par la neige; **it was all b. of a silly misunderstanding** tout ça à cause d'un *ou* tout provenait d'un petit malentendu; **he's ineligible b. of his age** il ne peut être élu à cause de son âge

bechamel ['beʃəmel] **N** *Culin (sauce)* béchamel

▸▸ ***bechamel sauce*** sauce *f* béchamel

beck [bek] **N 1** *(in Northern England) (stream)* ruisseau *m*, ru *m* **2** *(idioms)* **to be at sb's b. and call** être constamment à la disposition de qn; **she has him at her b. and call** elle le fait marcher à la baguette, il lui obéit au doigt et à l'œil

beckon ['bekən] **VI** faire signe; **to b. to sb** faire signe à qn; *Fig* **a glittering career beckoned for the young singer** la jeune chanteuse avait devant elle une brillante carrière; *Fig* **the bright lights of the city beckoned** les lumières de la ville étaient une tentation; **I can't stay, work beckons** il faut que je m'en aille, j'ai du travail

VT 1 *(motion)* faire signe à; **I beckoned them over (to me)** je leur ai fait signe d'approcher; **he beckoned me to follow him** il m'a fait signe de le suivre **2** *(attract, call)* attirer

become [bɪ'kʌm] *(pt* **became** [-'keɪm], *pp* **become**)

VI 1 *(grow)* devenir, se faire; **the noise became louder and louder** le bruit est devenu de plus en plus fort *ou* a continué à augmenter; **to b. old** vieillir; **to b. fat** grossir; **to b. weak** s'affaiblir; **it became clear that we were wrong** il s'est avéré que nous nous trompions; **we became friends** nous sommes devenus amis; **she's becoming a dreadful nuisance** elle est en train de devenir vraiment gênante; **to b. known** commencer à être connu **2** *(acquire post of)* devenir; **to b. president** devenir président; **she's b. an accountant** elle est devenue comptable

VT *Formal* **1** *(suit* ▸ *of hat, dress)* aller à; **that hat really becomes you** ce chapeau vous va vraiment bien **2** *(befit)* convenir à, être digne de; **such behaviour doesn't b. him** une telle conduite n'est pas digne de lui

▸ **become of VT INSEP whatever will b. of us?** qu'allons-nous devenir? **I wonder what became of that young man** je me demande ce qu'est devenu ce jeune homme

becoming [bɪ'kʌmɪŋ] **ADJ** *Formal* **1** *(fetching)* qui va bien, seyant; **that's a very b. hat** ce chapeau vous va très bien; **you look very b. in that dress** cette robe te va très bien **2** *(suitable)* convenable, bienséant; **such language is hardly b. for a young lady!** un tel langage n'est guère convenable chez une jeune fille!

becquerel [ˌbekə'rel] **N** *Phys* becquerel *m*

BEd [ˌbi:'ed] **N** *Br (abbr* **Bachelor of Education)** *(person)* = titulaire d'une licence de sciences de l'éducation; *(qualification)* licence *f* de sciences de l'éducation

BED [bed] *(pt & pp* **bedded,** *cont* **bedding)** **N 1** *(furniture)* lit *m*; **to be in b.** *(to rest)* être couché, être au lit; *(through illness)* être alité, garder le lit; **he's in b. with the flu** il est au lit avec la grippe; **to read in b.** lire au lit; **we asked for a room with two beds** nous avons demandé une chambre à deux lits; **they sleep in separate beds** ils font lit à part; **it's time to go to** *or* **time for b.** il est l'heure d'aller au lit *ou* de se coucher; **to get out of b.** se lever; **to get into b.** se mettre au lit; *Fam Fig* **to get into b. with sb** *(form partnership with)* travailler en collaboration avec qn□; **did I get you out of b.?** est-ce que je t'ai tiré du lit?; **she got** *or* **put the children to b.** elle a couché les enfants *ou* mis les enfants au lit; **to make the b.** faire le lit; **they made me up a b.** ils m'ont préparé un lit; **she took to her b. with pneumonia** elle a dû s'aliter à cause d'une pneumonie; **the doctor recommended complete b. rest** le médecin a conseillé l'immobilité totale; *Fam* **to go to b. with sb** coucher avec qn; *Fam* **he's/she's really great in b.** c'est vraiment un bon coup; **to get out of b. on the wrong side** se lever du pied gauche *ou* du mauvais pied; *Prov* **you've made your b., now you must lie in it** comme on fait son lit, on se couche; **life's not a b. of roses** la vie n'est pas toujours une partie de plaisir; **teaching in a secondary school isn't exactly a b. of roses** enseigner dans un lycée n'a rien d'une sinécure; *esp Br* **b. and breakfast** *(accommodation)* chambre *f* d'hôte *ou* chez l'habitant; **we stayed in a b. and breakfast** nous avons pris une chambre d'hôte; **b. and breakfast** *(sign)* chambres d'hôte; *St Exch* **b. and breakfasting** aller et retour *m*

2 *(plot ▸ of flowers)* parterre *m*, plate-bande *f*; *(▸ of vegetables)* planche *f*; *(▸ of coral, oysters)* banc *m*

3 *(bottom ▸ of river)* lit *m*; *(▸ of lake, sea)* fond *m*

4 *(layer ▸ of clay, rock)* couche *f*, lit *m*; *Miner (▸ of ore)* gisement *m*; *(▸ of ashes)* lit *m*; *Constr (▸ of mortar)* bain *m*; **b. of nails** lit *m* à clous; *Culin* **place the roast on a b. of vegetables** placez le rôti sur un lit de légumes

5 *(of machine)* base *f*, bâti *m*; *(of lorry)* plateau *m*; *(of printing press)* marbre *m*, plateau *m*; *Br Typ & Press* **to put a newspaper to b.** boucler un journal

VT 1 *(embed)* fixer, enfoncer; *Constr* asseoir

2 *Hort* repiquer

3 *Fam (have sex with)* coucher avec

▸▸ *bed bath* toilette *f (d'un malade)*; *Admin* ***bed blocking*** = indisponibilité de lits d'hôpital due au fait que certaines personne âgées ne peuvent être renvoyées à leur domicile, n'étant pas suffisamment autonomes pour vivre chez elles; ***bed board*** planche *f* à mettre sous le matelas; ***bed frame*** châlit *m*; *Br* ***bed jacket*** liseuse *f*; ***bed linen*** draps *mpl* de lit (et taies *fpl* d'oreiller)

▸ **bed down VI** *(go to bed)* se coucher; *(spend the night)* coucher

VT SEP *(children)* mettre au lit, coucher; *(animal)* installer pour la nuit

▸ **bed out VT SEP** *Hort* repiquer

bedbug ['bedbʌg] **N** punaise *f* des lits

bedchamber ['bed,tʃeɪmbə(r)] **N** *Arch* chambre *f*

bedclothes ['bedkləʊðz] **NPL** draps *mpl* et couvertures *fpl*; **to turn down the b.** ouvrir le lit

beddable ['bedəbəl] **ADJ** *Fam Hum* baisable

bedding ['bedɪŋ] **N 1** *(bedclothes)* draps *mpl* et couvertures *fpl*; *(including mattress)* literie *f*; *Mil* matériel *m* de couchage **2** *(for animals)* litière *f*

▸▸ *Hort* ***bedding out*** *(of plants)* repiquage *m*, dépotage *m*, dépotement *m*; *Hort* ***bedding plant*** plante *f* à repiquer

bedevil [bɪ'devəl] *(Br pt & pp* **bedevilled,** *cont* **bedevilling,** *Am pt & pp* **bedeviled,** *cont* **bedeviling)** **VT 1** *(plague ▸ plans, project)* déranger, gêner; *(▸ person)* harceler, tourmenter; **bedevilled by** *or* **with problems** assailli par les problèmes **2** *(confuse)* embrouiller

bedfellow ['bed,feləʊ] **N 1** *(bedmate)* **he was my b. when we were children** nous avons partagé le même lit dans notre enfance **2** *(associate)* associé(e) *m,f*, collègue *mf*; **they make strange bedfellows** ils forment une drôle d'association *ou* de paire

bedlam ['bedləm] **N 1** *(chaos)* tohu-bohu *m*; *(in classroom)* chahut *m*; **utter b. broke out after her speech** un véritable tumulte éclata après son discours; **it's absolute b. in town today!** quel cirque en ville, aujourd'hui!; **the meeting was absolute b.** la réunion était un véritable bazar **2** *Arch (asylum)* maison *f* de fous *ou* d'aliénés

bed-night **N** *Com (in hotel)* nuitée *f*

Bedouin ['beduɪn] *(pl inv or* **Bedouins)** **N** Bédouin (e) *m,f*

ADJ bédouin

bedpan ['bedpæn] **N** bassin *m* (hygiénique)

bedpost ['bedpəʊst] **N** colonne *f* de lit; *Hum* **(just) between you, me and the b.** entre nous

bedraggled [bɪ'drægəld] **ADJ** *(clothing, person)* débraillé; *(hair)* ébouriffé, échevelé

bedridden ['bed,rɪdən] **ADJ** alité, cloué au lit; *(permanently)* grabataire

bedrock ['bedrɒk] **N** *Geol* soubassement *m*, substratum *m*; *Fig* base *f*, fondation *f*; *Br* **to get down to b.** considérer l'essentiel

bedroll ['bedrəʊl] **N** matériel *m* de couchage *(enroulé)*

bedroom ['bedrʊm] **N** chambre *f* (à coucher); **spare b.** chambre *f* d'ami

COMP *(carpet, window)* de la chambre

▸▸ *Theat* ***bedroom comedy*** comédie *f* de boulevard; *Am* ***bedroom community*** cité-dortoir *f*

Beds *(written abbr* **Bedfordshire)** le Bedfordshire, = comté dans le sud de l'Angleterre

bedside ['bedsaɪd] **ADJ** *(lamp, table)* de chevet

N chevet *m*; **at** *or* **by your b.** à votre chevet; **to rush to sb's b.** courir au chevet de qn

▸▸ ***bedside manner*** comportement *m* envers les malades; **the doctor has a good b. manner** le médecin sait rassurer les malades

bedsit ['bed,sɪt], **bedsitter** ['bed,sɪtə(r)], **bedsitting room** [,bed'sɪtɪŋ-] **N** *Br* chambre *f* meublée, studette *f*

bedsocks ['bedsɒks] **NPL** chaussettes *fpl (que l'on porte au lit)*

bedsore ['bedsɔː(r)] **N** *Med* escarre *f*, eschare *f*

bedspace ['bedspeɪs] **N** *Com (in hotel)* capacité *f* d'accueil

bedspread ['bedspred] **N** dessus-de-lit *m inv*, couvre-lit *m*

bedstead ['bedsted] **N** châlit *m*

bedtick ['bedtɪk] **N** *Am (bug)* punaise *f*

bedtime ['bedtaɪm] **N** heure *f* du coucher; **b.!** c'est l'heure d'aller au lit *ou* de se coucher!; **what's his b.?** à quelle heure se couche-t-il?; **it's your b.** il est l'heure d'aller te coucher; **it's long past your b.** il y a longtemps que tu devrais être au lit; **they were allowed to stay up past their b.** on leur a permis de se coucher plus tard que d'habitude

▸▸ ***bedtime story*** histoire *f (qu'on lit à l'heure du coucher)*; **I'll read you a b. story** je vais te lire une histoire avant que tu t'endormes

bed-wetter [-'wetə(r)] **N** *(child)* enfant *mf* qui fait pipi au lit; **he's a b.** il fait pipi au lit

bed-wetting [-'wetɪŋ] **N** incontinence *f* nocturne, énurésie *f*

bee [biː] **N 1** *(insect)* abeille *f*; *Fam* **he's a busy (little) b.** *(is energetic)* il déborde d'énergie; *(has a lot of work)* il a énormément de choses à faire; **to have a b. in one's bonnet (about sth)** être obsédé (par qch); *Fam* **it's the b.'s knees!** c'est formidable *ou* super!; *Fam* **she thinks he's the b.'s knees** elle le trouve formidable; *Fam* **he thinks he's the b.'s knees** il ne se prend pas pour n'importe qui **2** *Am (social event)* réunion *f (de voisins ou d'amis pour des travaux en commun)*; **quilting b.** atelier *m* de patchwork

▸▸ *Bot* ***bee orchid*** ophrys *f* abeille; ***bee sting*** piqûre *f* d'abeille

Beeb [biːb] **N** *Br Fam* **the B.** = surnom courant de la BBC

beech [biːtʃ] *(pl inv or* **beeches)** *Bot* **N** *(tree)* hêtre *m*; *(wood)* (bois *m* de) hêtre *m*

COMP *(chair, table)* de hêtre

▸▸ ***beech grove*** hêtraie *f*; *Bot* ***beech mast*** *(UNCOUNT)* faines *fpl (tombées par terre)*; ***beech nut*** faine *f*; ***beech tree*** hêtre *m*

bee-eater **N** *Orn* guêpier *m*

beef [biːf] *(Br pl sense* **2 beeves** [biːvz], *Am pl sense* **2 beefs,** *pl sense* **3 beefs)** **N 1** *(UNCOUNT) (meat)* bœuf *m*; **joint of b.** rôti *m* (de bœuf), rosbif *m*

2 *(animal)* bœuf *m*

3 *Fam (complaint)* grief□ *m*; **what's your b.?** c'est quoi, ton problème?; **their main b. is high taxation** ils râlent surtout parce qu'ils trouvent les impôts élevés; *Am* **to have a b. with sb/sth** avoir des ennuis avec qn/qch

4 *Fam (muscle)* **put some b. into it!** allez, un peu de nerf!

COMP *Culin (sausage, stew)* de bœuf

VI *Fam* râler; **to b. about sth** râler contre qch

▸▸ *Agr* ***beef cattle*** bœufs *mpl* de boucherie *ou* d'embouche; ***beef farm*** élevage *m* de bœufs; ***beef farmer*** éleveur *m* de bœufs; *EU* ***beef mountain*** montagne *f* de bœuf; *Culin* ***beef olives*** = chair à saucisse enrobée de fines tranches de bœuf, cuite à la cocotte; *Culin* ***beef stroganoff*** bœuf *m* stroganoff; ***beef tea*** bouillon *m* de bœuf; ***beef tomato*** marmande *f*; *Culin* ***beef Wellington*** = bœuf en croûte

▸ **beef up VT SEP** *Fam (army, campaign)* renforcer; *(report, story)* étoffer

beefburger ['biːf,bɜːgə(r)] **N** hamburger *m*

beefcake ['biːfkeɪk] **N** *(UNCOUNT) Fam Hum (attractive men)* beaux mecs *mpl* musclés

Beefeater ['biːf,iːtə(r)] **N** = surnom des gardiens de la Tour de Londres

beefing ['biːfɪŋ] **N** *Fam (complaining)* ronchonnements *mpl*, rouspétances *fpl*

beefsteak ['biːf,steɪk] **N** *Culin* bifteck *m*, steak *m*

▸▸ ***beefsteak tomato*** marmande *f*

beefy ['biːfɪ] *(compar* **beefier,** *superl* **beefiest)** **ADJ 1** *(consistency, taste)* de viande, de bœuf **2** *Fam (brawny)* costaud; *(fat)* grassouillet

beehive ['biːhaɪv] **N 1** *(for bees)* ruche *f* **2** *(hairstyle)* = coiffure très haute maintenue avec de la laque

beekeeper ['biː,kiːpə(r)] **N** apiculteur(trice) *m,f*

beekeeping ['biː,kiːpɪŋ] **N** apiculture *f*

beeline ['biːlaɪn] **N** *Fam* **to make a b. for sb/sth** aller droit *ou* directement vers qn/qch□

Beelzebub [biː'elzɪ,bʌb] **PR N** *Bible* Belzébuth

beemer ['biːmə(r)] **N** *Fam (BMW® car)* BM *f*

been [biːn] *pp of* **be**

beep [biːp] **N** *(of car horn)* coup *m* de klaxon; *(of alarm, timer)* signal *m* sonore, bip *m*

VT 1 **to b. the** *or* **one's horn** klaxonner **2** *(person ▸ on pager)* appeler au récepteur d'appel

VI *(car horn)* klaxonner; *(alarm, timer)* sonner, faire bip

beeper ['biːpə(r)] **N** récepteur *m* d'appels

beeping ['biːpɪŋ] **N** *(UNCOUNT) (of alarm, timer)* bip-bip *m*; **a sudden b. of car horns woke me up** des coups de klaxon brutaux m'ont réveillé

beer [bɪə(r)] **N** bière *f*; **to go for a b.** aller boire une bière; *Br Fig* **his life is not all b. and skittles** sa vie n'est pas toujours rose

▸▸ ***beer barrel*** tonneau *m* à bière; *Am Fam* ***beer bash*** beuverie *f* à la bière entre étudiants; *Fam* ***beer belly*** brioche *f*; ***beer bottle*** canette *f ou* bouteille *f* de bière; *Am Fam* ***beer bust*** = soirée entre étudiants où l'on consomme beaucoup de bière; ***beer can*** canette *f* de bière *(en métal)*; ***beer cellar*** *(bar)* brasserie *f*; ***beer garden*** = jardin d'un pub, où l'on peut prendre des consommations; ***beer glass*** verre *m* à bière; *Fam* ***beer gut*** brioche *f*, bide *m*; ***beer mat*** sous-bock *m inv*; *Fam* ***beer money*** argent *m* de poche□; ***beer pump*** pompe *f* à bière; *Br* ***beer tent*** = grande tente abritant la buvette lors des manifestations sportives de plein air

beery ['bɪərɪ] *(compar* **beerier,** *superl* **beeriest)** **ADJ** *(atmosphere, smell, taste)* qui sent la bière; *(party)* où l'on boit beaucoup de bière; *(person)* qui a bu beaucoup de bière

beeswax ['biːzwæks] **N** cire *f* d'abeille; *Am Fam* **mind your own b.!** occupe-toi de tes oignons!

beet [biːt] N *Bot & Culin* betterave *f* (potagère); *Am* **(red) b.** betterave *f* (rouge)

▸▸ ***beet sugar*** sucre *m* de betterave

beetle [ˈbiːtəl] N **1** *(insect)* scarabée *m*, coléoptère *m* **2** *(game)* = jeu de dés où l'on essaye de dessiner un scarabée **3** *Constr (hammer)* mailloche *f*; *Tech (machine)* mouton *m*; *Constr (for paving)* hie *f*, demoiselle *f*

VI **1** *(cliff, crag)* surplomber **2** *Br Fam* courir précipitamment❑; **he beetled in/out of the house** il est entré dans/sorti de la maison à toute vitesse

• **Beetle**® N *Aut* **(Volkswagen) B.** Coccinelle *f*

▸▸ *Br* ***beetle drive*** = fête où l'on joue au "beetle"

beetle-browed [-braʊd] ADJ *Br (with overhanging eyebrows)* aux sourcils proéminents; *(with bushy eyebrows)* aux sourcils broussailleux; *(scowling)* renfrogné

beetle-crusher N *Fam* écrase-merde *m*

beetling [ˈbiːtlɪŋ] ADJ *(cliff, crag)* qui surplombe, surplombant; *(brow)* proéminent; *(eyebrows)* broussailleux

beetroot [ˈbiːtruːt] N *Bot & Culin* betterave *f* (potagère *ou* rouge); **to go (as red as a) b.** devenir rouge comme une tomate

befall [bɪˈfɔːl] *(pt* **befell** [-ˈfel], *pp* **befallen** [-ˈfɔːlən]) *Literary* VT arriver à, survenir à; **no harm will b. her** il ne lui sera fait aucun mal

VI *(happen)* arriver, se passer

befit [bɪˈfɪt] *(pt & pp* **befitted**, *cont* **befitting**) VT *Formal* convenir à, seoir à; **as befits a woman of her eminence** comme il sied à une femme de son rang; **it does not b. a man to...** ce n'est pas le fait d'un homme de...

befitting [bɪˈfɪtɪŋ] ADJ *Formal* convenable, seyant; **in a manner b. a statesman** d'une façon qui sied à un homme d'État; **with b. modesty** avec la modestie qui sied

BEFORE [bɪˈfɔː(r)]

- ADV
  - avant **1**
  - en avant **2**
- PREP
  - avant **1, 2**
  - devant **3–5**
- CONJ
  - avant de, avant que **1**
  - plutôt que de **2**
- ADJ
  - précédent

ADV **1** *(at a previous time)* avant; **you should have thought of that b.** tu aurais dû y penser avant; **haven't we met b.?** est-ce que nous ne nous sommes pas déjà rencontrés?; **I've never seen this film b.** c'est la première fois que je vois ce film; **I have/had seen it b.** je l'ai/l'avais déjà vu; **he's made mistakes b.** ce n'est pas la première fois qu'il se trompe; **such things have happened b.** c'est déjà arrivé; **she carries on driving as b.** elle continue de conduire comme auparavant *ou* avant

2 *Literary (ahead)* en avant, devant

PREP **1** *(in time)* avant; **the day b. the meeting** la veille de la réunion; **the day b. yesterday** avant-hier; **they arrived b. us** ils sont arrivés avant nous; **the couch won't be delivered b. next Tuesday** le divan ne sera pas livré avant mardi prochain; **it should have been done b. now** ça devrait déjà être fait; **b. that, she was a teacher** auparavant *ou* avant ça, elle était professeur; **that was b. your time** *(you weren't born)* vous n'étiez pas encore né; *(you hadn't arrived, joined etc)* vous n'étiez pas encore là; *Fam* **it's not b. time, and not b. time** ce n'est pas trop tôt

2 *(in order, preference)* avant; **ladies b. gentlemen** les dames avant les messieurs; **she puts family b. friends** pour elle, la famille est plus importante que les amis; **they put quality b. quantity** ils font passer la qualité avant la quantité; **the welfare of the people comes b. private concerns** le bien-être du peuple passe avant tout intérêt privé; **b. anything else, I would like to thank you** avant tout, je voudrais vous remercier

3 *(in space)* devant; *Formal* **on the table b. them** sur la table devant eux; *Fig* **we have a difficult task b. us** nous avons une tâche difficile devant nous; **b. my very eyes** sous mes propres yeux; *Naut* **to sail b. the wind** avoir le vent arrière *ou* en poupe; *Mil* **the troops fled b. the enemy** les troupes se sont enfuies devant l'ennemi

4 *(in the presence of)* devant, en présence de; **he said it b. witnesses** il l'a dit devant *ou* en présence de témoins; *Law* **to appear b. the court/judge** comparaître devant le tribunal/juge; **she appeared b. the committee** elle s'est présentée devant le comité

5 *(for the consideration of)* devant; **the problem b. us** la question qui nous occupe; *Law* **the case b. the court** l'affaire portée devant le tribunal, l'affaire dont le tribunal est saisi; **the matter went b. the council** l'affaire est passée devant le conseil

CONJ **1** *(in time)* avant de, avant que; **she hesitated b. answering** elle a hésité avant de répondre; **may I see you b. you leave?** puis-je vous voir avant que vous ne partiez *ou* avant votre départ?; **I saw him the day b. he died** je l'ai vu la veille de sa mort; **get out b. I call the police!** fichez le camp avant que je n'appelle la police *ou* sinon j'appelle la police!; **it'll be a long time b. he tries that again** il ne recommencera pas de sitôt, il n'est pas près de recommencer; **it'll be two years b. the school is built** l'école ne sera pas construite avant deux ans; **it was almost an hour b. the ambulance arrived** il a fallu presque une heure avant que l'ambulance n'arrive; **b. I forget, they expect you this evening** avant que je n'oublie, il faut que je te dise qu'ils comptent sur toi ce soir; **b. you know it** avant qu'on ait le temps de dire "ouf"; **it'll be Christmas b. we know it** le temps va passer vite jusqu'à Noël

2 *(rather than)* plutôt que de; **I'll die b. I let him marry my daughter** je mourrai plutôt que de le laisser épouser ma fille

ADJ d'avant, précédent; **the day b.** la veille; **the night b.** la veille au soir; **the week b.** la semaine d'avant *ou* précédente; **this summer and the one b.** cet été et celui d'avant *ou* le précédent

---

beforehand [bɪˈfɔːhænd] ADV auparavant, à l'avance; **she had prepared her speech b.** elle avait préparé son discours au préalable *ou* à l'avance; **if you're coming let me know b.** prévenez-moi si vous décidez de venir

ADJ *Fam Hum (early)* **you were a bit b. with the congratulations!** tu t'y es pris un peu tôt pour les félicitations!

before-tax ADJ *Fin* brut, avant impôts; **b. income** revenus *mpl* bruts

befriend [bɪˈfrend] VT *(make friends with)* prendre en amitié, se prendre d'amitié pour; *(assist)* venir en aide à, aider; **he was befriended by a colleague** un de ses collègues s'est pris d'amitié pour lui

befuddle [bɪˈfʌdəl] VT **1** *(confuse* ▸ *person)* brouiller l'esprit *ou* les idées de, embrouiller; *(*▸ *mind)* embrouiller **2** *(muddle with alcohol)* griser, enivrer; **his mind was befuddled with drink** il était étourdi par l'alcool

beg [beg] *(pt & pp* **begged**, *cont* **begging**) VT **1** *(solicit as charity)* mendier; **to b. food** mendier de la nourriture; **she begged money from the passers-by** elle mendiait auprès des passants; **to b., borrow or steal** se procurer par tous les moyens

2 *(ask for)* demander, solliciter; *(plead with)* supplier; **I begged the doctor not to say anything** j'ai supplié le médecin de ne rien dire; **she begged to be sent back to school** elle supplia qu'on la renvoie à l'école; **she begged a favour of her sister** elle a demandé à sa sœur de lui rendre un service; **to b. sb's forgiveness** *or* **pardon** demander pardon à qn; **I b. your pardon** *(I apologize)* je vous demande pardon; *(I didn't hear you)* pardon?; *(indignantly)* pardon!

3 *Formal (request politely)* **I b. to differ** permettez-moi de ne pas être de votre avis; **I b. to inform you that...** je tiens à *ou* j'ai l'honneur de vous informer que...; **to b. leave to do sth** demander la permission de faire qch

4 *(idiom)* **to b. the question** *(evade the issue)* éluder la question; *(assume something proved)* considérer que la question est résolue; **that begs the question of whether...** cela pose la question de savoir si..., c'est toute la question de savoir si...; **wanting to climb Mount Everest rather begs the question "why?"** on serait enclin à se demander pourquoi quelqu'un aurait envie d'escalader le Mont Everest

VI **1** *(solicit charity)* mendier; **to b. for food** mendier de la nourriture; **children begging (for money) in the street** des enfants qui mendient dans la rue

2 *(ask, plead)* supplier; **to b. for forgiveness/mercy** demander pardon/grâce

3 *(dog)* faire le beau

4 *Br (idioms)* **I'll have that last sandwich if it's going begging** je prendrai bien ce dernier sandwich si personne d'autre ne le veut; **there's a piece of cake going begging** il reste un morceau de gâteau; **these jobs are going begging** ce sont des emplois qui trouvent peu d'amateurs

▸**beg off** VI *Br* se soustraire; **our best player begged off pleading illness** notre meilleur joueur s'est fait excuser pour cause de maladie

beget [bɪˈget] *(pt* **begot** [-ˈgɒt] *or* **begat** [-ˈgæt], *pp* **begotten** [-ˈgɒtən], *cont* **begetting**) VT *Bible & Literary (father)* engendrer; *Fig (cause)* engendrer, causer; **Abraham begat Isaac** Abraham engendra Isaac; **the only begotten Son of the Father** le Fils unique du Père

beggar [ˈbegə(r)] N **1** *(mendicant)* mendiant(e) *m,f*; *(pauper)* indigent(e) *m,f*; *Prov* **beggars can't be choosers** nécessité fait loi **2** *Br Fam (person)* type *m*; **you lucky b.!** sacré veinard!; **poor b.!** pauvre diable!; **you naughty little b.!** petit coquin!

VT *(defy)* **to b. (all) description** défier toute description; **it beggars belief** c'est incroyable

beggarly [ˈbegəlɪ] ADJ *(conditions, life)* misérable, malheureux; *(meal)* maigre, piètre; *(salary, sum)* misérable, dérisoire

beggar-my-neighbour *Br* N *Cards* bataille *f*

ADJ *Com* protectionniste; **b. policies** politique *f* protectionniste *ou* du chacun pour soi

beggary [ˈbegərɪ] N misère *f*, mendicité *f*; **they were reduced to b.** ils étaient réduits à la mendicité

begging [ˈbegɪŋ] N mendicité *f*; **to live by b.** vivre d'aumône

▸▸ ***begging bowl*** sébile *f (de mendiant)*; *Fig* **many sports organizations have to approach the government with a b. bowl** de nombreuses associations sportives sont obligées de demander l'aumône au gouvernement; ***begging letter*** lettre *f* de requête *(demandant de l'argent)*

BEGIN [bɪˈgɪn] *(pt* **began** [bɪˈgæn], *pp* **begun** [bɪˈgʌn], *cont* **beginning**) VT **1** *(start)* commencer; *(career, term)* commencer, débuter; *(task)* entreprendre, s'attaquer à; *(work)* commencer, se mettre à; **to b. to do** *or* **doing sth** commencer à faire qch, se mettre à faire qch; **she began the first chapter** *(reading)* elle commença à lire le premier chapitre; *(writing)* elle commença à écrire le premier chapitre; **she began life as a waitress** elle a débuté comme serveuse; **he soon began to complain** il n'a pas tardé à se plaindre; **the film doesn't b. to compare with the book** le film est loin de valoir le livre; **he can't b. to compete with her** il ne lui arrive pas à la cheville; **I can't b. to explain** c'est trop difficile à expliquer

2 *(start to say)* commencer; **"this is unforgivable," she began** "c'est impardonnable", commença-t-elle

3 *(found* ▸ *institution, club)* fonder, inaugurer; *(initiate* ▸ *business, fashion)* lancer; *(*▸ *argument, fight, war)* déclencher, faire naître; *(*▸ *conversation)* engager, amorcer; *(*▸ *discussion, speech)* commencer, ouvrir

VI **1** *(start* ▸ *person, career, concert, project, speech)* commencer; **the day began badly/well** la journée s'annonçait mal/bien; **to b. again** *or* **afresh** recommencer (à zéro); **b. at the beginning** commencez par le commencement; **when does school b.?** quand est la rentrée?; **after the film begins** après le début du film; **her career began in Hollywood** sa carrière a débuté à Hollywood; **he began in politics** il a commencé par faire de la politique; **let me b. by thanking our host** permettez-moi tout d'abord de remercier notre hôte; **let's b. with a song** commençons par une chanson; **her name begins with (a) B** son nom commence par un B; **the play begins with a murder** la pièce débute par un meurtre; **I began with the idea of buying a house** au départ *ou* au début je voulais acheter une maison

2 *(originate* ▸ *club, country, institution)* être fondé; *(*▸ *fire, epidemic)* commencer; *(*▸ *war)* éclater, commencer; *(*▸ *trouble)* commencer; *(*▸ *river)* prendre sa source; *(*▸ *road)*

commencer; (▸ *fashion)* commencer, débuter; **the magazine began as a freesheet** la revue a débuté comme publication gratuite

• **to begin with** ADV **1** *(in the first place)* d'abord, pour commencer; **to b. with, it's too cold** d'abord, il fait trop froid; **to b. with, the statistics are wrong** pour commencer *ou* d'abord, les chiffres sont faux

2 *(initially)* au départ; **everything went well to b. with** tout s'est bien passé au début *ou* au départ; **the plate was cracked to b. with** l'assiette était déjà fêlée au départ

beginner [bɪ'gɪnə(r)] N débutant(e) *m,f*; **not bad for a b.** pas si mal pour un débutant; **it's b.'s luck!** on a toujours de la chance au début!; **French for beginners** français pour débutants; **complete** *or* **absolute b.** grand débutant; **b.'s class** cours *m* de débutants

beginning [bɪ'gɪnɪŋ] N **1** *(start* ▸ *of book, career, project)* commencement *m*, début *m*; **in** *or* **at the b.** au début, au commencement; **from the b.** dès le commencement *ou* le début; **this is just the b. of our troubles** nos ennuis ne font que commencer; **let's start again from the b.** reprenons depuis le début; **at the b. of the academic year** au début de l'année universitaire; **from b. to end** du début à la fin, d'un bout à l'autre; **it's the b. of the end** c'est le début de la fin **2** *(early part, stage* ▸ *of book, career, war)* commencement *m*, début *m*; (▸ *of negotiations)* début *m*, ouverture *f*; **the b. of the world** l'origine *ou* le commencement du monde; **since the b. of time** depuis la nuit des temps; **I have the beginnings of a cold** je couve un rhume, j'ai un début de rhume **3** *(origin* ▸ *of event)* origine *f*, commencement *m*; **Protestantism had its beginnings in Germany** le protestantisme a pris naissance en Allemagne; **his assassination signalled the b. of the war** son assassinat a marqué le déclenchement de la guerre

ADJ **b. student** débutant(e) *m,f*

begone [bɪ'gɒn] EXCLAM *Literary* hors d'ici!

begonia [bɪ'gəʊnɪə] N *Bot* bégonia *m*

begrudge [bɪ'grʌdʒ] VT **1** *(envy)* envier; **to b. sb sth** envier qch à qn; **she begrudges him his success** elle lui en veut de sa réussite **2** *(give grudgingly)* donner *ou* accorder à regret; **he begrudges every minute spent away from his family** il rechigne à passer une seule minute loin de sa famille; **you don't b. me the money, do you?** tu ne me donnes pas cet argent à contrecœur, n'est-ce pas?; **to b. doing sth** faire qch à contrecœur; **I b. spending so much on rent** ça me fait mal au cœur de payer un loyer aussi cher

beguile [bɪ'gaɪl] VT **1** *(charm)* envoûter, séduire **2** *(delude)* enjôler, tromper; **to b. sb into doing sth** amener qn à faire qch **3** *(pass pleasantly)* **to b. (away) the hours** faire passer le temps *(agréablement)*

beguiling [bɪ'gaɪlɪŋ] ADJ charmant, séduisant

begum ['beɪgəm] N bégum *f*

behalf [bɪ'hɑːf] N *Br* **on b. of sb,** *Am* **in b. of sb** *(as their representative)* de la part de *ou* au nom de qn; *(in their interest)* dans l'intérêt de *ou* pour qn; **on b. of everyone here, I thank you** au nom de tous ceux qui sont ici présents, je vous remercie; **I'm here on b. of the president** je viens de la part du président; **she accepted the award on his b.** elle a reçu le prix en son nom *ou* pour lui; **she acted on his b. when he was ill** c'est elle qui l'a représenté quand il était malade; **your lawyer acts on your b.** votre avocat agit en votre nom

behave [bɪ'heɪv] VI **1** *(act)* se comporter, se conduire; **why are you behaving this way?** pourquoi agis-tu de cette façon?; **to b. badly/well** mal/bien se comporter; **what a way to b.!** quelles manières!; **to know how to b.** savoir vivre; **he behaved badly towards her** il s'est mal conduit envers elle; **she's behaving very strangely** elle se comporte de façon bizarre **2** *(act properly)* se tenir bien; **will you b.!** sois sage!, tiens-toi bien! **3** *(function)* fonctionner, marcher; **she studies how matter behaves in extremes of cold and heat** elle étudie le comportement de la matière dans des conditions de froid ou de chaleur extrêmes; **the car behaves well on curves** la voiture tient bien la route dans les virages

VT **to b. oneself** se tenir bien; **b. yourself!** sois sage!, tiens-toi bien!; **to b. itself** *(machine, clock etc)* marcher, fonctionner

-behaved [bɪ'heɪvd] SUFF **well-b.** sage, qui se conduit *ou* se tient bien; **badly-b.** qui se conduit *ou* se tient mal

behaviour, *Am* **behavior** [bɪ'heɪvjə(r)] N **1** *(of person)* comportement *m*, conduite *f*; *(of animal)* comportement *m*; **her b. towards her mother was unforgivable** la façon dont elle s'est comportée avec sa mère était impardonnable; **to be on one's best b.** se tenir *ou* se conduire de son mieux **2** *Phys (of atom, chemical, light)* comportement *m*; *(of machine)* fonctionnement *m*

COMP *(modification, problem)* du comportement

▸▸ *Psy* ***behaviour pattern*** type *m* de comportement; *Psy* ***behaviour therapy*** thérapie *f* comportementale

behavioural, *Am* **behavioral** [bɪ'heɪvjərəl] ADJ *Psy* de comportement, comportemental; *(analysis, study)* de comportement

▸▸ ***behavioural pattern*** type *m* de comportement; ***behavioural science*** science *f* du comportement, comportementalisme *m*

behaviourism, *Am* **behaviorism** [bɪ'heɪvjərɪzəm] N *Psy* behaviorisme *m*

behaviourist, *Am* **behaviorist** [bɪ'heɪvjərɪst] *Psy* N behavioriste *mf*

ADJ behavioriste

behead [bɪ'hed] VT décapiter

beheading [bɪ'hedɪŋ] N décapitation *f*

behemoth [bɪ'hiːmɒθ] N *(monster)* monstre *m*

behest [bɪ'hest] N *Formal* commandement *m*, ordre *m*; **at the b. of the Queen** sur ordre de la reine

BEHIND [bɪ'haɪnd]

PREP
• derrière **1, 2, 4** • en retard sur **3**
ADV
• derrière **1** • en retard **2**
N
• derrière

PREP **1** *(at the back of)* derrière; **b. the house** derrière la maison; **she came out from b. the bushes** elle est sortie de derrière les buissons; **I sat down right b. him** je me suis assis juste derrière lui; **lock the door b. you** fermez la porte à clé (derrière vous); **his wife was b. the bar that night** sa femme était derrière le bar *ou* au bar ce soir-là

2 *(indicating past time)* derrière; **he has ten years' experience b. him** il a dix ans d'expérience derrière lui; **your troubles are b. you now** vos ennuis sont terminés maintenant; **let's put it all b. us** oublions tout cela, n'y pensons plus

3 *(indicating deficiency, delay)* en retard sur, derrière; **she is b. the other pupils** elle est en retard sur les autres élèves; **we're three points b. the other team** nous sommes à trois points derrière l'autre équipe; **the trains are running b. schedule** *or* **b. time** les trains ont du retard (sur l'horaire); **b. the times** *(country)* arriéré, attardé; **you're b. the times** *(old-fashioned)* tu n'es pas à la page; *(not aware of latest developments)* tu as un métro de retard

4 *(responsible for)* derrière; **who was b. the plot?** qui était derrière le complot *ou* à l'origine du complot?; **what's b. all this?** qu'est-ce que ça cache?

5 *(supporting)* **we're right b. you on this** vous avez tout notre soutien dans cette affaire; **the country is right b. the new policies** la population soutient tout à fait les nouvelles mesures

ADV **1** *(at, in the back)* derrière, en arrière; **look b.** regardez derrière; **he attacked them from b.** il les a attaqués par derrière; **they followed b.** ils arrivaient derrière, ils suivaient; **to stay** *or* **remain b.** *(be at the back)* rester *ou* demeurer en arrière; *(not leave)* ne pas partir; **I'll stay b. and wait for them** je resterai derrière pour les attendre; **the teacher kept him b.** *or* **made him stay b.** le professeur l'a retenu *ou* l'a mis en retenue; **I left my umbrella b.** *(at home)* j'ai oublié mon parapluie à la maison; *(at someone else's home)* j'ai oublié mon parapluie (chez lui/eux/*etc*); **disaster was not far b.** la catastrophe était imminente

2 *(late)* en retard; **I'm b. in** *or* **with my rent** je suis en retard sur mon loyer; **I'm b. in** *or* **with my work** j'ai du retard dans mon travail; **she's too far b. to catch up with the others** elle a pris trop de retard pour pouvoir rattraper les autres; **our team is three points b.** notre équipe a trois points de moins

N *Euph (buttocks)* derrière *m*, postérieur *m*; **to kick sb in the b.** botter le derrière à qn; **get up off your b. and find yourself a job!** remue-toi un peu et trouve du boulot!

behindhand [bɪ'haɪndhænd] ADV en retard; **we're b. with the rent** nous sommes en retard sur le loyer; **I'm getting b. with my work** je suis en train de prendre du retard dans mon travail

behind-the-scenes ADJ secret(ète); **a b. look at politics** un regard en coulisse sur la politique

behold [bɪ'həʊld] *(pt & pp* **beheld** [-'held]) VT *Arch or Literary (see)* regarder, voir; *(notice)* apercevoir; **b.!** voyez!; **a sight to b.** un spectacle à voir; **b. your king** voici votre roi

beholden [bɪ'həʊldən] ADJ *Formal* redevable; **I am deeply b. to him** je lui suis infiniment redevable

beholder [bɪ'həʊldə(r)] N *Prov* **beauty is in the eye of the b.** il n'y a point de laides amours

behove [bɪ'həʊv], *Am* **behoove** [bɪ'huːv] VT *Arch or Literary* **it behoves them to be prudent** il leur appartient d'être prudents; **it ill behoves her to criticize** ça lui va mal de critiquer

beige [beɪʒ] N beige *m*

ADJ beige

Beijing [,beɪ'dʒɪŋ] N Beijing

being ['biːɪŋ] N **1** *(creature)* être *m*, créature *f*; **a human b.** un être humain; **a b. from another planet** une créature (venue) d'une autre planète **2** *(essential nature)* être *m*; **her whole b. rebelled** tout son être se révoltait **3** *(existence)* existence *f*; **already in b.** déjà existant, qui existe déjà; **to bring** *or* **to call sth into b.** faire naître qch, susciter qch; **the movement came into b. in the 1920s** le mouvement est apparu *ou* fut créé dans les années 20

Beirut [,beɪ'ruːt] N Beyrouth

bejewelled, *Am* **bejeweled** [bɪ'dʒuːəld] ADJ *(person)* paré *ou* couvert de bijoux; *(box, purse)* incrusté de bijoux

belabour, *Am* **belabor** [bɪ'leɪbə(r)] VT **1** *(beat)* rouer de coups **2** *(criticize)* injurier, invectiver

Belarus [,belə'ruːs] N Biélorussie *f*

belated [bɪ'leɪtɪd] ADJ tardif; **to wish you a b. happy birthday** pour te souhaiter un bon anniversaire avec un peu de retard

belatedly [bɪ'leɪtɪdlɪ] ADV tardivement

belay [bɪ'leɪ] VT **1** *Naut* amarrer **2** *(in mountaineering)* assurer

▸▸ ***belay plate*** plaquette *f* d'assurage

belaying [bɪ'leɪɪŋ] N **1** *Naut* amarrage *m* **2** *(in mountaineering)* assurance *f*, assurage *m*

▸▸ ***belaying cleat, belaying pin*** cabillot *m*, taquet *m*

belch [beltʃ] N renvoi *m*, rot *m*; **to give a b.** roter

VT *(expel)* cracher, vomir; **the house was belching smoke and flames** la maison crachait de la fumée et des flammes

VI roter

▸ **belch forth, belch out** VT SEP *(flames, smoke etc)* cracher, vomir

VI **smoke and flames were belching out of the house** la maison crachait de la fumée et des flammes

beleaguer [bɪ'liːgə(r)] VT **1** *(harass)* harceler, assaillir; **reporters beleaguered him with questions** les journalistes le harcelèrent de questions; **she was beleaguered by problems** elle croulait sous les problèmes **2** *Mil (besiege* ▸ *city)* assiéger; (▸ *army, group)* encercler, cerner

beleaguered [bɪ'liːgəd] ADJ *Mil (city)* assiégé; *Fig (project, ideology)* très critiqué; *(government, politician)* assailli de toutes parts; *(parents, look, manner)* accablé

belfry ['belfrɪ] *(pl* **belfries)** N *(of church)* beffroi *m*, clocher *m*; *(of tower)* beffroi *m*

Belgian ['beldʒən] N Belge *mf*

ADJ belge

COMP *(embassy)* de Belgique; *(history)* de la Belgique

▸▸ *Formerly* ***Belgian franc*** franc *m* belge

Belgium ['beldʒəm] **N** Belgique *f*

belie [bɪ'laɪ] *(pt & pp* **belied,** *cont* **belying)** **VT** *Formal (misrepresent)* donner une fausse idée *ou* impression de; *(contradict* ▸ *hope, impression)* démentir, tromper; *(*▸ *promise)* démentir, donner le démenti à; **her youthful figure belied her age** la jeunesse de sa silhouette démentait son âge

belief [bɪ'li:f] **N 1** *(feeling of certainty)* croyance *f*; **b. in God** croyance en Dieu; **contrary to popular b.** contrairement à ce qu'on croit; **it's beyond b.** c'est incroyable; **he's lazy beyond b.** il est incroyablement paresseux

2 *(conviction, opinion)* conviction *f*, certitude *f*; **it's my b. he's lying** je suis certain *ou* convaincu qu'il ment; **in the b. that he would help them** certain *ou* persuadé qu'il allait les aider; **in the mistaken b. that...** persuadé à tort que...; **to the best of my b.** autant que je sache

3 *Rel (religious faith)* foi *f*, croyance *f*; *(political faith)* dogme *m*, doctrine *f*

4 *(confidence, trust)* confiance *f*, foi *f*

believable [bɪ'li:vəbəl] **ADJ** *(story, account)* croyable, crédible; *(character in novel, person)* crédible

BELIEVE [bɪ'li:v] **VT 1** *(consider as real or true)* croire; **don't b. a word she says** ne croyez pas un mot de ce qu'elle dit; **I don't b. a word of it** je n'en crois rien *ou* pas un mot; **don't you b. it!** détrompe-toi!; **he's getting married! – I don't b. it!** il va se marier! – c'est pas vrai!; **she's 50, would you b. it!** elle a 50 ans, figure-toi!; **he couldn't b. his ears/his eyes** il n'en croyait pas ses oreilles/ses yeux; **and, b. it or not, she left** et, crois-le si tu veux, elle est partie; **I can well b. it** je suis prêt à le croire, je veux bien le croire; **it has to be seen to be believed** il faut le voir pour le croire

2 *(accept statement or opinion of)* croire; **if she is to be believed, she was born a duchess** à l'en croire, elle est duchesse; **and b. (you) me, I know what I'm talking about!** et croyez-moi, je sais de quoi je parle!; *Fam* **you'd better b. it!** bien sûr que oui!

3 *(hold as opinion, suppose)* croire; **I don't b. we've met** je ne crois pas que nous nous connaissions; **I b. I've taken a wrong turning** je crois que je me suis trompé de route *ou* que j'ai pris la mauvaise route; **I don't know what to b.** je ne sais que croire, je ne sais pas à quoi m'en tenir; **it is widely believed that the prisoners have been killed** on pense généralement que les prisonniers ont été tués; **she is, I b., our greatest novelist** elle est, je crois *ou* à mon avis, notre meilleure romancière; **we have every reason to b. he's telling the truth** nous avons tout lieu de croire qu'il dit la vérité; **I b. not** je crois que non, je ne crois pas; **I b. so** je crois que oui, je crois; **I wouldn't have believed it of him** je n'aurais pas cru cela de lui

VI *(have religious faith)* être croyant, avoir la foi

▸ **believe in VT INSEP 1 to b. in miracles/God** croire aux miracles/en Dieu **2 I b. in free enterprise** je crois à la libre entreprise; **they b. in their president** il font confiance à leur président

believer [bɪ'li:və(r)] **N 1** *(supporter)* partisan *m*, adepte *mf*; **a b. in socialism** un partisan du socialisme; **he's a great b. in taking exercise** il est convaincu qu'il faut faire de l'exercice **2** *Rel* croyant(e) *m,f*; **are you a b.?** êtes-vous croyant?

Belisha beacon [bɪ'li:ʃə-] **N** *Br* = globe orange clignotant marquant un passage clouté

belittle [bɪ'lɪtəl] **VT** rabaisser, dénigrer; **he's always belittling her work** il dénigre toujours son travail; **to b. oneself** *(disparage)* se déprécier; *(demean)* se déconsidérer *(aux yeux de quelqu'un, auprès de quelqu'un)*

Belize [be'li:z] **N** Belize *m*; **in B.** au Belize

bell [bel] **N 1** *(in church)* cloche *f*; *(handheld)* clochette *f*; *(on bicycle)* sonnette *f*; *(for cows)* cloche *f*, clarine *f*; *(on boots, toys)* grelot *m*; *(sound)* coup *m* (de cloche); **there goes the dinner b.** c'est la cloche qui annonce le dîner; *Naut* **it sounded four/eight bells** cela a piqué quatre/huit coups (de cloche); **saved by the b.!** sauvé par le gong!; *Rel* **b., book and candle** instruments *mpl* du culte; **bells and whistles** accessoires *mpl*

2 *(electrical device* ▸ *on door)* sonnette *f*; **there's the b.** il y a quelqu'un à la porte, on sonne (à la porte); **to ring the b.** sonner

3 *Br Fam (telephone call)* **to give sb a b.** passer un coup de fil à qn

4 *Bot (of flower)* calice *m*, clochette *f*; *Mus (of oboe, trumpet)* pavillon *m*

5 *(of stag)* bramement *m*; *(of hound)* aboiement *m*

VI *(stag)* bramer; *(hound)* aboyer

VT *Fig* **to b. the cat** attacher le grelot

▸▸ *Naut* **bell buoy** bouée *f* à cloche; *Am* **bell captain** chef *m* chasseur; *Hort* **bell glass** cloche *f* de verre; *Bot* **bell heather** bruyère *f* cendrée; *Chem* **bell jar** cloche *f* de verre; *Am Sport* **bell lap** dernier tour *m (de piste, de circuit)*; *Am Bot & Culin* **bell pepper** poivron *m*; **bell push** bouton *m* de sonnette; **bell rope** *(to call servant)* cordon *m* de sonnette; *(in belfry)* corde *f* de cloche; **bell tent** tente *f* conique; **bell tower** clocher *m*

belladonna [ˌbelə'dɒnə] **N** *Bot & Pharm* belladone *f*

bell-bottomed [-'bɒtəmd] **ADJ** à pattes d'éléphant

bell-bottoms NPL pantalon *m* à pattes d'éléphant

bellboy ['belbɔɪ] **N** *(page)* chasseur *m*; *(porter)* porteur *m*

belle [bel] **N** belle *f*, beauté *f*; **the b. of the ball** la reine du bal

bellflower ['belˌflaʊə(r)] **N** *Bot* campanule *f*

bellhop ['belhɒp] **N** *Am (page)* chasseur *m*; *(porter)* porteur *m*

bellicose ['belɪkəʊs] **ADJ** belliqueux

bellicosity [ˌbelɪ'kɒsətɪ] **N** bellicisme *m*

-bellied ['belɪd] **SUFF round-/swollen-b.** au ventre rond/enflé

belligerence [bɪ'lɪdʒərəns], **belligerency** [bɪ'lɪdʒərənsɪ] **N** *Mil* belligérance *f*

belligerent [bɪ'lɪdʒərənt] **N 1** *(in dispute)* partie *f* **2** *Mil* belligérant(e) *m,f*

ADJ 1 *(aggressive* ▸ *person, tone of voice, attitude)* agressif, belliqueux **2** *Mil (at war* ▸ *country)* belligérant

bellow ['beləʊ] **VI** *(bull)* beugler, meugler; *(elephant)* barrir; *(person)* brailler; **to b. at sb** *(with rage)* brailler dans les oreilles de qn; **he bellowed with pain** il a hurlé de douleur; **the crowd bellowed with laughter** la foule hurlait de rire

VT to b. sth (out) brailler qch; *Fam (song)* beugler qch

N *(of bull)* beuglement *m*, meuglement *m*; *(of elephant)* barrissement *m*; *(of person)* braillement *m*

bellowing ['beləʊɪŋ] **N** *(of bull)* beuglement *m*, meuglement *m*; *(of elephant)* barrissement *m*; *(of person)* braillement *m*

bellows ['beləʊz] **NPL 1** *Tech (for fire)* soufflet *m*; **a pair of b.** un soufflet **2** *Mus (for accordion, organ)* soufflerie *f*

bell-ringer N *Mus* sonneur *m*, carillonneur *m*

bell-ringing N *Mus* carillonnement *m*

bell-shaped ADJ en forme de cloche

bellwether ['belˌweðə(r)] **N** *Agr (sheep)* sonnailler *m*; *Fig (person)* meneur(euse) *m,f*, chef *m*

belly ['belɪ] *(pl* **bellies,** *pt & pp* **bellied) N 1** *(stomach)* ventre *m*; **a big b.** un gros ventre; **he only thinks of his b.** il ne pense qu'à son estomac; *Fam Fig* **to go b. up** *(of company)* faire faillite ▫

2 *(of plane, ship)* ventre *m*; *(of sail)* creux *m*

3 *Mus (of cello, guitar)* table *f* d'harmonie

4 *Culin* **b. of pork, pork b.** poitrine *f* de porc

5 *Arch (womb)* ventre *m*

VI to b. (out) s'enfler, se gonfler

VT enfler, gonfler

▸▸ *Fam* **belly button** nombril ▫ *m*; **belly chain** chaîne *f* de taille; **belly dance** danse *f* du ventre; **belly dancer** danseuse *f* du ventre *ou* orientale; *Swimming* **belly flop** plat *m*; **to do a b. flop** faire un plat; *Fam* **belly laugh** gros rire ▫ *m*

bellyache ['belɪeɪk] *Fam* **N 1** *(pain)* mal *m* au *ou* de ventre ▫; **I've got (a) b.** j'ai mal au ventre **2** *(complaint)* rogne *f*, rouspétance *f*

VI râler; **stop bellyaching!** arrête de râler!

bellyaching ['belɪˌeɪkɪŋ] **N** *(UNCOUNT) Fam* ronchonnements *mpl*, rouspétances *fpl*; **I don't want any b.** je n'accepterai aucune rouspétance

bellyful ['belɪful] **N** *Fam (of food)* ventre *m* plein ▫; *Fig* **I've had a b.** j'en ai jusque-là; **I've had a b. of your complaints** j'en ai ras le bol de tes rouspétances

belly-land *Fam Aviat* **VT** atterrir sur le ventre ▫

VI atterrir sur le ventre ▫

belong [bɪ'lɒŋ] **VI 1** *(as property)* **to b. to sb** appartenir à *ou* être à qn; **the book belongs to her** le livre lui appartient *ou* est à elle; **the company belongs to a large conglomerate** l'entreprise appartient à un important conglomérat; *Law* **to b. to the Crown** *(land etc)* dépendre de la Couronne

2 *(as member)* **to b. to a society** faire partie d'une société; **do you b. to this club?** êtes-vous membre de ce cercle?; **he belongs to a trade union** il fait partie *ou* il est membre d'un syndicat, il est syndiqué

3 *(as part, component)* appartenir; **the field belongs to that house** le champ dépend de cette maison; **this key belongs to the car** cette clé est pour la voiture; **this jacket belongs with those trousers** cette veste va avec ce pantalon; **which species do they b. to?** à quelle espèce appartiennent-ils?; **she belongs in another era** elle est d'une autre époque

4 *(be in proper place)* être à sa place; **the dishes b. in that cupboard** les assiettes vont dans ce placard; **put the books back where they b.** remettez les livres à leur place; **the two of them b. together** ces deux-là sont faits pour être ensemble; **these gloves b. together** ces gants appartiennent à la même paire; **I don't b. here** je ne suis pas à ma place ici; **go back home where you b.** rentrez chez vous; **he belongs in teaching** sa place est dans l'enseignement; **these issues b. in a court of law** ces questions relèvent d'un tribunal

belonging [bɪ'lɒŋɪŋ] **N a sense of b.** un sentiment d'appartenance

• **belongings NPL** affaires *fpl*, possessions *fpl*; **she packed the few belongings she had** elle a emballé le peu (de choses *ou* d'affaires) qu'elle avait; **personal belongings** objets *mpl ou* effets *mpl* personnels

beloved [bɪ'lʌvɪd] **N** bien-aimé(e) *m,f*, amour *m*; **my b.** mon (ma) bien-aimé(e); *Rel* **dearly b., we are gathered here today...** mes bien chers frères, nous sommes ici aujourd'hui...

ADJ chéri, bien-aimé; **he was b. by** *or* **of all his friends** il était cher à tous ses amis; **my b. father** mon très cher père, mon père bien-aimé

below [bɪ'ləʊ] **PREP 1** *(at, to a lower position than)* au-dessous de, en dessous de; *(under)* sous; **the flat b. ours** l'appartement au-dessous *ou* en dessous du nôtre; **her skirt came to b. her knees** sa jupe lui descendait au-dessous du genou; **b. the surface** sous la surface; **b. (the) ground** sous (la) terre; **b. sea level** au-dessous du niveau de la mer

2 *(inferior to)* au-dessous de, inférieur à; **temperatures b. zero** des températures au-dessous de *ou* inférieures à zéro; his *Br* **marks** *or Am* **grades are b. average** ses notes sont au-dessous de *ou* inférieures à la moyenne; **b. the poverty line** en dessous du seuil de pauvreté; **children b. the age of five** des enfants de moins de cinq ans

3 *(downstream of)* en aval de

4 *(south of)* au sud de

ADV 1 *(in lower place, on lower level)* en dessous, plus bas; **we looked down onto the town b.** nous contemplions la ville à nos pieds; **down b. in the valley** en bas dans la vallée; **the flat b.** l'appartement d'en dessous *ou* du dessous; **seen from b.** vu d'en bas; *Arch or Literary* **here b.** *(on earth)* ici-bas

2 *(with numbers, quantities)* moins; *Fam* **it was 20 b.** il faisait moins 20; **children of five and b.** les enfants de cinq ans et moins

3 *(in text)* plus bas, ci-dessous; **see b.** voir plus bas *ou* ci-dessous; **the address given b.** l'adresse mentionnée ci-dessous

4 *Naut* en bas; **to go b.** descendre dans l'entrepont; **she went b. to her cabin** elle est descendue à sa cabine

below-the-line ADJ *Acct (expenses)* au-dessous de la ligne
▸▸ ***below-the-line accounts*** comptes *mpl* de résultats exceptionnels; *Acct* ***below-the-line costs*** coûts *mpl* hors-média

belt [belt] N **1** *(band of leather etc) & Sport* ceinture *f*; *Mil* ceinturon *m*, ceinture *f*; **a leather b.** une ceinture en cuir; **he had a gun at his b.** il portait un revolver à la ceinture; **to give sb the b.** *(at school)* donner une correction à qn *(avec une lanière de cuir)*; **to be a brown/black b.** *(in martial arts)* être ceinture marron/noire; *Fig* **to have sth under one's b.** *(move, project)* en avoir fini avec qch; *(driving licence, degree)* avoir qch en poche; **once you've got a few years' experience under your b.** une fois que tu as quelques années d'expérience à ton actif; *Boxing* **no hitting below the b.** il est interdit de porter des coups bas; *Fig* **that was a bit below the b.** c'était un peu déloyal comme procédé; **to pull in** *or* **to tighten one's b.** se serrer la ceinture
2 *Tech (of machine)* courroie *f*
3 *(area, zone)* région *f*; **belts of high unemployment** des régions à fort taux de chômage
4 *Fam (sharp blow ▸ with hand)* gifle□ *f*; *(▸ with bat, stick)* coup□ *m*; **he gave the ball a terrific b.** il a tapé un grand coup dans la balle; **to give sb a b. in the face** flanquer un gnon *ou* un pain dans la tronche à qn
5 *Fam (of whisky)* gorgée□ *f*
VT **1** *(dress, trousers)* ceinturer, mettre une ceinture à; **he had a gun belted to his waist** il avait un revolver à la ceinture **2** *(hit with belt)* donner des coups de ceinture à; *(as punishment)* donner une correction à *(avec une lanière de cuir)* **3** *Fam (hit with hand)* gifler□; *(hit with bat, stick ▸ ball)* frapper dans□, taper dans□; *(▸ person)* frapper□; **I belted him (one) in the eye** je lui en ai collé un dans l'œil; **she belted the ball** elle a donné un grand coup dans la balle
VI *Br Fam* filer; **they went belting along** ils fonçaient; **he belted into/out of the room** il est entré dans/sorti de la pièce à toute berzingue; **to b. down the stairs** descendre l'escalier quatre à quatre; **they were belting down the motorway** ils fonçaient sur l'autoroute
▸▸ ***belt buckle*** boucle *f* de ceinture; *Tech* ***belt conveyor*** transporteur *m* à courroie *ou* à ruban *ou* à bande; *Tech* ***belt drive*** transmission *f* par courroie; ***belt loop*** passant *m (de ceinture)*; *Tech* ***belt sander*** ponceuse *f* à courroie

▸**belt out** VT SEP *Fam (order, instructions)* gueuler; *(song)* gueuler, brailler

▸**belt up** VI **1** *(in car, plane)* attacher sa ceinture **2** *Br Fam (be quiet)* la fermer, la boucler; **b. up!** boucle-la!

belt-driven ADJ *Tech* actionné par courroie

belted ['beltɪd] ADJ ceinturé; **a b. raincoat** un imperméable à ceinture
▸▸ *Aut* ***belted tyre*** pneu *m* à ceinture

belter ['beltə(r)] N *Br Fam* **1** *(excellent thing)* **it was a real b.** c'était vraiment génial **2** *(singer)* = chanteur ou chanteuse qui chante à pleins poumons; *(song)* = chanson chantée à pleins poumons

belting ['beltɪŋ] N **1** *Tech (belts)* courroie(s) *f(pl)*; *Tex (material)* matériau *m* à courroies **2** *Fam* **to give sb a b.** *(as punishment)* donner des coups de ceinture *ou* administrer une correction à qn; *(in fight)* rouer qn de coups; *(in match, competition etc)* mettre la pâtée à qn

beltway ['beltweɪ] N *Am Transp* (boulevard *m*) périphérique *m*; *Fig Pol* **inside the b.** à Washington

beluga [bɪ'lu:gə] N *(fish)* bélouga *m*, béluga *m*; *(whale)* bélouga *m*, béluga *m*, baleine *f* blanche; *Culin (caviar)* caviar *m* de bélouga *ou* béluga

belvedere ['belvɪˌdɪə(r)] N *Archit* belvédère *m*

bemoan [bɪ'məʊn] VT pleurer, se lamenter sur; **he bemoaned the loss of his freedom** il pleura la perte de sa liberté; **to b. one's fate** pleurer sur son sort; **she was bemoaning the fact that they had no money** elle se lamentait de ce qu'ils n'avaient pas d'argent

bemuse [bɪ'mju:z] VT déconcerter, dérouter, rendre perplexe

bemused [bɪ'mju:zd] ADJ déconcerté, dérouté, perplexe; **he gave a b. smile** il sourit d'un air *ou* il eut un sourire déconcerté

ben [ben] N *Ir & Scot Geog* sommet *m*, mont *m*
▸▸ ***Ben Nevis*** = point culminant de la Grande-Bretagne, en Écosse (1343m)

bench [bentʃ] N **1** *(seat)* banc *m*; *(caned, padded)* banquette *f*; *(in auditorium)* gradin *m*; **park b.** banc *m* public
2 *Sport* banc *m (pour les joueurs qui ne sont pas sur le terrain)*; **on the b.** en réserve
3 *Br Parl* banc *m*; **the government benches** les bancs du gouvernement
4 *(work table)* établi *m*
5 *Law (seat)* banc *m*; **the b.** *(judge)* la cour, le juge; *(judges as group)* les juges, les magistrats; **address your remarks to the b.** adressez-vous à la cour; **he serves** *or* **sits on the b.** *(permanent office)* il est juge; *(for particular case)* il siège au tribunal
COMP *(lathe, vice)* d'établi
VT *Am Sport* retirer du jeu
▸▸ *Sport* ***bench press*** développé-couché *m*; ***bench seat*** *(in vehicle)* banquette *f*; *Am Law* ***bench trial*** procès *m* sans jury; *Law* ***bench warrant*** mandat *m* d'arrêt

benchmark ['bentʃˌmɑ:k] N repère *m*; *Constr (in surveying)* repère *m* de nivellement; *Fig* repère *m*, point *m* de référence
COMP *(decision)* de base, de référence
▸▸ *Can Admin* ***benchmark position*** poste-repère *m*; *Comput* ***benchmark programme*** programme *m* d'évaluation des performances; *Comput* ***benchmark test*** test *m* d'évaluation (de programme)

benchmarking ['bentʃmɑ:kɪŋ] N *Ind & Tech* benchmarking *m*

benchtest ['bentʃˌtest] *Tech* N banc *m* d'essai
VT faire passer au banc d'essai

BEND [bend]

VT	
• plier **1**	• courber **1, 2**
• tordre **2**	• diriger **4**
VI	
• se courber **1**	• céder **3**
N	
• virage **1**	• coude **1**
• pli **2**	

(pt & pp **bent** [bent]*)*
VT **1** *(arm, finger)* plier; *(knee, leg)* plier, fléchir; *(back, body)* courber; *(head)* pencher, baisser; **they bent their heads over their books** ils se penchèrent sur leurs livres; *Rel* **to b. one's head in prayer** baisser la tête pour prier; **to b. sb to one's will** plier qn à sa volonté; *Br Fam* **he likes to b. the elbow** il sait lever le coude, il aime bien picoler; *Fam* **to b. sb's ear** casser les oreilles à qn
2 *(pipe, wire)* tordre, courber; *(branch, tree)* courber, faire ployer; *(bow)* bander, arquer; **to b. sth at right angles** plier qch à angle droit; **he bent the rod out of shape** il a tordu la barre; **to b. the rules** faire une entorse au règlement
3 *(deflect ▸ light)* réfracter; *(▸ ray)* infléchir; *(▸ stream)* dériver, détourner
4 *Literary (direct, turn)* diriger; **they bent their steps towards home** ils se dirigèrent *ou* ils dirigèrent leurs pas vers la maison; **they bent themselves to the task** ils se sont attelés à la tâche
5 *Naut (fasten ▸ cable, rope)* étalinguer; *(▸ sail)* enverguer
VI **1** *(arm, knee, leg)* plier; *(person)* se courber, se pencher; *(head)* se pencher; *(rod, wire)* plier, se courber; *(branch, tree)* ployer, plier; **to b. under the burden/the weight** ployer sous le fardeau/le poids; **she bent over the counter** elle s'est penchée par-dessus le comptoir; **he bent backwards/forwards** il s'est penché en arrière/en avant
2 *(river, road)* faire un coude, tourner; **the road bends to the left** la route tourne à gauche
3 *(submit)* céder; **the people refused to b. to the colonial forces** le peuple a refusé de se soumettre aux forces coloniales; **the government bent to pressure from the unions** l'administration a cédé à la pression des syndicats
N **1** *(in road)* virage *m*, tournant *m*; *(in river)* méandre *m*, coude *m*; *(in pipe, rod)* coude *m*; **to take a b. at speed** prendre un virage à toute vitesse; **the road makes a b. to the right** la route fait un coude vers la droite; **bends for 7 miles** *(sign)* virages sur 10 km; *Fam* **to drive sb round the b.** rendre qn dingue; *Fam* **he's completely round the b.** il est complètement dingue
2 *(in arm)* pli *m*, saignée *f*; *(in knee)* pli *m*, flexion *f*; **she did a couple of forward bends** elle s'est penchée plusieurs fois en avant
3 *Naut (knot)* nœud *m* (de jonction)
• **bends** NPL *Med* **the bends** la maladie des caissons; **to get the bends** être atteint par la maladie des caissons

▸**bend back** VT SEP replier, recourber
VI **1** *(person)* se pencher en arrière **2** *(blade, tube)* se recourber

▸**bend down** VT SEP *(branch, tree)* faire ployer; *(blade, tube)* replier, recourber
VI **1** *(person)* se courber, se baisser **2** *(branch, tree)* plier, ployer

▸**bend over** VT SEP replier, recourber
VI se pencher; *Fig* **to b. over backwards to please (sb)** se donner beaucoup de mal pour faire plaisir (à qn)

bended ['bendɪd] ADJ *Literary* **on one's b. knees, on b. knee** *(ask for something)* à genoux; **to go down on b. knee** *or* **knees** *(kneel down)* se mettre à genoux, s'agenouiller; *Fig* **to go down on one's b. knees to sb** *(beg)* supplier qn

bender ['bendə(r)] N **1** *Fam (drinking session)* beuverie *f*; **to go on a b.** faire la noce **2** *very Fam (homosexual)* pédale *f*, tantouze *f*, = terme injurieux désignant un homosexuel **3** *Am Fam Sport* balle *f* à effet□

beneath [bɪ'ni:θ] PREP **1** *(under)* sous; **buried b. tons of rubble** enfoui sous des tonnes de gravats; **the ship sank b. the waves** le navire a sombré sous les vagues
2 *(below)* **the valley was spread out b. us** la vallée s'étalait sous nos pieds
3 *(unworthy of)* indigne de; **she thinks the work is b. her** elle estime que le travail est indigne d'elle; **b. contempt** parfaitement méprisable
4 *(socially inferior to)* inférieur *(socialement)*; **he married b. him** il a fait une mésalliance; **she thinks everybody's b. her** elle s'imagine que tout le monde lui est inférieur
ADV *(underneath)* dessous, en dessous; **from b.** d'en dessous

Benedictine N **1** [benɪ'dɪktɪn] *Rel* bénédictin(e) *m,f* **2** [benɪ'dɪkti:n] *(liqueur)* Bénédictine® *f*
ADJ [benɪ'dɪktɪn] *Rel* bénédictin

benediction [ˌbenɪ'dɪkʃən] N *Rel & Fig (blessing)* bénédiction *f*; *(service)* salut *m*

benefaction [ˌbenɪ'fækʃən] N **1** *(good deed)* acte *m* de bienfaisance **2** *Fin (donation)* don *m*, donation *f*

benefactor ['benɪfæktə(r)] N bienfaiteur *m*

benefice ['benɪfɪs] N *Rel* bénéfice *m*

beneficence [bɪ'nefɪsəns] N *Literary* **1** *(kindness)* bienveillance *f*, bienfaisance *f* **2** *(good deed)* acte *m* de bienfaisance, bienfait *m*

beneficent [bɪ'nefɪsənt] ADJ *Literary (person, regime)* bienfaisant, généreux; *(change, effect)* bienfaisant, salutaire

beneficial [ˌbenɪ'fɪʃəl] ADJ *(good, useful)* avantageux, profitable; *(effect)* salutaire; **legislation b. to the self-employed** des lois favorables aux travailleurs non-salariés; **the holiday proved highly b.** les vacances ont été extrêmement bénéfiques; **vitamins are b. to health** les vitamines sont bonnes pour la santé
▸▸ *Law* ***beneficial owner*** usufruitier(ère) *m,f*

beneficiary [ˌbenɪ'fɪʃərɪ] *(pl* **beneficiaries***)* N **1** *(of insurance policy, trust)* bénéficiaire *mf*; *Law (of will)* bénéficiaire *mf*, légataire *mf*; *(of family allowance)* allocataire *mf*; *Fig* **the main beneficiaries of the new law will be working mothers** ce sont les mères qui travaillent qui bénéficieront le plus de la nouvelle loi **2** *Rel* bénéficier *m*

benefit ['benɪfɪt] *(pt & pp* **benefited** *or* **benefitted**, *cont* **benefiting** *or* **benefitting***)* N **1** *(advantage)* avantage *m*; **to have the b. of sth** bénéficier de qch; **the benefits of a good education** les avantages *mpl* ou les bienfaits *mpl* d'une bonne éducation; **she is starting to feel the benefits of the treatment** elle commence à ressentir les bienfaits du traitement; **she did it for the b. of the whole family** elle a agi pour le bien-être de toute la famille; **I'm saying this for your b.** je dis cela pour toi *ou* pour ton bien; **the holiday wasn't of much b. to him** les vacances ne lui ont pas fait tellement de bien; **it's to your b. to watch your diet** il est dans votre intérêt de surveiller ce que vous mangez; **this law is to the b. of the wealthy** cette loi favorise les gens aisés; **to offer sb the b. of one's experience** faire profiter qn de son expérience; **with the b. of hindsight, I now see I was wrong** avec le recul *ou* rétrospectivement, je m'aperçois que j'avais tort; **to give sb the b. of the doubt** laisser *ou* accorder à qn le bénéfice du doute; *Fin* **benefits** *(to employee)* avantages *mpl* sociaux **2** *Fin (payment)* allocation *f*, prestation *f*; **social security benefits** prestations *fpl* sociales; *Am* **tax b.** dégrèvement *m*, allègement *m* fiscal **3** *(performance)* spectacle *m (au profit d'une association caritative)*

VT *(do good to)* faire du bien à; *(bring financial profit to)* profiter à; **a steady exchange rate benefits trade** un change stable est avantageux pour le commerce *ou* favorise le commerce; **whom does it b.?** qui en bénéficie?

VI **to b. by** *or* **from sth** bénéficier de qch, profiter de qch, tirer avantage de qch; **he will b. from the experience** l'expérience lui sera bénéfique; **the novel would b. greatly from judicious editing** le roman gagnerait beaucoup à être révisé de façon judicieuse; **you would b. from a stay in the country** un séjour à la campagne vous ferait du bien; **who benefits most from his death?** à qui sa mort profite-t-elle le plus?

►► *Rel & Hist* ***benefit of clergy*** bénéfice *m* de clergie; ***benefit concert*** concert *m (au profit d'une association caritative)*; *Sport* ***benefit match*** match *m (au profit d'un joueur auquel on rend hommage)*; *Fin* ***benefits package*** *(to employee)* avantages *mpl* sociaux; *Theat* ***benefit performance*** représentation *f* de bienfaisance; *Am Fin* ***benefit society*** société *f* de prévoyance, mutuelle *f*

Benelux ['benɪlʌks] **N** Bénélux *m*; **the B. countries** les pays du Bénélux

benevolence [bɪ'nevələns] **N 1** *(kindness)* bienveillance *f*, bienfaisance *f* **2** *(good deed)* acte *m* de bienfaisance, bienfait *m*

benevolent [bɪ'nevələnt] **ADJ 1** *(kindly)* bienveillant; **to feel b. towards sb** être bien disposé envers qn **2** *(donor)* généreux, charitable; *(organization)* de bienfaisance

►► *Hist* ***benevolent despot*** despote *m* éclairé; *Hist* ***benevolent despotism*** despotisme *m* éclairé; *Fin* ***benevolent fund*** fonds *m* de prévoyance; *Admin* ***benevolent society*** association *f* de bienfaisance

benevolently [bɪ'nevələntlɪ] **ADV** avec bienveillance

BEng [,bi:'eŋ] **N** *Br Univ* (*abbr* **Bachelor of Engineering**) *(person)* = titulaire d'une licence d'ingénierie; *(qualification)* licence *f* d'ingénierie

Bengal [,beŋ'gɔ:l] **N** Bengale *m*

►► *Br Tech* ***Bengal light*** feu *m* de Bengale; ***Bengal tiger*** tigre *m* du Bengale

Bengali [,beŋ'gɔ:lɪ], **Bengalese** [,beŋgə'li:z] **N 1** *(person)* Bengali *mf*, Bengalais(e) *m,f* **2** *(language)* bengali *m*

ADJ bengali, bengalais

COMP *(history)* du Bangladesh; *(teacher)* de bengali

benighted [bɪ'naɪtɪd] **ADJ** *Literary (ignorant* ► *person)* plongé dans (les ténèbres de) l'ignorance; (► *mind)* étroit; (► *policy)* aveugle

benign [bɪ'naɪn] **ADJ 1** *(kind* ► *person)* affable, aimable; (► *smile)* bienveillant; *Pol* (► *power, system)* bienfaisant, salutaire **2** *(harmless) & Med (illness, tumour)* bénin(igne) **3** *(temperate* ► *climate)* doux (douce), clément

Benin [be'ni:n] **N** Bénin *m*

Benjamin ['bendʒəmɪn] **PR N** *Bible* Benjamin

benny ['benɪ] (*pl* **bennies**) **N** *Fam Drugs slang* (comprimé *m* de) Benzédrine®□ *f*

bent [bent] *pt & pp of* **bend**

ADJ 1 *(curved* ► *tree, tube, wire)* tordu, courbé; (► *branch)* courbé; (► *back)* voûté; (► *person)* voûté, tassé; *(out of shape* ► *aerial, coathanger)* tordu; (► *axle, lever)* coudé; *Am Fam Fig* **b. out of shape** *(angry, upset)* dans tous ses états

2 *(dented)* cabossé, bosselé

3 *Br (determined)* **he's b. on becoming an actor** il est décidé à *ou* veut absolument devenir acteur; **to be b. on self-destruction** être porté à l'autodestruction

4 *Br Fam (dishonest)* pourri

5 *Br very Fam Pej (homosexual)* homo, gay; **as b. as a nine bob note** *or* **as a three pound note** pédé comme un phoque

N *(liking)* penchant *m*, goût *m*; *(aptitude)* aptitudes *fpl*, dispositions *fpl*; **they're of an artistic b.** ils sont tournés vers les arts; **she has a natural b. for music** *(liking)* elle a un goût naturel pour la musique; *(talent)* elle a des dispositions naturelles pour la musique; **he followed his (natural) b.** il a suivi son penchant *ou* son inclination

►► *Bot* ***bent grass*** agrostide *f*

bentwood ['bentwʊd] *Carp* **N** bois *m* courbé

COMP *(chair, table)* en bois courbé

benumbed [bɪ'nʌmd] **ADJ** *Literary* **b. by the** *or* **with cold** *(person)* transi de froid; *(fingers, toes)* engourdi par le froid; **her mind was b. with fear** elle était transie de *ou* paralysée par la peur

benzene ['benzi:n] *Chem* **N** benzène *m*

►► ***benzene ring*** noyau *m* benzénique

benzin ['benzi:n], **benzine** [ben'zi:n] **N** *Chem* benzine *f*

benzodiazepine [,benzəʊdaɪ'æzəpi:n] **N** *Pharm* benzodiazépine *f*

benzol ['benzɒl], **benzole** ['benzəʊl] **N** *Chem* benzol *m*

bequeath [bɪ'kwi:ð] **VT** *(pass on)* transmettre, léguer; *Law (in will)* léguer; **her father bequeathed her his fortune** son père lui a légué sa fortune; **they've bequeathed nothing to us but a ruined economy** ils ne nous ont légué qu'une économie en ruine

bequest [bɪ'kwest] **N** legs *m*; **she made a b. of £2,000 to her favourite charity** elle a légué 2000 livres à l'œuvre de bienfaisance qu'elle préférait

berate [bɪ'reɪt] **VT** réprimander; **he berated them for being late** il leur a reproché d'être en retard

Berber ['bɜ:bə(r)] **N 1** *(person)* Berbère *mf* **2** *(language)* berbère *m*

ADJ berbère

bereave [bɪ'ri:v] (*pt & pp* **bereaved** *or* **bereft** [-'reft]) **VT** priver, déposséder; **the war bereaved them of their two sons** la guerre leur a pris leurs deux fils, ils ont perdu leurs deux fils à la guerre

bereaved [bɪ'ri:vd] **ADJ** affligé, endeuillé; **a b. mother** une mère qui vient de perdre son enfant; **he's recently b.** il a perdu quelqu'un récemment

NPL **the b.** la famille du défunt

bereavement [bɪ'ri:vmənt] **N** deuil *m*; **owing to a recent b.** en raison d'un deuil récent; **she has suffered a b.** elle a été affligée par un deuil; **in his b.** dans son deuil; **a tragic b.** une perte cruelle

►► ***bereavement counselling*** = service d'aide psychologique aux personnes frappées par un deuil; ***bereavement counsellor*** = personne apportant une aide psychologique aux personnes frappées par un deuil

bereft [bɪ'reft] *Formal or Literary pt & pp of* **bereave**

ADJ privé; **b. of all hope** complètement désespéré; **I feel utterly b.** je me sens totalement seul; **to leave sb b. of speech** rendre qn muet

beret ['bereɪ] **N** béret *m*

berg [bɜ:g] **N** *(iceberg)* iceberg *m*

bergamot ['bɜ:gəmɒt] **N** *(fruit)* bergamote *f*; *(tree)* bergamotier *m*

►► ***bergamot oil*** essence *f* de bergamote

beriberi [,berɪ'berɪ] **N** *Med* béribéri *m*

berk [bɜ:k] **N** *Br Fam* andouille *f*, debile *mf*; **to make a complete b. of oneself** se conduire comme une andouille; **to feel a right b.** se sentir con

Berlin [bɜ:'lɪn] **N** Berlin; **East B.** Berlin-Est; **West B.** Berlin-Ouest

►► ***the Berlin airlift*** le pont aérien de Berlin; ***the Berlin Wall*** le mur de Berlin

Berliner [bɜ:'lɪnə(r)] **N** Berlinois(e) *m,f*

berm, berme [bɜ:m] **N** *Archit* berme *f*

Bermuda [bə'mju:də] **N** les Bermudes *fpl*

• **Bermudas** **NPL** *(shorts)* bermuda *m*

►► *Am* ***Bermuda Plan*** tarif *m* chambre avec petit déjeuner anglais; *Naut* ***Bermuda rig*** gréement *m* Marconi; ***Bermuda shorts*** bermuda *m*; ***the Bermuda Triangle*** le triangle des Bermudes

Bern [bɜ:n] **N** *Geog* Berne

Bernese [,bɜ:'ni:z] **N** Bernois(e) *m,f*

ADJ bernois

►► ***the Bernese Alps*** l'Oberland *m* bernois

berried ['berɪd] **ADJ 1** *Bot* à baies, couvert de baies **2** *Zool (crustacean)* œuvé

berry ['berɪ] (*pl* **berries**, *pt & pp* **berried**) **N 1** *Bot & Culin (fruit)* baie *f*; **to go b. picking** aller cueillir des baies **2** *Zool (of crustacean)* œuf *m*; **lobster in b.** homard *m* œuvé

VI **to go berrying** aller cueillir des baies

berserk [bə'zɜ:k] **ADJ** fou furieux (folle furieuse); **to go b.** *(person)* devenir fou furieux; *(crowd)* se déchaîner

berth [bɜ:θ] **N 1** *Naut & Rail (bunk)* couchette *f*

2 *Naut (in harbour)* mouillage *m*, poste *m* d'amarrage; *(distance)* distance *f*; **to give a ship a wide b.** éviter *ou* parer un navire, passer au large d'un navire

3 *Br Fam (job)* boulot *m*; **to find a soft** *or* **an easy b.** trouver un emploi pépère

4 *Br (idiom)* **to give sb a wide b.** éviter qn (à tout prix)

VI *Naut (at dock)* venir à quai, accoster; *(at anchor)* mouiller; **when do we b.?** quand accostons-nous?

VT *Naut (dock)* amarrer, faire accoster; *(assign place to)* donner un poste d'amarrage à

berthing ['bɜ:θɪŋ] **N** *Naut (of ship)* abordage *m* à quai

beryl ['berəl] **N** *Miner* béryl *m*

beryllium [be'rɪlɪəm] **N** *Chem* béryllium *m*

beseech [bɪ'si:tʃ] (*pt & pp* **beseeched** *or* **besought** [-'sɔ:t]) **VT** *Formal or Literary* **1** *(ask for)* solliciter, implorer **2** *(entreat)* implorer, supplier; **to b. sb to do sth** implorer *ou* supplier qn de faire qch; **please, I b. you** s'il vous plaît, je vous en supplie

beseeching [bɪ'si:tʃɪŋ] **ADJ** suppliant, implorant

beset [bɪ'set] (*pt & pp* **beset**, *cont* **besetting**) **VT** *(usu passive)* **1** *(assail)* assaillir, harceler; **I was b. by** *or* **with doubt** j'étais assailli par le doute; **the whole project is b. with financial difficulties** le projet pose énormément de problèmes sur le plan financier; **they are b. with problems** ils sont assaillis de problèmes **2** *(surround)* encercler; **b. by the enemy** cerné par l'ennemi

besetting [bɪ'setɪŋ] **ADJ** *Formal (idea, thought etc)* obsédant; **his b. sin was greed** la cupidité était son plus grand défaut

beside [bɪ'saɪd] **PREP 1** *(next to)* à côté de, auprès de; **walk b. me** marchez à côté de moi; **he wanted to keep his family b. him** il voulait garder sa famille auprès de lui; **a plate with a glass b. it** une assiette avec un verre à côté; **a house b. the sea** une maison au bord de la mer

2 *(as compared with)* à côté de, par rapport à; **b. him everyone else appears slow** à côté de lui, tous les autres paraissent lents

3 *(in addition to)* en plus de, outre; *(apart from)* à part, excepté; **other people b. ourselves** d'autres (personnes) que nous

4 *(wide of)* **that is b. the point** *or* **question** cela n'a rien à voir (avec l'affaire en question); **whether you arrived or not is b. the point** que tu sois arrivé ou non n'est pas le problème; **b. oneself (with joy/anger)** fou (folle) (de joie/colère); **b. oneself with enthusiasm** débordant d'enthousiasme

Attention: ne pas confondre avec **besides**.

besides [bɪ'saɪdz] **PREP 1** *(in addition to)* en plus de, outre; **there are three (other) candidates b. yourself** il y a trois (autres) candidats à part vous; **what other skills do you have b. languages?** quelles compétences avez-vous à part *ou* outre les langues?; **have you got it in anything b. black?** est-ce que vous l'avez dans d'autres couleurs qu'en noir?; **that's b. what you already owe me** c'est en plus de ce que tu me dois déjà; **b. being old, she's also extremely deaf** non seulement elle est vieille, mais elle est également très sourde; **b. which that book is out of print** sans compter que ce livre est épuisé **2** *(with negatives) (apart from)* hormis, excepté; **nobody b. me** personne à part moi; **she said nothing b. what we knew already** elle n'a rien dit que nous ne sachions déjà

ADV 1 *(in addition)* en plus, en outre; **and more b.** et d'autres encore; **he owns two flats and a country house b.** il est propriétaire de deux appartements ainsi que d'une maison à la campagne; **he knows the rudiments but little else b.** il connaît les rudiments mais pas grand-chose d'autre *ou* de plus **2** *(furthermore)* en plus; **it's an excellent play and, b., the tickets aren't expensive** la pièce est excellente et en plus, les billets ne coûtent pas cher

Attention: ne pas confondre avec **beside**.

besiege [bɪˈsiːdʒ] **VT 1** *Mil (surround ▸ town)* assiéger; *Fig (▸ person, office)* assaillir; **the tourists were besieged by beggars** les touristes étaient assaillis par des mendiants **2** *(harass)* assaillir, harceler; **besieged by doubt** rongé *ou* assailli par le doute; **we've been besieged by requests for help** nous avons été assaillis de demandes d'aide

besmirch [bɪˈsmɜːtʃ] **VT** *Literary (make dirty)* souiller; *Fig (tarnish)* souiller; **to b. sb's name** souiller *ou* ternir le nom de qn

besom **N 1** [ˈbiːzəm] *(broom)* balai *m* **2** [ˈbɪzəm] *Scot Fam Pej (woman)* bonne femme *f*; **she's a cheeky b.!** elle est gonflée!

besotted [bɪˈsɒtɪd] **ADJ 1** *(infatuated)* fou (folle), épris; **to be b. with sb** *(in love)* être fou *ou* follement épris de qn; **to be b. with sth** *(car, computer etc)* adorer qch; **she is b. with her grandchildren** elle est folle de ses petits enfants **2** *(foolish)* idiot; **b. with drink** abruti (par l'alcool), soûl

bespatter [bɪˈspætə(r)] **VT** *Literary (splash)* éclabousser; *Fig (tarnish)* souiller, éclabousser; **bespattered with mud** tout maculé de boue

bespeak [bɪˈspiːk] *(pt* **bespoke** [-ˈspəʊk], *pp* **bespoke** *or* **bespoken** [-ˈspəʊkən]) **VT** *Literary (be sign of)* démontrer, témoigner de; **her action bespeaks kindness** son geste témoigne de sa bonté; **their hesitation bespeaks moral weakness** leur hésitation révèle une faiblesse morale

bespectacled [bɪˈspektəkəld] **ADJ** qui porte des lunettes, à lunettes

bespoke [bɪˈspəʊk] *pt of* **bespeak**

ADJ *(shoemaker, tailor)* à façon; *(shoes, suit)* fait sur mesure

besprinkle [bɪˈsprɪŋkəl] **VT** *Literary (with sugar, talcum)* saupoudrer; *(with liquid)* asperger, arroser

Bess [bes] **PR N** *Fam* **Good Queen B.** = la reine Elisabeth Ière d'Angleterre

BEST [best]

ADJ	
• meilleur **1**	• plus beau **2**
ADV	
• mieux	
N	
• le meilleur **1, 2**	• le mieux **2**

ADJ 1 *(superl of* **good***)* meilleur; **it's one of the b. films I've ever seen** c'est un des meilleurs films que j'aie jamais vus; **she's my b. friend** c'est ma meilleure amie; **may the b. man win** que le meilleur gagne; **she gave him the b. years of her life** elle lui a sacrifié les plus belles années de sa vie; **I'm doing what is b. for the family** je fais ce qu'il y a de mieux pour la famille; **she knows what's b. for her** elle sait ce qui lui va *ou* convient le mieux; **I only want what's b. for you** je ne veux que ce qu'il y a de mieux pour toi; **they think it b. not to answer** ils croient qu'il vaut mieux ne pas répondre; **it's b. not to smoke at all** il est préférable de ne pas fumer du tout; **what's the b. thing to do?** quelle est la meilleure chose à faire?; **the b. thing (to do) is to keep quiet** le mieux, c'est de ne rien dire; **it would be b. to…, the b. plan would be to…** le mieux serait de…; **the b. thing about it is that it's free/is that she didn't even realize** le mieux, c'est que c'est gratuit/c'est qu'elle ne s'en est même pas rendu compte; **getting that job in Paris was the b. thing that ever happened to him** décrocher cet emploi à Paris est la meilleure chose qui lui soit arrivée; **b. of all** le meilleur de tout; *Com* **b. before October 2008** *(on packaging)* à consommer de préférence avant octobre 2008

2 *(reserved for special occasions)* plus beau (belle); **she was dressed in her b. clothes** elle portait ses plus beaux vêtements

3 *(idiom)* **the b. part of** la plus grande partie de; **she spent the b. part of the day working** elle a passé le plus clair de la journée à travailler; **I waited for the b. part of an hour** j'ai attendu près d'une heure *ou* presque une heure

ADV *(superl of* **well***)* mieux; **he does it b.** c'est lui qui le fait le mieux; **Tuesday would suit me b.** le mieux pour moi serait mardi; **the b.-kept garden in the village** le jardin le mieux entretenu du village; **the b.-looking women** les femmes les plus jolies; **which film did you like b.?** quel est le film que vous avez préféré?; **you know b.** c'est vous (qui êtes) le mieux placé pour en juger; **he's b. able to decide** il est le plus à même de décider; **do as you think b.** faites comme bon vous semble(ra); **I comforted her as b. I could** je l'ai consolée de mon mieux *ou* du mieux que j'ai pu; **you had b. apologize to her** vous feriez mieux de lui présenter vos excuses; **these things are b. left to the police** il vaut mieux laisser à la police le soin de s'occuper de ces choses-là

N 1 *(most outstanding person, thing, part etc)* le (la) meilleur(e) *m,f*; **it/she is the b. there is** c'est le meilleur/la meilleure qui soit; **he wants her to have the b.** il veut qu'elle ait ce qu'il y a de mieux, il veut ce qu'il y a de mieux pour elle; **your parents only want the b. for you** tes parents ne veulent que ce qu'il y a de mieux pour toi; **only the b. will do** ne fera l'affaire que ce qu'il y a de meilleur; **the b. of it is that…** le plus beau de l'affaire, c'est que…; **the b. you can say about him is that…** le mieux qu'on puisse dire à son sujet c'est que…; **even the b. of us can make mistakes** tout le monde peut se tromper; **to get** *or* **to have the b. of the bargain** avoir la part belle; **to get the b. of sb in an argument** l'emporter sur qn dans une discussion; **she wants the b. of both worlds** elle veut tout avoir

2 *(greatest, highest degree)* le mieux, le meilleur; **they're the b. of friends** ce sont les meilleurs amis du monde; **to the b. of my knowledge/recollection** autant que je sache/je me souvienne; **the b. of luck!** bonne chance!; **(even) at the b. of times** même dans les meilleurs moments; **she's not the calmest of people, (even) at the b. of times** ce n'est pas quelqu'un de très calme de toute façon; **it's journalism at its b.** c'est du journalisme de haut niveau; **the garden is at its b. in spring** c'est au printemps que le jardin est le plus beau; **he was at his b. last night** il était en pleine forme hier soir; **I'm not at my b. in the morning** je ne suis pas en forme le matin; **this is Shakespeare at his b.** voilà du meilleur Shakespeare; **I am in the b. of health** je me porte à merveille, je suis en excellente santé; **to do one's b.** faire de son mieux *ou* tout son possible; **do your b.!** faites de votre mieux!, faites pour le mieux!; **do your b. to finish on time** faites de votre mieux pour finir à temps; **it was the b. we could do** nous ne pouvions pas faire mieux; **do the b. you can** *(given the circumstances)* arrangez-vous; *(in exam)* faites de votre mieux; **to get the b. out of sb/sth** tirer un maximum de qn/qch; **to bring out the b. in people** faire ressortir les bons côtés des gens; **to look one's b.** *(gen)* être resplendissant; **she looks her b. with short hair** les cheveux courts l'avantagent; **we'll have to make the b. of the situation** il faudra nous accommoder de la situation (du mieux que nous pouvons); **to make the b. of a bad bargain** *or* **job** faire contre mauvaise fortune bon cœur

3 *(nicest clothes)* **they were (dressed) in their (Sunday) b.** ils étaient endimanchés *ou* portaient leurs habits du dimanche; **I keep it for b.** *(of dress, suit etc)* je le garde pour des occasions spéciales

4 *(good wishes)* **(I wish you) all the b.** (je vous souhaite) bonne chance

5 *Sport (winning majority)* **we played the b. of three (games)** le jeu consistait à gagner *ou* il fallait gagner deux parties sur trois; **let's make it the b. of five** le premier qui remporte trois jeux *ou* parties sur cinq a gagné

VT *Arch (get advantage over)* l'emporter sur; *(defeat)* vaincre

• **at best ADV** au mieux; **this is, at b., a temporary solution** c'est, au mieux, une solution temporaire

• **for the best ADV** pour le mieux; **it's all for the b.** c'est pour le mieux; **he meant it for the b.** il avait les meilleures intentions du monde; **we must hope for the b.** il faut être optimiste

▸▸ *TV & Cin* **best boy** aide-électricien *m*; **best man** garçon *m* d'honneur; *Com* **best practice** meilleure pratique *f*

BEST MAN

Dans les pays anglo-saxons, le garçon d'honneur présente l'alliance au marié et prononce un discours lors de la réception de mariage.

best-before date **N** *Culin (for foodstuffs)* date *f* limite de consommation; *(for batteries, car oil etc)* date *f* limite d'utilisation

bestial [ˈbestɪəl] **ADJ** bestial

bestiality [ˌbestɪˈælətɪ] *(pl* **bestialities***)* **N 1** *(of behaviour, character)* bestialité *f* **2** *(act)* acte *m* bestial **3** *(sexual practice)* bestialité *f*

bestially [ˈbestɪəlɪ] **ADV** avec bestialité, bestialement

best-in-class **N** *(at dog show)* meilleur *m* de groupe

bestir [bɪˈstɜː(r)] *(pt & pp* **bestirred**, *cont* **bestirring***)* **VT to b. oneself** s'activer

best-of-breed **N** *(at dog show)* meilleur *m* de race

bestow [bɪˈstəʊ] **VT** *Formal (favour, gift, praise)* accorder; *(award, honour)* conférer, accorder; **to b. sth on sb** accorder *ou* conférer qch à qn

bestowal [bɪˈstəʊəl] **N** *Formal (of favour, honour, title)* octroi *m*

bestride [bɪˈstraɪd] *(pt* **bestrode** [-ˈstrəʊd], *pp* **bestridden** [-ˈstrɪdən]) **VT** *Literary* **1** *(straddle ▸ bicycle, house)* enfourcher; *(▸ chair)* se mettre à califourchon *ou* à cheval sur **2** *(span ▸ river)* enjamber, franchir; *(▸ obstacle)* enjamber

best-seller **N 1** *(book)* best-seller *m*, succès *m* de librairie; *(hi-fi, record)* article *m* qui se vend bien; **to be on the b. list** être un best-seller **2** *(author)* auteur *m* à succès

best-selling **ADJ** *(book, item)* à fort tirage; *(author)* à succès

besuited [bəˈsuːtəd] **ADJ** qui porte/portait un costume

bet [bet] *(pt & pp* **bet** *or* **betted**, *cont* **betting***)* **N** pari *m*; **do you want to make a b.?** tu veux parier?; **to win/to lose a b.** gagner/perdre un pari; **he lay** *or* **put** *or* **placed a b. on the race** il a parié *ou* il a fait un pari sur la course; **place your bets!** faites vos jeux!; **all bets are off** les paris sont annulés; **they're taking bets** ils prennent des paris; *Fig* **it's a good** *or* **safe b. that they'll win** ils vont gagner à coup sûr; *Fam Fig* **your best b. is to take a taxi** tu ferais mieux de prendre un taxi

VT *also Fig* parier; **I b. her £5 he wouldn't come** j'ai parié 5 livres avec elle qu'il ne viendrait pas; **I'll b. you anything you want** je te parie tout ce que tu veux; **I'm willing to b. she's lying** je suis prête à parier qu'elle ment; *Fam* **I b. you won't do it!** (t'es pas) chiche!; *Fam* **I'll b. my bottom dollar** *or* **my boots he loses** il va perdre, j'en mettrais ma main au feu; *Fam* **b. you I will!** chiche (que je le fais)!

VI parier, miser; **to b. against/on sth** parier contre/sur qch; **which horse did you b. on?** quel cheval as-tu joué?, sur quel cheval as-tu misé?; **to b. 5 to 1** parier *ou* miser à 5 contre 1; **(do you) want to b.?** *(as challenge)* tu paries?; *Fam* **he said he'd phone me – well, I wouldn't b. on it!** il a dit qu'il me téléphonerait – à ta place, je ne me ferais pas trop d'illusions!; *Fam* **I wouldn't b. on getting your money back** à mon avis, tu n'es pas près de revoir ton argent; *Fam* **are you going to the party? – you b.!** tu vas à la soirée? – et comment! *ou* qu'est-ce que tu crois?; *Fam* **I'll tell him off – I'll**

b.! *(you will)* je vais lui dire ses quatre vérités – j'en doute pas!; *(you won't)* je vais lui dire ses quatre vérités – mon œil!

beta-blocker [-'blɒkə(r)] **N** *Med* bêtabloquant *m*

betacarotene [,bi:tə'kærəti:n] **N** bêtacarotène *m*

beta-test **VT** *Comput* conduire les bêta-tests sur, conduire les essais approfondis sur

beta-testing **N** *Comput* bêta-tests *mpl*

betel ['bi:təl] *Bot*
N bétel *m*
►► ***betel nut*** noix *f* d'arec; ***betel palm*** aréquier *m*, arec *m*

Bethlehem ['beθlɪhem] **N** *Bible* Bethléem

betide [bɪ'taɪd] **VI** *Literary* advenir

betimes [bɪ'taɪmz] **ADV** *Arch (early)* de bonne heure, tôt; *(in good time)* à temps; *(soon)* bientôt

betoken [bɪ'təʊkən] **VT** *Formal (indicate)* être l'indice de, révéler; *(augur)* présager, annoncer

betray [bɪ'treɪ] **VT** **1** *(be disloyal to* ► *friend, principle)* trahir; *(*► *husband, wife)* tromper, trahir; *(*► *country)* trahir, être traître à; *Fig* **my face betrayed me** mon visage m'a trahi
2 *(denounce)* trahir, dénoncer; *(hand over)* trahir, livrer; **he betrayed the rebels to the police** il a livré les rebelles à la police
3 *(confidence, hope, trust)* trahir, tromper
4 *(disclose* ► *secret, truth)* trahir, divulguer; *(*► *grief, happiness)* trahir, laisser voir; **her voice betrayed her nervousness** sa voix laissait deviner son inquiétude

betrayal [bɪ'treɪəl] **N** **1** *(of person, principle)* trahison *f*
2 *(act)* (acte *m* de) trahison *f*; **it's a b. of one's country** c'est une trahison envers son pays
3 *(of confidence, trust)* abus *m*, trahison *f*
4 *(of secret, truth)* trahison *f*, divulgation *f*

betrayer [bɪ'treɪə(r)] **N** traître(esse) *m,f*

betrothal [bɪ'trəʊðəl] **N** *Arch* fiançailles *fpl*; **her b. to the prince** ses fiançailles avec le prince

betrothed [bɪ'trəʊðd] *Arch* **ADJ** fiancé, promis; **she is b. to our son** elle est fiancée à *ou* avec notre fils
N fiancé(e) *m,f*, promis(e) *m,f*

BETTER ['betə(r)]

> **ADJ**
> • meilleur **1** • mieux **2**
> **ADV**
> • mieux **1–3**
> **N**
> • le meilleur **1** • supérieur **2**
> • parieur **3**
> **VT**
> • améliorer

ADJ **1** *(compar of* **good***) (superior)* meilleur; **you will find no b. hotel** vous ne trouverez pas mieux comme hôtel; **it's b. than nothing** c'est mieux que rien; **nothing could be b., it couldn't be b.** cela ne peut pas être mieux, c'est on ne peut mieux; **that's b.!** voilà qui est mieux!; **I'm b. at languages than he is** je suis meilleur *ou* plus fort en langues que lui; **he's a b. cook than you are** il cuisine mieux que toi; **she's a b. painter than she is a sculptor** elle peint mieux qu'elle ne sculpte; **fruit juice is b. for you than coffee** le jus de fruit est meilleur pour la santé que le café; **I had hoped for b. things** j'avais espéré mieux; **to get b.** *(at doing something)* faire des progrès; *(weather, situation etc)* s'améliorer; **the weather is b.** il fait meilleur; **business is (getting) b.** les affaires vont mieux; **he looks b. without his glasses** il est mieux sans lunettes; **you get a b. view from here** on voit mieux d'ici; **it's b. if I don't see them** il vaut mieux *ou* il est préférable que je ne les voie pas; **it's b. that way** c'est mieux comme ça; **it would be b. if you called me tomorrow** ce serait *ou* il vaudrait mieux que tu m'appelles demain; **it would have been b. to have waited a little** il aurait mieux valu attendre un peu; **you're far b. leaving now** il vaut beaucoup mieux que tu partes maintenant; **to be all the b. for having done sth** se trouver mieux d'avoir fait qch; **you'll be all the b. for a holiday** des vacances vous feront le plus grand bien; **all the b.!** tant mieux!; **they're b. off than we are** *(richer)* ils ont plus d'argent que nous; *(in a more advantageous position)* ils sont dans une meilleure position que nous; **she'd be b. off in hospital** elle serait mieux à l'hôpital; **he'd have been b. off staying where he was** il aurait mieux fait de rester où il était
2 *(compar of* **well***) (improved in health)* mieux; **to get b.** commencer à aller mieux; **now that he's b.** maintenant qu'il va mieux; **I hope you will soon be b.** j'espère que vous serez bientôt rétabli; **my cold is much b.** mon rhume va beaucoup mieux; **I'm feeling much b.** je me sens beaucoup mieux; **you're looking b.** tu as meilleure mine
3 *(morally)* **she's a b. person for it** ça lui a fait beaucoup de bien; *Hum* **you're a b. man than I am!** tu es (bien) du mérite; **he is no b. than his brother** il ne vaut pas mieux que son frère; **you're no b. than a liar!** tu n'es qu'un menteur!; *Euph Old-fashioned or Hum* **she's no b. than she should be** elle n'est pas d'une vertu farouche
4 *(idiom)* **the b. part of sth** la plus grande partie de qch; **I waited for the b. part of an hour** j'ai attendu presque une heure; **we haven't seen them for the b. part of a month** ça fait presque un mois *ou* près d'un mois que nous ne les avons pas vus
ADV **1** *(compar of* **well***) (more proficiently, aptly etc)* mieux; **he swims b. than I do** il nage mieux que moi; **she paints b. than she sculpts** elle peint mieux qu'elle ne sculpte; **the town would be b. described as a backwater** la ville est plutôt un coin perdu; **he held it up to the light, the b. to see the colours** il l'a mis dans la lumière afin de mieux voir les couleurs; **to go one b. (than sb)** renchérir (sur qn)
2 *(indicating preference)* **I liked his last book b.** j'ai préféré son dernier livre; **I'd like nothing b. than to talk to him** je ne demande pas mieux que de lui parler; **so much the b.** tant mieux; **or b. still** ou mieux encore; **the less he knows the b.** moins il en saura, mieux ça vaudra; **the more I know him the b. I like him** plus je le connais plus je l'aime; *Prov* **b. late than never** mieux vaut tard que jamais
3 *(with adj)* mieux, plus; **b. looking** plus beau (belle); **b. paid/prepared** mieux payé/préparé; **she's one of Canada's b.-known authors** c'est un des auteurs canadiens les plus *ou* mieux connus
4 *(idioms)* **we'd b. be going** *(must go)* il faut que nous partions; *(would be preferable)* il vaut mieux que nous partions; **you'd b. not** il ne vaudrait mieux pas; **hadn't you b. phone first?** est-ce qu'il ne vaudrait pas mieux que tu appelles avant?; **it'll be ready tomorrow – it'd b. be!** ce sera prêt demain – il vaudrait mieux!; **you'd b. be on time!** tu as intérêt à être à l'heure!
N **1** *(superior of two)* le (la) meilleur(e) *m,f*; **which is the b. of the two?** lequel des deux est le meilleur?; **what do you think of this wine? – I've tasted b.** comment trouvez-vous ce vin? – j'en ai bu de meilleurs; **there's been a change for the b. in his health** son état de santé s'est amélioré; **the situation has taken a turn for the b.** la situation a pris une meilleure tournure; **for b. or worse** pour le meilleur ou pour le pire; **I expected b. of you** je m'attendais à mieux de ta part
2 *(usu pl) (person)* supérieur(e) *m,f*
3 *(gambler)* parieur(euse) *m,f*
4 *(idioms)* **curiosity got the b. of me** ma curiosité l'a emporté; **we got the b. of them in the deal** nous l'avons emporté sur eux dans l'affaire
VT *(position, status, situation)* améliorer; *(achievement, sales figures)* dépasser; **can you b. that?** pouvez-vous faire mieux que cela?; **she's eager to b. herself** elle a vraiment envie d'améliorer sa situation
►► *Fam Hum* ***better half*** *(husband, wife)* moitié *f*

betterment ['betəmənt] **N** amélioration *f*; *Law (of property)* plus-value *f*

betting ['betɪŋ] **N** **1** *(bets)* pari *m*, paris *mpl*; **the b. was heavy** les paris allaient bon train; *Fig* **what's the b. they refuse to go?** je suis prêt à parier qu'ils ne voudront pas y aller **2** *(odds)* cote *f*; **the b. is 5 to 1 on Blackie** (la cote de) Blackie est à 5 contre 1, la cote est à 5 contre 1 sur Blackie
ADJ **I'm not a b. man** je n'aime pas parier
►► ***betting office*** (bureau *m* de) PMU *m*; ***betting shop*** bureau *m* de paris *(appartenant à un bookmaker)*; ***betting slip*** bulletin *m* de pari

bettor ['betə(r)] **N** *Am (gambler)* parieur(euse) *m,f*

BETWEEN [bɪ'twi:n] **PREP** **1** *(in space or time)* entre; **the crowd stood b. him and the door** la foule le séparait de la porte; **the distance b. the two towns** la distance entre *ou* qui sépare les deux villes; **it happened b. 3 and 4 a.m.** cela s'est passé entre 3 heures et 4 heures (du matin); **b. now and this evening** d'ici ce soir; **I'm b. jobs at the moment** je suis entre deux emplois en ce moment; **you'll have an hour b. trains** vous aurez une heure entre les deux trains; **you shouldn't eat b. meals** tu ne devrais pas manger entre les repas *ou* en dehors des repas
2 *(in the range that separates)* entre; **it will cost b. 5 and 10 million** ça coûtera entre 5 et 10 millions; **children b. the ages of 5 and 10** les enfants de 5 à 10 ans; **something b. a laugh and a groan** quelque chose entre un rire et un grognement
3 *(indicating connection, relation)* entre; **a bus runs b. the airport and the hotel** un bus fait la navette entre l'aéroport et l'hôtel; **it's a half-hour drive b. home and the office** il y a une demi-heure de route entre la maison et le bureau; **a treaty b. the two nations** un traité entre les deux États; **an argument b. two experts** une dispute entre deux experts; **the difference/distinction b. A and B** la différence/distinction entre A et B; **he felt things weren't right b. them** il sentait que ça n'allait pas entre eux; **no one can come b. us** personne ne peut nous séparer; **b. you and me, b. ourselves** entre nous; *Hum* **b. you, me and the gatepost** *or* **bedpost** entre nous; **this is strictly b. ourselves** *or* **b. you and me** que cela reste entre nous
4 *(indicating alternatives)* entre; **I had to choose b. going with them and staying at home** il fallait que je choisisse entre les accompagner et rester à la maison
5 *(added together)* **b. us we saved enough money for the trip** à nous tous nous avons économisé assez d'argent pour le voyage; **they have seven children b. them** à eux deux ils ont sept enfants; **the five groups collected £1,000 b. them** les cinq groupes ont recueilli 1000 livres en tout; **(in) b. painting, writing and looking after the children, she was kept very busy** entre la peinture, l'écriture et les enfants, elle était très occupée
6 *(indicating division)* entre; **he divided it b. his children** il l'a partagé entre ses enfants; **they shared the cake b. them** ils se sont partagé le gâteau
ADV = **in between**
• **in between** **ADV** **1** *(in intermediate position)* **a row of bushes with little clumps of flowers in b.** une rangée d'arbustes intercalés de petits bouquets de fleurs; **he's neither right nor left but somewhere in b.** il n'est ni de droite ni de gauche mais quelque part entre les deux
2 *(in time)* entre-temps, dans l'intervalle **PREP** entre

between-decks *Naut* **ADV** dans l'entrepont
N entrepont *m*

betweentimes [bɪ'twi:ntaɪmz] **ADV** dans l'intervalle, entre-temps

betwixt [bɪ'twɪkst] **ADV** **something b. and between** quelque chose entre les deux

bevel ['bevəl] *(Br pt & pp* **bevelled**, *cont* **bevelling**, *Am pt & pp* **beveled**, *cont* **beveling***)* **VT** biseauter, tailler en biseau *ou* de biais
N **1** *(surface)* surface *f* oblique; *Geom (angle)* angle *m* oblique **2** *Carp* fausse équerre *f*
►► *Carp* ***bevel edge*** biseau *m*; *Tech* ***bevel gear*** engrenage *m* conique; *Carp* ***bevel square*** fausse équerre *f*

bevelled, *Am* **beveled** ['bevəld] **ADJ** biseauté

bevelling, *Am* **beveling** ['bevəlɪŋ] **N** biseautage *m*

beverage ['bevərɪdʒ] **N** boisson *f*

bevvy ['bevɪ] *(pl* **bevvies**, *pt & pp* **bevvied***)* *Br Fam*
N **1** *(alcohol)* alcool□ *m* **2** *(alcoholic drink)* **to have a b.** boire un coup **3** *(drinking session)* beuverie *f*; **to go on the b.** aller se cuiter
VI picoler
VT **to get bevvied** se soûler la gueule

bevy ['bevɪ] *(pl* **bevies***)* **N** *(of people)* bande *f*, troupeau *m*; *(of larks, quails, swans)* volée *f*; *(of roe deer)* harde *f*

bewail [bɪ'weɪl] **VT** *Literary* pleurer; **to b. one's fate** se lamenter sur son sort

beware [bɪˈweə(r)] *(infinitive and imperative only)* VI prendre garde; **b.!** prenez garde!; **b. of getting lost** prenez garde de ne pas vous perdre; **b. of pickpockets** attention aux pickpockets; **b. of married men** méfiez-vous des hommes mariés; **b. of making hasty decisions** gardez-vous de prendre des décisions hâtives; **b. of the dog!** *(sign)* chien méchant!
VT prendre garde; **b. what you say to her** prenez garde *ou* faites attention à ce que vous lui dites

bewhiskered [bɪˈwɪskəd] ADJ *Literary (with side whiskers)* qui a des favoris; *(bearded)* barbu

bewilder [bɪˈwɪldə(r)] VT rendre perplexe, dérouter

bewildered [bɪˈwɪldəd] ADJ perplexe

bewildering [bɪˈwɪldərɪŋ] ADJ déconcertant, déroutant

bewilderingly [bɪˈwɪldərɪŋlɪ] ADV de manière déconcertante *ou* déroutante; **the problem is b. complex** le problème est d'une complexité déroutante; **even more b., she didn't tell anyone** chose encore plus ahurissante, elle ne l'a dit à personne

bewilderment [bɪˈwɪldəmənt] N confusion *f*, perplexité *f*; **"why?" she asked in b.** "pourquoi?", demanda-t-elle avec perplexité; **to my complete b., he refused** à mon grand étonnement, il a refusé

bewitch [bɪˈwɪtʃ] VT **1** *(cast spell over)* ensorceler, enchanter **2** *(fascinate)* enchanter, charmer

bewitching [bɪˈwɪtʃɪŋ] ADJ *(smile)* enchanteur, charmeur; *(beauty, person)* charmant, séduisant

bey [beɪ] N *Hist* bey *m*

beyond [bɪˈjɒnd] PREP **1** *(on the further side of)* au-delà de, de l'autre côté de; **the museum is a few yards b. the church** le musée se trouve à quelques mètres après l'église; **b. the mountains lies China** au-delà des montagnes se trouve la Chine; **the countries b. the sea** les pays d'outre-mer *ou* au-delà des mers
2 *(outside the range of)* au-delà de, au-dessus de; **do your duties extend b. teaching?** est-ce que vos fonctions s'étendent au-delà de l'enseignement?; **b. one's ability** au-dessus de ses capacités; **b. belief** incroyable; **b. question** indiscutablement, incontestablement; **b. repair** irréparable; **due to circumstances b. our control** dû à des circonstances indépendantes de notre volonté; **his guilt has been established b. (all reasonable) doubt** sa culpabilité a été établie sans aucun *ou* sans le moindre doute; **it's (gone) b. a joke** cela dépasse les bornes; **b. one's means** au-dessus de ses moyens; **I'm b. caring what they do next** peu m'importe ce qu'ils feront ensuite; **it's b. me** cela me dépasse, je n'y comprends rien; **economics is completely b. me** je ne comprends rien à l'économie; **why he wants to go there is b. me** je ne comprends pas pourquoi il veut y aller
3 *(later than)* au-delà de, plus de; **the deadline has been extended to b. 2008** l'échéance a été repoussée au-delà de 2008; **b. 2009 that law will no longer be valid** après *ou* à partir de 2009, cette loi ne sera plus applicable
4 *(apart from, other than)* sauf, excepté; **I know nothing b. what I've already told you** je ne sais rien de plus que ce que je vous ai déjà dit
ADV **1** *(on the other side)* au-delà, plus loin; **they crossed the mountains and the valleys b.** ils ont traversé les montagnes et les vallées au-delà **2** *(after)* au-delà; **major changes are foreseen for 2008 and b.** des changements importants sont prévus pour 2008 et au-delà
N **the (great) b.** l'au-delà *m*

bezel [ˈbezəl] N **1** *Tech (face ▸ of tool)* biseau *m*; *Miner (▸ of gem)* facette *f* **2** *Metal (rim ▸ for gem)* chaton *m*; *(▸ for watch crystal)* portée *f*

B-feature N *Cin* film *m* de série B

BFI [ˌbiːefˈaɪ] N *(abbr* **British Film Institute***)* = organisme britannique de promotion du cinéma (aide à la réalisation notamment)

BFPO [ˌbiːefˌpiːˈəʊ] N *Mil (abbr* **British Forces Post Office***)* = mention figurant dans l'adresse des militaires britannique

bhp [ˌbiːeɪtʃˈpiː] N *Aut (abbr* **brake horsepower***)* puissance *f* au frein

Bhutan [ˌbuːˈtɑːn] N Bhoutan *m*

bi [baɪ] *Fam* N bisexuel(elle)ᵓ *m,f*
ADJ bi *(inv)*

biannual [ˌbaɪˈænjʊəl] ADJ semestriel

biannually [ˌbaɪˈænjʊəlɪ] ADV deux fois par an

bias [ˈbaɪəs] *(pt & pp* **biased** *or* **biassed***)* N **1** *(prejudice)* préjugé *m*; **there is still considerable b. against women candidates** les femmes qui se présentent sont encore victimes d'un fort préjugé; **they are quite without b.** ils sont sans préjugés
2 *(tendency)* tendance *f*, penchant *m*; **the school has a scientific b.** l'école favorise les sciences
3 *Sewing* biais *m*; **cut on the b.** taillé dans le biais
4 *Sport (in bowls ▸ weight)* = poids ou renflement d'une boule qui l'empêche d'aller droit; *(▸ curved course)* déviation *f*
5 *Math* biais *m*
VT *(influence)* influencer; *(prejudice)* prévenir; **his experience biased him against/towards them** son expérience l'a prévenu contre eux/en leur faveur; **the course is biased towards the arts** l'enseignement est plutôt orienté sur les lettres
▸▸ *Sewing* ***bias binding*** biais *m (ruban)*

biased [ˈbaɪəst] ADJ **1** *(partial)* partial; **b. opinion** opinion *f* préconçue; **you're b. in her favour** tu as un parti pris pour elle **2** *Sport (ball)* décentré

bib [bɪb] N **1** *(for child)* bavoir *m*, bavette *f* **2** *(of apron, dungarees)* bavette *f*; *Br Fam* **in one's best b. and tucker** sur son trente et un, *Can* sur son trente-six **3** *Sport* dossard *m*

Bible [ˈbaɪbəl] N Bible *f*
• **bible** N *Fig (manual)* bible *f*, évangile *m*; **the gardener's b.** la bible du jardinier
▸▸ ***the Bible Belt*** = États du sud des États-Unis où l'évangélisme est très répandu; ***Bible class*** *(in school, church)* classe *f* d'instruction religieuse; *(in Catholic church)* catéchisme *m*; ***Bible school*** cours *m* d'instruction religieuse; ***Bible study*** étude *f* de la Bible

Bible-basher N *Br Fam Pej* évangéliste *m* extrémisteᵓ

Bible-bashing ADJ *Br Fam Pej* **B. preacher** évangéliste *m* extrémisteᵓ

Bible-thumper [-ˈθʌmpə(r)] N *Br Fam Pej* évangéliste *m* extrémisteᵓ

Bible-thumping ADJ *Br Fam Pej* **B. preacher** évangéliste *m* extrémisteᵓ

biblical, Biblical [ˈbɪblɪkəl] ADJ biblique; *Fam Hum* **to know sb in the b. sense** connaître qn au sens biblique du terme

bibliographer [ˌbɪblɪˈɒgrəfə(r)] N bibliographe *mf*

bibliographical [ˌbɪblɪəˈgræfɪkəl] ADJ bibliographique

bibliography [ˌbɪblɪˈɒgrəfɪ] *(pl* **bibliographies***)* N bibliographie *f*

bibliophile [ˈbɪblɪəˌfaɪl] N bibliophile *mf*

bibulous [ˈbɪbjʊləs] ADJ *Literary (person)* adonné à la boisson; *(celebration)* bien arrosé

bicameral [ˌbaɪˈkæmərəl] ADJ *Pol* bicaméral

bicarb [baɪˈkɑːb] N *Fam* bicarbonate *m* (de soude)ᵓ

bicarbonate [baɪˈkɑːbənət] N *Chem* bicarbonate *m*; **b. of soda** bicarbonate *m* de soude

bicentenary [ˌbaɪsenˈtiːnərɪ] *(pl* **bicentenaries***)* *Br* N bicentenaire *m*
ADJ bicentenaire

biceps [ˈbaɪseps] *(pl* **inv***)* N biceps *m*

bicker [ˈbɪkə(r)] VI se chamailler; **to b. about** *or* **over sth** se chamailler à propos de qch

bickering [ˈbɪkərɪŋ] N chamailleries *fpl*; **stop your b.!** arrêtez de vous chamailler!
ADJ chamailleur

bicoloured, *Am* **bicolored** [ˌbaɪˈkʌləd] ADJ *Zool* bicolore

bicultural [ˌbaɪˈkʌltʃərəl] ADJ biculturel

bicycle [ˈbaɪsɪkəl] N vélo *m*, bicyclette *f*; **I go to work by b.** je vais travailler à bicyclette *ou* à vélo; **do you know how to ride a b.?** sais-tu faire du vélo *ou* de la bicyclette?; **he went for a ride on his b.** il est allé faire un tour à vélo; **he was riding his b.** il était à bicyclette *ou* à vélo
COMP *(bell, lamp)* de vélo, de bicyclette
VI faire du vélo *ou* de la bicyclette; **she bicycles to work** elle va travailler à bicyclette *ou* à vélo
▸▸ ***bicycle chain*** chaîne *f* de vélo; *(for securing bike)* antivol *m inv*; ***bicycle clip*** pince *f* à vélo; *Ftbl* ***bicycle kick*** retourné *m* bicyclette; ***bicycle lock*** antivol *m*; ***bicycle path*** piste *f ou* bande *f* cyclable; ***bicycle pump*** pompe *f* à bicyclette *ou* à vélo; ***bicycle race*** course *f* de bicyclette; ***bicycle rack*** *(on pavement)* ratelier *m* à bicyclettes *ou* à vélos; *(on car)* porte-vélos *m inv*; ***bicycle shop*** magasin *m* de cycles; ***bicycle track*** piste *f* cyclable

BID [bɪd]

VI
- faire une offre **1**
- faire une soumission **2**

VT
- offrir **1**
- dire **3**
- demander **2**
- ordonner **4**

N
- offre **1**
- soumission **2**
- tentative **4**
- enchère **1**
- demande **3**

(pt & pp vi all senses and vt senses **1** *and* **2 bid,** *pt vt senses* **3** *and* **4 bade** [bæd], *pp vt senses* **3** *and* **4 bidden** [ˈbɪdən], *cont all senses* **bidding***)*
VI **1** *Fin (offer to pay)* faire une offre, offrir; **to b. for sth** faire une offre pour qch; **they b. against us** ils ont surenchéri sur notre offre
2 *Com (tender)* faire une soumission, répondre à un appel d'offres; **several firms b. on the project** plusieurs entreprises ont soumissionné pour le projet
3 *(make attempt)* **he's bidding for the presidency** il vise la présidence
4 *(idiom)* **to b. fair to do sth** promettre de faire qch; **the negotiations b. fair to succeed** les négociations s'annoncent bien *ou* sont en bonne voie
VT **1** *Fin (offer to pay)* faire une offre de, offrir; *(at auction)* faire une enchère de; **what am I b. for this table?** combien m'offre-t-on pour cette table?; **we b. £300 for the statue** nous avons fait une enchère de 300 livres pour la statue
2 *Cards* demander, annoncer
3 *Literary (say)* dire; **he bade them good day** il leur souhaita le bonjour; **they bade him farewell** ils lui firent leurs adieux; **she bade them welcome** elle leur souhaita la bienvenue
4 *Literary (order, tell)* ordonner, enjoindre; **he bade them enter** il les pria d'entrer; **do as you are bidden** faites ce qu'on vous dit
N **1** *Fin (offer to pay)* offre *f*; *(at auction)* enchère *f*; **I made a b. of £100** *(gen)* j'ai fait une offre de 100 livres; *(at auction)* j'ai fait une enchère de 100 livres; **a higher b.** une surenchère; **they made a higher b.** ils ont surenchéri; **to put a b. in on a flat** faire une offre pour un appartement
2 *Com (tender)* soumission *f*; **the firm made** *or* **put in a b. for the contract** l'entreprise a fait une soumission *ou* a soumissionné pour le contrat; **the State invited bids for** *or* **on the project** l'État a mis le projet en adjudication
3 *Cards* demande *f*, annonce *f*; **it's your b.** c'est à vous d'annoncer; **to make a b. of two hearts** demander *ou* annoncer deux cœurs; **I make no b.** je passe (parole); **he raised the b.** il a monté *ou* enchéri
4 *(attempt)* tentative *f*; **to make a b. for power** *(legally)* viser le pouvoir; *(illegally)* tenter un coup d'état; **they made a b. to gain control of the movement** ils ont tenté de prendre la tête du mouvement; **the prisoners made a b. for freedom** les prisonniers ont fait une tentative d'évasion; **a rescue b.** une tentative de sauvetage; **she failed in her b. to beat the record** elle a échoué dans sa tentative de battre le record
▸▸ *Fin* ***bid bond*** caution *f* d'adjudication *ou* de soumission; *St Exch* ***bid price*** cours *m* acheteur
▸ **bid up** VT SEP *Fin* enchérir *ou* surenchérir sur

biddable [ˈbɪdəbəl] ADJ **1** *Cards* demandable **2** *Br (docile)* docile, obéissant

bidder [ˈbɪdə(r)] N **1** *Fin & Com (at auction)* enchérisseur(euse) *m,f*; **there were no bidders** il n'y a pas eu de preneurs, personne n'a fait d'offre; **sold to the highest b.** vendu au plus offrant **2** *Com (tenderer)* soumissionnaire *mf*; **the highest / lowest b.** le soumissionnaire le plus/le moins offrant **3** *Cards* demandeur(euse) *m,f*

bidding ['bɪdɪŋ] N **1** *Fin & Com (at auction)* enchères *fpl*; **the b. went against me** on avait enchéri sur mon offre; **to start the b. at £5,000** commencer les enchères à 5000 livres; **to open the b.** ouvrir les enchères; **to raise the b.** faire monter les enchères; **b. was brisk** les enchères étaient vives
2 *Com (tenders)* soumissions *fpl*
3 *Cards* enchères *fpl*
4 *Literary (request)* demande *f*; *(order)* ordre *m*, ordres *mpl*; **he did his mother's b.** il respecta les volontés de sa mère; **at her brother's b.** sur la requête de son frère
▸▸ *Am St Exch* ***bidding price*** cours *m* acheteur; ***bidding war*** bataille *f* d'enchères

bide [baɪd] *(pt* **bided** *or* **bode** [bəʊd], *pp* **bided)** VT **to b. one's time** attendre son heure *ou* le bon moment

bidet ['bi:deɪ] N bidet *m*

bidirectional [ˌbaɪdə'rekʃənəl] ADJ bidirectionnel
▸▸ *Typ* ***bidirectional printing*** impression *f* bidirectionnelle

biennial [ˌbaɪ'enɪəl] ADJ **1** *(every two years)* biennal, bisannuel **2** *(lasting two years)* biennal
N **1** *(event)* biennale *f* **2** *Bot (plant)* plante *f* bisannuelle

biennially [ˌbaɪ'enɪəlɪ] ADV tous les deux ans

bier [bɪə(r)] N *(for corpse)* bière *f*; *(for coffin)* brancards *mpl*

biff [bɪf] *Fam* VT flanquer un coup de poing à
N coup *m* de poing[◻], gnon *m*; **she gave him a b. on the nose** elle lui a flanqué son poing dans *ou* sur la figure

bifidus ['bɪfɪdəs] N *Biol* bifidus *m*

bifocal [ˌbaɪ'fəʊkəl] ADJ bifocal
• **bifocals** NPL lunettes *fpl* bifocales *ou* à double foyer

bifurcate ['baɪfəkeɪt] VI bifurquer

bifurcation [ˌbaɪfə'keɪʃən] N bifurcation *f*

BIG [bɪg]

> **ADJ**
> • grand **1, 2, 4, 6, 7** • gros **1**
> • aîné **3** • important **5**
> • à la mode **8**

(compar **bigger**, *superl* **biggest)**
ADJ **1** *(in size* ▸ *car, hat, majority)* grand, gros (grosse); *(*▸ *crowd, field, room)* grand; *(*▸ *person)* grand, fort; **the crowd got bigger** la foule a grossi; **in b. letters** en (lettres) majuscules; **a b. A** un A majuscule; **to make sth bigger** *(garment, hole)* agrandir qch; **the new wallpaper makes the room look bigger** le nouveau papier peint agrandit la pièce; **we're not b. eaters** nous ne sommes pas de gros mangeurs; **to earn b. money** gagner gros; *Fig* **he has a b. head** il a la grosse tête; *Fam Fig* **he has a b. mouth** il faut toujours qu'il l'ouvre; *Fam* **why did you have to open your b. mouth?** tu ne pouvais pas la fermer, non?; *Bible or Literary* **to be b. with child** être enceinte, attendre un enfant; *Fam* **she's too b. for her boots** *or* **her breeches** elle ne se prend pas pour n'importe qui
2 *(in height)* grand; **to get** *or* **to grow bigger** grandir; **you're a b. boy now** tu es un grand garçon maintenant; **she's b. enough to look after herself** elle est assez grande pour se défendre
3 *(older)* aîné, plus grand; **my b. sister** ma grande sœur
4 *(as intensifier)* grand, énorme; **he's just a b. bully** ce n'est qu'une grosse brute; **you're the biggest fool of the lot!** c'est toi le plus bête de tous!
5 *(important, significant* ▸ *decision, problem)* grand, important; *(*▸ *drop, increase)* fort, important; *(*▸ *mistake)* grave; **the b. day** le grand jour; **you've got a b. day ahead of you tomorrow** tu as une journée importante devant toi demain; **he's b. in publishing, he's a b. man in publishing** c'est quelqu'un d'important dans l'édition; **we're onto something b.!** nous sommes sur une piste intéressante!; *Fam* **to be into sb/sth b. time** *or* **in a b. way** être dingue de qn/qch; *Fam* **he's been doing drugs b. time** *or* **in a b. way** depuis quelque temps il arrête pas de se droguer; *Fam* **it's going to cost them b. time** ça va leur revenir vachement cher; *Fam* **to be in the b. time, to have made the b. time** être en haut de l'échelle, être le dessus du panier, être arrivé; *Fam* **to hit** *or* **to make** *or* **to reach the b. time** arriver, réussir; *Fam* **b. deal!** tu parles!; *Fam* **it's no b. deal** il n'y a pas de quoi en faire un plat!
6 *(grandiose)* grand; **don't get any b. ideas about doing this yourself** ne crois pas que tu vas pouvoir faire ça tout seul; **I've got b. plans for you** j'ai de grands projets pour toi; **you really do things in a b. way** tu ne fais pas les choses à moitié; **they entertain in a b. way** ils font les choses en grand quand ils reçoivent; **b. words!** ce sont de bien grands mots!
7 *(generous)* grand, généreux; **he has a b. heart** il a du cœur *ou* bon cœur; **he's a b. spender** c'est un grand dépensier; *Ironic* **you know what he's like, the last of the b. spenders!** tu le connais, toujours à faire des frais; *Ironic* **that's b. of you!** quelle générosité!
8 *Fam (popular)* à la mode[◻]; **Japanese food is really b. just now** la cuisine japonaise est vraiment à la mode en ce moment
9 *Fam (enthusiastic)* **to be b. on sth** être fana de qch; **the company is b. on research** l'entreprise investit beaucoup dans la recherche
ADV **1** *(grandly)* **he talks b.** il se vante, il fanfaronne; **to think b.** voir grand
2 *Fam (well)* **their music goes over** *or* **down b. with teenagers** les adolescents adorent leur musique; **they made it b. in the pop world** ce sont maintenant des stars de la musique pop
▸▸ *Fam* ***the Big Apple*** = surnom donné à la ville de New York; *Mus* ***big band*** big band *m (grand orchestre de jazz typique des années 40–50)*; *Br Fam St Exch* ***the Big Bang*** = déréglementation de la Bourse de Londres en octobre 1986; *Fam Astron* ***the big bang*** le big-bang, le big bang; *Astron* ***the big bang theory*** la théorie du big-bang *ou* big bang; ***Big Ben*** Big Ben; *Am St Exch* ***the big board*** = la Bourse de New York; ***Big Brother*** Big Brother; **B. Brother is watching you** Big Brother vous surveille; *Com* ***big business*** *(UNCOUNT)* les grandes entreprises *fpl*; *Zool* ***big cat*** fauve *m*, grand félin *m*; *Fam Fig* ***big cheese*** gros bonnet *m*; *Cin & TV* ***big close-up*** très gros plan *m*; *Am Fam* ***big daddy*** = surnom donné au gouvernement américain; *Am Astron* ***the Big Dipper*** la Grande Ourse; ***big dipper*** *(in fairground)* montagnes *fpl* russes; *Br Aut* ***big end*** tête *f* de bielle; *Hunt* ***big game*** gros gibier *m*; *Br Fam Hum* ***big girl's blouse*** *(wimp)* femmelette *f*; *Am Pej Pol* ***Big Government*** = gouvernement interventionniste sur le plan social; *Fam Fig* ***big gun*** gros bonnet *m*; *Fam* ***big hair*** = coiffure volumineuse et apprêtée; *Fam Fig* ***big hitter*** poids *m* lourd; *Am Fam* ***big house*** *(prison)* taule *f*, placard *m*; **he's gone to the b. house** on l'a mis à l'ombre; *Fam Mktg* ***Big Idea, big idea*** idée-force[◻] *f*; *Br Press* ***The Big Issue*** = hebdomadaire vendu au profit des sans-logis par ces derniers, le Réverbère; *Am Sport* ***Big League*** *(gen)* première division *f*; *(in baseball)* = une des deux principales divisions de base-ball professionnel aux États-Unis; *Sport* ***big match*** grand match *m*; ***big name*** grand nom *m*; *Br Fam Fig* ***big noise*** gros bonnet *m*; *Cin* ***the big screen*** le grand écran, le cinéma; *Fam Fig* ***big shot*** gros bonnet *m*; **he thinks he's a real b. shot** il croit qu'il est vraiment quelqu'un; *Br Fam* ***the Big Smoke*** *(gen)* la grande ville[◻]; *(London)* = surnom donné à Londres; *Fam Fig* ***the big stick*** le bâton, la force; ***big stick diplomacy*** diplomatie *f* musclée; *Anat* ***big toe*** gros orteil *m*; ***big top*** *(tent)* grand chapiteau *m*; *(circus)* cirque *m*; *Fam Fig* ***big wheel*** gros bonnet *m*

▸ **big up** VT SEP *Br Fam* **1** *(publicize)* faire du battage à propos de de; **to b. oneself up** se faire mousser; **all the radio stations are bigging up his new album** toutes les stations de radio font un sacré battage autour de son dernier album **2** *(greet)* saluer; **I want to b. up all my friends back in London** un grand bonjour à tous mes amis à Londres

> **BIG BEN**
>
> Nom de la cloche de la Tour de l'horloge à Westminster, souvent donné à tort à la tour elle-même. Elle est considérée comme un des monuments principaux de Londres.

bigamist ['bɪgəmɪst] N bigame *mf*

bigamous ['bɪgəməs] ADJ bigame

bigamy ['bɪgəmɪ] N bigamie *f*; **to commit b.** être coupable de bigamie

big-bellied ADJ *(fat)* ventru, pansu; **she's b.** *(of pregnant woman)* elle a un gros ventre

big-boned ADJ fortement charpenté

big-game ADJ **b. hunter** chasseur *m* de gros gibier; **b. hunting** chasse *f* au gros gibier

biggie ['bɪgɪ] N *Fam (success* ▸ *song)* tube *m*; *(*▸ *film, record)* succès[◻] *m*; **his next book/film should be a b.** son prochain livre/film devrait faire un malheur; *Am* **no b.!** pas de problème!

biggish ['bɪgɪʃ] ADJ *(tall, large)* assez grand; *(fat)* assez gros (grosse)

bighead ['bɪghed] N *Fam* crâneur(euse) *m,f*

bigheaded [ˌbɪg'hedɪd] ADJ *Fam* crâneur; **to be b.** avoir la grosse tête

bigheadedness [ˌbɪg'hedɪdnɪs] N *Fam* suffisance[◻] *f*

bighearted [ˌbɪg'hɑ:tɪd] ADJ au grand cœur; **to be b.** avoir le cœur sur la main, avoir bon *ou* du cœur

bight [baɪt] N *Geog (of shoreline)* baie *f*; **the Great Australian B.** la Grande Baie Australienne, le Grand Golfe Australien *ou* de l'Australie

bigness ['bɪgnɪs] N *(of person* ▸ *tallness)* grande taille *f*; *(*▸ *fatness)* grosseur *f*; *(of thing)* grandes dimensions *fpl*

big-note VT *Austr & NZ Fam* **to b. oneself** faire le fanfaron

bigot ['bɪgət] N *(gen)* sectaire *mf*, intolérant(e) *m,f*; *Rel* bigot(e) *m,f*, sectaire *mf*

> Note that the French word **bigot** is a false friend. It is used to describe an excessively religious person but has no overtones of sectarianism.

bigoted ['bɪgətɪd] ADJ *(gen* ▸ *person)* sectaire, intolérant; *(*▸ *attitude, opinion)* fanatique; *Rel* bigot

bigotry ['bɪgətrɪ] N *(gen)* sectarisme *m*, intolérance *f*; *Rel* bigoterie *f*

big-shot ADJ *Fam* **a b. lawyer from London** un crack du barreau de Londres

big-ticket ADJ *Am (expensive)* cher

big-time ADJ *Fam (actor, singer)* à succès[◻]; *(businessman, politician)* de haut vol; *(project)* ambitieux[◻], de grande échelle[◻]

bigwig ['bɪgwɪg] N *Fam* gros bonnet *m*

bijou ['bi:ʒu:] ADJ *Br (flat, residence)* petit mais chic

bike [baɪk] N *(bicycle)* vélo *m*, bicyclette *f*; *(motorcycle)* moto *f*; **to ride a b.** *(bicycle)* faire du vélo *ou* de la bicyclette; *(motorcycle)* faire de la moto; *Br Fam* **on your b.!** *(go away)* dégage!; *(don't be ridiculous)* mais oui, c'est ça!
VI *(bicycle)* faire du vélo; *(motorcycle)* faire de la moto; **we biked there** nous y sommes allés à *ou* en vélo/moto
VT *(send by motorcycle courier)* envoyer par coursier; **to b. sth round to sb** envoyer qch à qn par coursier
▸▸ ***bike lane*** piste *f* cyclable; ***bike shed*** cabane *f ou* remise *f* à vélos

biker ['baɪkə(r)] N *Fam* motard(e) *m,f*, motocycliste[◻] *mf*

bikini [bɪ'ki:nɪ] N bikini *m*; **to have one's b. line done** se faire faire une épilation maillot

bilabial [ˌbaɪ'leɪbɪəl] *Ling* N bilabiale *f*
ADJ bilabial

bilateral [ˌbaɪ'lætərəl] ADJ bilatéral
▸▸ ***bilateral agreement*** accord *m* bilatéral; ***bilateral aid*** aide *f* bilatérale; ***bilateral talks*** pourparlers *mpl* bilatéraux; ***bilateral trade*** commerce *m* bilatéral

bilateralism [ˌbaɪ'lætərəlɪzəm] N bilatéralisme *m*

bilaterally [ˌbaɪ'lætərəlɪ] ADV bilatéralement

bilberry ['bɪlbərɪ] *(pl* **bilberries)** N *Bot* myrtille *f*

bile [baɪl] N **1** *Physiol* bile *f* **2** *Literary (irritability)* mauvaise humeur *f*, irascibilité *f*
▸▸ *Physiol* ***bile duct*** canal *m* biliaire

bilestone ['baɪl,stəʊn] N *Med* calcul *m* biliaire

bilge [bɪldʒ] N **1** *Naut (hull)* bouchain *m*, renflement *m*; *(hold)* fond *m* de cale, sentine *f*; *(water)* eau *f* de cale *ou* de sentine **2** *(UNCOUNT) Fam Fig (nonsense)* âneries *fpl*, idioties *fpl*; **he talks a load of b.** il raconte un tas de bêtises

►► *Naut* ***bilge keel*** quille *f* de bouchain; *Naut* ***bilge pump*** pompe *f* de drain *ou* de cale; ***bilge water*** *(UNCOUNT) Naut* eau *f* de cale *ou* de sentine; *Fam Fig (nonsense)* âneries *fpl*, idioties *fpl*

bilharzia [bɪl'hɑːtsɪə] N **1** *(UNCOUNT) Med (disease)* bilharziose *f* **2** *Biol (parasite)* bilharzia *f*, bilharzie *f*

biliary ['bɪlɪərɪ] ADJ *Anat* biliaire

►► *Med* ***biliary colic*** coliques *fpl* hépatiques

bilingual [baɪ'lɪŋgwəl] ADJ *Ling* bilingue; **to be b. in French and English** être bilingue français-anglais

►► ***bilingual dictionary*** dictionnaire *m* bilingue; ***bilingual secretary*** secrétaire *mf* bilingue

bilingualism [baɪ'lɪŋgwəlɪzəm] N *Ling* bilinguisme *m*

bilious ['bɪlɪəs] ADJ **1** *Med* bilié; **b. attack** crise *f* de foie **2** *(colour)* écœurant **3** *Literary (irritable)* bilieux, irascible

biliousness ['bɪlɪəsnɪs] N **1** *Med* affection *f* hépatique **2** *(of colour)* aspect *m* écœurant **3** *Literary (irritability)* mauvaise humeur *f*, irascibilité *f*

bilk [bɪlk] VT *Br* **1** *(thwart ► person)* contrecarrer, contrarier les projets de; *(► plan)* contrecarrer, contrarier **2** *(cheat)* escroquer; **they bilked her of her fortune** ils lui ont escroqué sa fortune

Bill [bɪl] N *Br Fam* **the (Old) B.** les flics *mpl*

bill [bɪl] N **1** *(for gas, telephone)* facture *f*, note *f*; *(for product)* facture *f*; *Br (in restaurant)* addition *f*, note *f*; *(in hotel)* note *f*; **to pay a b.** payer *ou* régler une facture; **to foot the b.** payer la note *ou* les dépenses; **may I have the b. please?** l'addition, s'il vous plaît; **have you paid the telephone b.?** as-tu payé le téléphone?; **put it on my b.** mettez-le sur ma note

2 *Law (draft of law)* projet *m* de loi; **to introduce a b. in Parliament** présenter un projet de loi au Parlement; **to pass/reject a b.** adopter/repousser un projet de loi

3 *(poster)* affiche *f*, placard *m*; **(stick) no bills!** défense d'afficher

4 *Theat* affiche *f*; **to head** *or* **to top the b.** être en tête d'affiche *ou* en vedette

5 *Com & Fin (promissory note)* effet *m* (de commerce), traite *f*; **b. made out to bearer** effet au porteur

6 *Am (banknote)* billet *m* (de banque); **a ten-dollar b.** un billet de dix dollars

7 *(beak)* bec *m*

8 *Geog* promontoire *m*, bec *m*

VT **1** *(invoice)* facturer; **he bills his company for his travel expenses** il se fait rembourser ses frais de voyage par son entreprise; **b. me for the newspaper at the end of the month** envoyez-moi la facture pour le journal à la fin du mois **2** *(advertise)* annoncer; **they're billed as the best band in the world** on les présente comme le meilleur groupe du monde **3** *Theat* mettre à l'affiche, annoncer; **he is billed to appear as Cyrano** il est à l'affiche dans le rôle de Cyrano

VI **to b. and coo** *(birds)* se becqueter; *(people)* roucouler

►► *Fin* ***bill book*** livre *m* d'échéance; *Fin* ***bill broker*** agent *m ou* courtier(ère) *m,f* de change; *Fin* ***bills for collection*** effets *mpl* à l'encaissement; *Customs* ***bill of entry*** déclaration *f* d'entrée (en douane); *Fin* ***bill of exchange*** lettre *f* de change, effet *m* de commerce; ***bill of fare*** carte *f* (du jour); ***bills in hand*** effets *mpl* en portefeuille; *Naut* ***bill of health*** patente *f* (de santé); *Fam* **the doctor gave him a clean b. of health** le médecin l'a trouvé en parfaite santé□; *Fam* **the investigators gave the engine a clean b. of health** les enquêteurs ont conclu que le moteur était en parfait état□; *Law* ***bill of indictment*** acte *m* d'accusation; *Com* ***bill of lading*** connaissement *m*; *Fin* ***bill payable at sight*** effet *m* payable à vue *ou* à présentation; ***bills payable*** effets *mpl* à payer; ***bills payable ledger*** livre *m ou* journal *m* des effets à payer; ***bills receivable*** effets *mpl* à recevoir; ***bills receivable ledger*** livre *m ou* journal *m* des effets à recevoir; ***the Bill of Rights*** *Br Hist* = loi de 1689 déterminant les droits du citoyen anglais; *Am* = les dix premiers amendements à la Constitution américaine garantissant, entre autres droits, la liberté d'expression, de religion et de réunion; ***bill of sale*** acte *m ou* contrat *m* de vente

billboard ['bɪlbɔːd] N *Mktg* panneau *m* (d'affichage)

►► ***billboard advertising*** publicité *f* sur panneaux; ***billboard site*** emplacement *m* d'affichage

billet ['bɪlɪt] N **1** *Mil (accommodation)* cantonnement *m* (chez l'habitant); *(document)* billet *m* de logement **2** *Br Old-fashioned Fam (job)* situation□ *f*

VT *(gen)* loger; *Mil* cantonner, loger; **the captain billeted his men on the mayor/on the town** le capitaine a cantonné ses hommes chez le maire/dans la ville

billeting ['bɪlɪtɪŋ] N *Mil (in private house)* logement *m* chez l'habitant; *(on town)* cantonnement *m*

►► ***billeting officer*** officier *m* de cantonnement

billfold ['bɪlfəʊld] N *Am* portefeuille *m*

billhead ['bɪlhed] N *Am Com* facture *f*

billhook ['bɪlhʊk] N serpe *f*, serpette *f*

billiard ['bɪljəd] COMP de billard

• **billiards** N *(UNCOUNT)* (jeu *m* de) billard *m*; **to play billiards** jouer au billard; **to have** *or* **to play a game of billiards** faire *ou* disputer une partie de billard

►► ***billiard ball*** boule *f* de billard; ***billiard cue*** queue *f* de billard; ***billiard hall*** (salle *f* de) billard *m*; ***billiard table*** (table *f* de) billard *m*

billing ['bɪlɪŋ] N **1** *Theat* affichage *m*; **to get** *or* **to have top/second b.** être en tête d'affiche/en deuxième place à l'affiche

2 *Am (advertising)* **to give sth advance b.** annoncer qch

3 *Fin* facturation *f*

4 *also Fig (sound)* **b. and cooing** roucoulements *mpl*

►► ***billing date*** date *f* de facturation; ***billing machine*** caisse *f* (enregistreuse); ***billing office*** bureau *m* de facturation

billion ['bɪljən] *(pl* **inv** *or* **billions)** N *(thousand million)* milliard *m*; *Br Old-fashioned (million million)* billion *m*

billionaire [,bɪljə'neə(r)] N milliardaire *mf*

billionth ['bɪljənθ] N **1** *(ordinal)* milliardième *mf* **2** *(fraction)* milliardième *m*

ADJ milliardième

billow ['bɪləʊ] N **1** *(of smoke)* tourbillon *m*, volute *f* **2** *(wave)* grosse vague *f*; *Literary* **the billows** les flots *mpl*

VI *(cloth, flag)* onduler; *(sail)* se gonfler; *(cloud, smoke)* tourbillonner, tournoyer; *(sea)* se soulever en vagues

billowy ['bɪləʊɪ] ADJ *(sea)* houleux, agité; *(wave)* gros (grosse); *(sail)* gonflé; *(skirt)* tourbillonnant; **b. clouds of smoke** de gros nuages de fumée

billposter ['bɪl,pəʊstə(r)], **billsticker** ['bɪl,stɪkə(r)] N afficheur(euse) *m,f*, colleur(euse) *m,f* d'affiches

billposting ['bɪl,pəʊstɪŋ], **billsticking** ['bɪl,stɪkɪŋ] N affichage *m*

billy ['bɪlɪ] *(pl* **billies)** N **1** *Am (weapon)* **b. (club)** matraque *f* **2** *Br & Austr (can)* gamelle *f*; *Austr* **to boil the b.** faire le thé *(dans une gamelle)* **3** *Fam (goat)* bouc□ *m*

►► ***billy goat*** bouc *m*

billycan ['bɪlɪkæn] N *Br & Austr* gamelle *f*

Billy No Mates N *Br Hum* = individu peu populaire; **nobody's called me for days, what a B....** ça fait des jours que personne m'a appelé; j'ai pas d'amis...

billy-o, billy-oh ['bɪlɪəʊ] N *Br Fam Old-fashioned* **he ran like b.** il a couru comme un dératé

BIM [,biːaɪ'em] N *Com (abbr* **British Institute of Management)** = organisme britannique dont la fonction est de renseigner et de conseiller les entreprises en matière de gestion, ainsi que de promouvoir l'enseignement de cette discipline

bimbette [bɪm'bet], **bimbo** ['bɪmbəʊ] *(pl* **bimbos** *or* **bimboes)** N *Fam Pej* = jeune femme sexy et un peu bête

bi-media ADJ bi-média

bimetallic [,baɪmɪ'tælɪk] ADJ bimétallique

►► ***bimetallic strip*** bilame *m*

bimetallism [,baɪ'metəlɪzəm] N *Fin* bimétallisme *m*

bimonthly [,baɪ'mʌnθlɪ] *(pl* **bimonthlies)** ADJ *(every two months)* bimestriel; *(twice monthly)* bimensuel

ADV *(every two months)* tous les deux mois; *(twice monthly)* deux fois par mois

N *Press* bimestriel *m*

bin [bɪn] *(pt & pp* **binned**, *cont* **binning)** N **1** *Br (for rubbish)* poubelle *f*, boîte *f* à ordures

2 *(for coal, grain)* coffre *m*; *(for bread)* huche *f*

3 *Br (for wine)* casier *m* (à bouteilles)

4 *Fam* **the b.** *(psychiatric hospital)* la maison de fous

VT *Br Fam (discard)* flanquer à la poubelle

►► *Br* ***bin bag*** sac *m* poubelle; *Br* ***bin end*** *(wine)* fin *f* de série; *Br* ***bin liner*** sac *m* poubelle

binary ['baɪnərɪ] ADJ *Math & Comput* binaire

N *Astron* binaire *f*

►► ***binary code*** code *m* binaire; ***binary file*** fichier *m* binaire; ***binary number*** nombre *m* binaire; ***binary search*** recherche *f* binaire *ou* dichotomique; *Astron* ***binary star*** binaire *f*; *Mil* ***binary weapon*** arme *f* binaire

bind [baɪnd] *(pt & pp* **bound** [baʊnd]) VT **1** *(tie)* attacher, lier; **b. him to his chair** attachez-le à sa chaise; **to b. sb hand and foot** ligoter qn; **he was bound hand and foot** il avait les pieds et les poings liés

2 *Med (dress ► wound)* bander, panser

3 *Sewing (provide with border)* border; *(buttonhole)* brider

4 *(book)* relier; **the book is bound in leather** le livre est relié en cuir

5 *(stick together)* lier, agglutiner; *Culin* **add eggs to b. the sauce** ajouter des œufs pour lier la sauce

6 *Fig (bond, unite)* lier, attacher; **they are bound by friendship** c'est l'amitié qui les unit; **they are very much bound up with each other** *(lovers)* ils sont très attachés l'un à l'autre; *(friends)* ils sont très liés; **the two companies are bound by commercial interests** des intérêts commerciaux lient les deux sociétés

7 *(oblige)* obliger, contraindre; **we are bound to tell the truth** nous sommes obligés *ou* tenus de dire la vérité; **they bound him to secrecy** ils lui ont fait jurer le secret; *Law* **to be bound by oath** être lié par serment

8 *(apprentice)* mettre en apprentissage

VI **1** *Law (agreement, promise)* engager; *(rule)* être obligatoire **2** *Culin (sauce)* se lier; *Constr (cement)* durcir, prendre **3** *(mechanism)* se gripper

N **1** *Mus* liaison *f* **2** *Fam (nuisance)* plaie *f*; **working at weekends is a real b.!** quelle corvée de devoir travailler le week-end!, c'est la plaie de devoir travailler le week-end!; **we're in a bit of a b.** nous sommes plutôt dans le pétrin

►**bind over** VT SEP *Br Law (order)* sommer; **they were bound over to keep the peace** ils ont été sommés de ne pas troubler l'ordre public

►**bind up** VT SEP *(tie ► gen)* attacher, lier; *Med (► wound)* bander, panser

binder ['baɪndə(r)] N **1** *(folder)* classeur *m*

2 *(bookbinder)* relieur(euse) *m,f*

3 *(glue)* colle *f*; *Tech & Chem* liant *m*, aggloméрant *m*

4 *Agr (machine)* lieuse *f*

bindery ['baɪndərɪ] *(pl* **binderies)** N atelier *m* de reliure

binding ['baɪndɪŋ] N **1** *(for book)* reliure *f*

2 *Sewing* extrafort *m*

3 *Constr* agglutination *f*, agrégation *f*; *(of road surface)* liant *m*, agglomérant *m*

4 *(on skis)* fixation *f*; **safety (release) bindings** fixations *fpl* de sécurité

ADJ **1** *(law)* obligatoire; *(contract, promise)* qui engage *ou* lie; **the agreement is b. on all parties** l'accord est opposable à *ou* engage chaque partie; *Com* **it is b. on the buyer to make immediate**

payment l'acheteur est tenu de payer immédiatement **2** *(food)* constipant

bindweed ['baɪndwi:d] N *Bot* liseron *m*

binge [bɪndʒ] *Fam* N **1** *(spree)* **to go on a b.** faire la bringue; **they went on a shopping b.** ils sont allés dépenser du fric dans les magasins; **an eating b.** une grosse bouffe **2** *(drinking bout)* beuverie *f*, bringue *f*

VI **1** *(overspend)* faire des folies□ **2** *(overeat)* faire des excès□ *(de nourriture)*; *(drink too much)* prendre une cuite; **to b. on sth** *(drink)* s'enfiler des litres de qch; *(food)* s'empiffrer de qch

►► ***binge drinking*** = fait de boire de très grandes quantités d'alcool en une soirée, de façon régulière

bingo ['bɪŋgəʊ] N bingo *m*, loto *m*

EXCLAM *Fam* ça y est!

►► ***bingo hall*** salle *f* de bingo

> **BINGO**
>
> Ce jeu d'argent très populaire en Grande-Bretagne est très proche du jeu de loto. Il est souvent pratiqué dans d'anciens cinémas ou des salles municipales. Les participants sont en grande majorité des dames d'un certain âge issues de la classe ouvrière.

Bin Laden [bɪn'lɑ:dən] PR N **Osama B.** Oussama Ben Laden

binman ['bɪnmæn] *(pl* **binmen** [-men]) N *Br* éboueur *m*

binnacle ['bɪnəkəl] N *Naut* habitacle *m*

binocular [bɪ'nɒkjʊlə(r)] ADJ *Opt* binoculaire

• **binoculars** NPL jumelles *fpl*; **visible through b.** visible aux jumelles

►► ***binocular vision*** vision *f* binoculaire

binomial [,baɪ'nəʊmɪəl] *Math* N binôme *m*

ADJ binomial

►► ***the binomial theorem*** le binôme de Newton, le théorème de Newton

bint [bɪnt] N *Br very Fam Pej* greluche *f*

bio[1] ['baɪəʊ] *(pl* **bios**) N *Fam* biographie□ *f*

bio[2] ['baɪəʊ] ADJ bio *inv*

►► ***bio yoghurt*** yaourt *m* bio

biochemical [,baɪəʊ'kemɪkəl] N produit *m* biochimique

ADJ biochimique

►► *Ecol* ***biochemical oxygen demand*** demande *f* biochimique en oxygène

biochemist [,baɪəʊ'kemɪst] N biochimiste *mf*

biochemistry [,baɪəʊ'kemɪstrɪ] N biochimie *f*

biochip ['baɪəʊ,tʃɪp] N biopuce *f*

biodegradability [,baɪəʊdɪ,greɪdə'bɪlɪtɪ] N biodégradabilité *f*

biodegradable [,baɪəʊdɪ'greɪdəbəl] ADJ biodégradable

biodegradation [,baɪəʊdegrə'deɪʃən] N biodégradation *f*

biodegrade [,baɪəʊdɪ'greɪd] VI biodégrader

biodiesel ['baɪəʊ,di:zəl] N *Chem* biodiesel *m*

biodiversity [,baɪəʊdaɪ'vɜ:sɪtɪ] N *Biol* biodiversité *f*

bioelectric [,baɪəʊɪ'lektrɪk] ADJ *Physiol* bioélectrique

bioelectricity [,baɪəʊɪlek'trɪsɪtɪ] N *Physiol* bioélectricité *f*

bioelement [,baɪəʊ'elɪmənt] N *Biol* bioélément *m*

bioethanol [,baɪəʊ'eθənɒl] N *Chem* bioéthanol *m*

bioethics [,baɪəʊ'eθɪks] N *(UNCOUNT) Med* bioéthique *f*

biofuel ['baɪəʊfjʊəl] N biocarburant *m*

biogenesis [,baɪəʊ'dʒenɪsɪs] N *Biol* biogenèse *f*

biogenetic [,baɪəʊ'dʒənetɪk] ADJ *Biol* biogénétique

biogeography [,baɪəʊdʒɪ'ɒgrəfɪ] N *Biol* biogéographie *f*

biographer [baɪ'ɒgrəfə(r)] N biographe *mf*

biographical [,baɪə'græfɪkəl] ADJ biographique; **b. novel** biographie *f* romancée

biography [baɪ'ɒgrəfɪ] N biographie *f*

biological [,baɪə'lɒdʒɪkəl] ADJ biologique

►► ***biological balance*** équilibre *m* biologique; ***biological clock*** horloge *f* interne *ou* biologique; **my b. clock is ticking away** *(of woman)* mon temps est compté si je veux avoir des enfants; ***biological control*** *(of insects)* élimination *f* des insectes par des méthodes biologiques; *Mil* ***biological warfare*** guerre *f* bactériologique

biologically [,baɪə'lɒdʒɪkəlɪ] ADV biologiquement

biologist [baɪ'ɒlədʒɪst] N biologiste *mf*

biology [baɪ'ɒlədʒɪ] N biologie *f*

COMP *(lesson, teacher)* de biologie

bioluminescent [,baɪəʊlu:mɪ'nesənt] ADJ *Bot, Entom & Ich* bioluminescent

biomarker ['baɪəʊ,mɑ:kə(r)] N *Biol & Physiol* biomarqueur *m*, marqueur *m* biologique

biomass ['baɪəʊmæs] N *Biol* biomasse *f*

biomaterial [,baɪəʊmə'tɪərɪəl] N *Med* biomatériau *m*

biometric [,baɪəʊ'metrɪk] ADJ biométrique

biometrics [,baɪəʊ'metrɪks] N *(UNCOUNT) Biol* biométrie *f*

bionic [baɪ'ɒnɪk] ADJ bionique

bionics [baɪ'ɒnɪks] N *(UNCOUNT)* bionique *f*

bio-organic ADJ *Biol & Chem* bio-organique

biophysicist [,baɪəʊ'fɪzɪsɪst] N biophysicien (enne) *m,f*

biophysics [,baɪəʊ'fɪzɪks] N *(UNCOUNT)* biophysique *f*

biopic ['baɪəʊpɪk] N *Fam Cin* film *m* biographique□

biopiracy [,baɪəʊ'paɪrəsɪ] N biopiratage *m*, biopiraterie *f*

biopsy ['baɪɒpsɪ] *(pl* **biopsies**) N *Med* biopsie *f*

biorhythm ['baɪəʊrɪðəm] N *Biol & Physiol* biorythme *m*

BIOS ['baɪɒs] N *Comput (abbr* **basic input/output system**) BIOS *m*

bioscience ['baɪəʊ,saɪəns] N bioscience *f*

bioscope ['baɪəʊskəʊp] N *Cin* **1** *Old-fashioned (projector)* bioscope *m* **2** *SAfr (cinema)* cinéma *m*

biosecurity [,baɪəʊsɪ'kjʊərətɪ] N biosécurité *f*

biosignature [,baɪəʊ'sɪgnətjə(r)] N signature *f* biologique

biosphere ['baɪəʊ,sfɪə(r)] N *Biol* biosphère *f*

biosynthesis [,baɪəʊ'sɪnθəsɪs] N *Chem & Biol* biosynthèse *f*

biotechnology [,baɪəʊtek'nɒlədʒɪ] N biotechnologie *f*; **the b. industry** la bioindustrie

biotherapy [,baɪəʊ'θerəpɪ] N *Biol & Med* biothérapie *f*

biotope ['baɪətəʊp] N *Ecol* biotope *m*

bioweapon ['baɪəʊ,wepən] N arme *f* biologique

bipartisan [,baɪpɑ:tɪ'zæn] ADJ *Pol* biparti, bipartite

bipartism [,baɪ'pɑ:tɪzəm] N *Pol* bipartisme *m*

bipartite [,baɪ'pɑ:taɪt] ADJ *Bot & Pol* biparti, bipartite

biped ['baɪped] *Zool* N bipède *m*

ADJ bipède

biplane ['baɪpleɪn] N *Aviat* biplan *m*

bipolar [,baɪ'pəʊlə(r)] ADJ **1** *Phys (having two poles)* bipolaire **2** *Am Psy* bipolaire

►► *Am Psy* ***bipolar disorder*** trouble *m* polaire

bipolarization, -isation [,baɪpəʊləraɪ'zeɪʃən] N *Pol* bipolarisation *f*

bipolarized, -ised [,baɪ'pəʊləraɪzd] ADJ *Pol* bipolarisé

birch [bɜ:tʃ] N **1** *Bot (tree)* bouleau *m*; *(wood)* (bois *m* de) bouleau *m* **2** *Br (rod for whipping)* verge *f*; **to give sb the b.** fouetter qn

COMP *(forest, furniture)* de bouleau

VT *Br* fouetter

►► ***birch plantation*** boulaie *f*, plantation *f* de bouleaux

birching ['bɜ:tʃɪŋ] N *Br* correction *f*; **to give sb a b.** fouetter qn, donner une correction à qn

bird [bɜ:d] N **1** *(gen)* oiseau *m*; *Culin* volaille *f*; **she eats like a b.** elle a un appétit d'oiseau; **a little b. told me** mon petit doigt me l'a dit; **strictly for the birds** bon pour les imbéciles; *Euph* **it's time you talked to him about the birds and the bees** *(facts of life)* il serait temps de lui expliquer que les bébés ne naissent pas dans les choux; **the b. has flown** l'oiseau s'est envolé; *Fam* **to give sb the b.** *(hiss)* huer *ou* siffler qn□; *(send packing)* envoyer qn paître; *Am (make fun of)* se foutre de la gueule de qn; *Am (gesture at)* faire un doigt d'honneur à qn; *Am Fam* **to flip sb the b.** faire un doigt d'honneur à qn; *Prov* **birds of a feather flock together** qui se ressemble s'assemble; **you and your father are birds of a feather** toi et ton père, vous ne valez pas mieux l'un que l'autre, toi et ton père, je vous mets dans le même sac; *Prov* **a b. in the hand is worth two in the bush** un tiens vaut mieux que deux tu l'auras

2 *Br Fam (woman)* nana *f*

3 *Fam (individual)* type *m*; **he's a strange b.** c'est un drôle d'oiseau; **a home b.** un(e) casanier(ère); *Fig* **night b.** noctambule *mf*

4 *Br Fam Crime slang* **to do b.** faire de la taule

►► *Fam Pej* ***bird brain*** tête *f* de linotte, écervelé(e) *m,f*; *Hunt* ***bird dog*** chien *m* d'arrêt *(pour le gibier à plumes)*; ***bird droppings*** fiente *f*; *Br* ***bird fancier*** *(interested in birds)* ornithologue *mf* amateur; *(breeder)* aviculteur(trice) *m,f*; *Med* ***bird flu*** grippe *f* aviaire; ***bird of paradise*** *(bird, flower)* oiseau *m* de paradis; *also Fig* ***bird of passage*** oiseau *m* de passage; ***bird of prey*** oiseau *m* de proie, rapace *m*; *Orn* ***bird sanctuary*** réserve *f ou* refuge *m* d'oiseaux

birdbath ['bɜ:dbɑ:θ, *pl* -bɑ:ðz] N vasque *f (pour les oiseaux)*

birdbox ['bɜ:dbɒks] N abri *m* pour les oiseaux

bird-brained [-breɪnd] ADJ *Fam (person)* écervelé, qui a une cervelle d'oiseau; *(idea)* insensé□

birdcage ['bɜ:dkeɪdʒ] N *(small)* cage *f* à oiseaux; *(large)* volière *f*

birdcatcher ['bɜ:dkætʃə(r)] N oiseleur *m*

birdhouse ['bɜ:dhaʊs, *pl* -haʊzɪz] N *Br (in garden)* abri *m* pour les oiseaux; *Am (aviary)* volière *f*

birdie ['bɜ:dɪ] N **1** *Fam (small bird)* petit oiseau□ *m*, oisillon□ *m*; *Phot* **watch the b.!** le petit oiseau va sortir! **2** *Golf* birdie *m*; **a b. 3** un birdie 3

VT *Golf* **to b. a hole** faire un birdie *(jouer un trou en un coup au-dessous du par)*

birdlike ['bɜ:dlaɪk] ADJ *(appetite)* d'oiseau; **b. movements/features** mouvements *mpl*/traits *mpl* semblables à ceux d'un oiseau

birdlime ['bɜ:dlaɪm] N glu *f*

bird-nesting N **to go b.** aller dénicher des oiseaux

birdseed ['bɜ:dsi:d] N graine *f* pour les oiseaux

bird's-eye ADJ **a b. view of sth** une vue panoramique de qch; *Fig* une vue d'ensemble de qch

►► *Cin & TV* ***bird's-eye shot, bird's-eye view*** plan *m* en plongée

bird-watcher N ornithologue *mf* amateur

bird-watching N ornithologie *f*; **to go b.** aller observer les oiseaux

biretta [bɪ'retə] N *Rel* barrette *f (d'un ecclésiastique)*

Biro® ['baɪrəʊ] *(pl* **Biros**) N *Br* stylo *m* (à) bille, Bic® *m*

birth [bɜ:θ] N **1** *(of child)* naissance *f*; **deaf from b.** sourd de naissance; *Fam Hum* **he should have been drowned at b.!** on aurait dû le noyer à la naissance!

2 *(act of bearing young* ► *of person)* accouchement *m*, couches *fpl*; (► *of animal)* mise *f* bas; **to give b.** *(woman)* accoucher; *(animal)* mettre bas; **she gave b. to a boy** elle a accouché d'un garçon; **a difficult b.** un accouchement difficile; **will the father be present at the b.?** le père assistera-t-il à l'accouchement *ou* à la naissance?

3 *Fig (origin* ► *of movement, nation)* naissance *f*, origine *f*; (► *of era, industry)* naissance *f*, commencement *m*; (► *of product, radio)* apparition *f*

4 *(ancestry, lineage)* naissance *f*, ascendance *f*; **he's Chinese by b.** il est chinois de naissance; **of high b.** de bonne famille, bien né; **of low b.** de basse extraction

►► ***birth certificate*** *Admin (original)* acte *m* de naissance; *(copy)* extrait *m* de naissance; *Astrol* ***birth chart*** thème *m* astral; *Press* ***births column*** carnet *m* rose ***birth control*** *(contraception)* contraception *f*; *(family planning)* contrôle *m* des naissances; **to practise b. control** utiliser un contraceptif *ou* un moyen de contraception; ***birth father*** père *m* biologique; ***birth mother*** mère *f* biologique; ***birth pangs*** douleurs *fpl* de l'accouchement; *Fig* **the b. pangs of democracy** la naissance difficile de la démocratie; ***birth parents*** parents *mpl* biologiques; ***birth rate*** (taux *m* de) natalité *f*

birthday ['bɜːθdeɪ] **N** anniversaire *m*; **her 21st b.** ses 21 ans; **let me buy the b. girl a drink** laisse-moi te payer un verre pour ton anniversaire; **they're giving him a b. party** ils organisent une fête pour son anniversaire

COMP *(cake, card, present)* d'anniversaire

▸▸ ***the Birthday Honours*** = titres honorifiques et autres distinctions décernés chaque année le jour de l'anniversaire officiel du souverain britannique; *Fam Hum* ***birthday suit*** *(of man)* costume *m* d'Adam; *(of woman)* costume *m* d'Ève

birthing ['bɜːθɪŋ] **N**

▸▸ *Br Obst* ***birthing pool*** piscine *f* d'accouchement; *Obst* ***birthing room*** salle *f* d'accouchement

birthmark ['bɜːθmɑːk] **N** tache *f* de naissance

birthplace ['bɜːθpleɪs] **N** *(town)* lieu *m* de naissance; *(house)* maison *f* natale; *Fig* berceau *m*

birthright ['bɜːθraɪt] **N** droit *m* (acquis à la naissance); **freedom of speech is every citizen's b.** la liberté d'expression constitue un droit pour chaque citoyen

birthstone ['bɜːθstəʊn] **N** pierre *f* porte-bonheur *(selon la date de naissance)*

biryani [ˌbɪrɪ'ɑːnɪ] **N** *Culin* biriani *m*; **chicken b.** poulet *m* biriani

Biscay ['bɪskeɪ] **N** Biscaye *f*

biscuit ['bɪskɪt] **N 1** *Br Culin* biscuit *m*, petit gâteau *m*; *Fam* **that really takes the b.!** ça, c'est vraiment le bouquet!

2 *Am Culin* = petit gâteau que l'on mange avec de la confiture ou avec un plat salé

3 *(colour)* beige *m*

4 *Cer* biscuit *m*

ADJ (de couleur) beige

▸▸ ***biscuit barrel*** boîte *f* à biscuits; ***biscuit cutter*** emporte-pièce *m*; ***biscuit factory*** biscuiterie *f*; ***biscuit tin*** boîte *f* à biscuits

bisect [baɪ'sekt] **VT** *(gen)* couper en deux; *Math* diviser en deux parties égales

VI *(of road etc)* bifurquer

bisection [ˌbaɪ'sekʃən] **N** *(action)* division *f* en deux; *Math* bissection *f*

bisector [ˌbaɪ'sektə(r)] **N** *Math* bissectrice *f*

bisexual [ˌbaɪ'sekʃʊəl] **N 1** *(person)* bisexuel(elle) *m,f* **2** *Biol & Zool* hermaphrodite *m*

ADJ 1 *(person, tendency)* bisexuel **2** *Biol & Zool* bisexué, hermaphrodite

bishop ['bɪʃəp] **N 1** *Rel* évêque *m*; **b.'s palace** palais *m* épiscopal, évêché *m* **2** *Chess* fou *m*

bishopric ['bɪʃəprɪk] **N** *Rel (position)* épiscopat *m*; *(diocese)* évêché *m*

bismuth ['bɪzməθ] **N** *Chem* bismuth *m*

bison ['baɪsən] **N** *Zool* bison *m*

bisque [bɪsk] **N 1** *(colour)* beige-rosé *m* **2** *Cer* biscuit *m* **3** *Culin (soup)* bisque *f*

bistre, *Am* **bister** ['bɪstə(r)] *Art* **N** bistre *m*

ADJ bistré

bistro ['biːstrəʊ] *(pl* **bistros**) **N** *Culin* bistro *m*

bisulphite [ˌbaɪ'sʌlfaɪt] **N** *Chem* bisulfite *m*; **sodium b.** bisulfite *m* de sodium *ou* de soude

bisync [ˌbaɪ'sɪŋk], **bisynchronous** [ˌbaɪ'sɪŋkrənəs] **ADJ** *Comput* bisynchrone

BIT[1] [bɪt]

N	
• bout **1**	• morceau **1**
• un peu de **2**	• pas mal de **2**
• numéro **3**	• mors **6**
• mèche **7**	• bit **8**

N 1 *(piece ▸ of paper, wood, string)* bout *m*; *(▸ of land)* morceau *m*; *(▸ of cake, meat, cheese)* morceau *m*; *(smaller)* bout *m*; *(▸ of book)* passage *m*; *(▸ of film)* séquence *f*; *(▸ of jigsaw puzzle)* pièce *f*; **you missed out the best bits** *(of story, joke)* tu as oublié le meilleur; **I liked the b. where they were in the cave** *(in book)* j'aime le passage où ils sont dans la caverne; *(in film)* j'aime la séquence où ils sont dans la caverne; **this is the difficult b.** c'est là où ça se complique; **bits and pieces of sth** des morceaux de qch; **she picked up her bits and pieces** elle a ramassé ses affaires; **in bits** en morceaux; *Fam* **she was in bits when they broke up** elle a eu le cœur brisé quand ils se sont séparés; **to take sth to bits** démonter qch; **the dog tore the paper to bits** le chien a complètement déchiré le journal; **to fall to bits** *(book, clothes)* tomber en lambeaux; **the wall was falling to bits** le mur tombait en morceaux *ou* en ruine; **to come to bits** *(dismantle)* se démonter; *(break)* tomber en morceaux; *Fam* **I love him to bits!** je l'adore!□

2 *(unspecified small quantity)* **a b. of dirt** une petite saleté; **a b. of advice** un (petit) conseil; **a b. of money/time** un peu d'argent/de temps; **a little b. of tact/patience** un tout petit peu de tact/de patience; **quite a b. of rain/trouble** pas mal de pluie/d'ennuis; **it's a b. of a problem** cela pose un problème; **it was a b. of a nuisance** c'était vraiment ennuyeux; **we got a b. of a shock** ça nous a fait un choc; **it's not a b. of use** cela ne sert absolument à rien; **he's a b. of a crook** il est un peu escroc sur les bords; **I've been a b. of a fool** j'ai été un peu bête; **to do one's b.** y mettre du sien, faire un effort; **we did our b. to help the children** nous avons fait ce qu'il fallait pour aider les enfants; **they ate up every b.** ils ont tout mangé jusqu'au dernier morceau; **I've had quite a b. to drink** j'ai un peu trop bu; **to make quite a b.** *(earn money)* gagner pas mal d'argent *ou* de fric; **to have a b. put away** avoir un petit pécule; **that must be worth quite a b.!** ça doit valoir pas mal d'argent!; **she's every b. as competent as he is** elle est tout aussi compétente que lui; *Fam* **to have a b. on the side** *(male lover)* avoir un amant; *(female lover)* avoir une maîtresse; *Br Fam* **to be a b. of all right** *(of woman)* être une jolie fille; *(of man)* être un beau mec; *Br Fam* **this is a b. of all right!** ça c'est chouette!; *Fam* **that takes a b. of doing** ça, c'est bien difficile

3 *Fam (role)* numéro *m*; **he's doing his perfect father b.** il nous fait son numéro du père parfait

4 *Fam (small coin)* pièce□ *f*; **a threepenny b.** une pièce de trois pence

5 *Am (coin)* = ancienne pièce de 12,5 cents; **two bits** vingt-cinq cents

6 *(for horse)* mors *m*; *Fig* **to take the b. between one's teeth** prendre le mors aux dents

7 *Tech (of drill)* mèche *f*

8 *Comput* bit *m*; **bits per second** bits *mpl* par seconde

9 *Am Fam (term of imprisonment)* peine *f* de prison□; **he did a b. in Fort Worth** il a fait de la taule à Fort Worth

• **a bit ADV 1** *(some time)* quelque temps; **let's sit down for a b.** asseyons-nous un instant *ou* un peu; **we waited a good/little b.** nous avons attendu un bon/un petit moment; **hold on** *or* **wait a b.!** attendez un peu *ou* un instant!; **he's away quite a b.** il est souvent absent; **after a b. we left** au bout de quelque temps nous sommes partis; **in a b.** dans quelques minutes

2 *(slightly)* un peu; **she's a good/little b. older than he is** elle est beaucoup/un peu plus âgée que lui; **it's a (little) b. more expensive** c'est un (tout petit) peu plus cher

3 *(at all)* **they haven't changed a b.** ils n'ont pas du tout changé; **I don't care a b.** cela m'est bien *ou* complètement égal; **are we bothering you? – not a b.!** on vous dérange? – pas du tout!; **not a b. of it!** pas le moins du monde!; **it's asking a b. much to expect her to apologize** il ne faut pas s'attendre à des excuses, c'est trop lui demander; **that's a b. much** *or* **a b. steep!** ça c'est un peu fort!

• **bit by bit ADV** petit à petit

▸▸ *Comput* ***bit command*** commande *f* binaire; *Cin & Theat* ***bit part*** petit rôle *m*; *Cin & Theat* ***bit player*** acteur(trice) *m,f* qui joue des petits rôles; *Comput* ***bit rate*** débit *f* binaire

bit[2] *pt of* **bite**

bitch [bɪtʃ] **N 1** *(female canine ▸ gen)* femelle *f*; *(dog)* chienne *f*; *(fox)* renarde *f*; *(wolf)* louve *f*; **a collie b.** un colley femelle

2 *very Fam Pej (woman)* garce *f*, **you b.!** espèce de garce!; *Br* **the poor b.** la pauvre; **the lucky b.** la veinarde

3 *Fam (thing)* saloperie *f*; **life's a b.!** chienne de vie!; **a b. of a job** une saloperie de boulot; **this problem's a real b.** c'est un vrai casse-tête!

4 *Fam (complaint)* motif *m* de râler; **what's their latest b.?** qu'est-ce qui les fait râler maintenant?

VT *Am Fam (spoil)* gâcher□; **that's really bitched my day** ça m'a vraiment fichu ma journée en l'air

VI *Fam* **1** *Br (say nasty things)* déblatérer (**about** contre) **2** *(complain)* râler, rouspéter; **to b. about sb/sth** râler *ou* rouspéter contre qn/qch

bitchin ['bɪtʃɪn] **ADJ** *Am Fam* super, génial

bitch-slap *Fam* **N** = gifle donnée avec la main grande ouverte

VT = gifler avec la main grande ouverte

bitchy ['bɪtʃɪ] *(compar* **bitchier**, *superl* **bitchiest**) **ADJ** *Fam* vache; **a b. remark** une vacherie; **she was very b. to the new girl** elle a été très vache avec la nouvelle

BITE [baɪt]

VT	
• mordre **1**	• piquer **1**
• agacer **2**	
VI	
• mordre **1–3**	• piquer **1**
N	
• morsure **1**	• piqûre **1**
• bouchée **2**	• touche **4**

(pt **bit** [bɪt], *pp* **bitten** ['bɪtən])

VT 1 *(of animal, person)* mordre; *(subj: insect, snake)* piquer, mordre; **I bit a piece out of the pear** j'ai mordu dans la poire; **the dog bit him on the leg** le chien l'a mordu à la jambe; **the dog bit the rope in two** le chien a coupé la corde en deux avec ses dents; **to b. one's nails** se ronger les ongles; **he bit his lip** il s'est mordu la lèvre; *Fig* **they've been bitten by the photography bug** ils sont devenus des mordus de photographie; *also Fig* **to b. one's tongue** se mordre la langue; *Fig* **to b. the bullet** serrer les dents; **we're going to have to b. the bullet and fire them** il va falloir prendre le taureau par les cornes et les renvoyer; **to b. the dust** mordre la poussière; **theirs is the latest plan to b. the dust** leur projet est le dernier à être tombé à l'eau; **to b. the hand that feeds one** montrer de l'ingratitude envers qn qui vous veut du bien; *Prov* **once bitten, twice shy** chat échaudé craint l'eau froide; *Am Fam* **b. me!** va te faire voir!

2 *Fam Fig (bother)* agacer, contrarier; **what's biting him?** quelle mouche l'a piqué?

VI 1 *(animal, person)* mordre; *(insect, snake)* piquer, mordre; *(fish)* mordre (à l'hameçon); **I bit into the apple** j'ai mordu dans la pomme; **does the dog b.?** il mord, votre chien?; **he bit through the cord** il coupa la ficelle avec ses dents; **are they** *or* **the fish biting (today)?** alors, ça mord?; *Fig* **don't worry, I don't b.!** n'ayez pas peur, je ne mords pas!

2 *(air, wind)* mordre, cingler

3 *Aut & Tech (clutch, screw)* mordre; *(tyre)* adhérer (à la route); **the acid bit into the metal** l'acide a attaqué le métal; **the rope bit into his wrists** la corde mordait dans la chair de ses poignets

4 *(take effect)* **the law is beginning to b.** les effets de la loi commencent à se faire sentir

N 1 *(of animal, person)* morsure *f*; *(of insect, snake)* piqûre *f*, morsure *f*; **mosquito bites** piqûres *fpl* de moustiques; *Am Fam* **to put the b. on sb** taper du fric à qn

2 *(piece)* bouchée *f*; **he swallowed the steak in three bites** il a avalé le bifteck en trois bouchées; **to take a b. of sth** *(bite into)* mordre dans qch; *(taste)* goûter (à) qch; *Fig* **the repairs took a big b. out of our savings** les réparations ont fait un trou dans nos économies; **do you want a b.?** tu veux (y) goûter?; *Br Fam* **to have** *or* **to get another** *or* **a second b. at the cherry** s'y reprendre à deux fois

3 *Fam (something to eat)* **we stopped for a b. (to eat)** nous nous sommes arrêtés pour manger un morceau; **I haven't had a b. all day** je n'ai rien mangé de la journée□

4 *Fishing* touche *f*; **did you get a b.?** ça a mordu?

5 *(sharpness ▸ of mustard, spice)* piquant *m*; *(▸ of speech, wit)* mordant *m*; *(▸ of air, wind)* caractère *m* cinglant *ou* mordant

6 *Med* articulé *m* dentaire

▸ **bite back** VT SEP **to b. sth back** se retenir de dire qch

▸ **bite off** VT SEP arracher d'un coup de dents; **she bit off a piece of toast** elle a mordu dans la tartine; **to b. off more than one can chew** avoir les yeux plus grands *ou* gros que le ventre; *Fam* **to b. sb's head off** enguirlander qn

biter ['baɪtə(r)] N *Br Prov* **it's a case of the b. bit** c'est l'arroseur arrosé, tel est pris qui croyait prendre

biting ['baɪtɪŋ] ADJ **1** *(insect)* piqueur, vorace **2** *Fig (remark, wit)* mordant, cinglant; *(wind)* cinglant, mordant; *(cold)* mordant, perçant

▸▸ *Aut* **biting point** *(of clutch)* point *m* d'attaque

bitmap ['bɪt,mæp] *Comput* N bitmap *m*

ADJ *(image, font)* bitmap, en mode point

bitmapped ['bɪtmæpt] ADJ *Comput (image, font)* bitmap, en mode point

bit-slice processor N *Comput* processeur *m* en tranches

bitten ['bɪtən] *pp of* **bit**

bitter ['bɪtə(r)] ADJ **1** *(taste)* amer, âpre; *Fig* **it's a b. pill (to swallow)** c'est difficile à avaler

2 *(resentful ▸ person)* amer; *(▸ look, tone)* amer, plein d'amertume; *(▸ reproach, tears)* amer; **to be b. about sth** être amer *ou* plein d'amertume au sujet de qch; *Fam Pej* **b. and twisted** aigri

3 *(unpleasant ▸ disappointment, experience)* amer, cruel; *(▸ argument, struggle)* violent; *(▸ blow)* dur; **the b. truth** l'amère vérité *f*; **we fought to the b. end** nous avons lutté jusqu'au bout

4 *(extreme ▸ enemy)* acharné; *(▸ opposition)* violent, acharné

5 *(cold ▸ wind)* cinglant, glacial; *(▸ weather)* glacial; *(▸ winter)* rude, dur

N *(beer)* = bière pression relativement amère, à forte teneur en houblon

• **bitters** NPL bitter *m*, amer *m*; *Pharm* amer *m*; **whisky and bitters** = cocktail au whisky et au bitter

▸▸ *Pharm* **bitter aloes** aloès *m* (médicinal); **bitter lemon** Schweppes® *m* au citron; *Bot* **bitter orange** orange *f* amère

bitterly ['bɪtəlɪ] ADV **1** *(speak)* amèrement, avec amertume; *(criticize)* âprement; *(weep)* amèrement **2** *(intensely ▸ ashamed, unhappy)* profondément; *(▸ disappointed)* cruellement; **it was a b. cold day** il faisait un froid de loup; **I've regretted it b. ever since** je n'ai cessé de le regretter amèrement

bittern ['bɪtən] N *Orn* butor *m*

bitterness ['bɪtənɪs] N **1** *(of disappointment, person, taste)* amertume *f*; *(of criticism, remark)* âpreté *f* **2** *(of opposition)* violence *f*

bittersweet ['bɪtəswi:t] ADJ *(memory, taste)* aigre-doux (aigre-douce), doux-amer (douce-amère)

N *Bot* douce-amère *f*

▸▸ *Am* **bittersweet chocolate** chocolat *m* noir *ou* à croquer

bitty ['bɪtɪ] (*compar* **bittier**, *superl* **bittiest**) ADJ **1** *Br Fam (disjointed)* décousu[□] **2** *Am (small)* **a little b. town** une toute petite ville

bitumen ['bɪtjumɪn] N bitume *m*

bituminous [bɪ'tju:mɪnəs] ADJ bitumineux; **b. coal** flambant *m*

bivalent [,baɪ'veɪlənt] ADJ *Chem* bivalent

bivalve ['baɪvælv] N bivalve *m*

ADJ bivalve

bivouac ['bɪvʊæk] (*pt & pp* **bivouacked**, *cont* **bivouacking**) *Mil* N bivouac *m*

VI bivouaquer

biweekly [,baɪ'wi:klɪ] (*pl* **biweeklies**) ADJ *(every two weeks)* bimensuel; *(twice weekly)* bihebdomadaire

ADV *(every two weeks)* tous les quinze jours; *(twice weekly)* deux fois par semaine

N *Press* bimensuel *m*

bizarre [bɪ'zɑ:(r)] ADJ bizarre

bizarrely [bɪ'zɑ:lɪ] ADV bizarrement

bizarreness [bɪ'zɑ:nɪs] N bizarrerie *f*

bizzies ['bɪzɪz] NPL *Br Fam* **the b.** *(the police)* les flics *mpl*

blab [blæb] (*pt & pp* **blabbed**, *cont* **blabbing**) *Fam*

VT laisser échapper[□], divulguer[□]

VI **1** *(tell secret)* vendre la mèche **2** *(prattle)* jaser, babiller; **she blabbed on about her holiday** elle n'en finissait pas de nous raconter ses vacances

blabber ['blæbə(r)] *Fam* N **1** *(person)* moulin *m* à paroles **2** *(prattle)* bavardage *m*, papotage *m*

VI jaser, babiller; **to b. on about sth** parler de qch à n'en plus finir

blabbermouth ['blæbə,maʊθ, *pl* -'maʊðz] N *Fam* pipelette *f*

black [blæk] ADJ **1** *(colour)* noir; **as b. as ink** noir comme du jais *ou* de l'encre; **b. and blue** *(bruised)* couvert de bleus; **they beat him b. and blue** ils l'ont roué de coups; **to be b. and blue all over** être couvert de bleus, être tuméfié

2 *(race)* noir; **the b. area of New York** le quartier noir de New York; **he won the b. vote** il a gagné les voix de l'électorat noir; **b. man** Noir *m*; **b. woman** Noire *f*; *Br Fam* **b. man's wheels** *(BMW ®)* BM *f*

3 *(coffee)* noir; *(tea)* nature *(inv)*

4 *(dark)* noir, sans lumière; **the room was as b. as** *Br* **pitch** *or Am* **tar** dans la pièce il faisait noir comme dans un four

5 *(gloomy ▸ future, mood)* noir; *(▸ despair)* sombre; **they painted a b. picture of our prospects** ils ont peint un sombre tableau de notre avenir; **the situation is not as b. as it looks** la situation n'est pas aussi désespérée qu'on pourrait le croire; **in a fit of b. despair** dans un moment d'extrême désespoir; **it's a b. day for the UN** c'est un jour noir pour l'ONU

6 *(angry)* furieux, menaçant; **he gave her a b. look** il lui a jeté *ou* lancé un regard noir

7 *(wicked)* noir, mauvais; **a b. deed** un crime, un forfait; **he's not as b. as he's painted** il n'est pas aussi mauvais qu'on le dit

8 *(dirty)* noir, sale; **her hands were b. with ink** elle avait les mains pleines d'encre

9 *Br Ind (factory, goods)* boycotté

N **1** *(colour)* noir *m*; **to be dressed in b.** *(gen)* être habillé de *ou* en noir; *(in mourning)* porter le deuil; **he'd argue** *or* **swear that b. is white** il refuse d'admettre l'évidence

2 *(darkness)* obscurité *f*, noir *m*

3 the b. *(in roulette)* le noir; *(in snooker)* la bille *ou* boule noire

4 *(idioms)* **to be in the b.** *(person)* être solvable; *(account)* être créditeur; **to get back into the b.** sortir du rouge; **to put sth down in b. and white** écrire qch noir sur blanc; **things aren't that b. and white** les choses ne sont pas si simples

VT **1** *(make black)* noircir; *(shoes)* cirer *(avec du cirage noir)*; **he blacked his attacker's eye** il a poché l'œil de son agresseur; *Theat* **the actors blacked their faces** les acteurs se sont noirci le visage **2** *Br Ind* boycotter

• **Black** N **1** *(person)* Noir(e) *m,f* **2** *Chess* noir *m*

▸▸ ***black Africa*** l'Afrique *f* noire; ***black American*** Afro-Américain(e) *m,f*; ***the black art, the black arts*** la magie noire; ***black bear*** ours *m* noir; *Entom* ***black beetle*** cafard *m*, blatte *f*; ***black belt*** *Sport* ceinture *f* noire; *Am Fam* = zone habitée par des Noirs; **she's a b. belt in judo** elle est ceinture noire de judo; ***black box*** boîte *f* noire; *Culin* ***black bread*** pain *m* de seigle; *Scot Culin* ***black bun*** = sorte de pain au raisin consommé au nouvel an; ***black cab*** taxi *m* londonien, taxi *m* anglais; ***black cherry*** *(fruit)* guigne *f* noire; *(tree)* merisier *m* américain, *Can* cerisier *m* tardif; ***black comedy*** comédie *f* noire; ***the Black Country*** le Pays noir; *Hist* ***Black Death*** peste *f* noire; *Com* ***black economy*** économie *f* noire; ***black eye*** œil *m* poché *ou* au beurre noir; ***the Black Forest*** la Forêt noire; ***Black Forest gateau*** forêt-noire *f*; *Petr* ***black gold*** or *m* noir; *Astron* ***black hole*** trou *m* noir; ***black humour*** humour *m* noir; ***black ice*** verglas *m*; *St Exch* ***black knight*** chevalier *m* noir; ***black magic*** magie *f* noire; ***black mamba*** mamba *m* noir; *Br Fam* ***Black Maria*** panier *m* à salade *(fourgon)*; ***black mark*** mauvais point *m*; **it's a b. mark against her** ça joue contre elle; ***black market*** N *Com* marché *m* noir; **on the b. market** au marché noir COMP *(cigarettes, whisky)* au marché noir; *Com* ***black marketeer*** vendeur(euse) *m,f* au marché noir; ***Black Mass*** messe *f* noire; *St Exch* ***Black Monday*** lundi *m* noir, jour *m* du krach (boursier) *(le lundi 19 octobre 1987)*; ***black money*** *(earned on black market)* argent *m* du marché noir; *(undeclared)* argent *m* non déclaré au fisc; *Rel* ***Black Muslim*** Black Muslim *mf (membre d'un mouvement séparatiste noir se réclamant de l'Islam)*; *Pol* ***Black Nationalism*** = mouvement nationaliste noir américain; *Am Pol* ***Black Panther*** Panthère *f* noire; ***black pepper*** poivre *m* gris; *Pol* ***Black Power*** Black Power *m (mouvement séparatiste noir né dans les années 60 aux États-Unis)*; *Br Culin* ***black pudding*** boudin *m* (noir); ***black rhinoceros*** rhinocéros *m* noir; *Parl* ***Black Rod*** = huissier chargé par la Chambre des lords britannique de convoquer les Communes; ***Black Russian*** *(cocktail)* black russian *m*; ***the Black Sea*** la mer Noire; ***black sheep*** brebis *f* galeuse; *Br Fig* ***black spot*** point *m* noir; *Hist* ***the Black and Tans*** = forces armées britanniques envoyées en Irlande en 1920 pour lutter contre le Sinn Fein; ***Black Thursday*** jeudi *m* noir *(jour du krach de Wall Street qui déclencha la crise de 1929)*; ***black tie*** = nœud papillon noir porté avec une tenue de soirée; **b. tie** *(on invitation card)* tenue de soirée exigée; ***black velvet*** *(cocktail)* = cocktail de champagne et de stout; *Br Mil* ***Black Watch*** = nom populaire d'un régiment de l'armée britannique, le Royal Highland Regiment; ***black widow (spider)*** latrodecte *m*, veuve *f* noire

▸ **black out** VT SEP **1** *(extinguish lights)* plonger dans l'obscurité; *Mil (in wartime)* faire le black-out dans **2** *Rad & TV (programme)* interdire la diffusion de **3** *(memory)* effacer (de son esprit), oublier

VI s'évanouir

▸ **black up** VI *Theat* se maquiller la peau en noir, se noircir le visage

> **THE BLACK COUNTRY**
>
> Le Pays noir désigne, en Grande-Bretagne, la région des West Midlands, autrefois riche en aciéries et en mines de charbon.

black-and-tan ADJ *(dog)* noir et feu *inv*

black-and-white ADJ **1** *(photograph, television)* noir et blanc; *Cin* **a b. film** un film en noir et blanc **2** *Fig (clear-cut)* précis, net; **there's no b. solution** le problème n'est pas simple; **he has very b. views on the war** il a des idées très arrêtées sur la guerre

N *Art (drawing, print)* dessin *m* en noir et blanc; *Phot (photograph)* photographie *f* en noir et blanc

blackball ['blæk,bɔ:l] N vote *m* contre

VT blackbouler

blackballing ['blæk,bɔ:lɪŋ] N blackboulage *m*

Blackberry® ['blækbərɪ] N Blackberry® *m*

blackberry ['blækbərɪ] (*pl* **blackberries**) N *Bot* mûre *f*

COMP *(jam)* de mûres; *(tart)* aux mûres

VI cueillir des mûres; **to go blackberrying** aller ramasser *ou* cueillir des mûres

▸▸ ***blackberry bush*** mûrier *m*

blackbird ['blæk,bɜ:d] N *Orn* merle *m*

blackboard ['blæk,bɔ:d] N tableau *m* (noir)

black-bordered [-'bɔ:dəd] ADJ *Art* à bordure noire

blackcock ['blæk,kɒk] N *Orn* coq *m* de bruyère

blackcurrant [,blæk'kʌrənt] N *(bush, fruit)* cassis *m*

blacken ['blækən] VT **1** *(make black ▸ house, wall)* noircir; *(▸ shoes)* cirer *(avec du cirage noir)*; **he blackened his face** il s'est noirci le visage **2** *(make dirty)* noircir, salir; **his fingers were blackened with ink** il avait les doigts couverts *ou* pleins d'encre; **smoke-blackened buildings** des bâtiments noircis par la fumée **3** *Fig (name, reputation)* noircir, ternir

VI *(cloud, sky)* s'assombrir, (se) noircir; *(colour, fruit)* (se) noircir, devenir noir

blackening ['blækənɪŋ] N noircissement *m*

black-eyed pea, black-eyed bean N dolique *m*, dolic *m*, niébé *m*

blackfly ['blæk,flaɪ] (*pl* **inv** *or* **blackflies**) N *Entom* puceron *m* noir

blackguard ['blægɑ:d] N *Old-fashioned* canaille *f*

blackhead ['blæk,hed] N point *m* noir

black-hearted ADJ méchant, malfaisant

blacking ['blækɪŋ] N (for shoes) cirage m noir; (for stove) pâte f à noircir

blackish ['blækɪʃ] ADJ noirâtre, tirant sur le noir

blackjack ['blæk,dʒæk] N 1 (card game) vingt-et-un m 2 Am (truncheon) matraque f

VT Am (beat) matraquer; (compel) contraindre (sous la menace); they blackjacked him into paying ils l'ont forcé à payer

blackleg ['blæk,leg] (pt & pp blacklegged, cont blacklegging) Br Pej N jaune m, briseur m de grève

VI briser la grève

blacklist ['blæklɪst] N liste f noire

VT mettre sur la liste noire

blackmail ['blæk,meɪl] VT faire chanter; to be blackmailed être victime d'un chantage; I'm being blackmailed for £5,000 je suis victime d'un chantage, on me réclame 5000 livres; he blackmailed them into meeting his demands il les a contraints par le chantage à satisfaire ses exigences

N chantage m

blackmailer ['blæk,meɪlə(r)] N maître chanteur m

blackness ['blæknɪs] N 1 (of colour) noir m, couleur f noire; Fig (of deed) atrocité f, noirceur f 2 (of night, room) obscurité f, noir m

blackout ['blækaut] N 1 (power failure) panne f d'électricité; Mil (in wartime) black-out m inv 2 (loss of consciousness) évanouissement m, étourdissement m; (amnesia) trou m de mémoire; I must have had a b. j'ai dû m'évanouir 3 Rad & TV black-out m inv, censure f

Blackshirt ['blæk∫ɜːt] N Hist Chemise f noire

blacksmith ['blæk,smɪθ] N (for horses) maréchal-ferrant m; (for tools) forgeron m

blackthorn ['blæk,θɔːn] N Bot prunelier m, épine f noire

black-tie ADJ it's b. il faut être en smoking

▸▸ black-tie dinner dîner m en smoking

blacktop ['blæk,tɒp] N Am route f goudronnée

blackwater fever ['blæk,wɔːtə-] N Med fièvre f bilieuse hémoglobinurique

bladder ['blædə(r)] N 1 Anat vessie f; to have a full b. avoir la vessie pleine 2 (of leather, skin, ball) vessie f 3 Bot & Med vésicule f

▸▸ Med bladder infection cystite f; Med bladder stone calcul m vésical

bladdered ['blædəd] ADJ Br Fam (drunk) bourré, beurré, pété

bladderwort ['blædə,wɜːt] N Bot utriculaire f

bladderwrack ['blædə,ræk] N Bot fucus m vésiculeux

blade [bleɪd] N 1 (cutting edge ▸ of knife, razor, tool) lame f; (▸ of guillotine) couperet m

2 Tech (of fan, propeller) pale f; (of helicopter) hélice f; (of turbine motor, water wheel) aube f; (of ice skates) lame f; (of oar, paddle) plat m, pale f; (of windscreen wiper) balai m, raclette f

3 Bot (of grass) brin m; (of wheat) pousse f; wheat in the b. blé m en herbe

4 Naut (in rowing ▸ oar) aviron m

5 Literary (sword) lame f

6 Arch (young man) gaillard m

7 Am Fam Crime slang (knife) lame f, surin m

VI Am Fam faire du roller

-bladed [bleɪdɪd] SUFF 1 (knife, razor) à lame…; sharp-b. knife couteau m aiguisé 2 (fan, propeller) à pale…; a five-b. fan un ventilateur à cinq pales

blader ['bleɪdə(r)] N Am Fam rolleur(euse) m,f

blag [blæg] Br Fam N (robbery) braquage m

VT 1 (steal) piquer 2 (con) to b. oneself sth obtenir qch au culot; to b. one's way in resquiller

blah [blɑː] Fam N 1 (meaningless remarks, nonsense) blabla m, baratin m 2 b., b., b. (to avoid repetition) etc etc; he went on for half an hour about how we all had to work harder, b., b., b. il nous a rabâché pendant une demi-heure qu'il fallait qu'on fasse tous plus d'efforts, etc etc

ADJ Am (uninteresting) insipide ▫, ennuyeux ▫

blame [bleɪm] N 1 (responsibility) responsabilité f, faute f; they laid or put the b. for the incident on the secretary ils ont rejeté la responsabilité de l'incident sur la secrétaire; we had to bear or to take the b. nous avons dû endosser la responsabilité; I got the b. for breaking the window c'est moi qu'on a accusé d'avoir cassé la fenêtre; to shift the b. onto sb rejeter la responsabilité sur qn; where does the b. lie? à qui la faute?; the b. lies with her c'est (de) sa faute

2 (reproof) blâme m, réprimande f; her conduct has been without b. sa conduite a été irréprochable

VT 1 (consider as responsible) rejeter la responsabilité sur; they b. inflation on the government or the government for inflation ils accusent le gouvernement d'être responsable de l'inflation; they blamed the early frost for the bad harvest ils ont attribué leur mauvaise récolte aux gelées précoces; he is/is not to b. c'est/ce n'est pas de sa faute; the bad weather was to b. c'était à cause du mauvais temps; don't b. me (for it)! inutile de m'accuser!; don't b. me if you're late tu ne viendras pas dire que c'est de ma faute si tu es en retard; you have only yourself to b. tu ne peux t'en prendre qu'à toi-même, tu l'as voulu ou cherché

2 (reproach) critiquer, reprocher; to b. sb for sth reprocher qch à qn; I b. myself for having left her alone je m'en veux de l'avoir laissée seule; you can't b. her for wanting a divorce tu ne peux pas lui reprocher de vouloir divorcer; I wouldn't b. you if you left him je te comprendrais si tu le quittais; he left in disgust – I don't b. him! il est parti dégoûté – ça se comprend!

blamed [bleɪmd] ADJ Am damné, maudit

blameless ['bleɪmlɪs] ADJ irréprochable, sans reproche; to lead a b. life avoir une vie irréprochable

blamelessly ['bleɪmlɪslɪ] ADV d'une façon irréprochable

blameworthy ['bleɪm,wɜːðɪ] ADJ (person) fautif, coupable; (action) répréhensible

blanch [blɑːntʃ] VT (gen) décolorer, blanchir; Agr & Culin blanchir; blanched almonds amandes fpl émondées ou épluchées

VI blêmir

blancmange [blə'mɒndʒ] N Culin = entremets généralement préparé à partir d'une poudre, flan m instantané

bland [blænd] ADJ 1 (flavour, food) fade, insipide; (diet) fade 2 (person ▸ dull) insipide, ennuyeux; (▸ ingratiating) mielleux, doucereux 3 (weather) doux (douce)

blandish ['blændɪʃ] VT amadouer

blandishment ['blændɪʃmənt] N (usu pl) (coaxing) cajoleries fpl; (flattery) flatterie f; neither threats nor blandishments had any effect on him mes menaces comme mes flatteries n'ont eu aucun effet sur lui

blandly ['blændlɪ] ADV (say ▸ dully) affablement, avec affabilité; (▸ ingratiatingly) d'un ton mielleux

blank [blæŋk] ADJ 1 (paper ▸ with no writing) vierge, blanc (blanche); (▸ unruled) blanc (blanche); Admin (form) vierge, à remplir; Admin fill in the b. spaces remplissez les blancs ou les (espaces) vides; Admin leave this line b. n'écrivez rien sur cette ligne; b. ballot paper bulletin m blanc, vote m blanc

2 (empty ▸ screen, wall) vide; (▸ cassette) vierge; (▸ cartridge) à blanc; Comput (▸ disk) vide; to go b. (screen) s'éteindre; (face) se vider de toute expression; my mind went b. j'ai eu un trou; Cards to be b. in clubs ne pas avoir de trèfles dans son jeu

3 (face, look ▸ expressionless) vide, sans expression; (▸ confused) déconcerté, dérouté; she looked b. (expressionless) elle avait le regard vide; (confused) elle avait l'air déconcerté

4 (absolute ▸ protest, refusal) absolu, net; (▸ dismay) absolu, profond

N 1 (empty space, void) blanc m, (espace m) vide m; fill in the blanks remplissez les blancs ou les (espaces) vides; she filled in the blanks of her education elle a comblé les lacunes de son éducation; the rest of his life is a b. on ne sait rien du reste de sa vie; my mind was a total b. j'ai eu un passage à vide complet; Fig to draw a b. (be unsuccessful in search) faire chou blanc; Am (be unable to remember) avoir un trou de mémoire; she searched everywhere for him but drew a b. elle l'a cherché partout mais sans succès; Cards to have a b. in clubs ne pas avoir de trèfles dans son jeu

2 (form) formulaire m (vierge ou à remplir), imprimé m

3 (cartridge) cartouche f à blanc; Fam Hum to shoot or to fire blanks (man) être stérile ▫

4 (in dominoes) blanc m

5 (metal disc ▸ in minting coins) flan m; Metal & Tech flan, masselotte f, galette f

6 Typ (to replace swear word etc) tiret m

VT Fam faire semblant de ne pas voir, ignorer; I said hello but he just blanked me je lui ai dit bonjour mais il m'a ignoré

▸▸ Fin blank cheque chèque m en blanc; Fig to write sb a b. cheque donner carte blanche à qn; Fin blank credit crédit m en blanc; Fin blank endorsement endossement m en blanc; Literature blank verse vers mpl blancs ou sans rime

▸**blank out** VT SEP (parts of text, tape) effacer; Phot her face had been blanked out (on negative) on avait effacé son visage; Typ (on print) on avait caché son visage; she's blanked out the memory elle a effacé cet événement de sa mémoire

VI (lose consciousness) tomber dans les pommes

blank-endorse VT Fin endosser en blanc

blanket ['blæŋkɪt] N 1 (for bed) couverture f 2 Fig (of clouds, snow) couche f; (of fog) manteau m, nappe f; (of smoke) voile m, nuage m; (of despair, sadness) manteau m 3 Typ blanchet m

VT 1 (of snow) recouvrir; (of fog, smoke) envelopper, voiler; blanketed with snow recouvert de neige 2 (noise) étouffer, assourdir

ADJ général, global; a b. rule for all employees un règlement qui s'applique à tout le personnel

▸▸ Com blanket agreement accord-cadre m; blanket bath grande toilette f (d'un malade alité); Rad & TV blanket coverage (of event) reportage m (très) complet; Ins our insurance policy guarantees b. coverage notre police d'assurance couvre tous les risques; Ins blanket policy police f globale (tous risques); Sewing blanket stitch point m de feston

blanking ['blæŋkɪŋ] N TV & Tech suppression f de faisceau; (erasing) effacement m

blankly ['blæŋklɪ] ADV 1 (look ▸ without expression) avec le regard vide; (▸ with confusion) d'un air ahuri ou interdit 2 (answer, state) carrément; (refuse) tout net, sans ambages

blankness ['blæŋknɪs] N 1 (of person) air m confus ou décontenancé 2 (of eyes, expression) vacuité f

blare [bleə(r)] N (gen) vacarme m; (of car horn, siren) bruit m strident; (of radio, television) beuglement m; (of trumpet) sonnerie f

VI (siren, music) beugler; (voice) brailler

▸**blare out** VT SEP (of radio, television) beugler, brailler; (of person) brailler, hurler

VI (radio, television) beugler, brailler; (person, voice) brailler, hurler

blarney ['blɑːnɪ] Fam N (smooth talk) baratin m; (flattery) flatterie ▫ f

VT (smooth talk) baratiner; (wheedle) embobiner; (flatter) flatter ▫

▸▸ Blarney Stone = au château de Blarney, en Irlande, pierre censée donner des dons d'éloquence à ceux qui l'embrassent; he's kissed the B. Stone il a la langue bien pendue

blasé [Br 'blɑːzeɪ, Am blɑː'zeɪ] ADJ blasé

blaspheme [blæs'fiːm] Rel VT blasphémer

VI blasphémer

blasphemer [blæs'fiːmə(r)] N Rel blasphémateur(trice) m,f

blasphemous ['blæsfəməs] ADJ Rel (poem, talk) blasphématoire; (person) blasphémateur

blasphemously ['blæsfəməslɪ] ADV Rel de façon impie, avec impiété

blasphemy ['blæsfəmɪ] (pl blasphemies) N Rel blasphème m; what you're saying is b. c'est blasphémer ce que vous dites là

blast [blɑːst] N 1 (explosion) explosion f; (shock wave) souffle m; the house was destroyed by the b. la maison a été soufflée par l'explosion

2 (of air) bouffée f; (of steam) jet m; (of wind) coup m de vent, rafale f

3 (sound ▸ of car horn, whistle) coup m strident; (▸ of trumpet) sonnerie f; (▸ of explosion) déto-

nation *f*; (▸ *of rocket*) rugissement *m*; **a whistle b.** un coup de sifflet; **he blew a couple of blasts on his whistle** il a donné plusieurs coups de sifflet

4 *Am Fam (fun)* **we had a b.** on s'est vraiment marrés; **he gets a b. out of teasing her** cela l'amuse de la taquiner; **it was a b.** c'était génial

5 *Fam* **a b. from the past** *(song)* un vieux tube; **that's a real b. from the past** *(fashion, behaviour etc)* c'est comme autrefois; *(brings back memories)* ça me ramène des années en arrière

6 *(idioms)* **she had the radio on (at) full b.** elle faisait marcher la radio à fond; **the machine was going at full b.** la machine avançait à toute allure

VT 1 *Constr & Mining (with explosives)* faire sauter; **they blasted a tunnel through the mountain** ils ont creusé un tunnel à travers la montagne avec des explosifs

2 *(with gun)* tirer sur; **the thieves blasted their way through the roadblock** les voleurs ont forcé le barrage routier en tirant des coups de feu

3 *(of radio, television)* beugler

4 *(criticize)* attaquer *ou* critiquer violemment

5 *(plan)* détruire; *(hope)* briser, anéantir

VI *(radio, television)* beugler; *(music)* retentir; **the radio was blasting away** la radio marchait à fond

EXCLAM *Fam* **b. (it)!** zut alors!; **b. that car!** il y en a marre de cette voiture!; **b. her!** ce qu'elle peut être embêtante!

▸▸ *Tech* ***blast furnace*** haut-fourneau *m*

▸ **blast off VI** *(rocket)* décoller

blasted ['blɑːstɪd] *Fam* **ADJ 1** *(as intensifier)* fichu, sacré; **you b. fool!** espèce d'imbécile! **2** *(drunk)* bourré, beurré; *(on drugs)* défoncé

ADV *(for emphasis)* **don't go so b. fast!** ne va pas si vite, bon sang!

blasting ['blɑːstɪŋ] **N 1** *(explosions)* travail *m* aux explosifs, explosions *fpl*; *Tech* minage *m* **2** *Br Fam (verbal attack)* engueulade *f*; **he got a b. from the boss** le patron lui a passé un sacré savon

blastoderm ['blæstəʊdɜːm] **N** *Biol* blastoderme *m*

blast-off N lancement *m*, mise *f* à feu *(d'une fusée spatiale)*; **ten seconds to b.** dix secondes avant la mise à feu

blastomere ['blæstəˌmɪə(r)] **N** *Biol* blastomère *m*

blatancy ['bleɪtənsɪ] **N** *(obviousness)* évidence *f*, caractère *m* flagrant

blatant ['bleɪtənt] **ADJ** *(discrimination, injustice)* évident, flagrant; *(lie)* manifeste; **it was a b. attempt to win him over** c'était une tentative évidente de s'assurer ses faveurs

blatantly ['bleɪtəntlɪ] **ADV** *(discriminate, disregard)* de façon flagrante; *(cheat, lie)* de façon éhontée; **it's b. obvious that...** il est évident que...; **yes, that's b. obvious** oui, évidemment

blather ['blæðə(r)] *Am* **N** *(UNCOUNT)* âneries *fpl*, bêtises *fpl*

VI raconter des bêtises *ou* des âneries

blaxploitation [ˌblæksplɔɪ'teɪʃən] **N** *Cin* = genre de cinéma qui exploitait les stéréotypes associés à l'identité noire américaine au cinéma, au cours des années 70

blaze [bleɪz] **N 1** *(flame)* flamme *f*, flammes *fpl*, feu *m*; *(large fire)* incendie *m*; **five die in b.** *(in headline)* un incendie a fait cinq morts

2 *(burst* ▸ *of colour)* éclat *m*, flamboiement *m*; (▸ *of light)* éclat *m*; (▸ *of eloquence, enthusiasm)* élan *m*, transport *m*; (▸ *of sunlight)* torrent *m*; **a b. of gunfire** des coups de feu, une fusillade; **in a sudden b. of anger** sous le coup de la colère; **he finished in a b. of glory** il a terminé en beauté

3 *Miner (of gem)* éclat *m*, brillance *f*

4 *Br Fam (idioms)* **what the blazes are you doing here?** qu'est-ce que tu fabriques ici?; **how the blazes would I know?** comment veux-tu que je le sache?; **we ran like blazes** nous avons couru à toutes jambes; **go** *or* **get to blazes!** va te faire voir!

VI 1 *(fire)* flamber; **the house was blazing (away)** *(on fire)* la maison flambait; **he suddenly blazed with anger** il s'est enflammé de colère; **his eyes were blazing with anger/passion** ses yeux lançaient des éclairs de colère/passion **2** *(colour, light, sun)* flamboyer; *(gem)* resplendir, briller; **the fields blazed with colour** les champs resplendissaient de mille couleurs

VT 1 *(proclaim)* proclamer, claironner; *(publish)* publier; **the news was blazed across the front page** la nouvelle faisait la une du journal **2** *(lead)* **to b. the way for sth** préparer le terrain pour qch **3** *(idiom)* **to b. a trail** frayer un chemin; **they're blazing a trail in biotechnology** ils font un travail de pionniers dans le domaine de la biotechnologie

▸ **blaze down VI** *(sun)* flamboyer, darder ses rayons

▸ **blaze up VI 1** *(fire)* prendre immédiatement *ou* rapidement **2** *(person)* s'enflammer de colère, s'emporter; *(anger, resentment)* éclater

blazer ['bleɪzə(r)] **N** blazer *m*

blazing ['bleɪzɪŋ] **ADJ 1** *(building, town)* en flammes, embrasé; **to sit in front of a b. fire** s'installer devant une bonne flambée

2 *(sun)* brûlant, ardent; *(heat)* torride; **a b. hot day** une journée de chaleur torride

3 *(light)* éclatant; *(colour)* très vif; *(gem)* brillant, étincelant; *(eyes)* qui jette des éclairs

4 *(argument)* violent

5 *(angry)* furieux

blazon ['bleɪzn] **VT** *(proclaim)* proclamer, claironner; **to b. sth abroad** proclamer qch, crier qch sur les toits; *Fig* **his name was blazoned over the front pages of all the newspapers** son nom s'étalait en grosses lettres à la une de tous les journaux

▸ **blazon forth, blazon out VT SEP** *Formal* annoncer *ou* proclamer à son de trompe

bldg *(written abbr* **building)** bât.

bleach [bliːtʃ] **N** *(gen)* décolorant *m*; **(household) b.** eau *f* de Javel

VT 1 *(clothes, linen)* passer à l'eau de Javel **2** *(of sun* ▸ *bones)* blanchir; (▸ *colour)* éclaircir **3** *(hair* ▸ *chemically)* décolorer, oxygéner; (▸ *with sun)* éclaircir; **to b. one's hair** se décolorer les cheveux; **a bleached blonde** une fausse blonde, une blonde décolorée

VI blanchir; **do not b.** *(washing instruction)* javel interdite

bleachers ['bliːtʃəz] **NPL** *Am Sport* gradins *mpl*

bleaching ['bliːtʃɪŋ] **N** blanchiment *m*; *(of hair)* décoloration *f*

▸▸ ***bleaching agent*** produit *m* blanchissant, décolorant *m*

bleak [bliːk] **ADJ 1** *(place, room)* froid, austère; *(landscape)* morne, désolé

2 *(weather)* morne, maussade; *(winter)* rude, rigoureux

3 *(situation)* sombre, morne; *(life)* morne, monotone; **the future looks b.** l'avenir se présente plutôt mal

4 *(mood, person)* lugubre, morne; *(smile)* pâle; *(tone, voice)* monocorde, morne

bleakly ['bliːklɪ] **ADV** *(speak)* d'un ton morne *ou* monocorde; *(stare)* d'un air triste, lugubrement

bleakness ['bliːknɪs] **N 1** *(of furnishings, room)* austérité *f*; *(of landscape)* caractère *m* morne *ou* désolé

2 *(of weather)* caractère *m* morne *ou* maussade; *(of winter)* rigueurs *fpl*

3 *(of situation)* caractère *m* sombre *ou* peu prometteur; *(of life)* monotonie *f*

4 *(of mood, person)* tristesse *f*; *(of voice)* ton *m* monocorde *ou* morne

blearily ['blɪərɪlɪ] **ADV** les yeux troubles

bleary ['blɪərɪ] *(compar* **blearier**, *superl* **bleariest)** **ADJ 1** *(eyes, vision)* trouble **2** *(indistinct)* indécis, vague

bleary-eyed ADJ *(from sleep)* aux yeux troubles

bleat [bliːt] **VI 1** *(sheep)* bêler; *(goat)* bêler, chevroter **2** *(person* ▸ *speak)* bêler, chevroter; (▸ *whine)* geindre, bêler

VT *(say)* dire d'un ton bêlant; *(whine)* geindre, bêler

N 1 *(of sheep)* bêlement *m*; *(of goat)* bêlement, chevrotement *m* **2** *(of person* ▸ *voice)* bêlement *m*; (▸ *complaint)* gémissement *m*

bleating ['bliːtɪŋ] **ADJ** *(voice)* chevrotant

N 1 *(of sheep)* bêlement *m*; *(of goat)* bêlement *m*, chevrotement *m* **2** *(of person* ▸ *voice)* bêlement *m*; (▸ *complaint)* gémissement *m*

bleed [bliːd] *(pt & pp* **bled** [bled]) **VI 1** *(lose blood)* saigner, perdre du sang; **to b. to death** saigner à mort; **my nose is bleeding** je saigne du nez; *Fig Ironic* **my heart bleeds for you!** tu me fends le cœur! **2** *Bot (plant)* pleurer, perdre sa sève **3** *(cloth, colour)* déteindre

VT 1 *(person)* saigner **2** *Fig Fin (extort money from)* saigner; **to b. sb dry** *or* **white** saigner qn à blanc **3** *Aut & Tech (brake, radiator)* purger

N *Comput & Typ* fond *m* perdu, plein papier *m*

bleeder ['bliːdə(r)] **N** *Br very Fam (person* ▸ *gen)* type *m*; (▸ *disagreeable)* salaud *m*; **poor b.** pauvre gars *m*; **lucky b.** sacré veinard *m*

bleeding ['bliːdɪŋ] **N 1** *Med (loss of blood)* saignement *m*; *(haemorrhage)* hémorragie *f*; *(taking of blood)* saignée *f*; **they stopped the b.** ils ont arrêté l'hémorragie; **b. from the nose** saignement *m* de nez **2** *Hort (of plant)* écoulement *m* de sève **3** *Aut & Tech (of brake, radiator)* purge *f*

ADJ 1 *(wound)* saignant, qui saigne; *(person)* qui saigne **2** *Br very Fam (as intensifier)* fichu, sacré; **b. idiot!** espèce d'imbécile!; **what a b. nuisance!** quelle saloperie!

ADV *very Fam* vachement; **you're b. (well) coming with me!** un peu, que tu vas venir avec moi!; **that was b. stupid!** c'est vraiment con, ce que tu as fait/dit!

▸▸ ***bleeding heart*** *Pej (person)* sentimental *m*; *Bot* cœur-de-Jeannette *m*

bleeding-heart ADJ *Pej* **he's a b. liberal** c'est un sentimental qui s'apitoie sur le sort des infortunés

bleep [bliːp] **N** bip *m*, bip-bip *m*

VI émettre un bip *ou* un bip-bip

VT 1 *(doctor)* appeler (au moyen d'un bip *ou* d'un bip-bip) **2** *Rad & TV* **to b. words (out)** masquer des paroles (par un bip)

bleeper ['bliːpə(r)] **N** *Br* bip *m*, bip-bip *m*

bleeping ['bliːpɪŋ] **N** *(of electronic device)* bip-bip *m*

blemish ['blemɪʃ] **N 1** *(flaw)* défaut *m*, imperfection *f*; *(on fruit)* tache *f* **2** *(on face* ▸ *pimple)* bouton *m* **3** *Fig (on name, reputation)* tache *f*, *Literary* souillure *f*; **her reputation is without b.** sa réputation est sans tache

VT 1 *(beauty, landscape)* gâter; *(fruit)* tacher **2** *Fig (reputation)* tacher, *Literary* souiller

> Note that the French verb **blêmir** is a false friend and is never a translation for the English verb **to blemish**. It means **to go pale.**

blench [blentʃ] **VI** *(recoil in fear)* reculer; *(turn pale)* blêmir; **she blenched at the idea** à cette pensée, elle pâlit *ou* blêmit; **without blenching** sans broncher *ou* sourciller

blend [blend] **VT 1** *(mix together* ▸ *gen)* mélanger, mêler; (▸ *cultures, races)* fusionner; (▸ *feelings, qualities)* joindre, unir; *Culin* **b. the butter and sugar (together), b. the sugar into the butter** mélangez le beurre au *ou* avec le sucre; **to b. old traditions with modern methods** faire un mélange de traditions anciennes et de méthodes modernes **2** *(colours* ▸ *mix together)* mêler, mélanger; (▸ *put together)* marier; **to b. white and black** mélanger du blanc avec du noir; *(in painting)* **to b. one colour into another** fondre une couleur dans une autre

VI 1 *(mix together* ▸ *gen)* se mélanger, se mêler; (▸ *cultures, races)* fusionner; (▸ *feelings, sounds)* se confondre, se mêler; (▸ *perfumes)* se marier; **their voices blended into one** leurs voix se confondaient **2** *(colours* ▸ *form one shade)* se fondre; (▸ *go well together)* aller ensemble

N 1 *(mixture* ▸ *of teas, whiskies, tobaccos etc)* mélange *m* **2** *Fig (of feelings, qualities)* alliance *f*, mélange *m*; **his speech was a b. of caution and encouragement** son discours était un mélange de prudence et d'encouragement

▸▸ *Comput* ***blended threat*** = attaque lancée contre un réseau, combinant plusieurs méthodes afin de causer le plus de dégâts possibles; ***blended whisky*** blend *m (whisky obtenu par mélange de whiskies de grain industriels et de whiskies pur malt)*

▸**blend in** VI *(harmonize)* s'harmoniser, se marier (**with** avec); *(of person)* s'intégrer; **that new building doesn't b. in with its surroundings** ce nouveau bâtiment ne se marie pas bien *ou* ne va pas bien avec ce qui l'entoure

VT SEP *Culin (mix)* incorporer

blender ['blendə(r)] N *Culin* mixer *m*

blending ['blendɪŋ] N **1** *(mixing)* mélange *m*; *Pharm* mixtion *f*; *(in winemaking)* coupage *m* **2** *Fig (of feelings, qualities)* alliance *f*

bless [bles] *(pt & pp* **blessed***)* VT **1** *Rel (of God, priest)* bénir; **God b. (you)!, b. you!** que Dieu vous bénisse!; **b. you!** *(after sneeze)* à vos/tes souhaits!, *Suisse* santé!; *(in thanks)* merci mille fois!; **Mary, b. her, has agreed to do it** Mary, Dieu soit loué, a accepté de le faire; **he remembered her birthday, b. his heart!** et il n'a pas oublié son anniversaire, le petit chéri!; **b. your heart!** que tu es gentil!; *Fam Old-fashioned* **b. my soul!** Seigneur!, mon Dieu!; *Br Fam Hum* **he's doing his mum's shopping for her? ah, b. (him** *or* **his little cotton socks)!** il fait les courses pour sa mère? comme il est gentil!; *Fam* **I'm blessed if I know!** que le diable m'emporte si je sais!; **God b. America** = phrase traditionnellement prononcée par le président des États-Unis pour terminer une allocution **2** *(usu passive) Formal (endow, grant)* douer, doter; **to be blessed with sth** jouir de qch, avoir le bonheur de posséder qch; **she is blessed with excellent health** elle a le bonheur d'avoir une excellente santé; **they have been blessed with two fine children** ils ont deux enfants adorables; *Fam* **he hasn't a penny to b. himself with** il n'a pas le sou **3** *Rel (glorify)* **to b. God** bénir *ou* adorer Dieu

blessed [blest] *pt & pp of* **bless**

ADJ [blesɪd] **1** *Rel (holy)* béni, sacré

2 *Rel (favoured by God)* bienheureux, heureux; *Bible* **b. are the poor in spirit** heureux les pauvres d'esprit

3 *(wonderful ▸ day, freedom, rain)* béni

4 *Fam (as intensifier)* sacré, fichu; **the whole b. day** toute la sainte journée; **I can't see a b. thing** je n'y vois rien

NPL [blest] *Rel* **the b.** les bienheureux *mpl*

▸▸ *Rel* ***the Blessed Virgin*** la Sainte Vierge

blessedly ['blesɪdlɪ] ADV parfaitement; **the speech was b. short** Dieu merci, le discours fut bref

blessedness ['blesɪdnɪs] N félicité *f*; *Rel* béatitude *f*

blessing ['blesɪŋ] N **1** *Rel (God's favour)* grâce *f*, faveur *f*; **the b. of the Lord be upon you** que Dieu vous bénisse

2 *Rel (prayer)* bénédiction *f*; *(before meal)* bénédicité *m*; **to give** *or* **to pronounce the b.** donner la bénédiction; **the priest said the b.** le prêtre a donné la bénédiction

3 *Fig (approval)* bénédiction *f*, approbation *f*; **with the b. of his parents** avec la bénédiction de ses parents

4 *(advantage)* bienfait *m*, avantage *m*; *(godsend)* aubaine *f*, bénédiction *f*; **it was a b. that no one was hurt** c'était une chance que personne ne soit blessé; **the rain was a b. for the farmers** la pluie était un don du ciel *ou* une bénédiction pour les agriculteurs; **it was a b. in disguise** c'était une bonne chose, en fin de compte

blest [blest] *Arch or Literary* = **blessed**

blether ['bleðə(r)] N **1** *(foolish talk)* âneries *fpl*, bêtises *fpl* **2** *Scot (chat)* causette *f*; **to have a b. (with sb)** bavarder (avec qn)

VI **1** *(talk foolishly)* dire des âneries *ou* des bêtises **2** *Scot (chat)* bavarder

blight [blaɪt] N **1** *Bot & Agr (of flowering plants)* rouille *f*; *(of fruit trees)* cloque *f*; *(of cereals)* rouille *f*, nielle *f*; *(of potato plants)* mildiou *m* **2** *(curse)* malheur *m*, fléau *m*; **the accident cast a b. on our holiday** l'accident a gâché nos vacances; **her illness was a b. on their happiness** sa maladie a terni leur bonheur

VT **1** *Bot & Agr (plants ▸ gen)* rouiller; *(cereals)* nieller, rouiller **2** *(spoil ▸ happiness, holiday)* gâcher; *(▸ career, life)* gâcher, briser; *(▸ hopes)* anéantir, détruire; *(▸ plans)* déjouer; **a marriage blighted by money problems** un mariage assombri par des problèmes d'argent

blighter ['blaɪtə(r)] N *Br Fam* type *m*; **you lucky b.!** sacré veinard!; **silly blighters!** les imbéciles!

blimey ['blaɪmɪ] EXCLAM *Br Fam* ça alors!, mon Dieu!

blimp [blɪmp] N *Aviat (airship)* dirigeable *m*

• **Blimp** N *Fam* vieux réac *m*

blind [blaɪnd] ADJ **1** *(sightless)* aveugle, non voyant; **to go b.** devenir aveugle; **b. from birth** aveugle de naissance; **he's b. in one eye** il est aveugle d'un œil, il est borgne; **I'm b. without my glasses** je ne vois rien sans mes lunettes; **as b. as a bat** myope comme une taupe; **to turn a b. eye to sth** fermer les yeux sur qch

2 *(unthinking)* aveugle; **b. loyalty/trust** loyauté *f*/confiance *f* aveugle; **he flew into a b. rage** il s'est mis dans une colère noire; **they were b. to the danger** le danger leur échappait; **she was b. to the consequences** elle ne voyait pas les conséquences; **love is b.** l'amour est aveugle

3 *(hidden from sight ▸ corner, turning)* sans visibilité

4 *Aviat (landing, take-off)* aux appareils; **b. flying** vol *m* sans visibilité, vol *m* en P.S.V.

5 *(as intensifier)* **he was b. drunk** il était ivre mort; *Fam* **it doesn't make a b. bit of difference to me** cela m'est complètement égal

6 *(without exit ▸ window, door)* feint, aveugle

VT **1** *(deprive of sight)* aveugler, rendre aveugle; *(of flash of light)* aveugler, éblouir; **blinded ex-servicemen** aveugles *mpl* de guerre; **we were blinded by the smoke** on était aveuglé par la fumée

2 *(deprive of judgement, reason)* aveugler; **love blinded her to his faults** aveuglée par l'amour, elle n'a pas vu ses défauts; *Hum* **to b. sb with science** éblouir qn par sa science

N **1** *(for window)* store *m*; **shop b.** *(over pavement)* banne *f* **2** *Br Fam (trick)* prétexte[□] *m*, feinte[□] *f*; **the trip was just a b. for his smuggling activities** le voyage a servi à masquer *ou* dissimuler ses activités de contrebande **3** *Am (hiding place)* cachette *f*; *Hunt* affût *m*

NPL **the b.** les aveugles *mpl*, les non-voyants *mpl*; **I was told to show him how the new photocopier works but it's like the b. leading the b.** on m'a demandé de lui montrer comment se servir de la nouvelle photocopieuse mais je n'en sais pas plus long que lui

ADV **1** *Aut & Aviat (drive, fly ▸ without visibility)* sans visibilité; *(▸using only instruments)* aux instruments **2** *(purchase)* sans avoir vu; *(decide)* à l'aveuglette **3** *(as intensifier)* **I would swear b. he was there** j'aurais donné ma tête à couper *ou* j'aurais juré qu'il était là

▸▸ *Br* ***blind alley*** impasse *f*, cul-de-sac *m*; *Fig* **the government's new idea is just another b. alley** encore une idée du gouvernement qui n'aboutira à rien *ou* ne mènera nulle part; ***blind date*** *(meeting)* rendez-vous *m ou* rencontre *f* arrangé(e) *(avec quelqu'un qu'on ne connaît pas)*; *(person)* inconnu(e) *m,f (avec qui on a rendez-vous)*; ***blind man's buff*** *(game)* colin-maillard *m*; ***blind side*** *Sport (in rugby)* côté *m* fermé; *Aut* angle *m* mort; **on my b. side** dans mon angle mort; ***blind spot*** *Aut (in mirror)* angle *m* mort; *(in road)* endroit *m* sans visibilité; *Med* point *m* aveugle; *Fig (weak area)* côté *m* faible, faiblesse *f*; **he has a b. spot about his daughter** quand il s'agit de sa fille, il refuse de voir la vérité en face; **I have a b. spot about maths** je ne comprends rien aux mathématiques; *Mktg* ***blind test*** test *m* aveugle; *Mktg* ***blind testing*** tests *mpl* aveugles

blinder ['blaɪndə(r)] N **1** *Br Fam* **to go on a b.** *(get drunk)* se bourrer (la gueule) **2** *Fam (outstanding feat)* **he played a b. (of a game)** il a eu un jeu spectaculaire; **the first goal was a b.** le premier but a été spectaculaire **3** *Am (for horse)* œillère *f*

blindfold ['blaɪndfəʊld] N bandeau *m*

VT bander les yeux à *ou* de

ADV les yeux bandés; **I could do the job b.** je pourrais faire ce travail les yeux bandés *ou* fermés

ADJ aux yeux bandés

blinding ['blaɪndɪŋ] ADJ **1** *(light)* aveuglant, éblouissant; *Fig (speed)* éblouissant; **a b. headache** un mal de tête effroyable; **it was a b. revelation** ça a été une véritable révélation; **the b. intensity of his criticism** l'intensité affolante de ses critiques **2** *Br Fam (excellent)* super, génial

N *(of person, animal)* aveuglement *m*; *(by bright light)* éblouissement *m*

blindingly ['blaɪndɪŋlɪ] ADV de façon aveuglante; **it was b. obvious** ça sautait aux yeux

blindly ['blaɪndlɪ] ADV *(unseeingly)* à l'aveuglette; *Fig (without thinking)* aveuglément

blindness ['blaɪndnɪs] N cécité *f*; *Fig* aveuglement *m*; **the government's b. to social problems** l'aveuglement du gouvernement face aux problèmes sociaux

blindside ['blaɪndsaɪd] VT **to b. sb** prendre qn au dépourvu

blindworm ['blaɪndwɜːm] N *Zool* orvet *m*

bling (bling) [blɪŋ('blɪŋ)] *Fam* N *(jewellery)* bijoux[□] *mpl*, quincaillerie *f*

ADJ *(ostentatious)* tape-à-l'œil, bling bling; **that car is so b.!** cette voiture est vraiment tape-à-l'œil!

blink [blɪŋk] VI **1** *(person)* cligner *ou* clignoter des yeux; *(eyes)* cligner, clignoter; *Fig* **without blinking** *(calmly, without surprise)* sans sourciller; *Fig* **she didn't even b. at the news** elle n'a même pas sourcillé en apprenant la nouvelle; *Fig* **to b. at the facts** fermer les yeux sur la vérité **2** *(light, cursor)* clignoter, vaciller

VT **1 to b. one's eyes** cligner les *ou* des yeux; **to b. away** *or* **to b. back one's tears** refouler ses larmes *(en clignant des yeux)* **2** *Am Aut* **to b. one's lights** faire un appel de phares

N **1** *(of eyelid)* clignement *m* (des yeux), battement *m* de paupières; **in the b. of an eye** en un clin d'œil, en un rien de temps **2** *(of light)* lueur *f*; *(of sunlight)* rayon *m* **3** *Br Fam (idiom)* **to be on the b.** *(machine, TV)* déconner

▸▸ *Comput* ***blink rate*** *(of cursor)* vitesse *f* de clignotement

blinker ['blɪŋkə(r)] N *Aut* **b. (light)** *(turn signal)* clignotant *m*; *(warning light)* feu *m* de détresse

VT mettre des œillères à; *Fig* **when it comes to her family she's very blinkered** elle a des œillères quand il s'agit de sa famille

• **blinkers** NPL *(for eyes)* œillères *fpl*

blinking ['blɪŋkɪŋ] *Br Fam* ADJ sacré, fichu; **b. idiot!** espèce d'idiot!; **the b. thing won't work!** pas moyen de faire marcher cette saloperie!

ADV sacrément, fichtrement

blintz, blintze [blɪnts] N *Culin* crêpe *f* fourrée

blip [blɪp] N **1** *(sound)* bip *m*; *(spot of light)* spot *m*; *(on graph)* sommet *m* **2** *(temporary problem)* mauvais moment *m* (à passer); **the company suffered a b. in February when it lost that contract** l'entreprise a subi un contretemps en février lorsqu'elle a perdu ce contrat

bliss [blɪs] N **1** *(happiness)* bonheur *m* (complet *ou* absolu), contentement *m*; **what b. to have a lie-in!** quel bonheur de pouvoir faire la grasse matinée!; **our holiday was absolute b.!** on a passé des vacances absolument merveilleuses *ou* divines!; **wedded b.** le bonheur conjugal **2** *Rel* béatitude *f*

blissful ['blɪsfʊl] ADJ **1** *(person ▸ happy)* bienheureux; *(▸ peaceful)* serein; *(holiday, weekend etc)* plein de bonheur; **we had a b. time in France** nous avons passé un merveilleux séjour en France; **...she said with a b. sigh** ...dit-elle en soupirant de bonheur; **she remained in b. ignorance** elle était heureuse dans son ignorance **2** *Rel* bienheureux

blissfully ['blɪsfʊlɪ] ADV *(agree, smile)* d'un air heureux; *(peaceful, quiet)* merveilleusement; **he was b. happy** il était comblé de bonheur; **we were b. unaware of the danger** nous étions dans l'ignorance la plus totale du danger

B-list ADJ *(star, celebrity, guest)* pas parmi les plus connus; **there were only B. stars among the guests** il n'y avait aucune vedette de stature internationale parmi les invités

blister ['blɪstə(r)] N **1** *(on skin)* ampoule *f*, cloque *f* **2** *(on painted surface)* boursouflure *f*; *(on metal surface)* soufflure *f*

VI **1** *(skin)* se couvrir d'ampoules **2** *(paint)* se boursoufler; *(metal)* former des soufflures

VT **1** *(skin)* donner des ampoules à **2** *(paint)* boursoufler; *(metal)* former des soufflures dans

▸▸ *Br* ***blister pack*** *(for light bulb, pens)* blister *m*; *(for pills)* plaquette *f*

blistered [ˈblɪstəd] **ADJ** couvert d'ampoules

blistering [ˈblɪstərɪŋ] **ADJ 1** *(sun)* brûlant, de plomb; *(heat)* torride **2** *(attack, criticism)* cinglant, virulent; *(remark)* caustique, cinglant; **she's setting a b. pace** elle mène un train d'enfer

N 1 *(on skin)* ampoules *fpl*; **b. is inevitable** la formation d'ampoules est inévitable **2** *(of paint)* cloquage *m*

blisteringly [ˈblɪstərɪŋlɪ] **ADV it was a b. hot day** c'était une journée d'une chaleur étouffante; **it was b. hot** il faisait une chaleur étouffante

blithe [blaɪð] **ADJ** *(cheerful)* gai, joyeux; *(carefree)* insouciant; **b. indifference** indifférence *f* insouciante

blithely [ˈblaɪðlɪ] **ADV** *(cheerfully)* gaiement, joyeusement; *(carelessly)* avec insouciance; **she b. ignored him** elle l'a ignoré avec une complète désinvolture; **he was b. unaware of the danger** il ne se doutait pas le moins du monde du danger qu'il courait

blithering [ˈblɪðərɪŋ] **ADJ** *Fam* sacré; **a b. idiot** un crétin fini; **you b. fool!** espèce d'imbécile!

BLitt [ˌbiːˈlɪt] **N** *Br Univ (abbr* **Bachelor of Letters**) *(person)* = titulaire d'une licence de littérature; *(qualification)* licence *f* de littérature

blitz [blɪts] **N** *Mil (attack)* attaque *f* éclair; *(bombing)* bombardement *m* aérien intense; *Fig* **to have a b. on sth** s'attaquer à qch; **let's have a b. and get this work done** attaquons-nous à ce travail pour en finir; *Fig* **the b. of holiday advertisements starts immediately after Christmas** dès que les fêtes sont finies, on est bombardé de publicité par les agences de voyage

VT *Mil (attack)* pilonner; *(bomb)* bombarder; **the house was blitzed** la maison a été endommagée/détruite par un bombardement; *Fam Fig* **to b. sb with letters/complaints** bombarder qn de lettres/plaintes

• **Blitz N** *Hist* **the B.** le Blitz

blitzed [blɪtst] **ADJ** *Fam (drunk)* bourré; *(on drugs)* défoncé

blizzard [ˈblɪzəd] **N** *Met* tempête *f* de neige, blizzard *m*

bloat [bləʊt] **VT** gonfler, bouffir

VI bouffir

bloated [ˈbləʊtɪd] **ADJ** *(gen)* gonflé, boursouflé; *(stomach)* gonflé, ballonné; **to feel b.** se sentir ballonné; **b. with pride** bouffi d'orgueil; **he suffers from a b. ego** sa suffisance n'a pas de limites

bloater [ˈbləʊtə(r)] **N** *Ich* bouffi *m*

blob [blɒb] **N** *(drop)* goutte *f*; *(stain)* tache *f*; **a b. on the horizon** une forme indistincte à l'horizon

bloc [blɒk] **N** *Pol & Com* bloc *m*

block [blɒk] **N 1** *(of ice, stone, wood)* bloc *m*; *(of chocolate)* grosse tablette *f*; *(for butcher, executioner)* billot *m*; *(for athletes)* bloc *m* de départ; *Am* **the painting was on the (auctioneer's) b.** le tableau était mis aux enchères; **to put** *or* **to lay one's head on the b.** prendre des risques

2 *(toy)* **(building) blocks** jeu *m* de construction, (jeu *m* de) cubes *mpl*

3 *(of seats)* groupe *m*; *St Exch (of shares)* paquet *m*; *(of tickets)* série *f*; *Comput* bloc *m*

4 *(area of land)* pâté *m* de maisons; **we walked round the b.** nous avons fait le tour du pâté de maisons; *Am* **the school is five blocks away** l'école est à cinq rues d'ici; **the new kid on the b.** le petit nouveau

5 *Br (building)* immeuble *m*; *(of barracks, prison)* quartier *m*; *(of hospital)* pavillon *m*; **b. of flats** immeuble *m* (d'habitation)

6 *(obstruction ▸ in pipe, tube)* obstruction *f*; *Am (▸ in traffic)* embouteillage *m*; *Med & Psy* blocage *m*; *Fin & Com* **to put a b. on sth** *(cheque, account, prices, imports)* bloquer qch; **to have a (mental) b. about sth** faire un blocage sur qch; **I have a (mental) b. about maths** je fais un blocage sur les maths; **he's suffering from writer's b.** il n'arrive pas à écrire, c'est le vide *ou* le blocage total

7 *Fam (head)* caboche *f*; **I'll knock your b. off!** je vais te démolir le portrait!

8 *Tech* **b. (and tackle)** palan *m*, moufles *mpl*

VT 1 *(obstruct ▸ pipe, tube)* boucher; *(▸ road)* bloquer, barrer; *(▸ view)* boucher, cacher; *(▸ artery)* obstruer; **to b. one's ears** se boucher les oreilles; **to b. sb's way** barrer le chemin à qn; **that building blocks the sun** ce bâtiment empêche le soleil d'entrer **2** *(hinder ▸ traffic)* bloquer, gêner; *(▸ progress)* gêner, enrayer; *Fin (▸ credit, deal, funds, account)* bloquer; *Sport (▸ ball)* bloquer; *(▸ opponent)* faire obstruction à; *Parl* **to b. a bill** faire obstruction à un projet de loi; **the goalkeeper blocked the shot** le gardien arrêta le tir; *Tennis* **she blocked the serve magnificently** elle fit un superbe retour de service **3** *Comput (text)* sélectionner

VI *Sport* faire de l'obstruction

▸▸ *Cin* ***block booking*** location *f* en bloc; *Typ* ***block capital*** (caractère *m*) majuscule *f*; **in b. capitals** en majuscules; *Comput* ***block copy*** copie *f* de bloc; ***block diagram*** *Comput & Geog* bloc-diagramme *m*; *Electron* schéma *m* (de principe); *Typ* ***block letter*** (caractère *m*) majuscule *f*; **in b. letters** en majuscules; *Am* ***block party*** fête *f* de rue; *Pol & Ind* ***block vote*** = mode de scrutin utilisé par les syndicats britanniques par opposition au mode de scrutin "un homme, une voix"

▸ **block in VT SEP 1** *(car)* bloquer; **I've been blocked in** ma voiture est bloquée **2** *(drawing, figure)* colorer; *Fig (plan, scheme)* ébaucher

▸ **block off VT SEP** *(road)* bloquer, barrer; *(door, part of road, window)* condamner

▸ **block out VT SEP 1** *(light, sun)* empêcher d'entrer; *(view)* cacher, boucher **2** *(ideas)* empêcher; *(information)* interdire, censurer; **to b. out the memory of sb/sth** refouler le souvenir de qn/qch **3** *(outline)* ébaucher

▸ **block up VT SEP 1** *(pipe, tube)* boucher, bloquer; *(sink)* boucher **2** *(hole)* boucher; *(door, window)* condamner **3** *(nose)* **my nose is blocked up** j'ai le nez bouché

blockade [blɒˈkeɪd] **N 1** *Mil* blocus *m*; **to lift** *or* **to raise a b.** lever un blocus; **to be under b.** être en état de blocus; *Hist* **to run the b.** forcer le blocus **2** *Fig (obstacle)* obstacle *m*

VT 1 *Mil* faire le blocus de **2** *Fig (obstruct)* bloquer, obstruer

blockage [ˈblɒkɪdʒ] **N** *(gen)* obstruction *f*; *(in pipe)* obstruction *f*, bouchon *m*; *Med (in heart, artery)* blocage *m*, obstruction *f*

blockbuster [ˈblɒkbʌstə(r)] **N** *Fam (success ▸ book)* best-seller[□] *m*, livre *m* à succès[□]; *(▸ film)* superproduction[□] *f*

blocked [blɒkt] **ADJ** *Fin & Com (account, cheque, market)* bloqué

blocked-up ADJ bouché; **I have a b. nose** j'ai le nez bouché

blockhead [ˈblɒkhed] **N** *Fam* imbécile *mf*, idiot(e) *m,f*

blockhouse [ˈblɒkhaʊs, *pl* -haʊzɪz] **N** *Hist & Mil* blockhaus *m*, casemate *f*

blocking [ˈblɒkɪŋ] **N 1** *(of street)* encombrement *m*, embouteillage *m*; *(of port)* blocus *m* **2** *Elec (of current)* blocage *m* **3** *(of bookbinding)* gaufrage *m*, frappe *f*

▸▸ *Comput* ***blocking software*** logiciel *m* de filtrage

block-oriented ADJ *Comput* orienté bloc

blog [blɒg] *(pt & pp* **blogged**, *cont* **blogging**) *Comput (abbr* **weblog**) **N** blog *m*

VI bloguer

blogger [ˈblɒgə(r)] **N** *Comput* bloggeur(euse) *m, f*, blogueur(euse) *m,f*

blogging [ˈblɒgɪŋ] **N** *Comput* blogging *m*, création *f* de blogs

blogosphere [ˈblɒgəsfɪə(r)] **N** blogosphère *f*

bloke [bləʊk] **N** *Br Fam* type *m*

blokeish, blokish [ˈbləʊkɪʃ], **blokey** [ˈbləʊkɪ] **ADJ** *Br Fam* = typique d'un style de vie caractérisé par de fréquentes sorties entre copains, généralement copieusement arrosées, et un goût prononcé pour le sport et les activités de groupe

blond [blɒnd] **N** blond *m*

ADJ blond

blonde [blɒnd] **N** blonde *f*

ADJ blonde; **to have a b. moment** avoir un passage à vide

blood [blʌd] **N 1** *Anat (fluid)* sang *m*; **to donate** *or* **to give b.** donner son sang; **to shed** *or* **to spill b.** verser *ou* faire couler du sang; **she bit him and drew b.** elle l'a mordu (jusqu')au sang; **the b. rushed to his head** le sang lui est monté à la tête; *Fig* **he has b. on his hands** il a du sang sur les mains; *Fig* **his b. is up** il est furieux; *Fam* **the mafia are after his b.** la mafia veut sa peau; *Fig* **the boss is after your b.** le patron en a après toi; **there is bad b. between the two families** le torchon brûle entre les deux familles; **his attitude makes my b. boil** son attitude me met hors de moi; **it's like getting b. out of a stone** ce n'est pas une mince affaire; **her b. froze** *or* **ran cold at the thought** rien qu'à y penser son sang s'est figé dans ses veines; **the film made my b. run cold** le film m'a donné des frissons; *Fam* **a film full of b. and guts** un film gore; **to do sth in cold b.** faire qch de sang-froid; **travelling is** *or* **runs in her b.** elle a le voyage dans le sang *ou* dans la peau; **what we need is new** *or* **fresh** *or* **young b.** nous avons besoin d'un *ou* de sang nouveau; **they're out for b.** ils cherchent à se venger; *Prov* **b. is thicker than water** la voix du sang est la plus forte **2** *(breeding, kinship)* **of noble/Italian b.** de sang noble/italien

VT 1 *Hunt (hound, hunter)* donner le goût du sang à **2** *Fig (beginner, soldier)* donner le baptême du feu à

▸▸ *Med* ***blood bank*** banque *f* du sang; ***blood blister*** pinçon *m*; ***blood brother*** frère *m* de sang; *Anat* ***blood cell*** cellule *f* sanguine, globule *m* (du sang); *Med* ***blood count*** numération *f* globulaire; ***blood diamond*** diamant *m* de la guerre; *Med* ***blood donor*** donneur(euse) *m,f* de sang; ***blood doping*** = transfusion sanguine utilisée comme méthode de dopage; *Med* ***blood group*** groupe *m* sanguin; ***blood heat*** température *f* du sang; ***blood money*** prix *m* du sang; ***blood orange*** (orange *f*) sanguine *f*; ***blood plasma*** plasma *m* sanguin; *Biol* ***blood poisoning*** septicémie *f*; *Med* ***blood pressure*** tension *f* (artérielle); **the doctor took my b. pressure** le médecin m'a pris la tension; **to have high/low b. pressure** faire de l'hypertension/de l'hypotension; *Fig* **her b. pressure goes up every time she talks politics** elle se met en colère chaque fois qu'elle parle politique; *Med* ***blood product*** dérivé *m* du sang; *Culin* ***blood pudding*** boudin *m* (noir); ***blood relation*** parent(e) *m,f* par le sang; *Med* ***blood sample*** prise *f* de sang; *Am Culin* ***blood sausage*** boudin *m* (noir); *Med* ***blood serum*** sérum *m* sanguin; *Br Hunt* ***blood sport*** sport *m* sanguinaire; ***blood sugar*** glycémie *f*; **to have low b. sugar** avoir une glycémie faible; ***blood sugar level*** taux *m* de glycémie; *Med* ***blood test*** analyse *f* de sang; **to have a b. test** faire faire une analyse de sang; *Med* ***blood transfusion*** transfusion *f* sanguine *ou* de sang; *Med* ***blood type*** groupe *m* sanguin; *Anat* ***blood vessel*** vaisseau *m* sanguin

blood-and-thunder ADJ *(adventure)* à sensation; *(melodramatic)* mélodramatique

bloodclot [ˈblʌdklɒt] **N** caillot *m* (de sang)

bloodcurdling [ˈblʌdˌkɜːdlɪŋ] **ADJ** terrifiant; **a b. scream** un cri à vous glacer *ou* figer le sang

-blooded [ˈblʌdɪd] **SUFF** de sang...; **blue-b.** de sang noble, aristocratique; **warm-b.** à sang chaud

bloodhound [ˈblʌdˌhaʊnd] **N 1** *(dog)* limier *m* **2** *Fam (detective)* limier *m*, détective[□] *m*

bloodiness [ˈblʌdɪnɪs] **N** état *m* sanglant; **the b. of war** les carnages de la guerre

bloodless [ˈblʌdlɪs] **ADJ 1** *(without blood)* exsangue **2** *(battle, victory, coup)* sans effusion de sang **3** *(cheeks, face)* pâle

bloodlessly [ˈblʌdlɪslɪ] **ADV** sans effusion de sang

bloodletting [ˈblʌdˌletɪŋ] **N 1** *(bloodshed)* carnage *m*, massacre *m* **2** *Med* saignée *f*

blood-red ADJ rouge sang *(inv)*

bloodshed [ˈblʌdʃed] **N** carnage *m*, massacre *m*; **without b.** sans effusion *f* de sang

bloodshot [ˈblʌdʃɒt] **ADJ** injecté (de sang); **her eyes became b.** ses yeux se sont injectés (de sang)

bloodstain [ˈblʌdsteɪn] **N** tache *f* de sang

bloodstained [ˈblʌdsteɪnd] **ADJ** taché de sang

bloodstock [ˈblʌdstɒk] **N** *Zool & Horseracing* chevaux *mpl* de race *ou* de sang

bloodstone ['blʌdstəʊn] **N** *Miner* héliotrope *m (pierre)*

bloodstream ['blʌdstri:m] **N** sang *m*, système *m* sanguin

bloodsucker ['blʌd,sʌkə(r)] **N** *Zool & Fig* sangsue *f*

bloodsucking ['blʌd,sʌkɪŋ] **ADJ** *Zool* hématophage; *Fig* vampirique

bloodthirsty ['blʌd,θɜ:stɪ] (*compar* **bloodthirstier**, *superl* **bloodthirstiest**) **ADJ** *(animal, person)* assoiffé *ou* avide de sang; *(film)* sanglant

bloody ['blʌdɪ] (*compar* **bloodier**, *superl* **bloodiest**) **ADJ 1** *(wound)* sanglant, saignant; *(bandage, clothing, hand)* taché *ou* couvert de sang; *(nose)* en sang; **he came home with a b. nose** il est rentré en saignant du nez; *Fig* **to give sb a b. nose** donner une raclée à qn **2** *(battle, fight)* sanglant, meurtrier **3** *Br very Fam (as intensifier)* foutu; **you b. fool!** espèce de crétin!; **b. hell!** et merde!; **I can't get the b. car to start** je n'arrive pas à faire démarrer cette foutue bagnole

ADV *Br very Fam* vachement; **it's b. hot!** quelle putain de chaleur!; **you can b. well do it yourself!** tu n'as qu'à te démerder (tout seul)!; **I wish he'd b. stop it!** quand est-ce qu'il va s'arrêter, merde!

VT ensanglanter, couvrir de sang; **they came out of it bloodied but unbowed** ils s'en sont sortis meurtris mais avec la tête haute

▸▸ ***Bloody Mary*** *Hist (queen)* = surnom de la reine Marie Tudor, donné par les protestants qu'elle persécuta; *(cocktail)* bloody mary *m inv*

bloody-minded **ADJ** *Br Fam (person)* vache; *(attitude, behaviour)* buté□, têtu□; **he's just being b.!** il le fait rien que pour emmerder le monde!

bloody-mindedness [-'maɪndɪdnɪs] **N** *Br Fam* caractère *m* difficile□; **it's sheer b. on your part** tu le fais uniquement pour emmerder le monde

bloom [blu:m] **N 1** *Bot (flower)* fleur *f*; **to be in b.** *(lily, rose)* être éclos; *(bush, garden, tree)* être en floraison *ou* en fleurs; **to be in full b.** *(lily, rose)* être épanoui; *(bush, garden, tree)* être en pleine floraison; **the roses are just coming into b.** les roses commencent tout juste à fleurir *ou* à s'épanouir **2** *(of cheeks, face)* éclat *m*; **in the b. of youth** dans la fleur de l'âge, en pleine jeunesse **3** *Bot (on fruit)* velouté *m*

VI 1 *Bot (flower)* éclore; *(bush, tree)* fleurir; *(garden)* se couvrir de fleurs **2** *Fig (person)* être en pleine forme; *(arts, industry)* prospérer

bloomer ['blu:mə(r)] **N 1** *Bot (plant)* plante *f* fleurie **2** *Fam (blunder)* gaffe *f*, faux pas□ *m*; **I made a terrible b.** j'ai fait une gaffe terrible

bloomers ['blu:məz] **NPL (a pair of) b.** une culotte bouffante

blooming ['blu:mɪŋ] **ADJ 1** *Bot (flower)* éclos; *(bush, garden, tree)* en fleur, fleuri **2** *(glowing ▸ with health)* resplendissant, florissant; *(▸ with happiness)* épanoui, rayonnant **3** *Br Fam (as intensifier)* sacré, fichu; **you b. idiot!** espèce d'imbécile!; **he's a b. nuisance** il est casse-pieds

ADV *Br Fam* sacrément, vachement; **you can b. well do it yourself!** tu n'as qu'à te débrouiller tout seul!

blooper ['blu:pə(r)] **N** *Am Fam* gaffe *f*, faux pas□ *m*; **he made such a b.!** la gaffe qu'il a faite!

blootered ['blu:təd] **ADJ** *Scot Fam (drunk)* pété, bourré

blossom ['blɒsəm] **N** *(flower)* fleur *f*; **to be in b.** être en fleurs; **the chestnut trees are in full b.** les marronniers sont en pleine floraison; **the cherry trees are just coming into b.** les cerisiers commencent tout juste à fleurir

VI 1 *(flower)* éclore; *(bush, tree)* fleurir **2** *Fig (person, friendship, relationship)* s'épanouir; *(arts, industry)* prospérer; **she blossomed into a talented writer** elle est devenue un écrivain doué

blossoming ['blɒsəmɪŋ] **N** *(of flower)* éclosion *f*; *(of bush, tree)* fleuraison *f*, floraison *f* **2** *Fig (of person, friendship, relationship)* épanouissement *m*

ADJ 1 *(flower)* qui commence à éclore; *(bush, tree)* qui commence à fleurir **2** *Fig (friendship, relationship)* en herbe

blot [blɒt] (*pt & pp* **blotted**, *cont* **blotting**) **N 1** *(spot ▸ gen)* tache *f*; *(▸ of ink)* tache *f*, pâté *m* **2** *Fig (on character, name, reputation)* tache *f*; *(on civilization, system)* tare *f*; **it's a b. on the landscape** ça gâche le paysage

VT 1 *(dry)* sécher **2** *(spot)* tacher; *(with ink)* tacher, faire des pâtés sur; **to b. one's copybook** salir sa réputation **3** *(letter)* passer un buvard sur; **to b. one's lipstick** fixer son rouge à lèvres *(en pressant les lèvres sur un mouchoir à papier)*

▸**blot out** **VT SEP** *(obscure ▸ light, sun)* cacher, masquer; *(▸ memory, thought)* effacer; *(▸ act, event)* éclipser

blotch [blɒtʃ] **N** *(spot ▸ of colour)* tache *f*; *(▸ of ink)* tache *f*, pâté *m*; *(▸ on skin)* tache *f*, marbrure *f*

VI 1 *(skin)* se couvrir de taches *ou* de marbrures **2** *(pen)* faire des pâtés

VT 1 *(clothing, paper)* tacher, faire des taches sur **2** *(skin)* marbrer; **her face was blotched with tears** son visage portait des traces de larmes

blotchy ['blɒtʃɪ] (*compar* **blotchier**, *superl* **blotchiest**) **ADJ** *(cloth, paper, report)* couvert de taches; *(complexion, skin)* marbré

blotter ['blɒtə(r)] **N** *(paper)* buvard *m*; *(desk pad)* sous-main *m inv*

blotting ['blɒtɪŋ] **N** *(of ink)* séchage *m (au buvard)*

▸▸ ***blotting paper*** (papier *m*) buvard *m*

blotto ['blɒtəʊ] **ADJ** *Fam (drunk)* parti

blouse [blaʊz] **N** *(for woman)* chemisier *m*, corsage *m*; *(for sailor)* vareuse *f*

> Note that the French word **blouse** is a false friend. Its most common meaning is **overall**.

BLOW [bləʊ]

N
- coup de poing **1**
- coup de vent **3**
- coup **1, 2, 5**
- souffle **4**

VI
- souffler **1–3**
- sauter **5**
- éclater **5**

VT
- faire bouger **1**
- jouer de **3**
- faire sauter **4**
- gâcher **8**
- souffler **2, 6**
- faire éclater **4**
- claquer **7**
- révéler **9**

(*pt* **blew** [blu:], *pp* **blown** [bləʊn])

N 1 *(hit)* coup *m*; *(with fist)* coup *m* de poing; **to come to blows, to exchange blows** en venir aux mains; *Fig* **to strike a b. for freedom** rompre une lance pour la liberté

2 *(setback)* coup *m*, malheur *m*; *(shock)* coup *m*, choc *m*; **her death came as a terrible b. (to them)** sa mort a été (pour eux) un choc terrible; **to soften** *or* **to cushion the b.** amortir le choc; **it was a big b. to her pride** son orgueil en a pris un coup

3 *(blast of wind)* coup *m* de vent; *(stronger)* bourrasque *f*

4 *(puff)* souffle *m*; **have a good b.** *(blow your nose)* mouche-toi bien

5 *(of whistle)* coup *m*

6 *Fam Drugs slang Br (cannabis)* shit *m*; *Am (cocaine)* coke *f*, neige *f*; *(heroin)* héro *f*, blanche *f*

VI 1 *(wind)* souffler; **the wind is blowing from the north** le vent souffle du nord; **it's blowing a gale out there** le vent souffle en tempête là-bas; *Fig* **let's wait and see which way the wind blows** attendons de voir de quel côté *ou* d'où souffle le vent

2 *(person)* souffler; **she blew on her hands/on her coffee** elle a soufflé dans ses mains/sur son café; **he blows hot and cold** il souffle le chaud et le froid

3 *(move with wind)* **the trees were blowing in the wind** le vent soufflait dans les arbres; **papers blew all over the yard** des papiers se sont envolés à travers la cour; **the window blew open/shut** un coup de vent a ouvert/fermé la fenêtre

4 *Mus (wind instrument)* sonner; *(whistle)* siffler

5 *(explode ▸ tyre)* éclater; *(▸ fuse)* sauter; *(▸ boiler)* exploser

6 *Am very Fam (be disgusting)* **this coffee really blows!** il est vraiment dégueulasse, ce café!

VT 1 *(of wind)* faire bouger; *(leaves)* chasser, faire envoler; **the wind blew the door open/shut** un coup de vent a ouvert/fermé la porte; **a gust of wind blew the papers off the table** un coup de vent a fait s'envoler les papiers de la table; **he was nearly blown off his feet** *(by wind, explosion)* il a failli être emporté

2 *(of person)* souffler; **b. your nose!** mouche-toi!; **he blew the dust off the book** il a soufflé sur le livre pour enlever la poussière; **to b. sb a kiss** envoyer un baiser à qn; **to b. bubbles/smoke rings** faire des bulles/ronds de fumée

3 *Mus (wind instrument)* jouer de; *(whistle)* faire retentir; **the policeman blew his whistle** le policier a sifflé *ou* a donné un coup de sifflet; *Fam* **to b. the gaff** vendre la mèche; *Fam* **to b. one's own trumpet** se vanter; *Fam* **to b. the whistle on sb** balancer qn; *Fam* **to b. the whistle on sth** dévoiler qch

4 *Aut (tyre)* faire éclater; *(fuse, safe)* faire sauter; **the house was blown to pieces** la maison a été entièrement détruite par l'explosion; **the gunman threatened to b. their heads off** l'homme au pistolet a menacé de leur faire sauter la cervelle

5 *(egg)* vider

6 *(glass)* souffler

7 *Fam (squander ▸ money)* claquer; **he blew all his savings on a new car** il a claqué toutes ses économies pour s'acheter une nouvelle voiture

8 *Fam (spoil ▸ chance)* gâcher□; **I blew it!** j'ai tout gâché!; **that's blown it!** ça a tout gâché *ou* bousillé!, ça a tout fait louper!

9 *Fam (reveal, expose)* révéler; **to b. sb's cover** griller qn; *Fam* **to b. the lid off sth** faire des révélations sur qch□

10 *Br Fam (disregard)* **b. the expense, we're going out to dinner** au diable l'avarice, on sort dîner ce soir

11 *Fam (idioms)* **the Grand Canyon blew my mind** quel pied le Grand Canyon!; *Br* **oh, b. (it)!** la barbe!, mince!; **to b. one's top** exploser de rage; **he blew a gasket** *or* **a fuse when he found out** quand il l'a appris, il a piqué une crise; **to b. sb out of the water** *(criticize)* descendre qn en flammes; *(beat)* battre qn à plates coutures; **b. me down!** ça par exemple!; *Br* **I'll be** *or* **I'm blowed if I'm going to apologize!** pas question que je fasse des excuses!

▸▸ *Vulg* ***blow job*** *(oral sex)* pipe *f*; **to give sb a b. job** tailler une pipe à qn

▸**blow away** **VT SEP 1** *(of wind)* chasser, disperser; *Br* **let's take a walk to b. away the cobwebs** allons nous promener pour nous changer les idées **2** *Fam (astound, impress)* emballer; **the film just blew me away** ce film m'a complètement retourné **3** *Fam (shoot dead)* flinguer, descendre

▸**blow down** **VT SEP** *(of wind)* faire tomber, renverser; *(of person)* faire tomber *ou* abattre (en soufflant)

VI être abattu par le vent, tomber

▸**blow in** **VT SEP** *(door, window)* enfoncer

VI *Fam* débarquer à l'improviste, s'amener

▸**blow off** **VT SEP 1** *(of wind)* emporter

2 *(release)* laisser échapper, lâcher

3 *Am Fam* **to b. sb off** *(not turn up)* poser un lapin à qn; *(ignore)* snober qn□

4 *Am Fam* **to b. sth off** *(not go to)* ne pas assister à qch; **let's b. off that meeting and go for a drink** oublions cette réunion et allons boire un verre à la place

VI *(hat, roof)* s'envoler

▸**blow out** **VT SEP 1** *(extinguish ▸ candle)* souffler; *Elec (▸ fuse)* faire sauter; **to b. one's brains out** se faire sauter *ou* se brûler la cervelle; **to b. sb's brains out** faire sauter la cervelle à qn **2** *(of storm)* **the hurricane eventually blew itself out** l'ouragan s'est finalement calmé **3** *(cheeks)* gonfler

VI *Elec (fuse)* sauter; *(candle)* s'éteindre; *Aut (tyre)* éclater

▸**blow over** **VT SEP** *(tree)* abattre, renverser

VI 1 *(storm)* se calmer, passer; *Fig* **the scandal soon blew over** le scandale fut vite oublié **2** *(tree)* s'abattre, se renverser

▸**blow up** **VT SEP 1** *(explode ▸ bomb)* faire exploser *ou* sauter; *(▸ building)* faire sauter **2** *(inflate)* gonfler **3** *(enlarge)* agrandir; *(exaggerate)* exagérer; **the whole issue was blown up out of all proportion** la question a été exagérée hors de (toute) proportion

VI 1 *(explode)* exploser, sauter; *Fig* **the plan blew up in their faces** le projet leur a claqué dans les doigts **2** *(begin ▸ wind)* se lever; *(▸ storm)* se préparer; (▸ *crisis*) se déclencher; **the argument blew up out of nowhere** la dispute a commencé sans raison **3** *Fam (lose one's temper)* exploser, se mettre en boule; **to b. up at sb** engueuler qn

blowback ['bləʊbæk] **N** retour *m* de souffle

blow-by-blow **ADJ** détaillé; **she gave me a b. account** elle m'a tout raconté en détail

blowcock ['bləʊkɒk] **N** *Tech* robinet *m* d'extraction *ou* de vidange

blowdart ['bləʊdɑːt] **N** petite flèche *f*

blow-dry **VT** *(hair)* sécher (avec un séchoir); **to b. sb's hair** faire un brushing à qn

N brushing *m*

blow-drying **N** **too much b. can damage your hair** à force d'être séchés au séchoir, les cheveux s'abîment

blower ['bləʊə(r)] **N 1** *Tech (device)* soufflante *f*; *(in ventilation system)* turbine *f* de ventilation **2** *Br Fam (telephone)* bigophone *m*; **to get on the b. to sb** passer un coup de fil à qn

blowfly ['bləʊflaɪ] (*pl* **blowflies**) **N** *Entom* mouche *f* à viande

blowgun ['bləʊgʌn] **N** *Am* sarbacane *f*

blowhard ['bləʊhɑːd] **N** *Am Fam* vantard(e) *m,f*, fanfaron(onne) *m,f*

blowhole ['bləʊhəʊl] **N 1** *(of whale)* évent *m* **2** *Tech* bouche *f* d'aération, évent *m* **3** *(in ice)* = trou où un phoque etc vient respirer

blowing ['bləʊɪŋ] **N 1** *(of wind)* souffle *m* **2** *(of glass)* soufflage *m*

blowlamp ['bləʊlæmp] **N** *Br Metal* lampe *f* à souder, chalumeau *m*

blown [bləʊn] *pp of* **blow**

ADJ b. glass verre *m* soufflé

blowout ['bləʊaʊt] **N 1** *Elec (of fuse)* **there's been a b.** les plombs ont sauté

2 *Aut (of tyre)* éclatement *m*; **I had a b.** j'ai un pneu qui a éclaté

3 *(of gas)* éruption *f*

4 *Br Fam (meal)* gueuleton *m*; **let's have a b.** faisons un gueuleton *ou* une grande bouffe

blowpipe ['bləʊpaɪp] **N 1** *Br (weapon)* sarbacane *f* **2** *Chem & Ind (tube)* chalumeau *m*; *(in glassmaking)* canne *f* de souffleur, fêle *f*

blowtorch ['bləʊtɔːtʃ] **N** *Metal* lampe *f* à souder, chalumeau *m*

blow-up **N 1** *(explosion)* explosion *f* **2** *Fam (argument)* engueulade *f* **3** *(enlargement)* agrandissement *m*

blow-valve **N** *Tech (on steam boiler)* reniflard *m*

blowy ['bləʊɪ] (*compar* **blowier**, *superl* **blowiest**) **ADJ** venté, venteux

blowzy, *Am* **blowsy** ['blaʊzɪ] (*compar* **blowzier**, *superl* **blowziest**) **ADJ** *Pej (untidy)* négligé; *(sluttish)* vulgaire

BLT [ˌbiːel'tiː] **N** (*abbr* **bacon, lettuce and tomato**) = sandwich avec du bacon, de la laitue et de la tomate

blub [blʌb] *Br Fam* (*pt & pp* **blubbed**, *cont* **blubbing**) **VI** pleurer comme un veau *ou* une Madeleine

N I had a bit of a b. at the end of the film j'ai un peu pleuré à la fin du film

blubber ['blʌbə(r)] **N 1** *(of whale)* blanc *m* de baleine; *Fam Pej (of person)* graisse▫ *f* **2** *Br Fam (cry)* **I had a bit of a b. at the end of the film** j'ai un peu pleuré à la fin du film

VI *Br Fam* pleurer comme un veau *ou* une Madeleine

blubbering ['blʌbərɪŋ] **N** *Br Fam* larmoiements *mpl*

bludgeon ['blʌdʒən] **N** gourdin *m*, matraque *f*

VT 1 *(beat)* matraquer; **he was bludgeoned to death** il a été matraqué à mort **2** *(force)* contraindre, forcer; **they bludgeoned him into selling the house** ils lui ont forcé la main pour qu'il vende la maison

blue [bluː] (*cont* **blueing** *or* **bluing**) **N 1** *(colour)* bleu *m*; **dressed in b.** habillé en bleu

2 *Pol* = membre du parti conservateur britannique; **a true b.** *(patriot)* un(e) patriote *mf*; *Pol* un(e) conservateur(trice) *m,f*

3 *Br Univ* **Cambridge/Oxford b.** = étudiant sélectionné dans l'équipe de l'Université de Cambridge/d'Oxford; **the Dark/Light Blues** l'équipe *f* universitaire d'Oxford/de Cambridge

4 *(idioms)* **out of the b.** sans prévenir; **he arrived out of the b.** il est arrivé à l'improviste; **her resignation was** *or* **came like a bolt from the b.** sa démission a été une véritable surprise

ADJ 1 *(colour)* bleu; **to go** *or* **to turn b.** *(of sky, litmus paper)* virer au bleu; *(of person* ▸ *because suffocating, near death)* devenir violacé *ou* bleu; **to be b. with cold** être bleu de froid; *Fam* **I've told you so until I'm b. in the face** je me tue à te le dire; *Fam* **she can complain until she's b. in the face** elle peut se plaindre autant qu'elle veut

2 *Fam (depressed)* triste▫, cafardeux; **to feel b.** avoir le cafard

3 *Fam (obscene* ▸ *language, joke)* obscène▫, cochon; (▸ *book, movie)* porno; *Br* **his jokes turn the air b.** ses plaisanteries sont affreusement cochonnes

4 *Br Fam (idioms)* **to scream b. murder** crier comme un putois; **once in a b. moon** tous les trente-six du mois; *Am* **he talks a b. streak** il n'arrête pas de jacasser

5 *Pol* conservateur(trice) *m,f*

• **blues** **N 1** *Fam (depression)* **the blues** le cafard; **to get** *or* **to have the blues** avoir le cafard **2** *Mus* le blues; **to sing the blues** chanter le blues; *Am Fig (complain)* pleurnicher

▸▸ *Med* ***blue baby*** enfant *mf* bleu(e), *Spéc* enfant *mf* cyanosé(e); *Mil* ***blue berets*** casques *mpl* bleus; ***blue blood*** sang *m* bleu *ou* noble; ***blue cheese*** (fromage *m*) bleu *m*; ***blue chip*** *St Exch (stock)* valeur *f* de père de famille *ou* de premier ordre; *Fin (investment)* placement *m* de bon rapport; *Fig* ***blue gold*** or *m* bleu; *Am* ***blue jeans*** jean *m*; ***blue rinse*** rinçage *m* à reflets bleus; *Zool* ***blue whale*** baleine *f* bleue, grand rorqual *m*

blue-arsed fly [-ɑːst-] **N** *Br very Fam* **to run about** *or* **around like a b.** courir dans tous les sens

Bluebeard ['bluːˌbɪəd] **PR N** Barbe-bleue

bluebell ['bluːbel] **N** jacinthe *f* des bois; *Scot (harebell)* campanule *f*

blueberry ['bluːbərɪ] (*pl* **blueberries**) **N** myrtille *f*, *Can* bleuet *m*

COMP *(jam)* de myrtilles; *(pie, tart)* aux myrtilles

bluebird ['bluːbɜːd] **N** *(in America)* rouge-gorge *m* bleu; *(in Australia)* langrayen *m* à face noire

blue-black **ADJ** bleu tirant sur le noir, bleu-noir

bluebottle ['bluːˌbɒtəl] **N** *(fly)* mouche *f* bleue *ou* à viande

blue-chip **ADJ** *Com* **b. company** affaire *f* de premier ordre; *St Exch* **b. stocks** *or* **shares** valeurs *fpl* de père de famille *ou* de premier ordre

blue-collar **ADJ** *Ind (gen)* ouvrier; *(area, background, union)* populaire, ouvrier

▸▸ ***blue-collar worker*** col *m* bleu

blue-eyed **ADJ** aux yeux bleus; *Br Fam* **his mother's b. boy** le chouchou de sa maman, le petit chéri de sa maman

bluegrass ['bluːgrɑːs] **N 1** *Bot (grass)* pâturin *m* des champs **2** *Mus* musique *f* bluegrass

blue-green **ADJ** bleu-vert *(inv)*

bluejack ['bluːdʒæk] **VT** *Tel* = envoyer un SMS anonyme à

bluejacking ['bluːdʒækɪŋ] **N** *Tel* bluejacking *m*, = envoi de SMS anonymes à d'autres propriétaires de portables utilisant le protocole Bluetooth®

blueness ['bluːnɪs] **N** bleu *m*

blueprint ['bluːprɪnt] **N 1** *Archit & Tech (photographic)* bleu *m* **2** *Fig (programme)* plan *m*, projet *m*; *Tech (prototype)* prototype *m*; **the b. for democratic government** le modèle démocratique

blue-ribbon **ADJ**

▸▸ *Am* ***blue-ribbon committee*** comité *m* constitué par des personnalités; *Sport* ***blue-ribbon event*** épreuve *f* phare; *Law* ***blue-ribbon jury*** jury *m* d'experts

bluestocking ['bluːˌstɒkɪŋ] **N** *Br Hist* bas-bleu *m*

Bluetooth® ['bluːtuːθ] **N** *Tel* (technologie *f*) Bluetooth® *m*

bluff [blʌf] **N** *(deception)* bluff *m*; **to call sb's b.** *(at poker)* inviter qn à mettre cartes sur table; *Fig* prendre qn au mot

VT bluffer; **don't try to b. me** n'essayez pas de m'en conter; **to b. one's way through things** marcher au bluff; **we'll just have to b. it out** nous n'aurons qu'à bluffer

VI bluffer

bluffer ['blʌfə(r)] **N** bluffeur(euse) *m,f*

blunder ['blʌndə(r)] **N** *(mistake)* bourde *f*; *(remark)* gaffe *f*, impair *m*; **I made a terrible b.** j'ai fait une gaffe épouvantable

VI 1 *(make a mistake)* faire une gaffe *ou* un impair **2** *(move clumsily)* avancer à l'aveuglette, tâtonner; **he was blundering about in the dark** il avançait à l'aveuglette *ou* à tâtons dans le noir; **he blundered through the interview** il s'embrouillait au cours de l'entretien

blunderbuss ['blʌndəbʌs] **N** *Hist* tromblon *m*

blunderer ['blʌndərə(r)] **N** gaffeur(euse) *m,f*

blundering ['blʌndərɪŋ] **N** *(UNCOUNT)* maladresse *f*, gaucherie *f*

ADJ *(person, action, remark)* maladroit

blunt [blʌnt] **ADJ 1** *(blade)* émoussé; *(point)* épointé; *(pencil)* mal taillé, épointé; *(instrument)* contondant **2** *(frank* ▸ *person, reply)* direct, franc (franche); *(refusal)* catégorique; **let me be b.** permettez que je parle franchement

VT *(blade)* émousser; *(pencil, point)* épointer; *Fig (feelings, senses)* émousser

bluntly ['blʌntlɪ] **ADV** carrément, franchement; **to put it b., …** (pour parler) franchement, …

bluntness ['blʌntnɪs] **N 1** *(of blade)* état *m* émoussé, manque *m* de tranchant **2** *(frankness)* franchise *f*, brusquerie *f*

blur [blɜː(r)] (*pt & pp* **blurred**, *cont* **blurring**) **N** *(vague shape)* masse *f* confuse, tache *f* floue; **without my glasses, everything is a b.** sans mes lunettes, je suis complètement dans le brouillard; **my childhood is all a b. to me now** maintenant mon enfance n'est plus qu'un vague souvenir; **when travelling so fast, the countryside is just a b.** quand on avance à une telle vitesse, le paysage n'est qu'une suite de formes confuses

VT 1 *(writing)* estomper, effacer; *(outline)* estomper **2** *(judgment, memory, sight)* troubler, brouiller; **tears blurred my eyes** mes yeux étaient voilés de larmes; **time had blurred the memory** le souvenir était devenu confus avec le temps **3** *Cin & TV (face etc)* flouter

VI 1 *(inscription, outline)* s'estomper; *(judgment, memory, sight)* se troubler, se brouiller **2** *(smudge* ▸ *ink)* s'estomper

blurb [blɜːb] **N** *Mktg* notice *f* publicitaire, argumentaire *m*; *(on book)* (texte *m* de) présentation *f*

blurred [blɜːd] **ADJ** flou, indistinct

blurring ['blɜːrɪŋ] **N** flou *m*

▸ **blurt out** [blɜːt] **VT SEP** *(secret)* laisser échapper

blush [blʌʃ] **VI 1** *(person* ▸ *gen)* rougir, devenir rouge; (▸ *with embarrassment)* rougir; **she blushed deeply** elle est devenue toute rouge; **I b. to think of it now** maintenant quand j'y pense, j'en rougis **2** *Literary (flower, dawn)* rougir

N rougeur *f*; **a b. rose to her cheeks** le sang lui est monté au visage; **to hide one's blushes** baisser les yeux d'embarras; *Hum* **please, spare our blushes!** ne nous faites pas rougir, s'il vous plaît!; **she was in the first b. of youth** elle était dans la prime fleur de l'âge

▸▸ ***blush wine*** vin *m* rosé très léger

blusher ['blʌʃə(r)] **N** *(make-up)* fard *m* à joues, blush *m*

blushing ['blʌʃɪŋ] **N** *(UNCOUNT)* rougissement *m*

ADJ *(person)* rougissant; **the b. bride** la mariée

bluster ['blʌstə(r)] **VI 1** *(wind)* faire rage, souffler en rafales; *(storm)* faire rage, se déchaîner **2** *(speak angrily)* fulminer, tempêter **3** *(boast)* se vanter, fanfaronner

VT *(person)* intimider; **he tried to b. his way out of doing it** il a essayé de se défiler avec de grandes phrases

N *(UNCOUNT)* **1** *(boasting)* fanfaronnades *fpl*; **his threats were no more than b.** ses menaces n'étaient en fait que du vent **2** *(wind)* rafale *f*

blustering ['blʌstərɪŋ] **N** *(UNCOUNT)* fanfaronnades *fpl*

ADJ fanfaron

blustery ['blʌstərɪ] **ADJ** *(weather)* venteux, à bourrasques; *(wind)* qui souffle en rafales, de tempête

Blvd *(written abbr* **boulevard***)* bd, boul

BMA [ˌbiːem'eɪ] **N** *Med (abbr* **British Medical Association***)* = ordre britannique des médecins

BMI [ˌbiːem'aɪ] **N** *Med (abbr* **body mass index***)* IMC *f*; **he has a B. of 21** son IMC est de 21, il a un IMC de 21

B-movie **N** *Cin* film *m* de série B

BMX [ˌbiːem'eks] **N** *(abbr* **bicycle motorcross***)* *(bicycle)* VTT *m*; *(sport, activity)* cyclo-cross *m inv*

BNP [ˌbiːen'piː] **N** *Pol (abbr* **British National Party***)* = parti d'extrême-droite britannique

BO [ˌbiː'əʊ] **N** *Fam (abbr* **body odour***)* odeur *f* corporelle□; **he's got BO** il sent mauvais

boa ['bəʊə] **N 1 (feather) b.** boa *m* **2** *Zool* boa *m*

▸▸ *Zool* ***boa constrictor*** boa constricteur *m*, constrictor *m*

boar [bɔː(r)] **N** *(male pig)* verrat *m*; *(wild pig)* sanglier *m*

board [bɔːd] **N 1** *(plank)* planche *f*; *Theat* **the boards** la scène, les planches *fpl*

2 *(cardboard)* carton *m*; **the boards** *(of book)* les plats *mpl*

3 *(for games)* tableau *m*; *(for draughts)* damier *m*; *(for chess)* échiquier *m*

4 *(notice board)* tableau *m*; *Sch* **to write sth on the b.** écrire qch au tableau

5 *Admin & Com* conseil *m*, commission *f*; **to be on the b.** faire partie *ou* être membre du conseil d'administration

6 *(meals provided)* pension *f*; *Arch (table)* table *f*; *Com Br* **b. and lodging,** *Am* **b. and room** (chambre *f* et) pension *f*

7 *Aviat & Naut* bord *m*; **to go on b.** monter à bord, embarquer; **we're on b.** nous sommes à bord; *Fig* **to be on b.** *(for a project)* s'être engagé à participer; **the environmental protesters have got the mayor on b.** les militants écologistes ont le soutien du maire; **they took provisions on b.** ils ont embarqué des provisions; *Br* **to go by the b.** être abandonné *ou* oublié; **his principles went by the b.** il a dû abandonner ses principes; *Fig* **to take sth on b.** tenir compte de qch

8 *Comput (in PC)* carte *f*; *(in mainframe)* panneau *m*; *(for messages, discussion)* forum *m*; **on b.** installé

9 *Fam (surfboard)* surf *m*, planche *f* (de surf); *(snowboard)* planche *f* (de snowboard)

COMP *Admin (decision)* du conseil d'administration

VT *(plane, ship)* monter à bord de; *(bus, train)* monter dans; *Mil & Naut (in attack)* monter *ou* prendre à l'abordage

VI 1 *(lodge)* être en pension; **to b. with sb** être pensionnaire chez qn **2** *(passenger)* monter à bord, embarquer; **the flight is now boarding at gate 3** embarquement immédiat du vol porte 3 **3** *Fam (to snowboard)* faire du snowboard

▸▸ ***board of directors*** conseil *m* d'administration; ***board of examiners*** jury *m* d'examen; ***board game*** jeu *m* de société; ***board of inquiry*** commission *f* d'enquête; *Com* ***board meeting*** réunion *f* du conseil d'administration; *Com* ***board member*** membre *m* du conseil d'administration; ***board shorts*** short *m* de surf; *Com* ***the Board of Trade*** *(in UK)* le ministère du Commerce; *(in US)* la chambre de commerce; ***board of trustees*** conseil *m* de gestion

▸**board up** **VT SEP** couvrir de planches; *(door, window)* boucher, obturer

boarder ['bɔːdə(r)] **N 1** pensionnaire *mf*; *Sch* interne *mf*, pensionnaire *mf* **2** *(snowboarder)* snowboarder *m*, snowboardeur(euse) *m,f*, surfeur(euse) *m,f* des neiges

boarding ['bɔːdɪŋ] **N 1** *(UNCOUNT) (gen)* planches *fpl*; *(floor)* planchéiage *m* **2** *(embarking)* *Aviat & Naut* embarquement *m*; *Naut & Mil (in attack)* abordage *m*

▸▸ *Aviat* ***boarding card*** carte *f* d'embarquement; ***boarding house*** pension *f*; *Sch* internat *m*; *Aviat* ***boarding pass*** carte *f* d'embarquement; ***boarding school*** internat *m*, pensionnat *m*; **to go to b. school** être interne; **they sent their children to b. school** ils ont mis leurs enfants en internat

> **BOARDING SCHOOLS**
>
> Les "boarding schools" existent depuis des siècles en Grande-Bretagne. Autrefois, elles accueillaient essentiellement la progéniture de la haute société britannique et se caractérisaient par une discipline très stricte, un confort inexistant, et la fréquence des brimades. Aujourd'hui encore, les "boarding schools" prônent des valeurs traditionnelles et sont fréquentées par des enfants issus de milieux aisés du fait de leur coût élevé. Ces établissements ont pourtant dû s'adapter à la société moderne: ils sont maintenant très souvent mixtes et acceptent des pensionnaires d'origine sociale un peu plus variée qu'autrefois.

boardroom ['bɔːdrʊm] **N** *Com* salle *f* de conférence; *Fig (management)* administration *f*; **to be promoted to the b.** être promu au conseil d'administration; **the decision was taken at b. level** la décision a été prise au niveau de la direction

boardwalk ['bɔːdwɔːk] **N** *Am* passage *m* en bois; *(on beach)* promenade *f* (en planches)

boast [bəʊst] **N** *(brag)* fanfaronnade *f*; **it's his proud b. that he has never lost a game** il se vante de n'avoir jamais perdu un jeu

VI se vanter, fanfaronner; **failing the exam is nothing to b. about** il n'y a pas de quoi se vanter d'avoir raté l'examen; **without boasting** *or* **wanting to b.** sans vouloir me vanter

VT 1 *(brag)* se vanter de; **he boasted that he could beat me** il s'est vanté de pouvoir me battre **2** *(possess)* être fier d'avoir; **the town boasts an excellent symphonic orchestra** la ville se glorifie d'avoir un excellent orchestre symphonique; **the entire town boasts just one pub** il n'y a qu'un seul pub dans toute la ville

boaster ['bəʊstə(r)] **N** fanfaron(onne) *m,f*, vantard(e) *m,f*

boastful ['bəʊstfʊl] **ADJ** fanfaron, vantard

boastfully ['bəʊstfʊlɪ] **ADV** en se vantant

boasting ['bəʊstɪŋ] **N** *(UNCOUNT)* vantardise *f*, fanfaronnade *f*, fanfaronnades *fpl*

boat [bəʊt] *Naut* **N** *(gen)* bateau *m*; *(for rowing)* barque *f*, canot *m*; *(for sailing)* voilier *m*; *(ship)* navire *m*, paquebot *m*; **to go by b.** prendre le bateau; **they crossed the Atlantic by b.** ils ont traversé l'Atlantique en bateau; *Fig* **we're all in the same b.** nous sommes tous logés à la même enseigne

VI voyager en bateau; **to go boating** aller se promener en bateau

▸▸ *Naut* ***boat deck*** pont *m* des embarcations; ***boat neck*** *(on dress, jumper)* encolure *f* bateau; *Hist* ***boat people*** boat people *mpl*; ***the Boat Race*** = course universitaire annuelle d'aviron sur la Tamise entre les universités d'Oxford et de Cambridge; ***boat race*** *(event)* course *f* d'avirons; *Naut* régates *fpl*; *SEng Fam (rhyming slang* **face***)* tronche *f*, trombine *f*; ***boat train*** = train qui assure la correspondance avec un bateau

boatbuilder ['bəʊtˌbɪldə(r)] **N** *Naut* constructeur *m* naval

boater ['bəʊtə(r)] **N** *(hat)* canotier *m*

boathook ['bəʊthʊk] **N** *Naut* gaffe *f*

boathouse ['bəʊthaʊs, *pl* -haʊzɪz] **N** *Naut* abri *m ou* hangar *m* à bateaux

boating ['bəʊtɪŋ] *Naut* **N** canotage *m*

COMP *(accident, enthusiast, trip)* de canotage; *(lake)* de plaisance

boatload ['bəʊtləʊd] **N** *(merchandise)* cargaison *f*; *(people)* plein bateau *m*; **six boatloads of refugees** six bateaux pleins de réfugiés

boatman ['bəʊtmən] *(pl* **boatmen** [-mən]*)* **N** *Naut (rower)* passeur *m*; *(renter of boats)* loueur *m* de canots

boatswain ['bəʊsən] **N** *Naut* maître *m* d'équipage

boatyard ['bəʊtjɑːd] **N** *Naut* chantier *m* de construction navale

Bob [bɒb] **N** *Fam* **B.'s your uncle!** et voilà le travail!

bob [bɒb] *(pt & pp* **bobbed,** *cont* **bobbing,** *pl sense* **3** *inv)* **VI** *(move)* **to b. up and down** *(in one's seat)* s'agiter **the buoy was bobbing up and down on the water** la bouée dansait sur l'eau; **I could see his head bobbing up and down behind the wall** je voyais par moments sa tête surgir de derrière le mur; **to b. in/out** entrer/sortir rapidement; **to b. for apples** = essayer d'attraper avec les dents des pommes flottant dans une bassine d'eau à Halloween

VT 1 *(move up and down)* faire monter et descendre; **she bobbed a curtsy** elle a fait une petite révérence **2** *(hair)* couper au carré; **to have one's hair bobbed** se faire couper les cheveux au carré

N 1 *(abrupt movement)* petit coup *m*, petite secousse *f*; *(of head)* hochement *m ou* salut *m* de tête; *(curtsy)* petite révérence *f*

2 *(hairstyle)* (coupe *f* au) carré *m*; **to wear one's hair in a b.** avoir les cheveux coupés au carré; **to have a b.** avoir une coupe au carré, avoir un carré

3 *Br Fam Old-fashioned (shilling)* shilling□ *m*; **that must cost a few b.** ça ne doit pas être donné; **he's not short of a b. or two** il n'est pas dans l'indigence, il a de quoi

4 *Fam (idioms)* **all my bits and bobs** toutes mes petites affaires; **I've brought a few bits and bobs for lunch** j'ai apporté quelques bricoles pour le déjeuner

bobbin ['bɒbɪn] **N 1** *Tex (gen)* bobine *f*; *(for lace)* fuseau *m* **2** *Elec* corps *m* de bobine

bobble ['bɒbəl] **N** *(pompom)* pompon *m*

▸▸ *Br* ***bobble hat*** chapeau *m* à pompon

bobby ['bɒbɪ] *(pl* **bobbies***)* **N** *Br Fam (policeman)* flic *m*

▸▸ *Am* ***bobby pin*** pince *f* à cheveux; *Am* ***bobby socks, bobby sox*** socquettes *fpl (de fille)*

bobby-dazzler [-'dæzlə(r)] **N** *Br Fam Old-fashioned* **she's a right b.!** c'est un beau brin de fille!; **his new car's a b.** sa nouvelle voiture est vraiment extra

bobby-soxer [-'sɒksə(r)] **N** *Am Fam* fille□ *f*, minette *f*

bobcat ['bɒbkæt] **N** *Zool* lynx *m* roux

bobo ['bəʊbəʊ] *Fam (abbr* **bourgeois bohemian***)*

N bobo

ADJ bobo

bobsled ['bɒbsled], **bobsleigh** ['bɒbsleɪ] **N** bobsleigh *m*, bob *m*

VI faire du bobsleigh

bobtail ['bɒbteɪl] **N** *(tail)* queue *f* écourtée; *(cat)* chat *m* écourté; *(dog)* chien *m* écourté

bock [bɒk] **N 1** *Am (beer)* bière *f* brune forte **2** *(glass)* bock *m*

bod [bɒd] **N** *Fam* **1** *Br (person)* type *m*; **he's a bit of an odd b.** c'est plutôt un drôle d'oiseau **2** *(body)* physique□ *m*, corps□ *m*; **he's got a great b.!** il est vachement bien (foutu)!

bode [bəʊd] *pt of* **bide**

VI *(presage)* augurer, présager; **to b. well/ill** être de bon/de mauvais augure (**for** pour)

bodge [bɒdʒ] **VT** *Br Fam* **1** *(spoil)* saboter, bousiller **2** *(mend clumsily)* rafistoler

bodice ['bɒdɪs] **N** *(of dress)* corsage *m*; *(corset)* corset *m*

-bodied ['bɒdɪd] **SUFF an able-b. man** un homme robuste *ou* solide; **a full-b. wine** un vin robuste

bodily ['bɒdɪlɪ] **ADJ** matériel; **to cause sb b. harm** blesser qn

ADV 1 *(carry, seize)* à bras-le-corps; **he was carried b. to the door** on l'a saisi (à bras-le-corps) et transporté jusqu'à la porte **2** *(entirely)* entièrement; **she threw herself b. into her work** elle s'est jetée à corps perdu dans son travail

▸▸ ***bodily fluids*** fluides *mpl* organiques; ***bodily functions*** fonctions *fpl* corporelles; ***bodily strength*** force *f* physique

bodkin ['bɒdkɪn] **N** *Sewing (needle)* grosse aiguille *f*; *(for tape)* passe-lacet *m*

body ['bɒdɪ] *(pl* **bodies***)* **N 1** *Anat & Zool (human, animal)* corps *m*; **he gave himself to her b. and soul** il s'est donné à elle corps et âme; *Fig* **to have just enough to keep b. and soul together** avoir tout juste de quoi vivre; **this obsession with the b. beautiful** cette obsession que tout le monde a d'avoir un corps parfait

2 *(corpse)* cadavre *m*, corps *m*; *Fam* **over my dead b.!** il faudra me passer sur le corps!

3 *(group)* ensemble *m*, corps *m*; *Admin (organi-*

zation) organisme *m*; **the main b. of voters** le gros des électeurs; **a large b. of people** une foule énorme; **taken as a b.** dans leur ensemble, pris ensemble; *Law* **legislative b.** corps *m* législatif
4 *(mass)* masse *f*; **a b. of water** un plan d'eau; **a growing b. of evidence** une accumulation de preuves; **there is a large b. of support for the policy** un grand nombre de personnes sont en faveur de cette politique
5 *(largest part ▸ of document, speech, e-mail)* fond *m*, corps *m*
6 *(of car)* carrosserie *f*; *(of plane)* fuselage *m*; *(of ship)* coque *f*; *(of dress)* corsage *m*; *(of building)* corps *m*; *(of musical instrument)* coffre *m*
7 *(fullness ▸ of wine)* corps *m*; *(▸ of hair)* volume *m*; **a wine with (a lot of) b.** un vin qui a du corps; **a shampoo that gives your hair b.** un shampooing qui donne du volume à vos cheveux
8 *Fam (man)* bonhomme *m*; *(woman)* bonne femme *f*
9 *(garment)* body *m*
10 *Phys* corps *m*
▸▸ ***body armour*** vêtements *mpl* pare-balles; ***body art*** body art *m*; ***body bag*** sac *m* mortuaire; *Boxing* ***body blow*** coup *m* dur; *Fig* **to be a real b. blow to sb's hopes** être un véritable coup porté aux espoirs de qn; *Sport* ***body building*** culturisme *m*; ***body clock*** horloge *f* interne *ou* biologique; ***body count*** pertes *fpl* en vies humaines; *Cin* ***body double*** doublure *f*; *Psy* ***body dysmorphic disorder*** dysmorphophobie *f*; ***body fascism*** culte *m* excessif de la beauté physique *(conduisant à un phénomène de discrimination)*; ***body fluids*** fluides *mpl* organiques; ***body hair*** poils *mpl*; ***body heat*** chaleur *f* animale; ***body image*** image *f* corporelle; ***body language*** langage *m* corporel, gestuelle *f*; **I could tell by his b. language** je le savais d'après la façon dont il se tenait; ***body lotion*** lait *m* corporel; *Med* ***body mass index*** indice *m* de masse corporelle; **he has a b. mass index of 21** son indice de masse corporelle est de 21, il a un indice de masse corporelle de 21; ***body odour*** odeur *f* corporelle; ***body paint*** peinture *f* pour le corps; ***body piercing*** piercing *m*; *Pol* ***body politic*** corps *m* politique; ***body popper*** smurfer(euse) *m,f*; ***body popping*** smurf *m*; *Med* ***body scan*** scanographie *f*; *Med* ***body scanner*** scanner *m*, scanographe *m*; ***body scrub*** produit *m* exfoliant pour le corps; ***body search*** fouille *f* corporelle; ***body shop*** *Aut (for vehicles)* atelier *m* de carrosserie; *Am Fam (gym)* club *m* de gym▫; *Typ* ***body size*** force *f* de corps; *Hist* ***body snatcher*** déterreur (euse) *m,f* de cadavres; ***body stocking*** body *m*; ***body swerve*** feinte *f*; *Scot Fam Fig* **to give sb/sth a b. swerve** éviter qn/qch▫; ***body warmer*** gilet *m* matelassé

bodycheck [ˈbɒdɪˌtʃek] *Sport* **N** *(in ice hockey, football)* interception *f*
VT *(in ice hockey, football)* intercepter

bodyguard [ˈbɒdɪgɑːd] **N** garde *m* du corps

bodyshell [ˈbɒdɪʃel] **N** *Aut* caisse *f*, coque *f*, carcasse *f*

body-surf **VI** *Sport* body-surfer

body-surfer **N** *Sport* body-surfer(euse) *m,f*, body-surfeur(euse) *m,f*

body-surfing **N** *Sport* body-surfing *m*

bodywork [ˈbɒdɪwɜːk] **N** *Aut* carrosserie *f*

Boer [bɔː] **N** Boer *mf*
ADJ boer
▸▸ *Hist* ***the Boer War*** la guerre des Boers

boffin [ˈbɒfɪn] **N** *Br Fam* chercheur *m* scientifique *ou* technique▫

bog [bɒg] *(pt & pp* **bogged**, *cont* **bogging)** **N 1** *(area)* marécage *m*, marais *m*; *(peat)* tourbière *f*
2 *Br very Fam (lavatory)* chiottes *fpl*
▸▸ *Br very Fam* ***bog paper, bog roll*** PQ *m*, papier-cul *m*

▸**bog down** **VT SEP** empêcher, entraver; *(vehicle)* embourber, enliser; *Fig* **I got bogged down in paperwork** je me suis laissé déborder par la paperasserie; **let's not get bogged down in details** ne nous perdons pas dans les détails

▸**bog off** **VI** *Br very Fam* **oh, b. off!** *(go away)* dégage!; *(expressing contempt, disagreement)* va te faire voir!

bogey [ˈbəʊgɪ] **N 1** *(monster)* démon *m*, fantôme *m*; *(source of fear)* spectre *m*, hantise *f*; *(pet worry)* bête *f* noire
2 *Golf* bogey *m*
3 *Br Fam (in nose)* crotte *f* de nez
4 *Rail* bogie *m*; *(trolley)* diable *m*
VT *Golf* **to b. a hole** faire un bogey *(jouer un trou en un coup au-dessus du par)*

bogeyman [ˈbəʊgɪmæn] *(pl* **bogeymen** [-men]) **N** *Br* croque-mitaine *m*, père *m* fouettard, *Can* bonhomme *m* Sept Heures; **the b. will get you** le croque-mitaine va t'attraper

boggle [ˈbɒgəl] **VI 1** *(be amazed)* être abasourdi; **the mind boggles!** ça laisse rêveur! **2** *(hesitate)* hésiter; **she boggles at the idea of marriage** elle n'est pas sûre de vouloir se marier

boggy [ˈbɒgɪ] *(compar* **boggier**, *superl* **boggiest)** **ADJ** *(swampy)* marécageux; *(peaty)* tourbeux

bogie [ˈbəʊgɪ] **N** *Rail* bogie *m*; *(trolley)* diable *m*

bogof [ˈbɒgɒf] *(abbr* **buy one, get one free)** = offre promotionnelle consistant à offrir un produit gratuit pour chaque produit acheté

bog-standard **ADJ** *Br Fam* tout ce qu'il y a d'ordinaire▫

bogus [ˈbəʊgəs] **ADJ** *(fake)* faux (fausse)
▸▸ *Com* ***bogus company*** société *f* fantôme

Bohemia [bəʊˈhiːmɪə] **N** Bohême *f*

bohemian [bəʊˈhiːmɪən] **N** bohème *mf*
ADJ bohème
• **Bohemian** **N** *(from Bohemia)* Bohémien (enne) *m,f*; *(gypsy)* bohémien(enne) *m,f* **ADJ** *(of Bohemia)* bohémien; *(gypsy)* bohémien

boho [ˈbəʊhəʊ] *Fam* **N** bohème *mf*
ADJ bohème
▸▸ ***boho chic*** look *m* bohémien

boil [bɔɪl] **N 1** *(on face, body)* furoncle *m* **2** *Phys (boiling point)* **bring the sauce to the b.** amenez la sauce à ébullition; **the water is coming to the b.** l'eau se met à bouillir; *Br* **the water's on the b.** l'eau bout *ou* est bouillante; *Br* **the pan has gone off the b.** l'eau de la casserole ne bout plus; *Fig* **their romance has gone off the b.** leur histoire tourne au ralenti, leur histoire ne marche plus très fort
VT 1 *(liquid)* faire bouillir, amener à ébullition **2** *(food)* cuire à l'eau, faire bouillir; **to b. the kettle** *(by gas)* mettre la bouilloire sur le feu; *(by electricity)* mettre la bouilloire en marche; *Br* **to b. the kettle dry** laisser s'évaporer l'eau dans la bouilloire; **I can't even b. an egg!** je ne sais même pas faire cuire un œuf!; *Br Fam* **go (and) b. your head!** va te faire cuire un œuf!
VI 1 *(liquid)* bouillir; **the kettle's boiling** l'eau bout (dans la bouilloire); **don't let the soup b.** ne laisse pas bouillir la soupe; *Br* **the pot boiled dry** toute l'eau de la casserole s'est évaporée; *Fam* **to keep the pot boiling** *(bring in enough money)* faire bouillir la marmite; *Fam* **I'm boiling!** *(very hot)* je crève de chaleur *ou* de chaud! **2** *(seethe ▸ ocean)* bouillonner; *(▸ person)* bouillir; **I was boiling with anger** je bouillais de rage

▸**boil away** **VI** *(continue boiling)* bouillir très fort; *(evaporate)* s'évaporer

▸**boil down** **VT SEP** *Culin* faire réduire; *Fig* réduire à l'essentiel; **he boiled the speech down to the basics** il a réduit son discours à l'essentiel
VI *Culin (sauce)* se réduire

▸**boil down to** **VT INSEP** revenir à; **it boils down to the same thing** ça revient au même

▸**boil over** **VI 1** *(overflow)* déborder; *(milk)* se sauver, déborder **2** *Fig (with anger)* bouillir; **he boiled over with rage** il bouillait de rage; **the unrest boiled over into violence** l'agitation a débouché sur la violence

▸**boil up** **VT SEP** *(milk, water)* faire bouillir
VI *(milk, water)* monter; *Fig* **frustration boiled up in her** elle commençait à s'énerver sérieusement

boiled [bɔɪld] **ADJ**
▸▸ *Culin* ***boiled egg*** œuf *m* à la coque; ***boiled ham*** jambon *m* blanc; ***boiled potatoes*** pommes de terre *fpl* à l'eau *ou* bouillies; *Br* ***boiled sweets*** bonbons *mpl* à sucer

boiler [ˈbɔɪlə(r)] **N 1** *(furnace)* chaudière *f*; *(domestic)* chaudière *f*; *(pot)* casserole *f* **2** *Culin (chicken)* poule *f* à faire au pot
▸▸ ***boiler room*** *(in building)* salle *f* des chaudières, chaufferie *f*; *Naut (in boat)* chaufferie *f*, chambre *f* de chauffe; *Am Fin* = organisation qui vend illégalement au public des produits financiers très spéculatifs ou sans valeur; *Br* ***boiler suit*** *(for work)* bleu *m* ou bleus *mpl* (de travail); *(fashion garment)* salopette *f*

boilerman [ˈbɔɪləˌmæn] *(pl* **boilermen** [-ˈmen]) **N** *Rail & Ind* chauffeur *m*

boiling [ˈbɔɪlɪŋ] **ADJ** *(very hot)* bouillant; **the weather here is b.** il fait une chaleur infernale ici
ADV **b. hot** tout bouillant; **a b. hot cup of tea** une tasse de thé bouillant; *Fam* **it's b. hot today** il fait une chaleur à crever aujourd'hui
N *(action)* ébullition *f*; *(bubbling)* bouillonnement *m*
▸▸ ***boiling point*** point *m* d'ébullition; **at b. point** à ébullition; **to reach b. point** arriver à ébullition; *Fig* être en ébullition

boiling-water reactor **N** *Nucl* réacteur *m* à eau bouillante

boil-in-the-bag **ADJ** *Culin* en sachet-cuisson

boisterous [ˈbɔɪstərəs] **ADJ 1** *(exuberant)* tapageur, plein d'entrain; **a b. meeting** une réunion houleuse **2** *Naut (sea)* tumultueux, turbulent; *(wind)* violent, furieux

boisterously [ˈbɔɪstərəslɪ] **ADV** bruyamment, tumultueusement

boisterousness [ˈbɔɪstərəsnɪs] **N 1** *(exuberance)* turbulence *f* **2** *Naut (of sea)* turbulence *f*; *(of wind)* violence *f*

bold [bəʊld] **ADJ 1** *(courageous)* intrépide, hardi; **a b. plan** un projet audacieux *ou* osé; **he grew bolder in his efforts** il s'est enhardi dans ses tentatives
2 *(not shy)* assuré; *(brazen)* effronté; **may I be so b. as to ask your name?** puis-je me permettre de vous demander qui vous êtes?; **he put a b. face on it, he put on a b. front** face à cela il a fait *ou* gardé bonne contenance; *Br Fam* **to do sth as b. as brass** faire qch avec un culot pas possible; **he's as b. as brass** il a un culot pas possible
3 *(vigorous)* puissant, hardi; **with b. strokes of the brush** avec des coups de brosse vigoureux *ou* puissants; **a b. style of writing** un style (d'écriture) hardi
4 *(colours)* vif, éclatant
5 *Typ* gras
N *Typ* caractères *mpl* gras, gras *m*; **in b.** en gras
▸▸ *Typ* ***bold character*** caractère *m* gras; ***bold face*** caractères *mpl* gras, gras *m*; **in b. face** en gras; ***bold italics*** caractères *mpl* italiques gras; ***bold print, bold type*** caractères *mpl* gras

boldly [ˈbəʊldlɪ] **ADV 1** *(bravely)* intrépidement, audacieusement **2** *(impudently)* avec impudence, effrontément **3** *(forcefully)* avec vigueur, vigoureusement

boldness [ˈbəʊldnɪs] **N 1** *(courage)* intrépidité *f*, audace *f* **2** *(impudence)* impudence *f*, effronterie *f* **3** *(force)* vigueur *f*, hardiesse *f*

bole [bəʊl] **N** *Bot* fût *m*, tronc *m* *(d'arbre)*

bolero *(pl* **boleros)** **N 1** [bəˈleərəʊ] *Mus (dance, music)* boléro *m* **2** [bəˈleərəʊ, ˈbɒlərəʊ] *(jacket)* boléro *m*

boletus [bəˈliːtəs] *(pl* **boletuses** *or* **boleti** [-taɪ]) **N** *Bot* bolet *m*

Bolivia [bəˈlɪvɪə] **N** Bolivie *f*

Bolivian [bəˈlɪvɪən] **N** Bolivien(enne) *m,f*
ADJ bolivien
COMP *(embassy)* de Bolivie; *(history)* de la Bolivie

boll [bəʊl] **N** *Bot* capsule *f* *(du cotonnier, du lin)*

bollard [ˈbɒlɑːd] **N** *(on wharf)* bollard *m*; *Br (on road)* borne *f*

bollock [ˈbɒlək] *Br very Fam* **ADV** **b. naked** à poil, le cul à l'air
• **bollocks** **N** *(UNCOUNT) (nonsense)* conneries *fpl*, couillonnades *fpl* **NPL** *(testicles)* couilles *fpl*; **it's the (dog's) b.** c'est super *ou* génial **EXCLAM** quelles conneries!; **oh, b., I've got no money on me!** quelle merde *ou* quelle connerie, je n'ai pas d'argent sur moi!

bollocking [ˈbɒləkɪŋ] **N** *Br very Fam* engueulade *f*; **he got/she gave him a right b.** il a reçu/elle lui a passé un sacré savon

▸**bollocks up** VT SEP *Br very Fam* foutre le bordel dans

Bollywood [ˈbɒlɪwʊd] N *Cin* = appellation de l'industrie du film en Inde, formée à partir de "Bombay" (où furent produits pendant longtemps la plupart des films) et "Hollywood"

BOLLYWOOD

La plupart des films de Bollywood suivent certaines conventions: ils sont généralement longs et de style mélodramatique, ils comprennent des chansons et des numéros de danse, les personnages sont habillés de costumes élaborés, et l'intrigue s'articule presque toujours autour d'une histoire d'amour conventionnelle. Ces films constituent un aspect important de la culture populaire indienne et au cours de ces dernières années ils ont également trouvé un certain public en Occident.

Bologna [bəˈləʊnjə] N Bologne

Bolognese [ˌbɒləˈneɪz] (*pl* inv) N Bolonais(e) *m,f*
ADJ bolonais; *Culin* **spaghetti B.** spaghettis *mpl* (à la) bolognaise

boloney = **baloney**

Bolshevik [ˈbɒlʃɪvɪk] *Hist & Pol* N bolchevik *mf*
ADJ bolchevique

Bolshevism [ˈbɒlʃɪvɪzəm] N *Hist & Pol* bolchevisme *m*

bolshie, bolshy [ˈbɒlʃɪ] *Br Fam* N *Pol* rouge *mf*
ADJ **1** *(intractable)* ronchon; **she's in a b. mood** elle est de très mauvais poil; **she was a bit b. about going to school** elle a un peu rechigné pour aller à l'école **2** *Pol* rouge

bolster [ˈbəʊlstə(r)] VT *(strengthen)* soutenir; **he bolstered my morale** il m'a remonté le moral; **it bolstered his ego** ça a fait du bien à son amour propre
N *(cushion)* traversin *m*

▸**bolster up** VT SEP *Fig (regime, government)* appuyer, soutenir; *(theory)* étayer; **he bolstered himself up with a few drinks** il a bu quelques verres pour se donner du courage; **bolstered up by recent successes** fort de ses récents succès; **these laws simply b. up the system** ces lois ne font que renforcer le système

bolt [bəʊlt] VI **1** *(move quickly)* se précipiter; **a rabbit bolted across the lawn** un lapin a traversé la pelouse à toute allure **2** *(escape)* déguerpir; *(horse)* s'emballer **3** *Bot (plants)* monter en graine
VT **1** *(lock)* fermer à clé, verrouiller; **did you b. the door?** avez-vous poussé *ou* mis les verrous? **2** *(food)* engloutir **3** *Tech (fasten)* boulonner
N **1** *(sliding bar to door, window)* verrou *m*; *(in lock)* pêne *m*
2 *(for nut)* boulon *m*
3 *(dash)* **we made a b. for the door** nous nous sommes rués sur la porte; **she made a b. for it** elle s'est sauvée à toutes jambes
4 *(lightning)* éclair *m*
5 *(of cloth)* rouleau *m*
6 *(of crossbow)* carreau *m*; *(of firearm)* culasse *f* mobile; *Fig* **to have shot one's b.** *(made final attempt)* avoir joué sa dernière carte
ADV **b. upright** droit comme un i; **he was standing b. upright** il était debout, raide comme la justice *ou* droit comme un i
▸▸ **bolt hole** abri *m*, refuge *m*; **he used the cottage as a b. hole** il s'est servi du cottage comme refuge

▸**bolt down** VT SEP *(food, meal)* avaler à toute vitesse

▸**bolt in** VT SEP enfermer au verrou

▸**bolt out** VI sortir en coup de vent

BOMAD [ˈbəʊmæd] N *(abbr* **Bank of Mum and Dad**) = les parents, envisagés par leurs enfants comme prêteurs de dernier recours

bomb [bɒm] N **1** *Mil (explosive)* bombe *f*; *Nucl* **the b.** la bombe atomique; **to drop a b.** lâcher *ou* larguer une bombe; *Fam* **this room looks as if a b.'s hit it** cette pièce est un véritable champ de bataille
2 *Br Fam (large sum of money)* fortune⁰ *f*; **the repairs cost a b.** les réparations ont coûté les yeux de la tête; **to make a b.** se faire un fric fou
3 *Am Fam (failure)* fiasco⁰ *m*, bide *m*
4 *Fam* **she's da** *or* **the b.** elle est super; **that's da b.!** c'est super!, c'est le top!
5 *(in swimming pool)* bombe *f*; **to do a b.** faire une bombe
6 *Fam (idioms)* **this car goes like a b.** elle fonce, cette voiture; *Br* **the show went like a b.** le spectacle a fait un malheur
VT **1** *Mil (drop a bomb on)* bombarder **2** *Am Fam Sch & Univ (test)* se planter complètement à
VI *Fam* **1** *(go quickly)* bomber, filer à toute vitesse; **we bombed down the motorway** on bombait sur l'autoroute **2** *(fail* ▸ *film, show)* être un fiasco⁰, être un bide; *Am Sch & Univ* (▸ *student)* se planter complètement
▸▸ *Mil* **bomb bay** soute *f* à bombes; **bomb disposal** déminage *m*; **bomb disposal expert** démineur *m*; **bomb disposal squad, bomb disposal team** équipe *f* de déminage; **bomb scare** alerte *f* à la bombe; **bomb shelter** abri *m*

▸**bomb along** *Br Fam* VT INSEP **to b. along the road** bomber sur la route
VI *(of car, driver)* bomber

▸**bomb out** VT SEP **1** *Mil (destroy)* détruire par bombardement; **the whole street had been bombed out** toute la rue avait été détruite par les bombardements; **he was bombed out (of his house)** il a perdu sa maison dans le bombardement **2** *Br Fam (fail to keep appointment with)* **to b. sb out** poser un lapin à qn

bombard [bɒmˈbɑːd] VT *Mil* bombarder; *Fig* **to b. sb with questions** bombarder *ou* assaillir qn de questions

bombardier [ˌbɒmbəˈdɪə(r)] N *Mil (in Air Force)* bombardier *m (aviateur)*; *Br (in Royal Artillery)* caporal-chef *m* d'artillerie, brigadier-chef *m* d'artillerie

bombardment [bɒmˈbɑːdmənt] N *Mil* bombardement *m*

bombast [ˈbɒmbæst] N grandiloquence *f*, boursouflure *f*

bombastic [bɒmˈbæstɪk] ADJ *(style)* ampoulé, grandiloquent; *(person)* grandiloquent, pompeux

bombastically [bɒmˈbæstɪkəlɪ] ADV *(speak)* avec grandiloquence; *(write)* dans un style ampoulé

bombazine [ˈbɒmbəziːn] N *Tex* bombasin *m*

bombe [bɒm] N *Culin (ice cream)* bombe *f* glacée

bomber [ˈbɒmə(r)] N **1** *Mil (aircraft)* bombardier *m* **2** *(terrorist)* plastiqueur(euse) *m,f*
▸▸ **bomber jacket** blouson *m* d'aviateur; *Aviat & Mil* **bomber pilot** pilote *m* de bombardier

bombing [ˈbɒmɪŋ] N *(by aircraft)* bombardement *m*; *(by terrorist)* attentat *m* à la bombe
COMP *(mission, raid)* de bombardement

bombproof [ˈbɒmpruːf] ADJ à l'épreuve des bombes

bombshell [ˈbɒmʃel] N **1** *Mil (explosive)* obus *m* **2** *Fig (shock)* **their wedding announcement came as a complete b.** l'annonce de leur mariage a fait l'effet d'une bombe; **to drop a b.** faire part d'une nouvelle qui fait l'effet d'une bombe **3** *Fam (woman)* **a blonde b.** une blonde incendiaire

bombsight [ˈbɒmsaɪt] N *Mil* viseur *m* de bombardement

bombsite [ˈbɒmsaɪt] N *Mil* lieu *m* bombardé; *Br* **to look like a b.** *(of untidy room)* ressembler à un champ de bataille

bombthrower [ˈbɒmˌθrəʊə(r)] N *Mil* **1** *(device)* lance-bombes *m inv* **2** *(person)* lanceur(euse) *m,f* de bombes

bona fide [ˌbəʊnəˈfaɪdɪ] ADJ *(genuine* ▸ *excuse, contract, reason)* valable; (▸ *agreement, offer)* sérieux; (▸ *charity, refugee)* vrai, authentique

bonanza [bəˈnænzə] N aubaine *f*, filon *m*; *Am Mining* riche filon *m*; **she had a real b. at the sales** elle a fait de véritables affaires pendant les soldes
ADJ exceptionnel; **2004 was a b. year for them** ils ont connu une année exceptionnelle en 2004

Bonapartist [ˈbəʊnəpɑːtɪst] N bonapartiste *mf*
ADJ bonapartiste

bonce [bɒns] N *Br Fam (head)* caboche *f*

bond [bɒnd] N **1** *(link)* lien *m*, liens *mpl*, attachement *m*; **there is a very close b. between us** nous sommes très liés
2 *Law (agreement)* engagement *m*, contrat *m*; **we entered into a b. to buy the land** nous nous sommes engagés à acheter la terre; **my word is my b.** je n'ai qu'une parole
3 *Law (for bail)* caution *f* financière
4 *Fin (certificate)* obligation *f*; **long/medium/short b.** obligation *f* longue/moyenne/courte
5 *Chem (link)* liaison *f*; *(adhesion)* adhérence *f*
6 *Typ (paper)* papier *m* de qualité supérieure
7 *Com* **in b.** en entrepôt; **he put the merchandise in b.** il a entreposé les marchandises en douane; **to take goods out of b.** dédouaner des marchandises, faire sortir des marchandises de l'entrepôt
VT **1** *(hold together)* lier, unir
2 *Com (goods)* entreposer
3 *Law (place under bond)* placer sous caution; *(put up bond for)* se porter caution pour
4 *Fin* lier (par garantie financière)
5 *Constr* liaisonner
6 *(people)* **the experience really bonded them (together)** cela a créé des liens très forts entre eux
VI **1** *Chem (with adhesive)* **the surfaces have bonded** les surfaces ont adhéré l'une à l'autre **2** *(of people)* former des liens affectifs; **we didn't really b.** on n'a pas vraiment accroché; *Hum* **the guys have been away bonding on a fishing trip** ils sont allés pêcher entre hommes
• **bonds** NPL *(fetters)* chaînes *fpl*, fers *mpl*; *Fig* liens *mpl*, contraintes *fpl*
▸▸ *Fin* **bond equivalent yield** = rendement équivalent à celui d'une obligation; *Fin* **bond fund** fonds *m* obligataire; *Fin* **bond investment** placement *m* obligataire; *Fin* **bond issue** emprunt *m* obligataire; **to make a b. issue** émettre un emprunt; *Fin* **bond market** marché *m* obligataire *ou* des obligations; *Fin* **bond note** titre *m* d'obligation; *Typ* **bond paper** papier *m* de qualité supérieure; *Fin* **bond trading** opérations *fpl* sur obligations; *Fin* **bond yield** rendement *m* de l'obligation

bondage [ˈbɒndɪdʒ] N **1** *(slavery)* esclavage *m*; *Fig* esclavage *m*, servitude *f* **2** *(sexual)* bondage *m (pratique sexuelle où l'un des partenaires est attaché)*

bonded [ˈbɒndɪd] ADJ **1** *Fin* titré **2** *Com* (entreposé) sous douane
▸▸ *Com* **bonded warehouse** entrepôt *m* sous douane

bonder [ˈbɒndə(r)] N *Com* entrepositaire *m*

bondholder [ˈbɒndhəʊldə(r)] N *Fin* obligataire *mf*, détenteur(trice) *m,f ou* porteur(euse) *m,f* d'obligations

bonding [ˈbɒndɪŋ] N **1** *(between people)* formation *f* des liens affectifs
2 *(of two objects)* collage *m*
3 *Elec* système *m ou* circuit *m* régulateur de tension
4 *Constr* liaison *f*
▸▸ *Chem* **bonding agent** agent *m* de collage *ou* d'adhésivité

bondstone [ˈbɒndstəʊn] N *Constr* parpaing *m*

bone [bəʊn] N **1** *Anat & Zool (of human, animal)* os *m*; *(of fish)* arête *f*; **she's got good b. structure** elle a les pommettes saillantes; **to work one's fingers to the b.** se tuer au travail; **to be as dry as a b.** *(earth)* être desséché; *(well)* être à sec; *(washing)* être complètement sec (sèche); **b. of contention** pomme *f* de discorde; **chilled** *or* **frozen to the b.** glacé jusqu'à la moelle (des os); **his comments were a bit close to** *or* **near the b.** ses commentaires frôlaient l'indécence; **I have a b. to pick with you** j'ai un compte à régler avec toi; **he hasn't got a suspicious/generous b. in his body** il n'est pas méfiant/généreux pour un sou; **there's trouble ahead, I can feel it in my bones** quelque chose me dit qu'il va y avoir du grabuge; **to make no bones about doing sth** ne pas hésiter à faire qch; **she made no bones about her displeasure** elle n'a pas caché son mécontentement; **he's nothing but skin and b.** *or* **bones, he's nothing but a bag of bones** il est maigre comme un clou **2** *(substance)* os *m*; *(in corset)* baleine *f*; **the handle was made from b.** le manche était en os **3** *(essential)* essentiel *m*; **the bare bones of sth** l'essentiel de qch

VT 1 *Culin (meat)* désosser; *(fish)* ôter les arêtes de **2** *Am Vulg (have sex with)* baiser
VI *Am Vulg (have sex)* baiser, s'envoyer en l'air
• **bones NPL** *(remains)* ossements *mpl*, os *mpl*; **to lay sb's bones to rest** enterrer qn
►► *Cer* ***bone china*** porcelaine *f* tendre; *Anat* ***bone marrow*** moelle *f*; *Agr* ***bone meal*** engrais *m* (de cendres d'os)

►**bone up on VT INSEP** *Fam (study)* **to b. up on sth** potasser qch

boned [bəʊnd] **ADJ 1** *Culin (meat, poultry)* désossé **2** *(corset)* baleiné

bone-dry ADJ *(earth)* desséché; *(well)* à sec; *(washing)* complètement sec (sèche)

bonehead ['bəʊn,hed] **N** *Fam* crétin(e) *m,f*, imbécile *mf*

boneless ['bəʊnlɪs] **ADJ** *Culin (meat)* désossé, sans os; *(fish)* sans arêtes

boner ['bəʊnə(r)] **N 1** *very Fam (erection)* **to have a b.** bander **2** *Am Fam (blunder)* gaffe *f*, bourde *f*

boneshaker ['bəʊn,ʃeɪkə(r)] **N** *Fam (car)* tacot *m*; *Hist (bicycle)* vélocipède[□] *m*

bonfire ['bɒn,faɪə(r)] **N** *(with fireworks)* feu *m* de joie; *(for burning leaves etc)* feu *m* de jardin; **to make** *or* **to build a b.** *(with wood, leaves etc)* faire un feu
►► *Br* ***Bonfire Night*** le 5 novembre *(commémoration de la tentative de Guy Fawkes de faire sauter le Parlement en 1605)*

bong[1] [bɒŋ] **N** *(droning sound)* bourdon *m*
VI *(drone)* bourdonner

bong[2] **N** *Fam Drugs slang* pipe *f* à eau[□], bang *m*

bongo ['bɒŋgəʊ] *(pl* **bongos** *or* **bongoes) N b. (drum)** bongo *m*

bonhomie ['bɒnəmiː] **N** bonhomie *f*

bonito [bə'niːtəʊ] *(pl* **bonitos) N** *Ich* bonite *f*

bonk [bɒŋk] *Br Fam* **VI** s'envoyer en l'air
VT s'envoyer en l'air avec
N partie *f* de jambes en l'air; **to have a b.** faire une partie de jambes en l'air

bonkers ['bɒŋkəz] **ADJ** *Br Fam* cinglé; **to go b.** devenir cinglé

bonnet ['bɒnɪt] **N 1** *(hat ► woman's)* bonnet *m*, chapeau *m* à brides; *(►child's)* béguin *m*, bonnet *m* **2** *Br Aut* capot *m*; **to have a look under the b.** jeter un coup d'œil sous le capot

bonny ['bɒnɪ] *(compar* **bonnier**, *superl* **bonniest)** **ADJ** *Scot & NEng (pretty)* joli, beau (belle)

bonsai ['bɒnsaɪ] **N** *Bot & Hort* bonsaï *m*

bonus ['bəʊnəs] **N 1** *(gen) & Com* prime *f*; **to work on a b. system** travailler à la prime; **Christmas b.** prime *f* de fin d'année; *Fig* **the holiday was an added b.** les vacances étaient en prime; **it's a real b. having a theatre close by** le fait qu'il y ait un théâtre tout près constitue vraiment un plus **2** *Br St Exch (dividend on shares)* dividende *m* supplémentaire, bonification *f*
►► ***bonus number*** *(in lottery)* numéro *m* complémentaire; *Mktg* ***bonus pack*** prime *f* produit en plus; *Br St Exch* ***bonus share*** action *f* gratuite *ou* donnée en prime

bony ['bəʊnɪ] *(compar* **bonier**, *superl* **boniest) ADJ 1** *Anat* osseux; *(knees, person)* anguleux, décharné; *(fingers, arms)* squelettique **2** *Culin (fish)* plein d'arêtes; *(meat)* plein d'os

bonzer ['bɒnzə(r)] *Austr & NZ Fam* **ADJ** vachement bien, super
EXCLAM super!

bonzo ['bɒnzəʊ] **ADJ** *Am Fam* cinglé, fêlé

boo [buː] **VT** huer, siffler; **the audience booed him off the stage** il a quitté la scène sous les huées *ou* les sifflets du public
VI pousser des huées, siffler; **to b. at sb** huer *ou* siffler qn
N huée *f*; **her arrival was greeted with boos** elle s'est fait huer à son arrivée
EXCLAM hou!; *Br Fam* **he wouldn't say b. to a goose** c'est un grand timide[□]

boob [buːb] *Fam* **N 1** *(breast)* nichon *m*; **to have a b. job** se faire refaire les nichons **2** *Br (mistake)* gaffe *f*, boulette *f*; **to make a b.** faire une gaffe *ou* une boulette
VI *Br (make mistake)* gaffer
►► *Fam* ***boob tube*** *(strapless top)* bustier *m* moulant[□]; *Am (TV)* télé *f*

boo-boo *(pl* **boo-boos) N** *Fam* **1** *(blunder)* gaffe *f*, bourde *f*; **to make a b.** faire une gaffe *ou* une bourde **2** *Am (injury)* bobo *m*

booby ['buːbɪ] *(pl* **boobies) N 1** *Fam (idiot)* nigaud (e) *m,f*, ballot *m* **2** *Orn* fou *m*
►► ***booby hatch*** *Naut* écoutillon *m*; *Am Fam (mental hospital)* asile *m* de dingues; *Sport* ***booby prize*** prix *m* de consolation *(attribué par plaisanterie au dernier)*; **to win** *or* **to get the b. prize** gagner *ou* recevoir le prix de consolation; ***booby trap*** *Mil* objet *m* piégé; *(practical joke)* traquenard *f*

booby-trap *(pt & pp* **booby-trapped**, *cont* **booby-trapping) VT** *Mil* piéger

booger ['buːgə(r)] **N** *Am Fam* crotte *f* de nez

boogie ['buːgɪ] *Fam* **VI 1** *(dance)* danser[□], guincher; *(party)* faire la fête **2** *Am (leave)* mettre les bouts, s'arracher; **let's b. on out of here** on met les bouts, on s'arrache
N 1 *(dance)* boogie *m*; **to have a b.** danser[□], guincher **2** *Am very Fam* nègre (négresse) *m,f*, = terme injurieux désignant un Noir
►► *Sport* ***boogie board*** boogie board *m*; *Sport* ***boogie boarding*** boogie boarding *m*; **to go b. boarding** faire du boogie boarding; *Am* ***boogie man*** croque-mitaine *m*, père *m* fouettard, *Can* bonhomme *m* Sept Heures

boogie-woogie [-'wuːgɪ] **N** *Mus* boogie-woogie *m*

booing ['buːɪŋ] **N** *(UNCOUNT)* huées *fpl*

BOOK [bʊk]

N	
• livre **1, 2**	• registre **1**
• carnet **3**	• pari **5**
VT	
• réserver **1**	• embaucher **2**
VI	
• réserver **1**	
NPL	
• comptes, comptabilité **1**	• registre **2**

N 1 *(gen)* livre *m*; *Com & Fin* registre *m*; *Sch* cahier *m*; **a b. on** *or* **about gardening** un livre de jardinage; *Tel* **I'm in the b.** *(listed in directory)* je suis dans l'annuaire; **not published in b. form** inédit en librairie; *Hum* **his little black b.** son carnet d'adresses; *Fig* **her face is an open b.** toutes ses émotions se voient sur son visage; **she's an open b.** on peut lire en elle comme dans un livre; **to read sb like a b.** *or* **an open b.** lire à livre ouvert dans la pensée de qn; **mathematics is a closed b. to me** je ne comprends rien aux mathématiques; *Br* **to bring sb to b.** obliger qn à rendre des comptes; **to do things** *or* **to go by the b.** faire les choses selon les règles; **to be in sb's good books** être dans les petits papiers de qn; **to be in sb's bad books** être mal vu de qn; *Fam* **in my b.** à mon avis[□]; **that's one for the b.** *or* **books!** il faudra marquer ça d'une pierre blanche!; **to throw the b. at sb** donner le maximum à qn
2 *(section of work)* livre *m*; *(of poem)* chant *m*
3 *(of stamps, tickets)* carnet *m*; *(of matches)* pochette *f*
4 *(of samples)* jeu *m*, album *m*
5 *(in betting)* pari *m*; **to make a b.** faire un pari; **we've opened a b. on how late he'll be** les paris sont ouverts sur le retard qu'il va avoir
VT 1 *(reserve)* réserver, retenir; *Br (tickets)* prendre; **I've booked you (a seat) on the next flight** je vous ai réservé une place sur le prochain vol; **have you booked your trip?** avez-vous fait les réservations pour votre voyage?; **the performance is booked up** *or* **fully booked** on joue à bureaux *ou* guichets fermés; **the restaurant is fully booked** le restaurant est complet; **I've booked myself into the best hotel in town** *(in advance)* j'ai réservé une chambre dans le meilleur hôtel de la ville; *(on the spur of the moment)* j'ai pris une chambre dans le meilleur hôtel de la ville
2 *Com (engage)* embaucher, engager; **he's booked solid until next week** il est complètement pris jusqu'à la semaine prochaine
3 *Law (of police)* **he was booked for speeding** il a attrapé une contravention pour excès de vitesse
4 *Sport* prendre le nom de
5 *Com (order)* enregistrer
6 *Am Fam* **to b. it** *(leave)* mettre les bouts, s'arracher; *(move quickly)* foncer
VI 1 *(make a reservation)* réserver; **to b. into a hotel** prendre une chambre d'hôtel; **to b. through to Nice** prendre tous les billets nécessaires pour Nice
2 *Am Fam (leave)* mettre les bouts, s'arracher; *(move quickly)* foncer
• **books NPL 1** *Acct, Com & Fin (accounts)* livre *m* de comptes; **to keep the books** tenir les comptes *ou* la comptabilité; **the books and records** la comptabilité; *Fam* **to cook the books** trafiquer les comptes
2 *Admin (of club)* registre *m*; **he's on our books** *(member of our club etc)* c'est un de nos membres; *(player in our team)* c'est un de nos joueurs; *(employee)* il est dans nos fichiers
►► ***book club*** club *m* du livre; *Acct* ***book debts*** comptes *mpl* fournisseurs, dettes *fpl* compte; ***book end*** serre-livres *m inv*; *Acct* ***book entry*** écriture *f* comptable; ***book fair*** salon *m* du livre; *(secondhand)* foire *f* aux livres; ***book group*** cercle *m* de lecture; ***the book industry*** l'industrie *f* du livre; ***book jacket*** jaquette *f*; ***book lover*** bibliophile *mf*; ***book number*** numéro *m* ISBN, numéro *m* de dépôt légal; ***book review*** critique *f* littéraire; ***book reviewer*** critique *mf* littéraire; *Br* ***book token*** bon *m* d'achat de livres, chèque-livre *m*; ***the book trade*** l'industrie *f* du livre; *Fin* ***book value*** valeur *f* comptable, valeur de bilan

►**book in VT SEP** inscrire; *(at hotel)* réserver une chambre pour
VI *Br* se faire enregistrer; *(at hotel)* prendre une chambre

►**book up VT SEP** réserver, retenir; **the restaurant is booked up** le restaurant est complet; **she's booked up (all) next week** elle est prise (toute) la semaine prochaine
VI réserver

BOOK GROUP

Depuis quelques années, on assiste à une explosion du nombre des cercles de lecture ("book groups") en Grande-Bretagne et aux États-Unis. Les membres de ces cercles de lecture sont le plus souvent des femmes, qui se retrouvent à intervalles réguliers pour discuter d'un livre qu'elles ont choisi ensemble. La popularité des "book groups" s'explique en partie par le fait que certains talk shows télévisés américains et britanniques ont lancé leur propres débats autour d'un livre, auxquels le public est invité à participer. Cette formule connaît un tel succès que les livres sélectionnés pour les discussions deviennent immédiatement des best-sellers.

bookable ['bʊkəbəl] **ADJ 1** *Br (seat)* qui peut être réservé d'avance **2** *Law (offence)* passible d'une contravention

bookbinder ['bʊk,baɪndə(r)] **N** relieur(euse) *m,f*

bookbinding ['bʊk,baɪndɪŋ] **N** reliure *f*

bookcase ['bʊkkeɪs] **N** bibliothèque *f (meuble)*

booker ['bʊkə(r)] **N** *(for model, actor)* agent *m*

bookie ['bʊkɪ] **N** *Fam* bookmaker[□] *m*

booking ['bʊkɪŋ] **N 1** *(reservation)* réservation *f*; **who made the b.?** qui a fait la réservation? **2** *(of actor, singer)* engagement *m*
►► ***booking agency*** agence *f* de réservation; ***booking clerk*** préposé(e) *m,f* aux réservations; ***booking fee*** frais *mpl* de réservation; ***booking office*** bureau *m* de location

bookish ['bʊkɪʃ] **ADJ** *(person)* qui aime la lecture, studieux; *(style)* livresque

bookkeeper ['bʊk,kiːpə(r)] **N** *Acct* comptable *mf*, teneur *m* de comptes

bookkeeping ['bʊk,kiːpɪŋ] **N** *Acct* tenue *f* de(s) livres, comptabilité *f*

book-learning N *(UNCOUNT)* connaissances *fpl* livresques

booklet ['bʊklɪt] **N** brochure *f*, plaquette *f*

bookmaker ['bʊk,meɪkə(r)] **N** bookmaker *m*

bookmark ['bʊkmɑːk] **N** signet *m*, marque-page *m*; *Comput (for Web page)* signet *m*

VT *Comput (Web page)* créer un signet sur; **don't forget to b. this page** n'oublie pas de créer un signet sur cette page

►► *Comput* ***bookmark list*** liste *f* de signets

bookmobile ['bukməbi:l] N *Am* bibliobus *m*

bookplate ['bukpleɪt] N ex-libris *m*

bookrest ['bukrest] N lutrin *m*, support *m* à livres

bookseller ['buk,selə(r)] N libraire *mf*

bookselling ['buk,selɪŋ] N librairie *f*, commerce *m* du livre

bookshelf ['bukʃelf] (*pl* **bookshelves** [-ʃelvz]) N étagère *f* à livres, rayon *m* (de bibliothèque)

bookshop ['bukʃɒp] N *Br* librairie *f*

bookstall ['bukstɔ:l] N étalage *m* de bouquiniste; *Br (in station)* kiosque *m* à journaux

bookstore ['bukstɔ:(r)] N *Am* librairie *f*

bookworm ['bukwɜ:m] N *Entom* ver *m* du papier; *Fig* rat *m* de bibliothèque

Boolean ['bu:lɪən] ADJ *Comput* booléen

►► ***Boolean algebra*** algèbre *f* booléenne; ***Boolean function*** fonction *f* booléenne; ***Boolean operator*** opérateur *m* booléen; ***Boolean search*** recherche *f* booléenne

boom [bu:m] VI **1** *(resonate ► gen)* retentir, résonner; *(► guns, thunder)* tonner, gronder; *(► voice)* tonner, tonitruer **2** *(prosper)* prospérer, réussir; **business is booming** les affaires sont en plein essor

VT *(say loudly)* tonner; **"nonsense!" he boomed** "quelles idioties!", dit-il d'une voix tonitruante

N **1** *(sound ► gen)* retentissement *m*; *(► of guns, thunder)* grondement *m*; *(► of waves)* grondement *m*, mugissement *m*; *Mus (► of organ)* ronflement *m*; *(► of voice)* rugissement *m*, grondement *m*

2 *(period of expansion)* (vague *f* de) prospérité *f*, boom *m*, période *f* d'essor; *(of trade)* forte hausse *f* ou progression *f*; *(of prices, sales)* brusque *ou* très forte hausse *f*, montée *f* en flèche; *(of product)* popularité *f*, vogue *f*

3 *Naut (spar)* bôme *f*, gui *m*

4 *TV & Cin (for camera, microphone)* perche *f*, girafe *f*; *Tech (for crane)* flèche *f*

►► *Am Fam* ***boom box*** radiocassette[□] *f*; *TV & Cin* ***boom microphone*** microphone *m* sur girafe, microphone *m* sur perche; *TV & Cin* ***boom operator*** perchiste *mf*; *TV & Cin* ***boom shot*** plan *m* en plongée; *Econ* ***boom town*** ville *f* en plein essor, ville-champignon *f*

►**boom out** VT SEP tonner; **"of course!" he boomed out** "bien sûr!", dit-il d'une voix tonitruante

VI *(guns, thunder)* gronder, tonner; *(voice)* tonner, tonitruer

boomerang ['bu:məræŋ] N boomerang *m*

VI faire boomerang; **his tricks will b. on him one day** un jour ses tours lui retomberont sur le nez

►► ***boomerang effect*** effet *m* boomerang

booming ['bu:mɪŋ] ADJ **1** *(sound)* retentissant **2** *(business)* prospère, en plein essor

N *(UNCOUNT) (gen)* retentissement *m*; *(of guns, thunder)* grondement *m*; *(of voice)* rugissement *m*, grondement *m*

boon [bu:n] N *(blessing)* aubaine *f*, bénédiction *f*; **the new industrial estate is a b. to the area** la nouvelle zone industrielle est une aubaine pour la région

►► ***boon companion*** bon compère *m*

boondocks ['bu:ndɒks], **boonies** ['bu:nɪz] NPL *Am Fam* **the b.** le bled, la cambrousse; **in the b.** à perpète(-les-oies), en pleine cambrousse

boondoggle ['bu:n,dɒgəl] VI *Am Fam* flemmarder, peigner la girafe

boor [buə(r)] N *(rough)* rustre *m*; *(uncouth)* goujat *m*, malotru *m*

boorish ['buərɪʃ] ADJ grossier, rustre

boorishly ['buərɪʃlɪ] ADV grossièrement; **he behaved b.** il s'est comporté en rustre

boorishness ['buərɪʃnɪs] N *(roughness)* rudesse *f*, manque *m* d'éducation *ou* de savoir-vivre; *(uncouthness)* goujaterie *f*

boost [bu:st] VT **1** *Com (sales)* faire monter, augmenter; *Ind (productivity)* développer, accroître; *(morale, confidence)* renforcer; *(economy)* relancer; **a policy designed to b. the economy** des mesures destinées à relancer l'économie

2 *Elec* survolter; *Aut* suralimenter

3 *Mktg (promote)* faire de la réclame *ou* de la publicité pour

4 *Am Fam (steal)* piquer, faucher

5 *Am Fam (break into)* cambrioler[□]

N **1** *(increase)* augmentation *f*, croissance *f*; *(improvement)* amélioration *f*; *Com* **a b. in sales** une brusque augmentation des ventes; **the success gave her morale a b.** le succès lui a remonté le moral **2** *(promotion)* **the review gave his play a b.** la critique a fait de la publicité pour *ou* du battage autour de sa pièce **3** *(leg-up)* **to give sb a b.** faire la courte échelle à qn; *Fig* donner un coup *m* de pouce à qn

booster ['bu:stə(r)] N **1** *Astron* **b. (rocket)** fusée *f* de lancement, moteur *m* auxiliaire

2 *Rad* amplificateur *m*

3 *Elec (device)* survolteur *m*; *(charge)* charge *f* d'appoint

4 *Med* piqûre *f* de rappel

►► ***booster cushion, booster seat*** réhausseur *m*; *Med* ***booster shot*** piqûre *f* de rappel; ***booster station*** *Tel* station *f* relais; *Tech* station *f* auxiliaire de pompage

boot [bu:t] N **1** botte *f*; *(ankle-length)* bottine *f*; *Sport (for football, rugby)* chaussure *f*; *Fam* **to give sb the b.** flanquer qn à la porte; *Fam* **she got the b.** elle a été flanquée à la porte, elle a été virée; *Br Fam* **they put the b. in** ils lui ont balancé des coups de pied; *Fig* ils ont enfoncé méchamment le clou

2 *Br Aut* coffre *m*, malle *f*

3 *Fam (kick)* coup *m* de pied[□]; **he needs a b. up the backside** il a besoin d'un bon coup de pied au derrière

4 *Br Fam Pej (ugly woman)* boudin *m*, cageot *m*

VT **1** *(kick)* donner des coups de pied à **2** *(equip with boots)* botter **3** *Comput* amorcer, faire démarrer; **to b. the system** initialiser le système

• **to boot** ADV en plus, par-dessus le marché; **she's beautiful and intelligent to b.** elle est belle, et intelligente par-dessus le marché

►► *Fam* ***boot camp*** *Am Mil* = camp d'entraînement pour nouvelles recrues; *Br (centre for young offenders)* = centre de redressement *(pour jeunes délinquants)*; **to go into b. camp** faire ses classes; *Comput* ***boot disk*** *(hard)* disque *m* de démarrage; *(floppy)* disquette *f* de démarrage; ***boot polish*** cirage *m*; *Br* ***boot sale*** = sorte de marché aux puces où des particuliers apportent dans leur voiture les objets de brocante qu'ils souhaitent vendre; *Comput* ***boot sector*** secteur *m* d'initialisation; *Comput* ***boot track*** piste *f* d'amorçage

►**boot up** *Comput*

VT SEP *(computer)* amorcer, faire démarrer

VI *(computer)* s'amorcer, démarrer; *(person)* démarrer

bootable ['bu:təbəl] ADJ *Comput* amorçable

bootblack ['bu:tblæk] N cireur *m* de chaussures

bootee ['bu:ti:] N *(for babies)* petit chausson *m*, bottine *f*

booth [bu:ð] N **1** *(at fair)* baraque *f*, stand *m*; *Am (at exhibition)* stand *m* **2** *(cubicle ► for telephone, language laboratory)* cabine *f*; *(► for voting)* isoloir *m* **3** *(in restaurant)* box *m*

bootjack ['bu:tdʒæk] N *Tech* tire-botte *m*

bootlace ['bu:tleɪs] N lacet *m* (de chaussure)

bootleg ['bu:t,leg] (*pt & pp* **bootlegged**, *cont* **bootlegging**) VI faire de la contrebande de boissons alcoolisées

VT *(make)* fabriquer illicitement; *(sell)* vendre en contrebande

N *(gen)* marchandise *f* illicite; *(cassette, video, software etc)* pirate *m*; *(remix)* remix *m* bootleg; *Am (liquor)* alcool *m* de contrebande

ADJ **1** *(illicit)* de contrebande; **b. cassette/record** cassette *f*/disque *m* pirate **2** *(trousers, jeans)* trompette

bootlegger ['bu:t,legə(r)] N *(of cassettes, videos, software etc)* = personne qui se livre au piratage; *Am (of liquor)* bootlegger *m*

bootlegging ['bu:t,legɪŋ] N *(of cassettes, videos, software etc)* piratage *m*; *Am (of liquor)* contrebande *f*

bootlick ['bu:tlɪk] VI *Fam* **he's always bootlicking** c'est un vrai lèche-bottes

bootlicker ['bu:t,lɪkə(r)] N *Fam* lèche-bottes *mf inv*

bootloader ['bu:t,ləudə(r)] N *Comput* chargeur-amorce *m*

bootmaker ['bu:t,meɪkə(r)] N bottier *m*

bootstrap ['bu:tstræp] N **1** *(on boot)* tirant *m* de botte; *Fig* **she pulled herself up by her own bootstraps** elle a réussi par ses propres moyens **2** *Comput* programme *m* amorce, amorce *f*

ADJ autonome

►► *Comput* ***bootstrap program*** programme *m* amorce, amorce *f*

booty ['bu:tɪ] N **1** *(loot)* butin *m* **2** *Am Fam (buttocks)* cul *m*, derche *m*; *very Fam* **to get some b.** *(have sexual intercourse)* s'envoyer en l'air; *Fam* **to make a b. call** = passer un coup de fil à son ami ou amie pour organiser une partie de jambes en l'air; *Fam* **to shake one's b.** s'éclater en dansant

booze [bu:z] *Fam* N *(UNCOUNT)* alcool[□] *m*, boissons *fpl* alcoolisées[□]; **bring your own b.** apportez à boire; **to go on the b.** picoler; **she's off the b.** elle a arrêté de picoler

VI picoler

►► *Br* ***booze cruise*** *(to France)* = excursion d'une journée pour aller s'approvisionner en alcool bon marché en France

boozehound ['bu:zhaund] N *Am Fam* poivrot(e) *m,f*

boozer ['bu:zə(r)] N *Fam* **1** *(drunkard)* poivrot(e) *m,f* **2** *Br (pub)* pub[□] *m*

booze-up N *Br Fam* beuverie *f*, soûlerie *f*; **to have a b.** prendre une cuite

boozily ['bu:zɪlɪ] ADV *Fam* **to look at sb b.** regarder qn à travers les vapeurs de l'alcool; **to say sth b.** dire qch d'une voix avinée

boozy ['bu:zɪ] (*compar* **boozier**, *superl* **booziest**) ADJ *Fam (party, evening)* bien arrosé; **her b. husband** son soûlard de mari

bop [bɒp] (*pt & pp* **bopped**, *cont* **bopping**) N **1** *(music)* bop *m* **2** *Fam (dance)* danse[□] *f*; **shall we have a b.?** on danse? **3** *Fam (punch)* coup *m* de poing[□]

VT *Fam (hit)* cogner[□]; **he bopped me on the nose!** il m'a allongé un marron sur le nez!

VI *Fam (dance)* danser[□]; **we bopped (away) all night** on a dansé toute la nuit

bo-peep [bəu-] N cache-cache *m inv*

• **Bo-Peep** PR N **Little B.** = dans une comptine anglaise, petite bergère qui a perdu son troupeau

boracic [bə'ræsɪk] ADJ **1** *Chem (acid)* borique **2** *Br Fam (rhyming slang* **boracic lint** = **skint**) fauché, raide

►► *Pharm* ***boracic lint*** coton *m* boriqué; *Pharm* ***boracic ointment*** pommade *f* boriquée

borage ['bɒrɪdʒ] N *Bot* bourrache *f*

borax ['bɔ:ræks] N *Miner & Pharm* borax *m*

Bordeaux [bɔ:'dəu] N **1** *(region)* le Bordelais; **he's/she's from B.** c'est un/une Bordelais/Bordelaise **2** *(wine)* bordeaux *m*

border ['bɔ:də(r)] N **1** *(boundary)* frontière *f*; **on the b. between Norway and Sweden** à la frontière entre la Norvège et la Suède; **they live near the Scottish b.** ils habitent près de la frontière écossaise; **to cross the b.** passer la frontière; **they tried to escape over the b.** ils ont tenté de s'enfuir en passant la frontière; **north of the B.** *(from viewpoint of England)* en Écosse; *(from viewpoint of Ireland)* en Irlande du nord; *(from viewpoint of the US)* au Canada; **south of the B.** *(from viewpoint of Scotland)* en Angleterre; *(from viewpoint of Northern Ireland)* en République d'Irlande; *(from viewpoint of Canada)* aux États-Unis; *(from viewpoint of the US)* au Mexique

2 *(outer edge ► of lake)* bord *m*, rive *f*; *(► of field)* bordure *f*, limite *f*; *(► of forest)* lisière *f*, limite *f*

3 *(edging ► of dress, handkerchief, plate, notepaper)* bord *m*, bordure *f*

4 *Hort (in garden)* bordure *f*, plate-bande *f*

5 *Comput (of paragraph, cell)* bordure *f*

COMP *(state)* frontière *(inv)*; *(zone)* frontière *(inv)*, frontalier; *(search)* à la frontière; *(dispute, patrol)* frontalier

VT **1** *(line edges of)* border; *(encircle)* entourer,

encadrer **2** *(be adjacent to)* toucher; **Mexico borders Texas** le Mexique touche *ou* a une frontière commune avec le Texas; **their garden is bordered on two sides by open fields** sur deux côtés, leur jardin est entouré de champs à perte de vue

• **Borders** NPL **the Borders** les Borders *fpl*, = région frontalière du sud-est de l'Écosse

▸▸ ***border controls*** contrôles *mpl* aux frontières; ***border crossing*** passage *m* de frontière; *Mil* ***border guard*** garde-frontière *m*; ***border police*** police *f* des frontières; *Customs* ***border post*** poste-frontière *m*; ***border region*** région *f* frontalière; ***border town*** ville *f* frontière *ou* frontalière; ***border trade*** commerce *m* frontalier

▸ **border on, border upon** VT INSEP **1** *(be adjacent to)* toucher, avoisiner; **my property borders on his** ma propriété touche la sienne; **Italy and Austria b. on each other** l'Italie et l'Autriche ont une frontière commune *ou* sont limitrophes **2** *(verge on)* friser, frôler; **to b. on a lie/the absurd** friser le mensonge/l'absurde; **his remark borders on slander** sa remarque frise la calomnie; **hysteria bordering upon madness** une crise de nerfs proche de *ou* qui frôle la folie

borderer ['bɔːdərə(r)] N frontalier(ère) *m,f*; *Br (in Scotland)* Écossais(e) *m,f* frontalier(ère); *(in England)* Anglais(e) *m,f* frontalier(ère)

bordering ['bɔːdərɪŋ] ADJ *(country)* contigu(ë), limitrophe

borderland ['bɔːdəlænd] N *(country)* pays *m* frontière; *also Fig (area)* région *f* limitrophe; **the b. between fantasy and reality** la frontière entre l'imagination et la réalité

borderline ['bɔːdəlaɪn] N limite *f*, ligne *f* de démarcation; **to be on the b.** être à la limite; **the b. between acceptable and unacceptable behaviour** ce qui sépare un comportement acceptable d'un comportement inacceptable

ADJ limite; **a b. case** un cas limite; *Psy* un borderline *inv*; **b. students** *(in exam)* les étudiants qui atteignent tout juste la moyenne

▸▸ *Psy* ***borderline personality disorder*** trouble *f* de la personnalité borderline

bore [bɔː(r)] *pt of* **bear**

N **1** *(person)* raseur(euse) *m,f*; *(event, thing)* ennui *m*, corvée *f*; **what a b. she is!** ce qu'elle peut être lassante *ou* fatigante!; **visiting them is such a b.!** quelle barbe de leur rendre visite!; **homework is a real b.!** quelle corvée, les devoirs!

2 *Constr (from drilling)* trou *m* de sonde; *Tech* alésage *m*

3 *Tech (diameter of gun, tube)* calibre *m*; **a twelve-b. shotgun** un fusil de calibre douze

4 *Mining (hole)* trou *m* de sonde, sondage *m*, forage *m*

VT **1** *(tire)* ennuyer; *Fam* **housework bores me stiff** *or* **rigid** *or* **to tears** *or* **to death** *or* **out of my mind** faire le ménage m'ennuie à mourir; *Fam* **he bores the pants off me** il me barbe profondément; **I won't b. you with the details** je vous passe les détails **2** *Tech (drill* ▸ *hole)* percer; *(*▸ *well)* forer, creuser; *(*▸ *tunnel)* creuser; *(*▸ *cylinder)* aléser

VI forer, sonder; **to b. through sth** percer qch; **they're boring for coal** ils forent pour extraire du charbon, ils recherchent du charbon par forage; *Fig* **I felt his eyes boring into me** je sentais son regard me transpercer

boreal ['bɔːrɪəl] ADJ *Literary (forest)* boréal

bored [bɔːd] ADJ *(person)* qui s'ennuie; *(expression, sigh)* d'ennui; **you look b.** tu as l'air de t'ennuyer; **to be** *or* **to get b.** s'ennuyer; **to be b. with doing sth** s'ennuyer à faire qch; **I'm b. with my job** j'en ai assez de mon travail; *Fam* **to be b. stiff** *or* **rigid** *or* **to tears** *or* **to death** *or* **out of one's mind** s'ennuyer ferme *ou* à mourir

boredom ['bɔːdəm] N ennui *m*

borehole ['bɔːhəʊl] N *Constr* trou *m* de sonde; *Mining (for mine)* trou *m* de mine

borer ['bɔːrə(r)] N *(person)* foreur *m*, perceur *m*; *(for wood)* vrille *f*, foret *m*; *(for metal)* alésoir *m*; *(for mine, well)* foret *m*, sonde *f*

boric ['bɔːrɪk] ADJ *Chem (acid)* borique

boring ['bɔːrɪŋ] ADJ *(tiresome)* ennuyeux; *(uninteresting)* sans intérêt; **the meeting was so b.** cette réunion était assommante

N *Tech (in wood)* perforation *f*, forage *m*; *(in metal)* alésage *m*; *(in ground)* forage *m*, sondage *m*

▸▸ *Tech* ***boring machine*** *(for wood)* perceuse *f*; *(for metal)* alésoir *m*

born [bɔːn] ADJ **1** *(gen)* né; **to be b.** naître; **she was b. blind/in 1975** elle est née aveugle/en 1975; **b. of an American father** né d'un père américain; **a child b. into this world** un enfant qui vient au monde; **b. and bred** né et élevé; **she was b. and bred in Boston** c'est une Bostonienne de souche; **they were b. to riches** ils sont nés riches; **she was b. Elizabeth Hughes, but writes under the name E. R. Johnson** elle est née Elizabeth Hughes mais écrit sous le nom d'E.R. Johnson; *Fig* **the place where communism was b.** le lieu où est né le communisme; **anger b. of frustration** une colère née de *ou* due à la frustration; *Fam* **in all my b. days** de toute ma vie❑; *Fam* **I wasn't b. yesterday!** je ne suis pas né d'hier *ou* de la dernière pluie!; **she was b. with a silver spoon in her mouth** elle est née avec une cuillère en argent dans la bouche; **she was b. lucky** elle est née coiffée, elle est née sous une bonne étoile **2** *(as intensifier)* **he's a b. musician** il est né musicien, c'est un musicien né; **you're a b. fool** tu es un parfait idiot; **he's a b. loser** il est né sous une mauvaise étoile

born-again ADJ *Rel & Fig* rené

▸▸ ***born-again Christian*** chrétien *m* rené

borne [bɔːn] *pp of* **bear**

Borneo ['bɔːnɪəʊ] N Bornéo

borough ['bʌrə] N **1** *(British town)* = ville représentée à la Chambre des communes par un ou plusieurs députés **2** *(in London)* = une des 32 subdivisions administratives de Londres **3** *(in New York)* = une des cinq subdivisions administratives de New York

▸▸ ***borough council*** = conseil municipal d'un "borough"

borrow ['bɒrəʊ] VT **1** *(gen) & Fin* emprunter; **to b. sth from sb** emprunter qch à qn; **she borrowed money from him** elle lui a emprunté de l'argent; **can I b. the car?** est-ce que je peux prendre la voiture?; **an artist who borrows his ideas from nature** un artiste qui trouve ses idées dans la nature; **we often b. books from the library** nous empruntons souvent des livres à la bibliothèque; **a word borrowed from Russian** un mot emprunté au russe **2** *Br Math (in subtraction)* **I b. one** je retiens un

VI emprunter (**from** à); **to b. from sb** *(borrow money)* faire un emprunt à qn, emprunter de l'argent à qn; **to b. on** *or* **at interest** emprunter à intérêt

▸ **borrow against** VT INSEP *Fin (salary, property)* emprunter sur; **the company borrowed against its assets** l'entreprise a emprunté de l'argent en utilisant son actif comme garantie

borrowed ['bɒrəʊd] ADJ *(gen) & Fin* emprunté, d'emprunt; **b. capital** capitaux *mpl* empruntés *ou* d'emprunt; **the company is living on b. time** les jours de l'entreprise sont comptés; **my grandfather is living on b. time** mon grand-père a de la chance d'être encore en vie; **he'd been living on b. time since he was caught stealing from his employer** il était en sursis depuis qu'on l'avait pris à voler son employeur

borrower ['bɒrəʊə(r)] N *(gen) & Fin* emprunteur (euse) *m,f*

borrowing ['bɒrəʊɪŋ] N *Fin & Ling* emprunts *mpl*; **financed by b.** financé par des emprunts

▸▸ ***borrowing power*** capacité *f* de crédit *ou* d'emprunt *ou* d'endettement; ***the borrowing rate*** le taux d'intérêt des emprunts; ***borrowing requirements*** besoins *mpl* de crédit

borsch [bɔːʃ], **borscht** [bɔːʃt] N *Culin* bortsch *m*, borchtch *m*

borstal ['bɔːstəl] N *Br Formerly* = ancien nom d'une institution pour jeunes délinquants, aujourd'hui appelée "young offender institution"

borzoi ['bɔːzɔɪ] N (lévrier *m*) barzoï *m*

bosh [bɒʃ] (UNCOUNT) *Br Fam* N bêtises❑ *fpl*, âneries *fpl*

EXCLAM n'importe quoi!, sottises!

bos'n ['bəʊsən] N *Naut* maître *m* d'équipage

Bosnia ['bɒznɪə] N Bosnie *f*

Bosnia-Herzegovina [-ˌheətsəgə'viːnə] N Bosnie-Herzégovine *f*

▸▸ ***Bosnia-Herzegovina Federation*** Fédération *f* croato-musulmane

Bosnian ['bɒznɪən] N Bosnien(enne) *m,f*, Bosniaque *mf*

ADJ bosnien, bosniaque

bosom ['bʊzəm] N **1** *(of woman)* seins *mpl*; *Fig Literary (of person)* poitrine *f*; **she took the child to her b.** elle prit l'enfant sous son aile **2** *(of dress)* corsage *m* **3** *Fig (centre)* sein *m*, fond *m*; **in the b. of the community** au sein de la communauté

▸▸ *Fam* ***bosom buddy*** meilleur pote *m*; ***bosom friend*** ami(e) *m,f* intime

bosomy ['bʊzəmɪ] ADJ *Fam (woman)* qui a une forte poitrine❑

Bosporus ['bɒspərəs], **Bosphorus** ['bɒsfərəs] N Bosphore *m*

boss [bɒs] N **1** *Fam (person in charge)* patron (onne)❑ *m,f*, chef *m*; **who's the b. around here?** qui est-ce qui commande ici?; **I'll show you who's b.!** je vais te montrer qui est le chef!; **she's the b.** c'est elle qui porte la culotte; **to be one's own b.** être son propre patron

2 *Fam (of gang)* caïd *m*; *Am (politician)* manitou *m* (du parti)

3 *Mil (knob)* bossage *m*; *(on shield)* ombon *m*

4 *Archit* bossage *m*

5 *Tech* mamelon *m*, bossage *m*; *Aviat & Naut (of propeller)* moyeu *m*

VT *Fam (person)* commander❑, donner des ordres à❑; *(organization)* diriger❑, faire marcher❑

▸ **boss about, boss around** VT SEP *Fam* mener à la baguette; **stop bossing me around!** j'en ai assez que tu me donnes des ordres!

boss-eyed ADJ *Br Fam* qui louche❑; **she's b.** elle louche

bossily ['bɒsɪlɪ] ADV *Fam* d'une manière autoritaire❑

bossiness ['bɒsɪnɪs] N *Fam* comportement *m* autoritaire❑

bossy ['bɒsɪ] *(compar* **bossier**, *superl* **bossiest)** ADJ *Fam* autoritaire❑, dictatorial❑; **don't be so b., don't be such a b. boots** arrête de jouer au petit chef

Boston ['bɒstən] N Boston

▸▸ *Mktg* ***Boston matrix*** matrice *f* BCG; *Hist* ***the Boston Tea Party*** la "Boston Tea Party"

bosun ['bəʊsən] N *Naut* maître *m* d'équipage

bot [bɒt] N *Comput* bot *m*

botanic [bə'tænɪk], **botanical** [bə'tænɪkəl] ADJ botanique

▸▸ ***botanic garden*** jardin *m* botanique

botanist ['bɒtənɪst] N botaniste *mf*

botanize, -ise ['bɒtənaɪz] VI herboriser

botany ['bɒtənɪ] N botanique *f*

botch [bɒtʃ] *Fam* N travail *m* salopé; **those workmen made a real b. of the job** ces ouvriers ont fait un travail de cochon *ou* ont tout salopé

VT *(job)* saloper; *(interview, speech)* rater

▸ **botch up** VT SEP *Fam (job)* saloper; *(interview, speech)* rater

botched [bɒtʃt] ADJ *Fam* **a b. suicide attempt** une tentative de suicide ratée; **a b. job** un travail de sagouin; **to make a b. job of sth** bousiller qch

botch-up N = **botch**

both [bəʊθ] PREDET les deux, l'un (l'une) et l'autre; **b. dresses are pretty** les deux robes sont jolies; **on b. sides of the road** des deux côtés de la route; **hold it in b. hands** tenez-le à *ou* des deux mains; **you can't have it b. ways!** il faut te décider, c'est soit l'un, soit l'autre!

PRON tous (toutes) (les) deux *mpl, fpl*; **b. (of them) are coming** ils viennent tous les deux; **b. are to blame** c'est leur faute à tous les deux; **why not do b.?** pourquoi ne pas faire les deux?; **from b. of us** de notre part à tous les deux; **we b. said yes** nous avons dit oui tous les deux; **b. you and I like to travel** nous aimons tous les deux voyager;

• **both... and...** CONJ **her job is b. interesting and well-paid** son travail est à la fois intéressant et bien payé; **I b. read and write Spanish** je sais lire et écrire l'espagnol

bother ['bɒðə(r)] N **1** *(trouble)* ennui *m*; *Br* **to be in** *or* **to have a spot of b. (with sb)** avoir des ennuis (avec qn); **I hear there was a bit of b. down at the**

pub last night il paraît qu'il y a eu du grabuge hier soir au pub; **he doesn't give her any b.** il ne la dérange pas; **the trip isn't worth the b.** le voyage ne vaut pas la peine; **if it's not too much b.** si cela ne vous dérange pas trop; **I hope I haven't put you to a lot of b.** j'espère que je ne vous ai pas trop dérangé; **I didn't go to the b. of cooking a meal** je n'ai pas pris la peine de cuisiner un repas; **thanks for babysitting – it's no b.!** merci pour le babysitting – de rien!

2 *(nuisance)* ennui *m*; **sorry to be a b.** excusez-moi de vous déranger

VT 1 *(irritate)* ennuyer, embêter; *(pester)* harceler; *(disturb)* déranger; **I'm sorry to b. you** excusez-moi de vous déranger; **would it b. you if I opened the window?** cela vous dérange *ou* ennuie si j'ouvre la fenêtre?

2 *(worry)* tracasser; **don't b. yourself** *or* **your head about it** ne vous tracassez pas à ce sujet; **it doesn't b. me whether they come or not** cela m'est bien égal qu'ils viennent ou pas

3 *(hurt)* faire souffrir; **his leg is bothering him again** sa jambe le fait de nouveau souffrir

VI prendre la peine; **don't b. to answer the phone** ce n'est pas la peine de répondre au téléphone; **please don't b. getting up!** ne vous donnez pas la peine de vous lever!; **don't b. about me** ne vous en faites pas *ou* ne vous inquiétez pas pour moi; **let's not b. with the housework** laissons tomber le ménage

EXCLAM *Br Fam* flûte!, mince!

botheration [ˌbɒðəˈreɪʃən] **EXCLAM** *Fam Old-fashioned* flûte!, mince!

bothersome [ˈbɒðəsəm] **ADJ** ennuyeux, gênant

Botox® [ˈbəʊtɒks] *Pharm* **N** Botox® *m*

VT *Fam* faire des injections de Botox® à; **to get Botoxed** se faire faire des injections de Botox®

bottle [ˈbɒtəl] **N 1** *(container, contents)* bouteille *f*; *(of perfume)* flacon *m*; *(of medicine)* flacon *m*, fiole *f*; *(jar)* bocal *m*; *(made of stone)* cruche *f*, cruchon *m*; **a wine b.** une bouteille à vin; **a b. of wine** une bouteille de vin; **he drank (straight) from the b.** il a bu au goulot; *Fam Fig* **he was too fond of the b.** il levait bien le coude, il aimait la bouteille; *Fam* **to hit the b.** picoler dur; *Fam* **they're on the b.** ils lèvent bien le coude; *Fam* **to be off the b.** s'abstenir *ou* s'arrêter de boire[□] **2** *(for baby)* biberon *m*; **her baby is on the b.** son bébé est nourri au biberon **3** *Br Fam (nerve)* cran *m*, culot *m*; **he lost his b.** il s'est dégonflé; **she's got a lot of b.** elle a un sacré cran

VT *Ind (drinks)* mettre en bouteille; *(fruit)* mettre en bocal *ou* conserve, conserver

►► ***bottle bank*** = conteneur pour la collecte du verre usagé; *Fam Pej* ***bottle blonde*** blonde *f* décolorée; ***bottle green*** vert *m* bouteille; ***bottle opener*** ouvre-bouteilles *m inv*, décapsuleur *m*; ***bottle rack*** casier *m* à bouteilles

►**bottle out VI** *Br Fam* se dégonfler; **he bottled out of the fight** il s'est dégonflé au dernier moment et a refusé de se battre; **he bottled out of telling her the truth** finalement il a eu la trouille de lui dire la vérité

►**bottle up VT SEP 1** *(emotions)* refouler, ravaler **2** *Mil (army)* embouteiller, contenir

bottlebrush [ˈbɒtəlbrʌʃ] **N** rince-bouteilles *m inv*, goupillon *m*

bottled [ˈbɒtəld] **ADJ** en bouteille *ou* bouteilles; **b. beer** bière *f* en bouteille *ou* bouteilles; **b. gas** gaz *m* en bouteille *ou* bouteilles

bottle-fed ADJ élevé *ou* nourri au biberon

bottle-feed VT nourrir au biberon

bottle-feeding N alimentation *f* au biberon

bottleful [ˈbɒtəlfʊl] **N a b. of sth** une pleine bouteille de qch; **by the b.** à pleine bouteille

bottleneck [ˈbɒtəlnek] **N** *(in road)* rétrécissement *m* de la chaussée, étranglement *m*; *(of traffic)* embouteillage *m*, bouchon *m*; *(in industry)* goulet *m ou* goulot *m* d'étranglement

bottlenosed dolphin [ˈbɒtəlˌnəʊzd-] **N** grand dauphin *m*, dauphin *m* à gros nez

bottle-washer N *(person)* laveur(euse) *m,f* de bouteilles; *(machine)* rince-bouteilles *m inv*

bottling [ˈbɒtəlɪŋ] **N** *(of drinks)* mise *f* en bouteille(s); *(of fruit)* mise *f* en bocaux, mise *f* en conserve

BOTTOM [ˈbɒtəm] **N 1** *(lowest part* ► *of garment, heap)* bas *m*; *(*► *of water)* fond *m*; *(*► *of hill, stairs)* bas *m*, pied *m*; *(*► *of outside of container)* bas *m*; *(*► *of inside of container)* fond *m*; *(*► *of chair)* siège *m*, fond *m*; *Naut (*► *of ship)* carène *f*; **at the b. of my bag** au fond de mon sac; **at the b. of the staircase** au pied *ou* bas de l'escalier; **at the b. of page one** au bas de la page un, en bas de page un; **the ship sank to the b.** le navire a coulé; **the ship touched (the) b.** le navire a touché le fond; *Fig* **I believe, at the b. of my heart, that...** je crois, au fond de moi-même, que...; **he thanked them from the b. of his heart** il les a remerciés du fond du cœur; **my reasoning knocked the b. out of his argument** mon raisonnement a démoli son argument; **the b. fell out of the grain market** le marché des grains s'est effondré; *Fam* **bottoms up!** cul sec!

2 *(last place)* **he's (at the) b. of his class** il est le dernier de sa classe; **you're at the b. of the list** vous êtes en queue de liste; **you have to start at the b. and work your way up** vous devez commencer au plus bas et monter dans la hiérarchie à la force du poignet

3 *(far end)* fond *m*, bas *m*; **at the b. of the street/garden** au bout de la rue/du jardin

4 *Fig (origin, source)* base *f*, origine *f*; **I'm sure she's at the b. of all this** je suis sûr que c'est elle qui est à l'origine de cette histoire; **I intend to get to the b. of this affair** j'entends aller au fin fond de cette affaire *ou* découvrir le pot aux roses

5 *(buttocks)* derrière *m*, fesses *fpl*

6 *(of two-piece garment)* bas *m*; **pyjama bottoms** bas *m* de pyjama; **bikini b.** bas *m* de maillot de bain

7 *(in billiards, snooker)* **to put b. on a ball** faire de l'effet à revenir *ou* de l'effet rétrograde

8 *Br Aut (gear)* première *f*

ADJ it's on the b. shelf il se trouve sur l'étagère du bas; **the b. book in the pile** le livre qui est en bas de la pile; **the b. half of the chart** la partie inférieure du tableau; **the b. floor** le rez-de-chaussée; **the b. stair** *(going up)* la marche du bas, la première marche; *(going down)* la dernière marche; *Br* **she's collecting things for her b. drawer** elle réunit des choses pour son trousseau

• **at bottom ADV** au fond; **at b., their motives are purely mercenary** au fond, leurs intentions sont purement intéressées

►► ***bottom feeder*** *Ich* poisson *m* de fond; *Fig Pej (unsuccessful person)* raté(e) *m,f*; *(team, company)* ratés *mpl*; *Br Aut* ***bottom gear*** première *f* (vitesse *f*); *Acct & Fin* ***bottom line*** résultat *m* net, solde *m* final, résultat *m* financier; **all he's interested in is the b. line** la seule chose qui l'intéresse c'est de faire de l'argent; *Fig* **the b. line is we can't afford it** le fait est que nous ne pouvons pas nous le permettre; *Comput & Typ* ***bottom margin*** marge *f* du bas, marge *f* inférieure

►**bottom out VI** *Fin (prices)* atteindre son niveau plancher; *Econ (recession, inflation, unemployment)* atteindre son plus bas niveau

bottomless [ˈbɒtəmlɪs] **ADJ** sans fond, insondable; *(unlimited* ► *funds, supply)* inépuisable

►► *Fig* ***bottomless pit*** gouffre *m*; **it's like pouring money into a b. pit** c'est comme jeter de l'argent par les fenêtres

bottom-line analysis N *Acct & Fin* analyse *f* des résultats financiers

bottommost [ˈbɒtəmˌməʊst] **ADJ** le plus bas

bottom-of-the-range N modèle *m* de base

ADJ bas de gamme

botty [ˈbɒtɪ] **N** *Br Fam* fesses[□] *fpl*

botulin [ˈbɒtjʊlɪn] **N** *Chem* toxine *f* botulique

botulism [ˈbɒtjʊlɪzəm] **N** *Med* botulisme *m*

bouclé [ˈbuːkleɪ] *Tex* **N** bouclé *m*

COMP *(sweater, fabric)* en bouclette

►► ***bouclé wool*** bouclette *f*

boudoir [ˈbuːdwɑː(r)] **N** boudoir *m*

bouffant [ˈbuːfɒn] **ADJ** *(hairstyle, sleeve)* bouffant

bougainvillaea, bougainvillea [ˌbuːgənˈvɪlɪə] **N** *Bot* bougainvillée *f*, bougainvillier *m*

bough [baʊ] **N** branche *f*

bought [bɔːt] *pt & pp of* **buy**

►► *Acct & Fin* ***bought ledger*** cahier *m ou* livre *m* des achats

bouillon [ˈbuːjɒn] **N** *Culin* bouillon *m*, consommé *m*

►► *Am* ***bouillon cube*** cube *m* de bouillon; *Am* ***bouillon cup*** tasse *f* à bouillon *ou* à consommé

boulder [ˈbəʊldə(r)] **N** bloc *m* de roche, *Spec* boulder *m*; *(smaller)* gros galet *m*

boulevard [ˈbuːləvɑːd] **N** boulevard *m*

bounce [baʊns] **N 1** *(rebound)* bond *m*, rebond *m*; *Sport* **he caught the ball on the b.** il a pris la balle au bond; *Sport* **you get a better b. on grass** cela rebondit mieux sur l'herbe

2 *(spring)* **there isn't much b. in this ball** cette balle ne rebondit pas beaucoup; **I'd like to put some b. in my hair** je voudrais donner du volume à mes cheveux; *Fig* **he's still full of b. at 70** à 70 ans il est encore plein d'énergie

3 *Am Fam (dismissal)* **to give sb the b.** virer qn; **he got the b.** il s'est fait virer

4 *Fam* **on the b.** *(in succession)* à la suite

VT 1 *(cause to spring)* faire rebondir; **she bounced the ball against** *or* **off the wall** elle fit rebondir la balle sur le mur; **he bounced the baby on his knee** il a fait sauter l'enfant sur son genou; **signals are bounced off a satellite** les signaux sont renvoyés *ou* retransmis par satellite; **to b. an idea off sb** soumettre une idée à qn

2 *Fam Banking (cheque)* refuser d'honorer[□]; **the bank bounced my cheque** la banque a refusé mon chèque

3 *Fam (throw out)* flanquer à la porte, vider

VI 1 *(object)* rebondir; **the ball bounced down the steps** la balle a rebondi de marche en marche; **the knapsack bounced up and down on his back** le sac à dos tressautait sur ses épaules; **the bicycle bounced along the bumpy path** le vélo faisait des bonds sur le chemin cahoteux; **the hailstones were bouncing off the roof** les grêlons rebondissaient sur le toit

2 *(person)* bondir, sauter; **we bounced up and down on the bed** nous faisions des bonds sur le lit; **she came bouncing into/out of the room** elle est entrée dans/sortie de la pièce d'un bond

3 *Fam Banking (cheque)* être refusé pour non-provision[□]; **I hope this cheque won't b.** j'espère que ce chèque ne sera pas refusé

4 *Comput (e-mail)* revenir à l'expéditeur

►► *Comput* ***bounce message*** = message électronique non délivré revenu à l'expéditeur

►**bounce back VI** *(ball)* rebondir; *(person* ► *after illness, disappointment)* se remettre rapidement; *(Stock Exchange)* reprendre, remonter; *Fin* **the pound has bounced back against the dollar** la livre a regagné du terrain par rapport au dollar

bouncer [ˈbaʊnsə(r)] **N** *Fam (doorman)* videur[□] *m*

bouncing [ˈbaʊnsɪŋ] **ADJ 1** *(healthy)* qui respire la santé; **a b. baby** un bébé en pleine santé **2** *(ball)* qui rebondit

bouncy [ˈbaʊnsɪ] *(compar* **bouncier**, *superl* **bounciest**) **ADJ 1** *(ball, bed)* élastique; *(hair)* souple, qui a du volume **2** *(person)* plein d'entrain, dynamique

►► *Br* ***bouncy castle*** château *m* gonflable

BOUND [baʊnd]

ADJ
• sûr **1** • obligé **2**
• lié **3, 5** • relié **6**
• à destination de **4**

N
• saut, bond **1**

VI
• sauter, bondir

VT
• borner, limiter

NPL
• borne, limite

pt & pp of **bind**

ADJ 1 *(certain)* sûr, certain; **it was b. to happen** c'était à prévoir; **it's b. to rain tomorrow** il pleuvra sûrement demain; **he's b. to apologize** il ne va pas manquer de s'excuser

2 *(compelled)* obligé; **they are b. by the treaty to take action** l'accord les oblige à prendre des mesures; **the teacher felt b. to report them** l'enseignant s'est cru obligé de les dénoncer

3 *(connected)* **b. up** lié; **his frustration is b. up with his work** sa frustration est directement liée à son travail

4 *(heading towards)* **b. for** *(person)* en route pour; *(shipment, cargo etc)* à destination de; *(train)* à destination *ou* en direction de; **to be homeward b.** être sur le chemin du retour; **where are you b. for?** où allez-vous?; **I'm b. for Chicago** je suis en route pour Chicago; **all shipments b. for Madrid** toutes cargaisons à destination de Madrid; **the train is b. for Rome** le train est à destination *ou* en direction de Rome; **on a plane b. for Tokyo** dans un avion à destination de *ou* en route pourTokyo

5 *(tied)* lié; **b. hand and foot** pieds et poings liés

6 *Typ (book)* relié; **b. in boards** cartonné

N *(leap)* saut *m*, bond *m*; **at one b., in a single b.** d'un seul bond *ou* saut

VI *(person)* sauter, bondir; *(animal)* faire un bond *ou* des bonds, bondir; **the children bounded into/out of the classroom** les enfants sont entrés dans/sortis de la salle de classe en faisant des bonds; **the dog bounded down the hill** le chien dévala la colline en bondissant

VT borner, limiter; **a country bounded on two sides by the sea** un pays limité par la mer de deux côtés

• **bounds NPL** limite *f*, borne *f*; **the situation has gone beyond the bounds of all reason** la situation est devenue complètement aberrante *ou* insensée; **her rage knew no bounds** sa colère était sans bornes; **within the bounds of possibility** dans la limite du possible; *Fig* **to keep within bounds** rester dans la juste mesure, pratiquer la modération; **out of bounds** *(gen)* dont l'accès est interdit; *(in golf)* hors du jeu; **the castle gardens are out of bounds to visitors** les jardins du château sont interdits au public

boundary ['baʊndərɪ] *(pl* **boundaries)** **N** limite *f*, frontière *f*; **b. (line)** limite *f*, *Sport* limites *fpl* du terrain; *(in basketball)* ligne *f* de touche; **to hit** *or* **to score a b.** *(in cricket)* envoyer la balle jusqu'aux limites du terrain

►► *Br Parl* ***boundary change*** *(of parliamentary constituency)* = modification des limites d'une circonscription; *Hort* ***boundary stone*** borne *f*, pierre *f* de bornage

bounden ['baʊndən] **ADJ** *Formal* **b. duty** devoir *m* impérieux

bounder ['baʊndə(r)] **N** *Fam Old-fashioned or Hum* goujat▫ *m*, malotru▫ *m*

boundless ['baʊndlɪs] **ADJ** *(energy, wealth)* illimité; *(ambition, gratitude)* sans bornes; *(space)* infini

bounteous ['baʊntɪəs] **ADJ** *Literary (person)* généreux, libéral; *(harvest, supply)* abondant

bounteousness ['baʊntɪəsnɪs] **N** *Literary (of person)* bonté *f*, générosité *f*; *(of harvest, supply)* abondance *f*

bountiful ['baʊntɪfʊl] **ADJ** *Literary (person)* généreux, libéral; *(harvest, supply)* abondant

bounty ['baʊntɪ] *(pl* **bounties)** **N 1** *Literary (generosity)* munificence *f* **2** *(gift)* don *m* **3** *(reward)* prime *f*

►► ***bounty hunter*** chasseur *m* de primes

bouquet [bʊ'keɪ] **N 1** *(of flowers)* bouquet *m*; *Fig* **to throw bouquets at sb** faire des compliments à qn; *TV* **b. of channels** bouquet *m* de chaînes **2** *(of wine)* bouquet *m*

Bourbon ['bʊəbən] *Hist* **N** Bourbon *mf*

ADJ bourbonien

bourbon ['bɜːbən] **N** *(whisky)* bourbon *m*

►► *Br* ***bourbon biscuit*** = biscuit au chocolat fourré de crème au chocolat

bourdon ['bʊədən] **N** *Mus (of organ, bagpipes)* bourdon *m*

bourgeois ['bɔːʒwɑː] **N** bourgeois(e) *m,f*

ADJ bourgeois

bourgeoisie [ˌbɔːʒwɑː'ziː] **N** bourgeoisie *f*

bout [baʊt] **N 1** *(of illness)* attaque *f*; *(of fever)* accès *m*; *(of rheumatism)* crise *f*; *(of coughing)* quinte *f*; *(of self-pity)* crise *f*; *(of depression, intense activity)* période *f*; **a b. of bronchitis/flu** une bronchite/grippe; **she's prone to frequent bouts of illness** elle est souvent malade; **a b. of drinking** une soûlerie, une beuverie **2** *Sport (in boxing, wrestling)* combat *m*

boutique [buː'tiːk] **N** *(shop)* boutique *f*; *(in department store)* rayon *m*

►► ***boutique hotel*** hôtel *m* de charme

bovine ['bəʊvaɪn] **N** bovin *m*

ADJ *also Fig* bovin

►► *Vet* ***bovine spongiform encephalopathy*** encéphalite *f* bovine spongiforme

Bovril® ['bɒvrɪl] **N** *Br* = préparation à base de suc de viande utilisée comme boisson ou comme condiment

bovver ['bɒvə(r)] **N** *(UNCOUNT) Br Fam Old-fashioned (fighting)* bagarre *f*

►► ***bovver boots*** brodequins *mpl*, rangers *mpl*; ***bovver boy*** loubard *m*

bow[1] [bəʊ] **N 1** *(curve)* arc *m*

2 *(for arrows)* arc *m*; **he drew the b.** il a tiré à l'arc

3 *Mus (stick)* archet *m*; *(stroke)* coup *m* d'archet

4 *(in ribbon)* nœud *m*, boucle *f*; **tie it in a b.** faites un nœud

VI *Mus* manier l'archet

►► ***bow legs*** jambes *fpl* arquées; ***bow tie*** nœud *m* papillon; *Br Archit* ***bow window*** fenêtre *f* en saillie, oriel *m*, bow-window *m*

bow[2] [baʊ] **N 1** *(gen)* salut *m (fait en inclinant le buste)*; **he made her a deep** *or* **low b.** il l'a saluée profondément *ou* bien bas; **to take a b.** *(of performer)* saluer **2** *Naut (of ship)* avant *m*, proue *f*; **on the port/starboard b.** par bâbord/tribord avant **3** *Naut (oarsman)* nageur *m* de l'avant

VT *(bend)* incliner, courber; *(knee)* fléchir; *(head ► in shame)* baisser; *(► in prayer)* incliner

VI 1 *(in greeting)* incliner la tête, saluer; **I bowed to him** je l'ai salué de la tête; **he refuses to b. and scrape to anyone** il refuse de faire des courbettes *ou* des salamalecs à qui que ce soit **2** *(bend)* se courber; *(under load)* ployer **3** *Fig (yield)* s'incliner; **to b. to the inevitable** s'incliner devant l'inévitable; **the government is bowing under** *or* **to pressure from the unions** l'administration s'incline sous la pression des syndicats

►► ***bow oar*** aviron *m* de l'avant; ***bow rope*** amarre *f* de bout *ou* de l'avant; ***bow wave*** lame *f* d'étrave

►**bow down VT SEP** faire plier; *Fig* écraser, briser

VI s'incliner; **he bowed down to her** il s'est incliné devant elle

►**bow out VI** *Fig (retire, withdraw)* tirer sa révérence

bowdlerize, -ise ['baʊdləraɪz] **VT** expurger; *Fig* **a bowdlerized version of the party** une version tronquée de la soirée

bowed [baʊd] **ADJ** *(back)* courbé; *(head)* baissé

bowel ['baʊəl] **N** *(usu pl)* **1** *(of human)* intestin *m*, intestins *mpl*; *(of animal)* boyau *m*, boyaux *mpl*, intestins *mpl*; **a b. disorder** troubles *mpl* intestinaux **2** *Fig* **the bowels of the earth** les entrailles *fpl* de la terre

►► *Med* ***bowel cancer*** cancer *m* de l'intestin; ***bowel movement*** selles *fpl*; **to have a b. movement** aller à la selle

bower ['baʊə(r)] **N 1** *Bot (arbour)* berceau *m* de verdure, charmille *f* **2** *Literary (cottage)* chaumière *f*; *(boudoir)* boudoir *m*

bowfronted [ˌbəʊ'frʌntɪd] **ADJ** *(piece of furniture)* pansu; *Archit (house)* à la façade arrondie

bowhead ['bəʊhed] **N** *Zool (whale)* baleine *f* boréale

bowing[1] ['baʊɪŋ] **N** *(UNCOUNT) (greeting)* saluts *mpl*; **b. and scraping** salamalecs *mpl*, courbettes *fpl*

bowing[2] ['bəʊɪŋ] **N** *Mus* technique *f* d'archet; **his b. is perfect** il a un coup d'archet parfait

bowl [bəʊl] **N 1** *(receptacle, contents)* bol *m*; *(larger)* bassin *m*, cuvette *f*; *(made of glass)* coupe *f*; *(for washing-up)* cuvette *f*; **a b. of rice** un bol de riz

2 *(rounded part ► of spoon)* creux *m*; *(► of pipe)* fourneau *m*; *(► of wine glass)* coupe *f*; *(► of sink, toilet)* cuvette *f*

3 *Geog* bassin *m*, cuvette *f*

4 *Am Sport (arena)* amphithéâtre *m*; *(championship)* championnat *m*, coupe *f*; *(trophy)* coupe *f*

5 *Sport (ball)* boule *f*

VT 1 *Sport (ball, bowl)* lancer, faire rouler; *(hoop)* faire rouler **2** *Sport (score)* **I bowled 160** j'ai marqué 160 points; **to b. the ball** *(in cricket)* servir; **he bowled (out) the batsman** il a mis le batteur hors jeu

VI 1 *Sport (play bowls)* jouer aux boules; *(play tenpin bowling)* jouer au bowling; *(in cricket)* lancer (la balle); **he bowls for England** *(in cricket)* il sert pour l'Angleterre; *(in bowls)* il joue pour l'Angleterre **2** *(move quickly)* filer, aller bon train; **the bus bowled along the country lanes** l'autocar roulait à toute vitesse sur les petites routes de campagne

• **bowls N** *Br Sport* (jeu *m* de) boules *fpl*; **let's play (a game of) bowls!** et si on jouait aux boules!

►**bowl out VT SEP** *Sport (in cricket)* mettre hors jeu

►**bowl over VT SEP 1** *(knock down)* renverser, faire tomber **2** *Fam Fig (amaze)* stupéfier▫, sidérer; **I was bowled over by the news** la nouvelle m'a abasourdi

bow-legged [bəʊ-] **ADJ** à jambes arquées

bowler ['bəʊlə(r)] **N 1** *Sport (in bowls)* joueur (euse) *m,f* de boules *ou* pétanque, bouliste *mf*; *(in tenpin bowling)* joueur(euse) *m,f* de bowling; *(in cricket)* lanceur(euse) *m,f* **2** *Br (hat)* (chapeau *m*) melon *m*

►► *Br* ***bowler hat*** (chapeau *m*) melon *m*

bowlful ['bəʊlfʊl] **N** bol *m*; **a b. of water** une cuvette d'eau

bowline ['bəʊlɪn] **N** *Naut (rope)* bouline *f*; *(knot)* nœud *m* de chaise

bowling ['bəʊlɪŋ] **N** *Sport (bowls)* jeu *m* de boules, pétanque *f*; *(tenpin)* bowling *m*; *(in cricket)* service *m*; **to go b.** *(play bowls)* (aller) jouer à la pétanque; *(play tenpin bowling)* (aller) faire du bowling

►► ***bowling alley*** *(building)* bowling *m*; *(single lane)* piste *f* de bowling; ***bowling ball*** boule *f* de bowling; ***bowling green*** terrain *m* de boules *(sur gazon)*

bowman[1] ['bəʊmən] *(pl* **bowmen** [-mən]) **N** *Literary (archer)* archer *m*

bowman[2] ['baʊmən] *(pl* **bowmen** [-mən]) **N** *Naut* nageur *m* de l'avant

bow-saw [bəʊ-] **N** *Carp* archet *m (scie)*

bowser ['baʊzə(r)] **N** camion-citerne *m*

bowsprit ['bəʊsprɪt] **N** *Naut* beaupré *m*

bowstring ['bəʊstrɪŋ] **N** *Mus* corde *f*

bow-wow [ˌbaʊ'waʊ] **N** *(in children's language)* toutou *m*

EXCLAM ouâ ouâ

box [bɒks] *(pl* **boxes)** **N 1** *(container, contents)* boîte *f*; *(with lock)* coffret *m*; *(cardboard box)* carton *m*; *(crate)* caisse *f*; **b. of chocolates** boîte *f* de chocolats; *Fig* **how can people live in these little boxes?** comment les gens font-ils pour vivre dans ces trous de souris?; *Fig* **in a pine** *or* **wooden b.** *(coffin)* dans un cercueil; *Hum* **the only way he's leaving here is in a wooden b.** il ne partira d'ici que les pieds devant; *Br Fam* **to be out of one's b.** *(extremely drunk)* être complètement pété; *Fam Fig* **to think outside the b.** être original dans sa façon de penser, être inventif

2 *(compartment)* compartiment *m*; *Theat* loge *f*; *Theat (on ground floor)* baignoire *f*; *Law (for jury, reporters)* banc *m*; *Br Law (for witness)* barre *f*; *Horseriding (in stable)* box *m*, stalle *f*; **the Royal b.** = loge réservée aux membres de la famille royale

3 *(designated area ► on form)* case *f*; *(► in newspaper)* encadré *m*; *(► frame around article)* cadre *m*; *(► on screen)* boîte *f*, case *f*; *Comput (► for graphic)* cadre *m*; *(► that can be drawn)* encadré *m*; *(► on road, sportsfield)* zone *f* quadrillée; *Ftbl (penalty box)* surface *f* de réparation

4 *Aut & Tech (casing)* boîte *f*, carter *m*; *(of axle, brake)* boîte *f*; *(of wheel)* moyeu *m*; *(of lock)* palâtre *m*, palastre *m*

5 *Fam TV (television)* **the b.** la télé; **what's on the b.?** qu'y a-t-il à la télé?

6 *(postal address)* boîte *f* postale

7 *(blow)* **a b. on the ears** une gifle, une claque

8 *Gym (for vaulting)* plinth *m*

9 *Bot* buis *m*

COMP *(border, hedge)* de *ou* en buis

VT 1 *(fight)* boxer avec, boxer; **to b. sb's ears** gifler qn; **she boxed his ears** elle l'a giflé **2** *(put in box)* mettre en boîte *ou* caisse

VI *(fight)* faire de la boxe, boxer

▸▸ ***box calf*** box *m*, box-calf *m*; *Phot* ***box camera*** appareil *m* photographique rudimentaire; *Am Geog* ***box canyon*** cañon *m ou* canyon *m* encaissé; ***box cutter*** cutter *m*; ***box file*** boîte *f* archive; *Br* ***box junction*** carrefour *m (matérialisé sur la chaussée par des bandes croisées)*; ***box kite*** cerf-volant *m* cellulaire; ***box number*** *(in newspaper)* numéro *m* d'annonce; *(at post office)* numéro *m* de boîte à lettres; **B. number 301** Référence 301, Réf. 301; *Theat & Cin* ***box office*** *(office)* bureau *m* de location; *(window)* guichet *m* (de location); **the play was a big success at the b. office** *or* **was good b. office** la pièce a fait beaucoup d'entrées; *Sewing* ***box pleat*** pli *m* creux; ***box spring*** sommier *m* à ressort; ***box of tricks*** sac *m* à malices

▸**box in** **VT SEP** *(enclose)* enfermer, confiner; *(pipes, bath, wash basin)* encastrer; **the car was boxed in between two vans** la voiture était coincée entre deux camionnettes; **to feel boxed in** se sentir à l'étroit; **don't b. me in!** de l'air!

boxcar [ˈbɒkskɑː(r)] **N** *Am Rail* wagon *m* de marchandises (couvert)

boxed [bɒkst] **ADJ** en boîte

▸▸ ***boxed set*** *(of CDs, videos, books)* coffret *m*

boxer [ˈbɒksə(r)] **N 1** *(fighter)* boxeur *m* **2** *(dog)* boxer *m*

• **boxers** **NPL** *(boxer shorts)* caleçon *m*

▸▸ *Aut* ***boxer engine*** moteur *m* à cylindres à plat, boxer *m*; ***boxer shorts*** caleçon *m*

boxful [ˈbɒksfʊl] **N** pleine boîte *f*; *(cardboard box)* plein carton *m*; *(crate)* pleine caisse *f*

boxing [ˈbɒksɪŋ] **N** boxe *f*

▸▸ *Br* ***Boxing Day*** = le 26 décembre; ***boxing glove*** gant *m* de boxe; ***boxing match*** match *m* de boxe; ***boxing ring*** ring *m*

box-pleated **ADJ** *Sewing* à plis creux

boxroom [ˈbɒksrʊm] **N** *Br* débarras *m*, capharnaüm *m*

boxwood [ˈbɒkswʊd] **N** *Bot* buis *m*

boy [bɔɪ] **N 1** *(male child)* garçon *m*, enfant *m*; **a little b.** un petit garçon, un garçonnet; **when I was a b.** quand j'étais petit *ou* jeune; **be a good b.!** sois sage!; **bad b.!** vilain!; **an Italian b.** un petit *ou* jeune Italien; **I've known them since they were boys** je les connais depuis leur enfance *ou* depuis qu'ils sont petits; **boys will be boys** les hommes et les garçons sont comme ça et on ne les changera pas; *Fig* **he's just a b. when it comes to women** ce n'est encore qu'un gamin quand il s'agit des femmes; **he's a mother's b.** c'est le petit garçon à sa maman

2 *(son)* fils *m*; **the Smiths' b.** le petit Smith

3 *Br Sch (student)* élève *m*

4 *Fam (term of address)* **that's my b.!** je te reconnais bien là!; **sit down, my b.** assieds-toi, mon petit *ou* mon grand; **my dear b.** mon cher ami; *Br* **how are you, old b.?** ça va mon vieux?

5 *(male adult)* **he likes to think he's one of the boys** il aime à croire qu'il fait partie de la bande; **a local b.** un gars du coin; **come on, boys!** allons-y les gars!; **a night out with the boys** une virée entre copains; *Fam* **the boys in blue** les flics *mpl*; **the backroom boys** ceux qui restent dans les coulisses; *Fam* **he threatened to send the boys round** il a menacé d'envoyer ses gars; *Fam* **the big boys** *(important men)* les grosses légumes *fpl*; *Fig* **to play with the big boys** jouer dans la cour des grands

6 *(used to address dog, horse etc)* mon beau; **down, b.!** couché, mon beau!

EXCLAM (oh) b.! dis donc!

▸▸ ***boy band*** boys band *m*; *Br Fam* ***boy racer*** jeune conducteur *m* imprudent⁻; ***Boy Scout, boy scout*** scout *m*; ***boy wonder*** petit génie *m*

boycott [ˈbɔɪkɒt] **N** boycottage *m*, boycott *m*

VT boycotter

boyfriend [ˈbɔɪˌfrend] **N** petit ami *m*, copain *m*

boyhood [ˈbɔɪhʊd] **N** *(when very young)* enfance *f*, première jeunesse *f*; *(in teens)* adolescence *f*; **b. friends** amis *mpl* d'enfance

boyish [ˈbɔɪɪʃ] **ADJ 1** *(youthful)* d'enfant, de garçon; *(childish)* enfantin, puéril **2** *(tomboyish* ▸ *behaviour)* de garçon manqué; **she's very b.** elle fait très garçon manqué

boyishly [ˈbɔɪɪʃlɪ] **ADV 1** *(youthfully, childishly)* comme un enfant **2** *(tomboyishly)* comme un garçon

boyishness [ˈbɔɪɪʃnɪs] **N 1** *(of young man)* air *m* juvénil **2** *(of girl)* airs *mpl* de garçon manqué

boy-meets-girl **ADJ a b. story** une histoire d'amour conventionnelle

boysenberry [ˈbɔɪzənˌberɪ] **N** mûre *f* de Boysen

bozo [ˈbəʊzəʊ] **N** *Am Fam* crétin(e) *m,f*, andouille *f*

bps [ˌbiːpiːˈes] *Comput (abbr* **bits per second***)* bits *mpl* par seconde

BR [ˌbiːˈɑː(r)] **N** *Formerly (abbr* **British Rail***)* = société des chemins de fer britanniques

bra [brɑː] **N** soutien-gorge *m*

▸▸ ***bra strap*** bretelle *f* de soutien-gorge; ***bra top*** brassière *f*

brace [breɪs] *(pl senses* **1** *to* **4 braces**, *pl sense* **5 inv)** **N 1** *Tech (supporting or fastening device)* attache *f*, agrafe *f*

2 *(for leg)* appareil *m* orthopédique; *(for teeth)* appareil *m* dentaire *ou* orthodontique; *(for torso)* corset *m*

3 *Constr* étai *m*

4 *(drill)* **b. (and bit)** vilebrequin *m* à main

5 *(of game birds, pistols)* paire *f*

VT 1 *(strengthen)* renforcer, consolider; *(support)* soutenir; *Constr* étayer; *(beam)* armer; *Aviat (wing)* croisillonner; **to b. a beam with sth** armer une poutre de qch **2** *(steady, prepare)* **he braced his body/himself for the impact** il raidit son corps/s'arc-bouta en préparation du choc; **the family braced itself for the funeral** la famille s'est armée de courage pour les funérailles; **b. yourself for some bad news** préparez-vous à de mauvaises nouvelles **3** *(of weather)* fortifier, tonifier

VI *Am (prepare)* se préparer; **they braced for the attack** ils se préparèrent à soutenir l'assaut

• **braces** **NPL 1** *Br (for trousers)* bretelles *fpl* **2** *(for teeth)* appareil *m* dentaire *ou* orthodontique

▸▸ ***brace position*** position *f* de sécurité

bracelet [ˈbreɪslɪt] **N** bracelet *m*

• **bracelets** **NPL** *Fam Crime slang (handcuffs)* menottes⁻ *fpl*, bracelets *mpl*

bracer [ˈbreɪsə(r)] **N** *Fam* remontant *m*

brachial [ˈbrækɪəl] **ADJ** *Anat* brachial

brachiopod [ˈbrækɪəpɒd] **N** *Zool (mollusc)* brachiopode *m*

brachycephalic [ˌbrækɪsɪˈfælɪk] **ADJ** *Anat, Méd & Zool* brachycéphale

bracing [ˈbreɪsɪŋ] **ADJ** fortifiant, tonifiant; **a b. wind** un vent vivifiant

N *Constr* entretoisement *m*

▸▸ *Constr* ***bracing strut*** jambe *f* de force

bracken [ˈbrækən] **N** *Bot* fougère *f*

bracket [ˈbrækɪt] **N 1** *Tech (L-shaped support)* équerre *f*, support *m*; *(for shelf)* équerre *f*, tasseau *m*; *(lamp fixture)* fixation *f*; *Archit* console *f*, corbeau *m* **2** *(category)* groupe *m*, classe *f*; *Fin (level of income, tax)* tranche *f*; **the 20–25 age b.** le groupe des 20–25 ans; **the high/low income b.** la tranche des gros/petits revenus **3** *Math & Typ (round)* parenthèse *f*; *(square)* crochet *m*; *(connecting two lines)* accolade *f*; **in** *or* **between brackets** entre parenthèses

VT 1 *(put in parentheses)* mettre entre parenthèses; *(put in square brackets)* mettre entre crochets; *(connect in vertical list)* réunir par une accolade **2** *Fig (categorize)* associer, mettre dans la même catégorie; **he is often bracketed with the Surrealists** on le range souvent parmi les surréalistes; **why b. together two such different companies?** pourquoi mettre deux entreprises aussi différentes dans la même catégorie?

bracketing [ˈbrækɪtɪŋ] **N** *(in parentheses)* mise *f* entre parenthèses; *(in square brackets)* mise *f* entre crochets; *(in a vertical list)* réunion *f* par une accolade

brackish [ˈbrækɪʃ] **ADJ** saumâtre

bract [brækt] **N** *Bot* bractée *f*

brad [bræd] **N** *Tech* semence *f*, clou *m* de tapissier

bradawl [ˈbrædɔːl] **N** *Tech* poinçon *m*

bradycardia [ˌbrædɪˈkɑːdɪə] **N** *Med* bradycardie *f*

brae [breɪ] **N** *Scot (hillside)* colline *f*; *(slope)* pente *f*, côte *f*

brag [bræg] *(pt & pp* **bragged**, *cont* **bragging)** **VI** se vanter; **to b. about sth** se vanter de qch; **he's always bragging about his salary** il faut toujours qu'il se vante de son salaire; **it's nothing to b. about** il n'y a pas là de quoi se vanter

N *Cards (card game)* = jeu de cartes qui ressemble au poker

braggadocio [ˌbrægəˈdəʊtʃɪəʊ] **N** *Literary* vantardise *f*

braggart [ˈbrægət] **N** vantard(e) *m,f*, fanfaron (onne) *m,f*

bragging [ˈbrægɪŋ] **ADJ** vantard, fanfaron

N vantardise *f*, fanfaronnades *fpl*

Brahman [ˈbrɑːmən] **N** *Rel (person)* brahmane *m*

Brahmanism [ˈbrɑːmənɪzəm] **N** *Rel* brahmanisme *m*

Brahmin [ˈbrɑːmɪn] *(pl* inv *or* **Brahmins) N 1** *Rel* brahmane *m* **2** *Am Fam* intellectuel(elle)⁻ *m,f*; **she's a Boston B.** elle est d'une vieille famille bostonienne⁻

braid [breɪd] **N 1** *(trimming)* ganse *f*, soutache *f*; *(on uniform)* galon *m* **2** *esp Am (of hair)* tresse *f*, natte *f*; **she wears her hair in braids** elle porte *ou* se fait des nattes

VT 1 *(decorate with)* soutacher, galonner **2** *esp Am (plait)* tresser, natter

braided [ˈbreɪdɪd] **ADJ 1** *(clothing)* passementé **2** *esp Am (hair)* tressé

braiding [ˈbreɪdɪŋ] **N 1** *(decoration) (on cushion, clothing)* galon *m*, passepoil *m* **2** *esp Am (of hair)* tressage *m*, nattage *m*

braille, Braille [breɪl] **N** braille *m*; **to read B.** lire le braille; **in B.** en braille

COMP *(reader, teacher)* de braille; *(book)* en braille

▸▸ ***Braille alphabet*** alphabet *m* braille

brain [breɪn] **N 1** *(part of body)* cerveau *m*; *(mind)* cerveau *m*, tête *f*; *Culin* cervelle *f*; *Med* **she had a b. scan** on lui a fait un scanner du cerveau

2 *Fam Fig* **to blow one's brains out** se faire sauter la cervelle; **you've got money on the b.** tu es obsédé par l'argent; **she's got it on the b.** elle ne pense qu'à ça, ça la tient

3 *(intelligence)* intelligence *f*; **he's got brains** il est intelligent; **you need a good b. to solve this puzzle** il faut être intelligent pour résoudre ce problème; **I haven't got the brains to become a doctor** je ne suis pas assez intelligent pour devenir médecin; **anyone with half a b.** n'importe qui d'un tant soit peu intelligent; **can I pick your brains for a minute?** j'ai besoin de tes lumières

4 *Fam (clever person)* cerveau *m*

VT *Fam (hit)* assommer⁻

• **brains** **N** *Fam (clever person)* cerveau *m*; **the brains** le cerveau; **she's the brains of the family/business** c'est elle le cerveau de la famille/de l'entreprise

▸▸ *Med* ***brain damage*** lésions *fpl* cérébrales; *Med* ***brain death*** mort *f* cérébrale; ***brain drain*** fuite *f ou* exode *m* des cerveaux; *Med* ***brain imaging*** imagerie *f* cérébrale; *Med* ***brain scanning*** imagerie *f* cérébrale; *Med* ***brain surgeon*** neurochirugien *m*; *Med* ***brain surgery*** neurochirurgie *f*; *Am* ***brain trust***, *Br* ***brains trust*** *(panel of experts)* groupe *m* d'experts, brain-trust *m*; *Med* ***brain tumour*** tumeur *f* au cerveau

> When translating **brain**, note that **cerveau** and **cervelle** are not interchangeable. **Cerveau** refers to the organ, whereas generally **cervelle** refers to brain matter.

brainbox [ˈbreɪnbɒks] **N** *Br Fam (skull)* crâne⁻ *m*; *(person)* cerveau *m*

brainchild [ˈbreɪnˌtʃaɪld] *(pl* **brainchildren** [-ˈtʃɪldrən]) **N** *Fam* bébé *m*; **the scheme is his b.** le projet est son bébé

brainless [ˈbreɪnlɪs] **ADJ** *(person)* écervelé, stupide; *(idea)* stupide

brainpower [ˈbreɪnˌpaʊə(r)] **N** intelligence *f*

brainstorm [ˈbreɪnstɔːm] **N 1** *Med* congestion *f* cérébrale **2** *Br Fam Fig (mental aberration)* idée *f* insensée *ou* loufoque **3** *Am Fam Fig (brilliant idea)* idée *f* géniale

VI faire du brainstorming
VT plancher sur

brainstorming ['breɪn,stɔːmɪŋ] N brainstorming *m*, remue-méninges *m inv*; **a b. session** un brainstorming, une réunion de remue-méninges

brainteaser ['breɪn,tiːzə(r)] N *Fam* énigme[□] *f*, colle *f*

brainwash ['breɪnwɒʃ] VT faire un lavage de cerveau à; **to b. sb into doing sth** faire un lavage de cerveau à qn pour qu'il fasse qch; **I won't be brainwashed into buying things I don't need** je refuse de me laisser manipuler pour acheter des choses dont je n'ai pas besoin

brainwashing ['breɪn,wɒʃɪŋ] N lavage *m* de cerveau

brainy ['breɪnɪ] (*compar* **brainier**, *superl* **brainiest**) ADJ *Fam* intelligent[□], futé

braise [breɪz] VT *Culin* braiser, cuire à l'étouffée

braising ['breɪzɪŋ] N *Culin* cuisson *f* à l'étouffée
▸▸ ***braising beef*** bœuf *m* à braiser

brake [breɪk] N **1** *(gen) & Aut* frein *m*; **to put on** *or* **to apply the brakes** freiner; **to slam on the brakes** écraser la pédale de frein; **release the b.** desserrez le frein; *Fig* **high interest rates acted as a b. on borrowing** des taux d'intérêt élevés ont freiné les emprunts **2** *(carriage)* break *m*
COMP *Aut (cable)* de frein
VI *Aut* freiner, mettre le frein; **to b. hard** freiner brusquement, écraser la pédale de frein
▸▸ *Aut* ***brake block*** sabot *m ou* patin *m* de frein; *Aut* ***brake fade*** fading *m*; *Aut* ***brake fluid*** liquide *m* de freins, Lockheed® *m*; *Aut* ***brake horsepower*** puissance *f* au frein; *Aut* ***brake lamp*** feu *m* de stop; *Aut* ***brake lever*** frein *m* à main; *Aut* ***brake light*** feu *m* de stop; *Aut* ***brake lining*** garniture *f* de frein; *Aut* ***brake pad*** plaquette *f* de frein; *Aut* ***brake pedal*** pédale *f* de frein; *Aut* ***brake shoe*** mâchoire *f* de frein; *Br Rail* ***brake van*** fourgon *m* à frein

braked trailer ['breɪkt-] N *Aut* remorque *f* freinée

brakelight function ['breɪklaɪt-] N *Am Rad & TV* signal *m* de fin de temps de parole

brakesman ['breɪksmən] (*pl* **brakesmen** [-mən]) N *Br Rail* garde-frein *m*

braking ['breɪkɪŋ] N *Aut* freinage *m*
▸▸ ***braking distance*** distance *f* de freinage

bramble ['bræmbəl] N *Bot* **1** *(prickly shrub)* roncier *m*, roncière *f*; **brambles** *(thorns)* ronces **2** *(blackberry bush)* ronce *f* des haies, mûrier *m* sauvage **3** *(berry)* mûre *f* sauvage
▸▸ ***bramble jelly*** gelée *f* de mûres

brambly ['bræmblɪ] ADJ *Bot* couvert de ronces

bran [bræn] N son *m* (de blé), bran *m*
▸▸ ***bran flakes*** son *m* en flocons; *Br* ***bran mash*** son *m ou* bran *m* mouillé; *Br* ***bran tub*** pêche *f* miraculeuse *(jeu)*

branch [brɑːntʃ] N **1** *(of tree)* branche *f*; **the branches** le branchage, les branches
2 *(secondary part* ▸ *of road)* embranchement *m*; (▸ *of river)* bras *m*; (▸ *of railway)* bifurcation *f*, raccordement *m*; (▸ *of candlestick, artery)* branche *f*
3 *(division* ▸ *gen)* division *f*, section *f*; (▸ *of family)* ramification *f*, branche *f*; (▸ *of science)* branche *f*; (▸ *of police force)* antenne *f*; (▸ *of government, civil service)* service *m*; *Mil* (▸ *of armed forces)* division *f*
4 *Com (of company)* agence *f*, succursale *f*, filiale *f*; *(of shop)* succursale *f*; *(of bank)* agence *f*, succursale *f*; **where's the nearest b. of Kookaï?** où se trouve le Kookaï le plus proche?
5 *Comput (of network)* branchement *m*
VI **1** *(tree)* se ramifier **2** *(road, river)* bifurquer
▸▸ ***branch banking*** banque *f* à réseau; *Rail* ***branch line*** ligne *f* secondaire; ***branch manager*** *(of bank)* directeur(trice) *m,f* d'agence; *(of shop)* directeur(trice) *m,f* de succursale; ***branch office*** *(of company)* succursale *f*; *Banking (of bank)* agence *f*, succursale *f*
▸ **branch off** VI **1** *(road)* bifurquer; **a smaller path branches off to the left** un chemin plus petit bifurque vers la gauche **2** *(digress)* **I'd like to b. off from my main topic for a moment** j'aimerais m'écarter un instant du sujet qui m'occupe
▸ **branch out** VI étendre ses activités; **they're branching out into the restaurant business** ils étendent leurs activités à *ou* se lancent dans la restauration; **I'm going to b. out on my own** je vais faire cavalier seul

branched [brɑːntʃt] ADJ **1** *Bot* branchu, rameux **2** *(candlestick)* à (plusieurs) branches

branchia ['bræŋkɪə] (*pl* **branchiae** [-kiiː]) N *Ich & Zool* branchie *f*

branchiate ['bræŋkɪət] ADJ *Ich & Zool* branchié

brand [brænd] N **1** *Com & Mktg (trademark)* marque *f* (de fabrique); **he always buys the same b. of cigars** il achète toujours la même marque de cigares; *Fig* **he has his own b. of humour** il a un sens de l'humour particulier
2 *(identifying mark* ▸ *on cattle)* marque *f*; *Hist* (▸ *on criminal)* flétrissure *f*
3 *Metal (branding iron)* fer *m* à marquer
4 *(burning wood)* tison *m*, brandon *m*
VT **1** *(with branding iron* ▸ *person, animal, goods)* marquer au fer rouge; *Hist* (▸ *criminal)* flétrir, marquer au fer rouge; *Hist* (▸ *slave)* marquer **2** *Fig (label)* étiqueter, stigmatiser; **she was branded (as) a thief** on lui a collé une étiquette de voleuse **3** *(impress indelibly)* **the experience was branded on his memory for life** l'expérience resta à jamais gravée dans sa mémoire
▸▸ *Mktg* ***brand advertising*** publicité *f* de marque *ou f* sur la marque; *Mktg* ***brand awareness*** mémorisation *f ou* notoriété *f* de la marque; *Mktg* ***brand image*** image *f* de marque; *Mktg* ***brand leader*** marque *f* dominante; *Mktg* ***brand loyalty*** fidélité *f* à la marque; *Com & Mktg* ***brand manager*** chef *m* de marque; *Com & Mktg* ***brand name*** marque *f* (de fabrique); *Mktg* ***brand name recall*** mémorisation *f* de la marque; *Mktg* ***brand recognition*** identification *f* de la marque

branded goods ['brændɪd-] NPL *Com & Mktg* produits *mpl* de marque

branding ['brændɪŋ] N **1** *(of cattle)* marquage *m* au fer rouge **2** *Mktg* marquage *m*
▸▸ ***branding campaign*** campagne *f* d'image de marque; ***branding iron*** fer *m* à marquer

brandish ['brændɪʃ] N brandissement *m*
VT brandir

brand-led ADJ *Mktg* conditionné par la marque, piloté par la marque

brand-loyal ADJ *Mktg* fidèle à la marque

brand-new ADJ tout *ou* flambant neuf

brandy ['brændɪ] (*pl* **brandies**) N *(cognac)* cognac *m*; *(made from fruit other than grapes)* eau-de-vie *f*; **b. and soda** fine *f* à l'eau
▸▸ *Br Culin* ***brandy butter*** = beurre mélangé avec du sucre et parfumé au cognac; ***brandy glass*** verre *m* à cognac; *Br Culin* ***brandy snap*** cigarette *f* russe au gingembre

brash [bræʃ] ADJ **1** *(showy)* exubérant; *(impudent)* effronté, impertinent **2** *(colour)* criard

brashly ['bræʃlɪ] ADV *(showily)* avec exubérance; *(with impudence)* effrontément, avec impertinence

brashness ['bræʃnɪs] N *(showiness)* exubérance *f*; *(impudence)* effronterie *f*, impertinence *f*

brass [brɑːs] N **1** *(metal)* cuivre *m* (jaune), laiton *m*
2 *(objects)* **b.**, **brasses** cuivres *mpl*; **the b. is cleaned once a week** les cuivres sont faits une fois par semaine
3 *Br (memorial)* plaque *f* mortuaire (en cuivre)
4 *Mus* **the b.** les cuivres *mpl*
5 *Fam Mil* **the (top) b.** les huiles *fpl*
6 *Br Fam (nerve)* toupet *m*, culot *m*; **he had the b. to accuse me of cheating** il a eu le toupet de m'accuser de tricher
7 *Br Fam (money)* pognon *m*
8 *(idioms)* **to get down to b. tacks** en venir au fait *ou* aux choses sérieuses; *Br very Fam* **it's b. monkeys** *(very cold)* on se les gèle, on se les caille; *Br Fam* **it's not worth a b. farthing** ça ne vaut pas un clou
COMP *(object, ornament)* de *ou* en cuivre; *(foundry)* de cuivre
▸▸ *Mus* ***brass band*** fanfare *f*, orchestre *m* de cuivres; *Br Fam Fig* ***brass hat*** gros bonnet *m*; *Am* ***brass knuckles*** coup-de-poing *m* américain; *Br Fam* ***brass neck*** *(nerve)* toupet *m*, culot *m*; **to have a b. neck** avoir du culot, être culotté; **I don't know how you have the b. neck to say that!** je ne sais pas comment tu peux avoir le culot de dire une chose pareille!; *Art* ***brass rubbing*** *(picture)* décalque *m*; *(action)* décalquage *m* par frottement; *Mus* ***the brass section*** les cuivres *mpl*
▸ **brass off** VT SEP *Br Fam* **to b. sb off** gonfler qn

brasserie ['bræsərɪ] N brasserie *f*

brassic ['bræsɪk] ADJ *Br Fam (poor)* fauché, à sec, sans un

brassica ['bræsɪkə] N *Bot* brassica *m*

brassie ['brɑːsɪ] N *Golf* brassie *m*

brassiere *Br* ['bræzɪə(r), *Am* brə'zɪər] N soutien-gorge *m*

brassiness ['brɑːsɪnɪs] N **1** *(of sound)* caractère *m* métallique **2** *Fam (brazenness)* effronterie[□] *f*, impertinence[□] *f*

brassware ['brɑːsweə(r)] N *(utensils)* chaudronnerie *f* d'art

brasswork ['brɑːswɜːk] N *Metal* dinanderie *f*

brassy ['brɑːsɪ] (*compar* **brassier**, *superl* **brassiest**)
ADJ **1** *(colour)* cuivré; *(sound)* cuivré, claironnant; *Pej (yellow, blonde)* artificiel; *(cheap jewellery)* qui fait toc **2** *Fam (brazen)* effronté[□], impertinent[□]
N *Golf* brassie *m*

brat [bræt] N *Pej* morveux(euse) *m,f*, galopin *m*; **that kid is a real b.** un vrai morveux, ce gamin; **she brought her brats** elle a amené sa marmaille

bravado [brə'vɑːdəʊ] N bravade *f*

brave [breɪv] ADJ **1** *(courageous)* courageux; **be b.!** sois courageux!, du courage!; **to put on a b. face, to put a b. face on it** faire bonne contenance; **it was a b. effort nonetheless** néanmoins c'était un bel effort **2** *Literary (splendid)* beau (belle), excellent; **a b. new world** une ère nouvelle
VT *(person)* braver, défier; *(danger, storm)* braver, affronter
NPL *(people)* **the b.** les courageux *mpl*; **the bravest of the b.** les plus braves d'entre les braves
N *Hist (Indian warrior)* brave *m*, guerrier *m* indien

> Note that the French adjective **brave** is a false friend. Its most common meaning is **kind**.

bravely ['breɪvlɪ] ADV courageusement, bravement

bravery ['breɪvərɪ] N courage *m*, vaillance *f*

bravo [,brɑː'vəʊ] (*pl* **bravos**) EXCLAM bravo!
N bravo *m*

bravura [brə'vʊərə] N *(gen) & Mus* bravoure *f*

brawl [brɔːl] N *(fight)* bagarre *f*, rixe *f*; **a drunken b.** une querelle d'ivrognes
VI *(fight)* se bagarrer

brawler ['brɔːlə(r)] N bagarreur(euse) *m,f*

brawling ['brɔːlɪŋ] N *(fighting)* bagarres *fpl*, rixes *fpl*

brawn [brɔːn] N *(UNCOUNT)* **1** *(muscle)* muscles *mpl*; *(strength)* muscle *m*; **all b. and no brains** tout dans les bras et rien dans la tête **2** *Br Culin* fromage *m* de tête

brawny ['brɔːnɪ] (*compar* **brawnier**, *superl* **brawniest**) ADJ *(arm)* musculeux; *(person)* musclé

bray [breɪ] N *(of donkey)* braiment *m*; *Pej (of person)* braillement *m*
VI *(donkey)* braire; *Pej (person)* brailler

braze [breɪz] VT *Metal* braser

brazen ['breɪzən] ADJ **1** *(bold)* effronté, impudent; **a b. lie** un mensonge audacieux *ou* effronté; **a b. hussy** une effrontée **2** *Metal (brass)* de cuivre (jaune), de laiton; *(sound)* cuivré
▸ **brazen out** VT SEP **you'll have to b. it out** il va falloir que tu t'en tires par des fanfaronnades

brazen-faced ADJ effronté, impudent

brazenly ['breɪzənlɪ] ADV effrontément, impudemment

brazenness ['breɪzənnɪs] N effronterie *f*

brazier ['breɪzɪə(r)] N **1** *(for fire)* brasero *m* **2** *Metal (brass worker)* chaudronnier *m*

Brazil [brə'zɪl] N Brésil *m*

brazil [brə'zɪl] N **b. (nut)** noix *f* du Brésil

Brazilian [brəˈzɪljən] **N** **1** *(person)* Brésilien(enne) *m,f* **2** *(wax)* épilation *f* maillot brésilienne
ADJ brésilien
COMP *(embassy, history)* du Brésil
▸▸ ***Brazilian wax*** épilation *f* maillot brésilienne

breach [briːtʃ] **N** **1** *(gap)* brèche *f*, trou *m*; *Mil* **our troops made a b. in the enemy lines** nos troupes ont percé les lignes ennemies; *Fig* **she stepped into the b. when I fell ill** elle m'a remplacé au pied levé quand je suis tombé malade **2** *(violation ▸ of law)* violation *f* (**of** de); *(▸ of discipline, order, rules)* infraction *f* (**of** de); *(▸ of etiquette, friendship)* manquement *m* (**of** à); *(▸ of confidence, trust)* abus *m* (**of** de); **a b. of faith** *(gen)* un manque de foi; *Law* un acte de déloyauté; **a b. of professional secrecy** une violation du secret professionnel **3** *(rift)* brouille *f*, désaccord *m*
VT **1** *(make gap in)* ouvrir une brèche dans, faire un trou dans; *Mil* **we breached the enemy lines** nous avons percé les lignes ennemies **2** *Com & Law (agreement)* violer, rompre; *(promise)* manquer à
▸▸ *Law* ***breach of contract*** rupture *f* de contrat; *Law* ***breach of the peace*** atteinte *f* à l'ordre public; *Parl* ***breach of privilege*** atteinte *f* aux privilèges parlementaires; ***breach of promise*** *(gen)* manque *m* de parole; *(of marriage)* violation *f* de promesse de mariage; *Law* ***breach of trust*** prévarication *f*

bread [bred] **N** *(UNCOUNT)* **1** *(foodstuff)* pain *m*; **a loaf of b.** un pain, une miche; **b. and butter** du pain beurré; **a slice of b. and butter** une tartine (beurrée); **translation is her b. and butter** la traduction est son gagne-pain; *Rel* **the b. and wine** les espèces *fpl*; **to earn one's daily b.** gagner sa vie *ou* sa croûte; *Fig* **to put b. on the table** *(of person)* faire bouillir la marmite; *Fig* **to take the b. out of sb's mouth** ôter le pain de la bouche à qn; **I know which side my b. is buttered (on)** je sais où est mon intérêt; *Bible* **give us each day our daily b.** donnez-nous aujourd'hui notre pain quotidien **2** *Fam (money)* pognon *m*, fric *m*
VT *Culin (coat in breadcrumbs)* passer à la chapelure
▸▸ *Br* ***bread bin***, *Am* ***bread box*** *(small)* boîte *f* à pain; *(larger)* huche *f* à pain; *Culin* ***bread pudding*** gâteau *m* de pain; *Br Culin* ***bread sauce*** sauce *f* à la mie de pain

bread-and-butter **ADJ** **1** *Fam (basic)* **a b. job** un travail qui assure le nécessaire▫; **the b. issues** les questions les plus terre-à-terre▫ **2** *Fam (reliable ▸ person)* sur qui l'on peut compter▫
▸▸ *Culin* ***bread-and-butter pudding*** pudding *m* au pain

breadbasket [ˈbredˌbɑːskɪt] **N** **1** *(basket)* corbeille *f* à pain **2** *Geog* région *f* céréalière **3** *Fam Old-fashioned (stomach)* estomac▫ *m*

breadboard [ˈbredbɔːd] **N** **1** *(for bread)* planche *f* à pain **2** *Electron* montage *m* expérimental

breadcrumb [ˈbredkrʌm] **N** miette *f* de pain
VT *Culin (coat in breadcrumbs)* passer à la chapelure
• **breadcrumbs** **NPL** *Culin* chapelure *f*, panure *f*; **fish fried in breadcrumbs** du poisson pané

breaded [ˈbredɪd] **ADJ** *Culin* pané; *(before cooking)* enrobé de chapelure

breadfruit [ˈbredfruːt] **N** *Bot (tree)* arbre *m* à pain; *(fruit)* fruit *m* à pain

breadline [ˈbredlaɪn] **N** = file d'attente pour recevoir des vivres gratuits; *Fig* **to live** *or* **to be on the b.** être sans le sou *ou* indigent

breadth [bredθ] **N** **1** *(width)* largeur *f*; **60 metres in b.** 60 mètres de large **2** *(scope ▸ of mind, thought)* largeur *f*; *(▸ of style)* ampleur *f*

breadthwise [ˈbredθˌwaɪz], **breadthways** [ˈbredθˌweɪz] **ADV** dans le sens de la largeur

breadwinner [ˈbredˌwɪnə(r)] **N** *Fin* soutien *m* de famille

BREAK [breɪk]

VT
• casser **1–3** • briser **1, 9, 10**
• fracturer **2** • enfoncer **5**
• enfreindre **6** • rompre **6, 8**
• couper **8** • ruiner **11**
• amortir **12** • annoncer **13**
• battre **15** • déchiffrer **14**

VI
• se casser **1** • se briser **1**
• se fracturer **2** • se disperser **4**
• se détériorer **6** • faire une pause **7**
• se lever **8** • être annoncé **8**
• éclater **8**

N
• cassure **1** • fracture **1**
• rupture **1, 3, 4** • fissure **2**
• ouverture **3** • interruption **4**
• pause **4, 5** • vacances **5**
• évasion **6** • chance **7**
• changement **8** • break **9, 11**

(*pt* **broke** [brəʊk], *pp* **broken** [ˈbrəʊkn])
VT **1** *(split into pieces ▸ glass, furniture)* casser, briser; *(▸ branch, lace, string, egg, toy)* casser; **b. the stick in two** cassez le bâton en deux; **to b. sth into pieces** mettre qch en morceaux; **to get broken** se casser; **to b. a safe** forcer un coffre-fort; *Rel* **to b. bread** *(priest)* administrer la communion; *(congregation)* recevoir la communion; *Fig* **to b. bread with sb** partager le repas de qn; *Fig* **to b. sb's heart** briser le cœur à qn; **he broke her heart** il lui a brisé le cœur; **it breaks my heart to see her unhappy** ça me brise le cœur de la voir malheureuse; *Fig* **to b. the ice** rompre *ou* briser la glace
2 *Med (fracture)* casser, fracturer; **to b. one's leg** se casser *ou* se fracturer la jambe; **to b. one's neck** se casser *ou* se rompre le cou; **the fall broke his back** la chute lui a brisé les reins; *Fam Fig* **to b. one's back** s'échiner; *Fam Fig* **they broke their backs trying to get the job done** ils se sont éreintés à finir le travail; *Fam* **we've broken the back of the job** nous avons fait le plus gros du travail; *Fam* **I'll b. his neck if I catch him doing it again!** je lui tords le cou si je le reprends à faire ça!; *Fam Fig* **b. a leg!** merde! *(pour souhaiter bonne chance)*
3 *(render inoperable ▸ appliance, machine)* casser; **you've broken the TV** tu as cassé la télé
4 *(cut surface of ▸ ground)* entamer; *(▸ skin)* écorcher; *Law (seals ▸ illegally)* briser; *(legally)* lever; **the seal on the coffee jar was broken** le pot de café avait été ouvert; **the skin isn't broken** la peau n'est pas écorchée; **to b. new** *or* **fresh ground** innover, faire œuvre de pionnier; **scientists are breaking new** *or* **fresh ground in cancer research** les savants font une percée dans la recherche contre le cancer
5 *(force a way through)* enfoncer; **the river broke its banks** la rivière est sortie de son lit; **to b. the sound barrier** franchir le mur du son
6 *Law (violate ▸ law, rule)* violer, enfreindre; *(▸ speed limit)* dépasser; *(▸ agreement, treaty)* violer; *(▸ contract)* rompre; *(▸ promise)* manquer à; **she broke her appointment with them** elle a annulé son rendez-vous avec eux; **he broke his word to her** il a manqué à la parole qu'il lui avait donnée; *Law* **to b. parole** = commettre un délit qui entraîne la révocation de la mise en liberté conditionnelle; *Mil* **to b. bounds** violer la consigne
7 *(escape from, leave suddenly) Law* **to b. jail** s'évader (de prison); **to b. cover** *(animal)* être débusqué; *(person)* sortir à découvert
8 *(interrupt ▸ fast, monotony, spell)* rompre; *Elec (▸ circuit, current)* couper; *Typ (▸ word, page)* couper; **we broke our journey at Brussels** nous avons fait une étape à Bruxelles; **a cry broke the silence** un cri a déchiré *ou* percé le silence; *Mil* **to b. step** rompre le pas
9 *(put an end to ▸ strike)* briser; *(▸ uprising)* mater; **the new offer broke the deadlock** la nouvelle proposition a permis de sortir de l'impasse; **he's tried to stop smoking but he can't b. the habit** il a essayé d'arrêter de fumer mais il n'arrive pas à se débarrasser *ou* se défaire de l'habitude; **to b. sb of a habit** corriger *ou* guérir qn d'une habitude; **to b. oneself of a habit** se corriger *ou* se défaire d'une habitude
10 *(wear down, destroy ▸ enemy)* détruire; *(▸ person, will, courage, resistance)* briser; *(▸ witness)* réfuter; *(▸ health)* abîmer; *(▸ alibi)* écarter; **torture did not b. him** *or* **his spirit** il a résisté à la torture; **this scandal could b. them** ce scandale pourrait signer leur perte; **the experience will either make or b. him** l'expérience lui sera ou salutaire ou fatale
11 *(bankrupt)* ruiner; **her new business will either make or b. her** sa nouvelle affaire la rendra riche ou la ruinera; **to b. the bank** *(exhaust funds)* faire sauter la banque; *Hum* **buying a book won't b. the bank!** acheter un livre ne te/nous/*etc* ruinera pas!
12 *(soften ▸ fall)* amortir, adoucir; **we planted a row of trees to b. the wind** nous avons planté une rangée d'arbres pour couper le vent
13 *(reveal, tell)* annoncer, révéler; **b. it to her gently** annonce-le lui avec ménagement
14 *(solve ▸ code)* déchiffrer
15 *Sport* **to b. a record** battre un record; **to b. sb's service** *(in tennis)* prendre le service de qn; **Williams was broken in the fifth game** Williams a perdu son service dans le cinquième jeu
16 *(divide into parts ▸ collection)* dépareiller; *(▸ bank note)* entamer; **can you b. a £10 note?** pouvez-vous faire de la monnaie sur un billet de 10 livres?
17 *(horse)* dresser
18 *Euph* **to b. wind** lâcher un vent
VI **1** *(split into pieces ▸ glass, furniture)* se casser, se briser; *(▸ branch, stick)* se casser, se rompre; *(▸ lace, string, egg, toy)* se casser; **to b. apart** se casser *ou* se briser (en morceaux); **the plate broke in two/into pieces** l'assiette s'est cassée en deux/en morceaux; *Fig* **her heart broke** elle a eu le cœur brisé
2 *Med (fracture ▸ bone, limb)* se fracturer; **is the bone broken?** y a-t-il une fracture?; *Hum* **any bones broken?** rien de cassé?
3 *(become inoperable ▸ lock, tool)* casser; *(▸ machine)* tomber en panne; **the dishwasher broke last week** le lave-vaisselle est tombé en panne la semaine dernière
4 *(disperse ▸ clouds)* se disperser, se dissiper; *Mil (▸ troops)* rompre les rangs; *(▸ ranks)* se rompre
5 *(escape)* **to b. free** se libérer; **the ship broke loose from its moorings** le bateau a rompu ses amarres
6 *(fail ▸ health, person, spirit)* se détériorer; **the witness broke under questioning** le témoin a craqué au cours de l'interrogatoire; **she** *or* **her spirit did not b.** elle ne s'est pas laissée abattre
7 *(take a break)* faire une pause; **let's b. for coffee** arrêtons-nous pour prendre un café
8 *(arise suddenly ▸ day)* se lever, poindre; *(▸ dawn)* poindre; *Press & TV (▸ news)* être annoncé; *(▸ scandal, war)* éclater
9 *(weather)* changer; *(storm)* éclater
10 *(voice ▸ of boy)* muer; *(▸ with emotion)* se briser
11 *(wave)* déferler; **the sea was breaking against the rocks** les vagues se brisaient sur les rochers
12 *Obst* **her waters have broken** elle a perdu les eaux
13 *Sport (boxers)* se dégager; **b.!** break!, stop!
14 *Sport (ball)* dévier; *(in billiards, snooker, pool)* donner l'acquit
15 *(idiom)* **to b. even** *(gen)* s'y retrouver; *Fin* rentrer dans ses frais
N **1** *(in china, glass)* cassure *f*, brisure *f*; *(in wood)* cassure *f*, rupture *f*; *Med (in bone, limb)* fracture *f*; *Fig (with friend, group)* rupture *f*; *(in marriage)* séparation *f*; **a clean b.** *(in object)* une cassure nette; *Med (in bone)* une fracture simple; **the b. with her husband was a painful experience** ça a été très pénible pour elle quand elle s'est séparée de son mari; **to make a clean b. with the past** rompre avec le passé
2 *(crack)* fissure *f*, fente *f*
3 *(gap ▸ in hedge, wall)* trouée *f*, ouverture *f*; *Geol (▸ in rock)* faille *f*; *(▸ in line)* interruption *f*, rupture *f*; *Typ (▸ in word)* césure *f*; *(▸ in pagination)* fin *f* de page; **a b. in the clouds** une éclaircie
4 *(interruption ▸ in conversation)* interruption *f*, pause *f*; *(▸ in trip)* arrêt *m*; *(▸ in production)* suspension *f*, rupture *f*; *(▸ in series)* interruption *f*; *Literature & Mus* pause *f*; **guitar b.** *(in rock)* (courte) improvisation *f* de guitare; *Elec* **a b. in the circuit** une coupure de courant; **a (commercial) b.** *Rad* un intermède de publicité; *TV* une page de publicité; *TV* **a b. in transmission** une interruption des programmes (due à un incident technique)
5 *(rest)* pause *f*; *(holiday)* vacances *fpl*; *Br Sch* récréation *f*; **let's take a b.** on fait une pause?; **we worked all morning without a b.** nous avons tra-

vaillé toute la matinée sans nous arrêter; **you need a b.** *(short rest)* tu as besoin de faire une pause; *(holiday)* tu as besoin de vacances; **an hour's b. for lunch** une heure de pause pour le déjeuner; **lunch b.** pause *f* de midi; **a weekend in the country makes a pleasant b.** un week-end à la campagne fait du bien; *Fam* **give me a b.!** *(don't talk nonsense)* dis pas n'importe quoi!; *(stop nagging)* fiche-moi la paix!

6 *(escape)* évasion *f*, fuite *f*; *Law* **jail b.** évasion *f* (de prison); **she made a b. for the woods** elle s'est élancée vers le bois; **to make a b. for it** prendre la fuite

7 *Fam (opportunity)* chance❑ *f*; *(luck)* (coup *m* de) veine *f*; **to have a lucky b.** avoir de la veine; **to have a bad b.** manquer de veine; **this could be your big b.** ça pourrait être la chance de ta vie; **she's never had an even b. in her life** rien n'a jamais été facile dans sa vie; **give him a b.** donne-lui une chance; *(he won't do it again)* donne-lui une seconde chance

8 *(change)* changement *m*; **a b. in the weather** un changement de temps; **a b. with tradition** une rupture avec la tradition

9 *(carriage)* break *m*

10 *Literary* **at b. of day** au point du jour, à l'aube

11 *Sport* **to have a service b.** *or* **a b. (of serve)** *(in tennis)* avoir une rupture de service *(de l'adversaire)*; **to have two b. points** *(in tennis)* avoir deux balles de break; **he made a 70 b.** *(in snooker, pool etc)* il a fait une série de 70

►► *Comput* ***break character*** caractère *m* d'interruption; *Comput* ***break key*** touche *f* d'interruption

► **break away** VI **1** *(move away)* se détacher; *(escape)* s'évader; **I broke away from the crowd** je me suis éloigné de la foule; **he broke away from her grasp** il s'est dégagé de son étreinte **2** *(end association)* rompre; *(province ► from State)* se séparer; **a group of MPs broke away from the party** un groupe de députés a quitté le parti **3** *Sport (in racing, cycling)* s'échapper, se détacher du peloton

VT SEP détacher; **they broke all the fittings away from the walls** ils ont décroché toutes les appliques des murs

► **break back** VI *(in tennis)* = gagner le service de son adversaire après avoir perdu son propre service

► **break down** VI **1** *(vehicle, machine)* tomber en panne; **the car has broken down** la voiture est en panne

2 *(fail ► health)* se détériorer; *(► authority)* disparaître; *(► argument, system, resistance)* s'effondrer; *(► negotiations, relations, plan)* échouer; **radio communications broke down** le contact radio a été coupé; **their marriage is breaking down** leur mariage se désagrège

3 *(lose one's composure)* s'effondrer; **to b. down in tears** fondre en larmes

4 *(divide)* se diviser; **the report breaks down into three parts** le rapport comprend *ou* est composé de trois parties

5 *Chem* se décomposer; **to b. down into sth** se décomposer en qch

VT SEP **1** *(destroy ► barrier)* démolir, abattre; *(► door)* enfoncer; *Fig (► resistance)* briser; **we must b. down old prejudices** il faut mettre fin aux vieux préjugés **2** *(analyse ► idea, statistics)* analyser; *(► reasons)* décomposer; *(► account, figures, expenses)* décomposer, ventiler; *(► bill, estimate)* détailler; *(► substance)* décomposer; **the problem can be broken down into three parts** le problème peut se décomposer en trois parties

► **break in** VT SEP **1** *(train ► person)* former; *(► horse)* dresser; **a month should be enough to b. you in to the job** un mois devrait suffire pour vous faire *ou* vous habituer au métier **2** *(clothing)* porter *(pour user)*; **I want to b. these shoes in** je veux que ces chaussures se fassent **3** *(knock down ► door)* enfoncer

VI **1** *Law (burglar)* entrer par effraction **2** *(speaker)* interrompre; **to b. in on sb/sth** interrompre qn/qch

► **break into** VT INSEP **1** *(of burglar)* entrer par effraction dans; *(drawer)* forcer; **they broke into the safe** ils ont fracturé *ou* forcé le coffre-fort; **they've been broken into three times** ils se sont fait cambrioler trois fois

2 *(begin suddenly)* **the audience broke into applause** le public s'est mis à applaudir; **to b. into a run/sprint** se mettre à courir/à sprinter

3 *(conversation)* interrompre

4 *(start to spend ► savings)* entamer; **I don't want to b. into a £20 note** je ne veux pas entamer un billet de 20 livres

5 *Com (market)* percer sur; **the firm has broken into the Japanese market** l'entreprise a percé sur le marché japonais

► **break off** VI **1** *(separate)* se détacher, se casser; **a branch has broken off** une branche s'est détachée (de l'arbre) **2** *(stop)* s'arrêter brusquement; **he broke off in mid-sentence** il s'est arrêté au milieu d'une phrase; **they broke off from work** *(for rest)* ils ont fait une pause; *(for day)* ils ont cessé le travail; **to b. off for lunch** s'arrêter pour déjeuner **3** *(end relationship)* rompre; **she's broken off with him** elle a rompu avec lui

VT SEP **1** *(separate)* détacher, casser; **to b. sth off sth** casser *ou* détacher qch de qch **2** *(end ► agreement, relationship)* rompre; **they've broken off their engagement** ils ont rompu leurs fiançailles; **to b. it off (with sb)** rompre (avec qn); **Italy had broken off diplomatic relations with Libya** l'Italie avait rompu ses relations diplomatiques avec la Libye

► **break open** VT SEP *(door)* enfoncer; *(lock, safe, till)* forcer; *Fam (bottle of wine etc)* ouvrir❑, déboucher❑; **to b. a desk open** ouvrir un bureau en forçant la serrure

► **break out** VI **1** *(begin ► war, storm)* éclater; *(► disease, fire)* se déclarer; *(► fight)* se déclencher **2** *(become covered)* **to b. out in spots** *or* **in a rash** avoir une éruption de boutons; **to b. out in a sweat** se mettre à transpirer **3** *(escape)* s'échapper; **to b. out from** *or* **of prison** s'évader (de prison); **we have to b. out of this vicious circle** il faut que nous sortions de ce cercle vicieux

VT SEP *(bottle, champagne)* ouvrir

► **break through** VT INSEP *(sun)* percer; *(barrier, enemy lines etc)* enfoncer; **I broke through the crowd** je me suis frayé un chemin à travers la foule; **the troops broke through enemy lines** les troupes ont enfoncé les lignes ennemies; **she eventually broke through his reserve** elle a fini par le faire sortir de sa réserve

VI percer; *Fig & Mil* faire une percée; *Fig* **his hidden feelings tend to b. through in his writing** ses sentiments cachés tendent à transparaître *ou* percer dans ses écrits

► **break up** VT SEP **1** *(divide up ► rocks)* briser, morceler; *Law (► property)* morceler; *(► soil)* ameublir; *(► bread, cake)* partager; **illustrations b. up the text** le texte est aéré par des illustrations

2 *(destroy ► house)* démolir; *(► road)* défoncer

3 *(end ► fight, party)* mettre fin à, arrêter; *Com & Law (► conglomerate, trust)* scinder, diviser; *Com (► company)* scinder; *Pol (► coalition)* briser, rompre; *Admin (► organization)* dissoudre; *(► empire)* démembrer; *(► family)* séparer; **his drinking broke up their marriage** le fait qu'il buvait a brisé *ou* détruit leur mariage

4 *(disperse ► crowd)* disperser; **b. it up!** *(people fighting or arguing)* arrêtez!; *(said by policeman)* circulez!

5 *Fam (distress)* bouleverser, retourner; **the news really broke her up** la nouvelle l'a complètement bouleversée

VI **1** *(split into pieces ► road, system)* se désagréger; *(► ice)* craquer, se fissurer; *(► ship)* se disloquer; **the ship broke up on the rocks** le navire s'est disloqué sur les rochers

2 *(come to an end ► meeting, party)* se terminer, prendre fin; *(► partnership)* cesser, prendre fin; *(► talks, negotiations)* cesser; **their marriage broke up** leur mariage n'a pas marché

3 *(boyfriend, girlfriend)* rompre; **she broke up with her boyfriend** elle a rompu avec son petit ami; **they've broken up** ils se sont séparés

4 *(disperse ► clouds)* se disperser; *(► group)* se disperser; *(► friends)* se quitter, se séparer

5 *Br Sch* **we b. up for Christmas on the 22nd** les vacances de Noël commencent le 22

6 *(lose one's composure)* s'effondrer

breakable ['breɪkəbəl] ADJ fragile, cassable

• **breakables** NPL **put away all breakables** rangez tout objet fragile

breakage ['breɪkɪdʒ] N **1** *(of metal)* rupture *f*; *(of glass)* casse *f*, bris *m* **2** *(damages)* casse *f*; **have there been any breakages?** est-ce qu'il y a eu de la casse?; **the insurance pays for all b.** *or* **breakages** l'assurance paye toute la casse

breakaway ['breɪkəweɪ] N *(of people)* séparation *f*; *(of group)* rupture *f*; *Sport (in cycling)* échappée *f*

ADJ séparatiste, dissident; *Pol* **a b. group** un groupe dissident; *Pol* **a b. republic** une république séparatiste et indépendante

breakbone fever ['breɪkbəʊn-] N *Med* dengue *f*

breakdance ['breɪkdɑːns] *Mus* N smurf *m*

VI danser le smurf

breakdancer ['breɪkˌdɑːnsə(r)] N *Mus* smurfeur (euse) *m,f*

breakdancing ['breɪkˌdɑːnsɪŋ] N *Mus* smurf *m*

breakdown ['breɪkdaʊn] N **1** *Tech (mechanical)* panne *f*; **to have a b.** tomber en panne

2 *(of communications, negotiations)* rupture *f*; *(of system, service)* arrêt *m* complet; *(of tradition, state of affairs)* détérioration *f*, dégradation *f*; *(of marriage, relationship)* échec *m*

3 *Psy (nervous)* dépression *f* nerveuse; *Med (physical)* effondrement *m*; **to have a b.** faire une dépression (nerveuse)

4 *(analysis ► of ideas, statistics)* analyse *f*; *(► of reasons)* décomposition *f*; *Com (► of costs, figures)* ventilation *f*; *Fin (► of account, expenses)* décomposition *f*, ventilation *f*; *(► of bill, estimate)* détail *m*; **a b. of the population by age** une répartition de la population par âge; **give me a b. of the annual report** faites-moi l'analyse du rapport annuel

►► *Aut* ***breakdown gang*** équipe *f* de dépannage; *BrAut* ***breakdown lorry*** dépanneuse *f*, camion *m* de dépannage; *Aut* ***breakdown and recovery service*** service *m* de remorquage et de dépannage; *Aut* ***breakdown service*** service *m* de dépannage; *Aut* ***breakdown truck, breakdown van*** dépanneuse *f*, camion *m* de dépannage

breaker ['breɪkə(r)] N **1** *(scrap merchant)* **the ship was sent to the b.'s** le navire a été envoyé à la démolition **2** *(wave)* déferlante *f* **3** *Elec* disjoncteur *m*

►► ***breaker's yard*** *(for cars, boats etc)* chantier *m* de démolition

break-even N *Fin* seuil *m* de rentabilité; *Acct* point *m* mort, point *m* d'équilibre; *Fin* **to reach b.** atteindre le seuil de rentabilité

►► *Fin* ***break-even analysis*** analyse *f* du point mort; ***break-even point*** *Fin* seuil *m* de rentabilité; *Acct* point *m* mort, point *m* d'équilibre; ***break-even price*** prix *m* minimum rentable

breakfast ['brekfəst] N petit déjeuner *m*; **to have b.** prendre le petit déjeuner; **what do you want for b.?** que veux-tu pour ton petit déjeuner?; *Fig* **she could have someone like you for b.** les gens comme toi, elle n'en fait qu'une bouchée

COMP *(service, set)* à petit déjeuner; *(tea, time)* du petit déjeuner

VI prendre le petit déjeuner, déjeuner

►► ***breakfast bar*** plan *m* snack; ***breakfast buffet*** buffet *m* du petit déjeuner; *Culin* ***breakfast cereal*** céréales *fpl*; ***breakfast meeting*** réunion *f* pendant le petit déjeuner; *Rad & TV* ***breakfast programme*** émission *f* du matin; ***breakfast room*** salle *f* du petit déjeuner; ***breakfast table*** table *f* pour le petit déjeuner; ***breakfast television*** télévision *f* du matin

break-in N cambriolage *m*

breaking ['breɪkɪŋ] N **1** *(shattering)* bris *m*; *Med (of bone)* fracture *f*; *Law (of seal ► illegal)* bris *m*; *(► legal)* levée *f*; *Aviat (of sound barrier)* franchissement *m*; *Law* **b. and entering** effraction *f*

2 *(violation ► of treaty, rule, law)* violation *f* (**of** de); *(► of promise)* manquement *m* (**of** à); *(► of commandment)* désobéissance *f* (**of** à)

3 *(interruption ► of journey)* interruption *f*; *(► of silence)* rupture *f*; *(► of strike)* action *f* de briser

4 *Ling* fracture *f*

5 *(of horse)* dressage *m*

6 *(of fall, force of something)* amortissement *m*

ADJ *(news, story)* de dernière minute

►► ***breaking in*** **1** *(of horse)* dressage *m*; *Fig (of new employee)* formation *f* **2** *(burglary)* effraction *f* **3** *(of door)* enfoncement *m*, défonçage *m*; ***breaking point*** point *m* de rupture; *Fig* **I've reached b. point** je suis à bout, je n'en peux plus; **the situation has reached b. point** la situation est devenue critique; ***breaking up*** **1** *(of building)* démolition *f*; *(of earth, field)* défoncement *m*, premier labourage *m*; *(of rocks, substance)* broyage *m*, décomposition *f*; *(of organization, assembly)* dissolution *f*; *(of crowd)* dispersion *f*; *(of family)* désagrégation *f*; *(of estate, property, country)* morcellement *m*; *(of ship)* dépècement *m* **2** *Sch* entrée *f* en vacances **3** *(of ice)* débâcle *f*

breakneck ['breɪknek] **ADJ at b. speed** à une allure folle, à tombeau ouvert

break-out **N** *(from prison)* évasion *f* (de prison)

breakpoint ['breɪkpɔɪnt] **N 1** *Sport (in tennis)* balle *f* de break **2** *Comput* point *m* de rupture

breakthrough ['breɪkθruː] **N 1** *(advance, discovery)* découverte *f* capitale, percée *f* (technologique); *(in negotiations)* progrès *m*; *(in market)* percée *f*; **their latest b. in computing technology** leur dernière découverte en technologie informatique; **to make a b.** *(discovery)* faire une percée; *(in negotiations)* progresser; **the b. came only after a week of deadlock** la situation ne s'est débloquée qu'après une semaine **2** *Mil (in enemy lines)* percée *f*

break-up **N 1** *(disintegration* ► *of association)* démembrement *m*, dissolution *f*; *(*► *of relationship)* rupture *f*; *Com (*► *of company)* scission *f*; **before our b.** avant que nous ne rompions

2 *(end* ► *of meeting, activity)* fin *f*

3 *(of ship)* dislocation *f*

4 *(of ice)* débâcle *f*

►► *Com* ***break-up bid*** = offre d'achat d'une entreprise en difficulté; *Fin* ***break-up price*** prix *m* de liquidation; *Com* ***break-up value*** valeur *f* de liquidation

breakwater ['breɪk,wɔːtə(r)] **N** digue *f*, briselames *m inv*

bream [briːm] *(pl* **inv** *or* **breams) N** *Ich* brème *f*

breast [brest] **N 1** *(chest)* poitrine *f*; *(of animal)* poitrine *f*, poitrail *m*; *(of bird)* gorge *f*; *Culin (of chicken)* blanc *m*; *Literary* **he held her to his b.** il la tint serrée contre sa poitrine **2** *(bosom* ► *of woman)* sein *m*, poitrine *f*; *Literary (*► *of man)* sein *m*; **she put the baby to her b.** elle porta le bébé à son sein; **a child at the b.** un enfant au sein

VT 1 *Literary (face* ► *waves, storm)* affronter **2** *(reach summit of)* atteindre le sommet de; **the runner breasted the tape** le coureur a franchi la ligne d'arrivée (en vainqueur)

►► ***breast cancer*** cancer *m* du sein; ***breast enlargement*** augmentation *f* mammaire; ***breast implants*** implants *mpl* mammaires; ***breast milk*** lait *m* maternel; ***breast pocket*** poche *f* de poitrine; ***breast pump*** tire-lait *m*; ***breast reduction*** réduction *f* mammaire

breastbone ['brestbəʊn] **N** *Anat* sternum *m*

breast-fed **ADJ** nourri au sein

breast-feed **VT** allaiter, donner le sein à

VI allaiter, nourrir au sein

breast-feeding **ADJ** *(woman)* allaitant

N allaitement *m* au sein

breastplate ['brestpleɪt] **N** *(armour)* plastron *m* (de cuirasse)

breaststroke ['breststrəʊk] **N** *Swimming* brasse *f*; **to swim (the) b.** nager la brasse

breastwork ['brest,wɜːk] **N** *Mil* parapet *m*

breath [breθ] **N 1** *(of human, animal)* haleine *f*, souffle *m*; **to have bad b.** avoir mauvaise haleine; *Fam* **to have onion/whisky b.** avoir l'haleine qui sent les oignons/le whisky; **take a b.** respirez; **he took a deep b.** il a respiré à fond; **I took a deep b. and started to explain** je respirai profondément et commençai d'expliquer; **let me get my b. back** laissez-moi retrouver mon souffle *ou* reprendre haleine; **she stopped for b.** elle s'est arrêtée pour reprendre haleine; **to be out of b.** être essoufflé *ou* à bout de souffle; **to be short of b.** avoir le souffle court; **he said it all in one b.** il l'a dit d'un trait; **they are not to be mentioned in the same b.** on ne saurait les comparer; **but in the next b. he said the opposite** mais quelques secondes plus tard il a dit le contraire; **under one's b.** à voix basse, tout bas; **she laughed under her b.** elle a ri sous cape; **with her dying b.** en mourant; **he drew his last b.** il a rendu l'âme *ou* le dernier soupir; **music is the b. of life to him** la musique est toute sa vie; **to hold one's b.** retenir son souffle; **don't hold your b. waiting for the money** si c'est l'argent que tu attends, ne compte pas dessus *ou* tu perds ton temps; **I'm wasting my b.** je perds mon temps, je me fatigue pour rien; **save your b.!** inutile de gaspiller ta salive!; **the sight took his b. away** la vue *ou* le spectacle lui a coupé le souffle; **it takes my b. away** je n'en reviens pas **2** *(gust)* souffle *m*; **we went out for a b. of fresh air** nous sommes sortis prendre l'air; *Fig* **it's/she's like a b. of fresh air** c'est/elle est comme une bouffée d'air frais **3** *(hint)* trace *f*; **the faintest b. of scandal** le plus petit soupçon de scandale

►► ***breath freshener*** purificateur *m* d'haleine, spray *m* buccal; ***breath test*** Alcootest® *m*

breathable ['briːðəbəl] **ADJ** *(fabric)* respirant

breathalyse, *Am* **breathalyze** ['breθəlaɪz] **VT** faire passer l'Alcootest® à

Breathalyser®, *Am* **Breathalyzer®** ['breθəlaɪzə(r)] **N** Alcootest® *m*

breathe [briːð] **VI 1** *(person)* respirer; **to b. hard** haleter; **to b. heavily** *or* **deeply** *(after exertion)* souffler *ou* respirer bruyamment; *(during illness)* il respirait péniblement; **you can't b. in here** *(it's too hot)* on ne peut pas respirer ici; **is he still breathing?** est-il toujours en vie?, vit-il encore?; *Fig* **I breathed more easily** *or* **again after the exam** après l'examen j'ai enfin pu respirer; *Fam* **to b. down sb's neck** *(supervise)* être sur le dos de qn; *(look over their shoulder)* regarder par-dessus l'épaule de qn; *Fig* **I need room to b.** *(in relationship)* j'ai besoin d'espace, il faut que je respire **2** *(wine)* respirer

VT 1 *(take in oxygen)* respirer; **she breathed a sigh of relief** elle poussa un soupir de soulagement; **to b. one's last** rendre le dernier soupir *ou* l'âme; **she breathed new life into the project** elle a insufflé de nouvelles forces au projet **2** *(whisper)* murmurer; **don't b. a word!** ne soufflez pas mot!; **they didn't b. a word about it** ils n'en ont pas soufflé mot **3** *Ling* aspirer

► **breathe in VT SEP** inhaler

VI inspirer

► **breathe out VT SEP** expirer

VI expirer

breathed [briːðd] **ADJ** *Ling (unvoiced)* sourd, non voisé

breather ['briːðə(r)] **N** *(rest)* moment *m* de repos *ou* de répit; **let's take a b.** prenons le temps de souffler un peu; **I went out for a b.** je suis sorti prendre l'air

►► *Aut* ***breather pipe*** (tuyau *m* de) reniflard *m*; *Tech* ***breather port*** orifice *m* de reniflard

breathing ['briːðɪŋ] **N** *(gen)* respiration *f*, souffle *m*; **heavy b.** respiration *f* bruyante

►► *Tech* ***breathing apparatus*** *(for fireman, miner etc)* masque *m* à oxygène; *(for diver)* scaphandre *m*; ***breathing space*** moment *m* de répit; *Fig* **I need some b. space** *(in relationship)* j'ai besoin de respirer *ou* d'espace

breathless ['breθlɪs] **ADJ 1** *(from exertion)* essoufflé, hors d'haleine; *(from illness)* oppressé, qui a du mal à respirer **2** *(from emotion)* **his kiss left her b.** son baiser lui a coupé le souffle; **we waited in b. excitement** nous attendions le souffle coupé par l'émotion *ou* en retenant notre haleine **3** *(atmosphere)* étouffant

breathlessly ['breθlɪslɪ] **ADV** *(gasping)* en haletant; *Fig (hurriedly)* en toute hâte

breathlessness ['breθlɪsnɪs] **N** essoufflement *m*

breathtaking ['breθ,teɪkɪŋ] **ADJ** impressionnant; **with a b. lack of tact** avec un manque de tact incroyable; **a b. view** une vue à (vous) couper le souffle

breathtakingly ['breθ,teɪkɪŋlɪ] **ADV** *(beautiful)* extraordinairement; *(stupid, tactless etc)* incroyablement

breathy ['breθɪ] *(compar* **breathier,** *superl* **breathiest) ADJ** qui respire bruyamment; *Mus* qui manque d'attaque; **she has a b. voice** elle respire bruyamment en parlant

breech [briːtʃ] **N 1** *Tech (of gun)* culasse *f* **2** *(of person)* derrière *m*

►► *Obst* ***breech birth, breech delivery*** accouchement *m* par le siège; *Obst* ***breech presentation*** présentation *f* par le siège

breeches, *Am* **britches** ['brɪtʃɪz] **NPL** pantalon *m*; *(knee-length)* haut-de-chausses *m*; *Horseriding (for riding)* culotte *f*; *Am* **to be too big for one's b.** avoir la grosse tête

breed [briːd] *(pt & pp* **bred** [bred]) **N 1** *Zool (race)* race *f*, espèce *f*; *(within race)* type *m*; *Bot (of plant)* espèce *f* **2** *Fig (kind)* sorte *f*, espèce *f*; **he's one of a dying b.** il fait partie d'une espèce en voie de disparition; **she is one of the new b. of executives** elle fait partie de la nouvelle race *ou* génération de cadres

VT 1 *(raise* ► *animals)* élever, faire l'élevage de; *Hort (*► *plants)* cultiver; *Literary or Hum (*► *children)* élever; **to b. in/out a characteristic** faire acquérir/éliminer une caractéristique (par la sélection); **they're specially bred for racing** ils sont élevés spécialement pour la course; *Prov* **what's bred in the bone will come out in the flesh** bon chien chasse de race **2** *Fig (cause)* engendrer, faire naître; **dirt breeds disease** la saleté entraîne des maladies

VI 1 *(animals, people)* se reproduire, se multiplier; **to b. like rabbits** se multiplier comme des lapins **2** *(animal breeder)* faire de l'élevage

breeder ['briːdə(r)] **N 1** *(farmer)* éleveur(euse) *m,f*; *(animal)* reproducteur(trice) *m,f* **2** *Pej or Hum (heterosexual)* hétéro *mf*

breeding ['briːdɪŋ] **N 1** *(raising* ► *of animals)* élevage *m*; *Hort (*► *of plants)* culture *f*

2 *Biol (reproduction)* reproduction *f*, procréation *f*

3 *(upbringing)* éducation *f*; **he lacks b.** il manque de savoir-vivre

4 *Phys* surgénération *f*, surrégénération *f*

►► ***the breeding season*** *(for animals)* la saison des amours; *(for birds)* la saison des nids; ***breeding stock*** animaux *mpl* élevés en vue de la reproduction

breeding-ground **N 1** *(for animals, birds)* lieu *m* de prédilection pour l'accouplement *ou* la ponte **2** *Fig* foyer *m*, terrain *m* propice; **a b. for terrorists** une pépinière de terroristes; **damp areas are a b. for germs** les zones humides sont des foyers de microbes *ou* constituent un terrain propice aux microbes

breeze [briːz] **N 1** *(wind)* brise *f*; **a gentle** *or* **light b.** une petite *ou* légère brise; **a stiff b.** un vent frais; **there's quite a b.** ça souffle **2** *Fam (easy task)* **it's a b.** c'est du gâteau

VI *(move quickly)* **the car breezed along the country lanes** la voiture roulait à vive allure sur les routes de campagne

►► *Br Constr* ***breeze block*** parpaing *m*

► **breeze in VI** *(quickly)* entrer en coup de vent; *(casually)* entrer d'un air désinvolte

► **breeze out VI** *(quickly)* sortir en coup de vent; *(casually)* sortir d'un air désinvolte

► **breeze through VT INSEP** *(exam)* réussir les doigts dans le nez; **to b. through life** se laisser vivre

VI *(pass exam with ease)* réussir les doigts dans le nez

breezeway ['briːzweɪ] **N** *Am* passage *m* couvert *(souvent entre la maison et le garage)*

breezily ['briːzɪlɪ] **ADV** *(casually)* avec désinvolture; *(cheerfully)* joyeusement, jovialement

breezy ['briːzɪ] *(compar* **breezier,** *superl* **breeziest) ADJ 1** *(weather, day)* venteux; *(place, spot)* éventé **2** *(person* ► *casual)* désinvolte; *(*► *cheerful)* jovial, enjoué

brekkie, brekky ['brekɪ] **N** *Br Fam (abbr* **breakfast)** petit déj *m*

Bremen ['breɪmən] **N** Brême

brent [brent] **N 1** *Orn* **b. (goose)** bernache *f* cravant **2** *(oil)* brent *m*

brethren ['breðrɪn] **NPL** *Formal (fellow members)* camarades *mpl*; *Rel* frères *mpl*

Breton ['bretən] **N 1** *(person)* Breton(onne) *m,f* **2** *(language)* breton *m*
ADJ breton

breve [bri:v] **N** *Mus & Typ* brève *f*

breviary ['bri:viəri] *(pl* **breviaries***)* **N** *Rel* bréviaire *m*

brevity ['breviti] **N 1** *(shortness)* brièveté *f* **2** *(succinctness)* concision *f*; *(terseness)* laconisme *m*; *Prov* **b. is the soul of wit** = la concision est le secret d'un bon mot d'esprit

brew [bru:] **N 1** *(infusion)* infusion *f*; *(herbal)* tisane *f*; **a witch's b.** un brouet de sorcière
2 *(beer)* brassage *m*; *(amount made)* brassin *m*
3 *Br Fam (tea)* thé□ *m*; **do you want a b.?** tu veux du thé?
4 *Am Fam (beer)* mousse *f*
VT 1 *(make ▸ tea)* préparer, faire infuser; *(▸ beer)* brasser **2** *Fig (scheme)* tramer, mijoter
VI 1 *(tea)* infuser; *(beer)* fermenter **2** *(make beer)* brasser, faire de la bière **3** *Fig (storm)* couver, se préparer; *(scheme)* se tramer, mijoter; **there's something brewing** il se trame quelque chose, il y a quelque chose qui se prépare; **I could tell by her face there was a storm brewing** j'ai vu sur son visage qu'il y avait de l'orage dans l'air; **there's trouble brewing** il y a de l'orage dans l'air
▸ **brew up VI 1** *(storm)* couver, se préparer; *(trouble)* se préparer, se tramer **2** *Br Fam (make tea)* préparer *ou* faire du thé□

brewer ['bru:ə(r)] **N** *Ind* brasseur(euse) *m,f*
▸▸ *Br Fam Hum* ***brewer's droop*** = impuissance temporaire due à l'alcool; **he had b.'s droop** il a bandé mou parce qu'il avait trop picolé; *Biol* ***brewer's yeast*** levure *f* de bière

brewery ['bruəri] *(pl* **breweries***)* **N** brasserie *f (fabrique)*

brewski ['bru:ski] **N** *Am Fam (beer)* mousse *f*

brew-up **N** *Br Fam* **to have a b.** faire du thé□; **we stopped work for a b.** nous avons fait une pause pour prendre un thé

briar ['braiə(r)] *Bot* **N 1** *(thorn)* épine *f*; *(wild rose)* églantier *m* **2** *(heather)* bruyère *f*; *(wood)* (racine *f* de) bruyère *f* **3** *(pipe)* pipe *f* de bruyère
▸▸ ***briar pipe*** pipe *f* de bruyère; *Bot* ***briar root*** racine *f* de bruyère

bribable ['braibəbəl] **ADJ** corruptible

bribe [braib] **VT** soudoyer, acheter; *(witness)* suborner; **to b. sb to do sth** *or* **into doing sth** soudoyer qn *ou* graisser la patte à qn pour qu'il fasse qch; **we bribed the guard to tell us** nous avons soudoyé le garde pour qu'il nous le dise; **I bribed him with sweets** je l'ai acheté avec des bonbons
N pot-de-vin *m*; **to take bribes** se laisser corrompre; **I offered him a b.** je lui ai offert un pot-de-vin

bribery ['braibəri] **N** corruption *f*; *(of witness)* subornation *f*; **open/not open to b.** corruptible/incorruptible; *Law* **b. and corruption** corruption *f*; *Hum* **that's b. and corruption!** c'est une tentative de corruption!

brick [brik] **N 1** *(for building)* brique *f*; **a house made of b.** une maison en brique; **to invest in bricks and mortar** investir dans l'immobilier; *Fam* **to come down on sb like a ton of bricks** passer un savon à qn; *Fam Fig* **to be one b. short of a load** ne pas être net; **a bricks-and-clicks shop** une société qui vend ses produits en magasin et sur Internet
2 *(of ice cream)* pavé *m*
3 *Br (toy)* cube *m* (de construction); **a box of bricks** un jeu de construction
4 *Br Fam Old-fashioned (man)* chic type *m*; *(woman)* chic fille *f*
COMP *(building)* en brique *ou* briques
VT *Br* **to b. it** les avoir à zéro; **they were absolutely bricking it when they saw the cops coming** ils les avaient vraiment à zéro quand ils ont vu les flics approcher
▸▸ ***brick red*** rouge *m* brique *inv*; ***brick wall*** mur *m* de brique; *Fig* **to come up against a b. wall** se heurter à un obstacle infranchissable; **it's like talking to a b. wall** autant (vaut) parler à un mur *ou* un sourd; **it's like banging your head against a b. wall** c'est peine perdue
▸ **brick up VT SEP** murer

brickbat ['brikbæt] **N** *(weapon)* morceau *m* de brique; *Fig (criticism)* critique *f*; **the government has been receiving more brickbats than bouquets** le gouvernement a été plus critiqué qu'applaudi

brickfield ['brik,fi:ld] **N** briqueterie *f*

bricklayer ['brik,leiə(r)] **N** *Constr* maçon *m*, ouvrier-maçon *m*

bricklaying ['brik,leiiŋ] **N** *Constr* briquetage *m*

brickmaker ['brik,meikə(r)] **N** briquetier *m*

brickwork ['brikwɜ:k] **N** *Constr (structure)* briquetage *m*, brique *f*
• **brickworks NPL** *Ind* briqueterie *f*

brickyard ['brikjɑ:d] **N** *Ind* briqueterie *f*

bridal ['braidəl] **ADJ** *(gown, veil)* de mariée; *(chamber, procession)* nuptial; *(feast)* de noce
▸▸ ***bridal party*** la noce *(les invités)*; ***bridal suite*** suite *f* nuptiale

bride [braid] **N** *(before wedding)* (future) mariée *f*; *(after wedding)* (jeune) mariée *f*; **the b. and groom** les (jeunes) mariés *mpl*; **his b. of four months** la femme avec qui il est/était marié depuis quatre mois

bridegroom ['braidgrum] **N** *(before wedding)* (futur) marié *m*; *(after wedding)* (jeune) marié *m*

bridesmaid ['braidzmeid] **N** demoiselle *f* d'honneur; **always the b., never the bride!** elle est toujours demoiselle d'honneur mais on ne l'a jamais demandée en mariage; *Fig* c'est l'éternel second!

bride-to-be **N** future mariée *f*

bridge [bridʒ] **N 1** *(structure)* pont *m*; **the engineers built** *or* **put a b. across the river** les ingénieurs ont construit *ou* jeté un pont sur le fleuve
2 *Fig (link)* rapprochement *m*; **building bridges between East and West** efforts *mpl* de rapprochement entre l'Est et l'Ouest
3 *Naut (of ship)* passerelle *f* (de commandement)
4 *(of nose)* arête *f*; *(of glasses)* arcade *f*
5 *Mus (of stringed instrument)* chevalet *m*
6 *(dentures)* bridge *m*
7 *Cards* bridge *m*; **what about a game of b.?** et si on faisait un bridge?; **they're playing b.** ils bridgent
8 *(in song)* pont *m* sonore; *Cin & TV (shot)* transition *f*
9 *(in billiards, snooker, pool)* chevalet *m*
10 *Sport (in wrestling)* pont *m*; **to make a b.** ponter
11 *Comput (in network)* pont *m*
COMP *Cards (party, tournament)* de bridge
VT *(river)* construire *ou* jeter un pont sur; *Fig* **a composer whose work bridged two centuries** un compositeur dont l'œuvre est à cheval sur deux siècles; **in order to b. the gap in our knowledge/in our resources** pour combler la lacune dans notre savoir/le trou dans nos ressources
▸▸ *Am Fin* ***bridge loan*** prêt-relais *m*; *Cards* ***bridge player*** bridgeur(euse) *m,f*

bridgehead ['bridʒhed] **N** *Mil* tête *f* de pont

bridgework ['bridʒwɜ:k] **N** *(UNCOUNT) (in dentistry)* **to have b. done** se faire faire un bridge

bridging ['bridʒiŋ] **N 1** *Fig (of gap)* comblement *m* **2** *Elec* shuntage *m* **3** *Chem* pontage *m*
▸▸ *Elec* ***bridging connection*** montage *m* en pont; *Br Fin* ***bridging loan*** prêt-relais *m*; *Constr* ***bridging piece*** entretoise *f*

bridle ['braidəl] **N** *(harness)* bride *f*; *Fig (constraint)* frein *m*, contrainte *f*
VT *(horse)* brider; *Fig (emotions)* refréner; **to b. one's tongue** tenir sa langue
VI *(horse)* redresser la tête; *Fig (person)* s'indigner, se scandaliser
▸▸ ***bridle path*** piste *f* cavalière

brief [bri:f] **ADJ 1** *(short in duration)* bref, court; **a b. interval** un court intervalle; **I caught a b. glimpse of her** je n'ai fait que l'entrevoir
2 *(succinct)* concis, bref; **we exchanged a few b. words** nous avons échangé quelques mots; **to be b., I think you're right** (en) bref, je crois que tu as raison; **a b. account** un exposé sommaire
3 *(terse ▸ person, reply)* laconique; *(abrupt)* brusque
4 *(short in length)* court; **a very b. pair of shorts** un short très court
VT 1 *(bring up to date)* mettre au courant; *Mil (give orders to)* donner des instructions à; **the boss briefed me on the latest developments** le patron m'a mis au courant des derniers développements; **the soldiers were briefed on their mission** les soldats ont reçu leurs ordres pour la mission **2** *Br Law (lawyer)* confier une cause à; *(case)* établir le dossier de
N 1 *Br Law* dossier *m*, affaire *f*; **he took our b.** il a accepté de plaider notre cause; **to hold a watching b. for sb/sth** veiller (en justice) aux intérêts de qn/qch; **to hold no b. for sb/sth** ne pas se faire l'avocat de qn/qch; *Fig* **he holds no b. for those who take drugs** il ne prend pas la défense de ceux qui se droguent **2** *(instructions)* briefing *m*; **my b. was to develop sales** la tâche *ou* la mission qui m'a été confiée était de développer les ventes **3** *Br Fam (lawyer)* avocat□ *m*
• **briefs NPL** *(underwear)* slip *m*
• **in brief ADV** en résumé

briefcase ['bri:fkeis] **N 1** serviette *f*, mallette *f* **2** *Comput (Windows® icon)* porte-documents *m*

briefing ['bri:fiŋ] **N 1** *Mil (for mission)* instructions *fpl*, directives *fpl*; *Admin (meeting)* réunion *f* d'information, briefing *m*; *Aviat* briefing *m*; **they gave me a final b.** ils m'ont donné les dernières directives **2** *Br Law (of lawyer)* constitution *f*
▸▸ ***briefing room*** salle *f* de réunion

briefly ['bri:fli] **ADV 1** *(for a short time)* un court instant; **we spoke b. on the telephone** nous avons échangé quelques mots au téléphone **2** *(succinctly)* brièvement; *(tersely)* laconiquement; **put b., the situation is a mess** en bref, la situation est très embrouillée

> Attention: ne pas confondre avec **shortly**.

briefness ['bri:fnis] **N 1** *(of time)* brièveté *f*, courte durée *f* **2** *(succinctness)* concision *f*; *(terseness)* laconisme *m*; *(abruptness)* brusquerie *f*

brier = **briar**

Brig. *Mil (written abbr* **brigadier***)* général *m* de brigade; **B. Smith** le général de brigade Smith

brig [brig] **N** *Naut* **1** *(ship)* brick *m* **2** *Am (prison on ship)* prison *f (à bord d'un navire)*

brigade [bri'geid] **N** *(gen) & Mil* brigade *f*; *Fig Hum Pej (group of people)* bande *f*; *Fig* **one of the old b.** un vieux de la vieille

brigadier [,brigə'diə(r)] **N** *Br Mil* général *m* de brigade
▸▸ *Am Mil* ***brigadier general*** *(in army)* général *m* de brigade; *(in air force)* général *m* de brigade aérienne

brigand ['brigənd] **N** brigand *m*, bandit *m*

brigandage ['brigəndidʒ] **N** brigandage *m*

bright [brait] **ADJ 1** *(weather, day)* clair, radieux; *(sunshine)* éclatant; *(room)* clair; *(fire, light)* vif; *(colour)* vif, éclatant; **the weather will get brighter later** le temps s'améliorera en cours de journée; **cloudy with b. intervals** nuageux avec des éclaircies; **to become brighter** s'éclaircir; **b. red** rouge *m* vif; *Fig* **b. and early** tôt le matin, de bon *ou* grand matin
2 *(shining ▸ diamond, star)* brillant; *(▸ metal)* poli, luisant; *(▸ eyes)* brillant, vif; **she likes the b. lights** elle aime la grande ville
3 *(clever)* intelligent; *(child)* éveillé, vif; **he's not very b.** ce n'est pas une lumière, il n'est pas très futé *ou* malin; **a b. idea** une idée géniale *ou* lumineuse
4 *(cheerful)* gai, joyeux; *(lively)* animé, vif; **you're very b. this morning!** tu es bien gai ce matin!; **to be b. and breezy** avoir l'air en pleine forme; **it was the only b. spot in the day** c'était la seule chose positive de la journée
5 *(promising)* brillant; **to have a b. future** avoir un brillant avenir; **the future's looking b.** l'avenir est plein de promesses *ou* s'annonce bien; **to look on the b. side** prendre les choses du bon côté, être optimiste
ADV *Literary (burn, shine)* avec éclat, brillamment
• **brights NPL** *Am Aut (headlights)* **to put the brights on** se mettre en pleins phares
▸▸ *Br Fam* ***bright spark*** *(clever person)* lumière *f*; *Ironic* **you're a b. spark!** gros malin!

brighten ['braitən] **VT 1** *(decorate ▸ place, person)* égayer; *(enliven ▸ conversation)* animer, égayer; *(colour)* aviver **2** *(prospects)* améliorer, faire paraître sous un meilleur jour
VI 1 *(weather)* s'améliorer **2** *(person)* s'animer; *(face)* s'éclairer; *(eyes)* s'allumer, s'éclairer; **their**

mood brightened ils se sont déridés 3 *(prospects)* s'améliorer

▸ **brighten up** = brighten

brightening ['braɪtənɪŋ] N 1 *(of sky, weather)* éclaircissement *m*; *Fig* **there was a momentary b. of her mood** elle s'est égayée un moment 2 *(of colours)* avivage *m*

bright-eyed ADJ aux yeux brillants; *Fig (eager)* enthousiaste; *Hum* **b. and bushy-tailed** frais comme la rosée

brightly ['braɪtlɪ] ADV 1 *(shine)* avec éclat; **the stars were shining b.** les étoiles scintillaient; **the fire burned b.** le feu flambait 2 *(cheerfully)* gaiement, joyeusement; **to smile b.** sourire d'un air radieux; **to answer b.** répondre gaiement

brightness ['braɪtnɪs] N 1 *(of sun)* éclat *m*; *(of light)* intensité *f*; *(of room)* clarté *f*, luminosité *f*; *(of colour)* éclat *m*; *TV* **b. (control)** (dispositif *m* de réglage de la) luminosité *f* 2 *(cheerfulness)* gaieté *f*, joie *f*; *(liveliness)* vivacité *f*; *(of smile)* éclat *m* 3 *(cleverness)* intelligence *f*

brill[1] [brɪl] *(pl* inv*)* N *Ich* barbue *f*

brill[2] ADJ *Br Fam (terrific)* super, sensass

brilliance ['brɪljəns], **brilliancy** ['brɪljənsɪ] N 1 *(of light, smile, performance, career)* éclat *m*, brillant *m* 2 *(cleverness)* intelligence *f*; **no one doubts her b.** il ne fait pas de doute qu'elle est d'une intelligence supérieure

brilliant ['brɪljənt] ADJ 1 *(light, sunshine)* éclatant, intense; *(smile)* éclatant, radieux; *(colour)* vif, éclatant

2 *(outstanding ▸ mind, musician, writer)* brillant, exceptionnel; *(▸ film, novel, piece of work)* brillant, exceptionnel; *(▸ success)* éclatant; **a b. career** une brillante carrière

3 *Fam (terrific)* sensationnel, super; **you were b.!** tu as été formidable *ou* magnifique!

4 *(intelligent)* brillant; **that's a b. idea** c'est une idée lumineuse *ou* de génie

N *Miner (diamond, cut)* brillant *m*

brilliantine ['brɪljəntiːn] N brillantine *f*

brilliantly ['brɪljəntlɪ] ADV 1 *(shine)* avec éclat; **b. coloured** d'une couleur vive; **b. lit** très bien éclairé 2 *(perform, talk)* brillamment; **to play b.** jouer avec brio

brim [brɪm] *(pp & pt* **brimmed**, *cont* **brimming**) N *(of hat)* bord *m*; *(of bowl, cup)* bord *m*; **full to the b.** plein à ras bord

VI déborder; **eyes brimming with tears** des yeux pleins *ou* noyés de larmes; *Fig* **the newcomers were brimming with ideas** les nouveaux venus avaient des idées à revendre

▸ **brim over** VI déborder; *Fig* **to be brimming over with enthusiasm** déborder d'enthousiasme

brimful [ˌbrɪm'fʊl] ADJ *Br (cup)* plein à déborder *ou* jusqu'au bord; *Fig* débordant; **b. of confidence** très *ou* excessivement confiant

brimless ['brɪmlɪs] ADJ *(hat)* sans bord *ou* bords

-brimmed [brɪmd] SUFF **wide-b.** à larges bords; **narrow-b.** à bords étroits

brimstone ['brɪmstəʊn] N 1 *Arch (sulphur)* soufre *m* 2 *Entom (butterfly)* citron *m*

brindle ['brɪndəl], **brindled** ['brɪndəld] ADJ moucheté, tavelé

brine [braɪn] N 1 *(salty water)* eau *f* salée; *Culin* saumure *f*; **mussels in b.** moules *fpl* en saumure 2 *Literary (sea)* mer *f*; *(sea water)* eau *f* de mer

BRING [brɪŋ]

- amener **1, 2, 4, 5**
- apporter **1**
- provoquer **3**
- mener **5**
- rapporter **7**

VT *(pt & pp* **brought** [brɔːt]) 1 *(take ▸ animal, person, vehicle)* amener; *(▸ object)* apporter; *(▸ fashion, idea, product)* introduire, lancer; **she brought a lot of luggage (with her)** elle a apporté beaucoup de bagages; **her father's bringing her home today** son père la ramène à la maison aujourd'hui; **what brings you here?** qu'est-ce qui vous amène?; **can you b. me a beer, please?** vous pouvez m'apporter une bière, s'il vous plaît?; **that brings the total to £350** cela fait 350 livres en tout; **he brought his dog with him** il a emmené son chien; **black musicians brought jazz to Europe** les musiciens noirs ont introduit le jazz en Europe; **this programme is brought to you by the BBC** ce programme est diffusé par la BBC

2 *(into specified state)* entraîner, amener; **to b. sth into play** faire jouer qch; **to b. sth into question** mettre *ou* remettre qch en question; **to b. sb to his/her senses** ramener qn à la raison; **to b. sth to an end** *or* **a close** *or* **a halt** mettre fin à qch; **to b. sth to sb's attention** *or* **knowledge** *or* **notice** attirer l'attention de qn sur qch; **to b. a child into the world** mettre un enfant au monde; **to b. sth to light** mettre qch en lumière, révéler qch; **to b. sth to mind** rappeler qch; **to b. sth onto the market** introduire qch sur le marché

3 *(produce)* provoquer, causer; **her performance brought wild applause** son interprétation a provoqué un tonnerre d'applaudissements; **to b. sth upon sb** attirer qch sur qn; **her foolhardiness brought misfortune upon the family** son imprudence a attiré le malheur sur la famille; **you've brought it on yourself** vous l'avez cherché; **you b. credit to the firm** vous faites honneur à la société; **it brings bad/good luck** ça porte malheur/bonheur; **to b. new hope to sb** redonner de l'espoir à qn; **the story brought tears to my eyes** l'histoire m'a fait venir les larmes aux yeux; **money does not always b. happiness** l'argent ne fait pas toujours le bonheur; **the winter brought more wind and rain** l'hiver a amené encore plus de vent et de pluie; **tourism has brought prosperity to the area** le tourisme a enrichi la région; **who knows what the future will b.?** qui sait ce que l'avenir nous/lui/*etc* réserve?

4 *(force)* amener; **she can't b. herself to speak about it** elle n'arrive pas à en parler; **her performance brought the audience to its feet** les spectateurs se sont levés pour l'applaudir

5 *(lead)* mener, amener; **the path brings you straight (out) into the village** ce chemin vous mène (tout) droit au village; **the shock brought him to the verge of a breakdown** le choc l'a mené au bord de la dépression nerveuse; **to b. sb into a discussion** faire participer qn à une discussion; **that brings us to the next question** cela nous amène à la question suivante

6 *Law* **to b. an action** *or* **a suit against sb** intenter un procès à *ou* contre qn; **to b. a charge against sb** porter une accusation contre qn; **the case was brought before the court** l'affaire a été déférée au tribunal, le tribunal a été saisi de l'affaire; **he was brought before the court** il a comparu devant le tribunal; **the murderer must be brought to justice** l'assassin doit être traduit en justice; **to b. evidence** avancer *ou* présenter des preuves

7 *(financially)* rapporter; **her painting only brings her a few thousand pounds a year** ses peintures ne lui rapportent que quelques milliers de livres par an

▸ **bring about** VT SEP 1 *(cause ▸ changes, war)* provoquer, amener, entraîner; *(▸ reconciliation)* amener; *(▸ person's downfall)* entraîner; *(▸ accident)* provoquer, causer 2 *Naut* faire virer de bord

▸ **bring along** VT SEP *(person)* amener; *(thing)* apporter

▸ **bring away** VT SEP *(memories, impressions)* garder

▸ **bring back** VT SEP 1 *(fetch ▸ person)* ramener; *(▸ thing)* rapporter; **no amount of crying will b. him back** pleurer ne le ramènera pas à la vie; *Law* **to b. a case back before the court** ressaisir le tribunal d'un dossier 2 *(restore)* restaurer; **the news brought a smile back to her face** la nouvelle lui a rendu le sourire; **they're bringing back miniskirts** ils relancent la minijupe; **to b. sb back to life** ranimer qn 3 *(evoke ▸ memory)* rappeler (à la mémoire); **that brings it all back to me** ça réveille tous mes souvenirs

▸ **bring down** VT SEP 1 *(fetch ▸ person)* amener; *(▸ thing)* descendre, apporter

2 *(reduce ▸ prices, temperature)* faire baisser; *(▸ currency)* déprécier, avilir; *(▸ inflation, unemployment, swelling)* réduire

3 *(cause to land ▸ kite)* ramener (au sol); *(▸ plane)* faire atterrir

4 *(cause to fall ▸ prey)* descendre; *(▸ plane, enemy, tree)* abattre; **her performance brought the house down** son interprétation lui a valu des applaudissements à tout rompre

5 *Pol (overthrow)* faire tomber, renverser

6 *Fam (depress)* déprimer[□], donner le cafard à

7 *Literary (provoke ▸ anger)* attirer; **to b. down the wrath of God on sb** attirer la colère de Dieu sur qn

▸ **bring forth** VT SEP *Formal* 1 *(produce ▸ fruit)* produire; *(▸ child)* mettre au monde; *(▸ animal)* mettre bas 2 *(elicit)* provoquer

▸ **bring forward** VT SEP 1 *(present ▸ person)* faire avancer; *(▸ argument)* avancer, présenter; *Law (▸ witness)* produire; *Law (▸ evidence)* avancer, présenter

2 *(chair etc)* avancer

3 *Admin (move ▸ date, meeting)* avancer; **the conference has been brought forward to the 28th** la conférence a été avancée au 28

4 *Acct* reporter; **brought forward** reporté

▸ **bring in** VT SEP 1 *(fetch in ▸ person)* faire entrer; *(▸ thing)* rentrer; **to b. in the harvest** rentrer la moisson; **they want to b. a new person in** ils veulent prendre quelqu'un d'autre; **to b. sb in for questioning** emmener qn au poste de police pour l'interroger

2 *(introduce ▸ laws, system)* introduire, présenter; *(▸ fashion)* lancer; **the government has brought in a new tax bill** le gouvernement a présenté *ou* déposé un nouveau projet de loi fiscal

3 *(yield, produce)* rapporter; **to b. in interest** rapporter des intérêts; **tourism brings in millions of dollars each year** le tourisme rapporte des millions de dollars tous les ans

4 *Law (verdict)* rendre; **they brought in a verdict of guilty** ils l'ont déclaré coupable

▸ **bring off** VT SEP 1 *Br Fam (trick)* réussir[□]; *(plan)* réaliser[□]; *Com (deal)* conclure[□], mener à bien[□]; **did you manage to b. it off?** avez-vous réussi votre coup? 2 *Sport (player)* faire sortir 3 *(person ▸ from ship)* débarquer; **the injured men will be brought off by helicopter** les blessés seront évacués en hélicoptère

▸ **bring on** VT SEP 1 *(induce)* provoquer, causer; **the shock brought on a heart attack** le choc a provoqué une crise cardiaque; *Hum* **what brought this on?** *(why are you offering to help?)* qu'est-ce que tu me caches?

2 *(encourage)* encourager; **the warm weather has really brought on the flowers** la chaleur a bien fait pousser les fleurs; **the idea is to b. on new tennis players** il s'agit d'encourager de nouveaux tennismen

3 *Theat (person)* amener sur scène; *(thing)* apporter sur scène; **b. on our next contestant** faites entrer le concurrent suivant

4 *Sport (substitute)* faire entrer

▸ **bring out** VT SEP 1 *(take out ▸ person)* faire sortir; *(▸ thing)* sortir

2 *Com (commercially ▸ product, style)* lancer; *(▸ record)* sortir; *(▸ book)* publier

3 *(accentuate)* souligner; **that colour brings out the green in her eyes** cette couleur met en valeur le vert de ses yeux; **to b. out the best/worst in sb** faire apparaître qn sous son meilleur/plus mauvais jour

4 *Br Med (in rash, spots)* **strawberries b. me out in spots** les fraises me donnent des boutons

5 *(encourage ▸ person)* encourager; **he's very good at bringing people out (of themselves)** il sait très bien s'y prendre pour mettre les gens à l'aise; **the sun has brought out the roses** le soleil a fait s'épanouir les roses

6 *Ind (workers)* appeler à la grève; **they're threatening to b. everyone out (on strike)** ils menacent d'appeler tout le monde à faire grève

▸ **bring over** VT SEP *(take ▸ person)* amener; *(▸ thing)* apporter

▸ **bring round** VT SEP 1 *(take ▸ person)* amener; *(▸ thing)* apporter; *Br Fig* **I brought the conversation round to marriage** j'ai amené la conversation sur le mariage 2 *(revive)* ranimer 3 *(persuade)* convaincre, convertir; **to b. sb round to a point of view** convertir *ou* amener qn à un point de vue

▸ **bring through** VT SEP **he brought the country through the depression** il a réussi à faire sortir le pays de la dépression; **the doctors brought me through my illness** grâce aux médecins, j'ai survécu à ma maladie

▸**bring to** VT SEP *(revive)* ranimer

▸**bring together** VT SEP **1** *(people)* réunir; *(facts)* rassembler **2** *(introduce)* mettre en contact, faire se rencontrer; **her brother brought them together** son frère les a fait se rencontrer **3** *(reconcile)* réconcilier; *Ind* **an arbitrator is trying to b. the two sides together** un médiateur essaie de réconcilier les deux parties

▸**bring up** VT SEP **1** *(take ▸ person)* amener; *(▸ thing)* monter

2 *(child)* élever; **to be well/badly brought up** être bien/mal élevé; **I was brought up to be polite** on m'a appris la politesse

3 *(mention ▸ fact, problem)* signaler, mentionner; *(▸ question)* soulever; **don't b. that up again** ne remettez pas cela sur le tapis; **we won't b. it up again** nous n'en reparlerons plus

4 *(vomit)* vomir, rendre

5 *Law* **to b. sb up before a judge** citer *ou* faire comparaître qn devant un juge

6 *(move forward ▸ troops)* faire avancer; *(▸ reinforcements, fresh supplies etc)* faire venir

7 *(raise)* **to b. sb/sth up to professional standard** élever qn/qch à un niveau professionnel

bring-and-buy N *Br Com* **b. (sale)** = brocante de particuliers

> **BRING-AND-BUY SALE**
>
> Ces brocantes sont en général destinées à réunir des fonds pour une œuvre de charité. On y vend des articles d'occasion et des produits faits maison.

bringing up [ˈbrɪŋɪŋ-] N *(of child)* éducation *f*

brink [brɪŋk] N *(of precipice, river)* bord *m*; **to be on the b. of sth** *(tears, war, success, starvation etc)* être au bord de qch; *(discovery)* être à la veille de qch; *(death)* être à deux doigts de qch; *(ruin)* être au bord *ou* à deux doigts de qch; **to be on the b. of doing sth** être sur le point de faire qch; **animals on the b. of extinction** les animaux en voie de disparition; *Fig* **to stand shivering on the b.** hésiter à faire le plongeon

brinkmanship [ˈbrɪŋkmənʃɪp], **brinksmanship** [ˈbrɪŋksmənʃɪp] N *Pol* politique *f* de la corde raide; **he's a master in the art of b.** c'est un maître dans l'art de savoir jusqu'où il peut aller; **the country is engaged in a tense game of diplomatic b. with the West** le pays a entamé un bras de fer diplomatique avec l'Ouest

briny [ˈbraɪnɪ] *(compar* **brinier**, *superl* **briniest)** ADJ saumâtre, salé

N *Literary* **the b.** la mer

briquet, briquette [brɪˈket] N *(of coal)* briquette *f*, aggloméré *m*; *(of ice cream)* pavé *m*

brisk [brɪsk] ADJ **1** *(person)* vif, alerte; *(curt)* sec (sèche); *(manner)* brusque

2 *(quick)* rapide, vif; **to go for a b. walk** se promener d'un bon pas; **at a b. pace** à vive allure

3 *Com* florissant; **business is b.** les affaires marchent bien; **we're doing a b. trade in this particular item** cet article se vend très bien; *St Exch* **b. trading** marché *m* actif

4 *(weather)* vivifiant, frais (fraîche); *(day, wind)* frais (fraîche)

brisket [ˈbrɪskɪt] N *(of animal)* poitrine *f*; *Culin* poitrine *f* de bœuf

briskly [ˈbrɪsklɪ] ADV **1** *(move)* vivement; *(walk)* d'un bon pas; *(speak)* brusquement, sèchement; *(act)* sans délai *ou* tarder **2** *Com* **cold drinks were selling b.** les boissons fraîches se vendaient très bien *ou* comme des petits pains

briskness [ˈbrɪsknɪs] N **1** *(of person)* vivacité *f*; *(of manner)* brusquerie *f*; *(of action)* rapidité *f* **2** *Com* activité *f* **3** *(of weather)* fraîcheur *f*

bristle [ˈbrɪsəl] N *(of beard, brush)* poil *m*; *(of boar, pig)* soie *f*; *Bot (of plant)* poil *m*, soie *f*; **a brush with nylon/natural bristles** une brosse en nylon/soie; **a pure b. brush** une brosse pur sanglier

VI **1** *(hair)* se redresser, se hérisser **2** *Fig (show anger)* s'irriter, se hérisser; **they bristled at any suggestion of incompetence** ils se hérissèrent lorsqu'on osa insinuer qu'ils étaient incompétents

▸**bristle with** VT INSEP *Br (swarm with)* grouiller de; **the whole subject bristles with difficulties** toute la question est hérissée de difficultés; **the town centre was bristling with police** le centre-ville grouillait de policiers

bristly [ˈbrɪslɪ] *(compar* **bristlier**, *superl* **bristliest)** ADJ *(beard ▸ in appearance)* aux poils raides; *(▸ to touch)* qui pique; *(chin)* piquant; **his face was all b.** il avait une barbe de trois jours

Bristol [ˈbrɪstəl] N *(city)* Bristol

• **bristols** NPL *Br Fam Old-fashioned* roberts *mpl*, nichons *mpl*

▸▸ ***Bristol board*** bristol *m*; ***the Bristol Channel*** le canal de Bristol

Brit [brɪt] N *Fam* Britannique ◻ *mf*, British *m*

• **the Brit Awards, the Brits** NPL *Mus* = distinction récompensant les meilleures œuvres musicales britanniques de l'année (classique exclue)

Britain [ˈbrɪtən] N **(Great) B.** Grande-Bretagne *f*; **in B.** en Grande-Bretagne

Britannia [brɪˈtænjə] N *(figure)* = femme assise portant un casque et tenant un trident, qui personnifie la Grande-Bretagne

Britannic [brɪˈtænɪk] ADJ *Formal* **His** *or* **Her B. Majesty** Sa Majesté Britannique

Britart [ˈbrɪtɑːt] N = appellation collective des jeunes artistes britanniques qui ont fait de Londres, depuis la fin des années 1970, un important centre d'art contemporain

britches *Am* = **breeches**

Briticism [ˈbrɪtɪsɪzəm] N *Ling* anglicisme *m*

British [ˈbrɪtɪʃ] NPL **the B.** les Britanniques *mpl*, les Anglais *mpl*

ADJ britannique, anglais; **B. goods** produits *mpl* anglais

▸▸ *Cin* ***British Board of Film Classification*** = organisme britannique délivrant les visas de sortie pour les films; *Rad & TV* ***the British Broadcasting Corporation*** la BBC; ***British Columbia*** la Colombie-Britannique ***the British Commonwealth*** le Commonwealth; *Admin* ***the British Council*** = organisme public chargé de promouvoir la langue et la culture anglaises; ***the British Embassy*** l'ambassade *f* de Grande-Bretagne; *Hist* ***the British Empire*** l'Empire *m* britannique; ***British English*** anglais *m* britannique; ***the British Isles*** les îles *fpl* Britanniques; **in the B. Isles** aux îles Britanniques; *Pol* ***the British National Party*** = parti d'extrême-droite britannique; *Formerly* ***British Rail*** = société des chemins de fer britanniques, SNCF *f*; ***British Standards Institution*** = association britannique de normalisation; *Formerly* ***British SummerTime*** = heure d'été britannique

> **BRITISH COUNCIL**
>
> Le British Council est chargé de promouvoir la langue et la culture anglaises, et de renforcer les liens culturels avec les autres pays.

Britisher [ˈbrɪtɪʃə(r)] N *Am* Britannique *m,f*, Anglais(e) *mf*

Briton [ˈbrɪtən] N Britannique *mf*, Anglais(e) *m,f*; *Hist* Breton(onne) *m,f* (d'Angleterre)

Britpop [ˈbrɪtpɒp] N *Mus* = la musique pop britannique du milieu des années 90

Brittany [ˈbrɪtənɪ] N Bretagne *f*

brittle [ˈbrɪtəl] ADJ **1** *(breakable)* cassant, fragile **2** *(person)* froid, indifférent; *(humour)* mordant, caustique; *(reply)* sec (sèche); **a b. tone of voice** un ton sec *ou* cassant **3** *(sound)* strident, aigu (uë)

▸▸ *Med* ***brittle bone disease*** ostéogenèse *f* imparfaite, fragilité *f* osseuse héréditaire

brittleness [ˈbrɪtəlnɪs] N **1** *(fragility)* fragilité *f* **2** *(of person)* froideur *f*, insensibilité *f*; *(of humour)* causticité *f*, mordant *m*; **the b. of her voice** sa voix crispée **3** *(of sound)* son *m* aigu

broach [brəʊtʃ] VT **1** *(subject)* aborder, entamer **2** *(barrel)* percer, mettre en perce; *(supplies)* entamer

N **1** *Am (jewellery)* broche *f (bijou)* **2** *Constr* perçoir *m*, foret *m*

broad [brɔːd] ADJ **1** *(wide)* large; **the road is 4 metres b.** la route a 4 mètres de large *ou* de largeur; **she has a b. back** elle a une forte carrure; **a b. grin** un large *ou* grand sourire; **to have b. shoulders** être large d'épaules; **to be b. in the beam** *(ship)* être ventru; *Fam (person)* être large des hanches ◻; *Br Fig* **it's as b. as it's long** c'est bonnet blanc et blanc bonnet, c'est du pareil *ou* ça revient au même

2 *(extensive)* vaste, immense; **we offer a b. range of products** nous offrons une large *ou* grande gamme de produits; **in b. daylight** au grand jour, en plein jour; *Fig* au vu et au su de tout le monde, au grand jour

3 *(general)* général; **here is a b. outline** voilà les grandes lignes; **in the broadest sense of the word** au sens le plus large du mot; **his books still have a very b. appeal** ses livres plaisent toujours à *ou* intéressent toujours un vaste public; **to be in b. agreement** être d'accord dans les grandes lignes

4 *(not subtle)* évident; **"surely not," she said with b. sarcasm** "pas possible", dit-elle d'un ton des plus sarcastiques; **he speaks with a b. Scottish accent** il a un accent écossais prononcé *ou* un fort accent écossais

5 *(liberal)* libéral; **to have b. views** avoir les idées larges; **she has very b. tastes in literature** elle a des goûts littéraires très éclectiques

6 *(coarse)* grossier, vulgaire; **b. humour** humour *m* grivois; **a b. joke** une plaisanterie osée *ou* leste

N **1** *Anat (widest part)* **the b. of the back** le milieu du dos **2** *Am Fam (woman)* gonzesse *f*

▸▸ ***broad bean*** fève *f*; *Rel* ***Broad Church*** = groupe libéral à l'intérieur de l'Église anglicane; *Fig* **the party is a b. church** le parti rassemble de nombreux courants différents; *Am Sport* ***broad jump*** saut *m* en longueur; *Am Sport* ***broad jumper*** sauteur(euse) *m,f* en longueur

broadband [ˈbrɔːdbænd] N **1** *Rad* diffusion *f* en larges bandes de fréquence **2** *Tel & Comput* connexion *f* à haut débit *ou* à large bande, ADSL *m*; **have you got b. at home?** est-ce que tu as l'ADSL chez toi?

ADJ **1** *Rad* à larges bandes **2** *Tel & Comput* à haut débit, à large bande

▸▸ ***broadband network*** réseau *m* à haut débit *ou* à large bande, réseau *m* ADSL

broadcast [ˈbrɔːdkɑːst] *(pt & pp* **broadcast** *or* **broadcasted)** N *Rad & TV* émission *f*; **live/recorded b.** émission *f* en direct/en différé; **repeat b.** rediffusion *f*

VT **1** *Rad & TV* diffuser; **the match will be b. live** le match sera diffusé en direct; *Fig* **you don't have to b. it!** ce n'est pas la peine de le crier sur les toits *ou* le carillonner partout! **2** *Agr* semer à la volée

VI *Rad & TV (station)* émettre; *(actor)* participer à une émission, paraître à la télévision; *(show host)* faire une émission

ADJ *Rad* radiodiffusé; *TV* télévisé

ADV *Agr* à la volée

▸▸ ***broadcast journalism*** journalisme *m* de radio et de télévision; *Comput* ***broadcast message*** message *m* système; ***broadcast satellite*** satellite *m* de radiodiffusion; ***broadcast signal*** signal *m* de radiodiffusion; *Mktg* ***broadcast sponsorship*** parrainage *m* audiovisuel

broadcaster [ˈbrɔːdkɑːstə(r)] N *Rad & TV (person)* personnalité *f* de la radio *ou* de la télévision; **independent b.** *Rad* station *f* de radio; *TV* chaîne *f* de télévision privée

broadcasting [ˈbrɔːdkɑːstɪŋ] N *Rad* radiodiffusion *f*; *TV* télévision *f*; **he wants to go into b.** il veut faire une carrière à la radio ou à la télévision

▸▸ *Cin & TV* ***broadcasting copy*** copie *f* antenne; ***Broadcasting House*** = siège de la BBC à Londres; *Cin & TV* ***broadcasting rights*** droits *mpl* de diffusion *ou* d'antenne; *Rad & TV* ***broadcasting station*** station *f* émettrice

broadcloth [ˈbrɔːdklɒθ] N *Tex* drap *m* fin

broaden [ˈbrɔːdən] VT élargir; **to b. sb's outlook** *or* **horizons** élargir l'horizon de qn; **travel broadens the mind** les voyages ouvrent de nouveaux horizons

VI s'élargir

▸**broaden out** VI *(river, road, valley)* s'élargir

broad-leaved ADJ *Bot* feuillu

broadloom ['brɔːdluːm] **ADJ** *Tex (carpet)* en grande largeur

broadly ['brɔːdlɪ] **ADV 1** *(widely)* largement; **to smile b.** faire un grand sourire **2** *(generally)* en général; **b. speaking** d'une façon générale, en gros

broad-minded ADJ to be b. avoir les idées larges; **he has very b. parents** ses parents sont très tolérants *ou* larges d'esprit

broad-mindedness [-'maɪndɪdnɪs] **N** largeur *f* d'esprit

broadness ['brɔːdnɪs] **N 1** *(width)* largeur *f* **2** *(coarseness)* grossièreté *f*, vulgarité *f* **3** *Ling* **the b. of his accent** son accent prononcé

Broads [brɔːdz] **NPL the (Norfolk) B.** = ensemble de lacs situés dans le Norfolk et le Suffolk

broadsheet ['brɔːdʃiːt] **N** *Press (newspaper)* journal *m* plein format; *Br* journal *m* de qualité

broad-shouldered [-'ʃəʊldəd] **ADJ** large d'épaules, aux larges épaules

broadside ['brɔːdsaɪd] **N 1** *Naut (of ship)* flanc *m* **2** *Mil (volley of shots)* bordée *f*; **the ship fired a b.** le navire a lâché une bordée **3** *Fig (tirade)* attaque *f* cinglante; *(of insults)* bordée *f* d'injures; **to fire a b. at sb/sth** s'en prendre violemment à qn/qch

ADV b. (on) par le travers; *Naut* **the ship is b. on to the wharf** le navire présente le flanc *ou* le travers au quai; *Br Aut* **the truck hit us b.** on le camion nous a heurtés sur le côté

broad-spectrum ADJ *Pharm* à large spectre

broadways ['brɔːdˌweɪz], **broadwise** ['brɔːdˌwaɪz] **ADV** dans le sens de la largeur

brocade [brə'keɪd] **N** brocart *m*; **b. curtains/skirt** rideaux *mpl*/jupe *f* en brocart

VT brocher; **brocaded gown** robe *f* de brocart

broccoli ['brɒkəlɪ] **N** *(UNCOUNT)* brocolis *mpl*

brochure [*Br* 'brəʊʃə(r), *Am* brəʊ'ʃʊr] **N** *(gen)* brochure *f*, dépliant *m*; *Sch & Univ* prospectus *m*

brochureware [brəʊ'ʃʊrweə(r)] **N** *Comput* sites *mpl* brochure

brogue [brəʊg] **N** *Ling (accent)* accent *m* du terroir; *(Irish)* accent *m* irlandais

• **brogues NPL** = chaussures basses assez lourdes ornées de petits trous

broil [brɔɪl] *Am* **VT** *Culin* griller, faire cuire sur le gril; *Fig* griller

VI *Culin* griller; **broiling sun** soleil *m* brûlant

broiler ['brɔɪlə(r)] **N** *Culin* **1** *(chicken)* poulet *m* (à rôtir) **2** *Am (grill)* gril *m*, rôtissoire *f*; *Fam Fig* **it's a b. today** il fait une chaleur à crever aujourd'hui

►► ***broiler house*** éleveuse *f* (de poulets)

broke [brəʊk] *pt of* **break**

ADJ *Fam* **1** *(with no money)* fauché, à sec; **to go b.** faire faillite; **to go for b.** jouer le tout pour le tout; **to be flat** *or* **dead** *or Br* **stony b.** être fauché comme les blés, être raide comme un passe-lacet **2** *(broken)* bousillé; **if it ain't b., don't fix it** s'il n'y a pas de problèmes particuliers, il ne faut rien changer

broken ['brəʊkən] *pp of* **break**

ADJ 1 *(damaged* ► *chair, toy, window)* cassé, brisé; *(*► *leg, rib)* fracturé, cassé; *(*► *back)* brisé, cassé; *(*► *biscuit)* brisé; *Fig (heart)* brisé; **are there any b. bones?** y a-t-il des fractures?; **to die of a b. heart** mourir de chagrin; **she's from a b. home** elle vient d'un foyer désuni; **a b. marriage** un mariage brisé, un ménage désuni

2 *(sleep* ► *disturbed)* interrompu; *(*► *restless)* agité

3 *(speech)* mauvais, imparfait; **he speaks b. English** il parle un mauvais anglais; **in b. French** en mauvais français; **in a voice b. with sobs** d'une voix entrecoupée de sanglots; **in a b. voice** d'une voix brisée

4 *(agreement, promise)* rompu, violé; *(appointment)* manqué

5 *(health)* délabré; **her spirit is b.** elle est abattue; **he's a b. man since his wife's death** il a le cœur brisé *ou* il est très abattu depuis la mort de sa femme

6 *(incomplete* ► *set)* incomplet(ète)

7 *(uneven* ► *ground)* accidenté; *(*► *coastline)* dentelé; *(*► *line)* brisé, discontinu

8 *(tamed* ► *animal)* dressé, maté

►► *Com* ***broken lots*** articles *mpl* dépareillés

broken-down ADJ 1 *(damaged* ► *machine)* détraqué; *(*► *car)* en panne **2** *(worn out)* fini, à bout

brokenhearted [ˌbrəʊkən'hɑːtɪd] **ADJ** au cœur brisé

brokenly ['brəʊkənlɪ] **ADV** *(speak)* de façon entrecoupée

broken-winded [-'wɪndɪd] **ADJ** *(horse)* poussif

broker ['brəʊkə(r)] **N 1** *Com (for goods)* courtier (ère) *m,f* (de commerce); *St Exch* courtier(ère) *m,f* (en Bourse), agent *m* de change; *Ins* **(insurance) b.** courtier(ère) *m,f ou* agent *m* d'assurances; *Com* **wine b.** négociant *m* en vins; *St Exch* **b.'s commission** (frais *mpl* de) courtage *m*; **b.'s contract** courtage *m* **2** *Com (second-hand dealer)* brocanteur *m*

VT *Fig* **to b. an agreement** négocier un accord en tant qu'intermédiaire

brokerage ['brəʊkərɪdʒ] **N** *Com* **1** *(fee)* (frais *mpl* de) courtage *m* **2** *(profession)* courtage *m*

►► ***brokerage house*** *(business)* maison *f* de courtage

broking ['brəʊkɪŋ] **N** *(profession)* courtage *m*

brolly ['brɒlɪ] *(pl* **brollies)** **N** *Br Fam* pépin *m* *(parapluie)*

bromeliad [brəʊ'miːlɪæd] **N** *Bot* broméliacée *f*

bromide ['brəʊmaɪd] **N** *Chem & Typ* bromure *m*; *Pharm (sedative)* bromure *m* (de potassium)

bronchial ['brɒŋkɪəl] **ADJ** *Anat* des bronches, bronchique

►► *Anat* ***bronchial tubes*** bronches *fpl*

bronchiole ['brɒŋkɪəʊl] **N** *Anat* bronchiole *f*

bronchitic [brɒŋ'kɪtɪk] *Med* **N** bronchiteux (euse) *m,f*, bronchitique *mf*

ADJ bronchiteux, bronchitique

bronchitis [brɒŋ'kaɪtɪs] **N** *(UNCOUNT) Med* bronchite *f*; **to have (an attack of) b.** avoir *ou* faire une bronchite

bronchopneumonia [ˌbrɒŋkəʊnjuː'məʊnɪə] **N** *Med* broncho-pneumonie *f*

bronchus ['brɒŋkəs] *(pl* **bronchi** [-kaɪ]) **N** *Anat* bronche *f*

bronco ['brɒŋkəʊ] *(pl* **broncos)** **N** *Am* cheval *m* sauvage *(de l'Ouest)*

broncobuster ['brɒŋkəʊˌbʌstə(r)] **N** *Am* = cow-boy qui dompte les chevaux sauvages

brontosaur ['brɒntəˌsɔː(r)], **brontosaurus** [ˌbrɒntə'sɔːrəs] *(pl* **brontosauruses** *or* **brontosauri** [-raɪ]) **N** *Zool* brontosaure *m*

bronze [brɒnz] **N 1** *(alloy)* bronze *m*

2 *(statue)* bronze *m*, statue *f* de *ou* en bronze

3 *(medal)* médaille *f* en bronze; **he's a b. medallist** il a remporté la médaille de bronze

4 *(colour)* (couleur *f* de) bronze *m inv*

COMP 1 *(lamp, medal, statue)* de *ou* en bronze **2** *(colour, skin)* (couleur *f* de) bronze *(inv)*

VT *(metal)* bronzer; *(skin)* faire bronzer, brunir

VI se bronzer, brunir

►► ***the Bronze Age*** l'âge *m* du bronze; ***bronze medal*** médaille *f* de bronze

bronzed [brɒnzd] **ADJ** bronzé, hâlé

bronzer ['brɒnzə(r)] **N** *(make-up)* poudre *f* de soleil

bronzing ['brɒnzɪŋ] **N** bronzage *m*

►► ***bronzing powder*** poudre *f* de soleil

brooch [brəʊtʃ] *(pl* **brooches)** **N** broche *f (bijou)*

brood [bruːd] **N 1** *Orn (of birds)* couvée *f*, nichée *f*; *Zool (of animals)* nichée *f*, portée *f* **2** *Hum (children)* progéniture *f*; *Pej* marmaille *f* **3** *Fig Pej (of scoundrels etc)* race *f*, engeance *f*

VI 1 *Orn (bird)* couver **2** *(danger, storm)* couver, menacer **3** *(person)* ruminer, broyer du noir; **to b. about things** ruminer; **all he does is sit there brooding** il passe son temps à broyer du noir; **it's no use brooding on** *or* **over the past** cela ne sert à rien de s'appesantir sur *ou* remâcher le passé

►► *Agr* ***brood mare*** (jument *f*) poulinière *f*

brooder ['bruːdə(r)] **N 1** *(hen)* (poule *f*) couveuse *f* **2** *(enclosure)* couveuse *f* (artificielle) **3** *Fig (person)* **he's such a b.** il est toujours à ruminer

broody ['bruːdɪ] *(compar* **broodier**, *superl* **broodiest) ADJ 1** *(gloomy)* mélancolique, cafardeux **2** *(motherly)* **a b. hen** une (poule) couveuse; *Br Fam Fig* **to feel b.** être en mal d'enfant

brook [brʊk] **N** *(stream)* ruisseau *m*

VT *(usu neg) (tolerate)* supporter, tolérer; *(answer, delay)* admettre, souffrir; **he will b. no insolence** il ne supporte pas d'impertinence

broom [bruːm] **N 1** *(brush)* balai *m* **2** *Bot* genêt *m*

►► ***broom handle*** manche *m* à balai

broomstick ['bruːmstɪk] **N** manche *m* à balai

Bros., bros. *(written abbr* **brothers)** Frères

broth [brɒθ] **N** *Culin* bouillon *m (de viande et de légumes)*

brothel ['brɒθəl] **N** maison *f* close *ou* de passe, *Fam* bordel *m*

►► *Br Fam* ***brothel creeper*** = chaussure de daim à semelle de crêpe pour hommes

brother ['brʌðə(r)] *(pl senses* **2** and **3 brethren** ['breðrɪn] *or* **brothers)** **N 1** *(relative)* frère *m*; **older/younger b.** frère *m* aîné/cadet

2 *Rel* frère *m*; **B. Damian** Frère Damian

3 *(fellow member* ► *of trade union)* camarade *m*; *(*► *of professional group)* collègue *m*; *Mil* **brothers in arms** compagnons *mpl ou* frères *mpl* d'armes; **his b. officers** les autres officiers de sa brigade *ou Mil* de son régiment

4 *Am Fam (term of address)* **hey, b.!** *(to stranger)* eh, camarade!; *(to friend)* eh, mon vieux!

5 *Fam Black Am slang (fellow black man)* = nom donné par les noirs américains à un homme noir

EXCLAM *Fam* **(oh) b.!** dis donc!, bigre!

brotherhood ['brʌðəhʊd] **N 1** *(relationship)* fraternité *f*; *Fig (fellowship)* fraternité *f*, confraternité *f*; *Rel* confrérie *f*; **the b. of man** la communauté humaine **2** *(association)* association *f*; *Rel* confrérie *f* **3** *Am Ind (entire profession)* corporation *f*

brother-in-law *(pl* **brothers-in-law)** **N** beau-frère *m*

brotherliness ['brʌðəlɪnɪs] **N** amour *m* fraternel

brotherly ['brʌðəlɪ] **ADJ** fraternel; **he felt very b. towards her** il la considérait un peu comme une sœur

brought [brɔːt] *pt & pp of* **bring**

brouhaha ['bruːhɑːhɑː] **N** brouhaha *m*, vacarme *m*

brow [braʊ] **N 1** *(forehead)* front *m*; **her troubled b.** son air inquiet **2** *(eyebrow)* sourcil *m* **3** *(of hill)* sommet *m*

browbeat ['braʊbiːt] *(pt* **browbeat**, *pp* **browbeaten** [-biːtən]) **VT** intimider, brusquer; **to b. sb into doing sth** forcer qn à faire qch en usant d'intimidation

browbeaten ['braʊˌbiːtən] **ADJ** persécuté

browbeating ['braʊˌbiːtɪŋ] **N** intimidation *f*

ADJ intimidant

brown [braʊn] **N** marron *m*; **dressed in b.** habillé en marron

ADJ 1 *(gen)* marron *(inv)*; *(leather)* marron *(inv)*; *(hair* ► *light)* châtain; *(*► *dark)* brun; *(eyes)* marron; **light b. hair** cheveux *mpl* châtain clair; **a light b. scarf** une écharpe marron clair; **in a b. study** plongé dans ses pensées, pensif **2** *(tanned)* bronzé, hâlé; **he's looking very b. after his holiday** il est rentré de vacances très bronzé; **as b. as a berry** tout bronzé

VT 1 *Culin* faire dorer; *(sauce)* faire roussir **2** *(tan)* bronzer, brunir

VI 1 *Culin* dorer **2** *(skin)* bronzer, brunir

►► ***brown ale*** bière *f* brune; *Zool* ***brown bear*** ours *m* brun; *Sport* ***brown belt*** *(in martial arts)* ceinture *f* marron; ***brown bread*** *(UNCOUNT) Com* ***brown goods*** produits *mpl* bruns; *Orn* ***brown owl*** chat-huant *m*, chouette *f* des bois, hulotte *f*; ***brown paper*** papier *m* d'emballage; ***brown paper bag*** sac *m* en papier kraft; *Zool* ***brown rat*** (rat *m*) surmulot *m*, rat *m* gris *ou* d'égout; ***brown rice*** riz *m* complet; *Pol* ***Brown Shirt*** fasciste *mf*; *Hist (Nazi)* chemise *f* brune; ***brown sugar*** *Culin* cassonade *f*, sucre *m* roux; *Fam Drugs slang* héro *f*

brownbag [ˌbraʊn'bæg] *(pp & pt* **brownbagged**, *cont* **brownbagging)** **VT** *Am Fam* **I b. it to work** j'apporte mon déjeuner tous les jours au travail; **to b. it** *(drink)* = boire de l'alcool au goulot, dans la rue, la bouteille étant enveloppée d'un sac en papier

brownbagger [ˌbraʊnˈbægə(r)] **N** *Am Fam* = personne qui apporte son déjeuner sur son lieu de travail

browned-off [braʊnd-] **ADJ** *Br Fam* **to be b.** *(bored)* en avoir marre; *(discouraged)* ne plus avoir le moral; **she's b. with her job** elle en a marre *ou* ras le bol de son travail

brown-eyed ADJ aux yeux marrons

brownfield site [ˈbraʊnfiːld-] **N** terrain *m* à bâtir *(après démolition de bâtiments préexistants)*

brown-haired ADJ *(light)* aux cheveux châtains; *(dark)* aux cheveux bruns

brownie [ˈbraʊnɪ] **N 1** *(elf)* lutin *m*, farfadet *m* **2** *Culin (cake)* brownie *m*; **chocolate brownies** brownies *mpl* au chocolat
• **Brownie (Guide) N** jeannette *f*; **to join the Brownies** s'inscrire aux jeannettes, devenir jeannette
►► *Fam Hum* ***brownie point*** bon point *m*; **to win** *or* **to get b. points** se faire bien voir; **doing the ironing should earn you a few b. points** tu seras bien vu si tu fais le repassage

Browning [ˈbraʊnɪŋ] **N** *Mil* **B. (automatic rifle)** browning *m*

browning [ˈbraʊnɪŋ] **N 1** *(by sun)* brunissement *m*, bronzage *m* **2** *Culin* **the b. of the meat is important** c'est important de faire rissoler la viande **3** *Br Culin (substance)* colorant *m* brun (pour les sauces)

brownish [ˈbraʊnɪʃ] **ADJ** qui tire sur le marron, brunâtre

brown-nose *very Fam* **N** lèche-cul *mf inv*
VT faire du lèche-cul à
VI faire du lèche-cul

brown-noser [-ˈnəʊzə(r)] **N** *very Fam* lèche-cul *mf inv*

brownout [ˈbraʊnaʊt] **N** *Am Elec (electric failure)* baisse *f* de tension

browsable [ˈbraʊzəbəl] **ADJ** *(book)* agréable à feuilleter; *(website)* agréable à parcourir

browse [braʊz] **VI 1** *(person)* regarder, jeter un œil; **she browsed through the book** elle a feuilleté le livre; **feel free to b.** *(in shop)* vous pouvez regarder si vous voulez; *(sign)* entrée libre **2** *Zool (animal)* brouter, paître
N *(look)* **I popped into the shop to have a b. around** je suis passé au magasin pour jeter un coup d'œil *ou* regarder
VT *Comput* **to b. the Net/Web** naviguer sur l'Internet/le Web
►► *Comput* ***browse mode*** mode *m* survol

► **browse through VT INSEP 1** *Fig* **to b. through a book/magazine** feuilleter un livre/un magazine; **to b. through sb's books/records** jeter un coup d'œil aux livres/disques de qn **2** *Comput* se promener dans, survoler

browser [ˈbraʊzə(r)] **N 1** *(in shop)* **browsers welcome** *(sign)* entrée libre **2** *Comput* navigateur *m*, logiciel *m* de navigation, *Can* fureteur *m*

brucellosis [ˌbruːsɪˈləʊsɪs] **N** *Med & Vet* brucellose *f*

bruise [bruːz] **N 1** *(on person)* bleu *m*, contusion *f*; **to be covered in** *or* **with bruises** être couvert de bleus **2** *(on fruit)* meurtrissure *f*, talure *f*
VT 1 *(person)* faire un bleu à, contusionner; *Fig* blesser; **to b. one's arm** se faire un bleu au bras; **to be bruised all over** être couvert de bleus; *Fig* **his ego was bruised** son amour-propre en a pris un coup **2** *(fruit)* taler, abîmer; *(lettuce)* flétrir
VI *Bot (fruit)* se taler, s'abîmer; **to b. easily** *(person)* se faire facilement des bleus; *Fig* être très sensible

bruised [bruːzd] **ADJ** *Med* meurtri; *Fig (pride)* blessé; **badly b.** couvert de bleus

bruiser [ˈbruːzə(r)] **N** *Fam (big man)* malabar *m*; *Boxing (fighter)* cogneur□ *m*; **their baby's a real b.!** leur bébé est vraiment costaud!

bruising [ˈbruːzɪŋ] **N** *(UNCOUNT)* contusions *fpl*, bleus *mpl*; **he suffered b. to his arm** il a eu le bras contusionné; *Fam Hum* **to be cruising for a b.** chercher les emmerdes
ADJ *Fig* pénible, douloureux; **it was a rather b. experience** ce fut une expérience plutôt douloureuse

Brummie, Brummy [ˈbrʌmɪ] *Br Fam* **N** = nom familier désignant un natif de Birmingham
ADJ de Birmingham□

brunch [brʌntʃ] **N** brunch *m*
VI prendre un brunch, bruncher

Brunei [bruːˈnaɪ] **N** Brunei *m*

brunette [bruːˈnet] **N** brune *f*, brunette *f*; **she's a b.** elle est brune
ADJ *(hair)* châtain

brunt [brʌnt] **N the car took the b. of the shock** c'est la voiture qui a tout pris; **she bore the b. of his anger** c'est elle qui a fait les frais de sa colère; **to bear the b. of the expense** supporter la plus grande partie des frais

brush [brʌʃ] *(pl* **brushes***)* **N 1** *(gen)* brosse *f*; *(for paint* ► *small)* pinceau *m*; *(*► *large)* brosse *f*; *(for paste)* pinceau *m*, brosse *f*; *(shaving brush)* blaireau *m*; *(scrubbing brush)* brosse *f* dure; *(broom)* balai *m*; *(with dustpan)* balayette *f*
2 *(act of brushing)* coup *m* de brosse; **to give sth a b.** *(clothes)* donner un coup de brosse à qch; *(floor)* donner un coup de balai à qch; **to give one's hair a b.** se donner un coup de brosse; **to give one's teeth a b.** se brosser les dents
3 *(encounter, skirmish)* accrochage *m*, escarmouche *f*; *Fig* **to have a b. with death** frôler la mort; **to have a b. with the law** avoir des démêlés avec la justice
4 *(light stroke)* effleurement *m*; **she felt the b. of his lips on her neck** elle a senti ses lèvres lui effleurer le cou
5 *(of fox)* queue *f*
6 *(UNCOUNT) Bot (undergrowth)* broussailles *fpl*; *Geog (scrubland)* brousse *f*
VT 1 *(clothes, carpet)* brosser; **to b. one's hair/teeth** se brosser les cheveux/les dents; **she brushed her hair back from her face** elle a brossé ses cheveux en arrière
2 *(sweep* ► *floor)* balayer
3 *(touch lightly)* effleurer, frôler; *(surface)* raser
4 *Tex (wool)* gratter
VI effleurer, frôler; **her hair brushed against his cheek** ses cheveux ont effleuré *ou* frôlé sa joue
►► ***brush fire*** *(fire)* feu *m* de brousse, incendie *m* de broussailles; *Mil (minor war)* conflit *m* armé; ***brush stroke*** *(gen)* coup *m* de brosse; *Art* coup *m ou* trait *m* de pinceau

► **brush aside VT SEP 1** *(move aside)* écarter, repousser **2** *(ignore* ► *remark)* balayer d'un geste; *(*► *report)* ignorer

► **brush away VT SEP 1** *(remove* ► *tears)* essuyer; *(*► *insect)* chasser; *(remove* ► *from clothes)* enlever d'un coup de brosse; *(*► *from floor)* enlever d'un coup de balai **2** *(person, difficulty)* écarter; **to b. away criticism** mépriser les critiques

► **brush down VT SEP** *(clothing)* donner un coup de brosse à; *(horse)* brosser

► **brush off VT SEP 1** *(remove)* enlever *(à la brosse ou à la main)*; *(insect)* chasser **2** *(dismiss* ► *plea, challenge)* rejeter; *(*► *person)* écarter, repousser
VI *(dirt)* s'enlever

► **brush past VT INSEP** frôler en passant

► **brush up VT SEP 1** *Fam (revise)* revoir□, réviser□; **I have to b. up my maths** il faut que je me remette à niveau en maths **2** *(sweep up)* ramasser à la balayette

brushdown [ˈbrʌʃdaʊn] **N to give sb a b.** donner un coup de brosse à qn; **to give a horse a b.** brosser *ou* panser un cheval

brushed [brʌʃt] **ADJ** *Tex* gratté; **b. cotton** pilou *m*, finette *f*

brushing [ˈbrʌʃɪŋ] **N 1** *(of clothes, carpet, hair)* brossage *m* **2** *(of floor)* balayage *m*

brush-off N *Fam* **to give sb the b.** envoyer promener *ou* balader qn; **I got the b.** on m'a envoyé sur les roses

brush-up N 1 *Br (clean-up)* coup *m* de brosse **2** *Fam (revision)* révision□ *f*; **my German could do with a b.** j'aurais besoin de me remettre à l'allemand

brushwood [ˈbrʌʃwʊd] **N** *(UNCOUNT) Bot (undergrowth)* broussailles *fpl*; *(cuttings)* menu bois *m*, brindilles *fpl*

brushwork [ˈbrʌʃwɜːk] **N** *(UNCOUNT) (gen)* travail *m* au pinceau; *Art* touche *f*

brusque [bruːsk] **ADJ** *(abrupt)* brusque; *(curt)* brusque, bourru

brusquely [ˈbruːsklɪ] **ADV** *(abruptly)* avec brusquerie; *(curtly)* avec brusquerie *ou* rudesse, brutalement

brusqueness [ˈbruːsknɪs] **N** *(abruptness)* brusquerie *f*; *(curtness)* brusquerie *f*, rudesse *f*

Brussels [ˈbrʌsəlz] **N** Bruxelles
►► ***Brussels sprout*** chou *m* de Bruxelles

brutal [ˈbruːtəl] **ADJ** *(cruel* ► *action, behaviour, person)* brutal, cruel; *(uncompromising* ► *honesty)* franc (franche), brutal; *(severe* ► *climate, cold)* rude, rigoureux

brutality [bruːˈtælətɪ] *(pl* **brutalities***)* **N 1** *(cruelty)* brutalité *f*, cruauté *f* **2** *(act of cruelty)* brutalité *f*

brutalize, -ise [ˈbruːtəlaɪz] **VT 1** *(ill-treat)* brutaliser **2** *(make brutal)* rendre brutal

brutally [ˈbruːtəlɪ] **ADV** *(attack, kill, treat)* brutalement, sauvagement; *(say)* brutalement, franchement; *(cold)* extrêmement; **to be b. frank** *or* **honest with sb** être d'une franchise brutale avec qn

brute [bruːt] **N 1** *(animal)* brute *f*, bête *f* **2** *(person* ► *violent)* brute *f*; *(*► *coarse)* brute *f* (épaisse), rustre *m*; **a great b. of a man** une grande brute
ADJ 1 *(animal-like)* animal, bestial **2** *(purely physical)* brutal; **b. force** *or* **strength** force *f* brutale; **by b. force** par la force; **you'll have to use b. force** il faudra user de la manière forte **3** *(mindless)* brut; **an act of b. stupidity** un acte d'une bêtise sans nom

brutish [ˈbruːtɪʃ] **ADJ 1** *(animal-like)* animal, bestial **2** *(cruel)* brutal, violent; *(coarse)* grossier

brutishly [ˈbruːtɪʃlɪ] **ADV 1** *(like an animal)* comme une brute **2** *(cruelly)* brutalement, violemment; *(coarsely)* grossièrement

Brylcreem® [ˈbrɪlkriːm] **N** = marque de brillantine

bryony [ˈbraɪənɪ] *(pl* **bryonies***)* **N** *Bot* bryone *f*

BS [ˌbiːˈes] **N 1** *Br (abbr* **British Standard/Standards***)* = indique que le chiffre qui suit renvoie au numéro de la norme fixée par l'Institut britannique de normalisation **2** *Am Univ (abbr* **Bachelor of Science***) (person)* = titulaire d'une licence de sciences; *(qualification)* licence *f* de sciences **3** *Am very Fam (abbr* **bullshit***)* conneries *fpl*

BSc [ˌbiːesˈsiː] **N** *Br (abbr* **Bachelor of Science***) (person)* = titulaire d'une licence de sciences; *(qualification)* licence *f* de sciences

BSE [ˌbiːesˈiː] **N** *Vet (abbr* **bovine spongiform encephalopathy***)* EBS *f*

B-share N *St Exch* action *f* ordinaire avec droit de vote, action *f* à dividende prioritaire

BSI [ˌbiːesˈaɪ] **N** *(abbr* **British Standards Institution***)* = association britannique de normalisation, AFNOR *f*

BSL [ˌbiːesˈel] **N** *(abbr* **British Sign Language***)* langue *f* des signes britannique

BST [ˌbiːesˈtiː] **N** *(abbr* **British SummerTime***)* = heure d'été britannique

BTW *Comput (written abbr* **by the way***) (in e-mail messages)* à propos

bubba [ˈbʌbə] **N** *Am Fam* **1** *(brother)* frangin *m* **2** *(Southern male)* plouc *m (du Sud des États-Unis)*

bubble [ˈbʌbəl] **N 1** *(of foam)* bulle *f*; *(in liquid)* bouillon *m*; *(in champagne)* bulle *f*; *(in glass)* bulle *f*, soufflure *f*; *(in paint)* boursouflure *f*, cloque *f*; *(in metal)* soufflure *f*; **soap bubbles** bulles *fpl* de savon
2 *(transparent cover)* cloche *f*
3 *Fig (illusion)* **to prick** *or* **to burst sb's b.** réduire à néant les illusions de qn, enlever ses illusions à qn; **the b. finally burst** finalement mes/ses *etc* illusions s'envolèrent
4 *(sound)* glouglou *m*
VI 1 *(liquid)* bouillonner, faire des bulles; *(champagne)* pétiller; *(gas)* barboter; *Fig* **her real feelings bubbled beneath the surface** ses sentiments véritables bouillonnaient en elle **2** *(gurgle)* gargouiller, glouglouter **3** *(brim)* déborder; **the children were bubbling with excitement** les enfants étaient tout excités *ou* surexcités
►► ***bubble bath*** bain *m* moussant; *Br Aut* ***bubble car*** = petite voiture à trois roues; ***bubble econo-***

my économie *f* de bulle; ***bubble gum*** bubble-gum *m*; *Comput* ***bubble memory*** mémoire *f* à bulles; ***bubble pack*** *Com (for toy, batteries)* blister *m*, emballage *m* bulle; *(for pills)* plaquette *f*; *Br Culin* ***bubble and squeak*** = plat à base de pommes de terre et de choux, servi réchauffé; *Com* ***bubble wrap*** bullpack® *m*

▸**bubble over** VI *also Fig* déborder; **to b. over with enthusiasm** déborder d'enthousiasme

bubble-jet printer N *Comput* imprimante *f* à bulles

bubbling ['bʌblɪŋ] ADJ bouillonnant

N *(UNCOUNT)* bouillonnement *m*; *Chem* barbotage *m*; *(in paintwork)* boursouflures *fpl*

bubbly ['bʌblɪ] *(compar* **bubblier**, *superl* **bubbliest**) ADJ **1** *Chem (liquid)* pétillant, plein de bulles **2** *(person)* pétillant, plein d'entrain; *(personality)* plein de vitalité

N *Br Fam (champagne)* champ' *m*

bubonic [bju:'bɒnɪk] ADJ *Med* bubonique

▸▸ ***bubonic plague*** peste *f* bubonique

buccal ['bʌkəl] ADJ *Anat* buccal

buccaneer [ˌbʌkə'nɪə(r)] N **1** *Hist* boucanier *m* **2** *(unscrupulous person)* flibustier *m*, pirate *m*

Bucharest [ˌbu:kə'rest] N Bucarest

buck [bʌk] N **1** *(male animal)* mâle *m*

2 *Fam (young man)* jeune mec *m*

3 *Am Fam (dollar)* dollar▫ *m*; **to be down to one's last b.** être fauché *ou* raide; **to make a b.** gagner sa croûte; **to make a fast** *or* **quick b.** faire du fric facilement; **to get more bang for one's b.** en avoir plus pour son argent

4 *Fam (responsibility)* **to pass the b. onto sb** *(blame)* faire porter le chapeau à qn; *(shift responsibility)* refiler le bébé à qn; **it's far too easy to pass the b.** c'est trop facile de rejeter la responsabilité sur quelqu'un d'autre; **the b. stops here** *(with me)* en dernier ressort, c'est moi le responsable; *(with you)* en dernier ressort, c'est toi le responsable

5 *(of horse)* ruade *f*

6 *Gym* cheval *m*, cheval-d'arçons *m inv*

COMP *(goat, hare, kangaroo, rabbit)* mâle

VI **1** *(horse)* donner une ruade **2** *Fam (resist)* **to b. against change** se rebiffer contre les changements

VT **1** *(of horse)* **the horse bucked his rider (off)** le cheval a désarçonné *ou* jeté bas son cavalier **2** *Fam (resist)* **to b. the system** se rebiffer contre le système; **it takes courage to b. public opinion** il faut du courage pour aller à l'encontre de l'opinion publique

▸▸ ***buck deer*** daim *m*, chevreuil *m*; *Br* ***buck's fizz*** = cocktail composé de champagne et de jus d'orange

▸**buck up** *Br Fam* VT SEP **1** *(cheer up)* remonter le moral à▫ **2** *(improve)* améliorer▫; **you'd better b. your ideas up** tu as intérêt à te remuer *ou* à en mettre un coup

VI **1** *(cheer up)* se secouer; **b. up! life goes on!** courage! la vie continue! **2** *(hurry up)* se grouiller, se magner

buckaroo ['bʌkəˌru:] N *Am* cow-boy *m*

bucket ['bʌkɪt] N **1** *(container, contents)* seau *m*; **a b. of water** un seau d'eau; *Fam* **it rained buckets** il a plu à seaux; *Fam* **to cry** *or* **to weep buckets** pleurer comme une Madeleine *ou* un veau; **a b. and spade** un seau et une pelle *(symbole, pour un Britannique, de vacances familiales au bord de la mer)* **2** *Tech (of dredger, grain elevator)* godet *m*; *(of pump)* piston *m*; *(of wheel)* auget *m*

VI *Br Fam* **1** *(rain)* pleuvoir à seaux **2** *(move hurriedly)* aller à fond de train; *(car)* rouler à fond la caisse; **we were bucketing along** nous roulions à fond la caisse

▸▸ *Tech* ***bucket elevator*** élévateur *m* à godets, noria *f*; ***bucket hat*** bob *m*; *Aut & Aviat* ***bucket seat*** baquet *m*, siège-baquet *m*, siège *m* cuve; ***bucket shop*** *Fin* bureau *m ou* maison *f* de contrepartie, bureau *m* de courtier marron; *Br Com (travel agency)* = organisme de vente de billets d'avion à prix réduit

▸**bucket down** VI *Br Fam* pleuvoir à seaux

bucketful ['bʌkɪtful] N plein seau *m*; **a b. of water** un seau plein d'eau; **in bucketfuls** à seaux

bucking ['bʌkɪŋ] N *(of horse)* ruades *fpl*

▸▸ ***bucking bronco*** *(horse)* cheval *m* de rodéo; *(mechanical)* rodéo *m* mécanique

buckle ['bʌkəl] N **1** *(clasp)* boucle *f* **2** *Metal (kink ▸ in metal)* gauchissement *m*, flambage *m*; *Aut (▸ in wheel)* voilure *f*

VI **1** *(fasten)* se boucler, s'attacher **2** *(distort ▸ metal)* gauchir, se déformer; *(▸ wheel)* se voiler; **the bridge buckled under the weight of traffic** le pont s'est déformé sous le poids des véhicules **3** *(give way ▸ knees, legs)* se dérober; *Fig (person ▸ under attack)* céder; *(▸ under criticism)* se décomposer; **his knees buckled** ses jambes se dérobèrent sous lui

VT **1** *(fasten ▸ suitcase, belt, shoe)* boucler; *(safety belt)* attacher **2** *(distort)* déformer, fausser; *(metal)* gauchir, fausser; *(wheel)* voiler

▸**buckle down** VI *Fam* s'appliquer▫; **to b. down to work** se mettre au travail; **come on now, b. down!** allez, au boulot!; **she'll have to b. down if she wants to pass** il faudra qu'elle en mette un coup si elle veut réussir

▸**buckle on** VT SEP *(armour)* revêtir, endosser; *(gunbelt, sword)* attacher, ceindre

▸**buckle to** VI *Fam* s'y mettre, s'y atteler

▸**buckle up** VI *Am Aut* **b. up!** attachez vos ceintures!

buckling ['bʌkəlɪŋ] N *(of metal)* déformation *f*, gauchissement *m*; *(of wheel)* voilure *f*

buckram ['bʌkrəm] N *Tex* bougran *m*

Bucks *(written abbr* **Buckinghamshire**) le Buckinghamshire, = comté dans le sud de l'Angleterre

bucksaw ['bʌksɔ:] N *Tech* scie *f* à bûches

buckshee [ˌbʌk'ʃi:] *Br Fam* ADJ gratis, à l'œil

ADV gratis, à l'œil

buckshot ['bʌkʃɒt] N chevrotine *f*, gros plomb *m*

buckskin ['bʌkskɪn] N peau *f* de daim

bucktoothed ['bʌkˌtu:θt] ADJ **to be b.** avoir des dents de lapin

buckwheat ['bʌkwi:t] N *Bot* sarrasin *m*, blé *m* noir

▸▸ *Culin* ***buckwheat flour*** farine *f* de blé noir *ou* de sarrasin; *Culin* ***buckwheat pancake*** galette *f* de blé noir *ou* de sarrasin

bucolic [bju:'kɒlɪk] ADJ bucolique, pastoral

N *Literature* bucolique *f*

bud [bʌd] *(pt & pp* **budded**, *cont* **budding**) N **1** *(on shrub, tree)* bourgeon *m*; *(of flower)* bouton *m*; **the trees are in b.** les arbres bourgeonnent; **the roses are in b.** les roses sont en bouton **2** *Biol & Anat* papille *f* **3** *Am Fam (term of address)* **hey, b.!** *(to stranger)* eh, vous là-bas!; *(to friend)* eh, mon vieux!

VI **1** *(plant)* bourgeonner; *(flower)* former des boutons **2** *Fig (talent)* (commencer à) se révéler *ou* percer

Budapest [ˌbju:də'pest, ˌbju:də'peʃt] N Budapest

Buddha ['budə] PR N *Rel* Bouddha

Buddhism ['budɪzəm] N *Rel* bouddhisme *m*

Buddhist ['budɪst] *Rel* N Bouddhiste *mf*

ADJ *(country, priest)* bouddhiste; *(art, philosophy, temple)* bouddhique

budding ['bʌdɪŋ] ADJ **1** *(plant)* bourgeonnant, couvert de bourgeons; *(flower)* en bouton **2** *Fig (artist, genius)* en herbe, prometteur; *(love, talent)* naissant

buddleia ['bʌdlɪə] N *Bot* buddleia *m*

buddy ['bʌdɪ] *(pl* **buddies**) N *esp Am Fam (friend)* copain (copine) *m,f*; **since when are they such buddies?** depuis quand sont-ils si copains?; **they're best** *or* **big buddies** ce sont les meilleurs copains du monde

▸▸ ***buddy film, buddy movie*** = film qui raconte les histoires de deux copains

▸**buddy up** VI *Am Fam* **to b. up to sb** faire de la lèche à qn

buddy-buddy ADJ *esp Am (close, friendly)* copain (copine) (**with** avec); **those two are very b.** ils sont très copain-copain

budge [bʌdʒ] VI **1** *(move)* bouger; **it won't b.** c'est coincé, c'est bloqué **2** *Fig (yield)* céder, changer d'avis; **she refused to b.** elle ne voulut pas en démordre; **he wouldn't b. an inch** il a tenu bon

VT **1** *(move)* faire bouger **2** *(convince)* convaincre, faire changer d'avis; **he won't be budged** il reste inébranlable, il n'y a pas eu moyen de le faire changer d'avis

▸**budge over, budge up** VI *Fam* se pousser▫

budgerigar ['bʌdʒərɪgɑ:(r)] N *Br Orn* perruche *f*

budget ['bʌdʒɪt] N *(gen) & Fin (financial plan)* budget *m*; *(allocated ceiling)* enveloppe *f* budgétaire; **to be on a tight b.** disposer d'un budget serré *ou* modeste; **it was finished well below** *or* **within b.** c'est revenu bien moins cher que prévu; **the project is already over b.** on a déjà dépassé le budget qui était alloué pour le projet

VT budgétiser, inscrire au budget; **to b. one's time** bien organiser son temps

VI dresser *ou* préparer un budget

ADJ **1** *(inexpensive)* économique, pour petits budgets; **b. prices** prix *mpl* avantageux *ou* modiques **2** *Econ & Fin* budgétaire

• **Budget** N *Pol* **the B.** le budget

▸▸ ***budget account*** *(with store)* compte-crédit *m*; *(with bank)* compte *m* permanent; ***budget allocation*** enveloppe *f* budgétaire; *Br Pol* ***budget box, budget briefcase*** = attaché-case que le chancelier de l'Échiquier brandit devant les photographes de presse lorsqu'il a établi le budget de l'année; ***budget committee*** commission *f* du budget; ***budget constraint*** contrainte *f* budgétaire; ***budget cuts*** coupes *fpl* budgétaires; ***Budget Day*** = jour de la présentation du budget par le chancelier de l'Échiquier britannique; ***budget deficit*** déficit *m* budgétaire; ***budget estimates*** prévisions *fpl* budgétaires; ***budget forecast*** prévisions *fpl* budgétaires; ***budget planning*** planification *f* budgétaire; *Br & Can Pol* ***Budget speech*** = discours à l'occasion de la présentation du budget au parlement; ***budget surplus*** excédent *m* budgétaire

▸**budget for** VT INSEP *(gen)* prévoir des frais de, budgétiser; **to b. for sth** *Acct (allow for in accounts)* inscrire qch au budget, prévoir des frais de qch; *Econ & Fin* inscrire *ou* porter au budget, budgétiser; **I'm budgeting for my holidays** je surveille mes dépenses pour pouvoir partir en vacances

budgetary ['bʌdʒɪtərɪ] ADJ *Fin & Econ* budgétaire

budgeting ['bʌdʒɪtɪŋ] N *Fin* **1** *(of person, company)* budgétisation *f*, planification *f* budgétaire **2** *Acct* comptabilité *f* budgétaire

budgie ['bʌdʒɪ] N *Br Fam* perruche▫ *f*

Buenos Aires [ˌbwenəs'aɪrɪz] N Buenos Aires

buff [bʌf] N **1** *(colour)* (couleur *f*) chamois *m*

2 *Tex (leather)* peau *f* de buffle; *(polishing cloth)* polissoir *m*

3 *(enthusiast)* **a wine b.** un amateur de vin; **a history b.** un(e) mordu(e) d'histoire

4 *Fam* **in the b.** *(naked)* à poil

VT polir; **to b. one's nails** se polir les ongles; **it just needs buffing up a bit** cela a juste besoin d'être un peu astiqué

ADJ **1** *(coloured)* (couleur) chamois; *(leather)* de *ou* en buffle **2** *Fam (good-looking)* canon *(inv)*

buffalo ['bʌfələʊ] *(pl* **inv** *or* **buffaloes**) *Zool* N *(male)* buffle *m*; *(female)* bufflesse *f*, bufflonne *f*; *(in US)* bison *m*; **a herd of b.** un troupeau de buffles

▸▸ ***buffalo hide*** peau *f* de buffle; *Culin* ***buffalo mozzarella*** mozzarella *f* au lait de bufflonne; *Culin* ***buffalo wings*** ailes *fpl* de poulet frites

buffer ['bʌfə(r)] N **1** *(protection)* tampon *m*; *Am Aut (on car)* pare-chocs *m inv*; *Rail (on train)* tampon *m*; *(at station)* butoir *m*, heurtoir *m*; *Comput* tampon *m*, mémoire *f* intermédiaire; *Chem* substance *f* tampon; *Fig Econ* **a b. against inflation** une mesure de protection contre l'inflation; *Fig* **to run into** *or* **to hit the buffers** tomber à l'eau; *Fam* **to act as a b.** *(between people)* faire tampon **2** *Br Fam (fool)* imbécile▫ *mf*; **an old b.** un vieux schnock **3** *(for polishing)* polissoir *m*

VT tamponner, amortir (le choc); **to be buffered against reality** être protégé de la réalité *ou* des réalités (de la vie)

▸▸ *Comput* ***buffer memory*** mémoire *f* tampon; *Pol* ***buffer state*** état *m* tampon; *Com* ***buffer stock*** stock *m* tampon; *Pol* ***buffer zone*** région *f* tampon

buffering ['bʌfərɪŋ] **N 1** *Comput (storage)* stockage *m* en mémoire tampon; *(use)* utilisation *f* de mémoire tampon **2** *Chem* tamponnage *m*

buffet¹ [*Br* 'bʊfeɪ, *Am* bə'feɪ] **N 1** *Culin (refreshments)* buffet *m*; **cold b.** buffet *m* froid **2** *(sideboard)* buffet *m* **3** *Com (restaurant)* buvette *f*, cafétéria *f*; *(in station)* buffet *m ou* café *m* de gare; *(on train)* wagon-restaurant *m*

COMP *Culin (lunch, dinner)* -buffet

►► *Rail* ***buffet car*** wagon-restaurant *m*

buffet² ['bʌfɪt] **VT 1** *(batter)* **buffeted by the waves** ballotté par les vagues; **the trees were buffeted by the wind** les arbres étaient secoués par le vent; *Fig Literary* **buffeted by misfortune** poursuivi par la malchance **2** *Literary (hit ► with hand)* souffleter; *(► with fist)* donner un coup de poing à

N *Literary (blow ► with hand)* soufflet *m*; *(► with fist)* coup *m* de poing

buffeting ['bʌfɪtɪŋ] **N 1** *(of rain, wind)* assaut *m*; **the waves gave the boat a real b., the boat took quite a b. from the waves** le navire a été violemment ballotté par les vagues **2** *Literary (beating)* bourrades *fpl*

ADJ violent

buffing ['bʌfɪŋ] **N** polissage *m*

buffoon [bə'fu:n] **N** bouffon *m*, pitre *m*; **to act** *or* **to play the b.** faire le clown *ou* le pitre

buffoonery [bə'fu:nərɪ] **N** *(UNCOUNT)* bouffonnerie *f*, bouffonneries *fpl*

bug [bʌg] *(pt & pp* **bugged**, *cont* **bugging) N 1** *Am (insect)* insecte *m*; *Entom (bedbug)* punaise *f*; *Fam Fig* **she's been bitten by the travel b.** elle a la passion des voyages

2 *Fam Biol & Med (germ)* microbe^◻ *m*; **to catch a b.** attraper un microbe; **I've got a stomach b.** j'ai des problèmes intestinaux^◻; **there's a b. going round** il y a un virus qui se balade *ou* qui traîne

3 *Fam Tech (defect)* défaut^◻ *m*, erreur^◻ *f*; **there are still a few bugs to be ironed out** il y a encore quelques petits trucs qui clochent

4 *Comput* bogue *m*

5 *Fam Tech (microphone)* micro *m* (caché)

VT 1 *Fam (bother)* taper sur les nerfs de; **what's bugging him?** qu'est-ce qu'il a?; **it really bugs me to think of her having all that money** ça m'énerve vraiment de savoir qu'elle a tout cet argent **2** *Tech (wiretap ► room)* poser *ou* installer des appareils d'écoute (clandestins) dans; *(► phone)* brancher sur table d'écoute

►**bug off VI** *Am Fam (leave hurriedly)* ficher le camp; **b. off!** dégage!, fiche le camp!

bugaboo ['bʌgəbu:] **N** loup-garou *m*, croque-mitaine *m*

bugbear ['bʌgbeə(r)] **N** *(monster)* épouvantail *m*, croque-mitaine *m*; *Fig (worry)* bête *f* noire, cauchemar *m*; **maths is my b.** les maths c'est mon cauchemar; *Econ* **inflation is the government's chief b.** l'inflation est le grand cauchemar du gouvernement

bug-eyed ADJ *Am Fam* aux yeux globuleux *ou* exorbités^◻; **she was b. in amazement** elle avait les yeux écarquillés d'étonnement

bug-free ADJ 1 *Comput (program)* exempt d'erreurs *ou* de bogues **2** *(room ► without listening devices)* sans micros clandestins; *(► having no insects)* d'où les insectes ont été chassés

bugger ['bʌgə(r)] *Br very Fam* **N 1** *(foolish person)* couillon *m*; *(unpleasant person)* salaud *m*; **silly b.!** pauvre connard!; **stop playing silly buggers!** arrête de faire le con!; **poor old b.** pauvre bougre *m*; **he can be a real b. sometimes** c'est un vrai saligaud *ou* salopard des fois **2** *(thing, job)* truc *m* chiant; **this job's a real b.** c'est une saloperie de boulot; **her house is a b. to find** sa maison est vachement dure à trouver **3** *(damn)* **I don't give a b.** je m'en tape

EXCLAM *Br very Fam* merde alors!

VT 1 *(sodomize)* sodomiser

2 *Br very Fam (damn)* **b. him!** je l'emmerde!; **well, b. me!** merde alors!; **oh, b. it!** oh, merde!

3 *Br very Fam (damage)* bousiller; **that's really buggered it!** *(broken it)* ça l'a complètement bousillé; *(spoilt things)* ça a tout gâché^◻

4 *Br very Fam (exhaust)* mettre sur les genoux^◻

• **bugger all ADJ** *Br very Fam* que dalle; **b. all money/thanks** pas un sou/un merci^◻; **that was b. all help** ça n'a servi à rien^◻

►**bugger about, bugger around** *Br very Fam* **VT SEP to b. sb about** *or* **around** *(treat badly)* se foutre de la gueule de qn; *(waste time of)* faire tourner qn en bourrique

VI glander

►**bugger off VI** *Br very Fam* foutre le camp; **b. off!** *(go away)* fous le camp!; *(leave me alone)* fous-moi la paix!; *(expressing contempt, disagreement)* va te faire foutre!

►**bugger up VT SEP** *Br very Fam* saloper

buggeration [bʌgə'reɪʃən] **EXCLAM** *Br very Fam* bordel!, putain!, merde!

buggered ['bʌgəd] **ADJ** *Br very Fam* **1** *(broken)* foutu

2 *(in surprise)* **well, I'll be b.!** merde alors!

3 *(in annoyance)* **I'm b. if I'll do anything to help** ils peuvent toujours courir pour que je les aide; **(I'm) b. if I know** j'en sais foutre rien

4 *(exhausted)* crevé, naze

5 *(in trouble)* foutu; **if we don't get the money soon, we're b.** si on a pas l'argent rapidement, on est foutus

buggery ['bʌgərɪ] **N 1** *(sodomy)* sodomie *f* **2** *very Fam* **to run like b.** courir ventre à terre; **my plans have been shot to b.** ça a foutu mes projets en l'air

bugging ['bʌgɪŋ] **N** *(of room)* utilisation *f* d'appareils d'écoute (clandestins); *(of telephone)* mise *f* sur écoute

►► ***bugging device*** appareil *m* d'écoute (clandestin)

buggy ['bʌgɪ] *(pl* **buggies) N 1** *(carriage)* boghei *m* **2** *(for baby)* poussette *f*, poussette-canne *f*; *Am (pram)* voiture *f* d'enfant

bughouse ['bʌghaus, *pl* -hauzɪz] *Am Fam Pej* **N** maison *f* de fous

ADJ dingue, cinglé

bugle ['bju:gəl] **N** clairon *m*; **to sound the b.** faire sonner le clairon

VI jouer du clairon, sonner le clairon

►► ***bugle call*** sonnerie *f* de clairon

bugler ['bju:glə(r)] **N** (joueur *m* de) clairon *m*

bugless ['bʌglɪs] **ADJ** *Comput* sans bogues

bug-ridden ADJ *Comput* bogué

build [bɪld] *(pt & pp* **built** [bɪlt]) **VT 1** *(dwelling)* bâtir, construire; *(temple)* bâtir, édifier; *(bridge, machine, ship)* construire; *(nest)* faire, bâtir; **houses are being built** des maisons sont en construction; **we are planning to b. a new garage** nous avons l'intention de faire construire un nouveau garage; **we're building an extension on the house** nous agrandissons la maison; *Fig* **to b. castles in the air** bâtir des châteaux en Espagne; *Mktg* **to b. a brand** créer une marque **2** *(found)* bâtir, fonder; **to b. one's hopes on sth** fonder ses espoirs sur qch

VI 1 *(construct)* bâtir; **developers are planning to b. on the land** les promoteurs envisagent de construire *ou* bâtir sur le terrain; *Fig* **to b. on sand** bâtir sur le sable; *Fig* **his success is built on hard work** sa réussite repose sur un travail acharné **2** *(increase)* augmenter, monter; **excitement/tension is building** l'excitation/la tension augmente *ou* monte

N 1 *Anat* carrure *f*, charpente *f*; **of strong b.** solidement bâti *ou* charpenté; **of heavy b.** de forte corpulence *ou* taille; **of medium b.** de taille *ou* corpulence moyenne; **of slight b.** fluet; **he has the b. of a rugby player** il est bâti comme un joueur de rugby **2** *(construction work)* travaux *mpl* de construction

►**build in VT SEP** *Constr (wardrobe, beam etc)* encastrer; *Fig (include ► special features)* intégrer

►**build into VT SEP** *(incorporate)* intégrer à

►**build on VT SEP** *Constr* ajouter

VT INSEP we need to b. on our achievements il faut consolider nos succès

►**build up VT SEP 1** *(develop ► business, theory)* établir, développer; *(► reputation)* établir, bâtir; *(► confidence)* donner, redonner; *(► strength)* prendre; **you need to b. up your strength, you need building up** vous avez besoin de prendre des forces

2 *Ind (increase ► production)* accroître, augmenter; *(► excitement)* faire monter, accroître; *(► pressure)* accumuler

3 *(promote)* faire de la publicité pour; **the film wasn't as good as it had been built up to be** le film n'était pas aussi bon qu'on le prétendait

4 *Constr (wall ► make higher)* rehausser; *(► rebuild)* réparer

VI 1 *(business)* se développer **2** *(excitement)* monter, augmenter; *(pressure)* s'accumuler; **traffic is building up** il commence à y avoir beaucoup de circulation

builder ['bɪldə(r)] **N 1** *Constr (contractor)* entrepreneur(euse) *m,f (en bâtiment)*; *(worker)* ouvrier(ère) *m,f* du bâtiment; *Com & Ind (of machines, ships)* constructeur(trice) *m,f* **2** *Fig (founder)* fondateur(trice) *m,f*; **the builders of the empire** les bâtisseurs *mpl* de l'empire

building ['bɪldɪŋ] **N 1** *(structure)* bâtiment *m*; *(monumental)* édifice *m*; *(apartment, office)* immeuble *m* **2** *Constr (work)* construction *f*; **b. is due to start on Monday** les travaux de construction doivent commencer lundi

COMP *Constr (land)* à bâtir; *(materials)* de construction

►► ***building block*** *(toy)* cube *m*; *Fig* composante *f*; *Constr* ***building contractor*** entrepreneur(euse) *m,f* (en bâtiment *ou* construction); ***building industry*** (industrie *f* du) bâtiment *m*; *Am Fin* ***building and loan association*** société *f* de crédit immobilier; ***building plot*** terrain *m* à bâtir; ***building site*** chantier *m* (de construction); *Br Fin* ***building society*** société *f* de crédit immobilier; ***building trade*** (industrie *f* du) bâtiment *m*; ***building worker*** ouvrier(ère) *m,f* du bâtiment

BUILDING SOCIETY

Les "building societies" fonctionnent comme des banques mais elles n'ont pas de système de compensation. Établissements consentant des prêts immobiliers aux particuliers, elles jouent un rôle important dans la vie en Grande-Bretagne. Au cours des dernières années, de nombreuses "building societies" ont abandonné leur statut de sociétés mutuelles pour devenir des banques cotées en Bourse.

build-up N 1 *(increase ► in pressure)* intensification *f*; *(► in excitement)* montée *f*; *(► in production)* accroissement *m*; *(► in stock)* accumulation *f*; *Mil (► in troops)* rassemblement *m* **2** *(publicity)* campagne *f* publicitaire *(avant le lancement d'un produit)*; **they gave the product a big b.** ils ont fait beaucoup de publicité pour le produit **3** *(preparatory period)* **the b. to the match** la période d'avant le match; **in the b. to the election, there will be...** pendant la période qui précédera les élections, il y aura...

built [bɪlt] *pt & pp of* **build**

ADJ *(building)* bâti, construit; *(person)* charpenté; **British b.** de construction britannique; **to be powerfully b.** *(person)* être puissamment *ou* solidement charpenté; **to be slightly b.** *(person)* être fluet

built-in ADJ *(beam, wardrobe)* encastré; *(device, safeguard)* intégré; *Fig (feature)* inné, ancré; *Comput* incorporé

►► ***built-in obsolescence*** obsolescence *f* programmée

built-to-order ADJ *Comput* construit sur mesure

built-up ADJ 1 *(land)* bâti; **the area is becoming very b.** ça se construit beaucoup *ou* on a beaucoup construit dans la région **2** *(in clothing)* **b. shoulders** épaules *fpl* surhaussées; **b. shoes** chaussures *fpl* à semelles compensées

►► ***built-up area*** agglomération *f* (urbaine)

bulb [bʌlb] **N 1** *Bot (tulip etc)* bulbe *m*, oignon *m*

2 *Elec* **(light) b.** ampoule *f*

3 *Tech (of thermometer)* réservoir *m*

4 *Anat* bulbe *m*

bulbous ['bʌlbəs] **ADJ** *Bot* bulbeux; *Anat* **a b. nose** un gros nez

Bulgaria [bʌl'geərɪə] **N** Bulgarie *f*

Bulgarian [bʌl'geərɪən] **N 1** *(person)* Bulgare *mf* **2** *(language)* bulgare *m*

ADJ bulgare

COMP *(embassy)* de Bulgarie; *(history)* de la Bulgarie; *(teacher)* de bulgare

bulge [bʌldʒ] **N 1** *(lump, swelling)* renflement *m*; *(on vase, jug)* panse *f*, ventre *m*; *Br Mil* saillant *m*; **he noticed a b. in her pocket** il remarqua que sa poche faisait un renflement; **this dress shows all my bulges** on voit tous mes bourrelets avec cette robe **2** *(increase)* poussée *f*; *Econ* **a population b.** une explosion démographique

VI *(swell)* se gonfler, se renfler; *(stick out)* faire saillie, saillir; **his suitcase was bulging with gifts** sa valise était bourrée de cadeaux; *Fig* **the town was bulging at the seams with holidaymakers** la ville était pleine à craquer de vacanciers; **his eyes bulged** il avait les yeux saillants *ou* globuleux

bulging [ˈbʌldʒɪŋ] **ADJ** *(forehead, wall, ceiling)* bombé; *(stomach)* ballonné; *(muscles, waist)* saillant; *(eyes)* protubérant, globuleux; *(cheeks)* bouffi; *(bag, wallet etc)* bourré, plein à craquer

bulgur [ˈbʌlgə(r)] **N** *Culin* **b. (wheat)** pilpil® *m*

bulimia [buˈlɪmɪə] **N** *Med* boulimie *f*

bulk [bʌlk] **N 1** *(mass)* masse *f*; *(stoutness)* corpulence *f*; **the great b. of the cathedral loomed out of the darkness** la silhouette massive de la cathédrale se dessina dans l'obscurité; **a man of enormous b.** un homme très corpulent **2** *(main part)* **the b.** la plus grande partie, la majeure partie; **she left the b. of her fortune to charity** elle légua le plus gros de sa fortune aux bonnes œuvres **3** *Comput (of information)* volume *m*, masse *f*

COMP *Com (order, supplies)* en gros

VT *Com (packages)* grouper

VI *Br* **to b. large** occuper une place importante; **the prospect of a further drop in prices bulked large in their minds** la perspective d'une autre baisse des prix les préoccupait vivement *ou* était au premier plan de leurs préoccupations

• **in bulk ADV** par grosses quantités; *Com* en gros; *Naut* en vrac

▸▸ *Com* ***bulk buying*** *(UNCOUNT)* achat *m* par grosses quantités; achat *m* en gros; *Naut* ***bulk carrier*** vraquier *m*, transporteur *m* de vrac; *Mktg* ***bulk mail*** *(UNCOUNT)* envois *mpl* en nombre; *Mktg* ***bulk mailing*** mailing *m ou* publipostage *m* à grande diffusion; *Com* ***bulk rate*** affranchissement *m* à forfait

bulkhead [ˈbʌlkhed] **N** *Aviat & Naut* cloison *f (d'avion, de navire)*

bulkiness [ˈbʌlkɪnɪs] **N** *(of object)* grosseur *f*, encombrement *m*, volume *m*; *(of person)* corpulence *f*

bulky [ˈbʌlkɪ] **ADJ 1** *(massive, large)* volumineux; *(cumbersome)* encombrant; **a b. sweater** un gros pull; **a b. package** un paquet encombrant *ou* volumineux **2** *(corpulent, stout)* corpulent, gros (grosse); *(solidly built)* massif

bull [bʊl] **N 1** *(male cow)* taureau *m*; **like a b. in a china shop** comme un éléphant dans un magasin de porcelaine; *Fig* **to take the b. by the horns** prendre le taureau par les cornes

2 *(male of a species* ▸ *elephant, whale)* mâle *m*

3 *Fam (large, strong man)* costaud *m*, malabar *m*; **a great b. of a man** un homme fort comme un bœuf

4 *St Exch* haussier *m*, spéculateur(trice) *m,f* à la hausse

5 *(centre of target)* mille *m*, centre *m* de la cible; **to hit the b.** faire mouche, mettre dans le mille

6 *very Fam (nonsense)* conneries *fpl*; **that's a lot** *or* **load of b.** c'est des conneries tout ça

7 *Br Fam Mil slang (polishing)* fourbissage▫ *m*

COMP *(elephant, whale)* mâle

VT *St Exch (market, prices, shares)* pousser à la hausse; **to b. the market** chercher à faire hausser les cours

VI *St Exch (person)* spéculer *ou* jouer à la hausse; *(stocks)* être en hausse

• **Bull N** *Astrol* **the B.** le Taureau

▸▸ *Aut* ***bull bars*** pare-buffles *m inv*; ***bull calf*** jeune taureau *m*, taurillon *m*; *St Exch* ***bull market*** marché *m* à la hausse *ou* haussier; ***bull mastiff*** = chien issu d'un métissage entre le bouledogue et le mastiff; *St Exch* ***bull position*** position *f* acheteur; *St Exch* ***bull speculation, bull trading*** spéculation *f* à la hausse; ***bull terrier*** bull-terrier *m*; *St Exch* ***bull transaction*** opération *f* à la hausse

bulldog [ˈbʊldɒg] **N 1** *(dog)* bouledogue *m* **2** *Br St Exch* **b. (bond)** obligation *f* bulldog *(obligation d'un emprunteur étranger à la Bourse de Londres, libellée en sterling)*

▸▸ ***bulldog clip*** pince *f* à dessin

bulldoze [ˈbʊldəʊz] **VT 1** *Constr (building)* démolir au bulldozer; *(earth, stone)* passer au bulldozer; **whole villages have been bulldozed** des villages entiers ont été rasés au bulldozer **2** *Fig (push)* **to b. sb into doing sth** forcer qn à faire qch, faire pression sur qn pour lui faire faire qch; **she bulldozed her way to the top** elle est arrivée au sommet à la force du poignet

bulldozer [ˈbʊldəʊzə(r)] **N** *Tech* bulldozer *m*

bulldyke [ˈbʊldaɪk] **N** *very Fam Pej* gouine *f* à l'allure masculine

bullet [ˈbʊlɪt] **N 1** *(from rifle, revolver)* balle *f*; *Br Fam Fig* **to get the b.** *(get fired)* se faire virer, se faire sacquer **2** *Typ & Comput* puce *f*

COMP *(hole)* de balle; *(wound)* par balle

▸▸ *Am Fin* ***bullet bond*** obligation *f* remboursable en une seule fois; *Typ & Comput* ***bullet point*** puce *f*; *Rail* ***bullet train*** train *m* à grande vitesse *(au Japon)*

bulleted list [ˈbʊlɪtɪd-] **N** *Typ & Comput* liste *f* à puces

bullet-headed ADJ 1 *(with a small, round head)* à tête ronde **2** *Am Fig (obstinate)* entêté, têtu

bulletin [ˈbʊlətɪn] **N** *Rad & TV (announcement)* bulletin *m*, communiqué *m*; *Press (newsletter)* bulletin *m*

▸▸ ***bulletin board*** *Am (gen)* tableau *m* d'affichage; *Comput* serveur *m* télématique, *Can* babillard *m*; *Comput* ***bulletin board service*** serveur *m* télématique, *Can* babillard *m*

bulletproof [ˈbʊlɪt,pruːf] **ADJ** *(glass, garment)* pare-balles *(inv)*; *(vehicle)* blindé

VT *(door, vehicle)* blinder

▸▸ ***bulletproof vest*** gilet *m* pare-balles

bullfight [ˈbʊlfaɪt] **N** corrida *f*, course *f* de taureaux

bullfighter [ˈbʊl,faɪtə(r)] **N** torero *m*, matador *m*

bullfighting [ˈbʊl,faɪtɪŋ] **N** *(UNCOUNT)* courses *fpl* de taureaux, corrida *f*; *(as art)* tauromachie *f*

bullfinch [ˈbʊlfɪntʃ] **N** *Orn* bouvreuil *m*

bullfrog [ˈbʊlfrɒg] **N** *Zool* grenouille *f* taureau, *Can* ouaouaron *m*

bull-headed ADJ *Fam* **1** *(impetuous)* d'une impétuosité de taureau; **to go at sth b.** foncer la tête la première dans qch **2** *(obstinate)* entêté▫, têtu▫

bullhorn [ˈbʊlhɔːn] **N** *Am* mégaphone *m*, porte-voix *m inv*

bullion [ˈbʊljən] **N** *(gold)* encaisse-or *f*, or *m* en lingots *ou* en barres; *(silver)* argent *m* en lingots *ou* en barres

bullish [ˈbʊlɪʃ] **ADJ 1** *St Exch (market, tendency)* à la hausse, haussier; **to be b.** *(of person)* spéculer *ou* jouer à la hausse **2** *Br Fam (optimistic)* **to be in a b. mood** être confiant *ou* optimiste▫

bull-necked ADJ au cou de taureau

bullock [ˈbʊlək] **N** *(castrated)* bœuf *m*; *(young)* bouvillon *m*

bullpen [ˈbʊlpen] **N** *Am (in police station)* = grande cellule commune

bullring [ˈbʊlrɪŋ] **N** arène *f (pour la corrida)*

bull's-eye N 1 *(centre of target)* mille *m*, centre *m* de la cible; **b.!** dans le mille!; **to hit the b.** faire mouche, mettre dans le mille; *Fig (person)* faire mouche, mettre dans le mille; *(remark)* faire mouche **2** *(sweet)* gros bonbon *m* à la menthe **3** *Archit (window)* œil-de-bœuf *m*, oculus *m*

bullshit [ˈbʊlʃɪt] *Vulg* **N** *(UNCOUNT)* conneries *fpl*; **don't give me that b.!** ne me raconte *ou* dis pas de conneries!

VT raconter des conneries à; **don't b. me!** ne me raconte pas de conneries!; **she bullshitted her way into the job** elle a eu le boulot au culot

VI déconner, raconter des conneries

EXCLAM des conneries, tout ça!

bullshitter [ˈbʊl,ʃɪtə(r)] **N** *Vulg (smooth talker)* baratineur(euse) *m,f*; **he's a b.** *(talks nonsense)* il raconte des conneries

bully [ˈbʊlɪ] **N 1** *(adult)* tyran *m*; *(child)* petite brute *f*; **don't be such a b.!** ne sois pas si tyrannique! **2** *Sport (in hockey)* bully *m*

VT *(intimidate* ▸ *spouse, employee)* brimer, persécuter; *(maltreat)* brutaliser; **she bullies her little sister** elle est tyrannique avec sa petite sœur; **they bullied me into going** ils m'ont forcé à y aller; **he gets bullied by the other children at school** il se fait persécuter par les autres enfants à l'école

EXCLAM *Fam Ironic* **b. for you!** quel exploit!, bravo!

▸ **bully off VI** *Sport (in hockey)* engager le jeu, mettre la balle en jeu

bullyboy [ˈbʊlɪbɔɪ] **N** *Br* brute *f*, voyou *m*; **b. tactics** manœuvres *fpl* d'intimidation

bullying [ˈbʊlɪɪŋ] **ADJ** *(intimidating)* agressif, brutal

N *(UNCOUNT)* brimades *fpl*; **the problem of b. in school** le problème des enfants persécutés par leurs camarades d'école

bully-off N *Sport (in hockey)* bully *m*

bulrush [ˈbʊlrʌʃ] **N** *Bot* jonc *m*

bulwark [ˈbʊlwək] **N** *Archit* rempart *m*, fortification *f*; *(breakwater)* digue *f*, môle *m*; *Fig (protection)* rempart *m*, protection *f*; **a b. against the harsh realities of life** un rempart *ou* une protection contre les dures réalités de la vie; **a b. against inflation** une mesure de protection contre l'inflation

• **bulwarks NPL** *Naut* bastingage *m*, pavois *m*

bum [bʌm] *(pt & pp* **bummed,** *cont* **bumming)** *Fam*

N 1 *Br (buttocks)* fesses▫ *fpl*; **to put bums on seats** attirer le public▫

2 *(tramp)* clochard(e)▫ *m,f*, clodo *m*; *(lazy person)* fainéant(e)▫ *m,f*, flemmard(e) *m,f*; *(worthless person)* minable *mf*, minus *m*; **to give sb the b.'s rush** *(dismiss)* envoyer paître qn; *(from work)* virer qn; **to give sth the b.'s rush** *(idea, suggestion)* rejeter qch▫; **my idea was given the b.'s rush** mon idée est passée à la trappe

3 *Sport (sports fanatic)* fana *mf*, mordu(e) *m,f*; **a beach b.** un(e) fana *ou* mordu(e) des plages

4 *Am (vagrancy)* **to be** *or* **to live on the b.** vagabonder; **he went on the b.** il s'est mis à dormir sous les ponts

ADJ *(worthless)* minable, nul; *(injured, disabled)* patraque, mal fichu; *(untrue)* faux (fausse)▫; **he got a bit of a b. deal** il a été très mal traité; *Am* **he was in jail on a b. rap** il était en prison pour un délit qu'il n'avait pas commis

VT *(beg, borrow)* **to b. sth off sb** emprunter qch à qn▫, taper qn de qch▫; **he's always bumming cigarettes** il est toujours à quémander *ou* mendier des cigarettes; **to b. a lift** *or* **a ride** se faire accompagner en voiture▫; **can I b. a lift** *or* **a ride to the station?** est-ce que tu peux me déposer à la gare?▫

VI *Am* **1** *(be disappointed)* l'avoir mauvaise **2** *(laze about)* traîner

▸▸ *Br* ***bum bag*** banane *f*; ***bum steer*** tuyau *m* percé; **to give sb a b. steer** donner un tuyau percé à qn

▸ **bum about, bum around** *Fam* **VT INSEP** *(spend time in)* **to b. around Australia/the country** parcourir l'Australie/le pays sac au dos▫; **to b. around the house** rester chez soi à glander

VI glander, glandouiller; *(travel)* vadrouiller; **they spent three months bumming around in Mexico** ils ont passé trois mois à se balader au Mexique

bumble [ˈbʌmbəl] **VI 1** *(speak incoherently)* bafouiller; **he bumbled through his speech** il a fait un discours décousu **2** *(move clumsily)* **he came bumbling in** il entra, l'air gauche

bumblebee [ˈbʌmbəlbiː] **N** *Entom* bourdon *m*

bumbler [ˈbʌmblə(r)] **N** empoté(e) *m,f*, maladroit(e) *m,f*

bumbling [ˈbʌmblɪŋ] **ADJ** *Fam (person)* empoté, maladroit; *(behaviour)* maladroit; **b. fool** *or* **idiot** andouille *f*

bumboat [ˈbʌmbəʊt] **N** *Naut* canot *m* d'approvisionnement

bumf [bʌmf] **N** *Br Fam* **1** *(documentation)* doc *f* **2** *Pej (useless papers)* paperasse *f* **3** *(toilet paper)* papier *m* cul

bumfreezer ['bʌm,fri:zə(r)] **N** *Br Fam (jacket)* blouson *m* court[□]; *(skirt)* jupe *f* ultra-courte[□], jupe *f* ras la touffe

bumhole ['bʌm,həʊl] **N** *very Fam* trou *m* de balle

bummed [bʌmd] **ADJ** *Am Fam* **to be b.** l'avoir mauvaise; **he's b. (out) with his job** il en a marre de son travail

bummer ['bʌmə(r)] **N** *Fam (bad experience)* poisse *f*; **the film's a real b.** ce film est vraiment nul *ou* un vrai navet; **what a b.!** quelle poisse!; **it's a real b. when you find out…** ça en fiche un coup quand on découvre que…

bump [bʌmp] **N 1** *(lump ▸ on head, in path, road surface)* bosse *f*; **he has a big b. on his head** il a une grosse bosse au crâne; **a b. in the road** une bosse sur la route; **to hit a b.** *(in car)* passer sur une bosse **2** *(blow, knock)* choc *m*, coup *m*; **he felt a b. as he reversed the car into the garage** il a senti un choc en reculant la voiture dans le garage; **her head hit the shelf with a b.** il y a eu un bruit sourd quand elle s'est cogné la tête contre l'étagère; *Fig* **to be brought down to earth with a b.** être ramené brutalement à la réalité **3** *Aviat (air current)* courant *m* ascendant

VT 1 *(hit)* heurter; *(elbow, head, knee)* cogner **2** *Fam* **to be bumped from a flight** perdre sa place sur un vol *(pour cause de sur-réservation)*

VI 1 *(move jerkily)* cahoter; **the old bus bumped along the country roads** le vieil autobus cahotait le long des petites routes **2** *(collide)* se heurter; **the boat bumped against the pier** le bateau a buté contre l'embarcadère **3** *Fam* **to b. and grind** *(dancer, striptease artist)* se déhancher *(en simulant l'acte sexuel)*

ADV things that go b. in the night les spectres *mpl*, les fantômes *mpl*

• **bumps NPL** *Br* **to give sb the (birthday) bumps** = à son anniversaire, tenir à plusieurs quelqu'un par les bras et les jambes, et lui faire toucher le sol un nombre de fois correspondant à son âge, *Can* donner la bascule à qn

▸▸ *Aut* ***bump start*** = démarrage d'un véhicule en le poussant

▸ **bump into VT INSEP** *(object)* rentrer dedans, tamponner; *(person)* rencontrer par hasard, tomber sur; **he bumped into a lamppost** il est rentré dans un réverbère; **I bumped into an old school friend this morning** je suis tombé sur un ancien camarade d'école ce matin

▸ **bump off VT SEP** *Fam (murder)* liquider, supprimer; *(with a gun)* descendre

▸ **bump up VT SEP** *Fam (increase)* faire grimper[□]; *Com (prices)* gonfler[□], faire grimper[□]

bumper ['bʌmpə(r)] **N 1** *Aut* pare-chocs *m inv*; **front/rear b.** pare-chocs *m inv* avant/arrière **2** *Am Rail (on train)* tampon *m*; *(at station)* butoir *m* **3** *(full glass)* rasade *f*

ADJ *(crop, harvest)* exceptionnel, formidable; *Br* **a b. issue** un numéro exceptionnel

▸▸ ***bumper car*** auto *f* tamponneuse, *Belg* autoscooter *m ou f*; *Aut* ***bumper sticker*** autocollant *m (pour voiture)*

bumpety-bump ['bʌmpɪtɪ-] **ADV** *Fam* en cahotant; **my heart went b.** mon cœur a battu à tout rompre

bumph = **bumf**

bumping ['bʌmpɪŋ] **N 1** *(collision)* heurt(s) *m(pl)*, choc(s) *m(pl)*; *(jolting)* cahotement *m* **2** *(of air passenger)* bumping *m*, refus *m* d'embarquer *(suite à sur-réservation)* **3** *Fam* **b. and grinding** *(of dancer, striptease artist)* déhanchements *mpl (simulant l'acte sexuel)*

bumpkin ['bʌmpkɪn] **N** *Fam Pej* plouc *m*, péquenaud *m*

bump-start VT *Aut* démarrer en poussant

bumptious ['bʌmpʃəs] **ADJ** suffisant, prétentieux

bumpy ['bʌmpɪ] *(compar* **bumpier**, *superl* **bumpiest)** **ADJ** *(road)* cahoteux; *(flight, ride)* agité (de secousses); *(surface, wall)* bosselé; **we had a b. flight** nous avons été secoués dans l'avion; *Fig* **we've got a b. ride ahead of us** on va traverser une mauvaise passe

bun [bʌn] **N 1** *(bread)* petit pain *m* (au lait); *Br Fam Fig* **she's got a b. in the oven** elle a un polichinelle dans le tiroir **2** *(in hair)* chignon *m*

• **buns NPL** *Am Fam (buttocks)* fesses[□] *fpl*, miches *fpl*

▸▸ *Br Fam Hum* ***bun fight*** *(gathering)* réception[□] *f*

bunch [bʌntʃ] **N 1** *(of flowers, straw)* bouquet *m*, botte *f*; *(of grapes)* grappe *f*; *(of bananas, dates)* régime *m*; *(of feathers, hair)* touffe *f*; *(of sticks, twigs)* faisceau *m*, poignée *f*; *(of keys)* trousseau *m*; *(of papers)* liasse *f*; *Br Fam* **do you want a b. of fives?** tu veux mon poing sur la gueule?

2 *Fam (of people)* bande[□] *f*; **they're a b. of idiots** c'est une bande d'imbéciles; **her family are a strange b.** elle a une drôle de famille; *Ironic* **you're a fine b.!** quelle équipe vous faites!; **he's the best of a bad b.** c'est le moins mauvais du lot

3 *(of cyclists)* peloton *m*

4 *Fam Ironic (idiom)* **thanks a b.!** merci beaucoup!

VT *(straw, vegetables)* mettre en bottes, botteler; *(flowers)* botteler, mettre en bouquets

• **bunches NPL** *Br* couettes *fpl*; **she wears her hair in bunches** elle porte des couettes

▸ **bunch together VT SEP** mettre ensemble; *(flowers)* botteler, mettre en bouquets

VI *(people)* se serrer, se presser

▸ **bunch up VT SEP** mettre ensemble; *(flowers)* mettre en bouquets, botteler; *(dress, skirt)* retrousser; **your dress is bunched up at the back** le derrière de ta robe est tout retroussé

VI 1 *(group of people)* se serrer **2** *(clothing)* se retrousser

bundle ['bʌndəl] **N 1** *(of clothes, linen)* paquet *m*; *(wrapped in a cloth)* paquet *m*; *Com (of goods)* paquet *m*, ballot *m*; *(of sticks, twigs)* faisceau *f*; *(of banknotes, papers)* liasse *f*; **he's a b. of nerves** c'est un paquet de nerfs; **a b. of firewood** un fagot; *Fam* **a b. of fun** *or* **laughs** marrant, amusant; *Fam* **the trip wasn't exactly a b. of laughs** le voyage n'était pas vraiment marrant; *Ironic* **b. of joy** *(baby)* bout *m* de chou

2 *Fam Fin (large sum of money)* **to cost a b.** coûter bonbon *ou* la peau des fesses; **to make a b.** faire son beurre

3 *Comput* plus produit *m*

4 *Br (idioms) Fam* **to go a b. on sth** s'emballer pour qch; *Fam Ironic* **thanks a b.!** merci beaucoup!

VT 1 *(clothes, linen, goods)* mettre en paquet; *(banknotes, papers)* mettre en liasses; *(sticks, twigs)* mettre en faisceaux; *(firewood)* mettre en fagots; *(straw)* botteler, mettre en bottes

2 *(shove)* **she bundled the papers into the drawer** elle fourra les papiers dans le tiroir; **he was bundled into the car** on l'a poussé dans la voiture brusquement *ou* sans ménagement; **he quickly bundled them out of the room** il les a poussés précipitamment hors de la pièce

3 *Comput* vendre en *ou* par lot

4 *Com & Mktg* **to b. sth with sth** offrir qch en plus de qch; **to come bundled with sth** être livré avec qch; *Comput* **bundled software** logiciel *m* livré avec le matériel

▸ **bundle off VT SEP they bundled me off the train** ils m'ont fait descendre du train en toute hâte; **the children were bundled off to school** les enfants furent envoyés *ou* expédiés à l'école vite fait

▸ **bundle up VT SEP 1** *(tie up)* mettre en paquet **2** *(dress warmly)* emmitoufler; **she bundled the baby up in a warm blanket** elle emmitoufla le bébé dans une grosse couverture

VI s'emmitoufler

bundling ['bʌndəlɪŋ] *Com*

N *(of products)* groupage *m*

▸▸ ***bundling selling*** vente *f* par lots

bung [bʌŋ] **N 1** *(stopper)* bondon *m*, bonde *f* **2** *(hole)* bonde *f* **3** *Fam (bribe)* pot-de-vin[□] *m*

VT 1 *(hole)* boucher **2** *Br Fam (put carelessly)* balancer; **just b. it in the bin** fiche-le à la poubelle **3** *Br Fam (add)* rajouter[□]; **b. it on the bill** rajoutez-le sur la note; **we'll b. in a few extras** on va rajouter quelques petits extras

▸ **bung up VT SEP** *Br Fam* boucher[□]; **my nose is/my eyes are bunged up** j'ai le nez bouché/les yeux gonflés

bungalow ['bʌŋgələʊ] **N** *(one-storey house)* maison *f* sans étage; *(in India)* bungalow *m*

bungee ['bʌndʒi:] **N** *(cord)* tendeur *m*

▸▸ ***bungee cord*** tendeur *m*; ***bungee jump*** saut *m* à l'élastique; ***bungee jumping*** saut *m* à l'élastique

bunghole ['bʌŋhəʊl] **N** bonde *f*

bungle ['bʌŋgəl] **VT** gâcher; **you bungled it** *or* **the job** tu as tout gâché

N *Br* **to make a b. of sth** gâcher qch

bungler ['bʌŋglə(r)] **N** incapable *mf*

bungling ['bʌŋglɪŋ] **ADJ** *(person)* incompétent, incapable; *(action)* maladroit, gauche

N incompétence *f*, *Fam* bousillage *m*; **your b. has cost us the contract** tes bourdes nous ont fait perdre le contrat

bunion ['bʌnjən] **N** oignon *m (cor)*

bunk [bʌŋk] **N 1** *(berth)* couchette *f*; *(bed)* lit *m* **2** *Br Fam* **to do a b.** se tirer, se faire la malle **3** *Fam (nonsense)* foutaises *fpl*; **that's a load of b.** ce sont des foutaises

VI *Fam* **1** *(sleep)* coucher[□]; *Am (spend the night)* dormir[□], passer la nuit[□] **2** *(escape)* se tailler

▸▸ ***bunk bed*** lit *m* superposé

▸ **bunk down VI** coucher *(dans un lit de fortune)*

▸ **bunk off VT INSEP to b. off school** sécher les cours

VI *Br Fam* **1** *(scram)* décamper, filer **2** *(from school)* sécher

bunker ['bʌŋkə(r)] **N 1** *Mil* blockhaus *m*, bunker *m*; **he was hiding in an underground b.** il se cachait dans un bunker enterré; **nuclear b.** abri *m* antiatomique **2** *(for coal)* coffre *m*; *Naut* soute *f* **3** *Golf* bunker *m*

VT 1 *Naut (coal, oil, ship)* mettre en soute **2** *Golf* envoyer la balle dans un bunker

bunkhouse ['bʌŋkhaus, *pl* -hauzɪz] **N** *Am* baraquement *m* (pour ouvriers)

bunkum ['bʌŋkəm] **N** *(UNCOUNT) Fam (nonsense)* foutaises *fpl*

bunny ['bʌnɪ] **N** *Fam* **b. (rabbit)** (petit) lapin[□] *m*, Jeannot lapin *m*

▸▸ *Fam* ***bunny boiler*** = femme obsessionnelle qui poursuit quelqu'un de ses assiduités; ***bunny girl*** hôtesse *f* de boîte de nuit *(habillée en lapin)*

Bunsen burner ['bʌnsən-] **N** (bec *m*) Bunsen *m*

bunt [bʌnt] **N** coup *m* retenu

VT *Sport* frapper doucement

VI *Sport* frapper doucement la balle

bunting ['bʌntɪŋ] **N 1** *Tex (fabric)* étamine *f* **2** *(UNCOUNT) (flags)* fanions *mpl*, drapeaux *mpl*; **the building was decorated with blue and white b.** le bâtiment était pavoisé de drapeaux bleus et blancs

buoy [*Br* bɔɪ, *Am* 'bu:ɪ] **N** *Naut* bouée *f*, balise *f*

VT *(waterway)* baliser; *(vessel, obstacle)* marquer d'une bouée

▸ **buoy up VT SEP 1** *Naut* faire flotter, maintenir à flot **2** *Fig (support, sustain)* soutenir; *(person)* remonter; *Fin (currency)* soutenir, maintenir; **her son's visit buoyed her up** *or* **buoyed up her spirits** la visite de son fils l'a remontée *ou* lui a remonté le moral

buoyancy ['bɔɪənsɪ] **N 1** *(ability to float)* flottabilité *f*; *Chem (of gas, liquid)* poussée *f* **2** *Fig (resilience)* ressort *m*, force *f* morale; *(cheerfulness)* entrain *m*, allant *m* **3** *Fin (of economy, sector)* robustesse *f*, vigueur *f*; *(of prices, currency)* stabilité *f*; *St Exch (of market)* fermeté *f*

▸▸ ***buoyancy aid*** = tout objet (bouée, flotteur, gilet etc) utilisé pour favoriser la flottabilité; ***buoyancy tank*** réservoir *m* de flottabilité

buoyant ['bɔɪənt] **ADJ 1** *(floatable)* flottable, capable de flotter; *(causing to float)* qui fait flotter; **sea water is very b.** l'eau de mer porte très bien **2** *Fig (cheerful)* plein d'allant *ou* d'entrain; *(mood)* gai, allègre; **her spirits were b. that morning** elle était pleine d'allant *ou* d'entrain ce matin-là **3** *Fin (economy, sector)* sain, robuste; *(prices, currency)* stable; *St Exch (market)* ferme

buoyantly ['bɔɪəntlɪ] **ADV** *(walk)* d'un pas allègre; *(float, rise)* légèrement; *(speak)* avec allant, avec entrain

BUPA ['bu:pə] **N** *(abbr* **British United Provident Association)** = association d'assurance-maladie privée

bupkis ['bʌpkɪs] **N** *Am Fam* que dalle; **he knows b. about it** il y connaît que dalle

bur [bɜː(r)] **N** *Bot* bardane *f*

Burberry® ['bɜːbərɪ] **N** *Br* gabardine *f*, imperméable *m* Burberry®

burble ['bɜːbəl] **VI 1** *(liquid)* glouglouter, faire glouglou; *(stream)* murmurer **2** *Pej (person)* jacasser; **he's always burbling on about moral values** il est toujours à jacasser *ou* dégoiser sur les valeurs morales

N 1 *(of a liquid)* glouglou *m*; *(of a stream)* murmure *m* **2** *Pej (chatter)* jacasserie *f*, jacassement *m*

burbot ['bɜːbət] **N** *Ich* lotte *f*

burbs [bɜːbz] **NPL** *Am Fam* **the b.** la banlieue□; **they live in the b.** ils habitent en banlieue

burden ['bɜːdən] **N 1** *Formal (heavy weight, load)* fardeau *m*, charge *f*

2 *Fig (heavy responsibility, strain)* fardeau *m*, charge *f*; **to be a b. to sb** être un fardeau pour qn; **his guilt was a heavy b. to bear** sa culpabilité était un lourd fardeau; **to increase/to relieve the tax b.** augmenter/alléger le fardeau *ou* le poids des impôts; *Law* **the b. of proof** la charge de la preuve; *Law* **the b. of proof rests with him** c'est à lui qu'il incombe d'apporter des preuves

3 *Naut* tonnage *m*, jauge *f*

4 *Br Mus (chorus, refrain)* refrain *m*; *Fig (theme, central idea)* fond *m*, substance *f*; **what is the main b. of her argument?** quel est le point essentiel de son argument?

VT 1 *(weigh down)* charger; **to be burdened with sth** être chargé de qch; *Fig* **to b. sb with taxes** accabler qn d'impôts **2** *(trouble)* ennuyer, importuner; **I don't want to b. you with my problems** je ne veux pas vous ennuyer avec mes problèmes; **she was burdened with guilt** elle était rongée par un sentiment de culpabilité

burdensome ['bɜːdənsəm] **ADJ** *Formal (load)* pesant; *Fin (taxes)* lourd

burdock ['bɜːdɒk] **N** *Bot* bardane *f*

bureau ['bjʊərəʊ] *(pl* **bureaus** *or* **bureaux** [-rəʊz]*)* **N 1** *Admin* service *m*, office *m*; *Com (in private enterprise)* bureau *m* **2** *Br (desk)* secrétaire *m*, bureau *m* **3** *Am (chest of drawers)* commode *f*

▸▸ ***bureau de change*** bureau *m* de change

bureaucracy [bjʊə'rɒkrəsɪ] *(pl* **bureaucracies***)* **N** bureaucratie *f*

bureaucrat ['bjʊərəkræt] **N** bureaucrate *mf*

bureaucratic [ˌbjʊərə'krætɪk] **ADJ** bureaucratique

burette, *Am* **buret** [bjʊ'ret] **N** *Chem* éprouvette *f* graduée, burette *f*

burg [bɜːg] **N** *Am Fam (village)* bled *m*; *(town)* ville□ *f*

burgeon ['bɜːdʒən] **VI** bourgeonner; *(leaf, flower)* éclore

burgeoning ['bɜːdʒənɪŋ] **ADJ** *(industry, population)* en expansion, en plein essor; **a b. talent** un talent en herbe; **the b. movement for independence** le mouvement naissant pour l'indépendance

burger ['bɜːgə(r)] **N** hamburger *m*

▸▸ ***burger bar*** fast-food *m (où l'on sert des hamburgers)*

burgess ['bɜːdʒɪs] **N** *Hist (elected representative)* député *m*, représentant *m*; *(citizen)* bourgeois (e) *m,f*

burgher ['bɜːgə(r)] **N** *Hist* bourgeois(e) *m,f*

burglar ['bɜːglə(r)] **N** cambrioleur(euse) *m,f*

▸▸ ***burglar alarm*** alarme *f* antivol

burglarize ['bɜːgləraɪz] **VT** *Am* cambrioler

burglary ['bɜːglərɪ] *(pl* **burglaries***)* **N** cambriolage *m*

burgle ['bɜːgəl] **VT** cambrioler

Burgundian [bɜː'gʌndɪən] **N** Bourguignon (onne) *m,f*

ADJ bourguignon

Burgundy ['bɜːgəndɪ] **N 1** *(region)* Bourgogne *f* **2** *(wine)* bourgogne *m*

• **burgundy N** *(colour)* bordeaux *m* **ADJ** *(colour)* bordeaux

burial ['berɪəl] **N** enterrement *m*, inhumation *f*; **a Christian b.** une sépulture ecclésiastique; **he was denied a Christian b.** il n'a même pas eu droit à un enterrement convenable

▸▸ ***burial chamber*** caveau *m*; ***burial ground*** cimetière *m*; ***burial mound*** tumulus *m*; ***burial place*** (lieu *m* de) sépulture *f*

burin ['bjʊərɪn] **N** *Tech* burin *m*

burk = **berk**

burka, burkha ['bɜːkə] **N** burka *f*, burqa *f*

Burkina-Faso [bɜːˌkiːnə'fæsəʊ] **N** Burkina *m*

burlap ['bɜːlæp] **N** *Tex* toile *f* à sac, gros canevas *m*

burlesque [bɜː'lesk] **N 1** *Literature & Theat* burlesque *m*, parodie *f* **2** *Am (bawdy comedy)* revue *f* déshabillée, striptease *m*

ADJ burlesque

VT parodier

burliness ['bɜːlɪnɪs] **N** *(of person)* forte carrure *f*

burly ['bɜːlɪ] *(compar* **burlier**, *superl* **burliest***)* **ADJ** de forte carrure

Burma ['bɜːmə] **N** *Formerly* Birmanie *f*

Burmese [ˌbɜː'miːz] *(pl* **inv***)* **N 1** *(person)* Birman (e) *m,f* **2** *(language)* birman *m*

ADJ birman

COMP *(embassy)* de Birmanie; *(history)* de la Birmanie; *(teacher)* de birman

▸▸ ***Burmese cat*** burmese *m*, chat *f* birman

BURN [bɜːn]

N	
• brûlure **1**	• combustion **2**
VI	
• brûler **1, 2**	• exploser **3**
VT	
• brûler **1**	• graver **2**

(Br pt & pp **burned** *or* **burnt** [bɜːnt], *Am pt & pp* **burned***)*

N 1 *(injury)* brûlure *f*

2 *Tech (in engine)* (durée *f* de) combustion *f*

3 *Fam* **to go for the b.** *(when exercising)* forcer jusqu'à ce que ça fasse mal□

VI 1 *(gen)* brûler; **there was a lovely fire burning in the sitting-room** un beau feu brûlait *ou* flambait au salon; **I can't get the wood to b.** je n'arrive pas à faire brûler *ou* flamber le bois; **the toast is burning** le pain grillé est en train de brûler; **she could see a cigarette burning in the dark** elle pouvait voir une cigarette qui brûlait *ou* se consumait dans l'obscurité; **this material won't b.** ce tissu est ininflammable; **the church burned to the ground** l'église a été réduite en cendres

2 *Fig (face, person)* **my face was burning** *(with embarrassment)* j'avais le visage en feu, j'étais tout rouge; **the wind made her face b.** le vent lui brûlait le visage; **I'm burning** *(from sun)* je brûle; *(from fever)* je suis brûlant, je brûle; **she burns easily** elle attrape facilement des coups de soleil; **she was burning with anger/impatience** elle bouillait de colère/d'impatience; **she was burning for adventure** elle brûlait du désir d'aventure

3 *Tech (mixture in engine)* exploser

VT 1 *(paper, logs, food)* brûler; *(car, crop, forest)* brûler, incendier; **to b. coal/oil/gas** *(boiler)* marcher au charbon/au mazout/au gaz; **three people were burnt to death** trois personnes sont mortes carbonisées *ou* ont été brûlées vives; **to be burnt alive** être brûlé vif; **suspected witches were burnt at the stake** les femmes soupçonnées de sorcellerie étaient brûlées vives; **his cigarette burnt a hole in the carpet** sa cigarette a fait un trou dans la moquette; **did you b. yourself?** est-ce que tu t'es brûlé?; **I burnt my mouth drinking hot tea** je me suis brûlé (la langue) en buvant du thé chaud; **I burnt my shoulders on holiday** j'ai attrapé des coups de soleil sur les épaules pendant les vacances; **I've burnt the potatoes** j'ai laissé brûler les pommes de terre; **the house was burnt to the ground** la maison fut réduite en cendres *ou* brûla entièrement; *Fig* **to b. one's boats** *or* **bridges** brûler ses vaisseaux *ou* les ponts; *Fig* **to b. one's fingers, to get one's fingers burnt** se brûler les doigts; *Fig* **to have money to b.** avoir de l'argent à ne pas savoir qu'en faire; **money burns a hole in his pocket** l'argent lui file entre les doigts

2 *Comput (CD)* graver

3 *Am Fam (swindle)* arnaquer

4 *Am Fam (anger)* foutre en rogne

▸▸ ***burn rate*** burn rate *m*

▸ **burn down VI 1** *(be destroyed by fire)* brûler complètement; **the building burned down** le bâtiment fut complètement détruit par le feu *ou* brûla complètement **2** *(die down)* **the fire in the stove has burned down** le feu dans le poêle est presque éteint; *(grow smaller)* diminuer, baisser; **the candle has burned down** la bougie a diminué

VT SEP *(building)* détruire par le feu, incendier

▸ **burn off VT SEP 1** *(vegetation)* brûler, détruire par le feu; *(gas)* brûler; *(paint)* décaper au chalumeau **2** *(calories)* brûler; **to b. off some energy** se dépenser

▸ **burn out VT SEP 1** *(destroy by fire* ▸ *building)* détruire par le feu **2** *(wear out* ▸ *bulb)* griller; *(*▸ *fuse)* faire sauter; *(*▸ *engine)* griller; *Fig* **to b. oneself out** s'épuiser **3** *(die down)* diminuer, éteindre; **after twelve hours the forest fire burnt itself out** au bout de douze heures l'incendie de forêt s'est éteint

VI *(bulb)* griller; *(fuse)* sauter; *(brakes, engine)* griller; *(candle, fire)* s'éteindre

▸ **burn up VT SEP 1** *(destroy by fire)* brûler

2 *Fig (person* ▸ *consume)* brûler, dévorer; **the desire for revenge was burning him up** il était dévoré par le désir de se venger

3 *(consume)* **this car burns up a lot of petrol** cette voiture consomme beaucoup d'essence; *Physiol* **to b. up a lot of calories/energy** dépenser *ou* brûler beaucoup de calories/d'énergie

4 *Am Fam (make angry)* **it really burns me up to see you like this** ça me rend dingue de te voir comme ça

VI 1 *(fire)* flamber **2** *Aviat* se consumer, se désintégrer

burner ['bɜːnə(r)] **N 1** *(on a stove)* brûleur *m*; *(on a lamp)* bec *m* **2** *(for essential oils)* brûle-parfums *m* **3** *Comput* graveur *m*

burn-in N *Comput (of machine)* rodage *m*

burning ['bɜːnɪŋ] **ADJ 1** *(on fire)* en flammes, en feu; *(arrow, torch)* enflammé; *Bible* **the b. bush** le buisson ardent

2 *(hot)* ardent, brûlant; **I have a b. sensation in my stomach** j'ai des brûlures d'estomac

3 *Fig (intense)* ardent, brûlant; **he had a b. desire to be a writer** il désirait ardemment être écrivain; **a b. thirst** une soif brûlante

4 *(crucial, vital)* brûlant; **a b. issue** une question brûlante

ADV b. hot coals des charbons; **her forehead is b. hot** elle a le front brûlant

N 1 *(sensation, smell)* **a smell of b.** une odeur de brûlé; **can anyone smell b.?** ça sent le brûlé ou quoi?; **he felt a b. in his chest** il sentit une brûlure à la poitrine **2** *(destruction by fire)* **he witnessed the b. of hundreds of books** il a été témoin de l'autodafé de centaines de livres **3** *Hist* **b. (at the stake)** supplice *m* du bûcher

burnish ['bɜːnɪʃ] **VT 1** *Metal* brunir, polir **2** *Literary* lustrer

N 1 *Metal* brunissure *f* **2** *Literary (shine)* brillant *m*, lustre *m*

burnisher ['bɜːnɪʃə(r)] **N** *Metal* **1** *(person)* brunisseur(euse) *m,f* **2** *(instrument)* brunissoir *m*, polissoir *m*

burnishing ['bɜːnɪʃɪŋ] **N** *Metal* brunissage *m*, polissage *m*

burnous, burnouse [bɜː'nuːs] **N** burnous *m*

burnout ['bɜːnaʊt] **N 1** *Astron (of rocket)* = arrêt par suite d'épuisement du combustible **2** *Elec* **what caused the b.?** qu'est-ce qui a fait griller les circuits? **3** *(exhaustion)* épuisement *m* total

Burns Supper [bɜːnz-] **N**

BURNS SUPPER

Le Burns Supper est une tradition écossaise vieille de deux cents ans, qui commémore la naissance du poète national, Robert Burns. Les célébrations prennent différentes formes, depuis la réunion d'amis à la bonne franquette jusqu'au dîner en grande cérémonie. Cette tradition fut initiée par les amis de Burns quelques années après sa mort en 1796 et ses composantes sont demeurées inchangées depuis. Le haggis, plat national écossais, est placé dans un grand plat et porté par une personne elle-même précédée par un joueur de cornemuse; le plat est alors déposé sur la table de l'hôte. L'un des invités récite le poème de Burns "Address to a Haggis". Le reste de la soirée est accompagné de lectures de poésie et de discours, le tout copieusement arrosé de whisky.

burnt [bɜ:nt] *pt & pp of* **burn**
ADJ **1** *(charred)* brûlé, carbonisé **2** *(sunburnt)* brûlé; **my nose is a bit b.** j'ai le nez un peu brûlé **3** *(dark)* **b. orange/red** orange/rouge foncé
▸▸ ***burnt offering*** *Rel (sacrifice)* holocauste *m*; *Hum (food)* plat *m* calciné *ou* carbonisé

burnt-out ADJ **1** *(destroyed by fire)* incendié, brûlé **2** *Fam (person)* lessivé, vidé; **she was b. by 30** elle était usée avant (l'âge de) 30 ans **3** *Tech (bearings)* grippé; *Elec (coil, light bulb)* grillé

burp [bɜ:p] *Fam* N rot *m*; **"cheers," he said with a b.** "à ta santé", dit-il en rotant
VI roter
VT **to b. a baby** faire faire son rot à un bébé

burqa = **burka**

burr [bɜ:(r)] N **1** *Metal (rough edge)* barbe *f*, bavure *f*
2 *Tech (tool)* fraise *f*
3 *Bot (on tree trunk)* broussin *m*; *(seed-case)* bardane *f*
4 *Ling (West Country accent)* grasseyement *m*; **he speaks with a soft b.** il a un léger accent du terroir

burro ['bʊrəʊ] N *Am* baudet *m*

burrow ['bʌrəʊ] N terrier *m*
VT **1** *(of person)* creuser; *(of animal, insect)* creuser, fouir; **he burrowed his way underneath the prison wall** il a creusé un tunnel sous le mur de la prison **2** *Fig (nestle)* enfouir; **the cat burrowed its head into my shoulder** le chat a blotti sa tête contre mon épaule
VI **1** *(dig)* creuser; **they found earthworms burrowing through the soil** ils ont trouvé des vers de terre qui creusaient des galeries dans le sol **2** *(search)* fouiller; **I've been burrowing through the files for clues** j'ai cherché *ou* fouillé dans les dossiers pour trouver des indices **3** *(nestle)* s'enfouir, s'enfoncer; **she burrowed under the sheets** elle s'est enfouie sous les draps

burrowing ['bʌrəʊɪŋ] ADJ *(animal)* fouisseur; *(insect)* fossoyeur, mineur

bursar ['bɜ:sə(r)] N **1** *Br Fin (treasurer)* intendant (e) *m,f*, économe *mf* **2** *Scot Univ (student)* boursier(ère) *m,f*

bursary ['bɜ:sərɪ] *(pl* **bursaries)** N **1** *Br Fin (treasury)* intendance *f*, économat *m* **2** *Univ (grant, scholarship)* bourse *f* (d'études)

bursitis [bɜ:'saɪtɪs] N *Med* bursite *f*; **I have b. in my shoulder** j'ai une bursite à l'épaule

BURST [bɜ:st]

N
• éclatement **1** • explosion **1, 2**
• éclat **2** • jaillissement **2**
VI
• crever, éclater **1** • entrer brusquement **2**
VT
• crever, faire éclater

(pt & pp **burst)**
N **1** *(explosion)* éclatement *m*, explosion *f*; *(puncture)* éclatement *m*, crevaison *f*
2 *(sudden eruption* ▸ *of laughter)* éclat *m*; *(*▸ *of emotion)* accès *m*, explosion *f*; *(*▸ *of ideas)* jaillissement *m*; *(*▸ *of thunder)* coup *m*; *(*▸ *of flame)* jet *m*, jaillissement *m*; *(*▸ *of applause)* salve *f*; *Mil* **a b. of gunfire** une rafale; **he had a sudden b. of energy** il a eu un sursaut d'énergie; **to put on** *or* **to have a sudden b. of speed** faire une pointe de vitesse, accélérer soudainement; **a b. of activity** une poussée d'activité; **to work in bursts** travailler par à-coups
VI **1** *(break, explode* ▸ *balloon, paper bag)* éclater; *Med (*▸ *abscess, bubble)* crever; *Aut (*▸ *tyre)* crever, éclater; *(*▸ *bottle)* éclater, voler en éclats; *(*▸ *dam)* éclater, céder; **to be bursting with pride** crever d'orgueil; **to be bursting with health** déborder de santé; **to be bursting with impatience** bouillir d'impatience; **I was bursting to tell him** je mourais d'envie de le lui dire; *Fig* **his heart felt as if it would b. with joy/grief** il crut que son cœur allait éclater de joie/se briser de chagrin; *Fam* **to be bursting (for the toilet)** avoir terriblement envie d'aller aux toilettes; *Hum* **I'll b. if I eat any more** je vais éclater si je mange une bouchée de plus
2 *(enter, move suddenly)* **two policemen b. into the house** deux policiers ont fait irruption dans la maison; **she b. through the door** elle est entrée brusquement; **the front door b. open** la porte d'entrée s'est ouverte brusquement; **the sun suddenly b. through the clouds** le soleil perça *ou* apparut soudain à travers les nuages
VT *(balloon, bubble)* crever, faire éclater; *(pipe)* faire éclater; *(boiler)* faire éclater, faire sauter; *Aut (tyre)* crever, faire éclater; *Med (abscess)* crever, percer; **the river is about to b. its banks** le fleuve est sur le point de déborder; **we've got a b. pipe** *(in house)* nous avons un tuyau qui a éclaté; **to b. a blood vessel** se faire éclater une veine, se rompre un vaisseau sanguin; *Br Fam Hum* **don't b. a blood vessel to get it done** ce n'est pas la peine de te crever pour finir, ce n'est pas la peine de te tuer à la tâche

▸**burst in** VI *(enter violently)* faire irruption; *(interrupt conversation)* interrompre brutalement la discussion; *(intrude)* entrer précipitamment; **it was very rude of you to b. in on us like that** c'était très mal élevé de ta part de faire irruption chez nous comme ça

▸**burst into** VT INSEP *(begin suddenly)* **to b. into laughter** éclater de rire; **to b. into tears** éclater en sanglots, fondre en larmes; **to b. into song** se mettre à chanter; **to b. into flames** prendre feu, s'enflammer

▸**burst open** VT SEP *(door* ▸ *open suddenly)* ouvrir brusquement; *(smash open)* enfoncer, briser; *(cover, lock)* faire sauter
VI *(of door)* s'ouvrir brusquement

▸**burst out** VI *(leave suddenly)* sortir précipitamment; **two men suddenly b. out of the room** deux hommes sortirent en trombe de la pièce
VT INSEP *(exclaim)* s'exclamer, s'écrier; **to b. out laughing** éclater de rire; **to b. out crying** fondre en larmes; **they all b. out singing** ils se sont tous mis à chanter d'un coup; **"I love you," he b. out** "je t'aime", lança-t-il

bursting ['bɜ:stɪŋ] ADJ **1** *(full)* plein à craquer; **to be b. at the seams** se défaire aux coutures, se découdre; *Fig* **the place was b. at the seams (with people)** l'endroit était plein à craquer; **to be b. with joy/pride** déborder de joie/d'orgueil; **to be b. with health** péter la santé **2** *(longing, yearning)* **to be b. to do sth** mourir d'envie de faire qch; **they were b. to tell us the news** ils mouraient d'envie de nous apprendre la nouvelle
• **to bursting** ADV **to be full to b.** être plein à craquer

burton ['bɜ:tən] N *Br Fam Old-fashioned* **to be gone for a b.** *(broken)* être fichu; *(lost)* avoir disparu; *(dead)* avoir cassé sa pipe; *(fallen)* avoir ramassé une bûche

Burundi [bʊ'rʊndɪ] N Burundi *m*

bury ['berɪ] *(pt & pp* **buried)** VT **1** *(in the ground)* enterrer, *Formal* inhumer; *(in water)* immerger; **to be buried alive** être enterré vivant; **he was buried at sea** son corps a été immergé en haute mer; **buried treasure** trésor *m* enterré *ou* enfoui; *Fig* **she's buried two husbands already** elle a déjà enterré deux maris; **we agreed to b. our differences** nous avons convenu d'oublier *ou* d'enterrer nos différends; *Fig* **to b. the hatchet** enterrer la hache de guerre, faire la paix
2 *(of snow, landslide* ▸ *town, house)* ensevelir; **she buried her feet in the sand** elle a enfoncé ses pieds dans le sable; *Fig* **to b. one's head in the sand** faire l'autruche
3 *(hide)* **she buried her face in the pillow** elle enfouit *ou* enfonça son visage dans l'oreiller; **to b. one's face in one's hands** enfouir son visage dans ses mains; **he always has his nose buried in a book** il a toujours le nez fourré dans un livre; *Fig* **to b. oneself in the country** s'enterrer à la campagne; **long-buried memories began to surface** des souvenirs oubliés depuis longtemps commencèrent à refaire surface; **it's buried in a drawer somewhere** c'est enfoui dans un tiroir quelque part
4 *(occupy)* **to b. oneself in (one's) work** se plonger dans son travail
5 *(thrust, plunge* ▸ *knife)* enfoncer, plonger; **he buried his hands in his pockets** il a fourré les mains dans ses poches

bus [bʌs] *(pl* **buses** *or* **busses**, *pt & pp* **bused** *or* **bussed**, *cont* **busing** *or* **bussing)** N **1** *(vehicle)* bus *m*, autobus *m*; *Am (coach)* car *m*; **by b.** en bus **2** *Br Fam (old car)* (vieille) bagnole *f*, guimbarde *f*
3 *Comput* bus *m*
COMP *(service, strike, ticket)* d'autobus, de bus
VI **we can walk or b. home** nous pouvons rentrer à pied ou en autobus
VT **1** *(transport)* emmener en autobus; **the children are bussed to school** les enfants vont à l'école en autobus **2** *Am (in restaurant)* **to b. tables** travailler comme aide-serveur; **he busses tables at the weekends** il travaille comme aide-serveur le week-end
▸▸ *Mktg* ***bus advertising*** publicité *f* sur les autobus; *Comput* ***bus board*** carte *f* bus; *Br* ***bus conductor*** receveur(euse) *m,f* d'autobus; *Comput* ***bus controller*** contrôleur *m* de bus; ***bus depot*** dépôt *m* d'autobus; *(long-distance bus station)* gare *f* routière; ***bus driver*** conducteur(trice) *m,f* d'autobus; ***bus lane*** voie *f ou* couloir *m* d'autobus; *Mktg* ***bus mailing*** publipostage *m* groupé, multipostage *m*; ***bus route*** itinéraire *m ou* trajet *m* d'autobus; **are you on a b. route?** est-ce qu'il y a un bus qui passe près de chez toi?; ***bus shelter*** Abribus® *m*; ***bus station*** gare *f* routière; ***bus stop*** arrêt *m* d'autobus *ou* de bus; ***bus way*** voie *f ou* couloir *m* d'autobus

busbar ['bʌsbɑ:(r)] N *Comput & Elec* bus *m*

busby ['bʌzbɪ] *(pl* **busbies)** N *Br Mil* bonnet *m* de hussard

bush [bʊʃ] N **1** *(shrub)* buisson *m*, arbuste *m*; **the children hid in the bushes** les enfants se cachèrent dans les fourrés; *Fig* **a b. of black hair** une tignasse de cheveux noirs
2 *Geog (in Africa, Australia)* **the b.** la brousse
3 *Aut & Tech* bague *f*; *(between bearing and shaft)* coussinet *m*
4 *Vulg (woman's pubic hair)* barbu *m*
ADV *Austr* **to go b.** aller dans la brousse
▸▸ ***bush jacket*** saharienne *f*; *Am Sport* ***bush league*** = petite équipe locale de base-ball; ***bush telegraph*** téléphone *m* de brousse; *Br Fig Hum (grapevine)* téléphone *m* arabe

bushbaby ['bʊʃ,beɪbɪ] N *Zool* galago *m*

bushed [bʊʃt] ADJ *Fam (exhausted)* crevé, claqué

bushel ['bʊʃəl] N **1** *(measure)* boisseau *m*; *Fig* **to hide one's light under a b.** cacher son talent **2** *Am Fam (great amount)* grande quantité *f*; **to have bushels of time** avoir vachement de temps; **there were bushels of people** il y avait des tas de gens

bushfire ['bʊʃ,faɪə(r)] N feu *m* de brousse

bushing ['bʊʃɪŋ] N *(UNCOUNT) Tech* bague *f*

Bushism ['bʊʃɪzəm] N *Fam* = faute de langue ou expression maladroite attribuée au président américain George W. Bush

Bushite ['bʊʃaɪt] *Pol* N = partisan de la politique menée par George W. Bush
ADJ = partisan de George W. Bush et de sa politique

Bushman ['bʊʃmən] *(pl* **inv** *or* **Bushmen** [-mən]) N *(in southern Africa)* Bochiman *m*

bushman ['bʊʃmən] *(pl* **bushmen** [-mən]) N *Austr & NZ* broussard *m*

bushmeat ['bʊʃmi:t] N = viande de gibier d'Afrique

bushwhacker ['bʊʃ,wækə(r)] N **1** *Am & Austr (backwoodsman)* broussard(e) *m,f* **2** *Am Mil (guerrilla)* guérillero *m*

bushy ['bʊʃɪ] *(compar* **bushier**, *superl* **bushiest)** ADJ **1** *(area)* broussailleux **2** *(tree)* touffu; *(beard, eyebrows, hair)* touffu, fourni

busily ['bɪzɪlɪ] ADV activement; **to be b. engaged in sth/in doing sth** être très occupé à qch/à faire qch; **she is b. collecting material for her next book** elle est très occupée à rassembler des matériaux pour son prochain livre; **he was b. scrib-**

bling in his notebook il griffonnait sur son calepin d'un air affairé

business ['bɪznɪs] N 1 *Com (company, firm)* affaire *f*, entreprise *f*; small businesses petites entreprises; he's got a mail-order b. il a une affaire *ou* entreprise de vente par correspondance; would you like to have *or* to run your own b.? aimeriez-vous travailler à votre compte?; b. for sale *(on sign, in advertisement)* commerce à vendre

2 *(UNCOUNT) Com & Ind (trade)* affaires *fpl*; *(commerce)* commerce *m*; b. is good/bad les affaires vont bien/mal; b. is slow les affaires ne vont pas; how's b.? comment vont les affaires?; b. as usual *(sign)* ouvert; hours of b. *(sign)* heures d'ouverture; to go to London on b. aller à Londres pour affaires; a profitable piece of b. une affaire rentable *ou* qui rapporte; we have lost b. to foreign competitors nous avons perdu une partie de notre clientèle au profit de concurrents étrangers; we can help you to increase your b. nous pouvons vous aider à augmenter votre chiffre d'affaires; the travel b. les métiers *ou* le secteur du tourisme; she's in the fashion b. elle est dans la mode; my b. is pharmaceuticals je travaille dans l'industrie pharmaceutique; she knows her b. elle connaît son métier; he's in b. il est dans les affaires; this firm has been in b. for 25 years cette entreprise tourne depuis 25 ans; she's in b. for herself elle travaille à son compte; to set up in b. ouvrir un commerce; he wants to go into b. il veut travailler dans les affaires; what's his line of b.?, what b. is he in? qu'est-ce qu'il fait (comme métier)?; the best in the b. le meilleur de tous; I'm not in the b. of solving your problems ce n'est pas à moi de résoudre tes problèmes; this shop will be open for b. from tomorrow ce magasin ouvrira demain; these high interest rates will put us out of b. ces taux d'intérêt élevés vont nous obliger à fermer; to go out of b. cesser une activité, faire faillite; he's got no b. sense il n'a pas le sens des affaires; she has a good head for b. elle a le sens des affaires; to do b. with sb faire affaire *ou* des affaires avec qn; *Fig* he's a man we can do b. with c'est un homme avec lequel nous pouvons traiter; a shop that does good b. un commerce qui marche bien; I've come on b. je suis venu pour le travail *ou* pour affaires; big b. is running the country les grandes entreprises gouvernent le pays; selling weapons is big b. la vente d'armes rapporte beaucoup d'argent; from now on I'll take my b. elsewhere désormais j'irai voir *ou* je m'adresserai ailleurs; they've put a lot of b. our way ils nous ont donné beaucoup de travail; it's bad b. to refuse credit c'est mauvais en affaires de refuser le crédit; *Univ* a degree in b., a b. degree un diplôme de gestion; let's get down to b. passons aux choses sérieuses; (now) we're in b.! nous voilà partis!; to talk b. parler affaires

3 *(concern)* it's my (own) b. if I decide not to go c'est mon affaire *ou* cela ne regarde que moi si je décide de ne pas y aller; what b. is it of yours? est-ce que cela vous regarde?; it's none of your b. cela ne vous regarde pas; tell him to mind his own b. dis-lui de se mêler de ses affaires; I was just walking along, minding my own b., when… je marchais tranquillement dans la rue quand…; what's your b. (with him)? que (lui) voulez-vous?; I'll make it my b. to find out je m'occuperai d'en savoir plus; people going about their b. des gens vaquant à leurs occupations; it's/it's not my b. to… c'est/ce n'est pas à moi de…; you had no b. reading that letter vous n'aviez pas à lire cette lettre; I could see she meant b. je voyais qu'elle ne plaisantait pas; I soon sent him about his b. je l'ai vite envoyé promener; *Fam* he drank like nobody's b. il buvait comme un trou; *Fam* she worked like nobody's b. to get it finished elle a travaillé comme un forçat pour tout terminer; *Br Fam* it's the b. *(excellent)* c'est impec

4 *(matter, task)* the b. of this meeting is the training budget l'ordre du jour de cette réunion est le budget de formation; any other b. *(on agenda)* points *mpl* divers; any other b.? d'autres questions à l'ordre du jour?; she had important b. to discuss elle avait à parler d'affaires importantes; that investigation of police misconduct was a dirty b. l'enquête sur la bavure policière a été une sale affaire; it's a bad *or* sad *or* sorry b. c'est une bien triste affaire; this strike b. has gone on long enough cette histoire de grève a assez duré; I'm tired of the whole b. je suis las de toute cette histoire

5 *(rigmarole)* it was a real b. getting tickets for the concert ça a été toute une affaire pour avoir des billets pour le concert

6 *Fam Euph* the dog did his b. and ran off le chien a fait ses besoins et a détalé

COMP d'affaires

▸▸ *Banking* ***business account*** compte *m* professionnel *ou* commercial; ***business accounting*** comptabilité *f* commerciale; ***business activity*** activité *f* commerciale; ***business acumen*** sens *m* des affaires; ***business address*** adresse *f* professionnelle; ***business administration*** gestion *f* commerciale; ***business angel*** business angel *m*, investisseur *m* providentiel; ***business area*** quartier *m* des affaires; ***business associate*** associé(e) *m,f*; ***business bank*** banque *f* d'affaires; ***business banking*** operations *fpl* des banques d'affaires; ***business buyer*** acheteur(euse) *m,f* industriel (elle); *Com* ***business card*** carte *f* de visite; ***business centre*** centre *m* des affaires; ***business class*** *(on aeroplane)* classe *f* affaires; to travel b. class voyager en classe affaires; *Br* ***business college*** école *f* de commerce; *(for management training)* école *f* (supérieure) de gestion; ***business computing*** informatique *f* de gestion; ***business concern*** entreprise *f* commerciale; ***business correspondence*** correspondance *f* *ou* communication *f* commerciale; *Journ* ***business correspondent*** correspondant(e) *m,f* financier(ère); ***business cycle*** cycle *m* des affaires, cycle *m* conjoncturel; ***business district*** quartier *m* des affaires; ***business economics*** économie *f* d'entreprise; ***business economist*** économiste *mf* d'entreprise; *Fam* ***business end*** *(of knife)* partie *f* coupante❑; *(of gun)* gueule❑ *f*; ***business ethics*** déontologie *f* *ou* morale *f* professionelle; ***business expenses*** *(for individual)* frais *mpl* professionnels; *(for firm)* frais *mpl* généraux; ***business failure*** défaillance *f* d'entreprise; ***business finance*** finance *f* d'entreprise; *Comput* ***business graphics*** graphiques *mpl* de gestion; ***business hours*** *(of office)* heures *fpl* de bureau; *(of shop, public service)* heures *fpl* d'ouverture; ***business incubator*** pépinière *f* d'entreprises; *Comput* ***business intelligence system*** réactique *f*; *Admin* ***business letter*** lettre *f* commerciale; ***business lounge*** *(in airport)* salon *m* classe affaires; ***business lunch*** déjeuner *m* d'affaires; ***business management*** gestion *f* d'entreprise; *(study)* économie *f* d'entreprise; ***business manager*** *Com & Ind* directeur(trice) *m,f* commercial(e); *Sport* manager *m*; ***business meeting*** rendez-vous *m* d'affaires; ***business operation*** opération *f* commerciale; ***business park*** zone *f* d'activités; ***business partner*** partenaire *mf*; ***business plan*** projet *m* commercial; ***business portfolio*** portefeuille *m* d'activités; ***business premises*** locaux *mpl* commerciaux; *Am* ***business reply***, *Br* ***business reply card*** carte-réponse *f*; ***business reply envelope*** enveloppe *f* préaffranchie; ***business school*** école *f* de commerce; ***business section*** *(of newspaper)* rubrique *f* des affaires; ***business sector*** secteur *m* tertiaire, secteur *m* d'affaires; ***business services*** services *fpl* du secteur tertiaire, services *fpl* aux entreprises; *Comput* ***business software*** logiciel *m* de bureau; ***business strategy*** stratégie *f* d'entreprise *ou* commerciale; *Sch & Univ* ***business studies*** études *fpl* commerciales *ou* de commerce; ***business suit*** complet *m*, complet-veston *m*; ***business taxation*** imposition *f* des entreprises; ***business transaction*** transaction *f* commerciale; ***business travel*** voyages *mpl* d'affaires; ***business traveller*** = personne qui voyage pour affaires; ***business trend*** courant *m* d'affaires; ***business trip*** voyage *m* d'affaires; to go on a b. trip voyager pour affaires; ***business world*** monde *m* des affaires

businesslike ['bɪznɪslaɪk] ADJ *(professional ▸ person, manner)* sérieux; *(systematic, methodical)* systématique, méthodique; I was amazed at the b. way in which she handled the funeral arrangements j'ai été étonné de voir avec quelle efficacité elle s'est occupée de l'enterrement; her manner was cold and b. son comportement était froid et direct

businessman ['bɪznɪsmæn] *(pl* businessmen [-men]) N homme *m* d'affaires; I'm not a very good b. je ne suis pas très doué en affaires

businesswoman ['bɪznɪs,wʊmən] *(pl* businesswomen [-'wɪmɪn]) N femme *f* d'affaires, businesswoman *f*

busing = bussing

busk [bʌsk] VI *Br* jouer de la musique *(dans la rue ou le métro)*; we earned money busking in the street/underground nous avons gagné de l'argent en jouant dans la rue/le métro

busker ['bʌskə(r)] N *Br* musicien(enne) *m,f* de rue

busload ['bʌsləʊd] N a b. of workers un autobus plein d'ouvriers; the tourists arrived by the b. *or* in busloads les touristes sont arrivés par cars entiers

busman ['bʌsmən] *(pl* busmen [-mən]) N *Br* to take a b.'s holiday = faire la même chose pendant ses loisirs que pendant son travail; that's a bit of a b.'s holiday vous appelez ça des vacances!

bussing ['bʌsɪŋ] N *Am Sch* = système de ramassage scolaire aux États-Unis, qui organise la répartition des enfants noirs et des enfants blancs dans les écoles afin de lutter contre la ségrégation raciale

bust [bʌst] *(pt & pp* busted *or* bust) ADJ *Fam* 1 *(broken)* fichu

2 *(bankrupt)* to go b. faire faillite❑

3 *(broke)* I'm b. je suis fauché

4 *(idiom)* or b.! = expression indiquant la détermination à arriver quelque part; New York or b.! destination New York, quoi qu'il arrive!

N 1 *(breasts)* poitrine *f*, buste *m*; a large b. une forte poitrine; she has a small b. elle a peu de poitrine; what (size) b. are you? combien est-ce que vous faites de tour de poitrine?

2 *Art* buste *m*

3 *Fam (by police ▸ arrest)* arrestation❑ *f*; *(▸ raid)* descente❑ *f*; *(▸ search)* perquisition❑ *f*; there was a big drugs b. in Chicago il y a eu un beau coup de filet chez les trafiquants de drogue de Chicago

4 *Am Fam (failure)* fiasco *m*

VT *Fam* 1 *(break)* bousiller; *Fig* to b. a gut *or* blood vessel se casser la nénette; *Am very Fam* to b. one's ass doing sth se crever *ou* se casser le cul à faire qch; *Am very Fam* I'm not going to b. my ass for him! je ne vais pas me casser le cul pour lui!

2 *Law (arrest, raid)* he was busted on a drugs charge il s'est fait choper *ou* embarquer pour une affaire de drogue; the police busted the house at 3 a.m. la police a fait une descente dans la maison à 3 heures du matin

3 *Am (tame ▸ horse)* dresser❑

4 *Am Fam Mil slang (demote)* rétrograder❑; he got busted to sergeant il est repassé sergent

5 *Am (catch)* découvrir❑; you're busted! je t'y prends!, je t'ai eu!

VI *Am* to be busting to do sth crever d'envie de faire qch

▸**bust out** VI *Fam (escape)* se tirer; three prisoners have busted out (of jail) trois prisonniers se sont fait la belle *ou* la paire

▸**bust up** *Fam* VT SEP 1 *(disrupt)* demonstrators busted up the meeting des manifestants sont venus semer la pagaïe dans la réunion 2 *(damage, destroy ▸ bar, flat)* saccager

VI 1 *(boyfriend, girlfriend)* rompre (après une dispute)❑; he's b. up with his girlfriend il a rompu avec sa copine après une engueulade 2 *Am (laugh)* éclater de rire❑

bustard ['bʌstəd] N *Orn* outarde *f*

buster ['bʌstə(r)] N *Fam Am (pal)* thanks, b. merci, mon pote; now listen, b.… écoute, mec…

bustle ['bʌsəl] N 1 *(activity)* agitation *f*; I enjoy the hustle and b. of working in a hospital j'aime bien travailler dans un hôpital à cause de tout le va-et-vient; the b. of New York l'animation des rues de New York 2 *(on dress)* tournure *f*

VT to b. sb out of the house faire sortir qn précipitamment

VI he bustled about *or* around the kitchen il s'affairait dans la cuisine; the nurse came bustling in l'infirmière entra d'un air affairé

bustline ['bʌstlaɪn] N tour *m* de poitrine

bustling ['bʌsəlɪŋ] **ADJ** *(person)* affairé; *(place)* animé; **the streets were b. with Christmas shoppers** les rues grouillaient de gens faisant leurs achats de Noël

N *(activity)* agitation *f*

bust-up **N** *Fam* **1** *(quarrel)* engueulade *f*; **Craig and Claire have had another b.** Craig et Claire se sont encore engueulés **2** *(brawl)* bagarre▫ *f*

busty ['bʌstɪ] *(compar* **bustier**, *superl* **bustiest)** **ADJ** *Fam* qui a une forte poitrine▫; **she was a big, b. woman** c'était une femme forte, à la poitrine plantureuse▫

busy ['bɪzɪ] *(compar* **busier**, *superl* **busiest**, *pt & pp* **busied)** **ADJ** **1** *(person)* occupé; **he was too b. to notice** il était trop occupé pour s'en apercevoir; **I'm b. enough as it is!** je suis déjà assez occupé!; **she was b. painting the kitchen** elle était occupée à peindre la cuisine; **he likes to keep b.** il aime bien s'occuper; **the packing kept me b. all afternoon** j'ai été occupé à faire les valises tout l'après-midi; **I'm afraid I'm b. tomorrow** malheureusement je suis pris demain; **the bank manager is b. with a customer** le directeur de l'agence est occupé avec *ou* en rendez-vous avec un client; **you HAVE been b.!** eh bien, tu n'as pas chômé!; *Fam* **she's as b. as a bee, she's a b. bee** elle est très occupée▫

2 *(port, road, street)* très fréquenté; *(time, period, schedule)* chargé, plein; **I've had a b. day** j'ai eu une journée chargée; **he has a b. schedule** il a un emploi du temps chargé *ou* bien rempli; *Com* **this is our busiest period** c'est la période où nous sommes en pleine activité; **the office is very b. at the moment** nous avons beaucoup de travail au bureau en ce moment; **the shops are very b. today** les magasins sont pleins (de monde) aujourd'hui

3 *Am (telephone line)* occupé; **I got the b. signal** ça sonnait occupé

4 *Pej (excessively elaborate)* chargé

VT **he busied himself with household chores** il s'est occupé à des tâches ménagères; **she busied herself by tidying the office** elle s'est occupée en faisant le ménage dans le bureau

▸▸ *Bot* ***busy lizzie*** balsamine *f*, impatiente *f*

busybody ['bɪzɪˌbɒdɪ] *(pl* **busybodies)** **N** *Fam* fouineur(euse) *m,f*, fouinard(e) *m,f*; **he's an awful b.** il se mêle des affaires de tout le monde

BUT [bʌt]

CONJ	
• mais **1–3, 5**	• absolument **4**
• sans que **6**	
ADV	
• ne... que	
PREP	
• sauf **1**	

CONJ **1** *(to express contrast)* mais; **my husband smokes, b. I don't** mon mari fume, mais moi non; **my husband doesn't smoke, b. I do** mon mari ne fume pas, mais moi si; **I speak Spanish b. not Italian** je parle espagnol mais pas italien; **she came home tired b. happy** elle est rentrée fatiguée mais heureuse

2 *(in exclamations)* mais; **b. that's absurd!** mais c'est absurde!

3 *(when addressing someone politely)* **sorry, b. I think that's MY umbrella** pardon, mais je crois que c'est mon parapluie; **excuse me, b. there's a call for you** excusez-moi, il y a un appel pour vous

4 *(used for emphasis)* **nobody, b. nobody, gets in without a ticket** personne, absolument personne, n'entre sans ticket

5 *(except, only)* mais; **it tastes like a grapefruit, b. sweeter** ça a le goût d'un pamplemousse, mais en plus sucré; **I'll do it, b. not right now** je vais le faire, mais pas tout de suite

6 *Literary* **she never hears his name b. she starts to weep** elle ne peut entendre son nom sans verser des larmes; **barely a day goes by b. he receives another invitation** il ne se passe pas un jour sans qu'il reçoive une nouvelle invitation

ADV *(only)* ne... que; **I can b. try** je ne peux qu'essayer; *Literary* **had I b. known!** si j'avais su!; *Formal* **his resignation cannot b. confirm such suspicions** sa démission ne fait que confirmer de tels soupçons; *Literary* **this life is b. transitory/b. a dream** cette vie n'est qu'éphémère/qu'un rêve

PREP **1** *(except)* sauf, à part; **she wouldn't see anyone b. her lawyer** elle ne voulait voir personne sauf *ou* à part son avocat; **who b. a fool would believe his story?** il n'y a qu'un imbécile pour croire son histoire; **nobody b. me knew about it** personne d'autre que moi n'était au courant; **anyone b. me** tout autre que moi; **anything b. that** tout plutôt que cela; **he's anything b. a hero** c'est loin d'être un héros; **where b. in Japan could you find such a gadget?** il n'y a qu'au Japon qu'on trouve un tel gadget; **nothing b. a miracle could have saved her** seul un miracle aurait pu la sauver; **he does nothing b. complain** il n'arrête pas de se plaindre; **there is nothing for it b. to obey** il n'y a qu'à obéir; **he is anything b. happy** il n'est pas du tout heureux; **is she lazy? – anything b.!** est-ce qu'elle est paresseuse? – bien au contraire!

2 *Br (with numbers)* **turn right at the next corner b. one** tournez à droite au deuxième carrefour; **I was the last b. two to finish** j'étais l'avant-avant-dernier à finir

N **you're coming and no buts** *or* **I don't want any buts!** tu viens, et pas de mais!

• **but for** **PREP** sans; **b. for her courage, many more people would have drowned** sans son courage, il y aurait eu beaucoup plus de noyés; **b. for the rain I should have gone out** s'il n'avait pas plu je serais sorti; **he wouldn't have left b. for me** *(it was my fault for being there)* il serait resté si je n'avais pas été là; *(it was for my sake)* il ne serait pas parti si ça n'avait pas été pour moi

• **but that** **CONJ** *Formal* **we should have been on time, b. that the train was delayed** nous aurions été à l'heure si le train n'avait pas été retardé

• **but then** **ADV** enfin; **b. then, that's just the way it goes** enfin, c'est comme ça

---

butane ['bju:teɪn] **N** *Chem* butane *m*

▸▸ ***butane gas*** gaz *m* butane, butane *m*

butch [bʊtʃ] *Fam* **ADJ** *(woman)* hommasse; *(man)* macho

N *(lesbian)* = lesbienne d'apparence masculine

butcher ['bʊtʃə(r)] **N** **1** *(gen)* boucher *m*; **she's gone to the b.'s** elle est partie chez le boucher; **b.'s shop** boucherie *f*; *Br* **b.'s boy** garçon *m* boucher

2 *(murderer)* boucher *m*

3 *Fam (surgeon, dentist)* boucher *m*, charcutier *m*

4 *SEng Fam (rhyming slang* **butcher's hook** = **look)** **to have a b.'s (at sb/sth)** mater (qn/qch); **let's have a b.'s (at it)!** montre un peu!

VT **1** *(animal)* abattre, tuer

2 *(person)* massacrer

3 *Fam (story, joke)* massacrer

4 *Fam (of surgeon, dentist* ▸ *patient)* charcuter

▸▸ ***butcher's block*** *(for professional use)* billot *m*; *(for domestic use)* planche *f* à découper

butchery ['bʊtʃərɪ] **N** **1** *Com (profession)* boucherie *f*; *Br (slaughterhouse)* abattoir *m* **2** *Fig (massacre)* boucherie *f*, massacre *m*

butler ['bʌtlə(r)] **N** maître *m* d'hôtel, majordome *m*

butt [bʌt] **N** **1** *(end)* bout *m*; *(of rifle)* crosse *f*; *(of cigarette)* mégot *m*; **the b. end** le bout

2 *esp Am Fam (buttocks)* fesses▫ *fpl*; **why don't you get off your b. and do something?** remue-toi un peu les fesses et fais quelque chose!; **move your b.!** bouge-toi!

3 *(in archery* ▸ *target)* but *m*; *(*▸ *mound)* butte *f*; *Mil* **the butts** le champ *ou* la butte de tir

4 *(person)* **she became the b. of their teasing** elle s'est trouvée en butte à leurs taquineries; **he was the b. of all the office jokes** il était la cible de toutes les plaisanteries du bureau

5 *(barrel)* tonneau *m*

VT **1** *(of animal)* donner un coup de corne à; *(of person)* donner un coup de tête à; **the goat butted its head against the gate** la chèvre donna un coup de corne à la barrière; *Fig* **he butted his way through the crowds** il s'est forcé un passage dans la foule **2** *Tech (abut)* abouter

ADV *Am Fam* **b. naked** à poil

▸▸ *Tech* ***butt joint*** joint *m* abouté, soudure *f* bout à bout; ***butt welding*** soudure *f* bout à bout

▸ **butt in** **VI** *(interrupt)* **excuse me for butting in** excusez-moi de m'en mêler *ou* de vous interrompre; **she's always butting in on people's conversations** elle s'immisce toujours dans les conversations des autres

▸ **butt out** **VI** *Fam* s'occuper de ses fesses; **b. out!** occupe-toi de tes fesses!; **just b. out of my life!** laisse-moi vivre!

butter ['bʌtə(r)] **N** beurre *m*; **she looked as if b. wouldn't melt (in her mouth)** on lui aurait donné le bon Dieu sans confession

VT **1** *(bread)* beurrer **2** *Culin (potatoes, vegetables)* mettre du beurre dans

▸▸ ***butter bean*** = sorte de haricot de Lima; *Br* ***butter biscuit***, *Am* ***butter cookie*** galette *f* au beurre; ***butter dish*** beurrier *m*; *Culin* ***butter icing*** glaçage *m* au beurre; ***butter knife*** couteau *m* à beurre; *EU* ***butter mountain*** montagne *f* de beurre

▸ **butter up** **VT SEP** *Fam* passer de la pommade à

butterball ['bʌtəbɔ:l] **N** *Am Fam* **he's a b.** il est un peu grassouillet

buttercup ['bʌtəkʌp] **N** *Bot* bouton *m* d'or

butterfat ['bʌtəfæt] **N** matière *f* grasse

butterfingered ['bʌtəˌfɪŋgəd] **ADJ** *Fam* maladroit▫, empoté; **a b. child** un enfant aux mains malhabiles▫

butterfingers ['bʌtəˌfɪŋgəz] **N** *Fam* maladroit (e)▫ *m,f (de ses mains)*

butterfly ['bʌtəflaɪ] *(pl* **butterflies)** **N** **1** *Entom* papillon *m*; **she always has** *or* **gets butterflies (in her stomach) before a performance** elle a toujours le trac avant une représentation **2** *Swimming* **(the) b.** la brasse papillon; **the 200 m b.** le 200 mètres papillon

▸▸ ***butterfly farm*** élevage *m* de papillons; ***butterfly net*** filet *m* à papillons; *Tech* ***butterfly nut*** papillon *m*, écrou *m* à ailettes; *Tech* ***butterfly valve*** (soupape *f* à) papillon *m*

buttermilk ['bʌtəmɪlk] **N** **1** *(sour liquid)* babeurre *m* **2** *Am (clabbered milk)* lait *m* fermenté

butterscotch ['bʌtəskɒtʃ] **N** *Culin* caramel *m* dur au beurre

▸▸ ***butterscotch sauce*** caramel *m* liquide

buttery ['bʌtərɪ] *(pl* **butteries)** **ADJ** **1** *(smell, taste)* de beurre; *(fingers)* couvert de beurre; *(biscuits)* fait avec beaucoup de beurre **2** *Fam Fig (obsequious)* mielleux▫

N *Br (in college, university* ▸ *storeroom)* office *m or f*; *(*▸ *snackbar)* buffet *m*, buvette *f*; *(*▸ *dining hall)* cantine *f*

butthead ['bʌtˌhed] **N** *Am Fam* crétin(e) *m,f*

butting ['bʌtɪŋ] **N** *(by animal)* coup(s) *m(pl)* de corne; *(by person)* coup(s) *m(pl)* de tête; **he was disqualified for b.** il a été disqualifié pour avoir donné un/des coup(s) de tête

buttock ['bʌtək] **N** fesse *f*; **buttocks** fesses *fpl*

button ['bʌtən] **N** **1** *(on clothing, bell, switch, sword)* bouton *m*; *Fam* **on the b.** exactement▫; **six o'clock on the b.** six heures tapantes; **as bright as a b.** vif, éveillé

2 *Am (badge)* badge *m*

3 *(sweet)* **chocolate buttons** pastilles *fpl* de chocolat

4 *Comput (on mouse)* bouton *m*; *(for menu selection)* case *f*

VT *(gen)* & boutonner; *Fam* **b. it** *or* **your lip** *or* **your mouth!** ferme-la!, boucle-la!

VI se boutonner; **the blouse buttons at the back** le chemisier se boutonne par derrière *ou* dans le dos

▸▸ *Ski* ***button lift*** téléski *m*, *Fam* tire-fesses *m inv*; ***button mushroom*** champignon *m* de couche *ou* de Paris

▸ **button up** **VT SEP** **1** *(piece of clothing)* boutonner **2** *Fam Fig (conclude)* régler▫

VI **1** *(piece of clothing)* se boutonner **2** *Fam (shut up)* **b. up!** ferme-la!, boucle-la!

button-down **ADJ** **1** *(collar)* boutonné; *(shirt)* à col boutonné **2** *Am Fig (conventional)* **a b. businessman** un homme d'affaires très comme il faut

buttoned-up ['bʌtənd-] **ADJ** *Fam (taciturn)* constipé, coincé

buttonhole ['bʌtənhəʊl] **N 1** *(in clothing)* boutonnière *f*; **she gave him a carnation for his b.** elle lui donna un œillet pour mettre à sa boutonnière **2** *Br (flower)* **she was wearing a pink b.** elle portait une fleur rose à la boutonnière
VT 1 *(make buttonholes in)* faire des boutonnières sur; *Sewing (sew with buttonhole stitch)* coudre au point de boutonnière **2** *Fam Fig (detain ▸ person)* retenir□, coincer
▸▸ *Sewing* **buttonhole stitch** point *m* de boutonnière

button-through **ADJ a b. dress** une robe-chemisier; **a b. skirt** une jupe boutonnée

buttress ['bʌtrɪs] **N 1** *Archit* contrefort *m* **2** *Geog (of mountain)* pilier *m* **3** *Fig (support)* pilier *m*
VT 1 *Archit* étayer; *(cathedral)* arc-bouter **2** *Fig (argument, system)* étayer, renforcer

butt-ugly **ADJ** hyper moche

butty ['bʌtɪ] *(pl* **butties***)* **N** *Br Fam (sandwich)* sandwich□ *m*, casse-croûte *m*

buxom ['bʌksəm] **ADJ** *(plump)* plantureux, bien en chair; *(busty)* à la poitrine plantureuse

BUY [baɪ] *(pt & pp* **bought** [bɔːt]*)* **VT 1** *Com (purchase)* acheter; **to b. sth for sb, to b. sb sth** acheter qch à *ou* pour qn; **I'll b. it for you** je te l'achète; **can I b. you a coffee?** puis-je t'offrir un café?; **she bought her car from her sister** elle a racheté la voiture de sa sœur; **I'll b. it from you** je te le rachète; **they bought it for £100** ils l'ont payé 100 livres; **have you bought the plane tickets?** avez-vous pris les billets d'avion?; **you'd better b. the theatre tickets today** tu devrais prendre *ou* louer les places de théâtre aujourd'hui; **we're out of coffee – I'll go and b. some more** nous n'avons plus de café – je vais aller en racheter; **to b. sth new/second-hand/on credit** acheter qch neuf/d'occasion/à crédit; **she bought herself a pair of skis** elle s'est acheté une paire de skis; **£20 won't b. you very much these days** avec 20 livres, on ne va pas très loin de nos jours
2 *(gain, obtain)* **to b. time** gagner du temps; **she bought their freedom with her life** elle paya leur liberté de sa vie; **money can't b. you love/happiness** l'amour/le bonheur ne s'achète pas
3 *(bribe)* acheter; **I won't be bought** on ne m'achètera pas
4 *Fam (believe)* **she'll never b. that story** elle n'avalera *ou* ne gobera jamais cette histoire; **do you think he'll b. it?** tu crois qu'il va marcher?; **OK, I'll b. that!** d'accord, je marche!
5 *Fam (idioms)* **to b. it,** *Am* **to b. the farm** *(die)* passer l'arme à gauche
N *Com (purchase)* affaire *f*; **a good/bad b.** une bonne/mauvaise affaire; **this car was a great b.** cette voiture était une très bonne affaire
VI acheter; *St Exch* **to b. spot** acheter au comptant; **to b. on credit** acheter à crédit *ou* à terme; **to b. on margin** acheter à découvert
▸▸ *St Exch* **buy order** ordre *m* d'achat

▸**buy back** **VT SEP** racheter

▸**buy in** **VT SEP 1** *Br (stockpile)* stocker, faire des provisions de; **we bought in plenty of coffee before the price increase** nous avons fait des provisions de café avant que les prix n'augmentent **2** *St Exch* acheter, acquérir

▸**buy into** **VT INSEP 1** *Fin* acheter une participation dans **2** *(believe)* **to b. into sth** gober qch; **there's no way I'm buying into this** pas question que je marche avec ça

▸**buy off** **VT SEP** *(bribe)* acheter; **they bought off the witness for £10,000** ils ont acheté le silence du témoin pour 10000 livres

▸**buy out** **VT SEP 1** *Fin* racheter la part de, désintéresser; **she bought out all the other shareholders** elle racheta les parts de tous les autres actionnaires; **he was bought out for £50,000** on lui a racheté sa part dans l'affaire pour 50 000 livres **2** *Mil* racheter; **he bought himself out (of the army)** il a payé pour pouvoir rompre son contrat avec l'armée

▸**buy up** **VT SEP** acheter en quantité; *(firm, shares, stock)* racheter; **the company bought up £50,000 worth of shares** la société racheta des actions pour une valeur de 50 000 livres

buy-back **N** *St Exch* rachat *m* d'actions

buyer ['baɪə(r)] **N** *Com* acheteur(euse) *m,f*; **I haven't found a b. for my house** je n'ai pas trouvé d'acheteur pour ma maison; **she's a b. at** *or* **for Harrods** elle est responsable des achats chez Harrods
▸▸ *Mktg* **buyer behaviour** comportement *m* de l'acheteur; *Fin* **buyer credit** crédit-acheteur *m*; *Com* **buyer's market** marché *m* à la baisse, marché *m* demandeur; *(for house buyers)* marché *m* d'offre *ou* offreur; *Mktg* **buyer readiness** prédisposition *f* à l'achat

buying ['baɪɪŋ] **N** *Com* achat *m*; *St Exch* exécution *f*; **b. and selling** l'achat et la vente
▸▸ *Mktg* **buying decision** décision *f* d'achat; *Fin* **buying power** pouvoir *m* d'achat; *St Exch* **buying quotation, buying rate** *(of shares)* cours *m* d'achat

buy-out **N** *Com* rachat *m*

buy-sell agreement **N** *Com & Law* protocole *m ou* accord *m* d'achat et de vente

buy-to-let **ADJ** relatif à l'achat de biens immobiliers en vue de les louer

buzz [bʌz] **N 1** *(of insect)* bourdonnement *m*, vrombissement *m*; *Fig* **there was a b. of conversation in the room** la pièce résonnait du bourdonnement des conversations; **the announcement caused a b. of excitement** l'annonce provoqua un murmure d'excitation
2 *(of buzzer)* coup *m* de sonnette
3 *Fam (telephone call)* coup *m* de fil; **to give sb a b.** donner un coup de fil à qn
4 *Fam (gossip)* **what's the b.?** quoi de neuf?
5 *(activity)* **I love the b. of London** j'adore l'animation de Londres
6 *Fam (strong sensation)* **I get quite a b. out of being on the stage** je m'éclate vraiment quand je suis sur scène; *Am Fam* **to get a b. on** *(take drugs)* se défoncer
VI 1 *(insect)* bourdonner, vrombir; *Fig* **the theatre buzzed with excitement** le théâtre était tout bourdonnant d'excitation; *Fam* **the town/party was really buzzing** la ville/la soirée était super animée
2 *(ears)* bourdonner, tinter; **her head was buzzing** elle avait des bourdonnements dans la tête; **his head was buzzing with ideas** les idées bourdonnaient dans sa tête
3 *(with buzzer)* **he buzzed for his secretary** il appela sa secrétaire (à l'interphone)
4 *Fam (be lively ▸ person)* tenir la forme; **he's really buzzing tonight** il tient vraiment la forme ce soir
VT 1 *(with buzzer)* **he buzzed the nurse** il appela l'infirmière d'un coup de sonnette **2** *Am Fam (telephone)* passer un coup de fil à **3** *Fam (building, town)* raser, frôler□; *(aircraft)* frôler□
▸▸ *Am* **buzz cut** coupe *f* à ras; *Tech* **buzz saw** scie *f* mécanique *ou* circulaire; *Cin* **buzz track** piste *f* de localisation

▸**buzz about** **VI** *(bees, flies)* voler en bourdonnant; *Fam (person)* s'affairer□, s'agiter□

▸**buzz off** **VI** *Fam* décamper, dégager; **b. off, will you!** dégage *ou* fiche le camp, tu veux!

buzzard ['bʌzəd] **N 1** *Br (bird of prey)* buse *f* **2** *Am (vulture)* urubu *m*

buzzer ['bʌzə(r)] **N** sonnette *f*; **there's the b.** *(on machine)* ça sonne; *(at door)* on sonne

buzzing ['bʌzɪŋ] **N** *(UNCOUNT) (of insects)* bourdonnement *m*, vrombissement *m*; *(in ears)* bourdonnement *m*, tintement *m*
ADJ *(insect)* bourdonnant, vrombissant; **a b. noise** *or* **sound** un bourdonnement *ou* vrombissement

buzz-kill **N** *Am Fam* rabat-joie□ *mf*

buzzword [bʌzwɜːd] **N** *Fam* mot *m* à la mode□

BY [baɪ]

ADV
- de côté **2**

PREP
- près de **1**
- devant **2**
- à **4, 16, 17**
- de **7, 13, 14**
- au bord de **1**
- par **3–6, 8, 15, 17**
- en **4, 6, 17**

ADV 1 *(past)* **she drove by without stopping** elle est passée (en voiture) sans s'arrêter; **he managed to squeeze by** il a réussi à passer (en se faufilant); **if you see him, just walk on by** si tu le vois, ne t'arrête pas; **two hours have gone by** deux heures ont passé; **as time went by he became less bitter** avec le temps il est devenu moins amer
2 *(aside, away)* de côté; **to lay** *or* **to put sth by** mettre qch de côté; **she put some money by for her old age** elle a mis de l'argent de côté pour ses vieux jours
3 *(nearby)* **is there a bank close by?** y a-t-il une banque près d'ici?; **she sat** *or* **stood by while they operated** elle est restée là pendant qu'ils opéraient; *Fig* **how can you just sit** *or* **stand by while he suffers?** comment peux-tu rester là sans rien faire alors qu'il souffre?; **stand by in case of an emergency** ne vous éloignez pas au cas où il y aurait une urgence
4 *(to, at someone's home)* **I'll stop** *or* **drop by this evening** je passerai ce soir; **your mother came by this morning** ta mère est passée ce matin
PREP 1 *(near, beside)* près de, à côté de; **by the sea** au bord de la mer; **she parked her car by the kerb** elle gara sa voiture au bord du trottoir; **come and sit by me** *or* **by my side** viens t'asseoir près *ou* auprès de moi; **by the fire** près du feu; **don't stand by the door** ne restez pas debout près de la porte
2 *(past)* devant; **she walked right by me** elle passa juste devant moi
3 *(through)* par; **she left by the back door** elle est partie par la porte de derrière
4 *(indicating means, method)* **to pay by cheque** payer par chèque; **by letter/phone** par courrier/téléphone; **to go by bus/car/plane/train** aller en autobus/voiture/avion/train; **send it by plane/ship** envoyez-le par avion/bateau; **by land and sea** par terre et par mer; **it's quicker by train** ça va plus vite en train; **I know her by name/sight** je la connais de nom/vue; *Literary* **he died by his own hand** il est mort de sa propre main; **you must wash it by hand** il faut le laver à la main; **was it made by hand/machine?** a-t-il été fait à la main/machine?; **by candlelight** à la lumière d'une bougie; **by moonlight** au clair de lune; **I can do it by myself** je peux le faire (tout) seul; **to be all by oneself** être tout seul
5 *(indicating agent or cause)* par; **it was built by the Romans** il fut construit par les Romains; **the house was surrounded by the police** la police a cerné la maison; **I was shocked by his reaction** sa réaction m'a choqué; **she has a daughter by her first marriage/husband** elle a une fille de son premier mariage/mari
6 *(as a result of)* par; *(with present participle)* en; **by chance/mistake** par hasard/erreur; **by working overtime he managed to pay off his debts** en faisant des heures supplémentaires il a réussi à rembourser ses dettes; **I'll lose by doing it** j'y perdrai
7 *(indicating authorship)* de; **a book by Toni Morrison** un livre de Toni Morrison; **a quartet by Schubert** un quatuor de Schubert
8 *(indicating part of person, thing held)* par; **carry it by the handle** prends-le par la poignée; **she took her by the hand** elle l'a prise par la main; **he seized him by the collar** il l'a saisi par le col
9 *(not later than, before)* **she'll be here by tonight/five o'clock** elle sera ici avant ce soir/pour cinq heures; **it must be done by tomorrow/Friday** ça doit être fait pour demain/vendredi; **by the end of the 21st century illiteracy should be stamped out** d'ici la fin du XXIème siècle l'analphabétisme devrait avoir disparu; **by 1960 most Americans had television sets** en 1960 la plupart des Américains avaient déjà un poste de télévision; **by the time you read this letter I'll be in California** lorsque tu liras cette lettre, je serai en Californie; **by the time the police came the thieves had left** le temps que la police arrive *ou* lorsque la police arriva, les voleurs étaient déjà partis; **he should be in India by now** il devrait être en Inde maintenant; **she had already married by then** à ce moment-là elle était déjà mariée
10 *(during)* **by daylight** au jour, à la lumière du jour; **he works by night and sleeps by day** il travaille la nuit et dort le jour
11 *(according to)* d'après; **to call sb by his/her**

name appeler qn par son nom; **they're rich, even by American standards** ils sont riches même par rapport aux normes américaines; **it's 6.15 by my watch** il est 6h15 à *ou* d'après ma montre; **you can tell he's lying by the expression on his face** on voit qu'il ment à l'expression de son visage

12 *(in accordance with)* selon, d'après; **by law** selon *ou* d'après la loi; *Sport & Fig* **to play by the rules** faire les choses dans les règles

13 *(with regard to)* de; **to do one's duty by sb** faire son devoir envers qn; **she's Canadian by birth** elle est canadienne de naissance; **cheerful by nature** gai par nature, d'un naturel gai; **he's an actor by trade** *or* **profession** il est acteur de profession; *Fam* **it's all right by me** moi, je suis d'accord *ou* je n'ai rien contre; *Fam* **if that's okay by you** si ça te va, si tu es d'accord□

14 *(indicating degree, extent)* de; *Sport* **she won by five points** elle a gagné de cinq points; **I missed the train by less than a minute** j'ai manqué le train de moins d'une minute; **she's older than her husband by five years** elle est plus âgée que son mari de cinq ans; **increase your income by half** augmentez vos revenus de 50 pour cent; **they overcharged me by ten percent** ils m'ont compté dix pour cent en trop; **his second book is better by far** son deuxième livre est nettement meilleur

15 *(in calculations, measurements)* **multiply/divide 12 by 6** multipliez/divisez 12 par 6; **the room is 6 metres by 3 (metres)** la pièce fait 6 mètres sur 3 (mètres)

16 *(indicating specific amount, duration)* **to be paid by the hour/week/month** être payé à l'heure/à la semaine/au mois; *Com* **they only sell by the kilo** ils ne vendent qu'au kilo; *Com* **it sold by the thousand** ça s'est vendu par milliers

17 *(indicating rate or speed)* **little by little** peu à peu; **day by day** jour par jour, de jour en jour; **year by year** d'année en année; **two by two** deux par deux

18 *(used with points of the compass)* quart; **north by west** nord-quart-nord-ouest

• **by and by** ADV *Literary* bientôt
• **by the by** ADV à propos ADJ **that's by the by** ça n'a pas d'importance

bye [baɪ] N *Sport* **1 to get a b.** = passer au tour suivant sans avoir à jouer *(lors d'un tournoi qui oppose un nombre impair de concurrents)*; **our team have got a b. into the second round** nous sommes passés directement au tour suivant, faute d'adversaire **2** *(in cricket)* balle *f* passée

EXCLAM *Fam* au revoir!□, salut!; **b. for now!** à bientôt!

bye-bye *Fam* EXCLAM au revoir□, salut; **say b.** *(to child)* dis au revoir

• **bye-byes** N *(in children's language)* dodo *m*; **go to bye-byes now** va faire dodo maintenant

byelaw = **bylaw**

by-election, bye-election N élection *f* (législative) partielle *(en Grande-Bretagne)*

Byelorussia [bɪˌeləʊˈrʌʃə] N Biélorussie *f*

Byelorussian [bɪˌeləʊˈrʌʃən] N **1** *(person)* Biélorusse *mf* **2** *(language)* biélorusse *m*

ADJ biélorusse

COMP *(embassy)* de Biélorussie; *(history)* de la Biélorussie; *(teacher)* de biélorusse

bygone [ˈbaɪgɒn] ADJ *Literary* passé, révolu; **the gallantry of a b. age** une galanterie qui n'a plus cours aujourd'hui; **in b. days** autrefois, jadis

N **1** *(object)* vieillerie *f* **2** *(idiom)* **let bygones be bygones** oublions le passé

bylaw [ˈbaɪlɔː] N **1** *Br (of local authority)* arrêté *m* municipal **2** *Am (of club, company)* statut *m*

by-line N *Press* signature *f (en tête d'un article)*

BYO [ˌbiːwaɪˈəʊ] N *(abbr* **bring your own**) = restaurant non autorisé à vendre des boissons alcoolisées mais où l'on a la possibilité d'apporter sa propre bouteille

BYOB [ˌbiːwaɪˌəʊˈbiː] N *(abbr* **bring your own bottle**) = "apportez une bouteille", inscription que l'on trouve sur un carton d'invitation à une soirée ou qui indique qu'un restaurant n'est pas autorisé à vendre d'alcool et que l'on peut donc en apporter soi-même pour accompagner son repas

bypass [ˈbaɪpɑːs] N **1** *(road)* rocade *f*; **the Oxford b.** la route qui contourne Oxford

2 *Tech (pipe)* conduit *m* de dérivation, by-pass *m*

3 *Elec* dérivation *f*

4 *Med* pontage *m*, by-pass *m*; **he's had a heart b.** il a subi un pontage coronarien

VT *(avoid* ► *town)* contourner, éviter; *(*► *problem, regulation)* contourner, éluder; *(*► *superior)* court-circuiter; **I bypassed the personnel officer and spoke directly to the boss** je suis allé parler directement au directeur sans passer par le chef du personnel

►► *Med* ***bypass operation, bypass surgery*** pontage *m*

byplay [ˈbaɪpleɪ] N *Theat* jeu *m* de scène secondaire

by-product N *Ind* sous-produit *m*, (produit *m*) dérivé *m*; *Fig* conséquence *f* indirecte, effet *m* secondaire

byre [ˈbaɪə(r)] N *Br* étable *f* (à vaches)

byroad [ˈbaɪrəʊd] N *(road)* chemin *m* détourné *ou* écarté

bystander [ˈbaɪˌstændə(r)] N spectateur(trice) *m,f*

byte [baɪt] N *Comput* octet *m*, byte *m*

byway [ˈbaɪweɪ] N **1** *(road)* chemin *m* détourné *ou* écarté **2** *Fig (of subject)* à-côté *m*; **the book explores the byways of Buddhist teaching** le livre explore les aspects peu connus *ou* les à-côtés de l'enseignement bouddhiste

byword [ˈbaɪwɜːd] N symbole *m*, illustration *f*; **the company has become a b. for inefficiency** le nom de cette entreprise est devenu synonyme d'inefficacité

Byzantine [*Br* bɪˈzæntaɪn, *Am* ˈbɪzəntiːn] N Byzantin(e) *m,f*

ADJ byzantin, de Byzance

Byzantium [bɪˈzæntɪəm] N Byzance

C

C¹, c¹ [siː] **N 1** *(letter)* C, c *m inv*; **two c's** deux c; **C for Charlie** C comme Célestin; *Fam* **the big C** *(cancer)* le cancer□

2 *Sch* **to get a C** avoir une note moyenne, avoir entre 10 et 13 sur 20

3 *Mus* do *m*, ut *m*; **in C sharp** en do dièse majeur

4 *(Roman numeral)* C *m*

ADJ *Mus (string)* de do

►► *Am Fam* ***C note*** billet *m* de cent dollars□; *Br Euph* ***the C word*** = le mot "cunt", le mot de Cambronne

C² **1** *(written abbr* **Celsius, Centigrade***)* C **2** *(written abbr* **century***)* s; **C16** XVIème s

c² **1** *(written abbr* **cent(s)***)* ct **2** *(written abbr* **circa***)* vers

CA¹ [ˌsiːˈeɪ] **N 1** *(abbr* **Consumers' Association***)* = association britannique des consommateurs **2** *Br (abbr* **chartered accountant***)* expert-comptable *m*

CA² **1** *(written abbr* **Central America***)* Amérique *f* centrale **2** *(written abbr* **California***)* Californie *f*

c/a *Banking (written abbr* **current** *or* **cheque** *or Am* **checking account***)* C/C *m*, CCB *m*

CAA [ˈsiːeɪˈeɪ] **N** *Br Aviat (abbr* **Civil Aviation Authority***)* = organisme britannique de réglementation de l'aviation civile

CAB [ˌsiːeɪˈbiː] **N** *Br (abbr* **Citizens' Advice Bureau***)* = en Grande-Bretagne, bureau où les citoyens peuvent obtenir des conseils d'ordre juridique, social etc

cab [kæb] **N 1** *(taxi)* taxi *m*; **let's go by c., let's take a c.** allons-y en taxi **2** *(of lorry, train)* cabine *f* **3** *(horse-drawn)* fiacre *m*

►► ***cab driver*** chauffeur *m* de taxi; ***cab rank*** station *f* de taxis

cabal [kəˈbæl] **N 1** *(plot)* cabale *f* **2** *(group)* coterie *f*

cabala [kəˈbɑːlə] **N** *Rel* cabale *f*

cabalism [ˈkæbəlɪzəm] **N** *Rel* cabalisme *m*

cabalistic [kæbəˈlɪstɪk] **ADJ** *Rel* cabalistique

cabana [kəˈbænə] **N** *Am* cabine *f (de plage)*

cabaret [ˈkæbəreɪ] **N** *(nightclub)* cabaret *m*; *(show)* spectacle *m*; **c. artist** artiste *mf* de cabaret

cabbage [ˈkæbɪdʒ] **N 1** *(vegetable)* chou *m* **2** *Br Fam (brain-damaged person)* légume *m*; *Pej (dull person)* larve *f*; **I'd rather die than be a c. for the rest of my life** plutôt mourir que vivre comme un légume jusqu'à la fin de mes jours **3** *Am Fam (money)* fric *m*, blé *m*, oseille *f*

►► ***cabbage lettuce*** laitue *f* pommée; ***cabbage patch*** carré *m* de salade; ***cabbage rose*** rose *f* centfeuilles; ***cabbage white*** *(butterfly)* piéride *f* du chou

cabbala, cabbalism *etc* = **cabala, cabalism** *etc*

cabbie, cabby [ˈkæbɪ] **N** *Fam (taxi-driver)* chauffeur *m* de taxi□; *(coachman)* cocher *m* (de fiacre)□

caber [ˈkeɪbə(r)] **N** *Sport* tronc *m*; **tossing the c.** = concours de lancement d'un tronc d'arbre *(dans les jeux des Highlands)*

cabin [ˈkæbɪn] **N 1** *(hut)* cabane *f*, hutte *f*

2 *Naut* cabine *f*

3 *Aviat* cabine *f*; **the first class c.** la cabine de première classe

4 *Br Rail (signal box)* cabine *f* d'aiguillage

5 *Br (of lorry, train)* cabine *f*

►► *Aviat* ***cabin attendant*** *(male)* steward *m*; *(female)* hôtesse *f* de l'air; *Naut* ***cabin boy*** mousse *m*; *Naut* ***cabin class*** deuxième classe *f*; *Aviat* ***cabin crew*** personnel *m* de cabine; *Naut* ***cabin cruiser*** cruiser *m*, yacht *m* de croisière; ***cabin fever*** = dépression ou mauvaise humeur dues à de longues périodes d'isolement; *Aviat* ***cabin staff*** personnel *m* de cabine; ***cabin trunk*** malle-cabine *f*

cabinet [ˈkæbɪnɪt] **N 1** *(furniture)* meuble *m* (de rangement); *(for bottles)* bar *m*; *(for television)* meuble *m* télé; *(for stereo)* meuble *m* hi-fi; *(for precious objects)* cabinet *m*; *(with glass doors)* vitrine *f* **2** *Pol* cabinet *m*; **to form a c.** former un cabinet *ou* un ministère

►► *Pol* ***cabinet meeting*** conseil *m* des ministres; *Pol* ***cabinet minister*** ministre *m* siégeant au cabinet; *Pol* ***cabinet reshuffle*** remaniement *m* ministériel

cabinet-maker **N** *Carp* ébéniste *mf*

cabinet-making **N** *Carp* ébénisterie *f*

cable [ˈkeɪbəl] **N 1** *(rope, wire)* câble *m*; **to lay a c.** poser un câble; **electric c.** câble *m* électrique

2 *(telegram)* télégramme *m*

3 *Naut (measure)* encablure *f*

4 *Knitting* point *m* de torsade

5 *TV* le cable; **it's only available on c.** ça n'existe que sur le câble

VT 1 *(lay cables in)* câbler **2** *(telegraph)* télégraphier à; **I cabled them to say I needed more money** je leur ai télégraphié que j'avais encore besoin d'argent

►► ***cable car*** téléphérique *m*; *TV* ***cable company*** câblo-opérateur *m*; *TV* ***cable distribution*** câblodistribution *f*, distribution *f* par câble; *Comput* ***cable modem*** modem-câble *m*; *Knitting* ***cable needle*** aiguille *f* à torsades; *TV* ***Cable News Network*** = réseau d'information américain par câble et satellite; *TV* ***cable operator*** câblo-opérateur *m*; ***cable railway*** funiculaire *m*; ***cable release*** déclencheur *m*; *Tel & Naut* ***cable ship*** câblier *m*; *Knitting* ***cable stitch*** point *m* de torsade; ***cable telephone*** téléphone *m* par câble; ***cable television*** câble *m*, télévision *f* par câble; ***cable television network*** réseau *m* câblé; ***cable transfer*** *(of money)* virement *m* télégraphique; ***cable TV*** câble *m*, télévision *f* par câble; **to have c. TV** avoir le câble

cabled [ˈkeɪbəld] **ADJ** câblé; *TV* **c. network** réseau *m* câblé

cablegram [ˈkeɪbəlgræm] **N** *Old-fashioned* câblogramme *m*

cableless [ˈkeɪbəllɪs] **ADJ** sans câble

cableway [ˈkeɪbəlweɪ] **N** téléphérique *m*

cabling [ˈkeɪbəlɪŋ] **N** câblage *m*; *Comput* câbles *mpl*

cabman [ˈkæbmən] *(pl* **cabmen** [-mən]*)* **N** *Br* chauffeur *m* de taxi

caboodle [kəˈbuːdəl] **N** *Fam* **the whole (kit and) c.** tout le bataclan *ou* bazar

caboose [kəˈbuːs] **N 1** *Am Rail* fourgon *m* de queue **2** *Naut* coquerie *f* **3** *Am very Fam (buttocks)* cul *m*, fesses□ *fpl*

cabotage [kæbəˈtɑːʒ] **N** *Aviat & Naut* cabotage *m*

►► ***cabotage fare*** tarif *m* de cabotage; ***cabotage route*** itinéraire *m* de cabotage

CAC 40 index [kækˈfɔːtɪ-] **N** *St Exch* indice *m* CAC 40

cacao [kəˈkɑːəʊ] *(pl* **cacaos***)* **N** *(bean)* cacao *m*; *(tree)* cacaoyer *m*, cacaotier *m*

cache [kæʃ] **N 1** *(hidden supply)* cache *f*; **a c. of weapons, an arms c.** une cache d'armes **2** *Comput* antémémoire *f*, mémoire-cache *f* **3** *(hiding place)* cachette *f*

VT 1 *(hide)* mettre dans une cachette **2** *Comput (data)* mettre en antémémoire *ou* en mémoire-cache

►► *Comput* ***cache memory*** antémémoire *f*, mémoire-cache *f*

cachet [ˈkæʃeɪ] **N** *also Fig* cachet *m*

cack [kæk] *Br very Fam* **N** *(excrement)* caca *m*

ADJ *(bad)* nul

cack-handed **ADJ** *Br Fam* maladroit□, gauche□

cackle [ˈkækəl] **N 1** *(of hen)* caquet *m*, caquètement *m* **2** *(of person* ► *chatter)* caquètement *m*, jacasserie *f*; (► *laugh)* gloussement *m*; **she gave a loud c.** elle gloussa bruyamment; *Fam* **cut the c.!** assez bavardé!, la ferme!

VT *(person)* glousser

VI 1 *(hen)* caqueter **2** *(person* ► *chatter)* caqueter, jacasser; (► *laugh)* glousser

cacophonous [kæˈkɒfənəs] **ADJ** cacophonique

cacophony [kæˈkɒfənɪ] *(pl* **cacophonies***)* **N** cacophonie *f*

cactus [ˈkæktəs] *(pl* **cactuses** *or* **cacti** [-taɪ]*)* **N** cactus *m*

►► *Bot* ***cactus flower*** fleur *f* de cactus

CAD¹ [ˌsiːeɪˈdiː] **N** *Com (abbr* **cash against documents***)* comptant *m* contre documents

CAD² [kæd] **N** *Comput (abbr* **computer-aided design, computer-assisted design***)* CAO *f*

cad [kæd] **N** *Br Old-fashioned* mufle *m*; **you c.!** vous êtes ignoble *ou* indigne!

cadaver [kəˈdævə(r)] **N** *Med* cadavre *m*

cadaverous [kəˈdævərəs] **ADJ** *Formal or Literary* cadavéreux, cadavérique

caddie [ˈkædɪ] **N 1** *Golf* caddie *m* **2** *Am (cart)* chariot *m*, Caddie® *m*

VI *Golf* **to c. for sb** être le caddie de qn

►► *Golf* ***caddie car, caddie cart*** chariot *m (pour clubs de golf)*

caddish [ˈkædɪʃ] **ADJ** *Br Old-fashioned (behaviour)* de mufle; *(person)* mufle; **that was a c. thing to do** c'est vraiment se comporter comme un mufle

caddy [ˈkædɪ] *(pl* **caddies***)* **N 1** *Br (container* ► *for tea)* boîte *f* **2** *Am (cart)* chariot *m*, Caddie® *m*

cadence [ˈkeɪdəns] **N** cadence *f*, rythme *m*; *Mus* cadence *f*

cadenza [kəˈdenzə] **N** *Mus* cadence *f*

cadet [kəˈdet] **N 1** *Mil* élève *mf* officier; *(police)* élève *mf* policier; *Br Sch* = élève qui reçoit une formation militaire **2** *(younger brother, son)* cadet *m* **3** *Austr (trainee journalist)* journaliste *mf* stagiaire

ADJ cadet

►► *Mil* ***cadet corps*** peloton *m* d'instruction militaire; *(for police training)* corps *m* d'élèves policiers

cadge [kædʒ] *Fam* N *Br* **1** *(person)* pique-assiette *mf inv*, parasite *m* **2** *(idiom)* **to be on the c.** chercher à se faire payer quelque chose
VT *(food, money)* se procurer *(en quémandant)*; **he cadged a meal from** *or* **off his aunt** il s'est invité à manger chez sa tante; **she cadged £10 off me** elle m'a tapé de 10 livres; **can I c. a lift?** ça ne t'ennuierait pas de me déposer?
VI **she's always cadging off her friends** elle est toujours en train de taper ses amis

cadger ['kædʒə(r)] N *Fam* pique-assiette *mf inv*, parasite *m*

Cadiz [kə'dɪz] N Cadix

cadmium ['kædmɪəm] N *Chem* cadmium *m*
▸▸ ***cadmium yellow*** jaune *m* de cadmium

cadre ['kɑːdə(r)] N cadre *m*

CAE [ˌsiːeɪ'iː] N *Comput (abbr* **computer-aided engineering, computer-assisted engineering***)* IAO *f*

caecum, *Am* **cecum** ['siːkəm] *(Br pl* **caeca** [-kə], *Am pl* **ceca** [-kə]*)* N *Anat* cæcum *m*

Caesar, *Am* **Cesar** ['siːzə(r)] PR N César; **Julius C.** Jules César
▸▸ *Culin* ***Caesar salad*** = salade à base de romaine, de croûtons et d'une vinaigrette additionnée d'œuf

Caesarean, *Am* **Cesarean** [sɪ'zeərɪən] N *Obst* césarienne *f*; **to be born** *or* **delivered by C.** naître par césarienne; **she has to have a C.** il va falloir lui faire une césarienne; **it was a C.** *(of delivery)* on lui a fait une césarienne
ADJ césarien
▸▸ *Obst* ***Caesarean birth*** césarienne *f*; *Obst* ***Caesarean section*** césarienne *f*

caesura [sɪ'zjʊərə] *(pl* **caesuras** *or* **caesurae** [-riː]*)* N *Literature* césure *f*

cafe, café ['kæfeɪ] N *(in UK)* snack *m*; *(in rest of Europe)* café *m*
▸▸ ***cafe society*** le beau monde

> **CAFÉ**
>
> En Grande-Bretagne, le mot "café" désigne une sorte de snack où l'on peut prendre un repas léger et boire du thé ou du café.

cafeteria [kæfɪ'tɪərɪə] N *(self-service restaurant)* restaurant *m* self-service, self *m*; *Am (canteen)* cantine *f*

caff [kæf] N *Br Fam* snack *m*

caffeinated ['kæfɪneɪtɪd] ADJ caféiné

caffeine ['kæfiːn] N caféine *f*

caffeine-free ADJ sans caféine

caftan ['kæftæn] N caftan *m*

cage [keɪdʒ] N **1** *(with bars)* cage *f* **2** *(lift)* cabine *f*; *Mining* cage *f* (d'extraction) **3** *Sport (in basketball)* panier *m*; *(in ice hockey)* cage *f*
VT mettre en cage, encager; **caged animal** animal en cage; **I feel caged in** je me sens enfermé
▸▸ ***cage bird*** oiseau *m* d'agrément *ou* d'appartement; ***cage diver*** = personne pratiquant la plongée en cage; ***cage diving*** plongée *f* en cage

cagey ['keɪdʒɪ] *(comp* **cagier**, *superl* **cagiest***)* ADJ *Fam (careful)* prudent; *(reticent)* réticent; **he was being c. about his salary** il s'est montré évasif lorsqu'il s'est agi de son salaire

cagily ['keɪdʒɪlɪ] ADV *Fam (carefully)* très prudemment; *(reticently)* avec réticence; **to answer c.** donner une réponse vague

caginess ['keɪdʒɪnɪs] N *Fam (carefulness)* prudence *f*; *(reticence)* réticence *f*; **there was a certain c. in her replies** elle évitait de répondre en restant dans le vague

Cagliari ['kæljərɪ] N Cagliari

cagoule [kə'guːl] N *Br* veste *f* imperméable *(à capuche)*

cahoots [kə'huːts] NPL *Fam (idiom)* **to be in c. (with sb)** être de mèche (avec qn)

CAI [ˌsiːeɪ'aɪ] N *Comput (abbr* **computer-aided instruction, computer-assisted instruction***)* EAO *m*

caiman = **cayman**

Cain [keɪn] PR N *Bible* Caïn; **to raise C.** *(make noise)* faire un bruit de tous les diables; *(make scene)* faire une scène terrible

cairn [keən] N cairn *m*
▸▸ ***cairn terrier*** cairn terrier *m*

cairngorm ['keəŋgɔːm] N *Miner* quartz *m* fumé
• **Cairngorm** N **the Cairngorms** les monts *mpl* Cairngorm
▸▸ ***the Cairngorm Mountains*** les monts *mpl* Cairngorm

Cairo ['kaɪərəʊ] N Le Caire

caisson ['keɪsɒn] N **1** *Constr (for working underwater)* caisson *m* **2** *Naut (in dry dock)* bateau-porte *m* **3** *Mil (for ammunition)* caisson *m*
▸▸ *Med* ***caisson disease*** maladie *f* des caissons

cajole [kə'dʒəʊl] VT enjôler; **to c. sb into doing sth** amadouer qn pour qu'il fasse qch

cajolery [kə'dʒəʊlərɪ] N *(UNCOUNT)* cajoleries *fpl*

Cajun ['keɪdʒən] N **1** Cajun *mf inv* **2** *(language)* cajun *m*
ADJ cajun *(inv)*

cake [keɪk] N **1** *(sweet)* gâteau *m*; *(pastry)* pâtisserie *f*; *(savoury)* croquette *f*; **a chocolate/cherry c.** un gâteau au chocolat/aux cerises; **to make** *or* **to bake a c.** faire un gâteau; *Fam* **it's a piece of c.** c'est du gâteau *ou* de la tarte; *Prov* **you can't have your c. and eat it** on ne peut pas avoir le beurre et l'argent du beurre **2** *(block ▸ of soap, wax)* pain *m*; *(▸ of chocolate)* plaquette *f*
COMP *(crumb)* de gâteau; *(dish)* à gâteau
VT **caked with mud/blood** couvert de boue/sang séché(e)
VI durcir; **the mud had caked on his boots** la boue avait séché sur ses bottes
▸▸ ***cake decoration*** décoration *f* pour gâteau; ***cake mix*** préparation *f* (instantanée) pour gâteau; *Am* ***cake pan*** moule *m* à gâteau; ***cake shop*** pâtisserie *f*; ***cake stall*** *(at fair)* stand *m* à gâteaux; ***cake stand*** plat *m* à gâteaux; *Br* ***cake tin*** moule *m* à gâteau

caked [keɪkt] ADJ *(mud, blood)* séché

cakehole ['keɪkhəʊl] N *Br Fam (mouth)* bouche *f*, clapet *m*; **shut your c.!** ferme-la!, ferme ton clapet!

cakewalk ['keɪkwɔːk] N **1** *(dance)* cake-walk *m* **2** *Am Fam Fig (easy task)* **the exam was a c.** l'examen, c'était du gâteau

CAL [ˌsiːeɪ'el, kæl] N *Comput (abbr* **computer-aided learning, computer-assisted learning***)* EAO *m*

calabash ['kæləbæʃ] N *Bot (fruit)* calebasse *f*; *(tree)* calebassier *m*

calaboose ['kæləbuːs] N *Am Fam* taule *f*, tôle *f*; **in the c.** en taule, en tôle

calamine ['kæləˌmaɪn] N *Chem* calamine *f*
▸▸ ***calamine lotion*** lotion *f* calmante à la calamine

calamitous [kə'læmɪtəs] ADJ calamiteux

calamity [kə'læmətɪ] *(pl* **calamities***)* N calamité *f*

calcareous [kæl'keərɪəs] ADJ *Chem* calcaire
▸▸ *Geol* ***calcareous schist*** calcschiste *m*

calceolaria [ˌkælsɪə'leərɪə] N *Bot* calcéolaire *f*

calcification [ˌkælsɪfɪ'keɪʃən] N *Chem* calcification *f*

calcify ['kælsɪfaɪ] *(pt & pp* **calcified***)* *Chem* VT calcifier
VI se calcifier

calcium ['kælsɪəm] N *Chem* calcium *m*
▸▸ ***calcium carbonate*** carbonate *m* de calcium; ***calcium chloride*** chlorure *m* de calcium; ***calcium deficiency*** carence *f* en calcium;

calculable ['kælkjʊləbəl] ADJ calculable

calculate ['kælkjʊleɪt] VT **1** *Math* calculer; *(estimate, evaluate)* calculer, évaluer; **he calculated that his chances of success were reasonably good** il calcula *ou* estima qu'il avait d'assez bonnes chances de réussir **2** *(design, intend)* **her remark was calculated to offend the guests** sa réflexion était destinée à offenser les invités; **words calculated to reassure us** paroles propres à nous rassurer
VI **1** *Math* calculer, faire des calculs **2** *Am (count, depend)* **I calculated on George lending me the money** je comptais sur George pour me prêter l'argent

calculated ['kælkjʊleɪtɪd] ADJ **1** *(considered)* calculé, mesuré; **a c. risk** un risque calculé **2** *(deliberate, intentional)* délibéré, voulu; **a c. insult** une insulte délibérée

calculating ['kælkjʊleɪtɪŋ] ADJ **1** *Pej (person)* calculateur **2** *(cautious)* prudent, mesuré
▸▸ *Math* ***calculating machine*** machine *f* à calculer

calculation [ˌkælkjʊ'leɪʃən] N **1** *Math & Fig* calcul *m*; **to make a c.** effectuer un calcul; **by** *or* **according to my calculations** selon *ou* d'après mes calculs **2** *(UNCOUNT) Pej (scheming)* **his offer of help was free of all c.** il a offert son aide sans la moindre arrière-pensée

calculator ['kælkjʊleɪtə(r)] N **1** *(machine)* calculateur *m*; *(small)* calculatrice *f* **2** *(table)* table *f*
COMP *(battery)* de calculatrice

calculus ['kælkjʊləs] N *Math & Med* calcul *m*

Calcutta [kæl'kʌtə] N Calcutta

Caledonia [ˌkælɪ'dəʊnjə] N *Hist* Calédonie *f*

Caledonian [ˌkælɪ'dəʊnjən] N Calédonien(enne) *m,f*
ADJ calédonien

calendar ['kælɪndə(r)] N **1** *(of dates)* calendrier *m* **2** *(register)* annuaire *m*; **the university c.** l'annuaire de l'université **3** *Am (planner)* agenda *m*
COMP *(day, month, year)* civil, calendaire
VT *(event)* inscrire sur le calendrier; *Am (put in planner)* noter *(dans son agenda)*
▸▸ ***calendar girl*** pin-up *f*

calender ['kælɪndə(r)] *Tech* N calandre *f*, laminoir *m*
VT calandrer

calendered ['kælɪndəd] ADJ *Tech (paper)* calandré, satiné

calends ['kælɪndz] NPL *Hist* calendes *fpl*

calf [kɑːf] *(pl* **calves** [kɑːvz]*)* N **1** *(young cow, bull)* veau *m*; **the cow is in c.** la vache est pleine
2 *(skin)* veau *m*, vachette *f*
3 *(buffalo)* bufflon *m*, buffletin *m*; *(elephant)* éléphanteau *m*; *(giraffe)* girafeau *m*, girafon *m*; *(whale)* baleineau *m*
4 *(part of leg)* mollet *m*
5 *Geol (of glacier)* glaçon *m*, veau *m*
▸▸ ***calf love*** premières amours *fpl*

calfskin ['kɑːfskɪn] N veau *m*, vachette *f*
COMP en veau, en vachette

Calgary ['kælgərɪ] N Calgary

caliber *Am* = **calibre**

calibrate ['kælɪbreɪt] VT *Tech (measuring instrument etc)* étalonner; *(bore)* calibrer; *(thermometer)* graduer; *Mil (piece of artillery)* vérifier le calibre de

calibration [ˌkælɪ'breɪʃən] N *Tech (of measuring instrument)* étalonnage *m*; *(of bore)* calibrage *m*; *(of thermometer)* graduation *f*

calibre, *Am* **caliber** ['kælɪbə(r)] N **1** *(of gun, tube)* calibre *m* **2** *(quality)* qualité *f*; **their work is of the highest c.** ils font un travail de grande qualité; **the two applicants are not of the same c.** les deux candidats ne sont pas du même calibre *ou* n'ont pas la même envergure

calico ['kælɪkəʊ] *(pl* **calicoes** *or* **calicos***)* *Tex* N *Br* calicot *m* blanc; *Am* calicot *m* imprimé, indienne *f*
COMP de calicot

California [ˌkælɪ'fɔːnjə] N la Californie; **Lower C.** la Basse-Californie

Californian [ˌkælɪ'fɔːnjən] N Californien(enne) *m,f*
ADJ californien

caliper *Am* = **calliper**

caliph, Caliph ['keɪlɪf] N *Rel* calife *m*

caliphate ['keɪlɪfɪt] N *Rel* califat *m*

calisthenics = **callisthenics**

calk [kɔːk] N *(on shoe, horseshoe)* crampon *m*
VT **1** *(shoe, horseshoe)* munir de crampons **2** *(make watertight)* calfeutrer; *Naut* calfater

CALL [kɔːl]

> **VI**
> • appeler **1, 2, 6** • pousser un cri **3**
> • passer **4** • s'arrêter **5**
>
> **VT**
> • appeler **1, 2, 4, 7** • réveiller **3**
> • annoncer **6, 10** • juger **9**
>
> **N**
> • appel **1–3** • visite **4**
> • demande **6, 8, 10** • jugement **9**
> • annonce **10**

VI 1 *(with one's voice)* appeler; **if you need me, just c.** si tu as besoin de moi, tu n'as qu'à (m')appeler; **she called to her son in the crowd** elle appela son fils dans la foule; **to c. for help** appeler à l'aide *ou* au secours

2 *(on the telephone)* appeler; **where are you calling from?** d'où appelles-tu?; **it's Alison calling** c'est Alison à l'appareil; **who's calling?** qui est à l'appareil?, c'est de la part de qui?; **may I ask who's calling?** qui est à l'appareil, je vous prie?

3 *(animal, bird)* pousser un cri

4 *Br (visit)* passer; **I'll c. at the butcher's on the way home** je passerai chez le boucher en revenant à la maison; **do c. again** n'hésitez pas à revenir; **I was out when they called** je n'étais pas là quand ils sont passés

5 *Br (stop)* s'arrêter; **to c. at** *(train)* s'arrêter à; *(ship)* faire escale à

6 *Cards (in bridge)* appeler (l'atout); *(in poker)* forcer l'adversaire à déclarer son jeu

VT 1 *(with one's voice)* appeler; **to c. sb's name** appeler qn; **"be careful!" he called** "attention!", cria-t-il; *Sch* **to c. the roll** faire l'appel

2 *(telephone)* appeler; **don't c. me at work** ne m'appelle pas au bureau; **we called his house** nous avons appelé chez lui; **to c. the police/fire brigade** appeler la police/les pompiers; *Hum Euph* **don't c. us, we'll c. you** on vous écrira

3 *(wake up)* réveiller

4 *(name or describe as)* appeler; **he has a cat called Felix** il a un chat qui s'appelle Félix; **what's this called?** comment est-ce qu'on appelle ça?, comment est-ce que ça s'appelle?; **are you calling me a thief?** me traitez-vous de voleur?; **to c. sb names** injurier qn, invectiver qn; **they called him all sorts of names** *or* **every name under the sun** ils l'ont traité de tous les noms

5 *(consider)* **he had no home to c. his own** il n'avait pas de chez lui; **(and you) c. yourself a Christian!** et tu te dis chrétien!; **I don't c. that clean** ce n'est pas ce que j'appelle propre; *Br* **let's c. it £10, shall we?** disons *ou* mettons 10 livres, d'accord?; **let's c. it a day** si on s'arrêtait là pour aujourd'hui?

6 *(announce)* **to c. an election** annoncer des élections; **to c. a meeting** convoquer une assemblée; **to c. a strike** appeler à la grève

7 *(summon)* appeler, convoquer; **he was called to the phone** on l'a demandé au téléphone; **to c. the doctor** faire venir le médecin, appeler le médecin; **she was suddenly called home** elle a été rappelée soudainement chez elle; **to be called away on an emergency** être appelé en urgence; **he's been called away, his mother is ill** il a dû s'absenter parce que sa mère est malade; **she was called as a witness** elle a été citée comme témoin; **he called me over** il m'a appelé; **to c. sth into question** remettre qch en question; **the scenery calls to mind certain parts of Brittany** le paysage rappelle un peu certaines parties de la Bretagne; **market forces will soon be called into play** on fera bientôt jouer les lois du marché

8 *Fin* **to c. a loan** exiger le remboursement d'un prêt

9 *Sport (declare, judge)* juger; **he called it out** il a jugé qu'elle était dehors

10 *Cards (in bridge)* annoncer; *(in poker)* demander

11 **to c. heads/tails** choisir face/pile; *Fam* **to c. the shots** *or Br* **tune** faire la loi

N 1 *(cry, shout)* appel *m*; *(of animal, bird)* cri *m*; *(of bugle, drum)* appel *m*; *Fig* **he showed dedication (above and) beyond the c. of duty** il a fait preuve d'un dévouement bien au-delà de ce qu'on était en droit d'attendre de lui; **a c. for help** un appel à l'aide *ou* au secours; **to give sb a c.** *(waken)* réveiller qn

2 *(on telephone)* appel *m*; **can I make a c.?** puis-je téléphoner?; **to put a c. through** passer une communication; **to make a c.** passer un coup de téléphone; **there's a c. for you** on vous demande au téléphone; **to take a c.** prendre un appel; **I'll give you a c. tomorrow** je t'appelle demain; **how much does a c. to Italy cost?** combien est-ce que ça coûte d'appeler en Italie *ou* l'Italie?; **he's on a c.** il est en ligne; **to return sb's c.** rappeler qn

3 *(summons)* appel *m*; **to come at/answer sb's c.** venir/répondre à l'appel de qn; **to be within c.** être à portée de voix; **this is the last c. for passengers for Bordeaux** ceci est le dernier appel pour les passagers à destination de Bordeaux; **c. for tenders** appel *m* d'offres; *Euph* **to obey** *or* **answer a c. of nature** satisfaire un besoin naturel

4 *(visit)* visite *f*; *Br* **to make** *or* **to pay a c. on sb** rendre visite à qn; *Br* **the doctor doesn't make house calls** le médecin ne fait pas de visites à domicile

5 *Br (stop)* **the ship made a c. at Genoa** le navire a fait escale à Gênes

6 *(demand, need)* **there have been renewed calls for a return to capital punishment** il y a des gens qui demandent à nouveau le rétablissement de la peine de mort; **there is little c. for unskilled labour** il n'y a qu'une faible demande de travailleurs non spécialisés; **there's no c. to shout** il n'y a aucune raison de crier; **there's no c. for rudeness!** pas besoin *ou* ce n'est pas la peine d'être impoli!; **you have first c. on my time** je m'occuperai de vous en premier lieu

7 *St Exch* option *f* d'achat, call *m*; **c. of more** option *f* du double

8 *Fin (for repayment)* demande *f* (d'argent); **c. for capital** appel *m* de fonds

9 *Sport (decision)* jugement *m*; *Fig Fam* **good c.!** bonne idée!

10 *Cards (in bridge)* annonce *f*; *(in solo, whist)* demande *f*

11 *Rel* vocation *f*; **he felt a c. (to the ministry)** il se sentait une vocation religieuse

12 *(heads or tails)* **your c.** pile ou face?; **it's your c.!** c'est à toi de décider

• **on call** **ADJ** *(doctor, nurse)* de garde; *(police, troops)* en éveil; *(car)* disponible; *Fin (loan)* remboursable sur demande

►► *Tel* **call barring** interdiction *f* d'appels; *Tel* **call box** *Br (telephone box)* cabine *f* téléphonique; *Am (on roadside)* borne *f* d'appel d'urgence; **call button** bouton *m* d'appel; *Com* **call centre** centre *m* d'appels; *Tel* **call connection** établissement *m* d'appel; *Tel* **call diversion** transfert *m* d'appel; *Tel* **call forwarding** redirection *f* d'appel; **call girl** *(prostitute)* call-girl *f*; *Tel* **call holding** mise *f* en attente d'appels; *Tel* **call key** touche *f* d'appel; *Am Rad* **call letters** indicatif *m* d'appel *(d'une station de radio)*; *St Exch* **call option** option *f* d'achat, call *m*; *St Exch* **call price** cours *m* du dont; *Tel* **call screening** filtrage *m* d'appels; *Comput* **call sequence** séquence *f* d'appel; *Rad* **call sign** indicatif *m* d'appel *(d'une station de radio)*; *Tel* **call waiting** signal *m* d'appel

► **call back** **VT SEP 1** *(on telephone)* rappeler **2** *(ask to return)* rappeler; **I was already at the door when she called me back** j'étais déjà près de la porte lorsqu'elle m'a rappelé

VI 1 *(on telephone)* rappeler; **can you c. back after five?** pourriez-vous rappeler après cinq heures? **2** *(visit again)* revenir, repasser

► **call by** **VI = call round**

► **call down** **VT SEP 1** *Literary (invoke)* **he called down the wrath of God on the killers** il appela la colère de Dieu sur la tête des tueurs **2** *Am Fam (reprimand)* engueuler

► **call for** **VT INSEP 1** *Br (collect)* **he called for her at her parents' house** il est passé la chercher chez ses parents; **whose is this parcel? – someone's calling for it later** à qui est ce paquet? – quelqu'un passera le prendre plus tard **2** *(put forward as demand)* appeler, demander; *(of agreement, treaty)* prévoir; **the opposition called for an official statement** l'opposition a exigé *ou* demandé une déclaration officielle; **the police are calling for tougher penalties** la police réclame des sanctions plus fermes **3** *(require)* exiger; **the situation called for quick thinking** la situation demandait *ou* exigeait qu'on réfléchisse vite; **this calls for a celebration/a drink!** il faut fêter/arroser ça!; **that wasn't called for** ça n'était vraiment pas nécessaire

► **call in** **VT SEP 1** *(send for)* faire venir; **c. Miss Smith in, please** faites entrer Mlle Smith, s'il vous plaît; **an accountant was called in to look at the books** on a fait venir un comptable pour examiner les livres de comptes; **she called the children in** *(back into the house)* elle a fait rentrer les enfants; **the army was called in to assist with the evacuation** on a fait appel à l'armée pour aider à l'évacuation **2** *(recall* ► *defective goods)* rappeler; *(*► *banknotes)* retirer de la circulation; *(*► *library books)* faire rentrer **3** *Fin (debt)* rappeler; **to c. in a loan** *(of bank)* demander le remboursement d'un prêt

VI 1 *Br (pay a visit)* passer; **she called in at her sister's to say goodbye** elle est passée chez sa sœur pour dire au revoir **2** *(telephone)* appeler, téléphoner; **to c. in sick** téléphoner pour prévenir qu'on est malade

► **call off** **VT SEP 1** *(appointment, meeting, match, holidays)* annuler; *(deal)* annuler, résilier; **to c. off a strike** *(before it takes place)* annuler un ordre de grève; *(when it has begun)* mettre fin à une grève; **to c. off one's engagement** rompre ses fiançailles; **the police called off their search** la police a arrêté ses recherches **2** *(dog, attacker)* rappeler

► **call on** **VT INSEP 1** *(summon)* faire appel à; **to c. on the experts/sb's services** faire appel aux *ou* avoir recours aux experts/services de qn; **the limited resources the police can c. on** les ressources limitées que la police peut mettre en œuvre

2 *(urge, invite)* **to c. on sb to do sth** demander à qn de faire qch; **I now c. on Mr Stewart** *(to speak)* je laisse la parole à M. Stewart

3 *(visit)* rendre visite à; **I'll c. on her this evening** je lui rendrai visite *ou* je passerai chez elle ce soir

4 *(invoke)* **to c. on God** invoquer le nom de Dieu

► **call out** **VT SEP 1** *(shout)* crier; **she called out the winning number** elle a annoncé le numéro gagnant **2** *(summon)* appeler, faire appel à; **the army was called out to help** on a fait appel à l'armée pour aider; **the union called out its members for 24 hours** le syndicat appela ses adhérents à une grève de 24 heures

VI *(shout)* appeler; **she called out to a policeman** elle appela un agent de police; **to c. out in anger/pain** crier de colère/douleur

► **call round** **VI** *Br* passer; **can I c. round this evening?** puis-je passer ce soir?; **your mother called round for the parcel** votre mère est passée prendre le paquet

► **call up** **VT SEP 1** *(telephone)* appeler

2 *Mil (for military service)* appeler; *(reservists)* mobiliser; **to be called up** être mobilisé/appelé

3 *(evoke)* évoquer, faire venir à l'esprit

4 *(summon)* appeler, convoquer

5 *Comput (help screen, menu)* rappeler

VI appeler

---

callable ['kɔːləbəl] **ADJ** *Fin (loan, debt)* remboursable sur demande

callboy ['kɔːlbɔɪ] **N 1** *Theat* avertisseur *m* **2** *Am (bellboy)* chasseur *m*, groom *m*

caller ['kɔːlə(r)] **N 1** *(visitor)* visiteur(euse) *m,f* **2** *Tel* personne *f* qui appelle; **the vast majority of callers just need someone to talk to** la plupart des gens qui nous appellent ont juste besoin de parler **3** *(in bingo)* animateur(trice) *m,f*

►► *Tel* **caller display** présentation *f* du numéro de l'appelant; *Tel* **caller identification, caller ID** identification *f* d'appel

calligrapher [kə'lɪgrəfə(r)] **N** calligraphe *mf*

calligraphy [kə'lɪgrəfɪ] **N** calligraphie *f*

call-in **N** *TV & Rad* émission *f* à ligne ouverte

calling ['kɔːlɪŋ] **N 1** *(vocation)* appel *m* intérieur, vocation *f*; **I felt no/a c. for a religious life** je n'avais pas/j'avais la vocation **2** *Formal (profession)* métier *m*, profession *f*

►► *Am* **calling card** *(visiting card)* carte *f* de visite; *Tel* carte *f* téléphonique; *Fin* **calling in** *(of debt, loan)* demande *f* de remboursement immédiat; *(of currency)* retrait *m*; **calling off** *(of appointment, meeting, match, holidays)* annulation *f*; *(of deal)* rupture *f*; *(of dog, attacker)* rappel *m*; **the c. off of the strike** l'annulation de l'ordre de grève; **calling up** *(of memory)* évocation *f*; *(by telephone)* appel *m* au téléphone; *Mil* appel *m* (sous les drapeaux)

calliper, *Am* **caliper** ['kælɪpə(r)] **N 1** *Math* **a pair of c. compasses** *or* **callipers** un compas **2** *Med* **c. (splint)** attelle-étrier *f* **3** *Tech (for brake)* étrier *m*

callisthenics [ˌkælɪs'θenɪks] **N** *(UNCOUNT) Sport* gymnastique *f* rythmique

callosity [kə'lɒsətɪ] *(pl* **callosities***)* **N** *Med & Bot* callosité *f*

callous ['kæləs] ADJ **1** *(unfeeling)* dur, sans cœur; *(behaviour, remark)* dur, impitoyable **2** *(skin)* calleux

calloused ['kæləst] ADJ *(feet, hands)* calleux, corné

callously ['kæləslı] ADV durement

callousness ['kæləsnıs] N dureté *f*

call-out N *(by maintenance man)* dépannage *m*
▸▸ ***call-out charge*** (frais *mpl* de) déplacement *m*

callow ['kæləʊ] ADJ sans expérience, sans maturité

callowness ['kæləʊnıs] N manque *m* d'expérience

call-up N *Br Mil (conscription)* convocation *f* (au service militaire), ordre *m* d'incorporation
▸▸ ***call-up papers*** ordre *m* d'incorporation; **to get one's c. papers** être appelé sous les drapeaux

callus ['kæləs] N *(on feet, hands)* cal *m*, durillon *m*

calm [kɑːm] N calme *m*; *(after upset, excitement)* accalmie *f*; **the government appealed for c.** le gouvernement appela au calme; **the c. before the storm** le calme qui précède la tempête
ADJ calme; **keep c.!** du calme!, restons calmes!; **she tried to keep c.** elle essaya de garder son calme *ou* sang-froid; **to be c. and collected** être maître de soi, garder son sang-froid
VT calmer; *(fears)* apaiser, calmer; **she tried to c. her nerves** elle essaya de se calmer
▸ **calm down** VT SEP calmer
VI se calmer; **c. down!** calmez-vous!, ne vous énervez pas!

calming ['kɑːmıŋ] ADJ calmant; **her words had a c. effect on him** ses paroles ont réussi à le calmer

calmly ['kɑːmlı] ADV calmement; **she received the news c.** elle a reçu la nouvelle calmement *ou* avec calme

calmness ['kɑːmnıs] N calme *m*

Calor gas® ['kælə-] N *Br* butane *m*, Butagaz® *m*
▸▸ ***Calor gas® heater*** radiateur *m* au butane; ***Calor gas® stove*** réchaud *m*

caloric [kə'lɒrık] ADJ *Phys & Physiol* calorique

calorie ['kælərı] N *Phys & Physiol* calorie *f*; **low-c. diet, c.-controlled diet** régime *m* hypocalorique *ou* basses calories *ou* faible en calories; *Fam* **to watch** *or* **to count the calories** surveiller sa ligne
▸▸ ***calorie count*** taux *m* de calorie

calorific [ˌkælə'rıfık] ADJ *Phys & Physiol* calorifique
▸▸ ***calorific value*** valeur *f* calorifique

calumniate [kə'lʌmnıeıt] VT *Formal* calomnier

calumny ['kæləmnı] (*pl* **calumnies**) N *Formal* calomnie *f*

calvary ['kælvərı] *Rel* N calvaire *m*
• **Calvary** N le Calvaire

calve [kɑːv] VI *(cow, glacier)* vêler

calving ['kɑːvıŋ] N *(of cow)* vêlage *m*, vêlement *m*; **at c. time** pendant le vêlement

Calvinism ['kælvınızəm] N *Rel* calvinisme *m*

Calvinist ['kælvınıst] *Rel* N calviniste *mf*
ADJ calviniste

calypso [kə'lıpsəʊ] (*pl* **calypsos**) N *Mus* calypso *m*

calyx ['keılıks] (*pl* **calyxes** *or* **calyces** [-siːz]) N *Bot* calice *m*

CAM [ˌsiːeı'em, kæm] N *Comput* (*abbr* **computer-aided manufacturing, computer-assisted manufacturing**) FAO *f*

cam [kæm] N *Tech* came *f*

camber ['kæmbə(r)] *Tech* N *(in road)* bombement *m*; *(in beam, girder)* cambre *f*, cambrure *f*; *(in ship's deck)* tonture *f*
VI *(road)* bomber, être bombé; *(beam, girder)* être cambré; *(ship's deck)* avoir une tonture

Cambodia [kæm'bəʊdjə] N Cambodge *m*

Cambodian [kæm'bəʊdjən] N Cambodgien(enne) *m,f*
ADJ cambodgien
COMP *(embassy, history)* du Cambodge

cambric ['keımbrık, 'kæmbrık] N *Tex* batiste *f*

Cambridge ['keımbrıdʒ] N Cambridge
▸▸ ***Cambridge Certificate*** = diplôme d'anglais langue étrangère administré par l'Université de Cambridge

Cambridgeshire ['keımbrıdʒʃıə] N le Cambridgeshire, = comté dans le sud de l'Angleterre

camcorder ['kæmˌkɔːdə(r)] N Caméscope® *m*

camel ['kæməl] N **1** *Zool* chameau *m*; *(with one hump)* dromadaire *m*; *(female)* chamelle *f* **2** *(colour)* fauve *m inv*
COMP **1** *(train)* de chameaux **2** *(coat, jacket* ▸ *of camel hair)* en poil de chameau; *(*▸ *coloured)* fauve *(inv)*
▸▸ ***camel driver*** chamelier *m*; ***camel ride*** promenade *f* à dos de chameau

camelhair ['kæməlheə(r)] N poil *m* de chameau
COMP *(coat, jacket)* en poil de chameau
▸▸ ***camelhair brush*** *(for watercolour painting)* pinceau *m* en petit-gris

camellia [kə'miːlıə] N *Bot* camélia *m*

cameo ['kæmıəʊ] (*pl* **cameos**) N **1** *(piece of jewellery)* camée *m* **2** *(piece of writing)* morceau *m* bref, court texte *m*; *Cin, Theat & TV (appearance)* brève apparition *f (par un acteur célèbre)*
COMP *(brooch, ring)* monté en broche
▸▸ *Cin, Theat & TV* ***cameo performance*** brève apparition *f (par un acteur célèbre)*; *Cin, Theat & TV* ***cameo role*** petit rôle *m (joué par un acteur célèbre)*

camera ['kæmərə] N **1** *(device* ▸ *for still photos)* appareil *m* (photographique), appareil photo *m*; *(*▸ *for film, video)* caméra *f*; **to be on c.** être à l'écran; **off c.** hors champ; **in front of the c.** devant les caméras **2** *Law* **in c.** à huis clos
COMP *(battery, case)* pour appareil photo; *(shop)* de photo
▸▸ *Cin & TV* ***camera angle*** angle *m* de prise de vue; *Cin & TV* ***camera crane*** grue *f* de prise de vue; ***camera crew*** équipe *f* de tournage; ***camera lens*** objectif *m*; *Cin & TV* ***camera loader*** clapman *m*; *Cin & TV* ***camera movement*** mouvement *m* d'appareil; *Opt* ***camera obscura*** chambre *f* noire; *Cin & TV* ***camera operator*** cadreur(euse) *m,f*; ***camera phone*** téléphone *m* portable avec appareil photo; *TV & Opt* ***camera tube*** tube *m* analyseur

cameraman ['kæmərəmæn] (*pl* **cameramen** [-men]) N cadreur *m*, cameraman *m*

camera-ready copy N *Typ & Comput* copie *f* prête pour la reproduction

camera-shy ADJ **he's c.** il n'aime pas être pris en photo

camerawork ['kæmərəwɜːk] N prise *f* de vue

Cameroon [ˌkæmə'ruːn] N Cameroun *m*

camiknickers ['kæmıˌnıkəz] NPL *Br* combinaison-culotte *f*

camisole ['kæmısəʊl] N caraco *m*, *Can & Suisse* camisole *f*

camomile ['kæməmaıl] N *Bot* camomille *f*
▸▸ ***camomile shampoo*** shampooing *m* à la camomille; ***camomile tea*** infusion *f* de camomille

camouflage ['kæməflɑːʒ] N camouflage *m*
COMP *(material, jacket, trousers)* de camouflage
VT camoufler
▸▸ *Mil* ***camouflage net*** filet *m* de camouflage

camp[1] [kæmp] N **1** *(place)* camp *m*; *(not permanent)* campement *m*; **to make** *or* **to pitch** *or* **to set up c.** établir un camp; **to break c.** lever le camp **2** *(group)* camp *m*, parti *m*; **the conservative c.** le parti *ou* camp conservateur, les conservateurs *mpl*; **to go over to the other c.** changer de camp; **to be in the same c.** être du même bord
VI camper; **are you going to c.?** allez-vous camper *ou* faire du camping?
▸▸ ***camp bed*** lit *m* de camp; ***camp chair*** pliant *m*, chaise *f* pliante; *Am* ***camp counselor*** moniteur (trice) *m,f*; ***camp follower*** *(gen)* = civil qui accompagne une armée pour rendre des services; *(prostitute)* prostituée *f*, fille *f* à soldats; *Fig (supporter)* compagnon *m* de route; ***camp stool*** pliant *m*, chaise *f* pliante

camp[2] N *(kitsch)* **(high) c.** kitsch *m*
ADJ **1** *(effeminate)* efféminé **2** *(affected)* affecté, maniéré; *(theatrical* ▸ *person)* cabotin; *(*▸ *manners)* théâtral **3** *(in dubious taste)* kitsch *(inv)*
▸ **camp out** VI camper, faire du camping; *Fig* **we camped out at my parents** nous avons campé chez mes parents

campaign [kæm'peın] N campagne *f*; **to conduct** *or* **to lead a c. against drugs** mener une campagne *ou* faire campagne contre la drogue; *Pol* **to be on the c. trail** être en pleine campagne électorale
VI mener une campagne, faire campagne; **to c. against/for sth** mener une campagne contre/en faveur de qch; **they campaigned for his release** ils ont mené une campagne pour sa libération
▸▸ *Pol* ***campaign manager*** chef *m* de campagne électorale; *Mil* ***campaign medal*** médaille *f* commémorative

campaigner [kæm'peınə(r)] N militant(e) *m,f*; *Mil* vétéran *m*; *Mil & Fig* **old c.** vétéran *m*; **campaigners in favour of/against nuclear power** des militants pronucléaires/antinucléaires

campanologist [ˌkæmpə'nɒlədʒıst] N carillonneur *m*

campanology [ˌkæmpə'nɒlədʒı] N art *m* des carillons

campanula [kəm'pænjʊlə] N *Bot* campanule *f*

camper ['kæmpə(r)] N **1** *(person)* campeur(euse) *m,f* **2** *(vehicle)* **c. (van)** camping-car *m*

campfire ['kæmpˌfaıə(r)] N feu *m* de camp

camphor ['kæmfə(r)] N *Chem* camphre *m*
▸▸ ***camphor oil*** essence *f* de camphre; ***camphor tree*** camphrier *m*

camphorated ['kæmfəreıtıd] ADJ *Chem* camphré

camping ['kæmpıŋ] N camping *m*; **to go c.** faire du camping, camper
COMP *(equipment)* de camping
▸▸ ***camping gas*** butane *m*; ***camping ground, camping grounds*** *(private)* camp *m*; *(commercial)* terrain *m* de camping, camping *m*; *(clearing)* emplacement *m* de camping, endroit *m* où camper; ***camping holiday*** vacances *fpl* (en) camping; ***camping site*** *(private)* camp *m*; *(commercial)* terrain *m* de camping, camping *m*; *(clearing)* emplacement *m* de camping, endroit *m* où camper; ***camping stool*** pliant *m*; ***camping stove*** camping-gaz *m*

camping-caravanning N campage-caravanage *m*, camping-caravaning *m*

campion ['kæmpjən] N *Bot* silène *m*, lychnis *m*

campus ['kæmpəs] (*pl* **campuses**) N *Univ (grounds)* campus *m*; *(buildings)* campus *m*, complexe *m* universitaire; **to live on c.** habiter sur le campus; **to live off c.** habiter en dehors du campus; **on-/off-c. housing** logements *mpl* sur le/en dehors du campus
▸▸ ***campus university*** université *f* regroupant sur un campus

camshaft ['kæmʃɑːft] N *Tech* arbre *m* à cames

CAN[1] [kən, *stressed* kæn]

• pouvoir **1, 4–7** • savoir **3**

(*pt* **could** [kəd, *stressed* kʊd], *negative forms* **cannot** ['kænət, *stressed* 'kænɒt], **could not**, *frequently shortened to* **can't** [kɑːnt], **couldn't** ['kʊdənt])

Le verbe **can** n'a ni infinitif, ni gérondif ni participe. Pour exprimer l'infinitif ou le participe, on aura recours à la forme correspondante de **be able to** (**he wanted to be able to speak English**; **she has always been able to swim**).

MODAL AUX V **1** *(be able to)* pouvoir; **c. you help me?** pouvez-vous m'aider?; **I'll come if I c.** je viendrai si je (le) peux; **I'll come as soon as I c.** je viendrai aussitôt que possible *ou* aussitôt que je pourrai; **we cannot possibly do it** nous ne pouvons absolument pas le faire; **we'll do everything we c. to help** nous ferons tout ce que nous pourrons *ou* tout notre possible pour aider; **she has everything money c. buy** elle a tout ce qu'elle veut; **she c. no longer walk** elle ne peut plus marcher; **I can't very well accept** il m'est difficile d'accepter; **you can't blame her for leaving him!** tu ne peux pas lui reprocher de l'avoir quitté!; **you'll have to leave, it can't be helped** il faudra que tu partes, il n'y a rien à faire **c. it be true?** serait-ce vrai?; **(it) could be** c'est possible; **can't we at least talk about it?** est-ce que nous pouvons au moins en discuter?; *Fam* **no c. do!** impossible!
2 *(with verbs of perception or understanding)* **c. you feel it?** tu le sens?; **we c. hear everything our**

neighbours say nous entendons tout ce que disent nos voisins; **I can't see anything** je ne vois rien; **I c. see his point of view** je comprends son point de vue; **there c. be no doubt about his guilt** sa culpabilité ne fait aucun doute

3 *(indicating ability or skill)* savoir; **c. you drive/sew?** savez-vous conduire/coudre?; **many people can't read or write** beaucoup de gens ne savent ni lire ni écrire; **she c. speak three languages** elle parle trois langues

4 *(giving or asking for permission)* pouvoir; **I've already said you can't go** je t'ai déjà dit que tu ne peux pas y aller; **c. I borrow your sweater? – yes, you c.** puis-je emprunter ton pull? – (mais oui,) bien sûr; **c. I sit with you?** puis-je m'asseoir avec vous?

5 *(used to interrupt, intervene)* pouvoir; **c. I just say something here?** est-ce que je peux dire quelque chose?

6 *(in offers of help)* pouvoir; **c. I be of any assistance?** puis-je vous aider?; **what c. I do for you?** que puis-je (faire) pour vous?

7 *(indicating possibility or likelihood)* pouvoir; **the contract c. still be cancelled** il est toujours possible d'annuler *ou* on peut encore annuler le contrat; **the job can't be finished in one day** il est impossible de finir le travail *ou* le travail ne peut pas se faire en un jour; **the cottage c. sleep six people** on peut loger six personnes dans ce cottage; **you c. always try again later** tu peux toujours réessayer plus tard; **he c. be very stubborn** il lui arrive d'être *ou* il peut être très têtu; **he could have done it** il aurait pu le faire; **what c. I have done with the keys?** qu'est-ce que j'ai bien pu faire des clés?; **she's as happy as c. be** elle est on ne peut plus heureux

8 *(indicating disbelief or doubt)* **you can't be serious!** (ce n'est pas possible!) vous ne parlez pas sérieusement!; **he can't possibly have finished already!** ce n'est pas possible qu'il ait déjà fini!; **the house can't have been that expensive** la maison n'a pas dû coûter si cher que ça; **how c. you say that?** comment pouvez-vous *ou* osez-vous dire ça?; **how COULD you!** comment avez-vous pu faire une chose pareille?; **you can't mean it!** tu ne penses pas ce que tu dis!; **what c. they want now?** qu'est-ce qu'ils peuvent bien vouloir maintenant?; **who on earth c. that be?** qui diable cela peut-il bien être?

9 *(expressing impatience or exasperation)* **I could have wept** j'avais envie de pleurer; **I could have smacked his face!** je l'aurais giflé!; **you could have warned me!** tu aurais pu me prévenir!

10 *Formal (idiom)* **his resignation cannot but confirm such suspicions** sa démission ne fait que confirmer de tels soupçons

can² [kæn] *(pt & pp* **canned**, *cont* **canning**) **N 1** *(container ▸ for liquid)* bidon *m*; *(▸ for tinned food)* boîte *f* (de conserve); *Am (▸ for rubbish)* poubelle *f*, boîte *f* à ordures; **a c. of beer/tuna** une boîte de bière/de thon; *Fig Fam* **a (real) c. of worms** un vrai casse-tête; *Fig Fam* **to open a c. of worms** mettre à jour toutes sortes d'histoires désagréables; *Fam* **the deal's in the c.** l'affaire est conclue

2 *Am Fam (prison)* taule *f*; **in the c.** en taule, au placard, à l'ombre

3 *Am Fam (toilet)* **the c.** les chiottes *fpl*

4 *Am Fam (buttocks)* fesses[▫] *fpl*; **to kick sb in the c.** botter les fesses à qn

5 *Br (idiom)* **to carry the c.** payer les pots cassés

VT 1 *(food)* mettre en boîte *ou* en conserve, conserver (en boîte) **2** *Am Fam (dismiss from job)* virer, renvoyer[▫] **3** *Am Fam* **c. it!** ferme-la!, la ferme!

• **cans NPL** *Fam (headphones)* casque *m (à écouteurs)*

▸▸ ***can opener*** ouvre-boîtes *m inv*

Canada ['kænədə] **N** Canada *m*

▸▸ *Orn* ***Canada goose*** bernache *f* du Canada

Canadian [kə'neɪdjən] **N** Canadien(enne) *m,f*

ADJ *(gen)* canadien

COMP *(embassy, history)* du Canada

▸▸ ***Canadian canoe*** canoë *m*; ***Canadian English*** anglais *m* du Canada; ***Canadian French*** français *m* canadien

Canadianism [kə'neɪdjəˌnɪzəm] **N** *(expression)* canadianisme *m*

canal [kə'næl] **N 1** *(waterway)* canal *m* **2** *Anat* canal *m*, conduit *m*

▸▸ ***canal barge, canal boat*** péniche *f*, chaland *m*; ***canal path*** chemin *m* de halage; *Geog* ***the Canal Zone*** *(of Panama)* la zone du canal de Panama; *(of Suez)* la zone du canal de Suez

canalization, -isation [ˌkænəlaɪ'zeɪʃən] **N** *Fig* canalisation *f*

canalize, -ise ['kænəlaɪz] **VT** *Fig* canaliser

canapé ['kænəpeɪ] **N** *Culin* canapé *m*

canard [kæ'nɑːd] **N** *(false report)* fausse nouvelle *f*, canard *m*

Canaries [kə'neərɪz] **NPL the C.** les Canaries *fpl*

canary [kə'neərɪ] *(pl* **canaries**) **N 1** *(bird)* canari *m*, serin *m* **2** *(colour)* jaune serin *m inv*, jaune canari *m inv*

ADJ *(colour)* jaune serin *(inv)*, jaune canari *(inv)*

▸▸ ***the Canary Islands*** les (îles *fpl*) Canaries *fpl*; *Bot* ***canary seed*** millet *m*; ***canary yellow*** jaune serin *m inv*, jaune canari *m inv*

canasta [kə'næstə] **N** *Cards* canasta *f*

cancan ['kænkæn] **N** cancan *m*, french cancan *m*

▸▸ ***cancan dancer*** danseuse *f* de cancan

cancel ['kænsəl] *(Br pt & pp* **cancelled**, *cont* **cancelling**, *Am pt & pp* **canceled**, *cont* **canceling**) **VT 1** *(call off ▸ event, order, reservation)* annuler; *(▸ appointment)* annuler, décommander; *(▸ goods)* décommander; **the flight has been cancelled** le vol a été annulé; **500, no c. that, 350...** 500, ou plutôt, 350...

2 *(revoke ▸ agreement, contract)* résilier, annuler; *(▸debt)* faire remise à; *(▸cheque)* faire opposition à

3 *(mark as no longer valid ▸ by stamping)* oblitérer; *(▸ by punching)* poinçonner

4 *(cross out)* barrer, rayer, biffer

5 *Math* éliminer

VI 1 *(having made booking)* se décommander **2** *Comput* s'annuler; **press "esc" to c.** appuyez sur "Echap" pour annuler

▸▸ *Comput* ***cancel button*** case *f* "annuler"

▸ **cancel out VT SEP 1** *(counterbalance)* neutraliser, compenser; **the factors c. each other out** les facteurs se neutralisent *ou* se compensent **2** *Math* éliminer, annuler

cancellation [ˌkænsə'leɪʃən] **N 1** *(calling off ▸ of event, reservation)* annulation *f*; *(annulment ▸ of agreement, contract)* résiliation *f*, annulation *f*; *(▸ of cheque)* opposition *f*; **we only got a table because there had been a c.** nous n'avons eu une table que parce que quelqu'un avait annulé sa réservation

2 *(act of invalidating ▸ by punching)* poinçonnage *m*; *(▸ by stamping)* oblitération *f*

3 *(crossing out)* biffage *m*

4 *Math* élimination *f*

▸▸ ***cancellation charge*** frais *mpl* d'annulation; ***cancellation clause*** clause *f* d'annulation *ou* de résiliation; ***cancellation fee*** frais *mpl* d'annulation

Cancer ['kænsə(r)] **N 1** *Astron* Cancer *m* **2** *Astrol* Cancer *m*; **he's a C.** il est (du signe du) Cancer

ADJ *Astrol* du Cancer; **he's C.** il est (du signe du) Cancer

cancer ['kænsə(r)] **N** *Med & Fig* cancer *m*; **to have c.** avoir un *ou* le cancer; **c. of the lung/skin, lung/skin c.** cancer *m* du poumon/de la peau; **to die of c.** mourir (à la suite) d'un cancer; **cigarettes cause c.** les cigarettes sont cancérigènes *ou* cancinogènes

▸▸ ***cancer cell*** cellule *f* cancéreuse; ***cancer patient*** cancéreux(euse) *m,f*; ***cancer research*** oncologie *f*, cancérologie *f*; **we're collecting money for c. research** nous recueillons des fonds pour la recherche contre le cancer; ***cancer research institute*** cancéropôle *m*; ***cancer screening*** dépistage *m* du cancer; *Fam Hum* ***cancer stick*** clope *f*

cancer-causing ADJ *Med* cancérigène, carcinogène

cancered ['kænsəd] **ADJ** *Med* cancérisé

Cancerian [ˌkæn'seərɪən] *Astrol* **N to be a C.** être (du signe du) Cancer

ADJ du Cancer; **the C. male** l'homme Cancer

cancerous ['kænsərəs] **ADJ** *Med* cancéreux

candelabra [ˌkændɪ'lɑːbrə] *(pl inv or* **candelabras**), **candelabrum** [ˌkændɪ'lɑːbrəm] **N** candélabre *m*

C&F, C and F [ˌsiːənd'ef] **N** *Com (abbr* **cost and freight**) C et F

C&I, C and I [ˌsiːənd'aɪ] **N** *Com (abbr* **cost and insurance**) C & A

candid ['kændɪd] **ADJ** *(person)* franc (franche), sincère; *(smile)* franc (franche); *(account, report)* qui ne cache rien; **I'd like your c. opinion** j'aimerais que vous me disiez franchement ce que vous en pensez; **to be quite c., I don't like it** pour parler franchement *ou* pour être franc, je ne l'aime pas

▸▸ ***candid camera*** appareil *m* photo à instantanés; ***candid camera shot*** = photo prise à l'insu de la personne photographiée

> Note that the French word **candide** is a false friend and is never a translation for the English word **candid**. It means **ingenuous**.

candida ['kændɪdə] **N** *Biol* candida *m*

candidacy ['kændɪdəsɪ] **N** candidature *f*

candidate ['kændɪdət] **N** candidat(e) *m,f*; **to be a** *or* **to stand as c. for mayor** être candidat à la mairie; **presidential c.** candidat aux élections présidentielles

candidature ['kændɪdətʃə(r)] **N** candidature *f*

candidiasis [ˌkandɪ'daɪəsɪs] **N** *Med* candidose *f*

candidly ['kændɪdlɪ] **ADV** *(speak)* franchement; *(smile)* candidement, avec candeur

candidness ['kændɪdnɪs] **N** franchise *f*

candied ['kændɪd] **ADJ** *Culin (piece of fruit, peel)* confit; *(whole fruit)* confit, glacé

▸▸ ***candied peel*** zeste *m* confit

candle ['kændəl] **N 1** *(of wax ▸ gen)* bougie *f*, chandelle *f*; *(▸ in church)* cierge *m*, chandelle *f*; *Fig* **he can't hold a c. to you** il ne vous arrive pas à la cheville; **to burn the c. at both ends** brûler la chandelle par les deux bouts **2** *Phys (former unit)* bougie *f*; *(candela)* candela *f*

▸▸ ***candle grease*** suif *m*

candlelight ['kændəllaɪt] **N** lueur *f* d'une bougie *ou* d'une chandelle; **she read by c.** elle lisait à la lueur d'une bougie

COMP *(dinner, supper)* aux chandelles

candlelit ['kændəllɪt] **ADJ** éclairé aux bougies *ou* aux chandelles

Candlemas ['kændəlməs] **N** *Rel* la Chandeleur

candlestick ['kændəlstɪk] **N** *(single)* bougeoir *m*; *(branched)* chandelier *m*

candlewick ['kændəlwɪk] *Tex* **N** *(yarn)* chenille *f* (de coton)

COMP *(bedspread)* en chenille (de coton)

can-do ADJ dynamique, entreprenant; **c. attitude** *or* **spirit** esprit *m* de battant *ou* de gagneur

candour, *Am* **candor** ['kændə(r)] **N** candeur *f*, franchise *f*

> Note that the French word **candeur** is a false friend and is never a translation for the English word **candour**. It means **ingenuousness**.

candy ['kændɪ] *(pl* **candies**, *pt & pp* **candied**) **N 1** *Am (piece)* bonbon *m*; *(UNCOUNT) (sweets in general)* bonbons *mpl*, confiserie *f* **2** *Culin (sugar)* sucre *m* candi **3** *Fam Drugs slang* came *f*

VT *(ginger, pieces of fruit, orange peel)* confire; *(whole fruit)* glacer, confire; *(sugar)* faire candir

VI se candir, se cristalliser

▸▸ *Am* ***candy apple*** pomme *f* d'amour; *Am* ***candy bar*** barre *f* chocolatée; *Br* ***candy floss*** barbe *f* à papa; *Am* ***candy store*** confiserie *f*

candy-striped ADJ à rayures multicolores

cane [keɪn] **N 1** *(stem of plant)* canne *f*; *(in making baskets, furniture)* rotin *m*, jonc *m* **2** *(rod ▸ for walking)* canne *f*; *(▸ for punishment)* verge *f*, baguette *f*; **to give sb the c.** fouetter qn; **to get the c.** être fouetté, recevoir le fouet **3** *Hort (for supporting plant)* tuteur *m*

COMP *(furniture)* en rotin; *(chair ▸ entirely in cane)* en rotin; *(▸ with cane back, seat)* canné

VT 1 *(beat with rod)* donner des coups de bâton à, fouetter **2** *Fam (defeat)* battre à plate couture **3** *Br Fam* **to c. it** *(get drunk)* se bourrer *ou* se pinter la gueule

▸▸ ***cane sugar*** sucre *m* de canne

caned [keɪnd] ADJ *Br Fam* bourré comme un coing; **to get c.** se cuiter, prendre une cuite

canine ['keɪnaɪn] ADJ *(gen)* canin; *Zool* de la famille des canidés
N **1** *Zool (animal)* canidé *m* **2** *Anat (tooth)* canine *f*
▸▸ *Anat* ***canine tooth*** canine *f*

caning ['keɪnɪŋ] N **1** *(beating)* **to give sb a c.** *(gen)* donner des coups de bâton *ou* de trique à qn; *Sch* fouetter qn à la baguette **2** *Fam (defeat)* **to get a c.** être battu à plate couture

canister ['kænɪstə(r)] N **1** *(for flour, sugar)* boîte *f*; **flour/sugar c.** boîte *f* à farine/sucre **2** *(for gas, shaving cream)* bombe *f*; **tear gas c.** bombe *f* lacrymogène

canker ['kæŋkə(r)] N **1** *(UNCOUNT) Med* ulcère *m*, chancre *m* **2** *Bot & Fig* chancre *m* **3** *Vet (of dog etc)* gale *f* de l'oreille; *(in horse's hoof)* crapaud *m*

cankerworm ['kæŋkəwɜːm] N ver *m* rongeur (des plantes)

cannabis ['kænəbɪs] N *(plant)* chanvre *m* indien; *(drug)* cannabis *m*
▸▸ ***cannabis resin*** résine *f* de cannabis

canned [kænd] ADJ **1** *(food)* en boîte, en conserve **2** *Fam (drunk)* paf *(inv)*, rond; **to get c.** se soûler
▸▸ ***canned goods*** conserves *fpl*; ***canned laughter*** rires *mpl* préenregistrés; ***canned music*** musique *f* enregistrée *ou* en conserve

cannelloni [ˌkænɪ'ləʊnɪ] N *(UNCOUNT) Culin* cannellonis *mpl*

cannery ['kænərɪ] *(pl* **canneries***)* N conserverie *f*, fabrique *f* de conserves

cannibal ['kænɪbəl] N cannibale *mf*, anthropophage *mf*
ADJ cannibale, anthropophage

cannibalism ['kænɪbəlɪzəm] N cannibalisme *m*, anthropophagie *f*

cannibalization, -isation [ˌkænɪbəlaɪ'zeɪʃən] N *Mktg & Tech* cannibalisation *f*

cannibalize, -ise ['kænɪbəlaɪz] VT *Tech (car, machine)* cannibaliser, récupérer des pièces détachées de; *(text)* récupérer des parties de; *Mktg (product)* cannibaliser

cannily ['kænɪlɪ] ADV *(cleverly ▸ assess)* avec perspicacité; *(▸ reason)* habilement, astucieusement; *(cautiously)* prudemment, avec circonspection

canning ['kænɪŋ] N mise *f* en boîte *ou* en conserve
COMP *(process)* de mise en boîte *ou* en conserve
▸▸ ***canning factory*** conserverie *f*, fabrique *f* de conserves; ***canning industry*** conserverie *f*, industrie *f* de la conserve

cannoli [kə'nəʊlɪ] NPL *Culin* cannoli *mpl*

cannon ['kænən] *(pl* **inv** *or* **cannons***)* N **1** *(weapon)* canon *m*; *Fig* **he's a loose c.** il n'en fait qu'à sa tête **2** *Tech (barrel of gun, syringe)* canon *m* **3** *Br (in billiards, snooker)* carambolage *m*
VI **1** *(bump)* **to c. into sb/sth** se heurter contre qn/qch **2** *Br (in billiards, snooker)* caramboler; **to c. off the cushion** *(of player)* jouer la bricole
▸▸ ***cannon fodder*** chair *f* à canon

cannonade [ˌkænə'neɪd] *Mil* N canonnade *f*
VT canonner

cannonball ['kænənbɔːl] N **1** *Mil (ammunition)* boulet *m* de canon **2** *Tennis* **a c. (serve)** un service en boulet de canon

cannot ['kænɒt] = **can not**

cannula = **canula**

canny ['kænɪ] *(compar* **cannier**, *superl* **canniest***)*
ADJ **1** *(clever)* astucieux, habile; *(shrewd)* malin (igne), rusé **2** *(cautious)* prudent, circonspect **3** *Br (person ▸ thrifty)* économe; *(▸ nice)* sympathique; *(bargain, deal)* avantageux

canoe [kə'nuː] *(cont* **canoeing***)* N canoë *m*; *(dugout)* pirogue *f*; *Sport* canoë *m*, canoë-kayak *m*; *Fig* **to paddle one's own c.** mener seul sa barque
VI *(gen)* faire du canoë; *Sport* faire du canoë *ou* du canoë-kayak; **we canoed down the river** nous avons descendu le fleuve en canoë

canoe-camping N canoë-camping *m*, *Can* canot-camping *m*

canoeing [kə'nuːɪŋ] N *Sport* canoë-kayak *m*; **to go c.** faire du canoë-kayak; **c. holiday** raid *m ou* randonnée *f* en canoë-kayak

canoeist [kə'nuːɪst] N *Sport* canoéiste *mf*

canon ['kænən] N **1** *Rel (decree, prayer)* canon *m*; *(clergyman)* chanoine *m*
2 *Literature* œuvre *f*
3 *Mus* canon *m*
4 *Fig (rule)* canon *m*, règle *f*
▸▸ *Rel* ***canon law*** droit *m* canon

canonical [kə'nɒnɪkəl] ADJ **1** *Rel (text)* canonique; *(practice)* conforme aux canons (de l'église); *(robe)* sacerdotal **2** *Mus* en canon **3** *Fig (accepted)* canonique, autorisé
▸▸ ***canonical dress*** vêtements *mpl* sacerdotaux; ***canonical hours*** *(Catholic)* heures *fpl* canoniales; *(Church of England)* = heures pendant lesquelles la célébration des mariages est autorisée (entre 8 heures et 18 heures)

canonization, -isation [ˌkænənaɪ'zeɪʃən] N *Rel & Fig* canonisation *f*

canonize, -ise ['kænənaɪz] VT *Rel & Fig* canoniser

canoodle [kə'nuːdəl] VI *Br Fam* se faire des mamours

canopy ['kænəpɪ] *(pl* **canopies***)* N **1** *(over bed)* baldaquin *m*, ciel *m* de lit; *(over balcony, doorway)* auvent *m*, marquise *f*; *(over throne, altar, statue)* dais *m*; *Archit (with columns)* baldaquin *m*
2 *(of parachute)* voilure *f*
3 *Aviat (of cockpit)* verrière *f*
4 *(in forest)* canopée *f*
5 *Fig (branches, sky)* voûte *f*; *Literary* **the c. of heaven** la voûte du ciel

cant[1] [kænt] N **1** *(UNCOUNT) (insincere talk)* paroles *fpl* hypocrites; *(clichés)* clichés *mpl*, phrases *fpl* toutes faites **2** *(jargon)* argot *m* de métier, jargon *m*
VI **1** *(talk ▸ insincerely)* parler avec hypocrisie; *(▸ in clichés)* débiter des clichés **2** *(use jargon)* parler en argot de métier, jargonner

can't [kɑːnt] = **can not**

cant[2] N **1** *(slope)* pente *f*, inclinaison *f*; *(oblique surface)* surface *f* oblique, plan *m* incliné **2** *Archit & Carp (edge)* chanfrein *m*, biseau *m* **3** *(movement)* secousse *f*, cahot *m*
VT **1** *(tip slightly)* pencher, incliner; *(overturn)* renverser *ou* retourner (d'un seul coup) **2** *Archit & Carp (edge)* biseauter, écorner
VI **1** *(tip slightly)* se pencher, s'incliner; *(overturn)* se renverser *ou* se retourner (d'un seul coup) **2** *(slope)* être incliné *ou* en pente

Cantab. *Univ (written abbr* **Cantabrigiensis***)* = de l'université de Cambridge

cantaloup, cantaloupe ['kæntəluːp] N cantaloup *m*
▸▸ ***cantaloup melon*** cantaloup *m*

cantankerous [kæn'tæŋkərəs] ADJ *(bad-tempered)* acariâtre, revêche, grincheux

cantata [kæn'tɑːtə] N *Mus* cantate *f*

canteen [kæn'tiːn] N **1** *(restaurant)* cantine *f*
2 *Am (flask)* flasque *f*, gourde *f*
3 *(box for cutlery)* coffret *m*; **c. of cutlery** ménagère *f*
4 *Mil (mess tin)* gamelle *f*

canter ['kæntə(r)] N petit galop *m*; **the horse set off at a c.** le cheval est parti au petit galop; *Fig* **to win in a c.** gagner haut la main
VT faire aller au petit galop
VI aller au petit galop

Canterbury ['kæntəbrɪ] N Cantorbéry
▸▸ ***Canterbury bell*** campanule *f*

canticle ['kæntɪkəl] N *Mus & Rel* cantique *m*

cantilever ['kæntɪliːvə(r)] N **1** *(beam, girder)* cantilever *m*; *(projecting beam)* corbeau *m*, encorbellement *m* **2** *Aviat* cantilever *m*
COMP *(girder)* en cantilever, cantilever *(inv)*
VT mettre en cantilever
▸▸ ***cantilever beam*** poutre *f* en porte-à-faux; ***cantilever bridge*** pont *m* cantilever

canto ['kæntəʊ] *(pl* **cantos***)* N *Literature* chant *m* *(d'un poème)*

canton N **1** ['kæntɒn] *Admin* canton *m* **2** ['kæntən] *Her* canton *m*
VT **1** [kæn'tɒn] *Admin (land)* diviser en cantons **2** [kæn'tuːn] *Mil (soldiers)* cantonner

cantonal ['kæntənəl] ADJ *Admin* cantonal

Cantonese [ˌkæntə'niːz] *(pl* **inv***)* N **1** *(person)* Cantonais(e) *m,f* **2** *(language)* cantonais *m*
ADJ cantonais

cantonization, -isation [ˌkæntənaɪ'zeɪʃən] N *Admin* morcellement *m (en cantons)*

cantonment [kæn'tuːnmənt] N *Mil* cantonnement *m*

cantor ['kæntɔː(r)] N *Rel* chantre *m*

Canuck [kə'nʌk] N *Am Fam (Canadian)* = terme injurieux ou humoristique désignant un Canadien (le plus souvent un Canadien français)

canula ['kænjələ] *(pl* **canulas** *or* **canulae** [-liː]*)* N *Med (for giving medication)* canule *f*, cathéter *m*; *(for draining)* sonde *f*

canvas ['kænvəs] *(pl* **inv** *ou* **canvasses***)* N **1** *(cloth)* toile *f*; *(for tapestry)* canevas *m*; **under c.** *(in a tent)* sous une tente; *Naut* sous voiles **2** *(painting)* toile *f*, tableau *m* **3** *Boxing* **the c.** le tapis
COMP *(bag, cloth)* de *ou* en toile

> Attention: ne pas confondre avec le verbe **to canvass**.

canvass ['kænvəs] VI **1** *(seek opinions)* faire un sondage **2** *Com (seek orders)* visiter la clientèle, faire la place; *(door to door)* faire du démarchage *ou* du porte-à-porte; **to c. for customers** prospecter la clientèle **3** *Pol (candidate, campaign worker)* faire campagne *(en faisant du porte-à-porte)*; **we're canvassing for the Greens** nous faisons campagne pour les Verts
VT **1** *(seek opinion of)* sonder; **to c. opinions (on sth)** sonder l'opinion (à propos de qch)
2 *Com (person)* démarcher, solliciter des commandes de; *(area)* prospecter
3 *Pol (person)* solliciter la voix de; *(area)* faire du démarchage électoral dans
4 *(for support in job application etc)* solliciter l'appui de
5 *Am Pol (ballots)* pointer
N = **canvassing**

> Attention: ne pas confondre avec le nom **canvas**.

canvasser ['kænvəsə(r)] N **1** *(pollster)* sondeur (euse) *m,f*, enquêteur(euse) *m,f*
2 *Com (salesman)* placier *m*; *(door to door)* démarcheur *m*; **no canvassers** *(sign)* démarchage interdit
3 *Pol* agent *m* électoral *(qui sollicite des voix)*
4 *Am Pol (of ballots)* scrutateur(trice) *m,f*

canvassing ['kænvəsɪŋ] N **1** *(gen) & Com* démarchage *m* **2** *Pol* démarchage *m* électoral **3** *(for support in job application etc)* sollicitation *f* d'appui **3** *Am Pol (of ballots)* pointage *m*

canyon ['kænjən] N cañon *m*, canyon *m*, gorge *f*

canyoner ['kænjənə(r)] N canyoniste *mf*

canyoning ['kænjənɪŋ] N *Sport* canyoning *m*

CAP [ˌsiːeɪ'piː, kæp] N *EU (abbr* **Common Agricultural Policy***)* PAC *f*

cap [kæp] *(pt & pp* **capped**, *cont* **capping***)* N **1** *(hat ▸ with peak)* casquette *f*; *(▸ without peak)* bonnet *m*; *(▸ of jockey, judge)* toque *f*; *(▸ of nurse, traditional costume)* coiffe *f*; *(▸ of soldier)* calot *m*; *(▸ of officer)* képi *m*; **c. and bells** marotte *f* (de bouffon); **in c. and gown** en costume d'apparat universitaire; *Fig* **if the c. fits, wear it** qui se sent morveux (qu'il) se mouche; *Fig* **to go to sb c. in hand** aller vers qn chapeau bas; *Old-fashioned* **to set one's c. at sb** jeter son dévolu sur qn; *Fig* **to put on one's thinking c.** réfléchir, méditer la question
2 *(cover, lid ▸ of bottle, container)* capsule *f*; *(▸ of lens)* cache *m*; *(▸ of tyre valve)* bouchon *m*; *(▸ of pen)* capuchon *m*; *(▸ of mushroom)* chapeau *m*; *(▸ of tooth)* couronne *f*; *(▸ of column, pedestal)* chapiteau *m*
3 *Br Sport* sélection *f*; **he has three England caps** il a été sélectionné trois fois dans l'équipe d'Angleterre
4 *Orn (of bird)* capuchon *m*
5 *(for toy gun)* amorce *f*; *Am (bullet)* bastos *f*
6 *(contraceptive device)* diaphragme *m*
7 *(spending limit)* plafond *m*
VT **1** *(cover)* couvrir, recouvrir; **the mountain was**

capped with snow le sommet de la montagne était recouvert de neige
2 *(tooth)* couronner, mettre une couronne à
3 *(outdo)* surpasser; **he capped that story with an even funnier one** il a raconté une histoire encore plus drôle que celle-là; **to c. it all** pour couronner le tout, pour comble
4 *Admin (impose limit on* ▸ *spending)* limiter, restreindre; *(*▸ *borough, region)* limiter les dépenses de; **these measures have been effective in capping overall expenditure** ces mesures ont permis de limiter les dépenses globales
5 *Br Sport* sélectionner (dans l'équipe nationale); **she was capped five times** elle a joué *ou* elle a été sélectionnée cinq fois
6 *Scot & NZ Univ (graduate)* conférer un diplôme à
7 *Am Fam (shoot)* descendre

capability [ˌkeɪpəˈbɪlətɪ] *(pl* **capabilities***)* **N 1** *(gen)* aptitude *f*, capacité *f*; **the work is beyond his capabilities** ce travail est au-dessus de ses capacités **2** *Mil* capacité *f*, potentiel *m*; **nuclear c.** puissance *f ou* potentiel *m* nucléaire; **we have the military c. to...** notre potentiel militaire est suffisant pour... **3** *Com* compétence *f*

capable [ˈkeɪpəbəl] **ADJ 1** *(able)* capable; **they are quite c. of looking after themselves** ils sont parfaitement capables de *ou* ils peuvent très bien se débrouiller tout seuls; **to show what one is c. of** montrer ce dont on est capable; **she's not c. of lying** elle est incapable de mentir; **that man's c. of anything** cet homme est capable de tout **2** *(competent)* capable, compétent; **the business is in c. hands** l'affaire est entre de bonnes mains

capably [ˈkeɪpəblɪ] **ADV** avec compétence, de façon compétente

capacious [kəˈpeɪʃəs] **ADJ** *Formal (room)* vaste, spacieux; *(clothing)* ample; *(container)* de grande capacité *ou* contenance

capacitance [kəˈpæsɪtəns] **N** *Elec* capacité *f*

capacitate [kəˈpæsɪteɪt] **VT** *Law* donner pouvoir *ou* qualité à (**to act** pour agir)

capacitor [kəˈpæsɪtə(r)] **N** *Elec* condensateur *m*

capacity [kəˈpæsɪtɪ] *(pl* **capacities***)* **N 1** *(size* ▸ *of container)* contenance *f*, capacité *f*; *(*▸ *of room)* capacité *f*; **the stadium has a c. of 50,000** le stade peut accueillir 50 000 personnes; **he has an amazing c. for beer** il peut boire une quantité étonnante de bière; **filled to c.** *(bottle, tank)* plein; *(ship, theatre)* plein, comble; **they played to a c. crowd** ils ont joué à guichets fermés
2 *(aptitude)* aptitude *f*, capacité *f*; **c. to learn** aptitude *f* à apprendre, capacité *f* d'apprendre; **she has a great c. for languages** elle a une grande aptitude *ou* capacité pour les langues, elle est douée pour les langues; **the work is well within our c.** nous sommes tout à fait en mesure *ou* capables de faire ce travail
3 *(position)* qualité *f*, titre *m*; *Law (legal competence)* pouvoir *m* légal; **she spoke in her c. as government representative** elle s'est exprimée en sa qualité de *ou* en tant que représentante du gouvernement; **he's acting in an advisory c.** il a un rôle consultatif; **they are here in an official c.** ils sont ici à titre officiel
4 *(of factory, industry)* moyens *mpl* de production; *(output)* rendement *m*; **the factory is (working) at full c.** l'usine produit à plein rendement; **the factory has not yet reached c.** l'usine n'a pas encore atteint son rendement maximum
5 *(of engine)* capacité *f*
6 *Elec* capacité *f*
▸▸ ***a capacity audience*** une salle comble; *Econ* ***capacity utilization*** utilisation *f* du potentiel de production

caparison [kəˈpærɪsən] *Arch or Literary* **N** caparaçon *m*
VT caparaçonner

cape¹ [keɪp] **N** *Geog (headland)* cap *m*; *(promontory)* promontoire *m*
▸▸ ***Cape Canaveral*** le cap Canaveral; ***Cape Cod*** le cap Cod; ***Cape Coloured*** métis(isse) *m,f* sud-africain(e); ***the Cape of Good Hope*** le cap de Bonne-Espérance; *Bot* ***cape gooseberry*** physalis *m*; ***Cape Horn*** le cap Horn; ***Cape Province*** la province du Cap; ***Cape Town*** Le Cap; ***Cape Verde*** le Cap-Vert; **in C. Verde** au Cap-Vert; ***the Cape Verde Islands*** les îles *fpl* du Cap-Vert; ***Cape Verdean*** **N** Capverdien(enne) *m,f* **ADJ** capverdien

cape² **N** *(cloak)* cape *f*, pèlerine *f*

caper¹ [ˈkeɪpə(r)] **VI 1** *(jump, skip)* **to c. (about)** faire des cabrioles, cabrioler, gambader **2** *(frolic)* faire le fou (la folle)
N 1 *(jump, skip)* cabriole *f*, gambade *f*
2 *(practical joke)* farce *f*
3 *Fam (nonsense)* **I haven't time for all that c.** je n'ai pas de temps à perdre avec des âneries pareilles; **what a c.!** *(fuss)* quel cirque!
4 *Fam (illegal activity)* coup *m*

caper² **N** câpre *f*; *(shrub)* câprier *m*
▸▸ ***caper sauce*** sauce *f* aux câpres

capercaillie, capercailzie [ˌkæpəˈkeɪlɪ] **N** *Orn* grand tétras *m*, coq *m* de bruyère

capful [ˈkæpfʊl] **N** *(of liquid)* (plein) bouchon *m*

capillary [kəˈpɪlərɪ] *(pl* **capillaries***)* *Biol* **N** capillaire *m*
ADJ capillaire
▸▸ ***capillary action*** capillarité *f*; ***capillary tube*** capillaire *m*

capital [ˈkæpɪtəl] **N 1** *(city)* capitale *f*; **the financial c. of the world** la capitale financière du monde
2 *(letter)* majuscule *f*, capitale *f*; **write in capitals** écrivez en (lettres) majuscules *ou* en capitales
3 *(UNCOUNT) Econ & Fin (funds)* capital *m*, capitaux *mpl*, fonds *mpl*; *(funds and assets)* capital *m* (en espèces et en nature); **to raise c.** réunir des capitaux; **c. invested, outlay of c.** mise *f* de fonds; **c. and labour** capital *m* et main-d'œuvre *f*; *Fig* **to try and make c. out of a situation** essayer de tirer profit *ou* parti d'une situation
4 *Fin (principal)* capital *m*, principal *m*
5 *Archit (of column)* chapiteau *m*
ADJ 1 *(chief, primary)* capital, principal; **it's of c. importance** c'est d'une importance capitale, c'est de la plus haute importance
2 *Law* capital
3 *(upper case)* majuscule; **c. D** D majuscule; **in c. letters** en majuscules, en capitales; **he's an idiot with a c. "I"** c'est un imbécile avec un grand "I"
4 *Br Fam Old-fashioned (wonderful)* épatant, fameux
COMP *Fin* de capital
▸▸ *Fin* ***capital assets*** actif *m* immobilisé, immobilisations *fpl*; *Fin* ***capital budget*** budget *m* d'investissement; ***capital charge*** intérêt *m* des capitaux (investis); ***capital city*** capitale *f*; *Fin & Acct* ***capital equipment*** biens *mpl* d'équipement, capitaux *mpl* fixes; *Fin* ***capital expenditure*** *(UNCOUNT)* mise *f* de fonds, investissements *mpl* (en immobilisations), dépenses *fpl* d'équipement; *Fin* ***capital gains*** plus-value *f*; *Fin* ***capital gains tax*** impôt *m* sur les plus-values; *Fin* ***capital goods*** biens *mpl* d'équipement *ou* d'investissement; *Fin* ***capital growth*** croissance *m* du capital; *Fin* ***capital income*** revenu *m* du capital; *Fin* ***capital investment*** mise *f* de fonds; *Fin* ***capital items*** biens *mpl* capitaux; *Fin* ***capital levy*** impôt *m ou* prélèvement *m* sur le capital; *Law* ***capital offence*** crime *m* passible de la peine de mort; *Fin* ***capital outlay*** dépenses *fpl* en capital; *Law* ***capital punishment*** peine *f* capitale, peine *f* de mort; *Fin* ***capital reserves*** profits *mpl* mis en réserve, réserves *fpl* non distribuées; *Formerly Fin* ***capital transfer tax*** droits *mpl* de mutation

capital-intensive **ADJ** à forte *or* intensité de capital, capitalistique

capitalism [ˈkæpɪtəlɪzəm] **N** capitalisme *m*

capitalist [ˈkæpɪtəlɪst] **ADJ** capitaliste
N capitaliste *mf*

capitalistic [ˌkæpɪtəˈlɪstɪk] **ADJ** capitaliste

capitalization, -isation [ˌkæpɪtəlaɪˈzeɪʃən] **N 1** *Fin (of interest)* capitalisation *f* **2** *Typ* emploi *m* des majuscules; *(putting into upper case)* mise *f* en majuscules
▸▸ *Fin* ***capitalization issue*** attribution *f* d'actions gratuites

capitalize, -ise [ˈkæpɪtəlaɪz] **VT 1** *Fin (convert into capital)* capitaliser; *(raise capital through issue of stock)* constituer le capital social de *(par émission d'actions)*; *(provide with capital)* pourvoir de fonds *ou* de capital; **under-/over-capitalized** sous-/sur-capitalisé; **capitalized value** valeur *f* capitalisée **2** *Fin (estimate value of)* capitaliser **3** *Typ (write in upper case* ▸ *first letter)* écrire avec une majuscule; *(*▸ *entire word)* écrire *ou* mettre en majuscules
VI to c. on sth *(take advantage of)* tirer profit ou parti de qch; *(make money on)* monnayer qch

capital-output ratio **N** ratio *m* capital-travail

capitation [ˌkæpɪˈteɪʃən] **N 1** *Fin* capitation *f* **2** *Br Sch* dotation *f* forfaitaire par élève *(accordée à un établissement scolaire)*
▸▸ *Br Sch* ***capitation allowance, capitation expenditure*** dotation *f* forfaitaire par élève *(accordée à un établissement scolaire)*; *Fin* ***capitation tax*** capitation *f*

Capitol [ˈkæpɪtəl] **N 1** *(in Rome)* **the C.** le Capitole **2** *(in US)* **the C.** *(national)* le Capitole *(siège du Congrès américain)*; *(state)* le Capitole *(siège du Congrès de l'État)*
▸▸ ***Capitol Hill*** = la colline du Capitole, à Washington, où se trouve le Congrès américain

> **CAPITOL HILL**
>
> Ce nom désigne, par extension, le Congrès américain, par exemple "The proposed bill is in danger of being rejected on Capitol Hill" ("La proposition de loi risque d'être rejétée par le Congrès américain").

capitulate [kəˈpɪtjʊleɪt] **VI** *Mil & Fig* capituler (**to** devant)

capitulation [kəˌpɪtjʊˈleɪʃən] **N** *Mil & Fig* capitulation *f*

capon [ˈkeɪpən] **N** chapon *m*

capper [ˈkæpə(r)] **N** *Am Fam* **that was the c.** *(the final straw)* c'est la goutte d'eau qui a fait déborder le vase

cappuccino [ˌkæpʊˈtʃiːnəʊ] *(pl* **cappuccinos***)* **N** cappuccino *m*

caprice [kəˈpriːs] **N** *(whim)* caprice *m*; *(change of mood)* saute *f* d'humeur

capricious [kəˈprɪʃəs] **ADJ** *(person)* capricieux, fantasque; *(weather)* capricieux, changeant

capriciously [kəˈprɪʃəslɪ] **ADV** capricieusement

Capricorn [ˈkæprɪkɔːn] **N 1** *Astron* Capricorne *m* **2** *Astrol* Capricorne *m*; **he's a C.** il est (du signe du) Capricorne
ADJ *Astrol* du Capricorne; **he's C.** il est (du signe du) Capricorne

caps [kæps] **NPL 1** *Typ & Comput (abbr* **capital letters***)* majuscules *fpl*; **put in small c.** à imprimer en petites capitales **2** *(abbr* **capsules***)* capsules *fpl*, gélules *fpl*
▸▸ *Typ & Comput* ***caps lock*** verrouillage *m* des majuscules; *Typ & Comput* ***caps lock key*** touche *f* de verrouillage des majuscules

capsicum [ˈkæpsɪkəm] **N** *(fruit, plant* ▸ *sweet)* poivron *m*, piment *m* doux; *(*▸ *hot)* piment *m*

capsize [kæpˈsaɪz] **VI** *(gen)* se renverser; *(boat)* chavirer; **we capsized** nous avons chaviré
VT *(gen)* renverser; *(boat)* faire chavirer

capstan [ˈkæpstən] **N** *Naut* cabestan *m*
▸▸ *Tech* ***capstan lathe*** tour *m* revolver

capsular [ˈkæpsjʊlə(r)] **ADJ** *Biol & Bot* capsulaire

capsule [ˈkæpsjuːl] **N 1** *(gen) & Aviat, Anat & Bot* capsule *f*; *(of coffee)* dosette *f*, minidose *f* **2** *Pharm* capsule *f*, gélule *f*
ADJ concis, bref

Capt. *(written abbr* **captain***)* cap

captain [ˈkæptɪn] **N 1** *(army rank)* capitaine *m*; *Mil (of ship)* capitaine *m*; *(navy rank)* capitaine *m* de vaisseau; **c. of the fleet** capitaine *m* de pavillon; **C. James Brown** *(in title)* le capitaine James Brown; **yes, c.!** oui, mon capitaine!
2 *(of group, team)* chef *m*, capitaine *m*; *Sport* capitaine *m* (d'équipe); **c. of industry** capitaine *m* d'industrie
3 *Am (of police)* commissaire *m* (de police) de quartier
4 *Am (head waiter)* maître *m* d'hôtel; *(of bellboys)* responsable *m* des grooms
VT 1 *(gen)* diriger; *Mil* commander **2** *Sport* être le capitaine de; **he captained the side in the World Cup** c'était lui le capitaine de l'équipe pour la Coupe du Monde

captaincy [ˈkæptɪnsɪ] *(pl* **captaincies***)* **N 1** *Naut & Mil* grade *m* de capitaine; **to receive one's c.** être promu *ou* passer capitaine **2** *Sport* poste *m* de capitaine; **under the c. of Rogers** avec Rogers comme capitaine

caption [ˈkæpʃən] **N 1** *(under illustration, photograph, cartoon)* légende *f* **2** *(in article, chapter)* sous-titre *m* **3** *Cin* sous-titre *m*

VT 1 *(illustration)* mettre une légende à, légender **2** *Cin* sous-titrer

captious [ˈkæpʃəs] **ADJ** *Formal (person)* qui trouve toujours à redire, chicanier; *(attitude)* chicanier

captivate [ˈkæptɪveɪt] **VT** captiver, fasciner

captivating [ˈkæptɪveɪtɪŋ] **ADJ** captivant, fascinant

captive [ˈkæptɪv] **N** captif(ive) *m,f*, prisonnier (ère) *m,f*; **to take sb c.** faire qn prisonnier; **to hold sb c.** garder qn en captivité

ADJ *(person)* captif, prisonnier; *(animal, balloon)* captif; *Mktg (audience, market)* captif; *Mktg (product)* lié; **a c. audience** *(of entertainer, show)* un public captif; **he had a c. audience** le public était forcé de l'écouter

captivity [kæpˈtɪvətɪ] **N** captivité *f*; **in c.** en captivité

captor [ˈkæptə(r)] **N** *(gen)* personne *f* qui capture; *(unlawfully)* ravisseur(euse) *m,f*

capture [ˈkæptʃə(r)] **VT 1** *(take prisoner ▸ animal, criminal, enemy)* capturer, prendre; *(▸ runaway)* reprendre; *(▸ city)* prendre, s'emparer de; *(in games)* prendre

2 *(gain control of ▸ market)* conquérir, s'emparer de; *(▸ attention, imagination)* captiver; *(▸ admiration, interest)* gagner

3 *(succeed in representing)* rendre, reproduire; **to c. the moment** *(photographer, photograph)* saisir l'instant; **to c. sb/sth (on film)** filmer qn/qch

4 *Comput (data)* saisir

N 1 *(of animal, criminal, enemy)* capture *f*, prise *f*
2 *Comput (of data)* saisie *f*

Capuchin [ˈkæpjʊtʃɪn] **N** *Rel* capucin *m*

ADJ *Rel* capucin; **a monk/nun of the C. order** un capucin/une capucine

• **capuchin N 1** *(cloak)* cape *f* (avec capuchon)
2 *Zool* **c. (monkey)** capucin *m*

▸▸ *Rel* ***Capuchin monk*** capucin *m*

car [kɑː(r)] **N 1** *(automobile)* voiture *f*, automobile *f*, auto *f*; **to go by c.** aller en voiture

2 *Am (of train)* wagon *m*, voiture *f*; *(in subway)* rame *f*

3 *Am (tram)* tramway *m*, tram *m*

4 *(of lift)* cabine *f (d'ascenseur)*

5 *(of airship, balloon)* nacelle *f*

COMP *(engine, tyre, wheel)* de voiture, d'automobile; *(journey, trip)* en voiture

▸▸ ***car alarm*** alarme *f* de voiture; ***car bomb*** voiture *f* piégée; ***car bomb attack*** attentat *m* à la voiture piégée; ***car bomber*** auteur *m* d'un attentat à la voiture piégée; *Br* ***car boot sale*** = sorte de marché aux puces où des particuliers apportent dans leur voiture les objets de brocante qu'ils souhaitent vendre; ***car chase*** course-poursuite *f*; ***car crash*** accident *m* de voitures; ***car dealer*** concessionnaire *m* automobile; ***car ferry*** ferry-boat *m*; *Br* ***car hire***

N location *f* de voitures

COMP *(company, firm)* de location de voitures; ***car industry*** industrie *f* (de l')automobile; ***car insurance*** assurance *f* auto; ***car keys*** clés *fpl* de voiture; ***car manufacturer*** constructeur *m* automobile; *Br* ***car park*** parking *m*, parc *m* de stationnement; *Br* ***car park attendant*** gardien (enne) *m,f* de parking; ***car pool*** *(of commuters)* = groupe de personnes qui s'organise pour utiliser la même voiture afin de se rendre à une destination commune; *(cars provided by company)* voitures *fpl* de fonction; ***car radio*** autoradio *f*; *Am* ***car rental*** **N** location *f* de voitures **COMP** *(company, firm)* de location de voitures; ***car salesman*** vendeur *m* de voitures; ***car sickness*** mal *m* des transports; **to suffer from c. sickness** être malade en voiture; ***car stereo*** autoradio *m*; ***car wash*** *(place)* portique *m* de lavage automatique (de voitures), *Can* lave-auto *m*; *(action)* lavage *m* de voitures; ***car worker*** ouvrier(ère) *m,f* de l'industrie automobile

> Note that the French word **car** is a false friend and is never a translation for the English word **car**. It means **coach**.

> **CAR BOOT SALE**
>
> On trouve des car boot sales partout en Grande-Bretagne; elles se tiennent souvent dans des parkings. Les participants louent un emplacement pour la journée et apportent toutes sortes d'articles dont ils veulent se débarrasser dans le coffre de leur voiture (d'où le nom de ce genre d'événement) et les exposent sur une table à côté de leur véhicule. C'est l'équivalent du vide-grenier français. De nombreux antiquaires et collectionneurs passent tous leurs week-ends à écumer les car boot sales à la recherche de bonnes affaires.

carafe [kəˈræf] **N** carafe *f*

caramel [ˈkærəmel] **N** caramel *m*

COMP *(ice cream, cake)* au caramel

▸▸ ***caramel cream*** crème *f* caramel; ***caramel custard*** crème *f* (renversée) au caramel; ***caramel flavouring*** arôme *m* caramel

caramelize, -ise [ˈkærəməlaɪz] **VT** caraméliser
VI se caraméliser

carapace [ˈkærəpeɪs] **N** *Zool* carapace *f*

carat, *Am* **karat** [ˈkærət] **N 1** *(for gold)* carat *m*; **an 18-c. gold ring** une bague en or 18 carats **2** *(for diamonds)* **metric c.** carat *m* (de 200 milligrammes)

caravan [ˈkærəvæn] *(Br pt & pp* **caravanned,** *cont* **caravanning,** *Am pt & pp* **caravanned** *or* **caravaned,** *cont* **caravanning** *or* **caravaning)** **N 1** *Br (vehicle)* caravane *f* **2** *(of gipsy)* roulotte *f* **3** *(in desert)* caravane *f*; **to travel in c.** voyager en convoi

VI to go caravanning faire du caravaning *ou Offic* du caravanage

▸▸ *Br* ***caravan site*** *(for campers)* camping *m* (pour caravanes); *(of gipsies)* campement *m*

caravanette [kærəvəˈnet] **N** camping-car *m*, *Offic* autocaravane *f*

caravanserai [ˌkærəˈvænsəraɪ] **N** *(inn)* caravansérail *m*

caraway [ˈkærəweɪ] **N** *(plant)* carvi *m*, cumin *m* des prés

▸▸ ***caraway seeds*** (graines *fpl* de) carvi *m*

carb [kɑːb] **N** *Fam* **1** *Aut (carburettor)* carburateur □ *m* **2** *(usu pl) (carbohydrate)* **carbs** glucides □ *mpl*

carbide [ˈkɑːbaɪd] **N** *Chem* carbure *m*

carbine [ˈkɑːbaɪn] **N** carabine *f*

carbohydrate [ˌkɑːbəʊˈhaɪdreɪt] **N 1** *Chem* hydrate *m* de carbone **2** *(usu pl) (foodstuff)* **carbohydrates** glucides *mpl*

carbolic [kɑːˈbɒlɪk] **ADJ** *Chem* phénique

▸▸ ***carbolic acid*** phénol *m*; ***carbolic soap*** savon *m* de Marseille

carbon [ˈkɑːbən] **N 1** *Chem* carbone *m* **2** *(copy, paper)* carbone *m*

▸▸ ***carbon copy*** *(of document)* carbone *m*; *Fig* réplique *f*; **she's a c. copy of her mother** c'est l'exacte réplique de sa mère; ***carbon credits*** crédits *mpl* de carbone; *Archeol* ***carbon dating*** datation *f* au carbone 14; *Chem* ***carbon dioxide*** gaz *m* carbonique, dioxyde *m* de carbone; ***carbon emissions*** émissions *fpl* de carbone; ***carbon fibre*** fibre *f* de carbone; *Aut* ***carbon filter*** filtre *m* au charbon; ***carbon footprint*** empreinte *f* carbone; *Chem* ***carbon monoxide*** monoxyde *m* de carbone; ***carbon monoxide poisoning*** empoisonnement *m* au monoxyde de carbone; ***carbon neutral*** neutre en CO_2, = ayant un bilan carbone neutre; ***carbon offsetting*** compensation *f* carbone, compensation *f* en CO_2; ***carbon paper*** (papier *m*) carbone *m*; *Metal* ***carbon steel*** acier *m* carburé

carbonaceous [ˌkɑːbəˈneɪʃəs] **ADJ** *Chem* carboné

carbonate [ˈkɑːbənɪt] **N** *Chem* carbonate *m*

carbonated [ˈkɑːbəneɪtɪd] **ADJ** *Chem* carbonaté; **c. soft drinks** boissons *fpl* gazeuses

carbonic [kɑːˈbɒnɪk] **ADJ** *Chem* carbonique

carboniferous [ˌkɑːbəˈnɪfərəs] *Geol* **ADJ** carbonifère

• **Carboniferous N the C.** le Carbonifère **ADJ the C. Period** le carbonifère

carbonization, -isation [ˌkɑːbənaɪˈzeɪʃən] **N** *Chem* carbonisation *f*

carbonize, -ise [ˈkɑːbənaɪz] **VT** *Chem* carboniser

Carborundum® [ˌkɑːbəˈrʌndəm] **N** carborundum® *m*

carboy [ˈkɑːbɔɪ] **N** bonbonne *f*, bombonne *f*

carbuncle [ˈkɑːˌbʌŋkəl] **N 1** *Med* furoncle *m* **2** *Miner (gemstone)* escarboucle *f*

carburation [ˌkɑːbjʊˈreɪʃən] **N** *Tech* carburation *f*

carburettor, *Am* **carburetor** [ˌkɑːbəˈretə(r)] **N** carburateur *m*

carcass, carcase [ˈkɑːkəs] **N 1** *(of animal)* carcasse *f*, cadavre *m*; *(for food)* carcasse *f* **2** *(of person ▸ dead)* cadavre *m*; *Fam Hum* **move** *or* **shift your c.!** pousse un peu ta viande! **3** *(of building)* carcasse *f*, charpente *f*; *(of car)* carcasse *f*

carcinogen [kɑːˈsɪnədʒən] **N** *Med* (agent *m*) carcinogène *m ou* cancérogène *m*

carcinogenic [ˌkɑːsɪnəˈdʒenɪk] **ADJ** *Med* carcinogène, cancérogène

carcinoma [ˌkɑːsɪˈnəʊmə] *(pl* **carcinomas** *or* **carcinomata** [-mətə]) **N** *Med* carcinome *m*

card[1] [kɑːd] **N 1** *(for game)* carte *f*; **how about a game of cards?** et si on jouait aux cartes?; **to play cards** jouer aux cartes; *Fig* **to play one's cards right** mener bien son jeu *ou* sa barque, bien se débrouiller; **play your cards right and you could get promoted** si tu te débrouilles bien, tu peux avoir une promotion; **to play one's best** *or* **strongest** *or* **trump c.** jouer sa carte maîtresse; **I still have a couple of cards up my sleeve** j'ai encore quelques atouts dans mon jeu; *Fig* **to keep one's cards close to one's chest** cacher son jeu; **to hold all the (winning** *or* **best) cards** avoir tous les atouts dans son jeu *ou* en main; **to lay** *or* **to place one's cards on the table** jouer cartes sur table; **it was** *Br* **on** *or Am* **in the cards that the project would fail** il était dit *ou* prévisible que le projet échouerait; **I don't think that's on the cards** je ne pense pas que ce soit possible

2 *(with written information ▸ gen)* carte *f*; *(▸ for business)* carte *f* (de visite); *(▸ for index)* fiche *f*; *(▸ for membership)* carte *f* de membre *ou* d'adhérent; *(▸ for library)* carte *f* (d'abonnement); *(postcard)* carte *f* (postale); *(programme)* programme *m*

3 *(credit card)* carte *f*; **to pay by c.** payer par carte

4 *(cardboard)* carton *m*

5 *Fam Old-fashioned (person)* plaisantin □ *m*; **he's a c.!** c'est un marrant *ou* un rigolo!

6 *Golf* carte *f* du parcours; *Sport (list of races)* programme *m* des courses

7 *Comput (circuit board)* cartet *f*

VT 1 *(information)* ficher, mettre sur fiche **2** *Am (ask for identity card)* demander sa carte (d'identité) à **3** *Golf (score)* marquer

COMP *Fin (payment, transaction)* par carte

• **cards NPL** *Br (idioms)* **to get one's cards** être mis à la porte; **the boss gave him his cards** le patron l'a renvoyé

▸▸ ***card catalogue*** fichier *m* (de bibliothèque); ***card file*** fichier *m*; ***card game*** jeu *m* de cartes; ***card index*** fichier *m*; ***card key*** carte-clé *f*; ***card reader*** lecteur *m* de cartes; *Comput* ***card slot*** emplacement *m* pour carte; ***card table*** table *f* de jeu; ***card trick*** tour *m* de cartes; *Br* ***card vote*** vote *m* sur carte *(chaque voix représentant le nombre de voix d'adhérents représentés)*

card[2] *Tex* **N** carde *f*
VT carder

cardamom, cardamon, cardamum [ˈkɑːdəməm] **N** cardamome *f*

▸▸ ***cardamom pod*** gousse *f* de cardamome; ***cardamom seeds*** (graines *fpl* de) cardamome *f*

cardan joint [ˈkɑːdən-] **N** *Tech* joint *m* de cardan

cardboard [ˈkɑːdbɔːd] **N** carton *m*

ADJ 1 *(container, partition)* de *ou* en carton **2** *Fig (unreal ▸ character, leader)* de carton-pâte, faux (fausse)

▸▸ ***cardboard box*** (boîte *f* en) carton *m*; ***cardboard city*** quartier *m* des sans-abri; ***cardboard cut-out*** découpage *m* en carton

card-carrying ADJ **c. member** membre *m*, adhérent(e) *m,f*; **c. Communist** membre *m* du parti communiste

cardholder ['kɑːdhəʊldə(r)] N *(of club, political party)* membre *m*, adhérent(e) *m,f*; *(of library)* abonné(e) *m,f*; *(of credit card)* titulaire *mf*; **c. not present** = transaction avec carte de crédit effectuée par téléphone ou par Internet

cardiac ['kɑːdɪæk] ADJ cardiaque
▸▸ *Med* ***cardiac arrest*** arrêt *m* cardiaque; *Med* ***cardiac massage*** massage *m* cardiaque

cardie ['kɑːdɪ] N *Br Fam* cardigan *m*

cardigan ['kɑːdɪgən] N *Br* cardigan *m*

cardinal ['kɑːdɪnəl] N **1** *Math & Rel* cardinal *m* **2** *Orn* cardinal *m* (rouge) **3** *(colour)* rouge cardinal *m inv*
ADJ **1** *(essential)* cardinal **2** *(colour)* rouge cardinal *(inv)*
▸▸ *Math* ***cardinal number*** nombre *m* cardinal; ***the cardinal points*** les (quatre) points *mpl* cardinaux; *Rel* ***cardinal sin*** péché *m* capital; ***the cardinal virtues*** les (quatre) vertus *fpl* cardinales

carding ['kɑːdɪŋ] N *Tex* cardage *m*

cardiogram ['kɑːdɪəgræm] N *Med* cardiogramme *m*

cardiograph ['kɑːdɪəgrɑːf] N *Med* cardiographe *m*

cardiography [ˌkɑːdɪ'ɒgrəfɪ] N *Med* cardiographie *f*

cardiologist [ˌkɑːdɪ'ɒlədʒɪst] N *Med* cardiologue *mf*

cardiology [ˌkɑːdɪ'ɒlədʒɪ] N *Med* cardiologie *f*

cardiovascular [ˌkɑːdɪəʊ'væskjʊlə(r)] ADJ *Med* cardio-vasculaire

cardphone ['kɑːdfəʊn] N *Br* téléphone *m* à carte

cardsharp ['kɑːdʃɑːp], **cardsharper** ['kɑːdʃɑːpə(r)] N tricheur(euse) *m,f* professionnel(elle) *(aux cartes)*

cardy *(pl* **cardies***)* = **cardie**

CARE [keə(r)]

VI
- s'intéresser à **1**
- aimer **2**
- vouloir **3**

N
- souci **1**
- soin **2, 3**
- charge **4**

VI **1** *(feel concern)* **to c. about sth** s'intéresser à *ou* se soucier de qch; **all you c. about is your work!** il n'y a que ton travail qui t'intéresse!; **a book for all those who c. about the environment** un livre pour tous ceux qui s'intéressent à l'environnement *ou* qui se sentent concernés par les problèmes d'environnement; **she didn't seem to c. at all** elle avait l'air de s'en moquer complètement; **I don't c. what people think** je me moque de ce que pensent les gens; **when do you want to tell them? – I don't c.** quand veux-tu leur dire? – ça m'est égal; *Fam* **as if I cared!, I couldn't c. less!** je m'en fiche éperdument, je m'en fous; **what do I c.?** qu'est-ce que ça peut me faire?; **we could be dead for all he cares** il se moque totalement de ce qui peut nous arriver; *Fam* **they don't c. a damn** ils s'en fichent éperdument *ou* comme de leur première chemise; **who cares?** qu'est-ce que ça peut bien faire?
2 *(feel affection)* **to c. about sb** aimer qn; **she cares a lot about her family** elle est très attachée *ou* elle tient beaucoup à sa famille
3 *Formal (like)* **would you c. to join us?** voulez-vous vous joindre à nous?; **I was more nervous than I cared to admit** j'étais plus intimidé qu'il n'y paraissait; **I've worked here longer than I c. to remember** ça fait une éternité que je travaille ici; **I wouldn't c. to go back there** cela ne me dit rien d'y retourner
N **1** *(worry)* souci *m*; **to be full of cares** avoir beaucoup de soucis; **you look as though you haven't a c. in the world** on dirait que tu n'as pas le moindre souci; **cares of State** responsabilités *fpl* d'État
2 *(UNCOUNT) (treatment* ▸ *of person)* soin(s) *m (pl)*, traitement *m*; *(looking after* ▸ *of teeth, hair etc)* soin(s) *m(pl)*; *(*▸ *of machine, material)* entretien *m*; **nursing c.** soins *mpl* à domicile; **you should take c. of that cough** vous devriez (faire) soigner cette toux; **he doesn't take c. of his bicycle** il ne prend pas soin de son vélo; **she needs special c.** elle a besoin de soins spécialisés
3 *(UNCOUNT) (attention)* attention *f*, soin *m*; **they worked with great c.** ils ont travaillé avec le plus grand soin; **handle with c.** *(on package)* fragile; **take c. not to offend her** faites attention à *ou* prenez soin de ne pas la vexer; **take c. not to spill the paint** prenez garde de *ou* faites attention à ne pas renverser la peinture; **drive with c.** conduisez prudemment; **he was charged with driving without due c. and attention** il a été accusé de conduite négligente; *Br Old-fashioned* **have a c.!** prenez garde!, faites attention!
4 *(protection, supervision)* charge *f*, garde *f*; **I'm leaving the matter in your c.** je vous confie l'affaire, je confie l'affaire à vos soins; **the children are in the c. of a nanny** on a laissé *ou* confié les enfants à une nurse *ou* à la garde d'une nurse; **he is under the c. of a heart specialist** c'est un cardiologue qui le traite *ou* qui le soigne; **to take c. of** *(invalid, child, customer, problem etc)* s'occuper de; **to take c. of one's health** ménager sa santé; **who will take c. of your cat?** qui va s'occuper *ou* prendre soin de ton chat?; **I'll take c. of the reservations** je me charge des réservations *ou* de faire les réservations, je vais m'occuper des réservations; **I have important business to take c. of** j'ai une affaire importante à expédier; **take c.!** salut!; **take (good) c. of yourself** fais bien attention à toi; **I can take c. of myself** je peux *ou* je sais me débrouiller (tout seul); **the problem will take c. of itself** le problème va s'arranger tout seul; **c. of** *(in address)* chez
5 *Br Admin* **the baby was put in c.** *or* **taken into c.** on a retiré aux parents la garde de leur bébé; **children in c.** enfants *mpl* confiés aux services sociaux
▸▸ *Br Admin* ***care assistant*** aide-soignant(e) *m,f*; *Br Admin* ***care in the community*** = système de soins prodigués aux malades mentaux en dehors du milieu hospitalier; ***care label*** *(on garment)* conseils *mpl* d'entretien; *Br Admin* ***care worker*** travailleur(euse) *m,f* social(e)

▸**care for** VT INSEP **1** *(look after* ▸ *child)* s'occuper de; *(*▸ *invalid)* soigner; **to look well cared for** *(animal, child, hair etc)* avoir l'air soigné *ou* une apparence soignée; *(car, garden etc)* avoir l'air bien entretenu **2** *(like)* aimer; **he still cares for her** *(loves)* il l'aime toujours; *(has affection for)* il est toujours attaché à elle, il tient toujours à elle; **I didn't c. for his last book** son dernier livre ne m'a pas plu, je n'ai pas aimé son dernier livre; **she didn't c. for the way he spoke** la façon dont il a parlé lui a déplu; *Formal* **would you c. for a cup of coffee?** aimeriez-vous *ou* voudriez-vous une tasse de café?

careen [kə'riːn] *Naut*
VI *(ship)* donner de la bande (de façon dangereuse); *(car, train)* tanguer
VT *(ship)* caréner; *(car, train)* faire tanguer

careening [kə'riːnɪŋ] N *Naut (of ship)* carénage *m*

career [kə'rɪə(r)] N **1** *(profession)* carrière *f*, profession *f*; **she made a c. (for herself) in politics** elle a fait carrière dans la politique; **it's a good/bad c. move** c'est bon/mauvais pour ta/sa/*etc* carrière; **good c. prospects** de bonnes possibilités d'avancement **2** *(life)* vie *f*, carrière *f*; **he spent most of his c. working as a journalist** il a travaillé presque toute sa vie comme journaliste; **her university c.** son parcours universitaire
COMP *(diplomat, soldier)* de carrière
VI *Br* **to c. along** aller à toute vitesse *ou* à toute allure; **to c. into a lorry** *(vehicle)* foncer dans un camion; **the car careered off the road** la voiture a quitté la route à vive allure
▸▸ ***career break*** interruption *f* de carrière; **to take a c. break** interrompre sa carrière *(pour élever des enfants, reprendre des études etc)*; ***career development*** évolution *f* professionnelle; *Sch & Univ Br* ***careers advisor, careers adviser***, *Am* ***career counselor*** conseiller(ère) *m,f* d'orientation professionnelle; ***careers guidance*** orientation *f* professionnelle; ***careers office*** centre *m* d'orientation professionnelle; *Br Sch & Univ* ***careers officer*** conseiller(ère) *m,f* d'orientation professionnelle; ***career path*** parcours *m* professionnel; ***careers service*** centre *m* d'orientation professionnelle; ***career woman*** femme *f* ambitieuse *ou* qui ne pense qu'à sa carrière

careerist [kə'rɪərɪst] N *Pej* carriériste *mf*

carefree ['keəfriː] ADJ *(person)* sans souci, insouciant; *(look, smile)* insouciant

careful ['keəfʊl] ADJ **1** *(cautious)* prudent; **be c.!** (faites) attention!; **be c. of the wet floor!** attention au sol mouillé!; **be c. to close the window before leaving** n'oubliez pas de fermer la fenêtre avant de partir; **be c. not to** *or* **be c. you don't hurt her feelings** faites attention à *ou* prenez soin de ne pas la froisser; **be c. (that) the boss doesn't find out** faites attention *ou* prenez garde que le patron n'en sache rien; **be c. crossing the road** fais attention en traversant *ou* quand tu traverses (la route); **you can never be too c.** *(gen)* on n'est jamais assez prudent; *(in double-checking something)* deux précautions valent mieux qu'une; **he was c. not to mention her name** il a pris soin de ne pas mentionner son nom; **to be c. with one's money** *(gen)* être économe; *Pej* être près de ses sous **2** *(thorough, painstaking* ▸ *person, work)* soigneux, consciencieux; *(*▸ *consideration, examination)* approfondi; **they showed c. attention to detail** ils se sont montrés très attentifs aux détails; **to be c. of one's appearance** être soucieux de son apparence

carefully ['keəfəlɪ] ADV **1** *(cautiously)* avec prudence *ou* précaution, prudemment; **she chose her words c.** elle a pesé ses mots **2** *(thoroughly* ▸ *work)* soigneusement, avec soin; *(*▸ *consider, examine)* de façon approfondie, à fond; *(*▸ *listen, watch)* attentivement

carefulness ['keəfʊlnɪs] N **1** *(caution)* prudence *f* **2** *(thoroughness)* attention *f*, soin *m*

careless ['keəlɪs] ADJ **1** *(negligent* ▸ *person)* négligent, peu soigneux; *(*▸ *work)* peu soigné; **a c. mistake** une faute d'inattention; **he's very c. about his appearance** il ne se soucie pas du tout de son apparence; **c. of the consequences** insouciant des conséquences; **to be c. with money** dépenser à tort et à travers **2** *(thoughtless* ▸ *remark)* irréfléchi **3** *(carefree* ▸ *person)* sans souci, insouciant; *(*▸ *look, smile)* insouciant
▸▸ *Law* ***careless driving*** conduite *f* imprudente; **accused of c. driving** accusé d'imprudence au volant

carelessly ['keəlɪslɪ] ADV **1** *(negligently* ▸ *work, write)* sans soin, sans faire attention; **to drive c.** conduire avec négligence **2** *(thoughtlessly* ▸ *act, speak)* sans réfléchir, à la légère; *(*▸ *dress)* sans soin, sans recherche **3** *(in carefree way)* avec insouciance, nonchalamment

carelessness ['keəlɪsnɪs] N *(UNCOUNT)* **1** *(negligence)* négligence *f*, manque *m* de soin *ou* d'attention **2** *(thoughtlessness* ▸ *of dress)* négligence *f*; *(*▸ *of behaviour)* désinvolture *f*; *(*▸ *of remark)* légèreté *f*

carer ['keərə(r)] N *(professional)* aide *mf* à domicile; *(relative)* = personne s'occupant d'un parent malade ou âgé

caress [kə'res] N caresse *f*
VT caresser

caret ['kærət] N *Typ* accent *m* circonflexe

caretaker ['keəˌteɪkə(r)] N *(of building)* concierge *mf*, gardien(enne) *m,f*
ADJ *(government, prime minister, manager)* intérimaire

careworn ['keəwɔːn] ADJ accablé de soucis, rongé par les soucis

cargo ['kɑːgəʊ] *(pl* **cargoes** *or* **cargos***)* N cargaison *f*, chargement *m*; **to take on** *or* **to embark c.** charger des marchandises; **c. outward** chargement *m* d'aller; **c. homeward** chargement *m* de retour
▸▸ ***cargo boat*** cargo *m*; ***cargo plane*** avion-cargo *m*; ***cargo ship*** cargo *m*; ***cargo pants, cargo trousers*** pantalon *m* cargo; ***cargo vessel*** cargo *m*

> Note that the French word **cargo** is a false friend and is never a translation for the English word **cargo**. It means **cargo ship**.

Caribbean [*Br* kærɪ'biːən, *Am* kə'rɪbɪən] N **the C.** *(area)* les Antilles *fpl*; *(sea)* la mer des Caraïbes *ou* des Antilles; **in the C.** dans les Caraïbes, aux Antilles

ADJ des Caraïbes
►► ***the Caribbean islands*** les Antilles *fpl*; ***the Caribbean Sea*** la mer des Caraïbes *ou* des Antilles

caribou [ˈkærɪbuː] (*pl* **inv** *or* **caribous**) **N** *Zool* caribou *m*

caricature [ˈkærɪkəˌtjʊə(r)] **N** *also Fig* caricature *f*
VT *(depict)* caricaturer; *(parody)* caricaturer, parodier

caricaturist [ˈkærɪkəˌtjʊərɪst] **N** caricaturiste *mf*

caries [ˈkeəriːz] (*pl* **inv**) **N** carie *f*

carillon [ˈkærɪljən] **N** carillon *m*

caring [ˈkeərɪŋ] **N** *(loving)* affection *f*; *(kindliness)* bienveillance *f*
ADJ 1 *(loving)* aimant; *(kindly)* bienveillant; **a more c. society** une société plus chaleureuse *ou* humaine; **a c. environment** un milieu chaleureux **2** *(organization)* à vocation sociale; **the c. professions** les métiers *mpl* du social

carjacking [ˈkɑːdʒækɪŋ] **N** = vol de voiture sous la menace d'une arme

carless [ˈkɑːlɪs] **ADJ** sans voiture

carload [ˈkɑːləʊd] **N a c. of boxes/people** une voiture pleine de cartons/de gens

Carmelite [ˈkɑːmɪlaɪt] *Rel* **N** *(nun)* carmélite *f*; *(friar)* carme *m*
ADJ carmélite

carmine [ˈkɑːmaɪn] **N** carmin *m*
ADJ carmin *(inv)*, carminé

carnage [ˈkɑːnɪdʒ] **N** carnage *m*

carnal [ˈkɑːnəl] **ADJ** charnel; **to have c. knowledge of sb** *Formal or Law* avoir des rapports sexuels avec qn; *Bible* connaître qn

carnation [kɑːˈneɪʃən] **N** œillet *m*
ADJ *(pink)* rose; *(reddish-pink)* incarnat

carnet [ˈkɑːneɪ] **N 1** *(book of tickets)* carnet *m* **2** *Com & Law* passavant *m*

carnival [ˈkɑːnɪvəl] **N 1** *(festival)* carnaval *m* **2** *(fun fair)* fête *f* foraine
COMP *(atmosphere, parade)* de carnaval

carnivore [ˈkɑːnɪvɔː(r)] **N** carnivore *m*, carnassier *m*

carnivorous [kɑːˈnɪvərəs] **ADJ 1** *(animal)* carnivore, carnassier **2** *(person, plant)* carnivore

carob [ˈkærəb] **N** *Bot & Culin (tree)* caroubier *m*; *(pod)* caroube *f*
►► ***carob bean*** caroube *f*; ***carob tree*** caroubier *m*

carol [ˈkærəl] (*Br pt & pp* **carolled**, *cont* **carolling**, *Am pt & pp* **caroled**, *cont* **caroling**) **N** chant *m* (joyeux); **to go c. singing** aller chanter des chants de Noël
VI *(person)* chanter (joyeusement); *(baby, bird)* gazouiller; **to go carolling** chanter des chants de Noël
VT 1 *(sing ► of person)* chanter (joyeusement); *(► of bird)* chanter **2** *(praise)* célébrer (par des chants)
►► ***carol service*** = office religieux qui précède Noël et qui se compose surtout de chants de Noël et de lectures de la Bible; ***carol singer*** = personne qui, à l'époque de Noël, va chanter et quêter au profit des bonnes œuvres

Carolina [ˌkærəˈlaɪnə] **N** Caroline *f*; **the Carolinas** la Caroline du Nord et la Caroline du Sud; **South/North C.** Caroline *f* du Sud/du Nord

Carolingian [ˌkærəˈlɪndʒɪən] *Hist* **N** Carolingien (enne) *m,f*
ADJ carolingien

carom [ˈkærəm] **N** carambolage *m*
VI caramboler

carotid [kəˈrɒtɪd] *Anat* **N** carotide *f*
ADJ *(artery)* carotide; *(nerve, system)* carotidien

carousal [kəˈraʊzəl] **N** *Literary* beuverie *f*, ribote *f*

carouse [kəˈraʊz] **VI** *Literary* faire ribote

carousel [ˌkærəˈsel] **N 1** *Phot (for slides)* carrousel *m* **2** *(for luggage)* carrousel *m*, tapis *m* roulant (à bagages) **3** *Am (merry-go-round)* manège *m* (de chevaux de bois)

carp[1] [kɑːp] (*pl* **inv** *or* **carps**) **N** *Ich* carpe *f*

carp[2] **VI** *(complain)* se plaindre; *(find fault)* critiquer; **he's always carping on about his work** il se plaint toujours de son travail

carpal [ˈkɑːpəl] *Anat* **N** carpe *m*
ADJ carpien
►► *Med* ***carpal tunnel syndrome*** syndrome *m* du canal carpien

Carpathian Mountains [kɑːˈpeɪθɪən-], **Carpathians** [kɑːˈpeɪθɪənz] **NPL the C.** les Carpates *fpl*; **in the C.** dans les Carpates

carpel [ˈkɑːpel] **N** *Bot* carpelle *m*

carpenter [ˈkɑːpəntə(r)] **N** *(for houses, large-scale works)* charpentier *m*; *(for doors, furniture)* menuisier *m*

carpentry [ˈkɑːpəntrɪ] **N** *(large-scale work)* charpenterie *f*; *(doors, furniture)* menuiserie *f*

carpet [ˈkɑːpɪt] **N 1** *(not fitted)* tapis *m*; *(fitted)* moquette *f*; *Fam Fig* **to be on the c.** *(of question)* être sur le tapis; *(of person)* être sur la sellette; *Fam* **to have** *or* **put sb on the c.** enguirlander qn, passer un savon à qn **2** *Br Fig (of leaves, snow)* tapis *m*
VT 1 *(floor)* recouvrir d'un tapis; *(with fitted carpet)* recouvrir d'une moquette, moquetter; *(house, room)* mettre de la moquette dans, moquetter; **carpeted hallway** couloir moquetté *ou* avec de la moquette; **all the rooms are carpeted** il y a de la moquette dans toutes les pièces; *Fig* **carpeted with leaves/snow** tapissé de feuilles/de neige **2** *Br Fam (scold)* enguirlander, passer un savon à
►► *Mil* ***carpet bombing*** bombardement *m* intensif; ***carpet shampoo*** shampooing *m* pour moquette; ***carpet slipper*** charentaise *f*; ***carpet sweeper*** *(mechanical)* balai *m* mécanique; *(electric)* aspirateur *m*; ***carpet tack*** fixe-tapis *m inv*; ***carpet tile*** carreau *m* de moquette

> Note that the French word **carpette** is a false friend and is never a translation for the English word **carpet**. It means **small rug**.

carpetbagger [ˈkɑːpɪtˌbægə(r)] **N** *Pej* **1** *Pol* candidat *m* étranger à la circonscription **2** *Am Hist* = nom donné aux nordistes qui s'installèrent dans le Sud des États-Unis après la guerre de Sécession pour y faire fortune

carpeting [ˈkɑːpɪtɪŋ] **N 1** *(carpets)* moquette *f* **2** *Br Fam (severe reprimand)* réprimande[□] *f*; **to give sb a c.** passer un savon à qn

carping [ˈkɑːpɪŋ] **N** *(UNCOUNT) (complaining)* plaintes *fpl* (continuelles); *(faultfinding)* chicanerie *f*, critiques *fpl* (malveillantes)
ADJ *(person ► complaining)* qui se plaint tout le temps; *(► faultfinding)* qui trouve toujours à redire, chicanier; *(attitude)* chicanier, grincheux; *(criticism, voice)* malveillant

carport [ˈkɑːpɔːt] **N** auvent *m* (pour voiture)

carpus [ˈkɑːpəs] **N** *Anat* carpe *m*

carriage [ˈkærɪdʒ] **N 1** *(vehicle ► horse-drawn)* calèche *f*, voiture *f* à cheval; *(► together with horses and driver)* équipage *m*; *Br* **c. and pair/four** voiture *f ou* équipage *m* à deux/quatre chevaux
2 *Br Rail* voiture *f*, wagon *m* (de voyageurs); **he was leaning out of the c. window** il se penchait par la fenêtre du compartiment
3 *Br Com (transportation)* transport *m*; *(cost of transportation)* transport *m*, fret *m*; *Com* **c. forward** (en) port dû; *Com* **c. free** franco de port; *Com* **c. insurance paid** port payé, assurance comprise; *Com* **c. paid** (en) port payé
4 *(bearing, posture)* port *m*, maintien *m*
5 *(of typewriter)* chariot *m*; *(of gun)* affût *m*
►► *Com* ***carriage charge, carriage charges*** frais *mpl* de port; *Br* ***carriage clock*** pendulette *f (à boîtier rectangulaire muni d'une poignée)*; *Sport* ***carriage driving*** course *f* de chevaux d'attelage; *Typ* ***carriage return*** retour *m* de chariot; *Br Com* ***carriage trade*** clientèle *f* riche

carriageway [ˈkærɪdʒweɪ] **N** *Br* chaussée *f*

carrier [ˈkærɪə(r)] **N 1** *(container ► on bicycle) (basket)* panier *m*; *(behind the saddle)* porte-bagages *m inv*; *Am (► on car)* galerie *f*; *(► for homing pigeon)* cartouche *f*
2 *Com (transporter ► company)* entreprise *f* de transport, transporteur *m*; *(► aeroplane)* appareil *m*, avion *m*; *(► ship)* navire *m*; **sent by c.** *(by road)* expédié par camion *ou* par transporteur; *(by rail)* expédié par chemin de fer; *(by air)* expédié par avion
3 *Med (of disease, germs)* porteur(euse) *m,f*
4 *(for signal)* opérateur *m*
►► *Br* ***carrier bag*** sac *m* en plastique; ***carrier pigeon*** pigeon *m* voyageur; *Comput* ***carrier signal*** signal *m* de détection de porteuse; *Rad* ***carrier wave*** onde *f* porteuse

carrier-based **ADJ** *Aviat & Naut* embarqué

carrion [ˈkærɪən] **N** charogne *f*
►► *Orn* ***carrion crow*** corneille *f* noire

carrot [ˈkærət] **N 1** *(plant & vegetable)* carotte *f* **2** *Fig (motivation)* carotte *f*; **the boss used the promise of promotion as a c.** le patron a promis une promotion pour nous encourager; **the c. and stick approach** la méthode de la carotte et du bâton **3** *Fam Hum* **carrots, c. top** *(redhead)* rouquin(e) *m,f*
COMP *(flavour, juice)* de carotte; *(soup, cake)* aux carottes

carroty [ˈkærətɪ] **ADJ** carotte *(inv)*, roux (rousse); **she has c. hair** elle est rousse *ou Hum* poil-de-carotte

carrousel = **carousel**

CARRY [ˈkærɪ]

VT	
• porter **1, 3–5, 8, 9**	• transporter **2**
• transmettre **2, 3, 6**	• adopter **11**
• vendre **12**	• retenir **13**
VI	
• porter	

(*pt & pp* **carried**)
VT 1 *(bear ► of person)* porter; *(► heavy load)* porter, transporter; **could you c. the groceries into the kitchen?** pourrais-tu porter les provisions jusqu'à la cuisine?; **the porter carried the suitcases downstairs/upstairs** le porteur a descendu/monté les bagages
2 *(convey, transport ► of vehicle)* transporter; *(► of river, wind)* porter, emporter; *(► of pipe)* acheminer, amener; *(► of airwaves, telephone wire)* transmettre, conduire; **she ran as fast as her legs would c. her** elle a couru à toutes jambes; **the current carried the raft out to sea** le courant a emporté le radeau au large; **she carries all the facts in her head** elle a tous les faits en mémoire; **he carried the secret to his grave** il a emporté le secret dans la tombe; **to c. a tune** chanter juste; *Fig* **to c. coals to Newcastle** porter de l'eau à la rivière
3 *(be medium for ► message, news)* porter, transmettre; *Med (► disease, virus)* porter; **rats c. diseases** les rats sont porteurs de maladies
4 *(have on one's person ► identity card, papers)* porter, avoir (sur soi); *(► cash)* avoir (sur soi); *(► gun)* porter; **I don't c. much money about** *or* **on me** je n'ai jamais beaucoup d'argent sur moi
5 *(comprise, include)* porter, comporter; *(have as consequence)* entraîner; **to c. a risk** comporter un risque; **to c. responsibility** comporter des responsabilités; **to c. a fine/penalty** être passible d'amende/d'une peine; **to c. (no) conviction** (ne pas) être convaincant; **our products c. a six-month warranty** nos produits sont accompagnés d'une garantie de six mois; **to c. weight/authority** *(of person, opinion)* avoir du poids/de l'autorité
6 *(of magazine, newspaper)* rapporter; *(of radio, television)* transmettre; **all the newspapers carried the story** l'histoire était dans tous les journaux
7 *(take, lead, extend)* **to c. an argument to its logical conclusion** aller au bout d'un raisonnement; **to c. sth too far** pousser qch trop loin; **to c. the battle** *or* **fight into the enemy's camp** *Mil* faire du territoire ennemi le lieu du conflit; *Fig* attaquer l'ennemi sur son propre terrain
8 *(bear, hold)* porter; **to c. oneself well** *(sit, stand)* se tenir droit; *(behave)* bien se conduire *ou* se tenir; **to c. one's head high** porter la tête haute
9 *(hold up, support ► roof, weight)* porter, supporter, soutenir
10 *(win)* **she carried the audience with her** le public était avec elle; **he carried all before him** ce fut un triomphe pour lui; **to c. the day** l'emporter
11 *(proposal ► pass)* adopter; *(► secure passage of)* faire adopter *ou* passer; **the motion was carried** la motion a été votée
12 *Com (deal in ► stock)* vendre, stocker
13 *Math* retenir; **add nine and c. one** ajoute neuf et retiens un
14 *(be pregnant with)* attendre; **she's carrying their fourth child** elle est enceinte de leur quatrième enfant

VI *(ball, sound)* porter; **her voice carries well** elle a une voix qui porte bien

▸**carry away VT SEP 1** *(remove)* emporter, enlever; *(of waves, wind)* emporter **2** *(usu passive) (excite)* **he was carried away by his enthusiasm/imagination** il s'est laissé emporter par son enthousiasme/imagination; **I got a bit carried away and spent all my money** je me suis emballé et j'ai dépensé tout mon argent; **don't get too carried away!** du calme!, ne t'emballe pas!

▸**carry back VT SEP 1** *(bring ▸ object)* rapporter; *(▸ person)* ramener **2** *(take ▸ object)* reporter; *(▸ person)* remmener; **that carries me back to my youth** cela me ramène à l'époque de ma jeunesse

▸**carry down VT SEP 1** *(from upstairs)* descendre **2** *(usu passive) (tradition)* transmettre

▸**carry forward VT SEP** *Acct* reporter; **carried forward** report, à reporter; **carried forward from the previous year/to the next year** report de l'exercice précédent/à l'exercice suivant

▸**carry off VT SEP 1** *(remove forcibly ▸ goods)* emporter, enlever; *(▸ person)* enlever; **the thieves carried off all their jewellery** les voleurs se sont enfuis avec tous leurs bijoux

2 *(award, prize)* remporter

3 *(do successfully ▸ aim, plan)* réaliser; *(▸ deal, meeting)* mener à bien; **to c.y it off** réussir le coup; **she carried it off beautifully** elle s'en est très bien tirée; **it's a difficult role and he didn't quite c. it off** c'est un rôle difficile, et il n'a pas su se montrer à la hauteur

4 *Euph (kill ▸ of disease)* emporter

▸**carry on VI 1** *Br (continue)* continuer; **I carried on working** *or* **with my work** j'ai continué à travailler, j'ai continué mon travail; **they carried on to the bitter end** ils sont allés jusqu'au bout **2** *Fam (make a fuss)* faire une histoire *ou* des histoires; **the way you c. on, you'd think I never did anything around the house** à t'entendre, je n'ai jamais rien fait dans cette maison **3** *Fam (have affair)* **he's carrying on with somebody else's wife** il a une liaison avec *ou* il couche avec la femme d'un autre

VT INSEP 1 *Br (continue ▸ conversation, work)* continuer, poursuivre; *(▸ tradition)* entretenir, perpétuer; **we can c. on this conversation later** nous pourrons poursuivre *ou* reprendre cette conversation plus tard **2** *(conduct ▸ work)* effectuer, réaliser; *(▸ negotiations)* mener; *(▸ discussion)* avoir; *(▸ correspondence)* entretenir

▸**carry out VT SEP 1** *(take away)* emporter **2** *(perform ▸ programme, raid)* effectuer; *(▸ idea, plan)* réaliser, mettre à exécution; *(▸ experiment)* effectuer, conduire; *(▸ investigation, research, survey)* conduire, mener; *(▸ instruction, order)* exécuter; **the police carried out a search** *(of house, premises)* la police a effectué une perquisition **3** *(fulfil ▸ obligation)* s'acquitter de; *(▸ wish)* satisfaire à; *(▸ responsibilities)* assumer; **he failed to c. out his promise** il a manqué à sa parole, il n'a pas tenu *ou* respecté sa promesse

▸**carry over VT SEP 1** *(transport)* faire traverser; *Fig (transfer)* reporter, transférer

2 *(defer, postpone)* reporter; **to c. over one's holiday entitlement/tax allowance to the next year** reporter ses congés/son abattement fiscal sur l'année suivante

3 *Acct* reporter; **to c. over a loss to the following year** reporter une perte sur l'année suivante

4 *St Exch (shares)* reporter, prendre en report

5 *Com* **to c. over goods from one season to another** stocker des marchandises d'une saison sur l'autre

▸**carry through VT SEP 1** *(accomplish)* réaliser, mener à bien *ou* à bonne fin **2** *(support)* soutenir (dans une épreuve); **her love of life carried her through her illness** sa volonté de vivre lui a permis de vaincre sa maladie

carryall ['kærɪ,ɔːl] **N** *Am* fourre-tout *m inv (sac)*

carrycot ['kærɪ,kɒt] **N** *Br* porte-bébé *m*

carrying ['kærɪɪŋ] **ADJ**

▸▸ *Tech* ***carrying axle*** *(of locomotive)* essieu *m* porteur; ***carrying capacity*** *(of vehicle)* charge *f* utile; *(of tourist attraction)* capacité *f* d'accueil; *Com* ***carrying charge*** *Am (extra charge)* supplément *m (que l'on paye lorsqu'on achète à crédit)*; *Br (transport costs)* frais *mpl* de transport; *Am Acct* ***carrying forward*** report *m*

carrying-on *(pl* **carryings-on)** **N** *Fam (of child)* cirque *m*; *(of unfaithful spouse, lover)* écart *m* de conduite[□], incartade(s)[□] *f(pl)*

carry-on **N** *Br Fam* **1** *(fuss)* histoires *fpl*; *(commotion)* tapage[□] *m*, agitation[□] *f*; **what a c.!** que d'histoires! **2** *(of child)* cirque *m*; *(of unfaithful spouse, lover)* écart *m* de conduite[□]

ADJ c. items bagages *mpl* à main

carry-out **N 1** *Am & Scot (restaurant)* = restaurant qui fait des plats à emporter; *(meal)* plat *m* à emporter **2** *Scot (drink)* = boissons alcoolisées à emporter

ADJ *Am & Scot (dish, food)* à emporter; *Scot (drink)* à emporter

▸▸ *Am & Scot* ***carry-out menu*** liste *f* des plats à emporter

carry-over **N 1** *(habit, influence, trace)* vestige *m* **2** *Fin (amount)* report *m*

carsick ['kɑː,sɪk] **ADJ to be** *or* **to feel c.** être malade en voiture

cart [kɑːt] **N 1** *(horse-drawn ▸ for farming)* charrette *f*; *(▸ for passengers)* charrette *f* (anglaise), voiture *f*; *Fig* **to put the c. before the horse** mettre la charrue avant les bœufs **2** *(handcart)* charrette *f* à bras **3** *Am (for shopping)* Caddie® *m*

VT 1 *(transport by cart)* charrier, charroyer, transporter en charrette **2** *Fam Fig (haul)* transporter[□], trimballer; **I've been carting this suitcase around all day** j'ai passé la journée à trimballer cette valise

▸▸ ***cart track*** chemin *m* de terre

▸**cart away, cart off VT SEP** *(rubbish, wood)* emporter; *Fam (person)* emmener

cartage ['kɑːtɪdʒ] **N** *Com* **1** *(transport ▸ in cart)* charroi *m*, charriage *m*; *(▸ in lorry)* camionnage *m* **2** *(cost ▸ by cart)* (coût *m* de) charriage *m*; *(▸ by lorry)* (coût *m* de) camionnage *m*

carte blanche [,kɑːt'blɑ̃ʃ] **N** carte *f* blanche; **to give sb c. (to do sth)** donner carte blanche à qn (pour faire qch)

cartel [kɑː'tel] **N** *Com & Pol* cartel *m*; **oil/steel c.** cartel *m* du pétrole/de l'acier

carter ['kɑːtə(r)] **N** charretier(ère) *m,f*

Cartesian [kɑː'tiːzɪən] **N** cartésien(enne) *m,f*

ADJ cartésien

▸▸ *Math* ***Cartesian coordinates*** coordonnées *fpl* cartésiennes

carthorse ['kɑːthɔːs, *pl* -hɔːsɪz] **N** cheval *m* de trait

Carthusian [kɑː'θjuːzjən] *Rel* **N** chartreux(euse) *m,f*

ADJ de *ou* des chartreux; **C. monastery** chartreuse *f (monastère)*

cartilage ['kɑːtɪlɪdʒ] **N** cartilage *m*

cartload ['kɑːtləʊd] **N** charretée *f*, voiturée *f* (of de); *(transported in tip cart)* tombereau *m*

cartographer [kɑː'tɒgrəfə(r)] **N** cartographe *mf*

cartographic [,kɑːtə'græfɪk], **cartographical** [,kɑːtə'græfɪkəl] **ADJ** cartographique

cartography [kɑː'tɒgrəfɪ] **N** cartographie *f*

cartomancy ['kɑːtəʊmænsɪ] **N** cartomancie *f*

carton ['kɑːtən] **N** *(cardboard box)* boîte *f* (en carton), carton *m*; *(of juice, milk)* carton *m*, brique *f*; *(of cream, yoghurt)* pot *m*; *(of cigarettes)* cartouche *f*

cartoon [kɑː'tuːn] **N 1** *(drawing)* dessin *m* humoristique; *(series of drawings)* bande *f* dessinée; *(animated film)* dessin *m* animé **2** *Art (sketch)* carton *m*

▸▸ ***cartoon character*** personnage *m* de bande dessinée/de dessin animé; ***cartoon strip*** bande *f* dessinée, BD *f*

cartoonist [kɑː'tuːnɪst] **N** *(of drawings)* dessinateur(trice) *m,f* humoristique; *(of series of drawings)* dessinateur(trice) *m,f* de bandes dessinées; *(for films)* dessinateur(trice) *m,f* de dessins animés, animateur(trice) *m,f*

cartridge ['kɑːtrɪdʒ] **N 1** *(for explosive, gun)* cartouche *f*

2 *(for pen, tape deck, typewriter)* cartouche *f*

3 *(for stylus)* cellule *f*

4 *Phot* chargeur *m* (d'appareil photo)

5 *Comput (disk)* cartouche *f*; **ink/toner c.** cartouche *f* d'encre/de toner

▸▸ ***cartridge belt*** *(for hunter, soldier)* cartouchière *f*; *(for machine gun)* bande *f* (de mitrailleuse); ***cartridge case*** *(for gun)* douille *f*, étui *m* (de cartouche); *(for cannon)* douille *f*; ***cartridge clip*** chargeur *m (d'une arme à feu)*; ***cartridge paper*** papier *m* à cartouche; ***cartridge pen*** stylo *m* à cartouche; ***cartridge player*** lecteur *m* de cartouche

cartwheel ['kɑːtwiːl] **N 1** *(of cart)* roue *f* de charrette **2** *(movement)* roue *f*; **to do** *or* **to turn cartwheels** faire la roue

VI faire la roue; **she cartwheeled across the floor** elle a traversé la pièce en faisant des roues

cartwright ['kɑːtraɪt] **N** charron *m*

carve [kɑːv] **VT 1** *(stone, wood)* tailler, sculpter; **to c. a statue in** *or* **out of marble** sculpter une statue dans le marbre; **she carved their names on the tree trunk** elle a gravé leurs noms sur le tronc de l'arbre; **the river had carved a channel through the rock** la rivière s'était creusé un lit dans le rocher **2** *(meat)* découper

▸**carve out VT SEP** *(piece)* découper, tailler; *(shape)* sculpter, tailler; **the company carved out a niche in the market** la société s'est taillé une place sur le marché; *Fig* **she carved out a career for herself in the arts** elle a fait carrière dans les arts

▸**carve up VT SEP 1** *(cut up ▸ meat)* découper; *Fig (▸ country, estate)* morceler, démembrer; **they carved up the profits among them** ils se sont partagé les profits **2** *Fam (disfigure ▸ person)* amocher à coups de couteau; *(▸ face)* balafrer[□], taillader[□] **3** *Fam (overtake dangerously)* faire une queue de poisson à[□]

carver ['kɑːvə(r)] **N 1** *(knife)* couteau *m* à découper; **carvers** service *m* à découper **2** *Br (chair)* fauteuil *m* de table *(qu'occupe le chef de famille)*

carvery ['kɑːvərɪ] *(pl* **carveries)** **N** = restaurant où l'on mange de la viande découpée à table

carving ['kɑːvɪŋ] **N 1** *(sculpture)* sculpture *f*; *(engraving)* gravure *f*; **wood c.** sculpture *f* sur bois **2** *(act)* taille *f*; *(skill)* taille *f*, art *m* de la taille **3** *(of meat)* découpage *m*

▸▸ ***carving fork*** fourchette *f* à découper; ***carving knife*** couteau *m* à découper

caryatid [,kærɪ'ætɪd] **N** *Archit* cariatide *f*

cascade [kæ'skeɪd] **N** cascade *f*, chute *f* d'eau; *Fig (of hair)* flot *m*

VI *(water, hair)* tomber en cascade; **the tins came cascading down** les boîtes de conserve sont tombées les unes après les autres

cascading menu [kæs'keɪdɪŋ-] **N** *Comput* menu *m* en cascade

CASE [keɪs] **N** *Comput (abbr* **computer-aided software engineering)** ingénierie *f* des systèmes assistée par ordinateur

CASE[1] [keɪs]

N	
• cas **1, 2, 6–8**	• affaire **3, 4**
• arguments **5**	

N 1 *(instance, situation)* cas *m*, exemple *m*; **it's a clear c. of mismanagement** c'est un exemple manifeste de mauvaise gestion; **if it's a c. of not having enough money** si c'est une question d'argent; **to put the c. clearly** exposer clairement le cas *ou* la situation; **in that c.** dans *ou* en ce cas; **in these cases it's best to wait** dans de telles circonstances, il vaut mieux attendre; **in this particular c.** en l'occurrence; **in which c.** auquel cas; **in your c.** en ce qui vous concerne, dans votre cas; **in many/most cases** dans beaucoup de/la plupart des cas; **in nine cases out of ten** neuf fois sur dix; **the current crisis is a c. in point** la crise actuelle est un exemple typique; **it's a c. of now or never** il s'agit de saisir l'occasion *ou* de faire vite

2 *(actual state of affairs)* cas *m*; **that is not the c. in Great Britain** ce *ou* tel n'est pas le cas en Grande-Bretagne; **as the c.** *or* **whatever the c. may be** selon le cas; **if such is indeed the c.** si tel est *ou* si c'est vraiment le cas

3 *(investigation)* affaire *f*; **a murder/fraud c.** une affaire de meurtre/fraude; **he's on the c.** *(working on it)* il s'en occupe; *(alert, informed)* il est très au courant; *Fam* **to be on sb's c.** être sur le dos de qn; *Fam* **get off my c.!** fiche-moi la paix!

4 *Law* affaire *f*, cause *f*, procès *m*; **a civil rights c.** une affaire de droits civils; **her c. comes up next week** son procès a lieu la semaine prochaine; **to try a c.** *Br (of judge)* juger une affaire; *Am (of lawyer)* = agir dans le cadre d'une action publique; **he won his c. for slander** *(barrister)* il a gagné le procès en diffamation; *(plaintiff)* il a gagné son procès *ou* il a eu gain de cause dans son procès en diffamation

5 *(argument)* arguments *mpl*; **there is no c. against him** aucune preuve n'a pu être retenue contre lui; **the c. against/for the defendant** les arguments contre/en faveur de l'accusé; **there is a good c. against/for establishing quotas** il y a beaucoup à dire contre/en faveur de l'établissement de quotas; **state your c.** présentez vos arguments; **there is a c. to be answered here** il ne faut pas négliger cette question; **to make (out) a c. for sth** présenter des arguments pour *ou* en faveur de qch

6 *Med (disease)* cas *m*; *(person)* malade *mf*; **there have been several cases of meningitis recently** il y a eu plusieurs cas de méningite récemment; **all burns cases are treated here** tous les grands brûlés sont traités ici

7 *Fam (person)* cas▫ *m*; **he's a real c.!** c'est un cas *ou* un phénomène!; **he's a sad c.** c'est vraiment un pauvre type

8 *Gram* cas *m*

• **in any case** ADV **1** *(besides)* en tout cas; **in any c. I shan't be coming** je ne viendrai pas en tout cas *ou* de toute façon

2 *(at least)* du moins, en tout cas

• **in case** ADV au cas où; **I'll take my umbrella (just) in c.** je vais prendre mon parapluie au cas où CONJ au cas où; **in c. you think I'm bluffing** au cas où tu croirais que je bluffe

• **in case of** PREP en cas de; **in c. of emergency/fire** en cas d'urgence/d'incendie

►► ***case history*** antécédents *mpl*; ***case law*** jurisprudence *f*, droit *m* jurisprudentiel; ***case load*** (nombre *m* de) dossiers *mpl* à traiter; ***case notes*** dossier *m*; ***case study*** étude *f* de cas

---

case² N **1** *(container)* caisse *f*, boîte *f*; *(for bottles)* caisse *f*; *(for fruit, vegetables)* cageot *m*; *(chest)* coffre *m*; *(for jewellery)* coffret *m*; *(for necklace, watch)* écrin *m*; *(for camera, guitar, spectacles, cigarettes)* étui *m*; *(for pencils, geometry etc instruments)* trousse *f*

2 *(for display)* vitrine *f*

3 *Br (suitcase)* valise *f*

4 *Typ* casse *f*; **lower c.** bas *m* de casse; **upper c.** haut *m* de casse; *Comptr* **this e-mail address is c. sensitive** cette adresse électronique tient compte des majuscules; **this URL is c. insensitive** le respect de majuscules et des minuscules n'est pas nécessaire pour cette URL

5 *Bot & Zool (covering)* enveloppe *f*

VT **1** *(put in box)* mettre en boîte *ou* caisse **2** *(cover)* couvrir, envelopper; **cased in ice** couvert de glace **3** *Fam (inspect)* examiner▫; **the robbers had thoroughly cased the joint** les voleurs avaient bien examiné les lieux (avant de faire leur coup)

►► ***case knife*** couteau *m* à gaine

casebook ['keɪsbʊk] N *(gen)* = recueil de comptes rendus de cas; *Law* recueil *m* de jurisprudence

casebound ['keɪsbaʊnd] ADJ cartonné

case-harden VT *Metal* cémenter; *Fig* endurcir

case-hardened ADJ *Metal* cémenté; *Fig* endurci

case-hardening N *Metal* cémentation *f*

casein ['keɪsi:n] N *Chem* caséine *f*

casement ['keɪsmənt] N *(window)* fenêtre *f* à battant *ou* battants, croisée *f*; *(window frame)* châssis *m* de fenêtre (à deux battants); *Literary* fenêtre *f*

►► ***casement window*** fenêtre *f* à battant *ou* battants, croisée *f*

casework ['keɪswɜ:k] N = travail social personnalisé

caseworker ['keɪsˌwɜ:kə(r)] N = travailleur social s'occupant de cas individuels et familiaux

cash [kæʃ] N **1** *(coins and banknotes)* espèces *fpl*, (argent *m*) liquide *m*; **I never carry much c.** je n'ai jamais beaucoup d'argent *ou* de liquide sur moi; **£3,000 in c.** 3000 livres en espèces *ou* en liquide; **hard** *or* **ready c.** liquide *m*; **to pay (in) c.** *(not credit)* payer comptant; *(money not cheque)* payer en liquide *ou* en espèces; **to buy/sell sth for c.** acheter/vendre qch comptant; **c. against documents** comptant contre documents; **to pay c. on the nail** payer rubis sur ongle; *Acct* **c. at bank** avoir *m* en banque; **c. in hand** fonds *mpl ou* espèces *mpl ou* argent *m* en caisse; *Acct* **c. in till** encaisse *f*, fonds *m* de caisse

2 *(money in general)* argent *m*; **to be short of c.** être à court (d'argent); **I haven't got any c.** *(no money)* je n'ai pas d'argent; *(no change)* je n'ai pas de monnaie; **I ran out of c.** je n'avais plus d'argent

3 *(immediate payment)* **discount for c.** escompte *m* de caisse; **c. down** argent *m* comptant; **to pay c. down** payer comptant; *Br* **c. on delivery** paiement *m* à la livraison, (livraison *f*) contre remboursement; **c. with order** payable à la commande

COMP **1** *(problems, worries)* d'argent **2** *(price, transaction)* (au) comptant

VT *(cheque)* encaisser, toucher; **could you c. this cheque for me?** *(to friend)* peux-tu me donner de l'argent contre ce chèque?; *(to bank employee)* voudriez-vous m'encaisser ce chèque?

►► ***cash account*** compte *m* de caisse; ***cash advance*** avance *m* en numéraire; *Br* ***cash and carry*** libre-service *m* de gros; ***cash balance*** *(status)* situation *f* de caisse; *(amount remaining)* solde *m* actif, solde *m* de caisse; *Acct* ***cash basis accounting*** comptabilité *f* de caisse *ou* de gestion; ***cash benefits*** avantages *mpl* en espèces; ***cash bonus*** prime *f* en espèces; ***cash book*** livre *m ou* journal *m* de caisse; ***cash budget*** budget *m* de trésorerie; ***cash card*** carte *f* de retrait; *Acct* ***cash contribution*** apport *m* en numéraire *ou* en espèces; ***cash cow*** vache *f* à lait; ***cash crop*** culture *f* de rapport *ou* commerciale; ***cash deficit*** déficit *m* de trésorerie; ***cash deposit*** versement *m* en espèces; ***cash desk*** caisse *f*; ***cash discount*** escompte *m* de caisse; ***cash dispenser*** distributeur *m* (automatique) de billets, DAB *m*, *Suisse & Belg* bancomat *m*; ***cash dividend*** dividende *m* en espèces; *Acct* ***cash expenditure*** dépenses *fpl* de caisse; *Fin* ***cash flow*** cash-flow *m*, trésorerie *f*; *Acct (in cash flow statement)* marge *f* brute d'autofinancement; *Hum* **to have c. flow problems** avoir des problèmes de trésorerie; ***cash incentive*** stimulation *f* financière; *Banking* ***cash machine*** distributeur *m* (automatique) de billets, DAB *m*, *Suisse & Belg* bancomat *m*; ***cash management*** gestion *f* de trésorerie; ***cash offer*** offre *f* d'achat avec paiement comptant; **she made us a c. offer for the flat** elle nous a proposé de payer l'appartement (au) comptant; ***cash payment*** *(immediate)* paiement *m* comptant; *(in cash)* paiement *m* en espèces *ou* en liquide; ***cash price*** prix *m* comptant; ***cash prize*** prix *m* en espèces; ***cash purchase*** achat *m* au comptant, achat contre espèces; *Acct* ***cash ratio*** ratio *m* de trésorerie; *Acct* ***cash received*** *(balance sheet item)* entrée *f* d'argent; ***cash register*** caisse *f* (enregistreuse); ***cash reserves*** réserves *fpl* en espèces; ***cash sale*** vente *f* au comptant; *Acct* ***cash statement*** état *m ou* relevé *m* de caisse; ***cash terms*** conditions *fpl* au comptant; ***cash transaction*** opération *f ou* transaction *f* au comptant; ***cash value*** valeur *f* vénale; *Banking* ***cash withdrawal*** retrait *m* d'espèces

► **cash in** VT SEP *(bond, certificate)* réaliser, se faire rembourser; *(coupon)* se faire rembourser; *Am Fam* **to c. in one's chips** *or* **checks** *(die)* casser sa pipe

VI *Fam* **1** *(take advantage)* **to c. in on a situation** profiter *ou* tirer profit d'une situation▫ **2** *Am (die)* casser sa pipe

► **cash up** VI *Br Com* faire ses comptes

cashable ['kæʃəbəl] ADJ encaissable, payable

cashback ['kæʃbæk] N *Br* **1** *(in mortgage lending)* = prime versée par une société de crédit immobilier au souscripteur d'un emprunt **2** *(in supermarket)* = espèces retirées à la caisse d'un supermarché lors d'un paiement par carte de crédit

cashew ['kæʃu:] N *(tree)* anacardier *m*; *(nut* (noix *f* de) cajou *m*

►► ***cashew nut*** (noix *f* de) cajou *m*

cashier¹ [kæ'ʃɪə(r)] N *Banking & Com* caissier (ère) *m,f*; *Am* **c.'s check** chèque *m* de banque; **c.'s desk** comptoir-caisse *m*

cashier² VT *Mil* casser; *Fig* renvoyer, congédier

cashless ['kæʃlɪs] ADJ *(society)* sans argent liquide; **we're moving towards a c. society** nous nous dirigeons vers une société où l'argent liquide ne sera plus utilisé; **c. transaction** transaction *f* sans argent

cashmere [kæʃ'mɪə(r)] N cachemire *m*

COMP *(coat, sweater)* de *ou* en cachemire

casing ['keɪsɪŋ] N **1** *(gen)* revêtement *m*, enveloppe *f*; *(for tyre)* enveloppe *f* extérieure; *(of pump)* enveloppe *f*, garniture *f*; *(of machine)* cage *f*, coquille *f*; *Constr (for reinforced concrete)* coffrage *m* **2** *(of window)* chambranle *m*, châssis *m*; *(of door)* encadrement *m*, chambranle *m*

casino [kə'si:nəʊ] *(pl* **casinos)** N casino *m*

cask [kɑ:sk] N *(barrel ► gen)* tonneau *m*, fût *m*; *(► large)* barrique *f*; *(► small)* baril *m*

casket ['kɑ:skɪt] N **1** *(small box)* coffret *m*, boîte *f* **2** *Am (coffin)* cercueil *m*

CASM ['kæzəm] N *Br Comput (abbr* **computer-aided sales and marketing, computer-assisted sales and marketing)** vente *f* et marketing *m* assistés par ordinateur

Caspian Sea ['kæspɪən-] N **the C.** la (mer) Caspienne

Cassandra [kə'sændrə] PR N *Myth & Fig* Cassandre

cassata [kə'sɑ:tə] N *Culin* cassate *f*

cassava [kə'sɑ:və] N *Bot (plant)* manioc *m*; *Culin (flour)* farine *f* de manioc

casserole ['kæsərəʊl] N **1** *(dish, pan)* cocotte *f* **2** *(stew)* ragoût *m*

VT (faire) cuire en ragoût

> Note that the French word **casserole** is a false friend and is never a translation for the English word **casserole**. It means **saucepan**.

cassette [kæ'set] N **1** *(tape)* cassette *f* **2** *Phot (cartridge)* chargeur *m*

►► ***cassette case*** étui *m* de cassette; ***cassette deck*** lecteur *m* de cassettes; ***cassette head cleaner*** cassette *f* autonettoyante; ***cassette library*** cassettothèque *f*; ***cassette player*** lecteur *m* de cassettes; ***cassette recorder*** magnétophone *m* à cassettes

cassock ['kæsək] N soutane *f*

cassowary ['kæsəweərɪ] *(pl* **cassowaries)** N *Orn* casoar *m*

CAST [kɑ:st]

VT	
• jeter **1, 2**	• projeter **2**
• perdre **3**	• distribuer les rôles de **4**
• mouler **5**	• couler **5**
N	
• acteurs **1**	• nuance **2**
• moulage **3**	• coulage **3**
• plâtre **4**	

(pt & pp **cast)**

VT **1** *(throw)* jeter, lancer; *Br* **to c. lots** tirer au sort; **to c. a spell on** *or* **over sb** *(witch)* jeter un sort à qn, ensorceler qn; *Fig* ensorceler *ou* envoûter qn; **to c. one's vote for sb** voter pour qn; **the number of votes c.** le nombre de voix *ou* de suffrages; *Naut* **to c. anchor** mouiller (l'ancre), jeter l'ancre; *Fig* **we'll have to c. our net wide to find the right candidate** il va falloir ratisser large pour trouver le bon candidat

2 *(direct ► light, shadow)* projeter; *(► look)* jeter, diriger; *(► doubt, suspicion)* jeter; **could you c. an eye over this report?** voulez-vous jeter un œil sur ce rapport?; **she c. a desperate glance at her mother** elle glissa à sa mère un regard désespéré, elle regarda sa mère avec désespoir; **to c. doubt on sth** jeter le doute sur qch; **this c. doubt on his ability** cela jeta un doute sur ses capacités; **to c. aspersions on sb's character** dénigrer qn; **the accident c. a shadow over their lives** l'accident a jeté une ombre sur leur existence

3 *(shed, throw off)* perdre; **the horse c. a shoe** le

cheval a perdu un fer; **to c. its skin** *(reptile)* muer
4 *(film, play)* distribuer les rôles de; **the director c. her in the role of the mother** le metteur en scène lui a attribué le rôle de la mère; *Fig* **to c. sb in the role of the villain** donner à qn le rôle du méchant
5 *Art & Tech (form, statue)* mouler; *(metal)* couler, fondre; *(plaster)* couler; *Fig* **they are all c. in the same mould** ils sont tous faits sur *ou* sont tous coulés dans le même moule
6 *Astrol (horoscope)* tirer
N 1 *Cin & Theat (actors)* distribution *f*, acteurs *mpl*; **the c. is Italian** tous les acteurs sont italiens; **Juliette Binoche heads a strong c.** Juliette Binoche est en tête d'une très bonne distribution; *Cin & TV* **c. and credits** générique *m*
2 *Art (colour, shade)* nuance *f*, teinte *f*; **white with a pinkish c.** blanc nuancé de rose
3 *Art & Tech (act of moulding ▸ metal)* coulage *m*, coulée *f*; *(▸ plaster)* moulage *m*; *(▸ coin, medallion)* empreinte *f*; *(mould)* moule *m*; *(object moulded)* moulage *m*; **to make a bronze c. of a statue** mouler une statue en bronze; *Fig Literary* **a man of his c.** un homme de sa trempe
4 *Med (for broken limb)* plâtre *m*; **her arm was in a c.** elle avait un bras dans le plâtre
5 *Med (squint)* strabisme *m*; **he had a c. in his eye** il louchait d'un œil, il avait un œil qui louchait
6 *Formal (type)* **the delicate c. of her features** la finesse de ses traits; **a peculiar c. of mind** une drôle de mentalité *ou* de tournure d'esprit
7 *(of earthworm)* déjections *fpl*
8 *(skin of insect, snake)* dépouille *f*
9 *(regurgitated food)* pelote *f* régurgitée *(par les hiboux, les faucons)*
▸▸ ***cast iron*** fonte *f*; ***cast list*** *Cin & TV* générique *m*; *Theat* distribution *f*; ***cast steel*** acier *m* moulé

▸ **cast about, cast around VI** *Br* **she c. about for an idea/an excuse to leave** elle essaya de trouver une idée/un prétexte pour partir

▸ **cast aside VT SEP** *Literary (book)* mettre de côté; *(shirt, shoes)* se débarrasser de; *Fig (person, suggestion)* rejeter, écarter; **to cast aside one's fears** oublier ses craintes

▸ **cast away VT SEP** *Naut* **to be c. away** être naufragé

▸ **cast back VT SEP c. your mind back to the day we met** souviens-toi du *ou* rappelle-toi le jour de notre première rencontre; **to c. one's thoughts back** se reporter en arrière

▸ **cast down VT SEP 1** *Formal (weapon)* déposer, mettre bas **2** *Fig Literary* **to be c. down** être démoralisé *ou* découragé

▸ **cast off VT SEP 1** *(undo)* défaire; *(untie)* délier, dénouer
2 *Knitting* rabattre
3 *Naut (lines, rope)* larguer, lâcher; *(boat)* larguer *ou* lâcher les amarres de
4 *Literary (rid oneself of ▸ clothing)* enlever, se débarrasser de; *Fig (▸ bonds)* se défaire de, se libérer de; *(▸ cares, habit, tradition)* se défaire de, abandonner
VI 1 *Naut* larguer les amarres, appareiller **2** *Knitting* rabattre les mailles

▸ **cast on** *Knitting* **VT SEP** *(stitches)* monter
VI monter les mailles

▸ **cast out VT SEP** *Arch or Literary (person)* renvoyer, chasser; *Fig (fear, guilt)* bannir

▸ **cast up VT SEP** *(of sea, tide, waves)* rejeter

---

castanets [ˌkæstəˈnets] **NPL** castagnettes *fpl*

castaway [ˈkɑːstəweɪ] *Naut* **N** naufragé(e) *m,f*; *Fig* naufragé(e) *m,f*, laissé-pour-compte (laissée-pour-compte) *m,f*

caste [kɑːst] **N** *(gen)* caste *f*, classe *f* sociale; *(in Hindu society)* caste *f*; *Br Fig* **to lose c.** déchoir, déroger
▸▸ ***caste system*** système *m* des castes

casteless [ˈkɑːstlɪs] **ADJ** sans caste

castellated [ˈkæstəleɪtɪd] **ADJ** *Archit* à tourelles; *Tech (filament, nut)* crénelé

caster [ˈkɑːstə(r)] **N 1** *(sifter)* saupoudroir *m*, saupoudreuse *f* **2** *(wheel)* roulette *f*
▸▸ *Br* ***caster sugar*** sucre *m* en poudre

castigate [ˈkæstɪgeɪt] **VT** *Formal* **1** *(punish)* corriger, punir; *(scold)* réprimander, tancer **2** *(criticize ▸ person)* critiquer sévèrement, fustiger; *(▸ book, play)* éreinter

castigation [ˌkæstɪˈgeɪʃən] **N** *Formal (punishment)* correction *f*, punition *f*; *(scolding)* réprimande *f*; *(criticism)* critique *f* sévère

Castile [kæsˈtiːl] **N** Castille *f*

Castilian [kæsˈtɪljən] **N 1** *(person)* Castillan(e) *m, f* **2** *(language)* castillan *m*
ADJ castillan

casting [ˈkɑːstɪŋ] **N 1** *Art (act & object)* moulage *m*; *Tech (act)* coulée *f*, coulage *m*, fonte *f*; *(object)* pièce *f* fondue **2** *Cin & Theat (selection of actors)* attribution *f* des rôles, casting *m*; *Fam Fig* **she denied having got the part on the c. couch** elle a nié avoir couché avec le metteur en scène pour obtenir le rôle **3** *Fishing* lancer *m*; **c. net** épervier *m*
▸▸ *Cin & Theat* ***casting director*** directeur(trice) *m,f* de casting, régisseur *m* de distribution; *Knitting* ***casting off*** arrêt *m* (de mailles); *Knitting* ***casting on*** montage *m* (de mailles); ***casting vote*** voix *f* prépondérante; **the president has a** *or* **the c. vote** le président a voix prépondérante

castle [ˈkɑːsəl] **N 1** *(building)* château *m* (fort); *Fig* **to build castles in the air** bâtir des châteaux en Espagne **2** *Chess* tour *f*
VI *Chess* roquer

castling [ˈkɑːslɪŋ] **N** *(UNCOUNT) Chess* roque *m*

cast-off N 1 *(piece of clothing)* vieux vêtement *m* **2** *Fig (person)* laissé-pour-compte (laissée-pour-compte) *m,f*; **I'm not going out with one of his cast-offs** je ne veux pas sortir avec une copine dont il ne veut plus **3** *Typ (in printing)* calibrage *m*
ADJ dont personne ne veut; **c. clothes** vieux vêtements *mpl*

castor[1] = **caster 2**

castor[2] **N** [ˈkɑːstə(r)] **1** *(secretion)* castoréum *m* **2** *Zool (beaver)* castor *m*
• **Castor** [ˈkæstə(r)] **PR N** *Myth, Astron* Castor
▸▸ ***castor oil*** huile *f* de ricin

castrate [kæˈstreɪt] **VT** châtrer, castrer; *Fig (weaken ▸ person, political movement)* émasculer

castration [kæˈstreɪʃən] **N** castration *f*; *Fig (of political movement)* émasculation *f*

castrato [kæˈstrɑːtəʊ] *(pl* **castratos** *or* **castrati** [-tiː]) **N** *Mus* castrat *m*

casual [ˈkæʒʊəl] **ADJ 1** *(unconcerned)* désinvolte, nonchalant; *(natural)* simple, naturel; **they're very c. about the way they dress** ils attachent très peu d'importance à leurs vêtements *ou* à la façon dont ils s'habillent; **I tried to appear c. when talking about it** j'ai essayé d'en parler avec désinvolture; **they were very c. about the danger** ils ne se sont pas souciés du danger
2 *(informal ▸ dinner)* simple, détendu; *(▸ clothing)* sport *(inv)*
3 *(superficial)* superficiel; **I took a c. glance at the paper** j'ai jeté un coup d'œil (rapide) au journal; **to the c. observer** pour un observateur non-averti; **to make c. conversation** parler de choses et d'autres, parler à bâtons rompus; **it was just a c. suggestion** c'était seulement une suggestion en passant; **she's just a c. acquaintance of mine** c'est quelqu'un que je connais très peu
4 *(happening by chance ▸ meeting)* de hasard; *(▸ onlooker)* venu par hasard
5 *(occasional ▸ job)* intermittent; *(▸ worker)* temporaire
N 1 *(farmworker ▸ for one day)* journalier(ère) *m, f*; *(▸ for harvest, season)* (travailleur(euse) *m,f*) saisonnier(ère) *m,f*; *(in construction work)* ouvrier(ère) *m,f* temporaire **2** *Br Fam (football supporter)* jeune supporter *m* de foot *(soucieux de sa mise et souvent responsable de violences)*
• **casuals NPL** *(clothing)* vêtements *mpl* sport; *(shoes)* chaussures *fpl* sport
▸▸ *Br* ***casual labourer*** *(for one day)* journalier (ère) *m,f*; *(for harvest, season)* (travailleur(euse) *m,f*) saisonnier(ère) *m,f*; *(in construction work)* ouvrier(ère) *m,f* temporaire; ***casual sex*** rapports *mpl* sexuels de rencontre

casualization, -isation [ˌkæʒʊəlaɪˈzeɪʃən] **N** *Br Ind* **the c. of labour** la précarisation de l'emploi

casually [ˈkæʒʊəlɪ] **ADV 1** *(unconcernedly)* avec désinvolture, nonchalamment
2 *(informally)* simplement; **to dress c.** s'habiller sport
3 *(glance, remark, suggest)* en passant; **they talked c. about this and that** ils ont parlé de choses et d'autres *ou* à bâtons rompus
4 *(by chance)* par hasard

casualness [ˈkæʒʊəlnɪs] **N 1** *(unconcern)* désinvolture *f*, nonchalance *f*
2 *(informality)* simplicité *f*; **the c. of their dress** l'allure décontractée *ou* sport de leur habillement
3 *(haphazardness)* hasard *m*, fortuité *f*
4 *(lack of seriousness)* manque *m* de sérieux

casualty [ˈkæʒjʊəltɪ] *(pl* **casualties) N 1** *(wounded)* blessé(e) *m,f*; *(dead)* mort(e) *m,f*; *(in accident, fire, earthquake etc)* victime *f*; **there were heavy casualties** *(gen)* il y avait beaucoup de victimes *ou* de morts et de blessés; *(dead)* il y avait beaucoup de pertes; **these children are the casualties of the divorce rate** ces enfants sont les victimes du divorce; *Fig* **truth is often a c. in political debates** la vérité est souvent sacrifiée dans les débats politiques; *Fig* **truth is the first c. of war** la première victime de la guerre, c'est la vérité **2** *(UNCOUNT) Br (hospital department)* urgences *fpl*; **she was taken to c.** elle a été emmenée aux urgences
▸▸ *Br* ***casualty department*** *(in hospital)* service *m* des urgences; ***casualty list, casualty return*** *(gen)* liste *f* des victimes; *Mil* état *m* des pertes; *Br* ***casualty ward*** *(in hospital)* service *m* des urgences

casuist [ˈkæzjʊɪst] **N** casuiste *m*

casuistry [ˈkæzjʊɪstrɪ] **N** *(philosophy)* casuistique *f*; *(UNCOUNT) (reasoning)* arguments *mpl* de casuiste

CAT[1] [kæt] **N** *Med (abbr* **computerized axial tomography)** TDM *f*
▸▸ ***CAT scan*** scanographie *f*; ***CAT scanner*** scanographe *m*

CAT[2] [ˌsiːeɪˈtiː] **N** *Comput* **1** *(abbr* **computer-aided trading, computer-assisted trading)** CAO *m* **3** *(abbr* **computer-aided translation, computer-assisted translation)** TAO *m* **3** *(abbr* **computer-aided teaching, computer-assisted teaching)** EAO *m*

cat [kæt] **N 1** *(animal)* chat *m*; *(female)* chatte *f*; **I'm not really a c. person** je n'aime pas beaucoup les chats; **the big cats** *(lions, tigers etc)* les grands félins
2 *(idioms)* **to let the c. out of the bag** révéler un secret par mégarde; **to be like a c. on a hot tin roof** *or Br* **on hot bricks** être sur des charbons ardents; **there isn't enough room to swing a c.** il n'y a pas la place de se retourner; **he looked like something the c. brought** *or* **dragged in** il ne ressemblait à rien; **has the c. got your tongue?** tu as perdu ta langue?; **to fight like c. and dog** se battre comme des chiffonniers; *Fam* **to be the c.'s pyjamas** être génial; *Br* **to put** *or* **to set the c. among the pigeons** jeter un pavé dans la mare; **to play (a game of) c. and mouse with sb** jouer au chat et à la souris avec qn; *Br* **to wait for the c. to jump** *or* **to see which way the c. will jump** attendre de voir d'où vient le vent; *Prov* **when the c.'s away the mice will play** quand le chat n'est pas là les souris dansent; *Prov* **a c. may look at a king** un chien regarde bien un évêque
3 *Pej (woman)* rosse *f*, chipie *f*
4 *Am Fam Old-fashioned (man)* mec *m*; **what a cool c.!** vraiment cool, ce type!
5 *Fam (boat)* catamaran *m*, cata *m*
6 *Fam Tech (catalytic converter)* pot *m* catalytique
COMP *(bowl, basket)* pour chats; *(breeder)* de chats; *(hair)* de chat
▸▸ ***cat burglar*** monte-en-l'air *m inv*; ***the cat family*** les félidés *mpl*; ***cat flap*** chatière *f*; ***cat food*** *(UNCOUNT)* nourriture *f* pour chats; ***cat litter*** litière *f* (pour chats); ***cat show*** exposition *f* féline

cataclysm [ˈkætəklɪzəm] **N** cataclysme *m*

cataclysmic [ˌkætəˈklɪzmɪk] **ADJ** cataclysmique

catacomb [ˈkætəkuːm] **N** *(usu pl)* catacombe *f*

catafalque [ˈkætəfælk] **N** catafalque *m*

Catalan [ˈkætəˌlæn] **N 1** *(person)* catalan(e) *m,f* **2** *Ling* catalan *m*
ADJ catalan

catalepsy [ˈkætəlepsɪ] **N** *Med* catalepsie *f*

cataleptic [ˌkætəˈleptɪk] **ADJ** *Med* cataleptique

catalogue, *Am* **catalog** [ˈkætəlɒg] **N** catalogue *m*; *(in library)* fichier *m*; *Fig* **his life story was a c. of disasters** l'histoire de sa vie a été un catalogue de malheurs

VT cataloguer, faire le catalogue de
▸▸ *catalogue number* référence *f*; *(for library book)* référence *f* bibliographique; *Com* **catalogue price** prix *m* catalogue

cataloguing, *Am* **cataloging** ['kætəlɒgɪŋ] N catalogage *m*

Catalonia [,kætə'ləʊnɪə] N Catalogne *f*

catalysis [kə'tæləsɪs] (*pl* **catalyses** [-si:z]) N *Chem* catalyse *f*

catalyst ['kætəlɪst] N *Chem & Fig* catalyseur *m*

catalytic [,kætə'lɪtɪk] ADJ *Chem* catalytique
▸▸ *Aut* ***catalytic converter*** pot *m* catalytique

catamaran [,kætəmə'ræn] N catamaran *m*

cataplasm ['kætəplæzəm] N *Med* cataplasme *m*

catapult ['kætəpʌlt] N **1** *Br (child's)* lance-pierres *m inv* **2** *Aviat & Mil* catapulte *f*
VT *(gen) & Aviat* catapulter; **he catapulted the stone over the wall** il a lancé la pierre par-dessus le mur; *Fig* **these reforms catapulted the country into the 20th century** ces réformes ont propulsé le pays dans le 20ème siècle; **to c. sb to stardom** *(of film etc)* propulser qn vers la célébrité
▸▸ ***catapult launcher*** catapulte *f*

cataract ['kætərækt] N **1** *Med* cataracte *f* **2** *(waterfall)* cataracte *f*, cascade *f* **3** *(downpour)* déluge *m*

catarrh [kə'tɑ:(r)] N *Med* catarrhe *m*; *Br* **to have bad c.** être très catarrheux

catarrhal [kə'tɑ:rəl], **catarrhous** [kə'tɑ:rəs] ADJ *Med* catarrheux

catastrophe [kə'tæstrəfi] N catastrophe *f*

catastrophic [,kætə'strɒfɪk] ADJ catastrophique

catastrophically [kætə'strɒfɪkəlɪ] ADV d'une façon catastrophique

catatonia [,kætə'təʊnɪə] N *Med* catatonie *f*

catatonic [,kætə'tɒnɪk] ADJ *Med* catatonique

catcall ['kætkɔ:l] *Theat* N sifflet *m*; **the actors were greeted with catcalls** les acteurs se sont fait siffler
VT *(actor)* siffler
VI *(audience)* siffler

CATCH [kætʃ]

VT	
• attraper **1–4**	• se prendre **5**
• saisir **6, 8**	• attirer **7**
• remarquer **10**	
VI	
• prendre **1**	• se prendre **4**
• s'accrocher **4**	
N	
• prise **1, 2**	• piège **3**
• loquet **4**	

(*pt & pp* **caught** [kɔ:t])
VT **1** *(ball, thrown object)* attraper; **to c. hold of sth** attraper qch; **c.!** attrape!; **to c. sb's arm** *(take hold of)* saisir *ou* prendre qn par le bras; **I caught him as he fell** je l'ai retenu *ou* attrapé au moment où il tombait
2 *(trap ▸ fish, mouse, thief)* attraper, prendre; **he got caught by the police** il s'est fait attraper par la police; **to get caught in a traffic jam** être pris dans un embouteillage; **we got caught in a shower/thunderstorm** nous avons été surpris par une averse/un orage; **to c. sb doing sth** surprendre qn à faire qch; **to c. oneself doing sth** se surprendre à faire qch; **they were caught trying to escape** on les a surpris en train d'essayer de s'évader; **don't get caught!** ne te fais pas prendre!; **if I c. you talking once more I'll throw you out!** si je te prends *ou* surprends encore une fois en train de parler, je te mets à la porte!; **you won't c. me doing the washing-up!** aucun danger de me surprendre en train de faire la vaisselle!; **don't let me c. you at it again!** que je ne t'y reprenne pas!; *Br Fam* **you'll c. it when you get home!** qu'est-ce que tu vas prendre en rentrant!; **to c. one's breath** reprendre son souffle; **to c. sb napping** prendre qn au dépourvu; **to c. sb in the act** *or* **red-handed** prendre qn sur le fait *ou* la main dans le sac
3 *(disease, infection)* attraper; *Fig (habit)* prendre; **to c. a cold** attraper un rhume; **to c. cold** attraper *ou* prendre froid; **I caught this cold from you** c'est toi qui m'as passé ce rhume; *Fam* **he'll c. his death (of cold)!** il va attraper la crève!
4 *(bus, train)* attraper, prendre; *(person)* attraper; *Br* **to c. the last post** arriver à temps pour la dernière levée (du courrier); **you're unlikely to c. her at home** je ne pense pas que tu la trouveras chez elle; **we caught him in a good mood** il était de bonne humeur quand nous l'avons vu; **I just caught the end of the film** j'ai juste vu la fin du film; *Fam* **let's go c. a movie!** allons au cinoche!; *Fam* **c. you later!** à plus tard!
5 *(on nail, obstacle)* **he caught his finger in the door** il s'est pris le doigt dans la porte; **she caught her skirt in the door** sa jupe s'est prise dans la porte; **he caught his coat on the brambles** son manteau s'est accroché aux ronces
6 *(hear clearly, understand)* saisir, comprendre; **I didn't quite c. what you said** je n'ai pas bien entendu ce que vous avez dit; **I don't c. your meaning** je ne vois pas ce que vous voulez dire
7 *(attract)* **to c. sb's attention** *or* **sb's eye** attirer l'attention de qn; **to try to c. sb's eye** essayer d'attirer le regard de qn; **their story caught the imagination of the public** leur histoire a passionné le public; *Br* **the house caught his fancy** la maison lui a plu; **to c. the light** refléter la lumière; **to c. the sun** *(person)* prendre des couleurs; **the garden catches the sun in the afternoon** le jardin est ensoleillé l'après-midi
8 *(in portrait, writing ▸ likeness, mood)* saisir; **the author has caught the mood of the time** l'auteur a su rendre l'atmosphère de l'époque
9 *(hit) Br* **to c. sb a blow** donner *ou* flanquer un coup à qn; **the punch caught me in the chest** j'ai reçu le coup de poing en plein dans la poitrine; **the wave caught her sideways** la vague l'a frappée de côté; **he fell and caught his head on the radiator** il est tombé et s'est cogné la tête contre le radiateur
10 *(notice)* remarquer; **did you c. the look on his face?** vous avez remarqué l'expression de son visage?; **I caught a hint of bitterness** *(in what she said)* j'ai senti un peu d'amertume dans ses paroles
VI **1** attraper; **(here,) c.!** tiens, attrape!
2 *(ignite ▸ fire, wood)* prendre; *(▸ engine)* démarrer
3 *(bolt, lock)* fermer; *(gears)* mordre
4 *(on obstacle ▸ in door, machinery etc)* se prendre; *(▸ on thorn, nail etc)* s'accrocher; **her skirt caught on a nail** sa jupe s'est accrochée à un clou
N **1** *(act)* prise *f*; **good c.!** bien rattrapé!
2 *(of fish)* prise *f*; **a fine c.** une belle prise; *Hum Fig* **he's a good c.** *(man)* c'est un beau parti
3 *(snag)* piège *m*; **there must be a c. in it somewhere** il doit y avoir un truc *ou* un piège quelque part, ça cache quelque chose; **where's** *or* **what's the c.?** qu'est-ce que ça cache?, où est le piège?
4 *(on lock, door)* loquet *m*; *(on window)* loqueteau *m*; *(on shoe–buckle)* ardillon *m*
5 *(in voice)* **with a c. in his voice** d'une voix entrecoupée
6 *(game)* jeu *m* de balle; **to play c.** jouer à la balle
7 *Mus* canon *m*
▸▸ *Agr* ***catch crop*** culture *f* dérobée; ***catch question*** question-piège *f*, colle *f*

▸**catch at** VT INSEP (essayer d')attraper

▸**catch on** VI **1** *(fashion, trend, slogan)* devenir populaire, prendre; **this dance style caught on in the fifties** cette danse a fait un tabac *ou* était très populaire dans les années cinquante; **the game never caught on in Europe** ce jeu n'a jamais pris en Europe *ou* eu de succès en Europe **2** *Fam (understand)* piger, saisir◻; **he still hasn't caught on** il n'y est toujours pas

▸**catch out** VT SEP *Br (by trickery)* prendre en défaut, piéger; *(in the act)* prendre sur le fait; **he tried to c. me out with a trick question** il a essayé de me coller *ou* prendre en défaut avec une question-piège; **to c. sb out in a lie** prendre *ou* surprendre qn à mentir; **I won't be caught out like that again!** on ne m'y prendra plus!

▸**catch up** VI **1** *(as verb of movement)* **to c. up with sb** rattraper qn; **I had to run to c. up with him** *or* **to c. him up** j'ai dû courir pour le rattraper *ou* le rejoindre; *Fig* **his past will c. up with him one day** il finira par être rattrapé par son passé **2** *(on lost time)* combler *ou* rattraper son retard; *(on studies)* rattraper son retard, se remettre au niveau **to c. up on** *or* **with one's work** rattraper le retard qu'on a pris dans son travail; **I need to c. up on some sleep** j'ai du sommeil à rattraper; **we had a lot of news to c. up on** nous avions beaucoup de choses à nous dire
VT SEP **1** *(entangle)* **the material got caught up in the machinery** le tissu s'est pris dans la machine; **they were caught up in a traffic jam for hours** ils ont été bloqués dans un embouteillage pendant des heures
2 *(absorb, involve)* **to get caught up in a wave of enthusiasm** être gagné par une vague d'enthousiasme; **he was too caught up in the film to notice what was happening** il était trop absorbé par le film pour remarquer ce qui se passait; **I refuse to get caught up in their private quarrel** je refuse de me laisser entraîner dans leurs querelles personnelles
3 *(seize ▸ object)* ramasser vivement, s'emparer de; *(▸ baby, child)* prendre dans ses bras
4 *(person, car in front etc)* rattraper

catch-all N fourre-tout *m inv*
ADJ fourre-tout *(inv)*, qui pare à toute éventualité; **c. phrase** expression *f* passe-partout

catch-as-catch-can N *Sport* catch *m*
ADJ *Am* improvisé

catcher ['kætʃə(r)] N *(gen) & Sport (in baseball)* attrapeur *m*; **c.'s mitt** gant *m* de baseball

catching ['kætʃɪŋ] N *(of ball)* **I'm no good at c.** je ne suis pas doué pour rattraper les balles qu'on m'envoie
ADJ **1** *Med* contagieux **2** *Fig (enthusiasm)* contagieux, communicatif; *(habit)* contagieux

catchline ['kætʃlaɪn] N accroche *f*; *(identification for story)* intitulé *m*

catchment ['kætʃmənt] N captage *m*
▸▸ ***catchment area*** *Geog (drainage area)* bassin *m* hydrographique; *Admin (for hospital)* = circonscription hospitalière; *(for school)* secteur *m* de recrutement scolaire; *Geog* ***catchment basin*** bassin *m* hydrographique

catchpenny ['kætʃ,penɪ] (*pl* **catchpennies**) *Br* N attrape-nigaud *m*
ADJ accrocheur

catchphrase ['kætʃfreɪz] N *(in advertising)* accroche *f*; *(set phrase)* formule *f* toute faite; *(of performer)* petite phrase *f*

catchword ['kætʃwɜ:d] N **1** *(slogan)* slogan *m*; *Pol* mot *m* d'ordre, slogan *m* **2** *Typ (in printing ▸ at top of page)* mot-vedette *m*; *(▸ at foot of page)* réclame *f* **3** *Theat* réclame *f*

catchy ['kætʃɪ] (*compar* **catchier**, *superl* **catchiest**) ADJ *(tune)* qui trotte dans la tête, facile à retenir; *(title)* facile à retenir

catechism ['kætəkɪzəm] N *Rel* catéchisme *m*

catechist ['kætəkɪst] N *Rel* catéchiste *mf*

catechize, -ise ['kætəkaɪz] VT **1** *Rel* catéchiser **2** *Fig (examine)* interroger, questionner

categoric [,kætɪ'gɒrɪk], **categorical** [,kætɪ'gɒrɪkəl] ADJ catégorique

categorically [,kætɪ'gɒrɪkəlɪ] ADV catégoriquement

categorization, -isation [,kætəgəraɪ'zeɪʃən] N catégorisation *f*

categorize, -ise ['kætəgəraɪz] VT catégoriser

category ['kætəgərɪ] (*pl* **categories**) N catégorie *f*
▸▸ *Mktg* ***category leader*** *(product)* chef *m* de file dans sa catégorie

cater ['keɪtə(r)] VI s'occuper de la nourriture, fournir des repas
VT *Am* s'occuper de la nourriture pour; **we're having the meal catered** nous faisons fournir le repas

▸**cater for,** *Am* **cater to** VT INSEP **1** *(with food)* s'occuper de la nourriture pour; **coach parties catered for** *(sign)* accueil de groupes **2** *(needs)* répondre à, satisfaire; *(tastes)* satisfaire; **we c. for the needs of small companies** nous répondons à la demande des petites entreprises; **the hotel doesn't c. for children** l'hôtel ne prévoit pas d'aménagements pour les enfants; **to c. for all tastes** satisfaire tous les goûts

cater-cornered *Am Fam* ADJ diagonal◻
ADV diagonalement◻

caterer ['keɪtərə(r)] N traiteur *m*

catering ['keɪtərɪŋ] N restauration *f*; **who did the c. for the wedding?** qui a fourni le repas pour le mariage?

COMP *(industry)* de la restauration; *(staff)* de restauration

▸▸ ***catering college*** école *f* de restauration, lycée *m* hôtelier; ***catering contract*** contrat *m* de restauration; ***catering firm*** traiteur *m*; ***catering manager*** chef *m ou* responsable *mf* de la restauration

caterpillar ['kætəpɪlə(r)] N *Zool & Tech* chenille *f*

▸▸ *Tech* ***caterpillar track*** chenille *f*; *Tech* ***caterpillar tractor*** tracteur *m* à chenilles

caterwaul ['kætəwɔːl] VI *(cat)* miauler; *(person)* brailler

N *(of cat)* miaulement *m*; *(of person)* braillement *m*

caterwauling ['kætəwɔːlɪŋ] N *(UNCOUNT)* *(of cat)* miaulements *mpl*; *(of person)* braillements *mpl*

catfish ['kætfɪʃ] *(pl* **inv** *or* **catfishes)** N *Ich* poisson-chat *m*

catgut ['kætgʌt] N **1** *(for musical instrument, racket)* boyau *m* (de chat) **2** *Med* catgut *m*

catharsis [kə'θɑːsɪs] *(pl* **catharses** [-siːz]) N catharsis *f*

cathartic [kə'θɑːtɪk] ADJ cathartique

N *Med* purgatif *m*, cathartique *m*

cathedral [kə'θiːdrəl] N cathédrale *f*

▸▸ ***cathedral city*** évêché *m*, ville *f* épiscopale

Catherine ['kæθrɪn] PR N **C. the Great** la Grande Catherine

catheter ['kæθɪtə(r)] N *Med* cathéter *m*, sonde *f* creuse; **he has to have a c.** il faut qu'on lui pose un cathéter

cathode ['kæθəʊd] *Elec* N cathode *f*

COMP *(beam, screen)* cathodique

▸▸ *Elec* ***cathode rays*** rayons *mpl* cathodiques; *Elec* ***cathode ray tube*** tube *m* cathodique; *Elec* ***cathode ray tube monitor*** moniteur *m* à tube cathodique

catholic ['kæθlɪk] ADJ **1** *(broad* ▸ *tastes)* éclectique **2** *(liberal* ▸ *views)* libéral **3** *(universal)* universel

• **Catholic** ADJ catholique; **the C. Church** l'Église *f* catholique N catholique *mf*

Catholicism [kə'θɒlɪsɪzəm] N catholicisme *m*

cathouse ['kæthaʊs, *pl* -haʊzɪz] N *Am Fam (brothel)* bordel *m*

catkin ['kætkɪn] N *Bot* chaton *m*

catmint ['kætmɪnt] N herbe *f* aux chats

catnap ['kætnæp] *Fam* N (petit) somme *m*; **to have a c.** faire un petit somme

VI sommeiller, faire un petit somme

catnip ['kætnɪp] N herbe *f* aux chats

cat-o'-nine-tails N chat à neuf queues *m*, martinet *m*

cats-eye® N *Br* catadioptre *m (marquant le milieu de la chaussée)*

cat's-paw N **1** *(person)* dupe *f* **2** *(on water)* = effet de vague produit par une légère brise

catsuit ['kætsuːt] N combinaison-pantalon *f*

catsup ['kætsəp] N *Am* ketchup *m*

cattery ['kætərɪ] *(pl* **catteries)** N pension *f* pour chats

cattiness ['kætɪnɪs] N *Fam* vacherie *f*, rosserie *f*

cattle ['kætəl] NPL *(UNCOUNT)* bétail *m*, bestiaux *mpl*, bovins *mpl*; **horned c.** bêtes *fpl* à cornes, bovins *mpl*; **we were herded onto trucks like c.** on nous a entassés dans des camions comme du bétail

▸▸ *Br* ***cattle breeder*** éleveur *m* (de bétail); ***cattle breeding*** élevage *m* (du bétail); *Agr* ***cattle cake*** tourteau *m*; *Fam* ***cattle class*** classe *f* éco; *Orn* ***cattle egret*** héron *m* garde-bœufs; ***cattle grid***, *Am* ***cattle guard*** = grille destinée à empêcher le passage du bétail mais non des voitures; ***cattle market*** marché *m ou* foire *f* aux bestiaux; *Br Fam Pej* **this beauty contest is just a c. market** ce concours de beauté n'est qu'un marché aux bestiaux; ***cattle prod*** aiguillon *m* électrique; ***cattle ranch*** ranch *m* (pour l'élevage du bétail); ***cattle rustler*** voleur *m* de bétail; ***cattle shed*** étable *f*; ***cattle show*** concours *m* agricole; ***cattle truck*** fourgon *m* à bestiaux

cattleman ['kætəlmən] *(pl* **cattlemen** [-mən]) N vacher *m*, bouvier *m*

catty ['kætɪ] *(compar* **cattier**, *superl* **cattiest)** ADJ *Fam (person, gossip)* méchant[□], vache; **a c. remark** une vacherie, une réflexion désagréable[□]

catty-corner, catty-cornered *Am* ADJ diamétralement opposé

ADV diamétralement opposé

catwalk ['kætwɔːk] N **1** *(at fashion show)* passerelle *f*; **on the c.** *(model)* sur la passerelle du défilé **2** *Naut* coursive *f*

▸▸ ***catwalk model*** mannequin *m* qui fait des défilés de mode

Caucasian [kɔː'keɪzjən], **Caucasic** [kɔː'keɪzɪk] N **1** *(from Caucasia)* Caucasien(enne) *m,f* **2** *(white person)* Blanc (Blanche) *m,f* **3** *Ling* caucasien *m*

ADJ **1** *(from Caucasia)* caucasien **2** *(white)* blanc (blanche); **the man is described as a C. male in his thirties** l'individu est de type européen et aurait entre trente et quarante ans **3** *Ling* caucasien, caucasique

Caucasus ['kɔːkəsəs] N *Geog* **the C.** le Caucase; **the C. mountains** le Caucase, la chaîne du Caucase

caucus ['kɔːkəs] N *Pol* **1** *Am (committee)* comité *m* électoral, caucus *m*; **the Democratic c.** le groupe *ou* le lobby démocrate **2** *Br (party organization)* comité *m*; **the Black c. of the Labour Party** = les personnalités noires du parti travailliste

▸▸ ***caucus meeting*** réunion *f* du comité électoral

caudal ['kɔːdəl] ADJ *Anat* caudal

▸▸ ***caudal fin*** (nageoire *f*) caudale *f*

caught [kɔːt] *pt & pp of* **catch**

caul [kɔːl] N coiffe *f (de nouveau-né)*; **born with a c.** né coiffé

cauldron ['kɔːldrən] N chaudron *m*; *Fig (hot place)* étuve *f*; *Fig* **a c. of unrest** un foyer de troubles

cauli ['kɒlɪ] N *Br Fam* chou-fleur[□] *m*

cauliflower ['kɒlɪˌflaʊə(r)] N chou-fleur *m*

▸▸ *Culin* ***cauliflower cheese*** chou-fleur *m* au gratin; ***cauliflower ear*** oreille *f* en chou-fleur

caulk [kɔːk] VT *(gen)* calfeutrer; *Naut* calfater

caulking ['kɔːkɪŋ] N *(gen)* calfeutrage *m*; *Naut* calfatage *m*

▸▸ ***caulking iron*** calfait *m*, burin *m*

causal ['kɔːzəl] ADJ *(gen)* causal; *Gram* causal, causatif

causality [kɔː'zælətɪ] N causalité *f*

causally ['kɔːzəlɪ] ADV **the two events are c. linked** les deux événements ont la même cause

causation [kɔː'zeɪʃən] N *(causing)* causalité *f*; *(cause-effect relationship)* relation *f* de cause à effet

causative ['kɔːzətɪv] ADJ *(gen)* causal; *Gram* causal, causatif

N *Gram* causatif *m*

cause [kɔːz] N **1** *(reason)* cause *f*; **to be the c. of sth** être (la) cause de qch; **he was the c. of all our trouble** c'est lui qui a été la cause *ou* qui a été à l'origine de tous nos ennuis; **the c. of the disease is not yet known** la cause de la maladie demeure inconnue; **she is the c. of his being in prison** c'est à cause d'elle qu'il est en prison; **the relation of c. and effect** la relation de cause à effet

2 *(justification)* raison *f*, motif *m*; **we mustn't give them c. for complaint** il ne faut pas leur donner de motif de se plaindre; **they have c. to be bitter** ils ont lieu d'être amers, ils ont de quoi être amers; **to have good c. for doing sth** avoir de bonnes raisons de faire qch; **with (good) c.** à juste titre; **without good c.** sans cause *ou* raison valable

3 *(principle)* cause *f*; **in the c. of justice** pour la cause de la justice; **her lifelong devotion to the c.** son dévouement de toujours à la cause; *Formal* **to make common c. with sb** faire cause commune avec qn; **it's all in a good c.!** c'est pour une bonne cause!

4 *Law* cause *f*; **to plead sb's c.** plaider la cause de qn

VT causer, provoquer; **smoking can c. cancer** le tabac peut provoquer des cancers; **to c. grief** causer du chagrin; **he has caused us a lot of trouble** il nous a créé beaucoup d'ennuis; **it will only c. trouble** cela ne servira qu'à semer la zizanie; **to c. sb/sth to do sth** faire faire qch à qn/qch; **what caused him to change his mind?** qu'est-ce qui l'a fait changer d'avis?; **this caused me to lose my job** à cause de cela, j'ai perdu mon emploi

causeway ['kɔːzweɪ] N chaussée *f*

caustic ['kɔːstɪk] ADJ *Chem & Fig* caustique

N *Chem* caustique *m*, substance *f* caustique

▸▸ *Chem* ***caustic soda*** soude *f* caustique

cauterization, -isation [ˌkɔːtəraɪ'zeɪʃən] N *Med* cautérisation *f*

cauterize, -ise ['kɔːtəraɪz] VT *Med* cautériser

caution ['kɔːʃən] N **1** *(care)* circonspection *f*, prudence *f*; **to proceed with c.** *(gen)* agir avec circonspection *ou* avec prudence; *(in car)* avancer lentement; **c.!** *(sign)* attention!; **to throw c. to the wind** faire fi de toute prudence

2 *(warning)* avertissement *m*; *(reprimand)* réprimande *f*

3 *Law* avertissement *m*; *Br* **I got off with a c.** je m'en suis tiré avec un avertissement

4 *Sport* avertissement *m*; **to give sb a c.** donner un avertissement à qn

5 *Br Fam Old-fashioned (person)* **he's a c.!** c'est un numéro *ou* un polisson!

VT **1** *(warn)* avertir, mettre en garde; **he cautioned them to be careful** il leur a conseillé d'être prudents; **to c. sb against doing sth** déconseiller à qn de faire qch; **he cautioned them against the evils of drink** il les a mis en garde contre les dangers de la boisson **2** *Law* **to c. sb** *(on arrest)* informer qn de ses droits; *(instead of prosecuting)* donner un avertissement à qn **3** *Sport (player)* donner un avertissement à

VI **to c. against sth** déconseiller qch

> Note that the French word **caution** is a false friend and is never a translation for the English word **caution**. Its most common meaning is **deposit, guarantee**.
> Note also that the French verb **cautionner** is a false friend. It never means **to warn**.

cautionary ['kɔːʃənərɪ] ADJ qui sert d'avertissement; **a c. tale** un récit édifiant

cautious ['kɔːʃəs] ADJ circonspect; *(driver, remark, optimism)* prudent; **to be c. about doing sth** faire qch avec circonspection; **c. optimism** optimisme *m* prudent

cautiously ['kɔːʃəslɪ] ADV avec prudence, prudemment; **to be c. optimistic** faire preuve d'un optimisme prudent

cautiousness ['kɔːʃəsnɪs] N *(care)* circonspection *f*, prudence *f*

cavalcade [ˌkævəl'keɪd] N cortège *m*; *(on horseback)* cavalcade *f*

cavalier [ˌkævə'lɪə(r)] N *(gen) & Mil* cavalier *m*

ADJ cavalier, désinvolte; **he treated me in a very c. fashion** il s'est comporté envers moi d'une façon très cavalière

• **Cavalier** *Hist* N Cavalier *m (partisan de Charles I*[er] *d'Angleterre pendant la guerre civile anglaise)*

ADJ royaliste, Cavalier

cavalry ['kævəlrɪ] N *Mil* cavalerie *f*

▸▸ *Mil* ***cavalry charge*** charge *f* de cavalerie; *Mil* ***cavalry officer*** officier *m* de cavalerie; ***cavalry twill*** = étoffe utilisée pour faire les culottes de cheval

cavalryman ['kævəlrɪmən] *(pl* **cavalrymen** [-mən]) N *Mil* cavalier *m (soldat)*

cave[1] [keɪv] N caverne *f*, grotte *f*

▸▸ ***cave art*** art *m* rupestre; ***cave dweller*** *(in prehistory)* homme *m* des cavernes; *(troglodyte)* troglodyte *m*; ***cave painting*** peinture *f* rupestre

> Note that the French word **cave** is a false friend and is never a translation for the English word **cave**. It means **cellar**.

cave[2] ['keɪvɪ] *Br Fam Old-fashioned School slang*

N **to keep c.** faire le guet

EXCLAM pet!

▸ **cave in** VI **1** *(ceiling, floor)* s'écrouler, s'effondrer, s'affaisser; *(wall)* s'écrouler, s'effondrer, céder **2** *Fam (person)* flancher, céder[□]; *(team, defence)* s'effondrer

caveat ['kævıæt] N avertissement *m*; *Br Law* notification *f* d'opposition; *Fig* **to insert a c.** ajouter une précision
►► *Com & Law* ***caveat emptor*** aux risques de l'acheteur

cave-in [keıv-] N **1** *(of ceiling, floor)* effondrement *m*, affaissement *m* **2** *Fam Fig* effondrement□ *m*, dégonflage *m*

caveman ['keıvmæn] *(pl* **cavemen** [-men]) N homme *m* des cavernes; *Fig* brute *f*

caver ['keıvə(r)] N spéléologue *mf*

cavern ['kævən] N caverne *f*

cavernous ['kævənəs] ADJ **1** *Fig* **a c. building** un bâtiment très vaste à l'intérieur; **c. depths** des profondeurs insondables; **a c. voice** une voix caverneuse

caviar, caviare ['kævıɑ:(r)] N caviar *m*

cavil ['kævəl] *(Br pt & pp* **cavilled,** *cont* **cavilling,** *Am pt & pp* **caviled,** *cont* **caviling)** N chicane *f*, ergotage *m*
VI chicaner, ergoter; **to c. at sth** chicaner *ou* ergoter sur qch

caving ['keıvıŋ] N spéléologie *f*; **to go c.** faire de la spéléologie

cavity ['kævətı] *(pl* **cavities)** N **1** *(in rock, wood)* cavité *f*, creux *m* **2** *Anat* cavité *f*; *(in tooth)* cavité *f*
►► ***cavity wall*** mur *m* creux *ou* à double paroi; ***cavity wall insulation*** isolation *f* en murs creux

cavort [kə'vɔ:t] VI **1** *(frolic)* cabrioler, gambader, faire des cabrioles **2** *Fig* batifoler; **while his wife was off cavorting around Europe** pendant que sa femme menait une vie de bâton de chaise en Europe

cavy ['keıvı] N *Zool (animal)* cobaye *m*, cochon *m* d'Inde

caw [kɔ:] N croassement *m*
VI croasser

cawing ['kɔ:ıŋ] N croassement *m*

cayenne pepper [ˌkeı'en-] N poivre *m* de cayenne

cayman ['keımən] N *Zool* caïman *m*

Cayman Islands ['keımən-] NPL **the C.** les îles *fpl* Caïmans

CB [ˌsi:'bi:] N **1** *(abbr* **Citizens' Band)** CB *f* **2** *(abbr* **Companion of (the Order of) the Bath)** = distinction honorifique britannique

CBE [ˌsi:bi:'i:] N *(abbr* **Companion of (the Order of) the British Empire)** = distinction honorifique britannique

CBI [ˌsi:bi:'aı] N *(abbr* **Confederation of British Industry)** = association du patronat britannique, Medef *m*

CBS [ˌsi:bi:'es] N *(abbr* **Columbia Broadcasting System)** = chaîne de télévision américaine

CC *(written abbr* **county council)** conseil *m* général

cc [ˌsi:'si:] N *(abbr* **cubic centimetre)** cm^3
VT *(abbr* **carbon copy)** pcc; **to cc sb sth, to cc sth to sb** envoyer une copie de qch à qn

CCA [ˌsi:si:'eı] N *Acct (abbr* **current cost accounting)** comptabilité *f* en coûts actuels

CCI [ˌsi:si:'aı] N *(abbr* **Chamber of Commerce and Industry)** CCI *f*

CCJ [ˌsi:si:'dʒeı] N *(abbr* **county court judgment)** jugement *m* de première instance

CCTV [ˌsi:si:ˌti:'vi:] N *(abbr* **closed-circuit television)** télévision *f* en circuit fermé

CD[1] [ˌsi:'di:] N **1** *(abbr* **compact disc)** CD *m*; **on CD** sur CD **2** *(abbr* **certificate of deposit)** certificat *m* de dépôt
►► ***CD burner*** graveur *m* de CD; ***CD library*** CDthèque *f*; ***CD player*** lecteur *m* de CD; ***CD rack*** casier *m* de rangement pour CD; ***CD rewriter*** graveur *m* de CD réinscriptibles; ***CD system*** chaîne *f* laser; ***CD video*** CD vidéo *m*; ***CD writer*** graveur *m* de CD

CD[2] *(written abbr* **Corps Diplomatique)** CD

CDI, CD-I [ˌsi:di:'aı] N *Comput (abbr* **compact disc interactive)** CDI *m*, CD-I *m*

CD-R [ˌsi:di:'ɑ:(r)] N **1** *(abbr* **compact disc recorder)** graveur *m* de disque compact **2** *(abbr* **compact disc recordable)** CD-R *m*

Cdr *Mil (written abbr* **commander)** Cdt

Cdre *(written abbr* **Commodore)** **1** *Mil* commodore *m (officier de rang inférieur au contre-amiral et supérieur au capitaine de vaisseau)* **2** *Naut (of merchant ships)* chef *m* de convoi; *(of shipping line)* doyen *m* (des capitaines); *(of yacht club)* président *m*

CD-ROM [ˌsi:di:'rɒm] *Comput*
N *(abbr* **compact disc read-only memory)** CD-ROM *m*, CD-Rom *m*, *Offic* DOC *m*, *Offic* cédérom *m*
►► ***CD-ROM burner*** graveur *m* de CD-ROM; ***CD-ROM drive*** lecteur *m* de CD-ROM, *Offic* lecteur *m* de disque optique; ***CD-ROM newspaper*** journal *m* sur CD-ROM; ***CD-ROM reader*** lecteur de CD-ROM

CD-RW [ˌsi:di:ˌɑ:'dʌbəlju:] N *Comput (abbr* **compact disc rewritable)** CD *m* réinscriptible

CDT [ˌsi:di:'ti:] N **1** *Am (abbr* **Central Daylight Time)** = heure d'été du centre des États-Unis **2** *Br Sch (abbr* **craft, design and technology)** = matière enseignée dans le secondaire qui comprend travaux manuels et technologie

CD-text N *(abbr* **compact disc text)** CD-texte *m*

CDV [ˌsi:di:'vi:] N *Comput (abbr* **compact disc video)** CDV *m*, CD vidéo *m*

cease [si:s] VI *Formal (activity, noise)* cesser, s'arrêter; **the rain eventually ceased** il a finalement cessé de pleuvoir; **we will not c. from campaigning for her release** nous ne cesserons pas de nous battre pour sa libération
VT *(activity, efforts, work)* cesser, arrêter; **to c. doing sth** cesser de *ou* arrêter de faire qch; **it never ceases to amaze me that…** cela m'étonne toujours que…; **to c. trading** cesser ses activités; **a county that ceased to exist in 1974** un comté qui n'existe plus depuis 1974; *Mil* **to c. fire** cesser le feu
N *Formal* **without c.** sans cesse

ceasefire [ˌsi:s'faıə(r)] N *Mil* cessez-le-feu *m inv*; **to declare a c.** déclarer un cessez-le-feu; **to agree to a c.** accepter un cessez-le-feu
►► ***ceasefire agreement*** accord *m* de cessez-le-feu

ceaseless ['si:slıs] ADJ incessant, continuel

ceaselessly ['si:slıslı] ADV sans cesse, continuellement

cecum *Am* = **caecum**

cedar ['si:də(r)] N cèdre *m*
COMP *(table, cupboard)* de *ou* en cèdre
►► ***cedar of Lebanon*** cèdre *m* du Liban; ***cedar tree*** cèdre *m*; ***cedar wood*** (bois *m* de) cèdre *m*

cede [si:d] VT céder (**to** à); **to c. a point** *(in argument)* concéder un point

cedilla [sı'dılə] N *Ling* cédille *f*

Ceefax® ['si:fæks] N *Br* Ceefax® *m*

ceilidh ['keılı] N = soirée de danse et de musique folklorique (en Irlande et en Écosse)

ceiling ['si:lıŋ] N **1** *(of room)* plafond *m*; *Fam* **to hit the c.** *(become angry)* sauter les plombs **2** *Aviat & Met* plafond *m*; **the cloud c.** le plafond de nuages; **to fly at the c.** plafonner **3** *Com & Econ* plafond *m*; **prices have reached their c.** les prix ont plafonné *ou* atteint leur plafond; **the government has set a three percent c. on wage rises** le gouvernement a limité à trois pour cent les augmentations de salaire
COMP *Com & Econ (charge, price)* plafond *(inv)*
►► ***ceiling fan*** ventilateur *m* de plafond; ***ceiling light*** plafonnier *m*; ***ceiling tile*** dalle *f* pour plafond

celadon ['selədɒn] N *Cer* céladon *m*
►► ***celadon green*** N (vert *m*) céladon *m* ADJ (vert) céladon

celandine ['seləndaın] N *Bot* chélidoine *f*

celeb [sə'leb] N *Fam* célébrité□ *f*

celebrant ['selıbrənt] N *Rel* célébrant *m*, officiant *m*

celebrate ['selıbreıt] VT **1** *(birthday, Christmas)* fêter, célébrer; *(event, victory)* célébrer; **to c. the memory of sth** commémorer qch; **the city is celebrating the anniversary of its founding** la ville fête l'anniversaire de sa fondation; **let's open a bottle of wine to c. the occasion** ouvrons une bouteille de vin pour fêter ça **2** *(praise* ► *person, someone's beauty)* célébrer, glorifier **3** *Rel* **to c. mass** célébrer la messe
VI faire la fête; **let's c. with a new car/a weekend in Paris** achetons une nouvelle voiture/allons passer un week-end à Paris pour fêter ça; **will you be celebrating tonight?** tu vas arroser ça ce soir?; **let's c. with some champagne** on va arroser ça au champagne; **let's c.!** *(gen)* il faut fêter ça!; *(with drinks)* il faut arroser ça!

celebrated ['selıbreıtıd] ADJ célèbre (**for** par)

celebration [ˌselı'breıʃən] N **1** *(of birthday, Christmas)* célébration *f*; *(of anniversary, past event)* commémoration *f*; **in c. of Christmas** pour fêter *ou* célébrer Noël; **in c. of 40 years of peace** pour commémorer 40 ans de paix
2 *Mus & Literature* éloge *m*, louange *f*; **he wrote the poem in c. of her beauty** il a écrit le poème pour célébrer sa beauté
3 *Rel (of communion, feast)* célébration *f*
4 *(often pl) (occasion* ► *of birthday, Christmas)* fête *f*, fêtes *fpl*; *(*► *of historical event)* cérémonies *fpl*, fête *f*; **this calls for a c.!** il faut fêter ça!, il faut arroser ça!; **to join in the celebrations** participer à la fête *ou* aux festivités; **birthday celebrations** fête *f* d'anniversaire
►► ***celebration dinner*** repas *m* de fête

celebratory [ˌselə'breıtərı] ADJ *(dinner)* de fête; *(marking official occasion)* commémoratif; *(atmosphere, mood)* de fête, festif

celebrity [sı'lebrətı] *(pl* **celebrities)** N **1** *(fame)* célébrité *f* **2** *(person)* vedette *f*, célébrité *f*
►► ***celebrity magazine*** magazine *m* people

celebutante [sı'lebjʊˌtɑ:nt] N *Fam* = jeune femme issue d'une famille riche, qui est l'objet d'une couverture médiatique importante

celeriac [sı'lerıæk] N céleri-rave *m*

celerity [sı'lerətı] N *Literary* célérité *f*, rapidité *f*

celery ['selərı] N céleri *m*; **head of c.** pied *m* de céleri; **stick of c.** branche *f* de céleri
COMP *(plant)* de céleri; *(soup)* au céleri
►► ***celery salt*** sel *m* de céleri

celestial [sı'lestıəl] ADJ *Astron & Fig* céleste
►► ***celestial body*** corps *m* céleste; *Astron* ***celestial sphere*** sphère *f* céleste

celiac *Am* = **coeliac**

celibacy ['selıbəsı] N *(sexual abstinence)* abstinence *f* sexuelle, chasteté *f*; *(not being married)* célibat *m*; *Rel* **to take a vow of c.** faire vœu de chasteté

celibate ['selıbət] ADJ *(person* ► *chaste)* qui n'a pas de rapports sexuels, chaste; *(life* ► *by choice)* de chasteté; *(*► *forced)* sans rapports sexuels
N personne *f* qui n'a pas de rapports sexuels

> Note that the French word **célibataire** is a false friend and is never a translation for the English word **celibate**. It means **unmarried**.

cell [sel] N **1** *(in prison)* cellule *f*; **he spent the night in the cells** il a passé la nuit en cellule
2 *(of monk, hermit)* cellule *f*
3 *Biol* cellule *f*; *(in beehive)* cellule *f*, alvéole *m*
4 *Elec* élément *m* (de pile)
5 *Am (mobile phone)* (téléphone *m*) portable *m*, *Belg* GSM *m*, *Suisse* Natel® *m*, *Can* cellulaire *m*
6 *Pol* cellule *f*
7 *Comput (on spreadsheet)* cellule *f*
COMP *Biol* cellulaire
►► *Biol* ***cell division*** division *f* cellulaire; *Biol* ***cell membrane*** membrane *f* cellulaire; *Biol* ***cell structure*** structure *f* cellulaire; *Biol* ***cell wall*** paroi *f* cellulaire

cellar ['selə(r)] N *(for wine)* cave *f*, cellier *m*; *(for coal, bric-a-brac)* cave *f*; *(for food)* cellier *m*; **he keeps a good c.** il a une bonne cave

> Note that the most common meaning of the French word **cellier** is **storeroom**.

cellarman ['seləmən] *(pl* **cellarmen** [-mən]) N sommelier *m*

cellist ['tʃelıst] N violoncelliste *mf*

cello ['tʃeləʊ] *(pl* **cellos)** N violoncelle *m*

Cellophane® ['seləfeın] N Cellophane® *f*

cellphone ['selfəʊn] N téléphone *m* cellulaire; *Am (mobile phone)* (téléphone *m*) portable *m*, *Belg* GSM *m*, *Suisse* Natel® *m*, *Can* cellulaire *m*

cellular ['seljʊlə(r)] ADJ **1** *Biol* cellulaire **2** *Constr* cellulaire **3** *Tex (blanket)* en cellular
►► ***cellular board*** *(cardboard)* carton *m* ondulé;

cellular logic logique *f* cellulaire; ***cellular radio*** radiotéléphonie *f* cellulaire; ***cellular (tele)phone*** téléphone *m* cellulaire

cellulite ['seljʊlaɪt] **N** *Physiol* cellulite *f*

celluloid® ['seljʊlɔɪd] **N** Celluloïd® *m*; *Fig* **to capture sb/sth on c.** filmer qn/qch
ADJ en Celluloïd®

cellulose ['seljʊləʊs] *Chem* **N** cellulose *f*
ADJ en *ou* de cellulose, cellulosique

Celsius ['selsɪəs] **ADJ** Celsius; **25 degrees C.** 25 degrés Celsius
►► ***Celsius thermometer*** thermomètre *m* de Celsius

Celt [kelt] **N** Celte *mf*

Celtic ['keltɪk] **N** *Ling* celtique *m*
ADJ celtique, celte

cement [sɪ'ment] **N 1** *Constr & Fig* ciment *m* **2** *(in dentistry)* amalgame *m* **3** *(glue)* colle *f*
VT 1 *Constr & Fig* cimenter **2** *(in dentistry)* obturer
►► ***cement mixer*** bétonnière *f*

cementation [ˌsiːmen'teɪʃən] **N** *Constr & Fig* cimentation *f*

cemetery ['semɪtrɪ] *(pl* **cemeteries***)* **N** cimetière *m*

cenotaph ['senətɑːf] **N** cénotaphe *m*

censer ['sensə(r)] **N** *Rel* encensoir *m*

censor ['sensə(r)] **N** censeur *m*; **to get past the c.** échapper à la censure
VT 1 *(ban ► book, film, article etc)* interdire, censurer; *(► scene)* supprimer, couper; *(► line, word)* supprimer **2** *(cut parts of ► film, article, newspaper)* censurer; *(► play, book, scenario)* censurer, expurger
►► *TV & Rad* ***censor bleep*** bip *m* de censure

> Attention: ne pas confondre avec le verbe **to censure**.

censoring ['sensərɪŋ] **N** censure *f*

censorious [sen'sɔːrɪəs] **ADJ** *Formal (comments, criticism)* sévère; *(person)* porté à la censure

censorship ['sensəʃɪp] **N 1** *(act, practice)* censure *f*; **there is no longer any c. of his films** ses films ne sont plus censurés **2** *(office of censor)* censorat *m*
►► ***censorship laws*** lois *fpl* de censure

censurable ['senʃərəbəl] **ADJ** *Formal* blâmable, qui mérite la réprobation

censure ['senʃə(r)] **N** blâme *m*, critique *f*
VT blâmer, critiquer

> Note that the French verb **censurer** is a false friend and is never a translation for the English verb **to censure**. It means **to censor**.
>
> Attention: ne pas confondre avec le verbe **to censor**.

census ['sensəs] **N** *Admin* recensement *m*; **to conduct** *or* **to take a c.** faire un recensement; **to conduct** *or* **to take a population c.** faire le recensement de la population, recenser la population
►► *Am* ***Census Bureau*** Bureau *m* des statistiques; ***census return*** formulaire *m* de recensement; ***census taker*** agent *m* recenseur

cent [sent] **N** *(coin)* cent *m*; **I haven't got a c.** je n'ai pas un sou; *Am* **to put one's two cents in** mettre son grain de sel

centaur ['sentɔː(r)] **N** *Myth* centaure *m*

centenarian [ˌsentɪ'neərɪən] **N** centenaire *mf*
ADJ centenaire

centenary [sen'tiːnərɪ] *(pl* **centenaries***)* **N** *(anniversary)* centenaire *m*, centième anniversaire *m*
COMP du centenaire

centennial [sen'tenjəl] **N** *Am* centenaire *m*, centième anniversaire *m*
ADJ 1 *(in age)* centenaire, séculaire **2** *(every hundred years)* séculaire

center, centering *etc Am* = **centre, centring** *etc*

centigrade ['sentɪgreɪd] **ADJ** centigrade; **25 degrees c.** 25 degrés centigrades
►► ***centigrade thermometer*** thermomètre *m* centigrade

centigram, centigramme ['sentɪgræm] **N** centigramme *m*

centilitre, *Am* **centiliter** ['sentɪˌliːtə(r)] **N** centilitre *m*

centimetre, *Am* **centimeter** ['sentɪˌmiːtə(r)] **N** centimètre *m*

centipede ['sentɪpiːd] **N** *Entom* mille-pattes *m inv*

central ['sentrəl] **ADJ 1** *(in location)* central; **c. Miami** le centre de Miami; **the office is very c.** *(in town)* le bureau est situé en plein centre **2** *(in importance)* central; **the c. character** le personnage central; **c. to the debate is the question of safety** la question de la sécurité se situe au cœur du débat; **this concept is c. to his theory** ce concept est au centre de sa théorie
N *Am Old-fashioned* central *m* téléphonique
►► ***Central African*** **N** Centrafricain(e) *m,f* **ADJ** centrafricain; ***the Central African Republic*** la République centrafricaine; ***Central America*** Amérique *f* centrale; ***Central American*** **N** Centraméricain(e) *m,f* **ADJ** centraméricain; *Geog* ***Central Asia*** Asie *f* centrale; ***central bank*** banque *f* centrale; ***Central Daylight Time*** heure *f* d'été du centre des États-Unis; ***Central Europe*** Europe *f* centrale; ***Central European*** **N** habitant (e) *m,f* de l'Europe centrale **ADJ** d'Europe centrale; ***Central European Time*** heure *f* de l'Europe centrale; ***central government*** gouvernement *m* central; ***central heating*** chauffage *m* central; *Am* ***Central Intelligence Agency*** CIA *f*; *Aut* ***central locking*** verrouillage *m* central; *Anat* ***central nervous system*** système *m* nerveux central; *Br Comput* ***central processing unit*** unité *f* centrale (de traitement), processeur *m* central; *Br* ***central reservation*** *(with grass)* terre-plein *m* central, *Belg & Suisse* berme *f* centrale; *(with barrier)* bande *f* médiane; ***Central Standard Time*** heure *f* d'hiver du centre des États-Unis

centralist ['sentrəlɪst] *Pol* **N** centraliste *mf*
ADJ centraliste

centralize, -ise ['sentrəlaɪz] **VT** centraliser
VI se centraliser

centralized, -ised ['sentrəlaɪzd] **ADJ** centralisé
►► *Comput* ***centralized data processing*** traitement *m* centralisé de l'information; ***centralized management*** gestion *f* intégrée; ***centralized purchasing*** achats *mpl* centralisés; *Comput* ***centralized storage*** mémoire *f* centrale

centralizing, -ising ['sentrəlaɪzɪŋ] **ADJ** centralisateur

centrally ['sentrəlɪ] **ADV** *(located)* au centre; *(organized)* de façon centralisée; **c. based** centralisé; **the flat is c. heated** l'appartement a le chauffage central; **the house is c. situated** la maison est située de façon centrale; *Econ* **a c. planned economy** une économie dirigée

centre, *Am* **center** ['sentə(r)] **N 1** *(gen)* centre *m*; **in the c.** au centre; **c. of gravity** centre *m* de gravité; *Med* **c. of infection** foyer *m* infectueux
2 *(of town)* centre *m*; **she lives in the city c.** elle habite dans le centre-ville
3 *Fig (of unrest)* foyer *m*; *(of debate)* cœur *m*, centre *m*; **at the c. of the debate** au cœur du débat; **the c. of attention** le centre d'attention
4 *(place, building)* centre *m*; **a sports/health c.** un centre sportif/médical
5 *Pol* centre *m*; **to be left/right of c.** être du centre gauche/droit
6 *Tech (of lathe)* pointe *f*; **to be off c.** *or* **out of c.** être décentré
7 *Sport (pass)* centre *m*
8 *(in rugby)* centre *m*
COMP 1 *(central)* central **2** *Pol* du centre
VT 1 *(place in centre)* centrer; **to c. a line** *(when keying)* centrer une ligne
2 *Cin & Phot (image)* cadrer; *Typ (text)* centrer
3 *Fig (attention)* concentrer, fixer; **to c. one's hopes on sth** mettre *ou* fonder tous ses espoirs sur qch
4 *Sport* **to c. the ball** centrer le ballon
►► *Ftbl* ***centre back*** arrière *m* central; *Ftbl* ***centre circle*** cercle *m* central; *Ftbl* ***centre forward*** avant-centre *m*; *Ftbl* ***centre half*** demi-centre *m*; *Tech* ***centre punch*** pointeau *m*; *Typ* ***centre spread*** double page *f* centrale; *Theat* ***centre stage*** centre *m* de la scène; *Fig* **his concerns always take c. stage** ses soucis à lui doivent toujours passer avant tout; *Sport* ***centre three-quarter*** *(in rugby)* trois-quarts *m* centre

► **centre on,** *Am* **center on VT INSEP** *(attention)* se concentrer sur; **the conversation centred on politics** la conversation tournait autour de la politique

centreboard, *Am* **centerboard** ['sentəbɔːd] **N** *Naut* dérive *f (d'un bateau)*

centrefold, *Am* **centerfold** ['sentəˌfəʊld] **N** *Press (in magazine, newspaper)* double page *f* centrale détachable; *(nude picture)* photo *f* de pin-up

centre-left, *Am* **center-left** **ADJ** *Pol (politician, party, views)* du centre gauche

centrepiece, *Am* **centerpiece** ['sentəpiːs] **N** *(outstanding feature)* joyau *m*; *(on table)* décoration *f* de table; *(of meal)* pièce *f* de résistance

centre-right, *Am* **center-right** **ADJ** *Pol (politician, party, views)* du centre droit

centrifugal [ˌsentrɪ'fjuːgəl] **ADJ** *Phys* centrifuge
►► ***centrifugal force*** force *f* centrifuge

centrifuge ['sentrɪfjuːdʒ] *Tech* **N** centrifugeur *m*, centrifugeuse *f*
VT centrifuger

centring, *Am* **centering** ['sentərɪŋ] **N 1** *(placing in centre)* centrage *m* **2** *Cin & Phot* cadrage *m*; *Typ (of text)* centrage *m*
►► ***centring tool*** centreur *m*

centripetal [ˌsentrɪ'piːtəl] **ADJ** *Phys* centripète
►► ***centripetal force*** force *f* centripète

centrist ['sentrɪst] *Pol* **N** centriste *mf*
ADJ centriste

centuries-old ['sentʃərɪz-] **ADJ** vieux (vieille) de plusieurs siècles

century ['sentʃʊrɪ] *(pl* **centuries***)* **N 1** *(time)* siècle *m*; **in the 20th c.** au 20ème siècle; **this house is five centuries old** cette maison a *ou* est vieille de cinq siècles; **these trees are centuries old** ces arbres sont plusieurs fois centenaires **2** *Sport (one hundred runs)* centaine *f*, série *f* de cent **3** *Antiq & Mil* centurie *f*
►► *Am Fam* ***century note*** billet *m* de cent dollars

CEO [ˌsiːiː'əʊ] **N** *(abbr* **chief executive officer***)* P-DG *m*

cephalic [sə'fælɪk, ke'fælɪk] **ADJ** *Anat* céphalique

ceramic [sɪ'ræmɪk] **N 1** *(objects)* céramique *f* **2** *(object)* (objet *m* en) céramique *f*
COMP *(art)* céramique; *(vase)* en céramique
►► *Br* ***ceramic hob*** plaque *f* vitrocéramique; ***ceramic tiles*** carrelage *m*

ceramics [sɪ'ræmɪks] **N** *(UNCOUNT)* céramique *f*

cereal ['sɪərɪəl] **N 1** *Agr (plant)* céréale *f*; *(grain)* grain *m* (de céréale) **2** *Culin* **(breakfast) c.** céréales *fpl*; **baby c.** bouillie *f*
COMP *Agr (farming)* céréalier
►► ***cereal bowl*** assiette *f* creuse, bol *m* à céréales; ***cereal crops*** céréales *fpl*

cerebellum [ˌserɪ'beləm] *(pl* **cerebellums** *or* **cerebella** [-lə]*)* **N** *Anat* cervelet *m*

cerebral **ADJ 1** ['serɪbrəl, *Am* sə'riːbrəl] *Anat* cérébral **2** ['serɪbrəl, sə'riːbrəl] *(intellectual)* cérébral
►► *Anat* ***cerebral cortex*** cortex *m* cérébral; *Med* ***cerebral death*** mort *f* cérébrale; *Med* ***cerebral palsy*** infirmité *f* motrice cérébrale, paralysie *f* cérébrale

cerebrospinal [ˌserəbrə'spaɪnəl] *Anat*
ADJ cérébro-spinal, céphalo-rachidien
►► ***cerebrospinal fluid*** liquide *m* céphalo-rachidien

cerebrum ['serɪbrəm] *(pl* **cerebrums** *or* **cerebra** [-brə]*)* **N** *Anat* cerveau *m*

ceremonial [ˌserɪ'məʊnjəl] **ADJ 1** *(rite, visit)* cérémoniel; *(robes)* de cérémonie **2** *Am (post)* honorifique
N cérémonial *m*; *Rel* cérémonial *m*, rituel *m*

ceremonially [ˌserɪ'məʊnjəlɪ] **ADV** selon le cérémonial d'usage

ceremonious [ˌserɪ'məʊnjəs] **ADJ** solennel; *(mock-solemn)* cérémonieux

ceremoniously [ˌserɪ'məʊnjəslɪ] **ADV** solennellement, avec cérémonie; *(mock-solemnly)* cérémonieusement

ceremony [*Br* 'serɪmənɪ, *Am* 'serəmaʊnɪ] (*pl* **ceremonies**) **N 1** *(UNCOUNT) (formality)* cérémonie *f*, cérémonies *fpl*; **with much c.** avec beaucoup de cérémonie; **without c.** sans cérémonie *ou* cérémonies; **we don't stand on c.** nous ne faisons pas de cérémonies **2** *(event)* cérémonie *f*

cert. (*written abbr* **certificate**) certificat *m*; **a c. 18 film** un film interdit aux moins de 18 ans

cert [sɜ:t] **N** *Br Fam* certitude *f*; **it's a dead c. that he'll win** il va gagner, ça ne fait pas un pli *ou* c'est couru d'avance; **he's a c. for the job** il est sûr d'obtenir le poste

certain ['sɜ:tən] **ADJ 1** *(sure)* certain, sûr; **to be c. of sth** être sûr de qch; **I'm c. of it!** j'en suis sûr!; **she was quite c. about what she had seen** elle était tout à fait sûre de ce qu'elle avait vu; **he was c. (that) she was there** il était certain qu'elle était là; **it's c. that she will get the job** il est sûr qu'elle aura le poste; **there is c. to be some opposition to the bill** il est sûr que la loi rencontrera une opposition; **to be c. to do sth** être sûr de faire qch; **he's c. to win** il est sûr qu'il va gagner; **he's c. to come** il ne manquera pas de venir, il viendra sûrement; **I'd better make c.** je ferais mieux de m'en assurer; **to make c. of sth** *(check)* vérifier qch, s'assurer de qch; *(be sure to have)* s'assurer qch; **he made c. that all the doors were locked** il a vérifié que toutes les portes étaient fermées; **I made c. of a good seat** je me suis assuré une bonne place

2 *(inevitable ▸ death, failure)* certain, inévitable; **the soldiers faced c. death** les soldats allaient à une mort certaine; **they face c. dismissal** ils seront renvoyés à coup sûr

3 *(definite, infallible ▸ cure)* sûr, infaillible

4 *(particular but unspecified)* certain; **in c. places** à certains endroits; **he has a c. something about him** il a un certain je ne sais quoi; **she has a c. charm** elle a un certain charme; **women of a c. age** les femmes d'un certain âge; **there's been a c. amount of confusion over this** il y a eu une certaine confusion à ce sujet; **to a c. extent** *or* **degree** dans une certaine mesure

5 *(not known personally)* certain; **a c. Mr Roberts** un certain M. Roberts

PRON certains (certaines) *mpl,fpl*; **c. of his colleagues** certains *ou* quelques-uns de ses collègues

• **for certain ADV I don't know for c.** je n'en suis pas certain; **I can't say for c.** je ne peux pas l'affirmer; **you'll have it tomorrow for c.** vous l'aurez demain sans faute

certainly ['sɜ:tənlɪ] **ADV 1** *(without doubt)* certainement, assurément; *(admittedly)* certes; **he is c. very handsome** il est très beau, ça ne fait pas de doute; **I will c. come** je ne manquerai pas de venir, je viendrai, c'est sûr; **it will c. won't be ready tomorrow** ça ne sera jamais prêt pour demain **2** *(of course)* certainement, bien sûr; **can you help me? – c.!** pouvez-vous m'aider? – bien sûr *ou* volontiers!; **are you angry? – I most c. am!** êtes-vous fâché? – oui, et comment!; **c. not!** bien sûr que non!, certainement pas!

> Note that the most common meaning of the French word **certainement** is **probably**.

certainty ['sɜ:təntɪ] (*pl* **certainties**) **N 1** *(conviction)* certitude *f*, conviction *f*; **I cannot say with any c. when I shall arrive** je ne peux pas dire exactement à quelle heure j'arriverai; **we can have no c. of success** nous ne sommes pas sûrs de réussir **2** *(fact)* certitude *f*, fait *m* certain; *(event)* certitude *f*, événement *m* certain; **I know for a c. that he's leaving** je sais à coup sûr qu'il part; **their victory is now a c.** leur victoire est maintenant assurée *ou* ne fait aucun doute; **it's an absolute c.** c'est une chose certaine, c'est une certitude absolue

certifiable [ˌsɜ:tɪ'faɪəbəl] **ADJ 1** *(gen)* qu'on peut certifier **2** *Psy (insane)* dont l'état nécessite l'internement psychiatrique; *Fam* **he's c.** il est fou à lier

certificate [sə'tɪfɪkət] **N 1** *(gen) & Admin* certificat *m* **2** *(academic)* diplôme *m*; *(vocational ▸ of apprenticeship)* brevet *m*

▸▸ *Aviat* ***certificate of airworthiness*** certificat *m* de navigabilité; *Com* ***certificate of incorporation*** certificat *m* d'enregistrement de société; ***certificate of insurance*** attestation *f* d'assurance; *Com* ***certificate of origin*** certificat *m* d'origine; *Br Formerly Sch* ***Certificate of Secondary Education*** = ancien brevet de l'enseignement secondaire en Grande-Bretagne, aujourd'hui remplacé par le "GCSE", BEPC *m*

certificated [sə'tɪfɪkeɪtɪd] **ADJ** diplômé

certification [ˌsɜ:tɪfɪ'keɪʃən] **N 1** *(act)* certification *f*, authentification *f* **2** *(certificate)* certificat *m*

certified ['sɜ:tɪfaɪd] **ADJ 1** *(having certificate)* diplômé **2** *(guaranteed)* **c. by a notary** notarié **3** *Psy (declared insane)* dont l'état nécessite l'internement psychiatrique

▸▸ ***certified accounts*** comptes *mpl* approuvés; *Am Fin* ***certified cheque*** chèque *m* certifié; ***certified copy*** copie *f* certifiée conforme, copie *f* authentique; *Am* ***certified letter*** lettre *f* recommandée; *Am* ***certified mail*** envoi *m* recommandé; **to send sth by c. mail** envoyer qch en recommandé avec accusé de réception; *Am* ***certified public accountant*** expert-comptable *m*; *Am Sch* ***certified teacher*** *(in state school)* professeur *m* diplômé; *(in private school)* professeur *m* habilité

certify ['sɜ:tɪfaɪ] (*pt & pp* **certified**) **VT 1** *(gen)* certifier, attester; *Med (death)* constater; *Am Fin (cheque)* certifier; *Acct* **to c. the books** viser les livres de commerce; **this is to c. that A. Gooch has...** *(on certificate, letter)* ce document certifie que A. Gooch a...; **to c. that sth is true** attester que qch est vrai **2** *Com (goods)* garantir **3** *Psy* **to c. sb (insane)** déclarer qn atteint d'aliénation mentale; *Fam* **he ought to be certified!** il est bon à enfermer!

VI to c. to sth attester qch

certitude ['sɜ:tɪtju:d] **N** *Formal* certitude *f*

cervical [sə'vaɪkəl, 'sɜ:rvɪkəl] **ADJ** *Anat* **1** *(of the cervix)* du col de l'utérus **2** *(of the neck)* cervical

▸▸ ***cervical cancer*** cancer *m* du col de l'utérus; ***cervical collar*** minerve *f*; ***cervical smear*** frottis *m* vaginal; ***cervical vertebra*** vertèbre *f* cervicale

cervix ['sɜ:vɪks] (*pl* **cervixes** *or* **cervices** [-ɪsi:z]) **N 1** *(of uterus)* col *m* de l'utérus **2** *(neck)* cou *m*

cessation [se'seɪʃən] **N** *Formal* cessation *f*, suspension *f*; *Mil* **c. of hostilities** cessation *f ou* suspension *f* des hostilités

cession ['seʃən] **N** *Law* cession *f*

cesspit ['sespɪt], **cesspool** ['sespu:l] **N** fosse *f* d'aisances; *Fig* cloaque *m*

CET [ˌsi:i:'ti:] **N 1** (*abbr* **Central European Time**) heure *f* de l'Europe centrale **2** *EU* (*abbr* **common external tariff**) tarif *m* externe commun

Ceylon [sɪ'lɒn] **N** *Formerly* Ceylan

CF [ˌsi:'ef] **N** *Am Com* (*abbr* **cost and freight**) C et F

cf. (*written abbr* **confer**) cf

CFC [ˌsi:ef'si:] **N** *Chem* (*abbr* **chlorofluorocarbon**) CFC *m*

CFO [ˌsi:ef'əʊ] **N** *Am* (*abbr* **Chief Financial Officer**) chef *m* comptable, chef *m* de la comptabilité

CFSP [ˌsi:efˌes'pi:] **N** *EU* (*abbr* **Common Foreign and Security Policy**) PESC *f*

cg (*written abbr* **centigram**) cg

CGI [ˌsi:dʒi:'aɪ] **N** *Comput* **1** (*abbr* **common gateway interface**) interface *f* commune de passerelle, CGI *f* **2** (*abbr* **computer-generated images**) images *fpl* de synthèse

CH [ˌsi:'eɪtʃ] **N 1** (*abbr* **Companion of Honour**) = décoration britannique remise aux citoyens qui ont rendu des services à l'État, chevalier *m* de la Légion d'honneur **2** *Banking & Fin* (*abbr* **clearing house**) chambre *f* de compensation

ch (*written abbr* **central heating**) ch. cent

cha [tʃɑ:] **N** *Br Fam Old-fashioned (tea)* thé ᵒ *m*

Chad [tʃæd] **N** Tchad *m*; **Lake C.** le lac Tchad

chaebol ['tʃeɪbɒl] **N** *Econ* chaebol *m*

chafe [tʃeɪf] **VT 1** *(rub)* frictionner, frotter **2** *(irritate)* frotter contre, irriter; **his shirt collar chafed his neck** son col de chemise lui irritait le cou **3** *(wear away ▸ collar)* élimer, user (par le frottement); *(▸ paint)* érafler; *(▸ rope)* raguer

VI 1 *(become worn ▸ gen)* s'user (par le frottement); *(▸ rope)* raguer **2** *(skin)* s'irriter; *Fig (person)* s'irriter, s'impatienter; **to c. at** *or* **under sth** s'irriter de qch; **the media chafed under the military censorship** soumis à la censure militaire, les médias rongeaient leur frein

chafed [tʃeɪft] **ADJ 1** *(skin)* irrité **2** *(worn ▸ collar)* usé; *(▸ paint)* éraflé; *(▸ rope)* ragué

chaff [tʃæf] **N 1** *(of grain)* balle *f*; *(hay, straw)* menue paille *f* **2** *Old-fashioned (teasing)* taquinerie *f*, raillerie *f* **3** *Electron* ruban *m* métallique antiradar

VT *Old-fashioned (tease)* taquiner

chaffinch ['tʃæfɪntʃ] **N** *Orn* pinson *m*

chafing ['tʃeɪfɪŋ] **N 1** *(warming ▸ of limbs)* friction *f* **2** *(of skin)* irritation *f*

▸▸ ***chafing dish*** chauffe-plats *m*

chagrin ['ʃægrɪn] **N** *Literary* (vif) dépit *m*, (vive) déception *f ou* contrariété *f*; **much to my c.** à mon grand dépit

VT contrarier, décevoir

chain [tʃeɪn] **N 1** *(gen)* chaîne *f*; *(small ▸ for medallion etc)* chaînette *f*; **we keep the dog on a c.** notre chien est toujours attaché; **to pull the c.** *(of toilet)* tirer la chasse d'eau; **to form a human c.** former une chaîne humaine; *Aut* **(snow) chains** chaînes *fpl* (à neige); *Am Fam* **to yank sb's c.** taquiner qn ᵒ

2 *Admin* **c. of office** écharpe *f* de maire

3 *(of mountains)* chaîne *f*; *(of islands)* chapelet *m*

4 *(of events)* série *f*, suite *f*; *(of ideas)* suite *f*

5 *Com (of shops, restaurants)* chaîne *f*; **fast food c.** chaîne *f* de restauration rapide; **c. of distribution** circuit *m* de distribution, réseau *m* de distribution

6 *Phys & Chem* chaîne *f*

7 *Tech (for surveying)* chaîne *f* d'arpenteur

8 *(unit of measurement)* 20,1 m, chaînée *f*

VT *also Fig* enchaîner; *(door)* mettre la chaîne à; **the dog was chained to the post** le chien était attaché au poteau (par une chaîne); **she chained herself to the railings** elle s'est enchaînée à la grille; *Fig* **to be chained to one's desk** être rivé à son bureau; *Fig* **she is chained to the kitchen sink** elle ne sort pas de sa cuisine

• **chains NPL** *(for prisoner)* chaînes *fpl*, entraves *fpl*; **a prisoner in chains** un prisonnier enchaîné; *Fig* **to break** *or* **burst one's chains** rompre ses chaînes

▸▸ ***chain armour*** mailles *fpl*; *(suit)* cotte *f* de mailles; *Tech* ***chain drive*** transmission *f* par chaîne; ***chain gang*** chaîne *f* de forçats; ***chain guard*** carter *m* (de bicyclette); *Aut* ***chain guide*** guide *m* chaîne; ***chain letter*** lettre *f* faisant partie d'une chaîne; ***chain lightning*** *(UNCOUNT)* éclairs *mpl* en zigzag; ***chain link*** chaînon *m ou* maillon *m* de chaîne; ***chain mail*** *(UNCOUNT)* mailles *fpl*; *(suit)* cotte *f* de mailles; *Phys, Chem & Fig* ***chain reaction*** réaction *f* en chaîne; **to set off a c. reaction** provoquer une réaction en chaîne; ***chain saw*** tronçonneuse *f*; ***chain smoker*** fumeur(euse) *m,f* invétéré(e), gros (grosse) fumeur(euse) *m,f*; ***chain stitch*** point *m* de chaînette; ***chain store*** magasin *m* à succursales (multiples); *(individual store)* succursale *f*

▸ **chain down VT SEP** enchaîner, attacher avec une chaîne

▸ **chain up VT SEP** *(prisoner)* enchaîner; *(dog)* mettre à l'attache, attacher; *(bike, gate)* mettre une chaîne à

chaining ['tʃeɪnɪŋ] **N** *Comput* chaînage *m*

chain-smoke VT he chain-smokes untipped cigarettes il fume des cigarettes sans filtre du matin au soir; **he was chain-smoking Gitanes** il fumait Gitane sur Gitane

VI fumer cigarette sur cigarette

chair [tʃeə(r)] **N 1** *(seat)* chaise *f*; *(armchair)* fauteuil *m*; **in the dentist's c.** dans le fauteuil du dentiste

2 *(chairperson)* président(e) *m,f*; **to be in the c.** présider; **to take the c.** prendre la présidence; **to address the c.** s'adresser au président

3 *Univ* chaire *f*; **to hold the c. in French** avoir *ou* occuper la chaire de français

4 *Fam (for execution)* **to go** *or* **to be sent to the c., to get the c.** passer à la chaise électrique ᵒ

VT 1 *Admin (meeting)* présider **2** *Br (hero, victor)* porter en triomphe

▸▸ ***chair back*** dossier *m* de chaise; ***chair leg*** pied *m* de chaise

chaircover ['tʃeəˌkʌvə(r)] **N** housse *f* de fauteuil

chairlift ['tʃeəlɪft] **N** télésiège *m*

chairman ['tʃeəmən] (*pl* **chairmen** [-mən]) **N 1** *(at meeting)* président *m (d'un comité)*; **to act as c.** présider la séance; **Mr C.** Monsieur le Président; **Madam C.** Madame la Présidente **2** *Com (of company)* président-directeur *m* général, P-D G *m*; **c. of the board** Président du conseil **3** *Pol* **C. Mao** le président Mao

chairmanship ['tʃeəmənʃɪp] **N** présidence *f (d'un comité)*; **under the c. of Mr Black** sous la présidence de M. Black

chairperson ['tʃeə,pɜːsən] **N** président(e) *m,f (d'un comité)*

chairwoman ['tʃeə,wʊmən] (*pl* **chairwomen** [-'wɪmɪn]) **N** présidente *f (d'un comité)*

chalet ['ʃæleɪ] **N** chalet *m*

▸▸ ***chalet park*** parc *m* résidentiel de loisirs

chalice ['tʃælɪs] **N 1** *Rel* calice *m* **2** *(goblet)* coupe *f*

chalk [tʃɔːk] **N 1** *(substance)* craie *f*; *(in rock-climbing)* magnésie *f*; **a piece of c.** un morceau de craie **2** *(piece)* craie *f*; **a set of coloured chalks** un assortiment de craies de couleur **3** *Br (idioms)* **by a long c.** de beaucoup, de loin; **not by a long c.** loin de là, tant s'en faut; **the best by a long c.** le meilleur, et de loin; **c. and talk** = méthode d'enseignement traditionnelle; **they're as different as c. and cheese** c'est le jour et la nuit

VT *(write)* écrire à la craie; *(mark)* marquer à la craie; *(rub with chalk ▸ gen)* frotter de craie; *(▸ cue)* enduire de craie; **to c. one's name on a wall** écrire son nom sur un mur à la craie; *Carp* **to c. a line** tringler une ligne

COMP *(hills, cliffs)* crayeux; *(drawing)* à la craie

▸▸ ***chalk dust*** poussière *f* de craie; ***chalk line*** *(drawn)* trait *m* à la craie; *Carp (string)* cordeau *m*; *(made by string)* ligne *f* faite au cordeau

▸ **chalk up VT SEP 1** *(write in chalk)* écrire à la craie

2 *(credit)* **c. that one up to me** mettez cela sur mon compte; *Fig* **to c. sth up to experience** mettre qch au compte de l'expérience; **they chalked their defeat up to lack of practice** ils ont mis leur défaite sur le compte du manque d'entraînement

3 *(add up ▸ points, score)* totaliser, marquer

4 *(attain ▸ victory)* remporter; *(▸ profits)* encaisser

chalkboard ['tʃɔːkbɔːd] **N** *Am* tableau *m* (noir)

chalkpit ['tʃɔːkpɪt] **N** carrière *f* de craie

chalky ['tʃɔːkɪ] (*compar* **chalkier**, *superl* **chalkiest**) **ADJ** *(earth, water)* calcaire; *(deposit)* calcique; *(hands)* couvert de craie; *(complexion)* crayeux, blafard; *(taste)* de craie; *(colour)* pâle, terreux

challenge ['tʃælɪndʒ] **VT 1** *(gen ▸ defy)* défier; **to c. sb** lancer un défi à qn; **to c. sb to do sth** défier qn de faire qch; **to c. sb to a game of tennis** inviter qn à faire une partie de tennis; **to c. sb to a duel** provoquer qn en duel

2 *(demand effort from)* mettre à l'épreuve; **she needs a job that really challenges her** elle a besoin d'un travail qui soit pour elle une gageure *ou* un challenge

3 *(contest ▸ authority, findings)* contester, mettre en cause; *(▸ statement)* protester contre, disputer; **to c. sb's right to do sth** contester à qn le droit de faire qch; **their position was challenged by younger artists** leur position a été remise en question par des artistes plus jeunes

4 *Mil (of sentry)* faire une sommation à

5 *Law (juror)* récuser

6 *Literary (require)* requérir

N 1 *(in contest)* défi *m*; **to issue a c.** lancer un défi; **to take up the c.** relever le défi; **Jackson's c. for the leadership of the party** la tentative de Jackson pour s'emparer de la direction du parti

2 *(in job, activity)* défi *m*; **to enjoy a c.** aimer les défis; **he needs a job that presents more of a c.** il a besoin d'un emploi plus stimulant; **environmental problems are the major c. for our generation** les problèmes d'environnement constituent la principale gageure *ou* le principal défi pour notre génération

3 *(to right, authority)* mise *f* en question, contestation *f*

4 *Law (of jury member)* récusation *f*

▸▸ *Sport* ***challenge cup*** coupe-challenge *f*; *Sport* ***challenge match*** challenge *m*

challenger ['tʃælɪndʒə(r)] **N** *(gen)* provocateur (trice) *m,f*; *Pol & Sport* challenger *m*; *Mktg (product, company)* challengeur *m*, prétendant(e) *m,f*

challenging ['tʃælɪndʒɪŋ] **ADJ 1** *(defiant ▸ look, remark)* provocateur **2** *(demanding ▸ ideas, theory)* provocateur, stimulant, exaltant; *(▸ job, activity)* stimulant, qui met à l'épreuve; **to find oneself in a c. situation** se trouver face à un défi

chamber ['tʃeɪmbə(r)] **N 1** *(hall, room)* chambre *f*; *Br Pol* **the upper/lower C.** la Chambre haute/basse

2 *Arch (lodgings)* logement *m*, appartement *m*

3 *(of gun)* chambre *f*

4 *Anat (of the heart)* cavité *f*; *(of the eye)* chambre *f*

5 *Metal (of furnace)* laboratoire *m*; *Phys (for ionization, expansion)* chambre *f*

6 *(of cave)* salle *f*

• **chambers NPL** *Law (of barrister, judge)* cabinet *m*; *(of solicitor)* cabinet *m*, étude *f*; **in chambers** en chambre du conseil; **the case was heard in chambers** l'affaire a été jugée en référé

▸▸ ***chamber concert*** concert *m* de musique de chambre; ***chamber music*** musique *f* de chambre; ***Chamber of Commerce*** Chambre *f* de commerce; *Parl* ***Chamber of Deputies*** Chambre *f* des députés; *Mus* ***chamber orchestra*** orchestre *m* de chambre; ***chamber pot*** pot *m* de chambre

chamberlain ['tʃeɪmbəlɪn] **N** chambellan *m*

chambermaid ['tʃeɪmbə,meɪd] **N** femme *f* de chambre

chameleon [kə'miːlɪən] **N** *Zool & Fig* caméléon *m*

chamfer ['tʃæmfə(r)] *Carp* **N** chanfrein *m*

VT 1 *(bevel)* chanfreiner **2** *(cut grooves in)* canneler

chammy ['ʃæmɪ] (*pl* **chammies**) **N** peau *f* de chamois

chamois (*pl inv*) **N 1** ['ʃæmwɑː] *Zool* chamois *m* **2** ['ʃæmɪ] *(hide)* peau *f* de chamois

VT ['ʃæmɪ] **1** *(leather, skin)* chamoiser **2** *(polish)* polir à la peau de chamois

▸▸ ***chamois leather*** *(cloth)* peau *f* de chamois

champ [tʃæmp] **VT** mâchonner

VI 1 *(munch)* mâchonner **2** *(idiom)* **to c. at the bit** ronger son frein

N *Fam (champion)* crack *m*

champagne [ʃæm'peɪn] **N 1** *(wine)* champagne *m* **2** *(colour)* champagne *m inv*

ADJ *(colour)* champagne *(inv)*; **a c.-coloured sofa** un canapé couleur champagne

▸▸ ***champagne cocktail*** cocktail *m* au champagne; ***champagne flute*** flûte *f* à champagne; ***champagne glass*** *(tall)* flûte *f* à champagne; *(broad)* coupe *f* à champagne; ***champagne reception*** réception *f* avec champagne

champers ['ʃæmpəz] **N** *Br Fam* champ' *m*

champion ['tʃæmpjən] **N 1** *(winner)* champion (onne) *m,f*; **the world chess c.** le champion du monde d'échecs; **she's a c. runner** elle est championne de course **2** *(supporter)* champion(onne) *m,f*; **he's a self-proclaimed c. of the working man** il se veut le champion des travailleurs

VT défendre, soutenir; **she championed the cause of birth control** elle s'est faite la championne de la régulation des naissances

ADJ *Scot & NEng Fam (excellent)* super, génial

▸▸ *Ftbl* ***the Champions' League*** la Ligue des Champions

championship ['tʃæmpjənʃɪp] **N 1** *(contest)* championnat *m*; **he plays c. tennis** il participe aux championnats de tennis **2** *(support)* défense *f*

▸▸ ***championship match*** match *m* de championnat

CHANCE [tʃɑːns]

N	
• chance **1**	• hasard **2**
• occasion **3**	• risque **4**
ADJ	
• fortuit	
VT	
• hasarder	

N 1 *(possibility, likelihood)* chance *f*; **is there any c. of seeing you again?** serait-il possible de vous revoir?; **there was little c. of him finding work** il y avait peu de chances qu'il trouve du travail; **we have an outside c. of success** nous avons une très faible chance de réussir; **she's got a good** *or* **strong c. of being accepted** elle a de fortes chances d'être acceptée *ou* reçue; **there's a fifty-fifty c. he won't turn up** il y a une chance sur deux qu'il ne vienne pas; *Fam* **no c.!** des clous!; **he's in with a c. of getting the job** il a une chance d'obtenir le poste; **(the) chances are (that) he'll never find out** il y a de fortes *ou* grandes chances qu'il ne l'apprenne jamais

2 *(fortune, luck)* hasard *m*; **games of c.** les jeux *mpl* de hasard; **there was an element of c. in his success** il y a eu une part de hasard dans sa réussite; **it was pure c. that I found it** je l'ai trouvé tout à fait par hasard; **to leave things to c.** laisser faire les choses; **to leave nothing to c.** ne rien laisser au hasard; *Fam* **c. would be a fine thing!** ah, si seulement je pouvais/il pouvait/*etc*!

3 *(opportunity)* occasion *f*; **I haven't had a c. to write to him** je n'ai pas trouvé l'occasion de lui écrire; **give him a c.!** donne-lui une chance!; **give her a c. to defend herself** donnez-lui l'occasion de se défendre; **it's a c. in a million** c'est une occasion unique; **I'm offering you the c. of a lifetime** je vous offre la chance de votre vie; **the poor man never had** *or* **stood a c.** le pauvre homme n'avait aucune chance de s'en tirer; **I go to the theatre when I get the c.** je vais au théâtre quand j'en ai l'occasion; **some children simply don't get a c. in life** pour certains enfants il n'y a tout simplement aucun avenir; **this is your last c.** c'est votre dernière chance; **there are no second chances, there is no second c.** tu n'as pas droit à l'erreur; *Fam* **given half a c. she'd play tennis every day** si elle pouvait elle jouerait au tennis tous les jours

4 *(risk)* risque *m*; **I don't want to take the c. of losing** je ne veux pas prendre le risque de perdre; **I'm taking no chances** je ne veux pas prendre de risques; **he took a c. on a racehorse** il a parié sur un cheval de course; **to take one's chances** tenter sa chance; *Fig* **take a c. on me** donne-moi une chance

ADJ *(encounter, meeting)* fortuit; **c. discovery** découverte *f* accidentelle *ou* fortuite; **I was a c. witness to the robbery** j'ai été un témoin accidentel du vol

VI *Formal or Literary (happen)* **I chanced to be at the same table as Sir Sydney** je me suis trouvé par hasard à la même table que Sir Sydney; **it chanced that no one else had heard of her** il s'est trouvé que personne d'autre n'avait entendu parler d'elle

VT *(risk) Literary* hasarder; **she chanced going out despite the curfew** elle s'est hasardée à sortir malgré le couvre-feu; **let's c. it** *or* **our luck** tentons notre chance; *Fam* **to c. one's arm** *(take a risk)* risquer le coup; *(push one's luck)* exagérer, pousser

• **by chance ADV** par hasard; **by pure** *or* **sheer c. we were both staying at the same hotel** il se trouvait que nous logions au même hôtel; **would you by any c. know who that man is?** sauriez-vous par hasard qui est cet homme?

▸ **chance on, chance upon VT INSEP** *(person)* rencontrer par hasard; *(thing)* trouver par hasard

> Note that the French noun **chance** is a false friend. Its most common meaning is **luck**.

chancel ['tʃɑːnsəl] **N** *Archit* chœur *m*

▸▸ ***chancel screen*** jubé *m*

chancellery ['tʃɑːnsələrɪ] (*pl* **chancelleries**) **N** chancellerie *f*

chancellor ['tʃɑːnsələ(r)] **N 1** *Pol* chancelier *m* **2** *Univ (in UK)* président(e) *m,f* honoraire; *(in US)* président(e) *m,f* (d'université)

▸▸ ***Chancellor of the Exchequer*** Chancelier *m* de l'Échiquier, ministre *m* des Finances *(en Grande-Bretagne)*

chancer ['tʃɑːnsə(r)] **N** *Br Fam* filou *m*

chancery ['tʃɑːnsərɪ] (*pl* **chanceries**) **N 1** *Law (in UK)* **C. (Division)** cour *f* de la chancellerie *(une des trois divisions de la Haute cour de justice en Angleterre)* **2** *Law (in US)* **Court of C.** cour *f* d'équité

chancre ['ʃæŋkə(r)] **N** *Med* chancre *m*

chancy ['tʃɑːnsɪ] (*compar* **chancier**, *superl* **chanciest**) **ADJ** *Fam* risqué

chandelier [ˌʃændə'lɪə(r)] **N** lustre *m* (*pour éclairer*)

> Note that the French word **chandelier** is a false friend and is never a translation for the English word **chandelier**. Its most common meaning is **candlestick** or **candelabra**.

chandler ['tʃɑːndlə(r)] **N 1** (*supplier*) fournisseur *m*; **ship's c.** shipchandler *m* **2** (*candlemaker*) chandelier *m*

CHANGE [tʃeɪndʒ]

> **N**
> • changement **1, 3** • correspondance **3**
> • monnaie **4**
> **VT**
> • changer (de) **1–4**
> **VI**
> • changer **1, 4** • se changer **2, 3**

N 1 (*alteration*) changement *m*; **we expect a c. in the weather** nous nous attendons à un changement de temps; **there's been a c. in the law** la loi a été modifiée; **a c. in public opinion** un revirement de l'opinion publique; **the party needs a c. of direction** le parti a besoin d'un changement de direction *ou* d'orientation; **a c. for the better/worse** un changement en mieux/pire, une amélioration/dégradation; **walking to work makes a pleasant c. from driving** c'est agréable d'aller travailler à pied plutôt qu'en voiture; **that makes a c.!** ça change un peu!; **yes, it makes a nice c., doesn't it?** oui, ça change un peu de l'ordinaire, n'est-ce pas?; **living in the country will be a big c. for us** cela nous changera beaucoup de vivre à la campagne; **there's been little c. in his condition** son état n'a guère évolué; **there are going to be some changes in this office!** il va y avoir du nouveau *ou* du changement dans ce bureau!; **to have a c. of heart** changer d'avis; *Fig* **I need a c. of scene** *or* **scenery** j'ai besoin de changer de décor *ou* d'air; **a c. is as good as a rest** changer de décor fait
autant de bien que de partir en vacances

2 (*fresh set or supply*) **a c. of clothes** des vêtements de rechange

3 (*in journey*) changement *m*, correspondance *f*; **if you go by underground you'll have to make two changes** si vous y allez en métro vous serez obligé de changer deux fois

4 (*money*) monnaie *f*; **small** *or* **loose c.** petite *ou* menue monnaie *f*; **she gave me two pounds in c.** elle m'a donné deux livres en monnaie; **can you give me c. for five pounds?** pouvez-vous me faire la monnaie de cinq livres?; **the machine doesn't give c.** la machine ne rend pas la monnaie; *Fam* **you won't get much c. out of £100** (*if you buy that*) il ne va pas te rester grand-chose sur tes 100 livres; *Br Fam Fig* **you'll get no c. out of him** on ne peut rien en tirer

5 *Euph* **the c.** (*menopause*) le retour d'âge

VT 1 (*substitute, switch*) changer, changer de; **to c. one's name** changer de nom; **she's going to c. her name to Parker** elle va prendre le nom de Parker; **to c. a fuse** changer un fusible; **to c. one's clothes** changer de vêtements, se changer; **to c. trains** changer de train; **they're going to c. the guard at 11 o'clock** ils vont faire la relève de *ou* relever la garde à 11 heures; **to c. sides** changer de côté; *Sport* **to c. ends** changer de camp; **this old desk has changed hands many times** ce vieux bureau a changé maintes fois de mains; **to c. one's mind** changer d'avis; **I've changed my mind about him** j'ai changé d'avis *ou* d'idée à son égard; **you'd better c. your ways** tu ferais bien de t'amender; **to c. the subject** changer de sujet; **don't c. the subject!** ne détourne pas la conversation!; **to c. gear** changer de vitesse; **to c. one's tune** changer de ton

2 (*exchange*) changer; **when are you thinking of changing your car?** quand pensez-vous changer de voiture?; **if the shoes are too small we'll c. them for you** si les chaussures sont trop petites nous vous les changerons; **to c. places with sb** changer de place avec qn; *Fig* **I wouldn't want to c. places with him!** je n'aimerais pas être à sa place!; **I'd like to c. my pounds into dollars** j'aimerais changer mes livres contre des *ou* en dollars; **does this bank c. money?** est-ce que cette banque fait le change?; **can you c. a ten-pound note?** (*into coins*) pouvez-vous me donner la monnaie d'un billet de dix livres?

3 (*modify, transform*) changer, transformer; **there's no point in trying to c. him** c'est inutile d'essayer de le changer; **the illness completely changed his personality** la maladie a complètement transformé son caractère; **to c. sb/sth into sth** changer qn/qch en qch; **the prince was changed into a frog** le prince fut changé en grenouille

4 (*baby, sheets, bed*) changer; **the baby needs changing** le bébé a besoin d'être changé

VI 1 (*alter, turn*) changer; (*luck, wind*) tourner; **to c. for the better/worse** changer en mieux/pire; **nothing will make him c.** rien ne le changera, il ne changera jamais; **wait for the lights to c.** attendez que le feu passe au vert; **winter changed to spring** le printemps a succédé à l'hiver; **the wind has changed** le vent a changé *ou* tourné

2 (*become transformed*) se changer, se transformer; **to c. into sth** se transformer en qch; **the ogre changed into a mouse** l'ogre s'est transformé en souris; **the country had changed from dictatorship to democracy overnight** en une nuit, le pays était passé de la dictature à la démocratie; **the lights changed from green to amber** les feux sont passés du vert à l'orange; **to c. from one system to another** passer d'un système à un autre

3 (*change clothing*) se changer; **she's gone upstairs to c.** elle est montée se changer; **they changed out of their uniforms** ils ont enlevé leurs uniformes; **he changed into a pair of jeans** il s'est changé et a mis un jean; **I'm going to c. into something warmer** je vais mettre quelque chose de plus chaud

4 (*transportation*) changer; **is it a direct flight or do I have to c.?** est-ce que le vol est direct ou faut-il changer?; **we had to c. twice** nous avons eu deux correspondances *ou* deux changements; **all c.!** (*announcement*) tout le monde descend!

5 *Br* **she changed into fourth gear** elle a passé la quatrième

6 (*moon*) entrer dans une nouvelle phase

• **for a change ADV it's nice to see you smiling for a c.** c'est bien de te voir sourire pour une fois; **he was early for a c.** pour une fois il était en avance

▸▸ *Euph* **the change of life** le retour d'âge; **change machine** distributeur *m* de monnaie; *Com* **change management** gestion *f* du changement; *Am* **change purse** porte-monnaie *m inv*

▸ **change down VI** *Aut* rétrograder; **he changed down into third** il est passé en troisième

▸ **change over VI 1** *Br* (*switch*) **he changed over from smoking cigarettes to smoking cigars** il s'est mis à fumer des cigares à la place de cigarettes; **the country has changed over to nuclear power** le pays est passé au nucléaire; *TV* **to c. over (to another channel)** passer sur une autre chaîne; *TV* **why don't we c. over to ITV?** et si on mettait ITV? **2** *Sport* (*change positions*) changer de côté

▸ **change up VI** *Aut* passer la vitesse supérieure; **he changed up into third** il a passé la troisième, il est passé en troisième

changeability [ˌtʃeɪndʒə'bɪlɪtɪ] **N 1** (*variability*) variabilité *f* **2** (*capriciousness, fickleness*) changements *mpl*

changeable ['tʃeɪndʒəbəl] **ADJ 1** (*variable*) variable; **c. weather** temps *m* variable *ou* instable **2** (*capricious, fickle*) changeant, inconstant

changeless ['tʃeɪndʒlɪs] **ADJ** immuable, inaltérable

changeling ['tʃeɪndʒlɪŋ] **N** = enfant substitué par les fées au véritable enfant d'un couple

changeover ['tʃeɪndʒˌəʊvə(r)] **N 1** (*switch*) changement *m*, passage *m*; (*after election*) relève *f*; **the c. to computers went smoothly** le passage à l'informatisation s'est fait en douceur **2** *Br Sport* changement *m* de côté; (*in relay race*) passage *m* du témoin

changing ['tʃeɪndʒɪŋ] **ADJ** qui change; **we're living in a c. world** nous vivons dans un monde en évolution
N changement *m*

▸▸ ***the Changing of the Guard*** la relève de la garde; *Br* ***changing room*** (*in sports centre, gym*) vestiaire *m*; (*in shop*) cabine *f* d'essayage; ***changing table*** table *f* à langer

channel ['tʃænəl] (*Br pt & pp* **channelled**, *cont* **channelling**, *Am pt & pp* **channeled**, *cont* **channeling**) **N 1** (*broad strait*) détroit *m*, bras *m* de mer; **the (English) C.** la Manche

2 (*river bed*) lit *m*; *Naut* (*navigable course*) chenal *m*, passe *f*

3 (*passage* ▸ *for gases, liquids*) canal *m*, conduite *f*; (▸ *for electrical signals*) piste *f*

4 (*furrow, groove*) sillon *m*; (*on a column*) cannelure *f*; (*in a street*) caniveau *m*

5 *TV* chaîne *f*; **the film is on C. 2** le film est sur la deuxième chaîne

6 *Rad* bande *f*

7 *Fig* (*means*) canal *m*, voie *f*; **to go through (the) official channels** suivre la filière officielle; **through diplomatic channels** par voie diplomatique; **channels of communication** canaux *mpl* de communication; **there were still channels of communication open** la communication n'était pas totalement interrompue

8 *Comput* (*of communication, data flow, for IRC*) canal *m*

VT 1 *Fig* (*direct*) canaliser, diriger; **the government wants to c. resources to those who need them most** le gouvernement veut affecter les ressources en priorité à ceux qui en ont le plus besoin; **she needs to c. her energies into some useful work** elle a besoin de canaliser son énergie à effectuer du travail utile **2** (*land*) creuser des rigoles dans; (*river*) canaliser; (*gas, water*) acheminer (par des conduites)

▸▸ *Com* ***channel of distribution*** circuit *m* de distribution, canal *m* de distribution; ***Channel Four*** = chaîne de télévision privée britannique à vocation culturelle; ***Channel ferry*** ferry *m* transmanche *inv*; *Fam* ***channel hopper*** zappeur(euse) *m,f*; *Fam* ***channel hopping*** zapping *m*; ***Channel Islander*** = habitant des îles Anglo-Normandes; ***the Channel Islands*** les îles *fpl* Anglo-Normandes; *Fam* ***channel surfing*** zapping *m*; ***the Channel Tunnel*** le tunnel sous la Manche, l'Eurotunnel *m*

channel-hop VI *TV Fam* zapper

chant [tʃɑːnt] **N 1** *Mus* mélopée *f*; *Rel* psalmodie *f* **2** (*slogan, cry*) chant *m* scandé

VT 1 *Mus* chanter; *Rel* psalmodier **2** (*slogans*) scander

VI 1 *Mus* chanter une mélopée; *Rel* psalmodier **2** (*crowd, demonstrators*) scander des slogans

> Note that the French verb **chanter** is a false friend and is never a translation for the English verb **to chant**. It means **to sing**.

chantey = **shanty**

chanting ['tʃɑːntɪŋ] **ADJ** (*voice*) monotone, traînant

N 1 *Mus* mélopée *f*; *Rel* chants *mpl*, psalmodie *f* **2** (*of slogans*) slogans *mpl* (scandés)

chantry ['tʃɑːntrɪ] **N** *Arch Rel* chantrerie *f*, chanterie *f*

chaos ['keɪɒs] **N** chaos *m*; **it'll be c. if you try to introduce these changes** ça va être la pagaille si tu fais ces changements; **the country is in a state of c.** le pays est dans un état de confusion totale; **our plans were thrown into c.** nos projets ont été bouleversés

▸▸ ***chaos theory*** théorie *f* du chaos

chaotic [keɪ'ɒtɪk] **ADJ** chaotique

chaotically [keɪ'ɒtɪklɪ] **ADV** chaotiquement; **clothes all c. piled into one drawer** vêtements tous mis en pagaille dans un tiroir

chap [tʃæp] (*pt & pp* **chapped**, *cont* **chapping**) **N 1** *Br Fam* (*man*) type *m*; **he's a nice c.** c'est un brave type; **be a good c. and tell him I'm not in** sois sympa et dis-lui que je ne suis pas là; **he's gone broke, poor c.** il a fait faillite, le pauvre; *Old-fashioned* **how are you, old c.?** comment allez-vous, mon vieux? **2** (*sore*) gerçure *f*, crevasse *f*

VT (*skin*) gercer, crevasser

VI (*skin*) (se) gercer, se crevasser

chapel ['tʃæpəl] **N 1** (*in church, school etc*) chapelle *f* **2** *Br* (*Nonconformist church*) temple *m*; *Scot* (*Catholic church*) église *f* catholique **3** *Br* (*of trade unionists*) = membres du syndicat dans une

maison d'édition ou la rédaction d'un journal
▸▸ ***chapel of rest*** = chambre mortuaire dans une entreprise de pompes funèbres

chaperon, chaperone ['ʃæpərəʊn] **N** chaperon *m*; **her aunt acted as her chaperone** sa tante lui servait de chaperon
VT chaperonner; *Fam* **don't worry, I'll chaperone you!** ne t'inquiète pas, je te servirai de chaperon

chaplain ['tʃæplɪn] **N** aumônier *m*; *(in private chapel)* chapelain *m*

chaplaincy ['tʃæplɪnsɪ] **N** aumônerie *f*
COMP *(work, duties)* de l'aumônier

chappie ['tʃæpɪ] *Old-fashioned* = **chap N 1**

chapter ['tʃæptə(r)] **N 1** *(of book)* chapitre *m*; **it's in c. three** c'est dans le troisième chapitre; **she can give** *or* **quote (you) c. and verse on the subject** elle peut citer toutes les autorités en la matière
2 *(era)* chapitre *m*; **this closed a particularly violent c. in our history** ceci marqua la fin d'un chapitre particulièrement violent de notre histoire
3 *(series)* succession *f*, cascade *f*; **a c. of accidents** une série d'accidents *ou* de malheurs, une série noire
4 *(of organization)* branche *f*, section *f*
5 *Rel* chapitre *m*
▸▸ *Rel* ***chapter house*** salle *f* capitulaire

char [tʃɑː(r)] *(pt & pp* **charred**, *cont* **charring)** **VT 1** *(reduce to charcoal)* carboniser, réduire en charbon **2** *(scorch)* griller, brûler légèrement
VI 1 *(scorch)* brûler; *(blacken)* noircir **2** *Br Fam Old-fashioned (clean)* faire des ménages
N 1 *Fam Old-fashioned (cleaner)* femme *f* de ménage **2** *Br Fam Old-fashioned (tea)* thé *m* **3** *Ich* omble *m* chevalier

charabanc ['ʃærəbæŋ] **N** *Old-fashioned* autocar *m* (de tourisme)

character ['kærəktə(r)] **N 1** *(nature, temperament)* caractère *m*; **the war completely changed his c.** la guerre a complètement transformé son caractère; **his remark was quite in/out of c.** cette remarque lui ressemblait tout à fait/ne lui ressemblait pas du tout
2 *(aspect, quality)* caractère *m*; **it was the vindictive c. of the punishment she objected to** c'était le caractère vindicatif du châtiment qu'elle désapprouvait
3 *(determination, integrity)* caractère *m*; **she's a woman of great c.** c'est une femme qui a beaucoup de caractère; **he lacks c.** il manque de caractère
4 *(distinction, originality)* caractère *m*; **to have c.** avoir du caractère; **the house had (great) c.** la maison avait beaucoup de caractère; **her face is full of c.** son visage a beaucoup de caractère
5 *(unusual person)* personnage *m*; **he's a bit of a c.** c'est un personnage; **she seems to attract all sorts of characters** elle semble attirer toutes sortes d'individus; **he's quite a c.!** c'est un phénomène *ou* un sacré numéro!
6 *Pej (person)* individu *m*; **there's a suspicious c. loitering outside** il y a un individu suspect qui rôde dehors
7 *Cin, Literature & Theat* personnage *m*; **the main c.** le personnage principal, le protagoniste; **Chaplin plays two different characters in 'The Great Dictator'** Chaplin joue deux rôles différents dans 'Le Dictateur'
8 *Typ* caractère *m*; **in Greek characters** en caractères grecs; *Typ & Comput* **characters per inch/second** caractères *mpl* par pouce/seconde
▸▸ *Cin & Theat* ***character actor*** acteur *m* de genre; ***character assassination*** diffamation *f*; *Comput* ***character code*** code *m* de caractère; *Cin & TV* ***character comedy*** comédie *f* de caractères; *Comput & Typ* ***character count*** nombre *m* de caractères; **to do a c. count** compter les caractères; *Comput & Typ* ***character font*** fonte *f* de caractère; *Comput* ***character generator*** générateur *m* de caractères; *Comput* ***character insert*** insertion *f* de caractère; *Cin & Theat* ***character part*** rôle *m* de composition; *Comput* ***character recognition*** reconnaissance *f* de caractères; *Br* ***character references*** références *fpl*; *Cin & Theat* ***character role*** rôle *m* de composition; *Comput* ***character set*** jeu *m* de caractères; ***character sketch*** portrait *m ou* description *f* rapide; *Comput* ***character space*** espace *m*; *Comput* ***character spacing*** espacement *m* des caractères; *Comput* ***character string*** chaîne *f* de caractères; *Law* ***character witness*** témoin *m* de moralité

character-forming, *Br* **character-building** **ADJ** qui forme le caractère; **it's c.** ça forme le caractère

characteristic [ˌkærəktəˈrɪstɪk] **ADJ** caractéristique; **she refused all honours with c. humility** elle refusa tous les honneurs avec l'humilité qui la caractérisait; **this attitude is c. of him** cette attitude lui correspond bien, c'est bien de lui
N 1 *(feature)* caractéristique *f*; **national characteristics** les caractères *mpl* nationaux **2** *Math (of logarithm)* caractéristique *f*

characteristically [ˌkærəktəˈrɪstɪklɪ] **ADV** de façon caractéristique; **he was c. generous with his praise** comme on pouvait s'y attendre, il fut prodigue de ses compliments *ou* il ne ménagea pas ses éloges; **c., she put her family first** elle fit passer sa famille en premier, ce qui était bien dans son caractère *ou* lui ressemblait bien

characterization, -isation [ˌkærəktəraɪˈzeɪʃən] **N 1** *Formal (description)* caractérisation *f* **2** *Cin, Literature & Theat* représentation *f ou* peinture *f* des personnages; **he's very poor at c.** *(writer)* ses personnages ne sont pas très convaincants; *(actor)* il n'a aucun talent pour l'interprétation

characterize, -ise ['kærəktəraɪz] **VT** caractériser; **the long pauses that c. his speech** les longs silences qui caractérisent son discours; **his music is characterized by a sense of joy** sa musique se caractérise par une impression de joie; **Shakespeare characterized Henry VI as a weak but pious king** Shakespeare a dépeint Henri VI comme un roi faible mais pieux

characterless ['kærəktəlɪs] **ADJ** sans caractère

charade [ʃəˈrɑːd] **N** *(pretence)* feinte *f*; **the trial was a complete c.!** c'était une véritable parodie de procès!
• **charades NPL** *(game)* charade *f* en action; **let's play charades** jouons aux charades

> Note that in most cases, the French word **charade** refers to a type of word game.

charcoal ['tʃɑːkəʊl] **N 1** *(fuel)* charbon *m* de bois **2** *Art* fusain *m* **3** *(colour)* gris *m* foncé *(inv)*
ADJ gris foncé *(inv)*
COMP 1 *(fuel)* à charbon **2** *Art* au charbon, au fusain
▸▸ ***charcoal burner*** charbonnier *m*; ***charcoal drawing*** croquis *m* au fusain; ***charcoal grey*** gris *m* foncé *inv*; ***charcoal pencil*** crayon *m* fusain; ***charcoal stove*** réchaud *m* à charbon de bois

charcoal-broiled **ADJ** *Am Culin* grillé au charbon de bois

chard [tʃɑːd] **N** *Bot & Culin* blette *f*, bette *inv*

Chardonnay ['ʃɑːdəˌneɪ] **N** *(wine)* chardonnay *m*, chardonnay *m*

CHARGE [tʃɑːdʒ]

N	
• frais **1**	• inculpation **2**
• accusation **3**	• responsabilité **4**
• charge **6, 7**	
VT	
• faire payer **1**	• accuser **3**
• inculper **4**	• charger **5, 7, 8**
VI	
• demander, prendre **1**	• se précipiter **2**
• charger **2, 3**	• se recharger **4**

N 1 *Com & Fin (fee, cost)* frais *mpl*; *(to an account)* imputation *f*; **administrative charges** frais *mpl* de dossier; **postal/telephone charges** frais *mpl* postaux/téléphoniques; **there's a c. of one pound for use of the locker** il faut payer une livre pour utiliser la consigne automatique; **is there any extra c. for a single room?** est-ce qu'il faut payer un supplément pour une chambre à un lit?; **what's the c. for delivery?** la livraison coûte combien?; **there's no c. for children** c'est gratuit pour les enfants; **it's free of c.** c'est gratuit; **there's a small admission c. to the museum** il y a un petit droit d'entrée au musée; *Am* **will that be cash or c.?** vous payez comptant ou vous le portez à votre compte?
2 *Law (accusation)* chef *m* d'accusation, inculpation *f*; *(judge's address to the jury)* réquisitoire *m*; **he was arrested on a c. of conspiracy** il a été arrêté sous l'inculpation d'association criminelle; **you are under arrest – on what c.?** vous êtes en état d'arrestation – pour quel motif?; **to bring** *or* **to file charges against sb** porter plainte *ou* déposer une plainte contre qn; **a c. of drunk driving was brought against the driver** le conducteur a été mis en examen pour conduite en état d'ivresse; **the judge threw out the c.** le juge a retiré l'inculpation; **she was acquitted on both charges** elle a été acquittée des deux chefs d'inculpation; **some of the charges may be dropped** certains des chefs d'accusation pourraient être retirés; **he pleaded guilty to the c. of robbery** il a plaidé coupable à l'accusation de vol
3 *(allegation)* accusation *f*; **the government rejected charges that it was mismanaging the economy** le gouvernement a rejeté l'accusation selon laquelle il gérait mal l'économie
4 *(command, control)* **who's (the person) in c. here?** qui est le responsable ici?; **she's in c. of public relations** elle s'occupe des relations publiques; **can I leave you in c. of the shop?** puis-je vous laisser la responsabilité du magasin?; **she was in c. of consumer protection** elle était responsable de la protection des consommateurs; **I was put in c. of the investigation** on m'a confié la responsabilité de l'enquête; **he was put in c. of 100 men** on a mis 100 hommes sous sa responsabilité; **to take c. of sth** prendre en charge qch, prendre *ou* assumer la direction de qch; **she took c. of organizing the festival** elle a pris en charge l'organisation du festival; **he took c. of his nephew** il a pris son neveu en charge
5 *Formal (dependent)* = personne confiée à la garde d'une autre; *(pupil)* élève *mf*; **the nanny is out for a walk with her charges** la nourrice est partie se promener avec les enfants qu'elle garde *ou* dont elle a la charge
6 *Mil (attack)* charge *f*; **soldiers made several charges against the demonstrators** les soldats ont chargé les manifestants à plusieurs reprises; *Br Hist* **the C. of the Light Brigade** la Charge de la brigade légère
7 *Elec & Phys* charge *f*; **I left it on c. all night** je l'ai laissé charger toute la nuit; *Am Fam Fig* **to get a c. out of sth/doing sth** *(thrill)* s'éclater *ou* prendre son pied avec qch/en faisant qch
8 *Her* meuble *m*
VT 1 *Com & Fin (person)* faire payer; *(sum)* faire payer, prendre; *(commission)* prélever; **how much would you c. to take us to the airport?** combien prendriez-vous pour nous emmener à l'aéroport?; **they didn't c. us for the coffee** ils ne nous ont pas fait payer les cafés; **you will be charged for postage** les frais postaux seront à votre charge
2 *Com & Fin (defer payment of)* **c. the bill to my account** mettez le montant de la facture sur mon compte; **I charged all my expenses to the company** j'ai mis tous mes frais sur le compte de la société; *Am* **can I c. this jacket?** *(with a credit card)* puis-je payer cette veste avec ma carte (de crédit)?
3 *(allege)* accuser; **to c. that sb has done sth** accuser qn d'avoir fait qch; **he charged his partner with having stolen thousands of pounds from the firm** il a accusé son associé d'avoir volé des milliers de livres à l'entreprise
4 *Law* inculper; **I'm charging you with the murder of X** je vous inculpe du meurtre de X
5 *(attack)* charger; **the police charged the crowd** les forces de l'ordre ont chargé la foule
6 *Formal (command, entrust)* **I was charged with guarding the prisoner** je fus chargé de la surveillance du prisonnier; **she was charged with the task of interviewing applicants** on lui confia la tâche d'interroger les candidats
7 *Elec* charger
8 *Formal (fill)* charger; **to c. sb's glass** remplir le verre de qn
VI 1 *(demand in payment)* demander, prendre; **do you c. for delivery?** est-ce que vous faites payer la livraison?; **he doesn't c.** il ne demande *ou* prend rien
2 *(rush ▸ person)* se précipiter; *(▸ animal)* charger; **the crowd charged across the square** la foule s'est ruée à travers la place; **she charged into/out of her office** elle entra dans son/sortit de son bureau au pas de charge

3 *Mil (attack)* charger, donner l'assaut; **c.!** à l'assaut!
4 *Elec* se charger, se recharger
▸▸ *Am Com & Fin* ***charge account*** compte *m* crédit d'achats, compte *m* accréditif; *Com & Fin* ***charge card*** carte *f* de paiement; *Br* ***charge hand*** sous-chef *m* d'équipe; *Br* ***charge nurse*** infirmier(ère) *m,f* en chef; *Br Law* ***charge sheet*** procès-verbal *m (établi par la police avant le passage d'un prévenu devant un tribunal)*

▸**charge down** VT SEP *Sport (ball)* contrer

▸**charge off** VT SEP *Am Fin (capital)* amortir, imputer à l'exercice; **we were obliged to c. off the whole operation** il a fallu imputer l'intégralité du coût de l'opération à l'exercice

▸**charge up** VT SEP **1** *Fin & Com (bill)* **to c. sth up to sb's account** mettre qch sur le compte de qn; **could you c. it up?** pourriez-vous le mettre sur mon compte? **2** *Elec* charger, recharger
VI *(battery)* se (re)charger

chargeable [ˈtʃɑːdʒəbəl] ADJ **1** *Com & Fin (to an account)* imputable; **to be c. to sb** *(payable by)* être à la charge de qn, être pris(e) en charge par qn; **travelling expenses are c. to the employer** les frais de déplacement sont à la charge de l'employeur **2** *Law* **a c. offence** un délit
▸▸ *Fin* ***chargeable expenses*** frais *mpl* facturables; *Fin* ***chargeable gain*** bénéfice *m* imposable

charge-cooled [-kuːld] ADJ *Aut (engine)* suralimenté refroidi

chargé d'affaires [ˌʃɑːʒeɪdæˈfeə(r)] *(pl* **chargés d'affaires**) N *Pol* chargé *m* d'affaires

charger [ˈtʃɑːdʒə(r)] N **1** *Elec* chargeur *m* **2** *Arch or Literary (horse)* cheval *m* de bataille

charily [ˈtʃeərəlɪ] ADV **1** *(cautiously)* précautionneusement **2** *(sparingly)* avec parcimonie

chariot [ˈtʃærɪət] N char *m*

charioteer [ˌtʃærɪəˈtɪə(r)] N aurige *m*

charisma [kəˈrɪzmə] N charisme *m*; **to have c.** avoir du charisme

charismatic [ˌkærɪzˈmætɪk] ADJ charismatique

charitable [ˈtʃærətəbəl] ADJ **1** *(generous, kind)* charitable **2** *(cause, institution)* de bienfaisance, de charité; **a c. donation** un don fait par charité; **c. works** les bonnes œuvres *fpl*
▸▸ ***charitable organization*** œuvre *f* de bienfaisance *ou* de charité; ***charitable status*** statut *m* d'organisation caritative; ***charitable trust*** fondation *f* d'utilité publique

charitably [ˈtʃærətəblɪ] ADV charitablement

charity [ˈtʃærətɪ] *(pl* **charities**) N **1** *Rel* charité *f*; *(generosity, kindness)* charité *f*; **he bought the painting out of c.** il a acheté le tableau par charité; **an act of c.** une action charitable, un acte de charité **2** *(help to the needy)* charité *f*; **to live on c.** vivre d'aumônes; **I don't want your c.** je ne veux pas que tu me fasses la charité; **they raised £10,000 for c.** ils ont collecté 10 000 livres pour les bonnes œuvres; *Prov* **c. begins at home** charité bien ordonnée commence par soi-même **3** *(association)* organisation *f* caritative; œuvre *f* de bienfaisance; **registered c.** œuvre *f* reconnue d'utilité publique; **we're not a c.!** nous ne sommes pas des philanthropes *ou* une organisation de bienfaisance!
▸▸ ***charity ball*** bal *m* de bienfaisance; ***the Charity Commission*** = commission gouvernementale britannique contrôlant les associations caritatives; *Br Ftbl Formerly* ***Charity Shield*** = match de football opposant l'équipe qui remporte la "FA Cup" à celle qui arrive en tête du championnat d'Angleterre; ***charity shop*** = magasin dont les employés sont des bénévoles et dont les bénéfices servent à subventionner une œuvre d'utilité publique; ***charity work*** bénévolat *m*

charlady [ˈtʃɑːˌleɪdɪ] *(pl* **charladies**) N *Br Old-fashioned* femme *f* de ménage

charlatan [ˈʃɑːlətən] N charlatan *m*
ADJ charlatanesque

charleston [ˈtʃɑːlstən] N charleston *m*; **to do the c.** danser le charleston

charley horse [ˈtʃɑːlɪ-] N *(UNCOUNT) Am Fam* crampe▫ *f*

charlie [ˈtʃɑːlɪ] N **1** *Br Fam (idiot)* cloche *f*; **I felt a right** *or* **proper c.** je me suis senti vraiment cloche **2** *Fam Drugs slang (cocaine)* coke *f*

charlotte [ˈʃɑːlət] N *Culin (baked)* charlotte *f*; **apple c.** charlotte *f* aux pommes

charm [tʃɑːm] N **1** *(appeal, attraction)* charme *m*; **he has great c.** il a beaucoup de charme; **to turn on the c.** faire du charme; *Ironic* **what c. school did you go to?** oh, comme tu parles bien! **2** *(spell)* charme *m*, sortilège *m*; *(talisman)* amulette *f*, fétiche *m*; **a lucky c.** un porte-bonheur; **to work like a c.** marcher à merveille *ou* à la perfection **3** *(piece of jewellery)* breloque *f*
VT **1** *(please, delight)* charmer, séduire; **I was charmed by his gentle manner** je fus charmé par ses douces manières; **she charmed him into accepting the invitation** elle l'a si bien enjôlé qu'il a accepté l'invitation **2** *(of magician)* charmer, ensorceler; *(of snake charmer)* charmer
• **charms** NPL charmes *mpl*
▸▸ ***charm bracelet*** bracelet *m* à breloques; ***charm offensive*** offensive *f* de charme

charmer [ˈtʃɑːmə(r)] N charmeur(euse) *m,f*

charming [ˈtʃɑːmɪŋ] ADJ charmant; *Ironic* **c.!** c'est charmant!

charmingly [ˈtʃɑːmɪŋlɪ] ADV de façon charmante; **he seemed c. innocent** il paraissait d'une innocence charmante

charring [ˈtʃɑːrɪŋ] N carbonisation *f*

chart [tʃɑːt] N **1** *Naut* carte *f* marine; *Astron* carte *f* (du ciel)
2 *(table)* tableau *m*; *(graph) & Med* courbe *f*
3 *Astrol* horoscope *m*
4 *Comput* graphique *m*
VT **1** *Naut (seas, waterway)* établir la carte de, faire un levé hydrographique de; *Astron (stars)* porter sur la carte **2** *(record* ▸ *on a table, graph)* faire la courbe de; *Fig* (▸ *progress, development)* rendre compte de; *Fig* **the book charts the rise of the labour movement** ce livre retrace la montée du mouvement travailliste; **this graph charts sales over the last ten years** ce graphique montre l'évolution des ventes au cours des dix dernières années
• **charts** NPL *Mus* hit-parade *m*; **she's (got a record) in the charts** elle est au hit-parade; **it's number one in** *or* **it's top of the charts** c'est le numéro un au hit-parade
▸▸ ***chart topper*** numéro *m* un

charter [ˈtʃɑːtə(r)] N **1** *(statement of rights)* charte *f*; *(of a business, organization, university)* statuts *mpl*; **the United Nations C.** la Charte de l'Organisation des Nations unies **2** *(lease, licence)* affrètement *m*; *(charter flight)* charter *m*; *Br* **we've hired three coaches on c.** nous avons affrété trois autocars
VT **1** *(establish)* accorder une charte à **2** *(hire, rent)* affréter
▸▸ ***charter company*** affréteur *m*; ***charter flight*** (vol *m*) charter *m*; ***charter plane*** (avion *m*) charter *m*

chartered [ˈtʃɑːtəd] ADJ *(plane, ship, coach)* affrété
▸▸ *Br* ***chartered accountant*** expert-comptable *m*; ***chartered surveyor*** expert *m* immobilier

charterer [ˈtʃɑːtərə(r)] N affréteur *m*, nolisateur *m*

chartering [ˈtʃɑːtərɪŋ] N *(of plane, ship, coach)* affrètement *m*; *(at reduced rates)* charterisation *f*

charwoman [ˈtʃɑːˌwʊmən] *(pl* **charwomen** [-ˈwɪmɪn]) N *Br Old-fashioned (cleaner)* femme *f* de ménage▫

chary [ˈtʃeərɪ] ADJ **1** *(wary)* précautionneux; **he's c. of allowing strangers into his home** il hésite à accueillir des gens qu'il ne connaît pas chez lui **2** *(ungenerous)* parcimonieux; **he was c. of praise** il faisait rarement des éloges, il était avare de compliments

chase [tʃeɪs] VT **1** *(pursue)* poursuivre; **two police cars chased the van** deux voitures de police ont pris la camionnette en chasse; **the dog chased the postman down the street** le chien a poursuivi le facteur jusqu'en bas de la rue; **the reporters were chased from** *or* **out of the house** les journalistes furent chassés de la maison
2 *(amorously)* courir (après); **he's always chasing young women** il est toujours à courir (après) les filles
3 *(try to obtain)* courir après; **there are thousands of applicants chasing only a few jobs** il y a des milliers de candidats qui courent après quelques postes seulement
4 *(engrave* ▸ *gold, silver)* ciseler
5 *Metal (emboss)* repousser
VI *(rush)* **she chased all around London to find a wedding dress** elle a parcouru *ou* fait tout Londres pour trouver une robe de mariée
N **1** *(pursuit)* poursuite *f*; **the hounds gave c. to the fox** la meute a pris le renard en chasse; **the prisoner climbed over the wall and the guards gave c.** le prisonnier escalada le mur et les gardiens se lancèrent à sa poursuite
2 *Cycling* poursuite *f*
3 *Hunt (sport, land, game)* chasse *f*
4 *Horseracing* steeple *m*
5 *(groove)* saignée *f*
6 *Typ* châssis *m*
▸▸ ***chase film, chase movie*** film *m* de poursuite; *Cin* ***chase scene*** scène *f* de poursuite

> Note that the French verb **chasser** is a false friend. Its most common meaning is **to hunt**.

▸**chase after** VT INSEP être à la poursuite de, poursuivre; *(amorously)* courir après; **we've been all over town chasing after that spare part** nous avons dû faire tout le tour de la ville pour trouver cette pièce détachée

▸**chase away, chase off** VT SEP chasser

▸**chase up** VT SEP *Br* **1** *(information)* rechercher **2** *(organization, person)* relancer; **can you c. up the manager for me?** pouvez-vous relancer le directeur à propos de ce que je lui ai demandé?; **I had to c. him up for the £50 he owed me** j'ai dû lui réclamer les 50 livres qu'il me devait; **I'll c. the matter up for you** je vais tenter d'activer les choses pour vous

chaser [ˈtʃeɪsə(r)] N **1** *(drink)* = alcool bu après une bière ou vice versa; **a pint of beer and a whisky c.** une pinte de bière suivie d'un whisky **2** *(pursuer)* chasseur *m* **3** *Horseracing* cheval *m* de course

chasing [ˈtʃeɪsɪŋ] N **1** *(engraving* ▸ *of gold, silver)* ciselage *m*, ciselure *f* **2** *Metal (embossing)* repoussage *m*

chasm [ˈkæzəm] N *also Fig* abîme *m*, gouffre *m*

chassis [ˈʃæsɪ] *(pl* **inv** [-sɪz]) N **1** *Aut* châssis *m*; *Aviat* train *m* d'atterrissage **2** *Fam (body)* châssis *m*
▸▸ ***chassis number*** numéro *m* de châssis

chaste [tʃeɪst] ADJ **1** *(sexually)* chaste **2** *(speech, taste, style)* sobre, simple

chastely [ˈtʃeɪstlɪ] ADV **1** *(sexually)* chastement **2** *(speak, dress)* sobrement

chasten [ˈtʃeɪsən] VT *Formal* **1** *(subdue, humble)* corriger, maîtriser; *(pride)* rabaisser **2** *(punish, reprimand)* châtier, punir

chasteness [ˈtʃeɪstnɪs] N caractère *m* chaste

chastening [ˈtʃeɪsənɪŋ] ADJ **prison had a c. effect on him** la prison l'a assagi; **it's a c. thought** c'est une pensée plutôt décourageante

chastise [tʃæˈstaɪz] VT **1** *(reprimand, criticize)* réprimander **2** *Formal (punish)* châtier; *(beat)* corriger

chastisement [ˈtʃæstɪzmənt] N *Formal (punishment)* châtiment *m*; *(beating)* correction *f*

chastity [ˈtʃæstətɪ] N chasteté *f*; **to take a vow of c.** faire vœu de chasteté
▸▸ ***chastity belt*** ceinture *f* de chasteté

chasuble [ˈtʃæzjʊbəl] N *Rel* chasuble *f*

chat [tʃæt] *(pt & pp* **chatted**, *cont* **chatting**) VI **1** bavarder, causer; **we were just chatting about this and that** nous causions de choses et d'autres; **he was chatting to the man next to him** il bavardait avec l'homme qui était à côté de lui **2** *Comput* bavarder, *Can* clavarder
N **1** *(conversation)* petite conversation *f*, causette *f*; **to have a c. with sb** bavarder avec qn; *(about a problem, work performance etc)* dire un mot à qn; **it's time we had a little c.** il est temps que nous ayons une petite discussion; **the c. at work is all about cars** au travail, on ne discute que de voitures; **we had a nice c. over lunch** nous

avons eu une conversation agréable pendant le déjeuner **2** *Comput (on Internet)* messagerie *f* de dialogue en direct, bavardage *m*, chat *m*, *Can* clavardage *m*

▸▸ *Comput* ***chat room*** site *m* de bavardage, salon *m* (de bavardage), *Can* bavardoir *m*; *Br TV* ***chat show*** causerie *f* télévisée, talk-show *m*; *Br TV* ***chat show host*** présentateur(trice) *m,f* de talk-show

▸ **chat up** **VT SEP** *Br Fam* baratiner, draguer; *Fig* **to c. up a client** baratiner un client

chattel [ˈtʃætəl] **N** *Law* bien *m* meuble; **goods and chattels** biens *mpl* et effets *mpl*

chatter [ˈtʃætə(r)] **VI 1** *(person)* papoter, bavarder; *(bird)* jaser, jacasser; *(monkey)* crier; **she sat quietly while Maria chattered away** elle restait tranquillement assise tandis que Maria palabrait **2** *(machine)* cliqueter **3** *(teeth)* claquer; **my teeth were chattering from** *or* **with the cold** j'avais tellement froid que je claquais des dents

N 1 *(of people)* bavardage *m*, papotage *m*; *(of birds)* jacassement *m*; *(of monkey)* cri *m* **2** *(of machines)* cliquetis *m* **3** *(of teeth)* claquement *m*

chatterbox [ˈtʃætəbɒks] **N** *Fam* moulin *m* à paroles

chatterer [ˈtʃætərə(r)] **N 1** *(talkative person)* bavard(e) *m,f* **2** *Zool* cotinga *m*

chattering [ˈtʃætərɪŋ] **N** *(of people)* bavardage *m*; *(of birds)* caquetage *m*; *(of monkeys)* babil *m*; *(of teeth)* claquement *m*; *(of machine-gun)* martèlement *m*

▸▸ *Pej* ***the chattering classes*** les intellectuels *mpl* qui s'écoutent parler

chatty [ˈtʃætɪ] **ADJ** *(person)* bavard; *(letter)* plein de bavardages; *(article)* écrit sur le ton de la conversation; **Mr Smith was very c.** *or* **in a very c. mood today** M. Smith était très bavard aujourd'hui

chat-up line **N** *Br Fam* = formule d'entrée en matière pour commencer à draguer quelqu'un; **that's his standard c.** c'est son baratin habituel quand il drague

chauffeur [ˈʃəʊfə(r)] **N** chauffeur *m*; **c.-driven** *(car)* avec chauffeur

VI travailler comme chauffeur, être chauffeur

VT conduire; **we were chauffeured to the airport** on nous a conduits à l'aéroport

chauvinism [ˈʃəʊvɪnɪzəm] **N** *(sexism)* machisme *m*, phallocratie *f*; *(nationalism)* chauvinisme *m*

chauvinist [ˈʃəʊvɪnɪst] **N** *(sexist)* phallocrate *m*, machiste *m*; *(nationalist)* chauvin(e) *m,f*

> Note that the French word **chauvin** only refers to patriotism.

chauvinistic [ʃəʊvɪˈnɪstɪk] **ADJ** *(sexist)* machiste, phallocrate; *(nationalist)* chauvin

> Note that the French word **chauvin** only refers to patriotism.

chav [tʃæv] **N** *Br Fam Pej* racaille *f*, lascar *m*

chavvy [ˈtʃævɪ] **ADJ** *Fam* qui fait racaille

cheap [tʃiːp] **ADJ 1** *(inexpensive)* bon marché *(inv)*, pas cher; **labour is cheaper in the Far East** la main-d'œuvre est moins chère en Extrême-Orient; **he bought a c. ticket to Australia** il a acheté un billet à prix *ou* tarif réduit pour l'Australie; **it works out cheaper to take a whole bottle** cela revient moins cher de prendre la bouteille entière; **it's c. to run** *(car)* elle est économique à l'entretien; *Fam* **he's very c.** *(shopkeeper)* il n'est pas cher; *Hum Ironic* **£100? it's c. at half the price!** 100 livres? c'est de l'arnaque!; **c. and cheerful** sans prétentions

2 *(poor quality)* de mauvaise qualité; *Br* **the furniture was c. and nasty** les meubles étaient de très mauvaise qualité

3 *(of little value)* de peu de valeur; **human life is c. in many countries** il y a beaucoup de pays où la vie humaine a peu de valeur

4 *(low, despicable)* **a c. joke** une plaisanterie de mauvais goût; **a c. remark** une remarque facile; **that was a c. shot** c'était vraiment mesquin comme critique; **she had made herself c. in her father's eyes** elle s'était rabaissée aux yeux de son père

5 *esp Am (stingy)* mesquin

ADV *(buy, get, sell)* bon marché; **I can get it for you cheaper** je peux vous le trouver pour moins cher; **clothes of that quality don't come c.** des vêtements de cette qualité coûtent cher; **it was going c.** c'était bon marché

• **on the cheap** **ADV** *Fam* **she furnished the house on the c.** elle a meublé la maison pour pas cher□; **they've got immigrants working for them on the c.** ils ont des immigrés qui travaillent pour eux au rabais□

▸▸ *Fin* ***cheap money*** argent *m* à bon marché; ***cheap rate*** tarif *m* réduit

cheapen [ˈtʃiːpən] **VT 1** *(lower, debase)* abaisser; **I wouldn't c. myself by accepting a bribe** je ne m'abaisserais pas à accepter un pot-de-vin **2** *(reduce the price of)* baisser le prix de

VI devenir moins cher

cheap-jack *Fam* **N** marchand *m* de bric-à-brac□, camelot□ *m*

ADJ 1 *(goods)* de pacotille **2** *(solution)* facile□; *(remark)* facile□, mesquin□

cheaply [ˈtʃiːplɪ] **ADV** à bon marché; **I can do the job more c.** je peux faire le travail à meilleur marché *ou* pour moins cher; **to eat out c.** manger dehors pour pas cher

cheapness [ˈtʃiːpnɪs] **N 1** *(low price)* bas prix *m* **2** *(poor quality)* mauvaise qualité *f*

cheapo [ˈtʃiːpəʊ] *Fam* **N** article *m* bas de gamme□

ADJ bas de gamme□, merdique

cheapskate [ˈtʃiːpskeɪt] **N** *Fam* radin(e) *m,f*, grippe-sou *m*

cheat [tʃiːt] **VT 1** *(defraud, swindle)* escroquer, léser; **to c. sb out of sth** escroquer qch à qn; **to feel cheated** se sentir lésé *ou* frustré; **to c. sb into doing sth** faire faire qch à qn en le trompant **2** *Fig Literary (deceive, trick)* duper; **to c. death** échapper à la mort

VI tricher; **she was expelled from university for cheating** elle fut renvoyée de l'université pour avoir triché aux examens

N 1 *(dishonest person)* tricheur(euse) *m,f*; *(crook, swindler)* escroc *m*, fraudeur(euse) *m,f* **2** *(dishonest practice)* tricherie *f*, tromperie *f* **3** *(in computer game)* cheat *m*

▸▸ *Am Fam* ***cheat sheet*** antisèche *m or f*

▸ **cheat on** **VT INSEP 1** *(falsify)* tricher sur **2** *(be unfaithful to)* tromper; **he cheats on his wife** il trompe sa femme

cheating [ˈtʃiːtɪŋ] **N 1** *(at cards, games)* tricherie *f*; *(at exams)* copiage *m*; **that's c.!** c'est de la triche! **2** *(fraud)* fraude *f* **3** *(UNCOUNT) (infidelity)* infidélité *f*, infidélités *fpl*

ADJ 1 *(dishonest)* malhonnête, trompeur **2** *(unfaithful, disloyal)* infidèle

CHECK [tʃek]

VT	
• contrôler **1**	• vérifier **1**
• enrayer **2**	• mettre au vestiaire **3**
• mettre à la consigne **3**	• cocher **4**
VI	
• vérifier **1**	• correspondre **2**
N	
• contrôle **1**	• enquête **2**
• frein **3**	• échec **4**
• addition **5**	• carreau **6**
• coche **7**	• chèque **8**
ADJ	
• à carreaux	

VT 1 *(inspect, examine)* contrôler, vérifier; *(confirm, substantiate)* vérifier; **she didn't c. her facts before writing the article** elle n'a pas vérifié les faits avant d'écrire son article; **the figures have to be checked** il faut vérifier les chiffres; **the doctor checked my blood pressure** le médecin a pris ma tension; **the inspector checked our tickets** le contrôleur a contrôlé nos billets; **to c. sth against sth** comparer qch à qch; **c. these names against the ones on the list** vérifie que ces noms sont les mêmes que ceux de la liste

2 *(contain, limit ▸ recession, inflation)* enrayer; *(▸ emotions, troops)* contenir; *(▸ urge)* réprimer; **to c. oneself** se retenir

3 *Am (coat, hat)* mettre au vestiaire; *(luggage)* mettre à la consigne

4 *Am (mark, tick)* cocher

5 *Chess* faire échec à

6 *Scot Fam (reprimand)* réprimander□

VI 1 *(confirm)* vérifier; **I'll have to c. with the accountant** je vais devoir vérifier auprès du comptable; **you'd better c. with her** vous feriez mieux de lui demander; **they usually have vacancies, but it's a good idea to c.** d'ordinaire, ils ont de la place, mais il vaut mieux s'en assurer *ou* vérifier

2 *(correspond)* correspondre, s'accorder (**with** avec)

3 *(pause, halt)* s'arrêter

N 1 *(examination, inspection)* contrôle *m*, vérification *f*; **the airline ordered checks on all their 747s** la compagnie aérienne a ordonné que des contrôles soient faits sur tous ses 747; **a routine c.** une vérification de routine

2 *(inquiry, investigation)* enquête *f*; **to do** *or* **to run a c. on sb** se renseigner sur qn; **to keep a c. on sb** observer qn

3 *(restraint)* frein *m*; **the House of Lords acts as a c. upon the House of Commons** la Chambre des lords met un frein au pouvoir de la Chambre des communes; *Pol* **(a system of) checks and balances** (un système d')équilibre *m* des pouvoirs; **he kept** *or* **held his anger in c.** il a contenu *ou* maîtrisé sa colère; **we could no longer hold** *or* **keep the enemy in c.** nous ne pouvions plus contenir l'ennemi

4 *Chess* échec *m*; **in c.** en échec; **c.!** échec au roi!

5 *Am (bill)* addition *f*; *(receipt for coats, luggage)* ticket *m*

6 *(square)* carreau *m*; **a skirt in black and white c.** une jupe à carreaux noirs et blancs

7 *Am (mark, tick)* coche *f*; **put a c. next to all the verbs** cochez tous les verbes

8 *Am (cheque)* chèque *m*

ADJ *(pattern, skirt)* à carreaux

▸▸ *Comput* ***check box*** case *f* de pointage, case *f* d'option; *Comput* ***check digit*** chiffre *m* de contrôle *ou* de vérification, clé *f*; *Mktg* ***check question*** question *f* de contrôle, question *f* filtre; *Mktg* ***check sample*** échantillon *m* témoin

▸ **check in** **VI 1** *(at airport)* se présenter à l'enregistrement **2** *(at hotel)* se présenter à la réception **3** *Am (phone)* **it's a little late, I'd better c. in with my parents** il se fait tard, il faudrait que je passe un coup de fil à mes parents

VT SEP 1 *(at airport ▸ baggage)* enregistrer

2 *(at hotel)* inscrire sur le registre

3 *(at cloakroom)* mettre au vestiaire; *(at left-luggage office)* mettre à la consigne

4 *Am (library book)* rapporter

▸ **check off** **VT SEP** *(names, numbers on list etc)* cocher

▸ **check on** **VT INSEP 1** *(facts)* vérifier **2** *(person)* **the doctor checked on two patients before leaving** le médecin est allé voir deux patients avant de partir; **would you mind checking on the baby?** tu peux aller voir si le bébé va bien?

▸ **check out** **VI 1** *(pay hotel bill)* régler sa note; *(leave hotel)* quitter l'hôtel **2** *(prove to be correct)* s'avérer exact; *(correspond, match)* s'accorder, correspondre **3** *Am Fam (die)* passer l'arme à gauche

VT SEP 1 *(library book)* faire tamponner; *(hotel guest)* faire régler sa note à

2 *(investigate ▸ person)* enquêter sur, se renseigner sur; *(▸ information, machine, place)* vérifier

3 *Fam (try)* essayer□; **why don't we c. out the restaurant that John told us about?** pourquoi ne pas essayer le restaurant dont John nous a parlé?

4 *Fam (look at)* **to c. sb/sth out** mater qn/qch; **c. this out** *(look)* vise un peu ça; *(listen)* écoute-moi ça

▸ **check over** **VT SEP** examiner, vérifier

▸ **check through** **VT SEP 1** *(examine ▸ baggage etc)* contrôler, examiner **2** *(send by plane)* faire envoyer (par avion); **I'd like my luggage checked through to Los Angeles** je voudrais faire envoyer directement mes bagages à Los Angeles

▸ **check up on** **VT INSEP** **to c. up on sb** enquêter *ou* se renseigner sur qn; **if you trusted me you wouldn't c. up on me all the time** si tu me faisais confiance tu ne serais pas toujours en train de m'espionner; **to c. up on sth** vérifier qch

checkbook *Am* = **chequebook**

check-control **N** *Aut* appareil *m* de signalisation des défauts

checked [tʃekt] **ADJ 1** *(pattern, tablecloth)* à carreaux, *Can* carreauté **2** *Ling (syllable)* fermé, entravé

checker ['tʃekə(r)] **N** *Am* **1** *(in draughts)* pion *m* **2** *(in supermarket)* caissier(ère) *m,f*; *(in left-luggage office)* préposé(e) *m,f* à la consigne; *(in cloakroom)* préposé(e) *m,f* au vestiaire

checkerboard ['tʃekəbɔ:d] **N** *Am Chess* échiquier *m*; *(in draughts)* damier *m*

checkered *Am* = **chequered**

checkers *Am* = **chequers**

check-in **N** *(at airport)* enregistrement *m*
►► ***check-in desk*** enregistrement *m*; ***check-in time*** *(at airport, hotel)* heure *f* d'enregistrement

checking ['tʃekɪŋ] **N** *(verification, examination)* contrôle *m*, vérification *f*; *(more detailed)* pointage *m*
►► *Am Banking* ***checking account*** compte *m* courant

checkless *Am* = **chequeless**

checklist ['tʃeklɪst] **N** liste *f* de contrôle; *Aviat* check-list *f*

checkmark ['tʃekmɑ:k] **N** *Am* coche *f*

checkmate ['tʃekmeɪt] **N 1** *Chess* échec et mat *m* **2** *Fig (deadlock, standstill)* impasse *f*; *(defeat)* échec *m* total
VT 1 *Chess* faire échec et mat à **2** *Fig (frustrate, obstruct)* contrecarrer; *(defeat)* vaincre

checkout ['tʃekaʊt] **N 1** *(in supermarket)* caisse *f* **2** *(in hotel)* heure *f* de départ; **c. (time) is 12 noon** les clients doivent libérer la chambre avant midi
►► *Am* ***checkout clerk*** caissier(ère) *m,f*; ***checkout desk*** caisse *f*; ***checkout display*** devant *m* de caisse, nez *m* de caisse; ***checkout girl*** caissière *f*; ***checkout operator*** caissier(ère) *m,f*

checkpoint ['tʃekpɔɪnt] **N** (poste *m* de) contrôle *m*
►► *Mil & Hist* ***Checkpoint Charlie*** checkpoint *m* Charlie

checkroom ['tʃekrum] **N** *Am (for coats, hats)* vestiaire *m*; *(for luggage)* consigne *f*

checksum ['tʃeksʌm] **N** *Comput* somme *f* de contrôle

check-up ['tʃekʌp] **N** *Med* bilan *m* de santé, check-up *m*; **to give sb a c.** faire le bilan de santé de qn; **to go for** *or* **to have a c.** se faire faire un check-up

Cheddar ['tʃedə(r)] **N C. (cheese)** cheddar *m*

cheek [tʃi:k] **N 1** *(of face)* joue *f*; **c. to c.** joue contre joue; **to be/to live c. by jowl with sb** être/vivre tout près de qn; **to turn the other c.** tendre *ou* présenter l'autre joue **2** *Fam (buttock)* fesse▫ *f* **3** *Br Fam (impudence)* culot *m*, toupet *m*; **he's got a c.!** il est culotté *ou* gonflé!, quel culot!; **he had the c. to ask her age!** il a eu le culot *ou* le toupet de lui demander son âge!; **what (a) c.!, of all the c.!** quel culot!, quel toupet!
VT *Br Fam* être insolent avec
►► *Horseriding* ***cheek piece*** montant *m*; *Zool* ***cheek pouch*** abajoue *f*

cheekbone ['tʃi:kbəʊn] **N** pommette *f*; **high/prominent cheekbones** pommettes *fpl* hautes/saillantes

cheekily ['tʃi:kɪlɪ] **ADV** *Br* avec effronterie *ou* impudence, effrontément

cheekiness ['tʃi:kɪnɪs] **N** *Br* effronterie *f*, audace *f*

cheeky ['tʃi:kɪ] *(compar* **cheekier**, *superl* **cheekiest)** **ADJ** *Br (person)* effronté, impudent; *(attitude, behaviour)* impertinent; **don't be c.!** pas d'impertinence!; *Fam* **a c. little wine** un bon petit pinard

cheep [tʃi:p] **N** pépiement *m*
VI pépier

cheer [tʃɪə(r)] **N 1** *(cry)* hourra *m*, bravo *m*; **I heard a c. go up** j'ai entendu des acclamations; **three cheers for the winner!** un ban *ou* hourra pour le gagnant!; **three cheers!** hourra! **2** *Fam* **cheers!** *(toast)* (à votre) santé!; *Br (at parting)* salut!, ciao!; *Br (thanks)* merci!▫ **3** *Literary (good spirits)* bonne humeur *f*, gaieté *f*; **words of good c.** paroles *fpl* d'encouragement; **be of good c.!** prenez courage!
VT 1 *(make cheerful* ► *person)* remonter le moral à, réconforter **2** *(encourage by shouts)* acclamer
VI pousser des acclamations *ou* des hourras

► **cheer on** **VT SEP** encourager (par des acclamations); **his supporters cheered him on to victory** les acclamations de ses supporters l'ont encouragé jusqu'à la victoire

► **cheer up** **VT SEP 1** *(person)* remonter le moral à, réconforter **2** *(house, room)* égayer
VI *(become more cheerful)* s'égayer, se dérider; **c. up!** courage!; **the weather's cheered up** le temps s'est arrangé

cheerful ['tʃɪəfʊl] **ADJ 1** *(happy* ► *person)* de bonne humeur; *(*► *remark, smile)* joyeux, gai; *(*► *atmosphere, mood, music)* gai, joyeux; *(*► *colour, wallpaper)* gai, riant; *(*► *news)* réjouissant; **she's always c.** elle est toujours de bonne humeur; *Ironic* **that's a c. thought!** voilà qui est réconfortant! **2** *(enthusiastic, willing* ► *helper, worker)* de bonne volonté; *(*► *dedication)* grand

cheerfully ['tʃɪəfʊlɪ] **ADV 1** *(happily)* joyeusement, avec entrain **2** *(willingly)* de plein gré, avec bonne volonté; **I could c. have hit him!** je l'aurais bien frappé!

cheerfulness ['tʃɪəfʊlnɪs] **N** *(of person)* bonne humeur *f*; *(of atmosphere, colour, music)* gaieté *f*; *(of remark, smile)* gaieté *f*, caractère *m* jovial

cheerily ['tʃɪərɪlɪ] **ADV** joyeusement, avec entrain

cheering ['tʃɪərɪŋ] **N** *(UNCOUNT)* acclamations *fpl*, hourras *mpl*
ADJ *(remark, thought)* encourageant, qui remonte le moral; *(news, sight)* encourageant, réconfortant

cheerio [ˌtʃɪərɪ'əʊ] **EXCLAM** *Br Fam* **1** *(goodbye)* salut!, ciao! **2** *Old-fashioned (toast)* à la tienne!

cheerleader ['tʃɪəˌli:də(r)] **N** *Sport* pom-pom girl *f*

cheerless ['tʃɪəlɪs] **ADJ** *(person)* triste, mélancolique; *(landscape)* morne

cheery ['tʃɪərɪ] *(compar* **cheerier**, *superl* **cheeriest)** **ADJ** *(person)* de bonne humeur; *(smile)* joyeux, gai

cheese [tʃi:z] **N 1** *(gen)* fromage *m*; **say c.!** *(when taking photo)* souriez!▫; **a c. and wine (evening)** = petite fête où l'on déguste du vin et du fromage **2** *(individual piece)* fromage *m*; **an assortment of different cheeses** un assortiment de fromages
COMP *(omelette, sandwich, sauce)* au fromage; *(knife)* à fromage
►► ***cheese biscuit*** *(for cheese)* biscuit *m* salé; *(cheese-flavoured)* biscuit *m* au fromage; ***cheese grater*** râpe *f* à fromage; ***cheese maker*** fromager (ère) *m,f*; ***cheese plant*** monstera *m*; ***cheese straw*** allumette *f* au fromage; ***cheese wire*** fil *m* à couper

► **cheese off** **VT SEP** *Fam* **to c. sb off** gonfler qn

cheeseboard ['tʃi:zbɔ:d] **N** *(board)* plateau *m* à fromage *ou* fromages; *(on menu)* plateau *m* de fromages

cheeseburger ['tʃi:zˌbɜ:gə(r)] **N** hamburger *m* au fromage, cheeseburger *m*

cheesecake ['tʃi:zkeɪk] **N 1** *(dessert)* gâteau *m* au fromage (blanc), cheesecake *m* **2** *(UNCOUNT) Fam Hum (attractive women)* belles nanas *fpl*; *(in photo)* pin-up *f inv*; *Br* **she's a real c.** elle est vraiment bien foutue

cheesecloth ['tʃi:zklɒθ] **N** *Culin & Tex* étamine *f*

cheeseparing ['tʃi:zˌpeərɪŋ] **N** parcimonie *f*
ADJ parcimonieux, pingre

cheesy ['tʃi:zɪ] *(compar* **cheesier**, *superl* **cheesiest)** **ADJ 1** *(flavour)* qui a un goût de fromage, qui sent le fromage; *(smell)* qui sent le fromage **2** *Fam (tasteless)* ringard **3** *Fam* **a c. grin** un large sourire▫

cheetah ['tʃi:tə] **N** *Zool* guépard *m*

chef [ʃef] *(pt & pp* **cheffed**, *cont* **cheffing)** **N** chef *m* cuisinier *ou* de cuisine, cuisinier(ère) *m,f*
VI être chef cuisinier
►► *Culin* ***chef's salad*** = salade à base de poulet, de jambon et de fromage

Chelsea tractor ['tʃelsɪ-] **N** *Fam Hum* = 4X4 utilisé en ville

chemical ['kemɪkəl] **N 1** *(product)* produit *m* chimique; **the c. industry** l'industrie *f* chimique **2** *(drug)* drogue *f* de synthèse
ADJ chimique
►► ***chemical element*** élément *m* chimique; ***chemical engineer*** ingénieur *m* chimiste; ***chemical engineering*** génie *m* chimique; ***chemical peel*** peeling *m* chimique; ***chemical reaction*** réaction *f* chimique; ***chemical toilet*** W-C *mpl* chimiques; ***chemical warfare*** guerre *f* chimique; ***chemical weapons*** armes *fpl* chimiques

chemically ['kemɪklɪ] **ADV** chimiquement

chemist ['kemɪst] **N 1** *(scientist)* chimiste *mf* **2** *Br (pharmacist)* pharmacien(enne) *m,f* **3** *(shop)* pharmacie *f*
►► *Br* ***chemist's shop*** pharmacie *f*

chemistry ['kemɪstrɪ] **N 1** *(science)* chimie *f* **2** *(affinity) Fig* **sexual c.** (bonne) entente *f* sexuelle; *Fig* **there was a certain c. between the members of the band** il y avait une certaine affinité entre les musiciens; *Fig* **there's no c., the c.'s missing** le courant ne passe pas, on n'a pas d'atomes crochus
COMP *(lesson, teacher, degree)* de chimie
►► ***chemistry set*** panoplie *f* de chimiste

chemotherapy [ˌki:məʊ'θerəpɪ] **N** *Med* chimiothérapie *f*

cheque, *Am* **check** [tʃek] **N** chèque *m*; **a c. for £7** *or* **to the amount of £7** un chèque de 7 livres; **will you take a c.?** est-ce que vous acceptez les chèques?; **who should I make the c. payable to?** à quel nom dois-je libeller le chèque?; **to pay by c.** payer par chèque; **to cash a c.** toucher un chèque; **to stop a c.** faire opposition à un chèque; **to write sb a c.** faire un chèque à qn; **a bad c.** un chèque sans provision; *Br* **a crossed/open c.** un chèque barré/non-barré
►► *Br* ***cheque account*** compte *m* chèques; *Br* ***cheque card*** = carte d'identité bancaire sans laquelle les chèques ne sont pas acceptés en Grande-Bretagne; ***cheque counterfoil*** talon *m* de chèque, souche *f*; *Br* ***cheque guarantee card*** = carte d'identité bancaire sans laquelle les chèques ne sont pas acceptés en Grande-Bretagne; ***cheque number*** numéro *m* de chèque; ***cheque stub*** talon *m* de chèque, souche *f*

chequebook, *Am* **checkbook** ['tʃekˌbʊk] **N** carnet *m* de chèques, chéquier *m*
►► ***chequebook journalism*** = dans les milieux de la presse, pratique qui consiste à payer des sommes importantes pour le témoignage d'une personne impliquée dans une affaire

chequeless, *Am* **checkless** ['kæʃlɪs] **ADJ** *(society)* sans chèques; **we're moving towards a c. society** nous nous dirigeons vers une société où les chèques ne seront plus utilisés

chequered, *Am* **checkered** ['tʃekəd] **ADJ 1** *(pattern)* à carreaux, à damiers, *Can* carreauté **2** *(varied)* varié; *(life)* plein de vicissitudes; **she's had a c. career** sa carrière a connu des hauts et des bas
►► ***chequered flag*** *(in motor racing)* drapeau *m* à damiers

cherish ['tʃerɪʃ] **VT** *(person)* chérir, aimer; *(ambition, hope)* caresser, nourrir; *(experience, memory, possession)* chérir; *(right, value)* tenir à; **one of my most cherished memories** un de mes souvenirs les plus chers

cheroot [ʃə'ru:t] **N** petit cigare *m (à bouts coupés)*

cherry ['tʃerɪ] *(pl* **cherries)** **N 1** *(fruit)* cerise *f*; *(tree)* cerisier *m*; *Prov* **life is just a bowl of cherries** = il faut voir la vie en rose
2 *(colour)* cerise *f inv*, rouge *m* cerise *(inv)*
3 *very Fam (virginity)* **to lose one's c.** perdre sa fleur
4 *very Fam (virgin)* puceau(elle) *m,f*
5 *Am Fam (newcomer)* bleu *m*
ADJ 1 *(colour)* cerise *(inv)*, rouge cerise *(inv)* **2** *Am Fam (in perfect condition)* en parfait état▫, impec
COMP *(blossom, wood)* de cerisier; *(pie, tart)* aux cerises
►► ***cherry brandy*** cherry *m*; ***cherry orchard*** cerisaie *f*; *Tech* ***cherry picker*** plate-forme *f* élévatrice; ***cherry red*** rouge *m* cerise *(inv)*; ***cherry stone*** noyau *m* de cerise; ***cherry tomato*** tomate *f* cerise; ***cherry tree*** cerisier *m*; *(wild)* merisier *m*

cherry-pick VT *Fig* écrémer

cherry-red ADJ (rouge) cerise *(inv)*; **c. lips** des lèvres *fpl* vermeilles

cherub ['tʃerəb] *(pl* **cherubs** *or* **cherubim** [-bɪm]) N *Bible* chérubin *m*; *Art* angelot *m*, ange *m* joufflu; *Fig* **a little c.** *(child)* un petit ange

cherubic [tʃe'ru:bɪk] ADJ *(face)* de chérubin; *(child, look, smile)* angélique

chervil ['tʃɜ:vɪl] N cerfeuil *m*

Cheshire ['tʃeʃə(r)] N le Cheshire, = comté dans le nord-ouest de l'Angleterre; *Fam* **to grin like a C. cat** avoir un sourire jusqu'aux oreilles▫
►► *Culin* **Cheshire cheese** fromage *m* de Chester, chester *m*

chess [tʃes] N *(UNCOUNT)* échecs *mpl*; **to play c.** jouer aux échecs; **let's play a game of c.** si on faisait une partie d'échecs?
►► **chess player** joueur(euse) *m,f* d'échecs; **chess tournament** tournoi *m* d'échecs

chessboard ['tʃesbɔ:d] N échiquier *m*

chessman ['tʃesmæn] *(pl* **chessmen** [-men]) N pion *m*, pièce *f (de jeu d'échecs)*

chest [tʃest] N **1** *Anat* poitrine *f*; *(of horse)* poitrail *m*; **to have a weak c.** être faible des bronches; *Fig* **to get something off one's c.** dire ce qu'on a sur le cœur **2** *(box)* coffre *m*, caisse *f*
COMP *(cold, measurement, pain)* de poitrine
►► **chest of drawers** commode *f*; **chest expander** extenseur *m (pour développer les pectoraux)*; **chest freezer** congélateur *m* coffre; **chest infection** infection *f* des voies respiratoires; **chest size** tour *m* de poitrine; **chest X-ray** radio *f* des poumons

chesterfield ['tʃestəfi:ld] N **1** *(coat)* pardessus *m* (de ville) **2** *(sofa)* canapé *m* Chesterfield

chestnut ['tʃesnʌt] N **1** *(tree)* châtaignier *m*; *(fruit)* châtaigne *f*; *(when cooked)* marron *m*; *Fig* **to pull sb's chestnuts out of the fire** tirer les marrons du feu à qn
2 **(horse) c.** marron *m* (d'Inde); **(horse) c. tree** marronnier *m* d'Inde
3 *(colour)* châtain *m inv*
4 *(wood)* châtaignier *m*
5 *(horse)* alezan(e) *m,f*
6 *Fam (joke)* **old c.** plaisanterie *f* rebattue *ou* éculée
ADJ *(colour, hair)* châtain *(inv)*; *(horse)* alezan
COMP *(blossom, wood)* de châtaignier; *(stuffing)* aux marrons
►► **chestnut brown** N châtain *m inv* ADJ châtain *(inv)*; **chestnut purée** crème *f* de marrons; **chestnut tree** châtaignier *m*

chesty ['tʃestɪ] *(compar* **chestier**, *superl* **chestiest**) ADJ *(cough)* de poitrine; **to be c.** être bronchitique

cheval glass [ʃə'væl-] N psyché *f (glace)*

chevron ['ʃevrən] N *Archit, Her & Mil* chevron *m*

Chevy ['ʃevɪ] N *Fam (Chevrolet® car)* Chevrolet▫ *f*

chew [tʃu:] VT mâcher, mastiquer; *(cigar, end of pen etc)* mâchonner; **to c. tobacco** chiquer, mâcher du tabac; **to c. one's nails** se ronger les ongles; *also Fig* **to c. the cud** ruminer; *Fam* **to c. the fat** *or* **the rag (with sb)** tailler une bavette (avec qn)
N **1** *(act)* mâchement *m*, mastication *f*; **to have a c. at sth** mâchonner qch
2 *(piece of tobacco)* chique *f*
3 *(sweet)* bonbon *m*
4 *(for cat, dog)* aliment *m* à mâcher

►**chew on** VT INSEP **1** *(food)* mâcher, mastiquer; *(bone)* ronger; *(tobacco)* chiquer; *(cigar, end of pen etc)* mâchonner; **he chewed on his pipe** il mâchouillait sa pipe **2** *Fam (problem, question)* ruminer▫, retourner dans sa tête▫

►**chew out** VT SEP *Am Fam* engueuler, passer un savon à

►**chew over** VT SEP *Fam (think over)* ruminer▫, retourner dans sa tête; *(discuss)* discuter de▫

►**chew up** VT SEP **1** *(food)* mâchonner, mastiquer **2** *(damage)* abîmer à force de ronger

chewing ['tʃu:ɪŋ] N mastication *f*
►► **chewing gum** chewing-gum *m*; **chewing tobacco** tabac *m* à chiquer

chewy ['tʃu:ɪ] *(compar* **chewier**, *superl* **chewiest**) ADJ **1** *Pej (meat)* difficile à mâcher **2** *(sweet)* mou (molle), tendre

chiaroscuro [kɪˌɑ:rəʊ'skʊərəʊ] *(pl* **chiaroscuros**) N *Art* clair-obscur *m*

chic [ʃi:k] N chic *m*, élégance *f*
ADJ chic, élégant

chicane [ʃɪ'keɪn] N **1** *Cards (in bridge)* main *f* à sans atout **2** *(barrier)* chicane *f*

chicanery [ʃɪ'keɪnərɪ] *(pl* **chicaneries**) N *(trickery)* ruse *f*, fourberie *f*; *(legal trickery)* chicane *f*

Chicano [tʃɪ'kɑ:nəʊ] *(pl* **Chicanos**) N Chicano *mf (Américain d'origine mexicaine)*

chichi ['ʃi:ʃi:] ADJ *(affected)* précieux

chick [tʃɪk] N **1** *(baby bird ► gen)* oisillon *m*; *(► of chicken)* poussin *m* **2** *Fam (woman)* poupée *f*, nana *f*
►► *Fam* **chick flick** = film qui plaît particulièrement aux femmes; *Fam* **chick lit** = genre romanesque destiné à un public de jeunes femmes et qui est censé refléter leurs préoccupations

chickadee ['tʃɪkədi:] N *Orn* mésange *f (d'Amérique du Nord)*

chicken ['tʃɪkɪn] N **1** *(bird)* poulet *m*; *(young)* poussin *m*; *Fam* **he's no (spring) c.** il n'est plus tout jeune▫; **which came first, the c. or the egg?** allez savoir quelle est la cause et quel est l'effet, l'œuf ou la poule?; *Fam* **it's a c.-and-egg situation** c'est le problème de l'œuf et de la poule, on ne sait pas lequel est à l'origine de l'autre; *Prov* **don't count your chickens before they are hatched** il ne faut pas vendre la peau de l'ours avant de l'avoir tué **2** *Fam (coward)* poule *f* mouillée, froussard(e) *m, f*
ADJ *Fam (cowardly)* froussard
COMP *(dish, stew)* de poulet; *(sandwich)* au poulet
►► **chicken breast** blanc *m* (de poulet); **chicken farm** élevage *m* de poulets, élevage *m* avicole; **chicken farmer** éleveur(euse) *m,f* de volailles, aviculteur(trice) *m,f*; **chicken leg** cuisse *f* (de poulet); **chicken liver** foie *m* de volaille; **chicken run** enclos *m (d'un poulailler)*; **chicken soup** *(clear)* potage *m* au poulet; *(creamy)* velouté *m ou* crème *f* de volaille; **chicken wire** grillage *m*

►**chicken out** VI *Fam* se dégonfler; **he chickened out of the race** il s'est dégonflé et n'a pas pris part à la course

chickenfeed ['tʃɪkɪnfi:d] N *(UNCOUNT)* **1** *(for poultry)* nourriture *f* pour volaille **2** *Fam Fig (small amount of money)* cacahuètes *fpl*; **£2,000 is c.** 2 000 livres, c'est pas grand-chose

chicken-hearted [-'hɑ:tɪd], **chicken-livered** [-'lɪvəd] ADJ poltron

chickenpox ['tʃɪkɪnpɒks] N *(UNCOUNT)* varicelle *f*

chickenshit ['tʃɪkɪnʃɪt] *Am very Fam* N *(person)* poule *f* mouillée
ADJ *(cowardly)* dégonflé

chickpea ['tʃɪkpi:] N *Br* pois *m* chiche

chickweed ['tʃɪkwi:d] N *Bot* mouron *m* blanc *ou* des oiseaux

chicory ['tʃɪkərɪ] *(pl* **chicories**) N *(for salad)* endive *f*; *(for coffee)* chicorée *f*

chide [tʃaɪd] *(pt* **chided** *or* **chid** [tʃɪd], *pp* **chid** [tʃɪd] *or* **chidden** ['tʃɪdən]) VT *Formal* gronder, réprimander

chief [tʃi:f] N **1** *(leader ► of tribe, group)* chef *m*; **in c.** en chef; **editor in c.** rédacteur(trice) *m,f* en chef; **too many chiefs and not enough Indians** trop de chefs et pas assez d'hommes de troupe *(pour exécuter les ordres et faire le travail)* **2** *Fam (boss)* patron(onne) *m,f*, boss *m*; **he's the big white c.** c'est lui le grand patron **3** *Her* chef *m*
ADJ **1** *(most important)* principal, premier; **one of the c. conflicts** un des principaux conflits; **the c. reason for doing sth** la raison majeure *ou* principale pour faire qch **2** *(head)* premier, en chef
• **in chief** ADV principalement, surtout
►► **Chief Constable** = en Grande-Bretagne, chef de la police d'un comté ou d'une région, commissaire *m* divisionnaire; *Am Admin* **chief executive** directeur(trice) *m,f*; *Com & Ind* **chief executive officer** président(e)-directeur(trice) général(e) *m,f*; **chief inspector** *(gen)* inspecteur(trice) *m,f* principal(e), inspecteur(trice) *m,f* en chef; *Br (of police)* commissaire *m* de police; *Br Sch* inspecteur(trice) *m,f* général(e); *Law* **chief justice** président(e) *m,f* de la Haute Cour de justice; *Am* président *m* de la Cour suprême; **chief of police** préfet *m* de police; *Mil* **chief of staff** chef *m* d'état-major; *Am (at White House)* secrétaire *m* général de la Maison Blanche; *Br* **chief superintendent** *(in police)* commissaire *m* principal; *Pol* **Chief Whip** = responsable du maintien de la discipline à l'intérieur d'un parti à la Chambre des communes

chiefly ['tʃi:flɪ] ADV principalement, surtout

chieftain ['tʃi:ftən] N chef *m (de tribu)*

chiffon ['ʃɪfɒn] *Tex*
N mousseline *f* de soie
ADJ **1** *(dress, scarf)* en mousseline (de soie)

chignon ['ʃi:njɒn] N chignon *m*

chihuahua [tʃɪ'wɑ:wə] N chihuahua *m*

chikungunya [tʃɪkən'gu:njə] N *Med* chikungunya *m*

chilblain ['tʃɪlbleɪn] N engelure *f*

child [tʃaɪld] *(pl* **children** ['tʃɪldrən]) N **1** *(boy or girl)* enfant *mf*; **ever since I was a c.** depuis mon enfance; **while still a c.** tout enfant; **children of the 60s** des enfants des années 60; **don't be such a c.!** ne fais pas l'enfant!; *Arch or Literary* **to be with c.** attendre un enfant, être enceinte; *Fam* **it's c.'s play for** *or* **to him** c'est un jeu d'enfant pour lui **2** *Literary (result)* fruit *m*
COMP *(psychology)* de l'enfant, infantile; *(psychologist)* pour enfants
►► **child abuse** mauvais traitements *mpl* à enfant; *(sexual)* sévices *mpl* sexuels infligés à un enfant; **child abuser** = personne coupable de mauvais traitements à enfant; *(sexual)* = personne coupable de sévices sexuels infligés à un enfant; *Cin & TV* **child actor** acteur *m* enfant; *Br Admin* **child benefit** *(UNCOUNT)* allocation *f* familiale *ou* allocations *fpl* familiales (pour un enfant); **child bride** femme *f* enfant; **she was his c. bride** c'était une enfant quand il l'a épousée; **child labour** travail *m* des enfants; **child molester** auteur *m* de sévices sexuels sur des enfants; **child pornography** pornographie *f* pédophile; **child poverty** pauvreté *f* des enfants, pauvreté *f* infantile; **child prodigy** enfant *mf* prodige; **child psychiatrist** pédopsychiatre *mf*; **child psychiatry** pédopsychiatrie *f*; **child seat** siège-auto *m (pour enfant)*; *Admin* **child support** pension *f* alimentaire, aliments *mpl* au profit de l'enfant; *Br Admin* **Child Support Agency** = organisme gouvernemental qui décide du montant des pensions alimentaires et les prélève au besoin; **child trust fund** = compte d'épargne ouvert par l'État au nom de chaque enfant britannique à sa naissance; **child welfare** protection *f* de l'enfance

childbearing ['tʃaɪldˌbeərɪŋ] N grossesse *f*
ADJ *(complications, problems)* de grossesse; **of c. age** en âge d'avoir des enfants; **she's got c. hips** elle est large des hanches

childbirth ['tʃaɪldbɜ:θ] N *(UNCOUNT)* accouchement *m*; **to die in c.** mourir en couches

childcare ['tʃaɪldkeə(r)] N **1** *(day care)* garde *f* d'enfants; **we haven't decided on c. arrangements yet** nous n'avons pas encore pris de décision quant à la garde des enfants **2** *Br Admin* protection *f* de l'enfance

child-friendly ADJ *(area, city)* aménagé pour les enfants; *(house, furniture)* conçu pour les enfants; *(restaurant)* pour les familles

childhood ['tʃaɪldhʊd] N enfance *f*; **to be in one's second c.** être retombé en enfance
COMP *(friend, memories)* d'enfance
►► **childhood sweetheart** amour *m* d'enfance

childish ['tʃaɪldɪʃ] ADJ **1** *(of children, childlike ► face, fears, voice)* d'enfant; *(► laughter, curiosity, innocence)* enfantin **2** *(immature)* enfantin, puéril; **don't be so c.** ne fais pas l'enfant, ne sois pas aussi puéril

childishness ['tʃaɪldɪʃnɪs] N *(UNCOUNT)* *(of person)* enfantillage *m*, puérilité *f*; *(of behaviour, remark)* puérilité *f*

childless ['tʃaɪldlɪs] ADJ sans enfants

childlike [ˈtʃaɪldlaɪk] ADJ enfantin; *(question)* naïf; *(smile)* d'enfant; **he was c. in his curiosity** il avait une curiosité enfantine *ou* d'enfant

childminder [ˈtʃaɪldˌmaɪndə(r)] N *Br (for very young children)* nourrice *f*; *(for older children)* assistante *f* maternelle

childminding [ˈtʃaɪldˌmaɪndɪŋ] N garde *f* d'enfants

childproof [ˈtʃaɪldpruːf] ADJ *(door)* ne pouvant pas être ouvert par les enfants, de sécurité; *(not breakable)* ne pouvant pas être cassé par les enfants

►► ***childproof lock*** serrure *f* de sécurité pour enfants

children [ˈtʃɪldrən] *pl of* **child**

►► ***children's book*** livre *m* pour enfants; ***children's home*** foyer *m* d'enfants; ***children's literature*** littérature *f* pour enfants; ***Children In Need*** = association caritative britannique de soutien aux enfants du monde entier, créée par la BBC, qui organise chaque année une grande soirée télévisée pour collecter des fonds; ***children's television*** télévision *f* pour enfants

Chile [ˈtʃɪlɪ] N Chili *m*

Chilean [ˈtʃɪlɪən] N Chilien(enne) *m,f*
ADJ chilien
COMP *(embassy, history)* du Chili

chili = **chilli**

chill [tʃɪl] VT **1** *(make cold* ► *food, wine, champagne)* mettre au frais; *(*► *glass, person)* glacer; **to be chilled to the bone/to the marrow** être glacé jusqu'aux os/jusqu'à la moelle **2** *Fig (enthusiasm)* refroidir **3** *Tech (metal)* tremper
VI **1** *(become cold)* se refroidir, rafraîchir **2** *Fam (relax)* décompresser; **c.!** relax!, calmos!
N **1** *(coldness)* fraîcheur *f*, froideur *f*; **there's a c. in the air** il fait assez frais *ou* un peu froid; **to take the c. off** *(room)* réchauffer un peu; *(wine)* chambrer; *Fig* **his remark cast a c. over the meeting** son observation a jeté un froid dans l'assemblée **2** *(feeling of fear)* frisson *m*; **the story sent chills down her spine** l'histoire lui a fait froid dans le dos **3** *(illness)* coup *m* de froid, refroidissement *m*; **to catch a c.** attraper *ou* prendre froid
ADJ *(air, weather)* frais (fraîche), froid; *(glance, response)* froid, glacial
►► ***chill cabinet*** armoire *f* réfrigérante

► **chill out** VI *Fam* décompresser; **I wish he'd c. out a bit** ça serait bien qu'il soit un peu plus cool; **he likes chilling out at home** il aime bien rester chez lui, peinard; **c. out!** relax!, calmos!

chilled [tʃɪld] ADJ **1** *(refrigerated)* **c. white wine** vin *m* blanc frais; **c. champagne** champagne *m* frappé; **c. meat** viande *f* réfrigérée *ou* frigorifiée; **c. products** produits *mpl* frigorifiés; **best served c.** *(on label)* servir glacé *ou* très frais **2** *Fam (relaxed)* cool *(inv)*

chilli [ˈtʃɪlɪ] N *(vegetable)* piment *m* (rouge); *(dish)* chili *m*
►► ***chilli con carne*** chili *m* con carne; ***chilli pepper*** piment *m* (rouge); ***chilli powder*** chili *m*; ***chilli sauce*** sauce *f* aux tomates et piments

chilliness [ˈtʃɪlɪnɪs] N *(of air, wind)* fraîcheur *f*; *Fig (of greeting, manner)* froideur *f*

chilling [ˈtʃɪlɪŋ] ADJ *(wind)* frais (fraîche), froid; *Fig (look, smile)* froid, glacial; *(news, story, thought)* qui donne des frissons

chill-out room N *(in nightclub)* espace *m* chill-out

chilly [ˈtʃɪlɪ] *(compar* **chillier**, *superl* **chilliest***)* ADJ **1** *(air, room)* (très) frais (fraîche), froid; **I feel c.** j'ai froid; **it's rather c. this morning** il fait plutôt frais *ou* frisquet ce matin **2** *Fig (greeting, look)* froid, glacial

chime [tʃaɪm] N *(bell)* carillon *m*; **to ring the chimes** carillonner; **(door) chimes** carillon *m* de porte
VT sonner; **the clock chimed six** l'horloge a sonné six heures
VI *(bell, voices)* carillonner; *(clock)* sonner
• **chimes** NPL *(for door)* carillon *m*, sonnette *f*

► **chime in** VI *Fam (say)* intervenir[□]; **all the children chimed in** tous les enfants ont fait chorus; **he chimed in with some silly remark** il est intervenu pour dire une bêtise[□]

chimera [kaɪˈmɪərə] N *Myth & Fig* chimère *f*

chiming [ˈtʃaɪmɪŋ] ADJ carillonnant; *(clock)* à carillon
N *(UNCOUNT)* carillonnement *m*, carillon *m*

chimney [ˈtʃɪmnɪ] N **1** *(in building)* cheminée *f*; *Fam* **to smoke like a c.** *(person)* fumer comme un sapeur *ou* un pompier **2** *(of lamp)* verre *m* **3** *Geol* cheminée *f*
►► ***chimney corner*** coin *m* du feu

> Note that the French word **cheminée** also means **fireplace** and **mantelpiece**.

chimneypiece [ˈtʃɪmnɪpiːs] N *Br* dessus *m ou* tablette *f* de cheminée

chimneypot [ˈtʃɪmnɪpɒt] N tuyau *m* de cheminée

chimneysweep [ˈtʃɪmnɪswiːp] N ramoneur *m*

chimp [tʃɪmp], **chimpanzee** [ˌtʃɪmpənˈziː] N *Zool* chimpanzé *m*

chin [tʃɪn] N menton *m*; **(keep your) c. up!** courage!; *Fam* **he took the news on the c.** il a encaissé la nouvelle (sans broncher)
►► ***chin strap*** *(on helmet)* jugulaire *f*

China [ˈtʃaɪnə] N Chine *f*; **the People's Republic of C.** la République populaire de Chine
►► ***the China Sea*** la mer de Chine; ***China tea*** thé *m* de Chine

china [ˈtʃaɪnə] N **1** *(material)* porcelaine *f*; **a piece of c.** une porcelaine **2** *(porcelain objects)* porcelaine *f*; *(porcelain dishes)* porcelaine *f*, vaisselle *f* (de porcelaine); *(crockery)* vaisselle *f* **3** *Br Fam (friend)* pote *m*; **my old c.!** mon vieux!
COMP *(cup, plate, doll)* de *ou* en porcelaine; *(shop)* de porcelaine
►► ***china cabinet*** dressoir *m*; ***china clay*** kaolin *m*

Chinagraph® [ˈtʃaɪnəgrɑːf] N *(pencil)* crayon *m* gras

Chinaman [ˈtʃaɪnəmən] *(pl* **Chinamen** [-mən]*)* N *Old-fashioned* Chinois *m*

Chinatown [ˈtʃaɪnətaʊn] N le quartier chinois

chinaware [ˈtʃaɪnəweə(r)] N *(UNCOUNT) (porcelain objects)* porcelaine *f*; *(porcelain dishes)* porcelaine *f*, vaisselle *f* (en porcelaine)

chinchilla [ˌtʃɪnˈtʃɪlə] N *Zool & (fur)* chinchilla *m*
COMP *(coat, wrap)* de chinchilla

chin-chin EXCLAM *Br Fam Old-fashioned (hello, goodbye)* salut!; *(in toast)* tchin-tchin!

chine [tʃaɪn] N *Anat & Culin* échine *f*

Chinese [ˌtʃaɪˈniːz] *(pl* **inv***)* NPL **the C.** les Chinois *mpl*
N **1** *(person)* Chinois(e) *m,f* **2** *(language)* chinois *m* **3** *Br Fam (meal)* repas *m* chinois[□]; **I feel like a C. tonight** j'ai envie de manger chinois ce soir
ADJ chinois
COMP *(embassy)* de Chine; *(history)* de la Chine; *(teacher)* de chinois
►► *Br* ***Chinese burn*** torture *f* indienne; *Bot & Culin* ***Chinese cabbage*** chou *m* chinois; ***Chinese chequers*** *(UNCOUNT)* dames *fpl* chinoises; *Bot & Culin* ***Chinese gooseberry*** kiwi *m (fruit)*; ***Chinese lantern*** lanterne *f* vénitienne; *Br Bot & Culin* ***Chinese leaves*** chou *m* chinois; ***Chinese water torture*** supplice *m* chinois; *Br* ***Chinese whispers*** téléphone *m* arabe

Chink [tʃɪŋk] N *Fam* Chinetoque *mf*, = terme injurieux désignant un Chinois

chink [tʃɪŋk] N **1** *(hole)* fente *f*, fissure *f*; *(of light)* rayon *m*; *Fig* **we found a c. in her armour** nous avons trouvé son point faible *ou* sensible **2** *(sound)* tintement *m (de pièces de monnaie, de verres)*
VI *(jingle)* tinter
VT *(jingle)* faire tinter

Chinky [ˈtʃɪŋkɪ] *(pl* **Chinkies***)* N *Fam* **1** *(restaurant)* (restaurant *m*) chinois[□] *m*; *(meal)* repas *m* chinois[□] **2** *(person)* Chinetoque *mf*, = terme injurieux désignant un Chinois

chinless [ˈtʃɪnlɪs] ADJ *(with receding chin)* au menton fuyant; *Fig (cowardly)* mou (molle)
►► *Br Fam Hum* ***chinless wonder*** = individu de bonne famille dépourvu de volonté et d'intelligence

chino [ˈtʃiːnəʊ] N *Tex* chino *m*; **chinos** *(trousers)* chinos *mpl*; **a pair of chinos** une paire de chinos

chintz [tʃɪnts] *Tex* N chintz *m*
COMP *(curtain)* de chintz; *(chair)* recouvert de chintz

chin-up N traction *f* (à la barre fixe); **to do chin ups** faire des tractions (à la barre fixe)

chinwag [ˈtʃɪnwæg] *(pt & pp* **chinwagged**, *cont* **chinwagging***)* *Fam* N causette *f*; **to have a c. (with sb)** tailler une bavette (avec qn)
VI bavarder

chip [tʃɪp] *(pt & pp* **chipped**, *cont* **chipping***)* N **1** *(piece)* éclat *m*; *(of wood)* copeau *m*, éclat *m*; *Fam* **she's a c. off the old block** elle est bien la fille de son père/de sa mère[□]; *Fam* **to have a c. on one's shoulder** en vouloir à tout le monde[□]; **he's got a c. on his shoulder about not having been to college** il n'a pas fait d'études et il en veut à tout le monde à cause de ça
2 *(flaw* ► *in dish, glass)* ébréchure *f*; *(*► *in chair, wardrobe)* écornure *f*; **this glass has a c. (in it)** ce verre est ébréché
3 *Br (French fry)* (pomme *f* de terre) frite *f*; *Am (crisp)* chips *f inv*, *Can* croustille *f*
4 *(for games, gambling)* jeton *m*, fiche *f*; **to cash in one's chips** se faire payer; *Fam Fig* casser sa pipe; *Fam* **when the chips are down** dans les moments difficiles[□]; *Br Fam* **to have had one's chips** être fichu *ou* cuit
5 *Comput* **(silicon) c.** puce *f*
6 *Golf* coup *m* coché
VT **1** *(dish, glass)* ébrécher; *(furniture)* écorner; *(paint, enamel)* écailler; *(tooth)* casser
2 *(cut into pieces)* piler; **to c. wood** faire des copeaux
3 *(shape by cutting)* tailler
4 *Br (potatoes)* couper en lamelles
5 *Sport (ball)* prendre en dessous, donner une pichenette à; **he chipped the ball over the net** d'une pichenette, il a envoyé la balle au-dessus du filet; *Golf* **to c. the ball** cocher
VI *(dish, glass)* s'ébrécher; *(furniture)* s'écorner; *(paint, enamel)* s'écailler
►► *Br* ***chip basket*** panier *m* à frites; ***chip pan*** friteuse *f*; *Br* ***chip and pin*** *(payment system)* paiement *m* par carte à puce; *Br* ***chip shop*** = boutique où l'on vend des frites ainsi que du poisson frit, des saucisses etc; *Golf* ***chip shot*** coup *m* d'approche roulé; *Br* ***chip van*** friterie *f (camionnette)*

> Note that the French word **chips** is a false friend for British English speakers. It means **crisps**.

► **chip away** VT SEP *(plaster)* décaper, enlever petit à petit
VI *(plaster)* s'écailler

► **chip away at** VT INSEP **to c. away at the old paintwork** enlever la vieille peinture petit à petit; **to c. away at sb's authority** grignoter l'autorité de qn; **just keep chipping away at him until he changes his mind** continuez à le travailler au corps jusqu'à ce qu'il change d'avis

► **chip in** *Fam* VI **1** *(contribute)* contribuer[□]; **we all chipped in with £5** nous avons tous donné 5 livres[□] **2** *(speak)* mettre son grain de sel; **he chipped in with a suggestion** il est intervenu pour faire une suggestion[□] **3** *Cards* miser[□]
VT INSEP **1** *(contribute)* contribuer[□], donner[□] **2** *(say)* dire[□]

► **chip off** VI *(fall off, break off* ► *paint, enamel etc)* s'écailler
VT SEP *(break off)* enlever; **somebody had chipped the nose off the statue** quelqu'un avait cassé le nez de la statue; **to c. a piece off a plate** ébrécher une assiette

chipboard [ˈtʃɪpbɔːd] N *(UNCOUNT) Br Constr* (panneau *m* d')aggloméré *m*, panneau *m* de particules

chipmunk [ˈtʃɪpmʌŋk] N *Zool* tamia *m*, *Can* suisse *m*

chipolata [ˌtʃɪpəˈlɑːtə] N *Br* chipolata *f*

chipped [tʃɪpt] ADJ *(dish, glass)* ébréché; *(furniture)* écorné; *(paint, enamel)* écaillé; *(tooth)* cassé
►► *Culin Am* ***chipped beef*** émincé *m* de bœuf; *Br* ***chipped potatoes*** (pommes *fpl* de terre) frites *fpl*

chipper [ˈtʃɪpə(r)] ADJ *Fam* **1** *(lively)* vif[□], fringant[□] **2** *(smartly dressed)* chic[□], élégant[□]

chippings [ˈtʃɪpɪŋz] NPL *(gen)* éclats *mpl*, fragments *mpl*; *(of wood)* copeaux *mpl*, éclats *mpl*; *(in roadwork)* gravillons *mpl*, *Can* gravelle *f*; **slow, loose c.** *(sign)* attention gravillons

chippy [ˈtʃɪpɪ] *(pl* **chippies***)* N **1** *Br Fam* = boutique où l'on vend des frites ainsi que du poisson frit, des saucisses etc **2** *Br & NZ Fam (carpenter)* charpentier□ *m*

chipset [ˈtʃɪpset] N *Comput* ensemble *m* de puces

chiromancer [ˈkaɪərəʊˌmænsə(r)] N chiromancien(enne) *m,f*

chiromancy [ˈkaɪərəʊˌmænsɪ] N chiromancie *f*

chiropodist [kɪˈrɒpədɪst] N *Br* pédicure *mf*

chiropody [kɪˈrɒpədɪ] N *(UNCOUNT) Br (treatment)* soins *mpl* du pied; *(science)* podologie *f*

chiropractic [ˌkaɪrəˈpræktɪk] N chiropraxie *f*, chiropractie *f*

chiropractor [ˈkaɪrəˌpræktə(r)] N chiropracteur (trice) *m,f*, chiropraticien(enne) *m,f*

chirp [tʃɜːp] VI *(bird)* pépier, gazouiller; *(insect)* chanter, striduler; *(person)* parler d'une voix flûtée

N *(of bird)* pépiement *m*, gazouillement *m*; *(of insect)* chant *m*, stridulation *f*; **c.-c.** *(sound of bird)* cri-cri

chirpily [ˈtʃɜːpɪlɪ] ADV *Fam* gaiement□

chirpiness [ˈtʃɜːpɪnɪs] N *Fam* humeur *f* joyeuse□, gaieté□ *f*

chirpy [ˈtʃɜːpɪ] *(compar* **chirpier**, *superl* **chirpiest***)* ADJ *Fam (person, voice)* gai□, plein d'entrain□; *(mood)* gai, enjoué□, joyeux□

chirrup [ˈtʃɪrəp] VI *(bird)* pépier, gazouiller; *(insect)* chanter, striduler; *(person)* parler d'une voix flûtée

N *(of bird)* pépiement *m*, gazouillement *m*; *(of insect)* chant *m*, stridulation *f*

chisel [ˈtʃɪzəl] *(Br pt & pp* **chiselled**, *cont* **chiselling**, *Am pt & pp* **chiseled**, *cont* **chiseling***)* N *(gen)* ciseau *m*; *(for engraving)* burin *m*

VT **1** *(carve)* ciseler; **to c. sth from** *or* **in** *or* **out of marble** ciseler qch dans du marbre; *Fig* **chiselled features** visage délicatement ciselé **2** *(engrave ▸ form, name)* graver au burin; *(▸ plate)* buriner **3** *esp Am Fam (cheat)* **to c. sb out of sth** carotter qch à qn

chiseller, *Am* **chiseler** [ˈtʃɪzələ(r)] N *Fam* **1** *esp Am (cheat)* carotteur(euse) *m,f*

chit [tʃɪt] N **1** *(memo, note)* note *f*; *(voucher)* bon *m*; *(receipt)* reçu *m*, récépissé *m* **2** *Fam Old-fashioned Pej (girl)* **a c. (of a girl)** une gamine

chitchat [ˈtʃɪtˌtʃæt] *(pt & pp* **chitchatted**, *cont* **chitchatting***)* N *(UNCOUNT)* bavardage *m*, papotage *m*

VI bavarder, papoter

chitterlings [ˈtʃɪtəlɪŋz] NPL *Culin* tripes *fpl*

chivalrous [ˈʃɪvəlrəs] ADJ **1** *(courteous)* chevaleresque, courtois; *(gallant)* galant **2** *(exploit, tournament)* chevaleresque

chivalrously [ˈʃɪvəlrəslɪ] ADV *(courteously)* de façon chevaleresque, courtoisement; *(gallantly)* galamment

chivalry [ˈʃɪvəlrɪ] N **1** *(courtesy)* conduite *f* chevaleresque, courtoisie *f*; *(gallantry)* galanterie *f*; *Hum* **the age of c. is not dead** la galanterie existe encore **2** *(knights, system)* chevalerie *f*

chives [tʃaɪvz] NPL ciboulette *f*, civette *f*; **add some c.** ajoutez de la ciboulette *ou* civette

chivvy, chivy [ˈtʃɪvɪ] *(pt & pp* **chivvied** *or* **chivied***)* VT **1** *Fam (nag)* harceler□; **to c. sb into doing sth** harceler qn jusqu'à ce qu'il fasse qch; **you'll have to c. them along** il faudra que tu les fasses se grouiller **2** *(hunt ▸ game)* chasser; *(▸ criminal)* pourchasser

chlamydia [kləˈmɪdɪə] N *Med* chlamydia *f*

chloral [ˈklɔːrəl] N *Chem* chloral *m*

chlorate [ˈklɔːreɪt] N *Chem* chlorate *m*

chloric [ˈklɔːrɪk] ADJ *Chem* chlorique

▸▸ ***chloric acid*** acide *m* chlorique

chloride [ˈklɔːraɪd] N *Chem* chlorure *m*

▸▸ ***chloride of lime*** chlorure *m* de chaux; ***chloride of silver*** chlorure *m* d'argent

chlorinate [ˈklɔːrɪneɪt] VT *(water)* javelliser; *Chem* chlorurer, chlorer

chlorinated [ˈklɔːrɪˌneɪtɪd] ADJ *(water)* chloré

chlorination [ˌklɔːrɪˈneɪʃən] N *(of water)* chloration *f*, javellisation *f*; *Chem* chloration *f*

chlorine [ˈklɔːriːn] N *Chem* chlore *m*

chlorite [ˈklɔːraɪt] N *Chem* chlorite *m*

chlorofluorocarbon [ˌklɔːrəˌflɔːrəʊˈkɑːbən] N *Chem* chlorofluorocarbone *m*, chlorofluorocarbure *m*

chloroform [ˈklɒrəfɔːm] *Chem & Med* N chloroforme *m*

VT chloroformer

chlorophyll, *Am* **chlorophyl** [ˈklɒrəfɪl] N *Bot* chlorophylle *f*

chloroquine [ˈklɔːrəʊkwiːn] N *Pharm* chloroquine *f*

choc [tʃɒk] N *Fam* chocolat□ *m*; **a box of chocs** une boîte de chocolats□

choc-ice N *Br* = glace individuelle rectangulaire enrobée de chocolat

chock [tʃɒk] N *Tech (for door, wheel)* cale *f*; *(for barrel)* cale *f*, chantier *m*; *Naut* chantier *m*, cale *f*

VT *Tech (barrel, door, wheel)* caler; *Naut* mettre sur un chantier *ou* sur cales

chocka [ˈtʃɒkə], **chock-a-block, chock-full** ADJ *Br Fam (room, theatre)* plein à craquer; *(container)* bourré, plein à ras bord; **the town is c. with tourists** la ville est archipleine de touristes

chocolate [ˈtʃɒkələt] N *(drink, sweet)* chocolat *m*; **a piece of c.** un morceau de chocolat; **a box of chocolates** une boîte de chocolats; **a cup of hot c.** une tasse de chocolat (chaud)

COMP *(biscuit, cake)* au chocolat, chocolaté

ADJ chocolat *(inv)*

▸▸ ***chocolate bar*** barre *f* chocolatée; ***chocolate brown*** N (couleur *f*) chocolat *m inv* ADJ chocolat *(inv)*; ***chocolate chip cookie*** biscuit *m* aux pépites de chocolat; ***chocolate factory*** chocolaterie *f*; ***chocolate manufacturer*** chocolatier-confiseur *m*

choice [tʃɔɪs] N **1** *(act of choosing)* choix *m*; **to make one's c.** faire son choix; **you'll have to make a c.** il faudra que tu choisisses *ou* que tu fasses un choix; **to have first c.** pouvoir choisir en premier; **it's your c.** c'est à vous de choisir *ou* décider; **by** *or* **from c.** de *ou* par préférence; **the holiday destination of c.** la destination de prédilection de bien des vacanciers

2 *(option)* choix *m*, option *f*; **they were given a c. between basketball and soccer** ils ont eu le choix entre le basket et le foot; **you have no c. (in the matter)** vous n'avez pas le choix; **I had no c. but to leave** je ne pouvais que partir

3 *(selection)* choix *m*, assortiment *m*; **a wide c. of goods** un grand choix de marchandises; **available in a c. of colours** disponible en plusieurs couleurs

4 *(thing, person chosen)* choix *m*; **he would be a good c. for president** il ferait un bon président; **Spain would be my c.** je choisirais l'Espagne; **you made the right/wrong c.** vous avez fait le bon/mauvais choix

ADJ **1** *(fruit, meat)* de choix, de première qualité; *(wine)* fin **2** *(well-chosen ▸ phrase, words)* bien choisi; **in a few c. words** en quelques mots bien choisis **3** *(coarse ▸ language)* grossier

choir [ˈkwaɪə(r)] N **1** *(group of singers)* chœur *m*, chorale *f*; *(in church)* chœur *m*, maîtrise *f*; **male voice c.** chœur *m ou* chorale *f* d'hommes; **we sing in the c.** *(gen)* nous faisons partie du chœur *ou* de la chorale; *(in church)* nous faisons partie du chœur, nous chantons dans la maîtrise **2** *Archit* chœur *m* **3** *(group of instruments)* chœur *m*

▸▸ ***choir practice*** répétition *f* de la chorale; **we have c. practice tonight** nous avons chorale ce soir; ***choir school*** maîtrise *f*; ***choir stall*** stalle *f*

choirboy [ˈkwaɪəbɔɪ] N jeune choriste *m*

choirmaster [ˈkwaɪəˌmɑːstə(r)] N *(gen)* chef *m* de chœur; *(in church)* maître *m* de chapelle

choke [tʃəʊk] VI étouffer, s'étouffer, s'étrangler; **to c. on sth** s'étouffer *ou* s'étrangler en avalant qch de travers; **to c. to death** mourir étouffé; **to c. with laughter** s'étouffer *ou* s'étrangler de rire; **to c. with rage** s'étouffer *ou* s'étrangler de rage

VT **1** *(asphyxiate)* étrangler, étouffer; **in a voice choked with emotion** d'une voix étranglée par l'émotion **2** *(strangle)* étrangler **3** *(clog)* boucher, obstruer; **choked with traffic** embouteillé, bouché; **choked with weeds** étouffé par les mauvaises herbes

N **1** *Aut* starter *m*; *Tech (in pipe)* buse *f*; *Aut* **to pull out the c.** mettre le starter **2** *(of artichoke)* foin *m*

▸▸ ***choke chain*** *(for dog)* collier *m* étrangleur

▸ **choke back, choke down** VT SEP *(anger)* refouler, étouffer; *(tears)* refouler, contenir; *(complaint, cry)* retenir

▸ **choke up** VT SEP **1** *(block ▸ road)* boucher, embouteiller; *(▸ pipe)* boucher, obstruer; **the drain is all choked up with leaves** la bouche d'égout est complètement obstruée par les feuilles **2** *Fam (emotionally)* émouvoir□, toucher profondément□; **she was all choked up** elle était bouleversée□ *ou* tout émue

choked [tʃəʊkt] ADJ **1** *(cry, voice)* étranglé **2** *Br Fam (person ▸ moved)* secoué; *(▸ sad)* peiné, attristé; *(▸ annoyed)* énervé, fâché

choker [ˈtʃəʊkə(r)] N *(necklace)* collier *m* (court); *(neckband)* tour *m* de cou

choking [ˈtʃəʊkɪŋ] N étouffement *m*, suffocation *f*

ADJ étouffant, suffocant; **he made a c. sound** il a fait un bruit comme quelqu'un qui s'étouffe

cholera [ˈkɒlərə] N *Med & Vet* choléra *m*

choleric [ˈkɒlərɪk] ADJ colérique, coléreux

cholesterol [kəˈlestərɒl] N *Med* cholestérol *m*; **to have high c.** avoir du cholestérol

▸▸ ***cholesterol level*** taux *m* de cholestérol, cholestérolémie *f*

chomp [tʃɒmp] *Fam* VT mastiquer bruyamment□

VI mastiquer bruyamment□

N mastication *f* bruyante□

choo-choo [ˈtʃuːˌtʃuː] *(pl* **choo-choos***)* N *(in children's language)* train□ *m*

chook [tʃʊk] N *Austr Fam (chicken)* poulet□ *m*

choose [tʃuːz] *(pt* **chose** [tʃəʊz], *pp* **chosen** [ˈtʃəʊzən]) VT **1** *(select)* choisir, prendre; **she chose a man as her assistant** elle a pris un homme pour assistant; **c. your words carefully** pesez bien vos mots; **there's little** *or* **not much to c. between the two parties** les deux partis se valent **2** *(elect)* élire **3** *(decide)* décider, juger bon; **they chose to ignore his rudeness** ils ont préféré ignorer sa grossièreté; **I didn't c. to invite her** *(invited unwillingly)* je l'ai invitée contre mon gré

VI choisir; **do as you c.** faites comme bon vous semble *ou* comme vous l'entendez *ou* comme vous voulez; **to c. from** *or* **between several people** choisir entre *ou* parmi plusieurs personnes; **there's not a lot to c. from** il n'y a pas beaucoup de choix

chooser [ˈtʃuːzə(r)] N *Comput* sélecteur *m*

choosing [ˈtʃuːzɪŋ] N choix *m*; **it was none of my c.** ce n'est pas moi qui l'ai choisi; **the circumstances were not of his c.** les circonstances n'étaient pas de son fait

choosy [ˈtʃuːzɪ] *(compar* **choosier**, *superl* **choosiest***)* ADJ *Fam* difficile□; **she's very c. about what she eats** elle ne mange pas n'importe quoi□, elle est très difficile sur la nourriture□; **you decide, I'm not c.** décide, cela m'est égal; **he can't afford to be c.** il ne peut pas se permettre de faire le difficile

chop [tʃɒp] *(pt & pp* **chopped**, *cont* **chopping***)* VT **1** *(cut ▸ gen)* couper; *(▸ wood)* couper; *Culin* hacher; **to c. sth finely** hacher qch menu; **to c. logic** couper les cheveux en quatre **2** *Fam (reduce ▸ budget, funding)* réduire□, diminuer□; *(▸ project)* mettre au rancart **3** *Sport (ball)* couper

VI **1** *(change direction)* varier; **to c. and change** changer constamment d'avis; **he's always chopping and changing** *(changing his mind)* il change d'opinion à tout bout de champ **2** *Fam* **c., c.!** vite, vite!

N **1** *(blow ▸ with axe)* coup *m* de hache; *(▸ with hand)* coup *m*; *Fam* **to get** *or* **to be given the c.** *Br (employee)* être viré; *(project)* être mis au rancart; *(chapter, part of text, film etc)* être supprimé□; **he's for the c.** il va y passer

2 *Culin (of pork, lamb)* côtelette *f*

3 *Golf* coup *m* piqué

4 *(in tennis)* volée *f* coupée *ou* arrêtée

• **chops** NPL *(jowls ▸ of person)* joue *f*; *(▸ of ani-*

mal) bajoues *fpl*; **to lick one's chops** se pourlécher les babines

▸**chop at VT INSEP 1** *(try to cut* ▸ *gen)* tenter de couper; *(*▸ *with axe)* donner des coups de hache à, tailler (à la hache) **2** *(try to hit)* essayer de frapper

▸**chop down VT SEP** abattre

▸**chop off VT SEP** trancher, couper; **they chopped off the king's head** ils ont coupé la tête au roi

▸**chop up VT SEP** couper en morceaux, hacher; *Culin* hacher

chophouse [ˈtʃɒphaʊs, *pl* -haʊzɪz] **N** *Old-fashioned* restaurant *m* spécialisé dans les grillades

chopper [ˈtʃɒpə(r)] **N 1** *Br (axe)* petite hache *f*; *Culin (cleaver)* couperet *m*, hachoir *m*

2 *Fam (helicopter)* hélico *m*

3 *Fam (motorcycle)* chopper *m*; *(bicycle)* vélo *m (à haut guidon)*

4 *Br Vulg (penis)* bite *f*

choppers [ˈtʃɒpəz] **NPL** *Fam (false teeth)* râtelier *m*; *(teeth)* ratiches *fpl*

chopping [ˈtʃɒpɪŋ] **N** *(of wood)* coupe *f*

▸▸ ***chopping block*** billot *m*; ***chopping board*** planche *f* à découper; ***chopping knife*** couperet *m*, hachoir *m*

choppy [ˈtʃɒpɪ] *(compar* **choppier**, *superl* **choppiest) ADJ 1** *(lake, sea)* un peu agité; *(waves)* clapotant **2** *(wind)* variable

chopstick [ˈtʃɒpstɪk] **N** baguette *f (pour manger)*

choral [ˈkɔːrəl] **ADJ** choral

▸▸ ***choral society*** chorale *f*; ***choral symphony*** symphonie *f* avec chœur

chorale [kəˈrɑːl] **N** *Mus* **1** *(hymn)* chœur *m*, choral *m* **2** *Am (choir)* chœur *m*, chorale *f*

chord [kɔːd] **N 1** *Anat & Geom* corde *f* **2** *Mus (group of notes)* accord *m*; *Fig* **to strike** *or* **to touch a c., to strike the right c.** toucher la corde sensible; **his words struck a c. with the audience** ses paroles ont trouvé un écho auprès du public

chore [tʃɔː(r)] **N** *(task* ▸ *routine)* travail *m* de routine; *(*▸ *unpleasant)* corvée *f*; **household chores** travaux *mpl* ménagers; *Am* **I have to do the chores** il faut que je fasse le ménage

choreograph [ˈkɒrɪəgrɑːf] **VT** *(ballet, dance)* chorégraphier, faire la chorégraphie de; *Fig (meeting, party)* organiser

choreographer [ˌkɒrɪˈɒgrəfə(r)] **N** chorégraphe *mf*

choreographic [ˌkɒrɪəˈgræfɪk] **ADJ** chorégraphique

choreography [ˌkɒrɪˈɒgrəfɪ] **N** chorégraphie *f*

chorister [ˈkɒrɪstə(r)] **N** choriste *mf*

chortle [ˈtʃɔːtəl] **VI** glousser; **to c. with delight at** *or* **over sth** glousser de plaisir à propos de qch

N gloussement *m*, petit rire *m*

chorus [ˈkɔːrəs] **N 1** *(choir)* chœur *m*, chorale *f*; **to sing in c.** chanter en chœur; **"no!," they shouted in c.** "non!," se sont-ils exclamés en chœur

2 *(piece of music)* chœur *m*, choral *m*

3 *(refrain)* refrain *m*; **to join in the c.** *(several people)* chanter le refrain en chœur; *(one person)* se joindre aux autres pour le refrain

4 *Theat & Mus (dancers, singers)* troupe *f*; *(speakers)* chœur *m*

5 *(of complaints, groans)* concert *m*; **a c. of praise** un concert de louanges; **a c. of criticism** une avalanche de critiques

VT *(song)* chanter en chœur; *(poem)* réciter en chœur; *(approval, discontent)* dire *ou* exprimer en chœur; **"yes please!" they chorused** "oui, s'il vous plaît!" ont-ils répondu en chœur

▸▸ *Theat & Mus* ***chorus girl*** girl *f*; *Theat & Mus* ***chorus line*** troupe *f*

chorusmaster [ˈkɔːrəsˌmɑːstə(r)] **N** *Theat & Mus* maître *m* de chant

chosen [ˈtʃəʊzən] *pp of* **choose**

ADJ choisi; **the c. few who were invited to the wedding** les quelques privilégiés qui ont été invités au mariage; **the c. people** le peuple élu

NPL the c. les élus *mpl*

chough [tʃʌf] **N** *Orn* crave *m*

choux [ʃuː] **N** *(pastry)* pâte *f* à choux

▸▸ ***choux bun*** chou *m* à la crème; ***choux pastry*** pâte *f* à choux

chow [tʃaʊ] **N 1** *(dog)* chow-chow *m* **2** *Fam (food)* bouffe *f*

▸**chow down** *Am Fam* **VT SEP** bouffer

VI bouffer

chow-chow N *(dog)* chow-chow *m*

chowder [ˈtʃaʊdə(r)] **N** *Culin* = potage épais contenant du poisson ou des fruits de mer

Christ [kraɪst] **PR N** le Christ, Jésus-Christ *m*; **the C. child** l'enfant *m* Jésus

EXCLAM *very Fam* Bon Dieu (de Bon Dieu)!; **C. Almighty!** nom de Dieu!; **for C.'s sake!** bon sang!

christen [ˈkrɪsən] **VT 1** *(gen)* appeler, nommer; *(nickname)* baptiser, surnommer; *Naut & Rel* baptiser; **to c. a child George** baptiser un enfant Georges; **she was christened Victoria but is known as Vicky** son nom de baptême est Victoria mais tout le monde l'appelle Vicky **2** *Fam (use for first time)* étrenner

Christendom [ˈkrɪsəndəm] **N** chrétienté *f*; **throughout C.** dans toute la chrétienté

christening [ˈkrɪsənɪŋ] **N** baptême *m*

COMP *(ceremony, robe)* de baptême

Christian [ˈkrɪstʃən] **N** chrétien(enne) *m,f*; **to become a C.** se convertir au christianisme

ADJ chrétien; *Fig (charitable)* charitable, bon; **C. burial** sépulture *f* en terre sainte; **the C. era** l'ère *f* chrétienne; **early C.** paléochrétien; **that wasn't very C. of you** ce n'était pas très charitable de ta part

▸▸ *Pol* ***Christian Democracy*** démocratie *f* chrétienne; *Pol* ***Christian Democrat*** **N** démocrate-chrétien(enne) *m,f* **ADJ** démocrate-chrétien; ▸▸ ***Christian name*** nom *m* de baptême, prénom *m*; **his C. name is Frank** il s'appelle Frank; ***Christian Science*** la Science chrétienne; ***Christian Scientist*** scientiste *mf* chrétien(enne)

Christianity [ˌkrɪstɪˈænətɪ] **N** christianisme *m*

christianize, -ise [ˈkrɪstʃənaɪz] **VT** christianiser, convertir au christianisme

Christmas [ˈkrɪsməs] **N** Noël *m*; **I'm staying with my parents over C.** je vais passer Noël chez mes parents; **at C.** à Noël; **for C.** pour Noël; **Merry C.!** joyeux Noël!

COMP *(party, present)* de Noël

▸▸ *Br* ***Christmas box*** étrennes *fpl (offertes à Noël)*; ***Christmas cake*** gâteau *m* de Noël *(cake décoré au sucre glace)*; ***Christmas card*** carte *f* de Noël; ***Christmas carol*** chant *m* de Noël, noël *m*; *Rel* cantique *m* de Noël; ***Christmas cracker*** = papillote contenant un pétard et une surprise traditionnelle au moment des fêtes; ***Christmas Day*** le jour de Noël; ***Christmas Eve*** la veille de Noël; ***Christmas Island*** l'île *f* Christmas; *Br* ***Christmas pudding*** pudding *m*, plum-pudding *m*; ***Christmas tree*** sapin *m ou* arbre *m* de Noël

CHRISTMAS CRACKER

Si vous êtes invité à un repas de Noël chez des Britanniques, vous trouverez très probablement un "Christmas cracker" à côté de votre assiette. Il s'agit d'une sorte de petit cylindre de carton en forme de papillote qui contient généralement un chapeau en papier, une blague ou une devinette, ainsi qu'un petit jouet ou un colifichet. Une personne tire de chaque côté du Christmas cracker qui s'ouvre alors en claquant – chaque cracker contenant un petit pétard – et seule une des deux personnes se retrouve avec la moitié de pétard qui contient les petites surprises. Ces dernières sont généralement médiocres et les blagues sont rarement très drôles, à tel point que pour faire allusion à la piètre qualité d'un objet ou d'une plaisanterie les gens diront "Did you get that in a Christmas cracker?" ("tu as trouvé ça dans un Christmas cracker?").

Christmassy [ˈkrɪsməsɪ] **ADJ** typique de Noël, qui rappelle la fête de Noël; **the town looks so C.** la ville a un tel air de fête; **those fairy lights make the town look very C.** les guirlandes lumineuses qui décorent la ville donnent vraiment le ton pour Noël; **I've just lost my job so I'm not feeling very C.** je viens juste de perdre mon travail alors je n'ai pas vraiment la tête à fêter Noël

Christmastide [ˈkrɪsməsˌtaɪd] **N** *Literary* la période de Noël *ou* des fêtes (de fin d'année) *(du 24 décembre au 6 janvier)*

Christopher [ˈkrɪstəfə(r)] **PR N C. Columbus** Christophe Colomb

chromatic [krəˈmætɪk] **ADJ** chromatique

▸▸ *Typ* ***chromatic printing*** impression *f* polychrome; *Mus* ***chromatic scale*** gamme *f* chromatique

chromatography [ˌkrəʊməˈtɒgrəfɪ] **N** *Chem* chromatographie *f*

chrome [krəʊm] **N** chrome *m*

COMP *(fittings, taps)* chromé

▸▸ ***chrome steel*** acier *m* chromé, chromé *m*; ***chrome tape*** bande *f* magnétique chromée; ***chrome yellow*** **N** jaune *m* de chrome **ADJ** jaune de chrome

chromium [ˈkrəʊmɪəm] **N** *Chem* chrome *m*

chromium-plated [-ˈpleɪtɪd] **ADJ** chromé

chromosome [ˈkrəʊməsəʊm] **N** *Biol* chromosome *m*

▸▸ ***chromosome abnormality*** aberration *f* chromosomique

chronic [ˈkrɒnɪk] **ADJ 1** *(long-lasting* ▸ *illness, unemployment)* chronique; **c. invalid** invalide *mf* chronique; **to suffer from c. ill health** être de santé fragile

2 *(habitual* ▸ *smoker, gambler)* invétéré

3 *(serious* ▸ *problem, situation)* difficile, grave

4 *Br Fam (very bad)* atroce[□], affreux[□]; **my back's hurting something c.** mon dos me fait un mal de chien

▸▸ *Med* ***chronic fatigue syndrome*** encéphalomyélite *f* myalgique, syndrome *m* de fatigue chronique

chronically [ˈkrɒnɪkəlɪ] **ADV 1** *(habitually)* chroniquement **2** *(severely)* gravement, sérieusement

chronicity [krɒˈnɪsɪtɪ] **N** *Med* chronicité *f*

chronicle [ˈkrɒnɪkəl] **N** chronique *f*

VT chroniquer, faire la chronique de

• **Chronicles N** *Bible* **the (Book of) Chronicles** le livre des Chroniques

chronicler [ˈkrɒnɪklə(r)] **N** chroniqueur(euse) *m,f*

chronological [ˌkrɒnəˈlɒdʒɪkəl] **ADJ** chronologique; **in c. order** par ordre *ou* dans un ordre chronologique

chronologically [ˌkrɒnəˈlɒdʒɪkəlɪ] **ADV** chronologiquement, par ordre chronologique

chronology [krəˈnɒlədʒɪ] **N** chronologie *f*

chronometer [krəˈnɒmɪtə(r)] **N** chronomètre *m*

chronometry [krəˈnɒmɪtrɪ] **N** chronométrie *f*

chrysalid [ˈkrɪsəlɪd] *(pl* **chrysalides** [-ˈsælɪdiːz]) **N** *Entom* chrysalide *f*

chrysanthemum [krɪˈsænθəməm] **N** chrysanthème *m*

chub [tʃʌb] *(pl* **inv** *or* **chubs) N** *Ich* chevaine *m*

chubbiness [ˈtʃʌbɪnɪs] **N** rondeur *f*

chubby [ˈtʃʌbɪ] *(compar* **chubbier**, *superl* **chubbiest) ADJ** *(fingers, person)* potelé; *(baby)* dodu; *(face)* joufflu; **c.-cheeked** joufflu

chuck [tʃʌk] **VT 1** *Fam (toss)* jeter[□], lancer[□]; **c. me that hammer** balance-moi le marteau; **they chucked him off the bus** ils l'ont vidé du bus

2 *Fam (give up* ▸ *activity, job)* laisser tomber[□], lâcher

3 *Fam (jilt* ▸ *boyfriend, girlfriend)* plaquer

4 *(tap)* tapoter; **she chucked the child under the chin** elle a tapoté le menton de l'enfant

5 *Scot Fam* **c. it!** *(stop it!)* arrête![□]

N *Br* **1** *(tap)* petite tape *f* **2** *Culin (steak)* morceau *m* de bœuf dans le paleron **3** *Fam (idiom)* **to give sb the c.** *(employee)* virer *ou* vider qn; *(boyfriend, girlfriend)* plaquer qn

▸▸ *Culin* ***chuck steak*** morceau *m* de bœuf dans le paleron; *Am* ***chuck wagon*** cantine *f* ambulante *(pour les cow-boys)*

▸**chuck away VT SEP** *Fam (old clothing, papers)* balancer; *(chance, opportunity)* laisser passer[□]; *(money)* jeter par les fenêtres

▸**chuck down VT SEP** *Br Fam* **it's chucking it down** *(raining)* il tombe des cordes

▸ **chuck in** VT SEP *Br Fam (give up ▸ activity, job)* lâcher; *(▸ attempt)* renoncer à; **he chucked it all in and bought a farm** il a tout plaqué pour acheter une ferme; **to c. one's hand in** *Cards* jeter ses cartes sur la table; *Fig (admit defeat)* s'avouer vaincu

▸ **chuck out** VT SEP *Fam (old clothing, papers)* balancer; *(person)* vider, sortir□; **he chucked the troublemakers out** il a flanqué les provocateurs à la porte

▸ **chuck up** *Fam* VT SEP *(give up)* laisser tomber□
VI *(vomit)* dégueuler

chucker-out ['tʃʌkər-] N *Br Fam* videur□ *m*

chucking-out time ['tʃʌkɪŋ-] N *Br Fam (in pub)* heure *f* de la fermeture□

chuckle ['tʃʌkəl] VI glousser, rire; **he chuckled to himself** il riait tout seul
N gloussement *m*, petit rire *m*; **they had a good c. over her mishap** sa mésaventure les a bien fait rire

chuddies ['tʃʌdɪz] NPL *Br Fam (underpants)* slibar *m*

chuff[1] [tʃʌf] VI souffler, haleter; **the train chuffed up the hill** le train a monté la pente en haletant

chuff[2] N *Br Vulg (vagina)* craquette *f*, fente *f*; *(anus)* trou *m* de balle; **to be as tight as a nun's c.** *(miserly)* avoir des oursins dans le porte-monnaie

chuffed [tʃʌft] ADJ *Br Fam* vachement *ou* super content, ravi□; **to be c. about** *or* **at sth** être ravi de qch; **I was c. to bits** j'étais vachement content; **I'm really c. with myself** je suis vachement content de moi

chuffing ['tʃʌfɪŋ] ADJ *Br very Fam* foutu, sacré; **that c. idiot** ce sombre crétin

chug [tʃʌg] *(pt & pp* **chugged**, *cont* **chugging)** N **1** *(of engine, car, train)* halètement *m* **2** *Br very Fam* **to have a c.** *(masturbate)* se branler
VT *Fam (drink quickly)* descendre
VI **1** *(make noise ▸ engine, car, train)* s'essouffler, haleter **2** *(move)* avancer en soufflant *ou* en haletant **3** *Br very Fam (masturbate)* se branler

▸ **chug along** VI *Fam (move slowly)* se traîner□; **the guy in front was chugging along at 30 km/h** le type devant moi se traînait à 30 km/h

chum [tʃʌm] *Fam* N copain (copine) *m,f*; **the game's up, c.** c'est fichu, mon vieux

▸ **chum up** *(pt & pp* **chummed**, *cont* **chumming)** VT INSEP *Fam* **to c. up with sb** devenir copain (copine) avec qn

chummy ['tʃʌmɪ] *(compar* **chummier**, *superl* **chummiest)** ADJ *Fam* amical□; **she's very c. with the boss** elle est très copine avec le patron

chump [tʃʌmp] N *Fam Old-fashioned* **1** *(dolt ▸ boy)* ballot *m*; *(▸ girl)* gourde *f* **2** *Br (head)* boule *f*; **you're off your c.!** tu as perdu la boule!
▸▸ *Br Culin* ***chump chop*** côtelette *f* d'agneau *(coupée dans le gigot)*

chunder ['tʃʌndə(r)] *Fam* N vomi□ *m*
VI dégueuler

chunk [tʃʌŋk] N *(of meat, wood)* gros morceau *m*; *(of budget, time)* grande partie *f*

chunky ['tʃʌŋkɪ] *(compar* **chunkier**, *superl* **chunkiest)** ADJ **1** *(person ▸ stocky)* trapu; *(▸ chubby)* potelé, enrobé; *(food, stew)* avec des morceaux **2** *Br (clothing, sweater)* de grosse laine; *(jewellery)* gros (grosse)

Chunnel ['tʃʌnəl] N *Br Fam* **the C.** le tunnel sous la Manche□, l'Eurotunnel□ *m*

chunter ['tʃʌntə(r)] VI *Br* râler, rouspéter; **what's he chuntering on about now?** qu'est-ce qu'il a encore à râler *ou* rouspéter?

church [tʃɜ:tʃ] N **1** *(building ▸ gen)* église *f*; *(▸ Protestant)* église *f*, temple *m*; **I saw her in c.** je l'ai vue à l'église
2 *(services ▸ Protestant)* office *m*; *(▸ Catholic)* messe *f*; **to go to c.** *(Protestants)* aller au temple *ou* à l'office; *(Catholics)* aller à la messe *ou* à l'église; **do you go to c.?** êtes-vous pratiquant?
3 *(denomination)* Église *f*; **churches all over the world have condemned this decision** toutes les Églises du monde ont condamné cette décision
4 *(UNCOUNT) (clergy)* **the c.** les ordres *mpl*; **to go into the c.** entrer dans les ordres; **to leave the c.** quitter les ordres
COMP *(bell, roof)* d'église
• **Church** N *(institution)* **the C.** l'Église *f*; **the Anglican C.** l'Église *f* anglicane; **the (Roman) Catholic C.** l'Église *f* catholique; **C. of England** Église *f* anglicane; **C. of Scotland/Ireland** Église *f* d'Écosse/d'Irlande
▸▸ ***Church Fathers*** Pères *mpl* de l'Église; ***church hall*** salle *f* paroissiale; ***church service*** office *m*, culte *m*; ***church wedding*** mariage *m* religieux

churchgoer ['tʃɜ:tʃ,gəʊə(r)] N pratiquant(e) *m,f*

churchgoing ['tʃɜ:tʃ,gəʊɪŋ] ADJ pratiquant; **the c. public** les gens qui vont à l'église
N fréquentation *f* des églises

Churchillian [,tʃɜ:'tʃɪlɪən] ADJ churchillien

churchman ['tʃɜ:tʃmən] *(pl* **churchmen** [-mən]) N *(clergyman)* ecclésiastique *m*; *(churchgoer)* pratiquant *m*

churchwarden [,tʃɜ:tʃ'wɔ:dən] N bedeau *m*, marguillier *m*

churchwoman ['tʃɜ:tʃ,wʊmən] *(pl* **churchwomen** [-,wɪmɪn]) N **1** *(clergywoman)* femme *f* d'église **2** pratiquante *f*

churchy ['tʃɜ:tʃɪ] *(compar* **churchier**, *superl* **churchiest)** ADJ **1** *(atmosphere, song)* qui rappelle l'église **2** *Fam Pej (person)* bigot

churchyard ['tʃɜ:tʃjɑ:d] N *(grounds)* terrain *m* autour de l'église; *(graveyard)* cimetière *m (autour d'une église)*

churl [tʃɜ:l] N *Literary (ill-bred person)* rustre *mf*, malotru(e) *m,f*; *(surly person)* ronchon(onne) *m,f*

churlish ['tʃɜ:lɪʃ] ADJ *(rude)* fruste, grossier; *(bad-tempered ▸ person)* qui a mauvais caractère, revêche; *(▸ attitude, behaviour)* revêche, désagréable; **it would be c. not to acknowledge the invitation** ce serait grossier *ou* impoli de ne pas répondre à l'invitation

churlishly ['tʃɜ:lɪʃlɪ] ADV *(rudely)* grossièrement; *(in bad-tempered manner)* hargneusement, de façon revêche

churlishness ['tʃɜ:lɪʃnɪs] N *(rudeness)* grossièreté *f*; *(bad temper ▸ habitual)* mauvais caractère *m*; *(▸ temporary)* mauvaise humeur *f*

churn [tʃɜ:n] VT **1** *(cream)* baratter **2** *(mud)* remuer; *(water)* faire bouillonner
VI *(sea, water)* bouillonner; *Fig* **the thought made my stomach c.** j'ai eu l'estomac tout retourné à cette idée
N **1** *(for butter)* baratte *f* **2** *Br (milk can)* bidon *m* **3** *Mktg* perte *f* de clients passés à la concurrence

▸ **churn out** VT SEP *Fam* **1** *(produce rapidly ▸ gen)* produire rapidement□; *(▸ novels, reports)* pondre à la chaîne *ou* en série **2** *(produce mechanically)* débiter

▸ **churn up** VT SEP *(mud)* remuer; *(sea, water)* faire bouillonner; *Fig* **I felt all churned up** *(nervous)* j'étais tout retourné; *(excited)* j'étais tout excité

churning ['tʃɜ:nɪŋ] N *(of cream)* barattage *m*

chute [ʃu:t] N **1** *(for parcels)* glissière *f*; *(for rubbish)* vide-ordures *m inv*
2 *(in playground, swimming pool)* toboggan *m*
3 *(in river)* rapide *m*
4 *Fam (parachute)* parachute□ *m*

chutney ['tʃʌtnɪ] N chutney *m (condiment à base de fruits)*

chutzpah ['hʊtspə] N *esp Am Fam* culot *m*

chyme [kaɪm] N *Physiol* chyme *m*

CIA [,si:aɪ'eɪ] N *Am (abbr* **Central Intelligence Agency)** CIA *f*

ciborium [sɪ'bɔ:rɪəm] *(pl* **ciboria**[-rɪə]) N *Rel (vessel)* ciboire *m*

cicada [sɪ'kɑ:də] *(pl* **cicadas** *or* **cicadae** [-di:]) N *Entom* cigale *f*

cicatrice ['sɪkətrɪs], **cicatrix** ['sɪkətrɪks] *(pl* **cicatrices** [-'traɪsi:z]) N *Med* cicatrice *f*

Cicero ['sɪsərəʊ] PR N Cicéron

cicerone [,tʃɪtʃə'rəʊnɪ] *(pl* **cicerones** *or* **ciceroni** [-ni:]) N cicérone *m*, guide *m*

CID [,si:aɪ'di:] N *(abbr* **Criminal Investigation Department)** = police judiciaire britannique, PJ *f*

cider ['saɪdə(r)] N **1** *Br (alcoholic drink)* cidre *m* **2** *Am (apple juice)* jus *m* de pommes
▸▸ ***cider apple*** pomme *f* à cidre; ***cider press*** pressoir *m* à cidre; ***cider vinegar*** vinaigre *m* de cidre

cif, CIF [,si:aɪ'ef] N *Com (abbr* **cost, insurance and freight)** CAF, caf

cigar [sɪ'gɑ:(r)] N cigare *m*
COMP *(box, case, tobacco)* à cigares; *(ash, smoke)* de cigare
▸▸ ***cigar cutter*** coupe-cigares *m inv*; ***cigar holder*** fume-cigare *m inv*; ***cigar lighter*** allume-cigares *m inv*

cigarette, *Am* **cigaret** [,sɪgə'ret] N cigarette *f*
COMP *(ash, butt, burn)* de cigarette; *(packet, smoke)* de cigarettes; *(paper, tobacco)* à cigarettes
▸▸ ***cigarette card*** = image offerte autrefois avec chaque paquet de cigarettes; ***cigarette case*** étui *m* à cigarettes, porte-cigarettes *m inv*; ***cigarette end*** mégot *m*; ***cigarette holder*** fume-cigarette *m inv*; ***cigarette lighter*** briquet *m*; ***cigarette machine*** *(vending machine)* distributeur *m* automatique de cigarettes; *(for rolling cigarettes)* rouleuse *f*; ***cigarette smoker*** fumeur(euse) *m,f* (de cigarettes)

ciggie, ciggy ['sɪgɪ] *(pl* **ciggies)** N *Fam* clope *m or f*, sèche *f*

CIM [,si:aɪ'em] N *Comput (abbr* **computer-integrated manufacturing)** CFAO *f*

CIM waybill N *Com* lettre *f* de voiture CIM

C-in-C *Mil (written abbr* **Commander-in-Chief)** commandant *m* en chef, généralissime *m*

cinch [sɪntʃ] N **1** *Fam* **it's a c.** *(easy to do)* c'est simple comme bonjour, c'est du gâteau; *(certainty)* c'est du tout cuit **2** *Am (for saddle)* sous-ventrière *f*, sangle *f*
VT *Am (horse)* sangler; *(saddle)* attacher par une sangle

cinder ['sɪndə(r)] N cendre *f*; **cinders** *(in fireplace)* cendres *fpl*; *(from furnace, volcano)* scories *fpl*; **burnt to a c.** réduit en cendres
▸▸ *Am* ***cinder block*** parpaing *m*; ***cinder track*** (piste *f*) cendrée *f*

Cinderella [,sɪndə'relə] PR N Cendrillon
N *Fig* parent *m* pauvre□

Cinders ['sɪndəz] N *Fam* Cendrillon□ *f*

cineaste, cineast ['sɪnɪæst] N cinéphile *mf*

cine camera ['sɪnɪ-] N *Br* caméra *f*

cine-film N *Br* film *m*

cinema ['sɪnəmə] N *Br (building)* cinéma *m*; *esp Br (industry)* (industrie *f* du) cinéma *m*; **to go to the c.** aller au cinéma
▸▸ *Mktg* ***cinema advertising*** publicité *f* au cinéma; *TV* ***cinema channel*** chaîne *f* de cinéma

cinema-goer N *Br* personne *f* qui fréquente les cinémas

cinema-going *Br* N fréquentation *f* des salles de cinéma
ADJ **the c. public** les cinéphiles *mfpl*

CinemaScope® ['sɪnəməskəʊp] N CinémaScope® *m*

cinematic [,sɪnɪ'mætɪk] ADJ *(tradition, style, technique)* cinématographique; **the novel has a very c. quality** le roman utilise des effets qui rappellent le cinéma

cinematograph [,sɪnə'mætəgrɑ:f] N *Br* cinématographe *m*

cinematographer [,sɪnəmə'tɒgrəfə(r)] N directeur(trice) *m,f* de la photographie, chef opérateur *m*

cinematographic [,sɪnəmætə'græfɪk] ADJ cinématographique

cinematography [,sɪnəmə'tɒgrəfɪ] N *Br* cinématographie *f*

cinéma vérité [sɪnəmə'verɪteɪ] N cinéma-vérité *m*

cinephile ['sɪnɪfaɪl] N *Am* cinéphile *mf*

Cinerama® [,sɪnə'rɑ:mə] N Cinérama® *m*

cineraria [,sɪnə'reərɪə] N *Bot* cinéraire *f*

cinnabar ['sɪnəbɑ:(r)] N *Miner* cinabre *m*

cinnamon ['sɪnəmən] N **1** *(spice)* cannelle *f* **2** *(tree)* cannelier *m* **3** *(colour)* cannelle *f*
COMP *(flavour, tea)* à la cannelle
ADJ cannelle *(inv)*
▸▸ ***cinnamon stick*** bâton *m* de cannelle

cinqfoil, cinquefoil ['sɪŋkfɔɪl] **N 1** *Bot* potentille *f* rampante, quintefeuille *f* **2** *Archit* quintefeuille *m*

cipher ['saɪfə(r)] **N 1** *(code)* chiffre *m*, code *m* secret; **written in c.** crypté, codé
2 *(monogram)* chiffre *m*, monogramme *m*
3 *(Arabic numeral)* chiffre *m*
4 *Literary (zero)* zéro *m*; *Fig* **they're mere ciphers** ce sont des moins que rien
VT 1 *(encode)* crypter, chiffrer, coder **2** *(calculate)* chiffrer

circa ['sɜːkə] **PREP** circa, vers

circadian [sɜː'keɪdɪən] **ADJ** *Biol* circadien

circle ['sɜːkəl] **N 1** *(gen) & Geom* cercle *m*; *(around eyes)* cerne *m*; **we stood in a c. around him** nous formions (un) cercle *ou* nous nous tenions en cercle autour de lui; **she had dark circles under her eyes** elle avait les yeux cernés, elle avait des cernes sous les yeux; **he had us going** *or* **running round in circles trying to find the information** il nous a fait tourner en rond à chercher les renseignements; **to come full c.** revenir au point de départ, boucler la boucle
2 *(group of people)* cercle *m*, groupe *m*; **the family c.** le cercle familial; **she has a wide c. of friends** elle a beaucoup d'amis *ou* un grand cercle d'amis; **his c. of advisers** son groupe de conseillers; **in artistic/political circles** dans les milieux artistiques/politiques
3 *Theat* balcon *m*
4 *Archeol* **stone c.** cromlech *m*
VT 1 *(draw circle round)* entourer (d'un cercle), encercler **2** *(move round)* tourner autour de; **the Moon circles the Earth** la lune est en orbite autour *ou* tourne autour de la Terre **3** *(surround)* encercler, entourer
VI 1 *(bird, plane)* faire *ou* décrire des cercles; **the plane circled overhead** l'avion a décrit des cercles dans le ciel; *Fig* **she circled round the issue** elle tournait autour du pot **2** *(planet)* tourner

circlet ['sɜːklɪt] **N** *(on head ▸ crown)* couronne *f*; *(▸ for hair)* bandeau *m*; *(on arm)* brassard *m*; *(on finger)* anneau *m*

circlip ['sɜːklɪp] **N** *Tech* circlip *m*
▸▸ ***circlip pliers*** pince *f* à circlip

circuit ['sɜːkɪt] **N 1** *(series of events, venues, places)* circuit *m*; **the tennis c.** le circuit des matches de tennis
2 *(periodical journey)* tournée *f*; *Law* tournée *f* *(d'un juge d'assises)*; **to be on the western c.** faire la tournée de l'ouest
3 *(journey around)* circuit *m*, tour *m*; **we made a c. of the grounds** nous avons fait le tour des terrains; **the Earth's c. around the Sun** l'orbite de la Terre autour du Soleil
4 *Elec* circuit *m*
5 *Sport (track)* circuit *m*, parcours *m*; **to make one c. of the track** faire un tour de circuit
▸▸ *Elec* ***circuit board*** plaquette *f* (de circuits imprimés); *Elec* ***circuit breaker*** disjoncteur *m*; *Law* ***circuit court*** = tribunal en service dans les principales villes de province lors du passage du "circuit judge"; *Law* ***circuit judge*** *Br* juge *m* itinérant; *Am* juge *m* de la Cour d'appel; *Sport* ***circuit training*** programme *m* d'exercices en salle

circuitous [sə'kjuːɪtəs] **ADJ** *(route)* qui fait un détour, détourné; *(journey)* compliqué; *Fig (reasoning, thinking)* contourné, compliqué; **by c. means** par des moyens détournés *ou* indirects

circuitously [sə'kjuːɪtəslɪ] **ADV** *(reach destination)* par le chemin le plus long; *(reason, argue)* avec beaucoup de circonvolutions

circuitry ['sɜːkɪtrɪ] **N** système *m* de circuits

circular ['sɜːkjʊlə(r)] **ADJ 1** *(movement, shape, ticket)* circulaire; **c. journey** voyage *m* circulaire, circuit *m* **2** *(reasoning)* faux (fausse), mal fondé
N *(letter, memo)* circulaire *f*; *(publicity material)* prospectus *m*
▸▸ ***circular argument*** pétition *f* de principe; ***circular letter*** circulaire *f*; *Tech* ***circular saw*** scie *f* circulaire

circularity [ˌsɜːkjʊ'lærətɪ] **N 1** *(of movement, shape)* forme *f* circulaire **2** *(of reasoning, argument)* circularité *f*

circularize, -ise ['sɜːkjʊləraɪz] **VT** *(send letters to)* envoyer des circulaires à; *(send publicity material to)* envoyer des prospectus à

circulate ['sɜːkjʊleɪt] **VT 1** *(book, bottle)* faire circuler; *(document ▸ from person to person)* faire circuler; *(▸ in mass mailing)* diffuser; *(news, rumour)* propager; **the memo was circulated to all members of staff** on a fait circuler le document parmi tout le personnel **2** *(banknotes)* mettre en circulation, émettre
VI circuler; *(at a party)* aller de groupe en groupe

circulating ['sɜːkjʊleɪtɪŋ] **ADJ** circulant
▸▸ *Math* ***circulating decimal*** fraction *f* périodique; ***circulating library*** *(mobile library)* bibliothèque *f* ambulante *ou* mobile; *Am (lending library)* bibliothèque *f* de prêt

circulation [ˌsɜːkjʊ'leɪʃən] **N 1** *(gen)* circulation *f*; **to be in c.** *(book, money)* être en circulation; *(person)* être dans le circuit; **notes in c.** billets en circulation; **the memo was for internal c. only** c'était une note de service à usage interne uniquement; **she's out of c. at the moment** elle a disparu de la circulation pour l'instant
2 *(of magazine, newspaper)* tirage *m*; **a newspaper with a large c.** un journal à grand tirage; **the Times has a c. of 200,000** le Times tire à 200 000 exemplaires
3 *Anat & Bot* circulation *f*; **to have good/poor c.** avoir une bonne/une mauvaise circulation
4 *(of traffic)* circulation *f*
▸▸ *Press* ***circulation figures*** chiffres *mpl* de diffusion

> Note that the French word **circulation** also means **traffic**.

circulatory [ˌsɜːkjʊ'leɪtərɪ] **ADJ** *Anat & Bot* circulatoire

circumcise ['sɜːkəmˌsaɪz] **VT** *(boy)* circoncire; *(girl)* exciser

circumcised ['sɜːkəmˌsaɪzd] **ADJ** *(boy, man)* circoncis

circumcision [ˌsɜːkəm'sɪʒən] **N** *(act)* circoncision *f*; *Rel* **the C.** la (fête de la) Circoncision; **female c.** excision *f*

circumference [sə'kʌmfərəns] **N** circonférence *f*; **to be 30 metres in c.** avoir 30 mètres de circonférence

circumflex ['sɜːkəmfleks] *Ling* **N** accent *m* circonflexe
ADJ circonflexe

circumlocution [ˌsɜːkəmlə'kjuːʃən] **N** circonlocution *f*, périphrase *f*; **without c.** sans ambages

circumlocutory [ˌsɜːkəm'lɒkjʊtərɪ] **ADJ** qui procède par circonlocutions, périphrastique

circumnavigate [ˌsɜːkəm'nævɪgeɪt] **VT** *(iceberg, island)* contourner; **to c. the world** faire le tour du monde

circumnavigation [ˌsɜːkəmˌnævɪ'geɪʃən] **N** circumnavigation *f*

circumscribe ['sɜːkəmskraɪb] **VT 1** *(limit)* restreindre, limiter **2** *Math* circonscrire

circumscribed ['sɜːkəmskraɪbd] **ADJ 1** *(limited)* restreint, limité **2** *Math* circonscrit

circumscription [ˌsɜːkəm'skrɪpʃən] **N 1** *(limitation)* restriction *f*, limitation *f* **2** *Math* circonscription *f*

circumspect ['sɜːkəmspekt] **ADJ** circonspect

circumspection [ˌsɜːkəm'spekʃən] **N** circonspection *f*

circumspectly ['sɜːkəmˌspektlɪ] **ADV** avec circonspection

circumstance ['sɜːkəmstəns] **N** *(UNCOUNT)* **1** *(events)* **force of c.** contrainte *f* *ou* force *f* des circonstances; **I am a victim of c.** je suis victime des circonstances **2** *Formal (ceremony)* **pomp and c.** grand apparat *m*, pompe *f*
• **circumstances NPL 1** *(conditions)* circonstance *f*, situation *f*; **in** *or* **under these circumstances** dans les circonstances actuelles, vu la situation actuelle *ou* l'état actuel des choses; **in** *or* **under normal circumstances** en temps normal; **under no circumstances** en aucun cas; **due to circumstances beyond our control** en raison de circonstances indépendantes de notre volonté **2** *(facts)* circonstance *f*, détail *m*; **the circumstances of her death** les circonstances de sa mort **3** *(financial situation)* **if his circumstances allowed** si ses moyens le permettaient; **in easy circumstances** à l'aise

circumstantial [ˌsɜːkəm'stænʃəl] **ADJ 1** *(incidental)* accidentel, fortuit **2** *Formal (description, report)* circonstancié, détaillé
▸▸ *Law* ***circumstantial evidence*** preuves *fpl* indirectes

circumstantiate [ˌsɜːkəm'stænʃɪeɪt] **VT** *(event, report)* donner des détails circonstanciés sur; *Law (evidence)* confirmer en donnant des détails sur

circumvent [ˌsɜːkəm'vent] **VT 1** *(law, rule)* tourner, contourner **2** *(outwit ▸ person)* circonvenir, manipuler; *(▸ plan)* faire échouer

circumvention [ˌsɜːkəm'venʃən] **N** *(of law, rule)* fait *m* de tourner *ou* contourner

circus ['sɜːkəs] **N 1** *(gen) & Antiq* cirque *m*; **to join a c.** entrer dans un cirque **2** *Br (roundabout)* rond-point *m*
COMP *clown, performer* de cirque

cirrhosis [sɪ'rəʊsɪs] **N** *(UNCOUNT) Med* cirrhose *f*; **c. of the liver** cirrhose *f* du foie; **to have c.** avoir une cirrhose

cirrus ['sɪrəs] *(pl* **cirri** [-raɪ]) **N 1** *Met* cirrus *m* **2** *Bot* vrille *f*

CIS [ˌsiːaɪ'es] **N** *(abbr* **Commonwealth of Independent States)** CEI *f*

cisalpine [sɪs'ælpaɪn] **ADJ** cisalpin
▸▸ ***Cisalpine Gaul*** Gaule *f* cisalpine

cissy = **sissy**

Cistercian [sɪ'stɜːʃən] *Rel* **N** cistercien(enne) *m,f*
ADJ cistercien
▸▸ ***the Cistercian Order*** l'ordre *m* de Cîteaux

cistern ['sɪstən] **N** *(tank)* citerne *f*; *(for toilet)* réservoir *m* de chasse d'eau

citadel ['sɪtədəl] **N** *also Fig* citadelle *f*

citation [saɪ'teɪʃən] **N 1** *(quotation)* citation *f* **2** *Am Law (summons)* citation *f*

cite [saɪt] **VT 1** *(quote)* citer; **he cited it as an example** il l'a cité en exemple **2** *(commend)* citer; **she was cited for bravery** elle a été citée pour sa bravoure **3** *Law* citer; **they were cited to appear as witnesses** ils étaient cités comme témoins

citizen ['sɪtɪzən] **N 1** *(of nation, state)* citoyen(enne) *m,f*; *Admin (national)* ressortissant(e) *m,f*; **to become a French c.** prendre la nationalité française; **c. of the world** citoyen(enne) *m,f* du monde **2** *(of town)* habitant(e) *m,f* **3** *(civilian)* civil(e) *m,f* *(par opposition à "militaire")*
▸▸ *Admin* ***Citizens' Advice Bureau*** = en Grande-Bretagne, bureau où les citoyens peuvent obtenir des conseils d'ordre juridique, social etc; ***citizen's arrest*** = arrestation par un citoyen d'une personne soupçonnée d'avoir commis un délit; *Rad* ***Citizens' Band*** citizen band *f*; ***Citizens' Band radio*** CB *f*; *Admin* ***Citizen's Charter*** = programme lancé par le gouvernement britannique en 1991 et qui vise à améliorer la qualité des services publics

citizenry ['sɪtɪzənrɪ] *(pl* **citizenries**) **N** *(of nation)* (ensemble *m* des) citoyens *mpl*; *(of town)* (ensemble *m* des) habitants *mpl*

citizenship ['sɪtɪzənʃɪp] **N** citoyenneté *f*, nationalité *f*; **to apply for French c.** demander la citoyenneté *ou* nationalité française; **c. papers** déclaration *f* de naturalisation; **good c.** civisme *m*

citrate ['sɪtreɪt] **N** *Chem* citrate *m*

citric ['sɪtrɪk] **ADJ** *Chem* citrique
▸▸ ***citric acid*** acide *m* citrique

citron ['sɪtrən] **N** *Bot (fruit)* cédrat *m*; *(tree)* cédratier *m*

citronella [ˌsɪtrə'nelə] **N** *Bot* citronnelle *f*
▸▸ ***citronella oil*** citronnelle *f*

citrus fruit ['sɪtrəs-] **N a c.** un agrume; **c., citrus fruits** agrumes *mpl*

city ['sɪtɪ] *(pl* **cities**) **N** *(town)* (grande) ville *f*; **life in the c.** la vie en ville, la vie citadine; **the whole c. turned out** toute la ville était présente, tous les habitants de la ville étaient présents
COMP *(lights, limits, streets)* de la ville; *(officers, police, services)* municipal; *(life)* en ville, citadin; *Am Press (news)* local; *(page, press)* des nouvelles locales

• **City** N *Fin (of London)* = centre d'affaires de Londres; **the C.** la City (de Londres); **he's something in the C.** il travaille à la City (de Londres)
COMP *Br Press (news, page, press)* financier
▸▸ ***city break*** *(holiday)* court séjour *m* en ville; *Br* ***city centre*** centre *m* de la ville, centre-ville *m*; ***city council*** conseil *m* d'arrondissement; *Press* ***city desk*** *Br* service *m* financier; *Am* service *m* des nouvelles locales; *Press* ***city editor*** *Br* rédacteur (trice) *m,f* en chef pour les nouvelles financières; *Am* rédacteur(trice) *m,f* en chef pour les nouvelles locales; ***city fathers*** édiles *mpl* locaux; *Br* ***city hall*** **1** *(building)* mairie *f*, hôtel *m* de ville **2** *Am (municipal government)* administration *f* (municipale); *Am Admin* ***city manager*** administrateur(trice) *m,f (payé(e) par la municipalité pour gérer ses affaires)*; ***city planner*** urbaniste *mf*; ***city planning*** urbanisme *m*; *Fam Pej* ***city slicker*** = citadin sophistiqué; ***city technology college*** = collège technique britannique, généralement établi dans des quartiers défavorisés

THE CITY

La City, quartier financier de la capitale, est une circonscription administrative autonome de Londres ayant sa propre police.

cityscape ['sɪtɪˌskeɪp] **N** paysage *m* urbain
city-state **N** *Hist* cité *f*
civet ['sɪvɪt] **N** *Zool (mammal, secretion)* civette *f*
▸▸ ***civet cat*** civette *f*
civic ['sɪvɪk] **ADJ** *(authority, building)* municipal; *(duty, right)* civique
▸▸ ***civic centre*** = centre administratif d'une ville, parfois complété par des équipements de loisirs, cité *f* administrative
civics ['sɪvɪks] **N** *(UNCOUNT)* instruction *f* civique
civies = **civvies**
civil ['sɪvəl] **ADJ** **1** *(of community)* civil **2** *(non-military)* civil **3** *(polite)* poli, courtois, civil; **she was very c. to me** elle s'est montrée très aimable avec moi; **keep a c. tongue in your head!** restez poli!
▸▸ *Law* ***civil action*** action *f* civile; ***civil aircraft*** avion *m* civil; ***civil aviation*** aviation *f* civile; ***Civil Aviation Authority*** = organisme de contrôle des compagnies aériennes; *Mil* ***civil defence*** protection *f* civile; ***civil disobedience*** résistance *f* passive (à la loi); ***civil engineer*** ingénieur *m* des travaux publics; ***civil engineering*** génie *m* civil; ***civil law*** *(system)* code *m* civil; *(study)* droit *m* civil; *Law* ***civil liability*** responsabilité *f* civile; ***civil liberties*** libertés *fpl* civiques; *Br* ***Civil List*** liste *f* civile *(allouée à la famille royale britannique)*; ***civil marriage*** mariage *m* civil; ***civil partnership*** union *f* civile *(d'un couple homosexuel)*, pacs *m (d'un couple homosexuel)*; ***civil rights*** droits *mpl* civils *ou* civiques; ***the civil rights movement*** la lutte pour les droits civils *ou* civiques; *Admin* ***civil servant*** fonctionnaire *mf*; *Admin* ***civil service*** fonction *f* publique, administration *f*; **to be in the c. service** être fonctionnaire *ou* dans l'administration *ou* dans la fonction publique; ***civil war*** guerre *f* civile; **the American C. War** la guerre de Sécession; **the English C. War** la guerre civile anglaise; ***civil wedding*** mariage *m* civil; **we had a c. wedding** nous nous sommes mariés à la mairie

CIVIL PARTNERSHIP

Le Civil Partnerships Act (loi sur le partenariat civil) a été voté par le parlement britannique en 2004. Il garantit aux couples homosexuels les mêmes droits qu'aux couples mariés en matière de succession, de retraite, ainsi que pour ce qui concerne la garde et l'éducation des enfants. Cette loi est entrée en application en décembre 2005; le chanteur Elton John et son compagnon David Furnish furent parmi les premiers couples à en bénéficier. Bien que le partenariat civil ne soit pas à proprement parler un mariage, les termes "gay marriage" et "same-sex marriage" (mariage unisexe) s'emploient couramment et de nombreux couples organisent des festivités comme pour un mariage traditionnel. Il faut noter que contrairement au pacs, les civil partnerships ne concernent que les couples homosexuels.

civilian [sɪ'vɪljən] **ADJ** civil *(par opposition à "militaire")*; **in c. clothes** en civil; **in c. life** dans le civil
N civil(e) *m,f (par opposition à "militaire")*
civility [sɪ'vɪlətɪ] *(pl* **civilities)** **N** **1** *(quality)* courtoisie *f*, civilité *f* **2** *(act)* civilité *f*, politesse *f*
civilization, -isation [ˌsɪvɪlaɪ'zeɪʃən] **N** civilisation *f*; *Fam* **it's miles from c.** c'est à des kilomètres du monde civilisé
civilize, -ise ['sɪvɪlaɪz] **VT** civiliser
civilized, -ised ['sɪvɪlaɪzd] **ADJ** *(person, society)* civilisé; **they have real coffee in their office – very c.!** ils ont du vrai café dans leur bureau – la classe!; **their divorce was a very c. affair** ils ont divorcé comme des gens civilisés; **let's be c. about this** tâchons d'être conciliants
civilizing, -ising ['sɪvɪlaɪzɪŋ] **ADJ** **the c. influence of…** l'influence civilisatrice de…
civvy ['sɪvɪ] *(pl* **civies** *or* **civvies)** *Br Fam* **N** *(civilian)* civil(e)[a] *m,f (par opposition à "militaire")*
ADJ civil[a]
• **civvies** **NPL** *(dress)* vêtements *mpl* civils[a]; **in civvies** (habillé) en civil
▸▸ *Br Fam* ***civvy street*** vie *f* civile[a]; **in c. street** dans le civil[a], dans la vie civile[a]
CJD [ˌsiːdʒeɪ'diː] **N** *Med (abbr* **Creutzfeldt-Jakob disease)** MCJ *f*; **new variant C.** nouveau variant *m* de MCJ
CJEC [ˌsiːdʒeiː'siː] **N** *EU (abbr* **Court of Justice of the European Communities)** CJCE *f*
cl *(written abbr* **centilitre)** cl
clack [klæk] **VI** *(make noise)* claquer; *(jabber)* jacasser, papoter
VT faire claquer
N **1** *(sound)* claquement *m* **2** *Tech (valve)* clapet *m*
clacking ['klækɪŋ] **N** *(noise)* claquement *m*
clad [klæd] *(pt & pp* **clad,** *cont* **cladding)** *pt & pp of* **clothe**
ADJ *Literary* habillé, vêtu; **c. in rags** habillé *ou* vêtu de haillons
VT *Tech* revêtir
cladding ['klædɪŋ] **N** *Tech* revêtement *m*, parement *m*

CLAIM [kleɪm]

VT	
• prétendre **1**	• revendiquer **2**
• réclamer **2, 4, 5**	• demander **3, 4**
• récupérer **5**	
N	
• affirmation **1**	• droit **2**
• demande **3**	• demande d'indemnité **4**

VT **1** *(assert, maintain)* prétendre, déclarer; **it is claimed that…** on dit *ou* prétend que… *+ indicative*; **to c. to be sth** se faire passer pour qch, prétendre être qch; **he claims to be an expert** il se prétend expert; **to c. acquaintance with sb** prétendre connaître qn
2 *(assert one's right to)* revendiquer, réclamer; *(responsibility, right)* revendiquer; **he claims all the credit** il s'attribue tout le mérite; **to c. damages/one's due** réclamer des dommages et intérêts/son dû; **no one has yet claimed responsibility for the hijacking** le détournement n'a pas encore été revendiqué
3 *(apply for ▸ money)* demander; *(▸ expenses)* demander le remboursement de
4 *(call for ▸ attention)* réclamer, demander; *(▸ respect, sympathy)* solliciter
5 *(collect, take ▸ baggage)* récupérer; *(▸ lost property)* réclamer; **has anyone arrived to c. her?** *(lost child)* est-ce que quelqu'un est venu la chercher?; **the storm claimed five lives** *or* **five victims** l'orage a fait cinq victimes
VI **to c. for** *or* **on sth** *(insurance)* demander le paiement de qch; *(travel expenses)* demander le remboursement de qch
N **1** *(assertion)* affirmation *f*, prétention *f*; **they have been making all sorts of claims about their new product** ils ont paré leur nouveau produit de toutes sortes de qualités; **I make no claims to understand why** je ne prétends pas comprendre pourquoi; **the town lays c. to being the place where golf was invented** les gens de cette ville prétendent que c'est ici que le golf fut inventé
2 *(right)* droit *m*, titre *m*; *(by trade unions)* demande *f* d'augmentation, revendication *f* salariale; **c. to property** droit *m* à la propriété; **what is her c. to the throne?** quel est son titre à la couronne?; **his only c. to fame is that he once appeared on TV** c'est à une apparition à la télévision qu'il doit d'être célèbre
3 *(demand)* demande *f*; **he has no claims on me** je ne lui suis redevable de rien; **she has many claims on her time** elle est très prise; **to have many claims on one's purse** avoir beaucoup de frais; **to lay c. to** *(property etc)* prétendre à, revendiquer son droit à; *(skills)* s'attribuer; **we put in a c. for better working conditions** nous avons demandé de meilleures conditions de travail; **pay c.** revendications *fpl* salariales
4 *Ins* demande *f* d'indemnité, déclaration *f* de sinistre; **to put in a c. for sth** demander une indemnité pour qch, faire une déclaration de sinistre pour qch; **the company pays 65 percent of all claims** la société satisfait 65 pour cent de toutes les demandes de dédommagement
5 *(piece of land)* concession *f*
▸▸ *Ins* ***claims adjuster*** répartiteur(trice) *m,f*; *Ins* ***claim form*** *(for insurance)* formulaire *m* de déclaration de sinistre; *(for expenses)* note *f* de frais
▸ **claim back** **VT SEP** *(expenses, cost)* se faire rembourser; *(VAT)* récupérer

claimant ['kleɪmənt] **N** **1** *Admin & Ins* demandeur (eresse) *m,f*; *Law* demandeur(eresse) *m,f*, requérant(e) *m,f* **2** *(to throne)* prétendant(e) *m,f*
clairvoyance [kleə'vɔɪəns] **N** voyance *f*, don *m* de seconde vue
clairvoyant [kleə'vɔɪənt] **N** voyant(e) *m,f*, extralucide *mf*
ADJ doué de seconde vue
clam [klæm] *(pt & pp* **clammed,** *cont* **clamming)** **N** **1** *Zool* palourde *f*, clam *m*; *Fam* **to shut up like a c.** refuser de parler[a] **2** *Am Fam (dollar)* dollar[a] *m*
VI *Am* **to go clamming** aller ramasser des clams
▸▸ *Culin* ***clam chowder*** = potage épais aux palourdes
▸ **clam up** **VI** *Fam* ne plus piper mot; **don't c. up on me** parle-moi
clambake ['klæmbeɪk] **N** *Am* = repas de fruits de mer sur la plage; *Fig* fête *f*
clamber ['klæmbə(r)] **VI** grimper (en s'aidant des mains); **to c. aboard a train** se hisser à bord d'un train; **he clambered over the rocks** il a escaladé les rochers
N escalade *f*
clamminess ['klæmɪnɪs] **N** *(of hands, skin)* moiteur *f* froide; *(of air)* humidité *f* froide
clammy ['klæmɪ] *(compar* **clammier,** *superl* **clammiest)** **ADJ** *(hands, skin)* moite (et froid); *(weather)* humide, lourd; *(walls)* suintant, humide
clamor *Am* = **clamour**
clamorous ['klæmərəs] **ADJ** **1** *(noisy)* bruyant **2** *(demands)* insistant
clamorously ['klæmərəslɪ] **ADV** bruyamment
clamour, *Am* **clamor** ['klæmə(r)] **N** **1** *(noise)* clameur *f*, vociférations *fpl* **2** *(demand)* revendication *f* bruyante; *(protest)* tollé *m*; **there was a great c.** ça a été un tollé général
VI vociférer, crier; **to c. for sth** demander *ou* réclamer qch à grands cris *ou* à cor et à cri; **the children clamoured to go out** les enfants ont demandé à sortir à grands cris
clamp [klæmp] **N** **1** *(fastener)* pince *f*, *Med* clamp *m*; *Tech* crampon *m*; *(on worktable)* valet *m* (d'établi)
2 *Agr* = tas de navets ou de pommes de terre couvert de paille
3 *(of bricks)* tas *m*, pile *f*
4 *Aut* sabot *m* de Denver
VT **1** *(fasten)* attacher, fixer; *Med (wound)* clamper; *Tech* serrer, cramponner; **to c. sth to sth** fixer qch sur qch (à l'aide d'une pince)
2 *(curfew, restrictions)* imposer
3 *Agr* entasser
4 *(vehicle)* mettre un sabot à; **my car has been clamped** on a mis un sabot à ma voiture
▸ **clamp down** **VI** donner un coup de frein; **to c. down on** *(expenses, inflation)* mettre un frein à; *(crime, demonstrations)* stopper; *(information)* censurer; *(the press)* bâillonner; *(person)* serrer

la vis à; **the police are clamping down on illegal parking** la police sévit contre *ou* devient plus sévère avec les automobilistes en stationnement interdit

clampdown ['klæmpdaun] **N** mesures *fpl* répressives, répression *f*; **there has been a c. on credit** il y a eu un resserrement du crédit; **a c. on crime** un plan de lutte contre la criminalité

clamping ['klæmpɪŋ] **N 1** *(of cars)* immobilisation *f* des voitures au moyen de sabots de Denver **2** *Med* clampage *m*, agrafage *m*

clamshell ['klæmʃel] **N 1** *(packaging)* coque *f* plastique **2** *(mobile phone)* téléphone *m* à clapet

clan [klæn] **N** clan *m*

clandestine [klæn'destɪn] **ADJ** clandestin

clandestinely [klæn'destɪnlɪ] **ADV** clandestinement

clang [klæŋ] **VI** retentir *ou* résonner (d'un bruit métallique); **the gate clanged shut** le portail s'est fermé avec un bruit métallique

VT faire retentir *ou* résonner

N bruit *m* métallique

clanger ['klæŋə(r)] **N** *Br Fam* gaffe *f*; **to drop a c.** faire une gaffe

clank [klæŋk] **N** cliquetis *m*, bruit *m* sec et métallique

VI cliqueter, faire un bruit sec

VT faire cliqueter

clannish ['klænɪʃ] **ADJ** *Pej (group)* fermé, exclusif; *(person)* qui a l'esprit de clan *ou* de corps

clansman ['klænzmən] *(pl* **clansmen** [-mən]) **N** membre *m* d'un clan

clanswoman ['klænz,wumən] *(pl* **clanswomen** [-,wɪmɪn]) **N** membre *m* d'un clan

clap [klæp] *(pt & pp* **clapped,** *cont* **clapping) VT 1 to c. one's hands** *(to get attention, to mark rhythm)* frapper dans ses mains, taper des mains; *(to applaud)* applaudir **2** *(pat)* taper, frapper; **the boss clapped her on the back** le patron lui a donné une tape dans le dos **3** *(put)* mettre, poser; **she clapped her hand to her forehead** elle s'est frappé le front; *Fam* **the judge clapped them in jail** le juge les a flanqués en prison; **he clapped his hat on his head** il a enfoncé son chapeau sur sa tête; *Fam* **the minute she clapped eyes on him** dès qu'elle eut posé les yeux sur lui□; *Fam* **I've never clapped eyes on her before** je ne l'ai jamais vue de ma vie□

VI *(to get attention, to mark rhythm)* frapper dans ses mains; *(in applause)* applaudir

N 1 *(sound ▸ gen)* claquement *m*; *(▸ of hands)* battement *m*; *(▸ of applause)* applaudissements *mpl*; **to give sb a c.** applaudir qn; **c. of thunder** coup *m* de tonnerre **2** *(pat)* tape *f*; **she gave him a c. on the back** elle lui a donné une tape dans le dos **3** *very Fam* **the c.** *(venereal disease)* la chaude-pisse; **to have (a dose of) the c.** avoir la chaude-pisse

clapboard ['klæpbɔːd] **N** *Constr* planche *f* à clin; **c. (house)** maison *f* à clins

Clapham ['klæpəm] **N** = quartier dans le sud de Londres; **the man on the C. omnibus** Monsieur Tout-le-Monde

clapometer [klæ'pɒmɪtə(r)] **N** applaudimètre *m*

clapped-out [klæpt-] **ADJ** *Br Fam (machine, TV)* fichu; *(person)* crevé

clapper ['klæpə(r)] **N** *(of bell)* battant *m*

• **clappers NPL** *Br Fam* **to go like the clappers** aller à toute pompe

▸▸ *Cin* **clapper boy** clapman *m*

clapperboard ['klæpəbɔːd] **N** *Cin* claquette *f*, claquoir *m*, clap *m*

clapping ['klæpɪŋ] **N** *(UNCOUNT) (to get attention, to mark rhythm)* battements *mpl* de mains; *(applause)* applaudissements *mpl*

claptrap ['klæptræp] **N** *(UNCOUNT) Fam (nonsense)* âneries□ *fpl*

claque [klæk] **N 1** *Theat (for applause)* claque *f* **2** *(group of admirers)* admirateurs(trices) *mpl,fpl*

claret ['klærət] **N 1** *Br* (vin *m* de) bordeaux *m* (rouge) **2** *(colour)* bordeaux *m inv*

ADJ bordeaux *(inv)*

clarification [,klærɪfɪ'keɪʃən] **N** *(UNCOUNT)* **1** *(explanation)* clarification *f*, éclaircissement *m*; **to ask for c.** demander des éclaircissements **2** *(of butter)* clarification *f*; *(of wine)* collage *m*

clarify ['klærɪfaɪ] *(pt & pp* **clarified) VT 1** *(explain)* clarifier, éclaircir; **to c. sb's mind on sth** expliquer qch à qn, éclaircir les idées de qn sur qch **2** *(butter)* clarifier; *(wine)* coller

VI 1 *(matter, situation)* s'éclaircir **2** *(butter)* se clarifier

clarinet [,klærə'net] **N** clarinette *f*

▸▸ **clarinet player** clarinettiste *mf*

clarinetist, clarinettist [,klærə'netɪst] **N** clarinettiste *mf*

clarion ['klærɪən] **N** clairon *m*

▸▸ **clarion call** appel *m* de clairon; **a c. call to action** un appel à l'action

clarity ['klærətɪ] **N 1** *(of explanation, of text)* clarté *f*, précision *f*; **c. of mind** lucidité *f*, clarté *f* d'esprit **2** *(of liquid)* clarté *f*

clash [klæʃ] **N 1** *(sound ▸ gen)* choc *m* métallique, fracas *m*; *(▸ of cymbals)* retentissement *m*

2 *(between people ▸ fight)* affrontement *m*, bagarre *f*; *(▸ disagreement)* dispute *f*, différend *m*; **clashes on the border** des affrontements *mpl* à la frontière

3 *(incompatibility ▸ of ideas, opinions)* incompatibilité *f*; *(▸ of interests)* conflit *m*; *(▸ of colours)* discordance *f*; **c. of personalities, personality c.** incompatibilité *f* de caractères

4 *(of appointments, events)* coïncidence *f* fâcheuse

VI 1 *(swords, metallic objects)* s'entrechoquer, se heurter; *(cymbals)* résonner

2 *(people ▸ fight)* se battre; *(▸ disagree)* se heurter; **to c. with sb over sth** avoir un différend avec qn à propos de qch; **police clashed with protesters** il y a eu des heurts entre la police et les manifestants

3 *(be incompatible ▸ ideas, opinions)* se heurter, être incompatible *ou* en contradiction; *(▸ interests)* se heurter, être en conflit; *(▸ colours)* jurer, détonner; **that shirt clashes with your trousers** cette chemise jure avec ton pantalon

4 *(appointments, events)* tomber en même temps

VT *(metallic objects)* heurter *ou* entrechoquer bruyamment; *(cymbals)* faire résonner

clashing ['klæʃɪŋ] **ADJ 1** *(sound)* bruyant, retentissant **2** *(opinions)* opposé; *(colours, styles)* discordant

clasp [klɑːsp] **VT** *(hold)* serrer, étreindre; *(grasp)* saisir; **to c. sb/sth in one's arms/to one's breast** serrer qn/qch dans ses bras/sur son cœur; **he clasped her hand** il lui a serré la main

N 1 *(fastening ▸ on handbag, dress, necklace)* fermoir *m*; *(▸ on belt)* boucle *f* **2** *(hold)* prise *f*, étreinte *f*; **hand c.** poignée *f* de mains

▸▸ **clasp knife** couteau *m* pliant

class [klɑːs] **N 1** *(category, division)* classe *f*, catégorie *f*; **what c. are you travelling in?** en quelle classe voyagez-vous?; **c. A eggs** œufs de catégorie A; **c. A drug** = drogue du type héroïne ou cocaïne; **he's just not in the same c. as his brother** il n'arrive pas à la cheville de son frère; **to be in a c. by oneself** *or* **in a c. of one's own** être unique, former une classe à part

2 *Biol, Bot & Zool* classe *f*

3 *(social division)* classe *f*

4 *Sch & Univ (group of students)* classe *f*; *(course)* cours *m*, classe *f*; **she's attending** *or* **taking a psychology c.** elle suit un cours de psychologie; *Am* **the c. of 1972** la promotion de 1972

5 *Br Univ (grade)* **what c. (of) degree did you get?** quelle mention est-ce que tu as eu (à ton diplôme)?; **first c. honours** licence *f* avec mention très bien

6 *(elegance)* classe *f*; **to have c.** avoir de la classe

ADJ *Fam (excellent)* classe *(inv)*; **a c. car/hi-fi** une voiture/chaîne classe; **she's a real c. act** elle est vraiment classe

VT classer, classifier; **classed first** classé premier; **to c. sb/sth with sb/sth** assimiler qn/qch à qn/qch

▸▸ *Am Law* **class action** recours *m* collectif en justice; **class distinctions** distinctions *fpl* entre les classes; **class struggle** lutte *f* des classes; **class system** système *m* de classes; **class war(fare)** lutte *f* des classes

class-conscious ADJ *(person ▸ aware)* conscient des distinctions sociales; *(▸ snobbish)* snob; *(attitude, manners)* snob

class-consciousness N *(awareness)* conscience *f* des distinctions sociales; *(snobbishness)* snobisme *m*

classic ['klæsɪk] **ADJ** *also Fig* classique; **it was a c case of xenophobia** c'était un cas typique de xénophobie; *Fam* **it was c.!** *(joke, situation, event)* ça payait!

N 1 *(gen)* classique *m*; **it's a c. of modern cinema** c'est un classique du cinéma moderne; *Fam* **it was a c.!** *(joke, situation, event)* ça payait! **2** *Sport* classique *f* **3** *Sch & Univ* **classics** les lettres *fpl* classiques

▸▸ **classic car** voiture *f* ancienne; **classics degree** licence *f* de lettres classiques

classical ['klæsɪkəl] **ADJ 1** *(gen)* classique **2** *(civilization)* de l'antiquité; *Sch & Univ* **c. education** études *fpl* de lettres; **c. Greece** la Grèce antique; **c. scholar** humaniste *mf*; **in c. times** dans l'antiquité

▸▸ **classical music** musique *f* classique

classically ['klæsɪkəlɪ] **ADV** classiquement, de façon classique; **a c. trained musician** un musicien de formation classique; **she's not c. beautiful** elle n'a pas une beauté classique

classicism ['klæsɪ,sɪzəm] **N** classicisme *m*

classicist ['klæsɪsɪst] **N** humaniste *mf*; *(advocate of classical studies)* partisan(e) *m,f* des études classiques

classification [,klæsɪfɪ'keɪʃən] **N 1** *(action ▸ of plants, animals)* classification *f*; *(▸ of papers, competitors, books etc)* classement *m* **2** *(category)* classification *f*, classe *f*

classified ['klæsɪfaɪd] **ADJ 1** *(arranged)* classifié, classé **2** *(secret ▸ document)* (classé) secret

N *(advertisement)* petite annonce *f*; **the classifieds** les petites annonces *fpl*

▸▸ **classified ad, classified advertisement** petite annonce *f*; **classified information** renseignements *mpl* (classés) secrets

classifier ['klæsɪ,faɪə(r)] **N** classeur *m*

classify ['klæsɪfaɪ] *(pt & pp* **classified) VT 1** *(categorize)* classer; **their music is classified as jazz** leur musique est classée comme étant du jazz **2** *(make secret ▸ document)* classer secret

classless ['klɑːslɪs] **ADJ** *(society)* sans classes; *(person, accent)* qui n'appartient à aucune classe (sociale)

classmate ['klɑːsmeɪt] **N** camarade *mf* de classe

classroom ['klɑːsrum] **N** (salle *f* de) classe *f*

▸▸ **classroom assistant** assistant(e) *m,f* scolaire; **classroom teaching** enseignement *m* en classe

classy ['klɑːsɪ] *(compar* **classier,** *superl* **classiest) ADJ** *Fam (hotel, restaurant)* chic□ *(inv)*, de luxe□ *(inv)*, classe *(inv)*; *(person)* chic□ *(inv)*, classe *(inv)*

clatter ['klætə(r)] **N** *(rattle)* cliquetis *m*; *(commotion)* fracas *m*; **the c. of dishes** le bruit d'assiettes entrechoquées

VT heurter *ou* entrechoquer bruyamment

VI *(typewriter)* cliqueter; *(dishes)* s'entrechoquer bruyamment; *(falling object)* faire du bruit; **the old cart clattered by** le vieux chariot est passé dans un bruit de ferraille

Claudius ['klɔːdɪəs] **PR N** *(emperor)* Claude

clause [klɔːz] **N 1** *Gram* proposition *f* **2** *Law (of treaty, law)* clause *f*, article *m*; *(of will)* disposition *f*; *Ins (of policy)* avenant *m*; *Pol* **C. 4** = article de la constitution du Parti travailliste britannique affirmant son attachement au principe de propriété publique des grands secteurs industriels (abrogé en 1995)

claused bill [klɔːzd-] **N** *Com* connaissement *m* clausé

claustrophobia [,klɔːstrə'fəubjə] **N** claustrophobie *f*

claustrophobic [,klɔːstrə'fəubɪk] **ADJ** *(person)* claustrophobe; *(feeling)* de claustrophobie; *(place, situation)* où l'on se sent claustrophobe; **I feel c.** j'ai un sentiment de claustrophobie

clavichord ['klævɪkɔːd] **N** clavicorde *m*

clavicle ['klævɪkəl] **N** *Anat* clavicule *f*

claw [klɔː] **N 1** *(of bird, cat, dog)* griffe *f*; *(of bird of prey)* serre *f*; *(of crab, lobster)* pince *f*; *Fam (hand)* patte *f*; *also Fig* **to draw in/to show one's claws** rentrer/sortir ses griffes; *Fam* **to get one's claws**

into sb mettre le grappin sur qn **2** *(of hammer)* pied-de-biche *m*

VT *(scratch)* griffer; *(grip)* agripper *ou* serrer (avec ses griffes); *(tear)* déchirer (avec ses griffes); *Fig* **he clawed his way to the top** il a employé tous les moyens nécessaires pour arriver en haut de l'échelle

VI to c. at sth *(of cat)* saisir qch avec ses griffes, s'accrocher à qch; *(try to grip)* essayer de s'accrocher à qch *ou* d'agripper qch

►► ***claw hammer*** marteau *m* à pied-de-biche, marteau *m* fendu

›**claw back VT SEP** *Br* **1** *Fin (expenditure)* récupérer **2** *(regain)* regagner péniblement; **she clawed her way back to a prominent position** à force de persévérance, elle a réussi à regagner une position influente

:lawback ['klɔːbæk] **N** *Fin (recovery)* récupération *f*; *(sum)* somme *f* récupérée

:lay [kleɪ] **N 1** *(gen)* argile *f*, (terre *f*) glaise *f*; *(for pottery)* argile *f*; **(modelling) c.** pâte *f* à modeler; *Fig* **to have feet of c.** avoir des pieds d'argile **2** *Sport (in tennis)* **to play on c.** jouer sur terre battue; **to be good on c.** jouer bien sur la terre battue

COMP *(brick, pot)* en argile, en terre; *(pipe)* en terre

►► *Sport* ***clay court*** court *m* en terre battue; ***clay pigeon*** pigeon *m* d'argile *ou* de ball-trap; *Am Fam Fig (sitting duck)* cible *f* facile❑; ***clay pigeon shooting*** ball-trap *m*; ***clay pit*** glaisière *f*; ***clay soil*** terre *f* glaise

clayey ['kleɪɪ] **ADJ** argileux, glaiseux

claymation [kleɪ'meɪʃən] **N** *Br Cin & TV* = animation de figurines en pâte à modeler

claymore ['kleɪmɔː(r)] **N** *Hist* claymore *f*

CLEAN [kliːn]

ADJ
- propre **1**
- net **1–5**
- vierge **1, 4**
- pur **2**
- habile **6**

VT
- nettoyer **1**
- laver **1**
- vider **2**

VI
- nettoyer **1**
- se nettoyer **2**

ADV
- carrément **1**

N
- nettoyage

ADJ 1 *(free from dirt* ► *hands, shirt, room)* propre, net; *(*► *animal, person)* propre; *(*► *piece of paper)* vierge, blanc (blanche); **my hands are c.** j'ai les mains propres, mes mains sont propres; **to keep sth c.** tenir qch propre; *Fig* j'ai la conscience nette *ou* tranquille; **he made a c. breast of it** il a dit tout ce qu'il avait sur la conscience, il a déchargé sa conscience; **he made a c. sweep of the medals/prizes** il a raflé toutes les médailles/tous les prix

2 *(free from impurities* ► *air)* pur, frais (fraîche); *(*► *water)* pur, clair; *(*► *sound)* net, clair

3 *(morally pure* ► *conscience)* net, tranquille; *(*► *joke)* qui n'a rien de choquant; **it was all good c. fun** c'était une façon innocente de nous amuser; **keep it c.!** pas de grossièretés!; **c. living** une vie saine

4 *(honourable* ► *fight)* loyal; *(*► *reputation)* net, sans tache; **he's got a c. driving licence** il n'a jamais eu de contraventions graves; **to have a c. record** avoir un casier (judiciaire) vierge; **the doctor gave him a c. bill of health** le docteur l'a trouvé en parfaite santé

5 *(smooth* ► *curve, line)* bien dessiné, net; *(*► *shape)* fin, élégant; *(*► *cut)* net, franc (franche); **the building has c. lines** le bâtiment a de belles lignes; **to make a c. break** en finir une bonne fois pour toutes; **we made a c. break with the past** nous avons rompu avec le passé, nous avons tourné la page

6 *(throw)* adroit, habile

7 *Fam* **to be c.** *(innocent)* n'avoir rien à se reprocher❑; *(without incriminating material)* n'avoir rien sur soi❑; *(not carrying drugs)* ne pas avoir de drogue sur soi❑; *(not carrying weapons)* ne pas être armé❑; *(no longer addicted to drugs)* avoir décroché

8 *Nucl (not radioactive)* non radioactif; **a c. bomb** une bombe propre *ou* sans retombées radioactives

VT 1 *(room, cooker)* nettoyer; *(clothing)* laver; **I cleaned the mud from my shoes** j'ai enlevé la boue de mes chaussures; **to c. one's teeth** se laver *ou* se brosser les dents; **to c. one's plate** *(eat everything on it)* finir son assiette; **to c. the windows** faire les vitres *ou* les carreaux

2 *(chicken, fish)* vider

VI 1 *(person)* nettoyer; **she spends her day cleaning** elle passe sa journée à faire le ménage

2 *(carpet, paintbrush)* se nettoyer; **this cooker cleans easily** ce four est facile à nettoyer *ou* se nettoie facilement

3 *(of cleaning product, detergent)* nettoyer

ADV *Fam* **1** *(completely)* carrément❑; **the handle broke c. off** l'anse a cassé net❑; **he cut c. through the bone** il a coupé l'os de part en part❑; **the bullet went c. through his chest** la balle lui a carrément traversé la poitrine❑; **the robbers got c. away** les voleurs se sont enfuis sans laisser de trace❑; **we c. forgot about the appointment** nous avions complètement oublié le rendez-vous❑

2 *(idiom)* **to come c. about sth** révéler qch❑; **the murderer finally came c.** l'assassin a fini par avouer❑

N nettoyage *m*; **the carpet needs a good c.** la moquette a grand besoin d'être nettoyée; **I gave my shoes a c.** j'ai nettoyé mes chaussures

►► *Typ* ***clean proof*** *(with few corrections)* épreuve *f* peu chargée; *(final)* épreuve *f* pour bon à tirer; ***clean room*** *Med* pièce *f* aseptisée; *Comput* salle *f* blanche

›**clean out VT SEP 1** *(tidy)* nettoyer à fond; *(empty)* vider **2** *Fam (person)* nettoyer, plumer; **we're completely cleaned out** nous sommes totalement fauchés; **he cleaned me out** il m'a plumé

›**clean up VT SEP 1** *(make clean)* nettoyer à fond; **I cleaned the children up as best I could** j'ai fait de mon mieux pour débarbouiller les enfants; **c. this mess up!** nettoyez-moi ce fouillis! **2** *(make orderly* ► *cupboard, room)* ranger; *(*► *affairs, papers)* ranger, mettre de l'ordre dans; **the police intend to c. up the city** la police a l'intention d'épurer *ou* de nettoyer cette ville

VI 1 *(tidy room)* nettoyer; *(tidy cupboard, desk)* ranger; *(wash oneself)* faire un brin de toilette **2** *Fam (make profit)* gagner gros❑; **we cleaned up on the deal** nous avons touché un gros paquet sur cette affaire, cette affaire nous a rapporté gros❑

clean-cut ADJ 1 *(lines)* net; *(shape)* bien délimité, net **2** *(person)* propre (sur soi), à l'apparence très soignée

cleaner ['kliːnə(r)] **N 1** *(cleaning lady)* femme *f* de ménage; *(man)* (ouvrier *m*) nettoyeur *m* **2** *(product* ► *gen)* produit *m* d'entretien; *(*► *stain remover)* détachant *m*; *(device)* appareil *m* de nettoyage **3** *(dry cleaner)* teinturier(ère) *m,f*; **I took the clothes to the c.'s** j'ai donné les vêtements à nettoyer *ou* au teinturier; *Fam* **to take sb to the cleaners** nettoyer *ou* plumer qn

cleaning ['kliːnɪŋ] **N** *(UNCOUNT) (activity* ► *gen)* nettoyage *m*; *(*► *household)* ménage *m*; **to do the c.** faire le ménage

COMP *(staff)* de nettoyage

►► ***cleaning fluid*** produit *m* nettoyant; ***cleaning lady*** femme *f* de ménage; ***cleaning materials*** produits *mpl* d'entretien; ***cleaning up*** *(of room) & Fig (of neighbourhood)* nettoyage *m*; *(of exhaust gases)* dépollution *f*

clean-limbed ADJ bien proportionné *ou* bâti

cleanliness ['klenlɪnɪs] **N** propreté *f*; *Prov* **c. is next to godliness** = la pureté de l'âme passe d'abord par celle du corps

clean-living ADJ qui mène une vie saine

cleanly[1] ['kliːnlɪ] **ADV 1** *(smoothly)* net; **the handle snapped off c.** l'anse s'est cassée net **2** *(fight, play)* loyalement

cleanly[2] ['klenlɪ] *(compar* **cleanlier**, *superl* **cleanliest**) **ADJ** *Literary* propre

cleanness ['kliːnnɪs] **N** *(of hands, habits, language, apartment)* propreté *f*, *(of water)* pureté *f*, *(of lines)* netteté *f*, pureté *f*

clean-out N nettoyage *m* à fond; **to give a room a c.** nettoyer une pièce

clean-room clothing N *(UNCOUNT) Comput* vêtements *mpl* de salle blanche

cleanse [klenz] **VT 1** *(clean* ► *gen)* nettoyer; *(*► *with water)* laver; *Med (*► *blood)* dépurer; *(*► *wound)* nettoyer **2** *Fig (purify)* purifier; **to c. sb of their sins** laver qn de ses péchés

cleanser ['klenzə(r)] **N 1** *(detergent)* détergent *m*, détersif *m* **2** *(for skin)* (lait *m*) démaquillant *m*

clean-shaven ADJ *(face, man)* rasé de près

cleansing ['klenzɪŋ] **N** nettoyage *m*

ADJ *(lotion, pads)* démaquillant; *(power, property)* de nettoyage

►► ***cleansing cream*** crème *f* démaquillante; *Br Admin* ***cleansing department*** service *m* du nettoyage; ***cleansing lotion, cleansing milk*** *(for skin)* lait *m* démaquillant

clean-up N nettoyage *m* à fond; **the house needs a good c.** la maison a besoin d'être nettoyée à fond; **to give sth a c.** nettoyer qch à fond

CLEAR [klɪə(r)]

ADJ
- transparent **1**
- clair **1–6**
- vif **3**
- net **4, 9, 13**
- évident **7**
- libre **10, 12**
- tranquille **11**

ADV
- distinctement **1**
- entièrement **3**

VT
- débarrasser **1, 2**
- dégager **2, 12, 13**
- clarifier **3**
- autoriser **4**
- innocenter **5**
- franchir **6**
- finir **8**
- liquider **8, 9**
- dédouaner **10**

VI
- s'éclaircir **1, 2**

ADJ 1 *(transparent* ► *glass, plastic)* transparent; *(*► *water)* clair, limpide; *(*► *air)* pur; **c. honey** miel *m* liquide; **c. soup** *(plain stock)* bouillon *m*; *(with meat)* consommé *m*

2 *(cloudless* ► *sky)* clair, dégagé; *(*► *weather)* clair, beau (belle); **on a c. day** par temps clair; **the sky grew clearer** le ciel se dégagea

3 *(not dull* ► *colour)* vif; *(*► *light)* éclatant, radieux; *(untainted* ► *complexion)* clair, frais (fraîche); **to have (a) c. skin** avoir la peau nette

4 *(distinct* ► *outline)* net, clair; *(*► *photograph)* net; *(*► *sound)* clair, distinct; *(*► *voice)* clair, argentin; *TV* **the picture was very c.** l'image était très nette; **make sure your writing is c.** efforcez-vous d'écrire distinctement *ou* proprement; **the lyrics are not very c.** je ne distingue pas très bien les paroles de la chanson

5 *(not confused* ► *mind)* pénétrant, lucide; *(*► *thinking, argument, style)* clair; *(*► *explanation, report)* clair, intelligible; *(*► *instructions)* clair, explicite; *(*► *message)* en clair; **I want to keep a c. head** je veux rester lucide *ou* garder tous mes esprits; **a c. thinker** un esprit lucide; **c. thinking is essential** il est essentiel de garder un esprit lucide; **I've got the problem c. in my head** je comprends *ou* saisis le problème

6 *(understandable)* clair; **is that c.?** est-ce que c'est clair?; **as c. as day** clair comme le jour *ou* comme de l'eau de roche; *Hum* **as c. as mud** clair comme l'encre; **to make one's meaning** *or* **oneself c.** se faire comprendre; **do I make myself c.?** est-ce que je me fais bien comprendre?, est-ce que c'est bien clair?; **he was unable to make his meaning c.** il n'arrivait pas à s'expliquer; **we want to make it c. that...** nous tenons à préciser que...+ *indicative*; **to make it c. to sb that...** bien faire comprendre à qn que...+ *indicative*; **now let's get this c. – I want no nonsense!** comprenons-nous bien *ou* soyons clairs – je ne supporterai pas de sottises!

7 *(obvious, unmistakable)* évident, clair; **it's c. that he's lying** il est évident *ou* clair qu'il ment; **a c. indication of a forthcoming storm** un signe certain qu'il va y avoir de l'orage; **it is a c. case of favouritism** c'est manifestement du favoritisme, c'est un cas de favoritisme manifeste; **it's c. from her letter that she's unhappy** sa lettre montre clairement qu'elle est malheureuse; **it was not c. who had won** on ne savait pas exactement qui avait gagné

8 *(certain)* **he is quite c. about what has to be done**

il sait parfaitement ce qu'il y a à faire; **I wasn't c. what she meant** je n'étais pas sûr de ce qu'elle voulait dire; **I want to be c. in my mind about it** je veux en avoir le cœur net

9 *(unqualified)* net, sensible; **it's a c. improvement over the other** c'est nettement mieux que l'autre, il y a un net progrès par rapport à l'autre; **they won by a c. majority** ils ont gagné avec une large majorité

10 *(unobstructed, free ▸ floor, path)* libre, dégagé; *(▸ route)* sans obstacles, sans danger; *(▸ view)* dégagé; **the roads are c. of snow** les routes sont déblayées *ou* déneigées; **c. of obstacles** sans obstacles; **his latest X-rays are c.** ses dernières radios ne montrent rien d'anormal; **c. space** espace *m* libre; **to be c. of sth** être débarrassé de qch; **once the plane was c. of the trees** une fois que l'avion eut franchi les arbres; **to be c. of debts** être libre de dettes; *Fig* **can you see your way c. to lending me £5?** auriez-vous la possibilité de me prêter 5 livres?; **all c.!** *(there's no traffic, no one is watching)* vous pouvez y aller, la voie est libre; *Mil* fin d'alerte!

11 *(free from guilt ▸ conscience)* tranquille; **is your conscience c.?** as-tu la conscience tranquille?; **I can go home with a c. conscience** je peux rentrer la conscience tranquille

12 *(time)* libre; **I have Wednesday c.** je n'ai rien de prévu pour mercredi; **we have four c. days to finish** nous avons quatre jours pleins *ou* entiers pour finir

13 *(net ▸ money, wages)* net; **he brings home £300 c.** il gagne 300 livres net; **a c. profit** un bénéfice net

ADV 1 *(distinctly)* distinctement, nettement; *Rad* **reading you loud and c.** je te reçois cinq sur cinq; **I can hear you as c. as a bell** je t'entends très clairement

2 *(away from, out of the way)* **when we got c. of the town** quand nous nous sommes éloignés de la ville; **we pulled him c. of the wrecked car** nous l'avons sorti de la carcasse de la voiture; **she was thrown c. of the car** elle a été éjectée de la voiture; **stand c.!** écartez-vous!; **stand c. of the doors!** attention à la fermeture automatique des portes!; **to keep** *or* **to steer c. of sth** éviter qch; *Naut* **to steer c. of a rock** passer au large d'un écueil

3 *(all the way)* entièrement, complètement; **you can see c. to the mountain** on peut voir jusqu'à la montagne; **the thieves got c. away** les voleurs ont disparu sans laisser de trace

N *(idiom)* **to be in the c.** *(out of danger)* être hors de danger; *(out of trouble)* être tiré d'affaire; *(free of blame)* être blanc comme neige; *(above suspicion)* être au-dessus de tout soupçon; *(no longer suspected)* être blanchi (de tout soupçon); *Sport* être démarqué

VT 1 *(remove ▸ object)* débarrasser, enlever; *(▸ obstacle)* écarter; *(▸ weeds)* arracher, enlever; **c. the papers off the desk** enlevez ces papiers du bureau, débarrassez le bureau de ces papiers; **she cleared the plates from the table** elle a débarrassé la table

2 *(remove obstruction from ▸ gen)* débarrasser; *(▸ entrance, road)* dégager, déblayer; *(▸ forest, land)* défricher; *(▸ streets, room)* faire évacuer; *(▸ pipe)* déboucher; **it's your turn to c. the table** c'est à ton tour de débarrasser la table *ou* de desservir; **to c. one's desk** *(tidy)* débarrasser son bureau; *(complete pending tasks)* régler les affaires en suspens; **he cleared a space on the floor** il a dégagé un espace sur le sol; **to c. one's throat** se racler la gorge; **this land has been cleared of trees** ce terrain a été déboisé; **c. the room!** évacuez la salle!; **the judge cleared the court** le juge a fait évacuer la salle; **the police cleared the way for the procession** la police a ouvert un passage au cortège; *Fig* **the talks cleared the way for a cease-fire** les pourparlers ont préparé le terrain *ou* ont ouvert la voie pour un cessez-le-feu; *also Fig* **to c. the ground** déblayer le terrain; **to c. the decks** *(make space)* faire de la place, faire le ménage

3 *(clarify ▸ liquid)* clarifier; *(▸ wine)* coller, clarifier; *(▸ skin)* purifier; *(▸ complexion)* éclaircir; **open the windows to c. the air** ouvrez les fenêtres pour aérer; *Fig* **his apology cleared the air** ses excuses ont détendu l'atmosphère; **I went for a walk to c. my head** *(from hangover)* j'ai fait un tour pour m'éclaircir les idées; *(from confusion)* j'ai fait un tour pour me rafraîchir les idées *ou* pour me remettre les idées en place

4 *(authorize)* autoriser, approuver; **the plane was cleared for take-off** l'avion a reçu l'autorisation de décoller; **the editor cleared the article for publication** le rédacteur en chef a donné son accord *ou* le feu vert pour publier l'article; **you'll have to c. it with the boss** il faut demander l'autorisation *ou* l'accord *ou* le feu vert du patron

5 *(vindicate, find innocent)* innocenter, disculper; **to c. sb of a charge** disculper qn d'une accusation; **the court cleared him of all blame** la cour l'a totalement disculpé *ou* innocenté; **to c. one's name** se justifier, défendre son honneur

6 *(avoid touching)* franchir; *(obstacle)* éviter; **to c. a ditch** sauter *ou* franchir un fossé; **the horse cleared the fence with ease** le cheval a sauté sans peine par-dessus *ou* a franchi sans peine la barrière; **the plane barely cleared the trees** l'avion a franchi les arbres de justesse; **hang the curtains so that they just c. the floor** accrochez les rideaux de façon à ce qu'ils touchent à peine le parquet

7 *(make a profit of)* **she cleared 10 percent on the deal** l'affaire lui a rapporté 10 pour cent net *ou* 10 pour cent tous frais payés; **I c. £1,000 monthly** je fais un bénéfice net de 1000 livres par mois

8 *(dispatch ▸ work)* finir, terminer; *Com (▸ stock)* liquider; **he cleared the backlog of work** il a rattrapé le travail en retard

9 *(settle ▸ account)* liquider, solder; *(▸ cheque)* compenser; *(▸ debt)* s'acquitter de; *(▸ dues)* acquitter

10 *(of customs officer ▸ goods)* dédouaner; *(▸ ship)* expédier

11 *(pass through)* **to c. customs** *(person)* passer la douane; *(shipment)* être dédouané; **the bill cleared the Senate** le projet de loi a été voté par le Sénat

12 *Med (blood)* dépurer, purifier; *(bowels)* purger, dégager

13 *Sport* **to c. the ball** dégager le ballon

14 *Tech (decode)* déchiffrer

15 *Comput* **to c. the screen** vider l'écran

VI 1 *(weather)* s'éclaircir, se lever; *(sky)* se dégager; *(fog)* se lever, se dissiper; **it's clearing** le temps se lève, le ciel se dégage

2 *(liquid, complexion)* s'éclaircir; *(skin)* devenir plus sain; *(expression)* s'éclairer; **her face cleared** son visage s'est éclairé

3 *(cheque)* être encaissé; **it takes three days for the cheque to c.** il y a trois jours de délai d'encaissement

4 *(obtain clearance)* recevoir l'autorisation

▸**clear away** VT SEP *(remove)* enlever, ôter; *(one's things)* ranger; **we cleared away the dishes** nous avons débarrassé (la table) *ou* desservi

VI 1 *(tidy up)* débarrasser, desservir **2** *(disappear ▸ fog, mist)* se dissiper

▸**clear off** VT SEP *(remove)* retirer, enlever

VI *Fam* filer; **c. off!** dégage!, fiche le camp!

▸**clear out** VT SEP **1** *(tidy)* nettoyer, ranger; *(empty ▸ cupboard)* vider; *(▸ room)* débarrasser

2 *(throw out ▸ rubbish, old clothes)* jeter; **he cleared everything out of the house** il a fait le vide dans la maison; **to c. everyone out of a room** faire évacuer une pièce

3 *Fam (leave without money)* nettoyer, plumer

4 *Fam (goods, stock)* épuiser[□]

VI *Fam (leave building, room etc)* filer, déguerpir[□]; *(leave home ▸ spouse, partner)* se tirer; **he told us to c. out** il nous a ordonné de disparaître; **c. out (of here)!** dégage!, fiche le camp!

▸**clear up** VT SEP **1** *(settle ▸ problem)* résoudre; *(▸ misunderstanding)* dissiper; *(▸ mystery)* éclaircir, résoudre **2** *(tidy up)* ranger, faire du rangement dans

VI 1 *(weather)* s'éclaircir, se lever; *(fog, mist)* se dissiper, se lever **2** *(spots, rash)* disparaître; **his cold is clearing up** son rhume tire à sa fin **3** *(tidy up)* ranger, faire le ménage; **I'm fed up with clearing up after you** j'en ai assez de faire le ménage derrière toi

clearance ['klɪərəns] **N 1** *(removal ▸ of buildings, litter)* enlèvement *m*; *(▸ of obstacles)* déblaiement *m*; *(▸ of people)* évacuation *f*; *Com (▸ of merchandise)* liquidation *f*; **land c.** *(clearing of vegetation)* défrichement *m*; *(removal of debris)* déblaiement *m ou* dégagement *m* de terrain; **slum c.** assainissement *m* des taudis

2 *(space)* jeu *m*, dégagement *m*; **there was a ten centimetre c. between the lorry and the bridge** il y avait un espace de dix centimètres entre le camion et le pont; **how much c. is there?** que reste-t-il comme place?

3 *(permission)* autorisation *f*, permis *m*; *(from customs)* dédouanement *m*; **the plane was given c. to land** l'avion a reçu l'autorisation d'atterrir; **they sent the order to headquarters for c.** ils ont envoyé la commande au siège pour contrôle; **c. inward(s)** déclaration *f* d'entrée; **c. outward(s)** déclaration *f* de sortie

4 *Banking (of cheque)* compensation *f*

5 *Sport* dégagement *m*

6 *Med* clairance *f*

▸▸ *Com* **clearance sale** liquidation *f*, soldes *mpl*

clear-cut ADJ **1** *(lines, shape)* nettement défini, net **2** *(decision, situation)* clair; *(difference)* clair, net; *(opinion, plan)* bien défini, précis

clear-headed ADJ lucide

clearing ['klɪərɪŋ] **N 1** *(in forest)* clairière *f*; *(in clouds)* éclaircie *f*

2 *(of land)* déblaiement *m*, défrichement *m*; *(of passage)* dégagement *m*, déblaiement *m*; *(of pipe)* débouchage *m*

3 *(removal ▸ of objects)* enlèvement *m*; *(▸ of people)* évacuation *f*

4 *(of name, reputation)* réhabilitation *f*; *Law (of accused)* disculpation *f*

5 *Banking & Fin (of cheque)* compensation *f*; *(of account)* liquidation *f*, solde *m*; *(of debt)* acquittement *m*

6 *(of debt)* acquittement *m*

7 *Br Univ* = système selon lequel les places restantes dans les universités sont attribuées aux étudiants qui n'ont pas été acceptés lors d'une première sélection

▸▸ *Br* **clearing bank** banque *f* de compensation; **clearing house** *Banking & Fin* chambre *f* de compensation; *(for information, materials)* bureau *m* central; *Mil* **clearing station** *(for wounded)* centre *m* de triage *ou* d'évacuation; *Banking & Fin* **clearing system** système *m* de compensation

clearly ['klɪəlɪ] **ADV 1** *(distinctly ▸ see)* clair, bien; *(▸ understand)* clairement, bien; *(▸ hear, speak)* distinctement; *(▸ describe, explain)* clairement, précisément; *(▸ think)* clairement, lucidement; **c. legible** bien lisible **2** *(obviously)* manifestement, à l'évidence; **they c. didn't expect us** il était clair *ou* évident qu'ils ne nous attendaient pas; **this is c. unacceptable** c'est tout à fait inacceptable

clearness ['klɪənɪs] **N 1** *(of air, glass)* transparence *f*; *(of water)* limpidité *f* **2** *(of speech, thought)* clarté *f*, précision *f*

clear-out **N** *Br Fam* rangement[□] *m*; **to have a c.** faire du rangement[□]

clear-sighted ADJ *Fig (person)* perspicace, lucide, clairvoyant; *(decision, plan)* réaliste

clear-sightedness [-'saɪtɪdnɪs] **N** *Fig (of person)* perspicacité *f*, lucidité *f*, clairvoyance *f*; *(of plan)* réalisme *m*

clearway ['klɪəweɪ] **N** *Br Aut* route *f* à stationnement interdit

cleat [kli:t] **N 1** *(on shoe)* clou *m* **2** *Carp (block of wood)* tasseau *m* **3** *Naut (for fastening ropes)* taquet *m*

cleavage ['kli:vɪdʒ] **N 1** *(of woman)* décolleté *m*; **to show a lot of c.** *(woman)* avoir un décolleté plongeant; *(dress)* être très décolleté **2** *Biol (of cell)* division *f* **3** *Chem & Geol* clivage *m*

cleave [kli:v] *(pt* **cleaved** *or* **clove** [kləʊv] *or* **cleft** [kleft], *pp* **cleaved** *or* **cloven** ['kləʊvən] *or* **cleft** [kleft]) **VT 1** *Literary (split)* fendre; *Fig* diviser, séparer **2** *Biol (cell)* diviser **3** *Chem & Geol (mineral)* cliver

▸**cleave to** *(pt* **cleaved** *or* **clove** [kləʊv] *or* **cleft** [kleft], *pp* **cleaved** *or* **clove** [kləʊv]) **VT INSEP** *Literary (person, party, principle)* être fidèle à; *(values, traditions)* être très attaché à

cleaver ['kli:və(r)] **N** couperet *m*

clef [klef] **N** *Mus* clef *f*, clé *f*

cleft [kleft] *pt & pp of* **cleave**

ADJ *(split ▸ gen)* fendu; *(▸ branch)* fourchu

N *(opening ▸ gen)* fissure *f*; *(▸ in rock)* fissure *f*, crevasse *f*

▸▸ *Med* ***cleft palate*** palais *m* fendu; ***cleft stick*** branche *f* fourchue; *Br Fig* **to be in a c. stick** être ou se trouver entre le marteau et l'enclume

clematis ['klemətɪs] **N** *Bot* clématite *f*

clemency ['klemənsɪ] *(pl* **clemencies)** **N 1** *(mercy)* clémence *f*, indulgence *f* (**to** envers); **to show c.** faire preuve de clémence **2** *(of weather)* douceur *f*, clémence *f*

clement ['klemənt] **ADJ 1** *(person)* clément, magnanime **2** *(weather)* doux (douce), clément

clementine ['kleməntaɪn] **N** clémentine *f*

clench [klentʃ] **VT** *(fist, jaw, buttocks)* serrer; *(grasp firmly)* empoigner, agripper; *(hold tightly)* serrer; **between clenched teeth** *(to say)* les dents serrées; **to c. sth in one's hand** serrer qch dans la main

Cleopatra [ˌkliːəˈpætrə] **PR N** Cléopâtre

▸▸ ***Cleopatra's Needle*** l'obélisque *m* de Cléopâtre

clerestory ['klɪəstɔːrɪ] *(pl* **clerestories)** **N** *Archit* claire-voie *f (dans une église)*

clergy ['klɜːdʒɪ] **N** *(UNCOUNT)* (membres *mpl* du) clergé *m*

clergyman ['klɜːdʒɪmən] *(pl* **clergymen** [-mən]) **N** *(gen)* ecclésiastique *m*; *(Catholic)* curé *m*, prêtre *m*; *(Protestant)* pasteur *m*

clergywoman ['klɜːdʒɪˌwʊmən] *(pl* **clergywomen** [-ˌwɪmɪn]) **N** (femme *f*) pasteur *m*

cleric ['klerɪk] **N** ecclésiastique *m*

clerical ['klerɪkəl] **ADJ 1** *(office ▸ staff, work)* de bureau; *(▸ position)* de commis; **to do c. work** travailler dans un bureau **2** *Rel* clérical, du clergé

▸▸ ***clerical assistant*** employé(e) *m,f* de bureau; ***clerical collar*** col *m* d'ecclésiastique; ***clerical error*** *(in document)* faute *f* de copiste; *(in accounting)* erreur *f* d'écriture

clericalism ['klerɪkəˌlɪzəm] **N** *Rel* cléricalisme *m*

clerk [*Br* klɑːk, *Am* klɜːrk] **N 1** *Admin & Com (in office)* employé(e) *m,f* (de bureau), commis *m*; *(in bank)* employé(e) *m,f* de banque

2 *Law* clerc *m*

3 *Am (sales assistant)* vendeur(euse) *m,f*

4 *Am (receptionist)* réceptionniste *mf*

5 *Rel* **c. in holy orders** ecclésiastique *m*

6 *Arch (scholar)* savant(e) *m,f*, clerc *m*

VI *Am* **1** *(as assistant)* **to c. for sb** être assistant(e) de qn **2** *(as sales assistant)* travailler comme vendeur(euse)

▸▸ *Sport* ***clerk of the course*** commissaire *m* de piste; ***Clerk of the Court*** greffier(ère) *m,f* (du tribunal); *Br Constr* ***clerk of works*** conducteur (trice) *m,f* de travaux

clever ['klevə(r)] **ADJ 1** *(intelligent)* intelligent, astucieux

2 *(skilful ▸ person)* adroit, habile; *(▸ work)* bien fait; **to be c. with one's hands** être adroit ou habile de ses mains; **to be c. at sth/at doing sth** être doué pour qch/pour faire qch; **to be c. at maths** être fort en maths

3 *(cunning)* malin(igne), astucieux; rusé; **he was too c. for us** il s'est montré plus malin que nous *Pej* **he's/she's too c. by half** il/elle est bien trop malin/maligne

4 *(ingenious ▸ book)* intelligemment ou bien écrit, ingénieux; *(▸ film)* ingénieux, intelligent; *(▸ idea, plan)* ingénieux, astucieux

▸▸ *Br Fam* ***clever clogs, clever Dick*** petit(e) malin (igne)[□] *m,f*

cleverly ['klevəlɪ] **ADV** *(intelligently)* intelligemment, astucieusement; *(skilfully)* adroitement, habilement; *(cunningly)* avec ruse; *(ingeniously)* ingénieusement; **she c. managed to avoid paying the fine** elle s'est débrouillée pour ne pas payer l'amende

cleverness ['klevənɪs] **N** *(intelligence)* intelligence *f*, astuce *f*; *(skilfulness)* habileté *f*, adresse *f*; *(cunning)* ruse *f*; *(ingenuity)* ingéniosité *f*

cliché [*Br* 'kliːʃeɪ, *Am* kliːˈʃeɪ] **N 1** *(idea)* cliché *m*; *(phrase)* cliché *m*, lieu *m* commun, banalité *f* **2** *Typ* cliché *m*

clichéd [*Br* 'kliːʃeɪd, *Am* kliːˈʃeɪd] **ADJ** banal; **a c. phrase** un cliché, une banalité, un lieu commun; **the end of the film is very c.** la fin du film est très conventionnelle

cliché-ridden **ADJ** bourré ou truffé de clichés

click [klɪk] **N 1** *(sound)* petit bruit *m* sec; *(of tongue)* claquement *m*; *Comput* clic *m*; *Ling* clic *m*, click *m*; *Com & Comput* **a clicks-and-mortar company** = une société qui vend ses produits en magasin et sur Internet **2** *(of ratchet, wheel)* cliquet *m* **3** *Am Fam Mil slang (kilometre)* borne *f*, kilomètre[□] *m*

VT 1 *(fingers, tongue)* faire claquer; **he clicked his heels (together)** il a claqué les talons **2** *Comput* cliquer (sur)

VI 1 *(make sound)* faire un bruit sec; **she clicked along the pavement in her high heels** ses hauts talons faisaient de petits bruits secs sur le trottoir; **cameras were clicking** on entendait le déclic des appareils; **the photographers were clicking away furiously** les photographes s'en donnaient à cœur joie; **to c. together** *(of two parts)* s'emboîter (avec un bruit sec); **to c. shut** *(door etc)* se refermer avec un bruit sec

2 *Fam (become clear)* **it suddenly clicked** tout à coup ça a fait tilt

3 *Fam (be a success)* bien marcher[□]; **they clicked from the beginning** *(got on well)* ils se sont bien entendus dès le début[□], ça a tout de suite collé entre eux; **to c. with the public** *(play, film)* avoir du succès auprès du public[□]

4 *Comput* cliquer; **to c. on sth** cliquer sur qch; **to c. and drag** cliquer et glisser

clickable ['klɪkəbəl] **ADJ** *Comput* cliquable, que l'on peut cliquer

▸▸ ***clickable image*** image *f* cliquable; ***clickable image map*** image *f* cliquable

clicking ['klɪkɪŋ] **N** *(sound)* cliquetis *m*

client ['klaɪənt] **N 1** *(customer)* client(e) *m,f* **2** *Comput* client *m*

▸▸ *Com & Mktg* ***client base*** clientèle *f*; *Pej* ***client state*** État *m* à la solde d'un autre

clientele [ˌkliːɒnˈtel] **N** *Com* clientèle *f*; *Theat* clientèle *f*, public *m* (habituel)

client-server **ADJ** *Comput* client-serveur

▸▸ ***client-server model*** modèle *m* client-serveur *(inv)*

cliff [klɪf] **N** escarpement *m*; *(on coast)* falaise *f*; *(in mountaineering)* à-pic *m*

cliffhanger ['klɪfˌhæŋə(r)] **N** *Fam (situation in film, story)* situation *f* à suspense[□]; *(moment of suspense)* moment *m* d'angoisse[□]; **it was a real c.** ça m'a/nous a/*etc* tenu en haleine jusqu'à la fin; **the election was a real c.** le résultat des élections est resté incertain jusqu'au dernier moment[□]

climacteric [klaɪˈmæktərɪk] **N** *(gen)* climatère *m*; *(women's)* ménopause *f*; *(men's)* andropause *f*

ADJ climatérique; *Fig* crucial, critique

climactic [klaɪˈmæktɪk] **ADJ** à son apogée, à son point culminant; **the c. moment of the film** le paroxysme du film

> Attention: ne pas confondre avec l'adjectif **climatic**.

climate ['klaɪmɪt] **N** *Met* climat *m*; *Fig* climat *m*, ambiance *f*; **the c. of opinion** (les courants *mpl* de) l'opinion *f*; **the economic c.** la conjoncture économique

▸▸ *Ecol* ***climate canary*** = phénomène naturel annonciateur des changements environnementaux causés par le réchauffement climatique; *Ecol* ***climate change*** changement *m* climatique; *Am Aut* ***climate control*** climatiseur *m*

climatic [klaɪˈmætɪk] **ADJ** *Met* climatique

> Attention: ne pas confondre avec l'adjectif **climactic**.

climatologist [ˌklaɪməˈtɒlədʒɪst] **N** *Met* climatologue *mf*

climatology [ˌklaɪməˈtɒlədʒɪ] **N** *Met* climatologie *f*

climax ['klaɪmæks] **N 1** *(highest point)* paroxysme *m*; *(of film, play, piece of music)* point *m* culminant; *(of career)* apogée *m*, point *m* culminant; **this brought matters to a c.** ceci a porté l'affaire à son point culminant; **as the battle reached its c.** lorsque la bataille fut à son paroxysme; **he worked up to the c. of his story** il amena le récit à son point culminant **2** *(sexual)* orgasme *m* **3** *(in rhetoric)* gradation *f*

VI 1 *(film, story)* atteindre son paroxysme ou son point culminant; **a tough election campaign climaxing in victory on polling day** une campagne électorale acharnée qui a été couronnée de succès le jour du scrutin **2** *(sexually)* atteindre l'orgasme

VT amener ou porter à son point culminant

climb [klaɪm] **VI 1** *(road, sun)* monter; *(plane)* monter, prendre de l'altitude; *(prices)* monter, augmenter; *(plant)* grimper; **the plane climbed 200 feet** l'avion a pris 60 mètres d'altitude **2** *(person)* grimper; **I climbed into bed/into the boat** j'ai grimpé dans mon lit/à bord du bateau; **to c. over an obstacle** escalader un obstacle; **he climbed (up) out of the hole/through the opening** il s'est hissé hors du trou/par l'ouverture; *Fam* **he climbed into his jeans** il a enfilé son jean, il a sauté dans son jean; **to c. to power** se hisser au pouvoir; **to c. (socially** *or* **in the world)** s'élever (au-dessus de sa condition) **3** *Sport* faire de l'escalade; *(on rocks)* varapper; **to go climbing** faire de l'escalade

VT 1 *(ascend ▸ stairs, steps)* monter, grimper; *(▸ hill)* escalader, grimper; *(▸ mountain)* gravir, faire l'ascension de; *(▸ cliff, wall)* escalader; *(▸ ladder, tree)* monter sur; *(▸ rope)* monter à **2** *Sport (rockface)* escalader, grimper sur

N 1 *(of hill, slope)* montée *f*, côte *f*; *(in mountaineering)* ascension *f*, escalade *f*; **it's quite a c.** ça monte dur; **it was an easy c. to the top (of the hill)** ça montait en pente douce jusqu'au sommet (de la colline); **there were several steep climbs along the route** il y avait plusieurs bonnes côtes sur le trajet **2** *(of plane)* montée *f*, ascension *f*; **rate of c.** vitesse *f* ascensionnelle ou de montée

▸**climb down** **VI 1** *(descend)* descendre; *Sport* descendre, effectuer une descente **2** *(back down)* en rabattre, céder

▸**climb up** **VT INSEP 1** *(ascend ▸ stairs, steps)* monter, grimper; *(▸ hill)* escalader, grimper; *(▸ mountain)* gravir, faire l'ascension de; *(▸ cliff, wall)* escalader; *(▸ ladder, tree)* monter sur; *(▸ rope)* monter à **2** *Sport (rockface)* escalader, grimper sur

climb-down **N** dérobade *f*, reculade *f*; **a government c. over the issue looks likely** il est probable que le gouvernement fera machine arrière à ce sujet

climber ['klaɪmə(r)] **N 1** *(person)* grimpeur(euse) *m,f*; *(mountaineer)* alpiniste *mf*; *Sport (rock climber)* varappeur(euse) *m,f*; *Fig Pej* **(social) c.** arriviste *mf* **2** *(plant)* plante *f* grimpante

climbing ['klaɪmɪŋ] **N 1** *(action)* montée *f*, escalade *f*; **the c. of Everest** l'escalade *f* de l'Everest **2** *(mountaineering)* alpinisme *m*; *Sport (rock climbing)* varappe *f*, escalade *f*

ADJ 1 *(plant)* grimpant **2** *(plane, star)* ascendant

▸▸ *Br* ***climbing frame*** cage *f* à poules *(jeu)*; ***climbing irons*** *(for mountaineer)* grappins *mpl*; *(on boots)* crampons *mpl*; *(for climbing trees, poles)* étriers *mpl*; *Sport* ***climbing wall*** mur *m* d'escalade

climes [klaɪmz] **NPL** *Literary or Hum* régions *fpl*, contrées *fpl*; **he's gone to sunnier c.** il est allé sous des climats plus souriants

clinch [klɪntʃ] **VT 1** *(settle ▸ deal)* conclure; *(▸ argument)* régler, résoudre; *(▸ agreement)* sceller; **that clinches it!** comme ça, c'est réglé!; **that was what clinched it for me** c'est ce qui m'a décidé **2** *Tech (nail)* river; *Naut* étalinguer

VI *Boxing* combattre corps à corps

N 1 *Tech* rivetage *m*; *Naut* étalingure *f* **2** *Boxing* corps-à-corps *m inv*; **they went into a c.** ils ont lutté corps à corps **3** *Fam (embrace)* étreinte[□] *f*, enlacement[□] *m*; **they were in a c.** ils étaient enlacés[□]

clincher ['klɪntʃə(r)] **N** *Fam* argument *m* décisif[□], argument *m* massue[□]

cling [klɪŋ] *(pt & pp* **clung** [klʌŋ]) **VI 1** *(hold on tightly)* s'accrocher, se cramponner; **they clung to one another** ils se sont enlacés, ils se sont cramponnés l'un à l'autre; *Fig* **to c. to a hope/to a belief/to the past** se raccrocher à un espoir/à une croyance/au passé; **she clings to her children even though they are now grown up** elle s'accroche à ses enfants bien qu'ils soient maintenant adultes **2** *(stick)* adhérer, coller; **a dress that clings to the body** une robe très près du corps *ou* très ajustée **3** *(smell)* persister

clingfilm [ˈklɪŋˌfɪlm] **N** *Br* film *m* alimentaire (transparent)

clinging [ˈklɪŋɪŋ] **ADJ** *(clothing)* collant, qui moule le corps; *Pej (person)* collant
▸▸ *Am Fam Fig* ***clinging vine*** pot *m* de colle

clingy [ˈklɪŋɪ] *(compar* **clingier,** *superl* **clingiest)** **ADJ** *(clothing)* moulant; *Pej (person)* collant; **she's so c.** *(child)* elle est toujours dans mes jupes; **he's the c. type** c'est le genre collant

clinic [ˈklɪnɪk] **N 1** *(part of hospital)* service *m*; **eye c.** clinique *f* ophtalmologique
2 *(treatment session)* consultation *f*
3 *Br (private hospital)* clinique *f*
4 *(consultant's teaching session)* clinique *f*
5 *(health centre)* centre *m* médico-social *ou* d'hygiène sociale
6 *Br (of MP)* permanence *f*
7 *Am Sport* séance *f* d'entraînement *(avec un spécialiste)*

clinical [ˈklɪnɪkəl] **ADJ 1** *Med (lecture, tests)* clinique **2** *Fig (attitude, tone)* froid, aseptisé
▸▸ *Med* ***clinical depression*** dépression *f* nerveuse; ***clinical psychologist*** spécialiste *mf* en psychologie clinique; *Med* ***clinical psychology*** psychologie *f* clinique; *Med* ***clinical thermometer*** thermomètre *m* médical; ***clinical trials*** tests *mpl* cliniques

clinically [ˈklɪnɪkəlɪ] **ADV 1** *Med* cliniquement **2** *Fig (act, speak)* objectivement, froidement

clinician [klɪˈnɪʃən] **N** *Med* clinicien(enne) *m,f*

clink [klɪŋk] **VT** faire tinter *ou* résonner; **they clinked (their) glasses** ils ont trinqué
VI tinter, résonner
N 1 *(sound)* tintement *m* (de verres) **2** *Fam (jail)* taule *f*; **in the c.** en taule

clinker [ˈklɪŋkə(r)] **N 1** *(UNCOUNT) (ash)* mâchefer *m*, scories *fpl* **2** *Constr (brick)* brique *f* vitrifiée

clinker-built **ADJ** *Naut (boat)* (bordé) à clin

clip [klɪp] *(pt & pp* **clipped,** *cont* **clipping)** **VT 1** *(cut)* couper (avec des ciseaux), rogner; *(hedge)* tailler; *(animal)* tondre; **c. the coupon out of the magazine** découpez le bon dans le magazine; **I clipped five seconds off my personal best** j'ai amélioré mon record de cinq secondes; **to c. a bird's wings** rogner les ailes d'un oiseau; *Fig* **to c. sb's wings** laisser moins de liberté à qn
2 *Br (ticket)* poinçonner
3 *(attach)* attacher; *(papers)* attacher (avec un trombone); *(brooch)* fixer; **to c. a microphone to sb's tie** attacher *ou* fixer un micro à la cravate de qn
4 *Br Fam (hit)* frapper◻, cogner; **to c. sb round the ear** flanquer une taloche à qn
5 *Br (skim, graze)* effleurer; **I clipped the gate as I drove in** j'ai effleuré la barrière en rentrant la voiture
6 *Am Fam (cheat)* escroquer, rouler
N 1 *(snip)* petit coup *m* de ciseaux
2 *(from film, TV programme)* court extrait *m*; *Am (from newspaper)* coupure *f*
3 *(clasp)* pince *f*; *(for paper)* trombone *m*, pince *f*; *(for pipe)* collier *m*, bague *f*; **bicycle** *or* **trouser c.** pince *f* à pantalon, pince-pantalon *m inv*
4 *(for bullets)* chargeur *m*
5 *(brooch)* clip *m*; *(for hair)* barrette *f*; *(for tie)* fixe-cravate *m*
6 *Br Fam (blow)* gifle◻ *f*, taloche *f*; **he got a c. round the ear** il s'est pris une taloche
7 *Fam (speed)* **at a (good) c.** à vive allure◻, à toute vitesse◻
▸▸ *Comput* ***clip art*** clipart *m*; *Fam* ***clip joint*** = boîte de nuit où l'on pratique des prix excessifs
▸**clip on** **VT SEP 1** *(document)* attacher (avec un trombone) **2** *(brooch, earrings)* mettre
VI s'attacher *ou* se fixer avec une pince

clipboard [ˈklɪpbɔːd] **N 1** *(writing board)* écritoire *f* à pince, clipboard *m* **2** *Comput* bloc-notes *m*
▸▸ ***clipboard file*** fichier *m* presse-papiers

clip-clop [-klɒp] *(pt & pp* **clip-clopped,** *cont* **clip-clopping)** **N** clip-clop *m*; **we heard the c. of horses' hooves** nous avons entendu les chevaux passer et le clip-clop de leurs sabots
VI faire clip-clop

clip-on **ADJ** amovible
• **clip-ons** **NPL** *(sunglasses)* = verres teintés amovibles; *(earrings)* clips *mpl (d'oreilles)*
▸▸ ***clip-on earrings*** clips *mpl (d'oreilles)*; ***clip-on microphone*** micro-cravate *m*; ***clip-on tie*** cravate *f* à système

clipped [klɪpt] **ADJ** *(speech, style)* heurté, saccadé; **a c. manner of speaking** un débit heurté

clipper [ˈklɪpə(r)] **N** *Naut (ship)* clipper *m*
• **clippers** **NPL** *(for nails)* pince *f* à ongles; *(for hair)* tondeuse *f*; *(for hedge)* sécateur *m* à haie

clippie [ˈklɪpɪ] **N** *Br Fam* receveuse◻ *f (de bus)*

clipping [ˈklɪpɪŋ] **N 1** *(from newspaper)* coupure *f* de presse **2 clippings** *(from nails)* rognures *fpl*; *(from hair)* mèches *fpl (de cheveux coupés)*; *(from hedge)* bouts *mpl* de branches; **grass clippings** herbe *f* coupée

clique [kliːk] **N** *Pej* clique *f*, coterie *f*

cliquey [ˈkliːkɪ], **cliquish** [ˈkliːkɪʃ] **ADJ** *Pej* exclusif, qui a l'esprit de clan

clitoral [ˈklɪtərəl] **ADJ** clitoridien

clitoridectomy [ˌklɪtərɪˈdektəmɪ] *(pl* **clitoridectomies)** **N** *Med* clitoridectomie *f*

clitoris [ˈklɪtərɪs] **N** clitoris *m*

Cllr *(written abbr* **Councillor)** conseiller(ère) *m,f*

cloak [kləʊk] **N** *(cape)* grande cape *f*; *Fig* **under the c. of darkness** sous le couvert de la nuit, à la faveur de l'obscurité; **as a c. for his illegal activities** pour cacher *ou* masquer ses activités illégales
VT 1 *(cover with cloak)* revêtir d'un manteau **2** *Fig* masquer, cacher; **cloaked with** *or* **in secrecy/mystery** empreint de secret/mystère

cloak-and-dagger **ADJ** *(affair, goings-on)* clandestin; **a c. story** un roman d'espionnage

cloakroom [ˈkləʊkrʊm] **N 1** *(for coats)* vestiaire *m* **2** *Br Euph (toilet* ▸ *public)* toilettes *fpl*; (▸ *in home)* cabinets *mpl*
▸▸ ***cloakroom attendant*** préposé(e) *m,f* au vestiaire; ***cloakroom ticket*** numéro *m* de vestiaire

clobber [ˈklɒbə(r)] *Fam* **VT 1** *(hit)* mettre une raclée à, tabasser, dérouiller **2** *(defeat)* battre à plate couture **3** *(penalize)* écraser◻, accabler◻; **the new tax legislation will c. small businesses** les nouvelles lois fiscales vont saigner à blanc les petites entreprises
N *Br (UNCOUNT) (clothes)* frusques *fpl*; *(belongings)* effets◻ *mpl*, barda *m*

clobbering [ˈklɒbərɪŋ] **N** *Fam* **to get a c.** *(be beaten up)* prendre une dérouillée *ou* une raclée, se faire tabasser; *(be defeated)* se prendre une pâtée, être battu à plate couture; **to give sb a c.** *(beat up)* tabasser qn, flanquer une raclée à qn; *(defeat)* flanquer une raclée à qn

cloche [klɒʃ] **N 1 c. (hat)** chapeau *m* cloche, cloche *f* **2** *Agr & Hort* cloche *f*

clock [klɒk] **N 1** *(gen)* horloge *f*; *(small)* pendule *f*; **it took us 15 minutes by the c.** il nous a fallu 15 minutes montre en main; *Fig* **the c. is ticking** le temps passe; **to put a c. back/forward** retarder/avancer une horloge; **to put** *or* **to turn the clocks back/forward** retarder/avancer les pendules; *Fig* **you can't turn the c. back** ce qui est fait est fait; **this law will put the c. back a hundred years** cette loi va nous ramener cent ans en arrière; **a race against the c.** une course contre la montre; **to work round the c.** travailler vingt-quatre heures sur vingt-quatre; *Fig* **to watch the c.** *(employee)* avoir les yeux rivés sur l'horloge, ne penser qu'à l'heure de la sortie
2 *(taximeter)* compteur *m*, taximètre *m*
3 *Fam (mileometer)* compteur *m* kilométrique; **a car with 30,000 miles on the c.** une voiture qui a 30 000 miles au compteur
4 *Comput* horloge *f*
VT 1 *(measure speed of)* enregistrer; *Sport (runner, driver)* chronométrer; **he was clocked at 185 mph** il a atteint les 300 km/h chrono; **the fastest time he's clocked this year** son meilleur temps cette année **2** *Fam (hit)* flanquer un marron à **3** *Fam (notice)* repérer◻; **she clocked him as soon as he walked in** elle l'a repéré dès qu'il est entré
▸▸ ***clock golf*** jeu *m* de l'horloge; ***clock radio*** radio-réveil *m*; *Comput* ***clock speed*** fréquence *f* d'horloge; *Comput* ***clock speed doubler*** doubleur *m* de fréquence (d'horloge); ***clock tower*** tour *f* (de l'horloge)
▸**clock in** **VI 1** *Ind (employee)* pointer (à l'arrivée) **2** *Sport (have a time of)* **for the 100 metres she clocked in at nine seconds** elle a fait neuf secondes aux 100 mètres
▸**clock off** **VI** *Ind* pointer (à la sortie), dépointer
▸**clock on** **VI** *Ind (employee)* pointer (à l'arrivée)
▸**clock out** **VI** *Ind* pointer (à la sortie), dépointer
▸**clock up** **VT SEP** *(work)* effectuer, accomplir; *(victory)* remporter; *Aut* **she clocked up 300 miles** elle a fait 300 miles au compteur

clock-doubled [-dʌbəld] **ADJ** *Comput* à fréquence d'horloge doublée

clocking [ˈklɒkɪŋ] **N** *Ind*
▸▸ ***clocking in*** pointage *m* à l'arrivée; ***clocking in card*** fiche *f* de pointage; ***clocking off*** pointage *m* à la sortie; ***clocking on*** pointage *m* à l'arrivée; ***clocking out*** pointage *m* à la sortie

clocklike [ˈklɒklaɪk] **ADJ** *(regularity)* d'horloge

clockmaker [ˈklɒkˌmeɪkə(r)] **N** horloger(ère) *m,f*

clock-watcher **N** **they're terrible clock-watchers** ils passent leur temps à guetter l'heure (de sortie)

clockwise [ˈklɒkwaɪz] **ADV** dans le sens des aiguilles d'une montre
ADJ **in a c. direction** dans le sens des aiguilles d'une montre

clockwork [ˈklɒkwɜːk] **N** *(of clock, watch)* mouvement *m* (d'horloge); *(of toy)* mécanisme *m*, rouages *mpl*; **to go** *or* **to run like c.** marcher comme sur des roulettes; **as regular as c.** réglé comme du papier à musique
ADJ *(toy)* mécanique; *(mechanism)* qui se remonte; **everything is done with c. precision** tout est réglé comme du papier à musique

clod [klɒd] **N 1** *(of earth)* motte *f* (de terre) **2** *Fam (idiot)* imbécile◻ *mf*, crétin(e) *m,f*

clodhopper [ˈklɒdˌhɒpə(r)] **N** *Fam* **1** *(clumsy person)* balourd(e)◻ *m,f* **2** *Hum (shoe)* godillot *m*

clog [klɒg] *(pt & pp* **clogged,** *cont* **clogging)** **N** *(wooden, leather)* sabot *m*; *Br Fam* **to pop one's clogs** *(die)* casser sa pipe
VT 1 *(pipe)* boucher, encrasser; *(street)* boucher, bloquer; *(wheel)* bloquer **2** *Fig (hinder)* entraver, gêner
VI *(pipe)* se boucher; *(firearm, machine)* s'encrasser
▸▸ ***clog dance*** = danse où les participants marquent le rythme avec leurs sabots
▸**clog up** **VT SEP** *(pipe)* boucher, encrasser; *(street)* boucher, bloquer; *(wheel)* bloquer
VI *(pipe)* se boucher; *(firearm, machine)* s'encrasser

cloister [ˈklɔɪstə(r)] **N** *Archit & Rel* cloître *m*; **cloisters** *(of convent, church)* cloître *m*
VT *Rel* cloîtrer; *Fig* éloigner *ou* isoler (du monde)

cloistered [ˈklɔɪstəd] **ADJ** *Fig (life)* de reclus; **she leads a c. life** elle mène une vie de recluse

clone [kləʊn] *Biol & Fig* **N** clone *m*; **a Tom Cruise/Marilyn Monroe c.** un clone de Tom Cruise/Marilyn Monroe
VT cloner

cloner [ˈkləʊnə(r)] **N** *Mktg* cloneur *m*

cloning [ˈkləʊnɪŋ] **N** *Biol* clonage *m*

CLOSE[1] [kləʊs]

ADJ
• proche **1, 2, 6** • serré **4, 7**
• attentif **5** • mal aéré **8**
ADV
• près **1** • étroitement **2**
N
• clos **1** • impasse **2**

(compar **closer,** *superl* **closest)**
ADJ 1 *(near in space or time)* proche; **the library is c. to the school** la bibliothèque est près *ou* proche de l'école; **in c. proximity to sth** dans le voisinage immédiat de *ou* tout près de qch; **they're very c. in age** ils ont presque le même âge; **his death brought the war closer to home** c'est avec sa mort que nous avons vraiment pris conscience de la guerre; **we are c. to an agreement** nous sommes presque arrivés à un accord; **at c. intervals** à intervalles rapprochés; **I saw him at c. quar-**

ters je l'ai vu de près; **at c. range** à bout portant; **to be c. at** *or* **to hand** *(shop, cinema etc)* être tout près; *(book, pencil etc)* être à portée de main; **to be c. to tears** être au bord des larmes; *Fam* **I came c. to thumping him one** j'ai bien failli lui en coller une; **he keeps things c. to his chest** il ne fait guère de confidences; **to give sb a c. shave** raser qn de près; *Fam* **that was a c. shave** *or* **call!** on l'a échappé belle!, on a eu chaud!

2 *(in relationship)* proche; **they're very c. (friends)** ils sont très proches; **he's a c. friend of mine** c'est un ami intime; **a c. relative** un parent proche; **I'm very c. to my sister** je suis très proche de ma sœur; **he has c. ties with Israel** il a des rapports étroits avec Israël; **sources c. to the royal family** des sources proches de la famille royale; **a subject c. to my heart** un sujet qui me tient à cœur; **to keep sth a c. secret** garder le secret absolu sur qch

3 *(continuous)* **they stay in c. contact** ils restent en contact en permanence

4 *(in competition, race etc)* serré; *(election)* vivement serré; **it was a c. contest** ce fut une lutte serrée; **to play a c. game** jouer serré; **c. finish** arrivée *f* serrée; **the bill was passed but it was a c. thing** la loi a été votée de justesse

5 *(thorough, careful)* attentif, rigoureux; **pay c. attention to what she says** faites très attention *ou* prêtez une grande attention à ce qu'elle dit; **have a c. look at these figures** examinez ces chiffres de près; **upon c. examination** après un examen détaillé *ou* minutieux; **to keep (a) c. watch** *or* **eye on sb/sth** surveiller qn/qch de près; **in c. confinement** en détention surveillée

6 *(roughly similar)* proche; **his version of events was c. to the truth** sa version des faits était très proche de la réalité; **he bears a c. resemblance to his father** il ressemble beaucoup à son père; **it's the closest thing we've got to an operating theatre** voilà à quoi se réduit notre salle d'opération

7 *(compact ▸ handwriting, print)* serré; *(▸ grain)* dense, compact; *Mil* **in c. formation** en ordre serré

8 *Br (stuffy ▸ room)* mal aéré, qui manque de ventilation *ou* d'air; **it's very c. in here** on manque vraiment d'air ici; **it's terribly c. today** il fait très lourd aujourd'hui

9 *Fam (miserly)* pingre[□], radin

10 *Ling (vowel)* fermé

ADV 1 *(near)* près; **I live c. to the river** j'habite près de la rivière; **don't come too c.** n'approche pas *ou* ne t'approche pas trop; **did you win? – no, we didn't even come c.** avez-vous gagné? – non, loin de là; **she came c. to losing her job** elle a failli perdre son emploi; **to come c. to death** frôler la mort; **to come c. to the world record** frôler le record du monde; **they walked c. behind us** ils nous suivaient de près; **she lives c. by** elle habite tout près; **I looked at it c. to** *or* **up** je l'ai regardé de près; **c. together** serrés les uns contre les autres; **sit closer together!** serrez-vous!; **it's brought us closer** ça nous a rapprochés

2 *(tight)* étroitement, de près; **he held me c.** il m'a serré dans ses bras

N 1 *(field)* clos *m*

2 *Br (street)* impasse *f*

3 *Br (of cathedral)* enceinte *f*

• **close on PREP it's c. on nine o'clock** il est presque neuf heures; **she must be c. on fifty** elle doit friser la cinquantaine *ou* doit avoir près de cinquante ans

• **close to PREP** *(almost, nearly)* presque; **the baby weighs c. to 7 pounds** le bébé pèse presque 3 kilos et demi

▸▸ *Am Law* ***close arrest*** arrêts *mpl* de rigueur; *Mil* ***close combat*** corps-à-corps *m inv*; *Mus* ***close harmony*** tessiture *f* limitée

---

CLOSE² [kləʊz]

VT
- fermer **1–4, 10**
- arrêter **6**
- conclure **5, 8**
- liquider **7**

VI
- fermer **1**
- se terminer **4**
- se refermer **2**
- clôturer **5**

N
- fin, conclusion

VT 1 *(shut ▸ door, window, shop, book)* fermer; *Fig* **to c. one's eyes to sth** fermer les yeux sur qch; **she closed her mind to anything new** elle s'est fermée à tout ce qui était neuf

2 *(opening, bottle)* fermer, boucher; *Fig* **we must c. the gap between the rich and the poor** nous devons combler le fossé entre riches et pauvres

3 *(block ▸ border, road)* fermer; **a road closed to motor traffic** une route interdite à la circulation automobile

4 *(shut down ▸ factory)* fermer

5 *(conclude ▸ matter)* conclure, terminer; *(▸ meeting, session)* lever, clore; *(▸ debate)* fermer; **the subject is now closed** l'affaire est close

6 *Com & Fin (account)* arrêter, clore; **to c. the books** balancer les comptes, régler les livres

7 *St Exch (operation)* liquider; *(position)* couvrir

8 *(settle ▸ deal)* conclure

9 *(move closer together)* serrer, rapprocher; *Fig* **the party closed ranks behind their leader** le parti a serré les rangs derrière le leader

10 *Elec (circuit)* fermer

VI 1 *(shut ▸ gate, window)* fermer, se fermer; *(▸ shop)* fermer; *(▸ cinema, theatre)* faire relâche; **this window doesn't c. properly** cette fenêtre ne ferme pas bien *ou* ferme mal; **the door closed quietly behind them** la porte s'est refermée sans bruit derrière eux; **the bakery closes on Fridays** la boulangerie ferme le vendredi

2 *(wound, opening)* se refermer; **the gap was closing fast** l'écart diminuait rapidement

3 *(cover, surround)* **the waves closed over him** les vagues se refermèrent sur lui; **my fingers closed around the gun** mes doigts se resserrèrent sur le revolver

4 *(meeting)* se terminer, prendre fin; *(speaker)* terminer, finir

5 *St Exch* clôturer; **the shares closed at 420p** les actions ont clôturé *ou* terminé à 420 pence; **the share index closed two points down** l'indice (boursier) a clôturé en baisse de deux points

N fin *f*, conclusion *f*; *(of day)* tombée *f*; *St Exch (on financial futures market)* clôture *f*; *(closing price)* cours *m* de clôture; **at c. of business** à la *ou* en clôture; **the year drew to a c.** l'année s'acheva; **towards the c. of the century** vers la fin du siècle; **at c. of play** *(in cricket)* à la fin du match

▸▸ *Comput* ***close box*** case *f* de fermeture; *Br* ***close season*** *Hunt* fermeture *f* de la chasse; *Fishing* fermeture *f* de la pêche; *Ftbl* intersaison *f*

▸ **close down VI 1** *(business, factory)* fermer **2** *Br TV & Rad* terminer les émissions

VT SEP *(business, factory)* fermer

▸ **close in VI 1** *(approach)* approcher, se rapprocher; *(encircle)* cerner de près; **the hunters closed in on their prey** les chasseurs se rapprochèrent de leur proie; **the police/his creditors are closing in** l'étau de la police/de ses créanciers se resserre **2** *(evening, night)* approcher, descendre; *(day)* raccourcir; *(darkness, fog)* descendre; **darkness closed in on us** la nuit nous enveloppa

▸ **close off VT SEP** isoler, fermer; **the area was closed off to the public** le quartier était fermé au public; *Acct* **to c. off an account** arrêter un compte

▸ **close out VT SEP 1** *Am (factory, shop, business)* liquider *(avant fermeture)* **2** *St Exch* **to c. out a position** boucler *ou* clore *ou* fermer une position

▸ **close up VT SEP 1** *(seal)* fermer; *(opening, pipe)* obturer, boucher; *(wound)* refermer, recoudre **2** *Typ (characters)* rapprocher; *Mil (ranks)* serrer **3** *(shop, house)* fermer

VI 1 *(wound)* se refermer **2** *(shopkeeper)* fermer

▸ **close with VT INSEP 1** *(finalize deal with)* conclure un marché avec **2** *Literary (fight with)* engager la lutte *ou* le combat avec

---

close-cropped ['kləʊs-] **ADJ** *(hair)* (coupé) ras; *(grass)* ras

closed [kləʊzd] **ADJ 1** *(shut ▸ shop, museum etc)* fermé; *(▸ eyes)* fermé, clos; *(▸ opening, pipe)* obturé, bouché; *(▸ road)* barré; *(▸ economy, mind)* fermé; **road c. to traffic** *(sign)* route interdite à la circulation; **c. on Tuesdays** *(sign)* fermé le mardi; *Theat* relâche le mardi; *Law* **in c. session** à huis clos; **to do sth behind c. doors** faire qch en cachette; **economics is a c. book to me** je ne comprends rien à l'économie

2 *(restricted)* exclusif; **a c. society** un cercle fermé

3 *Ling (sound, syllable)* fermé

4 *Elec (circuit, switch)* fermé

▸▸ ***closed circuit television*** télévision *f* en circuit fermé; *Br Hunt* ***closed season*** fermeture *f* de la chasse; ***closed set*** *Math* ensemble *m* fermé; *Cin & TV* plateau *m* fermé; *Ind* ***closed shop*** *(practice)* = système selon lequel une entreprise n'embauche que des travailleurs syndiqués; *(establishment)* = entreprise qui n'embauche que des travailleurs syndiqués

closedown ['kləʊzdaʊn] **N 1** *(of shop)* fermeture *f* (définitive) **2** *Br TV & Rad* fin *f* des émissions

close-fisted [ˌkləʊs'fɪstɪd] **ADJ** avare

close-fitting ['kləʊs-] **ADJ** ajusté, près du corps

close-knit ['kləʊs-] **ADJ** *Fig (community, family)* très uni

closely ['kləʊslɪ] **ADV 1** *(near)* de près; *(tightly)* en serrant fort

2 *(carefully ▸ watch)* de près; *(▸ study)* minutieusement, de près; *(▸ listen)* attentivement

3 *(connected, guarded)* étroitement; **he's c. related to him** il est l'un de ses proches parents; **c. connected with sth** étroitement lié à qch; **to work c. with sb** travailler en collaboration étroite avec qn

4 *(resemble)* beaucoup

5 *(evenly)* **c. contested elections** élections *fpl* très serrées *ou* très disputées

closeness ['kləʊsnɪs] **N 1** *(nearness)* proximité *f*

2 *(intimacy ▸ of relationship, friendship, family)* intimité *f*

3 *(compactness ▸ of weave)* texture *f ou* contexture *f* serrée; *(▸ of print)* resserrement *m* *(des caractères)*

4 *(similarity ▸ of copy, translation)* fidélité *f*

5 *(thoroughness ▸ of examination)* minutie *f*, rigueur *f*

6 *(of weather)* lourdeur *f*; *(of room)* manque *m* d'air

7 *(miserliness)* avarice *f*

close-range ['kləʊs-] **ADJ** *(weapon)* à courte portée

close-run ['kləʊs-] **ADJ** *(competition, race etc)* serré; **it was a c. contest** ce fut une lutte serrée

close-set ['kləʊs-] **ADJ** *(eyes)* rapproché

close-shaven ['kləʊs-] **ADJ** rasé de près

closet ['klɒzɪt] **N 1** *esp Am (cupboard)* placard *m*, armoire *f*; *(for hanging clothes)* penderie *f*; *Fam Fig* **to come out of the c.** *(homosexual)* révéler (publiquement) son homosexualité[□], faire son come-out **2** *Arch (small room)* cabinet *m* **3** *Old-fashioned* **(water) c.** waters *mpl*, cabinets *mpl*

ADJ secret(ète); **she's a c. gambler** elle n'ose pas avouer qu'elle joue[□]; **c. homosexual** = personne qui cache son homosexualité

VT enfermer *(pour discuter)*; **to be closeted with sb** être en tête-à-tête avec qn

close-up [kləʊs-] **N** *(photograph, in movie)* gros plan *m*; *(programme)* portrait *m*, portrait-interview *m*; **in c.** en gros plan; *Fig* **the programme gives us a c. of life in prison** l'émission nous donne une vision en gros plan de la vie carcérale

ADJ *(shot, photograph, picture)* en gros plan

▸▸ ***close-up lens*** bonnette *f*

closing ['kləʊzɪŋ] **N 1** *(shutting ▸ of factory, shop, business, theatre)* fermeture *f* **2** *(ending ▸ of meeting, session)* levée *f*; *(▸ of conference)* clôture *f* **3** *Fin & Admin (of account)* arrêté *m*, règlement *m*; *(of bank account)* fermeture *f*; *St Exch (of position)* clôture *f*

ADJ 1 *(concluding)* final, dernier **2** *(last)* de fermeture

▸▸ *Law Br* ***closing address***, *Am* ***closing argument*** *(to judges)* plaidoirie *f* de clôture; ***closing date*** *(for applications)* date *f* limite de dépôt; *(for project)* date *f* de réalisation *(d'une opération)*; ***closing down*** *(of factory, shop, business)* fermeture *f* (définitive); *St Exch* ***closing price*** cours *m* à la clôture; ***closing remarks*** observations *fpl* finales; ***closing speech*** discours *m* de clôture; ***closing time*** heure *f* de fermeture; **it's c. time!** on ferme!

closure ['kləʊʒə(r)] **N 1** *(gen)* fermeture *f*; *(of factory, shop, business)* fermeture *f* définitive

2 *(of meeting)* clôture *f*; *Parl* **to move the c.** demander la clôture

3 *(of crisis, conflict)* résolution *f*; **it gave him a sense of c.** ça lui a permis de tourner la page

4 *(for container)* fermeture *f*

5 *Ling* fermeture *f (d'une voyelle)*
►► *Br Parl* ***closure motion*** = motion présentée par un député à la Chambre des communes, visant à clore un débat de façon à procéder à un vote; *Am Parl* ***closure rule*** = règle du Sénat américain limitant le temps de parole

clot [klɒt] *(pt & pp* **clotted**, *cont* **clotting**) **N 1** *(of blood)* caillot *m*; *Med* **a c. on the lung/on the brain** une embolie pulmonaire/cérébrale **2** *Br Fam (fool)* cruche *f*
VT cailler, coaguler
VI (se) cailler, (se) coaguler

cloth [klɒθ] **N 1** *(material)* tissu *m*, étoffe *f*; *Naut (sail)* toile *f*, voile *f*; *(for bookbinding)* toile *f*; **c. of gold** drap *m* d'or **2** *(individual piece)* linge *m*; *(for cleaning)* chiffon *m*, linge *m*; *(tablecloth)* nappe *f*; *Theat* toile *f* (de décor) **3** *Rel* **the c.** *(the clergy)* le clergé; **a man of the c.** un membre du clergé
COMP *(clothing)* de *ou* en tissu, de *ou* en étoffe
►► ***cloth binding*** reliure *f* en toile; ***cloth boards*** *(of book)* cartonnage *m* pleine toile; ***cloth cap*** casquette *f (symbole de la classe ouvrière britannique)*

clothbound ['klɒθbaʊnd] **ADJ** *(book)* relié toile

clothe [kləʊð] *(pt & pp* **clothed** *or Literary* **clad** [klæd]) **VT** habiller, vêtir; *Fig* revêtir, couvrir; **three children to feed and c.** trois enfants à nourrir et à habiller; **clothed in furs** vêtu de fourrures

cloth-eared **ADJ** *Br Fam* dur de la feuille, sourdingue

clothes [kləʊðz] **NPL 1** *(garments)* vêtements *mpl*, habits *mpl*; **to put one's c. on** s'habiller; **to take one's c. off** se déshabiller; **with one's c. on** (tout) habillé; **with no c. on** déshabillé, (tout) nu; **dressed in one's best c.** sur son trente et un, endimanché **2** *Br (bedclothes)* draps *mpl*
►► ***clothes basket*** panier *m* à linge; ***clothes brush*** brosse *f* à habits; *Am* ***clothes closet*** penderie *f*; ***clothes hanger*** cintre *m*; ***clothes hook*** patère *f*; ***clothes moth*** mite *f*; *Br* ***clothes peg***, *Am* ***clothes pin*** pince *f* à linge; ***clothes prop*** perche *f* de corde à linge; ***clothes shop*** magasin *m* de vêtements

clotheshorse ['kləʊðzhɔːs, *pl* -hɔːsɪz] **N 1** *(for laundry)* séchoir *m* à linge **2** *Fig (model)* mannequin *m*; *Pej* **she's such a c.** elle ne pense qu'à ses toilettes

clothesline ['kləʊðzlaɪn] **N** corde *f* à linge

clothier ['kləʊðɪə(r)] **N 1** *(cloth dealer, maker)* drapier(ère) *m,f* **2** *(clothes seller)* marchand(e) *m,f* de vêtements *ou* de confection

clothing ['kləʊðɪŋ] **N** *(UNCOUNT)* **1** *(garments)* vêtements *mpl*, habits *mpl*; **an article** *or* **item of c.** un vêtement; **articles of c.** vêtements *mpl*; **warm c.** vêtements *mpl* chauds **2** *(act of dressing)* habillage *m*; *(providing with garments)* habillement *m*; *Rel (of monk, nun)* prise *f* d'habit
COMP *(industry, trade)* du vêtement, de l'habillement
►► ***clothing allowance*** indemnité *f* vestimentaire; ***clothing manufacturer*** confectionneur (euse) *m,f*

clotted cream ['klɒtɪd-] **N** = crème fraîche très épaisse typique du sud-ouest de l'Angleterre

clotting ['klɒtɪŋ] **N** *(of blood)* caillage *m*, caillement *m*, coagulation *f*

cloud [klaʊd] **N 1** *Met* nuage *m*, *Literary* nuée *f*; **he resigned under a c.** *(of suspicion)* en butte aux soupçons, il a dû démissionner; *(in disgrace)* tombé en disgrâce, il a dû démissionner; **to be on c. nine** être aux anges *ou* au septième ciel; **to have one's head in the clouds** être dans les nuages *ou* la lune; *Prov* **every c. has a silver lining** à quelque chose malheur est bon **2** *(of dust, smoke)* nuage *m*; *(of gas)* nappe *f*; *(of insects)* nuée *f*
VT 1 *(make hazy* ► *mirror)* embuer; *(*► *liquid)* rendre trouble; **a clouded sky** un ciel couvert *ou* nuageux **2** *(confuse)* obscurcir; **don't c. the issue** ne brouillez pas les cartes; **her anger is clouding her judgment** la colère l'empêche de voir clairement les choses **3** *(spoil* ► *career, future)* assombrir; *(*► *reputation)* ternir; *(*► *happiness)* troubler
VI 1 *(sky)* se couvrir (de nuages), s'obscurcir **2** *(face)* s'assombrir
►► *Nucl* ***cloud chamber*** chambre *f* de détente *ou* d'ionisation; ***cloud cover*** couverture *f* nuageuse; ***cloud formation*** formation *f* de nuages

►**cloud over** **VI** *(sky)* se couvrir *ou* se voiler (de nuages); *Fig (face)* s'assombrir; **it clouded over in the afternoon** ça s'est couvert dans l'après-midi

cloudburst ['klaʊdbɜːst] **N** grosse averse *f*

cloud-cuckoo-land **N** *Br Fam* **they're living in c.** ils planent complètement, ils n'ont pas les pieds sur terre

clouded ['klaʊdɪd] **ADJ 1** *(sky)* couvert (de nuages); *(liquid)* trouble; **to become c.** *(sky)* se couvrir; *(mind)* s'obscurcir **2** *Fig (judgement)* altéré

cloudiness ['klaʊdɪnɪs] **N** *(of sky)* nébulosité *f*; *(of liquid)* aspect *m* trouble

cloudless ['klaʊdlɪs] **ADJ** *(sky)* sans nuages; *Fig (days, future)* sans nuages, serein

cloudy ['klaʊdɪ] *(compar* **cloudier**, *superl* **cloudiest**) **ADJ 1** *Met* nuageux, couvert; **it will be c. today** le temps sera couvert aujourd'hui **2** *(liquid)* trouble; *(gem)* taché, nuageux; *(urine)* chargé **3** *Fig (confused)* obscur, nébuleux

clout [klaʊt] *Fam* **N 1** *(blow)* calotte *f*; **to give sb a c.** flanquer une calotte à qn; **to give sth a c.** flanquer un coup dans qch **2** *Fig (influence)* influence *f*, poids *m*; **to have** *or* **to carry a lot of c.** avoir le bras long **3** *NEng & Scot (cloth)* chiffon *m*; *(garment)* vêtement *m*
VT *(hit* ► *person)* flanquer une calotte à; *(*► *thing)* flanquer un coup dans

clove [kləʊv] *pt of* **cleave**
N 1 *(spice)* clou *m* de girofle; *(tree)* giroflier *m*; **oil of cloves** essence *f* de girofle **2** *(of garlic)* gousse *f*
►► ***clove hitch*** demi-clef *f*, nœud *m* de cabestan

cloven ['kləʊvən] *pp of* **cleave**
ADJ fendu, fourchu; **c. foot** *or* **hoof** *(of animal)* sabot *m* fendu; *(of devil)* pied *m* fourchu

cloven-footed, cloven-hoofed [-huːft] **ADJ** *(animal)* aux sabots fendus; *(devil)* aux pieds fourchus

clover ['kləʊvə(r)] **N** *Bot* trèfle *m*; *Fig* **to be in c.** être comme un coq en pâte

cloverleaf ['kləʊvəliːf] *(pl* **cloverleaves** [-liːvz]) **N** *Bot* feuille *f* de trèfle

clown [klaʊn] **N** *(entertainer)* clown *m*; *Theat* bouffon *m*; *Fig (fool)* pitre *m*, imbécile *mf*; **to act the c.** faire le clown; **to make a c. of oneself** se rendre ridicule
VI *(joke)* faire le clown; *(act foolishly)* faire le pitre *ou* l'imbécile

►**clown about, clown around** **VI** *(joke)* faire le clown; *(act foolishly)* faire le pitre *ou* l'imbécile

clowning ['klaʊnɪŋ] **N** *(UNCOUNT)* clowneries *fpl*, pitreries *fpl*

clownish ['klaʊnɪʃ] **ADJ** clownesque

cloy [klɔɪ] *also Fig* **VT** écœurer
VI devenir écœurant

cloying ['klɔɪɪŋ] **ADJ** écœurant

club [klʌb] *(pt & pp* **clubbed**, *cont* **clubbing**) **N 1** *(association)* club *m*, cercle *m*; **a tennis/football c.** un club de tennis/football; *Hum* **join the c.!** bienvenue au club!, tu n'es pas le seul!; **I've got a cold – join the c.!** j'ai un rhume – on est deux!; *Fam* **to be in the (pudding) c.** *(pregnant)* être en cloque
2 *(nightclub)* boîte *f* (de nuit); **the c. scene** = milieux branchés fréquentant les boîtes de nuit
3 *(weapon)* matraque *f*, massue *f*; *Sport* **(Indian) c.** massue *f* de gymnastique
4 *Golf* club *m* (de golf)
5 *Cards* trèfle *m*; **clubs** trèfles *mpl*; **the nine of clubs** le neuf de trèfle
VT matraquer, frapper avec une massue; **he was clubbed to death** il a été matraqué à mort
►► *Am Rail* ***club car*** wagon-restaurant *m*; ***club chair*** club *m*; *Aviat* ***club class*** classe *f* club, classe *f* affaires; ***club sandwich*** sandwich *m* mixte *(à trois étages)*; *Am* ***club soda*** eau *f* de Seltz; ***club tie*** = cravate aux couleurs d'une association sportive

►**club together** **VI** *(share cost)* se cotiser; **to c. together to buy sth** se cotiser pour acheter qch

CLUBS

Les "clubs" britanniques sont des lieux de rencontre et de détente très fermés, qui jouent un rôle important dans la vie sociale des milieux aisés en Grande-Bretagne. Traditionnellement ces institutions (notamment les "gentlemen's clubs" londoniens, tels que l'Athenaeum ou le Carlton Club) étaient interdites aux femmes, mais récemment cette tendance a commencé à changer.

clubbable ['klʌbəbəl] **ADJ** *Old-fashioned* sociable

clubber ['klʌbə(r)] **N** *Fam* **he's a real c.** il adore aller en boîte

clubbing ['klʌbɪŋ] **N** *Fam* **to go c.** aller en boîte

clubfooted [,klʌb'fʊtɪd] **ADJ** **to be c.** avoir un pied bot

clubhouse ['klʌbhaʊs, *pl* -haʊzɪz] **N** *Sport* pavillon *m*

clubland ['klʌblənd] **N** *Br* **1** *(area of gentlemen's clubs)* = quartier des alentours de Saint James's où se trouvent la plupart des clubs sélects de Londres **2** *(nightclub area)* = quartier des boîtes de nuit

cluck [klʌk] **VI** *(hen, person)* glousser; **she clucked in disapproval** elle a claqué sa langue de désapprobation
N *(of hen)* gloussement *m*; *(of person* ► *in pleasure)* gloussement *m*; *(*► *in disapproval)* claquement *m* de langue

clucking ['klʌkɪŋ] **N** *(of hen, person)* gloussement *m*

clue [kluː] **N 1** *(gen)* indice *m*, indication *f*; *(to crime)* indice *m*; **give me a c.** mettez-moi sur la piste; **her hat provides a c. to her profession** on devine sa profession à son chapeau; **where's John? – I haven't a c.!** où est John? – je n'en ai pas la moindre idée *ou* je n'en ai aucune idée!; *Fam* **he's useless at cooking, he hasn't got a c.!** il est nul en cuisine, il n'y connaît absolument rien!; *Fam* **he hasn't got a c. what he's doing** il fait n'importe quoi **2** *(in crosswords)* définition *f*; **what's the c. to 13 down?** quelle est la définition du 13 vertical? **3** *Naut* point *m* d'écoute

►**clue in** **VT SEP** *Fam (person)* mettre au courant

►**clue up** **VT SEP** *Fam (person)* renseigner, mettre au courant

clueless ['kluːlɪs] **ADJ** *Br Fam Pej* qui ne sait rien de rien

clump [klʌmp] **N 1** *(cluster* ► *of bushes)* massif *m*; *(*► *of trees)* bouquet *m*; *(*► *of hair, grass)* touffe *f* **2** *(mass* ► *of earth)* motte *f* **3** *(sound)* bruit *m* sourd
VI *(walk)* **to c. (about** *or* **around)** marcher d'un pas lourd; **with the neighbours clumping about upstairs** avec les voisins qui font du potin en haut
VT *(gather)* **to c. (together)** grouper; *(bushes, flowers)* planter en massif

clumsily ['klʌmzɪlɪ] **ADV 1** *(awkwardly)* maladroitement, gauchement **2** *(tactlessly)* sans tact **3** *(drawn)* grossièrement; **c. built** mal bâti

clumsiness ['klʌmzɪnɪs] **N 1** *(of person, movement)* maladresse *f*, gaucherie *f* **2** *(tactlessness)* gaucherie *f*, manque *m* de tact **3** *(awkwardness* ► *of tool)* caractère *m* peu pratique; *(*► *of design)* lourdeur *f*; *(*► *of shape)* grossièreté *f*, lourdeur *f*; *(*► *of sentence)* lourdeur *f*, maladresse *f*

clumsy ['klʌmzɪ] *(compar* **clumsier**, *superl* **clumsiest**) **ADJ 1** *(uncoordinated* ► *person, movement)* maladroit, gauche **2** *(tactless)* gauche, malhabile; **he made a c. apology** il s'est excusé de façon gauche **3** *(awkward* ► *tool)* peu commode *ou* pratique; *(*► *design)* lourd, disgracieux; *(*► *painting)* maladroit; *(*► *style)* lourd, maladroit

clung [klʌŋ] *pt & pp of* **cling**

clunk [klʌŋk] **N** *(sound)* bruit *m* sourd
VI faire un bruit sourd

cluster ['klʌstə(r)] **N 1** *(of fruit)* grappe *f*; *(of dates)* régime *m*; *(of flowers)* touffe *f*; *(of trees)* bouquet *m*; *(of stars)* amas *m*; *(of diamonds)* entourage *m*
2 *(group* ► *of houses, people)* groupe *m*; *(*► *of bees)* essaim *m*
3 *Ling* groupe *m*, agglomérat *m*
4 *Comput (of terminals)* grappe *f*
VI 1 *(people)* **to c. around sb/sth** se grouper autour de qn/qch **2** *(things)* former un groupe; **pretty cottages clustered around the church**

l'église était entourée de petites maisons coquettes; **to c. together** se grouper
▸▸ *Mktg* ***cluster analysis*** analyse *f* par segments; ***cluster bomb*** bombe *f* à fragmentation; *Mktg* ***cluster sampling*** échantillonnage *m* aréolaire, échantillonnage *m* par grappes

clutch [klʌtʃ] **VT1** *(hold tightly)* serrer fortement, étreindre **2** *(seize)* empoigner, se saisir de; **to c. hold of sth** s'agripper *ou* se cramponner à qch
VI to c. at sth se cramponner à qch, s'agripper à qch; *Fig* se cramponner à qch, se raccrocher à qch
N1 *(grasp)* étreinte *f*, prise *f*
2 *Aut (mechanism)* embrayage *m*; *(pedal)* pédale *f* d'embrayage; **to let in the c.** embrayer; **to let out** *or* **to release the c.** débrayer
3 *(of eggs, chicks)* couvée *f*; *Fig (group)* série *f*, ensemble *m*
4 *Am Fam (crisis)* crise ▫ *f*
• **clutches NPL** *Fig (control)* influence *f*; **to have sb in one's clutches** tenir qn en son pouvoir; **to fall into sb's clutches** tomber dans les griffes de qn
▸▸ ***clutch bag*** *(handbag)* pochette *f (sac à main)*; *Aut* ***clutch cable*** câble *m* de commande d'embrayage; *Aut* ***clutch disc*** disque *m* d'embrayage; *Aut* ***clutch fluid*** fluide *m* d'embrayage; *Aut* ***clutch housing*** carter *m* d'embrayage; *Aut* ***clutch pedal*** pédale *f* d'embrayage *ou* de débrayage; *Aut* ***clutch plate*** disque *m* d'embrayage

clutter ['klʌtə(r)] **N 1** *(mess)* désordre *m*; **the house is in a bit of a c.** la maison est plutôt en désordre **2** *(disordered objects)* désordre *m*, fouillis *m*; **among the c. on her desk** au milieu du désordre qu'il y a sur son bureau
VT *(room)* mettre en désordre; **a desk cluttered with papers** un bureau encombré de papiers; **his mind was cluttered with useless facts** son esprit était encombré d'informations inutiles
▸ **clutter up VT SEP** *(room)* mettre en désordre; **don't c. up the worktop** n'encombre pas le plan de travail

cluttered ['klʌtəd] **ADJ** encombré (**with** de)

cm *(written abbr* **centimetre***)* cm

Cmdr *Mil (written abbr* **Commander***)* Cdt

CMOS ['si:mɒs] **N** *Comput (abbr* **complementary metal oxide silicon***)* CMOS

CMR waybill [ˌsi:em'ɑ:-] **N** *Com* lettre *f* de voiture CMR

CMYK [ˌsi:em,waɪ'keɪ] **N** *Comput (abbr* **cyan, magenta, yellow, black***)* CMJN

CND [ˌsi:en'di:] **N** *Br (abbr* **Campaign for Nuclear Disarmament***)* = en Grande-Bretagne, mouvement pour le désarmement nucléaire

CNN [ˌsi:en'en] **N** *TV (abbr* **Cable News Network***)* = réseau d'informations américain diffusé par câble et satellite

C-note ['si:ˌnəʊt] **N** *Am Fam* billet *m* de 100 dollars ▫

CO[1] [ˌsi:'əʊ] **N** *Mil* **1** *(abbr* **commanding officer***)* commandant *m* **2** *(abbr* **conscientious objector***)* objecteur *m* de conscience

CO[2] *(written abbr* **Colorado***)* Colorado *m*

Co.[1] [kəʊ] **N** *(abbr* **company***)* Cie; *Fig* **Jane and co** Jane et compagnie

Co.[2] *(written abbr* **county***)* comté *m*

c/o [ˌsi:'əʊ] *(abbr* **care of***)* chez

> **co-** PRÉFIXE
>
> Le préfixe **co-** s'emploie avec des noms, des adjectifs et des verbes et véhicule deux notions très proches mais distinctes:
> • le fait d'être ou de faire quelque chose ENSEMBLE, comme dans les exemples suivants:
> **coexistence** coexistence; **to cosign** cosigner; **coeducational** mixte; **co-starring Tom Cruise** avec Tom Cruise.
> • la COOPÉRATION, comme dans les exemples suivants:
> **co-author** coauteur; **co-worker** collègue; **coproduction** coproduction; **they co-hosted the show** ils ont présenté l'émission ensemble.

.co ['dɒt'kəʊ] *Comput* = abréviation désignant les entreprises commerciales dans les adresses électroniques britanniques

coach [kəʊtʃ] **N 1** *(tutor)* répétiteur(trice) *m,f*; *Sport (trainer)* entraîneur(euse) *m,f*; *Ski (instructor)* moniteur(trice) *m,f*
2 *Br (bus)* car *m*, autocar *m*
3 *Br Rail* voiture *f*, wagon *m*
4 *(carriage)* carrosse *m*; **(stage) c.** diligence *f*, coche *m*; *Fig* **to drive a c. and horses through sth** démolir *ou* torpiller qch
COMP *(driver)* de car; *(tour, trip)* en car
VT *(tutor)* donner des leçons particulières à; *Sport* entraîner; **to c. sb for an exam** préparer qn à un examen; *Theat* **to c. sb for a part** faire répéter son rôle à qn; **the police coached the witness** la police a préparé le témoin à la déclaration; **he had been carefully coached in what to say** on lui avait bien expliqué quoi dire
VI *(tutor)* donner des leçons particulières; *Sport* être entraîneur(euse)
▸▸ *Am Aviat* ***coach class*** classe *f* économique; ***coach house*** remise *f (pour carrosse ou voiture)*; ***coach park*** emplacement *m* (de parking) réservé aux autocars; ***coach party*** groupe *m* voyageant en autocar; *Br* ***coach station*** gare *f* routière; ***coach tour*** circuit *m* (touristique) en car, voyage *m* en autocar; ***coach tour operator*** autocariste *m*

coachbuilder ['kəʊtʃˌbɪldə(r)] **N** carrossier *m*

coaching ['kəʊtʃɪŋ] **N** *(UNCOUNT) (tutoring)* leçons *fpl* particulières; *Sport (training)* entraînement *m*
▸▸ *Hist* ***coaching inn*** relais *m*

coachman ['kəʊtʃmən] *(pl* **coachmen** [-mən]*)* **N** cocher *m*

coachwork ['kəʊtʃwɜ:k] **N** carrosserie *f*

coagulant [kəʊ'ægjʊlənt] **N** coagulant *m*

coagulate [kəʊ'ægjʊleɪt] **VT** coaguler
VI (se) coaguler

coagulation [kəʊˌægjʊ'leɪʃən] **N** coagulation *f*

coal [kəʊl] **N1** *(gen)* charbon *m*; **a piece** *or* **lump of c.** un morceau de charbon; *Fig* **to carry coals to Newcastle** porter de l'eau à la rivière; *Fig* **to haul sb over the coals** réprimander qn vertement **2** *Ind (ore)* houille *f*; **soft c.** houille *f* grasse
VT *(supply with coal)* fournir *ou* ravitailler en charbon; *Naut* charbonner
VI *Naut* charbonner
COMP *(chute)* à charbon; *(depot, fire)* de charbon
▸▸ *Br* ***coal bunker*** coffre *m* à charbon; *Naut* soute *f* à charbon; ***coal cellar*** cave *f* à charbon; ***coal gas*** gaz *m* de houille; ***coal industry*** industrie *f* houillère; ***coal merchant*** charbonnier(ère) *m,f*, marchand(e) *m,f* de charbon; ***coal mine*** mine *f* de charbon *ou* de houille; ***coal miner*** mineur *m*; ***coal mining*** exploitation *f* du charbon *ou* de la houille; *Am* ***coal oil*** kérosène *m*, pétrole *m* (lampant); ***coal scuttle*** seau *m* à charbon; ***coal tar*** coaltar *m*, goudron *m* de houille; ***coal tit*** mésange *f* noire

coal-black ADJ noir comme du charbon

coalesce [ˌkəʊə'les] **VI** s'unir (en un groupe), se fondre (ensemble)

coalescence [ˌkəʊə'lesəns] **N** fusion *f*, union *f*

coalface ['kəʊlfeɪs] **N** front *m* de taille

coalfield ['kəʊlfi:ld] **N** bassin *m* houiller, gisement *m* de houille

coal-fired ADJ à charbon, qui marche au charbon

coalition [ˌkəʊə'lɪʃən] **N** coalition *f*; *Pol* **to form a c.** former une coalition, se coaliser
▸▸ *Pol* ***coalition government*** gouvernement *m* de coalition

coalman ['kəʊlmən] *(pl* **coalmen** [-men]*)* **N** charbonnier *m*, marchand *m* de charbon

coalshed ['kəʊlʃed] **N** hangar *m* à charbon

coarse [kɔ:s] **ADJ1** *(rough in texture, appearance)* gros (grosse), grossier; *(skin, hands)* rugueux, rêche; *(hair)* rêche; *(sandpaper)* épais(aisse); *(salt)* gros (grosse); *(features)* grossier, lourd **2** *(vulgar ▸ person, behaviour, remark, joke)* grossier, vulgaire; *(▸ laugh)* gros (grosse), gras; *(▸ accent)* commun, vulgaire **3** *(inferior ▸ food, drink)* ordinaire, commun
▸▸ ***coarse fishing*** pêche *f* à la ligne en eau douce; ***coarse grain*** gros grain *m*; ***coarse linen*** grosse toile *f*; ***coarse weave*** texture *f* grossière

coarsely ['kɔ:slɪ] **ADV1** *(roughly)* grossièrement; **c. chopped/ground** grossièrement haché/moulu; **c. woven** de texture grossière **2** *(uncouthly ▸ speak)* vulgairement, grossièrement; *(▸ laugh)* grassement; *(vulgarly)* indécemment, crûment

coarsen ['kɔ:sən] **VI1** *(texture, appearance)* devenir rude *ou* grossier; *(features)* s'épaissir **2** *(person)* devenir grossier *ou* vulgaire
VT1 *(texture, appearance)* rendre rude *ou* grossier; *(features)* épaissir **2** *(person, speech)* rendre grossier *ou* vulgaire

coarseness ['kɔ:snɪs] **N1** *(of skin)* rugosité *f*; *(of hair)* caractère *m* rêche; *(of fabric)* grossièreté *f*; *(of features)* grossièreté *f*, lourdeur *f* **2** *(uncouthness)* manque *m* de savoir-vivre; *(vulgarity)* grossièreté *f*, vulgarité *f*

coast [kəʊst] **N1** *(of sea)* côte *f*; *(extensive)* littoral *m*; *Br* **the c.** *(seaside)* la côte; **c. path** chemin *m* côtier; **we took the c. road** nous avons pris la route qui longe la mer; **off the c. of Ireland** *or* **the Irish c.** au large des côtes irlandaises; **from c. to c.** d'un bout à l'autre du pays, *Can* d'un océan à l'autre; **broadcast from c. to c.** diffusé dans tout le pays; *Fig* **the c. is clear** la voie est libre **2** *Am (act of coasting)* descente *f* en roue libre
VI *(vehicle)* avancer en roue libre; *(downhill)* descendre en roue libre; *Naut* caboter; *Fam Fig* **he coasted through the exam** il a eu l'examen les doigts dans le nez; *Fig* **you're coasting** *(not working hard)* tu te la coules douce

coastal ['kəʊstəl] **ADJ** littoral, côtier
▸▸ *Ecol* ***coastal erosion*** érosion *f* côtière; ***coastal navigation*** navigation *f* côtière, cabotage *m*; ***coastal traffic*** navigation *f* côtière, cabotage *m*; ***coastal waters*** eaux *fpl* littorales

coaster ['kəʊstə(r)] **N1** *(protective mat ▸ for glass)* dessous-de-verre *m inv*; *(▸ for bottle)* dessous-de-bouteille *m inv*; *(stand, tray)* présentoir *m* à bouteilles **2** *Naut (ship)* caboteur *m*

coastguard ['kəʊstgɑ:d] **N1** *(organization)* gendarmerie *f* maritime, *Can* Garde *f* côtière **2** *Br (person)* membre *m* de la gendarmerie maritime; *Hist* garde-côte *m*
▸▸ ***coastguard station*** bureau *m* de la gendarmerie maritime; ***coastguard vessel*** garde-côte *m*

coasting ['kəʊstɪŋ] **N** *Naut* navigation *f* côtière; **c. vessel** caboteur *m*

coastline ['kəʊstlaɪn] **N** littoral *m*

coat [kəʊt] **N1** *(overcoat ▸ gen)* manteau *m*; *(▸ man's)* manteau *m*, pardessus *m*; *(jacket)* veste *f*; *esp Am (of man's suit)* veston *m* **2** *(of animal)* pelage *m*, poil *m*; *(of horse)* robe *f* **3** *(covering ▸ of dust)* couche *f*; *(▸ of snow)* manteau *m*, couche *f*; *(▸ of paint, varnish, tar)* couche *f*, application *f*
VT1 *(cover)* couvrir, revêtir; *(with paint, varnish, tar)* enduire; *(cable)* revêtir, armer; *(paper)* coucher; **the shelves were coated with dust** les étagères étaient recouvertes de poussière; **my shoes were coated with mud** mes chaussures étaient couvertes de boue; **a coated tongue** une langue chargée **2** *Culin* **to c. sth with flour/with sugar** saupoudrer qch de farine/de sucre; **to c. sth with chocolate** enrober qch de chocolat; **to c. sth with egg** dorer qch à l'œuf
▸▸ *Her* ***coat of arms*** blason *m*, armoiries *fpl*; ***coat hanger*** cintre *m*; ***coat hook*** patère *f*; *Hist* ***coat of mail*** cotte *f* de mailles; ***coat rack, coat stand*** portemanteau *m*; ***coat tails*** queue-de-pie *f* *(costume)*; *Fig* **to ride (on) sb's c. tails, to hang on sb's c. tails** profiter de l'influence *ou* de la position de qn

coated ['kəʊtɪd] **ADJ** *(paper)* couché

coati [kəʊ'ɑ:tɪ] **N** *Zool* coati *m*

coating ['kəʊtɪŋ] **N** couche *f*; *(on pan)* revêtement *m*

co-author N coauteur *m*
VT *(book)* écrire en collaboration; **a book co-authored by Marsh and Brown** un livre écrit conjointement par Marsh et Brown

coax [kəʊks] **VT** cajoler, enjôler; **he coaxed us into going** à force de nous cajoler, il nous a persuadés d'y aller; **I coaxed the money out of him** j'ai obtenu l'argent de lui par des cajoleries

coaxial [ˌkəʊ'æksɪəl] ADJ *Geom & Elec* coaxial
►► *Comput* **coaxial cable** câble *m* coaxial

coaxing ['kəʊksɪŋ] N *(UNCOUNT)* cajolerie *f*, cajoleries *fpl*; **after a lot of c., he agreed** il s'est fait prier avant d'accepter; **no amount of c. would get him to agree** malgré les efforts pour l'enjôler, on n'a pas réussi à le faire accepter
ADJ enjôleur, cajoleur

cob [kɒb] N **1** *(horse)* cob *m*
2 *(swan)* cygne *m* mâle
3 *(of corn)* épi *m*
4 *Br (bread)* pain *m* rond, miche *f* de pain
5 *Br (nut)* noisette *f*
►► *Br* **cob loaf** pain *m* rond, miche *f* de pain

cobalt ['kəʊbɔːlt] N **1** *Chem* cobalt *m* **2** *(colour)* bleu *m* de cobalt
►► **cobalt blue** bleu *m* de cobalt; *Med* **cobalt bomb** bombe *f* au cobalt; **cobalt 60** cobalt *m* 60, cobalt *m* radioactif

cobber ['kɒbə(r)] N *Austr Fam* copain *m*, pote *m*

cobble ['kɒbəl] N *(stone)* pavé *m*
VT **1** *(road)* paver **2** *Br Old-fashioned (shoes)* réparer
►**cobble together** VT SEP bricoler, concocter; **they cobbled a compromise together** ils ont bricolé un compromis

cobbled ['kɒbəld] ADJ *(path, street)* pavé

cobbler ['kɒblə(r)] N **1** *(shoe repairer)* cordonnier (ère) *m,f*; *(shoemaker)* bottier *m* **2** *Am Culin (cake)* = dessert composé de fruits recouverts d'une couche de pâte; *(drink)* punch *m*
• **cobblers** *Br very Fam* NPL **1** *(testicles)* balloches *fpl*, boules *fpl* **2** *(nonsense)* foutaises *fpl*
EXCLAM n'importe quoi!, des foutaises, tout ça!

cobblestone ['kɒbəlˌstəʊn] N pavé *m (rond)*

cobnut ['kɒbnʌt] N noisette *f*

COBOL ['kəʊbɒl] N *Comput* (*abbr* **Common Business-Oriented Language**) cobol *m*

cobra ['kəʊbrə] N *Zool* cobra *m*, naja *m*

co-branding N *Mktg* alliance *f* de marque, co-branding *m*

cobweb ['kɒbweb] N toile *f* d'araignée; *(single thread)* fil *m* d'araignée; *Fig* **I'm going for a walk to clear away the cobwebs** *or* **to blow the cobwebs away** je vais faire un tour pour me rafraîchir les idées; *Fig* **to brush the cobwebs off sth** ressortir qch

coca ['kəʊkə] N *Bot (shrub)* coca *m*; *(leaf substance)* coca *f*

cocaine [kəʊ'keɪn] N cocaïne *f*
►► **cocaine addict** cocaïnomane *mf*; **cocaine addiction** cocaïnomanie *f*

coccyx ['kɒksɪks] *(pl* **coccyges** [ˌkɒk'saɪdʒiːz]) N *Anat* coccyx *m*

co-chair N coprésident(e) *m,f*
VT coprésider

cochineal ['kɒtʃɪniːl] N **1** *Entom* cochenille *f* **2** *(dye)* carmin *m*, cochenille *f* des teinturiers

cock [kɒk] N **1** *(rooster)* coq *m*; *(male bird)* (oiseau *m*) mâle *m*; *Fam Fig* **he thinks he's c. of the walk** il se prend pour le grand chef❑
2 *(tap)* robinet *m*
3 *(of gun)* chien *m*; **at full c.** armé
4 *Vulg (penis)* bite *f*, bitte *f*
5 *Br Fam (term of address)* pote *m*; **all right, c.?** ça va, mon pote?
6 *Agr (of hay)* meulon *m*
VT **1** *(gun)* armer
2 *(raise)* **the dog cocked its ears** le chien a dressé les oreilles; **the dog cocked its leg** le chien a levé la patte; *Br Fam* **to c. a snook at sb** faire un pied de nez à qn
3 *(head, hat)* pencher, incliner; *(thumb)* tendre
4 *(hay)* mettre en meulons
►► **cock lobster** homard *m* mâle; **cock pheasant** coq faisan *m*; **cock sparrow** moineau *m* mâle
►**cock up** *Br very Fam* VT SEP **to c. sth up** *(interview, exam)* foirer qch, se planter à qch; *(plan, arrangement)* faire foirer qch
VI **he's cocked up again** il a encore tout fait foirer

cockade [kɒ'keɪd] N *Hist* cocarde *f*

cock-a-doodle-doo [ˌkɒkəˌduːdəl'duː] *(pl* **cock-a-doodle-doos**) N cocorico *m*
EXCLAM cocorico!

cock-a-hoop ADJ *Fam* fier comme Artaban❑

cock-a-leekie [-'liːkɪ] N *Culin* **c. (soup)** = potage au poulet et aux poireaux

cock-and-bull story N histoire *f* à dormir debout

cockatoo [ˌkɒkə'tuː] *(pl* **cockatoos**) N *Orn* cacatoès *m*

cockchafer ['kɒkˌtʃeɪfə(r)] N *Entom* hanneton *m*

cockcrow ['kɒkkrəʊ] N aube *f*; **at c.** au chant du coq

cocker ['kɒkə(r)] N cocker *m*
►► **cocker spaniel** cocker *m*

cockerel ['kɒkərəl] N jeune coq *m*

cock-eyed [-aɪd] ADJ *Fam* **1** *(cross-eyed)* qui louche❑ **2** *(crooked)* de travers❑ **3** *(absurd* ► *idea, plan)* absurde❑; (► *story)* qui ne tient pas debout❑

cockfight ['kɒkfaɪt] N combat *m* de coqs

cockfighting ['kɒkˌfaɪtɪŋ] N *(UNCOUNT)* combats *mpl* de coqs

cockiness ['kɒkɪnɪs] N impertinence *f*

cockle ['kɒkəl] N *Zool* coque *f*; *Fig* **that will warm the cockles of your heart** voilà qui vous réchauffera le cœur

cockleshell ['kɒkəlˌʃel] N *(shell)* coquille *f*; *(boat)* coque *f*

Cockney ['kɒknɪ] N **1** *(person)* cockney *mf (Londonien né dans le "East End")* **2** *Ling* cockney *m*
ADJ cockney; **C. accent** accent *m* cockney

cockpit ['kɒkpɪt] N **1** *(of plane)* cabine *f* de pilotage, cockpit *m*; *(of racing car)* poste *m* du pilote; *(of yacht)* cockpit *m* **2** *(in cockfighting)* arène *f*; *Fig* arènes *fpl*

cockroach ['kɒkrəʊtʃ] N *Entom* cafard *m*, blatte *f*

cockscomb ['kɒkskəʊm] N **1** *(of rooster)* crête *f* **2** *Bot* crête-de-coq *f*

cocksure [ˌkɒk'ʃʊə(r)] ADJ *Pej* suffisant, outrecuidant

cocktail ['kɒkteɪl] N **1** *(mixed drink)* cocktail *m (boisson)* **2** *(gen* ► *mixture of things)* mélange *m*, cocktail *m*; **a c. of drugs** *(for recreational use)* un cocktail *ou* un mélange de drogues; *(medication)* un cocktail de médicaments
►► **cocktail bar** bar *m*; **cocktail cabinet** bar *m (meuble)*; **cocktail dress** robe *f* de cocktail; **cocktail lounge** bar *m*; **cocktail party** cocktail *m (fête)*; **cocktail sausage** petite saucisse *f* (à apéritif); **cocktail shaker** shaker *m*; **cocktail stick** pique *f* à apéritif

cock-up N *Br very Fam* foirade *f*; **to make a c. of sth** *(interview, exam)* foirer qch, se planter à qch; *(plan, arrangement)* faire foirer qch; **he made a c. of his exam** il s'est planté à l'examen

cocky ['kɒkɪ] *(compar* **cockier**, *superl* **cockiest**) *Fam* ADJ *(smug)* suffisant❑; **don't get c.!** ne prends pas ton air supérieur!❑

cocoa ['kəʊkəʊ] N **1** *(powder, drink)* cacao *m* **2** *(colour)* marron *m* clair
►► **cocoa bean** graine *f* de cacao; **cocoa butter** beurre *m* de cacao

coconut ['kəʊkənʌt] N noix *f* de coco
►► **coconut fibre** fibre *f* de coco, coir *m*; **coconut ice** = friandise à base de noix de coco; **coconut matting** tapis *m* en fibres de noix de coco; **coconut milk** lait *m* de coco; **coconut oil** huile *f* de coco; **coconut palm** cocotier *m*; **coconut shy** jeu *m* de massacre *(où l'on essaie d'abattre des noix de coco)*; **coconut tree** cocotier *m*

cocoon [kə'kuːn] N cocon *m*; *Fig* **wrapped in a c. of blankets** emmitouflé dans des couvertures
VT *(wrap)* envelopper avec soin; *Fig (overprotect* ► *child)* couver; **workers in the public sector have been cocooned from unemployment** les travailleurs du secteur public ont été protégés du chômage

cocooning [kə'kuːnɪŋ] N cocooning *m*

COD [ˌsiːəʊ'diː] ADV *Com* (*abbr Br* **cash on delivery**, *Am* **collect on delivery**) **to send sth C.** envoyer qch contre remboursement; **all goods are sent C.** toutes les marchandises doivent être payées à la livraison

cod [kɒd] *(pl* **inv** *or* **cods**) N *(fish)* morue *f*; *Culin* **dried c.** merluche *f*, morue *f* séchée; *Culin* **fresh c.** morue *f* fraîche, cabillaud *m*
►► *Culin* **cod fillet** filet *m* de cabillaud; *Culin* **cod roe** œufs *mpl* de morue; **the cod war** la guerre de la morue *(série de conflits ayant opposé la Grande-Bretagne et l'Islande au sujet de zones de pêche islandaises)*

coda ['kəʊdə] N *Mus* coda *f*

coddle ['kɒdəl] VT **1** *(pamper* ► *child)* dorloter, choyer **2** *Culin* (faire) cuire à feu doux; **a coddled egg** un œuf à la coque

code [kəʊd] N **1** *(cipher)* code *m*, chiffre *m*; *Biol & Comput* code *m*; **a message in c.** un message chiffré *ou* codé; **the letter was in c.** la lettre était codée
2 *(statement of rules)* code *m*; **c. of conduct** code *m* de conduite; **c. of ethics** *(gen)* sens *m* des valeurs morales, moralité *f*; *(professional)* code *m* de déontologie; **c. of honour** code *m* de l'honneur; **c. of practice** *(gen)* code *m* de déontologie; *(rules)* règlements *mpl* et usages *mpl*
3 *(postcode)* code *m* postal
4 *(dialling code)* code *m*, indicatif *m*
VT *(message)* coder, chiffrer
►► **code book** *(for encoding)* code *m ou* carnet *m* de chiffrement; *(for decoding)* code *m ou* carnet *m* de déchiffrement; **code name** nom *m* de code
►**code up** VT SEP *Typ (text)* insérer les codes dans

coded ['kəʊdɪd] ADJ **1** *(message)* codé, chiffré **2** *Comput* codé

co-defendant N *Law (in criminal law)* coaccusé(e) *m,f*; *(in civil law)* codéfendeur(eresse) *m,f*

codeine ['kəʊdiːn] N codéine *f*

coder ['kəʊdə(r)] N *(device)* codeur *m*

code-sharing N *Aviat* partage *m* de code, code-sharing *m*

codex ['kəʊdeks] *(pl* **codices** [-dɪˌsiːz]) N volume *m* de manuscrits anciens

codger ['kɒdʒə(r)] N *Fam* bonhomme *m*; **an old c.** un vieux bonhomme

codicil ['kɒdɪsɪl] N *Law* codicille *m*

codification [ˌkəʊdɪfɪ'keɪʃən] N codification *f*

codify ['kəʊdɪfaɪ] *(pt & pp* **codified**) VT codifier

coding ['kəʊdɪŋ] N **1** *(of message)* chiffrage *m* **2** *Comput* codage *m*
►► *Comput* **coding error** erreur *f* de codage; *Comput* **coding line** ligne *f* de programmation; *Comput* **coding sequence** séquence *f* programmée

co-director N codirecteur(trice) *m,f*

cod-liver oil N huile *f* de foie de morue

codominance [ˌkəʊ'dɒmɪnəns] N *Biol* codominance *f*

codominant [ˌkəʊ'dɒmɪnənt] ADJ *Biol* codominant

codpiece ['kɒdpiːs] N *Hist* braguette *f*

co-driver N *(in rally, race)* copilote *m*; *(of bus, coach)* deuxième chauffeur *m*

codswallop ['kɒdzˌwɒləp] N *(UNCOUNT) Br Fam* bêtises❑ *fpl*, âneries❑ *fpl*

co-ed *Fam Sch* ADJ *(school)* mixte❑; **to go c.** *(school)* devenir mixte❑
N **1** *Br (school)* école *f* mixte❑ **2** *Am (student)* étudiante❑ *f (dans un établissement scolaire mixte)*

coeducation [ˌkəʊedʒʊ'keɪʃən] N éducation *f* mixte

coeducational [ˌkəʊedʒʊ'keɪʃənəl] ADJ mixte

coefficient [ˌkəʊɪ'fɪʃənt] N *Math & Phys* coefficient *m*
►► *Phys* **coefficient of expansion** coefficient *m* de dilatation

coelacanth ['siːləkænθ] N *Ich* cœlacanthe *m*

coeliac, *Am* **celiac** ['siːlɪæk] *Med* N = personne atteinte de maladie cœliaque
ADJ cœliaque
►► **coeliac disease** maladie *f* cœliaque

coerce [kəʊ'ɜːs] VT contraindre, forcer; **we coerced them into confessing** nous les avons contraints à avouer

coercion [kəʊ'ɜːʃən] N *(UNCOUNT)* coercition *f*, contrainte *f*; *Law* coaction *f*; **to act under c.** agir sous la contrainte

coexist [ˌkəʊɪg'zɪst] VI coexister

coexistence [ˌkəʊɪg'zɪstəns] N coexistence *f*

coexistent [ˌkəʊɪg'zɪstənt] ADJ coexistant

C of E [ˌsiːəvˈiː] *(abbr* **Church of England)** N Église *f* anglicane
ADJ anglican; **he's C.** il appartient à l'Église anglicane

coffee [ˈkɒfɪ] N **1** *(drink)* café *m*; **we talked over c.** nous avons bavardé en prenant un café; **black c.** café *m* noir; *Br* **white c.,** *Am* **c. with cream/milk** *(gen)* café *m* au lait; *(in café)* café *m* crème, crème *m* **2** *(colour)* café au lait *m inv*
ADJ *(colour)* café au lait *(inv)*
COMP *(filter, jar, service)* à café; *(ice cream, icing)* au café
▸▸ *Br* ***coffee bar*** café *m*, cafétéria *f*; ***coffee bean*** grain *m* de café; ***coffee break*** pause-café *f*; ***coffee cake*** *Br (coffee-flavoured)* moka *m*; *Am (served with coffee)* gâteau *m (que l'on sert avec le café)*; ***coffee cream*** *(chocolate)* chocolat *m* fourré au café; ***coffee cup*** tasse *f* à café; ***coffee grinder*** moulin *m* à café; ***coffee grounds*** marc *m* de café; ***coffee house*** *(on the continent)* café *m*; *Br Hist* = café de type français ou viennois, qui était, au XVIIIème siècle, le lieu de rendez-vous des gens à la mode; ***coffee machine*** *(gen)* cafetière *f* électrique; *(in café)* percolateur *m*; *(drinks dispenser)* machine *f* à café; ***coffee mill*** moulin *m* à café; *Br* ***coffee morning*** = rencontre amicale autour d'un café, destinée souvent à réunir de l'argent au profit d'œuvres de bienfaisance; ***coffee mug*** = petite chope en faïence; ***coffee pot*** cafetière *f*; ***coffee shop*** *(small restaurant)* café-restaurant *m*; *(shop selling coffee)* magasin *m* spécialisé dans le café; ***coffee spoon*** cuillère *f ou* cuiller *f* à café, petite cuillère *f ou* cuiller *f*; *(smaller)* cuillère *f ou* cuiller *f* à moka; ***coffee table*** table *f* basse; ***coffee tree*** caféier *m*

coffee-coloured, *Am* **coffee-colored** ADJ café au lait *(inv)*

coffee-maker N cafetière *f* électrique

coffee-table book N = livre de grand format abondamment illustré (destiné à être feuilleté plutôt que véritablement lu)

coffer [ˈkɒfə(r)] N **1** *(strongbox)* coffre *m*, caisse *f* **2** *(watertight chamber)* caisson *m* **3** *Archit* caisson *m (de plafond)*
VT **1** *Mining & Constr (well)* coffrer **2** *Archit (ceiling)* diviser en caissons
• **coffers** NPL *Fin (funds ▸ of nation)* coffres *mpl*; *(▸ of organization)* caisses *fpl*, coffres *mpl*; **the Government hasn't got much left in the coffers** le gouvernement n'a plus grand-chose dans ses coffres

cofferdam [ˈkɒfədæm] N *Constr* batardeau *m*

coffering [ˈkɒfərɪŋ] N *Mining & Constr* coffrage *m*

coffin [ˈkɒfɪn] N *(box)* cercueil *m*, bière *f*

cofounder [ˌkəʊˈfaʊndə(r)] N cofondateur(trice) *m,f*

cog [kɒg] N **1** *(gearwheel)* roue *f* dentée **2** *(tooth)* dent *f (d'engrenage)*; *Fig* **you're only a (small) c. in the machine** *or* **the wheel** vous n'êtes qu'un simple rouage (dans *ou* de la machine)
▸▸ ***cog rail*** crémaillère *f*; *Am* ***cog railroad,*** *Br* ***cog railway*** chemin *m* de fer à crémaillère

cogency [ˈkəʊdʒənsɪ] N force *f*, puissance *f*

cogent [ˈkəʊdʒənt] ADJ *Formal (argument, reasons ▸ convincing)* convaincant, puissant; *(▸ pertinent)* pertinent; *(▸ compelling)* irrésistible

cogently [ˈkəʊdʒəntlɪ] ADV *Formal (argue ▸ convincingly)* puissamment; *(▸ pertinently)* pertinemment, avec à-propos; *(▸ compellingly)* irrésistiblement

cogitate [ˈkɒdʒɪteɪt] VI *Formal* méditer, réfléchir; **to c. about** *or* **on sth** méditer sur qch, réfléchir à qch

cogitation [ˌkɒdʒɪˈteɪʃən] N *(UNCOUNT)* réflexion *f*, méditation *f*; *Hum* cogitations *fpl*

cognac [ˈkɒnjæk] N cognac *m*

cognate [ˈkɒgneɪt] N **1** *Ling* mot *m* apparenté **2** *Law (person)* parent *m* proche, cognat *m*
ADJ **1** *Ling* apparenté, de même origine **2** *Law* parent

cognition [kɒgˈnɪʃən] N *(gen)* connaissance *f*; *Phil* cognition *f*

cognitive [ˈkɒgnɪtɪv] ADJ *Psy* cognitif
▸▸ ***cognitive psychology*** psychologie *f* cognitive; ***cognitive therapy*** thérapie *f* cognitive

cognizance, -isance [ˈkɒgnɪzəns] N **1** *Formal (knowledge)* connaissance *f*; **to take c. of sth** prendre connaissance de qch **2** *Formal (range, scope)* compétence *f*; *Law* **within the c. of this court** de la compétence de ce tribunal **3** *Her (badge)* emblème *m*

cognizant, -isant [ˈkɒgnɪzənt] ADJ **1** *Formal (aware)* ayant connaissance, conscient; **to be c. of a fact** être instruit d'un fait **2** *Law* compétent; **court c. of an offence** tribunal *m* compétent pour juger un délit

cognoscenti [ˌkɒnjəˈʃentiː] NPL connaisseurs *mpl*

COGS [ˌsiːəʊdʒiːˈes] N *Acct (abbr* **cost of goods sold)** coût *m* des produits vendus

cogwheel [ˈkɒgwiːl] N roue *f* dentée, roue *f* d'engrenage

cohabit [ˌkəʊˈhæbɪt] VI vivre maritalement (**with** avec)

cohabitation [kəʊˌhæbɪˈteɪʃən] N vie *f* maritale, union *f* libre (**with** avec)
▸▸ *Law* ***cohabitation agreement*** pacte *m* de concubinage *ou* de cohabitation

cohabitee [kəʊˌhæbɪˈtiː] N concubin(e) *m,f*

cohere [kəʊˈhɪə(r)] VI **1** *(stick together)* adhérer, coller **2** *(be logically consistent)* être cohérent; *(reasoning, argument)* (se) tenir

coherence [kəʊˈhɪərəns] N **1** *(cohesion)* adhérence *f* **2** *(logical consistency)* cohérence *f*

coherent [kəʊˈhɪərənt] ADJ *(logical ▸ person, structure)* cohérent, logique; *(▸ story, speech)* facile à suivre *ou* comprendre; *Fam* **the man wasn't c.** il racontait n'importe quoi, il était incohérent

coherently [kəʊˈhɪərəntlɪ] ADV de façon cohérente

cohesion [kəʊˈhiːʒən] N cohésion *f*
▸▸ *EU* ***cohesion policy*** politique *f* de cohésion

cohesive [kəʊˈhiːsɪv] ADJ cohésif; *Phys (force)* de cohésion

cohort [ˈkəʊhɔːt] N **1** *(group, band)* cohorte *f*
2 *Mil & Hist* cohorte *f*
3 *(follower)* acolyte *m*; *(supporter)* partisan *m*
4 *(in statistics)* cohorte *f*

coiffure [kwɑːˈfjʊə(r)] N *Formal* coiffure *f*

coil [kɔɪl] N **1** *(spiral ▸ of rope, wire)* rouleau *m*; *(▸ of hair)* rouleau *m*; *(in bun)* chignon *m*
2 *(single loop ▸ of rope, wire)* tour *m*; *(▸ of hair)* boucle *f*; *(▸ of smoke, snake)* anneau *m*
3 *Elec* bobine *f*
4 *(contraceptive device)* stérilet *m*
5 *Naut* glène *f*
VT **1** *(rope)* enrouler; *(hair)* enrouler, torsader; **the snake coiled itself up** le serpent s'est lové *ou* enroulé **2** *Elec* bobiner
VI **1** *(river, smoke, procession)* onduler, serpenter **2** *(rope)* s'enrouler; *(snake)* se lover, s'enrouler
▸▸ *Aut* ***coil ignition system*** circuit *m* d'allumage par bobine; *Tech* ***coil spring*** ressort *m* hélicoïdal

coiled [kɔɪld] ADJ *(rope)* enroulé, en spirale; *(spring)* en spirale; *(snake)* lové; *Fig* **like a c. spring** tendu, prêt à l'action

coin [kɔɪn] N **1** *(item of metal currency)* pièce *f* (de monnaie); **a 5p c.** une pièce de 5 pence; *Fig* **that's the other side of the c.** c'est le revers de la médaille **2** *(UNCOUNT) (metal currency)* monnaie *f*; **£50 in c.** 50 livres en espèces; *Fig* **to pay sb back in his own c.** rendre à qn la monnaie de sa pièce
VT **1** *(money)* **to c. money** battre monnaie; *Fam* **she's coining it (in)** elle se fait du fric **2** *(word)* fabriquer, inventer; *Ironic* **..., to c. a phrase ...,** comme on dit
▸▸ *Br Tel* ***coin box*** cabine *f* téléphonique (à pièces)

coinage [ˈkɔɪnɪdʒ] N **1** *(UNCOUNT) (creation ▸ of money)* frappe *f*; *Fig (▸ of word)* invention *f*
2 *(UNCOUNT) (coins)* monnaie *f*
3 *(UNCOUNT) (currency system)* système *m* monétaire
4 *(invented word, phrase)* invention *f*, création *f*; **the word is a recent c.** c'est un mot nouveau, c'est un néologisme

coincide [ˌkəʊɪnˈsaɪd] VI **1** *(in space, time)* coïncider **2** *(correspond)* coïncider, s'accorder

coincidence [kəʊˈɪnsɪdəns] N **1** *(accident)* coïncidence *f*, hasard *m*; **what a c.!** quelle coïncidence! **2** *(correspondence)* coïncidence *f*

coincidental [kəʊˌɪnsɪˈdentəl] ADJ **1** *(accidental)* de coïncidence; **our meeting was entirely c.** notre rencontre était une pure coïncidence; **this had the c. effect of...** par coïncidence, cela a eu le résultat de... **2** *(having same position)* coïncident

coincidentally [kəʊˌɪnsɪˈdentəlɪ] ADV par hasard

coiner [ˈkɔɪnə(r)] N *(of word, expression)* inventeur(trice) *m,f*

coin-op N *Fam* laverie *f* automatique

coin-operated [-ɒpəˌreɪtɪd] ADJ automatique

co-insurance N coassurance *f*

co-insurer N coassureur *m*

coitus [ˈkɔɪtəs] N coït *m*
▸▸ ***coitus interruptus*** coït *m* interrompu

Coke® [kəʊk] N *(cola)* Coca® *m*

coke [kəʊk] N **1** *(fuel)* coke *m* **2** *Fam Drugs slang (cocaine)* cocaïne *f*, coke *f*
VT *(coal)* cokéfier, convertir en coke
VI *(coal)* se cokéfier, se convertir en coke

cokehead [ˈkəʊkhed] N *Fam Drugs slang* **to be a c.** marcher à la coke

coking [ˈkəʊkɪŋ] N cokéfaction *f*, coké(i)fication *f*
ADJ *(coal)* cokéfiable

Col. *Mil (written abbr* **colonel)** Col

col[1] [kɒl] N **1** *Geol (pass)* col *m (d'une montagne)* **2** *Met* col *m* barométrique

col[2] *(written abbr* **column)** col

COLA [ˈkəʊlə] N *Am Fin (abbr* **cost-of-living adjustment)** augmentation *f* de salaire indexée sur le coût de la vie

colander [ˈkʌləndə(r)] N passoire *f*

cold [kəʊld] ADJ **1** *(body, object, food etc)* froid; **I'm c.** j'ai froid; **her hands are c.** elle a les mains froides; **my feet are c.** j'ai froid aux pieds; **he's getting c.** il commence à avoir froid; **eat it before it gets c.** mangez avant que cela refroidisse; *Fig* **the trail was c.** toute trace avait disparu; **is it over here? – no, you're getting colder** *(in children's game)* est-ce par ici? – non, tu refroidis; *Fig* **she poured c. water on our plans** sa réaction à l'égard de nos projets nous a refroidis; *Fig* **to get** *or* **to have c. feet** avoir la trouille; *Fam* **he's a c. fish** c'est un pisse-froid; *Fam* **to give sb the c. shoulder** snober qn; *Prov* **c. hands, warm heart** mains froides, cœur chaud
2 *(weather)* froid; **it's c.** il fait froid; **it's freezing c.** il fait un froid de loup *ou* de canard; **it's getting colder** la température baisse
3 *(unfeeling)* froid, indifférent; *(objective)* froid, objectif; *(unfriendly)* froid, peu aimable; **to be c. towards sb** se montrer froid envers qn; **the play left me c.** la pièce ne m'a fait ni chaud ni froid, la pièce m'a laissé froid; **to have a c. heart** avoir un cœur de pierre; **he murdered them in c. blood** il les a assassinés de sang-froid
4 *(unconscious)* **she was out c.** elle était sans connaissance; **he knocked him (out) c.** il l'a mis K-O
5 *(colour)* froid
N **1** *(cold weather, lack of heat)* froid *m*; **in this bitter c.** par ce froid intense; **the c. doesn't bother him** il ne craint pas le froid, il n'est pas frileux; **to feel the c.** être frileux; **come in out of the c.** entrez vous mettre au chaud; *Fig* **to come in from the c.** rentrer en grâce; *Fig* **the newcomer was left out in the c.** personne ne s'est occupé du nouveau venu **2** *Med* rhume *m*; **to have a** *or Scot* **the c.** être enrhumé; **to catch a** *or Scot* **the c.** s'enrhumer, attraper un rhume; **a c. in the chest/in the head** un rhume de poitrine/de cerveau; **a bad c.** un mauvais rhume
ADV **1** *(without preparation)* à froid; **she had to play the piece c.** elle a dû jouer le morceau sans avoir répété; *Med* **to operate c.** opérer à froid **2** *Am Fam (absolutely)* **she turned me down c.** elle m'a dit non carrément
▸▸ ***cold buffet*** buffet *m* froid; *Mktg* ***cold call*** visite

f à froid; *(on phone)* appel *m* à froid; *Tech* ***cold chisel*** ciseau *m* à froid; ***cold cream*** crème *f* de beauté, cold-cream *m*; *Am Culin* ***cold cuts*** *(gen)* viandes *fpl* froides; *(on menu)* assiette *f* anglaise; ***cold drink*** boisson *f* fraîche; *Hort* ***cold frame*** châssis *m* de couches *(pour plantes)*; *Met* ***cold front*** front *m* froid; *Phys* ***cold fusion*** fusion *f* froide, fusion *f* à froid; ***cold room*** chambre *f* froide *ou* frigorifique; *Mktg* ***cold selling*** vente *f* à froid; ***cold snap*** vague *f* de froid; ***cold sore*** bouton *m* de fièvre, *Can* feu *m* sauvage; *Aut & Comput* ***cold start, cold starting*** démarrage *m* à froid; ***cold steel*** arme *f* blanche; ***cold storage*** conservation *f* par le froid; **to put sth into c. storage** *(food)* mettre qch en chambre froide; *(furs)* mettre qch en garde; *Fig* mettre qch en attente; ***cold store*** *(room)* chambre *f* froide *ou* frigorifique; *(warehouse)* entrepôt *m* frigorifique; ***cold sweat*** sueur *f* froide; **to be in a c. sweat about sth** avoir des sueurs froides au sujet de qch; *Fam* **just thinking about my exams brings me out in a c. sweat** rien que de penser à mes examens, j'en ai des sueurs froides; ***cold tap*** robinet *m* d'eau froide; *Fam Drugs slang* ***cold turkey*** *(drugs withdrawal)* manque *m*; **to go c. turkey** décrocher d'un seul coup; *Pol* ***cold war*** guerre *f* froide; *Pol* ***cold warrior*** partisan *m* de la guerre froide

cold-blooded ADJ **1** *(animal)* à sang froid; **reptiles are c.** les reptiles sont des animaux à sang froid **2** *Fig (unfeeling)* insensible; *(ruthless)* sans pitié; **a c. murder** un meurtre commis de sang-froid; **a c. murderer** un meurtrier sans pitié

cold-bloodedly [-ˈblʌdɪdlɪ] ADV de sang-froid

cold-bloodedness [-ˈblʌdɪdnɪs] N *(of person)* manque *m* de sensibilité, dureté *f*; *(of crime)* cruauté *f*

coldcock [ˈkəʊldkɒk] VT *Am Fam (knock out)* assommer☐, estourbir

cold-hearted ADJ sans pitié, insensible

coldly [ˈkəʊldlɪ] ADV froidement, avec froideur

coldness [ˈkəʊldnɪs] N *also Fig* froideur *f*; **there is a c. between them** il y a un froid entre eux

cold-pressed [-prest] ADJ *(olive oil)* pressé à froid

cold-rivet VT *Tech* riveter à froid

cold-shoulder VT *Fam* snober; **we cold-shouldered them** nous leur avons battu froid *ou* les avons snobés

coleslaw [ˈkəʊlslɔː] N salade *f* de chou cru, coleslaw *m*

colic [ˈkɒlɪk] N *(UNCOUNT)* coliques *fpl*

coliform bacteria [ˈkɒlɪfɔːm-] NPL *Biol* colibacilles *mpl*

colitis [kɒˈlaɪtɪs] N *(UNCOUNT) Med* colite *f*

collaborate [kəˈlæbəreɪt] VI *also Pej* collaborer; **she collaborated with us on the project** elle a collaboré avec nous au projet

collaboration [kəˌlæbəˈreɪʃən] N collaboration *f* (**with sb** avec qn; **on sth** à qch); **in c. with** en collaboration avec

collaborator [kəˈlæbəˌreɪtə(r)] N collaborateur (trice) *m,f*

collage [ˈkɒlɑːʒ] N **1** *Art (picture, method)* collage *m* **2** *(gen ▸ combination of things)* mélange *m*

collagen [ˈkɒlədʒən] N *Biol* collagène *m*

collapse [kəˈlæps] VI **1** *(building, roof)* s'écrouler, s'effondrer; *(beam)* fléchir; *(land)* s'ébouler

2 *Fig (institution, plan)* s'effondrer, s'écrouler; *(government)* tomber, chuter; *(country, market, defence, economy, currency, prices)* s'effondrer

3 *(person)* s'écrouler, s'effondrer; *(health)* se délabrer, se dégrader; **he collapsed and died** il a eu un malaise et il est mort; **to c. with laughter** se tordre de rire; **I collapsed from the heat** je me suis évanoui tellement il faisait chaud; **he collapsed into an armchair** il s'effondra dans un fauteuil; **I feel like I'm about to c.** j'ai l'impression que je vais m'effondrer; *Med* **her lung has collapsed** elle a eu *ou* a fait un collapsus pulmonaire

4 *(fold up)* se plier; **the bicycle collapses so it can be stored away easily** la bicyclette se plie et peut ainsi être rangée facilement

VT **1** *(fold up ▸ table, chair)* plier **2** *(merge ▸ paragraphs, entries)* mettre ensemble, fusionner **3** *Comput (subdirectories)* réduire

N **1** *(of building, roof)* écroulement *m*, effondrement *m*; *(of beam)* rupture *f*; *(of land)* éboulement *m* **2** *Fig (of institution, plan)* effondrement *m*, écroulement *m*; *(of government)* chute *f*; *(of country)* effondrement *m*, débâcle *f*; *(of market, defence, economy, currency)* effondrement *m*; *(of prices)* effondrement *m*, chute *f* subite **3** *(of person)* écroulement *m*, effondrement *m*; *(of health)* délabrement *m*; *(of lung)* collapsus *m*

collapsed [kəˈlæpst] ADJ *Med* **c. lung** collapsus *m* pulmonaire; **to have a c. lung** avoir fait un collapsus pulmonaire

collapsible [kəˈlæpsəbəl] ADJ *(chair, boat)* pliant; *(handle)* rabattable; *Aut (steering column)* rétractile, rétractable

collar [ˈkɒlə(r)] N **1** *(on clothing)* col *m*; *(detachable ▸ for men)* faux col *m*; *(▸ for women)* col *m*, collerette *f*

2 *(for animal)* collier *m*; *(neck of animal)* collier *m*; *Culin (of beef)* collier *m*; *Culin (of mutton, veal)* collet *m*

3 *Tech (on pipe)* bague *f*

4 *Zool (marking ▸ on bird, animal)* collier *m*

VT **1** *Fam (seize)* prendre *ou* saisir au collet, colleter; *(criminal)* arrêter☐; *(detain)* intercepter☐, harponner **2** *Tech (pipe)* baguer

▸▸ ***collar size*** encolure *f*; ***collar stud*** bouton *m* de col

collarbone [ˈkɒləbəʊn] N clavicule *f*

collate [kəˈleɪt] VT **1** *(assemble ▸ information, texts, sheets)* collationner **2** *(compare ▸ text)* collationner (**with** avec) **3** *Rel* nommer *(à un bénéfice ecclésiastique)*

collateral [kɒˈlætərəl] N *Fin (guarantee)* nantissement *m*; **what can you provide as c.?** qu'est-ce que vous pouvez fournir en nantissement?

ADJ **1** *(secondary)* subsidiaire, accessoire; *Fin* subsidiaire **2** *(parallel)* parallèle; *(fact)* concomitant; *Law* collatéral **3** *(branch, family) & Med (artery)* collatéral

▸▸ *Mil* ***collateral damage*** dégâts *mpl ou* dommages *mpl* collatéraux; *Fin* ***collateral loan*** prêt *m* avec garantie; *Fin* ***collateral security*** nantissement *m*

collateralize, -ise [kəˈlætərəlaɪz] VT *Fin* garantir

collation [kəˈleɪʃən] N **1** *(of information, texts)* collation *f*; *(in bookbinding ▸ of sheets, signatures)* collationnure *f* **2** *(comparison ▸ of texts)* collation *f* **3** *Formal (light meal)* collation *f*

collator [kəˈleɪtə(r)] N **1** *(person)* collationneur (euse) *m,f*; *(machine)* assembleuse *f* **2** *Rel* collateur *m*

colleague [ˈkɒliːg] N *(in office, school)* collègue *mf*

collect[1] [kəˈlekt] VT **1** *(gather ▸ objects)* ramasser; *(▸ information, documents)* recueillir, rassembler; *(▸ evidence)* rassembler; *(▸ people)* réunir, rassembler; **to c. dust** prendre la poussière; **solar panels c. the heat** des panneaux solaires captent la chaleur

2 *Fig* **to c. oneself** *(calm down)* se reprendre, se calmer; *(reflect)* se recueillir; **let me c. my thoughts** laissez-moi réfléchir *ou* me concentrer; **to c. one's wits** rassembler ses esprits

3 *(as hobby)* collectionner, faire collection de; **she has collected more than 2,000 records** elle a une collection de plus de 2000 disques

4 *(money)* recueillir; *(taxes, fines, dues)* percevoir; *(pension, salary)* toucher; *(homework)* ramasser, relever; *(debt)* recouvrer

5 *Br (take away)* ramasser; **the council collects the rubbish** la commune se charge du ramassage des ordures; **when is the mail collected?** à quelle heure est la levée du courrier?

6 *(pick up ▸ people)* aller chercher, (passer) prendre; *(▸ luggage, ticket, car)* aller chercher, aller prendre; *(▸ goods)* enlever; **he'll c. us in his car** il viendra nous chercher *ou* passera nous prendre en voiture

VI **1** *(accumulate ▸ people)* se rassembler, se réunir; *(▸ things)* s'accumuler, s'amasser; *(▸ water, dirt)* s'accumuler **2** *(raise money)* **to c. for charity** faire la quête *ou* quêter pour une œuvre de bienfaisance **3** *Am Com* **c. on delivery** paiement *m* à la livraison, (livraison *f*) contre remboursement

ADV *Am Tel* **to call (sb) c.** téléphoner (à qn) en PCV, *Can* faire un appel à frais virés (à qn); *Com* **to send a parcel c.** envoyer un colis en port dû *ou* payable à destination

▸▸ *Am Tel* ***collect call*** appel *m* en PCV, *Can* appel *m* à frais virés

collect[2] [ˈkɒlekt] N *Rel (prayer)* collecte *f*

collectable [kəˈlektəbəl] ADJ **1** *(sought-after)* très recherché; *(valued by collectors)* prisé par les collectionneurs **2** *(debt)* recouvrable

N objet *m* de collection

collected [kəˈlektɪd] ADJ **1** *(calm, composed)* maître de soi, calme **2** *(complete)* complet(ète); **the c. works of Whitman** les œuvres complètes de Whitman

collectible = **collectable**

collecting [kəˈlektɪŋ] N collection *f*; **he does a lot of c. for the blind** il quête beaucoup *ou* il fait de nombreuses quêtes pour les aveugles

▸▸ *Banking & Fin* ***collecting agency, collecting bank*** banque *f* de recouvrement; ***collecting tin*** = boîte de collecte au profit d'une association caritative

collection [kəˈlekʃən] N **1** *(UNCOUNT) (collecting ▸ objects)* ramassage *m*; *(▸ information)* rassemblement *m*; *(▸ rent, money)* encaissement *m*; *(▸ debts)* recouvrement *m*; *(▸ taxes)* perception *f*; *(▸ data)* collecte *f*

2 *(things collected)* collection *f*; **Armani's winter c.** la collection d'hiver d'Armani

3 *(picking up ▸ of rubbish)* ramassage *m*; *Br (▸ of mail)* levée *f*; **your order is ready for c.** votre commande est prête; **c. times are 8.45 and 17.30** *(from letterbox)* les levées sont à 8h45 et 17h30

4 *(sum of money)* collecte *f*, quête *f*; **to take** *or* **to make a c. (for)** faire une quête *ou* collecte (pour)

5 *(group ▸ of people, things)* rassemblement *m*, groupe *m*; *(ordered)* assemblage *m*; **a c. of rubbish had built up outside the door** des ordures s'étaient amassées devant la porte; **a motley c.** un rassemblement hétéroclite

6 *(anthology)* recueil *m*

7 *Fin (of bill)* encaissement *m*; **a bill for c.** un effet à l'encaissement

▸▸ ***collection box*** *(gen)* caisse *f*; *(in church)* tronc *m*; *Fin* ***collection charges, collection fees*** frais *mpl* d'encaissement; ***collection plate*** *(in church)* corbeille *f*

collective [kəˈlektɪv] N coopérative *f*

ADJ collectif

▸▸ *Ind* ***collective agreement*** convention *f* collective; *Ind* ***collective bargaining*** = négociations pour une convention collective; *Agr* ***collective farm*** ferme *f* collective; *Ling* ***collective noun*** collectif *m*; *Law* ***collective ownership*** propriété *f* collective; *(of building)* copropriété *f*; *Psy* ***the collective unconscious*** l'inconscient *m* collectif

collectively [kəˈlektɪvlɪ] ADV collectivement

collectivism [kəˈlektɪˌvɪzəm] N *Econ* collectivisme *m*

collectivist [kəˈlektɪvɪst] *Econ* N collectiviste *mf*

ADJ collectiviste

collectivity [ˌkɒlekˈtɪvɪtɪ] N *Econ* collectivité *f*

collectivization, -isation [kəˌlektɪvaɪˈzeɪʃən] N *Econ* collectivisation *f*

collectivize, -ise [kəˈlektɪvaɪz] VT *Econ* collectiviser

collector [kəˈlektə(r)] N **1** *(as a hobby)* collectionneur(euse) *m,f* **2** *(of money)* encaisseur *m*; *(for charity)* quêteur(euse) *m,f*; *(of taxes)* percepteur *m*; *(of debts)* receveur *m* **3** *Tech (for oil, steam)* collecteur *m*; *(of overflow)* récepteur *m*

▸▸ ***collector's item, collector's piece*** pièce *f* de collection, collector *m*

colleen [ˈkɒliːn, kɒˈliːn] N *Ir* jeune fille *f*, *(Irish girl)* jeune Irlandaise *f*

college [ˈkɒlɪdʒ] N **1** *Br (institution of higher education)* établissement *m* d'enseignement supérieur; **I go to c.** je suis étudiant; **when you were at c.** quand tu étais à l'université; *Am* **to be c. bound** se destiner aux études supérieures; **agricultural c.** lycée *m* agricole; **c. of art** école *f* des beaux-arts; **c. of music** conservatoire *m* de musique; **a c. chum** un (une) copain (copine) de fac; **c. days** années *fpl* de fac

2 *Br (within university)* collège *m (dans les universités traditionnelles, communauté d'enseignants et*

d'étudiants disposant d'une semi-autonomie administrative)

3 *(for professional training)* école *f* professionnelle, collège *m* technique

4 *(organization)* société *f*, académie *f*; **the Royal C. of Physicians/Surgeons** l'Académie *f* de médecine/de chirurgie

▸▸ **the College of Cardinals** le Sacré Collège; **college education** études *fpl* supérieures; *Br* **College of Education** institut *m* de formation des maîtres; *Br* **College of Further Education** institut *m* d'éducation permanente; **college student** étudiant(e) *m,f*

collegiate [kəˈliːdʒɪət] **ADJ** *(life)* universitaire; *(university)* composé de collèges semi-autonomes

▸▸ *Rel* **collegiate church** collégiale *f*

collide [kəˈlaɪd] **VI 1** *(crash)* entrer en collision, se heurter; **to c. with** *(of vehicle)* heurter, tamponner, entrer en collision avec; **to c. with sb** *(of person)* se heurter à *ou* contre qn **2** *Fig (clash)* entrer en conflit, se heurter; **the two countries have collided over the issue of human rights** les deux pays se sont heurtés sur la question des droits de l'homme

collie [ˈkɒlɪ] **N** *(dog)* colley *m*

collier [ˈkɒlɪə(r)] **N** *Br* **1** *Mining* mineur *m* **2** *Naut* charbonnier *m*

colliery [ˈkɒljərɪ] *(pl* **collieries***)* **N** *Br Mining* houillère *f*, mine *f* (de charbon)

collision [kəˈlɪʒən] **N 1** *(crash)* collision *f*, choc *m*; *Rail* collision *f*, tamponnement *m*; **to come into c. with sth** entrer en collision avec *ou* tamponner qch; *Naut* **to be on a c. course** être sur un cap de collision; **the two planes were on a c. course** les deux avions risquaient d'entrer en collision; *Fig* **the government is on a c. course with the unions** le gouvernement va au-devant d'un conflit avec les syndicats **2** *Fig (clash)* conflit *m*, opposition *f* **3** *Phys (of particles)* choc *m*, collision *f*

▸▸ *Ins* **collision damage waiver** = suppression de franchise pour les dommages causés aux véhicules

colloid [ˈkɒlɔɪd] *Chem* **ADJ** colloïdal

N colloïde *m*

colloquial [kəˈləʊkwɪəl] **ADJ** *Ling (language, expression)* familier, parlé; *(style)* familier

colloquialism [kəˈləʊkwɪəˌlɪzəm] **N** *Ling* expression *f* familière

colloquially [kəˈləʊkwɪəlɪ] **ADV** *Ling* familièrement, dans la langue parlée; **known c. as...** communément appelé...

collude [kəˈluːd] **VI** être de connivence *ou* de mèche; **to c. with sb in sth** être de connivence avec qn dans *ou* pour qch

collusion [kəˈluːʒən] **N** collusion *f*; **to do sth in c. with sb** faire qch de connivence avec qn; **to be in c. with sb** être d'intelligence *ou* de connivence avec qn

collywobbles [ˈkɒlɪˌwɒbəlz] **NPL** *Br Fam (stomachache)* mal *m* au ventre[□]; *(nervousness)* trouille *f*; **I always get the c. before an exam** j'ai toujours la trouille avant un examen

Colo *(written abbr* **Colorado***)* Colorado *m*

cologne [kəˈləʊn] **N** eau *f* de Cologne

Colombia [kəˈlɒmbɪə] **N** Colombie *f*

Colombian [kəˈlɒmbɪən] **N** Colombien(enne) *m,f*

ADJ colombien

COMP *(embassy)* de Colombie; *(history)* de la Colombie

colon [ˈkəʊlən] **N 1** *(in punctuation)* deux-points *m inv* **2** *Anat* côlon *m*

colonel [ˈkɜːnəl] **N** *Mil* colonel *m*; **C. Jones** le colonel Jones

colonial [kəˈləʊnɪəl] **ADJ 1** *(power, life)* colonial; *Pej (attitude)* colonialiste; **c. days** époque *f* coloniale **2** *Archit* de style colonial; *(in America)* de style colonial *(du XVIIIème siècle)*

N colonial(e) *m,f*

colonialism [kəˈləʊnɪəˌlɪzəm] **N** colonialisme *m*

colonialist [kəˈləʊnɪəlɪst] **N** colonialiste *mf*

ADJ colonialiste

colonic [kəˈlɒnɪk] *Med* **ADJ** du côlon

N lavement *m*

▸▸ **colonic irrigation** lavement *m*

colonist [ˈkɒlənɪst] **N** colon *m*

colonization, -isation [ˌkɒlənaɪˈzeɪʃən] **N** colonisation *f*

colonize, -ise [ˈkɒlənaɪz] **VT** coloniser

colonizer, -iser [ˈkɒlənaɪzə(r)] **N** colonisateur (trice) *m,f*

colonnade [ˌkɒləˈneɪd] **N** *Archit* colonnade *f*

colony [ˈkɒlənɪ] *(pl* **colonies***)* **N** *(of people, animals, plants, bacteria)* colonie *f*; *Hist* **the Colonies** les Colonies *fpl*; **the English c. in Paris** la colonie anglaise de Paris

colophon [ˈkɒləfɒn] **N 1** *(logo)* logo *m*, colophon *m* **2** *(end text in book)* achevé *m* d'imprimer; *(end text in manuscript)* colophon *m*

color, colored *etc Am* = **colour, coloured** *etc*

Colorado [ˌkɒləˈrɑːdəʊ] **N** *(state, river)* le Colorado

▸▸ *Entom* **Colorado beetle** doryphore *m*, *Can* bête *f* à patates; **the Colorado River** le Colorado

coloration [ˌkʌləˈreɪʃən] **N** *(colouring)* coloration *f*; *(choice of colours)* coloris *m*

coloratura [ˌkɒlərəˈtʊərə] **N** *Mus* colorature *f*

▸▸ **coloratura aria** air *m* de colorature; **coloratura soprano** (soprano *f*) colorature *f*

colorectal [ˌkəʊləʊˈrektəl] **ADJ** *Med* colorectal

colossal [kəˈlɒsəl] **ADJ** colossal

colossus [kəˈlɒsəs] *(pl* **colossuses** *or* **colossi** [-saɪ]*)* **N** colosse *m*

▸▸ **the Colossus of Rhodes** le colosse de Rhodes

colostomic [ˌkɒləˈstɒmɪk] **ADJ** *Med* colostomique

colostomy [kəˈlɒstəmɪ] *(pl* **colostomies***)* **N** *Med* colostomie *f*; **to have a c.** subir une colostomie

▸▸ **colostomy bag** poche *f* (colostomique)

colour, *Am* **color** [ˈkʌlə(r)] **N 1** *(hue)* couleur *f*; **what c. is it?** de quelle couleur est-ce?; **what c. are his eyes?** de quelle couleur sont ses yeux?; **it's a sort of greenish c.** c'est d'une couleur un peu verdâtre; **the bleach took the c. out of it** l'eau de Javel l'a décoloré; **the movie is in c.** le film est en couleur *ou* couleurs; **he painted the room in bright/dark colours** il a peint la pièce de couleurs vives/sombres; *Fam* **we've yet to see the c. of his money** nous n'avons pas encore vu la couleur de son argent

2 *Fig* **the political c. of a newspaper** la couleur politique d'un journal

3 *Art (shade)* coloris *m*, ton *m*; *(paint)* peinture *f*; *(dye)* teinture *f*, matière *f* colorante; **box of colours** boîte *f* de couleurs

4 *(pigment)* matière *f* colorante, couleur *f*

5 *(complexion)* teint *m*, couleur *f (du visage)*; **to lose one's c.** pâlir, perdre ses couleurs; **to get one's c. back** reprendre des couleurs; **she had a lot of c. in her cheeks** ses joues avaient de belles couleurs; **to have a high c.** avoir le visage rouge; *Br* **to be off c.** ne pas être dans son assiette

6 *(race)* couleur *f*; **c. isn't an issue** ce n'est pas une question de couleur (de peau); **person of c.** personne *f* de couleur

7 *(interest)* couleur *f*; **to add c. to a story** colorer un récit

VT 1 *(give colour to ▸ with chemical, dye)* colorer; *(▸ with paint)* peindre; *(▸ with crayons, felt-tips)* colorier; **he coloured it blue** il l'a colorié en bleu; **to c. one's hair** se faire une couleur **2** *(distort ▸ judgement)* fausser; *(▸ fact)* influencer **3** *(exaggerate ▸ story, facts)* exagérer; *(enliven)* rendre plus vivant

VI *(person)* rougir; *(thing)* se colorer; *(fruit)* mûrir

• **colours NPL 1** *(of team)* couleurs *fpl*; **to get** *or* **to win one's colours** être sélectionné pour faire partie d'une équipe; *Fig* **to show one's true colours** se montrer sous son vrai jour; **to see sb in his/her true colours** voir qn sous son vrai jour **2** *(of school)* couleurs *fpl* **3** *Mil (flag)* couleurs *fpl*, drapeau *m*; *Naut* couleurs *fpl*, pavillon *m*; **to be called to the colours** être appelé sous les drapeaux; **to sail under false colours** naviguer sous un faux pavillon; *Fig* **to pass with flying colours** *(in exam)* être reçu brillamment *ou* haut la main; *Fig* **to nail one's colours to the mast** afficher ses opinions

COMP *(picture, slide, magazine)* en couleur(s)

▸▸ *Cin, Phot & TV* **colour balance** équilibre *m* des couleurs; *Br* **colour bar** discrimination *f* raciale; **colour bearer** porte-drapeau *m*; **colour blindness** daltonisme *m*; **colour chart** nuancier *m*; **colour code** code *m* coloré; *Comput* **colour display** affichage *m* couleur; **colour film** *(for camera)* pellicule *f* (en) couleur; *(movie)* film *m* en couleur; *Phot* **colour filter** filtre *m* coloré; *Comput* **colour graphics** graphisme *m* en couleur; *Phot* **colour graphics adapter** adaptateur *m* graphique couleur, CGA *m*; *Comput* **colour monitor** moniteur *m* couleur; *Mil* **colour party** garde *f* du drapeau; **colour photocopying** photocopie *f* en couleurs; **colour photography** photographie *f* en couleur(s); *Typ* **colour printer** imprimante *f* couleur; *Typ* **colour printing** impression *f* couleur; **colour scheme** palette *f ou* combinaison *f* de couleurs; **to choose a c. scheme** assortir les couleurs *ou* les tons; *Typ* **colour separation** séparation *f* des couleurs, séparation *f* quadrichromique; *Br Mil* **colour sergeant** sergent-chef *m (de la garde du drapeau)*; *Br Press* **colour supplement** supplément *m* illustré; **colour television** télévision *f* couleur; **colour television set** téléviseur *m* couleur; **colour therapy** chromothérapie *f*; *Art* **colour wheel** cercle *m* chromatique

▸ **colour in,** *Am* **color in VT SEP** colorier; **c. it in in blue** colorie-le en bleu

colour-blind, *Am* **color-blind ADJ** daltonien

colour-coded, *Am* **color-coded ADJ** dont la couleur correspond à un code; **the wires are c.** la couleur des fils correspond à un code

colour-coding, *Am* **color-coding N** système *m* de classement par couleurs; **what's their c.?** de quelle couleur sont-elles dans le classement?

coloured, *Am* **colored** [ˈkʌləd] **ADJ 1** *(having colour)* coloré; *(drawing)* colorié; *(pencils)* de couleur **2** *Pej (person ▸ gen)* de couleur; *(▸ in South Africa)* métis

• **coloureds NPL 1** *(clothes for washing)* couleurs *fpl* **2** *Pej (people ▸ gen)* gens *mpl* de couleur; *(▸ in South Africa)* métis *mpl*

colourful, *Am* **colorful** [ˈkʌləfʊl] **ADJ 1** *(brightly coloured)* coloré, vif **2** *Fig (person)* original, pittoresque; *(story)* coloré; **a c. character** un original; **c. language** langage *m* coloré

colouring, *Am* **coloring** [ˈkʌlərɪŋ] **N 1** *(act)* coloration *f*; *(of drawing)* coloriage *m*; **go and do some c.** *(to child)* va faire du coloriage

2 *(hue)* coloration *f*, coloris *m*

3 *(complexion)* teint *m*; **high c.** teint *m* coloré; **fair/dark c.** teint *m* clair/mat

4 *Fig (exaggeration)* travestissement *m*, dénaturation *f*

5 *(for food)* colorant *m*

▸▸ **colouring book** album *m* à colorier

colouring-in, *Am* **coloring-in N** coloriage *m*

▸▸ **colouring-in book** album *m* à colorier

colourist, *Am* **colorist** [ˈkʌlərɪst] **N 1** *Art* coloriste *mf* **2** *(hairdresser)* coloriste *mf*

colourization, -isation, *Am* **colorization** [ˌkʌləraɪˈzeɪʃən] **N** *Cin* colorisation *f*

colourize, -ise, *Am* **colorize** [ˈkʌləraɪz] **VT** *Cin* coloriser

colourless, *Am* **colorless** [ˈkʌləlɪs] **ADJ 1** *(clear)* sans couleur, incolore **2** *(pale)* terne, incolore; *(face)* blême; *(complexion)* pâle, délavé; *(light)* pâle, falot **3** *Fig (style)* sans intérêt, fade; *(voice)* terne; *(person)* insignifiant, falot

colourlessness, *Am* **colorlessness** [ˈkʌləlɪsnɪs] **N 1** *(paleness, transparency)* absence *f* de couleur; *(of complexion)* pâleur *f* **2** *Fig (of style)* fadeur *f*; *(of person)* manque *m* de personnalité

colourway, *Am* **colorway** [ˈkʌləweɪ] **N** coloris *m*

Colt® [kəʊlt] **N** *(revolver)* colt *m*, pistolet *m* (automatique)

colt [kəʊlt] **N 1** *(horse)* poulain *m* **2** *Fig (young person)* petit jeune *m*; *(inexperienced person)* novice *m*

coltish [ˈkəʊltɪʃ] **ADJ** *(gait, figure)* dégingandé; *(movement)* gauche

coltsfoot [ˈkəʊltsfʊt] **N** *Bot* pas-d'âne *m inv*, tussilage *m*

Columbia [kəˈlʌmbɪə] **N the District of C.** le district fédéral de Columbia
▸▸ ***the Columbia River*** la Columbia

columbine [ˈkɒləm,baɪn] **N** *Bot* ancolie *f*

Columbus [kəˈlʌmbəs] **PR N Christopher C.** Christophe Colomb
▸▸ ***Columbus Day*** = aux États-Unis, jour commémorant l'arrivée de Christophe Colomb en Amérique (deuxième lundi d'octobre)

column [ˈkɒləm] **N 1** *(gen) & Archit* colonne *f*
2 *Press (section of print)* colonne *f*; *(regular article)* rubrique *f*; **he writes the sports c.** il tient la rubrique des sports
3 *Comput & Typ* colonne *f*
4 *Mil & Naut (formation)* colonne *f*; **to march in c./in two columns** marcher en colonne/en deux colonnes; **supply/relief c.** colonne *f* de ravitaillement/de secours
▸▸ *Aut* ***column change*** levier *m* de vitesses sur colonne de direction; *Comput & Typ* ***column graph*** histogramme *m*; *Comput & Typ* ***column header*** en-tête *m* de colonnes; *Press* ***column inch*** = unité de mesure des espaces publicitaires équivalant à une colonne sur un pouce, centimètre-colonne *m*; **it got a lot of c. inches** *(story)* on y a consacré beaucoup d'espace dans le journal; *Comput & Typ* ***column mode*** mode *m* colonne; *Comput & Typ* ***column printing*** impression *f* en colonnes; *Comput & Typ* ***column width*** justification *f*

columnist [ˈkɒləmnɪst] **N** *Press & Journ* chroniqueur(euse) *m,f*, échotier(ère) *m,f*; **sports c.** chroniqueur(euse) *m,f* sportif(ive)

colza [ˈkɒlzə] **N** *Bot & Culin* colza *m*
▸▸ ***colza oil*** huile *f* de colza

.com [ˈdɒtˈkɒm] *Comput* = abréviation désignant les entreprises commerciales dans les adresses électroniques

coma[1] [ˈkəʊmə] **N** *Med* coma *m*; **in a c.** dans le coma

coma[2] *(pl* **comae** [-miː]*)* **N 1** *Bot* barbe *f* **2** *Astron* chevelure *f* **3** *Opt* coma *f*, comète *f*

co-management **N** cogérance *f*

comatose [ˈkəʊmətəʊs] **ADJ** *Med* comateux; **to be c.** être dans le coma; *Fam (fast asleep)* en écraser; *(drunk)* être ivre mort◻

comb [kəʊm] **N 1** *(for hair)* peigne *m*; *(large-toothed)* démêloir *m*; **to run a c. through one's hair, to give one's hair a c.** se donner un coup de peigne, se peigner
2 *(for horses)* étrille *f*
3 *Tex (for cotton, wool)* peigne *m*, carde *f*; *Elec* balai *m*
4 *(of fowl)* crête *f*; *(on helmet)* cimier *m*
5 *(honeycomb)* rayon *m* de miel
VT 1 *(hair)* peigner; **he combed his hair** il s'est peigné; **I combed the girl's hair** j'ai peigné la fille
2 *(horse)* étriller
3 *Tex (cotton, wool)* peigner, carder; **combed cotton** coton *m* peigné
4 *Fig (search)* fouiller, ratisser; **the police combed the area for clues** la police a passé le quartier au peigne fin *ou* a ratissé le quartier à la recherche d'indices
▸▸ *Typ* ***comb binding*** reliure *f* en spirale

▸ **comb out** **VT SEP 1** *(hair)* peigner; *(untangle)* démêler
2 *Tex (cotton, wool)* peigner
3 *(fleas)* retirer avec un peigne
4 *Fig (remove)* éliminer

combat [ˈkɒmbæt] *(pt & pp* **combated,** *cont* **combating)** *Mil* **N** combat *m*; **killed/lost in c.** tué/perdu au combat; **women are now used in a c. role** on envoie maintenant les femmes dans des situations de combat
VT combattre, lutter contre
VI combattre, lutter
COMP *(troops, mission)* de combat
▸▸ ***combat dress*** tenue *f* de combat; ***combat duty*** service *m* commandé; **on c. duty** en service commandé; *Psy* ***combat fatigue*** psychose *f* traumatique, syndrome *m* commotionnel; ***combat gear*** tenue *f* de combat; ***combat jacket*** veste *f* de treillis; *Am* ***combat pants*** battle-dress *m inv*, pantalon *m* multi-poches; ***combat stress*** psychose *f* (traumatique) du soldat; *Br* ***combat trousers*** battle-dress *m inv*, pantalon *m* multi-poches; *Mil* ***combat zone*** zone *f* de combat

combatant [ˈkɒmbətənt] *Mil* **N** combattant(e) *m,f*
ADJ combattant

combative [ˈkɒmbətɪv] **ADJ** combatif

combi [ˈkɒmbɪ] **N** *Austr Fam* **c. (van)** camping-car◻ *m*

combination [,kɒmbɪˈneɪʃən] **N 1** *(gen) & Chem & Math* combinaison *f*; *(of circumstances)* concours *m*; **nitrogen in c. with oxygen** l'azote combiné avec l'oxygène; **an attractive colour c.** une combinaison de couleurs attrayante; **an interesting c. of flavours** un mélange intéressant de parfums
2 *(of lock)* combinaison *f*
3 *(association, team)* association *f*, coalition *f*; **together they formed a winning c.** ensemble ils formaient une équipe gagnante
4 *Br Aut* side-car *m*
• **combinations** **NPL** *Br Old-fashioned (underclothing)* combinaison-culotte *f*
▸▸ ***combination lock*** serrure *f* à combinaison; ***combination skin*** peau *f* mixte; *Tech* ***combination spanner*** clé *f* mixte; *Med* ***combination therapy*** multithérapie *f*, trithérapie *f*

combine **VT** [kəmˈbaɪn] *(gen)* combiner, joindre; *Chem* combiner; **to c. work and studying** combiner le travail et les études; **let's c. forces** unissons *ou* joignons nos forces; **to c. business and** *or* **with pleasure** joindre l'utile à l'agréable; **this, combined with her other problems, made her ill** ceci, conjugué à ses autres problèmes, l'a rendue malade; **this furniture combines comfort with style** ces meubles allient confort et style
VI [kəmˈbaɪn] *(unite)* s'unir, s'associer; *(workers)* se syndiquer; *Pol (parties)* fusionner; *Chem* se combiner; **events combined to leave her penniless** les événements ont concouru à la laisser sans le sou
N [ˈkɒmbaɪn] **1** *(association)* association *f*; *Fin* trust *m*, cartel *m*; *Law* corporation *f* **2** *Agr* moissonneuse-batteuse *f*
▸▸ *Agr* ***combine harvester*** moissonneuse-batteuse *f*

combined [kəmˈbaɪnd] **ADJ** combiné, conjugué; **a c. effort** un effort conjugué; **c. operation** *(by several nations)* opération *f* alliée; *(by forces of one nation)* opération *f* interarmées
▸▸ *Naut* ***combined fleets*** flottes *fpl* combinées; *Mil* ***combined forces*** forces *fpl* alliées

combo [ˈkɒmbəʊ] *(pl* **combos)** **N 1** *Mus* combo *m* **2** *Fam (combination)* combinaison◻ *f*; *(mixture)* mélange◻ *m*

combust [kəmˈbʌst] **VI** brûler

combustible [kəmˈbʌstəbəl] **ADJ** combustible
N matière *f* inflammable; *(fuel)* combustible *m*

combustion [kəmˈbʌstʃən] **N** combustion *f*
▸▸ ***combustion chamber*** chambre *f* de combustion; ***combustion engine*** moteur *m* à combustion; ***combustion gases*** gaz *mpl* de combustion

COME [kʌm]

VI	
• venir **1, 2**	• se produire **3**
• exister **6**	• devenir **7**
• en venir à **8**	

(pt **came** [keɪm], *pp* **come** [kʌm]*)*
VI 1 *(move in direction of speaker)* venir; *arrive* venir, arriver; **c. here!** venez ici!; *(to dog)* au pied!; **here c. the children** voici les enfants qui arrivent; **coming!** j'arrive!; **c. with me** *(accompany me)* venez avec moi, accompagnez-moi; *(follow me)* suivez-moi; **please c. this way** par ici *ou* suivez-moi s'il vous plaît; **c. to the office tomorrow** passez *ou* venez au bureau demain; **would you like to c. for lunch/dinner?** voulez-vous venir déjeuner/dîner?; **I've got people coming** *(short stay)* j'ai des invités; *(long stay)* il y a des gens qui viennent; **he came to me for advice** il est venu me demander conseil; **he couldn't have c. at a worse time** il n'aurait pas pu tomber plus mal **you've c. to the wrong person** vous vous adressez à la mauvaise personne; **if you're looking for sun, you've c. to the wrong place** si c'est le soleil que vous cherchez, il ne fallait pas venir ici; **I c. this way every week** je passe par ici toutes les semaines; **c. and look,** *Am* **c. look** venez voir; *Fam* **c. and get it!** à la soupe!; *also Fig* **to c. running** arriver en courant; **we came to a small town** nous sommes arrivés dans une petite ville; **a car came hurtling round the corner** une voiture a pris le virage à toute vitesse; **I was coming to the end of my stay** mon séjour touchait à sa fin; **there will c. a point when…** il viendra un moment où…; **to c. and go** *(gen)* aller et venir; *Fig (pains, cramps etc)* être intermittent; **people are constantly coming and going** il y a un va-et-vient continuel; **fashions c. and go** la mode change tout le temps; *Fam* **I don't know whether I'm coming or going** je ne sais pas où j'en suis; **the computer industry has c. a very long way since then** l'informatique a fait énormément de progrès depuis ce temps-là; *Fig* **you could see it coming** on l'a vu venir de loin, c'était prévisible
2 *(occupy specific place, position)* venir, se trouver; **the address comes above the date** l'adresse se met au-dessus de la date; **my birthday comes before yours** mon anniversaire vient avant *ou* précède le tien; **Friday comes after Thursday** vendredi vient après *ou* suit jeudi; **that speech comes in Act 3/on page 10** on trouve ce discours dans l'acte 3/à la page 10; **what comes next?** qu'est-ce qu'il y a après?
3 *(occur, happen)* arriver, se produire; **such an opportunity only comes once in your life** une telle occasion ne se présente qu'une fois dans la vie; **he has a birthday coming** son anniversaire approche; **there's a storm coming** un orage se prépare; **success was a long time coming** la réussite s'est fait attendre; **take life as it comes** prenez la vie comme elle vient; **Christmas comes but once a year** il n'y a qu'un Noël par an; *Bible* **it came to pass that…** il advint que…; **c. what may** advienne que pourra, quoi qu'il arrive *ou* advienne
4 *(occur to the mind)* **the idea just came to me one day** l'idée m'est soudain venue un jour; **suddenly it came to me** *(I remembered)* tout d'un coup, je m'en suis souvenu; *(I had an idea)* tout d'un coup, j'ai eu une idée; **I said the first thing that came into my head** *or* **that came to mind** j'ai dit la première chose qui m'est venue à l'esprit; **the answer came to her** elle a trouvé la réponse
5 *(be experienced in a specified way)* **writing comes naturally to her** écrire lui est facile, elle est douée pour l'écriture; **a house doesn't c. cheap** une maison coûte *ou* revient cher; **the news came as a shock to her** la nouvelle lui a fait un choc; **her visit came as a surprise** sa visite nous a beaucoup surpris; **it comes as no surprise to learn he's gone** (le fait) qu'il soit parti n'a rien de surprenant; **he's as silly as they c.** il est sot comme pas un; **it'll all c. right in the end** tout cela va finir par s'arranger
6 *(be available)* exister; **this table comes in two sizes** cette table existe *ou* se fait en deux dimensions
7 *(become)* devenir; **it was a dream c. true** c'était un rêve devenu réalité; **to c. unhooked** se décrocher; **to c. undone** se défaire; **the buttons on my coat keep coming undone** mon manteau se déboutonne toujours
8 *(+ infinitive) (indicating gradual action)* en venir à, finir par; *(indicating chance)* arriver; **she came to trust him** elle en est venue à *ou* elle a fini par lui faire confiance; **we have c. to expect this kind of thing** nous nous attendons à ce genre de chose maintenant; **how did you c. to lose your umbrella?** comment as-tu fait pour perdre ton parapluie?; **(now that I) c. to think of it** maintenant que j'y songe, réflexion faite
9 *(be owing, payable)* **I still have £5 coming (to me)** on me doit encore 5 livres; *Fam* **you'll get what's coming to you** tu l'auras cherché *ou* voulu; *Fam* **he had it coming (to him)** il ne l'a pas volé
10 *(appear)* **a smile came to her lips** un sourire parut sur ses lèvres *ou* lui vint aux lèvres
11 *very Fam (have orgasm)* jouir
12 *(idioms)* **how c.?** comment ça?; *Fam* **c. again?** quoi?; **c. to that** à propos, au fait; **I haven't seen her in weeks, or her husband, c. to that** ça fait des semaines que je ne l'ai pas vue, son mari non plus d'ailleurs; **if it comes to that, I'd rather stay home** à ce moment-là *ou* à ce compte-là, je préfère rester à la maison; **don't c. the innocent!** ne

fais pas l'innocent!; *Br Fam* **you're coming it a bit strong!** tu y vas un peu fort!; *Br Fam* **don't c. it with me!** *(try to impress)* n'essaie pas de m'en mettre plein la vue!; *(lord it over)* pas la peine d'être si hautain avec moi!; **the days to c.** les prochains jours, les jours qui viennent; **in times to c.** à l'avenir; **for some time to c.** pendant quelque temps; **that will not be for some time to c.** ce ne sera pas avant quelque temps

PREP *(by)* **c. tomorrow/Tuesday you'll feel better** vous vous sentirez mieux demain/mardi; **I'll have been here two years c. April** ça fera deux ans en avril que je suis là; **c. the revolution, you'll all be out of a job** avec la révolution, vous vous retrouverez tous au chômage

EXCLAM c., c.!, c. now! allons!, voyons!

N *Vulg (semen)* foutre *m*

► **come about VI 1** *(occur)* arriver, se produire; **it came about that...** il arriva *ou* il advint que... + *indicative*; **the discovery of penicillin came about quite by accident** la pénicilline a été découverte tout à fait par hasard **2** *Naut (wind)* tourner, changer de direction; *(ship)* virer de bord

► **come across VI 1** *(walk, travel across* ► *field, street)* traverser; **as we stood talking she came across to join us** pendant que nous discutions, elle est venue se joindre à nous

2 *(create specified impression)* **to c. across well/badly** *(at interview)* faire une bonne/mauvaise impression, bien/mal passer; *(on TV)* bien/mal passer; **he never comes across as well on film as in the theatre** il passe mieux au théâtre qu'à l'écran

3 *(be communicated effectively)* **the author's message comes across well** le message de l'auteur passe bien

4 *Fam (do as promised)* s'exécuter□, tenir parole□

VT INSEP *(person)* rencontrer par hasard, tomber sur; *(thing)* trouver par hasard, tomber sur

► **come across with VT INSEP** *Fam (give* ► *information)* donner□, fournir□; *(*► *help)* offrir□; *(*► *money)* raquer, se fendre de; **he came across with the money he owed me** il m'a filé le fric qu'il me devait

► **come after VT INSEP** *(pursue)* poursuivre; **he came after me with a stick** il m'a poursuivi avec un bâton

► **come along VI 1** *(encouraging, urging)* **c. along, drink your medicine!** allez, prends *ou* bois ton médicament!; **c. along, we're late!** dépêche-toi, nous sommes en retard!

2 *(accompany)* venir, accompagner; **she asked me to c. along (with them)** elle m'a invité à aller avec eux *ou* à les accompagner

3 *(occur, happen)* arriver, se présenter; **an opportunity like this doesn't c. along often** une telle occasion ne se présente pas souvent; **don't accept the first job that comes along** ne prenez pas le premier travail qui se présente

4 *(progress)* avancer, faire des progrès; *(grow)* pousser; **the work isn't coming along as expected** le travail n'avance pas comme prévu; **the patient is coming along well** le patient se remet bien

► **come apart VI** *(object* ► *come to pieces)* se démonter; *(*► *break)* se casser; *(project, policy)* échouer; **to c. apart at the seams** *(garment)* se défaire aux coutures; *Fig* s'écrouler, craquer; **the book came apart in my hands** le livre est tombé en morceaux quand je l'ai pris

► **come at VT INSEP 1** *(attack)* attaquer, se jeter sur; **he came at me with a knife** il s'est jeté sur moi avec un couteau; *Fig* **questions came at me from all sides** j'ai été assailli de questions **2** *(approach)* **to c. at a problem from a different angle** aborder un problème sous un angle différent

► **come away VI 1** *(leave)* partir, s'en aller; **c. away from that door!** écartez-vous de cette porte!; **I came away with the distinct impression that all was not well** je suis reparti avec la forte impression que quelque chose n'allait pas; **he asked her to c. away with him** *(elope)* il lui a demandé de s'enfuir avec lui; *Br (go on holiday)* il lui a demandé de partir avec lui **2** *(separate)* partir, se détacher; **the page came away in my hands** la page m'est restée dans les mains

► **come back VI 1** *(return)* revenir; **to c. back home** rentrer (à la maison); **we'll c. back to that question later** nous reviendrons à cette question plus tard; **to c. back to what we were saying** pour en revenir à ce que nous disions

2 *(to memory)* **it's all coming back to me** tout cela me revient (à l'esprit *ou* à la mémoire); **her name will c. back to me later** son nom me reviendra plus tard

3 *(reply)* répondre; *Am (retort)* rétorquer, répliquer

4 *(recover)* remonter; **they came back from 3–0 down** ils ont remonté de 3 à 0

5 *(become fashionable again)* revenir à la mode; *(make comeback)* faire un come-back

► **come by VI** *(stop by)* passer, venir

VT INSEP *(acquire* ► *work, money)* obtenir, se procurer; **jobs are hard to c. by** il est difficile de trouver du travail; **how did you c. by this camera/those bruises?** comment as-tu fait pour avoir cet appareil photo/ces bleus?; **how did she c. by all that money?** comment s'est-elle procuré tout cet argent?

► **come down VT INSEP** *(descend* ► *ladder, stairs)* descendre; *(*► *mountain)* descendre, faire la descente de

VI 1 *(descend* ► *from ladder, stairs)* descendre; *(*► *from mountain etc)* descendre, faire la descente; *(plane* ► *crash)* s'écraser; *(*► *land)* atterrir; **to c. down to breakfast** descendre déjeuner *ou* prendre le petit déjeuner; **c. down from that tree!** descends de cet arbre!; **they came down to Paris** ils sont descendus à Paris; **hemlines are coming down this year** les jupes rallongent cette année; **he's c. down in the world** il a déchu; **you'd better c. down to earth** tu ferais bien de revenir sur terre *ou* de descendre des nues

2 *(fall)* tomber; **rain was coming down in sheets** il pleuvait des cordes; **the ceiling came down** le plafond s'est effondré

3 *(reach)* descendre; **her hair came down to her waist** les cheveux lui tombaient *ou* descendaient jusqu'à la taille

4 *(decrease)* baisser; **he's ready to c. down 10 percent on the price** il est prêt à rabattre *ou* baisser le prix de 10 pour cent

5 *(be passed down)* être transmis (de père en fils); **this custom comes down from the Romans** cette coutume nous vient des Romains; **the necklace came down to her from her great-aunt** elle tient ce collier de sa grand-tante

6 *(reach a decision)* se prononcer; **the majority came down in favour of/against abortion** la majorité s'est prononcée en faveur de/contre l'avortement; **to c. down on sb's side** décider en faveur de qn

7 *(be removed)* être défait *ou* décroché; **that wallpaper will have to c. down** il va falloir enlever ce papier peint; **the Christmas decorations are coming down today** aujourd'hui, on enlève les décorations de Noël; **the tree will have to c. down** *(be felled)* il faut abattre cet arbre; **these houses are coming down soon** on va bientôt démolir ces maisons

8 *Br Univ* obtenir son diplôme

9 *Fam Drugs slang* redescendre

► **come down on VT INSEP** *(rebuke)* s'en prendre à; **the boss came down hard on him** le patron lui a passé un de ces savons; **one mistake and he'll c. down on you like a ton of bricks** si tu fais la moindre erreur, il te tombera sur le dos

► **come down to VT INSEP** *(be a question of)* **to c. down to** se résumer *ou* se réduire à; **the whole difficulty comes down to this question** toute la difficulté se réduit à cette question; **it all comes down to money** ce n'est qu'une question d'argent

► **come down with VT INSEP** *(become ill with)* attraper; **he came down with a cold** il s'est enrhumé, il a attrapé un rhume

► **come forward VI** *(present oneself)* se présenter; **more women are coming forward as candidates** davantage de femmes présentent leur candidature; **no one has c. forward with any alternative ideas** personne n'a rien proposé d'autre; **the police have appealed for witnesses to c. forward** la police a demandé aux témoins de se faire connaître

► **come from VT INSEP** venir de; **she comes form China** elle vient *ou* elle est originaire de Chine; **to c. from a good family** être issu d' *ou* venir d'une bonne famille; **that's surprising coming from him** c'est étonnant de sa part; *Fam* **I can see where you're coming from** je vois ce que tu veux dire

► **come in VI 1** *(enter)* entrer; *(come inside)* rentrer; **c. in!** entrez!; **c. in now, children, it's getting dark** rentrez maintenant, les enfants, il commence à faire nuit

2 *(plane, train)* arriver

3 *(in competition)* arriver; **she came in second** elle est arrivée deuxième

4 *(be received* ► *money, contributions)* rentrer; **there isn't enough money coming in to cover expenditure** l'argent qui rentre ne suffit pas à couvrir les dépenses; **how much do you have coming in every week?** combien touchez-vous *ou* encaissez-vous chaque semaine?

5 *Press (news, report)* être reçu; **news is just coming in of a riot in Red Square** on nous annonce à l'instant des émeutes sur la place Rouge

6 *Rad & TV (begin to speak)* parler; **c. in, car number 1, over** j'appelle voiture 1, à vous

7 *(become seasonable)* être de saison; *(become fashionable)* entrer en vogue; **when do endives c. in?** quand commence la saison des endives?; **leather has c. in** le cuir est à la mode *ou* en vogue

8 *(prove to be)* **to c. in handy** *or* **useful** *(tool, gadget)* être utile *ou* commode; *(contribution)* arriver à point

9 *(be involved)* être impliqué; *(participate)* participer, intervenir; **where do I c. in?** quel est mon rôle là-dedans?; **this is where the law comes in** c'est là que la loi intervient; **I'd like to c. in on this** *(conversation)* j'aimerais dire quelques mots là-dessus *ou* à ce sujet

10 *(join an enterprise etc)* **to c. in with sb** s'associer à qn; **they were the founder members, the others didn't c. in till later** ce sont les membres fondateurs, les autres ne s'y sont associés que plus tard

11 *(tide)* monter

► **come in for VT INSEP** *(be object of* ► *abuse, reproach)* subir; **to c. in for criticism** être critiqué, être l'objet de critiques; **the government came in for a lot of criticism over its handling of the crisis** le gouvernement a été très critiqué pour la façon dont il gère la crise; **to c. in for praise** être félicité

► **come in on VT INSEP** *(be given a part in)* prendre part à; **they let him c. in on the deal** ils l'ont laissé prendre part à l'affaire

► **come into VT INSEP 1** *(inherit)* hériter de; *(acquire)* entrer en possession de; **to c. into some money** *(inherit it)* faire un héritage; *(win it)* gagner le gros lot; **they came into a fortune** *(won)* ils ont gagné une fortune; *(inherited)* ils ont hérité d'une fortune **2** *(play a role in)* jouer un rôle dans; **it's not simply a matter of pride, though pride does c. into it** ce n'est pas une simple question de fierté, bien que la fierté joue un certain rôle; **money doesn't c. into it!** l'argent n'a rien à voir là-dedans!

► **come of VT INSEP** résulter de; **what will c. of it?** qu'en adviendra-t-il?, qu'en résultera-t-il?; **no good will c. of it** ça ne mènera à rien de bon, il n'en résultera rien de bon; **that's what comes of being too ambitious** voilà ce qui arrive quand on est trop ambitieux **let me know what comes of the meeting** faites-moi savoir ce qui ressortira de la réunion

► **come off VT INSEP 1** *(fall off* ► *of rider)* tomber de; *(*► *of button)* se détacher de, se découdre de; *(*► *of handle, label)* se détacher de; *(of tape, wallpaper)* se détacher de, se décoller de; *(be removed* ► *of stain, mark)* partir de, s'enlever de

2 *(stop taking* ► *drug, medicine)* arrêter de prendre; *(*► *drink)* arrêter de boire; **to c. off the pill** arrêter (de prendre) la pilule

3 *(climb down from, leave* ► *wall, ladder etc)* descendre de; **to c. off a ship/off a plane** débarquer d'un navire/d'un avion; **I've just c. off the night shift** *(finished work)* je viens de quitter l'équipe de nuit; *(finished working nights)* je viens de finir le travail de nuit

4 *Ftbl (field)* sortir de

5 *Fam (idiom)* **oh, c. off it!** allez, arrête ton char!

VI 1 *(rider)* tomber; *(button)* se détacher, se découdre; *(handle, label)* se détacher; *(stain, mark)* partir, s'enlever; *(tape, wallpaper)* se détacher, se décoller; **the handle came off in his hand** la poignée lui est restée dans la main; **the colour came**

off on my dress la couleur a déteint sur ma robe; **the chain has c. off** *(of bicycle)* la chaîne a sauté

2 *Ftbl (leave the field)* sortir

3 *(fare, manage)* s'en sortir, s'en tirer; **you came off well in the competition** tu t'en es bien tiré au concours; **to c. off best** gagner

4 *Fam (happen)* avoir lieu□, se passer□; *(be carried through)* se réaliser□; *(succeed)* réussir□; **did the game c. off all right?** le match s'est bien passé?□; **my trip to China didn't c. off** mon voyage en Chine n'a pas eu lieu□; **his plan didn't c. off** son projet est tombé à l'eau

5 *Cin & Theat (film, play)* fermer

6 *very Fam (have orgasm)* décharger

▸**come on** **VI 1** *(follow)* suivre; **I'll c. on after (you)** je vous suivrai

2 *(in imperative)* **c. on!** *(with motion, encouraging, challenging)* vas-y!, allez!; *(hurry)* allez!; *Fam (expressing incredulity)* tu rigoles!; **c. on Scotland!** allez l'Écosse!; **c. on in/up!** entre/monte donc!; **oh, come on, for goodness sake!** allez, arrête!

3 *(progress)* avancer, faire des progrès; *(grow)* pousser, venir bien; **how is your work coming on?** où en est votre travail?; **my roses are coming on nicely** mes rosiers se portent bien; **her new book is coming on quite well** son nouveau livre avance bien

4 *(begin ▸ illness)* se déclarer; *(▸ storm)* survenir, éclater; *(▸ season)* arriver; **as night came on** quand la nuit a commençé à tomber; **it's coming on to rain** il va pleuvoir; **I feel a headache/cold coming on** je sens un mal de tête qui commence/que je m'enrhume

5 *(start functioning ▸ electricity, gas, heater, lights, radio)* s'allumer; *(▸ utilities at main)* être mis en service; **has the water c. on?** y a-t-il de l'eau?

6 *(behave, act)* **don't c. on all macho with me!** ne joue pas les machos avec moi!; *Fam* **you came on a bit strong** tu y es allé un peu fort

7 *Theat (actor)* entrer en scène; *(play)* être joué *ou* représenté; **his new play is coming on** on va donner sa nouvelle pièce

8 *Br Fam (start menstruating)* avoir ses ragnagnas

▸**come out** **VI 1** *(exit, go out socially)* sortir; **as we came out of the theatre** au moment où nous sommes sortis du théâtre

2 *(make appearance ▸ stars, sun)* paraître, se montrer; *(▸ flowers)* sortir, éclore; *Fig (▸ book)* paraître, être publié; *(▸ film)* paraître, sortir; *(▸ new product)* sortir; **to c. out in a rash** *(person)* se couvrir de boutons, avoir une éruption; **his nasty side came out** sa méchanceté s'est manifestée; **I didn't mean it the way it came out** ce n'est pas ce que je voulais dire

3 *(be revealed ▸ news, secret)* être divulgué *ou* révélé; *(▸ facts, truth)* émerger, se faire jour; **as soon as the news came out** dès qu'on a su la nouvelle, dès que la nouvelle a été annoncée

4 *(be removed ▸ stain)* s'enlever, partir; *(colour ▸ fade)* passer, se faner; *(▸ run)* déteindre

5 *(declare oneself publicly)* se déclarer; **to c. out strongly (for/against)** se prononcer avec vigueur (pour/contre); *Fam* **to c. out (of the closet)** *(homosexual)* révéler (publiquement) son homosexualité□, faire son come-out

6 *Br (on strike)* se mettre en *ou* faire grève

7 *(emerge, finish up)* se tirer d'affaire, s'en sortir; *(in competition)* se classer; **the government came out of the deal badly** le gouvernement s'est mal sorti de l'affaire; **I came out top in maths** j'étais premier en maths; *Fig* **everything will c. out (all) right in the end** tout finira par s'arranger

8 *(go into society)* faire ses débuts *ou* débuter dans le monde

9 *Math (yield solution)* **this sum won't c. out** je n'arrive pas à résoudre cette opération; **it comes out at …** le résultat est de …

10 *Phot* **the pictures came out well/badly** les photos étaient très bonnes/n'ont rien donné; **the house didn't c. out very well** la maison n'est pas très bien sur les photos

11 *Comput (exit)* sortir; **to c. out of a document** sortir d'un document

▸**come out with** **VT INSEP** *(say)* dire, sortir; **what will he c. out with next?** qu'est-ce qu'il va nous sortir encore?; **he finally came out with it** il a fini par le sortir

▸**come over** **VI 1** *(move, travel in direction of speaker)* venir; **at the party she came over to talk to me** pendant la soirée, elle est venue me parler; **do you want to c. over this evening?** tu veux venir à la maison ce soir?; **his family came over with the early settlers** sa famille est arrivée *ou* venue avec les premiers pionniers; **I met him in the plane coming over** je l'ai rencontré dans l'avion en venant

2 *(stop by)* venir, passer

3 *(change sides)* **they came over to our side** ils sont passés de notre côté; **he finally came over to their way of thinking** il a fini par se ranger à leur avis

4 *(make specified impression)* **her speech came over well** son discours a fait bon effet *ou* bonne impression; **he came over as honest** il a donné l'impression d'être honnête; **he doesn't c. over well on television** il ne passe pas bien à la télévision; **her voice comes over well** sa voix passe *ou* rend bien

5 *Fam (feel)* devenir□; **he came over all funny** *(felt ill)* il s'est senti mal tout d'un coup, il a eu un malaise□; **to c. over faint** être pris d'une faiblesse

VT INSEP affecter, envahir; **a change came over him** un changement se produisit en lui; **a feeling of fear came over him** il a été saisi de peur, la peur s'est emparée de lui; **what has c. over him?** qu'est-ce qui lui prend?

▸**come round** **VI 1** *(make a detour)* faire le détour; **we came round by the factory** nous sommes passés par *ou* nous avons fait le détour par l'usine

2 *(stop by)* passer, venir

3 *(occur ▸ regular event)* **don't wait for Christmas to c. round** n'attendez pas Noël; **when the championships/elections c. round** au moment des championnats/élections; **the summer holidays will soon be coming round again** bientôt, ce sera de nouveau les grandes vacances

4 *(change mind)* changer d'avis; **he finally came round to our way of thinking** il a fini par se ranger à notre avis; **they soon came round to the idea** ils se sont faits à cette idée; *(change to better mood)* **don't worry, she'll soon c. round** ne t'en fais pas, elle sera bientôt de meilleure humeur

5 *(recover consciousness)* reprendre connaissance, revenir à soi; *(get better)* se remettre, se rétablir

6 *Naut* venir au vent

▸**come through** **VI 1** *(be communicated)* **her enthusiasm comes through in her letters** son enthousiasme se lit dans ses lettres; **you're coming through loud and clear** je vous reçois cinq sur cinq

2 *(be granted, approved)* se réaliser; **did your visa c. through?** avez-vous obtenu votre visa?; **my request for a transfer came through** ma demande de mutation a été acceptée

3 *(survive)* survivre, s'en tirer

4 *Am Fam (do what is expected)* **he came through for us** il a fait ce qu'on attendait de lui□; **they came through with the money** ils ont rendu l'argent comme prévu□

VT INSEP 1 *(cross)* traverser; *Fig (penetrate)* traverser; **we came through marshland** nous sommes passés par *ou* avons traversé des marais; **the rain came through my coat** la pluie a traversé mon manteau; **water is coming through the roof** l'eau s'infiltre par le toit **2** *(survive)* **they came through the accident without a scratch** ils sont sortis de l'accident indemnes; **I'm sure you will c. through this crisis** je suis sûr que tu te sortiras de cette crise

▸**come to** **VI 1** *(recover consciousness)* reprendre connaissance, revenir à soi **2** *Naut (change course)* venir au vent, lofer; *(stop)* s'arrêter

VT INSEP 1 *(concern)* **when it comes to physics, she's a genius** pour ce qui est de la physique, c'est un génie; **when it comes to paying you can't see anyone for dust** quand il faut payer, il n'y a plus personne **2** *(amount to)* s'élever à, se monter à; **how much did dinner come to?** à combien s'élevait le dîner?; **her salary comes to £750 a month** elle gagne 750 livres par mois; **the plan never came to anything** le projet n'a abouti à rien; **that nephew of yours will never c. to anything** ton neveu n'arrivera jamais à rien **3** *Fig (arrive at, reach)* **what is the world** *or* **what are things coming to?** où va-t-on?; **I never thought it would c. to this** je ne me doutais pas qu'on en arriverait là; **if it comes to that …** à ce compte-là …; **let's hope it won't c. to that** espérons que nous n'en arrivions pas là

▸**come together** **VI 1** *(assemble)* se réunir, se rassembler; *(meet)* se rencontrer; **the two roads c. together at this point** les deux routes se rejoignent à cet endroit **2** *Fam (combine successfully)* **everything came together at the final performance** tout s'est passé à merveille pour la dernière représentation□

▸**come up** **VI 1** *(move upwards)* monter; *(moon, sun)* se lever

2 *(travel in direction of speaker)* **I c. up to town every Monday** je viens en ville tous les lundis; **they came up to Chicago** ils sont venus à Chicago; **to c. up for air** *(diver)* remonter à la surface; *Fig (take break)* faire une pause; **she came up the hard way** elle a réussi à la force du poignet; *Mil* **an officer who came up through the ranks** un officier sorti du rang

3 *(approach)* s'approcher; **to c. up to sb** s'approcher de qn, aborder qn; **it's coming up to five o'clock** il est presque cinq heures; **coming up now on Channel 4, the seven o'clock news** et maintenant, sur Channel 4, le journal de sept heures; *Fam* **one coffee, coming up!** et un café, un!

4 *(plant)* sortir, germer

5 *(come under consideration ▸ matter)* être soulevé, être mis sur le tapis; *(▸ question, problem)* se poser, être soulevé; *Law (▸ accused)* comparaître; *(▸ case)* être entendu; **the question of financing always comes up** la question du financement se pose toujours; **the subject came up twice in the conversation** le sujet est revenu deux fois dans la conversation; **your name came up twice** on a mentionné votre nom deux fois; **she comes up for re-election this year** son mandat prend fin cette année; **my contract is coming up for review** mon contrat doit être révisé; **her case comes up next Wednesday** elle passe au tribunal mercredi prochain

6 *(happen unexpectedly ▸ event)* survenir, surgir; *(▸ opportunity)* se présenter; **to deal with problems as they c. up** traiter les problèmes au fur et à mesure; **she's ready for anything that might c. up** elle est prête à faire face à toute éventualité; **I can't make it, something has c. up** je ne peux pas venir, j'ai un empêchement; **I'll let you know if anything comes up** *(further information)* s'il y a du nouveau, je vous tiendrai au courant; *(job vacancy etc)* je vous tiendrai au courant si je vois quelque chose qui vous convienne

7 *(intensify ▸ wind)* se lever; *(▸ light)* s'allumer; *(▸ sound)* s'intensifier; **when the lights came up at the interval** lorsque les lumières se rallumèrent à l'entracte

8 *(be vomited)* **everything she eats comes up (again)** elle vomit *ou* rejette tout ce qu'elle mange

9 *(colour, wood etc)* **the colour comes up well when it's cleaned** la couleur revient bien au nettoyage

10 *Fam (win)* gagner□; **did their number c. up?** *(in lottery)* ont-ils gagné au loto?; *Fig* est-ce qu'ils ont touché le gros lot?

11 *Fam Drugs slang (after taking drugs)* décoller

▸**come up against** **VT INSEP** *(be confronted with)* rencontrer; **they came up against some tough competition** ils se sont heurtés à des concurrents redoutables

▸**come up to** **VT INSEP 1** *(reach)* arriver à; **the mud came up to their knees** la boue leur montait *ou* arrivait jusqu'aux genoux; **she comes up to his shoulder** elle lui arrive à l'épaule; **we're coming up to the halfway mark** nous atteindrons bientôt la moitié **2** *(equal)* **to c. up to sb's expectations** répondre à l'attente de qn; **the play didn't c. up to our expectations** la pièce nous a déçus

▸**come up with** **VT INSEP** *(offer, propose ▸ money, loan)* fournir; *(think of ▸ plan, suggestion)* suggérer, proposer; *(▸ answer)* trouver; *(▸ excuse)* trouver, inventer; **they came up with a wonderful idea** ils ont eu une idée géniale; **what will she c. up with next?** qu'est-ce qu'elle va encore inventer?

▸**come upon** **VT INSEP** *(find unexpectedly ▸ person)* rencontrer par hasard, tomber sur; *(▸ object)* trouver par hasard, tomber sur

comeback [ˈkʌmbæk] **N** *Fam* **1** *(return ▸ of person)* retour□ *m*, come-back *m inv*; *Theat* rentrée□ *f*; **to make** *or* **to stage a c.** faire une rentrée□ *ou* un come-back; **70s fashions are making a c.** la mode des années 70 revient **2** *(retort)* réplique *f* **3** *(justification for complaint)* **to have no c.** n'avoir aucun recours

Comecon [ˈkɒmɪkɒn] **N** *(abbr* **Council for Mutual Economic Assistance***)* le Comecon

comedian [kəˈmiːdɪən] **N 1** *(comic)* comique *m*; *Fig (funny person)* clown *m*, pitre *m* **2** *Theat (comic actor)* comédien *m*

> Note that the French word **comédien** is a false friend. Its most common meaning is **actor**.

comedienne [kəˌmiːdɪˈen] **N 1** *(comic)* actrice *f* comique **2** *Theat (comic actress)* comédienne *f*

comedown [ˈkʌmdaʊn] **N** *Fam* déchéance□ *f*, dégringolade *f*; **he finds being a sales assistant a bit of a c.** il trouve plutôt humiliant de travailler comme vendeur

comedy [ˈkɒmədɪ] *(pl* **comedies***)* **N 1** *(genre)* comédie *f*; *Theat* genre *m* comique, comédie *f* **2** *(play, film)* comédie *f*; *(situation comedy)* sitcom *m ou f*; **the whole affair has been a c. of errors** toute cette affaire n'a été qu'une farce **3** *(of situation)* comique *m*

COMP *(act, duo)* comique

▸▸ ***comedy actor*** acteur *m* comique; ***comedy actress*** actrice *f* comique; ***comedy drama*** comédie *f* dramatique; ***comedy of manners*** comédie *f* de mœurs; ***comedy show*** spectacle *m* comique

come-hither **ADJ** *Fam* aguichant□; **a c. look** un regard aguichant

comely [ˈkʌmlɪ] *(compar* **comelier**, *superl* **comeliest***)* **ADJ** *Literary* charmant, beau (belle)

come-on **N** *Fam (enticement)* incitation□ *f*; **it was a c. to get buyers interested** c'était pour attirer les clients□; **to give sb the c.** *(sexually)* faire du gringue à qn

comer [ˈkʌmə(r)] **N** *(arrival)* arrivant(e) *m,f*; **the first comers** les premiers venus; **open to all comers** ouvert à tous *ou* au tout-venant; **I'm ready to take on all comers** je suis prêt à me battre avec n'importe qui

comestible [kəˈmestɪbəl] **ADJ** *Formal* comestible

• **comestibles** **NPL** comestibles *mpl*, denrées *fpl* comestibles

comet [ˈkɒmɪt] **N** comète *f*

come-to-bed **ADJ** *Fam* **c. eyes** regard *m* aguichant□ *ou* suggestif□

comeuppance [ˌkʌmˈʌpəns] **N** *Fam* **she got her c.** elle n'a eu que ce qu'elle méritait□

comfort [ˈkʌmfət] **N 1** *(well-being)* confort *m*, bien-être *m*; **to live in c.** vivre dans l'aisance *ou* à l'aise; **the boots are fur-lined for extra c.** les bottes sont fourrées pour plus de confort; **to do sth in the c. of one's own home** faire qch confortablement chez soi; *Fig* **the explosion was too close for c.** l'explosion a eu lieu un peu trop près à mon goût; **the deadline's getting a bit too close for c.** la date limite est un peu trop proche à mon goût; *Fig* **to step out of one's c. zone** s'aventurer en terrain inconnu **2** *(usu pl) (amenities)* aises *fpl*, commodités *fpl*; **every modern c.** tout le confort moderne; **I like my c.** *or* **comforts** j'aime bien mes aises *ou* mon confort **3** *(consolation)* réconfort *m*, consolation *f*; **to take c. in sth** trouver un réconfort dans qch; **she took c. from his words** elle a trouvé un réconfort dans ses paroles; **I took c. from** *or* **in the knowledge that it would soon be over** je me suis consolé en me disant que ce serait bientôt fini; **if it's any c. to you** si cela peut vous consoler; **you've been a great c. to me** vous avez été pour moi un grand réconfort; **some c. you are/that is!** tu parles d'une consolation!

VT 1 *(console)* consoler; *(relieve)* soulager; **they comforted the wounded** ils ont réconforté les blessés **2** *(cheer)* réconforter, encourager

▸▸ ***comfort eating*** = fait de manger pour se remonter le moral; ***comfort food*** = chose que l'on mange pour se remonter le moral; *Am* ***comfort station*** toilettes *fpl* publiques *(sur le bord d'une route)*

comfortable [ˈkʌmftəbəl] **ADJ 1** *(chair, shoes, bed, room)* confortable; *(temperature)* agréable **2** *(person)* à l'aise; **are you c.?** êtes-vous bien installé?; **make yourself c.** *(sit down)* installez-vous confortablement; *(feel at ease)* mettez-vous à l'aise, faites comme chez vous; **he couldn't get c. in bed** il ne savait pas comment se mettre dans le lit pour être à l'aise; **I'm not very c. about** *or* **I don't feel c. with the idea** l'idée ne me plaît pas particulièrement; **I wouldn't feel c. accepting that money** ça me mettrait mal à l'aise d'accepter cet argent **3** *(financially secure)* aisé, riche; *(easy ▸ job)* tranquille; **they're very c.** ils ont une vie aisée; **c. income** revenu *m* suffisant; **he makes a c. living** il gagne bien sa vie **4** *(not in pain)* **to be c.** *(after illness, operation, accident)* ne pas souffrir; **he had a c. night** il a passé une bonne nuit **5** *Fig (lead, win)* confortable; **that leaves us a c. margin** ça nous laisse une marge confortable

comfortably [ˈkʌmftəblɪ] **ADV 1** *(in a relaxed position ▸ sit, sleep)* confortablement, agréablement **2** *(in financial comfort)* à l'aise; **they live c.** ils vivent dans l'aisance *ou* à l'aise; **to be c. off** être à l'aise **3** *(easily)* facilement, à l'aise; **we should manage it c. in two hours** deux heures suffiront largement

comforter [ˈkʌmfətə(r)] **N 1** *(person)* consolateur(trice) *m,f* **2** *Br Old-fashioned (scarf)* cache-nez *m inv* **3** *(for baby)* tétine *f*, sucette *f* **4** *Am (quilt)* édredon *m*, *Can* confortable *m*; *(duvet)* couette *f*

comforting [ˈkʌmfətɪŋ] **ADJ** *(consoling ▸ remark, thought)* consolant, réconfortant, rassurant; *(encouraging)* encourageant

comfortless [ˈkʌmfətlɪs] **ADJ 1** *(room)* sans confort **2** *(dismal ▸ person)* triste, désolé; *(▸ thought)* peu rassurant, triste

comfy [ˈkʌmfɪ] *(compar* **comfier**, *superl* **comfiest***)* **ADJ** *Fam (chair, place, bed)* confortable□; **are you c.?** vous êtes bien installés?□

comic [ˈkɒmɪk] **ADJ** comique, humoristique

N 1 *(entertainer ▸ man)* acteur *m* comique *m*; *(▸ woman)* actrice *f* comique **2** *(magazine)* BD *f*, bande *f* dessinée

• **comics** **NPL** *Am (in newspaper)* bandes *fpl* dessinées

▸▸ ***comic actor*** acteur *m* comique; ***comic actress*** actrice *f* comique; ***comic book*** magazine *m* de bandes dessinées; ***comic opera*** opéra *m* comique; ***comic relief*** *Theat* intervalle *m* comique; *Fig* moment *m* de détente (comique); ***comic strip*** bande *f* dessinée

> **COMIC RELIEF**
>
> Comic Relief est le nom d'une association caritative fondée en 1985 par un groupe de comiques pour venir en aide aux victimes de la famine en Afrique. Afin de collecter des fonds, ils organisèrent "red-nose day", journée durant laquelle le public était invité à acheter un nez rouge en plastique et à s'en affubler. Cet événement a désormais lieu tous les deux ans et permet de recueillir des millions de livres sterling, et ce principalement au cours d'un téléthon auquel participent des comiques et des personnalités du monde de la télévision. Le public participe également en se faisant sponsoriser pour accomplir toutes sortes d'activités fantaisistes comme par exemple se raser la tête ou prendre un bain de haricots à la tomate (voir l'encadré **sponsored event**). L'argent est employé pour venir en aide aux plus démunis à l'étranger ainsi qu'en Grande-Bretagne.

comical [ˈkɒmɪkəl] **ADJ** drôle, comique

comically [ˈkɒmɪkəlɪ] **ADV** drôlement, comiquement

coming [ˈkʌmɪŋ] **ADJ 1** *(time, events)* à venir, futur; *(in near future)* prochain; **this c. Tuesday** mardi prochain; **the c. storm** l'orage qui approche **2** *Fam (promising ▸ person)* qui a de l'avenir□

N 1 *(gen)* arrivée *f*, venue *f*; **c. and going** va-et-vient *m inv*; **comings and goings** allées *fpl* et venues **2** *Rel* avènement *m*; **the Second C.** le second avènement

▸▸ ***coming of age*** majorité *f*; ***coming out*** *(of debutante)* entrée *f* dans la société; *(of homosexual)* coming out *m*, = fait de déclarer son homosexualité

comma [ˈkɒmə] **N 1** *Gram* virgule *f* **2** *Mus* comma *m*

command [kəˈmɑːnd] **N 1** *(order)* ordre *m*; *Mil* ordre *m*, commandement *m*; **to give a c.** donner un ordre; **the troops were withdrawn at** *or* **on his c.** les troupes ont été retirées sur ses ordres; **they are at your c.** ils sont à vos ordres; **at the word of c.** au commandement

2 *(authority)* commandement *m*; **who is in c. here?** qui est-ce qui commande ici?; **to be in c. of sth** avoir qch sous ses ordres, être à la tête de qch; **to be first/second in c.** commander en premier/en second; **he had/he took c. of the situation** il avait/il a pris la situation en main; **they are under her c.** ils sont sous ses ordres *ou* son commandement

3 *(control, mastery)* maîtrise *f*; **c. of the seas** maîtrise *f* des mers; **her c. of Spanish** sa maîtrise de l'espagnol; **she has a good c. of two foreign languages** elle possède bien deux langues étrangères; **all the resources at my c.** toutes les ressources à ma disposition *ou* dont je dispose; **I'm at your c.** je suis à votre disposition

4 *Mil (group of officers)* commandement *m*; *(troops)* troupes *fpl*; **to be responsible for one's c.** être responsable de ses troupes; **they were my first c.** c'est la première section que j'ai commandée

5 *Mil (area)* région *f* militaire; **Scottish/Northern c.** région *f* militaire d'Écosse/du Nord

6 *Comput* commande *f*

VT 1 *(order)* ordonner, commander; **she commanded that we leave immediately** elle nous a ordonné *ou* nous a donné l'ordre de partir immédiatement; **the general commanded his men to attack** le général a donné l'ordre à ses hommes d'attaquer

2 *(have control over ▸ army, ship, regiment)* commander; *(▸ emotions)* maîtriser, dominer

3 *(receive as due)* commander, imposer; **to c. respect** inspirer le respect, en imposer; **the translator commands a high fee** les services du traducteur valent cher; **this painting will c. a high price** ce tableau se vendra à un prix élevé

4 *(have use of)* disposer de; **all the skill he could c.** toute l'habileté qu'il possédait

5 *(of building, statue ▸ overlook)* dominer; **to c. a view of** avoir vue sur, donner sur

VI 1 *(order)* commander, donner des ordres **2** *(be in control)* commander; *Mil* commander, avoir le commandement

▸▸ *Comput* ***command code*** code *m* de commande; ***command economy*** économie *f* planifiée; *Comput* ***command file*** fichier *m* de commande; *Comput* ***command key*** touche *f* de commande; *Comput* ***command language*** langage *m* de commande; *Comput* ***command line*** ligne *f* de commande; ***command module*** *(of spacecraft)* module *m* de commande; *Br Theat* ***command performance*** = représentation (d'un spectacle) à la requête du monarque; *Mil* ***command post*** poste *m* de commandement

commandant [ˌkɒmənˈdænt] **N** *Mil* commandant *m*

commandeer [ˌkɒmənˈdɪə(r)] **VT 1** *Mil* réquisitionner **2** *(take for one's own use)* accaparer; **the boss commandeered our photocopier** le patron a fait main basse sur notre photocopieuse *ou* a réquisitionné notre photocopieuse

commander [kəˈmɑːndə(r)] **N 1** *(person in charge)* chef *m*; *Mil* commandant *m*; *Naut (rank)* capitaine *m* de frégate; *Aviat* chef *m* de bord **2** *Br (of police)* commissaire *m* divisionnaire, divisionnaire *m*

commander-in-chief **N** *Mil* commandant *m* en chef, généralissime *m*

commanding [kəˈmɑːndɪŋ] **ADJ 1** *(in command)* qui commande **2** *(overlooking ▸ view)* élevé; *(overlooking and dominant ▸ position)* dominant, important; **to have a c. lead** avoir une solide avance; **to be in a c. position** avoir une position dominante **3** *(tone, voice, look)* impérieux; *(air)*

imposant; *(beauty)* majestueux
▸▸ *Mil* ***commanding officer*** commandant *m*

commandment [kəˈmɑːndmənt] **N** commandement *m*; *Bible* **the Ten Commandments** les dix commandements, le Décalogue

commando [kəˈmɑːndəʊ] *(pl* **commandos** *or* **commandoes)** *Mil* **N** commando *m*
COMP *(raid, unit)* de commando

command-orientated, *Am* **command-oriented ADJ** *Comput (program)* orienté commande

commemorate [kəˈmeməˌreɪt] **VT** commémorer

commemoration [kəˌmeməˈreɪʃən] **N** commémoration *f*; *Rel* commémoraison *f*; **in c. of** en commémoration de

commemorative [kəˈmemərətɪv] **ADJ** commémoratif

commence [kəˈmens] *Formal* **VI** commencer
VT commencer; **she commenced speaking at two o'clock** elle a commencé à parler à deux heures; *Law* **to c. proceedings against sb** former un recours contre qn *(devant une juridiction)*

commencement [kəˈmensmənt] **N 1** *Fml (beginning)* commencement *m*, début *m*; *Law (of law)* date *f* d'entrée en vigueur **2** *Univ (in US, Canada, at Cambridge, in Trinity College, Dublin)* remise *f* des diplômes;
▸▸ *Univ* ***Commencement Day*** *(in US, at Cambridge)* jour *m* de la remise des diplômes

commend [kəˈmend] **VT 1** *(recommend)* recommander, conseiller; **he commended the proposal to the committee** il a recommandé le projet au comité; **the hotel has little to c. it apart from the cooking** il n'y a pas grand-chose de bien à dire sur cet hôtel à part la cuisine
2 *(praise)* louer, faire l'éloge de; **to c. sb for bravery** louer qn pour sa bravoure; **you are to be commended for your hard work** on doit vous féliciter pour votre dur labeur
3 *(entrust)* confier; **to c. sth to sb** confier qch à qn, remettre qch aux bons soins de qn; *Rel* **we c. our souls to God** nous recommandons notre âme à Dieu
4 *Arch or Formal (remember)* **c. me to Dr Smith** rappelez-moi au bon souvenir du Docteur Smith

commendable [kəˈmendəbəl] **ADJ** louable; **with c. promptness** avec une rapidité digne d'éloges

commendably [kəˈmendəblɪ] **ADV** de façon louable; **his speech was c. brief** son discours avait le mérite de la brièveté

commendation [ˌkɒmənˈdeɪʃən] **N 1** *(praise)* éloge *m*, louange *f*
2 *(recommendation)* recommandation *f*; *(award in competition)* mention *f* spéciale
3 *(award for bravery)* décoration *f*
4 *(entrusting)* remise *f*

commensurable [kəˈmenʃərəbəl] **ADJ** *Math* commensurable (**with** *or* **to** avec)

commensurate [kəˈmenʃərət] **ADJ** *Formal* **1** *(of equal measure)* de même mesure, commensurable **2** *(proportionate)* proportionné (**with** *or* **to** à); **the salary will be c. with your experience** le salaire sera en fonction de votre expérience; **there was no post c. with his abilities** aucun poste ne correspondait à ses compétences; **of c. value** d'une valeur équivalente

comment [ˈkɒment] **N 1** *(remark)* commentaire *m*, observation *f*; **to make a c. about sth** faire des observations sur qch; **she let it pass without c.** elle n'a pas relevé; **to refrain from c.** s'abstenir de faire des commentaires; *Fig* **it's a c. on our society** c'est une réflexion sur notre société; **no c.!** je n'ai rien à dire!; **(it's a) fair c.** c'est juste **2** *(UNCOUNT) (gossip, criticism)* **the decision provoked much c.** la décision a suscité de nombreux commentaires **3** *(note)* commentaire *m*, annotation *f*; *(critical)* critique *f*
VT to c. that... faire remarquer *ou* observer que... + indicative
VI 1 *(remark)* faire une remarque *ou* des remarques; **nobody commented on it** personne n'a fait de commentaire à ce sujet **2** *(give opinion)* **to c. on a text** commenter un texte, faire le commentaire d'un texte

commentary [ˈkɒməntrɪ] *(pl* **commentaries) N 1** *(remarks)* commentaire *m*, observations *fpl* **2** *Rad & TV* commentaire *m*; **with c. by Sue Barker** commenté par Sue Barker **3** *(on text)* commentaire *m*
▸▸ *Rad & TV* ***commentary box*** tribune *f* des journalistes

commentate [ˈkɒmənteɪt] *Rad & TV* **VT** commenter
VI faire le commentaire; **to c. on an event** faire le commentaire d'un *ou* commenter un événement

commentator [ˈkɒmənˌteɪtə(r)] **N 1** *Rad & TV* commentateur(trice) *m,f* **2** *Journ* journaliste *mf (de la presse écrite)*; **political c.** journaliste *mf* politique **3** *(analyst ▸ of text)* commentateur(trice) *m,f*

commerce [ˈkɒmɜːs] **N** *(UNCOUNT)* **1** *(trade)* commerce *m*, affaires *fpl*; *Am* **Secretary/Department of C.** ministre *m*/ministère *m* du Commerce **2** *Fig Literary (of ideas, opinions)* relations *fpl*, commerce *m*

commercial [kəˈmɜːʃəl] **ADJ 1** *(economic)* commercial; *(port, tribunal etc)* de commerce; **a c. venture** une entreprise commerciale
2 *(profitable)* commercial, marchand; **a c. success** un succès commercial
3 *Pej (profit-seeking ▸ record, book, pop group, film)* commercial; **their motives are purely c.** ils ont des motivations purement commerciales
4 *(television, radio)* commercial
N *TV & Rad* publicité *f*, spot *m* publicitaire
▸▸ ***commercial artist*** graphiste *mf*; ***commercial attaché*** attaché *m* commercial; ***commercial bank*** banque *f* commerciale; *TV & Rad* ***commercial break*** page *f* de publicité; ***commercial channel*** circuit *m* commercial; ***commercial college*** école *f* de commerce; ***commercial law*** droit *m* commercial; *Old-fashioned* ***commercial traveller*** voyageur *m ou* représentant *m* de commerce, VRP *m*; ***commercial value*** valeur *f* marchande; *Br* ***commercial vehicle*** véhicule *m* utilitaire, commerciale *f*

commercialism [kəˈmɜːʃəˌlɪzəm] **N** *(UNCOUNT)* **1** *(practice of business)* (pratique *f* du) commerce *m*, (pratique *f* des) affaires *fpl* **2** *Pej (profit-seeking)* mercantilisme *m*, esprit *m* commercial; *(on large scale)* affairisme *m*

commercialization, -isation [kəˌmɜːʃəlaɪˈzeɪʃən] **N** commercialisation *f*

commercialize, -ise [kəˈmɜːʃəlaɪz] **VT** commercialiser

commercially [kəˈmɜːʃəlɪ] **ADV** commercialement; **c. available** disponible dans le commerce

commie [ˈkɒmɪ] *Fam Pej* **ADJ** coco
N coco *mf*

commis [ˈkɒmɪ] **N**
▸▸ ***commis chef*** commis *m* (cuisinier *ou* de cuisine); ***commis waiter*** commis *m*

commiserate [kəˈmɪzəreɪt] **VI to c. with sb** *(feel sympathy)* éprouver de la compassion pour qn; *(show sympathy)* témoigner de la sympathie à qn; **we commiserated with him on his misfortune** nous avons compati à sa malchance

commiseration [kəˌmɪzəˈreɪʃən] **N** commisération *f*

commissariat [ˌkɒmɪˈseərɪət] **N 1** *Pol* commissariat *m* **2** *Mil (department)* intendance *f*; *(food supply)* ravitaillement *m*

commissary [ˈkɒmɪsərɪ] *(pl* **commissaries) N 1** *Am Mil (shop)* intendance *f*; *(officer)* intendant *m* **2** *Am Cin (cafeteria)* restaurant *m* (du studio) **3** *Rel* délégué *m (d'un évêque)*

commission [kəˈmɪʃən] **N 1** *(authority for special job)* mission *f*; *Art* commande *f*; **to give a c. to an artist** passer une commande à un artiste; **work done on c.** travail *m* fait sur commande
2 *(delegation of authority)* délégation *f* de pouvoir *ou* d'autorité, mandat *m*; *(formal warrant)* mandat *m*, pouvoir *m*; *Mil* brevet *m*; **to resign one's c.** démissionner; **when he received his c.** quand il a été élevé *ou* promu au grade d'officier
3 *(committee)* commission *f*, comité *m*
4 *Com (fee)* commission *f*, courtage *m*; **to work on a c. basis** travailler à la commission; **I get (a) five percent c.** je reçois une commission de cinq pour cent; **c. only** rémunération *f* à la commission
5 *Law (of crime)* perpétration *f*
6 *Naut (of ship)* armement *m*; **to put a ship into c.** armer un navire
VT 1 *(work of art, book)* commander; *(artist)* passer commande à; **we commissioned an architect to design a new house** nous avons engagé un architecte pour faire les plans d'une nouvelle maison
2 *(grant authority to)* donner pouvoir *ou* mission à, déléguer, charger; **to c. sb to do sth** charger qn de faire qch
3 *Mil (make officer)* nommer à un commandement; **he was commissioned general** il a été promu au grade de *ou* nommé général
4 *(make operative)* mettre en service; *Naut (ship)* mettre en service, armer
• **in commission ADJ** *(gen)* en service; *Naut (ship)* en armement, en service
• **out of commission ADJ** *(gen)* hors service; *(car)* en panne; *Naut (not working)* hors service; *(in reserve)* en réserve; **you'll be out of c. for six weeks** vous serez obligé de suspendre vos activités pendant six semaines **ADV** *Naut* **to take a ship out of c.** désarmer un navire
▸▸ *Com* ***commission agent*** commissionnaire *mf*; *Acct* ***commission note*** note *f* de commission

commissionaire [kəˌmɪʃəˈneə(r)] **N** *Br* portier *m (d'un hôtel etc)*

commissioned [kəˈmɪʃənd] **ADJ** *(operative)* en service; *Naut (ship)* armé
▸▸ *Mil* ***commissioned officer*** officier *m*

commissioner [kəˈmɪʃənə(r)] **N 1** *(member of commission)* membre *m* d'une commission, commissaire *m* **2** *(of police) Br* préfet *m* de police, *Am* (commissaire *m*) divisionnaire *m*; *(of government department)* haut fonctionnaire *m*
▸▸ *Br Law* ***commissioner for oaths*** = officier ayant qualité pour recevoir les déclarations sous serment

commissioning [kəˈmɪʃənɪŋ] **N 1** *Mil (of officer)* nomination *f* à un commandement **2** *Naut (of ship)* armement *m*; *(of new power plant)* mise *f* en service *ou* en exploitation
▸▸ ***commissioning editor*** directeur(trice) *m,f* éditorial(e) *(chargé(e) notamment de commander de nouveaux ouvrages aux auteurs)*

commit [kəˈmɪt] *(pt & pp* **committed,** *cont* **committing) VT 1** *(crime)* commettre, perpétrer; *(mistake)* faire, commettre; **to c. suicide** se suicider; **committing perjury is a crime** se parjurer *ou* faire un faux serment est un délit
2 *(entrust ▸ thing)* confier, remettre; *(▸ person)* confier; **to c. sth to sb's care** confier qch aux soins de qn *ou* à la garde de qn; **to c. a body to the earth** porter un corps en terre; **to c. sth to memory** apprendre qch par cœur; **to c. sth to paper** *or* **writing** coucher *ou* consigner qch par écrit
3 *(confine)* **to c. sb (to a mental hospital)** interner qn; **to c. sb to prison** incarcérer qn
4 *(promise)* engager; **to c. oneself (to sth/to doing sth)** s'engager (à qch/à faire qch); **he refused to c. himself** il s'est tenu sur la réserve, il a refusé de prendre parti *ou* de s'engager; *Mil* **he had committed 2,000 troops to the defence of the village** il avait assigné 2000 soldats à la défense du village
5 *Pol (legislative bill)* renvoyer en commission
6 *Law* **to c. sb for trial** mettre qn en accusation
VI *(emotionally)* s'engager, s'investir; **he can't c.** il ne peut pas s'engager

commitment [kəˈmɪtmənt] **N 1** *(promise, loyalty)* engagement *m*; **to make a c.** *(emotionally, intellectually)* s'engager; **his c. to the proposed reform of the tax system** son soutien pour la réforme du système fiscal qui a été proposée; **I found her lacking in c.** je trouvais qu'elle ne s'investissait pas assez; **so many men avoid c. in relationships** il y a tellement d'hommes qui refusent de s'investir dans les relations amoureuses
2 *(obligation)* obligations *fpl*, responsabilités *fpl*; **I cannot do it because of other commitments** d'autres obligations m'empêchent de le faire; **he has family commitments** il a des obligations familiales; **teaching commitments** charge *f* d'enseignement, enseignement *m*

3 *Com & Fin* engagement *m* financier; **c. of funds** engagement *m* de dépenses; **with no c.** sans obligation d'achat

4 *(to mental hospital)* internement *m*; *(to prison)* incarcération *f*, emprisonnement *m*

5 *Pol (of legislative bill)* renvoi *m* en commission

6 *Law (order)* mandat *m* de dépôt

▸▸ *Banking* ***commitment fee*** commission *f* d'engagement

committal [kəˈmɪtəl] **N 1** *(sending ▸ gen)* remise *f*; *(▸ to mental hospital)* internement *m*; *(▸ to prison)* incarcération *f*, emprisonnement *m* **2** *(of body to grave)* mise *f* en terre

▸▸ *Law* ***committal order*** mandat *m* de dépôt; *Law* ***committal proceedings, committal for trial*** mise *f* en accusation

committed [kəˈmɪtɪd] **ADJ** *(writer, artist)* engagé; **a c. Socialist/Christian** un socialiste/chrétien convaincu; **he didn't seem very c.** son engagement ne semblait pas être très ferme; **to be c. to an idea** être attaché à une idée

committee [kəˈmɪtɪ] **N** commission *f*, comité *m*; *(in government)* commission *f*; **to be** *or* **to sit on a c.** faire partie d'une commission *ou* d'un comité; *Parl* **in c.** en comité

COMP *(member)* d'une commission, d'un comité

▸▸ ***committee of inquiry*** commission *f* d'enquête; ***committee meeting*** réunion *f* de comité; *EU* ***Committee of Permanent Representatives*** Comité *m* des représentants permanents; *EU* ***Committee of the Regions*** Comité *m* des régions; *Br Parl* ***committee stage*** = stade de discussion d'un projet de loi par une commission

committeeman [kəˈmɪtɪmæn] *(pl* **committeemen** [-men]*)* **N** membre *m* d'une commission *ou* d'un comité

committeeperson [kəˈmɪtɪˌpɜːsən] *(pl* **committeepeople** [-ˌpiːpəl]*)* **N** membre *m* d'une commission *ou* d'un comité

committeewoman [kəˈmɪtɪˌwʊmən] *(pl* **committeewomen** [-ˌwɪmɪn]*)* **N** membre *m* d'une commission *ou* d'un comité

commode [kəˈməʊd] **N 1** *(chest of drawers)* commode *f* **2** *(for chamberpot)* chaise *f* percée

commodious [kəˈməʊdɪəs] **ADJ** *Formal (building, room)* spacieux, vaste; *(armchair)* grand et confortable

commodity [kəˈmɒdətɪ] *(pl* **commodities***)* **N 1** *(product)* marchandise *f*; *(consumer good)* produit *m*, article *m*; *(food item)* denrée *f*; **a basic** *or* **staple c.** un produit de base **2** *Econ (raw material)* produit *m* de base, matière *f* première; *St Exch* **to trade in commodities** faire le négoce de matières premières

▸▸ *St Exch* ***commodity broker, commodity dealer*** courtier(ère) *m,f* en matières premières; *St Exch* ***commodity exchange*** échange *m* des marchandises; *St Exch* ***commodity futures*** opérations *fpl* à terme sur matières premières; *St Exch* ***commodity market, commodities market*** marché *m* des matières premières; *St Exch* ***commodity prices*** prix *mpl* des marchandises, cours *mpl* des denrées; *Econ* ***commodity terms of trade*** termes *mpl* de l'échange

commodore [ˈkɒmədɔː(r)] **N 1** *(navy rank)* contre-amiral *m*, *Belg* amiral *m* de flotille, *Can* commodore *m* **2** *Naut (of merchant ships)* chef *m* de convoi; *(of shipping line)* doyen *m* (des capitaines); *(of yacht club)* président *m*

common [ˈkɒmən] **ADJ 1** *(ordinary)* courant, commun; *(plant, species)* commun; **it's quite c.** c'est courant *ou* tout à fait banal; **he's nothing but a c. criminal** ce n'est qu'un vulgaire criminel; **c. name** *(of plant)* nom *m* vulgaire; **a c. occurrence** une chose fréquente *ou* qui arrive souvent; **a c. sight** un spectacle familier; **in c. parlance** dans le langage courant; **the c. man** l'homme du peuple; **the c. people** le peuple, les gens du commun; **c. salt** sel *m* (ordinaire); **a c. soldier** un simple soldat; **it's only c. courtesy to reply** ce serait la moindre des politesses de répondre; *Br* **to have the c. touch** savoir parler aux gens simples

2 *(shared, public)* commun; **by c. consent** d'un commun accord; **the c. good** le bien public; **c. land** terrain *m* communal *ou* banal; **c. ownership** copropriété *f*; **c. staircase** escalier *m* commun; **c. wall** mur *m* commun *ou* mitoyen; **c. ground** *(in interests)* intérêt *m* commun; *(for discussion)* terrain *m* d'entente; *Br* **to make c. cause with sb** faire cause commune avec qn

3 *(widespread)* général, universel; **the c. belief** la croyance universelle; **in c. use** d'usage courant; **it's c. knowledge that…** tout le monde sait que… + *indicative*, il est de notoriété publique que… + *indicative*; **the agreement is c. knowledge** l'accord est connu de tous; **it's c. practice to thank your host** il est d'usage de remercier son hôte

4 *Pej (vulgar)* commun, vulgaire; **a c. little man** un petit homme vulgaire

5 *Gram (gender)* non marqué

6 *Mus* **c. time** *or* **measure** mesure *f* à quatre temps

N *(land)* terrain *m* communal; *Br Law* **right of c.** *(of land)* communauté *f* de jouissance; *(of pasture)* droit *m* de (vaine) pâture; *(of property)* droit *m* de servitude

• **Commons NPL** *Br & Can Pol* **the Commons** les Communes *fpl*

• **commons NPL 1** *Arch or Literary* **the commons** *(common people)* le peuple **2** *Old-fashioned (food)* chère *f*; **to be on short commons** faire maigre chère

• **in common ADV** en commun; **to have sth in c. with sb** avoir qch en commun avec qn; **we have nothing in c.** nous n'avons rien en commun; **they have certain ideas in c.** ils partagent certaines idées

▸▸ *EU* ***Common Agricultural Policy*** politique *f* agricole commune; *Law* ***common assault*** voie *f* de fait simple; *Com* ***common carrier*** transporteur *m* (public), entreprise *f* de transport public; ***common cold*** rhume *m*; *Fin* ***common currency*** monnaie *f* commune; *Fig* **to be c. currency** être monnaie courante; *Math & Fig* ***common denominator*** dénominateur *m* commun; *Math* ***common divisor*** commun diviseur *m*; *Br Sch* ***Common Entrance*** = examen de fin d'études primaires permettant d'entrer dans une "public school"; *EU* ***common external tariff*** tarif *m* externe commun; *Math* ***common factor*** facteur *m* commun; *EU* ***Common Fisheries Policy*** politique *f* commune de la pêche; *EU* ***Common Foreign and Security Policy*** politique *f* étrangère et de sécurité commune; *Comput* ***common gateway interface*** interface *f* commune de passerelle; *Orn* ***common gull*** goéland *m* cendré; ***common law*** common law *f*; *Formerly EU* ***the Common Market*** le marché commun; *Math* ***common multiple*** commun multiple *m*; *Gram* ***common noun*** nom *m* commun; ***common ownership*** copropriété *f*; *Br Sch & Univ* ***common room*** *(for students)* salle *f* commune; *(for staff)* salle *f* des professeurs; ***common sense*** bon sens *m*, sens *m* commun; **it's only c. sense** ça tombe sous le sens; *Am St Exch* ***common stock*** actions *fpl* ordinaires

> **COMMON LAW**
>
> On désigne ainsi l'ensemble des règles de droit qui constituent la base du système juridique des pays de langue anglaise. À l'opposé des systèmes issus du droit romain, qui s'appuie sur la loi telle qu'elle est fixée dans des Codes, ces règles, non écrites, sont établies par la jurisprudence.

commoner [ˈkɒmənə(r)] **N 1** *(not noble)* roturier (ère) *m,f* **2** *Br Law (with joint land rights)* = personne qui a droit de vaine pâture **3** *Br Univ* = étudiant ne bénéficiant pas de bourse (particulièrement à Oxford ou à Cambridge)

common-law ADJ c. husband concubin *m* (reconnu juridiquement); **c. marriage** concubinage *m*; **c. wife** concubine *f* (reconnue juridiquement)

commonly [ˈkɒmənlɪ] **ADV 1** *(usually)* généralement, communément; **what is c. known as…** ce que l'on appelle dans le langage courant… **2** *Pej (vulgarly)* vulgairement

commonness [ˈkɒmənnɪs] **N 1** *(usualness)* caractère *m* commun *ou* ordinaire

2 *(frequency)* fréquence *f*

3 *(universality)* généralité *f*, universalité *f*

4 *Pej (vulgarity)* vulgarité *f*

commonplace [ˈkɒmənˌpleɪs] **ADJ** banal, ordinaire; **DVDs have become c.** les DVD sont devenus courants *ou* sont maintenant monnaie courante

N *(thing)* banalité *f*; *(saying)* lieu *m* commun, platitude *f*

commonweal [ˈkɒmənwiːl] **N** *Literary* bien *m* commun

commonwealth [ˈkɒmənwelθ] **N 1** *(country)* pays *m*; *(state)* État *m*; *(republic)* république *f* **2** *(body politic)* corps *m* politique

• **Commonwealth N 1 the (British) C. (of Nations)** le Commonwealth; **Minister** *or* **Secretary of State for C. Affairs** ministre *m* du Commonwealth **2** *Hist* **the C.** = période de l'histoire britannique de 1649 (mort de Charles Ier) à 1660 (rétablissement de la monarchie) **COMP** *(country)* du Commonwealth

▸▸ ***the Commonwealth of Australia*** le Commonwealth d'Australie; ***Commonwealth Day*** = commémoration de la naissance de la reine Victoria, jour férié dans de nombreux pays du Commonwealth (deuxième lundi de mars); *Br* ***Commonwealth Development Group*** = organisme *m* gouvernemental dont le rôle est de répartir l'aide aux pays en voie de développement; *Br* ***the Commonwealth Games*** les jeux *mpl* du Commonwealth; ***the Commonwealth of Independent States*** la Communauté d'États indépendants

commotion [kəˈməʊʃən] **N 1** *(noise)* brouhaha *m*; **what's all the c. (about)?** qu'est-ce que c'est que ce brouhaha *ou* vacarme? **2** *(disturbance)* agitation *f*; **what a c.!** quel cirque!; **to be in a (state of) c.** *(crowd)* être agité; *(city)* être en émoi; **the news caused a real c.** la nouvelle a causé un véritable désordre **3** *(civil unrest)* insurrection *f*, troubles *mpl*

comms [kɒmz] **ADJ** *Br* de communication

▸▸ *Comput* ***comms package*** logiciel *m* de communication; *Comput* ***comms port*** port *m* de communication

communal [ˈkɒmjʊnəl] **ADJ 1** *(shared ▸ bathroom, changing room)* commun; **c. property** biens *mpl* en commun *ou* en copropriété; **c. room** pièce *f* commune **2** *(of community)* communautaire, collectif; **c. life** la vie commune *ou* communautaire; **a c. activity** une activité collective; **c. violence** violence *f* entre communautés

communally [ˈkɒmjʊnəlɪ] **ADV** collectivement, en commun; **c. owned** en copropriété

commune N [ˈkɒmjuːn] **1** *(group of people)* communauté *f*; **to live in a c.** vivre en communauté **2** *Admin (district)* commune *f*

VI [kəˈmjuːn] **1** *(communicate)* communier; **to c. with nature** communier avec la nature **2** *Rel* communier

• **Commune N** [ˈkɒmjuːn] *Hist* **the (Paris) C.** la Commune

communicable [kəˈmjuːnɪkəbəl] **ADJ** communicable; *Med (disease)* contagieux, transmissible

communicant [kəˈmjuːnɪkənt] **N** *Rel* communiant(e) *m,f*

communicate [kəˈmjuːnɪkeɪt] **VI 1** *(be in touch)* communiquer; *(contact)* prendre contact, se mettre en contact; **they c. with each other by phone** ils communiquent par téléphone; **I find it difficult to c. (with others)** j'ai du mal à entrer en relation avec les autres; **they c. well (with one another)** ils s'entendent bien; **we can't seem to c.** on ne se comprend pas; **we've stopped communicating** on a cessé de communiquer, on ne se parle plus **2** *(rooms ▸ connect)* communiquer **3** *Rel* communier, recevoir la communion

VT 1 *(impart ▸ news)* communiquer, transmettre; *(▸ feelings)* communiquer, faire partager; **she communicated the news to them** elle leur a fait part de la nouvelle **2** *(disease)* transmettre

communicating [kəˈmjuːnɪˌkeɪtɪŋ] **ADJ** *(room)* communicant

▸▸ ***communicating door*** porte *f* de communication

communication [kəˌmjuːnɪˈkeɪʃən] **N 1** *(UNCOUNT) (contact)* communication *f*; **are you in c. with her?** êtes-vous en contact *ou* en relation avec elle?; **to be in close c. with one another** être en relation constante; **we haven't had any c. for six months** nous ne sommes plus en relation(s) depuis six mois; **we broke off all c. with him** nous avons rompu tout contact avec lui; **to be in radio c. with sb** communiquer avec qn par radio, être en communication radio avec qn **2** *(UNCOUNT) (of thoughts, feelings)* communication *f*; **to be good at c., to have good c. skills** avoir des talents de communicateur, être un bon communicateur; **c. gap** manque *m* de communication; **c. problem** problème *m* de communication **3** *(message)* communication *f*, message *m*; **no official c. of his death has yet been received** on n'a encore reçu aucune communication officielle de sa mort

• **communications** NPL *(technology)* communications *fpl*; *(roads, telegraph lines etc)* communications *fpl*; *Mil* liaison *f*, communications *fpl*

▸▸ *Br* ***communication cord*** sonnette *f* d'alarme *(dans les trains)*; ***communications link*** liaison *f* de communications; *Astron* ***communications satellite*** satellite *m* de télécommunication; *Comput* ***communications software*** logiciel *m* de communication

communications-intensive ADJ = utilisant intensivement les moyens de communication

communicative [kəˈmjuːnɪkətɪv] ADJ **1** *(talkative)* communicatif, expansif; **he's not very c.** il est peu communicatif **2** *(ability, difficulty)* de communication

▸▸ *Ling* ***communicative competence*** compétence *f* de communication

communion [kəˈmjuːnjən] N **1** *(sharing)* communion *f*; **a c. of interests** une communauté d'intérêts; **c. with nature** communion *f* avec la nature **2** *Rel (group)* communion *f*; *(denomination)* confession *f*

• **Communion** N *Rel (sacrament)* communion *f*; **to give C.** donner la communion; **to take** *or* **to receive C.** recevoir la communion

▸▸ *Rel* ***communion cup*** calice *m*; *Rel* ***communion service*** célébration *f* de la communion; *Rel* ***communion wafer*** hostie *f*; *Rel* ***communion wine*** vin *m* de messe

communiqué [kəˈmjuːnɪkeɪ] N communiqué *m*

Communism [ˈkɒmjʊˌnɪzəm] N communisme *m*

Communist [ˈkɒmjʊnɪst] N communiste *mf*

ADJ communiste

▸▸ ***Communist International*** Komintern *m*; ***Communist Party*** parti *m* communiste

community [kəˈmjuːnətɪ] *(pl* **communities***)* N **1** *(group of people, animals)* communauté *f*, groupement *m*; **the American c. in Paris** la communauté américaine de Paris; **the business c.** le monde des affaires; **the international c.** la communauté internationale; **a sense of c.** un sens communautaire *ou* de la solidarité

2 *(locality)* communauté *f*; **a small mining c.** une petite communauté minière

3 *Rel* communauté *f*

4 *(sharing)* propriété *f* collective; *Law* communauté *f*; **c. of goods/interests** communauté *f* de biens/d'intérêts

• **Community** N *EU* **the (European) C.** la Communauté (européenne)

▸▸ ***community association*** = en Grande-Bretagne, association socioculturelle locale; *Admin* ***community care*** = système britannique de soins et d'aide au niveau local; ***community centre*** foyer *m* municipal, centre *m* social; *Am TV* ***community channel*** = chaîne du réseau câblé sur laquelle des particuliers peuvent diffuser leurs propres émissions; *Br Formerly Admin* ***community charge*** = impôt aboli en 1993, regroupant taxe d'habitation et impôts locaux, payable par chaque occupant adulte d'une même habitation; *Am Fin* ***community chest*** fonds *m* commun *(à des fins sociales)*; ***community leader*** = personne qui joue un rôle actif dans la vie d'une communauté; ***community policing*** îlotage *m*, *Can* services *mpl* de police communautaires, patrouille *f* pédestre de quartier; ***community relations*** relations *fpl* publiques; *Br* ***community school*** = école servant de maison de la culture; *Law* ***community service*** travail *m* d'intérêt général; ***community singing*** *(UNCOUNT)* chansons *fpl* populaires *(reprises en chœur)*; ***community spirit*** esprit *m* de groupe; ***community worker*** animateur(trice) *m,f* socioculturel(elle)

commutable [kəˈmjuːtəbəl] ADJ **1** *(exchangeable)* interchangeable, permutable **2** *Law (sentence)* commuable

commutation [ˌkɒmjuːˈteɪʃən] N **1** *Law (of penalty)* commutation *f*; **c. of sentence** commutation *f* de peine

2 *(UNCOUNT) (exchange)* échange *m*, substitution *f*

3 *(payment)* échange *m*

4 *Elec (of current)* redressement *m*

5 *Am (commuting)* migration *f* journalière

▸▸ *Am Transp* ***commutation ticket*** carte *f* d'abonnement

commutator [ˈkɒmjuːˌteɪtə(r)] N *Elec* commutateur *m*

commute [kəˈmjuːt] N trajet *m (entre travail et domicile)*; **it's an easy c.** c'est un trajet commode

VI faire un trajet régulier, faire la navette; **I c. from the suburbs** je viens tous les jours de banlieue; **to c. by train/car** se rendre à son travail en train/voiture

VT **1** *(exchange)* substituer, échanger **2** *(convert)* convertir; *Fin* **to c. an annuity into a lump sum** racheter une rente en un seul versement **3** *Law (sentence)* commuer; **a sentence commuted to life imprisonment** une peine commuée en emprisonnement à vie

commuter [kəˈmjuːtə(r)] N banlieusard(e) *m,f (qui fait un trajet journalier pour se rendre au travail)*, *Belg* navetteur(euse) *m,f*, *Suisse* pendulaire *mf*; **I've been a c. for 15 years** ça fait 15 ans que je fais la navette (entre chez moi et le travail); **the problems caused by c. traffic** les problèmes provoqués par l'utilisation de la voiture pour se rendre au travail; **c. traffic is very heavy this evening** la circulation en direction de la banlieue est très dense ce soir

COMP *(line, train)* de banlieue

▸▸ ***commuter airline*** compagnie *f* d'aviation court-courrier; *Br* ***the commuter belt*** la grande banlieue; ***commuter plane*** commuter *m*; ***commuter town*** cité-dortoir *f*

commuterland [kəˈmjuːtəlænd] N = grande banlieue considérée comme un pays à part, où l'on ne fait rien d'autre que dormir

commuting [kəˈmjuːtɪŋ] N *(UNCOUNT)* trajets *mpl* réguliers, migrations *fpl* quotidiennes *(entre le domicile, généralement en banlieue, et le lieu de travail)*

comp [kɒmp] N *Fam* **1** *Typ (compositor)* metteur *m* (en pages)◻ **2** *(ticket)* exonéré◻ *m*

compact ADJ [kəmˈpækt] **1** *(small)* compact, petit; *(person)* trapu; **the gadget is c. and easy to use** ce gadget ne prend pas de place et est facile à utiliser **2** *(dense)* dense, serré **3** *(concise)* concis, condensé

VT [kəmˈpækt] *(compress)* compacter, tasser; *Comput (file)* comprimer

N [ˈkɒmpækt] **1** *(for powder)* poudrier *m* **2** *Am (car)* (voiture *f*) compacte *f*, petite voiture *f* **3** *Formal (agreement)* convention *f*, contrat *m*; *(informal)* accord *m*, entente *f*

▸▸ ***compact disc*** (disque *m*) compact *m*, CD *m*; ***compact disc interactive*** CDI *m*; ***compact disc player*** platine *f* CD; ***compact disc recorder*** graveur *m* de disque compact; ***compact disc rewritable*** CD *m* réinscriptible; ***compact disc video*** CD vidéo *m*

compacting [kəmˈpæktɪŋ] N *Comput* compression *f*

compactly [kəmˈpæktlɪ] ADV **1** *(made)* de manière compacte; **c. designed** conçu sans perte de place **2** *(concisely)* de manière concise

compactness [kəmˈpæktnɪs] N **1** *(smallness)* compacité *f* **2** *(denseness)* compacité *f*, densité *f* **3** *(conciseness)* concision *f*

Companies Act [ˈkʌmpənɪz-] N *Br Law* Loi *f* sur les sociétés

companion [kəmˈpænjən] N **1** *(friend* ▸ *male)* compagnon *m*; *(*▸ *female)* compagne *f*; *(employee)* dame *f* de compagnie; **to be employed as a c. to sb** être employé pour tenir compagnie à qn; **a travelling c.** un compagnon de voyage; **a drinking c.** un compagnon de bistrot; **companions in arms/distress** compagnons *mpl* d'armes/d'infortune

2 *(one of pair)* pendant *m*; **to be a c. to sth** faire pendant à qch

3 *(handbook)* manuel *m*

4 *(in titles)* compagnon *m*; **C. to English Literature** *(title of book)* guide *m* de la littérature anglaise

5 *Naut* capot *m* (d'escalier)

▸▸ ***Companion of Honour*** = décoration britannique remise aux citoyens qui ont rendu des services à l'État, chevalier *m* de la Légion d'honneur; *Naut* ***companion ladder*** échelle *f* de commandement; ***companion volume*** *(book)* volume *m* qui va de pair

companionable [kəmˈpænjənəbəl] ADJ *(person)* sociable, d'une compagnie agréable; **they sat in c. silence** ils étaient assis tranquillement sans éprouver le besoin de parler

companionship [kəmˈpænjənʃɪp] N *(UNCOUNT) (fellowship)* compagnie *f*; *(friendship)* amitié *f*, camaraderie *f*; **he enjoys the c. of the football team** il aime la camaraderie qui règne au sein de l'équipe de football; **the dog provides c. for her** le chien lui fait de la compagnie *ou* lui tient compagnie

companionway [kəmˈpænjənweɪ] N *Naut* escalier *m* de descente; *(on smaller boat)* montée *f*, descente *f*

company [ˈkʌmpənɪ] *(pl* **companies***)* N **1** *(companionship)* compagnie *f*; **we enjoy one another's c.** nous aimons être ensemble; **I like his c.** j'aime sa compagnie, j'aime être avec lui; **she's good c.** elle est d'agréable compagnie; **to keep sb c.** tenir compagnie à qn; **to be fond of one's own c.** aimer être seul; **in c. with others** en compagnie d'autres; **we request the pleasure of your c. at dinner** nous ferez-vous le plaisir de venir dîner?; **here's where we part c.** voilà où nos chemins se séparent; *Fig* là, je ne suis plus d'accord avec vous

2 *(companions)* compagnie *f*, fréquentation *f*; **I don't like the c. he keeps** je n'aime pas ses fréquentations; **she has got into** *or* **she's keeping bad c.** elle a de mauvaises fréquentations; *Fig* **if I'm wrong, I'm in good c.** si j'ai tort, je ne suis pas le seul; *Prov* **a man is known by the c. he keeps** dis-moi qui tu fréquentes, je te dirai qui tu es

3 *(people present)* assemblée *f*, personnes *fpl* présentes; **to do sth in c.** faire qch en public; **you mustn't speak like that in c.** on ne dit pas ces choses-là en société; **present c. excepted** à part les personnes ici présentes

4 *(UNCOUNT) (guests)* invités *mpl*, compagnie *f*; **are you expecting c.?** attendez-vous de la visite?; *Fam* **we've got c.!** *(there's someone else here, we're being followed)* nous avons de la compagnie!

5 *Com (firm)* société *f*, compagnie *f*; **to form** *or* **to incorporate a c.** constituer une société; **Jones & C.** Jones et Compagnie; **to do sth on** *or* **in c. time** faire qch pendant les heures de travail

6 *(group of people)* compagnie *f*, assemblée *f*

7 *Theat (of actors)* troupe *f*, compagnie *f*

8 *Mil* compagnie *f*; *Naut (crew)* équipage *m*

9 *(of girl guides)* compagnie *f*

10 *(guild)* corporation *f* de marchands

COMP *(policy)* d'entreprise

• **Company** N *Am Fam* **the C.** la CIA◻

▸▸ ***company accounts*** comptes *mpl* sociaux; ***company car*** voiture *f* de fonction; ***company director*** directeur(trice) *m,f*; *Br* ***company law*** droit *m* des sociétés; ***company lawyer*** avocat(e) *m,f* d'une entreprise *ou* société; ***company policy*** politique *f* de l'entreprise; ***company secretary*** secrétaire *mf* général(e) *(d'une entreprise)*; *Mil* ***company sergeant-major*** adjudant *m*

comparability [ˌkɒmpərəˈbɪlətɪ] N comparabilité *f*

comparable [ˈkɒmpərəbəl] ADJ comparable; **to be c. to sth** être comparable à qch; **the salaries aren't at all c.** il n'y a pas de comparaison possible entre les salaires

comparative [kəmˈpærətɪv] ADJ **1** *(relative)* relatif; **the c. wealth of the two countries** la fortune relative des deux pays; **she's a c. stranger to me** je la connais relativement peu **2** *(study)* comparatif; *(field of study)* comparé **3** *Gram* comparatif

N *Gram* comparatif *m*; **in the c.** au comparatif

▸▸ ***comparative adverb*** adverbe *m* de comparaison *ou* comparatif; ***comparative grammar*** grammaire *f* comparée; ***comparative linguistics*** linguistique *f* comparée; ***comparative literature*** littérature *f* comparée

comparatively [kəmˈpærətɪvlɪ] ADV **1** *(quite)* relativement **2** *(study)* comparativement

compare [kəmˈpeə(r)] VT **1** *(contrast)* comparer, mettre en comparaison; **let's c. Fitzgerald with**

Hemingway comparons Fitzgerald à *ou* avec Hemingway; **compared with** *or* **to sth** en comparaison de *ou* par comparaison avec qch; **compared with the others she's brilliant** elle est brillante par rapport aux autres; **compared with last year's figures** par rapport aux chiffres de l'année dernière; **to c. notes** échanger ses impressions **2** *(liken)* comparer, assimiler; **to c. sth to sth** comparer qch à qch; **it's impossible to c. the two systems** il n'y a pas de comparaison possible entre les deux systèmes **3** *Gram* former les degrés de comparaison de

VI être comparable (**with** à); **to c. well** *or* **favourably (with sth)** soutenir la comparaison (avec qch); **how do the two candidates c.?** quelles sont les qualités respectives des deux candidats?; **how do the brands c. in (terms of) price?** les marques sont-elles comparables du point de vue prix?; **other kinds of washing powder just can't c.** les autres marques de lessive ne sont pas à la hauteur de celle-ci; **her cooking doesn't** *or* **can't c. with yours** il n'y a aucune comparaison entre sa cuisine et la tienne

N *Literary* **beauty beyond c.** beauté *f* sans pareille

comparison [kəm'pærɪsən] **N 1** *(gen)* comparaison *f*; **there's no c.** il n'y a aucune comparaison (possible); **to draw** *or* **to make a c. between sth and sth** faire la comparaison de qch avec qch *ou* entre qch et qch; **this book stands** *or* **bears c. with the classics** ce livre soutient la comparaison avec les classiques; **without c., beyond all c.** sans comparaison **2** *Gram* comparaison *f*; **degrees of c.** degrés *mpl* de comparaison

• **by comparison ADV** par comparaison

• **in comparison ADV** par comparaison

• **in comparison with PREP** en comparaison de, par rapport à

compartment [kəm'pɑːtmənt] **N 1** *(section)* compartiment *m* **2** *Naut & Rail* compartiment *m*

compartmentalize, -ise [ˌkɒmpɑːt'mentəlaɪz] **VT** compartimenter

compass ['kʌmpəs] **N 1** *(for direction)* boussole *f*; *Naut* compas *m*; **to take a c. bearing** prendre un relèvement au compas

2 *Geom* compas *m*

3 *(limits)* étendue *f*; *(range)* portée *f*; **within the narrow c. of this book** dans les limites restreintes de ce livre; **beyond the c. of the human mind** audelà de la portée de l'esprit humain

4 *Mus (of voice)* étendue *f*, portée *f*

VT 1 *(go round)* faire le tour de; *(surround)* encercler, entourer **2** *Literary (accomplish ▸ goal)* atteindre; *(▸ ends)* en venir à; *(▸ task)* accomplir

• **compasses NPL** *Geom* **(a pair of) compasses** un compas

COMP *(error)* du compas

►► *Naut* **compass card** rose *f* des vents; **compass course** route *f* magnétique; **compass point** aire *f* de vent; *Naut* **compass rose** rose *f* des vents; *Archit* **compass window** fenêtre *f* en saillie ronde

compassion [kəm'pæʃən] **N** compassion *f*, pitié *f*; **to arouse c.** faire pitié, exciter la compassion; **to show c.** montrer de la compassion; **you have no c.** tu n'as pas de pitié

►► **compassion fatigue** = lassitude du public à l'égard des nécessiteux

compassionate [kəm'pæʃənət] **ADJ** compatissant; **on c. grounds** pour des raisons personnelles *ou* familiales

►► **compassionate leave** congé *m* exceptionnel; *Mil* permission *f* exceptionnelle *(pour raisons personnelles)*

compassionately [kəm'pæʃənətlɪ] **ADV** avec compassion

compatibility [kəmˌpætə'bɪlətɪ] **N** compatibilité *f*

compatible [kəm'pætəbəl] **ADJ** compatible (**with** avec); *Comput* **IBM-c.** compatible IBM

compatibly [kəm'pætəblɪ] **ADV** d'une manière compatible (**with** avec)

compatriot [kəm'pætrɪət] **N** compatriote *mf*

compel [kəm'pel] *(pt & pp* **compelled,** *cont* **compelling)** **VT 1** *(force)* contraindre, obliger; **to c. sb to do sth** contraindre *ou* forcer qn à faire qch; **ill health compelled her to retire** pour des raisons de santé, elle a été obligée de prendre sa retraite **2** *(demand)* imposer, forcer; **the sort of woman who compels admiration** le genre de femme qu'on ne peut s'empêcher d'admirer *ou* qui force l'admiration; **a tone of voice that compels attention** un ton de voix qui retient l'attention

compelling [kəm'pelɪŋ] **ADJ 1** *(reason, desire, urge)* convaincant, irrésistible **2** *(book, film, performance)* envoûtant; **her book makes c. reading** son livre est captivant *ou* prenant; **a c. speaker** un orateur qui subjugue *ou* captive son auditoire

compellingly [kəm'pelɪŋlɪ] **ADV** irrésistiblement, d'une façon irrésistible

compendium [kəm'pendɪəm] *(pl* **compendiums** *or* **compendia** [-dɪə]) **N 1** *(summary)* abrégé *m*, précis *m* **2** *Br (collection)* collection *f*

►► **compendium of games** boîte *f* de jeux

compensable [kəm'pensəbəl] **ADJ** indemnisable; *Acct* **c. loss** perte *f* indemnisable

compensate ['kɒmpenseɪt] **VT 1** *(make amends to ▸ person)* dédommager, indemniser; **to c. sb for sth** *(for loss)* dédommager qn de qch; *(for injury)* dédommager qn pour qch **2** *(offset)* compenser, contrebalancer; *Tech* compenser, neutraliser

VI 1 *(make up)* être une *ou* servir de compensation, compenser; **she compensates for her short stature by wearing high heels** elle porte des talons hauts pour compenser sa petite taille **2** *(with money)* dédommager, indemniser **3** *Psy* compenser

compensating ['kɒmpenˌseɪtɪŋ] **ADJ** compensateur

►► **compensating magnet** aimant *m* correcteur *ou* de correction; *Fin* **compensating payment** règlement *m* en compensation

compensation [ˌkɒmpen'seɪʃən] **N 1** *(recompense)* indemnité *f*, dédommagement *m*; *(payment)* rémunération *f*; **all of the victims will receive c.** toutes les victimes recevront une indemnité; **working for oneself has its compensations** travailler à son compte a ses avantages; **in c. for** en compensation de; **by way of c. for your wasted time** pour compenser le temps perdu **2** *(adaptation)* compensation *f*; *(in weight)* contrepoids *m*; *Tech* compensation *f*, neutralisation *f*

►► *Br Law* **compensation order** = obligation de la part de l'accusé de réparer ses actions; *Br* **compensation package** *(for redundancy)* prime *f* de licenciement; *Am (when starting new job)* avantages *mpl* sociaux

compensator ['kɒmpenˌseɪtə(r)] **N**

►► *Tech* **compensator arm** bras *m* compensateur; **compensator valve** valve *f* de compensation

compensatory [ˌkɒmpen'seɪtərɪ] **ADJ** compensateur, compensatoire

►► *Law* **compensatory damages** dommages-intérêts *mpl* compensatoires; *EU* **compensatory levy** prélèvement *m* compensatoire

compere ['kɒmpeə(r)] *Br* **N** animateur(trice) *m,f*, présentateur(trice) *m,f*

VT animer, présenter

VI animer, présenter

compete [kəm'piːt] **VI 1** *(vie)* rivaliser; **to c. with sb for sth** rivaliser avec qn pour qch, disputer qch à qn; **seven candidates are competing for the position** sept candidats se disputent le poste; *Fig* **her cooking can't c. with yours** sa cuisine n'a rien de commun *ou* ne peut pas rivaliser avec la vôtre; **children here aren't encouraged to c.** ici, les enfants ne sont pas encouragés à la compétition **2** *Com (one company)* faire de la concurrence (**with** à); *(two or more companies)* se faire concurrence; **they c. with foreign companies for contracts** ils sont en concurrence avec des entreprises étrangères pour obtenir des contrats; **we have to c. on an international level** nous devons être à la hauteur de la concurrence sur le plan international **3** *Sport (take part)* participer; *(contend)* concourir; **to c. against sb for sth** concourir *ou* être en compétition avec qn pour qch; **there are only three teams competing** il n'y a que trois équipes sur les rangs

competence ['kɒmpɪtəns] **N 1** *(ability)* compétence *f* (**in** pour *ou* en), aptitude *f* (**in** à *ou* pour); **to have the c. to do sth** avoir les moyens *ou* la capacité de faire qch; **that's beyond my c.** c'est audelà de mes moyens, ça dépasse mes compétences **2** *Law (of court)* compétence *f*; *(of evidence)* admissibilité *f*; *(of witness)* habilité *f*; **to be within the c. of the court** être de la compétence du tribunal **3** *Ling* compétence *f*

competency ['kɒmpɪtənsɪ] *(pl* **competencies)** **N 1** *Law* **c. to stand trial** aptitude *f* à comparaître **2** *(ability)* compétence *f* (**in** pour *ou* en), aptitude *f* (**in** à *ou* pour)

competent ['kɒmpɪtənt] **ADJ 1** *(capable)* compétent, capable; *(qualified)* qualifié; **is she c. to handle the accounts?** est-elle compétente *ou* qualifiée pour tenir la comptabilité?; **he's quite c. at French** il a un bon niveau de français; **a c. piece of work** du bon travail **2** *(sufficient)* suffisant **3** *Law (witness)* habile; *(court)* compétent; *(evidence)* admissible, recevable; **c. to inherit** habilité à succéder

competently ['kɒmpɪtəntlɪ] **ADV 1** *(capably)* avec compétence **2** *(sufficiently)* suffisamment

competition [ˌkɒmpɪ'tɪʃən] **N 1** *(rivalry)* compétition *f*, rivalité *f*; **c. for the position is fierce** il y a beaucoup de concurrence pour le poste, on se dispute âprement le poste; **to be in c. (with sb)** être en compétition *ou* concurrence (avec qn); **to enter into c. with sb** concurrencer *ou* faire concurrence à qn

2 *Com & Econ* concurrence *f*; **unfair c.** concurrence *f* déloyale; **what's the c. doing?** que fait la concurrence?, que font nos rivaux *ou* concurrents?; **the company has to stay ahead of the c.** l'entreprise doit rester plus compétitive que les autres

3 *(opposition)* **you're up against some tough c.** *(in race)* vous êtes en face d'adversaires de taille; *(for job, university)* la concurrence est rude

4 *(contest)* concours *m*; *Sport* compétition *f*; *(race)* course *f*; **beauty/fishing c.** concours *m* de beauté/de pêche; **c. winner** gagnant(e) *m,f*; **to enter a c.** se présenter à un concours; **that's him out of the c.** le voilà hors compétition

5 *Biol* concurrence *f*

►► *Aut* **competition car** voiture *f* de compétition

competitive [kəm'petətɪv] **ADJ 1** *(involving competition)* de compétition **2** *(person)* qui a l'esprit de compétition; *(atmosphere, environment)* de compétition; **he's so c.** il a vraiment l'esprit de compétition **3** *Com & Econ (product, price)* concurrentiel, compétitif; *(company, industry)* compétitif; **in a c. marketplace** dans un marché de concurrence; **to offer c. terms** proposer des prix très compétitifs

►► *Com & Mktg* **competitive advantage** avantage *m* concurrentiel; *Com & Mktg* **competitive awareness** sensibilité *f* compétitive; **competitive bidding** appel *m* d'offres; **competitive edge** (léger) avantage *m* concurrentiel; **competitive examination** concours *m*; **competitive pricing** fixation *f* des prix compétitifs; **competitive sports** sports *mpl* de compétition; **competitive strategy** stratégie *f* concurrentielle

competitively [kəm'petətɪvlɪ] **ADV** avec un esprit de compétition; *Com* **c. priced goods** produits *mpl* au prix compétitif

competitiveness [kəm'petətɪvnɪs] **N** *(of product)* concurrence *f*, *(of company, price)* compétitivité *f*; *(of person)* esprit *m* de compétition

competitor [kəm'petɪtə(r)] **N** *(gen) & Com & Sport* concurrent(e) *m,f*; *(participant)* participant(e) *m,f*

compilation [ˌkɒmpɪ'leɪʃən] **N** compilation *f*

►► **compilation album** compilation *f*

compile [kəm'paɪl] **VT 1** *(gather ▸ facts, material)* compiler **2** *(compose ▸ list)* dresser; *(▸ dictionary)* rédiger *(par compilation)* **3** *Comput* compiler

compiler [kəm'paɪlə(r)] **N 1** *(gen)* compilateur (trice) *m,f* **2** *(of dictionary)* rédacteur(trice) *m,f* **3** *Comput* compilateur *m*

complacence [kəm'pleɪsəns], **complacency** [kəm'pleɪsənsɪ] **N** autosatisfaction *f*, complaisance *f*

complacent [kəm'pleɪsənt] **ADJ** *(person)* satisfait *ou* content de soi, suffisant, complaisant; *(look, remark)* très satisfait; **to be c. about sth** faire de l'autosatisfaction à propos de qch

Attention: ne pas confondre avec l'adjectif anglais **complaisant**.

complacently [kəm'pleɪsəntlɪ] ADV *(act, smile, reply)* d'un air suffisant, avec suffisance *ou* complaisance; *(speak)* d'un ton suffisant, avec suffisance

complain [kəm'pleɪn] VI **1** *(grumble)* se plaindre; **he's always complaining** il n'arrête pas de se plaindre; **he complained of a headache** il s'est plaint d'un mal de tête; *Fam* **how's it going? – can't c.** comment ça va? – je n'ai pas à me plaindre *ou* ça peut aller **2** *(make formal protest)* formuler une plainte *ou* une réclamation, se plaindre; **to c. to sb (about sth)** se plaindre à *ou* auprès de qn (au sujet de qch)

VT **to c. that...** se plaindre que... + *indicative*

complainant [kəm'pleɪnənt] N *Law* demandeur(eresse) *m,f*, plaignant(e) *m,f*

complaint [kəm'pleɪnt] N **1** *(official protest)* plainte *f*, récrimination *f*; *Com* réclamation *f*; *Law (in criminal law)* plainte *f*; *(in civil law)* demande *f* introductive d'instance; **to make** *or* **to lodge a c.** se plaindre; **to lodge a c. against sb** porter plainte contre qn **2** *(grievance)* sujet *m ou* motif *m* de plainte, grief *m*; **I have no c.** *or* **no cause for c.** je n'ai aucune raison de me plaindre; **do you have any complaints about the company?** est-ce que vous avez à vous plaindre de l'entreprise?; **this is her latest c.** c'est la dernière chose dont elle s'est plainte **3** *(illness)* maladie *f*, affection *f*; **she has a liver c.** elle souffre du foie

▸▸ ***complaints book*** cahier *m* de réclamations; ***complaints department*** service *m* des réclamations

complaisance [kəm'pleɪzəns] N *Formal* complaisance *f*, obligeance *f*

complaisant [kəm'pleɪzənt] ADJ *Formal* complaisant, obligeant

Attention: ne pas confondre avec l'adjectif **complacent**.

complement N ['kɒmplɪmənt] **1** *(gen)* complément *m*; **with a full c.** au grand complet; **the English department now has a full c. of staff** tous les postes du département d'anglais sont pourvus; **have we got a full c.?** *(in office, team etc)* est-ce que nous sommes au complet?

2 *Math* complément *m*

3 *Gram (of verb)* complément *m*; *(of subject)* attribut *m*

4 *Naut (ship's crew, staff)* personnel *m*, effectif *m* (complet)

5 *Mus* complément *m*

6 *Med* complément *m*

VT ['kɒmplɪ,ment] compléter, être le complément de; **they c. each other well** *(of two people)* ils se complètent parfaitement

complementary [,kɒmplɪ'mentərɪ] ADJ **1** *(gen)* complémentaire; **the two pieces are c.** les deux morceaux se complètent **2** *Math* complémentaire

▸▸ *Geom* ***complementary angle*** angle *m* complémentaire; ***complementary medicine*** médecine *f* douce

complete [kəm'pli:t] ADJ **1** *(entire)* complet(ète), total; **a c. set of golf clubs** un jeu complet de clubs; **Christmas wouldn't be c. without the traditional dinner** Noël ne serait pas Noël sans le repas traditionnel; **my happiness is c.** mon bonheur est total, rien ne manque à mon bonheur; **the c. works of Shakespeare** les œuvres complètes de Shakespeare **2** *(finished)* achevé, terminé **3** *(as intensifier)* complet(ète), absolu; **if the job is not done to your c. satisfaction** si vous n'êtes pas entièrement satisfait du travail effectué; **I need a c. break from teaching** j'ai besoin de vraies vacances où je ne penserai plus du tout à mes cours; **he's a c. fool** c'est un crétin fini *ou* un parfait imbécile; **he's a c. stranger** c'est un total inconnu; **a c. (and utter) failure** un échec total *ou* sur toute la ligne; **the project was a c. success** le projet a pleinement réussi

VT **1** *(make whole)* compléter; **I just need one more card to c. my collection** il me manque une seule carte pour compléter ma collection; *Com* **to c. an order** exécuter une commande **2** *(finish)* achever, finir; *(training, apprenticeship)* accomplir **3** *(form, questionnaire)* remplir

• **complete with** PREP avec, doté *ou* pourvu de; **c. with instructions** comprenant des instructions

completely [kəm'pli:tlɪ] ADV complètement; **I c. understand your frustration** je comprends tout à fait ta frustration

completeness [kəm'pli:tnɪs] N état *m* complet; **there's a c. to it** *(to novel, film etc)* il a un caractère abouti; **they added a final volume for c.** ils ont ajouté un dernier volume pour que l'ensemble soit complet

completion [kəm'pli:ʃən] N **1** *(of work)* achèvement *m*; **the bridge is due for c. in January** le pont doit être fini en janvier; **in the process of c.** en (cours d')achèvement; **the project is nearing c.** le projet est près de son terme *ou* s'achève **2** *Law (of sale)* exécution *f*; **payment on c. of contract** paiement *m* à l'exécution du contrat **3** *(of happiness, misfortune)* comble *m*

▸▸ ***completion date*** *(for building, repair work)* date *f* d'achèvement; *Com (for sale)* date *f* d'exécution

complex ['kɒmpleks] ADJ *(gen)* complexe

N **1** *(system)* complexe *m*, ensemble *m*; **housing c.** grand ensemble *m*; **shopping/industrial c.** complexe *m* commercial/industriel **2** *Psy* complexe *m*; **she has a c. about her weight** elle est complexée par son poids; **you'll give her a c.** tu vas lui donner un complexe

▸▸ *Math* ***complex number*** nombre *m* complexe; *Gram* ***complex sentence*** phrase *f* complexe

complexion [kəm'plekʃən] N **1** *(of face)* teint *m*; **to have a dark/fair c.** avoir le teint mat/clair; **to have a good** *or* **clear c.** avoir une belle peau **2** *(aspect)* aspect *m*; **that puts a different c. on things** voilà qui change la situation

complexity [kəm'pleksətɪ] *(pl* **complexities**) N complexité *f*

compliance [kəm'plaɪəns] N **1** *(conformity)* conformité *f* **2** *(agreement)* acquiescement *m*; *(submission)* complaisance *f* **3** *Tech (flexibility)* élasticité *f*

• **in compliance with** PREP conformément à; **in c. with the law** conformément à la loi; **she acted in c. with the terms of the contract** elle a agi en accord avec les stipulations du contrat

compliant [kəm'plaɪənt] ADJ **1** *(person)* accommodant, docile **2** *Comput* conforme *(***with** à)

complicate ['kɒmplɪkeɪt] VT compliquer, embrouiller; **that complicates matters** cela complique les choses; **why c. things?** pourquoi se compliquer la vie?; **her illness was complicated by an infection** sa maladie s'est compliquée d'une infection

complicated ['kɒmplɪkeɪtɪd] ADJ *(complex)* compliqué, complexe; *(muddled)* embrouillé; **to become** *or* **to get c.** se compliquer

complication [,kɒmplɪ'keɪʃən] N *(gen)* complication *f*; *Med* **if no complications set in** s'il ne survient pas de complications

complicity [kəm'plɪsətɪ] N complicité *f*; **his c. in the murder** sa complicité dans le meurtre

compliment N ['kɒmplɪmənt] *(expression of praise)* compliment *m*; **to pay sb a c.** faire *ou* adresser un compliment à qn; *Ironic* **she returned the c.** elle lui a retourné le compliment

VT ['kɒmplɪment] faire des compliments à, complimenter; **to c. sb on sth** féliciter qn de qch, faire des compliments à qn sur qch; **she complimented him on his English/haircut** elle l'a félicité *ou* elle lui a fait des compliments pour son anglais/sa coupe de cheveux

• **compliments** NPL ['kɒmplɪmənts] *Formal (respects)* compliments *mpl*, respects *mpl*; **to convey** *or* **present one's compliments to sb** présenter ses compliments *ou* hommages à qn; **give him my compliments** faites-lui mes compliments; **compliments of the season** *(greeting, on card)* meilleurs vœux; **with compliments** *(on compliments slip, card)* avec nos compliments; **my compliments to the chef** mes compliments au chef; *Com* **to send sth with one's compliments** envoyer qch à titre gratuit *ou* gracieux (avec ses compliments)

▸▸ *Com* ***compliments slip*** papillon *m (joint à un envoi)*

complimentary [,kɒmplɪ'mentərɪ] ADJ **1** *(approving)* flatteur; **they weren't very c. about my paintings** ils ne se sont pas montrés très flatteurs à l'égard de mes tableaux; **c. remarks** compliments *mpl*, félicitations *fpl* **2** *(given free)* gratuit, gracieux

▸▸ ***complimentary copy*** *(of book)* exemplaire *m* offert à titre gracieux; ***complimentary ticket*** billet *m* de faveur

comply [kəm'plaɪ] *(pt & pp* **complied**) VI **1** *(agree, consent)* accepter, consentir; **to c. with sth** *(obey* ▸ *code, specifications)* se conformer à qch; *(*▸ *contract)* respecter qch; *(*▸ *request)* accepter qch; *(*▸ *order)* obéir à qch; **to c. with the rules** observer *ou* respecter les règlements; **I will c. with your wishes** je me conformerai à vos désirs **2** *(machinery)* être conforme; **cars must c. with existing regulations** les voitures doivent être conformes aux normes en vigueur

component [kəm'pəʊnənt] N *(of program, education, system)* élément *m*; *Elec, Phys & Chem* composant *m*; *Aut & Tech* pièce *f*

ADJ composant, constituant

▸▸ ***component part*** *(of machine)* pièce *f* détachée; *(of theory)* composante *f*

comport [kəm'pɔ:t] *Formal* VT **to c. oneself** se comporter, se conduire

VI *(suit, be appropriate)* concorder (**with** avec)

comportment [kəm'pɔ:tmənt] N *Formal* comportement *m*, conduite *f*

compose [kəm'pəʊz] VT **1** *(make up)* **to be composed of sth** se composer *ou* être composé de qch

2 *(letter, musical or literary work)* composer; **I composed a reply to his letter** j'ai formulé une réponse à sa lettre

3 *Typ (set)* composer

4 *(make calm)* **c. yourself!** calmez-vous!; **she composed her features** elle a composé son visage; **I need to c. my thoughts** j'ai besoin de mettre de l'ordre dans mes idées

5 *Formal (settle* ▸ *quarrel)* arranger, régler

VI *(create music)* composer

composed [kəm'pəʊzd] ADJ calme, posé

composer [kəm'pəʊzə(r)] N *Mus* compositeur(trice) *m,f*

composing [kəm'pəʊzɪŋ] N **1** *(of letter, musical or literary work)* composition *f*, création *f* **2** *Typ* composition *f*

composite ['kɒmpəzɪt] ADJ **1** *(gen) & Archit & Phot* composite **2** *Bot & Math* composé

N **1** *(compound)* composite *m*; *Archit* (ordre *m*) composite *m* **2** *Bot* composée *f*, composacée *f* **3** *Pol* = proposition discutée au niveau national

▸▸ *St Exch* ***composite index*** indice *m* composé *ou* composite; *Cin & TV* ***composite print*** copie *f* standard

composition [,kɒmpə'zɪʃən] N **1** *(of letter, musical or literary work)* composition *f*, création *f*; **poetry of his own c.** poésie de sa composition

2 *(musical or literary work)* composition *f*, œuvre *f*

3 *Sch (essay)* dissertation *f*

4 *(constitution* ▸ *parts)* composition *f*, constitution *f*; *(*▸ *mixture)* mélange *m*, composition *f*; *Constr* stuc *m*; **the chemical c. of water** la composition chimique de l'eau

5 *Art (distribution of elements)* composition *f*

6 *Ling (of sentence)* construction *f*; *(of word)* composition *f*

7 *Typ* composition *f*

8 *Law (agreement* ▸ *with creditors)* arrangement *m*, accommodement *m*; *(on bankruptcy)* concordat *m* préventif

compositor [kəm'pɒzɪtə(r)] N *Typ* compositeur(trice) *m,f*

compos mentis [,kɒmpəs'mentɪs] ADJ *Law* sain d'esprit; *Fam* **to be c.** *(not drunk, not half asleep)* être en possession de toutes ses facultés; **I'm not c. yet** je suis encore à moitié endormi

compost [*Br* 'kɒmpɒst, *Am* 'kɒmpəʊst] N compost *m*

VT **1** *(treat with compost)* composter *(une terre)* **2** *(convert into compost)* faire du compost à partir de

▸▸ ***compost bin*** composteur *m*; ***compost heap*** tas *m* de compost

composter [*Br* ˈkɒmpɒstə(r), *Am* ˈkɒmpəʊstə(r)] **N** composteur *m*

composure [kəmˈpəʊʒə(r)] **N** calme *m*, sang-froid *m*; **to lose one's c.** perdre son calme; **to recover** *or* **regain one's c.** se ressaisir

compote [ˈkɒmpɒt] **N** *Culin (dessert)* compote *f*; *Am (dish)* compotier *m*

compound **ADJ** [ˈkɒmpaʊnd] **1** *(gen)* composé; *Chem* composé, combiné; *Tech (engine)* compound *(inv)*
2 *Gram (sentence)* complexe; *(tense, word)* composé
3 *Mus* composé
4 *Math (number)* complexe
N [ˈkɒmpaʊnd] **1** *(enclosed area)* enceinte *f*, enclos *m*; *(for prisoners of war)* camp *m*
2 *(in South Africa ▸ for workers)* quartier *m* des noirs; *(▸ for livestock)* parc *m* à bétail
3 *(mixture)* composé *m*, mélange *m*; *Chem* composé *m*; *Tech* compound *m*
4 *Gram* mot *m* composé
VT [kəmˈpaʊnd] **1** *Chem (combine)* combiner, mélanger; *(form by combining)* composer **2** *(make worse ▸ difficulties, mistake)* aggraver **3** *Law (settle)* régler à l'amiable; **to c. a debt** faire une transaction pour le règlement d'une dette
VI [kəmˈpaʊnd] *Law* composer, transiger; *(with one's creditors)* arriver à un concordat; **to c. with sb for sth** transiger avec qn au sujet de *ou* pour qch
▸▸ *Acct* ***compound entry*** *(in bookkeeping)* article *m* composé; *Biol* ***compound eye*** œil *m* composé *ou* à facettes; *Math* ***compound fraction*** fraction *f* composée; *Med* ***compound fracture*** fracture *f* multiple *ou* compliquée; *Fin* ***compound interest*** *(UNCOUNT)* intérêts *mpl* composés; *Mus* ***compound time*** mesure *f* composée

comprehend [ˌkɒmprɪˈhend] **VT 1** *(understand)* comprendre, saisir **2** *(include)* comprendre, inclure
VI *(understand)* comprendre, saisir

comprehensible [ˌkɒmprɪˈhensəbəl] **ADJ** compréhensible, intelligible

comprehensibly [ˌkɒmprɪˈhensəblɪ] **ADV** d'une manière compréhensible *ou* intelligible

comprehension [ˌkɒmprɪˈhenʃən] **N 1** *(understanding)* compréhension *f*; **things that are beyond our c.** des choses qui nous dépassent **2** *Sch (exercise)* exercice *m* de compréhension; **a reading/listening c.** un exercice de compréhension écrite/orale **3** *(inclusion)* inclusion *f*

comprehensive [ˌkɒmprɪˈhensɪv] **ADJ 1** *(thorough)* complet(ète), exhaustif; *(detailed)* détaillé, complet(ète); *(defeat, victory)* écrasant; *(knowledge)* vaste, étendu; **c. measures** mesures *fpl* d'ensemble **2** *Br Sch* polyvalent; **the schools went c.** les écoles ont abandonné les critères sélectifs d'entrée
N *Br Sch (school)* = établissement secondaire d'enseignement général
▸▸ *Br* ***comprehensive insurance*** assurance *f* tous risques; ***comprehensive policy*** police *f* tous risques, police *f* multirisque; ***comprehensive school*** = établissement secondaire d'enseignement général

> Note that the French word **compréhensif** is a false friend and is never a translation for the English word **comprehensive**. Its most common meaning is **understanding**.

> COMPREHENSIVE SCHOOLS
>
> Les "comprehensive schools" ont été introduites en Grande-Bretagne en 1965 par les travaillistes dans le but de démocratiser l'enseignement et d'assurer l'égalité des chances pour tous les enfants, quels que soient les revenus de leurs parents et leur origine sociale. En 1975 une série de lois fut votée pour promouvoir ce type d'éducation. Mais le changement est lent et les progrès sont entravés par des poches de résistance en faveur des traditionnelles "grammar schools" et "public schools", ainsi que par le niveau insuffisant de certaines "comprehensives" situées dans des quartiers déshérités. Aujourd'hui 90 pour cent des élèves du secondaire fréquentent les "comprehensive schools". Bien qu'il n'y ait pas de sélection, la qualité de l'enseignement varie énormément suivant les établissements.

comprehensively [ˌkɒmprɪˈhensɪvlɪ] **ADV** *(thoroughly)* complètement, exhaustivement; *(in detail)* en détail

comprehensiveness [ˌkɒmprɪˈhensɪvnɪs] **N** *(of answer, treatment of subject)* caractère *m* complet

compress **VT** [kəmˈpres] **1** *(squeeze together)* comprimer; **to c. one's lips** serrer *ou* pincer les lèvres
2 *Fig (condense ▸ ideas, facts, writing)* condenser, concentrer; **three centuries are compressed into two chapters** trois siècles sont concentrés en deux chapitres
3 *Tech (air)* refouler, comprimer
4 *Comput (file)* compresser
VI [kəmˈpres] **1** *Tech (material)* se comprimer **2** *Fig (be condensed)* se condenser, se concentrer
N [ˈkɒmpres] *Med* compresse *f*

compressed [kəmˈprest] **ADJ 1** *(lips)* serré, pincé **2** *(style)* condensé
▸▸ *Tech* ***compressed air*** air *m* comprimé

compression [kəmˈpreʃən] **N 1** *(of material)* compression *f*; *Tech* **in c.** comprimé **2** *Fig (condensing)* réduction *f* **3** *Comput (of file)* compression *f*
▸▸ *Tech* ***compression chamber*** chambre *f* de compression; *Aut* ***compression ignition*** allumage *m* par compression; ***compression pump*** pompe *f* de compression; *Tech* ***compression ratio*** taux *m* de compression; *Tech* ***compression stroke*** *(in engine)* (temps *m* de) compression *f*

compressive [kəmˈpresɪv] **ADJ** qui peut être comprimé, compressible
▸▸ *Tech* ***compressive strength*** résistance *f* à la compression; *Tech* ***compressive stress*** contrainte *f* de compression

compressor [kəmˈpresə(r)] **N** *Anat & Tech* compresseur *m*
▸▸ *Tech* ***compressor unit*** groupe *m* compresseur

comprise [kəmˈpraɪz] **VT 1** *(consist of)* comprendre, consister en; **the group comprises** *or* **is comprised of four women and two men** il y a quatre femmes et deux hommes dans le groupe, le groupe est formé de quatre femmes et deux hommes **2** *(constitute)* constituer; **women c. 60 percent of the population** les femmes représentent 60 pour cent de la population

compromise [ˈkɒmprəmaɪz] **N** compromis *m*; **to agree to a c.** accepter un compromis; **to reach** *or* **to arrive at a c.** aboutir *ou* parvenir à un compromis; **there must be no c.** il ne faut pas faire de compromis
COMP *(decision, solution)* de compromis
VI transiger, aboutir à *ou* accepter un compromis; **to c. with sb (on sth)** transiger avec qn *ou* aboutir à un compromis avec qn (sur qch)
VT 1 *(principles, reputation)* compromettre; **don't say anything to c. yourself** ne dites rien qui puisse vous compromettre **2** *(jeopardize)* mettre en péril, risquer; **the party's chances of electoral success were severely compromised by the character of their leader** la personnalité du leader a sérieusement compromis les chances de victoire du parti aux élections

compromising [ˈkɒmprəˌmaɪzɪŋ] **ADJ** compromettant

comptroller [kənˈtrəʊlə(r)] **N** *Admin* administrateur(trice) *m,f*, intendant(e) *m,f*; *Fin* contrôleur(euse) *m,f*
▸▸ *Am* ***Comptroller General*** président *m* de la Cour des comptes, *Can* Contrôleur *m* général

compulsion [kəmˈpʌlʃən] **N 1** *(force)* contrainte *f*, coercition *f*; **to act under c.** agir sous la contrainte; **there's no c. to do it** il n'y a pas d'obligation à le faire; **he is under no c. to sell** il n'est nullement obligé de vendre, rien ne l'oblige à vendre **2** *Psy (impulse)* compulsion *f*; **I felt a sudden c. to visit my grandmother** j'ai soudain ressenti un besoin urgent de rendre visite à ma grand-mère

compulsive [kəmˈpʌlsɪv] **ADJ 1** *Psy (behaviour)* compulsif; *(smoker, gambler)* invétéré; **he's a c. liar** il ne peut pas s'empêcher de mentir, mentir est un besoin chez lui **2** *(reason)* coercitif **3** *Fig (absorbing)* passionnant; **this TV series is c. viewing** quand on commence à regarder ce feuilleton, on ne peut plus s'en passer
▸▸ ***compulsive eater*** boulimique *mf*; ***compulsive eating disorder*** boulimie *f*; ***compulsive lying*** mythomanie *f*

compulsively [kəmˈpʌlsɪvlɪ] **ADV 1** *Psy (drink, steal, smoke)* d'une façon compulsive **2** *Fig* irrésistiblement; **it's c. readable/watchable** c'est passionnant

compulsorily [kəmˈpʌlsərəlɪ] **ADV** d'office; *Admin* **to be retired c.** être mis à la retraite d'office

compulsory [kəmˈpʌlsərɪ] **ADJ 1** *(obligatory)* obligatoire; **military service/Latin is c.** le service militaire/le latin est obligatoire
2 *(compelling)* irrésistible
3 *(law)* obligatoire
4 *(coercive)* coercitif
N *Sport (in ice-skating)* **the compulsories** les figures *fpl* imposées
▸▸ ***compulsory education*** enseignement *m* obligatoire; *Fin* ***compulsory liquidation*** liquidation *f* forcée; *Br Admin* ***compulsory purchase*** expropriation *f* pour cause d'utilité publique; ***compulsory purchase order*** ordre *m* d'expropriation; *Ind* ***compulsory redundancy*** licenciement *m* sec; ***compulsory retirement*** mise *f* à la retraite d'office; *Pol* ***compulsory voting*** vote *m* obligatoire

compunction [kəmˈpʌŋkʃən] **N** *(remorse)* remords *m*; *(misgiving)* scrupule *m*; *Rel* componction *f*; **he has no c. about stealing** il n'a aucun scrupule *ou* il n'hésite pas à voler; **without the slightest c.** sans le moindre scrupule

computation [ˌkɒmpjuːˈteɪʃən] **N 1** *(calculation)* calcul *m* **2** *(reckoning)* estimation *f*

computational [ˌkɒmpjuːˈteɪʃənəl] **ADJ** quantitatif, statistique
▸▸ ***computational linguistics*** linguistique *f* computationnelle

compute [kəmˈpjuːt] **VT** calculer
VI calculer

computer [kəmˈpjuːtə(r)] **N** *(electronic)* ordinateur *m*; **he's good at/he works in computers** il est bon en/il travaille dans l'informatique; **to be c. literate** avoir des connaissances en informatique; **to have sth on c.** avoir qch sur ordinateur
▸▸ ***the computer age*** l'ère *f* des ordinateurs *ou* de l'informatique; ***computer analyst*** analyste *mf*; ***computer animation*** animation *f* par ordinateur; ***computer art*** dessin *m* par ordinateur; *Am* ***computer camp*** colonie *f* de vacances centrée sur l'informatique; ***computer centre*** centre *m* informatique, infocentre *m*; ***computer code*** code *m* d'ordinateur; ***computer course*** cours *m* d'informatique; ***computer crime*** fraude *f* informatique; ***computer dating*** = rencontres sélectionnées par ordinateur; ***computer engineer*** ingénieur-informaticien(enne) *m,f*; ***computer equipment*** équipement *m* informatique; ***computer expert*** informaticien(enne) *m,f*; ***computer fraud*** fraude *f* informatique; ***computer game*** jeu *m* informatique; *Fam* ***computer geek*** allumé(e) *m,f* de l'informatique; ***computer graphics*** **NPL** *(function)* graphiques *mpl* **N** *(field)* infographie *f*; ***computer language*** langage *m* de programmation; ***computer literacy*** compétence *f* informatique; ***computer manufacturer*** constructeur *m* informatique; ***computer model*** modèle *m* informatique; ***computer nerd*** allumé(e) *m,f* de l'informatique; ***computer network*** réseau *m* informatique; ***computer operator*** opérateur(trice) *m,f* (sur ordinateur); ***computer printout*** sortie *f* papier; *(continuous)* listing *m*, listage *m*; ***computer processing*** traitement *m* sur ordinateur; ***computer program*** programme *m* informatique; ***computer programmer*** programmeur(euse) *m,f*; ***computer programming*** programmation *f*; ***computer science*** informatique *f*; ***computer scientist*** informaticien(enne) *m,f*; ***computer simulation*** simulation *f* par ordinateur; ***computer system*** système *m* informatique; ***computer technician*** technicien(enne) *m,f* en informatique; ***computer terminal*** terminal *m* informatique; ***computer typesetting*** composition *f* par ordinateur; ***computer virus*** virus *m* informatique

computer-aided, computer-assisted ADJ assisté par ordinateur
▸▸ ***computer-aided design*** conception *f* assistée par ordinateur; ***computer-aided engineering*** ingénierie *f* assistée par ordinateur; ***computer-aided instruction, computer-aided learning*** enseignement *m* assisté par ordinateur; ***computer-aided manufacturing*** fabrication *f* assistée par ordinateur; ***computer-aided translation*** traduction *f* assistée par ordinateur

computer-controlled ADJ contrôlé par ordinateur

computer-enhanced ADJ *(graphics, images)* amélioré par ordinateur

computer-generated ADJ généré par ordinateur
▸▸ ***computer-generated image*** image *f* de synthèse

computer-integrated manufacturing N fabrication *f* intégrée par ordinateur

computerizable, -isable [kəm'pju:tə,raɪzəbəl] ADJ informatisable

computerization, -isation [kəm,pju:təraɪ'zeɪʃən] N **1** *(of system, work, company)* informatisation *f* **2** *(of data* ▸ *inputting)* saisie *f* sur ordinateur; *(*▸ *processing)* traitement *m* (électronique)

computerize, -ise [kəm'pju:təraɪz] VT **1** *(system, work, company)* informatiser **2** *(data* ▸ *put on computer)* saisir sur ordinateur; *(*▸ *process by computer)* traiter par ordinateur

computerized, -ised [kəm'pju:təraɪzd] ADJ informatisé
▸▸ ***computerized accounts*** comptabilité *f* informatisée; ***computerized banking*** informatique *f* bancaire; ***computerized data*** données *fpl* informatiques; ***computerized key*** clé *f* magnétique; *Med* ***computerized axial tomography*** tomodensitométrie *f*; *St Exch* ***computerized trading system*** système *m* informatique de cotation

computer-to-computer ADJ *(transmission)* d'ordinateur à ordinateur

computer-typeset *(pt & pp* **computer-typeset,** *cont* **computer-typesetting)** VT composer sur ordinateur
VI composer sur ordinateur

computing [kəm'pju:tɪŋ] N **1** *(field)* informatique *f*; **she works in c.** elle travaille dans l'informatique **2** *(calculation)* calcul *m*; *(reckoning)* estimation *f*
▸▸ ***computing centre*** centre *m* de calcul; ***computing machine*** machine *f* à calcul; ***computing power*** puissance *f* de calcul

comrade ['kɒmreɪd] N camarade *mf*

comradeship ['kɒmreɪdʃɪp] N camaraderie *f*

Comsat® ['kɒmsæt] N *(abbr* **communications satellite)** satellite *m* de communication

Con. *Pol (written abbr* **conservative)** conservateur

con [kɒn] *(pt & pp* **conned,** *cont* **conning)** VT **1** *Fam (swindle)* arnaquer; *(trick)* duper[□]; **I've been conned!** je me suis fait avoir!, on m'a eu!; **he conned us into buying it** il nous a persuadés de l'acheter et nous nous sommes fait avoir; **they were conned out of £500** ils se sont fait arnaquer de 500 livres **2** *Arch (study)* étudier en détail; *(learn by heart)* apprendre par cœur
N **1** *Fam (swindle)* arnaque *f*; *(trick)* duperie[□] *f* **2** *Fam (convict)* taulard(e) *m,f*; **an ex-c.** un ancien taulard **3** *(disadvantage)* contre *m*; **the pros and cons** le pour et le contre
▸▸ *Fam* ***con artist*** arnaqueur *m*; ***con man*** arnaqueur *m*, escroc*m*; ***con trick*** arnaque *f*, escroquerie *f*

concatenated [kɒn'kætəneɪtɪd] ADJ **1** *(linked)* enchaîné, lié **2** *Comput & Ling* concaténé

concatenation [kɒn,kætə'neɪʃən] N **1** *(series)* série *f*, chaîne *f*; *(of circumstances)* enchaînement *m* **2** *Comput & Ling* concaténation *f*

concave [,kɒn'keɪv] ADJ *Phys & Opt* concave

concavity [kɒn'kævətɪ] *(pl* **concavities)** N *Phys & Opt* concavité *f*

conceal [kən'si:l] VT *(hide* ▸ *object, emotion, truth)* cacher, dissimuler; *(*▸ *news)* tenir secret (ète); *Fin & Law (*▸ *assets)* dissimuler; **to c. sth from sb** cacher qch à qn; **to c. oneself** se cacher; **in order to c. the fact that...** pour dissimuler le fait que... + *indicative*

concealed [kən'si:ld] ADJ *(lighting)* indirect; *(driveway, entrance, microphone)* caché; **danger! c. entrance** *(sign)* danger! sortie de véhicules

concealment [kən'si:lmənt] N *(act of hiding)* dissimulation *f*; *Law (of criminal)* recel *m*; *(of facts, truth)* non-divulgation *f*; *Fin & Law* **c. of assets** dissimulation *f* d'actif

concede [kən'si:d] VT **1** *(admit)* concéder, admettre; **to c. a point** concéder un point (important); **he conceded (that) he was wrong** il a admis *ou* reconnu qu'il avait tort; **to c. defeat** s'avouer vaincu **2** *(give up)* concéder, accorder; *Sport* concéder; *Ftbl* **they conceded a free kick/a goal** ils ont concédé un coup franc/un but **3** *(grant* ▸ *privileges)* concéder
VI céder

conceit [kən'si:t] N **1** *(vanity)* vanité *f*, suffisance *f* **2** *Literary (witty expression)* trait *m* d'esprit

conceited [kən'si:tɪd] ADJ vaniteux, suffisant; **I don't want to sound c. but...** je ne veux pas avoir l'air prétentieux mais...

conceitedly [kən'si:tɪdlɪ] ADV avec vanité *ou* suffisance; **he c. imagined that...** il a eu la prétention d'imaginer que... + *indicative*

conceivable [kən'si:vəbəl] ADJ concevable, imaginable; **every c. means** tous les moyens possibles et imaginables; **it's quite c. that it was an accident** il est tout à fait concevable que ç'ait été un accident; **what c. reason could I have?** quelle raison pourrais-je bien avoir?

conceivably [kən'si:vəblɪ] ADV **I don't see how it's c. possible** ce n'est pas concevable; **this might c. start a war** il est concevable que *ou* il se peut que cela déclenche une guerre; **she could c. have done it, it's c. possible that she did it** il n'est pas exclu qu'elle l'ait fait; **is he capable of it? – c.** en est-il capable? – c'est fort possible

conceive [kən'si:v] VT **1** *(idea, plan)* concevoir; **I can't c. why they did it** je ne comprends vraiment pas pourquoi ils l'ont fait **2** *(child)* concevoir; *Fig* **she conceived a passion for jazz** elle conçut une passion pour le jazz
VI **1** *(think)* concevoir; **I can c. of him having done it** je peux très bien imaginer qu'il l'ait fait **2** *(become pregnant)* concevoir

concentrate ['kɒnsəntreɪt] VI **1** *(pay attention)* se concentrer, concentrer *ou* fixer son attention; **I can't c. with all that noise** tout ce bruit m'empêche de me concentrer; **to c. on sth** se concentrer sur qch; **c. on your work!** appliquez-vous à votre travail! **2** *(focus)* **the government should c. on improving the economy** le gouvernement devrait s'attacher à améliorer la situation économique; **just c. on getting the suitcases ready!** occupe-toi seulement des valises! **3** *(gather)* se concentrer, converger; **the population tends to c. in cities** la population tend à se concentrer dans les villes
VT **1** *(focus)* concentrer; **to c. one's attention on sth** concentrer son attention sur qch; **it concentrates the mind** cela aide à se concentrer **2** *(bring together)* concentrer, rassembler; *Chem* concentrer; **Conservative support is concentrated in the South** le soutien du parti conservateur est concentré dans le Sud
N *(of tomatoes, fruit juice etc)* concentré *m*; *(mineral)* minerai *m* concentré; **made from c.** *(fruit juice)* fait à base de concentré

concentration [,kɒnsən'treɪʃən] N **1** *(mental)* concentration *f*, application *f*; **to lose one's c.** se déconcentrer; **c. span** concentration *f*; **he has a poor c. span** il n'arrive pas à se concentrer très longtemps **2** *(specializing)* spécialisation *f*; **in view of their recent c. on other areas of the market** étant donné qu'ils se sont récemment concentrés sur d'autres secteurs du marché **3** *(grouping* ▸ *of troops etc)* concentration *f*; **c. of effort** convergence *f* des efforts; *Chem* **(degree of) c.** *(of acid)* titre *m*
▸▸ ***concentration camp*** camp *m* de concentration

concentric [kən'sentrɪk] ADJ concentrique

concept ['kɒnsept] N concept *m*
▸▸ *Mus* ***concept album*** album *m* concept; ***concept car*** concept car *m*; *Mktg* ***concept test*** test *m* de concept

conception [kən'sepʃən] N **1** *(idea)* conception *f*; **to have a clear c. of sth** se représenter clairement qch; **she has no c. of time** elle n'a aucune notion du temps **2** *Biol* conception *f*

concept-testing N *(UNCOUNT) Mktg* tests *mpl* de concept

conceptual [kən'septʃuəl] ADJ conceptuel
▸▸ ***conceptual art*** art *m* conceptuel

conceptualize, -ise [kən'septʃuəlaɪz] VT concevoir, conceptualiser

CONCERN [kən'sɜ:n]

N	
• inquiétude **1**	souci **1, 2**
• affaire **3, 4**	intérêt **5**
VT	
• inquiéter **1**	• concerner **2**
• intéresser **3**	• traiter de **4**

N **1** *(worry)* inquiétude *f*, souci *m*; **his condition is giving cause for c.** son état est inquiétant; **there's no cause for c.** il n'y a pas de raison de s'inquiéter; **to express c. about sth** exprimer de l'inquiétude au sujet de qch; **there is growing c. for her safety** on est de plus en plus inquiet à son sujet *ou* sur son sort; **there is growing c. that...** on craint de plus en plus que... + *subjunctive*; **she showed great c. for their welfare** elle s'est montrée très soucieuse de leur bien-être; **a look of c.** un regard inquiet; **this is a matter of great c.** c'est un sujet très inquiétant
2 *(source of worry)* souci *m*, préoccupation *f*; **my main c. is the price** ce qui m'inquiète surtout, c'est le prix
3 *(affair, business)* affaire *f*; **what c. is it of yours?** en quoi est-ce que cela vous regarde?; **it's none of my c.** cela ne me regarde pas, ce n'est pas mon affaire
4 *Com (firm)* **a (business) c.** une affaire, une firme
5 *(share)* intérêt *m*; **we have a c. in the restaurant** nous avons des intérêts dans le restaurant
6 *Fam (object)* truc *m*, machin *m*
VT **1** *(worry)* inquiéter; **your health concerns me** je m'inquiète *ou* je suis inquiet pour votre santé; **they're concerned about her** ils s'inquiètent *ou* se font du souci à son sujet; **we were concerned to learn that...** nous avons appris avec inquiétude que... + *indicative*; **I'm only concerned with the facts** je ne m'intéresse qu'aux faits
2 *(involve)* concerner; **where the budget** *or* **as far as the budget is concerned** en ce qui concerne le budget; **to c. oneself in** *or* **with sth** s'occuper de *ou* s'intéresser à qch; **there is no need for you to c. yourself with my affairs** vous n'avez pas à vous occuper de mes affaires; **this doesn't c. you** cela ne vous regarde pas; **it concerns your mother** c'est au sujet de votre mère; **as far as I'm concerned** en ce qui me concerne, quant à moi; **to whom it may c.** à qui de droit
3 *(be important to)* intéresser, importer; **the outcome concerns us all** les résultats nous importent à tous
4 *(of book, report)* traiter de

concerned [kən'sɜ:nd] ADJ **1** *(worried)* inquiet (ète), soucieux; **he didn't seem at all c.** il n'avait pas du tout l'air inquiet *ou* de s'inquiéter **2** *(involved)* intéressé; **pass this request on to the department c.** transmettez cette demande au service compétent; **notify the person c.** avisez qui de droit; **the people c.** *(in question)* les personnes *fpl* en question *ou* dont il s'agit; *(involved)* les intéressés *mpl*

concerning [kən'sɜ:nɪŋ] PREP au sujet de, à propos de; **I wrote to her c. the lease** je lui ai écrit au sujet du bail

concert N ['kɒnsət] **1** *(performance)* concert *m*; **to give a c.** donner un concert; **Miles Davis in c.** Miles Davis en concert **2** *Br Fig Formal (agreement)* accord *m*, entente *f*
VT [kən'sɜ:t] concerter, arranger
• **in concert with** PREP ['kɒnsət] *Br Formal* de concert avec; **we acted in c. with the police** nous avons agi de concert avec la police
COMP ['kɒnsət] *(performer, pianist)* de concert
▸▸ ***concert grand*** piano *m* de concert; ***concert hall*** salle *f* de concert; *St Exch* ***concert party*** action *f* de concert; *Mus* ***concert pitch*** diapason *m*

(de concert); *Mus* **concert tour** tournée *f*; *Br* **concert venue** salle *f* de concert

concerted [kən'sɜ:tɪd] **ADJ** concerté; **a c. effort** un effort concerté; **c. action** action *f* d'ensemble *ou* concertée

concertgoer ['kɒnsətˌgəʊə(r)] **N** amateur *m* de concerts

concertina [ˌkɒnsə'ti:nə] **N** concertina *m*
VI se plier en accordéon; **the front of the car concertinaed** le devant de la voiture s'est plié en accordéon
▸▸ *Typ* ***concertina fold*** pliure *f* en accordéon

concertmaster ['kɒnsətˌmɑ:stə(r)] **N** *Am Mus* premier violon *m*

concerto [kən'tʃeətəʊ] (*pl* **concertos** *or* **concerti** [-ti:]) **N** *Mus* concerto *m*; **piano/violin c.** concerto *m* pour piano/violon

concession [kən'seʃən] **N 1** *(gen) & Law* concession *f*; **to make concessions** faire des concessions; **as a c. to sb/sth** comme concession à qn/qch; **the only c. the film makes to reality is...** la seule concession que le film fasse à la réalité est...
2 *Com (within store)* concession *f*
3 *Com (reduction)* réduction *f*; **price: £5 (concessions £3)** prix des billets: 5 livres (tarif réduit 3 livres)
4 *Mining & Petr* concession *f*; **an oil c.** une concession pétrolière
▸▸ *Am* ***concession stand*** buvette *f (dans un cinéma, un stade etc)*; *Br* ***concession ticket*** *(for theatre, cinema)* billet *m* à prix réduit

concessionaire [kənˌseʃə'neə(r)] **N** *Com* concessionnaire *mf*

concessionary [kən'seʃənərɪ] (*pl* **concessionaries**) **ADJ 1** *(gen) & Fin & Law* concessionnaire **2** *Com (fare, ticket)* à prix réduit
N concessionnaire *mf*

conch [kɒntʃ, kɒŋk] (*pl* **conches** ['kɒntʃɪz] *or* **conchs** [kɒŋks]) **N 1** *Zool* conque *f* **2** *Archit* (voûte *f* d')abside *f*

concierge ['kɒnsɪeɜ] **N** *Am* concierge *mf*

conciliate [kən'sɪlɪeɪt] **VT 1** *(appease)* apaiser; *(win over)* se concilier (l'appui de); **she managed to c. my mother** elle a réussi à se concilier les bonnes grâces de ma mère **2** *(reconcile)* concilier
VI *Formal* **to c. between two people/countries** réconcilier deux peuples/pays

conciliation [kənˌsɪlɪ'eɪʃən] **N 1** *(appeasement)* apaisement *m* **2** *(reconciliation)* conciliation *f* **3** *Ind (in dispute)* conciliation *f*, arbitrage *m*
▸▸ *Ind* ***conciliation board*** conseil *m* d'arbitrage; *EU* ***Conciliation Committee*** comité *m* de conciliation; *Ind* ***conciliation service*** service *m* de conciliation

conciliator [kən'sɪlɪˌeɪtə(r)] **N 1** *(appeaser)* conciliateur(trice) *m,f* **2** *Ind (in dispute)* médiateur *m*

conciliatory [kən'sɪlɪətərɪ] **ADJ 1** *(manner, words)* conciliant; *(person)* conciliateur, conciliant; **in a c. spirit** dans un esprit de conciliation **2** *Law & Pol (procedure)* conciliatoire

concise [kən'saɪs] **ADJ** *(succinct)* concis; *(abridged)* abrégé

concisely [kən'saɪslɪ] **ADV** avec concision

conciseness [kən'saɪsnɪs], **concision** [kən'sɪʒən] **N** concision *f*

conclave ['kɒŋkleɪv] **N 1** *(private meeting)* assemblée *f ou* réunion *f* à huis clos; **in c.** en réunion privée **2** *Rel* conclave *m*

conclude [kən'klu:d] **VT 1** *(finish)* conclure, terminer; *(meeting, session)* clore, clôturer; **to be concluded** *(serialized story)* suite et fin au prochain numéro; *(TV serial)* suite et fin au prochain épisode
2 *(settle ▸ deal, treaty)* conclure
3 *(deduce)* conclure, déduire
4 *(decide)* décider
VI 1 *(person)* conclure; **to c., I would just like to say...** en conclusion *ou* pour conclure, je voudrais simplement dire... **2** *(event)* se terminer, s'achever

concluding [kən'klu:dɪŋ] **ADJ** de conclusion, final; **he made a few c. remarks** il a fait quelques remarques finales

conclusion [kən'klu:ʒən] **N 1** *(end)* conclusion *f*, fin *f*; *(of meeting, session)* clôture *f*; **to bring sth to a c.** mener qch à sa conclusion *ou* à terme; **she brought the matter to a successful c.** elle a mené l'affaire à (bon) terme **2** *(decision, judgement)* conclusion *f*, décision *f*; **to come to** *or* **to reach the c. that...** conclure que... + *indicative*, (en) arriver à la conclusion que... + *indicative*; **the c. to be drawn from this matter** la conclusion à tirer de cette affaire; **it's up to you to draw your own conclusions** c'est à vous d'en juger **3** *(settling ▸ of deal, treaty)* conclusion *f*
• **in conclusion ADV** en conclusion, pour conclure

conclusive [kən'klu:sɪv] **ADJ** *(decisive ▸ proof, argument)* concluant, décisif; *(final)* final

conclusively [kən'klu:sɪvlɪ] **ADV** *(prove, argue, show)* de façon concluante *ou* décisive, définitivement

concoct [kən'kɒkt] **VT 1** *(prepare ▸ meal, dish)* confectionner **2** *Fig (invent ▸ excuse, scheme)* combiner, concocter; *(▸ plot)* machiner

concoction [kən'kɒkʃən] **N 1** *(action)* confection *f*, préparation *f* **2** *(meal, dish, drink)* mélange *m* **3** *Fig (scheme)* combinaison *f*

concomitant [kən'kɒmɪtənt] *Formal* **ADJ** concomitant; **adolescence with all its c. anxieties** l'adolescence et les angoisses qui l'accompagnent
N accessoire *m*; **ill health is a common c. of poverty** la mauvaise santé va souvent de pair avec la misère

concord ['kɒŋkɔ:d] **N 1** *Formal (harmony)* concorde *f*, harmonie *f*; **to live in c.** vivre en bon accord *ou* en harmonie
2 *(treaty)* accord *m*, entente *f*
3 *Gram* accord *m*; **to be in c. with sth** s'accorder avec qch
4 *Mus* accord *m*

concordance [kən'kɔ:dəns] **N 1** *Formal (agreement)* accord *m* **2** *(index)* index *m*; *(of Bible, of author's works)* concordance *f*
• **in concordance with PREP** en accord avec; **the policy is in c. with our declared aims** cette politique s'accorde *ou* est en accord avec les objectifs que nous nous sommes fixés

concordant [kən'kɔ:dənt] **ADJ** *Formal* concordant, s'accordant; **c. with** s'accordant avec

concordat [kɒn'kɔ:dæt] **N** concordat *m*

Concorde ['kɒnkɔ:d] **N** *Aviat* Concorde *m*

concourse ['kɒŋkɔ:s] **N 1** *(of people, things)* multitude *f*, rassemblement *m*; *(crowd)* foule *f*
2 *(of circumstances, events)* concours *m*
3 *(meeting place)* lieu *m* de rassemblement; *(in building)* hall *m*
4 *Am (street)* boulevard *m*; *(crossroads)* carrefour *m*

concrete ['kɒŋkri:t] **N 1** *Constr* béton *m* **2** *Phil* **the c.** le concret
ADJ 1 *(specific ▸ advantage)* concret(ète), réel; *(▸ example, proposal, term)* concret(ète); **he made us a c. offer** il nous a fait une offre précise *ou* concrète; **we need c. proof** il nous faut des preuves concrètes *ou* matérielles; **in c. terms** concrètement **2** *Gram, Math & Mus* concret(ète) **3** *Constr* en *ou* de béton; **c. monstrosity** horreur *f* architecturale; **c. slab** dalle *f* de béton
VT *Constr* bétonner
▸▸ *Fig* ***concrete jungle*** univers *m* de béton; *Constr* ***concrete mixer*** bétonnière *f*; *Gram* ***concrete noun*** nom *m* concret; ***concrete poetry*** *(UNCOUNT)* calligrammes *mpl*
▸ **concrete over VT SEP** *(garden, field etc)* bétonner

concreting ['kɒŋkri:tɪŋ] **N** *Constr* bétonnage *m*

concretion [kən'kri:ʃən] **N** concrétion *f*

concubinage [kɒn'kju:bɪnɪdʒ] **N** concubinage *m*

concubine ['kɒŋkjʊbaɪn] **N** concubine *f*

concur [kən'kɜ:(r)] (*pt & pp* **concurred**, *cont* **concurring**) **VI 1** *(agree)* être d'accord, s'entendre; **to c. with sb/sth** être d'accord avec qn/qch; **the experts' opinions c.** les avis des experts convergent; **he proposed a different approach and she concurred** il a proposé une approche différente et elle a approuvé **2** *(occur together)* coïncider, arriver en même temps; **events concurred to make it a miserable Christmas** tout a concouru à gâcher les fêtes de Noël **3** *(findings, results of experiment)* concorder (**with** avec)

concurrence [kən'kʌrəns] **N 1** *(agreement)* accord *m*, concordance *f* de vues **2** *(assent)* assentiment *m*, consentement *m* (**in** à) **3** *(simultaneous occurrence)* coïncidence *f*, concomitance *f*, simultanéité *f*; **c. of events** concours *m* de circonstances

concurrent [kən'kʌrənt] **ADJ 1** *(simultaneous)* concomitant, simultané; *Law* **two c. sentences** deux peines *fpl* confondues
2 *(acting together)* concerté
3 *(agreeing)* concordant, d'accord
4 *Math & Tech (intersecting)* concourant

concurrently [kən'kʌrəntlɪ] **ADV** simultanément; *Law* **the two sentences to run c.** avec confusion des deux peines

concuss [kən'kʌs] **VT 1** *Med (injure ▸ brain)* commotionner; **to be concussed** être commotionné **2** *(shake)* ébranler, secouer violemment

concussion [kən'kʌʃən] **N 1** *(UNCOUNT) Med (brain injury)* commotion *f* cérébrale **2** *(shaking)* ébranlement *m*, secousse *f* violente

condemn [kən'dem] **VT 1** *Law (sentence)* condamner; **condemned to death** condamné à mort; *Fig* **people who are condemned to live in poverty** les gens qui sont condamnés à vivre dans la misère
2 *(disapprove of)* condamner, censurer
3 *(declare unsafe ▸ building)* déclarer inhabitable, condamner; **this meat has been condemned** cette viande a été jugée impropre à la consommation
4 *Am Law (property)* exproprier pour cause d'utilité publique

condemnation [ˌkɒndem'neɪʃən] **N 1** *Law (sentence)* condamnation *f*
2 *(criticism)* condamnation *f*, censure *f*
3 *(of building)* condamnation *f*; *(of meat)* fait *m* de juger impropre à la consommation
4 *Am Law (of property)* expropriation *f* pour cause d'utilité publique

condemned [kən'demd] **ADJ 1** *Law (sentenced)* condamné; **the c. man** le condamné **2** *(building)* condamné; *(meat)* jugé impropre à la consommation
▸▸ ***condemned cell*** cellule *f* des condamnés

condensation [ˌkɒnden'seɪʃən] **N 1** *(of gas, liquid, vapour)* condensation *f* **2** *(on glass)* buée *f*, condensation *f* **3** *Phys (of beam)* concentration *f*

condense [kən'dens] **VT 1** *(make denser)* condenser, concentrer; *(gas, liquid, vapour)* condenser **2** *(report, book, text)* condenser, résumer **3** *Phys (beam)* concentrer
VI *(become liquid)* se condenser; *(become concentrated)* se concentrer

condensed [kən'denst] **ADJ** condensé, concentré; *Typ* **in c. print** en caractères étroits
▸▸ ***condensed book*** livre *m* condensé; ***condensed milk*** lait *m* concentré

condenser [kən'densə(r)] **N 1** *Elec & Tech* condensateur *m* **2** *(of gas)* condenseur *m* **3** *Phys (of beam, light source)* condensateur *m*

condensing [kən'densɪŋ] **N** condensation *f*

condescend [ˌkɒndɪ'send] **VI 1** *(behave patronizingly)* **to c. (to sb)** se montrer condescendant (envers qn *ou* à l'égard de qn) **2** *(lower oneself)* **to c. to do sth** condescendre à *ou* daigner faire qch

condescending [ˌkɒndɪ'sendɪŋ] **ADJ** condescendant

condescendingly [ˌkɒndɪ'sendɪŋlɪ] **ADV** avec condescendance; *(speak)* d'un ton condescendant; **he treated me very c.** il m'a traité de haut, il m'a pris de très haut

condescension [ˌkɒndɪ'senʃən] **N** condescendance *f* (**to** envers *ou* pour)

condiment ['kɒndɪmənt] **N** condiment *m*
▸▸ ***condiment set*** poivrier *m* et salière *f*

condition [kən'dɪʃən] **N 1** *(state ▸ mental, physical)* état *m*; **books in good/poor c.** livres en bon/mauvais état; **in your c.** *(to pregnant woman)* dans ton état; **you're in no c. to drive** vous n'êtes

pas en état de conduire; **the human c.** la condition humaine; **I'm out of c.** je ne suis pas en forme; **you should get yourself into c.** vous devriez faire des exercices pour retrouver la forme; **he's in excellent c.** sa condition physique est excellente; **in working c.** en état de marche
2 *(stipulation)* condition *f*; **to make a c. that…** stipuler que… + *indicative*; **you can borrow the book, on one c.** tu peux emprunter le livre, à une condition; **it was a c. of the lease that…** l'une des stipulations du bail était que…+ *subjunctive*; *Com* **conditions of sale** conditions *fpl* de vente; *Law* **the conditions of a contract** les conditions *fpl ou* stipulations *fpl* d'un contrat
3 *(illness)* maladie *f*, affection *f*; **he has a heart c.** il a une maladie de cœur
4 *Formal (social status)* situation *f*, position *f*
VT 1 *(train)* conditionner; *Psy* provoquer un réflexe conditionné chez, conditionner; **her upbringing conditioned her to believe in God** son éducation l'a automatiquement portée à croire en Dieu; **a conditioned reflex** un réflexe conditionné **2** *(make fit ▸ animal, person)* mettre en forme; *(▸ thing)* mettre en bon état; **to c. one's hair** mettre de l'après-shamp(o)oing **3** *(determine)* conditionner, déterminer; **the market is conditioned by the economic situation** le marché dépend de la conjoncture économique
• **conditions NPL** *(circumstances)* conditions *fpl*, circonstances *fpl*; **living/working conditions** conditions *fpl* de vie/de travail; **under these conditions** dans ces conditions; **road** *or* **driving conditions** état *m* des routes; **drive with particular care as conditions on the roads are hazardous** soyez prudents sur les routes: le mauvais temps rend la circulation très dangereuse; **the weather conditions** les conditions *fpl* météorologiques
• **on condition that CONJ** à condition que + *subjunctive*; **I'll tell you on c. that you keep it secret** je vais vous le dire à condition que vous gardiez le secret

conditional [kən'dɪʃənəl] **ADJ 1** *(dependent on other factors)* conditionnel; **to be c. on** *or* **upon sth** dépendre de qch **a c. promise** une promesse conditionnelle *ou* sous condition **2** *Gram* conditionnel
N *Gram* conditionnel *m*; **in the c.** au conditionnel
▸▸ ***conditional acceptance*** acceptation *f* sous réserve; ***conditional access television*** télévision *f* à accès conditionnel; *Br Law* ***conditional discharge*** mise *f* en liberté conditionnelle

conditionally [kən'dɪʃənəlɪ] **ADV** conditionnellement

conditioner [kən'dɪʃənə(r)] **N** *(for hair)* après-shampo(o)ing *m*; *(for fabric)* assouplisseur *m*

conditioning [kən'dɪʃənɪŋ] **N** *(gen)* conditionnement *m*; *(fitness)* mise *f* en forme
ADJ traitant
▸▸ ***conditioning shampoo*** shampo(o)ing *m* démêlant

condo ['kɒndəʊ] *(pl* **condos**) **N** *Am Fam (ownership)* copropriété[□] *f*; *(building)* immeuble *m* (en copropriété)[□]; *(flat)* appartement *m* en copropriété[□], *Can* condo *m*

condole [kən'dəʊl] **VI** *Literary* exprimer ses condoléances *ou* sa sympathie (**with** à)

condolence [kən'dəʊləns] **N** condoléances *fpl*; **a letter of c.** une lettre de condoléances; **to offer one's condolences to sb** présenter ses condoléances à qn

condom ['kɒndəm] **N** préservatif *m (masculin)*

condominium [ˌkɒndə'mɪnɪəm] *(pl* **condominiums**) **N 1** *(government)* condominium *m* **2** *(country)* condominium *m* **3** *Am (ownership)* copropriété *f*; *(building)* immeuble *m* (en copropriété); *(flat)* appartement *m* en copropriété

condone [kən'dəʊn] **VT** *(overlook)* fermer les yeux sur; *(forgive)* pardonner, excuser; **we cannot c. such immoral behaviour** nous ne pouvons excuser un comportement aussi immoral; **I am not condoning the crime** je ne cherche pas à excuser le crime

condor ['kɒndɔː(r)] **N** condor *m*

conduce [kən'djuːs] **VI** *Formal (action, thing)* contribuer (**to** à)

conducive [kən'djuːsɪv] **ADJ** favorable; **this weather is not c. to studying** ce temps n'incite pas à étudier

conduct N ['kɒndʌkt] **1** *(behaviour)* conduite *f*, comportement *m* (**towards sb** à l'égard de *ou* avec *ou* envers qn); **bad/good c.** mauvaise/bonne conduite *f*; **her c. towards me** son comportement envers moi *ou* à mon égard **2** *(handling ▸ of business, negotiations)* conduite *f*; **the lawyer's c. of the case** la manière dont l'avocat a mené l'affaire
VT [kən'dʌkt] **1** *(manage, carry out ▸ business, operations, religious service)* diriger; *(▸ campaign, survey)* mener; *(▸ inquiry)* conduire, mener; *(▸ experiment)* effectuer; **this is not the way to c. negotiations** ce n'est pas ainsi qu'on négocie; *Law* **to c. one's own case** plaider soi-même sa cause
2 *(guide)* conduire, mener; **the director conducted us through the factory** le directeur nous a fait visiter l'usine; **conducted tours** visites *fpl* guidées
3 *(behave)* **to c. oneself** se conduire, se comporter
4 *(musicians, music)* diriger
5 *Elec & Phys (transmit)* conduire, être conducteur de
VI [kən'dʌkt] *Mus* diriger; *(work as conductor)* être chef d'orchestre; **who's conducting?** qui est le chef d'orchestre?, qui dirige?
▸▸ *Sch* ***conduct report*** rapport *m (sur la conduite d'un élève)*; *Mil* ***conduct sheet*** feuille *f ou* certificat *m* de conduite

conducting [kən'dʌktɪŋ] **N 1** *(of business, people)* conduite *f* **2** *(of musicians, music)* art *m* de diriger

conduction [kən'dʌkʃən] **N** *Elec & Phys* conduction *f*

conductive [kən'dʌktɪv] **ADJ** *Elec & Phys* conducteur
▸▸ ***conductive education*** = enseignement adapté aux besoins des handicapés moteurs

conductivity [ˌkɒndʌk'tɪvətɪ] **N** *Elec & Phys* conductivité *f*

conductor [kən'dʌktə(r)] **N 1** *(of musicians, music)* chef *m* d'orchestre **2** *Transp (railway official)* chef *m* de train; *Br (on bus)* receveur *m* **3** *Elec & Phys* (corps *m*) conducteur *m*

> Note that the French word **conducteur** is not always a translation for the English word **conductor**.

conductress [kən'dʌktrɪs] **N** *Br (on bus)* receveuse *f*

conduit ['kɒndɪt] **N** *Tech (for fluid)* conduit *m*, canalisation *f*; *Elec* tube *m*; *Fig (for money)* intermédiaire *mf*

condyle ['kɒndɪl] **N** *Anat* condyle *m*

cone [kəʊn] **N 1** *(gen) & Math* cône *m*
2 **(traffic) c.** cône *m* de signalisation
3 *(for ice cream)* cornet *m*
4 *Anat (in retina)* cône *m*
5 *Bot (of pine, fir)* pomme *f*, cône *m*
▸ **cone off VT SEP** *Br* mettre des cônes de signalisation sur

cone-bearing ADJ *Bot* conifère

cone-shaped [-ʃeɪpt] **ADJ** en forme de cône, conique

confab ['kɒnfæb] *(pt & pp* **confabbed**, *cont* **confabbing**) *Fam* **N** causette *f*; **to have a c. (about sth)** causer (de qch)
VI causer, bavarder[□]

confection [kən'fekʃən] **N 1** *(act)* confection *f* **2** *(sweet)* sucrerie *f*, friandise *f*; *(pastry)* pâtisserie *f*; *(cake)* gâteau *m*

confectioner [kən'fekʃənə(r)] **N** *(of sweets)* confiseur(euse) *m,f*; *(of pastry, cakes)* pâtissier (ère) *m,f*; **c.'s (shop)** *(▸ for sweets)* confiserie *f*; *(▸ for pastry, cakes)* pâtisserie *f*
▸▸ ***confectioner's custard*** crème *f* pâtissière, *Can* costarde *f*; *Am* ***confectioner's sugar*** sucre *m* glace

confectionery [kən'fekʃənərɪ] *(pl* **confectioneries**) **N** *(sweets)* confiserie *f*; *(pastry)* pâtisserie *f*

confederacy [kən'fedərəsɪ] *(pl* **confederacies**) **N 1** *(alliance)* confédération *f* **2** *(conspiracy)* conspiration *f*
• **Confederacy N** *Hist* **the C.** les États *mpl* confédérés *(pendant la guerre de Sécession américaine)*

confederate N [kən'fedərət] **1** *(member of confederacy)* confédéré(e) *m,f* **2** *(accomplice)* complice *mf*
ADJ [kən'fedərət] confédéré
VT [kən'fedəreɪt] confédérer
VI [kən'fedəreɪt] se confédérer
• **Confederate** [kən'fedərət] **N** *Hist* sudiste *mf (pendant la guerre de Sécession américaine)*; **the Confederates** les Confédérés *mpl*
▸▸ *Hist* ***the Confederate States (of America)*** les États *mpl* confédérés *(pendant la guerre de Sécession américaine)*

confederation [kənˌfedə'reɪʃən] **N** confédération *f*
▸▸ ***Confederation of British Industry*** = patronat britannique, Medef *m*

confer [kən'fɜː(r)] *(pt & pp* **conferred**, *cont* **conferring**) **VT** *(title, rank, powers)* conférer, accorder (**on** à); *(degree, diploma)* remettre (**on** à); **to c. an award on sb** remettre une récompense *ou* un prix à qn
VI conférer, s'entretenir; **to c. with sb (about sth)** s'entretenir avec qn (de qch); **contestants are not allowed to c.** les concurrents n'ont pas le droit de se consulter

conference ['kɒnfərəns] **N 1** *(meeting)* conférence *f*; *(consultation)* conférence *f*, consultation *f*; **to be in c. (with)** *(with several people)* être en conférence (avec); *(with one or two people)* être en réunion (avec); **we hope to get management to the c. table** nous espérons réunir la direction en table ronde **2** *(convention)* congrès *m*, colloque *m*; *Pol* congrès *m*, assemblée *f*; **the Labour Party c.** le congrès du parti travailliste **3** *Am Sport (association)* association *f*, ligue *f*
▸▸ ***conference call*** téléconférence *f*; ***conference centre*** *(building)* centre *m* de congrès; *(town)* = ville pouvant accueillir des congrès; ***conference delegate*** congressiste *mf*; ***conference hall*** salle *f* de conférence; ***conference organizer*** organisateur(trice) *m,f* de conférences *ou* de congrès; ***conference pack*** = dossier offert aux conférenciers avec informations générales sur la conférence, petits cadeaux etc; ***Conference pear*** poire *f* conférence; ***conference room*** salle *f* de conférence

conferment [kən'fɜːmənt], **conferral** [kən'fɜːrəl] **N** action *f* de conférer; *(of degree, diploma)* remise *f* (de diplôme); *(of favour, title)* octroi *m*; **the c. of a title on sb** l'anoblissement *m* de qn

confess [kən'fes] **VT 1** *(admit ▸ fault, crime)* avouer, confesser; **to c. one's guilt** *or* **that one is guilty** avouer sa culpabilité, s'avouer coupable; **I must** *or* **I have to c. I was wrong** je dois reconnaître *ou* admettre que j'avais tort; **I don't understand either, I must c.** je dois avouer que je ne comprends pas non plus; **medical experts c. themselves helpless** les médecins s'avouent impuissants **2** *Rel (sins)* confesser, se confesser de; *(of priest)* confesser
VI 1 *(criminal)* avouer, faire des aveux; **the thief confessed** le voleur est passé aux aveux; **she confessed to five murders** elle a avoué *ou* confessé cinq meurtres **2** *(admit)* faire des aveux; **he confessed to having lied** il a reconnu *ou* avoué avoir menti; **I c. to not liking her** j'avoue que je ne l'aime pas **3** *Rel* se confesser

confession [kən'feʃən] **N 1** *(of guilt)* aveu *m*, confession *f*; **to make a full c.** faire des aveux complets; **I have a c. to make** j'ai un aveu à faire; **on my own c.** de mon propre aveu; **that would be a c. of failure** cela reviendrait à s'avouer vaincu **2** *Rel* confession *f*; *(sect)* confession *f*; **do you go to c.?** allez-vous vous confesser?; **she made her c.** elle s'est confessée; **the priest heard our c.** le prêtre nous a confessés; **a c. of faith** une confession de foi

confessional [kən'feʃənəl] *Rel* **N** confessionnal *m*; **the secrets of the c.** les secrets du confessionnal
ADJ confessionnel

confessor [kən'fesə(r)] **N** *Rel* confesseur *m*

confetti [kən'fetɪ] **N** *(UNCOUNT)* confettis *mpl*

confidant [ˌkɒnfɪ'dænt] **N** confident *m*

> Attention: ne pas confondre avec l'adjectif anglais **confident**.

confidante [ˌkɒnfɪˈdænt] N confidente *f*

confide [kənˈfaɪd] VT **1** *(reveal)* avouer en confidence, confier; **to c. a secret to sb** confier un secret à qn; **she confided to me that ...** elle m'a confié que ...; **she confided her fear to them** elle leur a avoué en confidence sa peur; **2** *(entrust)* confier; **to c. sth to sb's care** confier qch à la garde de qn

▸ **confide in** VT INSEP **1** *(talk freely to)* se confier à; **there's nobody I can c. in** il n'y a personne à qui je puisse me confier **2** *(trust)* avoir confiance en, se fier à; **you can c. in me!** vous pouvez me faire confiance!, fiez-vous à moi!

confidence [ˈkɒnfɪdəns] N **1** *(faith)* confiance *f*; **she has no c. in her own ability** elle n'a aucune confiance en elle; **I have every c. that you'll succeed** je suis absolument certain que vous réussirez; **to put one's c. in sb/sth** faire confiance à qn/qch; **to win sb's c.** gagner la confiance de qn; **the c. placed in me** la confiance qui m'a été témoignée; **with complete c.** en toute confiance

2 *(self-assurance)* confiance *f* (en soi), assurance *f*; **he spoke with c.** il a parlé avec assurance; **he lacks c.** il n'est pas très sûr de lui; **full of c.** *(person)* plein d'assurance *ou* de confiance en soi; *(performance)* plein d'assurance

3 *(certainty)* confiance *f*, certitude *f*; **I can say with c.** je peux dire avec confiance *ou* assurance

4 *(trust)* confiance *f*; **I was told in c.** on me l'a dit confidentiellement *ou* en confiance; **she told me in the strictest c.** elle me l'a dit dans la plus stricte confidence; **to take sb into one's c.** se confier à qn, faire des confidences à qn; **to be in sb's c.** partager les secrets de qn

5 *(private message)* confidence *f*; **to exchange confidences** échanger des confidences

▸▸ ***confidence trick*** escroquerie *f*, abus *m* de confiance; ***confidence trickster*** escroc *m*

> Note that the French word **confidence** never means **trust** or **self-assurance**.
>
> When translating **confidence**, note that the French words **confiance** and **confidence** are not interchangeable. **Confiance** means **trust** and **confidence** is only used in the sense of a **secret**.

confident [ˈkɒnfɪdənt] ADJ **1** *(self-assured)* sûr (de soi), assuré; **in a c. tone** d'un ton assuré *ou* plein d'assurance **2** *(certain)* assuré, confiant; **c. of success** sûr de réussir; **we are c. that the plan will work** nous sommes persuadés que le projet va réussir

> Attention: ne pas confondre avec le nom anglais **confidant**.

confidential [ˌkɒnfɪˈdenʃəl] ADJ **1** *(private)* confidentiel; *(on envelope)* confidentiel; **I would like you to treat this conversation as c.** j'aimerais que vous considériez cette conversation comme étant confidentielle; **keep it c.** n'en parlez à personne **2** *(attached to one person ▸ position)* de confiance

▸▸ ***confidential agent*** homme *m* de confiance; ***confidential secretary*** secrétaire *mf* particulier (ère)

confidentiality [ˌkɒnfɪˌdenʃɪˈælətɪ] N confidentialité *f*; **all inquiries treated with complete c.** *(in advertisement)* les demandes de renseignements sont traitées en toute discrétion

confidentially [ˌkɒnfɪˈdenʃəlɪ] ADV confidentiellement; **c., I don't trust him** entre nous, je ne lui fais pas confiance

confidently [ˈkɒnfɪdəntlɪ] ADV **1** *(with certainty)* avec confiance; **I can c. predict (that)...** je peux prédire avec assurance (que)... **2** *(assuredly)* avec assurance

confiding [kənˈfaɪdɪŋ] ADJ confiant, sans méfiance

configurable [kənˈfɪgjʊrəbəl] ADJ *(gen)* & *Comput* configurable, paramétrable

configuration [kənˌfɪgəˈreɪʃən] N *(gen)* & *Comput* configuration *f*, paramétrage *m*

configure [kənˈfɪgə(r)] VT *(gen)* & *Comput* configurer

confine [kənˈfaɪn] VT **1** *(restrict)* limiter, borner; **to c. oneself to sth** se borner *ou* s'en tenir à qch; **we confined ourselves to discussing the financial arrangements** nous nous en sommes tenus à discuter des dispositions financières; **please c. your remarks to the subject under consideration** veuillez vous limiter au sujet en question; **confined space** espace restreint **2** *(shut up)* confiner, enfermer; *(imprison)* incarcérer, enfermer; **her illness confined her to the house/to bed** sa maladie l'a obligée à rester à la maison/à garder le lit; *Mil* **to c. sb to barracks** consigner qn **3** *Old-fashioned (pregnant woman)* **to be confined** accoucher, être en couches

confinement [kənˈfaɪnmənt] N **1** *(detention)* détention *f*, réclusion *f*; *(imprisonment)* emprisonnement *m*, incarcération *f*; *Mil* **c. to barracks** consigne *f* (au quartier); **six months' c.** six mois de prison **2** *Old-fashioned (in childbirth)* couches *fpl*, accouchement *m*

confines [ˈkɒnfaɪnz] NPL confins *mpl*, limites *fpl*; **within the c. of reason** dans les limites de la raison; **within/beyond the c. of human knowledge** dans/au delà des limites de la connaissance humaine

confirm [kənˈfɜːm] VT **1** *(verify)* confirmer, corroborer; **to c. that...** confirmer que... + *indicative*; *Com* **we c. receipt of** *or* **that we have received your letter** nous accusons réception de votre lettre

2 *(finalize ▸ arrangement, booking)* confirmer; **c. our reservation with the restaurant** confirmez notre réservation auprès du restaurant; **to be confirmed** *(sign for concert, film etc)* à confirmer

3 *(strengthen ▸ position)* assurer, consolider; *(▸ belief, doubts, resolve)* confirmer, raffermir; **that confirms her in her opinion** cela la conforte dans son opinion

4 *(make valid ▸ treaty)* ratifier; *(▸ result)* confirmer; *(▸ election)* valider; *(▸ nomination)* approuver; *(▸ decision)* entériner; *Law* entériner, homologuer

5 *Rel* confirmer; **to be confirmed** recevoir la confirmation

VI confirmer; **please c. in writing** veuillez confirmer par écrit

confirmation [ˌkɒnfəˈmeɪʃən] N **1** *(verification)* confirmation *f*; **the report is still awaiting c.** cette nouvelle n'a pas encore été confirmée; **in c. of** en confirmation de

2 *(finalization ▸ of arrangements)* confirmation *f*; **all bookings subject to c.** *(in brochure, on form, website)* toute réservation doit être confirmée

3 *(strengthening ▸ of position)* consolidation *f*, raffermissement *m*; *(▸ of belief, doubts, resolve)* confirmation *f*

4 *(validation ▸ of treaty)* ratification *f*; *(▸ of result)* confirmation *f*; *(▸ of election)* validation *f*; *(▸ of nomination)* approbation *f*; *(▸ of decision)* entérinement *m*; *Law* entérinement *m*, homologation *f*

5 *Rel* confirmation *f*

▸▸ *Com* ***confirmation of receipt*** accusé *m* de réception

confirmed [kənˈfɜːmd] ADJ **1** *(long-established)* invétéré; **he's a c. bachelor** c'est un célibataire endurci; **he's a c. smoker** c'est un fumeur invétéré **2** *Fin (letter of credit)* irrévocable

▸▸ *Aviat* ***confirmed seat*** place *f* confirmée

confirming bank [kənˈfɜːmɪŋ-] N banque *f* confirmatrice

confiscate [ˈkɒnfɪskeɪt] VT confisquer; **to c. sth from sb** confisquer qch à qn

confiscation [ˌkɒnfɪˈskeɪʃən] N confiscation *f*

confiscatory [ˌkɒnfɪˈskeɪtərɪ] ADJ *(power)* de confiscation

conflagration [ˌkɒnfləˈgreɪʃən] N *Formal* incendie *m*

conflate [kənˈfleɪt] VT *Formal* réunir, regrouper

conflation [kənˈfleɪʃən] N *Formal* fusion *f*

conflict N [ˈkɒnflɪkt] **1** *(clash)* conflit *m*, lutte *f*; *Mil* conflit *m*, guerre *f*; **she often comes into c. with her mother** elle entre souvent en conflit *ou* se heurte souvent avec sa mère **2** *(disagreement)* dispute *f*; *Law* conflit *m*; **to be in c. (with)** être en conflit (avec); **this was in c. with her principles** c'était en conflit *ou* en contradiction avec ses principes; **our differing beliefs brought us into c.** nos croyances divergentes nous ont opposés; **there is a c. between the two statements** les deux déclarations ne concordent pas

VI [kənˈflɪkt] **1** *(ideas, interests)* s'opposer, se heurter; **the research findings c. with this view** les résultats des recherches sont en contradiction avec *ou* contredisent cette idée; **the policies c. (with one another)** ces politiques sont incompatibles **2** *(fight)* être en conflit *ou* en lutte

▸▸ ***conflict diamond*** diamant *m* de la guerre; ***conflict of interests*** conflit *m* d'intérêts

conflicting [kənˈflɪktɪŋ] ADJ *(opinions)* incompatible; *(advice, evidence, reports)* contradictoire

▸▸ ***conflicting interests*** des intérêts *mpl* qui s'opposent

confluence [ˈkɒnflʊəns] N **1** *(of rivers, glaciers ▸ place)* confluent *m*; *(▸ action)* confluence *f* **2** *(gathering together)* confluence *f*, *Fig (crowd)* rassemblement *m*

conform [kənˈfɔːm] VI **1** *(comply ▸ person)* se conformer, s'adapter; **to c. to** *or* **with sth** se conformer *ou* s'adapter à qch; **to c. to the law** obéir aux lois; **you are expected to c.** tu es supposé te conformer

2 *(action, thing)* être en conformité; **all cars must c. to** *or* **with the regulations** toute voiture doit être conforme aux normes

3 *(correspond)* correspondre, répondre; **she conforms to** *or* **with my idea of a president** elle correspond *ou* répond à ma conception d'un président; **this conforms with what we were told/we expected** ceci est conforme à ce que l'on nous avait dit/nos attentes

4 *Rel* être conformiste

VT *(ideas, actions)* conformer, rendre conforme

conformism [kənˈfɔːmɪzəm] N conformisme *m*

conformist [kənˈfɔːmɪst] ADJ conformiste

N *(gen)* & *Rel* conformiste *mf*

conformity [kənˈfɔːmətɪ] *(pl* **conformities***)* N **1** *(with rules, regulations)* conformité *f* **2** *(in behaviour, dress, attitude)* conformisme *m* **3** *Rel* conformisme *m*

• **in conformity with** PREP en accord avec, conformément à; **their action was in c. with the law** ce qu'ils ont fait était en conformité avec la loi

confound [kənˈfaʊnd] VT **1** *(perplex)* déconcerter; **to be confounded** être confondu; **he confounded his critics** il a fait mentir les gens qui le critiquaient

2 *(bring to nothing ▸ plans)* renverser; *(▸ hopes)* réduire à néant

3 *Formal (mix up)* confondre

4 *Fam Old-fashioned (curse)* **c. him!** qu'il aille au diable!; **c. it!** quelle barbe!

5 *Arch (defeat ▸ enemy)* confondre

confounded [kənˈfaʊndɪd] ADJ *Fam Old-fashioned (wretched)* maudit; **it's a c. nuisance!** c'est la barbe!, quelle barbe!; **this c. thing has broken again!** ce satané truc est encore cassé!

confraternity [ˌkɒnfrəˈtɜːnɪtɪ] N association *f*

confront [kənˈfrʌnt] VT **1** *(face)* affronter, faire face à; **the obstacles confronting us** les obstacles auxquels nous devons faire face; **the headmaster confronted him in the corridor** le directeur l'affronta dans le couloir; **the two groups of demonstrators confronted each other** les deux groupes de manifestants se sont affrontés; **to be confronted by** *or* **with sth** *(problem, risk)* se trouver en face de qch **2** *(present)* confronter; **she confronted him with the facts** elle l'a confronté avec les faits

confrontation [ˌkɒnfrʌnˈteɪʃən] N **1** *(conflict)* conflit *m*, affrontement *m*; *Mil* affrontement *m*; **he hates c.** il a horreur des situations de conflit **2** *(act of confronting)* confrontation *f*

confrontational [ˌkɒnfrʌnˈteɪʃənəl] ADJ *(situation)* d'affrontement; *(policy)* de confrontation; **to be c.** *(person)* aimer les conflits

Confucian [kənˈfjuːʃən] N confucéen(enne) *m,f*

ADJ confucéen

confuse [kənˈfjuːz] VT **1** *(muddle ▸ person)* embrouiller; *(▸ thoughts)* embrouiller, brouiller; *(▸ memory)* brouiller; **don't c. me!** ne m'embrouillez pas (les idées)!; **to c. the issue, to c. matters** embrouiller *ou* compliquer les choses

2 *(perplex)* déconcerter, rendre perplexe; *(fluster)* troubler; *(embarrass)* embarrasser
3 *(mix up)* confondre; **you're confusing me with my brother** vous me confondez avec mon frère; **don't c. the two issues** ne confondez pas les deux problèmes
4 *(disconcert ▸ opponent)* confondre

confused [kən'fjuːzd] **ADJ 1** *(muddled ▸ person)* désorienté; *(▸ sounds)* confus, indistinct; *(▸ thoughts)* confus, embrouillé; *(▸ memory)* confus, vague; **wait a minute, I'm getting c.** attends, là, je ne suis plus; **very old people often get c.** les personnes très âgées ont souvent les idées confuses **2** *(perplexed)* perplexe; *(flustered)* troublé; *(embarrassed)* confus; **I'm still a little c. as to why he did it** je ne comprends toujours pas très bien pourquoi il a fait cela **3** *(disordered)* en désordre; *(opponent)* confus

> Note that the most common meaning of the French word **confus** is **embarrassed**.

confusedly [kən'fjuːzɪdlɪ] **ADV** confusément

confusing [kən'fjuːzɪŋ] **ADJ** embrouillé, déroutant; **it's very c.** on s'y perd; **the plot is c.** on se perd dans l'intrigue; **I hope my explanation wasn't too c.** j'espère que mon explication ne vous a pas trop embrouillé; **there's a c. number of different makes** il y a tant de marques différentes qu'on s'y perd

confusingly [kən'fjuːzɪŋlɪ] **ADV** de façon embrouillée; **c., they both had the same name** ils avaient le même nom, ce qui provoquait souvent des confusions

confusion [kən'fjuːʒən] **N 1** *(bewilderment)* confusion *f*; *(embarrassment)* déconfiture *f*, trouble *m*, embarras *m*; **he stared at it in c.** il le fixa d'un regard perplexe; **she's in a state of c.** elle a l'esprit troublé; **this news added to her c.** cette nouvelle a ajouté à sa confusion; **in my c. I said yes** dans mon embarras, j'ai dit oui; **it will only lead to c.** ce ne va faire qu'embrouiller les choses **2** *(mixing up)* confusion *f*; **to avoid c.** pour éviter toute confusion; **there is some c. as to who won** il y a incertitude sur le vainqueur **3** *(disorder)* désordre *m*; *(of enemy)* désordre *m*, désarroi *m*; **everything was in c.** tout était en désordre *ou* sens dessus dessous

confute [kən'fjuːt] **VT** *Formal (argument)* réfuter; *(person)* réfuter les arguments de

conga ['kɒŋgə] *Mus* **N** conga *f*
VI danser la conga
▸▸ ***conga drum*** conga *f*

congeal [kən'dʒiːl] **VI** *(fat, oil)* (se) figer; *(blood)* (se) coaguler; *(milk)* (se) cailler
VT *(fat, oil)* (faire) figer; *(blood)* (faire) coaguler; *(milk)* (faire) cailler

congenial [kən'dʒiːnjəl] **ADJ** *(pleasant)* sympathique, agréable; **in c. surroundings** dans un cadre agréable; **to spend an afternoon in c. company** passer un après-midi en agréable compagnie

congenital [kən'dʒenɪtəl] **ADJ** *Med* congénital, de naissance; *Fig* **he's a c. liar** c'est un menteur né
▸▸ ***congenital defect*** vice *m* de conformation

congenitally [kən'dʒenɪtəlɪ] **ADV** de manière congénitale, congénitalement

conger ['kɒŋgə(r)] **N** *Zool* congre *m*, anguille *f* de mer
▸▸ ***conger eel*** congre *m*, anguille *f* de mer

congest [kən'dʒest] **VT 1** *(crowd)* encombrer **2** *Med (clog)* congestionner

congested [kən'dʒestɪd] **ADJ 1** *(area, town)* surpeuplé; *(road)* encombré, embouteillé; *(airport, communication lines)* encombré; **the roads are c. with traffic** il y a des embouteillages *ou* des encombrements sur les routes **2** *Med (clogged ▸ organ)* congestionné; *(▸ nose)* bouché; **I'm feeling really c.** j'ai les bronches très prises

congestion [kən'dʒestʃən] **N 1** *(of area)* surpeuplement *m*; *(of road, traffic)* encombrement *m*, embouteillage *m*; **the new road will relieve the c. in the town** la nouvelle route va décongestionner la ville **2** *Med (blockage ▸ in organ, nose)* congestion *f*
▸▸ *Br* ***congestion charge*** taxe *f* anti-embouteillages

conglomerate N [kən'glɒmərət] **1** *(mass)* conglomérat *m* **2** *Fin & Econ* conglomérat *m* **3** *Geol* conglomérat *m*
ADJ [kən'glɒmərət] **1** *(composed of various things)* congloméré, aggloméré **2** *Geol* congloméré **3** *(relating to a conglomerate)* congloméral
VI [kən'glɒməreɪt] s'agglomérer

conglomeration [kənˌglɒmə'reɪʃən] **N 1** *(mass)* groupement *m*, rassemblement *m*; *(of buildings)* agglomération *f*; *Fig* **a c. of ideas** un mélange d'idées **2** *(act, state)* agglomération *f*, conglomération *f*

Congo ['kɒŋgəʊ] **N** *(country, river)* **the C.** le Congo

Congolese [ˌkɒŋgə'liːz] *(pl* **inv) N** Congolais(e) *m,f*
ADJ congolais
COMP *(embassy, history)* du Congo

congrats [kən'græts] **EXCLAM** *Fam* chapeau!

congratulate [kən'grætʃʊleɪt] **VT** féliciter, complimenter; **I c. you** je vous félicite, (je vous fais) mes compliments; **she congratulated them on their engagement** elle leur a présenté ses félicitations à l'occasion de leurs fiançailles; **I congratulated myself for having kept my temper** je me suis félicité d'avoir gardé mon sang-froid; **they are to be congratulated** ils méritent d'être félicités

congratulations [kənˌgrætʃʊ'leɪʃənz] **EXCLAM** (toutes mes) félicitations!, je vous félicite!
NPL félicitations *fpl*; **congratulations on the new job/your engagement/passing your exams** félicitations pour votre nouveau poste/vos fiançailles/vos examens; **I hear congratulations are in order** il paraît qu'il faut vous féliciter; **give her my congratulations** transmets-lui mes félicitations, félicite-la de ma part

congratulatory [kən'grætʃʊlətərɪ] **ADJ** de félicitations

congregate ['kɒŋgrɪgeɪt] **VI** se rassembler, se réunir

congregation [ˌkɒŋgrɪ'geɪʃən] **N 1** *(group)* assemblée *f*, rassemblement *m* **2** *Rel (of worshippers)* assemblée *f* (de fidèles), assistance *f*; *(of priests)* congrégation *f*; **I'm not a member of your c.** je ne fais pas partie de votre paroisse, je ne viens pas à l'église ici **3** *Br Univ* assemblée *f* générale

congregational [ˌkɒŋgrɪ'geɪʃənəl] **ADJ 1** *(relating to a group)* d'une assemblée **2** *Rel* de l'assemblée (des fidèles); *(priests)* de *ou* d'une congrégation
• **Congregational ADJ** *Rel* congrégationaliste; **the C. Church** l'Église *f* congrégationaliste

congress ['kɒŋgres] **N 1** *(association, meeting)* congrès *m* **2** *(UNCOUNT) Formal (sexual intercourse)* rapports *mpl* sexuels
• **Congress N** *Pol* Congrès *m*; *(session)* = session du Congrès américain

> **CONGRESS**
>
> Le Congrès, organe législatif américain, est constitué du Sénat et de la Chambre des représentants. Une proposition de loi doit obligatoirement être approuvée séparément par ces deux Chambres. La Chambre des représentants compte 435 membres correspondant aux différentes circonscriptions qui constituent chaque État. Le Sénat est composé de 100 membres (deux par État).

congressional [kəŋ'greʃənəl] **ADJ** *(gen)* d'un congrès
• **Congressional ADJ** *Pol* du Congrès
▸▸ ***Congressional district*** = circonscription d'un représentant du Congrès américain; ***Congressional Record*** = journal officiel du Congrès américain

congressman ['kɒŋgresmən] *(pl* **congressmen** [-mən]) **N** *Pol* membre *m* du Congrès américain; **Mr C.** Monsieur le Député

congresswoman ['kɒŋgresˌwʊmən] *(pl* **congresswomen** [-ˌwɪmɪn]) **N** *Pol* membre *m* du Congrès américain; **Miss/Ms/Mrs C.** Madame le *ou* la député

congruence ['kɒŋgrʊəns], **congruency** ['kɒŋgrʊənsɪ] **N 1** *Formal (similarity)* conformité *f* **2** *Formal (correspondence)* correspondance *f*; *(suitability)* convenance *f* **3** *Math* congruence *f*

congruent ['kɒŋgrʊənt] **ADJ 1** *Formal (similar)* conforme; **c. with** *or* **to** conforme à **2** *Formal (corresponding)* en harmonie; *(suitable)* convenable **3** *Math (number)* congru, congruent; *(triangle)* congruent

congruity [kɒŋ'gruːətɪ] *(pl* **congruities) N** *Formal* convenance *f*

congruous ['kɒŋgrʊəs] **ADJ** *Formal* **1** *(corresponding)* qui s'accorde; **to be c. with sth** s'accorder avec qch **2** *(suitable)* convenable, qui convient

conic ['kɒnɪk] **ADJ** *Geom* conique
▸▸ ***conic projection*** *(in mapmaking)* projection *f* conique; *Geom* ***conic section*** section *f* conique

conical ['kɒnɪkəl] **ADJ** conique

conifer ['kɒnɪfə(r)] **N** conifère *m*

coniferous [kə'nɪfərəs] **ADJ** conifère; **a c. forest** une forêt de conifères

conjectural [kən'dʒektʃərəl] **ADJ** conjectural

conjecture [kən'dʒektʃə(r)] **N** conjecture *f*; **whether he knew or not is a matter for c.** savoir s'il était au courant ou pas relève de la conjecture; **it's sheer c.** ce ne sont que des conjectures
VT conjecturer, présumer
VI conjecturer, faire des conjectures

conjoin [kən'dʒɔɪn] *Formal* **VT** joindre, unir; *Med* **conjoined twins** *(male)* frères *mpl* siamois; *(female)* sœurs *fpl* siamoises
VI s'unir

conjoint [kənˌdʒɔɪnt] **ADJ** *Formal* conjoint, uni

conjointly [kənˌdʒɔɪntlɪ] **ADV** *Formal* conjointement

conjugal ['kɒndʒʊgəl] **ADJ** conjugal
▸▸ ***conjugal rights*** droits *mpl* conjugaux

conjugate VT ['kɒndʒʊˌgeɪt] *Gram (verb)* conjuguer
VI ['kɒndʒʊˌgeɪt] *Gram & Biol* se conjuguer
ADJ ['kɒndʒʊgɪt] **1** *(joined, connected)* conjoint, uni **2** *Chem* conjugué

conjugated ['kɒndʒəˌgeɪtɪd] **ADJ 1** *Gram (verb)* conjugated **2** *Biol & Chem* conjugué

conjugation [ˌkɒndʒʊ'geɪʃən] **N** *Gram & Biol* conjugaison *f*

conjunction [kən'dʒʌŋkʃən] **N 1** *(combination)* conjonction *f*, union *f*; **c. tickets** billets *mpl* complémentaires **2** *Astron & Gram* conjonction *f*; *Astron* **in c.** *(planets)* en conjonction
• **in conjunction with PREP** conjointement avec; **to work in c. with sb** travailler conjointement avec qn; **these factors, in c. with others, were responsible for…** ces facteurs combinés à d'autres furent responsables de…

conjunctive [kən'dʒʌŋktɪv] **ADJ** *(gen) & Anat & Gram* conjonctif

conjunctivitis [kənˌdʒʌŋktɪ'vaɪtɪs] **N** *Med* conjonctivite *f*; **to have c.** avoir de la conjonctivite

conjure VT 1 ['kʌndʒə(r)] *(produce ▸ gen)* faire apparaître, produire; *(▸ by magic)* faire apparaître *(par prestidigitation)*; **to c. a rabbit from a hat** faire sortir un lapin d'un chapeau; **they conjured a bottle of wine out of nowhere** *or* **thin air** ils ont fait apparaître une bouteille de vin comme par enchantement **2** [kən'dʒʊə(r)] *Arch (appeal to)* conjurer, implorer
VI ['kʌndʒə(r)] faire des tours de passe-passe; *Br Fig* **his is a name to c. with** c'est quelqu'un d'important

▸**conjure up VT SEP 1** *(call to mind ▸ images, memories)* évoquer **2** *(call up ▸ spirit etc)* faire apparaître **3** *(produce)* **they conjured up some armchairs** ils ont déniché des fauteuils d'on ne sait où; **she conjured up an incredible meal out of almost nothing** elle a réussi à préparer un repas fantastique avec presque rien

conjurer ['kʌndʒərə(r)] **N** *(magician)* prestidigitateur(trice) *m,f*; *(sorcerer)* sorcier(ère) *m,f*

conjuring ['kʌndʒərɪŋ] **N** prestidigitation *f*
▸▸ ***conjuring trick*** tour *m* de passe-passe *ou* de prestidigitation

conk [kɒŋk] *Fam* N **1** *(blow)* gnon *m* **2** *Br (head)* caboche *f* **3** *Br (nose)* pif *m*
VT *(hit)* cogner

▸ **conk out** VI *Fam* **1** *(machine, television etc)* tomber en panne[a]
2 *(lose consciousness)* tomber dans les pommes
3 *(go to sleep)* s'endormir[a], s'écrouler
4 *Am (die)* clamser, clamecer

conker ['kɒŋkə(r)] N *Br Fam* marron[a] *m*
• **conkers** N = jeu d'enfant qui consiste à tenter de casser un marron tenu au bout d'un fil par son adversaire

Conn *(written abbr* **Connecticut***)* Connecticut *m*

connect [kə'nekt] VT **1** *(join ▸ pipes, wires)* raccorder; *(▸ pinions, shafts, wheels)* engrener, coupler; *Elec (▸ circuits)* interconnecter; *Elec (▸ wires)* connecter; **to c. sth to sth** joindre *ou* relier *ou* raccorder qch à qch; **c. this wire to the other terminal** connectez ce fil à l'autre borne
2 *(join to supply ▸ machine, house, telephone)* brancher, raccorder; **the telephone/electricity hasn't been connected** le téléphone/l'électricité n'a pas été branché(e); **to be connected (up) to sth** être branché sur qch
3 *Tel* mettre en communication, relier; **I'm trying to c. you** j'essaie d'obtenir votre communication
4 *(link ▸ of path, railway, road, airline)* relier; **to c. with** *or* **to** relier à; **the new rail link connects Terminal 3 with** *or* **to the train station** la nouvelle liaison ferroviaire relie l'aérogare 3 à la gare
5 *(associate ▸ person, place, event)* associer; **to c. sb/sth with sb** associer qn/qch à qn; **to c. sb/sth with sth** faire le rapprochement entre qn et qch; **I'd never connected the two things before** je n'avais (encore) jamais fait le rapprochement entre les deux; **there is nothing to c. the two crimes** il n'y a aucun lien entre les deux crimes; **at first I didn't c. the name with the face** au début je n'ai pas fait le lien *ou* le rapprochement entre le nom et le visage; **to be connected with** *(of person)* avoir des relations *ou* un lien avec; *(of thing)* se rattacher *ou* se rapporter à
VI **1** *(bus, plane, train)* assurer la correspondance; **to c. with** assurer la correspondance avec
2 *(blow)* atteindre son but; *(boxer)* frapper *ou* atteindre son adversaire; *(tennis player, cricketer, racket, bat)* frapper la balle; *Fam* **my fist connected with his chin** je l'ai touché au menton[a]
3 *(wires)* être reliés (**with** à); *(roads)* se rejoindre; *(rooms)* communiquer (**with** avec); **this road connects with the motorway** cette route rejoint l'autoroute; **the tunnels don't c.** les deux tunnels ne sont pas reliés *ou* ne communiquent pas
4 *Comput (to Internet)* connecter
N *Comput* connexion *f*
▸▸ ***connect time*** durée *f* (d'établissement) de la connexion

▸ **connect up** VT SEP *(pipes)* raccorder; *Elec (wires)* connecter

connected [kə'nektɪd] ADJ **1** *(linked ▸ subjects, species)* connexe
2 *(coherent ▸ speech, sentences)* cohérent, suivi
3 *(associated)* **to be c. with** avoir un lien *ou* rapport avec
4 *(related)* **to be c. with** *or* **to** avoir un lien de parenté avec; **to be well c.** *(person)* avoir des relations

connecting [kə'nektɪŋ] ADJ *Elec (cable, wire)* de connexion
▸▸ ***connecting door*** porte *f* de communication; ***connecting flight*** correspondance *f*; *Tech* ***connecting pipe*** tuyau *m* de raccordement *ou* de jonction; *Tech* ***connecting rod*** bielle *f*; ***connecting rooms*** *(in hotel)* pièces *fpl* communicantes; ***connecting train*** correspondance *f*

connection [kə'nekʃən] N **1** *(link, association)* lien *m*, rapport *m*, connexion *f*; **to make a c. between** *or* **to** *or* **with sth** faire le lien avec qch; **does this have any c. with what happened yesterday?** ceci a-t-il un rapport quelconque avec ce qui s'est passé hier?; **in this** *or* **that c.** à ce propos, à ce sujet
2 *Tech* connexion *f*; *(of pipes, wires)* assemblage *m*, raccordement *m*; *(of machine parts)* accouplement *m*, engrenage *m*; *Elec* prise *f*, raccord *m*; *Comput* connexion *f*, liaison *f*; **there's a loose c.** il y a un faux contact
3 *Tel* communication *f*, ligne *f*; **a bad c.** une mauvaise communication *ou* ligne
4 *(transfer ▸ between buses, planes, trains)* correspondance *f*; **to miss one's c.** rater sa correspondance
5 *(transport)* liaison *f*; **the town enjoys excellent road and rail connections** la ville dispose d'excellentes liaisons routières et ferroviaires
6 *(personal relationship)* rapport *m*, relation *f*; **he has CIA connections** il a des liens avec la CIA; **family connections** parenté *f*; **to establish a business c. with a firm** établir des relations commerciales avec une entreprise
7 *(family relationship)* parenté *f*; **there's no c. with the Yorkshire Smythes** il n'y a pas de lien de parenté avec les Smythe du Yorkshire; **my family has Scottish connections** il y a des Écossais dans ma famille
8 *(colleague, business contact)* relation *f* (d'affaires); **she has some useful connections in the publishing world** elle a des relations utiles dans le monde de l'édition
• **in connection with** PREP à propos de
▸▸ *Tech* ***connection kit*** kit *m* d'accès *ou* de connexion

connective [kə'nektɪv] ADJ *Gram (word, phrase)* conjonctif
N conjonction *f*
▸▸ *Anat* ***connective tissue*** tissu *m* conjonctif

connectivity [ˌkɒnek'tɪvɪtɪ] N *Comput* connectivité *f*

connector [kə'nektə(r)] N *Elec* connecteur *m*; *Tech* raccord *m*
▸▸ *Tech* ***connector kit*** kit *m* d'accès *ou* de connexion

connexion = **connection**

conning tower ['kɒnɪŋ-] N *Naut (on submarine)* kiosque *m*; *(on warship)* centre *m* opérationnel

conniption [kə'nɪpʃən] N *(often pl) Am Fam* crise *f* d'hystérie[a]; **to be in a c., to have conniptions** piquer une crise

connivance [kə'naɪvəns] N *Pej* connivence *f*; **with the c. of, in c. with** de connivence avec; **to be in c. with sb** être de connivence avec qn

connive [kə'naɪv] VI *Pej (plot)* être de connivence; **they connived together to undermine government policy** ils étaient de connivence pour déstabiliser la politique du gouvernement; **to c. at** *(abuse, irregularity etc)* se rendre complice de

conniving [kə'naɪvɪŋ] ADJ *Pej* malhonnête, rusé, sournois

connoisseur [ˌkɒnə'sɜː(r)] N connaisseur(euse) *m,f*; **a c. of fine wine/good literature** un connaisseur en vins/littérature

connotation [ˌkɒnə'teɪʃən] N **1** *(association)* connotation *f*; **the name has connotations of quality and expertise** ce nom évoque la qualité et la compétence **2** *Ling* connotation *f* **3** *(in logic)* implication *f*

connote [kə'nəʊt] VT **1** *Formal (imply ▸ of word, phrase, name)* évoquer **2** *Ling* connoter **3** *(in logic)* impliquer

connubial [kə'njuːbɪəl] ADJ *Formal or Hum* conjugal, matrimonial; **c. bliss** bonheur *m* conjugal

conquer ['kɒŋkə(r)] VT **1** *(defeat ▸ person, enemy)* vaincre
2 *(take control of ▸ city, nation)* conquérir; *Com & Mktg (▸ market, market share)* conquérir
3 *(succeed in climbing, reaching etc)* conquérir; **Everest was conquered in 1953** l'Everest a été conquis en 1953
4 *(master ▸ feelings, habits)* surmonter; *(▸ disease, disability, fears)* vaincre, surmonter
5 *(win over ▸ someone's heart)* conquérir; *(▸ audience, public)* conquérir, subjuguer

conquering ['kɒŋkərɪŋ] ADJ victorieux

conqueror ['kɒŋkərə(r)] N **1** *(of country)* conquérant *m*; *Hist* **(William) the C.** Guillaume le Conquérant **2** *(victor)* vainqueur *m*

conquest ['kɒŋkwest] N **1** *(of land, person)* conquête *f*; *Com & Mktg (of market, market share)* conquête *f*; **the c. of space** la conquête de l'espace; *Hist* **the (Norman) C.** la conquête de l'Angleterre **2** *(land, person conquered)* conquête *f*; **he's her latest c.** c'est sa dernière conquête; **to make a c.** faire une conquête; **to make a c. of sb** faire la conquête de qn

conrod ['kɒnrɒd] N *Aut* bielle *f*

Cons *Pol (written abbr* **Conservative***)* conservateur(trice) *m,f*

consanguinity [ˌkɒnsæŋ'gwɪnətɪ] N consanguinité *f*

conscience ['kɒnʃəns] N **1** *(moral sense)* conscience *f*; **always let your c. be your guide** laissez-vous toujours guider par votre conscience; **a matter of c.** un cas de conscience; **to have a clear** *or* **an easy c.** avoir la conscience tranquille; **my c. is clear** j'ai la conscience tranquille; **to have a bad** *or* **guilty c.** avoir mauvaise conscience; **to have sth on one's c.** avoir qch sur la conscience; **I can't sleep with that on my c.** je ne peux pas dormir avec ça sur la conscience; **in all c.** en toute conscience **2** *(UNCOUNT) (scruples)* mauvaise conscience *f*, remords *m*, scrupule *m*; **to have no c. (about doing sth)** ne pas avoir de scrupules (à faire qch)
▸▸ ***conscience clause*** clause *f* de conscience; ***conscience money*** argent *m* restitué *(pour soulager sa conscience)*

conscience-stricken ADJ pris de remords; **to be c.** être pris de remords, être la proie des remords

conscientious [ˌkɒnʃɪ'enʃəs] ADJ consciencieux; **she was her usual c. self** elle était consciencieuse comme toujours; **to be c. about timekeeping** être très ponctuel
▸▸ ***conscientious objector*** objecteur *m* de conscience

conscientiously [ˌkɒnʃɪ'enʃəslɪ] ADV consciencieusement

conscientiousness [ˌkɒnʃɪ'enʃəsnɪs] N conscience *f*

conscious ['kɒnʃəs] ADJ **1** *(aware)* conscient; **to be c. of sth/of doing sth** être conscient de qch/de faire qch; **he's all too c. of his shortcomings as a writer** il n'est que trop conscient de ses défauts en tant qu'écrivain; **I wasn't c. of having annoyed you** je ne m'étais pas rendu compte que je t'avais énervé; **to become c. of sth** prendre conscience de qch; **politically c.** politisé
2 *(awake)* conscient; **to become c.** reprendre connaissance; **he's not c. yet** il n'a pas encore repris connaissance; *Fam Hum (he's still in bed)* il n'a pas encore fait surface
3 *(deliberate ▸ attempt)* conscient; *(▸ cruelty, rudeness)* intentionnel, délibéré; **it was not a c. decision** ce n'était pas une décision prise de façon consciente; **it required a c. effort to...** il fallait se forcer pour...
4 *(able to think ▸ being, mind)* conscient
N *Psy* **the c.** le conscient

-conscious ['kɒnʃəs] SUFF conscient de; **clothes-c.** qui fait attention à sa tenue; **fashion-c.** qui suit la mode; **safety-c.** soucieux de sécurité; **health-c.** soucieux de sa santé

consciously ['kɒnʃəslɪ] ADV consciemment, délibérément; **he would never c. do such a cruel thing** il ne ferait jamais une chose aussi cruelle délibérément

consciousness ['kɒnʃəsnɪs] N **1** *(awareness)* conscience *f*; **political c.** conscience *f* politique; **the organization aims to raise people's c. of these problems** l'organisme a pour objet de sensibiliser les gens à ces problèmes **2** *(state of being awake)* connaissance *f*; **to lose c.** perdre connaissance; **to regain c.** reprendre connaissance **3** *(mentality)* conscience *f*; **the national c.** la conscience nationale
▸▸ ***consciousness raising*** sensibilisation *f*

conscript VT [kən'skrɪpt] *(men, troops)* enrôler, recruter; *(workers, labourers)* recruter d'office; **to be conscripted** être appelé (sous les drapeaux); *Fig* **I've been conscripted to do the dishes** on m'a enrôlé *ou* réquisitionné pour faire la vaisselle
N ['kɒnskrɪpt] conscrit *m*, appelé *m*
ADJ ['kɒnskrɪpt] *(army)* de conscrits

conscription [kən'skrɪpʃən] N conscription *f*

consecrate ['kɒnsɪkreɪt] **VT** **1** *Rel (sanctify* ▸ *church, building, bread, wine)* consacrer **2** *Rel (ordain* ▸ *bishop)* consacrer, sacrer **3** *(dedicate)* consacrer, dédier; **to c. one's life to sth** consacrer sa vie à qch; **the day was consecrated to the memory of the country's dead** la journée a été dédiée à la mémoire des morts du pays

consecrated ['kɒnsɪˌkreɪtɪd] **ADJ** *Rel* consacré
▸▸ ***consecrated ground*** terre *f* sainte *ou* bénite

consecration [ˌkɒnsɪ'kreɪʃən] **N** **1** *Rel (sanctification)* consécration *f* **2** *Rel (ordination)* sacre *m* **3** *(dedication)* consécration *f*

consecutive [kən'sekjʊtɪv] **ADJ** **1** *(successive* ▸ *days, weeks)* consécutif; **for the third c. day** pour le troisième jour consécutif; **they have had five c. home wins** ils ont remporté cinq victoires consécutives sur leur terrain; **c. interpreting** interprétation *f* consécutive **2** *Gram (clause)* consécutif

consecutively [kən'sekjʊtɪvlɪ] **ADV** consécutivement; **for five years c.** pendant cinq années consécutives; *Law* **the sentences to be served c.** avec cumul de peines

consensual [kən'sensjʊəl] **ADJ** **1** *Law (contract, agreement)* consensuel **2** *Physiol* consensuel

consensus [kən'sensəs] **N** consensus *m*; **to reach a c.** arriver à un consensus; **what is the c. of opinion?** quelle est l'opinion général?; **they failed to reach a c. (of opinion)** ils n'ont pas obtenu de consensus (d'opinion); **the general c. was that the new road was unnecessary** l'opinion générale était que la nouvelle route n'était pas nécessaire
COMP *(politics)* de consensus; *(management)* par consensus

consent [kən'sent] **VI** consentir; **to c. to sth/to do sth** consentir à qch/à faire qch; **they consented to my request for compassionate leave** ils ont consenti à ma demande de congé exceptionnel
N consentement *m*, accord *m*; **to give/withhold one's c. to sth** donner/ne pas donner son consentement à qch; **we got married without my parents' c.** nous nous sommes mariés sans le consentement de mes parents; **he refused his c. to a divorce** il a refusé son consentement pour le divorce; **by common c.** d'un commun accord; **by mutual c.** par consentement mutuel

consenting [kən'sentɪŋ] **ADJ** *Law (adult)* consentant; *Fam Hum* **she is a c. adult, after all** elle est majeure et vaccinée, après tout

consequence ['kɒnsɪkwəns] **N** **1** *(result)* conséquence *f*, suite *f*; **as a c. of** à la suite de; **it all came about as a c. of that one brief meeting** tout est arrivé à la suite de cette courte réunion; **she acted regardless of the consequences** elle a agi sans se soucier des conséquences; **the policy had terrible consequences for the poor** cette mesure a eu des conséquences terribles pour les pauvres **2** *(importance)* conséquence *f*, importance *f*; **a person of no** *or* **little c.** une personne sans importance; **it is of some c. to me** ça a de l'importance pour moi; **a man of c.** un homme important; **it's of no c.** c'est sans conséquence, cela n'a pas d'importance
• **consequences** **NPL** *(results)* conséquences *fpl*; **to take** *or* **to suffer the consequences** accepter *ou* subir les conséquences; **to face the consequences** faire face aux conséquences **N** *Br (game)* cadavres *mpl* exquis
• **in consequence** **ADV** par conséquent
• **in consequence of** **PREP** **in c. of which, we have made the following decision** à la suite de quoi nous avons pris la décision suivante

consequent ['kɒnsɪkwənt] **ADJ** **1** *(resulting)* résultant; **to be c. upon sth** être la conséquence de qch, résulter de qch; **a glut and the c. drop in prices** un surplus et la baisse des prix qui en résulte **2** *(in logic)* conséquent

consequential [ˌkɒnsɪ'kwenʃəl] **ADJ** **1** *(resulting)* conséquent, consécutif (**to** à); **c. effects** *(of action)* répercussions *fpl* **2** *(self-important)* vaniteux, suffisant **3** *(significant, important)* important
▸▸ *Law* ***consequential damages*** dommages *mpl* indirects

consequently ['kɒnsɪkwəntlɪ] **ADV** par conséquent, donc

conservancy [kən'sɜːvənsɪ] (*pl* **conservancies**) **N** *Ecol* **1** *Br (commission)* administration *f* **2** *(of natural resources)* préservation *f*; **nature c.** défense *f* de l'environnement **3** *(protected area)* zone *f* protégée *(d'un point de vue écologique)*

conservation [ˌkɒnsə'veɪʃən] **N** **1** *(of works of art)* préservation *f* **2** *Ecol (of natural resources)* préservation *f* **3** *Phys* conservation *f*; **the c. of energy/mass/momentum** le principe de conservation de l'énergie/de la masse/du moment
▸▸ *Ecol* ***conservation area*** zone *f* protégée *(d'un point de vue architectural ou historique)*

conservationist [ˌkɒnsə'veɪʃənɪst] **N** *Ecol* défenseur *m* de l'environnement

conservatism [kən'sɜːvəˌtɪzəm] **N** *(traditionalism)* conservatisme *m*
• **Conservatism** **N** *Pol (policy of Conservative Party)* conservatisme *m*

conservative [kən'sɜːvətɪv] **N** *(traditionalist)* traditionaliste *mf*, conformiste *mf*
ADJ **1** *(traditionalist* ▸ *views)* conformiste
2 *(conventional* ▸ *suit, clothes)* classique
3 *(modest* ▸ *estimate)* prudent; **at a c. estimate** au minimum, au bas mot
4 *Phys* conservateur
• **Conservative** *Pol* **N** conservateur(trice) *m,f*
ADJ *(policy, government, MP)* conservateur
▸▸ *Br* ***the Conservative Party*** le parti conservateur

conservatively [kən'sɜːvətɪvlɪ] **ADV** *(dress)* de façon conventionnelle; **it was c. estimated at £5,000** selon des estimations prudentes, cela devrait coûter 5000 livres

conservatoire [kən'sɜːvəˌtwɑː(r)] **N** conservatoire *m*

conservatory [kən'sɜːvətərɪ] (*pl* **conservatories**) **N** **1** *(greenhouse)* jardin *m* d'hiver **2** *(attached to house)* véranda *f* **3** *(school)* conservatoire *m*

conserve **VT** [kən'sɜːv] **1** *(save* ▸ *energy, resources, battery)* économiser; **to c. one's strength** ménager ses forces **2** *(building, monument)* conserver, préserver
N ['kɒnsɜːv, kən'sɜːv] confiture *f*; **strawberry c.** confiture *f* de fraises

consider [kən'sɪdə(r)] **VT** **1** *(believe)* considérer, estimer, penser; **I've always considered her (to be) a good friend** je l'ai toujours considérée comme une bonne amie; **she considers it wrong to say such things** elle pense qu'il est mauvais de dire de telles choses; **c. it done** considérez cela comme fait; **c. yourself dismissed** tenez-vous pour congédié; **I c. myself lucky** je m'estime heureux; **I would c. it an honour** je m'estimerais honoré; **I c. it my duty to...** j'estime qu'il est de mon devoir de...; **we c. it likely that...** nous estimons qu'il est probable que... + *indicative*
2 *(ponder* ▸ *problem, offer, possibility)* considérer, examiner; *(*▸ *issue, question)* réfléchir à; **have you ever considered becoming an actress?** avez-vous jamais songé à devenir actrice?; **have you considered (buying) a larger model?** est-ce que vous avez envisagé d'acheter un modèle plus grand?; **he was considering whether to go out when...** il se demandait s'il allait sortir quand...; **I'm willing to c. your offer** je suis prêt à examiner votre proposition; **I'll c. it** je verrai, je réfléchirai; **the jury retired to c. its verdict** le jury se retira pour délibérer
3 *(bear in mind* ▸ *points, facts)* prendre en considération; *(*▸ *costs, difficulties, dangers)* tenir compte de; **we got off lightly, when you c. what might have happened** nous nous en sommes bien tirés, quand on pense à ce qui aurait pu arriver; **all things considered** tout bien considéré
4 *(show regard for* ▸ *feelings, wishes)* tenir compte de; **she never considers anybody but herself** elle ne fait jamais attention aux autres
5 *(discuss* ▸ *report, case)* examiner, considérer; **she's being considered for the post of manager** on pense à elle pour le poste de directeur
6 *(contemplate* ▸ *picture, scene)* examiner, observer
VI réfléchir; **I need time to c.** j'ai besoin de temps pour réfléchir

considerable [kən'sɪdərəbəl] **ADJ** **1** *(great)* considérable; **she showed c. courage** elle a fait preuve de beaucoup de courage; **a c. number (of)** un nombre considérable (de); **to a c. extent** dans une (très) large mesure; **with c. difficulty** avec beaucoup de difficulté **2** *(worthy of attention)* digne d'attention; *(person)* notable, important

considerably [kən'sɪdərəblɪ] **ADV** considérablement

considerate [kən'sɪdərət] **ADJ** *(person)* prévenant (**with** envers), plein d'égards (**with** envers *ou* pour), aimable (**with** envers); **that's very c. of you** c'est très aimable à vous; **try to be more c.** essaie d'être un peu plus prévenant; **he's always so c. of** *or* **towards others** il est toujours si prévenant envers les autres

considerately [kən'sɪdərətlɪ] **ADV** avec des égards

consideration [kənˌsɪdə'reɪʃən] **N** **1** *(thought)* considération *f*; **I'll give it some c.** j'y penserai; **the matter needs careful c.** le sujet demande une attention particulière; **to take sth into c.** prendre qch en considération, tenir compte de qch; **taking everything** *or* **all things into c.** tout bien considéré; **after due c.** après mûre réflexion
2 *(factor)* considération *f*, préoccupation *f*; **time is our main c.** le temps est notre principale préoccupation; **there is another c.** il y a autre chose dont il faut tenir compte; **money is always the first c.** la question d'argent vient toujours en premier; **money is no c.** l'argent n'entre pas en ligne de compte
3 *(thoughtfulness)* égard *m*; **to show c. for sb/sb's feelings** ménager qn/la sensibilité de qn; **show some c.!** fais preuve d'un peu de considération!; **have you no c. for other people?** n'as-tu donc aucun égard pour les autres?; **she remained silent out of c. for his family** elle se tut par égard pour sa famille
4 *(discussion)* étude *f*; **under c.** *(question, candidate etc)* à l'étude
5 *(importance)* **of no c.** sans importance
6 *Formal (payment)* rémunération *f*, finance *f*; **for a small c.** moyennant rémunération *ou* finance; **he'll do it for a c.** il le fera si vous le payez; **in c. of your services** en récompense de vos services

considered [kən'sɪdəd] **ADJ** **1** *(reasoned* ▸ *opinion, manner)* bien pesé, mûrement réfléchi; **it's my c. opinion that...** après mûre réflexion, je pense que... + *indicative*; **is that your c. opinion?** est-ce ainsi que vous voyez les choses? **2** *Formal (respected* ▸ *artist, writer)* considéré, respecté

considering [kən'sɪdərɪŋ] **CONJ** étant donné que, vu que; **c. she'd never played the part before, she did very well** pour quelqu'un qui n'avait jamais tenu ce rôle, elle s'est très bien débrouillée
PREP étant donné, vu; **c. his age/the circumstances** étant donné *ou* vu son âge/les circonstances
ADV *Fam* tout compte fait▫, finalement▫; **it's not so bad, c.** ce n'est pas si mauvais après tout▫ *ou* malgré tout▫

consign [kən'saɪn] **VT** **1** *Com (send* ▸ *goods)* envoyer, expédier; **to c. sth to sb** envoyer qch à qn **2** *(relegate* ▸ *thing)* reléguer; **I consigned his last letter to the rubbish bin** sa dernière lettre s'est retrouvée à la poubelle **3** *(entrust* ▸ *person)* confier; **as a child I was consigned to the care of my grandmother** enfant je fus confié aux soins de ma grand-mère

consignee [ˌkɒnsaɪ'niː] **N** *Com* consignataire *mf*

consignment [kən'saɪnmənt] **N** *Com* **1** *(despatch)* envoi *m*, expédition *f*; **goods for c.** marchandise *f* à expédier **2** *(batch of goods)* arrivage *m*, lot *m*; **a c. of heavy machinery** un arrivage de machines lourdes
▸▸ ***consignment note*** bordereau *m* d'expédition

▸ **consist in** [kən'sɪst-] **VT INSEP** *Formal* **to c. in sth/in doing sth** consister dans qch/à faire qch; **his "genius" consists in a mere talent for mimicry** son "génie" se résume à son talent d'imitateur

▸ **consist of** **VT INSEP** consister en, se composer de; **the panel consists of five senior lecturers** le jury se compose de cinq maîtres de conférence

consistency [kən'sɪstənsɪ] (*pl* **consistences** *or* **consistencies**) **N** **1** *(texture)* consistance *f*; **keep stirring until you get the right c.** remuez jusqu'à

ce que vous obteniez la consistance souhaitée **2** *(coherence ▸ of behaviour, argument, ideas etc)* cohérence *f*, logique *f*; **their policies lack c.** leur politique manque de cohérence
3 *(constancy ▸ of quality of work, ideas)* constance *f*; *(▸ of athlete, performances)* régularité *f*; **c. check** contrôle *m* d'uniformité
4 *(compatibility ▸ of result with theory)* concordance *f*
▸▸ *Acct* ***consistency concept*** principe *m* de la permanence (des méthodes)

consistent [kən'sɪstənt] **ADJ 1** *(having internal logic ▸ reasoning, behaviour, person)* conséquent, cohérent, logique; **she was c. in her choice of partners** elle a toujours fait preuve de cohérence dans le choix de ses partenaires **2** *(constant ▸ quality of work, ideas)* constant; *(▸ refusal, failure)* persistant; *(athlete, performer)* régulier **3** *(compatible)* compatible (**with** avec); **the results are c. with the theory** les résultats concordent avec la théorie; **this action is not c. with his character** cette action n'est pas en harmonie avec son caractère

Note that the French word **consistant** is a false friend and is never a translation for the English word **consistent**. Its most common meaning is **substantial**.

consistently [kən'sɪstəntlɪ] **ADV 1** *(with logic)* de manière cohérente *ou* conséquente **2** *(with regularity ▸ play, perform, work)* avec régularité; *(▸ fail, maintain)* constamment; **she has c. denied the accusation** elle a toujours nié cette accusation; **he has been c. better than the others** il a constamment été meilleur que les autres

consistory [kən'sɪstərɪ] *(pl* **consistories***)* **N** *Rel (pontifical)* consistoire *m*
▸▸ ***Consistory Court*** tribunal *m* ecclésiastique

consolation [ˌkɒnsə'leɪʃən] **N** consolation *f*, réconfort *m*; **that's one c.** c'est déjà une consolation; **if it's any c., the same thing happened to me** si cela peut te consoler, il m'est arrivé la même chose; **words of c.** mots *mpl* de réconfort
▸▸ *also Fig* ***consolation prize*** prix *m* de consolation

console **VT** [kən'səʊl] consoler; **he consoled me in my grief** il m'a consolé de ma peine; **c. yourself with the thought that it's Friday tomorrow** console-toi en pensant que demain c'est vendredi
N ['kɒnsəʊl] **1** *(control panel)* console *f*, pupitre *m*; *Aviat* tableau *m* de bord
2 *(cabinet)* meuble *m (pour téléviseur, chaîne hi-fi)*
3 *Mus (on organ)* console *f*
4 *Archit* console *f*
▸▸ ***console table*** console *f*

consolidate [kən'sɒlɪdeɪt] **VT 1** *(reinforce ▸ forces, power)* consolider; *(▸ knowledge)* consolider, renforcer; *Mil (position)* raffermir; **the company has consolidated its position as the market leader** la société a conforté *ou* renforcé sa position de leader sur le marché **2** *(combine ▸ companies, states)* réunir, fusionner; *Fin (▸ funds, loans, debt)* consolider; *St Exch (▸ shares)* regrouper; *Com (▸ orders, deliveries, consignments)* grouper
VI se consolider

consolidated [kən'sɒlɪˌdeɪtɪd] **ADJ 1** *Fin (funds, loan, debt)* consolidé; *St Exch (shares)* regroupé; *Com (orders, deliveries, consignments)* groupé **2** *(in name of company)* = désigne une société née de la fusion de deux entreprises
▸▸ *Acct* ***consolidated accounts*** comptes *mpl* consolidés; *Acct* ***consolidated balance sheet*** bilan *m* consolidé; *Pol* ***consolidated fund*** = "compte en banque" du gouvernement à la Banque d'Angleterre, qui sert à régler toutes les dépenses publiques; ***consolidated loan*** emprunt *m* consolidé

consolidation [kənˌsɒlɪ'deɪʃən] **N 1** *(reinforcement ▸ of power)* consolidation *f*; *(▸ of knowledge)* consolidation *f*, renforcement *m* **2** *(amalgamation ▸ of companies, states)* fusion *f*; *Fin (▸ of funds, loan, debt)* consolidation *f*; *St Exch (▸ of shares)* regroupement *m*; *Com (▸ of orders, deliveries, consignments)* groupage *m*

consolidator [kən'sɒlɪˌdeɪtə(r)] **N** *Com* groupeur *m*

consoling [kən'səʊlɪŋ] **ADJ** *(idea, thought)* réconfortant

consols ['kɒnsɒlz] **NPL** *Br Fin* (fonds *mpl*) consolidés *mpl*

consonance ['kɒnsənəns] **N 1** *Formal (of ideas)* accord *m*; **in c. with** en accord avec **2** *Literature, Ling & Mus* consonance *f*

consonant ['kɒnsənənt] **N** *Ling* consonne *f*
ADJ *Formal* en accord; **to be c. with** *or* **to sth** être en accord avec qch
▸▸ *Ling* ***consonant shift*** mutation *f* des consonnes

consort **N** ['kɒnsɔːt] **1** *(spouse)* époux *m*, épouse *f*; *(of monarch)* consort *m* **2** *Naut (ship)* escorteur *m*
VI [kən'sɔːt] **to c. with sb** fréquenter qn, frayer avec qn

consortium [kən'sɔːtjəm] *(pl* **consortiums** *or* **consortia** [-tjə]*)* **N** *Com, Fin & Law* consortium *m*

conspicuous [kən'spɪkjʊəs] **ADJ 1** *(visible)* bien visible; *(behaviour, hat, person)* voyant; **he felt c. in his new hat** il avait l'impression que son nouveau chapeau ne passait pas inaperçu; **to make oneself c.** se faire remarquer **2** *(obvious ▸ failure, lack)* manifeste, évident; *(▸ bravery, gallantry)* insigne; **to be c. by one's absence** briller par son absence
▸▸ ***conspicuous consumption*** consommation *f* ostentatoire

conspicuously [kən'spɪkjʊəslɪ] **ADV 1** *(visibly ▸ dressed)* de façon à se faire remarquer **2** *(obviously ▸ successful)* de façon remarquable *ou* évidente

conspicuousness [kən'spɪkjʊəsnɪs] **N 1** *(visibility)* caractère *m* bien visible; *(of behaviour, hat, person)* caractère *m* voyant **2** *(obvious nature ▸ of action)* caractère *m* insigne *ou* remarquable

conspiracy [kən'spɪrəsɪ] *(pl* **conspiracies***)* **N 1** *(plotting)* conspiration *f*, complot *m*; *(plot)* complot *m*; **he's been charged with c.** on l'a accusé de conspiration; **there's a c. against me** il y a un complot contre moi; **a c. of silence** une conspiration du silence **2** *Law (group of conspirators)* association *f* de malfaiteurs
▸▸ ***conspiracy theory*** thèse *f ou* théorie *f* du complot

conspirator [kən'spɪrətə(r)] **N** conspirateur(trice) *m,f*, comploteur(euse) *m,f*, conjuré(e) *m,f*

conspiratorial [kənˌspɪrə'tɔːrɪəl] **ADJ** *(smile, whisper, wink)* de conspirateur; *(group)* de conspirateurs

conspire [kən'spaɪə(r)] **VI 1** *(plot)* conspirer; **to c. (with sb) to do sth** comploter *ou* s'entendre (avec qn) pour faire qch; **to c. against sb** conspirer contre qn **2** *(combine ▸ events, the elements)* concourir, se conjurer; **to c. to do sth** concourir à faire qch; **everything conspired to make him late** tout a contribué à le mettre en retard; **circumstances conspired against me** les circonstances se sont liguées contre moi

constable ['kʌnstəbəl] **N** *Br* **(police) c.** agent *m* de police; **excuse me, C.** excusez-moi, monsieur l'agent

constabulary [kən'stæbjʊlərɪ] *(pl* **constabularies***)* **N the c.** la police
ADJ *(duties)* de policier

constancy ['kɒnstənsɪ] **N 1** *(steadfastness)* constance *f*; *(of feelings)* constance *f*, fidélité *f* **2** *(stability ▸ of temperature, light)* constance *f*; *(▸ of wind)* régularité *f*

constant ['kɒnstənt] **ADJ 1** *(continuous ▸ interruptions, noise, pain)* constant, continuel, perpétuel; *(▸ doubts, questions, complaining)* incessant; *(▸ care)* continuel, assidu, soutenu; **the entrance is in c. use** il y a un mouvement continuel à l'entrée; **through c. repetition** à force de répéter; **there was c. pressure for reform** il y avait une pression continuelle pour qu'une réforme soit mise en œuvre **2** *(unchanging ▸ pressure, temperature, light)* constant; *(▸ wind)* régulier **3** *(faithful ▸ affection, friend)* fidèle, loyal; **he was her c. companion** il était son fidèle compagnon
N *Math & Phys* constante *f*

constantly ['kɒnstəntlɪ] **ADV** constamment, sans cesse

constant-velocity joint **N** *Aut* joint *m* de cardan, joint *m* homocinétique

constellation [ˌkɒnstə'leɪʃən] **N 1** *Astron (of stars)* constellation *f* **2** *Fig (of celebrities)* constellation *f*

consternation [ˌkɒnstə'neɪʃən] **N** consternation *f*; **I watched in c.** je regardais avec consternation; **a look of c.** un air consterné; **the prospect filled me with c.** cette perspective m'a plongé dans la consternation

constipate ['kɒnstɪˌpeɪt] **VT** constiper

constipated ['kɒnstɪpeɪtɪd] **ADJ** *also Fig* constipé; *Fig* **his rather c. prose style** son style plutôt empesé *ou* guindé

constipation [ˌkɒnstɪ'peɪʃən] **N** constipation *f*

constituency [kən'stɪtjʊənsɪ] *(pl* **constituencies***)* *Pol* **N** *(area)* circonscription *f* électorale; *(people)* = habitants d'une circonscription électorale
COMP *(meeting, organization)* local; *Br* **the c. party** la section locale du parti

constituent [kən'stɪtjʊənt] **ADJ 1** *(component ▸ part, element)* constituant, composant **2** *Pol (assembly, power)* constituant
N 1 *Pol* administré(e) *m,f* **2** *(element)* élément *m* constitutif
▸▸ *Ling* ***constituent analysis*** analyse *f* en constituants; *Pol* ***constituent body*** corps *m* constitué

constitute ['kɒnstɪtjuːt] **VT 1** *(represent)* constituer; **what constitutes a state of emergency?** qu'est-ce que c'est qu'un état d'urgence?; **they c. a threat to the government** ils représentent une menace pour le gouvernement
2 *(make up)* constituer; **the countries that c. the EU** les pays qui constituent l'UE
3 *(set up ▸ committee)* constituer
4 *Formal (appoint ▸ chairman)* désigner; **to c. sb arbitrator** constituer qn arbitre

constituted ['kɒnstɪtjuːtɪd] **ADJ** *Pol* constitué

constitution [ˌkɒnstɪ'tjuːʃən] **N 1** *Pol (statute)* constitution *f*; *Am Pol* **the (United States) C.** la Constitution **2** *(health)* constitution *f*; **to have a strong/weak c.** avoir une constitution robuste/chétive **3** *(structure)* composition *f*

constitutional [ˌkɒnstɪ'tjuːʃənəl] **ADJ 1** *Pol (regime, reform)* constitutionnel; **the president's actions are not c.** les actions du président sont anticonstitutionnelles **2** *(official ▸ head, privilege)* constitutionnel **3** *(inherent ▸ weakness)* constitutionnel
N *Old-fashioned or Hum* **he's gone for his morning c.** il est allé faire sa petite promenade matinale
▸▸ ***constitutional law*** droit *m* constitutionnel; ***constitutional monarchy*** monarchie *f* constitutionnelle

constitutionalize, -ise [ˌkɒnstɪ'tjuːʃənəlaɪz] **VT** *Pol* constitutionnaliser

constitutionally [ˌkɒnstɪ'tjuːʃənəlɪ] **ADV 1** *Pol (act)* constitutionnellement **2** *(inherently ▸ strong, weak, lazy)* de *ou* par nature

constitutive ['kɒnstɪˌtjuːtɪv] **ADJ 1** *(body, organization)* constitutif **2** *Chem* constitutif **3** *(component ▸ part, element)* constituant, composant

constrain [kən'streɪn] **VT 1** *(force)* contraindre, forcer; **to c. sb to do sth** contraindre qn à faire qch **2** *(limit ▸ feelings, freedom)* contraindre, restreindre; *(of clothing)* gêner

constrained [kən'streɪnd] **ADJ 1** *(inhibited)* contraint; **to feel c. to do sth** se sentir contraint *ou* obligé de faire qch; **he felt c. by his clothes** il se sentait à l'étroit dans ses vêtements **2** *(tense ▸ manner, speech)* contraint; *(▸ atmosphere, smile)* contraint, gêné

constraint [kən'streɪnt] **N 1** *(restriction)* contrainte *f*; **there are certain constraints on their activities** ils subissent certaines contraintes dans leurs activités; **social constraints** contraintes *fpl* sociales; **to speak without c.** parler librement *ou* sans contrainte **2** *(pressure)* contrainte *f*; **to do sth under c.** agir *ou* faire qch sous la contrainte

constrict [kən'strɪkt] **VT 1** *(make narrower ▸ blood vessels, throat)* resserrer, serrer **2** *(hamper ▸ breathing, movement)* gêner

constricted [kən'strɪktɪd] **ADJ** *(opening, passage)* étroit; *(breathing, movement)* gêné, restreint; *also Fig* **to feel c. by sth** se sentir limité par qch

constriction [kən'strɪkʃən] **N 1** *(▸ in chest, throat)* constriction *f* **2** *(restriction)* restriction *f*

constrictive [kən'strɪktɪv] **ADJ** *Med* constrictif

constrictor [kən'strɪktə(r)] **N 1** *Anat* (muscle *m*) constricteur *m* **2** *Zool (snake)* constricteur *m*

construct VT [kən'strʌkt] **1** *(build ▸ building, bridge, dam, house, road)* construire; *(▸ nest, raft)* construire, bâtir; **to c. sth (out) of sth** construire qch à partir de qch **2** *(formulate ▸ sentence, play)* construire; *(▸ system, theory)* bâtir; **a beautifully constructed play** une pièce magnifiquement construite *ou* composée

N ['kɒnstrʌkt] **1** *Formal (thing constructed)* construction *f* **2** *Psy (idea)* concept *m*

construction [kən'strʌkʃən] **N 1** *(act of building ▸ of road, bridge, house)* construction *f*; *(▸ of machine)* construction *f*, réalisation *f*; **a building of simple/solid c.** un bâtiment de construction simple/solidement construit; **under c.** en construction; **to work in c.** travailler dans le bâtiment

2 *(thing constructed)* construction *f*

3 *(formulation ▸ of sentence, play)* construction *f*; *(▸ of system, theory)* construction *f*, élaboration *f*

4 *(interpretation)* interprétation *f*; **to put a wrong c. on sb's words** mal interpréter les paroles de qn

5 *Gram* construction *f*

6 *Geom* construction *f*

7 *Art* sculpture *f* constructiviste

COMP *(site, work)* de construction

▸▸ ***the construction industry*** le bâtiment; *Am* ***construction paper*** papier épais *m* de couleur; ***construction set*** jeu *m* de construction; ***construction worker*** ouvrier *m* du bâtiment

constructional [kən'strʌkʃənəl] **ADJ** de construction; *(technique)* mécanique

▸▸ *Tech* ***constructional engineering*** construction *f* mécanique

constructive [kən'strʌktɪv] **ADJ 1** *(criticism, remark)* constructif **2** *(relating to construction)* de construction

▸▸ *Ind* ***constructive dismissal*** = démission provoquée par la conduite de l'employeur

constructively [kən'strʌktɪvlɪ] **ADV** de manière constructive

constructor [kən'strʌktə(r)] **N 1** *(of building, road, machine)* constructeur *m* **2** *(of system, theory)* créateur *m*

construe [kən'struː] **VT 1** *(interpret, understand ▸ attitude, statement)* interpréter, expliquer; **the phrase can be construed to mean two things** on peut interpréter l'expression de deux manières différentes **2** *Gram (parse)* analyser, décomposer **3** *Old-fashioned Gram (translate)* traduire oralement

consul ['kɒnsəl] **N** consul *m*

▸▸ ***consul general*** consul *m* général

consular ['kɒnsjʊlə(r)] **ADJ** consulaire

▸▸ *Com* ***consular fees*** frais *mpl* consulaires; *Com* ***consular invoice*** facture *f* consulaire

consulate ['kɒnsjʊlət] **N** consulat *m*

consult [kən'sʌlt] **VT 1** *(ask ▸ doctor, expert)* consulter; **to c. sb about sth** consulter qn sur *ou* au sujet de qch **2** *(consider ▸ person's feelings)* prendre en considération **3** *(refer to ▸ book, map, watch)* consulter

VI consulter, être en consultation; **to c. together over sth** se consulter sur *ou* au sujet de qch; **to c. with sb** conférer avec qn

consultancy [kən'sʌltənsɪ] *(pl* **consultancies***)* **N 1** *(company)* cabinet *m* d'expert-conseil **2** *(advice)* assistance *f* technique; **to do c. work** être consultant **3** *Med (hospital post)* poste *m* de médecin/chirurgien consultant

▸▸ ***consultancy fees*** frais *mpl* de conseil; ***consultancy service*** service *m* d'assistance technique

consultant [kən'sʌltənt] **N 1** *Med (doctor ▸ specialist)* médecin *m* spécialiste, consultant *m*; *(▸ in charge of department)* consultant *m* **2** *(expert)* expert-conseil *m*, consultant *m*

COMP *(engineer)* conseil *(inv)*; *Med (doctor)* consultant

consultation [ˌkɒnsəl'teɪʃən] **N 1** *(discussion)* consultation *f*, délibération *f*; **a matter for c.** un sujet à débattre; **in c. with** en consultation *ou* en concertation avec; **to hold consultations about sth** avoir des consultations sur qch **2** *(reference)* consultation *f*; **the dictionary is designed for easy c.** le dictionnaire a été conçu pour être consulté facilement

consultative [kən'sʌltətɪv] **ADJ** consultatif; **I'm here in a purely c. capacity** je ne suis ici qu'à titre consultatif

consulting [kən'sʌltɪŋ] **ADJ** *(engineer)* conseil *(inv)*

▸▸ *Med* ***consulting room*** cabinet *m* de consultation

consumable [kən'sjuːməbəl] **ADJ** *(substance ▸ by fire)* consumable; *(foodstuffs)* consommable, de consommation

• **consumables NPL** *(food)* denrées *fpl* alimentaires, comestibles *mpl*; *(hardware)* consommables *mpl*

▸▸ *Com & Econ* ***consumable goods*** produits *mpl* de consommation

consume [kən'sjuːm] **VT 1** *(eat or drink)* consommer **2** *(use up ▸ energy, fuel)* consommer; *(▸ time)* dépenser **3** *(burn up ▸ of fire, flames)* consumer; **the city was consumed by fire** la ville a brûlé; *Fig* **to be consumed with desire/love** brûler de désir/d'amour; *Fig* **to be consumed with grief** être miné par le chagrin; *Fig* **to be consumed with hatred/jealousy** être dévoré par la haine/la jalousie

> When translating **to consume**, note that the French verbs **consommer** and **consumer** are not interchangeable. **Consommer** always refers to consumer activity, while **consumer** is used to describe the process of being eaten up or destroyed, especially by fire.

consumer [kən'sjuːmə(r)] **N** *(purchaser, user)* consommateur(trice) *m,f*; **gas/electricity c.** abonné(e) *m,f* au gaz/à l'électricité

COMP du consommateur, des consommateurs

▸▸ *Com* ***Consumers' Association*** = association britannique des consommateurs; *Mktg* ***consumer behaviour*** comportement *m* du consommateur; *Com & Mktg* ***consumer credit*** crédit *m* à la consommation; *Com & Econ* ***consumer debt*** endettement *m* des consommateurs; *Com & Mktg* ***consumer demand*** demande *f* des consommateurs; *Com & Econ* ***consumer durables*** biens *mpl* de consommation durables; ***consumer expenditure*** dépenses *fpl* de consommation; ***consumer goods*** biens *mpl* de consommation durables; ***consumer group*** groupe *m* de consommateurs; *Com* ***consumer organization*** organisme *m* de défense des consommateurs; *Com & Econ* ***consumer price index*** indice *m* des prix à la consommation; ***consumer products*** biens *mpl* de consommation; *Com & Econ* ***consumer protection*** défense *f* des consommateurs; ***consumer protection agency*** bureau *m* d'accueil des consommateurs; *Com & Econ* ***consumer society*** société *f* de consommation; *Com & Econ* ***consumer spending*** dépenses *fpl* de consommation; *Mktg* ***consumer survey*** étude *f* auprès des consommateurs finaux; ***consumer terrorism*** = actes de terrorisme perpétrés contre une entreprise par un client mécontent

consumerism [kən'sjuːməˌrɪzəm] **N** *Com & Econ* **1** *(consumer protection)* consumérisme *m* **2** *Pej (consumption)* consommation *f* à outrance

consummate ADJ ['kɒnsjʊmət, kən'sʌmət] *Formal* **1** *(very skilful ▸ artist, musician)* consommé, accompli; **she was c. in the art of concealing her feelings** elle était maître dans l'art de cacher ses sentiments **2** *(utter ▸ coward, fool, liar, snob)* accompli, parfait, fini

VT ['kɒnsəmeɪt] *(marriage, relationship)* consommer

consummation [ˌkɒnsə'meɪʃən] **N 1** *(of marriage, relationship)* consommation *f* **2** *(culmination ▸ of career, life's work)* couronnement *m* **3** *(achievement ▸ of ambitions, desires)* achèvement *m*

consumption [kən'sʌmpʃən] **N 1** *(eating, drinking)* consommation *f*; **unfit for human c.** non comestible; *Fig* **his words were not intended for public c.** ses paroles n'étaient pas destinées au public

2 *Com & Econ (purchasing)* consommation *f*

3 *(using up, amount used ▸ of gas, energy, oil)* consommation *f*, dépense *f*

4 *Old-fashioned Med (tuberculosis)* consomption *f* (pulmonaire), phtisie *f*

▸▸ *Com & Econ* ***consumption expenditure, consumption spending*** dépenses *fpl* de consommation

consumptive [kən'sʌmptɪv] *Old-fashioned Med*

ADJ *(disease, illness)* consomptif, destructif

N phtisique *mf*, tuberculeux(euse) *m,f*

cont. 1 *(written abbr* **contents***)* contenu *m*; *(in book)* table *f* des matières **2** *(written abbr* **continued***)* suite

contact ['kɒntækt] **N 1** *(UNCOUNT) (communication)* contact *m*, rapport *m*; **we don't have much c. with our neighbours** nous n'avons pas beaucoup de contacts avec nos voisins; **to be in c. with sb** être en contact *ou* en rapport avec qn; **the two leaders are in close c.** les deux dirigeants sont en contact étroit; **to come into c. with sb** entrer *ou* se mettre en contact *ou* en rapport avec qn; **anyone who has come into c. with the sick man** quiconque s'est trouvé au contact du malade; **she hadn't come into c. with poverty** elle ne s'était pas trouvée au contact de la pauvreté; **to make/lose c. with sb** prendre/perdre contact avec qn; **to stay in c. with sb** garder le contact *ou* rester en contact avec qn; **shall I give you a c. address/number?** voulez-vous que je vous donne l'adresse/le numéro où vous pouvez me joindre?

2 *(UNCOUNT) (touch)* contact *m*; **to come into c. with** entrer en contact avec, toucher; **the substance must not come into c. with the air** la substance ne doit pas être exposée à l'air; **always keep one foot in c. with the ground** gardez toujours un pied au sol; **physical c.** contact *m* physique; **eye c.** contact *m* visuel; **to make eye c. with sb** rencontrer le regard de qn

3 *(person)* relation *f*; **she has some useful business contacts** elle a quelques bons contacts (professionnels); **who's our c. in Paris?** qui est notre contact à Paris?

4 *Elec (connector, connection)* contact *m*; **to make/break (the) c.** mettre/couper le contact

5 *Med* = personne ayant approché un malade contagieux

6 *Phot (contact print)* planche *f* contact, épreuve *f* par contact

7 *(contact lens)* verre *m ou* lentille *f* de contact; **to wear contacts** porter des lentilles de contact

VT prendre contact avec, contacter; **we'll c. you later on this week** nous vous contacterons cette semaine

COMP 1 *Med (contagious ▸ dermatitis)* par contact **2** *(killing on contact ▸ herbicide, insecticide)* par contact

▸▸ *Elec* ***contact breaker*** disjoncteur *m*; *Pol* ***contact group*** groupe *m* de contact; ***contact lens*** verre *m ou* lentille *f* de contact; *Phot* ***contact print*** planche *f* contact, épreuve *f* par contact; ***contact sport*** sport *m* de contact

contactable [kɒn'tæktəbəl] **ADJ** que l'on peut joindre *ou* contacter, joignable; **I'm c. at this number** on peut me contacter *ou* m'appeler à ce numéro

contagion [kən'teɪdʒən] **N 1** *(contamination, disease)* contagion *f* **2** *Literary (moral corruption)* contamination *f*

contagious [kən'teɪdʒəs] **ADJ** *also Fig* contagieux; **he's no longer c.** il n'est plus contagieux

contagiousness [kən'teɪdʒəsnɪs] **N** contagion *f*, contagiosité *f*

contain [kən'teɪn] **VT 1** *(hold ▸ of bag, house, city)* contenir

2 *(include ▸ of pill, substance)* contenir; *(▸ of book, speech)* contenir, comporter; **the ore contains a high percentage of iron** le minerai a une forte teneur en fer; **the document contains a reference to...** le document contient une référence à...

3 *(restrain ▸ feelings)* contenir, cacher; **to c. one's anger** contenir sa colère; **he was unable to c. his laughter** il ne pouvait pas s'empêcher de rire; **I could barely c. myself** j'avais du mal à me contenir

4 *(curb ▸ enemy, growth, riot, inflation)* contenir, maîtriser
5 *(hold back ▸ fire, epidemic)* circonscrire; *(▸ flood waters)* contenir, endiguer
6 *(limit ▸ damage)* limiter
7 *Math* être divisible par

container [kən'teɪnə(r)] **N 1** *(bottle, box, tin etc)* récipient *m* **2** *Com (for transporting cargo)* conteneur *m*, container *m*
COMP *Com (port, ship, terminal)* porte-conteneurs *(inv)*; *(lorry, truck)* adapté au transport des conteneurs; *(dock, line, transport)* pour porte-conteneurs
▸▸ *Com* ***container depot*** entrepôt *m* de conteneurs, dépôt *m* pour conteneurs

containerization, -isation [kən,teɪnəraɪ'zeɪʃən] **N** *Com* **1** *(of cargo)* conteneurisation *f*, transport *m* par conteneurs **2** *(of port)* conteneurisation *f*

containerize, -ise [kən'teɪnəraɪz] **VT** *Com (cargo)* conteneuriser, transporter par conteneurs; *(port)* convertir à la conteneurisation

containment [kən'teɪnmənt] **N 1** *Pol* endiguement *m*, freinage *m*, retenue *f*; **a policy of c.** une politique d'endiguement **2** *Phys* confinement *m*

contaminate [kən'tæmɪneɪt] **VT 1** *(pollute ▸ food, river, water)* contaminer; *Fig (corrupt)* contaminer, souiller **2** *(irradiate ▸ land, person, soil)* contaminer

contamination [kən,tæmɪ'neɪʃən] **N 1** *(pollution, irradiation)* contamination *f* **2** *Fig* contamination *f*, corruption *f*

contango [kən'tæŋgəʊ] *(pl* **contangos***)* *Br St Exch* **N 1** *(postponement of payment)* report *m* **2** *(fee)* taux *m* de report

cont'd, contd *(written abbr* **continued***)* suite; **c. on p14** suite à la page 14; **to be c.** à suivre

contemplate ['kɒntempleɪt] **VT 1** *(ponder)* considérer, réfléchir sur **2** *(consider)* considérer, envisager; **it's too awful to c.** c'est insupportable rien que d'y penser; **to c. suicide** songer au suicide; **to c. doing sth** envisager de *ou* songer à faire qch **3** *(observe)* contempler
VI 1 *(ponder)* méditer, se recueillir **2** *(consider)* réfléchir

contemplation [,kɒntem'pleɪʃən] **N 1** *(thought)* réflexion *f*; **deep in c.** en pleine réflexion **2** *(observation)* contemplation *f* **3** *(meditation)* contemplation *f*, recueillement *m*, méditation *f*; **a period of c.** une période de recueillement

contemplative [kən'templətɪv] **ADJ** *(look, mood)* songeur, pensif; *(life)* contemplatif; *Rel (order, prayer)* contemplatif
N *Rel* contemplatif(ive) *m,f*

contemporaneous [kən,tempə'reɪnɪəs] **ADJ** *Formal* contemporain; **to be c. (with sb/sth)** être contemporain (de qn/ qch)

contemporaneously [kən,tempə'reɪnɪəslɪ] **ADV** *Formal (exist, live)* à la même époque; **c. with** à la même époque que

contemporary [kən'tempərərɪ] *(pl* **contemporaries***)* **ADJ 1** *(modern ▸ art, writer)* contemporain, d'aujourd'hui; *(▸ design, style)* moderne; **a study of c. Britain** une étude de la Grande-Bretagne d'aujourd'hui **2** *(of the same period ▸ account, report)* contemporain
N contemporain(e) *m,f*; **he was a c. of mine at university** nous étions ensemble *ou* en même temps à l'université

contempt [kən'tempt] **N 1** *(scorn)* mépris *m*; **to feel c. for sb/sth, to hold sb/sth in c.** mépriser qn/qch, avoir du mépris pour qn/qch; **to treat sb/sth with c.** traiter qn/qch avec dédain *ou* mépris; **I feel nothing but c. for him** je n'ai que du mépris pour lui; **to be beneath c.** être tout ce qu'il y a de plus méprisable **2** *Law* outrage *m*; **to charge sb with c. (of court)** accuser qn d'outrage (à magistrat *ou* à la Cour)

contemptible [kən'temptəbəl] **ADJ** *(action, attitude, person)* méprisable

contemptibly [kən'temptəblɪ] **ADV** dérisoirement; **a c. small sum** une somme dérisoire

contemptuous [kən'temptʃʊəs] **ADJ** *Formal (look, manner, remark)* méprisant, dédaigneux; **to be c. of sb/sth** dédaigner qn/qch, faire peu de cas de qn/qch

contemptuously [kən'temptʃʊəslɪ] **ADV** *(laugh, reject, smile)* avec mépris, avec dédain

contend [kən'tend] **VI 1** *(deal)* **to c. with sb** avoir affaire à qn; **to c. with sth** être aux prises avec qch; **this is just one of the difficulties we have to c. with** ce n'est que l'une des difficultés auxquelles nous devons faire face; **they still had the perimeter fence to c. with** il leur restait encore à régler le problème de la clôture d'enceinte; **if you do that again, you'll have me to c. with** si tu recommences, tu auras affaire à moi **2** *(compete)* combattre, lutter; **to c. with sb for** *or* **over sth** disputer *ou* contester qch à qn
VT *Formal (maintain, argue)* **to c. that...** soutenir que... + *indicative*

contender [kən'tendə(r)] **N** *(in boxing match)* adversaire *mf*; *(in race)* concurrent(e) *m,f*; *(for title)* prétendant(e) *m,f* (**for** à); *(for political office)* candidat(e) *m,f*

contending [kən'tendɪŋ] **ADJ** opposé
▸▸ *Law* ***contending party*** contestant(e) *m,f*

content N 1 ['kɒntent] *(amount contained)* teneur *f*; **gold/moisture c.** teneur *f* en or/humidité; **with a high iron c.** avec une forte teneur en fer, riche en fer; **peanut butter has a high protein c.** le beurre de cacahuètes est riche en protéines
2 ['kɒntent] *(substance ▸ of book, film, speech)* contenu *m*; *(meaning)* teneur *f*, fond *m*; **his films are all style and no c.** dans ses films, il y a la forme mais pas le fond
3 [kən'tent] *(satisfaction)* contentement *m*, satisfaction *f*
4 ['kɒntent] *Ling* contenu *m*
ADJ [kən'tent] content, satisfait (**with** de); **to be c. to do sth** ne pas demander mieux que de faire qch; **he seems quite c. with his lot in life** il semble assez content de son sort; **not c. with having ruined our evening, he came round next day** non content d'avoir gâché notre soirée, il revint le lendemain
VT [kən'tent] **to c. oneself with sth/doing sth** se contenter de *ou* se borner à qch/à faire qch
• **contents NPL** ['kɒntents] **1** *(of bag, bottle, house etc)* contenu *m* **2** *(of book, letter)* contenu *m*; **the contents (list), the list of contents** la table des matières
▸▸ ***contents insurance*** assurance *f* mobilier; ***contents page*** table *f* des matières; *Comput* ***content provider*** fournisseur *m* de contenu

contented [kən'tentɪd] **ADJ** *(person)* content, satisfait (**with** de); *(smile)* de contentement, de satisfaction

contentedly [kən'tentɪdlɪ] **ADV** avec contentement; **to live c.** vivre heureux

contentedness [kən'tentɪdnɪs] **N** contentement *m*, satisfaction *f*

contention [kən'tenʃən] **N 1** *Formal (belief)* affirmation *f*; **it is my c. that...** je soutiens que... + *indicative* **2** *(disagreement)* dispute *f*; **his morals are not in c.** sa moralité n'est pas ici mise en doute **3** *(competition)* **to be in c. for sth** être en compétition pour qch; **the teams in c.** les équipes concurrentes *ou* rivales

contentious [kən'tenʃəs] **ADJ 1** *(controversial ▸ issue, subject)* controversé **2** *(argumentative ▸ family, group, person)* querelleur, chicanier **3** *Law* contentieux

contentment [kən'tentmənt] **N** contentement *m*, satisfaction *f*; **a look of c.** un regard de satisfaction

contest N ['kɒntest] **1** *(competition)* concours *m*; **beauty c.** concours *m* de beauté; *Fig* **there's simply no c.** il n'y a aucune comparaison
2 *(struggle)* combat *m*, lutte *f*; **a c. for/between** un combat pour/entre
3 *Sport* rencontre *f*; *Boxing* combat *m*, rencontre *f*; **a c. with/between** un combat contre/entre
4 *Am Law* **no c.** pas de témoins à charge
VT [kən'test] **1** *(dispute ▸ idea, statement)* contester, discuter; **to c. a will** contester un testament **2** *Pol (fight for ▸ election, seat)* disputer; *Sport (▸ match, title)* disputer; **a keenly contested game** une partie très disputée
▸▸ *Fin* ***contested debt*** créance *f* litigieuse

contestant [kən'testənt] **N** concurrent(e) *m,f*, adversaire *mf*; *Boxing* combattant *m*

contestation [,kɒntes'teɪʃən] **N** contestation *f*

context ['kɒntekst] **N** contexte *m*; **out of/in c.** hors/en contexte; **the book places the writer in his social c.** le livre replace l'écrivain dans son contexte social; **her comments had been taken out of c.** ses commentaires avaient été retirés de leur contexte; **she was quoted out of c.** on a cité ses paroles hors de leur contexte

context-dependent ADJ to be c. dépendre du contexte

context-sensitive ADJ *Comput (spellchecker, help)* contextuel

contextual [kɒn'tekstjʊəl] **ADJ** contextuel

contextualize, -ise [kɒn'tekstjʊəlaɪz] **VT** *(events, facts)* contextualiser, remettre dans son contexte; *(word, expression)* contextualiser, utiliser en contexte

contextually [kɒn'tekstjʊəlɪ] **ADV** *(examine)* dans son contexte; **to be c. dependent** dépendre du contexte

contiguous [kən'tɪgjʊəs] **ADJ** *Formal* contigu(ë); **to be c. to** *or* **with sth** être contigu à qch

continence ['kɒntɪnəns] **N 1** *Med* continence *f* **2** *Formal (chastity)* continence *f*, chasteté *f*

continent ['kɒntɪnənt] **N** *Geog* continent *m*
ADJ 1 *Med* continent, qui n'est pas incontinent **2** *Formal (chaste)* continent, chaste
• **Continent N** *Br* **the C.** l'Europe *f* continentale; **on the C.** en Europe (continentale), outre-Manche

continental [,kɒntɪ'nentəl] **ADJ 1** *Br (European)* d'outre-Manche, européen, d'Europe continentale **2** *Geog* continental
N *Br* continental(e) *m,f*, habitant(e) *m,f* de l'Europe continentale
▸▸ ***continental breakfast*** petit déjeuner *m* à la française; *Met* ***continental climate*** climat *m* continental; *Geog* ***Continental Divide*** = ligne de partage des eaux entre l'Atlantique et le Pacifique; *Geol* ***continental drift*** dérive *f* des continents; *Am* ***continental plan*** *(at hotel)* tarif *m* chambre avec petit déjeuner continental; ***continental quilt*** couette *f*, duvet *m*; *Geol* ***continental shelf*** plateau *m* continental, plate-forme *f* continentale; *Am* ***continental United States*** = désigne les 48 États des États-Unis qui forment un bloc géographique (excluant Hawaii et l'Alaska)

> **CONTINENTAL BREAKFAST**
> Ce terme désigne un petit déjeuner léger, par opposition au breakfast anglais, beaucoup plus copieux et comportant un plat chaud.

contingency [kən'tɪndʒənsɪ] *(pl* **contingencies***)* **N** *Formal* **1** *(possibility)* éventualité *f*, contingence *f*; **to provide for all contingencies** parer à toute éventualité **2** *(chance)* événement *m* inattendu; *(uncertainty)* (cas *m*) imprévu *m*, éventualité *f* **3** *(in statistics)* contingence *f*
COMP *(plan)* d'urgence; *(table, coefficient)* des imprévus
• **contingencies NPL** *Fin* frais *mpl* divers
▸▸ *Law* ***contingency fee*** = aux États-Unis, principe permettant à un avocat de recevoir une part des sommes attribuées à son client si ce dernier gagne son procès; *Fin* ***contingency fund*** fonds *mpl* de prévoyance; *Acct* ***contingency theory*** théorie *f* de la contingence

contingent [kən'tɪndʒənt] **ADJ** *Formal* **1** *(dependent)* contingent; **to be c. on** *or* **upon sth** dépendre de qch
2 *(accidental)* accidentel, fortuit
3 *(uncertain)* éventuel
4 *Phil* contingent
N 1 *(gen) also Mil* contingent *m* **2** *(representative group)* groupe *m* représentatif
▸▸ *Acct* ***contingent liabilities, contingent liability*** passif *m* éventuel *ou* exigible

continual [kən'tɪnjʊəl] **ADJ 1** *(continuous ▸ pain, pleasure, struggle)* continuel **2** *(repeated ▸ nagging, warnings)* incessant, continuel

> Attention: ne pas confondre avec l'adjectif **continuous**.

continually [kən'tɪnjʊəlɪ] **ADV 1** *(continuously ▸ change, evolve)* continuellement **2** *(repeatedly ▸ complain, nag, warn)* sans cesse

> Attention: ne pas confondre avec l'adverbe **continuously**.

continuance [kən'tɪnjʊəns] **N 1** *(continuation)* continuation *f*, persistance *f*, durée *f* **2** *Am Law* ajournement *m (d'un procès)*

continuation [kənˌtɪnjʊ'eɪʃən] **N 1** *(sequel)* continuation *f*, suite *f* **2** *(resumption)* reprise *f* **3** *(prolongation)* prolongement *m*, suite *f*; *(of road)* prolongement *m*

continue [kən'tɪnju:] **VI 1** *(carry on)* continuer; **the situation cannot c.** la situation ne peut pas durer; **the situation continued into the 1960s** la situation s'est prolongée jusque dans le courant des années 60; **she will c. as director until December** elle gardera les fonctions de directrice jusqu'en décembre; **his bad luck continues** ses malheurs se poursuivent; **we continued on our way** nous avons poursuivi notre chemin, nous nous sommes remis en route; **the path continues on down to the river** le chemin continue jusqu'à la rivière; **to c. with a treatment** continuer un traitement **2** *(resume)* reprendre; **the talks will c. today** les entretiens reprendront aujourd'hui

VT 1 *(carry on ▸ education, work, activity)* poursuivre, continuer; *(▸ tradition)* perpétuer, continuer; *(▸ journey)* poursuivre; *(▸ conversation, treatment)* continuer; **to c. to do sth** *or* **doing sth** continuer à faire qch **2** *(resume ▸ conversation, performance, talks)* reprendre, continuer; **"furthermore," he continued...** "de plus", continua-t-il...; **to be continued** *(TV programme, serialized story)* à suivre; **continued on the next page** suite à la page suivante

continuing [kən'tɪnju:ɪŋ] **ADJ** continu; *(interest)* soutenu; **the c. story of a small American town** *(TV serial)* l'histoire *f* d'une petite ville américaine

▸▸ ***continuing education*** formation *f* permanente *ou* continue

continuity [ˌkɒntɪ'nju:ətɪ] *(pl* **continuities***)* **N 1** *(cohesion)* continuité *f*; **to ensure c.** assurer la continuité (**between** entre) **2** *Cin & TV* continuité *f*

COMP *Cin & TV (department, studio)* pour raccords

▸▸ *TV & Rad* ***continuity announcer*** speaker(ine) *m,f* (de transition); *Cin & TV* ***continuity girl*** scripte *f*

continuous [kən'tɪnjʊəs] **ADJ 1** *(uninterrupted ▸ noise, process)* continu, ininterrompu **2** *(unbroken ▸ line)* continu **3** *Gram (tense)* continu

▸▸ *Sch & Univ* ***continuous assessment*** contrôle *m* continu; *Comput* ***continuous mode*** mode *m* continu; *Comput* ***continuous paper*** papier *m* en continu; *Cin* ***continuous performances*** spectacle *m* permanent; *Comput* ***continuous stationery*** papier *m* en continu

> Attention: ne pas confondre avec l'adjectif **continual**.

continuously [kən'tɪnjʊəslɪ] **ADV** continuellement, sans arrêt

> Attention: ne pas confondre avec l'adverbe **continually**.

contort [kən'tɔ:t] **VT** *(body, features)* tordre; **face contorted by pain** visage *m* tordu par la douleur

VI his face contorted with rage/pain il grimaçait de rage/de douleur

contortion [kən'tɔ:ʃən] **N** *(of body)* contorsion *f*; *(of features)* crispation *f*; *Fig* **he went through all sorts of contortions to justify this decision** il a fait des pieds et des mains pour justifier cette décision

contortionist [kən'tɔ:ʃənɪst] **N** contorsionniste *mf*, homme *m* caoutchouc; *Fam* **you have to be a c. to get into this car!** il faut faire toute une gymnastique *ou* tout un tas de contorsions pour monter dans cette voiture!

contour ['kɒntʊə(r)] **N 1** *(line)* contour *m* **2** *(contour line)* courbe *f* de niveau **3** *(shape ▸ of body, car)* contour *m*; **the contours of the hill** les contours *mpl* de la colline

VT 1 *(map)* tracer les courbes de niveaux sur **2** *(shape ▸ dress, car)* tracer les contours de

▸▸ ***contour line*** courbe *f* de niveau; ***contour map*** carte *f* topographique

Contra ['kɒntrə] **N** *Pol (Nicaraguan)* contra *mf*

contra ['kɒntrə] *Acct* **N per c.** par contre; **as per c.** en contrepartie, porté ci-contre

VT contrepasser

▸▸ ***contra account*** compte *m* de contrepartie *ou* d'autre part; ***contra entry*** article *m ou* écriture *f* inverse, contre-passation *f*

contraband ['kɒntrəbænd] **N** *(UNCOUNT)* **1** *(smuggling)* contrebande *f* **2** *(smuggled goods)* (marchandises *fpl* de) contrebande *f*

ADJ *(activities, goods)* de contrebande

contrabass ['kɒntrəbeɪs] **N** *Mus* contrebasse *f*

contrabassoon [ˌkɒntrəbə'su:n] **N** *Mus* contrebasson *m*

contraception [ˌkɒntrə'sepʃən] **N** contraception *f*

contraceptive [ˌkɒntrə'septɪv] **N** contraceptif *m*

ADJ *(device, method)* contraceptif

▸▸ ***contraceptive advice*** conseils *mpl* sur la contraception; ***contraceptive pill*** pilule *f* contraceptive; ***contraceptive sponge*** éponge *f* contraceptive

contract N ['kɒntrækt] **1** *Com & Fin (agreement)* contrat *m*, convention *f*; *(to supply goods, services)* soumission *f*, adjudication *f*; *(document)* contrat *m*; **to draw up a c.** dresser *ou* rédiger un contrat; **to sign a c.** signer un contrat; **to be under c.** être sous contrat, avoir un contrat; **to put work out to c.** sous-traiter du travail; **they were given the c. to build the new road** ils se sont vu attribuer le contrat pour construire la nouvelle route; *Br* **to exchange contracts** *(when buying property)* finaliser l'achat d'un logement; *Fam* **to put out a c. on sb** mettre la tête de qn à prix; **c. of employment** contrat *m* de travail; **the police suspect it was a c. killing** la police soupçonne que c'est le travail d'un tueur à gages **2** *Cards (contract bridge)* bridge *m* contrat

VT [kən'trækt] **1** *Formal (agree)* **to c. to do sth** s'engager par contrat à faire qch; **she has contracted to make two films** elle a signé un contrat pour faire deux films

2 *Formal (agree to ▸ alliance, marriage)* contracter

3 *(acquire ▸ disease, illness, debt)* contracter

4 *(make tense ▸ features)* crisper; *Physiol (▸ muscle)* contracter; *(▸ tissues)* resserrer

5 *Ling (vowel, word)* contracter

VI [kən'trækt] **1** *(metal)* se contracter; *(opening, material)* rétrécir, se contracter; **the pupil contracts in bright light** la pupille se contracte à la lumière intense

2 *Physiol (muscle, pupil)* se contracter; *(tissues)* se resserrer

3 *Ling (vowel, word)* se contracter

4 *Com* **to c. for a supply of sth** s'engager à fournir qch; **to c. for work** entreprendre des travaux à forfait

COMP ['kɒntrækt] *(work)* à forfait, contractuel

▸▸ *Cards* ***contract bridge*** bridge *m* contrat; ***contract killer*** tueur *m* à gages; ***contract labour*** main-d'œuvre *f* contractuelle; ***contract law*** droit *m* des contrats; ***contract staff*** personnel *m* en contrat à durée déterminée *ou* en CDD; *(in public sector)* contractuels *mpl*

▸**contract in VI** *Br Com* s'engager (par contrat préalable)

▸**contract out VT SEP** *Com (work)* sous-traiter

VI *Br* **to c. out of sth** cesser de cotiser à qch

contracting [kən'træktɪŋ] **ADJ**

▸▸ ***contracting company*** *(party to a contract)* contractant *m*; *(subcontractor)* sous-traitant *m*; *Com & Fin* ***contracting parties*** contractants *mpl*

contraction [kən'trækʃən] **N 1** *(shrinkage ▸ of metal)* contraction *f*; *(▸ of opening, material)* rétrécissement *m*

2 *Physiol (of muscle, pupil)* contraction *f*; *(of tissues)* resserrement *m*

3 *Ling (of vowel, word)* contraction *f*; *(word)* mot *m* contracté; *(short form of word)* contraction *f*, forme *f* contractée; **"haven't" is a c. of "have not"** "haven't" est une forme contractée de "have not"

4 *Obst (in childbirth)* contraction *f* (utérine)

contractor [kən'træktə(r)] **N 1** *(firm of builders)* entrepreneur *m* (en bâtiment); *(building worker)* ouvrier *m* en bâtiment **2** *Com (company, supplier)* **haulage c.** entreprise *f* de transports; **arms c.** fournisseur *m* d'armement **3** *Law (party to a contract)* partie *f* contractante

contractual [kən'træktʃʊəl] **ADJ** *Com & Fin (agreement, obligation)* contractuel

contractually [kən'træktʃʊəlɪ] **ADV** *(binding, obliged)* par contrat; **I'm c. forbidden to...** le contrat m'interdit de...

contradict [ˌkɒntrə'dɪkt] **VT 1** *(challenge ▸ person, statement)* contredire; **she hates being contradicted** elle déteste qu'on la contredise; **to c. oneself** se contredire **2** *(conflict with ▸ of facts, stories)* contredire; **the statements of the witnesses c. each other** les dépositions des témoins se contredisent

contradiction [ˌkɒntrə'dɪkʃən] **N 1** *(inconsistency)* contradiction *f*; **he's full of contradictions** il est plein de contradictions; **in c. with** en désaccord avec **2** *(conflicting statement)* démenti *m*, contradiction *f*; **this was a c. of what they had previously said** c'était un démenti de ce qu'ils avaient dit auparavant; **a c. in terms** une contradiction dans les termes

contradictory [ˌkɒntrə'dɪktərɪ] **ADJ 1** *(statements, stories)* contradictoire, opposé **2** *(person)* qui a l'esprit de contradiction

contradistinction [ˌkɒntrədɪ'stɪŋkʃən] **N** *Formal* opposition *f*, contraste *m*; **in c. to** par opposition à, par contraste avec

contraflow ['kɒntrəˌfləʊ] **N** *Br Transp* circulation *f* à contre-courant

▸▸ ***contraflow system*** système *m* de circulation à contre-sens

contra-indication N *Med* contre-indication *f*

contralto [kən'træltəʊ] *(pl* **contraltos***)* *Mus* **N** *(voice)* contralto *m*; *(singer)* contralto *mf*

ADJ *(part, voice)* de contralto

contraption [kən'træpʃən] **N** *Fam* engin *m*, truc *m*

contrapuntal [ˌkɒntrə'pʌntəl] **ADJ** *Mus* en contrepoint, contrapuntique

contrarily ADV 1 [*Br* kən'treərɪlɪ, *Am* kɒn'trerəlɪ] *(obstinately)* par esprit de contradiction **2** [*Br* 'kɒntrərɪlɪ, *Am* kɒn'trerəlɪ] *(on the other hand)* contrairement

contrariness [kən'treərɪnɪs] **N** *(obstinacy)* esprit *m* de contradiction

contrariwise ADV 1 ['kɒntrərɪˌwaɪz] *(on the other hand)* d'autre part, en revanche **2** ['kɒntrərɪˌwaɪz] *(in the opposite direction)* en sens opposé **3** [kən'treərɪwaɪz] *(perversely)* par esprit de contradiction

contrary N ['kɒntrərɪ] contraire *m*

ADJ 1 ['kɒntrərɪ] *(opposed ▸ attitudes, ideas, opinions)* contraire, en opposition (**to** à) **2** [kən'treərɪ] *(obstinate ▸ attitude, person)* contrariant **3** ['kɒntrərɪ] *Formal (winds)* contraire

• **contrary to** ['kɒntrərɪ] **PREP** contrairement à; **c. to nature** contre nature; **c. to reason** contraire à la raison; **c. to the terms of the contract** contraire aux termes du contrat; **c. to popular belief** contrairement à ce que l'on croit généralement; **c. to what I had been told** contrairement à ce qu'on m'avait dit

• **on the contrary** ['kɒntrərɪ] **ADV** au contraire

• **to the contrary** ['kɒntrərɪ] **ADV the meeting will be at six, unless you hear to the c.** la réunion sera à six heures, sauf contrordre *ou* avis contraire

contrast VT [kən'trɑ:st] contraster, mettre en contraste; **to c. sb/sth with, to c. sb/sth to** mettre qn/qch en contraste avec

VI [kən'trɑ:st] contraster, trancher; **to c. with sth** contraster avec qch

N ['kɒntrɑ:st] **1** *(difference)* contraste *m*; *(person, thing)* contraste *m*; **as a c. to...** comme contraste à...; **life in Africa was a complete c. to life in Europe** la vie en Afrique présentait un contraste total avec la vie en Europe **2** *Art, Phot & TV* contraste *m*

• **by contrast, in contrast** ['kɒntrɑ:st] **ADV** par contraste

• **in contrast with, in contrast to** ['kɒntrɑ:st] **PREP** par opposition à, par contraste avec

▸▸ *Phot & TV* ***contrast button*** bouton *m* de contraste; *TV* ***contrast control*** réglage *m* du contraste

contrasting [kən'trɑ:stɪŋ], **contrastive** [kən'trɑ:stɪv] ADJ *(attitudes, lifestyles, responses)* qui fait contraste; *(colours)* opposé, contrasté

contrasty ['kɒntrɑ:stɪ] ADJ *Phot* contrasté

contravene [ˌkɒntrə'vi:n] VT **1** *(infringe ▸ law, rule)* transgresser, enfreindre, violer **2** *(dispute ▸ statement)* nier, opposer un démenti à

contravention [ˌkɒntrə'venʃən] N infraction *f*, violation *f*; **what he did was in c. of the law/regulations** ce qu'il a fait constitue une infraction par rapport à la loi/au règlement

contribute [kən'trɪbju:t] VT *(give ▸ money)* donner; *(▸ article, poem)* écrire; *(▸ ideas)* apporter (**to** à); **the government will c. a further two million pounds** le gouvernement ajoutera deux millions de livres à sa contribution; *Fin* **she contributes 10 percent of her salary to the pension scheme** elle verse 10 pour cent de son salaire dans son plan de retraite

VI **1** *(donate money)* contribuer; **we ask everyone to c. generously** nous demandons à chacun de contribuer généreusement; **to c. to a charity** donner à une association caritative

2 *(give)* donner; **he rarely contributes to discussions** il contribue rarement aux discussions

3 *(influence)* **to c. to sth** contribuer à qch; **to c. to the success of sth** contribuer au succès de qch

4 *(journalist, author)* **to c. to a newspaper/magazine** écrire pour un journal/magazine

5 *Fin (to pension scheme)* cotiser (**to** à)

contribution [ˌkɒntrɪ'bju:ʃən] N **1** *(of money, goods)* contribution *f*, cotisation *f*; *(of ideas, enthusiasm)* apport *m*; **I've already made a c.** j'ai déjà donné; **he made a valuable c. to the project** il a apporté une collaboration précieuse au projet; **the chocolate mousse was David's c.** c'est David qu'il faut remercier pour la mousse au chocolat

2 *(article)* article *m (écrit pour un journal)*

3 *Fin (to pension scheme, National Insurance)* cotisation *f*

4 *Acct (in management accounting)* marge *f* (brute); **c. in kind** apport *m* en nature

contributor [kən'trɪbjʊtə(r)] N **1** *(of money, goods)* donateur(trice) *m,f* **2** *(to magazine)* collaborateur(trice) *m,f*

contributory [kən'trɪbjʊtərɪ] *(pl* **contributories**) ADJ *(cause, factor)* contribuant, qui contribue; **to be a c. factor in sth** contribuer à qch

▸▸ *Law* ***contributory negligence*** faute *f* partagée; *Fin* ***contributory pension plan, contributory pension scheme*** système *m* de retraite par répartition

contrite [kən'traɪt] ADJ *(face, look)* contrit, repentant; **to look/be c.** avoir un air/être contrit

contritely [kən'traɪtlɪ] ADV d'un air contrit, avec contrition

contrition [kən'trɪʃən] N contrition *f*, pénitence *f*

contrivance [kən'traɪvəns] N **1** *(contraption)* dispositif *m*, mécanisme *m*

2 *(scheme)* manigance *f*

3 *(invention ▸ of scheme)* invention *f*

4 *Pej (scheme)* stratagème *m*

contrive [kən'traɪv] VT **1** *(engineer ▸ meeting)* combiner **2** *(invent ▸ device, machine)* inventer, imaginer

VI **to c. to do sth** trouver le moyen de faire qch; **she contrived to confuse matters still further** elle a réussi à embrouiller encore plus les choses

contrived [kən'traɪvd] ADJ **1** *(deliberate)* délibéré, arrangé **2** *(artificial)* forcé, peu naturel

CONTROL [kən'trəʊl]

N	
• direction **1**	• contrôle **1, 4, 5**
• maîtrise **1**	• réglage **2**
• commande **2**	• témoin **3**
• douane **4**	
VT	
• diriger **1**	• contrôler **1, 3, 4**
• régler **2**	• maîtriser **3**

(pt & pp **controlled**, *cont* **controlling**)

N **1** *(of country, organization)* direction *f*; *(of car, machine)* contrôle *m*; *(of one's life)* maîtrise *f*; *(of oneself)* maîtrise *f* (de soi); *Sport (of ball)* contrôle *m*; **to have c. of** *or* **over sb** avoir de l'autorité sur qn; **to have c. of** *or* **over sth** avoir le contrôle de qch; **to gain c. of sth** prendre le contrôle de qch; **the rebels have gained c. of the capital** les rebelles ont pris le contrôle de la capitale; **to be in c. of sth** être maître de qch; **to lose c. of** *(car)* perdre le contrôle de; *(situation)* ne plus être maître de; **to lose c. (of oneself)** ne plus être maître de soi; **to regain c. of oneself** se ressaisir; **the situation is under c.** nous maîtrisons la situation; **everything's under c.** *(organized, in hand)* tout est en bonne voie; *(there's no need to panic)* tout va bien; **to keep sth under c.** maîtriser qch; **dogs must be kept under c.** les chiens doivent être tenus en laisse; **the fire was finally brought under c.** l'incendie fut finalement maîtrisé; **under British/government c.** sous contrôle britannique/gouvernemental; **beyond** *or* **outside one's c.** indépendant de sa volonté; **due to circumstances beyond our c.** en raison de circonstances indépendantes de notre volonté; **the fire was out of c.** on n'arrivait pas à maîtriser l'incendie; **the car went out of c.** le chauffeur a perdu le contrôle de sa voiture; **things/the situation had got out of c.** la situation était devenue incontrôlable; **the crowd got out of c.** la foule s'est déchaînée; **her children are completely out of c.** ses enfants sont intenables

2 *(device)* **volume c.** réglage *m* du volume; **controls** *(on car, aircraft, machine)* commandes *fpl*; **the pilot was at the controls/took over the controls** le pilote était aux commandes/a pris les commandes

3 *(in experiment)* témoin *m*

4 *(checkpoint ▸ at border)* douane *f*; *(▸ in car rally)* contrôle *m*; **passport and customs controls** formalités *fpl* de douane

5 *(restraint, check)* contrôle *m*; **price/wage controls** contrôle *m* des prix/des salaires; **immigration controls** contrôle *m* de l'immigration; **there are to be new government controls on financial practices** il y aura de nouvelles réglementations gouvernementales sur les pratiques financières

VT **1** *(be in charge of, direct ▸ government, organization)* diriger; *Mil (▸ area)* contrôler

2 *(regulate ▸ machine, system, traffic)* régler; **this switch controls the central heating** ce commutateur règle *ou* commande le chauffage central

3 *(curb ▸ inflation, prices, spending, fire)* maîtriser; *(▸ imports)* limiter; *(▸ disease)* enrayer, juguler; *(master, restrain ▸ activities, emotions)* maîtriser; *(▸ one's passions)* dompter; *(▸ one's reactions)* contrôler, maîtriser; *(▸ animal, pupil)* tenir, se faire obéir de; *(▸ crowd)* contenir; **try to c. yourself** essaie de te contrôler *ou* maîtriser; **she could barely c. her anger** elle avait du mal à maîtriser sa colère; **he can't c. his pupils** il ne tient pas ses élèves, il manque d'autorité sur ses élèves

4 *(verify ▸ accounts)* contrôler; *(▸ experiment)* vérifier

COMP *(button, switch)* de commande, de réglage

▸▸ *Comput* ***control bit*** bit *m* de contrôle; *Comput* ***control character*** caractère *m* de contrôle; ***control column*** manche *m* à balai; ***control experiment*** expérience *f* de contrôle; ***control freak*** = personne qui veut tout contrôler; ***control group*** groupe *m* témoin; *Comput* ***control key*** touche *f* contrôle; ***control knob*** molette *f* de réglage; ***control panel*** *Aviat* tableau *m* de bord; *Comput* panneau *m* de configuration; *Sport & Aut* ***control point*** contrôle *m*; ***control room*** salle *f* des commandes; *Naut* poste *m* de commande; *Rad & TV* (cabine *f* de) régie *f*; ***control tower*** tour *f* de contrôle

controllable [kən'trəʊləbəl] ADJ *(animal, person, crowd)* discipliné; *(emotions, situation)* maîtrisable; *(expenditure, inflation, costs, mechanism)* contrôlable; *(speed, heat, brightness)* réglable; **the spread of the disease is c.** la progression de la maladie peut être maîtrisée *ou* enrayée; **the more easily c. aspects of the project** les aspects du projet les plus faciles à contrôler

controlled [kən'trəʊld] ADJ *(emotions, voice)* contenu; *(person)* calme; *(experiment)* contrôlé; *Med (diabetes)* équilibré; **she remained very c.** elle est restée très calme

▸▸ *Econ* ***controlled economy*** économie *f* dirigée *ou* planifiée; ***controlled explosion*** neutralisation *f (d'un explosif)*; **the bomb was let off in a c. explosion** la bombe a été neutralisée; *Br* ***controlled parking zone*** zone *f* à stationnement réglementé; *Econ* ***controlled price*** taxe *f*; ***controlled substance*** substance *f* réglementée

controller [kən'trəʊlə(r)] N **1** *(person in charge)* responsable *m*; **the new C. of BBC1** le nouveau responsable de BBC1 **2** *(accountant)* contrôleur *m* **3** *Comput* contrôleur *m*

controlling [kən'trəʊlɪŋ] ADJ *(power)* dirigeant; *(factor)* déterminant

▸▸ *Fin* ***controlling interest*** participation *f* majoritaire

controversial [ˌkɒntrə'vɜ:ʃəl] ADJ *(book, film, issue, subject)* controversé; *(decision, speech)* sujet à controverse; *(person)* controversé; **he's trying to be c.** il cherche la controverse

controversy ['kɒntrəˌvɜ:sɪ, *Br* kən'trɒvəsɪ] N controverse *f*, polémique *f*; **to be the subject of c.** être sujet à controverse; **her speech caused a lot of c.** son discours a provoqué beaucoup de controverses

contumacious [ˌkɒntju:'meɪʃəs] ADJ *Literary* insubordonné

contumacy ['kɒntjʊməsɪ] *(pl* **contumacies**) N **1** *Literary (disobedience)* insubordination *f* **2** *Law* contumace *f*

contumely ['kɒntju:mlɪ] *(pl* **contumelies**) N *Literary (language)* insolence *f*; *(insult)* offense *f*

contusion [kən'tju:ʒən] N *Med* contusion *f*

contusive [kən'tju:sɪv] ADJ *Med* contus

conundrum [kə'nʌndrəm] N **1** *(riddle)* devinette *f*, énigme *f* **2** *(problem)* énigme *f*

conurbation [ˌkɒnɜ:'beɪʃən] N conurbation *f*

convalesce [ˌkɒnvə'les] VI se remettre *(d'une maladie)*; **she's convalescing from a bad bout of flu** elle se remet d'une mauvaise grippe

convalescence [ˌkɒnvə'lesəns] N *(return to health)* rétablissement *m*; *(period of recovery)* convalescence *f*

convalescent [ˌkɒnvə'lesənt] N convalescent(e) *m,f*

ADJ convalescent

▸▸ ***convalescent home*** maison *f* de convalescence *ou* de repos

convection [kən'vekʃən] *Geol, Met & Phys* N convection *f*

COMP *(heating)* à convection; *(current)* de convection

convector [kən'vektə(r)] N radiateur *m* à convection, convecteur *m*

▸▸ ***convector heater*** radiateur *m* à convection, convecteur *m*

convene [kən'vi:n] VT *(conference, meeting)* convoquer

VI *(board, jury, members)* se réunir

convener [kən'vi:nə(r)] N **1** *Br Ind (in trade union)* = secrétaire des délégués syndicaux **2** *(of meeting)* président(e) *m,f*

convenience [kən'vi:njəns] N **1** *(ease of use)* commodité *f*; *(benefit)* avantage *m*; **for c., for c.'s sake** par commodité; **a bus service is provided for our customers' c.** un service d'autobus est à la disposition de nos clients; **our customers can now enjoy the c. of on-site parking** nous offrons désormais à notre clientèle la commodité d'un parking attenant; *Formal* **at your earliest c.** dans les meilleurs délais; **at your c.** quand cela vous conviendra **2** *(facility)* commodités *fpl*, confort *m*; **the house has every modern c.** la maison a tout le confort moderne **3** *Br Formal Euph (lavatory)* toilettes *fpl*; **public conveniences** toilettes *fpl* publiques

▸▸ ***convenience food*** aliment *m* prêt à consommer, plat *m* cuisiné; *Com* ***convenience goods*** produits *mpl* d'achat courant, produits *mpl* de consommation courante; *Am* ***convenience store*** = supérette de quartier qui reste ouverte tard le soir, *Can* dépanneur *m*

convenient [kən'vi:njənt] ADJ **1** *(suitable)* commode; **a c. place to stop** un endroit commode pour s'arrêter; **when would be c. for you?** quand cela vous arrangerait-il?; **2 o'clock isn't very c. (for me)** 14 heures ne m'arrange pas; **this isn't a very c. moment to talk** le moment n'est pas bien choisi pour parler **2** *(handy)* pratique; **the house is very**

c. for local shops and schools la maison est très bien située pour les magasins et les écoles; *Ironic* **the ticket collector wasn't there – how (very) c.!** le contrôleur n'était pas là – ça tombait très bien! **3** *(nearby)* **I grabbed a c. chair and sat down** j'ai saisi la chaise la plus proche et me suis assis

conveniently [kən'viːnjəntlɪ] **ADV** commodément; **the cottage is c. situated for the beach** le cottage est bien situé pour la plage; *Ironic* **they very c. forgot to enclose the cheque** comme par hasard, ils ont oublié de joindre le chèque

convenor = **convener**

convent ['kɒnvənt] **N 1** *Rel* couvent *m*; **to enter a c.** entrer au couvent **2** *(convent school)* école *f* tenue par des religieuses; **to have had a c. education** avoir été (à l'école) chez les religieuses

▸▸ ***convent school*** école *f* tenue par des religieuses

convention [kən'venʃən] **N 1** *(customs)* usage *m*, convenances *fpl*; **to defy c.** braver les usages; **according to c.** selon l'usage

2 *(accepted usage)* convention *f*, usage *m*; **to observe the conventions** respecter les convenances; **social conventions** conventions *fpl* sociales; **there is a c. that Ministers do not answer such questions** l'usage est que les ministres ne répondent pas à ce genre de questions

3 *(agreement)* convention *f*; **to sign a c. on sth** signer une convention sur qch

4 *(meeting)* convention *f*, congrès *m*; *Am Pol* convention *f*; **medical c.** congrès *m* médical

▸▸ ***convention centre*** palais *m* des congrès

conventional [kən'venʃənəl] **ADJ 1** *(customary ▸ behaviour, ideas, upbringing)* conventionnel; *(▸ person)* conformiste; *(▸ beauty, good looks)* classique; **c. wisdom** sagesse *f* populaire; **c. wisdom has it that…** d'aucuns disent que… + *indicative*
2 *(traditional ▸ medicine, methods, art)* classique, traditionnel **3** *Mil (non-nuclear)* conventionnel

▸▸ *Constr* ***conventional material*** matériau *m* traditionnel; *Comput* ***conventional memory*** mémoire *f* conventionnelle; ***conventional oven*** four *m* traditionnel *ou* classique; *Mil* ***conventional warfare*** guerre *f* conventionnelle; *Mil* ***conventional weapons*** armes *fpl* conventionnelles

conventionality [kən͵venʃə'nælətɪ] **N** conformisme *m*

conventionally [kən'venʃənəlɪ] **ADV 1** *(in accepted fashion)* conventionnellement; **she's not c. beautiful** elle n'est pas d'une beauté classique **2** *(traditionally)* d'une manière classique

conventioneer [kən͵venʃə'nɪə(r)] **N** *Am* participant(e) *m,f (à un congrès)*

converge [kən'vɜːdʒ] **VI 1** *(merge ▸ paths, lines)* converger; *(▸ ideas, tendencies)* converger **2** *(groups, people)* se rassembler; **thousands of fans converged on the stadium** des milliers de fans se sont rassemblés sur le stade **3** *Math* converger

convergence [kən'vɜːdʒəns] **N 1** *(of paths, lines)* convergence *f*, *(of ideas, tendencies)* convergence *f* **2** *Math* convergence *f*

▸▸ *EU* ***convergence criteria*** critères *mpl* de convergence; *EU* ***convergence process*** processus *m* de convergence

convergent [kən'vɜːdʒənt], **converging** [kən'vɜːdʒɪŋ] **ADJ 1** *(paths, tendencies)* convergent **2** *Math* convergent

▸▸ *Opt* ***convergent lens*** lentille *f* convexe *ou* convergente; ***convergent thinking*** raisonnement *m* convergent

conversant [kən'vɜːsənt] **ADJ to be c. with** *(language, regulations)* connaître; *(machinery, computers)* s'y connaître en; *(facts)* être au courant de; **we were expected to be fully c. with colloquial French** nous étions censés avoir une connaissance parfaite du français familier

conversation [͵kɒnvə'seɪʃən] **N** conversation *f*; **the art of c.** l'art *m* de la conversation; **to hold** *or* **have a c. with sb** avoir une conversation avec qn; **she was deep in c. with my sister** elle était en grande conversation avec ma sœur; **a telephone c.** une conversation téléphonique; **to get into c. with sb** engager la conversation avec qn; **to make c.** faire la conversation; **I'm not good at (making) c.** je ne suis pas très doué pour faire la conversation; **she was just making c.** elle parlait par politesse; **to run out of c.** n'avoir plus rien à dire; **she takes French c. classes** elle prend des cours de conversation française; *Fam* **that was a real c. stopper!** cela a arrêté net la conversation!

▸▸ ***conversation piece*** *(unusual object)* = objet qui suscite bien des commentaires; ***conversation skills*** l'art *m* de la conversation; **he has good/no c. skills** il est doué/n'est pas doué pour la conversation

conversational [͵kɒnvə'seɪʃənəl] **ADJ** *(tone, voice)* de la conversation; *(style)* familier; *Comput (mode)* dialogue; **c. Spanish** espagnol *m* courant

conversationalist [͵kɒnvə'seɪʃənəlɪst] **N** causeur(euse) *m,f*; **he's a brilliant c.** il brille dans la conversation

conversationally [͵kɒnvə'seɪʃənəlɪ] **ADV** *(mention, say)* sur le ton de la conversation

converse **VI** [kən'vɜːs] *Formal* converser; **to c. with sb** s'entretenir avec qn

ADJ ['kɒnvɜːs] *(opinion, statement, results)* contraire; *Math* réciproque

N ['kɒnvɜːs] **1** *(gen)* contraire *m*, inverse *m*; **I believe the c. to be true** je crois que l'inverse est vrai **2** *Phil* (proposition *f*) converse *f* **3** *Math* (proposition *f*) réciproque *f*

conversely [kən'vɜːslɪ] **ADV** inversement, réciproquement

conversion [kən'vɜːʃən] **N 1** *(process)* conversion *f*, transformation *f*; **the c. of water into wine** la transformation de l'eau en vin; **the c. of a house into flats** l'aménagement *m ou* la transformation d'une maison en appartements
2 *Math & Comput* conversion *f*
3 *Rel (change of beliefs)* conversion *f*
4 *Rugby* transformation *f*
5 *(in converted building)* = appartement aménagé dans un ancien hôtel particulier, entrepôt, atelier etc
6 *Law* conversion *f*
7 *Fin (of bonds, securities, loan stock)* conversion *f*

▸▸ *Fin* ***conversion issue*** émission *f* de conversion; *Comput* ***conversion program*** programme *m* de conversion; *Fin* ***conversion rate*** taux *m* de conversion; *Comput* ***conversion software*** logiciel *m* de conversion; ***conversion table*** table *f* de conversion

convert **VT** [kən'vɜːt] **1** *(building, car)* aménager, convertir; *(machine)* transformer; **to c. sth to** *or* **into sth** transformer *ou* convertir qch en qch; **the car has been converted to run on LPG** la voiture a été modifiée pour rouler au GPL; **her studio was a converted barn** son studio était une grange aménagée
2 *Math & Comput* convertir; **how do you c. pints into litres?** comment convertir des pintes en litres?
3 *Rel* convertir; **to be converted to Christianity** se convertir au christianisme; *Fig* **she converted them to her way of thinking** elle les a amenés à voir les choses à sa manière
4 *Sport* **to c. a try** *(in rugby)* transformer un essai
5 *Law* convertir; **to c. funds to another purpose** affecter des fonds à un autre usage
6 *Fin (bonds, securities, loan stock)* convertir

VI [kən'vɜːt] **1** *(vehicle, machine)* se convertir; **the settee converts into a bed** le canapé se transforme en lit **2** *Rel* se convertir (**to** à) **3** *Sport (in rugby)* transformer l'essai/un essai

N ['kɒnvɜːt] *(person)* converti(e) *m,f*; **to become a c. to sth** se convertir à qch; **to make a c. of sb** convertir qn; **she's made another c.** elle a encore converti quelqu'un

converter [kən'vɜːtə(r)] **N 1** *Metal, Phys & Comput* convertisseur *m*; *Rad* modulateur *m* de fréquence; **steel c.** convertisseur *m* Bessemer **2** *Nucl (converter reactor)* réacteur *m* convertisseur

▸▸ *Nucl* ***converter reactor*** réacteur *m* convertisseur

convertibility [kən͵vɜːtə'bɪlətɪ] **N 1** *(of money, currency)* convertibilité *f* **2** *(of building, machine)* convertibilité *f*

convertible [kən'vɜːtəbəl] **ADJ 1** *(money, currency)* convertible
2 *(machine, couch)* convertible
3 *(car)* décapotable
4 *Fin (bonds, securities, loan stock)* convertible; **c. money of account** monnaie *f* de compte convertible

N 1 *(car)* décapotable *f* **2** *(money, currency)* monnaie *f* convertible

convex [kɒn'veks] **ADJ** *Phys & Opt* convexe

convexity [kɒn'veksətɪ] *(pl* **convexities***)* **N** *Phys & Opt* convexité *f*

convey [kən'veɪ] **VT 1** *Formal (transport)* transporter
2 *(communicate)* transmettre; **to c. one's meaning** communiquer sa pensée; **I tried to c. to him the importance of the decision** j'ai essayé de lui faire comprendre l'importance de la décision; **no words can c. my gratitude** aucun mot ne peut traduire ma gratitude; **his writing conveys the mood of the country** sa manière d'écrire évoque l'atmosphère du pays; **please c. my thanks (to them)** veuillez leur transmettre mes remerciements
3 *(of air ▸ sound, smell)* transmettre
4 *Law* transférer (**to** à)

conveyance [kən'veɪəns] **N 1** *(transport)* transport *m* **2** *Old-fashioned (vehicle)* véhicule *m* **3** *Law (transfer of property)* cession *f*, transfert *m*; *(document)* acte *m* de cession

conveyancer [kən'veɪənsə(r)] **N** *Law* = personne qui rédige un acte translatif ou des actes translatifs de propriété immobilière

conveyancing [kən'veɪənsɪŋ] **N** *Law* **1** *(procedure)* procédure *f* translative de propriété **2** *(drawing up documents)* rédaction *f* des actes de cession *ou* des actes translatifs de propriété

conveyor [kən'veɪə(r)] **N 1** *(transporter)* transporteur *m*; *Mining* convoyeur *m* **2** *(belt)* tapis *m* roulant; **bucket c.** transporteur *m* à godets **3** *Formal (person ▸ of letter, parcel)* porteur(euse) *m,f*

▸▸ ***conveyor belt*** tapis *m* roulant

convict **VT** [kən'vɪkt] déclarer *ou* reconnaître coupable; **she was convicted** elle a été déclarée *ou* reconnue coupable; **to c. sb of** *or* **for sth** déclarer *ou* reconnaître qn coupable de qch; **you stand convicted by your own words** vos propres paroles vous condamnent

N ['kɒnvɪkt] *(convicted person)* détenu(e) *m,f*; *Old-fashioned (prisoner)* forçat *m*, bagnard *m*

VI [kən'vɪkt] rendre un verdict de culpabilité

> Attention: ne pas confondre avec le verbe **to convince**.

conviction [kən'vɪkʃən] **N 1** *(belief)* conviction *f*; **to act from c.** agir par conviction
2 *(UNCOUNT) (certainty)* certitude *f*, conviction *f*; **he lacks c.** il manque de conviction
3 *(UNCOUNT) (plausibility)* **to carry c.** *(voice, manner)* être convaincant; **the theory carries little c.** la théorie est peu convaincante
4 *Law* condamnation *f*; **the prosecution called for his c.** la partie plaignante a demandé sa condamnation; **she has several previous convictions** elle a déjà été condamnée plusieurs fois

convince [kən'vɪns] **VT** convaincre, persuader; **to allow oneself to be convinced** se laisser convaincre; **to c. sb of sth** convaincre *ou* persuader qn de qch; **to c. sb to do sth** convaincre *ou* persuader qn de faire qch

> Attention: ne pas confondre avec le verbe **to convict**.

convinced [kən'vɪnst] **ADJ** convaincu; **to be c. of sth** être convaincu de qch; **to be c. (that)…** être convaincu que… + *indicative*

convincing [kən'vɪnsɪŋ] **ADJ** *(argument, person, performance)* convaincant; *(victory, win)* décisif, éclatant; **she wasn't very c. as Juliet** elle n'était pas convaincante dans le rôle de Juliette; **the battle scenes were very c.** les scènes de bataille étaient très réalistes

convincingly [kən'vɪnsɪŋlɪ] **ADV** *(argue, speak, pretend)* de façon convaincante; *(beat, win)* haut la main

convivial [kən'vɪvɪəl] **ADJ** *(atmosphere, lunch)* convivial, joyeux; *(manner, person)* joyeux, plein d'entrain

conviviality [kən͵vɪvɪ'ælətɪ] **N** convivialité *f*, gaieté *f*, jovialité *f*

convocation [͵kɒnvə'keɪʃən] **N 1** *(summoning)* convocation *f* **2** *(meeting)* assemblée *f*, réunion *f*; *Br Rel* synode *m*

convoke [kən'vəʊk] VT *(assembly, meeting)* convoquer

convoluted [ˌkɒnvə'lu:tɪd] ADJ *(shape)* convoluté; *(prose, reasoning, argument)* alambiqué

convolution [ˌkɒnvə'lu:ʃən] N *Formal* **1** *(complication ▸ of prose, reasoning, argument)* méandre *m* **2** *(twist)* circonvolution *f* **3** *Anat (of brain)* circonvolution *f*

convolvulus [kən'vɒlvjʊləs] *(pl* **convolvuluses** *or* **convolvuli** [-laɪ]) N *Bot* liseron *m*

convoy ['kɒnvɔɪ] N convoi *m*; **to travel in c.** voyager en convoi

VT convoyer, escorter

convulse [kən'vʌls] VT **1** *(person)* secouer; *Fig (someone's life)* bouleverser; **to be convulsed with laughter/pain** se tordre de rire/douleur **2** *Med (muscle)* convulsionner

VI *Med (person)* avoir des convulsions; *(face, lungs, muscle)* se convulser, se contracter, se crisper

convulsion [kən'vʌlʃən] N **1** *Med* convulsion *f*; **to have convulsions** avoir des convulsions; *Fam* **to be in convulsions** *(laughing)* se tordre de rire **2** *(revolution, war)* bouleversement *m*; *(earthquake)* secousse *f*; *Fig* **political convulsions** bouleversements *mpl* politiques

convulsive [kən'vʌlsɪv] ADJ **1** *Med (movement)* convulsif **2** *(transition)* brutal; **the most c. years in the country's history** les années les plus agitées dans l'histoire du pays

convulsively [kən'vʌlsɪvlɪ] ADV *Med* convulsivement

coo [ku:] *(pl* **coos**) N roucoulement *m*

VI *(dove, pigeon)* roucouler; *(baby, person)* babiller, gazouiller; **the neighbours came to c. over the baby** les voisins sont venus s'extasier sur le bébé

VT *(endearments, sweet nothings)* roucouler

EXCLAM *Br Fam Old-fashioned* ça alors!

cooing ['ku:ɪŋ] N *(of dove, pigeon)* roucoulement *m*; *(of baby, person)* gazouillement *m*

cook [kʊk] N cuisinier(ère) *m,f*; **she's an excellent c.** c'est une excellente cuisinière; *Fam* **chief** *or* **head c. and bottle-washer** bonne *f* à tout faire; *Prov* **too many cooks spoil the broth** = si tout le monde met son grain de sel, on n'arrive à rien

VT **1** *(meal)* faire, préparer; *(food, meat)* (faire) cuire; **the meat should be cooked all the way through** la viande doit être bien cuite; *Fam* **to c. sb's goose** mettre qn dans le pétrin **2** *Br Fam* **to c. the accounts** *or* **the books** falsifier *ou* truquer les comptes

VI *(person)* cuisiner, faire la cuisine; *(food)* cuire; **can you c.?** est-ce que tu sais faire la cuisine?; **he cooks well** il cuisine bien; **it cooks in five minutes** ça cuit en cinq minutes; *Fam* **what's cooking?** qu'est-ce qui se mijote?; *Fam Fig* **now we're cooking!**, *Br* **now we're cooking with gas!** maintenant tout marche comme sur des roulettes!

▸▸ ***the Cook Islands*** les îles *fpl* Cook

▸ **cook up** VT SEP *Fam (plan)* mijoter; *(excuse, story)* inventer[□]

cookbook ['kʊkbʊk] N livre *m* de cuisine

cook-chill ADJ cuisiné (et réfrigéré)

cooked [kʊkt] ADJ *(food, meat)* cuit; **I always have a c. meal in the evening** je mange toujours un repas chaud le soir; *Br* **c. breakfast** petit déjeuner *m* anglais

cooker ['kʊkə(r)] N *Br* **1** *(stove)* cuisinière *f*; **electric/gas c.** cuisinière *f* électrique/à gaz **2** *Br Fam (apple)* pomme *f* à cuire[□]

cookery ['kʊkərɪ] N cuisine *f*

▸▸ ***cookery book*** livre *m* de cuisine; ***cookery course*** stage *m* de cuisine; ***cookery programme*** émission *f* de cuisine

cookhouse ['kʊkhaʊs, *pl* -haʊzɪz] N cuisine *f*

cookie ['kʊkɪ] N **1** *Am (biscuit)* biscuit *m*

2 *Fam (person)* **a tough c.** un dur à cuire; **a smart c.** un petit malin

3 *Comput* cookie *m*, cafteur *m*, *Can* témoin *m*

4 *(idioms)* **that's the way the c. crumbles!** c'est la vie![□]; *Fam* **to toss** *or Am* **shoot one's cookies** *(vomit)* gerber, dégueuler

▸▸ *Am* ***cookie cutter*** emporte-pièce *m*; *Am* ***cookie jar*** bocal *m* à biscuits; *Fig* **to be caught with one's hand in the c. jar** être pris en flagrant délit

cookie-cutter ADJ *Am (building, plan, approach)* qui manque d'originalité

cooking ['kʊkɪŋ] N **1** *(activity)* cuisine *f*; **to do the c.** faire la cuisine **2** *(food)* cuisine *f*; **French/home c.** cuisine *f* française/maison

COMP *(oil, sherry)* de cuisine

▸▸ ***cooking apple*** pomme *f* à cuire; ***cooking chocolate*** chocolat *m* à cuire; ***cooking fat*** matière *f* grasse pour la cuisine; ***cooking foil*** papier *m* d'aluminium; ***cooking time*** temps *m* de cuisson; ***cooking utensils*** batterie *f* de cuisine

cool [ku:l] ADJ **1** *(in temperature ▸ breeze, room, weather, drink)* frais (fraîche); *(▸ clothes, material)* léger; **it's c.** *(weather)* il fait frais; **it's getting cooler in the evenings** *(weather)* les soirées sont plus fraîches; **keep in a c. place** *(on packaging)* tenir au frais

2 *(colour ▸ blue, green)* clair

3 *(calm ▸ person, manner, voice)* calme; *Fam* **keep c.!** du calme![□]; **to keep a c. head** garder la tête froide, garder son sang-froid; *Fam* **she's a c. customer!** *(cheeky)* elle a du culot!, elle en prend à son aise!; *(self-possessed)* elle a beaucoup de sang-froid!; **to be c., calm and collected** être d'un calme olympien; **to be/look as c. as a cucumber** garder son sang-froid *ou* calme

4 *(unfriendly ▸ person, greeting, welcome)* froid

5 *Fam (sum of money)* **she earned a c. million dollars last year** elle a gagné la coquette somme d'un million de dollars l'année dernière; **I lost a c. thousand** j'ai perdu mille livres bien comptées

6 *Fam (fashionable, sophisticated)* branché; **Glasgow's a really c. city** Glasgow est une ville hyper-branchée; **he still thinks it's c. to smoke** il pense encore que ça fait bien de fumer

7 *Fam (great)* génial, super; **we had a really c. weekend** on a passé un super week-end; **that's a c. jacket** elle est cool *ou* super, cette veste; **I'll be there at eight – c.!** je serai là à huit heures – super!

8 *Fam (allowed, acceptable)* **is it c. to smoke in here?** on peut fumer ici?

9 *Fam (accepting, not upset)* **are you c. with that?** ça te va?; **I thought she'd be angry, but she was really c. about it** je pensais qu'elle se fâcherait, mais en fait elle a été très cool

ADV *Fam* **to play it c.** *(act calm)* jouer décontracté; *(be calm)* être décontracté[□]; **play it c.!** ne nous énervons pas![□]

N **1** *(coolness)* fraîcheur *f*; **the c. of the evening** la fraîcheur du soir **2** *(calm)* calme *m*, sang-froid *m*; **to keep/to lose one's c.** garder/perdre son calme

VT *(air, liquid, room)* rafraîchir, refroidir; *(brow, feet)* rafraîchir; **to c. sb's ardour** refroidir l'ardeur de qn; *Fig* **to c. one's heels** faire le pied de grue; **they left him to c. his heels in jail** ils l'ont laissé mijoter en prison; *Fam* **c. it!** du calme![□]

VI *(food, liquid)* (se) refroidir; *(friendship, relationship)* se refroidir; *(enthusiasm, passion, temper)* s'apaiser, se calmer

▸ **cool down** VI **1** *(weather)* se rafraîchir; *(liquid)* (se) refroidir, se rafraîchir; *(machine)* se refroidir **2** *(person)* se calmer; **give him time to c. down** donne-lui le temps de se calmer **3** *Fig (situation)* se détendre; **things have cooled down between them** les relations se sont refroidies entre eux

VT SEP **1** *(person)* calmer; *(situation)* calmer, détendre **2** *(of cold drink)* rafraîchir

▸ **cool off** VI **1** *(person ▸ become less hot)* se rafraîchir; *(▸ become calmer)* se calmer **2** *Fig (affection, enthusiasm)* se refroidir

coolant ['ku:lənt] N *Tech* liquide *m* de refroidissement

▸▸ *Tech* ***coolant inlet*** arrivée *f* de liquide de refroidissement; *Tech* ***coolant outlet*** sortie *f* de liquide de refroidissement

coolbag ['ku:lbæg] N glacière *f*

coolbox ['ku:lbɒks] N glacière *f*

cooler ['ku:lə(r)] N **1** *(for food)* glacière *f*

2 *Tech (device for cooling)* (appareil *m*) refroidisseur *m*

3 *Fam (prison)* taule *f*; **in the c.** en taule

4 *(drink)* **(wine) c.** = mélange de vin, de jus de fruit et d'eau gazeuse

cool-headed ADJ calme, imperturbable

coolhunter ['ku:lˌhʌntə(r)] N tendanceur *m*, = personne employée par une société commerciale pour identifier les nouvelles tendances de la mode telles qu'elles apparaissent dans la rue, les bars etc

coolie ['ku:lɪ] N coolie *m*

cooling ['ku:lɪŋ] N *(in temperature)* rafraîchissement *m*, refroidissement *m*; *(in relationships)* refroidissement *m*; **there had been a c. in their relationship** leurs relations s'étaient refroidies; *Fig* **c. off period** période *f* de réflexion

ADJ *(breeze, drink)* rafraîchissant; *Ind & Tech* réfrigérant

▸▸ *Tech* ***cooling fan*** ventilateur *m* de refroidissement; *Tech* ***cooling system*** système *m* de refroidissement; *Tech* ***cooling tower*** aéroréfrigérant *m*

coolly ['ku:lɪ] ADV **1** *(calmly ▸ react, respond)* calmement; **she walked c. out of the room** elle a calmement quitté la pièce **2** *(without enthusiasm ▸ greet, welcome)* froidement, fraîchement **3** *(impertinently ▸ behave, say)* avec impertinence

coolness ['ku:lnɪs] N **1** *(in temperature ▸ of air, water, weather)* fraîcheur *f*; *(▸ of clothes)* légèreté *f* **2** *(calmness)* calme *m*, sang-froid *m* **3** *(of welcome, manner)* froideur *f*

coon [ku:n] N **1** *Fam (raccoon)* raton *m* laveur[□] **2** *very Fam* nègre (négresse) *m,f*, = terme raciste désignant un Noir

coonskin ['ku:nskɪn] N **1** *(skin)* peau *f* de raton laveur **2** *(hat)* chapeau *m* en peau de raton laveur **3** *(coat)* manteau *m* en peau de raton laveur

COMP en peau de raton laveur

coop [ku:p] N poulailler *m*

co-op ['kəʊˌɒp] *(abbr* **co-operative society**) N coopérative *f*, coop *f*

• **Co-op** N *Br* **the C.** la Coop

▸ **coop up** VT SEP *(animal, person, prisoner)* enfermer; **we were cooped up for hours in a tiny room** nous sommes restés enfermés pendant des heures dans une pièce minuscule; **to feel cooped up** se sentir à l'étroit; **I've been cooped up at home all day** j'ai été cloîtré chez moi toute la journée

cooper ['ku:pə(r)] N tonnelier *m*

cooperage ['ku:pərɪdʒ] N tonnellerie *f*

cooperate [kəʊ'ɒpəˌreɪt] VI **1** *(work together)* collaborer, coopérer; **to c. with sb** collaborer avec qn **2** *(be willing to help)* se montrer coopératif

cooperation [kəʊˌɒpə'reɪʃən] N **1** *(collaboration)* coopération *f*, concours *m*; **in c. with** *or* **with the c. of sb** avec la coopération *ou* le concours de qn **2** *(willingness to help)* coopération *f*

▸▸ ***cooperation agreement*** accord *m* de coopération; *EU* ***cooperation in justice and home affairs*** coopération *f* en justice et affaires intérieures; *EU* ***cooperation procedure*** procédure *f* de coopération

cooperative [kəʊ'ɒpərətɪv] ADJ **1** *(joint ▸ activity, work)* coopératif **2** *(helpful ▸ attitude, person)* coopératif; **he has been most c.** il a été très coopératif

N *Com* coopérative *f*

▸▸ ***Cooperative for American Relief Everywhere*** = organisation humanitaire américaine; *Am Pol* ***cooperative federalism*** fédéralisme *m* coopératif; *Com* ***cooperative group*** coopérative *f* (de consommateurs); *Com* ***cooperative selling*** vente *f* en coopération; *Com* ***cooperative society*** société *f* coopérative

cooperatively [kəʊ'ɒpərətɪvlɪ] ADV coopérativement

co-opt VT **1** *(onto committee)* coopter, admettre; **I was co-opted as a member of the committee** on m'a coopté *ou* admis comme membre du comité; **to be co-opted into/onto sth** être coopté à qch **2** *Fam (commandeer)* réquisitionner[□]; **I've been co-opted to help with the spring cleaning** j'ai été réquisitionné pour le nettoyage de printemps

co-option [kəʊ'ɒpʃən] N cooptation *f*

coordinate VT [kəʊ'ɔ:dɪneɪt] coordonner

N [kəʊ'ɔ:dɪnət] *Geom* coordonnée *f*

ADJ [kəʊ'ɔ:dɪnət] *Gram & Geom* coordonné

• **coordinates** NPL [kəʊ'ɔ:dɪnəts] *(clothes)* coordonnés *mpl*

▸▸ *Chem* ***coordinate bond*** liaison *f* de coordination; *Gram* **coordinate clause** proposition *f* coordonnée; *Geom* **coordinate geometry** géométrie *f* analytique

coordinated [kəʊ'ɔ:dɪˌneɪtɪd] ADJ *(physically, in movements)* coordonné; **I'm not very c.** je ne suis pas très coordonné; **to give sth a more c. appearance** donner à qch une apparence plus harmonieuse

coordinating [kəʊ'ɔ:dɪˌneɪtɪŋ] ADJ *(body, officer)* de coordination
►► *Gram* ***coordinating conjunction*** conjonction *f* de coordination

coordination [kəʊˌɔ:dɪ'neɪʃən] N **1** *(harmonious combination)* coordination *f*; **we need greater c. between doctors and nurses** il nous faut une plus grande coordination entre médecins et infirmières **2** *(ease of movement)* coordination *f*; **she lacks c.** elle manque de coordination; **to have a c. problem** avoir des problèmes de coordination
►► ***coordination number*** coordinence *f*

coordinator [kəʊ'ɔ:dɪˌneɪtə(r)] N coordinateur (trice) *m,f*, coordonnateur(trice) *m,f*

coot [ku:t] N **1** *(bird)* foulque *f* (macroule) **2** *Fam Old-fashioned (fool)* bêta *m*; **silly old c.!** gros bêta!

cooties ['ku:tɪz] NPL *Am Fam* poux▫ *mpl*

co-owner N copropriétaire *mf*

co-ownership N copropriété *f*

cooze [ku:z] N *Am Vulg (female genitals)* craquette *f*, fente *f*; *(women)* nanas *fpl*, cuisse *f*

cop [kɒp] *(pt & pp* **copped**, *cont* **copping**) *Fam* N **1** *(policeman)* flic *m*; **to play cops and robbers** jouer aux gendarmes et aux voleurs; **to play good c.-bad c.** adopter la stratégie gentil flic/méchant flic **2** *Br (arrest)* **it's a fair c.!** je suis fait! **3** *Br (idiom)* **it's not much c.** ça ne vaut pas grand-chose, c'est pas terrible
VT *Fam (catch)* attraper▫, pincer; **to get copped** *(by police)* se faire pincer; *Br* **to c. it** *(be caught and punished)* se faire pincer; *(get injured)* être blessé▫; *(die)* clamser; **you'll c. it if he finds out!** qu'est-ce que tu vas prendre s'il s'en rend compte!; **to c. hold of sth** attraper qch; **c. this!** *(listen)* écoute-moi ça!; *(look)* regarde-moi ça!; *Law* **to c. a plea** plaider coupable▫ *(pour éviter une charge plus grave)*; **to c. some** *Br* **zeds** *or Am* **zees** roupiller
►► *Fam* ***cop shop*** *(police station)* poste *m* de police▫; *Fam TV* ***cop show*** série *f* policière▫

►**cop off** VI *Br Fam* **to c. off with sb** lever *ou* emballer qn; **did you c. off last night?** t'as réussi à lever quelqu'un hier soir?

►**cop out** VI *Fam (avoid responsibility)* se défiler; *(choose easy solution)* choisir la solution de facilité▫; **to c. out of doing sth** ne pas avoir le cran de faire qch

co-parent [kəʊ'peərənt] N coparent *m*
VT **to c. a child** partager l'éducation d'un enfant avec une autre personne
VI partager l'éducation d'un enfant avec une autre personne

co-parental [kəʊpə'rentəl] ADJ coparental

co-parenting [kəʊ'peərəntɪŋ] N = fait de partager l'éducation d'un enfant avec une autre personne

copartner [kəʊ'pɑ:tnə(r)] N coassocié(e) *m,f*

copartnership [kəʊ'pɑ:tnəʃɪp] N partenariat *m*

COPE [kəʊp] N *Br Journ (abbr* **Committee on Publication Ethics**) = comité de conseil en matière d'éthique dans l'édition scientifique

cope [kəʊp] VI *(person)* se débrouiller, s'en sortir; **I can't c. any more** je n'en peux plus; **that's all right, thanks, I can c.** ça va, merci, j'y arriverai; **she's coping very well on her own** elle s'en sort très bien toute seule; **to c. with** *(situation, danger, job, debt)* faire face à; *(difficulty)* venir à bout de; *(troublemaker)* se charger de; *(look after* ► *children)* s'occuper de; *(put up with* ► *children, noise)* supporter; **I can't c. with her when she gets angry** je ne sais pas comment la prendre quand elle se met en colère; **the system can't c. with this volume of work** le système ne peut pas supporter ce volume de travail; **the engine couldn't c. with the extra weight** le moteur n'était pas assez puissant pour supporter cette charge supplémentaire
N *Rel* chape *f*
VT *Constr* **1** *(provide with coping* ► *wall)* chaperonner **2** *(join* ► *timbers)* assembler

Copenhagen [ˌkəʊpən'heɪgən] N Copenhague

copiable ['kɒpɪəbəl] ADJ *Comput* copiable

copier ['kɒpɪə(r)] N photocopieuse *f*, copieur *m*

co-pilot N copilote *mf*

coping ['kəʊpɪŋ] N *Constr (of wall)* chaperon *m*
►► *Psy* ***coping mechanism*** stratégie *f* d'adaptation, coping *m*; *Tech* ***coping saw*** scie *f* à découper *ou* à chantourner; *Constr* ***coping stone*** couronnement *m*, chaperon *m*

copious ['kəʊpjəs] ADJ *(amount, food)* copieux; *(sunshine, notes)* abondant; **we drank c. amounts of beer** nous avons bu des quantités de bière

copiously ['kəʊpjəslɪ] ADV *(cry, produce, write)* en abondance, abondamment

co-plaintiff N *Law* codemandeur(eresse) *m,f*

cop-out N *Fam* dérobade *f*; **what a c.!** belle façon de se défiler!

copper ['kɒpə(r)] N **1** *(UNCOUNT) (colour, metal)* cuivre *m*
2 *Fam* **coppers** *(coins)* monnaie▫ *f*; **to give a beggar a few coppers** donner quelques sous à un mendiant
3 *Fam (policeman)* flic *m*
4 *(container)* lessiveuse *f*
COMP *(coin, kettle, wire)* en cuivre
ADJ *(colour, hair)* cuivré
VT *(in metalwork)* cuivrer
►► *Bot* ***copper beech*** hêtre *m* pourpre; *Chem* ***copper sulphate*** sulfate *m* de cuivre

copper-bottomed [-'bɒtəmd] ADJ *(saucepan)* à fond de cuivre; *Fig (deal, guarantee)* en béton

copper-coloured ADJ cuivré

copperhead ['kɒpəhed] N *Zool* trigonocéphale *m*

copperplate ['kɒpəpleɪt] N **1** *Typ (plate)* cuivre *m* **2** *(print)* plaque *f* (de cuivre) **3** *(handwriting)* écriture *f* moulée
COMP *(handwriting)* moulé
►► ***copperplate engraving*** taille-douce *f*

coppersmith ['kɒpəsmɪθ] N chaudronnier(ère) *m,f*

copperware ['kɒpəweə(r)] N *(UNCOUNT)* ustensiles *mpl* en cuivre

coppery ['kɒpərɪ] ADJ *(colour)* cuivré

coppice ['kɒpɪs] *Agr* N taillis *m*
VT couper en taillis
VI couper des arbres en taillis

copra ['kɒprə] N *Bot* coprah *m*

co-presenter N coprésentateur(trice) *m,f*

co-processor N *Comput* coprocesseur *m*

coproduce [ˌkəʊprə'dju:s] VT *Cin, Theat & TV* coproduire

coproducer [ˌkəʊprə'dju:sə(r)] N *Cin, Theat & TV* coproducteur(trice) *m,f*

coproduction [ˌkəʊprə'dʌkʃən] N *Cin, Theat & TV* coproduction *f*

copse [kɒps] N *Bot* taillis *m*

copter ['kɒptə(r)] N *Fam* hélico *m*

Coptic ['kɒptɪk] N *Ling* copte *m*
ADJ copte
►► ***the Coptic Church*** l'Église *f* copte

copublish [ˌkəʊ'pʌblɪʃ] VT coéditer

copublisher [ˌkəʊ'pʌblɪʃə(r)] N coéditeur *m*

copublishing [ˌkəʊ'pʌblɪʃɪŋ] N coédition *f*

copula ['kɒpjʊlə] *(pl* **copulas** *or* **copulae** [-li:]) N *Gram* copule *f*

copulate ['kɒpjʊleɪt] VI copuler

copulation [ˌkɒpjʊ'leɪʃən] N copulation *f*

copulative ['kɒpjʊlətɪv] ADJ **1** *Gram* copulatif **2** *Physiol* copulateur

copy ['kɒpɪ] *(pl* **copies**, *pt & pp* **copied**) N **1** *(duplicate* ► *of painting, statue)* copie *f*, reproduction *f*; *(*► *of document, letter, photograph)* copie *f*; **to make a c. of sth** faire une copie de qch
2 *(of book, magazine, record)* exemplaire *m*; *(of newspaper)* numéro *m*; **500 copies of the book were printed** le livre a été tiré à 500 exemplaires
3 *(UNCOUNT) Typ, Press & Journ (written material)* copie *f*; *(in advertisement)* texte *m*; **his story made good c.** son histoire a fait un bon papier; **he wrote some brilliant c.** *(one article)* il a écrit un article excellent; *(several articles)* il a écrit d'excellents articles
4 *Comput* **c. and paste** copier-coller *m*
VT **1** *(work of art, drawing etc)* copier, imiter
2 *(write out* ► *letter, notes)* copier
3 *(imitate* ► *person, movements, gestures)* copier, imiter; *(*► *style, system)* copier
4 *(in order to cheat)* copier (**from sb** sur qn; **from sth** dans qch)
5 *(photocopy)* photocopier
6 *Comput* copier; **to c. sth to disk** copier qch sur disquette; **to c. and paste sth** faire un copier-coller sur qch
7 *(send copy to)* envoyer une copie à; **to c. sb with sth** faire parvenir une copie de qch à qn
VI **1** *(cheat)* copier (**from sb** sur qn; **from sth** dans qch); **no copying!** on ne copie pas! **2** *Am Tel (hear)* **do you c.?** vous me recevez?
►► *Comput* ***copy command*** commande *f* de copie; *Press* ***copy deadline*** tombée *f*, dernière heure *f*; *Am Press* ***copy desk*** secrétariat *m* de rédaction; *Comput* ***copy disk*** disquette *f* de copie; ***copy editor*** *Press* secrétaire *mf* de rédaction; *(in publishing)* préparateur(trice) *m,f* de copie; *Comput* ***copy protection*** protection *f* contre la copie; ***copy taster*** premier lecteur *m*; ***copy typist*** dactylographe *mf*, dactylo *mf*

►**copy out** VT SEP recopier; **to c. out a passage from a book** transcrire *ou* recopier un passage d'un livre

copybook ['kɒpɪbʊk] N cahier *m*
ADJ *(sentiments)* commun; **a c. example** un exemple classique

copycat ['kɒpɪkæt] N *Fam* copieur(euse)▫ *m,f*
COMP *(killing, murder, crime)* inspiré par un autre

copy-edit VT *(manuscript)* corriger
VI préparer la copie

copy-editing N préparation *f* de copie

copyholder ['kɒpɪˌhəʊldə(r)] N **1** *Typ (reader)* lecteur(trice) *m,f*, teneur(euse) *m,f* de copie **2** *(device)* porte-copie *m*

copying ['kɒpɪɪŋ] N *(imitation)* imitation *f*; *Sch (cheating)* copiage *m*
►► ***copying machine*** duplicateur *m*; *(photocopier)* photocopieuse *f*; *Comput* ***copying program*** programme *m* de copie

copyist ['kɒpɪɪst] N copiste *mf*

copy-protect VT *Comput* protéger (contre la copie)

copy-protected ADJ *Comput* anticopie *(inv)*, protégé (contre la copie)

copyreader ['kɒpɪˌri:də(r)] N *Am Typ* secrétaire *mf* de rédaction

copyright ['kɒpɪraɪt] N copyright *m*, droit *m* d'auteur; **she has c. on the book** elle a des droits d'auteur sur le livre; **it's still subject to c.** c'est toujours soumis au droit d'auteur; **breach** *or* **infringement of c.** violation *f* du droit d'auteur; **c. Lawrence Durrell** copyright, Lawrence Durrell; **out of c.** dans le domaine public
VT obtenir les droits exclusifs *ou* le copyright de
ADJ *(book)* qui est protégé par des droits d'auteur; *(article)* dont le droit de reproduction est réservé
►► ***copyright deposit library*** bibliothèque *f* de dépôt légal; ***copyright law*** loi *f* du droit d'auteur; ***copyright library*** bibliothèque *f* de dépôt légal; ***copyright notice*** mention *f* de réserve

copyrighted ['kɒpɪˌraɪtɪd] ADJ *(book)* déposé

copytaker ['kɒpɪˌteɪkə(r)] N *Journ* opérateur *m*

copywriter ['kɒpɪˌraɪtə(r)] N *Journ* rédacteur (trice) *m,f* publicitaire

copywriting ['kɒpɪˌraɪtɪŋ] N *Journ* rédaction *f* publicitaire

coquetry ['kəʊkɪtrɪ, 'kɒkɪtrɪ] *(pl* **coquetries**) N coquetterie *f*

coquette [kəʊ'ket, kɒ'ket] *Literary* N coquette *f*

coquettish [kəʊ'ketɪʃ, kɒ'ketɪʃ] ADJ *(woman)* coquet; *(look, smile, behaviour)* charmeur, aguichant

cor [kɔ:(r)] EXCLAM *Br Fam* **c. (blimey)!** ça alors!

coracle ['kɒrəkəl] N coracle *m*

coral ['kɒrəl] **N 1** *(substance)* corail *m* **2** *(colour)* corail *m inv*
ADJ 1 *(pink, red, lipstick)* corail *(inv)*; *Literary (lips)* de corail **2** *(colour)* corail *(inv)*
COMP *(earrings, necklace)* de corail; *(island)* corallien
▸▸ ***coral reef*** récif *m* de corail; **the Coral Sea** la mer de Corail; *Zool* ***coral snake*** serpent *m* corail

corbel ['kɔ:bəl] **N** *Archit* corbeau *m*

cord [kɔ:d] **N 1** *(string)* cordon *m*; *(for climbing)* cordelette *f*
2 *(cable)* câble *m*
3 *(corduroy)* velours *m* côtelé
4 *Anat* **(umbilical) c.** cordon *m* (ombilical)
COMP *(skirt, trousers)* en velours côtelé
VT corder
• **cords NPL** *Fam* **(pair of) cords** pantalon *m* en velours côtelé

cordage ['kɔ:dɪdʒ] **N** *Naut* cordage *m*

corded ['kɔ:dɪd] **ADJ** *(material)* côtelé

cordial ['kɔ:dɪəl] **ADJ 1** *(warm* ▸ *greeting, welcome)* chaleureux **2** *(strong* ▸ *hatred)* cordial; **to have a c. dislike for sb** détester qn cordialement
N *(drink)* cordial *m*

cordiality [ˌkɔ:dɪ'ælətɪ] *(pl* **cordialities) N** cordialité *f*

cordially ['kɔ:dɪəlɪ] **ADV 1** *(warmly* ▸ *greet etc)* cordialement; *Am* **c. yours** *(at end of letter)* salutations amicales **2** *(completely* ▸ *hate, detest)* cordialement

cordite ['kɔ:daɪt] **N** cordite *f*

cordless ['kɔ:dlɪs] **ADJ** *(telephone, iron, kettle, mouse)* sans fil

cordon ['kɔ:dən] **N 1** *(barrier)* cordon *m*; **police c.** cordon *m* de police; **the police put a c. round the building** la police a encerclé le bâtiment **2** *Hort* cordon *m* **3** *(decoration)* cordon *m*
VT barrer, interdire l'accès à, isoler

▸ **cordon off VT SEP** barrer, interdire l'accès à, isoler

cordon bleu [-blɜ:] **ADJ** de cordon bleu; **c. cook** cordon-bleu *m*
N *(cookery, chef)* cordon-bleu *m*

corduroy ['kɒdərɔɪ] **N** velours *m* côtelé; **(pair of) corduroys** pantalon *m* de *ou* en velours côtelé
ADJ de velours côtelé

core [kɔ:(r)] **N 1** *(of mass)* centre *m*, partie *f* centrale; *(of apple, pear)* trognon *m*, cœur *m*; *(of organization)* noyau *m*; *(of argument)* essentiel *m*, centre *m*; *Fig* **to be French/a socialist to the c.** être français/socialiste jusqu'à la moelle; *Fig* **rotten to the c.** pourri jusqu'à l'os
2 *Geol (of earth)* noyau *m*
3 *Tech (of electric cable)* âme *f*, noyau *m*; *(of nuclear reactor)* cœur *m*; *(of magnet)* noyau *m*
4 *Med (of abscess, boil etc)* bourbillon *m*
VT *(apple, pear)* enlever le trognon de
▸▸ *Fin* ***core assets*** actif *m* principal; *Com & Mktg* ***core brand*** marque *f* phare; *Com* ***core business*** activité *f* principale; ***core competence*** noyau *m* de compétence; *Sch* ***core curriculum*** tronc *m* commun; ***core hours*** *(in flexitime scheme)* plage *f* fixe; *Mktg* ***core market*** marché *m* principal, marché *m* de référence; *Comput* ***core memory*** mémoire *f* à tores (magnétiques); *Com & Mktg* ***core message*** *(in advertising)* message *m* principal; ***core skills*** compétences *fpl* de base; *Sch* ***core subject*** matière *f* principale; *Ind* ***core time*** *(in flexitime)* plage *f* fixe; *Ling* ***core vocabulary*** vocabulaire *m* de base

coreligionist [ˌkəʊrɪ'lɪdʒənɪst] **N** coreligionnaire *mf*

corer ['kɔ:rə(r)] **N (apple) c.** vide-pomme *m*

co-respondent [ˌkəʊrɪ'spɒndənt] **ADJ** *(shoes)* bicolore *(style années 40)*
N *Law (in divorce suit)* complice *mf* de l'adultère

Corfu [kɔ:'fu:] **N** Corfou

corgi ['kɔ:gɪ] **N** corgi *m*

coriander [ˌkɒrɪ'ændə(r)] **N** coriandre *f*
▸▸ ***coriander seeds*** graines *fpl* de coriandre

Corinthian [kə'rɪnθɪən] **N** Corinthien(enne) *m,f*
ADJ 1 *Geog* corinthien **2** *Archit (column etc)* corinthien

cork [kɔ:k] **N 1** *(UNCOUNT) (substance)* liège *m* **2** *(stopper)* bouchon *m*; **he took** *or* **pulled the c. out of the bottle** il a débouché la bouteille; *Fam* **put a c. in it!** la ferme! **3** *Fishing (float)* flotteur *m*, bouchon *m*
COMP *(sole, tile, bath mat)* de *ou* en liège
VT 1 *(seal* ▸ *bottle)* boucher **2** *(blacken)* **to c. one's face** se noircir le visage avec un bouchon brûlé
▸▸ *Bot* ***cork oak*** chêne-liège *m*

▸ **cork up VT SEP 1** *(seal* ▸ *bottle)* boucher **2** *(suppress* ▸ *emotions, feelings)* réprimer

corkage ['kɔ:kɪdʒ] **N** *(UNCOUNT)* droit *m* de bouchon

corked [kɔ:kt] **ADJ** *(wine)* qui sent le bouchon

corker ['kɔ:kə(r)] **N** *Br Fam* **he's/she's a real c.** *(good-looking)* c'est un beau gars/un beau brin de fille; **that was a c. of a goal** c'était un super but; **it's a c.** *(car, bike etc)* c'est un (vrai) bijou

corking ['kɔ:kɪŋ] **ADJ** *Br Fam* épatant, fameux

corkscrew ['kɔ:kskru:] **N** tire-bouchon *m*
VI *(staircase)* tourner en vrille; *(plane)* vriller; **the plane corkscrewed out of the sky** l'avion est tombé en vrille
▸▸ ***corkscrew curl*** mèche *f* en tire-bouchon

cork-tipped [-tɪpt] **ADJ** *(cigarette)* (à bout) filtre

corkwood ['kɔ:kwʊd] **N** *Bot* liège *m*

corm [kɔ:m] **N** *Bot* bulbe *m*

cormorant ['kɔ:mərənt] **N** *Orn* cormoran *m*

corn [kɔ:n] **N 1** *(UNCOUNT) Br (cereal)* blé *m*
2 *(UNCOUNT) esp Am (maize)* maïs *m*; **c. on the cob** épi *m* de maïs
3 *(UNCOUNT) (seed)* grain *m (de plante céréalière)*
4 *(UNCOUNT) Fam (banality)* banalité *f*; *(sentimentality)* sentimentalité *f* bêbête; **the book/film is pure c.** le livre/film est d'un gnan gnan!
5 *(on foot)* cor *m*; *Fam Fig* **to tread on sb's corns** *Br (upset)* toucher qn à l'endroit sensible; *(trespass)* marcher sur les plates-bandes de qn
▸▸ ***corn bread*** pain *m* à la farine de maïs; *Orn* ***corn bunting*** bruant *m*; *Am Culin* ***corn dog*** = saucisse de Francfort enrobée de farine de maïs, frite et servie sur un bâtonnet; ***corn dolly*** figurine *f* en paille tressée; ***corn exchange*** halle *f* au blé; *Br Hist* **the Corn Laws** les lois *fpl* sur le blé; *Am* ***corn liquor*** whisky *m* à base de maïs; ***corn oil*** huile *f* de maïs; ***corn plaster*** pansement *m* (pour cors); *Am Culin* ***corn pone*** pain *m* de maïs; ***corn poppy*** coquelicot *m*; ***corn syrup*** sirop *m* de maïs; *Am* ***corn whiskey*** whisky *m* de maïs

cornball ['kɔ:nbɔ:l] *Am Fam* **N** sentimental(e) *m,f*
ADJ *(trite)* bateau *(inv)*, banal; *(sentimental)* sentimental, à l'eau de rose

corncob ['kɔ:nkɒb] **N** épi *m* de maïs; *(pipe)* pipe *f* en épi de maïs
▸▸ ***corncob pipe*** pipe *f* en épi de maïs

corncockle ['kɔ:nˌkɒkəl] **N** *Bot* nielle *f*

corncrake ['kɔ:nkreɪk] **N** *Orn* râle *m* des genêts

cornea ['kɔ:nɪə] **N** cornée *f*

corneal ['kɔ:nɪəl] **ADJ** cornéen
▸▸ *Med* ***corneal graft*** greffe *f* de la cornée

corned beef [kɔ:nd-] **N** corned-beef *m*

cornelian [kɔ:'ni:lɪən] **N** *Miner* cornaline *f*

CORNER ['kɔ:nə(r)]

N
• coin **1–4, 6** • virage **3**
• situation difficile **5** • corner **7**
VT
• coincer **1** • accaparer **2**
VI
• prendre un virage

N 1 *(of page, painting, table etc)* coin *m*; **to turn down the c. of a page** faire une corne à une page
2 *(inside room, house etc)* coin *m*; **to search every c. of the house** chercher dans tous les coins et recoins de la maison; **to put a child in the c.** mettre un enfant au coin; *Br* **to fight one's c.** *(argue one's case)* défendre sa position; **to be in sb's c.** être du côté de qn, soutenir qn; **with someone as powerful as her in your c., you can't lose** avec quelqu'un d'aussi puissant qu'elle derrière toi, tu ne peux pas perdre
3 *(of street)* coin *m*; *(bend in the road)* tournant *m*, virage *m*; **on** *or* **at the c.** au coin; **the house on** *or* **at the c.** la maison qui fait l'angle; **at the c. of Regent Street and Oxford Street** à l'intersection *ou* à l'angle de Regent Street et d'Oxford Street; **to hang around street corners** traîner dans les rues; **he/the car took the c. at high speed** il/la voiture a pris le tournant à toute allure; **to overtake on a c.** doubler dans un virage; **it's just around** *or Br* **round the c.** *(house, shop etc)* c'est à deux pas d'ici; *Fig (Christmas, economic recovery etc)* c'est tout proche; *Fig* **you never know what's round the c.** on ne sait jamais ce qui peut arriver; **to turn the c.** *(car)* prendre le tournant; *Fig (patient)* passer le moment *ou* stade critique; *(business, economy, relationship)* passer un cap critique; **to cut the c.** *(in car, on bike)* couper le virage, prendre le virage à la corde; *(on foot)* couper au plus court, prendre le plus court; *Fig* **to cut corners** *(economize excessively)* faire des économies exagérées; *(not follow rules)* contourner les règlements; **if you cut corners now you'll just have more work to do later on** si tu fais les choses trop vite maintenant, tu auras plus à faire plus tard
4 *(of eye)* coin *m*; *(of mouth)* coin *m*, commissure *f*; **to look at sb/sth out of the c. of one's eye** regarder qn/qch du coin de l'œil
5 *Fam (difficulty)* situation *f* difficile, mauvaise passe *f*; **to drive sb into a tight c.** acculer qn, mettre qn dans une situation difficile
6 *(remote place)* coin *m*; **the four corners of the earth** les quatre coins du monde; **they had created a little c. of France in Edinburgh** ils avaient recréé un petit coin de France à Édimbourg
7 *Ftbl* corner *m*
8 *Com* **to make a c. in sth** avoir le monopole de qch, accaparer qch
COMP *(cupboard, table etc)* d'angle
VT 1 *(animal, prey etc)* coincer, acculer; **she cornered me at the party** elle m'a coincé à la soirée
2 *Com (market)* accaparer; **to c. the market in sth** accaparer le marché de qch
VI *Aut* prendre un virage; **the car corners well** la voiture tient bien la route dans les virages
▸▸ *Sport* ***corner flag*** drapeau *m* de corner; *Ftbl* ***corner kick*** corner *m*; *Br* ***corner shop,*** *Am* ***corner store*** petite épicerie *f*, *Can* dépanneur *m*

cornered ['kɔ:nəd] **ADJ** *(animal, prey)* acculé, coincé; **we've got him c.** on l'a acculé *ou* coincé

cornering ['kɔ:nərɪŋ] **N 1** *Br Aut (of driver)* façon *f* de prendre les virages; *(of car)* stabilité *f* dans les virages; **the car is good at c.** la voiture prend bien les virages **2** *Com (of market)* accaparement *m*

cornerstone ['kɔ:nəstəʊn] **N** *Archit* pierre *f* d'angle *ou* angulaire; *Fig* pierre *f* angulaire, fondement *m*

cornet ['kɔ:nɪt] **N 1** *Mus (instrument)* cornet *m* à pistons; *(player)* cornettiste *mf* **2** *Br* **(ice-cream) c.** cornet *m* (de glace)

cornetist, cornettist [kɔ:'netɪst] **N** *Mus* cornettiste *mf*

cornfield ['kɔ:nfi:ld] **N** *Br* champ *m* de blé; *Am* champ *m* de maïs

cornflakes ['kɔ:nfleɪks] **NPL** corn flakes *mpl*

cornflour ['kɔ:nˌflaʊə(r)] **N** *Br* fécule *f* de maïs, Maïzena® *f*

cornflower ['kɔ:nˌflaʊə(r)] **N 1** *(plant)* bleuet *m*, bluet *m*, barbeau *m* **2** *(colour)* bleu *m* centaurée
ADJ *(colour)* bleu centaurée
▸▸ ***cornflower blue*** bleu *m* centaurée

cornice ['kɔ:nɪs] **N 1** *Archit* corniche *f* **2** *(snow)* corniche *f*

Cornish ['kɔ:nɪʃ] **NPL** *(people)* **the C.** les Cornouaillais *mpl*
N *(language)* cornique *m*
ADJ cornouaillais
▸▸ *Br Culin* ***Cornish pasty*** = chausson à la viande et aux légumes

Cornishman ['kɔ:nɪʃmən] *(pl* **Cornishmen** [-mən]) **N** Cornouaillais *m*

Cornishwoman ['kɔ:nɪʃˌwʊmən] *(pl* **Cornishwomen** [-ˌwɪmɪn]) **N** Cornouaillaise *f*

cornstarch ['kɔ:nstɑ:tʃ] **N** *Am* fécule *f* de maïs, Maïzena® *f*

cornucopia [ˌkɔ:njʊ'kəʊpjə] **N** *Myth & Fig* corne *f* d'abondance

Cornwall ['kɔːnwɔːl] **N** la Cornouailles, = comté dans le sud-ouest de l'Angleterre; **in C.** en Cornouailles

corny ['kɔːnɪ] *(compar* **cornier**, *superl* **corniest**) **ADJ** *(trite)* bateau *(inv)*, banal; *(sentimental)* sentimental, à l'eau de rose; **he's so c.** il est vraiment lourd; **a c. joke** une blague éculée, *Can* une farce plate

corolla [kə'rɒlə] **N** *Bot* corolle *f*

corollary [kə'rɒlərɪ] *(pl* **corollaries**) **N** *Formal* corollaire *m*; **as a c. to this** en corollaire à ceci

corona [kə'rəʊnə] *(pl* **coronas** *or* **coronae** [-niː]) **N 1** *Anat, Astron, Bot & Phys* couronne *f* **2** *Archit* larmier *m* **3** *(cigar)* corona *m*

▸▸ *Phys* ***corona discharge*** effluve *f* électrique

coronary ['kɒrənərɪ] *(pl* **coronaries**) *Med* **ADJ** coronaire

N infarctus *m* (du myocarde); **to have a c.** avoir un infarctus (du myocarde); *Fam* **I just about had a c. when I saw the bill** j'ai failli avoir une attaque quand j'ai vu l'addition

▸▸ ***coronary artery*** artère *f* coronaire; ***coronary bypass*** pontage *m* coronarien; ***coronary heart disease*** maladies *fpl* coronariennes; ***coronary thrombosis*** infarctus *m* du myocarde, thrombose *f* coronarienne

coronation [ˌkɒrə'neɪʃən] **N** *(of monarch)* couronnement *m*, sacre *m*

COMP *(robes, day)* du couronnement, du sacre

▸▸ *Culin* ***coronation chicken*** = morceaux de poulet froid à la mayonnaise parfumée au curry

coroner ['kɒrənə(r)] *Law*

N coroner *m*

▸▸ ***coroner's inquest*** enquête *f* judiciaire *(menée par le coroner)*

coronet ['kɒrənɪt] **N** *(of prince, duke)* couronne *f*; *(for woman)* diadème *m*

Corp. 1 *Com (written abbr* **corporation**) Cie **2** *Mil (written abbr* **corporal**) caporal *m*

corporal ['kɔːpərəl] **N 1** *Mil (in infantry, air force)* caporal-chef *m*; *(in artillery)* brigadier-chef *m* **2** *Rel* corporal *m*

ADJ corporel

▸▸ ***corporal punishment*** châtiment *m* corporel

corporate ['kɔːpərət] **ADJ 1** *Law (forming a single body)* constitué (en corps), formant (un) corps **2** *(of a specific company)* d'une société, de la société; *(of companies in general)* d'entreprise; *(taxation)* sur les sociétés; **to make one's way up the c. ladder** faire carrière dans l'entreprise; **we have a number of c. customers** certains de nos clients sont des entreprises; **one of our largest c. sponsors** un de nos plus importants sponsors **3** *(collective ▸ decision, responsibility)* collectif

▸▸ ***corporate advertising*** publicité *f* institutionnelle, publicité *f* d'entreprise; ***corporate assets*** biens *mpl* sociaux; ***corporate banking*** banque *f* d'entreprise; ***corporate body*** personne *f* morale; ***corporate bond*** obligation *f* de sociétés; *Fin* ***corporate buyout*** rachat *m* d'une entreprise par les salariés; ***corporate culture*** culture *f* d'entreprise; ***corporate hospitality*** = réceptions, déjeuners, billets de spectacles etc offerts par une entreprise à ses clients; ***corporate identity, corporate image*** image *f* de marque; **the company's c. image** l'image *f* de la société; **our c. image demands that...** notre image en tant que société exige que... + *subjunctive*; ***corporate law*** droit *m* des sociétés *ou* des entreprises; ***corporate lawyer*** juriste *m* spécialisé en droit des sociétés; *Fin* ***corporate lending*** crédit *m* aux entreprises; ***corporate name*** raison *f* sociale; *St Exch* ***corporate raider*** attaquant *m*; ***corporate sponsorship*** sponsoring *m*, parrainage *m* d'entreprises; ***corporate strategy*** stratégie *f* de l'entreprise; *Fin* ***corporate tax*** impôt *m* sur les sociétés

corporation [ˌkɔːpə'reɪʃən] **N 1** *(company)* compagnie *f*, société *f*; *Law Br* personne *f* morale; *Am* société *f* anonyme **2** *(municipal authorities)* municipalité *f* **3** *Fam (paunch)* bedaine *f*, brioche *f*

COMP *Br (bus, worker)* municipal, de la ville

▸▸ *Fin Am* ***corporation income tax***, *Br* ***corporation tax*** impôt *m* sur les sociétés

corporeal [kɔː'pɔːrɪəl] **ADJ** corporel, matériel

corps [kɔː(r)] *(pl* **inv** [kɔːz]) **N 1** *Mil* corps *m*; *Admin* service *m*; **medical/intelligence c.** service *m* de santé/de renseignements; **tank c.** blindés *mpl* **2** *(trained team of people)* corps *m*

▸▸ ***corps de ballet*** corps *m* de ballet

corpse [kɔːps] **N** cadavre *m*, corps *m*

VI *Fam (actor)* avoir une crise de fou rire□

corpulence ['kɔːpjʊləns] **N** corpulence *f*, embonpoint *m*

corpulent ['kɔːpjʊlənt] **ADJ** corpulent

corpus ['kɔːpəs] *(pl* **corpuses** *or* **corpora** [-pərə]) **N 1** *(collection of writings ▸ by author)* recueil *m*; *(▸ on specific subject)* corpus *m* **2** *(main body)* corpus *m*

corpuscle ['kɔːpʌsəl] **N** *Physiol* corpuscule *m*, globule *m*; **red/white blood corpuscles** globules *mpl* rouges/blancs

corral [kɒ'rɑːl] *(pt & pp* **corralled**, *cont* **corralling**) *Am* **N** corral *m*

VT *(cattle, horses)* enfermer dans un corral; *Fig* encercler; **to c. sb into doing sth** amener qn à faire qch

correct [kə'rekt] **ADJ 1** *(right ▸ answer, spelling etc)* correct; **do you have the c. time?** avez-vous l'heure exacte?; **to prove (to be) c.** s'avérer juste; **c. to four decimal places** exact à quatre chiffres après la virgule; **am I c. in thinking that...?** ai-je raison de penser que...?; **you must be Mr Jones – that's c.** vous devez être M. Jones – c'est exact; **she was quite c. in her assumptions** ses suppositions étaient parfaitement justes; **if my memory is c.** si j'ai bonne mémoire; **figures c. at time of going to press** chiffres exacts au moment de la publication **2** *(suitable, proper ▸ behaviour, manners etc)* correct, convenable, bienséant; *(▸ person)* correct, convenable; **the c. thing for him to do in the circumstances is to resign** dans ces circonstances la bienséance veut qu'il démissionne; **she was quite c. to do what she did** elle a fait ce qu'il convenait de faire; **the c. procedure** la procédure d'usage

VT 1 *(rectify ▸ mistake, spelling etc)* corriger, rectifier; *(▸ squint, bad posture, imbalance)* corriger; *(▸ situation)* rectifier; *(▸ instrument setting)* modifier

2 *(mark errors in ▸ exam, proofs, homework)* corriger

3 *(indicate error to ▸ person)* corriger, reprendre; **please c. me whenever I make a mistake** veuillez me corriger *ou* me reprendre si je fais des erreurs; **to c. sb on** *or* **about sth** corriger *ou* reprendre qn sur qch; **to c. sb's French** corriger le français de qn, reprendre qn sur son français; **c. me if I'm wrong, but...** corrigez-moi si je me trompe, mais...; **I stand corrected** je reconnais mon erreur; **to c. oneself** se reprendre, se corriger

4 *Arch (punish)* punir; *(physically)* corriger, infliger une correction à

correcting fluid [kə'rektɪŋ-] **N** liquide *m* correcteur

correction [kə'rekʃən] **N 1** *(action ▸ of exam paper, proofs, homework etc)* correction *f*; *(of error)* correction *f*, rectification *f* **2** *(alteration)* correction *f*; **to make corrections** faire des corrections; **to make corrections to a text** apporter des corrections à un texte **3** *Arch (punishment)* correction *f*, punition *f*, châtiment *m*; **house of c.** maison *f* de correction *ou* de redressement

▸▸ ***correction fluid*** liquide *m* correcteur

corrective [kə'rektɪv] **ADJ** *(action, measure)* rectificatif, correctif; *(exercises, treatment)* correctif; *(lens, make-up)* correcteur

N correctif *m* (**to** de); *Med (for teeth)* appareil *m* dentaire; *(for deformed limb)* appareil *m* orthopédique

correctly [kə'rektlɪ] **ADV 1** *(in the right way ▸ answer, pronounce, report)* correctement; **he c. predicted that...** il a prédit avec raison que... + *indicative*; **smileys, more c. known as emoticons** les smileys, ou si l'on veut être plus correct, les binettes **2** *(properly ▸ behave, dress, speak)* correctement

correctness [kə'rektnɪs] **N 1** *(of answer, prediction etc)* exactitude *f*, justesse *f* **2** *(of behaviour, dress etc)* correction *f*

correlate ['kɒrəleɪt] **VI to c. (with sth)** *(gen)* être en corrélation *ou* rapport (avec qch), correspondre (à qch); *(in statistics)* être en corrélation (avec qch)

VT *(gen)* mettre en corrélation *ou* en rapport, faire correspondre; *(in statistics)* corréler; **these two trends are closely correlated** ces deux tendances sont en rapport étroit

correlation [ˌkɒrə'leɪʃən] **N** corrélation *f*

correlative [kɒ'relətɪv] **N** corrélatif *m*

ADJ corrélatif

correspond [ˌkɒrɪ'spɒnd] **VI 1** *(tally ▸ dates, statements)* correspondre; **to c. with** *or* **to sth** correspondre à qch **2** *(be equivalent)* correspondre, équivaloir (**with** *or* **to** à); **this animal corresponds roughly with** *or* **to our own domestic cat** cet animal correspond à peu près à notre *ou* est à peu près l'équivalent de notre chat domestique **3** *(exchange letters)* correspondre; **they corresponded (with each other) for many years** ils ont correspondu *ou* ils se sont écrit pendant des années

correspondence [ˌkɒrɪ'spɒndəns] **N 1** *(relationship, similarity)* correspondance *f*, rapport *m*, relation *f* **2** *(letter-writing)* correspondance *f*; **to be in c. with sb** être en correspondance avec qn; **to keep up a c. with sb** rester en correspondance avec qn **3** *(letters)* correspondance *f*, courrier *m*; **to read/to do one's c.** lire/faire son courrier *ou* sa correspondance; **she doesn't get much c.** elle ne reçoit pas beaucoup de courrier

COMP par correspondance; *(school)* d'enseignement par correspondance

▸▸ *Press* ***correspondence column*** courrier *m* des lecteurs; ***correspondence course*** cours *m* par correspondance

correspondent [ˌkɒrɪ'spɒndənt] **N 1** *(reporter)* correspondant(e) *m,f*; **special c.** envoyé(e) *m,f* spécial(e); **war/environment/sports c.** correspondant(e) *m,f* de guerre/pour les questions d'environnement/sportif(ive); **our Moscow c.** notre correspondant à Moscou **2** *(letter-writer)* correspondant(e) *m,f*; **I am a very bad c.** j'écris très peu

corresponding [ˌkɒrɪ'spɒndɪŋ] **ADJ** correspondant; **unemployment/inflation is higher than in the c. period last year** le chômage/l'inflation a augmenté par rapport à la période correspondante de l'année dernière *ou* à la même période l'année dernière

▸▸ ***corresponding member*** *(of society, club)* membre *m* correspondant

correspondingly [ˌkɒrɪ'spɒndɪŋlɪ] **ADV** *(proportionally)* proportionnellement; *(as a consequence)* donc, par conséquent; **prices are c. more expensive** les prix sont proportionnellement plus élevés

corridor ['kɒrɪˌdɔː(r)] **N** *(in building)* corridor *m*, couloir *m*; *(in train)* couloir *m*; *Fig* **the corridors of power** les allées *fpl* du pouvoir; *(behind the scenes)* les coulisses *fpl* du pouvoir

▸▸ *Rail* ***corridor train*** train *m* à couloir

corroborate [kə'rɒbəreɪt] **VT** confirmer, corroborer

corroboration [kəˌrɒbə'reɪʃən] **N** confirmation *f*, corroboration *f*; **to provide c. of sth** confirmer *ou* corroborer qch; **evidence produced in c. of sth** des preuves fournies à l'appui de qch

corroborative [kə'rɒbərətɪv] **ADJ** *(evidence, statement)* à l'appui

corrode [kə'rəʊd] **VT** *(of acid, rust)* corroder, ronger, attaquer; *Fig (happiness)* entamer, miner

VI *(due to acid, rust)* se corroder

corroded [kə'rəʊdɪd] **ADJ** corrodé, attaqué; **badly c. metal** métal très corrodé *ou* attaqué

corrosion [kə'rəʊʒən] **N** *(of metal)* corrosion *f*

corrosion-resistant **ADJ** anticorrosion *(inv)*

corrosive [kə'rəʊsɪv] **N** corrosif *m*

ADJ corrosif; *Fig* destructeur

corrugated ['kɒrəˌgeɪtɪd] **ADJ** *(cardboard, paper)* ondulé

▸▸ ***corrugated iron*** tôle *f* ondulée; **a c. iron hut** une cabane en tôle ondulée

corrupt [kə'rʌpt] **ADJ 1** *(dishonest ▸ person, society)* corrompu; **c. practices** pratiques *fpl* malhonnêtes

2 *(depraved, immoral)* dépravé, corrompu

3 *(containing alterations ▸ text)* altéré

4 *Comput (containing errors ▸ disk, file)* altéré

VT 1 *(make dishonest)* corrompre

2 *(deprave, debase ▸ person, society)* dépraver,

corrompre; (▸ *language)* corrompre; **to c. sb's morals** dépraver qn
3 *(alter* ▸ *text)* altérer, corrompre
4 *Comput (disk, file)* altérer

corruptible [kəˈrʌptəbəl] **ADJ** corruptible

corrupting [kəˈrʌptɪŋ] **ADJ** dépravant, corrupteur; **c. influence** influence *f* corruptrice

corruption [kəˈrʌpʃən] **N 1** *(of official, politician etc* ▸ *action, state)* corruption *f*
2 *(depravity, debasement* ▸ *action, state)* dépravation *f*, corruption *f*; *Law* **the c. of minors** le détournement de mineurs
3 *(of text* ▸ *action)* altération *f*, corruption *f*; (▸ *state)* version *f* corrompue; *(of word* ▸ *action)* corruption *f*; (▸ *state)* forme *f* corrompue
4 *Comput (of disk, file)* altération *f*

corruptive [kəˈrʌptɪv] **ADJ** corrupteur

corruptly [kəˈrʌptlɪ] **ADV 1** *(dishonestly)* de manière corrompue **2** *(in a depraved way)* d'une manière dépravée *ou* corrompue

corsage [kɔːˈsɑːʒ] **N 1** *(flowers)* = petit bouquet de fleurs à accrocher au corsage ou au poignet
2 *(bodice)* corsage *m*

corsair [ˈkɔːseə(r)] **N** *Naut* corsaire *m*

corselet [ˈkɔːslɪt] **N** *(garment, body armour)* & *Zool* corselet *m*

corset [ˈkɔːsɪt] **N** corset *m*; **surgical c.** corset *m* orthopédique

Corsica [ˈkɔːsɪkə] **N** Corse *f*

Corsican [ˈkɔːsɪkən] **N 1** *(person)* Corse *mf* **2** *(language)* corse *m*
ADJ corse

cortège [kɔːˈteɪʒ] **N** cortège *m*; **funeral c.** cortège *m* funèbre

cortex [ˈkɔːteks] *(pl* **cortices** [-tɪˌsiːz]) **N** *Anat & Bot* cortex *m*

corticoid [ˈkɔːtɪkɔɪd], **corticosteroid** [ˌkɔːtɪkəʊˈsterɔɪd] **N** *Med* corticoïde *m*, corticostéroïde *m*

cortisone [ˈkɔːtɪzəʊn] **N** *Biol & Chem* cortisone *f*

corundum [kəˈrʌndəm] **N** *Miner* corindon *m*

Corunna [kəˈrʌnə] **N** *Geog* La Corogne

coruscate [ˈkɒrəˌskeɪt] **VI** *Formal* briller, scintiller

coruscating [ˈkɒrəˌskeɪtɪŋ] **ADJ** *Formal* brillant, scintillant; *Fig (wit)* brillant, étincelant

corvette [kɔːˈvet] **N** *Naut* corvette *f*

cos[1] [kɒs] **N** *Br* **c. (lettuce)** (laitue *f*) romaine *f*

cos[2] [kɒs] **N** *Math (abbr* **cosine)** cos

cos[3] [kɒz] **CONJ** *Fam (abbr* **because)** parce que[□]

cosh [kɒʃ] **N** gourdin *m*, matraque *f*
VT assommer, matraquer

cosignatory [ˌkəʊˈsɪgnətərɪ] *(pl* **cosignatories) N** *Formal* cosignataire *mf* **(to** de)

cosily, *Am* **cozily** [ˈkəʊzɪlɪ] **ADV** *(warmly)* confortablement; **c. wrapped up** bien emmitouflé

cosine [ˈkəʊsaɪn] **N** *Math* cosinus *m*

cosiness, *Am* **coziness** [ˈkəʊzɪnɪs] **N 1** *(warmness, comfort)* confort *m* **2** *Fig (intimacy)* **given the c. of their relationship** vu les rapports copain-copain qu'ils entretiennent

cosmetic [kɒzˈmetɪk] **ADJ 1** *(for beautifying)* cosmétique **2** *Fig (superficial* ▸ *change, measure)* superficiel, symbolique; **it's purely c.** c'est purement symbolique, c'est uniquement pour la forme; **the policy change is c. rather than real** le changement de politique est plutôt un changement de forme que de fond
N cosmétique *m*, produit *m* de beauté; **to wear a lot of cosmetics** se maquiller beaucoup
▸▸ ***cosmetics counter*** rayon *m* des cosmétiques; ***cosmetics industry*** industrie *f* des cosmétiques; ***cosmetic surgery*** chirurgie *f* esthétique; **to have c. surgery** se faire faire de la chirurgie esthétique

cosmetician [ˌkɒzməˈtɪʃən] **N** *(specialist)* esthéticien(enne) *m,f*

cosmetologist [ˌkɒzməˈtɒlədʒɪst] **N** cosmétologue *mf*

cosmetology [ˌkɒzməˈtɒlədʒɪ] **N** cosmétologie *f*

cosmic [ˈkɒzmɪk] **ADJ 1** *(relating to the universe)* cosmique **2** *(large, significant)* gigantesque; **of c. proportions** aux proportions gigantesques
▸▸ ***cosmic dust*** poussières *fpl* cosmiques; ***cosmic radiation*** rayonnement *m* cosmique; ***cosmic ray*** rayon *m* cosmique

cosmogony [kɒzˈmɒgənɪ] **N** cosmogonie *f*

cosmology [kɒzˈmɒlədʒɪ] **N** cosmologie *f*

cosmonaut [ˈkɒzmənɔːt] **N** cosmonaute *mf*

cosmopolitan [ˌkɒzməˈpɒlɪtən] **ADJ** *(city, person, restaurant)* cosmopolite
N *(person)* cosmopolite *mf*

cosmos [ˈkɒzmɒs] **N** cosmos *m*; *Fig* univers *m*

Cossack [ˈkɒsæk] **N** Cosaque *m*
ADJ cosaque

cosset [ˈkɒsɪt] **VT** *(person)* dorloter, choyer, câliner

cossie [ˈkɒzɪ] **N** *Br & Austr Fam* maillot *m* de bain[□]

COST [kɒst]

N	
• coût **1**	• prix **1, 2**
VT	
• coûter **1**	• évaluer le coût de **2**
VI	
• coûter cher	
NPL	
• frais et dépens	

(pt & pp vt sense **1** *& vi* **cost,** *pt & pp vt sense* **2 costed)**
N 1 *(amount charged or paid)* coût *m*; **the car was repaired at a c. of £50** la réparation de la voiture a coûté 50 livres; **think of the c. (involved)!** imagine un peu le prix que ça coûte!; **to bear the c. of sth** payer qch; *(with difficulty)* faire face aux frais *ou* aux dépenses de qch; **to buy/to sell sth at c.** *(cost price)* acheter/vendre qch au prix coûtant; **at little/at great c.** à peu de/à grands frais; **at no extra c.** sans frais supplémentaires; **the firm cut its costs by 30 percent** l'entreprise a réduit ses frais de 30 pour cent; *Com* **c., insurance and freight** coût, assurance et fret
2 *Fig* prix *m*; **whatever the c.** à tout prix, à n'importe quel prix; **whatever the c. to myself** quoi qu'il m'en coûte; **at the c. of her job/reputation/marriage** au prix de son travail/sa réputation/son mariage; **as I discovered to my c.** comme je l'ai appris *ou* découvert à mes dépens; **to count the c. of sth** faire le bilan de qch; **the c. in human life** le prix en vies humaines; **the c. in human terms** *(of unemployment, closure)* le coût humain
VT 1 *(gen)* coûter; **how much** *or* **what does it c.?** combien ça coûte?; **it costs £10** cela coûte 10 livres; **it c. me £200** cela m'est revenu à *ou* m'a coûté 200 livres; **did it c. much?** est-ce que cela a coûté cher?; **it costs nothing to join** l'inscription est gratuite; **it didn't c. me a penny** ça ne m'a rien coûté du tout, ça ne m'a pas coûté un sou; *Fam* **it'll c. you!** *(purchase)* tu vas le sentir passer!; *(help, favour)* ce ne sera pas gratuit![□]; **it c. her a lot of time and effort** cela lui a demandé beaucoup de temps et d'efforts; **it c. him his job** cela lui a coûté son travail, cela lui a fait perdre son travail; **it doesn't c. anything to be polite** ça ne coûte rien d'être poli; **whatever it costs, I'm not going to give up** quoi qu'il m'en coûte, je n'abandonnerai pas; *Fam* **to c. an arm and a leg, to c. the earth** coûter les yeux de la tête *ou* la peau des fesses
2 *(work out price of* ▸ *trip)* évaluer le coût de; (▸ *job, repairs)* établir un devis pour; *Com* (▸ *product)* établir le prix de revient de; **he costed the repairs at £150** il a établi un devis de 150 livres pour les réparations, il a évalué les réparations à 150 livres; **a carefully costed budget** un budget calculé avec soin
VI *Fam (be expensive)* coûter cher[□], ne pas être donné[□]; **we can do it but it will c.** on peut le faire mais ça ne sera pas donné
• **costs NPL** *Law* frais *mpl* (d'instance) et dépens *mpl*; **to be awarded costs** se voir accorder des frais et dépens; **to be ordered to pay costs** être condamné aux dépens
• **at all costs ADV** à tout prix
• **at any cost ADV** en aucun cas; **he should not be approached at any c.** en aucun cas il ne doit être approché
▸▸ ***cost accounting*** comptabilité *f* analytique *ou* d'exploitation; *Acct* ***cost allocation*** imputation *f* des charges; *Fin* ***cost analysis*** analyse *f* des coûts, analyse *f* du prix de revient; *Acct* ***cost centre*** centre *m* d'analyse; *Fin* ***cost curve*** courbe *f* des coûts; *Acct* ***cost of goods*** coût *m* des produits; *Acct* ***cost of goods purchased*** coût *m* d'achat; *Acct* ***cost of goods sold*** coût *m* des ventes; ***cost of living*** coût *m* de la vie; *Fin* ***cost price*** prix *m* coûtant *ou* de revient; **to buy/to sell sth at c. price** acheter/vendre qch à prix coûtant; *Acct* ***cost pricing*** méthode *f* des coûts marginaux
▸ **cost out VT SEP** *(work out price of* ▸ *trip)* évaluer le coût de; (▸ *job, repairs)* établir un devis pour; *Com* (▸ *product)* établir le prix de revient de

Costa Brava [ˌkɒstəˈbrɑːvə] **N** Costa Brava *f*

Costa del Crime N *Br Hum* = appellation humoristique de la Costa del Sol, par allusion au grand nombre d'anciens criminels britanniques qui y résident

Costa del Sol N Costa del Sol *f*

co-star *(pt & pp* **co-starred,** *cont* **co-starring) N** *(of actor, actress)* partenaire *mf*
VI *(in film, TV programme)* être l'une des vedettes principales; **to c. with sb** partager la vedette *ou* l'affiche avec qn
VT the film co-stars Harvey Keitel le film met en scène Harvey Keitel dans l'un des rôles principaux *ou* vedettes; **co-starring Gwyneth Paltrow** *(in credits)* avec Gwyneth Paltrow

Costa Rica [-ˈriːkə] **N** Costa Rica *m*

Costa Rican [-riːkən] **N** Costaricien(enne) *m,f*
ADJ costaricien
COMP *(embassy, history)* du Costa Rica

cost-benefit ADJ *Fin*
▸▸ ***cost-benefit analysis*** analyse *f* des coûts et rendements; ***cost-benefit ratio*** rapport *m* coût/profit

cost-competitive ADJ *Com (product)* à prix compétitif; **we're not c.** nos prix ne sont pas compétitifs

cost-conscious ADJ to be c. contrôler ses dépenses

cost-cutting N *(UNCOUNT)* compression *f ou* réduction *f* des coûts
ADJ de compression *ou* de réduction des coûts

cost-effective ADJ rentable

cost-effectiveness N rentabilité *f*

costermonger [ˈkɒstəˌmʌŋgə(r)] **N** *Br Old-fashioned* marchand(e) *m,f* de quatre-saisons

costing [ˈkɒstɪŋ] **N** *Com (of product)* estimation *f* du prix de revient; *(of job, repairs)* établissement *m* d'un devis; **based on detailed costings** basé sur des calculs détaillés

costive [ˈkɒstɪv] **ADJ** *Med* constipé

costliness [ˈkɒstlɪnɪs] **N** *(high price)* cherté *f*

costly [ˈkɒstlɪ] *(compar* **costlier,** *superl* **costliest) ADJ 1** *(expensive)* coûteux, cher; **this may be a c. mistake** cette erreur pourrait me/vous/*etc* coûter cher **2** *(of high quality)* somptueux, riche

cost-plus N taux *m* de marque
ADJ *Fin* à coût majoré; **on a c. basis** sur la base du prix de revient majoré

cost-push inflation N *Fin* inflation *f* par les coûts

cost-reduce VT *Com* réduire le coût de

costume [ˈkɒstjuːm] **N 1** *(in cinema, theatre, TV)* costume *m*; **to be (dressed) in c.** porter un costume (de scène)
2 *(fancy dress)* costume *m*, déguisement *m*; **to be (dressed) in c.** être costumé *ou* déguisé
3 *(traditional dress)* **national c.** costume *m* national
4 *(for swimming)* maillot *m* de bain
5 *Br Old-fashioned (woman's suit)* tailleur *m*
VT *(film, play)* réaliser les costumes pour
▸▸ *Theat* ***costume(s) department*** service *m* des costumes; ***costume designer*** costumier(ère) *m,f*; ***costume drama*** dramatique *f* en costumes d'époque; ***costume jewellery*** *(UNCOUNT)* bijoux *mpl* fantaisie; ***costume piece, costume play*** pièce *f* en costumes d'époque

costumier [kɒˈstjuːmɪə(r)], **costumer** [kɒˈstjuːmə(r)] **N** costumier(ère) *m,f*

cosy, *Am* **cozy** [ˈkəʊzɪ] *(Br compar* **cosier,** *superl* **cosiest,** *Am compar* **cozier,** *superl* **coziest) ADJ 1** *(warm, snug* ▸ *house, room, atmosphere)* douillet,

confortable; **it's nice and c. in here** on est bien ici; **to look/feel c.** avoir l'air bien confortable/se sentir bien; **isn't this c.?** on n'est pas bien ici? **2** *(intimate ▸ chat, evening)* intime; *(▸ novel)* à l'atmosphère douce; *Pej* **they've got a very c. relationship** ils sont très copain-copain; **a c. little job** *(undemanding)* un travail pépère
N *(for teapot)* couvre-théière *m*; *(for egg)* couvre-œuf *m*

▸**cosy up to**, *Am* ▸**cozy up to** **VT INSEP** *Fam* se mettre dans les petits papiers de

cot [kɒt] **N** *Br (for baby)* lit *m* d'enfant; *Am (camp bed)* lit *m* de camp; *Naut* cadre *m* à l'anglaise
▸▸ *Br* ***cot death*** mort *f* subite du nourrisson

cotangent [kəʊ'tændʒənt] **N** *Math* cotangente *f*

cotel ['kɒtel] **N** *Am* auberge *f* de jeunesse

coterie ['kəʊtərɪ] **N** cercle *m*, cénacle *m*; *Pej* coterie *f*, clique *f*

co-trustee **N** *Law* co-administrateur(trice) *m,f*

cottage ['kɒtɪdʒ] **N 1** *(in country)* petite maison *f* (à la campagne), cottage *m*; **thatched c.** chaumière *f* **2** *Am (holiday home)* maison *f* de campagne, *Can* chalet *m*
▸▸ ***cottage cheese*** fromage *m* blanc (égoutté), cottage cheese *m*; *Br* ***cottage flat*** = appartement situé dans un pavillon; *Br* ***cottage hospital*** petit hôpital *m* de campagne; ***cottage industry*** industrie *f* artisanale; *(small-scale, at home)* industrie *f* familiale; *Br* ***cottage loaf*** = miche de pain en forme de brioche; *Br* ***cottage pie*** hachis *m* parmentier

cottager ['kɒtɪdʒə(r)] **N** *Br* habitant(e) *m,f* d'un cottage; *Am (owner)* propriétaire *mf* d'une maison de campagne; *(tenant)* locataire *mf* d'une maison de campagne

cottaging ['kɒtɪdʒɪŋ] **N** *(UNCOUNT) Br very Fam* = rencontres homosexuelles dans les toilettes publiques

cotter ['kɒtə(r)] **N** *Tech (wedge)* goupille *f*; *(pin)* clavette *f*
▸▸ ***cotter pin*** clavette *f*

cotton ['kɒtən] **N 1** *(material, plant)* coton *m*; **to pick c.** cueillir le coton; **is this dress c.?** *(made of cotton)* cette robe est-elle en coton? **2** *Br (thread for sewing)* fil *m*
COMP *(garment)* en coton; *(industry, trade)* du coton; *(culture, field, grower, plantation)* de coton
▸▸ *Geog* ***the Cotton Belt*** = région du coton dans le sud des États-Unis; *Br* ***cotton bud*** Coton-Tige® *m*; *Bot* ***cotton bush*** cotonnier *m*; *Am* ***cotton candy*** barbe *f* à papa; *Tech* ***cotton gin*** égreneuse *f* de coton; ***cotton mill*** filature *f* de coton; ***cotton picker*** *(person)* cueilleur(euse) *m,f* de coton; *Br* ***cotton wool*** coton *m* hydrophile, ouate *f*; *Fam* **my legs feel like c. wool** j'ai les jambes en coton; *Fig* **to wrap sb in c. wool** être aux petits soins pour qn; ***cotton wool balls*** boules *fpl* de coton; *Fig* ***cotton wool clouds*** nuages *mpl* cotonneux

▸**cotton on** **VI** *Fam* piger; **to c. on to sth** piger qch

▸**cotton to** **VT INSEP** *Am Fam* **1** *(take a liking to ▸ person)* se prendre d'amitié pour[□] **2** *(approve of ▸ person)* avoir à la bonne; *(▸ behaviour, suggestion)* voir d'un bon œil; **I don't c. to that kind of behaviour** je n'approuve pas ce genre de comportement[□]

cotton-picking **ADJ** *Am very Fam* sale, sacré

cottonseed ['kɒtən,si:d] **N** graine *f* de coton
▸▸ ***cottonseed oil*** huile *f* de coton

cottontail ['kɒtən,teɪl] **N** *Am Zool* **c. (rabbit)** lapin *m* de garenne

cotyledon [,kɒtɪ'li:dən] **N** *Bot* cotylédon *m*

couch [kaʊtʃ] **N** *(sofa)* canapé *m*, divan *m*, sofa *m*; *(in psychiatrist's office)* divan *m*; *Fam* **to be on the c.** faire une psychanalyse[□], voir un psy; *Fam Pej* **he's a real c. potato** il passe son temps affalé devant la télé
VT *(express ▸ phrase, comment)* formuler; **to be couched in very polite terms/in jargon** *(letter, document)* être formulé en termes très polis/en jargon
▸▸ *Bot* ***couch grass*** chiendent *m*

couchette [ku:'ʃet] **N** *Rail & Naut* couchette *f*
▸▸ *Rail* ***couchette car*** voiture-couchette *f*

cougar ['ku:gə(r)] **N** *Zool* couguar *m*, cougouar *m*, puma *m*

cough [kɒf] **N** toux *f*; **to have a c.** tousser; **I can't get rid of this c.** cette toux ne me passe pas; **that's a nasty c. (you've got)** tu as une mauvaise toux; **to give a warning c.** tousser *ou* toussoter en guise d'avertissement
COMP pour *ou* contre la toux, *Spec* antitussif
VI tousser
VT *(blood)* cracher
▸▸ ***cough drop, cough lozenge*** pastille *f* contre la toux *ou* antitussive; ***cough mixture*** sirop *m* contre la toux *ou* antitussif; ***cough sweet*** pastille *f* contre la toux *ou* antitussive; ***cough syrup*** sirop *m* contre la toux *ou* antitussif

▸**cough up** **VT SEP 1** *(blood)* cracher (en toussant) **2** *Fam (money)* cracher, raquer
VI *Fam (pay up)* banquer, raquer

coughing ['kɒfɪŋ] **N** toux *f*; **your c. woke me up** tu m'as réveillé en toussant; **fit of c., c. fit** quinte *f* de toux

COULD [kʊd]

> La forme négative est **couldn't**. Dans les contextes où il est nécessaire d'utiliser une forme plus soignée, on écrit **could not**.

MODAL AUX V 1 *(be able to)* **I'd come if I c.** je viendrais si je (le) pouvais; **she c. no longer walk** elle ne pouvait plus marcher; **they couldn't very well refuse** il leur aurait été difficile de refuser; **five years ago I c. run a mile in four minutes but I couldn't any more** il y a cinq ans, je courais un mile en quatre minutes mais je ne pourrais plus maintenant; **how c. she have done such a thing?** comment a-t-elle pu faire une chose pareille?; **she c. have had the job if she'd wanted it** elle aurait pu obtenir cet emploi si elle l'avait voulu; **you c. have warned me!** tu aurais pu me prévenir!; **I c. kill him!** je pourrais le tuer!; **he c. have jumped for joy** il en aurait presque sauté de joie; **she was as kind as c. be** elle était on ne peut plus gentille
2 *(with verbs of perception or understanding)* **he c. see her talking to her boss** il la voyait qui parlait avec son patron; **I c. see his point of view** je comprenais son point de vue
3 *(indicating ability or skill)* **she c. read and write** elle savait lire et écrire; **she c. speak three languages** elle parlait trois langues
4 *(in polite requests)* **c. I borrow your sweater?** est-ce que je pourrais t'emprunter ton pull?; **c. you help me please?** pourriez-vous *ou* est-ce que vous pourriez m'aider, s'il vous plaît?; **if I c. just intervene here** est-ce que je peux me permettre d'intervenir ici?
5 *(indicating supposition or speculation)* **the stock market c. crash tomorrow** le marché pourrait s'effondrer demain; **you c. well be right** tu pourrais bien avoir raison; **c. he be lying?** se pourrait-il qu'il mente?
6 *(indicating unwillingness)* **I couldn't just leave him there, c. I?** je ne pouvais vraiment pas le laisser là; **I couldn't possibly do it before tomorrow** je ne pourrai vraiment pas le faire avant demain
7 *(in polite suggestions)* **you c. always complain to the director** tu pourrais toujours te plaindre au directeur; **couldn't we at least talk about it?** est-ce que nous ne pourrions pas au moins en discuter?
8 *(inviting agreement)* **he left, and you couldn't blame him** il est parti, et on ne peut pas lui en vouloir

couldn't ['kʊdənt] = **could not**

couldn't-care-less **ADJ** *Fam (attitude)* je-m'en-foutiste

could've ['kʊdəv] = **could have**

coulomb ['ku:lɒm] **N** *Elec* coulomb *m*

council ['kaʊnsəl] **N 1** *(group of people)* conseil *m*; **the UN Security C.** le Conseil de sécurité des Nations unies
2 *Br (elected local body ▸ people)* conseil *m*; *(▸ government)* municipalité *f*; **to be on the c.** être au conseil; **the c. are improving services** la municipalité est en train d'améliorer les services
3 *(meeting)* conseil *m*; **to hold a c. of war** tenir un conseil de guerre
4 *Rel* concile *m*
COMP 1 *(meeting)* du conseil **2** *Br (election, service, worker)* municipal; *(leader, meeting)* du conseil municipal
▸▸ *Br* ***council estate*** cité *f* ***Council of Europe*** Conseil *m* de l'Europe; ***Council of the European Union*** Conseil *m* de l'Union européenne; *Br* ***council flat/house*** habitation *f* à loyer modéré, HLM *f or m*; *EU* ***Council of Ministers*** Conseil *m* des ministres; *Br Fin* ***council tax*** *(UNCOUNT)* impôts *mpl* locaux; *Br Fam* ***council telly*** = surnom donné aux chaînes de télévision hertziennes, disponibles sans abonnement; *Br* ***council tenants*** = locataires d'un appartement ou d'une maison appartenant à la municipalité

> Attention: ne pas confondre avec le nom **counsel**.

councillor, *Am* **councilor** ['kaʊnsələ(r)] **N** conseiller(ère) *m,f*; **C. (John) Murray** Monsieur le Conseiller Murray

> Attention: ne pas confondre avec le nom **counsellor**.

councillorship, *Am* **councilorship** ['kaʊnsələʃɪp] **N 1** *(rank)* dignité *f* de conseiller **2** *(period in office)* période *f* d'exercice des fonctions de conseiller

counsel ['kaʊnsəl] *(Br pt & pp* **counselled**, *cont* **counselling**, *Am pt & pp* **counseled**, *cont* **counseling**) **N 1** *Formal (advice)* conseil *m*; **to take c. with sb about sth** prendre conseil auprès de qn sur qch; **to keep one's own c.** garder ses opinions *ou* intentions pour soi **2** *Law* avocat(e) *m,f*; **c. for the defence** avocat(e) *m,f* de la défense; **c. for the prosecution** procureur *m*; **if c. would approach the bench** si vous voulez bien vous approcher, maître; *Br* **King's c., Queen's c.** avocat(e) *m,f* de la Couronne
VT 1 *Formal* conseiller; **to c. sb to do sth** conseiller à qn de faire qch; **to c. caution** recommander la prudence **2** *(in therapy)* conseiller

> Attention: ne pas confondre avec le nom **council**.

counselling, *Am* **counseling** ['kaʊnsəlɪŋ] **N** *(gen)* assistance *f*, *Can* counseling *m*; *(psychological)* aide *f* psychologique; **you need c.** tu as besoin de voir un psychologue; **she does c. at the university** elle est conseillère auprès des étudiants à l'université

counsellor, *Am* **counselor** ['kaʊnsələ(r)] **N 1** *(gen)* conseiller(ère) *m,f*; *(in therapy)* psychologue *mf* **2** *Am Law* avocat(e) *m,f*

> Attention: ne pas confondre avec le nom **councillor**.

COUNT [kaʊnt]

N	
• compte **1**	• chef d'accusation **3**
• taux **4**	• comte **5**
VT	
• compter **1, 2**	• considérer **3**
VI	
• compter **1–3**	

N 1 *(gen)* compte *m*, comptage *m*; *(of ballot papers)* dépouillement *m*; **it took three/several counts** il a fallu faire trois/plusieurs fois le compte, il a fallu compter trois/plusieurs fois; **to have a second c.** refaire le compte, recompter; **to lose c.** perdre le compte; **I've lost c. of the number of times he's been late** je ne compte plus le nombre de fois où il est arrivé en retard; **to keep c. (of sth)** tenir le compte (de qch); **at the last c.** la dernière fois qu'on a compté; **on the c. of three, begin** à trois, vous commencez
2 *Boxing* **to take the c.** être mis K-O; **to be out for the c.** *(boxer, person in fight)* être K-O; *(fast asleep)* dormir comme une souche
3 *Law* chef *m* d'accusation; **guilty on three counts of murder** coupable de meurtre sur trois chefs d'accusation; *Fig* **the argument is flawed on both counts** l'argumentation est défectueuse sur les deux points
4 *Med* taux *m*; **blood (cell) c.** numération *f* globulaire
5 *(nobleman)* comte *m*
VT 1 *(add up)* compter; **I counted ten people in the room** j'ai compté dix personnes dans la pièce; **to c. the votes** dépouiller le scrutin; *Fig* **to c. sheep**

(when sleepless) compter les moutons
2 *(include)* compter; **counting Alan, there were ten of us** en comptant Alan, nous étions dix; **not counting public holidays** sans compter les jours fériés
3 *(consider)* considérer, estimer; **to c. sb among one's friends** compter qn parmi ses amis; **do you c. her as a friend?** la considères-tu comme une amie?; **student grants are not counted as taxable income** les bourses d'études ne sont pas considérées comme revenu imposable; **c. yourself lucky you've got good friends** estime-toi heureux d'avoir des amis sur qui compter
VI **1** *(add up)* compter; **to c. to twenty/fifty/a hundred** compter jusqu'à vingt/cinquante/cent; **to c. on one's fingers** compter sur ses doigts; **counting from tomorrow** à partir *ou* à compter de demain
2 *(be considered, qualify)* compter; **two children c. as one adult** deux enfants comptent pour un adulte; **unemployment benefit counts as taxable income** les allocations (de) chômage comptent comme revenu imposable; **this exam counts towards the final mark** cet examen compte dans la note finale; **that/he doesn't c.** ça/il ne compte pas; **his record counted in his favour/against him** son casier judiciaire a joué en sa faveur/l'a desservi
3 *(be important)* compter; **every second/minute counts** chaque seconde/minute compte; **experience counts more than qualifications** l'expérience compte davantage que les diplômes; **he counts for nothing** il n'est pas important, il ne compte pas; **a private education doesn't c. for much now** avoir reçu une éducation privée n'est plus un grand avantage de nos jours
►► *Gram* ***count noun*** nom *m* comptable
► **count against** VT INSEP jouer contre
► **count down** VI faire le compte à rebours
► **count in** VT SEP *(include)* compter, inclure; **to c. sb in on sth** inclure *ou* compter qn dans qch; **c. me in!** je suis partant!, j'en suis!
► **count on** VT INSEP **1** *(rely on)* compter sur; **we're counting on you** nous comptons sur toi; **I wouldn't c. on him turning up, if I were you** si j'étais vous, je ne m'attendrais pas à ce qu'il vienne; **you can always c. on him to be late** tu peux compter sur lui pour être en retard, tu peux être sûr qu'il sera en retard; **I wouldn't c. on it** je n'y compterais pas **2** *(expect)* compter; **I wasn't counting on my husband being here** je ne comptais *ou* pensais pas que mon mari serait ici
► **count out** VT SEP **1** *(money, objects)* compter **2** *(exclude)* **(you can) c. me out** ne compte surtout pas sur moi **3** *(in boxing)* **to be counted out** être déclaré K-O
► **count up** VT SEP compter, additionner

countable ['kaʊntəbəl] ADJ *Gram (noun)* comptable, dénombrable

countdown ['kaʊntdaʊn] N compte *m* à rebours; *Fig* **the c. to the wedding/to Christmas has begun** la date du mariage/de Noël se rapproche

countenance ['kaʊntənəns] N **1** *Formal or Literary (face)* visage *m*; *(facial expression)* expression *f*, mine *f*; **to keep one's c.** faire bonne contenance; **to lose c.** *(person)* perdre contenance; *(government)* perdre la face **2** *Formal (support, approval)* **to give** *or* **to lend c. to sth** approuver qch
VT *Formal (support, approve of* ► *terrorism, violence, lying)* approuver; *(*► *idea, proposal)* approuver, accepter; **the government will never c. (doing) a deal with the terrorists** le gouvernement n'approuvera *ou* n'acceptera jamais l'idée d'un marché avec les terroristes

counter ['kaʊntə(r)] N **1** *(in shop)* comptoir *m*; *(in supermarket)* rayon *m*, *Can* comptoir *m*; *(in bank, post office)* guichet *m*; **it's available over the c.** *(medication)* on peut l'acheter sans ordonnance; *St Exch* **to buy shares over the c.** acheter des actions sur le marché hors cote; *Br Fam* **to sell sth under the c.** vendre qch en douce *ou* sous le manteau
2 *(device, on Web page)* compteur *m*
3 *(in board game* ► *round)* jeton *m*; *(*► *square)* fiche *f*
4 *Am (in kitchen)* plan *m* de travail
5 *Fencing & Boxing* contre *m*
VT *(respond to* ► *increase in crime, proposal)* contrecarrer; *(*► *accusation, criticism, threat)* contrer; **he countered that the project couldn't go ahead without him** il a répliqué *ou* rétorqué que le projet ne pouvait pas continuer sans lui; *Boxing* **to c. a blow** contrer un coup; *(ward off)* parer un coup
VI riposter, contre-attaquer; *Fencing & Boxing* contrer; **then he countered with his left** puis il a contré du gauche *ou* fait un contre du gauche; **she countered with a suggestion that/by asking whether…** elle a riposté en suggérant que/en demandant si…
ADV **to go** *or* **to run c. to sth** aller à l'encontre de qch; **to act c. to sb's advice/wishes** agir à l'encontre des conseils/des souhaits de qn
►► *Br* ***counter hand*** vendeur(euse) *m,f*; *Med Banking* ***counter staff*** employés(ées) *mpl,fpl* du guichet, guichetiers(ères) *mpl,fpl*; *Banking* ***counter transactions*** opérations *fpl* de caisse

counteract [ˌkaʊntər'ækt] VT *(person)* contrebalancer l'influence de; *(influence)* contrebalancer; *(effects of drug, taste of something)* neutraliser; *(rising crime)* lutter contre

counter-appraisal N *Am Com* contre-expertise *f*

counterattack [ˌkaʊntərəˌtæk] N *Mil & Sport* contre-attaque *f*, contre-offensive *f*; *Fig (in business, election etc)* contre-offensive *f*
VI *Mil & Sport* contre-attaquer; *Fig* riposter, contrer

counterattraction [ˌkaʊntərə'trækʃən] N spectacle *m* rival

counterbalance [ˌkaʊntəˌbæləns] N contrepoids *m*
VT contrebalancer, faire contrepoids à; *Fig* contrebalancer, compenser

counterbid ['kaʊntəbɪd] N *Fin* suroffre *f*, surenchère *f*; *(during takeover)* contre-OPA *f*

counterblast ['kaʊntəˌblɑːst] N *Fam* vive riposte[□] *f*

countercharge ['kaʊntəˌtʃɑːdʒ] *Law* N contre-accusation *f*
VI faire une contre-accusation
VT **to c. that…** riposter que… + *indicative*

countercheck ['kaʊntəˌtʃek] VT vérifier (une seconde fois)

counterclaim ['kaʊntəˌkleɪm] *Law* N demande *f* reconventionnelle *(en dommages-intérêts)*
VI faire une demande reconventionnelle *(en dommages-intérêts)*

counterclockwise [ˌkaʊntə'klɒkwaɪz] *Am* ADJ dans le sens inverse *ou* contraire des aiguilles d'une montre
ADV dans le sens inverse *ou* contraire des aiguilles d'une montre

counterculture ['kaʊntəˌkʌltʃə(r)] N culture *f* alternative

counterespionage [ˌkaʊntər'espɪənɑːʒ] N contre-espionnage *m*

counterfeit ['kaʊntəfɪt] N *(banknote, document)* faux *m*, contrefaçon *f*; *(piece of jewellery)* faux *m*
ADJ *(banknote, document)* faux (fausse); *(piece of jewellery)* contrefait; *Fig (sympathy, affection)* feint
VT *(banknote, passport, document, piece of jewellery)* contrefaire; *Fig (sympathy, affection)* feindre

counterfeiter ['kaʊntəˌfɪtə(r)] N *(of banknote)* faux-monnayeur *m*; *(of document, jewellery)* faussaire *mf*

counterfoil ['kaʊntəfɔɪl] N *Br (of cheque, ticket)* talon *m*, souche *f*
►► ***counterfoil book*** carnet *m* à souches

counter-guarantee N *St Exch* contre-garantie *f*

counterinsurgency [ˌkaʊntərɪn'sɜːdʒənsɪ] N contre-insurrection *f*
ADJ *(activities, tactics etc)* de contre-insurrection

counterintelligence [ˌkaʊntərɪn'telɪdʒəns] N *(UNCOUNT)* contre-espionnage *m*; *(information)* renseignements *mpl* (provenant du contre-espionnage)

counterintuitive [ˌkaʊntərɪn'tjuːɪtɪv] ADJ qui va contre l'intuition

countermand [ˌkaʊntə'mɑːnd] VT *(order)* annuler

countermarketing ['kaʊntəˌmɑːkətɪŋ] N contremarketing *m*

countermeasure ['kaʊntəˌmeʒə(r)] N contremesure *f*

countermove ['kaʊntəmuːv] N contre-mesure *f*; **in a c.** en guise de contre-mesure

counteroffensive ['kaʊntərəˌfensɪv] N *Mil* contre-offensive *f*

counteroffer ['kaʊntərˌɒfə(r)] N *Com & Fin* offre *f*; *(higher)* surenchère *f*

counterorder ['kaʊntərˌɔːdə(r)] N contrordre *m*

counterpane ['kaʊntəpeɪn] N *Br* dessus-de-lit *m inv*, couvre-lit *m*

counterpart ['kaʊntəpɑːt] N homologue *mf*; *(thing, system)* équivalent *m*; *(piece that corresponds)* pièce *f* qui va de pair

counterparty risk ['kaʊntəˌpɑːtɪ-] N *Banking* risque *m* de contrepartie

counterplot ['kaʊntəplɒt] N contre-ruse *f*

counterpoint ['kaʊntəpɔɪnt] N *Mus* contrepoint *m*

counterpoise ['kaʊntəpɔɪz] N contrepoids *m*; *Fig* **to be in c.** être en équilibre
VT contrebalancer, faire contrepoids à; *Fig* contrebalancer, compenser

counterproductive [ˌkaʊntəprə'dʌktɪv] ADJ qui va à l'encontre du but recherché, contreproductif

counter-programming N *Cin & TV* contre-programmation *f*

counterproposal ['kaʊntəprəˌpəʊzəl] N contre-proposition *f*

counterpurchase ['kaʊntəˌpɜːtʃɪs] N contre-achat *m*

Counter-Reformation N *Hist* Contre-Réforme *f*

counter-revolution N contre-révolution *f*

counter-revolutionary *(pl* **counter-revolutionaries***)* N contre-révolutionnaire *mf*
ADJ contre-révolutionnaire

countersegmentation [ˌkaʊntəˌsegmen'teɪʃən] N *Mktg* contre-segmentation *f*, stratégie *f* d'indifférenciation

countershaft ['kaʊntəʃɑːft] N *Tech (layshaft)* arbre *m* intermédiaire

countersign ['kaʊntəsaɪn] VT contresigner

countersignature ['kaʊntəˌsɪgnətʃə(r)] N contreseing *m*

countersink ['kaʊntəsɪŋk] *(pt* **countersank** [-sæŋk], *pp* **countersunk** [-sʌŋk]) *Tech* VT *(screw)* noyer; *(hole)* fraiser
N *(tool)* **c. (bit)** fraise *f*

counterstroke ['kaʊntəstrəʊk] N *Mil & Fig* contre-offensive *f*

countersunk ['kaʊntəsʌŋk] *pp of* **countersink**
ADJ *Tech (screw)* noyé; *(hole)* fraisé

countertenor [ˌkaʊntə'tenə(r)] N *Mus (singer)* haute-contre *m*; *(voice)* haute-contre *f*

counterterrorism [ˌkaʊntə'terərɪzəm] N contre-terrorisme *m*

counterterrorist [ˌkaʊntə'terərɪst] ADJ contre-terroriste

countertop ['kaʊntəˌtɒp] N *Am* plan *m* de travail

countertrade ['kaʊntətreɪd] N *Com* commerce *m* d'échange, troc *m*

countertrading [ˌkaʊntə'treɪdɪŋ] N *Com* troc *m*

countervailing ['kaʊntəˌveɪlɪŋ] ADJ *Literary* compensatoire, compensateur
►► *Econ* ***countervailing duty*** droit *m* compensateur

countervaluation [ˌkaʊntəˌvæljuˈeɪʃən] N contre-expertise *f*

counterweight ['kaʊntəweɪt] N contrepoids *m*

countess ['kaʊntɪs] N comtesse *f*

counting ['kaʊntɪŋ] N *(gen)* calcul *m*, compte *m*; *(of votes)* dépouillement *m*; *(of people)* compte *m*, dénombrement *m*
►► *Arch Com* ***counting house*** salle *f* du trésor

countless ['kaʊntlɪs] **ADJ** innombrable; **c. letters/people** un nombre incalculable de lettres/personnes; **I've told you c. times not to do that** je t'ai répété des centaines de fois *ou* je ne sais combien de fois de ne pas faire ça

countrified ['kʌntrɪfaɪd] **ADJ 1** *Pej* campagnard, provincial **2** *(rural)* **it's quite c. round here** c'est vraiment la campagne ici

country ['kʌntrɪ] *(pl* **countries) N 1** *(land, nation)* pays *m*; *(homeland)* patrie *f*; **in this c.** dans ce pays; **the Prime Minister isn't in the c.** le Premier ministre est à l'étranger; **to fight/to die for one's c.** se battre/mourir pour sa patrie; **in my c.** dans mon pays, chez moi; *Br Pol* **to go to the c.** appeler le pays aux urnes

2 *(as opposed to the city)* campagne *f*; **to live in the c.** vivre à la campagne; **to travel** *Br* **across** *or Am* **cross c.** *(in car, on bike)* prendre *ou* emprunter les petites routes (de campagne); *(on foot)* aller à travers champs

3 *(area of land, region)* région *f*; **the c. around Gloucester** la région autour de Gloucester; **we passed through some beautiful c.** nous avons traversé de beaux paysages; **this is good farming c.** c'est une bonne région agricole; **Wordsworth/Constable c.** le pays de Wordsworth/Constable; **this is bear c.** il y a beaucoup d'ours par ici

4 *Mus* country *f*

COMP *(house, road, town, bus)* de campagne; *(people)* de la campagne; *(life)* à la campagne

▸▸ *Fam Pej* ***country bumpkin*** péquenaud(e) *m,f*, plouc *mf*; **I felt like a c. bumpkin** j'ai eu l'impression de débarquer de ma campagne; ***country club*** = club sportif ou de loisirs situé à la campagne; ***the country code*** = code de conduite à respecter lorsqu'on se promène dans la campagne, qu'on y pique-nique etc; *Pej* ***country cousin*** cousin(e) *m,f* de province; ***country dancing*** danse *f* folklorique; ***country gentleman*** gentilhomme *m* campagnard; ***country house*** = grande maison de campagne, souvent historique; *Comput* ***country keyboard*** clavier *m* national; ***country music*** country *f*; *Br* ***country park*** parc *m* naturel; ***country seat*** *(of noble family)* manoir *m*

countryfolk ['kʌntrɪfəʊk] **NPL** gens *mpl* de la campagne

countryman ['kʌntrɪmən] *(pl* **countrymen** [-mən]) **N 1** *(who lives in the country)* campagnard *m*, habitant *m* de la campagne **2** *(compatriot)* compatriote *m*

countryside ['kʌntrɪsaɪd] **N** campagne *f*; *(scenery)* paysage *m*; **in the c.** à la campagne; **there is some magnificent c. around here** il y a des paysages magnifiques par ici

▸▸ ***the Countryside Alliance*** = association britannique qui milite contre l'interdiction de la chasse à courre; ***the Countryside Commission*** = organisme britannique indépendant chargé de la protection du milieu rural et de la gestion des parcs nationaux

> **COUNTRYSIDE DEBATE**
>
> En Grande-Bretagne, de nombreux ruraux se considèrent comme des laissés-pour-compte par rapport aux citadins. Le secteur agricole est en crise, les infrastructures des zones rurales sont inadéquates, et nombreux sont ceux qui ont du mal à se loger à un prix abordable. Depuis peu, la polémique s'articule également autour des problèmes écologiques liés à l'utilisation massive d'engrais et de pesticides, au développement des cultures transgéniques, et aux sites d'enfouissement des déchets nucléaires. La réputation des agriculteurs a été ternie par la crise de la maladie de la vache folle et par le spectre d'une épidémie de la forme humaine de la maladie, ainsi que par l'épidémie de fièvre aphteuse de 2001. Enfin, suite à l'abolition de la chasse à courre au renard votée en 2005, des groupes de pression tels que la "Countryside Alliance" accusent le gouvernement de vouloir se faire le fossoyeur des traditions rurales.

country-specific **ADJ** *Comput (keyboard)* particulier à un pays

country-style **ADJ c. cooking** cuisine *f* campagnarde

countrywoman ['kʌntrɪˌwʊmən] *(pl* **countrywomen** [-ˌwɪmɪn]) **N 1** *(who lives in the country)* campagnarde *f*, habitante *f* de la campagne **2** *(compatriot)* compatriote *f*

county ['kaʊntɪ] *(pl* **counties) N** comté *m*; *Br* **the c. of Kent** le comté du Kent; *Am* **New York C.** le comté de New York

COMP *(boundary)* de comté

ADJ *Br Pej* **she's very c.** elle est de la haute; **the c. set** la noblesse campagnarde

▸▸ *Am* ***county clerk*** = élu qui s'occupe de l'organisation des élections au niveau du comté ainsi que des archives; *Br* ***county council*** conseil *m* général; *Br* ***county councillor*** conseiller(ère) *m,f* général(e); *Eng Law* ***county court*** tribunal *m* d'instance; *Law* ***county court judgment*** jugement *m* de première instance; *Br* ***county cricket*** = grands matches de cricket disputés par les équipes du comté; *Am* ***county fair*** fête *f* du comté; *Br* ***County Hall*** hôtel *m* du comté, siège *m* du conseil de comté; *Am* ***county line*** frontière *f* délimitant un comté; ***county seat*** *(in US)* chef-lieu *m* de comté; ***county town*** *(in England)* chef-lieu *m* de comté

coup [ku:] **N 1** *(feat)* (beau) coup *m*; **to pull off a c.** réussir un beau coup **2** *(overthrow of government)* coup *m* d'État

▸▸ ***coup d'état*** coup *m* d'État

coupé ['ku:peɪ] **N** *Aut* coupé *m*

couple ['kʌpəl] **N 1** *(pair)* couple *m*; **an engaged c.** un couple de fiancés; **they make a lovely c.** ils forment un beau couple; **the happy c.** les jeunes mariés; **they go everywhere as a c.** ils vont partout ensemble *ou* en couple **2** *(as quantifier)* **were there many mistakes? – only a c.** est-ce qu'il y avait beaucoup de fautes? – seulement quelques-unes; **a c. of** *(a few)* quelques; *(two)* deux; **a c. of drinks** un verre ou deux, quelques verres; *Am* **he's a c. years older** il a deux ou trois ans de plus **3** *Phys* couple *m*

VI *(animals, birds, humans)* s'accoupler

VT 1 *(join* ▸ *oxen)* (ac)coupler; *(two engines, batteries)* accoupler

2 *(tie up* ▸ *horse)* atteler; *Rail (*▸ *carriage)* atteler, accrocher

3 *Fig (associate)* associer; **to c. sth with sth** associer qch à qch; **the name of Freud is coupled with that of Vienna** le nom de Freud est associé à Vienne; **her name has been coupled with his** *(romantically)* son nom a été uni au sien

4 *(accompany)* **coupled with that,...** en plus de cela,..., venant s'ajouter à cela,...

coupler ['kʌplə(r)] **N** *Tech* coupleur *m*

couplet ['kʌplɪt] **N** *Literature* distique *m*; **rhyming couplets** distiques *mpl* qui riment

coupling ['kʌplɪŋ] **N 1** *(mating* ▸ *of animals, birds, humans)* accouplement *m*

2 *Tech (static device)* raccord *m*, joint *m*; *(device for transmitting motion)* accouplement *m*, embrayage *m*; *Rail (for carriages)* attelage *m*

3 *(joining) Rail (of carriages)* attelage *m*; *Tech (of batteries)* couplage *m*

4 *(bringing together)* accouplement *m*; *(of ideas, names)* association *f*

▸▸ *Aut* ***coupling bar*** barre *f* d'accouplement

couply ['kʌplɪ] **ADJ** *Fam* = caractéristique des couples; **I don't like going out with Claire and John, they always act so c.** je n'aime pas sortir avec Claire et John, j'ai toujours l'impression d'être de trop[a]; **I'm staying in this weekend, all my friends are doing c. things with their partners** je ne sors pas ce week-end car toutes mes amies restent avec leur copain[a]

coupon ['ku:pɒn] **N** *(to be filled in)* coupon *m*; *Com (exchangeable voucher)* bon *m*; *Fin (on bearer bond)* coupon *m*; *Com* **(money-off) c.** bon *m* de réduction

▸▸ *Fin* ***coupon bond*** obligation *f* au porteur; *Com* ***coupon offer*** offre *f* de bon de réduction; *Fin* ***coupon yield*** rendement *m* coupon

couponing ['ku:pənɪŋ] **N** *Mktg* couponing *m*, couponnage *m*

courage ['kʌrɪdʒ] **N** courage *m*; **to have the c. to do sth** avoir le courage de faire qch; **a woman of great c.** une femme d'un grand courage, une femme très courageuse; **to take one's c. in both hands** prendre son courage à deux mains; **to take c. from the fact that...** être encouragé par le fait que... + *indicative*; **to have the c. of one's convictions** avoir le courage de ses opinions

courageous [kə'reɪdʒəs] **ADJ** courageux

courageously [kə'reɪdʒəslɪ] **ADV** courageusement

courgette [kɔ:'ʒet] **N** *Br* courgette *f*

courier ['kʊrɪə(r)] **N 1** *(messenger)* coursier(ère) *m,f*, messager(ère) *m,f*; *(company)* messagerie *f*; **to send sth by c.** *(locally)* envoyer qch par coursier; *(long-distance)* envoyer qch par messagerie; **she was a c. for drug dealers** elle transportait de la drogue pour le compte de trafiquants **2** *(in tourism)* accompagnateur(trice) *m,f*

COURSE [kɔ:s]

> **N**
> • route **1**
> • ligne de conduite **2**
> • terrain **7**
> • cours **1, 3, 4**
> • plat **6**
>
> **ADV**
> • bien sûr

N 1 *(path, route* ▸ *of ship, plane)* route *f*; *(*▸ *of river)* cours *m*; **to change c.** *(ship, plane)* changer de cap; *Fig (argument, discussion)* changer de direction, dévier; *(company)* changer de cap; **to be on c.** *(ship, plane)* suivre le cap fixé; *Fig* être en bonne voie; *Fig* **the company is on c. to achieve a record profit** la société est bien partie pour atteindre des bénéfices record; **to be off c.** *(ship, plane)* dévier de son cap; **you're a long way off c.** *(walking, driving)* vous n'êtes pas du tout dans la bonne direction *ou* sur la bonne route; *(with project, workflow)* vous êtes en mauvaise voie; **to set a c. for Marseilles** *(ship, plane)* mettre le cap sur Marseille

2 *Fig (approach)* **c. (of action)** ligne *f* (de conduite); **what other c. is open to us?** quelle autre solution avons-nous?; **it is the only c. open to me** c'est la seule chose que je puisse faire; **your best c. of action is to sue** la meilleure chose que vous ayez à faire est d'intenter un procès

3 *(development, progress* ▸ *of history, war)* cours *m*; **the law must take its c.** la loi doit suivre son cours; **it's best to let the fever run its c.** il vaut mieux laisser la fièvre évoluer normalement; **in the c. of time** avec le temps; **you will forget him in the c. of time** tu finiras par l'oublier, avec le temps tu l'oublieras; **in the normal** *or* **ordinary c. of events** normalement, en temps normal; **a building in the c. of construction/demolition** un bâtiment en cours de construction/démolition

4 *Sch & Univ* cours *mpl*; **a geography/music c.** des cours *mpl* de géographie/musique; **he's giving a c. of lectures on romanticism** il fait un cours sur le romantisme; **it's a five-year c.** c'est un enseignement sur cinq ans; **he has published a French c.** il a publié une méthode de français; **to go on a (training) c.** faire un stage; **I'm taking** *or* **doing a computer c.** je suis des cours *ou* un stage d'informatique

5 *Med* **a c. of injections** une série de piqûres; **c. of treatment** *(for an illness)* traitement *m*

6 *(in meal)* plat *m*; **first c.** entrée *f*; **second c.** plat *m* principal; **four-c. dinner** dîner *m* de quatre plats

7 *Golf* terrain *m*; *Horseracing* champ *m* de courses; *(in athletics)* parcours *m*; *Fig* **to stay the c.** tenir le coup

8 *Constr (of bricks)* assise *f*

VI 1 *(flow)* **tears coursed down his cheeks** les larmes ruisselaient sur ses joues; **I could feel the blood coursing through my veins** je sentais le sang bouillonner dans mes veines

2 *Hunt (hunt rabbits, hares)* chasser *(surtout le lièvre)*

ADV *Fam (of course)* bien sûr[a]; **c. I believe you** bien sûr que je te crois

• **in the course of PREP** au cours de; **in the c. of the next few weeks** dans le courant des semaines qui viennent

• **of course ADV** bien sûr; **of c. I believe you/she loves you** bien sûr que je te crois/qu'elle t'aime; **no one believed me, of c.** évidemment *ou* bien sûr, personne ne m'a cru; **of c. I'll tell you** il va de soi que je vous le dirai; **may I use your phone? – of c.!**

puis-je utiliser votre téléphone? – mais bien sûr!; **of c. not!** bien sûr que non!

courseware ['kɔːsweə(r)] **N** *Comput* didacticiel *m*

coursing ['kɔːsɪŋ] **N** *Hunt* chasse *f* à courre au lièvre

court [kɔːt] **N 1** *Law (institution)* cour *f*, tribunal *m*; *(court room, people in room)* cour *f*; **to clear the c.** évacuer la salle; **to appear in c.** *(accused, witness)* comparaître au tribunal; **to come before a c.** *(person)* comparaître devant un tribunal; *(case)* être jugé; **to take sb to c.** poursuivre qn en justice, intenter un procès contre qn; **to go to c.** faire appel à la justice, aller en justice; **to go to c. over sth** faire appel à la justice pour régler qch; **tell the c. what you saw** veuillez dire à la cour ce que vous avez vu; **I'll see you in c. then!** alors nous réglerons cela au tribunal!; **to settle sth out of c.** régler qch à l'amiable; *Fig* **to put** *or* **to rule sth out of c.** exclure qch

2 *(of monarch ▸ people)* cour *f*; *(▸ building)* palais *m*; *Br* **to be presented at c.** être introduit à la cour; *Fig* **to hold c.** avoir une cour d'adorateurs

3 *Sport (for tennis, badminton)* court *m*, terrain *m*; *(for squash)* court *m*; **he was on c. for three hours** il a été sur le court pendant trois heures

4 *(courtyard)* cour *f*; *(in names of blocks of flats)* résidence *f*; *(in names of palaces)* château *m*, palais *m*

5 *Old-fashioned* **to pay c. to a woman** faire la cour à une femme

VT 1 *Old-fashioned (seek in marriage)* faire la cour à, courtiser **2** *Fig (voters)* courtiser, chercher à séduire; **to c. sb's approval/support** chercher à gagner l'approbation/le soutien de qn; **to c. danger/disaster** aller au devant du danger/désastre

VI *Old-fashioned (one person)* fréquenter; *(two people)* se fréquenter; **they had been courting for nearly a year** ils se fréquentaient depuis presque un an

▸▸ *Law* ***Court of Appeal****, Am* ***court of appeals*** cour *f* d'appel; *Law* ***court appearance*** *(of accused)* comparution *f* en justice; *Br Cards* ***court card*** figure *f*; *Law* ***court case*** procès *m*, affaire *f*; *Br Journ* ***court circular*** = rubrique d'un journal indiquant les engagements officiels de la famille royale; *Journ* ***court correspondent*** correspondant(e) *m,f* à la cour royale; *Br* ***court of inquiry*** *(body of people)* commission *f* d'enquête; *(investigation)* enquête *f*; ***court jester*** bouffon *m* de cour; ***court of law*** tribunal *m*; *Law* ***court order*** ordonnance *f* du tribunal; *Law* ***court ruling*** décision *f* de justice; *Br* ***court shoe*** escarpin *m*; *Am* ***court tennis*** jeu *m* de paume

courteous ['kɜːtjəs] **ADJ** *(person, gesture, treatment)* courtois (**to** *or* **towards** envers)

courteously ['kɜːtjəslɪ] **ADV** *(speak, reply etc)* avec courtoisie, courtoisement

courtesan [ˌkɔːtɪ'zæn] **N** courtisane *f*

courtesy ['kɜːtɪsɪ] *(pl* **courtesies***)* **N 1** *(politeness)* courtoisie *f*; **at least have the c. to apologize** aie au moins la courtoisie de t'excuser; **common c. dictates that you should thank her** la moindre des courtoisies *ou* des politesses serait que tu la remercies; **do her the c. of hearing what she has to say** aie l'obligeance d'écouter ce qu'elle a à dire **2** *(polite action, remark)* politesse *f*; **after a brief exchange of courtesies** après un bref échange de politesses; **to show sb every c.** faire montre d'une extrême courtoisie envers qn

COMP *(visit)* de politesse

• **(by) courtesy of PREP** avec l'aimable autorisation de

▸▸ ***courtesy call*** visite *f* de politesse; **to pay a c. call on sb, to pay sb a c. call** faire une visite de politesse à qn; ***courtesy car*** *(from hotel)* voiture *f* de courtoisie; *(from garage)* véhicule *m* de remplacement; ***courtesy coach*** *(at airport)* navette *f* gratuite; ***courtesy light*** plafonnier *m*, éclairage *m* intérieur; *Br* ***courtesy title*** titre *m* de courtoisie

courthouse ['kɔːthaʊs, *pl* -haʊzɪz] **N** *Am Law* palais *m* de justice, tribunal *m*

courtier ['kɔːtjə(r)] **N** courtisan *m*

courtly ['kɔːtlɪ] **ADJ 1** *(polite, refined ▸ person, manners)* plein de style et de courtoisie **2** *(of a royal court ▸ life, ritual, pursuits)* de la cour; *(▸ splendour)* majestueux

▸▸ *Hist* ***courtly love*** amour *m* courtois

court-martial *(pl* **courts-martial***, Br pt & pp* **court-martialled***, cont* **court-martialling***, Am pt & pp* **court-martialed***, cont* **court-martialing***)* *Mil* **N** tribunal *m* militaire; **to be tried by c.** être jugé par un tribunal militaire

VT faire comparaître devant un tribunal militaire; **he was court-martialled** il est passé au tribunal militaire

court-ordered ADJ *Law (sale)* judiciaire

courtroom ['kɔːtrʊm] **N** salle *f* d'audience; *(people)* auditoire *m* d'un/du tribunal

courtship ['kɔːtʃɪp] **N 1** *(of couple)* **they married after a brief c.** ils se sont mariés peu de temps après avoir commencé à se fréquenter; *Fig* **his c. of new financial backers was unsuccessful** ses tentatives pour attirer de nouveaux commanditaires n'ont rien donné **2** *(of animals)* période *f* nuptiale, période *f* des amours

ADJ *(dance, ritual)* nuptial

▸▸ ***courtship display*** parade *f* nuptiale

courtyard ['kɔːtjɑːd] **N** *(of building)* cour *f*

couscous ['kuːskuːs] **N** couscous *m*

couscoussier [kuːskuː'sjeɪ], **couscoussière** [ˌkuːskuː'sjeə(r)] **N** couscoussier *m*

co-user N *Comput* co-utilisateur(trice) *m,f*

cousin ['kʌzən] **N** cousin(e) *m,f*; **a distant c.** un (une) cousin(e) éloigné(e); *Fig* **a distant c. of the sparrow** un cousin éloigné du moineau; *Fig* **our American cousins** nos cousins américains

couth [kuːθ] **ADJ** *Br Hum* **he's not very c.** il n'est pas très raffiné

couture [kuː'tʊə(r)] **N** couture *f*

couturier [kuː'tʊərɪeɪ] **N** couturier(ère) *m,f*; *(head of company)* directeur(trice) *m,f* d'une maison de haute couture

covalent [kəʊ'veɪlənt] **ADJ** *Chem* covalent

cove [kəʊv] **N 1** *(bay)* crique *f* **2** *Br Old-fashioned* gars *m*

coven ['kʌvən] **N** ordre *m ou* réunion *f* de sorcières

covenant ['kʌvənənt] **N 1** *Fin (promise of money)* convention *f*, engagement *m*; **(deed of) c.** contrat *m* **2** *(agreement)* engagement *m* **3** *Bible (of Jews)* alliance *f*

VT *Fin (promise payment of)* s'engager (par contrat) à payer; **to c. to do sth** convenir de faire qch; **to c. money** s'engager par contrat à payer une somme d'argent

VI *Fin* **to c. with sb for sth** convenir (par contrat) de qch avec qn

Coventry ['kɒvəntrɪ] **N** Coventry; *Br Fig* **to send sb to C.** *(ostracize)* mettre qn en quarantaine

COVER ['kʌvə(r)]

N
- housse **1**
- couvercle **3**
- abri **5**
- reprise **10**
- couvre-lit **2**
- couverture **4, 6, 7**
- remplacement **8**

VT
- couvrir **1, 4, 6–10, 14**
- parcourir **4**
- avoir sous surveillance **11**
- faire une reprise de **13**
- recouvrir **2**
- traiter **5**
- marquer **12**

N 1 *(protective ▸ for cushion, typewriter)* housse *f*; *(▸ for umbrella)* fourreau *m*; **loose c.** *(for chair, sofa)* housse *f*

2 *(on bed ▸ bedspread)* couvre-lit *m*; **the covers** *(blankets)* les couvertures *fpl*

3 *(lid)* couvercle *m*

4 *(of book, magazine)* couverture *f*; **(front) c.** couverture *f*; **hard/soft covers** couverture *f* rigide/souple; **to read a book (from) c. to c.** lire un livre de la première à la dernière page *ou* d'un bout à l'autre

5 *(shelter, protection)* abri *m*; *Hunt (for birds, animals)* couvert *m*; *Mil (from gunfire etc)* couvert *m*, abri *m*; *(firing)* tir *m* de couverture *ou* de protection; **to take c.** se mettre à l'abri; **to take c. from the rain** s'abriter de la pluie; **to run for c.** courir se mettre à l'abri; **we'll give you c.** *(by shooting)* nous vous couvrirons; **to keep sth under c.** garder qch à l'abri; **to do sth under c. of darkness** faire qch à la faveur de la nuit; **to work under c.** travailler clandestinement; **to break c.** *(animal, person in hiding)* sortir à découvert

6 *Ins* couverture *f*; **to have c. against sth** être couvert *ou* assuré contre qch; **full c.** garantie *f* totale

7 *(disguise, front ▸ for criminal enterprise)* couverture *f*; *(▸ for spy)* fausse identité *f*, identité *f* d'emprunt; *Fam* **your c. has been blown** vous avez été démasqué; **to be a c. for sth** servir de couverture à qch; **it's just a c. for her shyness** c'est juste pour cacher *ou* masquer sa timidité

8 *(during a person's absence)* remplacement *m*; **to provide c. for sb** remplacer qn; **I provide emergency c.** je fais des remplacements d'urgence

9 *Fin* marge *f* de sécurité; **to operate with/without c.** opérer avec couverture/à découvert

10 *Mus (new version of song)* reprise *f*

11 *(in restaurant)* couvert *m*

12 *(envelope)* enveloppe *f*; **under plain/separate c.** sous pli discret/séparé

VT 1 *(in order to protect)* couvrir; *(in order to hide)* cacher, dissimuler; *(cushion, chair, settee)* recouvrir; *(in bookbinding ▸ book)* couvrir; **to c. sth with a sheet/blanket** recouvrir qch d'un drap/d'une couverture; **to c. one's eyes** se couvrir les yeux; **to c. one's ears** se boucher les oreilles; **to c. one's face with one's hands** *(in shame, embarrassment)* se couvrir le visage de ses mains; **to c. one's shyness/nervousness** dissimuler *ou* masquer sa timidité/nervosité

2 *(coat ▸ with dust, snow)* recouvrir; **to be covered in dust/snow** être recouvert de poussière/neige; **his face was covered in spots** son visage était couvert de boutons; **you're covering everything in dust/paint** tu mets de la poussière/peinture partout; *Fig* **I was covered in** *or* **with shame** j'étais mort de honte; *Fig* **to c. oneself in glory** se couvrir de gloire

3 *(extend over, occupy ▸ of city, desert etc)* couvrir une surface de; **water covers most of the earth's surface** l'eau recouvre la plus grande partie de la surface de la terre; **his interests c. a wide field** il a des intérêts très variés

4 *(travel over)* parcourir, couvrir; **we covered 100 kilometres before breakfast** nous avons fait 100 kilomètres avant le petit déjeuner; **to c. a lot of ground** *(travel great distance)* faire beaucoup de chemin; *(search etc over a wide area)* parcourir un champ très vaste; *Fig (book, author etc)* couvrir de nombreux domaines; *(meeting etc)* traiter bien des problèmes

5 *(deal with)* traiter; **there's one point we haven't covered** il y a un point que nous n'avons pas traité *ou* vu; **is that everything covered?** *(in discussion)* tout a été vu?; **the course covers the first half of the century** le cours couvre la première moitié du siècle; **to c. all eventualities** parer à toute éventualité; **the law doesn't c. that kind of situation** la loi ne prévoit pas ce genre de situation

6 *(report on)* couvrir, faire la couverture de

7 *(of salesman, representative)* couvrir

8 *(be enough money for ▸ damage, expenses)* couvrir; *(▸ meal)* suffire à payer; **£30 should c. it** 30 livres devraient suffire; **to c. a deficit** combler un déficit; *Acct* **to c. a loss** couvrir un déficit; **to c. one's costs** *(company)* rentrer dans ses frais

9 *Ins* couvrir, garantir; **to be covered against** *or* **for sth** être couvert *ou* assuré contre qch

10 *(with gun ▸ colleague)* couvrir; **I've got you covered** *(to criminal)* j'ai mon arme braquée sur toi; *Fig* **the president covered himself by saying that…** le président s'est couvert en disant que… + *indicative*

11 *(monitor permanently ▸ exit, port etc)* avoir sous surveillance; **I want all exits covered immediately** je veux que toutes les sorties soient mises sous surveillance immédiatement

12 *Sport* marquer

13 *Mus (song)* faire une reprise de

14 *(of male animal)* couvrir, s'accoupler avec

• **covers NPL** *Sport (in cricket)* = partie du terrain située sur l'avant et sur la droite du batteur, à mi-distance de la limite du terrain

▸▸ ***cover charge*** *(in restaurant)* couvert *m*; *Am (in bar)* entrée *f*, prix *m* d'entrée; ***cover girl*** cover-girl *f*; *Am* ***cover letter*** *(for job application)* lettre *f* de motivation; *(sent with invoice etc)* lettre *f* d'accompagnement; *Br Ins* ***cover note*** attestation *f* provisoire; ***cover page*** *(of fax)* page *f* de garde;

cover price** (of magazine)* prix *m*; ***cover sheet** (of fax)* page *f* de garde; *Press* ***cover story article *m* principal (faisant la couverture)

▸**cover for** VT INSEP *(replace)* remplacer; *(provide excuses for)* couvrir; **I refuse to c. for you with the boss** je refuse de te couvrir auprès du patron

▸**cover in** VT SEP *(hole)* remplir

▸**cover up** VT SEP **1** *(hide, conceal)* cacher, dissimuler; *(in order to protect)* recouvrir; *Pej (involvement, report etc)* dissimuler, garder secret(ète); *(affair)* étouffer; **they covered up the body with a sheet** ils ont recouvert le cadavre d'un drap; **c. yourself up!** *(for decency)* couvre-toi! **2** *(in order to keep warm)* couvrir

VI *(hide something)* **the government is covering up again** le gouvernement est encore en train d'étouffer une affaire; **to c. up for sb** couvrir qn, protéger qn; **they're covering up for each other** ils se couvrent l'un l'autre

coverage ['kʌvərɪdʒ] **N 1** *(UNCOUNT) (reporting)* couverture *f*; **his c. of the coup** le reportage qu'il a fait du coup d'État; **the c. given to the elections was biased** le compte rendu des élections était partial; **royal weddings always get a lot of c.** les mariages de la famille royale bénéficient toujours d'une importante couverture médiatique; **radio/television c. of the tournament** la retransmission radiophonique/télévisée du tournoi **2** *(in book, dictionary)* traitement *m*; **the author's c. of the years 1789 to 1815 is sketchy** l'auteur traite les années 1789 à 1815 de manière sommaire **3** *Ins* couverture *f*

coveralls ['kʌvərɔːlz] **NPL** *Am* bleu *m ou* bleus *mpl* (de travail)

covered ['kʌvəd] **ADJ** *(walkway, bridge, market)* couvert

▸▸ ***covered wagon*** chariot *m* (à bâche)

covering ['kʌvərɪŋ] **N 1** *(of snow, dust, chocolate)* couche *f* **2** *(protective ▸ for floor)* revêtement *m*; *(▸ for plants, object in trailer)* bâche *f*; *(▸ on furniture)* housse *f*

ADJ *Mil (forces, troops)* de couverture

▸▸ *Mil* ***covering fire*** tir *m* de couverture; ***covering letter*** *(for job application)* lettre *f* de motivation; *(sent with invoice etc)* lettre *f* d'accompagnement

coverlet ['kʌvəlɪt] **N** *(for bed)* dessus-de-lit *m inv*, couvre-lit *m*

coverline ['kʌvəlaɪn] **N** *Journ* titraille *f*, titre *m* de rappel

covert ['kəʊvɜːt, 'kʌvət] **ADJ** *(operation, payments, contacts)* secret(ète); *(threats)* voilé; *(glance, look)* furtif; **he stole a c. glance at her** il lui a jeté un regard furtif

N 1 *(hiding place for animals)* fourré *m*, couvert *m* **2** *(of bird)* tectrice *f*, plume *f* de couverture

covertly ['kəʊvɜːtlɪ, 'kʌvətlɪ] **ADV** *(sold, paid)* secrètement; *(threaten)* de manière voilée; *(signal)* furtivement

cover-up **N** **the government denied that there had been any c.** le gouvernement a nié avoir étouffé l'affaire; **it's a c.** c'est un complot

covet ['kʌvɪt] **VT** *(crave, long for)* convoiter; *(wish for)* avoir très envie de; **the much-coveted prix Goncourt** le prix Goncourt, objet de tant de convoitise

covetous ['kʌvɪtəs] **ADJ** *(person)* avide; *(look)* de convoitise; **to be c. of sth** convoiter qch

covetously ['kʌvɪtəslɪ] **ADV** avec convoitise

covetousness ['kʌvɪtəsnɪs] **N** convoitise *f*, avidité *f*

covey ['kʌvɪ] **N** *(of partridge, grouse)* compagnie *f*, vol *m*

cow [kaʊ] **N 1** *(farm animal)* vache *f*; *Fig Fam* **till the cows come home** *(to wait)* jusqu'à la Saint-Glinglin; *(to argue, talk)* à n'en plus finir **2** *(female elephant)* éléphant *m* femelle, éléphante *f*; *(female seal)* phoque *m* femelle; *(female whale)* baleine *f* femelle **3** *Br very Fam Pej (woman)* vache *f*, chameau *m*; **that old c. next door** la vieille bique d'à côté; **you silly c.!** espèce d'abrutie!; **poor c.!** la pauvre!; **lucky c.!** la veinarde!

VT effrayer, intimider; **to c. sb into submission** intimider qn jusqu'à ce qu'il se soumette; **a cowed look** un air de chien battu

▸▸ *Bot* ***cow parsley*** cerfeuil *m* sauvage

coward ['kaʊəd] **N** lâche *mf*, poltron(onne) *m,f*; **don't be such a c.** ne sois pas aussi lâche; **I'm an awful c. when it comes to physical pain** j'ai très peur de *ou* je redoute beaucoup la douleur physique

cowardice ['kaʊədɪs] **N** lâcheté *f*; **moral c.** manque *m* de force morale

cowardly ['kaʊədlɪ] **ADJ** lâche

cowbell ['kaʊbel] **N** clochette *f*, sonnaille *f*

cowboy ['kaʊbɔɪ] **N 1** *(in American West)* cow-boy *m*; **to play cowboys and Indians** jouer aux cow-boys et aux Indiens **2** *Br Fam Pej (workman)* petit rigolo *m*; **a bunch of cowboys** une bande de petits rigolos; **some c. builder/plumber** un petit rigolo d'entrepreneur/de plombier, un soi-disant entrepreneur/plombier

COMP de cow-boy

▸▸ ***cowboy boots*** bottes *fpl* de cow-boy, santiags *fpl*; ***cowboy film, cowboy movie*** film *m* de cow-boys

cowcatcher ['kaʊˌkætʃə(r)] **N** *Rail* chasse-pierres *m inv*

cower ['kaʊə(r)] **VI** *(person)* se recroqueviller; *(animal)* se tapir; **I cowered** *or* **was cowering in my seat** j'étais recroquevillé sur ma chaise; **the dog was cowering in a corner** tout tremblant, le chien était tapi dans un coin

cowhand ['kaʊhænd] **N** vacher(ère) *m,f*, *(in Western)* cow-boy *m*

cowherd ['kaʊhɜːd] **N** vacher(ère) *m,f*, bouvier (ère) *m,f*

cowhide ['kaʊhaɪd] **N** peau *f* de vache; *(leather)* cuir *m ou* peau *f* de vache

cowl [kaʊl] **N 1** *(of chimney)* capuchon *m* **2** *Rel (hood)* capuchon *m*; *(habit)* habit *m* à capuchon **3** *Tech (cowling)* capot *m*

▸▸ ***cowl neck, cowl neckline*** *(on sweater, dress)* col *m* boule

cowlick ['kaʊlɪk] **N** mèche *f* rebelle

cowling ['kaʊlɪŋ] **N** *Tech* capot *m*

cowman ['kaʊmən] *(pl* **cowmen** [-mən]) **N 1** *(who looks after cattle)* vacher *m*, bouvier *m* **2** *(who owns cattle ranch)* propriétaire *m* d'un ranch

co-worker **N** *esp Am* collègue *mf*

cowpat ['kaʊpæt] **N** bouse *f* de vache

cowpoke ['kaʊpəʊk] **N** *Am Fam* cow-boy[□] *m*

cowpox ['kaʊpɒks] **N** *Vet* vaccine *f*

cowpuncher ['kaʊˌpʌntʃə(r)] **N** *Am Fam Old-fashioned* cow-boy[□] *m*

cowrie, cowry ['kaʊrɪ] *(pl* **cowries**) **N** *Zool (mollusc)* porcelaine *f*, *(shell)* cauri *m*

cowshed ['kaʊʃed] **N** étable *f*

cowslip ['kaʊslɪp] **N** *Bot* primevère *f*, coucou *m*

cox [kɒks] *Sport* **N** *(of rowing team)* barreur(euse) *m,f*

VT barrer

VI barrer; **he has coxed for Cambridge** il a été barreur dans l'équipe de Cambridge

coxless ['kɒkslɪs] **ADJ** *Br Sport*

▸▸ ***coxless four*** quatre *m* de pointe sans barreur; ***coxless pair*** deux *m* de pointe sans barreur

coxswain ['kɒksən] **N** *Br* **1** *Sport (of rowing team)* barreur(euse) *m,f* **2** *(of lifeboat)* timonier *m*, homme *m* de barre

coy [kɔɪ] **ADJ 1** *(shy ▸ person)* qui fait le/la timide; *(▸ answer, smile)* faussement timide; **why be so c. about accepting?** pourquoi faire semblant d'hésiter?

2 *Pej (affectedly shy)* qui fait la sainte-nitouche; **a c. look** un air de sainte-nitouche

3 *(provocative, playful)* coquet; **with a c. little smile** avec un petit sourire séducteur

4 *(evasive)* évasif; **he was rather c. about the price** il était plutôt évasif quant au prix

coyly ['kɔɪlɪ] **ADV** *(timidly)* avec une timidité affectée *ou* feinte; *(provocatively)* coquettement

coyness ['kɔɪnɪs] **N** *(timidity)* timidité *f* affectée *ou* feinte; *(provocativeness)* coquetteries *fpl*

coyote [kɔɪ'əʊtɪ] **N** *Zool* coyote *m*

coypu ['kɔɪpuː] *(pl* **inv** *or* **coypus**) **N** *Zool* ragondin *m*

coziness, cozy *Am* = **cosiness, cosy**

CP [ˌsiː'piː] **N** *(abbr* **Communist Party**) PC *m*

CPA [ˌsiːpiː'eɪ] **N** *Am (abbr* **certified public accountant**) expert-comptable *m*

cpa [ˌsiːpiː'eɪ] **N** *(abbr* **critical path analysis**) analyse *f* du chemin critique

CPAP ['siːˌpæp] **N** *Med (abbr* **continuous positive airway pressure**) ventilation *f* en pression expiratoire positive

CPD [ˌsiːpiː'diː] **N** *(abbr* **continuing professional development**) formation *f* permanente *ou* continue

cpi [ˌsiːpiː'aɪ] *Comput (abbr* **characters per inch**) cpi

Cpl *Mil (written abbr* **corporal**) caporal *m*

CP/M [ˌsiːpiː'em] **N** *(abbr* **control program for microprocessors**) CP/M *m*

cps [ˌsiːpiː'es] *Comput (abbr* **characters per second**) cps

CPT [ˌsiːpiː'tiː] *(abbr* **carriage paid to**) CPT

CPU [ˌsiːpiː'juː] **N** *Comput (abbr* **central processing unit**) unité *f* centrale (de traitement)

CR [ˌsiː'ɑː(r)] **N** *Typ & Comput (abbr* **carriage return**) retour *m* chariot

crab [kræb] *(pt & pp* **crabbed**, *cont* **crabbing**) **N 1** *(crustacean)* crabe *m*

2 *Sport (in rowing)* **to catch a c.** faire (une) fausse pelle

3 *Astron* **the C.** le Cancer

4 *(irritable person)* grincheux(euse) *m,f*

VI 1 *Fam (grumble)* maugréer[□], rouspéter **2** *(hunt crabs)* pêcher des crabes

• **crabs** **NPL** *Fam (pubic lice)* morpions *mpl*; **to have crabs** avoir des morpions

▸▸ ***crab apple*** *(fruit)* pomme *f* sauvage; *(tree)* pommier *m* sauvage; *Culin* ***crab cake*** croquette de crabe; *Zool & Med* ***crab louse*** morpion *m*; *Culin* ***crab paste*** beurre *m* de crabe; *Entom* ***crab spider*** araignée-crabe *f*, thomise *m*

crabbed [kræbd] **ADJ 1** *(handwriting)* en pattes de mouche **2** *Fam Old-fashioned* grognon, ronchon

crabby ['kræbɪ] *(compar* **crabbier**, *superl* **crabbiest**) **ADJ** *Fam* grognon, ronchon

CRACK [kræk]

N
- fêlure **1**
- fissure **1, 2**
- crevasse **1**
- fente **2**
- craquement **3**
- claquement **3**
- coup **3, 4**
- tentative **5**
- blague **6**
- crack **7**

ADJ
- d'élite

VT
- fêler **1**
- fissurer **1**
- crevasser **1**
- casser **2**
- cogner **3**
- faire craquer **4**
- faire claquer **4**
- déchiffrer **5**
- résoudre **5**

VI
- se fêler **1**
- se fissurer **1**
- se crevasser **1**
- claquer **2**
- craquer **2, 3**

N 1 *(in cup, glass, egg)* fêlure *f*; *(in ceiling, wall)* lézarde *f*, fissure *f*; *(in rock)* fissure *f*; *(in ground)* crevasse *f*; *(in varnish, enamel)* craquelure *f*; *(in skin)* gerçure *f*, crevasse *f*; *(in bone)* fêlure *f*; *Fig (fault ▸ in policy, argument etc)* fissure *f*, faiblesse *f*; **did you know there was a c. in this glass?** avais-tu remarqué que ce verre était fêlé?; *Fig* **the cracks are beginning to show in their marriage** leur mariage commence à battre de l'aile

2 *(small opening or gap ▸ in floorboards, door etc)* fente *f*; *(▸ in wall)* fissure *f*; **open the window a c.** ouvrez la fenêtre un petit peu

3 *(noise ▸ of branches, ice etc)* craquement *m*; *(▸ of whip)* claquement *m*; *(▸ of thunder)* coup *m*

4 *(blow ▸ on head, knee etc)* coup *m*; **I gave myself a c. on the head** je me suis cogné la tête

5 *Fam (attempt)* tentative[□] *f*; **I'll have a c. (at it), I'll give it a c.** je vais tenter le coup, je vais essayer (un coup); **to give sb a fair c. of the whip** donner sa chance à qn[□]; **to get a fair c. of the whip** avoir l'occasion de montrer de quoi on est capable[□]

6 *(joke, witticism)* blague *f*, plaisanterie *f*; **to make a c.** faire une plaisanterie, lancer une vanne; **a cheap c.** une plaisanterie facile

7 *(drug)* crack *m*

8 *Comput (program)* = programme permettant de forcer un système informatique

9 *Vulg (woman's genitals)* chatte *f*, con *m*
10 *Vulg (anus)* troufignon *m*, trou *m* du cul
11 *(idioms)* **at the c. of dawn** au point du jour; *Old-fashioned Hum* **we'll be here until the c. of doom** on va être ici jusqu'aux calendes grecques
ADJ *Fam (regiment, team etc)* d'élite; **c. regiment** régiment *m* d'élite; **one of their c. players** un de leurs meilleurs joueurs
VT 1 *(damage ▸ cup, glass, egg)* fêler; *(▸ ice)* fendre; *(▸ ceiling, wall)* lézarder, fissurer; *(▸ ground)* crevasser; *(▸ varnish, enamel)* craqueler; *(▸ skin)* gercer, crevasser; *(▸ bone)* fêler
2 *(open ▸ eggs, nuts)* casser; **to c. a safe** fracturer un coffre-fort; *Fam* **to c. (open) a bottle** ouvrir *ou* déboucher une bouteille☐; *Fam* **she never cracked a smile the entire evening** elle n'a pas souri une seule fois de la soirée☐
3 *(bang, hit ▸ head, knee)* **to c. one's head/knee on sth** se cogner la tête/le genou contre qch
4 *(make noise with ▸ whip)* faire claquer; *(▸ knuckles)* faire craquer
5 *(solve)* **to c. a code** déchiffrer un code; **the police think they have cracked the case** la police pense qu'elle a résolu l'affaire; **I think we've cracked it** je pense que nous y sommes arrivés
6 *(market)* percer sur
7 *Chem* craquer
8 *Comput* craquer, déplomber
9 *Fam (idiom)* **to c. a joke** sortir une blague
VI 1 *(cup, glass, ice)* se fissurer, se fêler; *(ceiling, wall)* se lézarder, se fissurer; *(ground)* se crevasser; *(varnish, enamel)* se craqueler; *(skin)* se gercer, se crevasser; *(bone)* se fêler
2 *(make noise ▸ whip)* claquer; *(▸ twigs)* craquer; **a rifle cracked and he dropped to the ground** un coup de fusil a retenti et il s'est effondré
3 *(give way, collapse ▸ through nervous exhaustion)* s'effondrer, craquer; *(▸ under questioning, surveillance)* craquer; **their marriage cracked under the strain** leur mariage s'est détérioré sous l'effet du stress; **his voice cracked with emotion** sa voix se brisa sous le coup de l'émotion
4 *Fam (idiom)* **to get cracking** *(start work)* s'y mettre☐, se mettre au boulot; *(get ready, get going)* se mettre en route☐; **get cracking!, let's get cracking!** au boulot!
▸▸ ***crack cocaine*** crack *m*; ***crack shot*** tireur(euse) *m,f* d'élite

▸ crack down VI sévir; **to c. down on sb/sth** sévir contre qn/qch

▸ crack up VT SEP 1 *(make laugh)* **it really cracked me up when I heard about it** je me suis vraiment écroulé de rire quand j'ai entendu parler de ça **2** *(always passive) (say good things about)* **it's not all it's cracked up to be** ce n'est pas tout ce qu'on en dit **3** *Fam (destroy)* bousiller
VI 1 *(ice)* se fissurer; *(ground)* se crevasser
2 *Fam (through nervous exhaustion)* s'effondrer☐, craquer☐; **I must be cracking up** *(going mad)* je débloque
3 *Br Fam (get angry)* péter les plombs
4 *Fam (with laughter)* se tordre de rire

---

crackbrained ['krækbreɪnd] **ADJ** *Fam* débile, dingue

crackdown ['krækdaʊn] **N** mesures *fpl* énergiques (**on sth** contre qch); **they're going to have a c. on petty theft** on va sévir contre les petits larcins

cracked [krækt] **ADJ 1** *(damaged ▸ cup, glass)* fêlé; *(▸ ice)* fendu; *(▸ ceiling, wall)* lézardé; *(▸ ground)* crevassé; *(▸ varnish)* craquelé; *(▸ skin)* gercé, crevassé **2** *(crushed ▸ pepper, wheat)* concassé **3** *Fam (mad ▸ person)* fêlé, taré

cracker ['krækə(r)] **N 1** *(savoury biscuit)* biscuit *m* salé, cracker *m*
2 *Br (for pulling)* = papillote contenant un pétard, une blague, un chapeau en papier et une surprise, traditionnelle en Grande-Bretagne au moment des fêtes
3 *(firework)* pétard *m*
4 *Br Fam (good-looking person)* canon *m*
5 *Br Fam (excellent thing)* merveille☐ *f*; **that was a c. of a goal** c'était un but magnifique☐
6 *Am Fam Pej (redneck)* = Blanc pauvre du sud des États-Unis
7 *Comput* cracker *m*
▸▸ *Am* ***cracker barrel*** boîte *f* à biscuits

cracker-barrel ADJ *Am Fam (wisdom, philosophy etc)* de quatre sous

crackers ['krækəz] **ADJ** *Br Fam* cinglé, fêlé; **to drive sb c.** faire tourner qn en bourrique

crackhead ['krækhed] **N** *Fam Drugs slang* accro *mf* au crack

cracking ['krækɪŋ] **ADJ 1** *Br Fam (excellent)* génial, épatant **2** *(fast)* **to keep up a c. pace** aller à fond de train
ADV *Br Fam Old-fashioned* **c. good** *(match, meal)* de première
N 1 *(sound)* craquement *m*; *(of whip)* claquement *m* **2** *(of paint)* craquelure *f*, craquelage *m* **3** *Chem* craquage *m*

crackle ['krækəl] **N 1** *(of paper, twigs, dry leaves)* craquement *m*; *(of fire)* crépitement *m*, craquement *m*; *(of radio)* grésillement *m*; *(on telephone)* friture *f*; *(of something frying)* grésillement *m*; *(of machinegun fire)* crépitement *m* **2** *(finish ▸ of paint, porcelain)* craquelure *f*
VI *(paper, twigs, dry leaves)* craquer; *(fire)* crépiter, craquer; *(radio)* grésiller; *(something frying)* grésiller; *(machinegun fire)* crépiter; *Fig* **to c. with energy** pétiller d'énergie
▸▸ *Cer* ***crackle finish*** craquelage *m*

crackleware ['krækəl,weə(r)] **N** *Cer* poterie *f* craquelée

crackling ['kræklɪŋ] **N 1** *(of paper, twigs, dry leaves)* craquement *m*; *(of fire)* crépitement *m*, craquement *m*; *(of radio)* grésillement *m*; *(on telephone)* friture *f*; *(of something frying)* grésillement *m*; *(of machinegun fire)* crépitement *m* **2** *Culin (of roast pork)* couenne *f* rôtie

crackpot ['krækpɒt] *Fam* **N** *(person)* cinglé(e) *m,f*
ADJ *(idea, scheme)* tordu; *(person)* cinglé

cradle ['kreɪdəl] **N 1** *(for baby) & Fig* berceau *m*; **the c. of democracy/the trade union movement** le berceau de la démocratie/du mouvement syndical; **from the c. to the grave** du berceau au tombeau; *Br Hum* **to be a c. snatcher,** *Am* **to rob the c.** les prendre au berceau *ou* biberon **2** *(frame ▸ for painter, window cleaner)* pont *m* volant, échafaudage *m* volant; *(▸ in hospital bed)* arceau *m* **3** *(for telephone receiver, PDA)* support *m*
VT *(hold carefully ▸ baby, kitten)* bercer, tenir tendrement (dans ses bras); *(▸ delicate object)* tenir précieusement *ou* délicatement (dans ses bras); **to c. a child in one's arms** bercer un enfant dans ses bras; **he cradled the rifle in his arms** il serrait le fusil contre lui
▸▸ ***cradle cap*** dermite *f* séborrhéique; **to have c. cap** *(baby)* avoir des croûtes de lait

cradle-song N berceuse *f*

cradle-to-grave ADJ 1 *(health cover, welfare system)* qui prend l'individu en charge tout au long de sa vie **2** *(gen) & Comput (service, support)* de bout en bout

craft [krɑːft] *(pl sense* **3** *inv)* **N 1** *(art)* art *m*; *(occupation)* métier *m* (manuel); **crafts** *(activity)* activités *fpl* manuelles **2** *(UNCOUNT) (guile, cunning)* ruse *f*; **to obtain sth by c.** obtenir qch par la ruse **3** *(boat, ship)* bateau *m*; *(aircraft)* avion *m*; *(spacecraft)* engin *m ou* vaisseau *m* spatial
VT *(usu passive)* travailler; *Fig* **a beautifully crafted film** un film magnifiquement travaillé
▸▸ ***craft centre*** centre *m* d'artisanat; *Br Sch* ***craft, design and technology*** = matière enseignée dans le secondaire qui incorpore travaux manuels et technologie; ***craft(s) fair*** foire *f* d'artisanat; ***craft union*** syndicat *m* d'artisans

craftily ['krɑːftɪlɪ] **ADV** *(cleverly)* astucieusement, ingénieusement, *Pej* avec ruse *ou* roublardise astucieusement

craftiness ['krɑːftɪnɪs] **N** habileté *f*; *Pej* ruse *f*, roublardise *f*

craftsman ['krɑːftsmən] *(pl* **craftsmen** [-mən]*)* **N** artisan *m*, homme *m* de métier; *(writer, actor)* homme *m* de métier

craftsmanship ['krɑːftsmənʃɪp] **N** connaissance *f* d'un *ou* du métier; **this is French c. at its best** voici l'artisanat français au sommet de sa qualité; **the c. is superb** cela a été superbement travaillé

craftswoman ['krɑːfts,wʊmən] *(pl* **craftswomen** [-,wɪmɪn]*)* **N** artisane *f*

craftwork ['krɑːftwɜːk] **N** artisanat *m*

crafty ['krɑːftɪ] *(compar* **craftier,** *superl* **craftiest***)* **ADJ** *(person, idea, scheme)* malin(igne), astucieux; *Pej (person)* rusé, roublard; *(idea, scheme)* rusé; **you c. old devil!** espèce de vieux renard!

crag [kræg] **N** *(steep rock)* rocher *m* escarpé *ou* à pic

craggy ['krægɪ] *(compar* **craggier,** *superl* **craggiest***)* **ADJ** *(hill)* escarpé, à pic; *Fig (features)* anguleux, taillé à la serpe

cram [kræm] *(pt & pp* **crammed,** *cont* **cramming***)* **VT 1** *(objects)* fourrer; *(people)* entasser; **to c. sth into a drawer** fourrer qch dans un tiroir; **there were ten of us crammed into a tiny office** nous étions dix entassés dans un bureau minuscule; **to c. clothes into a suitcase** bourrer des vêtements dans une valise, bourrer une valise de vêtements; **you can't c. anything else in** tu ne peux plus rien y mettre, même en forçant; **to c. food into one's mouth** se bourrer de nourriture, se gaver; **we crammed a lot into one day** on en a fait beaucoup en une seule journée **2** *Fam (facts)* apprendre à toute vitesse☐; *(students)* faire bachoter **3** *Agr (poultry)* appâter, gaver
VI 1 *Fam (study hard)* bachoter **2** *(into small space)* **100 people crammed in** 100 personnes se *ou* s'y sont entassées; **we all crammed into his office** nous nous sommes tous entassés dans son bureau

cram-full ADJ *Br* **to be c. (of sth)** être plein à craquer *ou* bourré (de qch)

crammer ['kræmə(r)] **N** *Br Fam (teacher)* répétiteur(trice)☐ *m,f*; *(student)* bachoteur(euse) *m,f*; *(school)* boîte *f* à bac

cramming ['kræmɪŋ] **N** *Fam (intensive learning)* bachotage *m*; *(intensive teaching)* bourrage *m* de crâne

cramp [kræmp] **N 1** *(muscle pain)* crampe *f*; **to have c.** *or Am* **a c.** avoir une crampe; **I've got c. in my leg** j'ai une crampe à la jambe; *Am* **to have stomach c., to have cramps** avoir des crampes d'estomac **2** *Carp* serre-joint *m* **3** *Constr (cramp iron)* crampon *m*, happe *f*, clameau *m*
VT 1 *(hamper ▸ person)* gêner; *(▸ project)* entraver, contrarier; *Fam* **to c. sb's style** faire perdre tous ses moyens à qn☐, priver qn de ses moyens☐ **2** *Carp (secure with a cramp)* maintenir à l'aide d'un serre-joint **3** *Constr (stones etc)* cramponner, agrafer
▸▸ *Constr* ***cramp iron*** crampon *m*, happe *f*, clameau *m*

cramped [kræmpt] **ADJ 1** *(room, flat)* exigu; **they live in very c. conditions** ils vivent très à l'étroit; **we're a bit c. for space** nous sommes un peu à l'étroit **2** *(position)* inconfortable **3** *(handwriting)* en pattes de mouche, serré

crampon ['kræmpən] **N** crampon *m* (à glace)

cranberry ['krænbərɪ] *(pl* **cranberries***)* **N** airelle *f*, *Can* canneberge *f*
COMP *(juice, sauce)* d'airelle, *Can* de canneberge

crane [kreɪn] **N 1** *Orn* grue *f* **2** *Tech & Cin* grue *f*
VT to c. one's neck tendre le cou
VI to c. (forward) tendre le cou
▸▸ ***crane driver*** grutier(ère) *m,f*; *Entom* ***crane fly*** tipule *f*; ***crane operator*** grutier(ère) *m,f*; *Cin & TV* ***crane shot*** prise *f* de vue sur grue

craniology [,kreɪnɪ'ɒlədʒɪ] **N** *Med* craniologie *f*

cranium ['kreɪnɪəm] *(pl* **craniums** *or* **crania** [-nɪə]*)* **N** *Anat (skull ▸ gen)* crâne *m*; *(▸ part enclosing brain)* boîte *f* crânienne

crank [kræŋk] **N 1** *Fam (eccentric)* allumé(e) *m,f*; **a religious c.** un(une) fanatique religieux(euse) **2** *Am Fam (bad-tempered person)* grognon(onne) *m,f* **3** *Tech* manivelle *f*
VT *(engine)* démarrer à la manivelle; *(gramophone)* remonter à la manivelle;
▸▸ *Tech* ***crank handle*** manivelle *f*

▸ crank out VT SEP *Am Fam (books, plays etc)* produire en quantités industrielles☐; **this is the fourth novel he's cranked out this year** c'est le quatrième roman d'affilée qu'il sort cette année

▸ crank up VT SEP 1 *(engine)* démarrer à la manivelle; *(gramophone)* remonter à la manivelle **2** *Fig (increase)* augmenter; **c. up the volume** monte le son **3** *(idiom)* **to get things cranked up** mettre tout en place

crankcase ['kræŋkkeɪs] **N** *Tech* carter *m*

crankiness ['kræŋkɪnɪs] **N** *Fam* **1** *(eccentricity)* bizarrerie◻ *f* **2** *Am, Austr & Ir (bad temper)* caractère *m* de cochon; *(on one occasion)* mauvaise humeur◻ *f*

cranking ['kræŋkɪŋ]

▸▸ *Tech* ***cranking handle*** manivelle *f*; *Aut* ***cranking speed*** vitesse *f* du démarreur, régime *m* de démarrage; *Aut* ***cranking torque*** couple *m* de démarrage

crankpin ['kræŋkpɪn] **N** *Tech* maneton *m*

crankshaft ['kræŋkʃɑːft] **N** *Tech* vilebrequin *m*

cranky ['kræŋkɪ] *(compar* **crankier**, *superl* **crankiest)** **ADJ** *Fam* **1** *Br (eccentric ▸ person, behaviour, ideas)* bizarre◻, loufoque◻ **2** *Am, Austr & Ir (bad-tempered)* grognon **3** *(unreliable ▸ machine)* capricieux◻

cranny ['krænɪ] *(pl* **crannies)** **N** *(crack)* fente *f*

crap [kræp] *(pt & pp* **crapped**, *cont* **crapping)** **N** *(UNCOUNT)* **1** *very Fam (faeces)* merde *f*; **to have** *or* **to take a c.** chier, couler un bronze

2 *very Fam (nonsense)* conneries *fpl*; **to talk c.** raconter *ou* dire des conneries; **don't give me that c.!** arrête de me raconter des conneries!; **he's full of c.** il raconte n'importe quoi; **what a load of c.!** quelles conneries!; **cut the c.!** arrête tes conneries!, arrête de dire n'importe quoi!

3 *very Fam (rubbish)* merde *f*; **get all this c. off the table** enlève tout ce bordel *ou* toute cette merde de la table; **he eats nothing but c.** il ne bouffe que des saloperies; **you don't believe all that c. about witches, do you?** tu ne crois quand même pas à toutes ces conneries sur les sorcières, hein?; **to feel like c.** *(ill)* se sentir vraiment patraque

4 *very Fam (unfair treatment)* **I don't need this c.!** je me passerais bien de ce genre de conneries!

5 *Am (dice game)* = jeu de dés similaire au quatre-cent-vingt-et-un et où on parie sur le résultat; **c. game** partie *f* de dés

VI *very Fam (defecate)* chier, couler un bronze

VT *very Fam* **to c. oneself** *(defecate, be scared)* faire dans son froc

ADJ *Br very Fam (of poor quality)* de merde, merdique; *(nasty)* dégueulasse; **what a c. book** quel livre merdique *ou* de merde *ou* à la con; **she's a c. cook, her cooking is c.** sa cuisine, c'est de la merde; **to feel c.** *(ill)* se sentir vraiment mal fichu; *(guilty)* se sentir coupable◻

• **craps N** *Am (dice game)* = jeu de dés similaire au quatre-cent-vingt-et-un et où on parie sur le résultat; **to shoot craps** *(play game)* jouer aux dés, faire une partie de dés; *(throw dice)* lancer les dés

▸ **crap out VI 1** *Am (in game)* = ne pas obtenir le résultat sur lequel on a parié dans un jeu de dés **2** *very Fam (back out)* se dégonfler; **he crapped out of the fight** il s'est dégonflé au dernier moment et a refusé de se battre; **he crapped out of asking her for a date** il allait lui demander de sortir avec lui mais il s'est dégonflé

crape [kreɪp] **N 1** *(fabric)* crêpe *m* **2** *(for people in mourning)* crêpe *m* noir (de deuil)

crapper ['kræpə(r)] **N** *very Fam (toilet)* chiottes *fpl*, gogues *mpl*

crappy ['kræpɪ] *(compar* **crappier**, *superl* **crappiest)** **ADJ** *very Fam (of poor quality)* de merde, merdique, à la con; *(nasty)* dégueulasse; **to feel c.** *(ill)* se sentir vraiment mal fichu; *(guilty)* se sentir coupable◻

crapshoot ['kræpʃuːt] **N** *Am* **1** *(game)* = jeu de dés similaire au quatre-cent-vingt-et-un et où on parie sur le résultat **2** *Fig (risky venture)* pari *m* risqué

crapshooter ['kræpˌʃuːtə(r)] **N** *Am* joueur(euse) *m,f* de dés

crapulous ['kræpjʊləs], **crapulent** ['kræpjʊlənt] **ADJ** *Literary* intempérant

> Note that the French word **crapuleux** is a false friend. It means **villainous** or **dissolute.**

CRASH [kræʃ]

N	
• accident **1**	• fracas **2**
• krach **3**	• panne **4**
ONOMAT	
• patatras	
VI	
• avoir un accident **1**	• s'écraser **1, 2**
• retentir **2**	• s'effondrer **4**
• tomber en panne, planter **5**	• pieuter **6**
VT	
• avoir un accident avec **1**	• s'inviter à **2**

N 1 *(collision)* accident *m*; **car/plane/train c.** accident *m* de voiture/d'avion/ferroviaire; **we were in a c.** *(car accident)* nous avons eu un accident de voiture; **the car looks as though it has been in a c.** la voiture semble avoir été accidentée; **the force of the c.** la force de l'impact; *Rugby* **to do a c. tackle** plaquer violemment

2 *(loud noise)* fracas *m*; **a c. of thunder** un coup de tonnerre; **there was a loud c. as the plate hit the ground** cela a fait un bruit fracassant quand l'assiette est tombée par terre; **there was a loud c. from the kitchen** un grand fracas a retenti dans la cuisine; **he closed the lid with a c.** il a fermé le couvercle avec fracas

3 *Fin (slump)* krach *m*, débâcle *f*

4 *Comput* panne *f*

COMP *(programme)* intensif, de choc

ADV he ran c. into a wall il est rentré en plein dans le mur; **something went c. in the attic** quelque chose est tombé dans le grenier

ONOMAT patatras!

VI 1 *(car, train, driver)* avoir un accident; *(plane)* s'écraser, se crasher; **we're going to c.** *(plane)* on va s'écraser; *(car)* on va lui rentrer dedans/rentrer dans le mur/*etc*; *(train)* on va avoir un accident; **the cars crashed (head on)** les voitures se sont percutées (de plein fouet); **to c. into sth** percuter qch, rentrer dans qch; **the car crashed through the fence** la voiture est passée à travers la clôture; **to c. into sb** *(person)* rentrer dans qn; **I crashed into him** je lui suis rentré dedans

2 *(make loud noise ▸ thunder)* retentir; *(▸ waves)* s'écraser; **the thunder crashed** *(once)* il y eut un violent coup de tonnerre; *(repeatedly)* le tonnerre retentit; **what are you crashing about at this hour for?** pourquoi fais-tu autant de vacarme *ou* boucan à cette heure?; **the elephants crashed through the undergrowth** les éléphants ont traversé le sous-bois dans un vacarme terrible

3 *(fall, hit with loud noise or violently)* **the tree came crashing down** l'arbre s'est abattu avec fracas; **the bookcase came crashing down** la bibliothèque s'est écroulée avec fracas; *Fig* **her world came crashing down about her** *or* **her ears** tout son monde s'est écroulé; **the vase crashed to the ground** le vase s'est fracassé au sol

4 *St Exch* s'effondrer; **shares crashed from 750p to 110p** le cours des actions s'est effondré: de 750 pence il est passé à 110 pence

5 *Comput (computer network, system)* sauter; *(computer)* tomber en panne, planter

6 *Fam (spend night, sleep)* pieuter, pioncer; *(fall asleep)* s'endormir◻; **can I c. at your place?** je peux pieuter chez toi?; **I need somewhere to c. for the next week** j'ai besoin d'un endroit où crécher la semaine prochaine

VT 1 *(vehicle)* **to c. a car** avoir un accident avec une voiture; *(on purpose)* démolir une voiture; **she crashed the car into a wall** elle est rentrée dans *ou* a percuté un mur (avec la voiture)

2 *(make noise with)* **to c. the gears** faire grincer la boîte de vitesses; **he crashed the books down on the table** il a posé les livres sur la table avec fracas

3 *Fam (party)* s'inviter à◻, taper l'incruste à

4 *Comput* faire tomber en panne

▸▸ ***crash barrier*** glissière *f* de sécurité; ***crash course*** cours *m* intensif; ***crash diet*** régime *m* choc; ***crash dive*** *(of submarine)* plongée *f* raide; *(of plane)* plongeon *m*; ***crash helmet*** casque *m* (de protection); ***crash landing*** atterrissage *m* forcé *ou* en catastrophe; *Fam* ***crash pad*** piaule *f* de dépannage; **he let me use his place as a c. pad** il m'a laissé crécher chez lui pour me dépanner; ***crash test dummy*** mannequin-test *m*; ***crash victim*** victime *f* d'un accident

▸ **crash out VI** *Fam (fall asleep)* s'endormir◻; *(spend the night, sleep)* pieuter, pioncer; **I found him crashed out in the corner** je l'ai trouvé endormi◻ *ou* qui roupillait dans le coin

crash-dive VI *(submarine)* plonger; *(plane)* faire un plongeon

crashing ['kræʃɪŋ] **ADJ** *Br Fam* **a c. bore** *(person)* une personne assommante; *(task)* une besogne assommante; *(party)* une soirée assommante; **to be a c. bore** être assommant

crashingly ['kræʃɪŋlɪ] **ADV** *Br Fam (boring)* incroyablement, terriblement

crash-land VT *(aircraft)* poser *ou* faire atterrir en catastrophe

VI *(aircraft)* faire un atterrissage forcé, atterrir en catastrophe

crash-test VT to c. a car tester une voiture en situation d'accident

crashworthiness ['kræʃ,wɜːðɪnɪs] **N** *(of vehicle, helicopter)* résistance *f* aux chocs

crass [kræs] **ADJ** *(comment, person)* lourd; *(behaviour, stupidity)* grossier; *(ignorance)* grossier, crasse

crassly ['kræslɪ] **ADV** *(behave, comment)* lourdement

crassness ['kræsnɪs] **N** *(of comment, person)* lourdeur *f*, manque *m* de finesse; **the c. of his ignorance** son ignorance crasse; **the c. of his behaviour** son manque de finesse

crate [kreɪt] **N 1** *(for storage, transport)* caisse *f*; *(for fruit, vegetables)* cageot *m*, cagette *f*; *(for glass, china)* harasse *f*; *(for bottles)* casier *m* **2** *Fam (old car)* caisse *f*; *(plane)* coucou *m*

VT *(goods)* mettre dans une caisse *ou* en caisses; *(fruit, vegetables)* mettre dans un cageot *ou* en cageots

crateload ['kreɪtləʊd] **N** caisse *f*; *Fam Fig* **they're selling by the c.** ils se vendent comme des petits pains

crater ['kreɪtə(r)] **N** *(of volcano, moon etc)* cratère *m*; *(from bomb)* entonnoir *m*; **the explosion had left a c. 20 feet wide** l'explosion avait laissé un cratère de 6 mètres de large; **bomb c.** entonnoir *m*; **shell c.** entonnoir *m*, trou *m* d'obus

VT creuser; **a street cratered by shellfire** une rue défoncée par des éclats d'obus

cravat [krə'væt] **N** *Br* foulard *m*

crave [kreɪv] **VT 1** *(long for ▸ cigarette, drink)* avoir terriblement envie de; *(▸ affection, love)* avoir soif *ou* terriblement besoin de; *(▸ stardom)* avoir soif de; *(▸ luxury, wealth)* avoir soif *ou* être avide de; *Med & Psy* éprouver un besoin impérieux de **2** *Formal (beg)* implorer; **to c. sb's pardon** implorer le pardon de qn; **to c. sb's indulgence** faire appel à l'indulgence de qn

VI to c. for sth désirer ardemment qch, réclamer qch

craven ['kreɪvən] **ADJ** *Literary (person, attitude)* lâche, veule

cravenly ['kreɪvənlɪ] **ADV** *Literary* avec lâcheté, lâchement

craving ['kreɪvɪŋ] **N** *(longing)* envie *f* impérieuse *ou* irrésistible; *(physiological need)* besoin *m* impérieux; **pregnant women often get cravings** les femmes enceintes éprouvent souvent des envies irrésistibles; **to have a c. for sth** *(for chocolate, sweets, cigarette)* avoir terriblement envie de qch; *(of alcoholic, drug addict)* avoir un besoin impérieux de qch

craw [krɔː] **N** *(of bird)* jabot *m*; *(of animal)* estomac *m*; *Fam Fig* **it sticks in my c.** cela me reste en travers de la gorge, j'ai du mal à l'avaler

crawfish ['krɔːfɪʃ] *(pl* **inv** *or* **crawfishes)** **N** *Am* écrevisse *f*

crawl [krɔːl] **N 1** *(of person)* **it involved a laborious c. through the undergrowth** il a fallu ramper tant bien que mal à travers le sous-bois **2** *(of vehicle)* ralenti *m*; **to move at a c.** avancer au ralenti *ou* au pas; **the traffic/train has slowed to a c.** les voitures avancent/le train avance maintenant au pas *ou* au ralenti **3** *(swimming stroke)* crawl *m*; **to do the c.** nager le crawl

VI 1 *(move on all fours ▸ person)* ramper; *(▸ baby)* marcher à quatre pattes; **he crawled into bed** il se traîna au lit; **to c. on one's hands and knees** marcher *ou* se traîner à quatre pattes; **she crawled under the desk** elle s'est mise à quatre pattes sous le bureau

2 *(move slowly ▸ traffic, train)* avancer au ralenti

ou au pas; (► *insect, snake*) ramper; **there's a caterpillar crawling up your arm** il y a une chenille qui te grimpe sur le bras

3 *(be infested)* **the kitchen was crawling with ants** la cuisine grouillait *ou* était infestée de fourmis; *Fam Fig* **the streets were crawling with police/tourists** les rues grouillaient de policiers/touristes

4 *(come out in goose pimples)* **just the thought of it makes my skin** *or* **flesh c.** j'ai la chair de poule rien que d'y penser

5 *Fam (grovel)* **to c. to sb** ramper *ou* s'aplatir devant qn, lécher les bottes de qn; **he'll come crawling back** il reviendra te supplier à genoux

6 *(in swimming)* nager le crawl

►► *Am Constr* ***crawl space*** vide *m* sanitaire

crawler ['krɔːlə(r)] **N 1** *Fam Pej (groveller)* lèche-bottes *mf inv* **2** *Comput (on Internet)* araignée *f*

• **crawlers NPL** *(for baby)* grenouillère *f*

►► *Br Aut* ***crawler lane*** file *f ou* voie *f* pour véhicules lents

crawling ['krɔːlɪŋ] **ADJ 1** *Fam Pej (grovelling)* rampant, de lèche-bottes **2** *(on all fours)* **she's reached the c. stage** *(baby)* elle commence à marcher à quatre pattes **3** *(infested)* grouillant (**with** de); **the kitchen was absolutely c.** la cuisine était d'une saleté repoussante

N *Fam Pej (grovelling)* **that's just c.** c'est du lèche-botte

crayfish ['kreɪfɪʃ] *(pl* **inv** *or* **crayfishes) N** écrevisse *f*

crayon ['kreɪɒn] **N** *(coloured pencil)* crayon *m* de couleur; *(pastel)* pastel *m*; *(made of wax)* pastel *m*; **eye/lip c.** crayon *m* pour les yeux/à lèvres

VT *(draw)* dessiner avec des crayons de couleurs; *(colour)* colorier *(avec des crayons)*

craze [kreɪz] **N** engouement *m*, folie *f*; **the latest dance/music c.** la nouvelle danse/musique à la mode; **it's becoming a c.** ça devient une vraie folie; **this c. for video games** cet engouement pour les jeux vidéo

VT 1 *Literary (send mad)* rendre fou (folle) **2** *(damage* ► *windscreen, glass)* étoiler; *Cer* (► *glazed, varnished surface)* craqueler

VI *(windscreen, glass)* s'étoiler; *Cer (glazed, varnished surface)* se craqueler

-crazed [kreɪzd] **SUFF** rendu fou (folle) par; **drug-c.** rendu fou (folle) par la drogue; **power-c. dictators** des dictateurs fous de pouvoir; **he was half-c. with fear** il était à moitié fou de peur

crazed [kreɪzd] **ADJ 1** *(mad* ► *look, expression)* fou (folle); **c. with fear/grief** fou (folle) de peur/douleur **2** *Cer (glazed, varnished surface)* craquelé

crazily ['kreɪzɪlɪ] **ADV** follement; *(behave)* comme un fou (folle)

craziness ['kreɪzɪnɪs] **N** folie *f*

crazy ['kreɪzɪ] *(compar* **crazier**, *superl* **craziest** *pl* **crazies) ADJ 1** *(insane* ► *person, dream)* fou (folle); **that's a c. idea!, that's c.!** c'est de la folie!; **this is c.** c'est fou; **that's the craziest thing I've ever heard** c'est la chose la plus insensée que j'aie jamais entendue; **to drive** *or* **to send sb c.** rendre qn fou; **he went c.** *(insane)* il est devenu fou; *(angry)* il est devenu fou (de colère *ou* de rage); *Fam* **the fans went c.** les fans ne se sont plus sentis; **like c.** *(work, drive, run, spend money)* comme un fou

2 *Fam (very fond)* **to be c. about sb/sth** être fou (folle) *ou* dingue de qn/qch; **I'm not c. about the idea** l'idée ne m'emballe pas vraiment; **he's football c.** c'est un fana *ou* un cinglé de foot

3 *(strange, fantastic)* bizarre, fou (folle)

4 *Am (very good)* formidable, génial

N *esp Am (person)* original(e) *m,f*

►► *Am* ***crazy bone*** petit juif *m*; ***crazy golf*** minigolf *m*; *Br* ***crazy paving*** = dallage irrégulier en pierres plates; *Am* ***crazy quilt*** couette *f* en patchwork

CRB [ˌsiːɑːˈbiː] **N** *Br (abbr* **Criminal Records Bureau)** identité *f* judiciaire

CRC [ˌsiːɑːˈsiː] **N** *Typ (abbr* **camera-ready copy)** copie *f* prête pour la reproduction

CRE [ˌsiːɑːˈriː] **N** *(abbr* **Commission for Racial Equality)** = commission contre la discrimination raciale

creak [kriːk] **N** *(of chair, floorboard, person's joints)* craquement *m*; *(of door hinge)* grincement *m*; *(of shoes)* crissement *m*; **to give a c.** *(chair, floorboard, person's joints)* craquer; *(door hinge)* grincer; *(shoes)* crisser

VI *(chair, floorboard, person's joints)* craquer; *(door hinge)* grincer; *(shoes)* crisser; *Fig (plot etc)* être boiteux; **the chair creaked under his weight** la chaise a craqué sous son poids

creaking ['kriːkɪŋ] **N** *(of chair, floorboard, person's joints)* craquement *m*; *(of door hinge)* grincement *m*; *(of shoes)* crissement *m*

ADJ *(chair, floorboard, person's joints)* qui craque; *(door hinge)* grinçant; *(shoes)* qui crisse

creaky ['kriːkɪ] *(compar* **creakier**, *superl* **creakiest) ADJ** *(chair, floorboard, person's joints)* qui craque; *(door hinge)* grinçant; *(shoes)* qui crisse; *Fig (dialogue, plot etc)* boiteux; **a c. noise** un craquement, un grincement, un crissement

cream [kriːm] **N 1** *(of milk)* crème *f*; **strawberries and c.** des fraises *fpl* à la crème; **c. of tomato/asparagus soup** velouté *m* de tomates/d'asperges

2 *(filling for biscuits, chocolates)* fondant *m*; *(individual chocolate)* chocolat *m* fourré; **vanilla c.** *(biscuit)* biscuit *m* fourré à la vanille; *(dessert)* crème *f* à la vanille; *(individual chocolate)* chocolat *m* fourré à la crème

3 *(mixture)* mélange *m* crémeux

4 *Fig (best, pick)* crème *f*; **the c. of society** la crème *ou* le gratin de la société; **the c. of the crop** le dessus du panier

5 *(for face, shoes etc)* crème *f*

6 *(ointment)* pommade *f*

7 *(colour)* crème *m inv*

COMP *(jug)* à crème

ADJ *(colour)* crème *(inv)*

VT 1 *(skim* ► *milk)* écrémer

2 *Culin (beat)* écraser, travailler; **c. the butter and sugar** travailler le beurre et le sucre en crème

3 *(hands, face)* mettre de la crème sur

4 *(add cream to* ► *coffee)* mettre de la crème dans

5 *Fam (defeat)* battre à plate couture, mettre la pâtée à; *Am (beat up)* casser la figure à; **we got creamed 4–0** on s'est fait écraser 4–0

6 *Vulg* **to c. one's jeans** prendre son pied

VI 1 *Vulg (man* ► *ejaculate)* décharger, balancer la sauce; *(woman* ► *be aroused)* mouiller **2** *(milk)* crémer

►► ***cream bun*** = petit pain au lait servi avec de la crème Chantilly; ***cream cake*** gâteau *m* à la crème; ***cream cheese*** fromage *m* frais; *Br* ***cream cracker*** biscuit *m* sec; ***cream eyeshadow*** ombre *f* à paupières en crème; ***cream puff*** chou *m* à la crème; ***cream sherry*** sherry *m ou* xérès *m* doux; ***cream slice*** = sorte de mille-feuille; ***cream soda*** = boisson gazeuse aromatisée à la vanille; *Culin* ***cream of tartar*** crème *f* de tartre; *Br* ***cream tea*** = goûter composé de thé et de scones servis avec de la confiture et de la crème;

▸ **cream off VT SEP** *(profits)* accaparer; **to c. off the best students** sélectionner les meilleurs étudiants; **they have creamed off the elite** ils se sont accaparé l'élite

cream-coloured ADJ crème *(inv)*

creamed [kriːmd] **ADJ** *Culin (chicken etc)* à la crème

►► *Culin* ***creamed coconut*** lait *m* de coco solidifié; ***creamed potatoes*** purée *f* de pommes de terre

creamer ['kriːmə(r)] **N 1** *(machine)* écrémeuse *f* **2** *(for coffee)* succédané *m* de crème **3** *Am (jug)* pot *m* à crème

creamery ['kriːmərɪ] *(pl* **creameries) N 1** *(dairy)* laiterie *f* **2** *(shop)* crémerie *f*

creamy ['kriːmɪ] *(compar* **creamier**, *superl* **creamiest) ADJ 1** *(containing cream* ► *coffee, sauce)* à la crème; (► *milk)* qui contient de la crème; **it's too c.** il y a trop de crème **2** *(smooth* ► *drink, sauce etc)* crémeux; (► *complexion, voice)* velouté **3** *(colour)* **c. white** blanc *m* cassé

crease [kriːs] **N 1** *(in material, paper* ► *made on purpose)* pli *m*; (► *accidental)* faux pli *m*; *(in skin, on face)* pli *m*; **to put a c. in a pair of trousers** faire le pli d'un pantalon; **in order to get rid of the creases** *(in shirt, blouse etc)* pour le/la défroisser **2** *(in cricket)* limite *f* du batteur **3** *(of bullet* ► *scalp etc)* érafler

VT *(on purpose)* faire les plis de; *(accidentally)* froisser, chiffonner; **this shirt is all creased** cette chemise est toute froissée; **to c. one's brow** froncer les sourcils

VI *(clothes)* se froisser, se chiffonner; **his face creased with laughter** son visage s'est plissé de rire

▸ **crease up** *Fam* **VT SEP** faire mourir *ou* se tordre de rire

VI se tordre de rire

crease-resistant ADJ infroissable

create [kriːˈeɪt] **VT 1** *(employment, problem, difficulties, the world)* créer; *(fuss, noise, impression, draught)* faire; **to c. a stir** *or* **a sensation** faire sensation; **to c. a scene** *(fuss)* faire une scène; *Law* **to c. a disturbance** porter atteinte à l'ordre public **2** *(appoint)* **he was created (a) baron** il a été fait baron

VI 1 *(be creative)* créer **2** *Br Fam (cause a fuss)* faire des histoires

creation [kriːˈeɪʃən] **N 1** *(UNCOUNT) (process of creating)* création *f*; *Bible* **the C.** la Création **2** *(something created)* création *f*; **the latest creations** *(fashions)* les dernières créations **3** *(UNCOUNT) (universe)* création *f*; *Fam* **where in c. did you get that hat!** où diable as-tu trouvé ce chapeau!

creative [kriːˈeɪtɪv] **N** *(department, work)* création *f*; *(person)* créatif(ive) *m,f*

ADJ *(person, mind, skill)* créatif; **to encourage sb to be c.** encourager la créativité chez qn; **we need some c. thinking** nous avons besoin d'idées originales

►► *Euph* ***creative accounting*** *(manipulation of accounts)* comptabilité *f* fantaisiste; ***the creative instinct*** l'instinct *m* de création; ***creative writing*** techniques *fpl* de l'écriture; ***creative writing class*** atelier *m* d'écriture

creatively [kriːˈeɪtɪvlɪ] **ADV** de manière créative; **you're not thinking very c. about your future** tu n'as pas d'idées très originales pour ton avenir

creativeness [kriːˈeɪtɪvnɪs], **creativity** [ˌkriːeɪˈtɪvətɪ] **N** créativité *f*

creator [kriːˈeɪtə(r)] **N** créateur(trice) *m,f*; *Rel* **the C.** le Créateur

creature ['kriːtʃə(r)] **N 1** *(living being)* créature *f*, être *m* (vivant); **we are all God's creatures** nous sommes tous les créatures de Dieu; **creatures from outer space** des créatures *fpl* de l'espace

2 *(person)* créature *f*; **poor c.!** le/la pauvre!; **he's a c. of habit** il est esclave de ses habitudes

3 *(animal)* bête *f*; **dumb creatures** les bêtes *fpl*

4 *Literary Pej (dependent person)* créature *f*; **man is the c. of circumstances** l'homme dépend des circonstances

►► ***creature comforts*** confort *m* matériel; **I like my c. comforts** j'aime *ou* je suis attaché à mon (petit) confort

crèche [kreʃ] **N** *Br (nursery)* crèche *f*; *(in shopping centre, leisure complex)* garderie *f*

►► ***crèche facilities*** garderie *f*

cred [kred] **N** *Br Fam (credibility)* **to have (street) c.** être branché *ou* dans le coup

credence ['kriːdəns] **N 1** *(faith, belief)* croyance *f*, foi *f*; **to give** *or* **to attach c. to sth** ajouter foi à qch; **to give** *or* **to lend c. to sth** rendre qch crédible **2** *Rel* crédence *f (meuble)*

credential [krɪˈdenʃəl] *(pt & pp* **credentialed**, *cont* **credentialing) VT** *Am* fournir des références à

credentials [krɪˈdenʃəlz] **NPL 1** *(references, proof of ability)* références *fpl*; *Fig* **a film director with excellent c.** un metteur en scène aux excellents antécédents **2** *(identity papers)* papiers *mpl* d'identité; **to ask to see sb's c.** demander ses papiers (d'identité) à qn, demander une pièce d'identité à qn **3** *(of diplomat)* lettres *fpl* de créance

credibility [ˌkredəˈbɪlətɪ] **N 1** *(trustworthiness)* crédibilité *f*; **the party has lost c. with the electorate** le parti a perdu de sa crédibilité auprès de l'électorat; **he has a c. problem** il manque de crédibilité **2** *(belief)* **it's beyond c.** c'est invraisemblable, c'est difficile à croire

►► ***credibility gap*** manque *m* de crédibilité; **to narrow the c. gap** regagner de sa crédibilité; ***credibility rating*** crédibilité *f*

credible ['kredəbəl] **ADJ** *(person)* crédible; *(evidence, statement)* crédible, plausible; **it is hardly**

c. that… il est difficile à croire que… + *subjunctive*

credibly ['kredəblı] **ADV** *(argue)* de manière crédible

CREDIT ['kredıt]

N
- crédit **1**
- croyance **3**
- mérite **2**
- unité de valeur **4**

VT
- créditer **1**
- croire **3**
- supposer **2**

NPL
- générique

N 1 *Fin* crédit *m*; *(in an account)* avoir *m*; **to be in c.** *(person)* avoir de l'argent sur son compte; *(account)* être créditeur; **to get back into c.** *(person)* rembourser un découvert; *(account)* redevenir créditeur; **to enter** *or* **to place a sum to sb's c.** créditer le compte de qn d'une somme, porter une somme à l'actif de qn; **debit and c.** débit *m* et crédit *m*; **to give sb c., to give c. to sb** *(of bank)* accorder un découvert à qn; *(of shop, pub)* faire crédit à qn; **to run a c. check on sb** *(to ensure enough money in account)* vérifier la solvabilité de qn, vérifier que le compte de qn est approvisionné; *(to ensure no record of bad debts)* vérifier le passé bancaire de qn; **we do not give c.** *(sign)* la maison ne fait pas crédit; **to sell/to buy/to live on c.** vendre/acheter/vivre à crédit; **her c. is good** elle a une bonne réputation de solvabilité; *Fig (she is trustworthy)* elle est digne de confiance

2 *(merit, honour)* mérite *m*; **to take the c. for sth/doing sth** s'attribuer le mérite de qch/d'avoir fait qch; **I can't take all the c. for it** tout le mérite ne me revient pas; **to give sb the c. for sth/doing sth** attribuer à qn le mérite de qch/d'avoir fait qch; **management got all the c.** tout le mérite est revenu à la direction; **give her c. for what she has achieved** reconnais ce qu'elle a accompli; **with c.** *(perform)* honorablement; **nobody emerged with any c. except him** c'est le seul qui s'en soit sorti à son honneur; **it must be said to his c. that…** il faut dire en sa faveur que… + *indicative*; **to her c., she did finish the exam** il faut lui accorder qu'elle a fini l'examen; **she has five novels to her c.** elle a cinq romans à son actif; **to be a c. to one's family/school, to do one's family/school c.** faire honneur à sa famille/son école, être l'honneur de sa famille/son école; **it does her (great) c.** c'est tout à son honneur; **give me SOME c.** crédit! je ne suis quand même pas si bête!; **c. where c. is due** il faut reconnaître ce qui est

3 *(credence)* croyance *f*; **to give c. to sb/sth** ajouter foi à qn/qch; **to lend c. to sth** accréditer qch, rendre qch plausible; **the theory is gaining c.** cette théorie est de plus en plus acceptée; **he's cleverer than I gave him c. for** il est plus intelligent que je le pensais *ou* supposais

4 *Univ* unité *f* de valeur, UV *f*; **how many credits do you need?** combien d'UV faut-il que tu aies?

COMP *(boom)* du crédit; *(purchase, sale, transaction)* à crédit

VT 1 *Fin (account)* créditer; **to c. an account with £200, to c. £200 to an account** créditer un compte de 200 livres

2 *(accord)* **I credited her with more sense** je lui supposais plus de bon sens; **c. me with a bit more intelligence!** tu serais gentil de ne pas sous-estimer mon intelligence!; **he is credited with the discovery of DNA** on lui attribue la découverte de l'ADN

3 *(believe)* croire; **would you c. it!** tu te rends compte!; **you wouldn't c. some of the things he's done** tu n'en reviendrais pas si tu savais les choses qu'il a faites; **I could hardly c. it** j'avais du mal à le croire

• **credits NPL** *Cin & TV* générique *m*

►► ***credit account*** *Banking* compte *m* créditeur; *Br Com (with shop)* compte *m* client; ***credit advice*** avis *m* de crédit; ***credit agency*** institution *f* de crédit; ***credit agreement*** accord *m ou* convention *f* de crédit; *Acct & Banking* ***credit balance*** solde *m* créditeur; ***credit bank*** banque *f* de crédit; ***credit broker*** courtier(ère) *m,f* en crédits *ou* en prêts; ***credit card*** carte *f* de crédit; **to pay by c. card** payer avec une *ou* régler par carte de crédit; ***credit card fraud*** usage *m* frauduleux de cartes de crédit; ***credit card reader*** lecteur *m* de cartes; ***credit ceiling*** plafond *m* de crédit; *Acct* ***credit column*** colonne *f* créditrice; ***credit control*** *(government restrictions)* resserrement *m ou* encadrement *m* du crédit; *(monitoring)* surveillance *f* des crédits; ***credit controller*** contrôleur(euse) *m,f* du crédit; ***credit crunch*** resserrement *m* du crédit; ***credit entry*** *Banking* article *m* porté au crédit d'un compte; *Acct* écriture *f* au crédit; ***credit facilities*** facilités *fpl* de crédit; ***credit freeze*** blocage *m* du crédit; ***credit history*** profil *m* crédit; **to obtain information on sb's c. history** établir des renseignements de solvabilité sur qn; ***credit limit*** limite *f ou* plafond *m* de crédit; ***credit line*** *Br (loan)* autorisation *f* de crédit; *Am (limit)* limite *f ou* plafond *m* de crédit; *Br* ***credit note*** *(in business)* facture *f ou* note *f* d'avoir; *(in shop)* avoir *m*; ***credit rating*** *(of person, company)* degré *m* de solvabilité; *(awarded by credit reference agency)* notation *f*; ***credit rating agency, credit reference agency*** agence *f* de notation; ***credit risk*** risque *m* de crédit; **to be a good/bad c. risk** représenter un risque peu important/important; *Acct* ***credit side*** crédit *m*, avoir *m*; *Fig* **on the c. side, the proposed changes will cut costs** les changements projetés auront l'avantage de réduire les coûts; *Fig* **on the c. side, he's a good cook** il faut lui accorder qu'il cuisine bien; ***credit squeeze*** restriction *f ou* encadrement *m* du crédit; ***credit terms*** modalités *fpl* de crédit; *Banking* ***credit transfer*** virement *m*, transfert *m* (de compte à compte); ***credit union*** société *f ou* caisse *f* de crédit; ***credit voucher*** chèque *m* de caisse

creditable ['kredıtəbəl] **ADJ** honorable, estimable

creditably ['kredıtəblı] **ADV** honorablement

creditor ['kredıtə(r)] **N** *Fin* créancier(ère) *m,f*

►► ***creditor countries, creditor nations*** pays *mpl* créditeurs

creditworthiness ['kredıt,wɜːðınıs] **N** *Com & Fin* solvabilité *f*

creditworthy ['kredıt,wɜːðı] **ADJ** *Com & Fin* solvable

credo ['kreıdəʊ] *(pl* **credos***)* **N** credo *m inv*

credulity [krı'djuːlətı] **N** crédulité *f*

credulous ['kredjʊləs] **ADJ** crédule, naïf

creed [kriːd] **N** *(religious)* credo *m inv*, croyance *f*; *(political)* credo *m inv*; **people of every colour and c.** des gens de toutes races et de toutes croyances; *Rel* **the (Apostles') C.** le Credo

creek [kriːk] **N** *Br (of sea)* crique *f*, anse *f*; *Am, Austr & NZ (stream)* ruisseau *m*; *(river)* rivière *f*; *Fam* **to be up the c. (without a paddle)** être dans de beaux draps *ou* dans le pétrin

creel [kriːl] **N** *(for fish)* panier *m* à poisson; *(for catching lobsters)* casier *m*

CREEP [kriːp] *(pt & pp* **crept** [krept]*)* **N** *Fam (unpleasant person)* sale type *m*; *Br (obsequious person)* lèche-bottes *mf inv*; **I can't stand that c. she's married to** je ne peux pas sentir ce sale type avec qui elle est mariée

VI 1 *(person, animal)* se glisser; **to c. into a room** entrer sans bruit *ou* se glisser dans une pièce; **I crept upstairs** je suis monté sans bruit; **I can hear somebody creeping about downstairs** j'entends quelqu'un bouger en bas; **the dog crept under the chair** le chien s'est tapi sous la chaise; **the shadows crept across the lawn** l'ombre a peu à peu envahi la pelouse; **the hours crept slowly by** les heures se sont écoulées lentement; *Fig* **a moralizing tone has crept into her writing** un ton moralisateur s'est insidieusement glissé dans ses écrits; **a feeling of uneasiness crept over me** un sentiment de gêne commençait à me gagner

2 *(plant* ► *along the ground)* ramper; *(*► *upwards)* grimper

3 *(be obsequious)* **she's always creeping to the teacher** elle est toujours en train de ramper devant le professeur

4 *(idiom)* **to make sb's flesh c.** donner la chair de poule à qn, faire froid dans le dos à qn

• **creeps NPL** *Fam* **he gives me the creeps** *(is frightening)* il me fait froid dans le dos▫, il me donne la chair de poule▫; *(is repulsive)* il me dégoûte▫ *ou* répugne▫

► **creep along VI** *(stealthily)* s'avancer furtivement, marcher à pas de loup; *(move slowly, in car etc)* se traîner

► **creep away VI** s'éloigner à pas de loup

► **creep up VI 1** *(approach)* s'approcher sans bruit; **to c. up to sth** s'approcher sans bruit de qch; **to c. up behind sb** s'approcher doucement *ou* discrètement de qn par derrière **2** *(increase* ► *water, prices)* monter lentement; *(*► *sales)* monter petit à petit; **the speedometer crept up to 120** l'aiguille de l'indicateur de vitesse est montée tout doucement jusqu'à 120

► **creep up on VT INSEP 1** *(in order to attack, surprise)* s'approcher discrètement de, s'approcher à pas de loup de; **don't c. up on me like that!** ne t'approche pas de moi sans faire de bruit comme ça!; **old age crept up on me** je suis devenu vieux sans m'en rendre compte **2** *(catch up with* ► *in competition, business etc)* rattraper peu à peu; **the deadline is creeping up on us** la date limite se rapproche

creeper ['kriːpə(r)] **N 1** *(plant* ► *that creeps upwards)* plante *f* grimpante; *(*► *that creeps along the ground)* plante *f* rampante

2 *Br Fam (shoe)* chaussure *f* à semelles de crêpe▫

3 *Am* **creepers** *(crampons)* crampons *mpl* à verglas

4 *Am* **creepers** *(child's garment)* barboteuse *f*

creeping ['kriːpıŋ] **ADJ 1** *(plant* ► *upwards)* grimpant; *(*► *along the ground)* rampant

2 *(animal, insect)* rampant

3 *Fig (inflation)* rampant; *(change)* graduel

4 *Fam (obsequious)* servile▫, rampant▫

N *Fam (obsequiousness)* servilité▫ *f*

►► *Med* ***creeping paralysis*** paralysie *f* progressive

creepy ['kriːpı] *(compar* **creepier**, *superl* **creepiest***)* **ADJ** *Fam* qui donne la chair de poule▫, qui fait froid dans le dos▫; **he's/it's c.** il/ça vous donne la chair de poule

creepy-crawly [-'krɔːlı] *(pl* **creepy-crawlies***)*, *Am* **creepy-crawler** [-'krɔːlə(r)] *Fam* **N** petite bestiole *f*

ADJ a horrible c. feeling une très désagréable sensation de fourmillement▫

cremate [krı'meıt] **VT** incinérer

cremation [krı'meıʃən] **N** incinération *f*, crémation *f*

crematorium [,kremə'tɔːrıəm] *(pl* **crematoria** [-rıə] *or* **crematoriums***)* **N** *(establishment)* crématorium *m*; *(furnace)* four *m* crématoire

crematory ['kremə,tɔːrı] *(pl* **crematories***)* **N** *Am (establishment)* crématorium *m*; *(furnace)* four *m* crématoire

crenellated, *Am* **crenelated** ['krenə,leıtıd] **ADJ** *Archit* crénelé, à créneaux

Creole ['kriːəʊl] **N 1** *(person)* Créole *mf* **2** *(language)* créole *m*

ADJ créole

creosote ['krıəsəʊt] **N** créosote *f*

VT traiter à la créosote

crepe [kreıp, krep] **N 1** *Tex (fabric)* crêpe *m*

2 *(crepe rubber)* crêpe *m*

3 *(crepe paper)* papier *m* crépon

4 *Culin (pancake)* crêpe *f*

COMP *(skirt, blouse etc)* de *ou* en crêpe

►► ***crepe bandage*** bande *f* Velpeau®; ***crepe de Chine*** crêpe *m* de Chine; ***crepe paper*** papier *m* crépon; ***crepe rubber*** crêpe *m*; ***crepe soles*** semelles *fpl* de crêpe

crepe-soled ADJ à semelle(s) de crêpe

crept [krept] *pt & pp of* **creep**

Cres. *Br (written abbr* **Crescent***)* rue *f*

crescendo [krı'ʃendəʊ] *(pl* **crescendos** *or* **crescendi** [-dı]*)* **N** *Mus & Fig* crescendo *m*; *Mus* **to build up to a c.** aller crescendo; *Fig* **to reach a c.** atteindre son paroxysme

VI *(gen)* augmenter; *Mus* faire un crescendo

ADV *Mus* crescendo, en augmentant

crescent ['kresənt] **N 1** *(shape)* croissant *m*; *Rel* **the C.** *(Islamic emblem)* le Croissant **2** *Br (street)* rue *f (en arc de cercle)*

ADJ *(shaped)* **c.(-shaped)** en (forme de) croissant

►► **crescent moon** croissant *m* de lune; *Am Culin* **crescent roll** croissant *m*

cress [kres] **N** cresson *m*

crest [krest] **N 1** *(peak ► of hill, wave)* crête *f*; *(► of ridge)* arête *f*; *(► of road)* haut *m ou* sommet *m* de côte; *Fig* **she's (riding) on the c. of a wave just now** tout lui réussit *ou* elle a le vent en poupe en ce moment

2 *(on chicken, lizard)* crête *f*; *(of bird)* huppe *f*; *(of peacock)* aigrette *f*

3 *(on helmet)* cimier *m*

4 *Her (coat of arms)* timbre *m*; *(emblem)* armoiries *fpl*; **a family c.** des armoiries *fpl* familiales

5 *Anat (of bone)* crête *f*, arête *f*

VT 1 *(reach the top of)* franchir la crête de **2** *Her (provide with emblem)* armorier

crested ['krestɪd] **ADJ 1** *(chicken, lizard)* orné d'une crête; *(bird)* huppé **2** *(helmet)* orné d'un cimier; *(plumed)* panaché **3** *Her (with emblem)* armorié

►► *Orn* **crested tit** mésange *f* huppée

crestfallen ['krest,fɔːlən] **ADJ** découragé, déconfit; **he looked c.** il avait l'air abattu *ou* déconfit

cretaceous [krɪ'teɪʃəs] *Geol* **N the C.** le crétacé

ADJ crétacé

►► **the Cretaceous period** le crétacé

Cretan ['kriːtən] **N** Crétois(e) *m,f*

ADJ crétois

Crete [kriːt] **N** Crète *f*

cretin ['kretɪn] **N 1** *Med* crétin(e) *m,f* **2** *Fam (idiot)* crétin(e)ᵒ *m,f*, imbécileᵒ *mf*

cretinism ['kretɪnɪzəm] **N** *Med* crétinisme *m*

cretinous ['kretɪnəs] **ADJ** *Med & Fig* crétin

cretonne ['kretɒn] **N** *Tex* cretonne *f*

Creutzfeldt-Jakob disease ['krɔɪtsfelt-'jækɒb-] **N** *Med* maladie *f* de Creutzfeldt-Jakob

crevasse [krɪ'væs] **N** *Geol* crevasse *f*; *Am (in dam)* crevasse *f*, fissure *f*

crevice ['krevɪs] **N** fissure *f*, fente *f*

crew [kruː] *Br pt of* **crow**

N 1 *(in rowing)* équipe *f*; *(on plane, ship)* équipage *m*; *Cin & TV* équipe *f*; **ambulance/camera c.** équipe *f* d'ambulanciers/de cameramen **2** *Fam (crowd, gang)* bande *f*, équipeᵒ *f*; **what a c.!** (quelle) drôle d'équipe!; **they're a good c. to work with** c'est une bonne équipe avec qui travailler

VI to c. for sb être l'équipier de qn

VT *(ship)* armer d'un équipage; *(plane)* fournir un équipage à; **this yacht can't be crewed by fewer than six** ce yacht exige un équipage de six au moins; *Naut* **crewed charter** location *f* de bateau avec équipage

►► **crew cut** coupe *f* de cheveux en brosse; **c. cuts are in fashion again** les cheveux en brosse reviennent à la mode; **crew member** membre *mf* d'équipage; **crew neck** col *m* ras le *ou* du cou, ras-ducou *m inv*

crib [krɪb] *(pt & pp* **cribbed**, *cont* **cribbing**) **N 1** *esp Am (cot)* lit *m* d'enfant

2 *(bin)* grenier *m* (à blé); *(stall)* stalle *f*

3 *(manger)* mangeoire *f*, râtelier *m*; *Rel* crèche *f*

4 *Fam (plagiarism)* plagiatᵒ *m*; *Br Sch (list of answers)* antisèche *f*

5 *(UNCOUNT) Cards (cribbage)* = jeu de cartes où l'on marque les points à l'aide de fiches que l'on enfonce sur une planche de bois

VT 1 *Fam (plagiarize)* plagierᵒ, copierᵒ; *Sch* **he cribbed the answers from his friend** il a copié les réponses sur son amiᵒ, il a pompé sur son ami **2** *Tech (line with planks)* boiser

VI copier; **the author had cribbed from Shaw** l'auteur avait plagié Shaw; *Sch* **don't c. off me!** ne copie pas sur moi!

►► *Am* **crib death** mort *f* subite (du nourrisson)

cribbage ['krɪbɪdʒ] **N** *(UNCOUNT)* = jeu de cartes où l'on marque les points à l'aide de fiches que l'on enfonce sur une planche de bois

crick [krɪk] **N 1 to have a c. in one's neck** avoir un torticolis; **a c. in one's back** un tour de reins **2** *Am Fam (stream)* ruisseauᵒ *m*

VT to c. one's neck attraper un torticolis; **to c. one's back** se faire un tour de reins

cricket ['krɪkɪt] **N 1** *Entom* grillon *m* **2** *(game)* cricket *m*; **to play c.** jouer au cricket; *Br Fam* **that's not c.** ça ne se fait pasᵒ, ce n'est pas fair-playᵒ

COMP *(ball, bat, match)* de cricket

►► **cricket field, cricket pitch** terrain *m* de cricket

cricketer ['krɪkɪtə(r)] **N** joueur(euse) *m,f* de cricket

crier ['kraɪə(r)] **N** *Hist* crieur(euse) *m,f*; *(in court)* huissier *m* d'audience

crikey ['kraɪkɪ] **EXCLAM** *Br Fam Old-fashioned* mince alors!

crim [krɪm] **N** *Br & Austr Fam (criminal)* criminel (elle)ᵒ *m,f*

Crimbo ['krɪmbəʊ] **N** *Br Fam (Christmas)* Noëlᵒ *m*

crime [kraɪm] **N 1** *(act)* crime *m*; *(phenomenon)* criminalité *f*; **c. is on the decline** il y a une baisse de la criminalité; **a life of c.** une vie de criminel; **c. doesn't pay** le crime ne paie pas; **a minor** *or* **petty c.** un délit mineur; **a c. against humanity** un crime contre l'humanité; *Law* **a c. of passion** un crime passionnel; *Fig* **it's a c. that she died so young** c'est vraiment injuste qu'elle soit morte si jeune; *Fig* **it's not a c. to...** ce n'est pas un crime de... **2** *Mil* manquement *m* à la discipline, infraction *f*

►► **crime fiction** romans *mpl* policiers; **crime figures** chiffres *mpl* de la criminalité; **crime prevention** lutte *f* contre la délinquance; **crime prevention officer** = agent de police chargé d'informer le public sur les moyens de lutter efficacement contre la délinquance; **crime rate** taux *m* de (la) délinquance; **crime scene** lieu *m* du crime; **crime series** série *f* policière; **crime wave** vague *f* de delinquance; **crime writer** auteur *m* de romans policiers

Crimea [kraɪ'mɪə] **N** *Hist* **the C.** la Crimée

Crimean [kraɪ'mɪən] *Hist* **N** Criméen(enne) *m,f*

ADJ criméen

►► **the Crimean War** la guerre de Crimée

criminal ['krɪmɪnəl] **N** criminel(elle) *m,f*

ADJ criminel; *Fig* **it would be c. to cut down these trees** ce serait un crime d'abattre ces arbres; *Fig* **it's c. the way he treats her** il ne devrait pas avoir le droit de la traiter comme ça

►► *Law* **criminal assault** agression *f* criminelle, voie *f* de fait; *Am Law* **criminal code** code *m* pénal; *Law* **criminal conversation** adultère *m*; *Law* **criminal court** cour *f* d'assises; *Law* **criminal damage** = délit consistant à causer volontairement des dégâts matériels; *Law* **criminal intent** malveillance *f*; **criminal investigation** enquête *f* criminelle; *Br* **Criminal Investigation Department** = police judiciaire britannique, PJ *f*; **criminal justice system** justice *f* pénale; **criminal law** droit *m* pénal *ou* criminel; **criminal lawyer** avocat(e) *m,f* au criminel, pénaliste *mf*; *Law* **criminal liability** responsabilité *f* pénale, majorité *f* pénale; *Law* **criminal negligence** négligence *f* coupable *ou* criminelle; *Law* **criminal offence** délit *m* pénal; **drink-driving is a c. offence** la conduite en état d'ivresse est un crime puni par la loi; *Law* **criminal proceedings** poursuites *fpl* au pénal; **to take** *or* **institute c. proceedings against sb** poursuivre qn au pénal; *Law* **criminal record** casier *m* judiciaire; **she hasn't got a c. record** son casier judiciaire est vierge, elle n'a pas de casier judiciaire; *Br* **Criminal Records Bureau**, *Scot* **Criminal Records Office** identité *f* judiciaire

criminalization, -isation [,krɪmɪnəlaɪ'zeɪʃən] **N** criminalisation *f*

criminalize, -ise ['krɪmɪnəlaɪz] **VT** criminaliser

criminally ['krɪmɪnəlɪ] **ADV** criminellement; **to be c. insane** être dément; **the c. insane** les fous dangereux; **he's been c. negligent** sa négligence est criminelle; *Fig* **it's c. wasteful** c'est un crime de gaspiller comme ça

criminologist [,krɪmɪ'nɒlədʒɪst] **N** criminologiste *mf*

criminology [,krɪmɪ'nɒlədʒɪ] **N** criminologie *f*

crimp [krɪmp] **VT 1** *(hair)* friser; *(pie crust)* pincer; *(metal)* onduler **2** *Fam (pinch together)* pincerᵒ, sertirᵒ **3** *Am Fam (hinder)* gênerᵒ, entraverᵒ

N 1 *(wave in hair)* cran *m*, ondulation *f*; *(fold in metal)* ondulation *f* **2** *Am Fam (obstacle)* obstacleᵒ *m*, entraveᵒ *f* **3** *(in cloth)* pli *m*

Crimplene® ['krɪmpliːn] **N** *Br* crêpe *m* polyester

crimson ['krɪmzən] **ADJ** cramoisi; **she turned c. with** *or* **in embarrassment** elle a rougi *ou* est devenue cramoisie de confusion; **the evening sky turned c.** le ciel nocturne est devenu pourpre *ou* s'est empourpré

N cramoisi *m*

cringe [krɪndʒ] **N** *Pej* **the c. factor usually associated with that type of Hollywood film** le côté insupportablement mélo de ce genre de production hollywoodienne

VI 1 *(shrink back)* avoir un mouvement de recul, reculer; *(cower)* se recroqueviller; **to c. in terror** reculer de peur; **the dog cringed in the corner** le chien se blottit dans le coin **2** *Fam (wince)* avoir envie de rentrer sous terreᵒ; **to c. with embarrassment** être mort de honte; **it's so sentimental, it makes me c.!** un tel mélo, ça me fait fuir!; **I c. at the very thought** j'ai envie de rentrer sous terre rien que d'y penser **3** *(be servile)* s'humilier, ramper, s'aplatir (**before sb** devant qn)

cringe-making **ADJ** *Br Fam* embarrassantᵒ, gênantᵒ

cringing ['krɪndʒɪŋ] **ADJ** *(fearful)* craintif; *(servile)* servile, obséquieux

crinkle ['krɪŋkəl] **VT** froisser, chiffonner; **to c. one's nose** froncer le nez

VI se froisser, se chiffonner; **his nose crinkled at the smell** l'odeur lui fit froncer le nez

N 1 *(wrinkle)* fronce *f*, pli *m*; *(on face)* ride *f* **2** *(noise)* froissement *m*

crinkle-cut **ADJ** *(chips, crisps)* dentelé

crinkly ['krɪŋklɪ] *(compar* **crinklier**, *superl* **crinkliest**) **ADJ** *(material, paper)* gaufré; *(hair)* crépu, crêpelé; **my fingers have gone all c.** la peau de mes doigts est toute fripée

crinoline ['krɪnəliːn] **N** crinoline *f*

cripes [kraɪps] **EXCLAM** *Br Fam Old-fashioned* sapristi!, mince!

cripple ['krɪpəl] **VT 1** *(person)* estropier **2** *Fig (damage ► industry, country, system)* paralyser; *(► plane, ship)* désemparer; *(► machine)* empêcher de fonctionner; *(► tank)* mettre hors de combat

N 1 *Fam (lame person)* estropié(e) *m,f*; *(invalid)* invalide *mf*; *(maimed person)* mutilé(e) *m,f* **2** *Fig* **he's an emotional c.** il est incapable d'exprimer ses émotions

crippled ['krɪpəld] **ADJ 1** *(person)* estropié, infirme; **to be c. with rheumatism** être perclus de rhumatismes **2** *Fig (industry, country, system)* paralysé; *(plane, ship)* désemparé; *(machine)* hors d'usage; *(tank)* hors de combat; **the country is c. with debt** le pays est paralysé par les dettes

crippling ['krɪpəlɪŋ] **ADJ 1** *(disease)* invalidant **2** *Fig (strikes)* paralysant; *(prices, taxes)* écrasant; **the c. effect of the blockade** l'effet *m* paralysant du blocus

crisis ['kraɪsɪs] *(pl* **crises** [-siːz]) **N** crise *f*, **things have come to a c.** la situation est à un point critique; **a minor family c.** un petit problème familial; **the government has a c. on its hands** le gouvernement se trouve face à une crise; **to settle** *or* **to resolve a c.** dénouer *ou* résoudre une crise; **the oil c.** le choc pétrolier; **an emotional c.** un passage difficile *(nerveusement)*

►► **crisis centre** *(for disasters)* cellule *f* de crise; *(for personal help)* centre *m* d'aide; *(for battered women)* association *f* d'aide d'urgence; **crisis of confidence** crise *f* de confiance; **crisis management** gestion *f* des crises; **crisis point** point *m* critique

crisp [krɪsp] **ADJ 1** *(crunchy ► vegetable, apple, lettuce)* croquant; *(► cracker, biscuit, pastry)* croquant, croustillant; *(► bread, bacon)* croustillant; *(► snow)* craquant; **the snow was c. underfoot** la neige craquait sous mes/nos/*etc* pas

2 *(fresh ► clothing)* pimpant; *(► linen)* apprêté; *(► paper)* craquant, raide; **a c. five pound note** un billet de cinq livres tout neuf

3 *(air, weather)* vif, tonifiant

4 *(concise ► style)* précis, clair et net

5 *(brusque)* tranchant, brusque; *(manner)* brusque; *(tone)* acerbe

N 1 *Br* **(potato) c.** (pomme *f*) chips *f*, *Can* croustille *f* **2** *Fam* **to be burnt to a c.** être carbonisé

VT faire chauffer pour rendre croustillant

VI devenir croustillant

crispbread ['krɪspbred] **N** *Culin* pain *m* suédois

crisper [ˈkrɪspə(r)] **N** *(in refrigerator)* bac *m* à légumes

crisply [ˈkrɪsplɪ] **ADV 1** *(succinctly)* avec concision **2** *(sharply)* d'un ton acerbe *ou* cassant

crispness [ˈkrɪspnɪs] **N 1** *(of vegetable, apple, lettuce)* croquant *m*; *(of cracker, biscuit, pastry)* croquant *m*, croustillant *m*; *(of bread, bacon)* croustillant *m*; *(of snow)* caractère *m* craquant
2 *(of clothing, linen)* fraîcheur *f*; *(of paper)* raideur *f*
3 *(of air, weather)* fraîcheur *f* vivifiante
4 *(of style)* précision *f*
5 *(brusqueness)* tranchant *m*, brusquerie *f*

crispy [ˈkrɪspɪ] *(compar* **crispier**, *superl* **crispiest)** **ADJ** *(vegetable)* croquant, *(biscuit)* croquant, croustillant; *(bacon)* croustillant

crisscross [ˈkrɪsˌkrɒs] **VT** entrecroiser; **a network of streets crisscrosses the town** un réseau de rues quadrille la ville; **a brow crisscrossed with wrinkles** un front sillonné de rides
VI s'entrecroiser
ADJ *(lines)* entrecroisé; *(in disorder)* enchevêtré; **in a c. pattern** en croisillons
N entrecroisement *m*; **a c. of paths** un réseau de chemins
ADV en réseau

crit [krɪt] **N** *Fam (criticism)* critique□ *f*

criterion [kraɪˈtɪərɪən] *(pl* **criteria** [-rɪə]) **N** critère *m*; **what criteria do you apply** *or* **what are your criteria when selecting candidates?** sur quels critères vous fondez-vous *ou* quels sont vos critères lorsque vous sélectionnez des candidats?

critic [ˈkrɪtɪk] **N** *(reviewer)* critique *mf*; *(fault-finder)* critique *mf*, détracteur(trice) *m,f*; **film/art/theatre c.** critique *mf* de cinéma/d'art/de théâtre; **she has her critics** il y en a qui la critiquent; **there are few critics of the policy** peu de gens critiquent la politique

critical [ˈkrɪtɪkəl] **ADJ 1** *(crucial)* critique, crucial; *(situation)* critique; **at a c. time** à un moment critique *ou* crucial; **he's in a c. condition** *or* **on the c. list** il est dans un état critique; **the next few days will be c.** les prochains jours seront décisifs
2 *(analytical)* critique; *(disparaging)* critique, négatif; **to be c. of sb/sth** *(person)* se montrer *ou* être critique à l'égard de qn/qch; *(report, article etc)* être critique à l'égard de qn/qch; **he's very c. of others** il critique beaucoup les autres, il est très critique vis-à-vis des autres; **to look at sth with a c. eye** regarder qch d'un œil critique; **don't be so c.** ne soyez pas si négatif
3 *(analysis, edition)* critique; *(essay, study)* critique, de critique; *(from the critics)* des critiques; **the play met with c. acclaim** la pièce fut applaudie par la critique
4 *Phys* critique; **the nuclear reactor went c.** le réacteur a atteint le seuil critique
▸▸ *Phys* ***critical angle*** angle *m* critique; *Phys* ***critical mass*** masse *f* critique; *Com & Tech* ***critical path*** chemin *m* critique; *Com & Tech* ***critical path analysis*** analyse *f* du chemin critique; *Com & Tech* ***critical path method*** méthode *f* du chemin critique; *Phys* ***critical temperature*** température *f* critique

critically [ˈkrɪtɪkəlɪ] **ADV 1** *(analytically)* d'un œil critique, en critique; *(disparagingly)* sévèrement **2** *(seriously)* gravement; **she is c. ill** elle est gravement malade, elle est dans un état critique **3** *(crucially)* **c. important** d'une importance vitale

criticism [ˈkrɪtɪˌsɪzəm] **N 1** *(action, act of criticizing)* critique *f*; **to come in for c.** se faire *ou* se voir critiquer; **to lay oneself open to c.** s'exposer à la critique; **this isn't meant as a c., but…** ce n'est pas une critique, mais…, ce n'est pas pour critiquer, mais…; **the report contained strong c. of this department** le rapport contenait de graves critiques de ce service **2** *(of film, book, work of art etc)* critique *f*

criticize, -ise [ˈkrɪtɪsaɪz] **VT 1** *(find fault with)* critiquer, réprouver; **to c. sb for sth** critiquer qn pour qch; **to c. sb for doing sth** critiquer qn d'avoir fait qch; **they have been criticized for not trying** on leur a reproché de ne pas avoir essayé; **his report has been criticized for being too…** on a reproché à son rapport d'être trop… **2** *(film, book, work of art etc)* critiquer, faire la critique de
VI critiquer; **stop criticizing** arrête de critiquer *ou* de faire des critiques

critique [krɪˈtiːk] **N** critique *f*
VT faire une critique de

critter [ˈkrɪtə(r)] **N** *Am Fam (creature)* créature□ *f*; *(animal)* bête□ *f*, bestiole *f*

CRM [ˌsiːɑːˈrem] **N** *Com & Mktg (abbr* **customer relationship management)** gestion *f* de la relation client

CRN [ˌsiːɑːˈren] **N** *Com (abbr* **customs registered number)** numéro *m* d'enregistrement douanier

croak [krəʊk] **VI 1** *(frog)* coasser; *(crow)* croasser **2** *(person)* parler d'une voix rauque **3** *Fam (die)* crever
VT *(utter)* dire d'une voix rauque *ou* éraillée
N *(of frog)* coassement *m*; *(of crow)* croassement *m*; *(of person)* ton *m* rauque

croaking [ˈkrəʊkɪŋ] **N** *(of frog)* coassement *m*; *(of crow)* croassement *m*

croaky [ˈkrəʊkɪ] *(compar* **croakier**, *superl* **croakiest)** **N 1** *(person)* Croate *mf* **2** *(language)* croate *m*
ADJ enroué

Croat [ˈkrəʊæt] **ADJ** croate

Croatia [krəʊˈeɪʃə] **N** Croatie *f*

Croatian [krəʊˈeɪʃən] **N 1** *(person)* Croate *mf* **2** *(language)* croate *m*
ADJ croate
COMP *(embassy)* de Croatie; *(history)* de la Croatie; *(teacher)* de croate

croc [krɒk] **N** *Fam* crocodile □ *m*

crochet [ˈkrəʊʃeɪ] **N c. (work)** (travail *m* au) crochet *m*
VT faire au crochet
VI faire du crochet

crocheting [ˈkrəʊʃeɪɪŋ] **N** (travail *m* au) crochet *m*

crock [krɒk] **N 1** *(jar, pot)* cruche *f*, pot *m* de terre; *(broken earthenware)* morceau *m* de faïence, tesson *m*; *Am very Fam* **that's a c. (of shit)!** tout ça, c'est des conneries! **2** *Br Fam* **old c.** *(car)* tacot *m*, guimbarde *f*; *(person)* croulant(e) *m,f*
● **crocks NPL** *Fam* vaisselle□ *f*

crockery [ˈkrɒkərɪ] **N** *(pottery)* poterie *f*, faïence *f*, *(plates, cups, bowls etc)* vaisselle *f*

crocodile [ˈkrɒkədaɪl] **N 1** *(reptile)* crocodile *m* **2** *Br Sch* cortège *m* en rangs *(par deux)*; **to walk in a c.** marcher deux par deux
COMP *(shoes, handbag)* en crocodile
▸▸ ***crocodile clip*** pince *f* crocodile; ***crocodile skin*** peau *f* de crocodile; ***crocodile tears*** larmes *fpl* de crocodile

crocus [ˈkrəʊkəs] **N** crocus *m*

croft [krɒft] **N** petite ferme *f*

crofter [ˈkrɒftə(r)] **N** *(farmer)* petit fermier *m*

Crohn's disease [ˈkrəʊnz-] **N** *Med* maladie *f* de Crohn

crone [krəʊn] **N** *Fam* vieille bique *f*

crony [ˈkrəʊnɪ] *(pl* **cronies)** **N** *Fam* pote *m*, copain (copine) *m,f*
▸▸ ***crony capitalism*** capitalisme *m* de copinage

cronyism [ˈkrəʊnɪɪzəm] **N** *Pej* copinage *m*

crook [krʊk] **N 1** *Fam (thief)* escroc *m*, filou *m* **2** *(bend* ▸ *in road)* courbe *f*, coude *m*; *(*▸ *in river)* coude *m*, détour *m*; *(*▸ *in arm)* creux *m*; *(*▸ *in leg)* flexion *f*; **in the c. of her arm** dans le creux de son bras **3** *(staff* ▸ *of shepherd)* houlette *f*; *(*▸ *of bishop)* crosse *f*
ADJ *Austr & NZ Fam (ill)* mal fichu; *(not working)* détraqué
VT *(finger)* courber, recourber; *(arm)* plier

crooked [ˈkrʊkɪd] **ADJ 1** *(not straight, bent* ▸ *stick)* courbé, crochu, *Can* croche; *(*▸ *path)* tortueux; *(*▸ *person)* courbé; **his hat was on c.** son chapeau était de travers; **a c. smile** un sourire en coin **2** *Fam (dishonest)* malhonnête□, *Can* croche
ADV de travers

crookedly [ˈkrʊkɪdlɪ] **ADV 1** *(walk, stand)* de travers **2** *(smile)* **to smile c.** avoir un sourire en coin

crookedness [ˈkrʊkɪdnɪs] **N 1** *(of outlines etc)* irrégularité *f*; *(curvature)* courbure *f* **2** *Fam (dishonesty)* malhonnêteté□ *f*, fausseté□ *f*

croon [kruːn] **VI & VT 1** *(sing softly)* fredonner, chantonner; *(professionally)* chanter *(en crooner)* **2** *(speak softly, sentimentally)* susurrer
N fredonnement *m*

crooner [ˈkruːnə(r)] **N** crooner *m*, chanteur (euse) *m,f* de charme

crop [krɒp] *(pt & pp* **cropped**, *cont* **cropping)** **N 1** *(produce)* produit *m* agricole, culture *f*; *(harvest)* récolte *f*; *(of fruit)* récolte *f*, cueillette *f*; *(of grain)* moisson *f*; **food crops** cultures *fpl* vivrières; **to get in** *or* **to harvest the crops** faire la récolte, rentrer les récoltes; **a poor/good c.** une mauvaise/bonne récolte; **we had a good wheat c.** *or* **c. of wheat** le blé a bien donné
2 *Fig* fournée *f*; **what do you think of this year's c. of students?** que pensez-vous des étudiants de cette année?
3 *(of whip)* manche *m*; *(riding whip)* cravache *f*
4 *(of bird)* jabot *m*
5 *(haircut* ▸ *for man)* coupe *f* rase *ou* courte; *(*▸ *for woman)* coupe *f* courte *ou* à la garçonne; **the barber gave me a (close) c.** le coiffeur m'a coupé les cheveux ras
VT 1 *(cut* ▸ *hedge)* tailler, tondre; *(*▸ *hair)* tondre; *(*▸ *tail)* écourter; **cropped trousers** pantacourt *m*
2 *Phot* recadrer; *Comput & Typ (graphic)* rogner
3 *(of animal)* brouter, paître
4 *(farm)* cultiver; *(harvest)* récolter
VI *(land, vegetables)* donner *ou* fournir une récolte; **to c. well** donner une bonne récolte
▸▸ ***crop circle*** = motif circulaire tracé dans un champ, attribué par certains à l'intervention d'extraterrestres; *Agr* ***crop dusting*** pulvérisation *f* des cultures; *Comput & Typ* ***crop mark*** trait *m* de coupe; *Agr* ***crop rotation*** assolement *m*, rotation *f* des cultures; *Agr* ***crop spraying*** pulvérisation *f* des cultures; ***crop top*** top *m* court

▸ **crop up VI** survenir, se présenter; **his name cropped up in the conversation** son nom a surgi dans la conversation; **we'll deal with anything that crops up while you're away** on s'occupera de tout pendant votre absence; **something has cropped up** j'ai un empêchement

cropper [ˈkrɒpə(r)] **N** *Br Fam* **to come a c.** *(fall)* se casser la figure; *(fail)* se planter; **I came a c. in the exams** je me suis ramassé *ou* planté aux examens

cropping [ˈkrɒpɪŋ] **N** *Comput & Typ (of graphic)* rognage *m*, recadrage *m*

croquet [ˈkrəʊkeɪ] **N** croquet *m*; **to play c.** jouer au croquet
COMP *(hoop, lawn, mallet)* de croquet

croquette [krɒˈket] **N** *Culin* croquette *f*; **potato c.** croquette *f* de pomme de terre

crosier [ˈkrəʊʒjə(r)] **N** *Rel* crosse *f* *(d'évêque)*

CROSS [krɒs]

N
- croix **1, 2**
- hybride **3**
- biais **4**

VT
- traverser **1**
- croiser **2, 4**
- faire une croix **3**
- contrarier **5**

VI
- traverser **1**
- se croiser **2**

ADJ
- de mauvaise humeur **1**
- diagonal **2**

N 1 *(mark, symbol)* croix *f*; **he signed with a c.** il a signé d'une croix; **the Iron C.** la Croix de fer
2 *Rel & Fig (burden)* croix *f*; **the C.** la Croix; **to make the sign of the c.** faire le signe de (la) croix; **we each have our c. to bear** chacun porte sa croix
3 *(hybrid)* hybride *m*, croisement *m*; **a c. between a horse and a donkey** un croisement *ou* hybride du cheval et de l'ânesse; *Fig* **the novel is a c. between a thriller and a comedy** ce roman est un mélange de policier et de comédie
4 *(in sewing)* **on the c.** en biais; **to cut sth on the c.** couper qch dans le biais
VT 1 *(go across* ▸ *road, room, sea)* traverser; *(*▸ *bridge, river)* traverser, passer; *(*▸ *fence, threshold)* franchir; **the bridge crosses the river at Orléans** le pont franchit *ou* enjambe le fleuve à Orléans; **she crossed the Atlantic** elle a fait la traversée de l'Atlantique; **to c. a picket line** franchir un piquet de grève; **a look of distaste crossed her face** une expression de dégoût passa sur son visage; **it crossed my mind that…** j'ai pensé *ou* l'idée m'a effleuré que… + *indicative*; **didn't it c. your**

mind that she might have been lying? est-ce qu'il ne t'est pas venu à l'idée qu'elle ait pu mentir?; *Br Fig Parl* **to c. the floor (of the House)** changer de parti politique; *Fig* **I'll c. that bridge when I come to it** je m'occuperai de ce problème en temps voulu; *Naut* **to c. the line** passer l'équateur

2 *(place one across the other)* croiser; **to c. one's arms/one's legs** croiser les bras/les jambes; **c. your fingers** *or* **keep your fingers crossed for me** pense à moi et croise les doigts; **let's keep our fingers crossed** croisons les doigts; *also Fig* **to c. swords with sb** croiser le fer avec qn; **c. my palm (with silver)!** donnez-moi une petite pièce!

3 *(mark with cross)* faire une croix sur; *Rel* **to c. oneself** faire le signe de (la) croix, se signer; **c. your "t"s** barrez *ou* mettez des barres à vos "t"; *Br* **to c. a cheque** barrer un chèque; *Fam* **c. my heart (and hope to die)** croix de bois croix de fer (, si je mens je vais en enfer)

4 *(animals, plants)* croiser; *Fig (two styles)* mélanger, marier

5 *(oppose)* contrarier, contrecarrer; **to be crossed in love** avoir une déception amoureuse

6 *Tel* **we've got a crossed line** il y a des interférences sur la ligne

VI **1** *(go across)* traverser; **she crossed (over) to the door** elle est allée à la porte; **she crossed (over) to the other side of the road** elle a traversé la route; **we crossed from Belgium into France** nous sommes passés de Belgique en France; **they crossed from Dover to Boulogne** ils ont fait la traversée de Douvres à Boulogne

2 *(intersect ▸ lines, paths, roads)* se croiser, se rencontrer; **our letters crossed in the post** nos lettres se sont croisées; **our paths crossed again a few years later** nos chemins se sont à nouveau croisés quelques années plus tard

ADJ **1** *(angry)* de mauvaise humeur, en colère; **she's c. with me** elle est fâchée contre moi; **don't be c. with me** il ne faut pas m'en vouloir; **he makes me so c.!** qu'est-ce qu'il peut m'agacer!; **I got c. with them** je me suis fâché contre eux; **I never heard her utter a c. word** elle ne dit jamais un mot plus haut que l'autre; **we've never had a c. word** nous ne nous sommes jamais disputés

2 *(diagonal)* diagonal

▸▸ *Opt* ***cross hairs*** = fils croisés d'une lunette qui déterminent la ligne de visée; ***cross section*** coupe *f* transversale; **in c. section** en coupe transversale; *Fig* **a c. section of the population** un groupe représentatif de la population; *Am* ***cross street*** rue *f* transversale

▸ **cross off** VT SEP *(item)* barrer, rayer; *(person)* radier; **to c. sb off the list** radier qn

▸ **cross out** VT SEP barrer, rayer

▸ **cross over** VT INSEP *(street)* traverser

VI *(go across street, sea, frontier etc)* traverser; **they crossed over to Cherbourg in their yacht** ils ont fait la traversée jusqu'à Cherbourg dans leur yacht

---

crossbar ['krɒsbɑː(r)] N *(on bike)* barre *f*; *(on goalposts)* barre *f* transversale

crossbeam ['krɒsbiːm] N *Constr* traverse *f*, sommier *m*

crossbench ['krɒsbentʃ] N *(usu pl) Br Parl* = banc où s'assoient les députés non inscrits à un parti; **on the crossbenches** du côté des non-inscrits

crossbencher [ˌkrɒs'bentʃə(r)] N *Br Parl* = au Parlement britannique, membre non inscrit, assis sur les bancs transversaux

crossbill ['krɒsbɪl] N *Orn* bec-croisé *m*

crossbones ['krɒsbəʊnz] NPL os *mpl* en croix *ou* de mort

cross-border ADJ transfrontalier

▸▸ ***cross-border talks*** négociations *fpl* transfrontalières; ***cross-border trade*** commerce *m* transfrontalier

crossbow ['krɒsbəʊ] N arbalète *f*

▸▸ ***crossbow slit (window)*** arbalétrière *f*

crossbred ['krɒsbred] *pt & pp of* **crossbreed** N hybride *m*, métis(isse) *m,f*

ADJ hybride, métis

crossbreed ['krɒsbriːd] *(pt & pp* **crossbred** [-bred]) N *(animal, plant)* hybride *m*, métis(isse) *m,f*; *Pej (person)* métis(isse) *m,f*, sang-mêlé *mf inv*

VT *(animals)* croiser; *(humans)* métisser; *(plants)* hybrider

cross-Channel ADJ *Br (ferry, route)* trans-Manche

cross-check N contre-épreuve *f*, recoupement *m*

VT contrôler (par contre-épreuve *ou* par recoupement)

VI vérifier par recoupement

cross-checking N contrôle *m* (par contre-épreuve *ou* par recoupement), contre-épreuve *f*, recoupement *m*

cross-compiler N *Comput* compilateur *m* croisé

cross-contamination N contamination *f* croisée

cross-country N cross-country *m*, cross *m*

ADV à travers champs

▸▸ ***cross-country runner*** coureur(euse) *m,f* de cross; ***cross-country running*** cross *m*; ***cross-country skier*** fondeur(euse) *m,f*; ***cross-country skiing*** ski *m* de fond

cross-cultural ADJ interculturel

cross-currency ADJ

▸▸ *Fin* ***cross-currency interest rate*** taux *m* d'intérêt croisé; *St Exch* ***cross-currency swap*** crédit *m* croisé

cross-current N contre-courant *m*

crosscut ['krɒskʌt] *(pt & pp* **crosscut**, *cont* **cross-cutting**) *Carp* ADJ *(incision)* coupé en travers; *(tool)* qui coupe en travers

VT couper en travers

▸▸ ***crosscut chisel*** bédane *m*; ***crosscut saw*** scie *f* passe-partout

cross-dressing N travestisme *m*, transvestisme *m*

crossed [krɒst] ADJ croisé

▸▸ ***crossed cheque*** chèque *m* barré

cross-examination N contre-interrogatoire *m*

cross-examine VT *(gen)* soumettre à un interrogatoire serré; *Law* faire subir un contre-interrogatoire à

cross-eyed ADJ qui louche; **she's c.** elle louche

cross-fade N *Rad* fondu *m* enchaîné (sonore)

cross-fertilization, -isation N *Bot* croisement *m*; *Fig* osmose *f*, enrichissement *m* croisé

cross-fertilize, -ise VT *Bot* hybrider; *Fig (ideas)* échanger

VI *Bot* s'hybrider; *Fig (teams, people at conference etc)* échanger des idées

crossfire ['krɒsˌfaɪə(r)] N *(UNCOUNT)* feux *mpl* croisés; *Mil & Fig* **to be caught in the c.** être pris entre deux feux

cross-grained ADJ **1** *(wood)* à fibres torses **2** *(person)* revêche, acariâtre

crosshair pointer ['krɒsheə-] N *Comput* pointeur-croix *m*

cross-hatch VT *Art* hachurer en croisillons

cross-hatching N *(UNCOUNT) Art* hachures *fpl* croisées

crossheaded ['krɒsˌhedɪd] ADJ *Tech (screwdriver)* cruciforme

cross-holding N *Fin* participation *f* croisée

cross-impact analysis N *Mktg* analyse *f* d'interférence

crossing ['krɒsɪŋ] N **1** *(sea journey)* traversée *f*; *Mil (of river)* franchissement *m*; **we had a good c.** nous avons eu *ou* fait une belle traversée **2** *(intersection)* croisement *m*; *(of roads)* croisement *m*, carrefour *m* **3** *(interbreeding)* croisement *m*

cross-legged ADJ en tailleur

crossly ['krɒslɪ] ADV *(with annoyance)* avec mauvaise humeur; *(angrily)* d'un air/d'un ton fâché

cross-marketing N *Mktg* cross-marketing *m*

cross-member N *Aut* traverse *f*

crossover ['krɒsˌəʊvə(r)] N **1** *(of roads)* (croisement *m* par) pont *m* routier; *(for pedestrians)* passage *m* clouté; *Rail* voie *f* de croisement **2** *Biol* croisement *m*

ADJ *Mus (style, album)* hybride

▸▸ ***crossover network*** *(in audio)* circuit *m* de recoupement

cross-party ADJ *Pol*

▸▸ ***cross-party agreement*** accord *m* entre partis; ***cross-party support*** = soutien au-delà des clivages politiques; ***cross-party talks*** négociations *fpl* entre partis

crosspatch ['krɒspætʃ] N *Fam* grincheux (euse)[□] *m,f*

crosspiece ['krɒspiːs] N *Tech* traverse *f*

crossply ['krɒsplaɪ] ADJ *(tyre)* à carcasse biaise *ou* croisée

cross-pollination N *Bot* pollinisation *f* croisée

cross-post VT *Comput* faire un envoi multiple de

cross-posting N *Comput* envoi *m* multiple

cross-pricing N *Com* fixation *f* de prix croisés

cross-purposes NPL **to be at c. with sb** *(misunderstand)* comprendre qn de travers; *(oppose)* être en désaccord avec qn; **we were at c.** il y a eu un malentendu entre nous; **they were talking at c.** ils ne parlaient pas de la même chose

cross-question VT *(gen)* soumettre à un interrogatoire serré; *Law* faire subir un contre-interrogatoire à

cross-refer *(pt & pp* **cross-referred**, *cont* **cross-referring**) VI **to c. to sth** renvoyer à qch

VT renvoyer; **the reader is cross-referred to page 332** il y a un renvoi à la page 332

cross-reference N renvoi *m*, référence *f*

VT *(provide with cross-references)* introduire des renvois dans

crossroad ['krɒsrəʊd] N *Am (across a road)* = route qui en coupe une autre; *(between main roads)* route *f* secondaire, route *f* départementale

crossroads ['krɒsrəʊdz] *(pl* **inv**) N croisement *m*, carrefour *m*; *Fig* **the city is at the c. of Europe** la ville est au carrefour de l'Europe; **her career is at a c.** sa carrière va maintenant prendre un tournant décisif

cross-stitch *Sewing* N point *m* de croix

VT coudre au point de croix

crosstalk ['krɒstɔːk] N **1** *Rad & Tel* diaphonie *f* **2** *Br (witty exchange)* joutes *fpl* oratoires; *Am (trivial conversation)* banalités *fpl*, bavardages *mpl*

crosstown ['krɒstaʊn] *Am* ADJ qui traverse la ville

ADV à travers la ville

cross-trainer N *(gym equipment)* cross-trainer *m*

cross-training N *Sport* cross-training *m*

crosswalk ['krɒswɔːk] N *Am* passage *m* clouté

crossway ['krɒsweɪ] N *Am (across a road)* = route qui en coupe une autre; *(between main roads)* route *f* secondaire, route *f* départementale

crosswind ['krɒswɪnd] N vent *m* de travers

crosswise ['krɒswaɪz] ADJ *(shaped like a cross)* en croix; *(across)* en travers; *(diagonally)* en travers, en diagonale

ADV *(into the shape of a cross)* en croix; *(across)* en travers; *(diagonally)* en travers, en diagonale

crossword (puzzle) ['krɒswɜːd-] N mots *mpl* croisés; **to do a c.** faire des mots croisés

crotch [krɒtʃ] N *(of tree)* fourche *f*; *(of trousers)* entre-jambes *m inv*; **she kicked him in the c.** elle lui a donné un coup de pied entre les jambes

crotchet ['krɒtʃɪt] N *Br Mus* noire *f*

crotchety ['krɒtʃɪtɪ] ADJ *Fam* grognon, bougon

croton ['krəʊtən] N *Bot* croton *m*

crouch [kraʊtʃ] VI **to c. (down)** *(person)* s'accroupir; *(animal)* se tapir

N *(posture)* **to go into a c.** s'accroupir; **to be in a c.** être accroupi

croup [kruːp] N **1** *(of animal)* croupe *f* **2** *Med* croup *m*

croupier ['kruːpɪə(r)] N croupier *m*

crow [krəʊ] *(Br pt & pp* **crowed** *or* **crew** [kruː], *pp* **crowed** *or* **crown** [krəʊn], *Am pt* **crowed**) N **1** *(bird)* corbeau *m*; *(smaller)* corneille *f*; **it's three miles as the c. flies** c'est à trois miles à vol d'oiseau; *Am Fam* **he had to eat c.** il a dû admettre qu'il avait tort[□] **2** *(sound of cock)* chant *m* du coq, cocorico *m* **3** *(of baby)* gazouillis *m*

VI 1 *(cock)* chanter 2 *(baby)* gazouiller 3 *(boast)* fanfaronner; **it's nothing to c. about** il n'y a pas de quoi être fier; **to c. over sth** se vanter de qch
►► ***crow's feet*** *(wrinkles)* pattes *fpl* d'oie; *Naut* ***crow's nest*** nid-de-pie *m*

crowbar ['krəʊbɑː(r)] N (pince *f* à) levier *m*

crowd [kraʊd] N 1 *(throng)* foule *f*, masse *f*; **a c. of noisy children** une bande d'enfants bruyants; **a disorderly c.** une cohue; **there were crowds of people in town** il y avait foule en ville; **there was quite a c. at the match** il y avait beaucoup de monde au match; **the concert drew a good c.** le concert a attiré beaucoup de monde; **she stands out in a c.** elle se distingue de la masse 2 *Fam (social group)* bande *f*; **to be in with the wrong c.** avoir de mauvaises fréquentations; **they stick to their own c.** ils font bande à part 3 *Fig Pej (people as a whole)* **the c.** la foule, la masse du peuple; **she always goes with** *or* **follows the c.** elle suit toujours le mouvement; **she doesn't like to be one of the c.** elle n'aime pas faire comme tout le monde
VI se presser; **to c. round sb/sth** se presser autour de qn/qch; **they crowded round to read the poster** ils se sont attroupés pour lire l'affiche; **the reporters crowded into the room** les journalistes se sont entassés dans la pièce; **don't all c. together!** ne vous serrez pas comme ça!; **they came crowding through the door** ils se sont bousculés pour entrer
VT 1 *(cram)* serrer, entasser; **people crowded the streets/the shops** des gens se pressaient dans les rues/les magasins; **the tables are crowded together** les tables sont collées les unes aux autres; **the park was crowded with sunbathers** le parc était plein de gens qui prenaient des bains de soleil 2 *Fam (jostle)* bousculer; **stop crowding me!** arrêtez de me bousculer!ᵒ, ne me poussez pas!ᵒ; **I was crowded off the bus** la foule m'a éjecté du bus 3 *Naut* **to c. on sail** mettre toutes les voiles dehors
►► *Cin & TV* ***crowd scene*** scène *f* de foule; ***crowd surfing*** = pratique courante dans les concerts pop ou rock, qui consiste à se laisser transporter, allongé, au-dessus de la foule, slam *m*

► **crowd in** VI 1 *(enter)* entrer en foule, affluer 2 *Fig (flood in)* submerger; **gloomy thoughts kept crowding in on me** de sombres pensées m'assaillaient

► **crowd out** VT SEP **we were crowded out by a bunch of students** un groupe d'étudiants nous a poussés vers la sortie; **independent traders are being crowded out by bigger stores** les petits commerçants sont étouffés par les grands magasins
VI sortir en foule

crowded ['kraʊdɪd] ADJ 1 *(busy ► room, building, bus etc)* bondé, plein; *(► street)* plein (de monde); *(► town)* encombré (de monde), surpeuplé; **the c. streets of Bombay** les rues pleines de monde de Bombay; **a room c. with furniture/with people** une pièce encombrée de meubles/pleine de monde; **the shops are too c.** il y a trop de monde dans les magasins; **he has a c. schedule** son emploi du temps est surchargé 2 *(overpopulated)* surpeuplé; **c. inner-city areas** les quartiers surpeuplés du centre-ville

crowfoot ['krəʊfʊt] *(pl sense* 1 **crowfoots**, *pl sense* 2 **crowfeet** [-fiːt]) N 1 *Bot* renoncule *f* 2 *Naut* araignée *f*

crowing ['krəʊɪŋ] N *(UNCOUNT) (of cock)* chant *m*; *Fig* fanfaronnades *fpl*

crown¹ [krəʊn] *pp of* **crow**

crown² [kraʊn] N 1 *(of monarch, martyr, made of flowers etc)* couronne *f*; **she wears the c.** c'est elle qui règne; **c. of thorns** couronne *f* d'épines
2 *(award)* prix *m*; **she won the Wimbledon c. for the second year running** elle a remporté le tournoi de Wimbledon pour la seconde année consécutive
3 *(top ► of hill, tree)* sommet *m*, cime *f*; *(► of roof)* faîte *m*; *(► of hat)* fond *m*; *(► of road)* bombement *m*; *(► of tooth)* couronne *f*; *Archit (► of arch)* clef *f*; **the c. (of the head)** le sommet de la tête
4 *(coin)* couronne *f*
5 *(outstanding achievement)* couronnement *m*; **it was the c. of his career** ce fut le couronnement de sa carrière
6 *(paper size)* couronne *f*
7 *Naut (of anchor)* diamant *m*
VT 1 *(confer a title on)* couronner, sacrer; **she was crowned queen/champion** elle fut couronnée reine/championne; **the crowned heads of Europe** les têtes couronnées de l'Europe
2 *(top)* couronner; *Fig (person's happiness)* combler, couronner; *(person's efforts)* récompenser; **to c. a tooth** couronner une dent; **the woods that c. the hill** les bois qui couronnent la colline; **her election success crowned her career** son succès aux élections a couronné sa carrière; *Fig* **and to c. it all, it started to rain** et pour couronner le tout, il s'est mis à pleuvoir
3 *(in draughts)* damer; **to be crowned** aller à dame
4 *Br Fam (hit)* flanquer un coup (sur la tête) à; **I'll c. you!** je vais te flanquer un de ces coups sur la tête!
VI *Obst (baby's head)* apparaître *(dans l'ouverture du vagin)*
• **Crown** N **the C.** la Couronne, l'État *m* (monarchie)
►► *Pol* ***Crown Agent*** = fonctionnaire du ministère britannique du développement outre-mer chargé des pays étrangers et des organisations internationales; *Br* ***crown cap*** capsule *f* (de bouteille); *Br* ***crown colony*** colonie *f* de la Couronne; *Law* ***Crown Court*** Cour *f* d'assises *(en Angleterre et au pays de Galles)*; ***crown estates*** terres *fpl* domaniales *ou* appartenant à la Couronne; ***crown green*** terrain *m* (de boules) bombé; ***crown jewels*** *(crown, sceptre etc)* joyaux *mpl* de la Couronne; *very Fam Hum (man's genitals)* bijoux *mpl* de famille; ***crown land*** terres *fpl* domaniales; ***crown prince*** prince *m* héritier; ***crown princess*** *(heir to throne)* princesse *f* héritière; *(wife of crown prince)* princesse *f* royale; *Br Law* ***Crown Prosecution Service*** ministère *m* public; *Culin* ***crown roast*** rôti *m* en couronne; ***crown wheel*** *(gen)* couronne *f*; *Aut* grande couronne *f*; *Tech* ***crown wheel and pinion*** couronne *f* d'entraînement

crowning ['kraʊnɪŋ] N 1 couronnement *m* 2 *Obst* apparition *f* de la tête de l'enfant *(dans l'ouverture du vagin)*
ADJ *Fig* suprême
►► *Hum* ***crowning glory*** *(hair)* chevelure *f*; **the red hair that was her c. glory** la belle crinière rousse qui faisait l'admiration de tout le monde; **the c. glory of her career** *(peak)* le plus grand triomphe de sa carrière

crozier = **crosier**

CRT [ˌsiːɑːˈtiː] N *(abbr* **cathode-ray tube***) (in TV set)* tube *m* cathodique

crucial ['kruːʃəl] ADJ *(critical)* critique, crucial; *Med & Phil* crucial; **to be c. to sth** être crucial pour qch

crucible ['kruːsɪbəl] N *(vessel)* creuset *m*; *Fig (test)* (dure) épreuve *f*
►► ***crucible steel*** acier *m* fondu au creuset

crucifix ['kruːsɪfɪks] N christ *m*, crucifix *m*; **(roadside) c.** calvaire *m*

crucifixion [ˌkruːsɪˈfɪkʃən] N crucifiement *m*
• **Crucifixion** N *Rel* **the C.** la crucifixion, la mise en croix

cruciform ['kruːsɪfɔːm] ADJ *Tech* cruciforme, en croix

crucify ['kruːsɪfaɪ] *(pt & pp* **crucified***)* VT 1 *(execute)* crucifier, mettre en croix; *Rel* **Christ Crucified** le Crucifié 2 *Fig (treat harshly)* mettre au pilori; *(defeat)* mettre la pâtée à, démolir; **we were crucified** *(in match)* ils nous ont mis la pâtée; **my mum will c. us if she finds out!** ma mère va nous étriper si elle découvre ça!

crud [krʌd] N *Fam* 1 *(UNCOUNT) (dirt)* crasse *f* 2 *(UNCOUNT) (nonsense)* conneries *fpl* 3 *(person)* ordure *f*, saloperie *f*; **you c.!** espèce de minable!

cruddy ['krʌdɪ] *(compar* **cruddier**, *superl* **cruddiest***)* ADJ *Fam* 1 *(dirty)* crado 2 *(of poor quality)* dégueulasse 3 *(unwell)* **I feel c.** je ne me sens pas bienᵒ, je ne suis pas dans mon assiette

crude [kruːd] ADJ 1 *(vulgar ► person, behaviour)* vulgaire, grossier; *(► manners)* fruste, grossier; **a c. remark** une grossièreté
2 *(raw)* brut; *(sugar)* non raffiné
3 *(unsophisticated ► tool)* grossier, rudimentaire; *(► piece of work)* mal fini, sommaire; *(► drawing)* grossier; **it was a c. attempt at self-promotion** c'était une tentative grossière pour se mettre en avant
4 *(stark ► colour, light)* cru, vif
N *Petr (crude oil)* brut *m*
►► *Petr* ***crude oil*** (pétrole *m*) brut *m*

crudely ['kruːdlɪ] ADV 1 *(vulgarly)* grossièrement; *(bluntly)* crûment, brutalement; **to put it c.** *(bluntly)* pour être tout à fait franc 2 *(unsophisticatedly)* grossièrement, sommairement; **a c. built hut** une cabane grossière

crudeness ['kruːdnɪs] N 1 *(vulgarity)* grossièreté *f* 2 *(rawness ► of material)* état *m* brut 3 *(lack of sophistication ► of tool)* caractère *m* rudimentaire; *(► of drawing, work)* manque *m* de fini, caractère *m* sommaire

cruel [krʊəl] *(compar* **crueller**, *superl* **cruellest***)* ADJ 1 *(unkind)* cruel; **to be c. to sb** être cruel envers qn; *Prov* **you've got to be c. to be kind** qui aime bien châtie bien 2 *(painful)* douloureux, cruel; **it was a c. disappointment** ce fut une cruelle déception; **a c. wind** un vent mauvais *ou* cinglant

cruelly ['krʊəlɪ] ADV cruellement

cruelty ['krʊəltɪ] *(pl* **cruelties***)* N 1 *(gen)* cruauté *f*; **c. to animals** la cruauté envers les animaux; **an act of c.** une cruauté 2 *Law* sévices *mpl*; **divorce on the grounds of c.** divorce pour sévices 3 *(cruel act)* cruauté *f*

cruet ['kruːɪt] N 1 *(for oil, vinegar)* petit flacon *m* 2 *(set of condiments)* service *m* à condiments 3 *Rel* burette *f*

Crufts [krʌfts] N

> **CRUFTS**
>
> Crufts est le nom d'une célèbre exposition canine qui se tient annuellement en Angleterre. Ils s'agit de l'exposition canine la plus importante au monde. Les chiens sont jugés en différents groupes, mais le prix le plus prestigieux est le "Best in Show", qui est attribué au champion toutes catégories. Les chiens sont jugés pour leur aspect extérieur ainsi que pour leur aptitude à obéir, et pour leur agilité dans les parcours d'obstacles. Crufts attire des milliers de visiteurs chaque année et est retransmis à la télévision; cet événement témoigne de l'amour que les Britanniques portent aux animaux.

cruise [kruːz] N 1 *(sea trip)* croisière *f*; **they went on a c.** ils sont partis en *ou* ont fait une croisière; **to be on a c.** être en croisière 2 *(missile)* missile *m* de croisière
VI 1 *(ship)* croiser; *(tourists)* être en croisière
2 *(car)* rouler; *(police car, taxi)* marauder, être en maraude; *(plane)* voler; **we cruised along at 70 km/h** nous roulions tranquillement à 70 km/h; **I cruised through the exam** j'ai trouvé l'examen super facile; **a cruising taxi** un taxi en maraude; *Hum* **you're cruising for a bruising!** toi, tu cherches les emmerdes!
3 *Fam (for sexual partner)* draguer
4 *Am Fam (leave)* mettre les bouts, se casser, s'arracher; **ready to c.?** on y va?
VT 1 *(ocean)* croiser dans 2 *Fam (sexual partner)* draguer; *(place)* aller draguer dans; **he was out cruising the streets** il se baladait en voiture
►► *Aut* ***cruise control*** régulateur *m* d'allure; ***cruise liner*** paquebot *m* de croisière; ***cruise missile*** missile *m* de croisière; ***cruise ship*** bateau *m* de croisière

cruiser ['kruːzə(r)] N 1 *(warship)* croiseur *m*; *(pleasure boat)* yacht *m* de croisière 2 *Am (police patrol car)* voiture *f* de police (en patrouille)

cruiserweight ['kruːzəweɪt] N *Br Boxing* poids *m* mi-lourd

cruising ['kruːzɪŋ] N *(in boat)* croisière(s) *f(pl)*
►► ***cruising altitude*** altitude *f* de croisière; ***cruising holiday*** croisière *f*; *Aviat* ***cruising range*** autonomie *f* à vitesse de croisière; ***cruising speed*** vitesse *f* de croisière

crumb [krʌm] N 1 *(of bread)* miette *f*; *(inside loaf)* mie *f*; *Fig (small piece)* miette *f*, brin *m*; **a c. of comfort** un brin de consolation; **a few crumbs of information** des bribes *fpl* d'information; *Fig* **they make the profit and we get the crumbs from their table** ils réalisent les bénéfices et nous récupérons les miettes **2** *Fam Pej (person)* nul (nulle) *m,f*

VT *Culin (cutlet, fish)* paner, couvrir de chapelure

rumble ['krʌmbəl] **VT** *(bread, stock cube)* émietter; *(earth, plaster)* effriter

VI *(bread, stock cube)* s'émietter; *(plaster)* s'effriter; *(building)* tomber en ruines, se désagréger; *(earth, stone)* s'ébouler; *Fig (hopes, society)* s'effondrer, s'écrouler; **everything is crumbling to dust** tout tombe en poussière; *Fig* **his world was crumbling around him** tout son petit monde s'écroulait *ou* s'effondrait

N *Br Culin (dessert)* crumble *m (dessert composé d'une couche de compote de fruits recouverte de pâte)*

rumbling ['krʌmblɪŋ] **ADJ** *(stone, earth)* qui s'effrite; *(wall)* qui s'écroule, croulant; *Fig (empire, opposition, resistance)* qui s'effondre

N *(of stone, earth)* effritement *m*; *Fig (of empire, opposition, resistance, prices etc)* effondrement *m*

rumbly ['krʌmblɪ] *(compar* **crumblier**, *superl* **crumbliest**, *pl* **crumblies)** **ADJ** friable

N *Br Fam (old person)* croulant(e) *m,f*

rumbs [krʌmz] **EXCLAM** *Br Fam Old-fashioned* mince!, zut!

rummy ['krʌmɪ] *(compar* **crummier**, *superl* **crummiest)** **ADJ** *Fam* **1** *(bad)* minable, nul **2** *(unwell)* patraque; **I feel c.** je me sens patraque

rump [krʌmp] *Fam Mil slang* **VI** éclater□

VT bombarder□

N 1 *(noise)* éclatement□ *m* **2** *(shell)* obus□ *m*

rumpet ['krʌmpɪt] **N** *Br* **1** *Culin (cake)* = galette épaisse que l'on mange chaude et beurrée **2** *(UNCOUNT) very Fam (women)* jolies nanas *fpl*, pépées *fpl*; *(men)* beaux mecs *mpl*; **a nice bit of c.** *(woman)* une jolie nana, une belle pépée; *(man)* un beau gars *ou* garçon□

rumple ['krʌmpəl] **VT** froisser, friper; **be careful not to c. your dress** fais attention de ne pas froisser *ou* chiffonner ta robe; **to c. a piece of paper** chiffonner *ou* froisser du papier; *(make into a ball)* mettre un papier en boule; **to get crumpled** se froisser

VI 1 *(crease)* se froisser, se chiffonner **2** *(collapse)* s'effondrer, s'écrouler; *Fig* **his face crumpled and tears came to his eyes** son visage se contracta et ses yeux se remplirent de larmes

►► *Aut* **crumple zone** zone *f* d'absorption

►**crumple up VT SEP** *(paper)* faire une boule avec

VI *(person)* s'écrouler; *(car)* se plier

crumpled ['krʌmpəld] **ADJ** froissé; **his clothes were lying in a c. heap** ses vêtements étaient jetés en boule

crunch [krʌntʃ] **N 1** *(sound ► of teeth)* coup *m* de dents; *(► of food)* craquement *m*; *(► of gravel, snow)* craquement *m*, crissement *m*

2 *Fam (critical moment)* moment *m* critique□; **when it comes to the c.** dans une situation critique□, au moment critique□; **if it comes to the c.** en cas de besoin□

3 *(exercise)* exercice *m* pour les abdominaux, abdominaux *mpl*; **to do crunches** faire des abdominaux

4 *Fam (busy time)* **to have a c. on** être surchargé□

ADJ *Fam* critique□, décisif□; **a c. match** un match décisif□

VT 1 *(chew)* croquer; **the dog was crunching a bone** le chien mordait bruyamment un os **2** *(crush underfoot)* faire craquer *ou* crisser, écraser **3** *(process ► data, numbers)* traiter à grande vitesse

VI 1 *(gravel, snow)* craquer, crisser; **the snow crunched beneath my feet** la neige crissait sous mes pieds **2** *(chew)* croquer; **to c. on sth** croquer qch

►**crunch up VT SEP** broyer

crunching ['krʌntʃɪŋ] **N** *(sound ► of teeth)* coup *m* de dents; *(► of food)* craquement *m*; *(► of gravel, snow)* craquement *m*, crissement *m*

crunchy ['krʌntʃɪ] *(compar* **crunchier**, *superl* **crunchiest)** **ADJ** *(food)* croquant; *(snow, gravel)* qui craque *ou* crisse

crupper ['krʌpə(r)] **N** *Horseriding (on saddle)* croupière *f*; *Zool (of horse)* croupe *f (de cheval)*

crusade [kru:'seɪd] **N** *Hist & Fig* croisade *f*; *Hist* **to go on (a) c.** partir en croisade; *Fig* faire une croisade; **to start a c. (against)** lancer une croisade (contre); *Hist* **the Crusades** les Croisades *fpl*

VI *Hist* partir en croisade, être à la croisade; *Fig* faire une croisade; **to c. for/against sth** mener une croisade pour/contre qch; **she spent her life crusading against injustice** elle a passé sa vie à lutter contre l'injustice

crusader [kru:'seɪdə(r)] **N** *Hist* croisé *m*; *Fig* champion(onne) *m,f*, militant(e) *m,f*; **a c. against injustice** un (une) champion(onne) de la lutte contre l'injustice

crush [krʌʃ] **VT 1** *(smash ► gen)* écraser, broyer; *(grapes etc)* exprimer le jus de; *(of boa constrictor ► victim)* comprimer; **crushed ice** glace *f* pilée; **they were crushed to death** ils sont morts écrasés

2 *(crease)* froisser, chiffonner; **crushed velvet** velours *m* frappé

3 *(defeat ► enemy)* écraser; *(suppress ► revolt)* écraser, réprimer; *Fig (► hopes)* écraser; **she felt crushed by the news** elle a été accablée *ou* atterrée par la nouvelle; **he crushed any attempt at reconciliation** il a fait échouer toutes les tentatives de réconciliation

4 *(squash, press)* serrer; **to be crushed together** être tassés *ou* serrés les uns contre les autres; **too many things had been crushed into the box** on avait entassé trop de choses dans la boîte; **we were crushed in the race for the door** nous avons été écrasés dans la ruée vers la porte

VI 1 *(throng)* se serrer, s'écraser; **we all crushed into the lift** nous nous sommes tous entassés dans l'ascenseur **2** *(crease)* se froisser

N 1 *(crowd)* foule *f*, cohue *f*; **there was a terrible c.** il y avait un monde fou; **in the c. to enter the stadium** dans la bousculade pour entrer dans le stade **2** *Fam (infatuation)* béguin *m*; **to have a c. on sb** en pincer *ou* avoir le béguin pour qn **3** *Br (drink)* jus *m* de fruit; **lemon c.** citron *m* pressé

►► *Theat* **crush bar** bar *m* des spectateurs; **crush barrier** barrière *f* de sécurité

crushing ['krʌʃɪŋ] **ADJ** *(defeat)* écrasant; *(remark)* cinglant, percutant; **to be dealt a c. blow** *(army, hopes)* en prendre un sacré coup

N *(of grapes)* pressage *m*; *(of ore)* broyage *m*, concassage *m*; *(of rebellion, uprising)* écrasement *m*; *(of hopes)* anéantissement *m*

crust [krʌst] **N 1** *(of bread, pie)* croûte *f*; *(of snow, ice)* couche *f*; **a c. of bread** un croûton, une croûte; *Geol* **the earth's c.** la croûte *ou* l'écorce *f* terrestre; *Fam* **to earn a** *or* **one's c.** gagner sa croûte **2** *(on wound)* croûte *f*, escarre *f* **3** *(on wine)* dépôt *m*

VT couvrir d'une croûte

VI former une croûte

►**crust over VI** *(become covered with a crust)* se couvrir d'une croûte; *(wound etc)* former une croûte

crustacean [krʌ'steɪʃən] **N** crustacé *m*

ADJ crustacé

crusted ['krʌstɪd] **ADJ to be c. with ice** être couvert d'une croûte de glace

crusty ['krʌstɪ] *(compar* **crustier**, *superl* **crustiest)** **ADJ 1** *(bread)* croustillant **2** *(bad-tempered ► person)* hargneux, bourru; *(► remark)* brusque, sec (sèche)

crutch [krʌtʃ] **N 1** *(support)* support *m*, soutien *m*; *(for walking)* béquille *f*; *Archit* étançon *m*; *Naut* support *m*; **she uses crutches** elle marche avec des béquilles **2** *Fig* soutien *m*; **a c. to lean on** un soutien **3** *Br (of tree)* fourche *f*; *(of trousers)* entrejambes *m inv*

crux [krʌks] *(pl* **cruxes** *or* **cruces** ['kru:si:z]) **N 1** *(vital point)* point *m* crucial *ou* capital; *(of problem)* cœur *m*; **the c. of the matter** le nœud de l'affaire **2** *(in climbing)* passage-clef *m*

cry [kraɪ] *(pt & pp* **cried**, *pl* **cries)** **VI 1** *(weep)* pleurer; **she cried in** *or* **with frustration** elle pleurait d'impuissance; **to c. over sth** pleurer *ou* verser des larmes sur qch; **we laughed until we cried** nous avons pleuré de rire *ou* avons ri aux larmes; **the film made them c.** ils ont pleuré pendant le film; *Prov* **it's no use crying over spilt milk** = ce qui est fait est fait **2** *(call out)* crier, pousser un cri; **to c. (out) in pain** pousser un cri de douleur; **to c. for help** crier au secours; **to c. for mercy** demander grâce, implorer la pitié **3** *(bird, animal)* pousser un cri *ou* des cris; *(hounds)* donner de la voix, aboyer

VT 1 *(weep)* pleurer; **she cried herself to sleep** elle s'est endormie en pleurant; **he cried tears of joy** il versa des larmes de joie; **he was crying his heart** *or* **eyes out** il pleurait toutes les larmes de son corps **2** *(shout)* crier; **"look!" she cried** "regardez!" s'écria-t-elle; *Old-fashioned* **to c. one's wares** vendre sa marchandise à la criée; **to c. wolf** crier au loup

N 1 *(exclamation)* cri *m*; **to give** *or* **utter a c.** pousser un cri; **a c. of pain** un cri de douleur; *also Fig* **a c. for help** un appel au secours; **he heard a c. for help** il a entendu crier au secours; **there were cries of "down with the king!"** on criait "à bas le roi!"; **it's still a far c. from what I asked for** cela reste loin de ce que j'avais demandé **2** *(of birds, animals)* cri *m*; *(of hounds)* aboiements *mpl*, voix *f*; **to be in full c.** donner de la voix **3** *(weep)* **to have a good c.** pleurer un bon coup

►**cry down VT SEP** décrier

►**cry off VI** *(from meeting)* se décommander; *(from promise)* se rétracter, se dédire

►**cry out VI** pousser un cri; **I cried out to them** je les ai appelés; *Fig* **to c. out against** protester contre; *Fig* **the system is crying out for reform** le système a grand besoin d'être réformé; **that wall is crying out for a coat of paint** ce mur a besoin d'un bon coup de peinture; *Fam* **for crying out loud!** bon sang!

VT SEP s'écrier; **"listen!" she cried out** "écoutez!" s'écria-t-elle

►**cry up VT SEP** prôner, exalter

crybaby ['kraɪˌbeɪbɪ] *(pl* **crybabies)** **N** *Fam* pleurnichard(e)□ *m,f*

crying ['kraɪɪŋ] **ADJ 1** *(person)* qui pleure, pleurant **2** *Fam (as intensifier)* criant, flagrant; **there is a c. need for more teachers** on a un besoin urgent d'enseignants□; **it's a c. shame** c'est un scandale□

N *(UNCOUNT)* **1** *(shouting)* cri *m*, cris *mpl*; **we could hear the baby's c.** on entendait les cris du bébé **2** *(weeping)* pleurs *mpl*; **stop your c.** arrête de pleurer

cryogenically [ˌkraɪə'dʒenɪkəlɪ] **ADV to freeze** *or* **preserve c.** cryogéniser

cryogenics [ˌkraɪə'dʒenɪks] **N** *(UNCOUNT) Phys (science)* cryologie *f*; *(production)* cryogénie *f*

cryonics [kraɪ'ɒnɪks] **N** *(UNCOUNT) Biol* cryogénisation *f*

cryosurgery [ˌkraɪəʊ'sɜ:dʒərɪ] **N** *Med* cryochirurgie *f*

crypt [krɪpt] **N** crypte *f*

cryptic ['krɪptɪk] **ADJ** *(secret)* secret(ète); *(obscure)* énigmatique, sibyllin; **he was very c. about his future plans** il a été très mystérieux sur ses projets d'avenir

►► **cryptic crossword** = mots croisés dont les définitions sont des énigmes qu'il faut résoudre

cryptically ['krɪptɪkəlɪ] **ADV** *(secretly)* secrètement; *(obscurely)* énigmatiquement

crypto- ['krɪptəʊ] **PREF** crypto-; **crypto-fascist** cryptofasciste *mf*

cryptogram ['krɪptəʊgræm] **N** cryptogramme *m*

cryptographer [krɪp'tɒgrəfə(r)] **N** cryptographe *mf*

cryptographic [ˌkrɪptə'græfɪk] **ADJ** cryptographique

►► *Comput* **cryptographic key** *(on Internet)* clé *f* de chiffrement

cryptography [krɪp'tɒgrəfɪ], **cryptology** [krɪp'tɒlədʒɪ] **N** cryptographie *f*

crystal ['krɪstəl] **N 1** *(gen) & Miner* cristal *m*; **as clear as c.** clair comme le jour *ou* comme de l'eau de roche

2 *(chip)* cristal *m*; **salt/snow crystals** cristaux *mpl* de sel/de neige

3 *Am (of watch)* verre *m* (de montre)

4 *Electron* galène *f*

ADJ *(vase, glass, water)* de cristal

►► **crystal ball** boule *f* de cristal; **crystal factory** cristallerie *f*; **crystal healing** = utilisation de cristaux à des fins curatives; *Rad* **crystal set** poste *m* à galène

crystal-clear ADJ clair comme le jour *ou* comme de l'eau de roche; *(voice)* cristalline; **to make sth c.** rendre qch bien clair

crystalline ['krɪstəlaɪn] N *Chem & Miner* cristallin

▸▸ *Opt* ***crystalline lens*** cristallin *m*

crystallization, -isation [ˌkrɪstəlaɪ'zeɪʃən] N *(gen) & Chem* cristallisation *f*

crystallize, -ise ['krɪstəlaɪz] VT cristalliser; *(sugar)* (faire) candir

VI *also Fig* se cristalliser

▸▸ ***crystallized fruit*** *(UNCOUNT)* fruits *mpl* confits

crystallography [ˌkrɪstə'lɒgrəfɪ] N *Miner* cristallographie *f*

CS [ˌsiː'es] N *Cin & TV (abbr* **close shot**) gros plan *m*

CSD [ˌsiːes'diː] N *Banking & St Exch (abbr* **Central Securities Depository**) depositaire *m* national de titres

CSE [ˌsiːes'iː] N *Formerly Sch (abbr* **Certificate of Secondary Education**) = ancien brevet de l'enseignement secondaire en Grande-Bretagne, aujourd'hui remplacé par le "GCSE"

C-section N *Obst* césarienne *f*

CST [ˌsiːes'tiː] N *Am (abbr* **Central Standard Time**) heure *f* d'hiver du centre des États-Unis

CSV [ˌsiːes'viː] NPL *Comput (abbr* **comma-separated values**) valeurs *fpl* séparées par des virgules

CTF [ˌsiːtiː'ef] N *(abbr* **child trust fund**) = compte d'épargne ouvert par l'État au nom de chaque enfant britannique à sa naissance

cub [kʌb] N **1** *(animal ▸ gen)* petit(e) *m,f*; *(▸ of fox)* renardeau *m*; *(▸ of bear)* ourson *m*; *(▸ of lion)* lionceau *m*; *(▸ of wolf)* louveteau *m*; **a lioness and her cubs** une lionne et ses petits **2** *(youngster)* **young c.** jeune blanc-bec *m* **3** *(scout)* louveteau *m (scout)*; **he goes to Cubs on Fridays** il va à la réunion des louveteaux le vendredi

▸▸ ***cub master*** chef *m (des scouts)*; ***cub mistress*** cheftaine *f (des scouts)*; ***cub reporter*** jeune journaliste *mf*; ***cub scout, Cub Scout*** louveteau *m (scout)*

Cuba ['kjuːbə] N Cuba

▸▸ ***Cuba libre*** *(cocktail)* = cocktail contenant du Coca®, du rhum et du jus de citron vert

Cuban ['kjuːbən] N Cubain(e) *m,f*

ADJ cubain

COMP *(embassy, history)* de Cuba

▸▸ ***Cuban heel*** talon *m* cubain; ***the Cuban missile crisis*** la crise de Cuba *(conflit américano-soviétique dû à la présence de missiles soviétiques à Cuba en 1962)*

cubbyhole ['kʌbɪhəʊl] N **1** *(cupboard)* débarras *m*, remise *f*; *(small room)* cagibi *m*, réduit *m* **2** *(in desk)* case *f*; *Aut* vide-poches *m inv*

cube [kjuːb] N *(gen) & Math* cube *m*

VT **1** *(cut into cubes)* couper en cubes *ou* en dés **2** *Math* cuber; *Tech (measure)* cuber; **27 cubed** 27 au cube

▸▸ *Math* ***cube root*** racine *f* cubique

cubic ['kjuːbɪk] ADJ *Math (shape, volume)* cubique; *(measurement)* cube

▸▸ ***cubic capacity*** volume *m*; ***cubic centimetre*** centimètre *m* cube; ***cubic content*** capacité *f* cubique; ***cubic equation*** équation *f* du troisième degré; ***cubic metre*** mètre *m* cube

cubicle ['kjuːbɪkəl] N *(in dormitory, hospital ward)* alcôve *f*, box *m*; *(in swimming baths)* cabine *f*; *(in public toilets)* W-C *mpl*; *(for trying on clothes)* cabine *f* d'essayage

cubism, Cubism ['kjuːbɪzəm] N *Art* cubisme *m*

cubist, Cubist ['kjuːbɪst] *Art* N cubiste *mf*

ADJ cubiste

cuckold ['kʌkəʊld] N *(mari m)* cocu *m*

VT faire cocu, cocufier

cuckoo ['kʊkuː] *(pl* **cuckoos**) N *(bird, sound)* coucou *m*

ADJ *Fam (mad)* loufoque, toqué; **to go c.** perdre la boule

▸▸ ***cuckoo clock*** coucou *m (pendule)*; *Bot* ***cuckoo spit*** crachat *m* de coucou

cucumber ['kjuːkʌmbə(r)] N concombre *m*

cud [kʌd] N bol *m* alimentaire *(d'un ruminant)*; **to chew the c.** *(cow etc)* ruminer; *Fig (of person)* ruminer une idée, méditer

cuddle ['kʌdəl] VI se faire un câlin, se câliner; **they were cuddling on the sofa** ils se faisaient un câlin sur le divan

VT câliner; *(child)* bercer *(dans ses bras)*

N câlin *m*; **they were having a c.** ils se faisaient un câlin; **she gave the child a c.** elle a fait un câlin à l'enfant

▸ **cuddle up** VI se blottir, se pelotonner; **she cuddled up close to him** elle se blottit contre lui; **they cuddled up to each other for warmth** ils se sont pelotonnés *ou* blottis l'un contre l'autre pour se tenir chaud

cuddly ['kʌdlɪ] *(compar* **cuddlier**, *superl* **cuddliest**) ADJ *(child, animal)* mignon à croquer; *(soft toy)* tout doux (toute douce); *Euph (plump)* rond

▸▸ ***cuddly toy*** peluche *f*

cudgel ['kʌdʒəl] *(Br pt & pp* **cudgelled**, *cont* **cudgelling**, *Am pt & pp* **cudgeled**, *cont* **cudgeling**) N gourdin *m*, trique *f*; *Fig* **to take up** *or* **to carry the cudgels for sb/sth** prendre fait et cause pour qn/qch

VT battre à coups de gourdin; **to c. sb to death** tuer qn à coups de gourdin; *Fam Fig* **he cudgelled his brains** il s'est creusé la tête *ou* le cerveau

cue [kjuː] N **1** *Theat (verbal)* réplique *f*; *Cin & TV (action)* signal *m*; *Mus* signal *m* d'entrée; *Theat* **to give sb their c.** donner la réplique à qn; **to miss one's c.** *Theat* manquer la réplique; *Cin & TV* rater le signal; **he took his c.** il a entamé sa réplique

2 *Fig (signal)* signal *m*; **to take one's c. from sb** prendre exemple sur qn; **her yawn was our c. to leave** nous avons compris qu'il fallait partir quand elle s'est mise à bâiller; **right on c., the door opened** la porte s'est ouverte juste au bon moment *ou* à point nommé

3 *(for snooker, pool)* queue *f (de billard)*; **c. rack** porte-queue *m*

4 *(of hair)* queue *f (de cheval)*

VI *(in snooker, pool)* queuter

VT *(prompt)* donner le signal à; *Theat* donner la réplique à

▸▸ ***cue ball*** bille *f* de joueur; *Cards* ***cue bid*** = annonce qui montre un as ou un vide; *Cin & TV* ***cue card*** carton *m* aide-mémoire; ***cue rack*** porte-queues *m inv*; *Rad & TV* ***cue sheet*** feuille *f* de conducteur, feuille *f* de mixage

▸ **cue in** VT SEP *Theat* donner la réplique à; *Cin & TV* donner le signal à

cuff [kʌf] N **1** *(of sleeve)* poignet *m*; *(that takes cuff links)* manchette *f*; *(of glove)* poignet *m*; *(of coat)* parement *m*; *Am (of trousers)* revers *m*; **off the c.** à l'improviste; **she was speaking off the c.** elle improvisait son discours, elle faisait un discours improvisé; **I can't tell you off the c.** je ne peux pas te le dire comme ça *ou* tout de suite; *Am* **he bought it on the c.** il l'a acheté à crédit **2** *(blow)* gifle *f*, claque *f*; **I got a c. round the ear** j'ai reçu une claque *ou* une gifle

VT **1** *(hit)* gifler, donner une gifle *ou* une claque à **2** *Fam (handcuff)* mettre *ou* passer les menottes à ▫ **3** *Am (trousers)* faire un revers à

• **cuffs** NPL *Fam (handcuffs)* menottes *fpl* ▫, bracelets *mpl*

▸▸ ***cuff link*** bouton *m* de manchette

cuisine [kwɪ'ziːn] N cuisine *f*

cul-de-sac ['kʌldəsæk] *(pl* **cul-de-sacs**) N cul-de-sac *m*, impasse *f*; *Fig* impasse *f*; **c.** *(sign)* voie sans issue

culinary ['kʌlɪnərɪ] ADJ culinaire

cull [kʌl] VT **1** *(sample)* sélectionner **2** *(remove from herd ▸ animal)* éliminer, supprimer; **to c. a herd of deer** = abattre une partie d'un troupeau de daims pour en réduire la taille **3** *(gather ▸ flowers, fruit)* cueillir

N **1** *(killing)* élimination *f* **2** *(animal)* animal *m* à éliminer

culminate ['kʌlmɪˌneɪt] VI *Astron* culminer

culminating ['kʌlmɪneɪtɪŋ] ADJ culminant

culmination [ˌkʌlmɪ'neɪʃən] N **1** *(climax ▸ of career)* apogée *m*; *(▸ of efforts)* maximum *m*; *(▸ of disagreement)* point *m* culminant **2** *Astron* culmination *f*

culottes [kjuː'lɒts] NPL jupe-culotte *f*

culpability [ˌkʌlpə'bɪlətɪ] N *Formal* culpabilité *f*

culpable ['kʌlpəbəl] ADJ *Formal* coupable

▸▸ *Scot Law* ***culpable homicide*** homicide *m* involontaire; ***culpable negligence*** négligence *f* coupable

culprit ['kʌlprɪt] N *(guilty person)* coupable *mf*; **I'm the c.** c'est moi le coupable; **poor housing is the main c.** ce sont les mauvaises conditions de logement qui sont principalement responsables

cult [kʌlt] N *Fig or Rel* culte *m*; **personality c.** culte *m* de la personnalité; **to make a c. of sth** avoir un culte pour qch; **it's become something of a minor c.** cela a suscité un véritable engouement; **the film has a c. following** c'est un film culte

COMP *(book, film)* culte

▸▸ ***cult figure*** idole *f*

cultivate ['kʌltɪveɪt] VT **1** *(land)* cultiver, exploiter; *(crop)* cultiver **2** *Biol (bacillus)* faire une culture de **3** *Fig (idea, person, friendship)* cultiver; **reading is the best way to c. the mind** la lecture est le meilleur moyen de se cultiver (l'esprit)

cultivated ['kʌltɪˌveɪtɪd] ADJ *(land)* cultivé, exploité; *(person)* cultivé; *(voice)* distingué

cultivation [ˌkʌltɪ'veɪʃən] N **1** *(of land, crops)* culture *f*; **fields under c.** cultures *fpl* **2** *Fig (of taste)* éducation *f*; *(of relations)* entretien *m*

cultivator ['kʌltɪˌveɪtə(r)] N *(person)* cultivateur (trice) *m,f*; *(tool)* cultivateur *m*; *(power-driven)* motoculteur *m*

cultural ['kʌltʃərəl] ADJ **1** *(background, institute)* culturel; **the c. environment** le milieu culturel **2** *Agr* de culture, cultural

▸▸ ***cultural anthropology*** culturologie *f*; *Fig* ***a cultural desert*** un désert culturel; ***cultural event*** manifestation *f* culturelle; ***cultural heritage*** patrimoine *m* culturel; ***cultural integration*** acculturation *f*; ***the Cultural Revolution*** la Révolution culturelle

culture ['kʌltʃə(r)] N **1** *(civilization, learning)* culture *f*; **popular/youth c.** culture *f* populaire/des jeunes; **a man of c.** un homme cultivé *ou* qui a de la culture; **to have no c.** être inculte

2 *(ethos, environment)* **the system breeds a c. of nepotism** ce système favorise le copinage à tous les niveaux; **a society characterized by a c. of individualism** une société où l'individualisme règne en maître

3 *Sport* **physical c.** culture *f* physique

4 *Agr (of land, crops)* culture *f*; *(of animals)* élevage *m*; *(of fowl)* aviculture *f*

5 *Biol* culture *f*

VT *(bacteria)* faire une culture de

▸▸ *Biol* ***culture medium*** milieu *m* de culture; ***culture shock*** choc *m* culturel; *Fam Hum* ***culture vulture*** fana *mf* de culture, culturophage *mf*

cultured ['kʌltʃəd] ADJ **1** *(refined ▸ person)* cultivé, lettré **2** *(grown artificially)* cultivé

▸▸ ***cultured pearl*** perle *f* de culture

culvert ['kʌlvət] N *Tech (for water)* caniveau *m*; *(for cable)* conduit *m*

cum [kʌm] PREP avec; **a kitchen-c.-dining area** une cuisine avec coin-repas; **he's a teacher-c.-philosopher** il est philosophe et enseignant

N *Vulg (semen)* foutre *m*

cumbersome ['kʌmbəsəm] ADJ *(bulky)* encombrant, embarrassant; *Fig (process, system, style)* lourd, pesant

cumin ['kjuːmɪn] N cumin *m*

cummerbund ['kʌməbʌnd] N large ceinture *(de smoking)*

cumulative ['kjuːmjʊlətɪv] ADJ cumulatif

▸▸ *Law* ***cumulative evidence*** preuve *f* par accumulation de témoignages; *Fin* ***cumulative interest*** intérêts *mpl* cumulatifs; ***cumulative total*** cumul *m*; *Pol* ***cumulative voting*** vote *m* plural

cumulatively ['kjuːmjʊlətɪvlɪ] ADV de façon cumulée

cumulonimbus [ˌkjuːmjʊləʊ'nɪmbəs] *(pl* **cumulonimbi** [-baɪ] *or* **cumulonimbuses**) N *Met* cumulonimbus *m*

cumulus ['kjuːmjʊləs] *(pl* **cumuli** [-laɪ]) N *Met* cumulus *m*

cuneiform ['kjuːnɪfɔːm] N écriture *f* cunéiforme

ADJ cunéiforme

cunnilingus [ˌkʌnɪ'lɪŋgəs] N cunnilingus *m*

cunning ['kʌnɪŋ] ADJ **1** *(shrewd)* astucieux, malin(igne); *Pej* rusé, fourbe; **he's as c. as a fox** il est

rusé comme un renard **2** *(skilful)* habile, astucieux **3** *Am (cute)* mignon, charmant
N 1 *(guile)* finesse *f*, astuce *f*; *Pej* ruse *f*, fourberie *f* **2** *(skill)* habileté *f*, adresse *f*

cunningly [ˈkʌnɪŋlɪ] **ADV 1** *(shrewdly)* astucieusement, finement; *Pej* avec ruse *ou* fourberie **2** *(skilfully)* habilement, astucieusement

cunt [kʌnt] **N** *Vulg* **1** *(vagina)* con *m*, chatte *f* **2** *Pej (man)* enculé *m*; *(woman)* salope *f*

cup [kʌp] *(pt & pp* **cupped**, *cont* **cupping)** **N 1** *(for drinking, cupful)* tasse *f*; *Rel* calice *m*; **a c. of coffee** une tasse de café; **a coffee c.** une tasse à café; **add two cups of sugar** ajoutez deux tasses de sucre; **that's just her c. of tea** c'est tout à fait à son goût; *Fam* **he's not (really) my c. of tea** il n'est pas (tout à fait) mon genre; *Fam* **rap isn't everyone's c. of tea** tout le monde n'aime pas le rap; *Literary* **my c. runneth over** mon bonheur est complet *ou* parfait; *Fam Old-fashioned* **he was in his cups** il avait du vent dans les voiles
2 *Sport (trophy, competition)* coupe *f*
3 *(shape ▸ of plant)* corolle *f*; *(▸ of bone)* cavité *f* articulaire, glène *f*; *(▸ of bra)* bonnet *m*
4 *(drink)* **champagne/cider c.** cocktail *m* au champagne/cidre; **fruit c.** cocktail *m* aux fruits *(pouvant contenir de l'alcool)*
5 *Tech* godet *m*, cuvette *f*
6 *Golf* trou *m*
7 *Med (cupping glass)* ventouse *f*
COMP 1 *Sport (winners, holders, match)* de coupe **2** *(handle)* de tasse; *(rack)* pour tasses
VT 1 *(hands)* mettre en coupe; **to c. one's hands around sth** mettre ses mains autour de qch; **she scooped up the water with her cupped hands** elle a recueilli l'eau dans ses mains jointes; **he cupped a hand to his ear** il mit sa main derrière son oreille; **she cupped her hands around her mouth and shouted** elle mit ses mains en porte-voix et cria; **he sat with his chin cupped in his hand** il était assis, le menton dans le creux de sa main **2** *Med (with cupping glass)* appliquer des ventouses sur
▸▸ *Sport* ***cup final*** finale *f* de la coupe; *Br Ftbl* ***the Cup Final*** la finale de la Coupe de Football; *Sport* ***cup finalist*** finaliste *mf* de la coupe; ***cup holder*** *(in car)* support *m* de tasse; ***cup size*** *(of bra)* profondeur *f* de bonnet; *Sport* ***cup tie*** match *m* de coupe

cup-and-ball joint **N** *Tech* joint *m* à rotule

cupbearer [ˈkʌp,beərə(r)] **N** *Hist* échanson *m*

cupboard [ˈkʌbəd] **N** *(on wall)* placard *m*; *(free-standing ▸ for dishes, pans)* buffet *m*, placard *m*; *(▸ for clothes)* placard *m*, armoire *f*; *Fig* **the c. is bare** il n'y a rien à se mettre sous la dent
▸▸ *Br* ***cupboard love*** amour *m* intéressé

cupcake [ˈkʌpkeɪk] **N 1** *(cake)* petit gâteau *m (dans une caissette en papier)*
2 *(term of affection)* mon chou, ma puce
3 *Am Fam (eccentric person)* allumé(e) *m,f*
4 *Am (homosexual)* pédale *f*, tantouze *f*, = terme injurieux désignant un homosexuel

cupful [ˈkʌpfʊl] **N** tasse *f*; **a c. of sugar** une tasse de sucre

Cupid [ˈkju:pɪd] **PR N** *Myth* Cupidon *m*; *Fig* **to play C.** jouer les entremetteurs(euses)
• **cupid N** *Art (cherub)* chérubin *m*, amour *m*
▸▸ ***Cupid's arrow*** les flèches *fpl* de Cupidon; ***Cupid's bow*** bouche *f* en forme de cœur; ***Cupid's dart*** les flèches *fpl* de Cupidon

cupidity [kju:ˈpɪdɪtɪ] **N** cupidité *f*

cupola [ˈkju:pələ] **N 1** *Archit (ceiling, roof)* coupole *f*, dôme *m*; *(tower)* belvédère *m* **2** *Naut* coupole *f* **3** *Metal (furnace)* cubilot *m*

cuppa [ˈkʌpə] **N** *Br Fam* tasse *f* de thé☐

cupping [ˈkʌpɪŋ] **N** *Med* application *f* de ventouses
▸▸ ***cupping glass*** ventouse *f*

cupric [ˈkju:prɪk] **ADJ** *Chem* cuprique
▸▸ ***cupric oxide*** oxyde *m* de cuivre

cup-shaped **ADJ** *Bot* cupulaire

cur [kɜ:(r)] **N** *Old-fashioned or Literary* **1** *(dog)* (chien *m*) bâtard *m*, sale chien *m* **2** *(person)* malotru(e) *m,f*, roquet *m*

curable [ˈkjʊərəbəl] **ADJ** guérissable, curable

curacy [ˈkjʊərəsɪ] *(pl* **curacies)** **N** *Rel* vicariat *m*

curare, curari [kjʊˈrɑ:rɪ] **N** *Bot* curare *m*

curate **N** [ˈkjʊərət] *Rel* vicaire *m (de l'Église anglicane)*; *Br* **it's a c.'s egg** il y a du bon et du mauvais
VT [kjʊərˈeɪt] *(exhibition)* organiser

curative [ˈkjʊərətɪv] **ADJ** *Med* curatif

curator [,kjʊəˈreɪtə(r)] **N 1** *(of museum)* conservateur(trice) *m,f*; *(of exhibition)* commissaire *mf*, curateur(trice) *m,f* **2** *Scot (guardian)* curateur(trice) *m,f*

curb [kɜ:b] **N 1** *(restraint)* frein *m*; **a c. on trade** une restriction au commerce; **to put a c. on sth** mettre un frein à qch **2** *(of well)* margelle *f* **3** *Am* = **kerb**
VT 1 *(restrain ▸ emotion)* refréner, maîtriser; *(▸ expenses)* restreindre, mettre un frein à; *(▸ child)* modérer, freiner; **to curb sb's enthusiasm** mettre un frein à l'enthousiasme de qn; **c. your tongue!** mesure tes paroles! **2** *(horse)* mettre un mors à **3** *Am* **c. your dog** *(sign)* votre chien doit faire ses besoins dans le caniveau
▸▸ ***curb bit*** *(on harness)* mors *m*; ***curb chain*** gourmette *f*; ***curb reins*** rênes *fpl* de filet

curbstone *Am* = **kerbstone**

curd [kɜ:d] **N** *(usu pl) (of milk)* caillot *m*, grumeau *m*; **curds** lait *m* caillé, caillebotte *f*; **curds and whey** lait *m* caillé sucré
▸▸ ***curd cheese*** fromage *m* blanc battu

curdle [ˈkɜ:dəl] **VT** *(milk)* cailler; *(sauce)* faire tourner; *(mayonnaise)* faire tomber; *Fam* **he had a face that would c. milk** il avait l'air aimable comme une porte de prison
VI *(milk)* cailler; *(sauce)* tourner; *(mayonnaise)* tomber; *Fig* **his screams made my blood c.** ses cris m'ont glacé le sang

cure [kjʊə(r)] **VT 1** *(disease, person)* guérir; *Fig (problem)* éliminer, remédier à; **he was cured of cancer** il a été guéri du cancer; **the nap seems to have cured my headache** on dirait que la sieste m'a fait passer mon mal de tête; *Fig* **his experiences in politics cured him of all his illusions** son expérience de la politique lui a fait perdre toutes ses illusions; *Prov* **what can't be cured must be endured** il faut prendre son mal en patience **2** *(tobacco, meat, fish ▸ gen)* traiter; *(▸ with salt)* saler; *(▸ by smoking)* fumer; *(▸ by drying)* sécher
N 1 *(remedy)* remède *m*, cure *f*; **a c. for the common cold** un remède contre le rhume de cerveau; **there's no known c.** on ne connaît pas de remède; **to take** *or* **to follow a c.** faire une cure; *Fig* **a c. for all ills** la panacée **2** *(recovery)* guérison *f*; **to be beyond** *or* **past c.** *(person)* être incurable; *Fig (problem, situation)* être irrémédiable **3** *Rel* **the c. of souls** la charge d'âmes

cure-all **N** panacée *f*

curettage [,kjʊərɪˈtɑ:ʒ, ,kjʊəˈretɪdʒ] **N** *Med* curetage *m*

curfew [ˈkɜ:fju:] **N** couvre-feu *m*; **the authorities imposed a/lifted the c.** les autorités ont imposé/levé le couvre-feu; *Am Fig* **to be under c.** *(teenager)* devoir rentrer à une heure précise

curing [ˈkjʊərɪŋ] **N 1** *(of disease, patient)* guérison *f* **2** *(of meat, tobacco, fish ▸ gen)* traitement *m*; *(▸ by salting)* salaison *f*; *(▸ by smoking)* fumaison *f*; *(▸ by drying)* séchage *m*

curio [ˈkjʊərɪəʊ] *(pl* **curios)** **N** curiosité *f*, bibelot *m*

curiosity [kjʊərɪˈɒsɪtɪ] *(pl* **curiosities)** **N 1** *(interest)* curiosité *f*; **out of c.** par curiosité; *Prov* **c. killed the cat** la curiosité est un vilain défaut **2** *(novelty ▸ object)* curiosité *f*; *(▸ person)* bête *f* curieuse

curious [ˈkjʊərɪəs] **ADJ 1** *(inquisitive)* curieux; **I'm c. to see/know** je suis curieux de voir/savoir; **I'm c. as to what happened next** je serais curieux de savoir ce qui s'est passé après **2** *(strange)* curieux, singulier; **the c. thing (about it) is...** ce qui est curieux là-dedans *ou* dans tout ça, c'est...; **a c.-looking object** un objet bizarre

curiously [ˈkjʊərɪəslɪ] **ADV 1** *(inquisitively)* avec curiosité **2** *(strangely)* curieusement, singulièrement; **c. enough** chose bizarre *ou* curieuse

curl [kɜ:l] **VI 1** *(hair)* friser; *(loosely)* boucler
2 *(paper, leaf)* se recroqueviller, se racornir; *(lip)* se retrousser; **her lip curled in contempt** elle fit une moue de mépris
3 *(road)* serpenter; *(smoke)* monter en spirale; *(waves)* onduler, déferler; **to c. round sth** *(plant etc)* s'enrouler autour de qch; **to c. oneself into a ball** *(of animal, person)* se rouler en boule
4 *Sport* jouer au curling
VT 1 *(hair)* friser; *(loosely)* (faire) boucler **2** *(paper)* enrouler; *(ribbon)* faire boucler; *(lip)* retrousser; **he curled his lip in scorn** il a fait une moue de mépris **3** *Sport (ball)* donner une trajectoire courbe à
N 1 *(of hair)* boucle *f* (de cheveux); **her hair hung over her shoulders in curls** ses cheveux lui tombaient en boucles sur les épaules **2** *(spiral)* courbe *f*; *(of smoke)* spirale *f*; *(of wave)* ondulation *f*; *Fig* **with a scornful c. of the lip** avec une moue méprisante

▸ **curl up** **VI 1** *(leaf, paper)* s'enrouler, se recroqueviller; *(bread)* se racornir **2** *(person)* se pelotonner; *(cat)* se mettre en boule, se pelotonner; *(dog)* se coucher en rond; **curled up in bed** pelotonné dans son lit; **the cat was sleeping curled up in a ball** le chat dormait roulé en boule; **she curled up in front of the fire with a book** elle s'est pelotonnée devant le feu avec un livre; **to c. up with laughter** se tordre de rire; *Fig* **I just wanted to c. up and die** *(in shame)* j'aurais voulu rentrer sous terre
VT SEP enrouler; **to c. oneself up** *(person)* se pelotonner; *(cat)* se mettre en boule, se pelotonner; *(dog)* se coucher en rond

curler [ˈkɜ:lə(r)] **N 1** *(for hair)* bigoudi *m*; **in her curlers** en bigoudis **2** *Sport* joueur(euse) *m,f* de curling

curlew [ˈkɜ:lju:] **N** *Orn* courlis *m*

curlicue [ˈkɜ:lɪkju:] **N** *(in design, handwriting)* enjolivure *f*; *(in skating)* figure *f* (compliquée)

curliness [ˈkɜ:lɪnɪs] **N** *(of hair ▸ loose)* boucles *fpl*; *(▸ tight)* frisure *f*

curling [ˈkɜ:lɪŋ] **N** *Sport* curling *m*
▸▸ ***curling irons*** *(for hair)* fer *m* à friser; *Sport* ***curling stone*** pierre *f* de curling; ***curling tongs*** *(for hair)* fer *m* à friser

curly [ˈkɜ:lɪ] **ADJ** *(compar* **curlier**, *superl* **curliest)** *(hair ▸ tight)* frisé; *(▸ loose)* bouclé; *(long piece of paper etc)* en spirale; *(eyelashes)* recourbé
N *Fam* **1 to have sb by the short and curlies** pouvoir faire ce qu'on veut de qn☐; **they've got us by the short and curlies** ils nous tiennent☐ **2** *(person with curly hair)* **hi there, c.** salut, le/la frisé(e)
▸▸ *Typ* ***curly bracket*** accolade *f*; ***curly endive*** frisée *f*; ***curly kale*** chou *m* frisé; ***curly lettuce*** (laitue *f*) frisée *f*; *Br Typ* ***curly quotes*** guillemets *mpl* anglais

curly-headed, curly-haired **ADJ** *(with loose curls)* à la tête bouclée, aux cheveux bouclés; *(with tight curls)* aux cheveux frisés

currant [ˈkʌrənt] **N 1** *(fruit)* groseille *f* **2** *(dried grape)* raisin *m* de Corinthe
▸▸ ***currant bun*** petit pain *m* aux raisins; ***currant bush*** groseillier *m*

currency [ˈkʌrənsɪ] *(pl* **currencies)** **N 1** *Econ & Fin* monnaie *f*, devise *f*; **to buy foreign c.** acheter des devises étrangères; **he has no Swiss c.** il n'a pas d'argent suisse; **this coin is no longer legal c.** cette pièce n'a plus cours (légal) *ou* n'est plus en circulation **2** *Fig (prevalence)* cours *m*, circulation *f*; **to gain c.** *(news)* s'accréditer; *(expression, habit)* devenir de plus en plus courant; *(ideas)* se répandre; **I give no c. to that idea** je n'accrédite pas cette idée; **ideas which had c. in the 1960s** des idées qui avaient cours dans les années 60
▸▸ *Econ* ***currency appreciation*** appréciation *f* d'une monnaie; *Fin* ***currency conversion*** conversion *f* de monnaies; *Fin* ***currency dealer*** cambiste *mf*; *Econ* ***currency depreciation*** dépréciation *f* monétaire; *Econ* ***currency devaluation*** dévaluation *f* monétaire; *Econ* ***currency dumping*** dumping *m* de change; *Econ & Fin* ***currency market*** marché *m* monétaire; *Fin* ***currency note*** billet *m* de banque; *Econ* ***currency reserves*** réserves *fpl* de devises; *Econ & Fin* ***currency snake*** serpent *m* monétaire; *Fin & St Exch* ***currency speculation*** spéculation *f* sur les devises; *Fin & St Exch* ***currency swap*** échange *m* de devises; ***currency unit*** unité *f* monétaire

current [ˈkʌrənt] **N** *(gen) & Elec* courant *m*; *Fig (trend)* cours *m*, tendance *f*; **the boat drifts with the c.** le courant fait dériver le bateau; **the currents of opinion** les tendances *fpl* de l'opinion; *also Fig* **to go with the c.** suivre le courant; *Fig*

to go against the c. aller à contre-courant; **to swim against the c.** nager contre le courant *ou* à contre-courant

ADJ 1 *(widespread)* courant, commun; **the c. theory** la théorie actuelle; **to be c.** *(word, expression)* être courant; *(theory, fashion)* avoir cours; **it's in c. use** c'est d'usage courant; **words that are in c. use** des mots courants *ou* qui s'emploient couramment; **as c. rumour has it, she...** on dit qu'elle..., si l'on en croit les rumeurs, elle... **2** *(most recent ▸ fashion, trend)* actuel; *(▸ price)* courant; **the c. issue of this magazine** le dernier numéro de cette revue; **the c. month** le mois courant *ou* en cours; **the c. exhibition at the Louvre** l'exposition qui a lieu en ce moment au Louvre; **his c. girlfriend** la fille avec qui il est en ce moment, sa copine du moment

▸▸ *Br* ***current account*** *Banking* compte *m* courant; *St Exch* liquidation *f* courante; ***current affairs***

NPL l'actualité *f*, les questions *fpl* d'actualité

COMP *(programme, magazine)* d'actualités; *Acct* ***current assets*** actif *m* de roulement; *Acct* ***current cost accounting*** comptabilité *f* en coûts actuels; ***current events*** les événements *mpl* actuels, l'actualité *f*; *Acct* ***current liabilities*** passif *m* exigible à court terme; *Fin* ***current rate of exchange*** cours *m* actuel du change; *Acct* ***current value accounting*** comptabilité *f* en valeur actuelle; *Fin* ***current yield*** taux *m* de rendement courant

> Note that the most common meaning of the French adjective **courant** is **common**.

currently [ˈkʌrəntlɪ] **ADV** actuellement, à présent; **c. showing** *(at cinema)* à l'affiche

curriculum [kəˈrɪkjələm] *(pl* **curricula** [-lə] *or* **curriculums)** **N** programme *m* d'enseignement; **on the c.** au programme; **the maths c.** le programme de maths

▸▸ *Br* ***curriculum vitae*** curriculum *m* (vitae)

curry [ˈkʌrɪ] *(pl* **curries,** *pt & pp* **curried)** **N** *Culin* curry *m*, cari *m*; **chicken c.** curry *m ou* cari *m* de poulet

VT 1 *Culin* accommoder au curry **2** *(horse)* étriller; *(leather)* corroyer; **to c. favour with sb** s'insinuer dans les bonnes grâces de qn

▸▸ *Culin* ***curry powder*** curry *m*, cari *m*; *Culin* ***curry sauce*** sauce *f* au curry *ou* cari

currycomb [ˈkʌrɪˌkəʊm] **N** étrille *f*

curse [kɜːs] **N 1** *(evil spell)* malédiction *f*; **to call down** *or* **to put a c. on sb** maudire qn; **a c. on the day I met you!** maudit soit le jour où je vous ai connu!; **the town is under a c.** la ville est sous le coup d'une malédiction

2 *(swearword)* juron *m*, imprécation *f*; *Fam* **curses!** zut!, mince alors!

3 *Fig (bane)* fléau *m*, calamité *f*; **the c. of loneliness** le fléau de la solitude

4 *Fam Old-fashioned or Euph (menstruation)* **the c.** les règles□ *fpl*; **she's got the c.** elle a ses règles

VT 1 *(damn)* maudire; **c. him!** maudit soit-il!; **c. it!** le diable l'emporte! **2** *(swear at)* injurier **3** *(afflict)* affliger; **he's cursed with a bad temper** il est affligé d'un mauvais caractère

VI *(swear)* jurer, blasphémer

▸▸ *Am* ***curse word*** juron *m*

cursed [ˈkɜːsɪd] **ADJ** maudit

cursing [ˈkɜːsɪŋ] **N** jurons *mpl*

cursive [ˈkɜːsɪv] **N** (écriture *f*) cursive *f*

ADJ cursif

cursor [ˈkɜːsə(r)] **N** *Comput* curseur *m*; **move the c. to the right/left** déplacez le curseur vers la droite/gauche; **the word where the c. is** le mot pointé

▸▸ ***cursor blink rate*** vitesse *f* de clignotement du curseur; ***cursor control*** contrôle *m* du curseur; ***cursor key*** touche *f* de curseur; ***cursor movement*** déplacement *m* du curseur; ***cursor position*** position *f* du curseur

cursorily [ˈkɜːsərəlɪ] **ADV** *(superficially)* superficiellement; *(hastily)* hâtivement, à la hâte

cursoriness [ˈkɜːsərɪnɪs] **N** caractère *m* sommaire

cursory [ˈkɜːsərɪ] **ADJ** *(superficial)* superficiel; *(hasty)* hâtif; **she gave the painting only a c. glance** elle n'a jeté qu'un bref coup d'œil au tableau; **after a c. examination of the document** après avoir lu le document en diagonale

curt [kɜːt] **ADJ** *(person, reply, manner)* brusque, sec (sèche); **in a c. tone** d'un ton cassant *ou* sec; **with a c. nod** avec un bref signe de tête

curtail [kɜːˈteɪl] **VT 1** *(cut short ▸ story, visit, studies)* écourter **2** *(reduce ▸ expenses)* réduire, rogner; *(▸ power, freedom)* limiter, réduire

curtailment [kɜːˈteɪlmənt] **N 1** *(of studies, visit)* raccourcissement *m* **2** *(of expenses)* réduction *f*; *(of power, freedom)* limitation *f*, réduction *f*

curtain [ˈkɜːtən] **N 1** *(gen)* rideau *m*; *Fig* rideau *m*, voile *m*; **to draw the curtains** *(open)* ouvrir les rideaux; *(close)* tirer *ou* fermer les rideaux; *Fig* **a c. of smoke** un rideau de fumée; *Fam* **if she finds out, it's curtains for us** si elle apprend ça, on est fichus **2** *Theat (for actor)* rappel *m*

VT garnir de rideaux

▸▸ *Theat* ***curtain call*** rappel *m*; **she took four c. calls** elle a été rappelée quatre fois; ***curtain hook*** crochet *m* de rideau; ***curtain material*** tissu *m* à rideaux; ***curtain rail*** tringle *f* à rideau *ou* à rideaux; ***curtain raiser*** *Theat* lever *m* de rideau; *Fig* événement *m* avant-coureur, prélude *m*; ***curtain ring*** anneau *m* de rideau; ***curtain rod*** tringle *f* à rideau *ou* à rideaux; *Archit* ***curtain wall*** mur-rideau *m*

▸ **curtain off VT SEP** séparer par un rideau

curtainsider [ˈkɜːtənˌsaɪdə(r)] **N** *Aut* camion *m* bâché

curtly [ˈkɜːtlɪ] **ADV** *(bluntly ▸ say, reply)* avec brusquerie, sèchement, sans ménagement

curtness [ˈkɜːtnɪs] **N** *(bluntness ▸ of tone, reply, manner, person)* brusquerie *f*, sécheresse *f*

curtsey, curtsy [ˈkɜːtsɪ] *(pl* **curtseys** *or* **curtsies,** *pt & pp* **curtseyed** *or* **curtsied)** **N** révérence *f*; **she made** *or* **gave a c.** elle a fait une révérence

VI faire une révérence

curvaceous [kɜːˈveɪʃəs] **ADJ** *Hum (woman)* bien fait, plantureux

curvature [ˈkɜːvətjə(r)] **N** *(gen)* courbure *f*; *Med* déviation *f*; **c. of the spine** *(abnormal)* déviation *f* de la colonne vertébrale, scoliose *f*; **the c. of space** la courbure de l'espace

curve [kɜːv] **N 1** *(gen)* courbe *f*; *(in road)* tournant *m*, virage *m*; *Archit (of arch)* voussure *f*; *(of beam)* cambrure *f*; **the c. of the bay** la courbe de la baie; **a woman's curves** les rondeurs *fpl* d'une femme **2** *Math* courbe *f* **3** *Am Sport* balle *f* coupée; *Fig* **to throw sb a c.** prendre qn de court

VI *(gen)* se courber; *(road)* être en courbe, faire une courbe; **to c. down(wards)/up(wards)** descendre/monter en courbe; **the road curves up the mountainside** la route monte en lacets le long de la montagne; **the path curved round to the left** le chemin tournait vers la gauche

VT *(gen)* courber; *Tech* cintrer

curveball [ˈkɜːvbɔːl] **N** *Fig* **to throw a c. at sb, to throw sb a c.** prendre qn au dépourvu; **the interviewer threw me a c. and asked what I thought about the election** l'interviewer m'a pris au dépourvu quand il m'a posé une question sur les élections

curved [kɜːvd] **ADJ** *(gen)* courbe; *(edge)* arrondi; *(road)* en courbe; *(nose)* busqué; *(convex)* convexe; *Tech* cintré

curvilinear [ˌkɜːvɪˈlɪnɪə(r)] **ADJ** *Math* curviligne

curvy [ˈkɜːvɪ] *(compar* **curvier,** *superl* **curviest)** **ADJ 1** *(road, line)* sinueux **2** *Fam (woman)* bien roulé

cushion [ˈkʊʃən] **N 1** *(pillow)* coussin *m*; *Fig* tampon *m*; **on a c. of air** sur un coussin d'air; *Fig* **the annual increase in salary acts as a c. against inflation** l'augmentation annuelle des salaires amortit les effets de l'inflation **2** *(in snooker, billiards etc)* bande *f*; **to play off the c.** jouer par la bande; **stroke off the c.** doublé *m*

VT 1 *(sofa)* mettre des coussins à; *(seat)* rembourrer; *Tech* matelasser **2** *Fig (shock, blow)* amortir; **to c. a fall** amortir une chute; **these tax cuts will c. price rises** ces réductions d'impôts amortiront la hausse des prix; **they have been cushioned against unemployment** ils ont été protégés contre le chômage

cushioning [ˈkʊʃənɪŋ] **N** *Tech* matelassage *m*

cushy [ˈkʊʃɪ] *(compar* **cushier,** *superl* **cushiest)** **ADJ** *Fam* peinard, pépère; **a c. job** *or* **number** une bonne planque, un boulot peinard; **he has a c. life** il a une petite vie peinarde

cusp [kʌsp] **N** *Anat & Bot* cuspide *f*; *Astron (of moon)* cuspide *f*; *Astrol* corne *f*; **on the c. of the 20th century** au tout début du XXème siècle; **on the c. between the 19th and 20th centuries** à la charnière du XIXème et du XXème siècle

cuspidor [ˈkʌspɪdɔː(r)] **N** *Am* crachoir *m*

cuss [kʌs] *Fam* **VI** jurer□, blasphémer□

VT injurier□

N 1 *(oath)* juron□ *m* **2** *Pej (person)* type *m*; **an awkward c.** un mauvais coucheur

cussed [ˈkʌsɪd] **ADJ** *Fam* **1** *(obstinate)* têtu□, entêté□ **2** *(cursed)* sacré; **it's a c. nuisance** c'est bigrement embêtant

cussedness [ˈkʌsɪdnɪs] **N** *Fam* esprit *m* de contradiction□; **out of sheer c.** rien que pour embêter le monde

custard [ˈkʌstəd] **N 1** *(sauce)* crème *f* anglaise épaisse **2** *(dessert)* crème *f* renversée, flan *m*

▸▸ *Br* ***custard apple*** anone *f*, chérimole *f*; ***custard cream*** biscuit *m* fourré à la vanille; ***custard pie*** tarte *f* à la crème; ***custard powder*** crème *f* anglaise instantanée; ***custard tart*** tarte *f* à la crème

custodial [kʌˈstəʊdɪəl] **ADJ** *Law* de prison

▸▸ ***custodial sentence*** peine *f* de prison *ou* de détention; ***custodial staff*** personnel *m* de surveillance

custodian [kʌˈstəʊdɪən] **N 1** *(of building)* gardien(enne) *m,f*; *(of museum)* conservateur(trice) *m,f*; *(of prisoner)* gardien(enne) *m,f*, surveillant(e) *m,f* **2** *Am St Exch* dépositaire *mf*, conservateur(trice) *m,f* de titres **3** *Fig (of morals, tradition)* gardien(enne) *m,f*, protecteur(trice) *m,f*

custody [ˈkʌstədɪ] *(pl* **custodies)** **N 1** *(care)* garde *f*; **the son is in the c. of his mother** le fils est sous la garde de sa mère; **to be given** *or* **awarded c. of a child** obtenir la garde d'un enfant; **the court awarded c. (of the children) to the father** le tribunal a confié la garde des enfants au père; **in safe c.** sous bonne garde **2** *Law (detention)* garde *f* à vue; *(imprisonment)* emprisonnement *m*; *(before trial)* détention *f* préventive; **to be in c.** être en détention préventive; **he was taken into (police) c.** il a été mis en garde à vue

custom [ˈkʌstəm] **N 1** *(tradition)* coutume *f*, usage *m*; **it is the c. to eat fish on Friday** l'usage veut qu'on mange du poisson le vendredi; **as c. has it** selon la coutume *ou* les us et coutumes; **it's her c. to read before going to sleep** elle a l'habitude de lire avant de s'endormir **2** *Com (trade)* clientèle *f*; **they have a lot of foreign c.** ils ont beaucoup de clients étrangers; **he has lost all his c.** il a perdu toute sa clientèle; **I'll take my c. elsewhere** je vais me fournir ailleurs **3** *Law* coutume *f*, droit *m* coutumier

▸▸ ***custom car*** voiture *f* customisée, custom *m*; *Customs* ***custom house*** (poste *m ou* bureau *m* de) douane *f*

customarily [ˌkʌstəˈmerəlɪ] **ADV** d'habitude

customary [ˈkʌstəmərɪ] **ADJ** *Formal* **1** *(traditional)* coutumier, habituel; *(usual)* habituel; **as is c.** comme le veut l'usage; **it is c. to tip taxi drivers** l'usage *ou* la coutume veut que l'on donne un pourboire aux chauffeurs de taxi; **with her c. politeness** avec sa politesse habituelle *ou* coutumière **2** *Law* coutumier

▸▸ ***customary tenant*** tenancier *m* censitaire

custom-built **ADJ** (fait) sur commande

customer [ˈkʌstəmə(r)] **N 1** *(client)* client(e) *m,f*; **regular c.** *(of restaurant etc)* habitué(e) *m,f*; *Prov* **the c. is always right** le client a toujours raison, le client est roi **2** *Fam (character)* type *m*; **he's an awkward c.** il n'est pas commode; **an ugly c.** un sale type

▸▸ *Com & Mktg* ***customer base*** base *f* de clientèle; *Com & Mktg* ***customer care*** = qualité du service fourni à la clientèle; *Com & Mktg* ***customer loyalty*** fidélité *f* de la clientèle; *Com & Mktg* ***customer satisfaction*** satisfaction *f* de la clientèle; *Com & Mktg* ***customer service*** service *m* clientèle; *Com & Mktg* ***customer service department*** service *m* clientèle, service *m* clients

customer-centred, *Am* **customer-centered, customer-driven, customer-focused** ADJ tributaire du consommateur

customization, -isation [ˌkʌstəmaɪˈzeɪʃən] N personnalisation *f*

customize, -ise [ˈkʌstəmaɪz] VT *(make to order)* faire *ou* fabriquer *ou* construire sur commande; *(personalize)* personnaliser; *Comput* **customized software** logiciel *m* sur mesure

custom-made ADJ *(clothing)* (fait) sur mesure; *(other articles)* (fait) sur commande

customs [ˈkʌstəmz] NPL **1** *(authorities, checkpoint)* douane *f*; **to clear** *or* **go through c.** passer la douane; **at c.** à la douane **2** *(duty)* droits *mpl* de douane

►► ***customs agent*** commissionnaire *mf* en douane; ***customs allowance*** tolérance *f ou* franchise *f* douanière; ***customs clearance*** dédouanement *m*; ***customs declaration*** déclaration *f* de *ou* en douane; ***customs duty*** droit *m ou* droits *mpl* de douane; *Br* ***Customs and Excise*** la Régie; ***customs house*** (poste *m ou* bureau *m* de) douane *f*; ***customs inspection*** visite *f* douanière *ou* de douanes; ***customs officer*** douanier(ère) *m,f*; ***customs service*** service *m* des douanes; ***customs union*** union *f* douanière

CUT [kʌt]

VT	
• couper **1–6, 8, 10, 15, 16, 21**	• découper **2**
• tailler **3, 4**	• tondre **3**
• arrêter **7**	• interrompre **6**
• blesser **11**	• réduire **9, 10**
• percer **14**	• manquer **13**
• monter **19**	• graver **17**
VI	
• couper **1, 4, 5, 7**	• se couper **2**
• faire mal **3**	
N	
• coupure **1, 2, 6**	• coup **3, 7**
• morceau **4**	• réduction **5**
• coupe **8, 11, 13**	• part **9**
ADJ	
• coupé **1, 3**	• réduit **2**

(*pt & pp* **cut**, *cont* **cutting**)

VT **1** *(incise, slash, sever)* couper; **he fell and c. his knee (open)** il s'est ouvert le genou en tombant; **she c. her hand** elle s'est coupé la main *ou* à la main; **he c. his wrists** il s'est ouvert *ou* taillé les veines; **they c. his throat** ils lui ont coupé *ou* tranché la gorge, ils l'ont égorgé; **you're cutting your own throat** c'est du suicide; **they c. the prisoners free** *or* **loose** ils ont détaché les prisonniers; *Fig* **to c. oneself loose from sth** se libérer de qch; *Fig* **the atmosphere was so tense, you could c. it with a knife** l'atmosphère était extrêmement tendue

2 *(divide into parts)* couper, découper; *(meat)* découper; *(slice)* découper en tranches; **she c. articles from the paper** elle découpait des articles dans le journal; **c. the cake in half/in three pieces** coupez le gâteau en deux/en trois; **to c. sth to shreds** *or* **to ribbons** mettre qch en pièces; **to c. sth to pieces** *(object)* couper qch en morceaux; *(army)* tailler qch en pièces; *Fig* **the critics c. the play to pieces** les critiques ont esquinté la pièce

3 *(trim ► grass, lawn)* tondre; *(► bush, tree)* tailler; *(reap ► crop)* couper, faucher; **I c. my nails/my hair** je me suis coupé les ongles/les cheveux; **you've had your hair c.** vous vous êtes fait couper les cheveux

4 *(shape ► dress, suit)* couper; *(► diamond, glass, key)* tailler; *(► screw)* fileter; *(dig ► channel, tunnel)* creuser, percer; *(engrave)* graver; *(sculpt)* sculpter; **steps had been c. in the rock** on avait taillé des marches dans le rocher; **the advance c. a swath through the enemy's defences** l'avance des troupes ouvrit une brèche dans la défense ennemie; *Prov* **c. your coat according to your cloth** = il ne faut pas vivre au-dessus de ses moyens

5 *(cross, traverse)* couper, croiser; *Math* couper; **where the path cuts the road** à l'endroit où le chemin coupe la route

6 *(interrupt)* interrompre, couper; **to c. sb short** couper la parole à qn; **we had to c. our visit short** nous avons dû écourter notre visite; **to c. a long story short, I left** bref *ou* en deux mots, je suis parti

7 *(stop)* arrêter, cesser; **he c. working weekends** il a arrêté de travailler le week-end; *very Fam* **c. the crap!** arrête tes conneries!

8 *(switch off)* couper; **he c. the engine** il a coupé *ou* arrêté le moteur

9 *(reduce ► numbers, spending)* réduire; *(► production)* diminuer; *(► speech)* abréger, raccourcir; **we c. our costs by half** nous avons réduit nos frais de moitié; **to c. prices** casser les prix; **the athlete c. five seconds off the world record** *or* **c. the world record by five seconds** l'athlète a amélioré le record mondial de cinq secondes

10 *Cin & TV (edit out)* faire des coupures dans, réduire; *(drop)* couper; **the censors c. two scenes** la censure a coupé *ou* supprimé deux scènes; **the film was c. to 100 minutes** le film a été ramené à 100 minutes

11 *(hurt feelings of)* blesser profondément; **her remark c. me deeply** sa remarque m'a profondément blessé

12 *Fam (ignore, snub)* **they c. me (dead) in the street** dans la rue ils ont fait comme s'ils ne me voyaient pas□

13 *Fam (absent oneself from ► meeting, appointment etc)* manquer (volontairement)□, sauter□; **I had to c. lunch in order to get there on time** j'ai dû me passer de déjeuner pour arriver à l'heure; **to c. class/school** sécher les cours

14 *(tooth)* percer; **the baby is cutting his first tooth** le bébé perce sa première dent; *Fam Fig* **a pianist who c. her teeth on Bach** une pianiste qui s'est fait la main sur du Bach

15 *Comput* couper; **to c. and paste sth** couper-coller qch

16 *(dilute)* couper

17 *(record, track)* graver, faire

18 *Cards* **to c. the cards** couper

19 *Cin (edit ► film)* monter

20 *Med (incise)* inciser; *Vet (castrate)* châtrer

21 *Sport (ball)* couper

22 *(idioms)* **to c. the ground from under sb's feet** couper l'herbe sous le pied de qn; *Fam* **he couldn't c. it, he couldn't c. the mustard** il n'était pas à la hauteur□; **you're cutting it a bit fine** vous comptez un peu juste; **an hour is cutting it too fine** une heure, ce n'est pas suffisant; *Fam* **that argument cuts no ice with me** cet argument ne m'impressionne pas□; **to c. a fine figure** avoir fière allure; **to c. one's losses** sauver les meubles; **to c. a caper** *or* **capers** *(skip)* faire des cabrioles, gambader; *(fool around)* faire l'idiot; *Aut* **to c. a corner** prendre un virage à la corde, couper un virage

VI **1** *(incise, slash)* couper, trancher; **this knife doesn't c.** ce couteau ne coupe pas bien; **c. around the edge** découpez *ou* coupez en suivant le bord; **she c. into the bread** elle a entamé le pain; **the rope c. into my wrists** la corde m'a coupé *ou* cisaillé les poignets; *Fig* **he c. through all the red tape** il s'est dispensé de toutes les formalités administratives; *Fig* **the yacht c. through the waves** le yacht fendait les vagues; *Fig* **to c. loose** se libérer; **to c. and run** se sauver, filer; **that argument cuts both** *or* **two ways** c'est un argument à double tranchant

2 *(cloth, paper)* se couper; **this meat cuts easily** cette viande se coupe facilement; **the cake will c. into six pieces** ce gâteau peut se couper en six

3 *(hurtfully)* faire mal

4 *(cross)* traverser, couper; *Math (lines)* se couper; **to c. through the park** couper par le parc

5 *(in cards)* couper

6 *Comput* **to c. and paste** couper-coller

7 *Cin & TV (stop filming)* couper; **the film cuts straight from the love scene to the funeral** l'image passe directement de la scène d'amour à l'enterrement; *Fam Fig* **to c. to the chase** en venir au fait

N **1** *(slit)* coupure *f*; *(deeper)* entaille *f*; *(wound)* balafre *f*; *Med* incision *f*; **a c. on the arm** une coupure *ou* une entaille au bras; **to be a c. above (the rest)** être nettement mieux que les autres *ou* le reste

2 *(act of cutting)* coupure *f*, entaille *f*; **to make a c. in sth** *(with knife, scissors etc)* faire une entaille dans qch

3 *(blow, stroke)* coup *m*; **a knife/sword c.** un coup de couteau/d'épée; **a saw c.** un trait de scie; *Fig* **his treachery was the unkindest c. of all** sa trahison était le coup le plus perfide

4 *(meat ► piece)* morceau *m*; *(► slice)* tranche *f*; **a c. off the joint** un morceau de rôti; **prime c.** morceau *m* de (premier) choix; **cheap cuts** bas morceaux *mpl*

5 *(reduction ► in price, taxes)* réduction *f*, diminution *f*; *(► in staff)* compression *f*; **the cuts in the Health Service** la réduction *ou* diminution du budget de la santé; **she took a c. in pay** elle a subi une diminution *ou* réduction de salaire; *Fin* **the cuts** les compressions *fpl* budgétaires; **power** *or* **electricity c.** coupure *f* de courant; **to make the c.** *Golf* se qualifier; *Fig* passer au stade suivant

6 *(deletion)* coupure *f*

7 *(gibe, nasty remark)* trait *m*, coup *m*

8 *(shape, style ► of clothes, hair)* coupe *f*; *(► of jewel)* taille *f*; **the c. of a suit** la coupe d'un costume

9 *Fam (portion, share)* part□ *f*; **what's his c. (of the profits)?** à combien s'élève sa part?

10 *Am Fam (absence)* absence□ *f*

11 *Cards* coupe *f*

12 *Fam (on record)* plage□ *f*

13 *Cin & TV* coupe *f*; **the c. from the love scene to the funeral** le changement de séquence de la scène d'amour à l'enterrement

14 *Sport (in tennis ► backspin)* effet *m*; *(in cricket)* coup *m* tranchant

15 *Am Typ (block)* cliché *m*

16 *Br (body of water)* étendue *f* d'eau; *(canal)* canal *m*

17 *(of tobacco)* **I prefer a finer/coarser c. of tobacco** je préfère le tabac plus fin/grossier

18 *(idioms)* **the c. and thrust of parliamentary debate** les joutes oratoires des débats parlementaires; **the c. and thrust of the business world** la concurrence féroce qui règne dans le monde des affaires

ADJ **1** *(hand, flowers)* coupé; *(tobacco)* découpé

2 *(reduced)* réduit; *(shortened)* raccourci; **to sell sth at c. prices** vendre qch au rabais; **the c. version of the film** la version raccourcie du film

3 *(shaped ► clothing)* coupé; *(faceted ► gem)* taillé; **a well-c. suit** un costume bien coupé *ou* de bonne coupe

4 *Br Fam (drunk)* soûl, plein

5 *(idiom)* **c. and dried** *(opinions)* tout fait; **everything was c. and dried** *(decided)* tout était déjà décidé; **it's not as c. and dried as that** ce n'est pas aussi simple que ça

►► ***cut glass*** cristal *m* taillé; *Comput* ***cut sheet feed*** dispositif *m* d'alimentation feuille à feuille; *(act)* alimentation *f* feuille à feuille; *Comput* ***cut sheet feeder*** dispositif *m* d'alimentation feuille à feuille

▸ **cut across** VT INSEP **1** *(cross, traverse)* traverser, couper à travers; **it's quicker if you c. across the fields** c'est plus rapide si tu coupes à travers (les) champs; **they c. across country** ils ont coupé à travers champs **2** *(go beyond)* surpasser, transcender; **the issue cuts across party lines** la question transcende le clivage des partis

▸ **cut along** VI *Br Fam Old-fashioned* filer

▸ **cut away** VT SEP *(remove)* enlever *ou* ôter (en coupant); *(branch)* élaguer, émonder; **they had to c. away the wreckage to reach the victim** ils ont dû découper l'épave pour atteindre la victime

▸ **cut back** VI **1** *(financially)* économiser, réduire les dépenses **2** *Cin & TV* revenir en arrière **to c. back to sth** revenir à qch **3** *(return)* rebrousser chemin, revenir sur ses pas

VT SEP **1** *(reduce)* réduire, diminuer; **arms spending has been c. right back** les dépenses d'armement ont été nettement réduites **2** *(prune, trim)* tailler; *(shrub, tree)* élaguer, tailler

▸ **cut back on** VT INSEP *(financially)* économiser sur; *(time)* réduire; **the factory c. back on production** la fabrique a réduit la production; **to c. back on smoking** fumer moins

▸ **cut down** VT SEP **1** *(tree)* couper, abattre; *(person ► in battle)* abattre; *Fig* **he was c. down by malaria** *(killed)* il est mort de la malaria; *(incapacitated)* il était terrassé par la malaria; *Literary* **to be c. down in one's prime** être fauché à la fleur de l'âge **2** *(make smaller ► article, speech)* abréger; *(► clothing)* rendre plus petit;

to c. sth down to about 150,000 words réduire qch à environ 150 000 mots; **she cuts down her dresses for her daughter** elle ajuste ses robes pour sa fille; **to c. sb down to size** remettre qn à sa place **3** *(curtail)* réduire, diminuer; *(expenses)* réduire, rogner; **we've been asked to c. down the amount of time we devote to sports** on nous a demandé de consacrer moins de temps au sport; **he c. his smoking down to ten a day** il ne fume plus que dix cigarettes par jour

▸ **cut down on** VT INSEP *(expenditure)* réduire; **I'm going to c. down on drinking/smoking** je vais boire/fumer moins; **they have c. down on eating out in restaurants** ils vont moins souvent au restaurant; **to c. down on the amount of time spent doing sth** passer moins de temps à faire qch

▸ **cut in** VI **1** *(interrupt)* interrompre; **she c. in on their conversation** elle est intervenue dans leur conversation; **he c. in on me to ask a question** il m'a coupé la parole pour poser une question; *Fig* **the new store is cutting in on our business** le nouveau magasin nous fait perdre de la clientèle

2 *Aut* faire une queue de poisson; **the taxi c. in in front of them** le taxi leur a fait une queue de poisson

3 *(at a dance)* **mind if I c. in?** vous permettez que je vous emprunte votre partenaire?

4 *Tech (of mechanism, safety device)* entrer en action

VT SEP *(include)* **we should c. him in on the deal** nous devrions l'intéresser à l'affaire

▸ **cut into** VT INSEP **1** *(interrupt)* **to c. into a conversation** intervenir dans *ou* interrompre brusquement la conversation **2** *(use)* **to c. into one's savings** entamer ses économies; **this work cuts into my free time** ce travail empiète sur mes heures de loisir

▸ **cut off** VT SEP **1** *(hair, piece of meat, bread)* couper; *(arm, leg)* amputer, couper; **they c. off the king's head** ils ont décapité le roi; **he was c. off in his prime** il a été emporté à la fleur de l'âge; **she c. off her nose to spite her face** elle s'est fait du tort en voulant se venger

2 *(interrupt* ▸ *speaker)* interrompre, couper; **he was c. off in mid sentence** il a été interrompu au milieu de sa phrase

3 *(disconnect, discontinue)* couper; *Tel* **he's been c. off** *(during conversation)* il a été coupé; *(disconnected)* on lui a coupé le téléphone; **they c. off the electricity** *or* **power** ils ont coupé le courant; **they c. off his allowance** ils lui ont coupé les vivres; **her family c. her off without a penny** sa famille l'a déshéritée; **it c. off the supply of blood to the brain** cela a empêché l'irrigation du cerveau

4 *(separate, isolate)* isoler; **the house was c. off by snow drifts** la maison était isolée par des congères; **he c. himself off from his family** il a rompu avec sa famille; **I feel c. off** je me sens coupé du monde

5 *(bar passage of)* couper la route à; **the battalion c. off the enemy's retreat** le bataillon a coupé la retraite à l'ennemi

▸ **cut out** VT SEP **1** *(make by cutting* ▸ *coat, dress)* couper, tailler; **a valley c. out by the river** une vallée creusée par le fleuve; *Fig* **to be c. out for sth** être fait pour qch, avoir des dispositions pour qch; **I'm not c. out for living abroad** je ne suis pas fait pour vivre à l'étranger; **he's not c. out to be a politician** il n'a pas l'étoffe d'un homme politique; **you have your work c. out for you** vous avez du pain sur la planche *ou* de quoi vous occuper

2 *(remove by cutting* ▸ *article, picture)* découper; *Med (*▸ *tumour etc)* enlever; **advertisements c. out from** *or* **of the paper** des annonces découpées dans le journal

3 *(eliminate)* supprimer; *(stop)* arrêter; **they c. out all references to the president** ils ont supprimé toute référence au président; **the new building cuts out a lot of the light** le nouveau bâtiment coupe une bonne partie de la lumière; **he c. out smoking** il a arrêté de fumer; *Fam* **c. it out!** ça suffit!, ça va comme ça!

4 *Fam (rival)* supplanter□

5 *(deprive)* priver; **his father c. him out of his will** son père l'a rayé de son testament; **they c. him out of his share** ils lui ont escroqué sa part

6 *Phot & Typ* détourer

VI **1** *(machine, engine* ▸ *stop operating)* caler; *(*▸ *switch off)* s'éteindre **2** *Am Fam (leave)* mettre les bouts, calter

▸ **cut up** VT SEP **1** *(food, wood)* couper; *(meat* ▸ *carve)* découper; *(*▸ *chop up)* hacher; *(body)* couper en morceaux

2 *(usu passive) Fam (affect deeply)* **she's really c. up about her dog's death** la mort de son chien a été un coup pour elle□; **he's very c. up about it** ça l'a beaucoup affecté□

3 *Am Fam (amuse)* **that really c. me up!** ça m'a fait rire!□

4 *Br Aut* faire une queue de poisson de

VI *Fam* **1** *Am (fool around)* faire le pitre **2** *Br (idiom)* **to c. up rough** se mettre en rogne *ou* en boule

cut-and-paste *Comput* VT couper-coller
VI couper-coller
N couper-coller *m*

cutaneous [kju'temjəs] ADJ *Anat* cutané

cutaway ['kʌtəweɪ] N **1** *(coat)* jaquette *f (d'homme)* **2** *(drawing, model)* écorché *m* **3** *Cin & TV* changement *m* de plan

cutback ['kʌtbæk] N **1** *(reduction* ▸ *in costs)* réduction *f*, diminution *f*; *(*▸ *in staff)* compression *f*; **a c. in production** une réduction de production **2** *Am Cin & TV* retour *m* en arrière, flashback *m*

cute [kju:t] ADJ *Fam* **1** *(attractive)* mignon□; *Am Pej* affecté□ **2** *(clever)* malin(igne)□; *Pej* **don't get c. with me** ne fais pas le malin avec moi

cuteness ['kju:tnɪs] N *Fam* **1** *(attractiveness)* charme□ *m* **2** *(cleverness)* ruse□ *f*

cuticle ['kju:tɪkəl] N **1** *Anat (skin)* épiderme *m*; *(on nails)* petites peaux *fpl*, envie *f* **2** *Bot* cuticule *f*

▸▸ ***cuticle remover*** repousse-peaux *m*

cutie ['kju:tɪ] N *Fam* **1** *(child, baby)* mignon (onne)□ *m,f*; *(term of endearment)* mon chou **2** *(shrewd person)* malin(igne)□ *m,f*

cutie-pie N *Fam (child, baby)* mignon(onne)□ *m,f*; *(term of endearment)* mon chou

cutlass ['kʌtləs] N *Hist* coutelas *m*

cutler ['kʌtlə(r)] N coutelier(ère) *m,f*

cutlery ['kʌtlərɪ] N *(UNCOUNT)* **1** *(eating utensils)* couverts *mpl* **2** *(knives, trade)* coutellerie *f*

cutlet ['kʌtlɪt] N *Culin* **1** *(gen)* côtelette *f*; *(of veal)* escalope *f* **2** *Br (croquette)* croquette *f*; **vegetable cutlets** croquettes *fpl* de légumes

cutoff ['kʌtɒf] N **1** *(stopping point)* limite *f*; **$100 is our c. (point)** nous nous arrêtons à 100 dollars, nous n'irons pas au-delà de 100 dollars; **we've taken a score of 370 as the c. point in deciding who to interview** *(no less than)* les candidats doivent avoir au minimum 370 points pour pouvoir passer l'entretien; **the c. point for remedial lessons is 150** *(no more than)* seuls les élèves qui obtiennent 150 points ou en deçà pourront bénéficier de cours de rattrapage **2** *Am (short-cut)* raccourci *m*

• **cutoffs** NPL **(a pair of) cutoffs** = un jean coupé pour en faire un short

▸▸ ***cutoff date*** date *f* limite; *Tech* ***cutoff device*** système *m* d'arrêt; *Tech* ***cutoff switch*** interrupteur *m*

cutout ['kʌtaʊt] N **1** *(figure)* découpage *m* **2** *Elec* disjoncteur *m*, coupe-circuit *m*; *Aut* échappement *m* libre

▸▸ ***cutout book*** livre *m* de découpages; *Astron* ***cutout point*** *(of rocket)* point *m* de largage

cut-price ADJ *(articles)* à prix réduit, au rabais; *(shop)* à prix réduits; *(manufacturer)* qui vend à prix réduits
ADV à prix réduit

cutter ['kʌtə(r)] N **1** *(person* ▸ *of clothes)* coupeur (euse) *m,f*; *(*▸ *of jewels)* tailleur *m*; *(*▸ *of film)* monteur(euse) *m,f* **2** *(tool)* coupoir *m* **3** *(sailing boat)* cotre *m*, cutter *m*; *(motorboat)* vedette *f*; *(of coastguard)* garde-côte *m*; *(warship)* canot *m*

cut-throat ['kʌtθrəʊt] N **1** *(murderer)* assassin *m* **2** *(razor)* rasoir *m* à main
ADJ féroce; *(competition)* acharné; *(prices)* très compétitif; **publishing is a c. business** le milieu de l'édition est un panier de crabes

▸▸ *Cards* ***cut-throat game*** partie *f* à trois; ***cut-throat razor*** rasoir *m* à main

cutting ['kʌtɪŋ] N **1** *(act)* coupe *f*; *(of jewel, stone)* taille *f*; *(of film)* montage *m*; *(of trees)* coupe *f*, abattage *m* **2** *(piece* ▸ *of cloth)* coupon *m*; *(*▸ *from newspaper)* coupure *f*; *Agr (*▸ *of shrub, vine)* marcotte *f*; *Hort (*▸ *of plant)* bouture *f*; **to take a c.** faire une bouture; **to grow a plant from a c.** faire pousser une plante à partir d'une bouture **3** *(for railway, road)* tranchée *f*
ADJ **1** *(tool)* tranchant, coupant **2** *(wind)* glacial, cinglant; *(rain)* cinglant **3** *(hurtful* ▸ *remark)* mordant, tranchant; *(*▸ *word)* cinglant, blessant; **she was rather c. about them** elle a dit des choses un peu dures sur eux

▸▸ ***cutting back*** *(of tree)* élagage *m*; *(of production, budget)* réduction *f*; *Cin & TV* ***cutting copy*** copie *f* de montage; ***cutting edge*** tranchant *m*; *Fig* **to be at the c. edge of technological progress** être à la pointe du progrès en technologie; *Press* ***cuttings file*** fichier *m* de coupures; ***cutting pliers*** pinces *fpl* coupantes; *Cin* ***cutting room*** salle *f* de montage; **my best scenes ended up on the c. room floor** mes meilleures scènes ont été coupées (au montage); *Cin & TV* ***cutting table*** table *f* de montage

cuttingly ['kʌtɪŋlɪ] ADV *(say)* d'un ton caustique

cuttlebone ['kʌtəlbəʊn] N os *m* de seiche

cuttlefish ['kʌtəlfɪʃ] *(pl* **inv***)* N *Ich* seiche *f*

▸▸ ***cuttlefish ink*** sépia *f*

CV [ˌsi:'vi:] N *Br (abbr* **curriculum vitae***)* CV *m*
ADJ *(abbr* **cardiovascular***)* cardio-vasculaire; **a CV workout** une séance de cardio-training

CV joint [ˌsi:'vi:-] N *Aut (abbr* **constant velocity joint***)* joint *m* de cardan

CVP [ˌsi:vi:'pi:] N *Fin (abbr* **cost-volume-profit***)* étude *f* de coût-efficacité

CWD [ˌsi:dʌbəlju:'di:] N *Vet (abbr* **Chronic Wasting Disease***)* maladie *f* du dépérissement chronique

cwo, CWO *Com (written abbr* **cash with order***)* payable à la commande

cwt *(written abbr* **hundredweight***)* *Br* = 50,8 kg, (poids *m* de) 112 livres *fpl*; *Am* = 45,36 kg, (poids *m* de) 100 livres *fpl*

CWU [ˌsi:dʌbəlju:'ju:] N *(abbr* **Communication Workers Union***)* = syndicat britannique des travailleurs des télécommunications

cyan ['saɪən] *Comput & Typ* ADJ cyan *(inv)*
N cyan *m inv*

cyanide ['saɪənaɪd] N *Chem* cyanure *m*

▸▸ ***cyanide poisoning*** empoisonnement *m* au cyanure

cyanosis [ˌsaɪə'nəʊsɪs] N *(UNCOUNT) Med* cyanose *f*

cyber ['saɪbə(r)] N *Comput* cyber *m*

cyberbanking ['saɪbəˌbæŋkɪŋ] N *Comput* transactions *fpl* bancaires en ligne

cyberbullying ['saɪbəˌbʊlɪɪŋ] N harcèlement *m* électronique, cyberharcèlement *m*, *Can* cyber-intimidation *f*

cybercafé ['saɪbəˌkæfeɪ] N *Comput* cybercafé *m*

cybercrime ['saɪbəkraɪm] N *Comput* cybercrime *m*

cyberculture ['saɪbəˌkʌltʃə(r)] N *Comput* cyberculture *f*

Cyber Monday ['saɪbə-] N *Am* = le lundi après Thanksgiving quand les gens retournent au bureau et reprennent leurs achats sur Internet

cybernaut ['saɪbənɔ:t] N *Comput* cybernaute *m*

cybernetic [ˌsaɪbə'netɪk] ADJ *Biol & Comput* cybernétique

cybernetics [ˌsaɪbə'netɪks] N *(UNCOUNT) Biol & Comput* cybernétique *f*

cyberpirate ['saɪbəˌpaɪrət] N *Comput* cyberpirate *m*

cyberpunk ['saɪbəˌpʌŋk] N *Literature* cyberpunk *m*

cybersex ['saɪbəˌseks] N *Comput* cybersexe *m*

cyberslacker ['saɪbəˌslækə(r)] N *Fam Comput* cyberparesseux(euse) *m,f*, = employé qui se sert du courrier électronique et de l'Internet de sa société à des fins personnelles pendant les heures de travail

cyberslacking ['saɪbəˌslækɪŋ] N *Fam Comput* cyberparesse *f*, = fait pour un employé de se servir du courrier électronique et de l'Internet de sa société à des fins personnelles pendant les heures de travail

cyberspace ['saɪbə,speɪs] **N** *Comput* cyberespace *m*; **in c.** dans le cyberespace

cybersquatter ['saɪbə,skwɒtə(r)] **N** *Comput* cybersquatteur *m*

cybersquatting ['saɪbə,skwɒtɪŋ] **N** *Comput* cybersquatting *m*, *Offic* cybersquattage *m*

cyberstalker ['saɪbə,stɔːkə(r)] **N** *Comput* = personne qui en harcèle une autre par l'intermédiaire d'Internet

cyberstalking ['saɪbə,stɔːkɪŋ] **N** *Comput* cybertraque *f*, *Offic* cyberharcèlement *m*

cyberterrorism [,saɪbə'terərɪzəm] **N** *Comput* cyberterrorisme *m*

cyberterrorist [,saɪbə'terərɪst] **N** *Comput* cyberterroriste *mf*

cyberwar ['saɪbə,wɔː(r)] **N** *Comput* cyberguerre *f*

cyclamen ['sɪkləmən] *(pl* **inv***)* **N** *Bot* cyclamen *m*

cycle ['saɪkəl] **N 1** *(gen)* cycle *m*; **the c. of the seasons** le cycle des saisons **2** *(bicycle)* bicyclette *f*, vélo *m*; *(tricycle)* tricycle *m*; *(motorcycle)* motocyclette *f*, moto *f*

VI faire de la bicyclette *ou* du vélo; **she cycled into town every day** elle allait en ville à bicyclette *ou* à vélo chaque jour

▸▸ ***cycle lane*** piste *f* cyclable; ***cycle path*** piste *f ou* bande *f* cyclable; ***cycle racing track*** vélodrome *m*; ***cycle rack*** *(on pavement)* râtelier *m* à bicyclettes *ou* à vélos; *(on car)* porte-vélos *m inv*; ***cycle track*** piste *f ou* bande *f* cyclable

cycler ['saɪklə(r)] **N** *Am* cycliste *mf*

cyclic ['saɪklɪk] **ADJ** cyclique

cyclical ['saɪklɪkəl] **ADJ** cyclique

▸▸ *Econ* ***cyclical fluctuations*** fluctuations *fpl* cycliques; *St Exch* ***cyclical stocks*** valeurs *fpl* cycliques; *Econ* ***cyclical unemployment*** chômage *m* conjoncturel

cycling ['saɪklɪŋ] **N** cyclisme *m*; **I go c. every weekend** *(gen)* je fais du vélo tous les week-ends; *Sport* tous les week-ends, je fais du cyclisme; **we went on a c. holiday** nous avons fait du cyclotourisme

COMP *(magazine, shoes)* de cyclisme

▸▸ ***cycling club*** club *m* de cyclisme; ***cycling clothes*** tenue *f* cycliste; ***cycling shorts*** cuissard *m*; ***cycling tour*** circuit *m* à bicyclette *ou* à vélo

cyclist ['saɪklɪst] **N** cycliste *mf*

cyclone ['saɪkləʊn] **N** *Met* cyclone *m*

▸▸ *Met* ***cyclone cellar*** abri *m* anticyclone

cyclonic [saɪ'klɒnɪk] **ADJ** *Met* cyclonique, cyclonal

cyclorama [,saɪkləʊ'rɑːmə] **N** *Art & Theat* cyclorama *m*

cyclostyle ['saɪkləʊ,staɪl] *Old-fashioned* **N** machine *f* à polycopier

VT polycopier

cyclotron ['saɪklətrɒn] **N** *Phys* cyclotron *m*

cygnet ['sɪgnɪt] **N** jeune cygne *m*

cylinder ['sɪlɪndə(r)] **N 1** *Aut, Math & Tech* cylindre *m*; **four-c. engine** moteur *m* à quatre cylindres; **six-c. car** six-cylindres *f*; **oxygen/gas c.** bouteille *f* d'oxygène/de gaz; **to be firing on all cylinders** *(engine)* tourner rond; *Fig (company)* fonctionner à plein régime; *(person)* être en pleine forme **2** *(of typewriter)* rouleau *m*; *(of gun)* barillet *m*

▸▸ *Tech* ***cylinder block*** bloc-cylindres *m*; *Tech* ***cylinder head*** culasse *f (d'un moteur)*; ***cylinder vacuum cleaner*** aspirateur-traîneau *m*

cylindrical [sɪ'lɪndrɪkəl] **ADJ** cylindrique

cymbal ['sɪmbəl] **N** cymbale *f*

Cymru ['kʊmrɪ] **N** = nom gallois du pays de Galles

cynic ['sɪnɪk] *(gen) & Phil* **N** cynique *mf*

ADJ cynique

cynical ['sɪnɪkəl] **ADJ** *(gen) & Phil* cynique

cynically ['sɪnɪklɪ] **ADV** *(gen) & Phil* cyniquement, avec cynisme

cynicism ['sɪnɪsɪzəm] **N** *(gen) & Phil* **1** *(attitude)* cynisme *m* **2** *(cynical remark)* remarque *f* cynique

cypher = **cipher**

cypress ['saɪprəs] **N** *Bot* cyprès *m*; **false c.** faux cyprès *m*, *Spec* chamæcyparis *m*

Cypriot ['sɪprɪət] **N** Chypriote *mf*, Cypriote *mf*; **Greek C.** Chypriote *mf* grec (grecque); **Turkish C.** Chypriote *mf* turc (turque)

ADJ chypriote, cypriote

COMP *(embassy, history)* de Chypre

Cyprus ['saɪprəs] **N** Chypre

Cyrillic [sɪ'rɪlɪk] **N** alphabet *m* cyrillique

ADJ cyrillique

cyst [sɪst] **N 1** *Med* kyste *m* **2** *Biol* sac *m* (membraneux)

cystic ['sɪstɪk] **ADJ** *Med* kystique

▸▸ ***cystic fibrosis*** mucoviscidose *f*

cystitis [sɪs'taɪtɪs] **N** *Med* cystite *f*; **to have c.** avoir une cystite

cytologic [,saɪtə'lɒdʒɪk], **cytological** [saɪtə'lɒdʒɪkəl] **ADJ** *Biol* cytologique

cytology [saɪ'tɒlədʒɪ] **N** *Biol* cytologie *f*

cytomegalovirus [,saɪtəʊ'megələʊ,vaɪrəs] **N** *Med* cytomégalovirus *m*

czar [zɑː(r)] **N** *(monarch)* tsar *m*; *(top person)* éminence *f* grise, ponte *m*

czarevitch ['zɑːrəvɪtʃ] **N** tsarévitch *m*

czarina [zɑː'riːnə] **N** tsarine *f*

czarist ['zɑːrɪst] **N** tsariste *mf*

ADJ tsariste

Czech [tʃek] **N 1** *(person)* Tchèque *mf* **2** *(language)* tchèque *m*

ADJ tchèque

COMP *(embassy, history)* de la République tchèque; *(teacher)* de tchèque

▸▸ ***the Czech Republic*** la République tchèque

Czechoslovak [,tʃekə'sləʊvæk] *Formerly* **N** Tchécoslovaque *mf*

ADJ tchécoslovaque

Czechoslovakia [,tʃekəslə'vækɪə] **N** *Formerly* Tchécoslovaquie *f*

d

D[1], d[1] [diː] **N 1** *(letter)* D, d *m inv*; **D for dog** D comme Désiré; **in 3-D** en trois dimensions, en 3-D

2 *Sch* **to get a D** avoir une mauvaise note, avoir entre 7 et 9 sur 20

3 *Mus* ré *m*

4 *Sport* **the D** *(on soccer field)* l'arc *m* de cercle pour coup de réparation

ADJ *Mus (string)* de ré

D[2] *Am (written abbr* **democrat, democratic***)* démocrate

d[2] 1 *(written abbr* **penny***)* = symbole du penny anglais jusqu'en 1971 **2** *(written abbr* **died***)* **d 1913** mort en 1913

DA [ˌdiːˈeɪ] **N** *Am Law (abbr* **District Attorney***)* Procureur *m* de la République; **the DA's office** le parquet

DAB [ˌdiːeɪˈbiː] **N** *(abbr* **digital audio broadcasting***)* diffusion *f* audionumérique

dab [dæb] *(pt & pp* **dabbed**, *cont* **dabbing***)* **N 1** *(small amount)* **a d.** un petit peu; **a d. of perfume** une goutte de parfum; **just give it a d. of paint** mets-y un coup de peinture

2 *(touch)* petit coup *m*; **a d. with a cloth** un petit coup de chiffon

3 *Ich* limande *f*

4 *Br Fam (idiom)* **to be a d. hand at sth** être doué en *ou* pour qch□; **to be a d. hand at doing sth** être doué pour faire qch□

VT 1 *(touch lightly)* tamponner; **to d. one's eyes (with a handkerchief)** se tamponner les yeux; **she dabbed the graze with cotton wool** elle tamponna l'écorchure avec du coton **2** *(daub)* **he dabbed paint on the canvas** il posait la peinture sur la toile par petites touches

• **dabs NPL** *Br Fam (fingerprints)* empreintes *fpl* digitales□

▸**dab off VT SEP** ôter en tamponnant

▸**dab on VT SEP** *(paint, antiseptic etc)* appliquer par petites touches

dabble [ˈdæbəl] **VT** mouiller; **they dabbled their feet in the water** ils trempaient les pieds dans l'eau

VI *Fig* **she dabbles in politics** elle fait un peu de politique; **to d. in art/music** être un peu artiste/musicien; **to d. on the Stock Market** boursicoter

dabbler [ˈdæblə(r)] **N** dilettante *mf*

dace [deɪs] **N** *Ich* dard *m*, vandoise *f*

dacha [ˈdætʃə] **N** dacha *f*

dachshund [ˈdækshʊnd] **N** teckel *m*

Dacron® [ˈdækrɒn] **N** *Am Tex* Dacron® *m*, Tergal® *m*

dactyl [ˈdæktɪl] **N** *Literature* dactyle *m*

dad [dæd] **N** *Fam (father)* papa *m*

Dada [ˈdɑːdɑː] *Art & Literature* **N** dada *m*

ADJ dada *(inv)*, dadaïste

Dadaism [ˈdɑːdɑːɪzəm] **N** *Art & Literature* dadaïsme *m*

daddy [ˈdædɪ] *(pl* **daddies***)* **N** *Fam* papa *m*; *Am* **the d. of them all** le meilleur de tous□

daddy-long-legs N *Br, Austr & NZ (crane fly)* tipule *f*; *Am (harvestman)* faucheur *m*, faucheux *m*

dado [ˈdeɪdəʊ] *(pl* **dadoes***)* **N** *Constr (of wall)* lambris *m* d'appui; *Archit (of pedestal)* dé *m*

►► ***dado rail*** cimaise *f*

daemon [ˈdiːmən] **N 1** *(demigod)* demi-dieu *m* **2** *(devil, evil spirit)* démon *m*

daff [dæf] **N** *Br Fam (daffodil)* jonquille□ *f*

daffodil [ˈdæfədɪl] **N** jonquille *f*

►► ***daffodil yellow*** jaune *m* d'or

daffy [ˈdæfɪ] *(compar* **daffier**, *superl* **daffiest***)* *Fam* **ADJ** *(person, idea)* loufoque, timbré

daft [dɑːft] *Fam* **ADJ** *Br (foolish)* idiot□, bête□; **don't be d.!** (ne) fais pas l'idiot!; **he's d. about her** il est fou d'elle

ADV don't talk d. ne dites pas de bêtises

daftie [ˈdɑːftɪ] **N** *Br Fam* cruche *f*, andouille *f*

daftness [ˈdɑːftnɪs] **N** *Br Fam* stupidité□ *f*

dag [dæg] **N** *Austr Fam* **1** *(unfashionable person)* ringard(e) *m,f* **2** *(untidy man)* type *m* négligé; *(untidy woman)* bonne femme *f* négligée

dagger [ˈdægə(r)] **N 1** *(weapon)* poignard *m*; *(smaller)* dague *f*; *Fig* **to be at daggers drawn with sb** être à couteaux tirés avec qn; **to** *Br* **look** *or Am* **shoot daggers at sb** foudroyer qn du regard **2** *Typ* croix *f*

dago [ˈdeɪgəʊ] *(pl* **dagos** *or* **dagoes***)* **N** métèque *mf*, = terme injurieux désignant une personne d'origine espagnole, italienne ou portugaise

dahlia [ˈdeɪljə] **N** dahlia *m*

Dáil (Éireann) [dɔɪl(ˈeərən)] **N** *Ir Parl* = chambre des députés de la république d'Irlande

daily [ˈdeɪlɪ] *(pl* **dailies***)* **ADJ** *(routine, task)* quotidien, de tous les jours; *(output, wage)* journalier; **to be paid on a d. basis** être payé à la journée; **(to earn) one's d. bread** (gagner) son pain quotidien; *Bible* **give us this day our d. bread** donne-nous aujourd'hui notre pain de ce jour

ADV tous les jours, quotidiennement; **twice d.** deux fois par jour

N 1 *(newspaper)* quotidien *m* **2** *Br Fam (servant)* femme *f* de ménage *(qui vient tous les jours)* **3** *Cin & TV* **dailies** rushes *mpl*

►► *Br Fam Old-fashioned* ***daily dozen*** gym *f* quotidienne□; *Fam* ***the daily grind*** le train-train quotidien; *Br* ***daily help, daily maid*** femme *f* de ménage *(qui vient tous les jours)*; *St Exch* ***Daily Official List*** cours *mpl* de clôture quotidiens; ***daily paper*** quotidien *m*; ***the daily round*** la tournée quotidienne

daintily [ˈdeɪntɪlɪ] **ADV 1** *(eat, hold)* délicatement; *(walk)* avec grâce **2** *(dress)* coquettement

daintiness [ˈdeɪntɪnɪs] **N 1** *(of manner)* délicatesse *f*, raffinement *m* **2** *(of dress)* coquetterie *f*

dainty [ˈdeɪntɪ] *(pl* **dainties**, *compar* **daintier**, *superl* **daintiest***)* **N** *(food)* mets *m* délicat; *(sweet)* friandise *f*

ADJ 1 *(small)* menu, petit; *(delicate* ▸ *features, porcelain, ornament)* délicat; **to walk with d. steps** marcher à petits pas délicats **2** *(food)* de choix, délicat; **d. morsels** mets *mpl* de choix **3** *(fussy)* **she's a d. eater** elle est difficile pour *ou* sur la nourriture

dairy [ˈdeərɪ] *(pl* **dairies***)* **N 1** *(building on farm)* laiterie *f*; *(shop)* crémerie *f*, laiterie *f* **2** *NZ (shop)* petite épicerie *f*

COMP *(cow, farm, products)* laitier; *(butter, cream)* fermier

►► ***dairy cattle*** vaches *fpl* laitières, bovins *mp*[l] laitiers; ***dairy farmer*** producteur(trice) *m,f* d[e] lait *ou* laitier(ère); ***dairy farming*** industrie *f* lai[tière]; ***dairy herd*** troupeau *m* de vaches laitières; ***dairy ice cream*** glace *f* à la crème; ***dairy produc[e]*** produits *mpl* laitiers

dairymaid [ˈdeərɪmeɪd] **N** fille *f* de ferme *(qu[i] s'occupe de la laiterie)*

dairyman [ˈdeərɪmən] *(pl* **dairymen** [-mən]*)* **N** *(o[n] farm)* employé *m* de laiterie; *(in shop)* crémier *m*, laitier *m*

dais [ˈdeɪs] **N** estrade *f*

daisy [ˈdeɪzɪ] *(pl* **daisies***)* **N** *(smaller)* pâquerette *f*; *(bigger)* marguerite *f*; **as fresh as a d.** frais (fraî[-]che) comme une rose; *Fam* **he's pushing up th[e] daisies** il mange les pissenlits par les racines

►► ***daisy chain*** guirlande *f* de pâquerettes; *Com[-] put* ***daisy chaining*** connexion *f* en boucle; *Fa[m] Mil* ***daisy cutter*** daisy cutter *f*, = nom donné à la bombe la plus destructrice de l'arsenal conventionnel américain; *Typ & Comput* ***daisy whee[l]*** marguerite *f*; ***daisy wheel printer*** imprimante *f* à marguerite

daisy-chain VT *Comput* connecter en boucle

Dalai Lama [ˌdælaɪˈlɑːmə] **PR N** dalaï-lama *m*

dale [deɪl] **N** vallée *f*, vallon *m*

dalliance [ˈdælɪəns] **N** *Literary* badinage *m*

dally [ˈdælɪ] *(pt & pp* **dallied***)* **VI 1** *(dawdle)* lanter[-] ner, lambiner; **to d. over sth** s'attarder sur qch **2** *(toy)* badiner; *(▸ with affections)* jouer; **to d. wit[h] an idea** caresser une idée **3** *Arch (flirt)* flirter

Dalmatian [dælˈmeɪʃən] **N 1** *(dog)* dalmatien *m* **2** *(person)* habitant(e) *m,f* de la Dalmatie

ADJ dalmate

dam [dæm] *(pt & pp* **dammed**, *cont* **damming***)* **N 1** *(barrier)* barrage *m* (de retenue) **2** *(reservoir)* réservoir *m* **3** *(animal)* mère *f*

VT *(river, lake)* construire un barrage sur; *(val[-] ley)* construire un barrage dans

damage [ˈdæmɪdʒ] **N 1** *(UNCOUNT) (harm)* dom[-] mage *m*, dommages *mpl*; *(visible effects)* dégâts *mpl*, dommages *mpl*; *(to ship, shipment)* avarie *f*, avaries *fpl*; **d. to property** dégâts *mpl* matériels; **the storm did a lot of d.** l'orage a causé des dégâts importants; **he said he would make good the d.** il a dit qu'il allait réparer les dégâts **2** *Fig* tort *m*, préjudice *m*; **the scandal has done the government serious d.** le scandale a fait énormément de tort *ou* a énormément porté préjudice au gouvernement; **the d. is done** le mal est fait; *Fam* **what's the d.?** *(how much do I owe?)* ça fait combien?□

VT *(harm* ▸ *crop, object)* endommager, causer des dégâts à; *(▸ food)* abîmer, gâter; *(▸ eyes, health)* abîmer; *(▸ship, shipment)* avarier; *(▸ rep[-] utation)* porter atteinte à, nuire à; *(▸ cause)* faire du tort à, porter préjudice à; **the storm damaged a lot of trees** de nombreux arbres ont été endommagés par la tempête; **smoking can seriously d. your health** le tabac nuit gravement à la santé; **damaged goods** marchandises *fpl* avariées; *Fig (person)* personne *f* au passé chargé

• **damages NPL** *Law* dommages *mpl* et intérêts *mpl*, dommages-intérêts *mpl*; **to award damages to sb for sth** accorder des dommages et intérêts à qn pour qch; **to be awarded damages** obteni[r] des dommages et intérêts; **to sue sb for damages**

poursuivre qn en dommages et intérêts; **liable for damages** civilement responsable
►► ***damage limitation*** effort *m* pour limiter les dégâts

damaging ['dæmɪdʒɪŋ] ADJ dommageable, nuisible; *Law* préjudiciable; **psychologically d.** dommageable sur le plan psychologique; **it's a d. blow to his re-election prospects/career** cela compromet sérieusement ses chances d'être réélu/sa carrière

Damascus [də'mæskəs] N Damas

damask ['dæməsk] N **1** *(silk)* damas *m*, soie *f* damassée; *(linen)* damassé *m* **2** *Metal* **d. (steel)** (acier *m*) damasquiné *m* **3** *(colour)* vieux rose *m inv*
ADJ **1** *(cloth)* damassé **2** *(colour)* vieux rose *(inv)*
►► ***damask rose*** rose *f* de Damas

dame [deɪm] N **1** *Arch or Literary (noble)* dame *f*; *Br Theat* **(pantomime) d.** vieille femme *f* comique *(dont le rôle est joué par un homme)* **2** *Am Fam Old-fashioned (woman)* pépée *f*
• **Dame** N *Br (title)* = titre donné à une femme ayant reçu certaines distinctions honorifiques

dammit ['dæmɪt] EXCLAM *Fam* mince!; *Br* **as near as d.** à un cheveu près

damn [dæm] EXCLAM *Fam* mince!
N *Fam* **I don't give a d.** j'en ai rien à cirer, je m'en balance; **I don't give a d. about the money** je me fiche pas mal de l'argent; **it's not worth a d.** ça ne vaut pas un pet de lapin *ou* un clou
VT **1** *Rel* damner **2** *(condemn)* condamner; **they damned him with faint praise** ils l'ont éreinté sous couleur d'éloge; **you're damned if you do and damned if you don't** quoique tu fasses tu es perdant **3** *Fam* **damn it!** mince!; **d. you!** va te faire voir!; **d. the expense/the consequences** au diable l'avarice/tant pis pour les conséquences; **well I'll be damned!** ça, c'est le comble!; **I'll be damned if I'll apologize!** m'excuser? plutôt mourir!
ADJ *Fam* fichu, sacré; **you d. fool!** espèce d'idiot!; **he's a d. nuisance** il est vraiment casse-pied; **it's a d. nuisance!** ce que c'est casse-pied!, quelle barbe!; **it's one d. thing after another** quand ce n'est pas une chose c'est l'autre
ADV *Fam* **1** *(as intensifier)* vachement; **a d. good idea** une super bonne idée; **you're d. right** t'as parfaitement raison; **he knows d. well what I mean** il sait exactement *ou* très bien ce que je veux dire□ **2** *Br (idiom)* **d. all** que dalle; **there's d. all in the fridge** il y a que dalle dans le frigo; **it's got d. all to do with you** ça n'a absolument rien à voir avec toi□; **he knows d. all about it** il n'en sait fichtre rien

damnable ['dæmnəbəl] ADJ **1** *Rel* damnable **2** *Fam Old-fashioned (awful)* exécrable, odieux

damnably ['dæmnəblɪ] ADV *Fam Old-fashioned* rudement

damnation [dæm'neɪʃən] N *Rel* damnation *f*
EXCLAM *Fam* enfer et damnation!

damned [dæmd] ADJ **1** *Rel* damné, maudit **2** *Fam* fichu, sacré; **he's a d. nuisance** il est vraiment casse-pied
ADV *Fam* rudement, vachement; **you know d. well what I mean** tu sais très bien ce que je veux dire□; **do what you d. well like!** fais ce que tu veux, je m'en fiche
NPL *Rel or Literary* **the d.** les damnés *mpl*

damnedest ['dæmdəst] *Fam* N *(utmost)* **to do one's d. (to do sth)** faire tout son possible (pour faire qch)□; **he did his d. to ruin the party** il a vraiment fait tout ce qu'il pouvait pour gâcher la soirée□
ADJ *Am* incroyable□; **it was the d. thing!** il fallait voir ça!

damn-fool ADJ *Fam* débile

damning ['dæmɪŋ] ADJ *(evidence, statement)* accablant; **the report was a d. indictment of the government** le rapport constituait un témoignage accablant contre le gouvernement

Damocles ['dæmə,kli:z] PR N *Myth* Damoclès; **the sword of D.** l'épée *f* de Damoclès

damp [dæmp] ADJ *(air, clothes, heat)* humide; *(skin, hand)* moite; **a d. patch** une tache d'humidité
N **1** *(moisture)* humidité *f* **2** *Mining (air)* mofette *f*; *(gas)* grisou *m*
VT **1** *(wet)* humecter **2** *Aut, Elec & Tech* amortir; *Mus* étouffer; *Fig (spirits)* décourager, refroidir **3** *(fire)* couvrir
►► ***damp course*** revêtement *m* d'étanchéité; *Br Fam* ***damp squib*** déception□ *f*; *Br Fam* **to be a d. squib** faire l'effet d'un pétard mouillé

dampen ['dæmpən] VT **1** *(wet)* humecter **2** *(ardour, courage)* refroidir; **don't d. their spirits** ne les découragez pas

damper[1] ['dæmpə(r)], *Am* **dampener** ['dæmpənə(r)] N **1** *(in furnace)* registre *m*
2 *Fig* **that put a d. on things** ça a fait l'effet d'une douche froide; **the news put a d. on the party/his enthusiasm** la nouvelle a jeté un froid sur la fête/a refroidi son enthousiasme
3 *Aut, Elec & Tech* amortisseur *m*; *Mus* étouffoir *m*
4 *(for linen, stamps)* mouilleur *m*

damper[2] N *Austr* = sorte de pain cuit au feu de bois

damping ['dæmpɪŋ] N **1** *(wetting)* mouillage *m* **2** *Aut, Elec & Tech* amortissement *m*

dampish ['dæmpɪʃ] ADJ un peu humide

dampness ['dæmpnɪs] N humidité *f*; *(of skin)* moiteur *f*

damp-proof ADJ *Constr* protégé contre l'humidité, hydrofuge
►► ***damp-proof course*** revêtement *m* d'étanchéité

damp-proofing N *Constr* isolation *f* contre l'humidité

damsel ['dæmzəl] N *Arch or Literary* damoiselle *f*; *Hum* **a d. in distress** une belle éplorée

damson ['dæmzən] N *(tree)* prunier *m* de Damas; *(fruit)* prune *f* de Damas
COMP *(jam, wine)* de prunes (de Damas)

dance [dɑ:ns] N **1** *(gen)* danse *f*; **may I have the next d.?** voulez-vous m'accorder la prochaine danse?; **to lead sb a (merry** *or* **pretty) d.** *(exasperate)* donner du fil à retordre à qn; *(deceive)* faire marcher qn; *(in romantic context)* mener qn en bateau; **the d. of the seven veils** la danse des sept voiles
2 *(piece of music)* morceau *m* (de musique)
3 *(art)* danse *f*; **the world of d.** le milieu de la danse
4 *(social occasion)* soirée *f* dansante; *(larger)* bal *m*; **to hold a d.** donner une soirée dansante *ou* un bal
COMP *(class, school, step, studio)* de danse
VI *(person)* danser; *Fig (leaves, light, words)* danser; *(eyes)* scintiller; **to d. with sb** danser avec qn; **to ask sb to d.** inviter qn à danser; **it's not the type of music you can d. to** ce n'est pas le genre de musique sur lequel on peut danser; **she danced along the street** elle descendit la rue d'un pas joyeux; *Fig* **to d. to sb's tune** obéir à qn au doigt et à l'œil
VT *(waltz, polka)* danser; **they danced every d. together** ils n'ont pas arrêté de danser ensemble; **to d. a baby on one's knee** faire sauter un bébé sur ses genoux; *Br* **to d. attendance on sb** s'empresser auprès de qn
►► ***dance band*** orchestre *m* de bal; ***dance floor*** piste *f* de danse; ***dance hall*** salle *f* de bal; ***dance mat*** tapis *m* de danse, dance mat *m*; ***dance music*** musique *f* dansante; *(modern)* dance *f*

dancer ['dɑ:nsə(r)] N danseur(euse) *m,f*

dancing ['dɑ:nsɪŋ] N danse *f*; **to go d.** aller danser
COMP *(class, teacher, school)* de danse
ADJ *(eyes)* scintillant
►► ***dancing girl*** danseuse *f*; ***dancing partner*** cavalier(ère) *m,f*; ***dancing shoe*** *(for dance)* chaussure *f* de bal; *(for ballet)* chausson *m* de danse

D & C, D and C [,di:ən'si:] N *Med (abbr* **dilatation and curettage**) (dilatation *f* et) curetage *m*

dandelion ['dændɪlaɪən] N pissenlit *m*, dent-de-lion *f*
►► ***dandelion clock*** aigrettes *fpl* de pissenlits

dander ['dændə(r)] N *Fam* **to get one's/sb's d. up** se mettre/mettre qn en rogne

dandified ['dændɪfaɪd] ADJ *(person)* à l'allure de dandy; *(appearance)* de dandy

dandle ['dændəl] VT *Br (small child* ► *on knee)* faire sauter; *(*► *in arms)* bercer

dandruff ['dændrʌf] N *(UNCOUNT)* pellicules *fpl*; **to have d.** avoir des pellicules
►► ***dandruff shampoo*** shampooing *m* antipelliculaire

dandy ['dændɪ] *(pl* **dandies**) N dandy *m*
ADJ *esp Am Fam* extra, épatant; **everything's fine and d.** tout va très bien□; *Ironic* **that's just d.!** c'est vraiment génial!

Dane [deɪn] N Danois(e) *m,f*

dang [dæŋ] *Am Fam* = **damn** *exclam & adv*

danger ['deɪndʒə(r)] N danger *m*; **the dangers of smoking/making rash judgements** les dangers du tabac/des jugements hâtifs; **d., keep out!** *(sign)* danger, entrée interdite!; **d. of death** *(sign)* danger de mort; **fraught with d.** extrêmement dangereux; **to be out of/in d.** être hors de/en danger; **to put sb/sth in d.** mettre qn/qch en danger; **he was in no d.** il n'était pas en danger, il ne courait aucun danger; **to be in d. of doing sth** courir le risque *ou* risquer de faire qch; **to be a d. to sb/sth** être un danger pour qn/qch; **he's a d. to society** c'est un danger public; **there is no d. of that happening** il n'y a pas de danger *ou* de risque que cela se produise; *Med* **to be on the d. list** être dans un état critique; *Med* **to be off the d. list** être hors de danger
►► *Br* ***danger money*** prime *f* de risque; ***danger signal*** *Rail* signal *m* d'arrêt; *Fig* signal *m* d'alerte *ou* d'alarme; ***danger zone*** zone *f* dangereuse

dangerous ['deɪndʒərəs] ADJ *(job, sport, criminal, animal)* dangereux; *(illness)* dangereux, grave; *(operation)* délicat, périlleux; *(assumption)* risqué; *Fig* **to be on d. ground** être sur un terrain glissant
►► *Law* ***dangerous driving*** conduite *f* dangereuse

dangerously ['deɪndʒərəslɪ] ADV dangereusement; *(ill)* gravement; **to live d.** vivre dangereusement; **the car was d. near the edge of the cliff** la voiture était dangereusement près du bord de la falaise; **you're coming d. close to being fired/spanked** continue comme ça et tu es viré/tu as une fessée; **this firm is d. close to collapse/bankruptcy** cette entreprise est au bord de l'effondrement/la faillite

dangle ['dæŋgəl] VT *(legs, arms, hands)* laisser pendre; *(object on chain, string)* balancer; **to d. sth in front of sb** balancer qch devant qn; *Fig* faire miroiter qch aux yeux de qn
VI *(legs, arms, hands)* pendre; *(keys, earrings)* se balancer; **with his legs dangling** les jambes pendant dans le vide *ou* ballantes; **the climber was dangling at the end of the rope** l'alpiniste se balançait *ou* était suspendu au bout de la corde; *Fig* **to keep sb dangling** laisser qn dans le vague

Danish ['deɪnɪʃ] NPL **the D.** les Danois *mpl*
N **1** *(language)* danois *m* **2** *Culin (pastry)* = sorte de pâtisserie fourrée
ADJ danois
COMP *(embassy, history)* du Danemark; *(teacher)* de danois
►► ***Danish blue*** *(cheese)* bleu *m* du Danemark; *Culin* ***Danish pastry*** = sorte de pâtisserie fourrée

dank [dæŋk] ADJ *(weather, dungeon)* humide et froid

Dantean ['dæntɪən], **Dantesque** [dæn'tesk] ADJ *Literature* dantesque

Danube ['dænju:b] N **the D.** le Danube

dapper ['dæpə(r)] ADJ propre sur soi, soigné; **he was looking very d.** il était tiré à quatre épingles

dapple ['dæpəl] VT tacheter; **sunlight dappled the wall/water** le soleil faisait des taches sur le mur/l'eau

dapple-grey ADJ gris pommelé *(inv)*
N **1** *(colour)* gris *m* pommelé *(inv)* **2** *(horse)* cheval *m* gris pommelé; *(mare)* jument *f* gris pommelé

Darby and Joan [,dɑ:bɪən'dʒəʊn] N = couple uni de personnes âgées
►► ***Darby and Joan club*** club *m* du troisième âge *(en Grande-Bretagne)*

DARC [,di:eɪ,ɑ:'si:] N *(abbr* **data radio channel**) DARC *f*

dare [deə(r)] MODAL V *(venture)* oser; **to d. (to) do sth** oser faire qch; **I daren't think** *or* **don't d. (to) think about it** je n'ose (pas) y penser; **she didn't**

d. (to) *or* **dared not say a word** elle n'a pas osé dire un mot; **let them try it if they d.!** qu'ils essaient s'ils osent!; **d. I interrupt?** puis-je me permettre de vous interrompre?; **don't you d. tell me what to do!** ne t'avise surtout pas de me dire ce que j'ai à faire!; **don't you d.!** je te le déconseille!; **how d. you speak to me in that tone of voice!** comment oses-tu me parler sur ce ton! **d. I say it** si j'ose m'exprimer ainsi; **I d. say you're hungry after your journey** je suppose que vous êtes affamés après ce voyage; **I d. say she's right** elle a probablement raison; **he was most apologetic – I d. say!** il s'est confondu en excuses – j'imagine!

VT **1** *(challenge)* défier; **to d. sb to do sth** défier qn de faire qch; **I d. you!** chiche! **2** *Literary (death, dishonour)* braver, défier; *(displeasure)* braver

N *(challenge)* défi *m*; **to do sth for a d.** faire qch pour relever un défi

daredevil ['deəˌdevəl] N casse-cou *m inv*

ADJ casse-cou *(inv)*

daren't [deənt] = **dare not**

daring ['deərɪŋ] N *(of person)* audace *f*, hardiesse *f*; *(of feat)* hardiesse *f*; **of great d.** très audacieux

ADJ *(audacious)* audacieux, hardi; *(provocative)* audacieux, provocant

daringly ['deərɪŋlɪ] ADV audacieusement, hardiment; **a d. low neckline** un décolleté audacieux *ou* provocant; **to be d. different** afficher sa différence avec audace

Darjeeling [dɑː'dʒiːlɪŋ] N **1** *(city)* Darjeeling **2** *(tea)* (thé *m*) Darjeeling *m*

dark [dɑːk] N noir *m*; **before/after d.** avant/après la tombée de la nuit; **to be afraid of the d.** avoir peur du noir *ou* dans le noir; **everything suddenly went d.** soudain ce fut le noir complet; **I can't work in the d.!** je ne peux pas travailler sans savoir où je vais!; **to keep sb in the d. about sth** maintenir qn dans l'ignorance à propos de qch; **to be in the d. about sth** être dans l'ignorance à propos de qch

ADJ **1** *(without light ▸ night, room, street)* sombre, obscur; *Fig (thoughts)* sombre; *(ideas)* noir; **it's very d. in here** il fait très sombre ici; **it's getting d.** il commence à faire nuit, la nuit tombe; **it gets d. early** il fait nuit de bonne heure; **it won't be d. for another hour yet** il ne fera pas nuit avant une heure; **it's still d. (outside)** il fait encore nuit; **the d. days of the war** la sombre période de la guerre

2 *(colour)* foncé; *(dress, suit)* sombre; **she always wears d. colours** elle porte toujours des couleurs sombres; **I'd like some d. meat** *(of poultry)* je voudrais une aile ou une cuisse

3 *(hair, eyes)* foncé; *(skin, complexion)* foncé, brun; **to have d. hair** avoir les cheveux bruns, être brun; **his d. good looks** sa beauté ténébreuse

4 *(hidden, mysterious)* mystérieux, secret(ète); *(secret)* bien gardé; *(hint)* mystérieux, énigmatique; **the d. side of the moon** la face cachée de la lune; **to keep sth d.** tenir qch secret; **keep it d.!** garde-le pour toi!

5 *(sinister)* noir; **there's a d. side to her** il y a une part d'ombre en elle; **a d. chapter in the country's history** un chapitre peu glorieux de l'histoire du pays

▸▸ *Hist* ***Dark Ages*** Haut Moyen Âge *m*; ***dark chocolate*** chocolat *m* noir; *Old-fashioned* ***the Dark Continent*** le Continent noir; ***dark glasses*** lunettes *fpl* noires; ***dark horse*** *(competitor, horse)* participant(e) *m,f* inconnu(e); *Am Pol* candidat (e) *m,f* surprise; *Fig* **to be a d. horse** *(secretive person)* être très secret; **you're a d. horse!** tu caches bien ton jeu!; *Astron* ***dark matter*** matière *f* noire *ou* sombre

darken ['dɑːkən] VT *(sky)* assombrir; *(colour)* foncer; **a darkened room** une pièce sombre; **never d. my door again!** et que je ne te revoie plus ici!

VI *(sky, room)* s'assombrir, s'obscurcir; *(hair, wood)* foncer; *(face, brow)* s'assombrir; *(painting)* s'obscurcir

darkening ['dɑːkənɪŋ] ADJ *(sky, face)* qui s'assombrit; **he looked up at the d. sky** il regarda le ciel qui s'assombrissait

N *(of sky, painting)* assombrissement *m*

dark-eyed ADJ aux yeux sombres *ou* foncés

dark-haired ADJ aux cheveux foncés

darkie ['dɑːkɪ] N *Fam Old-fashioned* moricaud(e) *m,f*, = terme raciste désignant un Noir

darkish ['dɑːkɪʃ] ADJ *(colour, sky, wood)* plutôt *ou* assez sombre; *(hair, skin)* plutôt brun *ou* foncé; *(person)* plutôt brun

darkly ['dɑːklɪ] ADV *(hint)* énigmatiquement; *(say)* sur un ton sinistre

darkness ['dɑːknɪs] N **1** *(of night, room, street)* obscurité *f*; **d. had fallen** il faisait nuit; **the house was in d.** la maison était plongée dans l'obscurité **2** *(of hair, skin)* couleur *f* foncée; **I don't like the d. of the colours** je n'aime pas toutes ces couleurs foncées

darkroom ['dɑːkrum] N *Phot* chambre *f* noire

dark-skinned ADJ *(having a dark complexion)* au teint mat; *(black)* à la peau noire

darky *(pl* **darkies)** = **darkie**

darling ['dɑːlɪŋ] N **1** *(term of affection)* chéri(e) *m, f*; **yes, d.?** oui, (mon) chéri?; **Kate, d.** Kate, chérie; **she's a d.** c'est un amour; **he was an absolute d. about it** il a été absolument charmant; **be a d. and...** sois gentil *ou* un amour... **2** *(favourite ▸ of teacher, parents)* favori(ite) *m,f*, chouchou (oute) *m,f*; *(▸ of media, high society)* coqueluche *f*; **to be the d. of the media/public** être la coqueluche des média/du public

ADJ *(beloved)* chéri; *(delightful)* charmant, adorable; **you d. man!** tu es un amour!, tu es adorable!

darn [dɑːn] N *(in garment)* reprise *f*; **there was a d. in the elbow of his sweater** son pull était reprisé au coude

VT **1** *(garment)* repriser, raccommoder **2** *Fam (damn)* **d. it!** bon sang!; **he's late, d. him!** il est en retard, il fait vraiment chier!; **I'll be darned!** ça alors!, oh, la vache!

EXCLAM *Fam* bon sang!

ADJ *Fam* sacré; **the d. car won't start** cette sacrée bagnole ne veut pas démarrer; **you're a d. fool** t'es vraiment idiot

ADV *Fam* vachement; **we were d. lucky** on a eu une sacrée veine; **don't be so d. stupid!** ce que tu peux être bête!; **to have a d. good try** faire un sacré effort; **you know d. well what I mean!** tu comprends parfaitement ce que je veux dire!

darned [dɑːnd] *Am Fam* = **darn** ADJ & ADV

darning ['dɑːnɪŋ] N *(action)* reprise *f*, raccommodage *m*; *(items to be darned)* linge *m* à repriser *ou* raccommoder

▸▸ ***darning egg*** œuf *m* à repriser; ***darning needle*** aiguille *f* à repriser; ***darning wool*** laine *f* à repriser

dart [dɑːt] N **1** *(weapon)* flèche *f*; *(for playing darts)* fléchette *f* **2** *Sewing* pince *f* **3** *(sudden movement)* **to make a d. at sb/sth** se précipiter sur qn/qch

VT *(glance, look ▸ quickly)* lancer, jeter; *(▸ angrily)* darder

VI **to d. away** *or* **off** partir en *ou* comme une flèche; **to d. in/out** entrer/sortir comme une flèche; **her eyes darted from one face in the crowd to another** son regard passait rapidement d'un visage à l'autre dans la foule

• **darts** N *(game)* fléchettes *fpl*; **to play darts** jouer aux fléchettes

dartboard ['dɑːtˌbɔːd] N cible *f* (de jeu de fléchettes)

dash [dæʃ] N **1** *(quick movement)* mouvement *m* précipité; **to make a d. for freedom** s'enfuir vers la liberté; **to make a d. for it** *(rush)* se précipiter; *(escape)* saisir l'occasion de s'enfuir; **a quick d. across to Paris** un petit saut à Paris

2 *Am Sport* sprint *m*; **the 100-metre d.** le 100 mètres plat

3 *(small amount ▸ of water, soda)* goutte *f*, trait *m*; *(▸ of cream, milk)* nuage *m*; *(▸ of lemon juice, vinegar)* filet *m*; *(▸ of salt, pepper)* soupçon *m*; *(▸ of colour, humour)* pointe *f*

4 *Typ (punctuation mark)* tiret *m*; *(in Morse code)* trait *m*

5 *(style)* panache *m*; **to cut a d.** avoir fière allure

6 *Aut (dashboard)* tableau *m* de bord

VT **1** *(throw)* jeter (avec violence); **to d. sth to the ground** jeter qch par terre avec violence; **to d. sth to pieces** fracasser qch; **several boats were dashed against the cliffs** plusieurs bateaux ont été projetés *ou* précipités contre les falaises; *Fig* **to d. sb's hopes** réduire les espoirs de qn à néant **2** *Fam Old-fashioned (damn)* **d. it!** bon sang!

VI **1** *(rush)* se précipiter; *Br* **I must d.** je dois filer; **he dashed back to his room** il est retourné à sa chambre en vitesse, il s'est dépêché de retourner à sa chambre; **to come dashing in** entrer comme un bolide, entrer en trombe; *Br* **I'm just going to d. home and...** je vais faire un saut chez moi et...; **the dog dashed across the road in front of us** le chien a traversé la route à toute vitesse devant nous **2** *(waves)* se jeter

EXCLAM *Br Fam Old-fashioned* bon sang!

▸ **dash off** VT SEP *(letter, memo)* écrire en vitesse; *(drawing)* faire en vitesse

VI partir en flèche

dashboard ['dæʃbɔːd] N *Aut* tableau *m* de bord

dashed [dæʃt] *Br Fam Old-fashioned* ADJ de malheur; **he really is a d. nuisance** c'est vraiment enquiquinant

ADV rudement, drôlement

dashing ['dæʃɪŋ] ADJ pimpant, fringant; **a d. young man** un beau jeune homme

dashingly ['dæʃɪŋlɪ] ADV *(behave)* avec allant; *(be dressed)* dans un style fringant

dashpot ['dæʃpɒt] N *Aut* dash-pot *m*

dastardly ['dæstədlɪ] ADJ *Literary (act, person)* odieux, infâme

DAT [ˌdiːeɪ'tiː, dæt] N *(abbr* **digital audio tape)** DAT *m*

▸▸ ***DAT cartridge*** cartouche *f* DAT; ***DAT drive*** lecteur *m* DAT, lecteur *m* de bande audionumérique

data ['deɪtə] *(pl of* **datum**, *usu with sing vb)* N informations *fpl*, données *fpl*; *Comput* données *fpl*; **a piece** *or* **an item of d.** une donnée, une information; *Comput* une donnée; **what little d. we do have suggests that...** le peu d'informations que nous avons semble montrer que...

COMP *Comput* de données

▸▸ ***data acquisition*** collecte *f* de données, saisie *f* de données; ***data analysis*** analyse *f* de données; ***data bank*** banque *f* de données; ***data bus*** bus *m* de données; ***data capture*** saisie *f* de données; ***data carrier*** support *m* de données; ***data collection*** recueil *m* de données, collecte *f* de données; ***data compression*** compression *f* de données; ***data conversion*** conversion *f* de données; ***data encryption*** cryptage *m* ou codage *m* de données; ***data entry*** entrée *f* de données; ***data file*** fichier *m* informatique; ***data management*** gestion *f* de données; ***data privacy*** secret *m* ou protection *f* des données; ***data processing*** N traitement *m* de l'information COMP *(department, service)* de traitement des données *ou* de l'information, informatique; ***data processor*** *(machine)* ordinateur *m*; *(person)* informaticien(enne) *m,f*; ***data protection*** protection *f* de l'information; ***data storage*** stockage *m* de données; ***data transfer*** transfert *m ou* transmission *f* de données

database ['deɪtəbeɪs] *Comput* N base *f* de données

VT mettre sous forme de base de données

▸▸ ***database management*** gestion *f* de base de données; ***database management system*** système *m* de gestion de bases de données

datacasting ['deɪtəˌkɑːstɪŋ] N *Comput* datacasting *m*, diffusion *f* de données

datacomms ['deɪtəkɒms], **datacommunications** [ˌdeɪtəkəˌmjuːnɪ'keɪʃənz] N *Br Comput* communication *f ou* transmission *f* de données, télématique *f*

▸▸ ***datacomms linkup*** liaison *f* télématique; ***datacomms network*** réseau *m* de communication de données; ***datacomms software*** logiciel *m* de communication

dataglove ['deɪtəglʌv] N *Comput* gant *m* de données

DATE[1] [deɪt]

N	
• date **1**	• rendez-vous **2**
• ami **3**	• échéance **4**
VT	
• dater **1, 2**	• sortir avec **3**
VI	
• se démoder **1**	• sortir ensemble **2**
• dater **3**	

N 1 *(of letter, day of the week)* date *f*; *(on coins, books etc)* millésime *m*; **what's the d. today?, what's today's d.?** quelle est la date aujourd'hui?, le combien sommes-nous aujourd'hui?; **what's the d. of the coin/building?** de quelle année est cette pièce/ce bâtiment?; **would you be free on that d.?** est-ce que vous seriez libre ce jour-là *ou* à cette date?; **at a later** *or* **some future d.** plus tard, ultérieurement; **of an earlier/a later d.** plus ancien/récent; **to fix a d. for sth** prendre date *ou* fixer une date pour qch; **shall we fix a d. now?** est-ce que nous prenons date *ou* fixons une date maintenant?; **have you set a d. yet?** *(for wedding)* est-ce que vous avez déjà décidé de la date du mariage?; **to put a d. to sth** *(remember when it happened)* se souvenir de la date de qch; *(estimate when built, established etc)* attribuer une date à qch, dater qch; **d. of birth** date *f* de naissance

2 *(meeting)* rendez-vous *m*; **let's make a d. for lunch** prenons rendez-vous pour déjeuner ensemble; **I already have a d. on Saturday night** j'ai déjà un rendez-vous samedi soir; **to go out on a d.** sortir en compagnie de quelqu'un; **on our first d.** la première fois que nous sommes sortis ensemble

3 *(person)* ami(e) *m,f*; **who's your d. tonight?** avec qui sors-tu ce soir?; **my d. didn't show up** on m'a posé un lapin

4 *Fin (of bill)* échéance *f*, terme *m*; **d. of maturity, due d.** (date *f* d')échéance *f*; **three months after d., at three months' d.** à trois mois de date *ou* d'échéance

VT 1 *(write date on ▸ cheque, letter, memo)* dater; **a fax dated 6 May** un fax daté du 6 mai

2 *(attribute date to ▸ building, settlement etc)* dater; (▸ *bottle of wine etc)* millésimer; **to d. sb** *(show age of)* donner une idée de l'âge de qn; **gosh, that dates him!** eh bien, ça montre qu'il n'est plus tout jeune *ou* ça ne le rajeunit pas!

3 *esp Am (go out with)* sortir avec; **they're dating each other** ils sortent ensemble

VI 1 *(clothes, style)* se démoder; *(novel)* vieillir

2 *esp Am (go out on dates)* sortir avec des garçons/filles; **how long have you two been dating?** ça fait combien de temps que vous sortez ensemble *ou* que vous vous voyez?

3 *(originate)* dater (**from** de), remonter (**from** à); **church dating from** *or* **back to the 13th century** église qui remonte au *ou* qui date du XIIe siècle

• **out of date ADJ to be out of d.** *(dress, style, concept, slang)* être démodé *ou* dépassé; *(dictionary, encyclopedia)* ne pas être à jour *ou* à la page; *(passport, season ticket etc)* être périmé; **it's the kind of dress that will never go out of d.** c'est le genre de robe indémodable *ou* qui ne se démodera jamais

• **to date ADV** à ce jour, jusqu'à maintenant

• **up to date ADJ to be up to d.** *(dress, style, person)* être à la mode *ou* à la page; *(dictionary)* être à la page *ou* à jour; *(passport)* être valide *ou* valable; *(list)* être à jour; **I'm not up to d. on what's been happening** je ne suis pas au courant de ce qui s'est passé dernièrement; **to bring/keep sb up to d. on sth** mettre/tenir qn au courant de qch; **to bring one's diary up to d.** mettre à jour son journal

▸▸ ***date rape*** = viol commis par une connaissance, un ami etc

> **DATE**
>
> Pour donner une date en anglais, on n'emploie pas l'article à l'écrit. En anglais britannique, on écrira donc "Monday 25th December 2006" ou, de plus en plus souvent, "Monday 25 December 2006", et, en abrégé, "25.12.06". Notez cependant qu'à l'oral, on prononce "Monday the twenty-fifth of December". En anglais américain, le mois est indiqué avant le jour. On écrira ainsi "Monday December 25 2006" et, en abrégé, "12.25.06", et on prononcera "December twenty-five".

date[2] **N** *(fruit)* datte *f*

▸▸ *Bot* ***date palm*** palmier *m* dattier

datebook ['deɪtbʊk] **N** *Am* agenda *m*

dated ['deɪtɪd] **ADJ** *(clothes, style)* démodé; *(term, expression, concept)* vieilli, désuet(ète); *(novel)* qui a mal vieilli

dateless ['deɪtlɪs] **ADJ 1** *(timeless)* indémodable **2** *(not dated ▸ document, letter)* non daté

dateline ['deɪt,laɪn] **N 1** *Press* date *f* de rédaction **2** *(on world map)* ligne *f* de changement de date

date-stamp N tampon *m* dateur; *(used for cancelling)* oblitérateur *m*, timbre *m* à date; *(postmark)* cachet *m* de la poste

VT *(book)* tamponner, mettre le cachet de la date sur; *(letter)* oblitérer

date-stamping N compostage *m*

dating ['deɪtɪŋ] **N** *(of building, settlement etc)* datation *f*

▸▸ ***dating agency*** agence *f* matrimoniale

dative ['deɪtɪv] *Gram* **N** datif *m*; **in the d.** au datif

ADJ datif

datum ['deɪtəm] *(pl* **data**) **N** *Formal* donnée *f*, information *f*; *Comput* donnée *f*

daub [dɔːb] **N 1** *(of paint)* tache *f*, barbouillage *m*; *(done on purpose)* barbouillage *m* **2** *Pej (painting)* croûte *f* **3** *(for walls)* torchis *m*

VT enduire; *(with mud)* couvrir; **a wall daubed with slogans** un mur couvert de slogans

VI *Pej (paint badly)* peinturlurer, barbouiller

daughter ['dɔːtə(r)] **N** fille *f*

daughter-in-law N bru *f*, belle-fille *f*

daunt [dɔːnt] **VT** intimider; **nothing daunted** nullement découragé

daunting ['dɔːntɪŋ] **ADJ** intimidant

dauntless ['dɔːntlɪs] **ADJ** déterminé

dauntlessly ['dɔːntlɪslɪ] **ADV** sans se décourager

davenport ['dævənpɔːt] **N 1** *Br (desk)* secrétaire *m* **2** *Am (sofa)* canapé(-lit) *m*

davit ['dævɪt] **N** *Naut* bossoir *m*, portemanteau *m*

Davy ['deɪvɪ] **PR N in D. Jones's locker** *(person, ship)* au fond de la mer

▸▸ *Mining* ***Davy lamp*** lampe *f* de sécurité de mineur

dawdle ['dɔːdəl] **VI** *Pej* traîner, lambiner, traînasser; **to d. over sth** traînasser *ou* traîner en faisant qch

dawdler ['dɔːdlə(r)] **N** lambin(e) *m,f*, traînard(e) *m,f*

dawdling ['dɔːdlɪŋ] **N stop all this d.!** arrête de traînasser!

ADJ traînard

dawn [dɔːn] **N 1** *(part of day)* aube *f*; **at d.** à l'aube; **from d. till dusk** du matin au soir; **at the crack of d.** au point du jour; **(just) as d. was breaking** alors que l'aube pointait; **to watch the d.** regarder le jour se lever **2** *Fig (of civilization, era)* aube *f*; *(of hope)* naissance *f*, éclosion *f*; **since the d. of time** depuis la nuit des temps

VI 1 *(day)* se lever; *Fig* **when the truth dawned on him** quand il a compris la vérité; *Fig* **it dawned on me that...** j'ai commencé à me rendre compte que... **2** *Fig (new era, hope)* naître

▸▸ ***dawn chorus*** chant *m* des oiseaux à l'aube; ***dawn raid*** descente *f* à l'aube; *(by police)* descente *f ou* rafle *f* à l'aube; *St Exch* raid *m (mené dès l'ouverture de la Bourse)*; *St Exch* ***dawn raider*** raider *m (qui opère dès l'ouverture de la Bourse)*

dawning ['dɔːnɪŋ] **ADJ** naissant

N *Fig (of civilization, era)* aube *f*, *(of hope)* naissance *f*, éclosion *f*

DAY [deɪ]

> **N**
> • jour **1, 2** • journée **1–3**
> • époque **4**

N 1 *(period of twenty-four hours)* jour *m*; *(emphasizing duration)* journée *f*; **it's a nice** *or* **fine d.** c'est une belle journée, il fait beau aujourd'hui; **on a clear d.** par temps clair; **a summer's/winter's d.** un jour d'été/d'hiver; **to have a d. out** aller passer une journée quelque part; **we went to the country for the d.** nous sommes allés passer la journée à la campagne; **what d. is it (today)?** quel jour sommes-nous (aujourd'hui)?; **(on) that d.** ce jour-là; **(on) the d. (that** *or* **when) she was born** le jour où elle est née; **the d. after, (on) the next** *or* **following d.** le lendemain, le jour suivant; **the d. after the party** le lendemain de *ou* le jour d'après la fête; **two days after the party** le surlendemain de *ou* deux jours après la fête; **the d. after tomorrow** après-demain; **the d. before, (on) the previous d.** la veille, le jour d'avant; **I had first met him two days before** je l'avais rencontré l'avant-veille pour la première fois; **the d. before yesterday** avant-hier; **once/twice a d.** une fois/deux fois par jour; **good d.!** bonjour!; **have a nice d.!** bonne journée!; **the other d.** l'autre jour; *Rel* **D. of Judgement** (jour *m* du) jugement dernier; *Rel* **D. of Atonement** jour *m* du Grand Pardon; **d. of reckoning** jour *m* de vérité; **any d. now** d'un jour à l'autre; **d. after d., d. in d. out** jour après jour; **for days on end** *or* **at a time** pendant des jours et des jours; **from d. to d.** de jour en jour; **to live from d. to d.** vivre au jour le jour; **from one d. to the next** d'un jour à l'autre; **from that d. on** *or* **onwards** à partir de ce jour-là; **from that d. to this** depuis ce jour-là; *Literary* **from this d. forth** à partir *ou* à compter d'aujourd'hui; **from d. one** depuis le premier jour; **one d.** un jour; **one of these days** un de ces jours; **some d.** un jour; **she's 70 if she's a d.** elle a 70 ans bien sonnés; **he doesn't look a d. older than 40/you** il n'a pas l'air d'avoir plus de 40 ans/d'être plus vieux que toi; **it's been one of those days!** tu parles d'une journée!; **on this (d.) of all days!** justement aujourd'hui!; **let's make a d. of it** passons-y la journée; **that really made my d.!** ça m'a fait très plaisir; **it's not my (lucky) d.** ce n'est pas mon jour (de chance); *Fam* **that'll be the d.!** *(it's highly unlikely)* il n'y a pas de danger que ça arrive de sitôt!; **at the end of the d.** à la fin de la journée; *Fig* en fin de compte, au bout du compte

2 *(hours of daylight)* jour *m*, journée *f*; **all d. (long)** toute la journée; **we haven't got all d.** nous n'avons pas que ça à faire; **to travel during the** *or* **by d.** voyager pendant la journée *ou* de jour; **to sleep during the** *or* **by d.** dormir le jour; **d. and night, night and d.** jour et nuit, nuit et jour

3 *(working hours)* journée *f*; **paid by the d.** payé à la journée; **to work a seven-hour d.** travailler sept heures par jour, faire des journées de sept heures; **to be on days** *(of worker)* être de jour; **how was your d.?, what kind of d. have you had?** comment s'est passée ta journée?; **it's been a hard/long d.** la journée a été dure/longue; **d. off** jour *m* de congé; **d. of rest** jour *m* de repos; **let's call it a d.** *(stop work)* arrêtons-nous pour aujourd'hui; *(end relationship)* finissons-en; **it's all in a d.'s work!** ça fait partie du travail!

4 *(often pl) (lifetime, era)* époque *f*; **in the days of King Arthur, in King Arthur's d.** du temps du Roi Arthur; **in days to come** à l'avenir; **in days gone by** par le passé; **in those days** à l'époque; **what are you up to these days?** qu'est-ce que tu fais de beau ces temps-ci?; **honestly, teenagers these days!** vraiment, les adolescents d'aujourd'hui!; **in the good old days** dans le temps; **in my/our d.** de mon/notre temps; **in this d. and age** de nos jours, aujourd'hui; **he was well-known in his d.** il était connu de son temps *ou* à son époque; **her d. will come** son heure viendra; **to have had its d.** *(theory, fashion etc)* être démodé; *(car, TV)* avoir fait son temps; **he's/this chair has seen better days** il/cette chaise a connu des jours meilleurs; **those were the days** c'était le bon temps

5 *(battle, game)* **to win** *or* **to carry the d.** l'emporter; **to lose the d.** perdre la partie

• **days ADV to work days** travailler de jour

• **this day week ADV** *Br* dans huit jours aujourd'hui

• **to the day ADV** jour pour jour; **it's a year ago to the d.** il y a un an jour pour jour *ou* aujourd'hui

• **to this day ADV** à ce jour, aujourd'hui encore

▸▸ ***day of action*** journée *f* d'action; ***day bed*** lit *m* de repos; ***day care*** *(for elderly, disabled)* service *m* d'accueil de jour; *(for children)* service *m* de garderie; ***day centre*** *(for children)* garderie *f*, *(for elderly, disabled)* = centre d'animation et d'aide sociale; ***day job*** travail *m* principal; *Fam Hum* **don't give up the d. job** *(to aspiring artist etc)* je ne crois pas que tu es prêt pour une carrière professionnelle; ***day labourer*** journalier(ère) *m, f*; ***day nurse*** infirmier(ère) *m,f* qui est de service de jour; ***day nursery*** garderie *f*; ***day pass*** *(for skiing)* forfait *m* journalier; *Sch* ***day pupil*** (élève *mf*) externe *mf*; *Br Ind* ***day release*** formation *f* continue en alternance; **to be on d. release** être en formation continue en alternance; *Rail* ***day return*** aller-retour *m* valable pour la journée; ***day room*** salle *f* commune; ***day school*** externat *m*; ***day shift*** *(period worked)* service *m* de jour; *(workers)* équipe *f* de jour; **to work the d. shift** travailler de jour, être (dans l'équipe) de jour; ***day trip*** excursion *f*; ***day tripper*** excursionniste *mf*

> When translating **day**, note that **jour** and **journée** are not interchangeable. **Jour** is used to refer to a day as a distinct unit of time, while **journée** emphasizes duration.

day-after recall N *Mktg* mémorisation *f* un jour après

daybook ['deɪbʊk] N *Acct* brouillard *m*

dayboy ['deɪbɔɪ] N *Br Sch* = demi-pensionnaire, dans une école où de nombreux élèves sont internes

daybreak ['deɪbreɪk] N point *m* du jour; **at d.** au point du jour

day-care ADJ *(facilities ▸ for elderly, disabled)* d'accueil de jour; *(▸ for children)* de garderie
▸▸ ***day-care centre*** = centre d'animation et d'aide sociale; *Am (for children)* garderie *f*

daydream ['deɪdriːm] N rêverie *f*; *Pej* rêvasserie *f*
VI rêver; *Pej* rêvasser; **to d. about sth** rêver *ou* rêvasser à qch

daydreaming ['deɪdriːmɪŋ] N *(UNCOUNT)* rêveries *fpl*, rêvasseries *fpl*

daygirl ['deɪgɜːl] N *Br Sch* = demi-pensionnaire, dans une école où de nombreux élèves sont internes

Day-Glo® ['deɪgləʊ] N tissu *m* fluorescent
ADJ fluorescent

daylight ['deɪlaɪt] N **1** *(dawn)* aube *f*, point *m* du jour; **before d.** avant l'aube **2** *(light of day)* jour *m*, lumière *f* du jour; **it was still d.** il faisait encore jour; **in d.** de jour; **in broad d.** en plein jour; **d. hours** heures durant lesquelles il fait jour; *Fig* **to put d. between oneself and sb** distancer qn; *Fig* **to begin to see d.** *(approach end of task)* commencer à voir le bout (du tunnel); *(begin to understand)* commencer à voir clair; *Fam* **it's d. robbery** c'est du vol pur et simple **3** *Fam* **to beat** *or* **to thrash** *or* **to knock the living daylights out of sb** tabasser qn; *Fam* **to scare** *or* **to frighten the living daylights out of sb** flanquer une trouille bleue à qn
▸▸ ***daylight saving (time)*** heure *f* d'été

daylong ['deɪlɒŋ] ADJ *(meeting, journey)* d'une journée

day-old ADJ *(chick, baby)* d'un jour

daytime ['deɪtaɪm] N journée *f*; **in the d.** le jour, pendant la journée
ADJ de jour
▸▸ ***daytime television, daytime TV*** émissions *fpl* télévisées pendant la journée

day-to-day ADJ *(life, running of business)* quotidien; *(chores, tasks)* journalier, quotidien; **the d. management of a company** l'administration courante d'une entreprise; **on a d. basis** au jour le jour

daze [deɪz] N *(caused by blow)* étourdissement *m*; *(caused by emotional shock, surprise)* ahurissement *m*; *(caused by medication)* abrutissement *m*; **to be in a d.** *(because of blow)* être étourdi; *(because of emotional shock, surprise)* être abasourdi *ou* ahuri; *(because of medication)* être abruti
VT *(of blow)* étourdir; *(of emotional shock, surprise)* abasourdir, ahurir; *(of medication)* abrutir

dazed [deɪzd] ADJ *(by blow)* étourdi, hébété; *(by emotional shock, surprise)* abasourdi, ahuri, hébété; *(by medication)* abruti

dazzle ['dæzəl] N *(of headlights)* lueur *f* éblouissante *ou* aveuglante; *Fig* éclat *m*
VT *also Fig* éblouir; **she was quite dazzled by him** il l'a complètement éblouie

dazzling ['dæzlɪŋ] ADJ éblouissant

dazzlingly ['dæzlɪŋlɪ] ADV **a d. bright day** une journée d'une clarté éblouissante; **d. beautiful** d'une beauté éblouissante

dB *Phys (written abbr* **decibel***)* dB

DBMS [ˌdiːbiːˌem'es] N *Comput (abbr* **database management system***)* SGBD *m*

DBS [ˌdiːbiː'es] N *(abbr* **direct broadcasting by satellite***)* télédiffusion *f* directe par satellite

DC [ˌdiː'siː] N **1** *Elec (abbr* **direct current***)* CC **2** *Am Fam (abbr* **District of Columbia***)* DC **3** *Br (abbr* **Detective Constable***)* inspecteur(trice) *m,f* de police

DCI [ˌdiːsiː'aɪ] N *Br (abbr* **detective chief inspector***)* inspecteur(trice) *m,f* de police divisionnaire

DD [ˌdiː'diː] N **1** *Univ (abbr* **Doctor of Divinity***) (person)* = titulaire d'un doctorat en théologie; *(qualification)* doctorat *m* en théologie **2** *Comput (abbr* **double density***)* double densité *f* **3** *Am Mil (abbr* **dishonorable discharge***)* = exclusion de l'armée pour manquement à l'honneur

D-day N le jour J

DDE [ˌdiːdiː'iː] N *Comput (abbr* **dynamic data exchange***)* DDE *m*

DDT [ˌdiːdiː'tiː] N *Chem (abbr* **dichlorodiphenyltrichloroethane***)* DDT *m*

> **PRÉFIXE**
> **DE-**
> Le préfixe **de-** sert à construire des verbes et des dérivés et il exprime différents sens à dominante négative:
> • le fait d'ÔTER une chose comme dans les mots:
> **decaffeinated** décaféiné; **deforestation** déboisement; **to dethrone** détrôner; **to defrock** défroquer
> • l'INVERSION d'un processus ou d'une action comme dans les mots:
> **to deactivate** désamorcer; **decentralized** décentralisé; **to decode** décoder; **deindustrialization** désindustrialisation
> • la RÉDUCTION de quelque chose, comme dans les exemples:
> **to devalue** dévaluer; **to degrade an officer** dégrader un officier
> • plus rarement, ce préfixe exprime le fait de QUITTER UN LIEU, comme dans les exemples:
> **to decamp** lever le camp; **they detrained** ils sont descendus du train; **they deplaned** ils sont descendus de l'avion
> Le préfixe **de-** se traduit presque toujours par **dé-** ou **dés-**, sauf lorsqu'il exprime le fait de quitter un lieu, auquel cas il faut souvent avoir recours à une périphrase.

DEA [ˌdiːiː'eɪ] N *Am (abbr* **Drug Enforcement Administration***)* = agence américaine de lutte contre la drogue

deacon ['diːkən] N *Rel* diacre *m*

deaconess [ˌdiːkə'nes] N *Rel* diaconesse *f*

deactivate [ˌdiː'æktɪveɪt] VT désamorcer

deactivation [ˌdiːˌæktɪ'veɪʃən] N désamorçage *m*

DEAD [ded]

> **ADJ**
> • mort **1, 3–5, 7, 9** • engourdi **2**
> • éteint **3** • hors jeu **6**
> • terne **8** • foutu **11**
> **ADV**
> • exactement **1** • super **2**
> **NPL**
> • morts
> **N**
> • milieu

ADJ **1** *(not alive ▸ person, animal, plant)* mort; *(▸ flower)* fané; **d. man** mort *m*; **d. woman** morte *f*; **the d. woman's husband** le mari de la défunte; **he has been d. for five years** il est mort *ou* décédé il y a cinq ans, cela fait cinq ans qu'il est mort; **to be d. on arrival** être mort *ou* décédé avant l'arrivée à l'hôpital; **d. or alive** mort ou vif; **more d. than alive** plus mort que vif; **half d. with hunger/exhaustion** à demi mort de faim/d'épuisement; **stone d.** raide mort; **to drop (down)** *or* **to fall down d.** tomber raide mort; **to shoot sb d.** tuer qn (avec une arme à feu), abattre qn; **to leave sb for d.** laisser qn pour mort; *Fam Fig* **you're d.** *or* **d. meat if he finds out** s'il l'apprend, tu es mort; *Fam* **drop d.!** va te faire voir!; *Fam* **d. as a doornail** *or* **a dodo** on ne peut plus mort; **to step into a d. man's shoes** être promu à la suite du décès de son supérieur; *Fam* **I wouldn't be seen d. wearing something like that** jamais de la vie je ne mettrai quelque chose comme ça❑; *Fam* **I wouldn't be seen d. with him** plutôt mourir que de me montrer en sa compagnie❑; *Prov* **d. men tell no tales** les morts ne parlent pas; **d. in the water** mort dans l'œuf

2 *(lacking in sensation ▸ fingers, toes etc)* engourdi; **to go d.** s'engourdir; **she fell to the floor in a d. faint** elle tomba à terre, inconsciente; **he is d. to reason** il ne veut pas entendre raison; *Fam* **she's d. from the neck up** elle n'a rien dans la tête; *Fam* **to be d. to the world** dormir d'un sommeil de plomb

3 *(not alight ▸ fire)* mort, éteint; *(▸ coals)* éteint; *(▸ match)* usé

4 *(lacking activity ▸ town)* mort; *(▸ business, market)* très calme; *Banking & Fin (▸ account)* inactif; **this place is d. in winter** cet endroit est mort l'hiver

5 *(language)* mort

6 *Sport (out of play ▸ ball)* hors jeu *(inv)*

7 *Elec (battery)* mort, à plat; *(wire)* hors *ou* sans tension; *Tel (phone, line)* coupé; **the line went d.** la ligne a été coupée; **the phone is** *or* **has gone d.** il n'y a pas de tonalité

8 *(dull ▸ colour)* terne, fade; *(▸ sound)* sourd

9 *Fam (tired out)* mort, crevé

10 *(finished with ▸ cigar)* entièrement fumé; *Fam* **are these glasses d.?** est-ce que vous avez fini avec ces verres❑?

11 *Fam (no longer working ▸ TV, fridge etc)* foutu

ADV **1** *(precisely)* **d. ahead** tout droit; *Br* **to be d. level (with sth)** être exactement au même niveau (que qch); *Br* **to arrive d. on time** arriver à l'heure pile *ou* juste à l'heure; *Br* **d. on target** *(hit something)* en plein dans le mille; *Br Fam* **you're d. right** tu as entièrement raison❑; *Br Fam* **you're d. on** c'est exactement ça❑

2 *Fam (very)* super; **d. beat** crevé, mort; **d. broke** complètement fauché; **d. drunk** ivre mort; **d. easy** super facile, fastoche; *Br* **it was d. lucky** c'était un super coup de bol *ou* de pot

3 *(completely)* **the sea was d. calm** la mer était parfaitement calme; **to be d. set on doing sth** être fermement décidé à faire qch; **to be d. (set) against sth** être résolument opposé à qch

4 *Aut* **d. slow** *(sign)* au pas

5 *(idioms)* **to play d.** faire le mort; **to stop d.** s'arrêter net; **to stop sb d.** arrêter qn net

NPL **the d.** les morts; *Rel* **to rise from the d.** ressusciter d'entre les morts

N *(depth)* **in the d. of winter** au cœur de l'hiver; **in the** *or* **at d. of night** au milieu *ou* au plus profond de la nuit

▸▸ ***dead body*** cadavre *m*, corps *m*; *Fam* **(it'll be) over my d. body!** il faudra me tuer d'abord!, moi vivant, jamais!; *Naut* ***dead calm*** calme *m* plat; *Tech* ***dead centre*** point *m* mort; *(of lathe)* centre *m* fixe; *Br Fam* ***dead cert*** *(in race, competition)* valeur *f* sûre❑; **it's a d. cert that he'll be there** il sera là à coup sûr; *Fig* ***dead duck*** *(plan, proposal ▸ which will fail)* désastre *m* assuré❑, plan *m* foireux; *(▸ which has failed)* désastre *m*, fiasco *m*; **he's a d. duck** c'en est fini de lui; ***dead end*** *(road)* cul *m* de sac, voie *f* sans issue, impasse *f*; **to come to a d. end** *(street)* se terminer en cul de sac; *Fig* aboutir à une impasse; ***dead hand*** **1** *(influence)* mainmise *f*, emprise *f*; **the d. hand of tradition** le poids de la tradition **2** *Law* mainmorte *f*; ***dead heat*** = course dont les vainqueurs sont déclarés ex aequo; *(horse race)* dead-heat *m*; **it was a d. heat** *(athletics race)* les coureurs sont arrivés ex aequo; ***dead letter*** *Admin (letter that cannot be delivered)* lettre *f* non distribuée, (lettre *f* passée au) rebut *m*; *Br (law, rule)* loi *f ou* règle *f* caduque *ou* tombée en désuétude; *Br* **to become a d. letter** *(law, rule)* tomber en désuétude; *Br Com* ***dead loss*** perte *f* sèche; *Br Fam* **to be a d. loss** *(person, thing)* être complètement nul; *Rail* ***dead man's handle*** manette *f* d'homme-mort; *Fin* ***dead money*** argent *m* mort, argent *m* qui dort; *Naut* ***dead reckoning*** estime *f*; **to navigate by d. reckoning** naviguer à l'estime; *Fam* ***dead ringer*** sosie❑ *m*; **to be a d. ringer for sb** être le sosie de qn; ***the Dead Sea*** la mer Morte; ***the Dead Sea Scrolls*** les manuscrits *mpl* de la mer Morte; ***dead silence*** silence *m* complet *ou* de mort; ***dead stop*** arrêt *m* brutal; **to come to a d. stop** s'arrêter net; ***dead weight*** poids *m* mort; *Aut* poids *m* utile; *Fig* **he's a d. weight** c'est un poids mort; *Br* ***dead wood*** *(trees, branches)* bois *m* mort; *Fig (people)* personnel *m* inutile; **there is too much d. wood in this office** il y a trop de gens payés à ne rien faire dans ce bureau

dead-and-alive ADJ *Br* mort, triste; **it's a d. sort of place** c'est un vrai trou

deadbeat ['dedbi:t] N *Fam (good-for-nothing)* bon (bonne) *m,f* à rien; *(tramp)* épave *f*, loque *f*; *(parasite)* pique-assiette *mf*

deaden ['dedən] VT *(sound)* assourdir; *(sense, nerve, hunger pangs)* calmer; *(pain)* endormir, calmer; *(blow)* amortir; **they had become deadened to...** ils étaient devenus insensibles à...

deadening ['dedənɪŋ] ADJ *(boredom, task)* abrutissant; **the d. effects of alcohol** les effets insensibilisants *ou* anesthésiants de l'alcool

deadhead ['dedhed] N **1** *Fam (dull person)* nullité *f* **2** *(person using free ticket ▸ in theatre)* spectateur (trice) *m,f* ayant un billet de faveur; *(▸ on train)* voyageur(euse) *m,f* muni(e) d'un billet gratuit **3** *Am (empty vehicle)* = train, avion, camion etc circulant à vide

VT *(plants)* enlever les fleurs fanées de

VI *Am (train)* circuler à vide

deadline ['dedlaɪn] N *(day)* date *f* limite; *(time)* heure *f* limite; **Monday is the absolute d.** c'est pour lundi dernier délai *ou* dernière limite; **the d. for returning your essays** la date limite *ou* la dernière limite pour rendre vos dissertations; **to meet/to miss a d.** respecter/laisser passer une date limite; **I'm working to a d.** j'ai un délai à respecter

deadliness ['dedlɪnɪs] N *(of poison, snake)* caractère *m* mortel; *(of weapon)* caractère *m* meurtrier; *Fig (of wit, repartee)* mordant *m*, causticité *f*

deadlock ['dedlɒk] N **1** *(situation)* impasse *f*; **to reach (a) d.** arriver à une impasse; **to break the d.** *(negotiators)* sortir de l'impasse; *(concession)* apporter une solution à l'impasse **2** *Tech* serrure *f* à pêne dormant; *Aut* serrure *f* passive

VT **talks are deadlocked** les discussions ont atteint une impasse, les discussions en sont au point mort

deadly ['dedlɪ] *(compar* **deadlier**, *superl* **deadliest**)

ADJ **1** *(lethal ▸ poison, blow)* mortel; *(▸ snake)* au venin mortel; *(▸ weapon)* meurtrier; *Fig (hatred)* mortel; *(wit, satire)* mordant, caustique; *(silence, pallor)* de mort, mortel; *Fig* **they are d. enemies** ce sont des ennemis mortels; **the seven d. sins** les sept péchés *mpl* capitaux

2 *(precise)* **his aim is d.** il a un tir excellent; **with d. accuracy** avec une extrême précision; **to d. effect** de façon dévastatrice

3 *(extreme)* **in d. earnest** *(be)* très sérieux; *(say)* très sérieusement

4 *Fam (boring)* mortel, barbant

5 *Austr & Ir Fam (excellent)* d'enfer, super *(inv)*

ADV extrêmement, terriblement; **d. accurate** extrêmement précis; **to be d. serious** être tout à fait sérieux; **d. pale** pâle comme la mort, d'une pâleur de mort *ou* mortelle; **it was d. boring** *or* **dull** c'était mortellement ennuyeux

▸▸ *Bot* ***deadly nightshade*** belladone *f*

deadpan ['dedpæn] ADJ *(face, expression)* impassible; *(humour)* pince-sans-rire *(inv)*

ADV d'un air impassible

deadwood ['dedwʊd] N *Am (trees, branches)* bois *m* mort; *Fig (people)* personnel *m* inutile

deaf [def] ADJ sourd; **to go d.** devenir sourd; **d. in one ear** sourd d'une oreille; **d. people** les sourds *mpl*; *Old-fashioned* **d. and dumb** sourd-muet, *f* sourde-muette; *Fig* **to turn a d. ear to sb/sth** faire la sourde oreille à qn/qch; *Fig* **our complaints fell on d. ears** nos protestations n'ont pas été entendues; **(as) d. as a post** sourd comme un pot; *Prov* **there are none so d. as those who will not hear** il n'est pire sourd que celui qui ne veut entendre

NPL **the d.** les sourds *mpl*

deaf-aid N *Br* appareil *m* acoustique

deafen ['defən] VT rendre sourd; *Fig* casser les oreilles à; **you're deafening me** vous me cassez les oreilles

deafening ['defənɪŋ] ADJ *(music, noise, roar)* assourdissant; *(applause)* retentissant; *Hum* **the silence was d.** il y avait un grand silence *ou* un silence impressionnant

deaf-mute N sourd-muet (sourde-muette) *m,f*

ADJ sourd-muet

deafness ['defnɪs] N surdité *f*

DEAL [di:l]

N	
• affaire **1**	• donne **3**
VT	
• donner **1**	• revendre **3**
VI	
• faire la donne **1**	• négocier **2**
• dealer **3**	

(pt & pp **dealt** [delt])

N **1** *(agreement)* affaire *f*, marché *m*; *St Exch* opération *f*, transaction *f*; **to do** *or* **to make a d. with sb** conclure une affaire *ou* un marché avec qn; **I'll make a d. with you** je te propose un marché; **the d. is off** l'affaire est annulée, le marché est rompu; **the government does not do deals with terrorists** le gouvernement ne traite pas avec les terroristes; **no d.!** je ne marche pas!; **it's a d.!** marché conclu!; **that wasn't the d.** ce n'est pas ce qui était convenu; **a good/bad d.** une bonne/mauvaise affaire; **to get a good d.** faire une bonne affaire; *esp Am Fam* **what's the d.?** qu'est-ce qui se passe?

2 *(treatment)* **to give sb a fair d.** être juste avec qn; **the government promised (to give) teachers a better d.** le gouvernement a promis d'améliorer la condition des enseignants; *Pol* **the New D.** le New Deal, la Nouvelle Donne

3 *Cards* donne *f*, distribution *f*; **it's my d.** c'est à moi de donner

4 *(quantity)* **a (good) d. of, a great d. of** *(money, time etc)* beaucoup de; **he thinks a great d. of her** il l'estime beaucoup/énormément; **I didn't enjoy it a great d.** je n'ai pas trop *ou* pas tellement aimé; **there's a good** *or* **great d. of truth in what you say** il y a beaucoup de vrai dans ce que vous dites; **I didn't do a great d. last night** je n'ai pas fait grand-chose hier soir; **a good/great d. faster** beaucoup plus vite; *Fam Ironic* **big d.!** la belle affaire!; *Fam* **no big d.** ça ne fait rien; *Fam* **he made a big d. out of it** il en a fait tout un plat *ou* tout un cinéma; *Fam* **what's the big d.?** et alors?, et puis quoi?

5 *Carp (timber)* planche *f*; **a d. table** une table en bois

VT **1** *Cards* donner, distribuer

2 *(strike)* **to d. sb a blow** assener un coup à qn; *Fig* **the news of her death dealt him a heavy blow** ce fut pour lui un coup terrible que d'apprendre sa mort; *Fig* **to d. sth a blow, to d. a blow to sth** porter un coup à qch

3 *(drugs)* revendre

VI **1** *Cards* faire la donne, donner; **it's your turn** *or* **it's you to d.** c'est à toi de distribuer *ou* de donner

2 *Com* négocier, traiter; **to d. on the Stock Exchange** faire des opérations *ou* des transactions en bourse; **to d. in leather/in options** faire le commerce des cuirs/des primes; **to d. in drugs** revendre de la drogue; *Fig* **to d. in death/human misery** être un marchand de mort/de misère humaine

3 *(in drugs)* revendre de la drogue, dealer

▸**deal in** VT SEP *Cards (player)* donner *ou* distribuer des cartes à, servir; *Fig* **deal me in** tu peux compter sur moi

▸**deal out** VT SEP *(cards, gifts)* donner, distribuer; *(justice)* rendre; *(punishment)* distribuer; **to d. out criticism** critiquer à tour de bras; *Fig* **deal me out** ne compte pas sur moi

▸**deal with** VT INSEP **1** *(handle ▸ problem, situation, query, complaint)* traiter; *(▸ customer, member of the public)* traiter avec; *(▸ difficult situation, child)* s'occuper de; **a difficult child to d. with** un enfant difficile; **a job that involves dealing with the public** un travail qui implique un contact avec le public; **the author deals with the question very sensitively** l'auteur traite *ou* aborde ce sujet avec beaucoup de délicatesse; **I'll d. with it** *(problem, situation etc)* je m'en occupe, je m'en charge; **I know how to d. with him** je sais m'y prendre avec lui; **I'll d. with you later** *(to naughty child)* je vais m'occuper de toi *ou* de ton cas plus tard; **the culprits were dealt with severely** les coupables ont été sévèrement punis; **the switchboard deals with over 1,000 calls a day** le standard traite *ou* reçoit plus de 1000 appels par jour; **that's that dealt with** voilà qui est fait **2** *(do business with)* traiter *ou* négocier avec; *(get supplies from ▸ grocer etc)* se fournir chez; **she's not an easy woman to d. with** ce n'est pas facile de traiter *ou* négocier avec elle **3** *(be concerned with) (subject)* traiter de

dealbreaker ['di:l,breɪkə(r)] N = événement ou décision qui rend impossible toute poursuite des negociations

dealer ['di:lə(r)] N **1** *Com* marchand(e) *m,f*, négociant(e) *m,f* (**in** en); *(supplier)* fournisseur *m* (**in** de); *St Exch* courtier(ère) *m,f*; *(in foreign exchange)* cambiste *mf*; *Aut* concessionnaire *mf* **2** *(in drugs)* dealer *m* **3** *Cards* donneur(euse) *m,f*

▸▸ *Com* ***dealer brand*** marque *f* de revendeur; *Mktg* ***dealer test*** test *m* auprès des distributeurs

dealership ['di:ləʃɪp] N *Aut & Com* concession *f*

dealing ['di:lɪŋ] N **1** *(UNCOUNT) St Exch* opérations *fpl*, transactions *fpl*; *(trading)* commerce *m*

2 *(UNCOUNT) Cards* donne *f*, distribution *f*

3 dealings *(business)* affaires *fpl*, transactions *fpl*; *(personal)* relations *fpl*; **to have dealings with sb** *(in business)* traiter avec qn, avoir affaire à qn; *(personal)* avoir affaire à qn

4 *(in drugs)* vente *f*

▸▸ *St Exch* ***dealing room*** salle *f* de marchés

dean [di:n] N *Rel & Univ* doyen(enne) *m,f*

▸▸ *Am Univ* ***Dean's List*** = tableau d'honneur dans les universités américaines

deanery ['di:nərɪ] N *Rel* doyenné *m*; *Univ* résidence *f* du doyen

dear [dɪə(r)] ADJ **1** *(loved)* cher; *(precious)* cher, précieux; *(appealing)* adorable, charmant; **he is a d. friend of mine** c'est un ami très cher; **he/the memory is very d. to me** il/ce souvenir m'est très cher; *Formal or Literary* **to hold sb/sth d.** chérir qn/qch; **all that I hold d. (in life)** tout ce qui m'est cher; **my dearest wish is that...** mon vœu le plus cher est que...; **to run for d. life** courir à toute vitesse; **to hang on for d. life** s'accrocher désespérément; **my d. fellow** mon cher ami; **my d. girl** ma chère; **what a d. little child/cottage/frock!** quel enfant/quel cottage/quelle robe adorable! **2** *(in letter)* **D. Sir** Monsieur; **D. Madam** Madame; **D. Sir or Madam** Madame, Monsieur; **D. Sirs** Messieurs; **D. Mrs Baker** Madame; *(less formal)* Chère Madame; *(informal)* Chère Madame Baker; **D. Henry** Cher Henry; **D. Mum and Dad** Chers Maman et Papa; **Dearest Richard** Très cher Richard **3** *(expensive ▸ item, shop)* cher; *(▸ price)* haut, élevé; *esp Br* **things are getting dearer** la vie augmente

EXCLAM **d. d.!, d. me!, oh d.!** *(surprise)* oh mon Dieu!; *(regret)* oh là là!; **oh d.!** *(worry)* mon Dieu!; **oh d. no!** (oh) que non!

N **my d.** *(to child, spouse, lover)* mon (ma) chéri (e); *(to friend)* mon (ma) cher (chère); **my dearest** mon (ma) chéri(e); **she's such a d.** elle est tellement gentille; *Br Fam* **I gave the old d. my seat** j'ai laissé ma place à la vieille dame; **poor d.** pauvre chéri(e); **be a d. and answer the phone, answer the phone, there's a d.** sois gentil *ou* un amour, réponds au téléphone

ADV *(sell, pay, cost)* cher

▸▸ *Fam* ***Dear John (letter)*** lettre *f* de rupture

dearie ['dɪərɪ] *Fam* N chéri(e) *m,f*

EXCLAM **(oh) d. me!** oh mon Dieu!

dearly ['dɪəlɪ] ADV **1** *(very much)* beaucoup, énormément; **I love him d.** je l'aime tendrement *ou* de tout mon cœur; **I would d. love to live in the country** j'aimerais beaucoup *ou* j'adorerais vivre à la campagne; **d. beloved son of...** *(on gravestone)* fils bien-aimé de... **2** *(at high cost)* **to pay d. for sth** payer cher qch; **you shall pay d. for this** cela vous coûtera cher

dearness ['dɪənɪs] N **1** *(costliness)* cherté *f* **2** *(of loved one)* **her d. to him grew with every day that passed** l'affection qu'il avait pour elle croissait de jour en jour

dearth [dɜ:θ] N pénurie *f*

DEATH [deθ] **N** mort *f*; *Admin & Law* décès *m*; *Press* **deaths (column)** rubrique *f* nécrologique; **I was with him at the time of his d.** j'étais auprès de lui quand il est mort; **a d. in the family** un décès dans la famille; **to fall/to jump to one's d.** se tuer en tombant/se jetant dans le vide; **to freeze/to starve to d.** mourir de froid/de faim; **to be beaten to d.** être battu à mort; **to be burnt to d.** *(accidentally)* périr dans les flammes; *(as form of martyrdom)* périr sur le bûcher; **to bleed to d.** perdre tout son sang; **to fight to the d.** se battre à mort; **to meet one's d.** trouver la mort; **to die a violent d.** mourir de mort violente; **he died an easy d.** il n'a pas souffert; **condemned to** *or* **under sentence of d.** condamné à mort; **to sentence/to put sb to d.** condamner/mettre qn à mort; **to send sb to his/her d.** envoyer qn à la mort; **to smoke/to drink oneself to d.** se tuer à force de fumer/boire; **to stab sb to d.** tuer qn à coups de couteau; **to work sb to d.** tuer qn à force de surmenage; **till d. do us part** *(in marriage ceremony)* jusqu'à ce que la mort nous sépare; **this means the d. of the steel industry** cela sonne le glas de la sidérurgie; *Fig* **it's been done to d.** *(play, subject for novel etc)* ça a été fait et refait; *Fam* **to look like d. (warmed up)** avoir une mine de déterré; *Fam* **to feel like d. (warmed up)** être en piteux état□; *Fam* **to catch one's d. (of cold)** attraper la mort *ou* la crève; *Fam* **to be sick** *or* **tired to d. of sb/sth** en avoir ras le bol de qn/qch; *Fam* **to be bored to d.** s'ennuyer à mourir; *Fam* **to be worried/scared to d.** être mort d'inquiétude/de frousse; *Fam* **you'll be the d. of me!** *(with amusement)* tu me feras mourir (de rire)!; *(with irritation)* tu es tuant!; **to be at d.'s door** *(patient)* être à l'article de la mort; **d. by misadventure** mort *f* accidentelle

►► ***death camp*** camp *m* de la mort; ***death cell*** cellule *f* de condamné à mort; ***death certificate*** acte *m ou* certificat *m* de décès; *Br Formerly Fin* ***death duty*** droits *mpl* de succession; ***death knell*** glas *m*; *Fig* **to sound the d. knell for** *or* **of sth** sonner le glas de qch; ***death mask*** masque *m* mortuaire; ***death penalty*** peine *f* de mort, peine *f* capitale; ***death rate*** taux *m* de mortalité; ***death rattle*** râle *m* d'agonie; ***death row*** quartier *m* des condamnés à mort; **he's been on d. row for ten years** cela fait dix ans qu'il est au quartier des condamnés à mort; ***death sentence*** condamnation *f* à mort; ***death squad*** escadron *m* de la mort; *Am Fin* ***death taxes*** droits *mpl* de succession; ***death throes*** agonie *f*; *(painful)* affres *fpl* de la mort; *Fig* agonie *f*; **to be in one's d. throes** agoniser, être agonisant; *(suffering)* connaître les affres de la mort; ***death toll*** nombre *m* de morts; **the d. toll stands at 567** il y a 567 morts, le bilan est de 567 morts; ***death trap*** = véhicule ou endroit extrêmement dangereux; **the house is a d. trap** cette maison est extrêmement dangereuse; ***death warrant*** ordre *m* d'exécution; *Fig* **to sign one's own d. warrant** signer son propre arrêt de mort; *Psy* ***death wish*** désir *m* de mort; *Fig* **he seems to have a d. wish** il faut croire qu'il est suicidaire

deathbed ['deθbed] **N** lit *m* de mort; **on one's d.** sur son lit de mort

ADJ *(confession)* fait à l'article de la mort; *(repentance)* exprimé à l'article de la mort

►► *Theat* ***deathbed scene*** scène *f* du lit de mort

deathblow ['deθbləʊ] **N** coup *m* fatal *ou* mortel; *Fig* coup *m* fatal; **to be the d. for sth** porter un coup fatal à qch

deathless ['deθlɪs] **ADJ** immortel; *Hum* inimitable

deathlike ['deθlaɪk] **ADJ** de mort, mortel

deathly ['deθlɪ] **ADJ** *(silence, pallor)* de mort, mortel

ADV d. pale pâle comme la mort; **the house was d. quiet** *(silent)* la maison était plongée dans un profond silence; *(sinister)* la maison était plongée dans un silence de mort

death's-head **N** tête *f* de mort

►► *Entom* ***death's-head moth*** sphinx *m* tête-de-mort

deathwatch ['deθwɒtʃ] **N** veillée *f* mortuaire

►► *Entom* ***deathwatch beetle*** grande *ou* grosse vrillette *f*, horloger *m* de la mort

deb [deb] **N** *Br Fam* débutante□ *f*

debacle [de'bɑːkəl] **N** débâcle *f*

debag [ˌdiː'bæg] *(pt & pp* **debagged,** *cont* **debagging)** **VT** *Fam* déculotter de force

debar [ˌdiː'bɑː(r)] *(pt & pp* **debarred,** *cont* **debarring)** **VT** interdire à; **to d. sb from sth/doing sth** interdire qch à qn/à qn de faire qch

debase [dɪ'beɪs] **VT 1** *(degrade ► person, sport)* avilir, abaisser; *(► reputation)* ternir; *(► tradition, profession, politics)* dévaloriser **2** *(make less valuable ► object)* dégrader, altérer; *(► metal, currency, coinage)* déprécier

debasement [dɪ'beɪsmənt] **N 1** *(degradation ► of person, sport)* avilissement *m*, abaissement *m*; *(of tradition, profession, politics)* dévalorisation *f* **2** *(of object)* dégradation *f*, altération *f*; *(of metal, currency, coinage)* dépréciation *f*

debatable [dɪ'beɪtəbəl] **ADJ** discutable, contestable; **it is d. whether...** on peut se demander si..., on peut se poser la question de savoir si...

debate [dɪ'beɪt] **VT** *(question etc)* débattre, discuter, agiter; *(subject)* mettre en discussion; **a much debated question** une question très débattue; **to d. whether to do sth or not** se demander si on doit faire qch

VI discuter (**with sb** avec qn; **on sth** sur qch); *(take part in a debate)* prendre part à un débat

N *(gen)* discussion *f*; *(organized)* débat *m*; **there's been a lot of d. about it** cela a été très *ou* longuement débattu; **there has been some d. over the effectiveness of the treatment** l'efficacité du traitement a été mise en doute; **open to d.** discutable, contestable; **after much** *or* **lengthy d.** *(between two or more people)* après de longs débats; *(with oneself)* après de longs débats intérieurs; **to be the subject of d.** faire le thème de débats

debater [dɪ'beɪtə(r)] **N** débatteur *m*; **to be a skilled d.** exceller dans les débats

debating [dɪ'beɪtɪŋ] **N** art *m* du débat; **she took up d. at university** elle a pris part à des débats formels à l'université

►► ***debating society*** société *f* de débats contradictoires

debauch [dɪ'bɔːtʃ] **VT** débaucher; *Arch or Literary (woman)* séduire

N *Arch or Literary* partie *f* de débauche

debauched [dɪ'bɔːtʃt] **ADJ** *(person)* débauché; *(tastes)* dépravé; *(life)* de débauche

debauchee [dɪbɔː'tʃiː] **N** débauché(e) *m,f*

debauchery [dɪ'bɔːtʃərɪ] **N** débauche *f*

debenture [dɪ'bentʃə(r)] **N** *Fin* obligation *f*

►► ***debenture bond*** titre *m* d'obligation, *Can* débenture *f*; ***debenture holder*** obligataire *mf*, détenteur(trice) *m,f* d'obligations; ***debenture issue*** émission *f* d'obligations; ***debenture stock*** obligation *f* sans garantie

debilitate [dɪ'bɪlɪteɪt] **VT** débiliter

debilitating [dɪ'bɪlɪteɪtɪŋ] **ADJ** *(illness)* débilitant; *(climate)* anémiant; **it had a d. effect on her concentration** cela a provoqué une baisse de sa concentration

debility [dɪ'bɪlətɪ] **N** débilité *f*

debit ['debɪt] *Acct, Banking & Fin* **N** débit *m*; *Br* **your account is in d.** votre compte est déficitaire *ou* débiteur

COMP *(balance, account, item)* débiteur

VT *(account)* débiter; *(person)* porter au débit de qn; **to d. £50 from sb's account, to d. sb's account with £50** débiter 50 livres du compte de qn, débiter le compte de qn de 50 livres; **has this cheque been debited to my account?** est-ce que ce chèque a été débité de mon compte?

►► *Banking* ***debit card*** = carte de paiement à débit immédiat; *Acct* ***debit column*** colonne *f* débitrice *ou* des débits; ***debit entry*** *Acct* écriture *f* passée au débit; *Banking* article *m* porté au débit d'un compte; *Fin* ***debit note*** note *f* de débit; *Acct* ***debit side*** débit *m*; *Fig* **on the d. side, he is not very presentable** ce qui le dessert, c'est qu'il n'est pas très présentable

debonair [ˌdebə'neə(r)] **ADJ** *(person)* d'une élégance nonchalante; *(smile, charm)* nonchalant

debouch [dɪ'baʊtʃ] **VI** *Geog & Mil* déboucher

debrief [ˌdiː'briːf] **VT** faire faire un compte rendu verbal de mission à, débriefer; **pilots are debriefed after every flight** on fait faire un compte rendu verbal de mission aux pilotes *ou* on débriefe les pilotes après chaque vol

debriefing [ˌdiː'briːfɪŋ] **N** compte rendu *m* verbal de mission

►► ***debriefing room*** salle *f* de compte rendu de mission

debris [*Br* 'debriː, *Am* də'briː] **N** *(UNCOUNT)* débris *mpl*; *Fig (after party etc)* détritus *mpl*; *Fig* **to salvage something from the d. of one's marriage** sauver quelque chose des restes de son mariage

debt [det] **N** *Fin (gen)* dette *f*; *Admin (to be recovered)* créance *f*; **bad d.** mauvaise créance; **outstanding d.** dette *f ou* créance *f* à recouvrer; **to be in d., to have debts** avoir des dettes, être endetté; **to be £12,000 in d.** avoir 12 000 livres de dettes; **to be out of d.** s'être acquitté de ses dettes; **to get** *or* **to run into d.** s'endetter; **to get out of d.** s'acquitter de ses dettes; **to pay one's debts** régler ses dettes; *Fig* **I shall always be in your d.** je vous serai toujours redevable; *Fam* **to be up to the** *or* **one's ears in d.** être criblé de dettes; **to owe sb a d. of gratitude** avoir une dette de reconnaissance envers qn; **he has paid his d. to society** il s'est acquitté de sa dette envers la société;

COMP de la dette

►► ***debt collection agency*** bureau *m* de recouvrement *ou* récupération des créances; ***debt collector*** agent *m* de recouvrement; ***debt financing*** financement *m* par endettement; ***debt of honour*** dette *f* d'honneur; ***debt rescheduling, debt restructuring*** rééchelonnement *m* des dettes; *Am* ***debt service,*** *Br* ***debt servicing*** service *m* de la dette; ***debt swap*** échange *m* de créances

debtor ['detə(r)] **N** *Fin* débiteur(trice) *m,f*

►► *Acct* ***debtor account*** compte *m* débiteur; *Econ* ***debtor country, debtor nation*** pays *m* débiteur; *Acct* ***debtor side*** débit *m*, doit *m*

debug [ˌdiː'bʌg] *(pt & pp* **debugged,** *cont* **debugging)** **VT 1** *Comput (program)* déboguer; *(machine)* mettre au point **2** *(remove hidden microphones from)* débarrasser des micros (cachés)

debugger [ˌdiː'bʌgə(r)] **N** *Comput* (programme *m*) débogueur *m*

debugging [ˌdiː'bʌgɪŋ] **N 1** *Comput (of program)* débogage *m*; *(of machine)* mise *f* au point **2** *(removal of microphones)* élimination *f* des micros (cachés)

debunk [ˌdiː'bʌŋk] **VT** *Fam* **1** *(ridicule)* tourner en ridicule **2** *(show to be false)* démystifier

debut ['deɪbjuː] *(pt & pp* **debut'd** [-bjuːd]) **N** début *m*; **to make one's d.** faire ses débuts

VI débuter; **to d. as** débuter dans le rôle de

►► ***debut performance*** première apparition *f*

debutante ['debjʊtɑːnt] **N** débutante *f*

Dec. *(written abbr* **December)** déc

decade ['dekeɪd] **N 1** *(ten years)* décennie *f*; **over a d. ago** il y a plus de dix ans **2** *Rel (of rosary)* dizaine *f*

> Note that the French word **décade** is a false friend. It usually refers to a period of ten days.

decadence ['dekədəns] **N 1** *(of person, life, society etc)* décadence *f* **2** *Art & Literature* décadentisme *m*

decadent ['dekədənt] **ADJ** décadent; **to become d.** tomber dans la décadence; *Hum* **how d.!** quelle décadence!

N 2 *Art & Literature* décadent(e) *m,f*

decaf, decaff ['diːkæf] **N** *Fam (coffee)* déca *m*

decaffeinate [ˌdiː'kæfɪneɪt] **VT** décaféiner

decaffeinated [ˌdiː'kæfɪneɪtɪd] **ADJ** décaféiné

decagramme, *Am* **decagram** ['dekəgræm] **N** décagramme *m*

decal ['diːkæl] **N** *Am Fam* décalcomanie□ *f*

decalcification [diːˌkælsɪfɪ'keɪʃən] **N** décalcification *f*

decalcify [ˌdiː'kælsɪfaɪ] **VT** décalcifier

Decalogue ['dekəlɒg] **N** *Bible* décalogue *m*

decamp [dɪˈkæmp] VI **1** *Mil* lever le camp **2** *Fam (abscond)* décamper, ficher le camp; **to d. to another room** aller s'installer dans une autre pièce

decant [dɪˈkænt] VT **1** *(liquid)* transvaser; *(wine, brandy etc)* décanter dans une carafe **2** *Fam (move, transfer ▸ people)* transférer

decanter [dɪˈkæntə(r)] N carafe *f*

decapitate [dɪˈkæpɪteɪt] VT décapiter

decapitation [dɪˌkæpɪˈteɪʃən] N décapitation *f*

decapod [ˈdekəpɒd] N *Zool* décapode *m*

decarbonize, -ise [ˌdiːˈkɑːbənaɪz] VT **1** *Tech* décalaminer **2** *Metal* décarburer

decathlete [dɪˈkæθliːt] N *Sport* décathlonien (enne) *m,f*

decathlon [dɪˈkæθlɒn] N *Sport* décathlon *m*

decay [dɪˈkeɪ] VI **1** *(rot ▸ food, wood, flowers)* pourrir; *(▸ meat)* s'avarier, pourrir; *(▸ corpse)* se décomposer; *(▸ tooth)* se carier; *(▸ building)* se délabrer; *(▸ stone)* s'effriter, se désagréger **2** *Fig (beauty, civilization, faculties)* décliner; *(family, country)* tomber en décadence **3** *Phys* dépérir, se dégrader, se désintégrer

VT *(wood)* pourrir; *(stone)* désagréger; *(tooth)* carier

N **1** *(of food, wood, flowers)* pourriture *f*; *(of corpse)* décomposition *f*; *(of teeth)* carie *f*; *(of building)* délabrement *m*; *(of stone)* effritement *m*, désagrégation *f* **2** *Fig (of beauty, faculties)* délabrement *m*; *(of family, country)* décadence *f*, déchéance *f*; *(of civilization)* déclin *m*; *also Fig* **to fall into d.** se délabrer; **in an advanced state of d.** *(building)* dans un état de délabrement avancé; *(corpse)* dans un état de putréfaction avancé; **moral d.** déchéance *f* morale **3** *Phys* désintégration *f*, dégradation *f*

decayed [dɪˈkeɪd] ADJ **1** *(food, wood, flowers)* pourri; *(meat)* avarié, pourri; *(corpse)* décomposé; *(tooth)* carié; *(building)* délabré, en ruines; *(stone)* effrité, désagrégé **2** *Fig (beauty)* fané; *(civilization)* délabré, en ruines

decaying [dɪˈkeɪɪŋ] ADJ **1** *(food, wood, flowers)* pourrissant; *(meat)* en train de s'avarier; *(corpse)* en décomposition; *(tooth)* en train de se carier; *(building)* qui se délabre; *(stone)* en désagrégation **2** *Fig (beauty)* qui se fane; *(civilization)* sur le déclin

decease [dɪˈsiːs] *Law & Admin* N décès *m*

VI décéder

> Attention: ne pas confondre avec le nom **disease.**

deceased [dɪˈsiːst] *(pl inv) Law & Admin* N **the d.** le (la) défunt(e)

ADJ décédé, défunt; **son of Robert Martin, d.** fils de feu M. Robert Martin

decedent [dɪˈsiːdənt] N *Am Law* défunt(e) *m,f*

deceit [dɪˈsiːt] N **1** *(quality)* duplicité *f* **2** *(trick)* supercherie *f*, tromperie *f* **3** *Law* fraude *f*; **by d.** frauduleusement

deceitful [dɪˈsiːtfʊl] ADJ trompeur; *(behaviour)* trompeur, sournois; **it was very d. of her** c'était très malhonnête de sa part

deceitfully [dɪˈsiːtfʊlɪ] ADV trompeusement, avec duplicité; **to obtain sth d.** obtenir qch en usant de duplicité

deceitfulness [dɪˈsiːtfʊlnɪs] N tromperie *f*, duplicité *f*

deceive [dɪˈsiːv] VT tromper; **to d. sb into doing sth** amener qn à faire qch en le trompant; **she deceived me into believing that…** elle m'a fait croire que…; **don't be deceived** ne vous y fiez pas; **to be deceived by appearances** se laisser tromper par les apparences; **to d. oneself** se mentir à soi-même; **don't d. yourself that it will be easy** ne croyez pas que ce sera facile; **I thought my eyes were deceiving me** je ne pouvais pas en croire mes yeux

VI tromper; **it was not done with intent to d.** cela n'a pas été fait dans l'intention de tromper

> Note that the French verb **décevoir** is a false friend and is never a translation for the English verb **to deceive**. It means **to disappoint.**

deceiver [dɪˈsiːvə(r)] N trompeur(euse) *m,f*

decelerate [ˌdiːˈseləreɪt] VI ralentir

deceleration [ˈdiːˌseləˈreɪʃən] N ralentissement *m*

December [dɪˈsembə(r)] N décembre; *see also* **February**

decency [ˈdiːsənsɪ] *(pl* **decencies***)* N décence *f*; **for d.'s sake** pour respecter les convenances; *Br* **an offence against public d.** un outrage à la pudeur; **to have the (common) d. to do sth** avoir la décence de faire qch; **to observe the decencies** observer les convenances

decent [ˈdiːsənt] ADJ **1** *(proper, morally correct)* décent, convenable; **d., churchgoing folk** des gens comme il faut, qui vont à la messe tous les dimanches; **after a d. length of time** après une période de temps convenable; **to do the d. thing** se comporter *ou* agir dans les règles; *(marry woman one has made pregnant)* faire son devoir, réparer; **are you d.?** *(dressed)* es-tu habillé?

2 *(satisfactory, reasonable ▸ housing, wage)* décent, convenable; *(▸ price)* convenable, raisonnable; **wait until you have a d. amount of money** attends d'avoir suffisamment d'argent; **a d. meal** un bon repas; **a d. night's sleep** une bonne nuit de sommeil; **the rooms are a d. size** les pièces sont de bonne taille; **to speak d. French** parler assez bien *ou* parler convenablement le français

3 *Fam (kind, good)* bien[□], sympa; *Br* **he's a d. sort (of chap)** c'est un type bien; **that's very d. of you** c'est très sympa de ta part

4 *Am Fam (excellent)* super, dément

decently [ˈdiːsəntlɪ] ADV **1** *(properly)* décemment, convenablement; **you can't d. ask her to do that** tu ne peux pas décemment lui demander de faire cela **2** *(reasonably)* pas trop mal; **the job pays d.** le travail paie raisonnablement bien **3** *Fam (kindly)* de manière sympa; **he's treated me very d.** il m'a traité de façon très correcte

decentralization, -isation [diːˌsentrəlaɪˈzeɪʃən] N *Pol* décentralisation *f*

decentralize, -ise [ˌdiːˈsentrəlaɪz] VT *Pol* décentraliser

decent-sized ADJ *(house, room)* de bonnes dimensions

deception [dɪˈsepʃən] N **1** *(act of deceiving)* tromperie *f*, duperie *f*; **by d.** en usant de tromperie **2** *(trick)* subterfuge *m*, tromperie *f* **3** *(state of being deceived)* duperie *f*

> Note that the French word **déception** is a false friend and is never a translation for the English word **deception**. It means **disappointment.**

deceptive [dɪˈseptɪv] ADJ trompeur; **appearances can be d.** il ne faut pas se fier aux apparences, les apparences sont trompeuses

deceptively [dɪˈseptɪvlɪ] ADV **d. worded/written** trompeur; **it looks d. easy/near** cela donne l'illusion d'être facile/tout près, on a l'impression que c'est facile/tout près; **he has a d. calm exterior** il paraît calme mais il ne faut pas s'y tromper

deceptiveness [dɪˈseptɪvnɪs] N caractère *m* trompeur

decibel [ˈdesɪbel] N décibel *m*; **d. level** niveau *m* en décibels

decide [dɪˈsaɪd] VT **1** *(resolve)* décider; **to d. to do sth** décider de faire qch; **it was decided to alter our strategy** il a été décidé que nous devions modifier notre stratégie; **nothing has been decided** rien n'a été décidé; **what have you decided?** qu'avez-vous décidé?; **the weather hasn't decided what it's doing yet** le temps n'arrive pas à se décider **2** *(determine ▸ outcome, someone's fate, career)* décider de, déterminer; *(▸ person)* décider; **that was what decided me to leave him** c'est ce qui m'a décidé à le quitter **3** *(settle ▸ debate, war)* décider de l'issue de

VI **1** *(make up one's mind)* décider, se décider; **I can't d.** je n'arrive pas à me décider; **you d.** c'est toi qui décides; **to d. on doing sth** décider de faire qch; **I've decided on Greece for my holiday** j'ai décidé d'aller passer mes vacances en Grèce; **have you decided on a date/a name?** vous êtes-vous décidés sur une date/un nom?; **to d. against/in favour of doing sth** décider de ne pas/de faire qch; **we've decided against a holiday this year** nous avons décidé de ne pas prendre de vacances cette année; *Law* **to d. in favour of sb/sth** décider en faveur de qn/qch **2** *(determine)* **but circumstances decided otherwise** mais les circonstances en ont décidé autrement **3** *(choose)* choisir; **you'll have to d. between me and him** il va falloir choisir entre moi et lui

decided [dɪˈsaɪdɪd] ADJ **1** *(distinct ▸ improvement, difference)* net, incontestable; *(▸ success)* éclatant; **it's a d. improvement** c'est nettement mieux **2** *(resolute ▸ person, look)* décidé, résolu; *(▸ opinion, stance)* ferme; *(▸ effort)* résolu; *(▸ refusal)* ferme, catégorique; **I'm quite d. about leaving** je suis fermement décidé à partir

decidedly [dɪˈsaɪdɪdlɪ] ADV **1** *(distinctly ▸ better, different)* vraiment; **I feel d. unwell today** je ne me sens vraiment pas bien aujourd'hui **2** *(resolutely)* résolument, fermement

> Note that the French word **décidément** is a false friend and is never a translation for the English word **decidedly.**

decider [dɪˈsaɪdə(r)] N *(goal)* but *m* décisif; *(point)* point *m* décisif; *(match)* match *m* décisif, rencontre *f* décisive; *(factor)* facteur *m* décisif; **the d.** *(to determine winner)* la belle

deciding [dɪˈsaɪdɪŋ] ADJ décisif, déterminant; **the chairperson has the d. vote** la voix du président est prépondérante

deciduous [dɪˈsɪdjʊəs] ADJ *Bot & Biol (tree)* à feuilles caduques; *(leaves, antlers, teeth)* caduc

decilitre, *Am* **deciliter** [ˈdesɪˌliːtə(r)] N décilitre *m*

decimal [ˈdesɪməl] N chiffre *m* décimal

ADJ décimal; **to go d.** adopter le système décimal

▸▸ ***decimal currency*** monnaie *f* décimale; *Math* ***decimal fraction*** chiffre *m* décimal; *Math* ***decimal place*** décimale *f*; **correct to four d. places** exact jusqu'à la quatrième décimale *ou* jusqu'au quatrième chiffre après la virgule *ou* au dix millième près; *Math* ***decimal point*** virgule *f*; ***decimal system*** système *m* décimal

decimalization, -isation [ˌdesɪməlaɪˈzeɪʃən] N décimalisation *f*

decimate [ˈdesɪmeɪt] VT décimer

decimation [ˌdesɪˈmeɪʃən] N décimation *f*

decimetre, *Am* **decimeter** [ˈdesɪˌmiːtə(r)] N décimètre *m*

decipher [dɪˈsaɪfə(r)] VT *(code, handwriting)* déchiffrer

decipherable [dɪˈsaɪfərəbəl] ADJ déchiffrable

decision [dɪˈsɪʒən] N **1** *(choice, judgement)* décision *f*; **to make** *or* **to take a d.** prendre une décision, se décider; *Law & Admin* prendre une décision; **to come to** *or* **to arrive at** *or* **to reach a d.** parvenir à une décision; **to make the right/wrong d.** faire le bon/mauvais choix; **it's your d.** c'est toi qui décides; **is that your d.?** ta décision est prise?; **the referee's d. is final** la décision de l'arbitre est irrévocable *ou* sans appel **2** *Formal (decisiveness)* décision *f*, résolution *f*, fermeté *f* **3** *(decision-making)* **it's a matter for personal d.** c'est une affaire de choix personnel

▸▸ ***decision model*** modèle *m* décisionnel *ou* déterministe *ou* de décision; *Comput* ***decision table*** table *f* de décision; ***decision theory*** théorie *f* de la décision

decision-maker N décideur(euse) *m,f*, décisionnaire *mf*; **to be a good d.** savoir prendre des décisions; **to be a bad d.** ne pas savoir prendre de décisions

decision-making N prise *f* de décision; **the d. process** le processus de (prise de) décision; **he's no good at d.** il ne sait pas prendre des décisions

▸▸ ***decision-making tool*** outil *m* d'aide à la décision

decision-tree analysis N analyse *f* d'arbre décisionnel *ou* de décision

decisive [dɪˈsaɪsɪv] ADJ **1** *(manner, person, tone)* décidé, résolu; **be d.!** montre-toi décidé *ou* résolu! **2** *(factor, battle, argument, question)* décisif, déterminant

decisively [dɪˈsaɪsɪvlɪ] ADV **1** *(resolutely)* résolument, sans hésitation **2** *(conclusively)* de manière décisive

decisiveness [dɪˈsaɪsɪvnɪs] N **1** *(of manner, person, tone)* décision *f*; **to say sth with d.** dire qch d'un air décidé *ou* résolu **2** *(of factor, battle, argument, question)* caractère *m* décisif *ou* déterminant

deck [dek] N **1** *Naut* pont *m*; **upper/lower d.** pont *m* supérieur/inférieur; **on d.** sur le pont; **to go (up) on d.** monter sur le pont; **below d.** *or* **decks** sous le pont; *Fig* **to clear the decks** mettre de l'ordre avant de passer à l'action; *Fam* **to hit the d.** *(fall)* se foutre la gueule par terre; *(to avoid injury)* tomber à plat ventre; *(get out of bed)* se lever; *also Fig* **all hands on d.!** tous sur le pont!; **it's all hands on d. at the moment as the project enters its final phase** tout le monde doit mettre la main à la pâte maintenant que le projet est entré dans sa phase finale
2 *(of plane, bus)* étage *m*; **top** *or* **upper d.** *(of bus)* impériale *f*
3 *(of cards)* jeu *m*; *Fam Fig* **he's not playing with a full d.** *(is not very bright)* c'est pas une lumière, il n'a pas inventé l'eau chaude
4 *(in hi-fi system)* platine *f*
5 *Constr* tablier *m*; *(of bridge)* plancher *m*; *Am (terrace)* ponton *m*
• **decks** NPL *(for DJ)* platines *fpl*
COMP *Naut (officer, cabin, crane)* de pont
VT **1** *(decorate)* parer, orner (**with** de); **they were decked out in their best clothes** ils étaient sur leur trente et un **2** *Fam (knock to the ground)* envoyer au tapis **3** *Naut (ship)* ponter
▸▸ ***deck cargo, deck load*** pontée *f*; ***deck tennis*** = sorte de tennis joué sur le pont d'un navire

deckchair [ˈdektʃeə(r)] N chaise *f* longue, transat *m*

deckhouse [ˈdekhaus, *pl* -hauzɪz] N *Naut* rouf *m*

decking [ˈdekɪŋ] N plancher *m*

deckle [ˈdekəl] N cadre *m* volant *(utilisé dans la fabrication artisanale du papier)*
▸▸ ***deckle edge*** *(on paper)* bord *m* frangeux, barbes *fpl*

deckle-edged ADJ *(paper)* à bord frangeux, à barbes

declaim [dɪˈkleɪm] *Formal* VT déclamer
VI déclamer; **to d. against sth** récriminer *ou* se récrier contre qch

declamation [ˌdekləˈmeɪʃən] N *Formal* déclamation *f*

declamatory [dɪˈklæmətrɪ] ADJ *Formal (style)* déclamatoire

declaration [ˌdekləˈreɪʃən] N **1** *(gen)* déclaration *f*; **d. of love/war/income** déclaration *f* d'amour/de guerre/de revenu **2** *Cards* annonce *f*
▸▸ *Law & Fin* ***declaration of bankruptcy*** jugement *m* déclaratif de faillite, déclaration *f* de faillite; *Am Hist* ***the Declaration of Independence*** la Déclaration d'indépendance (américaine); ***declaration of intent*** déclaration *f* d'intention

declare [dɪˈkleə(r)] VT **1** *(proclaim ▸ independence, war etc)* déclarer; **the two countries have declared war** *(on each other)* les deux pays se sont déclaré la guerre; **to d. a moratorium** décréter un moratoire; **to d. a strike** proclamer la grève; **she was declared the winner** elle a été déclarée vainqueur; *Law & Fin* **to d. sb bankrupt** constater *ou* prononcer l'état de faillite *ou* la faillite de qn; *Fin* **to d. a dividend of ten percent** déclarer un dividende de dix pour cent; *Customs* **have you anything to d.?** avez-vous quelque chose à déclarer?; **I d. this meeting officially open** je déclare la séance ouverte **2** *(announce)* déclarer; **to d. oneself** *(proclaim one's love)* se déclarer; *Pol* se présenter, présenter sa candidature; **to d. oneself for/against sth** se déclarer pour/contre qch **3** *Cards (trumps, suit)* appeler; **to d. one's hand** annoncer son jeu; *Fig* avouer ses intentions
VI **1 to d. for/against sth** faire une déclaration en faveur de/contre qch; **well, I (do) d.!** eh bien ça alors! **2** *Cards* faire l'annonce, annoncer; *Sport (in cricket)* déclarer la tournée terminée *(avant sa fin normale)*

declared [dɪˈkleəd] ADJ *(intention, opponent)* déclaré, ouvert

declassification [diːˌklæsɪfɪˈkeɪʃən] N *(of information)* déclassement *m*

declassify [ˌdiːˈklæsɪfaɪ] *(pt & pp* **declassified***)* VT *(information)* déclassifier

declension [dɪˈklenʃən] N *Gram* déclinaison *f*

declinable [dɪˈklaɪnəbəl] ADJ *Gram* déclinable

declination [ˌdeklɪˈneɪʃən] N **1** *Astron* déclinaison *f* **2** *Am (refusal)* refus *m* poli

decline [dɪˈklaɪn] N *(decrease ▸ in prices, standards, crime, profits)* baisse *f*; *Fig (of civilization, empire)* déclin *m*; **there has been a d. in child mortality** il y a eu une baisse de la mortalité infantile; **sales have shown a rapid d. over the last six months** on a observé une forte chute des ventes au cours des six derniers mois; **to be in d.** être en déclin; **to be on the d.** *(prices, sales)* être en baisse; *(civilization, influence)* être sur le déclin; *Fig* **to fall into d.** dépérir
VT **1** *(refuse ▸ invitation, honour, offer of help)* décliner, refuser; *(▸ food, drink)* refuser; *(▸ responsibility)* décliner; **to d. to do sth** refuser de faire qch **2** *Gram* décliner
VI **1** *(decrease, diminish ▸ empire, health)* décliner; *(▸ prices, sales, population)* baisser, être en baisse, diminuer; *(▸ influence, enthusiasm, fame)* baisser, diminuer; **to d. in importance/value/significance** perdre de son importance/de sa valeur/de sa signification
2 *(refuse)* refuser
3 *(slope downwards)* être en pente, descendre
4 *Gram* se décliner

declining [dɪˈklaɪnɪŋ] ADJ *(health, industry, market)* sur le déclin; *(sales)* en baisse; **he is in d. health** sa santé décline *ou* faiblit; **she was in her d. years** elle était au déclin de sa vie

declivity [dɪˈklɪvətɪ] N déclivité *f*

declutch [dɪˈklʌtʃ] VI *Aut* débrayer

declutter [diːˈklʌtə(r)] VT *Fam (room, house)* débarrasser; *Fig* **you need to d. your life** il faut recentrer ta vie sur l'essentiel

decoction [dɪˈkɒkʃən] *Pharm* N **1** *(process)* décoction *f* **2** *(product)* décocté *m*

decode [ˌdiːˈkəud] VT décoder, déchiffrer; *Comput & TV* décoder; **the file is automatically decoded when it is received** le fichier est décodé automatiquement à la réception

decoder [ˌdiːˈkəudə(r)] N décodeur *m*

decoding [ˌdiːˈkəudɪŋ] N décodage *m*

decoke [ˌdiːˈkəuk] *Br Tech* N décalaminage *m*
VT décalaminer

décolletage [ˌdeɪkɒlˈtɑːʒ] N décolleté *m*

décolleté [deɪˈkɒlteɪ] N décolleté *m*
ADJ décolleté

decolonization, -isation [diːˌkɒlənaɪˈzeɪʃən] N décolonisation *f*

decolonize, -ise [diːˈkɒlənaɪz] VT décoloniser

decommission [ˌdiːkəˈmɪʃən] VT **1** *Nucl (shut down ▸ nuclear power station)* déclasser **2** *Mil (remove from active service ▸ warship, aircraft)* mettre hors service

decommissioning [ˌdiːkəˈmɪʃənɪŋ] N **1** *Nucl (of nuclear power station)* déclassement *m* **2** *Mil (of warship, aircraft)* mise *f* hors service

decompose [ˌdiːkəmˈpəuz] *Chem & Phys* VT décomposer
VI se décomposer

decomposition [ˌdiːkɒmpəˈzɪʃən] N *Chem & Phys* décomposition *f*

decompress [ˌdiːkəmˈpres] VT *(gas, air)* décomprimer; *(diver)* faire passer en chambre de décompression; *Comput* décompresser

decompression [ˌdiːkəmˈpreʃən] N décompression *f*
▸▸ *Med* ***decompression chamber*** chambre *f* de décompression; *Med* ***decompression sickness*** maladie *f* des caissons; *Comput* ***decompression software*** logiciel *m* de décompression

decompressor [ˌdiːkəmˈpresə(r)] N *Comput* logiciel *m* de décompression

decongestant [ˌdiːkənˈdʒestənt] *Med* N décongestif *m*
ADJ décongestif

decongestion [ˌdiːkənˈdʒestʃən] N *Med* décongestion *f*

deconsecrate [ˌdiːˈkɒnsɪkreɪt] VT *Rel* désaffecter

deconsignment [ˌdiːkənˈsaɪnmənt] N *Com* déconsignation *f*

decontaminate [ˌdiːkənˈtæmɪneɪt] VT décontaminer

decontamination [ˈdiːkənˌtæmɪˈneɪʃən] N décontamination *f*
COMP *(equipment, team, measures)* de décontamination; *(expert)* en décontamination

decontrol [ˌdiːkənˈtrəul] *Com & Econ* N *(of prices)* libération *f*
VT *(trade)* lever le contrôle gouvernemental sur; **to d. prices** libérer les prix

decor [ˈdeɪkɔː(r)] N décor *m*

decorate [ˈdekəreɪt] VT **1** *(house, room ▸ paint)* peindre; *(▸ wallpaper)* tapisser **2** *(dress, hat)* garnir, orner; *(cake, tree, street)* décorer **3** *(give medal to)* décorer, médailler; **to be decorated for bravery** être décoré pour son courage
VI *(paint)* peindre; *(wallpaper)* tapisser

decorating [ˈdekəreɪtɪŋ] N *(of house, room)* décoration *f*; **to do the d.** faire les travaux (de décoration); *Br* **painting and d.** peinture *f* et décoration *f*

decoration [ˌdekəˈreɪʃən] N **1** *(action ▸ of house, street, cake, tree)* décoration *f*; *(▸ of dress, hat)* ornementation *f*; **interior d.** décoration *f* intérieure **2** *(ornament ▸ for house, street, cake, tree)* décoration *f*; *(▸ for dress, hat)* garniture *f*, ornements *mpl*; **decorations** *(in town, for festival etc)* décorations **3** *(with medal)* remise *f* d'une décoration (**of sb** à qn); *(medal)* décoration *f*, médaille *f*

decorative [ˈdekərətɪv] ADJ décoratif, ornemental; **the house is in excellent d. order** la décoration de la maison est en excellent état
▸▸ ***decorative arts*** arts *mpl* décoratifs

decoratively [ˈdekərətɪvlɪ] ADV décorativement

decorator [ˈdekəreɪtə(r)] N décorateur(trice) *m,f*; *Br* **(painter and) d.** peintre *mf* décorateur(trice); *Br* **we're having the decorators in next week** les peintres viennent la semaine prochaine

decorous [ˈdekərəs] ADJ *Formal (behaviour)* bienséant, séant, convenable; *(person)* convenable, comme il faut

decorously [ˈdekərəslɪ] ADV *Formal (dressed)* convenablement, comme il faut

decorticate [ˌdiːˈkɔːtɪkeɪt] VT *Formal* décortiquer

decorum [dɪˈkɔːrəm] N bienséance *f*, décorum *m*; **to behave with d.** se comporter comme il faut *ou* avec bienséance; **to have a sense of d.** avoir le sens des convenances

decouple [dɪˈkʌpəl] VT *Elec* découpler

decoupling [dɪˈkʌplɪŋ] N *Elec* découplage *m*

decoy N [ˈdiːkɔɪ] **1** *(for catching birds ▸ live bird)* appeau *m*, chanterelle *f*; *(▸ artificial device)* leurre *m* **2** *Fig (person)* appât *m*; *(message, tactic, phone call)* piège *m*; **we want you to act as a d.** nous voulons que vous serviez d'appât
VT [dɪˈkɔɪ] *(bird ▸ using live bird)* attirer à l'appeau *ou* à la chanterelle; *(▸ using artificial means)* attirer au leurre; *(person)* appâter, attirer; **they decoyed him into leaving his house** ils l'ont appâté *ou* attiré hors de chez lui
▸▸ ***decoy duck*** *(live)* appeau *m*, chanterelle *f*; *(wooden)* leurre *m*

decrease N [ˈdiːkriːs] *(in size)* réduction *f*, diminution *f*; *(in popularity)* baisse *f*; *(in price)* réduction *f*, baisse *f*; **a d. in numbers** une baisse des effectifs; **to be on the d.** être en diminution *ou* en baisse
VI [dɪˈkriːs] *(number, enthusiasm, population, speed)* décroître, diminuer; *(value, price, crime, inflation)* diminuer, baisser; *(in knitting)* diminuer, faire des diminutions
VT [dɪˈkriːs] réduire, diminuer; *(prices ▸ of government)* baisser; *(▸ of economic forces)* faire baisser; *Knitting* **d. three stitches** diminuer de trois mailles, faire trois diminutions

decreasing [diːˈkriːsɪŋ] ADJ *(amount, energy, population)* décroissant; *(value, price, popularity)* en baisse; **in d. order of importance** par ordre d'importance décroissant; **a d. number of stu-**

dents are going into industry de moins en moins d'étudiants se dirigent vers l'industrie

decreasingly [di:'kri:sɪŋlɪ] ADV de moins en moins

decree [dɪ'kri:] N *Pol* décret *m*, arrêté *m*; *Rel* décret *m*; *Law* jugement *m*, arrêt *m*; **to issue a d.** promulguer un décret; **by royal d.** par décret du roi/de la reine

VT décréter; *Pol* décréter, arrêter; *Rel* décréter; *Law* ordonner (par jugement); **fate decreed that...** le sort avait voulu que...

►► *Law* ***decree absolute*** jugement *m* définitif (de divorce); *Law* ***decree nisi*** jugement *m* provisoire (de divorce)

decrepit [dɪ'krepɪt] ADJ *(building, furniture)* délabré; *(person, animal)* décrépit

decrepitude [dɪ'krepɪtju:d] N *(of building, furniture)* délabrement *m*; *(of person)* décrépitude *f*

decriminalization, -isation [ˌdi:ˌkrɪmɪnəlaɪ'zeɪʃən] N dépénalisation *f*

decriminalize, -ise [ˌdi:'krɪmɪnəˌlaɪz] VT dépénaliser

decry [dɪ'kraɪ] *(pt & pp* **decried***)* VT décrier, dénigrer; **the union has decried the suggested increase as an insult** le syndicat a qualifié l'augmentation proposée d'insulte

decrypt [dɪ'krɪpt] VT décrypter

decryption [dɪ'krɪpʃən] N déchiffrement *m*

dedicate ['dedɪkeɪt] VT **1** *(devote)* consacrer; **to d. oneself to sb/sth** se consacrer à qn/qch **2** *(book, record etc)* dédier; **to d. sth to sb** dédier qch à qn **3** *Rel (consecrate* ► *church, shrine)* consacrer

dedicated ['dedɪkeɪtɪd] ADJ **1** *(devoted)* dévoué; **to be d. to one's work** être dévoué à son travail; **she is d. to her family/to helping the poor** elle se dévoue pour sa famille/pour aider les pauvres; **she is a d. teacher/doctor** c'est un professeur/médecin dévoué à son travail; **you've got to be d. (to do this job)** il faut pouvoir tout donner (pour faire ce travail) **2** *(assigned for particular purpose)* dédié, spécialisé

►► *Tel* ***dedicated line*** ligne *f* spécialisée

dedication [ˌdedɪ'keɪʃən] N **1** *(devotion)* dévouement *m*; **a life of d.** une vie de dévouement; **his d. to his job** son dévouement à son travail; **d. is what is needed** il est essentiel de pouvoir tout donner **2** *(in book, on photograph etc)* dédicace *f*; **I've got a few dedications to play** *(records)* j'ai quelques dédicaces à passer **3** *Rel (of church, shrine)* consécration *f*; *Am (of building)* inauguration *f*

deduce [dɪ'dju:s] VT déduire; **to d. sth from sth** déduire qch de qch; **I deduced that she was lying** j'en ai déduit qu'elle mentait

deduct [dɪ'dʌkt] VT déduire, retrancher; *(tax)* prélever; **to d. £10 from the price** déduire *ou* retrancher 10 livres du prix; **to d. 25 percent from a salary** prélever 25 pour cent d'un salaire; **to be deducted at source** *(tax)* être prélevé à la source; **after deducting expenses** après déduction des frais

deductibility [dɪˌdʌktə'bɪlɪtɪ] N déductibilité *f*

deductible [dɪ'dʌktəbəl] ADJ déductible

deduction [dɪ'dʌkʃən] N **1** *(inference)* déduction *f*; **your d. is correct** vous avez fait une bonne déduction; **by (a process of) d.** par déduction **2** *(subtraction)* déduction *f*; *(from pay)* retenue *f*, prélèvement *m*; **how much is that after deductions?** combien reste-t-il après déductions?; **after deductions, I'm left with a salary of £20,000** une fois les prélèvements décomptés, il me reste un salaire de 20 000 livres; **d. at source** retenue *f* à la source; **tax deductions** prélèvements *mpl* fiscaux

deductive [dɪ'dʌktɪv] ADJ déductif

deed [di:d] N **1** *(action)* action *f*; **in word and d.** en parole et en fait *ou* action; **brave d.** acte *m* de bravoure; **to do one's good d. for the day** faire sa bonne action *ou* sa BA de la journée; **we want deeds not words** nous voulons du concret *ou* des actions, pas des discours **2** *Law* acte *m* notarié; **the deeds to the house** les titres *mpl* de propriété de la maison

VT *Am Law* transférer par acte notarié

►► ***deed box*** classeur *m* à documents; ***deed of covenant*** = déclaration par laquelle on s'engage à verser régulièrement une certaine somme à un particulier, une association caritative, etc; ***deed of partnership*** acte *m* constitutif *ou* de société; ***deed poll*** contrat *m* unilatéral; **to change one's name by d. poll** changer de nom par contrat unilatéral, changer de nom officiellement; ***deed of sale*** acte *m* de vente; ***deed of transfer*** acte *m* de cession

deejay ['di:dʒeɪ] N *Fam* DJ *mf*

deem [di:m] VT *Formal* juger, considérer, estimer; **it was deemed necessary/advisable to call an enquiry** on a jugé qu'il était nécessaire/opportun d'ordonner une enquête; **he deemed it a great honour** il considéra cela comme un grand honneur, il estima que c'était un grand honneur; **she was deemed (to be) the rightful owner** elle était considérée comme la propriétaire de droit

DEEP [di:p]

ADJ
- profond **1–6**
- foncé **6**
- grave **7**

ADV
- profondément

N
- océan **1**

ADJ **1** *(going far down* ► *water, hole, wound etc)* profond; **the water/the hole is five metres d.** l'eau/le trou a cinq mètres de profondeur; **the road was a foot d. in snow** la route était sous *ou* recouverte de trente centimètres de neige; **a hole ten feet d.** un trou de dix pieds de profondeur; **the d. blue sea** le vaste océan; **to be in a d. sleep** être profondément endormi; **d. in thought/study** plongé dans ses pensées/l'étude; **d. in debt** criblé de dettes; **to get deeper and deeper into debt** s'endetter de plus en plus; **a d. breath** une inspiration profonde; *Fig* **take a d. breath and just do it** respire un bon coup et vas-y; **we're in d. trouble** nous sommes dans de sales draps; **the d. end** *(of swimming pool)* le côté le plus profond; *Fam* **to go off the d. end** *(lose one's temper)* piquer une crise *ou* une colère; *(panic)* perdre tous ses moyens, paniquer à mort; *Fig* **to be thrown in at the d. end** être mis dans le bain tout de suite; **to be in d. water** être dans le pétrin, avoir des problèmes; **I think we're getting into d. water here** je crois que nous sommes en train de nous engager sur un terrain dangereux

2 *(going far back* ► *forest, cupboard, serve)* profond; **d. in the forest** au (fin) fond de la forêt; **the crowd stood 15 d.** la foule se tenait sur 15 rangées; *Hum* **d. in Buckinghamshire, in deepest Buckinghamshire** dans le Buckinghamshire profond; **d. space** profondeurs *fpl* de l'espace

3 *(strong* ► *feelings)* profond; **with deepest sympathy** avec mes plus sincères condoléances

4 *(profound* ► *thinker)* profond

5 *(mysterious, difficult to understand* ► *book)* profond; **he's a d. one** on ne peut jamais savoir ce qu'il pense

6 *(dark, vivid* ► *colour)* foncé, profond; **d. blue eyes** des yeux d'un bleu profond; **to be in d. mourning** être en grand deuil

7 *(low* ► *sound, note)* grave; *(*► *voice)* grave, profond

ADV profondément; **they went d. into the forest** ils se sont enfoncés dans la forêt; **the snow lay d. on the ground** il y avait une épaisse couche de neige sur le sol; **he looked d. into her eyes** *(romantically)* il a plongé ses yeux dans les siens; *(probingly)* il l'a regardée droit dans les yeux; **the goalkeeper kicked the ball d. into the opposition's half** le gardien de but a shooté loin dans le camp adverse; **to go** *or* **to run d.** *(emotions)* être profond; **d. down she knew she was right** au fond *ou* dans son for intérieur elle savait qu'elle avait raison; **he thrust his hands d. into his pockets** il plongea les mains au fond de ses poches; **d. into the night** tard dans la nuit; **don't go in too d.** *(in water)* n'allez pas où c'est profond, n'allez pas trop loin; **don't get in too d.** *(involved)* ne t'implique pas trop; *Fam* **she's in it pretty d.** elle est dedans jusqu'au cou

N *Literary* **1** *(ocean)* **the d.** l'océan *m*

2 *(depth)* **in the d. of winter** au plus profond *ou* au cœur de l'hiver

►► ***deep freeze*** *(in home, shop)* congélateur *m*; *(industrial)* surgélateur *m*; ***the Deep South*** *(of the USA)* le Sud profond; *Ling* ***deep structure*** structure *f* profonde

deep-dish ADJ

►► ***deep-dish pie*** tourte *f*; ***deep-dish pizza*** pizza *f* à pâte épaisse

deepen ['di:pən] VT **1** *(hole, river bed, knowledge)* approfondir; *(mystery)* épaissir; *(love, friendship)* faire grandir, intensifier **2** *(sound, voice)* rendre plus grave; *(colour)* rendre plus profond, intensifier

VI **1** *(sea, river)* devenir plus profond; *(silence, mystery)* s'épaissir; *(crisis)* s'aggraver, s'intensifier; *(knowledge)* s'approfondir; *(love, friendship)* s'intensifier, grandir **2** *(colour)* devenir plus profond, s'intensifier; *(sound)* devenir plus grave

deep-fat frying N cuisson *f* en bain de friture

deep-freeze VT *(at home)* congeler; *(industrially)* surgeler

deep-frozen ADJ *(at home)* congelé; *(industrially)* surgelé

deep-fry VT faire frire

deep-fryer N friteuse *f*

deep-laid ADJ *(plan, scheme)* secret(ète), machiné dans le secret

deeply ['di:plɪ] ADV **1** *(dig, breathe, sleep, admire, regret, think)* profondément; *(drink)* à grands traits; **to sigh d.** pousser un profond soupir; **they gazed d. into each other's eyes** leurs regards étaient plongés dans les yeux l'un de l'autre; **to fall d. in love with sb** tomber profondément amoureux de qn; **to care d. about sb** être profondément attaché à qn; **I care d. about your happiness/this country's future** ton bonheur/l'avenir de ce pays est très important pour moi; **she can't have looked into it very d.** elle n'a pas dû s'en occuper très sérieusement; **his forehead was d. lined** son front était creusé de rides profondes **2** *(relieved, grateful, religious)* profondément, extrêmement; **d. offended** gravement offensé; **to be d. insulting** être très insultant

deepness ['di:pnɪs] N *(of ocean, voice, writer, remark)* profondeur *f*; *(of note, sound)* gravité *f*

deep-rooted ADJ *(tree)* dont les racines sont profondes; *Fig (ideas, belief, prejudice)* profondément ancré *ou* enraciné; *(feeling)* profond

deep-sea ADJ *(creatures, exploration)* des grands fonds

►► ***deep-sea diver*** plongeur(euse) *m,f* sous-marin(e); ***deep-sea diving*** plongée *f* sous-marine; ***deep-sea fisherman*** pêcheur *m* hauturier *ou* en haute mer; ***deep-sea fishing*** pêche *f* hauturière *ou* en haute mer

deep-seated [-'si:tɪd] ADJ *(sorrow, dislike)* profond; *(idea, belief, complex, prejudice)* profondément ancré *ou* enraciné

deep-set ADJ enfoncé

deep-six VT *Am Fam (throw away)* balancer; **we deep-sixed the project** on a balancé cette idée de projet

deep-vein thrombosis N *Med* thrombose *f* veineuse profonde

deer [dɪə(r)] *(pl* **inv***)* N *(male)* cerf *m*; *(female)* biche *f*; **(red) d.** cerf *m* commun; **(fallow) d.** daim *m*; **(roe) d.** chevreuil *m*; **the different species of d.** les différents types de cervidés

COMP *(hunter)* de cerf *ou* cerfs

►► ***deer park*** chasse *f* gardée pour le cerf

deerhound ['dɪəhaʊnd] N limier *m*, lévrier *m* d'Écosse

deerskin ['dɪəskɪn] N peau *f* de daim

COMP *(coat, gloves)* en daim

deerstalker ['dɪəˌstɔ:kə(r)] N **1** *(hunter)* chasseur(euse) *m,f* de cerf **2** *(hat)* chapeau *m* à la Sherlock Holmes

deerstalking ['dɪəˌstɔ:kɪŋ] N chasse *f* au cerf

de-escalate [di:-] VT *(crisis)* désamorcer; *(tension)* faire baisser

VI *(crisis)* se désamorcer; *(tension)* baisser

de-escalation [di:-] N *(of crisis)* désescalade *f*, désamorçage *m*; *(of tension)* baisse *f*

def [def] ADJ *Fam (excellent)* super, génial

deface [dɪ'feɪs] VT *(statue, painting ▸ with paint, aerosol spray)* barbouiller; *(▸ by writing slogans)* dégrader par des inscriptions; *(book)* abîmer *ou* endommager par des gribouillages *ou* des inscriptions

de facto [deɪ'fæktəʊ] ADJ de facto, de fait; *Law* **d. possession** possession *f* de fait
ADV *Law* **d. and de jure** de droit et de fait
N *Austr (partner)* concubin(e) *m,f*

defamation [ˌdefə'meɪʃən] N *Law* diffamation *f*; **to sue sb for d. of character** poursuivre qn en justice pour diffamation

defamatory [dɪ'fæmətrɪ] ADJ *Law* diffamatoire

defame [dɪ'feɪm] VT *Law* diffamer, calomnier

default [dɪ'fɔːlt] N **1** *Law (non-appearance ▸ in civil court)* défaut *m*, non-comparution *f*; *(▸ in criminal court)* contumace *f*
2 *Formal (absence)* **in d. of** à défaut de
3 *Comput* défaut *m*; **the C drive is the d.** C est l'unité de disque par défaut
4 *Fin & St Exch* défaut *m* de paiement, manquement *m* à payer
VI **1** *Law (fail to appear ▸ in civil court)* ne pas comparaître; *(▸ in criminal court)* être en état de contumace
2 *Fin & St Exch* manquer *ou* faillir à ses engagements; **to d. on a payment** ne pas honorer un paiement; **to d. on alimony payments** manquer aux versements de pension alimentaire
3 *Sport* déclarer forfait
4 *Comput & Tech* **to d. to sth** sélectionner qch par défaut; **the computer automatically defaults to the C drive** l'ordinateur sélectionne l'unité de disque C par défaut
• **by default** ADV **1** *(through lack of action)* **you are responsible by d.** tu es responsable pour n'avoir rien fait
2 *Law* **judgment by d.** jugement *m* par défaut *ou* contumace
3 *Sport* par forfait; **to win/to lose by d.** gagner/perdre par forfait
4 *Comput & Tech* par défaut; **the machine sets itself to 1 by d.** la machine se réglera sur 1 par défaut
▸▸ *Comput* ***default drive*** lecteur *m* par défaut; *Comput* ***default font*** police *f* par défaut; *Comput* ***default setting(s)*** configuration *f* par défaut; *Comput* ***default value*** valeur *f* par défaut

defaulter [dɪ'fɔːltə(r)] N **1** *Law (defendant)* inculpé(e) *m,f* contumace *ou* défaillant(e); *(witness)* témoin *m* défaillant **2** *Fin & St Exch* débiteur (trice) *m,f* défaillant(e) **3** *Br Mil & Naut* = soldat ou marin qui a transgressé la discipline

defaulting [dɪ'fɔːltɪŋ] ADJ **1** *Law (defendant)* contumace; *(witness)* défaillant **2** *Fin & St Exch* défaillant

defeasance [dɪ'fiːzəns] N *Law* defeasance *m*

defeat [dɪ'fiːt] N **1** *(of army, opposition, team, government)* défaite *f*; **to suffer a d.** connaître une défaite, échouer; **to admit d.** s'avouer vaincu **2** *(of project, bill)* échec *m*; *Parl (of measure)* rejet *m*
VT **1** *(army, opposition)* vaincre; *(team, government)* battre; **they were defeated by their own lack of preparation** ils ont été battus *ou* vaincus à cause de leur manque de préparation; **it defeats me** *(I don't understand)* cela me dépasse **2** *(attempts, project, bill)* faire échouer; **we were defeated by the weather** nous avons échoué à cause du temps; **to d. the ends of justice** contrarier la justice; **that rather defeats the object of the exercise** ça va plutôt à l'encontre du but recherché de l'opération

defeatism [dɪ'fiːtɪzəm] N défaitisme *m*; **an air/mood of d.** un air/une atmosphère défaitiste *ou* de défaite

defeatist [dɪ'fiːtɪst] N défaitiste *mf*
ADJ défaitiste

defecate ['defəkeɪt] VI *Physiol* déféquer

defecation [ˌdefə'keɪʃən] N *Physiol* défécation *f*

defect N ['diːfekt] défaut *m*; **physical d.** malformation *f*; **hearing/speech d.** défaut *m* de l'ouïe/de prononciation
VI [dɪ'fekt] *Pol (to another country)* passer à l'étranger; *(to another party)* quitter son parti pour un autre; **to d. to the West** passer à l'Ouest; **he defected from his native Poland** il s'est enfui de sa Pologne natale; **she defected to the Labour Party** elle a rejoint le parti travailliste; *Fig* **she's defected to our main competitor** elle est passée chez notre concurrent principal

defection [dɪ'fekʃən] N *Pol (to another country)* passage *m* à un pays ennemi; *(to another party)* passage *m* à un parti adverse; **after his d. from his native Poland** après qu'il se fut enfui de sa Pologne natale

defective [dɪ'fektɪv] ADJ **1** *(machine, reasoning)* défectueux; *(hearing, sight, organ)* déficient; *(memory)* infidèle; *(brakes)* en mauvais état; *Ind* **d. part** pièce *f* défectueuse **2** *Gram* défectif

> Attention: ne pas confondre avec l'adjectif anglais **deficient**.

defector [dɪ'fektə(r)] N *Pol & Fig* transfuge *mf*

defence, *Am* **defense** [dɪ'fens] N **1** *(protection)* défense *f*; **how much is spent on d.?** combien dépense-t-on pour la défense?; **to carry a weapon for d.** porter une arme pour se défendre; **to come to sb's d.** venir à la défense de qn; **to act/to speak in d. of sth** *(following attack)* agir/parler en défense de qch; *(in support of)* agir/parler en faveur de qch; **to speak in d. of sb, to speak in sb's d.** *(following attack)* parler en défense de qn; *(in support of)* parler en faveur de qn
2 *(thing providing protection)* protection *f*, défense *f*; *(argument)* défense *f*; **defences** *(weapons)* moyens *mpl* de défense; *(fortifications)* défenses *fpl*, fortifications *fpl*; **to use sth as a d. against sth** se servir de qch comme défense *ou* protection contre qch, se servir de qch pour se défendre *ou* se protéger de qch; **the body's natural defences against infection** les défenses naturelles de l'organisme contre l'infection; **to put up a stubborn d.** se défendre avec entêtement; **to catch sb when his/her defences are down** prendre qn quand il/elle n'est pas en position de se défendre *ou* de faire face
3 *Law* défense *f*; **the d.** *(lawyers)* la défense; **to appear for the d.** comparaître pour la défense; **the case for the d.** la défense; **to conduct one's own d.** assurer sa propre défense; **it must be said in her d. that...** il faut dire à sa décharge *ou* pour sa défense que...
4 *Sport* défense *f*; **the d.** *(players)* la défense; **to turn d. into attack** faire *ou* lancer une contre-attaque
COMP **1** *(forces)* de défense; *(cuts, minister)* de la défense **2** *(lawyer)* de la défense
▸▸ *Law* ***defence counsel*** défenseur *m*; *(in civil law)* avocat(e) *m,f* de la défense; *Med* ***defence mechanism*** défenses *fpl* immunitaires; *Psy* mécanisme *m* de défense; ***defence spending*** dépenses *fpl* pour la défense; *Law* ***defence witness*** témoin *m* à décharge

defenceless, *Am* **defenseless** [dɪ'fenslɪs] ADJ sans défense, vulnérable

defend [dɪ'fend] VT **1** *(protect)* défendre; **to d. sb/sth from** *or* **against attack** défendre qn/qch contre une attaque; **to d. one's actions** justifier ses actions; **to d. oneself** se défendre
2 *(justify ▸ opinion)* justifier
3 *Sport (goalmouth, title)* défendre
4 *Law* défendre

defendable [dɪ'fendəbəl] ADJ *Law* défendable

defendant [dɪ'fendənt] N *Law (in civil court)* défendeur(eresse) *m,f*; *(in criminal court)* inculpé(e) *m,f*; *(accused of serious crimes)* accusé(e) *m,f*

defender [dɪ'fendə(r)] N **1** *(of a cause, rights)* défenseur *m*, avocat(e) *m,f* **2** *Sport (player)* défenseur *m*; *(of title, record)* détenteur(trice) *m,f*
▸▸ ***Defender of the Faith*** Défenseur *m* de la foi

defending [dɪ'fendɪŋ] ADJ **1** *Sport (champion)* en titre **2** *Law* de la défense
▸▸ *Law* ***defending counsel*** défenseur *m*

defense, defenseless *etc Am* = **defence, defenceless** *etc*
▸▸ ***defense attorney*** défenseur *m*

defensible [dɪ'fensəbəl] ADJ *(idea, opinion etc)* défendable

defensive [dɪ'fensɪv] ADJ *(strategy, weapon, game etc)* défensif; **to get d.** se mettre sur la défensive; **don't be so d.!** ne te mets pas sur la défensive comme ça!
N *Mil & Fig* défensive *f*; **to be on the d.** être *ou* se tenir sur la défensive; **to go on the d.** se mettre sur la défensive
▸▸ *Mil* ***defensive action*** action *f* défensive; *Sport* ***defensive end*** *(in American football)* defensive end *m*; ***defensive position*** position *f* de défense

defensively [dɪ'fensɪvlɪ] ADV *(say)* d'un ton défensif, sur la défensive; *(react)* d'une manière défensive; **they played very d.** ils ont eu un jeu très défensif

defensiveness [dɪ'fensɪvnɪs] N **when she reacted/spoke with such d.** quand elle a réagi/parlé d'une manière aussi défensive; **her d. in the face of criticism** la façon qu'elle a de se mettre sur la défensive quand on la critique

defer [dɪ'fɜː(r)] *(pt & pp* **deferred**, *cont* **deferring)**
VT **1** *(question, case)* différer, ajourner, remettre; *(decision, meeting)* remettre, reporter; *(payment, business, judgment)* différer, retarder; *(verdict)* suspendre; **to d. sth to a later date** remettre *ou* reporter qch à plus tard; **to d. doing sth** différer de faire qch; *Law* **to d. sentencing** différer la condamnation **2** *Mil (person)* mettre en sursis (d'appel); **to d. sb on medical grounds** réformer qn temporairement pour raisons médicales
VI *(give way)* **to d. to sb** s'en remettre à qn; **to d. to sb's judgment/knowledge** s'en remettre au jugement/aux connaissances de qn; **to d. to sb's wishes** agir conformément aux souhaits de qn, se soumettre à la volonté de qn

deference ['defərəns] N déférence *f*, égard *m*, considération *f*; **out of** *or* **in d. to sb/sb's wishes** par égard *ou* considération pour qn/les souhaits de qn; **to treat sb with d., to pay** *or* **to show d. to sb** traiter qn avec déférence *ou* égards

deferential [ˌdefə'renʃəl] ADJ *(air, tone)* de déférence, respectueux; *(behaviour)* respectueux; *(person)* déférent, respectueux; **to be d. to sb** faire montre de déférence *ou* d'égards envers qn

deferentially [ˌdefə'renʃəlɪ] ADV avec déférence

deferment [dɪ'fɜːmənt], **deferral** [dɪ'fɜːrəl] N **1** *(of decision, meeting, payment, sentence)* report *m*, ajournement *m* **2** *Mil (for health reasons)* réforme *f*; **to apply for d.** demander à être réformé

deferred [dɪ'fɜːd] ADJ *(gen)* ajourné, retardé; *Fin (payment, shares)* différé; *Fin (annuity)* à paiement différé, à jouissance différée
▸▸ *Fin* ***deferred income*** produit *m* constaté d'avance

deffo ['defəʊ] ADV *Br Fam* absolument[□]; **are you coming tonight? – d.!** tu viens ce soir? – je veux!

defiance [dɪ'faɪəns] N défi *m*; **your d. of my orders meant that people's lives were put at risk** en défiant mes ordres vous avez mis la vie d'autrui en danger; **gesture/act of d.** geste *m*/acte *m* de défi
• **in defiance of** PREP **in d. of sb/sth** au mépris de qn/qch

defiant [dɪ'faɪənt] ADJ *(gesture, remark, look)* de défi; *(person, reply)* provocateur

defiantly [dɪ'faɪəntlɪ] ADV *(act)* avec une attitude de défi; *(reply, look at)* d'un air de défi

defibrillation [diːˌfɪbrɪ'leɪʃən] N *Med* défibrillation *f*

defibrillator [ˌdiː'fɪbrɪleɪtə(r)] N *Med* défibrillateur *m*

deficiency [dɪ'fɪʃənsɪ] *(pl* **deficiencies)** N **1** *(lack)* manque *m*, insuffisance *f* (**of** de); *Med (shortage)* carence *f*, déficience *f*; **a d. in** *or* **of calcium, a calcium d.** une carence en calcium **2** *(flaw ▸ in character, system)* défaut *m* **3** *(deficit)* manquant *m*, déficit *m*; *Com* découvert *m*; *Pol* déficit *m* budgétaire
▸▸ *Med* ***deficiency disease*** maladie *f* de carence

deficient [dɪ'fɪʃənt] ADJ **1** *(insufficient)* insuffisant, déficient; **to be d. in sth** manquer de qch **2** *(defective)* défectueux

> Attention: ne pas confondre avec l'adjectif **defective**.

deficit ['defɪsɪt] N *Com & Fin* déficit *m*; **to be in d.** être en déficit, être déficitaire; **to make up the d.** combler le déficit

▸▸ *deficit spending* dépenses *fpl* financées par le déficit

defile VT [dɪˈfaɪl] *(grave, sacred place)* profaner; *(memory)* salir

VI [dɪˈfaɪl] *Mil* défiler

N [ˈdiːfaɪl] *(valley, passage)* défilé *m*

defilement [dɪˈfaɪlmənt] N *(of grave, memory)* profanation *f*

> Note that the French word **défilement** is a false friend and is never a translation for the English word **defilement**.

definable [dɪˈfaɪnəbəl] ADJ définissable

define [dɪˈfaɪn] VT **1** *(term, word)* définir

2 *(boundary, role, subject)* définir, délimiter; *(concept, idea, feeling)* définir, préciser; *(objectives)* formuler; *(scope, extent)* déterminer; *(powers)* délimiter; **to d. what it means to be French** définir ce qu'être français signifie; **well-defined limits** limites bien déterminées

3 *(object, shape)* définir; **the figures in the painting are not clearly defined** les formes humaines du tableau ne sont pas bien définies

4 *Comput (value)* déclarer

defining [dɪˈfaɪnɪŋ] ADJ **1** *(decisive)* décisif; **a d. moment in history** un tournant de l'histoire **2** *(distinctive)* déterminant

definite [ˈdefɪnɪt] ADJ **1** *(precise, clear)* précis; *(advantage, improvement, opinion)* net; *(answer)* définitif; *(orders, proof)* formel; *(price)* fixe; **their plans to marry are still not d.** leurs projets de mariage sont encore vagues; **it's a d. advantage being a woman** c'est décidément un avantage d'être une femme; **the boss was very d. about the need for punctuality** le patron a été très ferme en ce qui concerne la ponctualité; **he has very d. ideas on the subject** il a des idées bien arrêtées sur la question **2** *(certain)* certain, sûr; *(date)* définitif, certain; **it's not d. yet** ce n'est pas encore définitif *ou* sûr; **is it d. that the Pope is coming to England?** est-il certain *ou* sûr que le pape vienne en Angleterre?; **I've heard rumours of a merger, but nothing d.** j'ai entendu dire qu'il allait y avoir une fusion, mais rien de sûr pour l'instant; **and that's d.!** et c'est sûr!

▸▸ *Gram* ***definite article*** article *m* défini

> Attention: ne pas confondre avec l'adjectif **definitive**.

definitely [ˈdefɪnɪtlɪ] ADV **1** *(certainly)* certainement, sans aucun doute; **he has d. decided to resign** il ne fait aucun doute qu'il a décidé de démissionner; **she's d. innocent** elle est innocente, c'est sûr *ou* certain; **I'll d. call you** je te téléphonerai sans faute; **she's d. leaving, but I don't know when** je sais qu'elle part, mais je ne sais pas quand; **are you d. giving up your flat?** allez-vous vraiment quitter votre appartement?; **that's d. not the man I saw** je suis sûr que ce n'est pas l'homme que j'ai vu; **are you going to the show? – d.!** est-ce que tu vas au spectacle? – absolument!; **d. not!** certainement pas! **2** *(clearly, without ambiguity)* **he told me very d. that he didn't want to come** il m'a dit très clairement qu'il ne voulait pas venir

> Attention: ne pas confondre avec l'adverbe **definitively**.

definition [defɪˈnɪʃən] N **1** *(of term, word)* définition *f*; **by d.** par définition; **to give a d. of sth** donner une définition de qch, définir qch **2** *(of duties, powers, territory)* définition *f*, délimitation *f*; *(of objectives)* formulation *f* **3** *(of photograph, sound)* netteté *f*; *TV* définition *f*

definitive [dɪˈfɪnɪtɪv] ADJ **1** *(conclusive)* définitif; *(battle, victory)* définitif, décisif; *(result)* définitif, qui fait autorité **2** *(authoritative* ▸ *biography, edition)* qui fait autorité; **she was, for me, the d. Juliet** pour moi, c'est une Juliette inégalable **3** *Zool (fully developed)* définitif

> Attention: ne pas confondre avec l'adjectif **definite**.

definitively [dɪˈfɪnɪtɪvlɪ] ADV définitivement

> Attention: ne pas confondre avec l'adverbe **definitely**.

deflate [dɪˈfleɪt] VT **1** *(ball, balloon, tyre)* dégonfler; *Fig (person)* démonter; **to d. sb's ego** porter un coup à l'orgueil de qn; **I felt rather deflated** *(disappointed)* j'étais assez déçu **2** *Fin & Econ (prices)* faire baisser, faire tomber; **to d. the currency** provoquer la déflation de la monnaie; **the measure is intended to d. the economy** cette mesure est destinée à faire de la déflation

VI **1** *(ball, balloon, tyre)* se dégonfler **2** *Fin & Econ* provoquer la déflation de la monnaie

deflation [dɪˈfleɪʃən] N **1** *(of ball, balloon, tyre)* dégonflement *m* **2** *Fin & Econ* déflation *f* **3** *(anticlimax)* abattement *m*

deflationary [dɪˈfleɪʃənərɪ], **deflationist** [dɪˈfleɪʃənɪst] ADJ *Fin & Econ* déflationniste

deflect [dɪˈflekt] VT *(ball, bullet)* (faire) dévier; *Phys (light)* défléchir; *(sound)* renvoyer; *Fig (person, attention, criticism)* détourner; **he would not be deflected from his purpose** rien ne l'aurait détourné de son but; **the ball was deflected into the net** le ballon a rebondi dans le filet

VI *(projectile)* dévier; *Phys (light)* être défléchi; *(magnetic needle)* décliner; **the ball deflected off the post** le ballon a rebondi contre le poteau

deflection [dɪˈflekʃən] N déviation *f*; *(of magnetic needle)* déclinaison *f*; *Phys (of light)* déflexion *f*; **it was a lucky d. off the post** heureusement la balle a été déviée par le montant du but

deflector [dɪˈflektə(r)] N déflecteur *m*

deflexion = **deflection**

defloration [ˌdiːflɔːˈreɪʃən] N *Literary* défloration *f*

deflower [ˌdiːˈflaʊə(r)] VT *Literary or Hum (woman)* déflorer

deflowering [ˌdiːˈflaʊərɪŋ] N *Literary or Hum (of virgin)* défloration *f*

defocus [ˌdiːˈfəʊkəs] VI *Opt* passer au flou

defoliant [ˌdiːˈfəʊlɪənt] N *Bot* défoliant *m*

defoliate [ˌdiːˈfəʊlɪeɪt] VT *Bot* défolier

defoliation [ˌdiːfəʊlɪˈeɪʃən] N *Bot* défoliation *f*

deforest [ˌdiːˈfɒrɪst] VT *Agr* déboiser

deforestation [ˈdiːˌfɒrɪˈsteɪʃən] N *Agr* déboisement *m*, déforestation *f*

deform [dɪˈfɔːm] VT déformer; *Fig (distort, ruin)* défigurer

deformation [ˌdiːfɔːˈmeɪʃən] N déformation *f*

deformed [dɪˈfɔːmd] ADJ *(person)* malformé; *(limb)* difforme, malformé; **the baby was born d.** le bébé est né avec une malformation

deformity [dɪˈfɔːmɪtɪ] N difformité *f*

DEFRA [ˈdefrə] N *Br Pol (abbr* **Department for Environment, Food and Rural Affairs***)* ministère de l'Agriculture et de l'Environnement

defragment [ˌdiːfrægˈment] VT *Comput* défragmenter

defragmentation [ˈdiːˌfrægmenˈteɪʃən] N *Comput* défragmentation *f*

defragmenter [ˌdiːfrægˈmentə(r)] N *Comput* défragmenteur *m*

defraud [dɪˈfrɔːd] VT *(the State)* frauder; *(company, person)* escroquer, *Spec* frustrer; **to d. sb of sth** escroquer qch à qn, frustrer qn de qch

VI *Law* **conspiracy to d.** entente *f* délictueuse dans le but de frauder

defrauder [dɪˈfrɔːdə(r)] N fraudeur(euse) *m,f*

defray [dɪˈfreɪ] VT *Formal* rembourser, prendre en charge; **to d. sb's expenses** rembourser les frais de qn, défrayer qn; **we will d. the cost of your air fare** nous vous rembourserons le prix de votre billet d'avion

defrayal [dɪˈfreɪəl], **defrayment** [dɪˈfreɪmənt] N *Formal* remboursement *m*

defrock [ˌdiːˈfrɒk] VT *Rel* défroquer

defrost [ˌdiːˈfrɒst] VT **1** *(food)* décongeler; *(refrigerator)* dégivrer **2** *Am Aut (demist)* désembuer; *(de-ice)* dégivrer

VI *(food)* se décongeler; *(refrigerator)* se dégivrer

defroster [ˌdiːˈfrɒstə(r)] N dégivreur *m*

deft [deft] ADJ adroit, habile; *(fingers)* habile

deftly [ˈdeftlɪ] ADV adroitement, habilement

deftness [ˈdeftnɪs] N adresse *f*, habileté *f*

defunct [dɪˈfʌŋkt] ADJ *(person)* défunt, décédé; *Fig (industry, company)* disparu; *(project, practice, law)* révolu

defuse [ˌdiːˈfjuːz] VT *also Fig* désamorcer

> Attention: ne pas confondre avec le verbe **to diffuse**.

defy [dɪˈfaɪ] *(pt & pp* **defied***)* VT **1** *(disobey)* s'opposer à; *(law, rule)* braver; **the union defied the court order** le syndicat n'a pas tenu compte de la décision judiciaire **2** *(challenge, dare)* défier; **she defied him to justify his claims** elle l'a défié *ou* mis au défi de justifier ses revendications; **a death-defying feat** un exploit téméraire **3** *Fig (make impossible)* défier; **to d. description** échapper à toute description, défier toute description

degearing [ˌdiːˈgɪərɪŋ] N *Fin* désendettement *m*

degeneracy [dɪˈdʒenərəsɪ] N *(process)* dégénérescence *f*; *(state)* décadence *f*, corruption *f*

degenerate VI [dɪˈdʒenəreɪt] dégénérer (**from/into** en/de); *Fig* **the discussion degenerated into an argument** la discussion dégénéra en dispute

ADJ [dɪˈdʒenərət] *Literary* dégénéré; *(person)* dépravé

N [dɪˈdʒenərət] *Literary (person)* dépravé(e) *m,f*

degeneration [dɪdʒenəˈreɪʃən] N *(process, state)* dégénérescence *f*

degenerative [dɪˈdʒenərətɪv] ADJ dégénératif

deglaze [diːˈgleɪz] VT *Culin* déglacer

degradable [dɪˈgreɪdəbəl] ADJ *Ecol* dégradable

degradation [ˌdegrəˈdeɪʃən] N **1** *(deterioration)* dégradation *f*; *Geol* érosion *f*

2 *(debasement)* avilissement *m*, dégradation *f*

3 *(poverty)* misère *f* abjecte

4 *Chem* dégradation *f*

5 *Mil* dégradation *f*

degrade [dɪˈgreɪd] VT **1** *(deteriorate)* dégrader; *Geol* éroder

2 *(debase)* avilir, dégrader; **to d. oneself** s'avilir; **I refuse to d. myself by playing these silly games** je refuse de m'abaisser à ces jeux idiots

3 *Mil (officer)* dégrader, casser

4 *Euph Mil (destroy)* détruire; *(kill)* tuer

degrading [dɪˈgreɪdɪŋ] ADJ avilissant, dégradant

-degree [dɪˈgriː] SUFF **first/second/third-d. burns** brûlures *fpl* au premier/deuxième/troisième degré; *Am Law* **first-d. murder** homicide *m* volontaire

degree [dɪˈgriː] N **1** *(extent, amount)* degré *m*; **to some** *or* **a (certain) d.** à un certain degré, (jusqu')à un certain point; **she's right to a d.** elle a raison jusqu'à un certain point *ou* dans une certaine mesure; **to such a d. that...** à tel point que...; **by degrees** petit à petit, graduellement; **to feel a d. of optimism** ressentir un certain optimisme; **there was a certain d. of mistrust between them** il y avait un certain degré de méfiance entre eux; **there are varying degrees of opposition to the new law** il y a une opposition plus ou moins forte à la nouvelle loi; **an honour of the highest d.** un honneur du plus haut degré; **a d. of precision never before thought possible** un niveau de précision jusqu'à présent considéré comme inaccessible

2 *(unit of measurement)* degré *m*; **the temperature is 28 degrees in New York** la température est de 28 degrés à New York; **it's 3 degrees outside** il fait 3 degrés dehors; **Paris is about 2 degrees east of Greenwich** Paris est environ à 2 degrés de longitude est de Greenwich; *Geom* **a 90-d. angle** un angle de 90 degrés

3 *(academic qualification)* diplôme *m* universitaire; *(undergraduate)* licence *f*; **she has a d. in economics** elle a une licence en sciences économiques; **he's taking** *or* **doing a d. in biology** il fait une licence de biologie; **I'd like to go on and do a further d.** je voudrais continuer après la licence

4 *Gram & Mus* degré *m*

5 *Arch or Literary (rank, status)* rang *m*; **a man of high d.** un homme de haut rang

6 *Am Law* **murder in the first d.** homicide *m* volontaire

▸▸ *Univ* ***degree ceremony*** cérémonie *f* de remise des diplômes; *Gram* ***degree of comparison*** degré *m* de comparaison

dehire [ˌdiːˈhaɪə(r)] VT *Am Euph (dismiss)* remercier

dehumanize, -ise [ˌdiːˈhjuːmənaɪz] VT déshumaniser

dehumidification [ˈdiːhjuːˌmɪdɪfɪˈkeɪʃən] N déshumidification *f*

dehumidifier [ˌdiːhjuːˈmɪdɪfaɪə(r)] N déshumidificateur *m*

dehumidify [ˌdiːhjuːˈmɪdɪfaɪ] VT déshumidifier

dehydrate [ˌdiːhaɪˈdreɪt] VT déshydrater; **to become dehydrated** se déshydrater
VI *(person, skin)* se déshydrater

dehydrated [ˌdiːhaɪˈdreɪtɪd] ADJ *(person, foodstuffs, skin)* déshydraté; *(milk, eggs)* en poudre

dehydration [ˌdiːhaɪˈdreɪʃən] N déshydratation *f*

dehydrator [ˌdiːhaɪˈdreɪtə(r)] N déshydrateur *m*

de-ice [diː-] VT dégivrer

de-icer [diːˈaɪsə(r)] N dégivreur *m*

de-icing [diː-] N dégivrage *m*

deification [ˌdiːɪfɪˈkeɪʃən] N *Rel* déification *f*

deify [ˈdiːɪfaɪ] VT *Rel* déifier

deign [deɪn] VT daigner; *Formal or Hum* **he didn't d. to reply** il n'a pas daigné répondre

deindex [ˌdiːˈɪndeks] VT *Fin* désindexer

deindustrialization, -isation [ˈdiːɪnˌdʌstrɪəlaɪˈzeɪʃən] N désindustrialisation *f*

deinstall [ˌdiːɪnˈstɔːl] VT *Br Comput* désinstaller

deinstallation [ˌdiːɪnstəˈleɪʃən] N *Br Comput* désinstallation *f*

deinstaller [ˌdiːɪnˈstɔːlə(r)] N *Br Comput* désinstallateur *m*

deionization, -isation [ˈdiːˌaɪənaɪˈzeɪʃən] N *Chem* déionisation *f*

deionize, -ise [ˌdiːˈaɪənaɪz] VT *Chem* déioniser

deionized, -ised [ˌdiːˈaɪənaɪzd] ADJ *Chem (water)* déminéralisé

deism [ˈdiːɪzəm] N *Rel* déisme *m*

deity [ˈdiːɪtɪ] *(pl* **deities**) N **1** *Myth (god)* dieu (déesse) *m,f* **2** *Rel (divinity)* divinité *f*
• **Deity** N *Rel* **the D.** Dieu *m*, la Divinité

déjà vu [ˌdeʒɑːˈvuː] N déjà-vu *m inv*; **to have a feeling of d.** avoir une impression de déjà-vu

dejected [dɪˈdʒektɪd] ADJ abattu, découragé; **to become d.** se décourager **he looked sad and d.** il avait l'air triste et abattu

dejectedly [dɪˈdʒektɪdlɪ] ADV *(speak)* d'un ton abattu; *(look)* d'un air abattu

dejection [dɪˈdʒekʃən] N abattement *m*, découragement *m*

dejunk [ˌdiːˈdʒʌŋk] VT *Fam (room, house)* débarrasser; *Fig* **you need to d. your life** il faut recentrer ta vie sur l'essentiel

de jure [deɪˈdʒʊəreɪ] ADV *Law* de jure, en droit

dekko [ˈdekəʊ] *(pl* **dekkos**) N *Br Fam* **to have** *or* **to take a d. at sth** jeter un coup d'œil *ou* un œil à qch

Del *(written abbr* **Delete**) *(on keyboard)* Suppr

delay [dɪˈleɪ] VT **1** *(cause to be late)* retarder; *(person)* retarder, retenir; **the flight was delayed (for) three hours** le vol a été retardé de trois heures; **they've been delayed by fog** ils ont été retardés par le brouillard **2** *(postpone, defer)* reporter, remettre; **she delayed handing in her resignation** elle a tardé à donner sa démission; **he delayed leaving until the last possible moment** il a repoussé *ou* retardé son départ jusqu'au dernier moment; **he had a delayed reaction to the news of his mother's death** il a mis un certain temps à réagir à la nouvelle de la mort de sa mère; **she's suffering from delayed shock** elle souffre d'un choc après coup *ou* a posteriori
VI tarder; **don't d., write off today for your free sample** demandez aujourd'hui même votre échantillon gratuit
N **1** *(lateness)* retard *m*; **there are long delays on the M25** la circulation est très ralentie *ou* est très perturbée sur la M25; **all flights are subject to d.** tous les vols ont du retard; **there's a three-to-four-hour d. on all international flights** il y a trois à quatre heures de retard sur tous les vols internationaux **2** *(waiting period)* **without d.** sans tarder *ou* délai; **without (any) further d.** sans plus tarder; **after much d.** après un long moment; **the defence lawyer requested a d. in the hearing** l'avocat de la défense demanda un report de (la) séance

> Note that the French word **délai** is a false friend and is almost never a translation for the English word **delay**. Its most common meaning is **time allowed.**

delayed-action [dɪˈleɪd-] ADJ *(fuse, shutter)* à retardement

delayering [ˌdiːˈleɪərɪŋ] N suppression *f* d'échelons

del credere [delˈkreɪdərɪ] *Com* N ducroire *m*
COMP *(agent, clause)* ducroire

delectable [dɪˈlektəbəl] ADJ délectable

delectation [ˌdiːlekˈteɪʃən] N *Literary or Hum* délectation *f*; **for your d.** pour votre plus grand plaisir

delegate N [ˈdelɪgət] délégué(e) *m,f*
VT [ˈdelɪgeɪt] **1** *(person)* déléguer; **the parents delegated Mrs Parker to represent them at the meeting** les parents déléguèrent *ou* désignèrent Mme Parker pour les représenter à la réunion **2** *(work, powers)* déléguer
VI [ˈdelɪgeɪt] déléguer; **she's not very good at delegating** elle ne sait pas déléguer

delegation [ˌdelɪˈgeɪʃən] N **1** *(group of delegates)* délégation *f* **2** *(of work, power)* délégation *f*

delete [dɪˈliːt] VT **1** *(remove)* supprimer; *(erase)* effacer; *(cross out)* barrer, biffer; *Comput* effacer, supprimer; **d. where applicable, d. as appropriate** *(on form)* rayer les mentions inutiles **2** *Com (from stock, catalogue)* supprimer; **we have decided to d. this item from stock** nous avons décidé de ne plus faire cet article
VI *Comput* effacer
►► *Comput* ***delete key*** touche *f* d'effacement

deleterious [ˌdelɪˈtɪərɪəs] ADJ *Formal (effect)* nuisible; *(influence, substance)* nuisible, délétère

deletion [dɪˈliːʃən] N **1** *(action)* suppression *f*; *Comput* effacement *m*, suppression *f*; **I made a lot of deletions in the text** j'ai supprimé beaucoup de choses *ou* j'ai fait beaucoup de coupes dans le texte **2** *(passage)* passage *m* effacé *ou* supprimé; *(word)* mot *m* effacé *ou* supprimé

delft [delft] N *Cer* faïence *f* (de Delft)
►► ***delft blue*** bleu *m* de faïence

Delhi [ˈdelɪ] N Delhi
►► *Hum* ***Delhi belly*** turista *f*

deli [ˈdelɪ] N *Fam (abbr* **delicatessen**) **1** *(fine foods shop)* épicerie *f* fine; *(food shop)* traiteur *m* **2** *Am (restaurant)* restaurant *m* traiteur
►► ***deli counter*** *(in supermarket)* rayon *m* traiteur

deliberate ADJ [dɪˈlɪbərət] **1** *(intentional)* délibéré, volontaire, voulu; **it was a d. attempt to embarrass the minister** cela visait délibérément à embarrasser le ministre; **it was quite d.!** c'était voulu, c'était fait exprès! **2** *(unhurried, careful)* mesuré, posé; **her speech was slow and d.** elle parlait lentement et posément
VI [dɪˈlɪbəreɪt] délibérer; **to d. on** *or* **upon sth** délibérer sur qch; **they deliberated whether or not to expel him** ils ont délibéré pour savoir s'ils allaient l'expulser
VT [dɪˈlɪbəreɪt] délibérer sur *ou* de

deliberately [dɪˈlɪbərətlɪ] ADV **1** *(intentionally)* intentionnellement, volontairement; **I d. didn't invite her** c'est intentionnellement que je ne l'ai pas invitée; **I didn't hurt him d.** je n'ai pas fait exprès de le blesser; **you have d. lied to the court** vous avez menti délibérément *ou* sciemment à la cour **2** *(unhurriedly, carefully)* de façon mesurée, avec mesure; *(walk)* d'un pas ferme

deliberation [dɪˌlɪbəˈreɪʃən] N **1** *(consideration, reflection)* délibération *f*, réflexion *f*; **after much d.** après délibération *ou* mûre réflexion **2** *(care, caution)* attention *f*, soin *m*; **with d.** *(say)* posément; *(do something)* de façon réfléchie; *(walk)* d'un pas mesuré; *(act)* avec circonspection
• **deliberations** NPL délibérations *fpl*

deliberative [dɪˈlɪbərətɪv] ADJ **1** *(group, assembly)* délibérant **2** *(conclusion)* mûrement réfléchi

delicacy [ˈdelɪkəsɪ] *(pl* **delicacies**) N **1** *(fineness ► of lace, china, features, fingers)* délicatesse *f*, finesse *f*
2 *(fragility ► of person, health)* délicatesse *f*, fragilité *f*; *(difficulty)* délicatesse *f*
3 *(sensitivity ► of mechanism, situation, question)* délicatesse *f*; *(► of feelings)* sensibilité *f*; **it's a matter of great d.** c'est une affaire très délicate **the question must be handled with d.** la question doit être traitée avec délicatesse
4 *(gentleness, lightness ► of touch)* légèreté *f*
5 *(of smell, colour, flavour)* délicatesse *f*
6 *(fine food)* mets *m* délicat; **it's considered a great d. in China** c'est considéré comme un mets très délicat *ou* fin en Chine

delicate [ˈdelɪkət] ADJ **1** *(fine ► lace, china, features, fingers)* délicat, fin
2 *(fragile ► person, health)* délicat, fragile
3 *(sensitive ► mechanism, situation, question)* délicat, difficile; *(feelings)* sensible; *(person ► over refined, easily shocked)* précieux; **a d. international situation** une situation internationale délicate; **to tread on d. ground** toucher à des questions délicates
4 *(gentle, light ► touch)* délicat
5 *(smell, colour, flavour)* délicat
6 *(instrument)* sensible
• **delicates** NPL linge *m* délicat

delicately [ˈdelɪkətlɪ] ADV **1** *(finely ► carved, embroidered etc)* délicatement, finement
2 *(sensitively ► deal with, approach)* avec délicatesse; **the mechanism is very d. balanced** le réglage du mécanisme est très sensible
3 *(gently, lightly ► touch, hold, pick up etc)* délicatement
4 *(subtly ► coloured, flavoured)* délicatement

delicatessen [ˌdelɪkəˈtesən] N **1** *Br (fine food shop)* épicerie *f* fine ; *(food shop)* traiteur *m* **2** *Am (restaurant)* restaurant *m* traiteur
►► ***delicatessen counter*** *(in supermarket)* rayon *m* traiteur

delicious [dɪˈlɪʃəs] ADJ délicieux

deliciously [dɪˈlɪʃəslɪ] ADV délicieusement

delight [dɪˈlaɪt] N **1** *(pleasure)* joie *f*, (grand) plaisir *m*; **she listened with d.** elle écoutait avec délectation; **to the d. of the audience** à la plus grande joie *ou* pour le plus grand plaisir de l'auditoire; **her brother took (great) d. in teasing her** son frère prenait (un malin) plaisir à la taquiner **2** *(source of pleasure)* délice *m*; **the delights of gardening** les charmes *mpl ou* délices *fpl* du jardinage; **it is such a d. to...** c'est si bon de...; **the child was a d. to teach** c'était un plaisir d'enseigner à cet enfant
VT ravir, réjouir; **to d. the ear** charmer les oreilles; **to d. the eye** enchanter la vue; **her show has delighted audiences everywhere** son spectacle a partout conquis *ou* ravi le public
► **delight in** VT INSEP se délecter de, aimer beaucoup; **to d. in doing sth** se délecter à *ou* aimer beaucoup faire qch; **he delights in publicity** il adore faire parler de lui; **she delights in irritating people** elle prend plaisir *ou* se complaît à énerver les gens

delighted [dɪˈlaɪtɪd] ADJ ravi (**with** de); **I'm d. to see you again** je suis ravi de vous revoir; **I was d. at the news** la nouvelle m'a fait très plaisir; **could you come to dinner on Saturday? – I'd be d. (to)** pourriez-vous venir dîner samedi? – avec (grand) plaisir

delightedly [dɪˈlaɪtɪdlɪ] ADV avec joie, joyeusement

delightful [dɪˈlaɪtfʊl] ADJ *(person, place)* charmant; *(book, experience, film)* merveilleux; **this rose has a d. perfume** cette rose a un parfum délicieux; **she looked d. in her new dress** sa nouvelle robe lui allait à ravir

delightfully [dɪˈlaɪtfʊlɪ] ADV *(dance, perform, sing)* merveilleusement, à ravir; **the evenings were d. cool** les soirées étaient merveilleusement fraîches

delimit [ˌdiːˈlɪmɪt] VT *Comput* délimiter

delimitation [ˈdiːˌlɪmɪˈteɪʃən] N *Comput* délimitation *f*

delimiter [ˌdiːˈlɪmɪtə(r)] N *Comput* délimiteur *m*

delineate [dɪˈlɪnɪeɪt] VT *Formal* **1** *(outline, sketch)* tracer **2** *Fig (define, describe)* définir, décrire; *(character in novel)* faire le portrait de

delineation [dɪˌlɪnɪˈeɪʃən] N **1** *(outline, sketch)* tracé *m* **2** *(definition, description)* définition *f*, description *f*; *(of character in novel)* portrait *m*

delinquency [dɪˈlɪŋkwənsɪ] (*pl* **delinquencies**) N 1 *Law (criminal behaviour)* délinquance *f*; *(negligence)* faute *f* 2 *Fin* défaillance *f*, défaut *m* de paiement

delinquent [dɪˈlɪŋkwənt] N 1 *Law (law breaker)* délinquant(e) *m,f* 2 *Fin (bad debtor)* mauvais payeur *m*
ADJ 1 *Law (law breaking)* délinquant; *(negligent)* fautif 2 *Fin (person)* défaillant; *(taxes, bill)* impayé; *(account, debt, loan)* en souffrance

delirious [dɪˈlɪrɪəs] ADJ 1 *Med* en délire; **to become d.** se mettre à délirer, être pris de délire 2 *Fig (excited, wild)* délirant, en délire; **he was d. with joy** il était fou de joie; **I'm not exactly d. at the prospect** cette perspective ne m'enchante guère

deliriously [dɪˈlɪrɪəslɪ] ADV de façon délirante, frénétiquement; **d. happy** follement heureux

delirium [dɪˈlɪrɪəm] N 1 *Med* délire *m*; **to be in a d.** être en plein délire 2 *Fig (state of excitement)* délire *m*; *Literary* **to be in a d. of joy** être transporté de joie
►► *Med* ***delirium tremens*** delirium tremens *m*

delist [ˌdiːˈlɪst] VT *Com & Mktg (product)* déréférencer; *St Exch (company)* radier de la cote

delisting [ˌdiːˈlɪstɪŋ] N *Com & Mktg (of product)* déréférencement *m*; *St Exch (of company)* radiation *f* de la cote

deliver [dɪˈlɪvə(r)] VT 1 *(letter, parcel, telegram)* remettre, apporter (**to** à); *(mail)* distribuer (**to** à); *(goods)* livrer (**to** à); **was my message delivered to you?** est-ce qu'on t'a remis mon message?; **the letter was delivered by hand** on m'a/lui/*etc* remis la lettre en main propre; **do you have your milk delivered?** est-ce que vous vous faites livrer votre lait?, est-ce qu'on vous livre votre lait?; **the train delivered us safely home** nous sommes rentrés en train sains; *Fig* **to d. the goods** *(of person)* remplir ses engagements; *(of new product)* tenir ses promesses; *Com* **delivered free** livraison franco; **delivered at** *or* **to domicile** livré à domicile; **delivered at frontier** rendu à la frontière
2 *Formal or Literary (save, rescue)* délivrer; *Bible* **d. us from evil** délivre-nous du mal
3 *Obst* **to d. a baby** faire un accouchement; *Formal or Literary* **she was delivered of a daughter** elle accoucha d'une fille
4 *(pronounce, utter)* **to d. a sermon/speech** prononcer un sermon/discours; *Formal* **to d. oneself of an opinion** faire part de *ou* émettre son opinion; *Law* **the jury delivered a verdict of not guilty** le jury a rendu un verdict de non-culpabilité
5 *(provide* ▸ *service)* assurer; *Tech (of machine, dynamo* ▸ *power)* débiter, fournir; *Aut (horsepower)* développer; *Fin* **to d. a profit** rapporter *ou* faire un profit; *St Exch* **to d. shares** délivrer des valeurs
6 *Am Pol* **can he d. the Black vote?** est-ce qu'il peut nous assurer les voix des Noirs?
7 *(strike)* **to d. a blow (to the head/stomach)** porter *ou* asséner un coup (à la tête/à l'estomac); *Ftbl* **to d. a pass** faire une passe
8 *Mil (of rocket)* lancer
VI 1 *(make delivery)* livrer 2 *Fam (do as promised)* tenir parole❑, tenir bon❑; *(new product supplier, political party etc)* tenir ses promesses; **can Brown d. on reform?** est-ce que Brown pourra tenir ses promesses en ce qui concerne les réformes?
▸ **deliver up** VT SEP *(fugitive, town)* livrer

deliverance [dɪˈlɪvərəns] N 1 *Formal or Literary (release, rescue)* délivrance *f* 2 *(pronouncement)* déclaration *f*; *Law* prononcé *m*

deliverer [dɪˈlɪvərə(r)] N 1 *Formal or Literary (saviour)* sauveur *m* 2 *Com (of goods)* livreur *m*

delivery [dɪˈlɪvərɪ] (*pl* **deliveries**) N 1 *(of letter, parcel, telegram)* remise *f*; *(of mail)* distribution *f*; *(of goods)* livraison *f*; **mail deliveries are rather irregular** la distribution du courrier est assez irrégulière; **to take d. of sth** prendre livraison de qch; **allow two weeks for d.** *(on sign, in advertisement)* délai de livraison: deux semaines; **payment on d.** règlement *m ou* paiement *m* à la livraison; **to pay on d.** payer à *ou* sur livraison
2 *Obst* accouchement *m*; **it was an easy d.** l'accouchement a été facile
3 *(of speech)* prononciation *f*; *(of speaker)* débit *m*, élocution *f*; **to have a good d.** avoir un bon débit
4 *(of water, power etc)* débit *m*; *(of pump)* refoulement *m*
5 *Sport (in cricket, baseball)* lancer *m*
6 *Law (of property)* tradition *f*; *(of bequest etc)* délivrance *f* (**to** à)
7 *Mil (of rocket)* lancement *m*
8 *St Exch (of shares)* livraison *f*
COMP *Com* de livraison
►► ***delivery address*** adresse *f* de livraison; ***delivery charges*** frais *mpl* de livraison; ***delivery date*** date *f* de livraison; ***delivery man*** livreur *m*; ***delivery note*** bon *m ou* bordereau *m ou* bulletin *m* de livraison; *Obst* ***delivery room*** salle *f* de travail *ou* d'accouchement; ***delivery time*** délai *m* de livraison; ***delivery van*** camion *m* de livraison; *(smaller)* camionnette *f* de livraison

dell [del] N vallon *m*

delouse [ˌdiːˈlaʊs] VT *(animal, person)* épouiller; *(clothing, furniture)* enlever les poux de

delphinium [delˈfɪnɪəm] (*pl* **delphiniums** *or* **delphinia** [-nɪə]) N *Bot* delphinium *m*

delta [ˈdeltə] N 1 *(in Greek alphabet)* delta *m* 2 *(of river)* delta *m*
COMP en delta
►► *Aviat* ***delta wing*** aile *f* (en) delta; ***delta wing aircraft*** avion *m* à ailes delta

delude [dɪˈluːd] VT tromper, duper; **he deluded investors into thinking that the company was doing well** il a fait croire aux investisseurs que la société se portait bien; **to d. oneself** se faire des illusions; **let's not d. ourselves about his motives** ne nous leurrons pas sur ses motivations

deluded [dɪˈluːdɪd] ADJ 1 *(mistaken, foolish)* **a poor d. young man** un pauvre jeune homme qu'on a trompé *ou* induit en erreur 2 *Psy* sujet à des délires

deluge [ˈdeljuːdʒ] N *also Fig* déluge *m*; **a d. of rain** une pluie diluvienne
VT *also Fig* inonder; **we have been deluged with letters** nous avons été submergés *ou* inondés de lettres

delusion [dɪˈluːʒən] N 1 *(illusion, mistaken idea)* illusion *f*; **she's under the d. that her illness isn't serious** elle s'imagine à tort que sa maladie n'est pas grave 2 *Psy* délire *m*; **to suffer from delusions** être sujet à des hallucinations; *Fig* **he has delusions of grandeur** il a la folie des grandeurs

deluxe [dəˈlʌks] ADJ de luxe; *(apartment)* (de) grand standing

delve [delv] VI 1 *(investigate)* fouiller; **she preferred not to d. too deeply into the past** elle préférait ne pas fouiller trop profondément (dans) le passé 2 *(search)* fouiller; **to d. in(to) one's pocket** fouiller dans sa poche 3 *(dig, burrow)* creuser; *(animal)* fouiller

Dem. *Am (written abbr* **Democrat(ic)**) démocrate

demagnetize, -ise [ˌdiːˈmægnɪtaɪz] VT *Phys* démagnétiser

demagogic [ˌdeməˈgɒgɪk] ADJ démagogique

demagogue [ˈdeməgɒg] N démagogue *mf*

demand [dɪˈmɑːnd] VT 1 *(request firmly)* exiger; *(money)* réclamer; **to d. an apology/explanation** exiger des excuses/une explication; **I d. to see the manager** appelez-moi le gérant; **they're demanding payment** ils réclament le paiement; **to d. that...** exiger que... + *subjunctive*; **to d. one's rights** revendiquer ses droits; **he demanded to know/to be told the truth** il exigeait de connaître/qu'on lui dise la vérité 2 *(require, necessitate)* exiger, réclamer; **he doesn't have the imagination demanded of a good writer** il n'a pas l'imagination que l'on attend d'un bon écrivain
N 1 *(obligation, requirement)* exigence *f*; **the demands of motherhood** les exigences de la maternité; **to make demands on sb** exiger beaucoup de qn; **he makes a lot of emotional demands** il a une très grande demande affective; **I have many demands on my time** je suis très pris 2 *(firm request)* demande *f*, réclamation *f*; **d. for payment** demande de paiement; **payable on d.** payable sur demande; **wage demands** revendications *fpl* salariales; **there have been many demands for the minister's resignation** beaucoup de voix se sont élevées pour exiger la démission du ministre; **to give in to sb's demands** céder aux exigences de qn; **you make too many demands on her** tu exiges trop d'elle 3 *Com & Econ* demande *f*; **to be in (great) d.** être (très) demandé *ou* recherché; **due to public d.** à la demande du public; **there is not much d. for books on the subject** les livres sur ce sujet ne sont pas très demandés
• **on demand** ADV sur demande; **she's in favour of abortion on d.** elle est pour l'avortement libre
►► *Com & Mktg* ***demand analysis*** analyse *f* de la demande; ***demand curve*** courbe *f* (d'évolution) de la demande; *Am Banking* ***demand deposit*** dépôt *m* à vue; ***demand feeding*** *(of baby)* allaitement *m* à la demande; *Com* ***demand management*** contrôle *m* de la demande; *Fin* ***demand note*** bon *m* à vue

> Note that the most common meaning of the French word **demande** is **request**. Note that the most common meaning of the French verb **demander** is **to ask** or **to request**.

demanding [dɪˈmɑːndɪŋ] ADJ *(person)* exigeant; *(job, profession, task)* difficile, astreignant; **the work is not physically d.** ce travail ne demande pas beaucoup de force physique; **children are at their most d. between the ages of two and four** les enfants demandent le plus d'attention entre deux et quatre ans

demand-led ADJ *Econ* tiré par la demande

demand-pull inflation N *Econ* inflation *f* par la demande

demarcation [ˌdiːmɑːˈkeɪʃən] N 1 *(of boundary, border)* établissement *m*; *(of two pieces of land)* démarcation *f*, *(of several territories)* délimitation *f* 2 *Ind* attributions *fpl*
►► ***demarcation dispute*** conflit *m* d'attributions; ***demarcation line*** ligne *f* de démarcation

demarket [ˌdiːˈmɑːkɪt] VT *Com & Mktg* retirer du marché

demarketing [ˌdiːˈmɑːkɪtɪŋ] N *Com & Mktg* démarketing *m*

demean [dɪˈmiːn] VT *Formal* avilir, rabaisser; **she wouldn't d. herself by marrying him** elle refusait de se rabaisser en l'épousant; **your behaviour demeans the office you hold** votre comportement déshonore la charge que vous occupez

demeaning [dɪˈmiːnɪŋ] ADJ *Formal* avilissant; **it was very d. having to...** c'était très avilissant de devoir...

demeanour, *Am* **demeanor** [dɪˈmiːnə(r)] N *Formal (behaviour)* comportement *m*; *(manner)* allure *f*, maintien *m*; **he had the d. of a gentleman** il avait des allures d'homme raffiné *ou* de gentleman

demented [dɪˈmentɪd] ADJ dément; *Fig* fou (folle); **to be d. with grief/anger/worry** être fou de douleur/de colère/d'inquiétude; **to drive sb d.** rendre qn fou

dementia [dɪˈmenʃə] N démence *f*
►► *Old-fashioned Med* ***dementia praecox*** démence *f* précoce

demerara [ˌdeməˈreərə] N *(sugar)* cassonade *f*
►► ***demerara sugar*** cassonade *f*

demerger [ˌdiːˈmɜːdʒə(r)] N *Br Com* scission *f*

demerit [diːˈmerɪt] N 1 *Formal (flaw)* démérite *m*, faute *f* 2 *Am Sch & Mil* blâme *m*

demesne [dɪˈmeɪn] N 1 *Formal (land, estate)* domaine *m* 2 *Law (possession)* possession *f*; **land held in d.** terrain *m* possédé en toute propriété

demigod [ˈdemɪgɒd] N demi-dieu *m*

demijohn [ˈdemɪdʒɒn] N dame-jeanne *f*, bonbonne *f*

demilitarization, -isation [ˈdiːˌmɪlɪtəraɪˈzeɪʃən] N démilitarisation *f*

demilitarize, -ise [ˌdiːˈmɪlɪtəraɪz] VT démilitariser; **a demilitarized zone** une zone démilitarisée

demise [dɪˈmaɪz] N 1 *Formal (death)* mort *f*, disparition *f*; *(end* ▸ *of newspaper, empire etc)* fin *f*, mort *f* 2 *Law (transfer)* cession *f* 3 *Hist* **the d. of the Crown** la transmission de la Couronne
VT 1 *Law (lease)* louer à bail; *(bequeath)* léguer 2 *Hist (transfer)* transmettre

demisemiquaver [ˈdemɪsemɪˌkweɪvə(r)] N *Br Mus* triple croche *f*

demist [ˌdiːˈmɪst] **VT** *BrAut* désembuer

demister [ˌdiːˈmɪstə(r)] **N** *BrAut* dispositif *m* antibuée

demisting [ˌdiːˈmɪstɪŋ] **N** *BrAut* désembuage *m*

demo [ˈdeməʊ] (*pl* **demos**) **N** *Fam* (*abbr* **demonstration**) **1** *(protest)* manif *f* **2** *(of band, singer)* disque *m*/cassette *f*/vidéo *f* de démonstration□ **3** *(of device, system)* démonstration *f*

►► *Comput* ***demo disk*** disquette *f* de démonstration *ou* d'évaluation; ***demo tape*** cassette *f* démo; *Comput* ***demo version*** version *f* de démonstration *ou* d'évaluation

demob [ˌdiːˈmɒb] (*pt & pp* **demobbed**, *cont* **demobbing**) *Br Fam Mil* **N** *(demobilization)* démobilisation□ *f*

VT démobiliser□

►► ***demob suit*** tenue *f* civile□

demobilization, -isation [diːˌməʊbɪlaɪˈzeɪʃən] **N** *Mil* démobilisation *f*

demobilize, -ise [ˌdiːˈməʊbɪlaɪz] **VT** *Mil* démobiliser

democracy [dɪˈmɒkrəsɪ] (*pl* **democracies**) **N** démocratie *f*

democrat [ˈdeməkræt] **N** démocrate *mf*

• **Democrat N 1** *(in US)* démocrate *mf*; **the Democrats** le parti démocrate **2** *(in UK)* = membre des "Liberal Democrats"

democratic [ˌdeməˈkrætɪk] **ADJ** *(country, organization, principle)* démocratique; *(person)* démocrate

• **Democratic ADJ** *Am Pol* démocrate

►► ***democratic government*** la démocratie; ***the Democratic Party*** le parti démocrate (américain); ***the Democratic Republic of Congo*** la République démocratique du Congo; ***democratic socialism*** socialisme *m* démocratique

democratically [ˌdeməˈkrætɪkəlɪ] **ADV** démocratiquement

democratize, -ise [dɪˈmɒkrətaɪz] **VT** démocratiser

VI se démocratiser

demodulation [ˈdiːˌmɒdjʊˈleɪʃən] **N** *Phys & Rad* démodulation *f*

demodulator [ˌdiːˈmɒdjʊleɪtə(r)] **N** *Comput* démodulateur *m*

demographer [dɪˈmɒɡrəfə(r)] **N** démographe *mf*

demographic [ˌdeməˈɡræfɪk] **ADJ** démographique

►► ***demographic analysis*** analyse *f* démographique

demographics [ˌdeməˈɡræfɪks] **N** *(UNCOUNT) (science)* (étude *f* de la) démographie *f*

NPL *(statistics)* statistiques *fpl* démographiques

demography [dɪˈmɒɡrəfɪ] **N** démographie *f*

demolish [dɪˈmɒlɪʃ] **VT 1** *also Fig (destroy)* démolir; **to d. sb** *(in argument)* démolir qn; *(in competition, fight)* mettre la pâtée à qn **2** *Fam (devour)* dévorer□

demolition [ˌdeməˈlɪʃən] **N** *also Fig* démolition *f*

• **demolitions NPL** *Mil* explosifs *mpl*

►► ***demolition contractor*** démolisseur *m*; *Sport* ***demolition derby*** = course de voitures dans laquelle celles-ci sont délibérément détruites; *Br* ***demolitions expert*** expert *m* en explosifs; ***demolition squad*** équipe *f* de démolition

demon [ˈdiːmən] **N 1** *(devil, evil spirit)* démon *m* **2** *Fig* diable *m*; **that child's a little d.** cet enfant est un petit démon; **she works like a d., she's a d. for work** c'est un bourreau de travail; **he's a d. tennis player** il joue au tennis comme un dieu; **the d. drink** le démon de la boisson

demonetize, -ise [ˌdiːˈmʌnɪtaɪz] **VT** *Fin* démonétiser

demoniac [dɪˈməʊnɪæk] **N** démoniaque *mf*

ADJ démoniaque

demoniacal [ˌdiːməˈnaɪəkəl] **ADJ** démoniaque

demonic [diːˈmɒnɪk] **ADJ** diabolique

demonology [ˌdiːməˈnɒlədʒɪ] **N** démonologie *f*

demonstrable [dɪˈmɒnstrəbəl] **ADJ** démontrable

demonstrably [dɪˈmɒnstrəblɪ] **ADV** manifestement

demonstrate [ˈdemənstreɪt] **VT 1** *(prove, establish)* démontrer; **that just demonstrates how stupid he is** ça ne fait que démontrer à quel point il est stupide **2** *(appliance, machine)* faire une démonstration de; **he demonstrated how to use a sewing machine** il a montré comment se servir d'une machine à coudre **3** *(ability, quality)* faire preuve de

VI manifester; **to d. for/against sth** manifester pour/contre qch

demonstration [ˌdemənˈstreɪʃən] **N 1** *(proof)* démonstration *f*

2 *(of appliance, machine, skills)* démonstration *f*; **the salesman gave a d. of the word processor** le vendeur a fait une démonstration du traitement de texte

3 *(protest)* manifestation *f*; **to hold** *or* **to stage a d.** faire une manifestation

4 *(of emotion)* démonstration *f*, manifestation *f*

5 *Mil* démonstration *f*

COMP *(car, copy, lesson, model)* de démonstration

> Note that the French word **démonstration** is never used to describe a protest.

demonstrative [dɪˈmɒnstrətɪv] **ADJ 1** *(person)* démonstratif **2** *(argument, proof)* démonstratif **3** *Gram (adjective, pronoun)* démonstratif

N *Gram* démonstratif *m*

demonstrator [ˈdemənˌstreɪtə(r)] **N 1** *(of appliance, machine)* démonstrateur(trice) *m,f*

2 *(protester)* manifestant(e) *m,f*

3 *Br Univ* préparateur(trice) *m,f*

4 *Am (appliance, machine)* modèle *m* de démonstration; *(car)* voiture *f* de démonstration

demoralization, -isation [dɪˌmɒrəlaɪˈzeɪʃən] **N** démoralisation *f*

demoralize, -ise [dɪˈmɒrəlaɪz] **VT** démoraliser

demoralizing, -ising [dɪˈmɒrəˌlaɪzɪŋ] **ADJ** démoralisant

demote [ˌdiːˈməʊt] **VT** rétrograder; **she's been demoted to assistant manager** elle a été rétrogradée au poste de directeur-adjoint

demotic [dɪˈmɒtɪk] **ADJ 1** *(of the people)* populaire **2** *Ling* démotique

N *Antiq* démotique *m*

• **Demotic N** *Antiq* grec *m* démotique

demotion [ˌdiːˈməʊʃən] **N** rétrogradation *f*

demotivate [ˌdiːˈməʊtɪveɪt] **VT** démotiver

demotivation [diːˌməʊtɪˈveɪʃən] **N** démotivation *f*

demur [dɪˈmɜː(r)] (*pt & pp* **demurred**, *cont* **demurring**) **VI 1** *Formal* soulever une objection; **I suggested she join us but she demurred** j'ai proposé qu'elle se joigne à nous mais elle s'y est opposée **2** *Law* opposer une exception

N objection *f*; **without d.** sans sourciller *ou* faire d'objection

demure [dɪˈmjʊə(r)] **ADJ 1** *(modest)* modeste, pudique; *(well-behaved)* sage; *(reserved)* retenu **2** *Pej (coy)* d'une modestie affectée

demurely [dɪˈmjʊəlɪ] **ADV 1** *(modestly)* modestement; *(reservedly)* avec retenue; **she sipped her tea d.** elle buvait son thé à petites gorgées *ou* avec délicatesse **2** *Pej (coyly)* avec une modestie affectée

demureness [dɪˈmjʊənɪs] **N 1** *(modesty)* modestie *f*, pudeur *f*; *(reserve)* retenue *f* **2** *Pej (coyness)* modestie *f* affectée

demurrage [dɪˈmʌrɪdʒ] **N** *Com* surestarie *f*

demystify [ˌdiːˈmɪstɪfaɪ] (*pt & pp* **demystified**) **VT** démystifier

demythologize, -ise [ˌdiːmɪˈθɒlədʒaɪz] **VT** démythifier

den [den] **N 1** *(of animal)* repaire *m*, tanière *f*; *Fig (hideout)* repaire *m*, nid *m*; **a d. of thieves** un repaire de voleurs; **a d. of iniquity** un lieu de perdition **2** *(room, study)* bureau *m*, cabinet *m* de travail; **he uses the study as his d.** quand il veut se détendre, il va dans le bureau

►► *Am* ***den mother*** *(in scout group)* cheftaine *f*

denationalization, -isation [ˈdiːˌnæʃənəlaɪˈzeɪʃən] **N** dénationalisation *f*

denationalize, -ise [ˌdiːˈnæʃənəlaɪz] **VT** dénationaliser

denature [ˌdiːˈneɪtʃə(r)], **denaturize, -ise** [ˌdiːˈneɪtʃəraɪz] **VT** *Biol & Chem* dénaturer

dengue [ˈdeŋɡɪ] *Med*

N *(fever)* dengue *f*

►► ***dengue fever*** dengue *f*

denial [dɪˈnaɪəl] **N 1** *(of story, rumour)* démenti *m*; *(of wrongdoing)* dénégation *f*; **to issue a d.** publier un démenti; **the minister's d. of responsibility was greeted with outrage** c'est avec indignation qu'on a appris que le ministre rejetait toute responsabilité

2 *(of request, right)* refus *m*; *Law* **d. of justice** déni *m* de justice

3 *(disavowal, repudiation)* reniement *m*; *Bible* **Peter's d. of Christ** le reniement du Christ par Pierre

4 *(abstinence)* abnégation *f*

5 *Psy* déni *m*; **to be in d.** *Psy* être en déni; *Fig* refuser de se rendre à l'évidence

denier [ˈdenɪə(r), dəˈnɪə(r)] **N 1** *Br (measure)* denier *m*; **15-d. stockings** bas *m* de 15 deniers **2** *Hist (coin)* denier *m*

denigrate [ˈdenɪɡreɪt] **VT** dénigrer

denim [ˈdenɪm] **N** (toile *f* de) jean *m*, denim *m*

COMP *(skirt, jacket)* en jean

• **denims NPL** blue-jean *m*, jean *m*

denizen [ˈdenɪzən] **N 1** *Literary or Hum (inhabitant)* habitant(e) *m,f*, hôte *mf*; *(regular visitor)* habitué(e) *m,f*; *Fig* **the denizens of the deep** *(fish)* les poissons *mpl* **2** *Br (permanent resident)* résident(e) *m,f* **3** *Bot (non-native plant)* plante *f* allogène; *Zool (non-native animal)* animal *m* allogène

Denmark [ˈdenmɑːk] **N** Danemark *m*

denominate [dɪˈnɒmɪneɪt] **VT 1** *Formal (name)* dénommer **2** *Fin* libeller; **denominated in dollars** libellé en dollars

denomination [dɪˌnɒmɪˈneɪʃən] **N 1** *Fin* valeur *f*; *(of share, banknote)* coupure *f*; **small/large denominations** petites/grosses coupures *fpl*; **coins of different denominations** des pièces de différentes valeurs **2** *Rel* confession *f*, culte *m* **3** *Formal (designation, specification)* dénomination *f*

denominational [dɪˌnɒmɪˈneɪʃənəl] **ADJ** *Rel* confessionnel

►► ***denominational school*** école *f* confessionnelle

denominator [dɪˈnɒmɪneɪtə(r)] **N** *Math* dénominateur *m*

denotation [ˌdiːnəʊˈteɪʃən] **N** *(UNCOUNT)* **1** *(indication)* dénotation *f*; *(representation, symbol)* signes *mpl*, symboles *mpl* **2** *(specific meaning)* signification *f*

denote [dɪˈnəʊt] **VT 1** *(indicate)* dénoter **2** *(mean)* signifier

dénouement [deɪˈnuːmɑ̃] **N** *(of play, situation)* dénouement *m*

denounce [dɪˈnaʊns] **VT 1** *(inform against ► criminal, crime)* dénoncer; **to d. sb to the authorities** signaler qn à la justice; **to d. sb as an impostor** taxer qn d'imposture **2** *(protest about ► abuse, government action, drug-taking)* dénoncer, s'élever contre; *(modern art, exhibition)* dénigrer; **they have been denounced as nothing more than murderers** ils ont été accusés de n'être que de vulgaires assassins **3** *(declare termination of ► treaty, agreement)* dénoncer

dense [dens] **ADJ 1** *(body, metal etc)* dense

2 *(thick ► fog, smoke)* épais(aisse); (► *undergrowth, vegetation, population, traffic)* dense; (► *crowd)* compact, dense; *Phot* opaque

3 *(prose, text)* dense, ramassé

4 *Fam (stupid)* bouché, stupide□

densely [ˈdenslɪ] **ADV to be d. packed together** être serrés les uns contre les autres; **a d.-populated area** une région très peuplée *ou* à forte densité de population; **the book is very d. written** le livre est écrit d'une manière dense *ou* ramassée; **a d.-wooded valley** une vallée très boisée

denseness [ˈdensnɪs] **N 1** *(of undergrowth, vegetation, crowd, traffic)* densité *f* **2** *Fam (stupidity)* stupidité□ *f*

density [ˈdensɪtɪ] **N 1** *(of body, metal etc)* densité *f*; *Tech* masse *f* volumique; *Phys* **ion/neutron d.** densité *f* ionique/neutronique **2** *(of population)* densité *f*

►► *density chart (in hotel)* feuille *f* d'occupation journalière

dent [dent] **N 1** *(in metal, wall)* bosse *f*; *(in bed, pillow)* creux *m*; **he made a d. in his car** il a cabossé sa voiture; **the car has a d. in the bumper** la voiture a le pare-chocs cabossé **2** *Fig (reduction)* **to make a d. in one's savings** faire un trou dans ses économies; *Fig* **to make a d. in sb's self-confidence** entamer la confiance en soi *ou* l'assurance de qn

VT 1 *(metal, wall)* cabosser, bosseler **2** *Fig (pride)* froisser; *(self-confidence)* entamer

dental ['dentəl] **ADJ 1** *(concerned with dentistry)* dentaire **2** *Ling* dental

N *Ling* dentale *f*

►► ***dental appointment*** rendez-vous *m* chez le dentiste; ***dental care*** soins *mpl* dentaires; ***dental floss*** fil *m* dentaire; ***dental hygiene*** hygiène *f* dentaire; ***dental hygienist*** assistant(e) *m,f* de dentiste *(qui s'occupe du détartrage etc)*; ***dental nurse*** assistant(e) *m,f* dentaire; *Am* ***dental office*** cabinet *m* dentaire; *Br* ***dental surgeon*** chirurgien-dentiste (chirugienne-dentiste) *m,f*; ***dental surgery*** *(activity)* chirurgie *f* dentaire; *Br (office)* cabinet *m* dentaire; ***dental technician*** prothésiste *mf* (dentaire); ***dental treatment*** traitement *m* dentaire

dented ['dentɪd] **ADJ** *(metal)* cabossé

dentifrice ['dentɪfrɪs] **N** *(paste)* pâte *f* dentifrice; *(powder)* poudre *f* dentifrice

dentine ['denti:n], *Am* **dentin** ['dentɪn] **N** *Anat & Zool* dentine *f*

dentist ['dentɪst] **N** dentiste *mf*; **to go to the d.** *or* **dentist's** aller chez le dentiste

►► ***dentist's chair*** fauteuil *m* de dentiste; *Am* ***dentist's office***, *Br* ***dentist's surgery*** cabinet *m* dentaire

dentistry ['dentɪstrɪ] **N** dentisterie *f*

dentition [den'tɪʃən] **N** *Anat & Zool* dentition *f*

denture ['dentʃə(r)] **N** *(artificial tooth)* prothèse *f* dentaire

• **dentures NPL** dentier *m*; **to wear dentures** porter un dentier

> Note that the French word **denture** is a false friend and is never a translation for the English word **dentures**. It means **set of teeth**.

denude [dɪ'nju:d] **VT** dénuder; **a landscape denuded of trees** un paysage sans arbres

denunciation [dɪ,nʌnsɪ'eɪʃən] **N** dénonciation *f*

Denver boot ['denvə-] **N** *Am Aut* sabot *m* de Denver®

deny [dɪ'naɪ] *(pt & pp* **denied***)* **VT 1** *(declare untrue)* nier; *(report, rumour)* démentir; **the prisoner denied having conspired** *or* **conspiring against the government** le prisonnier nia avoir conspiré contre le gouvernement; **the accused denies the charge** l'accusé nie; **there's no denying that we have a problem** il est indéniable que nous avons un problème; **he denied all knowledge of the incident** il a nié être au courant de l'incident

2 *(refuse)* refuser, *Literary* dénier; **to d. sb sth** *or* **sth to sb** refuser qch à qn; **to be denied access to sb/sth** se voir refuser l'accès à qn/qch; **in many countries people are denied even basic human rights** dans beaucoup de pays les gens sont privés des droits les plus fondamentaux

3 *(deprive)* priver; **she thought that by denying herself she could help others** elle pensait qu'en se privant elle pourrait aider les autres

4 *Arch or Literary (disavow, repudiate)* renier

deodorant [di:'əʊdərənt] **N** déodorant *m*

deodorize, -ise [di:'əʊdəraɪz] **VT** désodoriser

deodorizer, -iser [di:'əʊdə,raɪzə(r)] **N** *(for home)* désodorisant *m*

deontology [,di:ɒn'tɒlədʒɪ] **N** déontologie *f*

de-orbit [,di:'ɔ:bɪt] **N** *(of space station)* désatellisation *f*

VT *(space station)* désatelliser

deoxidize, -ise [di:'ɒksɪdaɪz] **VT** *Chem* désoxyder

deoxyribonucleic acid ['di:ɒksɪ,raɪbəʊnju:'kli:ɪk-] **N** *Biol & Chem* acide *m* désoxyribonucléique

dep *(written abbr* **departure/departs***)* dép

depart [dɪ'pɑ:t] **VI** *Formal* **1** *(leave)* partir; **the train now departing from platform two is the express to Liverpool** le train en partance au quai numéro deux est l'express de Liverpool; **they departed for Canada from Portsmouth** ils sont partis pour le Canada depuis Portsmouth **2** *(deviate, vary)* s'écarter; **to d. from tradition** s'écarter de la tradition; **to d. from sb's wishes** ne pas respecter la volonté de qn

VT quitter; *Euph* **to d. this life** quitter ce monde

departed [dɪ'pɑ:tɪd] *Euph Formal* **N the d.** le (la) défunt(e), le (la) disparu(e)

ADJ *(dead)* défunt, disparu

department [dɪ'pɑ:tmənt] **N 1** *Admin & Pol (division)* département *m*; *(ministry)* ministère *m*; **she works in the housing d.** elle travaille à l'antenne logement de la commune

2 *(in company, organization)* service *m*; **the sales/personnel d.** le service commercial/du personnel

3 *(field, responsibility)* domaine *m*; **recruiting staff is not my d.** le recrutement du personnel n'est pas mon domaine *ou* de mon ressort; *Fig* **cooking's not really my d.** la cuisine n'est pas vraiment mon domaine *ou* ma spécialité

4 *(in shop)* rayon *m*; **the toy d.** le rayon des jouets

5 *(in university)* département *m*; **the French/maths d.** *(at school)* = ensemble des professeurs de français/de mathématique d'un établissement d'enseignement secondaire sous la responsabilité de l'un d'entre eux

6 *Geog* département *m*

►► *Am* ***Department of Agriculture*** ministère *m* de l'Agriculture; *Am* ***Department of Commerce*** ministère *m* du Commerce; *Am* ***Department of Defense*** ministère *m* de la Défense; *Am* ***Department of Education*** ministère *m* de l'Éducation nationale; *Br* ***Department of Education and Employment*** = ministère britannique de l'Éducation et de l'Emploi; *Br* ***Department for Education and Skills*** ministère *m* de l'Éducation nationale; *Br* ***Department of Health*** ministère *m* de la Santé; *Am* ***Department of Homeland Security*** = ministère de la Sécurité intérieure, aux États-Unis; *Am* ***Department of the Interior*** = ministère de l'Intérieur; *Am* ***Department of Justice*** ministère *m* de la Justice; *Am* ***Department of Labor*** = ministère de l'Emploi et de la Solidarité; *Br Formerly* ***Department of Social Security*** ministère *m* des Affaires sociales; *Am* ***Department of State*** Département *m* d'État, ministère *m* des Affaires étrangères; ***department store*** grand magasin *m*; *Br* ***Department of Trade and Industry*** ministère *m* du commerce et de l'industrie; *Br* ***Department of Work and Pensions*** ministère *m* du Travail

departmental [,di:pɑ:t'mentəl] **ADJ 1** *Admin & Pol* du département

2 *(in company, organization)* du service

3 *(in shop)* du rayon

4 *(in university)* du département

5 *Geog* du département, départemental

►► ***departmental head*** chef *m* de service; *Univ* chef *m* du département; ***departmental manager*** chef *m* de service; ***departmental meeting*** réunion *f* de service

departure [dɪ'pɑ:tʃə(r)] **N 1** *(leaving)* départ *m*; **the crew were preparing for d.** l'équipage se préparait au départ; **her unexpected d. from politics** son départ inattendu de la scène politique; *Formal* **to take one's d.** prendre congé

2 *(variation, deviation)* modification *f*; **a d. from standard company policy** une entorse à la politique habituelle de l'entreprise; **a d. from his usual habits** une action contraire à ses habitudes

3 *(orientation)* orientation *f*; **farming was an entirely new d. for him** l'agriculture était une voie *ou* orientation tout à fait nouvelle pour lui

4 *Arch (death)* disparition *f*, trépas *m*

►► ***departure date*** date *f* de départ; ***departure gate*** *(in airport)* porte *f* (d'embarquement); ***departure lounge*** salle *f* d'embarquement; ***departure tax*** taxe *f* de départ; ***departure time*** heure *f* de départ

depend [dɪ'pend] **VI** dépendre; **that depends, it all depends** ça dépend

• **depending on PREP** selon; **a degree takes three or four years of study, depending on the subject chosen** un diplôme demande trois ou quatre ans d'études, selon la matière choisie

► **depend on, depend upon VT SEP 1** *(be determined by)* dépendre de; **her future may d. on it** son avenir en dépend peut-être; **that depends entirely on you** cela ne tient qu'à vous; **it depends on whether she accepts** ça dépend si elle accepte; **his job depends on his** *or* **him getting the contract** il ne gardera son emploi que s'il obtient le contrat; **survival depended on their finding enough water** pour survivre, il leur fallait trouver suffisamment d'eau **2** *(rely on)* dépendre de; **the firm depends heavily on orders from abroad** l'entreprise dépend beaucoup des commandes de l'étranger; **she depends on the money her children give her** l'argent qu'elle reçoit de ses enfants est sa seule ressource; *Ironic* **you can d. on him to be late** on peut être sûr qu'il arrive en retard **3** *(trust, be sure of)* compter sur; **I'm depending on you to help me** je compte sur vous pour m'aider; **we need somebody who can be depended on to be discreet** il nous faut quelqu'un sur la discrétion de qui on puisse compter; **you can d. on it!** vous pouvez en être sûr *ou* compter là-dessus!

dependability [dɪ,pendə'bɪlətɪ] **N** *(of machine, information)* fiabilité *f*; *(of person)* fiabilité *f*, sérieux *m*; *(of organization)* sérieux *m*

dependable [dɪ'pendəbəl] **ADJ** *(machine, information)* fiable; *(person)* fiable, sérieux; *(organization)* sérieux; **to be a d. source of income** fournir un revenu régulier

dependance *Am* = **dependence**

dependant [dɪ'pendənt] **N** *Admin* personne *f* à charge; **do you have any dependants?** avez-vous des personnes à charge?

> Attention: ne pas confondre avec l'adjectif **dependent**.

dependence [dɪ'pendəns] **N 1** *(reliance)* dépendance *f* (**on** de); **the government hopes to reduce our d. on oil** le gouvernement espère diminuer notre dépendance vis-à-vis du pétrole; **her d. on her children increased with the years** elle devenait de plus en plus dépendante de ses enfants au fil des années **2** *(trust)* confiance *f* (**on** en) **3** *Med (on drug)* (état *m* de) dépendance *f* (**on** à l'égard de)

dependency [dɪ'pendənsɪ] *(pl* **dependencies***)* **N 1** *(country)* dépendance *f* **2** *esp Am* = **dependence**

►► ***dependency culture*** = situation d'une société dont les membres ont une mentalité d'assistés; *Econ* ***dependency theory*** théorie *f* de la dépendance

dependent [dɪ'pendənt] **ADJ 1** *(reliant)* dépendant; **to be d. on sb/sth** dépendre de qn/qch; **she's financially d. on her parents** elle dépend financièrement *ou* elle est à la charge de ses parents; *Admin* **he has two d. children** il a deux enfants à charge; **to be d. on heroin/drugs** être héroïnomane/toxicomane; **she's heavily d. on sleeping pills** elle ne peut se passer de somnifères

2 *(contingent)* **to be d. on sth** dépendre de qch; **the prosperity of his business was d. on the continuation of the war** la prospérité de son entreprise dépendait *ou* était tributaire de la poursuite de la guerre

3 *Gram (clause)* subordonné

4 *Math (variable)* dépendant

N *Gram* subordonnée *f*

> Attention: ne pas confondre avec le nom **dependant**.

depict [dɪ'pɪkt] **VT 1** *(describe)* dépeindre; **Shakespeare depicts Richard III as cruel and calculating** Shakespeare dépeint Richard III comme un homme cruel et calculateur **2** *(paint, draw)* représenter

depiction [dɪ'pɪkʃən] **N 1** *(description)* description *f* **2** *(picture)* représentation *f*

depilatory [dɪ'pɪlətrɪ] *(pl* **depilatories***)* **N** épilatoire *m*, dépilatoire *m*

ADJ épilatoire, dépilatoire

►► ***depilatory cream*** crème *f* dépilatoire

deplane [,di:'pleɪn] **VI** descendre d'avion

deplete [dɪˈpliːt] VT 1 *(reduce)* diminuer, réduire; **the illness depleted her strength** la maladie amoindrissait ses forces; **our stocks have become depleted** nos stocks ont beaucoup diminué 2 *(impoverish, exhaust)* épuiser; **overproduction has depleted the soil** la surproduction a épuisé *ou* appauvri la terre; **the stream is depleted of fish** la rivière est beaucoup moins poissonneuse qu'avant

depleted uranium [dɪˈpliːtɪd-] N *Chem* uranium *m* appauvri

depletion [dɪˈpliːʃən] N 1 *(reduction)* diminution *f*, réduction *f* 2 *(exhaustion)* épuisement *m*; *(of soil)* appauvrissement *m*

deplorable [dɪˈplɔːrəbəl] ADJ déplorable, lamentable

deplorably [dɪˈplɔːrəblɪ] ADV d'une manière déplorable, lamentablement

deplore [dɪˈplɔː(r)] VT 1 *(regret)* déplorer, regretter 2 *(condemn, disapprove of)* désapprouver, condamner; **the President deplored the use of force against unarmed civilians** le Président a condamné l'usage de la force envers des civils non armés

deploy [dɪˈplɔɪ] VT déployer; **I think your talents would be better deployed elsewhere** je pense que vos talents seraient mieux utilisés ailleurs
VI se déployer

deployment [dɪˈplɔɪmənt] N déploiement *m*

depolarization, -isation [diːˌpəʊləraɪˈzeɪʃən] N *Electron* dépolarisation *f*

depolarize, -ise [ˌdiːˈpəʊləraɪz] VT *Electron* dépolariser

depollute [ˌdiːpəˈluːt] VT *Ecol* dépolluer

deponent [dɪˈpəʊnənt] N 1 *Gram* déponent *m* 2 *Law* déposant(e) *m,f*
ADJ *Gram* déponent

depopulate [ˌdiːˈpɒpjʊleɪt] VT dépeupler

depopulation [diːˌpɒpjʊˈleɪʃən] N dépeuplement *m*

deport [dɪˈpɔːt] VT 1 *(expel)* expulser; *Hist (to colonies, camp)* déporter; **they were deported to Mexico** ils furent expulsés vers le Mexique 2 *Formal (behave)* **to d. oneself** se comporter, se conduire

deportation [ˌdiːpɔːˈteɪʃən] N expulsion *f*; *Hist (to colonies, camp)* déportation *f*
▸▸ ***deportation order*** arrêt *m* d'expulsion

deportee [ˌdiːpɔːˈtiː] N expulsé(e) *m,f*; *Hist (prisoner)* déporté(e) *m,f*

deportment [dɪˈpɔːtmənt] N *Formal (behaviour)* comportement *m*; *(carriage, posture)* maintien *m*

depose [dɪˈpəʊz] VT 1 *(remove)* destituer; *(sovereign)* déposer, destituer 2 *Law* déposer
VI *Law* faire une déposition

deposit [dɪˈpɒzɪt] VT 1 *(leave, place)* déposer; **she deposited her belongings in a locker at Victoria Station** elle déposa *ou* laissa ses affaires dans une consigne à la gare Victoria; **the bus deposited me in front of my house** le bus m'a déposé devant ma maison
2 *(document* ▸ *with a bank)* mettre en dépôt (**with** dans); *(*▸ *with a solicitor)* confier (**with** à)
3 *(of liquid, river)* déposer
4 *Banking* déposer, remettre; **I'd like to d. £500** j'aimerais faire un versement de 500 livres; **to d. a cheque** déposer *ou* remettre un chèque (à la banque)
5 *(pay)* verser; *Fin* **to d. sth as security** nantir qch, gager qch
N 1 *Banking* dépôt *m*; **to make a d.** déposer de l'argent; **to make a d. of £200** faire un versement de 200 livres; **on d.** en dépôt
2 *Com & Fin (down payment)* acompte *m*; *(not returnable, for contract)* arrhes *fpl*; **she put down a d. on a house** elle a versé un acompte *ou* a fait un premier versement pour une maison; **a £50 d.** 50 livres d'acompte/d'arrhes
3 *(guarantee against loss or damage)* caution *f*; *(on bottle)* consigne *f*; **is there a d. on the bottle?** est-ce que la bouteille est consignée?
4 *Br Parl* cautionnement *m*; **to lose one's d.** perdre son cautionnement
5 *Geol* gisement *m*; **oil deposits** gisements *mpl* de pétrole
6 *(sediment, silt)* dépôt *m*; *(in wine)* dépôt *m*
▸▸ *Br Banking* ***deposit account*** compte *m* livret, compte *m* de dépôt; *(when notice has to be given before withdrawal)* compte *m* à terme; *Banking* ***deposit bank*** banque *f* de dépôt; *Banking* ***deposit slip*** bulletin *m* de versement

deposition[1] [ˌdepəˈzɪʃən] N 1 *Law* déposition *f* 2 *(sediment, silt)* dépôt *m* 3 *(removal of leader)* déposition *f*

deposition[2] [ˌdiːpəˈzɪʃən] VT *Mktg (product)* dépositionner

depositor [dəˈpɒzɪtə(r)] N déposant(e) *m,f*

depository [*Br* dəˈpɒzɪtrɪ, *Am* dəˈpɒzɪtəʊrɪ] *(pl* **depositories***)* N dépôt *m*, entrepôt *m*; **furniture d.** garde-meubles *m inv*

depot N 1 [ˈdepəʊ] *(warehouse)* dépôt *m*; **supply/ammunition d.** dépôt *m* de ravitaillement/munitions
2 [ˈdepəʊ] *Br (garage)* dépôt *m*, garage *m*
3 [ˈdepəʊ] *Br Mil* caserne *f*
4 [ˈdiːpəʊ] *Am (bus station)* gare *f* routière; *(railway station)* gare *f*; **bus/freight d.** gare *f* routière/des marchandises

depravation [ˌdeprəˈveɪʃən] N dépravation *f*

deprave [dɪˈpreɪv] VT dépraver

depraved [dɪˈpreɪvd] ADJ dépravé, perverti

depravity [dɪˈprævətɪ] *(pl* **depravities***)* N dépravation *f*, corruption *f*

deprecate [ˈdeprɪkeɪt] VT 1 *Formal (disapprove of, deplore)* désapprouver 2 *(denigrate, disparage)* dénigrer

deprecating [ˈdeprɪkeɪtɪŋ] ADJ 1 *(disapproving)* désapprobateur; *(derogatory)* dénigrant; **to be d. about sb/sth** désapprouver qn/qch 2 *(apologetic)* navré

deprecatingly [ˈdeprɪkeɪtɪŋlɪ] ADV 1 *(disapprovingly* ▸ *say, speak)* d'un ton désapprobateur; *(*▸ *look)* avec désapprobation 2 *(apologetically)* avec remords

deprecatory [ˈdeprɪkətrɪ] = **deprecating**

depreciate [dɪˈpriːʃɪeɪt] VT 1 *Com (value of something)* déprécier, rabaisser; *Acct (property, equipment)* amortir; *Fin (currency)* dévaloriser, déprécier 2 *(denigrate)* dénigrer, déprécier
VI *Com (value of something)* diminuer de valeur; *Com & Ind (machinery)* se déprécier; *Fin (currency)* se dévaloriser, se déprécier; *(prices, shares etc)* baisser; **the pound has depreciated against the dollar** la livre a reculé par rapport au dollar; **the tractor depreciated by £2,000** la valeur du tracteur a baissé de 2000 livres

depreciated [dɪˈpriːʃɪeɪtɪd] ADJ *Com & Ind* amorti; *Fin (currency)* déprécié

depreciation [dɪˌpriːʃɪˈeɪʃən] N 1 *Com (of goods)* dépréciation *f*; *Acct (of property, equipment)* amortissement *m*; *Fin (of currency)* dévalorisation *f*, dépréciation *f*; *(amount)* moins-value *f* 2 *(disparagement)* dénigrement *m*, dépréciation *f*
▸▸ ***depreciation charges*** frais *mpl* d'amortissement; *Acct* ***depreciation rate*** taux *m* d'amortissement

depredation [ˌdeprɪˈdeɪʃən] N déprédation *f*

depress [dɪˈpres] VT 1 *(deject, sadden)* déprimer; **it depressed her to talk about her father** le fait de parler de son père la déprimait *ou* lui donnait le cafard 2 *Econ (price)* (faire) baisser; *(trade)* faire languir; *(economy, market)* affaiblir 3 *Formal (push down on* ▸ *button, lever)* appuyer sur

depressant [dɪˈpresənt] *Med* N dépresseur *m*
ADJ dépresseur

depressed [dɪˈprest] ADJ 1 *(dejected, sad)* déprimé, abattu; *Med* déprimé; **you mustn't get d. about your exam results** tu ne dois pas te laisser abattre *ou* perdre le moral à cause de tes résultats d'examen; **to make sb (feel) d.** déprimer qn 2 *Econ (area, industry)* en déclin, touché par la crise, déprimé; *(prices, profits, wages)* en baisse; *St Exch* **the market is d.** les cours sont en baisse 3 *(sunken, hollow)* creux

depressing [dɪˈpresɪŋ] ADJ déprimant; *(idea, place)* triste, sinistre; **what a d. thought!** quelle triste idée!; **the unemployment figures make for d. reading** les chiffres du chômage sont plutôt déprimants

depressingly [dɪˈpresɪŋlɪ] ADV *(say, speak)* d'un ton abattu; **unemployment is d. high** le taux de chômage est déprimant; **his meaning was d. clear** la signification de ses paroles était d'une clarté déprimante

depression [dɪˈpreʃən] N 1 *(dejection, sadness)* dépression *f*; *Med* dépression *f* (nerveuse); **she suffers from d.** elle fait de la dépression; **he's in a state of d.** il est dans un état dépressif
2 *Econ (slump)* dépression *f*, crise *f* économique; **the country's economy is in a state of d.** l'économie du pays est en crise; *Am Hist* **the Great D.** la grande dépression
3 *Tech (pressing down)* abaissement *m*; *Aut (of pedal)* enfoncement *m*
4 *(hollow, indentation)* creux *m*; *Geog (in landscape)* dépression *f*
5 *Met* dépression *f*

depressive [dɪˈpresɪv] *Med* N dépressif(ive) *m,f*
ADJ dépressif; **to have a d. effect on the economy** déprimer l'économie

depressor [dɪˈpresə(r)] N *Anat* abaisseur *m*; *Med* **a tongue d.** un abaisse-langue

depressurize, -ise [ˌdiːˈpreʃəraɪz] VT dépressuriser
VI se dépressuriser

deprivation [ˌdeprɪˈveɪʃən] N *(UNCOUNT)* privation *f*; **a life of d. and misery** une vie de souffrances et de privations; **emotional d.** carence *f* affective

deprive [dɪˈpraɪv] VT priver; **to d. sb of sth** priver qn de qch; **she deprives herself of nothing** elle ne se prive de rien; **he was deprived of his rank** il fut déchu de son grade; **the legitimate heir was deprived of his inheritance** l'héritier légitime fut frustré *ou* dépossédé de son héritage; **I won't d. you of the pleasure of telling him about it** je ne te priverai pas du plaisir de le lui dire

deprived [dɪˈpraɪvd] ADJ *(area, child, background)* défavorisé; **the boy is emotionally d.** le garçon souffre d'une carence affective

deprogram [ˌdiːˈprəʊgræm] VT déprogrammer

dept. *(written abbr* **department***)* service *m*

depth [depθ] N 1 *(distance downwards)* profondeur *f*; **the wreck was located at a d. of 200 metres** l'épave a été repérée à 200 mètres de profondeur *ou* par 200 mètres de fond; **the canal is about 12 metres in d.** le canal a environ 12 mètres de profondeur; **this submarine could dive to a d. of 500 feet** ce sous-marin pouvait descendre jusqu'à une profondeur de 500 pieds
2 *(in deep water)* **she swam too far and got out of her d.** elle a nagé trop loin et a perdu pied; **to be out of one's d.** ne plus avoir pied; *Fig* avoir perdu pied, ne plus être sur son terrain; **I think she's a bit out of her d. in the new job** je crois qu'elle est un peu dépassée dans son nouveau travail
3 *Phot* **d. of field/focus** profondeur *f* de champ/foyer
4 *(of voice, sound)* registre *m* grave
5 *(extent, intensity)* profondeur *f*; *(of colour)* intensité *f*; **he had not realized her d. of feeling on the matter** il ne s'était pas rendu compte à quel point ce sujet lui tenait à cœur; **we must study the proposal in d.** nous devons étudier à fond *ou* en profondeur cette proposition
• **depths** NPL **the ocean depths** les grands fonds *mpl*; **in the depths of the forest** au (fin) fond de la forêt; **in the depths of despair** dans le plus profond désespoir; **in the depths of winter** au cœur de l'hiver
▸▸ ***depth bomb, depth charge*** grenade *f* sous-marine; *Tech* ***depth finder*** sondeur *m*; *Mktg* ***depth interview*** *(in market research)* entretien *m* en profondeur; ***depth psychology*** psychologie *f* des profondeurs

deputation [ˌdepjʊˈteɪʃən] N 1 *(representatives)* députation *f*, délégation *f* 2 *(action)* députation *f*, délégation *f*

depute VT [dɪˈpjuːt] *Formal (person)* députer (**to do sth** pour faire qch); *(authority, power)* déléguer; **she deputed the running of the business to her eldest son** elle délégua la gestion de l'entreprise à son fils aîné
N [ˈdepjuːt] *Scot* = **deputy**

deputize, -ise [ˈdepjʊtaɪz] VT députer
VI **to d. for sb** représenter qn

deputy ['depjʊtɪ] (*pl* **deputies**) N **1** *(assistant)* adjoint(e) *m,f*
2 *(substitute)* remplaçant(e) *m,f*, suppléant(e) *m,f*; **to act as sb's d.** remplacer qn, suppléer qn
3 *Pol (elected representative)* député *m*
4 *Am (law enforcement agent)* shérif *m* adjoint
►► ***deputy chairman*** vice-président *m*; *Br* ***deputy head teacher, deputy head*** directeur(trice) *m,f* adjoint(e); ***Deputy Leader*** adjoint(e) *m,f* du chef; **he is the former D. Leader of the Labour/Conservative Party** c'est l'ancien adjoint du leader du parti travailliste/conservateur; ***deputy manager*** directeur(trice) *m,f* adjoint(e); ***deputy mayor*** adjoint (e) *m,f* au maire; ***Deputy Prime Minister*** vice-Premier-Ministre *m*; ***deputy sheriff*** shérif *m* adjoint

DEQ [ˌdiːiː'kjuː] ADJ *Com (abbr* **delivered ex quay***)* DEQ

derail [dɪ'reɪl] VT *(train)* faire dérailler; *Fig (plans, negotiations)* faire avorter; **to be derailed** *(train)* dérailler; *Fig (plans, negotiations)* avorter
VI dérailler

derailment [dɪ'reɪlmənt] N *(of train)* déraillement *m*; *Fig (of plans, negotiations etc)* échec *m*

derange [dɪ'reɪndʒ] VT **1** *(disarrange, disorder)* déranger **2** *(drive insane)* rendre fou (folle)

deranged [dɪ'reɪndʒd] ADJ dérangé, déséquilibré; **the killer must have been d.** le tueur devait être fou *ou* déséquilibré; **the old woman seemed slightly d.** la vieille femme semblait un peu dérangée *ou* avoir l'esprit un peu dérangé

derangement [dɪ'reɪndʒmənt] N **1** *(disorder, disarray)* désordre *m* **2** *(mental illness)* démence *f*

derby [*Br* 'dɑːbɪ, *Am* 'dɜːbɪ] N **1** *(match)* **(local) d.** derby *m* **2** *Am (race)* derby *m* **3** *Am (hat)* chapeau *m* melon
• **Derby** N *Horseracing* **the D.** = grande course annuelle de chevaux à Epsom, en Grande-Bretagne

deregulate [ˌdiː'regjʊleɪt] VT **1** *Econ (prices, wages)* libérer, déréguler **2** *(relax restrictions on)* assouplir les règlements de, déréglementer

deregulation [ˌdiːregjʊ'leɪʃən] N **1** *Econ (of prices, wages)* libération *f*, dérégulation *f*; **d. of trade** libération *f* des échanges commerciaux **2** *(relaxation of restrictions)* assouplissement *m* des règlements, déréglementation *f*

derelict ['derəlɪkt] ADJ **1** *(abandoned)* abandonné, délaissé; **a d. old building** un vieux bâtiment à l'abandon **2** *Formal (negligent, neglectful)* négligent
N **1** *(vagrant)* clochard(e) *m,f*, vagabond(e) *m,f* **2** *Naut* navire *m* abandonné

dereliction [ˌderə'lɪkʃən] N **1** *(abandonment)* abandon *m* **2** *Br (negligence)* négligence *f*; **d. of duty** manquement *m* au devoir

derestricted [ˌdiːrɪ'strɪktɪd] ADJ *Br (road)* sans limitation de vitesse

derestriction [ˌdiːrɪ'strɪkʃən] N exemption *f*
►► *Br* ***derestriction sign*** fin *f* de limitation de vitesse

deride [dɪ'raɪd] VT tourner en ridicule, railler

> Note that the French verb **dérider** is a false friend and is never a translation for the English verb **to deride**.

derision [dɪ'rɪʒən] N dérision *f*

derisive [dɪ'raɪsɪv] ADJ moqueur

derisively [dɪ'raɪsɪvlɪ] ADV avec dérision; *(say, speak)* d'un ton moqueur

derisory [də'raɪzərɪ] ADJ **1** *(ridiculous)* dérisoire **2** *(mocking, scornful)* moqueur

derivation [ˌderɪ'veɪʃən] N dérivation *f*; **what is the d. of…?** quelle est l'origine de…?

derivative [dɪ'rɪvətɪv] ADJ **1** *(gen)* dérivé **2** *Pej (unoriginal)* peu original, banal; **his work is very d.** il n'a pas encore trouvé son style propre, il emprunte beaucoup aux autres; **I find his paintings rather d.** je trouve que ses peintures ne sont pas très originales
N *(gen)* dérivé *m*; *Math* dérivée *f*; *St Exch* produit *m* dérivé
►► *St Exch* ***derivative market, derivatives market*** marché *m* à terme des instruments financiers

derive [dɪ'raɪv] VT **1** *(gain, obtain* ► *origin, income, profit)* tirer (**from** de); *(*► *satisfaction)* trouver, tirer; *(*► *ideas)* trouver, puiser; **she derives great pleasure from her garden** elle tire beaucoup de plaisir de son jardin; **the young man derived little benefit from his expensive education** le jeune homme n'a guère tiré profit de ses études coûteuses; **to d. courage/strength from sth** trouver du courage/des forces dans qch **2** *(deduce)* dériver de
VI **to d. from** provenir de, venir de; **the word "coward" derives originally from French** le mot "coward" vient du français

dermatitis [ˌdɜːmə'taɪtɪs] N *(UNCOUNT) Med* dermite *f*, dermatite *f*

dermatologist [ˌdɜːmə'tɒlədʒɪst] N *Med* dermatologiste *mf*, dermatologue *mf*

dermatology [ˌdɜːmə'tɒlədʒɪ] N *Med* dermatologie *f*

derogate ['derəgeɪt] VT *Formal (disparage)* dénigrer, déprécier
VI **to d. from sth** porter atteinte à qch; **the claims in no way d. from her reputation as an artist** ces affirmations n'ont en aucune manière altéré sa réputation d'artiste

derogation [ˌderə'geɪʃən] N *Formal* **1** *(of law, rule)* dérogation *f* (**of** à) **2 d. from a right** atteinte *f* portée à un droit

derogatory [dɪ'rɒgətrɪ] ADJ *(comment, remark)* désobligeant, critique; *(word)* péjoratif; **to be d. about sb/sth** critiquer qn/qch
►► *Law* ***derogatory clause*** clause *f* dérogatoire

derrick ['derɪk] N **1** *Tech (crane)* mât *m* de charge **2** *Petr* derrick *m*, tour *f* de forage

derring-do [ˌderɪŋ'duː] N *Literary or Hum* bravoure *f*; **deeds of d.** prouesses *fpl*

derv [dɜːv] N *Br* gas-oil *m*

dervish ['dɜːvɪʃ] N *Rel* derviche *m*; **a whirling d.** un derviche tourneur

DES [ˌdiːiː'es] *Com (written abbr* **delivered ex-ship***)* DES

desalinate [ˌdiː'sælɪneɪt] VT *Chem* dessaler

desalination [diːˌsælɪ'neɪʃən] N *Chem* dessalage *m*, dessalement *m*
►► *Chem* ***desalination plant*** usine *f* de dessalage *ou* de dessalement

desalinator [ˌdiː'sælɪneɪtə(r)] N *Chem* désalinisateur *m*

descale [ˌdiː'skeɪl] VT détartrer

descant ['deskænt] *Mus*
N déchant *m*
►► ***descant recorder*** flûte *f* à bec soprano

descend [dɪ'send] VI **1** *Formal (go, move down)* descendre
2 *(fall)* tomber, s'abattre; **a thick blanket of fog descended on the valley** une couche épaisse de brouillard tomba sur la vallée; *Fig* **an air of gloom descended on the whole house** un sentiment de tristesse envahit la maison
3 *(pass on by ancestry)* descendre; *(pass on by inheritance)* revenir; **dogs and wolves probably d. from a common ancestor** les chiens et les loups descendent probablement d'un ancêtre commun; **Lord Grey's title descended to his grandson** le titre de Lord Grey est revenu à son petit-fils
4 to d. on *(attack* ► *group of people)* s'abattre *ou* tomber sur; *(invade* ► *village, town)* faire une descente sur; **Henry's army descended on the French coast** l'armée de Henri s'abattit sur la côte française; *Hum* **my in-laws descended on us last weekend** ma belle-famille a débarqué chez nous le week-end dernier
5 *(sink, stoop)* s'abaisser, descendre; **I never thought she would d. to malicious gossip** je n'aurais jamais pensé qu'elle s'abaisserait à cancaner; **you don't want to d. to their level** tu ne vas quand même pas te rabaisser à leur niveau

descendant [dɪ'sendənt] N descendant(e) *m,f*

descender [dɪ'sendə(r)] N **1** *Typ (of character)* jambage *m* **2** *(in mountaineering)* descendeur *m*

descending [dɪ'sendɪŋ] ADJ descendant
►► ***descending order*** ordre *m* décroissant; **in d. order of importance** par ordre décroissant d'importance; *Comput* ***descending sort*** tri *m* en ordre décroissant

descent [dɪ'sent] N **1** *(move downward)* descente *f*; **the aircraft made a sudden d.** l'avion a fait une descente subite; **the stream makes a gentle d.** le lit du ruisseau est en pente douce
2 *Fig Literary (decline)* chute *f*; **a d. into hell** une descente aux enfers
3 *(origin)* origine *f*; **of Irish d.** d'origine irlandaise; **I've traced my d. back to a sixteenth-century noble family** j'ai retrouvé la trace de mes ascendants dans une famille noble du seizième siècle
4 *(succession, transmission)* transmission *f*
5 *(invasion)* descente *f*

descramble [ˌdiː'skræmbəl] VT *Tel, Electron & TV* décrypter; *Comput* désembrouiller

descrambler [ˌdiː'skræmblə(r)] N *Tel, Electron & TV* décodeur *m*

describe [dɪ'skraɪb] VT **1** *(recount, represent)* décrire; **how would you d. yourself?** comment vous décririez-vous?; **witnesses described the man as tall and dark-haired** des témoins ont décrit l'homme comme étant grand et brun; **she described her attacker to the police** elle a fait une description *ou* un portrait de son agresseur à la police; **the book describes how they escaped** le livre décrit la façon dont ils se sont évadés **2** *(characterize)* définir, qualifier; **the general described himself as a simple man** le général s'est défini comme un homme simple; **our relations with them could best be described as strained** nos relations avec eux pourraient être qualifiées de *ou* sont pour le moins tendues **3** *(outline, draw* ► *circle, line)* décrire; *(*► *triangle)* tracer

description [dɪ'skrɪpʃən] N **1** *(account, representation)* description *f*; *(physical)* portrait *m*; *Admin (for police purposes, on passport)* signalement *m*; **the brochure gives a detailed d. of the hotel** la brochure donne une description détaillée de l'hôtel; **can you give us a d. of the man?** pouvez-vous nous faire un portrait de l'homme?; **a man answering the police d.** un homme correspondant au signalement donné par la police; **to be beyond** *or* **past d.** être indescriptible **2** *(kind)* sorte *f*, genre *m*; **the police seized weapons of every d.** la police a saisi toutes sortes d'armes; **we were unable to find a vehicle of any d.** nous étions incapables de trouver un quelconque véhicule

descriptive [dɪ'skrɪptɪv] ADJ descriptif
►► ***descriptive geometry*** géométrie *f* descriptive; ***descriptive linguistics*** linguistique *f* descriptive

descriptor [dɪ'skrɪptə(r)] N *Comput* descripteur *m*

descry [dɪ'skraɪ] (*pt & pp* **descried**) VT *Literary* apercevoir, distinguer

desecrate ['desɪkreɪt] VT profaner, souiller

desecration [ˌdesɪ'kreɪʃən] N profanation *f*

desegregate [ˌdiː'segrɪgeɪt] VT abolir la ségrégation raciale dans; **desegregated schools** = écoles qui ne sont plus soumises à la ségrégation raciale

desegregation [ˌdiːsegrɪ'geɪʃən] N déségrégation *f*

deselect [ˌdiːsɪ'lekt] VT **1** *Br Pol (candidate)* ne pas resélectionner **2** *Comput* désactiver

deselection [ˌdiːsɪ'lekʃən] N *Br Pol (of candidate)* = fait de ne pas resélectionner

desensitize, -ise [ˌdiː'sensɪtaɪz] VT désensibiliser

desert[1] ['dezət] N *(wilderness)* désert *m*
COMP *(area, plant, sand)* désertique
►► ***desert boots*** = chaussures en daim à lacets; ***desert island*** île *f* déserte; ***desert rat*** *Zool* gerboise *f*; *Br Mil* = soldat britannique combattant en Afrique du Nord (pendant la Seconde Guerre mondiale)

desert[2] [dɪ'zɜːt] VT *(person)* abandonner, délaisser; *(place)* abandonner, déserter; *(organization, principle)* déserter; **the soldier deserted his post** le soldat déserta son poste; *Fig* **his wits deserted him** il a perdu son sang-froid
VI *Mil* déserter; **to d. from the army** déserter l'armée; **one of the officers deserted to the enemy** un des officiers est passé à l'ennemi

deserted [dɪ'zɜːtɪd] ADJ désert; **the streets were d.** les rues étaient désertes

deserter [dɪ'zɜːtə(r)] N *Mil* déserteur *m*; **to be shot as a d.** être fusillé pour désertion

desertification [dɪˌzɜːtɪfɪˈkeɪʃən] N *Ecol* désertification *f*

desertion [dɪˈzɜːʃən] N *Mil* désertion *f*, *Law (of spouse)* abandon *m* (du domicile conjugal); *(of cause, organization)* défection *f*, désertion *f*

deserts [dɪˈzɜːts] NPL *(reward)* **to get one's just d.** avoir ce que l'on mérite

deserve [dɪˈzɜːv] VT mériter; **he deserved to win** *(and did)* il méritait de gagner; *(but did not)* il aurait mérité de gagner; **he deserves to die** il mérite la mort; **the idea deserves serious consideration** cette idée mérite qu'on y réfléchisse sérieusement; **she's taking a much deserved holiday** elle prend des vacances bien méritées; **I think he got what he deserved** je pense qu'il a eu ce qu'il méritait; **frankly, they d. each other** franchement ils se valent l'un l'autre *ou* ils sont dignes l'un de l'autre

VI mériter; *Formal* **to d. well of sth** bien mériter de qch

deservedly [dɪˈzɜːvɪdlɪ] ADV à juste titre, à bon droit; **Mozart has been described as a genius, and d. so** on a décrit Mozart comme un génie, à juste titre

deserving [dɪˈzɜːvɪŋ] ADJ *(person)* méritant; *(cause, organization)* méritoire; *Br Old-fashioned Hum* **the d. poor** les pauvres méritants *mpl*; *Formal* **a musician d. of greater recognition** un musicien qui mérite d'être davantage reconnu du public

desiccate [ˈdesɪkeɪt] VT dessécher, sécher

desiderata [dɪˌzɪdəˈrɑːtə] NPL *Literary* desiderata *mpl*

design [dɪˈzaɪn] N **1** *(drawing, sketch)* dessin *m*; *Ind* dessin *m*, plan *m*; *Archit* plan *m*, projet *m*; *Tex* modèle *m*; *(of book, magazine)* maquette *f*; **the d. for the new museum has been severely criticized** les projets *ou* plans du nouveau musée ont été sévèrement critiqués

2 *Ind (composition, structure ▸ of car, computer etc)* conception *f*; **the problems were all due to poor d.** tous les problèmes viennent de ce que la conception est mauvaise

3 *(subject for study)* design *m*; **book d.** conception *f* graphique; **fashion d.** stylisme *m*; **industrial d.** design *m*

4 *(pattern ▸ on sweater, carpet, wallpaper etc)* motif *m*; **a geometric d.** un motif géométrique

5 *(purpose, intent)* dessein *m*; **to do sth by d.** faire qch à dessein *ou* exprès; **to have designs on sb/sth** avoir des vues sur qn/qch

COMP *(course)* de dessin

VT *(plan)* concevoir; *(on paper)* dessiner; *Archit* faire les plans de; *(clothes)* concevoir, créer; *(syllabus)* concevoir, mettre au point; **the system is designed to favour the landowners** le système est conçu pour *ou* vise à favoriser les propriétaires terriens; **it's specially designed for very low temperatures** c'est spécialement conçu pour les très basses températures; **she designs jewellery** elle dessine des bijoux

▸▸ ***design award*** prix *m* du meilleur design; ***design department*** bureau *m* d'études; ***design engineer*** ingénieur *m* d'études; ***design fault*** défaut *m* de conception; ***design stage*** phase *f* de conception; ***design studio*** cabinet *m* de design; ***design team*** équipe *f* des concepteurs

designate *Formal* VT [ˈdezɪgneɪt] **1** *(appoint, name)* désigner, nommer; **to d. sb as one's successor** désigner qn comme son successeur; **the town is a designated special development area** la ville a été désignée *ou* classée zone de développement; **this area has been designated a no-smoking zone** cette zone est destinée aux non-fumeurs; **the school was designated as a civil defence training centre** l'école fut choisie comme centre de défense civile **2** *(indicate, signify)* indiquer, montrer; **the flags on the map d. enemy positions** les drapeaux sur la carte indiquent *ou* signalent les positions ennemies

ADJ [ˈdezɪgnət] désigné; **the Prime Minister d.** le Premier ministre désigné

▸▸ ***designated driver*** = personne qui s'engage à ne pas boire pour pouvoir reconduire d'autres personnes en voiture

designation [ˌdezɪgˈneɪʃən] N **1** *(name)* désignation *f* **2** *Comput (of website)* nommage *m*

▸▸ *Com & Law* ***designation of origin*** appellation *f* d'origine

designedly [dɪˈzaɪnɪdlɪ] ADV à dessein

designer [dɪˈzaɪnə(r)] N *Art & Ind* dessinateur (trice) *m,f*; *Tex* modéliste *mf*, styliste *mf*; *Cin & Theat* décorateur(trice) *m,f*; *(of haute couture)* couturier(ère) *m,f*; *(of books, magazines)* maquettiste *mf*; *(of furniture)* designer *m*; **she's a jewellery d.** elle est dessinatrice en bijouterie

COMP *(jeans)* haute couture; *(glasses, handbag)* de marque; *(furniture)* design

▸▸ ***designer baby*** bébé *m* à la carte; *(selected to help a sick sibling)* bébé-médicament *m*; ***designer drug*** = drogue de synthèse conçue spécialement pour contourner la loi sur les stupéfiants; ***designer label*** griffe *f* de grande marque; *Hum* ***designer stubble*** barbe *f* de deux jours *(faisant partie d'un look étudié, faussement négligé)*

designing [dɪˈzaɪnɪŋ] ADJ *(cunning)* rusé; *(scheming)* intrigant

N *(design work)* conception *f*, dessin *m*, design *m*

desirability [dɪˌzaɪərəˈbɪlətɪ] N *(UNCOUNT)* **1** *(benefits)* intérêt *m*, avantage *m*, opportunité *f*; **no one questions the d. of lowering interest rates** personne ne conteste les avantages d'une baisse des taux d'intérêts **2** *(attractiveness)* charmes *mpl*, attraits *mpl*

desirable [dɪˈzaɪərəbəl] ADJ **1** *(advisable)* souhaitable, *Formal* désirable; **some knowledge of languages is d.** connaissances en langues étrangères souhaitées **2** *(attractive)* à désirer, tentant; **a d. residence** une belle propriété **3** *(sexually appealing)* désirable, séduisant

desire [dɪˈzaɪə(r)] N **1** *(wish)* désir *m*, envie *f*; **she had no d. to go back** elle n'avait aucune envie d'y retourner; **my one d. is that you should be happy** mon seul désir *ou* tout ce que je souhaite, c'est que vous soyez heureux; **it is your father's d. that you should become an officer** c'est le désir de votre père que vous deveniez officier **2** *(sexual)* désir *m*; **to feel d. for sb** désirer *ou* avoir envie de qn

VT **1** *(want, wish)* désirer; **if you so d.** si vous le désirez; *Formal* **your presence is desired at the palace** votre présence est requise au palais; *Formal* **the Prince desires that you should be his guest tonight** le Prince désire que vous soyez son invité ce soir; **it was clear that she desired him to leave** il était clair qu'elle voulait qu'il parte; **it leaves much** *or* **a lot to be desired** cela laisse beaucoup à désirer; **it leaves nothing to be desired** cela ne laisse rien à redire; **his words had the desired effect** ses paroles eurent l'effet désiré *ou* escompté **2** *(want sexually)* désirer; **she no longer desired him** elle ne le désirait plus, elle n'avait plus envie de lui

desirous [dɪˈzaɪərəs] ADJ *Formal* désireux; **he was d. of re-establishing friendly relations** il était désireux de rétablir des relations amicales

desist [dɪˈzɪst] VI *Formal* cesser; **he was asked to d. from his political activities** on lui a demandé de cesser ses activités politiques

desk [desk] N **1** *(in home, office)* bureau *m*; *(with folding top)* secrétaire *m*; *(for pupil)* pupitre *m*; *(for teacher)* bureau *m* **2** *(reception counter)* réception *f*; *(cashier)* caisse *f*; **please leave your keys at the d.** *(in hotel)* prière de laisser les clefs à la réception **3** *Press (section)* service *m*; **the sports d.** le service des informations sportives; *Br* **Latin America d.** direction *f* des affaires latino-américaines

COMP *(diary, job, lamp)* de bureau

▸▸ ***desk accessory*** accessoire *m* de bureau; *Br* ***desk blotter*** sous-main *m inv*; *Am* ***desk clerk*** réceptionniste *mf*; *Journ* ***desk editor*** rédacteur (trice) *m,f*; ***desk research*** recherche *f* documentaire; ***desk tidy*** accessoire *m* de rangement pour bureau

deskill [ˌdiːˈskɪl] VT *Ind (workforce)* déqualifier; *(process, job)* automatiser

deskman [ˈdeskmæn] *(pl* **deskmen** [-men]) N *Journ* deskman *m*

desktop [ˈdesktɒp] N *Comput* **1** *(screen area)* bureau *m*; **you will find the icon on your d.** l'icône se trouve sur le bureau **2** *(computer)* **d. (computer)** ordinateur *m* de bureau *ou* de table

ADJ *(computer, model)* de bureau, de table

▸▸ ***desktop calculator*** calculatrice *f*; *Comput* ***desktop publishing*** publication *f* assistée par ordinateur, microédition *f*; *Comput* ***desktop publishing operator*** opérateur(trice) *m,f* de publication assistée par ordinateur; *Comput* ***desktop publishing package*** logiciel *m* de mise en page

desolate ADJ [ˈdesələt] **1** *(area, place ▸ empty)* désert; *(▸ barren, lifeless)* désolé; *Fig (gloomy, bleak)* morne, sombre **2** *(person ▸ sorrowful)* consterné, abattu; *(▸ friendless)* délaissé

VT [ˈdesəleɪt] **1** *(area, place ▸ devastate)* dévaster, saccager; *(▸ depopulate)* dépeupler **2** *(person)* désoler, navrer; **he was desolated at** *or* **by the loss of his job** il était désolé *ou* navré d'avoir perdu son emploi

desolately [ˈdesələtlɪ] ADV *(say)* d'un ton désolé; *(look at)* d'un air désolé

desolation [ˌdesəˈleɪʃən] N **1** *(barrenness, emptiness)* caractère *m* désert, désolation *f*; *(devastation, ruin)* dévastation *f*, ravages *mpl* **2** *(despair, sorrow)* désolation *f*, consternation *f*; *(loneliness)* solitude *f*

despair [dɪˈspeə(r)] N **1** *(hopelessness)* désespoir *m*; **to be in d.** être au désespoir; **to be in d. over** *or* **about sth** être désespéré par qch; **..., she said in d.** ..., dit-elle, désespérée; **in d., she took her own life** de désespoir elle a mis fin à ses jours; **his d. at ever finding a job made him turn to crime** parce qu'il désespérait de trouver un emploi, il est tombé dans la délinquance; **to drive sb to d.** réduire qn au désespoir, désespérer qn **2** *(cause of distress)* désespoir *m*; **William was the d. of his teachers** William faisait *ou* était le désespoir de tous ses professeurs

VI désespérer; **she began to d. of ever finding her brother alive** elle commençait à désespérer de retrouver un jour son frère vivant; **don't d., help is on the way** ne désespérez pas, les secours arrivent; **I d. of you** tu me désespères; *Formal* **they d. of his life** ils craignent pour sa vie

despairing [dɪˈspeərɪŋ] ADJ *(cry, look)* de désespoir, désespéré; *(person)* abattu, consterné

despairingly [dɪˈspeərɪŋlɪ] ADV *(look, speak)* avec désespoir

despatch = **dispatch**

desperado [ˌdespəˈrɑːdəʊ] *(pl* **desperadoes** *or* **desperados**) N *Literary or Hum* desperado *m*, hors-la-loi *m inv*

desperate [ˈdesprət] ADJ **1** *(hopeless, serious)* désespéré; **the refugees are in d. need of help** les réfugiés ont désespérément besoin d'assistance **2** *(reckless)* désespéré; **he died in a d. attempt to escape** il est mort en essayant désespérément de s'évader; **we heard d. screams** nous avons entendu des cris désespérés *ou* de désespoir; **I'm afraid she'll do something d.** j'ai bien peur qu'elle ne tente un acte désespéré; **a d. criminal/man** un criminel/homme prêt à tout **3** *(intent, eager)* **to be d. for money** avoir un besoin urgent d'argent; **she was d. to leave home** elle voulait à tout prix partir de chez elle; *Fam Hum* **I'm d. to go to the loo** je ne tiens plus, ça urge

desperately [ˈdesprətlɪ] ADV **1** *(hopelessly, seriously)* désespérément; **their country is d. poor** leur pays est d'une pauvreté désespérante; **he was d. ill with malaria** il était gravement atteint par le paludisme; **they're d. in love** ils s'aiment éperdument **2** *(recklessly)* désespérément **3** *(as intensifier)* terriblement; **he d. wanted to become an actor** il voulait à tout prix devenir acteur; **we're d. busy at the moment** nous sommes terriblement occupés en ce moment; **he's d. sorry** il est affreusement désolé; **do you want to go? – not d.** tu veux y aller? – pas vraiment

desperation [ˌdespəˈreɪʃən] N désespoir *m*; **an act of d.** un acte de désespoir; **he agreed in d.** en désespoir de cause, il a accepté

despicable [dɪˈspɪkəbəl] ADJ *(person)* méprisable, détestable; *(action, behaviour)* méprisable, ignoble; **it was a d. thing to do** c'était un acte indigne

despicably [dɪˈspɪkəblɪ] ADV *(behave)* bassement, d'une façon indigne

espise [dɪ'spaɪz] **VT** *(feel contempt for)* mépri-er; **he despised himself for his cowardice** il se mé-risait d'avoir été lâche; **these things are not to e despised** cela n'est pas à dédaigner

espite [dɪ'spaɪt] **PREP** malgré, en dépit de; **d. the act that...** malgré le fait que...; **d. what she says** uoi qu'elle dise; **d. leaving early, I still missed the rain** bien que je sois parti de bonne heure, j'ai nanqué mon train; **he laughed d. himself** il n'a as pu s'empêcher de rire

espoil [dɪ'spɔɪl] **VT** *Formal or Literary (person)* polier, dépouiller; *(land, town)* piller

espondence [dɪ'spɒndəns], **despondency** dɪ'spɒndənsɪ] **N** découragement *m*, abattement *n*

espondent [dɪ'spɒndənt] **ADJ** découragé, battu; **to become d.** se laisser abattre

espondently [dɪ'spɒndəntlɪ] **ADV** d'un air dé-ouragé *ou* abattu; *(say, speak)* d'un ton décou-agé *ou* abattu; **he wrote d. of his failure to find work** il écrivit une lettre découragée où il disait u'il ne trouvait pas de travail

espot ['despɒt] **N** *also Fig* despote *m*

espotic [de'spɒtɪk] **ADJ** *also Fig* despotique

espotically [de'spɒtɪkəlɪ] **ADV** *also Fig* despoti-uement; **to govern/to rule d.** gouverner/régner n despote

espotism ['despətɪzəm] **N** despotisme *m*

es res [ˌdez'rez] **N** *Br Fam (abbr* **desirable resi-ence)** *(flat)* bel appartement[□] *m*; *(house)* belle naison[□] *f*

essert [dɪ'zɜːt] **N** dessert *m*; **what's for d.?** u'est-ce qu'il y a comme dessert?; **we had ice ream for d.** nous avons eu de la glace en dessert

COMP *(knife, dish, plate)* à dessert

▸ ***dessert apple*** pomme *f* à couteau; ***dessert nenu*** carte *f* des desserts; ***dessert trolley*** chariot *n* de desserts; ***dessert wine*** vin *m* doux

essertspoon [dɪ'zɜːtspuːn] **N** cuiller *f ou* uillère *f* à dessert

estabilization, -isation [diːˌsteɪbɪlaɪ'zeɪʃən] **N** léstabilisation *f*

estabilize, -ise [ˌdiː'steɪbɪlaɪz] **VT** déstabiliser

estabilizing, -ising [ˌdiː'steɪbɪlaɪzɪŋ] **ADJ** *(for ountry, regime)* déstabilisant

▸▸ ***destabilizing factor*** facteur *m* de déséquilibre

estination [ˌdestɪ'neɪʃən] **N** destination *f*; **to each one's d.** arriver à sa destination

COMP *(bar, restaurant)* qui attire une clientèle vertie

▸▸ *Comput* ***destination disk*** *(hard disk)* disque *m*; *floppy disk)* disquette *f* cible; *Comput* ***destination drive*** lecteur *m* de destination; *Mktg* ***destination purchase*** achat *m* prévu

estine ['destɪn] **VT** destiner (**for** à; **to do** de faire)

estined ['destɪnd] **ADJ 1** *(intended)* **she felt she was d. for an acting career** elle sentait qu'elle était destinée à une carrière d'actrice; **she was d. for greater things** elle était promise à un plus grand avenir; **their plan was d. to fail** *or* **for failure** leur projet était voué à l'échec; **she was d. never to have children** le destin a voulu qu'elle n'ait jamais d'enfant; **he was d. never to see her again** il ne de-vait plus la revoir **2** *(bound)* **the flight was d. for Sydney** le vol était à destination de Sydney

estiny ['destɪnɪ] **N** *(fate)* destin *m*; *(personal fate)* destinée *f*, destin *m*; **she felt it was her d. to become a writer** elle avait le sentiment que c'était son destin de devenir écrivain

estitute ['destɪtjuːt] **ADJ 1** *(extremely poor)* dans a misère, sans ressources; **to be utterly d.** être dans la misère **2** *Formal (lacking)* dépourvu, dé-nué (**of** de)

NPL the d. les indigents *mpl ou* démunis *mpl*

estitution [ˌdestrɪ'tjuːʃən] **N** misère *f*, indigence *f*

estock [ˌdiː'stɒk] **VT** *Com (goods)* déstocker

estocking [ˌdiː'stɒkɪŋ] **N** *Com (of goods)* dés-tockage *m*

estress [ˌdiː'stres] **VT to d. oneself/one's life** se déstresser

VI déstresser; **a massage is a good way to d.** les massages sont un bon moyen de déstresser

destressing [ˌdiː'stresɪŋ] **ADJ** *(treatment, experience)* déstressant

destroy [dɪ'strɔɪ] **VT 1** *(demolish, wreck)* détruire; **an explosion has completely destroyed the railway station** une explosion a dévasté *ou* complètement détruit la gare; **they threaten to d. our democratic way of life** ils menacent d'anéantir *ou* de détruire nos institutions démocratiques **2** *(ruin, spoil* ▸ *efforts)* réduire à néant; *(*▸ *hope, love)* détruire; *(*▸ *career, friendship, marriage)* briser; *(*▸ *health)* ruiner, détruire; **to d. sb's life** briser la vie de qn **3** *(kill* ▸ *farm animal)* abattre; *(*▸ *pet)* supprimer, (faire) piquer

destroyer [dɪ'strɔɪə(r)] **N 1** *Mil* destroyer *m*, contre-torpilleur *m* **2** *(person)* destructeur(trice) *m,f*

▸▸ *Mil* ***destroyer escort*** escorteur *m*

destruct [dɪ'strʌkt] **VT** détruire

VI s'auto-détruire

N destruction *f*

COMP *(button, mechanism)* de destruction

destructible [dɪ'strʌktəbəl] **ADJ** destructible

destruction [dɪ'strʌkʃən] **N 1** *(demolition, devastation)* destruction *f*; **the earthquake brought about the d. of whole villages** le tremblement de terre a entraîné la disparition de villages entiers; **a nuclear war would result in total d.** une guerre nucléaire mènerait à une destruction totale; **the d. caused by the fire/storm** les ravages du feu/de la tempête **2** *(elimination* ▸ *of evidence)* suppression *f*; *(*▸ *of life, hope)* anéantissement *m* **3** *Fig (ruin)* ruine *f*; **drink and drugs proved to be his d.** l'alcool et la drogue l'ont détruit *ou* mené à sa perte

destructive [dɪ'strʌktɪv] **ADJ** destructeur; **she's a d. child** c'est une enfant qui aime casser; **d. criticism** critique *f* négative

destructively [dɪ'strʌktɪvlɪ] **ADV** de façon destructrice

destructiveness [dɪ'strʌktɪvnɪs] **N** *(of bomb, weapon)* capacité *f* destructrice; *(of criticism)* caractère *m* destructeur; *(of person)* penchant *m* destructeur

desuetude [dɪ'sjuːɪtjuːd] **N** *Literary* désuétude *f*

desultorily ['desəltrɪlɪ] **ADV** *(converse)* d'une manière décousue; *(wander, stroll)* sans but; *(recite, perform)* sans conviction

desultory ['desəltrɪ] **ADJ** *Formal (conversation)* décousu, sans suite; *(attempt)* peu suivi, peu soutenu, sans suite; **he made only a d. attempt to learn Italian** il a essayé d'apprendre l'italien, mais sans conviction

detach [dɪ'tætʃ] **VT 1** *(handle, hood)* détacher; *(trailer)* décrocher; *(stamp etc)* décoller; **to d. sth from sth** détacher *ou* séparer qch de qch **2** *(person)* **she managed to d. herself from the rest of the group** elle a réussi à s'éloigner du reste du groupe; **he can't d. himself sufficiently from the conflict** il n'a pas assez de recul par rapport au conflit **3** *Mil (troops)* détacher

detachable [dɪ'tætʃəbəl] **ADJ** *(gen)* détachable; *(collar, lining, strap, handle, lens)* amovible

detached [dɪ'tætʃt] **ADJ 1** *(separate)* détaché, séparé; **to become d.** *(stamp, retina)* se décoller; *(price tag, carriage)* se détacher; *(trailer)* se décrocher **2** *(objective)* objectif; *(unemotional)* détaché

▸▸ *Br* ***detached house*** maison *f* individuelle, pavillon *m*; *Med* ***detached retina*** rétine *f* décollée

detachment [dɪ'tætʃmənt] **N 1** *(separation)* séparation *f* **2** *(indifference)* détachement *m*; *(objectivity)* objectivité *f*; **with an air of d.** avec un air distancié *ou* détaché **3** *Mil* détachement *m*

detail [*Br* 'diːteɪl, *Am* dɪ'teɪl] **N 1** *(item, element)* détail *m*; **there's no need to go into d.** *or* **details** ça ne sert à rien d'entrer dans les détails; **down to the last d.** jusqu'au moindre détail; **the author recounts his childhood in great d.** l'auteur raconte son enfance dans les moindres détails; **attention to d. is important** il faut être minutieux *ou* méticuleux; **that's just a minor d.** ça n'a pas d'importance; **the d. of the carving** le détail *ou* les détails de la sculpture **2** *Mil (group of soldiers)* détachement *m*

VT 1 *(enumerate, specify)* raconter en détail, détailler, énumérer; **operating instructions are fully detailed in the booklet** le mode d'emploi détaillé se trouve dans le livret **2** *Mil* détacher, affecter

• **details NPL** *(particulars)* renseignements *mpl*, précisions *fpl*; *(name, address etc)* coordonnées *fpl*; **for further details please contact...** pour plus de renseignements, veuillez contacter...; **I can't give you any details** je ne peux vous donner aucune précision; **let me take down your details** laissez-moi vos coordonnées; **I'll send you the details of the property** je vous enverrai les informations *ou* renseignements concernant la propriété

▸▸ *Constr* ***detail drawing*** épure *f*; *Cin & TV* ***detail shot*** plan *m* de détail

detailed [*Br* 'diːteɪld, *Am* dɪ'teɪld] **ADJ** détaillé; **a d. account** un compte rendu détaillé *ou* très précis

detailing ['diːteɪlɪŋ] **N** *Am (thorough cleaning)* nettoyage *m* complet

detain [dɪ'teɪn] **VT 1** *Formal (delay)* retenir; *(in hospital)* garder; *Sch (pupil)* consigner; **I won't d. you any longer than is necessary** je ne vous retiendrai pas plus longtemps que nécessaire *ou* qu'il n'est nécessaire; **I'm afraid I've been detained** *(when cancelling appointment)* je suis désolé, je suis retenu; **this question need not d. us** cette question ne nous retiendra pas **2** *Law (keep in custody)* détenir, garder à vue; **to d. sb for questioning** mettre *ou* placer qn en garde à vue

detainee [ˌdiːteɪ'niː] **N** *Law* détenu(e) *m,f*

detangle [ˌdiː'tæŋgəl] **VT** *(hair)* démêler

detangler [ˌdiː'tæŋglə(r)] **N** *(for hair)* démêlant *m*

detect [dɪ'tekt] **VT** *(change, emotion, trace of substance)* déceler; *(error, pattern)* découvrir; *Mil & Mining* détecter; *Med (disease)* dépister; **do I d. a certain lack of enthusiasm on your part?** je crois déceler un certain manque d'enthousiasme de ta part; **the thieves managed to enter the building without being detected** les cambrioleurs ont pénétré dans le bâtiment sans éveiller l'attention *ou* sans qu'on s'en aperçoive; **she could barely d. his pulse** elle sentait à peine son pouls

detectable [dɪ'tektəbəl] **ADJ** *Mil & Mining* détectable; *Med (disease)* que l'on peut dépister; **the poison is not d. in the bloodstream** on ne peut pas déceler la présence du poison dans le sang

detection [dɪ'tekʃən] **N 1** *(discovery)* découverte *f*; *Mil & Mining* détection *f*; *Med (of disease)* dépistage *m*; **to escape d.** *(mistake)* passer inaperçu; **crime d.** la recherche des criminels

COMP *Mil & Mining (device)* de détection; *Med* de dépistage

detective [dɪ'tektɪv] **N** *(on a police force)* inspecteur(trice) *m,f* de police; *(private)* détective *m* (privé)

COMP *(film, novel)* policier

▸▸ ***detective agency*** agence *f* de détectives privés; *Br* ***detective chief inspector*** inspecteur (trice) *m,f* de police divisionnaire; *Br* ***detective constable*** inspecteur(trice) *m,f* de police; *Br* ***detective inspector*** inspecteur(trice) *m,f* de police principal(e); *Br* ***detective sergeant*** inspecteur (trice) *m,f* de police; ***detective series*** série *f* policière; ***detective story*** roman *m* policier, polar *m*

detector [dɪ'tektə(r)] **N** détecteur *m*

▸▸ *Br* ***detector van*** = voiture-radar utilisée pour la détection des postes de télévision non déclarés

détente [deɪ'tɒnt] **N** *Pol* détente *f*

detention [dɪ'tenʃən] **N 1** *(captivity)* détention *f*; **in d.** *(gen)* en détention; *Mil* aux arrêts **2** *Sch* retenue *f*, consigne *f*; **the entire class was given an hour's d.** toute la classe a eu une heure de retenue; **to put a pupil in d.** consigner un élève, mettre un élève en retenue

▸▸ *Br Law* ***detention centre*** = jusqu'en 1988, centre de détention pour jeunes délinquants (aujourd'hui appelé "young offenders' institution")

deter [dɪ'tɜː(r)] *(pt & pp* **deterred**, *cont* **deterring)** **VT 1** *(discourage* ▸ *person)* dissuader; **to d. sb from doing sth** dissuader qn de faire qch; **why should that d. you from going?** pourquoi est-ce que ça t'empêche d'y aller? **2** *(prevent* ▸ *attack)* prévenir

detergent [dɪˈtɜːdʒənt] N détergent *m*, détersif *m*; *Am (washing powder)* lessive *f*
ADJ détersif, détergent
►► ***detergent ball*** boule *f* doseuse

deteriorate [dɪˈtɪərɪəreɪt] VI *(weather, economy, building, health)* se détériorer; *(work, situation, relations)* se dégrader; **the situation has deteriorated even further** la situation a encore empiré *ou* s'est encore dégradée; **the patient's condition deteriorated overnight** l'état du malade s'est aggravé pendant la nuit

deterioration [dɪˌtɪərɪəˈreɪʃən] N *(in economy, building, health)* détérioration *f*; *(in work, situation, relations)* dégradation *f*, détérioration *f*; **there has been a d. in living standards** le niveau de vie a baissé; **despite the continuing d. of the situation** bien que la situation continue à empirer

determinant [dɪˈtɜːmɪnənt] *Math* N déterminant *m*
ADJ déterminant

determination [dɪˌtɜːmɪˈneɪʃən] N **1** *(resolve)* détermination *f*, résolution *f*; **an air of d.** un air résolu *ou* décidé **2** *(establishment, fixing ► of prices, wages etc)* détermination *f*, fixation *f*; *(► of boundaries)* délimitation *f*, établissement *m* **3** *Law (termination ► of contract etc)* résiliation *f*

determine [dɪˈtɜːmɪn] VT **1** *(control, govern)* déterminer, décider de; **this set will d. the outcome of the match** cette manche va déterminer le résultat du match
2 *(establish, find out)* déterminer, établir; **the police were unable to d. the cause of death** la police n'a pas pu déterminer *ou* établir la cause du décès
3 *(settle ► date, price)* déterminer, fixer; *(► boundary)* délimiter, établir
4 *(resolve)* **she determined to prove her innocence** elle a décidé de prouver son innocence
5 *Law (terminate ► contract, lease)* résilier

determined [dɪˈtɜːmɪnd] ADJ **1** *(decided, resolved)* déterminé, décidé; **to be d. to do sth** être déterminé *ou* résolu à faire qch; **she was d. (that) her son would go to university** elle était bien décidée *ou* déterminée à ce que son fils fasse des études supérieures; **he's a very d. young man** c'est un jeune homme très décidé *ou* qui a de la suite dans les idées **2** *(resolute)* **they made d. efforts to find all survivors** ils ont fait tout ce qu'ils ont pu pour retrouver tous les survivants

determiner [dɪˈtɜːmɪnə(r)] N *Gram* déterminant *m*

determining [dɪˈtɜːmɪnɪŋ] ADJ *(factor)* déterminant

deterrence [dɪˈterəns] N *(gen)* dissuasion *f*; *Mil* force *f* de dissuasion

deterrent [dɪˈterənt] N **1** *(gen)* agent *m* de dissuasion; **to act as** *or* **to be a d. (to)** exercer un effet dissuasif (contre) **2** *Mil* arme *f* de dissuasion
ADJ dissuasif, de dissuasion

detest [dɪˈtest] VT détester; **I d. housework** j'ai horreur de *ou* je déteste faire le ménage

detestable [dɪˈtestəbəl] ADJ détestable, exécrable

detestably [dɪˈtestəblɪ] ADV détestablement

detestation [ˌdiːteˈsteɪʃən] N haine *f*, horreur *f*

dethrone [dɪˈθrəʊn] VT détrôner, déposer

dethronement [dɪˈθrəʊnmənt] N déposition *f* *(d'un souverain)*

detonate [ˈdetəneɪt] VT faire détoner *ou* exploser
VI détoner, exploser

detonation [ˌdetəˈneɪʃən] N détonation *f*, explosion *f*

detonator [ˈdetəneɪtə(r)] N **1** *(for explosive)* détonateur *m*, amorce *f* **2** *Rail (fog signal)* pétard *m*

detour [ˈdiːtʊə(r)] N *(in road, stream)* détour *m*; *(for traffic)* déviation *f*; **to make a d.** faire un détour
VT (faire) dévier
VI faire un détour

detox [ˈdiːtɒks] *Fam* N désintoxication *f*
VI se désintoxiquer
►► ***detox centre*** centre *m* de désintoxication; ***detox programme*** cure *f* de désintoxication

detoxification [ˈdiːˌtɒksɪfɪˈkeɪʃən] N *(of person)* désintoxication *f*
►► ***detoxification centre*** centre *m* de désintoxication; ***detoxification programme*** cure *f* de désintoxication

detoxify [diːˈtɒksɪfaɪ] *(pt & pp* **detoxified***)* *Med* VT détoxifier
VI se détoxifier

detract [dɪˈtrækt] VI **to d. from** *(someone's pleasure, beauty of something)* diminuer, porter atteinte à; *(someone's worth, achievements)* déprécier; **the bad weather did not d. from our enjoyment of the holiday** le mauvais temps ne nous a pas empêchés d'apprécier nos vacances; **the criticism in no way detracts from her achievements** la critique ne réduit en rien la portée de *ou* n'enlève rien à ce qu'elle a accompli

detractor [dɪˈtræktə(r)] N détracteur(trice) *m,f*

detrain [ˌdiːˈtreɪn] *Formal* VT débarquer *(d'un train)*
VI descendre *(d'un train)*

detriment [ˈdetrɪmənt] N **to the d. of** au détriment de; **without d. to the truth** sans porter atteinte *ou* sans nuire à la vérité

detrimental [ˌdetrɪˈmentəl] ADJ nuisible; **to be d. to, to have a d. effect on** *(health, reputation)* être nuisible à, être préjudiciable à, nuire à; **pollution has a d. effect on** *or* **is d. to plant life** la pollution nuit à la flore; **it would be d. to my interests** cela desservirait mes intérêts

detritus [dɪˈtraɪtəs] N *(UNCOUNT)* *Formal (debris)* détritus *m*; *Geol* roches *fpl* détritiques, pierrailles *fpl*

Dettol® [ˈdetɒl] N = solution antiseptique

detune [ˌdiːˈtjuːn] VT *Rad & TV* dérégler

detuning [ˌdiːˈtjuːnɪŋ] N *Rad & TV* déréglage *m*

deuce [djuːs] N **1** *(on card, dice)* deux *m* **2** *Sport (in tennis)* égalité *f* **3** *Fam Old-fashioned (as expletive)* **where the d. is it?** où diable peut-il bien être?; **what the d.!** bon sang!

deuced [djuːst] *Fam Old-fashioned* ADJ sacré, satané, fichu
ADV diablement, bigrement

devaluation [ˈdiːˌvæljʊˈeɪʃən] N *Econ* dévaluation *f*

devalue [ˌdiːˈvæljuː] VT *Econ* dévaluer; *Fig (person, achievements, efforts)* dévaloriser; **the dollar has been devalued by three percent** le dollar a été dévalué de trois pour cent

devastate [ˈdevəsteɪt] VT **1** *(country, town)* dévaster, ravager; *(enemy)* anéantir **2** *(overwhelm)* foudroyer, accabler, anéantir; **he was devastated by his mother's death** la mort de sa mère l'a complètement anéanti

devastating [ˈdevəsteɪtɪŋ] ADJ **1** *(disastrous ► passion, storm)* dévastateur, ravageur; *(► news)* accablant; *(► argument, effect)* accablant, écrasant; **to deal a d. blow to sb/sth** porter un rude coup à qn/qch **2** *(highly effective ► person, charm)* irrésistible

devastatingly [ˈdevəsteɪtɪŋlɪ] ADV **1** *(disastrously)* de manière dévastatrice **2** *(as intensifier)* **d. beautiful** d'une beauté irrésistible; **d. funny** d'une drôlerie irrésistible

devastation [ˌdevəˈsteɪʃən] N *(disaster)* dévastation *f*; **scenes of utter d.** des scènes de dévastation

develop [dɪˈveləp] VI **1** *(evolve ► country, person)* se développer, évoluer; *(► feeling)* se former, grandir; *(► plot)* se développer, se dérouler; **to d. into sth** devenir qch; **let's see how things d.** attendons de voir comment les choses évoluent *ou* tournent **2** *(become apparent ► disease)* se manifester, se déclarer; *(► talent, trend)* se manifester; *(► event)* se produire **3** *Phot* se développer
VT **1** *(form ► body, mind)* développer, former; *(► story)* développer; *(► feeling)* former; **to d. one's muscles** développer ses muscles, se muscler
2 *(expand ► business, market)* développer; *(► idea, argument)* développer, expliquer (en détail), exposer (en détail)
3 *(improve ► skill)* développer, travailler; *(► machine, process)* mettre au point
4 *(acquire ► disease)* contracter; *(► cold, tic)* attraper; *(► symptoms)* présenter; **she developed a habit of biting her nails** elle a pris l'habitude de se ronger les ongles; **he has developed cancer** il es[t] atteint de cancer; **to d. a temperature** *or* **a feve[r]** (se mettre à) avoir *ou* faire de la température; **the machine has developed a fault** la machin[e] s'est mise à mal fonctionner
5 *(land, resources)* exploiter, mettre en valeu[r], aménager; **the site is to be developed** on va cons[truire] truire sur ce terrain, on va aménager le site
6 *Math, Mus & Phot* développer

developer [dɪˈveləpə(r)] N **1** *(of land)* promoteu[r] *m* (de construction) **2** *(person)* **to be a late d.** s[e] développer sur le tard **3** *Phot* révélateur *m*, dé[]veloppateur *m*

developing [dɪˈveləpɪŋ] ADJ *(crisis, storm)* qui s[e] prépare, qui s'annonce; *(industry)* en expan[sion]; **a d. interest in...** un intérêt grandissan[t] pour...
N *Phot* développement *m*; **d. and printing** *(sign)* travaux photographiques, développement et ti[]rage
►► *Phot* ***developing bath*** (bain *m*) révélateur *m*; *Econ* ***developing country, developing nation*** pay[s] *m ou* nation *f* en voie de développement; *Pho[t]* ***developing tank*** cuve *f* à développement

development [dɪˈveləpmənt] N **1** *(of body, person, mind)* développement *m*, formation *f*; *(o[f] ideas, language)* développement *m*, évolution *(of argument, theme)* développement *m*, expos[é] *m*; *(of plot, situation)* déroulement *m*, dévelop[]pement *m*; *(of business)* développement *m*, ex[]pansion *f*; *(of invention, process)* mise *f* au point *(of region)* mise *f* en valeur, exploitation *f*; **the[y] propose the d. of this land as a residential area i[ls]** suggèrent d'aménager ce terrain en zone rési[]dentielle
2 *(incident, event)* fait *m* nouveau; **we're awai[t]ing further developments** nous attendons la suit[e] des événements *ou* les derniers développe[]ments; **a surprise d.** un rebondissement; **ther[e] has been an unexpected d.** l'affaire a pris un[e] tournure inattendue; **there are no new develop[]ments** il n'y a rien de nouveau; **the latest develop[]ments in medical research** les dernière[s] découvertes médicales
3 *(tract of land)* **housing d.** cité *f* (ouvrière); **in[]dustrial d.** zone *f* industrielle
4 *Math, Mus & Phot* développement *m*
►► ***development aid*** = aide aux pays en voie d[e] développement; *Br* ***development area*** = zon[e] économiquement sinistrée bénéficiant d'aide[s] publiques en vue de sa reconversion; ***develop[]ment grant*** subvention *f* pour le développe[]ment; ***development loans*** crédits *mpl* d[e] développement; *Mktg* ***development stage*** *(o[f] product)* phase *f* de développement; ***develop[]ment studies*** études *fpl* du développement

deviant [ˈdiːvɪənt] ADJ **1** *(behaviour)* déviant, qu[i] s'écarte de la norme; *(growth)* anormal; **sexual[ly] d.** perverti **2** *Ling* déviant
N déviant(e) *m,f*; **sexual d.** pervers(e) *m,f*

deviate [ˈdiːvɪeɪt] VI **1** *(differ)* dévier, s'écarter; **those who d. from the norm** ceux qui s'écarten[t] de la norme **2** *(plane, ship)* dévier, dériver; *(mis[]sile)* dévier

deviation [ˌdiːvɪˈeɪʃən] N **1** *(from custom, princ[i]ple)* déviation *f*; *(from social norm)* déviance; **there must be no d. from the party line** on ne doi[t] en aucun cas s'écarter de la ligne du parti
2 *(in statistics)* écart *m*
3 *(of plane, ship)* déviation *f*, dérive *f*; *(of missile)* déviation *f*, dérivation *f*
4 *Math, Med & Phil* déviation *f*

deviationism [ˌdiːvɪˈeɪʃənɪzəm] N déviation[]nisme *m*

deviationist [ˌdiːvɪˈeɪʃənɪst] *Pol* N déviation[]niste *mf*
ADJ déviationniste

device [dɪˈvaɪs] N **1** *(gadget)* appareil *m*, engin *m*; *(mechanism)* mécanisme *m*, dispositif *m*; **a cleve[r] d.** un gadget astucieux; **safety d.** dispositif *m* d[e] sécurité; **nuclear d.** engin *m* nucléaire
2 *Comput* (unité *f*) périphérique *m*
3 *(scheme)* ruse *f*, stratagème *m*; **it was just a c[lever way] to get attention** ce n'était qu'une ruse pour o[btenir…] c'était juste un moyen de se faire remarquer; **t[o] leave sb to their own devices** *(alone)* laisser q[n]

s'occuper comme bon lui semble; *(without help)* laisser qn se débrouiller
4 *Literary (figure of speech)* formule *f*
5 *Her* emblème *m*
►► *Comput* **device driver** pilote *m* de périphérique; *Comput* **device manager** gestionnaire *m* de périphériques

devil ['devəl] (*Br pt & pp* **devilled,** *cont* **devilling,** *Am pt & pp* **deviled,** *cont* **deviling**) **N 1** *(demon)* diable *m,* démon *m*; *Rel* **the D.** le Diable, Satan *m*; *Fam Old-fashioned* **go to the d.!** va te faire voir!, va au diable!
2 *Fam Fig (person)* **you little d.!** petit monstre!; **you lucky d.!** veinard!; *Br* **poor d.!** pauvre diable!; *Br Hum* **go on, be a d.!** allez, laisse-toi faire *ou* tenter!
3 *Fam (as intensifier)* **what the d. are you doing?** mais enfin, qu'est-ce que tu fabriques?; **where the d. is it?** où diable peut-il bien être?, mais où est-ce que ça pourrait bien être?; **how the d. should I know?** comment voulez-vous que je sache?❑; **who the d. are you?** qui diable êtes-vous?, et d'où est-ce que vous sortez, vous?; **they worked/ran like the d.** ils ont travaillé/couru comme des fous *ou* des malades; **he has a d. of a temper** il a un fichu caractère, il a un caractère de cochon; **I had a d. of a time getting here** j'ai eu un mal fou *ou* un mal de chien à arriver jusqu'ici; **there'll be the d. to pay when your father finds out** ça va barder quand ton père apprendra ça; **we had the d. of a job** *or* **the d.'s own job finding the house** on a eu un mal fou à trouver la maison; **to be (caught) between the d. and the deep blue sea** être pris entre deux feux, être entre le marteau et l'enclume; **to give the d. his due...** en toute honnêteté, il faut dire que..., rendons *ou* rendons-lui justice...; **he has the luck of the d.** *or* **the d.'s own luck** il a une veine de pendu *ou* de cocu; **speak** *or* **talk of the d. (and he's sure to appear)!** quand on parle du loup (on en voit la queue)!; *Prov* **better the d. you know (than the d. you don't)** mieux vaut se contenter de ce qu'on a que de risquer de trouver pire; *Prov* **the d. finds** *or* **makes work for idle hands (to do)** l'oisiveté est (la) mère de tous les vices; *Prov* **(every man for himself and) let the d. take the hindmost** chacun pour soi et Dieu pour tous
4 *(ghostwriter)* nègre *m (d'un écrivain)*; *Br Law* avocat(e) *m,f* stagiaire; *Typ* **printer's d.** apprenti(e) *m,f* imprimeur
VT *Culin* = accommoder à la moutarde et au poivre; **devilled egg** œuf *m* à la diable
VI *Br* **to d. for sb** *(author)* servir de nègre à qn; *(lawyer)* être avocat stagiaire auprès de qn; *Typ (printer)* être apprenti imprimeur chez qn
►► **devil's advocate** avocat *m* du diable; **to play d.'s advocate** se faire l'avocat du diable; *Am* **devil's food cake** gâteau *m* au chocolat noir; *Culin* **devils on horseback** pruneaux *mpl* au bacon

devilfish ['devəlfɪʃ] (*pl* **inv** *or* **devilfishes**) **N** *Ich* mante *f*, diable *m* de mer

devilish ['devəlɪʃ] **ADJ 1** *(fiendish)* diabolique, infernal; *(mischievous)* espiègle **2** *Fam Old-fashioned (extreme)* sacré, satané
ADV *Fam Old-fashioned* sacrément, rudement

devilishly ['devəlɪʃlɪ] **ADV 1** *(fiendishly)* diaboliquement; *(mischievously)* par espièglerie **2** *Fam Old-fashioned (as intensifier)* rudement, sacrément

devil-may-care **ADJ** *(careless)* insouciant; *(reckless)* casse-cou

devilment ['devəlmənt] **N** *(mischief)* espièglerie *f*; *(malice)* méchanceté *f*, malice *f*; **a piece of d.** une espièglerie, une diablerie; **out of sheer d.** par pure méchanceté

devious ['diːvɪəs] **ADJ 1** *(cunning ► person)* retors, sournois; *(► means, method)* détourné; *(► mind)* tortueux; **she can be very d.** elle est parfois très retorse *ou* sournoise **2** *(winding ► route)* sinueux

deviously ['diːvɪəslɪ] **ADV** sournoisement

deviousness ['diːvɪəsnɪs] **N** *(of person)* sournoiserie *f*; *(of plan)* complexité *f*

devise [dɪ'vaɪz] **VT 1** *(plan)* imaginer, inventer, concevoir, élaborer; *(plot)* combiner, manigancer **2** *Law (property)* léguer
N legs *m* (de biens immobiliers)

devising [dɪ'vaɪzɪŋ] **N a scheme of his own d.** un plan de son invention

devitalize, -ise [ˌdiː'vaɪtəlaɪz] **VT** affaiblir

devoid [dɪ'vɔɪd] **ADJ d. of** dépourvu de, dénué de; **d. of interest** dépourvu d'intérêt, sans intérêt

devolution [ˌdiːvə'luːʃən] **N 1** *(of duty, power)* délégation *f*; *Law (of property)* transmission *f*, dévolution *f* **2** *Pol* décentralisation *f* **3** *Biol* dégénérescence *f*

> **DEVOLUTION**
>
> Le projet de décentralisation pour l'Écosse et le pays de Galles ("devolution"), soumis à référendum dans les années 70, fut abandonné par le parti conservateur, à la tête de la Grande-Bretagne de 1979 à 1997. Cependant, à la suite de la victoire des travaillistes en 1997, Tony Blair honora sa promesse électorale et organisa un nouveau référendum dans les deux régions. Les Écossais se déclarèrent en faveur de la décentralisation à une écrasante majorité. Le "oui" l'emporta également au pays de Galles mais de façon moins convaincante. Moins de deux ans plus tard, le 6 mai 1999, l'Écosse retrouvait un parlement après 300 ans d'interruption et les Gallois disposaient d'une assemblée pour la première fois en 500 ans (voir aussi encadrés sous **Scottish Parliament** et **Welsh Assembly**).

devolutive [ˌdiːvə'luːtɪv] **ADJ** dévolutif

devolve [dɪ'vɒlv] **VI 1** *(duty, job)* incomber; *(by chance)* incomber, échoir; **it devolves on** *or* **upon me to decide** c'est à moi (qu'il incombe) de décider; **the responsibility devolves on** *or* **upon him** la responsabilité lui incombe *ou* lui échoit **2** *Law (estate)* passer; **the property devolves on** *or* **upon the son** les biens passent *ou* sont transmis au fils
VT déléguer; **to d. sth on** *or* **upon** *or* **to sb** déléguer qch à qn, transmettre qch à qn
►► *Pol* **devolved parliament** parlement *m* régional

devote [dɪ'vəʊt] **VT** consacrer; **to d. oneself to** *(study, work)* se consacrer *ou* s'adonner à; *(a cause)* se vouer *ou* se consacrer à; *(pleasure)* se livrer à; **she devotes all her energies to writing** elle se consacre entièrement à l'écriture; **all funds are devoted entirely to research** tous les crédits sont entièrement consacrés *ou* affectés à la recherche

devoted [dɪ'vəʊtɪd] **ADJ** *(friend, servant, service)* dévoué, fidèle; *(husband, wife, mother, father)* dévoué; *(admirer)* fervent; **they are d. to each other** ils sont dévoués l'un à l'autre

devotedly [dɪ'vəʊtɪdlɪ] **ADV** avec dévouement

devotee [ˌdevə'tiː] **N** *(of opera, sport etc)* passionné(e) *m,f*; *(of doctrine)* adepte *mf*, partisan(e) *m,f*; *(of religion)* adepte *mf*; **a d. of Haydn** un fervent *ou* un grand amateur de Haydn

devotion [dɪ'vəʊʃən] **N 1** *(to person)* dévouement *m*, attachement *m*; *(to cause)* dévouement *m*; **no one doubts her d. to her work** personne ne met en doute *ou* ne doute de son dévouement professionnel; **he showed great d. to duty** il a prouvé son sens du devoir **2** *Rel* dévotion *f*, piété *f*
• **devotions** **NPL** *Rel* dévotions *fpl*, prières *fpl*

> When translating **devotion**, note that the French words **dévotion** and **dévouement** are not interchangeable. **Dévotion** usually refers to religious fervour and **dévouement** expresses the idea of dedication.

devotional [dɪ'vəʊʃənəl] *Rel* **ADJ** *(book, work)* de dévotion *ou* piété; *(attitude)* de prière, pieux
N service *m* (religieux)

devour [dɪ'vaʊə(r)] **VT 1** *(food)* dévorer, engloutir; *Fig (book)* dévorer; **he devoured her with his eyes** il l'a dévorée des yeux **2** *(of fire)* dévorer, consumer; *Fig* **devoured by hatred** dévoré par la haine

devouring [dɪ'vaʊərɪŋ] **ADJ** *(hunger, jealousy)* dévorant; *(interest)* ardent; *(need)* urgent

devout [dɪ'vaʊt] **ADJ 1** *(person)* pieux, dévot; *(hope, prayer)* fervent; **a d. Catholic/Muslim** un catholique/musulman fervent **2** *Formal (wish etc)* fervent, sincère

devoutly [dɪ'vaʊtlɪ] **ADV 1** *(pray)* avec dévotion, dévotement **2** *Formal (earnestly)* sincèrement

devoutness [dɪ'vaʊtnɪs] **N** dévotion *f*

dew [djuː] **N** rosée *f*
►► *Met* **dew point** point *m* de rosée

dewclaw ['djuːklɔː] **N** *Zool* ergot *m*

dewdrop ['djuːdrɒp] **N** goutte *f* de rosée

dewlap ['djuːlæp] **N** *also Hum* fanon *m*

dewy ['djuːɪ] (*compar* **dewier,** *superl* **dewiest**) **ADJ** couvert *ou* humide de rosée; *Fig* **d. complexion** teint *m* frais

dewy-eyed **ADJ** *(innocent)* innocent; *(trusting)* naïf, ingénu; **she looked at him d.** elle l'a regardé d'un air ingénu; **she gets all d. about her husband/France** elle est tout émue quand elle parle de son mari/la France

dexterity [dek'sterətɪ] **N** adresse *f*, dextérité *f*; **manual d.** habileté *f* manuelle

dexterous ['dekstrəs] **ADJ 1** *(person)* adroit, habile; *(movement)* adroit, habile, agile **2** *Formal (right-handed)* droitier

dexterously ['dekstrəslɪ] **ADV** adroitement, habilement

dextrin ['dekstrɪn] **N** *Chem* dextrine *f*

dextrose ['dekstrəʊs] **N** *Chem* dextrose *m*

dextrous = **dexterous**

dextrously = **dexterously**

DFC [ˌdiːef'siː] **N** *Mil* (*abbr* **Distinguished Flying Cross**) = distinction honorifique des armées de l'air américaine et britannique

DfES [ˌdiːefiː'es] **N** *Br Pol* (*abbr* **Department for Education and Skills**) ministère *m* de l'Éducation nationale

DfID [ˌdiːefaɪ'diː] **N** *Br Pol* (*abbr* **Department for International Development**) = secrétariat d'État à la Coopération

DFM [ˌdiːef'em] **N** *Mil* (*abbr* **Distinguished Flying Medal**) = médaille des armées de l'air américaine et britannique

DG [ˌdiː'dʒiː] **N** (*abbr* **director-general**) directeur (trice) *m,f* général(e)

dhoti ['dəʊtɪ] **N** pagne *m*

dhow [daʊ] **N** *Naut* = petit bateau arabe à une voile

DHS [ˌdiːeɪtʃ'es] **N** *Am* (*abbr* **Department of Homeland Security**) = ministère de la Sécurité intérieure, aux États-Unis

DHSS [ˌdiːeɪtʃˌes'es] **N** *Br Formerly Admin* (*abbr* **Department of Health and Social Security**) = ancien nom du ministère britannique de la Santé et de la Sécurité sociale

DI [ˌdiː'aɪ] **N** *Br* (*abbr* **Detective Inspector**) inspecteur(trice) *m,f* de police principal(e)

diabetes [ˌdaɪə'biːtiːz] **N** diabète *m*; **to have d.** avoir du diabète
►► **diabetes mellitus** diabète *m* pancréatique

diabetic [ˌdaɪə'betɪk] **N** diabétique *mf*
ADJ diabétique; **to be in a d. coma** faire un *ou* être en coma diabétique
COMP *(biscuits, jam)* pour diabétiques

diabolic [ˌdaɪə'bɒlɪk] **ADJ** *(action, plan)* diabolique, infernal; *(look, smile)* diabolique, satanique

diabolical [ˌdaɪə'bɒlɪkəl] **ADJ 1** *(fiendish ► action, plan)* diabolique, infernal; *(► look, smile)* diabolique, satanique **2** *Br Fam (terrible)* nul; **the food was d.** la nourriture était infecte; **I think it's a d. liberty** il faut un toupet monstre *ou* un sacré culot pour faire une chose pareille

diabolically [ˌdaɪə'bɒlɪklɪ] **ADV 1** *(fiendishly)* diaboliquement, de manière diabolique **2** *Br Fam (for emphasis)* vachement, sacrément

diacritic [ˌdaɪə'krɪtɪk] *Ling* **N** signe *m* diacritique
ADJ diacritique

diacritical [ˌdaɪə'krɪtɪkəl] **ADJ** *Ling* diacritique

diadem ['daɪədem] **N** diadème *m*

diaeresis, *Am* **dieresis** [daɪ'erɪsɪs] (*Br pl* **diaereses,** *Am* **diereses** [-'siːz]) **1** *Ling & Literature* diérèse *f* **2** *Comput & Typ* tréma *m*

diagnose [ˈdaɪəgnəʊz] VT **1** *Med (illness)* diagnostiquer; **they diagnosed her illness as cancer** ils ont diagnostiqué un cancer; **she has been diagnosed as a schizophrenic** d'après le diagnostic, elle est schizophrène **2** *Fig (fault, problem)* déceler, discerner

diagnosis [ˌdaɪəgˈnəʊsɪs] (*pl* **diagnoses** [-siːz]) N *Med & Fig* diagnostic *m*; *Biol & Bot* diagnose *f*; **to make** *or* **give a d.** faire un diagnostic

diagnostic [ˌdaɪəgˈnɒstɪk] ADJ diagnostique; **d. skill/ability** talent *m*/capacité *f* à diagnostiquer
▸▸ *Com* ***diagnostic audit*** audit *m* de diagnostic; *Comput* ***diagnostic disk*** disquette *f* de diagnostic; *Comput* ***diagnostic program*** programme *m* de diagnostic

diagnostician [ˌdaɪəgnɒsˈtɪʃən] N diagnostiqueur *m*; **she's an excellent d.** elle fait de très bons diagnostics

diagnostics [ˌdaɪəgˈnɒstɪks] N *(UNCOUNT) Comput & Med* diagnostic *m*

diagonal [daɪˈægənəl] N diagonale *f*
ADJ diagonal

diagonally [daɪˈægənəlɪ] ADV en diagonale, diagonalement, obliquement; **we cut d. across the field** nous avons traversé le champ en diagonale *ou* en biais; **his desk is d. across from mine** son bureau est en diagonale par rapport au mien; **a ribbon worn d. across the chest** un ruban porté en écharpe sur la poitrine; **their house is d. opposite ours** leur maison est en face de la nôtre, en diagonale

diagonal-ply tyre N pneu *m* à carcasse diagonale

diagram [ˈdaɪəgræm] (*Br pt & pp* **diagrammed**, *cont* **diagramming**, *Am pt & pp* **diagramed** *or* **diagrammed**, *cont* **diagraming** *or* **diagramming**) N *(gen)* diagramme *m*, schéma *m*; *Geom & Math* diagramme *m*, figure *f*; **to draw** *or* **to make a d. of sth** faire un schéma *ou* un dessin de qch
VT donner une représentation graphique de

diagrammatic [ˌdaɪəgrəˈmætɪk] ADJ schématique

dial [ˈdaɪəl] (*Br pt & pp* **dialled**, *cont* **dialling**, *Am pt & pp* **dialed**, *cont* **dialing**) N **1** *(of clock, telephone)* cadran *m*; *(of radio, TV)* bouton *m* (de réglage) **2** *Br Fam Old-fashioned (face)* tronche *f*
VT *(number)* faire, composer; **the number you have dialled has not been recognized** il n'y a pas d'abonné au numéro que vous avez demandé; **to d. Spain direct** appeler l'Espagne par l'automatique; **d. the operator** appelez l'opératrice; **to d.** *Br* **999** *or Am* **911** appeler Police Secours
▸▸ *Am* ***dial code*** indicatif *m*; *Am* ***dial tone*** tonalité *f*

dialect [ˈdaɪəlekt] N *Ling (regional)* dialecte *m*, parler *m*; *(local, rural)* patois *m*

dialectic [ˌdaɪəˈlektɪk] *Ling* N dialectique *f*
ADJ dialectique

dialectical [ˌdaɪəˈlektɪkəl] ADJ *Phil* dialectique

dialectics [ˌdaɪəˈlektɪks] N *(UNCOUNT) Phil* dialectique *f*

dialler [ˈdaɪələ(r)] N composeur *m* de numéros

dialling, *Am* **dialing** [ˈdaɪəlɪŋ] N composition *f* du numéro, numérotation *f*
▸▸ *Br* ***dialling code*** indicatif *m*; *Br* ***dialling tone*** tonalité *f*; **I can't get a d. tone** je n'arrive pas à avoir la tonalité

dialogue, *Am* **dialog** [ˈdaɪəlɒg] N dialogue *m*
▸▸ *Comput* ***dialogue box*** zone *f ou* boîte *f* de dialogue; *Cin & TV* ***dialogue coach*** répétiteur(trice) *m,f* de dialogues; *Comput* ***dialogue mode*** mode *m* dialogue; *Cin & TV* ***dialogue track*** bande *f* parole

dial-up N *Comput & Tel*
▸▸ ***dial-up access*** accès *m* commuté; *Br* ***dial-up account*** compte *m* d'accès par ligne commutée; ***dial-up line*** ligne *f* commutée; ***dial-up modem*** modem *m* réseau commuté; ***dial-up service*** service *m* de télétraitement

dialyse, *Am* **dialyze** [ˈdaɪəlaɪz] VT *Chem* dialyser

dialysis [daɪˈælɪsɪs] (*pl* **dialyses** [-siːz]) N *Chem & Med* dialyse *f*; **to be on d.** être sous dialyse
▸▸ ***dialysis machine*** dialyseur *m*

diamanté [dɪəˈmɒnteɪ] N tissu *m* diamanté

diameter [daɪˈæmɪtə(r)] N **1** *(gen) & Geom* diamètre *m*; **the tree is two metres in d.** l'arbre fait deux mètres de diamètre **2** *(of microscope)* unité *f* de grossissement

diametric [ˌdaɪəˈmetrɪk], **diametrical** [ˌdaɪəˈmetrɪkəl] ADJ *Geom & Fig* diamétral

diametrically [ˌdaɪəˈmetrɪklɪ] ADV *Geom & Fig* diamétralement; **d. opposed** diamétralement opposé

diamond [ˈdaɪəmənd] N **1** *(gem)* diamant *m*; *esp Am* **he's a d. in the rough** il a un cœur d'or sous ses dehors frustes
2 *(shape)* losange *m*
3 *Cards* carreau *m*; **the ace/jack of diamonds** l'as *m*/le valet de carreau
4 *Sport (in baseball)* terrain *m* (de base-ball)
COMP *(brooch, ring etc)* de diamant *ou* diamants
▸▸ ***diamond anniversary*** noces *fpl* de diamant; ***diamond drill*** foreuse *f* à pointe de diamant; ***diamond jubilee*** (célébration *f* du) soixantième anniversaire *m*; ***diamond merchant*** diamantaire *m*; ***diamond mine*** mine *f* de diamants; ***diamond necklace*** collier *m ou* rivière *f* de diamants; ***diamond wedding*** noces *fpl* de diamant

diamond-shaped ADJ en forme de losange

diapason [ˌdaɪəˈpeɪsən] N *Mus* diapason *m*; *(of organ)* principaux jeux *mpl* de fond

diaper [ˈdaɪəpə(r)] N *Am (nappy)* couche *f (de bébé)*

diaphanous [daɪˈæfənəs] ADJ diaphane

diaphragm [ˈdaɪəfræm] N **1** *Anat* diaphragme *m* **2** *Phot* diaphragme *m* **3** *(contraceptive)* diaphragme *m*

diarist [ˈdaɪərɪst] N *(private)* auteur *m* d'un journal intime; *(of public affairs)* chroniqueur *m*

diarize, -ise [ˈdaɪəraɪz] VT consigner dans son agenda

diarrhoea, *Am* **diarrhea** [ˌdaɪəˈrɪə] N diarrhée *f*; **to have d.** avoir la diarrhée

diary [ˈdaɪərɪ] (*pl* **diaries**) N **1** *(personal)* journal *m* (intime); **to keep a d.** tenir un journal **2** *Br (for business)* agenda *m*

Diaspora [daɪˈæspərə] N *Hist & Fig* diaspora *f*

diastole [daɪˈæstəlɪ] N *Physiol* diastole *f*

diatom [ˈdaɪətɒm] N *Bot & Geol* diatomée *f*

diatonic [ˌdaɪəˈtɒnɪk] ADJ *Mus* diatonique
▸▸ ***diatonic scale*** gamme *f* diatonique

diatribe [ˈdaɪətraɪb] N diatribe *f*

dibber [ˈdɪbə(r)] N *Br Hort* plantoir *m*

dibble [ˈdɪbəl] *Hort*
N plantoir *m*
VT *(plant)* repiquer au plantoir; *(seeds)* semer au plantoir
VI *(plant plants)* repiquer au plantoir; *(plant seeds)* semer au plantoir

dibs [dɪbz] NPL **1** *(jacks)* osselets *mpl* **2** *Fam (claim)* **to have d. on sth** avoir des droits sur qch[□]

dice [daɪs] (*pl* **inv**) N **1** *(game)* dé *m*; **to throw the d.** lancer le(s) dé(s); **to play d.** jouer aux dés; *Am Fam* **no d.!** des clous! **2** *Culin* dé *m*, cube *m*
VT *Culin* couper en dés *ou* en cubes
VI *Br* jouer aux dés; **to d. with death** jouer avec sa vie

dicey [ˈdaɪsɪ] *Br* (*compar* **dicier**, *superl* **diciest**) ADJ *Fam* risqué

dichotomous [daɪˈkɒtəməs] ADJ dichotomique
▸▸ *Mktg* ***dichotomous question*** *(in survey)* question *f* dichotomique

dichotomy [daɪˈkɒtəmɪ] (*pl* **dichotomies**) N dichotomie *f*

dick [dɪk] N **1** *Vulg (penis)* bite *f*, queue *f* **2** *Am Fam (detective)* privé *m* **3** *very Fam (idiot)* con *m*

dickens [ˈdɪkɪnz] N *Fam* **what the d. are you doing?** mais qu'est-ce que tu fabriques?; **a d. of a noise** un bruit d'enfer; **we had the** *or* **a d. of a job getting a babysitter** ça a été la galère *ou* la croix et la bannière pour trouver une babysitter

Dickensian [dɪˈkenzɪən] ADJ *(scene, Christmas etc)* à la Dickens; *(conditions)* qui sort d'un roman de Dickens

dicker [ˈdɪkə(r)] VI marchander; **to d. with sb (for sth)** marchander avec qn (pour obtenir qch)

dickey [ˈdɪkɪ] N **1** *(shirt)* faux plastron *m* (de chemise) **2** *Br (in carriage)* siège *m* du cocher; *Au* spider *m*, strapontin *m* **3** *Br Fam (bow tie)* nœud *m* pap
▸▸ *Br Fam* ***dickey bow*** nœud *m* pap

dickface [ˈdɪkfeɪs] N *very Fam* trou *m* du cul trouduc *m*

dickhead [ˈdɪkhed] N *very Fam* trou *m* du cul trouduc *m*

dickless [ˈdɪkləs] ADJ *very Fam (worthless)* minable, nul; *(lacking courage)* dégonflé, pétochard *m*

dicky [ˈdɪkɪ] (*pl* **dickies**, *compar* **dickier**, *superl* **dickiest**) N = **dickey**
ADJ *Br Fam (ladder)* peu solide[□], branlant; *(situation)* peu sûr[□]; **to have a d. heart** avoir le palpitant fragile

dicotyledon [ˌdaɪkɒtɪˈliːdən] N *Bot* dicotylédone *f*

Dictaphone® [ˈdɪktəfəʊn] N Dictaphone® *m* machine *f* à dicter

dictate VT [dɪkˈteɪt] **1** *(letter)* dicter; **to d. sth to sb** dicter qch à qn **2** *(determine ▸ terms, conditions)* dicter, imposer; **our budget will d. the type of computer we buy** le type d'ordinateur que nous achèterons dépendra de notre budget
VI [dɪkˈteɪt] **1** *(lay down law)* faire la loi; **I won't be dictated to** on ne me donne pas d'ordres **2** *(give dictation)* dicter
N [ˈdɪkteɪt] **1** *(order)* ordre *m* **2** *(usu pl) (principle)* précepte *m*; **the dictates of fashion** les exigences de la mode; **the dictates of conscience/reason** la voix de la conscience/raison

dictating machine [dɪkˈteɪtɪŋ-] N machine *f* à dicter

dictation [dɪkˈteɪʃən] N *(of letter, story)* dictée *f*; **to take d.** écrire sous la dictée; **at d. speed** à la vitesse d'une dictée; *Sch* **to do d.** faire la dictée; **French d.** dictée *f* de français

dictator [dɪkˈteɪtə(r)] N dictateur *m*

dictatorial [ˌdɪktəˈtɔːrɪəl] ADJ **1** *(power)* dictatorial **2** *(tone)* impérieux, autoritaire; *(person)* tyrannique

dictatorially [ˌdɪktəˈtɔːrɪəlɪ] ADV dictatorialement, en dictateur

dictatorship [dɪkˈteɪtəʃɪp] N dictature *f*

diction [ˈdɪkʃən] N **1** *(pronunciation)* diction *f*, élocution *f*; **to have good d.** avoir une bonne diction **2** *(phrasing)* style *m*, langage *m*

dictionary [ˈdɪkʃənərɪ] (*pl* **dictionaries**) N dictionnaire *m*; **a French–English d.** un dictionnaire français–anglais; **look it up in the d.** cherchez dans le dictionnaire
COMP *(entry)* de dictionnaire
▸▸ ***dictionary definition*** définition *f* de dictionnaire; **the d. definition of love** l'amour tel que le définit le dictionnaire

dictum [ˈdɪktəm] (*pl* **dicta** [-tə] *or* **dictums**) N *Formal* **1** *(statement)* affirmation *f*; *Law* opinion *f* judiciaire incidente **2** *(maxim)* dicton *m*, maxime *f*

did [dɪd] *pt of* **do**

didactic [dɪˈdæktɪk] ADJ didactique
• **didactics** N *(UNCOUNT)* didactique *f*

didactically [dɪˈdæktɪklɪ] ADV didactiquement

diddle [ˈdɪdəl] VT *Br Fam* duper, rouler; **to d. sb out of sth** carotter qch à qn; **I've been diddled** je me suis fait avoir
VI *Am very Fam (have sex)* baiser

diddler [ˈdɪdlə(r)] N *Br Fam* escroqueur(euse) *m, f*

diddly [dɪdlɪ], **diddly-squat** N *Am Fam* que dalle; **that's not worth d.** ça ne vaut pas un clou; **I don't know d. about computers** l'informatique, j'y pige que dalle

didgeridoo [ˌdɪdʒərɪˈduː] N *Mus* didjeridoo *m*, didgeridoo *m*

didn't [ˈdɪdənt] = **did not**

DIE[1] [daɪ]

VI
- mourir **1, 2, 4**
- s'éteindre **4**
- caler **3**
- avoir envie **5**

VT
- mourir de

VI 1 *(person)* mourir, décéder; **she's dying** *(has incurable illness)* elle est condamnée; *(is in her death throes)* elle est mourante *ou* à l'agonie; **she died of cancer** elle est morte du *ou* d'un cancer; **he died from his wounds** il est mort des suites de ses blessures; **thousands are dying of hunger** des milliers de gens meurent de faim; *Literary* **she died by her own hand** elle s'est suicidée *ou* donné la mort, elle a mis fin à ses jours; **to d. a hero** mourir en héros; **he left us to d.** il nous a abandonnés à la mort; *Fam Fig* **to d. laughing** mourir de rire; *Fam* **I nearly died, I could have died** *(from fear)* j'étais mort de trouille; *(from embarrassment)* j'aurais voulu rentrer sous terre, je ne savais plus où me mettre; **he'll do it or d. in the attempt** il y arrivera coûte que coûte; **to d. with one's boots on** *or* **in harness** mourir debout *ou* en pleine activité; **never say d.!** *(don't give up)* il ne faut jamais désespérer!; *(stay cheerful)* courage!, tenez bon!
2 *(animal, plant)* mourir
3 *(engine)* caler, s'arrêter; *(battery)* se mettre à plat
4 *(fire, love, memory)* s'éteindre, mourir; *(tradition)* s'éteindre, disparaître, mourir; *(smile)* disparaître, s'évanouir; **old habits d. hard** les mauvaises habitudes ne se perdent pas facilement; **her secret died with her** elle a emporté son secret dans la tombe
5 *Fam* **to be dying for sth** *(want very much)* avoir une envie folle de qch; **I'm dying for a drink** j'ai une envie folle de boire qch; **to be dying to do sth** mourir d'envie de faire qch
VT to d. a natural/violent death mourir de sa belle mort/de mort violente

die[2] *(pl sense* **1 dice** [daɪs], *pl sense* **2 dies)** **N 1** *(dice)* dé *m* (à jouer); *Fig* **the d. is cast** les dés sont jetés **2** *Archit (dado)* dé *m (d'un piédestal)*; *Tech (stamp)* matrice *f*; *(in minting)* coin *m*; **stamping d.** étampe *f*; **as straight as a d.** franc comme l'or
▸▸ ***die sinker*** graveur *m* d'étampes *ou* de matrices

▸**die away VI** s'affaiblir, s'éteindre, mourir

▸**die back VI** *(plant)* dépérir

▸**die down VI 1** *(wind)* tomber, se calmer; *(fire* ▸ *in chimney)* baisser; *(*▸ *in building, forest)* s'apaiser, diminuer; *(noise)* diminuer; *(anger, protest)* se calmer, s'apaiser **2** *(plant)* se flétrir, perdre ses feuilles et sa tige

▸**die off VI** mourir les uns après les autres

▸**die out VI** *(family, tribe, tradition)* disparaître, s'éteindre; *(fire)* s'éteindre; **the panda is in danger of dying out** le panda est menacé d'extinction

die-cast *Tech* **VT** mouler sous pression *ou* en matrice
ADJ moulé sous pression *ou* en matrice

die-casting N *Tech* moulage *m* en matrice

diegesis [daɪˈdʒiːsɪs] **N** diégèse *f*

diehard [ˈdaɪhɑːd] **N** conservateur(trice) *m,f*, réactionnaire *mf*; **the party diehards** les durs *mpl* du parti
ADJ intransigeant; *Pol* réactionnaire; **a d. liberal** un libéral pur et dur

dieresis *(pl* **diereses** [-siːz]) *Am* = **diaeresis**

diesel [ˈdiːzəl] **N 1** *(vehicle)* diesel *m*; *(fuel)* gas-oil *m*, gazole *m* **2** *very Fam Pej* **d. (dyke)** gouine *f (à l'allure masculine)*
▸▸ ***diesel engine*** *Aut* moteur *m* diesel; *Rail* motrice *f*; ***diesel fuel, diesel oil*** gas-oil *m*, gazole *m*; ***diesel train*** autorail *m*

diesel-electric ADJ diesel-électrique

diet [ˈdaɪət] **N 1** *(regular food)* alimentation *f*, nourriture *f*; **they live on a d. of rice and fish** ils se nourrissent de riz et de poisson; **a balanced d.** un régime équilibré; **a poor d.** un régime mal équilibré, une alimentation mal équilibrée **2** *(for medical reasons)* régime *m*, diète *f*; *(to lose weight)* régime *m*; **to be on a d.** être au régime; **to go on a d.** faire *ou* suivre un régime; **to put sb on a d.** mettre qn au régime **3** *Hist (assembly)* diète *f*
COMP *(drink, food)* de régime, basses calories
VI suivre un régime
▸▸ ***diet pill*** pilule *f* pour maigrir

dietary [ˈdaɪətrɪ] *(pl* **dietaries)** **ADJ** *(supplement)* alimentaire; *(of special food)* de régime, diététique
N *Formal* régime *m* alimentaire *(d'un malade, d'une prison)*
▸▸ ***dietary fibre*** cellulose *f* végétale

dietetic [ˌdaɪəˈtetɪk] **ADJ** diététique

dietetics [ˌdaɪəˈtetɪks] **N** *(UNCOUNT)* diététique *f*

dietician, dietitian [daɪəˈtɪʃən] **N** diététicien (enne) *m,f*

differ [ˈdɪfə(r)] **VI 1** *(vary)* différer, être différent (**from** de); **in what way does this text d. from the first?** en quoi ce texte diffère-t-il du premier?; **the two approaches d. quite considerably** les deux approches n'ont pas grand-chose à voir l'une avec l'autre; **to d. in size/shape/colour** être de tailles/de formes/de couleurs différentes; **to d. in price** avoir des prix différents **2** *(disagree)* être en désaccord, ne pas être d'accord; **I beg to d.** permettez-moi d'être d'un autre avis; **to agree to d.** garder chacun son opinion; **he differs with me about the best solution to apply** il n'est pas d'accord avec moi *ou* il ne partage pas mon avis sur la meilleure solution à adopter

difference [ˈdɪfrəns] **N 1** *(dissimilarity)* différence *f*; *(in age, size, weight)* écart *m*, différence *f*; **there's a big d. between living with someone and marrying them** il y a une grande différence entre vivre ensemble et être mariés; **there are many differences between the two cultures** les deux cultures sont très différentes l'une de l'autre; **I can't tell the d. between the two** je ne vois pas la différence entre les deux; **there's a d. in height of six inches** il y a une différence de hauteur de quinze centimètres; **d. in temperature** écart *m* de température; **she says the age d. doesn't matter** elle dit que la différence d'âge n'a pas d'importance; **it makes no d., it doesn't make the slightest d.** ça n'a aucune importance, ça revient au même, ça ne change absolument rien; **it makes no d. to me (one way or the other)** (d'une manière ou d'une autre), cela m'est (parfaitement) égal; **to make a d.** *(improve society)* faire avancer les choses; **it made a big d. to him** cela a beaucoup compté *ou* a tout changé pour lui; **does it make any d. whether he comes or not?** est-ce que ça change quelque chose qu'il vienne ou pas?; **that makes all the d.** voilà qui change tout; **a lick of paint makes all the d.** un petit coup de peinture et ça n'a plus du tout la même allure; **to notice a (big) d. in sb** trouver que qn a (énormément) changé; **a computer/a skiing holiday with a d.** un ordinateur/des vacances de ski pas comme les autres **2** *(disagreement)* différend *m*; **we have our differences** nous ne sommes pas toujours d'accord; **a d. of opinion** une différence *ou* divergence d'opinion; **to have a d. of opinion with sb** se disputer avec qn **3** *(in numbers, quantity)* différence *f*; **I'll pay the d.** je paierai la différence *ou* le reste; *Fam* **(it's the) same d.!** cela revient au même!

different [ˈdɪfrənt] **ADJ 1** *(not identical)* différent, autre; **d. from** *or* **to** *or esp Am* **than** différent de; **it's very d. from any other city I've visited** ça ne ressemble en rien aux autres villes que j'ai visitées; **you look d. today** tu n'es pas comme d'habitude aujourd'hui; **he put on a d. shirt** il a mis une autre chemise; **she's a d. person since their wedding** elle a beaucoup changé depuis leur mariage; **let's do something d.** faisons quelque chose de nouveau *ou* de différent; **that's quite a d. matter** ça, c'est une autre affaire *ou* histoire **2** *(various)* divers, différents, plusieurs; **she visited d. schools** elle a visité diverses *ou* différentes écoles; **at d. times** à différentes *ou* diverses reprises; **I talked to d. people about it** j'en ai parlé à plusieurs personnes; **d. people say d. things** les avis diffèrent **3** *(unusual)* original; **I'm looking for something d.** je cherche quelque chose d'original *ou* qui sorte de l'ordinaire; **she always has to be d.** elle veut toujours se singulariser, elle ne peut jamais faire comme tout le monde; **it's certainly d.** c'est original
ADV *Fam* **she thinks he's a saint but I know d.** elle le prend pour un petit saint mais moi je sais que ce n'est pas vrai; **you can pretend it's your house, they won't know any d.** tu peux faire comme si c'était ta maison, ils ne s'en rendront pas compte

differential [ˌdɪfəˈrenʃəl] **N 1** *(in salary)* écart *m* salarial **2** *Math* différentielle *f* **3** *Aut* différentiel *m*, engrenage *m* différentiel
ADJ différentiel
▸▸ *Math* ***differential calculus*** calcul *m* différentiel; *Math* ***differential equation*** équation *f* différentielle; *Aut* ***differential gear*** différentiel *m*, engrenage *m* différentiel; ***differential pricing*** établissement *m* des prix différentiels, tarification *f* différentielle

differentially [ˌdɪfəˈrenʃəlɪ] **ADV** *(pay)* à des taux différentiels

differentiate [ˌdɪfəˈrenʃɪeɪt] **VT 1** *(distinguish)* différencier, distinguer; **what differentiates this product from its competitors?** qu'est-ce qui différencie *ou* distingue ce produit de ses concurrents? **2** *Math* différencier, calculer la différentielle de
VI faire la différence *ou* distinction; **I'm unable to d. between the two** je ne vois pas de différence entre les deux; **she differentiates between morality and religion** elle fait une distinction entre moralité et religion

differentiation [ˌdɪfərenʃɪˈeɪʃən] **N** *(gen)* différenciation *f*; *Math* différentiation *f*

differently [ˈdɪfrəntlɪ] **ADV** différemment, autrement; **if things had turned out d.** si les choses s'étaient passées autrement; **I do it d. from** *or esp Am* **than you** je le fais différemment de *ou* autrement que vous, je ne fais pas ça comme vous

differently-abled ADJ *(in politically correct usage)* handicapé

difficult [ˈdɪfɪkəlt] **ADJ 1** *(problem, task)* difficile, dur; *(book, question)* difficile; **it was a d. decision to make** ce n'était pas une décision facile à prendre; **he's had a d. life** il a eu une vie difficile; **that's not so d.** ce n'est pas si difficile que ça; **I find it d. to believe she's gone** j'ai du mal à *ou* il m'est difficile de croire qu'elle est partie; **the most d. part is over** le plus difficile *ou* le plus dur est fait **2** *(awkward)* difficile, peu commode; **don't be so d.!** ne fais pas le difficile!, ne fais pas la fine bouche!; **he's d. to get along with** il n'est pas commode, il a un caractère difficile; **we could make life/things very d. for you** on pourrait sérieusement vous compliquer la vie/les choses; **she's at a d. age** elle est à l'âge ingrat

difficulty [ˈdɪfɪkəltɪ] *(pl* **difficulties)** **N 1** *(UNCOUNT) (trouble)* difficulté *f*, difficultés *fpl*; **to have** *or* **experience d. (in) doing sth** avoir du mal *ou* de la peine *ou* des difficultés à faire qch; **she experienced d. breathing** elle avait du mal *ou* de la peine *ou* des difficultés à respirer, elle respirait difficilement; **degree of d.** niveau *m* de difficulté; **with d.** avec difficulté *ou* peine; **without d.** sans difficulté *ou* peine; **it can be done, but with d.** cela peut se faire, mais difficilement **2** *(obstacle, problem)* difficulté *f*, problème *m*; **the main d. is getting the staff** le plus difficile, c'est de trouver le personnel; **I don't foresee any difficulties** je ne prévois aucun problème *ou* aucune difficulté **3** *(predicament)* difficulté *f*, embarras *m*; **to get into difficulties** être en difficulté; **to be in financial difficulties** avoir des ennuis d'argent, être dans l'embarras

diffidence [ˈdɪfɪdəns] **N** manque *m* d'assurance *ou* de confiance en soi, timidité *f*

diffident [ˈdɪfɪdənt] **ADJ** *(person)* qui manque de confiance en soi *ou* d'assurance; *(remark, smile)* timide; *(tone)* hésitant; **he was d. about speaking out** il hésitait à parler (par timidité)

diffidently [ˈdɪfɪdəntlɪ] **ADV** *(smile)* timidement, d'un air peu assuré; *(express oneself, say something)* sur un ton peu assuré

diffract [dɪˈfrækt] **VT** *Phys* diffracter

diffraction [dɪˈfrækʃən] **N** *Phys* diffraction *f*

diffuse VT [dɪˈfjuːz] diffuser, répandre
VI [dɪˈfjuːz] se diffuser, se répandre
ADJ [dɪˈfjuːs] **1** *(light)* diffus; *(thought)* diffus, vague **2** *(wordy)* diffus, prolixe

> Attention: ne pas confondre avec le verbe **to defuse**.

diffused [dɪˈfjuːzd] **ADJ** diffus
▸▸ ***diffused lighting*** éclairage *m* diffus *ou* indirect

diffuseness [dɪˈfjuːsnɪs] **N** *(of style)* prolixité *f*, caractère *m* diffus

diffuser [dɪˈfjuːzə(r)] **N** *(gen)* & *Elec* diffuseur *m*

diffusion [dɪ'fju:ʒən] **N 1** *(of light, news)* diffusion *f* **2** *(of style)* prolixité *f* **3** *Phys* diffusion *f*

diffusive [dɪ'fju:sɪv] **ADJ 1** *(property, characteristic)* diffusif **2** *(style)* diffus, prolixe

dig [dɪg] *(pt & pp* **dug** [dʌg], *cont* **digging) VT 1** *(in ground ▸ hole)* creuser; *(▸ tunnel)* creuser, percer; *(with spade)* bêcher; **he dug his way under the fence** il s'est creusé un passage sous la clôture; **he's been out digging the garden** il a bêché le jardin; **to d. potatoes** arracher des pommes de terre; *Fig* **to d. one's own grave** creuser sa propre tombe **2** *(jab)* enfoncer; **she dug me in the ribs (with her elbow)** elle m'a donné un coup de coude dans les côtes **3** *Fam Old-fashioned (understand)* piger; *(appreciate, like)* aimer□; *(look at)* viser; **d. that music!** écoute-moi (un peu) cette musique!; **she really digs you** *(likes you)* elle en pince vraiment pour toi

VI 1 *(person)* creuser; *(animal)* fouiller, fouir; **to d. for gold** creuser pour trouver de l'or; *Fig* **he spends hours digging about in old junk shops** il passe des heures à fouiller dans les magasins de brocante; *Fig* **if you d. a bit deeper** si on creuse un peu **2** *Fam Old-fashioned (understand)* piger

N 1 *(in ground)* coup *m* de bêche

2 *Archeol* fouilles *fpl*; **to go on a d.** faire des fouilles

3 *(jab)* coup *m*; **to give sb a d. in the ribs** donner un coup de coude dans les côtes de qn

4 *Fam (snide remark)* pique□ *f*; **he made a nasty d. at the government** il a lancé une pique au gouvernement; **that was a d. at you** cette pique était pour toi

▸**dig in VI 1** *Mil (dig trenches)* se retrancher; *Fig* tenir bon **2** *Fam (eat)* commencer à manger□; **d. in!** allez-y, mangez!, attaquez!

VT SEP 1 *(mix with ground)* enterrer **2** *(jab)* enfoncer; **to d. one's heels in** se braquer, se buter; **to d. oneself in** se retrancher; *Fig* camper sur ses positions

▸**dig into VT INSEP 1** *(delve into)* fouiller dans; *Fig* **don't d. into your savings** n'entame pas tes économies, ne pioche pas dans tes économies **2** *(start eating)* attaquer **3** *(jab)* **your elbow is digging into me** ton coude me rentre dans les côtes

▸**dig out VT SEP 1** *(remove)* extraire; *(from ground)* déterrer; **they had to d. the car out of the snow** il a fallu qu'ils dégagent la voiture de la neige (à la pelle) **2** *Fam (find)* dénicher

▸**dig over VT SEP** *(ground, soil)* retourner

▸**dig up VT SEP 1** *(ground ▸ gen)* retourner; *(▸ with spade)* bêcher **2** *(plant)* arracher **3** *(unearth)* déterrer; *Fam Fig (find)* dénicher; **where did you d. him up?** où est-ce que tu l'as pêché *ou* dégoté?

digest VT[dɪ'dʒest] **1** *(food)* digérer; **I find cheese difficult to d.** je digère mal le fromage **2** *(idea)* assimiler, digérer; *(information)* assimiler, comprendre **3** *(classify)* classer; *(sum up)* résumer

VI[dɪ'dʒest] digérer

N['daɪdʒest] **1** *(of book, facts)* résumé *m*; **in d. form** en abrégé

2 *Law* digeste *m*

3 *(magazine)* digest *m*

4 *Comput (of newsgroup, mailing list)* synthèse *f*

digestible [dɪ'dʒestəbəl] **ADJ** *also Fig* digeste, facile à digérerp; **easily d.** digeste, facile à digérer

digestion [dɪ'dʒestʃən] **N** digestion *f*

digestive [dɪ'dʒestɪv] **ADJ** digestif; **d. trouble** troubles *mpl* de la digestion

N *(drink)* digestif *m*; *Br (biscuit)* = sorte de sablé

▸▸ *Br* ***digestive biscuit*** = sorte de sablé; ***digestive system*** système *m* digestif; ***digestive tract*** tube *m* digestif

digger ['dɪgə(r)] **N 1** *(miner)* mineur *m*; *Br Fam* terrassier□ *m* **2** *(machine)* excavatrice *f*, pelleteuse *f* **3** *Fam (Australian)* Australien(enne)□ *m,f*; *(New Zealander)* Néo-Zélandais(e)□ *m,f*

digging ['dɪgɪŋ] **N** *(of soil)* bêchage *m*, labour *m* à la bêche; *(of well, ditches etc)* creusement *m*; *Archeol* fouilles *fpl*

digibox ['dɪdʒɪbɒks] **N** décodeur *m* numérique

digicam ['dɪdʒɪkæm] **N** caméra *f* numérique

digit ['dɪdʒɪt] **N 1** *(number)* chiffre *m*; **three-d. number** nombre *m* à trois chiffres; **double-d. inflation** taux *m* d'inflation à deux chiffres **2** *Anat (finger)* doigt *m*; *(toe)* orteil *m* **3** *Astron* doigt *m*

digital ['dɪdʒɪtəl] **ADJ 1** *Comput* numérique; *(clock, watch)* à affichage numérique; *(display, readout)* numérique; **d. technology** le numérique **2** *Anat* digital

▸▸ *Comput* ***digital analog converter*** convertisseur *m* analogique numérique; ***digital audio tape*** cassette *f* numérique; ***digital camera*** appareil *m* photo numérique; ***digital recording*** enregistrement *m* numérique; ***digital rights management*** gestion *f* des droits numériques; ***digital signal*** signal *m* numérique; *Comput* ***digital signature*** signature *f* électronique; ***digital television*** *(technique)* télévision *f* numérique; *(appliance)* téléviseur *m* numérique; *Comput* ***digital versatile disk*** disque *m* vidéo numérique; ***digital video*** vidéo *f* numérique; ***digital video camera*** caméra *f* vidéo numérique;

digitalis [ˌdɪdʒɪ'teɪlɪs] **N** *Bot* digitale *f*; *Pharm* digitaline *f*

digitalization, -isation [ˌdɪdʒɪtəlaɪ'zeɪʃən] **N** *Math & Comput* numérisation *f*; *Med* digitalisation *f*

digitalize, -ise ['dɪdʒɪtəlaɪz] **VT** *Med* administrer de la digitoxine à

digitally ['dɪdʒɪtəlɪ] **ADV** numériquement, sous forme digitale; **d. controlled** à commande numérique; **d. recorded/remastered** enregistré/remixé en numérique

digitization, -isation [ˌdɪdʒɪtaɪ'zeɪʃən] **N** *Math & Comput* numérisation *f*

digitize, -ise ['dɪdʒɪtaɪz] **VT** *Math & Comput* numériser

digitized, -ised ['dɪdʒɪtaɪzd] **ADJ** *Math & Comput* numérisé, digitalisé

digitizer, -iser ['dɪdʒɪtaɪzə(r)] **N** *Math & Comput* numériseur *m*

diglossia [daɪ'glɒsɪə] **N** *Ling* diglossie *f*

dignified ['dɪgnɪfaɪd] **ADJ** *(person)* plein de dignité, digne; *(silence)* digne; **she is very d.** elle a beaucoup de dignité; **she wasn't very d.** elle manquait de dignité *ou* de tenue

dignify ['dɪgnɪfaɪ] *(pt & pp* **dignified) VT** donner de la dignité à; **to d. sb with the name of...** honorer qn du nom de...; **I refuse to even d. that question with an answer** cette question n'est même pas digne de réponse *ou* ne mérite même pas une réponse

dignitary ['dɪgnɪtrɪ] *(pl* **dignitaries) N** dignitaire *m*

dignity ['dɪgnətɪ] *(pl* **dignities) N 1** *(importance, poise)* dignité *f*; **it would be beneath my d. to accept** accepter serait indigne de moi *ou* serait m'abaisser; **she considered it beneath her d.** elle s'estimait au-dessus de ça; **to stand on one's d.** se draper dans sa dignité; **with d.** avec dignité, dignement **2** *(rank)* dignité *f*, haut rang *m*; *(title)* titre *m*, dignité *f*

digress [daɪ'gres] **VI** s'éloigner, s'écarter; **you're digressing from the subject** vous vous éloignez du sujet; **but I d.** mais je m'égare, revenons à nos moutons

digression [daɪ'greʃən] **N** digression *f*

digs [dɪgz] **NPL** *Br Fam Old-fashioned* chambre *f* meublée□; **to live in d.** loger dans une chambre meublée; **I'm in d. in Wimbledon** j'habite une chambre meublée à Wimbledon

dihedral [daɪ'hi:drəl] *Geom* **N** dièdre *m*

ADJ dièdre

dike = **dyke**

dilapidated [dɪ'læpɪdeɪtɪd] **ADJ** *(house)* délabré; *(car)* déglingué; **in a d. state** dans un état de délabrement *ou* de dégradation avancé

dilapidation [dɪˌlæpɪ'deɪʃən] **N 1** *(of building)* délabrement *m*, dégradation *f*; **in a state of d.** dans un état de délabrement *ou* de dégradation avancé **2** *(usu pl) Law* détérioration *f (causée par un locataire)*

dilate [daɪ'leɪt] **VI 1** *(eyes)* se dilater **2** *Formal (talk)* **to d. on** *or* **upon a topic** s'étendre sur un sujet

VT dilater

dilation [daɪ'leɪʃən] **N 1** *(gen) & Med* dilatation *f* **2** *Formal (talk)* exposition *f* en détail

dilatoriness ['dɪlətrɪnɪs] **N** *Formal* lenteur *f*

dilatory ['dɪlətrɪ] **ADJ** *Formal (action, method)* dilatoire; *(person)* lent; **to be d. in doing sth** tarder à faire qch

dildo ['dɪldəʊ] *(pl* **dildos) N 1** *(device)* godemiché *m* **2** *very Fam (person)* trou *m* du cul, trouduc *m*

dilemma [dɪ'lemə] **N** dilemme *m*; **to be in a d.** être pris dans un dilemme; **her decision leaves me in something of a d.** sa décision me pose un dilemme

dilettante [ˌdɪlɪ'tæntɪ] *(pl* **dilettantes** *or* **dilettanti** [-tɪ]) **N** dilettante *mf*

ADJ dilettante

dilettantism [ˌdɪlɪ'tæntɪzəm] **N** dilettantisme *m*

diligence ['dɪlɪdʒəns] **N 1** *(effort)* assiduité *f*, application *f*, zèle *m*; **she shows great d. in her work** elle fait preuve de beaucoup de zèle *ou* d'assiduité dans son travail **2** *(carriage)* diligence *f*

diligent ['dɪlɪdʒənt] **ADJ** *(person)* assidu, appliqué; *(work)* appliqué, diligent; **he is very d. in his work** il fait son travail avec beaucoup d'assiduité *ou* de zèle

diligently ['dɪlɪdʒəntlɪ] **ADV** avec assiduité *ou* soin *ou* application, assidûment

dill[1] [dɪl] **N** *(herb)* aneth *m*

▸▸ ***dill pickle*** cornichon *m* à l'aneth

dill[2] **N** *Austr & NZ Fam (fool)* andouille *f*

dilly-dally *(pt & pp* **dilly-dallied) VI** *Fam (dawdle)* lanterner□, lambiner; *(hesitate)* hésiter□, tergiverser□

dilute [daɪ'lu:t] **VT 1** *(liquid)* diluer, étendre; *(milk, wine)* mouiller, couper d'eau; *(sauce)* délayer, allonger; *(colour)* délayer; **d. to taste** *(on bottle)* diluer selon votre goût **2** *Chem & Pharm* diluer **3** *Fig (weaken)* diluer, édulcorer; **diluted socialism** socialisme *m* édulcoré

ADJ *(liquid)* dilué, coupé *ou* étendu (d'eau); *(colour)* délayé, adouci; *Fig* dilué, édulcoré

dilution [daɪ'lu:ʃən] **N 1** *(act, product)* dilution *f*; *(of milk, wine)* coupage *m*, mouillage *m*; *Fig* édulcoration *f* **2** *Fin & St Exch (of shareholding)* dilution *f*

dim [dɪm] *(pt & pp* **dimmed,** *cont* **dimming) ADJ 1** *(light)* faible, pâle; *(lamp)* faible; *(room)* sombre; **to grow d.** *(light)* baisser; *(room)* devenir sombre; **her eyes grew d. with tears** ses yeux se voilèrent de larmes

2 *(indistinct ▸ shape)* vague, imprécis; *(▸ sight)* faible, trouble; *(▸ sound)* vague, indistinct; **she has only a d. memory of it** elle n'en a qu'un vague souvenir; *Hum* **in the d. and distant past** au temps jadis

3 *(gloomy)* sombre, morne; **to take a d. view of sth** ne pas beaucoup apprécier qch, voir qch d'un mauvais œil

4 *Fam (stupid)* gourde

VT 1 *(light)* baisser; **I'll d. the lamp** je vais mettre la lampe en veilleuse; *Aut* **to d. one's headlights** se mettre en codes *ou* en feux de croisement **2** *(beauty, colour, hope, metal)* ternir; *(memory)* estomper, effacer; *(mind, senses)* affaiblir, troubler; *(sound)* affaiblir; *(sight)* baisser, troubler; **his eyes were dimmed with tears** ses yeux étaient voilés de larmes

VI *(light)* baisser, s'affaiblir; *(beauty, glory, hope)* se ternir; *(colour)* devenir terne *ou* mat; *(memory)* s'estomper, s'effacer; *(sound)* s'affaiblir; *(sight)* baisser, se troubler

dimbo ['dɪmbəʊ] **N** *Fam* ballot *m*, nigaud *m*

dim-dip **N** *Aut* veilleuses-codes *fpl*

dime [daɪm] **N** *Am* pièce *f* de dix cents; *Fam* **guys like that are a d. a dozen** des types comme lui, on en trouve à la pelle; *Fam* **it's not worth a d.** *or* **one thin d.** ça ne vaut pas un clou

▸▸ *Am* ***dime novel*** roman *m* à quatre sous; *Am* ***dime store*** supérette *f* de quartier

dimension [dɪ'menʃən] **N 1** *(measurement, size)* dimension *f*; *Archit & Geom* dimension *f*, cote *f*; *Math & Phys* dimension *f* **2** *Fig (scope)* étendue *f*; *(aspect)* dimension *f*; **the book opens up a whole new d. of thought** ce livre ouvre un nouveau champ de réflexion

• **dimensions NPL** *Tech (of bulky object)* encombrement *m*

dimensional [dɪ'menʃənəl] SUFF **two-/four-d.** à deux/quatre dimensions

diminish [dɪ'mɪnɪʃ] VT **1** *(number)* diminuer, réduire; *(effect, power)* diminuer, amoindrir; *(value)* réduire **2** *(person)* déprécier, rabaisser **3** *Archit (column)* amincir, diminuer; *Mus* diminuer
VI diminuer, se réduire; **their profits have diminished** leurs bénéfices ont diminué

diminished [dɪ'mɪnɪʃt] ADJ **1** *(number, power, speed)* diminué, amoindri; *(reputation)* diminué, terni; *(value)* réduit **2** *Mus* diminué
►► *Br Law* ***diminished responsibility*** responsabilité *f* atténuée

diminishing [dɪ'mɪnɪʃɪŋ] ADJ *(influence, number, speed)* décroissant, qui va en diminuant; *(price, quality)* qui baisse, en baisse
N diminution *f*, baisse *f*
►► *Econ & Fig* ***diminishing returns*** rendements *mpl* décroissants; *Econ & Fig* **the law of d. returns** la loi des rendements décroissants

diminuendo [dɪˌmɪnjʊ'endəʊ] *(pl* **diminuendos**) *Mus* N diminuendo *m*
ADV diminuendo

diminution [ˌdɪmɪ'nju:ʃən] N **1** *(in number, value)* diminution *f*, baisse *f*; *(in speed)* réduction *f*; *(in intensity, importance, strength)* diminution *f*, affaiblissement *m*; *(in temperature)* baisse *f*, abaissement *m*; *(in authority, price)* baisse *f* **2** *Mus* diminution *f*

diminutive [dɪ'mɪnjʊtɪv] ADJ *(tiny)* minuscule, tout petit; *Ling* diminutif
N *Ling* diminutif *m*

dimly ['dɪmlɪ] ADV *(shine)* faiblement, sans éclat; *(see)* indistinctement, à peine; *(remember)* vaguement, à peine; **d. lit** mal *ou* faiblement éclairée

dimmed [dɪmd] *Comput*
ADJ *(command)* en grisé, estompé
►► ***dimmed icon*** icône *f* estompée

dimmer ['dɪmə(r)] N **1** *(on lamp)* variateur *m* (de lumière) **2** *Am Aut (switch)* basculeur *m* (de phares)
• **dimmers** NPL *Am Aut (headlights)* phares *mpl* code; *(parking lights)* feux *mpl* de position
►► ***dimmer switch*** variateur *m* (de lumière)

dimness ['dɪmnɪs] N **1** *(of light, sight)* affaiblissement *m*; *(of room)* obscurité *f*; *(of colour, metal)* aspect *m* terne; *(of memory, shape)* imprécision *f* **2** *Fam (stupidity)* sottise❑ *f*

dimple ['dɪmpəl] N *(in cheek, chin)* fossette *f*; *(in surface of ground, water)* ride *f*, ondulation *f*
VT *(of smile ► somebody's cheeks)* creuser des fossettes dans; *(of wind ► surface of water)* rider
VI *(cheek)* se creuser de fossettes; *(surface of ground)* onduler, former des rides; *(surface of water)* onduler, se rider

dimpled ['dɪmpəld] ADJ *(cheek, chin)* à fossettes; *(arm, knee)* potelé; *(surface)* ridé, ondulé

dimwit ['dɪmwɪt] N *Fam* crétin(e) *m,f*

dimwitted ['dɪmˌwɪtɪd] ADJ *Fam* crétin, gourde

din [dɪn] *(pt & pp* **dinned**, *cont* **dinning**) N *(of people)* tapage *m*, tumulte *m*; *(in classroom)* chahut *m*; *(of industry, traffic)* vacarme *m*; *Fam* **they were kicking up** *or* **making a real d.** ils faisaient un boucan d'enfer *ou* monstre
VT *Fam* **to d. sth into sb** faire (bien) comprendre qch à qn❑, enfoncer qch dans le crâne à qn; **to d. manners/the rules of the road into sb** inculquer les bonnes manières/le code de la route à qn❑

dinar ['di:nɑ:(r)] N dinar *m*

dine [daɪn] VI dîner, *Belg, Can & Suisse* souper; **to d. off** *or* **on sth** *(eat)* dîner de qch; **she dined off** *or* **on trout and fresh strawberries** elle a dîné d'une truite et de fraises fraîches; **to d. off sth** *(porcelain, silver)* manger dans qch; **we're dining in tonight** nous dînons à la maison ce soir
VT offrir à dîner à
▸ **dine out** VI dîner dehors *ou* en ville; *Fig* **I dined out on that story for weeks** ça m'a fait une bonne histoire à raconter pendant des semaines

diner ['daɪnə(r)] N **1** *(person)* dîneur(euse) *m,f*; **there were only a few late diners left in the restaurant** il n'y avait plus que quelques clients attardés dans le restaurant **2** *Am* petit restaurant *m*; *Rail* wagon-restaurant *m*

dinette [daɪ'net] N coin-repas *m*

ding-a-ling ['dɪŋəˌlɪŋ] N **1** *(ring)* dring dring *m*, tintement *m* **2** *Am Fam (fool)* cloche *f*, andouille *f*

dingbat ['dɪŋbæt] N **1** *Am Fam (thing)* truc *m*, machin *m* **2** *Fam (fool)* crétin(e) *m,f*, gourde *f* **3** *Comput* symbole *m* Dingbat

ding-dong N **1** *(of bells)* tintement *m*, sonnerie *f*; *(of doorbell)* sonnerie *f*; **to go d.** faire ding-dingdong **2** *Fam (fight)* bagarre *f*
ADJ *Fam* **to have a d. argument** *(of two people)* se disputer violemment❑; **d. match** partie *f* vivement disputée

dinghy ['dɪŋgɪ] *(pl* **dinghies**) N *(rowing boat)* petit canot *m*, youyou *m*; *(sailboat)* dériveur *m*; *(made of rubber)* canot *m* pneumatique, dinghy *m*

> Attention: ne pas confondre avec le terme **dingy**.

dinginess ['dɪndʒɪnɪs] N *(shabbiness)* aspect *m* miteux *ou* douteux; *(drabness)* couleur *f* terne

dingo ['dɪŋgəʊ] *(pl* **dingoes**) N *Zool* dingo *m*

dingy ['dɪndʒɪ] *(compar* **dingier**, *superl* **dingiest**) ADJ *(shabby)* miteux; *(dirty)* douteux; *(colour)* terne

> Attention: ne pas confondre avec le terme **dinghy**.

dining ['daɪnɪŋ-] COMP
►► ***Rail dining car*** wagon-restaurant *m*; ***dining hall*** réfectoire *m*, salle *f* à manger; ***dining room*** salle *f* à manger; ***dining room suite*** salle *f* à manger *(meubles)*; ***dining table*** table *f* de salle à manger

dink [dɪŋk] N **1** *Fam (person)* crétin(e) *m,f* **2** *very Fam (penis)* queue *f*

dinkum ['dɪŋkəm] *Austr Fam* ADJ *(person)* franc (franche)❑, sincère❑; *(thing)* authentique❑; **fair d.** régulier, vrai de vrai

dinky[1] ['dɪŋkɪ] *(compar* **dinkier**, *superl* **dinkiest**) ADJ *Fam* **1** *Br (small, neat)* mignon, coquet **2** *Am Pej (insignificant)* de rien du tout

dinky[2] *(abbr* **double income no kids yet**) *Fam Hum*
N = membre d'un couple à deux revenus sans enfants
COMP *(lifestyle etc)* de couple sans enfants à deux revenus

dinner ['dɪnə(r)] N **1** *(evening meal)* dîner *m*; *Belg, Can & Suisse* souper *m*; *(very late)* souper *m*; **to be at** *or* **having d.** être en train de dîner; **what's for d.?** qu'y a-t-il au dîner?; **ask her round for d.** invite-la à venir dîner; **they went out to d.** *(in restaurant)* ils ont dîné au restaurant *ou* en ville; *(at friends)* ils ont dîné chez des amis; **d.'s on the table** *or* **ready!** le dîner est prêt!, c'est prêt!, à table!; **she rang the d. bell** elle a sonné pour annoncer le dîner; **did you give the cat its d.?** avez-vous donné à manger au chat?; **a formal d.** un grand dîner *ou* dîner officiel; *Br Fam* **he's had more girlfriends than I've had hot dinners** il a eu je ne sais combien de petites amies❑ **2** *Ir, Scot & NEng (lunch)* déjeuner *m*
COMP *(fork, knife)* de table
►► ***dinner dance*** dîner *m* dansant; ***dinner hour*** *(at work)* heure *f* du déjeuner; *(at school)* pause *f* de midi; ***dinner jacket*** smoking *m*; *Br* ***dinner lady*** = employée d'une cantine scolaire; *Br* ***dinner money*** argent *m* pour la cantine; ***dinner party*** dîner *m (sur invitation)*; **we're having** *or* **giving a d. party** nous avons du monde à dîner, nous donnons un dîner; ***dinner plate*** (grande) assiette *f*; ***dinner roll*** petit pain *m*; ***dinner service***, ***dinner set*** service *m* de table; ***dinner table*** table *f* de salle à manger; **at** *or* **over the d. table** pendant le dîner, au dîner; ***dinner time*** heure *f* du dîner; **(it's) d. time!** à table!

dinnerware ['dɪnəweə(r)] N *Am* vaisselle *f*

dinosaur ['daɪnəsɔ:(r)] N *(animal)* dinosaure *m*; *Mktg (product)* poids *m* mort, produit *m* dodo; *Fig* **the institute's become a bit of a d.** l'institut est le survivant d'une époque révolue *ou* a fait son temps

dint [dɪnt] N *Arch (mark of blow ► in metal, wall)* bosse *f*
• **by dint of** PREP à force de; **she succeeded by d. of sheer hard work** elle a réussi à force de travailler dur

diocese ['daɪəsɪs] N *Rel* diocèse *m*

diode ['daɪəʊd] N *Electron* diode *f*

dioptre, *Am* **diopter** [daɪ'ɒptə(r)] N *Opt* dioptrie *f*

dioxide [daɪ'ɒksaɪd] N *Chem* dioxyde *m*, bioxyde *m*

dioxin [daɪ'ɒksɪn] N *Chem* dioxine *f*

Dip. *(written abbr* **diploma**) diplôme *m*

dip [dɪp] *(pt & pp* **dipped**, *cont* **dipping**) VI **1** *(incline ► ground)* descendre, s'incliner; *(► road)* descendre, plonger; *(► head)* pencher, s'incliner; **the road dips sharply** la route descend brusquement **2** *(drop ► sun)* baisser, descendre à l'horizon; *(► price)* diminuer, baisser; *(► temperature)* baisser; *(► plane)* piquer; *(► boat)* tanguer, piquer; **the sun dipped below the horizon** le soleil est descendu derrière l'horizon; **shares dipped on the London Stock Market yesterday** les actions ont baissé à la Bourse des valeurs de Londres hier **3** *(during dance)* se renverser
VT **1** *(immerse)* tremper, plonger; *Tech* tremper; *(clean)* décaper; *(dye)* teindre; *Agr (sheep)* baigner *(dans un bain parasiticide)*
2 *(plunge)* plonger; *Fig* **to d. one's hand in one's pocket** mettre la main à la poche
3 *Br Aut* **to d. one's headlights** se mettre en codes; **dipped headlights** codes *mpl*, feux *mpl* de croisement; **to drive on** *or* **with dipped headlights** rouler en codes
4 *(flag)* baisser; *Naut* **to d. a flag** (faire) marquer un pavillon
N **1** *Fam (swim)* baignade❑ *f*, bain❑ *m (en mer, en piscine)*; **to go for a d.** aller se baigner, aller faire trempette
2 *(liquid)* bain *m*; *Agr (for sheep)* bain *m* parasiticide
3 *(slope ► in ground)* déclivité *f*; *(► in road)* descente *f*; *Geol* pendage *m*
4 *(bob)* inclinaison *f*; *(of head)* hochement *m*
5 *(drop ► in temperature)* baisse *f*; *(► in price)* fléchissement *m*, baisse *f*; **the winter months saw a sharp d. in profits** les bénéfices ont fortement baissé pendant l'hiver
6 *Culin* = sauce dans laquelle on trempe les crudités etc; **avocado d.** purée *f* d'avocat
►► *Br Aut* ***dip switch*** basculeur *m* de phares
▸ **dip into** VT INSEP **1** *(dabble)* **I've only really dipped into Shakespeare** j'ai seulement survolé *ou* feuilleté Shakespeare **2** *(draw upon)* puiser dans; **we've had to d. into our savings** nous avons dû puiser dans nos économies

DipEd [ˌdɪp'ed] N *Br Univ (abbr* **Diploma in Education**) CAPES *m*

diphtheria [dɪf'θɪərɪə] N *Med* diphtérie *f*; **to have d.** être atteint de la diphtérie, avoir la diphtérie
►► ***diphtheria vaccine*** vaccin *m* antidiphtérique

diphthong ['dɪfθɒŋ] N *Ling* diphtongue *f*

diploid ['dɪplɔɪd] ADJ *Biol* diploïde

diploma [dɪ'pləʊmə] N diplôme *m*; **she has a d. in business studies** elle est diplômée de *ou* en commerce; **teaching d.** diplôme *m* d'enseignement

diplomacy [dɪ'pləʊməsɪ] N *Pol & Fig* diplomatie *f*; **you have to use a bit of d.** vous devez user d'un peu de diplomatie, il faut être un peu diplomate

diploma-level ADJ diplômant

diplomat ['dɪpləmæt] N *Pol & Fig* diplomate *mf*

diplomatic [ˌdɪplə'mætɪk] ADJ **1** *Pol* diplomatique **2** *Fig (person)* diplomate; *(action, remark)* diplomatique; **you have to be d. when dealing with these people** il faut faire preuve de tact *ou* user de diplomatie pour traiter avec ces gens-là; **that wasn't very d.** ça manquait un peu de tact *ou* de diplomatie
►► *Pol* ***diplomatic bag*** valise *f* diplomatique; *Pol* ***diplomatic corps*** corps *m* diplomatique; *Pol* ***diplomatic immunity*** immunité *f* diplomatique; **to claim d. immunity** faire valoir l'immunité diplomatique; *Am Pol* ***diplomatic pouch*** valise *f* diplomatique; *Pol* ***diplomatic relations*** relations *fpl* diplomatiques; *Pol* ***the Diplomatic Service*** la diplomatie, le service diplomatique

diplomatically [ˌdɪplə'mætɪkəlɪ] ADV *Pol* diplomatiquement; *Fig* avec diplomatie, diplomatiquement

diplomatist [dɪ'pləʊmətɪst] N *Pol & Fig* diplomate *mf*

dipole ['daɪpəʊl] **N** *Phys* dipôle *m*

dipped [dɪpt] **ADJ** *(sloping)* incliné
▸▸ *BrAut* ***dipped headlights*** codes *mpl*, feux *mpl* de croisement

dipper ['dɪpə(r)] **N 1** *(ladle)* louche *f*
2 *(of machine)* godet *m* (de pelleteuse); *(for lake, river)* benne *f* (de drague), hotte *f* à draguer
3 *BrAut* basculeur *m* (de phares)
4 *Orn* cincle *m* (plongeur), merle *m* d'eau

dipping ['dɪpɪŋ] **N 1** *(plunging)* plongée *f*, immersion *f*; *Metal* décapage *m*; *Agr (of sheep)* baignage *m* **2** *BrAut (of headlights)* mise *f* en code

dippy ['dɪpɪ] *(compar* **dippier**, *superl* **dippiest)** **ADJ** *Fam* loufoque, loufedingue; **to be d. about sb/sth** être dingue de qn/qch

dipso ['dɪpsəʊ] **N** *Fam* alcoolo *mf*

dipsomania [,dɪpsə'meɪnjə] **N** dipsomanie *f*

dipsomaniac [,dɪpsə'meɪnɪæk] **N** dipsomane *mf*
ADJ dipsomane

dipstick ['dɪpstɪk] **N 1** *Aut* jauge *f* (de niveau d'huile) **2** *Fam (idiot)* empoté(e) *m,f*

DIP switch ['dɪp-] **N** *Comput* interrupteur *m* DIP

dir 1 *Admin (written abbr* **director)** directeur(trice) *m,f* **2** *Comput (written abbr* **directory)** répertoire *m*

dire ['daɪə(r)] **ADJ 1** *(fearful)* affreux, terrible; *(ominous)* sinistre; **d. warnings** avertissements *mpl* sinistres **2** *Fam (very bad)* **the film was pretty d.** le film était vraiment mauvais[▫] *ou* nul **3** *(extreme)* extrême; **he's in d. need of sleep** il a absolument besoin de sommeil; **only in cases of d. necessity** seulement en cas de necessité absolue; **to be in d. straits** être dans une situation désespérée

DIRECT [dɪ'rekt]

VT
- diriger **1, 2, 4**
- réaliser **2**
- mettre en scène **2**
- adresser **3**
- ordonner **5, 6**

VI
- faire de la réalisation
- faire de la mise en scène

ADJ
- direct **1–3**
- franc **3**
- exact **4**

ADV
- directement

VT 1 *(supervise* ▸ *business)* diriger, gérer, mener; *(*▸ *office, work)* diriger; *(*▸ *movements)* guider; *(*▸ *traffic)* régler
2 *Cin, Rad & TV (film, programme)* réaliser; *(actors)* diriger; *Theat (play)* mettre en scène; **directed by Danny Boyle** *Cin, Rad & TV* réalisation Danny Boyle; *Theat* mise *f* en scène Danny Boyle
3 *(address)* adresser; **please d. your remarks to the chairperson** veuillez adresser vos observations au président; **the accusation was directed at him** l'accusation le visait; **he directed my attention to the map** il a attiré mon attention sur la carte; **we should d. all our efforts towards improving our education service** nous devrions consacrer tous nos efforts à améliorer notre système scolaire
4 *(point)* diriger; **I directed my steps homewards** je me suis dirigé vers la maison; **can you d. me to the train station?** pourriez-vous m'indiquer le chemin de la gare?
5 *(instruct)* ordonner; **he directed them to leave at once** il leur a donné l'ordre de partir immédiatement; **I did as I was directed** j'ai fait comme on m'avait dit *ou* comme on m'en avait donné l'ordre; **take as directed** *(on drugs packaging)* se conformer à la prescription du médecin
6 *Law* **to d. the jury** ordonner le jury
VI *Cin, Rad & TV* faire de la réalisation; *Theat* faire de la mise en scène; **it's her first chance to d.** *Cin, Rad & TV* c'est la première fois qu'elle a l'occasion de faire de la réalisation; *Theat* c'est la première fois qu'elle a l'occasion de faire de la mise en scène
ADJ 1 *(straight)* direct; **d. flight/route** vol *m*/chemin *m* direct
2 *(immediate* ▸ *cause, effect)* direct, immédiat; **she has d. control over the finances** les questions financières relèvent directement de sa responsabilité; **he's a d. descendant of the King** il descend du roi en ligne directe; **keep out of d. sunlight** *(on packaging)* évitez l'exposition directe au soleil
3 *(frank)* franc (franche), direct; *(denial, refusal)* catégorique, absolu; **he was always very d. with us** il nous a toujours parlé très franchement; **she asked some very d. questions** elle a posé des questions parfois très directes
4 *(exact)* exact, précis; **d. quotation** citation *f* exacte; **it's the d. opposite of what I said** c'est exactement le contraire de ce que j'ai dit
ADV *(go)* directement, tout droit; **to travel d. from London to Edinburgh** prendre un train/un vol/*etc* direct de Londres à Edimbourg; **to dispatch goods d. to sb** expédier des marchandises directement à qn; **the concert will be broadcast d. from Paris** ce concert sera transmis en direct de Paris
▸▸ ***direct action*** action *f* directe; *Tel* ***direct broadcast satellite*** satellite *m* de télédiffusion directe; *Elec* ***direct current*** courant *m* continu; *Br Banking & Fin* ***direct debit*** prélèvement *m* automatique; *Tel* ***direct dialling*** automatique *m*; *Am Gram* ***direct discourse*** discours *m ou* style *m* direct; ***direct hit*** coup *m* au but; **to score a d. hit on sth** *(of bomber)* toucher qch en plein dans le mille; *(of bomb)* tomber en plein dans qch; **the ship suffered two d. hits from missiles** le bateau a été touché par deux missiles; *Tel* ***direct line*** ligne *f* directe; *Com & Mktg* ***direct mail*** publipostage *m*; ***direct marketing*** marketing *m* direct; *Gram* ***direct object*** complément *m* (d'objet) direct; *Gram* ***direct question*** question *f* au style direct; *Pol* ***direct rule*** = contrôle direct du maintien de l'ordre par le gouvernement britannique en Irlande du Nord imposé en 1972; ***direct selling*** vente *f* directe; *Br Gram* ***direct speech*** discours *m ou* style *m* direct; *Fin* ***direct taxation*** imposition *f* directe

direct-dial **ADJ** *Tel*
▸▸ ***direct-dial number*** numéro *m* direct; ***direct-dial telephone*** ligne *f* téléphonique directe, téléphone *m* direct

direction [dɪ'rekʃən] **N 1** *(way)* direction *f*, sens *m*; **in every d.** en tous sens, dans tous les sens; **in the opposite d.** dans la direction opposée, en sens inverse; **in the right/wrong d.** dans le bon/mauvais sens, dans la bonne/mauvaise direction; **we were travelling in the d. of Paris** nous allions dans la *ou* en direction de Paris; **I'm going in your d.** je vais dans la même direction que toi; **which d. are you going (in)?** vers où allez-vous?, quelle direction prenez-vous?; *Fig* **a step in the right d.** un pas dans la bonne voie *ou* direction; *Fig* **she lacks d.** elle ne sait pas très bien où elle va; **to have a good/bad sense of d.** avoir un bon/mauvais sens de l'orientation; **to lose one's sense of d.** perdre le sens de l'orientation **2** *(control, management)* direction *f* **3** *Cin, Rad & TV* réalisation *f*; *Theat* mise *f* en scène; **under the d. of...** *Cin, Rad & TV* réalisation de..., réalisé par...; *Theat* mise en scène de...; *(of orchestra)* sous la direction de...
• **directions** **NPL 1** *(instructions)* indications *fpl*, instructions *fpl*, mode *m* d'emploi; **read the directions** lisez le mode d'emploi; *Theat* **stage directions** indications *fpl* scéniques **2** *(to find location)* **I asked for directions to the station** j'ai demandé le chemin de la gare; **you've been given the wrong directions** on vous a mal renseigné
▸▸ ***direction finder*** radiogoniomètre *m*; *Aut* ***direction indicator*** clignotant *m*

directional [dɪ'rekʃənəl] **ADJ** *(gen) & Electron* directionnel
▸▸ ***directional microphone, directional mike*** microphone *m* directionnel

directive [dɪ'rektɪv] **N** directive *f*, instruction *f*
ADJ directeur

directly [dɪ'rektlɪ] **ADV 1** *(straight)* directement; **go d. to the police station** allez directement *ou* tout droit au poste de police; **to be d. descended from sb** descendre en droite ligne *ou* en ligne directe de qn; **the affair concerns me d.** cette affaire me concerne directement; **to come d. to the point** aller droit au fait
2 *(promptly)* immédiatement; **d. after lunch** tout de suite après le déjeuner; **I'll be there d.** j'arrive tout de suite
3 *(frankly)* franchement
4 *(exactly)* exactement; **d. opposite the station** juste en face de la gare
CONJ *Br* aussitôt que + *indicative*, dès que + *indicative*; **we'll leave d. the money arrives** nous partirons dès que l'argent sera arrivé

directness [dɪ'rektnɪs] **N 1** *(of person, reply)* franchise *f*; *(of remark)* absence *f* d'ambiguïté **2** *(of attack)* caractère *m* direct

director [dɪ'rektə(r)] **N 1** *(person* ▸ *of business)* directeur(trice) *m,f*, chef *m*; *(*▸ *of organization)* directeur(trice) *m,f*; *(board member)* administrateur(trice) *m,f* **3** *Cin, Rad & TV* réalisateur(trice) *m,f*; *Theat* metteur *m* en scène **2** *Mus* chef *m* d'orchestre
▸▸ *Cin & TV* ***director's chair*** régisseur *m*; *Cin* ***director's cut*** version *f* du réalisateur, director's cut *f*; *Cin & TV* ***director of photography*** directeur (trice) *m,f* de la photographie; *Rad & TV* ***director of programming*** directeur(trice) *m,f* des programmes; *Br Law* ***Director of Public Prosecutions*** procureur *m* général; *Br Univ* ***director of studies*** = enseignant qui suit la scolarité d'un étudiant tout au long de son cursus universitaire

directorate [dɪ'rektərət] **N 1** *(board)* conseil *m* d'administration **2** *(position)* direction *f*, poste *m* de directeur
▸▸ *EU* ***directorate general*** conseil *m* d'administration

directorial [,daɪrek'tɔːrɪəl] **ADJ** de mise en scène; *Cin* **his d. début** son premier film derrière le caméra

directorship [dɪ'rektəʃɪp] **N** direction *f*, poste *m ou* fonctions *fpl* de directeur; **she holds directorships in several companies** elle fait partie du conseil d'administration de plusieurs entreprises

directory [dɪ'rektərɪ] *(pl* **directories)** **N** *(of addresses)* répertoire *m* (d'adresses); *Tel* annuaire *m* (des téléphones), bottin *m*; *Comput* répertoire *m*
• **Directory** **N** *Hist* **the D.** le Directoire
▸▸ *Tel Am* ***directory assistance***, *Br* ***directory enquiries*** (service *m* des) renseignements *mpl* téléphoniques; *Comput* ***directory structure*** structure *f* arborescente, structure *f* du répertoire

dirge [dɜːdʒ] **N** *Mus* hymne *m ou* chant *m* funèbre; *Fig* chant *m* lugubre

dirigible ['dɪrɪdʒəbəl] **N** dirigeable *m*
ADJ dirigeable

dirk [dɜːk] **N** *Scot* dague *f*, poignard *m*

dirt [dɜːt] **N** *(UNCOUNT)* **1** *(grime)* saleté *f*, crasse *f*; *(mud)* boue *f*; *(excrement)* crotte *f*, ordure *f*; **don't tread d. into the carpet** ne ramène pas de boue sur la moquette; **this dress really shows the d.** cette robe fait vite sale *ou* est très salissante
2 *(soil)* terre *f*; **to treat sb like d.** traiter qn comme un chien; *Am Fam Fig* **to eat d.** ramper[▫]
3 *(obscenity)* obscénité *f*
4 *Fam (scandal)* ragots *mpl*, cancans *mpl*; **to dig/to dish the d. on sb** dénicher/colporter des ragots sur qn
▸▸ *Am* ***dirt bike*** moto *f* tout-terrain; ***dirt farmer*** petit fermier *m*; ***dirt road*** chemin *m* de terre *ou* non goudronné; ***dirt track*** *(gen)* chemin *m* de terre; *Sport* (piste *f*) cendrée *f*; ***dirt track racing*** courses *fpl* sur cendrée

dirtbag ['dɜːtbæg] **N** *Am Fam* nullard(e) *m,f*

dirt-cheap *Fam* **ADJ** très bon marché[▫]
ADV pour rien[▫]; **I bought it d.** je l'ai payé trois fois rien

dirtily ['dɜːtɪlɪ] **ADV 1** *(eat)* salement **2** *(speak)* grossièrement **3** *(play, fight)* déloyalement

dirtiness ['dɜːtɪnɪs] **N** malpropreté *f*

dirty ['dɜːtɪ] *(compar* **dirtier**, *superl* **dirtiest**, *pt & pp* **dirtied)** **ADJ 1** *(not clean* ▸ *clothes, hands, person)* sale, malpropre, crasseux; *(*▸ *wound)* infecté; *(muddy)* plein de boue, crotté; **don't get d.!** ne vous salissez pas!; *also Fig* **to get one's hands d.** se salir les mains
2 *(colour)* sale; **a d. green** un vert sale
3 *(nasty)* sale; **politics is a d. business** il est difficile de garder les mains propres quand on fait de la politique; **a d. campaign** une campagne sordide; **that's a d. lie** ce n'est absolument pas vrai; **he's a d. fighter** il se bat en traître; **to give sb a d. look** regarder qn de travers *ou* d'un sale

il; *Am* **that's d. pool!** c'est un tour de cochon!; *am* **you d. rat!** espèce de salaud!
4 *(weather)* sale, vilain
5 *(obscene)* grossier, obscène; **to have a d. mind** voir l'esprit mal tourné; **d. magazines** revues *fpl* ornographiques; *Fam* **a d. old man** un vieux co- hon *ou* vicelard; **a d. joke/story** une blague/his- oire cochonne; **a d. word** une grossièreté, un ros mot; **"middle class" is a d. word around here** terme "classe moyenne" est une insulte par ici
ADV *Fam* **1** *(fight, play)* déloyalement; **to talk d.** *swearing)* dire des gros mots; *(sexually)* dire es trucs cochons **2** *Br (as intensifier)* vache- nent; **a d. great skyscraper** un gratte-ciel énorme
VT *(soil)* salir; *also Fig* **to d. one's hands** se salir les nains
VI se salir, se souiller; **to d. easily** *(material, car tc)* se salir facilement, être salissant
N *Br Fam* **to do the d. on sb** jouer un sale tour *ou* aire une vacherie à qn
▸ *Mil* ***dirty bomb*** bombe *f* sale, bombe *f* radio- ctive; *Fin* ***dirty money*** argent *m* sale *ou* mal ac- uis; *Br Fam Hum* ***dirty stop-out*** débauché(e) *m,f qui découche)*; ***dirty trick*** *(malicious act)* sale tour n; **to play a d. trick on sb** jouer un sale tour *ou* un our de cochon à qn; *Pol* ***dirty tricks campaign*** = nanœuvres déloyales visant à discréditer un dversaire politique; *Fam* ***dirty weekend*** week- nd *m* coquin; ***dirty work*** *(UNCOUNT) (unpleas- nt)* travail *m* salissant; *Fam (dishonest)* sale bou- ot *m*; **to do sb's d. work** faire le sale boulot pour qn

is [dɪs] **VT** *esp Am Fam (disparage)* débiner

> **PRÉFIXE**
>
> **DIS-**
>
> Ce préfixe de négation s'emploie avec des noms et des adjectifs pour exprimer:
>
> • le CONTRAIRE d'une action ou d'un état. Les traductions varient selon les termes: **disadvantage** désavantage; **to disapprove** désapprouver; **disembark** débarquer; **dissimilar** dissemblable; **dissatisfied** mécontent; **dishonesty** malhonnêteté; **disabled** infirme; **dislike** aversion; **to dislike** ne pas aimer; **to disagree** ne pas être d'accord; **to distrust** se méfier de
>
> • l'INVERSION ou l'INTERRUPTION d'un processus. Dans la plupart des cas, **dis-** se traduira par **dé-** ou **dés-**, comme dans: **to disentangle** démêler; **to disinfect** désinfecter; **to disarm** désarmer. Il existe néanmoins des exceptions comme **to discontinue** interrompre
>
> • Le fait d'ÔTER quelque chose. Dans ce sens, **dis-** se traduit généralement par **dé-** ou **dés-**, comme dans: **dismast** démâter; **dismember** démembrer; **she disrobed** elle s'est déshabillée

isability [ˌdɪsəˈbɪlətɪ] *(pl* **disabilities)** **N 1** *(state* ▸ *physical)* incapacité *f*, invalidité *f*; **partial/total d.** ncapacité *f* partielle/totale **2** *(handicap)* infirmité *f*, handicap *m*; **her d. makes her eligible for a pension** son infirmité lui donne droit à une pension **3** *Law* **d. to do sth** incapacité *f ou* inhabilité *f* à faire qch
▸▸ *Admin* ***disability allowance*** pension *f* d'invalidité; *Admin* ***disability benefit*** allocation *f* d'invalidité; *Admin* ***disability pension*** pension *f* d'invalidité

isable [dɪsˈeɪbəl] **VT 1** *(accident, illness)* rendre nfirme; *(maim)* mutiler, estropier; **a disabling disease** une maladie invalidante
2 *Mil (army, battalion)* mettre hors de combat
3 *(machine)* mettre hors service; *(ship)* faire subir une avarie à, désemparer; *(gun, tank)* mettre hors d'action; *Comput (option)* désactiver
4 *Law* **to d. sb from doing sth** rendre qn inhabile à faire qch; *(pronounce)* prononcer qn inhabile à faire qch

isabled [dɪsˈeɪbəld] **ADJ 1** *(handicapped)* infirme, handicapé; *(maimed)* mutilé, estropié; **d. ex-servicemen** invalides *mpl ou* mutilés *mpl* de guerre
2 *Mil (army, battalion)* mis hors de combat
3 *(machine)* hors service; *(ship)* avarié, désemparé; *(gun, tank)* mis hors d'action; *Comput (option)* désactivé
4 *Law* **to be d. from doing sth** être incapable de *ou* inhabile à faire qch
NPL the d. les handicapés *mpl*
▸▸ ***disabled access*** facilité *f* d'accès pour personnes handicapées

disablement [dɪsˈeɪbəlmənt] **N 1** *(physical handicap)* invalidité *f*, infirmité *f* **2** *(action) Mil* mise *f* hors de combat; *(of machine)* mise hors service

disabuse [ˌdɪsəˈbjuːz] **VT** *Formal* détromper, ôter ses illusions à; **to d. sb of sth** détromper qn de qch

disadvantage [ˌdɪsədˈvɑːntɪdʒ] **N 1** *(condition)* désavantage *m*, inconvénient *m*; **to be at a d.** être désavantagé *ou* dans une position désavantageuse; **to put sb at a d.** désavantager *ou* défavoriser qn; **the situation works** *or* **is to her d.** la situation est un handicap *ou* un désavantage pour elle **2** *Com (loss)* perte *f*
VT désavantager, défavoriser

disadvantaged [ˌdɪsədˈvɑːntɪdʒd] **ADJ** *(gen)* défavorisé; *(economically)* déshérité; **socially/educationally d.** défavorisé sur le plan social/en matière d'éducation
NPL the d. les défavorisés *mpl*

disadvantageous [ˌdɪsædvɑːnˈteɪdʒəs] **ADJ** désavantageux, défavorable; **to be d. to sb** être désavantageux *ou* défavorable à qn

disaffected [ˌdɪsəˈfektɪd] **ADJ** *(discontented)* mécontent; *(rebellious)* rebelle; **d. youth** jeunesse *f* révoltée

disaffection [ˌdɪsəˈfekʃən] **N** *(discontent)* mécontentement *m* (**from** à l'égard de); **there is widespread d. in the country** *(rebelliousness)* le pays est au bord de la rébellion

disagree [ˌdɪsəˈgriː] **VI 1** *(person, people)* ne pas être d'accord, être en désaccord; **to d. with sb about** *or* **on sth** ne pas être d'accord avec *ou* ne pas être du même avis que qn sur qch; **I d. with everything they've done** je suis contre *ou* je désapprouve tout ce qu'ils ont fait; **we d. on everything** *(differ)* nous ne sommes jamais d'accord; **I can't say I d. with her** *(in opinion etc)* je ne peux pas dire que je ne suis pas de son avis; *(as regards an action)* je ne peux pas dire que je la désapprouve **2** *(figures, records)* ne pas concorder **3** *(food, weather)* ne pas convenir; **spicy food disagrees with him** les plats épicés ne lui réussissent pas, il digère mal les plats épicés; **I must have eaten something that disagreed with me** j'ai dû manger quelque chose qui n'est pas bien passé

disagreeable [ˌdɪsəˈgrɪəbəl] **ADJ** *(person, remark)* désagréable, désobligeant; *(experience, job)* désagréable, pénible; *(smell)* désagréable, déplaisant; **don't be so d.!** ne soyez pas si désagréable!

disagreeableness [ˌdɪsəˈgrɪəbəlnɪs] **N** *(of situation, job, experience, smell)* caractère *m* désagréable; *(of person)* mauvaise humeur *f*; *(of remark)* désobligeance *f* (**to** envers)

disagreeably [ˌdɪsəˈgrɪəblɪ] **ADV** désagréablement, d'une façon désagréable *ou* désobligeante; **he behaved so d.!** il a été tellement insupportable!

disagreement [ˌdɪsəˈgriːmənt] **N 1** *(of opinions, records)* désaccord *m*, conflit *m*; **to be in d. with sb** ne pas partager l'avis de qn, être en désaccord avec qn; **they are in d. about** *or* **on what action to take** ils ne sont pas d'accord sur les mesures à prendre **2** *(quarrel)* différend *m*, querelle *f*; **they've had a d. over** *or* **about money** ils se sont disputés à propos d'argent, ils ont eu une querelle d'argent

disallow [ˌdɪsəˈlaʊ] **VT** *(argument, opinion)* rejeter; *Sport (goal, try)* refuser; *Law* débouter, rejeter

disambiguate [ˌdɪsæmˈbɪgjʊeɪt] **VT** désambiguïser

disappear [ˌdɪsəˈpɪə(r)] **VI 1** *(vanish* ▸ *person, snow)* disparaître; *(*▸ *object)* disparaître, s'égarer; *Ling* s'amuïr; **she disappeared from sight** on l'a perdue de vue; **he disappeared into the crowd** il s'est perdu dans la foule; **to d. over the horizon** disparaître à l'horizon; **to make sth d.** *(gen)* faire disparaître qch; *(magician)* escamoter qch **2** *(cease to exist* ▸ *pain, tribe)* disparaître; *(*▸ *problem)* disparaître, s'aplanir; *(*▸ *memory)* s'effacer, s'estomper; *(*▸ *tradition)* disparaître, tomber en désuétude; **as a species, the turtle is fast disappearing** les tortues sont une espèce en voie de disparition

disappearance [ˌdɪsəˈpɪərəns] **N** *(gen)* disparition *f*; *Ling* amuïssement *m*

disappearing act [ˌdɪsəˈpɪərɪŋ-] **N to do a d.** *(conjurer* ▸ *make someone or something disappear)* faire disparaître quelqu'un/quelque chose; *(*▸ *make self disappear)* disparaître; *Fam Fig (*▸ *sneak away)* s'esquiver[□], s'éclipser[□]; **he's done his famous d. again** il s'est encore éclipsé; *Fam* **the scissors have done a d.** les ciseaux ont disparu[□]

disappoint [ˌdɪsəˈpɔɪnt] **VT 1** *(person)* décevoir; **you promised to come, so don't d. him** vous avez promis de venir, alors ne lui faites pas faux bond **2** *(hope)* décevoir; *(plan)* contrarier, contrecarrer

disappointed [ˌdɪsəˈpɔɪntɪd] **ADJ 1** *(person)* déçu; **d. customers** clients *mpl* insatisfaits; **I'm very d. in him** il m'a beaucoup déçu; **I was d. to hear you won't be coming** j'ai été déçu d'apprendre que vous ne viendrez pas; **are you d. at** *or* **with the results?** les résultats vous ont-ils déçu?, avez-vous été déçu par les résultats?; **to be d. in love** être malheureux en amour **2** *(ambition, hope)* déçu; *(plan)* contrarié, contrecarré

disappointing [ˌdɪsəˈpɔɪntɪŋ] **ADJ** décevant; **how d.!** quelle déception!, comme c'est décevant!

disappointingly [ˌdɪsəˈpɔɪntɪŋlɪ] **ADV d. low grades** des notes *fpl* d'une faiblesse décourageante *ou* décevante; **the unemployment figures are still d. high** il est décevant de constater que les chiffres du chômage restent élevés

disappointment [ˌdɪsəˈpɔɪntmənt] **N 1** *(state)* déception *f*, déconvenue *f*; **to her great d. she failed** à sa grande déception *ou* déconvenue, elle a échoué; **book early to avoid d.** réservez bien à l'avance pour ne pas être déçu **2** *(letdown)* déception *f*, désillusion *f*; **she has suffered many disappointments** elle a essuyé bien des déboires; **it was a bit of a d.** *(of film, holiday etc)* c'était un peu décevant; **he has been a great d. to me** il m'a beaucoup déçu

disapprobation [ˌdɪsæprəˈbeɪʃən] **N** *Formal* désapprobation *f*; *(strong)* réprobation *f*

disapproval [ˌdɪsəˈpruːvəl] **N** désapprobation *f*; *(strong)* réprobation *f*; **a look of d.** un regard désapprobateur *ou* de désapprobation; **to shake one's head in d.** faire un signe désapprobateur de la tête; **much to my d. she decided to get married** elle a décidé de se marier, ce que je désapprouve entièrement

disapprove [ˌdɪsəˈpruːv] **VI** désapprouver; **to d. of sth** désapprouver qch; **she disapproves of smoking** elle désapprouve *ou* elle est contre le tabac; **your mother disapproves of your going** votre mère n'est pas d'accord pour que vous y alliez; **her father disapproves of me** son père ne me trouve pas à son goût
VT désapprouver

disapproving [ˌdɪsəˈpruːvɪŋ] **ADJ** désapprobateur, de désapprobation; **he was a stern, rather d. man** c'était un homme sévère, qui portait sur toutes choses un œil désapprobateur

disapprovingly [ˌdɪsəˈpruːvɪŋlɪ] **ADV** *(look)* d'un air désapprobateur; *(speak)* d'un ton désapprobateur, avec désapprobation

disarm [dɪsˈɑːm] **VT 1** *(country, enemy, critic)* désarmer **2** *(of charm)* désarmer, toucher
VI désarmer

disarmament [dɪsˈɑːməmənt] **N** désarmement *m*
COMP *(conference, negotiations, talks)* sur le désarmement

disarming [dɪsˈɑːmɪŋ] **N** désarmement *m*
ADJ désarmant

disarmingly [dɪsˈɑːmɪŋlɪ] **ADV** de façon désarmante; **he was d. frank/friendly** il montrait une franchise/une amabilité désarmante

disarrange [ˌdɪsəˈreɪndʒ] **VT** *(order, room)* déranger, mettre en désordre; *(plans)* déranger, bouleverser; *(hair)* défaire

disarray [ˌdɪsəˈreɪ] N *(of person)* confusion *f*, désordre *m*; *(of clothing)* désordre *m*; **in total d.** *(person, political party)* en plein désarroi; *(objects, room, life)* en désordre; *(troops)* en déroute; **the group was thrown into d.** la confusion *ou* le désordre régnait dans le groupe; **her clothes were in d.** elle était débraillée

disassemble [ˌdɪsəˈsembəl] VT démonter, désassembler

disassociate [ˌdɪsəˈsəʊʃɪeɪt] VT **1** *(gen)* dissocier, séparer; **to d. oneself from sb/sth** se dissocier *ou* désolidariser de qn/qch **2** *Chem* dissocier
VI *Chem (chemist)* opérer une dissociation; *(molecules)* se dissocier

disassociation [dɪsəˌsəʊsɪˈeɪʃən] N dissociation *f*

disaster [dɪˈzɑːstə(r)] N désastre *m*, catastrophe *f*; *(natural)* catastrophe *f*, sinistre *m*; **air d.** catastrophe *f* aérienne; **financial d.** désastre *m* financier; **a series of disasters** une suite de désastres *ou* de malheurs; **it would be a d.!** ce serait le désastre!; **she's heading for** *or* **courting d.** elle court à sa perte *ou* à la catastrophe; **they were near the summit when d. struck** ils avaient presque atteint le sommet quand la catastrophe s'est produite; **as a manager, he's a d.!** en tant que directeur, ce n'est pas une réussite!; **my hair's a d. this morning!** mes cheveux sont dans un état épouvantable ce matin!
►► ***disaster area*** région *f* sinistrée; *Fig* champ *m* de bataille; **your sister's a walking d. area!** ta sœur est une vraie catastrophe ambulante!; ***disaster fund*** fonds *m* de secours; ***disaster movie*** film *m* catastrophe

disastrous [dɪˈzɑːstrəs] ADJ désastreux, catastrophique

disastrously [dɪˈzɑːstrəslɪ] ADV désastreusement; **the performance went d. wrong** la représentation a tourné au désastre; **the estimates were d. inaccurate** l'inexactitude des prévisions s'est révélée désastreuse

disavow [ˌdɪsəˈvaʊ] VT *Formal (child, opinion)* désavouer; *(responsibility, faith)* renier

disavowal [ˌdɪsəˈvaʊəl] N *Formal (of child, opinion)* désaveu *m*; *(of responsibility, faith)* reniement *m*

disband [dɪsˈbænd] VT *(army, club)* disperser; *(organization)* disperser, dissoudre
VI *(army, club)* se disperser; *(organization)* se dissoudre

disbar [dɪsˈbɑː(r)] *(pt & pp* **disbarred,** *cont* **disbarring)** VT *Law* rayer du barreau *ou* du tableau de l'ordre *(des avocats)*

disbarment [dɪsˈbɑːmənt] N *Law* radiation *f* (du barreau)

disbelief [ˌdɪsbɪˈliːf] N incrédulité *f*; **she looked at him in d.** elle l'a regardé avec incrédulité

disbelieve [ˌdɪsbɪˈliːv] VT *(person)* ne pas croire; *(news, story)* ne pas croire à; **I see no reason to d. his story** je ne vois pas pourquoi on ne croirait pas à ce qu'il dit
VI *also Rel* ne pas croire (**in** à)

disbeliever [ˌdɪsbɪˈliːvə(r)] N *(gen)* incrédule *mf*; *Rel* incroyant(e) *m,f*, incrédule *mf*

disbelieving [ˌdɪsbɪˈliːvɪŋ] ADJ incrédule

disbud [ˌdɪsˈbʌd] *(pt & pp* **disbudded,** *cont* **disbudding)** VT *Bot (fruit tree)* ébourgeonner

disburse [dɪsˈbɜːs] VT *Fin* débourser

disbursement [dɪsˈbɜːsmənt] N *Fin* **1** *(payment)* débours *m*, dépense *f* **2** *(action)* déboursement *m*

disc [dɪsk] N **1** *(flat circular object)* disque *m*; **the d. of the moon** le disque de la lune
2 *(record)* disque *m*
3 *Anat* disque *m* (invertébral); **to slip a d.** se faire une hernie discale
4 *(identity tag)* plaque *f* d'identité; *Aut* **parking d.** disque *m* de stationnement;
►► *Aut* ***disc brake*** frein *m* à disque; *Phot* ***disc camera*** appareil *m* photo à disque; *Phot* ***disc film*** disque *m*; *Agr* ***disc harrow*** pulvériseur *m*; ***disc jockey*** animateur(trice) *m,f*, *(on radio, at disco)* disc-jockey *m*; ***disc parking*** stationnement *m* à disque

discard VT [dɪˈskɑːd] **1** *(get rid of)* se débarrasser de, mettre au rebut; *(idea, system)* renoncer, abandonner; *(friend)* abandonner; **his discarded coat still lay on the sofa** son manteau était toujours sur le canapé, tel qu'il l'y avait jeté **2** *Cards* se défausser de, défausser; *(in cribbage)* écarter
VI [dɪˈskɑːd] *Cards* se défausser; *(in cribbage)* écarter
N [ˈdɪskɑːd] **1** *Com & Ind (reject)* pièce *f* de rebut **2** *Cards* défausse *f*; *(in cribbage)* écart *m*

discern [dɪˈsɜːn] VT *(see)* discerner, distinguer; *(understand)* discerner

discernible [dɪˈsɜːnəbəl] ADJ *(visible)* visible; *(detectable)* discernable, perceptible; **he left for no d. reason** il est parti sans raison apparente

discernibly [dɪˈsɜːnəblɪ] ADV *(visibly)* visiblement; *(perceptibly)* perceptiblement, sensiblement

discerning [dɪˈsɜːnɪŋ] ADJ *(person)* judicieux, sagace; *(taste)* fin, délicat; *(look)* perspicace; **with a d. eye** d'un œil averti; **a house/car for the d. buyer** une maison/voiture pour l'acheteur avisé; **for the d. reader** pour le lecteur averti

discernment [dɪˈsɜːnmənt] N discernement *m*, perspicacité *f*

discharge VT [ˈdɪstʃɑːdʒ] **1** *(release ► patient)* laisser sortir, libérer; *(► prisoner)* libérer, mettre en liberté; **he was discharged from hospital yesterday** il est sorti de l'hôpital hier; **the patient discharged herself** la malade a signé une décharge et est partie
2 *(dismiss ► employee)* renvoyer, congédier; *(► official)* destituer; *Law (► jury)* dessaisir; *(► accused)* acquitter, relaxer; *Mil (from service)* renvoyer à la vie civile; *(from active duty)* démobiliser; *(for lack of fitness)* réformer; *Fin* **discharged bankrupt** failli *m* réhabilité
3 *(unload ► cargo)* décharger; *(► passengers)* débarquer
4 *(emit ► liquid)* dégorger, déverser; *(► gas)* dégager, émettre; *(of gland ► hormones)* sécréter; *Elec* décharger; *Med* **to d. pus** *(abscess)* suppurer
5 *(perform ► duty)* remplir, s'acquitter de; *(► function)* remplir
6 *Fin (debt)* s'acquitter de, régler
7 *(gun)* décharger, tirer; *(arrow)* décocher
VI [ˈdɪstʃɑːdʒ] **1** *(ship)* décharger **2** *Med (wound)* suinter **3** *Elec* être en décharge
N [dɪsˈtʃɑːdʒ] **1** *(release ► of patient)* sortie *f* *(of prisoner)* libération *f*, mise *f* en liberté
2 *(dismissal ► of employee)* renvoi *m*; *(► of soldier)* libération *f*; *(after active duty)* démobilisation *f*; *Law (acquittal)* acquittement *m*
3 *(of cargo)* déchargement *m*
4 *(emission)* émission *f*; *(of liquid)* écoulement *m*; *Med (of wound)* suintement *m*; *(vaginal)* pertes *fpl* (blanches); *(of pus)* suppuration *f*
5 *Elec* décharge *f*
6 *(of duty)* exécution *f*, accomplissement *m*
7 *(of debt)* acquittement *m*
8 *(of gun)* décharge *f*
►► *Tech* ***discharge pipe*** tuyau *m* de décharge *ou* de débit

disciple [dɪˈsaɪpəl] N *(gen)* & *Rel* disciple *m*

disciplinarian [ˌdɪsɪplɪˈneərɪən] N partisan *m* de la manière forte; **he is a strict d.** il est strict en matière de discipline
ADJ disciplinaire

disciplinary [ˈdɪsɪplɪnərɪ] ADJ **1** *(corrective ► measure)* disciplinaire; *(► committee)* de discipline; **to take d. action** *(of employer)* prendre des mesures disciplinaires **2** *(relating to field)* relatif à une discipline
►► ***disciplinary board*** conseil *m* de discipline; ***disciplinary hearing*** séance *f* du conseil de discipline; ***disciplinary procedure*** procédure *f* disciplinaire

discipline [ˈdɪsɪplɪn] N **1** *(training, control)* discipline *f*; **to keep d.** *(of teacher)* maintenir la discipline; **with iron d.** avec une discipline de fer **2** *(area of study)* discipline *f*, matière *f*
VT **1** *(train ► person)* discipliner; *(► mind)* discipliner, former; **to d. oneself** se discipliner **2** *(punish)* punir

disciplined [ˈdɪsɪplɪnd] ADJ discipliné

disclaim [dɪsˈkleɪm] VT **1** *(deny ► responsibility)* rejeter, décliner; *(► knowledge)* nier; *(► news, remark)* démentir; *(► paternity)* désavouer **2** *Law* se désister de, renoncer à

disclaimer [dɪsˈkleɪmə(r)] N **1** *(denial)* démenti *m*, désaveu *m*; **to issue a d.** publier un démenti **2** *Law* désistement *m*, renonciation *f*

disclose [dɪsˈkləʊz] VT **1** *(reveal ► secret)* divulguer, dévoiler; *(► news)* divulguer; *(► feelings)* révéler **2** *(uncover)* exposer, montrer

disclosure [dɪsˈkləʊʒə(r)] N **1** *(revelation)* divulgation *f*, révélation *f* **2** *(fact revealed)* révélation *f* **3** *St Exch* information *f* aux actionnaires
►► *Acct* ***disclosure of accounts*** publication *f* des comptes

disco [ˈdɪskəʊ] *(pl* **discos)** N **1** *(place)* discothèque *f*, boîte *f* **2** *(music)* disco *m or f*
COMP *(dancing, music)* disco

discography [dɪsˈkɒgrəfɪ] N discographie *f*

discolour, *Am* **discolor** [dɪsˈkʌlə(r)] VT *(change colour of, fade)* décolorer; *(turn yellow)* jaunir
VI *(change colour, fade)* se décolorer; *(turn yellow)* jaunir

discolouration, *Am* **discoloration** [dɪsˌkʌləˈreɪʃən] N *(fading)* décoloration *f*, *(yellowing)* jaunissement *m*

discoloured, *Am* **discolored** [dɪsˈkʌləd] ADJ *(faded)* décoloré; *(yellowed)* jauni

discombobulate [ˌdɪskəmˈbɒbjʊleɪt] VT *Am Fam Hum (plans)* chambarder; *(person)* déconcerter, confondre

discomfit [dɪsˈkʌmfɪt] VT *Formal* **1** *(confuse, embarrass)* déconcerter, gêner **2** *(thwart ► plan, project)* contrecarrer, contrarier

discomfiture [dɪsˈkʌmfɪtʃə(r)] N *Formal (embarrassment)* embarras *m*, gêne *f*

discomfort [dɪsˈkʌmfət] N **1** *(pain)* malaise *m*, *(unease)* gêne *f*; **she's in some d.** elle a assez mal; **you may experience some d.** il se peut que vous ressentiez une gêne **2** *(cause of pain, unease)* incommodité *f*, inconfort *m*
VT incommoder, gêner

discomposure [ˌdɪskəmˈpəʊʒə(r)] N *Formal* embarras *m*, gêne *f*

disconcert [ˌdɪskənˈsɜːt] VT **1** *(fluster)* déconcerter, décontenancer **2** *(upset)* troubler, gêner

disconcerting [ˌdɪskənˈsɜːtɪŋ] ADJ **1** *(unnerving)* déconcertant, déroutant **2** *(upsetting)* gênant

disconcertingly [ˌdɪskənˈsɜːtɪŋlɪ] ADV de façon déconcertante *ou* déroutante; **she had a d. abrupt manner** elle était d'une brusquerie déconcertante

disconnect [ˌdɪskəˈnekt] VT **1** *(detach ► plug, pipe, radio, TV)* débrancher; *(► wire, battery)* déconnecter; *(► gas, electricity, telephone, water)* couper **2** *Rail (carriages)* décrocher

disconnected [ˌdɪskəˈnektɪd] ADJ **1** *(remarks, thoughts)* décousu, sans suite; *(facts)* sans rapport **2** *(detached ► wire, battery)* déconnecté; *(► plug, appliance)* débranché; *(► gas, electricity, telephone, water)* coupé; *Tel* **I've been d.** *(for non payment of bill)* ils m'ont coupé le téléphone *(conversation cut off)* on a coupé la communication; **to get the gas/electricity/telephone d.** faire couper le gaz/l'électricité/le téléphone

disconnection, disconnexion [ˌdɪskəˈnekʃən] N **1** *(action ► of phone, gas, water, in phone call)* coupure *f*; *(► of wire, battery)* déconnexion *f*; *(► of appliance)* débranchement *m* **2** *Rail (of carriages)* décrochage *m*

disconsolate [dɪsˈkɒnsələt] ADJ triste, inconsolable

disconsolately [dɪsˈkɒnsələtlɪ] ADV tristement, inconsolablement

discontent [ˌdɪskənˈtent] N **1** *(dissatisfaction)* mécontentement *m*; **general** *or* **public d.** malaise *m*; **a cause of d.** un grief **2** *(person)* mécontent(e) *m,f*
ADJ mécontent
VT mécontenter

discontented [ˌdɪskənˈtentɪd] ADJ mécontent

discontinue [ˌdɪskənˈtɪnjuː] VT **1** *(gen)* cesser, interrompre **2** *Com & Ind (production)* abandonner; *(product)* interrompre; *(publication)* interrompre la publication de; **this item/model has been discontinued** cet article/ce modèle n se fait plus; **discontinued** *(on label)* fin de série **3** *Law (action, suit)* abandonner

►► *Com & Ind* ***discontinued line*** fin *f* de série

discontinuity [ˌdɪskɒntɪˈnjuːətɪ] *(pl* **discontinuities)** **N 1** *(gen) & Math* discontinuité *f* **2** *Geol* zone de discontinuité

discontinuous [ˌdɪskənˈtɪnjʊəs] **ADJ** *(gen) & Ling & Math* discontinu

discord [ˈdɪskɔːd] **N 1** *(UNCOUNT) (conflict)* désaccord *m*, discorde *f*; **civil d.** dissensions *fpl* sociales **2** *Mus* dissonance *f*

discordant [dɪsˈkɔːdənt] **ADJ 1** *(opinions)* incompatible, opposé; *(colours, sounds)* discordant **2** *Mus* dissonant

discotheque [ˈdɪskəʊtek] **N** discothèque *f*

discount N [ˈdɪskaʊnt] **1** *Com (price reduction)* remise *f*, rabais *m*; **I bought it at a d.** je l'ai acheté au rabais; **she got a d.** on lui a fait une remise; **the store is currently offering a 5 percent d. on suitcases** le magasin fait (une réduction de) 5 pour cent sur les valises en ce moment **2** *Fin & St Exch (deduction)* escompte *m*; **d. for cash** escompte *m* au comptant; **to be at a d.** *(shares)* être en perte, se trouver en moins-value; *Fig (politeness etc)* être en défaveur

COMP [ˈdɪskaʊnt] *Com (price, tariff)* réduit

VT [ˈdɪskaʊnt, dɪsˈkaʊnt] **1** *(disregard)* ne pas tenir compte de; **you have to d. half of what she says** il ne faut pas croire la moitié de ce qu'elle raconte; **they did not d. the possibility** ils n'ont pas écarté cette possibilité **2** *Com (article)* faire une remise ou un rabais sur **3** *Fin (sum of money)* faire une remise de, escompter; *(bill, banknote)* prendre à l'escompte, escompter

►► *Com* ***discount card*** carte *f* de réduction; ***discount house*** *Br Fin (bank)* banque *f* d'escompte; *(organization)* = organisme qui escompte des traites ou des effets; *Am Com (shop)* solderie *f*, magasin *m* de vente au rabais; *Fin* ***discount rate*** taux *m* d'escompte; *Com* ***discount store*** solderie *f*, magasin *m* de vente au rabais; *Com* ***discount voucher*** bon *m* de réduction

discountable [dɪsˈkaʊntəbəl] **ADJ** *Fin* escomptable

discounted [dɪsˈkaʊntɪd] **ADJ**

►► *Fin* ***discounted rate*** taux *m* d'escompte; *Acct* ***discounted value*** valeur *f* actualisée

discounting [dɪsˈkaʊntɪŋ] **N** *Com* remise *f*, *Fin (of bill)* escompte *m*

discourage [dɪˈskʌrɪdʒ] **VT 1** *(dishearten)* décourager, abattre; **to become discouraged** se laisser décourager; **don't get discouraged** ne te décourage pas **2** *(dissuade)* décourager, dissuader; **to d. sb from doing sth** dissuader qn de faire qch; **they were discouraged from going by the weather/the price** le temps/le prix les a dissuadés d'y aller; **we are trying to d. smoking** nous essayons de dissuader les gens de fumer; **her parents tried to d. this friendship** ses parents ont essayé d'empêcher cette amitié

discouragement [dɪˈskʌrɪdʒmənt] **N 1** *(depressed state)* découragement *m* **2** *(attempt to discourage)* **I met with d. on all sides** tout le monde a essayé de me décourager **3** *(deterrent)* **I hope this won't be a d. to you** j'espère que ceci ne te découragera pas; **to act as a d.** avoir un effet dissuasif

discouraging [dɪˈskʌrɪdʒɪŋ] **ADJ** décourageant

discourse N [ˈdɪskɔːs] **1** *Formal (sermon)* discours *m*; *(dissertation)* discours *m*, traité *m* **2** *Ling* discours *m* **3** *(UNCOUNT) Literary (conversation)* conversation *f*, débat *m*

VI [dɪˈskɔːs] **1** *Formal (speak)* **to d. on** *or* **upon sth** traiter de *ou* parler de qch; **to d. at great length on sth** discourir longuement sur qch **2** *Literary (converse)* s'entretenir

►► *Ling* ***discourse analysis*** analyse *f* du discours

discourteous [dɪsˈkɜːtɪəs] **ADJ** discourtois, impoli; **to be d. to** *or* **towards sb** être discourtois *ou* impoli avec *ou* envers qn

discourteously [dɪsˈkɜːtɪəslɪ] **ADV** d'une façon discourtoise *ou* impolie; **to behave d. towards sb** manquer de politesse envers qn, se montrer impoli *ou* discourtois avec qn

discourtesy [dɪsˈkɜːtɪsɪ] *(pl* **discourtesies) N** manque *m* de courtoisie, impolitesse *f*; **I meant no d.** je ne voulais pas me montrer discourtois

discover [dɪˈskʌvə(r)] **VT 1** *(country, answer, reason)* découvrir; **I finally discovered my glasses in my desk** j'ai fini par trouver mes lunettes dans mon bureau **2** *(realize)* se rendre compte; **when did you d. that your wallet had been stolen?** quand vous êtes-vous rendu compte qu'on vous avait volé votre portefeuille? **3** *(actor, singer etc)* découvrir; **to be discovered** être découvert

discoverer [dɪˈskʌvərə(r)] **N** découvreur *m*; **the d. of penicillin** la personne qui a découvert la pénicilline

discovery [dɪˈskʌvərɪ] *(pl* **discoveries) N 1** *(act, event)* découverte *f*; **voyage of d.** voyage *m* d'exploration **2** *(actor, singer, place, thing)* révélation *f*; **he's quite a d.** *(new actor, soccer player etc)* c'est une vraie révélation **3** *Law (of documents)* divulgation *f*

discredit [dɪsˈkredɪt] **VT 1** *(person)* discréditer **2** *(report, theory* ► *cast doubt on)* discréditer, mettre en doute; *(*► *show to be false)* montrer l'inexactitude de; **this theory is now considered discredited** cette théorie est maintenant en discrédit

N *(loss of good reputation)* discrédit *m*; **to bring d. on** *or* **upon** jeter le discrédit sur; **to his great d., he told a lie** à sa grand honte, il a menti; **to be a d. to one's family/school** déshonorer sa famille/son école

discreditable [dɪsˈkredɪtəbəl] **ADJ** peu honorable, indigne

discreet [dɪˈskriːt] **ADJ** discret(ète); **can you trust him to be d.?** peut-on compter sur sa discrétion?; **to follow sb at a d. distance** suivre qn à une distance respectueuse

> Attention: ne pas confondre avec l'adjectif **discrete**.

discreetly [dɪˈskriːtlɪ] **ADV** discrètement, de manière discrète

discrepancy [dɪˈskrepənsɪ] *(pl* **discrepancies) N** *(in figures)* contradiction *f*; *(in statements)* contradiction *f*, désaccord *m*, divergence *f*; **there's a d. between these reports** ces rapports se contredisent *ou* divergent (sur un point); **there's a d. in the accounts** les comptes ne concordent pas

discrete [dɪˈskriːt] **ADJ** *(gen) & Tech & Math* discret(ète)

> Attention: ne pas confondre avec l'adjectif **discreet**.

discretion [dɪˈskreʃən] **N 1** *(tact, prudence)* discrétion *f*; **to be the soul of d.** être la discrétion même; *Prov* **d. is the better part of valour** prudence est mère de sûreté **2** *(judgment, taste)* jugement *m*; **I'll leave it to your d.** je laisse cela à votre discrétion *ou* jugement; **use your own d.** jugez par vous-même; **a woman of d.** une femme de raison; **the age of d.** l'âge *m* de raison; **at the manager's d.** à la discrétion du directeur; **the committee has d. to award more than one prize** à la discrétion du comité, plus d'un prix peut être accordé

discretionary [dɪˈskreʃənərɪ] **ADJ** *Law* discrétionnaire

discriminate [dɪsˈkrɪmɪneɪt] **VI 1** *(on grounds of race, sex etc)* **to d. in favour of** favoriser; **she was discriminated against** elle faisait l'objet *ou* était victime de discrimination **2** *(distinguish)* établir *ou* faire une distinction, faire une différence; **to d. between right and wrong** distinguer le bien du mal

VT distinguer

discriminating [dɪsˈkrɪmɪneɪtɪŋ] **ADJ 1** *(showing discernment)* judicieux; *(in matters of taste)* qui a un goût sûr; *(audience, eye)* averti; *(ear, judgment)* fin; **he is not very d. in his choice of friends** il n'est pas très difficile dans le choix de ses amis **2** *(tax, tariff)* différentiel

discrimination [dɪsˌkrɪmɪˈneɪʃən] **N 1** *(on grounds of race, sex etc)* discrimination *f*; **sexual d.** discrimination *f* sexuelle **2** *(good judgement)* discernement *m*; *(in matters of taste)* goût *m* **3** *(ability to distinguish)* **powers of d.** capacités *fpl* de distinction, discernement *m*

discriminatory [dɪsˈkrɪmɪnətrɪ] **ADJ** *(treatment, proposals)* discriminatoire

discursive [dɪsˈkɜːsɪv] **ADJ** *Formal (essay, report, person etc)* discursif

discus [ˈdɪskəs] *(pl* **discuses** *or* **disci** [-kaɪ]) **N 1** *Sport* disque *m*; **the d.** *(event)* le cer du disque **2** *(in Ancient Greece)* discobole *m*

►► *Sport* ***discus thrower*** lanceur(euse) *m,f* de disque

discuss [dɪsˈkʌs] **VT** *(talk about* ► *problem, price, subject etc)* discuter de, parler de; *(*► *person)* parler de; *(debate)* discuter de; *(examine* ► *of author, book, report etc)* examiner, parler de, traiter de; **I'll d. it with you later** nous en parlerons *ou* discuterons plus tard; **I don't want to d. it** je ne veux pas en parler; **I refuse to d. rumours** je refuse de commenter des rumeurs

discussion [dɪsˈkʌʃən] **N** *(talk)* discussion *f*; *(debate)* débat *m*; *(examination* ► *by author in report)* traitement *m*; *(*► *of report)* examen *m*; **there's been a lot of d. about it** on en a beaucoup parlé; *(in parliament, on board etc)* cela a été beaucoup débattu; *(in press, in media)* cela a été largement traité; **to come up for d.** *(report, proposal etc)* être discuté; **it is still under d.** c'est encore en cours de discussion

►► *Comput* ***discussion list*** *(on Internet)* liste *f* de diffusion; *TV & Rad* ***discussion programme*** table *f* ronde

disdain [dɪsˈdeɪn] **N** dédain *m*, mépris *m*; **with** *or* **in d.** avec dédain, dédaigneusement; **a look of d.** un regard dédaigneux

VT *Formal* dédaigner; **he disdained to reply to her letter/remark** il n'a pas daigné répondre à sa lettre/remarque

disdainful [dɪsˈdeɪnfʊl] **ADJ** dédaigneux; **to be d. of sb/sth** se montrer dédaigneux envers qn/qch, dédaigner qn/qch

disdainfully [dɪsˈdeɪnfʊlɪ] **ADV** avec dédain, dédaigneusement

disease [dɪˈziːz] **N 1** *(illness)* maladie *f*; **he suffers from a kidney d.** il a une maladie des reins, il est malade des reins; **to combat d.** combattre la maladie **2** *Fig* mal *m*, maladie *f*

> Attention: ne pas confondre avec le nom **decease**.

diseased [dɪˈziːzd] **ADJ 1** *(body)* malade **2** *Fig (mind)* malade, dérangé; *(imagination)* malade

disembark [ˌdɪsemˈbɑːk] **VT** *(passengers, cargo)* débarquer

VI débarquer

disembarkation [ˌdɪsembɑːˈkeɪʃən], **disembarkment** [ˌdɪsɪmˈbɑːkmənt] **N** *(of passengers, cargo)* débarquement *m*

disembodied [ˌdɪsɪmˈbɒdɪd] **ADJ** *(voice, spirit)* désincarné

disembowel [ˌdɪsɪmˈbaʊəl] **VT** éviscérer, éventrer

disenchant [ˌdɪsɪnˈtʃɑːnt] **VT** désillusionner; **a disenchanting experience/encounter** une expérience/rencontre décevante

disenchanted [ˌdɪsɪnˈtʃɑːntɪd] **ADJ** désillusionné; **to be d. with sb/sth** avoir perdu ses illusions sur qn/qch, être désillusionné par qn/qch; **to become d. with sb/sth** perdre ses illusions sur qn/qch

disenchantment [ˌdɪsɪnˈtʃɑːntmənt] **N** désillusion *f*

disencumber [ˌdɪsɪnˈkʌmbə(r)] **VT** *Formal* **to d. oneself of sth** *(of coat etc)* se débarrasser de qch; *(of one's responsibilities, burdens)* s'affranchir de qch

disenfranchise [ˌdɪsɪnˈfræntʃaɪz] **VT** priver du droit de vote

disenfranchisement [ˌdɪsɪnˈfræntʃɪzmənt] **N** *(of person)* déchéance *f* de ses droits civiques; *(of borough)* déchéance *f* de ses droits de représentation

disengage [ˌdɪsɪnˈgeɪdʒ] **VT 1** *Tech* désenclencher; *(cogwheel)* désengrener; *(part, component)* débrayer, désembrayer; *(lever, catch)* dégager; *Aut (handbrake)* desserrer; *Aut* **to d.**

the clutch débrayer 2 (release) dégager; to d. oneself from sb's embrace se dégager de l'étreinte de qn
VI 1 (disconnect) to d. from (process) se désintéresser de; (society, group) se détacher de 2 Mil cesser le combat 3 Tech se désenclencher

disengagement [ˌdɪsɪn'geɪdʒmənt] N 1 (from political group, organization) désengagement m 2 Mil cessez-le-feu m inv

disentangle [ˌdɪsɪn'tæŋgəl] VT (string, plot, mystery) démêler; I tried to d. myself from the net j'ai essayé de me dépêtrer du filet; to d. oneself from a difficult situation se sortir à grand-peine d'une situation difficile

disequilibrium [ˌdɪsekwɪ'lɪbrɪəm] N Formal déséquilibre m

disestablish [ˌdɪsɪ'stæblɪʃ] VT séparer; to d. the Church séparer l'Église de l'État

disestablishment [ˌdɪsɪ'stæblɪʃmənt] N séparation f

disfavour, Am **disfavor** [dɪs'feɪvə(r)] N désapprobation f, défaveur f; to regard sb/sth with d. considérer qn/qch avec désapprobation, voir qn/qch d'un mauvais œil; to be in d. with sb être en disgrâce auprès de qn; to fall into d. with sb tomber en défaveur auprès de qn; at the risk of incurring sb's d. au risque de déplaire à qn

disfigure [dɪs'fɪgə(r)] VT (person, statue etc) défigurer; (landscape) gâter, enlaidir; a disfiguring disease une maladie qui défigure

disfigured [dɪs'fɪgəd] ADJ (person, statue etc) défiguré; (landscape) enlaidi

disfigurement [dɪs'fɪgəmənt] N (of person, statue etc) défiguration f; (of landscape) enlaidissement m

disfranchise [ˌdɪs'fræntʃaɪz] VT = disenfranchise

disgorge [dɪs'gɔːdʒ] VT 1 (food) régurgiter, rendre; Fig (contents, passengers, pollutants) déverser; the chimneys are disgorging smoke les cheminées crachent de la fumée 2 (give unwillingly ▸ information) donner avec répugnance ou à contrecœur
VI (river) se jeter, se dégorger

disgrace [dɪs'greɪs] N 1 (dishonour) disgrâce f; it will bring d. on or to the family cela fera tomber la famille dans la disgrâce, cela déshonorera la famille; it's no d. to be poor il n'y a pas de honte à être pauvre 2 (disfavour) disgrâce f, défaveur f; to be in d. (with sb) être en disgrâce (auprès de qn) 3 (shameful example or thing) honte f; it's a d. c'est une honte, c'est honteux; these streets are a d. ces rues sont une honte; look at you, you're a d.! regarde-toi, tu fais honte (à voir)!; that jacket is a d.! cette veste est une vraie guenille!; he's a d. to his profession il déshonore sa profession
VT 1 (bring shame on) faire honte à, couvrir de honte, déshonorer; to d. oneself se couvrir de honte; you disgraced me in front of all those people tu m'as couvert de honte devant tous ces gens 2 (usu passive) (discredit) disgracier; to be disgraced être disgrâcié

disgraceful [dɪs'greɪsful] ADJ (behaviour) honteux, scandaleux; Fam (hat, jacket etc) miteux; it's d. c'est honteux; it's d. that he wasn't there il est honteux qu'il ne soit pas venu

> Note that the French word **disgracieux** is a false friend and is never a translation for the English word **disgraceful**. It means **ungainly**.

disgracefully [dɪs'greɪsfʊlɪ] ADV honteusement; (late, rude, expensive) scandaleusement

disgruntled [dɪs'grʌntəld] ADJ (discontented) mécontent; (sulky) maussade; to be d. at or about sth/doing sth être mécontent de qch/faire qch

disguise [dɪs'gaɪz] N déguisement m; in d. déguisé; to put on a d. se déguiser
VT 1 (voice, handwriting, person) déguiser; to be disguised as sb/sth être déguisé en qn/qch to d. oneself as a policeman se déguiser en agent de police 2 (feelings, disappointment etc) dissimuler, masquer; (truth, facts) dissimuler, cacher; (unsightly feature) cacher; (bad taste of food, cough mixture etc) couvrir; there's no disguising the fact that... il faut avouer que...

disgust [dɪs'gʌst] N (sick feeling) dégoût m, aversion f, répugnance f; (displeasure) écœurement m, dégoût m; to be filled with d. at sth être écœuré par qch; I resigned in d. dégoûté ou écœuré, j'ai démissionné; much to my d. à mon grand dégoût
VT (sicken) dégoûter; (displease) écœurer; I am disgusted with him/this government/his behaviour il/ce gouvernement/son comportement m'écœure; to be disgusted with oneself (displeased) s'en vouloir; I am disgusted with or at my own stupidity (displeased) je m'en veux d'être aussi stupide

disgusting [dɪs'gʌstɪŋ] ADJ 1 (sickening ▸ person, behaviour, smell) écœurant, dégoûtant; (▸ habit, language) dégoûtant; how d.! c'est écœurant!, c'est dégoûtant! 2 (very bad) écœurant, déplorable; you d. little boy! espèce de petit dégoûtant!

disgustingly [dɪs'gʌstɪŋlɪ] ADV 1 (sickeningly) a d. bad meal un repas épouvantable 2 Fam (for emphasis) to be d. rich être scandaleusement riche▫; she is d. clever/successful ça me rend malade de voir comme elle est intelligente/comme elle réussit; you look d. fit vous avez l'air vachement en forme

dish [dɪʃ] N 1 (for food) plat m; the dishes la vaisselle; to wash or to do the dishes faire la vaisselle; to wash dishes (in restaurant) faire la plonge
2 (food) plat m; it's not a d. I often make ce n'est pas une recette ou un plat que je prépare souvent
3 (amount of food) plat m; we ate two whole dishes of lasagne nous avons mangé deux plats entiers de lasagnes
4 Fam Old-fashioned (good-looking woman) belle plante f, belle fille▫ f; (good-looking man) beau type m
5 (of telescope) miroir m concave (de télescope)
6 (container) récipient m; Phot cuvette f
VT Fam 1 Br (chances, hopes) ruiner 2 Am (criticize) to d. sb critiquer qn
►► TV Br dish aerial, Am dish antenna antenne f parabolique; dish mop lavette f; dish rack égouttoir m (à vaisselle); Am dish soap liquide m vaisselle

▸ **dish out** VT SEP 1 (food) servir 2 Fam Fig (money, leaflets etc) distribuer▫; (advice) prodiguer▫; you can d. it out but you can't take it (criticism) tu es bon pour critiquer mais pour ce qui est d'accepter la critique, c'est un autre problème!; he's really dishing it out (boxer) il frappe vraiment à coups redoublés

▸ **dish up** VT SEP (food) servir ou verser ou mettre dans un plat; Fam (arguments, excuses etc) ressortir
VI (serve food) servir; shall I d. up? je sers?

disharmonious [ˌdɪshɑː'məʊnjəs] ADJ peu harmonieux

disharmony [ˌdɪs'hɑːmənɪ] N manque m d'harmonie

dishcloth ['dɪʃklɒθ] N (for washing) lavette f; (for drying) torchon m (à vaisselle)

dishearten [dɪs'hɑːtən] VT décourager, abattre, démoraliser; don't get disheartened ne te décourage pas, ne te laisse pas abattre

disheartening [dɪs'hɑːtənɪŋ] ADJ décourageant

dishearteningly [dɪs'hɑːtənɪŋlɪ] ADV de façon décourageante; d. brief d'une brièveté décourageante; d. few people turned up peu de monde est venu, ce qui était décourageant

dished [dɪʃt] ADJ (angled) non parallèle; (convex) lenticulaire

dishevelled, Am **disheveled** [dɪ'ʃevəld] ADJ (hair) ébouriffé, dépeigné; (clothes) débraillé, en désordre; (person, appearance) débraillé

dishonest [dɪs'ɒnɪst] ADJ malhonnête; you're being d. not telling him how you feel c'est malhonnête de ne pas lui dire ce que tu ressens

dishonestly [dɪs'ɒnɪstlɪ] ADV de manière malhonnête, malhonnêtement

dishonesty [dɪs'ɒnɪstɪ] N malhonnêteté f

dishonour, Am **dishonor** [dɪs'ɒnə(r)] N déshonneur m; to bring d. on sb/one's country déshonorer qn/son pays
VT 1 (family, country, profession etc) déshonorer 2 Fin (cheque) refuser d'honorer; dishonoured cheque chèque m impayé ou non honoré

dishonourable, Am **dishonorable** [dɪs'ɒnərəbəl] ADJ (person) sans honneur; (conduct) déshonorant; there's nothing d. about losing perdre n'a rien de honteux; Mil he was given a d. discharge il a été renvoyé pour manquement à l'honneur

dishonourably, Am **dishonourably** [dɪs'ɒnərəblɪ] ADV (behave) de façon ou manière déshonorante; Mil to be d. discharged être renvoyé de l'armée pour manquement à l'honneur

dishpan ['dɪʃpæn] N Am bassine f

dishrag ['dɪʃræg] N (for washing) lavette f; (for drying) torchon m (à vaisselle)

dishtowel ['dɪʃtaʊəl] N torchon m (à vaisselle)

dishwasher ['dɪʃˌwɒʃə(r)] N 1 (machine) lave-vaisselle m; d. safe (glass, plate etc) garanti lave-vaisselle 2 (person) plongeur(euse) m,f

dishwashing liquid ['dɪʃˌwɒʃɪŋ-] N Am produit m à vaisselle

dishwater ['dɪʃˌwɔːtə(r)] N eau f de vaisselle Fam this coffee is like d.! c'est du jus de chaussettes, ce café!

dishy ['dɪʃɪ] (compar dishier, superl dishiest) ADJ Br Fam sexy (inv), séduisant▫; what a d. guy! il est canon, ce mec!

disillusion [ˌdɪsɪ'luːʒən] VT faire perdre ses illusions à, désillusionner; I hate to d. you but he's really after your money je suis désolé de devoir t'ôter tes illusions mais c'est après ton argent qu'il en a
N désillusion f, désabusement m

disillusioned [ˌdɪsɪ'luːʒənd] ADJ désillusionné, désabusé; to be d. with sb/sth avoir perdu ses illusions sur qn/qch

disillusionment [ˌdɪsɪ'luːʒənmənt] N désillusion f, désabusement m; the fans' increasing d with club management la désillusion grandissante des fans envers la direction du club

disincentive [ˌdɪsɪn'sentɪv] N facteur m décourageant; taxes are a d. to expansion les impôts découragent l'expansion; this will act as a d. ceci aura un effet dissuasif ou de dissuasion

disinclination [ˌdɪsɪnklɪ'neɪʃən] N (of person) manque m d'inclination; her d. to believe him sa tendance à ne pas le croire; to show a d. for work montrer ou manifester peu d'inclination au travail

disinclined [ˌdɪsɪn'klaɪnd] ADJ to be d. to do sth être peu disposé ou enclin à faire qch

disinfect [ˌdɪsɪn'fekt] VT désinfecter

disinfectant [ˌdɪsɪn'fektənt] N désinfectant m

disinfection [ˌdɪsɪn'fekʃən] N désinfection f

disinflation [ˌdɪsɪn'fleɪʃən] N Econ désinflation f

disinflationary [ˌdɪsɪn'fleɪʃənərɪ] ADJ Econ désinflationniste

disinformation [ˌdɪsɪnfə'meɪʃən] N désinformation f

disingenuous [ˌdɪsɪn'dʒenjʊəs] ADJ peu sincère

disingenuously [ˌdɪsɪn'dʒenjʊəslɪ] ADV avec peu de sincérité

disingenuousness [ˌdɪsɪn'dʒenjʊəsnɪs] N manque m de sincérité

disinherit [ˌdɪsɪn'herɪt] VT déshériter

disintegrate [dɪs'ɪntɪgreɪt] VI 1 (break into pieces ▸ stone, wet paper) se désagréger; (▸ plane, rocket) se désintégrer 2 Fig (break down ▸ coalition, the family) se désagréger; (▸ calm, confidence) s'effriter; (▸ health) se dégrader, s'effriter 3 Nucl se désintégrer

disintegration [dɪsˌɪntɪ'greɪʃən] N 1 (of stone, wet paper) désagrégation f; (of plane, rocket) désintégration f 2 Fig (of coalition, the family) désagrégation f 3 Nucl désintégration f

disinter [ˌdɪsɪn'tɜː(r)] (pt & pp disinterred, cont disinterring) VT 1 (body) déterrer, exhumer 2 Fig (scandal, information) déterrer

disinterest [ˌdɪs'ɪntərest] N 1 (objectivity) désintéressement m 2 Fam (lack of interest) manque m d'intérêt▫

disinterested [ˌdɪsˈɪntərestɪd] **ADJ 1** *(objective)* désintéressé **2** *Fam (uninterested)* indifférent

> Attention: ne pas confondre avec l'adjectif **uninterested**.

disinterestedness [ˌdɪsˈɪntərestɪdnɪs] **N 1** *(objectivity)* désintéressement *m* **2** *Fam (lack of interest)* manque *m* d'intérêt

disintermediation [ˈdɪsɪntəˌmiːdɪˈeɪʃən] **N** *Fin* désintermédiation *f*

disinterment [ˌdɪsɪnˈtɜːmənt] **N** déterrement *m*, exhumation *f*

disinvest [ˌdɪsɪnˈvest] **VI** désinvestir

disinvestment [ˌdɪsɪnˈvestmənt] **N** désinvestissement *m*

disjointed [dɪsˈdʒɔɪntɪd] **ADJ** *(conversation, film, speech)* décousu, incohérent; *(movements)* désordonné

disk [dɪsk] **N 1** *Comput (hard)* disque *m*; *(floppy)* disquette *f*; **on d.** sur disque, sur disquette; **to write sth to d.** sauvegarder qch sur disque *ou* disquette **2** *Am* = **disc**

►► ***disk access time*** temps *m* d'accès disque; ***disk capacity*** capacité *f* de disque/disquette; ***disk controller*** contrôleur *m* de disque; ***disk drive*** lecteur *m* de disquettes; ***disk operating system*** système *m* d'exploitation de disques; ***disk space*** espace *m* disque

disk-based **ADJ** *Comput* conçu pour disque; *(for floppy)* conçu pour disquettes

diskette [dɪsˈket] **N** *Comput* disquette *f*

►► ***diskette drive*** lecteur *m* de disquettes

diskless [ˈdɪsklɪs] **ADJ** *Comput* sans disque, sans unité de disque

dislike [dɪsˈlaɪk] **VT** ne pas aimer, **I d. flying** je n'aime pas prendre l'avion; **why do you d. him so much?** pourquoi le détestes-tu autant?; **he is much disliked** il est loin d'être apprécié; **I don't d. him** je n'ai rien contre lui

N *(for person)* aversion *f*, antipathie *f*; *(for thing)* aversion *f*; **to have a d. for** *or* **of sth** détester qch; **mutual d.** antipathie *f* mutuelle; **to take a d. to sb/sth** prendre qn/qch en grippe; **we all have our likes and dislikes** on est tous pareils, il y a des choses qu'on aime et des choses qu'on n'aime pas

dislocate [ˈdɪsləkeɪt] **VT 1** *(shoulder, knee etc ► of person)* se démettre, se déboîter, se luxer; *(► of accident, fall)* démettre, déboîter, luxer; **he has dislocated his shoulder** il s'est démis *ou* déboîté *ou* luxé l'épaule **2** *(disrupt ► plans)* désorganiser, perturber

dislocation [ˌdɪsləˈkeɪʃən] **N 1** *(of shoulder, knee etc)* luxation *f*, déboîtement *m* **2** *(disruption ► of plans)* perturbation *f*

dislodge [dɪsˈlɒdʒ] **VT** *(fish bone, piece of apple etc)* dégager; *(large rock)* déplacer; *Fig (enemy, prey)* déloger; *(leader, title holder)* prendre la place de; **several bricks had become dislodged** plusieurs briques s'étaient détachées; *Fig* **nothing would d. him from his position on arms control** rien ne pouvait ébranler sa conviction sur le contrôle des armements

disloyal [ˌdɪsˈlɔɪəl] **ADJ** déloyal; **to be d. to sb/sth** être déloyal envers qn/qch

disloyalty [ˌdɪsˈlɔɪəltɪ] **N** déloyauté *f*; **your d. to the company** votre déloyauté envers la compagnie; **an act of d.** un acte déloyal

dismal [ˈdɪzməl] **ADJ** *(face, person)* lugubre, sombre, triste; *(day, weather)* horrible; *(streets, countryside)* lugubre; *(song)* mélancolique, triste; *Fig (result, performance)* lamentable; *(future, prospect)* sombre; **what are you looking so d. about?** pourquoi as-tu l'air aussi lugubre?; **to be a d. failure** *(person)* être un zéro sur toute la ligne; *(film, project)* échouer lamentablement

dismally [ˈdɪzməlɪ] **ADV** lugubrement; *(fail)* lamentablement

dismantle [dɪsˈmæntəl] **VT** *(object, scenery, exhibition)* démonter; *Fig (system, reforms, arrangement)* démanteler

VI se démonter

dismast [ˌdɪsˈmɑːst] **VT** *Naut (ship)* démâter

dismay [dɪsˈmeɪ] **N** consternation *f*; *(stronger)* désarroi *m*; **in** *or* **with d.** avec consternation *ou* désarroi; **to be filled with d. by sth** être consterné par *ou* rempli de désarroi à cause de qch; **(much) to my d.** à ma grande consternation, à mon grand désarroi

VT consterner; *(stronger)* emplir de désarroi, effondrer; **we were dismayed by the news** nous avons été effondrés par la nouvelle, la nouvelle nous a remplis de désarroi

dismember [dɪsˈmembə(r)] **VT** démembrer

dismemberment [dɪsˈmembəmənt] **N** démembrement *m*

dismiss [dɪsˈmɪs] **VT 1** *(from job ► employee)* licencier, congédier, renvoyer; *(► magistrate, official)* destituer, révoquer, relever de ses fonctions; *Mil* **to d. sb from the army** rayer qn des cadres de l'armée

2 *(not take seriously ► proposal, theory, explanation)* rejeter; *(► objection, warning, rumours)* ne pas tenir compte de, ne pas prendre au sérieux; *(► danger)* mépriser; *(► problem)* écarter, refuser de considérer; **you cannot go on dismissing the threats/evidence** vous ne pouvez pas continuer à ignorer ces menaces/preuves; **he dismissed him as a crank** il a déclaré que c'était un excentrique à ne pas prendre au sérieux; **she is dismissed as an intellectual lightweight** on la considère comme une non-valeur sur le plan intellectuel

3 *(send away)* congédier; *Fig (thought, possibility)* écarter; *(memory)* effacer; *(suggestion, idea)* rejeter; *Sch (class)* laisser partir; **d. him from your thoughts** chasse-le de tes pensées; *Sch* **class dismissed!** vous pouvez sortir!; *Mil* **dismissed!** rompez!

4 *Law (hung jury)* dissoudre; **to d. a charge** *(judge)* rendre une ordonnance de non-lieu; **the judge dismissed the case** le juge a rendu une fin de non-recevoir; **case dismissed!** affaire classée!

5 *Sport (in cricket ► batsman, team)* éliminer; **England were dismissed for 127** l'équipe d'Angleterre a été éliminée avec 127 points

VI *Mil* **d.!** rompez (les rangs)!

dismissal [dɪsˈmɪsəl] **N 1** *(from work ► of employee)* licenciement *m*, renvoi *m*; *(► of magistrate, official)* destitution *f*, révocation *f*; **unfair d.** licenciement *m* non justifié **2** *(of proposal, theory, explanation)* rejet *m*; *(of danger)* mépris *m* **3** *Law (of case)* fin *f* de non-recevoir; *(of request, appeal)* rejet *m*; **d. of the charge** non-lieu *m*

dismissive [dɪsˈmɪsɪv] **ADJ** *(tone of voice, gesture)* dédaigneux; **to be d. of sb/sth** ne faire aucun cas de qn/qch; **you're always so d. of my efforts** tu fais toujours si peu de cas de mes efforts

dismissively [dɪsˈmɪsɪvlɪ] **ADV** *(offhandedly)* d'un ton dédaigneux; *(in final tone of voice)* d'un ton sans appel

dismount [ˌdɪsˈmaʊnt] **VT 1** *(cause to fall ► from horse)* désarçonner, démonter; *(► from bicycle, motorcycle)* faire tomber **2** *(gun, device)* démonter

VI descendre

Disneyfication [ˌdɪznɪfɪˈkeɪʃən] **N** *(of story, history, place)* disneylandisation *f*

Disneyfy [ˈdɪznɪfaɪ] **VT** *(story, history, place)* disneylandiser

disobedience [ˌdɪsəˈbiːdjəns] **N** désobéissance *f*; **she was punished for (her) d.** elle a été punie pour avoir désobéi; **an act of d.** un acte de désobéissance

disobedient [ˌdɪsəˈbiːdjənt] **ADJ** désobéissant; **to be d. to sb** désobéir à qn; **that was very d. of you** c'était très désobéissant de ta part

disobey [ˌdɪsəˈbeɪ] **VT** désobéir à

disobliging [ˌdɪsəˈblaɪdʒɪŋ] **ADJ** *Formal* désobligeant

disobligingly [ˌdɪsəˈblaɪdʒɪŋlɪ] **ADV** avec désobligeance

disorder [dɪsˈɔːdə(r)] **N 1** *(untidiness ► of house, room, desk)* désordre *m*; **to be in (a state of) d.** être en désordre; **the meeting broke up in d.** la réunion s'est achevée dans le désordre *ou* la confusion; **the army is retreating in d.** l'armée se retire en désordre **2** *(unrest)* trouble *m*; **serious disorders have broken out** de graves désordres ont éclaté; **public d.** atteinte *f* à *ou* trouble *m* de l'ordre public **3** *Med* trouble *m*, troubles *mpl*; **nervous/blood d.** troubles *mpl* nerveux/de la circulation; *Psy* **personality d.** trouble *m* caractériel *ou* de la personnalité

VT *(make untidy ► files, papers)* mettre en désordre

disordered [dɪsˈɔːdəd] **ADJ** *(room)* en désordre; *(mind)* malade; *Br* **to be mentally d.** souffrir de troubles mentaux

disorderliness [dɪsˈɔːdəlɪnɪs] **N 1** *(untidiness)* désordre *m* **2** *(of mob)* turbulence *f*

disorderly [dɪsˈɔːdəlɪ] **ADJ 1** *(untidy ► room, house)* en désordre, désordonné **2** *(unruly ► crowd, mob)* désordonné, agité; *(► person, conduct)* désordonné; *(► meeting, demonstration)* désordonné, confus; **to lead a d. life** mener une vie désordonnée *ou* déréglée

►► *Law* ***disorderly conduct*** conduite *f* portant atteinte à l'ordre public; *Law* ***disorderly house*** maison *f* close

disorganization, -isation [dɪsˌɔːgənaɪˈzeɪʃən] **N** désorganisation *f*; **in a state of d.** désorganisé

disorganize, -ise [dɪsˈɔːgənaɪz] **VT** *(disrupt ► plans, schedule)* déranger

disorganized, -ised [dɪsˈɔːgənaɪzd] **ADJ** *(person)* désorganisé; *(room)* désordonné; *(memories, ideas)* confus, désordonné

disorient [dɪsˈɔːrɪənt], **disorientate** [dɪsˈɔːrɪənteɪt] **VT** désorienter; **to be disoriented** être désorienté; **it's easy to become disoriented** c'est facile de perdre son sens de l'orientation; *Fig* on a vite fait d'être désorienté

disorientation [dɪsˌɔːrɪənˈteɪʃən] **N** désorientation *f*

disorienting [dɪsˈɔːrɪəntɪŋ] **ADJ** déroutant

disown [dɪsˈəʊn] **VT** *(child, opinion, statement)* renier, désavouer; *(country)* renier; *Fam* **if you go out looking like that I'll d. you!** si tu sors habillé comme ça, je ne te connais plus!

disparage [dɪˈspærɪdʒ] **VT** dénigrer, décrier

disparagement [dɪˈspærɪdʒmənt] **N** dénigrement *m*

disparaging [dɪˈspærɪdʒɪŋ] **ADJ** *(person, newspaper report ► about person)* désobligeant, malveillant; *(► about proposals, ideas)* critique; **to make d. remarks about sb** faire des remarques désobligeantes à propos de *ou* sur qn; **the critics were very d. about his latest play** les critiques ont beaucoup dénigré sa dernière pièce

disparagingly [dɪˈspærɪdʒɪŋlɪ] **ADV** *(say)* d'un ton désobligeant; *(look at)* d'un air désobligeant; **to speak d. of sb** parler de qn en termes de mépris, faire des remarques désobligeantes à l'égard de qn

disparate [ˈdɪspərət] **ADJ** *Formal* disparate

disparity [dɪˈspærətɪ] *(pl* **disparities)** **N** *(in ages)* disparité *f*; *(in report, statement, story)* contradiction *f*; *(of wealth, status)* disparité *f*, écart *m*

dispassionate [dɪˈspæʃənət] **ADJ 1** *(calm)* sans passion, dépassionné, calme **2** *(impartial)* impartial; **to take a d. view of things** juger impartialement les choses

dispassionately [dɪˈspæʃənətlɪ] **ADV 1** *(calmly)* sans émotion, calmement **2** *(impartially)* objectivement, impartialement

dispatch [dɪˈspætʃ] **VT 1** *(send ► letter, merchandise, telegram)* envoyer, expédier; *(► messenger)* envoyer, dépêcher; *(► troops, envoy)* envoyer

2 *(complete ► task, work)* expédier, en finir avec

3 *Euph (kill ► person)* tuer; *(► animal)* achever

4 *Fam (food)* s'envoyer

N 1 *(of letter, merchandise, telegram)* envoi *m*, expédition *f*; *(of messenger, troops, envoy)* envoi *m*

2 *Mil & Press (report)* dépêche *f*; *Mil* **to be mentioned in dispatches** être cité à l'ordre du jour

3 *Old-fashioned (swiftness)* promptitude *f*; **with d.** avec promptitude, rapidement

4 *(completion ► of task, work)* expédition *f*

5 *(execution)* exécution *f*

►► ***dispatch box*** *(for documents)* boîte *f* à documents; *Br Pol* ***the dispatch box*** = tribune d'où parlent les membres du gouvernement et leurs homologues du cabinet fantôme; ***dispatch case*** serviette *f*, porte-documents *m inv*; ***dispatch department*** service *m* des expéditions; ***dispatch***

note bordereau *m* d'expédition; ***dispatch rider*** estafette *f*

dispatcher [dɪ'spætʃə(r)] N expéditeur(trice) *m,f*

dispel [dɪ'spel] *(pt & pp* **dispelled,** *cont* **dispelling)** VT *(clouds, mist ▸ of sun)* dissiper; *(▸ of wind)* chasser; *(doubts, fears, anxiety)* dissiper

dispensable [dɪ'spensəbəl] ADJ dont on peut se passer, superflu; **the rest of the employees were d.** les autres employés n'étaient pas indispensables

dispensary [dɪ'spensərɪ] *(pl* **dispensaries)** N *Pharm* pharmacie *f*; *(for free distribution of medicine)* = établissement dispensant gratuitement des médicaments

dispensation [ˌdɪspen'seɪʃən] N **1** *(handing out)* distribution *f*

2 *(administration ▸ of charity, justice)* exercice *m*

3 *Admin, Law & Rel (exemption)* dispense *f*; **to receive d. from military service** être exempté du service militaire; **as a special d. the prisoner was allowed to attend the funeral** le prisonnier a reçu une permission exceptionnelle pour assister à l'enterrement

4 *Pol & Rel (system)* régime *m*

dispensatory [dɪ'spensətərɪ] ADJ *Law* dérogatoire

dispense [dɪ'spens] VT **1** *(of vending machine)* distribuer

2 *(administer ▸ justice, charity)* exercer; **to d. advice** donner des conseils

3 *Pharm* préparer

4 *Formal (exempt)* dispenser; **to d. sb from sth/doing sth** dispenser qn de qch/de faire qch

▸ **dispense with** VT INSEP *(do without)* se passer de; *(get rid of)* se débarrasser de; **to d. with the formalities** couper court aux *ou* se dispenser des formalités; **to d. with the need for sth** rendre qch superflu; **credit cards d. with the need for cash** avec les cartes de crédit, on n'a plus besoin d'avoir de l'argent liquide

dispenser [dɪ'spensə(r)] N **1** *Pharm* pharmacien (enne) *m,f* **2** *(machine)* distributeur *m*; **soap/coffee d.** distributeur *m* de savon/café **3** *Rel (of alms)* dispensateur(trice) *m,f*, distributeur (trice) *m,f*

dispensing [dɪ'spensɪŋ] ADJ

▸▸ *Br Pharm* ***dispensing chemist*** *(person)* pharmacien(enne) *m,f*; *(establishment)* pharmacie *f*; ***dispensing machine*** distributeur *m*; ***dispensing optician*** opticien(enne) *m,f*

dispersal [dɪ'spɜːsəl] N *(of crowd, seeds)* dispersion *f*; *(of gas ▸ disappearance)* dissipation *f*; *(▸ spread)* dispersion *f*; *(of light ▸ by prism)* dispersion *f*, décomposition *f*

dispersant [dɪ'spɜːsənt] N *Chem* dispersant *m*

disperse [dɪ'spɜːs] VT **1** *(crowd, seeds)* disperser; *(clouds, mist, smoke ▸ of sun)* dissiper; *(▸ of wind)* chasser; *(gas, chemical ▸ cause to spread)* propager; *(▸ cause to vanish)* disperser; *(light ▸ of prism)* disperser, décomposer **2** *(place at intervals)* répartir

VI *(crowds, seeds)* se disperser; *(clouds, mist, smoke ▸ with sun)* se dissiper; *(▸ with wind)* être chassé; *(gas, chemicals ▸ spread)* se propager; *(▸ vanish)* se dissiper; *(light ▸ with prism)* se décomposer

dispersing agent [dɪ'spɜːsɪŋ-] N agent *m* dispersant

dispersion [dɪ'spɜːʃən] N **1** *(of crowd, seeds)* dispersion *f*; *(of gas ▸ disappearance)* dissipation *f*; *(▸ spread)* dispersion *f*; *(of light ▸ by prism)* dispersion *f*, décomposition *f* **2** *Rel* **the D.** la Diaspora

dispirit [dɪ'spɪrɪt] VT décourager, abattre

dispirited [dɪ'spɪrɪtɪd] ADJ abattu

dispiritedly [dɪ'spɪrɪtɪdlɪ] ADV *(say)* d'un ton découragé *ou* abattu; *(look)* d'un air découragé *ou* abattu; *(play, do something)* sans enthousiasme

dispiriting [dɪ'spɪrɪtɪŋ] ADJ décourageant

dispiritingly [dɪ'spɪrɪtɪŋlɪ] ADV de façon décourageante *ou* démoralisante; **d., no one had come to meet them** personne n'était venu à leur rencontre, ce qui les démoralisait

displace [dɪs'pleɪs] VT **1** *(refugees, population)* déplacer; **displaced persons** personnes *fpl* déplacées

2 *Med* **to d. a bone** se déplacer un os

3 *(supplant)* supplanter, remplacer

4 *Chem & Phys (water, air)* déplacer

displacement [dɪs'pleɪsmənt] N **1** *(of refugees, population)* déplacement *m*

2 *Med (of bone)* déplacement *m*

3 *(supplanting)* remplacement *m*

4 *Chem & Phys (of water, air)* déplacement *m*

5 *Naut* déplacement *m*; **a ship of 10,000 tons d.** un bateau de 10 000 tonnes de déplacement

6 *Psy* déplacement *m*

▸▸ *Psy* ***displacement activity*** activité *f* de déplacement; *Naut* ***displacement ton*** tonne *f*

displacer unit [dɪs'pleɪsə-] N *Aut* amortisseur *m* à déplacement de fluide

display [dɪ'spleɪ] VT **1** *(gifts, medals, ornaments etc)* exposer; *Pej* exhiber; *(items in exhibition)* mettre en exposition, exposer; *Com (goods for sale)* mettre en étalage, exposer

2 *(notice, poster, exam results, prices)* afficher

3 *(courage, determination, skill)* faire preuve de, montrer; *(anger, affection, friendship, interest)* manifester; **the country displayed its military might** le pays a montré sa puissance militaire; **to d. one's ignorance/talent** faire la preuve de son ignorance/talent

4 *Press & Typ* mettre en vedette

5 *Comput (of screen)* afficher; *(of user)* visualiser

VI *(animal, bird, fish)* faire la parade

N **1** *(of gifts, medals, ornaments)* exposition *f*; *Pej* exhibition *f*; *Com (of goods for sale)* mise *f* en étalage; *(goods for sale)* étalage *m*, exposition *f*; **to be on d.** être exposé; **to put sth on d.** exposer qch; **to be on public d.** être présenté au public; **for d. (only)** *(on book)* exemplaire de démonstration; **you'll have a fine d. of flowers** vous aurez un beau déploiement de fleurs

2 *(of notice, poster, exam results, prices)* affichage *m*

3 *(of courage, determination, skill)* démonstration *f*; *(of anger, affection, friendship, interest)* manifestation *f*; **an air d.** un meeting aérien; **a military d.** une parade militaire; **a d. of force** une démonstration de force; **to make a great d. of sth** faire parade de qch

4 *(event ▸ of works of art)* exposition *f*; *(▸ of dancing, handicraft)* démonstration *f*

5 *Comput (screen, device)* écran *m*; *(visual information)* affichage *m*, visualisation *f*; *(of calculator)* viseur *m*

6 *(by animal, bird, fish)* parade *f*

7 *Press & Typ* lignes *fpl* en vedette

▸▸ *Press & Typ* ***display advertisement*** encadré *m*; *Press & Typ* ***display advertising*** étalage *m* publicitaire; ***display cabinet*** *(in shop)* étalage *m*, vitrine *f*; *(in home)* vitrine *f*; ***display case*** *(in shop)* étalage *m*, vitrine *f*; *(in home)* vitrine *f*; ***display copy*** *(of book)* exemplaire *m* de démonstration; *Com & Mktg* ***display pack*** emballage *m* de présentation, emballage *m* présentoir; ***display panel*** tableau *m ou* panneau *m* d'affichage; ***display rack*** présentoir *m*; ***display screen*** écran *m* de visualisation; ***display shelf*** présentoir *m*; ***display stand*** présentoir *m*; ***display unit*** *Comput* unité *f* de visualisation *ou* d'affichage; *(for goods)* présentoir *m*; ***display window*** *(of shop)* vitrine *f*, étalage *m*; *(of calculator)* viseur *m*

displease [dɪs'pliːz] VT mécontenter

displeasing [dɪs'pliːzɪŋ] ADJ déplaisant, désagréable (**to** à)

displeasure [dɪs'pleʒə(r)] N mécontentement *m*; **to incur sb's d.** encourir *ou* s'attirer le mécontentement de qn

disport [dɪ'spɔːt] VT *Formal* **to d. oneself** s'ébattre, folâtrer

disposable [dɪ'spəʊzəbəl] ADJ **1** *(throwaway ▸ lighter, nappy, cup, syringe)* jetable; *(▸ bottle)* non consigné; *(▸ wrapping)* perdu **2** *(available ▸ money)* disponible

N *(nappy)* couche *f* jetable; *(lighter)* briquet *m* jetable

• **disposables** N *Com* biens *mpl* de consommation non durables

▸▸ *Fin* ***disposable assets*** fonds *mpl* disponibles; ***disposable camera*** appareil *m* photo jetable; *Com* ***disposable goods*** biens *mpl* de consommation non durables; *Fin* ***disposable income*** revenus *mpl* disponibles (après impôts); **people with high d. incomes** personnes disposant de hauts revenus

disposal [dɪ'spəʊzəl] N **1** *(taking away)* enlèvement *m*; *(of rubbish, by authority)* enlèvement *m*, ramassage *m*; **they arranged for the d. of the body** ils ont pris les dispositions nécessaires pour se débarrasser du corps; **waste** *or* **refuse d.** traitement *m* des ordures

2 *(sale)* vente *f*; *Law (of property)* disposition *f*; **she left no instructions for the d. of her property** elle n'a laissé aucune instruction quant à ce qui devait être fait de ses biens

3 *(resolution ▸ of problem, question)* résolution *f*; *(▸ of business)* exécution *f*, expédition *f*

4 *Am (disposal unit)* broyeur *m* d'ordures *(dans un évier)*

5 *(availability)* **to be at sb's d.** être à la disposition de qn; **I am entirely at your d.** je suis à votre entière disposition; **to have sth at one's d.** avoir qch à sa disposition; **to put sb/sth at sb's d.** mettre qn/qch à la disposition de qn; **in the time at your d.** dans le temps dont tu disposes

6 *Formal (arrangement)* disposition *f*, arrangement *m*; *(of troops)* déploiement *m*

dispose [dɪ'spəʊz] VT **1** *Formal (arrange ▸ ornaments, books)* disposer, arranger; *(▸ troops, forces)* déployer **2** *(incline)* disposer, porter; **I am not disposed to help him** je ne suis pas disposé à l'aider; **his moving testimonial disposed the jury to leniency** son témoignage émouvant a disposé le jury à l'indulgence

VI *Prov* **man proposes, God disposes** l'homme propose et Dieu dispose

▸ **dispose of** VT INSEP **1** *(get rid of ▸ waste, rubbish, problem)* se débarrasser de; *(by taking away ▸ refuse)* enlever, ramasser; *(by selling)* vendre; *(by throwing away)* jeter; *(workers)* congédier, renvoyer; **I can d. of this old table for you** je peux te débarrasser de cette vieille table

2 *(deal with ▸ problem, question)* résoudre, régler; *(▸ task, matter under discussion)* expédier, régler; **to d. of an argument** détruire un argument

3 *Fam (food)* s'envoyer

4 *(have at one's disposal)* disposer de, avoir à sa disposition

5 *Fam (kill ▸ person, animal)* liquider; *Fig (team, competitor)* se débarrasser de

> Note that the French **disposer de** only means **to have at one's disposal.**

disposed [dɪ'spəʊzd] ADJ **to be d. to do sth** être disposé à faire qch; **to be well/ill d. towards sb** être bien/mal disposé envers qn

disposition [ˌdɪspə'zɪʃən] N **1** *(temperament, nature)* naturel *m*; **to have** *or* **to be of a cheerful d.** être d'un naturel enjoué

2 *Formal (arrangement ▸ of ornaments, books)* disposition *f*, arrangement *m*; *(▸ of troops, forces)* disposition *f*

3 *(inclination, tendency)* disposition *f* (**to do sth** à faire qch)

4 *Law* aliénation *f*

dispossess [ˌdɪspə'zes] VT *(person)* déposséder; *Law (of house, land)* exproprier; **to d. sb of sth** déposséder qn de qch

dispossession [ˌdɪspə'zeʃən] N dépossession *f*; *Law* expropriation *f*

disproportion [ˌdɪsprə'pɔːʃən] N disproportion *f*

disproportionate [ˌdɪsprə'pɔːʃənət] ADJ *(excessive)* disproportionné; **to be d. to sth** être disproportionné à *ou* avec qch; **we spent a d. amount of time on it** on a passé plus de temps dessus que cela ne le méritait

disproportionately [ˌdɪsprə'pɔːʃənətlɪ] ADV d'une façon disproportionnée; **d. long/expensive** d'une longueur/d'un prix disproportionné(e); **a d. large sum** une somme disproportionnée

disprove [ˌdɪs'pruːv] *(pp* **disproved** *or* **disproven** [-'pruːvən]) VT *(theory)* réfuter

disputable [dɪ'spjuːtəbəl] ADJ discutable, contestable

disputant [dɪs'pjuːtənt] N **1** *Formal* personne *f* participant à un débat **2** *Am Law* partie *f* en litige

disputation [ˌdɪspjuːˈteɪʃən] N *Formal* **1** *(debate)* discussion *f* **2** *(argument)* controverse *f*, débat *m*

dispute [dɪˈspjuːt] VT **1** *(question ▸ claim, theory, statement etc)* contester, mettre en doute; *Law (will)* contester; **I'm not disputing that** je ne conteste pas cela, je ne mets pas cela en doute; **I would d. that** je ne suis pas d'accord **2** *(debate ▸ subject, motion)* discuter, débattre **3** *(fight for ▸ territory, championship, title)* disputer
VI *(argue)* se disputer; *(debate)* discuter, débattre; **to d. over** *or* **about sth** débattre qch *ou* de qch
N **1** *(debate)* discussion *f*, débat *m*; **there's some d. about the veracity of his statement** la véracité de sa déclaration fait l'objet de discussions *ou* est sujette à controverse; **your honesty is not in d.** votre honnêteté n'est pas mise en doute *ou* contestée; **he is beyond (all) d.** *or* **without d. the best player the team has got** c'est incontestablement *ou* indiscutablement le meilleur joueur de l'équipe; **open to d.** contestable **2** *(argument ▸ between individuals)* dispute *f*, différend *m*; *(▸ between management and workers)* conflit *m*; *Law* litige *m*; **these are the main areas of d.** ce sont là les questions les plus conflictuelles *ou* litigieuses; **to be in d. with sb over sth** être en conflit avec qn sur qch; **to be in d.** *(proposals, territory, ownership)* faire l'objet d'un conflit; **a border d.** un litige portant sur une question de frontière

disqualification [dɪsˌkwɒlɪfɪˈkeɪʃən] N **1** *(from standing for election)* exclusion *f*; *(from sporting event)* disqualification *f*; *(from exam)* exclusion *f*; **a year's d. (from driving)** un retrait de permis d'un an **2** *Law (of witness)* inhabilité *f*, incapacité *f*; *(of testimony)* exclusion *f* **3** *(disqualifying factor)* cause *f* d'incapacité (**for** à); **it's not necessarily a d.** cela ne vous exclut pas forcément

disqualify [ˌdɪsˈkwɒlɪfaɪ] *(pt & pp* **disqualified***)* VT **1** *(from standing for election, from exam)* exclure; *Sport* disqualifier; **her youth disqualifies her from participating** son jeune âge ne l'autorise pas à participer; **being a woman doesn't d. me from expressing an opinion** le fait que je suis une femme ne m'interdit pas de donner mon avis; **to d. sb from driving** retirer son permis (de conduire) à qn, infliger un retrait de permis (de conduire) à qn **2** *Law (witness)* rendre inhabile *ou* incapable; *(testimony)* exclure; *(juror)* empêcher de faire partie du jury

disquiet [dɪsˈkwaɪət] *Formal* N inquiétude *f*
VT inquiéter, troubler; **to be disquieted by sth** être inquiet *ou* s'inquiéter de qch

disquieting [dɪsˈkwaɪətɪŋ] ADJ *Formal* inquiétant, troublant

disregard [ˌdɪsrɪˈgɑːd] N *(for person, feelings)* manque *m* de considération; *(of order, warning, danger etc)* mépris *m*; *(of the law, convention)* inobservation *f*; **to show complete d. for the feelings of others** ne pas du tout prendre les sentiments des autres en considération; **with complete d. for her own safety** au mépris total de sa vie
VT *(person, order, law, rules)* ne tenir aucun compte de; *(feelings, instructions, remark, warning)* ne tenir aucun compte de, négliger; *(danger)* ne tenir aucun compte de, ignorer; **I'll d. what you just said** je ne tiendrai pas compte de ce que tu viens de dire

disremember [ˌdɪsrɪˈmembə(r)] VT *Am Fam* ne pas se rappeler, ne pas se souvenir de

disrepair [ˌdɪsrɪˈpeə(r)] N *(of building)* mauvais état *m*, délabrement *m*; *(of road)* mauvais état *m*; **in (a state of) d.** en mauvais état; **to fall into d.** *(building)* se délabrer; *(road)* se dégrader, s'abîmer

disreputable [dɪsˈrepjʊtəbəl] ADJ **1** *(dishonourable ▸ behaviour)* honteux; *(▸ action, methods)* déshonorant, peu honorable; *(▸ life)* peu honorable **2** *(not respectable ▸ person)* de mauvaise réputation, louche; *(▸ area, club)* mal famé, de mauvaise réputation; *Hum (▸ clothing)* miteux; **she has some d. friends** elle a des amis pas très fréquentables

disreputably [dɪsˈrepjʊtəblɪ] ADV *(behave)* d'une manière honteuse

disrepute [ˌdɪsrɪˈpjuːt] N discrédit *m*; **to bring sth into d.** discréditer qch; **to fall into d.** *(acquire bad reputation)* tomber en discrédit; *(become unpopular)* tomber en défaveur

disrespect [ˌdɪsrɪˈspekt] N irrespect *m*, irrévérence *f*; **I meant no d. (to your family)** je ne voulais pas me montrer irrespectueux *ou* irrévérencieux (envers votre famille); **to show d. towards sb/sth** manquer de respect à qn/qch; **to treat sb/sth with d.** traiter qn/qch irrespectueusement; **no d., but isn't that a bit stupid?** sans vouloir te vexer, est-ce que ce n'est pas un peu bête?

disrespectful [ˌdɪsrɪˈspektful] ADJ irrespectueux, irrévérencieux; **to be d. to sb** manquer de respect à qn; **it would be d. not to go to the funeral** ce serait manquer de respect que de ne pas assister à l'enterrement

disrespectfully [ˌdɪsrɪˈspektfulɪ] ADV irrespectueusement

disrobe [ˌdɪsˈrəub] *Formal* VT *(judge, priest)* aider à enlever sa robe; *(undress)* déshabiller
VI *(judge, priest)* enlever sa robe; *(undress)* se déshabiller

disrupt [dɪsˈrʌpt] VT *(lesson, meeting, transport services)* perturber; *(conversation)* interrompre; *(plans)* déranger, perturber

disruption [dɪsˈrʌpʃən] N *(of lesson, meeting, transport service, plans)* perturbation *f*; *(of conversation)* interruption *f*; **all the disruptions to everyday life caused by the earthquake** tous les bouleversements de la vie quotidienne provoqués par le tremblement de terre; **we apologize to viewers for the d. to this evening's programmes** nous prions les téléspectateurs de bien vouloir nous excuser pour les changements intervenus dans les programmes de la soirée

disruptive [dɪsˈrʌptɪv] ADJ *(factor, person, behaviour)* perturbateur; **he is** *or* **has a d. influence** il a une influence perturbatrice; **your presence would be d.** votre présence aurait un effet perturbateur

dissatisfaction [ˈdɪsˌsætɪsˈfækʃən] N mécontentement *m*; **there is growing d. with his policies** le mécontentement grandit à l'égard de sa politique

dissatisfied [ˌdɪsˈsætɪsfaɪd] ADJ mécontent; **to be d. with sb/sth** être mécontent de qn/qch; **I am very d. with the service I received** je suis très mécontent *ou* je ne suis pas du tout satisfait du service que j'ai reçu; **the meal/explanation left me d.** le repas/l'explication m'a laissé sur ma faim

dissaving [dɪsˈseɪvɪŋ] N *Econ* désépargne *f*

dissect [dɪˈsekt] VT *(animal, plant)* disséquer; *Fig (argument, theory)* disséquer; *(book, report)* éplucher

dissecting [dɪˈsektɪŋ] ADJ *(table, room)* de dissection; *(microscope)* à dissection
►► ***dissecting knife*** scalpel *m*

dissection [dɪˈsekʃən] N *(of animal, plant)* dissection *f*; *Fig (of argument, theory)* dissection *f*; *(of book, report)* épluchage *m*

dissemble [dɪˈsembəl] *Literary* VT *(feelings, motives)* dissimuler
VI dissimuler

disseminate [dɪˈsemɪneɪt] VT *(knowledge, ideas)* disséminer, propager; *(information, news)* diffuser, propager

disseminated sclerosis [dɪˈsemɪneɪtɪd-] N *Med* sclérose *f* en plaques

dissemination [dɪˌsemɪˈneɪʃən] N *(of knowledge, ideas)* propagation *f*, dissémination *f*; *(of information, news)* diffusion *f*, propagation *f*

dissension [dɪˈsenʃən] N dissension *f*, discorde *f*; **there is d. in the ranks** il y a de la dissension *ou* discorde dans les rangs

dissent [dɪˈsent] N **1** *(UNCOUNT) (gen)* désaccord *m*; **to voice** *or* **to express one's d.** exprimer son désaccord; **voices of d.** voix discordantes; *Ftbl* **he has been booked for d.** l'arbitre a pris son nom après qu'il eut refusé d'obtempérer **2** *Rel* dissidence *f* **3** *Am Law* avis *m* contraire *(d'un juge)*
VI **1** *(person)* différer; *(opinion)* diverger; **to d. from an opinion** être en désaccord avec une opinion **2** *Rel* être dissident *ou* en dissidence

dissenter [dɪˈsentə(r)] N **1** *(gen)* dissident(e) *m,f*
2 *Rel* = dissident de l'Église anglicane

dissenting [dɪˈsentɪŋ] ADJ *(opinion)* divergent
►► *Am Law* ***dissenting opinion*** opinion *f* dissidente

dissertation [ˌdɪsəˈteɪʃən] N **1** *Univ Br* mémoire *m*, *Am* thèse *f* **2** *Formal (essay)* dissertation *f*; *(speech)* exposé *m*

disservice [ˌdɪsˈsɜːvɪs] N mauvais service *m*; **to do sb a d.** faire du tort à qn, rendre un mauvais service à qn; **to do oneself a d.** se faire du tort

dissidence [ˈdɪsɪdəns] N *(disagreement)* désaccord *m*; *Pol* dissidence *f*

dissident [ˈdɪsɪdənt] N dissident(e) *m,f*
ADJ dissident

dissimilar [ˌdɪˈsɪmɪlə(r)] ADJ dissemblable; **they are not d.** ils se ressemblent; **the situation now is not d. to what was going on 20 years ago** la situation actuelle n'est pas sans rappeler ce qui s'est passé il y a 20 ans

dissimilarity [ˌdɪsɪmɪˈlærətɪ] *(pl* **dissimilarities***)* N différence *f*

dissimulate [dɪˈsɪmjʊleɪt] *Formal* VT dissimuler, cacher
VI dissimuler

dissimulation [dɪˌsɪmjʊˈleɪʃən] N *Formal* dissimulation *f*

dissipate [ˈdɪsɪpeɪt] VT **1** *(disperse ▸ cloud, fears)* dissiper; *(▸ hopes)* détruire **2** *(waste ▸ fortune)* dilapider, gaspiller; *(▸ energy)* disperser, gaspiller **3** *Phys (heat, energy)* dissiper
VI **1** *(cloud, crowd, fears)* se disperser; *(hopes)* s'évanouir **2** *Phys (heat, energy)* se dissiper

dissipated [ˈdɪsɪpeɪtɪd] ADJ *(person)* débauché; *(habit, life)* de débauche; *(society)* décadent; **to lead** *or* **to live a d. life** mener une vie de débauche

dissipation [ˌdɪsɪˈpeɪʃən] N **1** *(of cloud, fears, hopes)* dissipation *f*
2 *(of fortune)* dilapidation *f*; *(of energy)* dispersion *f*, gaspillage *m*
3 *Phys (of heat, energy)* dissipation *f*
4 *(debauchery)* débauche *f*; **to lead** *or* **to live a life of d.** mener une vie de débauche

dissociate [dɪˈsəusɪeɪt] VT **1** *(gen)* dissocier, séparer; **to d. oneself from sb/sth** se dissocier *ou* désolidariser de qn/qch **2** *Chem* dissocier
VI *Chem (chemist)* opérer une dissociation; *(molecules)* se dissocier

dissociation [dɪˌsəusɪˈeɪʃən] N dissociation *f*

dissolute [ˈdɪsəluːt] ADJ *(person)* débauché; *(life)* de débauche, dissolu

dissoluteness [ˈdɪsəluːtnɪs] N débauche *f*

dissolution [ˌdɪsəˈluːʃən] N **1** *(gen)* dissolution *f* **2** *Am Law (divorce)* divorce *m* **3** *Hist* **the D. of the Monasteries** = destruction des monastères en 1539 après la proclamation de Henri VIII comme chef suprême de l'Église d'Angleterre

dissolve [dɪˈzɒlv] VT **1** *(salt, sugar)* dissoudre **2** *(empire, marriage, Parliament)* dissoudre **3** *(cloud, illusion)* dissiper
VI **1** *(salt, sugar)* se dissoudre; *Fig (fear, hopes)* s'évanouir, s'envoler; *(apparition)* s'évanouir; *(crowd)* se disperser; *(clouds)* disparaître; **to d. into tears** fondre en larmes; **to d. into laughter** être pris de rire **2** *(marriage, Parliament)* être dissout; *(empire)* se dissoudre **3** *Cin & TV* faire un fondu enchaîné
N *Cin & TV* fondu *m* enchaîné

dissonance [ˈdɪsənəns] N *Mus* dissonance *f*; *Fig (of colours, opinions)* discordance *f*

dissonant [ˈdɪsənənt] ADJ *Mus* dissonant; *Fig (colours, opinions)* discordant

dissuade [dɪˈsweɪd] VT *(person)* dissuader; **to d. sb from doing sth** dissuader qn de faire qch; **to d. sb from sth** détourner qn de qch

dissuasion [dɪˈsweɪʒən] N dissuasion *f*

distaff [ˈdɪstɑːf] N *(for spinning)* quenouille *f*; *Fig* **on the d. side** du côté maternel

distance [ˈdɪstəns] N **1** *(between two places)* distance *f*; **at a d. of 50 metres** à (une distance de) 50 mètres; **within walking/cycling d. from the station** à quelques minutes de marche/en vélo de la gare; **is it within walking d.?** peut-on y aller à pied?; **it's some** *or* **quite a** *or* **a good d. from here** c'est assez loin d'ici; **a short d. away** tout près; **it's no d. (at all)** c'est tout près *ou* à deux pas; **we covered the d. in ten hours** nous avons fait le trajet en dix heures; **d. (is) no object** *(in advertisement)* toutes distances couvertes, toutes destinations; *Fig* **to keep sb at a d.** tenir qn à distance (respectueuse); **to keep one's d. (from sb)** garder ses distances (par rapport à qn); **to go** *or* **stay the d.** *(boxer, political campaigner)* tenir la distance

2 *(distant point, place)* **to see/to hear sth in the d.** voir/entendre qch au loin; **in the middle d.** au second plan; **to see sth from a d.** voir qch de loin; **you can't see it from** *or* **at this d.** on ne peut pas le voir à cette distance

3 *(separation in time)* **it's very hard for me to remember at this d. in time** c'est très difficile de m'en souvenir après tout ce temps

4 *(aloofness, reserve)* froideur *f*

VT distancer; *Fig* **to d. oneself (from sb/sth)** prendre ses distances (par rapport à qn/qch)

►► ***distance education, distance learning*** enseignement *m* à distance *ou* par correspondance; *Sport* ***distance race*** épreuve *f* de fond; *Sport* ***distance runner*** coureur(euse) *m,f* de fond; ***distance teaching*** enseignement *m* à distance

distant [ˈdɪstənt] **ADJ 1** *(faraway ► country, galaxy, place)* lointain, éloigné; **the d. sound of the sea** le bruit de la mer au loin

2 *(in past ► times)* lointain, reculé; *(► memory)* lointain; **in the (dim and) d. past** il y a bien *ou* très longtemps, dans le temps

3 *(in future ► prospect)* lointain; **in the d. future** dans un avenir lointain; **in the not too d. future** dans un avenir proche, prochainement

4 *(relation)* éloigné; *(resemblance)* vague

5 *(remote ► person, look)* distant; *(aloof)* froid; **to have a d. manner** être distant *ou* froid

ADV three miles d. from here à trois miles d'ici; **not far d.** pas très loin

►► *Rail* ***distant signal*** signal *m* à distance

distantly [ˈdɪstəntlɪ] **ADV 1** *(in the distance)* au loin **2** *(resemble)* vaguement; **to be d. related** *(people)* avoir un lien de parenté éloigné; *(ideas, concepts etc)* avoir un rapport éloigné **3** *(speak, behave, look)* froidement, d'un air distant *ou* froid

distaste [dɪsˈteɪst] **N** dégoût *m* **(for** de**)**, répugnance *f* **(for** pour**)**; **to feel d. for sth** ne pas aimer qch; *(stronger)* éprouver du dégoût *ou* de la répugnance pour qch

distasteful [dɪsˈteɪstfʊl] **ADJ** *(unpleasant ► task, thought)* désagréable; *(in bad taste ► joke, remark etc)* de mauvais goût; **to be d. to sb** déplaire à qn; **I find it extremely d.** je trouve ça tout à fait déplaisant

distastefulness [dɪsˈteɪstfʊlnɪs] **N** *(repugnance)* caractère *m* désagréable; *(bad taste)* mauvais goût *m*

distemper[1] [dɪˈstempə(r)] **N** *(paint)* détrempe *f*
VT peindre à la *ou* en détrempe

distemper[2] **N** *Vet* maladie *f* de Carré

distend [dɪˈstend] **VT** *(cheeks)* gonfler; *(nostrils)* dilater; *(stomach)* distendre, ballonner
VI *(cheeks)* se gonfler; *(nostrils)* se dilater; *(stomach)* se ballonner, se distendre; *(sails)* se gonfler

distension [dɪˈstenʃən] **N** *(of cheeks)* gonflement *m*; *(of nostrils)* dilatation *f*; *(of stomach)* ballonnement *m*

distich [ˈdɪstɪk] **N** *Literature (couplet)* distique *m*

distil, *Am* **distill** [dɪˈstɪl] *(pt & pp* **distilled,** *cont* **distilling) VT 1** *Chem (liquid)* distiller **2** *Fig* condenser
VI se distiller
►► ***distilled water*** eau *f* distillée

►**distil off, distil out VT SEP** *Chem* chasser par la distillation

distillate [ˈdɪstɪlət] **N** *Chem* distillat *m*

distillation [ˌdɪstɪˈleɪʃən] **N 1** *Chem (process)* distillation *f*; *(product)* produit *m* de la distillation **2** *Fig* condensé *m*

distiller [dɪˈstɪlə(r)] **N** *Chem* distillateur *m*

distillery [dɪˈstɪlərɪ] *(pl* **distilleries) N** distillerie *f*

distinct [dɪˈstɪŋkt] **ADJ 1** *(different)* distinct; **to be d. from** se distinguer de; **the two poems are quite d. from each other** les deux poèmes sont tout à fait différents l'un de l'autre **2** *(clear ► memory)* clair, net; *(► voice, announcement, place, object)* distinct **3** *(decided, evident ► accent)* prononcé; *(► difference)* net, clair; *(► preference)* marqué; *(► lack of respect, interest)* évident; *(► likeness)* clair, net, prononcé; *(► advantage, improvement, impression)* net; **I have the d. impression you're trying to avoid me** j'ai la nette impression que tu essaies de m'éviter; **there's a d. smell of smoke in here** cela sent vraiment la fumée ici; **a d. possibility** une forte possibilité; **it is a d. possibility** *(in answer to question)* c'est fort possible

• **as distinct from PREP** par opposition à

> Attention: ne pas confondre avec l'adjectif **distinctive**.

distinction [dɪˈstɪŋkʃən] **N 1** *(difference)* distinction *f*; **to make** *or* **to draw a d. between two things** faire *ou* établir une distinction entre deux choses

2 *(excellence)* distinction *f*; **a writer/artist of great d.** un écrivain/artiste très réputé; **to win** *or* **to gain d. (as)** se distinguer (en tant que); **she has the d. of being the only woman to become Prime Minister** elle se distingue pour être la seule femme à avoir été nommée Premier ministre

3 *Sch & Univ (mark)* mention *f*; **he got a d. in maths** il a été reçu en maths avec mention; **to pass with d.** réussir un examen avec mention très bien

4 *(honour, award)* honneur *m*

distinctive [dɪˈstɪŋktɪv] **ADJ** *(colour, feature, style)* distinctif; **to be d. of sth** être caractéristique de qch; **her car is quite d.** sa voiture se remarque facilement

►► *Ling* ***distinctive feature*** trait *m* pertinent

> Attention: ne pas confondre avec l'adjectif anglais **distinct**.

distinctively [dɪˈstɪŋktɪvlɪ] **ADV** de manière distinctive

> Attention: ne pas confondre avec l'adverbe **distinctly**.

distinctly [dɪˈstɪŋktlɪ] **ADV 1** *(clearly ► speak, hear)* distinctement, clairement; *(► remember)* clairement; **I d. told you not to do that** je t'ai bien dit de ne pas faire cela **2** *(very)* vraiment, franchement; **he was d. rude to the old lady** il a été vraiment grossier avec la vieille dame; **by now the weather was d. cold** à présent il faisait vraiment froid

> Attention: ne pas confondre avec l'adverbe **distinctively**.

distinctness [dɪˈstɪŋktnɪs] **N 1** *(clearness)* clarté *f*, netteté *f* **2** *(separate nature)* spécificité *f*

distinguish [dɪˈstɪŋgwɪʃ] **VT 1** *(set apart)* distinguer; **to d. oneself** se distinguer; **to d. sth from sth** distinguer qch de qch; **reason distinguishes man from the other animals** la raison sépare l'homme des autres animaux **2** *(tell apart)* distinguer **3** *(discern)* distinguer
VI faire *ou* établir une distinction; **to d. between two things/people** faire la distinction entre deux choses/personnes

distinguishable [dɪˈstɪŋgwɪʃəbəl] **ADJ 1** *(visible)* visible; **the horizon was hardly d.** on distinguait à peine l'horizon **2** *(recognizable)* reconnaissable; *(sound, difference)* perceptible; *(improvement)* sensible **3** *(that can be differentiated)* que l'on peut distinguer, qui se distingue **(from** de**)**; **to be easily d. from sb/sth** se distinguer facilement de qn/qch, être facile à distinguer de qn/qch; **the two ideas are barely d.** les deux idées diffèrent à peine

distinguished [dɪˈstɪŋgwɪʃt] **ADJ 1** *(eminent)* distingué **2** *(refined ► manners, voice)* distingué; **to look d.** avoir l'air distingué; **d.-looking** distingué

distinguishing [dɪˈstɪŋgwɪʃɪŋ] **ADJ** *(characteristic)* distinctif

►► ***distinguishing features, distinguishing marks*** *(on passport)* signes *mpl* particuliers

distort [dɪˈstɔːt] **VT 1** *(face, image, structure, limbs)* déformer **2** *Fig (facts, truth, account)* déformer, dénaturer; *(judgment)* fausser; **his upbringing distorted his view of life** son éducation a déformé *ou* faussé son image de la vie **3** *Electron, Rad & TV* déformer
VI 1 *(face, image, structure, limbs)* se déformer **2** *Electron, Rad & TV* se déformer

distorted [dɪˈstɔːtɪd] **ADJ 1** *(face, image, structure, limbs)* déformé **2** *Fig (facts, truth, account)* déformé, dénaturé; *(view of life)* déformé, faussé; *(judgment)* faussé **3** *Electron, Rad & TV* déformé

distorting [dɪˈstɔːtɪŋ] **ADJ** déformant

distortion [dɪˈstɔːʃən] **N 1** *(of face, image, structure, limbs)* déformation *f* **2** *Fig (of facts, truth, account)* déformation *f* **3** *Electron & Rad* distorsion *f*; *TV* déformation *f*

distract [dɪˈstrækt] **VT 1** *(break concentration of)* distraire; *(disturb)* déranger; **to d. sb from his/her work** distraire qn de son travail; **to d. sb** *or* **sb's attention** *(accidentally)* distraire l'attention de qn; *(on purpose)* détourner l'attention de qn; **d. her for a couple of minutes** détourne son attention pendant quelques minutes **2** *(amuse)* distraire **3** *(preoccupy)* préoccuper

distracted [dɪˈstræktɪd] **ADJ 1** *(with thoughts elsewhere)* distrait **2** *(upset)* affolé, bouleversé; **d. with worry/with grief** fou (folle) d'inquiétude/de chagrin

> Note that the French word **distrait** never means **upset**. Its meaning is **absent-minded**.

distractedly [dɪˈstræktɪdlɪ] **ADV 1** *(with thoughts elsewhere)* distraitement, d'un air absent **2** *(anxiously)* d'un air affolé *ou* bouleversé; **she was sobbing d.** elle sanglotait, éperdue de douleur

distracting [dɪˈstræktɪŋ] **ADJ 1** *(disruptive)* gênant; **I find it d.** ça m'empêche de me concentrer; **it's very d. having so many people in the office** c'est très difficile de se concentrer (sur son travail) avec autant de gens dans le bureau **2** *(amusing)* distrayant

distraction [dɪˈstrækʃən] **N 1** *(interruption ► of attention, from objective)* distraction *f*; **I need a place where I can work without d.** il me faut un endroit où je pourrais travailler sans être dérangé

2 *(amusement)* distraction *f*

3 *(anxiety)* affolement *m*; *(absent-mindedness)* distraction *f*

4 *(madness)* affolement *m*; **to drive sb to d.** rendre qn fou (folle); **to love sb to d.** aimer qn éperdument *ou* à la folie

distrain [dɪˈstreɪn] **VI** *Law* **to d. on sb's goods** saisir les biens de qn

distraint [dɪˈstreɪnt] **N** *Law* saisie *f*

distraught [dɪˈstrɔːt] **ADJ** *(with worry)* angoissé, fou (folle) d'angoisse; *(after death)* fou (folle) *ou* éperdu de douleur, désespéré; **to be d. with grief** être fou (folle) de douleur; **to be d. over sth** être angoissé à cause de *ou* désespéré par qch

distress [dɪˈstres] **N 1** *(suffering ► mental)* angoisse *f*; *(► physical)* souffrance *f*; *(hardship)* détresse *f*; **to cause sb d.** causer du tourment à qn; **to be in d.** *(horse, athlete)* souffrir; *(mentally)* être angoissé; *(ship)* être en détresse *ou* perdition; *(aircraft)* être en détresse; **to be in financial d.** avoir de sérieux problèmes financiers **2** *Law (action)* saisie *f*; *(goods)* biens *mpl* saisis

VT 1 *(upset)* faire de la peine à, tourmenter; **he was distressed by the animal's suffering** les souffrances de la bête lui faisaient de la peine **2** *(furniture, leather, clothing)* vieillir

►► *Am Com* ***distress sale*** soldes *fpl* avant fermeture; ***distress signal*** signal *m* de détresse; *Fig* **to send out d. signals** envoyer des signaux de détresse

distressed [dɪˈstrest] **ADJ 1** *(mentally)* tourmenté; *(very sorry)* affligé; *(physically)* souffrant; *(financially)* dans le besoin; **there's no need to get d.** ce n'est pas la peine de vous tourmenter; **we were d. to hear of his death** nous avons été affligés d'apprendre sa mort; **to be d. by** *or* **about sth** être affligé par qch **2** *(furniture, leather, clothing)* vieilli **3** *Law* saisi

istressing [dɪ'stresɪŋ] **ADJ** pénible

istribute [dɪ'strɪbjuːt] **VT 1** *(hand out ▸ money, eaflets, gifts etc)* distribuer
2 *(share out, allocate ▸ wealth, weight)* répartir; *▸ paint)* répandre
3 *Fin (dividend)* répartir
4 *Cin & Com (supply)* distribuer

istributed database [dɪ'strɪbjuːtɪd-] **N** *Comut* base *f* de données répartie

istribution [ˌdɪstrɪ'bjuːʃən] **N 1** *(of money, leafets, gifts etc)* distribution *f*
2 *Cin & Com (delivery, supply)* distribution *f*; *(of ooks)* diffusion *f*; *Com* **to have a wide d.** être largement distribué
3 *(of wealth)* répartition *f*, distribution *f*; *(of oad, population)* répartition *f*
4 *Math (in statistics)* distribution *f*
▸▸ *Elec* ***distribution box*** boîte *f* de dérivation *ou* le jonction; *Com* ***distribution channel*** canal *m* de listribution; ***distribution costs*** frais *mpl* de distriution, coût *m* de la distribution; *Com* ***distribution network*** réseau *m* de distribution, circuit *m* le distribution

istributive [dɪ'strɪbjʊtɪv] *Gram*
N *(pronoun)* pronom *m* distributif; *(adjective)* adjectif *m* distributif
ADJ distributif
▸▸ *Com* ***the distributive trades*** le secteur de la listribution

istributor [dɪ'strɪbjʊtə(r)] **N 1** *Cin & Com* distriouteur *m*; *(of particular make of car, product)* concessionnaire *m* **2** *Aut* distributeur *m*
▸▸ *Aut* ***distributor cap*** tête *f* de Delco® *ou* d'allumeur

istributorship [dɪ'strɪbjʊtəʃɪp] **N** *Com* **to have he d. for sth** distribuer qch

istrict ['dɪstrɪkt] **N** *(of country)* région *f*; *(of town)* quartier *m*; *(administrative area ▸ of country)* disrict *m*; *(▸ of city)* arrondissement *m*; *(surroundng area)* région *f*
▸▸ *Am Law* ***district attorney*** procureur *m* de la République; ***the District of Columbia*** le district fédéral de Columbia; *Br Admin* ***district council*** conseil *m* municipal; *Am Law* ***district court*** tribuhal *m* d'instance (fédéral); *Br* ***district nurse*** infirnière *f* visiteuse

istrust [dɪs'trʌst] **N** méfiance *f*; **to have a deep d. of sb/sth** éprouver une profonde méfiance à l'égard de qn/qch
VT se méfier de; **to d. one's own eyes** ne pas en croire ses propres yeux

istrustful [dɪs'trʌstfʊl] **ADJ** méfiant; **to be deeply d. of sb/sth** éprouver une extrême méfiance pour *ou* à l'égard de qn/qch

isturb [dɪ'stɜːb] **VT 1** *(interrupt ▸ person)* déranger; *(▸ silence, sleep)* troubler; *(▸ criminal)* surprendre; **(please) do not d.** *(sign)* (prière de) ne pas déranger; *Law* **to d. the peace** troubler l'ordre public
2 *(distress, upset)* troubler, perturber; *(alarm)* inquiéter
3 *(alter condition of ▸ water)* troubler; *(▸ mud, sediment)* agiter, remuer; *(▸ papers)* déranger
4 *Phys (magnetic field)* perturber
5 *Law (interfere with the rights of)* inquiéter *ou* troubler dans la jouissance d'un droit

isturbance [dɪ'stɜːbəns] **N 1** *(interruption, disruption)* dérangement *m*
2 *Pol* **disturbances** *(unrest)* troubles *mpl*, émeute *f*
3 *(noise)* bruit *m*, vacarme *m*; *Law* **to cause a d.** troubler l'ordre public; **they create such a d. when they leave the disco** ils font tant de chahut *ou* de tapage lorsqu'ils sortent de la discothèque; **police were called to a d. in the early hours of the morning** la police a été appelée au petit matin pour mettre fin à un tapage nocturne
4 *(distress, alarm)* trouble *m*, perturbation *f*
5 *Law (interference with rights)* trouble *m* de jouissance

isturbed [dɪ'stɜːbd] **ADJ 1** *(distressed, upset)* troublé, perturbé; *(alarmed)* inquiet; *(as a characteristic)* perturbé; **to be d. at** *or* **by sth** être troublé par *ou* perturbé par *ou* inquiet de qch; **mentally d.** qui souffre de troubles mentaux; **emotionally d. children** enfants *mpl* souffrant de troubles émotionnels *ou* affectifs **2** *(interrupted ▸ sleep)* troublé; **we had a d. night** notre sommeil a été troublé

disturbing [dɪ'stɜːbɪŋ] **ADJ** *(alarming)* inquiétant; *(distressing, upsetting)* troublant, perturbant; **some viewers may find the programme d.** cette émission pourrait troubler *ou* perturber certains spectateurs

disunite [ˌdɪsjuː'naɪt] **VT** désunir

disunited [ˌdɪsjuː'naɪtɪd] **ADJ** désuni

disunity [ˌdɪs'juːnətɪ] **N** désunion *f*

disuse [ˌdɪs'juːs] **N** *(of term)* désuétude *f*; *(of machine)* abandon *m*, mise *f* au rancart; **to fall into d.** *(word, custom, law)* tomber en désuétude

disused [ˌdɪs'juːzd] **ADJ** *(machine)* mis au rancart; *(public building)* désaffecté; *(mine, well, railway line)* abandonné

disyllabic [ˌdɪsɪ'læbɪk] **ADJ** *Ling* dissyllabe, dissyllabique

ditch [dɪtʃ] **N 1** *(by roadside)* fossé *m*; *(for irrigation, drainage)* rigole *f*; **he drove the car into the d.** il est tombé dans le fossé avec la voiture **2** *Fam Aviat* **the d.** la baille, la flotte
VT 1 *Fam (abandon ▸ car)* abandonner❑; *(▸ plan, idea)* abandonner❑, laisser tomber❑; *(▸ boyfriend, girlfriend)* plaquer, laisser tomber❑; *(throw out)* se débarrasser de❑ **2** *Aviat* **to d. a plane** faire un amerrissage forcé
VI *Aviat* faire un amerrissage forcé

ditching ['dɪtʃɪŋ] **N 1** *Agr* creusement *m* de fossés **2** *Fam (dumping ▸ of car, plan, idea)* abandon❑ *m* **3** *Aviat* amerrissage *m* forcé

ditchwater ['dɪtʃˌwɔːtə(r)] **N** *Fam (idiom)* **to be as dull as d.** être ennuyeux comme la pluie

dither ['dɪðə(r)] *Fam* **VI** *(be indecisive)* hésiter❑, tergiverser❑, se tâter❑; **to d. about** *or* **over whether to do sth** hésiter à *ou* se tâter pour faire qch; **stop dithering (about)!** *(decide)* décide-toi!; *(make a start)* arrête de tourner en rond!
N to be in a d. hésiter❑, tergiverser❑, se tâter❑; **he was in** *or* **all of a d. about his exams** il était dans tous ses états à cause de ses examens

ditherer ['dɪðərə(r)] **N** *Fam* **he's such a d.** il est toujours à hésiter sur tout❑

dithery ['dɪðərɪ] **ADJ** *Fam* **1** *(indecisive)* hésitant❑, indécis❑ **2** *(agitated)* nerveux❑, agité❑

ditto ['dɪtəʊ] **ADV** idem, de même; *Fam* **I feel like a drink – d.** j'ai bien envie de prendre un verre – idem
▸▸ *Ling* ***ditto mark*** guillemets *mpl* itératifs, signes *mpl* d'itération

ditty ['dɪtɪ] *(pl* **ditties***)* **N** *Fam* chanson❑ *f*

ditz [dɪts] **N** *Am Fam* courge *f*, andouille *f*, cruche *f*

ditzy ['dɪtsɪ] **ADJ** *Am Fam* étourdi❑

diuretic [ˌdaɪjʊ'retɪk] *Med* **N** diurétique *m*
ADJ diurétique

diurnal [daɪ'ɜːnəl] **N** *Rel* diurnal *m*
ADJ *Bot, Zool & Astron* diurne

div [dɪv] **N** *Br Fam (idiot)* abruti(e) *m,f*

diva ['diːvə] **N** diva *f*; *Fig* **she's a bit of a d.** elle est un peu comédienne

divan [dɪ'væn] **N** *(couch)* divan *m*
▸▸ ***divan bed*** divan-lit *m*

dive [daɪv] *(Br pt & pp* **dived,** *Am pt* **dove** [dəʊv] *or* **dived,** *pp* **dived)** **VI 1** *(person, bird, submarine)* plonger; *(aircraft)* plonger, piquer, descendre en piqué; **to d. for clams/pearls** pêcher la palourde/des perles *(en plongée)*; **to d. for the ball** *(goalkeeper)* plonger (pour attraper le ballon) **2** *(as sport)* faire de la plongée **3** *(rush)* **they dived for the exit** ils se sont précipités *ou* ils ont foncé vers la sortie; **he dived for his camera** il s'est rué sur son appareil photo; **the soldiers dived into the doorway** les soldats se sont engouffrés dans l'entrée; **he dived into his pocket/the bag** il a plongé la main dans sa poche/le sac; **to d. under the table** plonger *ou* se jeter sous la table; **he dived under the covers and shut his eyes** il s'est enfoui *ou* il a plongé sous les couvertures et a fermé les yeux
N 1 *(of swimmer, bird)* plongeon *m*; *(of submarine, diver)* plongée *f*; *(by aircraft)* piqué *m*; **to go into a d.** *(aircraft)* piquer, descendre en piqué; **to make a d. for the ball** plonger (pour attraper le ballon); *Fam Boxing* **to take a d.** feindre le K-O; *Ftbl* **he took a d. in the box** il a fait exprès de s'effondrer dans la surface de réparation **2** *(sudden movement)* **to make a d. for the exit** se précipiter vers la sortie; **I made a d. for the vase** *(to stop it breaking)* je me suis précipité vers le vase **3** *Fam Pej (bar, café)* bouge *m*; *(hotel)* hôtel *m* borgne

▸ **dive in VI 1** *(swimmer)* plonger **2** *Fam* **d. in!** *(eat)* attaquez!; **we can't just d. in without any preparation** nous ne pouvons pas nous lancer comme ça sans aucune préparation

dive-bomb **VT** *(of aircraft)* bombarder *ou* attaquer en piqué; *(of bird)* attaquer en piqué

diver ['daɪvə(r)] **N 1** *(from diving board, underwater)* plongeur(euse) *m,f*; *(deep-sea)* scaphandrier *m* **2** *Orn* plongeon *m*

diverge [daɪ'vɜːdʒ] **VI 1** *(paths, roads)* se séparer, diverger; *(rays, lines)* diverger **2** *Fig (people, opinions)* diverger; **to d. from the truth** s'écarter de la vérité
VT *(rays, lines)* faire diverger

divergence [daɪ'vɜːdʒəns] **N 1** *(of paths, roads)* séparation *f*, divergence *f*; *(of rays, lines)* divergence *f* **2** *Fig (of people, opinions)* divergence *f*

divergent [daɪ'vɜːdʒənt] **ADJ** *(opinions)* divergent

diverging beam [daɪ'vɜːdʒɪŋ-] **N** *Aut* faisceau *m* divergent

divers ['daɪvəz] **ADJ** *Arch or Literary (several)* divers, plusieurs

diverse [daɪ'vɜːs] **ADJ 1** *(different from each other)* divers, différent; **they are very d. in their approach** ils ont une approche très différente **2** *(varied)* divers, varié

diversely [daɪ'vɜːslɪ] **ADV** diversement

diversification [daɪˌvɜːsɪfɪ'keɪʃən] **N** diversification *f*; **the company's recent d. into cosmetics** la diversification qu'a récemment entreprise la société en pénétrant le marché des cosmétiques

diversify [daɪ'vɜːsɪfaɪ] *(pt & pp* **diversified)** **VI** *(company)* se diversifier; **to d. into software/banking** se diversifier en pénétrant le secteur du logiciel/le secteur bancaire
VT diversifier

diversion [daɪ'vɜːʃən] **N 1** *(of traffic)* déviation *f*; *(of river)* dérivation *f*, détournement *m* **2** *(distraction)* diversion *f*; **it was a welcome d.** cela a été une diversion agréable; **to create a d.** *(distract attention)* faire (une) diversion; *Mil* opérer une diversion **3** *(amusement)* distraction *f*; **to seek d. from sth** chercher à se distraire de qch

diversionary [daɪ'vɜːʃənrɪ] **ADJ 1** *(remark, proposal)* destiné à faire diversion; **d. tactics** tactique *f* de diversion **2** *Mil (manoeuvre)* de diversion

diversity [daɪ'vɜːsətɪ] **N** diversité *f*

divert [daɪ'vɜːt] **VT 1** *(reroute ▸ traffic)* dévier; *(▸ train, plane, ship)* dévier (la route de); *(▸ river, attention, conversation, blow)* détourner; *Elec (current)* dévier; **I managed to d. his attention from the problem** j'ai réussi à détourner son attention de ce problème; **the plane was diverted to London** l'avion a été dévié *ou* détourné sur Londres **2** *(money)* transférer; *(illegally)* détourner **3** *(amuse)* distraire; **to d. oneself by doing sth** faire qch pour se distraire

diverting [daɪ'vɜːtɪŋ] **ADJ** divertissant

divest [daɪ'vest] **VT** *Formal* **1** *(take away from)* priver; **to d. sb. of sth** priver qn de qch **2** *(rid)* **to d. oneself of** *(opinion, belief)* se défaire de; *(coat)* enlever; *(luggage)* se débarrasser de; *(authority)* se dévêtir de; *(duty)* se désinvestir de; *(right)* renoncer à

divestment [daɪ'vestmənt] **N** *Am* désinvestissement *m*; *Fin* **d. of assets** scission *f* d'actifs

divide [dɪ'vaɪd] **VT 1** *(split up ▸ territory, property, work, inheritance)* diviser; *(▸ kingdom)* démembrer; *(▸ land)* morceler; *(▸ family)* diviser, désunir; *(▸ party)* diviser, scinder; **to d. sth in** *or* **into two** couper *ou* diviser qch en deux; **she divided the cake into six equal portions** elle a partagé *ou* coupé le gâteau en six parts égales
2 *(share out)* partager, répartir; **they divided the work between them** ils se sont partagé *ou* réparti

le travail; **he divides his time between the office and home** il partage son temps entre le bureau et la maison

3 *(separate)* séparer; **the Berlin Wall used to d. East and West** le mur de Berlin séparait l'Est de l'Ouest

4 *Math* diviser; **40 divided by 5 equals 8** 40 divisé par 5 égale 8

5 *Br Pol* **to d. the House** faire voter la Chambre

VI 1 *(cells, group of people, novel)* se diviser; **the class divided into groups** la classe s'est divisée *ou* répartie en groupes

2 *(river, road)* se séparer

3 *Math* diviser; **we're learning to d.** nous apprenons à faire des divisions; **10 divides by 2** 10 est divisible par 2, 10 est un multiple de 2

4 *Br Pol* aller aux voix; **the House divided on the question** la Chambre a voté sur la question

N 1 *(gap)* fossé *m*; **the North-South d.** la division Nord-Sud **2** *Am Geog (watershed)* ligne *f* de partage des eaux; **the Great** *or* **Continental D.** la ligne de partage des eaux des Rocheuses; **to cross the Great D.** *(die)* passer de vie à trépas

▸ **divide off** **VT SEP** séparer; **to d. sth off from sth** séparer qch de qch

▸ **divide out** **VT SEP** partager, répartir (**between/among** entre)

▸ **divide up** **VT SEP** diviser; **they divided the area/work up between them** ils se sont partagés le secteur/travail

VI se diviser

divided [dɪˈvaɪdɪd] **ADJ 1** *(property, territory)* divisé; *(work)* partagé; *Bot* découpé **2** *(disunited ▸ family, party)* divisé; **the party is d. on the issue** le parti est divisé sur ce problème; **opinion is d. on the matter** les avis sont partagés sur ce problème; **a political party d. against itself** un parti divisé; **to have d. loyalties** être déchiré

▸▸ *Am* ***divided highway*** route *f* à quatre voies; ***divided skirt*** jupe-culotte *f*

dividend [ˈdɪvɪdend] **N** *Fin, Math & St Exch* dividende *m*; *(from cooperative society)* ristourne *f*; *Fin* **to pay a d.** *(company)* verser un dividende; *St Exch (shares)* rapporter un dividende; *Fig* **to pay dividends** porter ses fruits

▸▸ ***dividend announcement*** déclaration *f* de dividende; ***dividend share*** action *f* de jouissance; *Fin* ***dividend tax*** impôt *m* sur les dividendes

divider [dɪˈvaɪdə(r)] **N 1** *(in room ▸ partition)* cloison *f* amovible; *(▸ piece of furniture)* meuble *m* de séparation **2** *(for files)* intercalaire *m*

• **dividers** **NPL** *Math* **(a pair of) dividers** un compas à pointes sèches

dividing [dɪˈvaɪdɪŋ] **ADJ** *(fence)* de séparation

▸▸ *Elec* ***dividing box*** boîte *f* de dérivation; *Fig* **it's a very thin d. line** c'est une distinction très subtile; ***dividing line*** limite *f*; *Fig* distinction *f*; ***dividing wall*** mur *m* de séparation, cloison *f*

divination [ˌdɪvɪˈneɪʃən] **N** divination *f*

divine [dɪˈvaɪn] **ADJ 1** *Rel* divin; **it was d. retribution** c'était le châtiment de Dieu **2** *Fam (delightful)* divin; **you look simply d.!** tu es absolument divine!

N *Rel (priest)* théologien *m*

VT 1 *Literary (foretell ▸ the future)* présager, prédire **2** *Literary (conjecture, guess)* deviner **3** *(locate ▸ water)* détecter *ou* découvrir par la radiesthésie

VI **to d. for water** détecter *ou* découvrir de l'eau par la radiesthésie

▸▸ *also Fig* ***divine inspiration*** inspiration *f* divine; ***divine intervention*** intervention *f* divine; *Hist* ***the divine right of kings*** la monarchie de droit divin

divinely [dɪˈvaɪnlɪ] **ADV** divinement

diviner [dɪˈvaɪnə(r)] **N 1** *(of future ▸ male)* devin *m*; *(▸ female)* devineresse *f* **2** *(for water)* sourcier *m*, radiesthésiste *mf*

diving [ˈdaɪvɪŋ] **N** *(underwater)* plongée *f* sous-marine; *(from board)* plongeon *m*

▸▸ ***diving bell*** cloche *f* à plongeur *ou* de plongée; ***diving board*** plongeoir *m*; ***diving suit*** scaphandre *m*

divining [dɪˈvaɪnɪŋ] **N** divination *f*; *(for water)* radiesthésie *f*

▸▸ ***divining rod*** baguette *f* de sourcier

divinity [dɪˈvɪnətɪ] *(pl* **divinities***)* *Rel* **N 1** *(quality, state)* divinité *f* **2** *(god, goddess)* divinité *f*; **the D.** la Divinité **3** *(theology)* théologie *f*; *Sch* instruction *f* religieuse; **Faculty/Doctor of D.** faculté *f* de/docteur *m* en théologie

divisible [dɪˈvɪzəbəl] **ADJ** divisible; **d. by** divisible par

division [dɪˈvɪʒən] **N 1** *(splitting up ▸ of territory, property, family, work, inheritance)* division *f*; *(▸ of kingdom)* démembrement *m*; *(▸ of land)* morcellement *m*; *(▸ of party)* division *f*, scission *f*

2 *(sharing out)* partage *m*; **the d. of labour** la division du travail; **the d. of responsibility** le partage des responsabilités

3 *(section ▸ of company, organization)* division *f*; *(▸ of scale, thermometer)* graduation *f*; *Law (▸ of court)* section *f*; *(compartment ▸ in box, bag)* compartiment *m*

4 *Biol, Mil & Sport* embranchement *m*

5 *Math* division *f*

6 *(that which separates)* division *f*; *(dividing line)* division *f*, scission *f*; *(in room)* cloison *f*; **class divisions** divisions *fpl* entre les classes, divisions *fpl* sociales

7 *(dissension)* division *f*

8 *Br Pol* = vote officiel à la Chambre des communes (pour lequel les députés se répartissent dans les deux "division lobbies"); **the bill was passed without d.** le projet de loi a été adopté sans qu'on ait procédé à un vote; **to carry a d.** avoir *ou* remporter la majorité des voix; **to call a d.** annoncer un vote; **to call for a d. on sth** demander que qch soit soumis à un vote

▸▸ *Br Pol* ***division bell*** = sonnerie à la Chambre des communes prévenant les députés qu'il faut venir voter; *Br Pol* ***division list*** = liste des députés qui ont voté pour ou contre une motion; *Br Pol* ***division lobby*** = nom des deux salles dans lesquelles les députés britanniques se répartissent pour voter; *Math* ***division sign*** symbole *m* de division

divisional [dɪˈvɪʒənəl] **ADJ** de la division, de division

▸▸ *Br Law* ***Divisional Court*** = juridiction d'appel rattachée à chacune des divisions de la "High Court"

divisive [dɪˈvaɪsɪv] **ADJ** *(policy, issue)* qui crée des divisions

divisor [dɪˈvaɪzə(r)] **N** *Math* diviseur *m*

divorce [dɪˈvɔːs] **N 1** *(of married couple)* divorce *m*; **I want a d.** je veux divorcer, je veux le divorce; **one in three marriages ends in d.** un couple sur trois divorce; **to file** *or* **to sue for (a) d.** demander le divorce, intenter un procès en divorce; **to get** *or* **to obtain a d.** obtenir le divorce; **they're getting a d.** ils divorcent **2** *Fig* séparation *f*, divorce *m*

COMP *(case, proceedings)* de divorce

VT 1 *(of husband, wife)* divorcer d'avec; *(of judge)* prononcer le divorce de; **you should d. him** tu devrais divorcer (d'avec lui); **they got divorced a few years ago** ils ont divorcé il y a quelques années **2** *Fig* séparer; **to d. sth from sth** séparer qch de qch

VI divorcer

▸▸ ***divorce court*** = chambre spécialisée dans les affaires familiales au tribunal de grande instance; ***divorce law*** droit *m* du divorce; ***divorce lawyer*** avocat(e) *m,f* spécialisé(e) dans les affaires *ou* cas de divorce

divorced [dɪˈvɔːst] **ADJ 1** *(person, couple)* divorcé; **a d. woman** une (femme) divorcée **2** *Fig* **to be d. from reality** *(person)* être coupé de la réalité, ne pas avoir les pieds sur terre; *(suggestion, plan)* être irréaliste

divorcee [dɪvɔːˈsiː] **N** divorcé(e) *m,f*

divot [ˈdɪvət] **N** motte *f* de terre

divulge [daɪˈvʌldʒ] **VT** divulguer, révéler

divvy [ˈdɪvɪ] *(pl* **divvies***)* **N** *Br Fam* **1** *Fin* dividende□ *m* **2** *(idiot)* abruti(e) *m,f*

▸ **divvy up** *(pt & pp* **divvied**, *cont* **divvying***)* **VT SEP** *Fam* partager□

dixie [ˈdɪksɪ] **N** *Br Fam Mil slang* gamelle□ *f*

Dixieland [ˈdɪksɪlænd] **N** *Mus* jazz *m* dixieland

▸▸ ***Dixieland jazz*** le (jazz) dixieland

DIY [ˌdiːaɪˈwaɪ] *Br (abbr* **do-it-yourself***)* **N** bricolag *m*

COMP de bricolage

dizzily [ˈdɪzɪlɪ] **ADV 1** *(walk)* avec une sensatio de vertige **2** *(rise ▸ cliffs, prices etc)* vertigineuse ment **3** *(behave, laugh)* étourdiment

dizziness [ˈdɪzɪnɪs] **N** *(UNCOUNT)* vertiges *mpl*

dizzy [ˈdɪzɪ] *(compar* **dizzier**, *superl* **dizziest***)* **ADJ** *(giddy)* **to feel d.** avoir le vertige, avoir la tête qu tourne; **you'll make yourself d.** tu vas avoir la têt qui tourne; **it makes me (feel) d.** cela me donne l vertige; **a d. spell** *or* **turn** un éblouissement *(height, speed)* vertigineux; **the d. heights of fam** les sommets grisants de la célébrité *ou* gloire *Fam (scatterbrained)* étourdi; **a d. blonde** un blonde évaporée

DJ [ˌdiːˈdʒeɪ] **N 1** *(abbr* **disc jockey***)* DJ *m* **2** *Fam (abb* **dinner jacket***)* smoking□ *m*

VI *(work as DJ)* travailler comme DJ

Djibouti [dʒɪˈbuːtɪ] **N** (République *f* de) Djibou

DLitt [ˌdiːˈlɪt] **N** *Univ (abbr* **Doctor of Letters***)* *(per son)* = titulaire d'un doctorat ès lettres; *(qualif cation)* doctorat *m* ès lettres

DLP [ˌdiːelˈpiː] **N** *(abbr* **Digital Light Processing** technologie *f* de projection DLP

DLR® [ˌdiːelˈɑː(r)] **N** *(abbr* **Docklands Light Railway** = réseau de train automatique aérien desser vant l'est de Londres

DNA [ˌdiːenˈeɪ] **N** *Biol (abbr* **deoxyribonucleic acid** ADN *m*

▸▸ ***DNA fingerprinting*** analyse *f* de l'empreint génétique; ***DNA profiling*** séquençage *m* d l'ADN; ***DNA test*** test *m* ADN; ***DNA testing*** test *mpl* ADN

D-notice **N** *Press* = consigne donnée par l gouvernement britannique à la presse pou empêcher la diffusion d'informations touchan à la sécurité du pays

DNS [ˌdiːenˈes] **N** *Comput (abbr* **Domain Name Sys tem***)* système *m* de nom de domaine, DNS *m*

DO[1] [duː]

V AUX
- à la forme interrogative **1**
- dans les question tags **2**
- à la forme négative **3**
- usage emphatique **4**
- usage elliptique **5**

VT
- faire **1, 2, 4, 6–10, 13, 17**
- s'occuper de **3, 19**
- étudier **5**
- suffire **11**

VI
- s'en tirer **1**
- aller **2, 5**
- faire **3**
- suffire **4**

N
- fête **2**

(3rd person singular **does** [dʌz], *pt* **did** [dɪd], *p* **done** [dʌn])

Les formes négatives sont **don't/doesn't** et **didn't**, qui deviennent **do not/does not** et **did not** à l'écrit, dans un style plus soutenu.

V AUX 1 *(in questions)* **do you know her?** est-ce qu tu la connais?, la connais-tu?; **don't/didn't yo know?** vous ne le savez/saviez pas?; **did I under stand you correctly?** vous ai-je bien compris? est-ce que je vous ai bien compris?; **why don you tell her?** pourquoi est-ce que tu ne (le) lu dis pas?, pourquoi ne (le) lui dis-tu pas?; **bo do I hate paperwork!** nom d'un chien, qu'est-c que je peux avoir horreur des paperasses!

2 *(in tag questions)* **he takes you out a lot, doesn he?** il te sort souvent, n'est-ce pas *ou* hein?; **h doesn't take you out very often, does he?** il ne t sort pas souvent, n'est-ce pas *ou* hein?; **so yo want to be an actress, do you?** alors tu veux deve nir actrice?; **you didn't sign it, did you?** *(in disbe lief, horror)* tu ne l'as pas signé, quand même? **look, we don't want any trouble, do we?** *(encourag ing, threatening)* écoute, nous ne voulons pa d'histoires, hein?

3 *(with the negative)* **I don't believe you** je ne t crois pas; **please don't tell her** s'il te plaît, ne (le lui dis pas; *Br* **don't let's go out** ne sortons pas

4 *(for emphasis)* **I DO believe you** sincèrement, j vous crois; **do you mind if I smoke? – yes I DO min** cela vous dérange-t-il que je fume? – juste nent, oui, ça me dérange; **he DOES know where t is** il sait bien où c'est; **I DID tell you** *(refuting someone's denial)* mais si, je te l'ai dit, bien sûr que je te l'ai dit; *(emphasizing earlier warning)* je e l'avais bien dit; **if you DO decide to buy it** si tu lécides finalement de l'acheter; **let me know when you DO decide** dis-moi quand tu auras décidé; **DO sit down** asseyez-vous donc; **DO let us know how your mother is** surtout dites-nous comment va votre mère; **DO stop crying** mais arête de pleurer, enfin

5 *(elliptically)* **you know as much as/more than I do** tu en sais autant que/plus que moi; **so do I/ does she** moi/elle aussi; **he didn't know and neither did I** il ne savait pas et moi non plus; **do you smoke? – I do/don't** est-ce que vous fumez? – oui/non; **may I sit down? – please do** puis-je m'asseoir? – je vous en prie; **I'll talk to her about it – please do/don't!** je lui en parlerai – oh, oui/non s'il vous plaît!; **don't, you'll make me blush!** arrête, u vas me faire rougir!; **will you tell her? – I may do** (le) lui diras-tu? – peut-être; **I may come to Paris next month – let me know if you do** il se peut que je vienne à Paris le mois prochain – préviens-moi si tu viens; **you said eight o'clock – oh, so I did** tu as dit huit heures – oh, c'est vrai; **I liked her – you didn't!** *(surprised)* elle m'a plu – non! vraiment?; **it belongs/it doesn't belong to me – does/doesn't it?** cela m'appartient/ne m'appartient pas – vraiment?; **yes you do – no I don't** mais si – mais non; **yes it does – no it doesn't** mais si – mais non; **you know her, I don't** tu la connais, moi pas; **you don't know her – I do!** tu ne la connais pas – si (je la connais)!

6 *(in sentences beginning with adverbial phrase)* **not only did you lie…** non seulement tu as menti…; **little did I realize…** j'étais bien loin de m'imaginer…

VT 1 *(be busy or occupied with)* faire; *(carry out ▸ task, work)* faire; **what are you doing?** qu'est-ce que tu fais?, que fais-tu?, qu'es-tu en train de faire?; **are you doing anything next Saturday?** est-ce que tu fais quelque chose samedi prochain?; **what do you do for a living?** qu'est-ce que vous faites dans la vie?; **what are these files doing here?** qu'est-ce que ces dossiers font ici?; **somebody DO something!** que quelqu'un fasse quelque chose!; **there's nothing more to be done** il n'y a plus rien à faire; **he does nothing but sleep, all he does is sleep** il ne fait que dormir; **you'll have to do it again** il va falloir que tu le refasses; **what do I have to do to make you understand?** mais qu'est-ce que je dois faire pour que tu comprennes?; **have I done the right thing?** ai-je fait ce qu'il fallait?; **what can I do for you?** que puis-je (faire) pour vous?; **the doctors can't do anything more for him** la médecine ne peut plus rien pour lui; **that dress really does something/nothing for you** cette robe te va vraiment très bien/ne te va vraiment pas du tout; **what do you do for entertainment?** quelles sont vos distractions?, comment est-ce que vous vous distrayez?; **what shall we do for water to wash in?** où est-ce qu'on va trouver de l'eau pour se laver?; **who did this to you?** qui est-ce qui t'a fait ça?; **what have you done to your hair?** qu'est-ce que tu as fait à tes cheveux?; *Hum* **don't do anything I wouldn't do** ne fais pas de bêtises; **that does it!** cette fois c'en est trop!; **that's done it, the battery's flat** et voilà, la batterie est à plat

2 *(produce, provide ▸ copy, report)* faire; **I don't do portraits** je ne fais pas les portraits; *Br* **the pub does a good lunch** on sert un bon déjeuner dans ce pub; **could you do me a quick translation of this?** pourriez-vous me traduire ceci rapidement?; **do you do day trips to France?** *(to travel agent)* est-ce que vous avez des excursions d'une journée en France?

3 *(work on, attend to)* s'occuper de; **can you do Mrs Baker first?** *(in hairdresser's)* peux-tu t'occuper de Mme Baker d'abord?; **to do the garden** s'occuper du jardin; **they do you very well in this hotel** on est très bien dans cet hôtel

4 *(clean, tidy ▸ room, cupboard)* faire; *(decorate ▸ room)* faire la décoration de; *(arrange ▸ flowers)* arranger; **to do one's teeth** se brosser les dents

5 *Sch & Univ (subject)* étudier; *Br (course)* suivre; **to do medicine/law** étudier la médecine/le droit, faire sa médecine/son droit; **we're doing Tartuffe** nous étudions Tartuffe

6 *(solve ▸ sums, crossword, equation)* faire

7 *Aut & Transp (speed, distance)* faire; **the car will do over 100** la voiture peut faire du 160; **it does thirty-five miles to the gallon** elle fait sept litres aux cents (kilomètres); **we did the trip in under two hours** nous avons fait le voyage en moins de deux heures

8 *Cin, Theat & TV (produce ▸ play, film)* faire; *(appear in)* être dans; *(play part of)* faire; *Mus (perform)* jouer

9 *Culin (cook)* faire; *(prepare ▸ vegetables, salad)* préparer; **to do sth in the oven** faire (cuire) qch au four; **how would you like your steak done?** comment voulez-vous votre steak?

10 *Fam (spend time ▸ working, in prison)* faire□; **she's doing three years for robbery** elle fait trois ans pour vol

11 *(be enough or suitable for)* suffire; **will £10 do you?** 10 livres, ça te suffira?; **those shoes will have to do the children for another year** les enfants devront encore faire un an avec ces chaussures

12 *(finish)* **well that's that done, thank goodness** bon, voilà qui est fait, dieu merci; **have you done eating/crying?** tu as fini de manger/pleurer?; **it will never be done in time** ce ne sera jamais fini à temps; **done!** *(in bargain)* marché conclu!

13 *(imitate)* imiter, faire; **he does you very well** il t'imite très bien

14 *Br Fam (prosecute)* **she was done for speeding** elle s'est fait pincer pour excès de vitesse; **we could do you for dangerous driving** nous pourrions vous arrêter pour conduite dangereuse□

15 *Fam (rob, burgle ▸ bank, shop)* cambrioler□, se faire

16 *Fam (cheat)* rouler, avoir; **you've been done** tu t'es fait rouler *ou* avoir

17 *Fam (visit)* faire; **to do London/the sights** faire Londres/les monuments

18 *Fam (take)* **to do drugs** se camer; **let's do lunch** il faudrait qu'on déjeune ensemble un de ces jours

19 *Br Fam (beat up)* s'occuper de, en mettre une à; **I'll do you!** je vais m'occuper de toi, moi!

20 *Fam (kill)* zigouiller, buter

21 *Fam (have sex with ▸ of man)* baiser; *(of woman)* baiser avec, s'envoyer; **to do it (with sb)** faire crac-crac (avec qn)

VI 1 *(perform ▸ in exam, competition etc)* s'en tirer, s'en sortir; **you did very well** tu t'en es très bien tiré *ou* sorti; **the company's not doing too badly** l'entreprise ne se débrouille pas trop mal; **how are you doing in the new job/at school?** comment te débrouilles-tu dans ton nouveau travail/à l'école?; **how do you do?** *(on first introduction)* enchanté (de faire votre connaissance); **try to do better in future** essaie de mieux faire à l'avenir; **how are we doing with the corrections?** *(checking progress)* où en sommes-nous avec les corrections?; **well done!** bien joué!, bravo!

2 *(referring to health)* aller; **how is she doing, doctor?** comment va-t-elle, docteur?; **he's not doing too well** il ne va pas trop bien; **mother and baby are both doing well** la maman et le bébé se portent tous les deux à merveille

3 *(act, behave)* faire; **do as you please** fais ce qui te plaît, fais ce que tu veux; **do as you're told!** fais ce qu'on te dit!; **you would do well to listen to your mother** tu ferais bien d'écouter ta mère; **to do well** *or* **right by sb** bien traiter qn; *Br* **to be/to feel hard done by** être/se sentir lésé; *Prov* **do as you would be done by** = traite les autres comme tu voudrais être traité

4 *(be enough)* suffire; **will £20 do?** 20 livres, ça ira *ou* suffira?; **that will do!** *(stop it)* ça suffit comme ça!

5 *(be suitable)* aller; **that will do (nicely)** ça ira *ou* conviendra parfaitement, cela fera très bien l'affaire; **this won't do** ça ne peut pas continuer comme ça; **it wouldn't do to be late** ce ne serait pas bien d'arriver en retard; **will that do?** *(as alternative)* est-ce que ça ira?

6 *(always in continuous form) (happen)* **is there anything doing at the club tonight?** est-ce qu'il y a quelque chose au club ce soir?; **there's nothing doing here at weekends** il n'y a rien à faire ici le week-end; *Fam* **nothing doing** *(rejection, refusal)* rien à faire

7 *(always in perfect tense) (finish)* **have you done?** tu as fini?

8 *(be connected with)* **it has to do with your missing car** c'est au sujet de votre voiture volée; **that's got nothing to do with it!** *(is irrelevant)* cela n'a rien à voir!; **I want nothing to do with it/you** je ne veux rien avoir à faire là-dedans/avec toi; **it's nothing to do with me** je n'y suis pour rien; **we don't have much to do with the people next door** nous n'avons pas beaucoup de contacts avec les gens d'à côté; **what I said to him has got nothing to do with you** *(it's none of your business)* ce que je lui ai dit ne te regarde pas; *(it's not about you)* ce que je lui ai dit n'a rien à voir avec toi; **that has a lot to do with it** cela joue un rôle très important

9 *Br Fam (work as cleaner)* faire le ménage□; **to do for sb** faire le ménage chez qn

N 1 *(tip)* **the do's and don'ts of car maintenance** les choses à faire et à ne pas faire dans l'entretien des voitures

2 *Br Fam (party, celebration)* fête□ *f*; **he's having a do to celebrate his promotion** il donne une fête pour célébrer sa promotion; **leaving do** pot *m* de départ

3 *Fam (excrement)* **dog do** crotte *f* de chien□

▸ **do away with** VT INSEP **1** *(abolish ▸ institution, rule, restriction)* abolir; *(get rid of ▸ object)* se débarrasser de **2** *(kill)* se débarrasser de, faire disparaître; **to do away with oneself** mettre fin à ses jours

▸ **do down** VT SEP *Br Fam* **1** *(criticize, disparage)* rabaisser□, médire sur□, dire du mal de□; **to do oneself down** se rabaisser□ **2** *(cheat)* avoir, rouler

▸ **do for** VT INSEP *Fam* **1** *Br (murder)* zigouiller; *(cause death of)* tuer□ **2** *(ruin ▸ object, engine)* bousiller; *(cause failure of ▸ plan)* ruiner□; *(▸ company)* couler□; **I'm done for** je suis cuit; **the project is done for** le projet est tombé à l'eau *ou* foutu **3** *Br (exhaust)* tuer, crever; **shopping always does for me** je suis toujours crevé après les courses; **I'm done for** je suis mort *ou* crevé; **it was that last hill that did for me** c'est la dernière colline qui m'a épuisé□

▸ **do in** VT SEP *Br Fam* **1** *(murder, kill)* zigouiller, buter, butter **2** *(exhaust)* tuer, crever **3** *(injure)* **to do one's back/one's knee in** se bousiller le dos/le genou; *Fam* **that girl really does my head in** *(annoys me)* cette fille, elle me prend la tête

▸ **do out** VT SEP *Br Fam (clean thoroughly)* nettoyer à fond□; *(decorate)* refaire□

▸ **do out of** VT SEP *Fam (cheat)* **to do sb out of sth** soutirer□ *ou* carotter qch à qn; *(money)* refaire *ou* escroquer□ qn de qch; **to do sb out of a job** *(of person)* faire perdre son travail à qn□

▸ **do over** VT SEP **1** *(room)* refaire; **the whole house needs doing over** toute la maison a besoin d'être refaite

2 *Am (do again)* refaire

3 *Br Fam (beat up)* casser la gueule *ou* la tête à

4 *Br Fam (rob ▸ person)* dépouiller; *(▸ house, bank etc)* cambrioler□

▸ **do up** VT SEP **1** *(fasten ▸ dress, jacket)* fermer; *(▸ zip)* fermer, remonter; *(▸ buttons)* boutonner; *(▸ shoelaces)* attacher; **do me up will you?** tu peux fermer ma robe? **2** *(wrap, bundle up)* emballer **3** *Fam (renovate ▸ house, cottage etc)* refaire□, retaper; *(old dress, hat)* arranger; **to do oneself up** *(make more glamorous)* se faire beau/belle; **to be done up to the nines** être sur son trente et un

VI *(skirt, dress)* se fermer; *(zip)* se fermer, se remonter; *(buttons)* se fermer, se boutonner; **it does up at the side** cela se ferme sur le côté

▸ **do with** VT INSEP **1** *Br Fam (after "could") (need, want)* avoir besoin de□; **I could have done with some help** j'aurais eu bien besoin d'aide; **I could do with a drink** je prendrais bien un verre, j'ai bien envie de prendre un verre

2 *Br Fam (after "can't") (tolerate)* supporter□; **I can't do** *or* **be doing with all this noise** je ne supporte pas ce vacarme; **I can't be doing with her** je ne l'aime pas

3 *(after "what") (act with regard to)* faire de; **she didn't know what to do with herself** *(to keep busy)* elle ne savait que faire *ou* à quoi s'occuper; *(for joy)* elle ne se tenait pas de joie; *(for awkwardness)* elle était gênée, elle ne savait plus où se mettre; **what are we going to do with your father for two whole weeks?** qu'allons-nous faire de ton père pendant deux semaines entières?; **what**

have you done with the hammer? qu'as-tu fait du marteau?

4 *(with past participle) (finish with)* finir avec; **I'm done with men for ever** j'en ai fini pour toujours avec les hommes; **I haven't done with him yet!** *(haven't finished scolding him)* je n'en ai pas encore fini avec lui!; **I'm done with trying to be nice to her** je n'essaierai plus jamais d'être gentil avec elle; **can I borrow the ashtray if you've done with it?** puis-je emprunter le cendrier si tu n'en as plus besoin?

▸ **do without** VT INSEP se passer de; **I could have done without this long wait** j'aurais bien pu me passer de cette longue attente; **we can do without the sarcasm** on n'a pas besoin de ces sarcasmes

VI faire sans; **he'll have to do without** il devra s'en passer *ou* faire sans

---

do² [dəʊ] N *Mus (fixed)* do *m inv*, ut *m inv*

DOA [ˌdiːəʊ'eɪ] ADJ *Med (abbr* **dead on arrival***)* **to be D.** être mort avant son arrivée à l'hôpital

Dobermann (pinscher) ['dəʊbəmən ('pɪnʃə(r))] N doberman *m*

doc [dɒk] N *Fam (doctor)* toubib *m*; **morning, d.** bonjour, docteur□

docile [*Br* 'dəʊsaɪl, *Am* 'dɒsəl] ADJ docile

docility [də'sɪlətɪ] N docilité *f*

dock [dɒk] VI **1** *(ship)* se mettre à quai; **when do we d.?** quand arrivons-nous à quai?; **we'll be docking at New York** nous entrerons à quai à New York **2** *(two spacecraft)* s'amarrer, s'arrimer

VT **1** *(ship)* mettre à quai; *(spacecraft)* amarrer, arrimer **2** *Fam (money)* **to d. sb's pay/pocket money** faire une retenue sur la paye/réduire l'argent de poche de qn **3** *(animal's tail)* couper

N **1** *Naut* dock *m*, docks *mpl*; **the docks** les docks *mpl*; **to be in dry d.** *(ship)* être en cale sèche; *Fig* **to be in d.** *(car, plane)* être en réparation **2** *Br Law* banc *m* des accusés; **the prisoner in the d.** l'accusé(e) *m,f*; *Fig* **to be in the d.** être sur la sellette **3** *Br Bot* patience *f*

COMP *(manager)* des docks

▸▸ ***dock strike*** grève *f* des dockers; *Br* ***dock worker*** docker *m*

docker ['dɒkə(r)] N *Br* docker *m*

▸▸ ***dockers' strike*** grève *f* des dockers

docket ['dɒkɪt] N **1** *Br (on file, package)* fiche *f* (de renseignements) **2** *Law Br (summary)* compte-rendu *m* des jugements; *Am (list of cases)* liste *f* des affaires en instance **3** *Br Customs (document)* récépissé *m* de douane

VT **1** *(file, package)* mettre une fiche (indiquant le contenu) sur **2** *Law Br (make summary of)* résumer; *Am (register)* enregistrer

docking ['dɒkɪŋ] N **1** *(of ship)* mise *f* à quai **2** *(of two spacecraft)* amarrage *m*, arrimage *m*

▸▸ ***docking manoeuvre*** accostage *m*; *Comput* ***docking station*** *(for notebook)* station *f* d'accueil

dockland ['dɒklənd] N quartier *m* des docks

dockyard ['dɒkjɑːd] N chantier *m* naval *ou* de constructions navales; **naval d.** arsenal *m* maritime *ou* de la marine

doctor ['dɒktə(r)] N **1** *(of medicine)* docteur *m*, médecin *m*; **dear D. Cameron** *(in letter)* docteur; **I've an appointment with D. Cameron** j'ai rendez-vous avec le docteur Cameron; **thank you, d.** merci, docteur; **he/she is a d.** il/elle est docteur *ou* médecin; **to go to the d.** *or* **d.'s** aller chez le docteur *ou* médecin; *Fam* **to be under the d.** être sous traitement médical□; **woman d., female d.** femme *f* médecin; **army d.** médecin *m* militaire; *Fam* **that's just what the d. ordered!** c'est exactement ce qu'il me faut *ou* fallait! **2** *Univ* docteur *m*; **D. of Science** docteur *m* ès *ou* en sciences; **to do a** *or* **to take one's d.'s degree** faire un doctorat

VT **1** *(tamper with* ▸ *results, figures)* falsifier, trafiquer; *(*▸ *accounts, evidence)* falsifier, fausser; *(*▸ *dice, cards)* piper; *(*▸ *wine)* frelater; **we'll need to d. the figures a little** il va falloir un peu arranger ces chiffres

2 *(drug* ▸ *drink, food)* mettre de la drogue dans; *(*▸ *racehorse)* doper

3 *Br (castrate, sterilize* ▸ *cat, dog)* châtrer

4 *(treat)* soigner

▸▸ *Univ* ***Doctor of Divinity*** *(person)* = titulaire d'un doctorat en théologie; *(qualification)* doctorat *m* en théologie; ***doctor's note*** certificat *m* médical; *Univ* ***Doctor of Philosophy*** *(person)* = titulaire d'un doctorat de 3ème cycle; *(qualification)* doctorat *m* de 3ème cycle

doctoral ['dɒktərəl] ADJ *Univ (thesis, degree)* de doctorat

doctorate ['dɒktərət] N *Univ* doctorat *m*; **to have/to do a d. in sth** avoir/faire un doctorat en qch

doctoring ['dɒktərɪŋ] N **1** *(of results, figures, accounts, evidence etc)* falsification *f*

2 *(drugging* ▸ *of drink, food)* adjonction *f* de drogue (of à); *(of racehorse)* doping *m*

3 *Fam (profession)* profession *f* de médecin□

4 *Br (of cat, dog)* castration *f*

5 *(treatment)* soins *mpl* (**of sb** donnés à qn)

doctrinaire [ˌdɒktrɪ'neə(r)] N doctrinaire *mf*

ADJ doctrinaire

doctrinal [dɒk'traɪnəl] ADJ doctrinal

doctrine ['dɒktrɪn] N doctrine *f*

docudrama [ˌdɒkju'drɑːmə] N *TV* docudrame *m*

document N ['dɒkjʊmənt] document *m*; *Law* acte *m*; **to draw up a d.** rédiger un document; *Law* **the documents in the case** le dossier de l'affaire; *Com* **documents against acceptance/payment** documents *mpl* contre acceptation/paiement

VT ['dɒkjʊment] **1** *(write about in detail)* décrire (de façon détaillée); *(record on film* ▸ *of film)* montrer (en détail), présenter (de façon détaillée); *(*▸ *of photographer)* faire un reportage sur; **the book documents life in the 1920s** le livre décrit la vie dans les années 20; **his involvement in the affair is well documented** on dispose de nombreux témoignages montrant qu'il a été impliqué à cette affaire; **the first documented case of smallpox** le premier cas de variole qu'on ait enregistré **2** *(support* ▸ *with evidence or proof)* fournir des preuves à l'appui de, attester; *(*▸ *with citations, references)* documenter

▸▸ ***document case*** porte-documents *m inv*; ***document shredder*** destructeur *m* de documents; *Comput* ***document file*** fichier *m* document; ***document holder*** *(for keyboarder)* bras *m* porte-copies; ***document imager*** imageur *m* documentaire; *Comput* ***document reader*** lecteur *m* de documents; *Law* ***document of title*** acte *m* de propriété; ***document wallet*** porte-documents *m inv*

documentary [ˌdɒkju'mentərɪ] (*pl* **documentaries**) N *Cin & TV* documentaire *m*

ADJ *(factual* ▸ *film, programme)* documentaire

▸▸ *Com & Fin* ***documentary bill*** traite *f* documentaire; ***documentary evidence*** preuve *f* littérale; ***documentary letter of credit*** lettre *f* de crédit documentaire; *Cin & TV* ***documentary maker*** documentariste *mf*

documentation [ˌdɒkjumen'teɪʃən] N documentation *f*

docusoap ['dɒkjusəʊp] N *TV* docu-soap *m*

dodder¹ ['dɒdə(r)] VI *(walk)* marcher d'un pas hésitant

dodder² N *Bot* cuscute *f*, *Fam* cheveux *mpl* du diable

dodderer ['dɒdərə(r)] N *Fam Pej* croulant(e) *m,f*, gâteux(euse) *m,f*

doddering ['dɒdərɪŋ] ADJ *(walk)* hésitant, chancelant; *Pej (elderly person)* gâteux; **a d. old fool** un vieux gâteux

doddery ['dɒdərɪ] ADJ *Fam (walk)* hésitant□, chancelant□; *Pej (elderly person)* gâteux; **I still feel a bit d.** *(after illness)* je me sens encore un peu faible□ *ou* flagada; **a d. old man** un vieux gâteux

doddle ['dɒdəl] N *Br Fam* **it's a d.** c'est simple comme bonjour, c'est du gâteau

dodge [dɒdʒ] N **1** *(evasive movement)* écart *m*; *(by footballer, boxer)* esquive *f*; **to make a d.** faire un écart *ou* une esquive **2** *Br Fam (trick)* truc *m*, combine *f*; **to be up to all the dodges** connaître toutes les combines

VT *(blow)* esquiver; *(falling rock, ball)* éviter; *(bullets)* passer entre, éviter; *(pursuer, police)* échapper à; *(creditor, landlord etc)* éviter; *(question)* éluder; **he has dodged paying tax** *or Br* **the taxman all his life** il a échappé au fisc toute sa vie; **to d. the issue** éluder *ou* esquiver le problème; **to d. school** sécher l'école

VI *(make evasive movement)* s'écarter vivement; *(footballer, boxer)* faire une esquive; **he dodged into the doorway** il s'est esquivé *ou* il a disparu dans l'entrée; **to d. behind a tree** se glisser prestement derrière un arbre; **to d. in and out of the crowd** faire du slalom dans la foule; **to d. out of the way** s'écarter vivement

Dodgem® ['dɒdʒəm] N *Br* auto *f* tamponneuse, *Belg* auto-scooter *m or f*

dodger ['dɒdʒə(r)] N *Fam (workshy)* tire-au-flanc *m inv*; *(dishonest)* combinard(e) *m,f*, roublard(e) *m,f*; *Old-fashioned* **an artful d.** un fin matois; **fare d.** resquilleur(euse) *m,f*; **they're after tax dodgers** ils cherchent à coincer ceux qui fraudent le fisc

dodgy ['dɒdʒɪ] (*compar* **dodgier**, *superl* **dodgiest**) ADJ *Br Fam* **1** *(risky, dangerous* ▸ *plan, idea)* risqué□; **the house is nice, but it's in a really d. area** la maison est bien mais elle est dans un quartier vraiment craignos; **investing money in a scheme like that is just too d.** c'est vraiment trop risqué d'investir dans ce genre de truc; **the weather looks pretty d.** *(unreliable)* le temps a l'air plutôt douteux□ *ou* menaçant□ **2** *(untrustworthy* ▸ *person)* louche; *(*▸ *scheme)* douteux□, suspect□; **they were involved in a couple of d. business deals** ils ont été impliqués dans des transactions plutôt louches **3** *(not working properly, unstable)* merdique; **the brakes are really d.** les freins sont très douteux□; **the engine sounds a bit d.** le moteur fait un bruit suspect□; **my stomach's been a bit d. for the last couple of days** ça fait deux jours que j'ai l'estomac un peu dérangé□

dodo ['dəʊdəʊ] (*pl* **dodos** *or* **dodoes**) N **1** *(extinct bird)* dronte *m*, dodo *m* **2** *Fam (fool)* andouille *f* **3** *Mktg (product)* poids *m* mort, produit *m* dodo

DOE [ˌdiːəʊ'iː] N *Am Admin (abbr* **Department of Energy***)* = ministère américain de l'Énergie

doe [dəʊ] N *(deer)* biche *f*; *(fallow deer)* daine *f*; *(rabbit)* lapine *f*; *(wild rabbit, hare)* hase *f*

doe-eyed ADJ *(person)* aux yeux de biche

doer ['duːə(r)] N *(dynamic person)* personne *f* dynamique; **she's a real d.** c'est une femme très active; **she is more (of) a d. than a talker** elle préfère l'action à la parole

doeskin ['dəʊskɪn] N peau *f* de daim; **made of d.** en daim

COMP *(gloves, shoes etc)* en daim

doesn't ['dʌzənt] = **does not**

doff [dɒf] VT *(hat)* ôter; **to d. one's cap to sb** ôter son chapeau *ou* se découvrir devant qn; *Fig* faire preuve de respect envers qn

dog [dɒg] (*pt & pp* **dogged**, *cont* **dogging**) N **1** *(animal)* chien *m*; **to treat sb like a d.** traiter qn comme un chien; **to follow sb about like a d.** suivre qn comme un petit chien; **she's like a d. with a bone** elle est toute contente *ou* joyeuse; *Br* **this is a real d.'s dinner** *or* **breakfast** *(mess)* c'est un vrai torchon *ou* gâchis; *Br Fam* **to be dressed** *or* **done up like a d.'s dinner** *(gaudy, showy)* être habillé de façon extravagante□; **to lead sb a d.'s life** mener la vie dure à qn; **it's a d.'s life being a teacher** c'est une vie de chien que d'être professeur; *Br Fam* **he doesn't have** *or* **stand a d.'s chance** il n'a pas la moindre chance□, il n'a aucune chance□; **a d. in the manger** un empêcheur de danser *ou* tourner en rond; *Fam* **I'm going to see a man about a d.** = façon humoristique d'éviter de dire où l'on va; **it's (a case of) d. eat d.** c'est la loi de la jungle; *Prov* **every d. has its** *or* **his day** = tout le monde a son heure de gloire; *Prov* **give a d. a bad name (and hang him)** = il est très difficile de se débarrasser de sa mauvaise réputation, qu'elle soit méritée ou non; *Prov* **let sleeping dogs lie** n'éveillez pas le chat qui dort; *Prov* **you can't teach an old d. new tricks** = les vieilles habitudes ont la vie dure; *Br Fam* **the dogs** les courses *fpl* de lévriers□; **to go to the dogs** aller aux courses de lévriers; *Fam* **this country's going to the dogs** le pays va à sa ruine□; *Fam* **this restaurant has gone to the dogs since he took over** ce restaurant ne vaut plus rien du tout depuis qu'il l'a racheté□

2 *(male fox, wolf etc)* mâle *m*

3 *Fam (person)* **you lucky d.!** sacré veinard!; **dirty d.** sale type *m*; **sly d.** (vieux) malin *m*; **there's life in the old d. yet!** je ne suis/ce n'est pas encore un vieux croulant!

4 *very Fam Pej (ugly woman)* cageot *m*

5 *Am Fam (hopeless thing)* catastrophe□ *f*
6 *Mktg (product)* poids *m* mort, gouffre *m* financier
7 *Tech (pawl)* cliquet *m*; *(cramp)* crampon *m*
8 *Am (hot dog)* hot dog *m*
COMP *(bowl, basket)* pour chien
VT 1 *(follow closely)* suivre de près; **to d. sb's footsteps** ne pas lâcher qn d'une semelle **2** *(plague)* **to be dogged by bad health/problems** ne pas arrêter d'avoir des ennuis de santé/des problèmes; **the team has been dogged by injury** l'équipe n'a pas arrêté d'avoir des blessés; **she is dogged by misfortune** elle est poursuivie par la malchance
►► ***dog biscuit*** biscuit *m* pour chien; ***dog breeder*** éleveur(euse) *m,f* de chiens; ***dog breeding*** élevage *m* de chiens; ***dog collar*** *(for dog)* collier *m* pour *ou* de chien; *Fam (of clergyman)* col *m* d'ecclésiastique□; ***dog days*** canicule *f*; ***dog food*** *(UNCOUNT)* nourriture *f* pour chiens; ***dog fox*** renard *m* mâle; ***dog handler*** maître-chien *m*; ***dog Latin*** latin *m* de cuisine; *Br Formerly* ***dog licence*** = permis de posséder un chien; ***dog paddle*** nage *f* du petit chien; ***dog racing*** courses *fpl* de lévriers; ***dog rose*** églantine *f*; ***dog show*** exposition *f* canine; ***Dog Star*** Sirius *f*; ***dog tag*** *(for dog, soldier)* plaque *f* d'identification; ***dog team*** attelage *m* de chiens; ***dog track*** cynodrome *m*

dogcart ['dɒgkɑːt] **N** dog-cart *m*

dog-catcher **N** employé(e) *m,f* de la fourrière

doge [dəʊdʒ] **N** *Hist* doge *m*

dog-eared **ADJ** *(page)* corné; *(book)* aux pages cornées

dog-end **N** *Br Fam (of cigarette)* mégot□ *m*

dogfight ['dɒgfaɪt] **N** *(between dogs)* combat *m* de chiens; *Mil (between aircraft)* combat *m* rapproché

dogfish ['dɒgfɪʃ] **N** *Ich* roussette *f*, chien *m* de mer

dogged ['dɒgɪd] **ADJ** *(courage, perseverance, pursuit)* tenace; *(person, character)* tenace, déterminé, persévérant; *(refusal)* obstiné; *(attachment)* fidèle

doggedly ['dɒgɪdlɪ] **ADV** *(fight, persist)* avec ténacité *ou* persévérance; *(refuse)* obstinément; **to be d. intent on doing sth** avoir la ferme intention de faire qch

doggedness ['dɒgɪdnɪs] **N** *(of person)* ténacité *f*, persévérance *f*; *(of courage)* ténacité *f*

doggerel ['dɒgərəl] **N** *(silly and comical)* poésie *f* burlesque; *(mediocre)* vers *mpl* de mirliton

doggie = **doggy**

doggo ['dɒgəʊ] **ADV** *Br Fam* **to lie d.** se tenir coi□

doggone ['dɒgɒn] *Am Fam* **EXCLAM d. (it)!** zut!, nom d'une pipe!
ADJ fichu; **I've lost the d. car keys** j'ai perdu ces saletés de clés de bagnole
ADV vachement; **it's so d. hot!** il fait une chaleur à crever!

doggy ['dɒgɪ] *(pl* **doggies***)* *Fam* **N** *(in children's language)* toutou *m*
ADJ *(smell)* de chien; **he's a d. person** il adore les chiens
►► ***doggy bag*** = sachet ou boîte que l'on propose aux clients dans les restaurants pour qu'ils emportent ce qu'ils n'ont pas consommé; *very Fam* ***doggy position*** levrette *f*

doggy-fashion, doggy-style **ADV** *very Fam* en levrette; **to do it d.** faire l'amour en levrette

doghouse ['dɒghaus, *pl* -hauzɪz] **N 1** *Am (kennel)* chenil *m*, niche *f* **2** *Fam (idiom)* **to be in the d. (with sb)** ne pas être en odeur de sainteté *ou* être en disgrâce (auprès de qn)□; **you're in the d. with Mum** tu n'es pas en odeur de sainteté avec Maman

dogleg ['dɒgleg] **N** *(in pipe, road, on golf course)* coude *m*
VI *(pipe, road, golf course)* faire un coude
ADJ *(pipe, road, golf course)* qui fait un coude

doglike ['dɒglaɪk] **ADJ** *(devotion)* aveugle

dogma ['dɒgmə] **N** dogme *m*

dogmatic [dɒg'mætɪk] **ADJ** dogmatique; **to be d. about sth** être dogmatique au sujet de qch

dogmatically [dɒg'mætɪklɪ] **ADV** dogmatiquement

dogmatism ['dɒgmətɪzəm] **N** dogmatisme *m*

dogmatist ['dɒgmətɪst] **N** personne *f* dogmatique

do-gooder [-'gudə(r)] **N** *Pej* âme *f* charitable, bonne âme *f*

dogsbody ['dɒgz,bɒdɪ] *(pl* **dogsbodies***)* **N** *Br Fam* bonne *f* à tout faire□; **I'm not your d.** je ne suis pas ton chien *ou* ta bonne

dogsled ['dɒgsled] **N** luge *f* tirée par des chiens

dog-tired **ADJ** *Fam* épuisé

dogtooth ['dɒgtuːθ] **N** *(tooth)* canine *f*
►► *Tex* ***dogtooth check*** pied *m* de poule; *Bot* ***dogtooth violet*** érythrone *m*, dent-de-chien *f*

dogtrot ['dɒgtrɒt] **N** petit trot *m*; **at a d.** au petit trot

dogwatch ['dɒgwɒtʃ] **N** *Naut* petit quart *m*

dogwood ['dɒgwʊd] **N** *Bot* cornouiller *m*

DoH [,diːəʊ'eɪtʃ] **N** *Br Pol (abbr* **Department of Health***)* ministère *m* de la Santé

doh[1] = **do**[2]

doh[2] [dəʊ] **EXCLAM** que je suis bête!

doily ['dɔɪlɪ] *(pl* **doilies***)* **N** napperon *m*

doing ['duːɪŋ] **N 1** *(work, activity)* **it's all your d.** tout cela, c'est de ta faute; **is this your d.?** *(have you done this?)* c'est toi qui as fait cela?; *(are you behind this?)* c'est toi qui es derrière cela?; **it's none of my d.** je n'y suis pour rien; **that'll take some d.** cela ne va pas être facile; **a job like this is going to take a lot of d.** un tel travail ne se fera pas en un tour de main *ou* en un tournemain **2** *Fam (beating)* **to give sb a d. (over)** passer qn à tabac, tabasser qn

doings ['duːɪŋz] **N** *Br Fam (thing)* machin *m*, truc *m*
NPL 1 *(of person)* ce qu'on fait, *Pej* agissements *mpl*; **to be informed of sb's d.** être au courant des faits et gestes de qn **2** *Fam (events)* événements□ *mpl*

do-it-yourself **N** bricolage *m*; **a d. enthusiast** un bricoleur
COMP *(manual, shop)* de bricolage
►► ***do-it-yourself kit*** des éléments *mpl* en kit

do-it-yourselfer [-jə'selfə(r)] **N** *Fam* bricoleur (euse) *m,f*

dol *(written abbr* **dollar***)* dol(l)

Dolby® ['dɒlbɪ] **N** Dolby® *m*; **in D. stereo** en Dolby® stéréo
►► ***Dolby® system*** système *m* Dolby® stéréo

doldrums ['dɒldrəmz] **NPL 1** *Geog (zone)* zones *fpl* des calmes équatoriaux, pot *m* au noir; *(weather)* calme *m* équatorial **2** *(idiom)* **to be in the d.** *(person)* avoir le cafard, broyer du noir; *(activity, trade)* être en plein marasme

dole [dəʊl] **N** *(UNCOUNT) Br Fam Admin* (indemnités *fpl* de) chômage□ *m*; **to be/to go on the d.** être/s'inscrire au chômage; **the d. queues are getting longer** de plus en plus de gens pointent au chômage
►► *Br Fam* ***dole money*** (indemnités *fpl* de) chômage□ *m*

►**dole out** **VT SEP** *(distribute)* distribuer; *(in small amounts)* distribuer au compte-gouttes

doleful ['dəʊlfʊl] **ADJ** *(mournful ► look, voice)* malheureux; *(► person, song)* triste

dolefully ['dəʊlfʊlɪ] **ADV** d'un air malheureux

doll [dɒl] **N 1** *(for child)* poupée *f*; *(for ventriloquist)* marionnette *f* (de ventriloque); **to play with dolls** jouer à la poupée
2 *Fam (girl)* nana *f*, souris *f*; *(attractive woman)* poupée *f*
3 *Fam (term of address)* poupée *f*
4 *Am Fam (nice person)* trésor *m*, chou *m*; **you're a d.** tu es un amour
►► *also Fig Br* ***doll's house***, *Am* ***doll house*** maison *f* de poupée; ***doll's pram*** poussette *f* de poupée

►**doll up** **VT SEP** **to get dolled up, to d. oneself up** se faire beau (belle), se pomponner; **she was all dolled up** elle s'était faite toute belle, elle était toute pomponnée

dollar ['dɒlə(r)] **N 1** *(currency)* dollar *m*; *Fam* **you can bet your bottom d.** *or* **dollars to doughnuts that he'll be there** tu peux être sûr qu'il sera là; *Fam* **you look like a million dollars in that dress!** tu es magnifique dans cette robe!; **that's the sixty-four thousand d. question** c'est la question cruciale **2** *Br Fam Old-fashioned* = cinq shillings
►► *Fin & Econ* ***dollar area*** zone *f* dollar; ***dollar bill*** billet *m* d'un dollar; ***dollar diplomacy*** diplomatie *f* du dollar; *Fin* ***dollar rate*** cours *m* du dollar; ***dollar sign*** (signe *m* du) dollar *m*

dollarization, -isation [dɒlərаɪ'zeɪʃən] **N** *Fin & Econ* dollarisation *f*

dollarize, -ise ['dɒləraɪz] **VT** *Fin & Econ* dollariser

dollop ['dɒləp] *Fam* **N** *(of mashed potatoes, cream etc)* (bonne) cuillerée□ *f*; *(of mud, plaster, clay)* (petit) tas□ *m*; *(of butter, margarine)* (gros *ou* bon) morceau□ *m*
VT to d. food out onto plates balancer de la nourriture dans des assiettes

dolly ['dɒlɪ] *(pl* **dollies**, *pt & pp* **dollied***)* **N 1** *Fam (for child)* poupée *f*
2 *Cin & TV (for camera)* chariot *m*, dolly *m*
3 *Br Fam Old-fashioned (woman)* poupée *f*
4 *Sport (in cricket)* prise *f* au vol facile; *(in tennis)* coup *m* facile
5 *(for clothes)* agitateur *m*
VI *Cin & TV* **to d. in/out** faire un travelling avant/arrière
►► *Br Fam Old-fashioned* ***dolly bird*** poupée *f* *(femme)*; *Br* ***dolly mixtures*** *(sweets)* petits bonbons *mpl* assortis; *Cin & TV* ***dolly operator*** machiniste *mf* caméra; ***dolly tub*** *(for laundry)* baquet *m* à lessive

dolman ['dɒlmən] **N** dolman *m*
►► ***dolman sleeve*** manche *f* chauve-souris

dolmen ['dɒlmən] **N** *Archeol* dolmen *m*

dolomite ['dɒləmaɪt] **N** *Miner* dolomite *f*; *Geol (rock)* dolomie *f*, dolomite *f*

Dolomites ['dɒləmaɪts] **NPL the D.** les Dolomites *fpl*, les Alpes *fpl* dolomitiques

dolphin ['dɒlfɪn] **N** *Zool* dauphin *m*

dolphinarium [,dɒlfɪ'neərɪəm] **N** aquarium *m* à dauphins

dolt [dəʊlt] **N** *(stupid person)* lourdaud *m*, gourde *f*

doltish ['dəʊltɪʃ] **ADJ** *(person)* lourdaud; *(behaviour)* idiot

-DOM — SUFFIXE

• Le suffixe **-dom** sert à construire des noms qui expriment un ÉTAT ou un CONCEPT à partir de noms, d'adjectifs ou de verbes:
freedom (de *free* libre) la liberté; **martyrdom** (de *martyr* martyre) le martyre; **boredom** l'ennui; **wisdom** la sagesse; **singledom** le fait d'être célibataire

• Il s'emploie à la suite de titres pour créer la notion de RANG:
dukedom (de *duke* duc) dignité de duc; **earldom** (de *earl* comte) dignité de comte; **popedom** (de *pope* pape) papauté

• **-dom** s'emploie également pour véhiculer la notion de TERRITOIRE sous l'autorité de quelqu'un, comme dans les termes:
dukedom duché; **earldom** comté; **kingdom** royaume, et également **Christendom** la chrétienté (dans le sens de l'ensemble des pays de tradition chrétienne)

Il n'existe pas d'équivalence directe entre les cas décrits dans les deux paragraphes ci-dessus. À titre d'exemple, le terme **dukedom** peut s'employer pour parler du rang ou du territoire, mais le terme **kingdom** ne s'applique qu'au territoire.

• Le suffixe **-dom** s'utilise également pour désigner une COLLECTIVITÉ de personnes ayant quelque chose en commun. Bien souvent ces termes ont une connotation négative:
officialdom l'administration; **yuppiedom** le milieu yuppie; **fandom** les fans
Christendom s'emploie également pour désigner l'ensemble des chrétiens.

• Le suffixe **-dom** s'emploie fréquemment dans des néologismes ayant trait au monde de la politique. Les termes **Blairdom** (dérivé du nom *Blair*) et **Bushdom** (dérivé de *Bush*) en sont des exemples; ces termes ont deux sens distincts. En effet, ces termes peuvent désigner soit la politique menée par Tony

Blair et George Bush, soit désigner l'ensemble de leurs partisans respectifs, comme dans l'exemple **dissent within Blair-dom** (des désaccords parmi les partisans de Tony Blair).

domain [dəˈmeɪn] **N 1** *(territory, sphere of interest)* domaine *m*; *Fig* **that's your d.** c'est ton domaine; **to be in the public d.** *(information)* être dans le domaine public **2** *Math, Biol, Chem & Phys* domaine *m* **3** *Comput* domaine *m*
►► *Comput* ***domain name*** nom *m* de domaine; ***Domain Name System*** système *m* de nom de domaine

dome [dəʊm] **N 1** *Archit* dôme *m*, coupole *f*
2 *(of head, skull)* calotte *f*; *(of hill)* dôme *m*; *(of heavens, sky)* voûte *f*; **the d. of his bald head** le sommet de son crâne chauve
3 *Fam (head)* tête□ *f*
4 *Metal (of furnace)* dôme *m*, voûte *f*
►► *Am* ***dome fastener*** bouton-pression *m*, pression *f*

domed [dəʊmd] **ADJ 1** *Archit (building)* à coupole, à dôme **2** *(shaped like a dome* ► *roof)* en forme de dôme *ou* de coupole; *(*► *forehead)* bombé

Domesday Book [ˈduːmzdeɪ-] **N** *Hist* **the D.** = recueil cadastral établi à la fin du XIème siècle à l'initiative de Guillaume le Conquérant afin de permettre l'évaluation des droits fiscaux sur les terres d'Angleterre

domestic [dəˈmestɪk] **ADJ 1** *(household* ► *duty, chore)* ménager; **for d. use only** *(on packaging)* réservé à l'usage domestique
2 *(of the family* ► *duties, problems)* familial; *(*► *life)* familial, de famille; **they lived in d. bliss for many years** ça a été un ménage très heureux pendant de nombreuses années; **a minor d. crisis** un petit problème à la maison; **a d. sort of person** *(woman)* une femme d'intérieur; *(man)* un homme d'intérieur
3 *(not foreign* ► *affairs, flight, airline, trade, market, policy)* intérieur; *(*►*currency, economy, news, produce)* national
4 *(not wild* ► *animal)* domestique
N *Br Formal* domestique *mf*; *Am* femme *f* de ménage
►► ***domestic appliance*** appareil *m* ménager; ***domestic fowl*** volaille *f*; ***domestic help*** aide *f* ménagère; ***domestic refuse*** ordures *fpl* ménagères; *Br Formerly Sch* ***domestic science*** enseignement *m* ménager; ***domestic servant*** domestique *m*; ***domestic service*** domesticité *f*; **she was in d. service** elle était domestique; ***domestic staff*** employés *mpl* de maison, domestiques *mpl*;

domestically [dəˈmestɪklɪ] **ADV 1 to be d. inclined** être une personne d'intérieur **2 to be produced d.** être produit à l'intérieur du pays *ou* au niveau national

domesticate [dəˈmestɪkeɪt] **VT** *(animal)* domestiquer, apprivoiser; *Hum (person)* habituer aux tâches ménagères

domesticity [ˌdəʊmeˈstɪsətɪ] **N 1** *(liking for home)* attachement *m* au foyer **2** *(home life)* vie *f* de famille; **the cosy d. of their life** leur petite vie tranquille

domicile [ˈdɒmɪsaɪl] **N** *Admin, Fin & Law* domicile *m*
VT 1 *Admin & Law (usu passive) (person)* **domiciled at Leeds** domicilié *ou* demeurant à Leeds **2** *Fin* domicilier; **bills domiciled in France** traites *fpl* payables en France
►► ***domiciled bill*** effet *m* domicilié

domiciliary [ˌdɒmɪˈsɪljərɪ] **ADJ** *Admin (visit)* domiciliaire; *(care, services)* à domicile

domiciliation [ˌdɒmɪsɪlɪˈeɪʃən] **N** *Fin* domiciliation *f*
►► ***domiciliation papers*** dossier *m* de domiciliation

dominance [ˈdɒmɪnəns] **N 1** *(command, influence* ► *of race, person, football team, political party)* prédominance *f* **2** *Biol (*► *of animal, gene, disease)* dominance *f* **3** *(importance)* importance *f*

dominant [ˈdɒmɪnənt] **ADJ 1** *(most important)* dominant; *(race, team, political party etc)* prédominant
2 *Biol (animal, gene, disease)* dominant
3 *(person, personality)* dominateur
4 *(building, geographical feature* ► *most elevated)* dominant; *(*► *most striking)* le plus frappant
5 *Mus* de dominante
N 1 *Mus (note)* dominante *f* **2** *Biol (gene)* dominance *f*
►► *Mus* ***dominant chord*** accord *m* de dominante; *Mus* ***dominant seventh*** septième *f* de dominante

dominantly [ˈdɒmɪnəntlɪ] **ADV** d'une manière dominante

dominate [ˈdɒmɪneɪt] **VT 1** *(person, a people)* dominer (sur); **to d. a match/game** *(of player, team)* dominer un match/un jeu; **to be dominated by sb** être dominé par qn; **the wedding dominated his thoughts to the exclusion of everything else** le mariage prédominait sur toute autre chose dans ses pensées **2** *(of mountain etc* ► *landscape)* dominer; **the fortress dominates the town** la forteresse domine *ou* commande la ville
VI dominer

dominating [ˈdɒmɪneɪtɪŋ] **ADJ** *(feature, colour)* dominant; *(personality)* dominateur

domination [ˌdɒmɪˈneɪʃən] **N** domination *f*; *(of organization)* contrôle *m*; *(of conversation)* monopolisation *f*; **Spain was under Roman d. at the time** à cette époque, l'Espagne était sous la domination romaine; **Manchester United's d. of English football** la suprématie exercée par Manchester United sur le football anglais

domineer [ˌdɒmɪˈnɪə(r)] **VI** se montrer autoritaire; **to d. over sb** se montrer autoritaire avec qn

domineering [ˌdɒmɪˈnɪərɪŋ] **ADJ** autoritaire

Dominica [dəˈmɪnɪkə] **N** Dominique *f*

dominical [dəˈmɪnɪkəl] **ADJ** *Rel* dominical

Dominican [dəˈmɪnɪkən] **N 1** *(person from the Dominican Republic)* Dominicain(e) *m,f* **2** *(person from Dominica)* Dominiquais(e) *m,f* **3** *Rel* dominicain(e) *m,f*
ADJ 1 *(from the Dominican Republic)* dominicain **2** *(from Dominica)* dominiquais **3** *Rel* dominicain
►► ***the Dominican Republic*** la République Dominicaine

dominion [dəˈmɪnjən] **N 1** *(rule, authority)* domination *f*, empire *m*; **to have** *or* **to hold d. over a country** avoir un pays sous sa domination **2** *(territory)* territoire *m*; *(in British Commonwealth)* dominion *m*

domino [ˈdɒmɪnəʊ] *(pl* **dominoes***)* **N 1** *(for game)* domino *m*; **to play dominoes** jouer aux dominos **2** *(cloak, mask)* domino *m*
►► ***domino effect*** effet *m* d'entraînement; ***domino theory*** théorie *f* des dominos

don[1] [dɒn] *(pt & pp* **donned**, *cont* **donning***)* **VT** *Formal (put on)* mettre

don[2] **N 1** *Br Univ* = professeur d'université (en particulier à Oxford et Cambridge) **2** *(Spanish title)* don *m*

donate [dəˈneɪt] **VT** *(money, goods)* faire un don de; *(specific amount)* faire (un) don de; **to d. blood** donner son *ou* du sang
VI *(give money, goods)* faire un don, faire des dons

donation [dəˈneɪʃən] **N** *(action)* don *m*, donation *f*; *(money, goods or blood given)* don *m*; **would you care to make a d.?** voudriez-vous faire un don *ou* faire une donation *ou* donner quelque chose?; **to make a d. to a charity** faire un don *ou* une donation à une œuvre (de charité)

donator [dəˈneɪtə(r)] **N** donateur(trice) *m,f*

done [dʌn] *pp of* **do**
ADJ 1 *(finished)* fini; **are you d. yet?** est-ce que tu as fini?; **to get sth d.** *(completed)* finir qch
2 *(cooked* ► *food)* cuit
3 *Fam (exhausted)* crevé, claqué
4 *(fitting)* **it's not the d. thing, it's not d.** ça ne se fait pas; **it used to be the d. thing to send your hostess flowers** ça se faisait d'envoyer des fleurs à son hôtesse
►► *Com* ***done deal*** = transaction dans laquelle les invendus ne peuvent être retournés au fournisseur; *Fig* **the peace agreement/merger is not a d. deal yet** l'accord de paix/la fusion n'est pas encore chose faite

doner kebab [ˈdɒnə-, ˈdəʊnə-] **N** sandwich *m* grec

dong [dɒŋ] **N 1** *(noise of bell)* ding-dong *m* **2** *Vulg (penis)* queue *f*, bite *f*

dongle [ˈdɒŋgəl] **N** *Comput* fiche *f* gigogne, clé *f* gigogne

donkey [ˈdɒŋkɪ] **N 1** *(animal)* âne *m*, ânesse *f*; *Fam* **he could talk the hind legs off a d.** il est bavard comme une pie; **I haven't seen her for d.'s years** je ne l'ai pas vue depuis une éternité **2** *Fam (idiot)* âne *m*, imbécile□ *mf* **3** *Br Fam Pej (sportsman)* incapable□ *m*
►► *Br* ***donkey derby*** course *f* d'ânes; *Br* ***donkey jacket*** = veste longue en tissu épais, généralement bleu foncé; ***donkey ride*** promenade *f* à dos d'âne

DONKEY RIDE

Les promenades à dos d'âne sont l'une des attractions traditionnelles que proposent les stations balnéaires britanniques aux enfants. Avec les crèmes glacées et la pelle et le seau, elle sont l'un des symboles des vacances passées en famille au bord de la mer en Grande-Bretagne.

donkey-work **N** *(UNCOUNT) Fam* **to do the d.** *(drudgery)* faire le sale boulot; *(difficult part)* faire le gros du travail□

donnish [ˈdɒnɪʃ] **ADJ** *Br (person)* érudit, savant; *(look, speech)* d'érudit, cultivé; *Pej* pédant; **he's a bit d.** il a un petit air professoral

donor [ˈdəʊnə(r)] **N 1** *(to charity)* donateur(trice) *m,f* **2** *(of blood, organ)* donneur(euse) *m,f*
►► ***donor card*** carte *f* de don d'organe; *Med* ***donor insemination*** insémination *f* avec sperme de donneur, IAD *f*

don't [dəʊnt] = **do not**
N *(usu pl)* chose *f* à ne pas faire; **a list of do's and don'ts** une liste de choses à faire et à ne pas faire

donut [ˈdəʊnʌt] **N** *Am* beignet *m*, *Can* beigne *m*

doobie [ˈduːbɪ] **N** *Fam (cannabis cigarette)* joint□ *m*

doodah [ˈduːdɑː] **N** *Fam* truc *m*, bidule *m*

doodle [ˈduːdəl] **N** gribouillage *m*, griffonnage *m*
VT & VI gribouiller, griffonner

doodlebug [ˈduːdəlˌbʌg] **N 1** *Fam (bomb)* V1□ *m*, bombe *f* volante□ **2** *Am (insect)* larve *f* de cicindèle

doo-doo [ˈduːduː] **N 1** *(excrement)* crotte *f*, caca *m*; **the dog's done a d. on the doormat** le chien a fait sa crotte sur le paillasson **2** *(trouble)* pétrin *m*; **we're in deep d.!** on est vraiment dans le pétrin!

doofus [ˈduːfəs] **N** *Am Fam* andouille *f*

doolally [ˌduːˈlælɪ] **ADJ** *Fam* timbré

doom [duːm] **N** *(UNCOUNT) (terrible fate)* destin *m* (malheureux), sort *m* (tragique); *(ruin)* perte *f*, ruine *f*; *(death)* mort *f*; **to meet one's d.** trouver la mort; **an air/a feeling of d.** un air/sentiment funeste; *Fig* **to be full of** *or* **all d. and gloom** voir tout en noir; **the situation's not all d. and gloom** la situation n'est pas aussi sombre qu'il y paraît
VT condamner; **an attempt doomed to failure** une tentative condamnée à l'insuccès *ou* vouée à l'échec

doomed [duːmd] **ADJ** *(town)* condamné; *(person)* perdu; *(ship, aircraft)* marqué par le destin; **to be d. (to failure)** être voué à l'échec; **she is d. to a life of poverty** elle est condamnée à une vie de misère

doom-laden **ADJ** de mauvais augure, sinistre

Doomsday [ˈduːmzdeɪ] **N** jour *m* du Jugement dernier; **till D.** jusqu'à la fin du monde *ou* des temps
►► *Hist* ***the Doomsday Book*** = recueil cadastral établi à la fin du XIème siècle à l'initiative de Guillaume le Conquérant afin de permettre l'évaluation des droits fiscaux sur les terres d'Angleterre

door [dɔː(r)] **N 1** *(of building, room, refrigerator, wardrobe)* porte *f*; **they shut the d. in my face** ils m'ont fermé la porte au nez; **he lives two doors down** *or* **away** il habite deux portes plus loin; **out of doors** dehors, en plein air; **to go from d. to d.** aller de porte en porte; **the journey takes two hours d. to d.** le voyage prend deux heures de porte à porte; **can someone answer the d.?** est-ce que quelqu'un peut aller ouvrir?; **the business finally closes its doors tomorrow** l'entreprise ferme définitivement demain; **tickets available at** *or* **on the d.** *(in advertisement, on sign)* billets en vente à l'entrée; **the agreement leaves the d. open for further discussion** l'accord laisse la porte ouverte à des discussions ultérieures; **the discovery opens the d. to medical advances** la découverte ouvre la voie à des progrès médicaux; *Fig* **to lay sth at sb's d.** imputer qch à qn, reprocher qch à qn; **she closed** *or* **shut the d. on any further negotiations** elle a rendu toute nouvelle négociation impossible; **behind closed doors** *(discussions etc)* entre quatre murs, à huis-clos; **to show** *or* **see sb to the d.** conduire qn à la porte, reconduire qn; *Fig* **to show sb the d.** montrer la porte à qn; **the foot in the d. technique** *(of salesman)* = la vente (en porte-à-porte) forcée **2** *(of car)* porte *f*, portière *f*; *(of train)* portière *f*

►► ***door chain*** chaînette *f* de sûreté; ***door handle*** poignée *f* de porte; *Aut* poignée *f* de portière; ***door knocker*** marteau *m* de porte, heurtoir *m*

doorbell ['dɔːbel] **N** sonnette *f*; **to ring the d.** sonner à la porte; **the d. rang** on sonna à la porte

do-or-die **ADJ** *(chance, effort)* désespéré, ultime; *(attitude, person)* jusqu'au-boutiste

doorframe ['dɔːfreɪm] **N** chambranle *m*, châssis *m* de porte

doorjamb ['dɔːdʒæm] **N** montant *m* de porte, jambage *m*

doorkeeper ['dɔːˌkiːpə(r)] **N** *(at hotel)* portier *m*; *(at apartment building)* concierge *mf*

doorknob ['dɔːnɒb] **N** poignée *f* de porte

doorman ['dɔːmən] *(pl* **doormen** [-mən]) **N** *(at hotel)* portier *m*; *(at apartment building)* concierge *m*; *(at pub, nightclub)* videur *m*

doormat ['dɔːmæt] **N 1** *(for door)* paillasson *m*, essuie-pieds *m inv* **2** *Fig (person)* chiffe *f* molle; **don't be such a d.** ne te laisse pas marcher sur les pieds comme ça; **to treat sb like a d.** traiter qn comme un moins que rien

doornail ['dɔːneɪl] **N** clou *m* de porte

doorpost ['dɔːpəʊst] **N** montant *m* de porte, jambage *m*

doorstep ['dɔːstep] **N 1** *(step)* pas *m* de la porte, seuil *m* de porte; **leave the milk on the d.** laissez le lait devant la porte; **don't leave him standing on the d., ask him to come in!** ne le laisse pas à la porte, fais-le entrer!; *Fig* **there are shops and a library on your d.** tu as des boutiques et une bibliothèque à ta porte **2** *Br Hum (thick slice of bread)* grosse tranche *f* de pain

VT *Br (of politician)* démarcher; *(of journalists)* harceler jusque devant sa porte

►► *Br* ***doorstep salesman*** vendeur *m* à domicile, démarcheur *m*

doorstepping ['dɔːstepɪŋ] **N** *Br (by politician)* démarchage *m* électoral; *(by journalists)* = pratique journalistique qui consiste à harceler les gens jusque devant leur porte

doorstop ['dɔːstɒp] **N** *(fixed)* butoir *m*; *(wedge)* cale-porte *m*

door-to-door **ADJ**

►► ***door-to-door canvassing*** porte-à-porte *m*; ***door-to-door enquiries*** enquête *f* de voisinage; ***door-to-door salesman*** vendeur *m* à domicile, démarcheur *m*; **he's a d. salesman** il fait du porte-à-porte; ***door-to-door selling*** vente *f* à domicile, porte-à-porte *m inv*

doorway ['dɔːweɪ] **N** porte *f*; *(frame)* encadrement *m* de la porte; **standing in the d.** debout dans l'embrasure de la porte

dopamine ['dəʊpəmɪn] **N** *Biol & Chem* dopamine *f*

dope [dəʊp] **N 1** *(UNCOUNT) Fam (illegal drug)* drogue□ *f*, dope *f*; *(cannabis)* shit□ *m*

2 *(for athlete, horse)* dopant *m*

3 *Fam (idiot)* crétin(e) *m,f*, andouille *f*

4 *(UNCOUNT) Fam Old-fashioned (news, information)* tuyau *m*, renseignement□ *m*; **to give sb the d. on sth** rencarder qn sur qch

5 *Chem & Tech (varnish)* enduit *m*; *(for fuel)* dopant *m*

6 *(for dynamite)* absorbant *m*

ADJ *Am Fam (excellent)* génial, super *(inv)*

VT 1 *(drug* ► *horse, person) (to prevent from winning)* droguer; *(to increase chances)* doper; *(*► *drink, food)* mettre une drogue *ou* un dopant dans **2** *Chem & Tech (varnish)* enduire; *(fuel)* doper

►► *Fam* ***dope dealer, dope pusher*** revendeur (euse)□ *m,f* de drogue, dealer *m*; ***dope test*** test *m* antidopage *ou* antidoping; **to fail/take a d. test** être déclaré positif à/subir un test antidopage *ou* antidoping

dopehead ['dəʊphed] **N** *Fam* **1** *(drug user)* camé(e) *m,f* **2** *(heavy cannabis user)* = personne qui fume beaucoup de cannabis

dopey *(compar* **dopier**, *superl* **dopiest**) = **dopy**

doping ['dəʊpɪŋ] **N 1** *(to prevent from winning)* administration *f* d'un narcotique (**of** à); *(to increase chances of winning)* dopage *m*, doping *m* **2** *Chem & Tech (varnishing)* enduisage *m*; *(of fuel)* dopage *m*

Doppler effect ['dɒplə(r)-] **N** *Phys* effet *m* Doppler

dopy ['dəʊpɪ] *(compar* **dopier**, *superl* **dopiest**) **ADJ** **1** *(sleepy)* (à moitié) endormi; *(drugged)* drogué, dopé **2** *Fam (silly)* abruti

do-re-mi [dəʊ-] **N** *Am Fam (money)* fric *m*, blé *m*

Doric ['dɒrɪk] **N 1** *Archit* dorique *m* **2** *Ling (in Ancient Greece)* dorien *m*

ADJ *Archit* dorique

dork [dɔːk] **N** *Am Fam (idiot)* niais(e)□ *m,f*, *(studious person)* ringard(e) *m,f*

dorky ['dɔːkɪ] **ADJ** *Am Fam (idiotic)* niais□; *(studious)* ringard

dorm [dɔːm] **N** *Fam (abbr* **dormitory**) **1** *(room)* dortoir□ *m* **2** *Am Univ* résidence *f* universitaire□

dormant ['dɔːmənt] **ADJ 1** *(idea, passion)* qui sommeille; *(energy, reserves)* inexploité; *(disease)* à l'état latent; **to lie d.** sommeiller

2 *(animal)* endormi; *(plant)* dormant

3 *(volcano)* en repos, en sommeil

4 *Banking (account)* sans mouvement

5 *Her* dormant

dormer ['dɔːmə(r)] **N** *(window)* lucarne *f*

►► ***dormer window*** lucarne *f*

dormitory ['dɔːmətrɪ] *(pl* **dormitories**) **N 1** *(room)* dortoir *m* **2** *Am Univ* résidence *f* universitaire

►► *Am* ***dormitory suburb***, *Br* ***dormitory town*** ville-dortoir *f*

dormouse ['dɔːmaʊs] *(pl* **dormice** [-maɪs]) **N** *Zool* loir *m*

dorsal ['dɔːsəl] **N** dorsale *f*

ADJ dorsal

►► *Ich* ***dorsal fin*** nageoire *f* dorsale

dory ['dɔːrɪ] *(pl* **dories**) **N 1** *(saltwater fish)* saint-pierre *m inv*, dorée *f*; *(freshwater fish)* dorée *f* **2** *Am (boat)* doris *m*

DOS [dɒs] **N** *Comput (abbr* **disk operating system**) DOS *m*

►► ***DOS command*** commande *f* du DOS; ***DOS prompt*** indicatif *m* (du) DOS, invite *f* du DOS; ***DOS switch*** clé *f ou* paramètre *m* du DOS

dosage ['dəʊsɪdʒ] **N** *(giving of dose)* dosage *m*; *(amount)* dose *f*; *(directions)* posologie *f*

dose [dəʊs] **N 1** *(amount)* dose *f*; **in small/large doses** à faible/haute dose; **I can only take him in small doses** je ne peux le supporter qu'à petites doses; **with a strong d. of humour** avec beaucoup d'humour; **that curry went through me like a d. of salts** ce curry est passé tout droit **2** *(of illness)* attaque *f*; **a bad d. of flu** une mauvaise grippe **3** *very Fam (venereal disease)* bléno *f*; **to catch a d.** attraper une bléno

VT 1 *(of pharmacist)* doser **2** *(person)* administrer un médicament à; **she dosed herself (up) with pills** elle s'est bourrée de médicaments

doser ['dəʊsə(r)] **N** *(for washing powder etc)* dosette *f*

dosh [dɒʃ] **N** *Br Fam* fric *m*

doss [dɒs] *Br Fam* **N 1** *(bed)* lit□ *m*, pieu *m* **2** *(nap)* somme *m*, roupillon *m*; **to have a d.** faire un somme **3** *(easy thing)* **it was a real d.** c'était fastoche

VI *(sleep)* pieuter; *(in doss house)* coucher à l'asile de nuit

►**doss about, doss around** **VI** *Br Fam* glander

►**doss down** **VI** *Br Fam* coucher□, crécher□; **I need somewhere to d. down for the night** j'ai besoin d'un endroit où coucher cette nuit□

dosser ['dɒsə(r)] **N** *Br Fam* **1** *(homeless person)* sans-abri□ *mf inv*, clochard(e) *m,f* **2** *(house)* foyer *m* de sans-abri **3** *Ir Fam Pej (lazy person)* fainéant(e) *m,f*, glandeur(euse) *m,f*

dosshouse ['dɒshaʊs, *pl* -haʊzɪz] **N** *Br Fam* foyer *m* de sans-abri□

dossier ['dɒsɪeɪ] **N** dossier *m*; **to keep a d. on sb** avoir un dossier sur qn

dot [dɒt] *(pt & pp* **dotted**, *cont* **dotting**) **N** point *m*; *(on material)* pois *m*; *Mus* point *m* d'augmentation; **"www d. harrap d. com"** *(in URL)* "www point harrap point com"; **d., d., d.** *(in punctuation)* points *mpl* de suspension; **dots and dashes** *(Morse code)* points *mpl* et traits *mpl*; *Fam* **since the year d.** depuis des siècles; *Fam* **that was in the year d.** c'était il y a une éternité

VT 1 *(mark)* marquer avec des points, pointiller; *(an "i")* mettre un point sur; *Fig* **to d. one's i's and cross one's t's** mettre les points sur les i

2 *(spot)* parsemer; **the lake was dotted with boats** des bateaux étaient dispersés sur le lac; **his shirt was dotted with flecks of tomato sauce** sa chemise était tachetée de sauce tomate; **the islands are dotted all round the coast** les îles sont éparpillées tout autour de la côte; *Culin* **d. the surface with butter** mettez des morceaux de beurre sur le dessus

3 *Mus (note)* pointer

4 *Fam* **to d. sb one** *(hit)* flanquer un gnon à qn

• **on the dot** **ADV** *(arrive)* à l'heure tapante; **at 3 o'clock on the d., on the d. of three o'clock** à 3 heures pile *ou* tapantes

►► *Comput* ***dot com*** *(company)* start-up *f*

dotage ['dəʊtɪdʒ] **N** gâtisme *m*; **to be in one's d.** être gâteux, être retombé en enfance

dot-com [-'kɒm] **ADJ** *Comput* qui a trait à la netéconomie; **d. millionnaire** = personne qui a fait fortune en montant une start-up

dot-commer [-'kɒmə(r)] **N** = personne qui travaille dans le secteur de la netéconomie

dote [dəʊt] **VI** être gâteux

►**dote on, dote upon** **VT INSEP** **to d. on** *or* **upon sb** être fou (folle) de qn, aimer qn à la folie

doting ['dəʊtɪŋ] **ADJ** *(parents, grandparents)* qui montre une tendresse *ou* une indulgence exagérée; **he has a d. mother** sa mère l'aime à la folie

dot-matrix printer **N** *Comput* imprimante *f* matricielle

dotted ['dɒtɪd] **ADJ 1** *(shirt, tie)* à pois **2** *Mus* pointé

►► ***dotted line*** *(on form)* ligne *f* en pointillés; *Aut* ligne *f* discontinue; **to sign on the d. line** *(on form)* signer à l'endroit indiqué; *Fig* donner son consentement; **tear along the d. line** détachez suivant le pointillé

dottle ['dɒtəl] **N** culot *m (dans une pipe)*

dotty ['dɒtɪ] *(compar* **dottier**, *superl* **dottiest**) **ADJ** *Br Fam (crazy)* fou (folle)□, dingue; **she's slightly d.** elle travaille du chapeau, elle est toquée; **he's absolutely d. about her** il est fou d'elle

DOUBLE ['dʌbəl]

ADJ
- double **1–3, 7**
- deux fois **4**
- en double **5**
- pour deux personnes **6**

PREDET
- deux fois plus

N
- double **1, 2, 3**

ADV
- en deux

VT
- doubler **1, 3**
- plier en deux **2**
- contrer **4**

VI
- doubler **1**
- contrer **2**

ADJ 1 *(twice as large* ► *quantity, portion)* double; **a d. whisky** un double whisky

2 *Bot* double

3 *(line, row)* double; **to go into** *or* **reach d. figures** *(inflation, unemployment etc)* atteindre la barre des dix pour cent; **an egg with a d. yolk** un œuf à deux jaunes

4 *(with figures, letters)* deux fois; **d. five two one** *(figure)* deux fois cinq deux un; *(phone number)* cinquante-cinq, vingt et un; **"letter" is spelt with a d. "t"** "letter" s'écrit avec deux "t"; **to throw a d. six/three** faire un double six/trois
5 *(folded in two)* en double, replié; **d. thickness** double épaisseur *f*
6 *(for two people)* pour *ou* à deux personnes
7 *(dual ▸ purpose, advantage)* double; *(ambiguous)* double, ambigu(ë); **a word with a d. meaning** un mot à double sens; **to lead a d. life** mener une double vie; **to have d. standards** faire deux poids, deux mesures; *Fam* **to do a d. take** marquer un temps d'arrêt ▫ *(par surprise)*
PREDET *(twice)* deux fois plus; **she earns d. my salary** elle gagne deux fois plus que moi *ou* le double de moi; **we ordered d. the usual quantity** nous avons commandé le double de la quantité habituelle; **food here costs nearly d. what it does at home** la nourriture ici coûte presque le double de chez moi
N 1 *(twice the amount)* double *m*; *(of alcohol)* double *m*; **he charged us d.** il nous a fait payer le double; **they pay him d. if he works nights** on le paye (au tarif) double s'il travaille la nuit; **make mine a d.** un double pour moi; **at** *or* **on the d.** au pas de course; **d. or quits** quitte ou double
2 *(duplicate)* double *m*, réplique *f*; *(of person)* double *m*, sosie *m*; *Cin & TV (stand-in)* doublure *f*; *Theat (actor with two parts)* acteur(trice) *m,f* qui tient deux rôles
3 *Horseracing* pari *m* couplé; *Cards* contre *m*; *(in darts)* double *m*; *(in billiards)* doublé *m*
ADV *(in two)* en deux; **to fold sth d.** plier qch en deux; **I was bent d. with pain** j'étais plié en deux de douleur; **to see d.** *(two of the same)* voir double
VT 1 *(increase)* doubler; **to d. the stakes** doubler la mise
2 *(fold)* plier en deux, replier
3 *Cin & TV* doubler
4 *Cards (bid, opponent)* contrer
VI 1 *(increase)* doubler
2 *Cards* contrer; **d.!** *(in bridge)* contre!
3 *(serve two purposes)* **the dining room doubles as a study** la salle à manger sert également de bureau; *Theat* **he doubles as the priest and the servant** il joue les rôles du prêtre et du domestique
▸▸ ***double act*** duo *m* comique; ***double agent*** agent *m* double; *Mus* ***double bass*** contrebasse *f*; *Mus* ***double bassoon*** contrebasson *m*; ***double bed*** grand lit *m*, lit *m* à deux places; ***double bill*** *Cin* = séance avec deux longs métrages à la suite; *TV* = programmation de deux longs métrages à la suite; *Psy* ***double bind*** double contrainte *f*; **to be caught in a d. bind** se trouver dans une situation insoluble, être dans une impasse; *Br* ***double bluff*** = technique consistant à faire croire qu'on bluffe alors qu'on dit la vérité; **it was a d. bluff on her part** elle voulait lui/nous/*etc* faire croire qu'elle bluffait; *Golf* ***double bogey*** bogey *m* double; *Am* ***double boiler*** casserole *f* à double fond; ***double chin*** double menton *m*; *Br* ***double cream*** crème *f* épaisse, *Can* crème *f* à fouetter; ***double cross*** trahison *f*, traîtrise *f*; *Am* ***double date*** sortie *f* à quatre *(deux couples)*; ***double doors, a double door*** une porte à deux battants; ***double Dutch*** *Br Fam* charabia *m*, baragouin *m*; *Am (game)* double dutch *m*; **to talk d. Dutch** baragouiner; **it's all d. Dutch to me!** c'est de l'hébreu pour moi!; ***double entendre*** mot *m*/expression *f* à double sens; *Acct* ***double entry*** comptabilité *f* en partie double; *Phot* ***double exposure*** surimpression *f*; *Sport* ***double fault*** double faute *f*; *Cin* ***double feature*** = séance avec deux longs métrages à la suite; *Br Univ* ***double first*** mention *f* très bien *(dans deux disciplines à la fois)*; *Mus* ***double flat*** double bémol *m*; ***double helix*** double hélice *f*; *Br Univ* ***double honours*** = licence portant sur deux matières; *Am Ins* ***double indemnity*** = clause d'une assurance-vie qui stipule qu'en cas de mort accidentelle de l'assuré la prime est doublée; *Am Law* ***double jeopardy*** double incrimination *f*; ***double knitting*** = laine assez épaisse utilisée en tricot; ***double knot*** double nœud *m*; *Comput & Typ* ***double line*** trait *m* double; *Gram* ***double negative*** double négation *f*; ***double occupancy*** *(of hotel room)* occupation *f* double; ***double page spread*** page *f* centrale, double page *f*; *(advert)* pub *f* double page; ***double parking*** stationnement *m* en double file; *Med* ***double pneumonia*** pneumonie *f* double; *Typ* ***double quotes*** guillemets *mpl*; ***double room*** chambre *f* pour deux personnes; *Br* ***double saucepan*** casserole *f* à double fond; *Mus* ***double sharp*** double dièse *m*; ***double sink*** évier *m* à deux bacs; *Typ* ***double spacing*** double interligne *m*; ***double time*** *(pay)* salaire *m* double; *Mil* pas *m* redoublé; *Mus* mesure *f* double; **I get d. time on Sundays** je suis payé le double le dimanche; **to march in d. time** marcher à pas redoublés; *Mus* **in d. time** en mesure double; *Med* ***double vision*** double vision *f*; **to have d. vision** voir double; *Fam* ***double whammy*** double coup *m* de malchance ▫; *Br* ***double white line*** *(on road)* double ligne *f* blanche *(d'interdiction de doubler)*; *Am Mus* ***double whole note*** double ronde *f*; *Br* ***double yellow line*** *(on road)* double ligne *f* jaune *(qui indique une zone de stationnement interdit)*; **to be parked on a d. yellow line** être en stationnement interdit

▸**double back** **VI** *(animal, person)* revenir sur ses pas; **the road doubles back on itself** la route tourne en épingle à cheveux; **he doubled back down a side road** il a rebroussé chemin par une petite route
VT SEP *(sheet)* mettre en double

▸**double for** **VT INSEP** *Cin & Theat* doubler

▸**double over** **VI** *(bend over)* se plier, se courber; **he doubled over in pain** il se plia en deux de douleur

▸**double up** **VI 1** *(bend over)* se plier, se courber; **he doubled up in pain** il se plia en deux de douleur; **to d. up with laughter** se tordre de rire **2** *(share)* partager; **there weren't enough rooms so we doubled up** il n'y avait pas assez de place, alors nous nous sommes mis à deux par chambre
VT SEP plier en deux, replier

---

double-acting, double-action **ADJ** à double effet

double-barrelled, *Am* **double-barreled** [-'bærəld] **ADJ** *(gun)* à deux coups; *Fig (question, remark)* équivoque
▸▸ *Br* ***double-barrelled name*** = nom de famille composé (p.ex. Burnes-Jones) indiquant souvent une origine noble

double-blind **ADJ** *(experiment, test)* en double aveugle; *(method)* à double insu, à double anonymat

double-book **VT** *(seat, room)* réserver pour deux personnes différentes, sur-réserver; **we've been double-booked again** nous sommes encore en double réservation; **I've double-booked myself for next Friday** je me suis engagé à faire deux choses différentes vendredi prochain
VI *(of hotel, airline)* faire une/des double(s) réservation(s)

double-booking **N** double réservation *f*

double-bottomed **ADJ** *(saucepan, suitcase)* à double fond; *(dinghy)* à double coque

double-breasted [-'brestɪd] **ADJ** croisé

double-check **VT** revérifier
VI revérifier

double-click *Comput* **N** double-clic *m*
VT cliquer deux fois sur, double-cliquer
VI cliquer deux fois, faire un double-clic

double-clutch **VI** *Am Aut* faire un double débrayage

double-cross **VT** trahir, doubler

double-crosser [-'krɒsə(r)] **N** traître(esse) *m,f*, faux jeton *m*

double-dealer **N** fourbe *m*

double-dealing **N** *(UNCOUNT)* fourberie *f*, double jeu *m*
ADJ fourbe, faux (fausse) comme un jeton

double-decker [-'dekə(r)] **N 1** *Br (bus)* autobus *m* à impériale **2** *Am (aircraft)* deux-ponts *m* **3** *Fam (sandwich)* club sandwich ▫ *m*

double-declutch **VI** *Br Aut* faire un double débrayage

double-declutching **N** *Br Aut* double débrayage *m*

double-density **ADJ** *Comput (disk)* (à) double densité

double-edged **ADJ** *(blade, knife, sword)* à double tranchant, à deux tranchants; *Fig (compliment, remark)* à double tranchant; **globalization is a d. sword** la mondialisation est un phénomène à double tranchant

double-faced **ADJ 1** *(reversible)* réversible, à double face **2** *Am (hypocritical)* hypocrite

double-fault **VI** faire une double faute

double-glaze **VT** *Br* isoler *(par système de double vitrage)*; **to d. a window** poser un double vitrage; **they've just had their house double-glazed** ils viennent de faire poser du double vitrage chez eux

double-glazed **ADJ** *Br* à double vitrage

double-glazing *Br* **N** *(UNCOUNT)* double vitrage *m*; **to put in** *or* **to install d.** installer un double vitrage
COMP *(salesman)* de double vitrage

double-headed **ADJ** à deux têtes, *Spec* bicéphale; *TV (programme)* animé par deux présentateurs
▸▸ ***double-headed coin*** pièce *f* de monnaie à deux faces; *Her* ***double-headed eagle*** aigle *f* à deux têtes

double-header **N** *Am Fam* = deux matchs disputés l'un après l'autre

double-jointed **ADJ** désarticulé

double-lock **VT** fermer à double tour

double-page spread **N** *Press & Typ* double page *f*

double-park **VT** garer en double file
VI se garer *ou* stationner en double file

double-pointed **ADJ** *Knitting (needle)* à double pointe

double-quick **ADJ** très rapide; **in d. time** *(move)* au pas de course *ou* de gymnastique; *(finish, work)* en un rien de temps
ADV en un rien de temps

double-sided **ADJ**
▸▸ *Comput* ***double-sided disk*** disque *m* double face; ***double-sided tape*** bande *f* adhésive double-face

double-space **VT** *Typ* taper à double interligne; **the text is double-spaced** le texte est à double interligne

double-speak **N** propos *mpl* ambigus *ou* équivoques; **rationalization is just d. for more unemployment** rationalisation n'est qu'un euphémisme pour plus de chômage

double-speed **ADJ** *Comput (CD-ROM)* double vitesse

double-stop *(pt & pp* **double-stopped,** *cont* **double-stopping)** **VI** *Mus (on violin)* faire des doubles-cordes

doublet ['dʌblɪt] **N 1** *Hist (jacket)* pourpoint *m*, justaucorps *m*; **d. and hose** pourpoint *m* et haut-de-chausse *m* **2** *(of words)* doublet *m*

double-talk **N** *(UNCOUNT) Fam (ambiguous)* = propos ambigus et contournés; *(gibberish)* charabia *m*

doublethink ['dʌbəl,θɪŋk] **N** *(UNCOUNT)* = raisonnement de mauvaise foi qui contient des contradictions flagrantes; **it's another case of d.** c'est encore un raisonnement pervers

doubling ['dʌbəlɪŋ] **N** *(of letter, number)* redoublement *m*, doublement *m*

doubly ['dʌblɪ] **ADV** *(twice as much)* doublement, deux fois plus; *(in two ways)* doublement; **she's d. careful now** elle redouble de prudence maintenant; **we must make d. sure that...** il faut bien vérifier que...

doubt [daʊt] **N 1** *(uncertainty ▸ about fact)* doute *m*, incertitude *f*; **beyond all reasonable d.** à n'en pas douter, sans le moindre doute; **to raise doubts in sb's mind** soulever des doutes dans l'esprit de qn; **the whole thing raised doubts about his abilities** toute cette affaire a mis ses capacités en question; **to cast d. on sth** mettre en doute *ou* jeter le doute sur qch; **to be in d.** *(person)* être en *ou* dans le doute; *(future, event)* être douteux *ou* incertain; **her honesty is in d.** *or* **open to d.** *(generally)* on a des doutes sur son honnêteté, son honnêteté est sujette à caution; *(this time)* son honnêteté est mise en doute; **we are in no d. as to his competence** nous n'avons aucun doute sur ses compétences; **the future of the company is in some d.** l'avenir de l'entreprise est incertain; **when in d., do nothing** dans le doute, abstiens-toi; **there is some d. as to whether they paid** on n'est pas certain qu'ils aient payé; **there is no d. about it** cela ne fait pas de doute; **there's no d. (but) that it will be a difficult journey** il n'y a pas de doute que le voyage sera pénible; **no d.** sans doute; **he'll no d. be late** il sera sûrement en retard; **there is room for d.** il est permis de douter; **without (any) d.** sans aucun *ou* le moindre doute **2** *(feeling of distrust)* doute *m*; **I have my doubts about him** j'ai des doutes sur lui *ou* à son sujet; **she has her doubts (about) whether it's true** elle doute que cela soit vrai; **I have no d.** *or* **doubts about it** je n'en doute pas

VT 1 *(consider unlikely)* **I d. (whether) she'll be there** je doute qu'elle soit là; **she'll be there – I don't d. it** elle sera là – je n'en doute pas *ou* j'en suis certain; **I d. it** j'en doute; **I d. if it makes him happy** je doute que cela le rende heureux **2** *(distrust)* douter de; **there was no doubting their sincerity** on ne pouvait pas mettre en doute leur sincérité; **she began to d. the evidence of her own eyes** elle n'en croyait pas ses yeux

VI *(have doubts)* douter, avoir des doutes

doubter ['daʊtə(r)] **N** incrédule *mf*, sceptique *mf*

doubtful ['daʊtfʊl] **ADJ 1** *(unlikely)* improbable, douteux

2 *(uncertain ▸ person)* incertain, indécis; **to be d. of** *or* **about sth** avoir des doutes sur qch; **I'm d. about his chances** je doute de *ou* j'ai des doutes sur ses chances; **we're d. about accepting** nous hésitons à accepter; **it's d. whether they're really serious** il est douteux qu'ils soient vraiment sérieux, on ne sait pas s'ils sont vraiment sérieux; **she looked d.** elle avait l'air peu convaincu

3 *(questionable ▸ answer, results)* douteux, discutable

4 *(dubious ▸ person)* louche, suspect; *(▸ affair)* douteux, louche; **a joke in d. taste** une plaisanterie d'un goût douteux

▸▸ *Fin* ***doubtful debt*** client *m* douteux, créance *f* douteuse

doubtfully ['daʊtfʊlɪ] **ADV** *(uncertainly)* avec doute, d'un air de doute; *(indecisively)* avec hésitation, de façon indécise

doubting ['daʊtɪŋ] **ADJ** sceptique, incrédule

▸▸ ***doubting Thomas*** Thomas *m* l'incrédule; **don't be such a d. Thomas** ne fais pas l'incrédule, ne fais pas comme saint Thomas

doubtless ['daʊtlɪs], **doubtlessly** ['daʊtlɪslɪ] **ADV** *(certainly)* sans aucun *ou* le moindre doute; *(probably)* (très) probablement

douche [du:ʃ] *Med* **N** lavage *m* interne, douche *f*; *(instrument)* poire *f* à injections

VT doucher

dough [dəʊ] **N 1** *Culin* pâte *f*; **bread d.** pâte *f* à pain **2** *Fam (money)* blé *m*

doughboy ['dəʊ,bɔɪ] **N 1** *Culin* boulette *f* (de pâte) **2** *Am Fam Mil slang* sammy *m (soldat américain de la Première Guerre mondiale)*

doughnut ['dəʊnʌt] **N** beignet *m*, *Can* beigne *m*; **jam d.** beignet *m* à la confiture

doughty ['daʊtɪ] *(compar* **doughtier**, *superl* **doughtiest)** **ADJ** *Literary* vaillant

doughy ['dəʊɪ] *(compar* **doughier**, *superl* **doughiest)** **ADJ 1** *(consistency)* pâteux; *(bread)* mal cuit **2** *(complexion)* terreux

dour [dʊə(r)] **ADJ** *(sullen)* renfrogné; *(stern)* austère, dur

douse [daʊs] **VT 1** *(extinguish ▸ light, fire)* éteindre **2** *(drench)* tremper, inonder; *(plunge)* plonger, tremper; **he doused himself with** *or* **in aftershave** il s'est aspergé d'après-rasage

dove[1] [dʌv] **N 1** *(bird)* colombe *f*; **ring d.** (pigeon *m*) ramier *m*, palombe *f*; **d. of peace** colombe *f* de la paix; **d. grey** gris *m* perle *(inv)* **2** *Pol* colombe *f*; **the doves and the hawks** les colombes *fpl* et les faucons *mpl*

dove[2] [dəʊv] *Am pt of* **dive**

dovecot, dovecote ['dʌvkɒt] **N** colombier *m*, pigeonnier *m*

Dover ['dəʊvə(r)] **N** Douvres; **the Strait of D.** le pas de Calais

▸▸ ***Dover sole*** sole *f*

dovetail ['dʌvteɪl] **VT 1** *Tech* assembler à queue d'aronde **2** *Fig (combine)* faire concorder, raccorder

VI 1 *Tech* se raccorder; **to d. into** se raccorder à **2** *Fig (combine)* bien cadrer, concorder; **the two projects d. nicely** les deux projets se rejoignent parfaitement

N *Tech* queue-d'aronde *f*

▸▸ *Tech* ***dovetail joint*** assemblage *m* à queue-d'aronde

dovish ['dʌvɪʃ] **ADJ** *esp Am Pol (person)* partisan de la manière douce; *(speech)* conciliateur

dowager ['daʊədʒə(r)] **N** douairière *f*; **the d. duchess** la duchesse douairière

▸▸ ***dowager's hump*** déformation *f* ostéoporotique postménopausique, bosse *f* de sorcière

dowdiness ['daʊdɪnɪs] **N** manque *m* d'élégance *ou* de distinction

dowdy ['daʊdɪ] *(compar* **dowdier**, *superl* **dowdiest**, *pl* **dowdies)** **ADJ** *(person)* sans chic, inélégant; *(dress)* peu flatteur, sans chic

dowel ['daʊəl] *Carp*

N d. (pin) cheville *f* en bois, goujon *m*

VT assembler avec des goujons, goujonner

dowelling ['daʊəlɪŋ] **N** *Carp* **1** *(act)* assemblage *m* à goujons, goujonnage *m* **2** *(wood)* tourillon *m*

dower house ['daʊə-] **N** *Br* petit manoir *m* (de douairière)

Dow-Jones [,daʊ'dʒəʊnz] *Am St Exch* **N** l'indice *m* Dow Jones

▸▸ ***the Dow-Jones average, the Dow Jones index*** l'indice *m* Dow Jones

DOWN[1] [daʊn]

PREP
- en bas de **2**
- le long de **3**
- à travers **4**

ADV
- en bas **1, 2**
- vers le bas **1, 3**
- en panne **9**

ADJ
- déprimé **1**

VT
- mettre à terre **1**
- faire tomber **1**
- descendre **1, 2**
- avaler **2**

N
- revers **1**

PREP 1 *(towards lower level of)* **a line d. the middle of the page** une ligne verticale au milieu de la page; **to go d. the steps/the mountain** descendre l'escalier/la montagne; **she fell d. the stairs** elle est tombée dans l'escalier; **tears ran d. her face** des larmes coulaient le long de son visage; **her hair hung d. her back** les cheveux lui tombaient dans le dos; **to go d. the plughole** passer par le trou (de l'évier/de la baignoire/*etc*); **the rabbit disappeared d. its hole** le lapin a disparu dans son trou; *Fam* **get that d. you** *(food, drink)* avale ça!

2 *(at lower level of)* en bas de; **it's d. the stairs** c'est en bas de l'escalier; **to work d. a mine** travailler au fond d'une mine; **they live d. the street** ils habitent plus loin *ou* plus bas dans la rue

3 *(along)* le long de; **he walked d. the street** il a descendu la rue; **look d. the corridor** regardez le long du couloir

4 *(through)* à travers; **d. (through) the ages** à travers les âges

5 *Br Fam (to)* à[□]; **they went d. the shops** ils sont partis faire des courses[□]

ADV 1 *(downwards)* vers le bas, en bas; **d.!** *(to dog)* couché!, bas les pattes!; **d. and d.** de plus en plus bas; **to come** *or* **to go d.** descendre; **my trousers keep slipping d.** mon pantalon n'arrête pas de descendre *ou* tomber; **she's paralysed from the waist d.** elle est paraplégique

2 *(on lower level)* en bas; **d. at the bottom of the hill/page** en bas de la colline/de la page; **d. there** là-bas; **I'm d. here** je suis ici en bas; **she lives three floors d.** elle habite trois étages plus bas; **his office is three doors d. on the left** *(along passage)* son bureau est trois portes plus loin sur la gauche; **the socks are in the third drawer d.** les chaussettes sont dans le troisième tiroir en partant du haut; **the blinds are d.** les stores sont baissés; **the river is d.** la rivière est basse; **I'll be d. in a minute** *(downstairs)* je descends dans un instant; **they aren't d. yet** ils ne sont pas encore descendus; **he was d. for a count of eight** il est resté à terre le temps de compter jusqu'à huit; **d. with the system!** à bas le système!

3 *(facing downwards)* vers le bas, dessous; **he was lying face d.** il était couché sur le ventre; **smooth side d.** le côté lisse dessous

4 *(reduced, lower)* **prices are d.** les prix ont baissé; *Fin* **the pound is d. two cents against the dollar** la livre a baissé de deux cents par rapport au dollar

5 *(below expected, desired level)* **the tyres are d.** *(underinflated)* les pneus sont dégonflés; *(flat)* les pneus sont à plat; **the cashier is £10 d.** il manque 10 livres au caissier; **bookings are d. on last week's** les réservations sont en baisse par rapport à la semaine dernière; *Ftbl* **we were two goals d. at half-time** on avait deux buts de retard à la mi-temps

6 *(on paper)* **get it d. in writing** *or* **on paper** mettez-le par écrit; **he's d. to speak at the conference** il est inscrit en tant qu'intervenant à la conférence

7 *(from city, the north)* **she came d. from Berlin** elle est arrivée de Berlin; **we're going d. south** nous descendons vers le sud; *Fam* **to go/to live d. under** *(gen)* aller/vivre aux antipodes[□]; *(Australia)* aller/vivre en Australie[□]; *(New Zealand)* aller/vivre en Nouvelle-Zélande[□]

8 *(in crossword)* verticalement; **I can't get five d.** je ne trouve pas le cinq vertical

9 *(out of action ▸ machine, computer)* en panne; **the lines are d.** les lignes sont coupées; **the computer has gone d.** l'ordinateur est tombé en panne

10 *(paid)* **he paid** *or* **put £5 d.** *(whole amount)* il a payé 5 livres comptant; *(as deposit)* il a versé (un acompte de) 5 livres; **5 d. and 3 to go** ça fait 5, il en reste 3

11 *(ill)* **he's (gone) d. with flu** il est au lit avec la grippe

12 *(depressed) Fam* **that gets me d.** ça me déprime

ADJ 1 *(depressed)* déprimé, malheureux; **to feel d.** avoir le cafard

2 *Fam* **he's d., but not out** il connaît des difficultés mais il s'accroche

3 *Br (train)* = en provenance d'une grande ville

4 *(elevator)* qui descend

5 *(overcritical)* **to be d. on sb** être monté contre qn[□]

VT 1 *(knock down ▸ opponent)* mettre à terre; *(▸ object, target)* faire tomber; **the pilot downed two enemy aircraft** le pilote a descendu deux avions ennemis

2 *(drink)* descendre; *(eat)* avaler; **he downed three beers** il a descendu trois bières

3 *Ind* **to d. tools** cesser le travail

N 1 *(setback)* revers *m*, bas *m*

2 *(in American football)* = chacune des quatre tentatives pour avancer d'au moins 10 yards, au football américain; **first d.** premier "down"

3 *Fam (idiom)* **to have a d. on sb** avoir une dent contre qn

• down for PREP they've got me d. for the 200m hurdles ils m'ont inscrit au 200m haies; **the meeting is d. for today** la réunion est prévue pour aujourd'hui; **she's d. for 20 boxes** *(has reserved)* elle a réservé 20 boîtes; **she's d. for £20** *(has agreed to donate)* elle est inscrite pour une cotisation de 20 livres

• down to PREP 1 *(through to and including)* jusqu'à; **she sold everything right d. to the house** elle a tout vendu, y compris la maison; **from the boss d. to the office boy** depuis le patron jusqu'au garçon de bureau; **from the Middle Ages d. to the present** du *ou* depuis le Moyen Âge jusqu'à nos jours

2 *(reduced to)* **I'm d. to my last pound** il ne me reste qu'une livre; **the team was d. to 10 men** l'équipe était réduite à 10 hommes

3 *(indicating responsibility)* **it's d. to you now** c'est à toi de jouer maintenant; **this is all d. to you!** *(your fault)* tout cela est de ta faute!; **any breakages will be d. to you** si vous cassez quelque chose, c'est vous qui paierez les dégâts ▸▸ *Comput* ***down arrow*** flèche *f* vers le bas; *Comput* ***down arrow key*** touche *f* de déplacement vers le bas; *Fin* ***down payment*** acompte *m*; **to make a d. payment on sth** verser un acompte pour qch

down[2] **N 1** *(on bird, person, plant, fruit)* duvet *m* **2 downs** *(hills)* chaîne *f* de collines crétacées

down-and-out **N** clochard(e) *m,f*
ADJ indigent, sans ressources

down-at-heel **ADJ 1** *(person)* miteux **2** *(shoe)* éculé

downbeat ['daʊnbi:t] **N** *Mus* temps *m* frappé
ADJ 1 *(gloomy ▸ person)* abattu, triste; *(▸ story)* pessimiste **2** *(relaxed ▸ person)* décontracté, flegmatique; *(▸ situation)* décontracté

downcast ['daʊnkɑ:st] **ADJ 1** *(person)* abattu, démoralisé **2** *(eyes, look)* baissé

downdraught, *Am* **downdraft** ['daʊndrɑ:ft] **N** *Met* courant *m* d'air descendant

downer ['daʊnə(r)] **N 1** *Fam (experience)* expérience *f* déprimante⌑; **to be on a d.** avoir le cafard, être déprimé⌑; **it was a real d. to find out I hadn't even got an interview** ça m'a mis le moral complètement à zéro de savoir que je n'avais même pas obtenu d'entretien **2** *Fam (drug)* tranquillisant⌑ *m*, sédatif⌑ *m*

downfall ['daʊnfɔ:l] **N 1** *(of person, institution)* chute *f*, ruine *f*; *(of dream, hopes)* effondrement *m*; *(of government)* écroulement *m*, effondrement *m*; **drink was his d.** la boisson l'a perdu **2** *(of rain, snow)* chute *f*

downgrade ['daʊngreɪd] **VT 1** *(job)* déclasser; *(employee)* rétrograder; *(hotel)* déclasser; *(goods)* classer dans une catégorie inférieure; **he was downgraded to area manager** il a été rétrogradé au rang de responsable régional; **the hurricane has been downgraded to a storm** l'ouragan n'est maintenant plus qu'une tempête **2** *(devalue ▸ role, status, significance)* dévaloriser **3** *(belittle)* rabaisser
N descente *f*

downgrading ['daʊnˌgreɪdɪŋ] **N 1** *(of job)* déclassement *m*; *(of employee)* déclassement *m* à une échelle de salaire inférieure, rétrogradation *f*; *(of hotel)* déclassement *m*; *(of goods)* classement *m* dans une catégorie inférieure **2** *(devaluing ▸ of role, status, significance)* dévalorisation *f*

downhearted [ˌdaʊn'hɑ:tɪd] **ADJ** abattu, découragé; **don't be d.!** ne te décourage pas!, ne te laisse pas abattre!

downhill [ˌdaʊn'hɪl] **ADV to go d.** *(car, road)* descendre, aller en descendant; *Fig (business)* péricliter; *Fig* **he let himself go d. after he lost his job** il a dégringolé *ou* il s'est laissé aller après avoir perdu son travail; *Fig* **her health went rapidly d.** sa santé déclina *ou* baissa rapidement
ADJ *(road)* en pente, incliné; *(walk)* en descente; *Fig* **when you get to 40, it's d. all the way** passé la quarantaine, vous ne faites plus que décliner; **it should all be d. from now on** *(be easy)* maintenant ça devrait aller comme sur des roulettes
N *(of road) & Ski* descente *f*
▸▸ *Ski* ***downhill race*** descente *f*; ***downhill racer, downhill skier*** descendeur(euse) *m,f*; ***downhill skiing*** ski *m* alpin

Downing Street ['daʊnɪŋ-] **N** Downing Street, = rue de Londres où se trouve la résidence officielle du Premier ministre britannique; **there has been no confirmation from D.** le Premier ministre n'a pas apporté de confirmation

> **DOWNING STREET**
>
> C'est à Downing Street à Londres que se trouvent les résidences officielles du Premier ministre, au n°10, et du ministre des Finances, au n°11. Le terme "Downing Street" est souvent employé pour désigner le gouvernement.

download ['daʊnləʊd] *Comput* **N** téléchargement *m*
VT télécharger
VI effectuer un téléchargement; **graphic files take a long time to d.** le téléchargement de fichiers graphiques est très lent

downloadable [ˌdaʊn'ləʊdəbəl] **ADJ** *Comput* téléchargeable; **d. font** police *f* téléchargeable

downloading [ˌdaʊn'ləʊdɪŋ] **N** *Comput* téléchargement *m*

down-low **N** *Am Fam* **on the d.** *(confidential)* confidentiel⌑

downmarket [ˌdaʊn'mɑ:kɪt] **ADJ** *(product, car)* bas de gamme; *(book)* grande diffusion *(inv)*; **it's a rather d. area** ce n'est pas un quartier très chic
ADV to move d. passer au bas de gamme

downpipe ['daʊnpaɪp] **N** *Br Constr* (tuyau *m* de) descente *f*

downplay ['daʊnpleɪ] **VT** *(event, person)* minimiser l'importance de; *(situation)* dédramatiser

downpour ['daʊnpɔ:(r)] **N** averse *f*, déluge *m*

downright ['daʊnraɪt] **ADJ 1** *(complete ▸ lie)* effronté, flagrant; *(▸ refusal)* catégorique; **d. stupidity** bêtise crasse; **a d. fool** un (une) crétin(e) achevé(e) **2** *(blunt, frank ▸ person, speech)* franc (franche), direct
ADV *(as intensifier)* franchement, carrément; **the sales assistant was d. rude** la vendeuse a été franchement grossière

Down's [daʊnz] *Fam* = **Down's Syndrome**

downshift [ˌdaʊn'ʃɪft] **VI 1** *Am Aut (change gear)* rétrograder **2** *(change lifestyle)* travailler moins pour mieux profiter de la vie

downshifting [ˌdaʊn'ʃɪftɪŋ] **N** = adoption d'un style de vie où le travail et l'argent passent après le temps libre

downside ['daʊnsaɪd] **N 1** *(underside)* dessous *m*; *Am* **d. up** sens dessous dessus **2** *(disadvantage)* inconvénient *m*; **there's a d. to everything** toute médaille a son revers; **on the d., we'll have to sleep in the train** le désavantage, c'est que nous devrons dormir dans le train
▸▸ *St Exch* ***downside risk*** risque *m* de baisse

downsize ['daʊnsaɪz] **VT 1** *(company)* réduire les effectifs de; *Suisse* redimensionner; *(project)* réduire l'envergure de **2** *(of designers ▸ car)* réduire les dimensions de **3** *Comput* micromiser
VI *(of company)* réduire ses effectifs

downsizing ['daʊnsaɪzɪŋ] **N 1** *(of company)* réduction *f* d'effectifs; *Suisse* redimensionnement *m* **2** *Comput* micromisation *f*

downspout ['daʊnspaʊt] **N** *Am* (tuyau *m* de) descente *f*

Down's syndrome [daʊnz-] **N** trisomie 21 *f*; **D. baby** bébé *m* trisomique

downstage [ˌdaʊn'steɪdʒ] **ADJ** du devant de la scène
ADV vers le devant de la scène; **d. from her** vers le devant de la scène par rapport à elle; **to stand d. of sb** se tenir plus en avant que qn sur la scène
N avant-scène *f*

downstairs **ADJ** ['daʊnˌsteəz] **1** *(gen)* en bas; **I'm using the d. phone** j'utilise le téléphone d'en bas **2** *(of lower floor)* de l'étage au-dessous *ou* inférieur; *(of ground floor)* du rez-de-chaussée
ADV [ˌdaʊn'steəz] **1** *(gen)* en bas (de l'escalier); **to come** *or* **to go d.** descendre (les escaliers); **she ran d.** elle a descendu l'escalier *ou* elle est descendue en courant; **he fell d.** il a dégringolé l'escalier **2** *(on lower floor)* à l'étage en dessous *ou* inférieur; *(on ground floor)* au rez-de-chaussée; **the family d.** la famille du dessous
N ['daʊnˌsteəz] **the d.** *(ground floor)* le rez-de-chaussée; *(lower floors)* les étages *fpl* inférieures

downstate ['daʊnsteɪt] *Am* **ADJ** *(in the country)* de la campagne; *(in the south)* du sud de l'État; **in d. New York** dans le sud de l'État de New York
ADV *(go)* vers le sud; *(be)* dans le sud

downstream **ADJ** ['daʊnˌstri:m] (situé) en aval
ADV ['daʊnˌstri:m] *(live)* en aval; *(move)* vers l'aval; **the boat drifted d.** le bateau était poussé par le courant
▸▸ *Petr* ***downstream operations*** opérations *fpl* en aval

downstroke ['daʊnstrəʊk] **N 1** *Tech (of piston)* course *f* descendante **2** *(in handwriting)* plein *m* **3** *Orn (of wing)* abaissée *f*

downswept ['daʊnswept] **ADJ** surbaissé

downswing ['daʊnswɪŋ] **N 1** *(trend)* tendance à la baisse, baisse *f* **2** *Golf* mouvement *m* descendant

down-to-earth **ADJ** *(direct)* direct; *(unpretentious)* simple; **he's very d.** *(practical)* il a les pieds sur terre

downtown ['daʊnˌtaʊn] *Am* **N** centre-ville *m*
ADJ d. New York le centre *ou* centre-ville de New York; **d. theatres** théâtres *mpl* du centre-ville
ADV en ville; **to live d.** habiter en ville; **he gave me a lift d.** il m'a descendu en ville

downtrodden ['daʊnˌtrɒdən] **ADJ 1** *(person)* opprimé **2** *(grass)* piétiné

downturn ['daʊntɜ:n] **N** *(in inflation, unemployment figures)* baisse *f*; *(in economy)* ralentissement *m*

downward ['daʊnwəd] **ADJ** *(movement)* vers le bas; *(path)* descendant; **to take a d. glance** *or* **look at sth** jeter un coup d'œil par en dessous à qch; *Fig* **a d. trend** une tendance à la baisse; **the economy is on a d. path** l'économie est sur une mauvaise pente
ADV = **downwards**
▸▸ ***downward mobility*** régression *f* sociale

downward-compatible **ADJ** *Comput* compatible vers le bas

downwards ['daʊnwədz] **ADV** vers le bas, de haut en bas; *(on river)* en aval; *(look)* en bas; **she put the letter face d.** elle a posé la lettre à l'envers; **the garden slopes d. away from the house** le jardin descend en pente depuis la maison; *Fig* **everyone from the president d.** tout le monde depuis le président jusqu'en bas de la hiérarchie; **we will have to revise our estimates d.** il faudra que nous revoyions nos estimations à la baisse; **prices started to spiral d.** les prix commencèrent à dégringoler

downwind [ˌdaʊn'wɪnd] **ADV** sous le vent; **to sail d.** naviguer sous le vent; **to be d. of sth** être sous le vent de qch

downy ['daʊnɪ] *(compar* **downier,** *superl* **downiest)** **ADJ 1** *(leaf, skin)* couvert de duvet, duveté; *(fruit)* duveté, velouté **2** *(fluffy)* duveteux

dowry ['daʊərɪ] *(pl* **dowries)** **N** *(money, property)* dot *f*

dowse [daʊz] **VT** = **douse**
VI *(for water, minerals)* faire de la radiesthésie, prospecter à la baguette

dowser ['daʊzə(r)] **N** *(for water)* sourcier *m*, radiesthésiste *mf*; *(for minerals)* radiesthésiste *mf*

dowsing ['daʊzɪŋ] **N** radiesthésie *f*
▸▸ ***dowsing rod*** baguette *f* (de sourcier)

doyen ['dɔɪən] **N** doyen *m* (d'âge)

doyenne ['dɔɪen] **N** doyenne *f* (d'âge)

doz. *(written abbr* **dozen)** douz

doze [dəʊz] **N** somme *m*; **to have a d.** faire un petit somme
VI sommeiller
▸ **doze off** **VI** s'assoupir

dozen ['dʌzən] **N** douzaine *f*; **a d. eggs** une douzaine d'œufs; **30 pence a d.** 30 pence la douzaine; **half a d.** une demi-douzaine; **by the d.** à la douzaine; **I've told you a d. times!** je te l'ai déjà dit vingt fois!; **there are dozens of men like him** des hommes comme lui, on en trouve à la douzaine

dozenth ['dʌzənθ] **ADJ** douzième; **for the d. time** pour la douzième fois

dozily ['dəʊzɪlɪ] **ADV** *(watch)* d'un œil somnolent; *(say, answer)* d'une voix endormie

doziness ['dəʊzɪnɪs] **N 1** *(drowsiness)* somnolence *f* **2** *Br Fam (stupidity)* bêtise⌑ *f*

dozy ['dəʊzɪ] *(compar* **dozier,** *superl* **doziest)** **ADJ** *(drowsy)* à moitié endormi, assoupi; **to feel d.** avoir envie de dormir **2** *Br Fam (stupid)* lent⌑, engourdi

DP [ˌdi:'pi:] **N** *Comput (abbr* **data processing)** TD *m*

DPhil [ˌdi:'fɪl] **N** *(abbr* **Doctor of Philosophy)** *(person)* = titulaire d'un doctorat de 3ème cycle; *(qualification)* doctorat *m* de 3ème cycle

dpi [ˌdi:pi:'aɪ] *Comput (abbr* **dots per inch)** dpi, ppp

DPM [ˌdi:pi:'em] **N** *(abbr* **Deputy Prime Minister)** vice-Premier-ministre *m*

DPP [ˌdiːpiːˈpiː] N *Br Law* (*abbr* **Director of Public Prosecutions**) procureur *m* général

dpt (*written abbr* **department**) service *m*

Dr 1 (*written abbr* **Doctor**) **Dr Jones** (*on envelope*) Dr Jones; **Dear Dr Jones** (*in letter*) Monsieur, Madame; (*less formal*) Cher Monsieur, Chère Madame; (*if acquainted*) Cher Docteur **2** (*written abbr* **drive**) allée *f*

drab [dræb] (*compar* **drabber**, *superl* **drabbest**) ADJ **1** (*colour*) terne, fade; (*surroundings*) morne, triste; (*existence*) terne, monotone; (*person*) insignifiant **2** (*shabby*) miteux

N **1** (*colour*) gris-vert *m*, gris-beige *m* **2** (*cloth*) grosse toile *f* bise

drably [ˈdræblɪ] ADV de façon terne; **d. coloured** aux couleurs ternes *ou* mornes

drabness [ˈdræbnɪs] N (*of colour*) caractère *m ou* aspect *m* terne, fadeur *f*; (*of surroundings*) caractère *m ou* aspect *m* morne, tristesse *f*, grisaille *f*

drachm [dræm] N **1** (*gen*) *& Pharm* drachme *m* **2** (*currency*) drachme *f*

drachma [ˈdrækmə] (*pl* **drachmas** *or* **drachmae** [-miː]) N *Formerly* (*currency*) drachme *f*

draconian [drəˈkəʊnɪən] ADJ draconien

draft¹ [drɑːft] N **1** (*of letter*) brouillon *m*; (*of novel, speech*) premier jet *m*, ébauche *f*; (*of plan, treaty*) avant-projet *m*; **this is only the first d.** ceci n'est qu'une ébauche; **the first d. of a novel** le premier jet d'un roman

2 *Com & Fin* traite *f*, effet *m*; **a d. on my bank in England for £500** une traite de 500 livres sur ma banque en Angleterre

3 *Mil* (*detachment* ▸ *of troops*) détachement *m*; (▸ *of recruits*) contingent *m*

4 *Am Mil* conscription *f*; **he left in order to avoid the d.** il est parti pour éviter de faire son service

5 *Am* (*beer*) pression *f*

VT **1** (*draw up* ▸ *first version*) faire le brouillon de, rédiger; (▸ *diagram*) dresser; (▸ *plan*) esquisser, dresser; *Law* (▸ *contract, will*) rédiger, dresser; (▸ *bill*) préparer **2** (*recruit*) détacher, désigner; **to d. sb to sth/to do sth** détacher qn à qch/pour faire qch; *Fig* **could we d. in some outside help?** est-ce que nous pourrions obtenir de l'aide à l'extérieur? **3** *Am Mil* (*enlist*) appeler (sous les drapeaux), incorporer; **he was drafted into the army** il fut appelé sous les drapeaux

COMP (*agreement*) préliminaire

▸▸ *Am Mil* **draft board** conseil *m* de révision; **draft budget** projet *m* de budget; *Am Mil* **draft card** ordre *m* d'incorporation; *Am Mil* **draft dodger** réfractaire *m*; *Am Mil* **draft dodging** insoumission *f*; **draft legislation** projet *m* d'acte législatif; **draft letter** (*gen*) brouillon *m* de lettre; (*formal*) projet *m* de lettre; *Br Comput* **draft mode** mode *m* rapide *ou* brouillon; *Br Comput* **draft quality** qualité *f* brouillon; *Comput* **draft quality printing** impression *f* en qualité brouillon; **draft treaty** projet *m* de convention; *Comput* **draft version** version *f* brouillon

draft² *Am* = **draught**

draftsman, draftsmanship *etc Am* = **draughtsman, draughtsmanship** *etc*

drafty (*compar* **draftier**, *superl* **draftiest**) *Am* = **draughty**

drag [dræg] (*pt & pp* **dragged**, *cont* **dragging**) VT **1** (*pull*) traîner, tirer; **to d. sth on** *or* **along the ground** traîner qch par terre; **he dragged me to a concert** il m'a traîné *ou* entraîné à un concert; **to d. sb out of bed** tirer qn de son lit; **to d. sb through the courts** traîner qn devant les tribunaux; **don't d. me into this!** ne me mêlez pas à vos histoires!; **to drag the truth/a confession out of sb** arracher la vérité/des aveux à qn; *Naut* **to d. anchor** chasser sur ses ancres; **to d. one's feet** traîner les pieds; *Fig* **to d. one's feet** *or* **heels (over doing sth)** tarder (à faire qch); **the government has been accused of dragging its feet** *or* **heels over the issue** on a accusé le gouvernement de montrer peu d'empressement à s'occuper de la question; **to d. sb's name through the mud** traîner qn dans la boue **2** (*search* ▸ *pond, river*) draguer; **they dragged the lake for the body** ils ont dragué le lac à la recherche du corps **3** *Comput* (*with mouse*) faire glisser

VI **1** (*trail* ▸ *skirt, coat*) traîner (par terre); *Naut* (▸ *anchor*) chasser

2 (*hang behind*) traîner, rester à l'arrière

3 (*search*) draguer (**for sth** pour retrouver qch)

4 (*go on and on*) traîner, s'éterniser; (*conversation*) languir; **the minutes dragged by** les minutes s'étiraient; **the second act dragged** le deuxième acte n'en finissait plus

5 (*smoker*) **to d. on** *or* **at a cigarette** tirer des bouffées d'une cigarette

6 *Comput* **to d. and drop** faire un glisser-lâcher

7 *Aut* (*brakes*) frotter, gripper, se gripper

N **1** (*pull*) tirage *m*; *Aviat, Aut & Naut* résistance *f*, traînée *f*

2 (*dredge*) drague *f*; (*sledge*) traîneau *m*; *Agr* (*harrow*) herse *f*; *Naut* araignée *f*

3 (*brake*) sabot *m ou* patin *m* de frein

4 (*handicap*) entrave *f*, frein *m*; **unemployment is a d. on the economy** le chômage est un frein pour l'économie

5 (*trail of fox*) piste *f*

6 *Fam* (*bore*) **he's a real d.!** quel raseur!; **the exams are a real d.!** quelle barbe ces examens!; **what a d.!** quelle barbe!, c'est la barbe!

7 *Fam* (*puff on cigarette*) bouffée *f*, taffe *f*; **I had a d. on** *or* **of his cigarette** j'ai tiré une bouffée de sa cigarette

8 *Fam* (*women's clothing*) **in d.** en travesti ᵒ

9 *Am Fam* (*street*) **the main d.** la rue principale ᵒ

10 *Am Fam* (*influence*) piston *m*; **she has a lot of d.** elle a le bras long

COMP *Fam* (*disco, show*) de travestis ᵒ

▸▸ **drag act** numéro *m* de travesti(s); **drag artist** travesti *m*; *Aviat & Aut* **drag coefficient, drag factor** coefficient *m* de traînée; **drag hunt** drag *m*; *Fam* **drag queen** travelo *m*; *Aut* **drag race** course *f* de dragsters; *Aut* **drag racing** course *f* de dragsters

▸ **drag along** VT SEP (*chair, toy*) tirer, traîner; (*person*) traîner, entraîner; **to d. oneself along** se traîner

▸ **drag apart** VT SEP séparer de force

▸ **drag away** VT SEP emmener de force; **I couldn't d. him away from his work** je ne pouvais pas l'arracher à son travail; **I couldn't d. myself away** j'étais cloué sur place

▸ **drag behind** VT SEP traîner derrière (soi)

VI être à la traîne; **stop dragging behind** arrête de traîner comme ça

▸ **drag down** VT SEP **1** (*lower*) entraîner (en bas); **being rude only drags you down to his level** être grossier ne fait que vous rabaisser à son niveau **2** (*weaken*) affaiblir; (*depress*) déprimer, décourager

▸ **drag in** VT SEP apporter (de force); **he insisted on dragging in the issue of housing** il voulait à tout prix mettre la question du logement sur le tapis

▸ **drag on** VI se prolonger, s'éterniser; **don't let the matter d. on** ne laissez pas traîner l'affaire; **the day dragged on** la journée s'éternisait *ou* n'en finissait pas

VT INSEP **to d. on a cigarette** tirer sur une cigarette

▸ **drag out** VT SEP (*prolong*) faire traîner; **to drag out talks** faire traîner des négociations

▸ **drag up** VT SEP **1** (*affair, story*) remettre sur le tapis, ressortir **2** *Br Fam* (*child*) élever à la diable *ou* tant bien que mal ᵒ; *Hum* **where were you dragged up?** où donc as-tu été élevé?

drag-and-drop N *Comput* glisser-lâcher *m*

dragging [ˈdrægɪŋ] N **1** (*pulling*) traînement *m*; *Naut* **d. of the anchor** dérapage *m* **2** (*of pond, river*) dragage *m*

ADJ **d. step** pas *m* traînant

draggy [ˈdrægɪ] (*compar* **draggier**, *superl* **draggiest**) ADJ *Br Fam* (*boring*) ennuyeux ᵒ, assommant; (*listless*) mou (molle) ᵒ, avachi ᵒ

draglift [ˈdræglɪft] N *Ski* tire-fesses *m*

dragnet [ˈdrægnet] N **1** (*for fish*) seine *f*, drège *f*; (*for game*) tirasse *f* **2** (*for criminals*) rafle *f*

dragon [ˈdrægən] N *Myth, Zool & Fig* dragon *m*; *Fam Drugs slang* **to chase the d.** chasser le dragon

▸▸ *St Exch* **dragon bond** = titre émis en Asie mais libellé en dollars américains; *Fam* **dragon's teeth** = obstacles antichars en béton

dragonfly [ˈdrægənflaɪ] (*pl* **dragonflies**) N libellule *f*

dragoon [drəˈguːn] N *Mil* dragon *m*

VT (*force*) contraindre, forcer; **he dragooned us into going** il nous a contraints *ou* forcés à y aller

dragrope [ˈdrægrəʊp] N *Aviat* guiderope *m*

dragster [ˈdrægstə(r)] N *Aut* voiture *f* à moteur gonflé, dragster *m*

drain [dreɪn] N **1** (*in house*) canalisation *f ou* tuyau *m* d'évacuation; (*of dishwasher*) tuyau *m* de vidange; (*outside house*) puisard *m*; (*sewer*) égout *m*; (*grid in street*) bouche *f* d'égout; (*in field, marshland*) fossé *m* de drainage; **to pour sth down the d.** (dé)verser qch dans les égouts; *Fig* **the family business went down the d.** l'entreprise familiale a fait faillite; **that's five years' work down the d.** voilà cinq années de travail perdues; **to laugh like a d.** rire comme une baleine **2** *Agr & Med* drain *m* **3** (*depletion*) perte *f*, épuisement *m*; **the upkeep of the house is a continual d. on their resources** l'entretien de la maison entraîne constamment des dépenses; **all that travelling was a terrible d. on him** tous ces voyages l'ont terriblement épuisé

VT **1** (*dry* ▸ *dishes, vegetables*) égoutter; (▸ *land*) drainer, assécher; (▸ *reservoir*) vider, mettre à sec; (▸ *mine*) drainer; (▸ *oil tank*) vider, vidanger; **she drained her glass** elle a vidé son verre *ou* a tout bu jusqu'à la dernière goutte; *Com* **drained weight** poids *m* net égoutté **2** *Agr & Med* drainer; **well drained soil** sol *m* bien drainé **3** (*deplete*) épuiser; **to d. sb of his/her strength** épuiser qn; **to feel drained** (*of energy*) être épuisé; (*of emotions*) être vidé; **the war drained the country of its resources** la guerre a saigné le pays

VI **1** (*colour*) disparaître; (*blood*) s'écouler; **the colour drained from her face** son visage a blêmi **2** (*dishes, vegetables*) s'égoutter; **leave the dishes to d.** laisse égoutter la vaisselle

▸ **drain away** VT SEP faire écouler

VI (*liquid*) s'écouler; (*hope, strength*) s'épuiser

▸ **drain off** VT SEP **1** (*liquid*) faire écouler; (*dishes, vegetables*) égoutter **2** *Agr & Med* drainer

VI s'écouler

drainage [ˈdreɪnɪdʒ] N (*UNCOUNT*) **1** (*process*) drainage *m*, assèchement *m*; **soil with good d.** sol *m* perméable **2** (*system* ▸ *in house*) système *m* d'évacuation des eaux; (▸ *in town*) système *m* d'égouts; (▸ *of land*) système *m* de drainage; *Geol* système *m* hydrographique **3** (*sewage*) eaux *fpl* usées, vidanges *fpl*

▸▸ *Geol* **drainage area, drainage basin** bassin *m* hydrographique; *Agr* **drainage ditch** fossé *m* d'écoulement

drainer [ˈdreɪnə(r)] N égouttoir *m*

draining [ˈdreɪnɪŋ] N (*of swamp*) drainage *m*, assèchement *m*; *Agr* (*of land*) drainage, assainissement *m*; *Med* (*of wound*) drainage

ADJ (*person, task*) épuisant

▸▸ **draining board, draining rack** égouttoir *m*

drainpipe [ˈdreɪnpaɪp] N (*from roof*) (tuyau *m* de) descente *f*; (*from sink*) tuyau *m* d'écoulement; *Agr* (*on land*) drain *m*

▸▸ *Br* **drainpipe trousers** pantalon *m* étroit

drake [dreɪk] N canard *m* (mâle)

DRAM [ˈdiːræm] N *Comput* (*abbr* **dynamic random access memory**) DRAM *f*

dram [dræm] N **1** (*gen*) *& Pharm* drachme *m* **2** *Fam* (*drop*) goutte ᵒ *f*; **a d. (of whisky)** un petit verre (de whisky) ᵒ

drama [ˈdrɑːmə] N **1** (*theatre*) théâtre *m*; **she teaches d.** elle enseigne l'art dramatique; **Spanish d.** le théâtre espagnol

2 (*play*) pièce *f* (de théâtre), drame *m*

3 (*situation*) drame *m*; *Fig* **to make a d. out of sth** faire un drame de qch

4 (*excitement*) intensité *f*; **the d. of the situation is heightened by the fact that...** l'intensité de la situation est renforcée par le fait que...; **a moment of high d.** un moment d'émotion intense; **full of d.** (*film etc*) plein de rebondissements

▸▸ **drama critic** critique *mf* dramatique *ou* de théâtre; *TV* **drama documentary** docudrame *m*; *Fam Pej* **drama queen** comédien(enne) ᵒ *m,f*; **don't be such a d. queen!** arrête ton cinéma!; **drama school** école *f* d'art dramatique, école *f* de théâtre; *TV* **drama series** série *f* dramatique; **drama student** étudiant(e) *m,f* en art dramatique

> Note that the French word **drame** also means **tragedy, disaster.**

dramadoc ['drɑːmədɒk] **N** *TV* docudrame *m*

dramatic [drə'mætɪk] **ADJ 1** *Literature, Mus & Theat* dramatique; **the d. works of Racine** le théâtre de Racine **2** *Fig (theatrical ▸ effect, entry)* théâtral, dramatique; *(▸ gesture, effect)* théâtral; *(spectacular ▸ change)* remarquable, spectaculaire; *(rise in prices)* spectaculaire, vertigineux; *(▸ scenery)* spectaculaire, grandiose; **there's no need to be so d. about it** ce n'est pas la peine d'en faire un drame *ou* toute une histoire; **the story took a d. turn** l'histoire prit un tour dramatique

> Note that the most common meaning of the French word **dramatique is tragic.**

dramatically [drə'mætɪklɪ] **ADV 1** *Literature, Mus & Theat* du point de vue théâtral **2** *Fig (act, speak)* de façon théâtrale; *(change, increase, drop)* de manière spectaculaire

> Note that the French word **dramatiquement** is a false friend and is never a translation for the English word **dramatically.**

dramatics [drə'mætɪks] **N** *(UNCOUNT) Theat* art *m* dramatique, dramaturgie *f*

NPL *Fig (behaviour)* comédie *f*, cirque *m*; *Pej* **this is no time for d.** ce n'est pas le moment de jouer la comédie *ou* de faire ton cinéma

dramatis personae [ˌdrə'mætɪsˌpɜː'səʊnaɪ] **NPL** *Literature & Theat* personnages *mpl (d'une pièce ou d'un roman)*

dramatist ['dræmətɪst] **N** auteur *m* dramatique, dramaturge *mf*

dramatization, -isation [ˌdræmətaɪ'zeɪʃən] **N 1** *(for theatre)* adaptation *f* pour la scène; *(for film)* adaptation *f* pour l'écran; *(for television)* adaptation *f* pour la télévision **2** *(exaggeration)* dramatisation *f*

dramatize, -ise ['dræmətaɪz] **VT 1** *(for theatre)* adapter pour la scène; *(for film)* adapter pour l'écran; *(for television)* adapter pour la télévision **2** *(exaggerate)* faire un drame de, dramatiser; *(make dramatic)* rendre dramatique

VI dramatiser; **he tends to d.** il a tendance à dramatiser

dramedy ['drɑːmədɪ] **N** *TV* comédie *f* dramatique, dramédie *f*

drank [dræŋk] *pt of* **drink**

drape [dreɪp] **N** *(way something hangs)* drapé *m*

VT 1 *(adorn ▸ person, window)* draper; *(▸ altar, room)* tendre; **the stage was draped with** *or* **in black** la scène était tendue de noir **2** *(hang)* étendre; **she draped a leg over the chair arm** elle a étendu sa jambe sur l'accoudoir; **he draped himself over the sofa** il s'est allongé langoureusement sur le canapé

• **drapes NPL** *Br (drapery)* tentures *fpl*; *Am (curtains)* rideaux *mpl*

draper ['dreɪpə(r)] **N** *Br* marchand(e) *m,f* de tissus

drapery ['dreɪpərɪ] *(pl* **draperies) N 1** *(UNCOUNT) (material)* étoffes *fpl*; *(arrangement of material)* draperie *f* **2** *(usu pl) (hangings)* tentures *fpl*; *(curtains)* rideaux *mpl* **3** *Br (shop)* magasin *m* de tissus

drastic ['dræstɪk] **ADJ** *(measures)* sévère, draconien; *(change, effect)* radical; *(remedy)* énergique; *(decline, rise, improvement)* dramatique; **d. cutbacks** coupes *fpl* sombres; *Com* **d. reductions** réductions *fpl* massives; **to take d. steps** trancher dans le vif, prendre des mesures draconiennes *ou* énergiques; **that's a bit d.** *(of proposal etc)* c'est un peu exagéré

drastically ['dræstɪklɪ] **ADV** radicalement; *(cut, reduce)* radicalement, sévèrement; **prices rose d.** les prix ont augmenté considérablement; **d. reduced prices** prix *mpl* cassés

drat [dræt] **EXCLAM** *Fam* diable!, bon sang!; **oh, d.!** bon sang!, nom de nom!

dratted ['drætɪd] **ADJ** *Fam* sacré, fichu; **where's that d. brother of mine?** mais où est passé mon frangin?

draught, *Am* **draft** [drɑːft] **N 1** *(breeze)* courant *m* d'air; **I can feel a d.** je suis dans un courant d'air; *Fig Fam* **we're (all) feeling the d.** les choses vont mal (pour tout le monde)

2 *(in fireplace)* tirage *m*

3 *(drink ▸ swallow)* trait *m*, gorgée *f*; **a d. of water** une gorgée d'eau

4 *(medicine)* potion *f*, breuvage *m*

5 on d. *(beer)* à la pression

6 *(in game)* pion *m (de jeu de dames)*

7 *(pulling)* traction *f*, tirage *m*; *Naut (of ship)* tirant *m* (d'eau)

ADJ *(horse)* de trait

▸▸ ***draught beer*** bière *f* pression; *Br* ***draught excluder*** bourrelet *m* (de porte)

draughtboard ['drɑːftbɔːd] **N** *Br* damier *m*

draught-proof VT calfeutrer

ADJ calfeutré

draught-proofing [-'pruːfɪŋ] **N** calfeutrage *m*

draughts [drɑːfts] **N** *Br (game)* (jeu *m* de) dames *fpl*; **a game of d.** un jeu de dames; **to play d.** jouer aux dames

draughtsman, *Am* **draftsman** ['drɑːftsmən] *(Br pl* **draughtsmen** [-mən], *Am pl* **draftsmen** [-mən]) **N 1** *(artist)* dessinateur(trice) *m,f*; *Archit & Ind* dessinateur(trice) *m,f* industriel(elle) **2** *Br (in game)* pion *m (de jeu de dames)*

draughtsmanship, *Am* **draftsmanship** ['drɑːftsmənʃɪp] **N** *(of artist)* talent *m* de dessinateur, coup *m* de crayon; *(of work)* art *m* du dessin

draughtswoman, *Am* **draftswoman** ['drɑːftsˌwʊmən] *(Br pl* **draughtswomen** [-wɪmɪn], *Am pl* **draftswomen** [-wɪmɪn]) **N** dessinatrice *f*; *Archit & Ind* dessinatrice *f* industrielle

draughty, *Am* **drafty** ['drɑːftɪ] *(Br compar* **draughtier,** *superl* **draughtiest,** *Am compar* **draftier,** *superl* **draftiest) ADJ** *(house, room)* plein de courants d'air; *(street, corner)* exposé à tous les vents *ou* aux quatre vents

DRAW [drɔː]

VT	
• dessiner **1**	• tirer **2–4, 7, 9**
• conduire **5**	• attirer **6**
• gagner **8**	• établir **9**
VI	
• tirer **2, 5**	• tirer au sort **3**
• dessiner **4**	• être ex æquo **7**
• faire match nul **7**	
N	
• loterie **3**	• tirage (au sort) **3**
• attraction **4**	• match nul **5**

(pt **drew** [druː], *pp* **drawn** [drɔːn])

VT 1 *(sketch)* dessiner; *(line, triangle)* tracer; *(map)* faire; **to d. a picture of sb** faire le portrait de qn; **he drew us a map of the village** il nous a fait un plan du village; *Fig* **the author has drawn his characters well** l'auteur a bien dépeint ses personnages; *Fig* **I d. the line at lying** je refuse de mentir; *(referring to other people)* je ne tolère pas le mensonge; *Fig* **you have to d. the line somewhere** il faut fixer des limites, il y a des limites; *Fig* **he doesn't know where to d. the line** il ne sait pas où s'arrêter

2 *(pull)* tirer; **to d. the curtains** *(open)* tirer *ou* ouvrir les rideaux; *(shut)* tirer *ou* fermer les rideaux; **he drew the blankets round him** il a tiré les couvertures autour de lui; **he drew his hand wearily across his forehead** il se passa la main sur le front avec lassitude; **she drew his hand towards her** elle approcha sa main de la sienne; **to d. a bow** *(in archery)* tirer à l'arc

3 *(haul, pull behind ▸ car)* tirer, traîner, remorquer; *(▸ trailer)* remorquer; **a carriage drawn by two horses** un équipage attelé à *ou* tiré par deux chevaux

4 *(take out)* tirer, retirer; *(remove)* retirer, enlever; *(tooth)* arracher, extraire; **he drew his knife from** *or* **out of his pocket** il a tiré son couteau de sa poche; **the thief drew a gun on us** le voleur a sorti un pistolet et l'a braqué sur nous; **to d. a sword** dégainer une épée; **he drew the winning number** il a tiré le numéro gagnant; **to d. lots** tirer au sort

5 *(lead)* conduire, entraîner; **she drew me towards the door** elle m'a entraîné vers la porte; *Fig* **I was drawn into the controversy** j'ai été mêlé à *ou* entraîné dans la dispute; **the senator refused to be drawn** *(refused to answer)* le sénateur refusa de répondre; *(refused to be provoked)* le sénateur refusa de réagir

6 *(attract, elicit)* attirer; **to be drawn to sb** être attiré par qn; **his remarks drew a lot of criticism** ses observations lui ont attiré de nombreuses critiques; **to d. sb's attention to sth** faire remarquer qch à qn; *Fig* **to d. the enemy's fire** attirer le feu de l'ennemi sur soi; **to d. blood** *(weapon)* faire couler le sang; *(dog)* mordre jusqu'au sang; *(cat)* griffer jusqu'au sang; *Fig (remark, criticism)* avoir un effet dévastateur; **to d. a crowd** *(incident)* créer un attroupement; *(of play)* attirer le public

7 *(take from source)* tirer, puiser; **to d. water from a well** puiser de l'eau dans un puits; **to d. (out) money from the bank** retirer de l'argent à la banque; *Fin* **to d. a cheque on one's account** tirer un chèque sur son compte **we barely had time to d. (a) breath** nous avons à peine eu le temps de souffler; **our members are drawn from all walks of life** nos membres appartiennent à tous les milieux; **his confession drew tears from his mother** son aveu a arraché des larmes à sa mère; **I d. comfort from the fact that he didn't suffer** je me console en me disant qu'il n'a pas souffert; **Cézanne drew inspiration from the French countryside** Cézanne s'est inspiré de *ou* a tiré inspiration de la campagne française; *Cards* **to d. trumps** faire tomber les atouts

8 *(earn ▸ amount, salary)* gagner, toucher; *(▸ pension)* toucher; *Fin (▸ interest)* rapporter

9 *(formulate ▸ comparison, parallel, distinction)* établir, faire; *(▸ conclusion)* tirer

10 *(disembowel)* vider

11 *(tie)* **the game was drawn** *Sport* ils ont fait match nul; *Cards* ils ont fait partie nulle

12 *Hunt (game)* débusquer; *(covert)* battre

13 *Med (abscess)* crever, percer

14 *Naut* **the ocean liner draws 8 metres** le paquebot a un tirant d'eau de 8 mètres

15 *Tech (metal)* étirer; *(wire)* tréfiler

VI 1 *(move)* **the crowd drew to one side** la foule s'est rangée sur le côté *ou* s'est écartée; **the bus drew into the coach station** l'autocar est arrivé *ou* entré dans la gare routière; **the leading runner drew ahead of the others** le coureur de tête a pris de l'avance sur les *ou* s'est détaché des autres; **to d. to a halt** s'arrêter; **the police car drew alongside and signalled him to stop** la voiture de police a roulé à sa hauteur et lui a fait signe d'arrêter; **to d. near** *(elections, Christmas)* approcher; **they drew nearer to us** ils se sont approchés un peu plus de nous; **to d. to an end** *or* **to a close** tirer *ou* toucher à sa fin

2 *(pull out gun)* tirer; **the policeman drew and fired** le policier a dégainé *ou* sorti son pistolet et a tiré

3 *(choose at random)* tirer au sort; **they drew for partners** ils ont tiré au sort leurs partenaires

4 *(sketch)* dessiner

5 *(fireplace, pipe)* tirer; *(pump, vacuum cleaner)* aspirer

6 *(tea)* infuser

7 *Sport (be equal ▸ two competitors)* être ex æquo *(inv)*; *(▸ two teams)* faire match nul; **Italy drew against Spain** l'Italie et l'Espagne ont fait match nul; **they drew two all** ils ont fait deux partout

N 1 *(act of pulling)* **to be quick on the d.** dégainer vite, avoir la détente rapide; *Fig* avoir de la repartie; **to beat sb to the d.** dégainer plus vite que qn; *Fig* devancer qn

2 *(card)* carte *f* tirée; **it's your d.** c'est à vous de tirer une carte

3 *(raffle, lottery)* loterie *f*, tombola *f*; *(selection of winners, competitors)* tirage *m* (au sort); **the d. will take place tonight** le tirage aura lieu ce soir

4 *(attraction)* attraction *f*; **the polar bears are the main d. at the zoo** les ours polaires sont la grande attraction du zoo; **the show proved to be a big d.** le spectacle s'est révélé être un grand succès

5 *Sport* match *m* nul; *Cards* partie *f* nulle; **the chess tournament ended in a d.** le tournoi d'échecs s'est terminé par une partie nulle; **a one–all/nil–nil d.** un match nul un à un/zéro à zéro; **it's a d. so far** pour l'instant, ils sont à égalité

6 *Am (gully)* ravine *f*, *(drain)* rigole *f*

7 *Br Fam Drugs slang (cannabis)* shit *m*

▸ **draw apart VT SEP** prendre à l'écart

VI se séparer; **they drew apart when I entered the room** ils se sont éloignés *ou* écartés l'un de l'autre quand je suis entré dans la pièce

▸**draw aside** VT SEP *(person)* prendre *ou* tirer à l'écart; *(thing)* écarter
VI s'écarter, se ranger

▸**draw away** VI **1** *(move away ▸ person)* s'éloigner, s'écarter; *(▸ vehicle)* s'éloigner, démarrer **2** *(move ahead)* prendre de l'avance

▸**draw back** VT SEP **1** *(pull back ▸ person)* faire reculer; *(▸ one's hand, thing)* retirer; **to d. back the curtains** ouvrir les rideaux **2** *(attract back)* **I'm increasingly being drawn back to folk music** je reviens de plus en plus à la musique folk
VI **1** *(move backwards)* reculer, se reculer, avoir un mouvement de recul **2** *(avoid commitment)* se retirer; **to d. back from making a decision** ne pas vouloir prendre une décision

▸**draw in** VT SEP **1** *(claws)* rentrer
2 *(involve)* impliquer, mêler; **he drew me into the conversation** il m'a mêlé à la conversation; **I got drawn into the project** je me suis laissé impliquer dans le projet; **he listened to the debate but refused to be drawn in** il a écouté le débat mais a refusé d'y participer *ou* de s'y joindre
3 *(attract)* attirer; **the film is drawing in huge crowds** le film fait de grosses recettes
4 *(sketch)* ébaucher
5 *(air)* aspirer, respirer; **to d. in a deep breath** respirer profondément
VI **1** *(move)* **the train drew in** le train est entré en gare; **the bus drew in to the kerb** *(pulled over)* le bus s'est rapproché du trottoir; *(stopped)* le bus s'est arrêté le long du trottoir **2** *(day, evening)* diminuer, raccourcir; **the nights are drawing in** les nuits raccourcissent *ou* diminuent

▸**draw off** VT SEP **1** *Br (remove ▸ clothing)* enlever, ôter; *(▸ gloves)* retirer, ôter **2** *(liquid)* tirer; **to d. off blood** faire une prise de sang

▸**draw on** VT SEP *Br* **1** *(put on ▸ gloves, trousers, socks)* enfiler **2** *(entice, encourage)* encourager, entraîner
VT INSEP **1** *(as source)* faire appel à; **I drew on my own experiences for the novel** je me suis inspiré *ou* servi de mes propres expériences pour mon roman; **I had to d. on my savings** j'ai dû prendre *ou* tirer sur mes économies **2** *(suck) (pipe, cigarette)* tirer sur
VI *(time ▸ come near)* approcher; *(▸ go past)* avancer; **as the evening drew on** au fur et à mesure que le soir avançait; **winter was drawing on** l'hiver approchait

▸**draw out** VT SEP **1** *(remove)* sortir, retirer, tirer; *(money)* retirer; **how much money did you d. out (of the bank)?** combien d'argent as-tu retiré (de la banque)?
2 *(extend ▸ sound, visit)* prolonger; *(▸ meeting, speech)* prolonger, faire traîner; *Tech (▸ metal)* étirer; *(▸ wire)* tréfiler
3 *(cause to speak freely)* faire parler; **she has a way of drawing people out** elle sait faire parler les gens, elle sait faire sortir les gens de leur coquille
4 *(information, secret)* soutirer
VI *(vehicle)* sortir, s'éloigner; **the train drew out (of the station)** le train est sorti de la gare; *Aut* **to d. out in order to overtake** déboîter pour doubler

▸**draw together** VT SEP *(people, objects)* rassembler, réunir; **the child's illness had drawn them together** la maladie de l'enfant les avait rapprochés
VI se rassembler

▸**draw up** VT SEP **1** *Br (pull up)* tirer; **I drew the covers up around my neck** j'ai ramené les couvertures autour de mon cou; **to d. a boat up (on the beach)** tirer un bateau à sec; **she drew herself up (to her full height)** elle s'est redressée (de toute sa hauteur) **2** *Br (move closer ▸ chair)* approcher; *Mil (troops)* aligner, ranger; **d. your chair up to the table** approche ta chaise de la table **3** *(formulate ▸ deed, document, will)* dresser, rédiger; *(▸ bill, list)* dresser, établir; *(▸ plan)* préparer, établir; *(▸ budget, itinerary)* établir
VI *Br* **1** *(move)* se diriger; **the other boat drew up alongside us** l'autre bateau est arrivé à notre hauteur *ou* à côté de nous **2** *(stop ▸ vehicle)* s'arrêter, stopper; *(▸ person)* s'arrêter

drawback ['drɔːbæk] N **1** *(disadvantage)* inconvénient *m*, désavantage *m*; **the main d. to the plan is its cost** le principal inconvénient du projet est son coût **2** *Admin* drawback *m*

drawbar ['drɔːbɑː(r)] N *Aut* barre *f* d'attelage

drawbridge ['drɔːbrɪdʒ] N pont-levis *m*, pont *m* basculant *ou* à bascule

drawcord ['drɔːkɔːd] N *(of curtains)* cordon *m*

drawdown ['drɔːdaʊn] N **1** *Fin* tirage *m* **2** *(in a reservoir)* abaissement *m* du niveau

drawee [drɔː'iː] N *Banking & Fin* tiré *m*

drawer N **1** [drɔː(r)] *(in chest, desk)* tiroir *m* **2** [drɔː(r)] *Banking & Fin (of cheque)* tireur *m*; *(of bill)* souscripteur *m*; **to refer a cheque to d.** refuser d'honorer un chèque **3** ['drɔːə(r)] *(of pictures)* dessinateur(trice) *m,f*; **she's a good d.** *(of child, amateur)* elle dessine bien
▸▸ ***drawer liner*** = feuille de papier servant à tapisser les fonds de tiroirs

drawers [drɔːz] NPL *Old-fashioned (for men)* caleçon *m*; *(for women)* culotte *f*

drawing ['drɔːɪŋ] N **1** *(picture)* dessin *m*; **to make a d. of sth** dessiner qch; **to study d.** étudier le dessin; **a pen d.** un dessin à la plume **2** *Metal (shaping, tapering)* étirage *m* **3** *Culin (of poultry)* vidage *m*
COMP *(paper, table)* à dessin; *(lesson, teacher)* de dessin
▸▸ ***drawing board*** planche *f* à dessin; *Fig* **still on the d. board** *(plan, project)* encore à l'étude; **it's back to the d. board** il faudra tout recommencer; ***drawing book*** cahier *m* de dessin; ***drawing card*** *Com* valeur *f* sûre; *Am Fig (of festival etc)* attraction *f*, clou *m*; ***drawing off*** *(of liquid)* soutirage *m*; *Br* ***drawing pin*** punaise *f (à papier)*; *Fin* ***drawing rights*** droits *mpl* de tirage; ***drawing room*** *(living room)* salon *m*; *(reception room)* salle *f ou* salon *m* de réception; ***drawing up*** *(of deed, document, will)* rédaction *f*; *(of constitution, plan)* élaboration *f*; *(of bill, list, budget, plan, itinerary)* établissement *m*

drawl [drɔːl] N débit *m* traînant, voix *f* traînante; **a Southern d.** un accent du sud des États-Unis
VI parler d'une voix traînante
VT dire d'une voix traînante

drawling ['drɔːlɪŋ] ADJ *(voice, tone)* traînant
N = affectation de langueur dans le débit; **his d. gets on my nerves** sa voix traînante me porte sur les nerfs

drawn [drɔːn] *pp of* **draw**
ADJ **1** *(blind, curtain)* fermé, tiré **2** *(face, features)* tiré; **he looked tired and d.** il avait l'air fatigué et avait les traits tirés **3** *Sport & Cards (match, game)* nul
▸▸ *Sewing* ***drawn (thread) work*** ouvrage *m* à jours

drawsheet ['drɔːʃiːt] N alaise *f*

drawstring ['drɔːstrɪŋ] N cordon *m*; **d. hood** capuche *f* à lien coulissant; **d. trousers, trousers with a d. waist** pantalon *m* à taille coulissante

dray [dreɪ] N *(for barrels)* haquet *m*; *(for stones, wood)* binard *m*, fardier *m*

drayhorse ['dreɪhɔːs, *pl* -hɔːsɪz] N cheval *m* de roulage

drayman ['dreɪmən] *(pl* **draymen** [-mən]) N conducteur *m* de haquet

DRC [ˌdiːɑː'siː] N *(abbr* **Democratic Republic of Congo)** **the D.** la RDC

dread [dred] N terreur *f*, effroi *m*; **I have a d. of dentists** j'ai la hantise des dentistes; **she lives in d. of her ex-husband** elle vit dans la crainte de son ex-mari; **she waited in d. for the phone to ring** angoissée, elle attendait que le téléphone sonne
VT craindre, redouter; **I'm dreading Monday** je redoute la journée de lundi; **she's dreading the journey** elle redoute *ou* elle appréhende le voyage; **I d. to think!** je n'ose même pas y penser!; **I d. to think of what might happen** je n'ose pas imaginer ce qui pourrait arriver
ADJ redoutable, effrayant

dreadful ['dredfʊl] ADJ **1** *(terrible ▸ crime, pain)* affreux, épouvantable; *(▸ enemy, weapon)* redoutable; **how d.!** quelle horreur!; **I'm a d. dancer** je danse atrocement mal; **to be d. at maths** être nul en maths **2** *(unpleasant)* atroce, affreux; **what a d. child!** cet enfant est insupportable!; **they said some d. things about her** ils ont raconté des horreurs sur son compte; **I feel d.** *(ill)* je ne me sens pas du tout bien; *(embarrassed)* je suis vraiment gêné **3** *(as intensifier)* **he's a d. bore!** c'est un casse-pieds insupportable!, c'est un horrible casse-pieds!; **what a d. waste!** quel affreux gaspillage!

dreadfully ['dredfʊlɪ] ADV **1** *(very)* terriblement; **d. ugly** affreusement laid; **he was d. afraid** il avait horriblement peur *ou* une peur atroce; **I'm d. sorry** je regrette infiniment *ou* énormément; **his handwriting is d. untidy** son écriture est terriblement mauvaise, il écrit horriblement mal **2** *(badly)* affreusement; **the children behaved d.** les enfants se sont affreusement mal comportés; **she suffers d. from backache** son dos la fait atrocement souffrir

dreadlocks ['dredlɒks] NPL dreadlocks *fpl*

dream [driːm] *(pt & pp* **dreamt** [dremt] *or* **dreamed)** VI **1** *(in sleep)* rêver; **to d. of** *or* **about sb/sth** rêver de qn/qch; **it can't be true, I must be dreaming** ce n'est pas vrai, je rêve **2** *(daydream)* rêvasser, rêver; **he's always dreaming** il est toujours dans la lune; **for years she'd dreamt of having a cottage in the country** elle rêvait depuis des années d'avoir un cottage à la campagne; *Fam* **d. on!** tu peux toujours rêver! **3** *(imagine)* **to d. of doing sth** songer à faire qch; **don't tell anyone – I wouldn't d. of it!** ne le dis à personne – jamais je ne songerais à faire une chose pareille!; **she'd never d. of complaining** jamais elle ne songerait à se plaindre
VT **1** *(in sleep)* rêver; **he dreamt a d.** il a fait un rêve; **she dreamt we were in Spain** elle a rêvé que nous étions en Espagne; **you must have dreamt it** vous avez dû le rêver **2** *(imagine)* songer, imaginer; **I never dreamt you would take me seriously** je n'aurais jamais pensé que tu me prendrais au sérieux
N **1** *(during sleep)* rêve *m*; **to have a d. about sb/sth** rêver de qn/qch; **to see sth in a d.** voir qch en rêve; **the child had a bad d.** l'enfant a fait un mauvais rêve *ou* un cauchemar; **sweet dreams!** faites de beaux rêves!
2 *(wish, fantasy)* rêve *m*, désir *m*; **the woman of his dreams** la femme de ses rêves; **her d. was to become a pilot** elle rêvait de devenir pilote; **a job beyond my wildest dreams** un travail comme je n'ai jamais osé imaginer *ou* qui dépasse tous mes rêves; **even in her wildest dreams she never thought she'd win first prize** même dans ses rêves les plus fous, elle n'avait jamais pensé remporter le premier prix; **the American d.** le rêve américain; **may all your dreams come true** que tous vos rêves se réalisent; **the holiday was like a d. come true** les vacances étaient comme un rêve devenu réalité; *Fam* **in your dreams!** tu peux toujours rêver!
3 *(marvel)* merveille *f*; **it worked like a d.** cela a réussi à merveille; **my interview went like a d.** mon entretien s'est passé à merveille; **this car goes like a d.** cette voiture marche à merveille; *Fam* **a d. of a house** une maison de rêve
4 *(daydream)* rêverie *f*, rêve *m*; **he's always in a d.** il est toujours dans les nuages *ou* en train de rêver
COMP *(car, person, house)* de rêve
▸▸ *Cin* ***dream sequence*** séquence *f* onirique; ***dream team*** dream team *f*; *Pol* ***the dream ticket*** *(policies)* le programme utopique *ou* à faire rêver; *(candidates)* le couple idéal; ***a dream world*** *(ideal)* un monde utopique; *(imaginary)* un monde imaginaire; **she lives in a d. world** elle vit dans les nuages

▸**dream away** VT SEP passer *ou* perdre en rêveries; **he'll d. his whole life away** il passera sa vie à rêver

▸**dream up** VT SEP imaginer, inventer, concocter; **some wonderful new scheme that the government has dreamt up** encore un de ces merveilleux projets concoctés par le gouvernement; **where did you d. that up?** où es-tu allé pêcher ça?

dreamboat ['driːmbəʊt] N *Fam Old-fashioned* *(man)* beau gosse *m*

dreamer ['driːmə(r)] N rêveur(euse) *m,f*; *(idealist)* rêveur(euse) *m,f*, utopiste *mf*; *Pej* songe-creux *m inv*

dreamily ['dri:mılı] **ADV** *(act)* d'un air rêveur *ou* songeur; *(speak)* d'un ton rêveur *ou* songeur; *(wander)* comme dans un rêve; *(absent-mindedly)* d'un air absent

dreaming ['dri:mıŋ] **N** rêves *mpl*; **this d. will get you nowhere** ça ne te mènera à rien de rêver comme ça

dreamland ['dri:mlænd] **N** pays *m* imaginaire *ou* des rêves *ou* des songes

dreamless ['dri:mlıs] **ADJ** sans rêves

dreamlessly ['dri:mlıslı] **ADV** *(sleep)* d'un sommeil sans rêves

dreamlike ['dri:mlaık] **ADJ** irréel, onirique; **the music/the play has a d. quality** la musique/la pièce a quelque chose d'irréel

dreamt [dremt] *pt & pp of* **dream**

dreamy ['dri:mı] *(compar* **dreamier**, *superl* **dreamiest)** **ADJ 1** *(vague ▸ person)* rêveur, songeur; *(▸ expression)* rêveur; *(absent-minded)* rêveur, distrait; **the d. look in her eye** son regard rêveur

2 *(impractical ▸ person)* utopique, rêveur; *(▸ idea)* chimérique, utopique

3 *(music, voice)* langoureux

4 *Fam (wonderful)* magnifique▫, ravissant▫

drearily ['drıərəlı] **ADV** tristement; **d. furnished** tristement meublé; **the storyline is d. predictable** l'intrigue n'est que trop prévisible

dreariness ['drıərınıs] **N** *(of surroundings)* aspect *m* morne *ou* terne, monotonie *f*; *(of life)* monotonie *f*, tristesse *f*; **the d. of the weather** la grisaille

dreary ['drıərı] *(compar* **drearier**, *superl* **dreariest)** **ADJ** *(surroundings)* morne, triste; *(life)* morne, monotone; *(work, job)* monotone, ennuyeux; *(person)* ennuyeux (comme la pluie); *(weather)* maussade, morne

dreck [drek] **N** *(UNCOUNT) Am very Fam (rubbish)* ordures *fpl*; *(excrement)* merde *f*

dredge [dredʒ] **VT 1** *(river)* draguer; **they dredged the river for the body** ils ont dragué le fleuve à la recherche du corps **2** *Culin (with flour, sugar)* saupoudrer

N *Naut* drague *f*

▸ **dredge up VT SEP** draguer; *Fig (scandal, unpleasant news)* déterrer, ressortir; **to d. sth up out of one's memory** ressortir qch de sa mémoire; **where did you d. these old photographs up from?** où as-tu été repêcher ces vieilles photos?

dredger ['dredʒə(r)] **N 1** *Naut (ship)* dragueur *m*; *(machine)* drague *f* **2** *Culin* saupoudreuse *f*, saupoudroir *m*

dredging ['dredʒıŋ] **N** *Naut (of river)* dragage *m*

dregs [dregz] **NPL** *also Fig* lie *f*; **she drank the tea down to the d.** elle a bu le thé jusqu'à la dernière goutte; **the d. of society** la lie *ou* les bas-fonds *mpl* de la société

drench [drentʃ] **VT 1** *(soak)* tremper, mouiller; **to get drenched (with rain)** se faire tremper, *Fam* se faire saucer; **drenched to the skin** trempé jusqu'aux os; **to be drenched with sweat** être en nage; *Fig* **she had drenched herself with perfume** elle s'était aspergée de parfum **2** *Vet* donner *ou* faire avaler un médicament à

N *Vet* (dose *f* de) médicament *m*

drenching ['drentʃıŋ] **N** trempage *m*

ADJ d. rain pluie *f* battante *ou* diluvienne

Dresden ['drezdən] **N 1** *(city)* Dresde **2** *(china)* porcelaine *f* de Saxe, saxe *m*; **a piece of D. china** un saxe

dress [dres] **N 1** *(frock)* robe *f*; **a cotton/summer d.** une robe de coton/d'été **2** *(clothing)* habillement *m*, tenue *f* **3** *(style of dress)* tenue *f*, toilette *f*; **formal/informal d.** tenue *f* de cérémonie/de ville; **in Indian d.** en tenue indienne; **to wear Western d.** s'habiller à l'occidentale; **in full d.** *(of men)* en grande tenue; *(of women)* en grande toilette; *Mil* en grande tenue, en uniforme de parade; **to have good d. sense** savoir s'habiller; **she's got no d. sense** elle ne sait pas s'habiller

VT 1 *(clothe)* habiller; **she dressed herself** *or* **got dressed** elle s'est habillée; **to be dressed in black/silk** être vêtu de noir/soie; **dressed in rags** vêtu *ou* couvert de haillons; **dressed as a clown/a witch** *(for a party)* déguisé en clown/en sorcière; *Fam* **dressed to kill** sur son trente et un

2 *(arrange ▸ gen)* orner, parer; *(▸ shop window)* faire la vitrine de; *(▸ ship)* pavoiser; *(groom ▸ horse)* panser; *(▸ hair)* coiffer

3 *(wound)* panser; **he dressed my wound** il a fait mon pansement

4 *Culin (salad)* assaisonner, garnir; *(meat, fish)* parer; **dressed chicken** poulet *m* prêt à cuire; **dressed crab** crabe *m* tout préparé pour la table

5 *(treat ▸ cloth, skins)* préparer, apprêter; *(▸ leather)* corroyer; *(▸ stone)* tailler, dresser; *(▸ metal)* polir; *(▸ timber)* dégrossir

6 *(bush, tree)* tailler; *(woods)* dégrossir

7 *Agr (field)* façonner

8 *Mil (troops)* aligner; **to d. ranks** se mettre en rangs

9 *(neuter ▸ animal)* dresser

VI 1 *(get dressed, wear clothes)* s'habiller; **she always dresses very smartly** elle s'habille toujours avec beaucoup d'élégance; **to d. for dinner** *(gen)* se mettre en tenue de soirée; *(man)* se mettre en smoking; *(woman)* se mettre en robe du soir; **do we have to d. for dinner?** est-ce qu'il faut s'habiller pour le dîner? **2** *Mil (soldiers)* s'aligner

▸▸ *Theat* ***dress circle*** premier balcon *m*, corbeille *f*; ***dress coat*** habit *m*, queue-de-pie *f*; ***dress code*** code *m* vestimentaire; ***dress designer*** modéliste *mf*, dessinateur(trice) *m,f* de mode; *(famous)* couturier *m*; ***dress material*** tissu *m* pour robes; *Theat* ***dress rehearsal*** (répétition *f*) générale *f*; *Fig (practice)* répétition *f* générale; ***dress shield*** dessous-de-bras *m inv*; ***dress shirt*** chemise *f* de soirée; ***dress size*** taille *f*; **I want to drop a d. size** je veux perdre une taille (de vêtements); **she's gone up two d. sizes** elle a grossi de deux tailles (de vêtements); ***dress suit*** habit *m*, tenue *f* de soirée; *Mil* ***dress uniform*** tenue *f* de cérémonie

▸ **dress down** *Br* **VT SEP 1** *Fam (scold)* passer un savon à **2** *(make less smart)* donner un aspect plus décontracté à; **you could d. down your suit by wearing a T-shirt under it** tu pourrais donner un aspect plus décontracté à ton costume en portant un tee-shirt en dessous

VI s'habiller simplement

▸ **dress up VI 1** *(put on best clothes)* s'habiller, se mettre sur son trente et un **2** *(put on disguise)* se déguiser, se costumer; **she dressed up as a clown** elle s'est déguisée en clown

VT SEP 1 *(put on best clothes)* habiller; **to be all dressed up, to be dressed up to the nines** être sur son trente et un

2 *(disguise)* déguiser; **his mother had dressed him up as a soldier** sa mère l'avait déguisé en soldat

3 *(smarten)* rendre plus habillé

4 *(embellish)* orner; **you could d. up the outfit with a nice scarf** tu pourrais rendre la tenue plus habillée avec un joli foulard; **it's the same old clichés dressed up as new ideas** c'est toujours les mêmes clichés, mais présentés comme des idées novatrices

dressage ['dresɑ:ʒ] **N** *Horseriding* dressage *m*

dress-down Friday N = journée du vendredi, où, contrairement au reste de la semaine, les employés sont libres de s'habiller comme ils le souhaitent

dresser ['dresə(r)] **N 1** *(person)* **he's a smart/sloppy d.** il s'habille avec beaucoup de goût/avec négligence

2 *Theat* habilleur(euse) *m,f*

3 *(tool ▸ for wood)* raboteuse *f*; *(▸ for stone)* rabotin *m*

4 *(for dishes)* buffet *m*, dressoir *m*

5 *Am (for clothing)* commode *f*

dressing ['dresıŋ] **N 1** *(act of getting dressed)* habillement *m*, habillage *m*

2 *Culin (sauce)* sauce *f*, assaisonnement *m*; *Am (stuffing)* farce *f*; **an oil and vinegar d.** une vinaigrette

3 *(for wound)* pansement *m*; **to apply a d.** mettre *ou* faire un pansement

4 *Agr (fertilizer)* engrais *m*

5 *(for cloth, leather)* apprêt *m*

• **dressings NPL** *Constr* moulures *fpl*, parement *m*

▸▸ *Old-fashioned* ***dressing case*** trousse *f* de toilette, nécessaire *m* de toilette; ***dressing gown*** robe *f* de chambre, peignoir *m*; ***dressing room*** *(at home)* dressing-room *m*, dressing *m*, vestiaire *m*; *(at gymnasium, sports ground)* vestiaire *m*; *Theat* loge *f* (d'acteur); *Am (in shop)* cabine *f* d'essayage; *Mil* ***dressing station*** poste *m* de secours; ***dressing table*** coiffeuse *f*, (table *f* de) toilette *f*; ***dressing up*** *(children's activity)* déguisement *m*

dressing-down N *Br Fam* réprimande▫ *f*, semonce▫ *f*; **to give sb a d.** passer un savon à qn; **he got a d.** il s'est fait passer un savon

dressmaker ['dres,meıkə(r)] **N** couturier(ère) *m,f*

dressmaking ['dres,meıkıŋ] **N** couture *f*, confection *f* des robes

dress-run N *Theat* répétition *f* générale

dressy ['dresı] *(compar* **dressier**, *superl* **dressiest)** **ADJ** *(clothes)* (qui fait) habillé, élégant; *(person)* élégant, chic; *(event)* habillé; **the charity ball is always a very d. occasion** le bal de charité est toujours un événement très habillé

drew [dru:] *pt of* **draw**

drib [drıb] **N** *(idiom)* **in dribs and drabs** petit à petit

dribble ['drıbəl] **VI 1** *(liquid ▸ drop by drop)* dégoutter, tomber goutte à goutte; *(▸ in a trickle)* dégouliner; **the wine dribbled down his chin** le vin lui dégoulina le long du menton; *Fig* **to d. in/out** *(of people)* entrer/sortir par petits groupes **2** *(baby)* baver **3** *Sport* dribbler

VT 1 *(trickle)* laisser couler *ou* tomber lentement; **he was dribbling milk from his mouth** du lait dégoulinait de sa bouche; **you're dribbling water everywhere!** tu fais dégouliner de l'eau partout! **2** *Sport (ball, puck)* dribbler

N 1 *(of person, dog)* bave *f*

2 *(trickle)* filet *m*

3 *Fig (small amount)* **a d. of** un petit peu de

4 *Sport* dribble *m*

dribbler ['drıblə(r)] **N** *Sport* dribbleur *m*

dribbling ['drıblıŋ] **N 1** *(of baby)* écoulement *m* de bave **2** *Sport* dribbling *m*

driblet ['drıblıt] **N** *(of liquid)* gouttelette *f*, petite goutte *f*; **in driblets** goutte à goutte, au compte-gouttes; *Fig* au compte-gouttes

dried [draıd] *pp of* **dry**

ADJ *(fruit)* sec (sèche); *(meat)* séché; *(milk, eggs)* déshydraté

▸▸ *Culin* ***dried cod*** merluche *f*, stockfisch *m*

dried-up ADJ *(river bed, lake)* asséché; *(apple, person)* ratatiné, desséché; *(talent, well)* tari; *(beauty, love)* fané

drier ['draıə(r)] *compar of* **dry**

N *(for clothes)* séchoir *m* (à linge); *(for hair ▸ hand-held)* séchoir *m* (à cheveux), sèche-cheveux *m inv*; *(▸ helmet)* casque *m* (sèche-cheveux); **under the d.** sous le casque

drift [drıft] **VI 1** *(float ▸ on water)* aller à la dérive, dériver; *(▸ in current, wind)* être emporté; *Aviat* dériver; *Naut* **to d. off course** dévier de son cap; **the boat drifted downstream** le bateau descendait le fleuve à la dérive *ou* à vau-l'eau; **the clouds drifted** les nuages étaient poussés par le vent; **mist drifted in from the sea** il y avait de la brume qui venait de la mer; **the sound of music drifted up from the garden** on entendait de la musique qui montait du jardin

2 *(sand, snow)* s'amonceler, s'entasser

3 *(move aimlessly)* marcher nonchalamment; **people began to d. in/out** les gens commençaient à entrer/sortir d'un pas nonchalant; *Fig* **the conversation drifted from one topic to another** la conversation passait d'un sujet à un autre; **he just drifts along, he just drifts through life** il se laisse porter par les événements; **to d. apart** *(friends)* se perdre de vue; *(couple)* se séparer petit à petit; **he drifted into a life of crime** il a sombré dans la délinquance

4 *Electron* se décaler

VT 1 *(of current)* entraîner, charrier; *(of wind)* emporter, pousser **2** *(of sand, snow)* amonceler, entasser

N 1 *(flow)* mouvement *m*, force *f*; *(of air, water)* poussée *f*; **the d. of the current took us southwards** le courant nous a emportés vers le sud; **the d. of the tide** *(speed)* la vitesse de la marée; *(direction)* le sens de la marée; *Fig* **the d. from the land** l'exode *m* rural, la migration vers la ville;

the d. towards war la dérive vers la guerre
2 *(of leaves, sand)* amoncellement *m*, entassement *m*; *(of fallen snow)* amoncellement *m*, congère *f*; *(of falling snow)* rafale *f*, bourrasque *f*; *(of clouds)* traînée *f*; *(of dust, mist)* nuage *m*; *Geol (deposits)* apports *mpl*
3 *Aviat & Naut (of plane, ship)* dérivation *f*; *(of missile)* déviation *f*; *(deviation from course)* dérive *f*
4 *Electron* déviation *f*
5 *(trend)* tendance *f*; **the d. back towards the classics** le retour aux classiques
6 *(meaning)* sens *m*, portée *f*; **do you get my d.?** voyez-vous où je veux en venir?; *Fam* **I get the/your d.** je pige
7 *Ling* évolution *f (d'une langue)*
8 *Mining* galerie *f* chassante
►► *Naut* ***drift anchor*** ancre *f* flottante; ***drift ice*** *(UNCOUNT)* glaces *fpl* flottantes *ou* en dérive; *Fishing* ***drift net*** filet *m* dérivant

► **drift off** VI *(fall asleep)* s'assoupir; **I drifted off for a while** je me suis assoupi quelques instants

drifter ['drɪftə(r)] N **1** *(person)* = personne qui n'a pas de but dans la vie; **he's a bit of a d.** il n'arrive pas à se fixer **2** *Naut (boat)* drifter *m*

drifting ['drɪftɪŋ] ADJ *(ship)* à la dérive; *(cloud)* traînant; **d. snow** neige *f* soulevée par le vent; **d. banks of fog/cloud** des traînées *fpl* de brouillard/de nuages
N *(caused by current)* entraînement *m* par le courant; *(caused by wind)* entraînement *m* par le vent; *(formation of drifts ► of snow)* amoncellement *m*; **caused by the d. of the snow across the road** causé par la neige soulevée par le vent en travers de la route

driftwood ['drɪftwʊd] N *(UNCOUNT)* bois *mpl* flottants

drill [drɪl] N **1** *(manual)* porte-foret *m*; *(electric)* perceuse *f*; *(of dentist)* fraise *f (de dentiste)*, roulette *f*; *Petr (for oil well)* trépan *m*; *(pneumatic)* marteau *m* piqueur; *Mining* perforatrice *f*
2 *(bit)* **d. (bit)** foret *m*, mèche *f*
3 *(exercises)* exercice(s) *m(pl)*; *Mil* manœuvre(s) *f(pl)*, drill *m*; *Sch* **verb d.** exercices *mpl* oraux sur les verbes; *Mil* **firing d.** instruction *f* du tir; *Br Fam Fig* **I know the d.** je sais ce qu'il faut faire❑, je connais la marche à suivre❑; *Br Fam* **what's the d.?** *(what do you want me to do?)* qu'est-ce qu'il y a à faire?❑; *(for working the photocopier etc)* comment on fait?
4 *Tex* treillis *m*
5 *Agr (machine)* semoir *m*; *(furrow)* sillon *m*
6 *Zool* drill *m*
VT **1** *(metal, wood)* forer, percer; *(hole)* percer; *(dentist)* fraiser; *Petr* **to d. an oil well** forer un puits de pétrole
2 *(train)* faire faire des exercices à; *Mil* faire faire l'exercice à; **I drilled him in what to say** je lui ai fait la leçon sur ce qu'il fallait dire; **the troops are well drilled** les troupes sont bien entraînées; **to d. good manners into sb** apprendre les bonnes manières à qn; *Sch* **to d. pupils in French verbs** faire faire aux élèves des exercices oraux sur les verbes français
3 *Agr (seeds)* semer en sillon; *(field)* tracer des sillons dans
4 *Fam (ball)* **he drilled the ball into the back of the net** il envoya la balle droit au fond du filet❑
VI **1** *(bore)* forer; **they are drilling for oil** ils forent *ou* effectuent des forages pour trouver du pétrole **2** *(train)* faire de l'exercice, s'entraîner; *Mil* être à l'exercice, manœuvrer
►► *Mil* ***drill sergeant*** sergent *m* instructeur

drilling ['drɪlɪŋ] N *(UNCOUNT) (in metal, wood)* forage *m*, perçage *m*; *(by dentist)* fraisage *m*; **d. for oil** forage *m* pétrolier
►► *Petr* ***drilling platform*** plate-forme *f* (de forage); *Petr* ***drilling rig*** *(on land)* derrick *m*, tour *f* de forage; *(at sea)* plate-forme *f* (de forage); *Petr* ***drilling ship*** navire *m* de forage

drily ['draɪlɪ] ADV *(wryly)* d'un air pince-sans-rire; *(coldly)* sèchement, d'un ton sec

DRINK [drɪŋk]

VT	
• boire	• prendre
VI	
• boire	
N	
• boisson **1, 4**	• verre **2**
• gorgée **3**	• alcool **4**

(*pt* **drank** [dræŋk], *pp* **drunk** [drʌŋk])
VT boire, prendre; **would you like something to d.?** voulez-vous boire quelque chose?; **I never d. coffee** je ne prends jamais de café; **fit to d.** potable; **this coffee isn't fit to d.** ce café est imbuvable; **this wine is best drunk at room temperature** ce vin se boit chambré; **d. your soup** mange ta soupe; **to d. sb's health, to d. a toast to sb** boire à la santé de qn; **he drank himself into a stupor** il s'est soûlé jusqu'à l'hébétude; **he's drinking himself to death** l'alcool le tue peu à peu; **to d. sb under the table** faire rouler qn sous la table
VI **1** *(gen)* boire; **I don't d.** je ne bois pas; **to d. heavily** boire beaucoup; **she drank out of** *or* **(straight) from the bottle** elle a bu à la bouteille; **I only d. socially** je ne bois jamais seul; **don't d. and drive** boire ou conduire, il faut choisir; **he drinks like a fish** il boit comme un trou; **I'll d. to that!** je suis pour!; **we drank to their success** nous avons bu *ou* porté un toast à leur succès
2 *(of wine)* **it won't d. quite as well in two years' time** dans deux ans il aura perdu de sa saveur
N **1** *(non-alcoholic)* boisson *f*; **may I have a d.?** puis-je boire quelque chose?; **a d. of water** un verre d'eau; **to give sb a d.** donner à boire à qn; **there's plenty of food and d.** il y a tout ce qu'on veut à boire et à manger; **hot drinks** boissons *fpl* chaudes
2 *(alcoholic)* verre *m*; *(before dinner)* apéritif *m*; *(after dinner)* digestif *m*; **we invited them in for a d.** nous les avons invités à prendre un verre; **I need a d.!** vite, donnez-moi à boire!; **I haven't had a d. in six months** je n'ai pas bu d'alcool depuis six mois; **he likes** *or* **enjoys a d.** il aime bien boire un verre; **to buy** *or* **to stand a round of drinks** payer une tournée; **drinks are on the house!** la maison offre à boire!; **he'd had one d. too many** il avait bu un verre de trop, il avait un verre dans le nez
3 *(mouthful)* gorgée *f*
4 *(alcohol)* la boisson, l'alcool *m*; **she's taken to d.** elle s'est mise à boire; **to be the worse for d.** être en état d'ébriété; **he can't hold his d.** il ne tient pas l'alcool; **to drive under the influence of d.** conduire en état d'ivresse *ou* d'ébriété; **he has a d. problem** il boit trop, il s'adonne à la boisson
5 *Br Fam (sea)* flotte *f*; **to be in the d.** être dans la flotte *ou* à la baille
►► *Am* ***drinks machine, drink machine*** distributeur *m* de boissons

► **drink away** VT SEP *(troubles)* noyer; *(fortune)* boire

► **drink down** VT SEP avaler *ou* boire d'un trait

► **drink in** VT SEP **1** *(water)* absorber, boire **2** *Fig (story, words)* boire; *(atmosphere, surroundings)* s'imprégner de; **we drank in every word** pas un seul mot ne nous a échappé, nous avons bu ses paroles

► **drink up** VT SEP boire (jusqu'à la dernière goutte), finir
VI vider son verre; **d. up!** finissez vos verres!

drinkable ['drɪŋkəbəl] ADJ *(safe to drink)* potable; *(pleasant to drink)* buvable; **this wine's very d.** c'est un vin qui se laisse boire

drink-driver N *Br* conducteur(trice) *m,f* ivre; **he's a notorious d.** tout le monde sait qu'il conduit souvent en état d'ébriété

drink-driving N *Br* conduite *f* en état d'ivresse; **he was arrested for d.** il a été arrêté pour conduite en état d'ivresse

drinker ['drɪŋkə(r)] N buveur(euse) *m,f*; **I'm not a coffee d.** je ne suis pas un buveur de café; **he's a hard** *or* **heavy d.** il boit sec *ou* beaucoup; **we're not really drinkers** nous ne sommes pas des grands buveurs

drinking ['drɪŋkɪŋ] N fait *m* de boire; **eating and d.** manger et boire; **heavy d.** ivrognerie *f*; **d. bout** *or* **session** beuverie *f*; **I'm not used to d.** je n'ai pas l'habitude de boire; **it was her d. that destroyed the marriage** c'est son alcoolisme qui a détruit leur mariage; **I'm not a d. man** je n'ai pas l'habitude de boire
COMP *(habits)* de buveur; *(companion)* de beuverie
►► ***drinking chocolate*** chocolat *m* à boire; *(powder)* chocolat *m* en poudre; *(hot drink)* chocolat *m* chaud; ***drinking fountain*** *(in street)* fontaine *f* publique; *(in corridor, public conveniences)* jet *m* d'eau potable; ***drinking song*** chanson *f* à boire; ***drinking straw*** paille *f*; ***drinking trough*** abreuvoir *m*; ***drinking water*** eau *f* potable

drinking-up time N *Br* = moment où les clients doivent finir leur verre avant la fermeture du bar

drip [drɪp] (*pt & pp* **dripped**, *cont* **dripping**) VI **1** *(liquid)* tomber goutte à goutte, dégoutter; **the rain is dripping down my neck** la pluie me dégouline dans le cou; **sweat dripped from his brow** son front ruisselait de sueur; **I was dripping with sweat** j'étais en nage; *Fig* **she was dripping with diamonds** elle était couverte de diamants **2** *(tap)* fuir, goutter; *(nose)* couler; *(washing)* s'égoutter; *(walls)* suinter; *(hair, trees)* dégoutter, ruisseler
VT laisser tomber goutte à goutte; **the ceiling was dripping water** le plafond gouttait, des gouttes d'eau tombaient du plafond; **you're dripping coffee everywhere** tu mets du café partout
N **1** *(falling drops ► from tap, gutter, ceiling)* égouttement *m*, dégoulinement *m*; **the d. method of making coffee** la méthode filtre de faire le café
2 *(sound ► from trees, roofs)* bruit *m* de l'eau qui goutte; *(► from tap)* bruit *m* d'un robinet qui fuit *ou* goutte
3 *(drop)* goutte *f*
4 *Fam Pej (person)* nouille *f*, lavette *f*
5 *Med (device)* goutte-à-goutte *m inv*; *(solution)* perfusion *f*; **she's on a d.** elle est sous perfusion
6 *Archit* larmier *m*
►► *Mktg* ***drip advertising*** publicité *f* continue, publicité *f* goutte à goutte; ***drip mat*** dessous-de-verre *m inv*; ***drip pan, drip tray*** lèchefrite *f*

drip-dry ADJ qui ne nécessite aucun repassage
VI s'égoutter
VT (faire) égoutter

drip-feed N *Med (device)* goutte-à-goutte *m inv*; *(solution)* perfusion *f*
VT *Med* alimenter par perfusion; *Fig (company)* perfuser

drip-feeding N *Med* alimentation *f* par perfusion; *Fig (of company)* subventions *fpl* données au coup par coup

dripping ['drɪpɪŋ] N **1** *Culin (of meat)* graisse *f (de rôti)*; **bread and d.** tartine *f* à la graisse **2** *(of liquid)* égouttement *m*, égouttage *m*
ADJ **1** *(tap)* qui fuit *ou* goutte **2** *(very wet)* trempé
ADV **his clothes were d. wet** ses vêtements étaient trempés *ou* étaient à tordre
►► ***dripping pan*** lèchefrite *f*

drippy ['drɪpɪ] (*compar* **drippier**, *superl* **drippiest**) ADJ **1** *Fam Pej (person)* mou (molle)❑ **2** *(tap)* qui fuit *ou* goutte

DRIVE [draɪv]

VT	
• conduire **1**	• chasser **2**
• pousser **2, 4**	• percer **6**
• faire fonctionner **7**	
VI	
• conduire **1**	• aller en voiture **1**
• rouler **2**	• se ruer **3**
N	
• promenade en voiture **1**	• trajet (en voiture) **1**
• allée **2**	• dynamisme **3**
• besoin **4**	• campagne **5**
• lecteur **11**	

(*pt* **drove** [drəʊv], *pp* **driven** ['drɪvən])
VT **1** *(bus, car, train)* conduire; *(racing car)* piloter; **can you d. a minibus?** savez-vous conduire un minibus?; **I d. a Volvo** j'ai une Volvo; **he drives a taxi/lorry** il est chauffeur de taxi/camionneur; **he drove her into town** il l'a conduite *ou* emmenée en voiture en ville; **could you d. me home?** pourriez-vous me reconduire chez moi?; **she drove the car into a tree** elle a heurté un arbre avec la voiture; **I haven't driven all this way just to...** je n'ai pas fait tout ce chemin juste pour...
2 *(chase)* chasser, pousser; **to d. sb out of the**

house/of the country chasser qn de la maison/du pays; **we drove the cattle back into the shed** nous avons fait rentrer le bétail dans l'étable; **the waves drove the ship onto the rocks** les vagues ont jeté le navire contre les rochers; **the strong winds had driven the ship off course** les vents forts avaient dévié le navire de sa route; **they have driven us into a corner** ils nous ont mis au pied du mur

3 *(work)* **it doesn't pay to d. your workers too hard** on ne gagne rien à surmener ses employés; **he drives himself too hard** il se surmène

4 *(force)* pousser, inciter; **he was driven to it** on lui a forcé la main; **driven by jealousy, he killed her** il l'a tuée sous l'emprise de la jalousie; **it's enough to d. you to drink!** cela vous pousserait à boire!; **the situation is driving me to despair/distraction** la situation me pousse au désespoir/me rend fou (folle); *Fam* **to d. sb crazy** *or* **mad** *or* **up the wall** rendre qn fou (folle); *Fam* **his performance drove the audience wild** son spectacle a mis le public en délire

5 *(hammer)* **to d. a nail home** enfoncer un clou; *Fig* **to d. a point home** faire admettre son point de vue; **to d. a hard bargain** avoir toujours le dernier mot en affaires, être dur en affaires

6 *(bore ▸ hole)* percer; *(▸ tunnel)* percer, creuser

7 *(operate ▸ machine)* faire fonctionner; *Tech* entraîner; **driven by electricity** marchant à l'électricité

8 *Golf* **to d. a ball** driver

9 *Hunt (game)* rabattre; *(area)* battre

VI **1** *(operate a vehicle)* conduire; *(travel in vehicle)* aller en voiture; **do you** *or* **can you d.?** savez-vous conduire?; **I don't d.** *(I never learned)* je n'ai pas mon permis; **I was driving at 100 mph** je roulais à 160 km/h; **we drove home** nous sommes rentrés en voiture; **are you walking or driving?** êtes-vous à pied ou en voiture?; **who was driving?** qui était au volant?; **d. on the right** roulez à droite, tenez votre droite; **they drove straight through the town** ils ont traversé la ville sans s'y arrêter

2 *(car)* rouler; *Fam* **this car drives like a dream** c'est un plaisir de conduire cette voiture

3 *(dash)* se ruer; **rain was driving against the window** la pluie fouettait les vitres

N **1** *(trip in car)* promenade *f* en voiture, trajet *m* (en voiture); **we went for a d.** nous avons fait une promenade *ou* un tour en voiture; **it's an hour's d. from here** c'est à une heure d'ici en voiture; **it's a very pleasant d. to the coast** la route est très belle jusqu'à la côte; **a 50-km d.** un parcours *ou* un trajet de 50 km

2 *(leading to house)* allée *f*; **the car was parked in the d.** la voiture était garée dans l'allée

3 *(energy)* dynamisme *m*, énergie *f*; **we need someone with d.** il nous faut quelqu'un de dynamique *ou* d'entreprenant; **to have plenty of d.** être très dynamique; **he lacks d.** il manque d'allant *ou* de dynamisme

4 *Psy (urge)* besoin *m*, instinct *m*; *(sexual)* pulsions *fpl*

5 *(campaign)* campagne *f*; **the company is having a sales d.** la compagnie fait une campagne de vente

6 *Br Cards (for bridge, whist)* tournoi *m*

7 *Sport (in cricket, tennis)* coup *m* droit; *Golf* drive *m*; *Ftbl* tir *m*, shoot *m*

8 *(of animals)* rassemblement *m*; *Hunt* battue *f*; **cattle d.** rassemblement *m* du bétail

9 *Tech (power transmission)* transmission *f*, commande *f*; *Aut* **four-wheel d.** quatre roues motrices *f inv*, quatre-quatre *m inv ou f inv*

10 *Aut (location of steering wheel)* conduite *f*; **left-hand d.** conduite à gauche

11 *Comput (for disk)* unité *f*, lecteur *m*; *(for tape)* dérouleur *m*; **d. a:/b:** unité *f* de disque a:/b:

12 *Mil* poussée *f*, offensive *f*

COMP *Tech (mechanism, device)* d'entraînement, d'actionnement, de transmission

▸ **drive along** VI *(car)* rouler, circuler; *(person)* rouler, conduire

VT SEP *(of river, wind)* pousser, chasser

▸ **drive at** VT INSEP vouloir dire; **she didn't understand what he was driving at** elle ne comprenait pas où il voulait en venir; **I see what you're driving at** je vous vois venir

▸ **drive away** VI *(person)* s'en aller *ou* partir (en voiture); *(car)* démarrer

VT SEP *(car)* démarrer; *(person)* emmener en voiture; *Fig (animal, intruder)* chasser, éloigner; *(friend)* éloigner; *(doubt, suspicion)* écarter; *(fear)* chasser

▸ **drive back** VT SEP **1** *(person)* ramener *ou* reconduire en voiture; *(car)* reculer **2** *(repel)* repousser, refouler; *(of flames)* faire reculer; **the soldiers were driven back by heavy machine-gun fire** les soldats furent repoussés par un puissant tir de mitrailleuse; **fear drove them back** la peur leur a fait rebrousser chemin

VI *(person)* rentrer en voiture; *(car)* retourner

▸ **drive down** VT SEP **1** *Econ (prices, inflation etc)* faire baisser **2** *(in car)* **to d. sb down to London** conduire qn à Londres

VI *(in car)* se rendre en voiture; **how did you get here? – we drove down** comment êtes-vous venus? – nous sommes venus *ou* descendus en voiture; **to d. down to Marseilles** descendre à Marseille en voiture

▸ **drive in** VT SEP *(nail, stake)* enfoncer; *(screw)* visser; *(rivet)* poser

VI *(person)* entrer (en voiture); *(car)* entrer

▸ **drive off** VT SEP **1** *(frighten away)* éloigner, chasser **2** *Aut (person)* emmener en voiture; **they were driven off in a taxi** ils ont été conduits en taxi

VI **1** *(leave ▸ person)* s'en aller *ou* s'éloigner en voiture; *(▸ car)* démarrer; *(of car, bus)* s'éloigner **2** *Golf* driver

▸ **drive on** VT SEP *(push)* pousser, inciter (**to do sth** à faire qch)

VI *(continue trip)* poursuivre sa route; *(after stopping)* reprendre la route

▸ **drive out** VT SEP *(person)* chasser, faire sortir; *(thought)* chasser; **to d. out evil spirits** *(from a place)* chasser les mauvais esprits; *(from a person)* chasser le mauvais œil

VI *(person)* sortir (en voiture); *(car)* sortir

▸ **drive up** VI *(person)* arriver (en voiture); *(car)* arriver; **a car drove up to the door** une voiture vint s'arrêter devant la porte

driveability [ˌdraɪvəˈbɪlɪtɪ] N maniabilité *f*, manœuvrabilité *m*

drive-in N *(cinema)* drive-in *m inv*, *Can* ciné-parc *m*; *(restaurant)* = restaurant où l'on est servi dans sa voiture; *(bank)* = banque où l'on est servi dans sa voiture

ADJ où l'on reste dans sa voiture

▸▸ ***drive-in cinema*** drive-in *m inv*

drivel [ˈdrɪvəl] *(Br pt & pp* **drivelled,** *cont* **drivelling,** *Am pt & pp* **driveled,** *cont* **driveling)** *Fam* N *(UNCOUNT)* **1** *(nonsense)* bêtises *fpl*, radotage *m*; **to talk d.** radoter; **the film was absolute d.** le film n'était qu'un tas de balivernes **2** *(saliva)* bave *f*

VI **1** *(speak foolishly)* dire des bêtises, radoter; **what's he drivelling on about?** qu'est-ce qu'il radote? **2** *(dribble)* baver

driveline [ˈdraɪvlaɪn] N *Aut* chaîne *f* cinématique

drivelling, *Am* **driveling** [ˈdrɪvəlɪŋ] ADJ *Fam* radoteur; **you d. idiot!** espèce d'idiot!

driven [ˈdrɪvən] *pp of* **drive**

ADJ **1** *(person)* motivé, déterminé **2** *Tech* **electrically d.** actionné par l'électricité

▸▸ ***driven snow*** neige *f* vierge

driver [ˈdraɪvə(r)] N **1** *(of car)* conducteur(trice) *m,f*; *(of bus, taxi, lorry)* chauffeur *m*, conducteur (trice) *m,f*; *(of racing car)* pilote *m*; *(of train)* mécanicien *m*, conducteur(trice) *m,f*; *(of cart)* charretier(ère) *m,f*; *Sport (of horse-drawn vehicle)* driver *m*; **she's a good d.** elle conduit bien

2 *(of animals)* conducteur(trice) *m,f*

3 *Golf* driver *m*

4 *Comput (software)* programme *m* de gestion, pilote *m*; *(hardware)* unité *f* de contrôle

5 *(decisive factor)* facteur *m* prépondérant *ou* déterminant

▸▸ *Am* ***driver's license*** permis *m* de conduire; ***the driver's seat*** la place du conducteur

drive-time programme N *Rad* = émission aux heures de grande écoute en voiture

driveway [ˈdraɪvweɪ] N voie *f* privée, allée *f* *(menant à une habitation)*

driving [ˈdraɪvɪŋ] ADJ **1** *(rain)* battant; **d. snow** neige *f* fouettée par le vent **2** *(powerful)* fort; *(ambition)* ferme

N conduite *f*; **his d. is awful** il conduit affreusement mal; **I like d.** j'aime conduire; **bad d.** conduite *f* imprudente; *Br* **d. under the influence,** *Am* **d. while intoxicated** conduite *f* en état d'ivresse

▸▸ *Tech* ***driving belt*** courroie *f* de commande; *Tech* ***driving force*** force *f* motrice; *Fig* **she's the d. force behind the project** c'est elle le moteur du projet; *Br* ***driving instructor*** moniteur(trice) *m,f* de conduite *ou* d'auto-école; ***driving lesson*** leçon *f* de conduite; *Br* ***driving licence*** permis *m* de conduire; ***driving mirror*** rétroviseur *m*; ***driving offence*** infraction *f* au code de la route; *Golf* ***driving range*** practice *m*; ***driving school*** auto-école *f*; ***driving seat*** place *f* du conducteur; *Fig* **she's in the d. seat** c'est elle qui mène l'affaire *ou* qui tient les rênes; *Tech* ***driving shaft*** arbre *m* moteur; ***driving test*** examen *m* du permis de conduire; **I passed my d. test in 1992** j'ai eu mon permis en 1992; **he failed his d. test** il a raté son permis; *Tech* ***driving wheel*** roue *f* motrice

drizzle [ˈdrɪzəl] N bruine *f*, crachin *m*; **the rain came down in a steady d.** il tombait un crachin persistant

VI bruiner, crachiner

drizzly [ˈdrɪzlɪ] ADJ de bruine *ou* crachin, bruineux

DRM [ˌdiːɑːrˈem] N *(abbr* **digital rights management)** GDN *f*

drogue [drəʊg] N **1** *Aviat (parachute)* parachute *m* antivrille; *(windsock)* manche *f* à air **2** *Naut* ancre *f* flottante

droid [drɔɪd] N *(in science fiction)* droïde *m*

droll [drəʊl] ADJ *(comical)* drôle, comique; *(odd)* curieux, drôle

dromedary [ˈdrɒmədərɪ] *(pl* **dromedaries)** N dromadaire *m*

drone [drəʊn] N **1** *(sound ▸ of bee)* bourdonnement *m*; *(▸ of engine, aircraft)* ronronnement *m*; *(louder)* vrombissement *m*; *Fig* **the d. of his voice** le ronronnement de sa voix

2 *(male bee)* abeille *f* mâle, faux-bourdon *m*; *Pej (person)* fainéant(e) *m,f*

3 *Mus* bourdon *m*

4 *(plane)* avion *m* téléguidé, drone *m*

VI *(bee)* bourdonner; *(engine, aircraft)* ronronner; *(more loudly)* vrombir; **a droning voice** une voix monotone; **he droned on for hours (about his wife)** il radotait pendant des heures de sa voix monotone (sur sa femme)

drongo [ˈdrɒŋgəʊ] *(pl* **drongos)** N **1** *Zool* drongo *m* **2** *Austr Fam (idiot)* abruti(e) *m,f*

drool [druːl] N *(of person, dog)* bave *f*

VI baver; *Fig* **to d. over sth** baver d'admiration *ou* s'extasier devant qch

droop [druːp] VI *(head)* pencher; *(eyelids)* s'abaisser; *(body)* s'affaisser; *(shoulders)* tomber; *(flowers)* commencer à baisser la tête *ou* à se faner; **her spirits drooped** elle s'est démoralisée

N *(of eyelids)* abaissement *m*; *(of head)* attitude *f* penchée; *(of body, shoulders)* affaissement *m*; *(of spirits)* langueur *f*, abattement *m*; **he could tell from the d. of her shoulders/head** il savait à ses épaules tombantes/à la façon dont elle penchait la tête

drooping [ˈdruːpɪŋ] ADJ *(shoulders, moustache)* tombant; *(eyelids)* abaissé; *(flowers)* qui commence à se faner; *Fig (person)* languissant; **to revive sb's d. spirits** remonter le moral à qn

droopy [ˈdruːpɪ] *(compar* **droopier,** *superl* **droopiest)** ADJ *(moustache, shoulders)* tombant; *(flowers)* qui commence à se faner

DROP [drɒp]

VT	
• laisser tomber **1, 4**	• lâcher **1, 4, 9**
• baisser **2**	• déposer **3**
• laisser échapper **5**	• écrire **6**
• omettre **7**	• perdre **8**
VI	
• tomber **1, 2**	• s'écrouler **2**
• baisser **3**	

N
- goutte **1**
- baisse **2**
- chute **2, 3**
- bonbon **6**
- livraison **7**

(pt & pp **dropped**, *cont* **dropping***)*

VT 1 *(let fall ▸ accidentally)* laisser tomber; *(▸ liquid)* laisser tomber goutte à goutte; *(▸ trousers)* laisser tomber; *(▸ bomb)* lancer, lâcher; *(▸ stitch)* sauter, laisser tomber; *(release)* lâcher; **be careful not to d. it** fais attention à ne pas le laisser tomber; **d. it!** *(to dog)* lâche ça!; **he dropped it from the balcony to his accomplice** il l'a lancé à son complice depuis le balcon; **they dropped soldiers/supplies by parachute** ils ont parachuté des soldats/du ravitaillement; **to d. a curtsy** faire une révérence; *Naut* **to d. anchor** mouiller, jeter l'ancre; *Sport* **to d. a goal** *(in rugby)* marquer un drop; **she dropped the ball over the net** *(in tennis)* elle a placé un amorti juste derrière le filet; *Br Fam* **to d. a brick** *or* **a clanger** faire une gaffe

2 *(lower ▸ voice)* baisser; *(▸ speed)* réduire; *(▸ hem)* ressortir

3 *(deliver)* déposer; **could you d. me at the corner, please?** pouvez-vous me déposer au coin, s'il vous plaît?

4 *(abandon ▸ friend)* laisser tomber, lâcher; *(▸ discussion, work)* abandonner, laisser tomber; **I've dropped the idea of going** j'ai renoncé à y aller; **to d. everything** laisser tout tomber; **let's d. the subject** ne parlons plus de cela, parlons d'autre chose; **just d. it!** laissez tomber!, assez!

5 *(utter ▸ remark)* laisser échapper; **to d. a hint about sth** faire allusion à qch; **he dropped me a hint that she wanted to come** il m'a fait comprendre qu'elle voulait venir; **she let (it) d. that she had been there** *(accidentally)* elle a laissé échapper qu'elle y était allée; *(deliberately)* elle a fait comprendre qu'elle y était allée

6 *(send ▸ letter, note)* écrire, envoyer; **I'll d. you a line next week** je t'enverrai un petit mot la semaine prochaine; **I'll d. it in the mail** *or Br* **post** je le/la mettrai à la poste

7 *(omit ▸ when speaking)* ne pas prononcer; *(▸ when writing)* omettre; *(▸ intentionally)* supprimer; **we dropped the love scene** nous avons supprimé la scène d'amour; **he drops his h's** il n'aspire pas les h; **let's d. the formalities, shall we?** oublions les formalités, d'accord?; **to d. a player from a team** écarter un joueur d'une équipe

8 *Br (lose)* perdre; **they dropped one game** ils ont perdu un match

9 *Comput (icon)* lâcher

10 *Am Fam (spend)* claquer

11 *Fam (knock down ▸ with punch)* sonner; *(▸ with shot)* descendre▫

12 *Fam Drugs slang* **to d. acid** prendre *ou* avaler de l'acide▫

13 *Br (of DJ ▸ record)* mettre

VI 1 *(fall ▸ object)* tomber, retomber; *(▸ liquid)* tomber goutte à goutte; *(▸ ground)* s'abaisser; **the book dropped from** *or* **out of her hands** le livre lui tomba des mains; **his jaw dropped** il en est resté bouche bée; **the road drops into the valley** la route plonge vers la vallée

2 *(person ▸ sink down)* se laisser tomber, tomber; *(▸ collapse)* s'écrouler, s'affaisser; **she dropped to her knees** elle est tombée à genoux; **I dropped exhausted into a chair** je me suis écroulé exténué sur une chaise; **I'm ready** *or* **fit to d.** *(from fatigue)* je tombe de fatigue, je ne tiens plus sur mes jambes; *(from sleepiness)* je tombe de sommeil; **he'll work until he drops** il va travailler jusqu'à épuisement; **she dropped dead** elle est tombée raide morte; *Fam* **d. dead!** va te faire voir!; **the team dropped to third place** l'équipe est descendue à la troisième position

3 *(decrease ▸ price, speed)* baisser, diminuer; *(▸ temperature)* baisser; *(▸ wind)* se calmer, tomber; *(▸ voice)* baisser; **shares dropped a point** les actions ont reculé d'un point; **the pound dropped three points against the dollar** la livre a reculé de *ou* a perdu trois points par rapport au dollar

4 *(end)* cesser; *Fam* **let it d.!** n'en parlons plus!; **I'm not going to let it d.** *(grievance etc)* je ne vais pas laisser passer cela

5 *(give birth ▸ animal)* mettre bas

N 1 *(of liquid)* goutte *f*; **d. by d.** goutte à goutte; **there hasn't been a d. of rain for weeks** il n'y a pas eu une goutte de pluie depuis des semaines; **would you like a d. of wine?** que diriez-vous d'une goutte *ou* d'une larme de vin?; **there's a d. left in the bottle** il reste une goutte dans la bouteille; *Fam* **he's had a d. too much (to drink)** il a bu un verre de trop▫; **I haven't touched a d. since** je n'y ai pas touché depuis; **it's just a d. in the ocean** ce n'est qu'une goutte d'eau dans la mer

2 *(decrease ▸ in price)* baisse *f*, chute *f* (**in** de); *(▸ in temperature)* baisse *f* (**in** de); *(▸ in voltage)* chute *f* (**in** de)

3 *(fall)* chute *f*; *(in parachuting)* saut *m* (en parachute); **a sudden d. in the ground level** une soudaine dénivellation; **at the d. of a hat** sans hésiter, à tout moment

4 *(vertical distance)* hauteur *f* de chute; *(slope)* descente *f* brusque; *(abyss)* à-pic *m inv*, précipice *m*; *(in climbing)* vide *m*; **it's a 50-metre d. from the cliff to the sea** il y a (un dénivelé de *ou* une hauteur de) 50 mètres entre le haut de la falaise et la mer; **careful, it's a long d.** attention, c'est haut; *Am* **to have the d. on sb** avoir l'avantage sur qn

5 *(earring)* pendant *m*, pendeloque *f*; *(on necklace)* pendentif *m*; *(on chandelier)* pendeloque *f*

6 *(sweet)* bonbon *m*, pastille *f*; **lemon drops** bonbons *mpl* au citron

7 *(delivery)* livraison *f*; *(from plane)* parachutage *m*, droppage *m*; **to make a d.** déposer un colis

8 *(hiding place)* cachette *f*, dépôt *m* (clandestin)

9 *(place to leave something)* lieu *m* de dépôt

• **drops NPL** *Med* gouttes *fpl*

▸▸ *Metal* **drop forge** marteau-pilon *m*; *Sport* **drop goal** *(in rugby)* drop-goal *m*, drop *m*; *Tech* **drop hammer** marteau-pilon *m*; **drop handlebars** guidon *m* renversé; *Sport* **drop kick** *(in rugby)* coup *m* de pied tombé; *Br Culin* **drop scone** = sorte de crêpe épaisse; *Sport* **drop shot** *(in tennis)* amorti *m*; **drop zone** zone *f* de droppage

▸**drop away VI 1** *(interest, support)* diminuer, baisser **2** *(land)* s'abaisser

▸**drop back VI** retourner en arrière, se laisser devancer *ou* distancer

▸**drop behind VI** *(in race)* se laisser distancer; *(with work)* prendre du retard (**with** dans); **she dropped behind to talk to John** elle est passée vers l'arrière pour parler à John

VT INSEP *(in race)* **to d. behind sb** se laisser distancer par qn

▸**drop by VI** passer

▸**drop down VI** *(person)* tomber (par terre); *(table leaf)* se rabattre

▸**drop in VI** passer; **I just dropped in for a chat** je suis seulement passé bavarder un moment; **to d. in on sb** passer voir qn

VT SEP *(deliver)* déposer; **I'll d. it in on my way to work** je le déposerai demain en allant au travail; *Fam* **you dropped me right in it** tu m'as mis dans le pétrin

▸**drop off VT SEP** *(person)* déposer; *(package, thing)* déposer, laisser

VI 1 *(fall asleep)* s'endormir; *(have a nap)* faire un (petit) somme; **it was two o'clock before I finally dropped off** je ne me suis pas endormi avant deux heures du matin **2** *(decrease ▸ membership, attendance etc)* diminuer, baisser **3** *(fall off)* tomber; **all the flowers dropped off when I moved the plant** toutes les fleurs sont tombées lorsque j'ai déplacé la plante

▸**drop out VI 1** *(fall out)* tomber **2** *(withdraw)* renoncer; **she dropped out of the race** elle s'est retirée de la course; **he dropped out of school** il a abandonné ses études; **to d. out of university** laisser tomber l'université **3** *(person ▸ from society)* vivre en marge de la société

▸**drop round** *Br* **VI** *(visit)* passer

VT SEP *(deliver)* déposer

drop-dead gorgeous ADJ *Fam* hyper canon

drop-down ADJ *(door)* qui s'ouvre par le haut

▸▸ *Comput* **drop-down menu** menu *m* déroulant

drop-forge VT *Metal* forger au marteau-pilon

drop-forging N *Metal* **1** *(process)* estampage *m* **2** *(result)* pièce *f* emboutie *ou* étampée

drop-in centre N *Br* centre *m* d'assistance sociale *(où l'on peut aller sans rendez-vous)*

droplet [ˈdrɒplɪt] **N** gouttelette *f*

dropout [ˈdrɒpaʊt] **N** *Fam (from society)* marginal(e)▫ *m,f*; *(from studies)* étudiant(e) *m,f* qui abandonne ses études▫; *Am* **he's a high school d.** il a quitté le lycée avant le bac

▸▸ *dropout rate (at university, college)* taux *m* d'abandon des études

dropped [drɒpt] **ADJ**

▸▸ **dropped ceiling** plafond *m* suspendu; *Sport* **dropped goal** *(in rugby)* drop-goal *m*; *Br* **dropped kerb** bordure *f* inclinée

dropper [ˈdrɒpə(r)] **N** compte-gouttes *m inv*

dropping [ˈdrɒpɪŋ] **N 1** *(of object)* descente *f*, chute *f*; *Aviat (of parachutist, package)* largage *m*, droppage *m*

2 *(reduction ▸ of prices)* baisse *f*, chute *f*

3 *(omission ▸ of word)* suppression *f*

4 *(abandonment ▸ of project, course)* abandon *m*

5 *Aut (of chassis)* surbaissement *m*

6 *Vet* **d. (of young)** mise *f* bas

• **droppings NPL** *(of animal)* crottes *fpl*; *(of bird)* fiente *f*

▸▸ **dropping off** *(of membership, attendance etc)* diminution *f*; *Fam* **dropping out** *(of school, university)* abandon▫ *m*; *(from society)* désinsertion *f* sociale▫; *Aviat* **dropping zone** zone *f* de largage *ou* de droppage

dropsical [ˈdrɒpsɪkəl] **ADJ** *Med* hydropique

dropsy [ˈdrɒpsɪ] **N** *Med* hydropisie *f*

dross [drɒs] **N** *(UNCOUNT)* **1** *Metal* scories *fpl*, crasse *f*; *Ind (of minerals)* schlamm *m* **2** *(waste)* déchets *mpl*, impuretés *fpl*; *Fig* rebut *m*; **it's total d.** ça ne vaut rien

drought [draʊt] **N 1** *(lack of rain)* sécheresse *f* **2** *(shortage)* disette *f*, manque *m*

drove [drəʊv] *pt of* **drive**

N 1 *(of animals)* troupeau *m* en marche; *(of people)* foule *f*, multitude *f*; **droves of students** des foules *fpl* d'étudiants; **every summer the tourists come in droves** chaque été les touristes arrivent en foule **2** *Tech (chisel)* boucharde *f*

VT 1 *(animals)* chasser, conduire **2** *Tech (stone)* boucharder

drover [ˈdrəʊvə(r)] **N** toucheur *m* de bestiaux

drown [draʊn] **VT 1** *(person, animal)* noyer; **to be drowned** se noyer; *(in battle, disaster)* mourir noyé; **to d. oneself** se noyer **2** *(field, village)* noyer; **don't d. it!** *(my drink)* ne mets pas trop d'eau!; **the pie was absolutely drowned in cream** le gâteau baignait dans la crème; **to d. one's sorrows** noyer son chagrin (dans la boisson) **3** *(make inaudible)* noyer, couvrir; **his voice was drowned by the music** sa voix était couverte par la musique

VI se noyer; *(in battle, disaster)* mourir noyé

▸**drown out VT SEP** *(sound)* couvrir; *(person)* couvrir la voix de

drowned [draʊnd] **ADJ** noyé; **a d. man** un noyé; *Fig* **he came home like a d. rat** il est rentré trempé

drowning [ˈdraʊnɪŋ] **ADJ a d. man** un homme en train de se noyer; *Prov* **a d. man will clutch at a straw** = dans une situation désespérée on se raccroche à un rien

N noyade *f*; **four drownings** *or* **cases of d.** quatre noyades *fpl*; **to save sb from d.** sauver qn de la noyade

drowse [draʊz] **VI** somnoler

drowsily [ˈdraʊzɪlɪ] **ADV** d'un air somnolent

drowsiness [ˈdraʊzɪnɪs] **N** *(UNCOUNT)* somnolence *f*; **may cause d.** *(on drugs packaging)* peut provoquer des somnolences

drowsy [ˈdraʊzɪ] *(compar* **drowsier**, *superl* **drowsiest***)* **ADJ** *(person, voice)* somnolent, engourdi; *(place)* endormi; **to feel d.** être tout endormi; **to make sb feel d.** *(of atmosphere)* engourdir qn; *(of drug)* endormir qn, provoquer des somnolences chez qn

drub [drʌb] *(pt & pp* **drubbed**, *cont* **drubbing***)* **VT 1** *(defeat thoroughly)* anéantir, battre à plate couture **2** *Arch (beat with stick)* battre, rosser **3** *(instil forcefully)* **to d. sth into sb** faire entrer qch dans la tête de qn

drubbing ['drʌbɪŋ] **N** *(defeat, punishment)* raclée *f*; **to give sb a real d.** mettre une raclée *ou* donner une correction à qn; **to get a good d.** se faire battre à plate couture

drudge [drʌdʒ] **N 1** *(person)* bête *f* de somme; **the household d.** la bonne à tout faire **2** *(work)* besogne *f*
VI trimer

drudgery ['drʌdʒərɪ] **N** *(UNCOUNT)* travail *m* de bête de somme; **the sheer d. of it!** quelle corvée!

drug [drʌg] *(pt & pp* **drugged,** *cont* **drugging) N 1** *(medication)* médicament *m*; **to be put on drugs by the doctor** se voir prescrire des médicaments par le médecin **2** *(illegal substance)* drogue *f*; *Law* stupéfiant *m*; **hard/soft drugs** drogues *fpl* dures/douces; **to be on** *or Fam* **to do drugs** se droguer; **to take drugs** se droguer; *(athlete)* se doper; **I don't do drugs** je ne touche pas à la drogue; **to be arrested on drugs charges** *(possession)* être arrêté pour détention de drogue *ou* de stupéfiants; *(trafficking)* être arrêté pour trafic de drogue; **the whole question of drugs in sport** tout le problème du dopage dans le sport; **music is (like) a d. for him** la musique est (comme) une drogue pour lui; *Fig* **a d. on the market** un produit invendable *ou* qui ne se vend pas
COMP de drogue
VT droguer; *(athlete, horse)* doper; **to d. sb's drink** mettre de la drogue dans le verre de qn; *Fam* **he's drugged up to the eyeballs** *(after operation)* il est bourré de médicaments; *Fig* **to be drugged with sleep** être engourdi de sommeil
►► ***drug abuse*** usage *m* de stupéfiants; ***drug addict*** drogué(e) *m,f*, toxicomane *mf*; ***drug addiction*** toxicomanie *f*; ***drug baron*** gros bonnet *m* de la drogue; ***drug company*** société *f* de produits pharmaceutiques; ***drug czar*** = haut responsable de la lutte contre la drogue; ***drug dependency*** dépendance *f* à l'égard des drogues, toxicomanie *f*, *Spec* pharmacodépendance *f*; ***Drug Enforcement Administration*** = agence américaine de lutte contre la drogue; ***drug peddling*** trafic *m* de drogue; ***drug pusher*** revendeur(euse) *m,f* de drogue; ***drug pushing*** trafic *m* de drogue; ***drug rehabilitation centre*** centre *m* de désintoxication; ***Drug Squad*** *(police)* brigade *f* des stupéfiants; ***drug taker*** *(addict)* drogué(e) *m,f*; *(athlete)* consommateur(trice) *m,f* de produits dopants; ***drug taking*** dopage *m*; ***drugs test*** *(on athlete, horse)* contrôle *m* antidopage; ***drug traffic*** trafic *m* de drogue *ou* de stupéfiants; ***drug trafficker*** narco-trafiquant(e) *m,f*; ***drug trafficking*** trafic *m* de drogue, narcotrafic *m*; ***drug user*** drogué(e) *m,f*

druggie ['drʌgɪ] **N** camé(e) *m,f*

druggist ['drʌgɪst] **N** *Am (person)* pharmacien (enne) *m,f*; **d., d.'s** *(shop)* pharmacie *f*

druggy *(pl* **druggies)** = **druggie**

drugstore ['drʌgstɔ:(r)] **N** *Am* drugstore *m*

druid ['dru:ɪd] **N** druide(esse) *m,f*

drum [drʌm] *(pt & pp* **drummed,** *cont* **drumming) N 1** *(instrument ► gen)* tambour *m*; *(► African)* tam-tam *m*; **to play (the) drums** jouer de la batterie; **John Rae on drums** John Rae à la batterie; **to beat** *or* **to bang a d.** taper *ou* frapper sur un tambour; *Fig* **to beat the d. for sb/sth** faire de la publicité pour qn/qch **2** *(for fuel)* fût *m*, bidon *m*; *(for rope)* cylindre *m*; *Comput (cylinder)* tambour *m*; *Constr* **(concrete) mixing d.** tambour *m* mélangeur (de béton) **3** *Anat (eardrum)* tympan *m*
VI 1 *(on drum kit)* jouer de la batterie; *(on one drum)* jouer du tambour **2** *(rain, fingers)* tambouriner
VT 1 *(on instrument)* tambouriner **2 to d. one's fingers on the table** tambouriner de ses doigts sur la table
►► *Aut* ***drum brake*** frein *m* à tambour; ***drum kit*** batterie *f*; *Mus* ***drum machine*** boîte *f* à rythmes; *Mil* ***drum major*** tambour-major *m*; *esp Am* ***drum majorette*** chef-majorette *f*; ***drum roll*** roulement *m* de tambour; *Comput* ***drum scanner*** scanner *m* à tambour; *Am* ***drum set*** batterie *f*

► **drum into VT SEP to d. sth into sb** enfoncer qch dans la tête de qn; **we had it drummed into us that...** on nous a enfoncé dans la tête que...

► **drum out VT SEP** expulser; **he was drummed out of the club/the army** il a été expulsé du club/de l'armée

► **drum up VT INSEP** *(customers, support)* trouver; *(supporters)* battre le rappel de; *(enthusiasm)* chercher à susciter; **to d. up business** rechercher des clients

drumbeat ['drʌmbi:t] **N** battement *m* de tambour

drumhead ['drʌmhed] **N** *Mus* peau *f* de tambour
►► *Mil* ***drumhead court-martial*** conseil *m* de guerre *(tenu sur le champ de bataille)*

drumlin ['drʌmlɪn] **N** *Geol* drumlin *m*

drummer ['drʌmə(r)] **N** *(in band)* batteur *m*; *(tribal)* joueur *m* de tambour; *Mil* tambour *m*
►► ***drummer boy*** tambour *m*

drumming ['drʌmɪŋ] **N** *(UNCOUNT) (sound ► of one drum)* son *m* du tambour; *(► of set of drums)* son *m* de la batterie; *(► of fingers, rain, woodpecker, in the ears)* tambourinement *m*, tambourinage *m*; **I really like his d.** j'aime beaucoup sa façon de jouer de la batterie

drumstick ['drʌmstɪk] **N 1** *Mus* baguette *f* **2** *Culin* pilon *m*

drunk [drʌŋk] *pp of* **drink**
ADJ 1 *(intoxicated)* soûl, saoul, ivre; **to get d. (on beer/on wine)** se soûler (à la bière/au vin); **to get sb d.** soûler qn; *Law* **d. and disorderly** en état d'ivresse publique; **d. and incapable** en état d'ivresse manifeste; *Fam* **dead** *or* **blind d.** ivre mort; **as d. as a lord** soûl comme une grive **2** *Fig* **d. with power/success** ivre de pouvoir/succès
N *(habitual)* ivrogne *mf*; *(on one occasion ► man)* homme *m* soûl *ou* ivre; *(► woman)* femme *f* soûle *ou* ivre
►► *Am Fam* ***drunk tank*** cellule *f* de dégrisement

drunkard ['drʌŋkəd] **N** ivrogne *mf*

drunken ['drʌŋkən] **ADJ** *(person)* ivre; *(laughter, sleep)* d'ivrogne; *(evening, party)* très arrosé; **d. brawl** querelle *f* d'ivrognes; **d. debauchery** ivrognerie *f*; **d. orgy** beuverie *f*, soûlerie *f*

drunkenly ['drʌŋkənlɪ] **ADV** *(speak, sing, shout)* comme un ivrogne; **he slumped d. into an armchair** complètement soûl, il s'affala dans un fauteuil; **he staggered d. down the street/the stairs** il a descendu la rue/l'escalier en titubant

drunkenness ['drʌŋkənnɪs] **N** *(state)* ivresse *f*; *(habit)* ivrognerie *f*

drunkometer [drʌŋ'kɒmɪtə(r)] **N** *Am Fam* Alcootest®ᵔ *m*

drupe [dru:p] **N** *Bot* drupe *f*

dry [draɪ] *(compar* **drier,** *superl* **driest,** *pt & pp* **dried) ADJ 1** *(climate, season, clothing, skin)* sec (sèche); **a d. spell** une période sèche; **tomorrow will be d. and bright** demain sera une journée sans pluie et ensoleillée; **to go** *or* **to run d.** *(well, river)* s'assécher, se tarir; **to keep sth d.** garder qch au sec; **keep d.** *(on packaging)* conserver à l'abri de l'humidité; **shampoo for d. hair** shampoing *m* (pour) cheveux secs; **her mouth had gone** *or* **turned d. with fear** elle avait la bouche sèche de peur; **to be d.** *(be thirsty)* avoir soif; *(cow)* être tarie *ou* sèche; **to be (as) d. as a bone, to be bone d.** *(washing, earth etc)* être très sec (sèche); *Hum* **there wasn't a d. eye in the house** tout le monde pleurait
2 *(vermouth, wine)* sec (sèche); *(champagne)* brut; **medium d.** *(wine)* demi-sec
3 *(where alcohol is banned)* où l'alcool est prohibé; *(where alcohol is not sold)* où on ne vend pas d'alcool; **to go d.** *(prohibit alcohol)* prohiber la consommation des boissons alcoolisées
4 *(boring ► book, lecture)* aride; **d. as dust** ennuyeux comme la pluie
5 *(wit, sense of humour)* pince-sans-rire *(inv)*
6 *Br Fam Pol (hardline)* = en faveur de la politique extrémiste du Parti Conservateur
N 1 *Br Fam Pol (hardliner)* = conservateur en faveur de la politique extrémiste du Parti
2 *Austr Fam (dry season)* saison *f* sècheᵔ
3 *(dry place)* **come into the d.** viens te mettre au sec
4 *(with towel, cloth)* **to give sth a d.** essuyer qch; **give your hair a d.** sèche tes cheveux
VT *(clothes, fruit, leaves)* (faire) sécher; *(dishes)* essuyer; **to d. one's eyes** se sécher les yeux, sécher ses yeux; **to d. one's tears** sécher ses larmes; **to d. one's hair** se sécher les cheveux; **to d oneself** se sécher, s'essuyer
VI *(clothes, hair, fruit, leaves)* sécher; **to put sth out to d.** mettre qch à sécher dehors; **you wash I'll d.** *(dishes)* tu laves et moi j'essuie
►► ***dry battery*** pile *f* sèche; ***dry cell*** pile *f* sèche; ***dry cleaner*** *(person)* teinturier(ère) *m,f*; ***dry cleaner's*** *(shop)* teinturerie *f*, pressing *m*; **to take sth to the d. cleaner's** porter qch chez le teinturier *ou* à la teinturerie *ou* au pressing; *Naut* ***dry dock*** cale sèche; **in d. dock** en cale sèche; *Agr* ***dry farming*** culture *f* sèche, dry-farming *m*; ***dry ginger*** = boisson gazeuse aux extraits de gingembre; *Com* ***dry goods*** *Br* marchandises *fpl* sèches; *Am* tissus *mpl* et articles *mpl* de bonneterie; *Am* ***dry goods store*** magasin *m* de tissus et d'articles de bonneterie; ***dry ice*** neige *f* carbonique; ***dry land*** terre *f* ferme; ***dry martini*** martini *m* dry; ***dry measure*** = unité de mesure des matières sèches; ***dry riser*** colonne *f* sèche; ***dry rot*** *(UNCOUNT) (in wood, potatoes)* pourriture *f* sèche; ***dry run*** *(trial practice)* coup *m* d'essai, test *m*; *Mil* entraînement *m* avec tir à blanc; **to give sth a d. run** tester qch; **to have a d. run** faire un essai; ***dry ski slope*** piste *f* de ski artificielle

► **dry off VI** *(clothes)* sécher; *(person)* se sécher
VT SEP sécher; **to d. oneself off** se sécher

► **dry out VI 1** *(clothes)* sécher; *(person)* se sécher **2** *(alcoholic)* se faire désintoxiquer, faire une cure de désintoxication
VT SEP *(alcoholic)* désintoxiquer

► **dry up VI 1** *(well, river)* s'assécher, se tarir; *(puddle, street)* sécher; *(inspiration)* se tarir; *(cow)* se tarir
2 *(dry the dishes)* essuyer la vaisselle
3 *Fam (be quiet)* la fermer, la boucler; **d. up, will you?** ferme-la *ou* boucle-la, tu veux?
4 *Fam (actor, speaker)* avoir un trou (de mémoire)ᵔ

dryad ['draɪəd] *(pl* **dryads** *or* **dryades** [-di:z]) **N** *Myth* dryade *f*

dry-clean VT nettoyer à sec; **to have sth dry cleaned** faire nettoyer qch (à sec); **d. only** *(on garment label)* nettoyage à sec

dry-cleaning N *(UNCOUNT)* **1** *(action)* nettoyage *m* à sec **2** *(clothes ► being cleaned)* vêtements *mpl* laissés au nettoyage (à sec) *ou* chez le teinturier *ou* à la teinturerie; *(► to be cleaned)* vêtements *mpl* à emmener au nettoyage (à sec) *ou* chez le teinturier *ou* à la teinturerie

dryer = **drier**

dry-eyed ADJ to be d. ne pas pleurer

drying ['draɪɪŋ] **N** *(of clothes, hair)* séchage *m*; *(of skin, flowers, wood)* dessèchement *m*; *(with cloth)* essuyage *m*
ADJ *(wind)* desséchant
►► ***drying cupboard*** armoire *f* sèche-linge; ***drying out* 1** *Fam (of alcoholic)* désintoxicationᵔ *f* **2** *(of skin)* dessèchement *m*; *(of soil, wood, clothes)* séchage *m*; ***drying rack*** séchoir *m*; ***drying room*** séchoir *m*; ***drying up*** *(of stream, river etc)* tarissement *m*; *Br* **to do the d. up** *(dry the dishes)* essuyer la vaisselle

dryly = **drily**

dryness ['draɪnɪs] **N 1** *(of region, weather, skin)* sécheresse *f* **2** *(of humour)* mordant *m*, causticité *f*; **the d. of her wit** son humour pince-sans-rire

dry-roasted ADJ *(peanuts)* grillé à sec

DSB [ˌdi:es'bi:] **N** *(abbr* **direct satellite broadcasting)** diffusion *f* directe par satellite

DSC [ˌdi:es'si:] **N** *Br Mil (abbr* **Distinguished Service Cross)** = décoration de l'armée britannique

DSc [ˌdi:es'si:] **N** *Univ (abbr* **Doctor of Science)** *(person)* = titulaire d'un doctorat en sciences; *(qualification)* doctorat *m* en sciences

DSL [ˌdi:es'el] **N** *Comput (abbr* **Digital Subscriber Line)** ligne *f* d'abonné numérique, DSL *m*

DSM [ˌdi:es'em] **N** *Br Mil (abbr* **Distinguished Service Medal)** = décoration de l'armée britannique

DSO [ˌdi:es'əʊ] **N** *Br Mil (abbr* **Distinguished Service Order)** = décoration de l'armée britannique

DSS [ˌdi:es'es] N *Br Formerly Admin* (*abbr* **Department of Social Security**) = ministère britannique de la Sécurité sociale

DST [ˌdi:es'ti:] N *Am* (*abbr* **daylight saving time**) heure *f* d'été

DTI [ˌdi:ti:'aɪ] N *Br Admin* (*abbr* **Department of Trade and Industry**) = ministère britannique du Commerce et de l'Industrie

DTP [ˌdi:tɪ'pi:] N *Comput* (*abbr* **desktop publishing**) PAO *f*

▸▸ ***DTP operator*** opérateur(trice) *m,f* de PAO; ***DTP software*** logiciel *m* de PAO

DT's [ˌdi:'ti:z] NPL *Fam* (*abbr* **delirium tremens**) delirium tremens□ *m*; **to have the D.** avoir une crise de delirium tremens

DTT [ˌdi:ti:'ti:] N (*abbr* **digital terrestrial television**) TNT *f*

dual ['dju:əl] ADJ (*purpose, nationality*) double; **to have d. nationality** avoir la double nationalité; **to have a d. personality** souffrir d'un dédoublement de la personnalité; **to have a d. purpose** *or* **function** avoir une double fonction; **with the d. aim of reducing inflation and stimulating demand** dans le but à la fois de réduire l'inflation et de stimuler la demande

▸▸ *Br Aut* ***dual carriageway*** route *f* à quatre voies; *Aviat & Aut* ***dual controls*** double commande *f*; ***dual currency*** deux monnaies *fpl*; ***dual economy*** économie *f* duale; *Br* ***dual ownership*** copropriété *f*

> Attention: ne pas confondre avec le nom anglais **duel**.

dual-band ADJ *Tel* dual-band, bibande

dual-control ADJ *Aviat & Aut* à double commande

dualism ['dju:əˌlɪzəm] N *Phil & Rel* dualisme *m*

duality [dju:'ælɪtɪ] N dualité *f*

dual-mode ADJ *Tel* Dual Mode

dual-purpose ADJ à double fonction

dual-venturi ADJ *Tech* à double venturi

dub [dʌb] (*pt & pp* **dubbed**, *cont* **dubbing**) N *Mus* dub *m*

VT **1** (*nickname*) surnommer **2** *Cin & TV* (*add soundtrack, voice*) sonoriser; (*in foreign language*) doubler; **dubbed into French** doublé en français **3** *Arch or Literary* **to d. sb a knight** armer *ou* adouber qn chevalier

dubbin ['dʌbɪn] N graisse *f* à chaussures, dégras *m*

VT graisser

dubbing ['dʌbɪŋ] N *Cin & TV* (*addition of soundtrack*) sonorisation *f*; (*in a foreign language*) doublage *m*

▸▸ ***dubbing mixer*** mélangeur *m* de son, ingénieur *m* du son; ***dubbing suite*** studio *m* de doublage

dubiety [dju:'baɪətɪ] N *Formal* (*uncertainty* ▸ *in voice, of expression, reply*) incertitude *f*; (▸ *of outcome*) nature *f* incertaine

dubious ['dju:bɪəs] ADJ **1** (*unsure* ▸ *reply, voice*) dubitatif; (▸ *expression*) dubitatif, d'incertitude; (▸ *outcome, value*) incertain; **to look d.** (*person*) avoir l'air dubitatif; **I'm rather d. about the whole thing** j'ai des doutes sur toute cette affaire; **I'm a bit d. about whether it will work** je ne suis pas très sûr que ça marche; **to be d. about whether to do sth** hésiter à faire qch **2** (*suspect* ▸ *person, nature, reputation, decision, origin*) douteux; (▸ *advantage*) contestable; (▸ *compliment*) équivoque; **of d. character** douteux; **a d. distinction** *or* **honour** un triste honneur

dubiously ['dju:bɪəslɪ] ADV **1** (*doubtfully*) d'un air de doute **2** (*in suspect manner*) d'une manière douteuse

dubiousness ['dju:bɪəsnɪs] N **1** (*uncertainty* ▸ *in voice, of expression, reply*) incertitude *f*; (▸ *of outcome*) nature *f* incertaine **2** (*suspect nature* ▸ *of person, reputation, decision, origin*) caractère *m* douteux; (*of advantage*) caractère *m* contestable; (*of compliment*) caractère *m* équivoque

Dubliner ['dʌblɪnə(r)] N Dublinois(e) *m,f*

ducal ['dju:kəl] ADJ ducal

ducat ['dʌkət] N *Hist* ducat *m*

• **ducats** NPL *Am Fam* (*money*) fric *m*, blé *m*, oseille *f*

duchess ['dʌtʃɪs] N duchesse *f*

duchesse potatoes ['dju:ʃes-] NPL *Culin* pommes *fpl* (de terre) duchesse

duchy ['dʌtʃɪ] (*pl* **duchies**) N duché *m*

duck [dʌk] N **1** (*bird*) canard *m*; **to take to sth like a d. to water** (*become good at*) se mettre à qch comme si on avait fait ça toute sa vie; (*develop a liking for*) prendre tout de suite goût à qch, mordre à qch; **criticism runs off him like water off a d.'s back** les critiques glissent sur lui comme de l'eau sur les plumes d'un canard; *Br* **to play (at) ducks and drakes** (*game*) faire des ricochets (dans l'eau); **to play ducks and drakes with** (*money*) gaspiller; (*person, issue*) traiter à la légère

2 (*in cricket*) score *m* nul; **to be out for a d.** ne marquer aucun point, faire un score nul; **to break one's d.** marquer son premier point

3 *Mil* véhicule *m* amphibie

4 (*material*) coutil *m*

• **ducks** N *Br Fam* (*form of address*) mon canard; **what do you want, ducks?** (*to woman*) et pour vous, ma petite dame?; (*to man*) et pour vas, monsieur

NPL (*trousers*) pantalon *m* de coutil

VT **1** (*dodge* ▸ *blow*) esquiver; **to d. one's head (out of the way)** baisser vivement la tête **2** (*submerge in water*) faire boire la tasse à **3** (*evade* ▸ *responsibility, question*) se dérober à, esquiver; **to d. the issue** s'esquiver; (*in reply*) user de faux-fuyants

VI **1** (*drop down quickly*) se baisser vivement; *Boxing* esquiver un coup; **d.!** baisse-toi!; **to d. under the water** plonger sous l'eau; **to d. behind a hedge** se cacher derrière une haie **2** *Fam* **to d. out of doing sth** (*avoid*) se défiler pour ne pas faire qch

▸▸ *Br very Fam* ***duck's arse*** (*hairstyle*) = coiffure masculine populaire dans les années 50 (cheveux courts plaqués vers l'arrière); ***duck pond*** mare *f* aux canards

duck-billed platypus [-bɪld-] N ornithorynque *m*

duckboards ['dʌkbɔ:dz] NPL caillebotis *m*

duckie = **ducky**

ducking ['dʌkɪŋ] N bain *m* forcé; **he got** *or* **took a d.** on lui a fait boire la tasse; *Br Fam* **d. and diving** (*trickery*) combines *fpl*; (*prevarication*) faux-fuyants *mpl*

duckling ['dʌklɪŋ] N (*male*) caneton *m*; (*female*) canette *f*; (*older*) canardeau *m*

duckweed ['dʌkwi:d] N *Bot* lentille *f* d'eau

ducky ['dʌkɪ] *Fam* N *Br* (*term of endearment*) mon canard; **what can I get you, d.?** (*to woman*) qu'est-ce qu'elle voulait, la petite dame *ou* demoiselle?; (*to man*) qu'est-ce qu'il voulait, le petit monsieur?

ADJ *Am* (*cute*) tout mignon

duct [dʌkt] N (*for gas, liquid, electricity*) conduite *f*, canalisation *f*; *Anat* conduit *m*, canal *m*; *Bot* vaisseau *m*; **tear/hepatic d.** canal *m* lacrymal/hépatique

▸▸ ***duct tape*** ruban *m* adhésif en toile

ductile ['dʌktaɪl] ADJ (*metal, plastic*) ductile; *Fig* (*person*) malléable, influençable

ductility [dʌk'tɪlɪtɪ] N (*of metal, plastic*) ductilité *f*; *Fig* (*of person*) malléabilité *f*

dud [dʌd] *Fam* ADJ (*false* ▸ *coin, note*) faux (fausse)□; (*useless* ▸ *drill, video*) qui ne marche pas□; (▸ *shell, bomb*) qui a raté□; (▸ *idea*) débile

N (*person*) nullité *f*, tache *f*; (*cheque*) chèque *m* en bois; (*coin*) fausse pièce *f* de monnaie□; (*note*) faux billet *m*□; (*shell*) obus *m* qui a raté *ou* qui n'a pas explosé□; **it's a d.** (*firework*) ça a raté, ce n'est pas parti; **to be a d. at maths/sport** être nul en maths/sport

▸▸ ***dud cheque*** chèque *m* en bois; ***dud note*** faux billet□ *m*

dude [du:d] N *Am Fam* **1** (*man*) type *m*, mec *m*; **hi** *or* **hey, d.!** salut mon vieux!; **a cool d.** un mec cool; **d.! that car is so cool!** la vache! elle est super cette bagnole! **2** *Old-fashioned* (*dandy*) gommeux *m* **3** (*city dweller*) citadin(e)□ *m,f*

▸▸ *Am* ***dude ranch*** = ranch qui propose des activités touristiques

dudgeon ['dʌdʒən] N *Formal* **in high d.** fort en colère, fort indigné

duds [dʌdz] NPL *Fam* (*clothes*) fringues *fpl*

DUE [dju:] N (*what one deserves*) **to give him his d., he did apologize** pour lui rendre justice, il faut reconnaître qu'il s'est excusé

ADJ **1** (*owed, payable* ▸ *amount, balance, money*) dû; (*debt*) exigible; (*bill*) échu; **when's the next instalment d.?** quand le prochain versement doit-il être fait?; **d. and payable now** (*on bill*) payable dès maintenant; **I'm d. some money next week** on doit me verser de l'argent la semaine prochaine; **repayment d. on 1 December** remboursement à effectuer le 1er décembre; **to fall d.** (*bill*) arriver à échéance, échoir; **to be d. an apology** avoir droit à des excuses; **to be d. a bit of luck/some good weather** mériter un peu de chance/du beau temps; **I'm d. (for) a** *Br* **rise** *or* *Am* **raise** (*I will receive one*) je vais être augmenté, je vais recevoir une augmentation; (*I deserve one*) je suis en droit d'attendre une augmentation; **(to give) credit where credit's d.** pour dire ce qui est, pour être juste

2 (*expected*) **we're d. round there at 7.30** on nous attend à 7h30, nous devons y être à 7h30; **to be d. to do sth** devoir faire qch; **we were d. to meet at 10p.m.** nous devions nous retrouver à 22 heures; **the train is d. in** *or* **to arrive now** le train devrait arriver d'un instant à l'autre; **she's d. back next week** elle doit rentrer la semaine prochaine; **the next issue is d. out next week** le prochain numéro doit sortir la semaine prochaine; **her baby is** *or* **she's d. any day now** elle doit accoucher d'un jour à l'autre

3 (*proper*) **to give sth d. consideration** accorder mûre réflexion à qch; **after d. consideration** après mûre réflexion; **to give sb d. warning** prévenir qn suffisamment tôt; **in d. course** (*at the proper time*) en temps voulu; (*in the natural course of events*) à un certain moment; (*at a later stage, eventually*) plus tard; **all in d. time** chaque chose en son temps; **to treat sb with d. respect** traiter qn avec le respect qui lui est dû; **with (all) d. respect...** avec tout le respect que je vous dois..., sauf votre respect...; **with (all) d. respect to the Prime Minister** avec tout le respect qui est dû au Premier ministre

ADV (*east, west etc*) plein

• **dues** NPL **1** (*fees*) droits *mpl*; *Fig* **he's paid his dues, he deserves his promotion** il a travaillé dur, il a mérité son avancement

2 (*books ordered*) livres *mpl* en commande

• **due to** PREP **1** (*owing to*) à cause de, en raison de; **d. to bad weather they arrived late** ils sont arrivés en retard à cause du mauvais temps

2 (*because of*) grâce à; **it's all d. to you** c'est grâce à toi; **her success is d. in (large) part to hard work** elle doit sa réussite en grande partie à son travail acharné; **d. to circumstances beyond our control** en raison de circonstances indépendantes de notre volonté

▸▸ *Law* ***due care*** diligence *f* normale; **to fail to exercise d. care and attention** ne pas prêter l'attention nécessaire; ***due date*** (*of bill, payment*) échéance *f*, (*of baby*) date *f* prévue pour la naissance; **on the d. date** à l'échéance, à terme échu; *Am Law* ***due process (of law)*** application *f* régulière de la loi

duel ['dju:əl] (*Br pt & pp* **duelled**, *cont* **duelling**, *Am pt & pp* **dueled**, *cont* **dueling**) N duel *m*; **to fight a d.** se battre en duel; **to challenge sb to a d.** provoquer qn en duel

VI se battre en duel

> Attention: ne pas confondre avec l'adjectif **dual**.

duelling, *Am* **dueling** ['dju:əlɪŋ] N le duel

▸▸ ***duelling pistols*** pistolets *mpl* de duel

duellist, *Am* **duelist** ['dju:əlɪst] N duelliste *mf*

duet [dju:'et] N duo *m*; **to sing/to play a d.** chanter/jouer en duo; **piano d.** (*performed on different pianos*) duo *m* pour piano; (*performed on one piano*) morceau *m* à quatre mains

VI **to d. with sb** chanter/jouer en duo avec qn

duettist [dju:'etɪst] N duettiste *mf*

duff [dʌf] ADJ *Fam (useless)* qui ne marche pas▫; *(idea)* débile; **it was a d. idea** c'était nul comme idée

N **1** *Br Fam* **up the d.** *(pregnant)* en cloque; **to get sb up the d.** mettre qn en cloque **2** *Am Fam (buttocks)* cul *m*, derche *m*; **get up off your d.!** bouge ton cul! **3** *Culin* = variante du plum-pudding

▸**duff up** VT SEP *Br Fam (beat up)* tabasser, démolir; **to get duffed up** se faire tabasser

duffel [ˈdʌfəl] N **1** *(fabric)* tissu *m* de laine **2** *Am (bag)* sac *m* marin

▸▸ ***duffel bag*** sac *m* marin; ***duffel coat*** duffel-coat *m*, duffle-coat *m*

duffer [ˈdʌfə(r)] N *Br Fam* **1** *(useless person)* gourde *f*; *(academically)* nullité *f*, cancre *m*; **to be a d. at sth** être nul en qch **2** *(old man)* vieux bonhomme *m*

duffle = **duffel**

dug [dʌg] *pt & pp of* **dig**

N mamelle *f*; *(of cow, goat)* pis *m*

dug-in ADJ retranché; *Mil* **a d. position** une position retranchée

dugout [ˈdʌgaʊt] N **1** *Mil* tranchée-abri *f*; *Sport* banc *m* abri de touche **2** *(canoe)* canoë *m* creusé dans un tronc

duh [dɜː] EXCLAM *Fam Ironic* **d.! I've got the map upside down, no wonder we're lost!** que je suis bête! la carte est à l'envers, pas étonnant qu'on se soit perdus!; **ouch, that dish is really hot! – well, d.!, it's just come out of the oven!** aïe, ce plat est brûlant! – évidemment, il sort du four!

DUI [ˌdiːjuːˈaɪ] N *Am (abbr* **driving under the influence***)* conduite *f* en état d'ivresse

duke [djuːk] N **1** *(nobleman)* duc *m* **2** *Old-fashioned Slang* **dukes** *(fists)* poings *mpl*; **put up your dukes!** en garde!

▸**duke out** VT SEP *Am Fam Old-fashioned* **to d. it out (with sb)** se bagarrer (avec qn)

dukedom [*Br* ˈdjuːkdəm, *Am* ˈduːkdəm] N *(territory)* duché *m*; *(title)* titre *m* de duc

dulcet [ˈdʌlsɪt] ADJ *Literary* doux (douce), suave; **her d. tones** sa douce voix

dulcimer [ˈdʌlsɪmə(r)] N *Mus* dulcimer *m*, tympanon *m*

dull [dʌl] ADJ **1** *(slow-witted* ▸ *person)* peu intelligent; *(*▸ *reflexes)* ralenti; **to grow d.** *(intellectual capacities)* s'affaiblir, décliner

2 *(boring* ▸ *book, person, lecture)* ennuyeux, assommant; **things have been pretty d. since she left** c'est plutôt monotone depuis qu'elle est partie; **there's never a d. moment with him around** on ne s'ennuie jamais avec lui; **deadly d.** mortel, ennuyeux à mourir; **it's deadly d. here** on s'ennuie à mourir ici

3 *(not bright* ▸ *colour)* terne, fade; *(*▸ *light, eyes)* terne; *(*▸ *weather, sky)* sombre, maussade

4 *(not sharp* ▸ *blade)* émoussé; *(*▸ *pain)* sourd; *(*▸ *sound)* sourd, étouffé; **the knife is d.** le couteau ne coupe plus bien

5 *(listless* ▸ *person)* abattu

6 *Com & Fin (market)* calme, inactif; **business is d.** les affaires ne marchent pas fort

VT *(sound)* assourdir; *(colour, metal)* ternir; *(blade, pleasure, senses, impression)* émousser; *(grief)* endormir

VI *(colour)* se ternir, perdre son éclat; *(pleasure)* s'émousser; *(pain)* s'atténuer; *(eyes)* s'assombrir, perdre son éclat; *(mind)* s'affaiblir, décliner

dullard [ˈdʌlɑd] N *Literary* benêt *m*

dullness [ˈdʌlnɪs] N **1** *(slow-wittedness)* lenteur *f ou* lourdeur *f* d'esprit

2 *(tedium* ▸ *of book, person, lecture)* caractère *m* ennuyeux

3 *(dimness* ▸ *of light)* faiblesse *f*; *(*▸ *of weather)* caractère *m* maussade

4 *(of sound, pain)* caractère *m* sourd; *(of blade)* manque *m* de tranchant

5 *(listlessness)* apathie *f*

6 *Com & Fin (of business)* stagnation *f*; *(of market)* inactivité *f*

dully [ˈdʌlɪ] ADV **1** *(listlessly)* d'un air déprimé; **…, she said d.** …, dit-elle d'une voix terne

2 *(tediously)* de manière ennuyeuse

3 *(dimly)* faiblement

4 *(not sharply)* sourdement

Dulux dog [ˈdjuːlʌks-] N *Br Fam* bobtail▫ *m (par allusion au chien qui apparaît dans les publicités des peintures Dulux®)*

duly [ˈdjuːlɪ] ADV **1** *(properly)* comme il convient; *(in accordance with the rules)* dans les règles, dûment; **d. appointed/elected** nommé/élu dans les règles, dûment nommé/élu **2** *(as expected* ▸ *arrive, call)* comme prévu; **I was d. surprised** comme de bien entendu, j'ai été surpris; **and he d. did what he had promised** et il a bien fait ce qu'il avait promis

dumb [dʌm] ADJ **1** *(unable or unwilling to speak)* muet; **to be struck d. (with fear/ surprise)** rester muet (de peur/ surprise); **d. animal** bête *f*, animal *m*; **d. insolence** silence *m ou* mutisme *m* insolent **2** *Fam (stupid)* bête▫; **that was a d. thing to do** c'est bête *ou* idiot d'avoir fait ça; **he's really d.** il est complètement abruti; **to play** *or* **act d.** jouer les imbéciles; **I don't want to go to some d. theatre!** je ne veux pas aller au théâtre, c'est nul!

▸▸ *Pej* ***dumb blonde*** blonde *f* évaporée; ***dumb show*** = pantomime faisant partie d'une pièce de théâtre; *Comput* ***dumb terminal*** terminal *m* passif; *Br* ***dumb waiter*** *(lift)* monte-plats *m inv*; *(trolley)* table *f* roulante; *(revolving tray)* plateau *m* tournant

▸**dumb down** VT SEP *(population, youth, electorate)* infantiliser; *(media, programme)* faire baisser le niveau de

dumbass [ˈdʌmæs] *Am very Fam* N taré(e) *m,f*, débile *mf*

ADJ débile

dumbbell [ˈdʌmbel] N **1** *Sport* haltère *m* **2** *Fam (fool)* abruti(e) *m,f*

dumbfound [dʌmˈfaʊnd] VT abasourdir, interloquer

dumbfounded [dʌmˈfaʊndɪd] ADJ *(person)* muet de stupeur, abasourdi, interloqué; *(silence)* stupéfait; **we were d. at the news** la nouvelle nous frappa de stupeur

dumbing down [ˈdʌmɪŋ-] N *(of population, youth, electorate)* infantilisation *f*, crétinisation *f*; *(of media, programme)* baisse *f* de niveau

dumbly [ˈdʌmlɪ] ADV silencieusement, sans prononcer un mot

dumbness [ˈdʌmnɪs] N **1** *(inability to speak)* mutité *f*; *(unwillingness to speak)* mutisme *m* **2** *Fam (stupidity)* bêtise▫ *f*, stupidité▫ *f*, imbécillité▫ *f*

dumbo [ˈdʌmbəʊ] N *Fam (fool)* abruti(e) *m,f*

dumbstruck [ˈdʌmstrʌk] ADJ *(person)* muet de stupeur, abasourdi, interloqué

dumdum [ˈdʌmdʌm] N **1** *Mil (bullet)* balle *f* dumdum **2** *Fam (fool)* cloche *f*

dummy [ˈdʌmɪ] *(pl* **dummies***)* N **1** *(in shop window, for dressmaking)* mannequin *m*; *(of ventriloquist)* marionnette *f*; *Fin (representative)* prête-nom *m*, homme *m* de paille; *Fam* **standing there like a stuffed d.** planté comme un piquet

2 *(fake object)* objet *m* factice; *(book, model for display)* maquette *f*; **all the bottles are dummies** toutes les bouteilles sont factices

3 *Br (for baby)* tétine *f*

4 *(in bridge* ▸ *cards)* main *f* du mort; *(*▸ *player)* mort *m*; **he is d.** c'est lui le mort

5 *Pej (mute)* muet(ette) *m,f*

6 *Fam (fool)* imbécile▫ *mf*

7 *Sport* feinte *f*; **to sell sb a d.** feinter qn

ADJ *(fake)* factice; **this is just a d. version** ce n'est qu'un modèle factice

VT *Sport* feinter

VI *Sport* feinter

▸▸ ***dummy bridge*** bridge *m* à trois personnes; ***dummy company*** société *f* fictive; ***dummy run*** *(trial)* essai *m*; *Aviat & Mil* attaque *f* simulée *ou* d'entraînement; **to give sth a d. run** faire l'essai de qch

dump [dʌmp] VT **1** *(rubbish, waste)* déverser, déposer; *(sand, gravel)* déverser; *(car, corpse)* abandonner; *(oil* ▸ *of ship)* vidanger; **to d. waste at sea** rejeter *ou* immerger des déchets dans la mer; **he just dumped me off at the motorway exit** il m'a déposé à la sortie de l'autoroute

2 *Fam (get rid of* ▸ *boyfriend, girlfriend)* plaquer; *(*▸ *member of government, board)* se débarrasser de▫; **to d. sb/sth on sb** laisser qn/qch sur les bras de qn▫; **they've dumped the kids on her again** ils lui ont encore refilé les gamins

3 *(set down* ▸ *bags, shopping, suitcase)* poser; **d. your bags in the corner** déposez *ou* laissez vos sacs dans le coin; **I'm just going home to d. my suitcase** je vais déposer ma valise chez moi

4 *Com* **to d. goods** faire du dumping

5 *Comput (memory)* vider

6 *Am Fam (kill)* buter, zigouiller

N **1** *(rubbish heap)* tas *m* d'ordures; *(place)* décharge *f*, dépôt *m* d'ordures

2 *Mil* dépôt *m*

3 *Fam Pej (town, village)* trou *m*; *(messy room, flat)* dépotoir *m*; **what a d.!** *(place)* quel trou!, quel bled!; **it's a real d. here** *(town)* c'est vraiment mortel ici

4 *Comput* cliché *m* mémoire; **(memory) d.** vidage *m* (de) mémoire; **(screen) d.** capture *f* d'écran

5 *very Fam* **to have** *or* **to take a d.** *(defecate)* chier, couler un bronze

VI *very Fam (defecate)* chier, couler un bronze

▸▸ *Mktg* **dump bin** panier *m* de présentation en vrac, panier *m* présentoir; *Comput* ***dump tape*** bande *f* de vidage; ***dump truck*** dumper *m*, tombereau *m*

▸**dump on** VT INSEP *Am Fam* **1** *(criticize)* s'en prendre à▫ **2** *Pej (complain to)* se décharger de ses problèmes sur▫

dumper [ˈdʌmpə(r)] N **d. (truck)** dumper *m*, tombereau *m*

dumping [ˈdʌmpɪŋ] N **1** *(of rubbish, waste)* dépôt *m ou* décharge *f* d'ordures *ou* de déchets; *(of toxic or nuclear waste* ▸ *at sea)* déversement *m ou* immersion *f* de déchets; *(*▸ *underground)* entreposage *m* sous terre de déchets; *(of oil from ship)* vidange *f*; **no d.** *(sign)* dépôt d'ordures interdit, décharge interdite **2** *Com* dumping *m* **3** *Comput (of memory)* vidage *m*

▸▸ ***dumping ground*** *(for rubbish)* décharge *f*, dépôt *m* d'ordures; *Fig (for inferior goods)* dépotoir *m*

dumpling [ˈdʌmplɪŋ] N **1** *Culin (savoury)* boulette *f* de pâte, knödel *m*; *Scot (sweet)* = variante du plum-pudding; **apple d.** pomme *f* en chausson **2** *Fam (plump person)* boulot(otte) *m,f*

dumps [dʌmps] NPL *Fam* **to be down in the d.** avoir le cafard

Dumpster® [ˈdʌmpstə(r)] N *Am* benne *f* à ordures

dumpy [ˈdʌmpɪ] ADJ *Fam (person)* courtaud▫, boulot; *(bottle)* pansu

dun [dʌn] *(pt & pp* **dunned**, *cont* **dunning***)* ADJ brun gris *(inv)*

N *(colour)* brun *m* gris *(inv)*; *(horse)* cheval *m* louvet; *(mare)* jument *f* louvette

VT *Com* presser, harceler; **to d. sb for money** *or* **payment** presser *ou* harceler qn pour qu'il paye

dunce [dʌns] N âne *m*, cancre *m*; **to be a d. at sth** être nul en qch

▸▸ ***dunce cap, dunce's cap*** bonnet *m* d'âne

dunderhead [ˈdʌndəhed] N âne *m*; **(you) d.!** espèce d'âne!

dune [djuːn] N dune *f*

▸▸ ***dune buggy*** buggy *m*

dung [dʌŋ] N *(UNCOUNT)* crotte *f*; *(of cow)* bouse *f*; *(of horse)* crottin *m*; *(of wild animal)* fumées *fpl*; *(manure)* fumier *m*

▸▸ *Entom* ***dung beetle, dung chafer*** bousier *m*

dungarees [ˌdʌŋgəˈriːz] NPL *Br (with bib)* salopette *f*; *Am (overalls)* bleu *m* de travail; **a pair of d.** *Br* une salopette, *Am* un bleu de travail

dungeon [ˈdʌndʒən] N *(in castle)* cachot *m* souterrain; *(tower)* donjon *m*; **Dungeons and Dragons®** *(game)* Donjons et Dragons *m*

dunghill [ˈdʌŋhɪl] N gros tas *m* de fumier

dunk [dʌŋk] VT **1** *(dip)* tremper **2** *(in basketball)* **to d. the ball** faire un lancer coulé

N *(in basketball)* dunk *m*, lancer *m* coulé

Dunkirk [dʌnˈkɜːk] N **1** *Geog* Dunkerque **2** *Hist* = l'évacuation des troupes alliées de Dunkerque, en mai–juin 1940

▸▸ ***Dunkirk spirit*** esprit *m* de ténacité

dunlin [ˈdʌnlɪn] N *Orn* bécasseau *m* variable

dunno [dəˈnəʊ] EXCLAM *Fam (abbr* **I don't know***)* j'sais pas!

dunnock [ˈdʌnək] N *Orn* accenteur *m* mouchet, fauvette *f* d'hiver

dunny ['dʌnɪ] **N** *Austr Fam (toilet)* chiottes *mpl*

duo ['dju:əʊ] **N** *Mus & Theat* duo *m*; *(couple)* couple *m*

duodecimal [ˌdju:əʊ'desɪməl] **ADJ** duodécimal

duodenal [ˌdju:əʊ'di:nəl] **ADJ** *Anat* duodénal
▸▸ *Med* ***duodenal ulcer*** ulcère *m* duodénal

duodenum [ˌdju:əʊ'di:nəm](*pl* **duodenums** *or* **duodena** [-nə]) **N** *Anat* duodénum *m*

dupe [dju:p] **VT** duper, leurrer; **to d. sb into doing sth** duper *ou* leurrer qn pour qu'il fasse qch; **she duped him into believing that…** elle lui a fait gober que…
N dupe *f*

duple ['dju:pəl] **ADJ 1** *Formal (double)* double **2** *Mus* binaire, à deux temps
▸▸ *Mus* ***duple time*** rythme *m* binaire *ou* à deux temps

duplex ['dju:pleks] **ADJ 1** *(double, twofold)* double **2** *Elec & Tel* duplex **3** *Typ (printing, copying)* recto verso
N *(apartment)* (appartement *m* en) duplex *m*; *Am (house)* = maison convertie en deux appartements
▸▸ *Am* ***duplex apartment*** (appartement *m* en) duplex *m*; *Am* ***duplex house*** = maison convertie en deux appartements

duplicate **VT** ['dju:plɪkeɪt] **1** *(document)* dupliquer, faire un double/des doubles de; *(key)* faire un double *ou* des doubles de **2** *(repeat ▸ work)* refaire; *(▸ feat)* reproduire; **that's just duplicating what they've already done** cela revient à refaire ce qu'ils ont déjà fait
N ['dju:plɪkət] *(of key, document)* double *m*; *Admin & Law* duplicata *m*, copie *f* conforme; **in d.** en double, en deux exemplaires
ADJ ['dju:plɪkət] *(key, document)* en double; *(receipt, certificate)* en duplicata
▸▸ ***duplicate copy*** *(of key, document)* double *m*; *(of receipt, certificate)* duplicata *m*

duplicating machine ['dju:plɪˌkeɪtɪŋ-] **N** duplicateur *m*

duplication [ˌdju:plɪ'keɪʃən] **N 1** *(on machine)* reproduction *f*; *(result)* double *m* **2** *(repetition ▸ of work, efforts)* répétition *f*; **unnecessary d. of work** répétition *f* inutile du travail

duplicator ['dju:plɪˌkeɪtə(r)] **N** duplicateur *m*

duplicitous [dju:'plɪsɪtəs] **ADJ** fourbe, faux (fausse)

duplicity [dju:'plɪsɪtɪ] **N** fausseté *f*, duplicité *f*

durability [ˌdjʊərə'bɪlɪtɪ] **N** *(of construction, relationship, peace)* caractère *m* durable, durabilité *f*; *(of fabric, metal)* résistance *f*; *(of politician, athlete)* longévité *f*

durable ['djʊərəbəl] **ADJ** *(construction, relationship, peace)* durable; *(fabric, metal)* résistant; *(politician, athlete)* qui jouit d'une grande longévité
• **durables** **NPL** biens *mpl* durables *ou* non périssables
▸▸ *Com* ***durable goods*** biens *mpl* durables *ou* non périssables

duration [djʊ'reɪʃən] **N** durée *f*; **of short d.** de courte durée; **for the d. of the summer holiday** pendant toute la durée des grandes vacances; **are you here for the d.?** êtes-vous ici jusqu'à la fin?

duress [djʊ'res] **N** contrainte *f*; **under d.** sous la contrainte

Durex® ['djʊəreks] **N 1** *Br (condom)* préservatif *m* **2** *Austr* Scotch® *m (ruban adhésif)*

during ['djʊərɪŋ] **PREP** pendant; *(in the course of)* au cours de; **they met d. the war** ils se sont rencontrés pendant la guerre; **d. the journey** en cours de route; **d. the investigation it emerged that…** au cours de l'enquête, il est apparu que…

durum ['djʊərəm] **N** blé *m* dur
▸▸ ***durum (wheat) semolina*** semoule *f* de blé dur

dusk [dʌsk] **N** crépuscule *m*; **at d.** au crépuscule, à la nuit tombante

duskiness ['dʌskɪnɪs] **N** *(of complexion)* matité *f*

dusky ['dʌskɪ] *(compar* **duskier**, *superl* **duskiest)** **ADJ 1** *(light)* crépusculaire; *(colour)* sombre, foncé; *(room)* sombre **2** *(skin)* mat

dust [dʌst] **N 1** *(UNCOUNT) (on furniture, of gold, coal)* poussière *f*; **a speck of d.** une poussière, un grain de poussière; **thick d. covered the furniture** une poussière épaisse couvrait les meubles; **to gather d.** *(ornaments)* amasser la poussière; *Fig (plans, proposals)* rester en plan; **to take a d. bath** *(of bird)* s'ébrouer dans la poussière; **to lay** *or* **to settle the d.** mouiller la poussière; *Fig* **to allow the d. to** *or* **to let the d. settle** attendre que les choses se calment; *Fig* **once the d. has settled** quand les choses se seront calmées; *Fam* **to raise a d.** faire tout un cinéma *ou* foin; **to throw d. in sb's eyes** tromper qn; **we won't see him for d.** *(he'll leave)* il partira en moins de temps qu'il n'en faut pour le dire **2** *(action)* **to give sth a d.** épousseter qch
VT 1 *(furniture, room)* épousseter; *Fig* **everything should be done and dusted by next Friday** tout doit être bouclé pour vendredi **2** *(with powder, flour)* saupoudrer; **to d. a field with insecticide** répandre de l'insecticide sur un champ; **to d. sth for fingerprints** chercher des empreintes digitales sur qch
VI the police are dusting for fingerprints la police cherche des empreintes digitales
▸▸ ***dust bag*** *(for vacuum cleaner)* sac *m* à poussière; *Am* ***dust ball*** mouton *m (poussière)*; *Geog* ***dust bowl*** zone *f* semi-désertique; ***dust cover*** *(for book)* jaquette *f*; *(for machine)* housse *f* de rangement; *(for furniture)* housse *f* de protection; ***dust devil*** tourbillon *m* de poussière; ***dust jacket*** *(for book)* jaquette *f*; *Entom* ***dust mite*** acarien *m* de poussière; *Br* ***dust sheet*** housse *f* de protection; ***dust storm*** tempête *f* de poussière; ***dust trap*** nid *m* à poussière
▸ **dust down** *(with brush)* brosser; *(with hand)* épousseter

dustbin ['dʌstbɪn] **N** *Br (for rubbish)* poubelle *f*
▸▸ ***dustbin lid*** couvercle *m* de poubelle; ***dustbin liner*** sac-poubelle *m*; ***dustbin man*** éboueur *m*

dustcart ['dʌstkɑ:t] **N** *Br* camion *m* des éboueurs

dustcloud ['dʌstklaʊd] **N** nuage *m* de poussière

duster ['dʌstə(r)] **N 1** *(cloth)* chiffon *m* (à poussière); *(for blackboard)* tampon *m* effaceur
2 *Am (garment ▸ for doing housework)* blouse *f*, tablier *m*; *(▸ for driving)* cache-poussière *m inv*
3 *(lightweight coat)* manteau *m* léger
4 *Agr* poudreuse *f*; *(aircraft)* = avion servant à répandre de l'insecticide sur les champs

dustiness ['dʌstɪnɪs] **N** état *m* poussiéreux

dusting ['dʌstɪŋ] **N 1** *(of room, furniture)* époussetage *m*, dépoussiérage *m*; **to do the d.** enlever la poussière, faire la poussière *ou* les poussières **2** *(with sugar, insecticide)* saupoudrage *m*; **give the cake a d. of icing sugar** saupoudrez le gâteau de sucre glace
▸▸ ***dusting powder*** talc *m*

dustman ['dʌstmən] (*pl* **dustmen** [-mən]) **N** *Br* éboueur *m*

dustpan ['dʌstpæn] **N** pelle *f* à poussière

dustproof ['dʌstpru:f] **ADJ** imperméable *ou* étanche à la poussière

dust-up **N** *Fam* accrochage *m*, prise *f* de bec; **to have a bit of a d. with sb/over** *or* **about sth** avoir une prise de bec avec qn/à propos de qch

dusty ['dʌstɪ] *(compar* **dustier**, *superl* **dustiest)** **ADJ 1** *(room, furniture, road)* poussiéreux; **to get d.** s'empoussiérer, se couvrir de poussière; *Fam Fig Old-fashioned* **not so d.** pas si mal **2** *(colour)* cendré; **d. pink** vieux rose *m inv* **3** *Fam Old-fashioned (idiom)* **to get a d. answer** se faire envoyer balader *ou* paître, se faire recevoir

Dutch [dʌtʃ] **NPL the D.** les Hollandais *mpl*, les Néerlandais *mpl*
N *(language)* néerlandais *m*
ADJ *(cheese)* de Hollande; *(bulbs, city)* hollandais; **to talk (to sb) like a D. uncle** faire la morale (à qn)
COMP *(embassy, history)* des Pays-Bas; *(teacher)* de néerlandais
ADV to go D. (with sb) *(share cost equally)* partager les frais (avec qn); **let's go D.** payons chacun notre part
▸▸ ***Dutch auction*** vente *f* à la baisse; *Br* ***Dutch barn*** hangar *m* à récoltes; *Br* ***Dutch cap*** diaphragme *m (contraceptif)*; *Fam* ***Dutch courage*** = courage trouvé dans la boisson; **I need some D. courage** il faut que je boive un verre pour me donner du courage; *Am* ***Dutch door*** porte *f* à deux vantaux; ***Dutch elm disease*** *(UNCOUNT)* maladie *f* de l'orme, graphiose *f*; ***Dutch oven*** *(casserole)* marmite *f*, fait-tout *m inv*; *Fam* ***Dutch treat*** = sortie où chacun paye son écot

dutch [dʌtʃ] **N** *Br Fam Old-fashioned* **the old d.** *(wife)* la patronne

Dutchman ['dʌtʃmən] (*pl* **Dutchmen** [-mən]) **N** Hollandais *m*, Néerlandais *m*; *Fig* **(then) I'm a D.!** je mange mon chapeau!

Dutchwoman ['dʌtʃˌwʊmən] (*pl* **Dutchwomen** [-'wɪmɪn]) **N** Hollandaise *f*, Néerlandaise *f*

dutiable ['dju:tjəbəl] **ADJ** *(goods purchased abroad)* soumis aux droits de douane, taxable

dutiful ['dju:tɪful] **ADJ** *(child)* obéissant, respectueux; *(husband, wife)* dévoué; *(worker, employee)* consciencieux; *(laughter, applause)* poli

dutifully ['dju:tɪfəlɪ] **ADV** *(work)* consciencieusement; **they smiled d.** ils sourirent poliment; **he kissed his mother d.** il embrassa sa mère machinalement

duty ['dju:tɪ] **N 1** *(moral or legal obligation)* devoir *m*; **to do one's d.** faire *ou* remplir son devoir; **to do one's d. by sb** remplir son devoir envers qn; **to fail in one's d.** manquer à son devoir; **it is my painful d. to inform you that…** j'ai la douloureuse tâche de vous informer que…; **I shall make it my d. to…** je considérerai de mon devoir de…; **it is your d. to…** il est de ton devoir de…; *Hum* **I must go, d. calls** je dois y aller, le devoir m'appelle; **to do sth out of a sense of d.** faire qch par sens du devoir
2 *(usu pl) (responsibility)* fonction *f*; **to take up one's duties** entrer en fonction; **to carry out** *or* **perform one's duties** exercer ses fonctions; **to hand over one's duties (to sb)** transmettre ses fonctions (à qn); **in the course of one's duties** dans l'exercice de ses fonctions; **public duties** responsabilités *fpl* publiques *ou* envers la communauté
3 *(tax)* taxe *f*, droit *m*; **customs d.** droit(s) *m(pl)* de douane; **liable to d.** passible de droits; **to pay d. on sth** payer une taxe sur qch; **d. paid** *(on document)* franc de douane, droits acquittés
4 *(of employee)* **on d.** *(soldier, doctor)* de garde; *(policeman)* de service; **to go on/off d.** *(soldier)* prendre/laisser la garde; *(doctor)* prendre la/cesser d'être de garde; *(policeman)* prendre/quitter son service; *Mil* **to be off d.** avoir quartier libre; **to do d. for sb** remplacer qn (dans son service); *Fig* **to do d. for sth** faire office de qch
▸▸ ***duty call*** visite *f* de politesse; **to pay a d. call** faire une visite de politesse; ***duty doctor*** médecin *m* de garde; *Journ* ***duty editor*** rédacteur *m* en chef de service; ***duty manager*** directeur(trice) *m,f* de service; ***duty officer*** officier *m* de service; ***duty roster, duty rota*** tableau *m* de service

duty-bound **ADJ** *Br* tenu (par son devoir); **you are d. to do it** votre devoir vous y oblige, vous y êtes tenu; **I feel d. to…** je me sens tenu par mon devoir de…

duty-free **ADJ** *(goods)* hors taxe, en franchise; *(shop)* hors taxe
ADV hors taxe, en franchise; **how much can I bring back d.?** combien de marchandises puis-je rapporter hors taxe *ou* en franchise?
N marchandises *fpl* hors taxe *ou* en franchise
▸▸ ***duty-free allowance*** quantité *f* de marchandises hors taxe autorisée; **my d. allowance** les marchandises hors taxe auxquelles j'ai droit; ***duty-free goods*** marchandises *fpl* franches de douane, marchandises *fpl* hors taxe; ***duty-free shop*** magasin *m* hors taxe

duvet ['du:veɪ] **N** *Br* couette *f*
▸▸ ***duvet cover*** housse *f* de couette; *Fam* ***duvet day*** = journée de congé supplémentaire pouvant être prise de façon impromptue

dux [dʌks] **N** *Scot Sch* premier(ère) *m,f* de l'école

DVB [ˌdi:vi:'bi:] **N** *(abbr* **Digital Video Broadcasting)** diffusion *f* numérique, DVB *f*

DVD [ˌdi:vi:'di:] **N** *Comput (abbr* **Digital Versatile Disk, Digital Video Disk)** DVD *m*; **on D.** sur DVD
▸▸ ***DVD player*** lecteur *m* de DVD

DVD-R [ˌdi:vi:ˌdi:'ɑ:(r)] **N** *Comptr (abbr* **Digital Versatile Disk-recordable)** DVD-R *m*

DVD-ROM N (*abbr* **Digital Versatile Disk read-only memory**) DVD-ROM *m*, DVD-Rom *m*

DVD-RW [di:vi:di:ɑ:'dʌb(ə)lju:] N *Comptr* (*abbr* **digital video disk-rewritable**) DVD-RW *m*

DVT [ˌdi:vi:'ti:] N *Med* (*abbr* **deep-vein thrombosis**) TVP *f*

dwarf [dwɔ:f] (*pl* **dwarfs** *or* **dwarves** [dwɔ:vz]) N **1** *(person)* nain(e) *m,f* **2** *(tree)* arbre *m* nain **3** *Myth* nain(e) *m,f*

ADJ *(plant, animal)* nain; **d. variety** variété *f* naine

VT **1** *(building)* écraser; *(achievements)* éclipser; **the tower dwarfs the main building** le bâtiment principal paraît tout petit à côté de la tour; **the church is dwarfed by the skyscraper** l'église est écrasée par le gratte-ciel; **Jack was so tall that he dwarfed his classmates** Jack était tellement grand que ses camarades de classe avaient l'air de nains par rapport à lui **2** *(make small* ► *tree)* rabougrir

►► *Astron* ***dwarf planet*** planète *f* naine; ***dwarf star*** étoile *f* naine, naine *f*

dwarfish ['dwɔ:fɪʃ] ADJ *(hands, feet)* de nain; *(person)* de taille très petite

dwarves [dwɔ:vz] *pl of* **dwarf**

dweeb [dwi:b] N *Am Fam* ringard(e) *m,f*

dwell [dwel] (*pt & pp* **dwelt** [dwelt] *or* **dwelled**) VI *Literary* demeurer, habiter; **to d. in sb's mind** *(image, thought)* rester dans l'esprit de qn

► **dwell on, dwell upon** VT INSEP *(the past* ► *think about)* penser sans cesse à; (► *talk about)* parler sans cesse de; *(problem, fact, memories)* s'attarder sur; **don't dwell on it** *(in thought)* n'y pense pas trop

dweller ['dwelə(r)] N habitant(ante) *m,f* (**in, on** de); **city-d.** citadin(ine) *m,f*

-dwelling ['dwelɪŋ] SUFF **tree-d.** arboricole, qui vit sur les arbres; **ocean-d.** qui vit dans l'océan; **cave-d. people** troglodytes *mpl*

dwelling ['dwelɪŋ] N *Literary* demeure *f*; *Admin* domicile *m*

►► *Law* ***dwelling house*** maison *f* d'habitation; *Literary* ***dwelling place*** demeure *f*

dwelt [dwelt] *pt & pp of* **dwell**

DWEM [dwem] N (*abbr* **dead white European male**) = écrivain, musicien etc européen blanc mort depuis longtemps

DWI [ˌdi:dʌbəlju:'aɪ] N *Am* (*abbr* **driving while intoxicated**) conduite *f* en état d'ébriété

dwindle ['dwɪndəl] VI *(hopes, savings, population)* se réduire, diminuer; **the island's population has dwindled to 120** la population de l'île est descendue à 120 habitants; **to d. (away) to nothing** se réduire à rien

dwindling ['dwɪndlɪŋ] N *(of savings, hopes)* diminution *f*; *(of population, audience, membership)* baisse *f*, diminution *f*; *(of enthusiasm)* baisse *f*

ADJ *(savings, hopes)* décroissant; *(population, audience, membership)* en baisse, décroissant; *(enthusiasm)* faiblissant; **d. pupil numbers** le nombre décroissant d'élèves; **a d. number of people** de moins en moins de gens

DWP [ˌdi:dʌbəlju:'pi:] N *Br Pol* (*abbr* **Department for Work and Pensions**) ministère *m* du Travail

dye [daɪ] N *(substance)* teinture *f*; *(colour)* teinte *f*, couleur *f*; **fast d.** *(on label)* bon teint; **the d. will run in the wash** la couleur partira au lavage; **it's the d. from my shoes** ce sont mes chaussures qui déteignent; *Literary* **villain of the deepest d.** fieffé coquin *m*

VT *(fabric, hair)* teindre; **to d. sth yellow/green** teindre qch en jaune/en vert; **to d. one's hair** se teindre les cheveux

VI *(fabric)* se teindre; **nylon doesn't d. well** le nylon est difficile à teindre *ou* se teint difficilement

dyed-in-the-wool [ˌdaɪd-] ADJ bon teint *(inv)*, invétéré; **a d. conservative** un conservateur bon teint

dyeing ['daɪɪŋ] N *(action)* teinture *f*

dyer ['daɪə(r)] N teinturier(ère) *m,f*; **d. and cleaner** teinturier(ère) *m,f* dégraisseur(euse)

dyestuff ['daɪstʌf] N teinture *f*, colorant *m*

dyeworks ['daɪwɜ:ks] (*pl* **inv**) N teinturerie *f*

dying ['daɪɪŋ] ADJ **1** *(person, animal)* mourant; *Literary* agonisant; *(tree, forest)* mourant; *(species)* en voie de disparition; **the d. man** le mourant; **her d. words** les mots qu'elle a prononcés en mourant, ses derniers mots; **it was her d. wish that…** sa dernière volonté était que…; **to** *or* **till my d. day** jusqu'à ma mort, jusqu'à mon dernier jour; **men like him are a d. breed** des hommes comme lui, on n'en fait plus **2** *Fig (art, craft)* en train de disparaître; *(industry)* en train de disparaître, en voie de disparition

N *(death throes)* agonie *f*; *(death)* mort *f*

NPL **the d.** les mourants *mpl*, les agonisants *mpl*; **prayers for the d.** prières *fpl* pour les mourants

dyke [daɪk] N **1** *(against flooding)* digue *f*; *(for carrying water away)* fossé *m*; *(embankment)* chaussée *f* surélevée *ou* en remblai **2** *very Fam (lesbian)* gouine *f*, = terme injurieux désignant une lesbienne

VT *(river)* endiguer; *(land)* protéger par des digues

dynamic [daɪ'næmɪk] ADJ **1** *(person)* dynamique **2** *Tech* dynamique

N dynamique *f*

►► *Comput* ***dynamic data exchange*** échange *m* dynamique de données; *Comput* ***dynamic RAM*** mémoire *f* RAM dynamique

dynamically [daɪ'næmɪkəlɪ] ADV dynamiquement

dynamics [daɪ'næmɪks] NPL *(of a situation, group)* dynamique *f*

N *(UNCOUNT) (study)* dynamique *f*

dynamism ['daɪnəmɪzəm] N *Phys & Fig* dynamisme *m*

dynamite ['daɪnəmaɪt] N *(explosive)* dynamite *f*; **a stick of d.** un bâton de dynamite; *Fig* **this story is d.!** cette histoire, c'est de la dynamite!; **a subject that is political d.** un sujet explosif sur le plan politique; *Fig* **this band is d.!** ce groupe est génial!

VT *(blow up)* dynamiter

dynamiting ['daɪnəˌmaɪtɪŋ] N dynamitage *m*

dynamo ['daɪnəməʊ] N *Tech* dynamo *f*; *Fig* **he's a human d.** il déborde d'énergie

dynastic [dɪ'næstɪk] ADJ dynastique

dynasty [*Br* 'dɪnəstɪ, *Am* 'daɪnəstɪ] N dynastie *f*; **the Romanov/Bourbon d.** la dynastie des Romanov/des Bourbon

dyne [daɪn] N *Phys* dyne *f*

dysentery ['dɪsəntrɪ] N *(UNCOUNT) Med* dysenterie *f*; **to have d.** avoir la dysenterie

dysfunction [dɪs'fʌŋkʃən] N *Med* dysfonction *f*, dysfonctionnement *m*

dysfunctional [dɪs'fʌŋkʃənəl] ADJ dysfonctionnel; **a d. family** une famille à problèmes

dyslectic [dɪs'lektɪk] *Med* N dyslexique *mf*

ADJ dyslexique

dyslexia [dɪs'leksɪə] N *Med* dyslexie *f*; **to suffer from d.** être dyslexique

dyslexic [dɪs'leksɪk] *Med* N dyslexique *mf*

ADJ dyslexique

dysmenorrhoea, *Am* **dysmenorrhea** [ˌdɪsmenə'rɪə] N *(UNCOUNT) Med* dysménorrhée *f*; **to have d.** souffrir de dysménorrhée

dyspepsia [dɪs'pepsɪə] N *(UNCOUNT) Med* dyspepsie *f*; **to have d.** souffrir de dyspepsie

dyspeptic [dɪs'peptɪk] N *Med* dyspeptique *mf*, dyspepsique *mf*

ADJ **1** *Med* dyspeptique, dyspepsique **2** *Fig (irritable)* irritable

dysphasia [dɪs'feɪzɪə] N *Med* dysphasie *f*

dystrophy ['dɪstrəfɪ] N *Med* dystrophie *f*

E[1], **e** [iː] **N 1** *(letter)* E, e *m inv*; **two e's** deux e; *Fam* **to give sb the big E** *(partner)* plaquer qn; *(employee)* virer qn **2** *Sch* **to get an E** avoir une très mauvaise note, avoir une note inférieure à 7 sur 20 **3** *Mus* mi *m*; **in E flat** en mi bémol

E[2] **N** *Fam Drugs slang (abbr* **ecstasy***) (drug, pill)* ecsta *f*

E[3] *(written abbr* **East***)* E

each [iːtʃ] **ADJ** chaque; **e. child has a different name** chaque enfant a un nom différent; **e. day** chaque jour, tous les jours; **e. (and every) one of us/you/them** chacun/chacune d'entre nous/vous/eux (sans exception)

PRON *(every one)* chacun, chacune; **e. of his six children** chacun de ses six enfants; **a number of suggestions, e. more crazy than the last** un certain nombre de suggestions toutes plus folles les unes que les autres; **to e. his own, e. to his own** à chacun ses goûts

ADV *(apiece)* **we have a book/a room e.** nous avons chacun un livre/une pièce; **the tickets cost £20 e.** les billets coûtent 20 livres chacun

• **each other PRON to hate e. other** se détester (l'un l'autre); *(more than two people)* se détester (les uns les autres); **do you two know e. other?** est-ce que vous vous connaissez?; **the children took e. other's hand** les enfants se sont pris par la main; **they walked towards e. other** ils ont marché l'un vers l'autre; **we get on e. other's nerves** nous nous portons mutuellement sur les nerfs

• **each way ADJ e. way bet** pari sur un cheval gagnant, premier ou placé **ADV** *(in betting)* placé; **to put money e. way on a horse** jouer un cheval placé

eager [ˈiːɡə(r)] **ADJ** *(impatient, keen)* impatient; *(learner, helper)* enthousiaste, fervent; *(crowd, face, look)* passionné, enfiévré; **to be e. to do sth** *(impatient)* avoir hâte de faire qch; *(very willing)* faire preuve d'enthousiasme *ou* de ferveur pour faire qch; **I am e. to help in any way I can** je tiens absolument à apporter mon aide; **to be e. to please** avoir envie de faire plaisir; **he's e. for me to see his work** il a très envie que je voie son travail

▸▸ *Fam* ***eager beaver*** travailleur(euse) *m,f* acharné(e)[□], mordu(e) *m,f* du travail

eagerly [ˈiːɡəlɪ] **ADV** *(wait)* impatiemment; *(help, ask)* avec empressement; *(say, look at, study)* avec passion; **her e. awaited second album** son deuxième album impatiemment attendu

eagerness [ˈiːɡənɪs] **N** *(to know, see, find out)* impatience *f*; *(to help)* empressement *m*; **to show** *or* **have no e. for sth** n'avoir aucunement envie de qch; **his e. to please** sa volonté de plaire; **her e. to succeed** son ardent désir de réussir

eagle [ˈiːɡəl] **N 1** *(bird)* aigle *m*

2 *(standard, seal)* aigle *f*

3 *Am Mil* aigle *m (insigne de grade de colonel)*

4 *Golf* eagle *m*

▸▸ *Orn* ***eagle owl*** grand-duc *m*

eagle-eyed ADJ aux yeux d'aigle

ADV *(watch)* avec une grande attention

eaglet [ˈiːɡlɪt] **N** *Orn* aiglon(onne) *m,f*

E & OE, E and OE [ˌiːənˈdəʊiː] **N** *Com (abbr* **errors and omissions excepted***)* SEO

ear [ɪə(r)] **N 1** *(of person, animal)* oreille *f*; **to have a good e.** avoir de l'oreille; **to have an e. for music** avoir l'oreille musicale; **to keep an e.** *or* **one's ears open** ouvrir les oreilles, tendre l'oreille; **keep an e. open for the baby** ouvre l'oreille au cas où le bébé pleurerait; **it has reached my ears that...** j'ai entendu dire que…; **he closed his ears to her request for help** elle lui a demandé de l'aide mais il a fait la sourde oreille; *Fam* **I've heard that until it's coming out of my ears** je l'ai tellement entendu que ça me sort par les oreilles; **to have the e. of sb** *(have influence with)* avoir l'oreille de qn; **to be grinning from e. to e.** sourire jusqu'aux oreilles; *Fam* **to be all ears** être tout oreilles *ou* tout ouïe; *Fam* **to throw sb out on his/her e.** *(from job, school)* virer qn; *(from family home)* flanquer qn dehors; *Fam* **to be up to one's ears in work** *or* **in it** être débordé (de travail); **to be up to one's ears in debt** être endetté jusqu'au cou; **it just goes in one e. and out the other** ça entre par une oreille et ça ressort par l'autre; **to keep one's e. to the ground** ouvrir l'oreille, être à l'écoute; **my ears are burning!** j'ai les oreilles qui (me) sifflent!; *Mus* **to play by e.** jouer à l'oreille; *Fig* **to play it by e.** improviser

2 *Tech (of vase)* anse *f*, oreille *f*; *(of bell)* anse

3 *(of seashell)* oreillette *f*

4 *(of grain)* épi *m*

▸▸ ***ear flap*** *(on cap)* oreillette *f*; ***ear infection*** otite *f*; ***ear, nose and throat department*** service *m* d'oto-rhino-laryngologie; ***ear, nose and throat specialist*** oto-rhino *mf*, oto-rhino-laryngologiste *mf*; ***ear protector*** *(against cold)* protège-tympan *m inv*; *(against noise)* casque *m* anti-bruit; ***ear trumpet*** cornet *m* acoustique

earache [ˈɪəreɪk] **N** mal *m* d'oreille; **to have** *Br* **e.** *or Am* **an e.** avoir mal aux oreilles

earbashing [ˈɪəbæʃɪŋ] **N** *Br Fam* **to give sb an e.** passer un savon à qn, souffler dans les bronches à qn; **to get an e.** se faire passer un savon, se faire souffler dans les bronches

earbud [ˈɪəbʌd] **N** mini-écouteur *m*

eardrops [ˈɪədrɒps] **NPL** gouttes *fpl* pour les oreilles

eardrum [ˈɪədrʌm] **N** tympan *m*

-eared [ɪəd] **SUFF long/short-e.** à oreilles longues/courtes

earful [ˈɪəfʊl] **N** *Fam* **to get an e.** *(be told off)* se faire passer un savon; **get an e. of this!** écoute un peu ça!; **to give sb an e.** *(tell off)* passer un savon à qn; *Am Fam* **to give sb an e. about sth** *(say a lot to)* raconter qch à qn en long, en large et en travers

earhole [ˈɪəhəʊl] **N** *Br Fam (ear)* esgourde *f*

earl [ɜːl] **N** comte *m*

▸▸ ***Earl Grey*** *(tea)* Earl Grey *m*

earldom [ˈɜːldəm] **N** *(title)* titre *m* de comte; *(estates, land)* comté *m*

EARLY [ˈɜːlɪ]

ADJ	
• matinal **1**	• premier **2**
• en avance **3**	• de bonne heure **3**
• précoce **4**	• prochain **5**
ADV	
• de bonne heure **1, 3**	• tôt **1, 2, 5**
• en avance **3**	• prématurément **4**

(compar **earlier**, *superl* **earliest***)*

ADJ 1 *(morning)* matinal; **I had an e. breakfast** j'ai déjeuné de bonne heure; **to get off to an e. start** partir de bonne heure; **the e. shuttle to London** le premier avion/train pour Londres; **it's too e. to get up** il est trop tôt pour se lever; **it's earlier than I thought** il est plus tôt que je ne pensais; **to be an e. riser** être matinal *ou* un lève-tôt; **very e. in the morning** très tôt; **e. morning call** appel *m* matinal; **e. morning walk** promenade *f* matinale

2 *(belonging to the beginning of a period of time* ▸ *machine, film, poem)* premier; *(*▸ *Edwardian, Victorian etc)* du début de l'époque; **in the e. afternoon/spring/fifties** au début de l'après-midi/du printemps/des années cinquante; **in the e. nineteenth century** au début du XIXème siècle; **when was that? – e. September** quand était-ce? – début septembre; *Br* **it's e. days yet** *(difficult to be definite)* il est trop tôt pour se prononcer; *(might yet be worse, better)* il est encore tôt; **from the earliest times** depuis le début des temps; **I need an e. night** je dois me coucher de bonne heure; **it's too e. to tell** il est trop tôt pour se prononcer, on ne peut encore rien dire; **the e. Roman Empire** l'Empire romain naissant; **the e. American settlers** les premiers pionniers américains; **an e. Picasso** une des premières œuvres de Picasso; **he's in his e. twenties** il a une vingtaine d'années; **in his e. youth** quand il était très jeune; **from an e. age** dès l'enfance; **at an e. age** de bonne heure, très jeune; **my earliest recollections** mes souvenirs les plus lointains; **e. reports from the front indicate that...** les premières nouvelles du front semblent indiquer que…; **in the e. stages of the project** dans une phase initiale du projet

3 *(ahead of time)* **to be e.** *(person, train, flight, winter)* être en avance; **I am half an hour e.** je suis en avance d'une demi-heure; **let's have an e. lunch** déjeunons de bonne heure; **you're too e.** vous arrivez trop tôt, vous êtes en avance; **Easter is e. this year** Pâques est de bonne heure cette année

4 *(premature)* précoce, hâtif; *(death)* prématuré; **e. beans** haricots *mpl* de primeur; **e. vegetables/fruit/produce** primeurs *fpl*

5 *(relating to the future* ▸ *reply)* prochain; **at an e. date** de bonne heure; **at an earlier date** plus tôt; **we need an e. meeting** il faut que nous nous réunissions bientôt; *Com* **at your earliest convenience** dans les meilleurs délais; **what is your earliest possible delivery date?** quelle est votre première possibilité de livraison?

ADV 1 *(in the morning* ▸ *rise, leave)* tôt, de bonne heure; **let's set off as e. as we can** mettons-nous en route le plus tôt possible

2 *(at the beginning of a period of time)* **e. in the evening/in the afternoon** tôt le soir/(dans) l'après-midi; **e. in the year/winter** au début de l'année/de l'hiver; **as e. as the tenth century** dès le dixième siècle; **I can't make it earlier than 2.30** je ne peux pas avant 14h30; **what's the earliest you can make it?** *(be here)* quand pouvez-vous être ici?; **e. on** tôt; **e. on it was apparent that...** il est vite apparu que…; **earlier on** plus tôt

3 *(ahead of schedule)* en avance; *(earlier than usual)* de bonne heure; **I want to leave e. tonight** *(from work)* je veux partir de bonne heure ce soir; **shop/post e. for Christmas** faites vos achats/postez votre courrier à l'avance pour Noël

4 *(prematurely)* **to die e.** *(young)* mourir jeune;

(sooner than expected) mourir prématurément; **this flower blooms very e.** cette fleur s'épanouit très précocement

5 *(relating to the future)* **at the earliest** au plus tôt; **we can't deliver earlier than Friday** nous ne pouvons pas livrer avant vendredi

▸▸ *Mktg* ***early adopter*** réceptif *m* précoce, adopteur *m* précoce; ***early American*** = style de mobilier et d'architecture du début du XIXème siècle; ***early bird*** *(early riser)* lève-tôt *mf*; *(person who arrives early)* = personne qui arrive tôt; *Prov* **the e. bird catches the worm** *(it's good to get up early)* le monde appartient à ceux qui se lèvent tôt; *(it's good to arrive early)* les premiers arrivés sont les mieux servis; *Am Com* ***early bird special*** = dans un restaurant, prix avantageux accordés aux clients qui consomment avant une certaine heure; *Br Com* ***early closing*** = jour où l'on ferme tôt; **it's e. closing today** *(for all shops)* les magasins ferment de bonne heure aujourd'hui; *(for this shop)* on ferme de bonne heure aujourd'hui; *Br Pol* ***Early Day Motion*** = proposition de loi dont la discussion n'est pas à l'ordre du jour, présentée par un député qui recherche l'appui de collègues de façon à attirer l'attention du parlement sur une question; ***early English*** gothique *m* anglais primitif; *Mktg* ***early follower*** suiveur *m* immédiat; *Mktg* ***early majority*** majorité *f* innovatrice; ***early music*** *(baroque)* musique *f* ancienne; *Fin* ***early redemption*** amortissement *m* anticipé; ***early retirement*** retraite *f* anticipée; **to take e. retirement** prendre sa retraite anticipée, partir en retraite anticipée; *Med* ***early screening*** *(for disease)* dépistage *m* précoce

earmark ['ɪəmɑːk] **VT 1** *(assign)* réserver; *(money)* affecter, assigner; **this money has been earmarked for research** cet argent a été affecté à la recherche; **I'll just e. that for myself** je me le réserve; **this land is earmarked for development** ce terrain est réservé *ou* assigné à l'aménagement **2** *(animal, livestock)* marquer à l'oreille

N marque *f* à l'oreille; *Fig* **to have all the earmarks of embezzlement/another of her silly ideas** porter tous les signes d'un détournement de fonds/d'une de ses idées stupides

earmuffs ['ɪəmʌfs] **NPL** protège-oreille *m*

earn [ɜːn] **VT 1** *(money)* gagner; *(interest)* rapporter; **how much do you e.?** combien gagnez-vous?; **to e. a living** gagner sa vie; **to e. one's living by writing** gagner sa vie de sa plume; **their money is earning a high rate of interest** leur argent est rémunéré à un taux élevé **2** *(respect, punishment ▸ of activities)* valoir; *(▸ of person)* mériter; **it earned him ten years in prison** cela lui a valu dix ans de prison; **her attitude has earned her a lot of friends/supporters** son attitude lui a gagné de nombreux amis/partisans; **you've earned it!** tu l'as mérité!

VI *(person)* gagner de l'argent; *(investment)* rapporter

earned [ɜːnd] **ADJ**

▸▸ *Com* ***earned income*** revenus *mpl* salariaux; *Fin* ***earned interest*** revenu *m* des intérêts; *Acct* ***earned surplus*** bénéfices *mpl* non distribués

earner ['ɜːnə(r)] **N 1** *(person)* salarié(e) *m,f*; **she's not a big e.** elle ne gagne pas beaucoup; **she's the main e. in the family** c'est elle qui fait vivre la famille **2** *Br Fam (source of income)* **it's a nice little e.** *(business, shop)* c'est une bonne petite affaire▫

earnest ['ɜːnɪst] **ADJ 1** *(person, expression, tone)* sérieux **2** *(hope, request)* ardent, fervent; *(endeavour)* fervent; *(desire)* profond

• **in earnest ADV** *(seriously)* sérieusement, sincèrement; *(in a determined way)* sérieusement; **it's raining in e. now** il pleut pour de bon cette fois

ADJ to be in e. être sérieux; **are you in e.?** *(in what you're saying)* parlez-vous sérieusement?

earnestly ['ɜːnɪstlɪ] **ADV** *(behave)* sérieusement; *(study, work)* sérieusement, avec ardeur; *(speak, nod, look at)* gravement; *(desire)* profondément; **we e. hope that...** nous espérons sincèrement que... + *indicative*

earnestness ['ɜːnɪstnɪs] **N** *(of discussion)* caractère *m* sérieux; *(of tone, person)* gravité *f*, sérieux *m*; *(of hope, desire)* sincérité *f*; *(of request)* ferveur *f*

earning ['ɜːnɪŋ] **N** *(act)* gain *m*

▸▸ *Com* ***earning capacity, earning power*** *(of business)* rapport *m*; *(of person)* revenu *m* potentiel

earnings ['ɜːnɪŋz] **NPL** *(of person)* salaire *m*, revenus *mpl*; *(of company)* revenus *mpl*; **do you have e. from any other sources?** avez-vous d'autres sources de revenus?; **to live off immoral e.** gagner sa vie par des procédés immoraux; *Fin* **e. before interest and tax** bénéfices *mpl* avant impôts et charges

▸▸ *Fin* ***earnings forecast*** résultats *mpl* prévisionnels; *Fin* ***earnings growth*** accroissement *m ou* augmentation *f* des bénéfices; *Fin* ***earnings per share*** bénéfice *m* par action; *Fin* ***earnings retained*** bénéfices *mpl* non distribués

earnings-related ADJ proportionnel au revenu

▸▸ ***earnings-related pension*** retraite *f* indexée sur le revenu

earpiece ['ɪəpiːs] **N** *(of telephone receiver, personal stereo)* écouteur *m*

ear-piercing ['ɪəpɪəsɪŋ] **ADJ** *(scream)* à vous percer les tympans

N *(for earrings)* **do you know anywhere in town that does e.?** connais-tu un endroit en ville où l'on peut se faire percer les oreilles?

earplugs ['ɪəplʌgz] **NPL** *(for sleeping)* bouchons *mpl* d'oreilles; *(made of wax)* boules *fpl* Quiès®; *(for protection against water, noise)* protège-tympans *mpl*

earring ['ɪərɪŋ] **N** boucle *f* d'oreille

earshot ['ɪəʃɒt] **N out of/within e.** hors de/à portée de voix

ear-splitting ADJ *(noise)* assourdissant

earth [ɜːθ] **N 1** *(the world, the planet)* terre *f*; **the e.** *or* **E.** *(planet)* la Terre; **the e.'s crust/atmosphere** l'écorce *f*/l'atmosphère *f* terrestre; **on e.** sur terre; *Fam* **where/why on e....?** où/pourquoi diable...?; *Fam* **what on e. have you done to your hair?** que diable as-tu fait à tes cheveux?; *Fam* **how on e. should I know?** comment veux-tu que je le sache?; **there's no reason on e.** il n'y a absolument aucune raison; *Fam* **to look like nothing on e.** ne ressembler à rien; *Fam* **to feel like nothing on e.** ne vraiment pas être dans son assiette; **to pay the e. for sth** payer qch les yeux de la tête; **it wouldn't cost the e.** ça ne coûterait pas les yeux de la tête; **he promised people the e.** il a promis la lune aux gens

2 *(ground)* sol *m*; *Fig* **to come back to e. (with a bump)** revenir (brutalement) sur terre; **the e. moved** la terre a tremblé; *Hum* **did the e. move for you?** *(after making love)* est-ce que tu as eu le grand frisson?

3 *Agr (soil)* terre *f*; **loose/heavy e.** terre(s) *f(pl)* meuble(s)/lourde(s)

4 *Br Elec* terre *f*, masse *f*; *(terminal)* mise *f* à terre; **dead e.** contact *m* parfait avec le sol

5 *(of fox)* terrier *m*, tanière *f*; **to go to e.** *(fox, fugitive)* se terrer; **I've been trying to get in touch with him but he seems to have gone to e.** j'ai essayé de le joindre mais on dirait qu'il s'est volatilisé; **to run to e.** *(fox)* chasser jusqu'à son terrier; *(fugitive)* dépister; *(person)* dénicher; *(mistake in the figures)* découvrir la source de

VT 1 *Br Elec* mettre à la terre **2** *Hunt* poursuivre jusqu'à son terrier

COMP *(floor)* en terre battue

▸▸ ***earth cable*** câble *m* de terre; ***earth closet*** fosse *f* d'aisance; ***earth connection*** prise *f* de terre; ***earth creature*** *(in science fiction)* créature *f* terrestre; ***earth mother*** *Myth* déesse *f* de la terre; *Fam Fig* mère *f* nourricière▫; *Astron* ***earth orbit*** *(of satellite)* orbite *f* terrestre; *Astron* ***earth satellite*** satellite *m* terrestre; ***earth science*** sciences *fpl* de la terre; *Astrol* ***earth sign*** signe *m* de terre; *TV* ***earth station*** station *f* terrestre; *Br* ***earth tremor*** secousse *f* sismique; *Br Elec* ***earth wire*** fil *m* de terre

▸ **earth up VT SEP** *(plant)* chausser, enchausser, butter

earthbound ['ɜːθbaʊnd] **ADJ 1** *(insects)* non volant **2** *(spaceship)* progressant en direction de la terre; *(journey)* en direction de la terre **3** *(unimaginative)* terre à terre

earthen ['ɜːθən] **ADJ** *(dish)* en *ou* de terre (cuite); *(floor)* en terre

earthenware ['ɜːθənweə(r)] **N** *(pottery)* poteri *f*; *(glazed)* faïence *f*

ADJ en *ou* de terre (cuite), en *ou* de faïence

earthfall ['ɜːθfɔːl] **N** éboulement *m* de terre

earthiness ['ɜːθɪnɪs] **N 1** *(of humour)* truculenc *f*; *(of person, character)* nature *f* directe **2** *(of food* goût *m* de terre

earthlight ['ɜːθlaɪt] **N** *Astron (of moon)* lumière cendrée

earthling ['ɜːθlɪŋ] **N** terrien(enne) *m,f*

earthly ['ɜːθlɪ] **ADJ 1** *(worldly)* terrestre; **e. pos sessions** biens *mpl* matériels **2** *Fam (possible* **there's no e. reason why I should believe you** je n'a absolument aucune raison de te croire▫; **she hasn't an e. chance of succeeding** elle n'a pas l moindre chance *ou* la plus petite chance de réussir▫

N *Br Fam* **1** *(chance)* **he doesn't have an e. of pass ing the exam** il n'a aucune chance de réussir à l'examen▫ **2** *(idea)* **I haven't an e. where he is** je ne sais vraiment pas où il se trouve▫

▸▸ ***the Earthly Paradise*** le Paradis terrestre

earthman ['ɜːθmən] *(pl* **earthmen** [-mən]) **N** ter rien *m*

earthmover ['ɜːθˌmuːvə(r)] **N** bulldozer *m*, *Offi* bouteur *m*

earthmoving ['ɜːθˌmuːvɪŋ] **ADJ**

▸▸ ***earthmoving equipment*** engins *mpl* de terras sement

earthquake ['ɜːθkweɪk] **N** tremblement *m* d terre

earth-shaking [-ʃeɪkɪŋ], **earth-shattering** [-ʃætərɪŋ] **ADJ** *Fam* **1** *(discovery, news)* stupéfiant▫ *(defeat)* accablant▫ **2** *(explosion, crash etc)* assourdissant▫

earthwoman ['ɜːθwʊmən] *(pl* **earthwomen** [-wɪmɪn]) **N** terrienne *f*

earthworks ['ɜːθwɜːks] **NPL** *Constr* terrasse ment *m*; *Archeol & Mil* fortification *f* en terre

earthworm ['ɜːθwɜːm] **N** ver *m* de terre, lombric *m*

earthy ['ɜːθɪ] **ADJ 1** *(taste, smell)* de terre **2** *(humour)* truculent; *(person, character)* direct

earwax ['ɪəwæks] **N** cire *f* *(sécrétée par le oreilles)*, cérumen *m*

earwig ['ɪəwɪg] **N** perce-oreille *m*

VT *Fam* écouter de façon indiscrète▫

VI *Fam* écouter aux portes▫

earworm ['ɪəwɜːm] **N** *Fam* = chanson ou air qu trotte dans la tête et dont il est difficile de se défaire

ease [iːz] **N 1** *(comfort)* aise *f*; **to be** *or* **to feel at e./ ill at e.** être *ou* se sentir à l'aise/mal à l'aise; **to be at e. with oneself** être bien dans sa peau; **a nation at e. with itself** une nation qui s'accepte; **to se sb's mind at e.** tranquilliser qn; **set your mind at e.** rassurez-vous, soyez tranquille; **to put sb at (his** *or* **her) e.** mettre qn à l'aise; *Mil* **(stand) at e.!** repos!; *Old-fashioned* **to take one's e.** prendre se aises, se mettre à l'aise **2** *(facility)* facilité *f*; *(o movements)* aisance *f*; **to do sth with e.** faire qch facilement *ou* aisément; **the e. with which they adapted** la facilité avec laquelle ils se sont adaptés; **e. of access** facilité *f* d'accès; **e. of use** facilité d'emploi **3** *(affluence)* **to live a life of e.** avoir la belle vie, mener une vie facile

VT 1 *(alleviate ▸ anxiety, worry)* calmer; *(▸ pain)* calmer, soulager; *(▸ pressure, tension)* relâcher; *(▸ traffic flow)* rendre plus fluide; *(▸ workload)* alléger; **to e. sb's mind** rassurer qn; **to e. sb of a burden** décharger qn d'un fardeau, retirer un fardeau des épaules de qn; **to e. sb of their anxiety/pain** calmer l'inquiétude/la douleur de qn **2** *(move gently)* **to e. oneself into a chair** s'installer délicatement dans un fauteuil; *Aut* **to e. in the clutch** embrayer en douceur; **she eased the rucksack from her back** elle fit glisser le sac à dos de ses épaules; **they eased him out of the car** ils l'ont aidé à sortir de la voiture; **to e. sth out** faire sortir qch délicatement; **he eased himself through the gap in the hedge** il s'est glissé *ou* faufilé à travers le trou dans la haie

VI *(pain)* se calmer, s'atténuer; *(situation, tension, rain)* se calmer

▸**ease off** VT SEP **1** *(lid, bandage)* enlever délicatement **2** *Naut (let out* ▸ *rigging)* filer, choquer

VI *(rain)* se calmer; *(business)* ralentir; *(traffic)* diminuer; *(tension)* se relâcher; **work has eased off** il y a moins de travail

▸**ease up** VI *(slow down* ▸ *in car)* ralentir; *(rain)* se calmer; *(business, work)* ralentir; *(traffic)* diminuer; **to e. up on sb/sth** y aller doucement avec qn/qch

easel ['i:zəl] N chevalet *m*

easily ['i:zɪlɪ] ADV **1** *(without difficulty)* facilement; **that's e. said/done** c'est facile à dire/faire; **the car holds six people e.** six personnes tiennent à l'aise dans cette voiture; **she is e. pleased** elle n'est pas difficile

2 *(undoubtedly)* sans aucun doute; **she's e. the best** c'est de loin la meilleure; **it's e. two hours from here** c'est facilement à deux heures d'ici

3 *(very possibly)* **he could e. change his mind** il pourrait bien changer d'avis; **the information could e. be wrong** les informations pourraient très bien être fausses

4 *(in a relaxed manner* ▸ *talk)* de manière décontractée; *(*▸ *smile, answer)* d'un air décontracté

easiness ['i:zɪnɪs] N **1** *(lack of difficulty)* facilité *f* **2** *(relaxed nature)* décontraction *f*

easing ['i:zɪŋ] N **1** *(of suffering, pressure)* atténuation *f*; *(caused by medication)* soulagement *m* **2** *(relaxation* ▸ *of conflict, pressure)* atténuation *f*; *(*▸ *of restrictions)* allègement *m*; **e. of tension** *(political etc)* détente *f*; *Com* **e. of the market** détente *f* du marché

▸▸ ***easing off*** *(of pain)* atténuation *f*; *(from work)* relâchement *m*

east [i:st] N **1** *Geog* est *m*; **in the e.** à l'est, dans l'est; **two miles to the e.** trois kilomètres à l'est; **look towards the e.** regardez vers l'est; **I was born in the e.** je suis né dans l'Est; **in the e. of Austria** dans l'est de l'Autriche; **on the e. of the island** à l'est de l'île; **the wind is in the e.** le vent est à l'est; **the wind is coming from the e.** le vent vient *ou* souffle de l'est; **the e. of England** l'est de l'Angleterre; **the E.** *(the Orient)* l'Orient *m*; *(in US)* l'Est *m (États situés à l'est du Mississippi)*; **E.-West relations** relations *fpl* Est-Ouest **2** *Cards* est *m*

ADJ **1** *Geog* est *(inv)*, de l'est; *(country)* de l'Est; *(wall)* exposé à l'est; **the e. coast** la côte est; **in e. London** dans l'est de Londres; **on the e. side** du côté est **2** *(wind)* d'est

ADV à l'est; *(travel)* vers l'est, en direction de l'est; **the village lies e. of Swansea** le village est situé à l'est de Swansea; **the living room faces e.** la salle de séjour est exposée à l'est; **the path heads (due) e.** le chemin va *ou* mène (droit) vers l'est; **drive e. until you come to a main road** roulez vers l'est jusqu'à ce que vous arriviez à une route principale; **I travelled e.** je suis allé vers l'est; **to sail e.** naviguer cap sur l'est; **it's 20 miles e. of Manchester** c'est à 32 kilomètres à l'est de Manchester; **e. by north** est quart-nord-est; **e. by south** est-quart-sud-est; **further e.** plus à l'est; *Am Fam* **back e.** dans l'est□ *(des États-Unis)*

▸▸ ***East Africa*** Afrique *f* orientale; ***East African*** N Africain(e) *m,f* de l'est ADJ d'Afrique orientale; ***East End*** *(of city)* quartiers *mpl* est; **to live in the E. End of Glasgow** habiter dans l'est de Glasgow; ***the East End*** = quartier industriel de Londres, connu pour ses docks et, autrefois, pour sa pauvreté; *esp Am* ***East Europe*** Europe *f* de l'Est; ***East European*** N Européen(enne) *m,f* de l'Est ADJ d'Europe de l'Est; ***the East Frisian Islands*** les îles *fpl* Frisonnes orientales; ***East German*** N Allemand(e) *m,f* de l'Est ADJ est-allemand, d'Allemagne de l'Est; ***(the former) East Germany*** (l'ex-) Allemagne *f* de l'Est; *Hist* ***East India Company*** compagnie *f* des Indes Orientales; *Hist* ***East Indian*** N natif(ive) *m,f* des Indes orientales ADJ des Indes orientales; *Hist* ***the East Indies*** les Indes *fpl* orientales; *Hist* ***East Prussia*** Prusse-Orientale *f*; ***the East Side*** l'East Side *m (quartier situé à l'est de Manhattan)*; ***East Sussex*** le Sussex oriental, = comté dans le sud de l'Angleterre; **in E. Sussex** dans le Sussex oriental

eastbound ['i:stbaʊnd] ADJ *(traffic)* en direction de l'est; *(lane, carriageway)* de l'est; *(road)* vers l'est; **e. traffic is subject to delays** la circulation est ralentie dans le sens est; *Br* **the e. carriageway of the motorway is closed** l'axe est de l'autoroute est fermé (à la circulation); **there are roadworks on the e. carriageway of the motorway** il y a des travaux sur l'autoroute en direction de l'est

Easter ['i:stə(r)] N Pâques *fpl*; **Happy E.!** joyeuses Pâques!; **last/next E.** à Pâques l'année dernière/l'année prochaine

COMP *(holiday, weekend)* de Pâques; *(celebrations)* pascal

▸▸ *Am* ***Easter basket*** = panier de friandises dont on raconte aux enfants qu'il s'agit d'un cadeau du "Easter bunny"; ***Easter bunny*** lapin *m* de Pâques; *(in US)* = personnage imaginaire qui distribue des friandises aux enfants; ***Easter Day*** le jour *ou* le dimanche de Pâques; ***Easter egg*** œuf *m* de Pâques; ***Easter Island*** l'île *f* de Pâques; **in** *or* **on E. Island** à l'île de Pâques; ***Easter Monday*** le lundi de Pâques; *Hist* ***the Easter Rising*** = insurrection irlandaise contre la Grande-Bretagne en 1916; ***Easter Sunday*** le jour *ou* le dimanche de Pâques; ***Easter week*** *(following Easter)* la semaine de Pâques; *(Holy Week)* la semaine sainte

easterly ['i:stəlɪ] *(pl* **easterlies***)* N vent *m* d'est

ADJ **1** *Geog* est *(inv)*, de l'est; **to travel in an e. direction** aller vers l'est; **the most e. point of the island** le point situé le plus à l'est de l'île; **a room with an e. aspect** une pièce exposée à l'est; *Naut* **to steer an e. course** faire route vers l'est; *(when setting out)* mettre le cap à l'est **2** *(wind)* d'est

ADV vers l'est, en direction de l'est

eastern ['i:stən] ADJ **1** *Geog* est *(inv)*, de l'est; *(of Far East)* oriental; **the e. wing of the castle** l'aile est du château; **in e. Canada** dans l'est du Canada; **the e. side of the country** la partie est du pays **2** *(wind)* d'est

▸▸ ***the Eastern Bloc*** le bloc de l'Est; ***Eastern Cape*** Cap-Est *m*; **in the E. Cape** au Cap-Est; *Rel* ***the Eastern Church*** l'Église *f* d'Orient; ***Eastern Daylight Time*** heure *f* d'été de New York; ***Eastern Europe*** Europe *f* de l'Est; ***Eastern European*** N Européen(enne) *m,f* de l'Est ADJ d'Europe de l'Est; ***Eastern European countries*** pays *mpl* d'Europe de l'Est; ***Eastern European Time*** heure *f* d'Europe orientale; *Rel* ***the Eastern Orthodox Church*** l'Église *f* d'Orient; ***Eastern Standard Time*** heure *f* d'hiver de New York; ***the Eastern Townships*** *(of Canada)* les Cantons *mpl* de l'Est

Easterner, easterner ['i:stənə(r)] N **1** *(in US)* = personne qui vient de l'est des États-Unis **2** *(oriental)* Oriental(e) *m,f*

Eastertide ['i:stətaɪd] N *Literary* (saison *f* de) Pâques *fpl*

east-facing ADJ *(house, wall)* (exposé) à l'est

eastward ['i:stwəd] ADJ vers l'est, en direction de l'est

ADV vers l'est, en direction de l'est; **to sail e.** naviguer cap sur l'est

N est *m*

eastwards ['i:stwədz] ADV vers l'est, en direction de l'est; **to sail e.** naviguer cap sur l'est

easy ['i:zɪ] *(compar* **easier**, *superl* **easiest***)* ADJ **1** *(not difficult)* facile; **it's e. to see why/that...** on voit bien pourquoi/que... + *indicative*; **it's e. (for her) to say that...** c'est facile (pour elle) de dire que... + *indicative*; **this will make your job easier** ceci vous facilitera la tâche; **to be e. to live with** être facile à vivre; **to be e. to get on with** être facile à vivre; **she is e.** *or* **an e. person to please** *(gen)* c'est facile de lui faire plaisir; *(concerning food)* elle n'est pas difficile; **it's an e. mistake to make** c'est une erreur qui est facile à faire; **it's not e. being the eldest child** ce n'est pas facile d'être l'aîné; **it's far from e., it's none too e.** c'est loin d'être facile, ce n'est pas facile du tout; **in e. stages** *(travel)* par petites étapes; *(learn)* sans peine; **within e. reach of** près de; **the e. way out** *or* **option** la solution facile *ou* de facilité; **there are no e. answers** c'est un problème qui est loin d'être facile à résoudre; **to have an e. time (of it)** *(a good life)* avoir la belle vie *ou* la vie facile; *Fam* **it's e. money** c'est de l'argent gagné facilement *ou* sans se fatiguer□; **to come in an e. first** *(in a race)* arriver bon premier; **an e. prey** *or* **victim** une proie facile; *Fam* **e. game** *or* **meat** bonne poire *f*; *Fam* **as e. as pie** *or* **ABC** *or* **as falling off a log** simple comme bonjour *ou* tout; *Fam* **to be on e. street** rouler sur l'or

2 *(at peace)* **to feel e. in one's mind** être tranquille, avoir l'esprit tranquille

3 *(easy-going* ▸ *person, atmosphere)* décontracté; *(*▸ *disposition, nature)* facile; *(*▸ *manner)* décontracté, naturel; *(*▸ *style)* coulant, facile; *Fam* **I'm e.** *(I don't mind)* ça m'est égal□; **they're usually fairly e. about deadlines** d'habitude ils sont assez accommodants sur les délais; *Com* **on e. terms** avec facilités de paiement; **to go at an e. pace** aller tranquillement

4 *(sexually) very Fam Pej* **she's e.** *or* **an e. lay** elle couche avec tout le monde, c'est une Marie-couche-toi-là; *Literary* **a woman of e. virtue** une femme de petite vertu *ou* aux mœurs légères

5 *(pleasant)* **to be e. on the eye** *(film, painting)* être agréable à regarder; *(person)* être bien fait de sa personne; **to be e. on the ear** *(music)* être agréable à écouter

6 *St Exch (market)* calme

ADV *(in a relaxed or sparing way)* doucement; **to go e.** y aller doucement; **to go e. on** *or* **with sb** y aller doucement avec qn; **to go e. on** *or* **with sth** y aller doucement avec *ou* sur qch; *Fam* **he's got it e.** *(has an easy life)* il se la coule douce, il a la belle vie; **to take things** *or* **it** *or* **life e.** *(lead a life of ease)* mener une vie tranquille; *(not overdo things)* ralentir; **you'll have to take it e.** *or* **go e. for a bit** il va falloir ralentir *ou* freiner un peu; *Fam* **take it e.!** *(gen)* doucement!; *(don't get upset)* ne t'en fais pas!; *Am (on parting)* bon courage!; *Fam* **e. now!, e. does it!** doucement!; **to sleep e. in one's bed** dormir sur ses deux oreilles; *Mil* **stand e.!** repos!; **easier said than done** plus facile à dire qu'à faire; **(it's) e. come e. go** *(money)* l'argent, ça va ça vient; *Am Fam* **e. over** *(egg)* cuit des deux côtés

▸▸ ***easy chair*** fauteuil *m*; *Mus* ***easy listening*** variété *f*

easy-come-easy-go ADJ *Fam (attitude)* insouciant□

easy-going ADJ **1** *(not given to anger)* qui prend les choses tranquillement; *(not worrying)* qui ne se fait pas de bile, décontracté; *(undemanding)* accommodant, coulant, peu exigeant; *(permissive)* qui a la conscience élastique; **the police take an e. attitude to such cases** dans de tels cas, la police se montre assez conciliante **2** *(horse)* à l'allure douce

easy-peasy [-'pi:zɪ] ADJ *Fam Hum* **e.(, lemon squeezy)!** c'est fastoche!

eat [i:t] *(pt* **ate** [eɪt], *pp* **eaten** ['i:tən]*)* VT **1** manger; **to e. (one's) breakfast/lunch/dinner** prendre son petit déjeuner/déjeuner/dîner; **to e. one's fill** manger tout son soûl *ou* content; **I don't e. meat** je ne mange pas de viande; **there's nothing to e.** il n'y a rien à manger; **would you like something to e.?** voulez-vous manger quelque chose?; **it looks good enough to e.!** on en mangerait!; **he/she looks good enough to e.** il est beau/elle est belle à croquer; **go on, she's not going to e. you** va, elle ne va pas te manger; **I'll e. my hat if he gets elected** s'il est élu, je veux bien être pendu; **he eats people like you for breakfast** il ne fait qu'une bouchée des gens comme toi; **to e. one's words** ravaler ses mots; **they ate us out of house and home** ils ont dévalisé notre frigo; **she ate her way through six packets of biscuits** elle a réussi à engloutir six paquets de biscuits; *Am Fam Fig* **to e. sb's lunch** *(defeat)* battre qn à plates coutures; *Am Vulg* **e. shit!** va te faire voir! **2** *(of machine* ▸ *credit card, ticket)* avaler **3** *Fam* **what's eating you?** qu'est-ce que tu as?□

VI **1** *(consume food)* manger; **to e. like a horse** manger comme un ogre; **to e. like a bird** avoir un appétit d'oiseau, manger trois fois rien; **to e., drink and be merry** faire la fête, s'amuser; **he eats out of my hand** *(bird)* il vient manger dans ma main; *Fig (person)* il fait tout ce que je veux; **treat them right and you'll have them eating out of your hand** traite-les bien et ils te mangeront dans la main **2** *(have meal)* dîner; **we e. at seven** nous dînons à sept heures; **to e. well** bien manger; **let's e.!** on mange?

• **eats** NPL *Fam* bouffe *f*; **let's get some eats** allons chercher de la bouffe

▸**eat away** VT SEP **1** *(of waves)* ronger; *(of mice)* ronger; *(of acid, rust)* ronger, corroder **2** *Fig (confidence)* miner; *(support, capital, resources)* entamer

VI *(person)* manger

▸**eat away at** VT INSEP **1** *(of waves)* ronger; *(of mice)* ronger; *(of acid, rust)* ronger, corroder **2** *Fig (confidence)* miner; *(support, capital, resources)* entamer

▸**eat in** VI manger chez soi *ou* à la maison

▸**eat into** VT INSEP **1** *(destroy)* attaquer **2** *(use up* ▸ *savings)* entamer; *(*▸ *time)* empiéter sur

▸**eat out** VI sortir déjeuner *ou* dîner, aller au restaurant

VT SEP **to e. one's heart out** se morfondre; **e. your heart out!** dommage pour toi!

▸**eat up** VI manger; **e. up!** *(there's lots more)* vas-y, mange!

VT SEP *(food)* terminer, finir; *Fig (electricity, gas, petrol)* consommer beaucoup de; **to e. up the miles** dévorer *ou* avaler les kilomètres; *Fam* **this stove eats up the coal** cette poêle mange beaucoup de charbon; **to be eaten up with sth** *(jealousy, hate, ambition)* être rongé *ou* dévoré par qch

eatable ['i:təbəl] ADJ *(fit to eat)* mangeable; *(edible)* comestible

• **eatables** NPL *Hum* vivres *mpl*, victuailles *fpl*

eaten ['i:tən] *pp of* **eat**

eater ['i:tə(r)] N **1** *(person)* mangeur(euse) *m,f*; **he's a big/small e.** c'est un gros/petit mangeur; **to be a messy e.** manger salement; **to be a fussy e.** être difficile (sur la nourriture) **2** *Br Fam (apple)* pomme *f* à couteau

eatery ['i:tərɪ] *(pl* **eateries***)* N *Fam* café-restaurant *m*

eating ['i:tɪŋ] N manger *m*

▸▸ ***eating apple*** pomme *f* à couteau; ***eating disorder*** trouble *m* du comportement alimentaire; ***eating habits*** habitudes *fpl* alimentaires; ***eating place*** restaurant *m*

eau [əʊ] N

▸▸ ***eau de Cologne*** eau *f* de Cologne; ***eau de toilette*** eau *f* de toilette; ***eau de vie*** eau *f* de vie

eaves ['i:vz] NPL avant-toit *m*, corniche *f*

▸▸ *Am* ***eaves trough*** gouttière *f* pendante

eavesdrop ['i:vzdrɒp] *(pt & pp* **eavesdropped**, *cont* **eavesdropping***)* VI écouter aux portes; **to e. on a conversation** tendre l'oreille pour écouter une conversation privée; **I found myself eavesdropping on their conversation** j'ai entendu leur conversation sans le vouloir; **stop eavesdropping!** arrête d'espionner le monde!

eavesdropper ['i:vz,drɒpə(r)] N indiscret(ète) *m,f*, personne *f* qui écoute aux portes

ebb [eb] N *(of tide)* reflux *m*; *(of public opinion)* variations *fpl*; **e. and flow** flux *m* et reflux *m*; **the e. and flow of married life** les hauts et les bas de la vie conjugale; **to be at a low e.** *(person)* ne pas avoir le moral; *(patient, enthusiasm, spirits)* être bien bas; *(business)* aller mal, être *ou* tourner au ralenti; *(finances, relations)* aller mal; **to be at one's lowest e.** *(person)* avoir le moral à zéro; *(patient)* être au plus mal *ou* bas; **to be at its lowest e.** *(enthusiasm, spirits)* être au plus bas; *(business, finances, relations)* aller au plus mal

VI **1** *(tide)* baisser, descendre; **to e. and flow** monter et baisser *ou* descendre **2** *Fig (confidence, enthusiasm, strength etc* ▸ *diminish)* baisser peu à peu; *(*▸ *disappear)* disparaître; *(rage, indignation)* se calmer; *(support)* s'amenuiser; *(time, water)* s'écouler

▸▸ ***ebb tide*** marée *f* descendante

▸**ebb away** VI *(confidence, enthusiasm, strength etc* ▸ *diminish)* baisser peu à peu; *(*▸ *disappear)* disparaître; *(rage, indignation)* se calmer; *(support)* s'amenuiser; *(time, water)* s'écouler; **his life was ebbing away** il baissait d'heure en heure

ebbing ['ebɪŋ] ADJ **1** *(water)* qui reflue **2** *(fortunes etc)* sur le déclin; *(popularity)* en baisse; *(strength, enthusiasm)* faiblissant

EBIT ['ebɪt, 'i:bɪt] N *Fin (abbr* **earnings before interest and tax***)* EBIT *m*

EBITDA [e'bɪtdɑ:, i:'bɪtdɑ:] N *Fin (abbr* **earnings before interest, tax, depreciation and amortization***)* EBITDA *m*

ebonics [ə'bɒnɪks] N *(UNCOUNT) Ling* = anglais parlé par une partie de la communauté Noire américaine

ebony ['ebənɪ] N **1** *(tree)* ébénier *m* **2** *(wood)* ébène *f* **3** *Fig (colour)* ébène *f*

ADJ **1** *(chair, table, bracelet)* en ébène **2** *Fig (eyes, hair)* d'ébène

e-book N livre *m* numérique, livre *m* électronique

EBRD [,i:bi:,ɑ:'di:] N *Pol (abbr* **European Bank for Reconstruction and Development***)* BERD *f*

e-broker N *St Exch* courtier(ère) *m,f* électronique

e-broking N *St Exch* courtage *m* électronique

ebullience [ɪ'bʊlɪəns] N exubérance *f*

ebullient [ɪ'bʊlɪənt] ADJ exubérant; **they were in (an) e. mood** *or* **in e. spirits** ils étaient d'une humeur exubérante

e-business N *Comput* commerce *m* électronique

EC [,i:'si:] N *Pol (abbr* **European Community***)* CE *f*

e-card N carte *f* électronique

e-cash N *Comput* argent *m* électronique, argent *m* virtuel, e-cash *m*

ECB [,i:si:'bi:] N *Com (abbr* **European Central Bank***)* BCE *f*

ECC [,i:si:'si:] N *EU (abbr* **European Community Commission***)* CCE *f*

eccentric [ɪk'sentrɪk] ADJ **1** *(person, clothes, behaviour)* excentrique **2** *Astron, Math & Tech* excentrique, excentré

N **1** *(person)* excentrique *mf*, original(e) *m,f* **2** *Tech* excentrique *m*

eccentrically [ɪk'sentrɪkəlɪ] ADV **1** *(dress, talk)* de manière excentrique **2** *Astron, Math & Tech* excentriquement

eccentricity [,eksen'trɪsətɪ] *(pl* **eccentricities***)* N **1** *(of person, character, behaviour etc)* excentricité *f* **2** *Math (of ellipse)* excentricité *f*; *Tech* excentricité *f*, désaxage *m*

ecclesiastic [ɪ,kli:zɪ'æstɪk] ADJ *(robes, traditions, calendar)* ecclésiastique; *(history)* de l'Église; *(music)* d'église

N ecclésiastique *m*

ecclesiastical [ɪ,kli:zɪ'æstɪkəl] ADJ *(robes, traditions, calendar)* ecclésiastique; *(history)* de l'Église; *(music)* d'église

ECE [,i:si:'i:] N *(abbr* **Economic Commission for Europe***)* Commission *f* économique pour l'Europe

ECG [,i:si:'dʒi:] N *Med* **1** *(abbr* **electrocardiogram***)* ECG *m* **2** *(abbr* **electrocardiograph***)* ECG *m*

ECGD [,i:si:,dʒi:'di:] N *Com (abbr* **Export Credits Guarantee Department***)* = organisme d'assurance pour le commerce extérieur, COFACE *f*

echelon ['eʃəlɒn] N **1** *(level)* échelon *m*; **the higher** *or* **upper echelons of the Civil Service** les niveaux supérieurs de l'administration **2** *Mil* échelon *m*

echinacea [ekɪ'neɪʃə] N *Bot & Med* échinacée *f*

echo ['ekəʊ] *(pl* **echoes**, *pt & pp* **echoed***)* N **1** *(of sound)* écho *m*; **to cheer sb to the e.** applaudir qn à tout rompre; *Fig* **there were echoes of Proust in his novel** son roman avait des accents proustiens; **her words found an e. in many hearts** ses mots ont fait vibré la corde sensible dans beaucoup de cœurs **2** *(radio signal)* écho *m*

VT *(sound)* répéter; *Fig (colour, theme)* reprendre, rappeler; *(architecture, style)* rappeler, évoquer; **to e. sb's opinions** *(person)* se faire l'écho des opinions de qn; *(editorial)* reprendre les opinions de qn

VI *(noise, voice, music)* résonner; *(place)* faire écho, résonner; **the corridor echoed with shouts/footsteps** des cris/bruits de pas résonnèrent dans le couloir, le couloir résonna de cris/bruits de pas

▸▸ ***echo chamber*** chambre *f* de réverbération; ***echo sounder*** échosondeur *m*; ***echo sounding*** sondage *m* par ultrasons; *Med* ***echo virus*** virus *m* ECHO

ECHR [,i:si:eɪtʃ'ɑ:(r)] N *Law (abbr* **European Court of Human Rights***)* CEDH *f*

ECJ [,i:si:'dʒeɪ] N *Law (abbr* **European Court of Justice***)* CJCE *f*

éclair [eɪ'kleə(r)] N *Culin* éclair *m*

eclectic [ɪ'klektɪk] N éclectique *mf*

ADJ éclectique; **an e. blend** un mélange varié

eclecticism [ɪ'klektɪsɪzəm] N éclectisme *m*

eclipse [ɪ'klɪps] *Astron & Fig* N éclipse *f*; **an e. of the sun/moon** une éclipse de soleil/lune; **total/partial e.** éclipse *f* totale/partielle; **to be in e.** être éclipsé; *Fig* **his career went into e.** il a connu une traversée du désert

VT éclipser; *Fig* **his performance was only eclipsed in 1998** sa performance n'a été améliorée qu'en 1998

> **PRÉFIXE**
>
> **ECO-**
>
> • Le préfixe **eco-** s'emploie avec des substantifs et des adjectifs. Il se traduit généralement en français par **éco-**, mais dans certains cas il est nécessaire de recourir à une périphrase.
>
> • Il s'emploie dans des mots ayant trait à l'ÉCOLOGIE comme dans les termes **ecosystem** (écosystème) et **ecosphere** (écosphère).
>
> • Les termes **eco-friendly** (qui ne nuit pas à l'environnement) et **ecowarrior** (écoguerrier) eux, sont liés à la notion de RESPECT ET DÉFENSE DE L'ENVIRONNEMENT, tout comme **ecotourism** écotourisme, **eco-design** éco-design et **eco-house** éco-maison. Citons également le terme familier et péjoratif **ecofreak**, qui désigne un enragé du mouvement écologiste.

eco-chic ['i:kəʊ-] ADJ éco-chic

ECOFIN, Ecofin ['i:kəʊ,fɪn] N *EU (abbr* **Economic and Financial Council of Ministers***)* (Conseil *m*) Ecofin *m*

ecofreak ['i:kəʊfri:k] N *Fam* écologiste *mf* enragé(e)

eco-friendly ['i:kəʊ-] ADJ *Ecol (product)* qui ne nuit pas à l'environnement; *(lifestyle, person)* qui respecte l'environnement

E-coli [,i:'kəʊlaɪ] N *Med* E-coli *f*

ecological [,i:kə'lɒdʒɪkəl] ADJ écologique

▸▸ ***ecological balance*** équilibre *m* écologique; ***ecological footprint*** empreinte *f* écologique

ecologically [,i:kə'lɒdʒɪklɪ] ADV écologiquement; **e. (speaking)** du point de vue de l'écologie; **e. harmful/sound** qui est nuisible à/qui respecte l'environnement; **to be e. conscious** *or* **aware** se préoccuper *ou* se soucier de l'environnement

ecologist [ɪ'kɒlədʒɪst] N écologiste *mf*

ecology [ɪ'kɒlədʒɪ] N écologie *f*

e-commerce N *Comput* commerce *m* électronique

econometric [ɪ,kɒnə'metrɪk] ADJ *Econ* économétrique

▸▸ ***econometric model*** modèle *m* économétrique

econometrics [ɪ,kɒnə'metrɪks] N *(UNCOUNT) Econ* économétrie *f*

economic [,i:kə'nɒmɪk] ADJ **1** *Econ (growth, system, recovery)* économique **2** *(profitable)* rentable; **e. rent** loyer *m* rentable; **it isn't e., it doesn't make e. sense** ce n'est pas rentable *ou* avantageux; **to make sth e.** rentabiliser qch **3** *Fam (inexpensive)* économique

▸▸ ***economic activity*** activité *f* économique; ***economic adviser*** conseiller(ère) *m,f* économique; ***economic aid*** aide *f* économique; ***economic analysis*** analyse *f* économique; ***economic analyst*** analyste *mf* économique; ***economic appraisal*** évaluation *f* économique; ***economic blockade*** blocus *m* économique; ***economic boom*** essor *m* économique; ***economic climate*** climat *m* économique; *EU* ***Economic Commission for Europe*** Commission *f* économique pour l'Europe; ***economic convergence*** convergence *f* économique; ***economic cooperation*** coopération *f* économique; ***economic crisis*** crise *f* économique; ***economic cycle*** cycle *m* économique; ***economic development*** croissance *f* par habitant *ou* per capita; ***economic downturn*** ralentissement *m* économique; ***economic embargo*** embargo *m* économique; ***economic factor*** facteur *m* économique; *EU* ***Economic and Financial Council of Ministers*** (Conseil *m*) Ecofin *m*; ***economic forecast*** prévisions *fpl* économiques; ***economic geography*** géographie *f* économique; ***economic growth rate*** taux *m* d'expansion économique; ***economic indicator*** indicateur *m* économique; ***economic interest group*** groupement *m* d'intérêt économique; *Com* ***economic life*** durée *f* de vie utile; *Pol* ***economic mi-***

grant émigrant *m* pour des raisons économiques; ***economic model*** modèle *f* économique; *Pol & Fin* ***Economic and Monetary Union*** union *f* économique et monétaire; ***economic paradigm*** paradigme *m* économique; ***economic performance*** *(of country)* résultats *mpl* économiques; ***economic plan*** programme *m* économique; ***economic planner*** conjoncturiste *mf*; ***economic planning*** planification *f* économique; ***economic policy*** politique *f* économique; ***economic power*** puissance *f* économique; ***economic profit*** résultat *m* économique; ***economic programme*** programme *m* économique; ***economic prospects*** prévisions *fpl* conjoncturelles *ou* économiques; ***economic rate of return*** taux *m* de rentabilité économique; ***economic recovery*** reprise *f ou* redressement *m* économique; ***economic refugee*** migrant(e) *m,f* économique; ***economic restructuring*** reconversion *f* économique; ***economic revival*** relance *f* économique; ***economic sanctions*** sanctions *fpl* économiques; *Br* ***Economic Secretary*** secrétaire *mf* à l'économie; ***economic sector*** secteur *m* économique; ***economic situation*** conjoncture *f* économique; *EU* ***Economic and Social Committee*** Comité *m* Économique et Social; *Br* ***Economic and Social Research Council*** = organisme chargé de distribuer des subventions pour la recherche en sciences sociales; ***economic surplus*** plus-value *f* économique; ***economic test*** test *m* économique; ***economic trend*** tendance *f ou* conjoncture *f* économique; *Pol & Fin* ***economic union*** union *f* économique; ***economic weather*** conjoncture *f* économique; ***economic welfare*** bien-être *m* économique; ***economic zone*** zone *f* économique

> Il faut noter que les adjectifs **economic** et **economical** ne sont pas interchangeables. **Economic** signifie **qui se rapporte à l'économie**, alors que **economical** signifie **qui permet d'économiser.**

economical [ˌi:kəˈnɒmɪkəl] **ADJ 1** *(person)* économe; *(machine, method, approach)* économique; **it's more e. to buy in bulk** c'est plus économique *ou* avantageux d'acheter par grandes quantités; **to be e. to run** *(car, heating)* être économique; **to be e. with sth** économiser qch; *Euph* **to be e. with the truth** dire la vérité avec parcimonie **2** *(style)* concis, sobre

> Voir note ci-dessus.

economically [ˌi:kəˈnɒmɪklɪ] **ADV 1** *Econ* économiquement; **e. viable** *(campaign, project, product)* économiquement viable **2** *(live)* de manière économe; *(use)* de manière économe, avec parcimonie **3** *(write)* avec sobriété
▸▸ ***economically developed country*** pays *m* développé

economics [ˌi:kəˈnɒmɪks] **N** *(UNCOUNT) (science)* économie *f* (politique), sciences *fpl* économiques
NPL *(financial aspects)* aspects *mpl* financiers; *(profitability)* rentabilité *f*; **we must consider the e. of the project before making any decisions** nous devons considérer l'aspect financier du projet avant de prendre une décision
COMP *(teacher, class)* d'économie
▸▸ ***economics correspondent*** journaliste *mf* économique; ***economics journalist*** journaliste *mf* économique

economist [ɪˈkɒnəmɪst] **N** économiste *mf*

economize, -ise [ɪˈkɒnəmaɪz] **VT** *(time, money etc)* économiser, ménager
VI économiser, faire des économies; **to e. on sth** économiser sur qch

economy [ɪˈkɒnəmɪ] *(pl* **economies) N 1** *(system)* économie *f*; **(centrally) planned e.** économie *f* planifiée; *Old-fashioned* **political e.** économie *f* politique **2** *(saving)* économie *f*; **to make economies** faire des économies; **it's a false e.** ce n'est pas vraiment rentable; **e. of style** concision *f* de style
COMP *(pack)* économique
ADV *(fly, travel)* en classe touriste
▸▸ ***economy brand*** marque *f* économique; *Am* ***economy car*** = voiture de taille moyenne, consommant peu par rapport aux "grosses américaines"; ***economy class*** classe *f* touriste; ***economy drive*** *(of company, government)* politique *f* de réduction des dépenses; **I'm on an e. drive at the moment** j'essaie d'économiser en ce moment; ***economy fare*** tarif *m* économique; ***economy measure*** mesure *f* de réduction des dépenses; **as an e. measure** par mesure d'économie; *Aut* ***economy mode*** *(with automatic gears)* mode *m* économique; ***economies of scale*** économies *fpl* d'échelle

eco-packaging N écoemballage *m*

eco-product N *Ecol* écoproduit *m*

ECOSOC [ˈi:kəʊˌsɒk] **N** *(abbr* **Economic and Social Committee)** CES *m*

ecosphere [ˈi:kəʊˌsfɪə(r)] **N** *Ecol* écosphère *f*

ecosystem [ˈi:kəʊˌsɪstəm] **N** *Ecol* écosystème *m*

ecotax [ˈi:kəʊtæks] **N** *Ecol* taxe *f* écologique, écotaxe *f*

ecoterrorist [ˈi:kəʊˌterərɪst] **N** *Ecol* = militant écologiste ayant recours à des actions violentes

ecotourism [ˈi:kəʊˌtʊərɪzəm] **N** *Ecol* écotourisme *m*

ecovillage [ˈi:kəʊˌvɪlɪdʒ] **N** écovillage *m*

ecowarrior [ˈi:kəʊˌwɒrɪə(r)] **N** *Ecol* écologiste *mf* activiste, écoguerrier(ère) *m,f*

ecru [ˈeɪkru:] **N** écru *m*
ADJ écru

ECSC [ˌi:si:ˌesˈsi:] **N** *Pol (abbr* **European Coal & Steel Community)** CECA *f*

ecstasy [ˈekstəsɪ] *(pl* **ecstasies) N 1** *(pleasure)* extase *f*, ravissement *m*; **to go into/be in ecstasies over sth** s'extasier/être en extase devant qch; *(critics)* être dithyrambique à propos de qch; **to send sb into ecstasies** faire tomber qn en extase **2** *(drug)* ecstasy *m ou f* **3** *Rel & Psy* extase *f*

ecstatic [ekˈstætɪk] **ADJ** ravi; **he got an e. reception from the crowd** il a été accueilli par une foule en délire; **to be e. about sth** *(in admiration* ▸ *gen)* être en extase devant qch; *(*▸ *with joy)* être ravi de qch; **I'm not e. about it** cela ne m'enchante pas

ecstatically [ekˈstætɪklɪ] **ADV** avec extase; **to be e. happy** être dans un bonheur extatique

ECT [ˌi:si:ˈti:] **N** *Med (abbr* **electroconvulsive therapy)** traitement *m* par électrochocs

ectopic [ekˈtəʊpɪk] **ADJ** *Med (pregnancy)* extra-utérin, ectopique

ectoplasm [ˈektəʊplæzəm] **N** *Biol* ectoplasme *m*

ectopy [ˈektəpɪ] **N** *Med* ectopie *f*

ECU [ˈeɪkju:] **N 1** *Formerly EU (abbr* **European Currency Unit)** ECU *m*, écu *m* **2** *Aut (abbr* **electronic control unit)** UCE *f*

Ecuador [ˈekwədɔ:(r)] **N** Équateur *m*

Ecuadoran [ˌekwəˈdɔ:rən], **Ecuadorian** [ˌekwəˈdɔ:rɪən] **N** Équatorien(enne) *m,f*
ADJ équatorien
COMP *(embassy)* d'Équateur; *(history)* de l'Équateur

ecumenical [ˌi:kjuˈmenɪkəl] **ADJ** œcuménique

ecumenism [i:ˈkju:mənɪzəm], **ecumenicism** [ˌi:kju:ˈmenɪsɪzəm] **N** œcuménisme *m*

eczema [ˈeksɪmə] **N** *Med* eczéma *m*; **to have e.** avoir de l'eczéma

ed.[ed] **N 1** *(abbr* **editor)** éd., édit. **2** *(written abbr* **edition)** éd., édit.
ADJ *(written abbr* **edited)** sous la dir. de, coll.

Edam [ˈi:dæm] **N** *(cheese)* édam *m*

EDC [ˌi:di:ˈsi:] **N 1** *(abbr* **European Defence Community)** CED *f* **2** *(abbr* **economically developed country)** pays *m* développé

eddy [ˈedɪ] *(pl* **eddies) N** *(of water, wind)* remous *m*, tourbillon *m*; *(of leaves, dust)* tourbillon
VI *(water)* faire des remous; *(wind, smoke, snow)* tourbillonner, tournoyer; *(crowds)* tournoyer
▸▸ *Elec* ***eddy currents*** courants *mpl* de Foucault

edelweiss [ˈeɪdəlvaɪs] **N** *Bot* edelweiss *m*, immortelle *f* des neiges

edema *Am* = **oedema**

Eden [ˈi:dən] **N** *Bible* l'Éden *m*, le Paradis terrestre; *Fig* éden *m*

EDF [ˌi:di:ˈef] **N** *Pol (abbr* **European Development Fund)** FED *m*

edge [edʒ] **N 1** *(of blade)* fil *m*, tranchant *m*; **a knife with a sharp** *or* **keen e.** un couteau à la lame aiguisée *ou* affilée; **to put an e. on** *(knife, blade)* aiguiser, affiler, affûter; **to take the e. off** *(knife, blade)* émousser; *Fig (pleasure)* gâter; *(argument)* couper tout l'effet de; **the sandwich took the e. off my hunger** ce sandwich a calmé ma faim; **the walk gave an e. to his appetite** la promenade lui a ouvert l'appétit; **to have the e. on** *(be better than)* avoir légèrement le dessus *ou* l'avantage sur; *(have an advantage over)* avoir l'avantage sur; *Am Fam* **to have an e. on** *(be drunk)* être éméché *ou* pompette; **to give sb/sth that extra e.** donner un plus à qn/qch; **the performance lacked e.** le spectacle manquait de ressort *ou* d'énergie; **with an e. in one's voice** d'un ton légèrement agacé; **to speak with a sarcastic/nervous/contemptuous e. to one's voice** parler avec une pointe de sarcasme/de nervosité/de mépris dans la voix
2 *(outer limit* ▸ *of table, cliff, road)* bord *m*; *(*▸ *of page)* bord *m*, marge *f*; *(*▸ *of forest)* lisière *f*, orée *f*; *(*▸ *of cube, brick)* arête *f*; *(*▸ *of coin, book)* tranche *f*; *(*▸ *of ski)* carre *f*; **at** *or* **by the water's e.** au bord de l'eau; **to stand sth on its e.** *(coin, book)* mettre qch sur la tranche; *(brick, stone)* poser *ou* mettre qch de *ou* sur chant; **it fell off the e.** il est tombé; **pages with gilt edges** pages aux tranches dorées, pages dorées sur tranches; **to be on the e. of** *(war, disaster, madness)* être au bord de; *Fig* **I was on the e. of my seat** *(waiting for news)* j'étais sur des charbons ardents; *Fig* **this film will have you on the e. of your seat** ce film est d'un suspense à vous faire frémir; **to be close to the e.** être près du bord; *Fig* être au bord du précipice; *Fig* **to push sb over the e.** faire craquer qn; **to live on the e.** prendre des risques
VT 1 *(give a border to)* border; **to e. sth with sth** border qch de qch
2 *(sharpen)* aiguiser, affiler, affûter
3 *(move gradually)* **to e. one's way** avancer *ou* progresser lentement; **she edged her way out onto the window ledge** elle gagna le rebord de la fenêtre avec précaution; **to e. one's chair nearer sb/sth** approcher sa chaise de qn/qch
4 *(in skiing)* **to e. one's skis** planter ses carres
VI avancer *ou* progresser lentement; **to e. past sb/sth** se faufiler à côté de qn/qch; **to e. away (from sb/sth)** s'éloigner doucement *ou* discrètement (de qn/qch); **he edged a little closer** il s'est rapproché un peu; **the car edged forward/backward** la voiture avança/recula doucement
• **on edge ADJ to be on e.** être énervé *ou* sur les nerfs **ADV to set sb's teeth on e.** faire grincer les dents à qn; **to set sb's nerves on e.** mettre les nerfs de qn à fleur de peau
▸▸ ***edge cutter*** *(for grass)* coupe-bordure(s) *m*; *Cin* ***edge numbers*** numéros *mpl* de bord; ***edge tool*** outil *m* tranchant; ***edge trimmer*** *(for grass)* coupe-bordure(s) *m*

▸**edge out VT SEP** *Fig* **she was edged out of her job** elle a été évincée de son poste; **the runner was edged out of second place** le coureur, qui avait longtemps été en deuxième place, a été dépassé peu avant l'arrivée
VI sortir lentement; **to e. out of a room** se glisser hors d'une pièce; **the driver/car edged out** le conducteur/la voiture se dégagea lentement

▸**edge up VT SEP to e. prices up** faire monter les prix doucement
VI 1 *(prices)* monter doucement **2** *(approach slowly)* **to e. up to sb/sth** s'avancer lentement vers qn/qch

-edged [edʒd] **SUFF double-e.** à double tranchant; **sharp-e.** bien affilé *ou* aiguisé

edgeways [ˈedʒweɪz], **edgewise** [ˈedʒwaɪz] **ADV 1** *(on its edge)* de chant; **to lay** *or* **set a plank e.** placer une planche de chant; *Fam* **I can't get a word in e.** je n'arrive pas à placer un mot (dans la conversation) **2** *(from side)* latéralement, de côté; **seen e. (on)** vu de côté

edginess [ˈedʒɪnɪs] **N** nervosité *f*; **there was an e. about him** il était assez nerveux

edging [ˈedʒɪŋ] **N** *(border* ▸ *on dress, of flowers etc)* bordure *f*
▸▸ *Hort* ***edging shears*** cisaille *f* à gazon; *Hort* ***edging tool*** coupe-gazon *m inv*, molette *f*

edgy ['edʒɪ] (*compar* **edgier**, *superl* **edgiest**) ADJ **1** *(nervous)* nerveux, sur les nerfs; **to get e.** s'énerver **2** *Fam (daring, avant-garde)* avant-garde; **her new album has a much edgier sound** son nouvel album a un son beaucoup plus original; **the film is an e. black comedy** ce film est une comédie noire très originale

EDI [ˌiːdiː'aɪ] N **1** *Comput (abbr* **Electronic Data Interchange***)* EDI *m* **2** *Fin (abbr* **European Data Interchange***)* EED *m*

edible ['edɪbəl] ADJ *(mushroom, berry)* comestible; *(fit to eat)* bon à manger, mangeable; **is it e.?** c'est bon à manger?

• **edibles** NPL comestibles *mpl*

edict ['iːdɪkt] N *Pol* décret *m*; *Fig* ordre *m*

►► *Hist* ***the Edict of Nantes*** l'édit *m* de Nantes

edification [ˌedɪfɪ'keɪʃən] N *Formal* édification *f*, instruction *f*; *esp Ironic* **for your e.** pour votre édification

edifice ['edɪfɪs] N *also Fig* édifice *m*

edify ['edɪfaɪ] (*pt & pp* **edified**) VT *Formal* édifier

edifying ['edɪfaɪɪŋ] ADJ *Formal* édifiant; *Hum* **it was hardly an e. spectacle/experience** le spectacle/l'expérience était loin d'être édifiant(e)

Edinburgh ['edɪnbrə] N Édimbourg

►► ***the Edinburgh Festival*** le Festival d'Édimbourg; ***Edinburgh Rock*** *(sweet)* = sorte de confiserie, spécialité d'Édimbourg

> **THE EDINBURGH FESTIVAL**
>
> Le festival international d'arts d'Édimbourg, créé en 1947, est aujourd'hui l'un des plus grands événements culturels au monde; il se tient chaque année dans la capitale écossaise au mois d'août. Le festival "off" ("the Fringe") est une grande rencontre du théâtre expérimental et un lieu très important pour les acteurs et les comiques qui veulent se faire connaître. Des centaines de représentations sont données chaque jour et toutes sortes de lieux sont transformés en salles de spectacle le temps du festival.

edit ['edɪt] N **1** *(of text)* révision *f*, correction *f* **2** *Comput (menu heading)* Edition *f*

VT **1** *(correct ► article, text, book)* corriger, réviser; *(prepare for release ► book, article)* éditer, préparer pour la publication; *(► film, TV programme, tape)* monter; **the footnotes were edited from the book** les notes ont été coupées dans le *ou* retranchées du livre; **give me an edited version of what happened** dites-moi brièvement ce qui s'est passé; **edited highlights** *(on television)* résumé *m* en images **2** *(newspaper, magazine, series)* diriger la rédaction de; **edited by...** *(series, newspaper)* sous la direction de... **3** *Comput (text)* modifier, éditer

►► *Comput* ***edit keys*** touches *fpl* de modification; *Comput* ***edit mode*** mode *m* Edition; *TV* ***edit suite*** régie *f ou* salle *f* de montage

> Note that the French verb **éditer** is a false friend. Its most common meaning is **to publish**.

► **edit in** VT SEP insérer

► **edit out** VT SEP *(scene)* couper; *(from text)* supprimer; *(write out of TV series)* faire disparaître; **he was edited out of the film when he broke his contract** on a coupé toutes les scènes du film où il apparaissait quand il a rompu son contrat

editable ['edɪtəbəl] ADJ pouvant être édité

editing ['edɪtɪŋ] N **1** *(initial corrections)* révision *f*, correction *f*; *(in preparation for publication)* édition *f*, préparation *f* à la publication; *(of film, tape)* montage *m* **2** *(of newspaper, magazine)* rédaction *f* **3** *Comput (of file, text)* édition *f*

►► *TV* ***editing desk*** table *f ou* banc *m* de montage; *Comput* ***editing function*** fonction *f* d'édition; *TV* ***editing table*** table *f* de montage; *Comput* ***editing window*** fenêtre *f* d'édition

edition [ɪ'dɪʃən] N *(of book, newspaper)* édition *f*; **first e.** première édition *f*; **revised/limited e.** édition *f* revue et corrigée/à tirage limité; **in Tuesday's e. of the programme** dans l'émission de mardi

►► ***edition time*** *(for newspaper)* bouclage *m*, heure *f* de l'édition, tombée *f*

> Note that the French word **édition** also means **publishing**.

editor ['edɪtə(r)] N **1** *(of newspaper, magazine)* rédacteur(trice) *m,f* en chef; *(of author)* éditeur (trice) *m,f*; *(of dictionary)* rédacteur(trice) *m,f*; *(of book, article ► who makes corrections)* correcteur(trice) *m,f*; *(► who writes)* rédacteur(trice) *m,f*; *(of film)* monteur(euse) *m,f*; **series e.** directeur (trice) *m,f* de la publication; *Press* **political e.** rédacteur(trice) *m,f* politique; *Press* **sports e.** rédacteur(trice) *m,f* sportif(ive); *Press* **e.'s note** note *f* de la rédaction **2** *Comput (software)* éditeur *m (de texte)*

editorial [ˌedɪ'tɔːrɪəl] ADJ *(decision, comment)* de la rédaction; *(job, problems, skills)* de rédaction, rédactionnel

N **1** *(article)* éditorial *m* **2** *(department)* service *m* de la rédaction, rédaction *f*

►► ***editorial changes*** corrections *fpl*; ***editorial column*** colonne *f* rédactionnelle; ***editorial content*** contenu *m* rédactionnel; ***editorial department*** *(in press)* service *m* de la rédaction, rédaction *f*, direction *f* de la rédaction; ***editorial director*** *(of newspaper)* rédacteur(trice) *m,f* en chef, directeur(trice) *m,f* de la rédaction; *(of publishing company)* directeur(trice) *m,f* de la rédaction; ***editorial freedom*** liberté *f* des rédacteurs; ***editorial interference*** ingérence *f* rédactionnelle; ***editorial office*** (salle *f* de) rédaction *f*; ***editorial opinion*** *(in press)* avis *m* éditorial; ***editorial policy*** politique *f* éditoriale; *(in press)* politique *f* de la rédaction; ***the editorial staff*** la rédaction

editorialist [ˌedɪ'tɔːrɪəlɪst] N *Am* éditorialiste *mf*

editorialize, -ise [ˌedɪ'tɔːrɪəlaɪz] VI émettre des opinions personnelles, être subjectif; **as the Times editorialized,...** comme l'affirmait l'éditorial du Times,...

editorially [ˌedɪ'tɔːrɪəlɪ] ADV du point de vue de la rédaction

editor-in-chief N rédacteur(trice) *m,f* en chef

editorship ['edɪtəʃɪp] N rédaction *f*; **during her e.** quand elle dirigeait la rédaction; **the series was produced under the general e. of...** la série a été produite sous la direction générale de...

EDP [ˌiːdiː'piː] N *Comput (abbr* **electronic data processing***)* traitement *m* électronique de l'information

educable ['edʒʊkəbəl] ADJ *Formal* éducable

educate ['edjʊkeɪt] VT **1** *(pupil)* donner de l'instruction à, instruire; **he was educated in France/at Oxford** il a fait ses études en France/à Oxford; **to have one's child educated** faire faire des études à son enfant **2** *(train, develop ► person, someone's taste, mind)* former; **the campaign aims to e. young people about the risks of drugs** la campagne a pour objet de sensibiliser les jeunes aux dangers de la drogue

educated ['edʒʊkeɪtɪd] ADJ *(person)* instruit; *(voice)* distingué; *(palate)* fin; **to make an e. guess** faire une supposition bien informée

education [ˌedʒʊ'keɪʃən] N **1** *(teaching)* enseignement *m*; **a classical/scientific e.** une formation classique/scientifique; **he has had a good e.** il a reçu une bonne instruction; **to get oneself an e.** faire des études; **he never completed his e.** il n'a jamais fini *ou* terminé ses études; **standards of e.** niveau *m* scolaire; **it was an e.** cela m'a beaucoup appris; *Hum* c'était très édifiant **2** *(learning)* éducation *f*; **a man without e.** un homme sans éducation

COMP *(costs, budget)* de l'éducation

►► ***Education Act*** réforme *f* (de l'Éducation); *Br* ***education authority*** académie *f* régionale; *Press* ***education correspondent*** correspondant(e) *m,f* chargé(e) des questions d'enseignement; *Br Pol* ***Education Secretary*** ministre *m* de l'éducation; ***education supplement*** supplément *m* éducation; ***the education system*** le système éducatif

> Note that the French noun **éducation** refers both to education and to upbringing.

educational [ˌedʒʊ'keɪʃənəl] ADJ *(programme, system)* éducatif; *(establishment)* d'éducation, d'enseignement; *(books, publisher)* scolaire; *(method, film, visit, TV)* éducatif, pédagogique; **they talked about rising/falling e. standards** ils ont évoqué la hausse/baisse du niveau scolaire; **it was very e.** c'était très instructif; *Hum* c'était très édifiant; **it was an e. experience/visit** c'était une expérience/visite instructive

►► ***educational adviser*** conseiller(ère) *m,f* d'orientation; ***educational age*** niveau *m* scolaire; ***educational channel*** chaîne *f* du savoir; ***educational cruise*** croisière *f* culturelle; ***educational psychologist*** *(practical)* psychologue *mf* scolaire; *(academic)* psychopédagogue *mf*; ***educational qualification*** diplôme *m*; *Comput* ***educational software*** logiciel *m* didactique

educationalist [ˌedʒʊ'keɪʃənəlɪst] N pédagogue *mf*

educationally [ˌedʒʊ'keɪʃənəlɪ] ADV d'un point de vue éducatif; **e. deprived child** = enfant qui n'a pas suivi une scolarité normale; *Br Old-fashioned* **e. subnormal** en retard sur le plan scolaire

educationist [ˌedʒʊ'keɪʃənɪst] N éducateur (trice) *m,f*

educative ['edʒʊkətɪv] ADJ éducatif

educator ['edʒʊkeɪtə(r)] N *esp Am* éducateur (trice) *m,f*

edutainment [ˌedjuː'teɪnmənt] N loisirs *mpl* éducatifs

ADJ ludo-éducatif

Edward ['edwəd] PR N **E. the Confessor** Édouard le Confesseur; **Prince E.** le prince Edward

Edwardian [ed'wɔːdɪən] ADJ *(architecture, design)* édouardien, de style Édouard VII, des années 1900; *(society, gentleman)* de l'époque d'Édouard VII, des années 1900; **E. style** style *m* Édouard VII; **the E. era** la Belle Époque

N = Britannique qui vivait sous le règne d'Édouard VII

> **-EE** — SUFFIXE
>
> • Le suffixe **-ee** vient s'ajouter à un radical verbal pour former des substantifs. Il tire son origine de l'élément français **-é(e)**, qui n'est cependant pas toujours la bonne traduction.
>
> • Le suffixe **-ee** désigne habituellement la PERSONNE QUI EST L'OBJET DE L'ACTION effectuée par le verbe:
>
> **employee** employé(e); **payee** bénéficiaire; **trainee** stagiaire.
>
> Il intervient souvent dans des contextes juridiques, où il possède généralement un contraire se terminant en **-or**:
>
> **lessee** preneur(euse) (à bail) (contraire: **lessor**); **grantee** donataire, cessionnaire (contraire: **grantor**)
>
> Des néologismes souvent humoristiques peuvent être créés à partir de mots se terminant en **-er**:
>
> **biographee** (inspiré de **biographer**) personne qui fait l'objet d'une biographie; **photographee** personne photographiée; **sendee** destinataire
>
> • **-ee** peut également prendre la signification contraire et désigner la PERSONNE QUI FAIT OU EST QUELQUE CHOSE:
>
> **absentee** absent(e); **escapee** évadé(e); **a devotee of classical music** un passionné de musique classique; **standee** *(on a bus)* passager(ère) debout; **attendee** personne présente

EEA [ˌiːiː'eɪ] N *Pol (abbr* **European Economic Area***)* EEE *m*

EEC [ˌiːiː'siː] N *Formerly Pol (abbr* **European Economic Community***)* CEE *f*

e-economy N économie *f* en ligne

EEG [ˌiːiː'dʒiː] N *Med* **1** *(abbr* **electroencephalogram***)* EEG *m* **2** *(abbr* **electroencephalograph***)* EEG *m*

eejit ['iːdʒɪt] N *Ir & Scot Fam* idiot(e)[a] *m,f*, andouille *f*

eel [iːl] N anguille *f*; *Fig* **to be as slippery as an e.** glisser comme une anguille; *Br Culin* **jellied eels** anguilles *fpl* en gelée

eelskin ['iːlskɪn] N peau *f* d'anguille

COMP en peau d'anguille

eelworm [ˈiːlwɜːm] N *Zool* anguillule *f*

EEPROM [ˈiːprɒm] N *Comput* (*abbr* **electrically erasable programmable ROM**) EEPROM *f*

-EER SUFFIXE

• Le suffixe **-eer** s'emploie avec un nom pour former soit un nom, soit un verbe.

• Le nom ainsi formé se rapporte toujours à une PERSONNE EXERÇANT UNE ACTIVITÉ:

auctioneer commissaire-priseur; **mountaineer** alpiniste; **engineer** ingénieur.

Certains ont une connotation péjorative: **profiteer** profiteur(euse); **racketeer** racketteur(euse); **mutineer** mutiné(e); **black marketeer** trafiquant(e) au marché noir

• Le verbe, dérivé du nom, décrit l'activité correspondante:

to electioneer participer à la campagne électorale *ou* faire de la propagande électorale; **to profiteer** faire des bénéfices exorbitants; **to go mountaineering** faire de l'alpinisme

eerie [ˈɪərɪ] (*compar* **eerier**, *superl* **eeriest**) ADJ (*house, silence, sound*) inquiétant, sinistre; **an e. silence** (*after explosion, in empty house etc*) un silence de mort; **it was e. to think that…** cela donnait des frissons *ou* la chair de poule de penser que…

eerily [ˈɪərəlɪ] ADV sinistrement, d'une manière sinistre; **it was e. quiet in the house** un calme inquiétant régnait dans la maison

eeriness [ˈɪərɪnɪs] N caractère *m* étrange *ou* sinistre

eery [ˈɪərɪ] (*compar* **eerier**, *superl* **eeriest**) = **eerie**

eff [ef] VI *Br very Fam Euph* **to e. and blind** jurer à tout va

• **eff off** VI *Br very Fam Euph* **e. off!** va te faire voir!; **I told him to e. off** je lui ai dit d'aller se faire voir

efface [ɪˈfeɪs] VT *also Fig* effacer; **to e. oneself** s'effacer

effacement [ɪˈfeɪsmənt] N effacement *m*

effect [ɪˈfekt] N **1** (*of action, law*) effet *m*; (*of chemical, drug, weather*) effet *m*, action *f*; **to have an e. on** avoir *ou* produire un effet sur; **to have no e.** ne produire aucun effet; **the e. of the law will be to…** la loi aura pour effet de…; **the e. of all this is that…** tout cela a pour résultat que…; *Br* **with e. from 1 January** à partir *ou* à compter du 1er janvier; **with immediate e.** à compter d'aujourd'hui; **to no** *or* **little e.** en vain; **to use** *or* **to put sth to good e.** (*technique, talent*) utiliser qch avec succès; (*money, inheritance*) faire bon usage de qch; **to put sth into e.** (*plan*) mettre qch à exécution; (*decision*) donner suite à qch; **to come into** *or* **to take e.** (*law*) entrer en vigueur; **to take e.** (*drug*) (commencer à) faire effet

2 (*meaning*) sens *m*; **to this** *or* **that e.** dans ce sens; **letters to the same e.** des lettres allant dans le même sens; **a rumour to the e. that…** une rumeur selon laquelle…; **a telegram/an announcement to the e. that…** un télégramme/une annonce disant que…; **or words to that e.** ou quelque chose dans le genre

3 (*impression*) effet *m*; **the combination of colours creates a pleasing e.** le mélange des couleurs laisse une impression agréable; **(just) for e.** (juste) pour faire de l'effet

4 (*simulation*) **moonlight e.** effet *m* de lune; **clever use of lighting created the e. of a thunderstorm** une utilisation adroite de la lumière donnait l'impression qu'il y avait un orage; **stage effects** jeux *mpl* scéniques; *Cin & TV* **(special) effects** trucage *m*, effets *mpl* spéciaux; **sound effect** bruitage *m*; *TV* **effects microphone** microphone *m* d'ambiance

VT *Formal* (*reform, repair*) effectuer; (*sale, purchase*) réaliser, effectuer; (*improvement*) apporter; (*cure, rescue, reconciliation*) mener à bien; **to e. one's escape** s'échapper; **to e. an entry** entrer de force; **to e. a cure for sth** apporter un remède à qch; **to e. a solution to sth** apporter une solution à qch; *Mil* **to e. a retreat** battre en retraite

• **effects** NPL *Formal* **household effects** articles *mpl* ménagers; **personal effects** effets *mpl* personnels

• **in effect** ADJ (*law, system*) en vigueur ADV (*in fact*) en fait, en réalité; **that is, in e., a refusal** c'est de fait un refus

effective [ɪˈfektɪv] ADJ **1** (*which works well* ▸ *measure, treatment, advertising etc*) efficace; (▸ *worker, manager*) efficace; (▸ *argument*) qui porte; (▸ *service, system*) qui fonctionne bien; (▸ *disguise*) réussi; **an e. way of doing sth** un moyen efficace de faire qch; **the medicine was e.** le médicament a produit son effet

2 *Admin & Fin* **e. date** date *f* d'entrée en vigueur; **e. as from 1 January** (*law etc*) en vigueur *ou* applicable à compter du 1er janvier; **to cease to be e.** (*policy, law*) cesser d'être applicable; **to become e.** entrer en vigueur

3 (*actual*) véritable; **to assume e. command of a team** assumer la direction réelle d'une équipe; **this resulted in the e. silencing of all opposition** (*was tantamount to*) cela a eu en effet pour résultat de faire taire les opposants

4 *Fin* (*yield, return, production*) effectif; (*value*) réel

5 (*creating effect* ▸ *colour, illustration*) qui fait de l'effet

• **effectives** NPL *Mil* effectifs *mpl*

▸▸ *Fin* ***effective annual rate*** taux *m* annuel effectif; *Econ* ***effective demand*** demande *f* effective; *Fin* ***effective exchange rate*** taux *m* de change effectif; *Fin* ***effective income*** revenu *m* réel; *Com* ***effective life*** (*of product, structure*) durée *f* de vie effective; ***effective range*** (*of firearm, missile*) portée *f* utile; *Fin* ***effective tax rate*** taux *m* d'imposition effectif

effectively [ɪˈfektɪvlɪ] ADV **1** (*in fact*) en réalité, en fait; **the country was e. ruled by the military** en fait *ou* en réalité, le pays était dirigé par les militaires; **the game was e. over** c'était comme si le match était déjà terminé

2 (*efficiently* ▸ *work, run, manage*) efficacement

3 (*successfully*) avec succès

4 (*impressively*) d'une manière impressionnante

> Note that the French word **effectivement** is a false friend and is never a translation for the English word **effectively**. It means **actually**.

effectiveness [ɪˈfektɪvnɪs] N **1** (*efficiency* ▸ *of treatment, advertising*) efficacité *f*; (▸ *of undertaking, attempt*) succès *m* **2** (*effect* ▸ *of entrance, gesture, colour*) effet *m*; **to improve the e. of your backhand** pour améliorer votre revers

effectual [ɪˈfektʃʊəl] ADJ **1** *Formal* (*action, plan*) efficace **2** *Law* (*contract*) valide; (*ruling*) en vigueur

effectually [ɪˈfektjʊəlɪ] ADV *Formal* efficacement

effeminacy [ɪˈfemɪnəsɪ] N (*of man*) caractère *m* efféminé; **the e. of his voice** sa voix efféminée

effeminate [ɪˈfemɪnət] ADJ (*man, voice*) efféminé

effervesce [ˌefəˈves] VI (*liquid*) être en effervescence; (*wine*) pétiller; (*gas*) s'échapper par effervescence; *Fig* (*person*) déborder de vie; **when the mixture effervesces** quand le mélange entre en effervescence

effervescence [ˌefəˈvesəns] N (*of liquid*) effervescence *f*; (*of wine*) pétillement *m*; *Fig* (*of person*) vitalité *f*, pétulance *f*

effervescent [ˌefəˈvesənt] ADJ (*liquid*) effervescent; (*wine*) pétillant; *Fig* (*person*) débordant de vie, pétulant

effete [ɪˈfiːt] ADJ *Formal* (*weak* ▸ *person*) mou (molle); (▸ *civilization, society*) affaibli; (*decadent*) décadent

efficacious [ˌefɪˈkeɪʃəs] ADJ *Formal* efficace

efficacy [ˈefɪkəsɪ], **efficaciousness** [efɪˈkeɪʃəsnɪs] N *Formal* efficacité *f*

efficiency [ɪˈfɪʃənsɪ] N **1** (*of company, method*) efficacité *f*; (*of machine* ▸ *in operation*) fonctionnement *m*; (▸ *in output*) rendement *m*; (*of person*) capacité *f*, compétence *f* **2** *Am* (*apartment*) studio *m*

▸▸ *Am* ***efficiency apartment*** studio *m*; ***efficiency expert*** expert *m* en organisation

efficient [ɪˈfɪʃənt] ADJ (*method, company*) efficace; (*piece of work*) bien fait; (*machine* ▸ *in operation*) qui fonctionne bien; (▸ *in output*) qui a un bon rendement; (*person*) performant, capable, compétent; **to be e. at sth** faire qch avec compétence; **to be e. in one's work** se montrer capable dans son travail; **the machine is now at its most e.** (*functions well*) la machine a maintenant un fonctionnement optimal; (*has high output*) la machine a maintenant un rendement optimal; **to make more e. use of sth** utiliser qch de manière plus efficace; **it was an e. performance by the Australian team** ce fut une belle performance de la part de l'équipe australienne

▸▸ *Econ* ***efficient market*** marché *m* efficient

efficiently [ɪˈfɪʃəntlɪ] ADV (*effectively*) efficacement; (*competently*) avec compétence; **the machine works e.** (*functions well*) la machine fonctionne bien; (*has high output*) la machine a un bon rendement; **to organize one's time e.** utiliser son temps de manière rationnelle

effigy [ˈefɪdʒɪ] (*pl* **effigies**) N effigie *f*; **to burn sb in e.** brûler qn en effigie

effing [ˈefɪŋ] *Br very Fam Euph* ADJ de merde; **you e. idiot!** espèce de connard!

ADV foutrement; **don't be so e. stupid!** qu'est-ce que tu peux être con!

N **there was a lot of e. and blinding** on a eu droit à un chapelet de jurons

efflorescence [ˌefləˈresəns] N **1** *Bot* floraison *f* **2** *Chem* efflorescence *f*

efflorescent [ˌefləˈresənt] ADJ *Chem* efflorescent

effluence [ˈefluəns] N *Literary* émanation *f*, effluence *f*

effluent [ˈefluənt] ADJ effluent

N **1** (*waste*) effluent *m* **2** (*stream*) effluent *m*

effluvium [ɪˈfluːvjəm] (*pl* **effluviums** *or* **effluvia** [-vjə]) N effluve *m*, émanation *f*; *Pej* émanation *f* désagréable *ou* fétide

effort [ˈefət] N **1** (*exertion*) effort *m*; **it will be a bit of an e.** ce sera un peu difficile; **without much e.** sans trop d'effort *ou* de peine; **with an e.** en faisant un effort; **their efforts were rewarded** leurs efforts ont été récompensés; **it was an e. for me to stay awake** j'avais du mal à rester éveillé; (*stronger*) rester éveillé me coûtait; **put some e. into it!** fais un effort!; **I put a lot of e. into that project** je me suis donné beaucoup de mal *ou* de peine pour ce projet; **to make an e. to do sth** faire (un) effort pour faire qch; **he made no e. to contact us** il n'a fait aucun effort pour nous joindre; **in an e. to do sth** dans le but de faire qch; **to make every e. to do sth** faire tout son possible pour faire qch; **at least she made the e.** au moins elle a essayé; **it's not worth the e.** ça ne vaut pas la peine de se fatiguer

2 (*attempt*) essai *m*, tentative *f*; **it's only my first e.** ce n'est que la première fois que j'essaie; **it was a good e.** pour un essai, c'était bien; *Fam* **what do you think of his latest e.?** qu'est-ce que vous pensez de sa dernière performance?

3 *Phys* (*of traction etc*) effort *m*, poussée *f*, travail *m*

4 *Fam* (*thing, gadget*) truc *m*; **there's this sort of lever e.** il y a une espèce de levier[□]

effortless [ˈefətlɪs] ADJ (*win*) facile; (*style, movement*) aisé; **she won with an almost e. ease** elle a gagné avec une facilité presque absolue

effortlessly [ˈefətlɪslɪ] ADV facilement, sans effort *ou* peine; **to be e. graceful/skilful** être naturellement gracieux/talentueux

effrontery [ɪˈfrʌntərɪ] N effronterie *f*; **she had the e. to correct me!** elle a eu l'audace de me corriger!

effusion [ɪˈfjuːʒən] N *Literary* **1** (*of words*) effusion *f* **2** (*of liquid*) écoulement *m*; (*of blood*) hémorragie *f*

effusive [ɪˈfjuːsɪv] ADJ **1** (*person*) expansif; (*welcome, thanks*) chaleureux; *Pej* exagéré; **to be e. in one's thanks** se confondre en remerciements; **to be e. in one's praise/congratulations** louer/féliciter qn avec grand enthousiasme **2** *Geol* effusif

effusively [ɪˈfjuːsɪvlɪ] ADV avec effusion; *Pej* avec une effusion exagérée; **to thank sb e.** se confondre en remerciements

effusiveness [ɪ'fju:sɪvnɪs] **N** effusion *f*; *Pej* effusion *f* exagérée; **the e. of his praise** l'enthousiasme *m* de ses louanges

E-fit® ['i:fɪt] **N** *Comput* portrait-robot *m* électronique

EFL [ˌi:ef'el] **N** (*abbr* **English as a foreign language**) = anglais langue étrangère

EFT [eft] **N** *Comput* (*abbr* **electronic funds transfer**) transfert *m* de fonds électronique

EFTA ['eftə] **N** (*abbr* **European Free Trade Association**) AELE *f*, AEL-E *f*

EFTPOS ['eftpɒs] **N** *Comput* (*abbr* **electronic funds transfer at point of sale**) transfert *m* de fonds électronique sur point de vente

eg [ˌi:'dʒi:] **ADV** (*abbr* **exempli gratia**) par exemple, p. ex.

EGA [ˌi:dʒi:'eɪ] **N** *Comput* (*abbr* **enhanced graphics adapter**) EGA *m*

egalitarian [ɪˌgælɪ'teərɪən] **N** égalitariste *mf*
ADJ égalitaire

egalitarianism [ɪˌgælɪ'teərɪənɪzəm] **N** égalitarisme *m*

e-generation **N** *Comput* e-génération *f*, génération *f* électronique

egg [eg] **N 1** *(foodstuff)* œuf *m*; **bacon and eggs** œufs *mpl* au bacon; **fried e.** œuf *m* sur le plat; **hard-boiled e.** œuf *m* dur; **soft-boiled e.** œuf *m* à la coque; *Fig* **to be left with** *or* **to get e. on one's face** avoir l'air ridicule **2** *(of bird, insect, fish)* œuf *m*; *(of woman)* ovule *m*; **to lay an e.** *(bird)* pondre un œuf; *Fig (fail)* faire un bide; *Prov* **don't put all your eggs in one basket** il ne faut pas mettre tous ses œufs dans le même panier; *Fam* **as sure as eggs is eggs** aussi sûr que deux et deux font quatre **3** *Br Old-fashioned (person)* **he's/she's a good e.** c'est un brave garçon/une brave fille; **a bad e.** un sale individu
▸▸ *Am* ***Egg Beaters***® = ersatz d'œufs brouillés, sans cholestérol; ***eggs Benedict*** œufs *mpl* Benedict, = plat composé d'une tranche de pain grillé surmontée d'une tranche de jambon et d'un œuf poché, le tout recouvert de sauce hollandaise; *Biol* ***egg cell*** ovule *m*; *Am* ***egg crate*** boîte *f* à œufs; *Br Culin* ***egg custard*** crème *f* anglaise; ***egg flip*** *(with milk)* lait *m* de poule; *(with alcohol)* lait *m* de poule alcoolisé; ***egg mayonnaise*** œuf *m* mayonnaise; *Am Culin* ***egg roll*** pâté *m* impérial; ***egg slicer*** coupe-œufs *m inv*; ***egg spoon*** cuillère *f* à œufs (à la coque); ***egg timer*** sablier *m*; *Zool* ***egg tooth*** dent *f* d'éclosion; *Br* ***egg whisk*** fouet *m*; ***egg white*** blanc *m* d'œuf; ***egg yolk*** jaune *m* d'œuf
▸ **egg on** **VT SEP** encourager, inciter; **to e. sb on to do sth** encourager *ou* inciter qn à faire qch

egg-and-spoon race **N** = jeu consistant à courir en tenant un œuf dans une cuillère

eggbeater ['egˌbi:tə(r)] **N 1** *(whisk)* fouet *m* **2** *Am Fam (helicopter)* hélico *m*

eggbox ['egbɒks] **N** *Br* boîte *f* à œufs

egghead ['eghed] **N** *Fam* intello *mf*

egg-laying **ADJ** ovipare
N ponte *f*

eggplant ['egplɑ:nt] **N** *Am* aubergine *f*

egg-shaped **ADJ** en forme d'œuf, ovoïde

eggshell ['egʃel] **N 1** *(of bird's egg)* coquille *f* d'œuf; **we all walk around on eggshells when the boss is in a bad mood** on marche tous sur des œufs quand le patron est de mauvaise humeur **2** *(colour)* coquille *f* d'œuf **3** *(paint)* peinture *f* coquille d'œuf
ADJ *(finish, paint)* coquille d'œuf *(inv)*
▸▸ ***eggshell blue*** bleu *m* pâle; ***eggshell china, eggshell porcelain*** coquille *f* d'œuf

eggy ['egɪ] **ADJ** *Fam (stained)* taché *ou* souillé de jaune d'œuf ᵒ; **an e. taste/smell** un goût/une odeur d'œuf ᵒ
▸▸ ***eggy bread*** pain *m* perdu ᵒ

egis *Am* = **aegis**

eglantine ['egləntaɪn] **N** *Bot (bush)* églantier *m*; *(flower)* églantine *f*

EGM [ˌi:dʒi:'em] **N** *Com* (*abbr* **extraordinary general meeting**) AGE *f*

ego ['i:gəʊ] **N 1** *(self-esteem)* amour-propre *m*; **to have an enormous e.** être imbu de soi-même; **it gave my e. a boost** mon ego en est ressorti gonflé; **it's just your e. that's hurt** tu es seulement blessé dans ton amour-propre; *Fam* **she's just on an e. trip** c'est par vanité qu'elle le fait ᵒ; **he's been on an e. trip since his promotion** il ne se sent plus depuis sa promotion **2** *Psy* **the e.** le moi, l'ego
▸▸ *Psy* ***ego ideal*** moi *m* idéal

egocentric [ˌi:gəʊ'sentrɪk] **ADJ** égocentrique

egocentricity [ˌi:gəʊsen'trɪsətɪ], **egocentrism** [ˌi:gəʊ'sentrɪzəm] **N** égocentrisme *m*

egoism ['i:gəʊɪzəm] **N** *(selfishness)* égoïsme *m*

egoist ['i:gəʊɪst] **N** égoïste *mf*

egoistic [ˌi:gəʊ'ɪstɪk], **egoistical** [ˌi:gəʊ'ɪstɪkəl] **ADJ** égoïste

egoistically [ˌi:gəʊ'ɪstɪkəlɪ] **ADV** égoïstement

egomania [ˌi:gəʊ'meɪnjə] **N** manie *f* égocentrique

ego-surfing **N** *Fam Comput* ego-surfing *m*

egotism ['i:gətɪzəm] **N** égotisme *m*

egotist ['i:gətɪst] **N** égotiste *mf*

egotistic [ˌi:gə'tɪstɪk], **egotistical** [ˌi:gə'tɪstɪkəl] **ADJ** égotiste

egotistically [ˌi:gə'tɪstɪklɪ] **ADV** de manière égotiste

e-government **N** *Comput* administration *f* électronique

egregious [ɪ'gri:dʒəs] **ADJ** *Formal (blatant* ▸ *error, mistake)* monumental, énorme; (▸ *lie)* énorme; (▸ *cowardice, incompetence)* extrême

egress ['i:gres] **N** *Formal (way out, exit)* sortie *f*, issue *f*; *(action of going out)* sortie *f*; **means of e.** issue *f*

egret ['i:grɪt] **N** *Orn* aigrette *f*

Egypt ['i:dʒɪpt] **N** Égypte *f*; **Lower E.** Basse-Égypte *f*; **Upper E.** Haute-Égypte *f*

Egyptian [ɪ'dʒɪpʃən] **N 1** *(person)* Égyptien (enne) *m,f* **2** *Ling* égyptien *m*
ADJ égyptien
COMP *(embassy)* d'Égypte; *(history)* de l'Égypte
▸▸ ***Egyptian cotton*** coton *m* égyptien, coton *m* jumel

eh [eɪ] **EXCLAM 1** *(what did you say?)* **eh?** hein?
2 *(seeking agreement)* **eh?** hein?
3 *(in astonishment)* **eh?** quoi?
4 *(in doubt, hesitation)* heu

EHIC [ˌi:eɪtʃˌaɪ'si:] **N** (*abbr* **European Health Insurance Card**) CEAM *f*

EIB [ˌi:aɪ'bi:] **N** (*abbr* **European Investment Bank**) BEI *f*

eider ['aɪdə(r)] **N** *Orn* eider *m*
▸▸ ***eider duck*** eider *m*

eiderdown ['aɪdədaʊn] **N 1** *(feathers)* duvet *m* d'eider **2** *(for bed)* édredon *m*

EIF [ˌi:aɪ'ef] **N** (*abbr* **European Investment Fund**) FEI *m*

eight [eɪt] **N 1** *(number, numeral)* huit *m inv*; **to reach the last e.** *(in knockout competition)* être en quart de finale; *Br* **to have had one over the e.** avoir bu plus que son compte **2** *(in rowing)* huit *m* (de pointe)
PRON huit
ADJ huit; **to work an e.-hour day** travailler huit heures par jour, faire des journées de huit heures; *see also* **five**
▸▸ *Am* ***eight ball*** *(ball)* bille *f* numéro huit; *(game)* = variante du billard; *Fam Fig* **to be behind the e. ball** être dans la mouise; *Am* ***eight hundred number*** numéro *m* vert

eight-bit **ADJ** *Comput*
▸▸ ***eight-bit byte*** octet *m*; ***eight-bit character*** caractère *m* à huit bits

eighteen [ˌeɪ'ti:n] **N** dix-huit *m inv*
PRON dix-huit
ADJ dix-huit; *see also* **five**

eighteenth [ˌeɪ'ti:nθ] **N 1** *(fraction)* dix-huitième *m* **2** *(in series)* dix-huitième *mf* **3** *(of month)* dix-huit *m inv*
ADJ dix-huitième *see also* **fifth**

eightfold ['eɪtfəʊld] **ADJ** **there's been an e. increase in property prices in the past decade** le prix des logements a été multiplié par huit au cours des dix dernières années
ADV **to increase e.** être multiplié par huit

eighth [eɪtθ] **N 1** *(fraction)* huitième *m* **2** *(in series)* huitième *mf* **3** *(of month)* huit *m inv*
ADJ huitième
ADV huitièmement; *(in contest)* en huitième position, à la huitième place; *see also* **fifth**
▸▸ *Am Sch* ***eighth grade*** = classe de lycée (12–13 ans); *Am Mus* ***eighth note*** croche *f*

eightieth ['eɪtɪəθ] **N 1** *(fraction)* quatre-vingtième *m* **2** *(in series)* quatre-vingtième *mf*
ADJ quatre-vingtième; *see also* **fifth**

eighty ['eɪtɪ] (*pl* **eighties**) **N** quatre-vingt *m inv*
PRON quatre-vingt
ADJ quatre-vingts; **page e.** page quatre-vingt; **e. million** quatre-vingts millions
COMP **e.-one** quatre-vingt-un; **e.-two** quatre-vingt-deux; **e.-first** quatre-vingt-unième; **e.-second** quatre-vingt-deuxième; *see also* **fifty**

eighty-six *Am* **ADJ** **to be e. on sth** *(in restaurant, bar)* être à court de qch ᵒ; **tell the customer we're e. on the chicken** dis au client qu'il n'y a plus de poulet
VT 1 *(eject)* vider **2** *(kill)* buter, refroidir

Eire ['eərə] **N** Eire *f*

eisteddfod [aɪ'stedfɒd] **N** = festival annuel de musique, littérature et théâtre au pays de Galles

either [*esp Br* 'aɪðə(r), *esp Am* 'i:ðə(r)] **ADJ 1** *(one or the other)* l'un (l'une) ou l'autre; **if you don't agree with e. suggestion...** si vous n'approuvez ni l'une ni l'autre *ou* aucune de ces suggestions...; **you can take e. route** tu peux prendre l'un ou l'autre de ces chemins; **e. bus will get you there** les deux bus y vont; **he can write with e. hand** il peut écrire avec la main droite ou avec la main gauche **2** *(each)* chaque; **there were candles at e. end of the table** il y avait des bougies aux deux bouts *ou* à chaque bout de la table; **there were people standing on e. side of the road** il y avait des gens de chaque côté *ou* de part et d'autre de la route
PRON *(one or the other)* l'un (l'une) ou l'autre; **you can take e.** *(bus, train etc)* vous pouvez prendre l'un ou l'autre *ou* n'importe lequel (des deux); **don't like e. of them** je ne les aime ni l'un ni l'autre; **if e. of you two makes the slightest noise** si l'un de vous deux fait le moindre bruit; **which would you like? – e.** lequel voudriez-vous? – n'importe lequel
ADV 1 *(gen)* non plus; **we can't hear anything e.** nous n'entendons rien non plus **2** *(emphatic use)* **and don't take too long about it e.!** et ne traîne pas, surtout!; **he had a suggestion to make and not such a silly one e.** il avait une suggestion à faire et qui n'était pas bête en plus
• **either…or** **CONJ** ou…ou, soit…soit; *(with negative)* ni…ni; **e. you stop complaining or I go home!** ou tu arrêtes de te plaindre, ou je rentre chez moi; **they're e. very rich or very stupid** ils sont soit très riches soit très bêtes; **she usually goes out with e. Ian or Simon** d'habitude elle sort (ou) avec Ian ou avec Simon *ou* soit avec Ian soit avec Simon; **e. come in or go out!** entre ou sors!; **e. pay up or be taken to court!** tu payes ou sinon c'est le tribunal!; **I've not met e. him or his brother** je n'ai rencontré ni lui ni son frère
• **either way** **ADV 1** *(in either case)* dans les deux cas; **e. way I lose** dans les deux cas je suis perdant; **you can do it e. way** tu peux le faire d'une façon comme de l'autre; **there is no evidence e. way** les preuves manquent de part et d'autre; **it's fine by me e. way** n'importe *ou* ça m'est égal **2** *(more or less)* en plus ou en moins; **a few days e. way could make all the difference** quelques jours en plus ou en moins pourraient changer tout **3** *(indicating advantage)* **it could go e. way** on ne peut rien prévoir; **the match could have gone e. way** le match était ouvert

either-or **ADJ** **it's an e. situation** il n'y a que deux solutions possibles

ejaculate [ɪ'dʒækjʊleɪt] **VI 1** *Physiol* éjaculer **2** *Literary (call out)* s'écrier, s'exclamer
VT 1 *Physiol* éjaculer **2** *Literary (utter)* lancer, pousser

ejaculation [ɪˌdʒækjʊ'leɪʃən] **N 1** *Physiol* éjaculation *f* **2** *Literary (exclamation)* cri *m*, exclamation *f*

eject [ɪ'dʒekt] **VT 1** *(troublemaker)* expulser **2** *(CD, video, pilot)* éjecter; *(lava)* projeter
VI *(pilot)* s'éjecter

ejection [ɪ'dʒekʃən] **N 1** *(of troublemaker)* expulsion *f* **2** *(of CD, video, pilot)* éjection *f*; *(of lava)* projection *f*
►► *Am* ***ejection seat*** siège *m* éjectable

ejector [ɪ'dʒektə(r)] **N** *(on gun)* éjecteur *m*
►► *Br* ***ejector seat*** siège *m* éjectable

eke out [iːk-] **VT SEP 1** *(make last ► rations)* faire durer **2** *(scrape)* **to e. out a living** gagner tout juste sa vie; **they eked out a miserable existence on the barren land** ils tiraient leur maigre subsistance du sol aride **3** *(by adding something)* augmenter

el [el] **N** *Am Fam (abbr* **elevated railroad***)* métro *m* aérien▫

elaborate ADJ [ɪ'læbrət] *(system, preparations)* élaboré; *(style, costume)* recherché, travaillé; *(excuse)* alambiqué; *(pattern, design)* compliqué; *(map, description, plans)* détaillé; **in e. detail** de manière très détaillée; **the whole thing was an e. joke** c'était une vaste plaisanterie
VT [ɪ'læbəreɪt] *(work out in detail ► plan, scheme etc)* élaborer; *(describe in detail)* décrire en détail
VI [ɪ'læbəreɪt] *(go into detail)* donner des détails; **there's no need to e. further** inutile de donner plus de détails; **could you e.?** est-ce que vous pouvez être plus précis?

elaborately [ɪ'læbərətlɪ] **ADV** *(decorated, designed etc)* minutieusement, avec recherche; *(planned)* minutieusement; *(packaged)* de manière élaborée

elaboration [ɪˌlæbə'reɪʃən] **N** *(working out ► of scheme, plan)* élaboration *f*; *(details)* exposé *m* minutieux

élan [eɪ'læn] **N** vigueur *f*, énergie *f*

eland ['iːlənd] **N** *Zool* éland *m*

elapse [ɪ'læps] **VI** s'écouler, passer

elapsed time [ɪ'læpst-] **N** *Comput* temps *m* écoulé

elastic [ɪ'læstɪk] **ADJ 1** *(material)* élastique **2** *Fig (timetable, arrangements, concept)* souple; *(word, moral principles)* élastique, souple; *(working hours, price, demand)* élastique
N 1 *(material)* élastique *m* **2** *Am (rubber band)* élastique *m*, caoutchouc *m*
►► *Br* ***elastic band*** élastique *m*, caoutchouc *m*; ***elastic stockings*** bas *mpl* anti-varices

elasticated [ɪ'læstɪkeɪtɪd], *Am* **elasticized** [ɪ'læstɪsaɪzd] **ADJ** *(stockings, waist)* élastique

elasticity [iːlæs'tɪsɪtɪ] **N** *Phys (of body)* élasticité *f*; *(of wood, metal)* flexibilité *f*; *Med (of muscles)* tonicité *f*; *(of hair)* élasticité *f*; *Mktg (of price, demand)* élasticité *f*; **e. of interpretation** *(of law)* élasticité *f*

elasticized *Am* = **elasticated**

elastomer [ɪ'læstəmə(r)] **N** *Chem* élastomère *m*

Elastoplast® [ɪ'læstəplɑːst] **N** *Br* sparadrap *m*

elate [ɪ'leɪt] **VT** remplir de joie, rendre euphorique

elated [ɪ'leɪtɪd] **ADJ** fou (folle) de joie, exalté, euphorique; **to feel e.** être fou de joie, exulter

elation [ɪ'leɪʃən] **N** allégresse *f*, exaltation *f*, euphorie *f*

Elba ['elbə] **N** l'île *f* d'Elbe; **on E.** sur l'île d'Elbe

elbow ['elbəʊ] **N** *(of arm, jacket, pipe, river)* coude *m*; **out at the elbows** *(jacket)* troué aux coudes; **with his elbows on the bar** les coudes sur le bar, accoudé au bar; *Fig* **to stand e. to e.** être coude à coude; **to be at sb's e.** être *ou* se tenir aux côtés de qn; *Br Fam* **to give sb the e.** *(employee)* virer qn; *(boyfriend, girlfriend)* larguer *ou* jeter qn; *(tenant)* mettre qn à la porte; *Br Fam* **to get the e.** *(employee)* se faire virer; *(boyfriend, girlfriend)* se faire larguer *ou* jeter; *(tenant)* se faire mettre à la porte; *Br Fam* **to bend the** *or* **one's e.** picoler, lever le coude
VT *(hit)* donner un coup de coude à; *(push)* pousser du coude; **to e. one's way through the crowd** se frayer un passage à travers la foule en jouant des coudes; **he just elbowed me aside** il m'a écarté du coude
►► *Fam* ***elbow grease*** huile *f* de coude; ***elbow joint*** *Anat* articulation *f* de coude; *Tech* raccord *m* coudé; ***elbow pad*** coudière *f*, ***elbow patch*** coude *m*
► **elbow out VT SEP** *(from job)* se débarrasser de

elbow-length ADJ e. gloves gants *mpl* longs (montant jusqu'au coude)

elbow-rest N accoudoir *m*

elbow-room N I don't have enough e. je n'ai pas assez de place (pour me retourner); *Fig* je n'ai pas suffisamment de liberté d'action

El Cheapo [ˌel'tʃiːpəʊ] *Fam Hum* **N** article *m* bas de gamme▫
ADJ bas de gamme▫

elder[1] ['eldə(r)] **ADJ** *(brother, sister)* aîné; **Pitt the E.** le Premier Pitt; **Pliny the E.** Pline l'Ancien
N 1 *(of two children)* aîné(e) *m,f* **2** *(of tribe, the Church)* ancien *m* **3** *(senior)* **you should respect your elders (and betters)** vous devez le respect à vos aînés
►► ***elder statesman*** *(gen)* vétéran *m*; *(politician)* vétéran *m* de la politique

elder[2] **N** *Bot* sureau *m*

elderberry ['eldəˌberɪ] **N** *Bot & Culin* baie *f* de sureau
COMP *(wine)* de sureau

elderflower ['eldəˌflaʊə(r)] **N** *Bot & Culin* fleur *f* de sureau

elderly ['eldəlɪ] **ADJ** âgé; **my e. uncle** mon vieil oncle; **she's getting rather e.** elle se fait bien vieille
NPL the e. les personnes *fpl* âgées

eldest ['eldɪst] **ADJ** aîné; **my e. daughter** ma fille aînée, mon aînée; **their e. son** leur fils aîné
N aîné(e) *m,f*
►► *Cards* ***eldest hand*** premier *m* en cartes

elect [ɪ'lekt] **VT 1** *(by voting)* élire; **to e. sb President** élire qn président; **to get elected** être élu; **to e. sb to office** élire qn **2** *Formal (choose)* choisir; **to e. to do sth** choisir de faire qch
ADJ élu; **the President e.** le président élu
NPL *Rel* **the e.** les élus *mpl*

elected [ɪ'lektɪd] **ADJ** élu
►► ***elected dictatorship*** = gouvernement élu qui se comporte comme une dictature;

election [ɪ'lekʃən] **N** élection *f*; **to stand for e.** se présenter aux élections; **to hold an e.** procéder à une élection; **the elections** les élections
COMP *(agent, campaign, speech, promise)* électoral; *(day, results)* des élections
►► ***election observer*** observateur *m* électoral; ***election platform*** plate-forme *f* électorale; ***election programme*** programme *m* électoral; ***election trail*** tournée *f* électorale; **on the e. trail** en tournée électorale

electioneer [ɪlekʃə'nɪə(r)] **VI** participer à la campagne électorale; *Pej* faire de la propagande électorale

electioneering [ɪˌlekʃə'nɪərɪŋ] **N** *(UNCOUNT)* campagne *f* électorale; *Pej* propagande *f* électorale
COMP *(speech, campaign)* électoral; *Pej* propagandiste

elective [ɪ'lektɪv] **ADJ 1** *(with power to elect ► assembly)* électoral
2 *(chosen ► official, post)* électif
3 *Am & Scot Sch & Univ (optional ► course, subject)* optionnel, facultatif
4 *Br Univ (medical student)* qui effectue un stage pratique *(dans un centre hospitalier)*
N 1 *Am & Scot Sch & Univ (subject)* cours *m* optionnel *ou* facultatif; **I'm taking two electives in psychology** je suis deux cours facultatifs en psychologie **2** *Br Univ (of medical student)* stage *m* pratique *(effectué dans un centre hospitalier)*; **she is on e. in Peru** elle est en stage pratique au Pérou
►► ***elective surgery*** chirurgie *f* de confort

elector [ɪ'lektə(r)] **N** *(with power to elect)* électeur (trice) *m,f*; *(in US electoral system)* grand électeur *m*, membre *m* du collège électoral
• **Elector N** *Hist* Électeur *m*

electoral [ɪ'lektərəl] **ADJ** électoral
►► ***electoral alliance*** apparentement *m*, alliance *f* électorale; ***electoral body*** corps *m* électoral; ***electoral college*** collège *m* électoral *(qui élit le président des États-Unis)*; *Br* ***Electoral Commission*** commission *f* électorale; ***electoral committee*** comité *m* électoral; ***electoral district*** circonscription *f* électorale; ***electoral pact*** pacte *m* électoral; ***electoral platform*** plate-forme *f* électorale; ***electoral process*** processus *m* électoral; ***electoral programme*** programme *m* électoral; *Br* ***electoral reform*** réforme *f* électorale; *Br* ***electoral register*** liste *f* électorale; **on the e. register** sur la liste électorale; ***electoral returns*** résultats *mpl* des élections; *Br* ***electoral roll*** liste *f* électorale; **on the e. roll** sur la liste électorale; ***electoral system*** système *m* électoral, régime *m* électoral; *Am* ***electoral vote*** vote *m* collégial

electorate [ɪ'lektərət] **N** électorat *m*

electret [ɪ'lektrət] **N** *Elec* électret *m*

electric [ɪ'lektrɪk] **ADJ 1** *(cooker, cable, current, musical instrument)* électrique; *Fig* **the atmosphere of the meeting was e.** l'atmosphère de la réunion était électrique; **the effect of her words was e.** ses mots ont eu un effet électrisant **2** *Ich* électrogène
N *Br Fam* électricité▫ *f*
• **electrics NPL** *Br Fam (of car, machine)* installation *f* électrique▫
►► *Tech* ***electric arc*** arc *m* électrique; *Br* ***electric blanket*** couverture *f* chauffante; ***electric blue*** bleu *m* électrique; ***electric chair*** chaise *f* électrique; **to go to the e. chair** être envoyé à la chaise électrique; ***electric charge*** charge *f* électrique; *Ich* ***electric eel*** anguille *f* électrique; ***electric eye*** œil *m* électrique; ***electric fence*** clôture *f* électrique; ***electric field*** champ *m* électrique; ***electric fire*** appareil *m* de chauffage électrique; ***electric guitar*** guitare *f* électrique; ***electric heater*** appareil *m* de chauffage électrique; ***electric light*** *(individual appliance)* lumière *f* électrique; *(lighting)* éclairage *m ou* lumière *f* électrique; ***electric motor*** moteur *m* électrique; ***electric organ*** *Mus* orgue *f* électrique; *Ich* organe *m* électrogène; ***electric power station*** centrale *f* électrique; *Ich* ***electric ray*** torpille *f*; ***electric shock*** décharge *f* électrique; **I got an e. shock from the switch** j'ai reçu une décharge en touchant l'interrupteur; *Med* ***electric shock therapy, electric shock treatment*** traitement *m* par électrochocs; ***electric storm*** orage *m*; ***electric underblanket*** protège-matelas *m* chauffant; *Aut* ***electric window*** glace *f ou* vitre *f* électrique

electrical [ɪ'lektrɪkəl] **ADJ** électrique
►► ***electrical appliance*** appareil *m* électrique; ***electrical engineer*** ingénieur *m* électricien; ***electrical engineering*** électrotechnique *f*, ***electrical failure*** panne *f* d'électricité; ***electrical fault*** défaut *m* dans le système électrique; *Am* ***electrical shock*** décharge *f* électrique; ***electrical storm*** orage *m*

electrically [ɪ'lektrɪkəlɪ] **ADV** électriquement; **e. operated** *(machine)* fonctionnant à l'électricité; *(windows)* à commande électrique; **e. charged** chargé d'électricité; *Fig* **an e. charged atmosphere** une atmosphère électrique

electrician [ˌɪlek'trɪʃən] **N** électricien(enne) *m,f*

electricity [ˌɪlek'trɪsətɪ] **N** électricité *f*; **to turn** *or* **to switch the e. off/on** couper/mettre le courant; **to be without e.** *(because of power cut)* être privé d'électricité; *(not installed)* ne pas avoir l'électricité; *Fig* **there was e. in the air** il y avait de l'électricité dans l'air
COMP *(bill)* d'électricité; *(supply)* en électricité
►► *Br Formerly* ***electricity board*** agence *f* régionale de distribution de l'électricité; ***electricity showroom*** magasin d'électro-ménager *(où l'on peut aussi payer ses factures d'électricité)*

electrification [ɪˌlektrɪfɪ'keɪʃən] **N** électrification *f*

electrify [ɪ'lektrɪfaɪ] **VT 1** *(railway line)* électrifier; *(charge with electricity ► fence)* électriser **2** *Fig (audience)* électriser

electrifying [ɪ'lektrɪfaɪŋ] **ADJ** *Fig* électrisant

electroacoustic [ɪˌlektrəʊə'kuːstɪk] **ADJ** électroacoustique

electrocardiogram [ɪˌlektrəʊ'kɑːdɪəgræm] **N** *Med* électrocardiogramme *m*

electrocardiograph [ɪˌlektrəʊ'kɑːdɪəgrɑːf] **N** *Med* électrocardiographe *m*

electrocardiography [ɪˌlektrəʊˌkɑːdɪ'ɒgrəfɪ] **N** *Med* électrocardiographie *f*

electrochemical [ɪˌlektrəʊ'kemɪkəl] **ADJ** électrochimique

electrochemistry [ɪˌlektrəʊ'kemɪstrɪ] **N** électrochimie *f*

electroclash [ɪ'lektrəʊ,klæʃ] N *Mus* electroclash *m*

electroconvulsive therapy [ɪ,lektrəʊkən'vʌlsɪv-] N *Med* thérapie *f* par électrochocs

electrocute [ɪ'lektrəkju:t] VT électrocuter; **you'll e. yourself** *(give yourself a shock)* tu vas prendre une décharge

electrocution [ɪ,lektrə'kju:ʃən] N électrocution *f*

electrode [ɪ'lektrəʊd] N *Chem & Elec* électrode *f*
►► **electrode gap** écartement *m* des électrodes; **electrode holder** porte-électrodes *m inv*

electrodynamics [ɪ,lektrəʊdaɪ'næmɪks] N *(UNCOUNT) Phys* électrodynamique *f*

electroencephalogram [ɪ,lektrəʊen'sefələgræm] N *Med* électro-encéphalogramme *m*

electroencephalograph [ɪ,lektrəʊen'sefələgrɑ:f] N *Med* électro-encéphalographe *m*

electrolysis [,ɪlek'trɒləsɪs] N *Chem & Med* électrolyse *f*

electrolyte [ɪ'lektrəʊlaɪt] N *Chem* électrolyte *m*

electrolytic [ɪ,lektrəʊ'lɪtɪk] ADJ *Chem* électrolytique

electromagnet [ɪ,lektrəʊ'mægnɪt] N électro-aimant *m*

electromagnetic [ɪ,lektrəʊmæg'netɪk] ADJ électromagnétique

electromagnetism [ɪ,lektrəʊ'mægnɪtɪzəm] N électromagnétisme *m*

electromotive [ɪ,lektrəʊ'məʊtɪv] ADJ *Phys* électromoteur
►► **electromotive force** force *f* électromotrice

electron [ɪ'lektrɒn] N *Phys* électron *m*; **positive/negative e.** électron *m* positif/négatif
►► *Electron* **electron beam** faisceau *m* d'électrons; *Electron* **electron gun** canon *m* électronique *ou* à électrons; *Biol* **electron microscope** microscope *m* électronique; *Chem* **electron probe** sonde *f* électronique; *Astron* **electron telescope** télescope *m* électronique; *Elec* **electron tube** tube *m* électronique

electronic [,ɪlek'trɒnɪk] ADJ électronique
• **electronics** N *(UNCOUNT)* électronique *f* NPL *(of machine)* système *m* électronique COMP *(company)* d'électronique
►► *Comput* **electronic banking** transactions *fpl* bancaires électroniques, bancatique *f*; **electronic brain** cerveau *m* électronique; *Comput* **electronic cash** argent *m* électronique, argent *m* virtuel; *Comput* **electronic commerce** commerce *m* électronique; *Comput* **electronic computer** calculateur *m* électronique; **electronic crime** crime *m* informatique; *Comput* **electronic data interchange** échange *m* de données informatisé; *Comput* **electronic data processing** traitement *m* électronique de l'information; **electronics engineer** ingénieur *m* électronicien, électronicien (enne) *m,f*; *Phot* **electronic flash** flash *m* électronique; *Fin & Comput* **electronic funds transfer** transfert *m* de fonds électronique; **electronic funds transfer at point of sale** transfert *m* de fonds électronique au point de vente; **electronic funds transfer system** = système électronique de transfert de fonds; *Aut* **electronic ignition** allumage *m* électronique; **electronics industry** industrie *f* électronique; **electronic key** clef *f* électronique; *Comput* **electronic listening** écoute *f* électronique; *Comput* **electronic mail** courrier *m* électronique; *Comput* **electronic mailbox** boîte *f* à *ou* aux lettres électronique; *Comput* **electronic mall** galeries *fpl* électroniques; **electronic media** médias *mpl* électroniques; *Comput* **electronic money** argent *m* électronique, argent *m* virtuel; *(concept)* monétique *f*; **electronic music** musique *f* électronique; *TV* **electronic news gathering** journalisme *m* électronique de télévision; *Com* **electronic office** bureau *m* informatisé; *Mus* **electronic organ** orgue *m* électronique; *Com* **electronic payment** paiement *m* électronique; **electronic payment terminal** terminal *m* électronique de paiement; *Comput* **electronic point of sale** point *m* de vente électronique; *Comput* **electronic purse** porte-monnaie *m* électronique; *Comput* **electronic shopping** téléachat *m*, achats *mpl* en ligne; **electronic surveillance** surveillance *f* électronique; **electronic tag** bracelet *m* électronique *ou* de cheville *ou* de détention; **electronic tagging** étiquetage *m* électronique; *St Exch* **electronic trading** transactions *fpl* boursières electroniques; *Fin* **electronic transfer** transfert *m* de fonds électronique; *Mil* **electronic warfare** guerre *f* électronique

electronically [,ɪlek'trɒnɪkəlɪ] ADV électroniquement; *(operated)* par voie électronique

electroplate [ɪ'lektrəʊpleɪt] VT plaquer par galvanoplastie; *(with gold)* dorer par galvanoplastie; *(with silver)* argenter par galvanoplastie
N *(UNCOUNT)* articles *mpl* plaqués (par galvanoplastie); *(with silver)* articles *mpl* argentés

electroplated [ɪ'lektrəʊpleɪtɪd] ADJ plaqué *(par galvanoplastie)*
►► **electroplated nickel silver** rudz *m*

electropop [ɪ'lektrəʊ,pɒp] N pop *f* électronique, électropop *f*

electrosensitive [ɪ,lektrəʊ'sensɪtɪv] ADJ *Elec* électrosensible

electroshock [ɪ'lektrəʊʃɒk] N *Elec* électrochoc *m*
►► *Med* **electroshock therapy** thérapie *f* par électrochocs

electrostatic [ɪ,lektrəʊ'stætɪk] ADJ *Elec* électrostatique

electrostatics [ɪ,lektrəʊ'stætɪks] N *(UNCOUNT) Elec* électrostatique *f*

electrotechnic [ɪ,lektrəʊ'teknɪk], **electrotechnical** [ɪ,lektrəʊ'teknɪkəl] ADJ *Elec* électrotechnique

electrotherapy [ɪ,lektrəʊ'θerəpɪ] N *Med* électrothérapie *f*

electrotype [ɪ'lektrəʊtaɪp] *Typ* N galvanotype *m*
VT galvanotyper

elegance ['elɪgəns] N élégance *f*

elegant ['elɪgənt] ADJ *(person, style, solution)* élégant; *(building, furniture)* aux lignes élégantes

elegiac [elɪ'dʒaɪək] ADJ élégiaque
• **elegiacs** NPL vers *mpl* élégiaques

elegy ['elɪdʒɪ] *(pl* **elegies***)* N élégie *f*

element ['elɪmənt] N **1** *(water, air etc)* élément *m*; **the four elements** les quatre éléments *mpl*; **to be exposed to/to brave the elements** être exposé aux/affronter les éléments; *Fig* **to be in one's e.** être dans son élément
2 *(in kettle, electric heater)* résistance *f*
3 *(factor)* facteur *m*; *(small amount)* part *f*; **e. of uncertainty/danger/chance** part *f* d'incertitude/de danger/de chance; **there is an e. of risk involved** cela comporte un risque; **the e. of surprise** l'élément de *ou* le facteur surprise; **the personal/time e.** le facteur humain/temps; **the film has all the elements of a hit movie** le film a tous les ingrédients d'un film à succès
4 *(usu pl) (rudiment)* rudiment *m*; **the elements of computing** les rudiments de l'informatique
5 *(in society, group)* élément *m*; **the hooligan e.** l'élément hooligan de la société; **a disruptive e.** *(in class)* un élément perturbateur; **undesirable elements (in society)** éléments indésirables (de la société)
6 *Chem* élément *m*
7 *Rel* **the elements (of bread and wine)** les espèces *fpl*

elemental [,elɪ'mentəl] ADJ **1** *(basic)* fondamental, de base; **the e. needs of man** les besoins fondamentaux de l'homme; **to be e. to sth** être essentiel à qch
2 *(relating to the elements)* propre aux éléments; **the e. force of the storm** la force des éléments déchaînés dans la tempête
3 *(primitive)* élémentaire, primitif
4 *Chem & Phys* élémentaire

elementary [,elɪ'mentərɪ] ADJ élémentaire; **I only speak e. Russian** mon russe est rudimentaire
►► *Am* **elementary education** enseignement *m* primaire; *Chem & Phys* **elementary particle** particule *f* élémentaire; *Am* **elementary school** école *f* primaire

elephant ['elɪfənt] N éléphant *m*; **African/Indian e.** éléphant *m* d'Afrique/d'Asie; *Fam* **baby e.** éléphanteau *m*
►► *Zool* **elephant calf** éléphanteau *m*; *Zool* **elephant seal** éléphant *m* de mer

elephantiasis [,elɪfən'taɪəsɪs] N *Med* éléphantiasis *m*

elephantine [,elɪ'fæntaɪn] ADJ *(proportions, size)* éléphantesque; *(gait)* lourd, pesant; *(movement)* gauche, maladroit; *Fig (humour)* lourd

elevate ['elɪveɪt] VT **1** *(raise)* élever, hausser; *Mil (gun)* pointer en hauteur; *Rel (host, mind)* élever; **to e. sb to the peerage** élever qn à la pairie **2** *(exalt ► person)* exalter; *(someone's soul)* élever; **they had elevated their legends into a religion** ils avaient élevé leurs légendes au rang de religion

elevated ['elɪveɪtɪd] ADJ **1** *(height, position, rank)* haut, élevé; *(thoughts)* noble, élevé; *(style)* élevé, soutenu; **he has an e. opinion of himself** il a une haute opinion de lui-même **2** *(raised ► road, platform)* surélevé
►► *Am* **elevated railroad, elevated railway** métro *m* aérien; *TV & Cin* **elevated shot** plongée *f*

elevating ['elɪveɪtɪŋ] ADJ *(edifying)* édifiant; **the experience was far from e.** l'expérience n'a rien eu de bien inspirant
N élévation *f*, levage *m*

elevation [,elɪ'veɪʃən] N **1** *(raising ► of roof, in rank)* élévation *f*; *Rel (► of host)* élévation *f*; *(► of style, language)* caractère *m* élevé *ou* soutenu
2 *(height)* altitude *f*, hauteur *f*; **e. above sea level** altitude *f ou* hauteur *f* au-dessus du niveau de la mer
3 *Astron (of star)* élévation *f*
4 *(hill)* élévation *f*, hauteur *f*
5 *(of cannon)* hausse *f*
6 *Archit* élévation *f*; **viewed in e.** vu en élévation; **front e.** façade *f*; **side e.** façade *f* latérale; **rear e.** derrière *m*

elevator ['elɪveɪtə(r)] N **1** *Am (lift)* ascenseur *m*; *(for goods)* monte-charge *m inv*; *Fam Hum* **the e. doesn't go up to the top floor** c'est pas une lumière
2 *Aviat* gouvernail *m* de profondeur *ou* d'altitude
►► **elevator attendant, elevator operator** garçon *m* d'ascenseur; **elevator shaft** cage *f* d'ascenseur; **elevator shoes** chaussures *fpl* à semelles compensées

eleven [ɪ'levən] N **1** *(number, numeral)* onze *m inv*
2 *Sport (team)* onze *m*; **the French e.** le onze de France
PRON onze
ADJ onze; *see also* **five**

elevenses [ɪ'levənzɪz] N *Br* = boisson ou en-cas pour la pause de onze heures

eleventh [ɪ'levənθ] N **1** *(fraction)* onzième *m* **2** *(in series)* onzième *mf* **3** *(of month)* onze *m inv*
ADJ onzième; **at the e. hour** à la dernière minute
ADV onzièmement; *(in contest)* en onzième position, à la onzième place; *see also* **fifth**
►► *Am Sch* **eleventh grade** = classe de lycée (15–16 ans)

eleventh-hour ADJ de dernière minute; **e. talks** discussions *fpl* de dernière minute

elf [elf] *(pl* **elves** [elvz]*)* N elfe *m*, lutin *m*

elfin ['elfɪn] ADJ **1** *Fig (face, features)* délicat **2** *(music, dance)* féerique

elfish ['elfɪʃ] ADJ **1** *Fig (face, features)* délicat **2** *(music, dance)* féerique **3** *(mischievous)* espiègle

elicit [ɪ'lɪsɪt] VT *(information, explanation, response)* obtenir; *(facts, truth)* découvrir, mettre au jour; **to e. sth from sb** tirer qch de qn

elide [ɪ'laɪd] VT *Ling* élider

eligibility [,elɪdʒə'bɪlətɪ] N *(to vote)* éligibilité *f*; *(for a job)* admissibilité *f*; **there was no doubt as to his e.** *(for marriage)* c'était sans aucun doute un bon parti; **to determine sb's e. for promotion** décider si qn présente les conditions requises pour bénéficier d'une promotion

eligible ['elɪdʒəbəl] ADJ *(to vote)* éligible; *(for a job)* admissible; *(for promotion)* pouvant bénéficier d'une promotion; *(for marriage)* mariable; **to be e. for a pension/a tax rebate** avoir droit à une retraite/un dégrèvement fiscal; **to be e.** *(as possible husband or boyfriend)* être un bon *ou* beau parti; **there were lots of e. men at the party** il y avait beaucoup de bons *ou* beaux partis à la fête
►► **eligible bachelor** bon *ou* beau parti *m*

eliminate [ɪ'lɪmɪneɪt] **VT** *(competitor, alternative)* éliminer; *(stain, mark)* enlever, faire disparaître; *(item from diet)* supprimer, éliminer; *(possibility)* écarter, éliminer; *(kill)* éliminer, supprimer; *Math & Physiol* éliminer; **to e. hunger and poverty from the world** éliminer *ou* supprimer la faim et la pauvreté dans le monde; **the police have eliminated him from their enquiries** la police l'a écarté de son enquête; *Sport* **they were eliminated in the first round** ils ont été éliminés au premier round

eliminating [ɪ'lɪmɪneɪtɪŋ] **ADJ** éliminateur
▸▸ *Sport* ***eliminating heats, eliminating rounds*** épreuves *fpl* éliminatoires

elimination [ɪˌlɪmɪ'neɪʃən] **N 1** élimination *f*; **by (a process of) e.** par élimination **2** *Physiol* évacuation *f*

eliminator [ɪ'lɪmɪneɪtə(r)] **N** *Sport* éliminateur *m*; **the next match will be the e.** le prochain match décidera de qui sera éliminé

elision [ɪ'lɪʒən] **N** *Ling* élision *f*

elite [ɪ'liːt], **élite** [eɪ'liːt] **N** élite *f*; **to be one of the e.** faire partie de l'élite
ADJ d'élite

elitism [ɪ'liːtɪzəm] **N** élitisme *m*

elitist [ɪ'liːtɪst] **N** élitiste *mf*
ADJ élitiste

elixir [ɪ'lɪksə(r)] **N** élixir *m*; **e. of life** élixir *m* de vie

Elizabeth [ɪ'lɪzəbəθ] **PR N Queen E.** la reine Élisabeth

Elizabethan [ɪˌlɪzə'biːθən] **N** Élisabéthain(e) *m,f*
ADJ élisabéthain

elk [elk] *(pl* **inv** *or* **elks) N** *Zool* élan *m*; **North American e.** wapiti *m*, cerf *m* du Canada

ell [el] **N** *Arch* aune *f*

ellipse [ɪ'lɪps] **N** *Math* ellipse *f*
• **Ellipse N the E.** = endroit situé près de la Maison Blanche, à Washington, où ont lieu des cérémonies officielles ainsi que des manifestations

ellipsis [ɪ'lɪpsɪs] *(pl* **ellipses** [-siːz]) **N** *Gram* ellipse *f*

ellipsoid [ɪ'lɪpsɔɪd] **N** *Math* ellipsoïde *m*

elliptic [ɪ'lɪptɪk], **elliptical** [ɪ'lɪptɪkəl] **ADJ** elliptique

elliptically [ɪ'lɪptɪkəlɪ] **ADV** de manière elliptique, par ellipse

elm [elm] **N** orme *m*
▸▸ ***elm grove*** ormaie *f*

elocution [ˌelə'kjuːʃən] **N** élocution *f*, diction *f*
COMP *(lesson, teacher)* d'élocution, de diction

elocutionist [ˌelə'kjuːʃənɪst] **N** professeur *m* d'élocution *ou* de diction

elongate ['iːlɒŋgeɪt] **VT** allonger; *(line)* prolonger
VI s'allonger, s'étendre

elongated ['iːlɒŋgeɪtɪd] **ADJ** *(in space)* allongé; *(in time)* prolongé

elongation [ˌiːlɒŋ'geɪʃən] **N 1** *(lengthening)* allongement *m*; *(of line)* prolongement *m* **2** *Astron* élongation *f*

elope [ɪ'ləʊp] **VI** s'enfuir pour se marier; **to e. with sb** s'enfuir avec qn pour l'épouser

elopement [ɪ'ləʊpmənt] **N** fugue *f* amoureuse *(en vue d'un mariage)*

eloquence ['eləkwəns] **N** éloquence *f*

eloquent ['eləkwənt] **ADJ** éloquent; **to be an e. speaker** être éloquent, avoir de l'éloquence; *Fig* **an e. gesture** un geste éloquent; **the state of the economy is an e. indictment of this policy** la situation économique en dit long sur cette politique

eloquently ['eləkwəntlɪ] **ADV** éloquemment, avec éloquence

ELSE [els] **ADV 1** *(after indefinite pronoun)* d'autre; **anybody** *or* **anyone e.** *(at all)* n'importe qui d'autre, toute autre personne; *(in addition)* quelqu'un d'autre; **anyone e. would have phoned the police** n'importe qui d'autre aurait appelé la police; **I couldn't find anyone e. to help me** je n'ai pu trouver personne d'autre pour m'aider; **he's no cleverer than anybody e.** il n'est pas plus intelligent qu'un autre; **it couldn't be anyone e.'s** ça ne pouvait être celui de personne d'autre; **anything e.** *(at all)* n'importe quoi d'autre; *(in addition)* quelque chose d'autre; **would you like** *or* **will there be anything e.?** *(in shop)* vous fallait-il autre chose?; *(in restaurant)* désirez-vous autre chose?; **he wouldn't accept anything e.** il n'a rien voulu accepter d'autre; **I couldn't do anything e. but** *or* **except apologize** je ne pouvais (rien faire d'autre) que m'excuser; **anywhere e.** ailleurs; **I haven't got anywhere e.** *or* **I've got nowhere e. to go** je n'ai nulle part ailleurs où aller; **everybody e.** tous les autres; **everything e.** tout le reste; **everywhere e.** partout ailleurs; **everywhere e. was shut** *(other shops)* tous les autres magasins étaient fermés; **there is little e. we can do** nous ne pouvons pas faire grand-chose d'autre; **and much e. (besides)** et beaucoup de choses encore; **there isn't much e. to be done** il ne reste pas beaucoup à faire; *(we've no choice)* il n'y a pas grand-chose d'autre à faire; **nobody** *or* **no one e.** personne d'autre; **nothing e.** rien d'autre; **we're alive, nothing e. matters** nous sommes vivants, c'est tout ce qui compte; **there's nothing e. for it** il n'y a rien d'autre à faire; **nowhere e.** nulle part ailleurs; **somebody** *or* **someone e.** quelqu'un d'autre; **this is somebody e.'s** c'est à quelqu'un d'autre; **something e.** autre chose, quelque chose d'autre; **somewhere** *or Am* **someplace e.** ailleurs, autre part; **if all e. fails** en dernier recours; **it'll teach him a lesson, if nothing e.** au moins, ça lui servira de leçon; *Fam* **he's/she's/it's something e.!** il est/elle est/c'est incroyable!; *Fam* **the price of petrol is something e.!** bonjour le prix de l'essence!
2 *(after interrogative pronoun) (in addition)* d'autre; **what/who e.?** quoi/qui d'autre?; **what e. can I do?** que puis-je faire d'autre?; **who e. but Frank?** qui d'autre que Frank?; **how/why e. would I do it?** comment/pourquoi le ferais-je sinon?; **where e. would he be?** où peut-il être à part là?
3 *(otherwise)* autrement; *(if not, then)* ou bien; **come tomorrow or e. it will be too late** venez demain, autrement il sera trop tard; **he must be joking, or e. he's mad** il plaisante, ou bien alors il est fou; **do what I tell you or e.!** fais ce que je te dis, sinon!

---

elsewhere [els'weə(r)] **ADV** ailleurs; **to go e.** aller ailleurs; **e. in France** ailleurs en France; **her ambitions lie e.** ses ambitions se situent à un autre niveau

ELT [ˌiːel'tiː] **N** *(abbr* **English language teaching)** = enseignement de l'anglais

elucidate [ɪ'luːsɪdeɪt] **VT** *(point, question)* élucider, expliciter; *(reasons)* expliquer
VI expliquer, être plus clair; **could you e.?** pourrais-tu être plus clair?

elucidation [ɪˌluːsɪ'deɪʃən] **N** *(of point, question)* élucidation *f*, éclaircissement *m*; *(of reasons)* explication *f*

elude [ɪ'luːd] **VT** *(enemy, pursuers)* échapper à; *(question)* éluder; *(blow)* esquiver; *(someone's gaze)* éviter, fuir; *(obligation, responsibility)* se dérober à, se soustraire à; *(justice)* se soustraire à; **his name/that word eludes me** son nom/ce mot m'échappe; **to e. sb's grasp** échapper à (l'emprise de) qn; **success has always eluded him** la réussite lui a toujours échappé

elusive [ɪ'luːsɪv] **ADJ** *(enemy, prey, happiness, thought)* insaisissable; *(word, concept)* difficile à définir; *(answer)* élusif, évasif; **she's being rather e.** *(difficult to find)* elle se fait plutôt discrète ces derniers temps; *(vague)* elle se montre assez évasive

elusiveness [ɪ'luːsɪvnɪs] **N** *(of answer)* caractère *m* élusif *ou* évasif; *(of thoughts, happiness)* caractère *m* insaisissable

elver ['elvə(r)] **N** *Ich* civelle *f*, pibale *f*

elves [elvz] *npl of* **elf**

elvish ['elvɪʃ] **ADJ 1** *Fig (face, features)* délicat **2** *(music, dance)* féerique **3** *(mischievous)* espiègle

Elysian [ɪ'lɪzɪən] **ADJ** *Myth* élyséen
▸▸ ***Elysian fields*** champs *mpl* Elysées

'em [əm] *Br Fam* = **them**

em [em] **N** *Typ* cadratin *m*
▸▸ ***em dash*** tiret *m* cadratin; ***em space*** cadratin *m*

emaciated [ɪ'meɪʃɪeɪtɪd] **ADJ** émacié, décharné; **to become e.** s'émacier, se décharner

emaciation [ɪˌmeɪsɪ'eɪʃən] **N** émaciation *f*

e-mail, email ['iːmeɪl] *Comput* **N** *(UNCOUNT)* courrier *m* électronique, e-mail *m*, mél *m*, courriel *m*; **to contact sb by e.** contacter qn par courrier électronique; **to send sth by e.** envoyer qch par courrier électronique; **to check one's e.** consulter sa boîte à lettres électronique
VT *(message, document)* envoyer par courrier électronique; *(person)* envoyer un courrier électronique à; **can I e. you?** est-ce que je peux vous contacter par courrier électronique?; **e. us at...** envoyez-nous vos messages à l'adresse suivante...
▸▸ ***e-mail account*** compte *m* de courrier électronique; ***e-mail address*** adresse *f* électronique; ***e-mail application*** *(for job)* candidature *f* en-ligne; ***e-mail client*** client *m* de courrier électronique; ***e-mail program*** programme *m* de courrier électronique; ***e-mail software*** logiciel *m* de courrier électronique

emanate ['eməneɪt] **VI to e. from** émaner de
VT *(love)* rayonner de; *(concern)* respirer

emanation [ˌemə'neɪʃən] **N** émanation *f*

emancipate [ɪ'mænsɪpeɪt] **VT** émanciper; *(slaves)* affranchir

emancipated [ɪ'mænsɪpeɪtɪd] **ADJ** émancipé; *(slaves)* affranchi

emancipation [ɪˌmænsɪ'peɪʃən] **N** émancipation *f*; *(of slaves)* affranchissement *m*
▸▸ *Am Hist* ***the Emancipation Proclamation*** la proclamation d'émancipation

e-marketer N webmarketeur *m*, e-marketer *m*

e-marketing N e-marketing *m*, webmarketing *m*

emasculate [ɪ'mæskjʊˌleɪt] **VT** émasculer; *Fig* émasculer, affaiblir

emasculation [ɪˌmæskjʊ'leɪʃən] **N** émasculation *f*; *Fig* émasculation *f*, affaiblissement *m*

embalm [ɪm'bɑːm] **VT** *(body)* embaumer

embalmer [ɪm'bɑːmə(r)] **N** embaumeur *m*, thanatopracteur *m*

embalming [ɪm'bɑːmɪŋ] **N** embaumement *m*
▸▸ ***embalming fluid*** fluide *m* de thanatopraxie

embankment [ɪm'bæŋkmənt] **N** *(of concrete)* quai *m*; *(of earth)* berge *f*; *(to contain river)* digue *f*; *(along railway, road)* talus *m*
• **Embankment N the E.** = nom abrégé du "Victoria Embankment", rue de la rive nord de la Tamise à Londres

embargo [em'bɑːgəʊ] *(pl* **embargoes) N 1** *Com & Pol* embargo *m*; **to put** *or* **to place** *or* **to lay an e. on sth** mettre l'embargo sur qch; **to lift/to break an e.** lever/enfreindre un embargo; **there is still an e. on arms, arms are still under an e.** les armes sont encore sous embargo; **oil/arms e.** embargo *m* pétrolier/sur les armes; **trade e.** embargo *m* commercial **2** *Fig (on spending)* interdiction *f*; **to put an e. on sth** interdire *ou* bannir qch
VT *Com & Pol* mettre l'embargo sur; *Fig* interdire

embark [ɪm'bɑːk] **VT** *(passengers, cargo)* embarquer
VI embarquer, monter à bord

embarkation [ˌembɑː'keɪʃən], **embarkment** [ɪm'bɑːkmənt] **N** *(of passengers, cargo)* embarquement *m*
▸▸ ***embarkation card, embarkation papers*** carte *f* d'embarquement

embarrass [ɪm'bærəs] **VT** embarrasser, gêner; **to e. the government/one's family** mettre le gouvernement/sa famille dans l'embarras

embarrassed [ɪm'bærəst] **ADJ** embarrassé; **to feel e. (about sth)** être embarrassé *ou* se sentir gêné (à propos de qch); **to be (financially) e.** être gêné, avoir des problèmes d'argent

embarrassing [ɪm'bærəsɪŋ] **ADJ** *(experience, person)* embarrassant, gênant; *(situation)* embarrassant, délicat; **how e.!** comme c'est gênant *ou* embarrassant!; **this is rather e. but...** cela me gêne beaucoup mais...

embarrassingly [ɪm'bærəsɪŋlɪ] **ADV** de manière embarrassante; **it was e. obvious** c'était évident au point d'en être embarrassant; **he gave an e. bad performance** sa prestation était tellement mauvaise qu'on en était gêné pour lui; **e., we seem to have omitted the principal's name** il semble que nous ayons oublié le nom du directeur, ce qui est plutôt embarrassant

embarrassment [ɪm'bærəsmənt] **N 1** *(feeling)* embarras *m*, gêne *f*; **(much) to my e.** à mon grand embarras; **to cause sb e.** mettre qn dans l'embarras; **to be in a state of financial e.** avoir des problèmes *ou* embarras financiers; **an e. of riches** l'embarras du choix **2** *(person, thing)* source *f* d'embarras; **to be an e. to sb** être une source d'embarras pour qn, faire honte à qn

embassy ['embəsɪ] *(pl* **embassies)** **N** ambassade *f*; **the British/French E.** l'ambassade *f* de Grande-Bretagne/France

COMP *(staff, employee)* d'ambassade

►► ***embassy official*** fonctionnaire *mf* d'ambassade; ***embassy secretary*** secrétaire *mf* d'ambassade

embattled [ɪm'bætəld] **ADJ** *(army)* engagé dans la bataille; *(town)* ravagé par les combats; *Fig (leader, government)* en difficulté, aux prises avec des difficultés

embed [ɪm'bed] *(pt & pp* **embedded,** *cont* **embedding)** **VT 1** *(in wood)* enfoncer; *(in rock)* sceller; *(in cement)* sceller, noyer; *(jewels)* enchâsser, incruster; **to be embedded in sth** *(hook, tooth etc)* être enfoncé dans qch; **embedded in concrete** noyé dans le béton; **to be embedded in sb's memory** être gravé dans la mémoire de qn **2** *Comput* intégrer, imbriquer

embedded [ɪm'bedɪd] **ADJ** *(in wood)* enfoncé; *(in rock)* scellé; *(in cement)* scellé, noyé; *(jewels)* enchâssé, incrusté; *Fig (journalist, reporter)* embarqué, incorporé; **e. in my memory** gravé dans ma mémoire

►► *Gram* ***embedded clause*** proposition *f* enchâssée; *Comput* ***embedded command*** commande *f* intégrée

embellish [ɪm'belɪʃ] **VT** *(garment, building)* embellir, décorer, orner; *(account, story etc)* enjoliver, embellir

embellishment [ɪm'belɪʃmənt] **N** *(of building)* embellissement *m*; *(of garment)* décoration *f*; *(of account, story etc)* enjolivement *m*, embellissement *m*; *(in handwriting)* fioritures *fpl*

ember ['embə(r)] **N** charbon *m* ardent, morceau *m* de braise; **embers** braise *f*; *Literary* **the embers of a dying passion** les cendres d'une passion mourante

►► *Rel* ***the Ember days*** les Quatre-Temps *mpl*

embezzle [ɪm'bezəl] **VT** *(money)* détourner, escroquer; **to e. money from sb** escroquer de l'argent à qn

VI commettre des détournements de fonds; **to e. from a company** détourner les fonds d'une société

embezzlement [ɪm'bezəlmənt] **N** *(of funds)* détournement *m*; **to be convicted of e.** être reconnu coupable de détournement de fonds

embezzler [ɪm'bezlə(r)] **N** escroc *m*, fraudeur (euse) *m,f*, auteur *m* d'un détournement de fonds

embitter [ɪm'bɪtə(r)] **VT** *(person)* remplir d'amertume, aigrir; *(relations)* altérer, détériorer

embittered [ɪm'bɪtəd] **ADJ** aigri

embittering [ɪm'bɪtərɪŋ] **ADJ** *(experience)* qui aigrit

emblazon [ɪm'bleɪzən] **VT 1** *Her* blasonner; **the shield is emblazoned with dragons** le bouclier porte des dragons **2** *(display)* **the team strip had the name of their sponsors emblazoned across the front** le nom de leur sponsor était inscrit sur le devant du maillot de l'équipe; **she didn't want to see her name emblazoned across the front page of the 'Sun'** elle ne voulait pas voir son nom étalé en première page du 'Sun'

emblem ['embləm] **N** emblème *m*; *Her* emblème *m*, devise *f*; *Aut (on radiator)* écusson *m*; **he has become the e. of defiant youth** il est devenu l'incarnation de la jeunesse révoltée

emblematic [ˌemblə'mætɪk] **ADJ** emblématique; **to be e. of sth** être emblématique de qch

embodiment [ɪm'bɒdɪmənt] **N 1** *(epitome)* incarnation *f*, personnification *f*; **to be the e. of goodness/evil** *(person)* être la bonté même/le mal incarné; **the new building is the e. of modernity** ce nouveau bâtiment est la modernité même **2** *(inclusion)* intégration *f*, incorporation *f*

embody [ɪm'bɒdɪ] *(pt & pp* **embodied)** **VT 1** *(epitomize* ► *of person)* incarner; **she embodies the archetypal career woman** c'est le type même de la femme qui se consacre entièrement à sa carrière **2** *(include)* inclure, intégrer; **the principles embodied in the American Constitution** les principes inscrits dans la constitution américaine

embolden [ɪm'bəʊldən] **VT 1** *Formal* enhardir, donner du courage à; **to e. sb to do sth** enhardir qn à faire qch, donner à qn le courage de faire qch; **to feel emboldened to do sth** se sentir le courage de faire qch **2** *Typ (characters)* renforcer, graisser

embolism ['embəlɪzəm] **N** *Med* embolie *f*; **to suffer** *or* **to have an e.** faire *ou* avoir une embolie

embolus ['embələs] *(pl* **emboli** [-laɪ]) **N** *Med* embole *m*, embolus *m*

embonpoint [ˌɒmbɒn'pwɑ̃] **N** *Hum* embonpoint *m*, rondeurs *fpl*

emboss [ɪm'bɒs] **VT** *(metal)* repousser, estamper; *(leather)* estamper, gaufrer; *(cloth, paper)* gaufrer

embossed [ɪm'bɒst] **ADJ** *(metal)* repoussé; *(leather)* gaufré; *(cloth, wallpaper)* gaufré, à motifs en relief

embossing [ɪm'bɒsɪŋ] **N** *Typ* gaufrage *m*

embrace [ɪm'breɪs] **VT 1** *(friend, child)* étreindre; *(lover)* étreindre, enlacer; *(official visitor, statesman)* donner l'accolade à; **to e. one another tenderly** s'étreindre tendrement **2** *(include)* regrouper, comprendre, embrasser; **the view from the terrace embraces the whole valley** de la terrasse la vue s'étend sur toute la vallée *ou* embrasse toute la vallée **3** *(adopt* ► *religion, cause)* embrasser; *(*► *opportunity)* saisir

VI *(friends)* s'étreindre; *(lovers)* s'étreindre, s'enlacer; *(statesmen)* se donner l'accolade

N *(of friend, child)* étreinte *f*; *(of lover)* étreinte *f*, enlacement *m*; *(of official visitor, statesman)* accolade *f*; **to hold** *or* **to clasp sb in an e.** étreindre qn

> Note that the most common meaning of the French verb **embrasser** is **to kiss**.

embrasure [ɪm'breɪʒə(r)] **N 1** *Archit* embrasure *f*, ébrasement *m* **2** *Mil* embrasure *f*, sabord *m*

embrocation [ˌembrə'keɪʃən] **N** *Old-fashioned* embrocation *f*

embroider [ɪm'brɔɪdə(r)] **VT** *(garment, cloth)* broder; *Fig (story, truth)* embellir, enjoliver

VI *(with needle)* broder; *Fig (embellish)* broder, enjoliver

►**embroider on VT INSEP** *(story, truth)* enjoliver

embroidering [ɪm'brɔɪdərɪŋ] **N** *(on garment, cloth)* broderie *f*; *Fig (of story, truth)* enjolivement *m*, embellissement *m*

embroidery [ɪm'brɔɪdərɪ] *(pl* **embroideries)** **N** *(on garment, cloth)* broderie *f*; *Fig (of story, truth)* enjolivement *m*, embellissement *m*

►► ***embroidery frame*** métier *m* à broder; ***embroidery silk*** soie *f* à broder; ***embroidery thread*** fil *m* à broder

embroil [ɪm'brɔɪl] **VT** mêler, impliquer; **to e. sb in sth** mêler qn à qch, impliquer qn dans qch; **to get embroiled in sth** se retrouver mêlé à qch; **to get embroiled with sb** *(romantically)* avoir une liaison avec qn

embroilment [ɪm'brɔɪlmənt] **N** *Formal (in matter, situation)* implication *f*; *(with lover)* liaison *f*

embryo ['embrɪəʊ] *(pl* **embryos)** **N** *Biol & Fig* embryon *m*; **I have the e. of an idea** j'ai un embryon d'idée; **in e.** *(foetus, idea)* à l'état embryonnaire

►► ***embryo donation*** accueil *m* de l'embryon; ***embryo research*** recherche *f* portant sur les embryons; ***embryo sac*** sac *m* embryonnaire

embryogenesis [ˌembrɪəʊ'dʒenɪsɪs] **N** *Biol* embryogenèse *f*

embryogenic [ˌembrɪəʊ'dʒenɪk] **ADJ** *Biol* embryogénique

embryology [ˌembrɪ'ɒlədʒɪ] **N** *Biol* embryologie *f*

embryonic [ˌembrɪ'ɒnɪk] **ADJ** *Biol* embryonnaire; *Fig (plan, idea)* à l'état embryonnaire; **the plan is still at an e. stage** le projet est encore à l'état embryonnaire

►► *Biol* ***embryonic stem cell*** cellule *f* souche embryonnaire

embryoscopy [ˌembrɪ'ɒskəpɪ] **N** *Med* embryoscopie *f*

embus [ɪm'bʌs] *Mil* **VT** faire monter à bord d'un autocar

VI monter à bord d'un autocar

emcee [ˌem'siː] *Fam (abbr* **master of ceremonies)** **N** maître *m* de cérémonies; *Rad & TV* animateur (trice) *m,f*

VT animer

emend [ɪ'mend], **emendate** ['ɪmendeɪt] **VT** *Formal* corriger

emendation [ɪmen'deɪʃən] **N** *Formal* correction *f*

emerald ['emərəld] **N 1** *(gemstone)* émeraude *f* **2** *(colour)* (vert *m*) émeraude *m*

ADJ *(colour)* émeraude

COMP *(brooch, ring)* en émeraude; *(necklace)* d'émeraudes

►► ***emerald green*** **N** (vert *m*) émeraude *m* **ADJ** (vert *m*) émeraude; *Literary* ***the Emerald Isle*** l'Île *f* d'Émeraude

emerge [ɪ'mɜːdʒ] **VI** *(person, animal)* sortir; *(sun)* sortir, émerger; *(truth, difficulty)* émerger, apparaître; *(theory, new state)* émerger; *(new leader)* apparaître; **to e. from the water** *(diver, submarine, island)* émerger; **to e. from hiding** sortir de sa cachette; **new playwrights have emerged on the scene** de nouveaux dramaturges ont fait leur apparition; **to e. as favourite** apparaître comme le favori; **it later emerged that...** il est apparu par la suite que...; **to e. victorious** *or* **the winner** sortir vainqueur; **to e. unscathed** sortir indemne

emergence [ɪ'mɜːdʒəns] **N** *(of theory)* émergence *f*; *(of new state, new leader)* apparition *f*

emergency [ɪ'mɜːdʒənsɪ] *(pl* **emergencies)** **N 1** *(situation)* (cas *m* d')urgence *f*; **this is an e.!** c'est une urgence!; **in case of e., in an e.** en cas d'urgence; **to be prepared for any e.** être prêt à toutes les éventualités; **to declare a state of e.** déclarer l'état d'urgence; **national e.** catastrophe *f* nationale; **for e. use only** *(sign)* à n'utiliser qu'en cas d'urgence **2** *Med (department)* (service *m* des) urgences *fpl*

COMP *(measures, procedure, meeting)* d'urgence

►► ***emergency aid*** aide *f* d'urgence; ***emergency brake*** frein *m* de secours; *Am Aut (handbrake)* frein *m* à main; *Med* ***emergency case*** urgence *f*; *Br Parl* ***emergency debate*** débat *m* d'urgence; *Med* ***emergency doctor*** urgentiste *mf*, urgentologue *mf*; ***emergency exit*** sortie *f* ou issue *f* de secours; ***emergency food aid*** aide *f* alimentaire d'urgence; ***emergency fund*** fonds *m* de secours; *Aviat* ***emergency landing*** atterrissage *m* forcé; *Pol* ***emergency legislation*** loi *f* d'exception, loi *f* d'urgence; *Med* ***emergency operation*** opération *f* à chaud; *Med* ***emergency patient*** urgence *f*; ***emergency powers*** pouvoirs *mpl* extraordinaires; ***emergency rations*** vivres *mpl* de secours *ou* de réserve; ***emergency regulations*** mesures *fpl* d'exception; ***emergency repairs*** réparations *fpl* d'urgence; ***emergency response vehicle*** véhicule *m* d'urgence; *Am Med* ***emergency room*** salle *f* des urgences; ***emergency service*** *Aut* service *m* de dépannage; *Med* service *m* des urgences; ***emergency services*** services *mpl* d'urgence; *Aut* ***emergency stop*** arrêt *m* d'urgence; ***emergency supply*** réserve *f*; ***emergency surgery*** opération *f* à chaud; *Aviat* ***emergency tank*** réservoir *m* auxiliaire; *Fin* ***emergency tax*** impôt *m* extraordinaire; ***emergency telephone*** téléphone *m* d'urgence, poste *m* d'appel d'urgence; *Br Med* ***emergency ward*** salle *f* des urgences

emergent [ɪ'mɜːdʒənt] **ADJ** *(theory, nation)* naissant

emerging market [ɪ'mɜːdʒɪŋ-] **N** *Fin* marché *m* émergeant

emeritus [ɪ'merɪtəs] **ADJ** *Univ* honoraire

emery ['emərɪ] **N** *Miner* émeri *m*

►► ***emery board*** lime *f* à ongles; ***emery cloth*** toile *f* (d')émeri; ***emery paper*** papier *m* (d')émeri; ***emery powder*** poudre *f* d'émeri; ***emery wheel*** meule *f* (en) émeri

emetic [ɪ'metɪk] *Med & Pharm* N émétique *m*, vomitif *m*
ADJ émétique

emf, EMF [,iːem'ef] N **1** *Elec* (*abbr* **electromotive force**) force *f* électromotrice **2** (*abbr* **European Monetary Fund**) FME *m*

EMI [,iːem'aɪ] N (*abbr* **European Monetary Institute**) IME *m*

emigrant ['emɪgrənt] N émigrant(e) *m,f*; (*when established abroad*) émigré(e) *m,f*
COMP (*worker, population*) émigré

emigrate ['emɪgreɪt] VI émigrer (**to** à)

emigrating ['emɪgreɪtɪŋ] ADJ émigrant

emigration [,emɪ'greɪʃən] N émigration *f*

émigré ['emɪgreɪ] N émigré(e) *m,f*
COMP (*writer*) émigré

eminence ['emɪnəns] N **1** (*prominence*) rang *m* éminent; (*of office*) grandeur *f*, distinction *f*; **to occupy a position of e.** avoir un rang éminent; **to achieve e. in one's profession** atteindre un rang éminent dans sa profession **2** (*high ground*) éminence *f*, hauteur *f*
• **Eminence** N *Rel* (*title*) Éminence *f*; **Your/His E.** Votre/Son Éminence

eminent ['emɪnənt] ADJ **1** (*distinguished*) éminent **2** (*conspicuous*) éminent, remarquable, insigne; **in view of his e. suitability for the job** du fait qu'il convient tout à fait pour le poste
►► *Am Law* ***eminent domain*** droit *m* d'expropriation pour cause d'utilité publique

eminently ['emɪnəntlɪ] ADV (*very*) éminemment, tout à fait; **an e. likeable young man** un jeune homme tout à fait aimable; **e. suitable** qui convient parfaitement; **it is e. desirable that…** il est fort à souhaiter que…, il est éminemment souhaitable que…; *Hum* **an e. forgettable film** un film qui n'a rien d'inoubliable

emir [e'mɪə(r)] N émir *m*

emirate ['emərət] N émirat *m*

emissary ['emɪsərɪ] (*pl* **emissaries**) N émissaire *m*

emission [ɪ'mɪʃən] N **1** (*action* ► *of gas, heat*) émission *f*, dégagement *m*; (► *of pollutant, radiation, light, sound*) émission *f*; *Fin* (► *of bank notes*) émission *f* **2** (*substance*) émanation *f*; **nocturnal emissions** pollutions *fpl* nocturnes
►► *Aut* ***emission limit*** seuil *m* d'émission

emit [ɪ'mɪt] (*pt & pp* **emitted**, *cont* **emitting**) VT (*sound, radiation, light*) émettre; (*heat*) dégager, émettre; (*smell*) exhaler, dégager; (*gas*) dégager; (*sparks, cry*) lancer

emitter [ɪ'mɪtə(r)] N *Nucl, Phys & Electron* émetteur *m*

Emmental ['emən,tɑːl], **Emmentaler** ['emən,tɑːlə(r)] N *Culin* Emmental *m*

Emmenthal, Emmenthaler = **Emmental, Emmentaler**

Emmy ['emɪ] N **E. (award)** = distinction récompensant les meilleures émissions télévisées américaines de l'année

emo ['iːməʊ] N *Mus* emo *m*

emollient [ɪ'mɒlɪənt] *Pharm* ADJ émollient; *Fig* adoucissant, calmant
N émollient *m*

emolument [ɪ'mɒljʊmənt] N *Formal* (*usu pl*) **emoluments** émoluments *mpl*, rémunération *f*

e-money N argent *m* électronique, argent *m* virtuel

emote [ɪ'məʊt] VI (*on stage*) faire dans le genre tragique; (*in life*) avoir un comportement théâtral

emoticon [ɪ'məʊtɪkɒn] N *Comput (Internet)* émoticon *m*, émoticone *f*, *Can* binette *f*

emotion [ɪ'məʊʃən] N (*particular feeling*) sentiment *m*; (*faculty*) émotion *f*; **to be in control of one's emotions** contrôler *ou* maîtriser ses émotions; **to show no e.** ne laisser paraître aucune émotion; **to shake with e.** (*person, voice*) trembler d'émotion; **to appeal to the emotions** faire appel aux sentiments; **to express one's emotions** exprimer ses sentiments; **don't let your emotions get in the way** ne te laisse pas influencer par tes sentiments; **full of e.** ému

emotional [ɪ'məʊʃənəl] ADJ **1** (*stress*) émotionnel; (*life, problems*) affectif; **to have** *or* **carry a lot of e. baggage** avoir accumulé les échecs sentimentaux; **to be afraid of e. commitment** avoir peur de s'engager sur le plan émotionnel; **e. shock** choc *m* émotif *ou* émotionnel; **she's an e. wreck** elle a de gros problèmes émotionnels
2 (*person* ► *easily moved*) sensible, qui s'émeut facilement; (► *stronger*) émotif; (*appealing to the emotions* ► *plea, speech, music*) émouvant; **he got very e. at the funeral** il était très ému à l'enterrement; **why do you always have to get so e.?** pourquoi faut-il toujours que tu te mettes dans de tels états?; *Hum Euph* **to be tired and e.** être ivre mort
3 (*charged with emotion* ► *issue*) passionné, brûlant; (► *reunion, farewell, scene*) chargé d'émotion
4 (*governed by emotions* ► *person*) passionné, ardent; (► *reaction, state*) émotionnel; **you shouldn't be so e.** tu es vraiment trop sensible
►► ***emotional blackmail*** chantage *m* affectif; ***emotional deprivation*** carence *f* affective

emotionalism [ɪ'məʊʃənəlɪzəm] N *Pej* sensiblerie *f*; **it's a piece of e.** c'est du sentimentalisme; **the e. of his writing** son style sentimentaliste

emotionally [ɪ'məʊʃənəlɪ] ADV **1** (*immature, scarred*) sur le plan affectif; **to feel e. exhausted** *or* **drained** se sentir vidé (sur le plan émotionnel); **to be e. disturbed** souffrir de troubles affectifs; **to be e. involved with sb** avoir des liens affectifs avec qn; **I'm too e. involved with the whole situation** cette situation me touche de trop près **2** (*react, speak*) avec émotion; **an e. charged atmosphere** une atmosphère chargée d'émotion

emotionless [ɪ'məʊʃənlɪs] ADJ (*person*) indifférent; (*face, look*) impassible; (*style*) sobre

emotive [ɪ'məʊtɪv] ADJ qui déchaîne les passions; **e. speech/language** discours *m*/langage *m* sensationnaliste; **racism is a very e. issue** le racisme est un sujet qui déchaîne les passions; **an e. word** un mot chargé

empanel [ɪm'pænəl] (*Br pt & pp* **empanelled**, *cont* **empanelling**, *Am pt & pp* **empaneled**, *cont* **empaneling**) VT (*jury*) constituer; (*juror*) inscrire sur la liste *ou* le tableau du jury

empanelling, *Am* **empaneling** [ɪm'pænəlɪŋ] N (*of jury*) constitution *f*; (*of juror*) inscription *f* sur la liste *ou* le tableau du jury

empathetic [,empə'θetɪk] ADJ (*person*) compréhensif; *Psy* empathique

empathetically [,empə'θetɪkəlɪ] ADV avec compassion

empathize, -ise ['empəθaɪz] VI **to e. with sb** s'identifier à qn

empathy ['empəθɪ] N (*affinity* ► *gen*) affinité *f*, affinités *fpl*; *Phil & Psy* empathie *f*; (*power, ability*) capacité *f* à s'identifier à autrui; **the e. between them** les affinités qui existent entre eux; **our e. with her pain** notre sympathie à sa douleur

emperor ['empərə(r)] N empereur *m*; **E. Augustus** l'Empereur Auguste
►► *Zool* ***emperor moth*** saturnie *f*, paon *m* de nuit; *Orn* ***emperor penguin*** manchot *m* empereur

emphasis ['emfəsɪs] (*pl* **emphases** [-siːz]) N **1** (*importance*) accent *m*; **to place** *or* **to lay** *or* **to put e. on sth** mettre l'accent sur qch; **there is too much e. on materialism in our society** on accorde trop d'importance aux choses matérielles dans notre société; **this year the e. is on bright colours/steady growth** cette année, l'accent est mis sur les couleurs vives/sur une croissance régulière; **a change of e.** un changement de priorités; **the e. now is on winning votes** ce qui est important maintenant c'est de gagner des voix **2** (*stress* ► *in words*) force *f*, accentuation *f*; *Gram* mise *f* en relief; *Ling* accent *m*; **the e. comes on the last syllable** l'accent est placé *ou* tombe sur la dernière syllabe; **to say sth with e.** dire qch avec emphase *ou* emphatiquement; **he waved his arms around for e.** il faisait de grands gestes pour ponctuer son discours; **the word is only used in the sentence for e.** dans la phrase, le mot n'a qu'une valeur intensive

emphasize, -ise ['emfəsaɪz] VT **1** (*detail, need, importance*) insister sur; **she emphasized the need for caution** elle a bien insisté sur la nécessité d'être prudent; **I cannot e. this point enough** je ne saurais trop insister sur ce point **2** (*physical feature*) accentuer; **to e. the waist** (*garment*) marquer *ou* accentuer la taille **3** *Ling* (*syllable*) accentuer; (*word*) accentuer, appuyer sur

emphatic [ɪm'fætɪk] ADJ **1** (*refusal*) catégorique; (*speaker, manner, tone*) énergique, vigoureux; (*victory, defeat*) net; **she was e. that they must not be late** elle a bien insisté sur le fait qu'ils ne devaient pas être en retard; **to be e. in one's denials** nier catégoriquement; **an e. gesture** un grand geste **2** *Ling* emphatique

emphatically [ɪm'fætɪklɪ] ADV **1** (*forcefully*) énergiquement; (*deny*) catégoriquement; **they had been e. defeated** ils avaient été largement battus **2** (*definitely*) clairement; **I most e. do not agree with you** je ne suis absolument pas d'accord avec vous; **e. yes!** tout à fait, oui!

emphysema [,emfɪ'siːmə] N *Med* emphysème *m*

empire ['empaɪə(r)] N empire *m*; *Hist* **the (British) E.** l'Empire *m* britannique; *Fig* **a shipbuilding e.** un empire dans le monde de la construction navale
• **Empire** COMP (*costume, furniture, style*) Empire
►► ***the Empire State*** = surnom donné à l'État de New York; ***the Empire State Building*** l'Empire State Building *m*

empire-builder N *Fig* bâtisseur *m* d'empires

empire-building *Fig* ADJ de bâtisseur d'empires
N **there's too much e. going on** on joue trop les bâtisseurs d'empires

empiric [ɪm'pɪrɪk] ADJ empirique
N empiriste *mf*

empirical [ɪm'pɪrɪkəl] ADJ empirique
►► *Chem* ***empirical formula*** formule *f* empirique

empiricism [ɪm'pɪrɪsɪzəm] N empirisme *m*

emplacement [ɪm'pleɪsmənt] N *Mil* (*of cannon*) emplacement *m*

emplane [ɪm'pleɪn] VT embarquer (à bord d'un avion)
VI embarquer (à bord d'un avion)

employ [ɪm'plɔɪ] VT **1** (*give work to*) employer; **they e. 245 staff** ils ont 245 employés; **to e. sb as a receptionist** employer qn comme réceptionniste; **he has been employed with the firm for twenty years** il travaille pour cette entreprise depuis vingt ans **2** (*use* ► *means, method, word*) employer, utiliser; (► *skill, diplomacy*) faire usage de, employer; (► *force*) employer, avoir recours à **3** (*occupy*) **to e. oneself/to be employed in doing sth** s'occuper/être occupé à faire qch; **you'd be better employed doing your homework** tu ferais mieux de faire tes devoirs; **have you no better way of employing your time?** tu n'as rien de mieux à faire?
N *Formal* service *m*; **to be in sb's e.** travailler pour qn, être au service de qn; **to have sb in one's e.** employer qn, avoir qn à son service

employable [ɪm'plɔɪəbəl] ADJ (*person*) susceptible d'être employé; (*method*) utilisable; **a good education makes you more e.** une bonne formation donne plus de chances de trouver du travail

employed [ɪm'plɔɪd] ADJ employé; **I am not e. at the moment** je n'ai pas de travail en ce moment
NPL personnes *fpl* qui ont un emploi; **employers and e.** patronat *m* et salariat *m*

employee [ɪm'plɔɪiː] N employé(e) *m,f*, salarié(e) *m,f*; **she is an e. of Company X, she is a Company X e.** c'est une employée de la Société X; **management and employees** la direction et les employés *ou* le personnel; (*in negotiations*) les partenaires *mpl* sociaux
►► *Com* ***employee association*** comité *m* d'entreprise; *Com* ***employee benefits*** avantages *mpl* accordés aux employés; *Com* ***employee buyout*** reprise *f* de l'entreprise par les salariés, RES *f*; *Com* ***employee contributions, employee's contributions*** (*to benefits*) cotisations *fpl* salariales, charges *fpl* sociales salariales; *Com* ***employee incentive scheme*** système *m* de rémunération au rendement; *Com* ***employee profit-sharing scheme*** intéressement *m* aux résultats; *Com* ***employee representative*** délégué(e) *m,f* du personnel; *Com* ***employee shareholding*** actionnariat *m*

ouvrier; *Com Br* ***employee share ownership plan***, *Am* ***employee stock ownership plan*** plan *m* d'actionnariat des salariés

employer [ɪm'plɔɪə(r)] **N** patron(onne) *m,f*, *Formal* employeur(euse) *m,f*; **they are good employers** ce sont de bons employeurs *ou* patrons; **who is your e.?** pour qui travaillez-vous?; **this company is the town's largest e.** c'est cette entreprise qui emploie le plus de gens dans la ville; **employers** *(as a body)* patronat *m*

▸▸ ***employers' association*** organisation *f* patronale, syndicat *m* patronal; ***employer's contribution*** *(to employee benefits)* cotisation *f* patronale; ***employer cost index*** = rapport trimestriel du ministère de l'Emploi américain, indiquant le niveau des salaires et des prestations sociales, parfois considéré comme un indicateur du niveau d'inflation; ***employers' federation*** chambre *f* syndicale, syndicat *m* patronal; ***employer's liability*** responsabilité *f* patronale; ***employers' organization*** organisation *f* patronale, syndicat *m* patronal

employment [ɪm'plɔɪmənt] **N 1** *(work)* emploi *m*; **to be without e.** être sans emploi *ou* travail; **to be in e.** avoir un emploi *ou* du travail; **full e.** plein emploi *m*; **conditions of e.** conditions *fpl* de travail; **to look for** *or* **to seek e.** chercher du travail *ou* un emploi, être demandeur d'emploi; **to give** *or* **to provide e.** donner *ou* fournir du travail; **(the) e. figures** les chiffres *mpl* de l'emploi; *Br* **Secretary (of State) for** *or* **Minister of E.**, *Am* **Secretary for E.** ministre *m* du Travail **2** *(recruitment)* embauche *f*; *(providing work)* emploi *m* **3** *(use ▸ of method, word)* emploi *m*; *(▸ of force, skill)* usage *m*, emploi *m*

▸▸ ***employment agency, employment bureau*** agence *f ou* bureau *m* de placement; ***employment exchange*** ANPE *f*; ***employment law, employment legislation*** code *m ou* législation *f* du travail; ***employment protection*** protection *f* de l'emploi; *Law* ***employment tribunal*** conseil *m* de prud'hommes

emporium [em'pɔːrɪəm] *(pl* **emporiums** *or* **emporia** [-rɪə]) **N** grand magasin *m*

empower [ɪm'paʊə(r)] **VT 1** *Formal (give permission to)* habiliter, autoriser; **to e. sb to do sth** habiliter *ou* autoriser qn à faire qch **2** *(give power to)* **to e. sb** *(emotionally, psychologically)* donner à qn les moyens de s'assumer; **political involvement can e. minorities** l'action politique peut permettre aux minorités de s'émanciper **3** *(employee)* accorder davantage d'autonomie à

empress ['emprɪs] **N** impératrice *f*; **E. Josephine** l'Impératrice Joséphine

emptiness ['emptɪnɪs] **N** vide *m*; **a feeling of e.** un sentiment de vide

empty ['emptɪ] *(compar* **emptier**, *superl* **emptiest**, *pl* **empties**) **ADJ 1** *(glass, room, box etc)* vide; *(city, street)* désert; *(cinema)* désert, vide; *(job, post)* vacant, à pourvoir; **the house was e. of people** la maison était vide; **my stomach is e.** *(I'm hungry)* j'ai un creux (à l'estomac); **to do sth on an e. stomach** faire qch à jeun; *Med* **to be taken on an e. stomach** *(on packaging)* à prendre à jeun; **the fuel gauge was at** *or* **showing e.** le niveau du réservoir était à zéro; **to be running on e.** *(car)* avoir le réservoir presque vide; *Fig* ne plus avoir d'énergie, être à bout de souffle; *Prov* **e. vessels make most noise** = ce sont souvent les ignorants qui sont les plus bavards **2** *Fig (words, talk)* creux; *(promise)* en l'air, vain; *(gesture)* dénué de sens; *(threat)* en l'air; **e. of meaning** vide *ou* dénué de sens; **to feel e.** *(drained of emotion)* se sentir vidé (sur le plan émotionnel); *(after bereavement, trauma)* sentir un vide; **life feels e. now that you've gone** ma vie est vide maintenant que tu es partie

N *Fam (bottle)* bouteille *f* vide[□]; *(glass)* verre *m* vide[□]; *(crate)* caisse *f* vide[□]

VT *(glass, pocket, room)* vider; *(car, lorry)* décharger; *(cesspool, tank, barrel)* vidanger; *Comput (wastebasket, bin)* vider; **he emptied (the contents of) the bucket over her head** il a vidé le seau sur sa tête; **she emptied the cigarette butts into a plant pot** elle a versé les mégots dans un pot de fleurs

VI *(building, street, container)* se vider; *(water)* s'écouler; **to e. into the sea** *(river)* se jeter dans la mer; **the crowd emptied onto the streets** la foule s'est répandue dans les rues

▸▸ ***empty nester*** = parent déprimé après que ses enfants ont quitté le foyer familial; ***empty nest syndrome*** = dépression ressentie par les parents dont les enfants ont récemment quitté le foyer familial

▸ **empty out VT SEP** vider

VI *(tank, container)* se vider; *(water, liquid)* s'écouler

empty-handed [-'hændɪd] **ADJ** les mains vides; **to leave e.** repartir les mains vides; **to return e.** rentrer bredouille *ou* les mains vides

empty-headed ADJ écervelé, sans cervelle

emptying ['emptɪɪŋ] **N** *(of glass, pocket, room)* vidage *m*; *(of car, lorry)* déchargement *m*; *(of cesspool, tank, barrel)* vidange *f*; *(of streets)* dépeuplement *m*

EMS [ˌiːem'es] **N** *Formerly Fin (abbr* **European Monetary System**) SME *m*

EMU [ˌiːem'juː] **N** *Pol & Fin (abbr* **economic and monetary union**) UME *f*

emu ['iːmjuː] **N** *Orn* émeu *m*

emulate ['emjʊleɪt] **VT** *(person, action)* imiter; *Comput* émuler, simuler

emulation [ˌemjʊ'leɪʃən] **N** *(gen) & Comput* émulation *f*

emulator ['emjʊleɪtə(r)] **N** *Comput* émulateur *m*

emulsifier [ɪ'mʌlsɪfaɪə(r)] **N** *Chem* émulsifiant *m*, émulseur *m*

emulsify [ɪ'mʌlsɪfaɪ] **VT** *Chem* émulsionner, émulsifier

emulsion [ɪ'mʌlʃən] **N 1** *Chem & Phot* émulsion *f* **2** *(paint)* (peinture *f*) émulsion *f*

VT appliquer de la peinture émulsion sur

▸▸ ***emulsion paint*** peinture *f* émulsion *f*

en [en] **N** *Typ* demi-cadratin *m*

▸▸ ***en dash*** tiret *m* demi-cadratin; ***en space*** demi-cadratin *m*

enable [ɪ'neɪbəl] **VT 1 to e. sb to do sth** permettre à qn de faire qch; *Law* habiliter *ou* autoriser qn à faire qch **2** *Comput (option)* activer

enabled [ɪ'neɪbəld] **ADJ** *Comput (option)* activé

enabling [ɪ'neɪblɪŋ] **ADJ** *Law* habilitant

▸▸ ***enabling act*** loi *f* d'habilitation; ***enabling legislation*** décret *m* d'application

enact [ɪ'nækt] **VT 1** *Law (bill, law)* promulguer **2** *(scene, play)* jouer; **the political drama currently being enacted** le drame politique qui se joue *ou* se déroule actuellement

enactment [ɪ'næktmənt] **N 1** *Law (of bill, law etc)* promulgation *f* **2** *(of scene, play)* représentation *f*

enamel [ɪ'næməl] *(Br pt & pp* **enamelled**, *cont* **enamelling**, *Am pt & pp* **enameled**, *cont* **enameling**) **N 1** *Art (on clay, glass etc)* émail *m* **2** *(paint)* peinture *f* laquée *ou* vernie **3** *(on teeth)* émail *m*

COMP *(mug, saucepan)* en émail, émaillé

VT émailler

▸▸ ***enamel paint*** peinture *f* laquée *ou* vernie; ***enamel work*** émaillure *f*; *(painting on enamel)* peinture *f* sur émail

enamelled, *Am* **enameled** [ɪ'næməld] **ADJ 1** *(covered with enamel ▸ brick)* émaillé; *(▸ tile)* vernissé; **e. saucepan** casserole *f* émaillée **2** *(painted)* peint en émail

enamelling, *Am* **enameling** [ɪ'næməlɪŋ] **N** émaillage *m*

enamour, *Am* **enamor** [ɪ'næmə(r)] **VT** *Literary* **his behaviour did little to e. me of him** son comportement ne me l'a guère rendu plus sympathique

enamoured, *Am* **enamored** [ɪ'næməd] **ADJ** *Literary* **to be e. of** *(person)* être amoureux *ou* épris de; *(job, flat)* être enchanté *ou* ravi de; **to become e. of sb** s'éprendre de qn; **he wasn't exactly e. of our proposal** notre proposition ne l'enchantait guère

encage [ɪn'keɪdʒ] **VT** *Formal (animal)* encager

encamp [ɪn'kæmp] **VI** camper

VT faire camper; **to be encamped** camper

encampment [ɪn'kæmpmənt] **N** campement *m*

encapsulate [ɪn'kæpsjʊleɪt] **VT 1** *Pharm* mettre en capsule **2** *Ecol (waste)* inerter; **3** *(summarize)* résumer; **this film encapsulates the atmosphere of the times** ce film contient *ou* renferme l'atmosphère de l'époque

▸▸ *Comput* ***encapsulated PostScript*** EPS *m*

encase [ɪn'keɪs] **VT 1** *(provide with covering)* envelopper; **encased in concrete** noyé dans le béton; **encased in chocolate** enrobé de chocolat **2** *(put in case)* encaisser **(in** dans)

encash [ɪn'kæʃ] **VT** *Br Fin (cheque)* encaisser

encashment [ɪn'kæʃmənt] **N** *Br Fin* encaissement *m*

encaustic [en'kɔːstɪk] **ADJ** *(brick, tile)* émaillé; *Art (painting)* encaustique

N *Art (technique)* encaustique *f*

encephalitis [ˌensefə'laɪtɪs] **N** *Med* encéphalite *f*

▸▸ ***encephalitis lethargica*** encéphalite *f* épidémique

encephalopathy [enˌsefə'lɒpəθɪ] **N** *Med* encéphalopathie *f*

enchant [ɪn'tʃɑːnt] **VT 1** *(delight)* enchanter, ravir; **he was less than enchanted by the prospect** l'idée ne l'enchantait guère **2** *(put spell on)* enchanter, ensorceler

enchanted [ɪn'tʃɑːntɪd] **ADJ 1** *(delighted)* enchanté **(with** de) **2** *(under a spell, magic)* enchanté, ensorcelé; **an e. wood** une forêt enchantée

enchanter [ɪn'tʃɑːntə(r)] **N** enchanteur *m*

enchanting [ɪn'tʃɑːntɪŋ] **ADJ** *(smile, scenery)* enchanteur; *(voice, person)* ravissant, charmant; *(idea, thought)* délicieux; **an e. little cottage** une charmante petite maison de campagne

enchantingly [ɪn'tʃɑːntɪŋlɪ] **ADV** *(sing, play)* merveilleusement bien

enchantment [ɪn'tʃɑːntmənt] **N 1** *(delight)* enchantement *m*, ravissement *m* **2** *(casting of spell)* enchantement *m*, ensorcellement *m*

enchantress [ɪn'tʃɑːntrɪs] **N** enchanteresse *f*

enchilada [ˌentʃɪ'lɑːdə] **N** *Culin* enchilada *f*; *Fam* **big e.** *(person)* huile *f*; **the whole e.** *(everything)* tout le tremblement

encircle [ɪn'sɜːkəl] **VT** entourer; *Mil & Hunt* encercler, cerner

encirclement [ɪn'sɜːkəlmənt] **N** encerclement *m*

▸▸ *Mktg* ***encirclement strategy*** stratégie *f* d'encerclement

encircling [ɪn'sɜːkəlɪŋ] **N** encerclement *m*

ADJ *Mil* **e. movement** manœuvre *f* d'encerclement

encl. 1 *(written abbr* **enclosure**) PJ **2** *(written abbr* **enclosed**) ci-joint

enclave ['enkleɪv] **N** enclave *f*

enclose [ɪn'kləʊz] **VT 1** *(surround ▸ with wall)* entourer, ceinturer; *(▸ with fence)* clôturer; **a garden enclosed with** *or* **in** *or* **by high walls** un jardin entouré *ou* ceint de hauts murs **2** *(in letter)* joindre; **to e. sth with a letter** joindre qch à une lettre; **I e. a cheque for £20** je joins un chèque de 20 livres

enclosed [ɪn'kləʊzd] **ADJ 1** *(area)* clos; **an e. space** un espace clos **2** *Com (cheque)* ci-joint, ci-inclus; **please find e. my CV** veuillez trouver ci-joint *ou* ci-inclus mon CV

N the e. *(in letter ▸ cheque)* le chèque ci-joint; *(▸ cash)* la somme ci-jointe

▸▸ *Rel* ***enclosed order*** ordre *m* cloîtré

enclosure [ɪn'kləʊʒə(r)] **N 1** *(enclosed area)* enclos *m*; **the lions' e.** *(in zoo)* l'enclos *m* des lions; **public e.** aire *f* réservée au public; *(at racecourse)* pesage *m*

2 *(in letter)* pièce *f* jointe *ou* annexée *ou* incluse; **enclosures** pièces *fpl* jointes

3 *(action)* action *f* de clôturer

4 *Br Hist* enclosure *f*

encode [en'kəʊd] **VT** coder, chiffrer; *Comput* encoder

encoder [en'kəʊdə(r)] **N** *(gen) & Comput* encodeur *m*

encoding [en'kəʊdɪŋ] **N** codage *m*; *Comput* encodage *m*

encomium [en'kəʊmjəm] *(pl* **encomiums** *or* **encomia** [-mjə]) **N** *Formal* panégyrique *m*

encompass [ɪn'kʌmpəs] **VT 1** *(include)* englober, comprendre, regrouper; **their repertoire encom-**

passes most musical styles leur répertoire englobe la plupart des genres musicaux **2** *Formal (surround)* entourer, encercler

encore [ˈɒŋkɔː(r)] EXCLAM **e.! e.!** bis! bis!
N bis *m*; **to call for an e.** bisser; **to give an e.** *(performer)* donner un bis; **to give an e. of a song** rechanter *ou* rejouer une chanson en bis
VT *(singer, performer)* rappeler, bisser; *(song)* bisser

encounter [ɪnˈkaʊntə(r)] VT *(person, enemy)* rencontrer; *(difficulty, resistance, danger)* rencontrer, se heurter à
N *(gen)* & *Mil* rencontre *f*
▸▸ *Psy* ***encounter group*** = séance de psychothérapie de groupe

encourage [ɪnˈkʌrɪdʒ] VT **1** *(person)* encourager, inciter; **to e. sb to do sth** encourager *ou* inciter qn à faire qch; **don't e. him!** *(in bad behaviour)* ne l'encourage pas!; **to e. sb in his/her belief that…** renforcer qn dans sa conviction que…, conforter qn dans son idée que… **2** *(support ▸ good works)* appuyer; *(▸ the arts, commerce)* favoriser; *(▸ belief)* encourager; **they encouraged their daughter's ambition** ils ont encouragé leur fille à réaliser ses ambitions

encouragement [ɪnˈkʌrɪdʒmənt] N encouragement *m*; **to give sb e., to give e. to sb** donner des encouragements à *ou* encourager qn; **to get** *or* **to receive e. from sb** recevoir des encouragements de la part de qn; **without your e.** sans vos encouragements; **shouts/words of e.** cris *mpl*/mots *mpl* d'encouragement

encouraging [ɪnˈkʌrɪdʒɪŋ] ADJ encourageant; *(smile, words)* d'encouragement; **he wasn't very e. to me** il ne s'est pas montré très encourageant à mon égard; **it is e. to see the progress that has been made** c'est encourageant de constater les progrès qui ont été faits

encouragingly [ɪnˈkʌrɪdʒɪŋlɪ] ADV *(smile, speak)* de manière encourageante; **e., a working party has been set up** fait encourageant, un groupe de travail a été mis en place

encroachment [ɪnˈkrəʊtʃmənt] N *(on land, rights, time)* empiétement *m*; *(by sea, river)* envahissement *m*, *Spec* ingression *f*; *(by buildings)* envahissement *m*

encroach on, encroach upon [ɪnˈkrəʊtʃ-] VT INSEP *(land, rights, time)* empiéter sur; **the sea is encroaching on the land** la mer gagne sur les terres; **the new buildings are encroaching on the countryside** les nouveaux bâtiments envahissent la campagne; *Fig* **to e. on sb's territory** marcher *ou* empiéter sur les plates-bandes de qn

encrust [ɪnˈkrʌst] VT *(with jewels)* incruster; *(with mud, snow, ice)* couvrir; **to be encrusted with sth** être incrusté *ou* couvert *ou* recouvert de qch

encrypt [enˈkrɪpt] N *Comput* crypter, encrypter, chiffrer

encryption [enˈkrɪpʃən] N *Comput* chiffrement *m*
▸▸ ***encryption key*** clé *f* de chiffrement

encumber [ɪnˈkʌmbə(r)] VT *Formal (person, room)* encombrer (**with** de); **the party remains encumbered by the legacy of its Stalinist past** le parti pâtit encore du legs encombrant de son passé stalinien
▸▸ *Law* ***encumbered estate*** *(with debts)* propriété *f* grevée de dettes; *(with mortgage)* propriété *f* hypothéquée

encumbrance [ɪnˈkʌmbrəns] N *Formal* **1** *(hindrance)* embarras *m*; **to be an e. to sb** *(physically)* encombrer qn; *(financially)* être à la charge de qn; **the suitcase was something of an e.** la valise était plutôt encombrante **2** *Law (of inheritance)* charges *fpl*; **to free an estate from encumbrances** dégrever une propriété

encyclical [ɪnˈsɪklɪkəl] *Rel* ADJ encyclique
N encyclique *f*

encyclopaedia, encyclopaedic *etc* = **encyclopedia, encyclopedic** *etc*

encyclopedia [ɪnˌsaɪkləʊˈpiːdjə] N encyclopédie *f*

encyclopedic [ɪnˌsaɪkləʊˈpiːdɪk] ADJ encyclopédique

encyclopedist [ɪnˌsaɪkləʊˈpiːdɪst] N encyclopédiste *mf*

END [end]

N
• bout **1, 5** • côté **2**
• fin **3, 4** • but **4**
• mort **6**
VT
• terminer
VI
• se terminer

N **1** *(furthermost part, tip, edge)* bout *m*, extrémité *f*; **at the e. of the garden** au bout *ou* fond du jardin; **it's at the other e. of town** c'est à l'autre bout de la ville; **at the northern e. of the park/town/lake** à l'extrémité nord du parc/de la ville/du lac; **the rope is frayed at this e./at that e./at one e.** la corde est effilochée à ce bout-ci/à ce bout-là/au bout; **at either e. of the political spectrum** aux deux extrémités de l'éventail politique; *Tel* **at the other e. of the line** au bout de la ligne; **from one e. of the country/of the town to the other** d'un bout à l'autre du pays/de la ville; **third from the e.** troisième en partant de la fin; *Sport* **to change ends** changer de côté; **to come to the e. of the road** arriver au bout de la route; *Fig (in one's career)* arriver au bout de sa carrière; *(in one's life)* arriver au bout de sa vie; *(be unable to make progress)* être dans une impasse; *Fig* **this is the e. of the road** *or* **line** c'est fini; *Fig* **to get hold of the wrong e. of the stick** mal comprendre; *Br very Fam* **to get** *or* **have one's e. away** *(have sex)* tirer un *ou* son coup; **to go to the ends of the earth** aller jusqu'au bout du monde

2 *(area, aspect)* côté *m*; **how are things (at) your e.?** comment ça va de ton côté *ou* pour toi?; **what's the weather like at your e.?** *(in phone conversation)* quel temps fait-il chez vous?, quel temps est-ce que vous avez?; **the marketing/manufacturing e. of the operation** le côté marketing/fabrication de l'opération, tout ce qui est marketing/fabrication; **to keep one's e. of the bargain** tenir parole; **to keep one's e. up** tenir bon; **he doesn't know** *or* **can't tell one e. of a word processor from the other** il ne sait même pas à quoi ressemble un traitement de texte; **to make (both) ends meet** *(financially)* joindre les deux bouts

3 *(conclusion, finish)* fin *f*; **at the e. of July/of spring/of the year** à la fin du mois de juillet/du printemps/de l'année; **from beginning to e.** du début à la fin, de bout en bout; **to read to the e. of a book, to read a book to the e.** lire un livre jusqu'au bout *ou* jusqu'à la fin; **I waited until the e. of the meeting** j'ai attendu la fin de la réunion; **to be at an e.** être terminé *ou* fini; **my patience is at** *or* **has come to an e.** ma patience est à bout; **to be at the e. of one's resources/one's strength** avoir épuisé ses ressources/ses forces; *Fin* **e. of the financial year** clôture *f* de l'exercice; **to bring sth to an e.** *(meeting)* clore qch; *(situation)* mettre fin à qch; *(speech)* achever qch; **to come to an e.** s'achever, prendre fin; **to draw to an e.** arriver *ou* toucher à sa fin; **to put an e. to sth** mettre fin à qch; **we want an e. to the war** nous voulons que cette guerre cesse *ou* prenne fin; **the e. of the world** la fin du monde; *Fam* **it's not the e. of the world!** ce n'est pas la fin du monde!; **until the e. of time** jusqu'à la fin des temps; **the e. is nigh** la fin est proche; **and that was the e. of that** et ça s'est terminé comme ça; **let that be an e. to the matter!** qu'on en finisse là!, qu'on n'en parle plus!; *Fam* **he's/you're the e.!** *(impossible)* il est/tu es incroyable!; *(extremely funny)* il est/tu es trop (drôle)!; **to come to a bad e.** mal finir; *Fam* **e. of story!** *(stop arguing)* plus de discussions!; *(I don't want to talk about it)* un point, c'est tout!; **we'll never hear the e. of it** on n'a pas fini d'en entendre parler; **is there no e. to his talents?** a-t-il donc tous les talents?, n'y a-t-il pas de limite à ses talents?

4 *(aim)* but *m*, fin *f*; **to achieve** *or* **to attain one's e.** atteindre son but; **with this e. in view** *or* **mind, to this e.** dans ce but, à cette fin; *Formal* **to what e.?** dans quel but?, à quelle fin?; **for political ends** à des fins politiques; **an e. in itself** une fin en soi; **the e. justifies the means** la fin justifie les moyens

5 *(remnant ▸ of cloth, rope)* bout *m*; *(▸ of loaf)* croûton *m*; *(▸ of candle)* bout *m*; *(▸ of cigarette)* bout *m*, mégot *m*

6 *Euph or Literary (death)* mort *f*; **to meet one's e.** trouver la mort; **I was with him at the e.** j'étais auprès de lui dans ses derniers moments

7 *Sport (in American football)* moitié *f* de terrain

8 *Sport (in bowls, curling)* manche *f*

COMP *(seat, table)* du bout; **they live in the e. house** ils habitent la dernière maison, au bout de la rue

VT *(speech, novel)* terminer, conclure; *(meeting, discussion)* clore; *(day)* terminer, finir; *(war, speculation, relationship)* mettre fin *ou* un terme à; *(work, task)* terminer, finir, achever; **she ended the letter with a promise to write again soon** elle a terminé la lettre en promettant de récrire bientôt; **the war to e. all wars** la der des ders; **he decided to e. it all** *(life, relationship)* il décida d'en finir; **she ended her days in a retirement home** elle a fini ses jours dans une maison de retraite

VI *(story, film)* finir, se terminer, s'achever; *(path, road etc)* se terminer, s'arrêter; *(season, holiday)* se terminer, toucher à sa fin; **to e. happily** *(of story)* avoir une fin heureuse, bien se terminer; **how** *or* **where will it all e.?** comment tout cela finira-t-il *ou* se terminera-t-il?; **to e. in a point** se terminer en pointe; **the discussion ended in an argument** la discussion s'est terminée en dispute; **to e. in failure/divorce** se solder par un échec/un divorce; **the word ends in -ed** le mot se termine par *ou* en -ed; **the book ends with a quotation** le livre se termine par une citation; **it'll e. in tears** ça va mal finir

• **end on** ADV par le bout

• **end to end** ADV **1** *(with ends adjacent)* bout à bout
2 *(from one end to another)* d'un bout à l'autre

• **from end to end** ADV d'un bout à l'autre

• **in the end** ADV finalement; **we got there in the e.** finalement nous y sommes arrivés, nous avons fini par y arriver; **he always pays me back in the e.** il finit toujours par me rendre ce qu'il me doit; **you'll get used to it in the e.** tu finiras par t'y habituer

• **no end** ADV *Fam* **it upset her/cheered her up no e.** ça l'a bouleversée/ravie à un point (inimaginable); **it helped me no e.** ça m'a énormément aidé▫

• **no end of** ADJ *Fam* **it'll do you no e. of good** cela vous fera un bien fou; **to have no e. of trouble doing sth** avoir énormément de mal *ou* un mal fou *ou* un mal de chien à faire qch; **to think no e. of sb** porter qn aux nues

• **on end** ADV **1** *(upright)* debout; **to stand sth on e.** mettre qch debout; **her hair was standing on e.** elle avait les cheveux dressés sur la tête
2 *(in succession)* entier; **for hours/days on e.** pendant des heures entières/des jours entiers; **for four hours on e.** pendant quatre heures de suite *ou* d'affilée

▸▸ *Rail* ***end carriage*** wagon *m* de queue; *Comput* ***end key*** touche *f* fin; *Am Sport* ***end line*** ligne *f* de fond; *Typ* ***end matter*** parties *fpl* annexes; *Tech* ***end piece*** embout *m*; ***end product*** *Ind & Com* produit *m* final; *Fig* résultat *m*; ***end result*** résultat *m* final; *Am* ***end run*** faux-fuyant *m*; *TV & Cin* ***end titles*** générique *m* de fin; ***end zone*** *(in American football)* zone *f* d'en-but

▸**end up** VI finir; **they ended up in Manchester** ils se sont retrouvés à Manchester; **to e. up in hospital/in prison** finir à l'hôpital/en prison; **to e. up doing sth** finir par faire qch; **to e. up (as) the boss/on the dole** finir patron/chômeur

end-all *see* **be-all**

endanger [ɪnˈdeɪndʒə(r)] VT *(life, country)* mettre en danger; *(health, reputation, future, chances)* compromettre
▸▸ ***endangered species*** espèce *f* en voie de disparition

end-consumer N *Com* utilisateur *m* final; *(of foodstuffs)* consommateur *m* final, utilisateur *m* final

endear [ɪnˈdɪə(r)] VT faire aimer; **what endears him to me** ce qui le rend cher à mes yeux; **to e. oneself to sb** se faire aimer de qn; **the Chancellor's decision did not e. him to the voters** la décision du

Chancelier ne lui a pas gagné la faveur des électeurs

endearing [ɪn'dɪərɪŋ] **ADJ** *(personality, person)* attachant; *(smile)* engageant; **it's a very e. characteristic of his** c'est un trait de caractère qui le rend très attachant

endearingly [ɪn'dɪərɪŋlɪ] **ADV** de manière attachante; *(smile)* de manière engageante

endearment [ɪn'dɪəmənt] **N** **endearments, words of e.** mots *mpl* tendres; **term of e.** terme *m* affectueux

endeavour, *Am* **endeavor** [ɪn'devə(r)] *Formal* **N** effort *m*; **to wish sb good luck in their endeavours** souhaiter bonne chance à qn dans ses entreprises; **to make every e. to obtain sth** faire tout son possible pour obtenir qch; **in an e. to stop the strike** en tentant de mettre fin à la grève; **despite her best endeavours** malgré tous ses efforts; **a new field of human e.** une nouvelle perspective pour l'homme

VI to e. to do sth s'efforcer *ou* essayer de faire qch

endemic [en'demɪk] **ADJ** *Ecol, Med & Fig* endémique; *Fig* **the problem is e. to the region** c'est un problème endémique dans la région

N *Med* endémie *f*

endgame ['endgeɪm] **N** *Chess* fin *f* de partie; *Mktg* objectif *m* (marketing)

ending ['endɪŋ] **N 1** *(of nuclear tests etc)* cessation *f*; *(of restrictions)* levée *f* **2** *(of story, book)* fin *f*; **a story with a happy/sad e.** une histoire qui finit bien/mal **3** *Ling* terminaison *f*; **accusative/genitive e.** désinence *f* de l'accusatif/du génitif

endive ['endaɪv] **N 1** *(curly-leaved)* (chicorée *f*) frisée *f* **2** *esp Am (chicory)* endive *f*

endless ['endlɪs] **ADJ 1** *(speech, road, journey, list, job)* interminable, sans fin; *(patience)* sans bornes, infini; *(resources)* inépuisable, infini; *(desert)* infini; **it's an e. task, it's e.** cela n'en finit pas; **after what seemed like an e. wait** après une attente qui m'a/lui a/*etc* semblé une éternité; **the possibilities are e.** les possibilités sont innombrables; **to ask e. questions** poser des questions à n'en plus finir **2** *Tech (belt, screw)* sans fin

endlessly ['endlɪslɪ] **ADV** *(speak)* continuellement, sans cesse; *(extend)* à perte de vue, interminablement; **to be e. patient/generous** être d'une patience/générosité sans bornes

endnote ['endnəʊt] **N** *Comput* note *f* de fin de document, NfD *f*

endocardium [,endəʊ'kɑːdɪəm] **N** *Anat* endocarde *m*

endocarp ['endəʊkɑːp] **N** *Bot* endocarpe *m*

endocranium [,endəʊ'kreɪnɪəm] *(pl* **endocraniums** *or* **endocrania** [-nɪə]) **N** *Anat* endocrâne *m*

endocrinal [,endəʊ'kraɪnəl] **ADJ** *Physiol* endocrinien

endocrine ['endəʊkraɪn] **ADJ** *Physiol (disorders, system)* endocrinien

►► ***endocrine gland*** glande *f* endocrine

endocrinology [,endəʊkraɪ'nɒlədʒɪ] **N** *Med* endocrinologie *f*

end-of-month **ADJ** de fin de mois

►► *Fin* ***end-of-month balance*** solde *m* de fin de mois; *Fin* ***end-of-month payments*** échéances *fpl* de fin de mois; *Fin* ***end-of-month statement*** relevé *m* de fin de mois

end-of-year **ADJ** de fin d'année; *Fin* de fin d'exercice

►► *Fin* ***end-of-year balance sheet*** bilan *m* de l'exercice; *Com* ***end-of-year bonus*** gratification *f* de fin d'année

endogamy [en'dɒgəmɪ] **N** endogamie *f*

endogenous [en'dɒdʒɪnəs] **ADJ** *Biol, Bot & Med* endogène

endometrium [,endəʊ'miːtrɪəm] *(pl* **endometria** [-trɪə]) **N** *Anat* endomètre *m*

endomorph ['endəʊmɔːf] **N** endomorphe *m*

endorphin [en'dɔːfɪn] **N** *Biol & Chem* endorphine *f*

endorse [ɪn'dɔːs] **VT 1** *(cheque)* endosser; *(document* ▸ *sign)* apposer sa signature sur; *(*▸ *annotate)* apposer une remarque sur; *(passport)* viser; *Fin (bill of exchange)* avaliser, endosser, donner son aval à

2 *Br Law* **to e. a driving licence** faire état d'une infraction sur un permis de conduire

3 *(approve* ▸ *action, decision)* approuver; *(*▸ *opinion)* soutenir, adhérer à; *(*▸ *appeal, candidature)* appuyer, soutenir; **I e. all you have done** j'approuve tout ce que vous avez fait

4 *(product)* faire de la publicité pour; **sportswear endorsed by top athletes** des vêtements de sport recommandés par des sportifs de haut niveau

endorsee [,endɔː'siː] **N** *Fin* endossataire *mf*

endorsement [ɪn'dɔːsmənt] **N 1** *(of cheque)* endossement *m*, endos *m*; *(of document* ▸ *signature)* signature *f*; *(*▸ *annotation)* remarque *f*; *(of bill)* aval *m*; *(on passport)* mention *f* spéciale; *(in insurance)* avenant *m*

2 *Br Law (on driving licence)* = infraction dont il est fait état sur le permis de conduire

3 *(approval* ▸ *of action, decision)* approbation *f*; *(*▸ *of claim, candidature)* appui *m*

4 *(of product)* **the film star has made a fortune from her e. of cosmetic products** cette vedette du cinéma a gagné une fortune en faisant de la publicité pour des cosmétiques

►► *Fin* ***endorsement fee*** commission *f* d'endos

endorser [ɪn'dɔːsə(r)] **N** *Fin (of document, cheque)* endosseur *m*, cessionnaire *mf*; *(of bill of exchange)* avaliste *mf*, avaliseur *m*

endoscope ['endəʊskəʊp] **N** *Med* endoscope *m*

endoscopic [,endəʊ'skɒpɪk] **ADJ** *Med* endoscopique

endoscopy [en'dɒskəpɪ] **N** *Med* endoscopie *f*

endoskeleton [,endəʊ'skelɪtən] **N** *Zool* endosquelette *m*

endosperm ['endəʊspɜːm] **N** *Bot* endosperme *m*

endow [ɪn'daʊ] **VT 1** *(person, institution)* doter; *(university chair, hospital ward)* fonder; **to e. a hospice with £1 million** doter un hospice d'un million de livres **2** *(usu passive)* **to be endowed with sth** être doté de qch; **endowed with great talents** doué de grands talents; *Fam Hum* **to be well endowed** *(man, woman)* avoir tout ce qu'il faut

endowment [ɪn'daʊmənt] **N 1** *Fin (action, money)* dotation *f* **2** *(usu pl) Formal (talent, gift)* don *m*, talent *m*; **man's natural endowments** les qualités naturelles de l'être humain

►► ***endowment assurance*** assurance *f* en cas de vie, assurance *f* à dotation; ***endowment fund*** fonds *m* de dotation; ***endowment insurance*** assurance *f* en cas de vie, assurance *f* à dotation; ***endowment mortgage*** prêt-logement *m* lié à une assurance-vie; ***endowment policy*** assurance *f* en cas de vie, assurance *f* à dotation

endpaper ['end,peɪpə(r)] **N** *Typ* garde *f*, page *f* de garde

endue [ɪn'djuː] **VT** *Literary* doter

endurable [ɪn'djʊərəbəl] **ADJ** supportable, endurable

endurance [ɪn'djʊərəns] **N** endurance *f*; **to have great powers of e.** avoir une grande endurance; **it is beyond e.** c'est insupportable; **she was tried beyond e.** elle a été éprouvée au-delà des limites du supportable

►► *Sport* ***endurance race*** course *f* d'endurance; ***endurance test*** épreuve *f* d'endurance; *Fig* **this is a real e. test** c'est une véritable épreuve d'endurance

endure [ɪn'djʊə(r)] **VT** *(bear* ▸ *hardship)* endurer, subir; *(*▸ *pain)* endurer; *(*▸ *person, stupidity, laziness)* supporter, souffrir; **it was more than she could e.** c'était plus qu'elle ne pouvait supporter; **she can't e. being kept waiting** elle ne supporte *ou* ne souffre pas qu'on la fasse attendre; **he can't e. seeing** *or* **to see children mistreated** il ne supporte pas qu'on maltraite des enfants

VI *Formal (relationship, ceasefire, fame)* durer; *(memory)* rester; **their names will e. forever in our hearts** leurs noms resteront pour toujours dans nos cœurs

enduring [ɪn'djʊərɪŋ] **ADJ** *(friendship, fame, peace)* durable; *(democracy, dictatorship)* qui dure; *(actor, politician etc)* qui jouit d'une grande longévité *(en tant qu'acteur, homme politique etc)*

enduro [ɪn'djʊərəʊ] **N** *Sport* enduro *m*

end-user **N** *Com* utilisateur *m* final; *(of foodstuffs)* consommateur *m* final, utilisateur *m* final

endways ['endweɪz], **endwise** ['endwaɪz] **ADV 1** *(end up)* de chant, debout; **e. on** avec le bout en avant; **I could only see the object e. on** je ne voyais que la face latérale de l'objet; **the house stands e. on to the road** la maison est perpendiculaire à la route **2** *(end to end)* bout à bout; **to put things together e.** mettre des choses bout à bout **3** *(lengthways)* longitudinalement; **we'll have to take it through e.** il faudra que nous le passions dans le sens de la longueur

enema ['enɪmə] **N** *Med (act)* lavement *m*; *(liquid)* produit *m* à lavement; **to give sb an e.** administrer un lavement à qn

enemy ['enɪmɪ] *(pl* **enemies**) **N 1** *(foe)* ennemi(e) *m,f*; **to make enemies** se faire des ennemis; **I made an e. of her** je m'en suis fait une ennemie; **to be one's own worst e.** se nuire à soi-même **2** *Mil* **the e.** l'ennemi *m*; **the e. was** *or* **were advancing** l'ennemi avançait; **boredom is the e.** l'ennui, voilà l'ennemi

COMP *(forces, attack, missile, country)* ennemi; *(advance, strategy)* de l'ennemi

►► ***enemy alien*** ressortissant(e) *m,f* d'un pays ennemi; ***enemy fire*** feu *m* de l'ennemi

enemy-occupied **ADJ** *(territory)* occupé par l'ennemi

energetic [,enə'dʒetɪk] **ADJ** *(person, measures)* énergique; *(music)* vif, rapide; *(campaigner, supporter)* enthousiaste; **to feel e.** se sentir d'attaque *ou* en forme; **after a very e. day** après une journée très chargée; **I don't want to do anything too e.** je ne veux rien faire qui demande trop d'énergie; **it's a very e. game** c'est un jeu où l'on se dépense beaucoup

energetically [,enə'dʒetɪkəlɪ] **ADV** énergiquement

energetics [,enə'dʒetɪks] **N** *(UNCOUNT) Phys* énergétique *f*

energize, -ise ['enədʒaɪz] **VT** *(person)* donner de l'énergie à, stimuler; *Elec* alimenter

energy ['enədʒɪ] *(pl* **energies**) **N 1** *(vitality)* énergie *f*; **to be/to feel full of e.** être/se sentir plein d'énergie; **to have no e.** se sentir sans énergie; **she didn't have the e. for an argument** elle n'avait pas assez d'énergie pour se disputer; **glucose is full of e.** le glucose est très énergétique

2 *(effort)* énergie *f*; **to devote** *or* **to apply (all) one's e.** *or* **energies to sth** consacrer toute son énergie *ou* toutes ses énergies à qch; **to shout/work with all one's e.** crier/travailler de toutes ses forces

3 *Phys* énergie *f*; **kinetic e.** énergie *f* cinétique

4 *(power)* énergie *f*; **to save** *or* **to conserve e.** faire des économies d'énergie; **Minister of** *or* **Secretary (of State) for E.** ministre *m* de l'Énergie

COMP *(conservation, consumption)* d'énergie; *(supplies, programme, level, resource)* énergétique

►► ***energy audit*** = évaluation de la quantité d'énergie consommée dans un bâtiment; ***energy crisis*** crise *f* énergétique *ou* de l'énergie; ***energy gap*** pénurie *f* d'énergie

energy-saving **ADJ** *(device)* pour économiser l'énergie

enervate ['enəveɪt] **VT** amollir, débiliter

enervating ['enəveɪtɪŋ] **ADJ** amollissant, débilitant

enervation [,enə'veɪʃən] **N** *(state)* mollesse *f*

enfeeble [ɪn'fiːbəl] **VT** affaiblir

enfilade [,enfɪ'leɪd] *Mil* **N** enfilade *f*

VT prendre en enfilade

enfold [ɪn'fəʊld] **VT** *(embrace)* envelopper (**in** dans); **to e. sb in one's arms** étreindre qn, entourer qn de ses bras

enforce [ɪn'fɔːs] **VT** *(policy, decision)* mettre en œuvre, appliquer; *(law)* mettre en vigueur; *(order, police)* faire exécuter; *(one's rights)* faire valoir; *(one's will, discipline)* faire respecter; *(contract)* faire exécuter; **such a law would be impossible to e.** une telle loi serait impossible à appliquer; **to e. obedience** se faire obéir

enforceable [ɪn'fɔːsəbəl] **ADJ** exécutoire

►► *Law* ***enforceable judgment*** jugement *m* exécutoire

enforced [ɪn'fɔːst] **ADJ** forcé

enforcement [ɪnˈfɔːsmənt] **N** *(of policy, decision)* mise *f* en œuvre; *(of law)* application *f*, exécution *f*; *(by the police)* mise *f* à exécution; *(of one's rights)* exercice *m*; *(of one's will, discipline)* respect *m*; *(of contract)* exécution *f*
▸▸ *Law* ***enforcement notice*** = notification pour violation des règles de l'urbanisme

enfranchise [ɪnˈfræntʃaɪz] **VT 1** *(give vote to)* admettre au suffrage, accorder le droit de vote à **2** *(free ▸ slave)* affranchir

enfranchisement [ɪnˈfræntʃɪzmənt] **N 1** *Pol (of citizen)* admission *f* au suffrage **2** *(freeing ▸ of slave)* affranchissement *m*

ENG [ˌiːenˈdʒiː] **N** *(abbr* **electronic news gathering***)* journalisme *m* électronique de télévision

engage [ɪnˈgeɪdʒ] **VT 1** *(occupy, involve)* **to e. sb in conversation** *(talk to)* discuter avec qn; *(begin talking to)* engager la conversation avec qn; **to be engaged in doing sth** être occupé à faire qch; **while we were engaged in conversation** pendant que nous discutions
2 *Formal (employ ▸ staff)* engager; *(▸ lawyer)* engager les services de; *(▸ workers)* embaucher; **to e. the services of sb** employer les services de qn
3 *Formal (attract, draw ▸ interest, attention)* attirer; *(▸ sympathy)* susciter
4 *Aut & Tech* engager; **to e. the clutch** embrayer; **to e. a gear** engager une vitesse; **to e. gear** embrayer
5 *Mil* **to e. the enemy** engager (le combat avec) l'ennemi
VI 1 *(take part)* **to e. in sth** *(game)* prendre part à qch, participer à qch; *(activity)* se livrer à qch; **to be engaged in research** faire de la recherche; **to be engaged in warfare** être en guerre; **to e. in conversation** discuter; **to e. in sex** avoir des relations sexuelles
2 *Mil* **to e. in battle with the enemy** engager le combat avec l'ennemi
3 *Aut & Tech* s'engager; *(cogs)* s'engrener; *(machine part)* s'enclencher
4 *Formal (promise)* **to e. to do sth** s'engager à faire qch

engaged [ɪnˈgeɪdʒd] **ADJ 1** *(couple)* fiancé; **to be e. to be married** être fiancé; **to get e.** se fiancer; **the e. couple** les fiancés *mpl*
2 *(busy, occupied)* occupé; **I'm otherwise e.** je suis déjà pris; **to be e. in discussions with sb** être engagé dans des discussions avec qn; **to be e. in a conversation** être en pleine discussion
3 *Br (telephone)* occupé; **the line** *or* **number is e.** la ligne est occupée; **I got the e. tone** ça sonnait occupé
4 *(toilet)* occupé

engagement [ɪnˈgeɪdʒmənt] **N 1** *(betrothal)* fiançailles *fpl*; **they announced their e.** ils ont annoncé leurs fiançailles
2 *(appointment)* rendez-vous *m*; **dinner e.** rendez-vous *m* pour dîner; **public e.** engagement *m* à paraître en public; **she has many social engagements** elle est très demandée; **to have an e.** être pris, être occupé; **he couldn't come, owing to a prior** *or* **previous e.** il n'a pas pu venir car il était déjà pris
3 *Mil* engagement *m*
4 *Aut & Tech* engagement *m*
5 *(recruitment)* engagement *m*, embauche *f*
6 *Formal (promise)* obligation *f*, engagement *m*
7 *(for actor, performer)* engagement *m*, contrat *m*
▸▸ ***engagement diary*** agenda *m*; ***engagement party*** (fête *f* de) fiançailles *fpl*; ***engagement ring*** bague *f* de fiançailles

engaging [ɪnˈgeɪdʒɪŋ] **ADJ** *(smile, manner, tone)* engageant; *(person, personality)* aimable, attachant

engagingly [ɪnˈgeɪdʒɪŋlɪ] **ADV** de manière engageante

engender [ɪnˈdʒendə(r)] **VT** engendrer, créer; **to e. sth in sb** engendrer qch chez qn

engine [ˈendʒɪn] **N 1** *(in car, plane)* moteur *m*; *(in ship)* machine *f*; *Fig* **the e. of progress/reform**/*etc* le moteur du progrès/de la réforme/*etc* **2** (*Br* **railway** *or Am* **railroad**) **e.** locomotive *f*; **to sit with one's back to the e.** être assis dans le sens opposé à *ou* inverse de la marche; **to sit facing the e.** être assis dans le sens de la marche **3** *(in computer game)* moteur *m*
COMP *(failure, trouble)* de moteur *ou* machine
▸▸ *Aut* ***engine block*** bloc-moteur *m*; *Aut* ***engine bulkhead*** pare-feu *m* de moteur; *Aut* ***engine compartment*** compartiment *m* moteur; *Br Rail* ***engine driver*** mécanicien(enne) *m,f*, conducteur (trice) *m,f*; ***engine house*** bâtiment *m* des machines *ou* des moteurs; *(for fire engines)* dépôt *m*; *Aut* ***engine immobilizer*** (dispositif *m*) antidémarrage *m*; *Tech* ***engine mounting*** support *m* moteur; ***engine oil*** huile *f* à *ou* de moteur; *Naut* ***engine room*** salle *f* des machines; *Rail* ***engine shed*** dépôt *m* (des locomotives); *(circular)* rotonde *f*

> Note that the French word **engin** is a false friend and is rarely a translation for the English word **engine**. Its most common meaning is **machine**.

engineer [ˌendʒɪˈnɪə(r)] **N 1** *(for roads, machines, bridges)* ingénieur *m*, femme *f* ingénieur; *(mechanic, repairer)* dépanneur(euse) *m,f*; **civil e.** ingénieur *m* civil; **marine e.** ingénieur *m* du génie maritime; **mechanical e.** ingénieur *m* mécanicien; **mining e.** ingénieur *m* des mines; **consulting e.** ingénieur *m* conseil; **production e.** ingénieur *m* (chargé) de la production; *Tel* **telephone e.** technicien(enne) *m,f* des télécommunications *ou* du téléphone
2 *Naut* ingénieur *m*, mécanicien *m*; **chief e.** chef *m* mécanicien; **second e.** officier *m* mécanicien en second
3 *Aviat* **flight e.** *(on military aircraft)* mécanicien *m* navigant; *(on civil aircraft)* mécanicien *m* de bord; **aircraft e.** mécanicien *m* de piste
4 *Mil* soldat *m* du génie, sapeur *m*; **the engineers** le génie, l'arme *f* du génie; *Br* **the Royal Engineers**, *Am* **the Corps of Engineers** le Génie
5 *Am Rail (driver ▸ of locomotive)* conducteur (trice) *m,f*, mécanicien(enne) *m,f*
6 *Fig Pej (instigator ▸ of plan, plot)* âme *f*, instigateur(trice) *m,f*; **her ex-husband was the e. of her downfall** son ex-mari a été l'instigateur de sa ruine
VT 1 *(road, bridge, car)* concevoir; **the bridge has been superbly engineered** le pont est un superbe travail d'ingénierie **2** *Fig Pej (bring about ▸ coup, downfall, defeat)* machiner; *(▸ event, situation)* manigancer; **she engineered his escape** elle a organisé son évasion **3** *(work ▸ goal, victory)* amener
▸▸ ***engineer officer*** ingénieur *m* mécanicien

> Note that the French word **ingénieur** is never used to mean **repairman**.

engineering [ˌendʒɪˈnɪərɪŋ] **N 1** *Tech* ingénierie *f*, engineering *m*; **to study e.** faire des études d'ingénieur; **an incredible feat of e.** une merveille de la technique; **an intricate piece of e.** une mécanique très complexe; **agricultural e.** génie *m* agricole *ou* rural; **civil e.** génie *m* civil; **industrial e.** organisation *f* industrielle; **light e.** petite mécanique *f*; **marine e.** génie *m* maritime; **mechanical e.** mécanique *f*; **precision e.** mécanique *f* de précision; **production e.** technique *f* de la production **2** *Pej (planning)* machinations *fpl*, manœuvres *fpl*; **he had participated in the e. of her downfall** il avait participé aux machinations *ou* manœuvres qui ont conduit à sa ruine
▸▸ *Tech* ***engineering consultancy*** société *f* d'ingénieurs-conseils; ***engineering consultant*** ingénieur-conseil *m*; ***engineering department*** service *m* technique; ***engineering and design department*** bureau *m* d'études; ***engineering firm*** entreprise *f* de construction mécanique; *Rail* ***engineering work*** travail *m* d'ingénierie

engineman [ˈendʒɪnmən] (*pl* **enginemen** [-mən]) **N** *Am* mécanicien *m*

England [ˈɪŋglənd] **N** Angleterre *f*
COMP *(team)* d'Angleterre; *(player)* anglais; *(victory)* de *ou* pour l'Angleterre

English [ˈɪŋglɪʃ] **NPL the E.** les Anglais *mpl*
N *(language)* anglais *m*; **do** *or* **can you speak E.?** parlez-vous (l')anglais?; **to study E.** étudier *ou* apprendre l'anglais; **she speaks excellent E.** elle parle très bien (l')anglais; **we spoke (in) E. to each other** nous nous sommes parlé en anglais; **that's not good E.** ce n'est pas du bon anglais; **in plain** *or* **simple E.** clairement; **so what you mean, in plain** *or* **simple E., is that…** autrement dit *ou* en d'autres termes, ce que vous voulez dire, c'est que…; **can you put that in plain** *or* **simple E.?** pouvez-vous vous exprimer plus clairement?; **American/Australian E.** l'anglais *m* américain/australien; **the King's/Queen's E.** l'anglais *m* correct; **E. as a Foreign Language** anglais *m* langue étrangère; **E. Language Teaching** enseignement *m* de l'anglais; **E. as a Second Language** anglais *m* deuxième langue
ADJ anglais
COMP *(history)* de l'Angleterre; *(teacher)* d'anglais
▸▸ ***English breakfast*** petit déjeuner *m* anglais *ou* à l'anglaise, breakfast *m*; ***the English Channel*** la Manche; ***the English disease*** *(strikes)* = terme faisant référence à la fréquence des grèves avant les lois anti-syndicales en Grande-Bretagne; *(hooliganism)* = expression qui fait référence aux violences auxquelles se livrent les supporters anglais; ***English English*** l'anglais *m* d'Angleterre; ***English Heritage*** = organisme britannique de protection du patrimoine historique; *Am Mus* ***English horn*** cor *m* anglais, hautbois *m* alto; ***English law*** = la loi d'Angleterre, du Pays de Galles et de l'Irlande du Nord (soumise à la Couronne); *Am* ***English muffin*** muffin *m*; *Bot* ***English oak*** *(tree, wood)* chêne *m* pédonculé; ***English Riviera*** = surnom donné à Torbay en raison de la douceur de son climat et de la popularité de ses stations balnéaires; ***English rose*** = le type idéal de la femme anglaise; ***English setter*** setter *m* anglais; *Am* ***English sheepdog*** bobtail *m*; ***English speaker*** *(as native speaker)* anglophone *mf*; *(as non-native speaker)* personne *f* parlant anglais; *Am* ***English for Speakers of Other Languages*** = anglais langue étrangère; ***English for special purposes*** = anglais spécialisé

> **ENGLISH BREAKFAST**
>
> Le petit déjeuner traditionnel anglais se compose d'un plat chaud (des œufs au bacon, par exemple), de céréales ou de porridge, et de toasts à la marmelade d'oranges, le tout accompagné de café ou de thé; aujourd'hui il est généralement remplacé par une collation plus légère.

Englishman [ˈɪŋglɪʃmən] (*pl* **Englishmen** [-mən]) **N** Anglais *m*; *Prov* **an E.'s home is his castle** charbonnier est maître dans sa maison

English-speaking **ADJ** *(as native language)* anglophone; *(as learned language)* parlant anglais

Englishwoman [ˈɪŋglɪʃˌwʊmən] (*pl* **Englishwomen** [-ˌwɪmɪn]) **N** Anglaise *f*

engrave [ɪnˈgreɪv] **VT** graver; **engraved in her memory** gravé dans sa mémoire

engraver [ɪnˈgreɪvə(r)] **N** graveur *m*

engraving [ɪnˈgreɪvɪŋ] **N** gravure *f*

engross [ɪnˈgrəʊs] **VT 1** *(absorb)* absorber **2** *Br Law (make clear copy of ▸ manuscript, document)* grossoyer

engrossing [ɪnˈgrəʊsɪŋ] **ADJ** absorbant

engrossment [ɪnˈgrəʊsmənt] **N 1** *(absorption)* absorption *f* (in dans); **her total e. in the project meant she had almost no free time** ce projet l'absorbait tellement qu'elle n'avait pour ainsi dire plus une minute à elle **2** *Br Law* rédaction *f* de la grosse

engulf [ɪnˈgʌlf] **VT** engloutir; **to be engulfed by the waves** sombrer dans les flots; **engulfed by the flames** englouti par les flammes; **the house was suddenly engulfed in darkness** la maison a été soudain plongée dans l'obscurité; **a feeling of despair engulfed him** le désespoir l'a terrassé

enhance [ɪnˈhɑːns] **VT** *(quality, reputation, performance)* améliorer; *(value, chances, prestige)* augmenter, accroître; *(taste, beauty)* rehausser, mettre en valeur; *Fin (pension)* augmenter; *Comput (image, quality)* améliorer

enhancement [ɪnˈhɑːnsmənt] **N** *(of quality, reputation, performance)* amélioration *f*; *(of value, chances, prestige)* augmentation *f*, accroissement *m*; *(of taste, beauty)* rehaussement *m*, mise *f* en valeur; *Fin (of pension)* augmentation *f*; *Comput (of image, quality)* amélioration *f*

enharmonic [ˌenhɑːˈmɒnɪk] ADJ *Mus* enharmonique

enigma [ɪˈnɪgmə] N énigme *f*; **he remains an e. to us** il est encore une énigme pour nous

enigmatic [ˌenɪgˈmætɪk] ADJ énigmatique

enigmatically [ˌenɪgˈmætɪkəlɪ] ADV *(smile, speak)* d'un air énigmatique; *(worded)* énigmatiquement, d'une manière énigmatique

enjoin [ɪnˈdʒɔɪn] VT *Formal* **1 to e. sb to do sth** *(urge)* exhorter qn à faire qch, recommander fortement *ou* vivement à qn de faire qch; *(command)* enjoindre *ou* ordonner à qn de faire qch; **to e. sth on sb** enjoindre qch à qn **2** *Am (forbid)* **to e. sb from doing sth** interdire à qn de faire qch

enjoy [ɪnˈdʒɔɪ] VT **1** *(like ▸ in general)* aimer; *(▸ on particular occasion)* apprécier; **to e. sth/doing sth** aimer qch/faire qch; **to e. a glass of wine with one's meal** aimer boire un verre de vin avec son repas; **to e. life** aimer la vie; **he enjoys swimming/going to the cinema** il aime la natation/aller au cinéma; **I don't e. being made fun of** je n'aime pas qu'on se moque de moi; **e. your meal!** bon appétit!; **did you e. your meal, sir?** avez-vous bien mangé, monsieur?; **I enjoyed that** *(book, film)* cela m'a plu; *(meal)* je me suis régalé; **I thoroughly enjoyed the weekend/party** j'ai passé un excellent week-end/une excellente soirée; **I e. the various advantages the job has to offer** j'apprécie les divers avantages qu'offre ce poste; **did you e. it?** cela t'a plu?; **what did you e. most?** qu'avez-vous préféré?, qu'est-ce qui vous a le plus plu?; **to e. oneself** s'amuser; **e. yourselves!** amusez-vous bien!; **did you e. yourself?** alors, c'était bien?; **I enjoyed seeing them make fools of themselves** j'ai pris plaisir à les voir se ridiculiser **2** *(possess ▸ rights, respect, privilege, income, good health)* jouir de; *(▸ profits)* bénéficier de; **to e. good health/a high standard of living** jouir d'une bonne santé/d'un haut niveau de vie

EXCLAM *esp Am (enjoy yourself)* amusez-vous bien!; *(enjoy your meal)* bon appétit!

enjoyable [ɪnˈdʒɔɪəbəl] ADJ *(book, film, day)* agréable; *(match, contest)* beau (belle); *(meal)* excellent; **we had a most e. evening** nous avons passé une soirée des plus agréables

enjoyably [ɪnˈdʒɔɪəblɪ] ADV de manière agréable, agréablement; **we spent the week most e.** nous avons passé une semaine des plus agréables

enjoyment [ɪnˈdʒɔɪmənt] N **1** *(pleasure)* plaisir *m*; **to get e. from sth/doing sth** tirer du plaisir de qch/à faire qch; **to get e. out of life** jouir de la vie; **I don't do this for e.** je ne fais pas cela pour le *ou* mon plaisir **2** *(of privileges, rights etc)* jouissance *f*

enlarge [ɪnˈlɑːdʒ] VT **1** *(expand ▸ territory, house, business)* agrandir; *(▸ field of knowledge, group of friends)* étendre, élargir; *(▸ hole)* agrandir, élargir; *(▸ pores)* dilater; *Med (▸ organ)* hypertrophier **2** *Phot* agrandir

VI **1** *(gen)* s'agrandir, se développer; *(pores)* se dilater; *Med (organ)* s'hypertrophier **2** *Phot* **the photo won't e. well** la photo ne donnera pas un bon agrandissement *ou* ne rendra pas bien en agrandissement

enlarged [ɪnˈlɑːdʒd] ADJ *(majority)* accru; *(photograph)* agrandi; *Med (tonsil, liver)* hypertrophié; **e. edition** *(of reference book)* édition *f* augmentée

enlargement [ɪnˈlɑːdʒmənt] N **1** *(of territory, house, business)* agrandissement *m*; *(of group of friends, field of knowledge) & EU* élargissement *m*; *(of hole)* agrandissement *m*, élargissement *m*; *(of pore)* dilatation *f*; *Med (of organ)* hypertrophie *f* **2** *Phot* agrandissement *m*

▸▸ *EU* ***enlargement criteria*** critères *mpl* d'élargissement

enlarger [ɪnˈlɑːdʒə(r)] N *Phot* agrandisseur *m*

enlighten [ɪnˈlaɪtn] VT éclairer; **to e. sb about sth/as to why...** éclairer qn sur qch/sur la raison pour laquelle...; **can somebody e. me as to what is going on?** est-ce que quelqu'un peut m'expliquer ce qui se passe?

enlightened [ɪnˈlaɪtənd] ADJ *(person, view, policy)* éclairé; **e. self-interest** magnanimité *f* intéressée

▸▸ *Hist* ***enlightened despot*** despote *m* éclairé

enlightenment [ɪnˈlaɪtənmənt] N *(explanation, information)* éclaircissements *mpl*; *(state)* édification *f*, instruction *f*; **for your e.** pour votre édification *ou* instruction

• **Enlightenment** N *Hist* **the (Age of) E.** le Siècle des lumières

enlist [ɪnˈlɪst] VT *(supporters)* recruter; *Mil (soldier)* enrôler, engager; *(someone's support, help, sympathy)* s'assurer; **she enlisted the help of two bystanders** elle a obtenu de l'aide de la part de deux spectateurs

VI *Mil (of soldier)* s'engager

enlisted [ɪnˈlɪstɪd] ADJ *Am Mil* **e. man** (simple) soldat *m*; **e. woman** femme *f* soldat de deuxième classe

enlistment [ɪnˈlɪstmənt] N *Mil* enrôlement *m*, engagement *m*

enliven [ɪnˈlaɪvən] VT *(conversation, party)* animer

en masse [ɑ̃ˈmæs] ADV en masse, massivement

enmesh [ɪnˈmeʃ] VT prendre dans un filet; *Fig* mêler; **to become** *or* **get enmeshed in sth** s'empêtrer dans qch; **he got enmeshed in the plot** il s'est trouvé mêlé au complot

enmity [ˈenmətɪ] *(pl* **enmities***)* N *Formal* inimitié *f*, hostilité *f*; **e. for/towards sb** inimitié pour/envers qn

ennoble [ɪˈnəʊbəl] VT **1** *(confer title upon)* anoblir **2** *Fig (exalt, dignify)* ennoblir, grandir

ennoblement [ɪˈnəʊbəlmənt] N **1** *(of commoner)* anoblissement *m* **2** *Fig (of character)* ennoblissement *m*

ennobling [ɪˈnəʊblɪŋ] ADJ *Fig (effect, experience)* ennoblissant

ennui [ɒnˈwiː] N *Literary* ennui *m*

enormity [ɪˈnɔːmətɪ] *(pl* **enormities***)* N **1** *(of action, crime)* énormité *f* **2** *Formal (atrocity)* atrocité *f*; *(crime)* crime *m* très grave **3** *(great size)* énormité *f*; **they were aware of the e. of the task ahead of them** ils se rendaient compte de l'énormité de la tâche qui les attendait

enormous [ɪˈnɔːməs] ADJ **1** *(very large ▸ thing)* énorme; *(▸ amount, number)* énorme, colossal; **they've got an e. dog** ils ont un chien énorme; **e. amounts of food** une quantité énorme *ou* énormément de vivres; **an e. crowd had gathered** un monde fou s'était rassemblé; **there's an e. difference between the two estimates** il y a une énorme différence entre les deux estimations **2** *(as intensifier)* énorme, grand; **the operation was an e. success** l'opération a été un très grand succès; **it has given me e. pleasure** cela m'a fait énormément plaisir

enormously [ɪˈnɔːməslɪ] ADV énormément, extrêmement; **demand has increased e.** la demande a énormément augmenté; **it was e. successful** ce fut extrêmement réussi

ENOUGH [ɪˈnʌf]

ADJ
• assez de
PRON
• assez
ADV
• assez **1, 2** • suffisamment **1**

ADJ assez de; **e. money** assez *ou* suffisamment d'argent; **do you have e. money to pay?** avez-vous de quoi payer?; **you've had more than e. wine** tu as bu plus qu'assez de vin; **the report is proof e.** le rapport est une preuve suffisante; **she's not fool e. to believe that!** elle n'est pas assez bête pour le croire!

PRON assez; **do you need some money? – I've got e.** avez-vous besoin d'argent? – j'en ai assez *ou* suffisamment; **will this be e.?** est-ce que ça suffira?; **we earn e. to live on** nous gagnons de quoi vivre; **there's e. for everybody** il y en a assez pour tout le monde; **e./not e. is known for us to be able to make a prediction** on en sait assez/on n'en sait pas assez pour faire une prévision; **not e. of us are here to take a vote** on n'est pas assez nombreux pour voter; **he's had e. to eat** il a assez mangé; **more than e.** plus qu'il n'en faut; **there was more than e.** il y en avait largement; **e. is e.!** ça suffit comme ça!, trop c'est trop!; **after five years he decided that e. was e. and resigned** après cinq ans il en eut assez et donna sa démission; **e. is as good as a feast** mieux vaut assez que trop; *Fam* **e. said!** je vois!; **that's e.!** ça suffit!; **it's e. to drive you mad** c'est à vous rendre fou; **I can't get e. of his films** je ne me lasse jamais de ses films; **to have had e. (of sth)** en avoir assez (de qch); **she's had e. of working late** elle en a assez de travailler tard le soir

ADV **1** *(sufficiently)* assez, suffisamment; **he's old e. to understand** il est assez grand pour comprendre; **it's a good e. reason** c'est une raison suffisante; **you know well e. what I mean** vous savez très bien ce que je veux dire; **fair e.!** ça va!, d'accord!

2 *(fairly)* assez; **to do sth well e.** faire qch passablement bien; **she's honest e.** elle est assez honnête; **it's good e. in its own way** ce n'est pas mal dans le genre

3 *(with adverb)* **oddly** *or* **strangely e., nobody knows her** chose curieuse, personne ne la connaît

en passant [ɑ̃ˈpæsɑ̃] ADV en passant

enplane [ɪnˈpleɪn] VT embarquer (à bord d'un avion)

VI embarquer (à bord d'un avion)

enprint [ˈenprɪnt] N *Phot* format *m* normal

enquire = **inquire**

enquiry = **inquiry**

enrage [ɪnˈreɪdʒ] VT rendre furieux, mettre en rage; **she was enraged by the government's complacency** la complaisance du gouvernement la rendait furieuse

enrapture [ɪnˈræptʃə(r)] VT émerveiller, enchanter; **we were enraptured by the beauty of the island** nous étions en extase devant la beauté de l'île

enraptured [ɪnˈræptʃəd] ADJ émerveillé, ébloui

enrich [ɪnˈrɪtʃ] VT *(mind, person, life)* enrichir; *(soil)* fertiliser, amender; *Phys* enrichir; **breakfast cereals enriched with vitamins** céréales *fpl* enrichies en vitamines

▸▸ *Comput* ***enriched text*** texte *m* enrichi; *Chem* ***enriched uranium*** uranium *m* enrichi

enriching [ɪnˈrɪtʃɪŋ] ADJ enrichissant

enrichment [ɪnˈrɪtʃmənt] N *(of mind, person, life)* enrichissement *m*; *(of soil)* fertilisation *f*, amendement *m*; *Phys* enrichissement *m*

enrol, *Am* **enroll** [ɪnˈrəʊl] *(Br pt & pp* **enrolled**, *cont* **enrolling**, *Am pt & pp* **enroled**, *cont* **enroling***)* VT **1** *(student)* inscrire, immatriculer; *(member)* inscrire; *Mil (recruit)* enrôler, recruter **2** *Am Pol (prepare)* dresser, rédiger; *(register)* enregistrer

VI *(student)* s'inscrire; *Mil* s'engager, s'enrôler; **to e. on** *or* **for a course** s'inscrire à un cours; **to e. as a student** s'inscrire à la faculté

▸▸ *Am* ***enroled bill*** projet *m* de loi enregistré; *Br* ***enrolled nurse*** = infirmière diplômée

enrolment, *Am* **enrollment** [ɪnˈrəʊlmənt] N *(registration ▸ of members)* inscription *f*; *(▸ of students)* inscription *f*, immatriculation *f*; *(▸ of workers)* embauche *f*; *Mil* enrôlement *m*, recrutement *m*; **the club has an e. of 500 members** le club compte 500 membres; **a school with an e. of 300 students** une école avec un effectif de 300 élèves

Ens *(written abbr* **Ensign***)* **1** *Br Mil* (officier *m*) porte-étendard *m* **2** *Am Naut* enseigne *m* de vaisseau de deuxième classe

ensconce [ɪnˈskɒns] VT *Formal or Hum* installer; **she ensconced herself/was ensconced in the armchair** elle se cala/était bien calée dans le fauteuil

ensemble [ɒnˈsɒmbəl] N *(gen) & Mus* ensemble *m*

enshrine [ɪnˈʃraɪn] VT enchâsser; *Fig (cherish)* conserver pieusement *ou* religieusement; **our fundamental rights are enshrined in the constitution** nos droits fondamentaux font partie intégrante de la constitution

ensign [ˈensaɪn] N **1** *(flag)* drapeau *m*, enseigne *f*; *Naut* pavillon *m* **2** *Br Mil* (officier *m*) porte-étendard *m* **3** *Am Naut* enseigne *m* de vaisseau de deuxième classe

ensilage [ˈensaɪlɪdʒ] N *Agr* ensilage *m*, silotage *m*

enslave [ɪnˈsleɪv] VT réduire en esclavage, asservir; *Fig* asservir

enslavement [ɪnˈsleɪvmənt] N asservissement *m*, assujettissement *m*; *Fig* sujétion *f*, asservissement *m*, assujettissement *m*

ensnare [ɪnˈsneə(r)] VT *also Fig* prendre au piège; **ensnared by her charms** séduit par ses charmes; **she used her beauty to e. him into marrying her** elle s'est servi de sa beauté comme d'un appât pour qu'il l'épouse

ensue [ɪnˈsjuː] VI s'ensuivre, résulter; **a long silence ensued** il se fit un long silence; **the problems that have ensued from government cutbacks** les problèmes qui ont résulté des restrictions gouvernementales

ensuing [ɪnˈsjuːɪŋ] ADJ *(action, event)* qui s'ensuit; *(month, year)* suivant

en suite [ˌɒnˈswiːt] ADJ **with e. bathroom** avec salle de bain particulière
ADV **with bathroom e.** avec salle de bain particulière

ensure [ɪnˈʃʊə(r)] VT **1** *(guarantee)* assurer, garantir; **I did everything I could to e. that he would succeed** *or* **to e. his success** j'ai fait tout ce que j'ai pu pour m'assurer qu'il réussirait *ou* pour assurer son succès **2** *(protect)* protéger, assurer

ENT [ˌiːenˈtiː] *Med (abbr* **ear, nose & throat)** N ORL *f*
ADJ ORL

entail [ɪnˈteɪl] VT **1** *(imply ▸ consequence, expense)* entraîner; *(▸ difficulty, risk)* comporter; *(▸ delay, expense)* occasionner; *(▸ in logic)* entraîner; **it entailed my going to London** cela exigeait que je me rende à Londres; **starting a new job often entails a lot of work** prendre un nouveau poste exige souvent *ou* nécessite souvent beaucoup de travail **2** *Law* **to e. an estate** substituer un héritage; **an entailed estate** un bien grevé
N *Law* **1** *(act)* substitution *f* **2** *(property)* bien *m* substitué **3** *(inheritance)* héritage *m* inéluctable

entangle [ɪnˈtæŋgəl] VT **1** *(ensnare)* empêtrer, enchevêtrer; **to become** *or* **get entangled in sth** s'empêtrer dans qch; **the bird was entangled in the net** l'oiseau était empêtré dans le filet **2** *(snarl ▸ hair)* emmêler; *(▸ threads)* emmêler, embrouiller **3** *Fig (involve)* entraîner, impliquer; **she got entangled in the dispute** elle s'est retrouvée impliquée dans la dispute; **he became entangled with a group of drug dealers** il s'est retrouvé mêlé à un groupe de dealers

entanglement [ɪnˈtæŋgəlmənt] N **1** *(in net, undergrowth)* enchevêtrement *m* **2** *(of hair, thread)* emmêlement *m* **3** *Fig (involvement)* implication *f*; **emotional entanglements** complications *fpl* sentimentales; **his e. with Marie/with the police** son histoire avec Marie/avec la police

entente [ɒnˈtɒnt] N entente *f*
▸▸ ***entente cordiale*** entente *f* cordiale

ENTER [ˈentə(r)]

VT
• entrer dans **1, 2**
• s'inscrire à **2**
• inscrire **3, 4**
• présenter **5**

VI
• entrer **1**
• s'inscrire **2**

N
• entrée

VT **1** *(go into ▸ room)* entrer dans; *(▸ building)* entrer dans, pénétrer dans; **as I entered the building** comme j'entrais dans le bâtiment; **the ship entered the harbour** le navire est entré au *ou* dans le port; **where the river enters the sea** à l'embouchure du fleuve; **where the bullet entered the body** l'endroit où la balle a pénétré le corps; **as we e. a new decade** alors que nous entrons dans une nouvelle décennie; **the war entered a new phase** la guerre est entrée dans une phase nouvelle; **a note of sadness entered her voice** une note de tristesse s'est glissée dans sa voix; **the thought never entered my head** l'idée ne m'est jamais venue à l'esprit
2 *(join ▸ university)* s'inscrire à, se faire inscrire à; *(▸ profession)* entrer dans; *(▸ army)* s'engager *ou* entrer dans; *(▸ politics)* se lancer dans; **to e. the church/a convent** entrer dans les ordres/dans un couvent; **to e. the war** entrer en guerre
3 *(register)* inscrire; **the school entered the pupils for the exam/in the competition** l'école a présenté les élèves à l'examen/au concours; **to e. a horse for a race** engager *ou* inscrire un cheval dans une course
4 *(record ▸ on list)* inscrire; *(▸ in book)* noter; *Comput (▸ data)* entrer, introduire; *Acct (▸ item)* comptabiliser; **he entered the figures in the ledger** il a porté les chiffres sur le livre de comptes
5 *(submit)* présenter; **to e. a protest** protester officiellement; *Law* **to e. an appeal** interjeter appel
VI **1** *(come in)* entrer; *Theat* **e. Juliet** entre Juliette
2 *(register)* s'inscrire; **she entered for the race/for the exam** elle s'est inscrite pour la course/à l'examen
N *Comput (key)* (touche *f*) entrée *f*
▸▸ *Comput* ***enter key*** touche *f* entrée

▸**enter into** VT INSEP **1** *(begin ▸ conversation, relations)* entrer en; *(▸ negotiations)* entamer **2** *(become involved in)* **to e. into an agreement with sb** conclure un accord avec qn; **to e. into partnership with sb** s'associer avec qn; *Fig* **I entered into the spirit of the game** je suis entré dans le jeu **3** *(affect)* entrer dans; **money doesn't e. into it** l'argent n'entre pas en jeu *ou* en ligne de compte; **my feelings don't e. into my decision** mes sentiments n'ont rien à voir avec *ou* ne sont pour rien dans ma décision

▸**enter up** VT SEP *(amount)* inscrire, porter; *Acct* **to e. up an item/figures in the ledger** porter un article/des chiffres sur le livre des comptes

▸**enter upon** VT INSEP **1** *(career)* débuter *ou* entrer dans; *(negotiations)* entamer; *(policy)* commencer **2** *Law (inheritance)* prendre possession de

enteric [enˈterɪk] ADJ *Med* entérique
▸▸ ***enteric fever*** (fièvre *f*) typhoïde *f*

entering [ˈentərɪŋ] N *(of order)* enregistrement *m*; *Comput (of command, character)* entrée *f*; *(of data)* entrée *f*, introduction *f*

enteritis [ˌentəˈraɪtɪs] N *(UNCOUNT) Med* entérite *f*

enterprise [ˈentəpraɪz] N **1** *Com (business, project)* entreprise *f*; **private e.** l'entreprise *f* privée **2** *(initiative)* initiative *f*, esprit *m* entreprenant *ou* d'initiative; **she showed great e.** elle a fait preuve d'un esprit entreprenant; **to lack e.** manquer d'initiative; **to be full of e., to have a lot of e.** être très entreprenant
▸▸ *Br Admin & Com* ***enterprise allowance*** aide *f* à la création d'entreprises; *Br* ***enterprise area*** = zone d'encouragement à l'implantation d'entreprises dans les régions économiquement défavorisées; *Com* ***enterprise culture*** = attitude favorable à l'essor de l'esprit d'entreprise; *Econ* ***enterprise economy*** = type d'économie qui facilite la création d'entreprises; *Com* ***enterprise zone*** = zone d'encouragement à l'implantation d'entreprises dans les régions économiquement défavorisées

enterprising [ˈentəpraɪzɪŋ] ADJ *(person)* entreprenant, plein d'initiative; *(project)* audacieux, hardi; *(solution)* imaginatif, ingénieux; **she's very e.** elle fait preuve d'initiative

enterprisingly [ˈentəpraɪzɪŋlɪ] ADV *(boldly)* audacieusement, hardiment; *(independently)* de sa propre initiative

entertain [ˌentəˈteɪn] VT **1** *(amuse)* amuser, divertir; **I entertained them with a story** je leur ai raconté une histoire pour les distraire *ou* amuser; **to keep sb entertained** divertir *ou* amuser qn **2** *(show hospitality towards)* recevoir; **he entertained them to dinner** *(at restaurant)* il leur a offert le dîner; *(at home)* il les a reçus à dîner **3** *(idea)* considérer, penser à; *(hope)* caresser, nourrir; *(doubt)* entretenir; *(suggestion)* admettre; **she had never entertained hopes of becoming rich** elle n'avait jamais nourri *ou* caressé l'espoir de devenir riche
VI recevoir; **we e. quite often** nous recevons (du monde) assez souvent

Note that the French verb **entretenir** is a false friend and is almost never a translation for the English verb **to entertain**. Its most common meaning is **to maintain**.

entertainer [ˌentəˈteɪnə(r)] N **1** *(comedian)* comique *mf*, amuseur(euse) *m,f*; *(in music hall)* artiste *mf* (de music-hall), fantaisiste *mf*; **a well-known television e.** un artiste de télévision bien connu **2** *(of guests)* **they never were big entertainers** ils n'ont jamais beaucoup reçu

entertaining [ˌentəˈteɪnɪŋ] N **she enjoys e.** elle aime bien recevoir; **they do a lot of business e.** ils donnent pas mal de réceptions d'affaires
ADJ amusant, divertissant

entertainingly [ˌentəˈteɪnɪŋlɪ] ADV de façon amusante *ou* divertissante

entertainment [ˌentəˈteɪnmənt] N **1** *(amusement)* amusement *m*, divertissement *m*; **for your e., we have organized...** pour vous distraire *ou* amuser, nous avons organisé...; **much to the e. of the crowd** au grand amusement de la foule; **this film is** *or* **provides good family e.** ce film est un bon divertissement familial; **her favourite e. is reading** la lecture est sa distraction préférée; **we had to make our own e.** il a fallu que l'on se divertisse nous-mêmes **2** *(performance)* spectacle *m*, attraction *f*; **musical entertainments will be provided** des attractions musicales sont prévues; **the e. business** l'industrie *f* du spectacle; **this show is intended to be an e.** ce spectacle est censé être un divertissement
▸▸ *Com* ***entertainment allowance*** frais *mpl* de représentation; ***entertainment centre*** système *m* audio-vidéo; ***entertainments director*** *(at holiday centre etc)* directeur(trice) *m,f* de l'animation; ***entertainments listings*** chronique *f* des spectacles; ***entertainment magazine*** guide *m* des spectacles; ***entertainments officer*** *(on ship, in students' union)* responsable *mf* chargé de l'animation; *Comput* ***entertainment software*** logiciel *m* de loisir; ***entertainment system*** système *m* audio-vidéo; ***entertainment tax*** taxe *f* sur les spectacles

enthral, *Am* **enthrall** [ɪnˈθrɔːl] *(pt & pp* **enthralled,** *cont* **enthralling)** VT *(fascinate)* captiver, passionner; **she was enthralled by the idea** elle était séduite par l'idée

enthralling [ɪnˈθrɔːlɪŋ] ADJ *(book, film)* captivant, passionnant; *(beauty, charm)* séduisant

enthrallingly [ɪnˈθrɔːlɪŋlɪ] ADV d'une manière captivante; **e. beautiful** d'une beauté fascinante

enthrone [ɪnˈθrəʊn] VT *(monarch)* mettre sur le trône, introniser; *(bishop)* introniser

enthronement [ɪnˈθrəʊnmənt] N intronisation *f*

enthuse [ɪnˈθjuːz] VI s'enthousiasmer; **she enthused over the plan** elle parlait du projet avec beaucoup d'enthousiasme
VT enthousiasmer, emballer; **you don't seem very enthused about it** tu n'as pas l'air emballé par l'idée

enthusiasm [ɪnˈθjuːzɪæzəm] N **1** *(interest)* enthousiasme *m*; **she hasn't much e. for the project** elle n'a pas beaucoup d'enthousiasme pour le projet; **the discovery has aroused** *or* **stirred up considerable e. among historians** la découverte a suscité un grand enthousiasme chez les historiens **2** *(hobby)* passion *f*; **collecting beer mats is just one of my little enthusiasms** je collectionne les dessous de bock, c'est un de mes passe-temps

enthusiast [ɪnˈθjuːzɪæst] N enthousiaste *mf*, fervent(e) *m,f*; **she's a jazz e.** elle est passionnée de *ou* elle se passionne pour le jazz; **football enthusiasts** passionnés *mpl* de football

enthusiastic [ɪnˌθjuːzɪˈæstɪk] ADJ *(person, response)* enthousiaste; *(shout, applause)* enthousiaste, d'enthousiasme; **they gave me an e. welcome** ils m'ont accueilli chaleureusement; **he's an e. football player** c'est un footballeur passionné; **she's very e. about the project** elle est très enthousiaste à l'idée de ce projet; **to be e. about a suggestion** accueillir une proposition avec enthousiasme; **we're not very e. about moving** déménager ne nous dit pas grand-chose, nous ne sommes pas enchantés de déménager; *Ironic* **don't sound so e.!** tu pourrais te montrer un peu plus enthousiaste!

enthusiastically [ɪnˌθjuːzɪˈæstɪkəlɪ] ADV *(receive)* avec enthousiasme; *(speak, support)* avec enthousiasme *ou* ferveur; *(work)* avec zèle

entice [ɪn'taɪs] **VT** attirer, séduire; **to e. sb to do sth** convaincre *ou* persuader qn de faire qch; **to e. sb away from sth** éloigner qn de qch; **I managed to e. him away from the television** j'ai réussi à l'arracher à la télévision; **enticed by their offer** alléché *ou* attiré par leur proposition

enticement [ɪn'taɪsmənt] **N 1** *(attraction)* attrait *m*, appât *m*; **the government offered the Japanese company many enticements to locate their factory in Britain** le gouvernement a offert toutes sortes d'avantages à la société japonaise pour l'inciter à installer son usine en Grande-Bretagne **2** *(act)* séduction *f*

enticing [ɪn'taɪsɪŋ] **ADJ** *(offer)* attrayant, séduisant; *(person)* séduisant; *(food)* alléchant, appétissant; **the water doesn't look very e.** l'eau n'est pas très tentante

enticingly [ɪn'taɪsɪŋlɪ] **ADV** de façon séduisante; **delicious smells wafted e. from the kitchen** de délicieuses odeurs de cuisine mettaient l'eau à la bouche

entire [ɪn'taɪə(r)] **ADJ 1** *(whole)* entier, tout; **my e. life** toute ma vie, ma vie entière; **the e. world** le monde entier; **the e. day** toute la journée; **she read the e. book in an afternoon** elle a lu le livre en entier *ou* tout le livre en l'espace d'un après-midi; **the e. business had proved to be a complete waste of time** toute l'affaire s'est résumée à une pure perte de temps

2 *(total)* entier, complet(ète); *(absolute)* total, absolu; **she has my e. support** elle peut compter sur mon soutien sans réserve; **to enjoy sb's e. confidence** jouir de l'entière confiance de qn

3 *(intact)* entier, intact

4 *Bot* entier

5 *(uncastrated ▸ horse)* entier

entirely [ɪn'taɪəlɪ] **ADV** entièrement, totalement; **I agree with you e.** je suis entièrement d'accord avec vous; **that's e. unnecessary** c'est absolument inutile; **I'm not e. satisfied** je ne suis pas complètement satisfait; **they lived their lives e. in the jungle** ils passèrent toute leur vie dans la jungle; **it's e. my fault** c'est entièrement ma faute; **that's another matter e.** c'est une toute autre affaire; **it's not e. clear what happened** on n'est pas tout à fait sûr de ce qui s'est passé; **the disease has been largely, though not e., eliminated** la maladie n'a pas été complètement éradiquée, mais presque; **the news was not e. unexpected** la nouvelle n'a pas vraiment fait l'effet d'une surprise

entirety [ɪn'taɪrətɪ] *(pl* **entireties**) **N 1** *(completeness)* intégralité *f*; **in its e.** en (son) entier, intégralement; **the book tells the story in its e.** le livre raconte l'histoire dans son entier; **the skeleton had been preserved in its e.** le squelette avait été intégralement conservé **2** *(total)* totalité *f*; **the e. of his estate** la totalité de ses biens

entitle [ɪn'taɪtəl] **VT 1** *(give right to)* autoriser; **the results e. them to believe that...** les résultats les autorisent à croire que...; **his disability entitles him to a pension** son infirmité lui donne droit à une pension; **this ticket entitles the bearer to free admission** ce billet donne au porteur le droit à une entrée gratuite; **to be entitled to do sth** *(by status)* avoir qualité pour *ou* être habilité à faire qch; *(by rules)* avoir le droit *ou* être en droit de faire qch; **you're entitled to your own opinion but...** vous avez le droit d'avoir votre avis mais...; **you're quite entitled to say that...** vous pouvez dire à juste titre que...; **to be entitled to vote** avoir le droit de vote

2 *Law* habiliter; **to be entitled to act** être habilité à agir

3 *(film, book, painting etc)* intituler; **the book is entitled...** le livre s'intitule...

4 *(bestow title on)* donner un titre à

entitlement [ɪn'taɪtəlmənt] **N** droit *m*; **e. to social security** droit *m* à la sécurité sociale; *Com* **holiday e.** congé *m* annuel *(auquel on a droit)*

▸▸ *Admin* ***entitlement card*** = sorte de carte d'identité destinée aux résidents britanniques, donnant droit aux prestations sociales etc

entity ['entətɪ] *(pl* **entities**) **N** entité *f*; **legal e.** personne *f* morale; **a separate e.** une entité séparée

entomb [ɪn'tu:m] **VT** mettre au tombeau, ensevelir; *Fig* ensevelir

entombment [ɪn'tu:mmənt] **N** mise *f* au tombeau, ensevelissement *m*; *Fig* ensevelissement *m*

entomological [ˌentəmə'lɒdʒɪkəl] **ADJ** *Zool* entomologique

entomologist [ˌentə'mɒlədʒɪst] **N** *Zool* entomologiste *mf*

entomology [ˌentə'mɒlədʒɪ] **N** *Zool* entomologie *f*

entourage [ˌɒntʊ'rɑ:ʒ] **N** entourage *m*

entr'acte ['ɒntrækt] **N** entracte *m*

entrails ['entreɪlz] **NPL** *also Fig* entrailles *fpl*

entrain [ɪn'treɪn] **VT** *Formal (person)* embarquer *(dans un train)*

VI *Formal* monter *(dans un train)*

entrance[1] ['entrəns] **N 1** *(means of entry)* entrée *f*; *(large)* portail *m*; *(foyer)* entrée *f*, vestibule *m*; **the e. to the store** l'entrée *f* du magasin; **I'll meet you at the e.** je te retrouverai à l'entrée

2 *(arrival)* entrée *f*; **to make an e.** *(gen)* faire une entrée; *Theat* entrer en scène

3 *(admission)* admission *f*; **the management reserves the right to refuse e.** *(sign)* la direction se réserve le droit de refuser l'entrée; **to gain e. to** *(club, profession, college etc)* être admis à

4 *(access)* accès *m*, admission *f*; **the police gained e. to the building from the back** la police a accédé au bâtiment par derrière

▸▸ ***entrance card*** carte *f* d'entrée *ou* d'admission; ***entrance examination*** *(for school)* examen *m* d'entrée; *(for job)* concours *m* de recrutement; ***entrance fee*** *(to exhibition, fair etc)* droit *m* d'entrée; *Br (to club, organization etc)* droit *m ou* frais *mpl* d'inscription; ***entrance hall*** *(in house)* vestibule *m*; *(in hotel)* hall *m*; *Am* ***entrance ramp*** bretelle *f* d'accès; ***entrance requirements*** qualifications *fpl* exigées à l'entrée; ***entrance ticket*** billet *m* d'entrée

entrance[2] [ɪn'trɑ:ns] **VT 1** *(hypnotize)* hypnotiser, faire entrer en transe **2** *Fig (delight)* ravir, enchanter; **she was entranced by the beauty of the place** elle était en extase devant la beauté de l'endroit; **they all sat entranced** ils étaient tous fascinés

entrancing [ɪn'trɑ:nsɪŋ] **ADJ** enchanteur, ravissant

entrancingly [ɪn'trɑ:nsɪŋlɪ] **ADV** *(smile)* de façon ravissante *ou* séduisante; *(dance, sing)* à ravir

entrant ['entrənt] **N 1** *(in exam)* candidat(e) *m,f*; *(in race)* concurrent(e) *m,f*, participant(e) *m,f*; **all entrants for the exam/competition** tous les candidats à l'examen/participants à la compétition **2** *(to profession, society)* débutant(e) *m,f*; *Com (on market)* acteur *m*; **a training course for (new) entrants to the profession** un cours de formation pour ceux qui débutent dans la profession; *Fin* **stocks in two new entrants to the market performed well** les actions de deux sociétés nouvellement introduites en Bourse se sont bien comportées

entrap [ɪn'træp] *(pt & pp* **entrapped**, *cont* **entrapping**) **VT 1** *(animal, bird)* prendre au piège; *Fig* **he felt entrapped** il se sentait pris au piège **2** *(trick)* prendre au piège; **he claimed that his client had been entrapped into committing a crime** il prétendait que son client avait été piégé et forcé à commettre un crime

entrapment [ɪn'træpmənt] **N 1** *Law* = incitation au délit par un policier afin de justifier une arrestation; *(by journalist)* = fait, pour un journaliste, d'inciter quelqu'un à commettre un délit dans le cadre d'un reportage **2** *(confinement)* enfermement *m*; **a sense of e.** un sentiment d'enfermement

entreat [ɪn'tri:t] **VT** *Formal* implorer, supplier; **to e. sb to do sth** supplier qn de faire qch; **spare his life, I e. you** épargnez sa vie, je vous en conjure; **I entreated her not to be cross with him** je l'ai priée instamment de ne pas se fâcher contre lui

entreating [ɪn'tri:tɪŋ] **ADJ** *Formal* suppliant, implorant

entreatingly [ɪn'tri:tɪŋlɪ] **ADV** *Formal (look)* d'un air suppliant; *(ask)* d'un ton suppliant, d'une voix suppliante

entreaty [ɪn'tri:tɪ] *(pl* **entreaties**) **N** *Formal* supplication *f*, prière *f*; **no one responded to her urgent entreaties** personne ne répondit à ses prières insistantes

entrée ['ɒntreɪ] **N 1** *(right of entry)* entrée *f* (**to** *or* **into** dans) **2** *Culin (course preceding main dish)* entrée *f*; *Am (main dish)* plat *m* principal *ou* de résistance

entrench [ɪn'trentʃ] **VT** *Mil & Fig* retrancher

entrenched [ɪn'trentʃt] **ADJ 1** *Mil* retranché; **an e. position** une position retranchée **2** *Fig (person)* inflexible, inébranlable; *(idea)* arrêté; *(power, tradition)* implanté; **the two neighbours became e. in a long-running feud** les deux voisins se retrouvèrent engagés dans une longue querelle; **attitudes that are firmly e. in our society** des attitudes qui sont fermement ancrées dans notre société; **he became more and more e. in his views** il s'est de plus en plus retranché sur ses positions; **an e. position** une position de retranchement

entrenchment [ɪn'trentʃmənt] **N** *Mil & Fig* retranchement *m*

entrepôt ['ɒntrəpəʊ] **N** *Com* entrepôt *m*

▸▸ ***entrepôt port*** port *m* franc

entrepreneur [ˌɒntrəprə'nɜ:(r)] **N** entrepreneur (euse) *m,f (homme ou femme d'affaires)*

entrepreneurial [ˌɒntrəprə'nɜ:rɪəl] **ADJ** *(spirit, attitude)* d'entrepreneur; *(society, person)* qui a l'esprit d'entreprise; *(skills)* d'entrepreneur

entrepreneurship [ˌɒntrəprə'nɜ:ʃɪp] **N** entrepreneuriat *m*, esprit *m* d'entreprise

entropy ['entrəpɪ] **N** *Phys* entropie *f*

entrust [ɪn'trʌst] **VT** confier; **to e. sth to sb** confier qch à qn; **she entrusted her children to them** elle leur a confié ses enfants, elle a confié ses enfants à leur garde; **to e. sb with a job** charger qn d'une tâche, confier une tâche à qn; **she entrusted him with the responsibility of selling it** elle l'a chargé de le vendre, elle lui a confié le soin de le vendre

entry ['entrɪ] *(pl* **entries**) **N 1** *(way in)* entrée *f*; *(larger)* portail *m* (**to** de)

2 *(act)* entrée *f*; **to make an e.** *(gen)* faire une entrée; *Theat* entrer en scène; **Poland's e. into the EU** l'entrée de la Pologne dans l'UE

3 *(admission)* entrée *f*, accès *m*; **this ticket gives you free e. to the exhibition** ce billet te donne le droit d'entrer gratuitement à l'exposition; **she was refused e. to the country** on lui a refusé l'entrée dans le pays; **no e.** *(sign)* défense d'entrer, entrée interdite; *(in street)* sens interdit

4 *(in dictionary)* entrée *f*; *(in diary)* notation *f*; *(in encyclopedia)* article *m*; *(on list)* inscription *f*; *Comput (of data)* entrée *f*; *Acct (in account book, ledger)* écriture *f*, article *m*; *Acct (action)* passation *f* d'écriture, inscription *f*; *Acct* **to make an e.** *(in ledger)* porter un article à compte, passer une écriture; *(in journal etc)* inscrire quelque chose; *Naut* **an e. in the log** un élément du journal de bord

5 *(competitor)* inscription *f*; *(item submitted for competition)* participant(e) *m,f*, concurrent(e) *m,f*; *Sport* **a late e.** un(e) participant(e) de dernière minute

6 *(UNCOUNT) (number of entrants)* taux *m* de participation; **the e. is down this year** *(in competition)* le taux de participation est en baisse cette année; *(in exam)* les candidats sont moins nombreux cette année; *(at school, university)* le nombre d'inscriptions a baissé cette année; **a big/small e.** *(in competition)* une forte/faible participation

▸▸ *Am* ***entry blank*** feuille *f* d'inscription; ***entry card*** *(for entry to a country)* fiche *f* de police *(au débarquement)*; ***entry fee*** *(for show, museum)* prix *m* d'entrée; *(for club, competition)* droit *m* d'inscription; ***entry form*** feuille *f* d'inscription; ***entry level*** *(of job)* niveau *m* d'embauche; ***entry permit*** visa *m* d'entrée; ***entry talks*** pourparlers *mpl* d'adhésion; ***entry tax*** taxe *f* d'entrée; ***entry visa*** visa *m* d'entrée; ***entry wound*** point *m* d'entrée d'une balle

entryism ['entrɪɪzəm] **N** *Pol* entrisme *m*, noyautage *m*

entryist ['entrɪɪst] *Pol* **ADJ** d'entrisme, de noyautage

N personne *f* qui pratique l'entrisme *ou* le noyautage

entry-level ADJ 1 *(bottom-of-the-range)* bas de gamme, d'entrée de gamme; **an e. computer** un ordinateur d'entrée de gamme 2 *(job)* au bas de l'échelle; *(salary)* de début de carrière

Entryphone® ['entrɪfəʊn] N *Br* Interphone® *m* *(à l'entrée d'un immeuble ou de bureaux)*

ents [ents] NPL *Fam* animation *f*; **he's part of the e. team** il fait partie de l'équipe animation et divertissement

entwine [ɪn'twaɪn] VT **to e. sth round sth** enlacer qch autour de qch; **to become entwined** *(one thing, ribbon etc)* s'enlacer; *(two or more things, ribbons etc)* s'entrelacer; **with arms entwined** les bras entrelacés; **her hair was entwined with ribbons** ses cheveux étaient entrelacés de rubans
VI s'enlacer (**round** autour de); *(two or more things)* s'entrelacer

E number N *Br* additif *m* code E; **there are a lot of E numbers in this jam** il y a beaucoup d'additifs dans cette confiture

enumerate [ɪ'nju:məreɪt] VT énumérer, dénombrer

enumeration [ɪˌnju:mə'reɪʃən] N énumération *f*, dénombrement *m*

enunciate [ɪ'nʌnsɪeɪt] VT 1 *(articulate)* articuler, prononcer 2 *Formal (formulate ▸ idea, theory, policy)* énoncer, exprimer
VI articuler

enunciation [ɪˌnʌnsɪ'eɪʃən] N 1 *(articulation)* articulation *f*, prononciation *f* 2 *Formal (of idea, theory, policy)* énonciation *f*, exposition *f*; *(of problem)* énoncé *m*

enuresis [ˌenjʊə'ri:sɪs] N *Med* énurésie *f*

envelop [ɪn'veləp] VT envelopper (**in** dans *ou* de); **enveloped in a blanket** enveloppé dans une couverture; **enveloped in mystery** entouré *ou* voilé de mystère; **enveloped in mist** voilé de brume

envelope ['envələʊp] N 1 *(for letter)* enveloppe *f*; **put the letter in an e.** mettez la lettre sous enveloppe; **in a sealed e.** sous pli cacheté; **they came in the same e.** ils sont arrivés sous le même pli; **back of an e. calculations** calculs *mpl* effectués à la hâte; *esp Am Fam Fig* **to push the e.** innover▫; **this company is pushing the e. in Web design** cette entreprise est à l'avant-garde de la conception de sites Web▫ 2 *Biol* enveloppe *f*, tunique *f*; *Math* enveloppe *f*; *Electron* enveloppe *f*

envelopment [ɪn'veləpmənt] N enveloppement *m*

envenom [ɪn'venəm] VT *also Fig* envenimer

enviable ['envɪəbəl] ADJ enviable; **in the e. position of being offered two jobs** dans la position enviable de se voir proposer deux emplois

enviably ['envɪəblɪ] ADV d'une manière enviable; **e. rich/well-read** d'une richesse/culture enviable

envious ['envɪəs] ADJ *(person)* envieux, jaloux; *(look, tone)* envieux, d'envie; **she's e. of their new house** elle est envieuse de leur nouvelle maison; **my sister's got a big house but I'm not e.** ma sœur a une grande maison, mais je ne l'envie pas; **I am very e. of you!** comme je t'envie!; **her success only made people e.** son succès n'a fait que des envieux *ou* jaloux

enviously ['envɪəslɪ] ADV avec envie

environment [ɪn'vaɪərənmənt] N 1 *Ecol & Pol (nature)* environnement *m*; **the Secretary of State for the E., the E. Secretary** le ministre de l'Environnement 2 *(surroundings ▸ physical)* cadre *m*, milieu *m*; *(▸ social)* milieu *m*, environnement *m*; *(▸ psychological)* milieu *m*, ambiance *f*; *Biol, Bot & Geog* milieu *m*; **an animal in its natural e.** un animal dans son milieu naturel; **a hostile e.** un climat d'hostilité, une ambiance hostile; **the novel examines the effect of e. on character** le roman étudie les effets du milieu ambiant sur le caractère; **a pleasant working e.** des conditions de travail agréables 3 *Comput & Ling* environnement *m*
▸▸ *Br* ***Environment Agency*** agence *f* pour la protection de l'environnement

environmental [ɪnˌvaɪərən'mentəl] ADJ 1 *Ecol & Pol* écologique; *(change)* de l'environnement 2 *(of surroundings)* du milieu
▸▸ ***environmental art*** art *m* environnemental; ***environmental audit*** = rapport sur l'impact des activités d'une entreprise sur l'environnement; ***environmental damage*** dégâts *mpl* écologiques; *Jur* préjudice *m* écologique; **chemicals that cause e. damage** produits chimiques nuisibles à l'environnement; ***environmental disaster*** catastrophe *f* écologique; ***environmental economics*** économie *f* de l'environnement; *Br* ***Environmental Health Officer*** inspecteur *m* sanitaire; ***environmental impact*** impact *m* sur l'environnement; ***environmental impact assessment*** étude *f* d'impact sur l'environnement; ***environmental pressure group*** groupe *m* de pression pour la défense de l'environnement; *Am* ***Environmental Protection Agency*** = agence américaine pour la protection de l'environnement; ***environmental science*** science *f* de l'environnement; ***environmental studies*** science *f* de l'environnement

environmentalism [ɪnˌvaɪərən'mentəlɪzəm] N environnementalisme *m*

environmentalist [ɪnˌvaɪərən'mentəlɪst] N 1 *Ecol* écologiste *mf*, environnementaliste *mf* 2 *Psy* environnementaliste *mf*

environmentally [ɪnˌvaɪərən'mentəlɪ] ADV *Ecol* écologiquement; **e. aware** sensibilisé aux problèmes de l'environnement; **e. sensitive** *(technology)* non polluant; *(site)* écologiquement fragile; **e. sound** *(practice, policy)* respectueux de l'environnement
▸▸ ***Environmentally Sensitive Area*** = zone de protection de la nature désignée par l'Union européenne où les agriculteurs doivent utiliser des méthodes traditionnelles

environmentally-friendly, environment-friendly ADJ *Ecol (policy)* respectueux de l'environnement; *(technology, product)* non polluant

environs [ɪn'vaɪərənz] NPL *Formal* environs *mpl*, alentours *mpl*; **Paris and its e.** Paris et ses environs

envisage [ɪn'vɪzɪdʒ], *Am* **envision** [ɪn'vɪʒən] VT *(imagine)* envisager; *(predict)* prévoir; **I don't e. (that there will be) any difficulty** je n'envisage pas (qu'il puisse y avoir) la moindre difficulté

envoy ['envɔɪ] N 1 *(emissary)* envoyé(e) *m,f*, représentant(e) *m,f*; *Pol* **e. (extraordinary)** ministre *m* plénipotentiaire 2 *Literature* envoi *m*

envy ['envɪ] *(pl* **envies**, *pt & pp* **envied**) N 1 *(jealousy)* envie *f*, jalousie *f*; **out of e.** par envie *ou* jalousie; **to be green with e.** être dévoré d'envie; **filled with e.** dévoré de jalousie 2 *(object of jealousy)* objet *m* d'envie; **she was the e. of all her friends** elle excitait *ou* faisait l'envie de tous ses amis
VT envier; **I do e. her** je l'envie vraiment; **I don't e. you!** je ne t'envie pas!; **to e. sb sth** envier qch à qn; **I don't e. him having to catch such an early train** je ne l'envie pas d'avoir à prendre le train de si bonne heure

enzyme ['enzaɪm] N *Biol & Chem* enzyme *m or f*
▸▸ *Med* ***enzyme deficiency*** enzymopathie *f*

EOC [ˌi:əʊ'si:] N *Admin (abbr* **Equal Opportunities Commission**) = commission pour l'égalité des chances en matière d'emploi en Grande-Bretagne

Eocene ['i:əʊsi:n] *Geol* ADJ éocène
N éocène *m*

eon *Am* = **aeon**

EONIA [i:'əʊnɪə] N *St Exch (abbr* **Euro Overnight Index Average**) EONIA *m*, TEMPÉ *m*

EP [ˌi:'pi:] N 1 *(abbr* **extended play**) super 45 tours *m*, EP *m* 2 *Am (abbr* **European Plan**) chambre *f* sans pension

EPA [ˌi:pi:'eɪ] N *(abbr* **Environmental Protection Agency**) = agence américaine pour la protection de l'environnement

epaulette, *Am* **epaulet** [ˌepə'let] N *(gen) & Mil* épaulette *f*

EPC [ˌi:pi:'si:] N *EU (abbr* **European Political Cooperation**) coopération *f* en matière de politique étrangère

e-petition [ˌi:pə'tɪʃən] N *Comput* e-pétition *f*

ephedrin, ephedrine [*Br* 'efɪdrɪn, *Am* ɪ'fedrən] N *Pharm* éphédrine *f*

ephemera [ɪ'femərə] *(pl* **ephemeras** *or* **ephemerae** [-'ri:]) N 1 *(short-lived thing)* chose *f* éphémère 2 *Zool* éphémère *m*

ephemeral [ɪ'femərəl] ADJ 1 *(short-lived)* éphémère, fugitif 2 *Zool* éphémère

ephemerid [ɪ'femərɪd] N *Zool* éphémère *m*

epic ['epɪk] ADJ 1 *(impressive)* héroïque, épique; *Hum* épique, homérique 2 *Literature* épique
N 1 *Literature* épopée *f*, poème *m ou* récit *m* épique 2 *(film)* film *m* à grand spectacle
▸▸ ***epic film, epic movie*** film *m* à grand spectacle

epicarp ['epɪˌkɑ:p] N *Bot* épicarpe *m*

epicene ['epɪsi:n] ADJ 1 *(hermaphrodite)* hermaphrodite; *(sexless)* asexué 2 *(effeminate)* efféminé 3 *Gram* épicène

epicentre, *Am* **epicenter** ['epɪsentə(r)] N épicentre *m*

epicure ['epɪˌkjʊə(r)] N gourmet *m*, gastronome *mf*

epicurean [ˌepɪkjʊə'ri:ən] ADJ *(gen)* épicurien
N 1 *(gen)* épicurien(enne) *m,f* 2 *(gourmet)* gourmet *m*, gastronome *mf*
• **Epicurean** *Phil* ADJ épicurien N épicurien (enne) *m,f*

epicyclic [ˌepɪ'saɪklɪk] ADJ *Astron & Tech* épicycloïdal
▸▸ ***epicyclic gear, epicyclic train*** train *m* épicycloïdal

epidemic [ˌepɪ'demɪk] *Med & Fig* N épidémie *f*
ADJ épidémique; **of e. proportions** qui prend les proportions d'une épidémie

epidemiological [ˌepɪˌdi:mɪə'lɒdʒɪkəl] ADJ *Med (evidence, research, study)* épidémiologique

epidemiologist [ˌepɪˌdi:mɪ'ɒlədʒɪst] N *Med* épidémiologiste *mf*

epidemiology [ˌepɪˌdi:mɪ'ɒlədʒɪ] N *Med* épidémiologie *f*

epidermis [ˌepɪ'dɜ:mɪs] N *Anat* épiderme *m*

epidural [ˌepɪ'djʊərəl] *Med* ADJ épidural
N anesthésie *f* épidurale, péridurale *f*; **she had an e.** on lui a fait une péridurale

epiglottis [ˌepɪ'glɒtɪs] *(pl* **epiglottises** *or* **epiglottides** [-tɪdi:z]) N *Anat* épiglotte *f*

epigram ['epɪgræm] N épigramme *f*

epigrammatic [ˌepɪgrə'mætɪk] ADJ épigrammatique

epigraph ['epɪgrɑ:f] N épigraphe *f*

epilepsy ['epɪlepsɪ] N *Med* épilepsie *f*

epileptic [ˌepɪ'leptɪk] *Med* ADJ épileptique
N épileptique *mf*
▸▸ ***epileptic fit*** crise *f* d'épilepsie; **to have an e. fit** avoir une crise d'épilepsie

epilogue, *Am* **epilog** ['epɪlɒg] N épilogue *m*

Epiphany [ɪ'pɪfənɪ] N *Rel* Épiphanie *f*, fête *f* des rois
• **epiphany** N *Literary (revelation)* révélation *f*

epiphyte ['epɪˌfaɪt] N *Bot* épiphyte *m*

episcopacy [ɪ'pɪskəpəsɪ] *(pl* **episcopacies**) N *Rel* 1 *(church government)* gouvernement *m* d'une Église par les évêques 2 *(bishops collectively)* épiscopat *m*

episcopal [ɪ'pɪskəpəl] ADJ *Rel* épiscopal
▸▸ *Rel* ***the Episcopal Church*** l'Église *f* épiscopale; ***episcopal palace*** évêché *m*; ***episcopal ring*** anneau *m* pastoral

episcopalian [ɪˌpɪskəʊ'peɪljən] *Rel* ADJ épiscopal, épiscopalien
N épiscopalien(enne) *m,f*; **the Episcopalians** les épiscopaux *mpl*, les épiscopaliens *mpl*

episcopate [ɪ'pɪskəpət] N *Rel* épiscopat *m*

episiotomy [ɪˌpɪzɪ'ɒtəmɪ] *(pl* **episiotomies**) N *Med* épisiotomie *f*

episode ['epɪsəʊd] N 1 *(period, event)* épisode *m*; *(part of story)* épisode *m*; **an unhappy e. in my life** un épisode malheureux de ma vie; **the first e. will be broadcast on Sunday** le premier épisode sera diffusé dimanche 2 *Med* crise *f*

episodic [ˌepɪ'sɒdɪk] ADJ épisodique

epistemic [ˌepɪ'sti:mɪk] ADJ épistémique

epistemology [eˌpɪsti:'mɒlədʒɪ] N *Phil* épistémologie *f*

epistle [ɪ'pɪsəl] N 1 *Formal or Hum (letter)* lettre *f*, épître *f* 2 *Literature* épître *f*
• **Epistle** N *Bible* the E. to the Romans l'Épître *f* aux Romains

epistolary [ɪ'pɪstələrɪ] ADJ *Formal* épistolaire

epitaph ['epɪˌtɑːf] N épitaphe *f*; this, his last and greatest novel, is a fitting e. to his genius ce roman, qui fut son dernier et son meilleur, témoigne de son génie

epithelium [ˌepɪ'θiːljəm] (*pl* epitheliums *or* epithelia [-ljə]) N *Biol & Bot* épithélium *m*

epithet ['epɪθet] N épithète *f*

epitome [ɪ'pɪtəmɪ] N *(typical example)* modèle *m*, type *m ou* exemple *m* même; she's the e. of generosity elle est l'exemple même de la générosité *ou* la générosité même

epitomize, -ise [ɪ'pɪtəmaɪz] VT *(typify)* personnifier, incarner; this latest announcement epitomizes the government's attitude towards education cette dernière déclaration est caractéristique de l'attitude du gouvernement concernant l'éducation

epizootic [ˌepɪzəʊ'ɒtɪk] *Vet* ADJ *(disease)* épizootique
N épizootie *f*

EPO [ˌiːpiː'əʊ] N 1 *EU (abbr* European Patent Office) OEB *m* 2 *Physiol (abbr* erythropoietin) EPO *f*

epoch ['iːpɒk] N époque *f*; the discovery marked a new e. in the history of science cette découverte a fait date dans l'histoire de la science

epoch-making ADJ qui fait date

eponymous [ɪ'pɒnɪməs] ADJ du même nom, éponyme

EPOS ['iːpɒs] N *Comput (abbr* electronic point of sale) = point de vente électronique

epoxy [ɪ'pɒksɪ] (*pl* epoxies) *Chem* ADJ *(function, group)* époxy *(inv)*, époxydique
N époxyde *m*
▸▸ *Chem* epoxy resin résine *f* époxyde *ou* époxy

EPP [ˌiːpiː'piː] N *Pol (abbr* European People's Party) PPE *m*

eppy ['epɪ] N *Br Fam (abbr* epileptic fit) to have an e. avoir une crise d'épilepsie; *Fig (lose one's temper)* péter une durite, péter les plombs

EPROM ['iːprɒm] N *Comput (abbr* erasable programmable read-only memory) mémoire *f* morte effaçable

EPS [ˌiːpiː'es] N 1 *Fin (abbr* earnings per share) BPA *m* 2 *Comput (abbr* encapsulated PostScript) EPS *m*

Epsom ['epsəm] N = célèbre terrain de courses de chevaux en Angleterre
▸▸ Epsom salts sel *m* d'Epsom, epsomite *f*

e-publishing N édition *f* électronique

equability [ˌekwə'bɪlɪtɪ] N *(of character, person)* placidité *f*, égalité *f* d'humeur; *(of climate)* caractère *m* tempéré; *(of temperature)* constance *f*

equable ['ekwəbəl] ADJ *(character, person)* placide; *(climate)* tempéré; *(temperature)* constant

equably ['ekwəblɪ] ADV tranquillement, placidement

equal ['iːkwəl] (*Br pt & pp* equalled, *cont* equalling, *Am pt & pp* equaled, *cont* equaling) ADJ 1 *(of same size, amount, degree, type)* égal; they are about e. ils se valent; e. in number égal en nombre; in e. measure *(elements, ingredients)* en quantité égale; I was embarrassed and annoyed in e. measure j'étais aussi gêné qu'agacé; to be e. to sth égaler qch; mix e. parts of sand and cement mélangez du sable et du ciment en parts égales; an e. amount of money une même somme d'argent; she speaks French and German with e. ease elle parle français et allemand avec la même facilité; to be on an e. footing with sb être sur un pied d'égalité avec qn; to meet/to talk to sb on e. terms rencontrer qn/parler à qn d'égal à égal; this will allow European businesses to compete on e. terms with their American counterparts cela permettra aux entreprises européennes de pouvoir rivaliser avec leurs concurrentes américaines sur un pied d'égalité; other *or* all things being e. toutes choses égales par ailleurs 2 *(adequate)* he proved e. to the task il s'est montré à la hauteur de la tâche; to feel e. to doing sth se sentir le courage de faire qch
N égal(e) *m,f*, pair *m*; a man who is your intellectual e. un homme qui est votre égal intellectuellement; she's easily his e. at tennis/chemistry elle l'égale facilement au tennis/en chimie; to talk to sb as an e. parler à qn d'égal à égal; we worked together as equals nous avons travaillé ensemble sur un pied d'égalité; he has no e. il est hors pair, il n'a pas son pareil
VT 1 *(gen) & Math* égaler; 2 and 2 equals 4 2 et 2 égalent *ou* font 4; let x e. y si x égale y 2 *(match)* égaler; no one in parliament could e. his eloquence personne au parlement ne pouvait égaler son éloquence; there is nothing to e. it il n'y a rien de comparable *ou* de tel
▸▸ *Am* Equal Access Act = loi américaine de 1984, obligeant les écoles publiques à laisser se réunir les élèves avant et après les cours à des fins religieuses dans l'enceinte de l'école; *Admin* Equal Employment Opportunities Commission = commission pour l'égalité des chances en matière d'emploi, aux États-Unis; equal opportunities chances *fpl* égales, égalité *f* des chances; *Admin* Equal Opportunities Commission = commission pour l'égalité des chances en matière d'emploi, en Grande-Bretagne; equal opportunity employer = entreprise s'engageant à respecter la législation sur la non-discrimination dans l'emploi; *Am* Equal Protection Clause = clause de non-discrimination dans la constitution américaine; equal rights égalité *f* des droits; *Am* Equal Rights Amendment = projet de loi américain rejeté en 1982 qui posait comme principe l'égalité des individus quels que soient leur sexe, leur religion ou leur race; equal sign, equals sign signe *m* égal; *Rad & TV* equal time droit *m* de réponse

equality [iː'kwɒlətɪ] (*pl* equalities) N égalité *f*; e. of opportunity égalité *f* des chances

equalization, -isation [ˌiːkwəlaɪ'zeɪʃən] N 1 *(gen)* égalisation *f*; *Electron* régularisation *f* 2 *Fin (of taxes, wealth)* péréquation *f*; *(of dividends)* régularisation *f*
▸▸ *Fin* equalization fund fonds *m* de parité; *Fin* equalization payment soulte *f*

equalize, -ise ['iːkwəlaɪz] VT *(chances)* égaliser; *Fin (taxes, wealth)* faire la péréquation de; *(dividends)* régulariser
VI *Sport* égaliser

equalizer, -iser ['iːkwəlaɪzə(r)] N 1 *Sport* but *m ou* point *m* égalisateur 2 *Electron* égaliseur *m* 3 *Am Fam (handgun)* flingue *m*

equalizing, -ising ['iːkwəlaɪzɪŋ] ADJ *(current etc)* compensateur; *(pressure)* de compensation; *Sport* the e. goal le but égalisateur

equally ['iːkwəlɪ] ADV 1 *(evenly)* également; divided e. divisé en parts *ou* parties égales; e. spaced également espacé; to contribute e. to the expenses contribuer pour une part égale à la dépense 2 *(to same degree)* également, aussi; they were e. responsible ils étaient également responsables *ou* responsables au même degré; I was e. surprised j'ai été tout aussi surpris; it applies e. to both young and old cela concerne les jeunes comme les personnes âgées; e. well tout aussi bien; e. talented students élèves également *ou* pareillement doués 3 *(by the same token)* efficiency is important, but e. we must consider the welfare of the staff l'efficacité, c'est important, mais nous devons tout autant considérer le bien-être du personnel; e., managers have responsibilities towards workers de même, la direction a des obligations envers le personnel

equanimity [ˌiːkwə'nɪmɪtɪ] N *Formal* égalité *f* d'âme, équanimité *f*; to disturb sb's e. troubler la sérénité de qn; to recover one's e. se ressaisir; with e. d'une âme égale, avec équanimité

equate [ɪ'kweɪt] VT 1 *(regard as equivalent)* assimiler, mettre sur le même pied; some people wrongly e. culture with elitism certaines personnes assimilent à tort culture et élitisme; you can't e. Joyce with Homer on ne peut pas mettre Homère et Joyce sur le même pied 2 *(make equal)* égaler, égaliser; our aim is to e. exports and imports notre but est d'amener au même niveau les exportations et les importations; *Math* to e. sth to sth mettre qch en équation avec qch

equation [ɪ'kweɪʒən] N 1 *Formal (association)* assimilation *f*; the e. of fame with success l'assimilation de la célébrité au succès 2 *Formal (equalization)* égalisation *f* 3 *Chem & Math* équation *f*; *Fig* money doesn't even come into the e. les questions d'argent n'entrent même pas en ligne de compte

equator [ɪ'kweɪtə(r)] N équateur *m*; at *or* on the e. sous *ou* à l'équateur

equatorial [ˌekwə'tɔːrɪəl] ADJ équatorial

equerry ['ekwərɪ] (*pl* equerries) N *Br (of household)* intendant(e) *m,f (de la maison du roi ou de la reine)*; *(of stable)* écuyer(ère) *m,f*

equestrian [ɪ'kwestrɪən] ADJ *(event)* hippique; *(skills)* équestre; *(statue)* équestre; *(equipment, clothing)* d'équitation
N *(rider)* cavalier(ère) *m,f*; *(in circus)* & M[…] écuyer(ère) *m,f*

equidistant [ˌiːkwɪ'dɪstənt, ˌekwɪ'dɪstənt] AD[J] équidistant, à distance égale (from de)

equilateral [ˌiːkwɪ'lætərəl, ˌekwɪ'lætərəl] AD[J] équilatéral
▸▸ *Geom* equilateral triangle triangle *m* équilatéra[l]

equilibrium [ˌiːkwɪ'lɪbrɪəm, ˌekwɪ'lɪbrɪəm] [N] équilibre *m*; in e. en équilibre; how does the spinning top maintain its e.? comment la toupie garde-t-elle l'équilibre?; she lost her e. elle a perdu l'équilibre
▸▸ *Econ* equilibrium price prix *m* d'équilibre

equine ['ekwaɪn] ADJ *(disease, family)* équin; *(profile)* chevalin
▸▸ equine distemper gourme *f*

equinoctial [ˌiːkwɪ'nɒkʃəl, ˌekwɪ'nɒkʃəl] AD[J] *(flower, line, point)* équinoxial; *(storm, tide)* d'équinoxe

equinox ['iːkwɪnɒks, 'ekwɪnɒks] N équinoxe *m*; autumnal e. équinoxe *m* d'automne; spring *or* vernal e. équinoxe *m* de printemps, point *m* vernal

equip [ɪ'kwɪp] (*pt & pp* equipped, *cont* equipping) VT 1 *(fit out ▸ factory)* équiper, outiller; *(▸ laboratory, kitchen)* installer, équiper; *(▸ army, soldier, ship)* équiper; the hospital is not equipped to perform heart surgery l'hôpital n'est pas équipé pour pratiquer la chirurgie du cœur 2 *Fig (prepare)* to be well-equipped to do sth avoir tout ce qu'il faut pour faire qch; it won't e. her for life's hardships cela ne la préparera pas à affronter les épreuves de la vie; he is ill-equipped to handle the situation il est mal armé pour faire face à la situation 3 *(supply ▸ person)* équiper, pourvoir; *(▸ army, machine, factory)* équiper, munir; to e. sb with sth munir *ou* équiper qn de qch; the fighter plane is equipped with the latest technology l'avion de combat est doté des équipements les plus modernes; she equipped herself for the hike with a tent and a sleeping bag elle s'est munie pour la randonnée d'une tente et d'un sac de couchage; if your computer is equipped with a DVD drive si votre ordinateur est pourvu d'un lecteur de DVD

equipage ['ekwɪpɪdʒ] N *(carriage) & Mil* équipage *m*

equipment [ɪ'kwɪpmənt] N *(UNCOUNT)* 1 *(gen)* équipement *m*; *(in laboratory, office, school)* matériel *m*; *Mil & Sport* équipement *m*, matériel *m*; camping e. matériel *m* de camping; electrical e. appareillage *m* électrique; factory e. outillage *m*; kitchen e. ustensiles *mpl* de cuisine; laboratory e. matériel *m* de laboratoire; lifesaving e. matériel *m* de sauvetage; office e. matériel *m* de bureau; sports e. équipement *m* sportif
2 *Fig* intellectual e. capacité *f* intellectuelle
3 *(act)* équipement *m*
4 *Fam Hum (male genitalia)* service *m* trois pièces

equitable ['ekwɪtəbəl] ADJ équitable, juste
▸▸ *Law* equitable distribution répartition *f* des biens matrimoniaux

equitably ['ekwɪtəblɪ] ADV équitablement, avec justice

equitation [ˌekwɪ'teɪʃən] N *Formal* équitation *f*

equity ['ekwətɪ] (*pl* equities) N 1 *(fairness)* équité *f* 2 *Law (system)* équité *f*; *(right)* droit *m* équitable 3 *Fin (market value, of shareholders)* fonds *mpl ou* capitaux *mpl* propres; *(share)* action *f* ordinaire; *(of company)* capital *m* actions

▸▸ ***equity capital*** capital *m* actions; ***equity dilution*** dilution *f* du capital; ***equity financing*** financement *m* par actions, financement *m* par capitaux propres; ***equity investment*** placement *m* en actions; ***equity issue*** augmentation *f* du capital par émission d'actions; ***equity leader*** valeur *f* vedette; *Fin* ***equity loan*** prêt *m ou* titre *m* participatif; ***equity market, equities market*** marché *m* des actions ordinaires; ***equity risk premium*** prime *f* de risque de variation du prix des actions; ***equity share*** action *f* ordinaire; ***equity share capital*** capital *m* en actions ordinaires; ***equities trader*** courtier(ère) *m,f* sur actions; *St Exch* ***equity trading*** marché *m* des actions, courtage *m* sur actions; *St Exch* ***equity unit trust*** SICAV *f* actions; ***equity warrant*** bon *m* de souscription d'actions

equity-linked ADJ *Fin & St Exch (policy)* libellé, investi en actions

equivalence [ɪ'kwɪvələns] N équivalence *f*; *Fin* **equivalences of exchange** parités *fpl* de change

equivalent [ɪ'kwɪvələnt] ADJ équivalent; **to be e. to sth** être équivalent à qch, équivaloir à qch; **that would be e. to saying that…** cela reviendrait à dire que…

N équivalent *m*; **it costs the e. of £5 per week** cela coûte l'équivalent de 5 livres par semaine

▸▸ *Chem* ***equivalent weight*** poids *m* équivalent

equivocal [ɪ'kwɪvəkəl] ADJ **1** *(ambiguous ▸ words, attitude)* ambigu(uë), équivoque **2** *(dubious ▸ behaviour, person)* suspect, douteux; *(▸ outcome)* incertain, douteux

equivocally [ɪ'kwɪvəkəlɪ] ADV **1** *(ambiguously)* de manière équivoque *ou* ambiguë **2** *(dubiously)* de manière douteuse

equivocate [ɪ'kwɪvəkeɪt] VI *Formal* user d'équivoques *ou* de faux-fuyants, équivoquer

equivocation [ɪ,kwɪvə'keɪʃən] N *(UNCOUNT) Formal (words)* paroles *fpl* équivoques; *(prevarication)* tergiversation *f*

ER[1] [,iː'ɑː(r)] N *Am Med (abbr* **emergency room**) urgences *fpl*

ER[2] *(written abbr* **Elizabeth Regina**) = emblème de la reine Élisabeth

er [ɜː(r)] EXCLAM heu

SUFFIXE

-ER, -OR

• Employés avec une racine verbale, les suffixes **-er** et **-or** servent à créer des noms de PERSONNES SE LIVRANT À UNE ACTIVITÉ. La traduction en est généralement **-eur/-euse**. Il n'existe pas de règle régissant l'emploi de **-er** ou **-or**.

Il peut s'agir soit d'une activité de tous les jours: **reader** lecteur; **driver** conducteur, ou bien d'une activité professionnelle:

teacher professeur; **actor** acteur; **astronomer** astronome

Cependant ils servent également à former des mots plus abstraits:

a believer in socialism un partisan du socialisme; **she is no respecter of tradition** elle ne fait pas partie de ceux qui respectent la tradition

• Les noms d'objets se terminant en **-er** ou **-or** désignent généralement des appareils remplissant la fonction indiquée par le verbe qui en forme la racine:

heater radiateur; **cigarette lighter** briquet; **decanter** carafe; **vacuum cleaner** aspirateur

• Le suffixe **-er** (mais non **-or**) s'emploie avec des noms de lieux pour désigner une PERSONNE ORIGINAIRE de ce lieu:

Londoner Londonien; **New Yorker** New-Yorkais; **Berliner** Berlinois. Il sert également à former des termes plus généraux: **islander** insulaire; **villager** villageois; **foreigner** étranger

ERA ['ɪərə] N *Am (abbr* **Equal Rights Amendment**) = projet de loi américain rejeté en 1982 qui posait comme principe l'égalité des individus quels que soient leur sexe, leur religion ou leur race

era ['ɪərə] N *(gen)* époque *f*; *Geol & Hist* ère *f*; **the end of an e.** la fin d'une époque; **her election marked a new e. in politics** son élection a marqué un tournant dans la vie politique; **the e. of horse travel** l'époque *ou* le temps des voyages à cheval

eradicate [ɪ'rædɪkeɪt] VT *(disease)* éradiquer, faire disparaître; *(poverty, problem)* faire disparaître, supprimer; *(abuse, crime)* extirper, supprimer; *(practice)* bannir, mettre fin à; *(weeds)* détruire, déraciner

eradication [ɪ,rædɪ'keɪʃən] N *(of disease)* éradication *f*, *(of poverty, problem)* suppression *f*, *(of abuse, crime)* extirpation *f*, suppression *f*, *(of practice)* fin *f*, *(of weeds)* destruction *f*, déracinement *m*

erasable [ɪ'reɪzəbəl] ADJ effaçable

erase [*Br* ɪ'reɪz, *Am* ɪ'reɪs] VT *(writing)* effacer, gratter; *(with eraser)* gommer; *(from tape, disk, file)* effacer; *Fig* effacer; **I've erased it from my memory** je l'ai effacé de ma mémoire

VI s'effacer

▸▸ ***erase head*** tête *f* d'effacement

eraser [*Br* ɪ'reɪzə(r), *Am* ɪ'reɪsə(r)] N gomme *f*

erasing [*Br* ɪ'reɪzɪŋ, *Am* ɪ'reɪsɪŋ] N effacement *m*

erasure [ɪ'reɪʒə(r)] N **1** *(act)* effacement *m*, grattage *m* **2** *(mark)* rature *f*, grattage *m*

ERDF [,iːɑː,diː'ef] N *Fin (abbr* **European Regional Development Fund**) FEDER *m*

ere [eə(r)] *Arch or Literary* PREP avant; **e. long** sous peu; **e. now, e. this** déjà, auparavant

CONJ avant que; **e. I leave** avant que je ne parte

erect [ɪ'rekt] ADJ **1** *(upright)* droit; *(standing)* debout; **man walks e.** l'homme marche debout; **she holds herself very e.** elle se tient bien droite; **with head e.** la tête haute; **the dog sat with ears e.** le chien était assis les oreilles dressées **2** *Physiol (penis, nipples)* en érection

VT *(build ▸ building, wall)* bâtir, construire; *(▸ statue, temple)* ériger, élever; *(▸ equipment)* installer; *(▸ roadblock, tent, mast, scaffolding)* dresser; *Fig (system)* édifier; *(obstacle)* élever

erectile [ɪ'rektaɪl] ADJ *Physiol* érectile

▸▸ *Med* ***erectile dysfunction*** troubles *mpl* érectiles; *Anat* ***erectile tissue*** tissu *m* érectile

erection [ɪ'rekʃən] N **1** *(action ▸ of building, wall)* construction *f*, *(▸ of statue, temple)* érection *f*, *(▸ of equipment)* installation *f*, *(▸ of roadblock, tent, mast, scaffolding)* dressage *m*; *Fig (▸ of system, obstacle)* édification *f* **2** *(building)* bâtiment *m*, construction *f* **3** *Physiol* érection *f*; **to have** *or* **to get an e.** avoir une érection

erectness [ɪ'rektnɪs] N attitude *f* droite; **the e. of his bearing** sa posture droite

erector [ɪ'rektə(r)] N **1** *Physiol (muscle)* érecteur *m* **2** *(builder)* constructeur(trice) *m,f*

▸▸ *Am* ***erector set*** jeu *m* de construction

erg [ɜːg] N *Phys & Geog* erg *m*

ergo ['ɜːgəʊ] ADV *Formal or Hum* donc, par conséquent

ergonomic [,ɜːgəʊ'nɒmɪk] ADJ ergonomique

ergonomically [,ɜːgəʊ'nɒmɪkəlɪ] ADV du point de vue ergonomique; **e. designed** *(chair, car, office)* d'une conception ergonomique

ergonomics [,ɜːgəʊ'nɒmɪks] N *(UNCOUNT)* ergonomie *f*

ergot ['ɜːgət] N *Agr* ergot *m*; *Pharm* ergot *m* de seigle

ergotism ['ɜːgətɪzəm] N *Med* ergotisme *m*

erigeron [ɪ'rɪdʒərən] N *Bot (plant)* érigéron *m*

Erin ['erɪn] N *Arch or Literary* Irlande *f*

Eritrea [,erɪ'treɪə] N Erythrée *f*

Eritrean [,erɪ'treɪən] N Erythréen(enne) *m,f*

ADJ érythréen

ERM [,iːɑː'rem] N *Formerly Fin (abbr* **exchange rate mechanism**) mécanisme *m* de change (du SME)

erm [ɜːm] EXCLAM euh

ermine ['ɜːmɪn] N *(fur, robe, stoat)* hermine *f*

erode [ɪ'rəʊd] VT **1** *(of water, wind)* éroder, ronger; *(of acid, rust)* ronger, corroder; **the rock face had been eroded away** la paroi du rocher avait été érodée **2** *Fig (courage, power)* ronger, miner; *(confidence)* miner, entamer; **the party's traditional power base has been gradually eroded** la base traditionnelle du parti s'effrite

VI *(rock, soil)* s'éroder; **the cliff is slowly eroding (away)** la falaise est lentement en train de s'éroder

erogenous [ɪ'rɒdʒɪnəs] ADJ érogène

▸▸ ***erogenous zone*** zone *f* érogène

Eros ['ɪərɒs] PR N *Myth* Éros

N *Psy* l'éros *m*

erosion [ɪ'rəʊʒən] N *(of soil, rock)* érosion *f*, *(of metal)* corrosion *f*, *Fig (of courage, power)* érosion *f*, corrosion *f*, *Fig (of confidence, popularity)* détérioration *f*; **wind e.** érosion *f* éolienne; **soil e.** érosion *f* du sol; **e. of prices** effritement *m* des prix

erosive [ɪ'rəʊsɪv] ADJ érosif; *(corrosive)* corrosif

erotic [ɪ'rɒtɪk] ADJ érotique

erotica [ɪ'rɒtɪkə] NPL *Art* art *m* érotique; *Literature* littérature *f* érotique

erotically [ɪ'rɒtɪklɪ] ADV érotiquement; **to be e. charged** avoir un contenu érotique

eroticism [ɪ'rɒtɪsɪzəm], **erotism** ['erətɪzəm] N érotisme *m*

err [ɜː(r)] VI *Formal* **1** *(make mistake)* se tromper; **to e. in one's judgment** faire une erreur de jugement; **I erred on the side of caution** j'ai péché par excès de prudence; *Prov* **to e. is human(, to forgive divine)** l'erreur est humaine(, le pardon divin) **2** *(sin)* pécher, commettre une faute **3** *(stray)* s'égarer, s'écarter (**from** de); *also Hum* **to e. from the straight and narrow** s'égarer du droit chemin

errand ['erənd] N commission *f*, course *f*; **to go on** *or* **to do** *or* **to run an e. (for sb)** faire une course (pour qn); **to send sb on an e.** envoyer qn faire une commission *ou* une course; **an e. of mercy** une mission de charité

▸▸ ***errand boy*** garçon *m* de courses

errant ['erənt] ADJ *(wayward)* dévoyé; **e. ways** vie *f* dévoyée; **e. husband** mari *m* infidèle

errata [e'rɑːtə] *pl of* **erratum**

erratic [ɪ'rætɪk] ADJ **1** *(irregular ▸ results)* irrégulier; *(▸ performance)* irrégulier, inégal; *(▸ person)* fantasque, excentrique; *(▸ mood)* changeant; *(▸ movement, course)* mal assuré; **he is a bit e.** on ne sait jamais comment il va réagir; **e. driving** conduite *f* déconcertante; **her playing is e.** *(musician)* son jeu est inégal; **the road/river follows an e. course** la route/rivière suit un cours irrégulier **2** *Geol & Med* erratique

erratically [ɪ'rætɪkəlɪ] ADV *(act, behave)* de manière fantasque *ou* capricieuse; *(move, work)* irrégulièrement, par à-coups; **he drives e.** il conduit de façon déconcertante; **to play e.** *(sportsman, musician)* avoir un jeu inégal

erratum [e'rɑːtəm] *(pl* **errata** [-tə]) N erratum *m*

▸▸ *Typ* ***erratum*** *or* ***errata slip*** liste *f* des errata

erring ['ɜːrɪŋ] ADJ *(sinning)* dévoyé, égaré; *(mistaken)* tombé dans l'erreur; *(husband, wife)* infidèle; **e. ways** vie *f* dévoyée

erroneous [ɪ'rəʊnjəs] ADJ erroné, inexact

erroneously [ɪ'rəʊnjəslɪ] ADV erronément, à tort

erroneousness [ɪ'rəʊnjəsnɪs] N erreur *f*, fausseté *f*

error ['erə(r)] N **1** *(mistake)* erreur *f*, faute *f*; **to make** *or* **to commit an e.** faire (une) erreur; **an e. of judgment** une erreur de jugement; **it would be an e. to assume that…** ce serait une erreur *ou* on aurait tort de supposer que…; *Com* **errors and omissions excepted** sauf erreur ou omission **2** *Math (mistake)* faute *f*, *(deviation)* écart *m*; **degree of e.** marge *f* d'erreur **3** *(mistakenness)* erreur *f*; **it was done in e.** cela a été fait par erreur *ou* méprise; **he was in e. over** *or* **on this point of law** il était dans l'erreur *ou* il avait tort sur ce point de loi; **I've seen the e. of my ways** je suis revenu de mes erreurs; **to show sb the e. of his/her ways** montrer à qn qu'il/elle est dans le mauvais chemin; *Rel* **to be in/to fall into e.** être/tomber dans l'erreur

▸▸ *Comput* ***error code*** code *m* d'erreur; *Comput* ***error correction*** correction *f* d'erreur; *Comput* ***error message*** message *m* d'erreur; *Comput* ***error routine*** sous-programme *m* de correction d'erreurs

ersatz ['eəzæts] ADJ **this is e. coffee** c'est de l'ersatz *ou* du succédané de café; **this sugar is e.** ce

sucre est un ersatz *ou* un succédané
N ersatz *m*, succédané *m*

Erse [3:s] ADJ gaélique, erse
N gaélique *m*

erstwhile ['3:stwaɪl] ADJ *Literary or Hum* d'autrefois

eructate ['i:rʌkteɪt] VI *Formal or Med* éructer

eructation [ˌi:rʌk'teɪʃən] N *Formal or Med* éructation *f*

erudite ['erudaɪt] ADJ *(book, person)* érudit, savant; *(word)* savant

erudition [ˌeru'dɪʃən] N érudition *f*

erupt [ɪ'rʌpt] VI **1** *(volcano ▸ start)* entrer en éruption; *(▸continue)* faire éruption; **an erupting volcano** un volcan en éruption **2** *(pimples)* sortir, apparaître; *(tooth)* percer; **her face erupted in spots** elle a eu une éruption de boutons sur le visage **3** *Fig (laughter, war, violence)* éclater; *(fire)* se déclarer; *(anger)* exploser; **the city erupted into violence** il y eut une explosion de violence dans la ville; **the stadium erupted in a huge roar** un énorme rugissement a retenti dans le stade; **he erupted when I told him the news** il est devenu furieux quand je lui ai annoncé la nouvelle

eruption [ɪ'rʌpʃən] N **1** *(of volcano)* éruption *f* **2** *(of pimples)* éruption *f*, poussée *f*; *(of teeth)* percée *f* **3** *Fig (of laughter)* éclat *m*, éruption *f*; *(of anger)* accès *m*, éruption *f*; *(of violence)* explosion *f*, accès *m*

ERV [ˌi:ɑ:'vi:] N *(abbr* **emergency response vehicle**) véhicule *m* d'urgence

erysipelas [ˌerɪ'sɪpɪləs] N *Med* érysipèle *m*, érésipèle *m*

erythema [ˌerɪ'θi:mə] N *Med* érythème *m*

erythrocyte [ɪ'rɪθrəusaɪt] N *Biol* érythrocyte *m*

erythromycin [ɪˌrɪθrəʊ'maɪsɪn] N *Pharm* érythromycine *f*

ESA ['i:es'eɪ] N **1** *(abbr* **European Space Agency**) ESA *f*, ASE *f* **2** *Ecol (abbr* **Environmentally Sensitive Area**) = zone de protection de la nature désignée par l'Union européenne où les agriculteurs doivent utiliser des méthodes traditionnelles

escalate ['eskəleɪt] VI **1** *(prices etc)* monter (en flèche) **2** *(war, situation etc)* s'aggraver; **small incidents can easily e. into a world war** de simples incidents (militaires) peuvent facilement mener à une guerre mondiale
VT *(fighting)* intensifier; *(problem)* aggraver; *(prices)* faire grimper

escalation [eskə'leɪʃən] N **1** *(of prices etc)* augmentation *f* (rapide), montée *f* en flèche; *(of interest rates)* escalade *f* **2** *(of war, situation)* escalade *f*
▸▸ *Law* ***escalation clause*** clause *f* d'indexation

escalator ['eskəleɪtə(r)] N escalier *m* roulant *ou* mécanique, escalator *m*
▸▸ *Law* ***escalator clause*** clause *f* d'indexation

escalope ['eskəˌlɒp] N *Culin* escalope *f*

escapade [ˌeskə'peɪd] N *(adventure)* équipée *f*; *(scrape)* fredaine *f*, escapade *f*; *(prank)* frasque *f*

escape [ɪ'skeɪp] VI **1** *(get away ▸ person, animal)* échapper, s'échapper; *(▸prisoner)* s'évader; **they escaped from the enemy/from the hands of their kidnappers** ils ont échappé à l'ennemi/des mains de leurs ravisseurs; **the thieves escaped after a police chase** les voleurs ont pris la fuite après avoir été poursuivis par la police; **the lion escaped from the zoo** le lion s'est échappé du zoo; **she escaped from the camp** elle s'est échappée du camp; *Fig* **to e. from the crowd** fuir la foule; *Fig* **to e. from reality** s'évader *ou* s'échapper de la réalité; **he escaped to Italy** il s'est enfui en Italie **2** *(gas, liquid, steam)* s'échapper, fuir **3** *(survive, avoid injury)* s'en tirer, en réchapper; **she escaped uninjured** elle s'en est tirée sans aucun mal; **he escaped with a reprimand** il en a été quitte pour une réprimande
VT **1** *(avoid)* échapper à; **to e. doing sth** éviter de faire qch; **I narrowly escaped being killed** j'ai failli *ou* manqué me faire tuer; **they escaped punishment/justice** ils ont échappé à la punition/justice; **he escaped detection** il ne s'est pas fait repérer; **there's no escaping the fact that...** il n'y a pas moyen d'échapper au fait que... **2** *(elude notice, memory of)* échapper à; **to e. notice** échapper à l'attention, passer inaperçu; **her name escapes me** son nom m'échappe; **nothing escapes them** rien ne leur échappe
N **1** *(of person)* fuite *f*, évasion *f*; *(of prisoner)* évasion *f*; *(of animal)* fuite *f*; **I made my e.** je me suis échappé *ou* évadé; **to make good one's e.** réussir à s'échapper; **they planned their e.** ils ont combiné leur plan d'évasion; *Fig* **he had a narrow e.** *(from danger)* il l'a échappé belle, il a eu chaud; *(from illness)* il revient de loin
2 *(diversion)* évasion *f*; **an e. from reality** une évasion hors de la réalité; *Fig* **the cinema provided an e. from their daily routine** le cinéma leur offrait un moyen de s'évader de leur routine quotidienne
3 *(of gas, liquid)* fuite *f*; *(of exhaust fumes, steam)* échappement *m*
4 *Comput* échappement *m*; *(key)* touche *f* d'échappement *m*
COMP *(plot)* d'évasion; *(device)* de sortie, de secours
▸▸ *Law* ***escape clause*** clause *f* échappatoire; ***escape hatch*** trappe *f* de secours; *Comput* ***escape key*** touche *f* d'échappement, touche *f* Echap; ***escape mechanism*** *Tech* mécanisme *m* de secours; *Psy* fuite *f* (devant la réalité); ***escape pipe*** tuyau *m* d'échappement *ou* de refoulement, tuyère *f*; ***escape road*** talus *m* de protection; ***escape route*** *(from fire)* itinéraire *m* de sortie de secours; *(of criminal)* itinéraire *m* ménagé pour s'échapper; *Comput* ***escape routine*** procédure *f* d'échappement; *Tech* ***escape valve*** soupape *f* d'échappement; *Astron* ***escape velocity*** vitesse *f* de libération; *Tech* ***escape wheel*** roue *f* d'échappement

escapee [ɪˌskeɪ'pi:] N évadé(e) *m,f*

escapement [ɪ'skeɪpmənt] N *(of clock, piano etc)* échappement *m*

escaper [ɪs'keɪpə(r)] N fugitif(ive) *m,f*

escapism [ɪ'skeɪpɪzəm] N évasion *f* hors de la réalité, fuite *f* devant la réalité

escapist [ɪ'skeɪpɪst] N = personne cherchant à s'évader du réel
ADJ d'évasion

escapologist [ˌeskə'pɒlədʒɪst] N = virtuose de l'évasion dans les spectacles de magie

escapology [ˌeskə'pɒlədʒɪ] N = art de l'évasion dans les spectacles de magie

escarole ['eskərəul] N *Bot & Culin* scarole *f*, endive *f* vraie

escarpment [ɪ'skɑ:pmənt] N *Geog* escarpement *m*

ESCB [ˌi:essi:'bi:] N *(abbr* **European System of Central Banks**) SEBC *m*

eschatology [ˌeskə'tɒlədʒɪ] N eschatologie *f*

eschew [ɪs'tʃu:] VT *Formal (duty, work, activity)* éviter; *(alcohol)* s'abstenir de boire; *(publicity, temptation, involvement)* fuir; **they have eschewed the use of new technology in favour of traditional methods** ils ont évité d'employer des techniques nouvelles au profit de méthodes traditionnelles

e-science N e-science *f*

esc key [esk-] N *Comput* touche *f* d'échappement, touche *f* Echap

escort N ['eskɔ:t] **1** *(guard)* escorte *f*, cortège *m*; *Mil & Naut* escorte *f*; **under the e. of** sous l'escorte de; **under police e.** sous escorte policière; **they were given a police e.** on leur a donné une escorte de police **2** *(from agency ▸ woman)* hôtesse *f*, accompagnatrice *f*, escorte *f*; *(▸ man)* accompagnateur *m*, escort *m* **3** *Old-fashioned (for woman)* cavalier *m*; *(for man)* cavalière *f*
COMP ['eskɔ:t] d'escorte
VT [ɪ'skɔ:t] **1** *Formal (accompany)* accompagner, escorter; **may I e. you home?** permettez-moi de vous raccompagner; **kindly e. these gentlemen to the door** veuillez raccompagner ces messieurs jusqu'à la porte; **her uncle escorted her to the dance** son oncle l'a accompagnée au bal **2** *(of police) & Mil* escorter; *(prisoner)* conduire sous escorte; **they escorted him in/out** ils l'ont fait entrer/sortir sous escorte
▸▸ ***escort agency*** service *m* *ou* bureau *m* d'hôtesses; *Mil* ***escort duty*** service *m* d'escorte; *Mil & Aviat* ***escort fighter*** chasseur *m* d'escorte; ***escort vessel*** (vaisseau *m*) escorteur *m*

escrow ['eskrəu] N *Law* dépôt *m* fiduciaire *ou* conditionnel; **in e.** en dépôt fiduciaire, en main tierce
▸▸ *Law* ***escrow account*** compte *m* bloqué; ***escrow agent*** dépositaire *mf* légal(e)

escutcheon [ɪ'skʌtʃən] N **1** *(shield)* écu *m*, écusson *m* **2** *(on door, handle, light switch)* écusson *m*

> SUFFIXE
>
> **-ESE**
>
> • Ce suffixe sert à former des noms et des adjectifs se rapportant à UN PAYS ou à UNE VILLE. Il se trouve que les adjectifs ainsi formés se rapportent toujours à des lieux situés dans des pays non-anglophones.
>
> (1) Le nom ainsi formé désigne soit une personne originaire de ce lieu, comme dans **a Chinese** un Chinois; **a Maltese** un Maltais; **the Viennese** les Viennois, soit la langue parlée à cet endroit, comme dans **Japanese** le japonais ou **Portuguese** le portugais. La traduction est généralement **-ais(e)**, **-ois(e)** ou **-ien(enne)**. Notez que le pluriel de ces noms est toujours invariable. Il faut noter également qu'il ne s'agit pas du seul préfixe servant à former des noms de langues ou nationalités en anglais.
>
> (2) L'adjectif ainsi formé s'emploie pour désigner des personnes ou des choses liés à ce lieu:
>
> **Vietnamese art** l'art vietnamien; **Milanese history** l'histoire milanaise; **she is Chinese** c'est une Chinoise.
>
> Là encore, la traduction est généralement **-ais(e)**, **-ois(e)** ou **-ien(enne)**.
>
> • Employé de façon péjorative, le suffixe **-ese** sert à créer des noms désignant des jargons jugés inutilement compliqués, utilisés par des groupes donnés. Ces noms se traduisent généralement en employant le mot **jargon** suivi du domaine de spécialité concerné. Ainsi, le terme **legalese** (formé à partir de l'adjectif *legal*) désigne le jargon juridique, le terme **journalese** (formé à partir du nom *journal*) désigne le jargon journalistique, **computerese** (formé à partir du nom *computer*) désigne le jargon informatique et enfin le jargon administratif est désigné par le nom **officialese** (formé à partir de l'adjectif *official*)

ESF [ˌi:es'ef] N *(abbr* **European Social Fund**) FSE *m*

e-signature N *Comput* signature *f* électronique, e-signature *f*

Eskimo ['eskɪməu] *(pl* **inv** *or* **Eskimos**) N **1** *(person)* Esquimau(aude) *m,f* **2** *Ling* esquimau *m*
ADJ esquimau
▸▸ ***Eskimo dog*** chien *m* esquimau; *Sport* ***Eskimo roll*** esquimautage *m*

> **ESKIMO**
>
> Aux États-Unis et au Canada le terme "Eskimo" est souvent considéré comme injurieux; on préfère le terme "Inuit". Les Canadiens utilisent aussi les termes "First Nations" et "First Peoples" pour parler de leur communautés autochtones.

ESL [ˌi:es'el] N *(abbr* **English as a Second Language**) = l'anglais comme deuxième langue

ESOP [ˌi:esˌəu'pi:] N *(abbr* **employee** *Br* **share** *or Am* **stock ownership plan**) plan *m* d'actionnariat des salariés

esophagus *Am* = **oesophagus**

esoteric [ˌesə'terɪk] ADJ *(obscure)* esotérique; *(private)* secret(ète)

ESP [ˌi:es'pi:] N **1** *(abbr* **extrasensory perception**) perception *f* extrasensorielle **2** *(abbr* **English for special purposes**) = anglais spécialisé

esp. *(written abbr* **especially**) particulièrement

espadrille [ˌespə'drɪl] N espadrille *f*

espalier [ɪ'spæljə(r)] N *(tree)* arbre *m* en espalier; *(trellis)* espalier *m*; *(method)* culture *f* en espaliers

esparto [e'spɑːtəʊ] *(pl* **espartos)** **N** *Bot* **e. (grass)** alfa *m*

especial [ɪ'speʃəl] **ADJ** *Formal (notable)* particulier, exceptionnel; *(specific)* particulier; **of e. importance** d'une importance toute particulière

especially [ɪ'speʃəlɪ] **ADV 1** *(to a particular degree)* particulièrement, spécialement; *(particularly)* en particulier, surtout; **the condition usually affects women, e. those over 50** cette maladie touche généralement les femmes, et particulièrement celles de plus de 50 ans; **he likes birds, e. parrots** il aime les oiseaux, spécialement les perroquets; **I can't mention it, e. since** *or* **as I'm not supposed to know anything about it** je ne peux pas en parler d'autant que *ou* surtout que je ne suis pas censé savoir quoi que ce soit à ce sujet; **the food at this restaurant is e. good** la cuisine de ce restaurant est particulièrement bonne; **be e. careful with this one** faites particulièrement attention à celui-ci; **was it any good? – not e.** est-ce que c'était bien? – pas particulièrement **2** *(for a particular purpose)* exprès; **I did it e. for you** je l'ai fait spécialement *ou* exprès pour vous

Attention: ne pas confondre avec **specially**.

Esperanto [ˌespə'ræntəʊ] **N** espéranto *m*
ADJ en espéranto

espionage ['espɪəˌnɑːʒ] **N** espionnage *m*

esplanade [ˌesplə'neɪd] **N** esplanade *f*

espousal [ɪ'spaʊzəl] **N** *Formal (of belief, cause)* adoption *f*

espouse [ɪ'spaʊz] **VT** *Formal (belief, cause)* épouser, adopter

espresso [e'spresəʊ] *(pl* **espressos)** **N** (café *m*) express *m*
▸▸ ***espresso machine*** machine *f* à express

espy [ɪ'spaɪ] *(pt & pp* **espied)** **VT** *Literary* apercevoir, distinguer

Esq. *(written abbr* **Esquire)** **Gregor Clark, E.** M. Gregor Clark

-ESQUE SUFFIXE

• Ce suffixe s'emploie pour former des adjectifs.
• Lorsqu'on l'ajoute à un nom (le plus souvent celui d'un écrivain), le suffixe véhicule la notion d'une QUALITÉ PARTICULIÈRE à la personne en question:
Kafkaesque kafkaïen; **Dantesque** dantesque; **Disneyesque** disneyien; **Lincolnesque** qui évoque Abraham Lincoln
• Il existe un nombre limité de noms d'objets, qui employés avec le suffixe **-esque**, forment des adjectifs indiquant un CARACTÈRE DE SIMILITUDE avec le nom dont ils dérivent. Ainsi l'adjectif **picturesque** est dérivé du mot *picture* (image): **a picturesque village** un village pittoresque. De même, l'adjectif **statuesque** est dérivé de *statue*: **a statuesque woman** une femme d'une beauté sculpturale

Esquire [ɪ'skwaɪə(r)] **N Gregor Clark, E.** M. Gregor Clark

-ESS SUFFIXE

• Le suffixe **-ess** est un élément féminin qui s'applique aux personnes:
princess princesse; **heiress** héritière; **waitress** serveuse; **actress** actrice; **air hostess** hôtesse de l'air; **goddess** déesse
Sous l'influence du politiquement correct, ce suffixe est, depuis quelques années, considéré comme péjoratif et s'utilise moins fréquemment que par le passé. Actuellement, on applique souvent la version masculine du nom aux femmes comme aux hommes; p. ex. **actor** (et non **actress**) s'emploie souvent pour désigner les deux sexes. D'autres mots en **-ess** ont aujourd'hui une consonance désuète: c'est le cas de **authoress** femme auteur; **poetess** poétesse; **ambassadress** ambassadrice. On dit plutôt qu'une femme est **author**, **poet** ou **ambassador**.
Enfin, certains mots en **-ess** appartiennent au registre littéraire ou historique et, employés dans le bon contexte, restent parfaitement acceptables:
enchantress enchanteresse; **temptress** tentatrice; **adventuress** aventurière
D'autres mots, tels que **waitress** (serveuse), sont plus enracinés dans l'usage. Il semblerait étrange, même aujourd'hui, de dire d'une femme qu'elle est **waiter**
• Le suffixe **-ess** s'emploie également dans un nombre très réduit de noms d'animaux femelles. Les plus courants sont **lioness** (lionne) et **tigress** (tigresse)

essay **N** ['eseɪ] **1** *Literature* essai *m*; *Sch* composition *f*, dissertation *f*; *Univ* dissertation *f* **2** *Formal (attempt)* essai *m*, tentative *f*
VT [e'seɪ] *Formal (try)* essayer, tenter; **to e. a smile** tenter de sourire

essayist ['eseɪɪst] **N** essayiste *mf*

essence ['esəns] **N 1** *(gen)* essence *f*, essentiel *m*; **the e. of her speech was that...** l'essentiel de son discours tenait en ceci que...; **time is of the e.** il est essentiel de faire vite, la vitesse s'impose
2 *Phil* essence *f*, nature *f*; *Rel* essence *f*
3 *Chem* essence *f*; **e. of rosemary** essence *f* de romarin; **peppermint e.** essence *f* de menthe
4 *Culin* extrait *m*; **vanilla e.** extrait *m* de vanille
• **in essence** **ADV** essentiellement, surtout

essential [ɪ'senʃəl] **ADJ 1** *(vital ▸ action, equipment, services)* essentiel, indispensable; *(▸ point, role)* essentiel, capital; *(▸ question)* essentiel, fondamental; **a well-trained workforce is e. to the success of your business** un personnel qualifié est essentiel au succès de votre entreprise; **it is e. to know whether...** il est essentiel *ou* il importe de savoir si...; **the e. thing is to relax** l'essentiel est de rester calme; **a balanced diet is e. for good health** un régime équilibré est essentiel pour être en bonne santé; **e. information** *(on packaging)* mentions *fpl* obligatoires **2** *(basic)* essentiel, fondamental; **the e. goodness of man** la bonté essentielle de l'homme; **the e. difference between them is that...** la différence principale entre eux est que...
N objet *m* indispensable; **a dishwasher is an e. of a modern kitchen** un lave-vaisselle est un élément indispensable dans une cuisine moderne; **the essentials** l'essentiel *m*; **the essentials of astronomy** les rudiments *mpl* de l'astronomie; **in (all) essentials** essentiellement
▸▸ ***essential fatty acid*** acide *m* gras essentiel; ***essential goods*** biens *mpl* de première nécessité; ***essential oil*** huile *f* essentielle

essentially [ɪ'senʃəlɪ] **ADV** *(fundamentally)* essentiellement, fondamentalement; *(mainly)* essentiellement, principalement; **it's e. a question of taste** c'est avant tout une question de goût; **he was not e. a bad man** au fond, ce n'était pas quelqu'un de mauvais; **e., nothing has changed** pour l'essentiel, rien n'a changé

Essex ['esɪks] **N** l'Essex *m*, = comté dans le sud-est de l'Angleterre; **in E.** dans l'Essex
▸▸ *Br Fam Pej* ***Essex girl*** minette *f*; *Br Fam Pej* ***Essex man*** = stéréotype du réactionnaire bête et vulgaire, originaire de l'Essex

ESSEX GIRL, ESSEX MAN

Il s'agit de stéréotypes sociaux apparus au cours des années 80. L'"Essex Girl" (originaire de l'Essex, comté situé à l'est de Londres) est censée être une jeune femme d'origine modeste aux mœurs légères, vulgaire, bruyante, et peu intelligente. L'"Essex Man" est lui aussi vulgaire et bruyant; de plus, il est réactionnaire et inculte.

EST [ˌiːes'tiː] **N** *(abbr* **Eastern Standard Time)** heure *f* normale de l'Est

est [est] **N** *Psy (abbr* **Erhard Seminars Training)** = méthode de formation psychologique créée par Werner Erhard

establish [ɪ'stæblɪʃ] **VT 1** *(create, set up ▸ business)* fonder, créer; *(▸ government)* constituer, établir; *(▸ society, system)* constituer; *(▸ factory)* établir, monter; *(▸ contact)* établir; *(▸ relations)* établir, nouer; *(▸ custom, law)* instaurer; *(▸ precedent)* créer; *(▸ order, peace)* faire régner; **she has established a 6 percent lead in the polls** elle a une avance de 6 pour cent dans les sondages; **to e. telephone contact with sb** contacter qn par téléphone; *Comput* **to e. a connection** se connecter; **the police have been unable to e. a link between the two murders** la police n'a pas pu établir de lien entre les deux meurtres; **to e. close relations with sb** nouer des relations avec qn; **to e. oneself in business** s'établir dans les affaires
2 *(confirm ▸ authority, power)* affermir; *(▸ reputation)* établir; **she has already established her reputation as a physicist** elle s'est déjà fait une réputation de physicienne; **the film established her as an important director** avec ce film, elle s'est affirmée comme un metteur en scène important
3 *(prove ▸ identity, truth)* établir; *(▸ cause, nature)* déterminer, établir; *(▸ guilt, need)* établir, prouver; *(▸ innocence)* établir, démontrer; **it has been established that there is no case against the defendant** il a été démontré qu'il n'y a pas lieu de poursuivre l'accusé
4 *Rel & Pol (Church)* ériger en Église d'État

established [ɪ'stæblɪʃt] **ADJ 1** *(existing, solid ▸ order, system)* établi; *(▸ government)* établi, au pouvoir; *(▸ business)* établi, solide; *(▸ law)* établi, en vigueur; *(▸ tradition)* établi, enraciné; *(▸ reputation)* établi, bien assis; **once the company becomes e.** quand la société sera bien établie; *Com* **e. in 1890** maison fondée en 1890; *Rel* **the e. Church** l'Église *f* officielle **2** *(proven ▸ fact)* acquis, reconnu; *(▸ truth)* établi, démontré

establishing shot [ɪ'stæblɪʃɪŋ-] **N** *TV & Cin* plan *m* de situation *ou* de mise en place *ou* d'ensemble

establishment [ɪ'stæblɪʃmənt] **N 1** *(of business)* fondation *f*, création *f*; *(of government)* constitution *f*; *(of society, system)* constitution *f*, création *f*; *(of law)* instauration *f*
2 *(institution)* établissement *m*; **a business e.** un établissement commercial, une firme; **a research e.** un établissement de recherche; **a family e.** *(hotel, restaurant)* un établissement familial
3 *(of fact, guilt, innocence, cause, identity)* établissement *m*
4 *Formal (staff)* personnel *m*; *Mil & Naut* effectif *m*; **to be on the e.** faire partie du personnel; *Mil* **peacetime e.** effectifs *mpl* de paix
• **Establishment** **N** *(ruling powers)* **the E.** les pouvoirs *mpl* établis, l'ordre *m* établi, l'establishment *m*; **he's such an E. figure** il fait vraiment partie de l'establishment; **to be against the E., to be anti-E.** être anticonformiste

estate [ɪ'steɪt] **N 1** *(land)* propriété *f*, domaine *m*; **her country e.** ses terres *fpl*; **e. manager** régisseur *m*
2 *Br* **(housing) e.** *(of privately-owned houses)* lotissement *m*; *(of council houses)* grand ensemble *m*; *Br* **(industrial) e.** zone *f* industrielle
3 *Law (property)* biens *mpl*, fortune *f*; *(of deceased)* succession *f*; **she left a large e.** elle a laissé une grosse fortune (en héritage)
4 *Br (car)* break *m*
5 *Formal (state, position)* état *m*, rang *m*; **men of low/high e.** les hommes d'humble condition/de haut rang; **the three estates** les trois états *mpl*; **the fourth e.** le quatrième pouvoir; *Hist* **the Estates (of the Realm)** les états *mpl* *ou* les ordres *mpl* (de l'Ancien Régime)
▸▸ *Br* ***estate agency*** agence *f* immobilière; *Br* ***estate agent*** *(salesperson)* agent *m* immobilier; *(manager)* intendant *m*, régisseur *m*; *Br* ***estate car*** break *m*; *Br* ***estate duty***, *Am* ***estate tax*** droits *mpl* de succession

esteem [ɪ'stiːm] **VT 1** *(respect ▸ person)* avoir de l'estime pour, estimer; *(▸ quality)* estimer, apprécier **2** *Formal (consider)* estimer, considérer; **I e. it a great honour** je m'estime très honoré
N estime *f*, considération *f*; **to hold sb/sth in high e.** tenir qn/qch en haute estime; **to go up/down in sb's e.** monter/baisser dans l'estime *ou* la considération de qn

ester ['estə(r)] **N** *Chem* ester *m*

esthete, esthetic *etc Am* = **aesthete, aesthetic** *etc*

estimable ['estɪməbəl] **ADJ** estimable, digne d'estime

estimate N ['estɪmət] **1** *(evaluation)* évaluation *f*, estimation *f*; **give me an e. of how much you think it will cost** donnez-moi une idée du prix que cela coûtera, à votre avis; **it's only an e.** ce n'est qu'une estimation; **his e. of 500 tonnes is way off the mark** son estimation de 500 tonnes est très éloignée de la réalité; **at a rough e.** approximativement; **these figures are only a rough e.** ces chiffres ne sont que très approximatifs; **at the lowest e. it will take five years** il faudra cinq ans au bas mot; **at an optimistic e.** dans le meilleur des cas **2** *Com (quote)* devis *m*; **get several estimates before deciding who to employ** faites faire plusieurs devis avant de décider quelle entreprise choisir; **ask the garage to give you an e. for the repairs** demandez au garage de vous établir un devis pour les réparations

VT ['estɪmeɪt] *(calculate ▸ cost, number)* estimer, évaluer; *(▸ distance, speed)* estimer, apprécier; **the cost was estimated at £2,000** le coût était évalué à 2000 livres; **I e. (that) it will take at least five years** à mon avis cela prendra au moins cinq ans, j'estime que cela prendra au moins cinq ans

estimated ['estɪmeɪtɪd] ADJ estimé; **an e. 50,000 people attended the demonstration** environ 50 000 personnes auraient manifesté; **it will cost an e. £500,000** on estime que cela coûtera 500 000 livres; **it is only an e. figure** ce n'est qu'une estimation; **e. time of arrival/of departure** heure *f* probable d'arrivée/de départ

estimation [ˌestɪ'meɪʃən] N **1** *(calculation)* estimation *f*, évaluation *f* **2** *(judgment)* jugement *m*, opinion *f*; **in my e.** à mon avis, selon moi **3** *(esteem)* estime *f*, considération *f*; **he went down/up in my e.** il a baissé/monté dans mon estime

estimator ['estɪmeɪtə(r)] N *Fin* expert *m*

Estonia [e'stəʊnjə] N Estonie *f*

Estonian [e'stəʊnjən] N **1** *(person)* Estonien (enne) *m,f* **2** *(language)* estonien *m*

ADJ estonien

COMP *(embassy)* d'Estonie; *(history)* de l'Estonie; *(teacher)* d'estonien

estrange [ɪ'streɪndʒ] VT aliéner, éloigner

estranged [ɪ'streɪndʒd] ADJ *(couple)* séparé; **to become e. from sb** se brouiller avec *ou* se détacher de qn; **he is e. from his wife** il est séparé de sa femme; **an e. couple** des époux séparés; **her e. husband** son mari, dont elle est séparée; **their e. son** leur fils avec qui ils sont brouillés

estrangement [ɪ'streɪndʒmənt] N éloignement *m*; *(from spouse)* séparation *f*

estrogen *Am* = **oestrogen**

estrous *Am* = **oestrus**

estuary ['estjʊərɪ] *(pl* **estuaries)** N *Geog* estuaire *m*; **the Thames e.** l'estuaire *m* de la Tamise

▸▸ ***estuary English*** = accent standard teinté d'accent Cockney, prédominant à Londres et dans le sud-est de l'Angleterre, ne permettant pas d'identifier l'appartenance sociale du locuteur

ETA N **1** [ˌiːtiː'eɪ] *Aviat (abbr* **estimated time of arrival)** HPA *f*; **our E. is 2300 hours** l'heure d'arrivée prévue est 23 heures **2** ['etə] *Pol (abbr* **Euskadi Ta Askatasuna)** ETA *f*

e-tail ['iːteɪl] N vente *f* en ligne

e-tailer ['iːteɪlə(r)] N entreprise *f* de vente en ligne

e-tailing ['iːteɪlɪŋ] N vente *f* en ligne

et al. [ˌet'æl] ADV *(abbr* **et alia)** et autres

etc. *(written abbr* **et cetera)** etc

et cetera [ɪt'setərə] ADV et cetera, et cætera

N **the et ceteras** les et cætera *mpl*

etch [etʃ] VT graver; *Art* graver à l'eau-forte; *Fig* **etched on my memory** gravé dans ma mémoire

VI graver; *Art* graver à l'eau-forte

etcher ['etʃə(r)] N *Art* graveur(euse) *m,f* à l'eau-forte

etching ['etʃɪŋ] N *Art* **1** *(print)* (gravure *f* à l')eau-forte *f*; *Hum Euph* **come up and see my etchings** monte, je vais te montrer ma collection d'estampes japonaises **2** *(technique)* gravure *f* à l'eau-forte

ETD [ˌiːtiː'diː] N *Aviat (abbr* **estimated time of departure)** HPD *f*

eternal [ɪ'tɜːnəl] ADJ **1** *(gen) & Phil & Rel* éternel; **e. life** la vie éternelle **2** *Pej (perpetual)* continuel, perpétuel; *(arguments, problems)* éternel; *(discussion, wrangling)* continuel, sempiternel; **e. complaints** perpétuelles récriminations *fpl*; **he's an e. student** c'est l'étudiant éternel; **to my e. shame** à ma grande honte

N **the E.** l'Éternel *m*

▸▸ ***the Eternal city*** la Ville éternelle, Rome *f*; *Br* ***the eternal triangle*** l'éternel triangle *m (femme, mari, amant)*

eternally [ɪ'tɜːnəlɪ] ADV **1** *(forever)* éternellement; **I shall be e. grateful** je serai infiniment reconnaissant **2** *Pej (perpetually)* perpétuellement, continuellement

eternity [ɪ'tɜːnətɪ] *(pl* **eternities)** N *also Fig* éternité *f*; **it seemed like an e.** on aurait dit une éternité; **for all e.** pour l'éternité; **he kept me waiting for an e.** il m'a fait attendre une éternité *ou* des éternités

▸▸ ***eternity ring*** = bague entièrement sertie de pierres symbolisant l'éternité du mariage

ethane ['iːθeɪn] N *Chem* éthane *m*

ether ['iːθə(r)] N **1** *Chem & Phys* éther *m* **2** *Literary (sky)* **the e.** l'éther *m*, la voûte céleste; *Rad* **over** *or* **through the e.** sur les ondes

ethereal [ɪ'θɪərɪəl] ADJ *(fragile)* éthéré, délicat; *(spiritual)* éthéré, noble; **she had an e. beauty** elle était d'une beauté éthérée

ethereally [ɪ'θɪərɪəlɪ] ADV **e. beautiful** d'une beauté éthérée

etherize, -ise ['iːθəraɪz] VT *Med* éthériser

Ethernet® ['iːθənet] N *Comput* Ethernet® *m*

ethic ['eθɪk] N éthique *f*, morale *f*

ADJ moral, éthique

ethical ['eθɪkəl] ADJ moral, éthique; **it's not e.** c'est contraire à la morale; **an e. code** un code déontologique; **the doctor's behaviour was not e.** *(against professional ethics)* le comportement du médecin n'était pas conforme au code déontologique

▸▸ *Pharm* ***ethical drug*** = remède vendu uniquement sur l'ordonnance d'un médecin; *Fin* ***ethical investment*** investissement *m* éthique; *Fin* ***ethical investment fund*** fonds *m* d'investissement éthique, SICAV *f* éthique

ethically ['eθɪkəlɪ] ADV d'un point de vue éthique; **e. questionable** d'une éthique douteuse; **she has behaved quite e.** son comportement a été tout à fait éthique *ou* moral

ethics ['eθɪks] N *(UNCOUNT) (study)* éthique *f*, morale *f*

NPL *(principles)* morale *f*; *(morality)* moralité *f*; **dubious e.** morale *f* douteuse; **medical e.** code *m* déontologique *ou* de déontologie

Ethiopia [ˌiːθɪ'əʊpjə] N Éthiopie *f*

Ethiopian [ˌiːθɪ'əʊpjən] N **1** *(person)* Éthiopien (enne) *m,f* **2** *Ling* éthiopien *m*

ADJ éthiopien

COMP *(embassy)* d'Éthiopie; *(history)* de l'Éthiopie

ethnic ['eθnɪk] ADJ **1** *(of race)* ethnique; **e. Albanians/Russians** population *f* d'origine albanaise/russe; **e. pride** revendication *f* d'une appartenance ethnique; **e. unrest** tensions *fpl* ethniques **2** *(traditional)* folklorique, traditionnel **3** *(exotic ▸ food, furniture, clothes)* exotique

N *Am* membre *m* d'une minorité ethnique

▸▸ ***ethnic cleansing*** purification *f* ethnique, nettoyage *f* ethnique; ***ethnic group*** ethnie *f*; ***ethnic minority*** minorité *f* ethnique; ***ethnic origin*** origine *f* ethnique

ethnically ['eθnɪklɪ] ADV du point de vue ethnique, ethniquement; **an e. mixed** *or* **diverse region** une région peuplée de diverses ethnies; **the area has been e. cleansed** cette zone a été le théâtre de nettoyages ethniques

ethnicity [eθ'nɪsɪtɪ] N appartenance *f* ethnique

ethnobiology [ˌeθnəʊbaɪ'ɒlədʒɪ] N ethnobiologie *f*

ethnocentric [ˌeθnəʊ'sentrɪk] ADJ ethnocentrique

ethnocide ['eθnəʊsaɪd] N ethnocide *f*

ethnographer [eθ'nɒgrəfə(r)] N ethnographe *mf*

ethnography [eθ'nɒgrəfɪ] N ethnographie *f*

ethnological [ˌeθnə'lɒdʒɪkəl] ADJ ethnologique

ethnologically [ˌeθnə'lɒdʒɪkəlɪ] ADV ethnologiquement

ethnologist [eθ'nɒlədʒɪst] N ethnologue *mf*

ethnology [eθ'nɒlədʒɪ] N ethnologie *f*

ethological [iːθə'lɒdʒɪkəl] ADJ *Zool* éthologique

ethology [ɪ'θɒlədʒɪ] N *Zool* éthologie *f*, éthographie *f*

ethos ['iːθɒs] N philosophie *f*, valeurs *fpl*, esprit *m*

ethylene ['eθɪliːn] N *Chem* éthylène *m*

▸▸ ***ethylene glycol*** éthylène *m* glycol

e-ticket N billet *m* électronique

etiolate ['iːtɪəʊleɪt] VT *Bot* étioler

etiological, etiology *Am* = **aetiological, aetiology**

etiquette ['etɪket] N *(UNCOUNT) (code of practice)* étiquette *f*; *(customs)* bon usage *m*, convenances *fpl*; **according to e.** selon l'usage; **it's simply not e.** cela ne se fait pas; **e. demands that...** l'étiquette veut *ou* exige que…; **court e.** cérémonial *m* de cour; **medical e.** déontologie *f* médicale; **that's not professional e.** c'est contraire à la déontologie *ou* aux usages de la profession

Etonian [iː'təʊnjən] N élève *m* de l'école d'Eton; **Old E.** ancien élève *m* d'Eton

Etruscan [ɪ'trʌskən] N **1** *(person)* Étrusque *mf* **2** *Ling* étrusque *m*

ADJ étrusque

ETUC [ˌiːtiːjuː'siː] N *(abbr* **European Trade Union Confederation)** CES *f*

etymological [ˌetɪmə'lɒdʒɪkəl] ADJ étymologique

etymologically [ˌetɪmə'lɒdʒɪkəlɪ] ADV étymologiquement

etymologist [ˌetɪ'mɒlədʒɪst] N étymologiste *mf*

etymology [ˌetɪ'mɒlədʒɪ] N étymologie *f*

EU [ˌiː'juː] N *(abbr* **European Union)** UE *f*; **EU legislation** législation *f* européenne; **EU policy** politique *f* communautaire; **the EU member states** les États *mpl* membres de l'UE; **imports to the EU** les importations *fpl* vers l'UE

eucalyptus [ˌjuːkə'lɪptəs] *(pl* **eucalyptuses** *or* **eucalypti** [-taɪ]) N *Bot* eucalyptus *m*

▸▸ ***eucalyptus oil*** essence *f* d'eucalyptus

Eucharist ['juːkərɪst] N Eucharistie *f*

Euclid ['juːklɪd] PR N *Myth* Euclide

Euclidian [juː'klɪdɪən] ADJ *Geom* euclidien

▸▸ ***Euclidian geometry*** géométrie *f* euclidienne

eugenics [juː'dʒenɪks] N *(UNCOUNT) Biol* eugénique *f*, eugénisme *m*

eulogist ['juːlədʒɪst] N panégyriste *mf*

eulogize, -ise ['juːlədʒaɪz] VT faire l'éloge *ou* le panégyrique de

eulogy ['juːlədʒɪ] *(pl* **eulogies)** N **1** *(commendation)* panégyrique *m* **2** *(funeral oration)* éloge *m* funèbre

eunuch ['juːnək] N eunuque *m*

euphemism ['juːfəmɪzəm] N euphémisme *m*

euphemistic [ˌjuːfə'mɪstɪk] ADJ euphémique

euphemistically [ˌjuːfə'mɪstɪkəlɪ] ADV par euphémisme, *Formal* euphémiquement; **e. known as...** auquel on se réfère par euphémisme sous le terme de…

euphonious [juː'fəʊnɪəs] ADJ euphonique

euphonium [juː'fəʊnɪəm] N *Mus* euphonium *m*, saxhorn *m* basse

euphony ['juːfənɪ] N euphonie *f*

euphorbia [juː'fɔːbɪə] N *Bot* euphorbe *f*

euphoria [juː'fɔːrɪə] N euphorie *f*

euphoric [juː'fɒrɪk] ADJ euphorique

Eur. *(written abbr* **Europe)** l'Europe *f*

Eurasia [jʊə'reɪʒə] N Eurasie *f*

Eurasian [jʊə'reɪʒən] N Eurasien(enne) *m,f*

ADJ *(person)* eurasien; *(continent)* eurasiatique

eureka [jʊə'riːkə] EXCLAM eurêka!

eurhythmics [juː'rɪðmɪks] N *(UNCOUNT) Formal* gymnastique *f* rythmique

EURIBOR ['jʊərɪbɔː(r)] N *Fin (abbr* **Euro Interbank Offered Rate)** EURIBOR *m*, TIBEUR *m*

Euro- [ˈjʊərəʊ] PREF euro-

EURO- PRÉFIXE

On rajoute le plus souvent ce préfixe à des noms et à des adjectifs.

• À l'origine, il signifie EUROPE ou EUROPÉEN, comme dans **Eurocentric** eurocentrique; **Eurotunnel** Eurotunnel; **eurocurrency** eurodevise. Il peut s'écrire **Euro-** ou **euro-** et se traduit généralement par **Euro-** ou **euro-**

• Aujourd'hui, en revanche, il a pour sens principal RELATIF À L'UNION EUROPÉENNE, comme dans **Eurocrat** eurocrate; **Euro-MP** député européen; **Euroland** Eurolande; **Euroscepticism** euroscepticisme. Dans ce cas, il s'écrit normalement avec une majuscule (**Euro-** et non **euro-**) et se traduit par **euro-** ou **Euro-**

euro [ˈjʊərəʊ] N *(currency)* euro *m*
▸▸ *EU* **Euro area** zone *f* euro; *St Exch* **Euro Interbank Offered Rate** EURIBOR *m*, TIBEUR *m*; *St Exch* **Euro Overnight Index Average** EONIA *m*, TEMPÉ *m*; *St Exch* **Euro Stoxx** Euro Stoxx *m*; *EU* **Euro zone** zone *f* euro

Eurobank [ˈjʊərəʊbæŋk] N eurobanque *f*

Eurobarometer [ˈjʊərəʊbəˌrɒmɪtə(r)] N Eurobaromètre *m*

eurobond [ˈjʊərəʊbɒnd] N *Fin* euro-obligation *f*

Eurocard® [ˈjʊərəʊkɑːd] N *Banking* Eurocarte® *f*

Eurocheque [ˈjʊərəʊˌtʃek] N *Br Banking* eurochèque *m*

Eurocommunism [ˌjʊərəʊˈkɒmjʊˌnɪzəm] N eurocommunisme *m*

Eurocracy [jʊəˈrɒkrəsɪ] N eurocratie *f*

Eurocrat [ˈjʊərəʊkræt] N eurocrate *mf*

eurocredit [ˈjʊərəʊˌkredɪt] N *Com* eurocrédit *m*

eurocurrency [ˈjʊərəʊˌkʌrənsɪ] N *Banking* eurodevise *f*, euromonnaie *f*
▸▸ ***eurocurrency market*** marché *m* des eurodevises

eurodollar [ˈjʊərəʊˌdɒlə(r)] N *Fin* eurodollar *m*

Euro-election N **the Euro-elections** les élections *fpl* européennes

Eurofranc [ˈjʊərəʊfræŋk] N *Fin* eurofranc *m*

Euroland [ˈjʊərəʊlænd] N *Pol* Eurolande *f*

Euroloan [ˈjʊərəʊləʊn] N *Fin* eurocrédit *m*

Euromarket [ˈjʊərəʊˌmɑːkɪt] N *Fin* marché *m* des eurodevises, euromarché *m*

Euro-MP N *EU* (*abbr* **European Member of Parliament**) député *m ou* parlementaire *m* européen

Europe [ˈjʊərəp] N Europe *f*; *Br (continental Europe)* Europe *f* continentale; **in E.** en Europe; **in Britain, E. has become a sensitive political subject** en Grande-Bretagne, la question de l'Union européenne est un sujet très délicat; **when Britain went into E. in 1973** quand la Grande-Bretagne est devenue membre de la CEE en 1973
▸▸ ***Europe agreement*** accord *m* européen; *Br Pol* ***Europe Minister*** ministre *m* pour l'Europe

European [ˌjʊərəˈpiːən] N *(inhabitant of Europe)* Européen(enne) *m,f*; *(pro-Europe)* partisan *m* de l'Europe unie, Européen(enne) *m,f*
ADJ européen; **we must adopt a more E. outlook** nous devons adopter un point de vue plus européen *ou* plus ouvert sur l'Europe; **the Single E. Market** le marché unique (européen)
▸▸ ***European Atomic Energy Community*** Communauté *f* européenne de l'énergie atomique; ***European Bank for Reconstruction and Development*** Banque *f* européenne pour la reconstruction et le développement; ***European Broadcasting Union*** Union *f* européenne de radiodiffusion, UER *f*; ***European Central Bank*** banque *f* centrale européenne; *Pol* ***European Coal and Steel Community*** Communauté *f* européenne de charbon et de l'acier; ***European Commission*** Commission *f* européenne; ***European Commissioner*** commissaire *m* européen; *Am* ***European Common Market*** Marché *m* commun européen; *Pol* ***European Community*** Communauté *f* européenne; ***European Convention on Human Rights*** Convention *f* européenne des droits de l'homme; ***European Convention for the Protection of Human Rights and Fundamental Freedoms*** Convention *f* européenne de sauvegarde des droits de l'homme et des libertés fondamentales; *EU* ***European Court of Human Rights*** Cour *f* européenne des droits de l'homme; *EU* ***European Court of Justice*** Cour *f* européenne de justice; *Ftbl* ***European Cup*** Coupe *f* d'Europe; *Fin* ***European currency snake*** serpent *m* monétaire européen; *Formerly Fin* ***European Currency Unit*** Unité *f* monétaire européenne; *Fin* ***European Development Fund*** Fonds *m* européen de développement; *Pol* ***European Economic Area*** Espace *m* économique européen; *Formerly* ***European Economic Community*** Communauté *f* économique européenne; *Formerly Fin* ***European Exchange Rate Mechanism*** mécanisme *m* de change européen; ***European Free Trade Association*** Association *f* européenne de libre-échange; ***European Health Insurance Card*** carte *f* européenne d'assurance maladie; ***European Investment Bank*** Banque *f* européenne d'investissement; *Fin* ***European monetary agreement*** accord *m* monétaire européen; *Fin* ***European Monetary Fund*** Fonds *m* monétaire européen; *Fin* ***European Monetary Institute*** Institut *m* monétaire européen; *Formerly Fin* ***European Monetary System*** Système *m* monétaire européen; ***European Parliament*** Parlement *m* européen; *EU* ***European Patent Office*** Office *m* européen des brevets; *Am* ***European plan*** *(in hotel)* chambre *f* sans pension; ***European Regional Development Fund*** Fonds *m* européen de développement régional; *Fin* ***European Social Fund*** Fonds *m* social européen; ***European Space Agency*** Agence *f* spatiale européenne; ***European Standards Commission*** Comité *m* européen de normalisation; ***European Union*** Union *f* européenne

Europeanism [ˌjʊərəˈpiːənɪzəm] N européanisme *m*

Europeanist [ˌjʊərəˈpiːənɪst] N européaniste *mf*
ADJ européaniste

Europeanize, -ise [ˌjʊərəˈpiːənaɪz] VT européaniser

European-style option N *St Exch* option *f* européenne

Europhile [ˈjʊərəʊfaɪl] N europhile *mf*, partisan *m* de l'Europe unie

Europhobe [ˈjʊərəʊfəʊb] N europhobe *mf*

Europhobic [ˌjʊərəʊˈfəʊbɪk] ADJ europhobique

Europol [ˈjʊərəʊpɒl] N Europol *m*

Euro-rebel N *Br* = politicien qui s'oppose à la ligne pro-européenne de son parti

Eurosceptic [ˈjʊərəʊˌskeptɪk] N *Br* eurosceptique *mf*

Euroscepticism [ˈjʊərəʊˌskeptɪsɪzəm] N *Br* euroscepticisme *m*

Euroseat [ˈjʊərəʊsiːt] N = siège de député européen

Eurospeak [ˈjʊərəʊspiːk] N jargon *m* communautaire

Eurostar® [ˈjʊərəʊstɑː(r)] N Eurostar® *m*

Eurostat [ˈjʊərəʊstæt] N Eurostat *m*

Eurotourism [ˈjʊərəʊˌtʊərɪzəm] N eurotourisme *m*

Eurotunnel® [ˈjʊərəʊˌtʌnəl] N Eurotunnel® *m*

Eurovision® [ˈjʊərəʊˌvɪʒən] N Eurovision® *f*; **who won E. last year?** qui a gagné le concours de l'Eurovision l'année dernière?
▸▸ ***the Eurovision® Song Contest*** le concours Eurovision® de la chanson

euroyen [ˈjʊərəʊjen] N *Fin* euroyen *m*

eurozone [ˈjʊərəʊzəʊn] N *EU* zone *f* euro

Eustachian tube [juːˈsteɪʃən-] N *Anat* trompe *f* d'Eustache

euthanasia [ˌjuːθəˈneɪzjə] N euthanasie *f*; **voluntary e.** euthanasie *f* volontaire *ou* active

EVA [ˌiːviːˈeɪ] N (*abbr* **economic value added**) VAE *f*

evacuate [ɪˈvækjʊeɪt] VT *(place, population)* évacuer; *Tech (exhaust gases)* refouler; *Phys (create vacuum in)* faire le vide dans; **children were evacuated to the countryside** les enfants ont été évacués vers la campagne; *Physiol* **to e. the bowels** vider les intestins

evacuation [ɪˌvækjʊˈeɪʃən] N *(of place, people, bowels)* évacuation *f*; *Tech (of exhaust gases)* refoulement *m*; *Phys (creation of vacuum)* production *f* du vide

evacuee [ɪˌvækjuːˈiː] N évacué(e) *m,f*

evade [ɪˈveɪd] VT **1** *(escape from ▸ pursuers)* échapper à; *(▸ punishment)* échapper à, se soustraire à **2** *(avoid ▸ blow, responsibility)* éviter, esquiver; *(▸ question)* esquiver, éluder; *(▸ eyes, glance)* éviter; **he has so far evaded arrest/detection** jusqu'à présent il a échappé à toute arrestation/détection; **to e. the issue** éluder le problème; **to e. tax** frauder le fisc; **success evades him** le succès lui échappe

> Note that the French verb **s'évader** is a false friend and is never a translation for the English verb **to evade**. It means **to escape**.

evader [ɪˈveɪdə(r)] N **tax e.** fraudeur(euse) *m,f* du fisc

evaluate [ɪˈvæljʊeɪt] VT **1** *(damages, worth)* évaluer, déterminer le montant de **2** *(assess ▸ situation, success, work)* évaluer, former un jugement sur la valeur de; *(▸ evidence, reasons)* peser, évaluer; *(▸ quality)* évaluer; *(▸ importance, effect)* mesurer **3** *Math* évaluer

evaluation [ɪˌvæljʊˈeɪʃən] N **1** *(of damages, worth)* évaluation *f* **2** *(of situation, work)* évaluation *f*, jugement *m*; *(of evidence, reasons, quality, importance, effect)* évaluation *f*

evanescent [ˌiːvəˈnesənt] ADJ *Literary* évanescent, fugitif

evangelical [ˌiːvænˈdʒelɪkəl] *Rel* ADJ *(relating to Gospels)* évangélique; **e. preacher** évangéliste *mf*; **an e. Christian/church/sect** un chrétien/une église/une secte évangélique; **e. zeal** zèle *m* religieux; *Fig* **an e. vegetarian/communist** un végétarien/communiste à tout crin
N évangélique *m*

evangelicalism [ˌiːvænˈdʒelɪkəlɪzəm] N *Rel* évangélisme *m*

evangelism [ɪˈvændʒɪlɪzəm] N *Rel* évangélisme *m*

evangelist [ɪˈvændʒɪlɪst] N **1** *(preacher)* évangélisateur(trice) *m,f* **2** *Fig (zealous advocate)* prêcheur(euse) *m,f*
• **Evangelist** N *Bible* évangéliste *m*

evangelize, -ise [ɪˈvændʒɪlaɪz] VT *Rel* évangéliser, prêcher l'Évangile à
VI **1** *Rel* prêcher l'Évangile **2** *Fig (advocate)* prêcher; **he has been evangelizing about jazz for years** il prêche les mérites du jazz depuis des années

evaporate [ɪˈvæpəreɪt] VI *(liquid)* s'évaporer; *Fig (hopes, enthusiasm)* s'envoler, se volatiliser; *(doubts, fears)* se dissiper
VT faire évaporer

evaporation [ɪˌvæpəˈreɪʃən] N *(of liquid)* évaporation *f*; *Fig* **this meant the e. of their hopes** ceci marqua la fin de leurs espoirs

evaporator [ɪˈvæpəˌreɪtə(r)] N *Ind* évaporateur *m*

evasion [ɪˈveɪʒən] N **1** *(avoidance ▸ of duty, responsibility, question)* dérobade *f* (**of** devant) **2** *(deception, trickery)* détour *m*, faux-fuyant *m*, échappatoire *f*; **to answer without e.** répondre sans détours *ou* sans biaiser

> Note that the French word **évasion** is a false friend and is rarely a translation for the English word **evasion**. Its most common meaning is **escape**.

evasive [ɪˈveɪsɪv] ADJ évasif; **an e. answer** une réponse évasive *ou* de Normand; **to take e. action** *(gen)* louvoyer; *Mil* effectuer une manœuvre dilatoire

evasively [ɪˈveɪsɪvlɪ] ADV évasivement; **he replied e.** il a répondu en termes évasifs

evasiveness [ɪˈveɪsɪvnɪs] N caractère *m* évasif; **her e. increased our suspicions** ses propos évasifs ont renforcé nos soupçons

EVC [ˌiːviːˈsiː] N *Mktg* (*abbr* **economic value to the customer**) valeur *f* économique apportée au consommateur

Eve [iːv] PR N *Bible* Ève

eve [iːv] **N 1** *(day before)* veille *f*; **on the e. of the election** à la veille des élections **2** *Arch or Literary (evening)* soir *m*; **on a summer's e.** un soir d'été

EVEN [ˈiːvən]

ADJ
• plat **1** • égal **2–4**
• pair **5**
ADV
• même **1** • encore **2**
VT
• égaliser

ADJ 1 *(level)* plat, plan; *(smooth)* uni, égal; **to make sth e.** égaliser *ou* aplanir qch; **it's e. with the desk** c'est au même niveau que le bureau
2 *(steady ▸ breathing, temperature)* égal; *(▸ rate, rhythm)* régulier
3 *(equal ▸ distribution, spread)* égal; **the score is** *or* **the scores are e.** ils sont à égalité; **now we're e.** nous voilà quittes, nous sommes quittes maintenant; **there's an e. chance he'll lose** il y a une chance sur deux qu'il perde; **the odds** *or* **chances are about e.** les chances sont à peu près égales; *Am* **to lay e. odds** donner à égalité; *Am* **the bookmakers are offering e. odds** les bookmakers offrent un enjeu égal; **they are an e. match** ils sont à partie égale; **to bet e. money** *(gen)* donner chances égales; *(in betting)* parier le même enjeu; **to get e. with sb** se venger de qn; **I'll get e. with you for that!** je vous revaudrai ça!; *Fam* **to be e. Stevens** être quitte
4 *(calm ▸ temper)* égal; *(▸ voice)* égal, calme; **to have an e. disposition** être d'un naturel calme
5 *(number)* pair
ADV 1 *(indicating surprise)* même; **he e. works on Sundays** il travaille même le dimanche; **e. the teacher laughed** même le professeur a ri, le professeur lui-même a ri; **she's e. forgotten his name** elle a oublié jusqu'à son nom; **he e. said so** il a été jusqu'à le dire, il l'a même dit; **without e. apologizing** sans même *ou* sans seulement s'excuser; **not e.** même pas
2 *(with comparative) (still)* encore; **e. better** encore mieux; **e. more tired** encore plus fatigué; **e. less** encore moins
3 *(qualifying)* **he seemed indifferent, e. hostile** il avait l'air indifférent, hostile même
VT égaliser, aplanir; **to e. the odds** égaliser les chances
• **even as CONJ 1** *Formal (at the very moment that)* au moment même où; **e. as we speak** au moment même où nous parlons
2 *Arch or Literary (just as)* comme; **it came to pass e. as he had foretold** tout arriva comme il l'avait prédit
• **even if CONJ** même si; **e. if I say so myself** sans fausse modestie; **e. if he did say that, what does it matter?** et même s'il a dit ça, quelle importance est-ce que ça a?
• **even now ADV 1** *(despite what happened before)* même maintenant; **e. now, four years later, I still haven't got over it** aujourd'hui encore, quatre ans plus tard, je ne m'en suis pas encore remis
2 *Literary (at this very moment)* en ce moment même
• **even so ADV** *(nevertheless)* quand même, pourtant; **yes, but e. so** oui, mais quand même
• **even then ADV 1** *(in that case also)* quand même; **but e. then we wouldn't be able to afford it** mais nous ne pourrions quand même pas nous le permettre
2 *(at that time also)* même à ce moment-là; **things were difficult enough e. then** les choses étaient assez difficiles même à ce moment-là; **e. then she wouldn't believe me** elle ne m'a pas cru pour autant
• **even though CONJ e. though he tries** malgré ses efforts; **e. though she explained it in detail** bien qu'elle l'ait expliqué en détail
• **even with PREP** même avec, malgré
▸ **even out VT SEP** *(surface)* égaliser, aplanir; *(prices)* égaliser; *(supply)* répartir *ou* distribuer plus également
VI *(surface)* s'égaliser, s'aplanir; *(prices)* s'égaliser; *(supply)* être réparti plus également
▸ **even up VT SEP 1** *(make equal ▸ score etc)* égaliser; **to e. things up** rétablir l'équilibre **2** *(sum)* arrondir au chiffre supérieur; **let's e. it up to a pound** arrondissons la somme à une livre

even-handed ADJ équitable, impartial

evening [ˈiːvnɪŋ] **N 1** *(part of day)* soir *m*; **(good) e.!** bonsoir!; **in the e.** le soir; **it is 8 o'clock in the e.** il est 8 heures du soir; **I'm hardly ever at home** *Br* **in the e.** *orAm* **evenings** je suis rarement chez moi le soir; **this e.** ce soir; **that e.** ce soir-là; **yesterday e.** hier soir; **tomorrow e.** demain soir; **on the e. of the next day, on the following e.** le lendemain soir, le soir suivant; **(on) the previous e.** la veille au soir; **on the e. of the fifteenth** le quinze au soir; **on the e. of her departure** le soir de son départ; **one fine spring e.** (par) un beau soir de printemps; **every e.** tous les soirs, chaque soir; **every Friday e.** tous les vendredis soir *ou* soirs; **on the e. of Monday, 29 March** dans la soirée du lundi 29 mars; **the long winter evenings** les longues soirées *ou* veillées d'hiver; **I work evenings** je travaille le soir; *Sport* **an e. match** une nocturne; *Fig* **in the e. of her life** au soir *ou* au déclin de sa vie **2** *(length of time)* soirée *f*; **all e.** toute la soirée; **we spent the e. playing cards** nous avons passé la soirée à jouer aux cartes; **thank you for a lovely e.** merci pour cette charmante soirée **3** *(entertainment)* soirée *f*; **a musical e.** une soirée musicale
COMP *(newspaper, train)* du soir
▸▸ ***evening bag*** sac *m* à main de soirée; ***evening class*** cours *m* du soir; ***evening dress*** *(for men)* tenue *f* de soirée, habit *m*; *(for women)* robe *f* du soir; **in e. dress** *(man)* en tenue de soirée; *(woman)* en robe du soir, en toilette de soirée; ***evening fixture*** rencontre *f* sportive en nocturne; ***evening gown*** robe *f* de soirée *ou* du soir; ***evening meal*** dîner *m*; *Cin & Theat* ***evening performance*** soirée *f*; **the e. performance starts at 7.30** *Theat* en soirée la représentation débute à 19h30; *Cin* en soirée la séance débute à 19h30; *Rel* ***evening prayers*** office *m ou* service *m* du soir; *Bot* ***evening primrose*** onagre *f*, herbe *f* aux ânes; ***evening primrose oil*** huile *f* d'onagre; *Rel* ***evening service*** office *m ou* service *m* du soir; *Astron* ***evening star*** étoile *f* du berger; ***evening wear*** *(UNCOUNT) (for men)* tenue *f* de soirée, habit *m*; *(for women)* robe *f* du soir

> When translating **evening**, note that **soir** and **soirée** are not interchangeable. **Soir** is used to refer to the evening as part of the day as opposed to the morning or the afternoon. For **soirée**, the emphasis is on duration.

evenly [ˈiːvənlɪ] **ADV 1** *(breathe, move)* régulièrement; *(talk)* calmement, posément **2** *(equally ▸ divide)* également, de façon égale; *(▸ spread)* de façon égale, régulièrement; **they are e. matched** ils sont de force égale; **it was an e. contested game** c'est une partie qui a opposé des adversaires de force égale

evenness [ˈiːvənnɪs] **N 1** *(of surface)* égalité *f*, caractère *m* lisse **2** *(of competition, movement)* régularité *f*

even-numbered ADJ (portant un nombre) pair

evens [ˈiːvənz] **NPL** *Br* **to lay e.** donner à égalité; **the bookmakers are offering e.** les bookmakers offrent un enjeu égal
▸▸ ***evens favourite*** favori(ite) *m,f* à égalité

evensong [ˈiːvənsɒŋ] **N** *Rel (Anglican)* office *m* du soir; *(Roman Catholic)* vêpres *fpl*

event [ɪˈvent] **N 1** *(happening)* événement *m*; **a historical e.** un événement historique; **in the course of events** par la suite, au cours des événements; **in the normal course of events** normalement; **as recent events have shown** comme l'ont montré de récents événements; **I realized after the e.** j'ai réalisé après coup; **the party was quite an e.** la soirée était un véritable événement; **when's the happy e.?** *(birth)* quand l'heureux événement doit-il avoir lieu? **2** *(organized activity)* manifestation *f*; **the society organizes a number of social events** l'association organise un certain nombre de soirées *ou* de rencontres **3** *Sport (meeting)* manifestation *f*; *(competition)* épreuve *f*; *(in horseracing)* course *f*; **field events** épreuves *fpl* d'athlétisme; **track events** épreuves *fpl* sur piste; **what was your best e.?** quelle a été ta meilleure discipline?
• **at all events, in any event ADV** en tout cas, de toute façon
• **in either event ADV** dans l'un ou l'autre cas
• **in the event ADV** en fait, en l'occurence; **a result that in the e. was most satisfying** un résultat qui était en fait très satisfaisant
• **in the event of PREP in the e. of rain** en cas de pluie; **in the e. of her refusing** au cas où *ou* dans le cas où elle refuserait
• **in the event that CONJ** au cas où; **in the unlikely e. that he comes** au cas *ou* dans le cas fort improbable où il viendrait
▸▸ *Mktg* ***event advertising*** publicité *f* par l'événement; *Astron* ***event horizon*** horizon *m* des événements; ***event management*** organisation d'événements; ***event manager*** responsable *m* d'événements; *Mktg* ***event promotion*** communication *f* événementielle

even-tempered ADJ d'humeur égale; **of an e. disposition** d'humeur égale

eventer [ɪˈventə(r)] **N** *Horseriding* participant(e) *m,f* au concours complet

eventful [ɪˈventfʊl] **ADJ** *(busy ▸ day, holiday, life)* mouvementé, fertile en événements

eventide [ˈiːvəntaɪd] **N** *Literary* soir *m*, tombée du jour
▸▸ *Br* ***eventide home*** maison *f* de retraite

eventing [ɪˈventɪŋ] **N** *Horseriding* participation au concours complet

eventual [ɪˈventʃʊəl] **ADJ** *(final)* final, ultime; *(resulting)* qui s'ensuit; **bad management led to the e. collapse of the company** une mauvaise gestion a finalement provoqué la faillite de l'entreprise; **the disease causes deterioration of the muscles and e. paralysis** la maladie entraîne la dégénérescence des muscles et la paralysie qui en résulte *ou* qui s'ensuit

> Note that the French word **éventuel** is a false friend and is never a translation for the English word **eventual**. It means **possible**.

eventuality [ɪˌventʃʊˈælətɪ] *(pl* **eventualities) N** éventualité *f*

eventually [ɪˈventʃʊəlɪ] **ADV** finalement, en fin de compte; **I'll get around to it e.** je le ferai un jour ou l'autre; **he'll get tired of it e.** il s'en lassera à la longue, il finira par s'en lasser; **she e. became a lawyer** elle a fini par devenir avocat; **the people who will e. benefit from these changes** les personnes qui, en fin de compte *ou* en définitive, bénéficieront de ces changements; **our arguments e. persuaded him** nos arguments ont fini par le convaincre *ou* l'ont finalement convaincu

> Note that the French word **éventuellement** is a false friend and is never a translation for the English word **eventually**. It means **possibly**.

eventuate [ɪˈventʃʊeɪt] **VI** *Formal* arriver, se produire; **his illness eventuated in death** sa maladie a fini par l'emporter

EVER [ˈevə(r)]

• toujours **1** • jamais **2, 3**

ADV 1 *(always)* toujours; **e. more important** de plus en plus important; **e.-increasing influence** influence toujours croissante *ou* qui croît de jour en jour; **an e.-present fear** une peur constante; **e. hopeful/the pessimist, he...** toujours plein d'espoir/pessimiste, il...
2 *(at any time)* jamais; **have you e. met him?** l'avez-vous jamais rencontré?; **nothing e. happens** il n'arrive *ou* ne se passe jamais rien; **all they e. do is work** ils ne font que travailler; **he hardly** *or* **scarcely e. smokes** il ne fume presque jamais; **don't e. come in here again!** ne mettez plus jamais les pieds ici!; **she was as cheerful as e.** elle était aussi gaie qu'à l'habitude; *Am* **e. and again** de temps à autre, de temps en temps
3 *(with comparatives, superlatives)* **lovelier/more slowly than e.** plus joli/plus lentement que jamais; **he's as sarcastic as e.** il est toujours aussi sarcastique; **the first/biggest e.** le tout premier/plus grand qu'on ait jamais vu; **the worst earthquake e.** le pire tremblement de terre qu'on ait jamais connu; **the best** *Br* **holiday** *or Am* **vacation we've e. had** les meilleures vacances qu'on ait jamais eues
4 *Fam (in exclamations) Am* **is it e. big!** comme c'est grand!ᵁ; *Am* **was he e. angry!** qu'est-ce qu'il

était furax!; *Am* **do you enjoy dancing? – do I e.!** aimez-vous danser? – et comment!; *Am* **was I e. grateful for your help!** je te suis vraiment reconnaissant de m'avoir donné un coup de main!; **well, did you e.!** ça, par exemple!

5 *(as intensifier)* **as quickly as e. you can** aussi vite que vous pourrez; **before e. they** *or* **before they e. set out** avant même qu'ils partent

6 *(in questions)* **how e. did you manage that?** comment donc y êtes-vous parvenu?; **what e. is the matter with you?** mais qu'est-ce que vous avez donc?; **when will they e. stop?** quand donc arrêteront-ils?; **where e. can it be?** où diable peut-il être?; **where e. have you been?** d'où venez-vous donc?; **who e. told you that?** qui est-ce qui a bien pu vous dire cela?; **who e. can it be?** qui est-ce que ça peut bien être?; **why e. not?** mais enfin, pourquoi pas?

• **ever after** ADV pour toujours; **they lived happily e. after** ils vécurent heureux jusqu'à la fin de leurs jours

• **ever so** ADV **1** *Fam (extremely)* vraiment□; **she's e. so clever** elle est vraiment intelligente; **it's e. so kind of you** c'est vraiment aimable à vous; **e. so slightly off-centre** un tout petit peu décentré; **thanks e. so (much)** merci vraiment

2 *Formal (however)* **no teacher, be he e. so patient...** aucun enseignant, aussi patient soit-il...

• **ever such** ADJ *Fam* vraiment□; **they've got e. such pretty curtains in the shop** ils ont vraiment de jolis rideaux dans ce magasin

evergreen ['evəgriːn] N **1** *(tree)* arbre *m* à feuilles persistantes; *(conifer)* conifère *m*; *(bush)* arbuste *m* à feuilles persistantes **2** *Fig (song, story)* chanson *f* ou histoire *f* qui ne vieillit jamais

ADJ **1** *(bush, tree)* à feuilles persistantes **2** *Fig (song, story)* qui ne vieillit pas; **an e. topic** une question toujours d'actualité

▸▸ *Fin* ***evergreen fund*** fonds *m* de crédit permanent non confirmé

everlasting [ˌevə'lɑːstɪŋ] ADJ **1** *(eternal ▸ hope, mercy)* éternel, infini; *(▸ fame)* éternel, immortel; *(▸ God, life)* éternel; **Henry, to his e. credit, said nothing** Henry n'a rien dit, ce qui est tout à son honneur **2** *(incessant)* perpétuel, éternel; **a life of e. misery** une vie de misère

N *Bot* immortelle *f*

▸▸ *Bot* ***everlasting flower*** immortelle *f*

everlastingly [ˌevə'lɑːstɪŋlɪ] ADV **1** *(eternally)* éternellement **2** *(incessantly)* sans cesse, perpétuellement

evermore [ˌevə'mɔː(r)] ADV toujours; **for e.** pour toujours, à jamais

EVERY ['evrɪ]

• tout **1–3** • chaque **1**
• chacun **4**

ADJ **1** *(each)* tout, chaque; **e. room has a view of the sea** les chambres ont toutes vue *ou* toutes les chambres ont vue sur la mer; **not e. room is as big as this** toutes les chambres ne sont pas aussi grandes que celle-ci; **e. word he says** tout ce qu'il dit; **he drank e. drop** il a bu jusqu'à la dernière goutte; **e. one of these apples** chacune de *ou* toutes ces pommes; **I've read e. one** je les ai lus tous; **e. one of them arrived late** ils sont tous arrivés en retard; **e. (single) one of us was there** nous étions tous là (au grand complet); **e. (single) one of these pencils is broken** tous ces crayons (sans exception) sont cassés; **e. (single) person in the room** tous ceux qui étaient dans la pièce (sans exception); **e. day** tous les jours, chaque jour; **she's feeling a little better e. day** elle se sent un peu mieux chaque jour; **at e. opportunity** chaque fois que c'est/c'était possible; **from e. side** de tous (les) côtés; **e. time I go out** chaque fois que je sors; **that's what fools them e. time** c'est ce qui les trompe à tous les coups *ou* à chaque fois; **of e. age/e. sort/e. colour** de tout âge/toute sorte/toutes les couleurs; **in e. way** *(by any means)* par tous les moyens; *(from any viewpoint)* à tous (les) égards, sous tous les rapports; *Prov* **e. little helps** les petits ruisseaux font les grandes rivières; **I can only give you half an hour – e. little helps** je ne peux t'accorder qu'une demi-heure – c'est mieux que rien; **e. man for himself** chacun pour soi; *(in danger)* sauve qui peut!; **e. person has this right** chacun a ce droit; **e. man Jack of them** tous sans exception

2 *(with units of time, measurement etc)* tout; **e. two days, e. second day, e. other day** tous les deux jours, un jour sur deux; **e. quarter of an hour** tous les quarts d'heure; **e. few days** tous les deux ou trois jours; **e. few minutes** toutes les cinq minutes; **once e. month** une fois par mois; **e. ten miles** tous les dix miles; **e. third man** un homme sur trois; **three women out of** *or* **in e. ten, three out of e. ten women** trois femmes sur dix; **e. other Sunday** un dimanche sur deux; **write on e. other line** écrivez en sautant une ligne sur deux

3 *(indicating confidence, optimism)* tout; **I have e. confidence that...** je ne doute pas un instant que...; **there's e. chance that we'll succeed** nous avons toutes les chances de réussir; **you have e. reason to be happy** vous avez toutes les raisons *ou* tout lieu d'être heureux; **you have e. right to be angry** tu as tout à fait le droit d'être en colère; **we wish you e. success** nous vous souhaitons très bonne chance

4 *(with possessive adj)* chacun, moindre; **his e. action bears witness to it** chacun de ses gestes *ou* tout ce qu'il fait en témoigne; **they hung on his e. word** ils ne perdaient pas un seul mot de ce qu'il disait; **her e. wish** son moindre désir, tous ses désirs

• **every now and again, every once in a while, every so often** ADV de temps en temps, de temps à autre

• **every which way** ADV *Am (everywhere)* partout; *(from all sides)* de toutes parts; **he came home with his hair e. which way** il est rentré les cheveux en bataille

everybody ['evrɪˌbɒdɪ] = **everyone**

everyday ['evrɪdeɪ] ADJ *(daily)* de tous les jours, quotidien; *(ordinary)* banal, ordinaire; **my e. routine** mon train-train quotidien; **e. life** la vie quotidienne, la vie de tous les jours; **it's an e. occurrence** cela arrive tous les jours; **an e. expression** une expression courante; **in e. use** d'usage courant; **for e. wear** pour porter tous les jours

Everyman ['evrɪmæn] N l'homme *m* de la rue

everyone ['evrɪwʌn] PRON tout le monde, chacun; **as e. knows** comme chacun *ou* tout le monde le sait; **e. knows that!** tout le monde *ou* n'importe qui sait cela!; **not e. can do it** ce n'est pas tout le monde qui pourrait le faire; **e. here/in this room** tout le monde ici/dans cette pièce; **e. else** tous les autres; **e. who was anyone was there** tous les gens qui comptent étaient là

everyplace ['evrɪˌpleɪs] *Am* = **everywhere** ADV

everything ['evrɪθɪŋ] PRON **1** *(all things)* tout; **e. he says** tout ce qu'il dit; **they sell e.** ils vendent de tout; **she means e. to me** elle est tout pour moi, je ne vis que pour elle; **don't believe e. you hear** il ne faut pas croire tout ce que tu entends; **he's got e. going for him** il a tout pour lui; *Fam* **a party with clowns, cakes and e.** une fête avec des clowns, des gâteaux et tout; *Fam* **I like her and e., but I wouldn't want to live with her** je l'aime bien, ce n'est pas la question, mais je n'aimerais pas vivre avec elle□ **2** *(the most important thing)* l'essentiel *m*; **winning is e.** l'essentiel, c'est de gagner; **money/beauty isn't e.** il n'y a pas que l'argent/la beauté qui compte

everywhere ['evrɪweə(r)] ADV partout; **I looked for it e.** je l'ai cherché partout; **e. she went** partout où elle allait; **Internet cafés are e. these days** on trouve des cafés Internet partout de nos jours; **he's been e.** il est allé partout; **e. you look there is poverty** de quelque côté que l'on se tourne, on voit la pauvreté; *Fam* **the files were e.** *(in disorder)* les dossiers étaient rangés n'importe comment

PRON *Fam* tout□; **e.'s in such a mess** tout est sens dessus dessous

evict [ɪ'vɪkt] VT *(tenant)* expulser, chasser

evictee [ɪˌvɪk'tiː] N *(tenant)* expulsé

eviction [ɪ'vɪkʃən] N expulsion *f*

▸▸ ***eviction notice*** mandat *m* d'expulsion; ***eviction order*** ordre *m* d'expulsion

evidence ['evɪdəns] N **1** *(reason for belief)* preuve *f*; *(testimony)* témoignage *m*; **we have clear e. that...** on a la preuve manifeste que...; **on the e. of eye witnesses** à en croire les témoins; **on the e. of their past performances** à en juger par leurs performances passées **2** *Law (proof)* preuves *fpl*; *(testimony)* témoignage *m*; **a piece of e.** une preuve; **to give e. against/for sb** témoigner contre/en faveur de qn; **oral/written e.** preuve *f* orale/littérale *ou* par écrit; **whatever you say may be held in e. against you** tout ce que vous direz pourra être retenu contre vous; **the e. is against him** les preuves pèsent contre lui; *Br* **to turn King's** *or* **Queen's e.**, *Am* **to turn State's e.** témoigner contre ses complices *(sous promesse de pardon)* **3** *(indication)* signe *m*, marque *f*; **to bear e. of sth** porter la marque de qch; **to show e. of sth** laisser voir qch; **her face showed no e. of her anger** son visage ne témoignait pas de *ou* ne trahissait pas sa colère; **this problem is very much in e. in Scotland** c'est un problème réel en Écosse; **his daughter was nowhere in e.** sa fille n'était pas là *ou* n'était pas présente; **a politician very much in e. these days** un homme politique très en vue ces temps-ci

VT *Formal* manifester, montrer; **as evidenced by the report that's just been published** comme en témoigne le rapport qui vient d'être publié

> Note that the French word **évidence** is a false friend and is never a translation for the English word **evidence**. It means **obviousness**.

evident ['evɪdənt] ADJ évident, manifeste; **with e. pleasure** avec un plaisir manifeste; **it is e. from the way she talks** cela se voit à sa manière de parler; **it is quite e. that he's not interested** on voit bien qu'il ne s'y intéresse pas, il ne s'y intéresse pas, c'est évident; **he's lying, that's e.** il ment, c'est évident

evidently ['evɪdəntlɪ] ADV **1** *(apparently)* apparemment; **did he refuse? – e. not** a-t-il refusé? – non apparemment *ou* à ce qu'il paraît; **unemployment is e. rising again** de toute évidence le chômage est à nouveau en hausse **2** *(clearly)* de toute évidence, manifestement; **e. worried** manifestement inquiet; **he was e. in pain** il était évident *ou* clair qu'il souffrait

> Note that the French word **évidemment** is a false friend and is never a translation for the English word **evidently**. It means **of course**.

evil ['iːvəl] *(Br compar* **eviller**, *superl* **evillest**, *Am compar* **eviler**, *superl* **evilest)** ADJ **1** *(wicked ▸ person)* malveillant, méchant; *(▸ deed, plan, reputation)* mauvais; *(▸ influence)* néfaste; *(▸ doctrine, spell, spirit)* maléfique; **he's in an e. mood** il est d'une humeur massacrante; **to have an e. tongue** être mauvaise langue; **he had his e. way with her** il est arrivé à ses fins avec elle; **to put off the e. day** *or* **hour** repousser le moment fatidique; **of e. repute** *(place)* mal famé; **the E. One** le Malin **2** *(smell, taste)* infect, infâme

N mal *m*; **to speak e. of sb** dire du mal de qn; **social evils** plaies *fpl* sociales, maux *mpl* sociaux; **the evils of drink** les conséquences *fpl* funestes de la boisson; **a necessary e.** un mal nécessaire; **pollution is one of the evils of our era** la pollution est un fléau de notre époque; **it's the lesser e.** *or* **of two evils** c'est le moindre mal; **to give sb evils** fusiller qn du regard

▸▸ ***the evil eye*** le mauvais œil; **to give sb the e. eye** jeter le mauvais œil à qn

evildoer ['iːvəlˌduːə(r)] N méchant(e) *m,f*, scélérat(e) *m,f*

evil-looking ADJ *(person)* qui a l'air mauvais; *(weapon)* menaçant

evilly ['iːvəllɪ] ADV *(smile, say)* avec malveillance; *(look)* d'un mauvais œil, d'un air méchant

evil-minded ADJ malveillant, mal intentionné

evil-smelling ADJ *Br* nauséabond

evince [ɪ'vɪns] VT *Formal (show ▸ interest, surprise)* manifester, montrer; *(▸ quality)* faire preuve de, manifester

> Note that the French verb **évincer** is a false friend and is never a translation for the English verb **to evince**. It means **to oust**.

eviscerate [ɪ'vɪsəreɪt] VT *Formal* éventrer, étriper; *Med* éviscérer

evisceration [ɪ,vɪsə'reɪʃən] N *Formal & Med* éviscération *f*

evocation [,evəʊ'keɪʃən] N évocation *f*

evocative [ɪ'vɒkətɪv] ADJ *(picture, scent)* évocateur; **to be e. of sth** évoquer qch

evoke [ɪ'vəʊk] VT **1** *(summon up ▸ memory, spirit)* évoquer **2** *(elicit ▸ admiration)* susciter; *(▸ response, smile)* susciter, provoquer

evoked set [ɪ'vəʊkt-] N *Mktg* ensemble *m* évoqué

evolution [,iːvə'luːʃən] N **1** *(of language, situation)* évolution *f*; *(of art, society, technology)* développement *m*, évolution *f*; *(of events)* développement *m*, déroulement *m*
2 *Biol, Bot & Zool* évolution *f*; **the theory of e.** la théorie de l'évolution des espèces
3 *(of dancers, troops)* évolution *f*
4 *Math* extraction *f* (de la racine)

evolutionary [,iːvə'luːʃənərɪ] ADJ **1** *Biol* évolutionniste **2** *(process)* évolutif

evolutionism [,iːvə'luːʃənɪzəm] N évolutionnisme *m*

evolutionist [,iːvə'luːʃənɪst] ADJ évolutionniste
N évolutionniste *mf*

evolve [ɪ'vɒlv] VI *(events)* se dérouler; *(situation, race)* évoluer, se développer; *Biol, Bot & Zool* évoluer; **to e. from sth** se développer à partir de qch; **the theory has evolved over the years** la théorie a évolué au fil des années; **medicine has evolved into a sophisticated science** la médecine est devenue une science sophistiquée
VT *(system, theory)* développer, élaborer

ewe [juː] N brebis *f*; **a e. lamb** une agnelle

ewer ['juːə(r)] N aiguière *f*

ex [eks] PREP **1** *Com* départ, sortie; **ex quay** à quai; **ex ship** à bord; **ex warehouse** à (prendre à) l'entrepôt, en entrepôt; **ex works** départ usine, sortie d'usine; **price ex works** prix *m* départ *ou* sortie usine **2** *Fin* sans; **ex all, ex allotment** ex-répartition *f*; **ex bonus** ex-capitalisation *f*; **ex cap, ex capitalization** ex-capitalisation *f*; **ex coupon** ex-coupon *m*, coupon *m* détaché; **ex dividend** ex-dividende *m*, dividende *m* détaché; **ex interest** sans *ou* exonéré d'intérêts; **ex new, ex rights** ex-droit *m*
N *Fam (former partner, spouse)* ex *mf*

ex- [eks] PREF ex-, ancien; **his ex-wife** son ex-femme; **he's an ex-teacher** c'est un ancien enseignant; **the ex-president** l'ancien(enne) président (e) *m,f*, l'ex-président(e) *m,f*

exacerbate [ɪg'zæsəbeɪt] VT *Formal* **1** *(make worse)* exacerber, aggraver **2** *(annoy)* énerver, exaspérer

exact [ɪg'zækt] ADJ **1** *(accurate, correct)* exact, juste; **it's an e. copy** *(picture)* c'est fidèle à l'original; *(document)* c'est une copie conforme *ou* textuelle; **she told me the e. opposite** elle m'a dit exactement le contraire; **those were her e. words** ce furent ses propres paroles, voilà ce qu'elle a dit textuellement **2** *(precise ▸ amount, idea, value)* exact, précis; *(▸ directions, place, time)* précis; **is it 5 o'clock? – 5:03 to be e.** est-il 5 heures? – 5 heures 03 plus exactement *ou* précisément; **she likes music, or to be e., classical music** elle aime la musique, ou plus précisément la musique classique; **can you be more e.?** pouvez-vous préciser?; *Fam* **the e. same dress** exactement la même robe[□] **3** *(meticulous ▸ work)* rigoureux, précis; *(▸ mind)* rigoureux; *(▸ instrument)* de précision
VT **1** *(demand ▸ money)* extorquer **2** *(insist upon ▸ obedience, discipline)* exiger
▸▸ ***exact science*** science *f* exacte; *Fig* **it's not an e. science** ce n'est pas une science exacte

exacting [ɪg'zæktɪŋ] ADJ *(person)* exigeant; *(activity, job)* astreignant, exigeant

exaction [ɪg'zækʃən] N *(act)* exaction *f*, extorsion *f*

exactitude [ɪg'zæktɪtjuːd] N exactitude *f*

exactly [ɪg'zæktlɪ] ADV **1** *(accurately)* précisément, avec précision; **I followed her instructions e.** j'ai suivi ses instructions à la lettre *ou* avec précision; **the computer can reproduce this sound e.** l'ordinateur peut reproduire exactement ce son **2** *(entirely, precisely)* exactement, justement; **I don't remember e.** je ne me rappelle pas au juste; **that's not e. what I meant** ce n'est pas exactement ce que je voulais dire; **I'm not e. sure what you mean** je ne suis pas tout à fait sûr de ce que tu veux dire; **he did e. the opposite of what I told him** il a fait exactement le contraire de ce que je lui ai dit; **it's e. the same thing** c'est exactement la même chose; **it's e. 5 o'clock** il est 5 heures juste; **it's been six months e.** cela fait six mois jour pour jour; **the journey took e. three hours** le voyage a duré très exactement trois heures; **are you ill? – not e.** êtes-vous malade? – pas exactement *ou* pas vraiment; **she didn't e. agree, but…** elle n'était pas vraiment d'accord, mais…; **e.!** exactement!, parfaitement!

exactness [ɪg'zæktnɪs] N exactitude *f*, soin *m*

exaggerate [ɪg'zædʒəreɪt] VI exagérer; **don't e.!** n'exagère pas!
VT **1** *(overstate ▸ quality, situation, size)* exagérer; *(▸ facts)* amplifier; *(▸ importance)* s'exagérer; **he is exaggerating the seriousness of the problem** il exagère la gravité du problème **2** *(emphasize)* accentuer; **she exaggerates her weakness to gain sympathy** elle se prétend plus faible qu'elle ne l'est réellement pour s'attirer la compassion; **tight trousers will e. your thinness** des pantalons serrés accentueront ta minceur *ou* te feront paraître encore plus mince

exaggerated [ɪg'zædʒəreɪtɪd] ADJ **1** *(number, story)* exagéré; *(fashion, style)* outré; **to have an e. opinion of oneself** *or* **of one's own worth** avoir une trop haute opinion de soi-même **2** *Med* exagéré

exaggeratedly [ɪg'zædʒəreɪtɪdlɪ] ADV d'une manière exagérée, exagérément

exaggeration [ɪg,zædʒə'reɪʃən] N exagération *f*; **that's an e.!** vous exagérez!/ils exagèrent!/*etc*; **it would be no e. to say that…** on pourrait dire sans exagérer *ou* sans exagération que…

exalt [ɪg'zɔːlt] VT **1** *(praise highly)* exalter, chanter les louanges de **2** *(in rank)* élever (à un rang plus important)

exalted [ɪg'zɔːltɪd] ADJ **1** *(prominent ▸ person)* de haut rang, haut placé; *(▸ position, rank)* élevé **2** *(elated)* exalté

exam [ɪg'zæm] N *Sch & Univ* examen *m*; **to sit** *or* **to take an e.** passer un examen; **to pass/to fail an e.** réussir à/échouer à un examen; **to have e. nerves** avoir le trac avant les examens; **when do the e. results come out?** quand les résultats de l'examen seront-ils connus?; **they wrote the essay under e. conditions** ils ont fait la dissertation dans les conditions de l'examen
COMP *(question)* d'examen
▸▸ ***exam board*** commission *f* d'examen; ***exam paper*** *(set of questions)* sujet *m* d'examen; *(written answer)* copie *f* (d'examen)

examination [ɪg,zæmɪ'neɪʃən] N **1** *(of records, files, proposal etc)* examen *m*; *(of building ▸ by official)* inspection *f*; *(▸ by potential buyer)* visite *f*; **it doesn't stand up to e.** *(argument, theory)* cela ne résiste pas à l'examen; *(alibi)* cela ne tient pas; **to carry out** *or* **to make an e. of sth** procéder à l'examen de qch; **her latest novel is an e. of the generation gap** son dernier roman est une analyse du fossé entre les générations; **the device was removed for e.** on a enlevé le mécanisme afin de l'examiner; **on e.** après examen; **the proposal is still under e.** la proposition est encore à l'étude
2 *Med* examen *m* médical; *(at school, work)* visite *f* médicale; *(regular)* bilan *m* de santé; **I'm just going in for an e.** j'y vais juste pour passer un examen médical
3 *Formal Sch & Univ* examen *m*; **to sit** *or* **to take an e.** passer un examen; **they wrote the essay under e. conditions** ils ont fait la dissertation dans les conditions de l'examen
4 *Law (of witness)* audition *f*; *(of suspect)* interrogatoire *m*
COMP *(question, results)* d'examen
▸▸ ***examination board*** commission *f* d'examen; ***examination paper*** *(set of questions)* sujet *m* d'examen; *(written answer)* copie *f* (d'examen)

examine [ɪg'zæmɪn] VT **1** *(inspect ▸ records, files, proposal etc)* examiner, étudier; *(▸ building)* inspecter; *(▸ baggage)* fouiller, examiner; **the weapon is being examined for fingerprints** on est en train d'examiner l'arme pour voir si elle porte des empreintes digitales; **to e. one's conscience** faire son examen de conscience
2 *Med* examiner; *Fam Hum* **he needs his head examined** il est complètement fou *ou* cinglé
3 *Sch & Univ* faire passer un examen à; *(orally)* interroger, faire passer l'épreuve orale à; **you'll be examined in French/in all six subjects/on your knowledge of the subject** vous aurez à passer un examen de français/dans ces six matières/pour évaluer vos connaissances sur le sujet
4 *Law (witness)* entendre; *(suspect)* interroger; *(case)* instruire

examinee [ɪg,zæmɪ'niː] N candidat(e) *m,f* (à un examen)

examiner [ɪg'zæmɪnə(r)] N *(in school, driving test)* examinateur(trice) *m,f*; *Sch & Univ* **the examiners** les examinateurs *mpl*, le jury

examining [ɪg'zæmɪnɪŋ] ADJ
▸▸ ***examining body*** jury *m* d'examen; *Br Law* ***examining magistrate*** juge *m* d'instruction

example [ɪg'zɑːmpəl] N **1** *(illustration)* exemple *m*; **to give just one e.,…** pour ne donner *ou* citer qu'un exemple,…; **this is an excellent e. of what I meant** ceci illustre parfaitement ce que je voulais dire; **it's a classic e. of 1960s architecture** c'est un exemple classique de l'architecture des années 60
2 *(person or action to be imitated)* exemple *m*, modèle *m*; **you're an e. to us all** vous êtes un modèle pour nous tous; **to follow sb's e.** suivre l'exemple de qn; **I followed your e. and complained about the poor service** j'ai fait comme vous et me suis plaint de la médiocrité du service; **to set an e.** montrer l'exemple; **she sets us all an e.** elle nous montre l'exemple à tous; **to set a good/bad e.** montrer le bon/mauvais exemple; **you're setting your little brother a bad e.** tu montres le mauvais exemple à ton petit frère
3 *(sample, specimen)* exemple *m*, spécimen *m*; *(of work)* échantillon *m*
4 *(warning)* exemple *m*; **let this be an e. to you** que ça te serve d'exemple; **to make an e. of sb** punir qn pour l'exemple
• **for example** ADV par exemple; **large cities, (as) for e. London** les grandes villes, telles que Londres (par exemple)

exasperate [ɪg'zɑːspəreɪt] VT exaspérer

exasperating [ɪg'zɑːspəreɪtɪŋ] ADJ exaspérant

exasperatingly [ɪg'zɑːspəreɪtɪŋlɪ] ADV **the service is e. slow in this restaurant** le service est d'une lenteur exaspérante *ou* désespérante dans ce restaurant; **he's e. arrogant** son arrogance est exaspérante

exasperation [ɪg,zɑːspə'reɪʃən] N *(irritation, frustration)* exaspération *f*; **to look at sb in e.** regarder qn avec exaspération *ou* un air exaspéré; **"shut up!," she screamed in e.** "tais-toi!," cria-t-elle, exaspérée; **I did it out of sheer e.** j'ai fait cela parce que j'étais exaspéré *ou* je n'en pouvais plus

excavate ['ekskəveɪt] VT **1** *(hole, trench)* creuser, excaver **2** *Archeol (temple, building)* mettre au jour; **to e. a site** faire des fouilles
VI *Archeol* faire des fouilles; *Constr* procéder à une excavation/des excavations

excavation [,ekskə'veɪʃən] N **1** *(of hole, trench)* excavation *f*, creusement *m* **2** *Archeol (of temple, building)* mise *f* au jour; **the excavations at Knossos** les fouilles *fpl* de Knossos

excavator ['ekskə,veɪtə(r)] N **1** *(machine)* excavateur *m*, excavatrice *f* **2** *(archaeologist)* = personne qui conduit des fouilles

exceed [ɪk'siːd] VT **1** *(be more than)* dépasser, excéder; **demand exceeded supply** la demande a excédé l'offre; **her salary exceeds mine by £5,000 a year** son salaire annuel dépasse le mien de 5000 livres **2** *(go beyond ▸ expectations, hopes, fears)* dépasser; *(▸ budget)* excéder, déborder; **to e. one's authority** outrepasser ses pouvoirs; **to e. one's instructions** aller au-delà des instructions reçues; **to e. the speed limit** dépasser la limite de vitesse, faire un excès de vitesse; **to be fined for exceeding the speed limit** avoir une amende pour excès de vitesse; **do not e. the stat**

ed dose *(on medication)* ne pas dépasser la dose prescrite

xceedingly [ɪk'si:dɪŋlɪ] **ADV** *(extremely)* extrêmement

xcel [ɪk'sel] *(pt & pp* **excelled**, *cont* **excelling)** **VI** exceller; **to e. at** *or* **in music** exceller en musique; **I've never excelled at games** je n'ai jamais été très fort en sport; **the company excels in the export field** la société excelle dans l'exportation

VT surpasser; *also Ironic* **to e. oneself** se surpasser

xcellence ['eksələns] **N** *(high quality)* qualité *f* excellente; *(commercially)* excellence *f*; **to strive for e.** s'efforcer d'atteindre une qualité excellente; **e. is our hallmark** l'excellence est notre signe distinctif; **awards for e.** prix *mpl* d'excellence; **centre of e.** centre *m* d'excellence

xcellency ['eksələnsɪ] *(pl* **Excellencies)** **N** Excellence *f*; **Your/His E.** Votre/Son Excellence

xcellent ['eksələnt] **ADJ** excellent; *(weather)* magnifique; **e.!** formidable!, parfait!

xcellently ['eksələntlɪ] **ADV** de façon excellente, superbement; **she had done e. in her exams** elle avait obtenu d'excellents résultats à ses examens; **it was e. done** cela a été fait de main de maître

xcept [ɪk'sept] **PREP** *(apart from)* à part, excepté, sauf; **everybody was there e. him, everybody e. him was there** tout le monde était là à part *ou* excepté *ou* sauf lui; **any day e. Saturday and anywhere e. here** n'importe quel jour sauf le samedi et n'importe où sauf ici; **I know nothing about it e. what he told me** je n'en sais pas plus que ce qu'il m'a dit; **I remember nothing e. that I was scared** je ne me souviens de rien sauf que *ou* excepté que j'avais peur

CONJ 1 *(apart from)* **I'll do anything e. sell the car** je ferai tout sauf vendre la voiture; **e. if** sauf *ou* à part si; **e. when** sauf *ou* à part quand **2** *(only)* seulement, mais; **I would tell her e. she wouldn't believe me** je le lui dirais bien, mais *ou* seulement elle ne me croirait pas **3** *Arch or Bible (unless)* à moins que

VT *(exclude)* excepter, exclure; **all countries, France excepted** tous les pays, la France exceptée *ou* à l'exception de la France; **present company excepted** à l'exception des personnes présentes, les personnes présentes exceptées

• **except for PREP** sauf, à part; **the typing's finished e. for the last page** il ne reste plus que la dernière page à taper; **he would have got away with it e. for that one mistake** sans cette erreur il s'en serait tiré

xcepting [ɪk'septɪŋ] **PREP** à part, excepté, sauf; **not e....** y compris…; **e. really outstanding candidates** à l'exception *ou* en dehors des candidats vraiment brillants

xception [ɪk'sepʃən] **N 1** *(deviation, exemption)* exception *f*; **the e. proves the rule** l'exception confirme la règle; **to make an e. (of sth/for sb)** faire une exception (pour qch/qn); **without e.** sans exception; **but she's an e.** mais elle n'est pas comme les autres; **with the e. of Daniel** à l'exception de Daniel; **and you're no e.** et cela te concerne aussi; **most Western countries were feeling the effects of the recession, and Britain was no e.** la plupart des pays occidentaux ressentaient les effets de la crise, et la Grande-Bretagne n'était pas épargnée **2** *(idiom)* **to take e. to sth** *(object to)* trouver à redire à qch; *(be offended by)* s'offusquer de qch; **I take e. to that remark** je n'apprécie pas du tout ce commentaire

xceptionable [ɪk'sepʃənəbəl] **ADJ** *(objectionable)* offensant, outrageant

xceptional [ɪk'sepʃənəl] **ADJ** exceptionnel; **in e. circumstances** dans des circonstances exceptionnelles; **these are e. times we live in** nous vivons une époque exceptionnelle

▸▸ *Am Sch* ***exceptional child*** *(gifted child)* enfant *mf* surdoué(e); *(child with learning difficulties)* = enfant qui a des difficultés d'apprentissage; *Acct* ***exceptional item*** poste *m* extraordinaire

xceptionally [ɪk'sepʃənəlɪ] **ADV** exceptionnellement; **that's e. kind of you** c'est extrêmement gentil de votre part; **e., no bail was granted** à titre exceptionnel, il n'a pas été accordé de remise en liberté sous caution; **she's an e. bright child** c'est une enfant d'une intelligence exceptionnelle

excerpt ['eksɜ:pt] **N** *(extract)* extrait *m* (**from** de)

excess N [ɪk'ses] **1** *(unreasonable amount)* excès *m*; **an e. of salt/fat in the diet** un excès de sel/de graisses dans l'alimentation

2 *(difference between two amounts)* supplément *m*, surplus *m*; **an e. of supply over demand** un excès de l'offre sur la demande

3 *(over-indulgence)* excès *m*; **a life of e.** une vie d'excès

4 *(usu pl) (unacceptable action)* excès *m*, abus *m*; **the excesses of the occupying troops** les excès *ou* abus commis par les soldats pendant l'occupation

5 *Br Ins* franchise *f*

ADJ ['ekses] *(extra)* en trop, excédentaire; **you're carrying a lot of e. weight** tu as beaucoup de kilos en trop *ou* à perdre

• **in excess of PREP** *(a stated percentage, weight)* au-dessus de; **she earns in e. of £25,000 a year** elle gagne plus de 25 000 livres par an

• **to excess** [ɪk'ses] **ADV** **he does** *or* **carries it to e.** il exagère, il dépasse les bornes; **to eat/to drink to e.** manger/boire à l'excès

▸▸ ***excess baggage*** *(UNCOUNT) (on plane)* excédent *m* de bagages; **I had 10 kilos of e. baggage** j'avais 10 kilos d'excédent de bagages; ***excess capacity*** surcapacité *f*, capacité *f* excédentaire; ***excess demand*** demande *f* excédentaire; *Br* ***excess fare*** supplément *m* de prix; ***excess luggage*** *(UNCOUNT) (on plane)* excédent *m* de bagages; *Fin* ***excess profits*** surplus *m* des bénéfices; *(unexpected)* bénéfices *mpl* exceptionnels, bénéfices *mpl* extraordinaires; *St Exch* ***excess shares*** actions *fpl* détenues en surnombre; ***excess supply*** suroffre *f*

excessive [ɪk'sesɪv] **ADJ** *(unreasonable)* excessif; *(demand)* excessif, démesuré; **e. drinking** excès *mpl* de boisson; **that's a bit e.** c'est un peu excessif; **to show e. interest in sb/sth** s'intéresser de trop près à qn/qch; **in e. detail** avec trop de détails

excessively [ɪk'sesɪvlɪ] **ADV** excessivement; **to eat/drink e.** manger/boire à l'excès; **it was hot/damaged, but not e. so** il faisait chaud/il était endommagé, mais pas trop

exchange [ɪks'tʃeɪndʒ] **VT** échanger; **to e. glances** échanger des regards; **to e. views** échanger des vues; **we didn't e. more than a couple of words all evening** nous n'avons pas échangé plus de quelques mots de toute la soirée; *Euph* **to e. words** *(quarrel)* se disputer; **shots were exchanged** il y a eu un échange de coups de feu; **to e. sth with sb** échanger qch avec qn; **we exchanged places (with each other)** nous avons échangé nos places; **would you like to e. places?** voulez-vous changer de place avec moi?; **we exchanged addresses** nous avons échangé nos adresses; **to e. sth for sth** échanger qch contre qch; **to e. sterling for dollars** changer des livres contre des dollars; **I would not e. my happiness for anything** je n'échangerais *ou* ne donnerais mon bonheur contre rien au monde

N 1 *(swap)* échange *m*; **his old car for my new one didn't seem a fair e.** échanger sa vieille voiture contre ma neuve ne me semblait pas équitable; **e. of contracts** échange *m* de contrats à la signature; *Br Prov* **fair e. is no robbery** = donnant donnant

2 *(discussion)* échange *m*; **we had a heated e.** nous avons eu des mots

3 *(cultural, educational)* échange *m*; **he took part in an e. with a school in France** il a participé à un échange avec une école française; **the Spanish students are here on an e. visit** les étudiants espagnols sont en visite ici dans le cadre d'un échange

4 *Fin (of currency)* change *m*; *(of goods, shares, commodities)* échange *m*

5 *Tel* central *m* téléphonique

6 *Com* bourse *f*

• **exchanges NPL** *Am Fin (bills)* lettres *fpl* de change, traites *fpl*

• **in exchange ADV** en échange

• **in exchange for PREP** en échange de; **in e. for helping with the housework she was given food and lodging** elle aidait aux travaux ménagers et en échange *ou* en contrepartie elle était nourrie et logée

▸▸ *Fin* ***exchange broker*** cambiste *mf*, agent *m* de change, courtier(ère) *m,f* de change; *Br Fin* ***exchange control*** contrôle *m* des changes; *Fin* ***exchange dealer*** cambiste *mf*, agent *m* de change, courtier(ère) *m,f* de change; *Fin* ***exchange gain*** gain *m* de change; *Fin* ***exchange index*** indice *m* boursier; *Fin* ***exchange loss*** perte *f* de change; *Fin* ***exchange market*** marché *m* des changes; *Fin* ***exchange offer*** offre *f* publique d'échange; *Fin* ***exchange premium*** prime *f* de change; *Sch & Univ* ***exchange programme*** programme *m* d'échange; *Fin* ***exchange rate*** taux *m* de change, cours *m* de change; **at the current e. rate** au cours du jour; *Formerly Fin* ***Exchange Rate Mechanism*** mécanisme *m* (des taux) de change (du SME); ***exchange rate parity*** parité *f* du change; ***exchange rate stability*** stabilité *f* des changes; *Fin* ***exchange reserves*** réserves *fpl* en devises (étrangères); *Fin* ***exchange restrictions*** contrôle *m* des changes; *Sch & Univ* ***exchange student*** = étudiant qui participe à un échange; *Fin* ***exchange transaction*** opération *f* de change; *Fin* ***exchange value*** contre-valeur *f*, valeur *f* d'échange; *Sch* ***exchange visit*** échange *m*

exchangeable [ɪks'tʃeɪndʒəbəl] **ADJ** échangeable, qui peut être échangé; **goods are e. only when accompanied by a valid receipt** les articles ne peuvent être échangés que s'ils sont accompagnés du ticket de caisse

exchequer [ɪks'tʃekə(r)] **N** *Pol & Fin (finances)* finances *fpl*

• **Exchequer N** *Admin* **the E.** *(department)* l'Échiquier *m*, le Ministère des Finances *(en Grande-Bretagne)*; *(money)* le Trésor public

▸▸ *Fin* ***exchequer bill*** bon *m* du Trésor

excise[1] ['eksaɪz] **N 1** *Com (tax)* taxe *f*, contribution *f* indirecte **2** *Br (government office)* régie *f*, service *m* des contributions indirectes; **men from the e.** *(customs officers)* officiers *mpl* des douanes; *(VAT inspectors)* inspecteurs *mpl* de la TVA

▸▸ ***excise bond*** acquit-à-caution *m*; *Com* ***excise duty, excise tax*** contribution *f* indirecte

excise[2] [ek'saɪz] **VT 1** *Formal (remove from a text)* retrancher, supprimer **2** *Med* exciser

exciseman ['eksaɪz,mæn] *(pl* **excisemen** [-men]**)** **N** *Br* employé *m* de la régie *ou* des contributions indirectes

excision [ek'sɪʒən] **N 1** *Formal (of piece of text)* coupure *f*, retranchement *m* **2** *Med* excision *f*

excitable [ɪk'saɪtəbəl] **ADJ** *(gen) & Med & Physiol* excitable

excite [ɪk'saɪt] **VT 1** *(agitate)* exciter, énerver; **the doctor said you weren't to e. yourself** le docteur a dit qu'il ne te fallait pas d'excitation *ou* qu'il ne fallait pas que tu t'énerves; **the sight of the rabbit had excited the dogs** la vue du lapin avait excité les chiens

2 *(fill with enthusiasm)* enthousiasmer; **I'm very excited by this latest development** ce fait nouveau me remplit d'enthousiasme

3 *(sexually)* exciter

4 *(arouse ▸ interest, curiosity)* susciter

5 *Phys, Physiol & Elec* exciter

excited [ɪk'saɪtɪd] **ADJ 1** *(enthusiastic, eager)* excité; **to be e. about** *or* **at sth** être excité par qch; **the children were e. at the prospect of going to the seaside** les enfants étaient tout excités à l'idée d'aller au bord de la mer; **you must be very e. at being chosen to play for your country** vous devez être fou de joie d'avoir été choisi pour jouer pour votre pays; **doctors are e. by this discovery** les médecins sont enthousiasmés par cette découverte; **it's nothing to get e. about** il n'y a pas de quoi en faire un plat, ça n'a rien d'extraordinaire; **don't get too e.** ne t'excite *ou* t'emballe pas trop; *Ironic* **well, don't sound too e.!** eh bien, quel enthousiasme!

2 *(agitated)* **don't go getting e., don't get e.** ne va pas t'énerver

3 *(sexually)* excité

4 *Phys, Physiol & Elec* excité

excitedly [ɪk'saɪtɪdlɪ] **ADV** *(behave, watch)* avec agitation; *(say)* sur un ton animé; *(wait)* fébrilement; **she was jumping up and down e.** elle sautait dans tous les sens, tout excitée

excitement [ɪk'saɪtmənt] **N 1** *(enthusiasm)* excitation *f*, animation *f*, enthousiasme *m*; **in her e. at the news she knocked over a vase** les nouvelles l'ont mise dans un tel état d'excitation *ou* d'enthousiasme qu'elle a renversé un vase; **an atmosphere of intense e.** une grande effervescence *ou* animation; **when the e. had died down** quand l'agitation *ou* l'effervescence fut retombée
2 *(agitation)* excitation *f*, agitation *f*; **the doctor advised her to avoid e.** le médecin lui a déconseillé toute agitation *ou* toute surexcitation *ou* tout énervement; **the e. of departure** l'émoi *m* du départ; **to cause great e.** faire sensation; *Hum Ironic* **I don't think I could stand the e.** je ne crois pas que je supporterais des sensations *ou* émotions aussi fortes; **the e. would kill her** une telle émotion lui serait fatale; **I've had quite enough e. for one day** j'ai eu assez de sensations fortes pour une seule journée
3 *(sexual)* excitation *f*
4 *(exciting events)* animation *f*; **there should be plenty of e. in today's match** le match d'aujourd'hui devrait être très animé; **we don't get much e. round here** il n'y a pas beaucoup d'animation par ici; **all the e. seemed to have gone out of their marriage** leur mariage semblait maintenant totalement dénué de passion; **he needs a bit of e. in his life** il lui faudrait ajouter un peu de piquant à son existence; **what's all the e. about?** mais que se passe-t-il?; **you shouldn't have had yesterday off, you missed all the e.** c'est dommage que tu n'aies pas travaillé hier, il y a eu beaucoup d'animation *ou* c'était très animé

exciting [ɪk'saɪtɪŋ] **ADJ 1** *(day, life, events, match, novel, film)* passionnant, palpitant; *(prospect)* palpitant; *(news)* sensationnel; **we've had an e. time (of it) recently** ces derniers temps ont été mouvementés; **nothing e. ever happens around here** il ne se passe jamais rien d'excitant *ou* de palpitant par ici; **it was e. to think that we'd soon be in New York** c'était excitant de penser que nous serions bientôt à New York; **it was an e. place to live** c'était passionnant de vivre là-bas
2 *(sexually)* excitant

excitingly [ɪk'saɪtɪŋlɪ] **ADV** d'une manière sensationnelle; *(dress)* avec originalité; **e. different** d'une originalité enthousiasmante *ou* électrisante; **the match finished as e. as it had started** le match s'est terminé de façon aussi palpitante qu'il avait commencé

exclaim [ɪk'skleɪm] **VT "but why?" he exclaimed** "mais pourquoi?" s'écria-t-il
VI s'écrier, s'exclamer

exclamation [ˌekskləˈmeɪʃən] **N** exclamation *f*
▸▸ *Br* ***exclamation mark**, Am **exclamation point*** point *m* d'exclamation

exclamatory [ek'sklæmətrɪ] **ADJ** exclamatif

exclude [ɪk'sklu:d] **VT 1** *(bar)* exclure; **to e. sb from sth** exclure qn de qch; **women were excluded from power** les femmes étaient exclues du pouvoir; **I felt that I was being excluded from the conversation** je sentais qu'on m'excluait de la conversation; **his disability excluded him from many leisure pursuits** son infirmité l'empêchait de pratiquer de nombreux loisirs **2** *(not take into consideration)* exclure; **to e. sb/sth from sth** exclure qn/qch de qch; **the figures e. deaths from other causes** ces chiffres ne tiennent pas compte des morts provoquées par d'autres causes; **submarine-launched missiles were excluded from the arms talks** les missiles sous-marins n'entraient pas dans le cadre des négociations sur les armements

exclusion [ɪk'sklu:ʒən] **N 1** *(barring)* exclusion *f*; **the e. of sb from a society/conversation** l'exclusion de qn d'une société/conversation; **the e. of women from voting** le fait que les femmes n'aient pas le droit de vote **2** *(omission)* exclusion *f*; **the e. of her name from the list** l'exclusion de son nom de la liste; **to the e. of everything** *or* **all else** à l'exclusion de toute autre chose
▸▸ ***exclusion clause*** clause *f* d'exclusion; ***exclusion order*** ordre *m* d'exclusion; **to serve an e. order on sb** frapper qn d'un ordre d'exclusion; *Mil* ***exclusion zone*** zone *f* d'exclusion

exclusive [ɪk'sklu:sɪv] **ADJ 1** *(select ▸ restaurant, neighbourhood)* chic; *(▸ club)* fermé; *(▸ shop)* de luxe; *(▸ school)* élitiste; **they live at a very e. address** ils vivent dans un quartier très chic
2 *(deal, contract)* exclusif; **to have e. rights in a production** avoir l'exclusivité d'une production; **e. to** réservé (exclusivement) à; **an interview e. to this magazine** une interview exclusive accordée à notre magazine
3 *(not including)* **e. of VAT** TVA non comprise; **e. of tax** hors taxe(s); **the rent is £200 a week e.** le loyer est de 200 livres par semaine sans les charges; **from 14 to 19 October, e.** du 14 au 19 octobre exclu; **all prices are e. of postage and packing** les prix indiqués ne tiennent pas compte des frais d'envoi et d'emballage
4 *(incompatible)* exclusif; **the two propositions are/are not mutually e.** les deux propositions sont/ne sont pas incompatibles
5 *(sole)* unique; **their e. concern** leur seul souci; **the e. use of gold** l'emploi exclusif d'or
N *Press* exclusivité *f*; *(interview)* interview *f* exclusive; **a Tribune e.** une exclusivité de la Tribune
▸▸ *Com* ***exclusive distribution*** distribution *f* exclusive; *Com* ***exclusive licence*** licence *f* exclusive

exclusively [ɪk'sklu:sɪvlɪ] **ADV** *(only)* exclusivement; **published e. in the Times** publié en exclusivité dans le Times

exclusivity [ˌeksklu:'sɪvətɪ] **N 1** *(of restaurant, district)* caractère *m* huppé; *(of club, social circle)* caractère *m* fermé **2** *(of contract)* exclusivité *f*
▸▸ ***exclusivity agreement*** accord *m* d'exclusivité; ***exclusivity clause*** clause *f* d'exclusivité

excommunicate *Rel* **VT** [ˌekskəˈmju:nɪkeɪt] excommunier
N [ekskəˈmju:nɪkət] excommunié(e) *m,f*
ADJ [ekskəˈmju:nɪkət] excommunié

excommunication [ˈekskəˌmju:nɪˈkeɪʃən] **N** *Rel* excommunication *f*

ex-con **N** *Fam* ancien(enne) taulard(e) *m,f*

excrement [ˈekskrɪmənt] **N** *(UNCOUNT) Formal* excréments *mpl*

excrescence [ɪk'skresəns] **N** *Formal (growth)* excroissance *f*

excrescent [ɪk'skresənt] **ADJ** *Formal* **1** *(outward-growing)* qui forme une excroissance **2** *(superfluous)* superflu, redondant

excreta [ek'skri:tə] **NPL** *Formal (faeces)* excréments *mpl*; *(waste matter)* excrétions *fpl*

excrete [ek'skri:t] **VT** *Physiol & Bot* excréter; *(of plant)* sécréter

excretion [ek'skri:ʃən] **N** *Physiol & Bot* **1** *(action)* excrétion *f* **2** *(substance)* sécrétion *f*

excruciating [ɪk'skru:ʃɪeɪtɪŋ] **ADJ 1** *(pain, sight)* atroce, insoutenable; *(death)* atroce; *(noise)* infernal; **the pain was e.** la douleur était atroce **2** *Fam (extremely bad)* atroce, abominable; **it was e.** *(embarrassing)* c'était affreux; *(boring)* c'était atroce

excruciatingly [ɪk'skru:ʃɪeɪtɪŋlɪ] **ADV** *(painful)* atrocement, affreusement; *Fam* **it was e. funny/boring** c'était à mourir de rire/d'ennui

exculpate [ˈekskʌlpeɪt] **VT** *Formal* disculper; **to e. sb from sth** disculper qn de qch

exculpation [ˌekskʌlˈpeɪʃən] **N** *Formal* disculpation *f*

excursion [ɪk'skɜ:ʃən] **N 1** *(organized trip)* excursion *f*; **to make** *or* **to go on an e.** faire une excursion **2** *(short local journey)* expédition *f*; **a shopping e.** un tour dans les magasins **3** *(into a different field)* incursion *f*; **after a brief e. into politics** après une brève incursion dans la politique
▸▸ *Br Formerly Rail* ***excursion ticket*** billet *m* circulaire *(bénéficiant de tarifs réduits)*; ***excursion train*** train *m* spécial

excursionist [ɪk'skɜ:ʃənɪst] **N** excursionniste *mf*

excusable [ɪk'skju:zəbəl] **ADJ** excusable, pardonnable

excusably [ɪk'skju:zəblɪ] **ADV e., perhaps, she refused to speak to them** elle a refusé de leur parler, ce qui est peut-être excusable *ou* pardonnable

excuse **N** [ɪk'skju:s] **1** *(explanation, justification)* excuse *f*; **a feeble e.** une mauvaise excuse; **her e. for not coming** *(in the past)* son excuse pour n'être pas venue; *(in the future)* son excuse pou[r] ne pas venir; **to give sth as one's e.** donner qc[h] comme excuse; **that's no e.** ce n'est pas une ex[cuse] *ou* une raison; **that's no e. for being rude** c[e] n'est pas une raison *ou* une excuse pour êtr[e] grossier; **there's no e. for it** c'est sans excuse c'est inexcusable; **he has no e. for not finishin[g] the job on time** il n'a pas d'excuse pour ne pa[s] avoir terminé le travail à temps; **I don't want (t[o] hear) any excuses!** je ne veux pas d'excuse!; **you'[d] better have a good e.!** tu as intérêt à avoir un[e] bonne excuse!; **excuses, excuses!** des excuses toujours des excuses!; **he's always finding ex[cuses] for them/for their behaviour** il est tout l[e] temps en train de leur trouver des excuses d'excuser leur comportement; **stop making ex[cuses] for him** arrête de lui trouver des excuses **I'm not making excuses for them** je ne les excus[e] pas; **make my excuses to them** présente-leur me[s] excuses; **ignorance of the law is no e.** nul n'es[t] censé ignorer la loi; **by way of (an) e.** en guis[e] d'excuse **2** *(example)* **a poor e. for a father** un pèr[e] lamentable; **this is a poor e. for a bus service** c[e] service d'autobus est lamentable **3** *(pretext)* ex[cuse] *f*, prétexte *m*; **an e. to do** *or* **for doing sth** un[e] excuse *ou* un prétexte pour faire qch; **it's only a[n] e.** ce n'est qu'un prétexte; **the government keep[s] finding excuses for not introducing reforms** le gou[]vernement n'arrête pas de trouver des excuse[s] pour retarder l'introduction de réformes; **he'[s] looking for an e. not to go to the party** il cherch[e] une excuse pour ne pas aller à la soirée; **any e[.] for a drink!** toutes les excuses sont bonnes pou[r] boire un verre!
VT [ɪk'skju:z] **1** *(justify ▸ bad behaviour)* excuse[r]; **his youth excuses him** sa jeunesse l'excuse *o[u]* peut lui servir d'excuse; **he tried to e. himself b[y] saying that...** il a essayé de se justifier en disan[t] que...
2 *(forgive ▸ bad behaviour, person)* excuser, par[]donner; **you can e. that in someone of his age** c'es[t] pardonnable chez quelqu'un de son âge; **I'll e[.] your lateness (just) this once** je te pardonne to[n] retard pour cette fois; **he is unable to attend th[e] meeting and asks to be excused** il lui est impos[]sible d'assister à la réunion et vous prie de bie[n] vouloir l'en excuser; **now, if you will e. me** main[]tenant, si vous voulez bien m'excuser; **one coul[d] be excused for thinking that he was much younge[r]** on dirait *ou* croirait qu'il est beaucoup plu[s] jeune; **e. me** *(to get past)* pardon; *(as interruption to attract someone's attention)* pardon, excusez-moi; *Am (as apology)* pardon, excusez-moi; **e[.] me, (but) aren't you...?** excusez-moi, vous ne se[]riez pas...?; *Ironic* **e. me for asking!** oh, ça va, j[e] ne faisais que demander!, ce n'était qu'un[e] question!; *Ironic* **well, e. me for mentioning it** oh, ça va, je n'en parlerai plus!; **to e. oneself** s'ex[]cuser; **if you'll e. the expression** si vous voulez m[e] pardonner l'expression
3 *(exempt)* dispenser; **to e. sb from sth/doing st[h]** dispenser qn de qch/de faire qch; **he is excuse[d] gym** il est dispensé de gymnastique
4 *(allow to go)* excuser; **please may I be excused** *(to go to lavatory)* puis-je sortir, s'il vous plaît? *(from table)* puis-je sortir de table, s'il vous plaît

excuse-me [ɪk'skju:z-] **N** = danse pendant la[]quelle on peut prendre le ou la partenaire d[e] quelqu'un d'autre

ex-directory *Br* **ADJ** sur la liste rouge; **an e[x-directory] number** un numéro ne figurant pas dans l'an[]nuaire *ou* figurant sur la liste rouge
ADV to go e. se mettre sur la liste rouge

execrable [ˈeksɪkrəbəl] **ADJ** *Formal* exécrable

execrably [ˈeksɪkrəblɪ] **ADV** *Formal* exécrable[]ment

execrate [ˈeksɪkreɪt] **VT** *Formal* **1** *(loathe)* exécre[r] **2** *(denounce)* condamner, s'élever contre **3** *(curse)* maudire

execration [ˌeksɪˈkreɪʃən] **N** *Formal* **1** *(loathing)* exécration *f* **2** *(denunciation)* condamnation *f* accusation *f*

executable file [ˈeksɪkju:təbəl-] **N** *Comput* fi[]chier *m* exécutable

execute [ˈeksɪkju:t] **VT 1** *(put to death)* exécuter **executed for murder/treason** exécuté pour meur[]tre/trahison
2 *Formal (carry out ▸ task)* exécuter; *(▸ plan*

metter à exécution; *Mus* (▸ *piece*) exécuter; **a superbly executed carving** une sculpture superbement exécutée

3 *Law (will, sentence, law)* exécuter; *(deed)* signer, souscrire

4 *Comput* exécuter

▸▸ *Comput* **execute cycle** cycle *m* d'exécution; *Comput* **execute file** fichier *m* exécutable

execution [ˌeksɪˈkjuːʃən] **N 1** *(of person)* exécution *f*

2 *Formal (of task, plan)* exécution *f*; *Mus (of piece)* exécution *f*; *(by musician)* interprétation *f*; **in the e. of one's duty** dans l'exercice de ses fonctions; **to put sth into e.** mettre qch à exécution

3 *Law (of will, sentence, law)* exécution *f*; *(of deed)* signature *f*, souscription *f*

4 *Comput* exécution *f*

executioner [ˌeksɪˈkjuːʃənə(r)] **N** bourreau *m*

executive [ɪgˈzekjʊtɪv] **N 1** *(person)* cadre *m*; **a business e.** un cadre commercial **2** *(body)* corps *m* exécutif; *Pol (branch of government)* exécutif *m*; *Am Pol* **the e.** l'exécutif *m*, le pouvoir exécutif **3** *(of political party, union)* bureau *m*, comité *m* central; **the union's national e.** le bureau national du syndicat

ADJ 1 *(dining room, washroom etc)* des cadres, de la direction; *(desk, chair)* de luxe; **e. model** *or* **version** *(of car)* modèle *m* grand luxe **2** *(function, role)* exécutif; **an e. officer in the civil service** un cadre de l'administration; **he's not good at making e. decisions** il n'est pas doué pour prendre des décisions importantes; *Hum* **you'll have to make an e. decision** il va falloir que tu prennes une décision capitale *ou* déterminante

▸▸ *Am Pol* **executive agreement** accord *m* en forme simplifiée *(qui ne nécessite pas l'approbation du Sénat)*; *Com* **executive board** directoire *m*; *Am Pol* **the executive branch** l'exécutif *m*; **executive briefcase** attaché-case *m*; *Aviat* **executive class** classe *f* affaires; **executive committee** comité *m* exécutif; *Com* **executive director** directeur *m* exécutif; **executive jet** jet *m* privé; **executive lounge** salon *m* classe affaires; *Com* **executive officer** cadre *m* supérieur; **executive power** pouvoir *m* exécutif; *Am Pol* **executive privilege** privilège *m* de l'exécutif *(droit dont bénéficie l'exécutif de limiter l'accès du Congrès, des tribunaux et du public à l'information, pour des raisons d'intérêt national)*; *Cin* **executive producer** producteur *m* délégué; *Comput* **executive program** programme *m* d'exécution; *Com* **executive secretary** secrétaire *mf* de direction; *Am* **executive session** *(of Senate)* séance *f* à huis clos; **executive suite** *(in hotel)* suite *f* de luxe; *(in company)* bureaux *mpl* de la direction; **executive toy** gadget *m* pour cadres

executor [ɪgˈzekjʊtə(r)] **N** *Law (of will)* exécuteur (trice) *m,f* testamentaire; **to make sb one's e.** désigner qn comme son exécuteur testamentaire

executrix [ɪgˈzekjʊtrɪks] **N** *Law (of will)* exécutrice *f* testamentaire

exegesis [ˌeksɪˈdʒiːsɪs] **N** exégèse *f*

exegetic [ˌeksɪˈdʒetɪk], **exegetical** [ˌeksɪˈdʒetɪkəl] **ADJ** exégétique

exemplary [ɪgˈzemplərɪ] **ADJ 1** *(very good* ▸ *behaviour, pupil)* exemplaire; **he's an e. student/husband** c'est un étudiant/mari modèle **2** *(serving as a warning)* exemplaire; **e. punishment** châtiment *m* exemplaire

▸▸ *Law* **exemplary damages** dommages-intérêts *mpl* exemplaires *ou* à titre exemplaire; *Law* **exemplary sentence** peine exemplaire

exemplification [ɪgˌzemplɪfɪˈkeɪʃən] **N** illustration *f*, illustrations *fpl*, exemplification *f*; **in e. of his remarks** pour exemplifier ses remarques

exemplify [ɪgˈzemplɪfaɪ] **VT 1** *(give example of)* illustrer, exemplifier **2** *(be example of)* illustrer

exempt [ɪgˈzempt] **ADJ** exempt, exempté, dispensé (**from** de); **to be e. from sth** être exempt de qch; **he was declared e. from any blame** il a été établi qu'il n'était en aucun responsable de ce qui s'était passé; **e. from taxes** exonéré d'impôt, exempt d'impôt

VT *(gen)* exempter, dispenser (**from** de); *(from tax)* exonérer, exempter (**from** de); *(from military service)* exempter (**from** de); **to e. sb/sth from sth** exempter qn/qch de qch; **to e. sb from blame** n'avoir rien à reprocher à qn

exemption [ɪgˈzempʃən] **N** *(action, state)* exemption *f*, dispense *f*; *(from tax)* exonération *f*, exemption *f*; **tax e.** exonération *f* fiscale

▸▸ *Law* **exemption clause** clause *f* de non-responsabilité

exercisable [ˈeksəˌsaɪzəbəl] **ADJ 1** *(right, authority, power)* que l'on peut exercer **2** *St Exch (option)* exerçable

exercise [ˈeksəsaɪz] **N 1** *(physical)* exercice *m*; **to take e.** prendre de l'exercice; **it's good e.** c'est un bon exercice; **I don't get much e.** je ne fais pas beaucoup d'exercice; **I'll walk, I need the e.** j'y vais à pied, j'ai besoin d'exercice; **physical exercises** exercices *mpl* physiques; **he does (physical) exercises every morning** il fait de la gymnastique tous les matins; **breathing exercises** gymnastique *f* respiratoire, exercices *mpl* respiratoires

2 *(mental, in education)* exercice *m*; **grammar exercises** exercices *mpl* de grammaire; **piano exercises** exercices *mpl* de piano

3 *(use)* exercice *m*; **in the e. of one's duties** dans l'exercice de ses fonctions; **by the e. of a little imagination** en usant d'un peu d'imagination, avec un peu d'imagination

4 *Mil* exercice *m*; **they're on exercises** ils sont à l'exercice

5 *(activity, operation)* **a fact-finding e.** une mission d'enquête; **it was an interesting e.** cela a été une expérience intéressante; **it was a pointless e.** cela n'a servi absolument à rien

6 *St Exch (of option)* levée *f*

7 *Am (ceremony)* cérémonie *f*; **graduation exercises** cérémonie *f* de remise des diplômes

VT 1 *(body, muscle)* exercer, faire travailler; *(horse)* faire faire de l'exercice à; **to e. a dog** *(take for a walk)* promener un chien

2 *(troops)* entraîner

3 *(use, put into practice* ▸ *right, authority, power)* exercer; **we must e. caution/restraint** nous devons user de prudence/de retenue

4 *St Exch (option)* lever

5 *Formal (preoccupy)* préoccuper

VI 1 *(take exercise)* faire de l'exercice **2** *(train* ▸ *in gymnasium etc)* s'exercer, s'entraîner; **he was exercising on the rings** il s'exerçait *ou* s'entraînait aux anneaux

▸▸ **exercise bike** vélo *m* d'appartement; **exercise book** *(for writing in)* cahier *m* d'exercices; *(containing exercises)* livre *m* d'exercices; **exercise class** cours *m* de gymnastique; *St Exch* **exercise date** date *f* d'échéance; *St Exch* **exercise notice** assignation *f*; *St Exch* **exercise price** *(of share)* prix *m* d'exercice, cours *m* de base; **exercise yard** *(in prison)* cour *f*, préau *m*

exert [ɪgˈzɜːt] **VT 1** *(pressure, force)* exercer; **they were willing to e. their influence on behalf of our campaign** ils étaient d'accord pour mettre leur influence au service de notre campagne **2 to e. oneself** *(make effort)* se donner de la peine *ou* du mal; *Ironic* **don't e. yourself!** ne te donne pas trop de mal, surtout!

exertion [ɪgˈzɜːʃən] **N 1** *(of force)* exercice *m*; **the e. of pressure on sb/sth** la pression exercée sur qn/qch **2** *(effort)* effort *m*; **after the day's exertions** après les efforts de la journée; **by one's own exertions** par ses propres moyens

exeunt [ˈeksɪʌnt] **VI** *Theat (in stage directions)* **e. the Queen and her attendants** la reine et sa suite sortent

exfoliant [eksˈfəʊlɪənt] **N** exfoliant *m*

exfoliate [eksˈfəʊlɪeɪt] **VT** exfolier

VI s'exfolier

exfoliating [eksˈfəʊlɪeɪtɪŋ] **ADJ** exfoliant

▸▸ **exfoliating cream** crème *f* exfoliante; **exfoliating scrub** crème *f* exfoliante, gommage *m* exfoliant

exfoliation [eksˌfəʊlɪˈeɪʃən] **N** exfoliation *f*

ex gratia [eksˈgreɪʃə] **ADJ** *Com (payment)* à titre gracieux, à titre de faveur

ex-growth **N** *Com (decline)* baisse *f*; **to go e.** être en déclin

exhalation [ˌeksəˈleɪʃən] **N 1** *(breathing out* ▸ *of air)* expiration *f*; (▸ *of smoke, fumes)* exhalation *f* **2** *(air breathed out)* exhalaison *f*

exhale [eksˈheɪl] **VT** *(air)* expirer; *(gas, fumes)* exhaler

VI *(breathe out)* expirer

exhaust [ɪgˈzɔːst] **N 1** *Aut (on vehicle* ▸ *system)* échappement *m*; (▸ *pipe)* pot *m ou* tuyau *m* d'échappement **2** *(UNCOUNT) (fumes)* gaz *mpl* d'échappement

VT 1 *(use up* ▸ *supplies, possibilities)* épuiser; **you're exhausting my patience** tu mets ma patience à bout **2** *(tire out)* épuiser, exténuer; **to e. oneself (doing sth)** s'épuiser (en faisant qch)

▸▸ **exhaust fumes** gaz *mpl* d'échappement; *Aut* **exhaust manifold** collecteur *m* d'échappement; *Br Aut* **exhaust pipe** pot *m ou* tuyau *m* d'échappement; *Aut* **exhaust stroke** *(in internal combustion engine)* temps *m* d'échappement; *Aut* **exhaust system** échappement *m*; *Aut* **exhaust valve** soupape *f* d'échappement

exhausted [ɪgˈzɔːstɪd] **ADJ 1** *(person, smile)* épuisé, exténué; **I'm e.** je n'en peux plus, je suis épuisé *ou* exténué **2** *(used up* ▸ *mine, land)* épuisé; **my patience is e.** je suis à bout de patience

exhaustible [ɪgˈzɔːstɪbəl] **ADJ** limité; **her patience is easily e.** elle est vite à bout de patience

exhausting [ɪgˈzɔːstɪŋ] **ADJ** *(job, climb, climate)* épuisant, exténuant, éreintant; *(person)* fatigant, excédant

exhaustion [ɪgˈzɔːstʃən] **N 1** *(tiredness)* épuisement *m*, éreintement *m*, grande fatigue *f*; **to be suffering from e.** être dans un état d'épuisement; **they worked to the point of e.** ils ont travaillé jusqu'à épuisement **2** *(of supplies, resources, topic)* épuisement *m*

exhaustive [ɪgˈzɔːstɪv] **ADJ** *(analysis, treatment)* exhaustif; *(investigation, enquiry)* approfondi, poussé; **the list is not e.** cette liste n'est pas exhaustive; **to make an e. study of a subject** traiter un sujet à fond

exhaustively [ɪgˈzɔːstɪvlɪ] **ADV** exhaustivement

exhibit [ɪgˈzɪbɪt] **VT 1** *(of artist)* exposer **2** *(show, display* ▸ *identity card, passport)* montrer; (▸ *in shop window)* exposer; *Law* (▸ *items of supporting evidence)* exhiber, produire **3** *(manifest* ▸ *courage, self-control)* montrer, faire preuve de

VI *(artist)* exposer

N 1 *(in an exhibition)* objet *m* (exposé); **one of the most interesting exhibits at the fair** l'une des pièces les plus intéressantes en exposition à la foire **2** *Law (in criminal proceedings)* pièce *f* à conviction; *(attached to contract)* annexe *f*; **e. A** *(in criminal proceedings)* première pièce *f* à conviction **3** *Am (exhibition)* exposition *f*

exhibition [ˌeksɪˈbɪʃən] **N 1** *(of paintings, products)* exposition *f*; *(of film)* présentation *f*; **he's having an e. at the new gallery** il expose à la nouvelle galerie; **the Klee e.** l'exposition *f* Klee; **trade e.** exposition *f* commerciale **2** *(of bad manners, ingenuity)* démonstration *f*; **to give sb an e. of sth** faire une démonstration de qch à qn; **to make an e. of oneself** se donner en spectacle **3** *Br Univ (award)* bourse *f* d'études

▸▸ **exhibition centre** centre *m* d'expositions; **exhibition hall** salle *f ou* hall *m* d'exposition; *Sport* **exhibition match** match-exhibition *m*; **exhibition stand** stand *m* (d'exposition)

> Note that the French word **exhibition** is a false friend and is never a translation for the English word **exhibition**.

exhibitionism [ˌeksɪˈbɪʃənɪzəm] **N 1** *(gen)* besoin *m ou* volonté *f* de se faire remarquer **2** *Psy* exhibitionnisme *m*

exhibitionist [ˌeksɪˈbɪʃənɪst] **N 1** *(gen)* = personne qui cherche toujours à se faire remarquer; **he's a terrible e.** il faut toujours qu'il cherche à se faire remarquer **2** *Psy* exhibitionniste *mf*

exhibitor [ɪgˈzɪbɪtə(r)] **N 1** *(at gallery, trade fair)* exposant(e) *m,f* **2** *Am (cinema owner)* exploitant (e) *m,f*

exhilarate [ɪgˈzɪləreɪt] **VT** *(of experience)* griser, exalter; *(of mountain air)* vivifier

exhilarated [ɪgˈzɪləreɪtɪd] **ADJ** *(mood, laugh)* exalté; **to feel e.** se sentir exalté; **to be e. at the idea of doing sth** être exalté à l'idée de faire qch

exhilarating [ɪg'zɪləreɪtɪŋ] **ADJ** *(experience)* exaltant, grisant; *(mountain air)* vivifiant

exhilaration [ɪg,zɪlə'reɪʃən] **N** exaltation *f*, griserie *f*

exhort [ɪg'zɔːt] **VT** *Formal* exhorter; **to e. sb to do sth** exhorter qn à faire qch

exhortation [,egzɔː'teɪʃən] **N** *Formal (act, words)* exhortation *f*

exhumation [,ekshjuː'meɪʃən] **N** *Formal* exhumation *f*

▸▸ ***exhumation order*** permis *m* d'exhumer

exhume [eks'hjuːm] **VT** *Formal* exhumer

ex-husband **N** ex-mari *m*

exigency ['eksɪdʒənsɪ] *(pl* **exigencies***)*, **exigence** ['eksɪdʒəns] **N** *Formal* **1** *(usu pl) (demand)* exigence *f*; **the exigencies of the situation** les exigences *fpl* de la situation **2** *(urgent situation)* situation *f* urgente

exigent ['eksɪdʒənt] **ADJ** *Formal* **1** *(urgent)* urgent, pressant **2** *(demanding, exacting)* exigeant

exiguity [eksɪ'gjuːətɪ] *(pl* **exiguities***)* **N** *Formal* exiguïté *f*

exiguous [eg'zɪgjʊəs] **ADJ** *Formal (means, income, quarters)* exigu(ë)

exile ['eksaɪl] **N 1** *(banishment)* exil *m*; **his self-imposed e.** son exil volontaire; **to live in e.** vivre en exil; **to send sb into e.** envoyer qn en exil; **to go into e.** partir en exil; **government in e.** gouvernement en exil; **to return from e.** rentrer d'exil **2** *(person)* exilé(e) *m,f*

VT exiler, expatrier; **he was exiled from his native Poland** il a été exilé *ou* expatrié de sa Pologne natale

exist [ɪg'zɪst] **VI** exister; **do ghosts e.?** les fantômes existent-ils?; **they e. in three sizes** elles existent en trois tailles; **there exists an ancient tradition which...** il existe une tradition ancienne qui...; **she treats me as if I don't e.** elle fait comme si je n'existais pas; **that's not living, that's just existing!** je n'appelle pas ça vivre, j'appelle ça subsister *ou* survivre; **can life e. under these conditions?**; la vie est-elle possible dans ces conditions?; **he earns enough to e. on** il gagne suffisamment pour vivre; **we can't e. without oxygen** nous ne pouvons pas vivre sans oxygène

existence [ɪg'zɪstəns] **N 1** *(being)* existence *f*; **ever since the e. of man** depuis que l'homme existe; **the continued e. of life on this planet/of these old-fashioned procedures** la survivance de la vie sur la planète/de ces procédures arriérées; **to come into e.** *(species)* apparaître; *(the earth)* se former; *(law, institution)* naître, être créé; **to be in e.** exister; **the oldest manuscript in e.** le plus ancien manuscrit existant; **it's the only one still in e.** c'est le seul qui existe encore; **to go out of e.** cesser d'exister **2** *(life)* existence *f*; **to lead a pleasant/wretched e.** mener une existence agréable/misérable

existent [ɪg'zɪstənt] **ADJ** *Formal* existant

existential [,egzɪ'stenʃəl] **ADJ** *Phil* existentiel

existentialism [,egzɪ'stenʃəlɪzəm] **N** *Phil* existentialisme *m*

existentialist [,egzɪ'stenʃəlɪst] *Phil* **N** existentialiste *mf*

ADJ existentialiste

existing [ɪg'zɪstɪŋ] **ADJ** *(gen)* actuel; *(law, legislation)* en vigueur; **most of the e. building dates from the 18th century** la plus grande partie du bâtiment date du XVIIIème siècle

exit ['eksɪt] **N 1** *(way out ▸ from room, building, motorway)* sortie *f*; **let's turn off at the next e.** prenons la prochaine sortie; **e. ramp** bretelle *f* de sortie; **e. only** *(sign)* réservé à la sortie **2** *(act of going out ▸ from a room)* sortie *f*; *Theat* sortie *f*, exit *m inv*; **to make a hurried e.** sortir en vitesse; *Theat or Fig* **to make one's e.** faire sa sortie **3** *Comput* sortie *f*

VI 1 *Theat* sortir; **e. Ophelia** *(as stage direction)* exit Ophélie, Ophélie sort **2** *(go out, leave)* sortir; *(bullet)* ressortir; **he exited through the rear door** il est sorti *ou* parti par la porte de derrière **3** *Comput* sortir

VT *(leave)* quitter, sortir de; *Comput* sortir de

▸▸ *Fin* ***exit charges*** frais *mpl* de sortie; *Com* ***exit interview*** = entretien entre un employeur et son employé lors du départ de ce dernier; *Br* ***exit permit*** permis *m* de sortie; *Br Pol* ***exit poll*** = sondage réalisé auprès des votants à la sortie du bureau de vote; *Com & Pol* ***exit strategy*** stratégie *f* de retrait; ***exit visa*** visa *m* de sortie; ***exit wound*** point *m* de sortie

exocrine ['eksəʊkraɪn] **ADJ** *Physiol* exocrine

exodus ['eksədəs] **N** exode *m*; **the e. of capital** la fuite des capitaux; **there was a general e. to the bar** il y a eu un mouvement de masse en direction du bar; **a mass e. towards the beaches** un exode en direction des plages

• **Exodus** **N** *Bible* **(the Book of) E.** l'Exode

ex officio [eksə'fɪʃɪəʊ] **ADJ** *(member)* de droit

ADV *(act, decide etc)* de droit

exonerate [ɪg'zɒnəreɪt] **VT 1** *(absolve)* disculper, innocenter; **to e. oneself** se disculper **2** *(exempt)* exonérer, décharger (**from** de)

exoneration [ɪg,zɒnə'reɪʃən] **N 1** disculpation *f* **2** *(exemption)* exonération *f*, décharge *f* (**from** de)

exoplanet ['eksəʊplænɪt] **N** *Astron* exoplanète *f*

exorbitance [ɪg'zɔːbɪtəns] **N** *(of price, demands, claims)* énormité *f*, démesure *f*

exorbitant [ɪg'zɔːbɪtənt] **ADJ** *(price, demands, claims)* exorbitant, démesuré, excessif; **£85 for that? that's e.!** 85 livres pour ça? c'est exorbitant!

exorbitantly [ɪg'zɔːbɪtəntlɪ] **ADV** *(priced, expensive)* excessivement, démesurément

exorcism ['eksɔːsɪzəm] **N** exorcisme *m*; **to carry out** *or* **to perform an e.** pratiquer un exorcisme

exorcist ['eksɔːsɪst] **N** exorciste *m*

exorcize, -ise ['eksɔːsaɪz] **VT** *(evil spirits, place, fears)* exorciser

exoskeleton ['eksəʊ,skelɪtən] **N** *Zool* exosquelette *m*, cuticule *f*

exotic [ɪg'zɒtɪk] **ADJ** exotique; **an e.-sounding name** un nom à consonance exotique; **e.-looking** exotique

N *Bot* plante *f* exotique

exotica [ɪg'zɒtɪkə] **NPL** objets *mpl* exotiques; **a collection of literary e.** une collection de pièces littéraires rares

exotically [ɪg'zɒtɪkəlɪ] **ADV** *(dressed, decorated)* avec exotisme; **e. perfumed** *(flower)* aux senteurs exotiques

exoticism [ɪg'zɒtɪsɪzəm] **N** exotisme *m*

expand [ɪk'spænd] **VT 1** *(empire, army, staff)* agrandir; *(company, business)* agrandir, développer; *(chest, muscles, ideas)* développer; *(knowledge, influence)* élargir, étendre; *Phys & Constr* dilater; **it's an idea that could easily be expanded into a novel** c'est une idée qu'on pourrait facilement développer pour en faire un roman; **the police force is to be expanded** les effectifs de la police doivent être augmentés **2** *Math (equation)* développer **3** *Comput (memory)* étendre

VI 1 *(empire, army, staff)* s'agrandir; *(company, business)* s'agrandir, se développer; *(chest, muscles, market)* se développer; *(knowledge, influence)* s'étendre, s'élargir; *(gas, metal)* se dilater; *(volume of traffic)* augmenter; **we are looking to e. into the cosmetics industry** nous envisageons de nous diversifier en nous lançant dans l'industrie des cosmétiques **2** *(talk, write at greater length)* préciser sa pensée; **could you e.?** est-ce que vous pourriez préciser ce que vous voulez dire par là?

▸ **expand on** **VT INSEP** *(talk, write at greater length about)* développer

expandable [ɪk'spændɪbəl] **ADJ 1** *(gas, material)* expansible; *(idea, theory)* qui peut être développé; *(basic set)* qui peut être complété **2** *Comput (memory)* extensible

expanded [ɪk'spændɪd] **ADJ** *Phys & Constr* expansé

▸▸ *Comput* ***expanded keyboard*** clavier *m* étendu; ***expanded memory*** mémoire *f* paginée *ou* expansée; ***expanded polystyrene*** polystyrène *m* expansé; *Typ* ***expanded type*** caractères *mpl* larges

expander [ɪk'spændə(r)] **N 1** *Gym* **(chest) e.** extenseur *m* **2** *Aut (in brake drum)* came *f* de frein

expanding [ɪk'spændɪŋ] **ADJ 1** *(company, empire, gas, metal)* en expansion; *(influence)* grandissant; *(industry, market)* en expansion, qui se développe; *(interests, circle of friends)* qui s'élargit; **the e. universe** l'univers *m* en expansion **2** *(extendable ▸ watchstrap, briefcase, suitcase)* extensible

▸▸ *Aut* ***expanding brake*** frein *m* à extension

expanse [ɪk'spæns] **N** étendue *f*; **a vast e.** *(of water, snow etc)* une vaste étendue; **the vast e. of the plain** l'immensité *f* de la plaine; **she was showing a large e. of thigh** on lui voyait une bonne partie des cuisses

expansion [ɪk'spænʃən] **N** *(of empire)* expansion *f*, élargissement *m*; *(of army, staff)* augmentation *f*, accroissement *m*; *(of chest, muscles, ideas)* développement *m*; *(of knowledge, influence)* élargissement *m*; *(of gas, metal)* expansion *f*, dilatation *f*; *Comput (of memory)* extension *f*; *(of business)* développement *m*, agrandissement *m*, extension *f*; **colonial/territorial e.** expansion *f* coloniale/territoriale

▸▸ *Comput* ***expansion board*** carte *f* d'extension; ***expansion bolt*** *Constr* boulon *m* de scellement *ou* d'expansion; *(in mountaineering)* cheville *f* *ou* piton *m* d'expansion; *Comput* ***expansion card*** carte *f* d'extension; *Tech* ***expansion joint*** joint *m* de dilatation; *Comput* ***expansion slot*** emplacement *m ou* logement *m* pour carte d'extension; *Aut* ***expansion stroke*** course *f* de détente; *Constr* ***expansion tank*** réservoir *m* d'expansion; *Am Sport* ***expansion team*** nouvelle équipe *f*

expansionism [ɪk'spænʃə,nɪzəm] **N** expansionnisme *m*

expansionist [ɪk'spænʃənɪst] **ADJ** expansionniste

N expansionniste *mf*

expansive [ɪk'spænsɪv] **ADJ** *(person, mood, gesture)* expansif; **in an e. mood** d'humeur loquace

> Attention: ne pas confondre avec l'adjectif **expensive**.

expansively [ɪk'spænsɪvlɪ] **ADV** *(talk)* de manière expansive; **she gestured e. towards the skyline/paintings** elle a désigné l'horizon/les tableaux d'un grand geste

expansiveness [ɪk'spænsɪvnɪs] **N** *(of person)* expansivité *f*

expat [,eks'pæt] *Fam (abbr* **expatriate***)* **N** expatrié(e)[□] *m,f*

ADJ *(Briton, American etc)* expatrié[□]; *(bar, community)* d'expatriés[□]

expatiate [eks'peɪʃɪeɪt] **VI** *Formal* s'étendre, discourir (longuement); **to e. on sth** s'étendre *ou* discourir (longuement) sur qch

expatriate **N** [eks'pætrɪət] expatrié(e) *m,f*

ADJ [eks'pætrɪət] *(Briton, American etc)* expatrié; *(bar, community)* d'expatriés

VT [eks'pætrɪeɪt] expatrier, exiler

expatriation [eks,pætrɪ'eɪʃən] **N** expatriation *f*

expect [ɪk'spekt] **VT 1** *(anticipate)* s'attendre à; **we e. rain/bad weather** nous nous attendons à de la pluie/du mauvais temps; **we expected that it would be much bigger** nous nous attendions à ce qu'il soit beaucoup plus gros, nous pensions qu'il allait être beaucoup plus gros; **to e. sb to do sth** s'attendre à ce que qn fasse qch; **we expected you to bring your own** nous pensions que vous alliez apporter le vôtre; **I hadn't expected them to be French** je ne m'attendais pas à ce qu'ils soient français; **to e. the worst** s'attendre au pire; **I expected as much!** je m'en doutais!, c'est bien ce que je pensais!; **that's only to be expected** ce n'est pas du tout surprenant; **it was better/worse than I expected** c'était mieux/pire que je ne m'y attendais; **she is as well as can be expected** elle va aussi bien que sa condition le permet; **I had expected better of** *or* **from you** je n'aurais pas cru ça de vous; **she played with the brilliance (which) we have come to e. (from her)** elle a joué avec le brio auquel elle nous a maintenant habitués; **what can you e. from a government like that?** que voulez-vous, avec un gouvernement pareil!; **she was angry – well, what did you e.?** elle était en colère – et alors, ça t'étonne?; **as might have been expected, as was to be expected** comme on pouvait s'y attendre; **I knew what to e.** je savais à quoi m'attendre; **I never know what to e. with you** je ne sais jamais à quoi m'attendre *ou* m'en tenir avec vous

2 *(count on)* **we're expecting you to help us** nous

comptons sur votre aide; **don't e. me to be there!** ne t'attends pas à ce que j'y sois!

3 *(demand)* **to e. sb to do sth** demander à qn de faire qch; **I e. complete obedience** je demande une obéissance totale; **I e. something to be done** j'exige qu'on fasse quelque chose à ce sujet; **you e. too much of him** tu lui en demandes trop; **it is expected that the candidate will be willing to undertake some travel** on attend du candidat qu'il soit disposé à voyager; **I'm expected to write all his speeches** je suis censé *ou* supposé rédiger tous ses discours

4 *(suppose, imagine)* imaginer, penser, supposer; **I e. so** je pense, j'imagine; **I don't e. so** je ne pense pas, j'imagine que non; **I e. you're right** tu dois avoir raison; **I e. it's where you left it** il doit être là où tu l'as laissé; **I e. you'll be wanting something to drink** vous boirez bien quelque chose; *(grudgingly)* j'imagine que vous voulez quelque chose à boire

5 *(baby)* attendre

6 *(await ▸ guest, letter, phone call)* attendre; **I'm expecting friends for dinner** j'attends des amis à dîner; **(at) what time should we e. you then?** à quelle heure devons-nous vous attendre alors?; *Br Fam* **I'll e. you when I see you then** bon, alors tu rentreras quand tu rentreras; **we're expecting them back any minute now** nous attendons leur retour d'une minute à l'autre

VI to be expecting *(be pregnant)* être enceinte, attendre un enfant

expectancy [ɪk'spektənsɪ], **expectance** [ɪk'spektəns] **N** *(anticipation)* **the look of e. on his face** l'attente qui se lisait sur son visage; **in a tone of eager e.** sur un ton plein d'espérance *ou* d'espoir

expectant [ɪk'spektənt] **ADJ** *(full of anticipation)* impatient; **the e. look on the children's faces** l'attente qui se lisait sur le visage des enfants; **in an e. tone of voice** la voix chargée d'espoir

▸▸ ***expectant mother*** future maman *f*

expectantly [ɪk'spektəntlɪ] **ADV** *(enquire, glance)* avec l'air d'attendre quelque chose; **fans waiting e. at the stage door** des fans qui attendent à la sortie des artistes, pleins d'espoir

expectation [,ekspek'teɪʃən] **N 1** *(UNCOUNT) (anticipation)* **with eager e.** avec l'air d'espérer quelque chose; **to live in e.** vivre dans l'expectative *ou* l'attente; **beyond all e.** au-delà de toute espérance; **there is every e. that we shall be seeing them again soon** il y a de grandes chances pour que nous les revoyions bientôt; **in e. of** dans l'attente de

2 *(usu pl) (hope, aspiration)* attente *f*; *Econ* **expectations** anticipations *fpl*; **to come up to sb's expectations** remplir *ou* répondre à l'attente de qn; **his performance fell short of** *or* **did not live up to their expectations** il n'a pas été à la hauteur de leurs espérances, il n'a pas répondu à leur attente; **to exceed sb's expectations** dépasser l'attente *ou* les espérances de qn; **the performance did not confirm the City expectations** les résultats n'ont pas répondu à l'attente de la City; **this merely confirms our worst expectations** cela ne fait que confirmer nos prévisions les plus noires; **contrary to expectations** contrairement à *ou* contre toute attente; **to have high expectations of sb/sth** attendre beaucoup de qn/qch

3 *(usu pl) (requirement)* exigence *f*; **we have certain expectations of our employees** nous avons certaines exigences envers nos employés; **what are your expectations?** *(for salary, job prospects)* quelles sont vos conditions *ou* exigences?

4 *Formal (prospects)* **to have great expectations** avoir de grandes espérances; **uncle from whom one has expectations** oncle *m* à héritage

expected [ɪk'spektɪd] **ADJ** attendu; *(hoped for)* espéré; **please state e. salary** indiquez vos prétentions

▸▸ *Fin* ***expected value*** valeur *f* attendue

expectorant [ɪk'spektərənt] **N** *Med* expectorant *m*

expectorate [ɪk'spektəreɪt] *Med or Formal* **VT** expectorer

VI rejeter des expectorations

expectoration [ɪk,spektə'reɪʃən] **N** *Med & Formal* expectoration *f*

expediency [ɪk'spi:djənsɪ] *(pl* **expediencies***)*, **expedience** [ɪk'spi:djəns] **N 1** *(advisability ▸ of measure, policy etc)* opportunité *f*; **on grounds of e.** pour des raisons de convenance **2** *(self-interest)* opportunisme *m*; **a measure that smacks of political e.** une mesure politique opportuniste

expedient [ɪk'spi:dɪənt] **ADJ 1** *(advisable)* indiqué, convenable, opportun **2** *(involving self-interest)* commode; **a politically e. measure** une mesure politique opportuniste

N expédient *m*

expedite ['ekspɪdaɪt] **VT** *Formal (work, legal process)* hâter, activer, accélérer; *(completion of contract, deal)* hâter; **to e. matters** accélérer *ou* activer les choses

expedition [,ekspɪ'dɪʃən] **N 1** *(journey)* expédition *f*; **one (member) of the e.** un des membres de l'expédition; **to go on an e.** aller *ou* partir en expédition, aller faire une expédition; **getting here was quite an e.!** ça a été toute une expédition pour arriver jusqu'ici!; **e. leader** chef *m* d'expédition **2** *Arch or Literary (speed)* diligence *f*; **with all possible e.** avec la plus grande diligence

expeditionary [,ekspɪ'dɪʃənərɪ] **ADJ**

▸▸ *Mil* ***expeditionary force*** force *f* expéditionnaire; ***expeditionary mission*** mission *f* d'expédition

expeditious [,ekspɪ'dɪʃəs] **ADJ** *Formal* diligent

expeditiously [,ekspɪ'dɪʃəslɪ] **ADV** *Formal* diligemment

expel [ɪk'spel] **VT 1** *(from school)* renvoyer; *(from party, country, club)* expulser **2** *(gas, liquid)* expulser; *(breath)* exhaler

expend [ɪk'spend] **VT 1** *(time, energy)* consacrer (**on** à); *(money)* dépenser (**on** sur); *(resources)* utiliser, employer **2** *(use up ▸ ammunition, supply)* épuiser

expendable [ɪk'spendəbəl] **ADJ** *(person, workforce, equipment)* superflu; *(troops, spies)* qui peut être sacrifié; **they decided I'm e.** ils ont décidé qu'ils pouvaient se passer de moi; **he thinks people are e.** il pense qu'il peut se débarrasser des gens comme bon lui semble

expenditure [ɪk'spendɪtʃə(r)] **N 1** *(act of spending ▸ money, energy etc)* dépense *f*; *(▸ resources, ammunition)* consommation *f* **2** *(UNCOUNT) (money spent)* dépenses *fpl* (**on** en); **arms/defence e.** dépenses *fpl* en armes/liées à la défense; **this will involve us in fairly heavy e.** cela va nous entraîner dans des dépenses assez considérables

expense [ɪk'spens] **N 1** *(cost)* dépense *f*, frais *mpl*; **at great/little e.** à grands/peu de frais; **at no extra e.** sans supplément de frais; **regardless of e.** sans regarder à la dépense; **the huge e. of moving house** le coût énorme qu'entraîne un déménagement; **to go to considerable e. to do sth** faire beaucoup de frais pour faire qch; **they didn't want to go to the e. of hiring a car** ils ne voulaient pas faire les frais de louer une voiture; **I don't want to put you to any e.** je ne veux pas vous faire faire des dépenses; **no e. was spared** on n'a pas regardé à la dépense; **without any thought for the e.** sans penser au coût que cela représentait; **to do sth at great personal e.** faire qch à grands frais personnels; **at (one's) own e.** à (ses) propres frais; **she had the book published at her own e.** elle a publié le livre à ses frais *ou* à compte d'auteur; **it's not worth the e.** c'est trop cher pour ce que c'est

2 *Fig* **a joke at somebody else's e.** une plaisanterie aux dépens de quelqu'un d'autre; **at the e. of sth** au détriment de qch; **to succeed at other people's e.** réussir aux dépens des autres; **not at my e., you won't** pas à mes dépens, il n'en est pas question

3 *Com* **no, that's my e.** non, c'est sur mon compte

• **expenses NPL** *Com & Law* frais *mpl*; **to meet/cover sb's expenses** rembourser/couvrir les frais de qn; **it's on expenses** c'est l'entreprise qui paie, cela passe dans les notes de frais; **to live on expenses** vivre sur ses notes de frais, vivre aux frais de son entreprise; **to incur expenses** faire des dépenses; **to put sth on expenses** mettre qch dans les notes de frais; **to cut down on expenses** réduire les frais; **to get expenses** *(be paid expenses)* être indemnisé de ses frais; **all expenses paid** tous frais payés; **to have all expenses paid** être défrayé de tout; **travelling expenses** frais *mpl* de déplacement; **accommodation expenses** frais *mpl* d'hôtel *ou* de séjour; **entertainment expenses** frais *mpl* de représentation; **incidental expenses** faux frais *mpl*

▸▸ *Com* ***expense account*** **N** note *f* de frais; **the firm gives him an e. account for basic entertaining** l'entreprise lui attribue une allocation pour ses frais de représentation; **to put sth on the e. account** mettre qch sur la note de frais **COMP** *(lunch, dinner)* qui passe dans les notes de frais; ***expense budget, expenses budget*** budget *m* des dépenses; ***expenses claim form*** note *f* de frais

expensive [ɪk'spensɪv] **ADJ** cher; **it's an e. hobby** c'est un passe-temps coûteux *ou* qui coûte cher; **the central heating became too e. to run** le chauffage central a commencé à revenir trop cher; **to have e. tastes** avoir des goûts de luxe; **London is an e. place to live** la vie est chère à Londres; **exactly how e. was it?** combien cela a-t-il coûté exactement?; *also Fig* **that could be an e. mistake** c'est une erreur qui pourrait coûter cher

> Attention: ne pas confondre avec l'adjectif **expansive**.

expensively [ɪk'pensɪvlɪ] **ADV** *(educated, trained, redecorated)* à grands frais; *(furnished)* luxueusement; **to be e. dressed** porter des vêtements chers; **if we could all try to live less e.** si nous essayions tous de vivre à moindres frais; **try not to have it done too e.** essaie de ne pas le faire faire à trop grands frais

expensiveness [ɪk'spensɪvnɪs] **N** cherté *f*, *(of mistake)* coût *m*; **the e. of her tastes** ses goûts de luxe

experience [ɪk'spɪərɪəns] **N 1** *(in life, in a subject)* expérience *f*; **he has lots of e.** il a beaucoup d'expérience *ou* une grande expérience; **I had no previous e.** je n'avais aucune expérience préalable; **I had no e. of looking after disabled people** je ne m'étais jamais occupé de personnes handicapées; **do you have any e. of working with animals?** avez-vous déjà travaillé avec des animaux?; **she has considerable management e.** elle a une expérience considérable de *ou* dans la gestion; **to lack e.** manquer d'expérience *ou* de pratique; **to gain e. of life** faire l'apprentissage de la vie; **e. shows** *or* **proves that...** l'expérience démontre *ou* montre *ou* prouve que...; **I know from e. that he's not to be trusted** je sais par expérience qu'il ne faut pas lui faire confiance; **to know from bitter e.** savoir pour en avoir fait la cruelle expérience; **to speak from e.** parler en connaissance de cause; **in** *or* **from my (own) e., (speaking) from personal e.** d'après mon expérience personnelle; **my e. has been** *or* **it has been my e. that...** d'après mon expérience...; **to put sth down to e.** tirer un enseignement *ou* une leçon de qch; **it's all good e.** *(as consolation)* à quelque chose malheur est bon; **the black e. in America** la condition des Noirs en Amérique

2 *(event)* expérience *f*; **I had so many exciting experiences** j'ai vécu tant d'aventures passionnantes; **after this stressful e.** après cette expérience stressante; *Hum* **bad weather is all part of the Scottish e.** le mauvais temps fait partie intégrante des joies de l'Écosse; **my first e. of French cooking/of a real Scottish New Year** la première fois que j'ai goûté à la cuisine française/que j'ai assisté à un vrai réveillon écossais; **it was his first e. of love** c'était la première fois qu'il tombait amoureux; **the crossing promises to be quite an e.** la traversée promet d'être une expérience mémorable; **I hope it wasn't a nasty e. for you** j'espère que cela n'a pas été trop désagréable pour toi; **it was not an e. I would care to repeat** je ne voudrais pas renouveler l'expérience

VT 1 *(undergo ▸ hunger, hardship, recession)* connaître; **to e. military combat** faire l'expérience du combat militaire; **he experienced great difficulty in raising the money** il a eu beaucoup de mal à trouver l'argent nécessaire **2** *(feel ▸ thrill, emotion, despair)* sentir, ressentir; **she experienced a certain feeling of fear** elle a ressenti une certaine frayeur; **he is experiencing a great deal of anxiety at the moment** il est très angoissé en ce moment **3** *(have personal knowledge of)* **come**

and e. Manhattan venez découvrir Manhattan; **if you've never experienced French cooking** si vous n'avez jamais goûté à la cuisine française; **to e. a real Scottish New Year** assister à un vrai réveillon écossais

▸▸ *Com* ***experience curve*** courbe *f* d'expérience

experienced [ɪk'spɪərɪənst] **ADJ** *(person)* expérimenté; *(observer)* averti; *(eye)* exercé; **we're looking for someone a bit more e.** nous recherchons quelqu'un qui ait un peu plus d'expérience; **to be e. in sth** avoir l'expérience de qch; **to be e. at doing sth** avoir l'habitude de faire qch; **at 15 he was already sexually e.** à 15 ans, il avait déjà couché avec plusieurs filles

experiment [ɪk'sperɪmənt] **N** *also Fig* expérience *f*; **to carry out** *or* **to conduct an e.** réaliser *ou* effectuer une expérience; **an e. in sth** une expérience de qch; **experiments on animals** des expériences *fpl* sur les animaux; **as an e., by way of e.** à titre d'expérience *ou* d'essai

VI faire une expérience *ou* des expériences; **to e. with a new technique** expérimenter une nouvelle technique; **to e. with drugs** essayer la drogue; **to e. on animals** faire des expériences sur les animaux

experimental [ɪkˌsperɪ'mentəl] **ADJ** expérimental; **this programme is still at the e. stage** ce programme est à l'essai *ou* en cours d'expérimentation

experimentally [ɪkˌsperɪ'mentəlɪ] **ADV** *(by experimenting)* expérimentalement; *(as an experiment)* à titre expérimental *ou* d'essai

experimentation [ɪkˌsperɪmen'teɪʃən] **N** expérimentation *f*; **recent e. has shown that...** des expériences récentes ont montré que...

expert ['ekspɜːt] **N** expert *m*, spécialiste *mf*; **to be an e. in one's field** être un expert dans son domaine; **he's an e. at archery** c'est un expert au tir à l'arc; **to ask an e.** consulter un spécialiste; **I'm no e., but...** je ne suis pas expert *ou* spécialiste en la matière, mais...; **do it yourself, you're the e.!** fais-le toi-même, c'est toi l'expert!

ADJ *(person)* expert; *(advice, opinion)* autorisé, d'expert; **to be e. at doing sth** être expert à faire qch; **to be e. at sth** être expert en qch; **to run** *or* **to cast an e. eye over sth** jeter un œil expert sur qch

▸▸ ***expert panel*** commission *f* d'experts; *Comput* ***expert system*** système *m* expert; *Law* ***expert testimony*** témoignage *m* d'expert; *Law* ***expert witness*** expert *m (appelé comme témoin)*; **to appear** *or* **to be called as an e. witness** paraître *ou* être appelé à la cour comme expert

expertise [ˌekspɜː'tiːz] **N** compétence *f*, savoir-faire *m*; **to do sth with great e.** faire qch avec beaucoup de compétence

expertly ['ekspɜːtlɪ] **ADV** d'une manière experte, expertement

expiate ['ekspɪeɪt] **VT** *Formal* expier

expiation [ˌekspɪ'eɪʃən] **N** *Formal* expiation *f*; **in e. of one's sins** pour expier *ou* en expiation de ses péchés

expiration [ˌekspɪ'reɪʃən] **N 1** *Formal (of contract, lease, visa)* expiration *f*, échéance *f*; *(of insurance policy, passport)* expiration *f* **2** *Formal (exhalation)* expiration *f*

▸▸ *Am* ***expiration date*** *(of product)* date *f* limite de consommation

expire [ɪk'spaɪə(r)] **VI 1** *(contract, lease, insurance policy)* expirer, arriver à terme; *(visa, passport)* expirer **2** *(exhale)* expirer **3** *Arch or Literary (die)* expirer

expiring [ɪk'spaɪərɪŋ] **ADJ 1** *(contract, lease, insurance policy)* qui expire, qui est à son terme; *(visa, passport)* sur le point d'expirer **2** *Arch or Literary (dying)* expirant, qui se meurt; **with an e. voice** d'une voix mourante

expiry [ɪk'spaɪərɪ] **N** *(of contract, lease, insurance policy)* expiration *f*, échéance *f*; *(of visa, passport)* expiration *f*

▸▸ ***expiry date*** *(of contract, lease, insurance policy)* date *f* d'expiration *ou* d'échéance; *(of visa, passport)* date *f* d'expiration; *(of product)* date *f* limite de consommation; *(on ticket, on voucher)* à utiliser avant le, valable jusqu'au; *(on bank card)* valable jusqu'au

explain [ɪk'spleɪn] **VT 1** *(clarify)* expliquer; **he explained to us how the machine worked** il nous a expliqué comment la machine marchait; **she explained that she was a tourist in the city** elle a expliqué qu'elle était dans la ville en touriste; **that is easily explained, that is easy to e.** c'est facile à expliquer, cela s'explique facilement; **that explains everything** voilà qui explique tout **2** *(account for)* expliquer; **she's got a cold, which explains** *or* **will e. why she's off work today** elle a un rhume, ce qui explique pourquoi elle ne travaille pas aujourd'hui; **I think you'd better e. yourself** je crois que tu ferais mieux de t'expliquer

VI *(clarify)* expliquer; **I don't understand, you'll need to e.** je ne comprends pas, il va falloir que tu m'expliques; **you've got a bit of** *or* **a little** *or* **some explaining to do** il va falloir que tu t'expliques

▸**explain away VT SEP** *(justify, excuse)* justifier; **e. that away if you can!** essayez donc de justifier cela!; **how did he manage to e. away the broken vase?** quelle raison a-t-il trouvée pour expliquer que le vase soit cassé?

explainable [ɪk'spleɪnəbəl] **ADJ** *(explicable)* **it's easily e.** cela s'explique facilement, c'est facilement explicable

explanation [ˌeksplə'neɪʃən] **N** explication *f*; **to give** *or* **to offer an e. for sth** donner une explication à qch; **to find an e. for sth** trouver une explication à qch; **the lecturer gave an e. of the term** le professeur a donné une explication de ce terme; **one e. is that...** l'une des explications est que...; **the minister is demanding a full e.** le ministre exige une explication; **I want an e.!** je veux une explication!; **you'd better have a good e.!** j'espère que tu as une bonne excuse *ou* une explication valable!

explanatory [ɪk'splænətrɪ] **ADJ** explicatif

expletive [ɪk'spliːtɪv] **N 1** *(swearword)* juron *m*; **a string of expletives** un chapelet de jurons **2** *Gram* explétif *m*

ADJ *Gram* explétif

explicable [ɪk'splɪkəbəl] **ADJ** explicable; **this phenomenon is not e. by sociological factors alone** ce phénomène ne peut s'expliquer par les seuls facteurs sociologiques

explicit [ɪk'splɪsɪt] **ADJ** *(denial, meaning, support)* explicite; *(instructions)* explicite, clair; *(details)* clair; **he was e. on this point** il a été très clair à ce sujet; **I can't be more e. at this stage** je ne peux pas en dire plus pour l'instant; **e. sex and violence on the television** le sexe et la violence montrés ouvertement à la télévision; **sexually e.** cru

explicitly [ɪk'splɪsɪtlɪ] **ADV** explicitement

explode [ɪk'spləʊd] **VT** *(detonate)* faire exploser *ou* sauter; *Fig (theory, myth etc)* détruire, anéantir

VI *(bomb, mine etc)* exploser, éclater, sauter; *Fig (person)* exploser; **to e. with laughter** éclater de rire; **to e. with anger** exploser de colère; **the game exploded into life** le match s'est animé d'un seul coup; **the boxer exploded into action** le boxeur est entré en action d'une manière fulgurante; **when the punk movement exploded onto the scene in the 1970s** quand le mouvement punk a pris la scène musicale d'assaut dans les années 70; **the population exploded with the advent of the industrial revolution** l'avènement de la révolution industrielle a provoqué une explosion démographique

exploded [ɪk'spləʊdɪd] **ADJ** *(bomb, mine etc)* qu'on a fait exploser; *Fig (theory, myth etc)* détruit, anéanti

▸▸ *Tech* ***exploded diagram, exploded view*** éclaté *m*

exploit N ['eksplɔɪt] exploit *m*

VT [ɪk'splɔɪt] **1** *(workers)* exploiter **2** *(natural resources)* exploiter

exploitation [ˌeksplɔɪ'teɪʃən] **N** *(of workers, of natural resources)* exploitation *f*

exploration [ˌeksplə'reɪʃən] **N 1** *(of place, problem)* exploration *f*; **voyage of e.** voyage *m* d'exploration **2** *Med* exploration *f*

explorative [ɪk'splɒrətɪv] **ADJ** explorateur

exploratory [ɪk'splɒrətrɪ] **ADJ** *(journey)* d'exploration; *(talks, discussions)* exploratoire; **e. drilling** forage *m* d'exploration; *Med* **to have e. surgery** subir une exploration

explore [ɪk'splɔː(r)] **VT 1** *(country)* explorer; *(town)* découvrir, explorer **2** *(issue, possibility, problem)* étudier, examiner; *(market)* prospecter; *Fig* **to e. every avenue** explorer toutes les voies *ou* solutions possibles; *Fig* **to e. the ground** tâter le terrain **3** *Med* explorer, sonder

VI faire une exploration; **let's go exploring** *(in the woods, countryside etc)* partons en exploration; *(in a city)* allons découvrir la ville

explorer [ɪk'splɔːrə(r)] **N** *(person)* explorateur(trice) *m,f*

explosion [ɪk'spləʊʒən] **N 1** *(of bomb, gas)* explosion *f*; **an e. ripped through the building** une explosion a ébranlé le bâtiment; *Fig* **an e. of anger** une explosion de colère; **there was an e. of laughter from the dining room** une explosion *ou* une tempête de rires est arrivée de la salle à manger **2** *(act of exploding)* explosion *f*

explosive [ɪk'spləʊsɪv] **ADJ 1** *(causing an explosion)* explosif; *(gas)* explosible; *Fig* **an e. situation** une situation explosive; *Fig* **an e. combination** un mélange explosif **2** *Ling* explosif

N 1 *(in bomb)* explosif *m*; **high e.** explosif *m* puissant **2** *Ling* explosive *f*

▸▸ ***explosive device*** dispositif *m* explosif; ***explosives expert*** expert(e) *m,f* en explosifs

exponent [ɪk'spəʊnənt] **N 1** *(of idea, theory)* apôtre *m*, avocat(e) *m,f*; *(of skill)* représentant(e) *m,f*; **he is a leading e. of this theory** il est l'un des plus fervents apôtres de cette théorie **2** *Math* exposant *m*

exponential [ˌekspə'nenʃəl] **ADJ** exponentiel

▸▸ *Math* ***exponential curve*** courbe *f* exponentielle

exponentially [ˌekspə'nenʃəlɪ] **ADV** de manière exponentielle

export N ['ekspɔːt] *Com* **1** *(action)* exportation *f*; **for e. only** réservé à l'exportation **2** *(product)* exportation *f*; **visible/invisible exports** exportations *fpl* visibles/invisibles

COMP ['ekspɔːt] *Com (goods, price)* à l'export

VT [ɪk'spɔːt] **1** *Com & Fig* exporter; **to e. goods to other countries** exporter des marchandises vers d'autres pays **2** *Comput* exporter (**to** vers)

VI [ɪk'spɔːt] *Com* exporter

▸▸ ***export agent*** commissionnaire *m* exportateur; ***export aid*** aide *f* à l'exportation; ***export ban*** interdiction *f* d'exporter; **to impose an e. ban on sth** interdire qch d'exportation; ***export bid*** offre *f* export; ***export company*** société *f* d'exportation, entreprise *f* exportatrice; ***export credit*** crédit *m* à l'exportation; ***export credit guarantee*** garantie de crédit à l'exportation; ***export drive*** campagne *f* visant à stimuler l'exportation; ***export duty*** droit *m* de sortie *ou* d'exportation; ***export earnings*** revenus *mpl ou* recettes *fpl* de l'exportation; ***export incentive*** prime *f* à l'exportation; ***export levy*** prélèvement *m* à l'exportation; ***export licence*** permis *m* d'exportation; ***export market*** marché *m* à l'export; ***export permit*** permis *m* d'exportation; ***export quotas*** contingents *mpl* d'exportation; ***export reject*** produit *m* impropre à l'exportation; ***export restrictions*** restrictions *fpl* à l'exportation; ***export revenue*** revenus *mpl* de l'exportation; ***export sales*** ventes *fpl* export *ou* à l'exportation; ***export subsidy*** prime *f ou* subvention *f* à l'exportation; ***export tariff*** tarif *m* export; ***export tax*** taxe *f* à l'exportation; ***export trade*** commerce *m* d'exportation

exportable [ɪk'spɔːtəbəl] **ADJ** *Com & Comput* exportable

exportation [ˌekspɔː'teɪʃən] **N** *Com & Fig* exportation *f*

exporter [ek'spɔːtə(r)] **N** *Com* exportateur(trice) *m,f*

exporting [ɪk'spɔːtɪŋ] **N** exportation *f*

ADJ exportateur

▸▸ ***exporting company*** société *f* exportatrice; ***exporting country*** pays *m* exportateur

expose [ɪk'spəʊz] **VT 1** *(uncover)* découvrir; *Phot* exposer; **her low-cut dress leaves her shoulders exposed** sa robe décolletée découvre *ou* laisse voir ses épaules; **to e. sb/sth to sth** exposer qn/qch à qch; **to be exposed to attack** être exposé aux attaques; **to be exposed to the elements** être ex posé aux intempéries; **he was exposed to German from the age of five** il a été au contact de l'allemand depuis l'âge de cinq ans; **to e. sth to view** exposer qch à la vue; **to e. oneself** *(exhibitionist)* s'exhiber; *Law* commettre un outrage à la pudeur; **to e. oneself to sth** *(to criticism, ridicule, risk)* s'exposer à qch **2** *(reveal, unmask ▸ plot)* découvrir; *(▸ spy)* découvrir, démasquer; **they're trying to e. him as...** ils essaient de démontrer que c'est... **3** *(abandon ▸ baby)* abandonner, exposer

exposé [eks'pəuzeɪ] **N** *Press* révélations *fpl*; **the newspaper's e. of the MP's activities** les révélations du journal sur les activités du parlementaire

exposed [ɪk'spəuzd] **ADJ** *(location, house, position etc)* exposé; *Tech (parts, gears)* apparent, à découvert; *(wires)* à nu; *Archit (beam)* apparent; **the house is in an e. position** la maison est très exposée; **the troops are in an e. position** les soldats sont à découvert; *Fig* **the government is in an e. position** le gouvernement est dans une position précaire

exposition [ˌekspə'zɪʃən] **N 1** *(explanation)* exposé *m* **2** *(exhibition)* exposition *f*

expostulate [ɪk'spɒstjuleɪt] **VI** *Formal* vitupérer; **to e. with sb about sth** faire des remontrances à qn à propos de qch

expostulation [ɪkˌspɒstjʊ'leɪʃən] **N** *Formal* vitupérations *fpl*, remontrances *fpl*

exposure [ɪk'spəuʒə(r)] **N 1** *(to harm, radiation)* exposition *f*; *Fin* risque *m*

2 *(to cold)* **to suffer from the effects of e.** souffrir des effets d'une exposition au froid; **to die of e.** mourir de froid

3 *(unmasking, revealing ▸ of crime, scandal)* révélation *f*, divulgation *f*

4 *Phot* pose *f*; **a 36-e. film** une pellicule (de) 36 poses; **time e.** pose *f*

5 *(position of house)* exposition *f*; **the building has a southern e.** le bâtiment est exposé au sud

6 *(media coverage)* couverture *f*; **to receive a lot of e.** *(book, person)* faire l'objet d'une couverture médiatique importante; **pop stars suffer from too much media e.** les stars de la musique pop sont l'objet d'une attention excessive des média

7 *(abandonment ▸ of baby)* abandon *m*, exposition *f*

▸▸ *Phot* ***exposure counter*** compteur *m* de prises de vue; *Phot* ***exposure meter*** exposimètre *m*, posemètre *m*; *Phot* ***exposure time*** temps *m* de pose

expound [ɪk'spaund] *Formal* **VT** exposer

VI to e. on sth disserter sur qch

express [ɪk'spres] **N 1** *Rail* express *m*; **to travel by e.** voyager en express **2** *(system of delivery)* exprès *m*

ADJ 1 *(clear ▸ instructions)* clair; **with the e. purpose of** dans le seul but de **2** *(fast ▸ delivery, messenger)* express

ADV *(send)* en exprès

VT 1 *(voice, convey)* exprimer; **to e. an interest in sth** manifester de l'intérêt pour qch; **to e. a wish** formuler un souhait; **to e. an opinion** exprimer *ou* émettre une opinion; **the two men expressed optimism that a peaceful solution would be found** les deux hommes se sont montrés optimistes quant à un règlement pacifique; **to e. oneself** s'exprimer; **to e. oneself through sth** s'exprimer par *ou* à travers qch

2 *(render in a different form)* exprimer; **it's difficult to e. this idea in Russian** cette idée est difficile à exprimer en russe; *Math* **to e. sth as a fraction** exprimer qch sous la forme d'une fraction

3 *Formal (juice)* extraire, exprimer; *(milk)* tirer

4 *(send)* envoyer en exprès

▸▸ *Am* ***express company*** entreprise *f* de livraison exprès; *Law* ***express consent*** consentement *m* exprès; ***express delivery*** envoi *m* par exprès; ***express freight*** fret *m* express; ***express letter*** lettre *f* exprès; *Am* ***Express Mail*** = service de distribution exprès du courrier, Chronopost® *m*; ***express messenger*** messager *m* exprès; **by e. messenger** par exprès; *Rail* ***express train*** train *m* express, express *m*

expression [ɪk'spreʃən] **N 1** *(of feelings, thoughts, friendship)* expression *f*; **to give e. to sth** exprimer qch; **her feelings found e. in music** ses sentiments trouvèrent leur expression dans la musique; **we'd like you to have it as an e. of our gratitude** nous vous l'offrons en témoignage de notre reconnaissance; **freedom of e.** liberté *f* d'expression

2 *(feeling ▸ in art, music)* expression *f*; **to play/to paint with e.** jouer/peindre avec expression; **he puts a lot of e. into what he plays** il met beaucoup d'expression dans ce qu'il joue

3 *(phrase)* expression *f*; *Ling* **set** *or* **fixed e.** expression *f ou* locution *f* figée *ou* toute faite; *Math* **algebraic e.** expression *f* algébrique

4 *(facial)* expression *f*; **I could tell by her e.** je voyais bien à son expression

5 *Biol (of gene)* expression *f*

▸▸ *Mus* ***expression mark*** signe *f* d'expression

expressionism, Expressionism [ɪk'spreʃənɪzəm] **N** *Art & Literature* expressionnisme *m*

expressionist, Expressionist [ɪk'spreʃənɪst] *Art & Literature* **ADJ** expressionniste

N expressionniste *mf*

expressionless [ɪk'spreʃənlɪs] **ADJ** *(face, person)* inexpressif, sans expression; *(voice)* inexpressif, éteint, terne; **the accused sat e. in the dock** l'inculpé était assis sans expression au banc des accusés

expressive [ɪk'spresɪv] **ADJ** *(face, gesture, smile)* expressif; **to be e. of sth** être indicatif de qch

expressively [ɪk'spresɪvlɪ] **ADV** *(gesture, smile)* avec expression

expressiveness [ɪk'spresɪvnɪs] **N** *(of face, gesture, smile)* expressivité *f*

expressly [ɪk'spreslɪ] **ADV** expressément; **I e. forbid you to leave** je vous interdis formellement de partir

expressway [ɪk'spresweɪ] **N** *Am* autoroute *f*

expropriate [eks'prəuprɪeɪt] **VT** exproprier

expropriation [eksˌprəuprɪ'eɪʃən] **N** expropriation *f*

expulsion [ɪk'spʌlʃən] **N 1** *(from school)* renvoi *m*; *(from party, country, club)* expulsion *f* **2** *(of breath)* expulsion *f*

expunge [ɪk'spʌndʒ] **VT** *Formal (delete)* supprimer, effacer; *(from memory)* effacer

expurgate ['ekspəgeɪt] **VT** *(book, play, text)* expurger; **expurgated edition** édition *f* expurgée

expurgation [ˌekspə'geɪʃən] **N** *(of book, play, text)* expurgation *f*

exquisite [ɪk'skwɪzɪt] **ADJ 1** *(food, beauty, manners)* exquis; *(jewellery, craftsmanship)* raffiné; **to have e. taste** avoir un goût exquis **2** *(intense ▸ pleasure, pain, thrill)* intense

exquisitely [ɪk'skwɪzɪtlɪ] **ADV 1** *(delightfully)* de façon exquise; **an e. warm afternoon** un après-midi délicieusement chaud; **an e. timed interjection** une exclamation tout à fait opportune **2** *(intensely)* intensément

exquisiteness [ɪk'skwɪzɪtnɪs] **N 1** *(delicacy, subtlety ▸ of work of art)* raffinement *m*, finesse *f*; *(▸ of hearing)* finesse *f* **2** *(intense degree ▸ of pleasure)* intensité *f*; *(▸ of pain)* acuité *f*

ex-serviceman *(pl* **ex-servicemen** [-mən]) **N** *Br Mil* retraité *m* de l'armée

ex-servicewoman *(pl* **ex-servicewomen** [-wɪmɪn]) **N** *Br Mil* retraitée *f* de l'armée

ext. *(written abbr* **extension)** poste *m*; **e. 4174** poste 4174

extant [ek'stænt] **ADJ** *Formal* encore existant; **only one of these manuscripts/buildings is still e.** seul l'un des manuscrits/bâtiments existe toujours

extemporaneous [ɪkˌstempə'reɪnɪəs] **ADJ** *Formal* improvisé, impromptu

extemporaneously [ɪkˌstempə'reɪnɪəslɪ] **ADV** *Formal* impromptu

extemporary [ɪkˌstempərərɪ] = **extemporaneous**

extempore [ɪk'stempərɪ] *Formal* **ADJ** improvisé, impromptu

ADV *(speak)* impromptu

extemporization, -isation [ɪkˌstempəraɪ'zeɪʃən] **N** *Formal* improvisation *f*

extemporize, -ise [ɪk'stempəraɪz] *Formal* **VT** *(speech, piece of music)* improviser

VI *(speaker, musician)* improviser

extend [ɪk'stend] **VT 1** *(stretch out ▸ arm, leg)* étendre, allonger; *(▸ wings)* ouvrir, déployer; *(▸ aerial)* déplier, déployer; **to e. one's hand to sb** tendre la main à qn

2 *(in length, duration ▸ guarantee, visa, news programme)* prolonger; *(▸ road, runway)* prolonger, allonger; **they extended his visa by six months** on a prolongé son visa de six mois; **the deadline has been extended until 25 May** la date limite a été repoussée au 25 mai

3 *(make larger, widen ▸ frontiers, law, enquiry, search)* étendre; *(▸ building)* agrandir; *(▸ vocabulary)* enrichir, élargir; **the company decided to e. its activities into the export market** la société a décidé d'étendre ses activités au marché de l'exportation

4 *(offer ▸ friendship, hospitality)* offrir; *(▸ thanks, condolences, congratulations)* présenter; *(▸ credit)* accorder; **to e. an invitation to sb** faire une invitation à qn; **to e. a welcome to sb** souhaiter la bienvenue à qn; **to e. one's sympathy to sb** présenter ses condoléances à qn

5 *(stretch ▸ horse, person)* pousser au bout de ses capacités *ou* à son maximum; **to e. oneself in a race** se donner à fond dans une course

VI 1 *(protrude ▸ wall, cliff)* avancer, former une avancée **2** *(stretch ▸ country, forest, hills etc)* s'étendre; *(▸ period of time)* se prolonger; **the queue extended all the way down the street** il y avait la queue jusqu'au bout de la rue; **the parliamentary recess extends into October** les vacances parlementaires se prolongent jusqu'en octobre; **the legislation does not e. to single mothers** la législation ne concerne pas les mères célibataires

extendable [ɪk'stendəbəl] **ADJ 1** *(aerial, pole)* télescopique; **e. ladder** échelle *f* à coulisse **2** *(in time ▸ contract, visa)* renouvelable; **the tenancy is e. by one year** le contrat de location peut être prolongé d'un an

extended [ɪk'stendɪd] **ADJ 1** *(in time ▸ contract, visit)* prolongé; **e. holiday** des vacances *fpl* prolongées; **the firm gave him an e. contract** la société a reconduit son contrat; **to be on e. leave** être en arrêt prolongé; **owing to the e. news bulletin** en raison de la prolongation du bulletin d'informations **2** *(larger, wider ▸ frontiers, enquiry, search)* étendu; **the bank granted him e. credit** la banque lui a accordé un crédit à long terme **3** *(in space ▸ body, arm)* étendu, allongé; *(building)* agrandi; *Mil* **in e. order** en ordre dispersé

▸▸ *Am Med* ***extended care*** soins *mpl* prolongés; ***extended coverage*** *Ins* couverture *f* multirisque; *Rad & TV* = informations détaillées sur un événement; ***extended family*** famille *f* élargie; *Am Met* ***extended forecast*** = prévisions météorologiques sur plus de deux jours; *Comput* ***extended keyboard*** clavier *m* étendu; *Comput* ***extended memory*** mémoire *f* étendue; *Horseriding* ***extended trot*** trot *m* allongé; ***extended warranty*** garantie *f* prolongée

extender lens [ɪk'stendə-] **N** bague *f* rallonge

extending [ɪk'stendɪŋ] **ADJ** *(table)* à rallonge *ou* rallonges; *(ladder)* à coulisse

N 1 *(of arm, leg, freedom)* extension *f* **2** *(of motorway)* prolongement *m* **3** *(of contract, visa)* prolongation *f*

extension [ɪk'stenʃən] **N 1** *(of arm, legislation, frontiers)* extension *f*

2 *(of house, building)* **to build an e. onto sth** agrandir qch; **do you like the new e.?** *(to the house)* la nouvelle partie de la maison vous plaît-elle?; *(of library, museum etc)* la nouvelle aile vous plaît-elle?

3 *(of motorway)* prolongement *m*

4 *(of contract, visa, time period)* prolongation *f*; **to ask for/to get an e.** *(to pay, hand in work)* demander/obtenir un délai; **the bar's been granted an e.** le bar a obtenu une prolongation de ses heures d'ouverture

5 *(telephone ▸ in office building)* poste *m*; *(▸ in house)* poste *m* supplémentaire; **can I have e. 946?** pouvez-vous me passer le poste 946?; **you can reach me on e. 231** vous pouvez me joindre au poste 231

6 (hair) extensions rajouts *mpl*
7 *Elec* prolongateur *m*, rallonge *f*
8 *Comput (of file)* extension *f*
9 *Acct (of balance)* transport *m*, report *m*
• **by extension** ADV par extension
►► ***extension cable*** câble *m* de raccordement; ***extension college*** institut *m* de formation permanente; ***extension cord*** prolongateur *m*, rallonge *f*; ***extension course*** cours *m* de formation permanente; ***extension ladder*** échelle *f* à coulisse; *Br* ***extension lead*** prolongateur *m*, rallonge *f*; *Tel* ***extension number*** numéro *m* de poste

extensive [ɪk'stensɪv] ADJ **1** *(desert, powers, knowledge)* étendu, vaste; *(damage, repairs)* important, considérable; *(tests, research, investigation)* approfondi; **the area is remarkable for its e. tree cover** cette région se distingue par l'étendue considérable de ses bois; **the issue has been given e. coverage in the media** ce problème a été largement traité dans les médias; **to make e. use of sth** beaucoup utiliser qch, faire un usage considérable de qch **2** *Agr (farming)* extensif

extensively [ɪk'stensɪvlɪ] ADV *(damaged, altered, revised)* considérablement; *(quote)* abondamment; *(travel, read)* beaucoup; *(discuss)* en profondeur; **the car has been e. tested** la voiture a subi des tests approfondis *ou* poussés; **to research sth e.** faire des recherches approfondies sur qch; **to use sth e.** beaucoup utiliser qch, faire un usage considérable de qch

extensor [ɪk'stensə(r)] N *Anat* extenseur *m*

extent [ɪk'stent] N **1** *(size, range ► of ground, knowledge, influence)* étendue *f*; *(► of debts, damage)* importance *f*; **trees ran along the entire e. of the boulevard** des arbres longeaient le boulevard sur toute sa longueur; **he has debts to the e. of £1,000** il a des dettes d'une valeur *ou* d'un montant de 1000 livres **2** *(degree)* mesure *f*, degré *m*; **these figures show the e. to which tourism has been affected** ces chiffres montrent à quel point le tourisme a été affecté; **to what e.?** dans quelle mesure?; **to that e.** sur ce point, à cet égard; **to the e. that..., to such an e. that...** à tel point que... + *indicative* **3** *(in publishing ► of book)* nombre *m* de pages
• **to a large extent, to a great extent** ADV dans une grande mesure, à un haut point *ou* degré
• **to an extent, to some extent, to a certain extent** ADV dans une certaine mesure, jusqu'à un certain point *ou* degré

extenuate [ɪk'stenjʊeɪt] VT atténuer

Note that the French verb **exténuer** is a false friend and is never a translation for the English verb **to extenuate**. It means **to exhaust.**

extenuating [ɪk'stenjʊeɪtɪŋ] ADJ **e. circumstances** circonstances *fpl* atténuantes

extenuation [ɪk,stenjʊ'eɪʃən] N atténuation *f*; **to say sth in e. of an offence/an act** dire qch pour atténuer la gravité d'un délit/d'un acte

exterior [ɪk'stɪərɪə(r)] ADJ extérieur (**to** à)
N *(of house, building)* extérieur *m*; *(of person)* apparence *f*, dehors *m*; **on the e.** à l'extérieur; **the house had a whitewashed e.** la maison avait une façade blanchie à la chaux; **underneath his stern e. he is very sensitive** sous des dehors sévères, c'est un sensible
►► *Math* ***exterior angle*** angle *m* externe

exteriorize, -ise [ɪk'stɪərɪəraɪz] VT extérioriser

exterminate [ɪk'stɜːmɪneɪt] VT *(pests)* exterminer; *(race, people)* exterminer, anéantir

extermination [ɪk,stɜːmɪ'neɪʃən] N *(of pests)* extermination *f*; *(of race, people)* extermination *f*, anéantissement *m*

exterminator [ɪk'stɜːmɪneɪtə(r)] N *(person ► gen)* exterminateur(trice) *m,f*; *(► of vermin)* dératiseur *m*; *(poison)* mort-aux-rats *f inv*

extern ['ekstɜːn] N *Am Med* externe *mf*

external [ɪk'stɜːnəl] ADJ *(events, relations, trade, wall, reality)* extérieur; *(injury)* externe; *(interference, pressure)* du dehors, de l'extérieur; *Comput* externe; *Pharm* **for e. use only** *(on packaging)* à usage externe uniquement
N *(usu pl)* **externals** extérieur *m*, formes *fpl* extérieures, dehors *mpl*; **to judge by externals** juger les choses selon les apparences
►► *Banking* ***external account*** *(of nation)* compte *m* des opérations extérieures; *(of individual)* compte *m* d'étranger, *Can* compte *m* de non-résident; *Fin* ***external audit*** audit *m* externe; *Fin* ***external auditing*** vérification *f* externe, audit *m* externe; *Fin* ***external auditor*** audit *m ou* auditeur(trice) *m,f* externe; *Econ* ***external balance*** balance *f* extérieure; *Econ* ***external debt*** dette *f* extérieure; *Fin* ***external deficit*** déficit *m* extérieur; *Univ* ***external degree*** = diplôme obtenu en examen final, sans que l'étudiant ait assisté aux cours; *Comput* ***external device*** dispositif *m* externe, périphérique *m*; *Comput* ***external drive*** unité *f* (de disque) externe; *Anat* ***external ear*** oreille *f* externe; *Univ* ***external examiner*** examinateur(trice) *m,f* venant de l'extérieur; *Fin* ***external financing*** financement *m* externe, fonds *mpl* extérieurs; *Econ* ***external foreign debt*** dette *f* extérieure; *Econ* ***external growth*** croissance *f* externe; *Econ* ***external labour market*** marché *m* du travail externe; *Comput* ***external modem*** modem *m* externe; *Univ* ***external student*** = étudiant qui passe un examen dans un établissement où il n'a pas étudié

externality [,ekstɜː'nælɪtɪ] N extériorité *f*

externalize, -ise [ɪk'stɜːnəlaɪz] VT extérioriser

externally [ɪk'stɜːnəlɪ] ADV à l'extérieur; *Pharm* **to be used e.** *(on packaging)* à usage externe

extinct [ɪk'stɪŋkt] ADJ *(species, race)* disparu, qui n'existe plus; **the horse and plough are nearly e.** le cheval et la charrue sont en voie d'extinction; **to become e.** *(species, tradition)* s'éteindre, disparaître; *(method)* disparaître
►► ***extinct volcano*** volcan *m* éteint

extinction [ɪk'stɪŋkʃən] N *(of species, race)* extinction *f*, disparition *f*; *(of fire, candle)* extinction *f*; **to be threatened with e.** être menacé d'extinction, être en voie de disparition; **to hunt an animal to e.** chasser un animal jusqu'à extinction de l'espèce

extinguish [ɪk'stɪŋgwɪʃ] VT *(fire, candle)* éteindre; *Fig (memory)* effacer

extinguisher [ɪk'stɪŋgwɪʃə(r)] N extincteur *m*

extirpate ['ekstəpeɪt] VT *Formal* extirper

extirpation [,ekstə'peɪʃən] N *Formal* extirpation *f*

extn. *(written abbr* **extension***)* poste *m*; **e. 421** poste 421

extol, *Am* **extoll** [ɪk'stəʊl] *(pt & pp* **extolled,** *cont* **extolling***)* VT *Formal (person, deed, talents)* faire l'éloge de; **to e. the virtues of the system** vanter les mérites du système, faire l'éloge du système; **to e. the beauty of nature** chanter les louanges de la nature

extort [ɪk'stɔːt] VT *(money)* extorquer, soutirer; *(confession, promise)* extorquer, arracher; **to e. money from sb** extorquer *ou* soutirer de l'argent à qn

extortion [ɪk'stɔːʃən] N *(of money, promise, confession)* extorsion *f*; **that's sheer e.!** *(very expensive)* c'est du vol pur et simple!

extortionate [ɪk'stɔːʃənət] ADJ *(price, demand)* exorbitant, démesuré; **that's e.!** *(very expensive)* c'est exorbitant *ou* du vol!

extortioner [ɪk'stɔːʃənə(r)], **extortionist** [ɪk'stɔːʃənɪst] N extorqueur(euse) *m,f*

extra ['ekstrə] ADJ **1** *(additional)* supplémentaire; **there are some e. questions overleaf** il y a des questions supplémentaires au dos; **I put an e. jumper on** j'ai mis un pull en plus; **he made an e. effort to get there on time** il a redoublé d'efforts pour y arriver à l'heure; **as an e. precaution** pour plus de précaution; **an e. helping of cake** une autre part de gâteau; **service/VAT is e.** le service/la TVA est en supplément; **e. pay** supplément *m* de salaire; **she asked for an e. £50** elle a demandé 50 livres de plus; **at no e. charge** sans supplément de prix **2** *(spare)* en plus; **an e. sheet of paper** une feuille en plus
ADV **1** *(extremely ► polite, kind)* extrêmement; *(► strong, white)* super-; **to work e. hard** travailler d'arrache-pied; **e. smart** *(dress, outfit)* superchic, ultrachic **2** *(in addition)* plus, davantage; **to pay e. for a double room** payer plus *ou* un supplément pour une chambre double
N **1** *(addition)* supplément *m*; **the paper comes with a business e.** le journal est vendu avec un supplément affaires; **a car with many extras** une voiture avec de nombreux accessoires en option
2 *Cin & TV* figurant(e) *m,f*
3 *(additional charge)* supplément *m*
4 *(luxury)* **little extras** petits extras *mpl ou* luxe *mpl*
►► *Cin* ***extra feature*** *(on DVD)* bonus *m*; ***extra point*** *(in American football)* transformation *f*; ***extra time*** *(to pay, finish)* délai *m*; *Sport* prolongations *fpl*; **the game has gone into e. time** on joue les prolongations

extra- ['ekstrə] PREF extra-; **e.-large** grande taille; **e.-strong** extra-solide

EXTRA- PRÉFIXE

En tant que préfixe accolé à un adjectif, **extra-** peut avoir deux sens:

• Il peut signifier PLUS QUE LA NORMALE et peut se joindre, dans ce sens, à pratiquement n'importe quel adjectif. On trouve parfois dans la traduction le préfixe **extra-**, mais le plus souvent on a recours à un adverbe comme **très** ou **particulièrement**. On compte parmi les combinaisons les plus lexicalisées:

extra-dry wine vin très sec; **extra-large eggs** de très gros œufs ; **extra-thin paper** du papier extrafin; **you'll have to take extra-special care over it** il faudra que tu y fasses particulièrement attention

• Il peut signifier EN DEHORS ou AU-DELÀ. Dans ce cas, la traduction est **extra-**:

extrasensory extrasensoriel; **extraterrestrial** extraterrestre; **extracurricular activities** activités extrascolaires; **extramarital sex** rapports extraconjugaux

extract VT [ɪk'strækt] **1** *(take out ► juice, oil, bullet)* extraire; *(► tooth)* arracher, extraire; *(► cork)* ôter, enlever; *(► letter from pocket etc)* tirer (**from** de); **to e. a quotation from a passage** extraire *ou* tirer une citation d'un passage
2 *(obtain ► information)* soutirer, arracher; *(► money)* soutirer; **to e. a confession from sb** soutirer *ou* arracher un aveu à qn
3 *Math* **to e. the square root of a number** extraire la racine carrée d'un nombre
4 *Comput (zipped file)* décompresser
N ['ekstrækt] **1** *(from book, piece of music)* extrait *m*; **selected extracts** *(from author, works)* morceaux *mpl* choisis **2** *(substance)* extrait *m*, concentré *m*; *Pharm* extrait *m*, essence *f*; *Culin* **beef/malt/vegetable e.** extrait *m* de bœuf/de malt/de légumes

extraction [ɪk'strækʃən] N **1** *(removal ► of juice, oil, bullet)* extraction *f*; *(► of tooth)* extraction *f*, arrachage *m*; **the e. of stone from the quarry** l'extraction de la pierre de la carrière; **she needs two extractions and three fillings** il faut lui arracher deux dents et en plomber trois **2** *(descent)* extraction *f*; **of noble/humble e.** de noble/modeste extraction; **he is of Scottish e.** il est d'origine écossaise

extractor [ɪk'stræktə(r)] N *(machine, tool)* extracteur *m*; *(fan)* ventilateur *m*, aérateur *m*
►► ***extractor fan*** ventilateur *m*, aérateur *m*; ***extractor hood*** *(on stove)* hotte *f* aspirante

extracurricular [,ekstrəkə'rɪkjʊlə(r)] ADJ *Sch* hors programme, extrascolaire; *Univ* hors programme
►► ***extracurricular activities*** activités *fpl* extrascolaires; *Fig Hum* frasques *fpl*

extraditable ['ekstrə,daɪtəbəl] ADJ *(person)* passible d'extradition; *(crime, offence)* qui justifie l'extradition

extradite ['ekstrədaɪt] VT *(send back)* extrader; *(procure extradition of)* obtenir l'extradition de; **the authorities were unable to e. him from the USA** les autorités n'ont pas réussi à obtenir son extradition des États-Unis

extradition [,ekstrə'dɪʃən] N extradition *f*; **to request/to obtain the e. of sb** demander/obtenir l'extradition de qn

COMP *(order, warrant)* d'extradition
▸▸ ***extradition treaty*** accord *m* d'extradition

extra-dry ADJ *(wine)* très sec(sèche); *(champagne, vermouth)* extra-dry *(inv)*

extra-fine ADJ *(flour, sugar)* extrafin, surfin

extrajudicial [ˌekstrədʒuːˈdɪʃəl] ADJ *Law* extrajudiciaire

extramarital [ˌekstrəˈmærɪtəl] ADJ extraconjugal
▸▸ ***extramarital relations*** relations *fpl* extraconjugales; ***extramarital sex*** rapports *mpl* extraconjugaux

extramural [ˌekstrəˈmjʊərəl] ADJ **1** *Br Univ* **e. lecturer** = enseignant qui donne des cours d'éducation permanente; **e. course** = cours donné dans le cadre de l'éducation permanente; **Department of E. Studies** = service d'une université qui s'occupe de l'éducation permanente, Institut *m* d'éducation permanente **2** *Am Univ (agency, funding)* extérieur à l'université; *(match, tournament)* inter-universitaire

extraneous [ɪkˈstreɪnjəs] ADJ **1** *(irrelevant ▸ idea, point, consideration, issue)* étranger, extérieur; **to be e. to sth** *(idea, point, issue)* être étranger à qch; *(detail)* être sans rapport avec qch **2** *(from outside ▸ noise, force)* extérieur

extraordinarily [ɪkˈstrɔːdənrəlɪ] ADV **1** *(as intensifier)* extraordinairement, incroyablement; **that play was e. badly acted** cette pièce était incroyablement mal jouée; **it took an e. long time to get there** nous avons mis un temps incroyable pour arriver **2** *(unusually)* extraordinairement, d'une manière inhabituelle; **e., they escaped unscathed/he made no reference to the event in his speech** fait extraordinaire, ils s'en sont sortis sans une égratignure/il n'a pas fait référence à l'événement dans son discours

extraordinary [ɪkˈstrɔːdənrɪ] ADJ **1** *(remarkable)* extraordinaire; **that's** *or* **how e.!** c'est extraordinaire *ou* incroyable!; **I find it e. that you did not inform the police** je trouve incroyable *ou* extraordinaire que vous n'ayez pas prévenu la police **2** *(surprising, unusual ▸ person)* bizarre, singulier; *(▸ house)* bizarre, curieux; *(▸ appearance, outfit)* insolite, singulier; *(▸ event)* bizarre, invraisemblable; *(▸ behaviour, speech)* étonnant, surprenant **3** *(additional ▸ meeting, session)* extraordinaire
▸▸ *Acct* ***extraordinary expenses*** frais *mpl* extraordinaires, dépenses *fpl* extraordinaires; *Com* ***extraordinary general meeting*** assemblée *f* générale extraordinaire; *Com* **to call an e. general meeting of the shareholders** convoquer d'urgence les actionnaires; *Acct* ***extraordinary income*** produits *mpl* exceptionnels; *Acct* ***extraordinary item*** poste *m* extraordinaire; *Acct* ***extraordinary loss*** résultats *mpl* exceptionnels *(pertes)*; ***extraordinary profit*** résultats *mpl* exceptionnels *(profits)*; ***extraordinary rendition*** transfert *m* illégal de détenus

extrapolate [ɪkˈstræpəleɪt] VT *(infer from facts)* déduire par extrapolation; *Math* établir par extrapolation; **if we e. these figures** *(use them as a basis)* si nous extrapolons à partir de ces chiffres; *(arrive at by extrapolation)* si nous déduisons ces chiffres par extrapolation
VI extrapoler; **to e. from sth** extrapoler à partir de qch

extrapolation [ɪkˌstræpəˈleɪʃən] N *(gen) & Math* extrapolation *f*

extrasensory [ˌekstrəˈsensərɪ] ADJ extrasensoriel
▸▸ ***extrasensory perception*** perception *f* extrasensorielle

extraterrestrial [ˌekstrətəˈrestrɪəl] N extraterrestre *mf*
ADJ extraterrestre

extraterritorial [ˈekstrəˌterɪˈtɔːrɪəl] ADJ *(possessions)* situé hors du territoire national; *(rights)* d'exterritorialité, d'extra-territorialité

extravagance [ɪkˈstrævəgəns] N **1** *(wasteful spending)* folles dépenses *fpl*, prodigalités *fpl*; **she accused the government of e.** elle a accusé le gouvernement de dilapider le trésor public; **the e. of his tastes** ses goûts dispendieux *ou* de luxe **2** *(extravagant purchase)* folie *f*; **to allow oneself little extravagances** se permettre des petites folies **3** *(exaggerated nature ▸ of behaviour, comparison)* extravagance *f*

> Note that the most common meaning of the French word **extravagance** is **eccentricity**.

extravagant [ɪkˈstrævəgənt] ADJ **1** *(wasteful, profligate ▸ person)* dépensier, prodigue; *(▸ tastes)* de luxe, dispendieux; *(▸ lifestyle)* dispendieux; **that was much too e. of you** tu as fait des folies; **I think you're being a bit e., having the central heating on all the time** je trouve que c'est du gaspillage de laisser le chauffage central allumé en permanence comme tu le fais; **to be e. with one's money** être gaspilleur *ou* dépensier, gaspiller son argent **2** *(exaggerated ▸ idea, opinion)* extravagant; *(▸ claim, comparison)* exagéré; *(▸ behaviour, prices)* extravagant, excessif; *(▸ praise)* outré; **to make e. claims** avoir des prétentions exagérées; **e. claims have been made for the drug** certaines propriétés ont été attribuées abusivement à ce médicament; **his e. prose style** le style excessif de sa prose

> Note that the most common meaning of the French word **extravagant** is **eccentric**.

extravagantly [ɪkˈstrævəgəntlɪ] ADV **1** *(lavishly)* **to spend money e.** jeter l'argent par les fenêtres; **to live e.** mener grand train; **to entertain e.** recevoir sans regarder à la dépense; **an e. furnished room** une pièce meublée à grands frais *ou* luxueusement meublée **2** *(exaggeratedly ▸ behave, act, talk)* de manière extravagante; *(▸ praise)* avec excès; **e. worded claims** des affirmations *fpl* exagérées *ou* excessives

extravaganza [ɪkˌstrævəˈgænzə] N *(lavish production)* grand spectacle *m*; *(literary work, piece of music)* œuvre *f* fantaisiste; **jazz e.** grand festival *m* de jazz; **the castle is a Baroque/Gothic e.** le château est construit dans un style baroque/gothique fantaisie

extravasation [ekˌstrævəˈseɪʃən] N *Med* épanchement *m*

extravert = **extrovert**

extreme [ɪkˈstriːm] ADJ **1** *(heat, pain, views, measures)* extrême; **they live in e. poverty** ils vivent dans une misère extrême; **to be in e. pain** souffrir terriblement *ou* atrocement; **to be e. in one's beliefs** être extrême dans ses convictions; **the e. left wing of the party** l'aile d'extrême gauche du parti; **e. old age** grand âge *m*; **an e. case** un cas exceptionnel **2** *(furthest away)* extrême; **at the e. end of the platform** à l'extrémité du quai; **on the e. right of the screen** à l'extrême droite de l'écran
N extrême *m*; **extremes of temperature** extrêmes *mpl* de température; **to go to extremes** exagérer; **to take** *or* **to carry sth to extremes, to go to extremes with sth** pousser qch à l'extrême; **to be driven to extremes** être poussé à bout; **to go from one e. to the other** aller *ou* passer d'un extrême à l'autre; **don't go to the opposite e.** ne tombe pas dans l'extrême inverse
• **in the extreme** ADV à l'extrême; **polite/careful in the e.** poli/soigneux à l'extrême
▸▸ *Cin & TV* ***extreme close-up*** plan *m* très rapproché; *Cin & TV* ***extreme long shot*** plan *m* très éloigné; *Formal* ***the extreme penalty*** le dernier supplice; ***extreme sports*** sports *mpl* extrêmes; *Rel* ***extreme unction*** extrême-onction *f*

extremely [ɪkˈstriːmlɪ] ADV *(very)* extrêmement

extremism [ɪkˈstriːmɪzəm] N *Pol* extrémisme *m*

extremist [ɪkˈstriːmɪst] *Pol* N extrémiste *mf*
ADJ extrémiste

extremity [ɪkˈstremətɪ] *(pl* **extremities***)* N **1** *(furthermost tip)* extrémité *f*; **at the southernmost e. of the peninsula** à l'extrémité sud de la péninsule
2 *(usu pl) (hand, foot)* **the extremities** les extrémités *fpl*
3 *(extreme nature ▸ of belief, view etc)* extrémité *f*
4 *(adversity, danger)* extrémité *f*; **to be reduced to the last e.** en être réduit à la dernière extrémité; **to help sb in his/her e.** aider qn dans son malheur
5 *(usu pl) (extreme measure)* extrémité *f*; **to resort to extremities** en venir à des extrêmes; **to drive sb to extremities** pousser *ou* conduire qn à des extrêmes

extricate [ˈekstrɪkeɪt] VT *(thing)* extirper, dégager; *(person)* dégager; **to e. oneself from a tricky situation** se sortir *ou* se tirer d'une situation délicate; **to e. oneself from a boring conversation** s'échapper d'une conversation ennuyeuse

extrinsic [ekˈstrɪnsɪk] ADJ extrinsèque
▸▸ *Fin* ***extrinsic value*** valeur *f* extrinsèque

extrovert [ˈekstrəvɜːt] N extraverti(e) *m,f*, extroverti(e) *m,f*; **he's an e.** c'est un extraverti
ADJ extraverti, extroverti

extrude [ɪkˈstruːd] VT **1** *Tech (metals, plastics)* extruder **2** *Formal (force out ▸ lava)* extruder

extrusion [ɪkˈstruːʒən] N **1** *Tech (of metal, plastic)* extrusion *f* **2** *Formal (action)* extraction *f*

exuberance [ɪgˈzjuːbərəns] N **1** *(of person, writing)* exubérance *f*; **to be full of e.** être plein d'exubérance; **youthful/natural e.** exubérance *f* juvénile/naturelle **2** *(of vegetation)* exubérance *f*, luxuriance *f*

exuberant [ɪgˈzjuːbərənt] ADJ **1** *(person, mood, style)* exubérant; *(health, vitality)* débordant; **she felt e. at the news** la nouvelle la remplit d'une joie exubérante **2** *(vegetation)* exubérant, luxuriant

exuberantly [ɪgˈzjuːbərəntlɪ] ADV avec exubérance; **e. cheerful** d'une gaieté exubérante; **e. healthy** débordant de santé

exude [ɪgˈzjuːd] VT *(blood, sap)* exsuder; *Fig (confidence, love)* déborder de; **she exudes health** elle respire la santé; **he exudes (an air of) confidence/well-being** un halo de confiance en soi/de bien-être se dégage de tout son être
VI exsuder

exult [ɪgˈzʌlt] VI *(rejoice)* exulter, jubiler; *(triumph)* exulter; **to e. at** *or* **in one's success** *(rejoice)* se réjouir de son succès; **to e. over defeated opponents** *(triumph)* exulter de la défaite de ses adversaires

exultant [ɪgˈzʌltənt] ADJ *(feeling, shout, look)* d'exultation; *(mood, crowd)* jubilant; **to look e.** avoir l'air d'exulter; **to be** *or* **to feel e. (at)** exulter (de)

exultantly [ɪgˈzʌltəntlɪ] ADV avec exultation

exultation [ˌegzʌlˈteɪʃən] N exultation *f*

ex-wife N ex-femme *f*

EYE [aɪ] *(cont* **eyeing** *or* **eying***)* N **1** *(organ)* œil *m*; **to have green eyes** avoir les yeux verts; **a girl with green eyes** une fille aux yeux verts; **before your very eyes!** sous vos yeux!; **look me in the e. and say that** regarde-moi bien dans les yeux et dis-le moi; **I saw it with my own eyes** je l'ai vu de mes yeux vu *ou* de mes propres yeux; **to open/close one's eyes** ouvrir/fermer les yeux; **with one's eyes closed/open** les yeux fermés/ouverts; *Fig* **she can't keep her eyes open** elle dort debout; **he went into it with his eyes open** il s'y est lancé en toute connaissance de cause; **to have the sun/the light in one's eyes** avoir le soleil/la lumière dans les yeux; **to look sb straight in the e.** regarder qn droit dans les yeux; **at e. level** au niveau des yeux
2 *(gaze)* regard *m*; **her eyes fell on the letter** son regard est tombé sur la lettre; **the film looks at the world through the eyes of a child** dans ce film, on voit le monde à travers les yeux d'un enfant; **with a critical e.** d'un œil critique; **I couldn't believe my eyes** je n'en croyais pas mes yeux; **all eyes were upon her** elle était au centre de tous les regards, tous les regards étaient posés sur elle
3 *Mil* **eyes left/right!** tête à gauche/à droite!; **eyes front!** fixe!
4 *Sewing (of needle)* chas *m*, œil *m*; *(eyelet)* œillet *m*
5 *(of potato, twig)* œil *m*
6 *(of hurricane)* œil *m*, centre *m*; **the e. of the storm** l'œil du cyclone; *Fig* **at the e. of the storm** dans l'œil du cyclone
7 *(photocell)* œil *m* électrique
8 *(for hammer handle)* emmanchure *f*; *(for axe blade)* toyère *f*
9 *(idioms)* **as far as the e. can see** à perte de vue; **to keep one's eyes and ears open** avoir l'œil et l'oreille aux aguets; **to open sb's eyes (to sth)**

ouvrir les yeux à qn (sur qch), dessiller les yeux à qn (sur qch); **the incident opened his eyes to the truth about her** l'incident lui ouvrit les yeux sur ce qu'elle était vraiment; **we can't close** *or* **shut our eyes to the problem** on ne peut pas fermer les yeux sur ce problème; **they can't close their eyes to the fact that the company's at fault** ils sont bien obligés d'admettre que la société est en faute; **I could do it with my eyes closed** *or* **shut** je pourrais le faire les yeux fermés; **for your eyes only** ultra-confidentiel; **in this job you need to have a good e. for detail** dans ce métier il faut être très méticuleux; **to have an e. for a bargain** savoir reconnaître une bonne affaire; *Br* **to get one's e. in** prendre ses repères; **he only has eyes for her** il n'a d'yeux que pour elle; **the boss has his e. on Smith for the job** le patron a Smith en vue pour le poste; **he has his e. on the gold medal/the mayor's position** il vise la médaille d'or/la mairie; **the police have had their e. on him for some time** cela fait un certain temps que la police l'a à l'œil; **he wants to buy an apartment, in fact he's already got his e. on one** il veut acheter un appartement, et d'ailleurs il en a déjà un en vue; **he always has an e. for** *or* **to the main chance** il ne perd jamais de vue ses propres intérêts; **in my/her eyes** à mes/ses yeux; **in the eyes of the law/of the Church** aux yeux *ou* au regard de la loi/de l'Église; **to run** *or* **to cast one's e. over sth** jeter un coup d'œil à qch; **she ran an e. over the contract** elle a parcouru le contrat; **to try to catch sb's e.** essayer d'attirer le regard de qn; **this article caught my e.** cet article a retenu mon attention; **could you keep your e. on the children/the house?** pourriez-vous surveiller les enfants/la maison?; **I have to keep an e. on him** il faut que je l'aie à l'œil; **I couldn't keep my eyes off him/it** je ne pouvais pas en détacher mes yeux; **she keeps an e. on things** elle a l'œil à tout; **keep an e. on the situation** suivez de près la situation; **to keep one's e. on the ball** *(gen)* ne pas quitter la balle des yeux; *Golf* fixer la balle; *Fig* être vigilant; **to take one's e. off the ball** *(gen)* perdre la balle des yeux; *Fig* cesser d'être vigilant; **keep your eyes on the road** regarde la route; **to keep one's e. open for sth** être attentif à qch; **keep your eyes open** *or* **an e. out for a filling station** essayez de repérer une station service; *Fam* **keep your eyes skinned** *or* **peeled** restez vigilant[□]; **anyone with half an e. can see it's a fake** du premier coup d'œil n'importe qui verrait que c'est un faux; **with half an e. on the weather** sans quitter le ciel des yeux; **the children were all eyes** les enfants n'en perdaient pas une miette; **an e. for an e. (and a tooth for a tooth)** œil pour œil(, dent pour dent); **his eyes are too big for his stomach** il a les yeux plus grands que le ventre; *Fam* **to give sb the e.** *(flirt)* faire de l'œil à qn; *(give signal)* faire signe à qn (d'un clin d'œil)[□]; **he has eyes in the back of his head** il a des yeux derrière la tête; **to set** *or* **lay eyes on sth** poser les yeux sur qch, apercevoir qch; **it was the biggest fish I'd ever laid eyes on** c'était le plus gros poisson que j'aie jamais vu; **I've never set** *or* **laid** *or Fam* **clapped eyes on her** je ne l'ai jamais vue de ma vie; **to make eyes at sb** faire de l'œil à qn; *Fam* **my e.!** mon œil!; **she and I don't see e. to e.** *(disagree)* elle ne voit pas les choses du même œil que moi, elle n'est pas de mon avis; *(dislike one another)* elle et moi, nous ne nous entendons pas; *Fam* **that's one in the e. for him!** ça lui fera les pieds!; **there's more to this than meets the e.** *(suspicious)* on ne connaît pas les dessous de l'affaire; *(difficult)* c'est moins simple que cela n'en a l'air; **there's more to her than meets the e.** elle gagne à être connue; **we're up to our eyes in it!** *(overworked)* on a du travail jusque là!; *(in deep trouble)* on est dans les ennuis jusqu'au cou!

VT regarder, mesurer du regard; **the child eyed the man warily** l'enfant dévisagea l'homme avec circonspection; **she stood eyeing the sweets** elle restait là à lorgner les bonbons; **to e. sth hungrily** dévorer qch du regard; **to e. sb up and down** regarder qn de la tête aux pieds

• **with an eye to** PREP **with an e. to sth/to doing sth** en vue de qch/de faire qch; **with an e. to the future** en vue *ou* en prévision de l'avenir

▸▸ ***eye bank*** banque *f* des yeux; ***eye camera*** caméra *f* oculaire; *Fam* ***eye candy*** *(men)* beaux mecs *mpl*; *(women)* belles nanas *fpl*; **his latest piece of e. candy** sa dernière nana; ***eye contact*** croisement *m* des regards; **to establish e. contact (with sb)** croiser le regard (de qn); **to maintain e. contact with sb** regarder qn dans les yeux; **she always avoids e. contact (with me)** elle évite tout le temps mon regard; *Am* ***eye doctor*** ophtalmologue *mf*; ***eye drops*** gouttes *fpl* pour les yeux; ***eye hospital*** centre *m* hospitalier d'ophtalmologie; ***eye make-up*** maquillage *m* pour les yeux; ***eye make-up remover*** démaquillant *m* pour les yeux; ***eye movement camera*** caméra *f* oculaire; ***eye rhyme*** rime *f* pour l'œil; ***eye socket*** orbite *f*; ***eye specialist*** ophtalmologue *mf*; ***eye test*** examen *m* de la vue

▸ **eye up** VT SEP *Fam* **1** *(with sexual interest)* **to e. up the girls/boys** reluquer les filles/les garçons; **he eyed her up** il l'a regardée de la tête aux pieds **2** *(estimate strength of* ▸ *opponent)* jauger (d'un coup d'œil)

---

eyeball [ˈaɪbɔːl] N globe *m* oculaire; *Fig* **doped** *or* **drugged (up) to the eyeballs** drogué à mort; **e. to e. (with)** nez à nez (avec)

VT *Fam* regarder fixement[□], reluquer

eyebath [ˈaɪbɑːθ, *pl* -bɑːðz] N *Br Med* œillère *f*

eyebrow [ˈaɪbraʊ] N sourcil *m*; **to raise one's eyebrows** lever les sourcils; *Fig* **(some) eyebrows were raised at this suggestion** *(in disapproval)* cette proposition a suscité des grimaces de désapprobation; *(in astonishment)* cette proposition a suscité de l'étonnement; **her behaviour raised a few eyebrows** son comportement en a fait tiquer quelques-uns; **to be up to one's eyebrows in sth** être dans qch jusqu'au cou

▸▸ ***eyebrow pencil*** crayon *m* à sourcils; ***eyebrow tweezers*** pince *f* à épiler

eyebrow-raising ADJ qui laisse perplexe

eye-catching ADJ *(colour, dress)* qui attire l'œil; *(poster, title)* accrocheur, tapageur

eyecup [ˈaɪkʌp] N *Am Med* œillère *f*

-eyed [aɪd] SUFF aux yeux...; **blue-e.** aux yeu bleus; **she stared at him, wide-e.** elle le regardait les yeux écarquillés; **one-e.** borgne, qui n' qu'un œil

eyeful [ˈaɪfʊl] N **1** *(of dirt, dust)* **I got an e. of san** j'ai reçu du sable plein les yeux **2** *Fam* **to get an e (of sb/sth)** mater (qn/qch); **get an e. of that** mate un peu ça!; **she's quite an e.!** elle est vache ment bien foutue!

eyeglass [ˈaɪglɑːs] N *(monocle)* monocle *m*

• **eyeglasses** NPL *Am (spectacles)* lunettes *fpl*

eyehole [ˈaɪhəʊl] N **1** *(peephole* ▸ *in mask)* trou *n* pour les yeux; *(*▸ *in door, wall)* judas *m* **2** *(eyele* œillet *m* **3** *Fam (eye socket)* orbite[□] *f*

eyelash [ˈaɪlæʃ] N cil *m*

▸▸ ***eyelash curlers*** recourbe-cils *m inv*

eyelet [ˈaɪlɪt] N *(gen) & Sewing* œillet *m*

eyelid [ˈaɪlɪd] N paupière *f*

eye-line N *TV & Cin* direction *f* du regard

eyeliner [ˈaɪˌlaɪnə(r)] N eye-liner *m*

eye-opener N *Fam* **1** *(surprise)* révélation[□] *f* surprise[□] *f*; **her behaviour was a real e. for hir** son comportement lui a ouvert les yeux; **the ex perience proved a bit of an e.!** l'expérience a été assez révélatrice! **2** *Am (drink)* = petit verre pri au réveil

eye-opening ADJ *Fam* qui ouvre les yeux[□], ré vélateur[□]; **it was very e.** ça a été très révélateur

eyepatch [ˈaɪpætʃ] N *(after operation)* cache *m* pansement *m (sur l'œil)*; *(permanent)* bandeau *n*

eyepiece [ˈaɪpiːs] N oculaire *m*

eye-popping ADJ *Am Fam* sensationnel

eyeshade [ˈaɪʃeɪd] N visière *f*

eyesight [ˈaɪsaɪt] N vue *f*; **to have good e.** avoi une bonne vue *ou* de bons yeux; **his e. is failin** sa vue baisse; **to lose one's e.** perdre la vue

eyesore [ˈaɪsɔː(r)] N horreur *f*; **the building is an e** le bâtiment est une horreur

eyespot [ˈaɪspɒt] N **1** *Bot* stigmate *m* **2** *Zool* ocell *m*

eyestalk [ˈaɪstɔːk] N *Zool (of crustacean)* pédi cule *m*, pédoncule *m*

eyestrain [ˈaɪstreɪn] N fatigue *f* des yeux; **compu ter screens can cause e.** les ordinateurs fatiguen les yeux; **to suffer from e.** avoir la vue fatiguée

eyetooth [ˈaɪtuːθ] *(pl* **eyeteeth** [-tiːθ]) N canine supérieure; *Fam* **I'd give my eyeteeth for a bike lik that** je donnerais n'importe quoi pour avoir u vélo comme ça

eyewash [ˈaɪwɒʃ] N *Med* collyre *m*; *Br Fam Fi* **that's a load of e.!** *(nonsense)* c'est de la foutaise! *(boasting)* ce n'est que de la frime!

eyewitness [ˌaɪˈwɪtnɪs] N témoin *m* oculaire

COMP *(description)* d'un témoin oculaire

▸▸ ***eyewitness account*** récit *m* de témoin ocu laire

eyrie [ˈɪərɪ] N aire *f (d'aigle)*

e-zine, ezine [ˈiːziːn] N *Comput* ezine *m*, e-zine *m*, magazine *m* électronique

F¹, f [ef] **N 1** *(letter)* F, f *m inv*; **two f's** deux f **2** *Sch* **to get an F** être recalé **3** *Mus* fa *m*; **in F** en fa
▸▸ *Br Euph* ***the F word*** = le mot "fuck", le mot de Cambronne

F² **1** (*written abbr* **Fahrenheit**) F
2 (*written abbr* **franc**) F
3 *Chem* (*written abbr* **fluorine**) F
4 *Phys* (*written abbr* **force**) F
5 *Phys* (*written abbr* **frequency**) F

FA [e'feɪ] **N** (*abbr* **Football Association**) **the FA** = la Fédération britannique de football
▸▸ ***the FA cup*** = le championnat de football

fa = **fah**

fab [fæb] **ADJ** *Fam* super, génial

Fabian ['feɪbjən] **N** *Pol* Fabien(enne) *m,f*
ADJ temporisateur; *Pol* Fabien
▸▸ *Pol* ***the Fabian Society*** = groupe socialiste de la fin du XIXème siècle en Grande-Bretagne

fable ['feɪbəl] **N 1** *(legend)* fable *f*, légende *f*; *Literature* fable *f* **2** *(false account)* fable *f*

fabled ['feɪbəld] **ADJ** *(famous)* légendaire, célèbre; *(fictitious)* légendaire, fabuleux

fabric ['fæbrɪk] **N 1** *(cloth)* tissu *m*, étoffe *f*; **silk, woollen and cotton fabrics** soieries *fpl*, lainages *mpl* et cotonnades *fpl* **2** *(framework, structure)* structure *f*; *Fig* **the f. of society** le tissu social
▸▸ ***fabric conditioner, fabric softener*** assouplissant *m* (textile)

> Note that the French word **fabrique** is a false friend and is never a translation for the English word **fabric**. Its most common meaning is **factory**.

fabricate ['fæbrɪkeɪt] **VT 1** *(manufacture)* fabriquer; *(produce)* produire **2** *(story)* inventer, fabriquer; *(document)* faire un faux de, contrefaire

fabrication [,fæbrɪ'keɪʃən] **N 1** *(manufacture)* fabrication *f*; *(production)* production *f* **2** *(falsehood)* fabrication *f*; **it's pure f.** c'est de la pure invention; **a pure f.** *(lie)* une histoire inventée de toutes pièces

fabulous ['fæbjʊləs] **ADJ 1** *(astounding)* fabuleux, incroyable; **f. wealth** une fortune fabuleuse *ou* incroyable **2** *Fam (marvellous)* génial; **we had a f. time** on s'est amusés comme des fous; **it's f.!** c'est super! **3** *(mythical ▸ beast, character, city)* fabuleux

fabulously ['fæbjʊləslɪ] **ADV** fabuleusement; **f. rich** fabuleusement riche

facade, façade [fə'sɑːd] **N** *Archit & Fig* façade *f*

FACE [feɪs]

N
- visage **1, 3, 4**
- figure **1**
- expression **2**
- apparence **3**
- façade **5**
- face **5–7**
- surface **7**

VT
- faire face à **1–4**
- être menacé de **5**
- se présenter à **6**
- revêtir **7**

VI
- se tourner **1**
- être orienté **2**

N 1 *(part of body)* visage *m*, figure *f*; **a handsome f.** un beau visage; **injuries to the f.** blessures *fpl* à la face *ou* au visage; **I know that f.** je connais cette tête-là, cette tête me dit quelque chose; **I have a good memory for faces** j'ai une bonne mémoire des visages, je suis très physionomiste; **she was lying f. down** *or* **downwards** elle était étendue à plat ventre *ou* face contre terre; **she was lying f. up** *or* **upwards** elle était étendue sur le dos; **he told her to her f. what he thought of her** il lui a dit en face *ou* sans ambages ce qu'il pensait d'elle; **to look sb in the f.** regarder qn en face *ou* dans les yeux; *Fig* **I'll never be able to look him in the f. again!** je n'oserai plus jamais le regarder en face!; *Fam* **to put on one's f.** *(put make-up on)* se maquiller

2 *(expression)* mine *f*, expression *f*; **to make** *or* **to pull a f. at sb** faire une grimace à qn; **to pull a funny f.** faire des simagrées, faire le singe; **she put on a brave** *or* **bold f.** elle a fait bon visage *ou* bonne contenance; **put a good** *or* **brave f. on it** vous n'avez qu'à faire *ou* faites contre mauvaise fortune bon cœur

3 *(appearance)* apparence *f*, aspect *m*; **it changed the f. of the town** cela a changé la physionomie de la ville; **this is the ugly f. of capitalism** voici l'autre visage *ou* le mauvais côté du capitalisme; **the f. of Britain is changing** le visage de la Grande-Bretagne est en train de changer; **Communism with a human f.** le communisme à visage humain

4 *(in advertising)* visage *m*; **she's the new f. of Lancôme** c'est le nouveau visage de Lancôme

5 *(front ▸ of building)* façade *f*, devant *m*; *(▸ of cliff)* paroi *f*; *(▸ of mountain)* face *f*

6 *Geom* face *f*

7 *(of clock, watch)* cadran *m*; *(of coin)* face *f*; *(of page)* recto *m*; *(of playing card)* face *f*, dessous *m*; *(of the earth)* surface *f*; *(of bat, golf club, tennis racquet)* surface *f* de frappe; *(of crystal)* facette *f*, plan *m*; *(of hammer)* plat *m*; **it fell f. down/up** *(gen)* c'est tombé du mauvais/bon côté; *(card, coin)* c'est tombé face en dessous/en dessus; *Fig* **she has vanished off the f. of the earth** elle a complètement disparu de la circulation; **my keys can't just have disappeared off the f. of the earth!** mes clés n'ont pas pu se volatiliser tout de même!

8 *Br Fam (impudence)* culot *m*, toupet *m*

9 *Mining* front *m* de taille

10 *Typ (typeface)* œil *m*; *(font)* fonte *f*

11 *(idioms)* **she laughed/shut the door in his f.** elle lui a ri/fermé la porte au nez; **to lose/to save f.** perdre/sauver la face; **he set his f. against our marriage** il s'est élevé contre notre mariage; **he won't show his f. here again!** il ne risque pas de remettre les pieds ici!; **her plans blew up in her f.** tous ses projets se sont retournés contre elle; *Br Fam* **to be off one's f.** *(drunk)* être pété *ou* bourré; *(on drugs)* être défoncé

VT 1 *(turn towards)* faire face à; **I turned and faced him** je me retournai et lui fis face; **f. the wall** tournez-vous vers le mur

2 *(be turned towards)* faire face à, être en face de; **he faced the blackboard** il était face au *ou* faisait face au tableau; **she was facing him** elle était en face de lui; **facing one another** l'un en face de l'autre, en vis-à-vis; **we were facing one another** nous étions face à face, nous nous faisions face; **to f. the front** regarder devant soi; **a room facing the courtyard** une chambre sur cour *ou* donnant sur la cour; **my chair faced the window** ma chaise était *ou* faisait face à la fenêtre; **facing page 9** en regard *ou* en face de la page 9

3 *(confront)* faire face *ou* front à, affronter; **he dared not f. me** il n'a pas osé me rencontrer face à face; **to f. sb with sth** confronter qn à qch; **to be faced with sth** être obligé de faire face à qch, être confronté à qch; **I was faced with having to pay for the damage** j'ai été obligé *ou* dans l'obligation de payer les dégâts; **he was faced with a difficult choice** il était confronté à un choix difficile; **to be faced with a decision** être confronté à une décision; **faced with the evidence** devant l'évidence, confronté à l'évidence; **we'll just have to f. the music** il va falloir affronter la tempête *ou* faire front

4 *(deal with)* faire face à; **to f. a problem** faire face à *ou* s'attaquer à un problème; **I can't f. telling her** je n'ai pas le courage de le lui dire; **we must f. facts** il faut voir les choses comme elles sont; **let's f. it, we're lost** admettons-le, nous sommes perdus

5 *(risk ▸ disaster)* être menacé de; *(▸ defeat, fine, prison)* encourir, risquer; **she faces the possibility of having to move** elle risque d'être obligée de déménager; **faced with eviction, he paid his rent** face à *ou* devant la perspective d'une expulsion, il a payé son loyer; **thousands f. unemployment** des milliers de personnes sont menacés de chômage

6 *(of problem, situation)* se présenter à; **the problem facing us** le problème qui se pose (à nous) *ou* devant lequel on se trouve; **the difficulties facing the EU** les difficultés que rencontre l'UE *ou* auxquelles l'UE doit faire face

7 *(cover)* revêtir (**with** de)

VI 1 *(turn)* se tourner; *(be turned)* être tourné; **she was facing towards the camera** elle était tournée vers *ou* elle faisait face à l'appareil photo; *Am Mil* **right f.!** à droite, droite!; *Am Mil* **about f.!** demi-tour!

2 *(house, window)* être orienté; *(look over)* faire face à, donner sur; **a terrace facing south** une terrasse orientée au sud; **the terrace faces towards the mountain** la terrasse donne sur la montagne; **facing forwards** *(in bus, train)* dans le sens de la marche; **facing backwards** dans le mauvais sens

• **in the face of PREP** **she succeeded in the f. of fierce opposition** elle a réussi malgré une opposition farouche; **in the f. of danger** devant le danger

• **on the face of it ADV** à première vue

• **face to face ADV** face à face; **she brought him f. to f. with her father** elle l'a confronté avec son père; **it brought us f. to f. with the problem** cela nous a mis directement devant le problème

▸▸ *Am* ***face amount*** *(of bank note, traveller's cheque)* valeur *f* nominale; *(of stamp)* valeur *f* faciale; ***face card*** figure *f (de jeu de cartes)*; ***face cream*** crème *f* pour le visage; *Br* ***face flannel*** gant *m* de toilette; *Metal* ***face hardening*** trempe *f* superficielle; ***face mask*** *(cosmetic)* masque *m* (de beauté); *Sport* masque *m*; ***face pack*** masque *m* (de beauté); ***face powder*** poudre *f*; ***face scrub*** *(cosmetic)* exfoliant *m*; *TV & Cin* ***face shot*** plan *m* de visage; *Am* ***face time*** *(meeting)* = rencontre en face à face entre deux personnes *(par opposition aux contacts par téléphone ou courrier électronique)*; *(on TV)* temps *m* de présence à l'écran; **we need some f. time to solve this** il faut qu'on se voie pour régler ça; ***face towel*** serviette *f* de toilette; ***face value*** *(of bank note, traveller's cheque)* valeur *f* nominale; *(of stamp)* valeur *f* faciale; *Fig* **I took her remark at f. value** j'ai pris sa remarque au pied de la lettre *ou* pour argent comptant; **don't take him at f. value** ne le jugez pas sur les apparences

▸ **face about** **VI** *Mil* faire demi-tour

▸ **face down** **VT SEP** tenir tête à

▸ **face on to** **VT INSEP** *(garden, street)* donner sur

▸ **face out** **VT SEP** *Br (problems, difficult situation)* surmonter; *(person)* résister à; **to f. it out** ne pas broncher

▸ **face up to** **VT INSEP** faire face à, affronter; **he won't f. up to the fact that he's getting older** il ne veut pas admettre qu'il vieillit

faceless ['feɪslɪs] **ADJ** anonyme

face-lift **N 1** *(surgery)* lifting *m*; **to have a f.** se faire faire un lifting **2** *Fam (renovation)* restauration ◻ *f*; **the house could do with a f.** la maison a besoin d'être ravalée *ou* retapée

facer ['feɪsə(r)] **N 1** *Tech (tool)* planeuse *f* **2** *Br Fam (problem)* os *m*, tuile *f*

face-saving **ADJ** qui sauve la face

facet ['fæsɪt] **N 1** *(gen) & Entom* facette *f* **2** *(aspect)* aspect *m*, facette *f*

facetious [fə'siːʃəs] **ADJ** *(person)* facétieux, moqueur; *(remark)* facétieux, comique; **I was being f.** je plaisantais; **there's no need to be so f.** il n'y a pas de quoi se moquer

facetiously [fə'siːʃəslɪ] **ADV** de manière facétieuse, facétieusement

facetiousness [fə'siːʃəsnɪs] **N** caractère *m* facétieux *ou* comique

face-to-face **ADJ** *(discussion, confrontation)* face à face; **a f. meeting** un face-à-face

facetted ['fæsɪtɪd] **ADJ** à facettes

facia = **fascia**

facial ['feɪʃəl] **ADJ** facial

N soin *m* du visage; **to have a f.** se faire faire un soin du visage

▸▸ ***facial hair*** poils *mpl* du visage; **to remove f. hair** enlever les poils disgracieux (du visage); ***facial sauna*** sauna *m* facial; ***facial scrub*** exfoliant *m*

facialist ['feɪʃəlɪst] **N** visagiste *mf*

facile [*Br* 'fæsaɪl, *Am* 'fæsəl] **ADJ** *Pej (simplistic ▸ remark, argument)* facile, simpliste; *(solution, victory)* trop facile; *(person)* superficiel, complaisant

facilitate [fə'sɪlɪteɪt] **VT** faciliter

facilitator [fə'sɪlɪteɪtə(r)] **N** animateur(trice) *m,f* de groupe

facility [fə'sɪlətɪ] *(pl* **facilities***)* **N 1** *(area, building)* installation *f*; **training/research f.** établissement *m* de formation/recherche; **nuclear f.** *(power station)* centrale *f* nucléaire; *(weapons plant)* installations *fpl* nucléaires

2 *(device)* mécanisme *m*; *Comput* fonction *f*; **the clock also has a radio f.** ce réveil fait aussi radio; **the computer has a spellcheck f.** l'ordinateur est équipé d'un correcteur orthographique

3 *(service)* service *m*; **we offer easy credit facilities** nous offrons des facilités de paiement *ou* crédit; *Br* **an overdraft f.** une autorisation de découvert

4 *(skill)* facilité *f*, aptitude *f*; **to have a f. for** *or* **with languages** avoir beaucoup de facilité pour les langues

5 *(ease)* facilité *f*; **with great f.** avec beaucoup de facilité

• **facilities** **NPL** *(equipment)* équipements *mpl*; *(place, building)* installations *fpl*, aménagements *mpl*; *(means)* moyens *mpl*; **play/sports/educational facilities** équipements *mpl* récréatifs/sportifs/scolaires; **military/port facilities** installations *fpl* militaires/portuaires; **storage/cooking facilities** installations *fpl* de stockage/cuisine; **a house/kitchen with no proper storage facilities** une cuisine/maison dépourvue de rangements *ou* d'espaces de rangement; **there are facilities for cooking** il y a la possibilité de *ou* il y a ce qu'il faut pour faire la cuisine; **the lack of sanitary facilities** le manque d'installations sanitaires; **the area has inadequate transport facilities** le quartier est mal desservi; **the university has excellent research facilities** l'université est très bien équipé pour la recherche; **there are no facilities for the disabled** il n'y a pas d'aménagements spéciaux prévus pour les handicapés; **feel free to use the facilities** n'hésitez pas à utiliser toutes les installations; **we don't have the facilities to hold a conference here** nous ne sommes pas équipés pour organiser une conférence ici; *Euph* **the facilities** les toilettes *fpl*

▸▸ ***facilities management*** *Comput* infogérance *f*; *(maintenance of buildings)* entretien *m* de bâtiments *(par une entreprise sous-traitante)*

facing ['feɪsɪŋ] **N** *Constr* revêtement *m*; *Sewing* revers *m*

▸▸ ***facing page*** page *f* ci-contre; ***facing pages*** pages *fpl* en regard

facsimile [fæk'sɪmɪlɪ] **N** fac-similé *m*; **in f.** en fac-similé

▸▸ ***facsimile edition*** *(of book)* fac-similé *m*; ***facsimile machine*** télécopieur *m*; ***facsimile transmission*** télécopie *f*

FACT [fækt] **N 1** *(gen)* fait *m*; **it's a (well-known) f. that...** tout le monde sait (bien) que...; **just stick to the facts** tenez-vous en aux faits; **let's get the facts straight** mettons les choses au clair; **ten facts about whales** dix choses à savoir sur les baleines; **I'll give you all the facts and figures** je vous donnerai tous les détails voulus; **the f. that he left is in itself incriminating** le fait qu'il soit parti est compromettant en soi; **he broke his promise, there's no getting away from the f.** disons les choses comme elles sont, il n'a pas tenu sa promesse; **I'm her friend, a f. you seem to have overlooked** vous semblez ne pas tenir compte du fait que je suis son ami; **I know for a f. that they're friends** je sais pertinemment qu'ils sont amis; **I know it for a f.** je le sais de source sûre, c'est un fait certain; **it's a f. of life** c'est une réalité; **to teach sb the facts of life** *(sex)* apprendre à qn comment les enfants viennent au monde; *(hard reality)* apprendre à qn la réalité des choses, mettre qn devant la réalité de la vie; **there's something strange going on, (and) that's a f.** il se passe quelque chose de bizarre, c'est sûr; **is that a f.?** c'est pas vrai?; **owing to the f. that...** du fait que...

2 *(UNCOUNT) (reality)* faits *mpl*, réalité *f*; **based on f.** *(argument)* basé sur des faits; *(book, film)* basé sur des faits réels; **f. and fiction** le réel et l'imaginaire; **the f. (of the matter) is that I forgot all about it** la vérité, c'est que j'ai complètement oublié

3 *Law (act)* fait *m*, action *f*; **the jury only decides issues of f.** les jurés ne sont juges que du fait

• **in fact** **ADV 1** *(giving extra information)* **he asked us, in f. ordered us, to be quiet** il nous a demandé, ou plutôt ordonné, de nous taire

2 *(correcting)* en fait; **he claims to be a writer, but in (actual) f. he's a journalist** il prétend être écrivain mais en fait c'est un journaliste

3 *(emphasizing, reinforcing)* **did she in f. say when she was going to arrive?** est-ce qu'elle a dit quand elle arriverait en fait?; **he said it'd take two days and he was in f. correct** il a dit que cela mettrait deux jours et en fait, il avait raison

▸▸ ***fact sheet*** fiche *f* d'informations

fact-finding **ADJ** d'information; **a f. mission** une mission d'information; **he's on a f. tour of the disaster area** il enquête sur la région sinistrée

faction[1] ['fækʃən] **N 1** *(group)* faction *f* **2** *(strife)* dissension *f*, discorde *f*

faction[2] **N** *(book, programme)* docudrame *m*

factious ['fækʃəs] **ADJ** factieux

factitious [fæk'tɪʃəs] **ADJ** *Literary* factice, artificiel

factor ['fæktə(r)] **N 1** *(element)* facteur *m*, élément *m*; **age is an important f.** l'âge joue un rôle important; **a determining f.** un facteur décisif *ou* déterminant; **the human f.** le facteur humain; **the safety f.** le facteur de sécurité; **the chill f.** le coefficient de froid

2 *Biol & Math* facteur *m*; **sales increased by a f. of ten** les ventes sont dix fois plus élevées, l'indice des ventes est dix fois plus haut; *Econ* **f. of production** facteur *m* de production

3 *(in suntan cream)* indice *m*; **f. 6** indice 6

4 *(agent)* agent *m*

5 *Scot (building manager)* syndic *m*

▸▸ ***factor analysis*** analyse *f* factorielle; *Biol* ***factor 8*** facteur *m* VIII

factorage ['fæktərɪdʒ] **N** *Fin* courtage *m*, commission *f* (d'affacturage)

factoring ['fæktərɪŋ] **N 1** *Fin* affacturage *m* **2** *Scot (management of building)* = administration d'un immeuble par l'association de copropriétaires

▸▸ ***factoring agent*** agent *m* d'affacturage; ***factoring company*** société *f* d'affacturage

factory ['fæktərɪ] *(pl* **factories***)* **N** usine *f*; *(smaller)* fabrique *f*; **a car f.** une usine d'automobiles; **an arms/munitions f.** une fabrique d'armes/de munitions; **a porcelain f.** une manufacture de porcelaine; **a biscuit f.** une biscuiterie *f*; **on the f. floor** dans les ateliers, parmi les ouvriers; **prices at the f. gate** prix *mpl* départ usine

COMP *(chimney, manager)* d'usine

▸▸ ***factory farm*** ferme *f* industrielle; ***factory farming*** élevage *m* industriel; ***factory inspection*** inspection *f* du travail; ***factory inspector*** inspecteur(trice) *m,f* du travail; ***factory outlet*** magasin *m* d'usine; ***factory overheads*** frais *mpl* généraux de fabrication; ***factory price*** prix *m* usine, prix *m* sortie usine; ***factory ship*** navire-usine *m*; ***factory shop*** magasin *m* d'usine; ***factory unit*** unité *f* de fabrication; ***factory work*** travail *m* en usine *ou* d'usine; ***factory worker*** ouvrier(ère) *m,f* d'usine

factotum [fæk'təʊtəm] **N** factotum *m*; **general f.** *(man)* homme *m* à tout faire; *(woman)* femme *f* à tout faire

factual ['fæktʃʊəl] **ADJ** *(account, speech)* factuel, basé sur les *ou* des faits; *(event)* réel

factually ['fæktʃʊəlɪ] **ADV** en se tenant aux faits; **f. inaccurate** inexact dans les faits

facultative ['fækəltətɪv] **ADJ** *(optional)* facultatif

faculty ['fækəltɪ] *(pl* **faculties***)* **N 1** *(of mind, body)* faculté *f*; **she's in full command of her faculties** elle a *ou* elle jouit de toutes ses facultés; **his critical faculties** son sens critique; **the f. of reason** la raison; **the f. of speech** le don de la parole **2** *Univ (section)* faculté *f*; *(staff)* corps *m* enseignant; **the F. of Arts/of Medicine** la faculté de lettres/de médecine

COMP *Univ (member, staff)* de faculté

fad [fæd] **N** *Fam (craze)* mode ◻ *f*, vogue ◻ *f*; *(personal)* lubie ◻ *f*, (petite) manie ◻ *f*; **it's just a (passing) f.** ce n'est qu'une lubie, ce n'est qu'un engouement passager

faddiness ['fædɪnɪs] **N** *Fam* goûts *mpl* difficiles ◻

faddy ['fædɪ] *(compar* **faddier**, *superl* **faddiest***)* **ADJ** *Fam (idea, taste)* capricieux ◻; *(person)* maniaque ◻, capricieux ◻; **he's f. about his food, he's a f. eater** il est difficile sur la nourriture

fade [feɪd] **VI 1** *(colour)* pâlir, passer; *(material)* se décolorer, passer; *(light)* baisser, diminuer; **the light is fading** *(daylight)* le jour baisse; *Tex* **guaranteed not to f.** garanti bon teint

2 *(wither ▸ flower)* se faner, se flétrir; *Fig (▸ beauty)* se faner

3 *(disappear ▸ figure)* disparaître; *(▸ memory, sight)* baisser; *(▸ thing remembered, writing)* s'effacer; *(▸ sound)* baisser, s'éteindre; *(▸ anger, interest)* diminuer; *(▸ hope, smile)* s'éteindre; **to f. from memory** s'effacer de la mémoire; **to f. from sight** disparaître aux regards; **the sound keeps fading** *(of radio, TV)* il y a du fading, le son s'en va

4 *Literary (die)* dépérir, s'éteindre; **he's fading fast** il dépérit à vue d'œil

5 *Am Fam (leave)* s'esbigner, calter

VT 1 *(discolour ▸ material, curtains)* décolorer; *(▸ colour)* faner **2** *(reduce)* baisser; *Cin & TV* faire disparaître en fondu **3** *Golf (ball)* faire dévier légèrement à droite

N 1 *Cin & TV* disparition *f* en fondu **2** *Golf* = coup qui fait dévier la balle légèrement à droite

▸ **fade away** **VI** *(gen)* disparaître; *(memory, sight)* baisser; *(thing remembered, writing)* s'effacer; *(sound)* s'éteindre; *(anger, interest)* diminuer; *(hope, smile)* s'éteindre; **he faded away** il a peu à peu dépéri

▸ **fade in** **VT SEP** *Cin & TV (picture)* faire apparaître en fondu; *Rad (sound)* monter

VI *Cin & TV (picture)* apparaître en fondu

▸ **fade out** VT SEP *Cin & TV (picture)* faire disparaître en fondu; *Rad (music, dialogue)* couper par un fondu sonore
VI **1** *(sound)* disparaître, s'éteindre **2** *Cin & TV (picture)* disparaître en fondu; *Rad (music, dialogue)* être coupé par un fondu sonore

faded ['feɪdɪd] ADJ *(material)* décoloré, déteint; *(jeans)* délavé; *(flower)* fané, flétri; *(beauty)* défraîchi, fané

fade-in N *Cin* fondu *m* en ouverture; *TV* apparition *f* graduelle; *Rad* fondu *m* sonore

fade-out N *Cin* fondu *m* en fermeture; *TV* disparition *f* graduelle; *Rad* fondu *m* sonore

fader ['feɪdə(r)] N *Cin & TV* potentiomètre *m*

fading ['feɪdɪŋ] N **1** *(of plant)* flétrissure *f*; *(of material)* décoloration *f* **2** *Rad* fading *m* **3** *Cin & TV* fondu *m*
ADJ *(flower)* qui se fane; *(light)* pâlissant

faecal, Am fecal ['fi:kəl] ADJ *Biol* fécal; **f. matter** matières *fpl* fécales, déjections *fpl*

faeces, Am feces ['fi:si:z] NPL *Physiol* fèces *fpl*

Faeroe ['feərəʊ] N **the F. Islands, the Faeroes** les îles *fpl* Féroé

faff [fæf] *Br Fam* VI **1** *(waste time)* **to f. (about** *or* **around)** glander; **stop faffing (about** *or* **around)!** arrêtez de tourner en rond! **2** *(potter)* s'occuper□, bricoler
N **1** *(panic)* panique□ *f* **2** *(effort)* **it's too much of a f.** c'est trop compliqué□

fag [fæg] *(pt & pp* **fagged**, *cont* **fagging)** N **1** *Br Fam (cigarette)* clope *f*
2 *Am very Fam (homosexual)* pédé *m*, = terme injurieux désignant un homosexuel
3 *Br (at school)* = jeune élève d'une "public school" assujetti à un "ancien"
4 *Br Fam (task)* corvée *f*, barbe *f*
VI *Br* **1** *(at public school)* **to f. for sb** faire les corvées de qn **2** *Fam Old-fashioned (work hard)* travailler dur□, s'échiner
VT *Fam (exhaust)* crever
▸▸ *Br Fam* ***fag end*** *(of cigarette)* mégot *m*; *Fig (remainder)* reste□ *m*; *(of material, winter)* bout□ *m*; *(of conversation)* dernières bribes□ *fpl*; *very Fam* ***fag hag*** fille *f* à pédés
▸ **fag out** VT SEP *Br Fam (of work, task)* crever

fagged [fægd] ADJ *Br Fam* **1 f. (out)** *(exhausted)* crevé, claqué **2** *(bothered)* **I can't be f.** j'ai trop la flemme

faggot ['fægət] N **1** *Br (of sticks)* fagot *m* **2** *Br Culin* boulette *f* de viande **3** *Am very Fam (homosexual)* pédé *m*, = terme injurieux désignant un homosexuel

faggy ['fægɪ] ADJ *Am very Fam Pej* qui fait pédé

fah [fɑ:] N *Br Mus* fa *m*

Fahrenheit ['færənhaɪt] ADJ Fahrenheit *(inv)*
▸▸ ***Fahrenheit scale*** échelle *f* Fahrenheit

faience [faɪ'jɑ:ns] N faïence *f*

FAIL [feɪl]

VT
- échouer à **1, 2**
- recaler **2**
- décevoir **3**
- négliger **4**

VI
- échouer **1, 2**
- être recalé **2**
- tomber en panne **3**
- baisser **4**
- manquer **5**

N
- échec

VT **1** *(not succeed in)* échouer à, ne pas réussir à; **he failed his driving test** il n'a pas eu son permis; **to f. a drugs test** être positif au contrôle antidopage; **to f. to do sth** ne pas arriver à faire qch
2 *Sch & Univ (exam)* échouer à, être recalé à; *(candidate)* refuser, recaler; **he failed the exam/history** il a échoué à l'examen/en histoire
3 *(let down)* décevoir, laisser tomber; **I won't f. you** je ne vous laisserai pas tomber, vous pouvez compter sur moi; **his heart failed him** le cœur lui a manqué; **my memory fails me** la mémoire me fait défaut, ma mémoire me trahit; **her courage failed her** le courage lui a fait défaut *ou* lui a manqué; **words f. me** je ne sais pas quoi dire
4 *(neglect)* **to f. to do sth** négliger de faire qch; **he failed to mention he was married** il a omis de signaler qu'il était marié; **they never f. to call** ils ne manquent jamais d'appeler; **she failed to answer his letter** elle n'a pas répondu à sa lettre; **I f. to see how I can help** je ne vois pas comment je peux aider; **I f. to understand why she came** je n'arrive pas à comprendre pourquoi elle est venue; **such success never fails to arouse jealousy** une telle réussite ne va jamais sans provoquer des jalousies; *Law* **to f. to appear** faire défaut
VI **1** *(not succeed* ▸ *attempt, plan)* échouer, ne pas réussir; *(▸ negotiations)* échouer, ne pas aboutir; *(▸ play)* faire fiasco; *(▸ person)* échouer; **he failed in his efforts to convince us** il n'a pas réussi *ou* il n'est pas arrivé à nous convaincre; **her attempt was bound to f.** sa tentative était vouée à l'échec; **it never fails** ça ne rate jamais; **if all else fails** en désespoir de cause
2 *Sch & Univ* échouer, être recalé; **I failed in maths** j'ai été collé *ou* recalé en maths
3 *(stop working)* tomber en panne, céder; *(brakes)* lâcher; *(engine)* caler; **his heart failed** son cœur s'est arrêté; **the power failed** il y a eu une panne d'électricité; **his parachute failed** son parachute ne s'est pas ouvert
4 *(grow weak* ▸ *eyesight, health, memory)* baisser, faiblir; *(▸ person, voice)* s'affaiblir; *(▸ light, strength)* baisser
5 *(be insufficient)* manquer, faire défaut; **their crops failed because of the drought** ils ont perdu les récoltes à cause de la sécheresse; **she failed in her duty** elle a manqué *ou* failli à son devoir
6 *(go bankrupt)* faire faillite
N *Sch & Univ* échec *m*; **he only had one f. and that was in maths** il n'a échoué *ou* été recalé qu'en maths; **out of a class of 25, I had 23 passes and 2 fails** sur une classe de 25, 23 ont été reçus et 2 ont été recalés
• **without fail** ADV *(for certain)* sans faute, à coup sûr; *(always)* inévitablement, immanquablement

failed [feɪld] ADJ qui n'a pas réussi, raté; **she's a f. artist** c'est une artiste manquée; **a f. marriage** un mariage manqué *ou* raté

failing ['feɪlɪŋ] N défaut *m*
PREP à défaut de; **f. this** à défaut; **f. which** faute *ou* à défaut de quoi; **f. any advice/evidence to the contrary** sauf avis contraire, sauf preuve du contraire
ADJ *(strength)* défaillant; *(business)* qui fait faillite; *(marriage)* qui va à la dérive; *(school)* en état d'échec; *Am (student)* faible, mauvais; **to be in f. health** avoir une santé défaillante

fail-safe ADJ *(device, machine)* à sûreté intégrée; *(plan)* infaillible
N dispositif *m* de sécurité *ou* de sûreté (intégrée)

failure ['feɪljə(r)] N **1** *(lack of success)* échec *m*, insuccès *m*; **to end in f.** se solder *ou* se terminer par un échec; **the f. of his new film** l'échec de son nouveau film
2 *Sch & Univ* échec *m*; **f. in an exam/in maths** échec à un examen/en maths; **there are too many failures** trop de candidats ont été recalés
3 *(fiasco)* échec *m*, fiasco *m*; *(plan)* échec *m*, avortement *m*; **the party was a total f.** la soirée a été un fiasco complet; **the play was a dismal f.** la pièce a été *ou* a fait un four noir
4 *(person)* raté(e) *m,f*; **he's a f. as a father** il fait un mauvais père, il n'est pas doué pour la paternité; **I feel a complete f.** je me sens vraiment nulle, j'ai l'impression d'être complètement nulle; **I'm a complete f. at maths** je suis totalement nul en maths
5 *(breakdown)* panne *f*; **a power f.** une panne d'électricité
6 *(lack)* manque *m*; **a f. of nerve** un manque de courage; **crop f.** perte *f* des récoltes
7 *(neglect, omission)* manquement *m*, défaut *m*; **his f. to keep his word** son manquement à sa parole; **f. to pay a bill** défaut *m* de paiement d'un effet; **his f. to arrive on time** le fait qu'il soit arrivé en retard; **the press criticized the government's f. to act** la presse a critiqué l'immobilisme du gouvernement; **f. to observe the rules will result in a fine** le manquement au règlement est passible d'une amende; *Law* **f. to appear** défaut *m* de comparution
8 *(bankruptcy)* faillite *f*
▸▸ *Am Com* ***failure investment*** investissement *m* en valeurs de redressement *ou* de retournement

fain [feɪn] ADV *Arch* volontiers; **I would f. be a father to your children** je serais trop heureux d'être un père pour vos enfants

faint [feɪnt] ADJ **1** *(slight* ▸ *breeze, feeling, sound, smell)* faible, léger; *(▸ idea)* flou, vague; *(▸ hope)* léger, faible; *(▸ possibility)* vague; *(▸ breathing, light)* faible; *(▸ voice)* faible, éteint; **there was a f. glow on the horizon** il y avait une faible lueur à l'horizon; **he hasn't the faintest chance of winning** il n'a pas la moindre chance de gagner; **I haven't the faintest idea** je n'en ai pas la moindre idée; **the sound of the footsteps grew fainter** le bruit des pas s'affaiblit; **her cries grew fainter** ses cris s'estompaient *ou* diminuaient
2 *(colour)* pâle, délavé
3 *(half-hearted)* faible, sans conviction; **a f. smile** *(feeble)* un vague sourire; *(sad)* un pauvre *ou* triste sourire; **to damn sb/sth with f. praise** ne pas se montrer très élogieux envers qn/à propos de qch
4 *(dizzy)* prêt à s'évanouir, défaillant; **to feel f.** se sentir mal, être pris d'un malaise; **he was f. with exhaustion** la tête lui tournait de fatigue
5 *Br Prov* **f. heart never won fair lady** = la pusillanimité n'a jamais conquis de cœur féminin
VI s'évanouir; **a fainting fit** un évanouissement; **to be fainting from** *or* **with hunger** défaillir de faim; *Fig* **I almost fainted when they told me I'd got the job** j'ai failli m'évanouir quand on m'a dit que j'avais le poste
N évanouissement *m*, syncope *f*; **she fell to the floor in a (dead) f.** elle s'est évanouie *ou* est tombée en syncope

faint-hearted [-'hɑ:tɪd] ADJ *(person)* timoré, pusillanime; *(attempt)* timide, sans conviction
NPL **not for the f.** à déconseiller aux âmes sensibles

faint-heartedly [-'hɑ:tɪdlɪ] ADV avec pusillanimité

faint-heartedness [-'hɑ:tɪdnɪs] N pusillanimité *f*

fainting ['feɪntɪŋ] N évanouissement *m*
▸▸ ***fainting fit*** évanouissement *m*

faintly ['feɪntlɪ] ADV **1** *(breathe, shine)* faiblement; *(mark, write)* légèrement; *(say, speak)* d'une voix éteinte, faiblement; **f. visible** à peine visible **2** *(slightly)* légèrement, vaguement; **the taste is f. reminiscent of cinnamon** cela rappelle vaguement la cannelle; **f. absurd/ridiculous** quelque peu absurde/ridicule

faintness ['feɪntnɪs] N **1** *(of light, sound, voice)* faiblesse *f*; *(of breeze)* légèreté *f*; *(of image, writing)* manque *m* de clarté **2** *(dizziness)* malaise *m*, défaillance *f*

FAIR [feə(r)]

ADJ
- juste **1**
- équitable **1**
- correct **1**
- blond **2**
- beau **3, 4**
- passable **5**
- considérable **6**
- véritable **7**

ADV
- équitablement **1**
- vraiment **2**

N
- foire **1, 2**

ADJ **1** *(just* ▸ *person, decision)* juste, équitable; *(▸ wage)* équitable; *(▸ contest, match, player)* loyal, correct; *(▸ deal, exchange)* équitable, honnête; *(▸ price)* correct, convenable; *(▸ criticism, profit)* justifié, mérité; **it's not f.** ce n'est pas juste; **it isn't f. to expect children to...** ce n'est pas raisonnable de demander à des enfants de...; **that's a f. point** c'est une remarque pertinente; **to be f. (to them), they did contribute their time** rendons-leur cette justice, ils ont donné de leur temps; **it's only f. to let him speak** ce n'est que justice de le laisser parler; **it is only f. to say that...** il faut dire que...; **as is only f.** ce n'est que justice, comme de juste; **I gave him f. warning** je l'ai prévenu à temps; **a f. sample** un échantillon représentatif; **he got his f. share of the property** il a eu tous les biens qui lui revenaient (de droit); **she's had more than her f. share of problems** elle a largement eu sa part de problèmes; *Br* **to have a f. crack of the whip** avoir toutes ses chances; *Fam* **the boss gave her a f. shake (of the dice)** *or* **a f. deal** *or Am & Austr* **a f. go** le patron l'a traitée équitablement *ou* a été fair-play avec elle❑; *Austr Fam* **f. go!** donne-moi/nous/*etc* une chance!❑; **it's all f. and above board, it's all f. and square** tout est régulier *ou* correct; *Prov* **all's f. in love and war** = en amour comme à la guerre, tous les coups sont permis; **by f. means or foul** par tous les moyens, d'une manière ou d'une autre; *Br Fam* **f. do's (for all!)** à chacun son dû!❑; **f. enough!** très bien!, d'accord!; **that's f. enough but don't you think that...** très bien *ou* d'accord, mais est-ce que vous ne pensez pas que...; **f.'s f., it's her turn now** il faut être juste, c'est son tour maintenant

2 *(light ► hair)* blond; *(► skin)* clair, blanc (blanche); **he's very f.** il est très blond

3 *Literary (lovely)* beau (belle); **his f. lady** sa belle; *Hum* **written in her own f. hand** écrit de sa main blanche

4 *(weather)* beau (belle); *(tide, wind)* favorable, propice; **the wind's set f. for France** le temps est au beau fixe sur la France

5 *(adequate)* passable, assez bon; **in f. condition** en assez bon état; **you have a f. chance of winning** vous avez des chances de gagner; **f. to middling** passable, pas mal; **how are you? – f. to middling** comment allez-vous? – comme çi comme ça; **in a f. way to recovering** en bonne voie de rétablissement

6 *(substantial)* considérable; **he makes a f. amount of money** il gagne pas mal d'argent; **she reads a f. amount** elle lit pas mal; **I have a f. idea (of) why** je crois bien savoir pourquoi; **a f. number** un nombre respectable; **at a f. pace** à une bonne allure

7 *Br Fam (real)* véritable❑; **I had a f. old time getting here** j'ai eu pas mal de difficultés à arriver jusqu'ici

ADV 1 *(act)* équitablement, loyalement; **to play f.** jouer franc jeu; **he told us f. and square** il nous l'a dit sans détours *ou* carrément; **you can't say fairer than that** il n'y a pas plus équitable

2 *Br Fam (completely)* tout à fait❑, vraiment❑; **you f. scared me to death** tu m'as vraiment fait une peur atroce

3 *(idiom)* **the play bids f. to being a success** cette pièce a de grandes chances d'être *ou* sera probablement un succès

N 1 *(entertainment)* foire *f*, fête *f* foraine; *(for charity)* kermesse *f*, fête *f*

2 *Com* foire *f*; **the Book F.** la Foire du livre

►► *Am Sport* ***fair catch*** arrêt *m* de volée; *Br* ***fair copy*** copie *f* au propre *ou* au net; **I made a f. copy of the report** j'ai recopié le rapport au propre; ***fair game*** proie *f* idéale; *Fig* **after such behaviour he was f. game for an attack** après s'être comporté de cette façon, il méritait bien qu'on s'en prenne à lui; ***Fair Isle*** **N** *(sweater)* = pull avec des motifs de couleurs vives **ADJ** = tricoté avec des motifs de couleurs vives; *Fin* ***fair market value*** valeur *f* vénale; ***fair play*** fair-play *m inv*; *Offic* franc-jeu *m*; *Br* ***fair rent*** = loyer fixé après un examen officiel du logement par l'administration; ***the fair sex*** le beau sexe; *Com* ***fair trade*** commerce *m* équitable; ***fair trial*** procès équitable; **to get a f. trial** être jugé de façon équitable

fairground ['feəgraʊnd] **N** champ *m* de foire

►► ***fairground ride*** attraction *f (de fête foraine)*

fair-haired **ADJ** *(blond)* blond, aux cheveux blonds; **the f. girl** la blonde; *Am Fam* **the boss's f. boy** le chouchou du patron

fairing ['feərɪŋ] **N** *(on vehicle)* carénage *m*

fairish ['feərɪʃ] **ADJ 1** *(chances, salary, weather)* assez bon; *(number)* respectable; **there's a f. amount of work still to do** il y a encore pas mal de travail **2** *(blondish)* plutôt blond

fairly ['feəlɪ] **ADV 1** *(justly ► treat)* équitablement, avec justice; *(► compare, judge)* impartialement, avec impartialité

2 *(honestly)* honnêtement, loyalement; **to fight/to play f.** se battre/jouer loyalement; **f. priced goods** articles à un prix honnête *ou* raisonnable; **to come by sth f. (and squarely)** obtenir qch par des moyens honnêtes; **to win f. and squarely** *(clearly, easily)* remporter une nette victoire; *(without dishonest means)* vaincre honnêtement

3 *(moderately)* assez, passablement; **a f. good book** un assez bon livre; **I'm f. certain** je suis à peu près certain; **she sings f. well** elle chante passablement bien; **he works f. hard** il travaille plutôt dur

4 *Br (positively)* absolument, vraiment; **he was f. beside himself with worry** il était dans tous ses états; **we f. raced through the work** nous avons fait notre travail à bonne allure

fair-minded **ADJ** équitable, impartial

fairness ['feənɪs] **N 1** *(justice)* justice *f*, honnêteté *f*; **in all f.** en toute justice; **in f.** *or* **out of f. to you** pour être juste envers *ou* avec vous, pour vous rendre justice **2** *(of hair)* blondeur *f*, blond *m*; *(of skin)* blancheur *f*

fair-sized **ADJ** assez grand

fairway ['feəweɪ] **N 1** *(in golf)* fairway *m* **2** *Naut* chenal *m*, passe *f*

fair-weather **ADJ** *(clothing, vessel)* qui convient seulement au beau temps; **a f. friend** un ami des beaux *ou* bons jours

fairy ['feərɪ] *(pl* **fairies)** **N 1** *(sprite)* fée *f*; **the bad f.** la fée Carabosse; *Fam* **to be away with the fairies** *(senile)* être complètement gaga; *(eccentric)* être farfelu; *(daydreaming)* être dans les nuages **2** *very Fam (homosexual)* pédé *m*, tapette *f*, = terme injurieux désignant un homosexuel

ADJ *(enchanted)* magique; *(fairylike)* féerique, de fée; **f. footsteps** des pas *mpl* légers

►► ***fairy cake*** petit gâteau *m (dans une caissette en papier)*; *Br* ***fairy cycle*** bicyclette *f* d'enfant; *Austr* ***fairy floss*** barbe *f* à papa; *Literature & Fig* ***fairy godmother*** bonne fée *f*; ***fairy lights*** guirlande *f* électrique; ***fairy queen*** reine *f* des fées; ***fairy ring*** cercle *m ou* rond *m* des sorcières; ***fairy story, fairy tale*** conte *m* de fées; *(untruth)* histoire *f* à dormir debout

fairyland ['feərɪlænd] **N** *Literature* royaume *m* des fées, féerie *f*; *Fig* féerie *f*

faith [feɪθ] **N 1** *(trust)* confiance *f*; **I have f. in him** je lui fais confiance; **she has lost (all) f. in the doctors** elle n'a plus aucune confiance dans les médecins; **to put one's f. in sth** mettres ses espoirs dans qch

2 *Rel (belief)* foi *f*; **f. in God** foi en Dieu; **to lose one's f.** perdre la foi; **F., Hope and Charity** la foi, l'espérance et la charité

3 *(particular religion)* foi *f*, religion *f*; **the Buddhist f.** la religion bouddhiste

4 *(honesty)* **he did it in good f.** il l'a fait en toute bonne foi; **he acted in bad f.** il a agi de mauvaise foi

5 *(loyalty)* fidélité *f*; **you must keep f. with the movement** il faut tenir vos engagements envers le mouvement; **to break f. with sb** manquer à sa parole envers qn

►► *Am* ***faith cure*** guérison *f* par la prière; ***faith healer*** guérisseur(euse) *m,f* spirituel(elle); ***faith healing*** guérison *f* par la foi; *Br Sch* ***faith school*** école *f* confessionnelle

faith-based *Am* **ADJ** à caractère religieux

►► ***faith-based school*** école *f* confessionnelle

faithful ['feɪθfʊl] **ADJ 1** *(believer, friend, lover)* fidèle (**to** à) **2** *(reliable)* sûr, solide; **he's a f. employee** c'est quelqu'un de sérieux *ou* sur qui on peut compter **3** *(accurate ► account, translation)* fidèle, exact; *(► copy)* conforme

NPL **the f.** *(supporters)* les fidèles *mpl*; *Rel* les fidèles *mpl*, les croyants *mpl*; *Pol* **the party f.** les fidèles *mpl* du parti

faithfully ['feɪθfʊlɪ] **ADV 1** *(loyally)* fidèlement, loyalement; **yours f.** *(in letter)* veuillez agréer mes salutations distinguées **2** *(accurately)* exactement, fidèlement

faithfulness ['feɪθfʊlnɪs] **N 1** *(loyalty)* fidélité *f*, loyauté *f*; **f. to the cause** fidélité *f* à *ou* loyauté *f* envers la cause **2** *(of report, translation)* fidélité *f*, exactitude *f*; *(of copy)* conformité *f*

faithless ['feɪθlɪs] **ADJ 1** *(dishonest, unreliable)* déloyal, perfide; *(to spouse, partner)* infidèle **2** *Rel* infidèle, non-croyant

faithlessness ['feɪθlɪsnɪs] **N 1** *(dishonesty, unreliability)* déloyauté *f*, perfidie *f*; *(to spouse, partner)* infidélité *f* **2** *Rel* manque *m* de foi

fake [feɪk] **VT 1** *(make ► document, painting)* faire un faux de, contrefaire; *(► style, furniture)* imiter

2 *(alter ► document)* falsifier, maquiller; *(► account)* falsifier; *(► election, interview, photograph)* truquer; **it's all faked** *(in cinema etc)* c'est du trucage

3 *(simulate)* feindre; **he faked a headache/sadness** il a fait semblant d'avoir mal à la tête/d'être triste; **she faked her own death** elle a fait croire à sa propre mort; *Sport* **to f. a pass** feinter la passe

4 *(ad-lib)* improviser

VI faire semblant; *Sport* feinter

N 1 *(thing)* article *m ou* objet *m* truqué; *(antique, painting)* faux *m* **2** *(person)* imposteur *m*; **she's a f.** elle essaie de se faire passer pour ce qu'elle n'est pas

ADJ *(antique, painting)* faux (fausse); *(account, document)* falsifié, faux (fausse); *(elections, interview, photograph)* truqué; **the pearls are f.** les perles sont fausses

►► ***fake tan*** *(product)* autobronzant *m*

faker ['feɪkə(r)] **N** *Fam* comédien(enne)❑ *m,f*

faking ['feɪkɪŋ] **N** **it's just f.** c'est de la comédie

fakir ['feɪˌkɪə(r)] **N** fakir *m*

falcon ['fɔːlkən] **N** faucon *m*

falconer ['fɔːlkənə(r)] **N** fauconnier *m*

falconry ['fɔːlkənrɪ] **N** fauconnerie *f*

Falkland ['fɔːlklənd] **N** **the F. Islands, the Falklands** les (îles *fpl*) Falkland *fpl*, les (îles *fpl*) Malouines *fpl*; **in the F. Islands** aux (îles) Falkland, aux (îles) Malouines

►► ***the Falklands War*** la guerre des Malouines

FALL [fɔːl]

> **N**
> - chute **1, 2, 4, 5, 11**
> - baisse **6, 7**
> - automne **10**
>
> **VI**
> - tomber **1, 6–8, 10–13, 15, 16**
> - se laisser tomber **2**
> - s'écrouler **3**
> - s'assombrir **9**
>
> **NPL**
> - cascade, chute

(pt **fell** [fel], *pp* **fallen** ['fɔːln])

N 1 *(tumble)* chute *f*; **have you had a f.?** êtes-vous tombé?, avez-vous fait une chute?; **a f. from a horse** une chute de cheval; *Literary* **the f. of night** la tombée de la nuit; **to be heading** *or* **riding for a f.** courir à l'échec

2 *(of rain, snow)* chute *f*; **there was a heavy f. of snow overnight** il y a eu de fortes chutes de neige dans la nuit

3 *Theat (of curtain)* baisser *m*

4 *(collapse ► of building, wall)* chute *f*, effondrement *m*; *(► of dirt, rock)* éboulement *m*, chute *f*; *(► of city, country)* chute *f*, capitulation *f*; *(► of regime)* chute *f*, renversement *m*; **the f. of the Roman Empire** la chute de l'Empire romain; **the f. of the Bastille** la prise de la Bastille

5 *(ruin ► of person)* perte *f*, ruine *f*; *Rel* **the F. (of Man)** la chute (de l'homme)

6 *(decrease ► in price, income, shares, temperature)* baisse *f* (**in** de); *(► in currency)* dépréciation *f*, baisse *f* (**in** de); *(more marked)* chute *f* (**in** de); *(► of barometer, in pressure)* chute *f* (**in** de)

7 *(lowering ► of water)* décrue *f*, baisse *f*; *(► of voice)* cadence *f*

8 *(drape)* **the f. of her gown** le drapé de sa robe, la façon dont tombe sa robe

9 *(slope)* pente *f*, inclinaison *f*

10 *Am (autumn)* automne *m*; **in the f.** en automne

11 *Sport (in judo)* chute *f*; *(in wrestling)* chute *f*

VI 1 *(barrier, cup, napkin, water, person)* tomber; **the napkin fell to the floor** la serviette est tombée par terre; **the child fell into the pond** l'enfant est tombé dans la mare; **she fell off the stool/out of the window** elle est tombée du tabouret/par la fenêtre; **to f. 20 feet** faire une chute de six mètres; **he fell over the pile of books** il est tombé en butant contre le tas de livres; **just let your arms f. to your sides** laissez simplement vos bras pendre *ou* tomber sur les côtés; **he fell full length** il est tombé de tout son long; **the crowd fell on** *or* **to their knees** la foule est tombée à genoux; **she did let f. a few hints** elle a fait effectivement quelques allusions; **the book fell open at page 20** le livre s'est ouvert à la page 20; *also Fig* **to f. on one's feet** retomber sur ses pieds; **I fell flat on**

my face je suis tombé à plat ventre *ou* face contre terre; *Fam Fig* je me suis planté; *Am very Fam also Fig* **he fell flat on his ass** il s'est cassé la gueule; **his only joke fell flat** la seule plaisanterie qu'il a faite est tombée à plat; **the scheme fell flat** le projet est tombé à l'eau; **despite all their efforts, the party fell flat** en dépit de leurs efforts, la soirée a fait un flop; **to f. to bits** *or* **to pieces** tomber en morceaux; **all her good intentions fell by the wayside** toutes ses bonnes intentions sont tombées à l'eau; **the job fell short of her expectations** le poste ne répondait pas à ses attentes

2 *(move deliberately)* se laisser tomber; **I fell into the armchair** je me suis laissé tomber dans le fauteuil; **they fell into one another's arms** ils sont tombés dans les bras l'un de l'autre

3 *(bridge, building)* s'écrouler, s'effondrer

4 *(err, go astray)* s'écarter du droit chemin; *Rel (sin)* pécher; **to f. from grace** *Rel* perdre la grâce; *Fig* tomber en disgrâce

5 *(ground)* descendre, aller en pente

6 *(government)* tomber, être renversé; *(city, country)* tomber; **after a long siege the city fell** après un long siège, la ville a capitulé; **Constantinople fell to the Turks** Constantinople est tombée aux mains des Turcs

7 *(darkness, light, night, rain, snow)* tomber; **as night fell** à la tombée de la nuit; **the tree's shadow fell across the lawn** l'arbre projetait son ombre sur la pelouse

8 *(land ▸ eyes, blow, weapon)* tomber; **my eyes fell on the letter** mon regard est tombé sur la lettre

9 *(face, spirits)* s'assombrir; **my spirits fell** tout d'un coup, j'ai perdu le moral

10 *(hang down)* tomber, descendre; **the fabric falls in gentle folds** ce tissu retombe en faisant de jolis plis; **his hair fell to his shoulders** ses cheveux lui descendaient *ou* tombaient jusqu'aux épaules; **his hair keeps falling into his eyes** ses cheveux n'arrêtent pas de lui tomber dans les yeux

11 *(decrease in level, value ▸ price, temperature)* baisser, tomber; *(▸ pressure)* baisser, diminuer; *(▸ wind)* tomber; **the thermometer/temperature has fallen ten degrees** le thermomètre/la température a baissé de dix degrés; **their voices fell to a whisper** ils se sont mis à chuchoter

12 *(issue forth)* tomber, s'échapper; **curses fell from her lips** elle laissa échapper des jurons; **the tears started to f.** il/elle se mit à pleurer

13 *(occur)* tomber; **May Day falls on a Tuesday this year** le Premier Mai tombe un mardi cette année; **the accent falls on the third syllable** l'accent tombe sur la troisième syllabe

14 *(descend)* **a great sadness fell over the town** une grande tristesse s'abattit sur la ville; **a hush fell among** *or* **over the crowd** tout d'un coup, la foule s'est tue

15 *(become)* **to f. asleep** s'endormir; **the child fell fast asleep** l'enfant est tombé dans un profond sommeil; **the bill falls due on the 6th** la facture arrive à échéance le 6; **to f. ill** *or* **sick** tomber malade; **to f. pregnant** tomber enceinte; **to f. in love (with sb)** tomber amoureux (de qn); **to f. silent** se taire; **it falls vacant in February** *(job)* il se trouvera vacant au mois de février; *(apartment)* il se trouvera libre *ou* il se libérera au mois de février; **to f. victim to sth** être victime de qch; **she fell victim to depression** elle a fait une dépression

16 *(die)* mourir; **the young men who fell in battle** les jeunes tombés au champ d'honneur

17 *(be classified)* **the athletes f. into two categories** les sportifs se divisent en deux catégories; **that falls outside my area of responsibility** cela ne relève pas de ma responsabilité; **that does not f. within the scope of our agreement** ceci n'entre pas dans le cadre de *ou* ne fait pas partie de notre accord

18 *(inheritance)* **the fortune fell to his niece** c'est sa nièce qui a hérité de sa fortune

19 *Sport (in cricket)* **two English wickets fell on the first day** deux batteurs anglais ont été éliminés le premier jour

COMP *Am (colours, weather)* d'automne, automnal

• **falls NPL** *(waterfall)* cascade *f*, chute *f* d'eau; **Niagara Falls** les chutes *fpl* du Niagara

▸▸ *Fam* **fall guy** *(dupe)* pigeon *m*; *(scapegoat)* bouc *m* émissaire□

▸ **fall about VI** *Br Fam* **to f. about (laughing)** se tordre de rire

▸ **fall apart VI 1** *(book, furniture)* tomber en morceaux; *Fig (nation)* se désagréger; *(conference)* échouer; *(system)* s'écrouler, s'effondrer; **her plans fell apart at the seams** ses projets sont tombés à l'eau; **her life was falling apart** toute sa vie s'écroulait; **their marriage is falling apart** leur mariage est en train de se briser *ou* va à vau-l'eau **2** *(person)* s'effondrer; **he more or less fell apart after his wife's death** il a plus ou moins craqué après la mort de sa femme

▸ **fall away VI 1** *(paint, plaster)* s'écailler

2 *(diminish in size ▸ attendance, figures)* diminuer; *(▸ fears)* se dissiper, fondre

3 *(defect)* déserter; **support for his policies is beginning to f. away** dans la politique qu'il mène il commence à perdre ses appuis

4 *(land, slope)* s'affaisser

▸ **fall back VI 1** *(fall)* tomber à la renverse *ou* en arrière

2 *(retreat, recede)* reculer, se retirer; *Mil* se replier, battre en retraite

3 *(lag, trail)* se laisser distancer, être à la traîne

4 *St Exch & Fin* **to f. back two points** se replier de deux points

▸ **fall back on VT INSEP to f. back on sth** avoir recours à qch; **it's good to have something to f. back on** *(skill)* c'est bien de pouvoir se raccrocher à quelque chose; *(money)* il vaut mieux avoir d'autres ressources

▸ **fall behind VI** se laisser distancer, être à la traîne; *Sport* se laisser distancer; *(in cycling)* décrocher; **she fell behind in** *or* **with her work** elle a pris du retard dans son travail; **we can't f. behind in** *or* **with the rent** nous ne pouvons pas être en retard pour le loyer

VT INSEP prendre du retard sur; **he's fallen behind the rest of the class** il a pris du retard sur le reste de la classe

▸ **fall down VI 1** *(book, person, picture)* tomber (par terre); *(bridge, building)* s'effondrer, s'écrouler **2** *(argument, comparison)* s'écrouler, s'effondrer; **where the whole thing falls down is…** là où plus rien ne tient debout *ou* où tout s'écroule c'est…

▸ **fall for VT INSEP** *Fam* **1** *(become infatuated with)* tomber amoureux de□; **they fell for each other** ils sont tombés amoureux l'un de l'autre; **they really fell for Spain in a big way** ils ont vraiment été emballés par l'Espagne **2** *(be deceived by)* se laisser prendre par□; **they really fell for it!** ils ont vraiment mordu!, ils se sont vraiment fait avoir!; **don't f. for that hard luck story of his** ne te fais pas avoir quand il te raconte qu'il a la poisse; **I'm not falling for that one!** ça ne prend pas!, à d'autres!

▸ **fall in VI 1** *(tumble)* tomber; **you'll f. in!** tu vas tomber dedans! **2** *(roof)* s'effondrer, s'écrouler **3** *(line up)* se mettre en rang, s'aligner; *Mil (troops)* former les rangs; *(one soldier)* rentrer dans les rangs; **f. in!** à vos rangs!

▸ **fall in with VT INSEP 1** *(frequent)* **to f. in with sb** se mettre à fréquenter qn; **she fell in with a bad crowd** elle s'est mise à fréquenter des gens louches **2** *Br (agree with ▸ suggestion)* accepter; *(▸ request)* accéder à; **I'll f. in with whatever you decide to do** je me rangerai à ce que tu décideras

▸ **fall off VI 1** *(drop off)* tomber; *(in mountain climbing)* dévisser; **she fell off the bicycle/horse** elle est tombée du vélo/de cheval **2** *(diminish ▸ attendance, exports, numbers, sales)* diminuer, baisser; *(▸ profits)* diminuer; *(▸ enthusiasm, production)* baisser, tomber; *(▸ population, rate)* baisser, décroître; *(▸ speed)* ralentir; *(▸ interest, zeal)* se relâcher; *(▸ popularity)* baisser; *(▸ wind)* tomber

▸ **fall on VT INSEP 1** *(drop on)* tomber sur; **something fell on my head** j'ai reçu quelque chose sur la tête

2 *(attack)* attaquer, se jeter sur; **the starving children fell on the food** les enfants, affamés, se sont jetés sur la nourriture; *Mil* **the guerrillas fell on the unsuspecting troops** les guérilleros ont fondu sur *ou* attaqué les troupes sans qu'elles s'y attendent

3 *(meet with)* tomber sur, trouver; **they fell on hard times** ils sont tombés dans la misère, ils ont subi des revers de fortune

4 *(of responsibility)* revenir à, incomber à; **suspicion falls on them** c'est eux que l'on soupçonne; **responsibility for looking after them falls on me** c'est à moi qu'il incombe de prendre soin d'eux

▸ **fall out VI 1** *(drop out)* tomber; **the keys must have fallen out of my pocket** les clés ont dû tomber de ma poche; **his hair is falling out** ses cheveux tombent, il perd ses cheveux

2 *(quarrel)* se brouiller, se disputer; **she's fallen out with her boyfriend** elle est *ou* s'est brouillée avec son petit ami

3 *(happen)* se passer, advenir; **as things fell out** en fin de compte

4 *Mil* rompre les rangs; **f. out!** rompez!

5 *Am Fam (fall asleep)* s'endormir□

▸ **fall over VI 1** *(lose balance ▸ person)* tomber (par terre); *(▸ thing)* se renverser, être renversé **2** *Fam (idioms)* **she was falling over herself to make us feel welcome** elle se mettait en quatre pour nous faire bon accueil; **the men were falling over each other to help her** les hommes ne savaient pas quoi inventer pour l'aider

▸ **fall through VI** *(fail)* échouer; **the deal fell through** l'affaire n'a pas abouti; **all our plans fell through at the last minute** tous nos projets sont tombés à l'eau au dernier moment

▸ **fall to VT INSEP 1** *Br (begin)* se mettre à; **we fell to work** nous nous sommes mis à l'œuvre; **we all fell to talking about the past** nous nous sommes tous mis à parler du passé **2** *(devolve upon)* appartenir à, incomber à; **the task that falls to us is not an easy one** la tâche qui nous incombe *ou* revient n'est pas facile; **it fell to her to break the news to him** ce fut à elle de lui annoncer la nouvelle

VI *(eat)* **he brought in the food and they fell to** il a apporté à manger et ils se sont jetés dessus; **she fell to as if she hadn't eaten for a week** elle a attaqué comme si elle n'avait rien mangé depuis huit jours

▸ **fall upon VT INSEP 1** *(attack)* attaquer, se jeter sur; *Mil* **the army fell upon the enemy** l'armée s'est abattue *ou* a fondu sur l'ennemi; **they fell upon the food** ils se sont jetés sur la nourriture **2** *(meet with)* tomber sur, trouver; **the family fell upon hard times** la famille a subi des revers de fortune

---

fallacious [fə'leɪʃəs] **ADJ** *(statement)* fallacieux, faux (fausse); *(hope)* faux (fausse), illusoire

fallacy ['fæləsɪ] *(pl* **fallacies)** **N** *(misconception)* erreur *f*, idée *f* fausse; *(false reasoning)* mauvais raisonnement *m*, sophisme *m*; *(in logic)* sophisme *m*; **it is a f. that…** ce serait une erreur de croire que…; **the f. of this argument is that…** ce qui est faux dans ce raisonnement, c'est que…

fallback ['fɔːlbæk] **N 1** *(retreat)* retraite *f*, recul *m* **2** *(reserve)* réserve *f*; **what's our f. position?** sur quoi est-ce qu'on peut se rabattre?

fallen ['fɔːlən] *pp of* **fall**

ADJ 1 *(gen)* tombé; *(hero, soldier)* tombé, mort; *(idol)* tombé en disgrâce; *(leaf)* mort **2** *(immoral)* perdu; **f. woman** fille *f* perdue

NPL *Literary* **the f.** ceux qui sont tombés au champ d'honneur

▸▸ *Rel & St Exch* ***fallen angel*** ange *m* déchu; *Med* ***fallen arches*** affaissement *m* de la voûte plantaire

fallibility [ˌfælə'bɪlətɪ] **N** faillibilité *f*

fallible ['fæləbəl] **ADJ** faillible; **everyone is f.** tout le monde peut se tromper

falling ['fɔːlɪŋ] **ADJ** *(piece of masonry, tile)* qui tombe; *(population)* décroissant; *(prices, temperature, standards, value)* en baisse

▸▸ ***falling rocks*** chute *f* de pierres; ***falling star*** étoile *f* filante

falling-off, fall-off **N** réduction *f*, diminution *f*; **a f. in production** une baisse de production; **a gradual f. of interest/of support** une baisse progressive d'intérêt/de soutien

Fallopian tube [fə'ləʊpɪən-] **N** *Anat* trompe *f* utérine *ou* de Fallope

fallout ['fɔːlaʊt] **N** *(UNCOUNT)* *(radioactive)* retombées *fpl* (radioactives); *Fam Fig (conse-

quences) retombées□ *fpl*, répercussions□ *fpl*
►► ***fallout shelter*** abri *m* antiatomique

fallow [ˈfæləʊ] **ADJ** *Agr (field, land)* en jachère, en friche; **to lie f.** être en jachère; *Fig* **a f. period** un passage à vide
N jachère *f*, friche *f*
►► *Zool* ***fallow deer*** daim *m*

false [fɔːls] **ADJ 1** *(wrong)* faux (fausse); *(untrue)* erroné, inexact; **a f. idea** une idée fausse *ou* erronée; **a f. statement** une fausse déclaration; **to give sb a f. impression of sth** donner à qn une fausse impression sur qch; **in a f. position** dans une position fausse; **don't make any f. moves** ne faites pas de faux pas
2 *(fake)* faux (fausse); *(artificial)* artificiel; **f. identity** fausse identité *f*; **f. name** faux nom *m*
3 *(deceptive)* faux (fausse), mensonger; **f. promises** promesses *fpl* mensongères, fausses promesses *fpl*; **a f. report** *or* **rumour** une fausse rumeur; *Law* **under f. pretences** par des moyens frauduleux; *Fig* **you've got me here under f. pretences** tu m'as bien piégé; *Law* **to bear f. witness** porter un faux témoignage
4 *(insincere)* perfide, fourbe; *(disloyal)* déloyal; **f. modesty** fausse modestie *f*
ADV faux; **her story rings f.** son histoire sonne faux; **to play sb f.** trahir qn
►► ***false alarm*** fausse alerte *f*; *Am* ***false arrest*** arrestation *f* illégale; ***false bottom*** *(of box etc)* double fond *m*; **a suitcase with a f. bottom** une valise à double fond; ***false dawn*** lueurs *fpl* annonciatrices de l'aube; *Fig* **it was a f. dawn** ce n'était qu'un faux espoir; *Acct* ***false entry*** fausse écriture *f*; ***false eyelashes*** faux cils *mpl*; ***a false friend*** *(gen)* un ami déloyal; *Ling* un faux ami; *Psy* ***false memory syndrome*** syndrome *m* des faux souvenirs; *Mus* ***false note*** fausse note *f*; *Fig* **to strike a f. note** ne pas être crédible; ***false positive*** *(test result)* résultat *m* faussement positif; ***false pregnancy*** grossesse *f* nerveuse; ***false ribs*** fausses côtes *fpl*; *Sport* ***false start*** faux départ *m*; ***false teeth*** dentier *m*

false-hearted [-ˈhɑːtɪd] **ADJ** *Literary* fourbe

falsehood [ˈfɔːlshʊd] **N** *Formal* **1** *(lie)* mensonge *m*; **to tell** *or* **to utter a f.** mentir, dire des mensonges **2** *(lying)* faux *m*; **truth and f.** le vrai et le faux

falsely [ˈfɔːlslɪ] **ADV** *(claim, state)* faussement; *(accuse, judge)* à tort, injustement; *(interpret)* mal; *(act)* déloyalement

falseness [ˈfɔːlsnɪs] **N 1** *(of belief, statement)* fausseté *f* **2** *(of friend, lover)* infidélité *f* **3** *(insincerity)* fausseté *f*, manque *m* de sincérité

falsers [ˈfɔːlsəz] **NPL** *Br Fam Hum (teeth)* râtelier *m*, dentier□ *m*

falsetto [fɔːlˈsetəʊ] *(pl* **falsettos)** *Mus* **N** fausset *m*
ADJ *(voice)* de fausset, de tête

falsies [ˈfɔːlsɪz] **NPL** *Fam (padding for breasts)* soutien-gorge *m* rembourré□; *(false breasts)* faux seins□ *mpl*; *(false eyelashes)* faux-cils□ *mpl*

falsifiable [ˌfɔːlsɪˈfaɪəbəl] **ADJ** *Phil* falsifiable

falsification [ˌfɔːlsɪfɪˈkeɪʃən] **N** falsification *f*

falsify [ˈfɔːlsɪfaɪ] *(pt & pp* **falsified) VT 1** *(document)* falsifier; *(evidence)* maquiller; *(accounts, figures)* truquer **2** *(misrepresent)* déformer, dénaturer

falsity [ˈfɔːlsətɪ] *(pl* **falsities) N** *(falseness)* fausseté *f*, erreur *f*

falter [ˈfɔːltə(r)] **VI 1** *(speaker)* hésiter, parler d'une voix mal assurée; **his voice faltered** il hésita **2** *(waver)* vaciller, chanceler; *(courage, memory)* faiblir; **his steps faltered as he neared the room** ses pas se firent hésitants tandis qu'il s'approchait de la pièce; **demand for luxury goods has begun to f.** la demande de produits de luxe a commencé à baisser **3** *(stumble)* chanceler, tituber
VT balbutier, bredouiller; **"I don't… I can't…," he faltered** "je... non... non…", bredouilla-t-il *ou* balbutia-t-il

faltering [ˈfɔːltərɪŋ] **ADJ** *(attempt)* timide, hésitant; *(voice)* hésitant, mal assuré; *(steps)* chancelant, mal assuré; *(courage, memory)* défaillant

fame [feɪm] **N** célébrité *f*, renommée *f*; **the film brought her f. and fortune** le film l'a rendue riche et célèbre; **to rise to f.** se faire un nom; **Mick Jagger of Rolling Stones f.** Mick Jagger, le chanteur du célèbre groupe The Rolling Stones

famed [feɪmd] **ADJ** célèbre, renommé; **f. for his generosity** connu *ou* célèbre pour sa générosité

familiar [fəˈmɪljə(r)] **ADJ 1** *(well-known)* familier; **a f. face** un visage familier *ou* connu; **his name is f.** j'ai déjà entendu son nom (quelque part), son nom me dit quelque chose; **there's something f. about the place** il me semble connaître cet endroit; **a f. feeling** un sentiment bien connu; **an all too f. story of drug addiction and homelessness** (c'est) toujours ce même problème de drogue et de sans-abris; *Fig* **we're on f. territory** nous voilà en terrain de connaissance
2 *(acquainted)* **to be f. with sth** bien connaître qch; **she's f. with the situation** elle est au courant *ou* au fait de la situation; **to become f. with sth** se familiariser avec qch
3 *(informal)* familier, intime; **to be on f. terms with sb** entretenir des rapports amicaux avec qn; **f. language/tone** langage *m*/ton *m* familier
4 *Pej (presumptuous* ► *socially)* familier; *(*► *sexually)* trop entreprenant; **don't let him get too f. (with you)** ne le laissez pas devenir trop entreprenant
N 1 *(friend)* familier *m*, ami(e) *m,f* **2** *(in witchcraft* ► *spirit)* démon *m* familier

familiarity [fəˌmɪlɪˈærətɪ] *(pl* **familiarities) N 1** *(of face, place)* caractère *m* familier
2 *(with book, rules, language)* connaissance *f*; **her f. with his work** sa connaissance de ses œuvres; *Prov* **f. breeds contempt** = la familiarité engendre le mépris
3 *(intimacy)* familiarité *f*, intimité *f*
4 *(usu pl) Pej (undue intimacy)* familiarité *f*, privauté *f*

familiarization, -isation [fəˌmɪljəraɪˈzeɪʃən] **N** familiarisation *f*
►► ***familiarization training*** initiation *f*; *Com* ***familiarization trip*** voyage *m* d'études *ou* de familiarisation

familiarize, -ise [fəˈmɪljəraɪz] **VT 1** *(inform)* familiariser; **to f. oneself with sth** se familiariser avec qch; **she familiarized him with the rules** elle l'a initié aux règles **2** *(make widely known)* répandre, vulgariser

familiarly [fəˈmɪljəlɪ] **ADV** familièrement; **the Victoria theatre, f. known as the Old Vic** le "Victoria theatre", que l'on appelle familièrement "Old Vic"

family [ˈfæmlɪ] *(pl* **families) N** *(gen) & Biol, Bot & Ling* famille *f*; **have you any f.?** *(relatives)* avez-vous de la famille?; *(children)* avez-vous des enfants?; **to raise a f.** élever des enfants; **a large f.** une famille nombreuse; **to start a f.** avoir un (premier) enfant; **she's (just like) one of the f.** elle fait (tout à fait) partie *ou* elle est (tout à fait) de la famille; **it runs in the f.** cela tient de famille; **of good f.** de bonne famille; **a f. audience** un public *ou* auditoire familial; **a f. business** une entreprise familiale; **f. butcher** boucher *m* de quartier; **f. doctor** docteur *m* de famille; **a f. hotel** une pension de famille; **f. portraits** portraits *mpl* d'ancêtres; *Old-fashioned Fam Euph* **to be in the f. way** attendre un enfant□; **we'll keep it in the f.** *(heirloom, land)* ça restera dans la famille; *(scandal)* ça ne sortira pas de la famille; **he's a f. man** il aime la vie de famille, c'est un bon père de famille; **unsuitable for f. viewing** non approprié aux enfants
COMP *(life)* familial, de famille; *(car, friend)* de la famille; *(dinner, likeness, quarrel)* de famille; *(programme)* pour les familles
►► *Br Formerly Admin* ***family allowance*** allocations *fpl* familiales; ***family Bible*** Bible *f* familiale *ou* de famille; ***family circle*** cercle *m* de (la) famille; *Am Law* ***family court*** = tribunal pour toute affaire concernant le droit de la famille; *Br Admin* ***family credit*** = prestation complémentaire pour familles à faibles revenus ayant au moins un enfant; *Br Law* ***Family Division*** = division de la "High Court" s'occupant des affaires matrimoniales; *Am* ***family fare*** *(on public transport)* tarif *m* familles; *Br Formerly Admin* ***family income supplement*** complément *m* familial; *Fam Hum* ***family jewels*** *(man's genitals)* bijoux *mpl* de famille; ***family law*** droit *m* de la famille; ***family leave*** congé *m* parental; ***family liaison officer*** = agent de police chargé d'aider les familles victi[mes] d'un incident grave; ***family name*** nom *m* d[e] famille; ***family planning*** planning *m* familial; ***fam[ily] planning clinic*** centre *m* de planning familia[l]; *Am* ***family practice*** médecine *f* générale; *Am* ***fa[mily] practitioner*** médecin *m* de famille, (méde[cin] *m*) généraliste *mf*; ***family room*** *(in hotel)* chambre *f* familiale; *Am (in house)* salle *f* de sé[jour]; *Br (in pub)* salle *f* réservée aux familles; ***family saloon*** berline *f* familiale; *Law* ***family set[tlement]*** arrangement *m* de famille; *Psy* ***famil[y] therapy*** thérapie *f* familiale; ***family tree*** arbre *m* généalogique

family-run **ADJ** *(hotel, restaurant)* géré en fa[mille], familial

famine [ˈfæmɪn] **N** famine *f*

famished [ˈfæmɪʃt] **ADJ** affamé; *Fam* **I'm f.!** je meurs de faim!, j'ai une faim de loup!

famous [ˈfeɪməs] **ADJ 1** *(renowned)* célèbre, re[n]nommé; **the stately home is f. for its gardens** le château est connu *ou* célèbre pour ses jardins; **a f. victory** une victoire célèbre; **f. last words** c'est ce que tu crois! **2** *Old-fashioned (first-rate)* fameux, formidable
NPL the f. les gens célèbres, les célébrités *fpl*

famously [ˈfeɪməslɪ] **ADV 1** *Fam (very well)* fa[meusement] (bien), rudement bien; **they get o[n] f.** ils s'entendent à merveille *ou* comme larron[s] en foire; **the project is coming along f.** l'opératio[n] marche comme sur des roulettes **2** *(with re[nown])* **the castle has often been the scene of im[portant] events, most f. when…** le château a souvent été la scène d'événements importants, le plus célèbre d'entre eux ayant eu lie[u] quand…; **as Oscar Wilde once f. said…** pour cite[r] la formule célèbre d'Oscar Wilde…

fan [fæn] *(pt & pp* **fanned**, *cont* **fanning) N 1** *(sup[porter])* enthousiaste *mf*, passionné(e) *m,f*; *(of ce[lebrity]) & Sport* fan *mf*; **a football f.** un fan *ou* u[n] passionné de football; **a crowd of football fans** une foule de supporters de football; **she's a chess/rap f.** elle se passionne pour les échecs, le rap; **he's a f. of Thai cooking** c'est un amateu[r] de cuisine thaïlandaise; **I'm not a great f. of hers, I'm not her biggest f.** je suis loin d'être un de se[s] admirateurs **2** *(ventilator* ► *mechanical)* ventila[teur] *m*; *(*► *hand-held)* éventail *m*; **shaped like a f.** en éventail; *Fam* **when it hits the f.** quand ça va nous tomber dessus **3** *Agr (machine)* tarare *m*; *(basket)* van *m*
VT 1 *(face, person)* éventer; **to f. oneself** s'évente[r] **2** *(fire)* attiser, souffler sur; *(passions)* attiser, ex[c]iter; *Fig* **to f. the flames** jeter de l'huile sur le feu; **these remarks had fanned the flames of nationalis[t] feeling** ces remarques avaient exacerbé le sen[timent] nationaliste; **to f. the embers of sb's pas[sion]** raviver les flammes de la passion de qn **3** *Agr (grain)* vanner
►► ***fan base*** public *m*; *Aut* ***fan belt*** courroie *f* d[e] ventilateur; ***fan club*** cercle *m* ou club *m* de fans; *Fig* **her f. club is here** ses admirateurs sont là; ***fan dance*** danse *f* des éventails; ***fan heater*** radiateu[r] *m* soufflant; ***fan jet*** *(engine)* turboréacteur *m*; *(plane)* avion *m* à turboréacteurs; ***fan letter*** lettre *f* d'un admirateur; ***fan mail*** courrier *m* des admirateurs; ***fan oven*** four *m* à chaleur tournante; *Archit* ***fan vaulting*** *(UNCOUNT)* voûte *f* ou voûtes *fpl* en éventail

►**fan out VT SEP** étaler (en éventail)
VI *(spread out)* s'étaler *ou* se déployer (en éven[tail]); *(army, search party)* se déployer

fan-assisted oven **N** four *m* à chaleur tour[nante]

fanatic [fəˈnætɪk] **N** fanatique *mf*
ADJ fanatique

fanatical [fəˈnætɪkəl] **ADJ** fanatique

fanatically [fəˈnætɪkəlɪ] **ADV** fanatiquement

fanaticism [fəˈnætɪˌsɪzəm] **N** fanatisme *m*

fanciable [ˈfænsɪəbəl] **ADJ** *Br Fam (person)* plutô[t] bien□, pas mal du tout□

fancied [ˈfænsɪd] **ADJ 1** *(imagined)* imaginaire **2** *Sport (favoured)* coté, en vogue

fancier [ˈfænsɪə(r)] **N** *(of animals, birds* ► *lover)* amateur(trice) *m,f*; *(*► *breeder)* éleveur(euse) *m,f*

fanciful [ˈfænsɪfʊl] **ADJ 1** *(whimsical* ► *person)* capricieux, fantaisiste; *(*► *notion)* fantasque; *(*►

roject) chimérique; (▸*clothing*) extravagant; **he was being rather f.** *(being unrealistic)* il se faisait des idées, il rêvait; *(indulging his imagination)* il se laissait porter par son imagination **2** *(imaginative)* imaginatif, plein d'imagination **3** *(imaginary)* imaginaire

ancifully [ˈfænsɪfʊlɪ] ADV **1** *(act)* capricieusement; *(dress)* d'une façon extravagante *ou* fantaisiste; **somewhat f. described as…** désigné sous le terme plutôt fantaisiste de… **2** *(draw, write)* avec imagination

an-cooled [-kuːld] ADJ refroidi par ventilateur

ancy [ˈfænsɪ] *(compar* **fancier**, *superl* **fanciest**, *pl* **fancies**, *pt & pp* **fancied**) ADJ **1** *(elaborate* ▸ *clothes)* recherché, raffiné; (▸*style)* recherché, travaillé; (▸ *excuse)* recherché, compliqué; **f. cakes** pâtisseries *fpl*; **just a bottle of ordinary wine, nothing f.** juste une bouteille de vin ordinaire, rien de spécial; **to cut out the f. stuff** arrêter les chichis

2 *(upmarket* ▸ *neighbourhood)* chic; (▸*shop, car)* de luxe; **f. food** plats *mpl* compliqués

3 *Pej (affected, pretentious* ▸ *talk, words)* extravagant; **with all her f. ways** avec ses grands airs

4 *(high* ▸ *price)* exorbitant

5 *Zool (breed)* d'agrément

N **1** *(whim)* caprice *m*, fantaisie *f*; **as the f. takes him** comme ça lui chante; **it's just a passing f.** ce n'est qu'une lubie

2 *Br (liking)* goût *m*, penchant *m*; **I've taken a f. to avocados lately** je me suis mis depuis quelque temps à aimer les avocats; **to take a f. to sb** *(become fond of)* se prendre d'affection pour qn; *(become sexually attracted to)* s'éprendre *ou* s'enticher de qn; **the dress took** *or* **caught her f.** la robe lui a fait envie *ou* lui a tapé dans l'œil; *Fam* **the idea tickled my f.** l'idée m'a séduit▫

3 *(imagination)* imagination *f*, fantaisie *f*; *Literary* **the realm of f.** le domaine de l'imaginaire, le royaume des chimères

4 *(notion)* idée *f* fantasque, fantasme *m*; **I have a f. that…** j'ai idée que…; **idle fancies** chimères *fpl*

VT **1** *Br Fam (want)* avoir envie de▫; *(like)* aimer▫; **do you f. a cup of tea?** ça te dirait une tasse de thé?; **I f. a bit of chicken** je mangerais volontiers un morceau de poulet, j'ai envie d'un morceau de poulet; **I don't f. travelling in this weather** cela ne me dit rien *ou* je n'ai pas envie de voyager par ce temps; **she wasn't sure if she fancied the idea** elle n'était pas sûre que l'idée la tentait; **to f. sb** s'enticher de qn

2 *Fam (imagine)* imaginer▫, s'imaginer▫; **f. meeting you here!** tiens! je ne m'attendais pas à vous voir ici!▫; **f. anyone wanting to do that!** qu'est-ce que les gens vont chercher!; **f. her coming!** qui aurait cru qu'elle allait venir!▫; **f. that!** tiens! voyez-vous cela!

3 *Fam (have good opinion of)* **to f. oneself** être infatué de sa petite personne, se gober; **she really fancies herself** elle ne se prend vraiment pas pour rien; **she fancies herself as an intellectual** elle se prend pour une intellectuelle▫; **I don't f. their chances of winning** je ne crois pas qu'ils aient des chances de gagner▫, j'imagine mal qu'ils puissent gagner▫; *Sport* **which horse do you f.?** à votre avis, quel sera le cheval gagnant?▫, quel cheval donnez-vous gagnant?▫

4 *Literary (believe)* croire, se figurer; **he fancies he knows everything** il se figure tout savoir; **she fancied she heard the baby crying** elle a cru entendre pleurer le bébé

▸▸ *Br* ***fancy dress*** déguisement *m*, costume *m*; **in f. dress** déguisé; **I didn't realise it was f. dress** je ne savais pas qu'il fallait se déguiser; ***fancy dress ball*** bal *m* masqué *ou* costumé; ***fancy dress party*** fête *f* déguisée; *Br* ***fancy goods*** articles *mpl* de fantaisie; *Br Fam Pej* ***fancy man*** jules *m*; **he's her new f. man** c'est son nouveau jules *ou* mec; *Br Fam Pej* ***fancy woman*** maîtresse▫ *f*, poule *f*

ancy-free ADJ sans souci

ancywork [ˈfænsɪwɜːk] N *(UNCOUNT)* ouvrages *mpl* d'agrément

anfare [ˈfænfeə(r)] N *Mus* fanfare *f*; *Fig* **with much f.** *(ostentation)* avec des roulements de tambour, avec éclat

anfic [ˈfænfɪk] N *Fam* fanfic *f*, fanfiction *f*

anfold [ˈfænfəʊld] ADJ

▸▸ *Comput* ***fanfold paper*** papier *m* continu plié en accordéon

fang [fæŋ] N *(of snake)* crochet *m*; *(of wolf, vampire)* croc *m*, canine *f*

fanlight [ˈfænlaɪt] N *Archit* imposte *f* (semi-circulaire)

fanny [ˈfænɪ] *(pl* **fannies**) N **1** *Br Vulg (female genitals)* chatte *f* **2** *Am Fam (buttocks)* fesses▫ *fpl*

▸▸ *Am* ***fanny bag, fanny pack*** banane *f (sac)*

▸ **fanny about, fanny around** VI *Br very Fam* perdre son temps à des bricoles, glander

fan-shaped ADJ en éventail

fantabulous [fænˈtæbjʊləs] ADJ *Fam* chic, chouette

fantail (pigeon) [ˈfænteɪl-] N *Orn* pigeon *m* paon

fantailed [ˈfænteɪld] ADJ *Orn*

▸▸ ***fantailed pigeon*** pigeon *m* paon

fantasia [fænˈteɪzjə] N *Literature & Mus* fantaisie *f*

fantasize, -ise [ˈfæntəsaɪz] VI fantasmer, se livrer à des fantasmes; **she fantasized about becoming rich and famous** elle rêvait de devenir riche et célèbre

VT rêver, imaginer (**that** que)

fantastic [fænˈtæstɪk] ADJ **1** *Fam (wonderful)* fantastique, sensationnel; **we had a f. time** nous nous sommes vraiment bien amusés; **what a f. goal!** quel but fantastique *ou* superbe! **2** *Fam (very great* ▸ *success)* inouï▫, fabuleux▫; (▸ *amount, sum, rate)* phénoménal▫, faramineux▫ **3** *(preposterous, strange* ▸ *idea, plan, story)* fantastique, bizarre; **it sounds f., but it's true** ça paraît inouï mais c'est vrai

fantastically [fænˈtæstɪklɪ] ADV **1** *Fam (greatly)* fantastiquement▫, extraordinairement▫; **it's f. expensive** c'est incroyablement *ou* terriblement cher **2** *(preposterously)* **somewhat f., the story ends with…** l'histoire se termine d'une manière un peu invraisemblable avec…

fantasy [ˈfæntəsɪ] *(pl* **fantasies**) N **1** *(dream)* fantasme *m*; *Psy* fantasme *m*; *(notion)* idée *f* fantasque; **sexual f.** fantasme *m* (sexuel) **2** *(imagination)* imagination *f*, fantaisie *f*; **f. and reality** l'imaginaire *m* et la réalité; **to live in a f. world** vivre dans un monde à soi **3** *Literature & Mus* fantaisie *f*

▸▸ ***fantasy football*** = jeu dans lequel les participants composent leur équipe idéale et marquent des points en fonction des performances réelles des joueurs choisis au cours de la saison

> Note that the French word **fantaisie** is a false friend.

fanzine [ˈfænziːn] N revue *f* spécialisée, fanzine *m*

FAO [ˌefeɪˈəʊ] N *(abbr* **Food and Agriculture Organization**) FAO *f*

FAQ [ˌefeɪˈkjuː] ADV *Br Com (abbr* **free alongside quay**) FLQ

N *Comput (abbr* **frequently asked questions**) FAQ

▸▸ *Comput* ***FAQ file*** fichier *m* FAQ

FAR [fɑː(r)]

ADV	
• loin **1, 2**	beaucoup **3**
ADJ	
• lointain **1**	• éloigné **1**
• autre **2**	• extrême **3**

(compar **farther** [ˈfɑːðə(r)] *or* **further** [ˈfɜːðə(r)], *superl* **farthest** [ˈfɑːðɪst] *or* **furthest** [ˈfɜːðɪst])

ADV **1** *(distant in space)* loin; **is it f.?** est-ce (que c'est) loin?; **how f. is it to town?** combien y a-t-il jusqu'à la ville?; **how f. is he going?** jusqu'où va-t-il?; **have you come f.?** êtes-vous venu de loin?; **the police are looking for them, they won't get very f.** la police est à leur recherche, ils n'iront pas très loin; **he went as f. north as Alaska** il est allé au nord jusqu'en Alaska; **f. away** *or* **off in the distance** au loin, dans le lointain; **he doesn't live f. away** *or* **off** il n'habite pas loin; **it isn't f. from the station** ce n'est pas loin de la gare; **f. above/below** loin au-dessus/au-dessous; **f. out at sea** en pleine mer; *Fig* **his thoughts are f. away** son esprit est ailleurs; **how f. can you trust him?** jusqu'à quel point peut-on lui faire confiance?; **how f. (on) are you in the book?** où en es-tu dans le livre?; **how f. have you got with the translation?** où en es-tu de la traduction?; **f. and wide** de tous côtés; **they came from f. and wide** ils sont venus de partout; **he travels f. and wide** il court le monde; **they searched f. and wide for a suitable site** ils ont cherché partout un emplacement convenable; **f. be it from me to interfere!** loin de moi l'idée d'intervenir!; **to be** *Br* **f. out** *or Am* **f. off** *(person)* se tromper complètement; *(report, survey)* être complètement erroné; *(guess)* être loin du compte; **he's not f. off** *or* **wrong** il n'a pas tout à fait tort; **she's not f. off being finished** elle n'est pas loin d'avoir fini; **to carry** *or* **to take sth too f.** pousser qch trop loin; **have you got f. to go?** avez-vous encore beaucoup de chemin à faire?; *Fig* êtes-vous loin du but?; **you won't get f. with that attitude** vous n'irez pas loin avec ce genre de comportement; **sincerity won't get you very f.** la sincérité ne vous mènera pas loin

2 *(distant in time)* loin; **as f. back as 1800** déjà en 1800, dès 1800; **as f. back as I can remember** aussi loin que je m'en souvienne; **she worked f. into the night** elle a travaillé très avant *ou* jusque tard dans la nuit; **the holidays aren't f. off** les vacances ne sont plus loin *ou* approchent; **he's not f. off sixty** il n'a pas loin de la soixantaine

3 *(with comparatives) (much)* beaucoup, bien; **this is f. better** c'est beaucoup *ou* bien mieux; **a f. greater problem** un problème bien *ou* autrement *ou* beaucoup plus grave; **she is f. more intelligent than I am** elle est bien *ou* beaucoup plus intelligente que moi

4 *(idioms)* **to go f.** *(person, idea)* aller loin, faire son chemin; **this has gone f. enough** trop, c'est trop; **his policy doesn't go f. enough** sa politique ne va pas assez loin; **I would even go so f. as to say…** j'irais même jusqu'à dire…, je dirais même…; **I wouldn't go so f. as to say he's lying** je n'irais pas jusqu'à dire qu'il ment; **things went so f. that…** les choses sont allées si loin que…; **to go too f.** *(exaggerate)* dépasser les bornes, exagérer; **that's going too f.** cela passe la mesure; **she's gone too f. to back out** elle s'est trop engagée pour reculer; **£5 doesn't go f. nowadays** on ne va pas loin avec 5 livres de nos jours

ADJ **1** *(distant)* lointain, éloigné; *(remote)* éloigné; **in the f. distance** tout au loin; **it's a f. cry from what she expected** ce n'est pas du tout *ou* c'est loin de ce qu'elle attendait

2 *(more distant)* autre, plus éloigné; **on the f. side** de l'autre côté; **the f. end of** l'autre bout de, l'extrémité de; **at the f. end of the room** au fond de la salle

3 *(extreme)* extrême; **the f. north** l'extrême nord *m*; *Pol* **the f. left/right** l'extrême gauche *f*/droite *f*

• **as far as** PREP jusqu'à; **I'll walk with you as f. as the end of the lane** je vais vous accompagner jusqu'au bout du chemin CONJ **1** *(distance)* **as f. as the eye can see** à perte de vue; **that's fine as f. as it goes** c'est très bien, jusqu'à un certain point

2 *(to the extent that)* autant que; **as f. as possible** autant que possible, dans la mesure du possible; **as f. as I can** dans la mesure de mon possible; **as f. as I can judge** (pour) autant que je puisse (en) juger; **as f. as I know** (pour) autant que je sache; **as f. as she's/I'm concerned** en ce qui la/me concerne, pour sa/ma part; **as f. as money goes** *or* **is concerned** pour ce qui est de l'argent

• **by far** ADV de loin, de beaucoup; **she's by f. the cleverest** *or* **the cleverest by f.** c'est de loin *ou* de beaucoup la plus intelligente

• **far and away** ADV de loin

• **far from** ADV *(not at all)* loin de; **f. from clean** loin d'être propre; **the report was f. from complimentary** le rapport était loin d'être flatteur; **he's not rich, f. from it** il n'est pas riche, loin de là *ou* tant s'en faut PREP *(rather than)* loin de; **f. from being generous, he is rather stingy** loin d'être généreux, il est plutôt radin; **f. from improving, the situation got worse** loin de s'améliorer, les choses ont empiré

• **in so far as** CONJ dans la mesure où

• **so far** ADV jusqu'ici, jusqu'à présent; **so f. this month** depuis le début du mois; **so f. so good** jusqu'ici ça va; **have you seen him? – not so f.** l'avez-vous vu? – pas encore; **the story so f.** résumé *m* des chapitres précédents

• **so far as** = **as far as** CONJ

▸▸ *the Far East* l'Extrême-Orient *m*; *the Far North* le Grand Nord; *the Far South* l'Antarctique *m*

farad ['færəd] N *Elec* farad *m*

faraway ['fɑːrəweɪ] ADJ *(distant)* lointain, éloigné; *(isolated)* éloigné; *(sound, voice)* lointain; *(look)* absent; **her eyes had a f. look** son regard était perdu dans le vague

farce [fɑːs] N **1** *Theat & Fig* farce *f*; **this law is a f.** cette loi est grotesque; **the trial degenerated into (a) f.** le procès a tourné à la farce **2** *Culin* farce *f*

farcical ['fɑːsɪkəl] ADJ risible, ridicule; **the election was completely f.** les élections furent une véritable farce

farcically ['fɑːsɪkəlɪ] ADV d'une manière ridicule *ou* grotesque

fare [feə(r)] N **1** *(charge ▸ for bus, underground)* prix *m* du billet *ou* ticket; *(▸ for boat, plane, train)* prix *m* du billet; *(▸ in taxi)* prix *m* de la course; **what is the f.?** *(gen)* combien coûte le billet?; *(in taxi)* combien je vous dois?; **fares are going up** les tarifs des transports augmentent; **have you got the f.?** avez-vous de quoi payer le billet?; **fares, please!** *(in bus, train)* tickets, s'il vous plaît! **2** *(taxi passenger)* client(e) *m,f* **3** *(food)* nourriture *f*; **good f.** bonne chère *f*; **traditional f.** cuisine *f* traditionnelle; **hospital/prison f.** régime *m* d'hôpital/de prison

VI **how did you f. at the booking office?** comment ça s'est passé au bureau de réservation?; **she fared badly** elle ne s'en est pas bien tirée, elle ne s'est pas bien débrouillée; **she fared well** elle s'en est bien tirée, elle s'est bien débrouillée; **the company has fared better in recent months** la société s'en tire mieux depuis quelques mois; **he fared better in last year's tournament** il s'en est mieux tiré *ou* il s'est mieux débrouillé lors du tournoi de l'année dernière; **his films have fared better in Europe than in America** ses films ont eu plus de succès en Europe qu'en Amérique

▸▸ *Fam Am* ***fare beater,*** *Br* ***fare dodger*** resquilleur(euse) *m,f*; ***fare stage*** *(of bus)* section *f*

farewell [ˌfeə'wel] N adieu *m*; **to bid sb f.** dire adieu à qn; **to say** *or* **to make one's farewells** faire ses adieux; **you can say f. to your chances of winning!** tu peux dire adieu à tes chances de victoire!, tu n'as plus aucune chance de gagner!

EXCLAM adieu!

COMP *(dinner, party)* d'adieu

far-fetched [-'fetʃt] ADJ farfelu; **a f. alibi** un alibi tiré par les cheveux; **a f. story** une histoire à dormir debout

far-flung ADJ **1** *(widespread)* étendu, vaste **2** *(far)* lointain; *(villages, places)* éloigné

farinaceous [ˌfærɪ'neɪʃəs] ADJ farinacé

farm [fɑːm] N ferme *f*, exploitation *f* (agricole); **to work on a f.** travailler dans une ferme; *Am Fam Fig* **to buy the f.** *(die)* clamser, claquer; *Am Fam Fig* **I'd bet the f. that...** je te parie tout ce que tu veux que...; **you can bet the f. that taxes will go up under the new government** je te parie tout ce que tu veux que le nouveau gouvernement va augmenter les impôts

COMP *(equipment)* agricole

VT *(land)* cultiver, exploiter; *(animals)* élever

VI être fermier, être cultivateur

▸▸ ***farm animals*** animaux *mpl* de ferme; ***farm belt*** zone *f* agricole; ***farm buildings*** bâtiments *mpl* de la ferme; *(outhouses)* dépendances *fpl*; ***farm labourer*** ouvrier(ère) *m,f* agricole; ***farm machinery*** machines *fpl* agricoles; ***farm produce*** produits *mpl* agricoles *ou* de ferme; ***farm shop*** = magasin qui vend des produits de la ferme; ***farm worker*** ouvrier(ère) *m,f* agricole

▸**farm out** VT SEP **1** *(shop)* mettre en gérance; *(work)* donner *ou* confier à un sous-traitant; **she farms some work out to local people** elle cède du travail à des sous-traitants locaux **2** *(child)* **she farms her children out to an aunt** elle confie (la garde de) ses enfants à une tante

farmable ['fɑːməbəl] ADJ *(land)* cultivable

farmer ['fɑːmə(r)] N *(of land)* fermier(ère) *m,f*, agriculteur(trice) *m,f*; *(of animals)* éleveur(euse) *m,f*; **sheep f.** éleveur(euse) *m,f* de moutons; **poultry f.** aviculteur(trice) *m,f*

▸▸ ***farmers' market*** marché *m* fermier

farmhouse ['fɑːmhaʊs, *pl* -haʊzɪz] N (maison *f* de) ferme *f*; **f. Cheddar** Cheddar *m* fermier

farming ['fɑːmɪŋ] N agriculture *f*; **fish/mink f.** élevage *m* de poisson/vison; **fruit/vegetable f.** culture *f* fruitière/maraîchère

COMP *(methods)* de culture, cultural; *(equipment, machines)* agricole; *(community, region)* rural

farmland ['fɑːmlænd] N *(UNCOUNT)* terre *f* arable, terres *fpl* arables

farmstead ['fɑːmsted] N ferme *f (et ses dépendances)*

farmyard ['fɑːmjɑːd] N cour *f* de ferme

▸▸ ***farmyard animal*** animal *m* de (la) ferme; ***farmyard smells*** odeurs *fpl* de ferme

Faroe = **Faeroe**

far-off ADJ *(place, time)* lointain, éloigné

far-out *Fam* ADJ **1** *(odd)* bizarre[□], farfelu; *(avant-garde)* d'avant-garde[□] **2** *(excellent)* génial, super

EXCLAM super!, génial!

far-reaching [-'riːtʃɪŋ] ADJ d'une grande portée; **to have f. consequences** avoir des conséquences considérables *ou* d'une portée considérable

farrier ['færɪə(r)] N *Br (blacksmith)* maréchal-ferrant *m*

farrow ['færəʊ] N *(piglets)* portée *f* (de cochons)

VT *(piglets)* mettre bas

VI *(sow)* mettre bas

far-seeing ADJ *(person)* prévoyant, perspicace; *(action)* prévoyant; *(decision)* pris avec clairvoyance

far-sighted ADJ **1** *(shrewd ▸ person)* prévoyant, perspicace; *(▸ action)* prévoyant; *(▸ decision)* pris avec clairvoyance **2** *Am (long-sighted)* hypermétrope

far-sightedness [-'saɪtɪdnɪs] N **1** *(of person)* prévoyance *f*, perspicacité *f*; *(of action, decision)* clairvoyance *f* **2** *Am (long-sightedness)* hypermétropie *f*, presbytie *f*

fart [fɑːt] *Fam* N **1** *(gas)* pet *m* **2** *(person)* birbe *m*; **he's a boring old f.** il est rasoir, c'est un raseur

VI péter

▸**fart about, fart around** VI *Fam* **1** *(play the fool)* déconner **2** *(waste time)* glander; **he's been farting about with the car for days** il a passé des journées entières à trifouiller la voiture; **if you hadn't spent so much time farting about with your make-up** si tu n'avais pas autant traîné en te maquillant

farther ['fɑːðə(r)] *(compar of* **far***)* ADV **1** *(more distant)* plus loin; **f. north** plus (loin) au nord; **how much f. is it?** c'est encore à combien?; **f. than the shop** plus loin que le magasin; **f. along the corridor** plus loin dans le couloir; **f. away, f. off** plus éloigné, plus loin; **to move f. and f. away** s'éloigner de plus en plus; **f. back** plus (loin) en arrière; **move f. back** reculez(-vous); **f. back than 1900** avant 1900; **f. down/up** plus bas/haut; **f. on** *or* **forward** plus loin; **f. on in the book** plus loin dans le livre **2** *(in addition)* en plus, de plus

ADJ plus éloigné, plus lointain; **on the f. side of the room** de l'autre côté *ou* au fond de la salle; **the f. end of the tunnel** l'autre bout du tunnel

farthest ['fɑːðɪst] *(superl of* **far***)* ADJ le plus lointain, le plus éloigné; **in the f. depths of Africa** au fin fond de l'Afrique

ADV le plus loin; **it's 3 km at the f.** il y a 3 km au plus *ou* au maximum

farthing ['fɑːðɪŋ] N *Br Hist (coin)* = pièce de monnaie qui valait le quart d'un ancien penny; *Fam Fig* **we haven't a f.** nous n'avons pas le sou

farthingale ['fɑðɪŋgeɪl] N *Hist* vertugadin *m*

FAS [ˌefer'es] ADV *Br Com (abbr* **free alongside ship***)* FLB, FLQ

fascia *(pl* **fasciae** [-ʃiː]*)* N **1** ['feɪʃə] *Archit* bandelette *f*, bande *f*; *(on shop front)* panneau *m*

2 ['feɪʃə] *Br Aut* tableau *m* de bord

3 ['fæʃɪə] *Anat* fascia *m*

4 ['feɪʃə] *(for mobile phone)* façade *f*

fascicle ['fæsɪkəl] N **1** *(gen) & Anat & Bot* faisceau *m* **2** *(of book)* fascicule *m*

fascinate ['fæsɪneɪt] VT **1** *(delight)* fasciner, captiver; **insects f. him** les insectes le fascinent; **she was fascinated by** *or* **with his story** elle était fascinée par son histoire **2** *(prey)* fasciner

fascinating ['fæsɪneɪtɪŋ] ADJ fascinant

fascination [ˌfæsɪ'neɪʃən] N fascination *f*, attra[it] *m*; **I don't understand the f. of tennis** je ne com[prends] pas l'attrait que peut avoir le tennis; **h[e] has always had a f. for dinosaurs** les dinosaure[s] ont toujours exercé une fascination sur lui, il [a] toujours été fasciné par les dinosaures; **sh[e] watched/listened in f.** elle regardait/écoutai[t] fascinée; **it holds a f. for him** ça le fascine

fascism ['fæʃɪzəm] N fascisme *m*

fascist ['fæʃɪst] N fasciste *mf*

ADJ fasciste

fashion ['fæʃən] N **1** *(current style)* mode *f*; **in f.** à la mode, en vogue; **to come back into f.** revenir [à] la mode; **big weddings are no longer in f.** ça ne s[e] fait plus, les grands mariages; **she dresses in th[e] latest f.** elle s'habille à la dernière mode; **th[e] Paris fashions** les collections *fpl* (de mode) par[i]siennes; **to set the f.** donner le ton, lancer l[a] mode; **it's the f. to take a year out before unive[r]sity** il est bien vu *ou* de bon ton de prendre un[e] année avant d'entrer à l'université; **out of f.** dé[]modé, passé de mode; **to go out of f.** se démo[]der; *Fam* **I've been spending money/eatin[g] chocolate as if it were going out of f.** je dépens[e] des sommes d'argent/mange des quantités d[e] chocolat incroyables **2** *(manner)* façon *f*, ma[]nière *f*; **in an orderly f.** d'une façon méthodique[,] méthodiquement; **we rubbed noses, Eskimo f[.]** nous nous sommes frotté le nez à la manièr[e] des esquimaux; **after the f. of Shakespeare** à l[a] manière de Shakespeare; **after the French f.** à l[a] française; **after a f.** tant bien que mal; **he ca[n] paint after a f.** il peint à sa manière

COMP *(editor, magazine)* de mode; *(industry)* d[e] la mode

VT *(gen)* fabriquer, modeler; *(carving, sculpture)* façonner; *(dress)* confectionner; *Fig (characte[r], person)* former, façonner; **to f. sth out of clay** fa[]çonner qch en argile; **to f. a log into a canoe** fa[]çonner un tronc d'arbre en canot

▸▸ ***fashion designer*** modéliste *mf*; **the great f. de[]signers** les grands couturiers; ***fashion house*** mai[]son *f* de (haute) couture; ***fashion mode[l]*** mannequin *m*; ***fashion photography*** photo *f* d[e] mode; ***fashion plate*** gravure *f* de mode; *Fig* élé[]gant(e) *m,f*; ***fashion show*** présentation *f* des mo[]dèles *ou* des collections, défilé *m* de mode; *Hu[m]* ***fashion victim*** esclave *mf* de la mode

fashionable ['fæʃənəbəl] ADJ *(clothing)* à l[a] mode; *(café, neighbourhood)* chic, à la mode[;] *(subject, writer)* à la mode, en vogue; **grey is f. thi[s] year** le gris se porte beaucoup cette année; [a] **café f. with writers** un café fréquenté par de[s] écrivains; **it is f. to say that...** il est de bon to[n] *ou* bien vu de dire que...; **it is no longer f. t[o] eat red meat** cela ne se fait plus de mange[r] de la viande rouge; **f. society** les gens *mpl* à l[a] mode

fashionably ['fæʃənəblɪ] ADV élégamment, à l[a] mode; **her hair is f. short** elle a les cheveux cou[]pés court selon la mode

fashionista [fæʃə'niːstə] N modeux(euse) *m,f*

FAST [fɑːst]

ADJ	
• rapide **1**	• en avance **2**
• solide **3**	• bon teint **4**
• libertin **5**	
ADV	
• vite **1**	• en avance **2**
• solidement **3**	• profondément **4**
N	
• jeûne	
VI	
• jeûner	

ADJ **1** *(quick)* rapide; **a f. film** une pellicule rapide[;] **she's a f. runner** elle court vite; **a f. time** *(in rac[e] etc)* un bon temps, un bon chrono; **at a f. pac[e]** d'un pas vif *ou* rapide; *Cin & TV* **in f. motion** e[n] accéléré; **he's a f. worker** il va vite en besogne[;] *Fig* il ne perd pas de temps; **he's on the f. trac[k] (to the top)** il gravit les échelons rapidement[;] **they see independence as the f. track to democrac[y]** ils considèrent que l'indépendance les mèner[a] rapidement à la démocratie; *Fam* **to pull a f. one on sb** jouer un mauvais tour à qn

2 *(clock)* en avance; **my watch is** *or Fam* **I'm (three minutes) f.** ma montre avance (de trois minutes)

3 *(secure ▸ knot, rope)* solide; *(▸ door, window, lid)* bien fermé; *(▸ grip)* ferme, solide; *(▸ friend)* sûr, fidèle; **to make a boat f.** amarrer un bateau

4 *(colour)* bon teint *(inv)*, grand teint *(inv)*; **the colour is not f.** la couleur déteint *ou* s'en va

5 *(wild)* libertin; **f. living** vie *f* dissolue *ou* de dissipation

ADV 1 *(quickly)* vite, rapidement; **how f. is the car going?** à quelle vitesse roule la voiture?; **he needs help f.** il lui faut de l'aide de toute urgence; **she ran off as f. as her legs would carry her** elle s'est sauvée à toutes jambes, elle a pris ses jambes à son cou; **the insults came f. and furious** les insultes volaient *ou* pleuvaient dru; **as f. as I ate he gave me more** il me resservait à mesure que je mangeais; **not so f.!** doucement!, pas si vite!

2 *(ahead of correct time)* en avance; **my watch is running f.** ma montre avance

3 *(securely)* ferme, solidement; **shut f.** bien fermé; **to hold f. (on) to sth** tenir fermement qch; *Fig* **to play f. and loose (with sb)** jouer double jeu (avec qn); **to play f. and loose with sb's emotions** se jouer des émotions de qn; **to play f. and loose with the statistics** truquer *ou* falsifier les statistiques

4 *(soundly)* profondément; **to be f. asleep** dormir à poings fermés *ou* profondément

N jeûne *m*; **to break one's f.** rompre le jeûne; *Rel* **a f. day** un jour maigre *ou* de jeûne

VI *(gen)* jeûner, rester à jeun; *Rel* jeûner, faire maigre

▸▸ ***fast bowler*** *(in cricket)* lanceur *m* rapide; ***fast break*** *(in basketball)* contre-attaque *f*; *Nucl* ***fast breeder reactor*** surrégénérateur *m*, surgénérateur *m*; ***fast food*** fast-food *m*, prêt-à-manger *m*; ***fast lane*** *(in UK)* voie *f* de droite; *(in Europe, US etc)* voie *f* de gauche; *Fig* **to live life in the f. lane** vivre à cent à l'heure; *Mktg* ***fast mover*** *(product)* article *m* à forte rotation; *Med* ***fast pulse*** pouls *m* fréquent; *Fam* ***fast talk*** baratin *m*; *Br* ***fast train*** rapide *m*

---

fastback [ˈfɑːstbæk] **N** voiture *f* à l'arrière profilé

fasten [ˈfɑːsən] **VT 1** *(attach)* attacher; *(close)* fermer; **to f. sth with glue/nails/string to sth** coller/clouer/lier qch à qch; **f. your seatbelt** attachez votre ceinture; **he fastened the two ends together** il a attaché les deux bouts ensemble *ou* l'un à l'autre; **to f. one's coat** boutonner son manteau

2 *(attention, eyes)* fixer; **he fastened his eyes on the door** il a fixé la porte des yeux *ou* a fixé son regard sur la porte; **to f. one's attention on sth** fixer son attention sur qch **3** *(ascribe ▸ guilt, responsibility)* attribuer; *(▸ crime)* imputer; **to f. sth on sb** attribuer qch à qn; **they fastened the blame on him** ils ont rejeté la faute sur lui

VI *(bra, dress)* s'attacher; *(bag, door, window)* se fermer; **the trousers f. at the side** le pantalon s'attache sur le côté

▸ **fasten down VT SEP** *(flap, shutter)* fermer; *(tent, furniture)* fixer au sol; *(envelope, sticker)* coller

▸ **fasten on VT SEP** *(belt, holster)* fixer

▸ **fasten up VT SEP** fermer, attacher

▸ **fasten upon VT INSEP 1** *(gaze at)* fixer; **her eyes fastened upon the letter** elle fixait la lettre du regard *ou* des yeux **2** *(seize upon)* saisir; **she fastened upon the idea of escaping** elle s'est mis en tête de s'échapper *ou* de s'évader

fastener [ˈfɑːsənə(r)], **fastening** [ˈfɑːsənɪŋ] **N** *(gen)* attache *f*; *(on box, door, window)* fermeture *f*; *(on bag, purse, necklace)* fermoir *m*; *(on clothing)* fermeture *f*; *(button)* bouton *m*; *(hook)* agrafe *f*; *(press stud)* pression *f*, bouton-pression *m*; *(zip)* fermeture *f* Éclair®; **what kind of f. is it?** comment cela se ferme-t-il *ou* s'attache-t-il?

fast-forward VI se dérouler en avance rapide

VT to f. a tape faire avancer *ou* défiler une cassette

N *(button)* touche *f* d'avance rapide

▸▸ ***fast-forward button*** touche *f* d'avance rapide

fast-growing ADJ 1 *(plant)* à pousse rapide **2** *Com (business, industry, market)* en pleine expansion

fastidious [fəˈstɪdɪəs] **ADJ 1** *(meticulous ▸ person)* méticuleux, minutieux; *(▸ work)* minutieux; **he is f. about the way he dresses** il est d'une coquetterie méticuleuse; **she is f. about protocol** elle est pointilleuse *ou* à cheval sur le protocole **2** *(fussy about details)* tatillon, pointilleux; *(fussy about cleanliness)* méticuleux, maniaque

> Note that the French word **fastidieux** is a false friend and is never a translation for the English word **fastidious**. It means **tedious**.

fastidiously [fəˈstɪdɪəslɪ] **ADV 1** *(meticulously)* méticuleusement, minutieusement **2** *(fussily)* **he f. examined the fork** il examina la fourchette avec un soin maniaque

fastidiousness [fəˈstɪdɪəsnɪs] **N 1** *(meticulousness)* minutie *f* **2** *(fussiness about detail)* caractère *m* pointilleux *ou* tatillon; *(fussiness about cleanliness)* méticulosité *f*

fasting [ˈfɑːstɪŋ] **N** jeûne *m*; *Med* diète *f* (absolue)

fast-moving ADJ *(film)* plein d'action; **f. events** des évènements *mpl* rapides

▸▸ *Mktg* ***fast-moving consumer goods*** biens *mpl* de consommation à forte rotation

fastness [ˈfɑːstnɪs] **N 1** *(secureness)* solidité *f* **2** *(of colour, dye)* solidité *f*, résistance *f* **3** *(stronghold)* place *f* forte, repaire *m*

fat [fæt] *(compar* **fatter**, *superl* **fattest**, *pt & pp* **fatted**, *cont* **fatting**) **ADJ 1** *(heavy, overweight ▸ person)* gros (grosse), gras; *(▸ cheeks, limb)* gros (grosse); *(▸ face)* joufflu; **to get** *or* **to grow f.** grossir, engraisser; **she's getting f.** elle prend de l'embonpoint; *Fig* **they had grown f. on their investments** ils s'étaient enrichis *ou* engraissés grâce à leurs investissements

2 *(meat)* gras

3 *(thick, hefty)* gros (grosse); *(book)* gros (grosse), épais; **a f. wallet** un portefeuille bien garni

4 *Fam (cheque, salary)* gros (grosse)[□]; **he made a f. profit** il a fait de gros bénéfices

5 *(productive ▸ year)* gras, prospère; *(▸ land, soil)* fertile, riche; *Am Fam* **to be in f. city** être plein aux as

6 *Fam (idioms)* **get this into your f. head** mets-toi ça dans la tête une fois pour toutes; **I reckon you'll get it back – f. chance!** je pense qu'on te le rendra – tu parles!; **that was a f. lot of good** *or* **use!** on est bien aidé avec ça!; **a f. lot of good it did him!** ça l'a bien avancé!, le voilà bien avancé!; **a f. lot of difference that has made!** ça a bien avancé les choses!; **a f. lot he cares!** il s'en fout pas mal!; **a f. lot you know about it!** comme si tu en savais quelque chose!; **it's not over till the f. lady sings** il ne faut jamais perdre espoir[□]

N 1 *(gen) & Anat* graisse *f*; **rolls of f.** des bourrelets *mpl* de graisse **2** *Culin (on raw meat)* graisse *f*, gras *m*; *(on cooked meat)* gras *m*; *(as cooking medium)* matière *f* grasse; *(as part of controlled diet)* lipide *m*; **we are trying to eat less f.** nous nous efforçons de manger moins de matières grasses *ou* corps gras; **this margarine is low in f.** cette margarine est pauvre en matières grasses *ou* allégée; **beef/mutton f.** graisse *f* de bœuf/de mouton; **pork f.** saindoux *m*; **fry in deep/shallow f.** faites frire/revenir; *Fam Fig* **the f.'s in the fire** ça va chauffer; **to live off the f. of the land** vivre comme un coq en pâte

VT engraisser; *Fig* **to kill the fatted calf** tuer le veau gras

▸▸ *Am Fam* ***fat camp*** = colonie de vacances où les enfants suivent une cure d'amaigrissement; *Fam Fig* ***fat cat*** *(rich, prosperous)* richard *m*; *(in industry)* = personne touchant un salaire extrêmement élevé de façon injustifiée; ***fat content*** (teneur *f* en) matières *fpl* grasses; *Am Fam* ***fat farm*** centre *m* d'amaigrissement[□]; ***fat intake*** ration *f* de corps gras; *Agr* ***fat stock*** bétail *m* d'engraissement; ***fat suit*** fat suit *m*, = costume rembourré destiné à faire paraître celui qui le porte plus gros qu'il n'est réellement; ***fat tax*** = taxe sur les aliments à teneur élevée en graisse, sucre et sel

fatal [ˈfeɪtəl] **ADJ 1** *(deadly ▸ disease, injury, accident)* mortel; *(▸ blow)* fatal, mortel; *(▸ result)* fatal; **this condition can prove f.** cela peut être mortel **2** *(ruinous ▸ action, consequences)* désastreux, catastrophique; *(▸ influence)* néfaste, pernicieux; *(▸ mistake)* fatal, grave; **such a decision would be f. to our plans** une décision de ce type porterait un coup fatal *ou* le coup de grâce à nos projets **3** *Literary (ordained by fate)* fatal, fatidique; **the f. hour** l'heure *f* fatale

▸▸ *Law* ***fatal accident enquiry*** enquête *f* à la suite d'un accident mortel; *Comput* ***fatal error*** erreur *f* fatale

fatalism [ˈfeɪtəlɪzəm] **N** fatalisme *m*

fatalist [ˈfeɪtəlɪst] **N** fataliste *mf*

ADJ fataliste

fatalistic [ˌfeɪtəˈlɪstɪk] **ADJ** fataliste

fatality [fəˈtælətɪ] *(pl* **fatalities**) **N 1** *(accident)* accident *m* mortel; *(person killed)* mort(e) *m,f*; **road fatalities** morts *fpl* sur la route; **a child was one of the fatalities** il y avait un enfant parmi les victimes **2** *Literary (destiny)* fatalité *f*

▸▸ ***fatality rate*** taux *m* de mortalité

> Note that the most common meaning of the French word **fatalité** is **fate**.

fatally [ˈfeɪtəlɪ] **ADV 1** *(mortally)* mortellement; **f. ill** condamné, perdu **2** *(inevitably)* fatalement; **the plan was f. flawed** le projet était fatalement *ou* forcément imparfait

> Note that the French word **fatalement** never means **mortally**.

fate [feɪt] **N 1** *(power)* destin *m*, sort *m*; **what does f. have in store for them?** qu'est-ce que le destin *ou* le sort leur réserve?; **stroke of f.** coup *m* du destin *ou* du sort **2** *(destiny of person, thing)* sort *m*; **I left her to her f.** je l'ai abandonnée à son sort; **to meet one's f.** trouver la mort; **the new project met with a similar f.** le nouveau projet a connu un destin semblable; *Fig* **a f. worse than death** un sort pire que la mort

• **Fates NPL the Fates** les Parques *fpl*

fated [ˈfeɪtɪd] **ADJ 1** *(destined)* destiné; **they seem f. to be unhappy** ils semblent destinés *ou* condamnés à être malheureux; **he was f. never to return** il devait ne plus jamais revenir **2** *(doomed)* voué au malheur

fateful [ˈfeɪtfʊl] **ADJ 1** *(decisive ▸ day, decision)* fatal, décisif; *(disastrous)* désastreux, catastrophique **2** *(prophetic)* fatidique

fathead [ˈfæthed] **N** *Fam* andouille *f*, courge *f*

fat-headed ADJ *Fam* idiot[□], imbécile[□]

father [ˈfɑːðə(r)] **N 1** *(parent)* père *m*; **he's a good f.** c'est un bon père; **he's a f. of three** il est père de trois enfants; **he's like a f. to me** il est comme un père pour moi; **from f. to son** de père en fils; **on my f.'s side** du côté de mon père; **yes, f.** oui, père, oui, papa; **she's her f.'s daughter** c'est bien la fille de son père; *Prov* **like f., like son** tel père, tel fils

2 *(usu pl) (ancestor)* ancêtre *m*, père *m*

3 *(founder)* père *m*, fondateur *m*; **the f. of cubism/modernism** le père du cubisme/du modernisme

4 *(leader)* dirigeant *m*

VT 1 *(child)* engendrer; *Fig (idea, science)* concevoir, inventer **2** *(impose)* attribuer; **to f. sth on sb** attribuer qch à qn

• **Father N 1** *Rel (priest)* père *m*; **F. Brown** le (révérend) père Brown; **yes, F.** oui, mon père **2** *Rel (God)* Père *m*; **God the F.** Dieu le Père; **the F., the Son and the Holy Ghost** le Père, le Fils et le Saint Esprit; **to say the Our F.** dire le Notre Père **3** *Pol* **the F. of the House** = titre traditionnel donné au doyen (par l'ancienneté) des parlementaires britanniques

▸▸ *Br* ***Father Christmas*** le Père Noël; ***father confessor*** directeur *m* de conscience, père *m* spirituel; ***Father's Day*** fête *f* des pères; ***father figure*** = personne qui joue le rôle du père; **he was a f. figure for all the employees** le personnel le considérait un peu comme un père; *Psy* ***father fixation*** fixation *f* au père; ***(Old) Father Time*** le Temps

fatherhood [ˈfɑːðəhʊd] **N** paternité *f*

father-in-law N beau-père *m*

fatherland [ˈfɑːðəlænd] **N** patrie *f*, mère *f* patrie

fatherless [ˈfɑːðəlɪs] **ADJ** sans père

fatherly [ˈfɑːðəlɪ] **ADJ** paternel

fathom [ˈfæðəm] *(pl* **inv** *or* **fathoms**) **N** *Naut* brasse *f (mesure)*; **the ship lies 50 fathoms down** le navire repose par 91 mètres de fond

VT 1 *(measure depth of)* sonder **2** *(understand)* sonder, pénétrer; **I just can't f. it** je n'y comprends rien; **I can't f. him (out)** je ne le comprends pas

fatigue [fəˈtiːg] **N 1** *(exhaustion)* fatigue *f*, épuisement *m*; **to be suffering from f.** être épuisé **2** *Tech (in material)* fatigue *f*; **metal f.** fatigue *f* du métal **3** *Mil (chore)* corvée *f*; **I'm on fatigue(s)** je suis de corvée

COMP *Mil (shirt, trousers)* de corvée

VT 1 *Formal (person)* fatiguer, épuiser; **he felt fatigued after a long day in the office** il se sentait las après une longue journée de bureau **2** *Tech (material)* fatiguer

• **fatigues NPL** *Mil (clothing)* treillis *m*, tenue *f* de corvée

►► *Mil* ***fatigue dress*** treillis *m ou* tenue *f* de corvée; *Mil* ***fatigue duty*** corvée *f*; *Mil* ***fatigue party*** corvée *f*; *Tech* ***fatigue test*** essai *m* de fatigue; *Mil* ***fatigue uniform*** treillis *m ou* tenue *f* de corvée

fatiguing [fəˈtiːgɪŋ] **ADJ** fatigant, épuisant

fatness [ˈfætnɪs] **N 1** *(of person)* embonpoint *m*, corpulence *f* **2** *(of meat)* teneur *f* en graisse

fatso [ˈfætsəʊ] *(pl* **fatsos** *or* **fatsoes)** **N** *Fam Pej* gros lard *m*

fatten [ˈfætən] **VT** *(animal, person)* engraisser; *(ducks, geese)* gaver

VI *(animals)* engraisser; *(person)* engraisser, prendre de l'embonpoint

► **fatten up VT SEP** *(person)* engraisser, faire grossir; *Agr (animal)* mettre à l'engrais; **we'll have to fatten you up a bit** il va falloir qu'on t'engraisse un peu

fattening [ˈfætənɪŋ] **ADJ** qui fait grossir

N *(of animals)* engraissement *m*; *(of ducks, geese)* gavage *m*

fatty [ˈfætɪ] *(pl* **fatties**, *compar* **fattier**, *superl* **fattiest)** **N** *Fam Pej (man)* gros *m* (bonhomme *m*); *(woman)* grosse *f* (bonne femme *f*); **hey, f.!** ohé, mon gros!/ma grosse!

ADJ 1 *(food)* gras; **avoid f. food** évitez les matières grasses *ou* les aliments gras **2** *(tissue)* adipeux

►► *Chem* ***fatty acid*** acide *m* gras; *Med* ***fatty degeneration*** dégénérescence *f* graisseuse

fatuity [fəˈtjuːətɪ] *(pl* **fatuities)** **N** sottise *f*, niaiserie *f*

fatuous [ˈfætjʊəs] **ADJ** *(person, remark)* sot (sotte), niais; *(look, smile)* niais, béat

fatuously [ˈfætjʊəslɪ] **ADV** *(say)* sottement, niaisement; *(smile)* niaisement, béatement

fatuousness [ˈfætjʊəsnɪs] **N** sottise *f*, niaiserie *f*

faucet [ˈfɔːsɪt] **N** *Am* robinet *m*

fault [fɔːlt] **N 1** *(UNCOUNT) (blame, responsibility)* faute *f*; **it's my f.** c'est (de) ma faute; **it's not my f.** ce n'est pas (de) ma faute; **whose f. is it?** à qui la faute?, qui est fautif?; **whose f. is it if you're unhappy?** et à qui la faute si vous êtes malheureux?; **it's nobody's f. but your own** vous n'avez à vous en prendre qu'à vous-même; **it's through no f. of mine** ce n'est absolument pas (de) ma faute; **to be at f.** être fautif *ou* coupable; **she's at f. for not having taken action** elle est coupable de ne pas avoir agi *ou* de ne pas être intervenue; **his memory was at f.** sa mémoire lui a fait défaut; **the judge found him to be at f.** le juge lui a donné tort

2 *(mistake)* erreur *f*; **a f. in the addition** une erreur d'addition

3 *(flaw ► in person)* défaut *m*; *(► in machine)* défaut *m*, anomalie *f*; **an electrical f.** un défaut électrique; **a mechanical f.** une défaillance mécanique; **for all her faults, in spite of her faults** malgré tous ses défauts; **honest/scrupulous to a f.** honnête/scrupuleux à l'excès; **to find f. with sth** trouver à redire à qch, critiquer qch; **to find f. with sb** critiquer qn

4 *Geol* faille *f*

5 *Sport (in tennis, badminton, squash, show jumping)* faute *f*

VT critiquer; **to f. sb/sth** trouver des défauts chez qn/à qch; **you can't f. her on her work** il n'y a rien à redire à son travail, vous ne pouvez pas prendre son travail en défaut; **I can't f. her logic** je ne trouve aucune faille à sa logique

►► *Geol* ***fault line*** ligne *f* de faille; *Geol* ***fault plane*** plan *m* de faille; *Com* ***fault tree*** arbre *m* de défaillances

> Note that the most common meaning of the French word **faute** is **error**.

faultfinder [ˈfɔːltˌfaɪndə(r)] **N 1** *Pej (person)* mécontent(e) *m,f*, chicaneur(euse) *m,f* **2** *(device)* détecteur *m* de défauts

faultfinding [ˈfɔːltˌfaɪndɪŋ] **N** *(UNCOUNT)* **1** *Pej (criticism)* critiques *fpl* **2** *(in machinery, equipment)* localisation *f* des défauts

ADJ *Pej (critical)* chicanier, grincheux

faultiness [ˈfɔːltɪnɪs] **N** *(of machine, logic, reasoning)* défectuosité *f*; *(of work, performance)* imperfection *f*; *(of grammar)* incorrection *f*

faultless [ˈfɔːltlɪs] **ADJ** *(performance, work)* impeccable, irréprochable; *(behaviour, person)* irréprochable; *(logic, reasoning)* sans faille

faultlessly [ˈfɔːltlɪslɪ] **ADV** impeccablement, parfaitement

fault-tolerant ADJ *Comput* quasi insensible aux défaillances, tolérant les pannes

faulty [ˈfɔːltɪ] *(compar* **faultier**, *superl* **faultiest)** **ADJ** *(machine)* défectueux; *(work)* défectueux, mal fait; *(logic, reasoning)* défectueux, erroné; *(grammar)* incorrect; **the wiring is f.** il y a un défaut dans l'installation électrique

faun [fɔːn] **N** *Myth* faune *m*

fauna [ˈfɔːnə] *(pl* **faunas** *or* **faunae** [-niː]) **N** *Zool* faune *f*

faux pas [ˌfəʊˈpɑː] *(pl* **inv** [-ˈpɑːz]) **N** bévue *f*, impair *m*

FAVOUR, *Am* **favor** [ˈfeɪvə(r)]

N	
• faveur **1, 3–6**	• service **2**
VT	
• préférer **1**	• être partisan de **2**
• favoriser **3, 4**	• ressembler à **5**

N 1 *(approval)* faveur *f*, approbation *f*; **to be in f.** *(person)* être bien en cour, être bien vu; *(artist, fashion)* être à la mode *ou* en vogue; **to be out of f.** *(person)* être mal en cour, ne pas être bien vu; *(artist, book)* ne pas être à la mode *ou* en vogue; *(fashion)* être démodé *ou* dépassé; **she's in f. with the boss** elle est bien vue du patron; **he speaks in their f.** il parle en leur faveur; **to fall out of f. with sb** perdre les bonnes grâces de qn; **this method has rather fallen out of f. in recent years** cette méthode a été plus ou moins abandonnée au cours de ces dernières années; **to find f. with sb** trouver grâce aux yeux de qn, gagner l'approbation de qn; **he is prepared to look with f. upon the suggestion** il est prêt à approuver *ou* à examiner favorablement la proposition; **to be in f. of sth** être partisan de qch, être pour qch; **to be in f. of doing sth** être d'avis de *ou* être pour faire qch

2 *(act of goodwill)* service *m*; **will you do me a f.** *or* **do a f. for me?** voulez-vous me rendre (un) service?; **may I ask a f. of you** *or* **ask you a f.?** puis-je vous demander un service?; **I did it as a f. to her** je l'ai fait pour lui rendre service; **do me a f. and play somewhere else** soyez gentil, allez jouer ailleurs; **she's not doing herself any favours by being so arrogant** son arrogance la dessert; *Br Fam* **are you going to buy it? – do me a f.!** tu vas l'acheter? – tu rigoles?

3 *(advantage)* **everything is in our f.** tout joue en notre faveur, nous avons tout pour nous; **a point in her f.** un bon point pour elle, un point en sa faveur; **the magistrates ruled in his f.** les juges lui ont donné raison *ou* gain de cause; **all those in f. raise your hand** que tous ceux qui sont pour lèvent la main; **he dropped the idea in f. of our suggestion** il a laissé tomber l'idée au profit de notre suggestion; **a will in f. of the children** un testament en faveur des enfants; **credit in your f.** à votre crédit

4 *(partiality)* faveur *f*, partialité *f*

5 *Hist (badge, ribbon)* faveur *f*

6 *Literary* **a woman's favours** les faveurs *fpl* d'une femme; **she was rather too free with her favours** elle était un peu trop prodigue de ses faveurs

VT 1 *(prefer)* préférer; *(show preference for)* montrer une préférence pour

2 *(support ► suggestion, team)* être partisan de, être pour; *(► candidate, project)* favoriser, appuyer; *(► theory)* soutenir; **I f. allowing more time for the planning stage** je suis partisan d'accorder plus de temps au stade préparatoire

3 *(benefit)* favoriser, faciliter; **the ground is quite firm, which favours this horse** le terrain est très ferme, ce qui est favorable à ce cheval *ou* ce qui avantage ce cheval; **circumstances that would f. a June election** des circonstances (qui seraient) favorables à une élection en juin

4 *(honour)* favoriser, gratifier; **she favoured him with a smile** elle l'a gratifié d'un sourire; **he favoured us with his company** il nous a fait l'honneur de se joindre à nous; **favoured with good looks** avantagé par la nature

5 *(resemble)* ressembler à; **he favours his mother** il ressemble à *ou* tient de sa mère

favourable, *Am* **favorable** [ˈfeɪvrəbəl] **ADJ** *(answer, comparison, impression)* favorable; *(time, terms)* bon, avantageux; *(reception)* bienveillant; *(weather, wind)* propice; **in a f. light** sous un jour favorable; **to be f. to an idea** approuver une idée; **the election will be held at the time most f. to the government** les élections auront lieu au moment (qui sera) le plus favorable au gouvernement

favourably, *Am* **favorably** [ˈfeɪvrəblɪ] **ADV** *(compare, react)* favorablement; *(consider)* d'un bon œil; **to be f. disposed to** *or* **towards sth** voir qch d'un bon œil; **to be f. disposed to** *or* **towards sb** être bien disposé envers qn; **she speaks very f. of you** elle parle de vous en très bons termes; **I hope everything goes f. for you** j'espère que tout ira bien pour toi; **to compare f. with sth** n'avoir rien à envier à qch; **I was f. impressed** j'ai été favorablement impressionné

favoured, *Am* **favored** [ˈfeɪvəd] **ADJ** favorisé; **he is one of our most f. clients** c'est un de nos clients privilégiés; **the f. few** les privilégiés *mpl*

favourite, *Am* **favorite** [ˈfeɪvrɪt] **ADJ** favori, préféré; **he's not one of my f. people** je ne le porte pas dans mon cœur

N 1 *(gen)* favori(ite) *m,f*, préféré(e) *m,f*; **chocolate cake is a firm f. with children** c'est vraiment le gâteau au chocolat que les enfants préfèrent; **he's the teacher's f.** c'est le chouchou du professeur; **he's a great f. with the old ladies** les vieilles dames l'affectionnent particulièrement; **roast duck? (that's) my f.!** du canard rôti? c'est mon plat préféré!; **that book is one of my favourites** c'est un de mes livres préférés; **let's listen to some old favourites** écoutons de vieilles chansons à succès; *Am* **to play favourites** faire du favoritisme **2** *Sport* favori *m*; **to back the f.** jouer le favori

• **favorites NPL** *Comput (Web sites)* favoris *mpl*

►► *Am Pol* ***favorite son*** = candidat favorisé par les électeurs du même état que lui; ***favourite son*** *(family member)* enfant *m* chéri

favouritism, *Am* **favoritism** [ˈfeɪvrɪtɪzəm] **N** favoritisme *m*

fawn [fɔːn] **N 1** *(animal)* faon *m* **2** *(colour)* fauve *m*

ADJ (de couleur) fauve

VI 1 to f. on sb *(person)* ramper devant qn, passer de la pommade à qn; *(dog)* faire fête à qn **2** *(deer)* mettre bas

fawning [ˈfɔːnɪŋ] **N** *(adulation, flattery)* adulation *f*

ADJ *(attitude, person)* servile, obséquieux; *(dog)* trop affectueux

fax [fæks] **N** *(machine)* fax *m*, *Offic* télécopieur *m*; *(document, message)* fax *m*, *Offic* télécopie *f*; **to send sb a f.** envoyer un fax *ou Offic* une télécopie à qn; **to send sth by f.** envoyer qch par fax *ou Offic* télécopie

VT *(document)* faxer, *Offic* télécopier, envoyer par fax *ou Offic* télécopie; *(person)* envoyer un fax *ou Offic* une télécopie à

►► *Comput* ***fax card*** carte *f* fax; ***fax cover sheet*** feuille *f* de garde *(pour fax)*; ***fax machine*** fax *m*, *Offic* télécopieur *m*; ***fax message*** fax *m*, *Offic* télécopie *f*; *Comput* ***fax modem*** modem-fax *m*; ***fax number*** numéro *m* de fax *ou Offic* de télécopie

► **fax back VT SEP** *(return by fax)* renvoyer par fax *ou Offic* par télécopie **(to** à); **I'll f. you back** je vous réponds par fax

faxable ['fæksəbəl] ADJ *(document)* faxable, *Offic* télécopiable; **are you f.?** est-ce qu'on peut vous joindre par fax?

faze [feɪz] VT *Fam* démonter□

FBI [ˌefbiː'aɪ] N *Am (abbr* **Federal Bureau of Investigation)** **the F.** le FBI

▸▸ ***FBI agent*** agent *m* du FBI

FBU [ˌefbiː'juː] N *Br (abbr* **Fire Brigades Union)** = syndicat britannique de pompiers

FC [ˌef'siː] N *(abbr* **Football Club)** FC *m*

FCL-FCL *Com (written abbr* **full container load-full container load)** FCL-FCL

FCL-LCL *Com (written abbr* **full container load-less than container load)** FCL-LCL

FD[1] [ˌef'diː] N *Am (abbr* **Fire Department)** brigade *f* des pompiers

FD[2] **1** *Br (written abbr* **Fidei Defensor)** = Défenseur de la foi **2** *Comput (written abbr* **floppy disk)** disquette *f*

FDA [ˌefdiː'eɪ] N *(abbr* **Food and Drug Administration)** = organisme officiel chargé de contrôler la qualité des aliments et de délivrer les autorisations de mise sur le marché pour les produits pharmaceutiques

FDD *Comput (written abbr* **floppy disk drive)** unité *f* de disquette

FDF [ˌefdiː'ef] N *Br (abbr* **Food and Drink Federation)** = fédération britannique de l'agro-alimentaire

FDI [ˌefdiː'aɪ] N *Econ (abbr* **foreign direct investment)** IED *m*

FDNY [ˌefdiːen'waɪ] N *Am (abbr* **Fire Department of New York)** brigade *f* des pompiers de New York

fealty ['fiːəltɪ] *(pl* **fealties)** N *Hist* fidélité *f*, allégeance *f*

fear [fɪə(r)] N **1** *(dread)* crainte *f*, peur *f*; **many people have an irrational f. of snakes** beaucoup de personnes ont une peur irrationnelle des serpents; **have no f.** ne craignez rien, soyez sans crainte; **he expressed his fears about their future** il a exprimé son inquiétude en ce qui concerne leur avenir; **to be** *or* **to go in f. for one's life** craindre pour sa vie; **she lives in a state of constant f.** elle vit dans la peur; **f. drove him to desperate action** sous l'effet de la peur, il a commis un acte désespéré; **for f. of what people would think** par peur du qu'en-dira-t-on; **for f. that she might find out** de peur qu'elle ne l'apprenne; **without f. or favour** impartialement; **(a) f. of heights** (le) vertige **2** *(awe)* crainte *f*, respect *m*; **the f. of God** la crainte *ou* le respect de Dieu; *Fam* **I put the f. of God into him** *(scared)* je lui ai fait une peur bleue; *(scolded)* je lui ai passé un savon **3** *(risk)* risque *m*, danger *m*; **there is no f. of her leaving** elle ne risque pas de partir, il est peu probable qu'elle parte; **there's no f. of that** ça ne risque pas d'arriver; *Fam* **will you tell him? – no f.!** lui direz-vous? – pas de danger *ou* pas question!

VT **1** *(be afraid of)* craindre, avoir peur de, redouter; **she fears nothing/no one** elle n'a peur de rien/de personne; **he fears failure above all else** l'échec est ce qu'il craint *ou* redoute par-dessus tout; **to f. the worst** craindre le pire; **he is a man to be feared** c'est un homme redoutable; **I f. he's in danger** je crains *ou* j'ai peur qu'il ne soit en danger; *Formal* **it is to be feared that...** il est à craindre que... + *subjunctive* **2** *Formal (be sorry)* regretter; **I f. it's too late** je crois bien qu'il est trop tard **3** *(revere* ▸ *God)* révérer, craindre

VI **I f. for my children** je crains *ou* je tremble pour mes enfants; **I was beginning to f. for her sanity** je commençais à m'inquiéter pour son état mental; **he fears for his life** il craint pour sa vie; **they f. for the future** ils craignent *ou* sont inquiets pour l'avenir; *Formal or Old-fashioned* **never f., f. not** ne craignez rien, soyez tranquille; **we'll be here tomorrow, never f.** nous serons là demain, n'aie pas peur

feared [fɪəd] ADJ redouté

fearful ['fɪəful] ADJ **1** *(very bad)* épouvantable, affreux; **he has a f. temper** il a un caractère épouvantable **2** *Fam Old-fashioned (as intensifier)* affreux□; **he's a f. bore!** c'est un raseur de première!; **they were making a f. din** ils faisaient un bruit épouvantable *ou* un boucan infernal **3** *(afraid)* peureux, craintif; **she is f. of angering him** elle craint de le mettre en colère

fearfully ['fɪəfulɪ] ADV **1** *(look, say)* peureusement, craintivement **2** *Fam Old-fashioned (as intensifier)* affreusement□, horriblement; **he's f. nasty** il est méchant à faire peur

fearfulness ['fɪəfulnɪs] N **1** *(frightening nature)* caractère *m* terrifiant; **the f. of his appearance** son aspect terrifiant **2** *(fear)* crainte *f*; *(concern)* appréhension *f*

fearless ['fɪəlɪs] ADJ intrépide, sans peur; **they set off, f. of the danger** ils se mirent en route sans crainte du danger *ou* bravant le danger

fearlessly ['fɪəlɪslɪ] ADV avec intrépidité

fearlessness ['fɪəlɪsnɪs] N intrépidité *f*, absence *f* de peur

fearsome ['fɪəsəm] ADJ **1** *(frightening)* effroyable, terrifiant **2** *(formidable* ▸ *opponent)* redoutable; *(*▸ *performance, car, motorbike)* impressionnant

feasibility [ˌfiːzə'bɪlətɪ] N faisabilité *f*; **to show the f. of a plan** démontrer qu'un plan est réalisable *ou* faisable; **the f. of doing sth** la possibilité de faire qch

▸▸ ***feasibility report*** rapport *m* de faisabilité; ***feasibility stage*** phase *f* de faisabilité; ***feasibility study*** étude *f* de faisabilité; ***feasibility test*** essai *m* probatoire

feasible ['fiːzəbəl] ADJ *(plan, suggestion)* faisable, réalisable

feast [fiːst] N **1** *(large meal)* festin *m*; **midnight f.** festin *m* nocturne; *Fig* **a f. for the eyes** un régal *ou* une fête pour les yeux; *Fig* **a f. of music/poetry** une véritable fête de la musique/poésie **2** *Rel* fête *f*

VI festoyer; **to f. on** *or* **off sth** se régaler de qch

VT **1** *Fig* **to f. oneself on sth** se régaler de qch; **to f. one's eyes on sth** se délecter à la vue de qch **2** *Old-fashioned (give feast to)* donner un banquet en l'honneur de

▸▸ ***feast day*** (jour *m* de) fête *f*; *Rel* ***Feast of Tabernacles*** fête *f* des Tabernacles; *Rel* ***Feast of Weeks*** Pentecôte *f (juive)*

feasting ['fiːstɪŋ] N festin *m*

feat [fiːt] N exploit *m*, prouesse *f*; **it was quite a f. getting the boss to agree to the idea** ça a été un véritable exploit *ou* une véritable prouesse que de faire accepter cette idée au chef; **f. of arms** fait *m* d'armes; **f. of strength/of skill** tour *m* de force/d'adresse; **a f. of engineering** une (véritable) prouesse technique, un chef-d'œuvre de la technique

feather ['feðə(r)] N *(of bird)* plume *f*; *(on tail, wing, of arrow)* penne *f*; **as light as a f.** léger comme une plume; **in fine f.** en pleine forme; *Fig* **to smooth sb's ruffled feathers** rasséréner qn; *Fig* **to show the white f.** manquer de courage; **that's a f. in his cap** il peut en être fier; **to make the feathers fly** mettre le feu aux poudres; **you could have knocked me down with a f.** les bras m'en sont tombés

COMP *(mattress)* de plume; *(headdress)* de plumes

VT **1** *(put feathers on* ▸ *arrow)* empenner; *Pej* **to f. one's (own) nest** faire son beurre **2** *Aviat (propeller)* mettre en drapeau **3** *(in rowing)* ramener à plat; **f. your oars!** avirons à plat!

VI *(in rowing)* plumer

▸▸ ***feather bed*** lit *m* de plumes; ***feather boa*** boa *m* de plumes; ***feather cut*** *(hairstyle)* coupe *f* en dégradé; ***feather duster*** plumeau *m*

featherbed ['feðəbed] *(pt & pp* **featherbedded**, *cont* **featherbedding)** VT *Pej (industry, business)* protéger (excessivement)

featherbedding ['feðəbedɪŋ] N *Pej (of industry, business)* protection *f* excessive

featherbrain ['feðəbreɪn] N *Fam* tête *f* de linotte

featherbrained ['feðəbreɪnd] ADJ *Fam* étourdi, tête en l'air

feather-edge N *Tech* biseau *m*

feather-edged ADJ *Tech* taillé en biseau, biseauté

feathering ['feðərɪŋ] N **1** *(of birds)* plumage *m* **2** *(of arrow)* empennage *m* **3** *(in rowing)* nage *f* plate **4** *Aviat (of propeller)* mise *f* en drapeau

featherstitch ['feðəstɪtʃ] N *Sewing* point *m* d'épines

featherweight ['feðəweɪt] N **1** *Boxing* poids *m* plume *inv*; **he started at f.** il a commencé (dans les) poids plume **2** *Fig (person of little importance)* poids *m* plume *inv*; **he's a (political/literary) f.** il n'a pas beaucoup de poids (sur le plan politique/littéraire)

ADJ *Boxing (contest, championship)* poids plume *inv*; *(champion)* de la catégorie *ou* des poids plume

feathery ['feðərɪ] ADJ *(light and soft* ▸ *snowflake)* duveteux; **f. strokes** *(with pencil)* traits *mpl* légers

feature ['fiːtʃə(r)] N **1** *(facial)* trait *m*; **a woman with delicate features** une femme aux traits fins **2** *(characteristic* ▸ *of style, landscape, play etc)* caractéristique *f*, particularité *f*; *(*▸ *of personality)* trait *m*, caractéristique *f*; *(*▸ *of car, machine, house, room)* caractéristique *f*; **safety features** dispositifs *mpl* de sécurité; **this is a f. of the novel** c'est un élément caractéristique du roman; **the most interesting f. of the exhibition** l'élément *ou* l'aspect le plus intéressant de l'exposition; **seafood is a special f. of the menu** les fruits de mer sont l'un des points forts du menu; **to make a f. of sth** mettre qch en valeur

3 *Rad & TV* reportage *m*; *Press (special)* article *m* de fond; *(regular)* chronique *f*

4 *Cin* film *m*, long métrage *m*; **full-length f.** long métrage *m*; **double-f. (programme)** programme *m* proposant deux films

VT **1** *Cin (star* ▸ *actor, actress)* avoir pour vedette; **also featuring Mark Williams** avec Mark Williams

2 *Press (display prominently)* **the story/the picture is featured on the front page** le récit/la photo est en première page

3 *Com (promote)* promouvoir, mettre en promotion

4 *(have as special feature* ▸ *of car, appliance)* comporter, être équipé *ou* doté de; *(*▸ *of house, room)* comporter; **all our cars f. twin airbags** toutes nos voitures sont équipées de deux airbags

VI **1** *Cin* figurer, jouer **2** *(appear, figure)* figurer; **meat does not f. on the menu** la viande ne figure pas au menu; **the millionaire featured prominently in the scandal** le millionnaire était très impliqué dans le scandale; **do I f. in your plans?** est-ce que je figure dans tes projets?

▸▸ *Press* ***feature article*** article *m* de fond; *Press* ***features editor*** = journaliste responsable d'une rubrique; *Cin* ***feature film*** long métrage *m*; *Cin* ***feature player*** acteur(trice) *m,f* de composition; *Cin* ***feature presentation*** long métrage *m*; *Press* ***feature story*** article *m* de fond; *Press* ***features writer*** journaliste *mf (qui écrit des articles de fond)*

feature-length ADJ *Cin*

▸▸ ***feature-length cartoon*** film *m* d'animation; ***feature-length film, feature-length movie*** long métrage *m*

featureless ['fiːtʃəlɪs] ADJ *(desert, city etc)* sans traits distinctifs *ou* marquants

featurette [ˌfiːtʃə'ret] N *Cin (on DVD)* bonus *m*

Feb. *(written abbr* **February)** févr

febrile ['fiːbraɪl] ADJ *Med & Literary* fébrile, fiévreux

February ['februərɪ] N février *m*; **this has been the wettest F. on record** cela a été le mois de février le plus pluvieux qu'on ait jamais vu; **in F.** en février, au mois de février; **the first/ninth of F., F. the first/ninth,** *Am* **F. first/ninth** le premier/neuf février; **during (the month of) F.** pendant le mois de février; **last/next F.** en février dernier/prochain; **at the beginning/end of F.** au début/à la fin février; **in the middle of F.** au milieu du mois de février, à la mi-février; **early/late in F., in early/late F.** au début/à la fin du mois de février; **every** *or* **each F.** tous les ans en février

COMP *(evening, weather, weekend)* de février, du mois de février

fecal, feces *Am* = **faecal, faeces**

feckless ['feklɪs] ADJ **1** *(irresponsible)* inconscient, irresponsable **2** *(ineffectual* ▸ *person)* propre à rien, incapable; *(*▸ *attempt)* inepte

fecklessness ['feklɪsnɪs] N **1** *(irresponsibility)* irresponsabilité *f*, inconscience *f* **2** *(ineffectuality)* manque *m* d'efficacité

fecund ['fekənd] ADJ *Literary* **1** *(woman, female animal)* fécond **2** *Fig (author)* fécond; *(imagination)* fécond, fertile

fecundity [fɪ'kʌndətɪ] N **1** *Biol & Literary (of woman, female animal)* fécondité *f* **2** *Fig Literary (of author)* fécondité *f*; *(of imagination)* fécondité *f*, fertilité *f*

Fed[1] [fed] N *Am* **1** *Fin (abbr* **Federal Reserve Board***)* banque *f* centrale (des États-Unis)
2 *Fin (abbr* **Federal Reserve (System)***)* (système *m* de) Réserve *f* fédérale
3 *Fin (abbr* **Federal Reserve Bank***)* banque *f* membre de la Réserve fédérale
4 *Fam (abbr* **Federal Agent***)* agent *m* du FBI
►► ***Fed bias*** = rapport de la banque centrale américaine sur le niveau d'inflation de l'économie nationale, considéré comme un indicateur de sa politique à venir en matière de taux d'intérêt; ***Fed funds*** fonds *mpl* fédéraux

Fed[2] *Am* **1** *(written abbr* **federal***)* fédéral **2** *(written abbr* **federation***)* fédération *f*

fed [fed] *pt & pp of* **feed**

federal ['fedərəl] ADJ **1** *(republic, police, system)* fédéral **2** *(responsibility, funding)* du gouvernement fédéral; *(taxes)* fédéral
N *Am Hist* nordiste *mf*
►► ***the Federal Bureau of Investigation*** le FBI; *Am* ***federal case*** = affaire du ressort d'un tribunal fédéral; *Am Fig* **there's no need to make a f. case out of it** il n'y a pas de quoi en faire une affaire d'État; *Am* ***federal court*** tribunal *m* fédéral; *Am* ***Federal Debt*** dette *f* publique *ou* de l'État; *Am* ***federal district court*** tribunal *m* de grande instance; *Am* ***Federal funds*** fonds *mpl* fédéraux; *Am* ***federal question*** = question qui relève d'un tribunal fédéral; ***the Federal Republic of Germany*** la République fédérale d'Allemagne; *Formerly* ***the Federal Republic of Yugoslavia*** la République fédérale de Yougoslavie; *Am* ***Federal Reserve*** Réserve *f* fédérale; *Am* ***Federal Reserve Bank*** banque *f* membre de la Réserve fédérale; *Am* ***Federal Reserve Board*** banque *f* centrale (des États-Unis); *Am* ***Federal Reserve System*** système *m* de Réserve *f* fédérale

federalism ['fedərəlɪzəm] N *Pol* fédéralisme *m*

federalist ['fedərəlɪst] *Pol* N fédéraliste *mf*
ADJ fédéraliste

federalize, -ise ['fedərəlaɪz] VT **1** *(states)* fédéraliser **2** *(subject to federal control)* soumettre à l'autorité d'un gouvernement fédéral
VI se fédéraliser

federate VT ['fedəreɪt] fédérer
VI ['fedəreɪt] se fédérer
ADJ ['fedərət] fédéré

federation [ˌfedə'reɪʃən] N fédération *f*

fedora [fɪ'dɔːrə] N *(hat)* feutre *m*

fed up ADJ *Fam* **to be f.** en avoir marre, en avoir ras le bol; **she's f. with him** elle en a marre de lui; **she's f. with it** elle en a marre; **to be f. (to the back teeth) with sb/with sth/with doing sth** en avoir (vraiment) marre *ou* ras le bol de qn/de qch/de faire qch; **I'm f. with the way you don't pay any attention to me** j'en ai marre *ou* ras le bol que tu ne fasses pas attention à moi; **you sound f.** tu as l'air d'en avoir marre *ou* ras le bol

fee [fiː] N **1** *(for doctor, lawyer)* honoraires *mpl* **2** *(for speaker, performer)* cachet *m*; *(retainer* ► *for company director)* jetons *mpl* de présence; *(for private tutor)* appointements *mpl*; *(for translator)* tarif *m*; *(for agency)* commission *f*; *(for private school)* frais *mpl* de scolarité; **(transfer) f.** *(of footballer)* indemnité *f* de transfert; **is there a f. for joining?** est-ce que l'inscription est payante?; **for a small f.** pour une somme modique **3** *Law* **property held in f. simple** propriété *f* inconditionnelle

feeb [fiːb] N *Am Fam* crétin(e) *m,f*

Feebie ['fiːbɪ] N *Am Fam* agent *m* du FBI

feeble ['fiːbəl] ADJ **1** *(lacking strength* ► *physically, morally)* faible; **don't be so f.!** ne sois pas une telle mauviette! **2** *(lacking conviction, force* ► *attempt, excuse)* piètre; *(*► *argument)* faible, peu convaincant; *(*► *smile)* timide; *(*► *joke)* qui manque de finesse, bête; *(*► *film, book, play)* faible, médiocre; **that's a pretty f. excuse** c'est une bien piètre excuse, c'est une excuse bien peu convaincante

feeble-minded ADJ faible d'esprit
NPL *Old-fashioned* **the f.** les débiles *mpl* mentaux

feeble-mindedness [-'maɪndɪdnɪs] N faiblesse *f* d'esprit

feebleness ['fiːbəlnɪs] N *(of person)* faiblesse *f*; *(of excuse, argument)* pauvreté *f*, faiblesse *f*; *(of film, book, play)* médiocrité *f*, faiblesse *f*; *(of smile)* timidité *f*; *(of joke)* manque *m* de finesse

feebly ['fiːblɪ] ADV *(say, shine)* faiblement; *(smile)* timidement; *(suggest)* sans (grande) conviction

feed [fiːd] *(pt & pp* **fed** [fed]*)* VT **1** *(provide food for* ► *person, family)* nourrir; *(*► *country)* approvisionner; *(*► *army)* ravitailler; **she insisted on feeding us** elle a tenu à nous faire manger; **there are ten mouths to f.** il y a dix bouches à nourrir; *Hum* **there's enough here to f. an army** il y a de quoi nourrir toute une armée; **the country is no longer able to f. itself** le pays n'est plus capable de subvenir à ses besoins alimentaires; **he earns just enough money to f. himself** il gagne juste de quoi se nourrir
2 *(give food to* ► *person, animal)* donner à manger à; *(*► *of bird)* donner la becquée à; *(*► *livestock)* affourager; *(breast-feed)* allaiter; *(bottle-feed)* donner le biberon à; *(fertilize* ► *plant, soil, lawn etc)* nourrir; **to f. sth to sb, to f. sb sth** donner qch à manger à qn; **to f. the birds** donner à manger aux oiseaux, nourrir les oiseaux; *Fam* **to f. one's face** s'en mettre plein la lampe, se goinfrer; **she's so ill she isn't even able to f. herself** elle est si malade qu'elle n'est pas capable de se nourrir *ou* de manger toute seule; **please do not f. the animals** *(sign)* prière de ne pas donner à manger aux animaux; **how much do you f. your cats?** quelle quantité de nourriture donnez-vous à vos chats?; **the chimps are fed a diet of nuts and bananas** on donne des noix et des bananes à manger aux chimpanzés; **they were fed to the lions** ils ont été jetés en pâture aux lions
3 *Fig (supply* ► *fire, furnace)* alimenter; *(*► *lake, river)* se jeter dans; *(*► *imagination, hope, rumour)* alimenter, nourrir; **to f. a parking meter** mettre des pièces dans un parcmètre
4 *(transmit)* **to f. information to sb, to f. sb information** donner des informations à qn; *(in order to mislead)* donner de fausses informations à qn *(afin de le tromper)*; *Fam* **to f. sb a line** faire avaler une histoire à qn
5 *Tech (introduce* ► *liquid)* faire passer; *(*► *solid)* faire avancer; *(insert* ► *paper, wire etc)* introduire; *Comput (*► *paper)* faire avancer, alimenter; **to f. data into a computer** entrer des données dans un ordinateur
6 *Theat (give cue to)* donner la réplique à
7 *Sport (pass to)* passer la balle à, servir; **she keeps feeding her backhand** elle n'arrête pas de lui envoyer des balles qu'elle renvoie de son revers
VI *(person, animal)* manger; *(baby* ► *gen)* manger; *(*► *breast-feed)* téter; **to put the cattle out to f.** mettre le bétail en *ou* au pâturage
N **1** *(foodstuff for animal)* nourriture *f*; *(hay, oats etc)* fourrage *m*
2 *(meal for baby* ► *breast milk)* tétée *f*; *(*► *bottled milk)* biberon *m*; **the baby gets its last f. at midnight** le bébé boit sa dernière tétée/son dernier biberon à minuit; *Fam* **the baby's off his f.** le bébé boude son biberon
3 *(meal for animal)* **the dog gets two feeds a day** le chien a à manger deux fois par jour
4 *Fam (meal)* repas *m*; **that was the best f. I've ever had!** je n'ai jamais aussi bien bouffé!
5 *Tech (introduction* ► *of liquid)* alimentation *f*; *(*► *of solid)* avancement *m*; *(device)* dispositif *m* d'alimentation/d'avancement; **petrol f.** alimentation *f* en essence
6 *Fam (actor)* acteur(trice) *m,f* qui donne la réplique; *(comedian's partner)* faire-valoir *m inv*; *(cue)* réplique *f*
►► ***feed belt*** *(of machinegun)* bande-chargeur *f* (souple); *Tech* ***feed hopper*** trémie *f*; ***feed line*** *(of comedian)* réplique *f*; *Tech* ***feed pipe*** tuyau *m* d'alimentation; *Tech* ***feed pump*** pompe *f* d'alimentation

►**feed back** VT SEP *(information, results)* renvoyer

►**feed in** VT SEP *(paper, wire)* introduire; *Comput (data)* entrer

►**feed up** VT SEP *(animal)* engraisser; *(goose)* gaver; **he needs feeding up** *(person)* il a besoin d'engraisser un peu

feedback ['fiːdbæk] N **1** *Electron* rétroaction *f*; *(in microphone)* effet *m* Larsen; *Comput* réaction *f*, rétroaction *f*; *Biol* rétroaction *f*; *Electron* **positive/negative f.** réactions *fpl* positives/négatives **2** *(UNCOUNT) (information)* réactions *fpl*, échos *mpl*; **we haven't had much f. from them** nous n'avons pas eu beaucoup de réactions *ou* d'échos de leur part; **we welcome f. from customers** nous sommes toujours heureux d'avoir les impressions *ou* les réactions de nos clients; **we need more f.** nous avons besoin de plus d'information *ou* d'informations en retour

feedbag ['fiːdbæg] N **1** *(container)* sac *m* à nourriture; *(containing food)* sac *m* de nourriture **2** *Am (for horse)* musette *f*, mangeoire *f* portative; *Fam Fig* **to put on the (old) f.** bouffer

feeder ['fiːdə(r)] N **1** *(eater)* mangeur(euse) *m,f*; **to be a heavy f.** *(person, animal)* manger beaucoup
2 *(person* ► *of machine)* alimenteur(euse) *m,f*; *(*► *of furnace)* chargeur(euse) *m,f*
3 *(child's bottle)* biberon *m*; *Br (bib)* bavette *f*, bavoir *m*
4 *(feeding device* ► *for cattle)* nourrisseur *m*, mangeoire *f* automatique; *(*► *for poultry)* mangeoire *f* automatique; *(*► *for machine)* chargeur *m*
5 *(river)* affluent *m*; *(road)* voie *f ou* bretelle *f* de raccordement; *(air route)* ligne *f* régionale de rabattement *(regroupant les passagers vers un aéroport principal)*
6 *Elec (power line)* câble *m ou* ligne *f* d'alimentation
7 *Comput (for printer, scanner, photocopier)* chargeur *m*
►► ***feeder airline*** compagnie *f* aérienne d'apport; ***feeder flight*** vol *m* d'apport; ***feeder network*** *(for airport)* réseau *m* d'apport; *Br Sch* ***feeder (primary) school*** = école primaire fournissant des élèves à un collège; ***feeder road*** voie *f ou* bretelle *f* de raccordement; ***feeder route*** *(in air transport)* ligne *f* régionale de rabattement *(regroupant les passagers vers un aéroport principal)*

feeding ['fiːdɪŋ] N *(of person, baby, animal, machine)* alimentation *f*; *Bible* **the F. of the Five Thousand** la multiplication des pains; **to be in a f. frenzy** *(sharks)* être rendu fou *ou* frénétique par la présence de nourriture; *Fig* **there was a f. frenzy on the stock market as investors rushed to buy up shares in the new company** la Bourse a connu une activité intense lors de la ruée des investisseurs sur les actions de la nouvelle société
►► ***feeding bottle*** biberon *m*; *Med* ***feeding cup*** canard *m*; *Zool* ***feeding ground, feeding grounds*** = lieux où viennent se nourrir des animaux; *Ind* ***feeding mechanism*** mécanisme *m* d'avance *ou* d'avancement; *(for liquid)* mécanisme *m* d'alimentation; ***feeding stuff*** nourriture *f ou* aliments *mpl* pour animaux; ***feeding time*** *(for child, animal)* heure *f* des repas; **it must be (his) f. time** ce doit être l'heure de son repas

FEEL [fiːl]

VT	
• toucher **1**	• sentir **2**
• ressentir **2, 3**	• penser **4**
VI	
• avoir **1**	• être **2, 4**
• se sentir **2**	• sentir **5**
• fouiller **6**	• avoir envie de **7**
N	
• toucher **1**	• atmosphère **4**

(pt & pp **felt** [felt]*)*
VT **1** *(touch)* toucher; *(explore)* tâter, palper; **f. it, it's so soft** touche-le, c'est tellement doux; **f. the quality of this cloth** apprécie la qualité de ce tissu; **I felt the lump on my arm** j'ai tâté *ou* palpé la grosseur sur mon bras; **he felt his pockets** il tâta ses poches; **to f. one's way** avancer à tâtons; *(in new job, difficult situation etc)* avancer avec pré-

caution; **to f. one's way into/out of/up** entrer/sortir/monter à tâtons; **I'm still feeling my way** je suis en train de m'habituer tout doucement

2 *(be aware of ▸ wind, sunshine, atmosphere, tension)* sentir; *(▸ pain)* sentir, ressentir; *(be sensitive to ▸ cold, beauty)* être sensible à; **I can't f. anything in my foot** je ne sens plus rien dans mon pied; **I felt the floor tremble** *or* **trembling** j'ai senti trembler le sol; **I could f. myself blushing** je me sentais rougir; **f. the weight of it!** soupèse-moi ça!; **he felt the full force of the blow** il a reçu le coup de plein fouet; **I bet he felt that!** il a dû le sentir passer!; **to make one's authority felt** affirmer son autorité, faire sentir son autorité; **I can f. a cold coming on** je sens que je suis en train de m'enrhumer; **I can f. it in my bones** j'en ai le pressentiment

3 *(experience ▸ sadness, happiness, joy, relief)* ressentir, éprouver; *(be affected by ▸ someone's absence, death)* être affecté par; **to f. fear/regret** avoir peur/des regrets; **he feels things very deeply** il ressent les choses très profondément; **do you f. anything for her?** est-ce que tu éprouves *ou* ressens quelque chose à son égard?; **to f. the effects of sth** ressentir les effets de qch

4 *(think)* penser, estimer; **I f. it is my duty to tell you** j'estime qu'il est de mon devoir de te le dire; **I felt it necessary to intervene** j'ai jugé nécessaire d'intervenir; **she feels very strongly that...** elle est tout à fait convaincue que... + *indicative*; **I can't help feeling that...** je ne peux pas m'empêcher de penser que...; **what do you f. about...?** qu'est-ce que vous pensez de...?; **you mustn't f. you have to do it** il ne faut pas que tu te sentes obligé de le faire

VI *(with complement)* **1** *(physically)* **to f. hot/cold/hungry/thirsty** avoir chaud/froid/faim/soif; **my hands/feet f. cold** j'ai froid aux mains/pieds; **my leg feels numb** j'ai la jambe engourdie, ma jambe est engourdie; **to f. good/old/full of energy** se sentir bien/vieux/plein d'énergie; **how do you f.** *or* **are you feeling today?** comment te sens-tu aujourd'hui?; *also Hum* **are you feeling all right?** *(physically)* est-ce que tu te sens bien?; **she's feeling a lot better** elle se sent beaucoup mieux; **my foot feels better** mon pied va mieux; **to f. as though** *or* **as if** *or* **like** croire que + *indicative*, avoir l'impression que + *indicative*; **my arm feels as if it's broken** j'ai l'impression que je me suis cassé le bras; **he's not feeling himself today** il n'est pas en forme aujourd'hui; **you'll soon be feeling (more) yourself** *or* **your old self again** tu iras bientôt mieux, tu seras bientôt remis; **you're as old as you f.** on a l'âge que l'on veut bien avoir; **I f. ten years younger** je me sens dix ans de moins

2 *(emotionally)* **to f. glad/sad/undecided** être heureux/triste/indécis; **to f. (like) a failure** avoir l'impression d'être un raté; **to f. (like) a new woman/man** se sentir comme neuve/neuf; **I felt like a criminal** j'ai eu l'impression d'être un criminel; **I f. really stupid** je me sens vraiment stupide; **I know how you f.** je sais ce que tu ressens; **if that's how you f....** si c'est comme ça que tu vois les choses...; **how would you f. if it happened to you?** comment te sentirais-tu *ou* qu'est-ce que ça te ferait si ça t'arrivait à toi?; **how would you f. if I were to offer you a job?** qu'est-ce que vous diriez si je vous offrais un emploi?; **how do you f. about him/the plan?** qu'est-ce que tu penses de lui/ce projet?, comment le trouves-tu/trouves-tu ce projet?; **I felt really bad about it** j'étais dans mes petits souliers; **he felt really bad about leaving her** ça l'ennuyait vraiment de la laisser; **she feels very strongly about it** elle a une position très arrêtée là-dessus

3 *(in impersonal constructions)* **it feels good to be alive/home** c'est bon d'être en vie/chez soi; **it feels strange to be back** ça fait drôle d'être de retour; **does that f. better?** est-ce que c'est mieux comme ça?; **it feels all wrong for me to be doing this** ça me gêne de faire ça; **it feels like (it's going to) rain/snow** on dirait qu'il va pleuvoir/neiger; **it feels like spring** ça sent le printemps; **what does it f. like** *or* **how does it f. to be Prime Minister?** quelle impression ça fait d'être Premier ministre?

4 *(give specified sensation)* **to f. hard/soft/smooth/rough** être dur/doux/lisse/rêche (au toucher); **the room felt hot/stuffy** il faisait chaud/l'atmosphère était étouffante dans la pièce; **the room feels damp** la pièce (me) paraît humide; **the atmosphere felt tense** on sentait une certaine tension dans l'air; **your neck feels swollen** on dirait que ton cou est enflé

5 *(be capable of sensation)* sentir

6 *(grope ▸ in drawer, pocket)* fouiller; **we had to f. in the dark for the light switch** il a fallu que nous cherchions l'interrupteur à tâtons dans l'obscurité

7 *(idiom)* **to f. like sth** *(want)* avoir envie de qch; **I f. like a cup of coffee/something to eat** j'ai envie d'une tasse de café/de manger quelque chose; **I felt like crying** j'avais envie de pleurer; **do you f. like going out tonight?** ça te dit de sortir ce soir?; **don't do it if you don't f. like it** ne le fais pas si tu n'en as pas envie *ou* si ça ne te dit rien

N 1 *(tactile quality, sensation)* **I could tell by the f. of it** je m'en étais rendu compte rien qu'au toucher; **this garment has a really nice f. to it** ce vêtement est vraiment agréable au toucher; **I like the f. of cotton next to** *or* **against my skin** j'aime bien le contact du coton sur ma peau

2 *(act of feeling, touching)* **to have a f. of sth** toucher qch; *very Fam* **he's always trying to have a quick f.** *(sexually)* il a la main baladeuse

3 *(knack)* **to get the f. of sth** s'habituer à qch; **to have a real f. for translation/music** avoir la traduction/la musique dans la peau

4 *(atmosphere)* atmosphère *f*; **the room has a nice homely f. (to it)** on se sent vraiment bien dans cette pièce; **his music has a really Latin f. (to it)** il y a vraiment une influence latino-américaine dans sa musique

5 *Sport (skill)* **he's got great f.** il est très doué *ou* habile

▸ **feel about, feel around** **VI** *(in drawer, pocket)* fouiller; **to f. about** *or* **around in the dark for sth** chercher qch à tâtons dans le noir, tâtonner dans le noir pour trouver qch

▸ **feel for** **VT INSEP 1** *(sympathize with)* **I f. for you** je compatis; *Ironic* comme je te plains!; **that poor woman, I f. for her** la pauvre, ça me fait de la peine pour elle **2** *(in drawer, handbag, pocket)* chercher

▸ **feel up** **VT SEP** *Fam (sexually)* peloter, tripoter

▸ **feel up to** **VT INSEP** **to f. up to doing sth** *(feel like)* se sentir le courage de faire qch; *(feel physically strong enough)* se sentir la force de faire qch; *(feel qualified, competent)* se sentir capable *ou* à même de faire qch; **I don't really f. up to it** *(feel like)* je ne m'en sens pas le courage; *(feel strong enough)* je ne m'en sens pas la force; *(feel qualified, competent enough)* je ne me sens pas à la hauteur; **if you f. up to it, how about a weekend in London?** si tu t'en sens le courage, que dirais-tu d'un week-end à Londres?

---

feeler ['fiːlə(r)] **N** *(of insect)* antenne *f*; *(of snail)* corne *f*; *(of mollusc)* tentacule *m*; *Fig* **to put out feelers** tâter le terrain

▸▸ *Tech* ***feeler gauge*** jauge *f* d'épaisseur

feel-good **ADJ** *Fam* **it's a real f. film** c'est un film qui donne la pêche; **the f. factor** l'optimisme *m* ambiant, le climat *m* d'optimisme

feeling ['fiːlɪŋ] **N 1** *(sensation)* sensation *f*; **she gets a tingling f. in her fingers** elle a une sensation de fourmillement dans les doigts; **I don't have any f. in my left foot** je n'ai plus aucune sensation dans le pied gauche; **there's a f. of spring in the air** ça sent le printemps

2 *(opinion)* avis *m*, opinion *f*; **she has very strong feelings about it** elle a des opinions très arrêtées là-dessus; **what is your f. about...?** que pensez-vous de...?; **the f. I have is that...** à mon avis...; **the general f. is that..., there is a general f. that...** l'opinion générale est que... + *indicative*

3 *(awareness ▸ relating to the future)* pressentiment *m*; *(▸ caused by external factors)* impression *f*; **I had a f. he would write** j'avais le pressentiment qu'il allait écrire; **I had a f. you'd say that** j'étais sûr que tu allais dire ça; **I have a strong f. that...** j'ai bien l'impression que...; **it's just a f.** c'est un pressentiment, ce n'est qu'une impression; **a f. of unease came over her** elle a commencé à se sentir mal à l'aise; **I have a f. that somebody's watching us** j'ai l'impression que quelqu'un nous observe; **I have the f. you're trying to avoid me** j'ai l'impression que tu essaies de m'éviter

4 *(sensitivity, understanding)* émotion *f*, sensibilité *f*; **a writer/a person of great f.** un écrivain/une personne d'une grande sensibilité; **to play the piano/to sing with f.** jouer du piano/chanter avec cœur *ou* sentiment; **to have a f. for poetry/music** être sensible à *ou* apprécier la poésie/la musique; **to show f. for sb** faire preuve de sympathie pour qn; **you have no f. for other people** les autres te sont indifférents; **to appeal to sb's better feelings** faire appel aux bons sentiments de qn

5 *(often pl) (emotion)* sentiment *m*; **to have mixed feelings about sb/sth** avoir des sentiments mitigés à l'égard de qn/qch; **feelings are running high** les passions sont déchaînées; **to hurt sb's feelings** blesser qn; **to show one's feelings** extérioriser ses émotions; **it has caused a lot of bad f.** cela a provoqué une grande hostilité; **I know the f.** je sais ce que c'est; **the f. is mutual** c'est réciproque; **to say sth with f.** dire qch avec émotion; **no hard feelings?** sans rancune?

ADJ *(person, look)* sympathique

feelingly ['fiːlɪŋlɪ] **ADV** avec émotion

feet [fiːt] *pl of* **foot**

feign [feɪn] **VT** *(surprise, innocence)* feindre; *(madness, death)* simuler; **to f. sleep** faire semblant *ou* mine de dormir; **to f. illness/interest** faire semblant *ou* mine d'être malade/intéressé

feigned [feɪnd] **ADJ** *(surprise, innocence)* feint; *(illness, madness, death)* simulé; **with feigned surprise/innocence** avec une surprise/innocence feinte

feint [feɪnt] *Mil & Sport* **N** feinte *f*

VI faire une feinte

feint-ruled **ADJ** *(paper)* à réglure légère

feistiness ['faɪstɪnɪs] **N** *Fam (liveliness)* entrain[□] *m*; *(combativeness)* cran *m*

feisty ['faɪstɪ] *(compar* **feistier**, *superl* **feistiest)** **ADJ** *Fam (lively)* plein d'entrain[□]; *(combative)* qui a du cran

feldspar ['feldspɑː(r)] **N** *Miner* feldspath *m*

felicitous [fɪ'lɪsɪtəs] **ADJ** *Literary* **1** *(happy)* heureux **2** *(word, term)* bien trouvé, heureux; *(choice, decision, colour combination)* heureux

felicity [fɪ'lɪsətɪ] **N** *Literary* **1** *(happiness)* félicité *f* **2** *(aptness ▸ of word, term)* à-propos *m*, justesse *f*; *(▸ of choice, decision, colour combination)* caractère *m* heureux

feline ['fiːlaɪn] **ADJ** félin

N félin *m*

fell [fel] *pt of* **fall**

VT *(tree)* abattre, couper; *Fig (opponent)* abattre, terrasser

N 1 *Br Geog* montagne *f*, colline *f*; **the fells** *(high moorland)* les landes *fpl* des plateaux

2 *(hide, pelt)* fourrure *f*, peau *f*

3 *(in forestry)* nombre *m* d'arbres abattus (en une fois), abattis *m*

4 *Sewing (seam)* couture *f* rabattue *ou* plate

ADJ 1 *Arch or Literary (fierce ▸ person)* féroce, cruel; *(deadly ▸ disease)* cruel **2** *(idiom)* **in** *or* **at one f. swoop** d'un seul coup

▸▸ ***fell runner*** coureur(euse) *m,f* en basse montagne; ***fell running*** course *f* en basse montagne; ***fell walker*** randonneur(euse) *m,f* de basse montagne; ***fell walking*** randonnée *f* en basse montagne

fella ['felə] **N** *Fam (man)* mec *m*, type *m*; *Br (boyfriend)* copain *m*, mec *m*

fellatio [fe'leɪʃɪəʊ] **N** fellation *f*

felling ['felɪŋ] **N** *(of tree, forest)* abattage *m*

fellow ['feləʊ] **N 1** *Fam Old-fashioned (man)* gars *m*, type *m*; **a good f.** un type *ou* gars bien; **an old f.** un vieux bonhomme; **the poor f.'s just lost his job** le pauvre vient juste de perdre son travail; **hello, old f.** salut, mon vieux; **my dear f.** mon cher ami; **give a f. a chance!** donne-moi une chance!

2 *Literary (comrade)* ami(e) *m,f*, camarade *mf*; *(other human being)* semblable *mf*; *(person in same profession ▸ man)* confrère *m*; *(▸ woman)* consœur *f*; **fellows in misfortune** compagnons (compagnes) *mpl,fpl* d'infortune; **school f.** camarade *mf* d'école

3 *Univ (professor)* professeur *m (faisant également partie du conseil d'administration)*; *(postgraduate student)* étudiant(e) *m,f* de troisième cycle *(souvent chargé de cours)*

4 *(of learned society)* membre *m*; **F. of the Royal Society** = membre de la Société royale (de Londres)

5 *(one of a pair)* **where is the f. to this sock/glove?** où est la chaussette/le gant qui va avec celle-là/celui-là?

ADJ f. prisoner/student camarade *mf* de prison/ d'études; **f. passenger/sufferer/soldier** compagnon (compagne) *m,f* de voyage/d'infortune/ d'armes; **f. being** *or* **creature** semblable *mf*, pareil(eille) *m,f*; **one's f. man** son semblable; **f. worker** *(in office)* collègue *mf* (de travail); *(in factory)* camarade *mf* (de travail), compagnon (compagne) *m,f* de travail; **f. citizen** concitoyen (enne) *m,f*; **f. countryman/countrywoman** compatriote *mf*; **it's rare to meet a f. hang-glider** c'est rare de rencontrer un autre adepte du deltaplane

▸▸ ***fellow feeling*** sympathie *f*; ***fellow traveller*** *(companion on journey)* compagnon (compagne) *m,f* de voyage *ou* de route; *Fig* compagnon (compagne) *m,f* de route; *Pol* communisant(e) *m,f*

fellowship ['feləʊʃɪp] **N 1** *(friendship)* camaraderie *f*; *(company)* compagnie *f* **2** *(organization)* association *f*, société *f*, *Rel* confrérie *f* **3** *Univ (scholarship)* bourse *f* d'études de l'enseignement supérieur; *(position)* poste *m* de chercheur

felon[1] ['felən] **N** *Law* criminel(elle) *m,f*

felon[2] **N** *Med* panaris *m*

felonious [fɪ'ləʊnjəs] **ADJ** *Law* criminel

felony ['felənɪ] **N** *Law* crime *m*; **to compound a f.** pactiser avec un crime

felspar ['felspɑː(r)] = **feldspar**

felt[1] [felt] *pt & pp of* **feel**

felt[2] **N** *Tex* feutre *m*; **roofing f.** feutre *m* bitumé

COMP de *ou* en feutre

VT *Tex (wool, hairs)* feutrer; *Constr (roof)* couvrir de feutre bitumé

▸▸ ***felt hat*** (chapeau *m* de *ou* en) feutre *m*; ***felt pen*** feutre *m*

felt-tip (pen) **N** (stylo *m*) feutre *m*

female ['fiːmeɪl] **ADJ 1** *(animal, plant, egg)* femelle; *(sex, quality, voice, employee)* féminin; *(vote)* des femmes; *(equality)* de la femme, des femmes; **a traditionally f. job** un travail traditionnellement réservé aux femmes; **f. slave** femme *f* esclave; **a study of the f. character** une étude du caractère de la femme; **f. company** la compagnie féminine *ou* des femmes; **the f. sex organs** les organes sexuels féminins *ou* de la femme; **male and f. clients** des clients et des clientes; **there are not enough f. politicians** il n'y a pas assez de femmes sur la scène politique **2** *Tech* femelle

N 1 *(animal, plant)* femelle *f*; *(person)* femme *f*; **the f. of the species** la femelle **2** *Pej (woman)* bonne femme *f*; **some f. called for you** il y a une bonne femme qui t'a demandé au téléphone

▸▸ ***female circumcision*** excision *f*; ***female condom*** préservatif *m* féminin; ***female impersonator*** travesti *m (dans un spectacle)*

> Note that the French word **femelle** is never used to refer to human beings.

feminine ['femɪnɪn] **ADJ 1** *(dress, woman, hands etc)* féminin; **the bedroom is very f.** c'est une vraie chambre de femme; **this flat needs the f. touch** cet appartement a besoin de la présence d'une femme **2** *Gram (ending, form)* féminin

N *Gram* féminin *m*; **in the f.** au féminin

femininity [ˌfemɪ'nɪnɪtɪ] **N** féminité *f*

feminism ['femɪnɪzəm] **N** féminisme *m*

feminist ['femɪnɪst] **N** féministe *mf*

ADJ féministe

feminization, -isation [ˌfemɪnaɪ'zeɪʃən] **N** féminisation *f*

feminize, -ise ['femɪnaɪz] **VT** *(boy)* féminiser, rendre efféminé; *(writing)* féminiser

VI se féminiser

feminizing, -ising ['femɪnaɪzɪŋ] **N** féminisation *f*

ADJ féminisant

femme fatale ['fæmfə'tɑːl] *(pl* **femmes fatales** ['fæmfə'tɑːl]) **N** *Cin* femme *f* fatale

femoral ['femərəl] **ADJ** *Anat* fémoral

femur ['fiːmə(r)] **N** *Anat* fémur *m*

fen [fen] **N** *Geog* marais *m*, marécage *m*

• **Fens NPL the Fens** = région de plaines anciennement marécageuses dans le sud-est de l'Angleterre

fence [fens] **N 1** *(gen)* barrière *f*; *(completely enclosing)* barrière *f*, clôture *f*; *(high and wooden)* palissade *f*; **electric/barbed-wire f.** clôture *f* électrique/en fil barbelé

2 *(in showjumping)* obstacle *m*; **to rush one's fences** *(horse)* arriver trop vite sur l'obstacle; *Fig* aller trop vite en besogne

3 *Fam Crime slang (of stolen goods)* receleur (euse)[□] *m,f*

4 *Tech (guard)* protection *f*

5 *(idioms)* **to come down on the right/wrong side of the f.** choisir le bon/mauvais parti; **to be on the other side of the f.** être de l'autre côté de la barricade; **to mend one's fences with sb** *(fans, electorate)* se refaire une réputation auprès *ou* regagner les faveurs de qn; *(friends, colleagues)* se réconcilier avec qn; **to sit on the f.** ne pas se prononcer, rester neutre; **stop sitting on the f., come down off the f.** prononce-toi

VT 1 *(land)* clôturer **2** *Fam Crime slang (stolen goods)* receler[□]

VI 1 *Sport* faire de l'escrime **2** *(evade question)* se dérober; *(joust verbally)* s'affronter verbalement **3** *Fam Crime slang (handle stolen goods)* faire du recel[□]

▸▸ ***fence post*** piquet *m* de clôture

▸ **fence in VT SEP 1** *(garden)* clôturer **2** *Fig (restrict* ▸ *person)* enfermer, étouffer; **he feels fenced in** il se sent enfermé, il étouffe

▸ **fence off VT SEP** séparer à l'aide d'une clôture

fence-mending **N** *Fig* reprise *f* des relations

fencer ['fensə(r)] **N 1** *Sport* escrimeur(euse) *m,f* **2** *(workman)* poseur(euse) *m,f* de clôtures

fencing ['fensɪŋ] **N** *(UNCOUNT)* **1** *Sport* escrime *f* **2** *Fig (verbal)* joutes *fpl* oratoires **3** *(fences)* clôture *f*, barrière *f*; *(material)* matériaux *mpl* pour clôture **4** *(action) (of land)* action *f* de clôturer **5** *Fam Crime slang (handling stolen goods)* recel[□] *m*

COMP *Sport (lesson)* d'escrime

▸▸ *Sport* ***fencing match*** assaut *m*

fend [fend] **VI to f. for oneself** se débrouiller tout seul; *(financially)* s'assumer, subvenir à ses besoins

▸ **fend off VT SEP** *(blow)* parer; *(attack, attacker)* repousser; *(takeover bid)* se défendre contre; *Fig (question)* éluder, se dérober à; *(person at door, on telephone)* éconduire

fender ['fendə(r)] **N 1** *(for fireplace)* garde-feu *m inv* **2** *Naut* défense *f* **3** *Am (on car)* aile *f*; *(on bicycle)* garde-boue *m inv*; *(on train, tram* ▸ *shock absorber)* pare-chocs *m inv*; (▸ *for clearing track)* chasse-pierres *m inv*

fender-bender **N** *Am Fam (minor accident)* petit accrochage[□] *m*

feng shui ['fəŋ'ʃweɪ] **N** feng shui *m*

fenland ['fenlænd] **N** *Geog* pays *m* marécageux

fennel ['fenəl] **N** *Bot & Culin* fenouil *m*

feral ['fɪərəl] **ADJ** *(animal)* féral

ferment **VT** [fə'ment] faire fermenter; *Fig* **to f. trouble** fomenter des troubles

VI [fə'ment] fermenter

N ['fɜːment] **1** *(agent)* ferment *m*; *(fermentation)* fermentation *f* **2** *Fig (unrest)* agitation *f*; **to be in (a state of) f.** être en effervescence

fermentation [ˌfɜːmən'teɪʃən] **N** fermentation *f*

fern [fɜːn] **N** *Bot* fougère *f*

ferocious [fə'rəʊʃəs] **ADJ** *(animal, appetite, criticism, fighting)* féroce; *(weapon)* meurtrier; *(competition)* acharné; *(heat)* terrible, intense; *(climate)* rude; **a f. war** une guerre sanguinaire

ferociously [fə'rəʊʃəslɪ] **ADV** *(bark, criticize, attack)* avec férocité, férocement; *(look at someone)* d'un œil féroce; **this business is f. competitive** ce secteur est caractérisé par une concurrence acharnée

ferociousness [fə'rəʊʃəsnɪs], **ferocity** [fə'rɒsɪtɪ] **N** *(of person, animal, attack, criticism)* férocité *f*; *(of climate)* rudesse *f*; *(of heat)* intensité *f*, caractère *m* torride; **the f. of the competition for a place at university** la concurrence acharnée pour entrer à l'université

ferret ['ferɪt] **N** *Zool* furet *m*

VT *(hunt with ferrets)* chasser au furet

VI 1 *(hunt with ferrets)* chasser au furet; **to go ferreting** aller à la chasse au furet **2** *Fig (in pocket, drawer)* fouiller; *(in room)* fouiller, fureter

▸ **ferret out VT SEP 1** *(animal)* déloger **2** *(information, truth)* dénicher

ferreting ['ferɪtɪŋ] **N** chasse *f* au furet

ferrety ['ferɪtɪ] **ADJ** de furet; *Pej (eyes, face)* de fouine

ferric ['ferɪk] **ADJ** *Chem* ferrique

Ferris wheel ['ferɪs-] **N** *(at fairground)* grande roue *f*

ferrite ['feraɪt] **N** *Chem* ferrite *f*

ferroconcrete [ˌferəʊ'kɒŋkriːt] **N** *Constr* béton *m* armé

ferromagnetic [ˌferəʊmæg'netɪk] **ADJ** *Phys* ferromagnétique

ferrous ['ferəs] **ADJ** *Chem* ferreux

ferrule ['feruːl] **N** *(of umbrella, walking stick)* virole *f*

ferry ['ferɪ] *(pl* **ferries**, *pt & pp* **ferried**) **N** *(large)* ferry *m*; *(small)* bac *m*; **to take the f.** prendre le ferry/le bac; **we took the f. to France** nous sommes allés en France en ferry; **passenger f.** ferry *m* pour passagers piétons; **car f.** car-ferry *m*

VT 1 *(of company* ▸ *by large boat)* transporter en ferry; (▸ *by small boat)* faire traverser en bac; *(of boat)* transporter; **Donald will f. you across in his rowing boat** Donald vous fera traverser dans sa barque **2** *Fig (by vehicle* ▸ *goods)* transporter; (▸ *people)* conduire; **he spends most of his time ferrying the kids around** il passe la majeure partie de son temps à conduire les enfants à droite et à gauche

▸▸ ***ferry crossing*** traversée *f* en ferry *ou* bac; ***ferry service*** ligne *f* de ferry; ***ferry terminal*** gare *f* maritime

ferryboat ['ferɪbəʊt] **N** *(large)* ferry *m*; *(small)* bac *m*

ferrying ['ferɪɪŋ] **N** *(in large boat)* transport *m* en ferry; *(in small boat)* transport *m* par bac

ferryman ['ferɪmən] *(pl* **ferrymen** [-mən]) **N** passeur *m*

fertile ['fɜːtaɪl] **ADJ** *(land, soil)* fertile; *(person, couple, animal)* fécond; *Fig (imagination)* fertile, fécond; **a f. egg** un œuf fécondé; *Fig* **to fall on f. ground** trouver un terrain propice

▸▸ *Geog* ***the Fertile Crescent*** le Croissant fertile

fertility [fɜː'tɪlətɪ] **N** *(of land, soil)* fertilité *f*; *(of person, animal)* fécondité *f*; *Fig (of imagination)* fertilité *f*, fécondité *f*

COMP *(rate)* de fécondité; *(rite, symbol)* de fertilité

▸▸ *Med* ***fertility clinic*** centre *m* de traitement de la stérilité; *Med* ***fertility drug*** médicament *m* pour le traitement de la stérilité; ***fertility rate*** taux *m* de fécondité; ***fertility symbol*** symbole *m* de fertilité; *Med* ***fertility treatment*** traitement *m* de la stérilité

fertilization, -isation [ˌfɜːtɪlaɪ'zeɪʃən] **N 1** *Biol (of animal, plant, egg)* fécondation *f* **2** *Agr (of land, soil)* fertilisation *f*

fertilize, -ise ['fɜːtɪlaɪz] **VT 1** *Biol (animal, plant, egg)* féconder **2** *Agr (land, soil)* fertiliser

fertilizer, -iser ['fɜːtɪlaɪzə(r)] **N** *Agr* engrais *m*

fervent ['fɜːvənt] **ADJ** *(desire, supporter etc)* fervent, ardent; **he is a f. believer in reincarnation** il croit ardemment à la réincarnation

fervently ['fɜːvəntlɪ] **ADV** *(beg, desire, speak)* avec ferveur; *(believe)* ardemment

fervid ['fɜːvɪd] *Formal* = **fervent**

fervour, *Am* **fervor** ['fɜːvə(r)] **N** ferveur *f*

fess up [fes-] **VI** *Fam* cracher le morceau

> **-FEST** — SUFFIXE
>
> Il s'agit d'un suffixe d'origine allemande surtout utilisé en anglais américain. Ce suffixe très générateur sert à former des noms familiers à partir de noms ou de verbes. Il dénote l'ABONDANCE du référent du nom auquel il est accolé :
>
> **a slugfest** (formé à partir de *slug* = gnon) une bagarre; **a gabfest** (formé à partir de

to gab = papoter) une longue conversation; **the show was a real yawnfest** (formé à partir de *to yawn* = bâiller) le spectacle était ennuyeux à mourir; **the sea got choppy and the cruise turned into a pukefest** (formé à partir de *to puke* = dégueuler) la mer a commencé à s'agiter et les passagers de la croisière se sont mis à dégueuler à qui mieux mieux

fester ['festə(r)] VI **1** *(wound)* suppurer; *Fig (situation)* s'envenimer; **resentment within the company continues to f.** le mécontentement continue de croître dans l'entreprise **2** *Br Fam (do nothing)* buller

festering ['festərɪŋ] ADJ *(wound)* suppurant; *Fig* **his f. resentment finally came to the surface** sa rancune accumulée finit par se manifester

festival ['festɪvəl] N *(of music, film etc)* festival *m*; *Rel* fête *f*; **street f.** festival *m* de rue; **the Cannes Film F.** le Festival de Cannes
►► *Am* ***festival seating*** *(in theatre)* placement *m* libre

festive ['festɪv] ADJ *(atmosphere)* de fête; **their golden wedding celebration was a very f. occasion** ils ont fait une grande fête pour célébrer leurs noces d'or; **there was a really f. atmosphere** l'atmosphère était vraiment à la fête; **the f. season** la période des fêtes; **to be in f. mood** *(person)* se sentir d'une humeur de fête

festivity [fes'tɪvətɪ] N *(merriness)* fête *f*; **an air/atmosphere of f.** un air/une atmosphère de fête
• **festivities** NPL *(celebrations)* festivités *fpl*; **the Christmas festivities** les fêtes *fpl* de Noël

festoon [fe'stu:n] N feston *m*, guirlande *f*
VT orner de festons, festonner; *Fig* **to be festooned in sth** *(draped with)* être couvert de qch
►► ***festoon blind*** store *m* autrichien

feta ['fetə] N **f. (cheese)** feta *f*

fetal *Am* = **foetal**

fetch [fetʃ] VT **1** *(go to get)* aller chercher; **to f. sb from the airport** aller chercher qn à l'aéroport; **I'll f. you** je viendrai te chercher; **f.!** *(to dog)* va chercher!; **run and f. him** va vite le chercher
2 *Com (be sold for)* rapporter; *(specific price)* atteindre; **it fetched a high price** cela s'est vendu cher; **it fetched £100,000** cela a atteint les 100 000 livres; **I'd be surprised if it fetched that much** cela m'étonnerait que cela rapporte autant *ou* que cela se vende aussi cher
3 *Br Fam (deal)* **to f. sb a blow** flanquer un coup à qn; **move or I'll f. you one!** dégage ou je t'en mets une!
4 *(generate ► response, laugh)* susciter; **the speech fetched a round of applause** le discours a été reçu par des applaudissements
5 *Literary (utter ► sigh, moan)* pousser
VI **I'm not going to f. and carry for you!** je ne vais pas être ta bonne à tout faire!

►**fetch back** VT SEP *(bring back ► person)* ramener; *(► thing)* rapporter

►**fetch up** VI *(reach)* **to f. up at a port** parvenir *ou* arriver à un port; **the kite fetched up in the branches of a tree** le cerf-volant est resté accroché dans les branches d'un arbre; *Fam* **they finally fetched up at our house** ils ont finalement abouti chez nous□; *Fam* **the car fetched up against a wall** la voiture s'est (finalement) arrêtée en heurtant un mur□
VT SEP **1** *(bring from lower place ► person)* faire monter; *(► thing)* remonter **2** *Fam (vomit)* dégueuler

fetching ['fetʃɪŋ] ADJ *(smile, person, look)* séduisant; *(hat, dress)* seyant

fête [feɪt, fet] N fête *f*, kermesse *f*; **village f.** fête *f* du village
VT fêter

> **FÊTE**
>
> En Grande-Bretagne, les "village fêtes" sont des manifestations en plein air où l'on vend des produits faits maison et où l'on organise des manifestations sportives et des jeux pour enfants; elles sont généralement destinées à réunir des fonds pour une œuvre de charité.

fetid ['fetɪd, 'fi:tɪd] ADJ fétide

fetish ['fetɪʃ] N *Psy & Rel* fétiche *m*; **to have a f. for** *or* **to make a f. of sth** être obsédé par qch, être un(e) maniaque de qch; *Fam* **he's got a bit of a shoe f.** il est un peu fétichiste des chaussures

fetishism ['fetɪʃɪzəm] N *Psy & Rel* fétichisme *m*; **food f.** obsession *f* pour la nourriture; **foot f.** fétichisme *m* du pied

fetishist ['fetɪʃɪst] N *Psy & Rel* fétichiste *mf*; **food f.** personne *f* obsédée par la nourriture; **foot f.** fétichiste *mf* du pied

fetishistic [,fetɪ'ʃɪstɪk] ADJ *Psy* fétichiste

fetlock ['fetlɒk] N *Zool (of horse ► part of leg)* partie *f* postérieure du pied; *(► joint)* boulet *m*; *(► hair)* fanon *m*

fetter ['fetə(r)] VT *(slave, prisoner)* enchaîner; *(horse)* entraver; *Fig* entraver
• **fetters** NPL *(of prisoner)* fers *mpl*, chaînes *fpl*; *(of horse)* entraves *fpl*; *Fig (of marriage, job)* chaînes *fpl*, sujétions *fpl*; **in fetters** *(prisoner)* enchaîné; *Fig* entravé; **to put sb in fetters** mettre qn aux fers; *Fig* entraver qn

fettle ['fetəl] N *Fam* **to be in fine** *or* **good f.** aller bien□

fetus *Am* = **foetus**

feud [fju:d] N *(between people, families)* querelle *f*; *(more aggressive ► between families)* vendetta *f*; **a bloody f.** une vendetta; **to have a f. with sb** être à couteaux tirés avec qn
VI se quereller, se disputer; **to f. with sb (over sth)** se quereller *ou* se disputer avec qn (pour qch); **they were feuding with each other over who owned the property** ils se disputaient la possession de la propriété

feudal ['fju:dəl] ADJ **1** *Hist (society, system)* féodal **2** *Pej (extremely old-fashioned)* moyenâgeux
►► *Hist* ***feudal lord*** seigneur *m*

feudalism ['fju:dəlɪzəm] N *Hist* féodalisme *m*

feudally ['fju:dəlɪ] ADV féodalement

fever ['fi:və(r)] N **1** *Med (illness)* fièvre *f*; **a bout of f.** un accès *ou* une poussée de fièvre; **to have a f.** *(high temperature)* avoir de la température *ou* de la fièvre **2** *Fig* excitation *f* fébrile; **a f. of anticipation** une attente fiévreuse *ou* fébrile; **football/election/gold f.** fièvre *f* du football/des élections/de l'or; **to be in a f. about sth** *(nervous, excited)* être tout excité à cause de qch; **things are at f. pitch here** l'excitation ici est à son comble

fevered ['fi:vəd] ADJ *(brow)* fiévreux; *Fig (imagination)* enfiévré

feverish ['fi:vərɪʃ] ADJ *Med* fiévreux; *Fig (activity, atmosphere)* fébrile, fiévreux

feverishly ['fi:vərɪʃlɪ] ADV *Fig* fébrilement, fiévreusement

feverishness ['fi:vərɪʃnɪs] N *Med* état *m* fébrile, fébrilité *f*

FEW [fju:]

> ADJ
> • peu de **1** • quelques **2**
> PRON
> • peu

ADJ **1** *(not many)* peu de; **f. people have done that** peu de gens ont fait cela; **so/too f. books to read** si/trop peu de livres à lire; **there are four books too f.** il manque quatre livres; **we are f. (in number)** nous sommes peu nombreux; **with f. exceptions** à peu d'exceptions près, sauf de rares exceptions; **on the f. occasions that I have met him** les rares fois où je l'ai rencontré; **her f. remaining possessions** le peu de biens qui lui restaient; **it is one of the f. surviving examples of...** c'est un des rares exemples qui restent de...; **she is one of the f. women to have held the post** c'est une des rares femmes à avoir assumé ces fonctions; **visitors are f. and far between** les visiteurs sont rares
2 *(indicating an unspecified or approximate number)* **every f. minutes** toutes les deux ou trois minutes; **the first f. copies** les deux ou trois premiers exemplaires; **in the past/next f. days** pendant les deux ou trois derniers/prochains jours; **he's been living in London for the past f. years** ça fait quelques années qu'il habite à Londres; **these past f. weeks have been wonderful** ces dernières semaines ont été merveilleuses
PRON *(not many)* peu; **how many of them are there? – very f.** combien sont-ils? – très peu nombreux; **there are very/too f. of us** nous sommes très peu/trop peu nombreux; **there are so f. of them** ils sont tellement peu nombreux; **I didn't realize how f. there were** je ne m'étais pas rendu compte qu'ils étaient aussi peu nombreux; **f. could have predicted the outcome** peu de personnes *ou* rares sont ceux qui auraient pu prévoir le résultat; **f. of them could speak French** peu parmi eux parlaient français; **the f. who knew her** les quelques personnes qui la connaissaient; **the chosen f.** les heureux élus
• **a few** ADJ quelques; **I have a f. ideas** j'ai quelques idées; **he has a f. more friends than I have** il a un peu plus d'amis que moi; **a f. more days/months/years** quelques jours/mois/années de plus; **a f. more days should see the job done** encore quelques jours et le travail devrait être fini
PRON quelques-uns (quelques-unes) *mpl, fpl*; **do you have many friends? – I have a f.** est-ce que tu as beaucoup d'amis? – (j'en ai) quelques-uns; **we need a f. more/less** il nous en faut un peu plus/moins; **a f. of these cakes/the survivors** quelques-uns de ces gâteaux/des survivants; **a f. of you** quelques-uns d'entre vous; **there are only a f. of us who attend regularly** seuls quelques-uns parmi nous y vont régulièrement; *Fam* **he's had a f. (too many)** *(drinks)* il a bu un coup (de trop); **to name but a f.** pour n'en citer que quelques-uns; **not a f.** pas peu
• **a good few, quite a few** ADJ un assez grand nombre de; **quite a f. minutes passed** un bon moment s'est écoulé PRON un assez grand nombre; **quite a f. agreed with me** ils étaient assez nombreux à être d'accord avec moi; **quite a f. of us/of the books** un assez grand nombre d'entre nous/de livres; **I hadn't seen all her films, but I'd seen a good f.** je n'avais pas vu tous ses films, mais j'en avais vu un assez grand nombre

fewer ['fju:ə(r)] *(compar of* **few***)* ADJ moins de; **there have been f. accidents than last year** il y a eu moins d'accidents que l'an dernier; **f. and f. people** de moins en moins de gens; **the f. people turn up the better** moins il y aura de monde et mieux ce sera; **no f. than** pas moins de
PRON moins; **there are f. of you than I thought** vous êtes moins nombreux que je ne le pensais; **I've got even/far** *or* **a lot f. than you** j'en ai encore/beaucoup moins que toi; **the f. the better** moins il y en a mieux c'est

fewest ['fju:ɪst] *(superl of* **few***)* ADJ le moins de; **the f. mistakes possible** le moins d'erreurs possible
PRON **I had the f.** c'est moi qui en ai eu le moins

fey [feɪ] ADJ **1** *(whimsical ► person, behaviour)* bizarre **2** *Scot (clairvoyant)* extralucide **3** *Scot (having feeling of impending death)* qui a des pressentiments de mort

fez [fez] N fez *m*

fiancé [fɪ'ɒnseɪ] N fiancé *m*

fiancée [fɪ'ɒnseɪ] N fiancée *f*

fiasco [fɪ'æskəʊ] *(pl* **fiascos** *or* **fiascoes***)* N fiasco *m*; **it was a f.** ça a été un véritable fiasco

fiat ['faɪæt] N *(decree)* décret *m*
►► *Am Fin* ***fiat money*** monnaie *f* fiduciaire

fib [fɪb] *(pt & pp* **fibbed**, *cont* **fibbing***)* *Fam* N petit mensonge□ *m*; **to tell fibs** raconter des histoires; **what a f.!** c'est des histoires!; **I told them a f. about having to do some work** je leur ai raconté qu'il fallait que je travaille□
VI raconter des histoires; **I'm sure he was fibbing about how much he earns** je suis sûr qu'il a menti□ *ou* raconté des histoires à propos de l'argent qu'il gagne; **I fibbed to them about having to do some work** je leur ai raconté qu'il fallait que je travaille□

fibber ['fɪbə(r)] N *Fam* menteur(euse)□ *m,f*

fiber, fiberboard *etc Am* = **fibre, fibreboard** *etc*

Fibonacci [,fɪbə'nætʃɪ] PR N
►► *Math* ***Fibonacci number*** nombre *m* de Fibonacci; ***Fibonacci series*** série *f* de Fibonacci

fibre, *Am* **fiber** ['faɪbə(r)] N **1** *(of cloth, wood)* fibre *f*; **artificial/natural fibres** fibres *fpl* artificielles/naturelles; *Fig* **moral f.** force *f* morale; *Fig* **to love sb/sth with every f. of one's being** aimer qn/qch de tout son être **2** *(UNCOUNT) (in diet)* fibres *fpl*; **to be high in f.** *(foodstuff)* être riche en fibres; **high-f. diet** régime *m ou* alimentation *f* riche en fibres

▸▸ *Comput* ***fibre optics*** fibre *f* optique, fibres *fpl* optiques

fibreboard, *Am* **fiberboard** ['faɪbəbɔːd] **N** panneau *m* de fibres

fibreglass, *Am* **fiberglass** ['faɪbəglɑːs] **N** fibre *f* de verre; **it's (made of) f.** c'est en *ou* de la fibre de verre

COMP *(boat, hull)* en fibre de verre

fibre-optic, *Am* **fiber-optic ADJ**

▸▸ ***fibre-optic cable*** câble *m* optique, câble *m* en fibres optiques; *Med* ***fibre-optic endoscopy*** fibroscopie *f*

fibrescope, *Am* **fiberscope** ['faɪbəskəʊp] **N** *Med & Opt* fibroscope *m*

fibrillation [ˌfaɪbrɪ'leɪʃən] **N** *Med* fibrillation *f*

fibroid ['faɪbrɔɪd] *Med* **N** *(tumour)* fibrome *m*

ADJ *(tissue)* fibreux

▸▸ ***fibroid tumour*** fibrome *m*

fibroma [faɪ'brəʊmə] (*pl* **fibromata** [-mətə]) **N** *Med* fibrome *m*

fibrosis [faɪ'brəʊsɪs] **N** *(UNCOUNT) Med* fibrose *f*

fibrositis [ˌfaɪbrə'saɪtɪs] **N** *(UNCOUNT) Med* fibrosite *f*

fibrous ['faɪbrəs] **ADJ** *Anat & Bot* fibreux

fibula ['fɪbjʊlə] (*pl* **fibulas** *or* **fibulae** [-liː]) **N** *Anat* péroné *m*

fickle ['fɪkəl] **ADJ** *(friend, fan)* inconstant; *(weather)* changeant, instable; *(lover)* inconstant, volage

fickleness ['fɪkəlnɪs] **N** *(of friend, fan, public, lover)* inconstance *f*; *(of weather)* instabilité *f*

fiction ['fɪkʃən] **N 1** *(UNCOUNT) Literature* ouvrages *mpl ou* œuvres *fpl* de fiction; **first prize for f.** premier prix *m* de fiction; **a work** *or* **piece of f.** un ouvrage *ou* une œuvre de fiction **2** *(invention)* fiction *f*; **she has difficulty separating fact from f.** elle a du mal à distinguer la réalité de la fiction; **it's pure f.** c'est de la pure fiction

▸▸ ***fiction writer*** auteur *m* d'ouvrages de fiction

fictional ['fɪkʃənəl] **ADJ** fictif; **a well-known f. character** un célèbre personnage de la littérature

fictionalize, -ise ['fɪkʃənəlaɪz] **VT** romancer

fictitious [fɪk'tɪʃəs] **ADJ** *(imaginary, invented)* fictif

▸▸ *Fin* ***fictitious assets*** actif *m* fictif; *Fin* ***fictitious person*** personne *f* fictive

fictitiously [fɪk'tɪʃəslɪ] **ADV** fictivement

fiddle ['fɪdəl] **N 1** *(musical instrument)* violon *m*; **to be as fit as a f.** être en pleine forme, être frais comme un gardon; *Fig* **to play second f. (to sb)** jouer les seconds violons *ou* rôles (auprès de qn) **2** *Fam (swindle)* truc *m*, combine *f*; *Br* **to work a f.** combiner quelque chose; **it's a f.** c'est un attrape-nigaud; **to be on the f.** traficoter; **tax f.** fraude *f* fiscale□

VI 1 *(be restless)* **stop fiddling!** tiens-toi tranquille!, arrête de remuer!; **to f. with sth** *(aimlessly, nervously)* jouer avec qch; *(interfere with)* jouer avec *ou* tripoter qch; **don't f. with the switch** laisse l'interrupteur tranquille, ne tripote pas l'interrupteur

2 *(tinker)* bricoler; **he fiddled with the knobs on the television** il a tourné les boutons de la télé dans tous les sens

3 *(play the fiddle)* jouer du violon; *Fig* **to f. while Rome burns** s'occuper de futilités alors qu'il est urgent d'agir

4 *Fam (cheat)* trafiquer

VT 1 *Fam (falsify* ▸ *results, financial accounts)* truquer□, falsifier□; *(*▸ *election)* truquer□; **to f. one's income tax** falsifier sa déclaration d'impôts; **he fiddled it so that he got the results he wanted** il a trafiqué pour obtenir les résultats qu'il voulait **2** *Fam (gain dishonestly* ▸ *money, time off)* carotter **3** *(play* ▸ *tune)* jouer au violon

fiddlededee [ˌfɪdəldiː'diː] **EXCLAM** *Fam Old-fashioned (in disagreement)* balivernes!

fiddle-faddle [-fædəl] *Fam Old-fashioned* **N 1** *(nonsense)* balivernes *fpl*, fadaises *fpl* **2** *(triviality)* bagatelles *fpl*

EXCLAM balivernes!

fiddler ['fɪdlə(r)] **N 1** *(fiddle player)* joueur(euse) *m,f* de violon, violoniste *mf* **2** *Fam (swindler)* arnaqueur(euse) *m,f* **3** *Fam (fidget)* = personne qui gigote tout le temps

▸▸ *Zool* ***fiddler crab*** crabe *m* violoniste

fiddlesticks ['fɪdəlstɪks] **EXCLAM** *Fam Old-fashioned (in disagreement)* balivernes!; *(in annoyance)* bon sang de bonsoir!

fiddling ['fɪdəlɪŋ] **ADJ** *(trivial, insignificant)* futile, insignifiant

N 1 *(fidgeting)* **stop your f.!** arrête de gigoter! **2** *Fam (swindling)* trafic□ *m*, falsification□ *f*; **his f. of the books** sa falsification des livres de comptes; **in spite of all his f.** malgré toutes ses combines

fiddly ['fɪdlɪ] **ADJ** *Br Fam (awkward* ▸ *job, task)* délicat□, minutieux□; *(*▸ *small object)* difficile à manier□, difficile à tenir entre les doigts□; **it's a bit f.** ça demande de la minutie□

fidelity [fɪ'delɪtɪ] **N 1** *(of people)* fidélité *f*; **they vowed f. to one another** ils se sont juré fidélité **2** *(of translation)* fidélité *f* **3** *Electron* fidélité *f*; **high f.** haute fidélité *f*

fidget ['fɪdʒɪt] **VI** *(be restless)* avoir la bougeotte, gigoter; **stop fidgeting!** arrête de gigoter!; **to f. with sth** jouer avec qch, tripoter qch

N 1 *(restless person)* **she's such a f.** elle ne tient pas en place, elle gigote tout le temps; **don't be such a f.!** arrête de gigoter! **2** *(idiom)* **to have** *or* **to get the fidgets** *(be restless, nervous)* ne pas tenir en place

fidgetiness ['fɪdʒɪtɪnɪs] **N** agitation *f* nerveuse

fidgety ['fɪdʒɪtɪ] **ADJ** qui ne tient pas en place; **I feel f.** je ne tiens plus en place

fiduciary [fɪ'duːʃjərɪ] (*pl* **fiduciaries**) *Law & Fin* **ADJ** fiduciaire

N fiduciaire *mf*

▸▸ *Law & Fin* ***fiduciary account*** compte *m* fiduciaire; ***fiduciary issue*** émission *f* fiduciaire

fief [fiːf] **N** *Hist & Fig* fief *m*

field [fiːld] **N 1** *(piece of land)* champ *m*; **to work in the fields** travailler dans les *ou* aux champs; **f. of wheat** champ *m* de blé; **strawberry f.** plantation *f* de fraisiers

2 *Sport (pitch)* terrain *m*; **the f.** *(defenders* ▸ *in baseball)* les défenseurs *mpl*; *(*▸ *in cricket)* les chasseurs *mpl*; **Smith is way ahead of the (rest of the) f.** Smith est loin devant *ou* devance largement les autres; **there's a very strong f. for the 100 metres** il y a une très belle brochette de concurrents *ou* participants au départ du 100 mètres; **sports** *or* **games f.** terrain *m* de sport; **to take the f.** entrer sur le terrain; **to lead the f.** *(in race)* mener la course, être en tête; *Fig (in sales, area of study)* être en tête; *(of theory)* faire autorité; **our company leads the f. when it comes to fitted kitchens** notre entreprise est en tête du marché pour ce qui est des cuisines encastrées; *Fam* **to play the f.** *(romantically)* avoir autant de liaisons amoureuses que l'on veut□

3 *(of oil, minerals etc)* gisement *m*; **oil/coal/gas f.** gisement *m* de pétrole/de charbon/de gaz

4 *Mil* **f. (of battle)** champ *m* de bataille; **bravery in the f.** bravoure *f* sur le champ de bataille; **to die on the f. of honour** mourir *ou* tomber au champ d'honneur; **the French now held the f.** les Français étaient maintenant maîtres du champ de bataille; **f. of fire** champ *m* de tir

5 *(sphere of activity, knowledge)* domaine *m*; **experts from every f.** des experts provenant de tous les domaines; **to be an expert in one's f.** être expert dans son domaine; **in the political f., in the f. of politics** dans le domaine politique; **what's your f.?, what f. are you in?** quel est ton domaine?; **that's not my f.** ce n'est pas de mon domaine *ou* dans mes compétences

6 *(practice rather than theory)* terrain *m*; **to work/to study in the f.** travailler/étudier sur le terrain; **to go out into the f.** aller sur le terrain

7 *Phys & Opt* champ *m*; **f. of force** champ *m* de force; **f. of vision** champ *m* visuel *ou* de vision; **magnetic f.** champ *m* magnétique

8 *Comput* champ *m*

9 *Her (on coat of arms, coin)* champ *m*; *(on flag)* fond *m*

VT 1 *(team)* présenter; *(player)* faire jouer; *Mil (men, hardware)* réunir; *Pol (candidate)* présenter **2** *(in cricket, baseball* ▸ *ball)* arrêter (et renvoyer); *Fig* **to f. a question** savoir répondre à une question

VI *(in cricket, baseball)* être en défense

▸▸ *Mil* ***field ambulance*** ambulance *f*; *Mil* ***field artillery*** artillerie *f* de campagne; *Mil* ***field battery*** batterie *f* de campagne; *Mil* ***field colours*** *(regimental flags)* couleurs *fpl* du régiment; *Am* ***field corn*** maïs *m* de grande culture; ***field day*** *Sch* journée *f* en plein air; *Mil* jour *m* des grandes manœuvres; *Fam Fig* **to have a f. day** s'en donner à cœur joie; *(do good business)* faire recette□; **if the press find out about this they'll have a f. day!** si les journaux l'apprennent, ils vont s'en donner à cœur joie!; ***field engineer*** ingénieur *m* de chantier *ou* sur le terrain; *Sport* ***field events*** concours *mpl* de saut et de lancer; *Mil* ***field exercise*** exercice *m* en campagne, manœuvre *f*; ***field glasses*** jumelles *fpl*; ***field goal*** *(in American football)* but *m*; *(in basketball)* panier *m*; *Mil* ***field gun*** canon *m*; *Am* ***field hockey*** hockey *m* (sur gazon); *Mil* ***field hospital*** antenne *f* chirurgicale, hôpital *m* de campagne; ***field ice*** banquise *f*; *Mil* ***field kitchen*** cuisine *f* roulante; ***field label*** *(in dictionary)* rubrique *f*, indicateur *m* de domaine; *Mil* ***field marshal*** maréchal *m*; ***field mushroom*** agaric *m* champêtre, rosé *m* des prés; *Mil* ***field officer*** officier *m* supérieur; *Mil* ***field rations*** ration *f* de guerre; ***field sports*** = la chasse et la pêche; ***field study*** étude *f* sur le terrain; *Mil* ***field telegraph*** télégraphe *m* militaire; ***field test*** essai *m* sur le terrain; ***field trials*** *(for machine)* essais *mpl* sur le terrain; *Sch & Univ* ***field trip*** voyage *m* d'études; *(of one afternoon, one day)* sortie *f* d'études; **a geography f. trip** une excursion d'études de géographie; ***field worker*** *(social worker)* travailleur(euse) *m,f* social(e); *(researcher)* chercheur(euse) *m,f* de terrain

fielder ['fiːldə(r)] **N** *(in cricket, baseball)* joueur *m* de l'équipe défendante

fieldmouse ['fiːldmaʊs] (*pl* **fieldmice** [-maɪs]) **N** *Zool* mulot *m*

fiend [fiːnd] **N 1** *(demon)* démon *m*, diable *m* **2** *(evil person)* monstre *m* **3** *Fam (fanatic, freak)* mordu(e) *m,f*, fana *mf*; **tennis f.** fana *mf ou* mordu(e) *m,f* de tennis; **a health f.** un(e) maniaque de la santé; **dope** *or* **drug f.** toxico *mf*; **sex f.** satyre□ *m*; *(in newspaper headline)* maniaque *mf* sexuel

fiendish ['fiːndɪʃ] **ADJ 1** *(fierce* ▸ *cruelty, look)* diabolique, démoniaque **2** *Fam (cunning* ▸ *plan)* diabolique□; *(very difficult* ▸ *problem)* abominable□, atroce□; **to take a f. delight** *or* **pleasure in doing sth** prendre un plaisir diabolique à faire qch

fiendishly ['fiːndɪʃlɪ] **ADV 1** *(cruelly)* diaboliquement **2** *Fam (extremely)* **f. clever** d'une intelligence diabolique; **f. difficult** abominablement *ou* atrocement difficile

fierce [fɪəs] **ADJ 1** *(aggressive* ▸ *animal, person, look, words)* féroce; **to give sb a f. look** jeter un regard féroce à qn **2** *(heat)* torride; *(sun)* ardent, brûlant; *(competition, fighting, loyalty, resistance)* acharné; *(battle, criticism, hatred, temper)* féroce; *(desire)* ardent; **she was f. in her defence of him** elle le défendait avec acharnement **3** *Fam (unpleasant)* désagréable□; **the weather has been f.** il a fait un temps de chien

fiercely ['fɪəslɪ] **ADV 1** *(aggressively)* férocement; **to look f. at sb** regarder qn d'un air féroce **2** *Fig (argue, attack, criticize, fight)* violemment; *(resist)* avec acharnement; *(independent)* farouchement; **to be f. opposed to sth** être ardemment opposé à qch; **it is a f. competitive business** c'est un secteur où la concurrence est acharnée; **to be f. loyal to sb** faire preuve d'une loyauté farouche *ou* à toute épreuve envers qn

fierceness ['fɪəsnɪs] **N 1** *(of animal, look, person)* férocité *f* **2** *Fig (of desire, sun)* ardeur *f*; *(of resistance)* acharnement *m*; *(of criticism)* férocité *f*

fieriness ['faɪərɪnɪs] **N 1** *(of sun)* ardeur *f* **2** *(of speech)* fougue *f*; *(of character)* ardeur *f*, fougue *f*, impétuosité *f*

fiery ['faɪərɪ] **ADJ 1** *(as though on fire* ▸ *heat, sun, coals)* ardent; *(*▸*sky, sunset)* embrasé; **a f. red colour** une couleur rouge feu; **f. red hair** cheveux *mpl* d'un roux flamboyant **2** *(passionate, volatile* ▸ *speech)* passionné, enflammé; *(*▸ *character)* fougueux, impétueux; **f. temper** tempérament *m* fougueux *ou* emporté **3** *(with a hot taste* ▸ *alcoholic drink)* extrêmement fort, brûlant; *(*▸ *curry)* très épicé

▸▸ *Am* ***the fiery cross*** la croix en flammes *(symbole du Ku Klux Klan)*

FIFA ['fi:fə] **N** *(abbr* **Fédération Internationale de Football Association***)* FIFA *f*

fife [faɪf] **N** *Mus* fifre *m*

FIFO ['faɪfəʊ] **N** *Comput & Ind (abbr* **first in, first out***)* PEPS

fifteen [fɪf'ti:n] **N 1** *(number, numeral)* quinze *m inv* **2** *(in rugby)* quinze *m*; **the school/Scottish f.** le quinze de l'école/d'Écosse

PRON quinze; **about f.** une quinzaine

ADJ quinze; **about f. people** une quinzaine de personnes; **his f. minutes of fame** son quart d'heure de célébrité; *see also* **five**

fifteenth [fɪf'ti:nθ] **N 1** *(fraction)* quinzième *m* **2** *(in series)* quinzième *mf* **3** *(of month)* quinze *m inv*

ADJ quinzième; *see also* **fifth**

fifth [fɪfθ] **N 1** *(fraction)* cinquième *m*

2 *(in series)* cinquième *mf*

3 *(of month)* cinq *m inv*; **the f.** le cinq; **on the f.** le cinq; **the f. of July, July the f.**, *Am* **July f.** le cinq juillet; **today is the f.** nous sommes le cinq aujourd'hui; **the f. of November** = jour anniversaire de la Conspiration des poudres aussi appelé "Guy Fawkes' Day"

4 *Mus* quinte *f*

5 *Aut* cinquième *f*; **in f.** en cinquième

6 *Am (Fifth Amendment)* Cinquième Amendement *m (de la Constitution des États-Unis, permettant à un accusé de ne pas répondre à une question risquant de jouer en sa défaveur)*; *Hum* **I plead the F.** je ne parlerai qu'en présence de mon avocat

ADJ cinquième; **f. finger** petit doigt *m*; *Aut* **f. gear** cinquième vitesse *f*; *Aut* **to go** *or* **to change into f. gear** passer en cinquième *f*; **a f. part** un cinquième; **on the f. day of the month** le cinq du mois; **in f. place** en cinquième position, à la cinquième place; **f. from the end/right** cinquième en partant de la fin/droite; **on the f. floor** *Br* au cinquième étage; *Am* au quatrième étage; *Am* **to feel like a f. wheel** avoir l'impression d'être la dernière roue du carrosse; **George the F.** Georges Cinq

ADV cinquièmement; *(in contest)* en cinquième position, à la cinquième place; **she came** *or* **was f.** *(in race, exam etc)* elle est arrivée cinquième

▸▸ ***Fifth Amendment*** Cinquième Amendement *m (de la Constitution des États-Unis, permettant à un accusé de ne pas répondre à une question risquant de jouer en sa défaveur)*; ***Fifth Avenue*** la Cinquième avenue; **she's very F. Avenue** elle est très Cinquième avenue *(fait référence à l'élite sociale new-yorkaise)*; *Pol* ***fifth column*** cinquième colonne *f*; *Pol* ***fifth columnist*** membre *m* de la cinquième colonne; *Br Sch* ***fifth form*** classe *f* de seconde; *Am Sch* ***fifth grade*** = classe de l'école primaire (9 à 10 ans); ***the Fifth Republic*** la Cinquième *ou* Vème République

fifth-generation **ADJ** *Comput* de cinquième génération

fifthly ['fɪfθlɪ] **ADV** cinquièmement, en cinquième lieu

fifth-rate **ADJ** *Fam* médiocre

fiftieth ['fɪftɪəθ] **N 1** *(fraction)* cinquantième *m* **2** *(in series)* cinquantième *mf*

ADJ cinquantième; *see also* **fifth**

fifty ['fɪftɪ] *(pl* **fifties***)* **N 1** *(number, numeral)* cinquante *m inv*; **I'm waiting for a number f. (bus)** j'attends le (bus numéro) cinquante; *Aut* **to do f.** faire du quatre-vingts; **to be f.** *(in age)* avoir cinquante ans; **he must be close to** *or* **getting on for f.** il doit approcher de la cinquantaine; **the fifties** les années cinquante; **in the early/late fifties** au début/à la fin des années cinquante; **the temperature will be in the high fifties** la température sera environ de quinze degrés; **she is in her fifties** elle a entre cinquante et soixante ans; **to be in one's early/late fifties** avoir une petite cinquantaine/la cinquantaine bien sonnée **2** *Am (money)* billet *m* de cinquante (dollars)

PRON cinquante; **about f.** une cinquantaine; **I need f. (of them)** il m'en faut cinquante, j'en ai besoin de cinquante; **there are f. (of them)** *(people)* ils sont cinquante; *(objects)* il y en a cinquante; **all f. of them left** tous les cinquante sont partis, ils sont partis tous les cinquante

ADJ cinquante; **f. people** cinquante personnes; **about f. people** une cinquantaine de personnes; **on page f.** (à la) page cinquante; **they live at number f.** ils habitent au numéro cinquante; **to be f. years old** avoir cinquante ans; **he works a f.-hour week** il travaille cinquante heures par semaine

COMP f.-one cinquante et un; **f.-two** cinquante-deux; **f.-first** cinquante et unième; **f.-second** cinquante-deuxième

fifty-fifty **ADJ on a f. basis** moitié-moitié, fifty-fifty; **his chances of winning/surviving are f.** il a une chance sur deux de gagner/de s'en tirer; **the animal's chances of survival are no more than f.** les chances de survie de l'animal ne dépassent pas cinquante pour cent

ADV moitié-moitié, fifty-fifty; **to split the profits f.** partager les bénéfices à parts égales; **to go f. (with sb on sth)** faire moitié-moitié *ou* fifty-fifty (avec qn pour qch); **I went f. with my brother** je me suis mis de moitié avec mon frère

fig [fɪg] **N** *(fruit)* figue *f*; *(tree)* figuier *m*; *Fam Old-fashioned* **I don't give** *or* **care a f.** je m'en moque comme de ma première chemise; **I don't give** *or* **care a f. what she thinks** je me contrefiche de ce qu'elle pense

▸▸ ***fig leaf*** *Bot* feuille *f* de figuier; *(on statue, in painting)* feuille *f* de vigne; *Fig* camouflage *m*; ***fig tree*** figuier *m*

FIGHT [faɪt]

N
- bagarre **1**
- combat **1**
- dispute **1**
- combativité **2**

VT
- se battre contre
- lutter contre

VI
- se battre
- se disputer
- combattre

(pt & pp **fought** [fɔ:t]*)*

N 1 *(physical)* bagarre *f*; *(verbal)* dispute *f*; *(of army, boxer)* combat *m*, affrontement *m*; *(against disease, poverty etc)* lutte *f*, combat *m*; **the f. for life** la lutte pour la vie; **her f. against cancer** sa lutte contre le cancer; **the f. for the leadership of the party** la lutte pour la tête du parti; **do you want a f.?** tu veux te battre?; **he enjoys a good f.** *(physical)* il aime la bagarre *ou* les bagarres; *(verbal)* il aime les disputes; *(boxing match)* il aime les bons combats de boxe; **to have** *or* **to get into a f. with sb** *(physical)* se battre avec qn; *(verbal)* se disputer avec qn; **to pick a f. (with sb)** chercher la bagarre (avec qn); **are you trying to pick a f. (with me)?** tu me provoques?, tu cherches la bagarre?; **a f. to the death** une lutte à mort; **are you going to the f.?** *(boxing match)* est-ce que tu vas voir le combat?; **to put up a (good) f.** (bien) se défendre; **to make a f. of it** se défendre avec acharnement; **to give in without (putting up) a f.** capituler sans (opposer de) résistance

2 *(fighting spirit)* combativité *f*; **there's not much f. left in him** il a perdu beaucoup de sa combativité; **he still has a lot of f. left in him** il n'a pas dit son dernier mot; **the news of the defeat took all the f. out of us** la nouvelle de la défaite nous a fait perdre tout cœur à nous battre *ou* nous a enlevé le courage de nous battre; **to show f.** montrer de la combativité, ne pas se laisser faire

VT *(person, animal)* se battre contre; *(boxer)* combattre (contre), se battre contre; *(match)* disputer; *(disease, terrorism, fire etc)* lutter contre, combattre; *(new measure, decision)* combattre; *(illness, temptation)* lutter contre; **to f. a duel** se battre en duel; **to f. a battle** livrer (une) bataille; *Fig* **I'm not going to f. your battles for you** c'est à toi de te débrouiller; **to f. a court case** *(lawyer)* défendre une cause; *(plaintiff, defendant)* être en procès; **to f. an election** *(politician)* se présenter à une élection; *Br* **I'll f. you for it** on réglera ça par une bagarre; **I'll f. you for custody** je me battrai contre toi pour obtenir la garde des enfants; **to f. a losing battle (against sth)** livrer une bataille perdue d'avance (contre qch); *Rel* **to f. the good f.** combattre pour la bonne cause; **she fought the urge to laugh** elle essayait de réprimer une forte envie de rire; **don't f. it** *(pain, emotion)* n'essaie pas de lutter; **you've got to f. it** il faut que tu te battes; **to f. one's way through the crowd/the undergrowth** se frayer un passage à travers la foule/les broussailles; **to f. one's way to the top of one's profession** se battre pour atteindre le sommet de sa profession

VI *(physically* ▸ *person, soldier)* se battre; *(*▸ *boxer)* combattre; *(*▸ *two boxers)* s'affronter; *(verbally)* se disputer; *(against disease, injustice, sleep etc)* lutter; **to f. against the enemy** combattre l'ennemi; **to f. to the death/the last** se battre à mort/jusqu'à la fin; **he fought in the war** il a fait la guerre; **they were fighting with each other** *(physically)* ils étaient en train de se battre; *(verbally)* ils étaient en train de se disputer; **they were fighting over some islands/who would sleep where** ils se battaient pour des îles/pour décider qui allait dormir où; **the children were fighting over the last biscuit** les enfants se disputaient (pour avoir) le dernier biscuit; **to f. for one's country** se battre pour sa patrie; **to f. for one's rights/to clear one's name** lutter pour ses droits/pour prouver son innocence; **they fought for the leadership of the party** ils se sont disputé la direction du parti; **he fought for breath** il se débattait *ou* il luttait pour respirer; **to f. for one's life** *(ill person)* lutter contre la mort; *Fig (in race, competition)* se battre avec la dernière énergie, se démener; **to go down fighting** se battre jusqu'au bout; **to f. shy of doing sth** tout faire pour éviter de faire qch; **to f. shy of sb** éviter qn

▸▸ ***the fight game*** la boxe

▸ **fight back** **VT SEP** *(tears)* refouler; *(despair, fear, laughter)* réprimer

VI *(in physical or verbal dispute)* se défendre, riposter; *(in boxing, football match)* se reprendre; *(in race)* revenir

▸ **fight down** **VT SEP** *(passion, resistance)* vaincre; *(impulse, urge)* réprimer

▸ **fight off** **VT SEP** *(attack, enemy, advances)* repousser; *(sleep)* combattre; *(disease)* résister à; **she has to f. men off** *(has a lot of admirers)* elle a des admirateurs à la pelle *ou* à ne plus savoir qu'en faire

▸ **fight out** **VT SEP just leave them to f. it out** laisse-les se bagarrer et régler cela entre eux

fighter ['faɪtə(r)] **N 1** *(person who fights)* combattant(e) *m,f*; *(boxer)* boxeur(euse) *m,f*; *Fig* **he's a f.** c'est un battant **2** *(plane)* avion *m* de chasse, chasseur *m*

COMP *(pilot)* de chasseur, d'avion de chasse; *(squadron)* de chasseurs, d'avions de chasse; *(plane)* de chasse

fighter-bomber **N** *Mil* chasseur *m* bombardier

fighting ['faɪtɪŋ] **N** *(UNCOUNT) (physical)* bagarre *f*, bagarres *fpl*; *(verbal)* dispute *f*, disputes *fpl*, bagarre *f*, bagarres *fpl*; *Mil* combat *m*, combats *mpl*; **f. broke out between police and fans** une bagarre s'est déclenchée entre la police et les fans; **there has been fierce f. in all parts of the country** des combats acharnés ont eu lieu dans l'ensemble du pays; **f. is not allowed in the playground** il est interdit de se bagarrer dans la cour; **to be in with** *or* **to have a f. chance** avoir de bonnes chances; **to be f. fit** être dans une forme éblouissante, avoir la forme olympique; **f. spirit** esprit *m* combatif; **that's f. talk!** c'est un langage offensif!

COMP *(forces, unit)* de combat

▸▸ ***fighting cock*** coq *m* de combat; *Ich* ***fighting fish*** poisson *m* combattant; ***fighting fund*** fonds *m* de solidarité; *Mil* ***fighting men*** combattants *mpl*; *Boxing* ***fighting weight*** poids *m* optimal *(pour un boxeur)*

figment ['fɪgmənt] **N a f. of the imagination** un produit *ou* une création de l'imagination

figurative [*Br* 'fɪgərətɪv, *Am* 'fɪgjərətɪv] **ADJ 1** *(language, meaning)* figuré; **in the f. sense** au (sens) figuré **2** *Art* figuratif

figuratively [*Br* ˈfɪgərətɪvlɪ, *Am* ˈfɪgjərətɪvlɪ] **ADV 1** *(speak, write)* au (sens) figuré, métaphoriquement; **f. speaking,...** métaphoriquement parlant,... **2** *Art* figurativement

FIGURE [*Br* ˈfɪgə(r), *Am* ˈfɪgjər]

N	
• chiffre **1**	• ligne **2**
• silhouette **3**	• personnage **4, 5**
• figure **6, 7, 9**	• figurine **10**
VT	
• penser **1**	• arriver à comprendre **2**
VI	
• figurer **1**	• sembler logique **2**

N 1 *(number, symbol)* chiffre *m*; *(amount)* somme *f*; **six-f. number** nombre *m* de six chiffres; **figures** *(for project etc)* détails *mpl* chiffrés; *(statistics)* statistiques *fpl*; **the figures for 2005** les statistiques de 2005; **his salary is in** *or* **runs to six figures** il gagne plus d'un million d'euros; **our takings have reached four figures** nous avons décroché les quatre chiffres; **in round figures** en chiffres ronds; **to be in double figures** *(inflation, unemployment)* dépasser la barre *ou* le seuil des 10 pour cent; **to get inflation down to single figures** réduire l'inflation à un taux inférieur à dix pour cent; **to put a f. on sth** *(give cost)* évaluer le coût de *ou* chiffrer qch; **I couldn't put a f. on the number of people there** je ne pourrais pas dire combien de personnes il y avait; **she's good at figures** elle est bonne en calcul; **he has no head for figures** il n'est pas doué en calcul; **name your f.** *(to purchaser, seller)* quel est votre prix?; **to find a mistake in the figures** trouver une erreur de calcul

2 *(human shape)* ligne *f*; **she has a good f.** elle a une jolie silhouette, elle est bien faite; **to look after one's f.** faire attention à sa ligne; **to keep/to lose one's f.** garder/perdre la ligne; **a fine f. of a woman/man** une femme/un homme qui a de l'allure; **to cut a fine f.** avoir beaucoup d'allure; **to cut a sorry f.** faire piètre figure; **he was a sorry f. standing there on the doorstep** *(wet, dirty etc)* il faisait piètre figure, debout sur le pas de la porte

3 *(human outline)* silhouette *f*; **a f. appeared on the horizon** une silhouette est apparue à l'horizon

4 *(character in novel, film, painting etc)* personnage *m*; **the group of figures on the left** le groupe de personnes à gauche; **key f.** personnage *m* central; **f. of fun** objet *m* de risée; **a hate f., a f. of hate** un objet de haine

5 *(person)* personnage *m*; **a distinguished f.** une personnalité

6 *(in geometry, skating, dancing)* figure *f*

7 *(illustration, diagram)* figure *f*

8 *(pattern ▸ on material)* dessin *m*

9 *(rhetorical)* **f. of speech** figure *f* de rhétorique; **it was just a f. of speech** ce n'était qu'une façon de parler

10 *(statuette)* figurine *f*

VT 1 *Fam (reckon)* penser❑; **we figured something like that must have happened** nous pensions *ou* nous nous doutions bien que quelque chose de ce genre était arrivé❑

2 *Am Fam (understand)* arriver à comprendre❑; **we couldn't f. it** nous n'arrivions pas à comprendre *ou* saisir❑

3 *(decorate ▸ material, velvet etc)* façonner; *(▸ silk)* brocher

4 *Mus* chiffrer

VI 1 *(appear)* figurer, apparaître; **does he f. in your plans?** est-ce qu'il figure dans tes projets?; **where do I f. in all this?** quelle est ma place dans tout cela?; **guilt figures quite a lot in his novels** la culpabilité a *ou* tient une place relativement importante dans ses romans; **she figured prominently in the scandal** elle a été très impliquée dans le scandale

2 *Fam (make sense)* sembler logique *ou* normal❑; **that figures!** *(I'm not surprised)* tu m'étonnes!; *(that makes sense)* c'est logique❑; **it figures that he'd do that** ça paraît logique *ou* normal qu'il ait fait ça❑; *Am* **it just doesn't f.** ça n'a pas de sens❑; *Am* **go f.!** qui aurait imaginé ça?❑

▸▸ *Br* ***figure of eight***, *Am* ***figure eight*** huit *m*; *(knot)* (nœud *m* en) huit *m*; ***figure skater*** patineur(euse) *m,f* artistique; ***figure skating*** **N** patinage *m* artistique **COMP** *(champion, championship)* de patinage artistique

▸**figure on** **VT INSEP** *Fam* **1** *(plan on)* compter sur❑; **to f. on doing sth** compter faire qch❑; **you didn't f. on that (happening), did you?** tu ne comptais *ou* pensais pas que ça arriverait, hein?❑, tu ne comptais pas là-dessus, hein?❑ **2** *Am (anticipate)* s'attendre à, prévoir; **with the roadworks you should f. on an hour's delay** il faut compter une heure de plus avec les travaux

▸**figure out** **VT SEP 1** *(understand)* arriver à comprendre; **we couldn't f. it out** nous n'arrivions pas à comprendre *ou* saisir **2** *(work out ▸ sum, cost etc)* calculer; **f. it out for yourself** réfléchis donc un peu; **she still hasn't figured out how to do it** elle n'a toujours pas trouvé comment faire

▸**figure up** **VT SEP** *Am Fam* faire le total de❑

> Note that when referring to the human body, the French noun **figure** means **face**.

figured [*Br* ˈfɪgəd, *Am* fɪgjəd] **ADJ 1** *(material, velvet etc)* façonné; *(silk)* broché **2** *Mus (counterpoint)* figuré; *(bass)* chiffré

figurehead [*Br* ˈfɪgəhed, *Am* ˈfɪgjəhed] **N** *Naut* figure *f* de proue; *Fig (of organization, society)* représentant(e) *m,f* nominal(e); *Pej* homme *m* de paille

figure-hugging [-ˈhʌgɪŋ] **ADJ** *Br (garment)* moulant

figurine [*Br* ˈfɪgəriːn, *Am* ˌfɪgjəˈriːn] **N** figurine *f*

Fiji [ˈfiːdʒiː] **N** Fidji; **the F. Islands** les îles *fpl* Fidji

Fijian [ˌfiːˈdʒiːən] **N 1** *(person)* Fidjien(enne) *m,f* **2** *Ling* fidjien *m*

ADJ fidjien

filament [ˈfɪləmənt] **N 1** *Elec* filament *m* **2** *Biol* filament *m*, filet *m*

▸▸ ***filament lamp*** lampe *f* à incandescence

filbert [ˈfɪlbət] **N** *(nut)* = espèce de grosse noisette

filch [fɪltʃ] **VT** *Fam (steal)* piquer

FILE [faɪl]

N	
• chemise **1**	• classeur **1**
• dossier **2**	• fichier **2, 3**
• file **4**	• lime **5**
VT	
• classer **1**	• intenter **2**
• limer **4**	
VI	
• faire du classement **1**	• entrer/sortir/*etc* à la file **2**

N 1 *(folder)* chemise *f*; *(box)* classeur *m*; **accordion f.** classeur *m* accordéon

2 *(dossier, documents)* dossier *m*; *(series or system of files)* fichier *m*; **the f. on James Brown, the James Brown f.** le dossier James Brown; **this letter belongs in the customer f.** cette lettre va dans le fichier clients; **to have/to keep sth on f.** avoir/garder qch dans ses dossiers; **it's on f.** c'est dans les dossiers, c'est classé; **we have placed your CV on f.** *or* **in our files** nous avons classé votre CV dans nos dossiers; **to have/to keep a f. on** avoir/garder un dossier sur; **to open/to close a f. on** ouvrir/fermer un dossier sur; **the police have closed their f. on the case** la police a classé l'affaire; **he's been on our f.** *or* **files for a long time** cela fait longtemps qu'il est dans nos dossiers

3 *Comput* fichier *m*; **data on f.** données *fpl* sur fichier; **data f.** fichier *m* de données

4 *(row, line)* file *f*; **in single** *or* **Indian f.** en *ou* à la file indienne

5 *(for metal, fingernails)* lime *f*

VT 1 *(documents, information)* classer; **it's filed under B** c'est classé à la lettre B; **it's filed under "invoices"** c'est classé dans le dossier "factures"

2 *Law* **to f. a suit against sb** intenter un procès à qn; **to f. a complaint (with the police/the manager)** déposer une plainte (au commissariat/auprès du directeur); **to f. a claim** déposer une demande; **to f. a claim for damages** intenter un procès en dommages-intérêts; **to f. a petition in bankruptcy** déposer son bilan; *Am* **to f. one's tax return** remplir sa déclaration d'impôts

3 *Journ* **to f. a story** boucler un sujet; **to f. copy** rapporter une copie

4 *(metal)* limer; **to f. one's fingernails** se limer les ongles; **to f. through sth** limer qch

VI 1 *(classify documents, information)* faire du classement

2 *(walk one behind the other)* **they filed up the hill** ils ont monté la colline en file (indienne) *ou* les uns derrière les autres; **the troops filed past the general** les troupes ont défilé devant le général; **the crowd filed slowly past the coffin** la foule a défilé lentement devant le cercueil; **to f. into a room** entrer dans une pièce à la *ou* en file; **to f. out of a room** sortir d'une pièce à la *ou* en file; **they all filed in/out** ils sont tous entrés/sortis à la file

▸▸ *Am* ***file cabinet*** classeur *m*; ***file card*** fiche *f* (de classeur); *Am* ***file clerk*** documentaliste *mf*; *Comput* ***file compression*** compression *f* de fichiers; *Comput* ***file conversion*** conversion *f* de fichiers; ***file copy*** copie *f* à classer; ***file divider*** carte-guide *f*; *Comput* ***file extension*** extension *f* du nom de fichier; *Am TV* ***file footage*** images *fpl* d'archive; *Comput* ***file format*** format *m* de fichier; *Comput* ***file management*** gestion *f ou* tenue *f* des fichiers; *Comput* ***file management system*** système *m* de gestion de fichiers; *Comput* ***file manager*** gestionnaire *m* des fichiers; *Comput* ***file name*** nom *m* de fichier; *Comput* ***file name extension*** extension *f* du nom de fichier; ***file number*** *(of document in file)* cote *f*; *Comput* ***file protection*** protection *f* de fichiers; ***file separator*** carte-guide *f*; *Comput* ***file server*** serveur *m* de fichiers; *Comput* ***file sharing*** partage *m* de fichiers; *Comput* ***file structure*** structure *f* de fichiers; *Comput* ***file transfer*** transfert *m* de fichiers; *Comput* ***file transfer protocol*** protocole *m* de transfert de fichiers; ***file trolley*** bac *m* roulant; *Comput* ***file viewer*** visualiseur *m*

▸**file away** **VT SEP 1** *(documents)* classer **2** *(rough edges)* polir à la lime; *(excess material)* enlever à la lime

▸**file down** **VT SEP 1** *(remove by filing ▸ rough edge)* enlever à la lime, limer **2** *(smooth by filing ▸ metal, nails, surface)* polir à la lime, limer; *(▸ horseshoe)* raboter

▸**file off** **VT SEP** *(remove by filing ▸ rough edge)* enlever à la lime, limer

file-compatible **ADJ** *Comput* compatible du point de vue des fichiers

filer [ˈfaɪlə(r)] **N** *Comput* classeur *m*, gestionnaire *m* de fichiers et de répertoires

file-sharing **ADJ** d'échange de fichiers

filial [ˈfɪljəl] **ADJ** filial

filibuster [ˈfɪlɪˌbʌstə(r)] **N 1** *Pol* obstruction *f* (parlementaire) **2** *Hist (pirate)* flibustier *m*

VI faire de l'obstruction

filigree [ˈfɪlɪgriː] **N** filigrane *m*

COMP en *ou* de filigrane

filing [ˈfaɪlɪŋ] **N 1** *(of documents)* classement *m*; *(for long-term storage)* archivage *m*; **I do the f.** je m'occupe du classement; **I still have a lot of f. to do** j'ai encore beaucoup de choses à classer **2** *Law (of complaint, claim)* dépôt *m*; *(of petition)* enregistrement *m* **3** *(of metal)* limage *m*

• **filings** **NPL** *(of metal)* limaille *f*

▸▸ ***filing cabinet*** classeur *m*; ***filing clerk*** documentaliste *mf*; ***filing system*** méthode *f* de classement; ***filing tray*** corbeille *f* pour correspondance à classer

Filipino [ˌfɪlɪˈpiːnəʊ] *(pl* **Filipinos***)* **N 1** *(person)* Philippin(e) *m,f* **2** *(language)* tagalog *m*, tagal *m*

ADJ philippin

FILL [fɪl]

VT	
• remplir **1**	• boucher **2**
• occuper **3, 4**	• répondre à **5**
VI	
• se remplir	

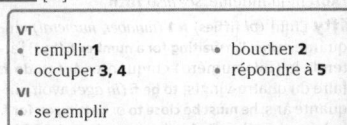

N to eat one's f. manger à sa faim, se rassasier; **to drink one's f.** boire tout son soûl; **when they had eaten their f.** quand ils eurent mangé tout leur content; *Fam* **I've had my f. of it/her** j'en ai assez/assez d'elle❑

VT 1 *(cup, glass, bottle)* remplir; *(room, streets* ▸ *of people, smoke, laughter)* envahir; *(chocolates)* fourrer; *(cake, pie)* garnir; *(vegetables)* farcir; *(pipe)* bourrer; *(cart etc)* charger; **to f. a page with writing** remplir une page d'écriture; **wind filled the sails** le vent a gonflé les voiles; **she filled his head with nonsense** elle lui a bourré le crâne de bêtises; **to be filled with people** *(room, street)* être plein *ou* rempli de gens; **to be filled with horror/admiration** être rempli d'horreur/d'admiration; **she was filled with horror at the news** cette nouvelle l'a remplie d'horreur; **to be filled with hope** être plein d'espoir; **to be filled with fear/envy** être dévoré de peur/d'envie; **it filled me with sorrow** cela m'a profondément peiné; **such were the thoughts that filled his mind** telles étaient les pensées qui occupaient son esprit

2 *(plug* ▸ *hole)* boucher; *(*▸ *tooth)* plomber; **to have a tooth filled** se faire plomber une dent; **the product filled a gap in the market** le produit a comblé un vide sur le marché; *Fam* **to f. sb full of lead** *(shoot)* plomber qn

3 *(position, vacancy* ▸ *of employee)* occuper; *(*▸ *of employer)* pourvoir; **to f. the office of president** remplir les fonctions de président; **the post has been filled** le poste a été pris *ou* pourvu

4 *(occupy* ▸ *time)* occuper; **reading fills my evenings** la lecture remplit mes soirées

5 *(meet* ▸ *requirement)* répondre à; *Fam* **to f. the bill** faire l'affaire

6 *(supply)* **to f. an order** *(in bar, restaurant)* apporter ce qui a été commandé; *(for stationery, equipment etc)* livrer une commande; **to f. a prescription** préparer une ordonnance

VI *(room, bath, bus)* se remplir; *(sail)* se gonfler; **her eyes filled with tears** ses yeux se sont remplis de larmes

▸▸ *Cin* ***fill light*** éclairage *m* d'appoint

▸ **fill in VT SEP 1** *(hole, window, door)* boucher, combler; *(ditch)* remblayer; **he filled it in in green** *(outline)* il l'a colorié *ou* rempli en vert; **to f. in the gaps in one's knowledge** combler ses lacunes

2 *(complete* ▸ *form, questionnaire, cheque stub)* compléter, remplir; *(insert* ▸ *name, missing word)* insérer; **to f. in the blanks** remplir les blancs

3 *(bring up to date)* mettre au courant; **to f. sb in on sth** mettre qn au courant de qch

4 *(use* ▸ *time)* occuper; **he's just filling in time** il fait ça pour s'occuper *ou* pour occuper son temps; **I've got a couple of months to f. in** je dois occuper mon temps pendant environ deux mois

VI faire un remplacement; **to f. in for sb** remplacer qn

▸ **fill out VT SEP 1** *(complete* ▸ *form, questionnaire, cheque stub)* compléter, remplir **2** *(pad out* ▸ *essay, speech)* étoffer

VI 1 *(cheeks)* se remplir; *(person)* s'étoffer **2** *(sails)* se gonfler

▸ **fill up VT SEP 1** *(make full)* remplir; *(person with food)* rassasier; **he filled the car up** il a fait le plein (d'essence); *Aut* **f. her** *or* **it up, please** le plein, s'il vous plaît **2** *(fill in* ▸ *hole)* boucher; *(*▸ *ditch)* remblayer **3** *(use* ▸ *day, time)* occuper

VI se remplir; **to f. up with petrol** faire le plein d'essence; **don't f. up on biscuits, you two!** ne vous gavez pas de biscuits, vous deux!

filler ['fɪlə(r)] **N 1** *(for holes, cracks)* mastic *m*; *(for cavity, open space)* matière *f* de remplissage

2 *(funnel)* entonnoir *m*

3 *(in quilt, beanbag etc)* matière *f* de rembourrage; *(in cigar)* tripe *f*

4 *Press & TV* bouche-trou *m*

5 *Ling* **f. (word)** mot *m* de remplissage

▸▸ *Aut* ***filler cap*** bouchon *m* du réservoir d'essence; *Tech* ***filler metal*** métal *m* d'apport; *Tech* ***filler rod*** baguette *f* de soudure

fillet ['fɪlɪt] **N 1** *(of meat, fish)* filet *m*

2 *(for hair)* ruban *m*

3 *Tech (strip* ▸ *of metal, wood)* ruban *m*, bande *f*; *(*▸ *raised projection)* collet *m*, bourrelet *m*

4 *Tech* **f. (weld)** soudure *f* d'angle

5 *Archit* congé *m*, filet *m*

6 *Typ* filet *m*

VT *(prepare* ▸ *meat, fish)* préparer; *(cut into fillets* ▸ *fish)* faire des filets dans, lever les filets de; *(*▸ *meat)* faire des steaks dans; **filleted sole** filets *mpl* de sole

▸▸ ***fillet steak*** filet *m* de bœuf; **two pieces of f. steak, two f. steaks** deux biftecks dans le filet

filling ['fɪlɪŋ] **N 1** *(in tooth)* plombage *m*; **I had to have a f.** il a fallu qu'on me fasse un plombage **2** *Culin (for cake, pie, sandwich)* garniture *f*; *(for vegetables, poultry* ▸ *savoury)* farce *f*; **they all have different fillings** *(chocolates)* ils sont tous fourrés différemment **3** *(of hole)* comblement *m*

ADJ *(foodstuff)* bourratif; **it was very f.** cela m'a rassasié

▸▸ ***filling in 1*** *(of hole, window, door)* comblement *m*; *(of ditch)* remblayage *m* **2** *(of form, questionnaire)* rédaction *f*; ***filling out*** *(of sails, balloon)* gonflement *m*; ***filling station*** station-service *f*, station *f* d'essence; ***filling up 1*** *(of container)* remplissage *m* **2** *(of hole)* bouchage *m*; *(of ditch)* remblayage *m* **3** *(of form)* rédaction *f*

fillip ['fɪlɪp] **N** coup *m* de fouet; **to give sb/sth a f.** donner un coup de fouet à qn/qch

fill-up **N** *Aut* plein *m*; **do you want a f.?** *(more to drink)* je te remplis ton verre?

filly ['fɪlɪ] *(pl* **fillies***)* **N 1** *(horse)* pouliche *f* **2** *Fam Old-fashioned (girl)* fille ◻ *f*

film [fɪlm] **N 1** *esp Br Cin* film *m*; **the f. of the book** le film tiré du livre; **full-length/short-length f.** (film *m*) long/court métrage *m*; **to shoot** *or* **to make a f. (about sth)** tourner *ou* faire un film (sur qch); **the f.'s on at the local cinema** le film passe au cinéma du coin; **to be in films** faire du cinéma

2 *Phot* pellicule *f*; **I left a f. to be developed** j'ai laissé une pellicule à développer; **a roll of f.** une pellicule

3 *(thin layer* ▸ *of oil, mist, dust)* film *m*, pellicule *f*; *Med (over eye)* taie *f*

4 *(sheet)* film *m*; **plastic f.** film *m* plastique

5 *(UNCOUNT) Typ* films *mpl*; **a piece of f.** un film

COMP *Cin (critic, star, producer)* de cinéma; *(clip)* d'un film; *(sequence)* de film; *(archives, award, rights)* cinématographique

VT *(event, person)* filmer; *Cin (scene)* filmer, tourner; *(novel)* porter à l'écran

VI *(record)* filmer; *Cin* tourner; **we start filming next week** on commence à tourner la semaine prochaine; **her novels don't f. well** ses romans ne se prêtent pas à l'adaptation cinématographique

▸▸ ***film actor*** acteur *m* de cinéma; ***film actress*** actrice *f* de cinéma; ***film buff*** cinéphile *mf*; ***film buyer*** acheteur(euse) *m,f* de films; ***film camera*** caméra *f*; ***film classification*** classification *f* des films; ***film club*** ciné-club *m*; ***film crew*** équipe *f* de tournage; ***film director*** metteur *m* en scène; ***film editor*** monteur(euse) *m,f*; ***film festival*** festival *m* cinématographique *ou* du cinéma; ***the film industry*** l'industrie *f* cinématographique *ou* du cinéma; ***film laboratory, film lab*** laboratoire *m* de film, labo *m* de film; ***film leader*** amorce *f*; ***film library*** cinémathèque *f*; ***film maker*** cinéaste *mf*; ***film noir*** film *m* noir; ***film premiere*** première *f*; ***film producer*** producteur(trice) *m,f* de cinéma; ***film projector*** appareil *m* de projection; ***film review*** critique *f* cinématographique; ***film reviewer*** critique *mf* de cinéma; ***film school*** école *f* de cinéma; ***film script*** scénario *m*; ***film set*** plateau *m* de tournage; *Phot* ***film speed*** sensibilité *f* d'une pellicule; ***film stock*** film *m* vierge; ***film strip*** bande *f* (de film) fixe; ***film studies*** filmologie *f*; ***film studio*** studio *m* (de cinéma); ***film synchronizer*** synchroniseuse *f*; ***film test*** bout *m* d'essai

▸ **film over VI** s'embuer, se voiler; **to f. over with tears** s'embuer de larmes

filmgoer ['fɪlm,gəʊə(r)] **N** amateur *m* de cinéma, cinéphile *mf*; **she is a regular f.** elle va régulièrement au cinéma

filmic ['fɪlmɪk] **ADJ** *Cin* cinématographique

filming ['fɪlmɪŋ] **N** *Cin* tournage *m*

filmless camera ['fɪlmlɪs-] **N** *Phot* caméra *f* sans film

film-making **N** production *f* cinématographique

filmography [fɪl'mɒgrəfɪ] **N** filmographie *f*

filmset ['fɪlmset] *(pt & pp* **filmset**, *cont* **filmsetting***)* **VT** *Br Typ* photocomposer

filmsetter ['fɪlm,setə(r)] **N** *Br Typ (machine)* photocomposeuse *f*; *(person)* photocompositeur (trice) *m,f*

filmsetting ['fɪlm,setɪŋ] **N** *Br Typ* photocomposition *f*

filmy ['fɪlmɪ] *(compar* **filmier**, *superl* **filmiest***)* **ADJ** *(material)* léger, vaporeux, aérien

Filofax® ['faɪləʊfæks] **N** organiseur *m*

filter ['fɪltə(r)] **N 1** *Chem, Comput, Tech & Phot* filtre *m*

2 *Br Aut* flèche *f* lumineuse *(autorisant le dégagement des voitures à droite ou à gauche)*

3 *(on cigarette)* filtre *m*

4 *Elec & Electron* filtre *m*; **frequency f.** filtre *m* de fréquences

VT *(coffee, oil, water, light etc)* filtrer; *(air)* épurer

VI 1 *(coffee, oil, water, light, air etc)* filtrer **2** *Br Aut* suivre la voie de dégagement; **the cars filtered to the left** les voitures ont suivi la voie de dégagement vers la gauche

▸▸ *Constr* ***filter bed*** couche *f* de filtration; ***filter coffee*** café *m* filtre; *Aut* ***filter element*** cartouche *f* filtrante; *Br Aut* ***filter lane*** voie *f* de dégagement; ***filter paper*** papier *m* filtre; ***filter tip*** *(tip)* (bout *m*) filtre *m*; *(cigarette)* cigarette *f* (bout) filtre

▸ **filter down VI** filtrer; **the information finally filtered down to them** les informations ont fini par filtrer jusqu'à eux

▸ **filter out VT SEP** *(sediment, impurities)* éliminer par filtrage *ou* filtration; *Fig (in selection procedure etc)* éliminer

VI *(people)* sortir petit à petit; *(news, information)* filtrer

▸ **filter through VT INSEP the light filtered through the branches** la lumière filtrait à travers les branches

VI *(pass slowly)* passer lentement; **the news soon filtered through** les nouvelles n'ont pas tardé à filtrer

filterable ['fɪltərəbəl] **ADJ** *Med (virus)* filtrant

filtering ['fɪltərɪŋ] **N** filtrage *m*, filtration *f*

▸▸ *Comput* ***filtering software*** logiciel *m* de filtrage

filth [fɪlθ] **N** *(UNCOUNT)* **1** *(on skin, clothes)* crasse *f*; *(in street)* saleté *f* **2** *(obscene books, films etc)* obscénités *fpl*; *(obscene words, jokes)* grossièretés *fpl*, obscénités *fpl*; **it's sheer f.** *(film, book)* c'est un ramassis d'obscénités **3** *Br Fam Pej* **the f.** *(police)* les flics *mpl*

filthy ['fɪlθɪ] *(compar* **filthier**, *superl* **filthiest***)* **ADJ 1** *(dirty)* dégoûtant, crasseux; **your hands are f.!** tes mains sont dégoûtantes! **2** *(obscene, smutty* ▸ *language, talk, jokes)* grossier, obscène, ordurier; *(*▸ *person)* grossier, dégoûtant; *(*▸ *film, book, photograph)* obscène, dégoûtant; *(*▸ *habit)* dégoûtant; **to have a f. mind** avoir l'esprit mal tourné **3** *Fam (nasty* ▸ *temper, day)* atroce◻, abominable◻; *(*▸ *trick)* vicieux◻, méchant◻; **he's in a f. mood** *or* **temper** il est de sale humeur, il est d'une humeur massacrante; **he gave me a f. look** il m'a jeté un sale regard, il m'a regardé d'un sale œil; *Br* **it's f. weather** il fait un temps de chien

ADV *Fam* **f. dirty** dégoûtant◻; **to be f. rich** être plein aux as

filtration [fɪl'treɪʃən] **N** *Chem* filtrage *m*, filtration *f*

▸▸ *Tech* ***filtration plant*** station *f* d'épuration

fin [fɪn] **N 1** *(of fish, whale)* nageoire *f*; *(of shark)* aileron *m*

2 *(of aircraft, spacecraft)* empennage *m*; *(of boat)* dérive *f*; *(of rocket, bomb)* ailette *f*

3 *Tech (of cylinder, pump, radiator)* ailette *f*; **cooling fins** ailettes *fpl* de refroidissement

4 *Am Fam (five-dollar bill)* billet *m* de cinq dollars◻

• **fins NPL** *(for swimming)* palmes *fpl*

▸▸ ***fin whale*** rorqual *m* commun

finagle [fɪ'neɪgəl] **VT** *Am Fam (obtain* ▸ *through cleverness)* se débrouiller pour avoir; *(*▸ *through devious means)* obtenir par subterfuge◻, carotter

final ['faɪnəl] **ADJ 1** *(last)* dernier; **the f. instalment** *(of hire purchase agreement)* le dernier versement, le versement libératoire; **f. warning** dernier avertissement *m* **2** *(definitive)* définitif; *(score)* final; **that's my f. offer** c'est ma dernière offre; **I'm not moving, and that's f.!** je ne bouge pas, un point c'est tout!; **the referee's decision is f.** la décision de l'arbitre est sans appel; **is that**

your f. answer? c'est ta réponse définitive?; **nothing's f. yet** il n'y a encore rien de définitif, rien n'est encore arrêté **3** *Phil (cause)* final; *Gram (clause)* de but, final

N 1 *(of competition)* finale *f*; **to get to the f.** *or* **finals** arriver en finale; **are they in the f.** *or* **finals?** est-ce qu'ils sont en finale? **2** *Press* dernière édition *f*; **late f.** dernière *f* édition du soir

• **finals NPL** *Univ* examens *mpl* de dernière année; **to sit one's finals** passer ses examens de dernière année

▸▸ *Fin* ***final accounts*** compte *m* définitif; *Aviat* ***final approach*** approche *f* finale; *Cin* ***final cut*** final cut *m*; ***final date*** date *f* limite; *Com* ***final demand*** dernier rappel *m*; *St Exch* ***final dividend*** dividende *m* définitif *ou* final; ***final edition*** *(of newspaper)* dernière édition *f*; *Univ* ***final examinations*** examens *mpl* de dernière année; *Typ* ***final proof*** morasse *f*; *Fin* ***final settlement*** solde *m* de tout compte; *Hist* **the Final Solution** la solution finale; *Sport* ***final whistle*** coup *m* de sifflet final

finale [fɪ'nɑːlɪ] **N** *Mus* finale *m*; *Fig* final *m*, finale *m*

finalist ['faɪnəlɪst] **N** *(in competition)* finaliste *mf*

finality [faɪ'nælətɪ] **N 1** *(of decision, death)* irrévocabilité *f*, caractère *m* définitif; **there was a note of f. in his voice** il y avait quelque chose d'irrévocable dans sa voix **2** *Phil* finalité *f*

finalization, -isation [ˌfaɪnəlaɪ'zeɪʃən] **N** *(of details, plans, arrangements)* mise *f* au point; *(of deal, decision, agreement)* conclusion *f*; **the work involved in the f. of the screenplay** le travail nécessaire pour mettre la dernière main *ou* la dernière touche *ou* la touche finale au scénario

finalize, -ise ['faɪnəlaɪz] **VT** *(details, plans, arrangements)* mettre au point; *(deal, decision, agreement)* mener à bonne fin; *(preparations)* mettre la dernière main *ou* touche à, mettre la touche finale à; *(date)* arrêter; **that hasn't been finalized yet** cela n'a pas encore été décidé *ou* arrêté; **nothing has been finalized** rien n'a encore été décidé *ou* arrêté; **details of the visit have yet to be finalized** les détails de la visite restent à préciser

finally ['faɪnəlɪ] **ADV 1** *(eventually)* finalement, enfin; **when he f. arrived** finalement, quand il est arrivé; **she f. agreed to come** elle a fini par accepter de venir; **f.!** enfin! **2** *(lastly)* enfin; **and, f., I would like to say...** et pour finir je voudrais dire que... **3** *(irrevocably)* définitivement; **"no," she said f.** "non", dit-elle fermement

finance **N** ['faɪnæns] *(UNCOUNT) (money management)* finance *f*; *(financing)* financement *m*; **it's a problem of f.** c'est un problème de financement; **through lack of f.** à cause d'un manque de financement; **we don't have the necessary f.** nous n'avons pas les fonds nécessaires; **high f.** la haute finance; **Minister/Ministry of F.** ministre *m*/ministère *m* de l'Économie et des Finances

VT [faɪ'næns] financer; *(project, enterprise)* financer, trouver les fonds pour; *(person, company)* financer, commanditer

• **finances NPL** ['faɪnænsəs] finances *fpl*, fonds *mpl*; **what state are your finances in?** comment vont tes finances?; **my finances are a bit low just now** je ne suis pas très en fonds en ce moment; **the company's finances are a bit low just now** les finances de l'entreprise sont un peu basses en ce moment

▸▸ *Pol* ***finance bill*** projet *m* de loi de finances; ***finance capital*** capital *m* financier; ***finance charges*** frais *mpl* financiers; ***finance company*** société *f* financière; ***finance costs*** frais *mpl* financiers *ou* de trésorerie; ***finance department*** direction *f* financière; ***finance director*** directeur(trice) *m,f* financier(ère); *Br* ***finance house*** société *f* financière, = société britannique de financement pour les achats à crédit; *Pol* ***Finance Minister*** ministre *m* de l'Économie et des Finances

financial [faɪ'nænʃəl] **ADJ 1** financier; **but does it make f. sense?** mais est-ce que c'est avantageux *ou* intéressant du point de vue financier? **2** *Austr & NZ Fam (possessing money)* **are you f.?** tu as assez de fric?

▸▸ ***financial accountant*** comptable *mf* financier (ère); ***financial accounting*** comptabilité *f* générale *ou* financière; ***financial adviser*** conseiller (ère) *m,f* financier(ère); ***financial aid*** aide *f* financière; ***financial analyst*** analyste *mf* financier (ère); ***financial appraisal*** évaluation *f* financière; ***financial assistance*** appui *m* financier, aide *f* financière; ***financial backer*** bailleur(eresse) *m,f* de fonds; ***financial backing*** financement *m*, aide *f* financière; ***financial capital*** capital *m* financier; ***financial centre*** place *f* financière; ***financial consultant*** conseiller(ère) *m,f* financier(ère), conseil *m* financier; ***financial control*** contrôle *m* financier; ***financial controller*** contrôleur(euse) *m,f* financier(ère); *Acct* ***financial costs*** frais *mpl* financiers; ***financial deal*** opération *f* financière; ***financial director*** directeur(trice) *m,f* financier (ère); ***financial engineering*** ingénierie *f* financière; ***financial expenses*** charges *fpl* financières; *St Exch* ***financial future*** instrument *m* financier à terme; *St Exch* ***financial futures exchange*** bourse *f* d'instruments financiers à terme; ***financial gearing*** effet *m* de levier financier; ***financial healthcheck*** diagnostic *m* financier; ***financial institution*** établissement *m* financier; ***financial instrument*** instrument *m* financier; ***financial intermediary*** intermédiaire *mf* financier(ère); ***financial management*** direction *f* *ou* gestion *f* financière; ***financial manager*** directeur(trice) *m, f* financier(ère); ***financial market*** marché *m* financier; *Rad & TV* ***financial news*** chronique *f* financière; ***financial ombudsman*** arbitre *m* financier; ***financial pages*** pages *fpl* financières; ***financial partner*** partenaire *mf* financier(ère); ***financial period*** période *f* comptable; ***financial plan*** plan *m* de financement; ***financial planning*** planification *f* financière; ***financial position*** position *f* *ou* situation *f* financière; ***financial pressure*** problèmes *mpl* financiers; ***financial product*** produit *m* financier; ***financial resources*** ressources *fpl*; ***financial services*** services *mpl* financiers; ***Financial Services Authority*** = organisme gouvernemental britannique chargé de contrôler les activités du secteur financier; ***financial situation*** situation *f* financière; ***financial statement*** état *m* financier, déclaration *f* de résultats; *Press* ***The Financial Times*** = quotidien britannique d'information financière; *Fin* ***Financial Times-Stock Exchange 100 Share Index*** = principal indice boursier du 'Financial Times' basé sur la valeur de 100 actions cotées à la Bourse de Londres; ***financial transaction*** opération *f* financière; *Br* ***the financial year*** *(in business)* l'exercice *m* financier; *(in politics)* l'année *f* budgétaire

> **FINANCIAL YEAR**
>
> Pour les impôts sur le revenu en Grande-Bretagne, l'année fiscale commence le 6 avril.

financially [faɪ'nænʃəlɪ] **ADV** financièrement; **are they f. sound?** est-ce qu'ils ont une bonne assise financière?; **he's f. naive** il est naïf sur les questions d'argent

financier [faɪ'nænsɪə(r)] **N** financier *m*

financing [faɪ'nænsɪŋ] **N** *(of project etc)* financement *m*

▸▸ ***financing capacity*** capacité *f* de financement; ***financing gap*** déficit *m* de financement; ***financing plan*** plan *m* de financement; ***financing terms*** modalités *fpl* de financement

finch [fɪntʃ] **N** *Orn* fringillidé *m*; *(goldfinch)* chardonneret *m*; *(chaffinch)* pinson *m*; *(bullfinch)* bouvreuil *m*

FIND [faɪnd]

> **VT**
> • trouver **1–4** • retrouver **1**
> • chercher **2** • constater **5**
> • déclarer **6** • se trouver **8**
>
> **VI**
> • prononcer
>
> **N**
> • trouvaille • merveille

(pt & pp **found** [faʊnd]*)*

VT 1 *(by searching)* trouver; *(lost thing, person)* retrouver; **I can't f. it anywhere** je ne le trouve nulle part; **she couldn't f. anything to say** elle ne trouvait rien à dire; **the police could f. no reason** *or* **explanation for his disappearance** la police n'arrivait pas à expliquer sa disparition; **the missing airmen were found alive** les aviateurs disparus ont été retrouvés sains et saufs; **I can't f. my place** *(in book)* je ne sais plus où j'en suis; **my wallet/he was nowhere to be found** mon portefeuille/il était introuvable

2 *(look for, fetch)* chercher; *Comput* **to f. and replace** trouver et remplacer; **he went to f. help/a doctor** il est allé chercher de l'aide/un médecin; **go and f. me a pair of scissors** va me chercher une paire de ciseaux; **could you f. me a cloth?** tu peux me trouver un chiffon?; **he said he'd try to f. me a job** il a dit qu'il essaierait de me trouver un travail; **to f. the time/money to do sth** trouver le temps de/l'argent nécessaire pour faire qch; **to f. the courage/strength to do sth** trouver le courage/la force de faire qch; **to f. one's feet** *(in new job, situation)* prendre ses repères; **I'm still finding my feet** je ne suis pas encore complètement dans le bain; **she couldn't f. it in her heart** *or* **herself to say no** elle n'a pas eu le cœur de dire non; **the bullet found its mark** la balle a atteint son but; **to f. one's way** trouver son chemin; **I'll f. my own way out** je trouverai la sortie tout seul; **she found her way back home** elle a réussi à rentrer chez elle

3 *(come across by chance)* trouver; **we left everything as we found it** nous avons tout laissé dans l'état où nous l'avions trouvé; **we found this wonderful little bistro on our last visit** nous avons découvert un adorable petit bistro lors de notre dernière visite; **you won't f. a better bargain anywhere** nulle part, vous ne trouverez meilleur prix; **this bird is found all over Britain** on trouve cet oiseau dans toute la Grande-Bretagne; **I found him at home** je l'ai trouvé chez lui; **I found her waiting outside** je l'ai trouvée qui attendait dehors; **they found him dead** on l'a trouvé mort; **you'll f. someone else** tu trouveras quelqu'un d'autre; **to f. happiness/peace** trouver le bonheur/la paix; **I take people as I f. them** je prends les gens comme ils sont; **I hope this letter finds you in good health** j'espère que vous allez bien

4 *(expressing an opinion, personal view)* trouver; **I don't f. that funny at all** je ne trouve pas ça drôle du tout; **I f. her very pretty** je la trouve très jolie; **she finds it very difficult/impossible to talk about it** il lui est très difficile/impossible d'en parler; **he finds it very hard/impossible to make friends** il a beaucoup de mal à/il n'arrive pas à se faire des amis; **I f. it hot/cold in here** je trouve qu'il fait chaud/froid ici; **how did you f. your new boss/your steak?** comment avez-vous trouvé votre nouveau patron/votre steak?; **Rovers have been found wanting** *or* **lacking in defence** les Rovers ont fait preuve de faiblesse au niveau de la défense

5 *(discover, learn)* constater; **I found (that) the car wouldn't start** j'ai constaté que la voiture ne voulait pas démarrer; **they came back to f. the house had been** *Br* **burgled** *or Am* **burglarized** à leur retour, ils ont constaté que la maison avait été cambriolée; **I f. I have time on my hands now that I am no longer working** je m'aperçois que j'ai du temps à moi maintenant que je ne travaille plus; **I think you'll f. I'm right** je pense que tu t'apercevras que j'ai raison

6 *Law* **to f. sb guilty/innocent** déclarer qn coupable/non coupable; **how do you f. the accused?** déclarez-vous l'accusé coupable ou non coupable?

7 *Old-fashioned or Formal (provide* ▸ *one's own tools, uniform)* fournir

8 *(reflexive use)* **to f. oneself** *(one's true self)* se trouver; **I woke up to f. myself on a ship** je me suis réveillé sur un bateau; **he found himself out of a job** il s'est retrouvé sans emploi; **I f./found myself in an impossible situation** je me trouve/me suis retrouvé dans une situation impossible; *Formal* **I f. myself unable to agree to your request** je me vois dans l'impossibilité d'accéder à votre demande; **she found herself forced to retaliate** elle s'est trouvée dans l'obligation de riposter

VI *Law* **to f. for/against the plaintiff** prononcer en faveur de l'accusation/de la défense

N *(object)* trouvaille *f*; *(person)* merveille *f*

▸▸ *Comput* ***find command*** commande *f* de recherche

▸ **find out VT SEP 1** *(learn, discover* ▸ *truth, real identity)* découvrir; *(*▸ *answer, phone number)* trouver; *(*▸ *by making enquiries, reading instructions)* se renseigner sur; **we found out that she**

was French nous avons découvert qu'elle était française; **what have you found out about him/it?** qu'est-ce que tu as découvert sur lui/là-dessus?; **can you f. out the date of the meeting for me?** est-ce que tu peux te renseigner sur la date de la réunion?; **when I found out the date of the meeting** quand j'ai appris la date de la réunion; **to f. out how to do sth/what sb is really like** découvrir comment faire qch/la véritable nature de qn; **I found out where he'd put it** j'ai trouvé où il l'avait mis **2** *(catch being dishonest)* prendre; *(show to be a fraud)* prendre en défaut; **make sure you don't get found out** veille à ne pas te faire prendre; **you've been found out** tu as été découvert; **she had been found out transferring money into her own account** on avait découvert qu'elle transférait de l'argent sur son propre compte

VI 1 *(investigate, make enquiries)* se renseigner; **to f. out about sth** se renseigner sur qch **2** *(learn, discover)* **his wife/his boss found out** sa femme/son chef a tout découvert; **his wife found out about his affair** sa femme a découvert qu'il avait une liaison; **what if the police f. out?** et si la police l'apprend?; **I didn't f. out about it in time** je ne l'ai pas su à temps

finder ['faɪndə(r)] **N 1** *(person)* **it becomes the property of the f.** celui/celle qui l'a trouvé en devient propriétaire; **finders keepers(, losers weepers)** celui qui le trouve le garde **2** *(of camera)* viseur *m*; *(of telescope)* chercheur *m*

▸▸ ***finder's fee*** commission *f* de démarcheur

finding ['faɪndɪŋ] **N** *Law* verdict *m*

• **findings NPL** *(of scientist, enquiry, investigation etc)* résultat *m*; *(of tribunal, committee, report)* conclusions *fpl*; **he published his findings in a scientific journal** il a fait publier les résultats de ses recherches dans un journal scientifique

FINE [faɪn]

> **ADJ**
> • excellent **1** • beau **1, 6**
> • fin **2, 3** • bien **4, 5**
> • subtil **7**
> **ADV**
> • bien
> **N**
> • amende
> **VT**
> • condamner à une amende

(compar **finer**, *superl* **finest)**

ADJ 1 *(of high quality* ▸ *meal, speech, view)* excellent; *(beautiful and elegant* ▸ *clothes, house)* beau (belle); *(*▸ *fabric)* précieux; *Fam (attractive, sexy)* canon *inv*; **she is a very f. athlete** c'est une excellente athlète; **this is a very f. wine** c'est un vin vraiment excellent; *Br* **a f. chap** un bon gars; **she is a f. lady** *(admirable character)* c'est une femme admirable; *(elegant)* c'est une femme élégante; **to appeal to sb's finer feelings** faire appel aux nobles sentiments de qn; **that was a f. effort by Webb** superbe effort de la part de Webb; **a f. example** un bel exemple; **of the finest quality** de première qualité; **made from the finest barley** fabriqué à base d'orge de la meilleure qualité; **her finest hour was winning the gold** elle a eu son heure de gloire quand elle a remporté la médaille d'or

2 *(very thin* ▸ *hair, nib, thread)* fin; **in this case there is a f. line between fact and fiction** dans le cas présent la frontière est très mince entre la réalité et la fiction; **it's a f. line** la différence *ou* la distinction est infime *ou* très subtile

3 *(not coarse* ▸ *powder, grain, drizzle)* fin; *(*▸ *features, skin)* fin, délicat; **to chop** *or* **to cut sth (up) f.** hacher qch menu; *Fig* **that's cutting it a bit f.** tu calcules un peu juste

4 *(good, OK)* **how is everyone? – oh, they're all f.** comment va tout le monde? – tout le monde va bien; **how are you? – f., thanks** comment ça va? – bien, merci; **more coffee? – no thanks, I'm f.** encore du café? – non, ça va, merci; **the tent's f. for two, but too small for three** la tente convient pour deux personnes, mais elle est trop petite pour trois; **I'll be back in about an hour or so – f.** je serai de retour d'ici environ une heure – d'accord *ou* entendu *ou* très bien; **I was a bit worried about the new job, but it turned out f. in the end** j'étais un peu inquiet à propos de mon nouveau travail mais ça s'est finalement bien passé; **(that's) f.** très bien, parfait; **that's f. by** *or* **with me** ça me va; **that's all very f., but what about me?** tout ça c'est bien joli, mais moi qu'est-ce que je deviens dans l'affaire?

5 *(well)* **that looks f. to me** cela m'a l'air d'aller; **he looks f. now** *(in health)* il a l'air de bien aller maintenant; **you look just f., it's a very nice dress** tu es très bien, c'est une très jolie robe; **that sounds f.** *(suggestion, idea)* très bien, parfait; *(way of playing music)* cela rend très bien

6 *Br (weather)* beau (belle); **a f. day** une belle journée; **there will be f. weather** *or* **it will be f. in all parts of the country** il fera beau *ou* il y aura du beau temps dans tout le pays; **it's turned out f. again** il fait encore beau; **I hope it keeps f. for you** j'espère que tu auras du beau temps; **one of these f. days** un de ces jours; **one f. day** un beau jour

7 *(subtle* ▸ *distinction, language)* subtil; *(precise* ▸ *calculations)* minutieux, précis; **f. detail** petit détail *m*; **to make some f. adjustments to sth** *(to text, plan)* peaufiner qch; *(to engine)* faire des petits réglages sur qch; **not to put too f. a point on it** pour parler carrément

8 *Fam Ironic (awful, terrible)* **that's a f. thing to say!** c'est charmant de dire ça!; **she was in a f. state** elle était dans un état épouvantable; **you picked a f. time to leave me/tell me!** tu as bien choisi ton moment pour me quitter/me le dire!; **this is a f. time to start that again!** c'est bien le moment de remettre ça sur le tapis!; **you're a f. one to talk!** ça te va bien de dire ça!, tu peux parler!; **here's another f. mess you've got me into!** tu m'as encore mis dans un beau pétrin!; **a f. friend you are!** eh bien, tu fais un bon copain/une bonne copine!

ADV *(well)* bien; **yes, that suits me f.** oui, cela me va très bien; **the baby is doing f.** le bébé va très bien; **we get along f. together** on s'entend très bien

N *(punishment)* amende *f*, contravention *f*; **to impose a f. on sb** infliger une amende à qn; **a parking f.** une contravention *ou* amende pour stationnement illégal; **a £25 f.** une amende de 25 livres

VT *(order to pay)* condamner à une amende, donner une contravention à; **she was fined heavily** elle a été condamnée à une lourde amende *ou* contravention; **she was fined for speeding** elle a reçu une contravention pour excès de vitesse; **they fined her £25 for illegal parking** ils lui ont donné *ou* elle a eu une amende *ou* contravention de 25 livres pour stationnement illégal

▸▸ ***fine art*** *(UNCOUNT)* beaux-arts *mpl*; *Fig* **he's got it down to a f. art** il est expert en la matière; ***fine arts*** beaux-arts *mpl*

▸ **fine down VT SEP** *(smooth* ▸ *wood)* polir, poncer; *Fig (hone* ▸ *theory, text)* affiner

fine-cut ADJ *(tobacco)* haché fin

fine-drawn ADJ *Fig* **1** *(distinction)* subtil **2** *(features)* fin **3** *(wire)* finement étiré; *(thread)* délié

fine-grained [-greɪnd] **ADJ** *(wood)* à fibres fines, à fil fin; *(leather)* à grain peu apparent

fine-looking ADJ beau (belle)

finely ['faɪnlɪ] **ADV 1** *(grated, ground, sliced)* finement; **f. chopped** haché menu, finement haché; **f. powdered** en poudre fine **2** *(delicately, subtly* ▸ *tuned)* avec précision; **the situation is very f. balanced** la situation est caractérisée par un équilibre précaire **3** *(carved, sewn etc)* délicatement

fineness ['faɪnnɪs] **N 1** *(of clothes, manners)* raffinement *m*; *(of work of art, features, handwriting)* finesse *f*

2 *(of sand, sugar, material)* finesse *f*

3 *(purity* ▸ *of metal)* pureté *f*

4 *(thinness* ▸ *of thread, hair, nib)* finesse *f*; *Fig (of detail, distinction)* subtilité *f*

finery ['faɪnərɪ] **N** *(UNCOUNT)* parure *f*; **the princess in all her f.** la princesse dans *ou* parée de ses plus beaux atours; **to be dressed in all one's f.** porter sa tenue d'apparat

fine-spun ADJ 1 *Tex (yarn, wool)* (filé) fin **2** *Fig (argument, logic)* subtil

finesse [fɪ'nes] **N 1** *(skill)* finesse *f* **2** *Cards* impasse *f*

VT *Cards* **to f. a card** faire l'impasse en jouant une carte

VI *Cards* **to f. against a card** faire l'impasse à une carte

fine-tooth(ed) comb N peigne *m* fin; *Fig* **to go through sth with a f.** passer qch au peigne fin

fine-tune VT *(machine, engine, radio)* régler avec précision; *Fig (plan)* peaufiner; *(economy)* = régler grâce à des mesures fiscales et monétaires

fine-tuning [-'tjuːnɪŋ] **N** *(of machine, engine, radio)* réglage *m* fin; *Fig (of plan)* peaufinage *m*; *(of economy)* = réglage obtenu par des mesures fiscales et monétaires

finger ['fɪŋgə(r)] **N 1** *(part of body)* doigt *m*; **to wear a ring on one's f.** porter une bague au doigt; **she ran her fingers through her/his hair** elle s'est passé les/ses doigts *ou* la/sa main dans les/ses cheveux; **to lick one's fingers** se lécher les doigts; **to eat with one's fingers** manger avec les doigts; **to hold sth between f. and thumb** tenir qch entre le pouce et l'index; **a f.'s breadth** un doigt; **to point a f. at sb/sth** montrer qn/qch du doigt; **I can twist him round my little f.** j'en fais ce que je veux; **to be all fingers and thumbs** avoir des mains de beurre, avoir deux mains gauches; *Br Fam* **get** *or* **pull your f. out!** remue-toi!; **to have a f. in every pie** jouer sur tous les tableaux; **if you lay a f. on her** si tu touches à un seul de ses cheveux; **to keep one's fingers crossed** croiser les doigts *(pour souhaiter bonne chance)*; **I'll keep my fingers crossed for you** je croiserai les doigts pour toi; **you could count them on the fingers of one hand** on pourrait les compter sur les doigts de la main; **to point the f. (of suspicion) at sb** diriger les soupçons sur qn; **the f. of suspicion points at the accountant** les soupçons pèsent sur le comptable; *Fam* **to put the f. on sb** *(inform on)* balancer qn; **to put one's f. on sth** *(identify)* mettre le doigt sur qch; **something has changed but I can't put my f. on it** il y a quelque chose de changé mais je n'arrive pas à dire ce que c'est; **to have one's f. on the pulse** *(person)* être très au fait de ce qui se passe; *(magazine, TV programme)* être à la pointe de l'actualité; *Fam* **to give sb the f.**, *Br Fam* **to stick two fingers up at sb** faire un bras d'honneur à qn; **success/happiness/the suspect slipped through his fingers** le succès/le bonheur/le suspect lui a glissé entre les doigts; **to work one's fingers to the bone** s'épuiser à la tâche; **you never lift** *or* **raise a f. to help** tu ne lèves jamais le petit doigt pour aider

2 *(of glove)* doigt *m*

3 *(of alcohol)* doigt *m*; *(of land)* bande *f*; **to cut a cake into fingers** couper un gâteau en petits morceaux rectangulaires

4 *Comput* = utilitaire de l'Internet permettant d'obtenir des informations sur un utilisateur du réseau

5 *Tech* doigt *m*; *(of dial)* index *m*

VT 1 *(feel)* tâter du doigt; *Pej* tripoter; **stop fingering that food!** arrête de tripoter la nourriture! **2** *Mus* doigter, indiquer le doigté de **3** *Fam (inform on)* balancer, donner

▸▸ *Culin* ***finger biscuit*** biscuit *m* à la cuiller; ***finger bowl*** rince-doigts *m inv*; ***finger buffet*** = buffet où sont servis des petits sandwiches, des petits-fours et des légumes crus; *Mus* ***finger exercises*** exercices *mpl* de doigté; ***finger food*** = petits-fours, petits sandwiches et légumes crus, servis à un buffet et que l'on mange avec les doigts; *Mus* ***finger hole*** trou *m*; ***finger paint*** peinture *f* pour peindre avec les doigts; ***finger painting*** peinture *f* avec les doigts; **children love f. painting** les enfants adorent peindre avec leurs doigts; ***finger puppet*** marionnette *f* à doigt

fingering ['fɪŋgərɪŋ] **N 1** *Mus (technique, numerals)* doigté *m* **2** *Pej (touching)* tripotage *m*

fingermark ['fɪŋgəˌmɑːk] **N** trace *f ou* marque *f* de doigt

fingernail ['fɪŋgəneɪl] **N** ongle *m* (de la main); **to hang on by one's fingernails** se retenir du bout des doigts; *Fig* se raccrocher comme on peut

fingerprint ['fɪŋgəprɪnt] **N** empreinte *f* digitale; **his fingerprints are all over it** c'est couvert de ses empreintes digitales; *Fig* tout indique que c'est lui; **to take sb's fingerprints** prendre les empreintes digitales de qn

VT *(person)* prendre les empreintes digitales de; **to f. sb genetically** identifier l'empreinte *ou* le code génétique de qn

▸▸ ***fingerprint expert*** spécialiste *mf* en empreintes digitales *ou* en dactyloscopie; ***fingerprint recognition*** reconnaissance *f* des empreintes digitales

fingerstall ['fɪŋgəstɔːl] **N** doigtier *m*

fingertip ['fɪŋgətɪp] **N** bout *m* du doigt; **to be Irish to one's fingertips** être irlandais jusqu'au bout des ongles; **to have information at one's fingertips** *(be conversant with)* connaître des informations sur le bout des doigts; *(readily available)* avoir des informations à portée de main

▸▸ ***fingertip controls*** commandes *fpl* à touches; ***fingertip search*** passage *m* au peigne fin, examen *m* minutieux

finial ['fɪnɪəl] **N** *Archit* fleuron *m*

finicky ['fɪnɪkɪ] **ADJ 1** *(person)* pointilleux, *Pej* tatillon; *(habit)* tatillon; **to be f. about sth** être pointilleux *or Pej* tatillon sur qch; **to be a f. eater** être difficile sur la nourriture **2** *(job, task)* minutieux; *(device, recipe)* compliqué; **this is a f. dish to make** c'est un plat très délicat à préparer

FINISH ['fɪnɪʃ]

N
- fin **1**
- finitions **2**
- finition **3**
- finish **4**

VT
- terminer **1**
- finir **1, 4**
- détruire **2**

VI
- finir, se terminer

N 1 *(end, closing stage ▸ of life, game etc)* fin *f*; *(▸ of race)* arrivée *f*; **a close f.** *(in race)* une arrivée serrée *ou* dans un mouchoir; **it was a fight to the f.** la partie fut serrée; **to be in at the f.** voir la fin; **she was exhausted by the f.** sur la fin elle était épuisée; **that was the f. of him** ce fut le coup de grâce; *St Exch* **price at the f.** prix *m* de clôture; *St Exch* **shares were up at the f.** les actions étaient en hausse à la clôture

2 *(created with paint, varnish, veneer)* finitions *fpl*; **paint with a gloss/matt f.** peinture *f* vernie/mate; **paper with a gloss/matt f.** papier *m* glacé/mat; **car with a metallic/silver f.** voiture *f* métallisée/argentée

3 *(quality of workmanship, presentation etc)* finition *f*; **his prose/acting lacks f.** sa prose/son jeu manque de poli

4 *Sport (of athlete)* finish *m inv*

5 *(shot at goal)* but *m*; **a superb f.** un but magnifique

VT 1 *(end, complete ▸ work, meal, school)* finir, terminer, achever; *(▸ race)* finir, terminer; *(consume ▸ supplies, food, drink)* finir, terminer; **to f. doing sth** finir *ou* terminer de faire qch; **when do you f. work?** *(time)* à quelle heure est-ce que tu finis?; *(date)* quand *ou* à quelle date finis-tu?; **to f. what one was saying** finir ce qu'on avait à dire; **to be in a hurry to get sth finished** être pressé de finir *ou* terminer qch; **f. your drinks** finissez *ou* videz vos verres

2 *(ruin ▸ someone's career)* mettre un terme à; *(▸ someone's chances)* détruire, anéantir; **that was the scandal that finished him** c'est le scandale qui l'a achevé

3 *(exhaust)* achever, tuer

4 *(put finish on ▸ wood, garment)* finir, mettre les finitions à; *Metal (part)* usiner; *Sewing* **to f. a buttonhole** brider une boutonnière; **the paintwork hasn't been very well finished** la peinture n'a pas été très bien faite

VI *(come to an end ▸ concert, film etc)* (se) finir, se terminer, s'achever; *(complete activity ▸ person)* finir, terminer; **to f. by doing sth** finir *ou* terminer en faisant qch; **when do you f.?** *(leave work)* quand est-ce que tu finis?; **please let me f.** *(speaking)* s'il te plaît, laisse-moi finir *ou* terminer; **to f. first/third** *(in race)* arriver premier/troisième; **where did he f.?** *(in race)* en quelle position est-il arrivé *ou* a-t-il fini?; **the runner finished strongly/well** *(in race)* le coureur a fini fort/a bien fini; **the book finishes with him returning to the family house** à la fin du livre il retourne à la maison familiale

▸▸ *Am Sport* ***finish line*** ligne *f* d'arrivée

▸**finish off VT SEP 1** *(complete ▸ work, letter)* finir, terminer, achever; *(▸ passing move in sport)* terminer, finir, conclure **2** *(consume ▸ drink)* finir, terminer **3** *(kill ▸ person, wounded animal)* achever; *Fig (exhaust ▸ person)* achever, tuer; *Fig* **fierce competition finished the industry off** une concurrence féroce a eu raison de cette industrie

VI *(in speech, meal)* finir, terminer; **they finished off with a coffee/by singing the national anthem** ils ont terminé par un café/en chantant l'hymne national

▸**finish up VT SEP** *(meal, food, drink)* finir, terminer; **f. up your drink** finissez *ou* terminez *ou* videz votre verre

VI *(end up)* finir; **to f. up in jail/hospital** finir en prison/à l'hôpital; **they finished up arguing** ils ont fini par se disputer; **she finished up a nervous wreck** à la fin c'était une vraie boule de nerfs, elle a fini à bout de nerfs

▸**finish with VT INSEP 1** *(have no further use for)* ne plus avoir besoin de; **have you finished with the paper/milk?** tu n'as plus besoin du journal/du lait?, tu as fini avec le journal/le lait?; **I haven't finished with it yet** j'en ai encore besoin

2 *(stop doing)* en finir avec; **I've finished with journalism for good** j'en ai fini à jamais avec le journalisme, moi et le journalisme, c'est fini; **I've finished with trying to help people** plus jamais je n'essaierai d'aider les gens

3 *(end relationship with)* rompre avec

4 *(stop punishing)* régler son compte à; **just wait till I f. with him** attends que je lui règle son compte, attends que j'en aie fini avec lui; **I haven't finished with you yet** je n'en ai pas encore fini avec toi

finished ['fɪnɪʃt] **ADJ 1** *(completed ▸ work, job)* fini, terminé, achevé; *(consumed ▸ wine, cake)* fini; **the butter is f.** il n'y a plus de beurre; **the plumber was f. by 4 p.m.** le plombier avait terminé *ou* fini à 16 heures; **f. product** *or* **article** produit *m* fini

2 *Fam (exhausted)* mort, crevé

3 *(ruined ▸ career)* fini, terminé; **he's f. as a politician** sa carrière d'homme politique est terminée *ou* finie, il est fini en tant qu'homme politique; **you're f.** c'est fini *ou* terminé pour vous

4 *(consummate)* fini; *Fig (performance)* parfaitement exécuté; *(appearance)* raffiné; **it's beautifully f.** les finitions sont magnifiques, c'est magnifiquement fini

5 *(over)* fini; **you and I are f.** toi et moi, c'est fini; **I'm f. with my boyfriend** mon petit ami et moi, c'est fini; **I'm f. with politics/journalism** la politique/le journalisme et moi, c'est fini, j'en ai fini avec la politique/le journalisme; **the headmaster was not f. with him yet** le principal n'en avait pas encore fini avec lui

finisher ['fɪnɪʃə(r)] **N 1** *Sport* finisseur(euse) *m,f*; *Ftbl* marqueur *m*; **he's a fast f.** *(athlete)* il finit vite, il est rapide au finish **2** *(thorough person)* **he's not a f.** il ne finit jamais complètement son travail **3** *Ind* finisseur(euse) *m,f*

finishing ['fɪnɪʃɪŋ] **ADJ** dernier; **f. coat** *(of paint, varnish etc)* dernière couche *f*; **the f. stroke** le coup de grâce

N 1 *(completion ▸ of task etc)* achèvement *m* **2** *Tech* finition *f*; *(of leather, paper)* apprêtage *m*

▸▸ *Br Sport* ***finishing line*** ligne *f* d'arrivée; ***finishing school*** = école privée de jeunes filles surtout axée sur l'enseignement des bonnes manières; *Ind* ***finishing shop*** atelier *m* de finitions; ***finishing touches*** finitions *fpl*; **to put the f. touches to sth** mettre la dernière main à qch

finite ['faɪnaɪt] **ADJ** limité; *Phil & Math (number, universe)* fini; *Gram (verb)* à aspect fini

N *Phil* **the f. and the infinite** le fini et l'infini

fink [fɪŋk] *Am Fam* **N 1** *(strikebreaker)* jaune *mf* **2** *(informer)* mouchard(e) *m,f*; *(to police)* indic *m*, balance *f* **3** *(nasty man)* salaud *m*; *(nasty woman)* salope *f*

VI to f. on sb *(to police)* donner *ou* balancer qn; *(to teacher, parent)* moucharder qn

Finland ['fɪnlənd] **N** Finlande *f*

Finn [fɪn] **N 1** *(inhabitant of Finland)* Finlandais(e) *m,f* **2** *Hist* Finnois(e) *m,f*

Finnish ['fɪnɪʃ] **N** *(language)* finnois *m*

ADJ 1 *(gen)* finlandais **2** *Hist* finnois

COMP *(embassy)* de Finlande; *(history)* de la Finlande; *(teacher)* de finnois

fiord [fjɔːd] **N** *Geog* fjord *m*

fir [fɜː(r)] **N** *(tree, wood)* sapin *m*

▸▸ *Br* ***fir cone*** pomme *f* de pin; ***fir tree*** sapin *m*

FIRE ['faɪə(r)]

N
- incendie **1**
- feu **1–4**
- appareil de chauffage **5**

VT
- tirer **1**
- décharger **1**
- virer **2**
- enflammer **3, 5**

VI
- tirer **1**
- tourner **2**

N 1 *(destructive)* incendie *m*; **f.!** au feu!; **to catch f.** prendre feu; **to set f. to sth, to set sth on f.** mettre le feu à qch; **be careful or you'll set f. to yourself** fais attention ou tu vas mettre le feu à tes vêtements; **to cause** *or* **to start a f.** *(person, faulty wiring)* provoquer un incendie; **all those empty boxes are a f. hazard** toutes ces boîtes vides constituent *ou* représentent un risque d'incendie; **on f.** en feu; **the building/village was set on f.** le bâtiment/village a été incendié; *Fig* **my throat's on f.** j'ai la gorge en feu; *Fam Hum* **where's the f.?** *(what's the rush?)* il n'y a pas le feu!; *Fig* **to play with f.** jouer avec le feu; *Fig* **to fight f. with f.** combattre le mal par le mal; *Fig* **he would go through f. and water for her** il se jetterait au feu pour elle; *Fam* **this novel is not going to set the world** *or Br* **the Thames on f.** ce roman ne casse pas des briques; *Fam* **he'll never set the world** *or Br* **the Thames on f.** il n'a jamais cassé trois pattes à un canard

2 *(in hearth, campsite)* feu *m*; **to light** *or* **to make a f.** allumer un feu, faire du feu; **to throw sth into** *or* **onto the f.** jeter qch au feu; **open f.** feu *m* de cheminée; **wood/coal f.** feu *m* de bois/de charbon

3 *(element)* feu *m*; **before man discovered f.** avant que l'homme ait découvert le feu; **to be afraid of f.** avoir peur du feu

4 *Mil* feu *m*; **open f.!** ouvrez le feu!; **to open/to cease f.** ouvrir/cesser le feu; **to open f. on sb** ouvrir le feu *ou* tirer sur qn; **to draw the enemy's f.** faire diversion en attirant le feu de l'ennemi; **to return (sb's) f.** riposter au tir (de qn); **hold your f.** *(don't shoot)* ne tirez pas; *(stop shooting)* cessez le feu; **to come under f.** essuyer le feu de l'ennemi; *Fig* être vivement critiqué *ou* attaqué; **under enemy f.** sous le feu de l'ennemi; *Fig* **between two fires** entre deux feux

5 *Br (heater)* appareil *m* de chauffage; **to turn the f. on/off** allumer/éteindre le chauffage

6 *(passion, ardour)* flamme *f*; **the f. of youth** la fougue de la jeunesse

7 *(of diamond)* lumière *f*, éclat *m*

VT 1 *(shot, bullet)* tirer; *(gun, cannon, torpedo)* décharger; *(arrow)* décocher; **to f. a gun at sb** tirer un coup de fusil sur qn; **only three bullets had been fired from the gun** seulement trois balles avaient été tirées avec le pistolet; **without a shot being fired** sans un seul coup de feu; **to f. a twenty-one-gun salute** tirer vingt et un coups de canon; *Fig* **to f. questions at sb** bombarder qn de questions

2 *Fam (dismiss)* virer; **you're fired!** vous êtes viré!

3 *(inspire ▸ person, audience, supporters, the imagination)* enflammer; **to f. sb with enthusiasm/desire** remplir qn d'enthousiasme/de désir

4 *Cer* cuire

5 *Tech (boiler, furnace)* chauffer, charger; *(fuel mix in engine)* enflammer

VI 1 *(shoot ▸ person)* tirer, faire feu; **the rifle failed to f.** le coup n'est pas parti; *Mil* **f.!** feu!; *Mil* **f. at will!** feu à volonté!; **to f. at** *or* **on sb** tirer sur qn; **we were fired on** nous avons reçu des coups de feu, on nous a tiré dessus

2 *(engine)* tourner; *(spark plug)* s'allumer; **the engine is only firing on two cylinders** le moteur ne tourne que sur deux cylindres; **to f. on all cylinders** *(engine)* tourner rond; *Fig (person)* être au mieux de sa forme; *(company)* fonctionner à plein régime

▸▸ ***fire alarm*** alarme *f* d'incendie; ***fire blanket*** couverture *f* pare-flamme; *Br* ***fire brigade*** brigade *f* des pompiers *ou* sapeurs-pompiers, *Suisse* service *m* du feu; **have you called the f. brigade?** as-tu appelé les pompiers?; *Comput* ***fire button*** *(on joystick)* bouton *m* feu; ***fire chief*** capitaine *m* des pompiers *ou* sapeurs-pompiers; ***fire clay*** argile *f* réfractaire; *Theat* ***fire curtain*** rideau *m* de fer; ***fire damage*** dégâts *mpl* causés par le feu; *Am* ***fire department*** brigade *f* des pompiers *ou* sapeurs-pompiers, *Suisse* service *m* du feu; ***fire door*** porte *f* coupe-feu; ***fire drill*** exercice *m* de sécurité *(en cas d'incendie)*; ***fire engine*** voiture *f* de pompiers; ***fire escape*** escalier *m* de secours *ou* d'incendie; ***fire exit*** sortie *f* de secours; ***fire extinguisher*** extincteur *m*; ***fire fighter*** pompier *m*, sapeur-pompier *m* (volontaire), *Suisse* homme *m* du feu; ***fire hose*** tuyau *m* de pompe à incendie; *Br* ***fire hydrant*** bouche *f* d'incendie, *Suisse* hydrant *m*; ***fire insurance*** *(UNCOUNT)* assurance-incendie *f*; ***fire irons*** accessoires *mpl* de cheminée; *Am* ***fire marshal*** capitaine *m* des pompiers *ou* sapeurs-pompiers; ***fire notice*** *(in hotel etc)* consignes *fpl* en cas d'incendie; *Am* ***fire plug*** *(fire hydrant)* bouche *f* d'incendie, *Suisse* hydrant *m*; *Fam (person)* = personne petite et grosse; ***fire practice*** exercice *m* d'incendie; ***fire prevention*** mesures *fpl* de sécurité contre l'incendie; ***fire regulations*** consignes *fpl* en cas d'incendie; ***fire safety*** sécurité *f* incendie; ***fire sale*** = vente au rabais de marchandises ayant subi de légers dégâts à la suite d'un incendie; ***fire screen*** écran *m* de cheminée; ***fire service*** brigade *f* des pompiers *ou* sapeurs-pompiers, *Suisse* service *m* du feu; *Astrol* ***fire sign*** signe *m* de feu; ***fire station*** caserne *f* de pompiers; ***fire tender*** voiture *f* de pompiers; *Am* ***fire truck*** voiture *f* de pompiers; ***fire walker*** = personne en transe qui marche sur des braises; ***fire walking*** = rituel consistant à marcher sur des braises; ***fire warden*** *(in forest)* guetteur *m* d'incendie; ***fire worship*** culte *m* du feu

▸ **fire away** **VI** *Fam (go ahead)* **f. away!** allez-y!

▸ **fire off** **VT SEP** *(round of ammunition)* tirer; *Fig (facts, figures)* balancer; **to f. off questions at sb** bombarder qn de questions; **she fired off a letter of complaint** elle a envoyé une lettre de réclamation sur-le-champ

fire-and-brimstone **ADJ** *(preacher, sermon)* menaçant des feux de l'enfer

firearm ['faɪrɑːm] **N** arme *f* à feu

COMP *(expert)* en armes à feu

▸▸ *Law* ***firearms offence*** délit *m* lié à la détention d'armes à feu; ***firearms training*** entraînement *m* à l'utilisation des armes à feu

fireball ['faɪəbɔːl] **N 1** *Met* éclair *m* en boule **2** *Astron* bolide *m* **3** *Fig* **she's a real f.** elle déborde d'énergie

fireboat ['faɪəbəʊt] **N** bateau-pompe *m*

firebox ['faɪəbɒks] **N** *Rail* foyer *m*

firebrand ['faɪəbrænd] **N 1** *(burning wood)* tison *m*, brandon *m* **2** *Fig (agitator)* brandon *m* de discorde

firebreak ['faɪəbreɪk] **N** *(in forest)* coupe-feu *m inv*

firebrick ['faɪəbrɪk] **N** brique *f* réfractaire

firebug ['faɪəbʌg] **N** *Fam* incendiaire *mf*, pyromane *mf*

firecracker ['faɪəˌkrækə(r)] **N** pétard *m*

firedamp ['faɪədæmp] **N** *Mining* grisou *m*

▸▸ ***firedamp explosion*** coup *m* de grisou

firedog ['faɪədɒg] **N** chenet *m*

fire-eater **N** *(in circus)* cracheur(euse) *m,f* de feu; *Fig* personne *f* belliqueuse, bagarreur (euse) *m,f*

fire-fighting **N** *(UNCOUNT)* lutte *f* contre les incendies

COMP *(equipment, techniques)* de lutte contre les incendies

firefly ['faɪəflaɪ] *(pl* **fireflies**) **N** *Zool* luciole *f*

fireguard ['faɪəgɑːd] **N** *(for open fire)* pare-feu *m inv*, garde-feu *m*

firehouse ['faɪəhaʊs, *pl* -haʊzɪz] **N** *Am* poste *m* d'incendie; *(with living quarters)* caserne *f* de (sapeurs-)pompiers

firelight ['faɪəlaɪt] **N** lueur *f ou* lumière *f* du feu; **in the f.** à la lueur *ou* lumière du feu

firelighter ['faɪəˌlaɪtə(r)] **N** allume-feu *m*

fireman ['faɪəmən] *(pl* **firemen** [-mən]) **N 1** *(firefighter)* pompier *m*, sapeur-pompier *m*, *Suisse* homme *m* du feu; **to give sb a f.'s lift** porter qn sur son épaule, la tête en bas **2** *Rail (of steam engine)* chauffeur *m* de locomotive

fireplace ['faɪəpleɪs] **N** cheminée *f*

fireproof ['faɪəpruːf] **ADJ** *(door, safe)* à l'épreuve du feu; *(clothing, toys)* ininflammable; *(dish)* allant au feu

VT ignifuger, rendre ininflammable

fire-retardant **ADJ** ignifuge

fireside ['faɪəsaɪd] **N** coin *m* du feu; **sitting by the f.** assis au coin du feu

▸▸ ***fireside chair*** fauteuil *m*; ***fireside chat*** *(by politician)* causerie *f* au coin du feu

firestorm ['faɪəstɔːm] **N** tempête *f* de feu

firetrap ['faɪətræp] **N this building's a real f.** ce bâtiment est un véritable piège (en cas d'incendie)

firewall ['faɪəwɔːl] **N 1** *Tech* cloison *f* pare-feu **2** *Comput* mur *m* coupe-feu, pare-feu *m inv*

VT *Comput* protéger par mur coupe-feu *ou* pare-feu

firewatcher ['faɪəˌwɒtʃə(r)] **N** *Br* guetteur(euse) *m,f* d'incendies

firewatching ['faɪəˌwɒtʃɪŋ] **N** *Br* surveillance *f* contre les incendies

firewater ['faɪəˌwɔːtə(r)] **N** *Fam* gnôle *f*

FireWire® ['faɪəwaɪə(r)] **N** *Comput* FireWire® *m*

firewood ['faɪəwʊd] **N** bois *m* à brûler; *(for use in home)* bois *m* de chauffage; **to chop sth up for f.** couper qch en morceaux pour en faire du bois de chauffage

firework ['faɪəwɜːk] **N** pièce *f* d'artifice; **fireworks** *(display)* feu *m* d'artifice; *Fam Fig* **there were fireworks at the meeting** il y a eu des étincelles à la réunion

▸▸ ***firework display, fireworks display*** feu *m* d'artifice

firing ['faɪərɪŋ] **N 1** *(UNCOUNT) Mil* tir *m*; **f. has been heavy** de nombreux coups de feu ont été tirés; **burst of f.** fusillade *f*

2 *Fam (dismissal)* renvoi *m*

3 *Aut (of engine, spark plug)* allumage *m*

4 *(in kiln)* cuite *f*, cuisson *f*; **they'll be given a second f.** elles seront cuites une deuxième fois

5 *Tech (of boiler furnace)* chauffage *m*, chargement *m*

▸▸ *Mil* ***firing line*** ligne *f* de tir; *Fig* **to be in the f. line** être dans la ligne de tir; *Aut* ***firing order*** *(of engine)* ordre *m* d'allumage; ***firing pin*** percuteur *m*; ***firing position*** *(of weapon)* position *f* de tir; *(of person)* position *f* du tireur; ***firing practice*** exercice *m* de tir; ***firing range*** champ *m* de tir; **within f. range** à portée de fusil; *Aut* ***firing sequence*** *(of engine)* ordre *m* d'allumage; ***firing squad*** peloton *m* d'exécution; **to be executed by f. squad** passer devant le peloton d'exécution

firm[1] [fɜːm] **N** *(company)* entreprise *f*; *(of solicitors)* étude *f*; *(of lawyers, barristers, consultants)* cabinet *m*; **it's a good f. to work for** cette entreprise est un bon employeur

firm[2] **ADJ 1** *(solid, hard* ▸ *flesh, fruit, mattress etc)* ferme; **on f. ground** sur la terre ferme; *Fig* sur un terrain solide

2 *(stable, secure* ▸ *basis)* solide; *(*▸ *foundations)* stable; *Com & Fin (*▸ *currency, market)* stable; *(*▸ *offer, sale, deal)* ferme; **these shares remain f. at 370p** ces actions se maintiennent à 370 pence; **the dollar remained f. against the yen** le dollar est resté fort contre le yen

3 *(strong* ▸ *handshake, grip, leadership)* ferme; **to have a f. hold** *or* **grasp** *or* **grip of sth** tenir qch fermement

4 *(unshakeable, definite* ▸ *belief, evidence, friendship)* solide; *(*▸ *view, opinion)* déterminé, arrêté; *(*▸ *intention, voice, agreement, offer)* ferme; *(*▸ *date)* définitif; **they are f. friends** ce sont de bons amis; **he was very f. about this** il a été très ferme à ce propos; **a f. favourite for the Derby/with the crowd** un grand favori dans le Derby/auprès de la foule; **I am a f. believer in female equality** je crois fermement à l'égalité de la femme; **to be f. with a child/dog** être ferme avec un enfant/chien

ADV to stand f. on sth ne pas céder sur qch

VT to f. the soil tasser le sol

VI *(muscles, prices)* se raffermir

▸ **firm up** **VT SEP** *(make firm* ▸ *muscles, prices)* raffermir; **to f. up an agreement** régler les derniers détails d'un accord

VI *(muscles, prices)* se raffermir

firmament ['fɜːməmənt] **N** *Arch or Literary (sky)* firmament *m*

firmly ['fɜːmlɪ] **ADV 1** *(tightly* ▸ *hold, grasp something)* fermement; *(*▸ *closed, secured)* bien; *Fig* **to keep one's feet f. on the ground** bien garder les pieds sur terre, rester fermement ancré dans la réalité **2** *(say, deny, refuse, deal with)* fermement, avec fermeté; **I f. believe that...** j'ai la ferme conviction que... + *indicative*

firmness ['fɜːmnɪs] **N 1** *(hardness* ▸ *of flesh, fruit, mattress)* fermeté *f*

2 *(stability* ▸ *of basis)* solidité *f*; *(*▸ *of foundations)* stabilité *f*; *Com & Fin (*▸ *of currency, market, prices)* stabilité *f*

3 *(strength* ▸ *of handshake, grip, leadership, character, belief)* fermeté *f*

4 *(of voice, denial, refusal)* fermeté *f*

firmware ['fɜːmweə(r)] **N** *Comput* firmware *m*, microprogramme *m*

FIRST [fɜːst]

ADJ	
• premier **1, 3**	
ADV	
• le premier **1**	• d'abord **2**
• en premier **1**	• pour la première fois **3**
N	
• le premier **1, 4**	• première **2, 6**

ADJ 1 *(in series)* premier; **the f. few days** les deux ou trois premiers jours; **the f. six months** les six premiers mois; **Louis the F.** Louis Premier *ou* Ier; **one hundred and f.** cent unième; **to be f. in the queue** être le (la) premier(ère) de la queue; **I'm f.** je suis *ou* c'est moi le premier; **she was f. in English Literature** elle était première en littérature anglaise; **she's in f. place** *(in race)* elle est en tête; **to win f. prize** gagner le premier prix; **this is the f. time I've been to New York** c'est la première fois que je viens à New York; **f. floor** *Br* premier étage *m*; *Am* rez-de-chaussée *m*; *Aut* **f. gear** première *f* (vitesse *f*); **put the car into f. gear** passe la première (vitesse); *Br* **f. year** *Univ* première année *f*; *Sch* sixième *f*; *Br* **a f.-year university student** un étudiant de première année à l'université; **I learnt of it at f. hand** je l'ai appris de la bouche de l'intéressé/l'intéressée, c'est lui-même/elle-même qui me l'a appris; **I haven't (got) the f. idea** je n'en ai pas la moindre idée; **I don't know the f. thing about cars** je n'y connais absolument rien en voitures; **I'll pick you up f. thing (in the morning)** je passerai te chercher demain matin à la première heure; **I'm not at my best f. thing in the morning** je ne suis pas au mieux de ma forme très tôt le matin; **there's a f. time for everything** il y a un début à tout; **to be the f. person to do sth** être le (la) premier(ère) à faire qch

2 *(immediately)* **f. thing after lunch** tout de suite après le déjeuner

3 *(most important* ▸ *duty, concern)* premier; **the f. priority** la priorité des priorités; **f. things f.!** prenons les choses dans l'ordre!; **to go back to f. principles** repartir sur des bases saines

ADV 1 *(before the others* ▸ *arrive, leave, speak)* le (la) premier(ère), en premier; **I saw it f.!** c'est moi qui l'ai vu le (la) premier(ère) *ou* en premier!; **you go f.** vas-y en premier; **ladies f.** les dames d'abord; *Comput & Ind* **f. in, f. out** premier entré, premier sorti; *Admin* **last in, f. out** dernier entré, premier sorti; **to come f.** *(in race)* arriver premier; *(in exam)* avoir la première place, être premier; **her career comes f.** sa carrière passe d'abord *ou* avant tout; **to put one's family f.** faire passer sa famille d'abord *ou* avant tout; *Prov* **f. come f. served** les premiers arrivés sont les premiers servis; **tickets were handed out on a f. come f. served basis** les billets ont été distribués par ordre d'arrivée

2 *(firstly, before anything else)* d'abord; **f., I want to say thank you** tout d'abord, je voudrais vous remercier, je voudrais d'abord vous remercier;

f. prepare the meat préparez d'abord la viande; **what should I do f.?** qu'est-ce que je dois faire en premier?; **she says f. one thing then another** elle dit d'abord une chose, et puis une autre; **I'm a mother f. and a wife second** je suis une mère avant d'être une épouse

3 *(for the first time)* pour la première fois; *(initially)* au début; **we f. met in London** nous nous sommes rencontrés à Londres; **when I f. knew him** quand je l'ai connu

4 *(sooner, rather)* **I'd die f.!** plutôt mourir!

N 1 *(before all others)* **the f.** le (la) premier(ère); **we were the very f. to arrive** nous sommes arrivés les tout premiers; **she was the f. in our family to go to university** c'était la première de la famille à aller à l'université; **he came in an easy f.** *(in race)* il est arrivé premier haut la main

2 *(achievement)* première *f*; **that's a notable f. for France** c'est une grande première pour la France

3 *(first time)* **the f. we heard/knew of it was when...** nous en avons entendu parler pour la première fois/l'avons appris quand...; **it's the f. I've heard of it!** première nouvelle!

4 *(in dates)* **the f. of May/the month** le premier mai/du mois

5 *Br Univ* **he got a f. in economics** il a eu mention très bien en économie; **she got a double f. in French and Russian** elle a eu mention très bien en français et en russe

6 *Aut* première *f*; **in f.** en première; **to put the car into f.** se mettre en première, passer la première

• **at first** **ADV** au début

• **first and foremost** **ADV** d'abord et surtout

• **first and last** **ADV** avant tout

• **first of all** **ADV** tout d'abord, pour commencer

• **first off** **ADV** *Fam* pour commencer▫

• **from first to last** **ADV** du début à la fin

• **from the (very) first** **ADV** dès le début

• **in the first instance** **ADV** d'abord; **apply in the f. instance to the personnel department** adressez d'abord votre demande au service du personnel

• **in the first place** **ADV 1** *(referring to a past action)* d'abord; **why did you do it in the f. place?** et puis d'abord, pourquoi as-tu fait cela?

2 *(introducing an argument)* d'abord; **in the f. place... and in the second place** d'abord... et ensuite

►► ***first aid*** **N** *(UNCOUNT) (technique)* secourisme *m*; *(attention)* premiers soins *mpl*; **to give/to receive f. aid** donner/recevoir les premiers soins **COMP** *(class, manual)* de secourisme; ***first aid box*** trousse *f* à pharmacie; ***first aid certificate*** brevet *m* de secourisme; ***first aid kit*** trousse *f* à pharmacie; *Br* ***first aid post, first aid station*** poste *m* de secours; *Am* ***the First Amendment*** le premier amendement *(de la Constitution des États-Unis garantissant la liberté d'expression, de culte et de réunion ainsi que la liberté de la presse)*; ***first class*** *(on train, plane)* première classe *f*; *Br (for letter, parcel)* tarif *m* normal; ***first cousin*** cousin(e) *m,f* germain(e); *Br* ***first eleven*** *(in soccer, cricket)* = les onze meilleurs joueurs sélectionnés pour former l'équipe la plus forte dans un club; *Am* ***the First Family*** *(presidential family)* la famille présidentielle; *(in a State)* la famille du gouverneur; *Br Sch* ***first form*** sixième *f*; *also Fig* ***first fruits*** premiers fruits *mpl*; *Am Sch* ***first grade*** = classe de l'école primaire (5 à 6 ans); *Sport* ***first half*** première mi-temps *f*; ***First Lady*** *(in US)* = femme du président des États-Unis; *Fig* **the f. lady of rock/of the detective novel** la grande dame du rock/du roman policier; ***first language*** langue *f* maternelle; ***first lieutenant*** *Naut* lieutenant *m* de vaisseau; *Am Mil & Aviat* lieutenant *m*; ***first love*** premier amour *m*; *Naut* ***first mate*** second *m*; *Pol* ***First Minister*** *(of Scottish Parliament)* Premier ministre *m*; ***first name*** prénom *m*; **to be on f. name terms with sb** appeler qn par son prénom; *Theat* ***first night*** première *f*; *Law* ***first offence*** premier délit *m*; *Law* ***first offender*** délinquant(e) *m,f* primaire; *Naut* ***first officer*** second *m*; *Theat* ***first performance*** première *f*; *Gram* ***first person*** première personne *f*; **in the f. person** à la première personne; ***first principle*** principe *m* fondamental *ou* de base; *Fin* ***first quarter*** *(of financial year)* premier trimestre *m*; ***first refusal*** préférence *f*; **to give sb f. refusal on sth** donner la préférence à qn pour qch; *Cin* ***first showing*** première exclusivité *f*; *Am* ***the First State*** = surnom donné au Delaware; *Sport* ***first string*** les meilleurs joueurs *mpl (d'une équipe)*; *Sport* ***first team*** (équipe *f*) première *f*; *Mus* ***first violin*** *(person, instrument)* premier violon *m*; ***the First World*** les pays *mpl* industrialisés; ***the First World War*** la Première Guerre mondiale

first-born **N** premier-né (première-née) *m,f* **ADJ** premier-né

first-degree **ADJ**

►► *Med* ***first-degree burn*** brûlure *f* au premier degré; *Am Law* ***first-degree murder*** meurtre *m* avec préméditation

first-foot *Scot* **N** = premier visiteur venant souhaiter la bonne année, la nuit de la Saint-Sylvestre

VT to f. sb = être le premier à rendre visite à quelqu'un pour lui souhaiter la bonne année la nuit de la Saint-Sylvestre

firsthand [fɜːst'hænd] **ADJ** *(knowledge, information, news)* de première main; **I know from f. experience what it is like to be poor** je sais d'expérience ce que c'est que d'être pauvre

ADV *(hear of something)* de première main

first-in first-out **ADJ** *Comput & Ind* premier entré, premier sorti

firstly ['fɜːstlɪ] **ADV** premièrement, en premier lieu

first-night **ADJ f. nerves** trac *m (du soir de la première)*

first-nighter [-'naɪtə(r)] **N** *Theat* spectateur (trice) *m,f* assistant *ou* ayant assisté à la première

first-notice day **N** *St Exch* premier jour *m* de notification

first-off **N** *Mktg* produit *m* vedette

first-past-the-post **ADJ** *Br Pol (system)* majoritaire à un tour; **the f. electoral system** le scrutin majoritaire à un tour

first-rate **ADJ** *(excellent ► wine, meal, restaurant)* de première qualité, excellent; *(► idea, performance, student)* excellent; **he's a f. badminton/chess player** il est excellent au badminton/aux échecs; *Br* **that's absolutely f.!** *(idea, news etc)* c'est formidable!

first-strike **ADJ** *Mil (missile)* de première frappe; **a f. capability** une force de frappe importante *(permettant d'attaquer en premier)*

first-time **ADJ f. visitors to the country** les personnes visitant le pays pour la première fois

►► ***first-time buyer*** *(of property)* primo-accédant *m*

firth [fɜːθ] **N** *Scot* estuaire *m*

fiscal ['fɪskəl] **ADJ** fiscal

N *Scot Law* **(procurator) f.** procureur *m* de la République

►► *Econ* ***fiscal austerity*** austérité *f* fiscale; *Econ* ***fiscal balance*** équilibre *m* fiscal; *Econ* ***fiscal drag*** frein *m* fiscal, érosion *f* fiscale; *Fin* ***fiscal measure*** mesure *f* fiscale; *Am Acct* ***fiscal period*** période *f* comptable; *Fin* ***fiscal policy*** politique *f* budgétaire; *Am* ***fiscal year*** *Fin* exercice *m* (financier), année *f* fiscale *ou* d'exercice; *Admin* année *f* budgétaire

> **FISCAL YEAR**
>
> En Grande-Bretagne, l'année fiscale commence le 1er avril pour les entreprises et le 6 avril pour les particuliers. Aux États-Unis, l'année fiscale correspond à l'année civile pour les particuliers.

fiscality [fɪ'skælətɪ] **N** fiscalité *f*

fish [fɪʃ] *(pl* **inv** *or* **fishes) N 1** *(aquatic creature)* poisson *m*; *Astrol* **the F.** les Poissons *mpl*; **he caught three f.** il a attrapé *ou* pris trois poissons; **I eat a lot of f.** je mange beaucoup de poisson; *Br* **f. and chips** poisson *m* frit avec des frites **2** *(idioms) Fam* **he's a queer f.** c'est un drôle de type; **to feel like a f. out of water** ne pas se sentir dans son élément; *Fam* **to drink like a f.** boire comme un trou; **there are plenty more f. in the sea** un de perdu, dix de retrouvés; **to have other f. to fry** avoir d'autres chats à fouetter; **to be a big f. in a small pond** être grand parmi les petits; **to be a little f. in a big pond** être perdu dans la masse; **neither f. nor fowl (nor good red herring)** ni chair ni poisson

COMP *(course, restaurant)* de poisson

VI 1 *Sport* pêcher; **to f. with a line/a rod** pêcher à la ligne/avec une canne; **to go fishing** aller à la pêche; **to go trout fishing** *or* **fishing for trout** aller à la pêche à la truite, aller pêcher la truite; *Fig* **to f. in troubled waters** pêcher en eau trouble; *Am Fam Fig* **to f. or cut bait** se décider▫ **2** *(search, seek)* **he fished around for his pen under the papers** il a fouillé sous ses papiers pour trouver son crayon; **to f. for information** essayer de soutirer des informations; **to f. for compliments** rechercher les compliments

VT *(river, lake etc)* pêcher dans

►► *Am Orn* ***fish eagle*** balbuzard *m*, *Can* aigle *m* pêcheur; ***fish farm*** établissement *m* piscicole; ***fish farmer*** pisciculteur(trice) *m,f*; ***fish farming*** pisciculture *f*; *Br* ***fish finger*** bâtonnet *m* de poisson pané; ***fish glue*** colle *f* de poisson; *Orn* ***fish hawk*** balbuzard *m*, *Can* aigle *m* pêcheur; ***fish hook*** hameçon *m*; ***fish kettle*** poissonnière *f*; ***fish knife*** couteau *m* à poisson; ***fish ladder*** échelle *f* à poissons; ***fish market*** marché *m* au poisson; ***fish meal*** farine *f* de poisson; ***fish paste*** pâte *f* de poisson; ***fish shop*** poissonnerie *f*; ***fish slice*** pelle *f* à poisson; *Am* ***fish stick*** bâtonnet *m* de poisson pané; *Scot* ***fish supper*** poisson *m* frit avec des frites *(à emporter)*; ***fish tank*** *(in house)* aquarium *m*; *(on fish farm)* vivier *m*

► **fish out** **VT SEP** *(from water)* repêcher; *Fig* **he fished out his wallet** il a sorti son portefeuille; *(with difficulty)* il a extrait son portefeuille; **she fished her keys out of her bag** elle a fouillé dans son sac et en a extrait ses clés

► **fish up** **VT SEP** *(from water)* repêcher; **to f. up sth from one's memory** ressortir qch de sa mémoire; *Fam* **where did you f. that up from?** *(object)* où est-ce que tu as été dénicher ça?; *(idea)* où est-ce que tu as été pêcher ça?

fish-and-chip shop **N** *Br* = boutique où l'on vend des frites ainsi que du poisson frit, des saucisses etc

fisherman ['fɪʃəmən] *(pl* **fishermen** [-mən]) **N** pêcheur *m*

►► ***fisherman's bend*** *(knot)* nœud *m* de grappin

fishery ['fɪʃərɪ] *(pl* **fisheries) N** *(fishing ground)* pêcherie *f*; *(fishing industry)* industrie *f* de la pêche

►► ***fishery protection vessel*** vedette *f* garde-pêche

fish-eye lens **N** *Phot* fish-eye *m*

fishing ['fɪʃɪŋ] **N** pêche *f*; **trout/salmon f.** pêche *f* à la truite/au saumon; **there is some good f. to be had along this river** il y a de bons coins de pêche dans cette rivière; **no f.** *(sign)* pêche interdite

COMP *(vessel, permit, port)* de pêche; *(season)* de la pêche; *(village, party)* de pêcheurs

►► ***fishing boat*** bateau *m* de pêche; ***fishing ground*** zone *f* de pêche; ***fishing line*** ligne *f* de pêche; ***fishing net*** filet *m* de pêche; *Am* ***fishing pole*** canne *f* à pêche, gaule *f*; ***fishing rod*** canne *f* à pêche, gaule *f*; ***fishing tackle*** articles *mpl* de pêche

fishmonger ['fɪʃˌmʌŋgə(r)] **N** *Br* poissonnier (ère) *m,f*; **f.'s** *(shop)* poissonnerie *f*; **to go to the f.'s** aller à la poissonnerie *ou* chez le poissonnier

fishnet ['fɪʃnet] **N** *Am (for catching fish)* filet *m* (de pêche)

►► ***fishnet stockings*** bas *mpl* résille; ***fishnet tights*** collant *m* résille

fishplate ['fɪʃpleɪt] **N** *Rail* éclisse *f*

fishwife ['fɪʃwaɪf] *(pl* **fishwives** [-waɪvz]) **N** poissonnière *f*, marchande *f* de poisson; *Fig* **she's a real f.** elle a un langage de charretier, elle parle comme un charretier

fishy ['fɪʃɪ] *(compar* **fishier**, *superl* **fishiest) ADJ 1** *(smell, taste)* de poisson **2** *Fam (suspicious)* louche▫; **there's something f. going on** il se passe quelque chose de louche; **there's something f. about her alibi** il y a quelque chose qui ne colle pas dans son alibi

fissile ['fɪsaɪl] **ADJ** *Phys* fissible, fissile

fission ['fɪʃən] **N** *Phys* fission *f*, *Biol* scissiparité *f*; **nuclear f.** fission *f* nucléaire

►► ***fission bomb*** bombe *f* atomique; *Nucl* ***fission reactor*** pile *f* atomique

fissure ['fɪʃə(r)] *Geol* N *(crevice, crack)* fissure *f*; *Fig* fissure *f*, brèche *f*
VT fissurer, fendre
VI se fissurer, se fendre

fist [fɪst] N poing *m*; **to clench one's fists** serrer les poings; **he shook his f. at me** il m'a menacé du poing; **to put one's fists up** se mettre en garde; **make a f.** serrez le poing

fistful ['fɪstfʊl] N poignée *f*

fisticuffs ['fɪstɪkʌfs] NPL *Br Hum* bagarre *f*

fistula ['fɪstjʊlə] N *Med* fistule *f*

FIT [fɪt]

ADJ	
• convenable **1**	• en forme **3**
N	
• crise **2**	• accès **3**
VT	
• aller à **1**	• correspondre à **2**
• installer **4**	• fixer **5**
• équiper **6**	
VI	
• correspondre **2**	

(*compar* **fitter**, *superl* **fittest**, *Br pt & pp* **fitted**, *cont* **fitting**, *Am pt & pp* **fit**, *cont* **fitting**)

ADJ **1** *(suitable)* convenable; **that dress isn't f. to wear** cette robe n'est pas mettable; **f. to eat** *(edible)* mangeable; *(not poisonous)* comestible; **f. to drink** *(water)* potable; **this coffee is not f. to drink** ce café est imbuvable; **a meal f. for a king** un repas digne d'un roi; **she's not f. to look after children** elle ne devrait pas avoir le droit de s'occuper d'enfants; **she's not a f. mother** c'est une mère indigne; **he's not f. to polish my boots** il n'est même pas bon à cirer mes chaussures; **my grandmother is no longer f. to drive** ma grand-mère n'est plus capable de conduire; **I'm not f. to be seen** je ne suis pas présentable; **these programmes aren't f. for children** ce ne sont pas des programmes pour les enfants; **throw it in the bin, that's all it's f. for** jette-le à la poubelle, c'est tout ce que ça mérite; **that's all he's f. for** c'est tout ce qu'il mérite; **to think** *or* **to see f. to do sth** trouver *ou* juger bon de faire qch; **do as you see** *or* **think f.** fais comme tu penses *ou* juges bon

2 *Fam (ready)* **to be f. to drop** être mort de fatigue; **I feel f. to burst** je me sens prêt à éclater; *Am* **I was f. to be tied** *(extremely angry)* j'étais furax

3 *(healthy)* en forme; *Br* **to get f.** retrouver la forme; *Br* **I've never felt fitter in my life** je ne me suis jamais senti en meilleure forme; **as f. as a fiddle** en pleine forme; **to keep** *or* **to stay f.** entretenir sa forme; **she is not a f. woman** *(well)* elle n'est pas en bonne santé; **the fittest member of the team** la personne la plus en forme de l'équipe; **it's a case of the survival of the fittest** ce sont les plus forts qui survivent; **f. for duty** bon pour le service; *Mil* valide

4 *Br Fam (good-looking)* bien foutu

N **1** *(size)* **it's a perfect f.** *(item of clothing)* cela me/vous/*etc* va à merveille; *(fridge, stove, piece of furniture)* cela s'adapte parfaitement; *(two interlocking pieces)* cela s'emboîte bien; **it's not a very good f.** *(too large)* c'est trop grand; *(too tight)* c'est trop juste; **tight/loose/comfortable f.** *(item of clothing)* coupe *f* ajustée/ample/confortable; **these trousers are a bit of a tight f.** ce pantalon est un peu juste; **it was a bit of a tight f.** *(in room, car)* on était un peu à l'étroit; *(parking car)* il n'y avait pas beaucoup de place

2 *Med (of apoplexy, epilepsy, hysterics)* crise *f*; **f. of coughing, coughing f.** quinte *f* de toux; **f. of crying** crise *f* de larmes; *Med* **to have a f.** avoir une crise; *Fig* **she'll have a f. when she finds out** elle va faire une crise quand elle le saura; *Fam* **to throw a f.** piquer une crise; **he nearly threw a f. when he heard the news** il a failli exploser quand il a appris la nouvelle

3 *(outburst ► of anger)* mouvement *m*, accès *m*, moment *m*; *(► of depression)* crise *f*; *(► of pique, generosity)* moment *m*; *(► of madness)* accès *m*; **he did it in a f. of rage/temper** il a fait cela dans un mouvement de rage/colère; **to be in fits (of laughter)** avoir le fou rire; **he had us all in fits** il nous a fait hurler *ou* mourir de rire; **to get a f. of the giggles** être pris d'un *ou* piquer un fou rire; **in a sudden f. of energy** dans un sursaut d'énergie; **to work by** *or* **in fits and starts** travailler par à-coups

VT **1** *(be the correct size for)* **to f. sb** aller à qn; **none of the keys fitted the lock** aucune des clés n'entrait dans la serrure; **doesn't the lid f. the box/jar?** le couvercle ne va-t-il pas sur la boîte/le bocal?; **the lid doesn't f. the pot very well** ce couvercle n'est pas très bien adapté à la casserole

2 *(correspond to, match ► description)* correspondre à; **to make the punishment f. the crime** adapter le châtiment au crime; **the music fitted the occasion** la musique était de circonstance; **to f. the bill** faire l'affaire

3 *(make suitable for)* **what do you think fits you for the job?** en quoi estimez-vous correspondre au profil de l'emploi?

4 *(install ► lock, door, window etc)* installer; *Br (carpet)* poser; *Br* **to have double-glazing fitted** se faire installer *ou* mettre le double vitrage; *Br* **to f. a kitchen** installer une cuisine; *Br* **I've got special tyres fitted** je me suis fait mettre des pneus spéciaux

5 *(attach, fix on)* fixer; **to f. a nozzle on the end of a pipe** adapter un ajutage à l'extrémité d'un tuyau; **then you f. the parts together** puis vous assemblez les différentes pièces

6 *(equip)* équiper; **to f. sth with sth** équiper qch de qch; **fitted with electronic security devices** équipé de dispositifs de sécurité électroniques

7 *(take measurements of ► person)* **to be fitted for a new suit** faire un essayage pour un nouveau costume

8 *(adjust ► idea, theory)* adapter; **I'll f. the dress on you** j'essaierai la robe sur vous

VI **1** *(be the correct size)* **the dress doesn't f.** la robe ne lui/me/*etc* va pas; **this lid/key doesn't f.** ce couvercle/cette clé n'est pas le bon/la bonne; **the key won't f. in the lock** la clé n'entre pas dans la serrure; **do these pieces f. together?** est-ce que ces morceaux vont ensemble?; **it won't f.** cela n'ira pas; **we won't all f. round one table** nous ne tiendrons pas tous autour d'une table; **the photos just f. onto the page** les photos tiennent juste sur la page; **cut the pieces to f.** couper les morceaux aux mesures adéquates

2 *(correspond, match ► description)* correspondre; **it all fits** tout concorde; **to f. with sth** correspondre à qch; *Fam* **my face didn't f.** je n'avais pas le profil de l'emploi▫

► **fit in** VI **1** *(go in space available)* tenir; **we won't all f. in** nous ne tiendrons pas tous; **that piece fits in here** *(jigsaw)* ce morceau va là **2** *(in company, group etc)* s'intégrer; **you don't f. in here** tu n'es pas à ta place ici; **I feel that I don't f. in** j'ai l'impression de ne pas être à ma place; **to f. in with** *(statement)* correspondre à; *(colour scheme)* s'accorder avec; **your plans don't f. in with mine** vos projets ne cadrent pas avec les miens; **she doesn't f. in easily with other people** elle a du mal à s'entendre avec les autres

VT SEP **1** *(install)* installer **2** *(find room for ► clothes in suitcase)* faire entrer; **can you f. one more in?** *(in car)* peux-tu prendre une personne de plus?; **how on earth are you going to f. everyone in?** *(in room, car etc)* comment diable vas-tu réussir à faire tenir tout le monde? **3** *(find time for ► patient)* prendre; *(► friend)* trouver du temps pour; **could you f. in this translation by the end of the week?** est-ce que vous pourriez faire cette traduction d'ici la fin de la semaine?; **could you f. in lunch this week?** *(with me)* est-ce que tu seras libre pour déjeuner avec moi cette semaine?; **I hope we've got time to f. in a visit to the Louvre** j'espère que nous aurons le temps de visiter le Louvre; **I don't know how he fits it all in** je me demande comment il trouve le temps de tout faire

► **fit out** VT SEP *(ship)* armer; *(person ► with equipment)* équiper; **to f. a child out with new clothes** renouveler la garde-robe d'un enfant

► **fit up** VT SEP **1** *(equip ► house, car)* équiper; *(► person)* munir; **to f. sb/sth up with sth** munir qn/équiper qch de qch; **they fitted me up with an artificial leg** ils m'ont mis une jambe artificielle **2** *Br Fam Crime slang* monter un coup contre; **I've been fitted up** c'est un coup monté

fitful ['fɪtfʊl] ADJ *(sleep)* intermittent; *(night)* agité, *(cough)* quinteux; **to make f. progress** progresser par à-coups; **attendance has been f.** les gens ne sont pas venus régulièrement

fitfully ['fɪtfʊlɪ] ADV *(work)* par à-coups; *(attend)* irrégulièrement; *(sleep)* de manière intermittente

fitment ['fɪtmənt] N *Br (in bathroom, kitchen etc)* élément *m* démontable

fitness ['fɪtnɪs] N **1** *(health)* forme *f* physique **2** *(suitability ► of person for job)* aptitude *f*; **your f. as a mother is not in question** vos compétences de mère ne sont pas en cause
►► *Br* ***fitness centre*** club *m* de gym; *Fam* ***fitness freak*** fana *mf* d'exercice physique; ***fitness room*** salle *f* de musculation; ***fitness training*** entraînement *m* physique

fitted ['fɪtəd] ADJ **1** *(garment)* ajusté
2 *Br (made to measure)* **the house has f. carpets in every room** il y a de la moquette dans toutes les pièces de la maison
3 *Br (built-in ► cupboard)* encastré
4 *(suited)* **to be f. for sth/doing sth** être apte à qch/à faire qch
►► ***fitted kitchen*** cuisine *f* intégrée; ***fitted sheet*** drap-housse *m*

fitter ['fɪtə(r)] N **1** *(of machine)* monteur(euse) *m,f*; *(of carpet)* poseur(euse) *m,f* **2** *(of clothes)* essayeur(euse) *m,f*

fitting ['fɪtɪŋ] ADJ *(suitable ► conclusion, remark)* approprié; *(socially correct)* convenable; **it was a f. tribute to a great athlete** c'était un hommage mérité rendu à un grand athlète; **it was only f. he should score the winning goal** ce n'était que justice qu'il marque le but gagnant
N **1** *(trying on ► of clothes)* essayage *m*; **I'm going for a f. tomorrow** j'ai rendez-vous pour un essayage demain **2** *Br (of shoe)* **have you got it in a wider/narrower f.?** l'avez-vous en plus large/plus étroit?
• **fittings** NPL *Br (of office)* installations *fpl*; *(of bathroom)* accessoires *mpl*; **electrical fittings** appareillage *m* électrique
►► ***fitting out*** *(of expedition etc)* équipement *m*; *(of ship)* armement *m*; ***fitting room*** salon *m ou* salle *f* d'essayage; *(cubicle)* cabine *f* d'essayage

fittingly ['fɪtɪŋlɪ] ADV convenablement; **f., he was buried in his home town** comme il convenait, il a été enterré dans sa ville natale

five [faɪv] N *(number, numeral)* cinq *m inv*; **f. times table** table *f* des cinq; **f. and f. are ten** cinq et cinq font dix; **I'm waiting for a number f. (bus)** j'attends le (bus numéro) cinq; *Cards* **the f. of hearts** le cinq de cœur; **to be f.** *(in age)* avoir cinq ans; **it's f. o'clock** il est cinq heures; **it's f. to/past f.** il est cinq heures moins cinq/cinq heures cinq; **come at f.** venez à cinq heures; **to get f. out of ten** avoir cinq sur dix; **a table for f.** une table pour cinq (personnes)
PRON cinq; **I need f. (of them)** il m'en faut cinq, j'en ai besoin de cinq; **there are f. (of them)** *(people)* ils sont cinq; *(objects)* il y en a cinq; **all f. of them left** tous les cinq sont partis, ils sont partis tous les cinq; *Fam* **to take f.** faire un break de cinq minutes▫; *Fam* **give me f.!** tope là! *(pour conclure un marché, dire bonjour ou manifester son approbation)*
ADJ cinq; **on page f.** (à la) page cinq; **they live at number f.** ils habitent au numéro cinq; **trains leave at f. minutes to the hour** le train part toutes les heures à moins cinq; **to be f. years old** avoir cinq ans
• **fives** N = sorte de squash où l'on utilise ses mains ou des battes en guise de raquettes
►► *Am Hist* ***the Five Nations*** les Cinq Nations iroquoises; *Formerly Sport* ***the Five Nations (Championship)*** le Tournoi des Cinq Nations; *Am Fam* ***five spot*** billet *m* de cinq dollars▫

five-day week N *Br* semaine *f* de cinq jours

five-door model N *Aut* (version *f*) cinq portes *f*

five-finger discount N *Fam Hum* **I got a f. on this CD** j'ai fauché ce CD

fivefold ['faɪvfəʊld] ADJ quintuple
ADV par cinq, au quintuple; **to increase f.** être multiplié par cinq, augmenter au quintuple, quintupler

fiver ['faɪvə(r)] N *Fam (five-pound note)* billet *m* de cinq livres□; *(five-dollar bill)* billet *m* de cinq dollars□; *Br* **it'll cost you a f.** ça te coûtera cinq livres□

five-seater N *Aut* cinq places *f*

five-speed gearbox N *Aut* boîte *f* cinq-vitesses, boîte *f* de vitesses cinq rapports

five-star ADJ *(hotel)* cinq étoiles

five-year ADJ *(plan)* quinquennal

FIX [fɪks]

VT	
• fixer **1, 2, 11, 12**	• s'occuper de **3, 4**
• préparer **5**	• arranger **6**
• réparer **7**	
N	
• pétrin **1**	• dose **2**

VT **1** *(fasten in position ▸ mirror, sign)* fixer; *(attention, gaze)* fixer; *(something in mind)* inscrire, graver; **to f. a post in the ground** enfoncer un poteau dans le sol; *Mil* **f. bayonets!** baïonnettes aux canons!; **to f. the blame on sb** attribuer *ou* imputer la faute à qn; **to f. one's hopes on sb/sth** mettre tous ses espoirs en qn/qch
2 *(set ▸ date, price, rate, limit)* fixer; *(▸ meeting place)* convenir de; **nothing has been fixed yet** rien n'a encore été fixé; **have you (got) anything fixed for Friday?** as-tu quelque chose de prévu pour vendredi?
3 *(arrange, sort out)* s'occuper de; **I'll f. it** je vais m'en occuper; **try to f. it so you don't have to stay overnight** essaye de t'arranger pour que tu ne sois pas obligé de passer la nuit là-bas; **I'll f. it with your teacher** j'arrangerai cela avec ton professeur; **I've fixed it for them to come tomorrow** je me suis arrangé pour qu'ils viennent demain
4 *Fam (settle a score with)* s'occuper de, régler son compte à; **I'll f. him** je vais m'occuper de lui, je vais lui régler son compte; **that'll f. him** ça devrait lui régler son compte
5 *Am Fam (prepare ▸ meal, drink)* préparer□; **can I f. you a drink?** puis-je te servir un verre?□
6 *Fam (adjust ▸ make-up, tie)* arranger□; **to f. one's hair** se coiffer□; *(redo)* se recoiffer□
7 *(mend, repair ▸ car, puncture etc)* réparer; **I've been meaning to get that fixed for ages** ça fait une éternité que j'ai l'intention de faire réparer ça
8 *Fam (rig ▸ race, fight, election, result)* truquer; *(set up ▸ interview)* arranger□; *(bribe ▸ jury, official, security guard etc)* acheter
9 *Am Fam (intend, plan)* prévoir de□; *(be determined)* être résolu à□; **he's fixing to go on holiday** *(planning)* il a prévu de partir en vacances; *(determined)* il est résolu à partir en vacances
10 *Aviat & Naut (position)* déterminer
11 *Chem (nitrogen)* fixer
12 *Art & Phot (drawing, photo)* fixer
13 *Fam Euph (neuter)* châtrer□
N **1** *Fam (tight spot, predicament)* pétrin *m*; **to be in a f.** être dans une mauvaise passe; **to get into/out of a f.** se mettre dans une/sortir d'une mauvaise passe; **you've put me in a bit of a f.** tu me mets dans l'embarras; **I'm in a bit of a f. financially** j'ai quelques difficultés financières□
2 *Fam Drugs slang* dose *f*, fix *m*; **to give oneself a f.** prendre un fix, se piquer; *Hum* **to get one's f. of coffee/news** avoir sa dose de café/d'informations
3 *Aviat & Naut* **to get a f. on** *(ship)* déterminer la position de; *Fig (get clear idea of)* se faire une idée de
4 *Fam (unfair arrangement)* **the result was a f.** le résultat avait été truqué□

▸ **fix on** VT SEP *(attach)* fixer
VT INSEP *(decide on ▸ date, candidate)* choisir

▸ **fix up** VT SEP **1** *(install, erect)* mettre en place, installer **2** *Fam (arrange ▸ date, meeting)* fixer□; *(▸ deal, holiday)* organiser□, mettre au point□; **it's all fixed up** c'est une affaire réglée, tout est arrangé; **f. me up with an appointment with the dentist** prends-moi un rendez-vous chez le dentiste; **he'll try to f. something up for us** il va essayer de nous arranger quelque chose; **have you got anything fixed up for this evening?** as-tu quelque chose de prévu pour ce soir?; **I've managed to f. him up with some work** j'ai réussi à lui trouver du travail; **you can stay here until you get fixed up (with a place to stay)** tu peux loger ici jusqu'à ce que tu trouves un endroit où habiter; **to f. sb up with a date** trouver un/une partenaire à qn **3** *(room)* refaire; *(flat, house)* refaire, retaper; **we could always f. the smallest bedroom up as a study** on pourrait toujours transformer la plus petite chambre en bureau
VI s'arranger pour que + *subjunctive*; **I've fixed up for us to see the flat tomorrow** je me suis arrangé pour que nous visitions l'appartement demain; **I've already fixed up to go out tonight** j'ai déjà prévu de sortir ce soir

fixated [fɪk'seɪtɪd] ADJ obsédé; **to be f. on sth** faire une fixation sur qch, être obsédé par qch

fixation [fɪk'seɪʃən] N **1** *(obsession)* fixation *f*; **to have a f. about sth** faire une fixation sur qch **2** *Chem* fixation *f*

fixative ['fɪksətɪv] N *Phot* fixateur *m*; *Art* fixatif *m*

fixed [fɪkst] ADJ **1** *(immovable ▸ glare)* fixe; *(▸ idea)* arrêté; *(▸ smile)* figé; **the seats are f. to the floor** les sièges sont fixés au sol **2** *(set, unchangeable ▸ price, rate, plans)* fixe; **people on f. incomes** des gens disposant de revenus fixes; *Law* **of no f. abode** sans domicile fixe **3** *Fam (placed)* **how are you f. for time/money?** *(how much do you have?)* combien de temps/d'argent as-tu?□; *(do you have enough?)* as-tu suffisamment de temps/d'argent?□; **how are you f. for accommodation/transport?** est-ce que tu as un endroit où loger/un moyen de transport?□
▸▸ *Fin* ***fixed assets*** immobilisations *fpl*, actif *m* immobilisé; *Cin & TV* ***fixed camera*** caméra *f* fixe; *Fin* ***fixed charge*** frais *mpl* fixes; *Fin* ***fixed cost*** coût *m* fixe *ou* constant, charge *f* fixe; *Com* ***fixed deposit*** dépôt *m* à terme (fixe) *ou* à échéance fixe; *Comput* ***fixed disk*** disque *m* fixe; *Fin* ***fixed exchange rate*** taux *m* de change fixe; *Cin & TV* ***fixed focus lens*** focale *f* fixe; *Fin* ***fixed income*** revenu *m* fixe; *Fin* ***fixed interest*** intérêt *m* fixe; *Fin* ***fixed investment*** immobilisations *fpl*; *Law* ***fixed penalty*** pénalité *f* fixe; ***fixed point*** point *m* fixe, point *m* de repère; *Math* ***fixed point arithmetic*** arithmétique *f* en virgule fixe; *Fin* ***fixed property*** immeubles *mpl*; *Fin* ***fixed rate*** taux *m* fixe; *Com* ***fixed salary*** salaire *m* fixe; *Astron* ***fixed satellite*** satellite *m* géostationnaire; *Comput & Typ* ***fixed space*** espace *m* fixe; *Comput & Typ* ***fixed spacing*** espacement *m* fixe; *Astron* ***fixed star*** étoile *f* fixe; *Com* ***fixed wage*** salaire *m* fixe

fixed-income ADJ *Fin* à revenu fixe
▸▸ ***fixed-income investment*** placement *m* à revenu fixe; ***fixed-income securities*** valeurs *fpl* à revenu fixe

fixed-interest ADJ *Fin* à intérêt fixe
▸▸ ***fixed-interest market*** marché *m* des obligations; ***fixed-interest securities*** valeurs *fpl* à intérêt fixe

fixedly ['fɪksɪdlɪ] ADV *(stare)* fixement

fixed-penalty ADJ *Law (crime, offence)* à pénalité fixe

fixed-price menu N menu *m* à prix fixe

fixed-rate ADJ *Fin (loan, mortgage)* à taux fixe; *(investment)* à revenu fixe
▸▸ ***fixed-rate bond*** obligation *f* à revenu fixe; ***fixed-rate borrowing*** emprunts *mpl* à taux fixe

fixed-term ADJ *Com* à terme fixe, à date fixe
▸▸ *Fin* ***fixed-term bill*** effet *m* à date fixe; *Com* ***fixed-term contract*** contrat *m* à durée déterminée, CDD *m*; *Fin* ***fixed-term credit*** crédit *m* à durée déterminée; *Fin* ***fixed-term deposit*** dépôt *m* à terme fixe *ou* à échéance fixe

fixer ['fɪksə(r)] N **1** *Fam (person)* combinard(e) *m,f* **2** *Phot* fixateur *m* **3** *(adhesive)* adhésif *m*

fixer-upper N *Fam* = maison ou appartement vendu(e) à bas prix en raison des travaux de rénovation nécessaires

fixing ['fɪksɪŋ] N **1** *(repairing)* réparation *f* **2** *Com (of prices etc)* établissement *m* **3** *St Exch* fixage *m*
• **fixings** NPL *Am (trimmings)* accessoires *mpl*; *(food)* accompagnements *mpl*, garnitures *fpl*; **roast turkey with all the fixings** dinde *f* rôtie avec tout ce qui s'ensuit
▸▸ *Phot* ***fixing bath*** *(container)* cuvette *f* de fixage; *(solution)* bain *m* de fixage; *Phot* ***fixing solution*** solution *f* de fixage

fixity ['fɪksətɪ] N *(of gaze)* fixité *f*; **f. of purpose** détermination *f*

fixture ['fɪkstʃə(r)] N **1** *(in building)* installation *f* fixe; *Fig* **she's become a f. here** elle fait partie des meubles à présent; *Fig* **she was something of a f. at his parties** elle apparaissait inévitablement à chacune de ses soirées; **bathroom fixtures** installations *fpl* sanitaires; **fixtures and fittings** agencements *mpl*, installations *fpl* fixes; *Acct* **fixtures and fittings £2,000** *(on balance sheet)* reprise 2000 livres **2** *Sport* rencontre *f*
▸▸ *Sport* ***fixture list*** calendrier *m*

fizz [fɪz] VI *(drink)* pétiller; *(firework)* crépiter; **the champagne fizzed out of the bottle** le champagne est sorti de la bouteille en pétillant
N **1** *(of drink)* pétillement *m*; **the champagne has lost its f.** le champagne est éventé; *Fig* **their marriage has lost its f.** leur mariage a perdu de son piment **2** *(sound)* sifflement *m* **3** *Fam (soft drink)* boisson *f* à bulles□; *Br (champagne)* champ' *m*; *(sparkling wine)* mousseux□ *m*

fizzle ['fɪzəl] VI *(drink)* pétiller; *(fire, firework)* crépiter; *(gas burner)* siffler

▸ **fizzle out** VI *Fig (interest, enthusiasm, desire)* tomber; *(plan, project)* tomber à l'eau; *(book, film, party, strike etc)* tourner *ou* partir en eau de boudin; *(career)* tourner court

fizzy ['fɪzɪ] *(compar* **fizzier**, *superl* **fizziest***)* ADJ *(soft drink)* gazeux; *(wine)* pétillant, mousseux

fjord = **fiord**

FL, Fla *(written abbr* **Florida***)* Floride *f*

flab [flæb] N *Fam (of person)* graisse□ *f*, lard *m*; *(in text)* délayage□ *m*, verbiage□ *m*; **to fight the f.** essayer de perdre sa graisse□

flabbergasted ['flæbəˌgɑːstɪd] ADJ *Fam* sidéré; **I was f. at** *or* **by the news** j'ai été sidéré par la nouvelle, la nouvelle m'a sidéré; **I was f. by how much he had improved** j'ai été sidéré *ou* époustouflé par ses progrès

flabbiness ['flæbɪnɪs] N *(of skin)* manque *m* de fermeté; *(of skin, arms, stomach, flesh)* manque *m* de fermeté, mollesse *f*; *(of person)* empâtement *m*; *(of person's grip)* mollesse *f*; *Fig (of prose, writing, novel)* prolixité *f*; *(of argument, idea)* faiblesse *f*

flabby ['flæbɪ] *(compar* **flabbier**, *superl* **flabbiest***)* ADJ *(skin)* flasque; *(arms, stomach, flesh)* flasque, mou (molle); *(person)* empâté; *(grip)* mou (molle); *Fig (prose, writing, novel)* prolixe; *(argument, speech)* peu convaincant, faible

flaccid ['flæsɪd] ADJ flasque

flag [flæg] *(pt & pp* **flagged**, *cont* **flagging***)* N **1** *(emblem of country, signal)* drapeau *m*; *(for celebration)* banderole *f*, fanion *m*; *Naut* pavillon *m*; **all the flags are out in the city** la ville est pavoisée; **black f.** *(of pirate ship)* drapeau *m* noir; *Naut* **yellow f.** pavillon *m* de quarantaine; **to fly the f.** défendre les couleurs de son pays; **to go down with all flags flying** *Naut* couler pavillon haut; *Fig* échouer la tête haute; **to keep the f. flying** faire front; **to put out the flags for sb** organiser une fête en l'honneur de qn
2 *(for charity)* = badge ou autocollant que l'on obtient lorsque l'on verse de l'argent à une œuvre de charité
3 *(in taxi)* **the f. was down/up** le taxi était pris/libre; **the driver put the f. down** le chauffeur a éteint son signal lumineux pour indiquer qu'il n'était plus libre
4 *Comput* drapeau *m*, fanion *m*
5 *(on floor)* dalle *f*
6 *Bot* iris *m*
7 *(for file, folder)* papillon *m*
8 *(in golf)* drapeau *m*
VT **1** *(put marker on ▸ page of book)* marquer; *Comput (highlight)* sélectionner; *Comput* **to f. an error** indiquer *ou* signaler une erreur par un drapeau *ou* un fanion **2** *(floor)* daller
VI *(strength)* faiblir; *(energy, enthusiasm, interest, spirits)* faiblir, tomber; *(efforts)* se relâcher; *(conversation)* tomber, s'épuiser; **I'm flagging** *(becom-*

ing physically or mentally tired) je fatigue; *(unable to eat any more)* je commence à être rassasié, je cale

▸▸ **flag airline** compagnie *f* aérienne nationale; *Naut* **flag captain** commandant *m* du navire amiral; **flag carrier** *(airline)* compagnie *f* aérienne nationale; *(shipping company)* compagnie *f* maritime nationale; *Naut* **flag of convenience** pavillon *m* de complaisance; *Am* **Flag Day** le 14 juin *(fête nationale des États-Unis)*; *Br* **flag day** = jour de quête d'une œuvre de charité; *Naut* **flag of distress** pavillon *m* de détresse; *Am* **flag football** = sorte de football américain où le fait d'enlever le foulard qu'un joueur porte autour de la taille tient lieu de placage; *Naut* **flag officer** contre-amiral *m*; *Am* **flag station** gare *f* d'arrêt facultatif; *Naut* **flag of truce** pavillon *m* parlementaire

▸ **flag down** VT SEP *(bus, motorist etc)* faire signe de s'arrêter à; *(taxi)* héler

▸ **flag out** VT SEP *Sport (racetrack)* jalonner

▸ **flag up** VT SEP *(mark, indicate)* marquer; *(mistake)* signaler, marquer

flagellate ['flædʒəleɪt] VT *Formal* flageller; *Fig* fustiger

ADJ *Biol & Bot* flagellé

N *Biol & Bot* flagellé *m*

flagellation [ˌflædʒə'leɪʃən] N *Formal* flagellation *f*

flageolet¹ ['flædʒəlet, ˌflædʒə'let] N *Mus* flageolet *m*

flageolet² ['flæʒəleɪ] N *Bot & Culin* (haricot *m*) flageolet *m*

flagged [flægd] ADJ *(floor)* dallé

flagging¹ ['flægɪŋ] ADJ *(enthusiasm, spirits, strength)* qui baisse; *(courage, determination, attention)* faiblissant; *(conversation)* qui tombe *ou* s'épuise

flagging² N *(paving)* dallage *m*

flagon ['flægən] N **1** *(large bottle)* grosse bouteille *f* (ventrue), bonbonne *f* **2** *(jug)* pot *m* (à anse)

flagpole ['flægpəʊl] N mât *m*; *Fam Fig* **let's run it up the f.** soumettons-le et voyons les réactions▫

flagrant ['fleɪgrənt] ADJ *(injustice, lie, abuse)* flagrant; **a f. disregard for the safety of others** un mépris flagrant *ou* évident pour la sécurité d'autrui

flagrante delicto [flə'græntɪdɪ'lɪktəʊ] ADV *Law & Fig* **to be caught in f.** être surpris en flagrant délit

flagrantly ['fleɪgrəntlɪ] ADV *(abuse, disregard, defy etc)* d'une manière flagrante; **f. unfair** d'une injustice criante; **f. dishonest** d'une malhonnêteté flagrante

flagship ['flægʃɪp] N *Naut* vaisseau *m ou* bâtiment *m* amiral; *Fig Com (product)* tête *f* de gamme; **the London store is the f. of the chain** le magasin de Londres est le plus important de la chaîne; **this latest model is the f. of their new range** ce dernier modèle est le produit vedette de leur nouvelle gamme

▸▸ *Com* **flagship brand** marque *f* étendard, marque *f* fer de lance; *Com* **flagship product** produit *m* fer de lance, produit *m* vedette; *Com* **flagship store** magasin *m* vitrine

flagstaff ['flægstɑːf] N mât *m*

flagstone ['flægstəʊn] N dalle *f*

▸▸ **flagstone pavement** dallage *m* en pierre

flag-waving N *(UNCOUNT) Fam Fig* discours *mpl* cocardiers▫

flail [fleɪl] N *Agr* fléau *m*

VT **1** *Agr* battre au fléau **2** *(limbs)* agiter

VI **1** *(person, limbs)* s'agiter violemment **2** *(rope, cable)* se balancer violemment

▸ **flail about** VI *(person, limbs)* s'agiter dans tous les sens; **she was flailing about in the water** elle se débattait des mains et des pieds dans l'eau

VT SEP *(arms, legs)* battre

flair [fleə(r)] N **1** *(stylishness)* style *m*; **to dress/write with f.** s'habiller/écrire avec style **2** *(gift)* don *m*; **to have a f. for sth** avoir un don pour qch; **to have a f. for languages/cooking** avoir le don des langues/pour cuisiner; **he had no f. for business** il n'avait pas le sens des affaires; **they have a real f. for making the right choices** ils ont vraiment le don de faire les bons choix

flak [flæk] N **1** *(gunfire)* tir *m* antiaérien *ou* de DCA **2** *(UNCOUNT) Fam Fig (criticism)* critiques▫ *fpl*; **I took a lot of f. over it** on m'a beaucoup critiqué pour cela; **to come in for a lot of f.** se heurter à beaucoup de critiques

▸▸ **flak jacket** gilet *m* pare-balles

flake [fleɪk] N **1** *(of snow)* flocon *m*; *(of metal)* paillette *f*; *(of paint, plaster)* écaille *f*; **flakes of dandruff** pellicules *fpl*; **a f. of skin** un bout de peau morte

2 *Am Fam (person)* allumé(e) *m,f*

3 *Fam Drugs slang (cocaine)* neige *f*

4 *Austr Culin* = chair de requin ou de raie

VI *(plaster)* s'effriter, s'écailler; *(paint)* s'écailler; *(skin)* peler; *(rock)* s'effriter; *Culin (fish)* s'émietter

VT *Culin (fish)* émietter; **flaked almonds** amandes *fpl* effilées

▸ **flake out** VI *Fam (collapse)* s'écrouler▫; *(fall asleep)* s'endormir▫; **I just want to f. out on the sofa** j'ai envie de m'effondrer sur le canapé et de roupiller

flaking ['fleɪkɪŋ] ADJ *(paint, plaster)* qui s'écaille; *(skin)* qui pèle; *(rock)* qui s'effrite

flaky ['fleɪkɪ] *(compar* **flakier**, *superl* **flakiest**) ADJ **1** *(paint, plaster)* écaillé; *(rock)* effrité; *(skin)* qui pèle; *(scalp)* sujet aux pellicules **2** *Fam (person)* allumé; *(idea)* loufoque

▸▸ *Br Culin* **flaky pastry** pâte *f* feuilletée

flamboyance [flæm'bɔɪəns], **flamboyancy** [flæm'bɔɪənsɪ] N *(of behaviour, lifestyle, personality)* extravagance *f*; *(of colour)* éclat *m*

flamboyant [flæm'bɔɪənt] ADJ *(behaviour, lifestyle, personality)* extravagant; *(colour)* éclatant; *(clothes)* aux couleurs éclatantes; *Pej* voyant; *Archit* flamboyant

flamboyantly [flæm'bɔɪəntlɪ] ADV de manière extravagante

flame [fleɪm] N **1** *(of fire, candle)* flamme *f*; **to be in flames** *(building, car)* être en flammes; **to burst into flames** prendre feu, s'enflammer; **to go up in flames** s'embraser; *Fig (hopes, chances)* s'envoler, partir en fumée; *also Fig* **to be shot down in flames** être descendu en flammes **2** *Literary (of passion, desire)* flamme *f* **3** *Comput* message *m* injurieux

VI **1** *Fig (face, cheeks)* s'empourprer; *(passion, anger)* brûler **2** *Comput* incendier

VT **1** *Culin* flamber **2** *Comput* descendre en flammes

▸▸ *Tech* **flame cutter** chalumeau *m* à découper; *Agr* **flame gun** agriflamme *m*; **flame red** rouge *m* feu; **flame retardant** retardateur *m* de flamme, ignifuge *m*; *Bot* **flame tree** flamboyant *m*; *Comput* **flame war** guerre *f* d'insultes

▸ **flame up** VI *(fire)* s'embraser; *Fig (person)* s'enflammer

flame-coloured, *Am* **flame-colored** ADJ ponceau *(inv)*, couleur de feu *(inv)*

flamenco [flə'meŋkəʊ] *(pl* **flamencos**) N flamenco *m*

COMP de flamenco

▸▸ **flamenco dancing** flamenco *m*; **flamenco music** flamenco *m*

flameproof ['fleɪmˌpruːf] ADJ *(clothing)* ininflammable, à l'épreuve des flammes; *(dish)* allant au feu

flamer ['fleɪmə(r)] N **1** *Am Fam (stupid or obnoxious person)* enflure *f* **2** *Comput* auteur *m* d'un message injurieux

flame-resistant = **flameproof**

flamethrower ['fleɪmˌθrəʊə(r)] N lance-flammes *m inv*

flaming ['fleɪmɪŋ] ADJ **1** *(sun, sky)* embrasé; *(fire)* flamboyant **2** *Br Fam (extremely angry)* **to be in a f. temper** être d'une humeur massacrante, être furax; **we had a f. row about it** nous avons eu une belle engueulade là-dessus **3** *Br Fam (as intensifier)* fichu; **you f. idiot!** espèce d'abruti!; **where are my f. keys?** où sont mes fichues clés?

ADV *Br Fam (as intensifier)* fichtrement; **don't be so f. stupid!** ne sois donc pas aussi bête!; **you know f. well what I mean** tu sais fichtrement bien ce que je veux dire

N *Comput* envoi *m* de messages injurieux

flamingo [flə'mɪŋgəʊ] *(pl* **flamingos** *or* **flamingoes**) N *Orn* flamant *m* rose

flammable ['flæməbəl] ADJ *(material, substance)* inflammable

flan [flæn] N *Culin* tarte *f*; *(savoury)* quiche *f*

▸▸ **flan case** fond *m* de tarte

Flanders ['flɑːndəz] N Flandre *f*, Flandres *fpl*

flange [flændʒ] *Tech* N *(on pipe, tube)* bride *f*, collerette *f*; *(of piece of sheet metal)* collet *m*, rebord *m*; *(of wheel)* boudin *m*, rebord *m*; *(of beam)* aile *f*; *(on rail)* patin *m*; *Aut (on radiator)* ailette *f*

VT brider; **to f. a piece of sheet metal** border une tôle, rabattre un collet sur une tôle; **to f. a wheel** bourreler une roue

▸▸ **flange coupling** raccordement *m* à bride; **flange girder** poutre *f* en I

flanged [flændʒd] ADJ *Tech (pipe, tube)* à bride(s); *(piece of sheet metal)* à bord tombé; *(wheel)* à boudin; *(beam)* à aile; *(rail)* à patin; *Aut (radiator)* à ailettes

flank [flæŋk] N **1** *(of person, animal)* flanc *m*; *Culin (of beef)* flanchet *m*

2 *(of mountain etc)* côté *m*, flanc *m*

3 *Mil (of army etc)* flanc *m*; **left/right f.** aile *f* gauche/droite; **to protect one's flanks** se couvrir sur les flancs; **to launch a f. attack** lancer une attaque de côté

4 *Sport* aile *f*

VT **1** *(be on either side of)* encadrer; **flanked by two policemen** encadré de deux gendarmes; **flanked by his wife and son** entouré de sa femme et de son fils **2** *Mil* flanquer

flanker ['flæŋkə(r)] N **1** *Sport (in rugby)* ailier *m*, flanqueur *m*; *(in American football)* = joueur qui se tient derrière la ligne de mêlée de façon à pouvoir réceptionner la balle **2** *Archit* ouvrage *m* flanquant **3** *Mil* flanc-garde *f*

flannel ['flænəl] *(Br pt & pp* **flannelled**, *cont* **flannelling**, *Am pt & pp* **flanneled**, *cont* **flanneling**) N **1** *(UNCOUNT) Tex* flanelle *f* **2** *Br (for washing)* gant *m* de toilette **3** *(UNCOUNT) Br Fam (empty words)* baratin *m*, bla-bla *m*, bla-bla-bla *m*; **to talk a lot of f.** faire beaucoup de baratin *ou* de bla-bla

COMP *Tex (nightgown, sheet, trousers, suit)* en *ou* de flanelle

VI *Br Fam (use empty words)* faire du baratin *ou* du bla-bla *ou* du bla-bla-bla; **stop flannelling!** arrête ton baratin *ou* ton bla-bla!

• **flannels** NPL pantalon *m* en *ou* de flanelle

flannelette [flænə'let] *Tex* N pilou *m*

COMP *(nightgown, sheet)* en *ou* de pilou

flap [flæp] *(pt & pp* **flapped**, *cont* **flapping**) N **1** *(of sails)* claquement *m*; *(of wings)* battement *m*; **the bird gave a f. of its wings** l'oiseau a battu des ailes

2 *(of counter, desk, table ▸ hinged)* abattant *m*; *(▸ sliding)* rallonge *f*; *(of pocket, tent, envelope, book jacket)* rabat *m*; *(in floor, door)* trappe *f*; *(of aircraft)* volet *m* (hypersustentateur); **a f. of skin** un morceau de peau décollée

3 *Fam (panic)* panique▫ *f*; **to be in a f.** être dans tous ses états, être paniqué; **to get into a f.** se mettre dans tous ses états

4 *Ling* battement *m*

VI **1** *(wings)* battre; *(sails, shutters, washing, curtains)* claquer; **the seagull flapped away** la mouette est partie dans un battement d'ailes **2** *Fam (panic)* paniquer▫, s'affoler▫; **stop flapping!** du calme!, calmos!

VT *(wings)* battre de; *(hands, piece of paper)* agiter; **the bird flapped its wings** l'oiseau a battu des ailes; **he was flapping his arms about to keep warm** il agitait ses bras pour se tenir chaud

flapjack ['flæpdʒæk] N *Culin Br* biscuit *m* à l'avoine, *Am* = petite crêpe épaisse

flapper ['flæpə(r)] N *(person)* = jeune fille dans le vent (dans les années 20)

flapping ['flæpɪŋ] N *(of wings)* battement *m*; *(of sail)* claquement *m*

flare [fleə(r)] N **1** *(bright flame ▸ of fire, match)* flamboiement *m*; *(▸ of jet engine)* flammes *fpl*

2 *(signal)* signal *m* lumineux; *(rocket)* fusée *f* éclairante

3 *(in clothes)* évasement *m*; **a skirt with a f. in it** une jupe évasée; **trousers with a f.** un pantalon à pattes d'éléphant

4 *Chem & Petr (in chemical plant, oil refinery)* torche *f*

VI 1 *(flame, match)* flamboyer

2 *(tempers)* s'échauffer; **tempers flared** les esprits se sont échauffés

3 *(nostrils)* frémir

4 *(clothes)* s'évaser

VT 1 *(nostrils)* dilater **2** *(clothes)* évaser

• **flares NPL** *Br* **(a pair of) flares** un pantalon à pattes d'éléphant

▸▸ ***flare gun*** pistolet *m* de détresse, lance-fusées *m inv*; *Br* ***flare path*** piste *f* à balises lumineuses; *Petr* ***flare stack*** torchère *f*

▸ **flare up VI** *(fire)* s'embraser; *Fig (dispute, quarrel, violence)* éclater; *(disease, epidemic, crisis)* apparaître, se déclarer; *(person)* s'emporter; **he flared up at me** il s'est emporté contre moi

flared [fleəd] **ADJ** *(trousers)* à pattes d'éléphant; *(dress)* évasé; *(skirt)* évasé, à godets

flare-up N *(of fire, light)* flamboiement *m*; *Fig (of anger, violence)* explosion *f*; *(of tension)* montée *f*; *(of disease, epidemic)* apparition *f*; *(quarrel)* dispute *f*

FLASH [flæʃ]

N
- éclat **1**
- flash **2, 5**
- torche **6**

VI
- clignoter **1**
- briller **1**
- filer comme l'éclair **2**

VT
- faire clignoter **1**
- montrer rapidement **2**
- diffuser **3**

ADJ
- tape-à-l'œil **1**

N 1 *(of light, diamond)* éclat *m*; *(of metal)* reflet *m*, éclat *m*; **we saw a f. of light in the distance** nous avons vu l'éclat d'une lumière au loin; **give three flashes of the torch** allume la torche trois fois; **f. of wit/humour** pointe *f* d'esprit/d'humour; **f. of inspiration** éclair *m* de génie; **in a f.** *(very quickly)* en un éclair, en un clin d'œil; **it came to me in a f.** cela m'est venu d'un seul coup; **f. of lightning** éclair *m*; **a f. in the pan** un feu de paille; **(as) quick as a f.** aussi rapide que l'éclair, rapide comme l'éclair

2 *(of news)* flash *m* (d'information)

3 *Mil (on uniform)* écusson *m*

4 *(of colour)* tache *f*

5 *Phot* flash *m*; **are you going to use a f. for this one?** est-ce que tu vas la prendre au flash, celle-ci?

6 *Am Fam (flashlight)* torche ◻ *f*

VI 1 *(light, torch, sign)* clignoter; *(diamond)* briller, lancer des éclats; **lightning flashed directly overhead** il y a eu des éclairs juste au-dessus; **his eyes flashed with anger** ses yeux lançaient des éclairs de colère; *Aut* **to f. at sb** faire un appel de phares à qn

2 *(move fast)* filer comme l'éclair, aller à la vitesse de l'éclair; **to f. in/out/past** *(person, car)* entrer/sortir/passer comme un éclair; **to f. past** *or* **by** *(time)* passer à toute vitesse; **the day/the days seemed to f. by** la journée a semblé passer/les jours ont semblé défiler à toute vitesse; **the thought flashed through** *or* **across her mind that...** la pensée que... lui a traversé l'esprit; **information flashed onto** *or* **up on the screen** des informations sont apparues sur l'écran; **my life flashed before me** ma vie a défilé devant mes yeux

3 *Fam (expose oneself)* s'exhiber◻; **to f. at sb** s'exhiber devant qn

VT 1 *(torch ▸ turn on and off)* faire clignoter; **to f. a light in sb's face** *or* **eyes** diriger une lumière dans les yeux de qn; *Aut* **to f. (one's headlights at) sb** faire un appel de phares à qn; *Fig* **to f. a smile at sb** lancer *ou* adresser un sourire à qn; *Fig* **she flashed me a look of contempt** elle m'a décoché un regard méprisant

2 *(give brief glimpse of ▸ passport, photograph etc)* montrer rapidement; **he flashed a £50 note at them** il leur passa un billet de 50 livres sous le nez

3 *(news, information)* diffuser; **to f. a message up on the screen** faire apparaître un message sur l'écran; **she flashed a report to head office** elle a envoyé un rapport-éclair au siège social

4 *Am Fam (expose oneself to)* s'exhiber devant◻

ADJ *Br Fam* **1** *(showy ▸ car, clothes, jewellery)* tape-à-l'œil *(inv)*; *(▸ person)* frimeur

2 *(expensive-looking)* chic ◻

▸▸ ***flash burn*** brûlure *f (causée par un éclat très violent et brûlant, comme celui d'une bombe)*; *Sch* ***flash card*** = carte portant un mot, une image etc utilisée dans l'enseignement comme aide à l'apprentissage; *Comput* ***flash drive*** clé *f* USB; ***flash flood*** crue *f* subite; ***flash freezing*** surgélation *f*; *Phot* ***flash gun*** flash *m*; *Br Fam* ***flash Harry*** frimeur *m*; ***flash mob*** flash mob *m*, attroupement *m* éclair; ***flash mobber*** = personne qui participe à un flash mob; *Com & Mktg* ***flash pack*** *(discounted)* emballage *m* portant une réduction de prix; ***flash photography*** photographie *f* au flash; ***flash welding*** soudure *f* par étincelage

▸ **flash around VT SEP** *Fam (show off)* montrer◻, exhiber◻; **he likes flashing his money around** il aime étaler sa richesse◻; **don't f. your money around here!** ne montre *ou* n'exhibe pas ton argent ici!◻

▸ **flash back VI** *(in novel, film etc)* **to f. back to sth** revenir en arrière sur *ou* faire un flash-back sur qch; **my mind flashed back to 1942** l'année 1942 m'est soudain revenue à l'esprit

▸ **flash forward VI** *(of film)* faire un saut en avant

flashback ['flæʃbæk] **N** *(in novel, film etc)* flash-back *m inv*, retour *m* en arrière; *Fam Drugs slang (hallucination)* flash-back *m inv*; **their story is told in f.** leur histoire est racontée par flash-back *ou* par retours en arrière; **a f. to the war** un flash-back sur la guerre; **I had a f. to when I was a child** mon enfance m'est revenue à l'esprit

flashbulb ['flæʃbʌlb] **N** *Phot* ampoule *f* de flash

flashcube ['flæʃkjuːb] **N** *Phot* cube *m* de flash

flasher ['flæʃə(r)] **N 1** *Aut (indicator)* clignotant *m* **2** *Fam (man)* exhibitionniste◻ *m*

flashforward ['flæʃ,fɔːwəd] **N** *Cin & TV* projection *f* en avant

flashily ['flæʃɪlɪ] **ADV** *Fam Pej* d'une manière tapageuse◻ *ou* tape-à-l'œil, tapageusement◻

flashing ['flæʃɪŋ] **ADJ** *(indicator, light, torch)* clignotant; *(diamonds)* étincelant; *Aut* **f. emergency lights** feux *mpl* de détresse; **f. light** *(on police car)* gyrophare *m*

N 1 *Fam (indecent exposure)* exhibitionnisme◻ *m* **2** *(of diamond)* éclat *m* **3** *(UNCOUNT) Constr (on roof)* noue *f*

flashlight ['flæʃlaɪt] **N 1** *Phot* ampoule *f* de flash **2** *esp Am (torch)* torche *f* électrique, lampe *f* électrique *ou* de poche

▸▸ ***flashlight photography*** photographie *f* au flash

flashover ['flæʃ,əʊvə(r)] **N** *Elec* étincelle *f* de rupture

flashy ['flæʃɪ] *(compar* **flashier**, *superl* **flashiest)** **ADJ** *Fam Pej (person)* frimeur; *(car, clothes, taste)* tape-à-l'œil *(inv)*, clinquant; *(colour)* voyant◻, criard◻

flask [flɑːsk] **N** *Pharm* fiole *f*; *Chem* ballon *m*; *(for water, wine)* gourde *f*; **(vacuum** *or* **Thermos®) f.** (bouteille *f*) Thermos® *f*

FLAT [flæt]

ADJ
- plat **1**
- dégonflé **1**
- crevé **1**
- à plat **1, 4**
- éventé **2**
- monotone **3**
- en dessous du ton **5**
- bémol **5**
- catégorique **6**
- fixe **7**

ADV
- catégoriquement **1**
- pile **2**
- en dessous du ton **3**

N
- appartement **1**
- plat **2, 3**
- bémol **5**
- crevaison **6**

VI
- partager un appartement

(compar **flatter**, *superl* **flattest)**

ADJ 1 *(countryside, feet, stomach, chest, shoes)* plat; *(surface)* plan; *(roof)* plat, en terrasse; *(nose)* épaté, camus; *(curve)* aplati; *(tyre ▸ deflated)* à plat, dégonflé; *(▸ punctured)* crevé; *(ball, balloon)* dégonflé; *(picture)* sans relief; *(in painting ▸ colour)* mat; *Archit (vault)* plat; *(arch)* déprimé; **to stretch out f.** *(person)* s'allonger à plat; **to stand f. against the wall** *(person)* se plaquer contre le mur; *(item of furniture)* être adossé contre le mur; **it folds up f.** c'est pliable; **he was lying f. on his back** il était allongé à plat sur le dos; *Fig* **to be f. on one's back** *(with illness)* être alité; **lay the book f. on the desk** pose le livre à plat sur le bureau; *also Fig* **to knock sb f.** faire tomber qn à la renverse; **the blow laid him f.** le coup l'a assommé; **to fall f. on one's back** tomber sur le dos; **to fall f.** *(joke)* tomber à plat; *(play etc)* faire un four; **to fall f. on one's face** tomber la tête la première; *Fig* se casser le nez; **the city had been bombed f.** les bombardements avaient rasé la ville

2 *(soft drink, beer, champagne)* éventé; **to go f.** *(beer, soft drink)* s'éventer, perdre ses bulles

3 *Fig (monotonous ▸ style, voice)* monotone, terne; *(without emotion ▸ voice)* éteint; *(stock market, business)* au point mort; *(social life)* peu animé; **business has been a bit f. lately** les affaires sont calmes ces derniers temps

4 *(battery)* à plat

5 *Mus* en dessous du ton, trop bas; **to be f.** *(singer)* chanter en dessous du ton *ou* trop bas; *(instrumentalist)* jouer en dessous du ton *ou* trop bas; **E f.** mi *m* bémol

6 *(categorical ▸ refusal, denial)* catégorique; **to give a f. refusal** refuser catégoriquement; **you're not going, and that's f.!** tu n'iras pas, un point c'est tout!

7 *Com (rate, fare, fee)* fixe

ADV 1 *(categorically)* catégoriquement; **she turned me down f.** elle m'a opposé un refus catégorique

2 *(exactly)* **in thirty seconds f.** en trente secondes pile

3 *Mus* en dessous du ton, trop bas

4 *Fam (idiom)* **f. broke** complètement fauché

N 1 *Br (apartment)* appartement *m*; **(block of) flats** immeuble *m* (d'habitation)

2 *(of hand, blade)* plat *m*

3 *Horseracing* **the f.** *(races)* le plat; *(season)* la saison des courses de plat

4 on the f. *(horizontally)* horizontalement; *Rail (track)* en palier; *Sport* sur le plat

5 *Mus* bémol *m*

6 *Fam (puncture)* crevaison◻ *f*; *(punctured tyre)* pneu *m* crevé◻; *(deflated tyre)* pneu *m* à plat◻; **we got a f.** *(puncture)* nous avons crevé

7 *Theat* ferme *f*

VI *Austr & NZ* **to f. with sb** partager un appartement avec qn

• **flats NPL 1** *Geog* **salt flats** marais *mpl* salants **2** *(shoes)* chaussures *fpl* plates

• **flat out ADJ** *(exhausted)* à plat, vidé; *(drunk)* fin saoul; *(knocked out)* K-O **ADV to work f. out** travailler d'arrache-pied; **to be going f. out** *(car)* être à sa vitesse maximum; *(driver, runner, horse)* être au maximum *ou* à fond; **the car does 100 mph f. out** la vitesse maximale *ou* de pointe de la voiture est de 160 km/h; **she's going f. out to win the chairmanship** elle met tout en jeu pour obtenir la présidence

▸▸ ***flat bed*** *(of lorry)* plateau *m*; ***flat blade screwdriver*** tournevis *m* à lame plate, tournevis *m* plat; *Naut* ***flat calm*** calme *m* plat; *Br* ***flat cap*** casquette *f*; *Comput* ***flat file*** fichier *m* de données non structurées; *Comput & TV* ***flat monitor*** écran *m* plat; *Comput* ***flat panel display*** moniteur *m* à écran plat; *Horseracing* ***flat race*** course *f* de plat; *Horseracing* ***flat racing*** *(races)* plat *m*; *(season)* saison *f* des courses de plat; *Comput & TV* ***flat screen*** écran *m* plat; *Horseracing* ***flat season*** saison *f* des courses de plat; ***flat top*** *(haircut)* brosse *f*; *Am Fam (aircraft carrier)* porte-avions◻ *m inv*; *Austr* ***flat white*** *(coffee)* café *m* au lait

flat-bed ADJ

▸▸ *Br* ***flat-bed lorry*** semi-remorque *f* à plateau; *Comput* ***flat-bed scanner*** scanner *m ou* scanneur *m* à plat; *Am* ***flat-bed truck*** semi-remorque *f* à plateau

flat-bottomed [-'bɒtəmd] **ADJ** *(boat)* à fond plat

flatcar ['flætkɑː(r)] **N** *Am Rail* wagon *m* en plate-forme

flat-chested [-'tʃestɪd] **ADJ to be f.** ne pas avoir de poitrine

flatfish ['flætfɪʃ] **N** *Ich* poisson *m* plat

flatfoot ['flætfʊt] **N 1** *Med* pied *m* plat **2** *Fam Old-fashioned (policeman)* poulet *m*

flat-footed **ADJ 1** *Med* aux pieds plats **2** *Fam (clumsy)* empoté; *(tactless)* maladroit□, lourdaud□ **3** *Fam (idiom)* **to catch sb f.** prendre qn par surprise□

flatiron ['flætaɪən] **N** fer *m* à repasser *(non électrique)*

flat-leaf parsley **N** *Bot & Culin* persil *m* plat

flatlet ['flætlɪt] **N** *Br* studio *m*

flatline ['flætlaɪn] *Med* **N** électrocardiogramme *m* plat

VI avoir un électrocardiogramme plat

flatly ['flætlɪ] **ADV 1** *(categorically ▸ deny, refuse)* catégoriquement **2** *(without emotion ▸ say, speak)* d'une voix éteinte; *(monotonously)* avec monotonie

flatmate ['flætmeɪt] **N** *Br* colocataire *mf (d'un même appartement)*; **she and I were flatmates in London** elle et moi partagions un appartement à Londres

flatness ['flætnɪs] **N 1** *(of surface etc)* nature *f* plate; *(of countryside)* absence *f* de relief; *(of curve etc)* aplatissement *m* **2** *(of refusal)* netteté *f* **3** *(of existence etc)* monotonie *f*; *(of style etc)* insipidité *f*, platitude *f*; *(of beer etc)* évent *m*; *(of colour)* caractère *m* terne; *(of sound)* caractère *m* sourd; **the f. in his voice** l'absence d'émotion dans sa voix

flat-rate **ADJ** à tarif forfaitaire

►► *Comput* ***flat-rate connection*** *(to Internet)* connexion *f* à tarif forfaitaire

flatten ['flætən] **VT 1** *(path, road, ground)* aplanir; *(dough, metal)* aplatir; *(animal, person ▸ of vehicle)* écraser; *(house, village ▸ of bulldozer, earthquake)* raser; *(crop ▸ of wind, storm)* écraser, aplatir; *(piece of paper)* étaler; **to f. oneself against a wall** se plaquer *ou* se coller contre un mur

2 *Fam (defeat thoroughly)* écraser, battre à plate couture

3 *Fam (knock to the ground)* démolir□

4 *Fam (subdue ▸ person)* clouer le bec à; **that'll f. her** ça lui clouera le bec, ça la remettra à sa place

5 *Mus (note)* baisser d'un demi-ton, bémoliser

VI *(countryside)* s'aplanir

▸ **flatten out** **VI 1** *(countryside, hills)* s'aplanir **2** *Aviat (plane)* se redresser; *(pilot)* redresser l'appareil

VT SEP *(piece of paper, cloth)* étaler à plat; *(bump, path, road)* aplanir

flattened ['flætənd] **ADJ 1** *(smoothed out)* aplati; *(nose)* épaté **2** *Mus (note)* bémolisé

flatter ['flætə(r)] **VT** *(of person)* flatter; *(of dress, photo, colour)* avantager; **I'm flattered to have been chosen** je suis flatté d'avoir été choisi *ou* que l'on m'ait choisi; **don't f. yourself!, you f. yourself!** non mais tu rêves!; **we f. ourselves on offering a more efficient service** nous nous flattons d'offrir un service plus efficace; **he flatters himself (that) he's a good singer** il a la prétention d'être un bon chanteur

VI flatter

flatterer ['flætərə(r)] **N** flatteur(euse) *m,f*

flattering ['flætərɪŋ] **ADJ** *(remark, person, offer)* flatteur; *(picture, colour)* avantageux, flatteur; *(dress)* seyant; **it is f. to be asked to give this speech** c'est flatteur d'être sollicité pour faire ce discours; **I didn't get a very f. impression of the city/your boss** la ville/ton patron ne m'a pas fait une impression très favorable

flatteringly ['flætərɪŋlɪ] **ADV** *(speak of, describe)* en termes flatteurs, flatteusement; **the photograph had been f. lit** la photo avait été prise dans une lumière flatteuse

flattery ['flætərɪ] **N** *(UNCOUNT)* flatterie *f*; **to use f.** employer la flatterie *ou* des flatteries; **f. will get you nowhere** la flatterie ne vous mènera nulle part, vous n'obtiendrez rien par la flatterie

flatulence ['flætjʊləns] **N** flatulence *f*

flatulent ['flætjʊlənt] **ADJ** flatulent

flatware ['flætweə(r)] **N** *(UNCOUNT) Am (cutlery)* couverts *mpl*; *(serving dishes)* plats *mpl*; *(plates)* assiettes *fpl*

flaunt [flɔːnt] **VT** *(wealth, beauty, knowledge)* étaler, faire étalage de; *(car, jewellery)* faire parade de, exhiber; *(bad manners, ignorance)* afficher; **to f. oneself** s'afficher; **if you've got it, f. it** si tu as ce qu'il faut, ne t'en cache pas

> Attention: ne pas confondre avec le verbe **to flout**.

flautist ['flɔːtɪst] **N** *Br Mus* flûtiste *mf*

flavour, *Am* **flavor** ['fleɪvə(r)] **N** *(of food, drink)* goût *m*; *(of ice-cream, tea, yoghurt)* parfum *m*; **it comes in six different flavours** il existe en six parfums différents; **chocolate/coffee f. ice-cream** glace *f* au chocolat/au café; **this coffee keeps its f. well** ce café garde bien sa saveur; **it doesn't have much f.** cela n'a pas beaucoup de goût; **it's got quite a spicy f.** c'est assez épicé; *Fig* **it gives the film a South American f.** cela donne une note sud-américaine au film; **to be f. of the month** *(in vogue)* être au goût du jour; *Fam* **you're not exactly f. of the month at the moment** tu n'es pas comme qui dirait en odeur de sainteté en ce moment, tu n'as pas vraiment la cote en ce moment

VT *(with spices, herbs)* assaisonner; *(with fruit, alcohol)* parfumer

►► ***flavour enhancer*** agent *m* de sapidité

flavouring, *Am* **flavoring** ['fleɪvərɪŋ] **N** *(savoury)* assaisonnement *m*; *(sweet)* parfum *m*, arôme *m*; **no artificial flavourings** *(on tin, package)* sans arômes artificiels

flavourless, *Am* **flavorless** ['fleɪvəlɪs] **ADJ** sans goût, insipide

flaw [flɔː] **N 1** *(in material, plan, character)* défaut *m* **2** *Law* vice *m* de forme

VT *(object)* endommager; *(someone's character, beauty)* altérer

flawed [flɔːd] **ADJ** *(reasoning)* défectueux; *(novel, film)* qui a des défauts; *(sweater, scarf, fabric)* qui a un/des défaut(s); *(wood)* gercé; *(diamond)* qui a un crapaud *ou* un défaut; **the argument is, however, f.** cette argumentation a cependant un défaut *ou* des défauts

flawless ['flɔːlɪs] **ADJ** parfait

flawlessly ['flɔːlɪslɪ] **ADV** parfaitement

flawlessness ['flɔːlɪsnɪs] **N** perfection *f*

flax [flæks] **N** lin *m*

►► ***flax field*** linière *f*

flaxen ['flæksən] **ADJ** *(hair)* blond pâle *ou* filasse *(inv)*

flay [fleɪ] **VT** *(animal)* dépouiller, écorcher; *(person)* fouetter; *Fig (criticize)* éreinter; **to f. sb alive** faire la peau à qn

flea [fliː] **N** puce *f*; **to have fleas** avoir des puces; *Fam* **to send sb off with a f. in his/her ear** *(dismiss)* envoyer balader qn; *(scold)* passer un savon à qn

►► ***flea circus*** cirque *m* de puces savantes; ***flea collar*** collier *m* antipuces; ***flea market*** marché *m* aux puces; ***flea powder*** poudre *f* antipuce

fleabag ['fliːbæg] **N** *Fam* **1** *Br (animal, person)* sac *m* à puces **2** *Am (cheap hotel)* hôtel *m* miteux

fleabite ['fliːbaɪt] **N** piqûre *f ou* morsure *f* de puce; *Fig (trifle)* broutille *f*

flea-bitten **ADJ** couvert de puces; *Fig (shabby)* miteux

fleapit ['fliːpɪt] **N** *Br Fam* cinéma *m* miteux; *Hum* **the local f.** le cinéma du coin

fleck [flek] **N 1** *(of colour)* moucheture *f*, tacheture *f*; *(of sunlight)* moucheture *f* **2** *(of dust)* particule *f*

VT *(with colour)* moucheter, tacheter; *(with sunlight)* moucheter; **hair flecked with grey** cheveux *mpl* grisonnants; **white flecked with brown** blanc *m* moucheté *ou* tacheté de marron

fled [fled] *pt & pp of* **flee**

fledged [fledʒd] **ADJ** *(bird)* emplumé

fledgling, fledgeling ['fledʒlɪŋ] **N 1** *(young bird)* oisillon *m* **2** *Fig* novice *mf*, débutant(e) *m,f*

COMP *(company, industry, political party etc)* naissant; *(doctor, lawyer)* débutant

flee [fliː] *(pt & pp* **fled** [fled]*)* **VI** s'enfuir, fuir; **to f. from sb/sth** fuir qn/qch; **to f. from a house/country** s'enfuir d'une maison/d'un pays; **to f. from temptation** fuir la tentation

VT *(person, danger, temptation)* fuir; *(country, town)* s'enfuir de

fleece [fliːs] **N 1** *(of sheep)* toison *f* **2** *Tex (sheepskin)* peau *f* de mouton; *(synthetic)* laine *f* polaire, tissu *m* polaire **3** *(garment)* fourrure *f* polaire, polaire *f*

COMP *Tex (made of sheepskin)* en peau de mouton; *(synthetic)* en laine polaire, en tissu polaire

VT 1 *Fam (cheat)* escroquer□; *(overcharge)* écorcher **2** *(shear ▸ sheep)* tondre

fleece-lined **ADJ** *(with sheepskin)* doublé de peau de mouton; *(with synthetic material)* doublé de laine polaire *ou* de tissu polaire

fleecing ['fliːsɪŋ] **N** *(UNCOUNT) Fam (overcharging)* escroquerie *f (fait de faire payer trop cher)*

fleecy ['fliːsɪ] *(compar* **fleecier**, *superl* **fleeciest***)* **ADJ** *(material)* laineux; *(clouds)* cotonneux

fleeing ['fliːɪŋ] **ADJ** *(army etc)* en fuite

fleet [fliːt] **N 1** *Naut* flotte *f*; *(smaller)* flottille *f*; **the F.** = la Marine nationale **2** *(of buses, cars, taxis)* parc *m*; **a f. of ambulances took the injured to hospital** plusieurs ambulances ont transporté les blessés à l'hôpital; **car f.** parc *m* automobile

ADJ *Literary* rapide; **f. of foot** aux pieds ailés

►► *Naut* ***fleet admiral*** amiral *m* de France; *Naut* ***the Fleet Air Arm*** = l'aéronavale britannique; ***Fleet Street*** = rue de Londres, dont le nom sert à désigner les grands journaux britanniques; **the F. Street papers** les journaux *mpl* nationaux; ***Fleet Street journalist*** journaliste *mf* de la presse nationale

> **FLEET STREET**
>
> Traditionnellement, cette rue de la City était celle des journaux. Aujourd'hui, beaucoup de journaux ont établi leur siège dans d'autres quartiers, notamment les Docklands. Cependant, le terme "Fleet Street" est encore employé pour désigner la presse et le monde du journalisme.

fleet-footed **ADJ** *Literary* au pied léger

fleeting ['fliːtɪŋ] **ADJ** *(memory)* fugace; *(beauty, pleasure)* passager; **for a f. moment** pendant un bref instant; **to catch a f. glimpse of** apercevoir, entrevoir; **to give sb a f. glance** lancer un regard rapide à qn; **to give sth a f. glance** jeter un coup d'œil rapide à qch

fleetingly ['fliːtɪŋlɪ] **ADV** *(glimpse, appear)* rapidement

Fleming ['flemɪŋ] **N** Flamand(e) *m,f*

Flemish ['flemɪʃ] **N** *Ling* flamand *m*

NPL the F. les Flamands *mpl*

ADJ flamand

flesh [fleʃ] **N 1** *(of person, animal, fruit)* chair *f*; **there's not much f. on her** elle n'est pas très grasse; **she looks better on TV than she does in the f.** elle est plus jolie à la télé qu'en chair et en os; **I'm only f. and blood, you know** je suis comme tout le monde, tu sais; **she's my own f. and blood** c'est ma chair et mon sang; *Fam* **to press the f.** *(politicians, royalty etc)* serrer des mains□, faire un bain de foule□ **2** *Rel* chair *f*; **to mortify the f.** mortifier sa chair; **pleasures/sins of the f.** plaisirs *mpl* de la/péchés *mpl* de chair; **the spirit is willing but the f. is weak** l'esprit est prompt mais la chair est faible; **to go the way of all f.** retourner à la *ou* redevenir poussière **3** *(colour)* couleur *f* chair

►► *Theat* ***flesh tights*** collant *m* chair; *Art* ***flesh tints*** carnations *fpl*; ***flesh wound*** blessure *f* superficielle *ou* légère

▸ **flesh out** **VT SEP** *(essay, report, character etc)* étoffer

VI *(person)* s'étoffer, prendre de la carrure

flesh-coloured, *Am* **flesh-colored** **ADJ** (couleur) chair *(inv)*; **f. tights** collants *mpl* chair

fleshpots ['fleʃpɒts] **NPL** *Hum Pej* lieux *mpl* de plaisir

fleshy ['fleʃɪ] *(compar* **fleshier**, *superl* **fleshiest***)* **ADJ** *(person)* bien en chair; *(part of the body, fruit, leaf)* charnu

fleur-de-lis, fleur-de-lys [ˌflɜːdəˈliː] (*pl* **fleurs-de-lis, fleurs-de-lys**) **N** *Her* fleur *f* de lis *ou* lys

flew [fluː] *pt of* **fly**

flex [fleks] **VT** *(one's arms, knees)* fléchir; **to f. one's muscles** bander *ou* faire jouer ses muscles; *Fig* faire étalage de sa force

N *esp Br (wire)* fil *m*; *(heavy-duty)* câble *m*

▸▸ ***flex holder*** enrouleur *m* pour fil électrique

flexibility [ˌfleksəˈbɪlətɪ] **N** *(of object)* flexibilité *f*, souplesse *f*; *Fig (of plan, approach)* flexibilité *f*; *(of person's character)* souplesse *f*; **he has always shown a lot of f.** *(in timing, arrangements)* il s'est toujours montré très disponible *ou* arrangeant; **what I like about this software is its f.** ce qui me plaît dans ce logiciel, c'est sa flexibilité *ou* souplesse d'emploi

flexible [ˈfleksəbəl] **ADJ** flexible, souple; *Fig (approach, plans, timetable etc)* flexible; *(person's character)* souple; *(as regards timing, arrangements)* arrangeant; **f. working hours** horaires *mpl* (de travail) à la carte *ou* flexibles; **my working hours are very f.** j'ai des horaires de travail très libres *ou* souples

▸▸ *Fin* ***flexible mortgage*** emprunt *m* immobilier à échéances variables; *Mil* ***flexible response*** riposte *f* graduée

flexicurity [ˌfleksɪˈkjʊərətɪ] **N** flexisécurité *f*

flexion [ˈflekʃən] **N** *Gram* flexion *f*

flexitime [ˈfleksɪtaɪm] **N** *(UNCOUNT) Br* horaires *mpl* à la carte *ou* flexibles; **to be on** *or* **to work f.** avoir des horaires à la carte

flexor [ˈfleksə(r)] **N** *Anat* fléchisseur *m*

flextime [ˈflekstaɪm] *Am* = **flexitime**

flibbertigibbet [ˌflɪbətɪˈdʒɪbɪt] **N** *Fam* écervelé(e) *m,f*, tête *f* de linotte

flick [flɪk] **N 1** *(with finger)* chiquenaude *f*; *(with wrist)* petit *ou* léger mouvement *m*; *(with tail, whip, duster)* petit *ou* léger coup *m*; *Sport* petit coup *m*; **with a f. of his finger** d'une chiquenaude; **give the table a quick f. with a duster** donne un petit coup de chiffon à *ou* sur la table; **at the f. of a switch** en appuyant simplement sur un interrupteur **2** *Br Fam Old-fashioned (film)* film *m*

VT *(switch)* appuyer sur; **he flicked the horse with his whip** il a donné un petit coup de fouet au cheval; **he had to keep flicking the hair out of his eyes** il n'arrêtait pas de chasser du doigt les cheveux qui lui tombaient dans les yeux; **don't f. your ash on the floor** ne mets pas tes cendres par terre; **she flicked the ash off the table** *(with duster)* d'un coup de chiffon, elle a enlevé la cendre de la table; *(with finger)* d'une chiquenaude, elle a enlevé la cendre de la table

• **flicks NPL** *Br Fam Old-fashioned* **the flicks** le ciné, le cinoche

▸▸ *Br* ***flick knife*** (couteau *m* à) cran *m* d'arrêt; *Aut* ***flick wipe*** balayage *m* unique

▸ **flick away VT SEP** chasser; *(with fingers)* repousser d'une chiquenaude

▸ **flick off VT SEP** *(with finger* ▸ *ash, paper etc)* envoyer promener *ou* enlever d'une chiquenaude; *(*▸ *light, computer)* éteindre; **to f. sth off with a duster** faire envoler qch d'un coup de torchon; **he flicked the dandruff off his collar** il secoua les pellicules qui se trouvaient sur son col

▸ **flick on VT SEP 1** *(light, computer)* allumer **2** *Ftbl* **to f. the ball on** prolonger une passe

▸ **flick out VI** sortir; **the snake's tongue was flicking in and out** la langue du serpent sortait et rentrait à petits coups rapides

▸ **flick through VT INSEP** *(book, newspaper)* feuilleter; *(photographs)* jeter un œil parmi; *TV* **to f. through the channels** passer rapidement d'une chaîne à une autre

flicker [ˈflɪkə(r)] **VI** *(flame, light)* vaciller, trembler; *(eyelids, TV picture)* trembler; *(instrument needle etc)* osciller; **the candle was flickering** la flamme de la bougie vacillait; **a smile flickered on his lips** un sourire erra sur ses lèvres

N *(of flame, light)* vacillement *m*, tremblement *m*; *(of eyelids)* tremblement *m*; *(of TV screen)* scintillement *m*; **a f. of recognition** une lueur de reconnaissance; **a f. of hope/a smile** l'ombre *f* d'un espoir/d'un sourire; **a f. of interest/annoyance** une pointe d'intérêt/d'énervement

flicker-free ADJ *(screen)* anti-scintillements *(inv)*

flickering [ˈflɪkərɪŋ] **ADJ** *(light, flame)* vacillant; *(image)* tremblotant

N 1 *(of light, flame)* vacillement *m* **2** *(of image)* scintillement *m*

flier [ˈflaɪə(r)] **N 1** *Aviat (pilot)* aviateur(trice) *m,f*; **she's a good/bad f.** *(passenger)* elle supporte bien/ne supporte pas l'avion

2 *Fam (start of race)* départ *m* lancé; *(false start)* faux départ *m*; **to get a f.** *(good start)* partir comme un boulet de canon

3 *Fam (fall)* vol *m* plané; **to take a f.** faire un vol plané

4 *Am Fam (speculative venture)* entreprise *f* à risques; **to take a f.** *(financial risk)* prendre un risque financier

5 *(leaflet)* prospectus *m*

VT to f. an area distribuer des prospectus dans un quartier

VI *(hand out fliers)* distribuer des prospectus

flies [flaɪz] **NPL 1** *(of trousers)* braguette *f*; **your f. are undone** *or* **open** ta braguette est ouverte **2** *Theat* dessus *mpl*, cintres *mpl*

flight [flaɪt] **N 1** *(act of flying* ▸ *of bird, plane)* vol *m*; *(*▸ *of projectile, star)* course *f*; **capable of f.** capable de voler; **to be in f.** être en vol

2 *(journey* ▸ *of bird, spacecraft, plane, missile)* vol *m*; **manned f.** *(of spacecraft)* vol *m* habité

3 *Aviat (journey in plane* ▸ *by passenger)* voyage *m*; *(*▸ *by pilot)* vol *m*; *(plane itself)* vol *m*; **I don't want to miss my f.** je ne veux pas rater mon avion; **my f. is at 2.15** mon avion est à 2h15; **how was your f.?** as-tu fait bon voyage?; **f. BA 314 to Paris** le vol BA 314 à destination de Paris; **when is the next f. to Newcastle?** à quelle heure part le prochain vol pour *ou* à destination de Newcastle?; **all flights out of Gatwick** tous les vols en provenance de Gatwick

4 *(group of birds)* vol *m*, volée *f*; *(group of aircraft)* flotte *f* aérienne; **the Queen's/King's F.** = avions au service de la famille royale; *Fig* **to be in the first** *or* **top f.** faire partie de l'élite

5 *(fleeing)* fuite *f*; **to be in full f.** être en pleine retraite; **to take f.** prendre la fuite; **to put sb/the enemy to f.** mettre qn/l'ennemi en fuite; *Fig* **f. of capital** évasion *f ou* fuite *f* des capitaux; *Bible* **the F. into Egypt** la fuite en Égypte

6 *(of stairs)* **f. (of stairs** *or* **steps)** escalier *m*; **I had to walk up all ten flights** j'ai dû monter les dix étages à pied; **it's another three flights up** c'est trois étages plus haut

7 *Fig* **a f. of the imagination** une envolée de l'imagination; **it was just a f. of fancy** ce n'était qu'une idée folle

8 *(on arrow, dart)* penne *f*, empennage *m*

▸▸ ***flight attendant*** *(male)* steward *m*; *(female)* hôtesse *f* de l'air; **one of our f. attendants** un des membres de l'équipage; *Fin* ***flight capital*** capitaux *mpl* flottants *ou* fébriles; ***flight clearance*** autorisation *f* de vol; ***flight control*** *(action* ▸ *of individual aircraft)* conduite *f*; *(*▸ *from ground)* contrôle *m* de la navigation aérienne; *Mil* contrôle *m* des missions aériennes; *(place)* contrôle *m* aérien; *(people)* contrôleurs *mpl* aériens; ***flight crew*** équipage *m (d'un avion)*; ***flight deck*** *(of aircraft)* poste *m ou* cabine *f* de pilotage, habitacle *m*; *(of aircraft carrier)* pont *m* d'envol; ***flight engineer*** mécanicien(enne) *m,f* navigant (e) *(d'avion)*, ingénieur *m* de vol; *Orn* ***flight feather*** *(of bird)* penne *f*; ***flight formation*** formation *f* de vol; ***flight lieutenant*** = capitaine de l'armée de l'air britannique; ***flight log*** journal *m* de vol; ***flight mechanic*** mécanicien(enne) *m,f* navigant (e); ***flight number*** numéro *m* de vol; ***flight path*** trajectoire *f* de vol; ***flight pattern*** formation *f* de vol; ***flight personnel*** personnel *m* navigant; ***flight plan*** plan *m* de vol; ***flight recorder*** enregistreur *m* de vol; ***flight sergeant*** = sergent-chef de l'armée de l'air britannique; ***flight simulator*** simulateur *m* de vol; ***flight socks*** chaussettes *fpl* de contention; ***flight time*** *(duration)* durée *f* de vol; *(take-off time)* heure *f* du vol

flightiness [ˈflaɪtɪnɪs] **N** inconstance *f*

flightless [ˈflaɪtlɪs] **ADJ** *(bird)* coureur

flighty [ˈflaɪtɪ] (*compar* **flightier**, *superl* **flightiest**) **ADJ** inconstant; *(in romantic relationships)* volage, inconstant

flimsily [ˈflɪmzɪlɪ] **ADV** *(built, constructed)* d'une manière peu solide, peu solidement

flimsiness [ˈflɪmzɪnɪs] **N 1** *(of cloth, garment shoes)* légèreté *f*; *(of building, plane, walls, wood en beams)* manque *m* de solidité; *(of paper, toys books)* fragilité *f* **2** *(of argument, case, excuse, evidence, alibi)* minceur *f*; *(of novel, plot)* faiblesse

flimsy [ˈflɪmzɪ] (*compar* **flimsier**, *superl* **flimsiest** *pl* **flimsies**) **ADJ 1** *(cloth, garment)* fin, léger *(shoes)* léger; *(building, plane, walls, wooden beams)* peu solide; *(paper)* peu résistant, fragile *(toys, books)* fragile **2** *(argument, case, excuse, evidence, alibi)* mince; *(novel, plot)* faible

N *(paper)* papier *m* pelure; *(with typing on it)* double *m* sur pelure

flinch [flɪntʃ] **VI 1** *(wince)* tressaillir; **without flinching** sans broncher **2** *(shy away)* **to f. from one's duty/obligations** reculer devant son devoir/ses obligations

fling [flɪŋ] (*pt & pp* **flung** [flʌŋ]) **VT** lancer, jeter; **to f. one's arms around sb's neck** jeter ses bras au tour du cou de qn; **f. it in the dustbin** jette-le à la poubelle; **he flung himself into an armchair** il s'est jeté dans un fauteuil; **to f. oneself into a task** se lancer dans une tâche; **I flung a few things into a suitcase** j'ai fourré quelques affaires dans une valise; **to f. sb into jail** jeter qn en prison; **don't just f. yourself at him** ne te jette pas dans ses bras; **he flung himself off the top of the cliff** il s'est jeté du haut de la falaise; **with his coat casually flung over his shoulders** avec son manteau négligemment jeté sur ses épaules; *Fig* **to f. sth in sb's face** envoyer qch à la figure de qn

N 1 *Fam (attempt, try)* **to give sth a f., to have a f. at sth** essayer qch; **to have a f. at doing sth** essayer de faire qch; **let's give it a f.** essayons un coup

2 *Fam (wild behaviour)* **youth must have its f.** il faut que jeunesse se passe; **to have a final f.** s'éclater une dernière fois

3 *Fam (affair)* **to have a f. with sb** avoir une aventure avec qn; **the two of them are having a f.** ils ont une aventure

4 *(dance)* = danse traditionnelle écossaise

▸ **fling about VT SEP** *(objects)* lancer; **he flung his arms about wildly** *(fighting)* il se démenait violemment; *(gesticulating)* il gesticulait violemment; *Fig* **to f. one's money about** mener grand train

▸ **fling away VT SEP** *(discard)* jeter (de côté); **that's just flinging your money away** c'est jeter ton argent par les fenêtres

▸ **fling back VT SEP** *(ball)* renvoyer; *(curtains)* ouvrir brusquement; *(sheets, blanket)* rejeter; **she flung back her head** elle a rejeté sa tête en arrière

▸ **fling down VT SEP** *(object)* jeter par terre; **to f. down a challenge** lancer *ou* jeter un défi; **f. down my keys, will you?** lance-moi mes clés, s'il te plaît

▸ **fling off VT SEP 1** *(coat, dress etc)* jeter **2** *(attacker)* repousser violemment **3** *(casual remarks)* dire avec désinvolture

▸ **fling open VT SEP** *(door, window)* ouvrir toute grande; **she flung the windows wide open** elle ouvrit les fenêtres en grand

▸ **fling out VT SEP 1** *(throw out)* jeter dehors; *(get rid of* ▸ *unwanted object)* jeter, balancer; *(*▸ *bill, legislation, case)* rejeter; *Fam* **to f. sb out** flanquer qn à la porte; **she flung him out of the house** elle l'a flanqué à la porte, elle l'a viré de chez elle **2** *(extend)* **to f. out one's arm** étendre le bras d'un grand geste; **he flung out a foot and turned the ball into the net** il tendit le pied et dévia la balle vers le filet

▸ **fling up VT SEP** *(throw* ▸ *in air)* jeter en l'air; *(*▸ *to someone in higher position)* lancer, envoyer; **he flung up his hands in horror** horrifié, il leva les bras au ciel

flint [flɪnt] **N** *(substance)* silex *m*; *(for cigarette lighter)* pierre *f* à briquet

COMP *(tools, axe)* en silex

▸▸ ***flint glass*** flint(-glass) *m*

flinty [ˈflɪntɪ] (*compar* **flintier**, *superl* **flintiest**) **ADJ** *(rocks, soil)* siliceux; *Fig (heart)* de pierre

flip [flɪp] (*pt & pp* **flipped**, *cont* **flipping**) **N 1** *(little push, flick)* petit coup *m*; **to give sth a f.** donner un petit coup à qch

2 *(turning movement)* demi-tour *m* *(sur soi-*

même); (somersault ▸ in diving) saut m périlleux; (▸ in gymnastics) flip-flap m
3 (drink) = boisson alcoolisée à l'œuf
4 Am (of hair) petite boucle f
VT1 (move with a flick) donner un petit coup sec à; (switch) basculer; **he flipped the packet open/shut** d'un petit coup sec il a ouvert/refermé le paquet
2 (throw) envoyer, balancer; **to f. a coin (for sth)** décider (qch) à pile ou face
3 Am (shares, property) = revendre rapidement pour réaliser un bénéfice
4 Fam (idiom) **to f. one's** Br **lid** or Am **wig** (get angry) exploser, piquer une crise; (go mad) devenir dingue, perdre la boule; (under effects of stress) craquer; (become ecstatic) être emballé, flasher
VI Fam (get angry) exploser, piquer une crise; (go mad) devenir dingue, perdre la boule; (under effects of stress) craquer; (become ecstatic) être emballé, flasher
ADJ Fam (flippant) désinvolte□
EXCLAM Fam mince!, zut!
▸▸ **flip chart** tableau m à feuilles; **flip phone** téléphone m à clapet; **flip side** Fam (of record) face f B□; Fig face f cachée; **there is, of course, a f. side to the expansion of industry** l'expansion de l'industrie a, comme toute médaille, son revers; **flip top** (of packet) couvercle m à rabat

▸**flip out** **VI 1** Fam (get angry) exploser, piquer une crise; (go mad) devenir dingue, perdre la boule; (under effects of stress) craquer; (become ecstatic) être emballé, flasher **2** (trailer of vehicle, racing car) faire un écart

▸**flip over** **VI** (turn over ▸ plane, boat, fish) se retourner; (▸ page) tourner tout seul
VT SEP (turn over ▸ stone, person, record) retourner; (▸ page) tourner

▸**flip through** **VT INSEP** (magazine) feuilleter; (photos, posters, wallpaper samples etc) jeter un coup d'œil à

flip-flop (pt & pp **flip-flopped**, cont **flip-flopping**)
N1 (sandal) tong f
2 Electron bascule f
3 (somersault) saut m périlleux avec appui sur les mains
4 Am Fam (in attitude, policy) volte-face□ f inv, revirement□ m; **to do a f. (over sth)** faire volte-face (sur qch)□, retourner sa veste (sur qch)
VI Fam Am (change one's opinion) faire volte-face□, retourner sa veste; (repeatedly) changer d'avis (on à propos de); **her feelings towards him f. between love and hate** ses sentiments pour lui oscillent entre l'amour et la haine

flippancy ['flɪpənsɪ] **N** (of person, attitude) légèreté f, désinvolture f; (of remark) désinvolture f

flippant ['flɪpənt] **ADJ** désinvolte; **he was just being f.** il ne parlait pas sérieusement

flippantly ['flɪpəntlɪ] **ADV** avec désinvolture

flipper ['flɪpə(r)] **N1** (for swimming) palme f **2** (of seal, penguin, whale) nageoire f

flipping ['flɪpɪŋ] Br Fam **ADJ** (as intensifier) fichu; **you've got a f. nerve!** tu as un fichu ou sacré culot!; **you f. idiot!** espèce d'idiot!
ADV (as intensifier) sacrément; **he's so f. annoying!** ce qu'il peut être embêtant!; **not f. likely!** il n'y a pas de risque!; Ironic **isn't it just f. marvellous!** c'est pas formidable!; **you can f. well do it yourself!** tu n'as qu'à le faire toi-même si c'est comme ça!

flip-top **ADJ** (carton, pack) à rabat; (mobile phone) à clapet

flirt [flɜːt] **VI1** (sexually) flirter **2** Fig **to f. with danger/death** frayer avec le danger/la mort; **to f. with an idea** jouer avec une idée
N (person) charmeur(euse) m,f

flirtation [flɜː'teɪʃən] **N** badinage m amoureux; **to have a f. with sb** flirter avec qn; Fig **his f. with danger/the idea ended in disaster** il a frayé avec le danger/joué avec cette idée et cela a tourné au désastre

flirtatious [flɜː'teɪʃəs] **ADJ** charmeur; (look, smile) enjôleur; **to be f. with sb** faire du charme à qn

flirtatiously [flɜː'teɪʃəslɪ] **ADV** d'un air charmeur; **she smiled f. at him** elle lui fit un sourire enjôleur

flit [flɪt] (pt & pp **flitted**, cont **flitting**) **VI1** (bird, bat etc) voleter; **bats were flitting about** des chauves-souris voletaient de-ci de-là; **people were constantly flitting in and out of his office** les gens n'arrêtaient pas d'entrer et de sortir de son bureau; **to f. from one subject to another** sauter d'un sujet à un autre, passer du coq à l'âne; **to f. from woman to woman/job to job** passer continuellement d'une femme à une autre/d'un emploi à un autre **2** Scot & NEng (move house) déménager **3** Br Fam (leave stealthily) déménager à la cloche de bois
N Scot & NEng déménagement m

flitch [flɪtʃ] **N** (of pork) flèche f

float [fləʊt] **N1** (for fishing line) bouchon m, flotteur m; (on raft, seaplane, fishing net, in carburettor, toilet cistern) flotteur m
2 (raft) radeau m; (floating logs) train m (de bois); (for swimming) planche f
3 (vehicle ▸ in parade, carnival) char m; (▸ for milk delivery) voiture f du livreur de lait
4 (cash advance) avance f; (business loan) prêt m de lancement; (money in cash register) fond m de caisse
5 (drink) = soda, jus de fruit ou milk-shake avec une boule de glace
6 St Exch flottant m; **clean f.** taux mpl de change libres ou flottants; **dirty f.** taux mpl de change concertés
7 Theat **the floats** (footlights) la rampe
VI1 (on water) flotter; (be afloat ▸ boat) flotter, être à flot; **the raft/log floated down the river** le radeau/le tronc d'arbre a descendu la rivière au fil de l'eau; **the bottle floated out to sea** la bouteille a été emportée vers le large; **the diver floated slowly up to the surface** le plongeur est remonté lentement à la surface; **we floated downstream** (in boat) le courant nous a portés **2** (in the air ▸ balloon, piece of paper) voltiger; (▸ mist, clouds) flotter; (▸ ghost, apparition) flotter, planer; **music/the sound of laughter floated in through the open window** de la musique est entrée/des bruits de rires sont entrés par la fenêtre ouverte; **she floated out of the room** elle est sortie de la pièce d'un pas léger **3** Fin (currency) flotter
VT1 (put on water ▸ ship, raft, platform) mettre à flot; (▸ paper boat, toy) faire flotter; **the timber is then floated downstream to the mill** le bois est ensuite flotté jusqu'à l'usine située en aval
2 (company) lancer, créer; St Exch (on Stock Market) introduire en Bourse; Fin (bonds, share issue) émettre; (loan) émettre, lancer
3 Fin (currency) faire flotter, laisser flotter
4 Fig (idea) lancer, proposer; (plan) proposer
▸▸ Br **float chamber**, Am **float bowl** (in carburettor) cuve f; **float glass** verre m flotté

▸**float about, float around** **VI** Fam (rumours) courir□; (unoccupied person) traîner; **there were rumours floating about that...** le bruit courait que...; **she's/it's floating about somewhere** elle/il traîne dans les parages

▸**float off** **VT SEP** (free ▸ boat) remettre à flot
VI (be carried away ▸ log, ship etc) partir ou être emporté au fil de l'eau; (in the air ▸ balloon, piece of paper) s'envoler

floating ['fləʊtɪŋ] **ADJ1** (on water) flottant
2 (not fixed) **there's a fairly large f. vote** les indécis sont assez nombreux; **the f. vote will determine the outcome** les voix des indécis détermineront le résultat
3 Fin (currency, exchange rate) flottant
4 Comput (accent) flottant
5 Tech (bearing) flottant
N1 (putting on the water) mise f à flot; (getting afloat again) remise f à flot
2 (of new company) lancement m, création f; (onto Stock Market) introduction f en Bourse; Fin (of loan, bonds, share issue) émission f, lancement m
3 Fin (of currency) flottement m
4 (of new idea, plan) proposition f
▸▸ Acct **floating assets** actif m circulant; **floating bridge** pont m de bateaux ou de radeaux; Fin **floating capital** capital m circulant; Banking **floating charge** nantissement m général; **floating crane** ponton-grue m; **floating dam** barrage m flottant; Fin **floating debt** dette f flottante ou non consolidée; **floating dock** dock m flottant; Culin **floating island** île f flottante; Med **floating kidney** rein m flottant; **floating off** (of wrecked ship etc) renflouage m; Comput **floating point** virgule f flottante; **floating population** (within country) population f flottante; Fin **floating rate** taux m flottant; Anat **floating rib** côte f flottante; **floating voter** électeur(trice) m,f indécis(e); Comput **floating window** fenêtre f flottante

floating-point **ADJ** Comput à ou en virgule flottante
▸▸ **floating-point arithmetic** arithmétique f en virgule flottante; **floating-point notation** notation f en virgule flottante; **floating-point processor** coprocesseur m arithmétique

floating-rate **ADJ** Fin à taux flottant
▸▸ **floating-rate bond** obligation f à taux flottant ou variable; **floating-rate interest** intérêt m à taux flottant; **floating-rate investment** investissement m à taux flottant ou variable; Banking **floating-rate note** effet m à taux flottant; **floating-rate securities** titres mpl à taux flottant ou variable

flock[1] [flɒk] **N** (of sheep) troupeau m; (of birds) vol m, volée f; (of people) foule f; Rel ouailles fpl
VI aller ou venir en foule ou en masse, affluer; **people are flocking to see it** les gens vont le voir en foule ou en masse, les gens affluent pour le voir; **the people flocked around him** les gens se sont massés ou attroupés autour de lui; **in summer people f. to the sea** en été les gens vont en foule au bord de la mer

flock[2] **N** Tex bourre f
▸▸ **flock wallpaper** papier m tontisse

▸**flock together** **VI** (sheep) se regrouper, s'attrouper

floe [fləʊ] **N** (ice) **f.** glace f flottante

flog [flɒg] (pt & pp **flogged**, cont **flogging**) **VT1** (beat) fouetter; Fam **to f. an idea/a joke to death** accommoder une idée/blague à toutes les sauces **2** Br Fam (sell) vendre□; (sell off quickly) bazarder; (stolen goods) fourguer

▸**flog off** **VT SEP** Br Fam (sell off quickly) bazarder; **they're flogging them off cheap** ils les bazardent pour pas cher

flood [flʌd] **N1** (of water) inondation f; Bible **the F.** le Déluge; **to be in f.** (river) être en crue
2 Fig (of applications, letters, offers) déluge m; (of light) flot m; **to be in floods (of tears)** pleurer à chaudes larmes
3 (tide) marée f montante
4 (floodlight) projecteur m
VT 1 (unintentionally) inonder; (deliberately) inonder, noyer; **the river flooded its banks** la rivière est sortie de son lit, la rivière a débordé; **you've flooded the bathroom** tu as inondé la salle de bains; **to be flooded** (ship) être envahi par l'eau; (house) être inondé
2 Aut (carburettor) noyer; (engine) étouffer, noyer
3 (river ▸ of rain) faire déborder
4 (usu passive) Fig (person ▸ with letters, replies) inonder, submerger; **to be flooded with applications/letters** être submergé de demandes/lettres; **to be flooded in light** (room, valley) être inondé de lumière
5 Agr (for irrigation) irriguer
6 Com **to f. the market (with sth)** inonder le marché (de qch)
VI1 (river) être en crue; (overflow) déborder
2 (land, area) être inondé
3 Fig (move in large quantities) **to f. into the streets** envahir les rues; **spectators were flooding into the stadium** les spectateurs affluaient dans le stade; **refugees are still flooding across the border** les réfugiés continuent à passer la frontière en foule ou en masse; **light was flooding through the window** la lumière entrait à flots par la fenêtre
4 (woman ▸ menstruate heavily) saigner abondamment
▸▸ **flood barrier** digue f de retenue; **flood control** contrôle m des crues; **flood plain** plaine f d'inondation, lit m majeur; **flood tide** marée f montante; **flood wall** mur m de protection contre les

crues; **flood warning** avis *m* de crue; **flood water** inondation *f*; **the f. waters have receded** les inondations ont diminué

▸**flood back** VI *(people)* revenir en foule *ou* en masse; *(strength, memories)* revenir à flots, affluer; **suddenly it all came flooding back** soudain tout m'est revenu en mémoire

▸**flood in** VI *(people)* entrer en foule *ou* en masse, affluer; *(applications, letters)* affluer; *(light, sunshine)* entrer à flots

▸**flood out** VT SEP inonder; **hundreds of families have been flooded out** *(from homes)* l'inondation a forcé des centaines de familles à quitter leurs maisons

VI *(people)* sortir en foule *ou* en masse; *(words)* sortir à flots; *(ideas)* se bousculer, affluer; **light flooded out of the open casement** des flots de lumière s'échappaient de la fenêtre ouverte; **money flooded out of the country** il y eut d'énormes fuites de capitaux

flooded ['flʌdɪd] ADJ *(land, house)* inondé; *Aut (carburettor, engine)* noyé

floodgate ['flʌdgeɪt] N vanne *f*, porte *f* d'écluse; *Fig* **the new law will open the floodgates to all kinds of fraudulent practices** cette nouvelle loi est la porte ouverte à toutes sortes de pratiques frauduleuses

flooding ['flʌdɪŋ] N *(UNCOUNT)* inondation *f*; **f. is a major problem** les inondations sont un grand problème

floodlight ['flʌdlaɪt] *(pt & pp* **floodlit** [-lɪt] *or* **floodlighted**) N *(lamp)* projecteur *m*; *(light)* lumière *f* des projecteurs; **to play under floodlights** jouer à la lumière des projecteurs

VT *(football pitch, stage)* éclairer (aux projecteurs); *(building)* illuminer

floodlighting ['flʌdlaɪtɪŋ] N *(UNCOUNT) (of pitch, stage)* éclairage *m* (aux projecteurs); *(of building)* illumination *f*

floodlit ['flʌdlɪt] *(pt & pp of* **floodlight**) ADJ *(pitch, match, stage)* éclairé (aux projecteurs); *(building)* illuminé

floor [flɔː(r)] N **1** *(ground ▸ gen)* sol *m*; *(▸ wooden)* plancher *m*, parquet *m*; *(▸ tiled)* carrelage *m*; **earthen f.** sol *m* en terre battue; **to put sth/to sit on the f.** poser qch/s'asseoir par terre; **the forest f.** le sol de la forêt, la couverture; *Fig* **to wipe the f. with sb** *(in match, fight)* battre qn à plate couture, réduire qn en miettes; *(in argument)* descendre qn

2 *(bottom part ▸ of lift, cage)* plancher *m*; *(▸ of sea, ocean)* fond *m*

3 *(storey)* étage *m*; **we live ten floors up** nous habitons au dixième étage; **their offices are two floors down** leurs bureaux sont deux étages plus bas; **on the same f.** au même étage; **on the f. below** à l'étage en-dessous; **on the second f.** *Br* au deuxième étage; *Am* au premier étage

4 *(for dancing)* piste *f* (de danse); **to take the f.** aller sur la piste (de danse)

5 *(in parliament, assembly etc)* enceinte *f*; *Br Parl* **the f. of the House** l'hémicycle *m*; **to have/to take the f.** *(speaker)* avoir/prendre la parole; **Mr Taylor has the f.** la parole est à M. Taylor; **questions from the f.** questions *fpl* du public; **to cross the f.** *(in parliament)* changer de parti

6 *(of stock exchange)* parquet *m*; **trading on the f. was quiet today** la journée n'a pas été très animée à la Bourse

7 *TV (of studio)* plateau *m*

VT **1** *(building, house)* faire le sol de; *(with linoleum)* poser le revêtement de sol dans; *(with parquet)* poser le parquet *ou* plancher dans, parqueter; *(with tiles)* poser le carrelage dans, carreler

2 *Fam (opponent)* terrasser; **that virus really floored me** ce virus m'a complètement terrassé

3 *Fam (puzzle, baffle)* dérouter; *(surprise, amaze)* abasourdir

4 *Fam* **to f. it** *(drive fast)* mettre le pied au plancher

▸▸ ***floor area*** *(of room, office)* surface *f*; *TV* ***floor assistant*** assistant(e) *m,f* de plateau; ***floor cleaner*** (produit *m*) nettoyant *m* pour sols; ***floor cloth*** serpillière *f*; *(old rag)* chiffon *m*; ***floor covering*** *(linoleum, fitted carpet)* revêtement *m* de sol; *(rug)* tapis *m*; *TV* ***floor crew*** personnel *m* de plateau; ***floor exercise*** *(in gymnastics)* exercice *m* au sol; *Am* ***floor lamp*** lampadaire *m*; *Pol* ***floor leader*** = chef de file d'un parti siégeant au Sénat ou à la Chambre des représentants aux États-Unis; ***floor manager*** *(in department store)* chef *m* de rayon; *TV* régisseur(euse) *m,f* de plateau; ***floor plan*** plan *m*; ***floor polish*** encaustique *f*, cire *f*; ***floor polisher*** *(machine)* cireuse *f*; *Com* ***floor price*** prix *m* seuil; ***floor show*** spectacle *m* de cabaret; ***floor tile*** carreau *m*; *St Exch* ***floor trader*** commis *m*; *St Exch* ***floor trading*** cotation *f* à la corbeille; ***floor wax*** cire *f*, encaustique *f*; ***floor work*** exercices *mpl* au sol

floorboard ['flɔːbɔːd] N lame *f* de parquet; **to take the floorboards up** enlever les lames du parquet; **we're going to sand the floorboards** nous allons poncer le parquet

flooring ['flɔːrɪŋ] N *(UNCOUNT)* **1** *(act)* **the f. has still to be done** il reste encore les sols à faire **2** *(material)* revêtement *m* de sol

▸▸ ***flooring tiles*** carreaux *mpl*

floorspace ['flɔːspeɪs] N espace *m*

floorwalker ['flɔːˌwɔːkə(r)] N *Am* chef *m* de rayon

floozie, floozy ['fluːzɪ] *(pl* **floozies**) N *Fam* traînée *f*

flop [flɒp] *(pt & pp* **flopped**, *cont* **flopping**) VI **1** *(fall slackly ▸ head, arm etc)* tomber; *(▸ person)* s'affaler, s'effondrer **2** *Fam (attempt, idea, recipe)* louper; *(fail ▸ play, film)* faire un four *ou* un bide; *(▸ actor)* faire un bide

N *Fam* **1** *(failure)* fiasco *m*, bide *m*; **this cake is a f.** ce gâteau est complètement loupé; **he was a f. as Othello** il était complètement nul dans le rôle d'Othello *ou* en Othello **2** *Am Fam (hotel)* hôtel *m* borgne; *(hostel)* asile *m* de nuit

ADV *Fam* **it went f. into the water** ça a fait plouf *ou* floc en tombant dans l'eau

flophouse ['flɒphaʊs, *pl* -haʊzɪz] N *Am Fam (hotel)* hôtel *m* borgne; *(hostel)* asile *m* de nuit

floppy ['flɒpɪ] *(compar* **floppier**, *superl* **floppiest**) ADJ *(ears, tail, plant)* pendant; *(collar, brim of hat)* mou (molle); *(trousers, sweater)* flottant, large; **the jumper went all f. when I washed it** le pull s'est complètement déformé au lavage; **he has f. hair** il a les cheveux qui lui tombent sur la figure

N *Comput* disquette *f*; **on f.** sur disquette

▸▸ *Comput* ***floppy disk*** disquette *f*; *Comput* ***floppy (disk) drive*** unité *f* de disquettes

floptical ['flɒptɪkəl] ADJ *Comput*

▸▸ ***floptical disk*** *(hard)* disque *m* optique; *(floppy)* disquette *f* optique; ***floptical drive*** *(hard)* unité *f* de disque optique; *(floppy)* unité *f* de disquette optique

flora ['flɔːrə] NPL flore *f*

floral ['flɔːrəl] ADJ *(arrangement, display)* floral; *(pattern, fabric, dress)* à fleurs, fleuri

▸▸ ***floral tribute*** *(gen)* bouquet *m ou* gerbe *f* de fleurs; *(funeral wreath)* couronne *f* de fleurs

floret ['flɔːrɪt] N fleuron *m*

florid ['flɒrɪd] ADJ **1** *(complexion)* coloré **2** *(style, architecture)* chargé; *(speech)* fleuri; *(music)* qui comporte trop de fioritures

Florida ['flɒrɪdə] N la Floride

florin ['flɒrɪn] N *(British, Dutch)* florin *m*

florist ['flɒrɪst] N fleuriste *mf*; **f.'s (shop)** fleuriste *m*

floss [flɒs] N **1** *(for embroidery)* fil *m* de schappe *ou* de bourrette **2** *(for teeth)* fil *m ou* soie *f* dentaire

VT *(teeth)* nettoyer au fil *ou* à la soie dentaire

VI *(floss teeth)* se nettoyer les dents au fil *ou* à la soie dentaire

flotation [fləʊ'teɪʃən] N **1** *(of ship ▸ putting into water)* mise *f* à flot; *(▸ off sandbank)* remise *f* à flot; *(of logs)* flottage *m* **2** *(of new company)* lancement *m*, création *f*; *(onto Stock Market)* introduction *f* en Bourse; *(of loan, bonds, share issue)* émission *f*, lancement *m* **3** *Fin (of currency)* flottement *m*

▸▸ ***flotation rings*** flotteurs *mpl*; ***flotation tank*** caisson *m* à isolation sensorielle; ***flotation therapy*** thérapie *f* par isolation sensorielle; ***flotation vest*** gilet *m* de sauvetage

flotilla [flə'tɪlə] N flottille *f*

flotsam ['flɒtsəm] N *(UNCOUNT)* morceaux *mpl* d'épave; **f. and jetsam** morceaux *mpl* d'épave et détritus; *Fig* **the f. and jetsam of society** les laissés-pour-compte *mpl* de la société

flounce [flaʊns] N **1** *(in garment)* volant *m* **2** *(of indignation, impatience)* mouvement *m* vif; **with a f. of her long skirt, she marched out of the room** elle sortit de la pièce d'un pas ferme en faisant voltiger sa longue jupe

VI **to f. into/out of a room** entrer dans une/sortir d'une pièce de façon très théâtrale; **she's been flouncing around all morning** elle s'est agitée toute la matinée

flouncy ['flaʊnsɪ] *(compar* **flouncier**, *superl* **flounciest**) ADJ *(dress, skirt)* froufroutant

flounder ['flaʊndə(r)] VI **1** *(in water, mud)* patauger péniblement; **the dolphin was floundering about in a few inches of water** le dauphin se débattait dans quelques centimètres d'eau **2** *(in speech, lecture etc)* perdre pied, s'empêtrer; **somehow he floundered through his speech** il est allé tant bien que mal jusqu'à la fin de son discours; **the economy is still floundering** l'économie est encore instable

N *Ich* flet *m*

flour ['flaʊə(r)] N farine *f*; **to dust sth with f.** (en)fariner qch

VT saupoudrer de farine, fariner

▸▸ ***flour bin*** boîte *f* à farine; ***flour dredger*** saupoudreuse *f* à farine; ***flour shaker*** saupoudreuse *f* à farine

flourish ['flʌrɪʃ] VI *(business, economy, plant)* prospérer; *(arts, literature etc)* fleurir, s'épanouir; *(in health)* être en pleine forme *ou* santé

VT *(wave, brandish ▸ sword, diploma)* brandir

N **1** *(in lettering, design)* ornement *m*, fioriture *f*; *(in signature)* paraphe *m*, parafe *m* **2** *(wave)* grand geste *m* de la main; **to carry things off with a f.** faire les choses avec panache; **with a f. of his sword** en faisant un moulinet avec son épée **3** *(in musical or written style)* fioriture *f*; **a f. of trumpets** une fanfare; **a little literary f.** un petit effet de style

flourishing ['flʌrɪʃɪŋ] ADJ *(business, economy)* florissant, prospère; *(plant)* qui prospère; *(trader)* prospère; *(in health)* en pleine forme *ou* santé

floury ['flaʊərɪ] ADJ **1** *(covered in flour ▸ hands)* enfariné; *(▸ clothes)* couvert de farine; *(rolls)* saupoudré de farine **2** *(texture, potatoes)* farineux

flout [flaʊt] VT *(orders, instructions)* passer outre à; *(tradition, convention)* se moquer de; *(laws of physics)* défier

> Attention: ne pas confondre avec le verbe **to flaunt**.

FLOW [fləʊ]

N
- circulation **1, 2**
- flux **2, 5**
- flot **4**
- écoulement **1**
- mouvement **2**

VI
- couler **1, 4, 5**
- provenir **7**
- circuler **2, 8**

N **1** *(of liquid)* circulation *f*; *(volume of liquid)* volume *m*; *(of river)* écoulement *m*; *(of lava)* coulée *f*; *(of tears)* ruissellement *m*; *(of blood ▸ in veins)* circulation *f*; *(▸ from wound)* écoulement *m*; *(of air, fuel etc)* passage *m*, arrivée *f*; *Elec (of current)* passage *m*; **the decreasing f. of oil from the North Sea** la quantité décroissante de pétrole en provenance de la mer du Nord

2 *(amount ▸ of traffic, people, information, work)* flux *m*; *(▸ of ideas)* flot *m*; *(movement ▸ of work)* acheminement *m*; *(▸ of information)* circulation *f*; *Fin (▸ of capital)* mouvement *m*; **there is normally a very heavy f. of traffic here** il y a généralement beaucoup de circulation *ou* une circulation intense par ici; **a steady f. of immigrants** un courant ininterrompu d'immigration; *Fig* **to go with the f.** suivre le mouvement; **f. of funds** mouvement *m* de fonds; **f. of money** flux *m* monétaire

3 *(of dress, cape)* drapé *m*

4 *(of prose, novel, piece of music)* flot *m*; **to be in full f.** *(orator)* être en plein discours; **there's no stopping him once he's in full f.** il n'y a pas moyen de l'arrêter quand il est lancé; **to follow the f. of sb's argument** suivre le fil de l'argumentation de qn
5 *(of the tide)* flux *m*
VI 1 *(liquid)* couler; *(electric current, air, blood in veins)* circuler; **the river flows into the sea** la rivière se jette dans la mer; **I let the waves f. over me** j'ai laissé les vagues glisser sur moi; **blood was still flowing from the wound** le sang continuait à couler *ou* s'écouler de la blessure; **the tears flowed down her cheeks** les larmes coulaient sur ses joues; *Fig* **I let the sound of the music just f. over me** j'ai laissé la musique m'envahir
2 *(traffic, crowd)* circuler, s'écouler; **new measures designed to enable the traffic to f. more freely** de nouvelles mesures destinées à rendre la circulation plus fluide
3 *(hair, dress)* flotter
4 *(prose, style, novel)* couler; *(work, project)* avancer, progresser; **this essay doesn't f. very well** cette dissertation n'est pas très fluide; **in order to keep the conversation flowing** pour entretenir la conversation
5 *(appear in abundance)* **the whisky flowed freely** le whisky a coulé à flots; **ideas flowed fast and furious** les idées fusaient de tous côtés
6 *(tide)* monter
7 *(emanate)* provenir; **decisions flowing from head office** les décisions qui proviennent *ou* émanent du siège social
8 *Fin (capital, money)* circuler
▸▸ ***flow diagram*** organigramme *m*, graphique *m* d'évolution; *Comput* ordinogramme *m*; *Comput* ***flow path*** branche *f* de traitement; ***flow pipe*** conduite *f* montante; *Acct* ***flow sheet*** feuille *f* d'avancement
▸ **flow away VI** *(liquid)* s'écouler
▸ **flow back VI** *(water)* refluer; *(in pipe etc)* regorger
▸ **flow in VI** *(water, liquid)* entrer, s'écouler; *(contributions, messages of sympathy, people)* affluer
▸ **flow out VI** *(water, liquid)* sortir, s'écouler; *(people, crowds)* s'écouler; **the sewage then flows out of the pipe into the lake** les égouts se déversent ensuite du conduit dans le lac

flower ['flaʊə(r)] **N 1** *Bot* fleur *f*; **to be in f.** être en fleur *ou* fleurs; **to come into f.** fleurir; **no flowers by request** *(at funeral)* ni fleurs ni couronnes; **to do the flowers** *(arrange)* s'occuper des compositions florales **2** *Fig (best part)* fine fleur *f*, crème *f*; *Literary* **the f. of the youth of Athens/of the army** la fine fleur de la jeunesse athénienne/de l'armée; **in the full f. of youth** dans la fleur de la jeunesse **3** *Chem* **flowers of sulphur** fleur *f* de soufre
VI 1 *(plant, tree)* fleurir; *(state)* être en fleur **2** *Literary (artistic movement, genre)* fleurir, s'épanouir
▸▸ ***flower arrangement*** *(art)* art *m* floral; *(example)* composition *f* florale; ***flower arranging*** *(UNCOUNT)* art *m* floral; **the f. arranging took no time at all** la composition florale a été réalisée en un rien de temps; ***flower child*** hippy *mf*, hippie *mf* *(surtout des années soixante)*; ***flower garden*** jardin *m* d'agrément; ***flower girl*** *(selling flowers)* marchande *f* de fleurs; *(at wedding)* = petite fille qui porte des fleurs dans un mariage, demoiselle *f* d'honneur; ***flower head*** capitule *m*; ***flower market*** marché *m* aux fleurs; ***flower people*** hippies *mpl (surtout des années soixante)*; ***flower power*** = pacifisme prôné par les hippies, surtout dans les années soixante; ***flower shop*** fleuriste *m*; **she owns two f. shops** elle est propriétaire de deux boutiques de fleurs; ***flower show*** exposition *f* de fleurs; *(outdoors, on a large scale)* floralies *fpl*; ***flower vase*** vase *m* à fleurs

flowerbed ['flaʊəbed] **N** parterre *m* de fleurs

flowered ['flaʊəd] **ADJ** *(dress, pattern)* fleuri, à fleurs

flowering ['flaʊərɪŋ] **N 1** *(of plant, tree)* floraison *f* **2** *(of artistic movement, talents)* épanouissement *m*
ADJ *(plant, tree ▸ which flowers)* à fleurs; *(▸ which is in flower)* en fleurs
▸▸ *Bot* ***flowering ash*** orne *m*; *Bot* ***flowering cherry*** cerisier *m* à fleurs

flowerpot ['flaʊəpɒt] **N** pot *m* de fleurs

flowery ['flaʊərɪ] **ADJ 1** *(fields, perfume)* fleuri; *(smell)* de fleurs; *(pattern, dress, carpet)* à fleurs **2** *(language, speech, compliments)* fleuri

flowing ['fləʊɪŋ] **ADJ** *(style, prose)* fluide; *(beard, hair, robes)* flottant; *(movement)* fluide, coulant

flowline ['fləʊlaɪn] **N** *(on organization chart)* ligne *f* de jonction de symboles

flowmeter ['fləʊˌmiːtə(r)] **N** *(for liquid etc)* débitmètre *m*, indicateur *m* d'écoulement *ou* de débit

flown [fləʊn] *pp of* **fly**

flu [fluː] **N** grippe *f*; **to have the f.** *or Br* **f.** avoir la grippe, être grippé
▸▸ ***flu epidemic*** épidémie *f* de grippe; ***flu jab*** vaccin *m* contre la grippe; ***flu virus*** virus *m* de la grippe

flub [flʌb] *(pt & pp* **flubbed**, *cont* **flubbing**) *Am Fam*
N gaffe *f*, bourde *f*
VT rater, louper
VI faire une gaffe, gaffer

fluctuate ['flʌktʃʊeɪt] **VI** *(rate, temperature, results etc)* fluctuer; *(interest, enthusiasm, support)* être fluctuant *ou* variable; *(person ▸ in enthusiasm, opinions etc)* être fluctuant *ou* changeant; *Fin (exchange rate, share prices)* fluctuer; **our production fluctuates from week to week** notre production est fluctuante *ou* varie d'une semaine sur l'autre

fluctuating ['flʌktʃʊeɪtɪŋ] **ADJ** *(rate, figures, prices etc)* fluctuant; *(enthusiasm, support etc)* fluctuant, variable; *(needs, opinions etc)* fluctuant, changeant

fluctuation [ˌflʌktʃʊ'eɪʃən] **N** fluctuation *f*

flue [fluː] **N 1** *(chimney)* conduit *m*; *(for stove, boiler)* tuyau *m* **2** *Mus (of organ)* tuyau *m*
▸▸ ***flue brush*** hérisson *m*; *Mus* ***flue pipe*** *(of organ)* tuyau *m*

fluency ['fluːənsɪ] **N 1** *(in speaking, writing)* facilité *f*, aisance *f*; **to speak with f.** avoir la parole facile **2** *(in a foreign language)* **f. in French is desirable** la connaissance du français parlé est souhaitable; **I doubt whether I'll ever achieve complete f.** je doute d'arriver un jour à parler couramment **3** *Sport (of play, strokes)* facilité *f*, aisance *f*

fluent ['fluːənt] **ADJ 1** *(prose, style)* fluide; **he's a f. speaker** il s'exprime aisément *ou* avec facilité **2** *(in a foreign language)* **to be f. in French, to speak f. French** parler couramment (le) français; **he replied in f. Urdu** il a répondu dans un ourdou aisé *ou* coulant; **I'll never be f.** je ne parlerai jamais couramment **3** *Sport (play, strokes)* facile, aisé

fluently ['fluːəntlɪ] **ADV 1** *(speak, write)* avec facilité *ou* aisance **2** *(speak a foreign language)* couramment **3** *Sport (play)* avec facilité *ou* aisance

fluff [flʌf] **N 1** *(UNCOUNT) (on baby animal, baby's head)* duvet *m*; *(from pillow, material etc)* peluches *fpl*; *(collected dust)* moutons *mpl*; **a bit of f.** une peluche; *Br Old-fashioned Fam (pretty girl)* nana *f*, gonzesse *f* **2** *Br Fam (mistake)* raté *m*; **he made a complete f. of the line** il a complètement raté sa réplique
VT *Br Fam (lines, entrance, interview)* rater, louper; **to f. it** se planter; *Sport* **to f. a shot** rater un coup
▸ **fluff out VT SEP** *(feathers)* hérisser, ébouriffer; *(hair)* faire bouffer; *(pillows, cushions)* secouer

fluffy ['flʌfɪ] *(compar* **fluffier**, *superl* **fluffiest**) **ADJ 1** *(material, sweater)* pelucheux; *(chick, kitten, hair)* duveteux; *(mousse, sponge, mashed potatoes)* léger; *(clouds)* cotonneux **2** *(covered in fluff, dust)* couvert de moutons
▸▸ *Br* ***fluffy toy*** (jouet *m* en) peluche *f*

fluid ['fluːɪd] **ADJ 1** *(substance)* fluide, liquide **2** *(flowing ▸ style, play, match)* fluide **3** *(liable to change ▸ situation)* indécis, indéterminé; *(▸ plans)* indéterminé
N fluide *m*, liquide *m*; **body** *or* **bodily fluids** sécrétions *fpl* corporelles; **to be on fluids** *(patient)* ne prendre que des liquides
▸▸ ***fluid dram*** drachme *f*; ***fluid mechanics*** *(UNCOUNT)* mécanique *f* des fluides; ***fluid ounce*** *(in UK)* = 0,028 l; *(in US)* = 0,03 l

fluidity [fluː'ɪdətɪ] **N 1** *(of substance)* fluidité *f* **2** *(of style, play, match)* fluidité *f* **3** *(liability to change ▸ of situation, plans)* indétermination *f*

fluke[1] [fluːk] **N** *(piece of good luck)* coup *m* de bol *ou* pot; *(coincidence)* hasard *m*; **by (a) sheer f.** *(coincidence)* par un pur hasard
COMP *(shot)* heureux

fluke[2] **N** *(on anchor)* patte *f*, bras *m*; *(on whale's tail)* lobe *m* de la nageoire caudale

fluke[3] **N** *Entom* douve *f*

fluky ['fluːkɪ] *(compar* **flukier**, *superl* **flukiest**) **ADJ** *Fam* **1** *(lucky ▸ shot, guess)* heureux□; *(▸ person)* chanceux□; **what a f. goal!** quel coup de bol, ce but! **2** *Am (strange)* bizarre□

flume [fluːm] **N 1** *(channel)* buse *f* **2** *(at swimming pool)* toboggan *m* **3** *Am (ravine)* ravin *m*

flummox ['flʌməks] **VT** *Fam* démonter□

flung [flʌŋ] *pt & pp of* **fling**

flunk [flʌŋk] *esp Am Fam* **VI** *(in exam, course)* se planter
VT *(of student ▸ French, maths)* se planter en; *(▸ exam)* se planter à; *(of teacher ▸ student)* recaler, coller; **the professor flunked her paper in geography** le prof ne lui a pas mis la moyenne à sa dissert' de géo

flunkey, flunky ['flʌŋkɪ] *(pl* **flunkeys** *or* **flunkies**) **N** *(manservant)* laquais *m*; *Pej (assistant)* larbin *m*

fluorescence [flʊə'resəns] **N** fluorescence *f*

fluorescent [flʊə'resənt] **ADJ** fluorescent
▸▸ ***fluorescent lighting*** éclairage *m* au néon; ***fluorescent tube*** néon *m*

fluoridation [ˌflʊərɪ'deɪʃən] **N** fluoration *f*, fluoruration *f*

fluoride ['flʊəraɪd] **N** fluorure *m*
COMP *(toothpaste)* au fluor

fluorine ['flʊəriːn] **N** fluor *m*

fluoroscope ['flʊərəskəʊp] **N** *Med* fluoroscope *m*

flurry ['flʌrɪ] *(pl* **flurries**, *pt & pp* **flurried**, *cont* **flurrying**) **N 1** *(of snow, wind)* rafale *f* **2** *Fig* **a f. of activity** un branle-bas de combat; **there has been a late f. of activity on the Stock Market** on a assisté à une reprise soudaine de l'activité boursière en fin de journée; **to be in a f. of excitement** être tout excité
VT *(usu passive)* agiter, troubler

flush [flʌʃ] **N 1** *(facial redness)* rougeur *f*; **to bring a f. to sb's cheeks** *(compliment, crude joke)* faire rougir qn; *(wine)* mettre le feu aux joues à qn
2 *(of beauty, youth, light)* éclat *m*; *(of emotion etc)* accès *m*; *(of enthusiasm)* élan *m*; **in the full f. of youth** dans tout l'éclat de la jeunesse; **in the first f. of victory/success** dans l'ivresse de la victoire/du succès
3 *(on toilet)* chasse *f* (d'eau); **to pull the f.** tirer la chasse (d'eau); **to give sth a (good) f. (out)** *(drains, pipes etc)* nettoyer qch à grande eau
4 *(in card games)* flush *m*
VI 1 *(face, person)* rougir; **to f. with embarrassment** rougir d'embarras; **I can't drink punch, it makes me f.** je ne peux pas boire de punch, ça me met le feu aux joues **2** *(toilet)* **it's not flushing properly** la chasse d'eau ne marche pas bien; **the toilet flushes automatically** la chasse d'eau fonctionne automatiquement
VT 1 *(cheeks, face)* empourprer; **the exercise had flushed their cheeks** l'exercice leur avait fait monter le sang au visage **2** *(with water)* **to f. the toilet** tirer la chasse (d'eau); **to f. sth down the toilet/sink** jeter qch dans les toilettes/l'évier **3** *Hunt* lever, faire sortir
ADJ 1 *(level ▸ surface)* de niveau; *(▸ door, lock)* encastré; *(▸ screw, nail)* noyé; *(▸ rivet)* à tête noyée *ou* perdue; **f. mounted** monté à fleur; **f. with the side of the cupboard** dans l'alignement du placard; **f. with the ground** au niveau du sol, à ras de terre **2** *Fam (with money)* en fonds□; **feeling f. today, are you?** tu es en fonds aujourd'hui?□
3 *Typ* justifié; **f. left/right** justifié à gauche/droite
ADV 1 *(fit, be positioned)* **this piece has to fit f. into the frame** ce morceau doit être de niveau avec la charpente **2** *Typ* **set f. left/right** justifié à gauche/droite
▸ **flush away VT SEP** *(in toilet)* jeter dans les toilettes; *(in sink)* jeter dans l'évier

VI *(down toilet)* partir; **it wouldn't f. away** ça ne voulait pas partir

▸**flush out VT SEP 1** *(clean out ▸ container, sink etc)* nettoyer à grande eau; *(▸ dirt, waste)* faire partir **2** *Hunt (animal)* faire sortir, lever; *Fig (person)* faire sortir; *(undercover agents)* forcer à se trahir; *(truth)* faire éclater

flushed [flʌʃt] **ADJ 1** *(person)* rouge; *(cheeks)* rouge, en feu; **he was looking rather f.** il était plutôt rouge; **f. with anger/joy** rouge de colère/plaisir **2** *Fig* **f. with success** enivré *ou* grisé par le succès

fluster [ˈflʌstə(r)] **N to be in a f.** être troublé *ou* nerveux; **to get into a f.** se troubler, devenir nerveux

VT *(make agitated, nervous)* troubler, rendre nerveux; **to get flustered** se troubler, perdre contenance

flustered [ˈflʌstəd] **ADJ** troublé; **you're looking a bit f.** tu as l'air un peu agité

flute [fluːt] **N 1** *Mus* flûte *f* **2** *Archit (groove on column)* cannelure *f* **3** *(glass)* flûte *f*

fluted [ˈfluːtɪd] **ADJ 1** *Archit (column)* cannelé **2** *(baking tin, pastry cutter, vase, dish)* à cannelures

fluting [ˈfluːtɪŋ] **N** *Archit* cannelures *fpl*

flutist [ˈfluːtɪst] **N** *Am Mus* flûtiste *mf*

flutter [ˈflʌtə(r)] **VI 1** *(wings)* battre; *(flag)* flotter; *(heart)* palpiter; *(pulse)* battre irrégulièrement; *Fig* **to make sb's heart f.** faire tressaillir le cœur de qn **2** *(butterfly, bird ▸ fly)* voleter, voltiger; *(▸ flap wings)* battre des ailes; *(leaf, paper)* voltiger; **to f. away** *(bird, butterfly)* s'envoler en voletant *ou* voltigeant; **the letter fluttered to the ground** la lettre a volé par terre; **her mother kept fluttering in and out of the room** sa mère entrait et sortait de la pièce sans arrêt

VT *(fan, piece of paper)* agiter; *(wings)* battre; **to f. one's eyelashes at sb** aguicher qn en battant des cils

N 1 *(of wings)* battement *m*; *(of heart)* battement *m* irrégulier, pulsation *f* irrégulière; *(of pulse)* battement *m* irrégulier; **with a f. of her eyelashes** avec un battement de cils aguichant **2** *Fam (nervous state)* **to be all in** *or* **of a f.** être dans tous ses états **3** *Br Fam (gamble)* pari *m*; **I have a little f. from time to time** *(on horse)* je fais un petit pari *ou* je parie de petites sommes de temps en temps; **to have a f. on the Stock Exchange** tenter sa chance à la Bourse, boursicoter

▸▸ ***flutter kick*** *(in swimming)* battement *m* des jambes

fluvial [ˈfluːvjəl] **ADJ** *Formal* fluvial

flux [flʌks] **N** *(UNCOUNT)* **1** *(constant change)* **to be in a state of (constant) f.** *(universe)* être en perpétuel devenir; *(government, private life etc)* être en proie à des changements permanents

2 *Med* flux *m*

3 *Metal* fondant *m*

4 *Phys* flux *m*

fluxion [ˈflʌkʃən] **N** *Med* fluxion *f*

fluxmeter [ˈflʌksˌmiːtə(r)] **N** *Phys* fluxmètre *m*

FLY [flaɪ]

> **N**
> • mouche **1** • braguette **2**
> **VI**
> • voler **1, 3** • prendre l'avion **1**
> • filer **2**
> **VT**
> • piloter **1** • transporter en avion **2**
> • parcourir en avion **2** • fuir **4**

(*pl* **flies**, *pt* **flew** [fluː], *pp* **flown** [fləʊn])

N 1 *Entom & Fishing* mouche *f*; *Fam* **they're dropping like flies** *(dying, fainting)* ils tombent comme des mouches; *Fam* **the recession is killing companies off like flies** la récession fait une véritable hécatombe parmi les entreprises; *Fig* **the f. in the ointment** *(person)* l'empêcheur(euse) *m,f* de tourner en rond; *(problem)* l'os *m*; *Fig* **there's a f. in the ointment** il y a un os; *Fam* **there are no flies on him** il n'est pas fou; *Fig* **he wouldn't hurt a f.** il ne ferait pas de mal à une mouche; *Br Fam* **I wouldn't mind being a f. on the wall** j'aimerais bien être une petite souris; *Fam* **to be catching flies** *(yawn, have mouth open)* gober les mouches; *Am Fam* **to live on the f.** vivre à cent à l'heure

2 *(often pl) (on trousers)* braguette *f*; **your flies are** *or* **f. is undone** *or* **open** ta braguette est ouverte

3 *(entrance to tent)* rabat *m*; *(flysheet)* auvent *m*

4 *Tech (flywheel)* volant *m*

5 *(in aeroplane)* **to go for a f.** faire un tour en avion

6 *Br Fam (idiom)* **to do sth on the f.** *(craftily, secretively)* faire qch en douce

VI 1 *(bird, insect, plane, pilot)* voler; *(passenger)* prendre l'avion; *(arrow, bullet, missile)* voler, filer; **I'm flying to Berlin tomorrow** *(passenger)* je prends l'avion pour Berlin demain; *(pilot)* je vole à Berlin demain; **he flies to Paris about twice a month** *(passenger)* il va à Paris en avion environ deux fois par mois; **we f. to Berlin four days a week** *(airline)* nous avons des vols pour Berlin quatre jours par semaine; **we f. to over a dozen destinations** *(airline)* nous desservons plus d'une douzaine de destinations; **soon we'll be flying over Manchester** nous allons bientôt survoler Manchester; **to f. across the Channel** traverser la Manche en avion; **to f. via London** faire escale à Londres; **those who have flown** *Br* **in** *or Am* **with Concorde** ceux qui ont voyagé en Concorde, ceux qui ont pris le Concorde; **which airline did you f. with?** avec quelle compagnie aérienne as-tu voyagé?; **they don't f. from Heathrow any more** ils n'ont plus de vols au départ de Heathrow; **the trapeze artist flew through the air** le trapéziste a voltigé; *Fig* **the bird had already flown** l'oiseau s'était envolé

2 *(move quickly ▸ person)* filer; *(▸ time)* passer à toute vitesse; *(flee)* s'enfuir; *(shoot into air ▸ sparks, dust, cork, shavings)* voler; *Fam* **I really must f.!** il faut vraiment que je file! *ou* que je me sauve!; **she flew out of the room** elle est sortie de la pièce comme un bolide; **he came flying round the corner** il a débouché du coin comme un bolide; **he flew to her rescue** il a volé à son secours; **the past two years have just flown** les deux dernières années ont passé à toute vitesse *ou* se sont envolées; **time flies!, doesn't time f.!** comme le temps passe!; **the door flew open and there stood...** la porte s'est ouverte brusquement sur...; **to f. into a rage** *or* **temper** s'emporter, sortir de ses gonds; **to knock** *or* **to send sb flying** envoyer qn rouler à terre; **to knock** *or* **to send sth flying** envoyer qch voler; **the insults were really flying** les insultes fusaient de toutes parts

3 *(kite)* voler; *(flag)* être déployé; *(in wind ▸ flag, coat)* flotter; *(▸ hair)* voler

4 *Am Fam (be accepted)* être accepté; **that idea isn't going to f. with the more senior members of staff** les employés les plus haut placés vont rejeter cette idée

5 *(idioms)* **to let f.** *(physically)* envoyer *ou* décocher un coup; *(verbally)* s'emporter; **she then let f. with a string of accusations** elle a alors lancé un flot d'accusations; **to (let) f. at sb** *(physically)* sauter *ou* se jeter sur qn; *(verbally)* s'en prendre violemment à qn; **to f. in the face of sth** *(reason, evidence, logic)* défier qch; **this flies in the face of our agreement** cela contrecarre notre accord

VT 1 *(plane, helicopter ▸ of pilot)* piloter

2 *(passengers, people, goods)* transporter en avion; *(route ▸ of pilot, passenger)* emprunter; *(airline)* voyager avec; *(distance ▸ of passenger, pilot, plane)* parcourir; *(combat mission)* effectuer; **to f. the Atlantic** *(pilot, passenger)* traverser l'Atlantique en avion; *(plane)* traverser l'Atlantique; **her employers flew her to the States** ses employeurs l'ont envoyée aux États-Unis en avion; **we're flying them home on the first flight** nous les rapatrions par le premier vol

3 *(flag ▸ of ship)* arborer; *(kite)* faire voler; **a flag is flown on public buildings when...** tous les bâtiments publics arborent un drapeau quand...

4 *(flee from ▸ the country)* fuir; *Fam* **to f. the coop** se faire la malle; **to f. the nest** *(baby bird)* quitter le nid; *Fig (person)* quitter le foyer familial

ADJ 1 *Br Old-fashioned (sharp)* malin(igne), rusé; **a f. guy** un malin, un rusé

2 *Black Am slang (excellent)* génial, super *(inv)*, géant; *(stylish, attractive)* chouette

▸▸ ***fly agaric*** amanite *f* tue-mouches; ***fly ball*** *(in baseball)* chandelle *f*; ***fly cruise*** forfait *m* avion et croisière; *Sport* ***fly half*** *(in rugby)* demi *m* d'ouverture; **to play f. half** jouer (en) demi d'ouverture; *Sport* ***fly kick*** *(in rugby)* coup *m* de pied à suivre; *Fishing* ***fly rod*** canne *f* à mouche; ***fly spray*** bombe *f* insecticide

▸**fly about, fly around VI** *(bird, insect)* voleter, voltiger; *(plane, pilot)* voler dans les parages, survoler les parages; *Fig (rumours)* courir; **there are lots of figures flying about** *or* **around** on entend tellement de chiffres différents

▸**fly away VI** *(bird, insect, plane)* s'envoler

▸**fly by VI 1** *(time)* passer à toute vitesse; **the time has flown by!** comme le temps a passé!; **as the days flew by** à mesure que les jours s'enfuyaient **2** *(plane)* passer

▸**fly in VT SEP** *(troops, reinforcements, food)* envoyer en avion; *(of pilot ▸ to an area)* emmener; *(▸ from an area)* amener

VI 1 *(person)* arriver en avion; *(plane)* arriver **2** *(bird, insect)* entrer

▸**fly off VT SEP 1** *(from oil rig, island)* évacuer en avion *ou* hélicoptère **2** *(transport by plane ▸ to an area)* emmener en avion; *(▸ from an area)* amener en avion

VI 1 *(bird, insect)* s'envoler; *(plane)* décoller; *(person)* partir en avion; **when do you f. off to Paris?** quand prenez-vous l'avion pour Paris? **2** *(hat, lid)* s'envoler; *(button)* sauter

▸**fly out VT SEP** *(person, supplies ▸ to an area)* envoyer par avion; *(▸ from an area)* évacuer par avion; **they flew the President out** *(to a place)* ils ont emmené le président en avion; *(from a place)* ils ont ramené le président en avion

VI 1 *(person)* partir (en avion), prendre l'avion; *(plane)* s'envoler; **which airport did you f. out of?** de quel aéroport es-tu parti?; **a medical team flew out to the disaster area** une équipe médicale s'est rendue en avion sur la région sinistrée; **I'll f. out to join you next Monday** je prendrai l'avion pour te rejoindre lundi prochain **2** *(come out suddenly ▸ from box, pocket)* s'échapper; **the knife flew out of his hand** le couteau lui a échappé de la main **3** *(bird)* sortir en volant

▸**fly past VI 1** *(plane, bird)* passer; *(plane ▸ as part of display, ceremony)* défiler; *Fig* **he flew past on a bicycle** il est passé à toute vitesse en bicyclette **2** *(time, days)* passer à toute vitesse

▸**fly up VI 1** *(plane, bird)* s'envoler; **the plane flew up to 10,000 metres** l'avion est monté à 10000 mètres; **I flew up from London on Saturday** j'ai pris l'avion depuis Londres samedi **2** *(end of plank, lid)* se soulever; **glass flew up into the air** des éclats de verre ont été projetés en l'air

flyable [ˈflaɪəbəl] **ADJ** *(plane)* pilotable

flyaway [ˈflaɪəweɪ] **ADJ 1** *(hair)* indiscipliné **2** *(person)* frivole, étourdi; *(idea)* frivole

flyblown [ˈflaɪbləʊn] **ADJ 1** *(of meat ▸ with eggs)* couvert *ou* plein d'œufs de mouches; *(▸ with maggots)* couvert *ou* plein d'asticots **2** *Fig (dirty, shabby)* en piteux état

flyby [ˈflaɪˌbaɪ] (*pl* **flybys**) **N 1** *(of plane, spacecraft)* = passage d'un avion ou d'un engin spatial à proximité d'un objectif **2** *Am (flypast)* défilé *m* aérien

fly-by-night *Fam* **ADJ** *(unreliable)* peu fiable, sur qui on ne peut pas compter; *(firm, operation)* véreux, louche

N 1 *(person ▸ irresponsible)* écervelé(e) *m,f*; *(▸ in debt)* débiteur(trice) *m,f* qui décampe en douce **2** *(nightclubber)* fêtard(e) *m,f*, couche-tard *mf inv*

flycatcher [ˈflaɪˌkætʃə(r)] **N** *Orn* gobe-mouches *m inv*

fly-drive N formule *f* avion plus voiture

▸▸ ***fly-drive holiday, fly-drive package*** formule *f* avion plus voiture

flyer = **flier**

fly-fishing N pêche *f* à la mouche; **to go f.** aller à la pêche à la mouche

flying [ˈflaɪɪŋ] **N 1** *(piloting plane)* pilotage *m*; *(travelling by plane)* voyage *m* en avion; **I love f.** *(as pilot)* j'adore piloter; *(as traveller)* j'adore prendre l'avion; **to be afraid of f.** avoir peur de prendre l'avion; **he goes f. at the weekends** le week-end, il fait de l'aviation **2** *(of flag)* déploiement *m*

ADJ 1 *(animal, insect)* volant; **they were hurt by f. glass** ils ont été blessés par des bris de verre
2 *(school)* d'aviation; *(staff)* navigant
3 *(fast)* rapide; **she took a f. leap over the fence** elle a sauté par-dessus la barrière
4 *(idiom)* **to pass with f. colours** réussir brillamment
▸▸ ***flying ambulance*** avion-ambulance *m*; ***flying boat*** hydravion *m*; ***flying bomb*** bombe *f* volante; *Constr* ***flying buttress*** arc-boutant *m*; ***flying circus*** *(exhibition)* voltige *f* aérienne; *(group)* groupe *m* de voltige aérienne; ***flying club*** aéro-club *m*; *Mil* ***flying column*** colonne *f* mobile, groupement *m* mobile; *Am Aviat* ***flying corps*** corps *m* d'armée aérien; ***flying doctor*** médecin *m* volant; ***the Flying Dutchman*** *(legend)* le Hollandais volant; *Ich* ***flying fish*** poisson *m* volant, exocet *m*; *Aviat* ***flying fortress*** forteresse *f* volante; *Zool* ***flying fox*** roussette *f*; *Zool* ***flying lemur*** galéopithèque *m*; ***flying lessons*** leçons *fpl* de pilotage (aérien); *Zool* ***flying lizard*** dragon *m* volant; ***flying machine*** machine *f* volante; *Aviat* ***flying officer*** lieutenant *m* de l'armée de l'air; *Ind* ***flying picket*** piquet *m* de grève volant; ***flying saucer*** soucoupe *f* volante; *Zool* ***flying snake*** serpent *m* volant; ***the Flying Squad*** = brigade de détectives britanniques spécialisés dans la grande criminalité; *Zool* ***flying squirrel*** écureuil *m* volant, polatouche *m*; *Sport* ***flying start*** départ *m* lancé; **the runner got off to a f. start** le coureur est parti comme une flèche; *Fig* **the campaign got off to a f. start** la campagne a démarré sur les chapeaux de roues; ***flying suit*** combinaison *f* d'aviateur; *Sport* ***flying tackle*** = plongeon pour plaquer ou stopper quelqu'un; ***flying time*** heures *fpl ou* temps *m* de vol; **200 hours' f. time** 200 heures de vol; ***flying visit*** visite *f* éclair; **to pay a f. visit to London** faire une visite éclair à Londres

flyleaf ['flaɪliːf] *(pl* **flyleaves** [-liːvz]) **N** page *f* de garde

Flymo® ['flaɪməʊ] **N** = tondeuse à gazon sur coussin d'air

flyover ['flaɪ,əʊvə(r)] **N 1** *Br Aut* pont *m* routier **2** *Am (flypast)* défilé *m* aérien

flypaper ['flaɪ,peɪpə(r)] **N** papier *m* tue-mouches, *Can* collant *m* à mouches

flypast ['flaɪpɑːst] **N** *Br* défilé *m* aérien

flypost ['flaɪpəʊst] **VI** coller illicitement des affiches

flyposter ['flaɪ,pəʊstə(r)] **N** = personne qui colle illicitement des affiches

flyposting ['flaɪ,pəʊstɪŋ] **N** affichage *m* illégal

flysheet ['flaɪʃiːt] **N 1** *(on tent)* auvent *m* **2** *(leaflet)* feuille *f* volante; *(instructions)* mode *m* d'emploi

fly-tipping **N** dépôt *m* d'ordures illégal

flyweight ['flaɪweɪt] **N** *Boxing* poids *m* mouche
ADJ de poids mouche

flywheel ['flaɪwiːl] **N** *Tech* volant *m*

FM [,ef'em] **N 1** *(abbr* **frequency modulation**) FM *f*; **FM radio** (radio *f*) FM *f*; **broadcast on FM only** diffusion en FM seulement **2** *Br Mil (abbr* **field marshal**) maréchal *m*

f-number **N** *Phot* échelle *f* d'ouverture

FO [,ef'əʊ] **N 1** *Mil (abbr* **field officer**) officier *m* supérieur **2** *Br Mil (abbr* **flying officer**) lieutenant *m* de l'armée de l'air **3** *Br (abbr* **Foreign Office**) **the FO** le Foreign Office, = le ministère britannique des Affaires étrangères

foal [fəʊl] **N** *(of horse* ▸ *male)* poulain *m*; *(*▸ *female)* pouliche *f*; *(of donkey)* ânon *m*; **the mare is in f.** la jument est pleine
VI mettre bas, pouliner

foam [fəʊm] **N 1** *(on beer)* mousse *f*; *(of mouth, sea)* écume *f*; **waves white with f.** vagues moutonneuses **2** *(artificial substance)* mousse *f*; *(in fire-fighting)* mousse *f* (carbonique); **polystyrene f.** mousse *f* en polystyrène
VI *(soapy water)* mousser, faire de la mousse; *(sea)* écumer, moutonner; **to f. at the mouth** *(animal)* baver, écumer; *(person)* baver, avoir l'écume aux lèvres; *Fig (be furious)* écumer (de rage)
▸▸ ***foam bath*** bain *m* moussant; ***foam fire extinguisher*** extincteur *m* à mousse carbonique; ***foam rubber*** caoutchouc *m* Mousse®

▸ **foam up** **VI** mousser, faire de la mousse

foaming ['fəʊmɪŋ] **ADJ** *(liquid)* mousseux; *(sea)* écumeux; *(blood, saliva)* spumeux; *(beer etc)* moussant

foamy ['fəʊmɪ] *(compar* **foamier**, *superl* **foamiest**) **ADJ** *(liquid)* mousseux; *(sea)* écumeux; *(blood, saliva)* spumeux; *(beer etc)* moussant

fob[1] [fɒb] **N** *(pocket)* gousset *m*; *(chain)* chaîne *f* (de gousset)
▸▸ ***fob watch*** montre *f* de gousset

fob[2], **FOB** [,efəʊ'biː] **ADV** *Com & Naut (abbr* **free on board**) FOB

▸ **fob off** *(pt & pp* **fobbed**, *cont* **fobbing**) **VT SEP** se débarrasser de; **to f. sb off** se débarrasser de qn; **he fobbed her off with promises** il s'est débarrassé d'elle avec de belles promesses; **don't try to f. that rubbish off on me!** n'essayez pas de me refiler cette camelote!

focal ['fəʊkəl] **ADJ** focal
▸▸ *Opt* ***focal distance*** distance *f* focale, focale *f*; *Opt* ***focal length*** distance *f* focale, focale *f*; *Opt* ***focal plane*** plan *m* focal; *Phot* ***focal plane shutter*** obturateur *m* focal *ou* à rideau; ***focal point*** *Opt* foyer *m*; *Fig (of room)* point *m* de convergence; *Fig* **the f. point of the debate** le point central du débat; *Opt* ***focal ratio*** diaphragme *m*

focalization, -isation [,fəʊkəlaɪ'zeɪʃən] **N 1** *(of heat, light)* convergence *f*; *(of beam, ray)* focalisation *f* **2** *Opt* mise *f* au point

fo'c'sle ['fəʊksəl] **N** *Naut* gaillard *m* d'avant; *(in merchant navy)* poste *m* d'équipage

focus ['fəʊkəs] *(pl* **focuses** *or* **foci** [-saɪ], *pt & pp* **focused** *or* **focussed**, *cont* **focusing** *or* **focussing**) **N 1** *Opt* foyer *m*; **the picture is in/out of f.** l'image est nette/floue, l'image est/n'est pas au point; **the binoculars are in/out of f.** les jumelles sont/ne sont pas au point; **bring the image into f.** fais la mise au point, mets l'image au point **2** *(centre* ▸ *of interest)* point *m* central; *(*▸ *of trouble)* foyer *m*, siège *m*; **she was the f. of attention** elle était le centre d'attention; **taxes are currently the f. of attention** en ce moment, les impôts sont au centre des préoccupations; **the government is trying to shift the f. of the debate** le gouvernement tente de déplacer le débat; **let's try and get the problem into f.** essayons de préciser le problème; **the organization will provide some kind of a f. for opposition to the project** l'organisation fournira un point de ralliement à l'opposition au projet **3** *Med* siège *m*, foyer *m*
VT 1 *Opt (camera, microscope etc)* mettre au point; **to f. a camera on sth** faire la mise au point d'un appareil photo sur qch **2** *(eyes)* fixer; **all eyes were focussed on him** tous les regards étaient rivés sur lui **3** *(direct* ▸ *heat, light)* faire converger; *(*▸ *beam, ray)* diriger; *Fig (*▸ *attention, energies)* concentrer; *(*▸ *interest, concern)* centrer
VI 1 *Opt* mettre au point **2** *(eyes)* se fixer, *Spec* accommoder; **to f. on sth** *(eyes)* se fixer sur qch; *(person)* fixer le regard sur qch **3** *(converge* ▸ *light, rays)* converger; *Fig (*▸ *attention)* se concentrer; **the debate focussed on unemployment** le débat était centré sur le problème du chômage; **his speech focussed on the role of the media** son discours a porté principalement sur le rôle des médias
▸▸ *Mktg & Pol* ***focus group*** groupe *m* témoin; *Cin* ***focus puller*** pointeur *m*

focusing, focussing ['fəʊkəsɪŋ] **N 1** *(of beams, rays etc)* convergence *f* **2** *(of microscope, lens etc)* mise *f* au point **3** *Opt* focalisation *f*; *Electron* focalisation *f*, concentration *f*
▸▸ ***focusing eyepiece*** loupe *f* de mise au point; ***focusing ring*** anneau *m* de mise au point; ***focusing screen*** loupe *f* de mise au point; ***focusing screw*** vis *f* de mise au point, écrou *m* de réglage du foyer; ***focusing viewer*** viseur *m* focimétrique *ou* focométrique

fodder ['fɒdə(r)] **N** *(UNCOUNT) (feed)* fourrage *m*; *Fig Pej (material)* substance *f*, matière *f*
VT *(animal)* donner le fourrage à, affourager

foe [fəʊ] **N** *Literary or Formal* ennemi(e) *m,f*, adversaire *mf*

foetal, *Am* **fetal** ['fiːtəl] **ADJ** fœtal; **in the f. position** en position fœtale, dans la position du fœtus
▸▸ ***foetal alcohol syndrome*** syndrome *m* d'alcoolisation fœtale; ***foetal heartbeat*** rythme *m* cardiaque du fœtus

foetid = **fetid**

foetus, *Am* **fetus** ['fiːtəs] **N** fœtus *m*

fog [fɒg] *(pt & pp* **fogged**, *cont* **fogging**) **N 1** *(mist)* brouillard *m*, brume *f* **2** *Fig (mental)* brouillard *m*, confusion *f*; **my mind is in a f. today** je suis dans le brouillard *ou* je ne sais plus où j'en suis aujourd'hui; **she was in a complete f. about what she was supposed to be doing** elle ignorait complètement ce qu'elle était censée faire **3** *Phot (on film, negative)* voile *m*
VT 1 *(glass, mirror)* embuer; *Phot (film, negative)* voiler **2** *(confuse)* embrouiller; **studying for too long just fogs the mind** quand on travaille trop longtemps, ça embrouille les idées
VI to f. (over *or* **up)** *(glass, mirror)* s'embuer; *Phot (film, negative)* se voiler
▸▸ ***fog bank*** banc *m* de brume; *Br* ***fog lamp***, *Am* ***fog light*** feu *m* de brouillard; ***fog signal*** *Naut* signal *m* de brume; *Rail* pétard *m*

fogbound ['fɒgbaʊnd] **ADJ** pris dans le brouillard *ou* la brume

fogey ['fəʊgɪ] **N** *Fam* schnock *m*; **he's an old f.** c'est un vieux schnock; *Hum* **he's a young f.** il est jeune mais très vieux jeu

fogginess ['fɒgɪnɪs] **N 1** *(weather)* temps *m* brumeux **2** *(of ideas)* confusion *f* **3** *Phot* voile *m*

foggy ['fɒgɪ] *(compar* **foggier**, *superl* **foggiest**) **ADJ 1** *(misty)* brumeux; **it's f.** il y a du brouillard *ou* de la brume; **it's getting f.** le brouillard commence à tomber; **on a f. day** par un jour de brouillard **2** *Phot (film, negative)* voilé **3** *Fam (idiom)* **I haven't the foggiest (idea** *or* **notion)** je n'ai aucune idée▫, je n'en ai pas la moindre idée▫

foghorn ['fɒghɔːn] **N** corne *f ou* sirène *f* de brume; **a voice like a f.** une voix tonitruante *ou* de stentor

foible ['fɔɪbəl] **N** *(quirk)* marotte *f*, manie *f*; *(weakness)* faiblesse *f*

foil [fɔɪl] **N 1** *(metal sheet)* feuille *f ou* lame *f* de métal; *Culin* **(silver) f.** (papier *m*) aluminium *m*, papier *m* alu; **cooked in f.** en papillote; **f. container** barquette *f* en papier aluminium
2 *(complement)* repoussoir *m*; *(person)* faire-valoir *m inv*; **he's the perfect f. to his wife** il sert de faire-valoir à sa femme; **it acts as a f. to her beauty** cela met en valeur sa beauté
3 *(sword)* fleuret *m*; **foils** *(fencing)* escrime *f* au fleuret
4 *(in jewellery)* paillon *m*
5 *Aviat & Naut (of hydrofoil)* patin *m*, aile *f*
6 *Archit (of arch etc)* lobe *m*
VT *(thwart* ▸ *attempt)* déjouer; *(*▸ *plan, plot)* contrecarrer; **foiled again!** encore raté!

foist on [fɔɪst-] **VT SEP 1** *(pass on)* **you're not foisting your old rubbish on** *or* **onto me** il n'est pas question que j'hérite de ta vieille camelote **2** *(impose on)* **she foisted her ideas on us** elle nous a imposé ses idées; **he foisted himself on us for the weekend** il s'est imposé *ou* invité pour le week-end

-fold [fəʊld] **SUFF a ten-f. increase** une multiplication par dix; **your investment should multiply six-f.** votre investissement devrait vous rapporter six fois plus

fold [fəʊld] **VT 1** *(bend)* plier; **f. the blanket in two** pliez la couverture en deux; **she sat with her legs folded under her** elle était assise, les jambes repliées sous elle; **he folded his arms** il s'est croisé les bras; **the bird folded its wings** l'oiseau replia ses ailes; **he folded her in his arms** il l'a serrée dans ses bras, il l'a enlacée **2** *Culin* incorporer
VI 1 *(bed, chair)* se plier, se replier **2** *Fam (fail* ▸ *business)* faire faillite▫, fermer (ses portes)▫; *(*▸ *newspaper)* disparaître▫, cesser de paraître▫; *(*▸ *play)* être retiré de l'affiche▫; **the bakery folded last year** le boulanger a mis la clef sous la porte l'année dernière
N 1 *(crease)* pli *m*; **folds of fat** bourrelets *mpl* de graisse
2 *(enclosure)* parc *m* à moutons; *(flock)* troupeau *m*
3 *Fig (group)* **the f. of the Party/the Church** le sein du Parti/de l'Église; **to return to the f.** rentrer au bercail; **to welcome sb back to the f.** accueillir l'enfant prodigue

4 *Geol* pli *m*
• **folds** NPL *Geol* plissement *m*
▸ **fold away** VT SEP plier et ranger; **fold your clothes away neatly** plie tes affaires et range-les; **I slept on a camp bed which I folded away every morning** je dormais sur un lit de camp que je repliais tous les matins
VI *(chair, table)* se plier, se replier
▸ **fold back** VT SEP *(sheet, sleeve)* replier, rabattre; *(door, shutter)* rabattre
VI se rabattre, se replier
▸ **fold down** VT SEP *(sheet)* replier, rabattre; *(chair, table)* plier; **he folded down a corner of the page** il a corné la page
VI se rabattre, se replier
▸ **fold in** VT SEP *Culin* incorporer
▸ **fold over** VT SEP *(newspaper)* plier, replier; *(sheet)* replier, rabattre
VI se rabattre, se replier
▸ **fold under** VT SEP *(edges)* replier en dessous
▸ **fold up** VT SEP plier, replier
VI *(chair, table)* se plier, se replier

foldaway ['fəʊldəweɪ] ADJ pliant

foldback ['fəʊldbæk] N *TV* ré-injection *f*, retour *m*, play-back *m inv*

folder ['fəʊldə(r)] N **1** *(cover)* chemise *f*; *(binder)* classeur *m*; *(for drawings)* carton *m*; **where's the f. on the new project?** où est le dossier sur le nouveau projet? **2** *Typ (machine)* plieuse *f* **3** *Comput (directory)* répertoire *m*, dossier *m*

folding ['fəʊldɪŋ] ADJ pliant; *(joint, shutter)* brisé
N **1** *(of material etc)* pliage *m*
2 *Typ (of pages)* pliure *f*
3 *Geol (of land)* plissement *m*
4 *Br Fam (paper money)* biffetons *mpl*, fafiots *mpl*, talbins *mpl*
▸▸ ***folding camera*** appareil *m* à soufflet; ***folding chair*** *(without arms)* chaise *f* pliante; *(with arms)* fauteuil *m* pliant; ***folding door*** porte *f* (en) accordéon; *Fam* ***folding money*** billets *mpl* de banque; ***folding seat, folding stool*** *(gen)* pliant *m*; *Aut & Theat* strapontin *m*; ***folding table*** table *f* pliante *ou* escamotable; *(with extending sections)* table *f* à battants; ***folding tray*** *(in plane, train)* tablette *f* *(qui se relève)*

foldout ['fəʊld,aʊt] N encart *m*

foliage ['fəʊlɪɪdʒ] N feuillage *m*
▸▸ ***foliage plant*** plante *f* cultivée pour son feuillage

foliate ['fəʊlɪeɪt] ADJ *Bot (plant)* feuillagé, feuillé

foliation [,fəʊlɪ'eɪʃən] N **1** *Typ (of book)* foliotage *m*
2 *(of metal)* battage *m*; *(of mirror)* étamage *m*
3 *Bot & Geol* foliation *f*
4 *Archit (decoration)* rinceaux *mpl*

folic acid ['fəʊlɪk-] N acide *m* folique

folio ['fəʊlɪəʊ] *(pl* **folios***)* N **1** *(of paper)* folio *m*, feuillet *m*; *Typ (page number)* numéro *m* **2** *(book)* livre *m* in-folio, in-folio *m inv* **3** *(paper size)* format *m* in-folio, in-folio *m inv*
▸▸ ***folio book*** livre *m* in-folio, in-folio *m inv*

folk [fəʊk] NPL **1** *(people)* gens *mpl*; **what will f. think?** qu'est-ce que les gens vont penser?, qu'est-ce qu'on va penser?; **the old f.** les vieux *mpl*; **the young f.** les jeunes *mpl*; **city/country f.** les gens *mpl* de la ville/de la campagne **2** *(race, tribe)* race *f*, peuple *m*
N *(music ▸ traditional)* musique *f* folklorique; *(▸ contemporary)* musique *f* folk, folk *m*
COMP *(concert, festival)* de folk
• **folks** NPL *Fam* **1** *(family)* famille *f*, parents *mpl*; **my folks are from Chicago** ma famille est de Chicago **2** *(people)* **the old folks** les vieux *mpl*; **the young folks** les jeunes *mpl*; **hi folks!** salut tout le monde!
▸▸ ***folk art*** art *m* populaire, arts *mpl* populaires; ***folk dancing*** *(UNCOUNT)* danse *f* folklorique; ***folk etymology*** étymologie *f* populaire; ***folk hero*** héros *m* populaire; ***folk medicine*** *(UNCOUNT)* remèdes *mpl* de bonne femme; ***folk memory*** tradition *f* populaire; ***folk music*** *(traditional)* musique *f* folklorique; *(contemporary)* musique *f* folk, folk *m*; ***folk rock*** folk-rock *m*; ***folk singer*** *(traditional)* chanteur(euse) *m,f* de chansons folkloriques; *(contemporary)* chanteur(euse) *m,f* folk; ***folk song*** *(traditional)* chanson *f ou* chant *m* folklorique; *(contemporary)* chanson *f* folk; ***folk tale*** conte *m* folklorique

folklore ['fəʊklɔː(r)] N folklore *m*

folksy ['fəʊksɪ] *(compar* **folksier**, *superl* **folksiest***)* ADJ *Fam* **1** *Am (friendly)* sympa **2** *(casual ▸ person)* sans façon; *(▸ speech)* populaire **3** *(dress, manners)* simple; *(tale)* populaire

foll. *(written abbr* **following***)* suiv

follicle ['fɒlɪkəl] N *Anat & Bot* follicule *m*

FOLLOW ['fɒləʊ] VT **1** *(come after)* suivre; *(in procession)* aller *ou* venir à la suite de, suivre; **f. me** suivez-moi; **he left, followed by his brother** il est parti, suivi de son frère; **the dog follows her (about *or* around) everywhere** le chien la suit partout *ou* est toujours sur ses talons; **to f. sb in/out** entrer/sortir à la suite de qn; **he followed me into the house** il m'a suivi dans la maison; **she always follows the crowd** elle suit toujours la foule *ou* le mouvement; **his talk will be followed by a discussion** son exposé sera suivi d'une discussion; **she followed this remark with a rather feeble joke** elle agrémenta cette remarque d'une plaisanterie un peu facile; **in the days that followed the accident** dans les jours qui suivirent l'accident; **he followed his father into politics** il est entré en politique sur les traces de son père; **George IV was followed by William IV** Guillaume IV a succédé à George IV; *Fam* **she'll be a hard act to f.** il sera difficile de lui succéder; **to f. suit** *(in cards)* fournir; *Fig* **she sat down and I followed suit** elle s'est assise, et j'en ai fait autant *ou* j'ai fait de même; **just f. your nose** *(walk)* continuez tout droit; *(act)* suivez votre instinct
2 *(pursue)* suivre, poursuivre; *(suspect)* filer; **she had her husband followed** elle a fait filer son mari; **f. that car!** suivez cette voiture!; **I'm being followed** on me suit; **we're continuing to f. this line of enquiry** nous continuons l'enquête dans la même direction
3 *(go along)* suivre, longer; **f. the path** suivez le chemin; **f. the arrows** suivez les flèches; **the border follows the river** la frontière suit *ou* longe le fleuve
4 *(conform to ▸ diet, instructions, rules)* suivre; *(▸ orders)* exécuter; *(▸ fashion)* suivre, se conformer à; *(▸ someone's advice, example)* suivre
5 *(understand)* suivre, comprendre; **do you f. me?** vous me suivez?; **I didn't f. why they killed him** je n'ai pas compris pourquoi ils l'ont tué
6 *(watch)* suivre *ou* regarder attentivement; *(listen to)* suivre *ou* écouter attentivement; *Mus* **to f. a score** suivre une partition
7 *(take an interest in)* suivre, se tenir au courant de; **she followed the murder case in the papers** elle a suivi l'affaire de meurtre dans les journaux; **have you been following that nature series on TV?** avez-vous suivi ces émissions sur la nature à la télé?
8 *(accept ▸ ideas)* suivre; *(▸ leader)* appuyer, être partisan de; *(▸ cause, party)* être partisan de, être pour; **to f. a football team** être supporter d'une équipe de foot
9 *(practise ▸ profession)* exercer, suivre; *(▸ career)* poursuivre; *(▸ religion)* pratiquer; *(▸ method)* employer, suivre
VI **1** *(come after)* suivre; *(in mountaineering)* grimper en second; **my husband is following later** mon mari viendra plus tard; **in the years that followed** dans les années qui suivirent; **he answered as follows** il a répondu comme suit; **my theory is as follows** ma théorie est la suivante; **a long silence followed** un long silence s'ensuivit; **roast beef with strawberries to f.** du rosbif suivi par des fraises
2 *(ensue)* s'ensuivre, résulter; **it doesn't necessarily f. that he'll die** cela ne veut pas forcément dire qu'il va mourir; **it follows from this that...** il en résulte que... + *indicative*; **that doesn't f.** ce n'est pas forcément *ou* nécessairement vrai
3 *(understand)* suivre, comprendre
4 *(imitate)* suivre, faire de même; **Paris sets the trend and the world follows** Paris donne le ton et le reste du monde suit
▸ **follow on** VI **1** *(come after)* suivre; **you go ahead, we'll f. on** partez en avant, nous vous suivons; **she said she would f. on later** elle a dit qu'elle nous rejoindrait plus tard **2** *(result)* **it follows on from this that...** il en résulte que... + *indicative* **3** *(in cricket)* = reprendre la garde du guichet au début de la seconde partie faute d'avoir marqué le nombre de points requis
▸ **follow through** VT SEP *(idea, plan)* poursuivre jusqu'au bout *ou* jusqu'à sa conclusion; **he didn't f. our proposal through** il n'a pas donné suite à notre proposition
VI *Sport* accompagner son coup *ou* sa balle; *(in billiards)* faire *ou* jouer un coulé
▸ **follow up** VT SEP **1** *(pursue ▸ advantage, success)* exploiter, tirer parti de; *(▸ offer)* donner suite à; *(▸ tip-off)* suivre; **to f. up a clue** suivre une piste **2** *(maintain contact)* suivre; *(of doctor)* suivre, surveiller **3** *(continue, supplement)* faire suivre, compléter; **f. up your initial phone call with a letter** confirmez votre coup de téléphone par écrit; **I followed up your suggestion for a research project** j'ai repris votre suggestion pour un projet de recherche
VI exploiter un avantage, tirer parti d'un avantage; **he followed up with a right to the jaw** il a continué avec un droit à la mâchoire

follower ['fɒləʊə(r)] N **1** *(devotee, disciple)* disciple *m*, partisan(e) *m,f*; **a f. of fashion** quelqu'un qui suit la mode
2 *Sport (supporter)* partisan(e) *m,f*, fan *mf*; **a f. of tennis** quelqu'un qui s'intéresse au tennis
3 *(attendant)* domestique *mf*; **the king and his followers** le roi et sa suite
4 *Mktg (company, product)* suiveur *m*

following ['fɒləʊɪŋ] ADJ **1** *(next)* suivant; **the f. day** le jour suivant, le lendemain; **the f. Monday** le lundi suivant; **the f. names** les noms suivants, les noms que voici **2** *(wind)* arrière *(inv)*
PREP après, suite à; **f. our conversation** suite à notre entretien; *Com* **f. your letter** suite à *ou* en réponse à votre lettre
N **1** *(supporters)* partisans *mpl*, disciples *mpl*; *(entourage)* suite *f*; **she has a large f.** elle a de nombreux partisans *ou* fidèles **2** *(about to be mentioned)* **he said the f.** il a dit ceci; **her reasons are the f.** ses raisons sont les suivantes; **the f. have been selected from among the candidates** les personnes suivantes ont été choisies parmi les candidats **3** *(of king, prince)* suite *f*

follow-me product N *Mktg* produit *m* tactique

follow-my-leader N *Br* = jeu où tout le monde doit imiter tous les mouvements d'un joueur désigné

follow-on N *(in cricket)* = reprise de la garde du guichet par une équipe au début de la deuxième partie faute d'avoir marqué assez de points

follow-the-leader N *Am* = jeu où tout le monde doit imiter tous les mouvements d'un joueur désigné

follow-through N **1** *(to plan)* suite *f*, continuation *f* **2** *Sport* accompagnement *m* *(d'un coup)* **3** *(in billiards)* coulé *m*

follow-up N **1** *(to event, programme)* suite *f*; *(on case, file)* suivi *m*; *Med (appointment)* visite *f ou* examen *m* de contrôle; **this meeting is a f. to that held in May** cette réunion est la suite de celle tenue en mai **2** *(bill, letter)* rappel *m*
ADJ *(action, survey, work)* complémentaire
▸▸ *Med* ***follow-up care*** soins *mpl* post-hospitaliers; ***follow-up interview*** *(for job, research)* deuxième entretien *m*; ***follow-up letter*** lettre *f* de rappel *ou* de relance; *Comput* ***follow-up message*** *(in newsgroups)* suivi *m* d'article; ***follow-up phone call*** coup *m* de téléphone de rappel *ou* de relance; *Mktg* ***follow-up publicity*** publicité *f* de rappel; ***follow-up visit*** visite *f* de contrôle

folly ['fɒlɪ] *(pl* **follies***)* N **1** *(UNCOUNT) Formal (foolishness)* folie *f*, sottise *f*; **an act of f., a f.** une folie; **it would be f. to continue** ce serait folie de continuer **2** *Archit (building)* folie *f*

foment [fəʊ'ment] VT **1** *(discord, discontent)* fomenter **2** *Med (wound)* fomenter

fomentation [,fəʊmen'teɪʃən] N **1** *(of discord, discontent)* fomentation *f* **2** *Med (of wound)* fomentation *f*

fond [fɒnd] **ADJ 1 to be f. of sb** aimer beaucoup qn, avoir de l'affection pour qn; **to be f. of sth** aimer beaucoup qch, être amateur de qch; **they're f. of each other** ils s'aiment bien; **he's f. of reading** il aime lire; **I'm not f. of being told I'm an idiot** je n'apprécie pas qu'on me traite d'idiot; **he was f. of the odd whisky** il aimait bien prendre un petit whisky de temps à autre

2 *(loving* ▸ *friend, wife, embrace)* affectueux, tendre; *(*▸ *parent)* indulgent, bon; *(*▸ *look)* tendre; **with fondest love** *(in letter)* affectueusement

3 *(hope)* fervent; *(ambition, wish)* cher; *(memory)* agréable; **my fondest dream** mon rêve le plus cher

4 *(foolish)* naïf; **in the f. hope of catching a glimpse of my idol** dans le fol espoir d'apercevoir mon idole

fondant ['fɒndənt] **N** *Culin* fondant *m*

▸▸ ***fondant icing*** glaçage *m* fondant

fondle ['fɒndəl] **VT** caresser; **he was fondling her leg under the table** il lui caressait la jambe sous la table

fondly ['fɒndlɪ] **ADV 1** *(lovingly)* tendrement, affectueusement **2** *(foolishly)* naïvement; **he f. believed she would accept** il avait la naïveté de croire *ou* il croyait naïvement qu'elle accepterait

fondness ['fɒndnɪs] **N** *(for person)* affection *f*, tendresse *f* (**for** pour *ou* envers); *(for things)* prédilection *f*, penchant *m* (**for** pour); **to have a f. for drink** avoir un penchant pour la boisson

fondue ['fɒndu:, 'fɒndju:] **N** *Culin* fondue *f*

▸▸ ***fondue set*** service *m* à fondue

font [fɒnt] **N 1** *Rel* fonts *mpl* baptismaux **2** *Typ & Comput* police *f*, fonte *f*

▸▸ *Typ & Comput* ***font cartridge*** cartouche *f* de polices; *Typ & Comput* ***font cassette*** cassette *f* de polices de caractères, cassette *f* de fontes; *Typ & Comput* ***font size*** taille *f* de police *ou* de fontes

fontanelle, *Am* **fontanel** [ˌfɒntə'nel] **N** *Anat* fontanelle *f*

food [fu:d] **N 1** *(nourishment)* nourriture *f*; *(as opposed to drink)* manger *m*; *(for expedition)* vivres *mpl*; *Agr (for animals)* pâture *f*; *(for poultry)* mangeaille *f*; **is there any f.?** y a-t-il de quoi manger?; **do you have enough f. for everyone?** avez-vous assez à manger *ou* assez de nourriture pour tout le monde?; **they like spicy f.** ils aiment la cuisine épicée; **we need to buy some f.** il faut qu'on achète à manger *ou* qu'on fasse des provisions; **we gave them f.** nous leur avons donné à manger; **take some f. for the journey** prenez de quoi manger pendant le voyage; **the f. here is especially good** la cuisine est particulièrement bonne ici; **he's off his f.** il n'a pas d'appétit, il a perdu l'appétit; **the cost of f.** le prix de la nourriture *ou* des denrées (alimentaires); **foods recommended for diabetics** aliments *mpl* conseillés aux diabétiques **2** *Fig (material)* matière *f*; **the accident gave her much f. for thought** l'accident l'a fait beaucoup réfléchir **3** *Hort* engrais *m*

COMP *(industry, product)* alimentaire; *(crop)* vivrier

▸▸ ***food additive*** additif *m* alimentaire; ***Food and Agriculture Organization*** Organisation *f* des Nations unies pour l'alimentation et l'agriculture; ***food aid*** aide *f* alimentaire; ***food allergy*** allergie *f* alimentaire; *Am* ***food bank*** banque *f* alimentaire; *Ecol* ***food chain*** chaîne *f* alimentaire; ***food combining*** combinaisons *fpl* alimentaires; ***food court*** = partie d'un centre commercial où se trouvent les restaurants; ***food critic*** critique *mf* gastronomique; *Am* ***the Food and Drug Administration*** = organisme officiel chargé de contrôler la qualité des aliments et de délivrer les autorisations de mise sur le marché pour les produits pharmaceutiques; ***food hall*** *(in shop)* rayon *m* d'alimentation; ***food hygiene regulations*** réglementation *f* sur l'hygiène alimentaire; ***food labelling*** étiquetage *m* des produits alimentaires; ***food manufacturer*** fabricant *m* de produits comestibles; ***food miles*** kilomètre *m* alimentaire; ***food mixer*** mixeur *m*; ***food packaging*** emballage *m* des produits alimentaires; ***food parcel*** colis *m* de vivres; ***food poisoning*** intoxication *f* alimentaire; ***food processing*** *(preparation)* traitement *m* industriel des aliments; *(industry)* industrie *f* alimentaire; ***food processor*** robot *m* ménager *ou* de cuisine; ***food products*** produits *mpl* alimentaires, comestibles *mpl*, denrées *fpl*; *Am* ***food stamp*** bon *m* alimentaire *(accordé aux personnes sans ressources)*; ***the Food Standards Agency*** = organisme britannique de contrôle de la sécurité alimentaire; ***food technology*** technologie *f* alimentaire; ***food value*** valeur *f* nutritive; *Ecol* ***food web*** réseau *m* alimentaire

foodie ['fu:dɪ] **N** *Fam* fin gourmet▫ *m*

foodstore ['fu:dstɔ:(r)] **N** magasin *m* d'alimentation

foodstuff ['fu:dstʌf] **N** aliment *m*

foo fighter [fu:-] **N** OVNI *m*

fool [fu:l] **N 1** *(idiot)* idiot(e) *m,f*, imbécile *mf*; **you stupid f.!** espèce d'imbécile *ou* d'abruti!; **what a f. I am!** suis-je idiot *ou* bête!; **don't be a f.!** ne fais pas l'idiot!; **she was a f. to go** elle a été idiote d'y aller; **I felt such a f.** je me suis senti bête; **he's no f.** *or* **nobody's f.** il n'est pas bête, il n'est pas né d'hier; **some f. of a politician** un imbécile *ou* un abruti de politicien; **to make a f. of sb** *(ridicule)* ridiculiser qn, se payer la tête de qn; *(trick)* duper qn; **she doesn't want to make a f. of herself** elle ne veut pas passer pour une imbécile *ou* se ridiculiser; **more f. you!** tu n'as qu'à t'en prendre à toi-même!; *Prov* **a f. and his money are soon parted** aux idiots l'argent brûle les doigts; **to go on a f.'s errand** y aller pour des prunes *ou* pour le roi de Prusse; **to send sb on a f.'s errand** envoyer qn décrocher la lune **2** *(jester)* bouffon *m*, fou *m* **3** *Culin* = sorte de mousse aux fruits; **raspberry f.** mousse *f* aux framboises

VT *(deceive)* duper, berner; **(I) fooled you!** je t'ai eu!; **don't try to f. me** n'essayez pas de me faire marcher; **your excuses don't f. me** vos excuses ne prennent pas avec moi; **he fooled me into believing it** il a réussi à me le faire croire; **they had me completely fooled** ils m'ont bien eu; *Ironic* **her, a socialist? you could've fooled me!** elle, une socialiste? je ne l'aurais pas cru!

VI 1 *(joke)* faire l'imbécile *ou* le pitre; **I'm only fooling** je ne fais que plaisanter, c'est pour rire; **stop fooling!** arrête de faire l'imbécile! **2** *(trifle)* **to f. with sb/sth** traiter qn/qch à la légère; **you'd better not f. with him** on ne plaisante pas avec lui

ADJ *Am* idiot, sot (sotte); **that's just the kind of f. thing he'd do** c'est tout à fait le genre de bêtise *ou* d'ânerie qu'il ferait; **that f. son of yours** ton imbécile de fils; *Fam* **what's all this (damn) f. nonsense about getting married?** se marier? qu'est-ce que c'est que ces foutaises?

▸▸ *Miner* ***fool's gold*** pyrite *f* de fer; *Bot* ***fool's parsley*** petite ciguë *f*

▸ **fool about, fool around VI 1** *(act foolishly)* faire l'imbécile *ou* le pitre; **I'm only fooling around** je ne fais que plaisanter, c'est pour rire; **she fooled around with drugs** elle a touché à la drogue

2 *(waste time)* perdre du temps; **stop fooling around and get up!** arrête de traîner et lève-toi!

3 *Fam (have affair)* avoir *ou* se payer des aventures▫; **he's been fooling around with a married woman** il batifole avec une femme mariée

4 *(fiddle)* **to f. around with sth** tripoter qch; **stop fooling around with that computer!** arrête de jouer avec cet ordinateur!

5 *Fam (of couple)* se bécoter

foolery ['fu:lərɪ] *(pl* **fooleries) N** *(behaviour)* bouffonnerie *f*, pitrerie *f*, pitreries *fpl*; *(act, remark)* bêtise *f*, sottise *f*; *(joke)* farce *f*, tour *m*

foolhardiness ['fu:lˌhɑ:dɪnɪs] **N** *(of act, person)* témérité *f*, imprudence *f*; *(of remark)* imprudence *f*

foolhardy ['fu:lˌhɑ:dɪ] **ADJ** *(act, person)* téméraire, imprudent; *(remark)* imprudent

foolish ['fu:lɪʃ] **ADJ 1** *(unwise)* insensé, imprudent; **it would be f. to leave now** ce serait de la folie de partir maintenant; **that was very f. of her** ce n'était pas très malin de sa part; **I was f. enough to believe her** j'ai été assez bête pour la croire; **don't do anything f.** ne faites pas de bêtises; **a f. hope** un fol espoir **2** *(ridiculous)* ridicule, bête; **I felt rather f.** je me sentais plutôt idiot *ou* ridicule; **the question made him look f.** la question l'a ridiculisé

foolishly ['fu:lɪʃlɪ] **ADV** *(stupidly)* bêtement, sottement; *(unwisely)* imprudemment; **f., I believed him** comme un idiot *ou* un imbécile je l'ai cru

foolishness ['fu:lɪʃnɪs] **N** bêtise *f*, sottise *f*; *(of plan, decision, idea etc)* stupidité *f*

foolproof ['fu:lpru:f] **ADJ** *(machine, mechanism)* indéréglable; *(plan, scheme)* infaillible, à toute épreuve

foolscap ['fu:lzkæp] **N** papier *m* ministre

COMP *(paper, size)* ministre *(inv)*

▸▸ ***foolscap envelope*** enveloppe *f* longue; ***foolscap pad*** bloc *m* de papier ministre

FOOT [fʊt] *(pl* **feet** [fi:t]) **N 1** *(of person, cow, horse, pig)* pied *m*; *(of bird, cat, dog)* patte *f*; **I came on f.** je suis venu à pied; **to be on one's feet** *(standing)* être *ou* se tenir debout; *(after illness)* être sur pied *ou* rétabli *ou* remis; **she's on her feet all day** elle est debout toute la journée; **on your feet!** debout!; **the speech brought the audience to its feet** l'auditoire s'est levé pour applaudir le discours; **to get** *or* **to rise to one's feet** se mettre debout, se lever; **put your feet up** reposez-vous un peu; **to put** *or* **to set sb on their feet again** *(cure)* remettre qn d'aplomb; *(in business)* remettre qn en selle; **I've never set f. in her house** je n'ai jamais mis les pieds dans sa maison; **never set f. in this house again!** ne remettez plus les pieds dans cette maison!; *Fig* **we got the project back on its feet** on a relancé le projet; **it's slippery under f.** c'est glissant par terre; *Fig* **the children are always under my feet** les enfants sont toujours dans mes jambes; *Fig* **to sit at sb's feet** être le disciple de qn

2 *(of chair, glass, lamp)* pied *m*

3 *(lower end* ▸ *of bed, stocking, cliff, mountain)* pied *m*; *(*▸ *of table)* bout *m*; *(*▸ *of page, stairs)* bas *m*; *(*▸ *of column)* base *f*; **at the f. of the page** au bas *ou* en bas de la page; **at the f. of the stairs** en bas de l'escalier; **at the f. of the ladder/mountain** au pied de l'échelle/de la montagne

4 *(unit of measurement)* = 30,48 cm, pied *m* (anglais); **to be five f.** *or* **feet high/thick** avoir cinq pieds de haut(eur)/d'épaisseur; **a 40-f. fall, a fall of 40 feet** une chute de 40 pieds; *Fam* **to feel ten feet tall** être aux anges *ou* au septième ciel

5 *Literature* pied *m*

6 *Br Mil* infanterie *f*; **the 42nd F.** le 42ème d'infanterie

7 *(idioms) Fam* **the only way I'll leave this house is feet first** je ne quitterai cette maison que les pieds devant; **to run** *or* **to rush sb off their feet** accabler qn de travail, ne pas laisser à qn le temps de souffler; **I've been rushed off my feet all day** je n'ai pas arrêté de toute la journée; *Fam* **he claims he's divorced – divorced, my f.!** il prétend être divorcé – divorcé, mon œil!; **to fall** *or* **to land on one's feet** retomber sur ses pieds; *Fig* **to find one's feet** s'adapter; *Fig* **to get a f. in the door** poser des jalons, établir le contact; *Fig* **to have a f. in the door** être dans la place; **to have a f. in both camps** avoir un pied dans chaque camp; *Fam* **to have one f. in the grave** avoir un pied dans la tombe; *Fig* **to have one's** *or* **both feet (firmly) on the ground** avoir les pieds sur terre; *Fam* **to have two left feet** être pataud *ou* empoté; **to have feet of clay** avoir un point faible *ou* vulnérable, avoir une faiblesse de caractère; **to put one's best f. forward** *(hurry)* se dépêcher, presser le pas; *(do one's best)* faire de son mieux; *Fig* **to put one's f. down** faire acte d'autorité; *Aut* accélérer; *Fam* **to put one's f.** *Br* **in it** *or Am* **in one's mouth** faire une gaffe; *Br* **she didn't put a f. wrong** elle n'a pas commis la moindre erreur; *Br Fig* **I never seem able to put a f. right** j'ai l'impression que je ne peux jamais rien faire comme il faut; **to catch sb on the wrong f.** prendre qn au dépourvu; *Sport* prendre qn à contre-pied; **to get** *or* **to start off on the right/wrong f.** être bien/mal parti; *Fig* **the** *Br* **boot** *or Am* **shoe is on the other f.** les rôles sont inversés

VT *Fam* **1** *(walk)* **he decided to f. it home** il a décidé de rentrer à pied▫

2 *(pay)* **to f. the bill** payer l'addition▫

▸▸ ***foot control*** commande *f* au pied; *Am* ***foot doctor*** podologue *mf*; *Tennis* ***foot fault*** faute *f* de pied; ***foot passenger*** piéton *m (passager sans* *véhicule); Br Mil* ***foot patrol*** patrouille *f* à pied; ***foot powder*** poudre *f* pour pieds; ***foot pump*** pompe *f* à pied; *Bot & Vet* ***foot rot*** piétin *m*; ***foot soldier*** *Mil* fantassin *m*; *(of political party)* militant (e) *m,f* de base; ***foot spa*** bain *m* de pieds à remous

▸ **foot up** **VT SEP** *Am Fam (add up* ▸ *bill)* additionner❏

footage ['fʊtɪdʒ] **N** *(UNCOUNT)* **1** *(length)* longueur *f* en pieds **2** *Cin (length)* métrage *m*; *(material filmed)* séquences *fpl*; **the film contains previously unseen f. on** *or* **about the war** le film contient des séquences inédites sur la guerre

▸▸ *Cin* ***footage meter*** métreuse *f*

foot-and-mouth disease **N** *Vet* fièvre *f* aphteuse

football ['fʊtbɔ:l] **N 1** *(game) Br* football *m*; *Am* football *m* américain **2** *(ball)* ballon *m* (de football), balle *f*; *Fig* **the abortion issue has become a political f.** les partis politiques se renvoient la balle à propos de l'avortement

▸▸ *Br* ***the Football Association*** = la Fédération britannique de football; ***football boot*** chaussure *f* de football; *Br* ***football club*** club *m* de football; *Br* ***football coupon*** grille *f* de Loto sportif; ***football fan*** *Br* fan *mf* de foot; *Am* fan *mf* de football américain; *Am* ***football field*** terrain *m* de football; *Am* ***football game*** match *m* de football américain; *Br* ***football ground*** terrain *m* de football; ***football hooligan*** hooligan *m*; ***football hooliganism*** vandalisme *m*, hooliganisme *m*; ***the Football League*** = association réunissant la majorité des clubs de football professionnels en Angleterre; *Br* ***football match*** match *m* de football; *Br* ***football pitch*** terrain *m* de football; ***football player*** *Br* joueur(euse) *m,f* de football, footballeur(euse) *m,f*; *Am* joueur(euse) *m,f* de football américain; *Br* ***football pools*** Loto *m* sportif; **to do the f. pools** jouer au Loto sportif; **he won £20 on the f. pools** il a gagné 20 livres au Loto sportif; *Br* ***football scarf*** = écharpe aux couleurs d'une équipe de football; ***football season*** saison *f* de football; *Br* ***football shirt*** maillot *m* de foot; *Br* ***football strip*** tenue *f* de foot; ***football supporter*** supporter *m* (de football); ***football team*** *Br* équipe *f* de football; *Am* équipe *f* de football américain; ***football widow*** = femme délaissée par un mari fan de football

footballer ['fʊtbɔ:lə(r)] **N** *Br* joueur(euse) *m,f* de football, footballeur(euse) *m,f*, *Am* joueur (euse) *m,f* de football américain

footbath ['fʊtbɑ:θ, *pl* -bɑ:ðz] **N** bain *m* de pieds

footbrake ['fʊtbreɪk] **N** frein *m* à pied

footbridge ['fʊtbrɪdʒ] **N** passerelle *f*

footer ['fʊtə(r)] **N 1** *Br Fam (football)* foot *m* **2** *Comput & Typ* bas *m* de page

footfall ['fʊtfɔ:l] **N 1** *(sound)* (bruit *m* de) pas *m*; **I heard a light f.** j'ai entendu un pas léger **2** *Mktg (people entering shop, airport etc)* taux *m* de fréquentation

foot-fault *Sport* **VT** *(of umpire)* **to f. a player** pénaliser un joueur pour faute de pied

VI faire une faute de pied

footgear ['fʊtgɪə(r)] **N** *(UNCOUNT)* chaussures *fpl*

foothills ['fʊthɪlz] **NPL** collines *fpl* basses *ou* avancées; *(of mountain range)* avant-monts *mpl*

foothold ['fʊthəʊld] **N** prise *f* de pied; *Fig* position *f* avantageuse; *also Fig* **to gain** *or* **to get a f.** prendre pied; **he gained a f. in the jazz world** il a su s'imposer dans le monde du jazz; *Com* **to get** *or* **to secure a f. in a market** prendre pied sur un marché

footie ['fʊtɪ] **N** *Br & Austr Fam (football)* foot *m*

footing ['fʊtɪŋ] **N 1** *(balance)* prise *f* de pied; **to get one's f.** prendre pied; **to keep/to lose one's f.** garder/perdre l'équilibre; **to miss one's f.** poser le pied à faux **2** *(position* ▸ *of person)* position *f*, condition *f*; *(*▸ *of institution etc)* condition *f*, état *m*; **to be on an equal f.** être sur un pied d'égalité; **let's try to keep things on a friendly f.** essayons de rester en bons termes; **on a war f.** sur le pied de guerre; **the business is now on a firm f.** l'affaire est maintenant en bonne voie

footle about, footle around ['fu:təl] **VI** *Fam (potter)* bricoler, s'occuper❏; **to f. about** *or* **around with sth** jouer avec qch, tripoter qch

footlights ['fʊtlaɪts] **NPL** rampe *f*; *Fig* **the f.** *(theatre)* le théâtre, les planches *fpl*

footling ['fu:tlɪŋ] **ADJ** *Fam (trivial)* insignifiant❏, futile❏

footloose ['fʊtlu:s] **ADJ** *Fam* **f. and fancy-free** libre comme l'air

footman ['fʊtmən] *(pl* **footmen** [-mən]) **N** valet *m* de pied

footnote ['fʊtnəʊt] **N** *(on page)* note *f* en bas de page; *(in speech)* remarque *f* supplémentaire; **as a f. I should just mention...** en dernière remarque, je signalerai que... + *indicative*; *Fig* **he was doomed to become just a f. in the history of events** il était destiné à rester en marge de l'histoire des événements *ou* à ne jouer qu'un rôle secondaire dans l'histoire des événements

footpath ['fʊtpɑ:θ, *pl* -pɑ:ðz] **N** *(path)* sentier *m*; *(paved)* trottoir *m*

footplate ['fʊtpleɪt] **N** *Br Rail* plate-forme *f* *(d'une locomotive)*

footplateman ['fʊtpleɪtmən] *(pl* **footplatemen** [-mən]) **N** *Br Rail* agent *m* de conduite

foot-pound *(pl* **foot-pounds)** **N** *Phys (measurement)* pied-livre *m*

footprint ['fʊtprɪnt] **N 1** *(of foot)* empreinte *f* (de pied) **2** *(of satellite)* empreinte *f* **3** *Comput* encombrement *m*

footrest ['fʊtrest] **N** *(gen)* repose-pieds *m inv*; *(stool)* tabouret *m*

foot-second *(pl* **foot-seconds)** **N** *Phys (measurement)* pied *m* par seconde

FOOTSIE, Footsie ['fʊtsɪ] **N** *St Exch (abbr* **Financial Times-Stock Exchange 100 Index)** = principal indice boursier du 'Financial Times' basé sur la valeur de 100 actions cotées à la Bourse de Londres

footsie ['fʊtsɪ] **N** *Fam* **to play f. with sb** *(rub feet)* faire du pied à qn; *Am (collaborate with)* être le (la) complice de qn❏

footslog ['fʊtslɒg] *(pt & pp* **footslogged**, *cont* **footslogging)** **VI** *Fam* marcher (d'un pas lourd)❏

footsore ['fʊtsɔ:(r)] **ADJ I was tired and f.** j'étais fatigué et j'avais mal aux pieds

footstall ['fʊtstɔ:l] **N** *Archit* socle *m*

footstep ['fʊtstep] **N 1** *(sound)* pas *m*; **I hear footsteps** j'entends des pas *ou* un bruit de pas **2** *(footprint)* (empreinte *f* de) pied *m ou* pas *m*; *Fig* **to follow** *or* **tread** *or* **walk in sb's footsteps** marcher sur les traces *ou* pas de qn; *Fig* **to follow in one's father's footsteps** suivre les traces de son père

footstool ['fʊtstu:l] **N** tabouret *m*

foot-tapping **ADJ** *(music)* entraînant, rythmé

footway ['fʊtweɪ] **N** *Br (path)* sentier *m*; *(paved)* passerelle *f*

footwear ['fʊtweə(r)] **N** *(UNCOUNT)* chaussures *fpl*; **he works in the f. department** il travaille au rayon chaussures

footwell ['fʊtwel] **N** *Aut* place *f* aux pieds

footwork ['fʊtwɜ:k] **N 1** *Sport* jeu *m* de jambes; *Fig* **it took some fancy f. to avoid legal action** il a fallu manœuvrer adroitement pour éviter un procès **2** *(walking)* marche *f*; **the job entails a lot of f.** le travail oblige à beaucoup marcher

footy = **footie**

fop [fɒp] **N** dandy *m*

foppish ['fɒpɪʃ] **ADJ** *(man)* dandy; *(dress, manners, elegance)* de dandy

FOR [,efəʊ'ɑ:(r)] **ADV** *Com (abbr* **free on rail)** franco wagon

FOR [fɔ:(r)]

> **PREP**
> - pour **A1–4, B1, 2, 4, C2–5, 7, 8**
> - dans la direction de **A4**
> - pendant **B3**
> - de **C6**
> - à l'intention de **A3**
> - à **A5**
> - en raison de **C5**
>
> **CONJ**
> - car

PREP A. 1 *(expressing purpose or function)* pour; **we were in Vienna f. a holiday/f. work** nous étions à Vienne en vacances/pour le travail; **what f.?** pourquoi?; **I don't know what she said that f.** je ne sais pas pourquoi elle a dit ça; **what's this knob f.?** à quoi sert ce bouton?; **it's f. adjusting the volume** ça sert à régler le volume; **can you give me something f. the pain?** est-ce que vous pouvez me donner quelque chose pour ou contre la douleur?; **an instrument f. measuring temperature** un instrument pour mesurer la température

2 *(in order to obtain)* pour; **f. further information write to...** pour de plus amples renseignements, écrivez à...; **they play f. money** ils jouent pour de l'argent

3 *(indicating recipient or beneficiary)* pour, à l'intention de; **these flowers are f. her** ces fleurs sont pour elle; **I've got some news f. you** j'ai une nouvelle à vous annoncer; **he left a note f. them** il leur a laissé un mot, il a laissé un mot à leur intention; **opera is not f. me** l'opéra, ça n'est pas pour moi; **you are the man f. me/the job** vous êtes l'homme qu'il me faut/qui convient pour ce poste; **equal pay f. women** un salaire égal pour les femmes; **parking f. customers only** *(sign)* parking réservé à la clientèle; **what can I do f. you?** que puis-je faire pour vous?; **a collection f. the poor** une quête pour les *ou* en faveur des pauvres; **it's f. your own good** c'est pour ton bien; **he often cooks f. himself** il se fait souvent la cuisine; **see f. yourself!** voyez par vous-même!; **she writes f. a sports magazine** elle écrit des articles pour un magazine de sport; **I work f. an advertising agency** je travaille pour une agence de publicité

4 *(indicating direction, destination)* pour, dans la direction de; **they left f. Spain** ils sont partis pour l'Espagne; **before leaving f. the office** avant de partir au bureau; **she ran f. the door** elle s'est précipitée vers la porte en courant; **he made f. home** il a pris la direction de la maison; **the train f. London** le train pour *ou* à destination de *ou* en direction de Londres; **change trains here f. Beaune** changez de train ici pour Beaune; **flight 402 bound f. Chicago is now boarding** les passagers du vol 402 à destination de Chicago sont invités à se présenter à l'embarquement

5 *(available for)* à; **f. rent** *(sign)* à louer; **f. sale** *(sign)* à vendre; **these books are f. reference only** ces livres sont à consulter sur place

B. 1 *(indicating span of time* ▸ *past, future)* pour, pendant; *(*▸ *action uncompleted)* depuis; **they're going away f. the weekend** ils partent pour le week-end; **they will be gone f. some time** ils seront absents (pendant *ou* pour) quelque temps; **they were in Spain f. two weeks** ils étaient en Espagne pour deux semaines; **she won't be back f. a month** elle ne sera pas de retour avant un mois; **I lived there f. one month** j'y ai vécu pendant un mois; **I've lived here f. two years** j'habite ici depuis deux ans; **you haven't been here f. a long time** il y a *ou* voilà *ou* ça fait longtemps que vous n'êtes pas venu; **we've known them f. years** nous les connaissons depuis des années, il y a des années que nous les connaissons; **I have not seen him f. three years** il y a trois ans que je ne l'ai vu; **can you stay f. a while?** pouvez-vous rester un moment?; **it's the worst accident f. years** c'est le pire accident qui soit arrivé depuis des années; **we have food f. three days** nous avons des vivres pour trois jours

2 *(indicating a specific occasion or time)* pour; **I went home f. Christmas** je suis rentré chez moi pour Noël; **he took me out to dinner f. my birthday** il m'a emmené dîner au restaurant pour mon anniversaire; **we made an appointment f. the 6th** nous avons pris rendez-vous pour le 6; **it's time f. bed** c'est l'heure de se coucher *ou* d'aller au lit; **there's no time f. that** il n'y a pas de temps pour ça; **f. the last/third time** pour la dernière/troisième fois

3 *(indicating distance)* pendant; **you could see f. miles around** on voyait à des kilomètres à la ronde; **we walked f. several miles** nous avons marché pendant plusieurs kilomètres; **they drove f. miles without seeing another car** ils ont roulé (pendant) des kilomètres sans croiser une seule voiture

4 *(indicating amount)* **they paid him £100 f. his**

services ils lui ont donné 100 livres pour ses services; **you can hire a car f. £20 a day** on peut louer une voiture pour 20 livres par jour; **it's £2 f. a ticket** c'est 2 livres le billet; **he's selling it f. £200** il le vend 200 livres; **I wrote a cheque f. £15** j'ai fait un chèque de 15 livres; **three f. £5** trois pour 5 livres **C. 1** *(indicating exchange, equivalence)* **do you have change f. a pound?** vous avez la monnaie d'une livre?; **he exchanged the bike f. another model** il a échangé le vélo contre *ou* pour un autre modèle; **what will you give me in exchange f. this book?** que me donnerez-vous en échange de ce livre?; **what's the Spanish f. "good"?** comment dit-on "good" en espagnol?; **what's the M f.?** qu'est-ce que le M veut dire?; **he has cereal f. breakfast** il prend des céréales au petit déjeuner; **to have sb f. a teacher** avoir qn comme professeur; **I know it f. a fact** je sais que c'est vrai; **I f. one don't care** pour ma part, je m'en fiche; **do you take me f. a fool?** me prenez-vous pour un imbécile?

2 *(indicating ratio)* pour; **there's one woman applicant f. every five men** sur six postulants il y a une femme et cinq hommes; **f. every honest politician there are a hundred dishonest ones** pour un homme politique honnête, il y en a cent qui sont malhonnêtes

3 *(representing, on behalf of)* pour; **I'm speaking f. all parents** je parle pour *ou* au nom de tous les parents; **the lawyer was acting f. his client** l'avocat agissait au nom de *ou* pour le compte de son client; **I'll go to the meeting f. you** j'irai à la réunion à votre place; **he plays rugby f. Scotland** il joue au rugby dans l'équipe d'Écosse; *Fam Hum* **she could talk/eat f. England!** elle n'arrête pas de parler/de manger!

4 *(in favour of)* pour; **I'm all f. it** je suis tout à fait pour; **vote f. Smith!** votez (pour) Smith!; **they voted f. the proposal** ils ont voté en faveur de la proposition; **he's f. the ecologists** il est pour les écologistes; **I'm f. shortening the hunting season** je suis pour une saison de chasse plus courte; **who's f. a drink?** qui veut boire un verre?; **I'm f. bed** je vais me coucher; *Law* **judgement f. the plaintiff** arrêt *m* en faveur du demandeur

5 *(because of)* pour, en raison de; **candidates were selected f. their ability** les candidats ont été retenus en raison de leurs compétences; **she couldn't sleep f. the pain** la douleur l'empêchait de dormir; **the region is famous f. its wine** la région est célèbre pour son vin; **she's in prison f. treason** elle est en prison pour trahison; **he couldn't speak f. laughing** il ne pouvait pas parler tellement il riait; **you'll feel better f. a rest** vous vous sentirez mieux quand vous vous serez reposé; **if it weren't f. you, I'd leave** sans vous, je partirais; **f. this reason** pour cette raison; **f. fear of waking him** de crainte de le réveiller; **do it f. my sake** faites-le pour moi

6 *(indicating cause, reason)* de; **the reason f. his leaving** la raison de son départ; **there are no grounds f. believing it's true** il n'y a pas de raison de croire que c'est vrai; **she apologized f. being late** elle s'est excusée d'être en retard; **I thanked him f. his kindness** je l'ai remercié de *ou* pour sa gentillesse

7 *(concerning, as regards)* pour; **so much f. that** voilà qui est classé; **f. my part, I refuse to go** pour ma part *ou* quant à moi, je refuse d'y aller; **I'm very happy f. her** je suis très heureux pour elle; **what are her feelings f. him?** quels sont ses sentiments pour lui?; **f. sheer impudence his remarks are hard to beat** pour ce qui est de l'effronterie, ses commentaires sont imbattables

8 *(given normal expectations)* pour; **it's warm f. March** il fait bon pour un mois de mars; **she looks very young f. her age** elle fait très jeune pour son âge

9 *(in phrases with infinitive verbs)* **it's not f. him to decide** il ne lui appartient pas *ou* ce n'est pas à lui de décider; **it's not f. her to tell me what to do** ce n'est pas à elle de me dire ce que je dois faire; **it was difficult f. her to apologize** il lui était difficile de s'excuser; **I have brought it f. you to see** je l'ai apporté pour que vous le voyiez; **this job is too complicated f. us to finish today** ce travail est trop compliqué pour que nous le finissions aujourd'hui; **there is still time f. her to finish** elle a encore le temps de finir; **it took an hour f. the taxi to get to the station** le taxi a mis une heure pour aller jusqu'à la gare; **the easiest thing would be f. you to lead the way** le plus facile serait que vous nous montriez le chemin; **there's no need f. you to worry** il n'y a pas de raison de vous inquiéter; **it is usual f. the mother to accompany her daughter** il est d'usage que la mère accompagne sa fille **D.** *(idioms)* **oh f. a holiday!** ah, si je pouvais être en vacances!; **oh f. some peace and quiet!** que ne donnerais-je pour la paix!; *Fam* **you'll be (in) f. it if your mother sees you!** ça va être ta fête si ta mère te voit!; *Fam* **now we're (in) f. it!** qu'est-ce qu'on va prendre!; **there's nothing f. it but to pay him** il n'y a qu'à *ou* il ne nous reste qu'à le payer; **that's the postal service f. you!** ça c'est bien la poste!

CONJ *Formal* car, parce que; **I was surprised when he arrived punctually, f. he was usually late** je fus surpris de le voir arriver à l'heure, car il était souvent en retard

• **for all PREP 1** *(in spite of)* malgré; **f. all their efforts** malgré tous leurs efforts

2 *(considering)* **f. all the use he is he might as well go and play** pour ce qu'il fait d'utile il peut aussi bien aller jouer; **f. all the sense it made** pour ce que c'était clair **CONJ f. all she may say** quoi qu'elle en dise; **f. all the good it does** pour tout l'effet que ça fait; **it may be true f. all I know** c'est peut-être vrai, je n'en sais rien

• **for all that ADV** pour autant, malgré tout **CONJ** *esp Literary* **f. all that he wanted to believe them** pour autant qu'il veuille les croire

• **for ever ADV** *(last, continue)* pour toujours; *(leave)* pour toujours, sans retour; **f. ever and a day** jusqu'à la fin des temps; **f. ever and ever** à tout jamais, éternellement; **to live f. ever** vivre éternellement; **Scotland f. ever!** vive l'Écosse!

fora ['fɔːrə] *pl of* **forum**

forage ['fɒrɪdʒ] **N 1** *(search)* fouille *f*; **to go on the f.** *(for provisions)* chercher de la nourriture; **to have a f. for sth** fouiller *ou* fourrager pour trouver qch **2** *(food)* fourrage *m* **3** *Mil (raid)* raid *m*, incursion *f*

VI 1 *(search)* fourrager, fouiller; **to f. for sth** fouiller *ou* fourrager pour trouver qch **2** *Mil (raid)* faire un raid *ou* une incursion

►► *Mil* ***forage cap*** calot *m*; *Agr* ***forage harvester*** fourragère *f*

▸ **forage about, forage around VI** *(rummage)* fourrager, fouiller (**in** dans)

foray ['fɒreɪ] **N** *Mil (raid)* raid *m*, incursion *f*; *(excursion)* incursion *f*; **she was on one of her forays round the bookshops** elle procédait à l'une de ses excursions dans les librairies; **he made a brief f. into politics** il a fait une courte incursion dans la politique

VI faire un raid *ou* une incursion

forbad, forbade [fə'bæd] *pt of* **forbid**

forbear *(pt* **forbore** [-'bɔː(r)], *pp* **forborne** [-'bɔːn]) *Formal* **VI** [fɔː'beə(r)] *(abstain)* s'abstenir; **to f. from doing** *or* **to do sth** se garder *ou* s'abstenir de faire qch; **she forbore to make any comment** elle s'abstint de tout commentaire

N ['fɔːbeə(r)] ancêtre *m*; **our forbears** nos aïeux *mpl*

forbearance [fɔː'beərəns] **N 1** *(patience)* patience *f*, indulgence *f*; **to show f. towards sb** montrer de l'indulgence envers qn **2** *(restraint)* abstention *f*

forbearing [fɔː'beərɪŋ] **ADJ** patient, indulgent

forbid [fə'bɪd] *(pt* **forbad** *or* **forbade** [-'bæd], *pp* **forbidden** [-'bɪdən]) **VT 1** *(not allow)* interdire, défendre; **to f. sb alcohol** interdire l'alcool à qn; **to f. sb to do sth** défendre *ou* interdire à qn de faire qch; **students are forbidden to talk during exams** les étudiants n'ont pas le droit de parler pendant les examens; **he was forbidden from seeing her again** on lui a interdit de la revoir; **it is strictly forbidden to smoke, smoking is strictly forbidden** il est formellement interdit de fumer **2** *(prevent)* empêcher; **my condition forbids strenuous exercise** mon état ne me permet pas de me livrer à des exercices violents; **God f.!** pourvu que non!; **if she were to die, Heaven** *or* **God f., I don't know what I'd do** si elle venait à mourir, Dieu (m'en) préserve, je ne sais pas ce que je ferais

forbidden [fə'bɪdən] *pp of* **forbid**

ADJ interdit, défendu; **to tread on f. ground** empiéter sur un terrain défendu; *Fig* toucher à un sujet tabou

►► ***the Forbidden City*** la Cité interdite; *Law* ***forbidden degrees*** = degrés de consanguinité au sein desquels le mariage est interdit; *Bible & Fig* ***forbidden fruit*** fruit *m* défendu

forbidding [fə'bɪdɪŋ] **ADJ** *(building, look, sky)* menaçant; *(person)* sévère, menaçant; *(weather)* sombre; *(face, aspect)* sinistre

forbiddingly [fə'bɪdɪŋlɪ] **ADV the castle towered f. over the town** le château, menaçant, dominait la ville; **f. difficult/complex** d'une difficulté/complexité rébarbative

forbore [fɔː'bɔː(r)] *pt of* **forbear**

forborne [fɔː'bɔːn] *pp of* **forbear**

FORCE [fɔːs]

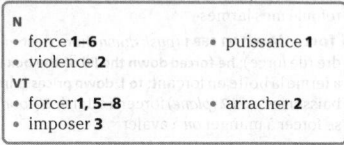

N	
• force **1–6**	• puissance **1**
• violence **2**	
VT	
• forcer **1, 5–8**	• arracher **2**
• imposer **3**	

N 1 *(power)* force *f*, puissance *f*; **forces of evil/nature** forces *fpl* du mal/de la nature; **moral f.** force *f* morale; **Europe is becoming a powerful economic f.** l'Europe devient une grande puissance économique; **television could be a f. for good** la télévision pourrait avoir une bonne influence; **to be a f. for change** être le moteur du changement; **she's a f. to be reckoned with** il faudra compter avec elle; **there are several forces at work** il y a plusieurs forces en jeu

2 *(strength)* force *f*; *(violence)* force *f*, violence *f*; **I'm against the use of f.** je suis contre le recours à la force; **the f. of the blow laid him out** la violence du coup l'a mis K-O; **they used f. to control the crowd** ils ont employé la force pour contrôler la foule; **I hit it with as much f. as I could muster** je l'ai frappé aussi fort que j'ai pu

3 *(of argument, word)* force *f*, poids *m*; **I don't see the f. of her argument** je ne perçois pas la force de son argument

4 *Phys* force *f*; **the f. of gravity** la pesanteur; *Met* **f. 10 on the Beaufort scale** force 10 sur l'échelle de Beaufort; **a f. 9 gale** un vent de force 9

5 *(of people)* force *f*; *Com* **our sales f.** notre force de vente; *Mil* **the allied forces** les armées *fpl* alliées, les alliés *mpl*; *Mil* **the (armed) forces** les forces *fpl* armées; **the (police) f.** les forces *fpl* de police; **he was in the forces** il était dans l'armée; **forces slang** argot *m* militaire

6 *(idioms)* **f. of circumstances** force *f* des choses; **by** *or* **from f. of habit** par la force de l'habitude; **by sheer f.** de vive force; **she managed it through sheer f. of will** elle y est arrivée uniquement à force de volonté; **the law comes into f. this year** la loi entre en vigueur cette année

VT 1 *(compel)* forcer, obliger; **to f. sb to do sth** contraindre *ou* forcer qn à faire qch; **I forced myself to be nice to them** je me suis forcé à être aimable avec eux; **no one's forcing you!** personne ne t'y force *ou* oblige!; *Ironic* **don't f. yourself!** ne te force surtout pas!; **they were forced to admit I was right** ils ont été obligés de reconnaître que j'avais raison; **he was forced to retire** il a été mis à la retraite d'office; **to f. sb's hand** forcer la main à qn

2 *(wrest)* arracher, extorquer; **I forced a confession from** *or* **out of him** je lui ai arraché une confession

3 *(impose)* imposer; **to f. sth on** *or* **upon sb** imposer qch à qn; **to f. oneself on sb** imposer sa présence à qn; **he forced himself** *or* **his attentions on her** il l'a poursuivie de ses assiduités

4 *(push)* **to f. one's way into a building** entrer *ou* pénétrer de force dans un immeuble; **I forced my way through the crowd** je me suis frayé un chemin *ou* passage à travers la foule; **to f. sth into sth** faire entrer qch de force dans qch; **don't f. it** ne force pas; **the car forced us off the road** la voiture nous a forcés à quitter la route; **to f. sb into a corner** pousser qn dans un coin; *Fig* mettre qn au pied du mur; **compressed air forces the liquid up the pipe** l'air comprimé fait monter le liquide dans le tuyau

5 *(break open)* forcer; **to f. (open) a door/lock** forcer une porte/une serrure
6 *(answer, smile)* forcer; **she managed to f. a smile** elle eut un sourire forcé
7 *(hurry)* forcer, hâter; *Hort* **to f. flowers/plants** forcer des fleurs/des plantes; **we forced the pace** nous avons forcé l'allure *ou* le pas; **I felt I had to f. the issue** j'ai senti qu'il fallait que je force la décision
8 *(strain ▸ metaphor, voice)* forcer; *(▸ word)* forcer le sens de
• **in force** ADJ en application, en vigueur; **the rules now in f.** le règlement en vigueur ADV en force; **the demonstrators arrived in f.** les manifestants sont arrivés en force; **the students were there in f.** les étudiants étaient venus en force *ou* en grand nombre; **in full f.** au grand complet

▸**force back** VT SEP **1** *(push back)* repousser, refouler; *Mil* faire reculer, obliger à reculer **2** *(repress)* réprimer; **I forced back my tears** j'ai refoulé mes larmes

▸**force down** VT SEP **1** *(push down)* faire descendre (de force); **he forced down the lid of the box** il a fermé la boîte en forçant; **to f. down prices** faire baisser les prix **2** *(plane)* forcer à atterrir **3** *(food)* se forcer à manger *ou* à avaler

▸**force out** VT SEP **1** *(push out)* faire sortir (de force); **hunger eventually forced them out** la faim les a finalement obligés à sortir; **to be forced out of business** être forcé à fermer boutique; *Fig* **the opposition forced him out** l'opposition l'a poussé dehors **2** *(remark)* **he forced out an apology** il s'est excusé du bout des lèvres

▸**force up** VT SEP faire monter (de force); **to f. prices up** faire monter les prix

forced [fɔːst] ADJ **1** *(compulsory)* forcé **2** *(smile)* forcé, artificiel; **he gave a f. laugh** il a ri du bout des lèvres **3** *(plant, fruit, vegetables)* forcé
▸▸ ***forced feeding*** *(of person)* alimentation *f* de force; *(of livestock)* gavage *m*; ***forced labour*** travail *m* forcé; *Aviat* ***forced landing*** atterrissage *m* forcé; *Fin* ***forced loan*** emprunt *m* forcé; *Mil* ***forced march*** marche *f* forcée; ***forced migration*** migration *f* forcée; ***forced sale*** vente *f* forcée; *Fin* ***forced saving*** épargne *f* forcée

force-feed *(pt & pp* **force-fed***)* VT *(person)* nourrir de force; *(animal)* gaver

forceful ['fɔːsful] ADJ *(person, personality)* énergique, fort; *(argument, style, impression)* puissant; *(language)* musclé; **he's not very f.** il n'est pas très énergique

forcefully ['fɔːsfʊlɪ] ADV *(speak, act)* énergiquement; *(express oneself, reason, write)* avec vigueur; *(argue)* énergiquement, avec force

forcefulness ['fɔːsfulnɪs] N vigueur *f*

force-land VI *Aviat* faire un atterrissage forcé

forcemeat ['fɔːsmiːt] N *Culin* farce *f*

forceps ['fɔːseps] NPL **(a pair of) f.** un forceps
▸▸ *Obst* ***forceps delivery*** accouchement *m* au forceps

forcible ['fɔːsəbəl] ADJ **1** *(by force)* de *ou* par force **2** *(powerful ▸ argument, style)* puissant; *(▸ personality)* puissant, fort; *(▸ speaker)* puissant; *(▸ reminder)* brutal
▸▸ *Law* ***forcible entry*** effraction *f*

forcibly ['fɔːsəblɪ] ADV **1** *(by force)* de force, par la force; **they were f. removed from the house** on les a fait sortir de force de la maison **2** *(argue, speak)* énergiquement, avec vigueur *ou* force; **they put their case very f.** ils se sont défendus avec force *ou* vigueur **3** *(recommend, remind)* fortement; **we were all f. reminded of our own mortality** nous avons été brutalement rappelés à notre condition de mortels

forcing ['fɔːsɪŋ] N **1** *(of lock, door)* forcement *m* **2** *Hort (in gardening)* forçage *m*, culture *f* forcée
▸▸ *Culin* ***forcing bag*** poche *f* à douille; *Hort* ***forcing frame*** châssis *m*; *Hort* ***forcing house*** *(for plants)* forcerie *f*; *Fam Fig* **it's just an academic f. house** dans cette boîte, tout ce qui compte ce sont les résultats aux examens

ford [fɔːd] N gué *m*
VT passer *ou* traverser à gué

fordable ['fɔːdəbəl] ADJ guéable

fore [fɔː(r)] ADJ **1** *(front)* à l'avant, antérieur; **the f. and hind legs** les pattes *fpl* de devant et de derrière **2** *Naut* à l'avant
N *Naut* avant *m*, devant *m*; **at the f.** au mât de misaine; *Fig* **to come to the f.** *(person)* percer, commencer à être connu; *(courage)* se manifester, se révéler; **the revolt brought these issues to the f.** la révolte a mis ces problèmes en évidence, la révolte a attiré l'attention sur ces problèmes; **this question has been very much to the f. in the talks** cette question a été au tout premier plan au cours des discussions
ADV *Naut* à l'avant; **f. and aft** de l'avant à l'arrière
EXCLAM *(in golf)* attention!, gare!
▸▸ *Typ* ***fore edge*** *(of book)* petit fond *m*, gouttière *f*; *Naut* ***fore hatch*** panneau *m* avant

> **PRÉFIXE**
> **FORE-**
> Lorsqu'il est suivi d'un nom ou d'un verbe, ce préfixe a deux significations principales, l'une liée à l'espace et l'autre au temps.
> • **Fore-** peut signifier PLACÉ DEVANT, comme dans **forelegs** pattes de devant; **forecourt** avant-cour; **forename** prénom; **foreground** premier plan
> Dans des mots tels que **forearm** (avant-bras) ou **forehead** (front), le préfixe désigne le devant de la partie du corps représentée par le nom
> • **Fore-** peut également signifier EN AVANCE. Dans ce sens, la traduction commence le plus souvent par **pré-**. Quelques exemples courants:
> **to foresee** prévoir; **forewarn** prévenir; **forerunner** précurseur; **forefather** ancêtre; **foreplay** préliminaires amoureux

fore-and-aft ADJ *Naut* aurique
▸▸ *Naut* ***fore-and-aft rig*** gréement *m* aurique; *Naut* ***fore-and-aft sail*** voile *f* aurique

forearm N ['fɔːrɑːm] avant-bras *m inv*
VT [fɔːr'ɑːm] prémunir; **he came forearmed** il est venu prémuni *ou* préparé

forebear ['fɔːbeə(r)] N ancêtre *m*; **our forebears** nos aïeux *mpl*

forebode [fɔː'bəʊd] VT *Formal* augurer

foreboding [fɔː'bəʊdɪŋ] N *(feeling)* mauvais pressentiment *m*; *(omen)* présage *m* de malheur, mauvais augure *m*; **she was filled with (a sense of) f.** elle était envahie par un mauvais pressentiment; **she had a f. that things would go seriously wrong** elle a eu le pressentiment que les choses allaient très mal tourner; **her laughter filled me with f.** ses rires m'ont rendu très appréhensif

forecast ['fɔːkɑːst] *(pt & pp* **forecast** *or* **forecasted***)* VT **1** *(gen) & Met* prévoir **2** *(in betting)* pronostiquer
N **1** *(gen) & Met* prévision *f*; **the f. is not good** *(gen)* les prévisions ne sont pas bonnes; *(weather)* la météo n'est pas bonne; *Com* **sales forecasts** prévisions *fpl* de ventes; **economic f.** prévisions *fpl* économiques; **the (weather) f.** le bulletin météorologique, la météo **2** *(in betting)* pronostic *m*; **racing f.** pronostic *m* des courses
▸▸ *Acct* ***forecast balance sheet*** bilan *m* prévisionnel

forecaster ['fɔːkɑːstə(r)] N pronostiqueur(euse) *m,f*; **weather f.** météorologiste *mf*, météorologue *mf*

forecasting ['fɔːkɑːstɪŋ] N *(of result etc)* pronostication *f*; *(of weather, economic matters, sports)* prévision *f*
▸▸ ***forecasting firm*** société *f* de prévisions; ***forecasting model*** modèle *m* de prévisions

forecastle ['fəʊksəl] N *Naut* gaillard *m* d'avant; *(in merchant navy)* poste *m* d'équipage

foreclose [fɔː'kləʊz] *Law* VT **to f. the mortgage** saisir le bien hypothéqué
VI saisir le bien hypothéqué; **to f. on sb** saisir les biens de qn; **to f. on a mortgage** saisir un bien hypothéqué

foreclosure [fɔː'kləʊʒə(r)] N *Law* forclusion *f*, saisie *f*

forecourt ['fɔːkɔːt] N avant-cour *f*, cour *f* de devant; *(of petrol station)* devant *m*; **f. prices** prix *mpl* à la pompe

foredoomed [fɔː'duːmd] ADJ *Literary* voué à l'échec

forefather ['fɔːfɑːðə(r)] N ancêtre *m*; **our forefathers** nos aïeux *mpl*

forefeet ['fɔːfiːt] *pl of* **forefoot**

forefinger ['fɔːfɪŋgə(r)] N index *m*

forefoot ['fɔːfʊt] *(pl* **forefeet** [-fiːt]*)* N *(of cow, horse)* pied *m* de devant *ou* antérieur; *(of cat, dog, bird)* patte *f* de devant *ou* antérieure

forefront ['fɔːfrʌnt] N premier rang *m*; **to be at** *or* **in the f. of sth** *(country, firm)* être au premier rang de qch; *(person)* être une sommité dans qch

foregather [fɔː'gæðə(r)] VI *Formal* se réunir, s'assembler

forego [fɔː'gəʊ] *(pt* **forewent** [-'went], *pp* **foregone** [-'gɒn]*)* VT renoncer à, se priver de

foregoing [fɔː'gəʊɪŋ] ADJ précédent, susdit; **the f. study** la susdite étude
N précédent(e) *m,f*; **if we are to believe the f.** si nous devons croire ce qui précède

foregone [fɔː'gɒn] *pp of* **forego**
▸▸ ***foregone conclusion*** issue *f* certaine *ou* prévisible; **it was a f. conclusion** c'était prévu d'avance

foreground ['fɔːgraʊnd] N *(gen) & Art, Phot & Comput* premier plan *m*; **in the f.** au premier plan; *Fig* **the Mayor is in the f.** le maire est bien en évidence; **they must be hoping that this issue will fade from the f.** ils doivent espérer que ce problème ne restera pas longtemps au premier plan
VT *Art, Phot & Comput* mettre au premier plan; *Fig* privilégier
▸▸ *TV & Cin* ***foreground matte*** cache *m* d'avant-plan

forehand ['fɔːhænd] N **1** *Sport* coup *m* droit; **to have a strong/weak f.** avoir un coup droit puissant/faible; **to play a f.** jouer un coup droit; **to serve to one's opponent's f.** servir sur le coup droit adverse **2** *(of horse)* avant-main *m*
▸▸ *Sport* ***forehand drive*** drive *m* de coup droit; ***forehand stroke*** coup *m* droit; ***forehand volley*** volée *f* de face

forehead ['fɔːhed] N front *m*

foreign ['fɒrən] ADJ **1** *(country, language, person, food)* étranger; *(aid, visit ▸ to country)* à l'étranger; *(▸ from country)* de l'étranger; *(products)* de l'étranger; *(trade)* extérieur; **she looked f.** elle paraissait étrangère; **a f.-sounding name** un nom aux consonances étrangères; **students from f. countries** des étudiants venant de l'étranger; **relations with f. countries** les relations avec l'étranger; **f. competition** concurrence *f* étrangère; **f. investment** investissement *m* étranger; **f. travel** voyages *mpl* à l'étranger **2** *(alien)* étranger; **such thinking is f. to them** un tel raisonnement leur est étranger
▸▸ *Fin* ***foreign account*** compte *m* étranger; ***foreign affairs*** affaires *fpl* étrangères; ***foreign agent*** *(spy)* agent *m* étranger; *Com* représentant(e) *m,f* à l'étranger; *Fin* ***foreign bill*** effet *m ou* traite *f* sur l'extérieur; *Med* ***foreign body*** corps *m* étranger; ***the Foreign and Commonwealth Office*** le Foreign Office, = le ministère britannique des Affaires étrangères; ***the Foreign and Commonwealth Secretary*** = le ministre britannique des Affaires étrangères; *Press* ***foreign correspondent*** correspondant(e) *m,f* à l'étranger; *Fin* ***foreign currency*** devises *fpl* étrangères; **to buy f. currency** acheter des devises étrangères; *Fin* ***foreign currency account*** compte *m* en devises étrangères; *Fin* ***foreign currency earnings*** apport *m* de devises étrangères; *Fin* ***foreign currency holding*** avoir *m* en devises étrangères; *Fin* ***foreign currency loan*** prêt *m* en devises étrangères; *Fin* ***foreign currency option*** option *f* de change; *Fin* ***foreign currency reserves*** réserves *fpl* de change, réserves *fpl* en devises; *Fin* ***foreign debt*** dette *f* extérieure; *Econ* ***foreign direct investment*** investissement *m* étranger direct; *Fin* ***foreign exchange*** devises *fpl* étrangères; *Fin* ***foreign exchange broker, foreign exchange dealer*** cambiste *mf*, courtier(ère) *m,f* en devises; *Fin* ***foreign exchange gain*** gain *m* de change; *Fin* ***foreign exchange loss*** perte *f* de

change; *Fin* ***foreign exchange market*** marché *m* des changes; *Fin* ***foreign exchange option*** option *f* sur devises; *Fin* ***foreign exchange rate*** cours *m* des devises; *Fin* ***foreign exchange reserves*** réserves *fpl* de change, réserves *fpl* en devises; *Fin* ***foreign exchange risk*** risque *m* de change; ***the Foreign Legion*** la Légion (étrangère); ***foreign market*** marché *m* extérieur; *Med* ***foreign matter*** corps *m* étranger; *Pol* ***foreign minister*** ministre *m* des affaires étrangères; ***the Foreign Office*** le Foreign Office, = le ministère britannique des Affaires étrangères; ***foreign policy*** politique *f* étrangère *ou* extérieure; ***the Foreign Secretary*** = le ministre britannique des Affaires étrangères; *Am* ***foreign service*** service *m* diplomatique

foreign-built ADJ *(car)* de marque étrangère; *(ship)* construit à l'étranger

foreigner ['fɒrənə(r)] N étranger(ère) *m,f*

> Attention: ne pas confondre avec **stranger**.

foreignness ['fɒrɪnnɪs] N air *m* étranger; *(of place)* caractère *m* étranger; *(exotic nature)* exotisme *m*; **the f. of the food/their way of life** la nourriture/leur mode de vie bien à part; **given the f. of this concept to our culture** étant donné que ce concept est étranger à notre culture

foreknowledge [fɔː'nɒlɪdʒ] N *Formal (advance knowledge)* **to have f. of sth** savoir qch à l'avance; **I had no f. of her plans** je ne savais pas à l'avance quels étaient ses projets

foreland ['fɔːlənd] N promontoire *m*, cap *m*

foreleg ['fɔːleg] N *(of horse)* jambe *f* de devant *ou* antérieure; *(of dog, cat)* patte *f* de devant *ou* antérieure

forelock ['fɔːlɒk] N *(of person)* mèche *f*, toupet *m*; *(of horse)* toupet *m*; **to touch** *or* **to tug one's f.** saluer en portant la main au front; *Fig* faire des courbettes

foreman ['fɔːmən] (*pl* **foremen** [-mən]) N *Ind* contremaître *m*, chef *m* d'équipe; *Law* président(e) *m,f*

foremast ['fɔːmɑːst] N *Naut* mât *m* de misaine

forementioned ['fɔːˌmenʃənd] ADJ *Law & Admin* précité

foremost ['fɔːməʊst] ADJ *(first ▸ in position)* le plus en avant; *(▸ in importance)* principal, le plus important; **of the f. importance** de la plus haute importance
ADV en avant

forename ['fɔːneɪm] N *Br* prénom *m*

forenoon ['fɔːnuːn] N *Arch or Literary or Scot* matinée *f*

forensic [fə'rensɪk] ADJ **1** *(chemistry)* légal; *(expert)* légiste **2** *(term)* du barreau; **he showed great f. skill at the trial** il a fait une plaidoirie remarquable
• **forensics** N *(UNCOUNT)* art *m* de la discussion *ou* du débat
▸▸ ***forensic department*** *(in hospital)* institut *m* médico-légal; ***forensic evidence*** expertise *f* criminalistique; ***forensic laboratory*** laboratoire *m* de criminalistique; ***forensic linguistics*** *(UNCOUNT)* linguistique *f* appliquée à la criminalistique; ***forensic medicine*** médecine *f* légale; ***forensic science*** criminalistique *f*; ***forensic scientist*** expert *m* légiste *ou* en criminalistique; ***forensic test*** = test effectué par un expert en criminalistique; **f. tests showed him to be the killer** les tests médico-légaux ont prouvé qu'il était l'assassin

foreordain [ˌfɔːrɔː'deɪn] VT *Formal* prédestiner

foreplay ['fɔːpleɪ] N *(UNCOUNT)* préliminaires *mpl* (amoureux)

forequarters ['fɔːkwɔːtəz] NPL *(of animal)* avant-train *m*; *(of carcass)* quartiers *mpl* de devant

forerunner ['fɔːrʌnə(r)] N **1** *(precursor ▸ person)* précurseur *m*; *(▸ invention, model)* ancêtre *m* **2** *(omen)* présage *m*, signe *m* avant-coureur

foresail ['fɔːseɪl] N *Naut* (voile *f* de) misaine *f*

foresee [fɔː'siː] (*pt* **foresaw** [-'sɔː], *pp* **foreseen** [-'siːn]) VT prévoir, présager

foreseeable [fɔː'siːəbəl] ADJ prévisible; **in the f. future** dans un avenir prévisible

foreseen [fɔː'siːn] *pp of* **foresee**

foreshadow [fɔː'ʃædəʊ] VT présager, annoncer; **her first novel foreshadowed this masterpiece** son premier roman a laissé prévoir ce chef-d'œuvre

foreshore ['fɔːʃɔː(r)] N *(beach)* plage *f*; *Geog* laisse *f* de mer

foreshorten [fɔː'ʃɔːtən] VT *Art* faire un raccourci de; *Phot (horizontally)* réduire; *(vertically)* écraser

foreshortening [fɔː'ʃɔːtənɪŋ] N *Art* raccourci *m*; *Phot (horizontal)* réduction *f*; *(vertical)* écrasement *m*

foresight ['fɔːsaɪt] N prévoyance *f*; **lack of f.** imprévoyance *f*; **with f. this could all have been avoided** avec un peu de prévoyance tout ceci aurait pu être évité

foreskin ['fɔːskɪn] N prépuce *m*

forest ['fɒrɪst] N forêt *f*; **oak/coniferous f.** forêt *f* de chênes/de conifères; **hills covered with forests, f.-covered hills** collines *fpl* boisées; *Fig* **a f. of aerials** une forêt d'antennes
VT *(region)* boiser (**with** de)
▸▸ ***forest fire*** incendie *m* de forêt; ***forest floor*** sol *m* de la forêt; ***forest management*** gestion *f* des forêts; ***forest park*** parc *m* forestier; *Am* ***forest ranger*** garde *m* forestier; *Am* ***the Forest Service*** = organisme américain de gestion des forêts domaniales, les eaux et forêts *fpl*

forestall [fɔː'stɔːl] VT **1** *(prevent)* empêcher, retenir; **she wanted to leave but he forestalled her** elle voulut partir mais il l'en empêcha **2** *(anticipate ▸ desire, possibility)* anticiper, prévenir; *(▸ person)* devancer, prendre les devants sur **3** *Com & Hist* accaparer

forestay ['fɔːsteɪ] N *Naut* étai *m* de misaine

forested ['fɒrɪstɪd] ADJ boisé (**with** de)

forester ['fɒrɪstə(r)] N forestier(ère) *m,f*

forestry ['fɒrɪstrɪ] N sylviculture *f*
▸▸ *Br* ***the Forestry Commission*** = organisme britannique de gestion des forêts domaniales, les eaux et forêts *fpl*

foretaste ['fɔːteɪst] N avant-goût *m*; **to give** *or* **offer sb a f. of sth** donner un avant-goût de qch à qn

foretell [fɔː'tel] (*pt & pp* **foretold** [-'təʊld]) VT prédire

forethought ['fɔːθɔːt] N *(premeditation)* préméditation *f*; *(foresight)* prévoyance *f*; **if you had given it some f.** si tu y avais un peu réfléchi à l'avance

foretold [fɔː'təʊld] *pt & pp of* **foretell**

forever [fər'evə(r)] ADV **1** *(eternally)* (pour) toujours, éternellement; **it won't last f.** ça ne durera pas toujours; **I'll love you f.** je t'aimerai toujours; **United f.!** vive United!
2 *(incessantly)* toujours, sans cesse; **he's f. finding fault** il trouve toujours à redire
3 *(for good)* pour toujours; **dinosaurs have vanished f.** les dinosaures ont disparu pour toujours
4 *Fam (a long time)* très longtemps[□]; **it'll take f.!** ça va prendre des lustres!; **he took f. to get ready** il a mis des heures à se préparer; **we can't wait f.** nous ne pouvons pas attendre jusqu'à la saint-glinglin

forewarn [fɔː'wɔːn] VT prévenir, avertir; **he forewarned them that life there would be difficult** il les a prévenus que là-bas la vie serait difficile; *Prov* **forewarned is forearmed** un homme averti en vaut deux

forewent [fɔː'went] *pt of* **forego**

forewoman ['fɔːwʊmən] (*pl* **forewomen** [-'wɪmɪn]) N **1** *Ind* contremaîtresse *f* **2** *Law (of jury)* présidente *f*

foreword ['fɔːwɜːd] N avant-propos *m inv*, préface *f*

forex ['fɔːreks] N *Fin (abbr* **foreign exchange**) devises *fpl* étrangères
▸▸ ***forex trading*** transactions *fpl* en devises étrangères

forfaiting ['fɔːfɪtɪŋ] N *Banking* forfaitage *m*, forfaitisation *f*

forfeit ['fɔːfɪt] VT **1** *(lose)* perdre; *(give up)* renoncer à, abandonner; **to f. one's rights** perdre *ou* être déchu de ses droits; **to f. one's life** payer de sa vie; *Fin* **to f. a deposit** perdre les arrhes **2** *Law (lose)* perdre (par confiscation); *(confiscate)* confisquer
N **1** *(penalty)* prix *m*, peine *f*; *Com (sum)* amende *f*, dédit *m* **2** *Law (loss)* perte *f* (par confiscation) **3** *(game)* **to play forfeits** jouer aux gages; **to pay a f.** avoir un gage
ADJ *Formal (subject to confiscation)* susceptible d'être confisqué; *(confiscated)* confisqué
▸▸ *Law* ***forfeit clause*** clause *f* de dédit

forfeiture ['fɔːfɪtʃə(r)] N **1** *Law (loss)* perte *f* (par confiscation); *Fig (surrender)* renonciation *f*; **f. of rights** renonciation *f* aux droits **2** *St Exch (of shares)* déchéance *f*, forfaiture *f*

forgather = **foregather**

forgave [fəˌgeɪv] *pt of* **forgive**

forge [fɔːdʒ] VT **1** *(metal, sword)* forger; *Fig* **to f. an alliance/a friendship** sceller une alliance/une amitié **2** *(counterfeit ▸ money, signature)* contrefaire; *(▸ picture, document)* faire un faux de, contrefaire; **a forged passport** un faux passeport; **a forged £20 note** un faux billet de 20 livres
VI *(go forward)* avancer; **we forged on, hoping to reach the village by nightfall** nous avons continué à toute allure dans l'espoir d'arriver au village avant la tombée de la nuit; **to f. into the lead** prendre la tête
N *(machine, place)* forge *f*

> Note that the French verb **forger** never means **to counterfeit**.

▸ **forge ahead** VI *(press forward)* faire des progrès; *(in race, election campaign)* prendre de l'avance; *(in business, undertaking)* aller de l'avant; **to f. ahead with one's plans** aller de l'avant dans ses projets, mener ses projets de l'avant

forged [fɔːdʒd] ADJ **1** *Metal* forgé **2** *(document, banknote, signature)* faux (fausse), contrefait; **f. document** faux *m*; *(identity paper)* faux papier *m*

forger ['fɔːdʒə(r)] N *(gen)* faussaire *mf*; *(of money)* faux-monnayeur *m*, faussaire *mf*

forgery ['fɔːdʒərɪ] (*pl* **forgeries**) N **1** *(of money, picture, signature)* contrefaçon *f*; *(of document)* falsification *f*; **to prosecute sb for f.** poursuivre qn pour faux (et usage de faux) **2** *(object)* faux *m*; **it's a f.** *(of signature)* c'est une fausse signature

forget [fə'get] (*pt* **forgot** [-'gɒt], *pp* **forgotten** [-'gɒtən]) VT **1** *(be unable to recall)* oublier; **he'll never f. her** il ne l'oubliera jamais; **have you forgotten all your Latin?** avez-vous oublié tout votre latin?; **I'll never f. seeing him play Lear** je ne l'oublierai jamais *ou* je le reverrai toujours dans le rôle de Lear; **I forgot (that) you had a sister** j'avais oublié que tu avais une sœur; **he's forgotten how to type** il ne sait plus (comment) taper; **I've forgotten which house is his** je ne sais plus *ou* j'ai oublié quelle maison est la sienne; **I never f. a face** j'ai la mémoire des visages; **she'll never let him f. his mistake** elle n'est pas près de lui pardonner son erreur; **I forgot the time** j'ai oublié l'heure; **to f. one's manners** oublier ses manières; **to f. oneself** s'oublier; **he was so overwhelmed by emotion that he quite forgot himself** il était tellement ému qu'il perdit toute retenue; **it's my idea and don't you f. it!** c'est moi qui ai eu cette idée, tâchez de ne pas l'oublier!; **such things are best forgotten** il vaut mieux ne pas penser à de telles choses; **that never-to-be-forgotten day** ce jour inoubliable *ou* mémorable
2 *(neglect, overlook)* oublier, omettre; **she forgot to mention that she was married** elle a oublié *ou* a omis de dire qu'elle était mariée; **he seems to have forgotten his old friends** il semble avoir oublié ses anciens amis; **the forgotten man of Scottish football** le laissé-pour-compte du football écossais; **not forgetting...** sans oublier...; **let's f. our differences** oublions nos différends; *Fam* **f. it!** *(in reply to thanks)* de rien![□]; *(in reply to apology)* ce n'est pas grave!, ne t'en fais pas!; *(in irritation)* laisse tomber!; *(in reply to question)* cela n'a aucune importance![□], peu importe![□]; **they can f. it!** *(they're being unreasonable, they've no chance)* ils peuvent faire une croix dessus!
3 *(leave behind)* oublier, laisser; **don't f. your umbrella!** n'oublie pas ton parapluie!
4 *(give up ▸ idea, plan)* abandonner, renoncer à; **if we don't get financial backing, we'll just have to f. the whole thing** si nous n'obtenons pas de sou-

tien financier il nous faudra renoncer au projet

VI oublier; **before I f.** *(can you do something?)* avant que j'oublie *ou* que je n'oublie; **to f. about sb/sth** oublier qn/qch; **sorry, I completely forgot about it** désolé, j'avais complètement oublié; **and you can f. about going to London!** et ce n'est pas la peine de songer à aller à Londres!

forgetful [fəˈgetfʊl] ADJ *(absent-minded)* distrait; *(careless)* négligent, étourdi; **to be f. of sth** être oublieux de qch

forgetfulness [fəˈgetfʊlnɪs] N *(absent-mindedness)* manque *m* de mémoire; *(carelessness)* négligence *f*, étourderie *f*; **in a moment of f.** dans un moment d'étourderie

forget-me-not N *Bot* myosotis *m*

forging [ˈfɔːdʒɪŋ] N *Metal (activity)* travail *m* de forge; *(forged item)* pièce *f* forgée

▸▸ ***forging mill*** forge *f*; ***forging press*** marteau-pilon *m*

forgivable [fəˈgɪvəbəl] ADJ pardonnable

forgivably [fəˈgɪvəblɪ] ADV **she was, quite f., rather annoyed with him!** elle était plutôt en colère contre lui, et on la comprend!

forgive [fəˈgɪv] *(pt* **forgave** [-ˈgeɪv], *pp* **forgiven** [-ˈgɪvən]) VT **1** *(pardon)* pardonner; **to f. sb (for) sth** pardonner qch à qn; **he asked me to f. him** il m'a demandé pardon; **f. my ignorance, but who exactly was Galsworthy?** pardonnez mon ignorance, mais qui était Galsworthy exactement?; **f. me, but haven't we met before?** pardonnez-moi *ou* excusez-moi, mais est-ce qu'on ne s'est pas déjà rencontrés?; **one might be forgiven for thinking that…** on pourrait pardonner de penser que… + *indicative*; **f. and forget** pardonner et oublier **2** *(debt, payment)* **to f. (sb) a debt** faire grâce (à qn) d'une dette

forgiveness [fəˈgɪvnɪs] N **1** *(pardon)* pardon *m*; **to ask sb's f.** demander pardon à qn **2** *(tolerance)* indulgence *f*, clémence *f*

forgiving [fəˈgɪvɪŋ] ADJ indulgent, clément

forgo *(pt* **forwent** [-ˈwent], *pp* **forgone** [-ˈgɒn]) = **forego**

forgot [fəˌgɒt] *pt of* **forget**

forgotten [fəˈgɒtən] *pp of* **forget**

fork [fɔːk] N **1** *(for eating)* fourchette *f*

2 *Agr* fourche *f*

3 *(junction* ▸ *in road, railway)* bifurcation *f*, embranchement *m*; **take the right f.** tournez *ou* prenez à droite à l'embranchement

4 *(on bicycle, motorbike)* fourche *f*

5 *(fork-shaped object* ▸ *of water diviner)* baguette *f* divinatoire; *(*▸ *to support branch)* poteau *m* fourchu; **f. of lightning** zigzag *m* (d'éclair)

VT *Agr* fourcher; **they were forking hay onto the truck** ils chargeaient du foin à la fourche dans le camion

VI **1** *(river, road)* bifurquer, fourcher; **the road forks at Newton** la route fait une fourche à Newton **2** *(car, person)* bifurquer, tourner; **he forked left** il a pris *ou* a tourné à gauche; **f. right for the airport** prenez à droite pour l'aéroport

> When translating **fork**, note that **fourchette** and **fourche** are not interchangeable. **Fourchette** is an item of cutlery, whereas **fourche** is an agricultural implement.

▸ **fork in** VT SEP *(compost)* enfouir en fourchant

▸ **fork off** VI *(road, driver)* bifurquer

▸ **fork out** *Fam* VT SEP *(provide, often unwillingly)* **to f. out money** allonger *ou* abouler de l'argent

VI *(pay out money)* **to f. out for sth** casquer pour qch; **he had to f. out (for it)** il a dû allonger la monnaie, il a dû casquer; **come on, f. out** *(what you owe me)* allez, aboule

▸ **fork over** VT SEP *(flower bed)* retourner légèrement à la fourche

forked [fɔːkt] ADJ *(tongue)* fourchu; *(river, road)* à bifurcation

▸▸ ***forked lightning*** éclair *m* en zigzags

forkful [ˈfɔːkfʊl] N **1** *(of food)* fourchetée *f* **2** *(of hay)* fourchée *f*

forklift [ˈfɔːklɪft] N **f. (truck)** chariot *m* élévateur

forlorn [fəˈlɔːn] ADJ **1** *(wretched)* triste, malheureux; **a f. cry** un cri de désespoir **2** *(lonely* ▸ *person)* abandonné, délaissé; *(*▸ *place)* désolé, désert; **the empty house had a f. look about it** la maison vide avait l'air abandonné **3** *(desperate)* désespéré; **I went there in the f. hope that she'd see me** j'y suis allé dans le fol espoir qu'elle accepterait de me voir; **they made one last f. attempt to contact her** ils ont fait un dernier effort désespéré pour la contacter

FORM¹ [fɔːm]

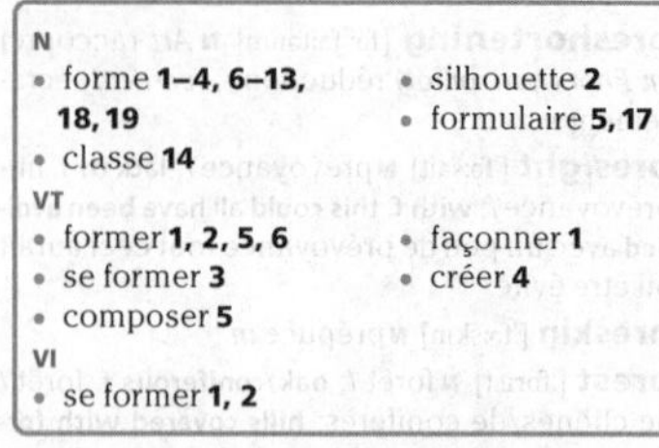

N	
• forme **1–4, 6–13, 18, 19**	• silhouette **2**
• classe **14**	• formulaire **5, 17**
VT	
• former **1, 2, 5, 6**	• façonner **1**
• se former **3**	• créer **4**
• composer **5**	
VI	
• se former **1, 2**	

N **1** *(shape)* forme *f*; **in the f. of a heart** en forme de cœur; **her plan began to take f.** son projet a commencé à prendre tournure *ou* forme

2 *(body, figure)* forme *f*, silhouette *f*; **a slender f. appeared at the door** une silhouette élancée apparut à la porte; **the human f.** la forme humaine

3 *(aspect, mode)* forme *f*; **it's written in the f. of a letter** c'est écrit sous forme de lettre; **the Devil appeared in the f. of a goat** le diable apparut sous la forme d'une chèvre; **the same product in a new f.** le même produit présenté différemment; **what f. should my questions take?** comment devrais-je formuler mes questions?; **the interview took the f. of an informal chat** l'entrevue prit la forme d'une discussion informelle

4 *(kind, type)* forme *f*, sorte *f*; **one f. of cancer** une forme de cancer; **we studied three different forms of government** nous avons examiné trois systèmes de gouvernement *ou* trois régimes différents; **all forms of sugar** le sucre sous toutes ses formes

5 *(document)* formulaire *m*; *(for bank, telegram)* formule *f*; **to fill in** *or* **out a f.** remplir un formulaire; **printed f.** imprimé *m*

6 *(condition)* forme *f*, condition *f*; **in good f.** en pleine forme, en excellente condition; *Br* **on f.**, *Am* **in f.** en forme; **John was** *Br* **on** *or Am* **in good f. at lunch** John était en forme *ou* plein d'entrain pendant le déjeuner; **I'm** *Br* **on** *or Am* **in top f.** je suis en pleine forme; *Br* **on** *or Am* **in their current f. they're unlikely to win** étant donné leur forme actuelle ils ont peu de chances de gagner; **he's** *Br* **off** *or Am* **out of f.** il n'est pas en forme; **to study (the) f.** *(in horse racing)* examiner le tableau des performances des chevaux

7 *(gen) & Art, Literature & Mus* forme *f*; **f. and content** la forme et le fond; **his writing lacks f.** ce qu'il écrit n'est pas clair

8 *(standard practice)* forme *f*, règle *f*; **to do sth as a matter of f.** faire qch pour la forme; **what's the usual f. in these cases?** que fait-on d'habitude *ou* quelle est la marche à suivre dans ces cas-là?; *Fam* **to know the f.** *(what to do)* savoir ce qu'il faut faire▫; *Law* **in due f.** en bonne et due forme

9 *Old-fashioned (etiquette)* forme *f*, formalité *f*; **it's good f.** c'est de bon ton, cela se fait; **it's bad f.** cela ne se fait pas; **it is bad f. to ask a lady her age** ce n'est pas poli de demander son âge à une dame

10 *(formula)* forme *f*, formule *f*; **f. of address** formule *f* de politesse; **the correct f. of address for a senator** la manière correcte de s'adresser à un sénateur; **it's only a f. of speech** ce n'est qu'une façon de parler; **the f. of the marriage service** les rites *mpl* du mariage

11 *(mould)* forme *f*, moule *m*

12 *Gram & Ling* forme *f*; **the masculine f.** la forme du masculin, le masculin

13 *Phil (structure)* forme *f*; *(essence)* essence *f*

14 *Br Sch (class)* classe *f*; **she's in the first/sixth f.** elle est en sixième/première

15 *Br (bench)* banc *m*

16 *Br Fam (criminal record)* casier *m* judiciaire▫; **has he got f.?** est-ce qu'il a un casier judiciaire?

17 *Comput (on Internet)* formulaire *m*

18 *Am Typ* forme *f*

19 *(of hare)* gîte *m*, forme *f*

VT **1** *(shape)* former, construire; *(character, mind)* former, façonner; *(sentence)* construire; *Metal* former, façonner; **he formed the model out of** *or* **from clay** il a sculpté *ou* façonné le modèle dans l'argile; **f. the dough into a ball** pétrissez la pâte en forme de boule; **she has trouble forming certain words** elle a du mal à prononcer certains mots

2 *(take the shape of)* former, faire; **the children formed a circle** les enfants formèrent un cercle; **f. a line please** faites la queue s'il vous plaît; **the applicants formed a queue** les candidats firent la queue

3 *(develop* ▸ *opinion)* se former, se faire; *(*▸ *plan)* concevoir, élaborer; *(*▸ *habit)* contracter; **he's wary of forming friendships** il hésite à nouer des amitiés; **to f. an impression** avoir une impression

4 *(organize* ▸ *association, club)* créer, fonder; *(*▸ *committee, government)* former; *Com (*▸ *company)* fonder, créer; **they formed themselves into a committee** ils se constituèrent en comité

5 *(constitute)* composer, former; **to f. the basis of sth** constituer la base de *ou* servir de base à qch; **to f. (a) part of sth** faire partie de qch; **the countries forming the alliance** les pays qui constituent l'alliance

6 *Gram* former; **how to f. the past tense** comment former le passé composé

VI **1** *(materialize)* se former, prendre forme; **doubts began to f. in his mind** des doutes commencèrent à prendre forme dans son esprit, il commença à avoir des doutes

2 *(take shape)* se former; **f. into a line!** alignez-vous!; **we formed into groups** nous nous sommes mis en groupes, nous avons formé des groupes

▸▸ *Ling* ***form class*** catégorie *f* grammaticale; *Comput* ***form document*** document *m* canevas; *Comput* ***form feed*** avancement *m* du papier; ***form letter*** lettre *f* circulaire; *Br Sch* ***form master*** professeur *m* principal; *Br Sch* ***form mistress*** professeur *m* principal; *Br Sch* ***form room*** salle *f* de classe, classe *f*; *Br Sch* ***form teacher, form tutor*** professeur *m* principal

▸ **form up** VI *Br* se mettre en ligne, s'aligner

form² *Am Typ* = **forme**

FORMAL [ˈfɔːməl]

ADJ	
• officiel **1, 2**	• solennel **1, 3**
• formel **2, 7, 8**	• formaliste **4, 7**
• de forme **5, 6**	
N	
• bal **1**	• habit *ou* robe de soirée **2**

ADJ **1** *(conventional* ▸ *function)* officiel, solennel; *(*▸ *greeting)* solennel, cérémonieux; **a f. dance** un grand bal; **a f. dinner** un dîner officiel; **is it f.?** *(the party, dance etc)* est-ce que c'est habillé?; **I only wear it on f. occasions** je ne le/la porte que pour les grandes occasions

2 *(official* ▸ *announcement, approval)* officiel; *(*▸ *order)* formel, explicite; **f. agreement/contract** accord *m*/contrat *m* en bonne et due forme; **a f. denial** un démenti formel *ou* catégorique; **she had no f. education** elle n'a jamais fait d'études; **no f. training is required** aucune formation spécifique n'est exigée; **we gave him a f. warning** nous l'avons averti officiellement *ou* dans les règles

3 *(correct* ▸ *person)* solennel; *(*▸ *behaviour, style)* soigné, solennel, *Pej* guindé; **she's very f.** elle est très à cheval sur les conventions; **don't be so f.** ne sois pas si sérieux, sois un peu plus détendu; **in f. language** dans un style soigné *ou* soutenu; **"vous" is the f. form** "vous" est la formule de politesse

4 *(ordered)* formaliste, méthodique

5 *(nominal)* de forme; **f. agreement** accord *m* de forme; **she is the f. head of State** c'est elle le chef d'État officiel

6 *(relating to form)* de forme; **a f. similarity** une similarité de forme

7 *Gram & Ling* formaliste, formel

8 *Phil* formel

N *Am* **1** *(dance)* bal *m*

2 *(suit)* habit *m* de soirée; *(dress)* robe *f* de soirée

▸▸ ***formal dress*** *(for ceremony)* tenue *f* de cérémonie; *(for evening)* tenue *f* de soirée; ***formal garden*** jardin *m* à la française

formaldehyde [fɔːˈmældɪhaɪd] N *Chem* formaldéhyde *m*

formalin [ˈfɔːməlɪn] N *Chem* formol *m*

formalism [ˈfɔːməlɪzəm] N *Phil & Art* formalisme *m*

formality [fɔːˈmælətɪ] (*pl* **formalities**) N **1** (*ceremoniousness*) cérémonie *f*; (*solemnity*) solennité *f*, gravité *f*; (*stiffness*) froideur *f*, raideur *f*; (*convention*) formalité *f*, étiquette *f*; **the f. of the dance** le caractère cérémonieux du bal **2** (*procedure*) formalité *f*; **it's a mere f.** c'est une simple formalité; **let's forget the formalities** dispensons-nous des formalités

formalize, -ise [ˈfɔːməlaɪz] VT officialiser

formally [ˈfɔːməlɪ] ADV **1** (*with formality*) solennellement, cérémonieusement; **f. dressed** (*for ceremony*) en tenue de cérémonie; (*for evening*) en tenue de soirée

2 (*officially*) officiellement, dans les règles; **the organization f. renounced violence** l'organisation a officiellement renoncé à la violence

3 (*speak*) de façon soignée; (*behave*) de façon solennelle, *Pej* de façon guindée

4 (*arrange*) de façon régulière

5 (*nominally*) pour la forme; **he did consult his father before proceeding, if only f.** il a demandé conseil à son père avant d'agir, ne serait-ce que pour la forme

> Note that the French word **formellement** is a false friend. Its most common meaning is **strictly** or **categorically**.

format [ˈfɔːmæt] (*pt & pp* **formatted**, *cont* **formatting**) N **1** (*size*) format *m* **2** (*layout*) présentation *f*; **the TV news now has a new f.** le journal télévisé a adopté une nouvelle présentation **3** *Comput* format *m*

VT **1** (*layout*) composer la présentation de **2** *Comput* (*disk*) formater; (*page, text*) mettre en forme, formater

formation [fɔːˈmeɪʃən] N **1** (*establishment* ▸ *of club*) création *f*, fondation *f*; (▸ *of committee, company*) formation *f*, fondation *f*; (▸ *of government*) formation *f*

2 (*development* ▸ *of character, person*) formation *f*; (▸ *of idea*) développement *m*, élaboration *f*; (▸ *of plan*) élaboration *f*, mise *f* en place

3 *Bot, Geol & Med* formation *f*

4 (*arrangement*) formation *f*, disposition *f*; *Mil* (*unit*) formation *f*, dispositif *m*; **battle f.** formation *f* de combat; **in close f.** en ordre serré

▸▸ ***formation dancing*** danse *f* en formation; ***formation flying*** vol *m* en formation

formative [ˈfɔːmətɪv] ADJ formateur; **the f. years** les années *fpl* formatrices

N *Gram* formant *m*, élément *m* formateur

formatted [ˈfɔːmætɪd] ADJ *Comput* (*disk*) formaté; (*page, text*) mis en forme, formaté

formatting [ˈfɔːmætɪŋ] N *Comput* (*of disk*) formatage *m*; (*of page, text*) mise *f* en forme, formatage *m*

forme, *Am* **form** [fɔːm] N *Typ* forme *f*

formed [fɔːmd] ADJ formé

-former [ˈfɔːmə(r)] SUFF *Br* élève *mf* de; **first-f.** élève *mf* de sixième

former [ˈfɔːmə(r)] ADJ **1** (*time*) passé; **in f. times** *or* **days** autrefois, dans le passé **2** (*earlier, previous*) ancien, précédent; **my f. boss** mon ancien patron; **I'm a f. student of his** je suis un de ses anciens élèves; **my f. wife** mon ex-femme; **in a f. life** dans une vie antérieure; **he's only a shadow of his f. self** il n'est plus que l'ombre de lui-même; **the f. Yugoslavia** l'ex-Yougoslavie *f* **3** (*first*) premier; **I prefer the f. idea to the latter** je préfère la première idée à la dernière

N **1** (*first*) premier(ère) *m,f*, celui-là *m*, celle-là *f*; **of the two methods I prefer the f.** des deux méthodes je préfère la première **2** *Tech* gabarit *m*

formerly [ˈfɔːməlɪ] ADV autrefois, jadis; **Mr Martin, f. a Liberal** M. Martin, autrefois libéral; **Mrs McBride, f. Miss Kane** Madame McBride, auparavant Mademoiselle Kane; **f. of London** résidant auparavant à Londres; **Burkina Faso, f. Upper Volta** le Burkina Faso, ancienne Haute-Volta

formic [ˈfɔːmɪk] ADJ *Chem* formique

▸▸ ***formic acid*** acide *m* formique

Formica® [fɔːˈmaɪkə] N Formica® *m*, plastique *m* laminé

COMP (*worktop, surface*) en Formica®, en plastique laminé

formidable [ˈfɔːmɪdəbəl] ADJ **1** (*inspiring fear*) redoutable, terrible; (*inspiring respect*) remarquable; **she's a f. athlete** c'est une athlète remarquable; **a f. intellect** un esprit brillant **2** (*difficult*) ardu; **a f. problem** un problème difficile

> Note that the most common meaning of the French word **formidable** is **fantastic, excellent**.

formidably [ˈfɔːmɪdəblɪ] ADV (*armed, difficult*) redoutablement; (*talented, thorough*) formidablement, remarquablement

forming [ˈfɔːmɪŋ] N **1** (*of company etc*) création *f*, fondation *f* **2** *Metal* formage *m*, façonnage *m*

formless [ˈfɔːmlɪs] ADJ (*shape*) informe; (*idea*) vague

Formosa [fɔːˈməʊsə] N *Formerly* Formose *m*

formula [ˈfɔːmjʊlə] (*pl sense* **1 formulas** *or* **formulae** [-liː], *pl senses* **2–4 formulas**) N **1** (*gen*) & *Chem & Math* formule *f*; **a f. for happiness** une recette qui assure le bonheur; **these romantic novels are all written to the same f.** ces romans à l'eau de rose sont tous écrits selon la même formule

2 (*expression*) formule *f*

3 *Aut* formule *f*

4 *Am* (*for baby*) bouillie *f* (*pour bébé*)

▸▸ ***Formula 1*** (*racing*) la formule 1; ***Formula 1 car*** voiture *f* de formule 1

formulaic [ˌfɔːmjʊˈleɪɪk] ADJ *Pej* (*plot*) stéréotypé; **f. expression** expression *f* toute faite

formulate [ˈfɔːmjʊleɪt] VT **1** (*express*) formuler; **difficult to f. in words** difficile à formuler (en paroles) **2** (*plan, policy*) élaborer

formulation [ˌfɔːmjʊˈleɪʃən] N **1** (*of idea*) formulation *f*, expression *f* **2** (*of plan, policy*) élaboration *f*

formwork [ˈfɔːmwɜːk] N *Constr* (*for reinforced concrete*) coffrage *m*

fornicate [ˈfɔːnɪkeɪt] VI *Formal* forniquer

fornication [ˌfɔːnɪˈkeɪʃən] N *Formal* fornication *f*

fornicator [ˈfɔːnɪkeɪtə(r)] N *Formal* (*man*) fornicateur *m*, coureur *m* de jupons; (*woman*) coureuse *f*

forsake [fəˈseɪk] (*pt* **forsook** [-ˈsʊk], *pp* **forsaken** [-ˈseɪkən]) VT *Formal* **1** (*abandon* ▸ *family, spouse*) abandonner; (▸ *friend*) délaisser; (▸ *place*) quitter; **her customary patience forsook her** sa patience habituelle lui fit défaut **2** (*give up*) renoncer à; **to f. one's religion** faire acte d'apostasie

forsooth [fəˈsuːθ] *Arch* ADV à vrai dire, en vérité

EXCLAM ma foi!, par exemple!

forswear [fɔːˈsweə(r)] (*pt* **forswore** [-ˈswɔː(r)], *pp* **forsworn** [-ˈswɔːn]) VT *Formal* **1** (*renounce*) abjurer **2** (*deny*) désavouer; **to f. oneself** se parjurer

forsythia [fɔːˈsaɪθɪə] N *Bot* forsythia *m*

fort [fɔːt] N fort *m*; (*smaller*) fortin *m*; *Fam Br* **to hold the f.**, *Am* **to hold down the f.** (*look after house*) garder la maison□; (*look after office, shop*) tenir la boutique□

▸▸ ***Fort Knox*** = fort militaire dans le Kentucky contenant les réserves d'or des États-Unis; *Fig Hum* **it's like F. Knox here** c'est une vraie forteresse ici

forte[1] [ˈfɔːteɪ] N (*strong point*) fort *m*; **patience is hardly his f.** la patience n'est pas vraiment son (point) fort

forte[2] [ˈfɔːtɪ] *Mus* ADJ forte

ADV forte

N forte *m*

forth [fɔːθ] ADV **1** *Literary* (*out, forward*) en avant; **to go** *or* **to set f.** se mettre en route; **to bring f.** produire; **to send f.** envoyer; **the ferry goes back and f. between…** le ferry fait la navette entre…; **to walk back and f.** marcher de long en large, faire les cent pas **2** *Literary* (*forwards in time*) **from this moment f.** dorénavant, désormais; **from this day f.** à partir d'aujourd'hui *ou* de ce jour **3** (**and so on**) **and so f.** (*etcetera*) et ainsi de suite, et cetera

forthcoming [ˌfɔːθˈkʌmɪŋ] ADJ **1** (*imminent* ▸ *event*) à venir; (▸ *book*) à paraître; (▸ *film*) qui va sortir prochainement; **the f. elections** les prochaines élections *fpl*; **f. attractions** (*film, theatre advertisement*) prochainement **2** (*made available*) **no answer was f.** il n'y a eu aucune réponse; **no information/support was f.** on ne nous a fourni aucune information/apporté aucun soutien; **the funds were not f.** les fonds n'ont pas été débloqués **3** (*verbally*) **he wasn't very f.** il n'a pas été très bavard

forthright [ˈfɔːθraɪt] ADJ (*person, remark*) franc (franche), direct; **he's a f. critic of the government** il critique le gouvernement ouvertement

forthrightness [ˈfɔːθraɪtnɪs] N franchise *f* (**about** au sujet de)

forthwith [ˌfɔːθˈwɪθ] ADV *Formal* sur-le-champ

fortieth [ˈfɔːtɪɪθ] N **1** (*fraction*) quarantième *m* **2** (*in series*) quarantième *mf*

ADJ quarantième; *see also* **fifth**

fortification [ˌfɔːtɪfɪˈkeɪʃən] N fortification *f*

fortified [ˈfɔːtɪfaɪd] ADJ fortifié

▸▸ *Br* ***fortified wine*** vin *m* de liqueur, vin *m* doux naturel

fortify [ˈfɔːtɪfaɪ] (*pt & pp* **fortified**) VT **1** (*place*) fortifier, armer; *Fig* (*person*) réconforter, remonter; **to f. oneself for the coming struggle** rassembler ses forces pour la lutte à venir; **have a drink to f. yourself** prenez un verre pour vous remonter **2** (*wine*) augmenter la teneur en alcool, alcooliser; (*food*) renforcer en vitamines

fortifying [ˈfɔːtɪfaɪɪŋ] ADJ fortifiant; (*drink etc*) remontant

fortissimo [fɔːˈtɪsɪməʊ] (*pl* **fortissimos** *or* **fortissimi** [-miː]) *Mus* N fortissimo *m*

ADJ fortissimo

ADV fortissimo

fortitude [ˈfɔːtɪtjuːd] N courage *m*, force *f* morale

fortnight [ˈfɔːtnaɪt] N *Br* quinzaine *f*, quinze jours *mpl*; **for a f.** pour quinze jours; **a f. ago** il y a quinze jours; **a f. tomorrow** demain en quinze; **a f.'s holiday** quinze jours de vacances; **it's been postponed for a f.** cela a été remis à quinzaine

fortnightly [ˈfɔːtnaɪtlɪ] (*pl* **fortnightlies**) *Br* N bimensuel *m*

ADJ bimensuel

ADV tous les quinze jours

Fortran, FORTRAN [ˈfɔːtræn] N *Comput* fortran *m*

fortress [ˈfɔːtrɪs] N (*fort*) fort *m*; (*prison*) forteresse *f*; (*castle*) château *m* fort; (*place, town*) place *f* forte

▸▸ ***fortress city*** cité *f* fortifiée; ***Fortress Europe*** forteresse *f* Europe

fortuitous [fɔːˈtjuːɪtəs] ADJ fortuit, imprévu

fortuitously [fɔːˈtjuːɪtəslɪ] ADV fortuitement, par hasard

fortunate [ˈfɔːtʃənət] ADJ (*person*) heureux, chanceux; (*choice, meeting*) heureux, propice; **you are f.** vous avez de la chance; **I was f. enough to get the job** j'ai eu la chance d'obtenir le travail; **how f.!** quelle chance!; **the less f. among them** les plus infortunés d'entre eux; **we should help those less f. than ourselves** nous devons aider ceux qui n'ont pas eu notre chance

> Note that the French adjective **fortuné** is a false friend. It means **wealthy**.

fortunately [ˈfɔːtʃənətlɪ] ADV heureusement, par bonheur

fortune [ˈfɔːtʃuːn] N **1** (*wealth*) fortune *f*; **he came to London to make his f.** il est venu à Londres pour faire fortune; **she makes a f.** elle gagne beaucoup d'argent *ou* un argent fou; **he made a f. on the house** il a gagné beaucoup d'argent en vendant la maison; **to come into a f.** hériter d'une fortune, faire un gros héritage; **a man of f.** un homme fortuné; **her jewels are worth a f.** ses bijoux valent une fortune; **to cost/to pay/to spend a (small) f.** coûter/payer/dépenser une (petite) fortune; **her face is her f.** son visage est son grand atout

2 (*future*) destin *m*; **to tell sb's f.** dire la bonne aventure à qn; **she tells fortunes** elle dit la bonne aventure

3 (*chance, fate*) sort *m*, fortune *f*; **f. smiled upon**

him *or* **has been kind to him** la chance lui a souri; **the novel traces its hero's changing fortunes** le roman retrace les tribulations de son héros; **the fortunes of war** les hasards *mpl* de la guerre
4 *(luck)* fortune *f*, chance *f*; **piece of good f.** coup *m* de chance, bonheur *m*; **ill f.** malchance *f*, mauvais sort *m*; **he had the good f. to win** il a eu la chance de gagner; **by good f.** par chance, par bonheur
►► ***fortune cookie*** = biscuit chinois dans lequel est caché un horoscope

fortune-hunter **N** *Pej (man)* coureur *m* de dot; *(woman)* aventurière *f*, femme *f* intéressée

fortune-teller **N** *(gen)* diseur(euse) *m,f* de bonne aventure; *(with cards)* tireur(euse) *m,f* de cartes, cartomancien(enne) *m,f*

fortune-telling **N** *(gen)* = fait de dire la bonne aventure; *(with cards)* cartomancie *f*

forty [ˈfɔːtɪ] *(pl* **forties***)* **N** quarante *m inv*
PRON quarante; **about f.** une quarantaine
ADJ quarante; *Fam* **to have f. winks** faire un petit somme; *see also* **fifty**

forty-five **N 1** *(record)* quarante-cinq tours *m* **2** *Am (pistol)* quarante-cinq *m*

fortyish [ˈfɔːtɪɪʃ] **ADJ** d'une quarantaine d'années; **I'd say she was f.** je lui donne la quarantaine *ou* une quarantaine d'années; **he was balding, f. and plump** il perdait ses cheveux et avait la quarantaine rondouillarde

forum [ˈfɔːrəm] *(pl* **forums** *or* **fora** [-rə]*)* **N 1** *(gen) & Fig* forum *m*, tribune *f*; *Hist* forum *m*; **a f. in which workers can put forward their views** un forum permettant aux ouvriers d'exprimer leurs opinions **2** *Comput (on Internet)* forum *m* (de discussion)

forward [ˈfɔːwəd] **ADJ 1** *(towards front ► movement)* en avant, vers l'avant; *(► position)* avant; **the seat is too far f.** le siège est trop avancé *ou* en avant
2 *(advanced)* **the project is no further f.** le projet n'a pas avancé
3 *(brash)* effronté, impertinent
4 *Fin & Com* à terme
ADV 1 *(in space)* en avant; *Naut* à l'avant; **to move f.** avancer; **keep going straight f.** continuez tout droit; **he reached f.** il a tendu le bras en avant; *Fig* **three witnesses came f.** trois témoins se sont présentés; *Mil* **f., march!** en avant, marche!; **clocks go f. one hour at midnight** il faut avancer les pendules d'une heure à minuit **2** *Formal (in time)* **from this moment f.** à partir de maintenant; **from this day f.** désormais, dorénavant **3** *Acct* **to carry the balance f.** reporter le solde à nouveau; **(carried) f.** report
VT 1 *(send on)* faire suivre; *Com* expédier, envoyer; **to f. sth to sb** faire parvenir qch à qn; **we'll f. your report to the relevant department** nous transmettrons votre rapport au service correspondant; **I've arranged to have my mail forwarded** j'ai fait le nécessaire pour qu'on fasse suivre mon courrier; **please f.** *(on envelope)* faire suivre SVP, prière de faire suivre **2** *(advance, promote)* avancer, favoriser
N avant *m*
►► *Fin* ***forward account*** compte *m* à terme; *Fin* ***forward buying*** achat *m* à terme; *Fin* ***forward contract*** contrat *m* à terme; *Fin & Com* ***forward dealing*** opérations *fpl* à terme; *Com* ***forward delivery*** livraison *f* à terme; *Fin* ***forward exchange market*** marché *m* des changes à terme; *Aut* ***forward gears*** marches *fpl* avant; *Econ* ***forward integration*** intégration *f* en aval, intégration *f* descendante; *Sport* ***forward line*** ligne *f* des avants; *Fin & Com* ***forward market*** marché *m* à terme; *Sport* ***forward pass*** *(in rugby)* passe *f* en avant; ***forward planning*** planification *f* à long terme; *Fin & Com* ***forward price*** prix *m* à terme; *Fin & Com* ***forward purchase*** achat *m* à terme; *Fin* ***forward rate*** cours *m* à terme, taux *m* pour les opérations à terme; *Gym* ***forward roll*** cabriole *f*, culbute *f*; *Com & St Exch* ***forward sale*** vente *f* à terme; *Comput* ***forward search*** recherche *f* avant; *Br Comput* ***forward slash*** barre *f* oblique; *Fin & Com* ***forward trading*** opérations *fpl* à terme

forwardation [ˌfɔːwəˈdeɪʃən] **N** *Fin* report *m*

forwarder [ˈfɔːwədə(r)] **N** *Com* transitaire *m*; **f. and consolidator** transitaire-groupeur *m*

forwarding [ˈfɔːwədɪŋ] **N 1** *(sending)* expédition *f*, envoi *m* **2** *Typ* collage *m* et endossage *m*
►► ***forwarding address*** adresse *f* pour faire suivre le courrier; *Com* adresse *f* pour l'expédition; **he left no f. address** il est parti sans laisser d'adresse; *Com* ***forwarding agent*** transitaire *m*; *Com* ***forwarding charges*** frais *mpl* d'expédition; *Com* ***forwarding office*** bureau *m* d'expédition

forward-looking **ADJ** *(person)* tourné vers *ou* ouvert sur l'avenir; *(plans)* tourné vers l'avenir *ou* le progrès; *(company, policy)* qui va de l'avant, dynamique, entreprenant

forwardness [ˈfɔːwədnɪs] **N 1** *(presumption)* effronterie *f*, impertinence *f*; *(eagerness)* empressement *m* **2** *Br (of child, season)* précocité *f*; *(of project)* état *m* avancé

forwards [ˈfɔːwədz] = **forward** *adv* 1, 2

forwent [fɔːˈwent] *pt of* **forgo**

Fosbury flop [ˈfɒzbərɪ-] **N** *Sport* fosbury-flop *m*

fossil [ˈfɒsəl] **N** fossile *m*; *Fam Pej* **an old f.** *(person)* une vieille croûte, un vieux fossile
ADJ fossilisé
►► ***fossil fuel*** combustible *m* fossile; ***fossil man*** l'homme *m* fossile

fossilization, -isation [ˌfɒsɪlaɪˈzeɪʃən] **N** fossilisation *f*

fossilize, -ise [ˈfɒsɪlaɪz] **VT** fossiliser
VI se fossiliser

fossilized, -ised [ˈfɒsɪlaɪzd] **ADJ** fossilisé; *Ling & Fig* figé

foster [ˈfɒstə(r)] **VT 1** *Br Law (of family, person)* accueillir; *(of authorities, court)* placer; **the children were fostered (out) at an early age** les enfants ont été placés dans une famille tout jeunes **2** *(idea, hope)* nourrir, entretenir **3** *(promote)* favoriser, encourager
►► ***foster brother*** frère *m* adoptif; ***foster child*** enfant *m* placé dans une famille d'accueil; ***foster father*** père *m* de la famille d'accueil; ***foster home*** famille *f* d'accueil; ***foster mother*** mère *f* de la famille d'accueil; ***foster parents*** famille *f* d'accueil; ***foster sister*** sœur *f* adoptive

fostering [ˈfɒstərɪŋ] **N 1** *(of child)* prise *f* en famille d'accueil; *(fostering out)* mise *f* en famille d'accueil **2** *(of the arts etc)* patronage *m*, encouragement *m*

fought [fɔːt] *pt & pp of* **fight**

foul [faʊl] **ADJ 1** *(food, taste)* infect; *(smell)* infect, fétide; *(breath)* fétide; **to smell f.** puer; **to taste f.** avoir un goût infect
2 *(filthy ► linen)* sale, souillé; *(► place)* immonde, crasseux; *(► air)* vicié, pollué; *(► water)* croupi
3 *Fam (horrible ► weather)* pourri; *(► person)* infect, ignoble[□]; **I've had a f. day** j'ai eu une sale journée; **she's in a f. mood** elle est d'une humeur massacrante; **he has a f. temper** il a un sale caractère *ou* un caractère de chien; **f. weather** *(gen)* sale temps *m*, temps *m* de chien; *Naut* gros temps *m*; **he's being really f. to me** il est absolument odieux[□] *ou* ignoble[□] avec moi
4 *(language)* grossier, ordurier; **he has a f. mouth** il est très grossier
5 *Literary (vile)* vil, infâme; *(unfair)* déloyal; **f. deed** infamie *f*; **murder most f.** horrible assassinat *m*
6 *(clogged)* obstrué, encrassé
7 *(idioms)* **to fall** *or* **to run f. of sb** se brouiller avec qn; **he fell f. of the boss** il s'est mis le patron à dos; **they fell f. of the law** ils ont eu des démêlés avec la justice; **to fall f. of a reef/ship** entrer en collision avec un récif/un navire
N *Sport (in boxing)* coup *m* bas; *(in football, baseball etc)* faute *f*
VT 1 *(dirty)* salir; *(air, water)* polluer, infecter; *(of dog)* salir; *(spark plugs)* encrasser; *Br* **it is an offence to allow a dog to f. the pavement** il est contraire à la loi de laisser son chien souiller le trottoir; *Fig* **to f. one's own nest** se nuire à soi-même
2 *(clog)* obstruer, encrasser; *(entangle)* embrouiller, emmêler; *(nets)* se prendre dans; **to f. pipes** engorger *ou* obstruer des canalisations
3 *(collide with)* entrer en collision avec
4 *Sport* commettre une faute contre
5 *Fig (reputation)* salir
VI 1 *(tangle)* s'emmêler, s'embrouiller **2** *Sport* commettre une faute
►► *Sport* ***foul ball*** *(in baseball)* sortie *f*; *Sport* ***foul line*** *(in baseball)* ligne *f* de jeu; *(in basketball)* ligne *f* de lancer franc; *(in bowling)* ligne *f* de faute; *Sport* ***foul play*** jeu *m* irrégulier *ou* déloyal *(in cards, games)* tricherie *f*; *Fig* **the police suspect f. play** la police croit qu'il y a eu meurtre *ou* croit au meurtre

►**foul up** **VI 1** *Fam (person)* merder; **don't f. up again/this time!** tâche de ne plus merder/ne pas merder cette fois! **2** *(gun barrel etc)* s'encrasser; *(pump)* s'engorger
VT SEP 1 *(contaminate)* polluer; *(clog)* obstruer, encrasser **2** *Fam (bungle)* ficher en l'air, flanquer par terre

fouler [ˈfaʊlə(r)] **N** *Sport* **he's a persistent f.** il commet des fautes sans arrêt

fouling [ˈfaʊlɪŋ] **N 1** *(of pipes)* engorgement *m* *(of spark plugs)* encrassement *m* **2** *Sport* **a lot of f.** beaucoup de jeu déloyal

foully [ˈfaʊlɪ] **ADV 1** *(speak)* grossièrement **2** *Literary (behave)* bassement, ignoblement; **he was f. murdered** il fut ignoblement assassiné

foul-mouthed **ADJ** grossier

foulness [ˈfaʊlnɪs] **N 1** *(dirtiness)* saleté *f*; *(of air)* fétidité *f*; **the f. of the smell** l'odeur *f* infecte, la puanteur **2** *(of language etc)* grossièreté *f*, obscénité *f* **3** *(of act, behaviour)* infamie *f*, ignominie *f*

foul-tempered **ADJ** **to be f.** avoir un sale caractère

foul-up **N** *Fam (mix-up)* cafouillage *m*; *(mechanical difficulty)* problème *m* *ou* difficulté *f* mécanique[□]; **there's been a f.** quelque chose a cloché *ou* cafouillé, il y a eu un cafouillage

found [faʊnd] *pt & pp of* **find**
ADJ *Br Old-fashioned* **£30 a week all f.** 30 livres la semaine tout compris
VT 1 *(establish ► organization, town)* fonder, créer; *(► business)* fonder, établir **2** *(base)* fonder, baser; **to be founded on** *(principle, belief, theory, suspicions)* être fondé *ou* basé sur; **founded on fact** *(of story, novel, film)* qui est basé sur des faits véridiques **3** *(cast)* fondre
►► *Art* ***found object*** objet *m* trouvé

foundation [faʊnˈdeɪʃən] **N 1** *(of business, town)* fondation *f*, création *f*
2 *(institution)* fondation *f*, institution *f* dotée; *(endowment)* dotation *f*, fondation *f*; **a charitable f.** une institution charitable
3 *(basis)* base *f*, fondement *m*; **the f.** *or* **foundations of our society** les fondements *mpl* de notre société; **his work laid the f.** *or* **foundations of modern science** son œuvre a jeté les bases de la science moderne; **the rumour is entirely without f.** la rumeur est dénuée de tout fondement
4 *(make-up)* fond *m* de teint
5 *Am (of building)* fondations *fpl*
• **foundations** **NPL** *Constr* fondations *fpl*; **to lay the foundations** poser les fondations
►► *Br* ***foundation course*** cours *m* introductif; ***foundation cream*** fond *m* de teint; *Old-fashioned* ***foundation garment*** *(girdle)* gaine *f*, combiné *m*; *(bra)* soutien-gorge *m*; *Br* ***foundation hospital*** = hôpital faisant partie du système de sécurité sociale britannique, mais géré par une équipe privée; ***foundation scholar*** élève *mf* boursier (ère); *Br* ***foundation school*** école *f* privée subventionnée *(acceptant en échange un droit de regard de l'État sur la gestion de ses affaires)*; *Constr* ***foundation stone*** pierre *f* commémorative; **to lay the f. stone** poser la première pierre

founder [ˈfaʊndə(r)] **N** fondateur(trice) *m,f*
VI 1 *(ship)* sombrer; **to f. on the rocks** s'échouer sur les rochers **2** *Fig (fail)* s'effondrer, s'écrouler; **the project foundered for lack of financial support** le projet s'est effondré faute de soutien financier **3** *(horse ► in mud)* s'embourber; *(► go lame)* se mettre à boiter
►► *Br* ***founder member*** membre *m* fondateur; ***founder's share*** part *f* bénéficiaire *ou* de fondateur

foundering [ˈfaʊndərɪŋ] **N** *(of hopes)* effondrement *m*

founding [ˈfaʊndɪŋ] **N 1** *(of business, organization, town)* fondation *f*, création *f* **2** *Metal* fonderie *f*, moulage *m*
ADJ fondateur
►► ***founding father*** père *m* fondateur; **one of the**

f. fathers of the Society l'un des pères fondateurs de la société; *Hist* ***the Founding Fathers*** les pères *mpl* fondateurs *(aux États-Unis)*

foundling ['faʊndlɪŋ] **N** *Formal* enfant *mf* trouvé(e); **f. hospital** hospice *m* pour enfants trouvés

foundry ['faʊndrɪ] *(pl* **foundries)** **N** *(place)* fonderie *f*; *(of articles)* fonderie *f*, fonte *f*; *(articles)* fonte *f*

fount [faʊnt] **N 1** *Br Typ* fonte *f* **2** *Literary (spring)* source *f*; **a f. of knowledge** un puits de science

fountain ['faʊntɪn] **N 1** *(natural)* fontaine *f*, source *f*; *(man-made)* fontaine *f*, jet *m* d'eau **2** *Fig* source *f*; **the f. of youth** la fontaine de jouvence

►► ***fountain pen*** stylo *m* à encre

fountainhead ['faʊntɪnhed] **N 1** *(spring)* source *f* **2** *Fig (source)* source *f*, origine *f*

four [fɔː(r)] **N 1** *(number, numeral)* quatre *m inv*; **on all fours** à quatre pattes; **to get** *or* **to go down on all fours** se mettre à quatre pattes **2** *(in rowing)* quatre *m*

PRON quatre

ADJ quatre; **the f. corners of the earth** les quatre coins du monde; **open to the f. winds** ouvert à tous les vents *ou* aux quatre vents; *see also* **five**

►► *Cards* ***four flush*** flush *m* de quatre cartes; *Am* ***the four hundred*** l'élite *f* sociale

four-colour, *Am* **four-color** **ADJ** *Typ* quadrichrome

►► ***four-colour printing*** impression *f* en quadrichromie; ***four-colour (printing) process*** quadrichromie *f*

four-cornered **ADJ** à quatre coins; *(quadrangular)* quadrangulaire

four-cycle **ADJ** *Am (engine, cylinder)* à quatre temps

four-door **ADJ** à quatre portes

four-engined **ADJ** à quatre moteurs

four-eyes **N** *Fam* binoclard(e) *m,f*

four-figure **ADJ** *Math (number, sum)* à quatre chiffres; *(logarithm)* à quatre décimales

fourfold ['fɔːfəʊld] **ADJ** quadruple

ADV au quadruple; **to increase f.** quadrupler

four-footed **ADJ** *(animal)* quadrupède, à quatre pattes; *Fam* **a f. friend** un ami à quatre pattes

four-handed **ADJ** *Cards & Mus* à quatre mains

four-in-hand **N** *(carriage)* attelage *m* à quatre

four-leaf clover, four-leaved clover **N** *Bot* trèfle *m* à quatre feuilles

four-legged [-'legɪd] **ADJ** quadrupède, à quatre pattes; *Hum* **our f. friends** nos compagnons à quatre pattes

four-letter word **N** gros mot *m*, obscénité *f*

four-part **ADJ** *Mus* à quatre parties; *(singing)* à quatre voix

four-phase **ADJ** *Elec (system)* tétraphasé

four-poster (bed) **N** lit *m* à baldaquin *ou* à colonnes

fourscore [,fɔː'skɔː(r)] *Arch* **ADJ** quatre-vingts; **f. years and ten** quatre-vingt-dix ans

N quatre-vingts *m inv*

four-seasons **ADJ** *(pizza)* quatre-saisons *(inv)*

four-seater **N** *Aut* voiture *f* à quatre places

foursome ['fɔːsəm] **N 1** *(people)* groupe *m* de quatre personnes; *(two couples)* deux couples *mpl*; **we went as a f.** nous y sommes allés à quatre **2** *(game)* partie *f* à quatre; **will you make up a f. for bridge?** voulez-vous faire le quatrième au bridge?

four-speed **ADJ** *Aut* à quatre vitesses

foursquare [,fɔː'skweə(r)] **ADJ 1** *(square)* carré **2** *(position, style)* solide; *(approach, decision)* ferme, inébranlable **3** *(forthright)* franc (franche)

ADV *(solidly)* fermement

four-star **ADJ** à quatre étoiles

►► *Mil* ***four-star general*** général *m* d'armée; ***four-star hotel*** hôtel *m* quatre étoiles *ou* de première catégorie; *Br* ***four-star petrol*** super *m*, supercarburant *m*

four-stroke *Aut* **N** moteur *m* à quatre temps

ADJ à quatre temps

fourteen [,fɔː'tiːn] **N** quatorze *m inv*

PRON quatorze

ADJ quatorze; *see also* **five**

fourteenth [,fɔː'tiːnθ] **N 1** *(fraction)* quatorzième *m* **2** *(in series)* quatorzième *mf* **3** *(of month)* quatorze *m inv*; **the F. of July** le quatorze juillet *(fête nationale française)*

ADJ quatorzième; *see also* **fifth**

►► ***the Fourteenth Amendment*** = amendement à la constitution américaine reconnaissant les anciens esclaves noirs comme citoyens à part entière

fourth [fɔːθ] **N 1** *(fraction)* quart *m*

2 *(in series)* quatrième *mf*

3 *(of month)* quatre *m inv*; **the F. of July** le quatre juillet *(fête nationale de l'Indépendance aux États-Unis)*

4 *Mus* quarte *f*

5 *Aut* quatrième *f*

6 *Cards* **to make a f.** faire le quatrième

ADJ quatrième

ADV quatrièmement; *(in contest)* en quatrième position, à la quatrième place; *see also* **fifth**

►► ***the fourth dimension*** la quatrième dimension; ***the fourth estate*** le quatrième pouvoir, la presse; ***fourth finger*** annulaire *m*; *Aut* ***fourth gear*** quatrième vitesse *f*; *Am Sch* ***fourth grade*** = classe d'école primaire pour les 8 à 9 ans; ***fourth quarter*** *(of financial year)* quatrième trimestre *m*; ***the Fourth World*** le quart-monde

fourthly ['fɔːθlɪ] **ADV** quatrièmement, en quatrième lieu

four-wheel **VI** *Am* faire du quatre-quatre

►► *Aut* ***four-wheel drive*** *(system)* propulsion *f* à quatre roues motrices; *(car)* quatre-quatre *m inv*; **with f. drive** à quatre roues motrices; ***four-wheel steering*** quatre roues *fpl* directrices

four-wheeled **ADJ** à quatre roues

four-wheeler **N** véhicule *m* à quatre roues

fowl [faʊl] *(pl* **inv** *or* **fowls)** **N 1** *(for eating* ► *collectively)* volaille *f*; *(*► *one bird)* volaille *f*, volatile *m* **2** *Arch or Literary (bird)* oiseau *m*; **all the fowls of the air** tous les oiseaux

VI chasser le gibier à plumes

►► ***fowl pest*** peste *f* aviaire

fowling ['faʊlɪŋ] **N to go f.** aller à la chasse au gibier à plumes

►► ***fowling piece*** carabine *f*, fusil *m* de chasse léger

fox [fɒks] *(pl* **inv** *or* **foxes)** **N 1** *(animal, fur)* renard *m*; *Fig* **he's a sly old f.** c'est un vieux renard; **as sly as a f.** rusé comme un renard **2** *Am Fam (woman)* jolie pépée *f*

VT 1 *(outwit)* duper, berner **2** *Fam (baffle)* désarçonner; **you've got me foxed** je suis perplexe ▫ **3** *(paper)* marquer *ou* tacher de rousseurs

►► ***fox brush*** queue *f* de renard; ***fox cub*** renardeau *m*; ***fox fur*** (peau *f* de) renard *m*; ***fox terrier*** fox *m inv*, fox-terrier *m*

foxglove ['fɒksglʌv] **N** *Bot* digitale *f* (pourprée)

foxhole ['fɒkshəʊl] **N 1** *(of fox)* terrier *m* de renard, renardière *f* **2** *Mil* gourbi *m*

foxhound ['fɒkshaʊnd] **N** fox-hound *m*, chien *m* courant

foxhunt ['fɒkshʌnt] **N** chasse *f* au renard

foxhunting ['fɒkshʌntɪŋ] **N** chasse *f* au renard; **to go f.** aller chasser le renard *ou* à la chasse au renard

foxiness ['fɒksɪnɪs] **N 1** *(craftiness)* ruse *f* **2** *Am Fam (of woman)* air *m* sexy

foxtail ['fɒksteɪl] **N** *Bot (grass)* vulpin *m*; *(flower)* queue-de-renard *f*

foxtrot ['fɒkstrɒt] *(pt & pp* **foxtrotted**, *cont* **foxtrotting)** **N** fox-trot *m inv*

VI danser le fox-trot

foxy ['fɒksɪ] *(compar* **foxier**, *superl* **foxiest)** **ADJ 1** *(wily)* rusé, malin(igne)

2 *(colour)* roux (rousse)

3 *(paper)* marqué *ou* taché de rousseurs

4 *Am Fam (sexy)* sexy *(inv)*; **a f. lady** une nana sexy

foyer ['fɔɪeɪ] **N 1** *(of cinema, hotel)* hall *m*, vestibule *m*; *(of theatre)* foyer *m* **2** *Am (of house)* entrée *f*, vestibule *m*

FPA [,efpiː'eɪ] **N** *Br (abbr* **Family Planning Association)** = association pour le planning familial

FPU [,efpiː'juː] **N** *Comput (abbr* **floating-point unit)** FPU *f*, coprocesseur *m* arithmétique

Fr **1** *Rel (written abbr* **Father)** P **2** *(written abbr* **France)** France *f* **3** *Fin (written abbr* **franc)** F *m inv*

FRA ['efɑː'reɪ] **N** *Fin (abbr* **Future Rate Agreement, Forward Rate Agreement)** ATF *m*

fracas [*Br* 'frækɑː, *Am* 'freɪkæs] *(Br pl* **inv** [-kɑːz], *Am pl* **fracases** [-kəsɪz]) **N** *(brawl)* rixe *f*, bagarre *f*; *(noise)* fracas *m*

fractal ['fræktəl] **N** *Geom* fractale *f*

fraction ['frækʃən] **N 1** *Math* fraction *f*

2 *Fig (bit)* fraction *f*, petite partie *f*; **at a f. of the cost** pour une fraction du prix; **for a f. of a second** pendant une fraction de seconde; **he escaped death by a f. of a second** il a été à deux doigts de la mort; **move back just a f.** reculez un tout petit peu

3 *Fin (of share)* fraction *f*, rompu *m*

4 *Chem (of distillation)* fraction *f*

5 *Pol (of communist party)* fraction *f*, groupe *m* fractionnaire

fractional ['frækʃənəl] **ADJ 1** *Math* fractionnaire **2** *Fig (tiny)* tout petit, infime; **f. part** fraction *f*; **a f. difference** une différence minime

►► *Fin* ***fractional currency*** monnaie *f* divisionnaire; *Chem* ***fractional distillation*** distillation *f* fractionnée

fractionally ['frækʃənəlɪ] **ADV 1** *(slightly)* un tout petit peu **2** *Chem* par fractionnement

fractionate ['frækʃəneɪt] **VT** *Chem & Ind (petroleum etc)* fractionner

fractionize, -ise ['frækʃənaɪz] **VT** *Math* fractionner

fractious ['frækʃəs] **ADJ 1** *(unruly)* indiscipliné, turbulent **2** *(irritable* ► *child)* grognon, pleurnicheur; *(*► *adult)* irascible, revêche, irritable; **to be f.** *or* **in a f. mood** être de mauvaise humeur; *(baby)* pleurnicher

fractiousness ['frækʃəsnɪs] **N 1** *(unruliness)* indiscipline *f* **2** *(irritableness)* irritabilité *f*; *(of baby)* caractère *m* grognon

fracture ['fræktʃə(r)] **N** fracture *f*

VT *(break)* fracturer; **he fractured his arm** il s'est fracturé le bras; **fractured skull** crâne *m* fracturé; **fractured ribs** côtes *fpl* cassées; *Fig* **their withdrawal fractured the alliance** leur retrait brisa l'alliance

VI *(break)* se fracturer

fragile [*Br* 'frædʒaɪl, *Am* 'frædʒəl] **ADJ 1** *(china, glass)* fragile; *Fig (peace, happiness)* précaire, fragile; **a f. relationship** des relations *fpl* fragiles *ou* précaires; **f.: handle with care** *(on package)* fragile: manipuler avec précaution **2** *(person* ► *physically)* fragile, frêle; *(*► *emotionally)* fragile; *Hum* **I'm feeling a bit f. this morning** je ne suis pas dans mon assiette ce matin

fragilely ['frædʒaɪllɪ] **ADV** fragilement

fragility [frə'dʒɪlətɪ] **N** fragilité *f*

fragment **N** ['frægmənt] *(of china, text)* fragment *m*, morceau *m*; *(of bomb)* éclat *m*; *Fig (of conversation)* bribe *f*; **the window shattered into fragments** la fenêtre a volé en éclats; **the report contains not a f. of truth** le rapport ne contient pas un atome *ou* une once de vérité

VT [fræg'ment] *(break)* fragmenter, briser; *(divide)* fragmenter, morceler

VI [fræg'ment] se fragmenter

fragmentary ['frægməntərɪ] **ADJ** fragmentaire

fragmentation [,frægmen'teɪʃən] **N** *(breaking)* fragmentation *f*; *(division)* fragmentation *f*, morcellement *m*; *Comput (of hard disk)* fragmentation *f*

►► ***fragmentation bomb*** bombe *f* à fragmentation; ***fragmentation grenade*** grenade *f* offensive

fragrance ['freɪgrəns] **N** parfum *m*

fragrant ['freɪgrənt] **ADJ** parfumé; **to be** *or* **smell f.** sentir bon; **f. pine woods** des pinèdes *fpl* odorantes

fraidy cat ['freɪdɪ-] **N** *Am Fam* poule *f* mouillée

frail [freɪl] **ADJ 1** *(object)* fragile; *(person)* fragile, frêle; *(health)* délicat, fragile; **she's rather f.** elle a une petite santé **2** *(happiness, hope)* fragile, éphémère

frailness ['freɪlnɪs] N **1** *(of object, person)* fragilité *f*; **the f. of his health** sa santé délicate **2** *(of happiness, hope)* fragilité *f*

frailty ['freɪltɪ] *(pl* **frailties***)* N *(of health, hope, person)* fragilité *f*; *(of character)* faiblesse *f*; **human f.** la faiblesse des hommes

frame [freɪm] N **1** *(border ► gen)* cadre *m*; *(► of canvas, picture etc)* cadre *m*, encadrement *m*; *(► of window)* cadre *m*, châssis *m*; *(► of door)* encadrement *m*; *(► for spectacles)* monture *f*; **glasses with red frames** des lunettes *fpl* avec une monture rouge

2 *(support, structure ► gen)* cadre *m*; *(► of bicycle)* cadre *m*; *(► of car)* châssis *m*; *(► of lampshade, racket, tent)* armature *f*; *(► of machine)* bâti *m*; *(► of ship)* charpente *f*, carcasse *f*; *(► in gardening)* châssis; *(► for walking)* déambulateur *m*; *Constr* charpente *f*; *Tex* métier *m*; **the bed has a wooden f.** le lit est muni d'un cadre en bois

3 *(in snooker, pool etc ► game)* partie *f*; *(► wooden device)* triangle *m*

4 *(body)* corps *m*; **his huge f. filled the doorway** sa large carrure s'encadrait dans la porte

5 *(setting, background, area, scope)* cadre *m*; **f. of mind** état *m* d'esprit; **I'm not in the right f. of mind for celebrating** je ne suis pas d'humeur à faire la fête; **f. of reference** système *m* de référence

6 *Phot* image *f*; *Cin* image *f*, photogramme *m*; *TV* trame *f*

7 *(in embroidery ► floor-standing)* métier *m* (à broder); *(► hand-held)* tambour *m* (à broder)

8 *Comput (of Web page)* cadre *m*

VT **1** *(enclose, encase)* encadrer; **she's had the photograph framed** elle a fait encadrer la photo; *Fig* **her face was framed by a white silk scarf** un foulard de soie blanc encadrait son visage

2 *Formal (design, draft)* élaborer; *(formulate, express)* formuler; **to f. a plan/system** élaborer un projet/système; **the contract was framed in legal jargon** le contrat était formulé en jargon juridique

3 *Phot & TV (subject)* cadrer

4 *Fam (incriminate falsely)* **to f. sb** monter un (mauvais) coup contre qn□; **I've been framed** j'ai été victime d'un coup monté□

►► *Am* ***frame backpack*** sac *m* à dos à armature; *Cin* ***frame counter*** compteur *m* d'images; *Comput* ***frame format*** *(of network)* protocole *m*; *Am* ***frame house*** maison *f* en bois; ***frame rucksack*** sac *m* à dos à armature

framer ['freɪmə(r)] N encadreur(euse) *m,f*

frame-up N *Fam (false incrimination)* coup *m* monté□

framework ['freɪmwɜːk] N **1** *(structure)* cadre *m*, structure *f*; *Constr* charpente *f*; *Tech* bâti *m* **2** *Fig* cadre *m*; **the bill seeks to provide a legal f. for divorce** le projet de loi vise à instaurer un cadre juridique pour les procédures de divorce; **within the f. of the UN/the EU** dans le cadre de l'ONU/ l'UE

framing ['freɪmɪŋ] N **1** *(of picture, photograph)* encadrement *m* **2** *Cin & Phot* cadrage *m*

franc [fræŋk] N franc *m*

►► ***franc area*** zone *f* franc

France [frɑːns] N France *f*

franchisable [ˌfræntʃaɪzəbəl] ADJ franchisable, qui peut être franchisé

franchise ['fræntʃaɪz] N **1** *Pol* suffrage *m*, droit *m* de vote **2** *Com & Law (granted by public body)* concession *f*; *(granted by manufacturer)* franchise *f* **3** *Com (shop, outlet)* boutique *f* franchisée, magasin *m* franchisé

VT accorder une franchise à

►► *Com* ***franchise agreement*** accord *m* de franchise; *Com* ***franchise outlet*** boutique *f* franchisée, magasin *m* franchisé

franchisee [ˌfræntʃaɪ'ziː] N *Com* franchisé(e) *m,f*

franchising ['fræntʃaɪzɪŋ] N franchisage *m*

franchisor ['fræntʃaɪzə(r)] N *Com* franchiseur (euse) *m,f*

Franciscan [fræn'sɪskən] *Rel* N franciscain(e) *m,f*

ADJ franciscain

franco ['fræŋkəʊ] *Com* ADJ franco

ADV franco

Francophile ['fræŋkəfaɪl] N francophile *mf*

ADJ francophile

Francophobe ['fræŋkəfəʊb] N francophobe *mf*

ADJ francophobe

Francophone ['fræŋkəfəʊn] N francophone *mf*

ADJ francophone

frangible ['frændʒɪbəl] ADJ cassant, fragile

frangipane ['frændʒɪpeɪn] N frangipane *f*

Franglais ['frɒŋgleɪ] N franglais *m*

Frank [fræŋk] N *Hist* Franc (Franque) *m,f*

frank [fræŋk] ADJ franc (franche); **I'll be f. with you** je vais vous parler franchement *ou* être franc avec vous; **to be (perfectly) f.,...** franchement,..., sincèrement,...

VT *Br* affranchir *(à la machine)*

N **1** *Br (on letter)* affranchissement *m* **2** *Am Fam (sausage)* saucisse *f* (de Francfort)□; *(hot dog)* hot dog□ *m*

Frankenstein ['fræŋkənstaɪn] PR N Frankenstein

►► *Fam* ***Frankenstein food*** = surnom donné aux aliments génétiquement modifiés par leurs détracteurs

Frankfurt ['fræŋkfɜːt] N **F. (am Main)** Francfort(-sur-le-Main)

frankfurter ['fræŋkfɜːtə(r)] N saucisse *f* de Francfort

frankincense ['fræŋkɪnsens] N encens *m*

franking ['fræŋkɪŋ] N *Br (of letter)* affranchissement *m (à la machine)*

►► ***franking machine*** machine *f* à affranchir

Frankish ['fræŋkɪʃ] N francique *m*

ADJ franc (franque)

Franklin stove ['fræŋklɪn-] N *Am* poêle *m* à bois

frankly ['fræŋklɪ] ADV franchement, sincèrement; **can I speak f.?** puis-je parler franchement *ou* en toute franchise?

frankness ['fræŋknɪs] N franchise *f*; **I admire his f.** j'admire sa franchise *ou* son franc-parler

frantic ['fræntɪk] ADJ **1** *(distraught, wild)* éperdu, affolé; **she was f. with worry** elle était folle d'inquiétude; **f. screams** des cris *mpl* éperdus *ou* d'affolement; **it drives him f.** cela le met hors de lui **2** *(very busy)* **a scene of f. activity** une scène d'activité frénétique; *Fam* **things are pretty f. at the office** il y a un travail fou au bureau

frantically ['fræntɪkəlɪ] ADV désespérément; **she worked f. to finish the dress** elle travailla comme une forcenée pour terminer la robe

frat [fræt] N *Am Fam (abbr* **fraternity***)* = confrérie d'étudiants

►► ***frat boy*** = étudiant américain membre d'une confrérie d'étudiants, s'adonnant à la boisson et aux conquêtes féminines; ***frat party*** = soirée organisée par une confrérie d'étudiants; ***frat rat*** = membre d'une confrérie d'étudiants

fraternal [frə'tɜːnəl] ADJ fraternel; **f. twins** des faux jumeaux *mpl*

fraternally [frə'tɜːnəlɪ] ADV fraternellement

fraternity [frə'tɜːnətɪ] *(pl* **fraternities***)* N **1** *(friendship)* fraternité *f* **2** *(association)* confrérie *f*; **the medical f.** la confrérie des médecins; *Pej* **the sailing/hunting f.** la clique des amateurs de voile/ des chasseurs **3** *Am Univ* = confrérie d'étudiants

►► *Am Univ* ***fraternity house*** maison *f* communautaire (où résident des étudiants appartenant à une même confrérie); *Am Univ* ***fraternity pin*** insigne *m* de confrérie

fraternization, -isation [ˌfrætənaɪ'zeɪʃən] N fraternisation *f*

fraternize, -ise ['frætənaɪz] VI fraterniser

fraud [frɔːd] N **1** *Law* fraude *f*; *Fin* escroquerie *f*; **she's been charged with f.** elle a été inculpée de fraude; **tax f.** fraude *f* fiscale; **credit card f.** usage *m* frauduleux de cartes de crédit; **to obtain sth by f.** obtenir qch frauduleusement *ou* par fraude **2** *(dishonest person)* imposteur *m*; **she's a f.** elle essaie de se faire passer pour ce qu'elle n'est pas **3** *(product, work)* supercherie *f*; **the whole thing is a f.!** c'est une vaste supercherie!

►► *Br* ***the Fraud Squad*** brigade *f* de répression des fraudes

fraudulence ['frɔːdjʊləns], **fraudulency** ['frɔːdjʊlənsɪ] N *(of transaction)* caractère *m* frauduleux; *(of concerns, sentiments)* fausseté *f*

fraudulent ['frɔːdjʊlənt] ADJ *(bankrupt, trading, transaction)* frauduleux; *(sympathy, feelings)* faux (fausse), affecté; *(charge, accusation)* faux (fausse)

►► ***fraudulent bankruptcy*** faillite *f* frauduleuse

fraudulently ['frɔːdjʊləntlɪ] ADV frauduleusement

fraught [frɔːt] ADJ **1** *(filled)* chargé, lourd; **an atmosphere f. with emotion/tension** une atmosphère chargée d'émotion/de tension; **f. with danger** rempli de dangers **2** *esp Br (tense)* tendu; **I'm feeling a bit f.** je me sens un peu angoissé *ou* tendu; **things got rather f. at work today** l'atmosphère était plutôt tendue au bureau aujourd'hui **3** *(distressing)* pénible; **it's a f. subject** c'est un thème ardu

fray [freɪ] VT *(usu passive)* **1** *(clothing, fabric, rope)* effilocher **2** *(nerves)* mettre à vif; **her nerves were frayed** elle avait les nerfs à vif

VI **1** *(clothing, fabric, rope)* s'effilocher; **her dress is fraying at the hem** l'ourlet de sa robe s'effiloche **2** *Fig* **tempers began to f.** les gens commençaient à s'énerver *ou* perdre patience; **to f. around** *or* **at the edges** *(agreement)* battre de l'aile; **after ten months of hard work the team were starting to f. around the edges** après dix mois de dur labeur l'équipe commençait à montrer des signes de fatigue nerveuse

N **the f.** la mêlée; **to enter** *or* **to join the f.** se jeter dans la mêlée

frayed [freɪd] ADJ **1** *(garment)* élimé; **her jacket was f. at the cuffs** sa veste était élimée aux poignets **2** *Fig* **tempers were getting f.** les gens étaient de plus en plus irritables; **to be f. around** *or* **at the edges** battre de l'aile

frazzle ['fræzəl] *Fam* VT *(exhaust)* tuer, crever

N **worn to a f.** crevé; **burnt to a f.** carbonisé□, calciné□; **you look burnt to a f.** *(by sun)* tu as l'air d'avoir pris un de ces coups de soleil

frazzled ['fræzəld] ADJ *Fam* **1** *(mentally)* à bout de nerfs; *(exhausted)* crevé; **his nerves were still f.** il était encore à bout de nerfs **2** *(burnt)* carbonisé□, calciné□; **I got f. on the beach** je me suis pris un gros coup de soleil sur la plage□

freak [friːk] N **1** *(abnormal event)* caprice *m* de la nature, aberration *f*; *(abnormal person)* phénomène *m* de foire, monstre *m*; *(eccentric person)* phénomène *m*, farfelu(e) *m,f*; **by a f. of nature** par un caprice de la nature; **by some f. (of chance)** par un hasard inouï; **just because I choose not to eat meat, that doesn't make me a f.** ce n'est pas parce que je ne mange pas de viande que je suis anormal; **f. show** exhibition *f* de monstres *(à la foire)* **2** *Fam (fanatic)* fana *mf*; *(addict)* accro *mf*; **a fitness f.** un (une) fana de la forme; **a speed/cocaine f.** un (une) accro au speed/à la cocaïne **3** *Fam (hippie)* hippie□ *mf*

ADJ *(storm)* anormal; *(accident)* insolite, bizarre; **f. weather conditions** des conditions *fpl* atmosphériques anormales

VI *Fam* **1** *(on drugs)* flipper **2** *(lose control of one's emotions)* perdre les pédales; *(become angry)* piquer une crise, péter les plombs

► **freak out** *Fam* VI **1** *(on drugs)* flipper **2** *(lose control of one's emotions)* perdre les pédales; *(become angry)* piquer une crise, péter les plombs **3** *(abandon restraint)* s'éclater

VT SEP **1** *(cause to hallucinate)* faire flipper **2** *(upset emotionally)* déboussoler

freaking ['friːkɪŋ] *Am very Fam* ADJ *(for emphasis)* sacré, foutu; **where are those f. kids?** mais où sont passés ces foutus gamins?

ADV *(for emphasis)* vachement; **it's f. cold out there** ça pince vachement dehors; **I don't f. know!** j'en sais foutre rien!

freakish ['friːkɪʃ] ADJ **1** *(strange)* étrange, bizarre; **a f.-looking man** un homme à l'allure étrange *ou* bizarre **2** *(abnormal ► weather)* anormal

freaky ['friːkɪ] *(compar* **freakier**, *superl* **freakiest***)* ADJ *Fam* bizarre□, insolite□

freckle ['frekəl] N tache *f* de rousseur; **she's got freckles** elle a des taches de rousseur

freckled ['frekəld], **freckly** ['frekəlɪ] *(compar* **frecklier**, *superl* **freckliest***)* ADJ taché de son, marqué de taches de rousseur; **a f. face/nose** un visage/nez couvert de taches de rousseur

-free [friː] SUFF **additive-f.** sans additifs; **salt-f.** sans sel; **trouble-f.** sans ennuis *ou* problèmes

FREE [friː]

ADJ
• libre **1–3, 5, 7** • gratuit **4**
• franco **9**
ADV
• gratuitement **1** • librement **2**
VT
• libérer **1, 3, 4** • dégager **2**
• déboucher **3**

ADJ **1** *(unconfined, unrestricted ▸ person, animal, passage, way)* libre; **as f. as the air** *or* **a bird** libre comme l'air; **the hostage managed to get f.** l'otage a réussi à se libérer; **to cut sb f.** délivrer qn en coupant ses liens; **to let sb go f.** relâcher qn, remettre qn en liberté; **to set f.** *(prisoner, animal)* remettre en liberté; *(slave)* affranchir; *(hostage)* libérer; **you are f. to leave** vous êtes libre de partir; **you are f. to refuse** libre à vous de refuser; **they gave us f. access to their files** ils nous ont donné libre accès à leurs dossiers; **to make a f. choice** décider librement *ou* en toute liberté; **feel f. to visit us any time** ne vous gênez pas pour nous rendre visite quand vous voulez; **feel f. to speak your mind** n'hésitez pas à dire ce que vous pensez; **can I use the phone? – yes, feel f.** puis-je téléphoner? – mais certainement
2 *(unattached)* libre, sans attaches; **with his f. hand** avec sa main libre; **grab the f. end of the rope** attrape le bout libre de la corde
3 *(democratic)* libre; **it's a f. country!** on est en démocratie!; **a f. press** une presse libre
4 *(at no cost)* gratuit; **f. admission** entrée *f* gratuite *ou* libre; **f. demonstration** démonstration *f* gracieuse; *Fig* **there's no such thing as a f. lunch** on n'a jamais rien pour rien; *Hum* **f., gratis and for nothing** complètement gratuitement
5 *(not in use, unoccupied)* libre; **is that seat f.?** est-ce que ce siège est libre?; **she doesn't have a f. moment** elle n'a pas un moment de libre; **are you f. for lunch today?** êtes-vous libre pour déjeuner aujourd'hui?; **could you let us know when you're f.?** pourriez-vous nous faire savoir quand vous êtes libre *ou* disponible?; **what do you do in your f. time?** que faites-vous pendant vos loisirs?; **she has very little f. time** elle a peu de temps libre
6 *(unhampered)* **the jury was not entirely f. of** *or* **from prejudice** les jurés n'étaient pas entièrement sans préjugés *ou* parti pris; **to be f. from care** être sans souci; **to be f. from pain** ne pas souffrir; **I just want to be f. of him!** je veux être débarrassé de lui!
7 *(approximate ▸ translation, interpretation)* libre; *Pej* approximatif
8 *(uninhibited)* **f. and easy** désinvolte, décontracté
9 *Com* **f. carrier** franco transporteur; **f. overside** franco allège; **f. in and out** bord à bord; **f. alongside ship, f. at quay** franco long du quai, franco long du bord; **f. at frontier** franco frontière; **f. of all average** franc (franche) de toute avarie; **f. on board** franco à bord; *Customs* **f. of duty** exempt de droits d'entrée; **f. on rail** franco wagon; **f. of tax** franc (franche) d'impôts; **f. on truck** franco camion; **f. on wharf** franco long du quai, franco long du bord
10 *(generous)* **to be f. with one's time** être généreux de son temps; **to be f. with one's money** être prodigue de son argent; **he was very f. with his advice** il a été très prodigue en conseils; **she's very f. with her criticism** elle ne ménage pas ses critiques
11 *(disrespectful)* trop familier; **he's a bit f. in his manners for my liking** il est un peu trop sans gêne à mon goût
12 *Chem* libre, non combiné; **f. nitrogen** azote *m* à l'état libre
ADV**1** *(at no cost)* gratuitement; **they will deliver f. of charge** ils livreront gratuitement; **children travel (for) f.** les enfants voyagent gratuitement; **it came f. with the magazine** c'était en prime pour l'achat du magazine
2 *(without restraint)* librement; **wolves roamed f. through the forests** les loups rôdaient librement à travers les forêts; **to make f. with sth** se servir de qch sans se gêner; **he made very f. with his wife's money** il ne se gênait pas pour dépenser l'argent de sa femme
VT **1** *(release ▸ gen)* libérer; *(▸ prisoner)* libérer, relâcher; *(▸ tied-up animal)* détacher; *(▸ caged animal)* libérer; *(▸ slave, colony)* affranchir; **to f. sb's hands** *(untie)* détacher les mains de qn; **giving up work has freed me to get on with my painting** arrêter de travailler m'a permis de continuer à peindre
2 *(disengage, disentangle)* dégager; **it took two hours to f. the driver from the wreckage** il a fallu deux heures pour dégager le conducteur de sa voiture; **she tried to f. herself from his grasp** elle essaya de se libérer *ou* se dégager de son étreinte; *Fig* **to f. sb from an obligation** libérer qn d'une obligation
3 *(unblock ▸ pipe)* déboucher; *(▸ passage)* libérer
4 *Com (prices, trade)* libérer; *(funds)* débloquer
▸▸ ***free agent*** personne *f* libre *ou* indépendante; *(sports player)* joueur(euse) *m,f* indépendant(e); **I'm a f. agent** je ne dépends de personne; *Psy* ***free association*** association *f* libre; *Econ* ***free banking*** banque *f* libre; ***Free Church*** Église *f* protestante d'Écosse; *Sport* ***free climbing*** escalade *f* libre; ***free competition*** libre concurrence *f*; *Sch* ***free composition*** composition *f* libre; ***free diver*** plongeur(euse) *m,f* autonome; ***free diving*** plongée *f* sous-marine autonome; *Golf* ***free drop*** free drop *m*, drop *m* sans pénalité; *Econ* ***free enterprise*** libre entreprise *f*; ***free fall*** chute *f* libre; ***free flight*** vol *m* ballistique; *Hist* ***Free France*** la France libre; *Hist* ***the Free French*** les Français *mpl* libres; *Com* ***free gift*** cadeau *m*; ***free hand*** liberté *f* d'action; **to give sb a f. hand to do sth** donner carte blanche à qn pour faire qch; **they gave me a completely f. hand** ils m'ont donné toute liberté d'action; *Br* ***free house*** = pub libre de ses approvisionnements (et non lié à une brasserie particulière); *St Exch* ***free issue*** attribution *f* d'actions gratuites; *Mus* ***free jazz*** free-jazz *m inv*; *Sport* ***free kick*** coup *m* franc; ***free love*** union *f* libre; *Econ* ***free market*** économie *f* de marché; *EU* ***free movement*** *(of goods, people)* libre circulation *f*; *Law* ***free pardon*** grâce *f*; *Customs* ***free port*** port *m* franc; ***free press*** liberté *f* de la presse; *Med* ***free radical*** radical *m* libre; *Sport* ***free running*** parkour *m*; *Com* ***free sample*** échantillon *m* gratuit; ***free skating*** figures *fpl* libres; ***free speech*** liberté *f* de parole *ou* d'expression; ***free spirit*** non-conformiste *mf*; ***Free State*** *(in South Africa)* État *m* libre; *Hist (Ireland)* État *m* libre d'Irlande; ***free thought*** libre pensée *f*; *Sport* ***free throw*** *(in basketball)* lancer *m* franc; *Econ* ***free trade*** libre-échange *m*; *Econ* ***free trader*** libre-échangiste *mf*; *Com* ***free trial*** essai *m* gratuit; *Com* ***free trial period*** période *f* d'essai gratuit; ***free verse*** vers *m* libre; ***free vote*** vote *m* libre; ***free will*** libre arbitre *m*; **to do sth of one's own f. will** faire qch de son plein gré; *Pol* ***the Free World*** le monde libre; *Econ* ***free zone*** zone *f* franche
▸ **free up** VT SEP *(funds)* dégager; *(time, space)* libérer; **this will f. up sales people to do more actual selling** cela donnera plus de temps au personnel de vente pour se consacrer à la vente même

freebie, freebee ['friːbɪ] *Fam* N *(for customer etc)* cadeau[□] *m*; *(perk)* à-côté[□] *m*; *Comput* produit *m* gratuit[□]; **it was a f. with the magazine** c'était un cadeau offert avec le magazine
ADJ gratis *(inv)*

freeboard ['friːbɔːd] N *Naut* franc-bord *m*

freeborn ['friːbɔːn] ADJ né libre, libre de naissance

freedom ['friːdəm] N liberté *f*; **the journalists were given complete f. to talk to dissidents** les journalistes ont pu parler aux dissidents en toute liberté; **f. from hunger** le droit de manger à sa faim; **f. from persecution** le droit de vivre sans persécution; **f. from responsibility** l'absence *f* de responsabilités; **she had the f. of the whole house** elle avait la maison à son entière disposition; **to be given** *or* **granted the f. of the city** être nommé citoyen d'honneur de la ville; **f. of the seas** liberté *f* de la haute mer
▸▸ ***freedom of association*** liberté *f* de réunion; ***freedom of conscience*** liberté *f* de conscience; ***freedom of entry*** liberté *f* d'entrée; ***freedom of exit*** liberté *f* de sortie; ***freedom fighter*** guérillero *m*, révolutionnaire *mf*; ***freedom of information*** liberté *f* d'information; *Law* ***Freedom of Information Act*** = loi sur la communication aux citoyens des informations de source gouvernementale; ***freedom of religion*** liberté *f* de culte; ***freedom of speech*** liberté *f* d'expression; ***freedom of trade*** liberté *f* du commerce; ***freedom of worship*** liberté *f* du culte

free-enterprise ADJ *Econ* libéral
▸▸ ***free-enterprise economy*** économie *f* de libre entreprise

free-flowing ADJ **1** *(river, stream)* qui coule librement; *(traffic, substance)* fluide **2** *(information)* librement accessible; *Fin (capital)* flottant

Freefone® ['friːfəʊn] N *Br Tel* = appel gratuit, numéro *m* vert; **call F. 800** appelez le numéro vert 800

free-for-all N mêlée *f* générale; **when the food arrived the queue quickly turned into a f.** quand la nourriture est arrivée la file d'attente a tourné en mêlée générale

free-form ADJ de forme libre
▸▸ *Mus* ***free-form jazz*** free-jazz *m inv*

freegan ['friːgən] N = personne qui consomme de la nourriture récupérée dans les poubelles des restaurants et des magasins

freehand ['friːhænd] ADJ à main levée
ADV à main levée

freehanded [ˌfriː'hændɪd] ADJ libéral, large

freehold ['friːhəʊld] N propriété *f* foncière inaliénable
ADV **to buy/to sell sth f.** acheter/vendre qch en propriété inaliénable
ADJ **f. property** propriété *f* inaliénable

freeholder ['friːhəʊldə(r)] N propriétaire *mf* foncier(ère) *(à perpétuité)*

freeing ['friːɪŋ] N *(of prisoner)* libération *f*, délivrance *f*; *(of slave)* affranchissement *m*; *(of funds, resources)* déblocage *m*

freelance ['friːlɑːns] N travailleur(euse) *m,f* indépendant(e), free-lance *mf*; *(journalist, writer)* pigiste *mf*
ADJ indépendant, free-lance *(inv)*
ADV en free-lance, en indépendant
VI travailler en free-lance *ou* indépendant; *(journalist, writer)* faire de la pige, travailler comme pigiste *ou* en indépendant

freelancer ['friːlɑːnsə(r)] N travailleur(euse) *m,f* indépendant(e), free-lance *mf*

freeload ['friːləʊd] VI *Fam* vivre aux crochets des autres

freeloader ['friːləʊdə(r)] N *Fam* pique-assiette *mf*, parasite[□] *mf*

freely ['friːlɪ] ADV **1** *(without constraint)* librement; **can I speak f.?** puis-je parler librement?; **I f. admit that...** j'avoue sans peine que... + *indicative*; **traffic is moving f. again** la circulation est redevenue fluide; **the book is now f. available** on peut se procurer le livre facilement maintenant; **the wine was flowing f.** le vin coulait à flots
2 *(liberally ▸ spend)* largement; *(▸ perspire, weep)* abondamment

freeman ['friːmən] *(pl* **freemen** [-mən]) N *Hist* homme *m* libre; *(citizen)* citoyen *m*; **he's a f. of the city** il est citoyen d'honneur de la ville

free-marketeer [-ˌmɑːkɪ'tɪə(r)] N *Econ* libéral (e) *m,f*

freemason, Freemason ['friːˌmeɪsən] N franc-maçon *m*

freemasonry, Freemasonry ['friːˌmeɪsənrɪ] N franc-maçonnerie *f*

freemen ['friːmən] *pl of* **freeman**

freenet ['friːnet] N *Comput* libertel *f*

Freepost® ['friːpəʊst] N *Br* port *m* payé

free-range ADJ *(chicken)* fermier
▸▸ ***free-range eggs*** œufs *mpl* de poules élevées en plein air

free-running N parkour *m*

freesheet ['friːʃiːt] N journal *m* gratuit

freesia ['friːziə] N *Bot* freesia *m*

free-spoken ADJ franc (franche)

freestanding [ˌfriːˈstændɪŋ] ADJ non encastré; *Gram* indépendant

freestyle [ˈfriːstaɪl] N *(in swimming)* nage *f* libre; *(skateboarding, skiing, snowboarding, rap music)* freestyle *m*
ADJ *(skateboarding, skiing, snowboarding, rap music)* freestyle
VI *(rap artist)* improviser

freethinker [ˌfriːˈθɪŋkə(r)] N libre-penseur *m*

free-to-air ADJ *TV (channel)* en clair

free-trade ADJ *Econ* libre-échangiste
▸▸ ***free-trade agreement*** accord *m ou* association *f* de libre-échange; ***free-trade area*** zone *f* de libre-échange; ***free-trade association*** association *f* de libre-échange; ***free-trade policy*** politique *f* antiprotectionniste, politique *f* de libre-échange; ***free-trade zone*** zone *f* de libre-échange

freeware [ˈfriːweə(r)] N *Comput* logiciel *m* (du domaine) public, logiciel libre, gratuiciel *m*
▸▸ ***freeware programs*** freewares *mpl*, logiciels *mpl* publics

freeway [ˈfriːweɪ] N *Am* autoroute *f*

freewheel [ˌfriːˈwiːl] N *(on bicycle)* roue *f* libre
VI **1** *(cyclist)* être en roue libre; **to f. down a slope** descendre une pente en roue libre **2** *(motorist)* rouler au point mort **3** *esp Am (travel in carefree fashion)* se laisser aller, aller sans but précis

freewheeling [ˌfriːˈwiːlɪŋ] ADJ *Fam* désinvolte, sans-gêne *(inv)*; **to lead a f. existence** rouler sa bosse

freeze [friːz] (*pt* **froze** [frəʊz], *pp* **frozen** [ˈfrəʊzən])
VI **1** *(earth, pipes, water)* geler; *(food)* se congeler; **the river has frozen** la rivière est prise *ou* a gelé; **the earth had frozen hard** la terre avait gelé; **the mud/food had frozen solid** la boue/nourriture avait gelé; **to f. to death** mourir de froid; **we'll f. if you open the window!** nous allons geler si vous ouvrez la fenêtre! **2** *Fig (stop moving)* **(everybody) f.!** que personne ne bouge!; **she froze (in her tracks)** elle est restée figée sur place; **her blood froze** son sang se figea *ou* se glaça dans ses veines; **the smile froze on his lips** le sourire se figea sur ses lèvres **3** *Comput (screen, computer)* être bloqué
VT **1** *(water)* geler, congeler; *(food)* congeler; *(at very low temperatures)* surgeler; *Med (blood, human tissue)* congeler; *Fig* **she froze them with a look** d'un regard elle les glaça sur place; **to be frozen to death** mourir de froid **2** *Econ & Fin (credit, wages)* geler, bloquer; *(currency, prices, assets)* geler **3** *Cin* **f. it!** arrêtez l'image!
N *Met* gel *m*; *Econ & Fin (of credit, wages)* gel *m*, blocage *m*; *(of currency, prices, assets)* gel *m*; **we're in for another big f.** *Met* il va y avoir une période de très grand froid; *Econ* il va y avoir une crise économique; **they called for a f. in the production of nuclear weapons** ils ont appelé à un gel de la production d'armes nucléaires; **wage f.** gel *m ou* blocage *m* des salaires
▸**freeze out** VT SEP *Fam (exclude)* exclure; *(snub)* snober
▸**freeze over** VI geler
▸**freeze up** VI **1** *(turn to ice)* geler **2** *Fam (person)* rester pétrifié

freeze-dried ADJ lyophilisé

freeze-dry (*pt & pp* **freeze-dried**) VT lyophiliser

freeze-frame N *Cin* arrêt *m* sur image

freezer [ˈfriːzə(r)] N congélateur *m*; *(in refrigerator)* freezer *m*; **in the f. section of your supermarket** au rayon surgelés de votre supermarché
▸▸ ***freezer bag*** sac *m* congélation; ***freezer compartment*** compartiment *m* congélateur *(d'un réfrigérateur)*

freeze-up N *Fam* gel *m*

freezing [ˈfriːzɪŋ] ADJ *Met* glacial; *(person)* gelé, glacé; **I'm f.** je suis gelé; **a f. wind was blowing** un vent glacial soufflait; **it's f. in this room!** on gèle *ou* ça caille dans cette pièce!; **your hands are f.** vous avez les mains gelées *ou* glacées
N **1** *(temperature)* **it's two degrees above/below f.** il fait deux degrés au-dessus/au-dessous de zéro **2** *Econ & Fin (of credit, wages)* blocage *m*, gel *m*; *(of currency, prices, assets)* gel *m*
ADV **a f. cold day** une journée glaciale; **it's f. cold outside** il fait un froid glacial dehors
▸▸ ***freezing instructions*** *(for food)* consignes *fpl* pour la congélation; ***freezing point*** point *m* de congélation; *Met* ***freezing rain*** neige *f* fondue

freight [freɪt] N **1** *(goods)* fret *m*; **to take in f.** *(load, cargo)* prendre du fret **2** *(transport)* **to send goods by f.** envoyer des marchandises en régime ordinaire
COMP *(transport)* de fret
VT **1** *(load ▸ vessel)* charger **2** *(hire ▸ ship)* (af)fréter; *(▸ of owner)* donner à fret **3** *esp Am (transport)* transporter
▸▸ *Am* ***freight car*** wagon *m* de marchandises, fourgon *m*; ***freight charges*** fret *m*, frais *mpl* de transport; ***freight depot*** gare *f* de marchandises; *Am* ***freight elevator*** monte-charge *m inv*; ***freight forward*** port *m* avancé; ***freight forwarder*** agent *m* de fret, transitaire *m*; ***freight forwarding*** transit *m*; ***freight insurance*** assurance *f* sur fret; ***freight note*** bordereau *m* d'expédition; ***freight plane*** avion-cargo *m*, avion *m* de fret; ***freight shipping*** messageries *fpl* maritimes; ***freight terminal*** terminal *m* de fret; ***freight ton*** tonne *f* d'affrètement; *Am* ***freight train*** train *m* de marchandises; ***freight vehicle*** véhicule *m* de transport de marchandises; *Am* ***freight yard*** dépôt *m* de marchandises

freightage [ˈfreɪtɪdʒ] N fret *m*, frais *mpl* de transport

freighter [ˈfreɪtə(r)] N *Naut* navire *m* de charge; *Aviat* avion-cargo *m*, avion *m* de fret

Freightliner® [ˈfreɪtlaɪnə(r)] N train *m* de transport de conteneurs

French [frentʃ] NPL **the F.** les Français *mpl*
N *(language)* français *m*; *Hum* **pardon** *or* **excuse my F.!** passez-moi l'expression!
ADJ français; *Br Fam* **to take F. leave** filer à l'anglaise
COMP *(embassy, history)* de France; *(teacher)* de français
▸▸ ***French bean*** haricot *m* vert; ***French bread*** baguette *f*; *Geog* ***French Canada*** le Canada français; ***French Canadian*** N Canadien(enne) *m,f* français (e) ADJ canadien français; ***French chalk*** craie *f* de tailleur; ***French cricket*** = jeu pour enfants qui se joue avec une balle et une batte de cricket; *Tech* ***French curve*** pistolet *m* (de dessinateur); *Am* ***French dip*** = sandwich à la viande accompagné d'un bouillon ou d'une sauce à base de la même viande, dans lesquels on trempe le sandwich; *Am* ***French door*** porte-fenêtre *f*; *Culin* ***French dressing*** *(in UK)* vinaigrette *f*; *(in US)* = sauce de salade à base de mayonnaise et de ketchup; ***the French Foreign Legion*** la Légion étrangère; *Formerly* ***French franc*** franc *m* français; ***French fried potatoes*** pommes *fpl* frites; ***French fries*** frites *fpl*; ***French Guiana*** la Guyane française; ***French horn*** cor *m* d'harmonie; *Fam* ***French kiss*** N patin *m* VT rouler un patin à VI se rouler un patin; *Br* ***French knickers*** caleçon *m* *(culotte pour femme)*; *Br Fam* ***French letter*** *(condom)* capote *f* anglaise; *Br* ***French loaf*** baguette *f*; ***French maid*** femme *f* de chambre française *(attachée au service particulier d'une dame)*; *Theat* soubrette *f*; ***French maid's outfit*** costume *m* de soubrette; ***French mustard*** moutarde *f* de Dijon; ***French plait*** *(hairstyle)* natte *f* africaine; *Br* ***French polish*** vernis *m* (à l'alcool); ***the French Quarter*** *(in New Orleans)* le quartier français, le Vieux Carré; *Hist* ***the French Revolution*** la Révolution (française); ***the French Riviera*** la Côte d'Azur; ***French roll*** *(hairstyle)* chignon *m* banane; *Sewing* ***French seam*** couture *f* anglaise; *Br* ***French stick*** baguette *f*; ***French Switzerland*** la Suisse romande; ***French toast*** pain *m* perdu; ***the French Triangle*** = région du sud des États-Unis comprise entre La Nouvelle-Orléans, Alexandria et Cameron; ***French West Africa*** l'Afrique-Occidentale *f* française; ***the French West Indies*** les Antilles *fpl* françaises; *Br* ***French window*** porte-fenêtre *f*

Frenchie [ˈfrentʃɪ] *Fam* N **1** *(French person)* Français(e) *m,f* **2** *(French kiss)* patin *m* **3** *(French letter)* capote *f* anglaise
ADJ français

Frenchified [ˈfrentʃɪfaɪd] ADJ *Fam* francisé, à la française

Frenchify [ˈfrentʃɪfaɪ] (*pt & pp* **Frenchified**) VT *Fam* franciser

Frenchman [ˈfrentʃmən] (*pl* **Frenchmen** [-mən]) N Français *m*

French-polish VT *Br* vernir (à l'alcool)

French-speaking ADJ francophone; **the F. world** le monde francophone, la francophonie

Frenchwoman [ˈfrentʃwʊmən] (*pl* **Frenchwomen** [-wɪmɪn]) N Française *f*

Frenchy (*pl* **Frenchies**) = **Frenchie**

frenetic [frəˈnetɪk] ADJ frénétique

frenetically [frəˈnetɪkəlɪ] ADV frénétiquement

frenzied [ˈfrenzɪd] ADJ *(activity)* frénétique, forcené; *(crowd)* déchaîné; *(person)* forcené, déchaîné

frenzy [ˈfrenzɪ] (*pl* **frenzies**) N **1** *(fury, passion)* frénésie *f*; **to work oneself (up) into a f.** *(get angry)* se mettre dans une colère noire; *(get upset)* se mettre dans tous ses états; *(get very excited)* se mettre dans un état de surexcitation folle **2** *(fit, outburst)* accès *m*, crise *f*; **in a f. of anger** dans un accès *ou* une crise de colère

frequency [ˈfriːkwənsɪ] (*pl* **frequencies**) N fréquence *f*; **the increasing f. of his absences** ses absences de plus en plus fréquentes
▸▸ *Rad* ***frequency band*** bande *f* de fréquences; *Rad* ***frequency changer*** changeur *m* de fréquence; *Math* ***frequency distribution*** distribution *f* des fréquences; *Rad* ***frequency modulation*** modulation *f* de fréquence; *Rad* ***frequency response*** réponse *f* en fréquence

frequent ADJ [ˈfriːkwənt] *(visits etc)* fréquent; *(customer)* habituel; *(practice, custom)* très répandu; *(explanation, state of affairs etc)* commun, habituel; **it is a f. occurrence** cela se produit souvent; **he became a f. visitor to our house** il est devenu un habitué de la maison; **this bird is a f. visitor to our shores** cet oiseau visite régulièrement nos rivages
VT [frɪˈkwent] *Formal* fréquenter
▸▸ ***frequent flyer club*** club *m* de fidélité de compagnie aérienne; ***frequent flyer programme*** programme *m* de fidélisation des passagers de compagnies aériennes; ***frequent use shampoo, frequent wash shampoo*** shampo(o)ing *m* pour lavages fréquents

frequenter [frɪˈkwentə(r)] N *(of a house etc)* habitué(e) *m,f*, familier *m*; **a great f. of public houses** un pilier de bar

frequently [ˈfriːkwəntlɪ] ADV fréquemment, souvent; **how f.?** avec quelle fréquence?, *Fam* tous les combien?; **I can't say how f. it happened** je ne saurais pas dire à quelle fréquence cela se produisait; *Comput* **f. asked questions** foire *f* aux questions

fresco [ˈfreskəʊ] (*pl* **frescoes** *or* **frescos**) N *Art* fresque *f*; **f. painter** fresquiste *mf*

fresh [freʃ] ADJ **1** *(recently made or produced)* frais (fraîche); **f. bread/butter** pain *m*/beurre *m* frais; **I'll make some f. coffee** je vais refaire du café; **f. flowers** fleurs *fpl* fraîches; **the bread was f. from the oven** le pain sortait du four; **there were f. tracks in the snow** il y avait des traces toutes fraîches dans la neige; **f. from** *or* **out of university** (tout) frais émoulu de l'université
2 *(new ▸ idea, problem)* nouveau(elle), original; *(▸ news, paint)* frais (fraîche); *(▸ impression)* frais (fraîche); **a f. approach** une approche nouvelle; **f. capital** nouveaux capitaux *mpl*; **they have agreed to f. talks** ils ont accepté de reprendre leurs négociations; **to make a f. start** prendre un nouveau départ; **he put on a f. shirt** il mit une chemise propre; **start on a f. page** prenez une nouvelle page; **the incident was still f. in his mind** le souvenir de l'incident était encore tout frais dans sa mémoire
3 *(rested)* frais (fraîche); **I felt fresher after a shower** une douche m'a rafraîchi; **as f. as a daisy** frais (fraîche) comme un gardon
4 *(air)* frais (fraîche), pur; *(taste)* rafraîchissant; *(cool)* frais (fraîche); **I need some f. air** j'ai besoin de prendre l'air; **in the f. air** au grand air, en plein air; **it's f. this morning** il fait frais ce matin; **a f. complexion** un teint frais; **f. colours** des couleurs *fpl* fraîches
5 *Met (gen)* frais (fraîche); *(on Beaufort scale)* **f. breeze** bonne brise *f*; **f. gale** coup *m* de vent
6 *(not salt ▸ water)* doux (douce)

7 *Am Fam (impudent)* insolent□; *(child)* mal élevé□; **don't you get f. with me, young man!** pas d'insolence avec moi, jeune homme!

8 *Am Fam (sexually forward)* effronté□; **he started to get f. so she hit him** il a commencé à prendre des libertés avec elle alors elle l'a frappé□

ADV fraîchement; **f. cut flowers** des fleurs *fpl* fraîchement cueillies; *Fam* **to be f. out of sth** être en panne de qch

freshen ['freʃən] **VT** rafraîchir; *(colour)* raviver; *esp Am* **can I f. your drink?** est-ce que je vous sers un autre verre?

VI *Naut (wind)* fraîchir

▸ **freshen up VI** faire un brin de toilette

VT SEP 1 *(person)* faire un brin de toilette à; **to f. oneself up** faire un brin de toilette; **to f. up one's lipstick** se remettre du rouge à lèvres **2** *(house, room)* donner un petit coup de peinture à **3** *Am (drink)* **let me f. up your drink** laisse-moi te resservir à boire

fresher ['freʃə(r)] **N** *Br Fam Univ* bizut *m*, bizuth *m*, étudiant(e) *m,f* de première année□

▸▸ ***freshers' week*** = semaine d'accueil des étudiants de première année

FRESHERS' WEEK

Dans les universités britanniques, les étudiants de première année ("freshers") arrivent généralement une semaine avant le début des cours afin de se familiariser avec leur nouvel environnement et achever les formalités administratives. Durant cette semaine, baptisée "freshers' week", les nouveaux étudiants ont l'occasion de faire connaissance lors de rencontres organisées par leur université. Il y a également une "freshers' fair" durant laquelle les étudiants sont invités à s'inscrire à toutes sortes de clubs proposant des activités sportives ou culturelles et où ils peuvent obtenir des informations sur les services qui leur sont proposés. Dans la plupart des universités, la semaine se termine par une grande soirée, le "freshers' ball".

freshly ['freʃlɪ] **ADV** récemment; **f. made coffee** du café qui vient d'être fait; **f. squeezed orange juice** jus *m* d'oranges pressées; **the grave had been f. dug** la fosse avait été fraîchement creusée

freshman ['freʃmən] *(pl* **freshmen** [-mən]) *Am Univ* étudiant(e) *m,f* de première année

freshness ['freʃnɪs] **N** fraîcheur *f*

freshwater ['freʃwɔːtə(r)] **ADJ**

▸▸ ***freshwater fish*** poisson *m* d'eau douce; ***freshwater fishing*** pêche *f* en eau douce

fret [fret] *(pt & pp* **fretted**, *cont* **fretting**) **VI** *(worry)* tracasser; **to f. about** *or* **over sb** se faire du souci pour qn; **don't f., I'll be all right** ne te tracasse pas *ou* ne t'inquiète pas, tout ira bien; **the little boy was fretting for his mother** le petit garçon réclamait sa mère en pleurant

VT 1 *(worry)* **to f. one's life away** passer sa vie à se tourmenter *ou* à se faire du mauvais sang **2** *(erode, wear down)* ronger; **a fretted rope** une corde effilochée **3** *(decorate* ▸ *metal, wood)* chantourner

N 1 *Fam (state)* **to get in a f. about sth** se faire du mauvais sang *ou* se ronger les sangs à propos de qch **2** *(on guitar)* touchette *f*, frette *f*

fretful ['fretfʊl] **ADJ** *(anxious)* inquiet(ète); *(irritable, complaining)* grincheux, maussade; **a f. child** un enfant grognon

fretfully ['fretfʊlɪ] **ADV 1** *(anxiously* ▸ *ask, say)* avec inquiétude; **the dog waited f. by the door** le chien attendait impatiemment à la porte **2** *(irritably)* d'une manière maussade; *(ask, say)* d'un ton grincheux *ou* maussade

fretfulness ['fretfʊlnɪs] **N 1** *(anxiousness)* inquiétude *f* **2** *(irritability)* irritabilité *f*

fretting ['fretɪŋ] **N 1** *(worrying)* inquiétude *f* (**over** à propos de); *(being upset)* agitation *f*; **I wish he'd stop his f.!** si seulement il pouvait arrêter de se faire du mauvais sang! **2** *(of rope etc)* usure *f*

fretwork ['fretwɜːk] **N** *Carp (technique)* découpage *m*, chantournement *m*; *(finished work)* travail *m* ajouré, bois *m* découpé *ou* chantourné

Freudian ['frɔɪdɪən] **ADJ** freudien

N disciple *mf* de Freud

▸▸ ***Freudian slip*** lapsus *m* (révélateur)

Freudianism ['frɔɪdɪənɪzəm] **N** freudisme *m*

FRG [,efɑː'dʒiː] **N** *Formerly (abbr* **Federal Republic of Germany**) RFA *f*

Fri. *(written abbr* **Friday**) ven

friable ['fraɪəbəl] **ADJ** friable

friar ['fraɪə(r)] **N** frère *m*, moine *m*; **Grey Friars** Franciscains *mpl*; **Black Friars** Dominicains *mpl*; **White Friars** Carmes *mpl*

▸▸ ***friar's balsam*** baume *m* de benjoin

friary ['fraɪərɪ] *(pl* **friaries**) **N** monastère *m*

fricassee ['frɪkəsiː] *Culin* **N** fricassée *f*

VT fricasser

fricative ['frɪkətɪv] *Ling* **N** fricative *f*

ADJ fricatif

friction ['frɪkʃən] **N 1** *Phys* friction *f*; *(of two bodies)* frottement *m*; *(of scalp etc)* friction *f* **2** *(discord)* friction *f*, conflit *m*; **it's an issue that often causes f. between neighbours** c'est un problème qui est souvent cause de frictions entre voisins

▸▸ *Aut* ***friction clutch*** embrayage *m* à friction; *Aut* ***friction drive*** entraînement *m* par friction; *Comput* ***friction feed*** avancement *m* par friction; ***friction glove*** *(for massage)* gant *m* de crin; *Aut* ***friction lining*** garniture *f* de friction; *Am* ***friction tape*** chatterton *m*

Friday ['fraɪdɪ] **N** vendredi *m*; **it's F. today** nous sommes *ou* on est vendredi aujourd'hui; **I'll see you (on) F.** je te verrai vendredi; **the cleaning woman comes on Fridays** la femme de ménage vient le vendredi; **I work Fridays** je travaille le vendredi; **there's a market each F.** *or* **every F.** il y a un marché tous les vendredis *ou* chaque vendredi; **every other F., every second F.** un vendredi sur deux; **the first/last F. of every month** le premier/dernier vendredi de chaque mois; **we arrive on the F. and leave on the Sunday** nous arrivons le vendredi et repartons le dimanche; **the programme's usually shown on a F.** généralement cette émission passe le vendredi; **the following F.** le vendredi suivant; **she saw the doctor last F.** elle a vu le médecin vendredi dernier; **I have an appointment next F.** j'ai un rendez-vous vendredi prochain; **the F. after next** vendredi en huit; **the F. before last** l'autre vendredi; **a week from F.**, *Br* **a week on F.**, *Br* **F. week** vendredi en huit; *Br* **a fortnight on F., F. fortnight** vendredi en quinze; **a week/fortnight ago F.** il y a eu huit/quinze jours vendredi; **F. morning** vendredi matin; **F. afternoon** vendredi après-midi; **F. evening** vendredi soir; **we're going out (on) F. night** nous sortons vendredi soir; **she spent F. night at her friend's house** elle a passé la nuit de vendredi chez son amie; **we caught the F. morning boat** nous avons pris le bateau du vendredi matin; **F. 26 February** vendredi 26 février; **they were married on F. 12 June** ils se sont mariés le vendredi 12 juin; **F. the thirteenth** vendredi treize

fridge [frɪdʒ] **N** réfrigérateur *m*

▸▸ ***fridge magnet*** aimant *m* décoratif, magnet *m*

fridge-freezer **N** réfrigérateur-congélateur *m*

fried [fraɪd] **ADJ 1** *(cooked in frying pan)* frit; **f. egg** œuf *m* poêlé *ou* sur le plat; **f. food** friture *f*; **f. potatoes** pommes *fpl* frites; **(special) f. rice** riz *m* cantonais **2** *Am Fam (drunk)* bourré, pété; *(on drugs)* raide, parti

friend [frend] **N 1** *(gen)* ami(e) *m,f*; **to make friends** se faire des amis; **he tried to make friends with her brother** il essaya d'être ami avec son frère; **shall we be friends?** on est amis?; *(after a quarrel)* on fait la paix?; **his school friends** ses camarades *mfpl* d'école; **Lesley's a good f. of mine** Lesley est une grande amie à moi; **we're just good friends** nous sommes bons amis sans plus; **my best f.** mon meilleur ami, ma meilleure amie; **we're the best of friends** nous sommes les meilleurs amis du monde; **he's a f. of the family** c'est un ami de la famille; **he's always been a real f. to us** il a toujours été là quand on a eu besoin de lui; **she's no f. of mine** elle ne fait pas partie de mes amis; **I tell you this as a f.** je vous dis ça en ami; **they wanted to part friends** ils voulaient se quitter bons amis; **you're among friends here** tu es entre amis ici; **a f. of yours is a f. of mine** tes amis sont mes amis; **she has friends in high places** elle a des amis en haut lieu *ou* bien placés; *Prov* **a f. in need is a f. indeed** = c'est dans le besoin qu'on reconnaît ses vrais amis; **f. or foe?** *(said by sentry)* qui va là?

2 *(supporter* ▸ *of law and order etc)* ami(e) *m,f*, partisan(e) *m,f*; (▸ *of the arts)* mécène *m*, ami(e) *m,f*; **f. of the poor** bienfaiteur(trice) *m,f* des pauvres; **she's no f. of trade unionism** elle n'est pas favorable au syndicalisme; **the Friends of the Tate Gallery** les Amis de la Tate Gallery; *Rel* **the (Society of) Friends** la Société des Amis, les Quakers *mpl*

3 *(addressing someone)* **my dear f.** mon (ma) cher(ère); **listen, f.** écoute, mon vieux

4 *(colleague)* collègue *mf*; **friends, we are gathered here tonight...** chers amis *ou* collègues, nous sommes réunis ici ce soir...

▸▸ ***Friends of the Earth*** les Amis de la Terre

friendless ['frendlɪs] **ADJ** sans amis

friendliness ['frendlɪnɪs] **N** gentillesse *f*; **an atmosphere of warmth and f.** une ambiance chaleureuse et sympathique

friendly ['frendlɪ] *(compar* **friendlier**, *superl* **friendliest**) **ADJ 1** *(person)* aimable, gentil; *(animal)* gentil; *(smile, advice, game)* amical; *(city, neighbours, face)* sympathique; **to be f. to** *or* **towards sb** être gentil *ou* aimable avec qn; **a f. welcome** *or* **reception** un accueil chaleureux; **that wasn't very f. of him!** ce n'était pas très gentil de sa part!; **someone ought to have a f. word with him and explain that...** quelqu'un devrait lui expliquer gentiment que... + *indicative* **2** *(close, intimate, allied)* ami; **they've become very f. lately** elles sont devenues très amies dernièrement; **she's very f. with the boss all of a sudden** elle est très copine avec le patron tout d'un coup; **to be on f. terms with sb** être en bons termes avec qn; **a f. nation** un pays ami; **to get too f. with sb** se montrer trop familier avec qn; *Fam* **don't let him get too f.** garde tes distances avec lui; **a f. plane** un avion allié

N *(game)* match *m* amical

▸▸ *Mil* ***friendly fire*** feu *m* allié, tirs *mpl* amis *ou* fratricides; **to come under f. fire** tomber sous le feu allié; ***the Friendly Islands*** Tonga *m*, les îles *fpl* des Amis; *Sport* ***friendly match*** match *m* amical; *Br Fin* ***friendly society*** société *f* de mutualité; *Fin* ***friendly takeover bid*** OPA *f* amicale

-FRIENDLY SUFFIXE

Ce suffixe sert à former des adjectifs sans équivalent direct en français.

• Au sens de PRATIQUE pour la personne ou la chose désignée par le nom, **-friendly** est apparu pour la première fois dans un mot du vocabulaire informatique: **user-friendly** (convivial). Depuis, il s'est étendu à d'autres domaines:

a child-friendly restaurant un restaurant pour les familles; **dog-friendly hotels** des hôtels où les chiens sont les bienvenus; **a bicycle-friendly city** une ville où l'on peut facilement rouler à bicyclette

• Le sens originel de **-friendly** s'est élargi jusqu'à couvrir celui de NON NUISIBLE, notamment à l'environnement:

an environment-friendly product un produit non polluant; **ozone-friendly** qui préserve la couche d'ozone; **wildlife-friendly fertilizer** un engrais qui ne détruit pas la faune et la flore

friendship ['frendʃɪp] **N** amitié *f*; **to form a f. with sb** se lier d'amitié avec qn, nouer une amitié avec qn; **he did it out of f. for her** il l'a fait par amitié pour elle; **to live in peace and f.** vivre en bonne intelligence; **the aim is to promote f. between nations** le but est de promouvoir l'amitié entre les nations

fries [fraɪz] *pl of* **fry**

frieze [friːz] **N 1** *Archit* frise *f* **2** *Tex* ratine *f*

frig [frɪg] (*pt & pp* **frigged**, *cont* **frigging**) *Vulg* VT *(have sex with)* baiser avec
VI *(masturbate)* s'astiquer le bouton, se branler
▸ **frig about, frig around** VI *very Fam (waste time)* traînailler, glandouiller; *(play the fool)* déconner
▸ **frig off** VI *very Fam* **f. off!** va te faire foutre!

frigate ['frɪgət] N frégate *f*
▸▸ *Orn* ***frigate bird*** frégate *f*

frigging ['frɪgɪŋ] *very Fam* ADJ fichu, foutu; **this f. car** cette foutue bagnole, cette putain de bagnole; **what a f. waste of time!** putain, quelle perte de temps!; **shut your f. mouth!** ferme-la!, ferme ta gueule!
ADV **don't f. lie to me!** ne me mens pas, bordel!; **I'm f. freezing!** je me les gèle!

fright [fraɪt] N **1** *(sudden fear)* frayeur *f*, peur *f*; **his face was pale with f.** il était vert de peur; **to take f. (at)** s'effrayer (de); **to give sb a f.** faire une frayeur à qn, faire peur à qn; **I got the f. of my life when he said that** j'ai eu la peur de ma vie quand il a dit ça **2** *Fam (mess)* **you look an absolute f.** tu fais vraiment peur à voir

frighten ['fraɪtən] VT effrayer, faire peur à; **stop it, you're frightening me!** arrête, tu me fais peur!; **to f. sb out of doing sth** dissuader qn de faire qch en lui faisant peur; **to f. sb into doing sth** faire peur à qn pour qu'il fasse qch; **he is easily frightened** il s'effraie pour un rien; **these animals are easily frightened** ces animaux s'effarouchent d'un rien; **to f. sb to death** *or* **out of their wits, to f. the life out of sb** faire une peur bleue à qn
▸ **frighten away** VT SEP faire fuir (par la peur); *(animal)* effaroucher; **the burglars were frightened away by the police siren** effrayés par la sirène de police, les cambrioleurs ont pris la fuite

frightened ['fraɪtənd] ADJ effrayé; **to be f. of sth** avoir peur de qch; **I was too f. to speak** je n'arrivais pas à parler tellement j'avais peur; **there's nothing to be f. of** il n'y a rien à craindre; **he looked f.** il avait l'air d'avoir peur; **f. faces/children** des visages *mpl*/des enfants *mpl* apeurés

frighteners ['fraɪtənəz] NPL *Fam* **to put the f. on sb** filer la trouille à qn

frightening ['fraɪtənɪŋ] ADJ effrayant; **the consequences are too f. to think of** on n'ose pas imaginer les conséquences; **it's f. to think what might have happened** ça fait peur de penser à ce qui aurait pu arriver

frighteningly ['fraɪtənɪŋlɪ] ADV à faire peur; **the story was f. true to life** l'histoire était d'un réalisme effrayant

frightful ['fraɪtfʊl] ADJ **1** *(horrible)* atroce, horrible, effroyable; **the soldier had f. wounds** le soldat avait des blessures atroces **2** *Br Fam (unpleasant)* **we had a f. time parking the car** on a eu un mal fou à garer la voiture **3** *Br Fam (as intensifier)* **he's a f. bore** il est horriblement *ou* affreusement casse-pieds

frightfully ['fraɪtfʊlɪ] ADV *Br* **he's a f. good dancer** il danse remarquablement bien; **it was f. generous of you to buy me lunch** c'était vraiment très généreux à vous de m'inviter à déjeuner; **I'm f. sorry** je suis absolument désolé; *Fam Hum* **f. f.** = maniérisme utilisé pour décrire les manières et l'accent de la haute bourgeoisie britannique

frightfulness ['fraɪtfʊlnɪs] N atrocité *f*

frigid ['frɪdʒɪd] ADJ **1** *(sexually)* frigide **2** *(smile, style, atmosphere)* glacial **3** *Geog & Met* glacial
▸▸ ***Frigid Zone*** régions *fpl* polaires

frigidity [frɪ'dʒɪdətɪ] N **1** *(coldness)* froideur *f* **2** *Psy* frigidité *f*

frigidly ['frɪdʒɪdlɪ] ADV *(answer, comment etc)* d'un ton glacial; **f. polite** d'une politesse glaciale

frill [frɪl] N *Tex* ruche *f*, volant *m*; *Culin* papillote *f*; *Zool* collerette *f*; **shirt f.** jabot *m*
• **frills** NPL *(ornamentation, luxuries)* **without frills** sans façon; **a cheap, basic package holiday with no frills** des vacances organisées simples et pas chères

frilled [frɪld] ADJ *(ribbon etc)* froncé, ruché; *(shirt)* à jabots
▸▸ *Zool* ***frilled lizard*** lézard *m* à collerette

frilly ['frɪlɪ] (*compar* **frillier**, *superl* **frilliest**) ADJ **1** *Tex* orné de fanfreluches **2** *(style)* affecté, apprêté

fringe [frɪndʒ] N **1** *(decorative edge ▸ on rug, carpet)* frange *f*; **a f. of trees** une bordure d'arbres
2 *(of hair)* frange *f*
3 *(periphery)* périphérie *f*, frange *f*; **on the f. of** *or* **fringes of** en bordure de; *Fig* en marge de; **to live on the f. of society** vivre en marge de la société; **to be on the radical f. of a party** appartenir à la frange radicale d'un parti
4 *Br Theat* **the F. (festival)** le festival off
5 *(of golf green)* lisière *f*
VT *(rug, carpet)* franger; **the path was fringed with rosebushes** le sentier était bordé de rosiers; **palm-fringed beaches** des plages *fpl* bordées de palmiers
▸▸ ***fringe benefits*** avantages *mpl* accessoires *ou* annexes; ***fringe group*** frange *f*; ***fringe market*** marché *m* marginal; *Br* ***fringe theatre*** théâtre *m* d'avant-garde *ou* expérimental

frippery ['frɪpərɪ] (*pl* **fripperies**) N **1** *(showy objects)* colifichets *mpl*, babioles *fpl*; *(on clothing)* fanfreluches *fpl* **2** *(UNCOUNT) (ostentation)* mignardises *fpl*, chichi *m*

Frisbee® ['frɪzbɪ] N Frisbee® *m inv*

Frisco ['frɪskəʊ] N *Fam* = surnom donné à San Francisco

frisk [frɪsk] VI *(play)* gambader; **the two kittens frisked about in the garden** les deux chatons gambadaient dans le jardin
VT *(search)* fouiller
N *(search)* fouille *f*; **to give sb a f.** fouiller qn

friskiness ['frɪskɪnɪs] N **1** *(liveliness)* vivacité *f* **2** *(sexual)* excitation *f* sexuelle

frisking ['frɪskɪŋ] N *(of suspect, traveller)* fouille *f*

frisky ['frɪskɪ] (*compar* **friskier**, *superl* **friskiest**) ADJ **1** *(animal)* fringant, vivace **2** *(person ▸ sexually)* gaillard; **to be feeling f.** être excité

fritillary [frɪ'tɪlərɪ] (*pl* **fritillaries**) N *Bot & Entom* fritillaire *f*

fritter ['frɪtə(r)] N *Culin* beignet *m*; **banana fritters** beignets *mpl* de banane
VT *(money, time)* gaspiller; *(fortune)* dissiper
▸ **fritter away** VT SEP *(money, time)* gaspiller; *(fortune)* dissiper; **I feel as if I've just frittered away the day** j'ai l'impression d'avoir perdu ma journée

frivolity [frɪ'vɒlətɪ] (*pl* **frivolities**) N frivolité *f*

frivolous ['frɪvələs] ADJ frivole

frivolously ['frɪvələslɪ] ADV de manière frivole

frizz [frɪz] N **she had a f. of blond hair** elle avait des cheveux blonds frisottés *ou* tout frisés
VT frisotter
VI frisotter

frizziness ['frɪzɪnɪs] N **the f. of my hair** mes cheveux *mpl* crépus

frizzle ['frɪzəl] VT **1** *Culin (overcook)* griller; *(burn)* calciner, carboniser **2** *(curl)* faire friser
VI **1** *(cook noisily)* grésiller **2** *(curl)* friser

frizzy ['frɪzɪ] (*compar* **frizzier**, *superl* **frizziest**) ADJ *(hair)* crêpelé, crépu

FRN [ˌefɑː'ren] N *Banking (abbr* **floating-rate note**) effet *m* à taux flottant

fro[1] [frəʊ] *see* **to and fro**

fro[2] [frəʊ] (*pl* **fros**) *Fam (abbr* **Afro**) ADJ *(hairstyle)* afro *(inv)*
N coiffure *f* afro, afro *m*

frock [frɒk] N *(dress)* robe *f*; *Rel* froc *m*
▸▸ ***frock coat*** redingote *f*

frog [frɒg] N **1** *Zool* grenouille *f*; *Fam* **to have a f. in one's throat** avoir un chat dans la gorge **2** *(on uniform)* brandebourg *m*; *(on women's clothing)* soutache *f* **3** *Vet (part of horse's hoof)* fourchette *f*
• **Frog** *Br Fam* N *(French person)* = terme xénophobe, souvent employé de manière humoristique, désignant un Français ADJ français[□]; **they've got some F. footballer playing for them** il y a un joueur français dans leur équipe[□]
▸▸ *Culin* ***frog's legs*** cuisses *fpl* de grenouille; ***frog pond*** grenouillère *f*

frogged [frɒgd] ADJ à brandebourgs

Froggie = **Froggy**

frogging ['frɒgɪŋ] N *(UNCOUNT) (on clothing)* soutaches *fpl*

Froggy ['frɒgɪ] *Br Fam* (*pl* **Froggies**) N = terme xénophobe, souvent employé de manière humoristique, désignant un Français
ADJ français[□]; **I hate F. food** j'ai horreur de la cuisine française[□]

frogman ['frɒgmən] (*pl* **frogmen** [-mən]) N homme-grenouille *m*

frogmarch ['frɒgmɑːtʃ] VT *Br (person)* emmener de force; **they frogmarched her out of the room** ils l'ont fait sortir de la pièce de force; **the protesters were frogmarched to a police van** les manifestants furent entraînés jusqu'au fourgon de police

frogmen ['frɒgmən] *pl of* **frogman**

frogspawn ['frɒgspɔːn] N *Br* frai *m* de grenouilles

frolic ['frɒlɪk] (*pt & pp* **frolicked**, *cont* **frolicking**) VI s'ébattre, gambader; **the children frolicked about on the grass** les enfants gambadaient sur la pelouse
N *(run)* gambades *fpl*, ébats *mpl*; *(game)* jeu *m*; **we let the dogs have a f. in the park** on a laissé les chiens s'ébattre dans le parc

FROM [frəm, *stressed* frɒm]

- de **1, 2, 4, 6, 10, 11**
- depuis **2**
- d'après **9**
- à partir de **2, 3**
- à base de **8**

PREP **1** *(indicating starting point ▸ in space)* de; **Einstein came to this country f. Germany** Einstein a quitté l'Allemagne pour s'établir ici; **her parents came f. Russia** ses parents venaient de Russie; **where's your friend f.?** d'où est *ou* vient votre ami?; **I've just come back f. there** j'en reviens; **there are no direct flights f. Hobart** il n'y a pas de vol direct à partir d'Hobart; **the 11.10 train f. Cambridge** le train de 11h10 en provenance de Cambridge; **the airport is about 15 kilometres f. the city centre** l'aéroport se trouve à 15 kilomètres environ du centre-ville; **it rained all the way f. Calais to Paris** il a plu pendant tout le trajet de Calais à Paris; **it takes 15 minutes f. here to my house** il faut 15 minutes pour aller d'ici à chez moi; **f. town to town** de ville en ville
2 *(indicating starting point ▸ in time)* de, à partir de, depuis; **f. now on** désormais, dorénavant; **f. that day** depuis ce jour, à partir de ce jour; **f. morning till night** du matin au soir; **f. the age of four** à partir de quatre ans; **she was unhappy f. her first day at boarding school** elle a été malheureuse dès son premier jour à l'internat; **f. the start** dès *ou* depuis le début; **a week f. today** dans huit jours; **she remembered him f. her childhood** elle se souvenait de lui dans son enfance; **we've got food left over f. last night** nous avons des restes d'hier soir
3 *(indicating starting point ▸ in price, quantity)* à partir de; **knives f. £2 each** des couteaux à partir de 2 livres la pièce; **the price has been increased f. 50 pence to 60 pence** on a augmenté le prix de 50 pence à 60 pence; **6 f. 14 is 8** 6 ôté de 14 donne 8; **we went f. three employees to fifteen in a year** nous sommes passés de trois à quinze employés en un an; **the bird lays f. four to six eggs** l'oiseau pond de quatre à six œufs; **every flavour of ice-cream f. vanilla to pistachio** tous les parfums de glace de la vanille à la pistache
4 *(indicating origin, source)* de; **who's the letter f.?** de qui est la lettre?; **f....** *(on letter, parcel)* expéditeur/expéditrice...; **don't tell her that the flowers are f. me** ne lui dites pas que les fleurs viennent de moi; **tell her that f. me** dites-lui cela de ma part; **I got a phone call f. her yesterday** j'ai reçu un coup de fil d'elle hier; **he got the idea f. a book he read** il a trouvé l'idée dans un livre qu'il a lu; **where did you get the ring f.?** où avez-vous eu la bague?; **you can get a money order f. the post office** vous pouvez avoir un mandat à la poste; **I bought my piano f. a neighbour** j'ai acheté mon piano à un voisin; **you mustn't borrow money f. them** vous ne devez pas leur emprunter de l'argent; **she stole some documents f. the ministry** elle a volé des documents au ministère; **I heard about it f. the landlady** c'est la propriétaire qui m'en a parlé; **a scene f. a play** une scène d'une

pièce; **a quotation f. Shakespeare** une citation tirée de Shakespeare; **he translates f. English into French** il traduit d'anglais en français; **she still has injuries resulting f. the crash** elle a encore des blessures qui datent de l'accident; **she's been away f. work for a week** ça fait une semaine qu'elle n'est pas allée au travail; **they returned f. their holidays yesterday** ils sont rentrés de vacances hier; **the man f. the Inland Revenue** le monsieur du fisc

5 *(off, out of)* **she took a book f. the shelf** elle a pris un livre sur l'étagère; **he drank straight f. the bottle** il a bu à même la bouteille; **she drew a gun f. her pocket** elle sortit un revolver de sa poche; **he took a beer f. the fridge** il a pris une bière dans le frigo

6 *(indicating position, location)* de; **f. the top you can see the whole city** du haut on voit toute la ville; **you get a great view f. the bridge** on a une très belle vue du pont; **the rock juts out f. the cliff** le rocher dépasse de la falaise

7 *(indicating cause, reason)* **you can get sick f. drinking the water** vous pouvez tomber malade en buvant l'eau; **his back hurt f. lifting heavy boxes** il avait mal au dos après avoir soulevé de gros cartons; **I guessed she was Australian f. the way she spoke** j'ai deviné qu'elle était australienne à sa façon de parler; **I know him f. seeing him at the club** je le reconnais pour l'avoir vu au cercle; **he died f. grief** il est mort de chagrin; **to act f. conviction** agir par conviction

8 *(using)* **they are made f. flour** ils sont faits à base de farine; **Calvados is made f. apples** le calvados est fait avec des pommes; **she played the piece f. memory** elle joua le morceau de mémoire; **I speak f. personal experience** je sais de quoi je parle

9 *(judging by)* d'après; **f. the way she sings you'd think she were a professional** à l'entendre chanter on dirait que c'est son métier; **f. his looks you might suppose that...** à le voir on dirait que… + *indicative*; **f. what I can see...** à ce que je vois…; **f. what I gather...** d'après ce que j'ai cru comprendre…

10 *(in comparisons)* de; **it's no different f. riding a bike** c'est comme faire du vélo; **how do you tell one f. the other?** comment les reconnais-tu l'un de l'autre?

11 *(indicating prevention, protection)* de; **she saved me f. drowning** elle m'a sauvé de la noyade; **we sheltered f. the rain in a cave** nous nous sommes abrités de la pluie dans une caverne; **they were hidden f. view** on ne les voyait pas

frond [frɒnd] **N** *Bot (of fern)* fronde *f*; *(on palm tree)* feuille *f*

FRONT [frʌnt]

> **N**
> • devant **1** • avant **1**
> • façade **1, 5, 6, 8** • bord de mer **2**
> • front **3, 4, 7**
> **ADJ**
> • de devant **1**
> **ADV**
> • par devant
> **VI**
> • être orienté **1** • faire front **2**
> **VT**
> • diriger **3**

N 1 *(forward part)* devant *m*; *(of vehicle)* avant *m*; *(of queue)* début *m*; *(of stage)* devant *m*; *(of building)* façade *f*; *(of shop)* devanture *f*; **I'll be at the f. of the train** je serai en tête de *ou* à l'avant du train; **he sat up f. near the driver** il s'est assis à l'avant près du conducteur; **our seats were at the f. (of the theatre)** nous avions des places aux premiers rangs (du théâtre); **come to the f. of the class** venez devant; **she went to the f. of the queue** elle alla se mettre au début de la queue; **to push one's way to the f.** se frayer un chemin jusqu'au premier rang; *Fig* se pousser (en avant); **The Times's theatre critic is out f. tonight** le critique dramatique du Times est dans la salle ce soir; **at the f. of the book** au début du livre; **she wrote her name on the f. of the envelope** elle écrivit son nom sur le devant de l'enveloppe; **he got wine down his f.** *or* **the f. of his shirt** du vin a été renversé sur le devant de sa chemise

2 *(seashore)* bord *m* de mer, front *m* de mer; **the hotel is on the f.** l'hôtel est au bord de la *ou* sur le front de mer; **a walk along** *or* **on the f.** une promenade au bord de la mer

3 *Mil* front *m*; **on the Eastern/Western f.** sur le front Est/Ouest; **he fought at the f.** il a combattu au front; *Fig* **the Prime Minister is being attacked on all fronts** on s'en prend au Premier ministre de tous côtés; **little had been achieved on the domestic** *or* **home f.** on avait accompli peu de choses sur le plan intérieur

4 *(joint effort)* front *m*; **to present a united f. (on sth)** faire front commun (devant qch)

5 *(appearance)* façade *f*; **his apparent optimism was only a f.** son optimisme apparent n'était qu'une façade; **to put on a bold** *or* **brave f.** faire preuve de courage

6 *(cover)* façade *f*, couverture *f*; **the shop is just a f. for a drugs ring** le magasin n'est qu'une couverture pour des trafiquants de drogue

7 *Met* front *m*; **cold/warm f.** front *m* froid/chaud

8 *Archit* façade *f*; **the north/south f.** la façade nord/sud

9 *Br Fam (nerve)* **to have the f. to do sth** avoir l'effronterie *ou* le front de faire qch[□]

10 *Fam (idioms)* **to pay up f.** payer d'avance[□]; **they want £5,000 up f.** ils veulent 5000 livres d'avance[□]; **he was very up f. about it** il a été franc sur ce point[□]

ADJ 1 *(in a forward position)* de devant; *Aut* **f. seat/wheel** siège *m*/roue *f* avant; **she was sitting in the f. row** elle était assise au premier rang; *Press* **the f. page** la première page; **his picture is on the f. page** sa photo est en première page; **to be f. page news** faire la une; **he came in through a f. window** il est entré par une fenêtre de devant; **I'll be in the f. end of the train** je serai en tête de *ou* à l'avant du train; **the f. part of the brain** la partie antérieure du cerveau; **a f. view** une vue de face; *Archit* une élévation du devant

2 *Ling* **a f. vowel** une voyelle avant *ou* antérieure

3 *Am Fam (idiom)* **to put sth on the f. burner** traiter qch en priorité[□]

ADV par devant; *Mil* **eyes f.!** fixe!

VI 1 *Br (face)* **the hotel fronts onto the beach** l'hôtel donne sur la plage; **the house fronts north** la maison est exposée *ou* orientée au nord

2 *Mil* faire front; **left f.!** à gauche front!, à gauche, gauche!

3 *(cover)* **the newspaper fronted for a terrorist organization** le journal servait de façade à une organisation terroriste

4 *Fam Black Am slang (show off)* frimer; *(tell lies)* baratiner, raconter des craques

VT 1 *(stand before ▸ building)* **lush gardens fronted the building** il y avait des jardins luxuriants devant le bâtiment

2 *Constr (cover the front of ▸ building)* donner une (nouvelle) façade à; **the house was fronted with stone** la maison avait une façade en pierre

3 *(lead)* être à la tête de, diriger; *TV (present)* présenter; *Mus* **to f. a band** *(lead it)* diriger un orchestre

4 *Am Fam (pay in advance)* avancer[□]; **the cashier can f. you the money** le caissier peut vous faire une avance *ou* vous avancer l'argent[□]

5 *Am Fam (give, lend money to)* filer; **can you f. me five bucks?** tu pourrais pas me filer cinq dollars?

• **in front ADV** *(in theatre, vehicle)* à l'avant; *(ahead, leading)* en avant; **there was a very tall man in the row in f.** il y avait un très grand homme assis devant moi; **the women walked in f. and the children behind** les femmes marchaient devant et les enfants derrière; **to send sb on in f.** envoyer qn devant; *Sport* **to be in f.** être en tête *ou* premier; **Manchester United are five points in f.** Manchester United mène par cinq points

• **in front of PREP** devant; **she was sitting in f. of the TV** elle était assise devant la télé; **he was right in f. of me** il était juste devant moi; **not in f. of the children!** pas devant les enfants!

▸▸ ***front cover*** *(of book, magazine)* couverture *f*; **his name is on the f. cover** son nom est en couverture; ***front desk*** réception *f*; ***front door*** *(of house)* porte *f* d'entrée; *(of vehicle)* portière *f* avant; *Theat* ***front of house*** = partie d'un théâtre où peuvent circuler les spectateurs; *Mil* ***the front line*** la première ligne; *Fig* **she is in the f. line in the fight against drug abuse** elle joue un rôle important dans la lutte contre la toxicomanie; *Am* ***front lot*** cour *f (devant un immeuble)*; ***front man*** *(representative, spokesman)* porte-parole *m inv*, représentant *m*; *Pej (figurehead)* prête-nom *m*; *TV (presenter)* présentateur *m*; ***front matter*** = pages préliminaires (avant le texte) d'un livre; *Am Fam* ***front money*** capital *m* initial[□] *ou* de départ[□], mise *f* de fonds initiale[□]; *Banking* ***front office*** front-office *m*; *Cin* ***front projection*** projection *f* frontale; ***front room*** *(at front of house)* = pièce qui donne sur le devant de la maison; *(sitting room)* salon *m*; *Am* ***front yard*** jardin *m (devant une maison)*

frontage [ˈfrʌntɪdʒ] **N 1** *(of house, building)* façade *f*; *(shopfront)* devanture *f* **2** *(of river etc)* terrain *m* en bordure; **garden with river f.** jardin *m* en bordure de rivière **3** *(land at front of building etc)* espace *m* sur le devant d'un immeuble

▸▸ *Am* ***frontage road*** contre-allée *f*

frontal [ˈfrʌntəl] **ADJ** *Mil (assault, attack)* de front; *Anat & Med* frontal

N *Rel* parement *m* d'autel

▸▸ *Aut* ***frontal impact*** choc *m* frontal; *Met* ***frontal system*** système *m* de fronts

frontbench [ˌfrʌntˈbentʃ] **N** *Br Pol (members of the government)* ministres *mpl*; *(members of the opposition)* ministres *mpl* du cabinet fantôme; **he's never been on the f.** *(government)* il n'a jamais été ministre; *(opposition)* il n'a jamais été membre du cabinet fantôme; **the frontbenches** *(in Parliament)* = à la Chambre des communes, bancs situés à droite et à gauche du président et occupés respectivement par les ministres du gouvernement en exercice et ceux du gouvernement fantôme

▸▸ ***frontbench spokesman, frontbench spokesperson*** *(of cabinet)* porte-parole *m inv* du gouvernement; *(of shadow cabinet)* porte-parole *m inv* du cabinet fantôme; ***frontbench team*** *(cabinet)* équipe *f* ministérielle; *(shadow cabinet)* cabinet *m* fantôme

frontbencher [ˌfrʌntˈbentʃə(r)] **N** *Br Pol (member of the government)* ministre *m*; *(member of the opposition)* membre *m* du cabinet fantôme

front-end **N** *Comput* interface *f*

▸▸ *Comput* ***front-end computer*** ordinateur *m* frontal; *Fin* ***front-end fee*** frais *mpl* d'entrée; *Fin* ***front-end loading*** = système de prélèvement des frais sur les premiers versements; *Comput* ***front-end processor*** processeur *m* frontal

frontier [*Br* ˈfrʌntɪə(r), *Am* frʌnˈtɪər] **N 1** *also Fig (border)* frontière *f*; **the frontiers of science** les frontières *fpl ou* limites *fpl* de la science **2** *Am* **the F.** la Frontière *(nom donné à la limite des terres habitées par les colons pendant la colonisation de l'Amérique du Nord)*

COMP 1 *(dispute)* de frontière; *(post)* frontière **2** *Am (spirit)* de pionnier

▸▸ ***frontier town*** = ville de l'Ouest américain, à l'époque des pionniers

frontispiece [ˈfrʌntɪspiːs] **N** frontispice *m*

front-line **ADJ** *Mil (soldiers, troops)* en première ligne; *(ambulance)* de zone de combat

▸▸ *Am Sport* ***front-line player*** avant *m*; *Pol* ***the front-line states*** les États *mpl* limitrophes *(d'un pays en guerre)*

front-loader **N** *(washing machine)* machine *f* à laver à chargement frontal

front-loading **ADJ** *(washing machine)* à chargement frontal

front-row [-rəʊ] **ADJ** *Sport* **f. forward** *(in rugby)* avant *m* de première ligne, première ligne *f*; **to have a f. seat** *Theat* être assis au premier rang; *Fig* être aux premières loges

front-runner **N 1** *Sport (horse)* cheval *m* de tête; *(athlete)* coureur(euse) *m,f* de tête **2** *(in election etc)* favori(ite) *m,f*

front-wheel drive **N** *Aut* traction *f* avant

frosh [frɒʃ] **N** *Am Fam Univ* étudiant(e) *m,f* de première année[□]

frost [frɒst] **N 1** *(freezing weather)* gel *m*, gelée *f*; **there was a f. last night** il a gelé hier soir; **heavy/light f.** grosse/petite gelée *f*; **a late f.** des gelées *fpl* tardives; **eight degrees of f.** huit degrés au-dessous de zéro **2** *(frozen dew)* givre *m*, gelée *f* blanche; **the grass was covered in f.** le gazon était couvert de givre **3** *Am Fam (fiasco)* four *m*, fiasco *m*

VT 1 *(freeze)* geler; *(cover with frost)* givrer; **the rim of the glass was frosted with sugar** le bord du verre avait été givré avec du sucre **2** *Am (cake)* glacer **3** *Tech (glass pane)* dépolir

VI *(freeze)* geler; *(become covered with frost)* se givrer

▸ **frost over, frost up VT SEP** givrer

VI se givrer

frostbite ['frɒstbaɪt] **N** *(UNCOUNT)* gelure *f*, froidure *f*; **he got f. in his toes** il a eu les orteils gelés; **the climber died of f.** l'alpiniste est mort gelé

frostbitten ['frɒstbɪtən] **ADJ** *(hands, nose)* gelé; *(plant)* gelé, grillé par le gel

frostbound ['frɒstbaʊnd] **ADJ** *(earth)* gelé

frosted ['frɒstɪd] **ADJ 1** *(frozen)* gelé; *(covered with frost)* givré

2 *(pane of glass)* dépoli

3 *Am (cake* ▸ *iced)* glacé; *(*▸ *sugared)* recouvert de sucre

4 *(lipstick, nail varnish)* nacré

frost-free ADJ *(refrigerator, freezer)* à dégivrage automatique

frostily ['frɒstɪlɪ] **ADV** *(greet)* de manière glaciale, froidement; *(say)* sur un ton glacial

frostiness ['frɒstɪnɪs] **N 1** *(of weather, air, morning)* froid *m* glacial **2** *(of person)* manière *f* glaciale; **the f. of her smile/behaviour** son sourire *m*/comportement *m* glacial

frosting ['frɒstɪŋ] **N** *Am (for icing)* glaçage *m*, glace *f*

frostproof ['frɒstpruːf] **ADJ** résistant à la gelée

frosty ['frɒstɪ] *(compar* **frostier**, *superl* **frostiest)** **ADJ 1** *(weather, air)* glacial; **we had several f. nights** il a gelé plusieurs nuits **2** *(ground, window)* couvert de givre **3** *(answer, manner)* glacial, froid

froth [frɒθ] **N** *(UNCOUNT)* **1** *(foam)* écume *f*, mousse *f*; *(on beer, coffee, chocolate)* mousse *f*; *(on lips)* écume *f* **2** *(trivialities, empty talk)* futilités *fpl*

VI *(liquid)* écumer, mousser; *(beer, soap)* mousser; **to f. at the mouth** écumer, baver; *Fam* **he was so angry he was practically frothing at the mouth** il écumait de rage

VT faire mousser; **she's frothing (up) some milk for the cappuccinos** elle fait mousser du lait pour les cappuccinos

frothy ['frɒθɪ] *(compar* **frothier**, *superl* **frothiest)** **ADJ 1** *(liquid)* mousseux, écumeux; *(beer, coffee, chocolate)* mousseux; *(sea)* écumeux **2** *(entertainment, literature)* creux, futile, sans substance **3** *(dress, lace)* léger, vaporeux

frown [fraʊn] **VI** froncer les sourcils, se renfrogner; **she frowned at my remark** mon observation lui a fait froncer les sourcils; **to f. at sb** regarder qn en fronçant les sourcils

N froncement *m* de sourcils; **he gave a f.** il fronça les sourcils

▸▸ ***frown lines*** rides *fpl* intersourcilières

▸ **frown on, frown upon VT INSEP** désapprouver; **her parents f. upon their friendship** ses parents voient leur amitié d'un mauvais œil; **such behaviour is rather frowned upon** ce type de comportement n'est pas vu d'un très bon œil *ou* n'est pas très bien vu

frowning ['fraʊnɪŋ] **ADJ** *(expression)* renfrogné

frowsty ['fraʊstɪ] *(compar* **frowstier**, *superl* **frowstiest)** **ADJ** *Br Fam* qui sent le renfermé▫

frowsy, frowzy ['fraʊzɪ] *(compar* **frowsier, frowzier**, *superl* **frowsiest, frowziest)** **ADJ** *Br Fam* **1** *(shabby* ▸ *person)* négligé▫; *(*▸ *clothing)* élimé▫, râpé▫ **2** *Fam (stuffy* ▸ *room)* qui sent le renfermé▫

froze [frəʊz] *pt of* **freeze**

frozen ['frəʊzən] *pp of* **freeze**

ADJ 1 *(ground, lake, pipes)* gelé; *(person)* gelé, glacé; **f. peas** petits pois *mpl* surgelés; **the lake is f. solid** le lac est complètement gelé; **my hands are f.** j'ai les mains gelées *ou* glacées; **I'm f. stiff** je suis gelé jusqu'à la moelle (des os); *Fig* **f. with terror** mort de peur **2** *(credit, wages)* gelé, bloqué; *(currency, prices, assets)* gelé; *(account)* bloqué **3** *Comput (screen)* bloqué

▸▸ ***frozen food*** *(in refrigerator)* aliments *mpl* congelés; *(industrially frozen)* surgelés *mpl*; ***frozen food compartment*** congélateur *m*; *Med* ***frozen shoulder*** épaule *f* ankylosée; ***frozen yoghurt*** yaourt *m* glacé

fructify ['frʌktɪfaɪ] *(pt & pp* **fructified)** *Formal* **VT** faire fructifier

VI fructifier

fructose ['frʌktəʊs] **N** *Chem* fructose *m*

frugal ['fruːgəl] **ADJ 1** *(person)* économe, frugal; *(life)* frugal, simple; **she's very f. with her money** elle est près de ses sous **2** *(meal)* frugal

frugality [fruː'gælətɪ] **N 1** *(of person)* parcimonie *f*, frugalité *f*; *(of life)* frugalité *f*, simplicité *f* **2** *(of meal)* frugalité *f*

frugally ['fruːgəlɪ] **ADV** *(live)* simplement, frugalement; *(distribute, give)* parcimonieusement; **we dined f. on bread and cheese** nous avons dîné simplement de pain et de fromage

fruit [fruːt] *(pl sense* **1 inv** *or* **fruits)** **N 1** *(gen)* fruit *m*; **to eat f.** manger des fruits; **a piece of f.** un fruit; **we eat a lot of f.** nous mangeons beaucoup de fruits; **a tree in f.** un arbre qui porte des fruits; **the f.** *or* **fruits of the earth** les fruits *mpl* de la terre; *Fig* **the f. of her womb** le fruit de ses entrailles; **their plans have never borne f.** leurs projets ne se sont jamais réalisés; **his book is the f. of much research** son livre est le fruit de longues recherches

2 *Br Fam Old-fashioned (term of address)* **old f.** mon vieux

3 *Am very Fam Pej (homosexual)* pédé *m*, tante *f*

4 *Am Fam (strange person)* **he's a real f.** il est vraiment loufoque

COMP *(basket)* à fruits; *(diet, farm, stall)* fruitier; *(flavouring)* de *ou* aux fruits

VI *Bot* donner

▸▸ *Zool* ***fruit bat*** chauve-souris *f* frugivore; ***fruit bowl*** coupe *f* à fruits, compotier *m*; ***fruit cocktail*** macédoine *f* de fruits; ***fruit cup*** *(dessert)* coupe *f* de fruits; *(drink)* boisson *f* aux fruits *(parfois alcoolisée)*; ***fruit dish*** *(individual)* coupe *f*, coupelle *f*; *(large)* coupe *f* à fruits, compotier *m*; ***fruit drop*** bonbon *m* aux fruits; ***fruit farmer*** arboriculteur (trice) *m,f* (fruitier(ère)); ***fruit farming*** arboriculture *f* (fruitière); *Entom* ***fruit fly*** mouche *f* du vinaigre, drosophile *f*; ***fruits of the forest*** fruits *mpl* des bois, *Suisse* petits fruits *mpl*; *Br* ***fruit gum*** boule *f* de gomme; ***fruit juice*** jus *m* de fruits; ***fruit knife*** couteau *m* à fruit(s); *Br* ***fruit machine*** machine *f* à sous; ***fruit salad*** salade *f* de fruits; ***fruit sugar*** fructose *m*; ***fruit tree*** arbre *m* fruitier

fruit-bearing ADJ *(tree etc)* frugifère, fructifère

fruitcake ['fruːtkeɪk] **N 1** *(cake)* cake *m* **2** *Fam (lunatic)* cinglé(e) *m,f*

fruit-eating ADJ *(animal)* frugivore

fruiterer ['fruːtərə(r)] **N** *Br* marchand(e) *m,f* de fruits, fruitier(ère) *m,f*

fruitful ['fruːtfʊl] **ADJ 1** *(discussion, suggestion)* fructueux, utile; *(attempt, collaboration)* fructueux **2** *(soil)* fertile, fécond; *(plant, tree)* fécond, productif

fruitfully ['fruːtfʊlɪ] **ADV** fructueusement

fruitfulness ['fruːtfʊlnɪs] **N 1** *(of work, discussion etc)* caractère *m* fructueux **2** *(of soil)* fertilité *f*; *(of tree etc)* productivité *f*

fruiting ['fruːtɪŋ] **ADJ** *(tree etc)* frugifère, fructifère

fruition [fruː'ɪʃən] **N** *Formal* réalisation *f*; **to come to f.** se réaliser; **to bring sth to f.** réaliser qch, concrétiser qch

fruitless ['fruːtlɪs] **ADJ 1** *(discussion, effort)* infructueux; **at least the trip won't have been entirely f.** au moins le voyage n'aura pas tout à fait servi à rien **2** *(plant, tree)* stérile, infécond; *(soil)* stérile

fruity ['fruːtɪ] *(compar* **fruitier**, *superl* **fruitiest)** **ADJ 1** *(flavour, sauce)* fruité, de fruit; *(perfume, wine)* fruité; **the wine has a f. taste** le vin a un goût fruité; **it has a f. smell** ça a une odeur fruitée **2** *(voice)* étoffé, timbré **3** *Fam (joke, story)* corsé▫, salé

frump [frʌmp] **N** femme *f* mal fagotée; **she looks a bit of a f. these days** elle se fagote vraiment mal ces temps-ci

frumpish ['frʌmpɪʃ] **ADJ** mal fagoté; **she wears rather f. clothes** elle s'habille plutôt mal

frustrate [frʌ'streɪt] **VT** *(person)* frustrer, agacer, contrarier; *(efforts, plans)* contrecarrer, faire échouer, contrarier; *(plot)* déjouer, faire échouer; **the rain frustrated our plans** la pluie a contrarié nos projets; **the prisoner was frustrated in his attempt to escape** le prisonnier a raté sa tentative d'évasion

frustrated [frʌ'streɪtɪd] **ADJ 1** *(annoyed)* frustré, agacé; *(disappointed)* frustré, déçu; *(sexually)* frustré; **a f. poet** un poète manqué **2** *(attempt, effort)* vain

frustrating [frʌ'streɪtɪŋ] **ADJ** agaçant, frustrant, pénible; **it's very f. having to wait** c'est vraiment pénible de devoir attendre; **a f. person** une personne agaçante *ou* pénible

frustration [frʌ'streɪʃən] **N** *(gen)* & *Psy* frustration *f*; **it's one of the frustrations of the job** c'est un des aspects frustrants du travail

fry [fraɪ] *(pt & pp* **fried**, *pl* **fries)** **VT 1** *(cook in frying pan)* faire frire, frire; **he fried himself an egg** il s'est fait un œuf sur le plat; *Am Fam* **go f. an egg!** va te faire cuire un œuf! **2** *Am Fam (convict)* faire passer à la chaise électrique▫

VI 1 *(food)* frire; *Fig (person)* griller **2** *Am Fam (convict)* passer à la chaise électrique▫

N 1 *(UNCOUNT) (fish)* fretin *m*; *(frogs)* têtards *mpl* **2** *Am (picnic)* = sorte de pique-nique où on mange de la friture **3** *(offal)* issues *fpl*; *(of lamb, pig)* fressure *f*

• **fries NPL** frites *fpl*

fryer ['fraɪə(r)] **N 1** *(pan)* poêle *f* (à frire); *(for deep-fat frying)* friteuse *f* **2** *(chicken)* poulet *m* à frire

frying ['fraɪɪŋ] **N** friture *f*

▸▸ ***frying pan*** poêle *f* (à frire); **to jump out of the f. pan into the fire** tomber de Charybde en Scylla, changer un cheval borgne pour un cheval aveugle

fry-pan N *Am* poêle *f* à frire

fry-up N *Br Fam* = bacon, saucisses, tomates etc cuits à la poêle, généralement consommés au petit déjeuner

FSA [ˌefes'eɪ] **N 1** *Fin (abbr* **Financial Services Authority)** = organisme gouvernemental britannique chargé de contrôler les activités du secteur financier **2** *(abbr* **Food Standards Agency)** = organisme britannique de contrôle de la sécurité alimentaire

f-stop N *Phot* ouverture *f* (du diaphragme)

ft *(written abbr* **foot)** pied *m*

FT 100 index [ef'tiː-] **N** *St Exch (abbr* **Financial Times-Stock Exchange 100 Index)** = principal indice boursier du 'Financial Times' basé sur la valeur de 100 actions cotées à la Bourse de Londres

FTP [ˌeftiː'piː] *Comput* **N** *(abbr* **FileTransfer Protocol)** protocole *m* de transfert de fichiers

VT télécharger par FTP

▸▸ ***FTP server*** serveur *m* FTP; ***FTP site*** site *m* FTP

FTSE index ['fʊtsɪ-] **N** *St Exch (abbr* **Financial Times-Stock Exchange 100 Index)** = principal indice boursier du 'Financial Times' basé sur la valeur de 100 actions cotées à la Bourse de Londres

fuchsia ['fjuːʃə] **N 1** *Bot* fuchsia *m* **2** *(colour)* fuchsia *m*

fuck [fʌk] *Vulg* **VT** *(of man)* baiser; *(of woman)* baiser avec; **f. you!, go f. yourself!** va te faire enculer!; **f. it!** putain de merde!; **f. me!** putain!

VI baiser; *Fig* **don't f. with me!** essaie pas de te foutre de ma gueule!

N 1 *(act)* baise *f*; **to have a f.** baiser, s'envoyer en l'air

2 *(sexual partner)* **he's a good f.** il baise bien

3 *(as intensifier)* **what the f. do you expect?** mais qu'est-ce que tu veux, putain de merde?; **who the f. left the window open?** quel est le con qui a laissé la fenêtre ouverte?; **I can't really afford it, but what the f.!** c'est un peu cher pour moi, mais je m'en fous!; **she'd like you to apologize – like f. I will!** elle voudrait que tu t'excuses – qu'elle aille se faire foutre!; **did you invite them? – like f. I did!**

tu les as invités? – tu déconnes ou quoi?; **shut the f. up!** ferme ta gueule!; **get the f. out of here!** fous-moi le camp!, dégage!

4 *(expressing surprise, disbelief)* **for f.'s sake!** merde!, putain!; *Br* **f. knows where he is!** j'ai pas la moindre idée d'où il peut être!

5 *(in comparisons)* **as stupid as f.** con comme la lune; **he ran like f.** il a pris ses jambes à son cou

6 not to give a (flying) f. (about) se foutre complètement (de); **I don't give a f.** j'en ai rien à branler; **who gives a f.!** tout le monde s'en fout!; **are you going to apologize? – am I f.!** est-ce que tu vas t'excuser? – des clous!

EXCLAM putain de merde!

• **fuck all** **PRON** *(nothing)* que dalle; **it's got f. all to do with you!** occupe-toi donc de tes fesses!; *Br* **f. all money/time** pas un flèche/une minute; **she's done f. all today** elle a rien foutu de la journée; **she knows f. all about it** elle y connaît que dalle

▸▸ ***fuck buddy*** copain (copine) *m,f* de baise, = partenaire avec qui on a des relations sexuelles hors du cadre d'une relation amoureuse

▸ **fuck about, fuck around** *Vulg* **VT SEP to f. sb about** *or* **around** *(treat badly)* se foutre de la gueule de qn; *(waste time of)* faire perdre son temps à qn

VI *(act foolishly)* déconner, faire le con; *(waste time)* glander, glandouiller; **to f. about** *or* **around with sth** tripoter qch

▸ **fuck off** *Vulg* **VT SEP to f. sb off** faire chier qn; **to be fucked off (with)** en avoir plein le cul (de)

VI *(leave)* se casser, calter; **f. off!** *(go away)* casse-toi!; *(expressing contempt, disagreement)* va te faire foutre!

▸ **fuck over** **VT SEP** *Vulg* **to f. sb over** *(cheat)* baiser qn, arnaquer qn; **I really got fucked over on that one** là je me suis vraiment fait baiser *ou* arnaquer; **he'd been fucked over for 1,000 dollars** il s'était fait baiser de 1000 dollars

▸ **fuck up** *Vulg* **VT SEP** *(plan, project)* foutre la merde dans; *(person)* foutre dans la merde; **he's really fucked up emotionally** il est complètement paumé; **they really fucked up their kids** ils ont complètement perturbé leurs gosses

VI merder

fucked [fʌkt] **ADJ** *Vulg* **1** *(car, stereo etc)* foutu, naze; **I'm f.!** *(exhausted)* je suis mort *ou* crevé!; **his knee/heart/eye is f.** son genou/cœur/œil est foutu; **his chances of winning the race were completely f.!** il n'avait plus une chance de gagner cette putain de course! **2** *Br (drunk)* bourré, pété

fucker [ˈfʌkə(r)] **N** *Vulg* **1** *(man)* enculé *m*, enfoiré *m*; *(woman)* connasse *f*; **some f.'s stolen my bike** il y a un enculé qui m'a piqué mon vélo; **you lazy f.!** espèce de grosse feignasse!; **you stupid f.!** pauvre con! **2** *(thing)* **I can't get the f. to start** j'arrive pas à faire démarrer cette saloperie

fuckface [ˈfʌkfeɪs] **N** *Vulg* tête *f* de con

fucking [ˈfʌkɪŋ] *Vulg* **ADJ** **I'm fed up with this f. car!** j'en ai plein le cul de cette putain de bagnole!; **you f. idiot!** pauvre con!; **f. hell!** putain de merde!; **where the f. hell have you been?** où est-ce que t'étais passé, bordel?; **she's here all the f. time!** elle est toujours fourrée ici!

ADV **he's so f. stupid!** tu parles d'un con!; **it was a f. awful day!** tu parles d'une putain de journée!; **I don't f. know!** j'en sais foutre rien!; **it's f. freezing!** on se les gèle!; **I'm f. well going home!** merde! moi je rentre chez moi!

fuck-up **N** *Vulg* **1** *(situation)* merde *f*; **to make a f. of sth** foirer qch **2** *Am (bungler)* bousilleur(euse) *m,f*; **he's a real f.** il fout sa merde partout

fuckwit [ˈfʌkwɪt] **N** *Vulg* connard (connasse) *m,f*

fuddle [ˈfʌdəl] **VT** *(confuse* ▸ *ideas, person)* embrouiller; *(intoxicate)* griser

fuddled [ˈfʌdəld] **ADJ** *(ideas, mind)* embrouillé, confus; *(person* ▸ *confused)* confus; *(*▸ *tipsy)* gris, éméché

fuddy-duddy [ˈfʌdɪˌdʌdɪ] *(pl* **fuddy-duddies***)* *Fam* **N** vieux schnock *m ou* schnoque *m*

ADJ vieux jeu *inv*

fudge [fʌdʒ] **N 1** *(UNCOUNT) (sweet)* caramel *m*; **a piece of f.** un caramel; **I made some f.** j'ai fait des caramels **2** *(dodging)* faux-fuyant *m*, échappatoire *f*; **the law/agreement is a f.** le texte de loi/de l'accord est délibérément flou **3** *(UNCOUNT) (nonsense)* balivernes *fpl*, âneries *fpl*

VI *(evade, hedge)* esquiver le problème; **the President fudged on the budget issue** le président a esquivé les questions sur le budget

VT 1 *(make up* ▸ *excuse)* inventer; *(*▸ *story)* monter; *(*▸ *figures, results)* truquer **2** *(avoid, dodge)* esquiver **3** *Am (ruin)* rater; **I totally fudged it** je l'ai complètement raté

fuel [fjʊəl] *(Br pt & pp* **fuelled**, *cont* **fuelling**, *Am pt & pp* **fueled**, *cont* **fueling***)* **N 1** *(gen) & Aviat* combustible *m*; *(coal)* charbon *m*; *(oil)* mazout *m*, fuel *m*, fioul *m*; *(wood)* bois *m*; *Aut* carburant *m*; **what f. do you use?** quel combustible utilisez-vous?; **coal is not a very efficient f.** le charbon n'est pas une source d'énergie très efficace; **nuclear f.** combustible *m* nucléaire **2** *Fig* **to add f. to the flames** jeter de l'huile sur le feu; **his words were merely f. to her anger** ses paroles n'ont fait qu'attiser *ou* qu'aviver sa colère

COMP *(costs)* de chauffage

VT 1 *(furnace)* alimenter (en combustible); *(car, plane, ship)* ravitailler en carburant **2** *Fig (controversy)* aviver; *(speculation)* nourrir; **his words only fuelled their anger/their suspicions** ses paroles n'ont servi qu'à aviver leur colère/leurs soupçons

▸▸ ***fuel bill*** *(of household)* facture *f* de chauffage; *(of region)* dépenses *fpl* énergétiques; *Elec* ***fuel cell*** élément *m* de conversion; ***fuel consumption*** consommation *f* d'énergie; *(of car)* consommation *f* de carburant; ***fuel element*** élément *m* combustible; ***fuel gauge*** jauge *f* d'essence; *Tech* ***fuel injection*** alimentation *f* par injection, injection *f* (de carburant); *Tech* ***fuel injection system*** système *m* d'injection (de combustible); *Tech* ***fuel injector*** injecteur *m* de carburant; ***fuel oil*** mazout *m*, fuel *m*, fioul *m*; ***fuel pipe*** tuyau *m* d'alimentation en carburant; ***fuel pressure*** pression *f* de carburant; ***fuel pump*** pompe *f* d'alimentation; ***fuel tank*** *(in home)* cuve *f* à mazout; *(in car)* réservoir *m* de carburant *ou* d'essence; *(in ship)* soute *f* à mazout *ou* à fuel; ***fuel tax*** taxe *f* sur les carburants; ***fuel temperature gauge*** jauge *f* de température du carburant

fuel/air **ADJ** air/carburant

▸▸ ***fuel/air explosive*** bombe *f* thermobarique; ***fuel/air mixture*** mélange *m* air/carburant

fueling *Am* = **fuelling**

fuel-injected **ADJ** à injection

fuelling, *Am* **fueling** [ˈfjʊəlɪŋ] **N** ravitaillement *m* en carburant

▸▸ ***fuelling stop*** escale *f* de ravitaillement (en carburant)

fug [fʌg] **N** *Br* **there's a terrible f. in here** *(stuffy)* ça sent vraiment le renfermé ici, on étouffe; *(smoky)* c'est complètement enfumé ici

fuggy [ˈfʌgɪ] *(compar* **fuggier**, *superl* **fuggiest***)* **ADJ** *Br (stuffy)* qui sent le renfermé; *(smoky)* enfumé

fugitive [ˈfjuːdʒətɪv] **N** *(escapee)* fugitif(ive) *m,f*, évadé(e) *m,f*; *(refugee)* réfugié(e) *m,f*; **she's a f. from justice** elle fuit la justice, elle est recherchée par la justice

ADJ 1 *(debtor, slave)* fugitif **2** *Literary (beauty, happiness)* éphémère, passager; *(impression, thought, vision)* fugitif, passager

fugue [fjuːg] **N** *Mus & Psy* fugue *f*

Führer [ˈfjʊərə(r)] **N 1** *Hist* Führer *m* **2** *Fam (dictator, boss)* tyran *m*

> **SUFFIXE**
>
> **-FUL**
>
> • Le suffixe **-ful** vient s'ajouter à un substantif pour produire un autre substantif. Il désigne alors la QUANTITÉ CONTENUE dans l'objet en question lorsque celui-ci est plein. En français on a tendance à mentionner simplement l'objet lui-même:
>
> **a cupful of flour** une tasse de farine; **three teaspoonfuls of sugar** trois cuillers à café de sucre; **six sackfuls of coal** six sacs de charbon; **two carfuls of people** deux voitures pleines de passagers
>
> • Lorsqu'il est accolé à une partie du corps, **-ful** se traduit généralement par **-ée**:
>
> **an armful of books** une brassée de livres; **a mouthful of bread** une bouchée de pain; **a handful of sweets** une poignée de bonbons
>
> Remarque: le pluriel se termine en **-fuls** (p. ex. **bucketfuls** et non **bucketsful**).

fulcrum [ˈfʊlkrəm] *(pl* **fulcrums** *or* **fulcra** [-krə]*)* **N** *(pivot)* pivot *m*, point *m* d'appui; *Fig (prop, support)* point *m* d'appui

fulfil, *Am* **fulfill** [fʊlˈfɪl] *(pt & pp* **fulfilled**, *cont* **fulfilling***)* **VT 1** *(carry out* ▸ *ambition, dream, plan)* réaliser; *(*▸ *prophecy, task)* accomplir, réaliser; *(*▸ *promise)* tenir; *(*▸ *duty, obligation)* remplir, s'acquitter de

2 *(satisfy* ▸ *condition)* remplir; *(*▸ *norm, regulation)* répondre à, obéir à; *(*▸ *desire, need)* satisfaire, répondre à; *(*▸ *prayer, wish)* exaucer; **to f. oneself** se réaliser, s'épanouir; **it's important to feel fulfilled** il est important de se réaliser (dans la vie)

3 *(complete, finish* ▸ *prison sentence)* achever, terminer

4 *Com (order)* exécuter; *(contract)* remplir, respecter

fulfilling [fʊlˈfɪlɪŋ] **ADJ** *(life, career, experience)* épanouissant

fulfilment, *Am* **fulfillment** [fʊlˈfɪlmənt] **N 1** *(of ambition, dream, wish)* réalisation *f*; *(of desire)* satisfaction *f*; *(of plan, condition, contract)* exécution *f*; *(of duty, prophecy, promise)* accomplissement *m*; *(of prayer)* exaucement *m*

2 *(satisfaction)* (sentiment *m* de) contentement *m ou* satisfaction *f*; **to find** *or* **to achieve f.** se réaliser, s'épanouir; **to seek f.** rechercher l'épanouissement; **she gets a sense** *or* **feeling of f. from her work** son travail la comble

3 *(of prison sentence)* achèvement *m*, fin *f*

4 *Com (of order)* exécution *f*

FULL [fʊl]

> **ADJ**
> • plein **1–3, 6, 8**
> • complet **3, 5**
> • détaillé **7**
> • rempli **1**
> • rassasié **4**
> • large **9**
>
> **ADV**
> • complètement **1**
> • carrément **2**
> • entièrement **1**

ADJ 1 *(completely filled)* plein, rempli; **the cup was f. to the brim** *or* **f. to overflowing with coffee** la tasse était pleine à ras bord de café; **this box is only half f.** cette boîte n'est remplie qu'à moitié *ou* n'est qu'à moitié pleine; **will you open the door for me, my hands are f.** vous voulez bien m'ouvrir la porte, j'ai les mains occupées; **don't talk with your mouth f.** ne parle pas la bouche pleine; **you shouldn't go swimming on a f. stomach** tu ne devrais pas nager après avoir mangé; **I've got a f. week ahead of me** j'ai une semaine chargée devant moi

2 *Fig* **(to be) f. of** *(filled with)* (être) plein de; **her arms were f. of flowers** elle portait des brassées de fleurs, elle avait des fleurs plein les bras; **her eyes were f. of tears** elle avait les yeux pleins de larmes; **a look f. of gratitude** un regard plein *ou* chargé de reconnaissance; **the children were f. of excitement** les enfants étaient très excités; **her parents were f. of hope** ses parents étaient remplis d'espoir; **she's f. of good ideas** elle est pleine de bonnes idées; **her letters are f. of spelling mistakes** ses lettres sont truffées de fautes d'orthographe; **f. of energy** *or* **of life** plein de vie; **to be f. of oneself** être plein de soi-même *ou* imbu de sa personne; **he's f. of his own importance** il est pénétré de sa propre importance; **they/the papers were f. of news about China** ils/les journaux ne parlaient que de la Chine; *Fam* **to be f. of it** raconter n'importe quoi; *Vulg* **to be f. of shit** déconner à pleins tubes

3 *(crowded* ▸ *room, theatre)* comble, plein; *(*▸ *hotel, restaurant, train)* complet(ète); **the hotel was f. (up)** l'hôtel était complet; *Theat* **house f.** *(sign)* complet

4 *(satiated)* rassasié, repu; *Br* **I'm f. (up)!** je n'en peux plus!

5 *(complete, whole)* tout, complet(ète) **she listened to him for three f. hours** elle l'a écouté pendant trois heures entières; **the house is a f. 10**

miles from town la maison est à 15 bons kilomètres *ou* est au moins à 15 kilomètres de la ville; **in f. sunlight** en plein soleil; **the f. amount** la somme totale; **she received her f. share of the money** elle a reçu tout l'argent qui lui revenait; **he rose to his f. height** il s'est dressé de toute sa hauteur; **to fall f. length** tomber de tout son long; **he leads a very f. life** il a une vie bien remplie; **the f. horror of the situation** toute l'horreur de la situation; **I don't want a f. meal** je ne veux pas un repas entier; **give him your f. name and address** donnez-lui vos nom, prénom et adresse; **in f. uniform** en grande tenue; **in f. view of the cameras/of the teacher** devant les caméras/le professeur; **I got f. marks in my maths test** j'ai eu 20 sur 20 à mon examen de maths; *Fig* **f. marks for observation!** bravo, vous êtes très observateur!; *Phot* **in f. colour** tout en couleur; *Naut* **f. sail** toutes voiles dehors; *Fig* **in f. sail** toutes voiles dehors, à toute vapeur

6 *(maximum)* plein; **make f. use of this opportunity** mettez bien cette occasion à profit, tirez bien profit de cette occasion; **they had the music on f. volume** ils avaient mis la musique à fond; **on f. beam** en feux de route, en pleins phares; **peonies in f. bloom** des pivoines épanouies; **it was going f. blast** *(heating)* ça chauffait au maximum; *(radio, TV)* ça marchait à pleins tubes; *(car)* ça roulait à toute allure; **the orchestra was at f. strength** l'orchestre était au grand complet; **she caught the f. force of the blow** elle a reçu le coup de plein fouet

7 *(detailed)* détaillé; **I didn't get the f. story** je n'ai pas entendu tous les détails de l'histoire; **he gave us a f. report** il nous a donné un rapport détaillé; **I asked for f. information** j'ai demandé des renseignements complets

8 *(plump ▸ face)* plein, rond; *(▸ figure)* rondelet, replet; *(▸ lips)* charnu

9 *(ample, wide ▸ clothes, skirt)* large, ample; *(▸ sleeve)* large, bouffant

10 *(sound)* timbré; *(voice)* étoffé, timbré

11 *(flavour)* parfumé; *(wine)* robuste, qui a du corps

12 *(brother, sister)* germain

ADV 1 *(entirely, completely)* complètement, entièrement; **I turned the heat on f.** *or Br* **f. on** j'ai mis le chauffage à fond; *Br* **he put the radio f. on** il a mis la radio à fond; **to turn a tap on f.** *or Br* **f. on** ouvrir un robinet en grand

2 *(directly, exactly)* carrément; **the blow caught her f. in the face** elle a reçu le coup en pleine figure; **lying f. in the sun** couché en plein (au) soleil

3 *(idioms)* **you know f. well I'm right** tu sais très bien *ou* parfaitement que j'ai raison; *Br* **f. out** à toute vitesse, à pleins gaz; **to ride f. out** filer à toute vitesse, foncer

• **in full ADV** intégralement; **to pay in f.** payer intégralement; **we paid the bill in f.** nous avons payé la facture dans son intégralité; **they refunded my money in f.** ils m'ont entièrement remboursé; **write out your name in f.** écrivez votre nom en toutes lettres; **they published the book in f.** ils ont publié le texte intégral *ou* dans son intégralité

• **to the full ADV** au plus haut degré, au plus haut point; *Br* **enjoy life to the f.** profitez de la vie au maximum

▸▸ ***full board*** pension *f* complète; *Fin* ***full consolidation*** intégration *f* globale; *Acct* ***full cost accounting (method)*** méthode *f* de capitalisation du coût entier; *Fin* ***full costing*** méthode *f* du coût complet; *Law* ***full court*** Assemblée *f* plénière; *Fin* ***full discharge*** quitus *m*; ***full dress*** *(evening clothes)* tenue *f* de soirée; *(uniform)* grande tenue *f*; *Tel* ***full duplex*** bidirectionnel *m* simultané, full duplex *m*; **to send sth f. duplex** transmettre qch en full duplex; *Econ* ***full employment*** plein emploi *m*; ***full fare*** *(for adult)* plein tarif *m*; *(for child)* une place entière; ***full frontal*** = photographie montrant une personne nue de face; ***full house*** *Cards* full *m*; *Theat* salle *f* comble; *Theat* **to play to a f. house** jouer à guichets fermés; *Comput* ***full Internet access*** accès *m* à tout l'Internet; *Law* ***full jurisdiction*** pleine juridiction *f*; *Aut* ***full licence*** permis *m* tous véhicules; *Br St Exch* ***full listing*** = description d'une société qui apparaît à la cote officielle de la Bourse de Londres; ***full member*** membre *m* à part entière; *Fam* ***the full monty*** *(everything)* la totale; **to do a F. Monty** *(strip)* faire un strip-tease intégral[▫]; ***full moon*** pleine lune *f*; **at f. moon** à la pleine lune; ***full pay*** paie *f* entière; *Fin* ***full payment*** paiement *m* intégral; *Typ* ***full point*** *(in punctuation)* point *m*; ***full price*** prix *m* fort; *Am* ***full professor*** professeur *m* d'université *(titulaire d'une chaire)*; *Mus* ***full score*** partition *f*; ***full session*** *(of a committee etc)* réunion *f* plénière; *Br* ***full stop*** *(pause)* arrêt *m* complet; *Gram* point *m*; *Comput* point *m* final; **the parade came to a f. stop** le défilé s'est arrêté; **the whole airport came to a f. stop** toute activité a cessé dans l'aéroport; **I won't do it, f. stop!** je ne le ferai pas, un point c'est tout!; *Br Univ* ***full term*** *(at Oxford and Cambridge)* = période pendant laquelle ont lieu les cours; ***full text*** texte *m* intégral; ***full time*** *(of working week)* temps *m* complet; *Sport* fin *f* de match; *Sport* ***full toss*** *(in cricket)* coup *m* plein; *Com* ***full weight*** poids *m* juste

---

fullback ['fʊlbæk] **N** *Sport* arrière *m*

full-blooded [-'blʌdɪd] **ADJ 1** *(hearty ▸ person)* vigoureux, robuste; *(▸ effort)* vigoureux, puissant; *(▸ argument)* violent; **you have our f. support** vous avez notre soutien inconditionnel **2** *(purebred ▸ horse)* pur sang; *(racially ▸ person)* de race pure; *Fig* **a f. Socialist** un socialiste pur et dur

full-blown ADJ 1 *(flower)* épanoui **2** *Fig (complete) Br* **a f. doctor** un médecin diplômé; **a f. crisis** une crise de la plus grande envergure; **f. war** la guerre généralisée; **the discussion developed into a f. argument** la discussion a dégénéré en véritable dispute **3** *Br Med* **to have f. Aids** avoir un Sida avéré

full-bodied [-'bɒdɪd] **ADJ** *(wine)* qui a du corps, corsé

full-colour ADJ *Typ* en couleur(s)

full-cost pricing N *Mktg* fixation *f* du prix en fonction du coût

full-cream milk N lait *m* entier

full-dress ADJ *(parade)* en habit de cérémonie

▸▸ ***full-dress debate*** débat *m* de fond; *Theat* ***full-dress rehearsal*** répétition *f* générale; ***full-dress uniform*** tenue *f* de cérémonie, grande tenue *f*

full-face(d) ADJ 1 *(person)* au visage rond **2** *(photograph)* de face **3** *Typ* gras

full-fashioned *Am* = **fully-fashioned**

full-fledged *Am* = **fully-fledged**

full-frontal ADJ

▸▸ ***full-frontal nudity*** *(in show)* nu *m* intégral; ***full-frontal photograph*** nu *m* de face *(photographie)*

full-grown ADJ adulte

full-length ADJ *(portrait)* en pied; *(curtain, dress)* long (longue); **a f. feature (film), a f. movie** un long métrage

ADV he was stretched out f. on the floor il était étendu de tout son long par terre

▸▸ ***full-length mirror*** glace *f* en pied; *TV & Cin* ***full-length shot*** plan *m* général

fullness ['fʊlnɪs] **N 1** *(state)* état *m* plein, plénitude *f*; *Med (of stomach)* plénitude *f*; **in the f. of time** avec le temps

2 *(of details, information)* abondance *f*

3 *(of face, figure)* rondeur *f*; **the f. of his lips** ses lèvres *fpl* charnues

4 *(of skirt, sound, voice)* ampleur *f*

full-out ADJ *Typ* au fer, sans alinéa

full-page ADJ pleine page

▸▸ ***full-page advertisement*** annonce *f* pleine page; *Comput* ***full-page display*** écran *m* pleine page

full-scale ADJ 1 *(model, plan)* grandeur nature *(inv)* **2** *(all-out ▸ strike, war)* total; *(▸ attack, investigation)* de grande envergure; **the factory starts f. production this week** l'usine commence à tourner à plein rendement cette semaine

▸▸ *Mil* ***full-scale fighting*** bataille *f* rangée

full-screen menu N *Comput* menu *m* plein écran

full-size(d) ADJ *(animal, plant)* adulte; *(drawing, model)* grandeur nature *(inv)*; *(keyboard, wheel)* aux dimensions standard; *Am* **f. car** grosse voiture *f*

full-strength ADJ *(solution, bleach)* non dilué; *(cigarette, aspirin)* très fort; *(team)* qui comprend les meilleurs joueurs

full-time ADJ *(job)* à plein temps; *(work, contract, employee)* à temps complet, à plein temps; **she's a f. translator** elle est traductrice à plein temps; **it's a f. job taking care of a baby!** s'occuper d'un bébé ne laisse pas une minute de libre!

ADV à plein temps, à temps plein

▸▸ *Sport* ***full-time score*** score *m* final

fully ['fʊlɪ] **ADV 1** *(totally ▸ automatic, dressed, satisfied, trained)* complètement, entièrement; *(▸ furnished)* entièrement; *(▸ paid)* intégralement; **I f. understand** je comprends très bien *ou* parfaitement; **I f. agree** je suis tout à fait d'accord; **I f. intend to return** j'ai la ferme intention de revenir; **I am f. aware of the implications** je suis tout à fait conscient des implications; **he is f. qualified** il a toutes les qualifications nécessaires; **f. licensed** *(hotel, restaurant etc)* autorisé à vendre de l'alcool; **f. loaded** *(van, plane etc)* en pleine charge **2** *(thoroughly ▸ answer, examine, explain)* à fond, dans le détail; **this topic is dealt with more f. below** ce thème est traité plus en détail ci-après; **I'll write more f. next week** j'écrirai plus longuement la semaine prochaine **3** *(at least)* au moins, bien; **it was f. two hours before he arrived** au moins deux heures ont passé avant qu'il n'arrive

full-year ADJ *(profits, results)* de l'exercice

fully-fashioned, *Am* **full-fashioned** [-'fæʃənd] **ADJ** moulant

fully-fledged, *Am* **full-fledged ADJ 1** *(bird)* qui a toutes ses plumes **2** *Fig* à part entière; **a f. doctor** un médecin diplômé; **a f. member** un membre à part entière; **a f. atheist** un athée pur et dur

fully-paid capital N *Fin* capital *m* entièrement versé

fulmar ['fʊlmə(r)] **N** *Orn* fulmar *m*

fulminate ['fʌlmɪneɪt] **VI** fulminer, pester; **he fulminated against** *or* **at his students** il fulminait *ou* pestait contre ses étudiants; **the preacher fulminated against the abuse of drugs** le pasteur fulminait contre l'abus de stupéfiants

fulmination [ˌfʌlmɪ'neɪʃən] **N** malédiction *f*, imprécation *f*

fulsome ['fʊlsəm] **ADJ** *(apology, thanks)* excessif, exagéré, outré; *(welcome)* plein d'effusions; *(compliments, praise)* dithyrambique, outré; **to be f. in one's praise of sb/sth** porter qn/qch aux nues

fulsomely ['fʊlsəmlɪ] **ADV** *(welcome)* avec effusion; **to apologize f.** se répandre en excuses; **she thanked/complimented us f.** elle s'est répandue en remerciements/compliments; **to praise sb/sth f.** porter qn/qch aux nues

fumarole ['fju:mərəʊl] **N** *Geol* fumerolle *f*

fumble ['fʌmbəl] **VI 1** *(grope ▸ in the dark)* tâtonner; *(▸ in pocket, purse)* fouiller; **he fumbled (about** *or* **around) in the dark for the light switch** il a cherché l'interrupteur à tâtons dans l'obscurité; **she fumbled in her bag for a pen** elle a fouillé dans son sac pour trouver un stylo; *Fig* **to f. for words** chercher ses mots **2** *Sport (drop the ball)* laisser tomber la balle

VT 1 *(handle awkwardly)* manier gauchement *ou* maladroitement; **she fumbled her way down the dark corridor** elle chercha son chemin à tâtons le long du couloir sombre; **he fumbled his lines** il récita son texte en bafouillant **2** *Sport (miss ▸ catch)* attraper *ou* arrêter maladroitement; **to f. the ball** laisser tomber la balle

N 1 *(grope)* tâtonnements *mpl* **2** *Sport (bad catch)* prise *f* de balle maladroite; *(dropping of the ball)* échappé *m*

fumbling ['fʌmbəlɪŋ] **ADJ** maladroit, gauche

N *(groping)* tâtonnements *mpl*

fume [fju:m] **VI 1** *(gas)* émettre *ou* exhaler des vapeurs; *(liquid)* fumer **2** *(person)* rager; **I'm fuming because I haven't been invited** je suis furieux de ne pas avoir été invité; **the boss is fuming** le patron est furieux

VT 1 *(treat with fumes)* fumer, fumiger **2** *(rage)* **"this is your fault," she fumed** "c'est de ta faute", dit-elle d'un ton rageur

• **fumes** NPL *(gen)* exhalaisons *fpl*, émanations *fpl*; *(of gas, liquid)* vapeurs *fpl*; **factory fumes** fumées *fpl* d'usine; **tobacco fumes** fumée *f* (de cigarette)
▸▸ ***fume cupboard*** sorbonne *f* (de laboratoire)

> Note that the French verb **fumer** is a false friend and is rarely a translation for the English verb **to fume**. It means **to smoke**.

fumigate ['fju:mɪgeɪt] VT désinfecter par fumigation

fumigation [ˌfju:mɪ'geɪʃən] N fumigation *f*

fumigator ['fju:mɪgeɪtə(r)] N *(device)* appareil *m* fumigatoire

fumitory ['fju:mɪtərɪ] (*pl* **fumitories**) N *(plant)* fumeterre *f*

fun [fʌn] (*pt & pp* **funned**, *cont* **funning**) N **1** *(amusement)* amusement *m*; *(pleasure)* plaisir *m*; **to have f.** s'amuser; **we had f. at the party** nous nous sommes bien amusés à la soirée; **have f.!** amusez-vous bien!; **what f.!** ce que c'est drôle *ou* amusant!; **I don't see the f. in kicking a ball round a field** je ne trouve pas ça drôle de faire le tour d'un terrain en donnant des coups de pied dans un ballon; **skiing is good** *or* **great f.** c'est très amusant de faire du ski; **it's f. to go cycling** c'est marrant de faire du vélo; **her brother is a lot of f.** son frère est très drôle; **I'm learning Chinese for f.** *or* **for the f. of it** j'apprends le chinois pour mon plaisir; **he only went for the f. of it** il n'y est allé que pour s'amuser; **just for the f. of it he pretended to be the boss** histoire de rire, il a fait semblant d'être le patron; **it wasn't much f. walking home in the rain** rentrer à pied sous la pluie n'avait rien d'une partie de plaisir; **his sister spoiled the f.** sa sœur a joué les trouble-fête *ou* les rabat-joie; **I don't want to spoil your f., but could you keep the noise down?** je ne veux pas jouer les trouble-fête, mais est-ce que vous pourriez faire un peu moins de bruit?; **having to wear a crash helmet takes all the f. out of motorcycling** devoir porter un casque gâche tout le plaisir qu'on a à faire de la moto; *Ironic* **her boyfriend walked in and that's when the f. began** son copain est entré et c'est là qu'on a commencé à rire; **the president has become a figure of f.** le président est devenu la risée de tous; **to make f. of** *or* **to poke f. at sb** se moquer de qn; **we'll have a children's party with lots of f. and games** on va organiser une fête pour les enfants avec des tas de jeux *ou* divertissements; **I've had enough of your f. and games** *(foolish behaviour)* j'en ai assez de tes blagues *ou* farces; **there'll be some f. and games if his wife finds out** *(trouble)* ça va mal aller si sa femme l'apprend **2** *(playfulness)* enjouement *m*, gaieté *f*; **to be full of f.** être plein d'entrain *ou* très gai; **he said it in f.** il l'a dit pour rire *ou* en plaisantant
ADJ *Fam* rigolo, marrant; **he's a f. guy** *or* **person** il est rigolo *ou* marrant
VI *Am Fam* plaisanter▫, badiner; **I was just funning!** c'était pour rire!
▸▸ ***fun fur*** fourrure *f* synthétique; ***fun run*** course *f* à pied pour amateurs *(pour collecter des fonds)*

funboard ['fʌnbɔ:d] N *Sport* funboard *m*

function ['fʌŋkʃən] N **1** *(role* ▸ *of machine, organ, institution)* fonction *f*; *(*▸ *of person)* fonction *f*, charge *f*; *Med* **vital functions** fonctions *fpl* vitales; **it is the f. of a lawyer to provide sound legal advice** l'avocat a pour fonction *ou* tâche de donner de bons conseils juridiques; **he combines the functions of servant and gardener** il tient le double emploi de domestique et de jardinier; **to discharge one's functions** s'acquitter de ses fonctions; **my f. in life** ma raison d'être
2 *(working)* fonctionnement *m*; **they tested the heart f.** ils ont examiné le fonctionnement du cœur
3 *(ceremony)* cérémonie *f*; *(reception)* réception *f*; *(meeting)* réunion *f*
4 *(gen) & Ling & Math* fonction *f*; **x is a f. of y** x est une fonction de y
5 *Comput* fonction *f*
VI fonctionner, marcher; **this room functions as a study** cette pièce sert de bureau *ou* fait fonction de bureau
▸▸ *Comput* ***function key*** touche *f* de fonction; ***functions manager*** *(in hotel)* responsable *mf* des réceptions; ***function room*** salle *f* de réception; *Ling* ***function word*** mot *m* fonctionnel

functional ['fʌŋkʃənəl] ADJ **1** *(utilitarian* ▸ *furniture, building, machine etc)* fonctionnel **2** *(in working order)* **to be f.** fonctionner; **the machine is no longer f.** la machine ne marche plus *ou* ne fonctionne plus; *Fam* **I'm barely f. before ten o'clock** je ne suis guère opérationnel avant dix heures **3** *Math & Med* fonctionnel
▸▸ ***functional illiterate*** illettré(e) *m,f*

functionality [ˌfʌŋkʃə'nælɪtɪ] N fonctionnalité *f*

functionally ['fʌŋkʃənəlɪ] ADV **to be f. illiterate** être illettré; **to be f. equivalent to sth** avoir la même fonction que qch

functionary ['fʌŋkʃənərɪ] (*pl* **functionaries**) N *Pej (employee)* employé(e) *m,f (dans une administration)*; *(civil servant)* fonctionnaire *mf*

functioning ['fʌŋkʃənɪŋ] N *(of machine etc)* fonctionnement *m*

fund [fʌnd] N **1** *(reserve of money)* fonds *m*, caisse *f*; **they've set up a f. for the earthquake victims** ils ont ouvert une souscription en faveur des victimes du séisme **2** *Fig* fond *m*, réserve *f*; **she has a large f. of amusing anecdotes** elle a tout un répertoire d'anecdotes amusantes; **a f. of knowledge** un trésor de connaissances
VT **1** *(project)* financer; *(company)* pourvoir de fonds; *Acct* **funded from cashflow** autofinancé; **to f. money** placer de l'argent dans les fonds publics **2** *Fin (debt)* consolider
• **funds** NPL *(cash resources)* fonds *mpl*; **public funds** fonds *mpl* publics; **secret funds** une caisse noire; **we spent all of our scarce funds on housing** nous avons dépensé le peu de capitaux dont nous disposions pour le logement; **for all other countries, remit $37 US funds** autres pays: envoyer 37 dollars US; **to be in/out of funds** être/ne pas être en fonds; **funds are low** les fonds sont bas; **I'm a bit short of funds** je n'ai pas beaucoup d'argent; *Banking* **insufficient funds** *(on returned cheque)* défaut *m* de provision; *Br* **the Funds** les bons *mpl* du Trésor; **to make a call for funds** faire un appel de capital
▸▸ *Fin* ***funds flow statement*** tableau *m* des emplois et ressources; *Fin* ***fund of funds*** fonds *m* de fonds; *Fin* ***fund management*** gestion *f* de fonds; *Fin* ***fund manager*** gestionnaire *mf* de fonds

fundamental [ˌfʌndə'mentəl] ADJ **1** *(basic* ▸ *concept, rule, principle)* fondamental, de base; *(*▸ *difference, quality)* fondamental, essentiel; *(*▸ *change, mistake)* fondamental; **a knowledge of economics is f. to a proper understanding of this problem** il est essentiel *ou* fondamental d'avoir des connaissances en économie pour bien comprendre ce problème; **f. research** recherche *f* fondamentale **2** *(central)* fondamental, principal; **it's of f. importance** c'est d'une importance capitale **3** *Mus* fondamental
N **1** *(usu pl)* **the fundamentals of chemistry** les principes *mpl* de base *ou* les fondamentaux *mpl* de la chimie; **when it comes to the fundamentals** quand on en vient à l'essentiel **2** *Mus* fondamentale *f*
▸▸ *Pol & Law* ***fundamental law*** loi *f* fondamentale; *Phys* ***fundamental particle*** particule *f* élémentaire; *Phys* ***fundamental unit*** unité *f* fondamentale

fundamentalism [ˌfʌndə'mentəlɪzəm] N *(gen) & Rel* fondamentalisme *m*; *(Muslim)* intégrisme *m*

fundamentalist [ˌfʌndə'mentəlɪst] N *(gen) & Rel* fondamentaliste *mf*, *(Muslim)* intégriste *mf*
ADJ *(gen) & Rel* fondamentaliste; *(Muslim)* intégriste

fundamentally [ˌfʌndə'mentəlɪ] ADV **1** *(essentially)* fondamentalement, essentiellement; **she seems hard but f. she's good-hearted** elle a l'air dure, mais au fond elle a bon cœur; **f., there's nothing wrong with the idea** l'idée en soi n'est pas mauvaise; **f., it's a question of who's got more money** au fond, ce qui importe c'est qui a le plus d'argent **2** *(completely)* **I disagree f. with his policies** je suis radicalement *ou* fondamentalement opposé à sa politique

funded ['fʌndɪd] ADJ *Fin (assets)* en rentes
▸▸ ***funded capital*** capitaux *mpl* investis; ***funded debt*** dette *f* consolidée; ***funded pension scheme*** régime *m* de retraite par capitalisation

fundholder ['fʌndhəʊldə(r)] N **1** *(person)* rentier (ère) *m,f* **2** *(medical practice)* = cabinet médical ayant obtenu le droit de gérer son propre budget auprès du système de sécurité sociale britannique

funding ['fʌndɪŋ] N *(UNCOUNT) Fin* **1** *(for project)* financement *m*; **BP will put up half of the f.** BP financera le projet à 50 pour cent **2** *(of debt)* consolidation *f*; *(of annuity, income)* assiette *f*
▸▸ ***funding loan*** emprunt *m* de consolidation; ***funding operation*** opération *f* de financement; ***funding plan*** plan *m* de financement

fundraiser ['fʌndreɪzə(r)] N *(person)* collecteur (trice) *m,f* de fonds; *(event)* = projet organisé pour collecter des fonds

fundraising ['fʌndreɪzɪŋ] N collecte *f* de fonds
ADJ *(dinner, project, sale)* organisé pour collecter des fonds

funeral ['fju:nərəl] N *(service)* enterrement *m*, obsèques *fpl*; *(more formal)* funérailles *fpl*; *(in announcement)* obsèques *fpl*; *(burial)* enterrement *m*; *Fam* **it's** *or* **that's your f.!** débrouille-toi!, c'est ton affaire!
COMP funèbre
▸▸ ***funeral ceremony*** cérémonie *f* funèbre; ***funeral director*** entrepreneur(euse) *m,f* de pompes funèbres; *Am* ***funeral home*** entreprise *f* de pompes funèbres; ***funeral march*** marche *f* funèbre; ***funeral parlour*** entreprise *f* de pompes funèbres; ***funeral procession*** cortège *m* funèbre; ***funeral pyre*** bûcher *m* (funéraire); ***funeral service*** service *m ou* office *m* funèbre

funereal [fju:'nɪərɪəl] ADJ *(atmosphere, expression)* funèbre, lugubre; *(voice)* sépulcral, lugubre; *(pace)* lent, mesuré

funfair ['fʌnfeə(r)] N fête *f* foraine

fungal ['fʌŋgəl] ADJ fongique
▸▸ *Med* ***fungal infection*** mycose *f*

fungi ['fʌŋgaɪ] *pl of* **fungus**

fungible ['fʌndʒɪbəl] *Law & St Exch* N **fungibles** fongibles *mpl*
ADJ fongible

fungicidal [ˌfʌndʒɪ'saɪdəl] ADJ antifongique, fongicide

fungicide ['fʌndʒɪsaɪd] N fongicide *m*

fungoid ['fʌŋgɔɪd] ADJ fongique
▸▸ ***fungoid growth*** fongosité *f*

fungus ['fʌŋgəs] (*pl* **fungi** [-gaɪ]) N **1** *Bot* champignon *m*; *(mould)* moisissure *f* **2** *Med* fongus *m*
▸▸ *Med* ***fungus infection*** mycose *f*

funicular [fju:'nɪkjʊlə(r)] ADJ funiculaire
N funiculaire *m*
▸▸ ***funicular railway*** funiculaire *m*

funk [fʌŋk] N **1** *Mus* musique *f* funk, funk *m inv*
2 *Fam Old-fashioned (fear)* trouille *f*, frousse *f*; *(depression)* découragement▫ *m*; **to be in a f.** *(afraid)* avoir la trouille; *(depressed)* avoir le cafard; **to be in a blue f.** avoir une peur bleue
3 *Fam Old-fashioned (coward)* froussard(e) *m,f*
4 *Am Fam (stink)* puanteur▫ *f*, odeur *f* infecte▫; **what a f.!** ce que ça pue!
VT **1** *(be afraid of)* **to f. doing sth** ne pas avoir le courage de faire qch; **she had her chance and she funked it** elle a eu sa chance mais elle s'est dégonflée **2** *(usu passive) (make afraid)* ficher la frousse à

funky ['fʌŋkɪ] (*compar* **funkier**, *superl* **funkiest**) ADJ **1** *esp Am Fam (excellent)* génial, super *(inv)*; *(fashionable)* branché, cool *(inv)* **2** *Mus* funky *(inv)*; **f. jazz** jazz *m* funky **3** *Am Fam (smelly)* puant▫

fun-loving ADJ qui aime s'amuser *ou* rire

funnel ['fʌnəl] (*Br pt & pp* **funnelled**, *cont* **funnelling**, *Am pt & pp* **funneled**, *cont* **funneling**) N **1** *(utensil)* entonnoir *m* **2** *(smokestack)* cheminée *f* **3** *(for ventilation)* tuyau *m ou* cheminée *f* d'aération
VT **1** *(liquid)* (faire) passer dans un entonnoir **2** *(crowd, funds)* canaliser; **complaints are funnelled to the head office** les réclamations sont canalisées vers le bureau central
VI **the crowd funnelled out of the gates** la foule

s'est écoulée par les grilles

►► *Met* ***funnel cloud*** tornade *f*

funnily ['fʌnılı] **ADV 1** *(strangely)* curieusement, bizarrement; **f. enough, I was just thinking of you** c'est drôle *ou* chose curieuse, je pensais justement à toi **2** *(amusingly)* drôlement, comiquement

funniness ['fʌnınıs] **N 1** *(strangeness)* bizarrerie *f* **2** *(amusing nature)* caractère *m* amusant *ou* drôle

funny ['fʌnı] (*compar* **funnier**, *superl* **funniest**, *pl* **funnies**) **ADJ 1** *(amusing)* amusant, drôle, comique; **it's not f.** ce n'est pas drôle; **you looked so f. in that hat** tu étais si drôle *ou* amusant avec ce chapeau; **she didn't see the f. side of it** elle n'a pas vu le côté comique de la situation; **he's trying to be f.** il cherche à faire de l'esprit; **stop trying to be f.!** ce n'est pas le moment de plaisanter!; *Br Fam* **was it f. ha-ha or f. peculiar?** c'était drôle-rigolo ou drôle-bizarre?

2 *(odd)* bizarre, curieux, drôle; **she has some f. ideas about work** elle a de drôles d'idées sur le travail; **the wine tastes f.** le vin a un drôle de goût; **it feels f.** ça fait drôle; **the engine sounds f.** le moteur fait un drôle de bruit; **I think it's f. that he should turn up now** je trouve (ça) bizarre qu'il arrive maintenant; **the f. thing (about it) is that she claimed she was away** ce qu'il y a de bizarre *ou* de curieux c'est qu'elle ait prétendu ne pas être là; *Fam* **she's f. that way** elle est comme ça; **(that's) f., I thought I heard the phone ring** c'est curieux *ou* drôle, j'ai cru entendre le téléphone; **(it's) f. you should say that** c'est drôle que vous disiez cela; **I've got a f. feeling that's not the last we've seen of her** j'ai comme l'impression qu'on va la revoir; *Fam* **I feel a bit f.** *(odd)* je me sens tout drôle *ou* tout chose; *(ill)* je ne suis pas dans mon assiette, je suis un peu patraque; *Fam* **he went all f. when he heard the news** la nouvelle l'a rendu tout chose; *Fam* **the computer went all f.** l'ordinateur s'est détraqué; *Fam* **f. money** des sommes *fpl* mirobolantes *ou* astronomiques

3 *(dubious, suspicious)* louche; *Fam* **none of your f. business!, don't try anything f.!** ne fais pas le malin!; *Fam* **there's some f. business** *or* **there's something f. going on** il se passe quelque chose de louche *ou* de pas très catholique; **there's something f. about that man** cet homme n'a pas l'air très catholique

4 *Br Fam (mentally)* dérangé; **he went a bit f. in his old age** il s'est mis à débloquer un peu en vieillissant

N *Am Fam (joke)* blague▫ *f*; **to make a f.** raconter une blague; **to pull a f. on sb** jouer un tour à qn▫, faire une farce à qn▫

ADV *Fam (walk, talk)* bizarrement▫

• **funnies NPL** *Am Fam* **the funnies** les bandes *fpl* dessinées▫ *(dans un journal)*

►► *Fam* ***funny bone*** petit juif *m*; *Fam Euph* ***funny farm*** maison *f* de fous; *Am Fam* ***funny papers*** supplément *m* bande dessinée▫

fur [fɜː(r)] (*pt & pp* **furred**, *cont* **furring**) **N 1** *(on animal)* poil *m*, pelage *m*, fourrure *f*; *Fam* **her remark made the f. fly** *or* **set the f. flying** ça a fait du grabuge quand elle a dit ça; *Fam* **the f. really flew!** ça a bardé!

2 *(coat, pelt)* fourrure *f*; **she was dressed in expensive furs** elle portait des fourrures de prix

3 *(in kettle, pipe)* incrustation *f*, (dépôt *m* de) tartre *m*

4 *Med (on tongue)* enduit *m*

VT 1 *(kettle, pipe)* entartrer, incruster **2** *Med (tongue)* empâter

VI to f. (up) *(kettle, pipe)* s'entartrer, s'incruster

►► ***fur coat*** (manteau *m* de) fourrure *f*; *Fam Hum* **to be all f. coat and no knickers** avoir fière allure tout en étant vide de substance▫; ***fur farm*** élevage *m* d'animaux à fourrure; *Zool* ***fur seal*** phoque *m*; ***fur skins*** peaux *fpl*; ***fur trade*** commerce *m* de fourrures, pelleterie *f*; ***fur trapper*** trappeur *m*

furbish ['fɜːbıʃ] **VT** *(polish)* fourbir, astiquer; *(renovate)* remettre à neuf

furious ['fjʊərıəs] **ADJ 1** *(angry)* furieux; **to be f. with sb/oneself** être furieux contre qn/soi-même; **she was f. with me for being late** elle était furieuse que je sois en retard; **he was f. when he saw the car** il s'est mis en colère quand il a vu la voiture; **a f. look** un regard furibond **2** *(raging, violent ► sea, storm)* déchaîné; *(► effort, struggle)* acharné; *(► pace, speed)* fou (folle)

furiously ['fjʊərıəslı] **ADV 1** *(answer, look)* furieusement **2** *(fight, work)* avec acharnement; *(drive, run)* à une allure folle; **the fire was blazing f.** l'incendie faisait rage

furl [fɜːl] **VT** *(flag, umbrella)* rouler; *Naut (sail)* ferler, serrer

furlong ['fɜːlɒŋ] **N** *(unit of measurement)* = 201,17 m, furlong *m*

furlough ['fɜːləʊ] **N 1** *Mil (leave of absence)* permission *f*, congé *m*; **to be on f.** être en permission **2** *Am (laying off)* mise *f* à pied provisoire

furnace ['fɜːnıs] **N** *(for central heating)* chaudière *f*; *Ind* fourneau *m*, four *m*; *Fig* **the office was like a f.** le bureau était une vraie fournaise

furnish ['fɜːnıʃ] **VT 1** *(supply ► food, provisions)* fournir; *(► information, reason)* fournir, donner; *(► funds)* pourvoir; *(opportunity)* offrir, présenter, fournir; **they furnished us with the translation** il nous ont donné la traduction; **they furnished the ship with provisions** ils ont ravitaillé le navire **2** *(house, room)* meubler; **she furnished her house with antiques** elle a meublé sa maison avec des antiquités; **a comfortably furnished house** une maison confortablement aménagée

furnished ['fɜːnıʃt] **ADJ** *(room, apartment)* meublé

furnishing fabric ['fɜːnıʃıŋ-] **N** tissu *m* d'ameublement

furnishings ['fɜːnıʃıŋz] **NPL 1** *(furniture)* meubles *mpl*, mobilier *m*, ameublement *m* **2** *Am (clothing)* habits *mpl*, vêtements *mpl*; *(accessories)* accessoires *mpl*

furniture ['fɜːnıtʃə(r)] **N** (UNCOUNT) **1** *(for house)* meubles *mpl*, mobilier *m*, ameublement *m*; **a piece of f.** un meuble; **antique f.** des meubles *mpl* anciens, du mobilier *m* ancien; **living room f.** un salon, des meubles *mpl ou* du mobilier *m* de salon; **Louis XV f.** du mobilier *m ou* des meubles *mpl* Louis XV; *Fam* **she feels as though she's just part of the f.** elle a l'impression de faire partie des meubles; **he treats me as if I were part of the f.** pour lui, je fais partie des meubles **2** *Naut & Typ* garniture *f* **3** *(accessories)* **street f.** mobilier *m* urbain; **door f.** = éléments décoratifs pour portes d'entrée

COMP *(shop, store)* d'ameublement, de meubles

►► *Entom* ***furniture beetle*** vrillette *f*; ***furniture polish*** encaustique *f*, cire *f*; ***furniture remover*** déménageur *m*; ***furniture showroom*** magasin *m* de meubles; ***furniture van*** camion *m* de déménagement

> Note that the French noun **fourniture** is a false friend. Its most common meaning is **supplies**.

furore [fjʊ'rɔːrı], *Am* **furor** ['fjʊrɔːr] **N** scandale *m*, tumulte *m*; **to cause** *or* **to create a f.** faire un scandale; **there's been a great f. over those scenes** ces scènes ont provoqué un énorme tumulte

furred [fɜːd] **ADJ 1** *(animal)* à poils **2** *(kettle, pipe)* entartré; *(tongue)* pâteux, chargé

furrier ['fʌrıə(r)] **N** fourreur *m*

furring ['fɜːrıŋ] **N** *(in kettle, pipe)* tartre *m*; *(on tongue)* enduit *m*

furrow ['fʌrəʊ] **N** *(in field)* sillon *m*; *(in garden)* rayon *m*, sillon *m*; *(on forehead, brow)* ride *f*, sillon *m*; *(on sea)* sillage *m*

VT 1 *(soil, surface)* sillonner **2** *(forehead, brow)* rider

VI *(forehead, brow)* se plisser; **her brow furrowed** son front se plissa

furrowed ['fʌrəʊd] **ADJ** *(forehead, brow)* ridé, sillonné de rides

furry ['fɜːrı] (*compar* **furrier**, *superl* **furriest**) **ADJ 1** *(animal)* à poils; *(tail, ears)* poilu; *(fabric)* qui ressemble à de la fourrure; *(toy)* en peluche; **the husky has a f. coat** le husky a de longs poils **2** *(kettle, pipe)* entartré; *(tongue)* pâteux, chargé

FURTHER ['fɜːðə(r)]

ADV	
• plus loin **1**	• plus **2**
• de plus **4**	
ADJ	
• plus éloigné **1**	• additionnel **2**
• supplémentaire **2**	
VT	
• avancer	

ADV (*compar of* **far**) **1** *(at a greater distance in space, time)* plus loin; **I walked f. than I intended to** je suis allé plus loin que je n'en avais l'intention; **f. to the south** plus au sud; **she's never been f. north than Leicester** elle n'est jamais allée plus au nord que Leicester; **f. along the beach** plus loin sur la plage; **how much f. is it?** c'est encore loin?; **have you much f. to go?** vous allez encore loin?; **he got f. and f. away from the shore** il a continué à s'éloigner de la rive; **to move f. away** s'éloigner; **she moved f. back** elle a reculé encore plus; **f. back than 1960** avant 1960; **f. forward, f. on** plus en avant, plus loin; *Fig* **she's f. on than the rest of the students** elle est en avance sur les autres étudiants; **I've got no f. with finding a nanny** mes recherches pour trouver une nourrice n'ont pas beaucoup avancé; **that doesn't get us much f.** cela ne nous avance pas beaucoup; **nothing could be f. from the truth** rien n'est moins vrai; **nothing could be f. from my mind** j'étais bien loin de penser à ça

2 *(more)* plus, davantage; **I have nothing f. to say** je n'ai rien à ajouter, je n'ai rien d'autre *ou* rien de plus à dire; **don't try my patience any f.** ne pousse pas ma patience à bout, n'abuse pas de ma patience; **the police want to question him f.** la police veut encore l'interroger; **she heard nothing f. from her sister** elle n'a pas eu d'autres nouvelles de sa sœur; **I want nothing f. to do with him** je ne veux plus avoir affaire à lui; **add water to the wine to make it go f.** allongez le vin d'eau; **until you hear f.** jusqu'à nouvel avis; **unless you hear f.** sauf avis contraire

3 *(to a greater degree)* **her arrival only complicated things f.** son arrivée n'a fait que compliquer les choses; **play was f. interrupted by rain** le jeu fut à nouveau interrompu par la pluie

4 *Formal (moreover)* de plus, en outre; **and f. I think it best we don't see each other again** et de plus *ou* et en outre je crois qu'il vaut mieux que nous ne nous voyions plus

5 *(idioms)* **I would go even f. and say he's a genius** j'irais même jusqu'à dire que c'est un génie; **we need to go f. into the matter** il faut approfondir davantage la question; **I'll go no f.** *(move)* je n'irai pas plus loin; *(say nothing more)* je vais en rester là; **this information must go no f.** cette information doit rester entre nous *ou* ne doit pas être divulguée

ADJ (*compar of* **far**) **1** *(more distant)* plus éloigné, plus lointain; **she walked to the f. end of the room** elle est allée à l'autre bout de la pièce

2 *(additional ► comments, negotiations)* additionnel, autre; *(► information, news)* supplémentaire, complémentaire; **do you have any f. questions?** avez-vous d'autres questions à poser?; **I need a f. £900** j'ai encore besoin de 900 livres; **upon f. consideration** à la réflexion, après plus ample réflexion; **I have no f. use for it** je ne m'en sers plus, je n'en ai plus besoin *ou* l'usage; **I would like f. details of the programme** j'aimerais avoir quelques précisions *ou* indications supplémentaires sur le programme; **for f. information, phone this number** pour tout renseignement complémentaire, appelez ce numéro; **please send me f. information concerning the project** veuillez m'envoyer de plus amples renseignements sur *ou* concernant le projet; *esp Mil* **to await f. orders** attendre les ordres; **without f. delay** sans autre délai, sans plus attendre; **until f. notice** jusqu'à nouvel ordre; **without f. ado** sans plus de cérémonie; **without f. warning** sans plus d'avertissement

VT *(cause, one's interests)* avancer, servir, favoriser; *(career)* servir, favoriser; *(chances)* augmenter

• **further to PREP** *Formal* suite à; **f. to your letter of 12 July** suite à votre lettre du 12 juillet; **f. to our discussion/conversation** suite à notre discussion/conversation

►► *Br* ***further education*** **N** enseignement *m* postscolaire **COMP** *(class)* d'éducation permanente; ***further education college*** centre *m* de formation continue

furtherance ['fɜːðərəns] **N** *Formal* **in f. of their policy** pour servir leur politique

furthermore [ˌfɜːðəˈmɔː(r)] ADV en outre, par ailleurs

furthermost [ˈfɜːðəməʊst] ADJ *Literary* le plus éloigné, le plus lointain; **to the f. ends of the earth** jusqu'au bout du monde

furthest [ˈfɜːðɪst] (*superl of* **far**) ADV le plus loin; **her house is the f. away** sa maison est la plus éloignée; **when it's f. from the sun** lorsqu'il se trouve le plus éloigné du soleil; **this is the f. north I've ever been** c'est le plus au nord que j'aie jamais été

ADJ le plus lointain, le plus éloigné; **it's 10 miles at the f.** il y a 16 kilomètres au plus *ou* au maximum

furtive [ˈfɜːtɪv] ADJ *(behaviour, look, smile)* furtif; *(person)* sournois

furtively [ˈfɜːtɪvlɪ] ADV furtivement, en douce

fury [ˈfjʊərɪ] (*pl* **furies**) N **1** *(anger)* fureur *f*, furie *f*; **to be in a f.** être dans une colère noire *ou* en furie; **he was beside himself with f.** il était hors de lui **2** *(violence ▸ of storm, wind)* violence *f*; (▸ *of fight, struggle)* acharnement *m*; *Br* **to work like f.** travailler d'arrache-pied *ou* avec acharnement; *Br* **to run like f.** courir ventre à terre **3** *(frenzy)* frénésie *f*; **a f. of activity** une période d'activité débordante

• **Furies** NPL *Myth* **the Furies** les Furies *fpl*, les Érinyes *fpl*

furze [fɜːz] N *(UNCOUNT) Bot* ajoncs *mpl*

fuse, *Am* **fuze** [fjuːz] VI **1** *(melt)* fondre; *(melt together)* fusionner; **the two metals fused (together)** les deux métaux ont fusionné **2** *(join)* s'unifier, fusionner; **at some point the aims of the parties fused** à un moment donné les objectifs des partis se sont rejoints *ou* confondus **3** *Br Elec* **the lights/the appliance fused** les plombs ont sauté

VT **1** *(melt)* fondre; *(melt together)* fondre, mettre en fusion; **to f. two pieces together** réunir deux pièces par fusion

2 *(unite)* fusionner, unifier, amalgamer; **an attempt to f. traditional and modern methods** une tentative pour associer les méthodes modernes et traditionnelles

3 *Br Elec (circuit)* faire sauter les plombs de; **to f. the lights** faire sauter les plombs

4 *(explosive)* amorcer

N **1** *Elec* plomb *m*, fusible *m*; **to blow a f.** faire sauter un plomb *ou* un fusible; *Fam Fig (lose one's temper)* se mettre dans une colère noire, exploser; **there's a f. blown** un des fusibles a sauté **2** *(of explosive)* amorce *f*; *Mining* cordeau *m*; *Fam* **to have a short f.** être soupe au lait, se mettre facilement en rogne; *Fig* **the incident which lit the f. of the revolution** l'incident qui a déclenché la révolution

▸▸ ***fuse box*** boîte *f* à fusibles, coupe-circuit *m*; *Aut* porte-fusible *m*; ***fuse wire*** fusible *m*

fused [fjuːzd] ADJ *(kettle, plug)* avec fusible incorporé

fuselage [ˈfjuːzəlɑːʒ] N fuselage *m*

fusilier [ˌfjuːzəˈlɪə(r)] N *Mil* fusilier *m*

fusillade [ˌfjuːzəˈleɪd] N *Mil* **a f. (of shots)** une fusillade; *Fig* **a f. of criticism/questions** une avalanche de critiques/questions

fusion [ˈfjuːʒən] N **1** *Metal* fonte *f*, fusion *f*; *Phys* fusion *f* **2** *Fig (of ideas, parties)* fusion *f*, fusionnement *m*; **their new sound is a f. of disco and rap** leur nouveau son est un mélange de disco et de rap

▸▸ *Nucl* ***fusion bomb*** bombe *f* thermonucléaire *ou* à hydrogène; *Culin* ***fusion food*** = cuisine qui mêle saveurs d'orient et d'occident; *Nucl* ***fusion reactor*** réacteur *m* nucléaire

fuss [fʌs] N **1** *(UNCOUNT) (bother)* histoires *fpl*; **what a lot of f. about nothing!** que d'histoires pour rien!; **all that f. over a game of football!** tout ça pour un match de foot!; **after a great deal of f. she accepted** après avoir fait toutes sortes de manières, elle a accepté; **can you have him ejected from the studio without too much f.?** est-ce que vous pouvez le faire évacuer du studio discrètement? **2** *(state of agitation)* panique *f*; **don't get into a f. over it!** ne t'affole pas pour ça!; **I don't see what all the f. is about** je ne vois pas pourquoi on fait un tel cinéma **3** *(idioms)* **to kick up** *or* **to make a f. about** *or* **over sth** faire des histoires *ou* tout un plat au sujet de qch; **he kicked up quite a f. about the bill** il a fait toute une histoire pour la facture; **I don't want any f. made when I retire** je ne veux pas qu'on fasse tout un cinéma quand je prendrai ma retraite; **you should have made a f. about it** tu n'aurais pas dû laisser passer ça; **to make a f. of** *or* **over sb** être aux petits soins pour qn; **he likes to be made a f. over** il aime bien qu'on fasse grand cas de lui

VI *(become agitated)* s'agiter; *(worry)* s'inquiéter, se tracasser; *(rush around)* s'affairer; **she kept fussing with her hair** elle n'arrêtait pas de tripoter ses cheveux; **to f. over sb** être aux petits soins pour qn; **stop fussing over me!** laisse-moi tranquille!; **don't f., we'll be on time** ne t'en fais pas, on sera à l'heure

VT **1** *esp Am (make nervous)* agacer, embêter **2** *Br Fam (idioms)* **I'm not fussed** ça m'est égal ◻; **I don't think he's particularly fussed whether we go or not** je crois que cela lui est égal qu'on y aille ou pas ◻

▸ **fuss about, fuss around** VI *(rush around)* s'affairer

fussbudget [ˈfʌsbʌdʒɪt] *Am* = **fusspot**

fussily [ˈfʌsɪlɪ] ADV **1** *(fastidiously)* de façon méticuleuse *ou* tatillonne; *(nervously)* avec anxiété **2** *(over-ornately)* de façon tarabiscotée; **f. dressed** vêtu avec trop de recherche; **the room was rather f. decorated** la décoration de la pièce était surchargée

fussiness [ˈfʌsɪnɪs] N **1** *(fastidiousness)* côté *m* tatillon; **his f. about food is ridiculous** il est si difficile sur la nourriture que c'en est ridicule **2** *(ornateness ▸ of decoration)* tarabiscotage *m*, manque *m* de simplicité; (▸ *of clothes, style)* manque *m* de simplicité

fusspot [ˈfʌspɒt], *Am* **fussbudget** [ˈfʌsbʌdʒɪt] N *Fam* **1** *(worrier)* anxieux(euse) ◻ *m,f*; **don't be such a f.** arrête de te faire du mauvais sang **2** *(fastidious person)* tatillon(onne) *m,f*; **she's such a f.!** qu'est-ce qu'elle peut être difficile!; **don't be such a f., leave the housework for one day** ne sois pas aussi tatillon, laisse tomber le ménage pour aujourd'hui

fussy [ˈfʌsɪ] (*compar* **fussier**, *superl* **fussiest**) ADJ **1** *(fastidious)* tatillon, pointilleux; **her daughter is very f. about what she eats** sa fille est très difficile sur la nourriture; **he's f. about what he wears** il fait très attention à ce qu'il porte; **we can't afford to be too f.** nous ne pouvons pas nous permettre d'être trop difficiles; **where shall we go? – I'm not f.** où est-ce qu'on va? – ça m'est égal **2** *(over-ornate ▸ decoration)* trop chargé, tarabiscoté; (▸ *style)* ampoulé, qui manque de simplicité; (▸ *clothes)* trop recherché

fustian [ˈfʌstɪən] N **1** *(fabric)* futaine *f* **2** *Fig Literary (bombast)* grandiloquence *f*

fustiness [ˈfʌstɪnɪs] N **1** *(of room, clothes)* odeur *f* de moisi **2** *Fig (of theory, idea, outlook etc)* caractère *m* démodé

fusty [ˈfʌstɪ] (*compar* **fustier**, *superl* **fustiest**) ADJ **1** *(room, clothes)* qui sent le moisi; *(smell)* de moisi **2** *Fig (theory, idea, outlook etc)* vieux jeu *(inv)*

futile [*Br* ˈfjuːtaɪl, *Am* ˈfuːtəl] ADJ *(action, effort)* vain, inutile; *(remark, question)* futile, vain; *(idea)* futile, creux; **it's f. trying to reason with him** il est inutile d'essayer de lui faire entendre raison; **all our attempts were f.** toutes nos tentatives ont été inutiles *ou* vaines

futility [fjuːˈtɪlətɪ] (*pl* **futilities**) N *(of action, effort)* inutilité *f*; *(of remark, question, idea)* futilité *f*

futon [ˈfuːtɒn] N futon *m*

future [ˈfjuːtʃə(r)] N **1** *(time ahead)* avenir *m*; **in (the) f.** à l'avenir; **sometime in the near f.** *or* **in the not so distant f.** *(gen)* bientôt; *(more formal)* dans un avenir proche; **in the distant f.** dans un avenir lointain; **I'll have to see what the f. holds** *or* **has in store** on verra ce que l'avenir me réserve; **you have to think of the f.** il faut songer à l'avenir **2** *(prospects)* avenir *m*; **young people today don't have much of a f.** les jeunes d'aujourd'hui n'ont pas beaucoup d'avenir; **he has a great f. ahead of him as an actor** c'est un comédien plein d'avenir; **she wants to assure her son's f.** elle veut assurer un bon avenir à son fils; **there's no f. in farming** l'agriculture n'est pas un métier d'avenir **3** *Gram* futur *m*; **the f. of the verb "to be"** le futur du verbe "to be"; **in the f.** au futur

ADJ **1** *(yet to happen, become)* futur; **f. generations** les générations *fpl* futures *ou* à venir; **my f. wife** ma future épouse *ou* femme; **at a f. date** à une date ultérieure; **I kept it for f. reference** je l'ai conservé comme document **2** *Com (delivery, estate)* à terme; **goods for f. delivery** marchandises *fpl* livrables ultérieurement

• **in future** ADV à l'avenir; **I shan't offer my advice in f.!** je ne donnerai plus de conseils désormais!; **in f., please ask before taking anything** à l'avenir, je vous prie de demander la permission avant de prendre quoi que ce soit

▸▸ *Gram* ***future perfect*** futur *m* antérieur; *Fin* ***Future Rate Agreement*** accord *m* de taux à terme; *Gram* ***future tense*** futur *m*, temps *m* futur; *Fin* ***future value*** valeur *f* capitalisée

future-proof *esp Comput* ADJ évolutif

VT rendre évolutif

futures [ˈfjuːtʃəz] NPL *St Exch (contracts)* contrats *mpl* à terme; *(transactions)* opérations *fpl* à terme; *(securities)* titres *mpl ou* valeurs *fpl* à terme; **sugar f.** sucre *m* (acheté) à terme

▸▸ *Fin* ***futures contract*** contrat *m* à terme; ***futures exchange*** marché *m* à terme; ***futures market*** marché *m* à terme; ***futures option*** option *f* sur contrats à terme; ***futures trading*** négociations *fpl* à terme; ***futures transaction*** opération *f* à terme

futurism [ˈfjuːtʃərɪzəm] N *Art & Literature* futurisme *m*

futurist [ˈfjuːtʃərɪst] *Art & Literature* N futuriste *mf*

ADJ futuriste

futuristic [ˌfjuːtʃəˈrɪstɪk] ADJ futuriste

futurologist [ˌfjuːtʃəˈrɒlədʒɪst] N futurologue *mf*

futurology [ˌfjuːtʃəˈrɒlədʒɪ] N futurologie *f*, prospective *f*

fuze *Am* = **fuse**

fuzz [fʌz] N *(UNCOUNT)* **1** *(down ▸ on peach)* duvet *m*; (▸ *on body)* duvet *m*, poils *mpl* fins; (▸ *on head)* duvet *m*, cheveux *mpl* fins

2 *(frizzy hair)* cheveux *mpl* crépus *ou* frisottants

3 *(on blanket, sweater)* peluches *fpl*

4 *very Fam (police)* **the f.** les flics *mpl*

5 *Am (lint)* peluches *fpl*

fuzziness [ˈfʌzɪnɪs] N **1** *(of image, picture)* flou *m*; *(of outline, recording etc)* manque *m* de netteté

2 *(of ideas)* confusion *f*

3 *(of cloth, garment)* caractère *m* pelucheux

4 the f. of my hair mes cheveux *mpl* crépus

fuzzy [ˈfʌzɪ] (*compar* **fuzzier**, *superl* **fuzziest**) ADJ **1** *(image, picture)* flou; *(outline, recording etc)* qui manque de netteté

2 *(confused ▸ ideas)* confus; **my head feels a bit f. today** j'ai un peu la tête qui tourne aujourd'hui

3 *(cloth, garment)* pelucheux

4 *(hair)* crépu, frisottant

▸▸ *Comput* ***fuzzy logic*** logique *f* floue

FX[1] [ˌefˈeks] NPL *Cin* effets *mpl* spéciaux *(du cinéma de science-fiction)*

FX[2] N *Fin (abbr* **foreign exchange***)* devises *fpl* étrangères

▸▸ ***FX broker***, ***FX dealer*** cambiste *mf*, courtier (ère) *m,f* en devises; ***FX market*** marché *m* des changes; ***FX option*** option *f* sur devises; ***FX transfer*** transfert *m* de devises

> **SUFFIXE**
>
> **-FY, -FICATION**
>
> Ces suffixes se combinent avec des adjectifs ou des noms pour former des verbes et des noms verbaux.
>
> • Le sens principal véhiculé par ces suffixes est celui de la TRANSFORMATION jusqu'à l'état indiqué par le mot auquel il s'attache:
>
> **to purify** épurer, purifier; **simplification** simplification; **clarification** clarification
>
> • Ces suffixes s'emploient également parfois sur un mode légèrement péjoratif, comme dans les cas suivants:
>
> **dandified** à l'allure de dandy; **the Disneyfication of culture** la Disneylandisation de la culture

FYI *(written abbr* **for your information***)* à titre indicatif

G¹, g¹ [dʒi:] **N1** *(letter)* G, g *m inv*; **two g's** deux g; **G for George** G comme Gaston **2** *Mus (note)* sol *m inv*; **G clef** clef *f* de sol; **in G minor** en sol mineur **3 G7** G7 *m*, groupe *m* des 7; **G7 summit** sommet *m* du G7; **G8** G8 *m*, groupe des 8

G² **N1** *Phys* conductance *f* **2** *Am Fam (abbr* **grand)** *($1,000)* 1000 dollars *mpl*; **he earns 50G a year** il gagne 50000 dollars par an

G³ **1** *(written abbr* **good)** B **2** *Austr Cin (written abbr* **general (audience)**) = tous publics

g² **1** *(written abbr* **gramme)** g **2** *(written abbr* **gravity)** g

G25 [ˌdʒi:twentɪˈfaɪv] **N** *Econ & Pol* le G25, le groupe des 25

G7 [ˌdʒi:ˈsevən] **N** *Econ & Pol* le G7, le groupe des 7

G8 [ˌdʒi:ˈeɪt] **N** *Econ & Pol* le G8, le groupe des 8

GAAP [ˌdʒi:eɪ,eɪˈpi:] **NPL** *Acct (abbr* **generally accepted accounting principles)** PCGR *mpl*

gab [gæb] *(pt & pp* **gabbed**, *cont* **gabbing)** *Fam* **N1** *(chatter)* parlotte *f*, parlote *f*; **we had a good g. on the phone** on a taillé une bonne bavette au téléphone **2** *(idiom)* **to have the gift of the g.** avoir la langue bien pendue; *(be convincing talker)* avoir du bagou(t)

VI *(chat)* bavarder, papoter; *(gossip)* caqueter, jaser

gabardine = **gaberdine**

gabble [ˈgæbəl] **VI1** *(idly)* faire la parlote, papoter; **they g. (away) for hours** ils papotent pendant des heures **2** *(inarticulately)* bredouiller, balbutier

VT bredouiller, bafouiller; **she gabbled (out) her story** elle a raconté son histoire en bredouillant

N baragouin *m*, flot *m* de paroles; **a g. of voices** un bruit confus de conversations; **to talk at a g.** bredouiller, parler vite *ou* avec volubilité

gaberdine [ˌgæbəˈdi:n] **N** gabardine *f*

gable [ˈgeɪbəl] **N** *(wall)* pignon *m*; *(over arch, door etc)* gâble *m*, gable *m*

►► ***gable end*** pignon *m*; ***gable roof*** comble *m* sur pignon(s); ***gable window*** fenêtre *f* sur pignon

gabled [ˈgeɪbəld] **ADJ** *(house)* à pignon *ou* pignons; *(wall)* en pignon; *(roof)* sur pignon *ou* pignons; *(arch)* à gâble

Gabon [gæˈbɒn] **N** Gabon *m*

Gabonese [ˌgæbɒˈni:z] **NPL the G.** les Gabonais *mpl*

ADJ gabonais

COMP *(embassy, history)* du Gabon

gad [gæd] *(pt & pp* **gadded**, *cont* **gadding)** **VI to g. about** *or* **around** se balader; **she's been out gadding about (town) all night** elle a passé toute la nuit à faire la fête (en ville); **she goes gadding all over the world** elle court le vaste monde

gadfly [ˈgædflaɪ] *(pl* **gadflies)** **N1** *(insect)* taon *m* **2** *(annoying person)* enquiquineur(euse) *m,f*, casse-pieds *mf inv*

gadget [ˈgædʒɪt] **N** gadget *m*; **a kitchen with all the latest gadgets** une cuisine avec tous les derniers gadgets; **what's that g. for?** à quoi sert ce truc-là?

gadgetry [ˈgædʒɪtrɪ] **N** *(UNCOUNT)* gadgets *mpl*

Gaelic [*Ir* ˈgeɪlɪk, *Scot* ˈgælɪk] **ADJ** gaélique

N *Ling* gaélique *m*

►► ***Gaelic coffee*** irish coffee *m*; ***Gaelic football*** football *m* gaélique, = jeu de balle irlandais à quinze où il est interdit de taper dans le ballon avec la main

Gaeltacht [ˈgeɪltæχt] **N the G.** = les régions d'Irlande où l'on parle le gaélique

gaff [gæf] **N1** *(fishhook)* gaffe *f*

2 *Naut (spar)* corne *f*

3 *Br (UNCOUNT) (nonsense)* foutaise *f*, foutaises *fpl*

4 *Br Fam (home)* baraque *f*

5 *Fam (idiom)* **to blow the g.** vendre la mèche; **to blow the g. on sb** dénoncer qn▫, vendre qn

VT *(fish)* gaffer

►► *Naut **gaff topsail*** voile *f* de flèche

gaffe [gæf] **N** *(blunder)* bévue *f*; **to commit** *or* **to make a g.** commettre une bévue

gaffer [ˈgæfə(r)] **N1** *Br Fam* **the g.** *(boss)* le patron▫, le chef▫; *(foreman)* le contremaître▫, le chef d'équipe▫ **2** *Fam (old man)* **an old g.** un vieux bonhomme *m* **3** *Cin* chef *m* électricien, gaffer *m*

►► *TV & Cin **gaffer grip*** pince *f* pour projecteur; ***gaffer tape*** ruban *m* adhésif en toile

gag [gæg] *(pt & pp* **gagged**, *cont* **gagging)** **N1** *(over mouth)* bâillon *m*; *Fig* **they want to put a g. on the press** ils veulent bâillonner la presse **2** *Fam (joke)* blague▫ *f*; *(visual)* gag▫ *m* **3** *Med* ouvre-bouche *m*

VT *(silence)* bâillonner; *Fig* bâillonner, museler

VI1 *(retch)* avoir un haut-le-cœur; **to make sb g.** donner envie de vomir à qn; **he gagged on a fishbone** il a failli s'étrangler avec une arête de poisson; *Br Vulg* **to be gagging for it** avoir envie de se faire tirer **2** *Fam (joke)* blaguer▫, rigoler▫ **3** *Theat (actor, comedian)* faire des improvisations comiques

►► *Am **gag law*** = toute loi limitant la liberté de la presse ou la liberté d'expression, *Can* loi *f* du bâillon; *Am **gag resolution, gag rule*** règle *f* du bâillon *(procédure parlementaire permettant de limiter le temps de parole et d'éviter l'obstruction systématique)*

gaga [ˈgɑ:gɑ:] **ADJ** *Fam (senile, crazy)* gaga; **to go g.** devenir gaga *ou* gâteux

gage¹ [geɪdʒ] **N1** *Arch (pledge)* gage *m* **2** *(challenge)* défi *m* **3** *Arch (glove)* gant *m*

gage² *Am* = **gauge**

gagging [ˈgægɪŋ] **N** *(of person, press)* bâillonnement *m*

►► ***gagging order*** = décision de justice visant à interdire à la presse de publier tout article à propos d'une affaire, *Can* ordonnance *f* imposant le secret

gaggle [ˈgægəl] **N** *(of geese) & Fig* troupeau *m*; **a g. of young schoolgirls** un troupeau de jeunes élèves

VI cacarder

gagman [ˈgægmən] *(pl* **gagmen** [-men]) **N** *Am Cin & Theat* auteur *m* de gags, gagman *m*

gaiety [ˈgeɪətɪ] **N** gaieté *f*

• **gaieties** **NPL** *Literary (merry-making)* réjouissances *fpl*

gaily [ˈgeɪlɪ] **ADV 1** *(brightly)* gaiement; **g. coloured** aux couleurs vives **2** *(happily)* gaiement, allègrement

gain [geɪn] **N1** *(profit)* gain *m*, profit *m*, bénéfice *m*; *Fig* avantage *m*; **to do sth for personal g.** faire qch par intérêt; **your loss is my g.** le profit de l'un est le dommage de l'autre

2 *(acquisition)* gain *m*; **there were large Conservative gains** le Parti conservateur a gagné de nombreux sièges

3 *(increase)* augmentation *f*, accroissement *m*; *(in value)* hausse *f*; **a g. in weight** une prise de poids; **there has been a net g. in their income** leurs revenus ont nettement augmenté; *St Exch* **there has been a g. of 100 points on the Dow Jones** l'indice Dow Jones a gagné 100 points; *Fin* **g. in value** plus-value *f*

4 *Electron* gain *m*

VT1 *(earn, win, obtain)* gagner; *(reputation)* acquérir; **you will g. nothing by it** vous n'y gagnerez rien; **what would we (have to) g. by joining?** quel intérêt avons-nous à adhérer?; **to g. friends (by doing sth)** se faire des amis (en faisant qch); **they managed to g. entry to the building** ils ont réussi à s'introduire dans le bâtiment; **to g. the impression that...** avoir l'impression que... + *indicative*; **to g. an advantage** obtenir un avantage; **to g. the upper hand** prendre le dessus; **we've not so much lost a daughter as gained a son** nous n'avons pas perdu une fille mais gagné un fils

2 *(increase)* gagner; *St Exch* **the share index has gained two points** l'indice des actions a gagné deux points

3 *(obtain more)* gagner, obtenir; **to g. weight/speed** prendre du poids/de la vitesse; **to g. experience** acquérir de l'expérience; **to g. time** gagner du temps; **to g. popularity** devenir plus populaire; **he has gained prestige through this action** cette action a rehaussé son prestige; **to g. ground (on)** *(of racer, pursuer)* gagner du terrain (sur); **to g. ground** *(of custom)* se répandre, se développer

4 *(of clock, watch)* avancer de; **my watch gains two minutes a day** ma montre avance de deux minutes par jour

5 *Literary (reach)* atteindre, gagner; **we finally gained the shore** nous avons fini par atteindre la rive

VI 1 *(profit)* profiter, gagner; **who stands to g. by this deal?** qui y gagne dans cette affaire?; **we have all gained by his hard work** nous avons tous bénéficié de son labeur **2** *(increase)* **to g. in popularity** gagner en popularité; **to g. in self confidence** gagner *ou* prendre de l'assurance; **to g. in number** devenir plus nombreux **3** *(clock)* avancer

▸ **gain on, gain upon** **VT INSEP** *(catch up)* rattraper, gagner du terrain sur

gainer [ˈgeɪnə(r)] **N** gagnant(e) *m,f*

gainful [ˈgeɪnfʊl] **ADJ1** *(profitable)* profitable, rémunérateur **2** *(paid)* rémunéré; **to be in g. employment** avoir un emploi rémunéré

gainfully [ˈgeɪnfʊlɪ] **ADV** de façon profitable, avantageusement; **to be g. employed** avoir un emploi rémunéré

gainsay [geɪnˈseɪ] *(pt & pp* **gainsaid** [-ˈsed]) **VT** *Formal (deny)* nier; *(contradict)* contredire; **you can't g. the facts** tu ne peux pas nier l'évidence; **there's no gainsaying her skill as an artist** on ne peut pas nier son talent artistique, son talent artistique est indéniable

gain-sharing N *Com* participation *f* aux bénéfices, intéressement *m*

gait [geɪt] N démarche *f*, allure *f*; *(of horse)* train *m*; **to walk with an unsteady g.** marcher d'un pas chancelant

gaiters ['geɪtəz] NPL guêtres *fpl*

gal [gæl] N **1** *Fam Old-fashioned (girl)* fille *f* **2** *Phys (unit of acceleration)* gal *m*

gala ['gɑːlə] N **1** *(festivity)* gala *m* **2** *Br Sport* réunion *f* sportive; **swimming g.** grand concours *m* de natation

COMP *(day, evening)* de gala

►► ***gala dress*** habit *m* de gala; ***a gala occasion*** une grande occasion; ***gala performance*** représentation *f* de gala

galactic [gə'læktɪk] ADJ *Astron* galactique

Galahad ['gæləhæd] PR N *Myth* **Sir G.** Galaad

Galapagos Islands [gə'læpəgəs-] NPL **the G.** les (îles *fpl*) Galapagos *fpl*

galaxy ['gæləksɪ] *(pl* **galaxies)** N **1** *Astron* galaxie *f*; **the G.** la Galaxie **2** *(gathering)* constellation *f*, pléiade *f*; **a g. of film stars** une pléiade de vedettes de cinéma

gale [geɪl] N **1** *(wind)* coup *m* de vent, grand vent *m*; *Met* **a force nine g.** un vent de force neuf; **the roof was blown off in a g.** le toit a été emporté par la tempête; **it's blowing a g.** le vent souffle en tempête **2** *(outburst)* éclat *m*; **gales of laughter** des éclats *mpl* de rire

►► *Met* ***gale force*** force *f* 8 à 9; *Met* ***gale warning*** avis *m* de coup de vent, avis *m* de tempête

gale-force ADJ *Met* **g. winds** vents *mpl* forts

galena [gə'liːnə] N *Miner* galène *f*

Galilean [gælɪ'liːən] ADJ galiléen

N Galiléen(enne) *m,f*

Galilee ['gælɪliː] N Galilée *f*; **the Sea of G.** le lac de Tibériade, la mer de Galilée

Galileo [gælɪ'leɪəʊ] PR N Galilée

gall [gɔːl] N **1** *Anat (human)* bile *f*; *(animal)* fiel *m*

2 *(bitterness)* fiel *m*, amertume *f*

3 *(nerve)* culot *m*, toupet *m*, effronterie *f*; **he had the g. to say it was my fault!** il a eu le culot *ou* le toupet de dire que c'était de ma faute!

4 *Bot* galle *f*, cécidie *f*

5 *Med & Vet* écorchure *f*, excoriation *f*; *Fig* **the criticism was a g. to his pride** la critique l'a piqué au vif

VT **1** *(annoy)* énerver; **it galled him to have to admit he was wrong** ça l'a énervé de devoir reconnaître qu'il avait tort **2** *Med & Vet* excorier

►► *Anat* ***gall bladder*** vésicule *f* biliaire

gallant ADJ **1** ['gælənt] *(brave)* courageux, vaillant; **g. deeds** des actions *fpl* d'éclat, des prouesses *fpl* **2** [gə'lænt, 'gælənt] *(chivalrous)* galant

N ['gælənt] *Literary* galant *m*

gallantly ['gæləntlɪ] ADV **1** *(bravely)* courageusement, vaillamment **2** *(chivalrously)* galamment

gallantry ['gæləntrɪ] *(pl* **gallantries)** N **1** *(bravery)* courage *m*, vaillance *f*, bravoure *f*; **a medal for g.** une médaille de bravoure **2** *(chivalry, amorousness)* galanterie *f*

galleon ['gælɪən] N *Naut* galion *m*

gallery ['gælərɪ] *(pl* **galleries)** N **1** *(of art)* musée *m* (des beaux-arts); **private g.** galerie *f*; **g. owner** galeriste *mf*

2 *(balcony)* galerie *f*; *(for spectators)* tribune *f*; **the press g.** la tribune de la presse; **strangers'** *or* **public g.** *(in Houses of Parliament)* tribune *f* du public

3 *(covered passageway)* galerie *f*

4 *Theat (upper balcony)* dernier balcon *m*; *(audience)* galerie *f*; *Fig* **to play to the g.** poser pour la galerie

5 *(tunnel)* galerie *f*

6 *Golf (spectators)* public *m*

7 *Am (veranda)* véranda *f*; *(balcony)* balcon *m*

galley ['gælɪ] N **1** *(ship)* galère *f*

2 *(rowing boat)* yole *f*

3 *(ship's kitchen)* coquerie *f*; *(aircraft kitchen)* office *m or f*

4 *Typ (container)* galée *f*; *(proof)* placard *m*

►► ***galley kitchen*** kitchenette *f*, cuisinette *f*; *Typ* ***galley proof*** (épreuve *f* en) placard *m*; ***galley slave*** galérien *m*

Gallic ['gælɪk] ADJ **1** *(French)* français; **G. charm** charme *m* typiquement français **2** *Hist (of Gaul)* gaulois

►► ***the Gallic Wars*** la guerre des Gaules

Gallicism ['gælɪsɪzəm] N gallicisme *m*

Gallicize, -ise ['gælɪsaɪz] VT franciser

galling ['gɔːlɪŋ] ADJ *(annoying)* irritant; *(humiliating)* humiliant, vexant; **it was g. to reflect that...** ça me/la/*etc* rendait malade de penser que... + *indicative*

gallium ['gælɪəm] N *Chem* gallium *m*

gallivant about, gallivant around VI *Hum* se balader; **he's gallivanting around the South of France** il se balade *ou* il est parti en vadrouille dans le Midi

gallon ['gælən] N *(in UK)* = 4,54 l, gallon *m*; *(in US)* = 3,78 l, gallon *m*; *Aut* **miles per g.** consommation *f* d'essence aux 100 kilomètres; *Fam* **they drink gallons of beer** ils boivent de la bière à tire-larigot

gallop ['gæləp] VI *(horse)* galoper; *(horse, rider)* aller au galop; **to g. away** *or* **off** partir au galop; *Fig* **he came galloping down the stairs** il a descendu l'escalier au galop;*Fig* **to g. through one's work/a task** expédier un travail/une tâche

VT *(horse)* faire galoper

N galop *m*; **at a g.** au galop (allongé); **(at) full g.** au grand galop; *Fig* **to do sth at a g.** faire qch à toute vitesse; **the pony broke into a g.** le poney a pris le galop

galloping ['gæləpɪŋ] ADJ *(horse)* au galop; *Fig* galopant

►► *Old-fashioned Med* ***galloping consumption*** phtisie *f* galopante; ***galloping inflation*** inflation *f* galopante

Gallo-Roman ['gæləʊ-] ADJ *(dialects)* gallo-roman; *(civilization, remains)* gallo-romain

N *Ling* gallo-roman *m*

gallows ['gæləʊz] *(pl* **inv)** N potence *f*, gibet *m*

►► *Br* ***gallows humour*** humour *m* noir; ***gallows tree*** potence *f*, gibet *m*

gallstone ['gɔːlstəʊn] N *Med* calcul *m* biliaire; **to have gallstones** avoir des calculs

Gallup Poll ['gæləp-] N sondage *m* (d'opinion) *(réalisé par l'institut Gallup)*

galore [gə'lɔː(r)] ADV en abondance, à gogo; **books/money g.** des livres/de l'argent à gogo

galoshes [gə'lɒʃɪz] NPL caoutchoucs *mpl (pour protéger les chaussures)*

galumph [gə'lʌmf] VI *Fam* courir lourdement *ou* comme un pachyderme; **he came galumphing down the stairs** il a descendu l'escalier avec la légèreté d'un éléphant *ou* d'un hippopotame

galvanic [gæl'vænɪk] ADJ **1** *Elec* galvanique **2** *Med (convulsive)* convulsif **3** *(stimulating)* galvanisant

galvanism ['gælvənɪzəm] N *Med* galvanisme *m*

galvanization, -isation [,gælvənaɪ'zeɪʃən] N *Med, Metal & Fig* galvanisation *f*

galvanize, -ise ['gælvənaɪz] VT *Med, Metal & Fig* galvaniser; **it galvanized the team into action** ça a poussé l'équipe à agir

galvanized, -ised ['gælvənaɪzd] ADJ galvanisé

►► ***galvanized iron*** fer *m* galvanisé

galvanizing, -ising ['gælvənaɪzɪŋ] ADJ

►► ***galvanizing effect*** effet *m* de galvanisation; *Fig* **the imminent danger had a g. effect on us** la proximité du danger nous a galvanisés

galvanometer [,gælvə'nɒmɪtə(r)] N *Elec* galvanomètre *m*

Gambia ['gæmbɪə] N **(the) G.** (la) Gambie

Gambian ['gæmbɪən] N Gambien(enne) *m,f*

ADJ gambien

gambit ['gæmbɪt] N *Chess* gambit *m*; *Fig* tactique *f*, stratagème *m*; *Chess* **king's/queen's g.** gambit *m* du roi/de la reine; *Fig* **opening g.** manœuvre *f* d'approche

gamble ['gæmbəl] VI jouer; **I don't g.** je ne joue pas pour de l'argent; **to g. on a throw of the dice** miser sur un coup de dé(s); **to g. on the Stock Exchange** jouer à la Bourse, boursicoter; *Fig* **Napoleon gambled and lost** Napoléon a joué et perdu

VT parier, miser; **to g. one's money on horses** jouer son argent aux courses; *Fig* **the government has gambled its political future on the plan's success** le gouvernement a joué son avenir sur le succès du projet

N **1** *(wager)* pari *m*; **I like an occasional g. on the horses** j'aime bien jouer aux courses de temps en temps **2** *(risk)* coup *m* de poker; **I know it's a g. but...** je sais que c'est risqué mais...; **his g. paid off** son coup de poker a payé; **it's a g. we have to take** c'est un risque qu'il faut prendre; **it's a bit of a g. whether it'll work or not** nous n'avons aucun moyen de savoir si ça marchera

▸**gamble away** VT SEP *(fortune)* perdre au jeu

gambler ['gæmblə(r)] N joueur(euse) *m,f*

gambling ['gæmblɪŋ] N *(UNCOUNT)* jeu *m*, jeux *mpl* d'argent; **g. on the Stock Exchange** la spéculation en Bourse

ADJ joueur; **I'm not a g. man but I would guess that they will accept the offer** je ne suis pas homme à parier mais je crois qu'ils vont accepter la proposition

►► ***gambling debts*** dettes *fpl* de jeu; *Pej* ***gambling den*** maison *f* de jeu, tripot *m*

gambol ['gæmbəl] *(Br pt & pp* **gambolled,** *cont* **gambolling,** *Am pt & pp* **gamboled,** *cont* **gamboling)** VI gambader, cabrioler

N gambade *f*, cabriole *f*

game [geɪm] N **1** *(gen)* jeu *m*; **card/party games** jeux *mpl* de cartes/de société; **a g. of chance/of skill** un jeu de hasard/d'adresse; **the children were playing a g. of cowboys and Indians** les enfants jouaient aux cow-boys et aux Indiens; **it's only a g.!** ce n'est qu'un jeu!; **I'm off my g. today** je joue mal aujourd'hui; **it put me right off my g.** ça m'a complètement déconcerté; **politics is just a g. to him** pour lui, la politique n'est qu'un jeu

2 *(contest)* partie *f*; *(esp professional)* match *m*; *(part of a game of cards)* manche *f*; **she plays a good g. of chess** c'est une bonne joueuse d'échecs, elle joue bien aux échecs; *Chess* **opening/middle/end g.** début *m*/milieu *m*/fin *f* de partie; **tonight's big g.** le grand match de ce soir; **he played 65 games for England** il a joué 65 fois pour l'Angleterre; **we had a good g.** *(played well)* nous avons bien joué; **g. over** *(in computer game)* game over, fin de partie

3 *(division of match ▸ in tennis, bridge)* jeu *m*; **g., set and match** jeu, set et match; **(one) g. all** un jeu partout

4 *(playing equipment, set)* jeu *m*

5 *Fam (scheme, trick)* ruse *f*, stratagème *m*; **what's your (little) g.?** qu'est-ce que tu manigances?, à quel jeu joues-tu?; **I know your (little) g.!** je sais bien où vous voulez en venir!; **the g.'s up!** tout est perdu!; **two can play at that g.** moi aussi je peux jouer à ce petit jeu-là; **that's not playing the g.** ce n'est pas loyal; **let's stop playing games and come to the point** trêve de plaisanteries, passons aux choses sérieuses; **don't play** *or* **come that g. with me!** tu ne m'auras pas à ce petit jeu-là!

6 *Fam (undertaking, operation)* **at this stage in the g.** à ce stade des opérations; **to be ahead of the g.** mener le jeu

7 *(activity)* travail *m*; **I'm new to this g.** je suis novice en la matière; **when you've been in this g. as long as I have, you'll understand** quand tu auras fait ça aussi longtemps que moi, tu comprendras

8 *(UNCOUNT) Culin & (in hunting)* gibier *m*; **small g.** menu gibier *m*; **big g.** les grands fauves *mpl*

9 *(idioms)* **to beat sb at his/her own g.** battre qn sur son propre terrain; **to give the g. away** vendre la mèche; **that gave the g. away** c'est comme ça qu'on a découvert le pot aux roses; *Br Fam* **to be on the g.** *(prostitute)* faire le tapin *ou* le trottoir; *Br* **the g. is not worth the candle** le jeu n'en vaut pas la chandelle; **to play sb's g.** entrer dans le jeu de qn

ADJ **1** *(plucky)* courageux, brave **2** *(willing)* prêt, partant; **he's g. for anything** il est toujours partant; *Pej* il est prêt à tout *ou* capable de tout; **I'm g. if you are!** si tu es partant, moi aussi!

VI **1** *Formal (gamble)* jouer (de l'argent) **2** *(play computer games)* faire des jeux électroniques

• **games** NPL *(international)* jeux *mpl*; *Br Sch* sport *m*; **he's good at games** il est bon en sport, c'est un sportif

►► ***game birds*** gibier *m* à plumes; ***game fish*** poisson *m* noble *(saumon, truite, brochet)*; **game laws** réglementation *f* de la chasse; ***game licence*** permis *m* de chasse; ***game park*** *(in Africa)* réserve *f*; *Culin* ***game pie*** tourte *f* au gibier, pâté *m* en croûte; ***game plan*** *Chess & Fig* stratégie *f*; *Mktg* stratégie *f* (de marketing); ***game point*** *(in tennis)* balle *f* de jeu; *Comput* ***games port*** port *m* (de connexion pour) jeux, sortie *f* jeux; ***game reserve*** réserve *f (pour animaux sauvages)*; ***game show*** *TV* jeu *m* télévisé; *Rad* jeu *m* radiophonique; *Math* ***game theory*** théorie *f* des jeux; ***game warden*** *(gamekeeper)* garde-chasse *m*; *(in safari park)* garde *m (d'une réserve)*

gamecock [ˈgeɪmkɒk] **N** *Br* coq *m* de combat

gamekeeper [ˈgeɪmkiːpə(r)] **N** garde-chasse *m*

gamely [ˈgeɪmlɪ] **ADV** courageusement, vaillamment

gamepad [ˈgeɪmpæd] **N** manette *f* de jeu

gamer [ˈgeɪmə(r)] **N 1** *(who plays computer games)* = amateur de jeux vidéo **2** *Am (athlete, sportsperson)* = sportif très compétitif

gamesmanship [ˈgeɪmzmənʃɪp] **N** = art de gagner (aux jeux) en déconcertant son adversaire; **this is just g.** ce n'est qu'une astuce pour déstabiliser son adversaire

gamete [ˈgæmiːt] **N** *Biol* gamète *m*

gameware [ˈgeɪmweə(r)] **N** *Comput* ludiciel *m*

gamey *(compar* **gamier**, *superl* **gamiest)** = **gamy**

gaming [ˈgeɪmɪŋ] **N 1** *(UNCOUNT) Old-fashioned (gambling)* jeu *m*, jeux *mpl* d'argent **2** *(playing of computer games)* (pratique *f* des) jeux *mpl* électroniques

►► ***gaming laws*** = lois réglementant les jeux de hasard; ***gaming table*** table *f* de jeu

gamma [ˈgæmə] **N** gamma *m*

►► ***gamma globulin*** gammaglobuline *f*; ***gamma radiation*** *(UNCOUNT)* rayons *mpl* gamma; ***gamma ray*** rayon *m* gamma

gamma-ray therapy **N** *Med* gammathérapie *f*

gammon [ˈgæmən] **N** *Br (cut)* jambon *m*; *(meat)* jambon *m* fumé

►► *Br* ***gammon steak*** = épaisse tranche de jambon fumé

gammy [ˈgæmɪ] *(compar* **gammier**, *superl* **gammiest)** **ADJ** *Br Fam* estropié; **to have a g. leg** avoir une patte folle

gamp [gæmp] **N** *Br Fam Arch* pébroque *m*, pépin *m*

gamut [ˈgæmət] **N** *Mus & Fig* gamme *f*; **this character runs the whole g. of emotions** ce personnage passe par toute la gamme des émotions

gamy [ˈgeɪmɪ] *(compar* **gamier**, *superl* **gamiest)** **ADJ** *(meat)* faisandé

gander [ˈgændə(r)] **N 1** *(goose)* jars *m* **2** *Br Fam (look)* **to have** *or* **to take a g. at sth** jeter un coup d'œil sur qch

G&T, G and T [ˌdʒiːənˈtiː] **N** *Fam* gin-tonic *m*

gang [gæŋ] **N 1** *(gen)* bande *f*; *(of criminals)* gang *m*; *Fam* **the whole g.** *(of friends, colleagues)* toute la bande; *Pol & Hist* **the G. of Four** la Bande des Quatre **2** *(of workmen)* équipe *f*, *(of convicts)* convoi *m*

►► ***gang rape*** viol *m* collectif; ***gang warfare*** guerre *f* des gangs

► **gang up** **VI** se mettre à plusieurs; **to g. up with sb** s'allier avec qn; **to g. up against** *or* **on sb** se liguer contre qn

ganga [ˈgændʒə] **N** *Fam (marijuana)* herbe *f*

gang-bang **N** *Vulg* **1** *(rape)* viol *m* collectif **2** *(orgy)* partouze *f*

ganger [ˈgæŋə(r)] **N** *Br (foreman)* contremaître *m*, chef *m* d'équipe

Ganges [ˈgændʒiːz] **N the (River) G.** le Gange

gangland [ˈgæŋlænd] **N** le milieu

►► ***gangland boss*** chef *m* de gang; ***gangland killing*** règlement *m* de comptes *(dans le milieu)*; ***gangland warfare*** guerre *f* des gangs

ganglia [ˈgæŋglɪə] *pl of* **ganglion**

gangling [ˈgæŋglɪŋ] **ADJ** dégingandé

ganglion [ˈgæŋglɪən] *(pl* **ganglia** [-lɪə]) **N** *Anat* ganglion *m*

gangmaster [ˈgæŋˌmɑːstə(r)] **N** contremaître *m*

gangplank [ˈgæŋplæŋk] **N** passerelle *f* (d'embarquement)

gang-rape **VT** commettre un viol collectif sur; **women who have been gang-raped** les femmes qui ont été victimes de viols collectifs; **they gang-raped her** ils l'ont violée

gangrene [ˈgæŋgriːn] **N** *(UNCOUNT) Med & Fig* gangrène *f*; **to have g.** avoir la gangrène

gangrenous [ˈgæŋgrɪnəs] **ADJ** gangreneux; **the wound went g.** la blessure s'est gangrenée

gangster [ˈgæŋstə(r)] **N** gangster *m*

COMP *(film, story)* de gangsters

gangsterism [ˈgæŋstərɪzəm] **N** gangstérisme *m*

gangway [ˈgæŋweɪ] **N 1** *Naut* passerelle *f* (d'embarquement) **2** *(passage)* passage *m*; *(of bus etc)* couloir *m* central; *Br (in theatre)* allée *f*

EXCLAM dégagez le passage!

►► ***gangway port*** sabord *m* de coupée

ganja = **ganga**

gannet [ˈgænɪt] **N 1** *Orn* fou *m* de Bassan **2** *Br Fam (greedy person)* glouton(onne) *m,f*

gantry [ˈgæntrɪ] *(pl* **gantries)** **N 1** *(for crane)* portique *m*; **(launching) g.** *(for rocket)* portique *m* (de lancement); *Rail* **(signal) g.** portique *m* (à signaux) **2** *(for barrel)* chantier *m* **3** *(for drinks)* étagères *fpl* à bouteilles *(dans un bar)*

►► ***gantry crane*** grue *f* (à) portique

gaol, gaolbird *etc Br* = **jail, jailbird** *etc*

gap [gæp] **N 1** *(hole, opening* ► *which needs mending)* trou *m*; *(*► *in floorboards)* interstice *m*; *(*► *created deliberately)* trouée *f*, ouverture *f*; *(*► *in a wall)* brèche *f*; *(*► *in clouds)* trou *m*; *(*► *in trees)* trouée *f*; *(*► *of spark plug, points)* écartement *m*; *(*► *in piston ring)* jeu *m* à la coupe (des segments); **a g. in the wall** un trou dans le mur; **the sun shone through a g. in the clouds** le soleil perça à travers les nuages

2 *(space between objects)* espace *m*; *(narrower)* interstice *m*, jour *m*; **a g. of 2 cm** un intervalle de 2 cm; **there was a g. of a few metres between each car** il y avait une distance de quelques mètres entre chaque voiture; **he has a g. between his front teeth** il a les dents de devant écartées; **I could see through a g. in the curtains** je voyais par la fente entre les rideaux

3 *(blank)* blanc *m*; **fill in the gaps with the missing letters** remplissez les blancs avec les lettres manquantes

4 *(in time)* intervalle *m*; **she returned to work after a g. of six years** elle s'est remise à travailler après une interruption de six ans

5 *(lack)* vide *m*; *(in memory etc)* trou *m*, lacune *f*; **to bridge** *or* **to fill a g.** combler un vide; **his death left a g. in our lives** sa mort a laissé un vide dans notre vie; **a g. in the market** un créneau sur le marché

6 *(omission)* lacune *f*; **there are several gaps in his story** il y a plusieurs trous dans son histoire

7 *(silence)* pause *f*, silence *m*

8 *(disparity)* écart *m*, inégalité *f*; **there's a technology g. between our two countries** il y a un fossé technologique entre nos deux pays; **to close the g.** réduire l'écart; **age g.** différence *f* d'âge

9 *Geog (opening in hills, mountains)* trouée *f*; *(mountain pass)* col *m*

10 *(in recording)* blanc *m* sonore; *(in recorded tape)* plage *f* de silence

►► ***gap site*** terrain *m* vague (entre deux bâtiments); *Br* ***gap year*** = année, souvent passée à voyager, que s'accorde un étudiant avant son entrée à l'université ou à la fin de ses études

gape [geɪp] **VI 1** *(stare)* regarder bouche bée; **he gaped at me** il m'a regardé bouche bée; **to g. in admiration/astonishment** être bouche bée d'admiration/d'étonnement; **what are you gaping at?** qu'est-ce que tu regardes avec cet air bête? **2** *(open one's mouth wide)* ouvrir la bouche toute grande **3** *(be open)* être béant, béer; **to g. (open)** *(thing)* s'ouvrir (tout grand); *(seam etc)* bâiller; *(hole)* être béant; **a chasm gaped at our feet** un gouffre béant s'ouvrait à nos pieds

N *(stare)* regard *m* ébahi

gaping [ˈgeɪpɪŋ] **ADJ 1** *(staring)* bouche bée *(inv)* **2** *(wide open) (hole, wound)* béant

gappy [ˈgæpɪ] *(compar* **gappier**, *superl* **gappiest)** **ADJ 1** *(account, knowledge)* plein de lacunes **2 g. teeth** des dents *fpl* écartées; **g. smile** sourire *m* édenté

gap-toothed **ADJ** *(with spaces between teeth)* aux dents écartées; *(with missing teeth)* à qui il manque des dents

garage **N 1** [*Br* ˈgærɑːʒ, ˈgærɪdʒ, *Am* gəˈrɑːʒ] *(for cars)* garage *m*; **there is g. space for two cars** il y a de la place pour garer deux voitures **2** [ˈgærɪdʒ] *Mus* garage *m*

VT [*Br* ˈgærɑːʒ, *Am* gəˈrɑːʒ] mettre au garage

►► ***garage door*** porte *f* de garage; ***garage mechanic*** garagiste *mf*, mécanicien(enne) *m,f*; ***garage sale*** = vente d'occasion chez un particulier, vide-grenier *m*

garb [gɑːb] *Literary* **N** costume *m*, mise *f*; **she was in gipsy g.** elle était en costume de gitane, elle était déguisée en gitane

VT vêtir

garbage [ˈgɑːbɪdʒ] **N** *(UNCOUNT)* **1** *Am (waste matter)* ordures *fpl* (ménagères), détritus *mpl*; **throw it in the g.** jette-le à la poubelle

2 *Fam (nonsense)* bêtises *fpl*, âneries *fpl*; **you're talking g.!** tu racontes n'importe quoi!

3 *Fam (worthless things)* **their new album is a load of g.** leur dernier album est vraiment nul; **I've been eating too much g. lately** je mange trop de cochonneries en ce moment

4 *Comput* données *fpl* erronées; **g. in, g. out** la qualité des résultats est fonction de la qualité des données à l'entrée

►► *Am* ***garbage can*** poubelle *f*; *Am* ***garbage collector*** éboueur *m*; *Am* ***garbage disposal unit*** broyeur *m* d'ordures; *Am* ***garbage dump*** décharge *f*; *Am* ***garbage heap*** tas *m* d'ordures; *Am* ***garbage man*** éboueur *m*; *Am* ***garbage truck*** camion *m* des éboueurs

garbanzo [gɑːˈbænzəʊ] *(pl* **garbanzos)** **N** *Am* **g. (bean)** pois *m* chiche

garble [ˈgɑːbəl] **VT** *(involuntarily* ► *story, message)* embrouiller; *(*► *quotation)* déformer; *(deliberately* ► *facts)* dénaturer, déformer; **a garbled account** un compte rendu trompeur *ou* mensonger; **a garbled message** un message confus

Garda [ˈgɑːdə] **N Lake G.** le lac de Garde

garden [ˈgɑːdən] **N 1** *(with flowers)* jardin *m*; *(with vegetables)* (jardin *m*) potager *m*; **back/front g.** jardin *m* de derrière/de devant; **to do the g.** jardiner, faire du jardinage

2 *(park)* **public g.** *or* **gardens** jardin *m* public, parc *m*; **g. of remembrance** = jardin en souvenir des défunts

3 *(fertile region)* jardin *m*

4 *(in street names)* **Gardens** = nom donné à certaines rues en Grande-Bretagne

5 *(idiom)* **everything in the g. is rosy** *or* **lovely** tout va bien

COMP de jardinage, de jardin

VI jardiner, faire du jardinage

• **gardens** **NPL** *(park)* jardin *m* public

►► *Am* ***garden apartment*** rez-de-jardin *m inv*; ***garden centre*** jardinerie *f*; ***garden chair*** chaise *f* de jardin; ***garden city*** cité-jardin *f*; ***the Garden of Eden*** le jardin d'Éden, l'Éden *m*; ***the Garden of England*** = surnom du comté de Kent, célèbre pour ses vergers et ses champs de houblon; *Br* ***garden flat*** rez-de-jardin *m inv*; ***garden furniture*** mobilier *m* de jardin; ***garden gnome*** nain *m* de jardin; *Br* ***garden party*** garden-party *f*; ***garden path*** allée *f (dans un jardin)*; *Fig* **she was led up the g. path** elle a été dupée, on l'a fait marcher; ***garden produce*** produits *mpl* maraîchers; ***garden shed*** resserre *f*; ***the Garden State*** = surnom donné au New Jersey; ***garden suburb*** banlieue *f* verte; ***garden tools*** outils *mpl* de jardinage; ***garden wall*** mur *m* du jardin

gardener [ˈgɑːdənə(r)] **N** jardinier(ère) *m,f*

gardenia [gɑːˈdiːnɪə] **N** *Bot* gardénia *m*

gardening [ˈgɑːdənɪŋ] **N** jardinage *m*; **he's fond of g.** il aime jardiner

COMP *(book, programme)* de *ou* sur le jardinage; *(tools, gloves)* de jardinage

gargantuan [gɑːˈgæntjʊən] **ADJ** gargantuesque

gargle [ˈgɑːgəl] **VI** se gargariser, faire des gargarismes

N gargarisme *m*

gargoyle ['gɑːgɔɪl] N gargouille *f*

garish ['geərɪʃ] ADJ *(colour)* voyant, criard; *(clothes)* voyant, tapageur; *(light)* cru, aveuglant

garishly ['geərɪʃlɪ] ADV **g. dressed** vêtu de manière tapageuse; **g. made-up** outrageusement fardé *ou* maquillé

garishness ['geərɪʃnɪs] N *(of appearance)* tape-à-l'œil *m inv*; *(of colour)* crudité *f*, violence *f*

garland ['gɑːlənd] N *(on head)* couronne *f* de fleurs; *(round neck)* guirlande *f ou* collier *m* de fleurs; *(hung on wall)* guirlande *f*

VT *(decorate)* parer de guirlandes, enguirlander; *(crown)* couronner de fleurs; **garlanded with flowers** paré de guirlandes de fleurs

garlic ['gɑːlɪk] N ail *m*; **clove of g.** gousse *f* d'ail; **head of g.** bulbe *m* d'ail

▸▸ ***garlic bread*** = pain chaud au beurre d'ail; ***garlic butter*** beurre *m* d'ail; ***garlic powder*** ail *m* en poudre; ***garlic press*** presse-ail *m inv*; ***garlic salt*** sel *m* d'ail; ***garlic sausage*** saucisson *m* à l'ail

garlicky ['gɑːlɪkɪ] ADJ *(taste)* d'ail; *(breath)* qui sent l'ail

garment ['gɑːmənt] N vêtement *m*; **the g. industry** la confection

▸▸ ***garment bag*** housse *f* pour vêtements

garner ['gɑːnə(r)] VT *(grain)* rentrer, engranger; *Fig (information)* glaner, recueillir; *(compliments)* recueillir

garnet ['gɑːnɪt] N *(stone, colour)* grenat *m*

ADJ **1** *(in colour)* grenat *(inv)* **2** *(jewellery)* de *ou* en grenat

garnish ['gɑːnɪʃ] VT *Culin* garnir; *(decorate)* embellir, orner (**with** de); **garnished with parsley** garni de persil

N *Culin* garniture *f*

garnishee [,gɑːnɪ'ʃiː] N *Law* tiers *m* saisi

▸▸ ***garnishee order*** ordonnance *f* de saisie-attribution

garnishing ['gɑːnɪʃɪŋ] N *Culin* garniture *f*; *Fig* embellissement *m*

garret ['gærət] N *(room)* mansarde *f*; **to live in a g.** habiter une chambre sous les combles

garrison ['gærɪsən] N garnison *f*

VT **1** *(troops)* mettre en garnison; **they were garrisoned in Scotland** ils étaient en garnison en Écosse **2** *(town)* placer une garnison dans

▸▸ ***garrison town*** ville *f* de garnison; ***garrison troops*** (troupes *fpl* de) garnison *f*

garrote, garrotte [gə'rɒt] N **1** *(execution)* (supplice *m* du) garrot *m* **2** *(collar)* garrot *m*

VT garrotter

garrotting, *Am* **garroting** [gə'rɒtɪŋ] N **1** *(strangling)* strangulation *f (avec un fil ou une corde)* **2** *(execution)* supplice *m* du garrot

garrulity [gæ'ruːlɪtɪ] N loquacité *f*

garrulous ['gærələs] ADJ **1** *(person)* loquace, bavard **2** *(style)* prolixe, verbeux

garrulously ['gærələslɪ] ADV verbeusement

garter ['gɑːtə(r)] N **1** *Br (for stockings)* jarretière *f*; *(for socks)* fixe-chaussette *m*; **Knight of the (Order of the) G.** chevalier *m* de l'ordre de la Jarretière **2** *Am (suspender)* jarretelle *f*

▸▸ *Am* ***garter belt*** porte-jarretelles *m inv*; *Knitting* ***garter stitch*** point *m* mousse

gas [gæs] *(pl* **gasses**, *pt & pp* **gassed**, *cont* **gassing)**

N **1** *(domestic)* gaz *m*; **to pay the g. bill** payer le gaz; **to use g. for cooking** faire la cuisine *ou* cuisiner au gaz

2 *Chem* gaz *m*

3 *Mining* grisou *m*

4 *Med* gaz *m* anesthésique *ou* anesthésiant; **to have g.** subir une anesthésie gazeuse *ou* par inhalation; **the dentist gave me g.** le dentiste m'a endormi au gaz; **g. and air** *(mask)* masque *m* à oxygène

5 *Am Aut* essence *f*; *Fam* **step on** *or* **hit the g.!** *(in car)* appuie sur le champignon!; *Fig* grouille!, grouille-toi!

6 *Am Fam (amusing person, thing, situation)* **the party was a real g.** on s'est bien marrés *ou* on a bien rigolé à la soirée; **what a g.!** quelle rigolade!

7 *Br Fam (chatter)* bavardage[□] *m*; **they had a good g. on the phone** ils ont taillé une bonne bavette au téléphone

8 *(UNCOUNT) Am (in stomach)* gaz *mpl*

VT **1** *(poison)* asphyxier *ou* intoxiquer au gaz; **to g. oneself** *(poison)* s'asphyxier au gaz; *(suicide)* se suicider au gaz **2** *Mil* gazer

VI *Fam (chatter)* bavarder[□], jacasser

▸▸ *Admin* ***Gas Board*** compagnie *f* du gaz; ***gas bracket*** applique *f* à gaz; ***gas burner*** brûleur *m* à gaz; ***gas central heating*** chauffage *m* central au gaz; ***gas chamber*** chambre *f* à gaz; *Br* ***gas cooker*** cuisinière *f* à gaz, gazinière *f*; ***gas cylinder*** bouteille *f* de gaz; ***gas explosion*** *(in home or street)* explosion *f* due à une fuite de gaz; *(in mine)* coup *m* de grisou; *Br* ***gas fire*** (appareil *m* de) chauffage *m* au gaz; ***gas fitter*** installateur(trice) *m,f* d'appareils à gaz; ***gas furnace*** fourneau *m* à gaz; *Am Fam* ***gas guzzler*** = voiture qui consomme beaucoup; ***gas heater*** *(radiator)* radiateur *m* à gaz; *(for water)* chauffe-eau *m inv* à gaz; ***gas industry*** industrie *f* du gaz; ***gas jet*** brûleur *m*; *Br* ***gas lamp*** *(in street)* bec *m* de gaz; ***gas lighter*** *(for cooker)* allume-gaz *m inv*; *(for cigarettes)* briquet *m* à gaz; ***gas main*** conduite *f* de gaz; *(big)* gazoduc *m*; ***gas mantle*** manchon *m* à incandescence; ***gas mask*** masque *m* à gaz; ***gas meter*** compteur *m* à gaz; ***gas oil*** gas-oil *m*, gazole *m*; ***gas oven*** *(domestic)* four *m* à gaz; *(cremation chamber)* four *m* crématoire; **to put one's head in a g. oven** se suicider en mettant la tête dans un four à gaz; *Am* ***gas pedal*** accélérateur *m*; ***gas pipe*** tuyau *m* à gaz; ***gas pipeline*** gazoduc *m*; *Br* ***gas ring*** *(part of cooker)* brûleur *m*; *(small cooker)* réchaud *m* à gaz; *Am* ***gas station*** poste *m* d'essence, station-service *f*; *Br* ***gas stove*** *(in kitchen)* cuisinière *f* à gaz, gazinière *f*; *(for camping)* réchaud *m* à gaz; ***gas tank*** *(domestic)* cuve *f* à gaz; *Am Aut (petrol tank)* réservoir *m* à essence; ***gas tap*** *(on cooker)* bouton *m* de cuisinière à gaz; *(at mains)* robinet *m* de gaz; ***gas turbine*** turbine *f* à gaz

gasbag ['gæsbæg] N *Br Fam Pej (chatterbox)* moulin *m* à paroles, pie *f*; *(boaster)* fanfaron(onne)[□] *m,f*

Gascony ['gæskənɪ] N Gascogne *f*

gas-cooled reactor N réacteur *m* à refroidissement par gaz

gaseous ['gæsɪəs] ADJ *Phys* gazeux

gas-fired ADJ *(boiler, heater, oven etc)* à gaz; *Br* **g. central heating** chauffage *m* central au gaz

gash [gæʃ] VT **1** *(knee, hand)* entailler; *(face)* balafrer, taillader; **she fell and gashed her knee** elle est tombée et s'est entaillé *ou* ouvert le genou **2** *(material)* déchirer, lacérer

N **1** *(on knee, hand)* entaille *f*; *(on face)* balafre *f*, estafilade *f*; **there was a great g. in the side of the ship** il y avait une profonde entaille *ou* une large brèche dans le flanc du navire **2** *(in material)* (grande) déchirure *f*, déchiqueture *f* **3** *Vulg (woman's genitals)* craquette *f*, fente *f*

gasholder ['gæshəʊldə(r)] N gazomètre *m*

gasify ['gæsɪfaɪ] *(pt & pp* **gasified)** VT gazéifier

VI se gazéifier

gasket ['gæskɪt] N **1** *Tech* joint *m* (d'étanchéité); *Aut* **(cylinder) head g.** joint *m* de culasse; **to blow a g.** *Aut* faire sauter un joint de culasse; *Fam Fig* piquer une colère **2** *Naut* raban *m* de ferlage

gaslight ['gæslaɪt] N lumière *f* du gaz; **by g.** à la lumière d'une lampe à gaz

gasman ['gæsmæn] *(pl* **gasmen** [-men]) N employé *m* du gaz

gasoline, gasolene ['gæsəliːn] N *Am Aut* essence *f*

gasometer [gæ'sɒmɪtə(r)] N gazomètre *m*

gasp [gɑːsp] VI **1** *(be short of breath)* haleter, souffler; **to g. for breath** *or* **for air** haleter, suffoquer **2** *(in shock, surprise)* avoir le souffle coupé; **to g. in** *or* **with amazement** avoir le souffle coupé par la surprise **3** *Br Fam Fig* **I'm gasping for a cigarette** je meurs d'envie de fumer une cigarette; **I'm gasping (for a drink)** je meurs de soif

VT **"what?" he gasped** "quoi?", dit-il d'une voix pantelante

N halètement *m*; *(of surprise)* hoquet *m*, sursaut *m*; **she gave** *or* **she let out a g. of surprise** elle a eu un hoquet de surprise; **there were gasps of admiration from the audience** il y a eu des sursauts d'admiration dans le public; **to give a g. of horror** avoir le souffle coupé par l'horreur; **he was at his last g.** *(dying)* il allait rendre son dernier souffle *ou* soupir; *(exhausted)* il était à bout de souffle

gasper ['gɑːspə(r)] N *Br Fam Old-fashioned* sèche *f*, clope *m or f*

gas-permeable ADJ **g. (contact) lenses** lentilles *fpl* semi-rigides

gassed, *Am* **gassed up** [gæst] ADJ *Fam (drunk)* bourré, pété

gassing ['gæsɪŋ] N **1** *(of person ▸ deliberate)* gazage *m* **2** *Fam (talk)* bavardage[□] *m*

gassy ['gæsɪ] *(compar* **gassier**, *superl* **gassiest)** ADJ **1** *(drink)* trop gazeux **2** *Fam (person)* bavard[□]

gastrectomy [gæs'trektəmɪ] *(pl* **gastrectomies)** N gastrectomie *f*

gastric ['gæstrɪk] ADJ gastrique

▸▸ ***gastric bypass*** by-pass *m* gastrique, dérivation *f* gastrique; *Med* ***gastric flu*** *(UNCOUNT)* grippe *f* intestinale *ou* gastro-intestinale; ***gastric juices*** sucs *mpl* gastriques; *Med* ***gastric ulcer*** ulcère *m* de l'estomac, gastrite *f* ulcéreuse

gastritis [gæs'traɪtɪs] N *(UNCOUNT) Med* gastrite *f*

gastroenteritis [,gæstrəʊ,entə'raɪtɪs] N *(UNCOUNT) Med* gastro-entérite *f*; **to have g.** avoir une gastro-entérite

gastroenterology [,gæstrəʊ,entə'rɒlədʒɪ] N *Med* gastro-entérologie *f*

gastrointestinal [,gæstrəʊ,ɪntes'taɪnəl] ADJ gastro-intestinal

gastronome ['gæstrənəʊm] N gastronome *mf*

gastronomic [,gæstrə'nɒmɪk] ADJ gastronomique

gastronomy [gæs'trɒnəmɪ] N gastronomie *f*

gastropod ['gæstrəpɒd] N gastéropode *m*, gastropode *m*

gastropub ['gæstrəʊpʌb] N *Br* pub *m* gastronomique

gasworks ['gæswɜːks] *(pl* **inv)** N usine *f* à gaz

gate [geɪt] N **1** *(into garden)* porte *f*; *(into driveway, field)* barrière *f*; *(bigger ▸ of mansion)* portail *m*; (▸ *into courtyard)* porte *f* cochère; *(low)* portillon *m*; *(wrought iron)* grille *f*; **the main g.** la porte *ou* l'entrée *f* principale; **the gates of heaven/hell** les portes *fpl* du paradis/de l'enfer; **to pay at the g.** *(for match)* payer à l'entrée

2 *(at airport)* porte *f*; **proceed to g. 22** embarquement porte 22

3 *(on ski slope)* porte *f*

4 *(on canal)* **lock gates** écluse *f*, portes *fpl* d'écluse

5 *Sport (spectators)* nombre *m* de spectateurs (admis); *(money)* recette *f*, entrées *fpl*; **there was a good/poor g.** il y a eu beaucoup/peu de spectateurs

6 *Electron* gâchette *f*

7 *Phot* fenêtre *f*

8 *(in horse racing)* **(starting) g.** starting-gate *f*

9 *Aut (for gearstick)* grille *f (de changement de vitesse)*

VT *Br Sch* consigner, mettre en retenue; **to be gated** se faire consigner

▸▸ ***gate lodge*** loge *f* du portier; ***gate money*** recette *f*, montant *m* des entrées

-GATE

Le scandale du Watergate qui secoua les États-Unis en 1972 a eu un effet non seulement sur la politique américaine mais également sur la langue anglaise. En effet, le terme "Watergate" a engendré toute une série de dérivés où le suffixe "-gate" est associé à un nom ou incident synonyme de scandale public. "Irangate" et "Contragate" renvoient respectivement à la vente illégale d'armes par le gouvernement Reagan au gouvernement iranien au milieu des années 80, et au financement de la campagne terroriste menée contre l'État nicaraguayen grâce à l'argent ainsi obtenu. Parmi les autres termes ainsi créés, citons "Monicagate", qui désigna la mise en accusation et le procès du président américain Clinton en 1998 à la suite de sa liaison avec la jeune assistante Monica Lewinsky et "Cheriegate", qui est le nom donné en Grande-Bretagne à une polémique impliquant Cherie Blair (femme de l'ancien Premier ministre britannique Tony Blair) et un promoteur immobilier véreux en 2002.

gateau ['gætəʊ] *(pl* **gateaux** [-təʊz]) **N** gros gâteau *m (décoré et fourré à la crème)*

gatecrash ['geɪtkræʃ] *Fam* **VI** *(at party)* s'inviter; jouer les pique-assiette; *(at paying event)* resquiller

VT to g. a party aller à une fête sans invitation; **to g. a concert** aller à un concert sans payer

gatecrasher ['geɪtkræʃə(r)] **N** *Fam (at party)* pique-assiette *mf*; *(at paying event)* resquilleur (euse) *m,f*

gatecrashing ['geɪtkræʃɪŋ] **N** *Fam* resquillage *m*

gated community ['geɪtɪd-] **N** = quartier de riches, sous la surveillance de vigiles, dans une ville où il y a beaucoup de ghettos pauvres

gatefold ['geɪtfəʊld] **N** encart *m* dépliant *(dans un magazine)*

gatehouse ['geɪthaʊs, *pl* -haʊzɪz] **N** *(of estate)* loge *f* du portier; *(of castle)* corps *m* de garde

gatekeeper ['geɪtki:pə(r)] **N** *(person)* gardien (enne) *m,f*; *Rail* garde-barrière *mf*

gate-leg table, gate-legged table N table *f* à abattant

gatepost ['geɪtpəʊst] **N** montant *m* de barrière *ou* de porte; *Br Fam* **between you, me and the g.** soit dit entre nous

gateway ['geɪtweɪ] **N 1** *(entrance)* porte *f*, entrée *f*; *Fig* porte *f*; **Istanbul, g. to the East** Istanbul, la porte de l'Orient; **the g. to success/happiness** la porte du succès/du bonheur **2** *Comput* passerelle *f* (de connexion)

gather ['gæðə(r)] **VT 1** *(pick, collect* ▸ *mushrooms, wood)* ramasser; (▸ *flowers, fruit)* cueillir; **to g. the harvest** rentrer la moisson; **to g. honey from the flowers** *(of bees)* butiner les fleurs

2 *(bring together* ▸ *information)* recueillir; (▸ *taxes)* percevoir, recouvrer; (▸ *belongings)* ramasser; **we are gathered here today...** nous sommes rassemblés ici aujourd'hui...

3 *(gain)* prendre; **to g. strength** prendre des forces; **to g. speed** *or* **momentum** prendre de la vitesse

4 *(prepare)* **to g. one's thoughts** se concentrer; **to g. one's wits** rassembler ses esprits

5 *(embrace)* serrer; **he gathered the children to him** il serra les enfants dans ses bras *ou* sur son cœur

6 *(clothes)* ramasser; **she gathered her skirts about her** elle ramassa ses jupes; **to g. one's hair into a bun/a ponytail/bunches** se faire un chignon/une queue de cheval/des couettes

7 *(deduce)* déduire, comprendre; **from what she told me, I g. there will be an inquiry** à l'en croire, il y aura une enquête; **I g. he isn't coming then** j'en déduis qu'il ne vient pas, donc il ne vient pas?; **as far as I can g.** d'après ce que j'ai cru comprendre; **I had (already) gathered as much** *(it was not news to me)* j'avais déjà compris; **prices have gone up – so I g.** les prix ont augmenté – c'est bien ce qu'il me semble

8 *Sewing* froncer; **the dress is gathered at the waist** la robe est froncée à la taille

9 *Typ (signatures)* assembler

VI 1 *(people)* se regrouper, se rassembler; *(crowd)* se former; *(troops)* se masser **2** *(clouds)* s'amonceler; *(darkness)* s'épaissir; *(storm)* menacer, se préparer; **tears were gathering in her eyes** ses yeux se remplissaient de larmes **3** *Med (abscess)* mûrir; *(pus)* se former

• **gathers NPL** *Sewing* fronces *fpl*

▸ **gather in VT SEP 1** *(harvest)* rentrer; *(wheat)* récolter; *(money, taxes)* recouvrer; *(books, exam papers)* ramasser **2** *Sewing* **gathered in at the waist** froncé à la taille

▸ **gather round VI** se regrouper, se rassembler; **g. round and listen** approchez(-vous) et écoutez

▸ **gather together VT SEP** *(people)* rassembler, réunir; *(books, belongings)* rassembler, ramasser

VI se regrouper, se rassembler

▸ **gather up VT SEP 1** *(objects, belongings)* ramasser; **he gathered her up in his arms** il l'a prise dans ses bras **2** *(skirts)* ramasser, retrousser; *(hair)* ramasser, relever; **her hair was gathered up into a bun** ses cheveux étaient ramassés *ou* relevés en chignon

gathered ['gæðəd] **ADJ** *Sewing* froncé, à fronces

gathering ['gæðərɪŋ] **N 1** *(group)* assemblée *f*, réunion *f*; **a g. of top scientists** une réunion de scientifiques de haut niveau; **a social g.** une fête; **a small g. was listening to him** quelques personnes attroupées l'écoutaient

2 *(accumulation)* accumulation *f*; *(of clouds)* amoncellement *m*

3 *(bringing together* ▸ *of people)* rassemblement *m*; (▸ *of objects)* accumulation *f*, amoncellement *m*; **the g. of the clans** le rassemblement des clans

4 *(harvesting)* récolte *f*; *(picking)* cueillette *f*

5 *(UNCOUNT) Sewing* froncis *m*, fronces *fpl*

ADJ *Literary* **the g. darkness** l'obscurité grandissante; **the g. storm** l'orage qui se prépare *ou* qui menace

gator ['geɪtər] **N** *Am Fam* alligator *m*

GATS [gæts] **N** *Econ (abbr* **General Agreement on Trade in Services)** AGCS *m*

GATT [gæt] **N** *Fin (abbr* **General Agreement on Tariffs and Trade)** GATT *m*

gauche [gəʊʃ] **ADJ** gauche, maladroit

gaucheness ['gəʊʃnɪs] **N** gaucherie *f*, maladresse *f*

gaudily ['gɔ:dɪlɪ] **ADV** *(dress)* de manière voyante, tapageusement; *(decorate)* de couleurs criardes

gaudiness ['gɔ:dɪnɪs] **N** *(of colours)* éclat *m* criard, violence *f*; *(of clothes, decor)* style *m* voyant, mauvais goût *m*

gaudy ['gɔ:dɪ] *(compar* **gaudier**, *superl* **gaudiest)** **ADJ** *(dress)* voyant; *(colour)* voyant, criard, tape-à-l'œil *(inv)*; *(display)* tapageur

gauge, *Am* **gage** [geɪdʒ] **N 1** *(instrument)* jauge *f*, indicateur *m*; **water/oil g.** indicateur *m ou* jauge *f* de niveau d'eau/d'huile; **pressure g.** manomètre *m*; *Aut* **(fuel** *or Br* **petrol** *or Am* **gas) g.** jauge *f* d'essence

2 *(standard measurement)* calibre *m*, gabarit *m*; *(diameter* ▸ *of wire, cylinder, gun)* calibre *m*

3 *Rail (of track) & Aut (of wheels)* écartement *m*

4 *Tech (of steel)* jauge *f*

5 *Cin (of film)* pas *m*

6 *Fig* **the survey provides a g. of current trends** le sondage permet d'évaluer les tendances actuelles

VT 1 *(screw etc)* calibrer; *(oil)* jauger, mesurer; *(measure, calculate)* mesurer, jauger; **to g. the temperature of the political situation** jauger la situation politique; **to g. a situation** évaluer une situation; **it was difficult to g. how interested they were/their enthusiasm** il était difficile de juger dans quelle mesure ils étaient intéressés/de juger de leur enthousiasme **2** *(predict)* prévoir; **he tried to g. what her reaction would be** il essaya de prévoir sa réaction **3** *(standardize)* normaliser

gauging rod, gauging stick ['geɪdʒɪŋ-] **N** jauge *f*

Gaul [gɔ:l] **N 1** *Geog* Gaule *f* **2** *(person)* Gaulois(e) *m,f*

Gaullist ['gəʊlɪst] *Pol* **ADJ** gaulliste

N gaulliste *mf*

gaunt [gɔ:nt] **ADJ 1** *(emaciated* ▸ *face)* hâve, creux, émacié; (▸ *body)* décharné, émacié **2** *(desolate* ▸ *landscape)* morne, lugubre, désolé; (▸ *building)* lugubre, désert

gauntlet ['gɔ:ntlɪt] **N** *(medieval glove)* gantelet *m*; *(for motorcyclist, fencer)* gant *m* (à crispin *ou* à manchette); **to throw down/to take up the g.** jeter/relever le gant; *Mil* **to run the g.** passer par les baguettes; *Fig* se faire fustiger; **to run the g. of an angry mob** se forcer *ou* se frayer un passage à travers une foule hostile; **she had to run the g. of their anger** elle a dû affronter leur colère

gauntness ['gɔ:ntnɪs] **N 1** *(of face, body)* maigreur *f*, aspect *m* émacié **2** *(of landscape)* aspect *m* morne *ou* lugubre, désolation *f*; *(of building)* aspect *m* lugubre

gauze [gɔ:z] **N** gaze *f*

gave [geɪv] *pt of* **give**

gavel ['gævəl] **N** marteau *m (de magistrat etc)*

gavotte [gə'vɒt] **N** gavotte *f*

Gawd [gɔ:d] **EXCLAM** *Br Fam* mon Dieu!

gawk [gɔ:k] *Fam* **VI** être *ou* rester bouche bée; **to g. at sb** regarder qn bouche bée

N *(person)* godiche *f*, grand dadais *m*

gawker ['gɔ:kə(r)] **N** *Fam* badaud(e) *m,f*, curieux(euse) *m,f*

gawkiness ['gɔ:kɪnɪs] **N** gaucherie *f*, air *m* emprunté

gawky ['gɔ:kɪ] *(compar* **gawkier**, *superl* **gawkiest)** **ADJ** gauche, emprunté

gawp [gɔ:p] **VI** *Br Fam* être *ou* rester bouche bée; **don't just stand there gawping, do something!** ne reste pas planté là, fais quelque chose

gay [geɪ] **ADJ 1** *(cheerful, lively* ▸ *appearance, party, atmosphere)* gai, joyeux; (▸ *laughter)* enjoué, joyeux; (▸ *music, rhythm)* gai, entraînant allègre; **to have a g. old time** prendre du bon temps; **with g. abandon** avec insouciance, sans retenue

2 *(bright* ▸ *colours, lights)* gai, vif, éclatant; **the streets were g. with coloured flags** les rues étaient égayées de drapeaux aux couleurs vives

3 *(homosexual)* gay, homosexuel

4 *Fam (stupid, pathetic)* nul

N homosexuel(elle) *m,f*, gay *mf*

COMP *(club, disco, magazine)* pour homosexuels

▸▸ ***the gay community*** la communauté homosexuelle *ou* gay; ***gay marriage*** mariage *m* homosexuel; ***gay parenting*** homoparentalité *f*; *Fam Pej* ***gay plague*** sida *m*; ***gay pride*** = revendication par les homosexuels de leur orientation sexuelle; ***gay rights*** les droits *mpl* des homosexuels

gay-friendly ADJ *(bar, hotel)* qui accueille volontiers les homosexuels

gayness ['geɪnɪs] **N** *(homosexuality)* homosexualité *f*

Gaza ['gɑ:zə] **N** Gaza

▸▸ ***the Gaza Strip*** la bande de Gaza

gaze [geɪz] **VI to g. at sb/sth** regarder qn/qch fixement *ou* longuement; **to g. into space** avoir le regard perdu dans le vague, regarder dans le vide

N regard *m* fixe; **to meet sb's g.** regarder qn dans les yeux; **exposed to the public g.** exposé aux regards inquisiteurs de tous

gazebo [gə'zi:bəʊ] *(pl* **gazebos)** **N** belvédère *m*

gazelle [gə'zel] *(pl inv or* **gazelles)** **N** gazelle *f*

gazette [gə'zet] **N** *(newspaper)* journal *m*; *(official publication)* journal *m* officiel

VT *Br* publier *ou* faire paraître au journal officiel

gazetteer [gæzɪ'tɪə(r)] **N** index *m ou* nomenclature *f* géographique

gazillion [gə'zɪljən] **N** *Fam* **I've got a g. things to do** j'ai un million de choses à faire

gazump [gə'zʌmp] **VT** *Br Fam* = rompre une promesse de vente (d'une maison) à la suite d'une surenchère; **we've been gazumped** le propriétaire de la maison est revenu sur sa promesse de vente pour accepter l'offre plus élevée d'une tierce personne

gazumping [gə'zʌmpɪŋ] **N** *Br Fam* = fait de revenir sur une promesse de vente pour accepter une offre plus élevée

GB[1] [ˌdʒi:'bi:] **N** *(abbr* **Great Britain)** G-B *f*; **GB plate** plaque *f* GB; *Aut* **GB sticker** autocollant *m* GB

GB[2] *Comput (written abbr* **gigabyte)** Go

GBH [ˌdʒi:bi:'eɪtʃ] **N** *(UNCOUNT) Law (abbr* **grievous bodily harm)** coups *mpl* et blessures *fpl*

GCE [ˌdʒi:si:'i:] **N** *Formerly Br Sch (abbr* **General Certificate of Education)** = certificat britannique de fin d'études secondaires en deux étapes ("O level" et "A level") dont la première est aujourd'hui remplacée par le "GCSE"

GCHQ [ˌdʒi:si:ˌeɪtʃ'kju:] **N** *Br (abbr* **Government Communications Headquarters)** = centre d'interception des télécommunications étrangères en Grande-Bretagne

GCSE [ˌdʒi:si:ˌes'i:] **N** *Br Sch (abbr* **General Certificate of Secondary Education)** = premier examen de fin de scolarité en Grande-Bretagne

GCSE

Cet examen a remplacé les "O levels", ou le "GCE O level", et le "CSE". On le passe après cinq ans de scolarité dans l'enseignement secondaire. Chaque élève choisit les matières dans lesquelles il veut se présenter (généralement entre cinq et dix) selon un système d'unités de valeur. Le nombre d'unités et les notes obtenues déterminent le passage dans la classe supérieure. Les élèves qui sont admis au "GCSE" peuvent ensuite préparer les "A levels" (l'équivalent du baccalauréat français). En Écosse, l'examen équivalent au "GCSE" s'appelle le "Standard Grade".

GDP [ˌdʒiːdiːˈpiː] **N** *Econ* (*abbr* **gross domestic product**) PIB *m*
►► ***GDP per capita*** PIB *m* par habitant

GDR [ˌdʒiːdiːˈɑː(r)] **N** *Formerly* (*abbr* **German Democratic Republic**) RDA *f*

Gds (*written abbr* **Gardens**) = abréviation écrite du terme "Gardens", qui est le nom donné à certaines rues en Grande-Bretagne

gear [gɪə(r)] **N 1** *(UNCOUNT) (accessories, equipment* ► *for photography, camping)* équipement *m*, matériel *m*; (► *for manual work)* outils *mpl*, matériel *m*; (► *for household)* ustensiles *mpl*; **he brought along all his skiing g.** il a apporté tout son équipement *ou* toutes ses affaires de ski
2 *(UNCOUNT) (personal belongings)* effets *mpl* personnels, affaires *fpl*; *(luggage)* bagages *mpl*; **he arrived with all his g.** *(his belongings)* il est arrivé avec tout son attirail;
3 *(UNCOUNT) (clothes)* vêtements *mpl*, tenue *f*; **she was in her jogging/swimming g.** elle était en (tenue de) jogging/en maillot de bain
4 *(UNCOUNT) Br Fam (fashionable clothes)* fringues *fpl*
5 *(UNCOUNT) (apparatus)* mécanisme *m*, dispositif *m*
6 *(in car, on bicycle)* vitesse *f*; **to** *Br* **change** *or Am* **shift g.** changer de vitesse; **out of g.** *(car)* au point mort; **to throw** *or* **put out of g.** *(car)* débrayer; *Fig (plan, process)* perturber; **put the car in g.** passez une vitesse; **to be in first/second g.** être en première/seconde; **in g.** *(car)* embrayé, en prise; *Am Fig* **to get into g.** se magner; **we're not operating in top g.** nous ne sommes pas à notre maximum *ou* au top de notre forme; *Br very Fam* **get your arse in g.!** remue-toi!
7 *(cogwheel)* roue *f* dentée, pignon *m*; *(system of cogs)* engrenage *m*
8 *(UNCOUNT) Br Fam (drugs)* dope *f*
VT 1 *(adapt)* adapter; **the army was not geared for modern warfare** l'armée n'était pas prête pour la guerre moderne; **her work schedule is geared to fit in with her holiday plans** son programme de travail concorde avec ses projets de vacances; **the city's hospitals were not geared to cater for such an emergency** les hôpitaux de la ville n'étaient pas équipés pour répondre à une telle situation d'urgence **2** *Aut & Tech* engrener **3** *Fin (link)* indexer; **salaries are geared to the cost of living** les salaires sont indexés au coût de la vie
►► ***gear change*** changement *m* de vitesse; ***gear lever*** levier *m* (de changement) de vitesse; ***gear ratio*** rapport *m* du changement de vitesse; ***gear shift*** *Am Aut* levier *m* (de changement) de vitesse; *(on bicycle)* changement *m* de vitesse; ***gear stick*** levier *m* (de changement) de vitesse

► **gear down VT SEP 1** *(reduce)* réduire **2** *Tech* démultiplier

► **gear up VT SEP 1** *(prepare)* **to be geared up** être paré *ou* fin prêt; **businesses were getting geared up for the single European market** les entreprises se préparaient en vue du marché unique européen **2** *(increase)* augmenter; **we must g. up production to meet the demand** il nous faut augmenter la production pour faire face à la demande
VI *(prepare)* se préparer; **the shops are gearing up for Christmas** les magasins se préparent pour Noël

gearbox [ˈgɪəbɒks] **N** boîte *f* de vitesses

gearing [ˈgɪərɪŋ] **N 1** *Tech* engrenage *m* **2** *Br Fin (leverage)* effet *m* de levier; *(as percentage)* ratio *m* d'endettement
►► ***gearing adjustment*** redressement *m* financier

gecko [ˈgekəʊ] (*pl* **geckos** *or* **geckoes**) **N** *Zool* gecko *m*

gee [dʒiː] **EXCLAM 1** *(to horse)* **g. up!** hue! **2** *Am Fam* **g. (whizz)!** ça alors!

gee-gee N *Br (in children's language)* dada *m*

geek [giːk] **N** *Am Fam Pej* **1** *(strange man)* mec *m* zarbi, allumé *m* **2** *(misfit)* ringard *m*, bouffon *m*

geeky [ˈgiːkɪ] (*compar* **geekier**, *superl* **geekiest**) **ADJ** *Am Fam Pej* ringard

geese [giːs] *pl of* **goose**

geezer [ˈgiːzə(r)] **N** *Fam* **1** *Br (man)* bonhomme *m*, coco *m*; **old g.** vieux type *m*; **funny old g.** drôle *m* de bonhomme **2** *Am (old person)* vioc (vioque) *m,f*

Geiger counter [ˈgaɪgə-] **N** compteur *m* Geiger

geisha (girl) [ˈgeɪʃə-] **N** geisha *f*

gel[1] [dʒel] (*pt & pp* **gelled**, *cont* **gelling**) **N 1** *Chem (gen)* gel *m* **2** *Theat* filtre *m* coloré **3** *(for hair)* gel *m*
VI 1 *(idea, plan* ► *take shape)* prendre forme *ou* tournure, se cristalliser; *(team)* se souder **2** *(jellify)* se gélifier

gel[2] [gel] **N** *Br Old-fashioned or Hum* fille *f*

gelatin [ˈdʒelətɪn], **gelatine** [ˈdʒelətiːn] **N** gélatine *f*
►► ***gelatine paper*** papier *m* gélatine

gelatinize, -ise [dʒɪˈlætɪnaɪz] **VT** gélatiniser
VI se gélatiniser

gelatinous [dʒɪˈlætɪnəs] **ADJ** gélatineux

geld [geld] **VT** *(bull)* châtrer; *(horse)* hongrer

gelding [ˈgeldɪŋ] **N** (cheval *m*) hongre *m*

gelignite [ˈdʒelɪgnaɪt] **N** gélignite *f*

gem [dʒem] **N 1** *(precious stone)* gemme *f*, pierre *f* précieuse; *(semiprecious stone)* gemme *f*, pierre *f* fine
2 *(masterpiece)* joyau *m*, bijou *m*, merveille *f*; **the Petit Trianon is an architectural g.** le Petit Trianon est un joyau architectural; **the g. of the collection** le joyau de la collection
3 *(person)* **you're a g.!** tu es un ange!; **our babysitter is a real g.** notre baby-sitter est une perle
4 *(in printing)* diamant *m*

Gemini [ˈdʒemɪnaɪ] **N 1** *Astron* Gémeaux *mpl* **2** *Astrol* Gémeaux *mpl*; **he's a G.** il est (du signe des) Gémeaux
ADJ *Astrol* des Gémeaux; **he's G.** il est (du signe des) Gémeaux

gemstone [ˈdʒemstəʊn] **N** *(precious)* gemme *f*, pierre *f* précieuse; *(semiprecious)* gemme *f*, pierre *f* fine

Gen (*written abbr* **general**) Gᵃˡ

gen [dʒen] **N** *(UNCOUNT) Br Fam* tuyaux *mpl*, renseignements *mpl*; **what's the g. on the new neighbours?** qu'est-ce qu'on raconte sur les nouveaux voisins?

► **gen up** (*pt & pp* **genned**, *cont* **genning**) *Br Fam* **VT SEP** rencarder, mettre au parfum
VI se rencarder (**on** sur)

gender [ˈdʒendə(r)] **N 1** *Gram* genre *m*; **common g.** genre *m* commun **2** *(sex)* sexe *m*; **the male/female g.** le sexe masculin/féminin
►► ***gender bias*** *(discrimination)* discrimination *f* sexuelle; *(favouritism)* = préjugé favorable à l'un ou l'autre des sexes; ***the gender gap*** = les différences entre les hommes et les femmes dans la société; ***gender reassignment*** réassignation *f* sexuelle; ***gender studies*** = à l'université, matière qui formule une critique des rôles de l'homme et de la femme tels qu'ils sont établis par la société

gender-bender N *Fam* **1** *(cross-dresser)* travelo *m* **2** *Comput* commutateur *m*, changeur *m* de genre

gender-changer [-ˌtʃeɪndʒə(r)] **N** *Comput* commutateur *m*, changeur *m* de genre

gene [dʒiːn] **N** *Biol & Med* gène *m*; *Fig* **music's in his genes** chez lui la musique, c'est héréditaire; **it's in his genes** c'est inné, il est né comme ça
►► ***gene bank*** génothèque *f*, banque *f* génomique; ***gene mapping*** cartographie *f* génétique; ***gene pool*** patrimoine *m* génétique; ***gene therapy*** thérapie *f* génique, génothérapie *f*

genealogical [ˌdʒiːnɪəˈlɒdʒɪkəl] **ADJ** généalogique
►► ***genealogical tree*** arbre *m* généalogique

genealogist [ˌdʒiːnɪˈælədʒɪst] **N** généalogiste *mf*

genealogy [ˌdʒiːnɪˈælədʒɪ] **N** généalogie *f*

genera [ˈdʒenərə] *pl of* **genus**

general [ˈdʒenərəl] **ADJ 1** *(common)* général; **as a g. rule** en règle générale, en général; **in g. terms** en termes généraux; **in the g. interest** dans l'intérêt de tous; **the g. feeling was that he should have won** le sentiment général était qu'il aurait dû gagner; **there was a g. movement to leave the room** la plupart des gens se sont levés pour sortir
2 *(approximate)* général; **a g. resemblance** une vague ressemblance; **to go in the g. direction of sth** se diriger plus ou moins vers qch
3 *(widespread)* général, répandu; **to be in g. use** être d'usage courant *ou* répandu; **to come into g. use** se généraliser; **there is g. agreement on the matter** il y a consensus sur la question
4 *(overall* ► *outline, plan, impression)* d'ensemble; **the g. effect is quite pleasing** le résultat général est assez agréable; **I get the g. idea** je vois en gros; **he gave her a g. idea** *or* **outline of his work** il lui a décrit son travail dans les grandes lignes; **the g. tone of her remarks was that...** ce qui ressortait de ses remarques c'est que… + *indicative*; **he made himself a g. nuisance** il a été embêtant à tout point de vue
5 *(ordinary)* **this book is for the g. reader** ce livre est destiné au lecteur moyen; **the g. public** le grand public
N 1 *(in reasoning)* **to go from the g. to the particular** aller du général au particulier **2** *Mil* général *m*
• **in general ADV** en général
►► ***General Agreement on Tariffs and Trade*** accord *m* général sur les tarifs douaniers et le commerce; *Med* ***general anaesthetic*** anesthésie *f* générale; ***General Assembly*** assemblée *f* générale; *Formerly Br Sch* ***General Certificate of Education*** = certificat de fin d'études secondaires en deux étapes ("O level" et "A level") dont la première est aujourd'hui remplacée par le "GCSE"; *Br Sch* ***General Certificate of Secondary Education*** = premier examen de fin de scolarité en Grande-Bretagne; *see also* **GCSE**; *Univ* ***general degree*** = licence comportant plusieurs matières; ***general election*** élections *fpl* législatives; ***general expenses*** frais *mpl* généraux; ***general headquarters*** (grand) quartier *m* général; ***general hospital*** centre *m* hospitalier; ***general knowledge*** culture *f* générale; ***general manager*** directeur(trice) *m,f* général(e); *Br* ***General Medical Council*** conseil *m* de l'ordre des médecins; ***general meeting*** assemblée *f* générale; *Br Sch* ***General National Vocational Qualification*** = formation professionnelle sur deux ans que l'on peut suivre à partir de 16 ans; ***General Post Office*** *(in Britain)* = titre officiel de la Poste britannique avant 1969; *(in US)* = les services postaux américains; ***general practice*** médecine *f* générale; ***general practitioner*** médecin *m* généraliste, *Can* omnipraticien(enne) *m,f*; ***general secretary*** *(of trade union, political party)* secrétaire *mf* général(e); *Mil* ***general staff*** état-major *m*; ***general store*** bazar *m*; ***general strike*** grève *f* générale; ***the General Strike*** = la grève de mai 1926 en Grande-Bretagne, lancée par les syndicats par solidarité avec les mineurs; *Sch* ***General Studies*** cours *m* de culture générale; ***General Synod*** = le Synode général de l'Église anglicane

general-interest ADJ généraliste
►► *TV* ***general-interest channel*** chaîne *f* généraliste; ***general-interest press*** presse *f* généraliste; *TV* ***general-interest station*** station *f* généraliste

generalissimo [ˌdʒenərəˈlɪsɪməʊ] (*pl* **generalissimos**) **N** généralissime *m*

generality [ˌdʒenəˈrælətɪ] (*pl* **generalities**) **N 1** *(generalization)* généralité *f*; **to confine oneself to generalities** s'en tenir aux généralités; **a principle of great g.** un principe très général **2** *Formal (majority)* plupart *f*; **the g. of mankind** la plupart des hommes

generalization, -isation [ˌdʒenərəlaɪˈzeɪʃən] **N 1** *(general comment)* généralisation *f*; **to make**

generalizations généraliser **2** *(spread)* généralisation *f*

generalize, -ise [ˈdʒenərəlaɪz] **VT** généraliser; **to become generalized** *(practice)* se généraliser
VI 1 *(person)* généraliser **2** *Med (disease)* se généraliser

generalized, -ised [ˈdʒenərəlaɪzd] **ADJ 1** *(involving many)* généralisé **2** *(non-specific)* général

generally [ˈdʒenərəlɪ] **ADV 1** *(usually)* en général, d'habitude; **he g. comes in the afternoon** d'habitude, il vient l'après-midi
2 *(in a general way)* en général, de façon générale; **g. speaking** en général, en règle générale
3 *(widely)* généralement; **the word is g. understood to mean...** le mot veut généralement dire...; **this information is not g. available** le public n'a pas accès à ces informations; **it is not g. known that...** beaucoup de gens ignorent que... + *indicative*
4 *(taken overall)* dans l'ensemble; **to make oneself g. useful** se rendre généralement utile

general-purpose **ADJ** *(tool, adhesive)* universel; *(knife)* tous usages; *(dictionary)* général

generalship [ˈdʒenərəlʃɪp] **N** *(UNCOUNT) Mil (skill, duties)* tactique *f*

generate [ˈdʒenəreɪt] **VT 1** *(produce ▸ electricity, power)* produire, générer; *Fig (▸ income)* créer; *(▸ emotion, interest)* susciter; **tourism generated three million pounds for the region** le tourisme a rapporté trois millions de livres à la région **2** *Ling & Comput* générer

generating [ˈdʒenəreɪtɪŋ] **ADJ** générateur
▸▸ *generating station* centrale *f* électrique; ***generating unit*** groupe *m* électrogène

generation [ˌdʒenəˈreɪʃən] **N 1** *(age group)* génération *f*; **the younger/older g.** la jeune/l'ancienne génération; **the rising g.** la jeune *ou* nouvelle génération; **a new g. of writers** une nouvelle génération d'écrivains; **from g. to g.** de génération en génération, de père en fils
2 *(by birth)* **she is second g. Irish** elle est née de parents irlandais
3 *(period of time)* génération *f*; **the house has been in the family for three generations** la maison est dans la famille depuis trois générations
4 *(model ▸ of machine)* génération *f*; **a third g. microprocessor** un microprocesseur de la troisième génération
5 *(UNCOUNT) (of electricity)* génération *f*, production *f*; *(of ideas etc)* génération *f*, formation *f*; *Ling* génération *f*
▸▸ *generation gap* écart *m* entre les générations; *(conflict)* conflit *m* des générations

generative [ˈdʒenərətɪv] **ADJ** génératif
▸▸ *Ling generative grammar* grammaire *f* générative

generator [ˈdʒenəreɪtə(r)] **N 1** *(electric ▸ in power station)* générateur *m*; *(backup device ▸ in factory, hospital etc)* groupe *m* électrogène; *(of steam)* générateur *m*, chaudière *f* (à vapeur); *(of gas)* gazogène *m*; **tourism is a major g. of income** le tourisme est une source importante de revenus **2** *Comput* (programme *m*) générateur *m*; *Tech (of heat etc)* générateur *m* **3** *(person)* générateur (trice) *m,f*

generatrix [ˈdʒenəˌreɪtrɪks] (*pl* **generatrices** [-trɪsiːz]) **N** génératrice *f*

generic [dʒɪˈnerɪk] **ADJ** générique
N *Mktg* produit *m* générique
▸▸ *generic advertising* publicité *f* générique; ***generic brand*** marque *f* générique; ***generic drug*** médicament *m* générique, générique *m*; ***generic market*** marché *m* générique; ***generic name*** *Biol* nom *m* du genre; *(of product, drug)* nom *m* générique; ***generic product*** produit *m* générique

generically [dʒɪˈnerɪkəlɪ] **ADV** génériquement

generosity [ˌdʒenəˈrɒsətɪ] **N** générosité *f*

generous [ˈdʒenərəs] **ADJ 1** *(with money, gifts)* généreux; **he has a g. nature** c'est une âme généreuse; **he was very g. in his praise** il ne tarissait pas d'éloges; **he's a bit too g. with his advice** il n'est pas avare de conseils
2 *(in value ▸ gift)* généreux; *(in quantity ▸ sum, salary)* généreux, élevé; **g. mark** *(for homework etc)* note *f* généreuse
3 *(copious)* copieux, abondant; *(large)* bon, abondant; **a g. portion** une part copieuse *ou* généreuse; **she cut him a g. slice of cake** elle lui a servi une bonne tranche de gâteau; **they serve g. helpings of cream** ils ne lésinent pas sur la crème; **a g. harvest** une récolte abondante
4 *Br (strong ▸ wine)* généreux
5 *(physically ▸ size)* généreux, ample; *Euph* **to have g. curves** avoir des formes généreuses

generously [ˈdʒenərəslɪ] **ADV 1** *(unsparingly)* généreusement, avec générosité
2 *(with magnanimity ▸ agree, offer)* généreusement; *(▸ forgive)* généreusement, avec magnanimité; **she g. offered to help** elle a généreusement proposé son aide; **he g. congratulated her on her victory** beau joueur, il l'a félicitée pour sa victoire
3 *(copiously)* **the soup was rather g. salted** *(oversalted)* la soupe était très généreusement salée
4 *(in size)* amplement; *Euph* **to be g. built** *or* **proportioned** avoir des formes généreuses

genesis [ˈdʒenəsɪs] (*pl* **geneses** [-siːz]) **N** genèse *f*, origine *f*
• Genesis **N** *Bible* la Genèse

genetic [dʒɪˈnetɪk] **ADJ** génétique
▸▸ *genetic code* code *m* génétique; ***genetic counselling*** conseil *m* génétique; ***genetic engineering*** génie *m* génétique; ***genetic fingerprint*** empreinte *f* génétique; ***genetic fingerprinting*** analyse *f* de l'empreinte génétique; ***genetic imprinting*** empreinte *f* génomique; ***genetic screening*** dépistage *m* des maladies génétiques

genetically [dʒɪˈnetɪkəlɪ] **ADV** génétiquement

genetically-modified **ADJ** *(plant, food, organism)* génétiquement modifié

geneticist [dʒɪˈnetɪsɪst] **N** généticien(enne) *m,f*

genetics [dʒɪˈnetɪks] **N** *(UNCOUNT)* génétique *f*

Geneva [dʒɪˈniːvə] **N** Genève; **Lake G.** le lac Léman
▸▸ *the Geneva Convention* la Convention de Genève

Genghis Khan [ˌgeŋgɪsˈkɑːn] **PR N** Gengis Khan

genial [ˈdʒiːnɪəl] **ADJ 1** *(friendly ▸ person)* aimable, affable; *(▸ expression, voice)* cordial, chaleureux; *(▸ face)* jovial **2** *Literary (clement ▸ weather)* clément

> Note that the French word **génial** is a false friend and is never a translation for the English word **genial**. It means **brilliant**.

geniality [ˌdʒiːnɪˈælətɪ] **N 1** *(of person, expression)* cordialité *f*, amabilité *f* **2** *Literary (of weather)* clémence *f*

genially [ˈdʒiːnɪəlɪ] **ADV** affablement, cordialement, chaleureusement

genie [ˈdʒiːnɪ] (*pl* **genii** [-nɪaɪ]) **N** génie *m*, djinn *m*

genii [ˈdʒiːnɪaɪ] *pl of* **genie, genius**

genital [ˈdʒenɪtəl] **ADJ** génital; **the g. organs** les organes *mpl* génitaux
• genitals **NPL** organes *mpl* génitaux
▸▸ *genital herpes* herpès *m* génital

genitalia [ˌdʒenɪˈteɪlɪə] **NPL** organes *mpl* génitaux, parties *fpl* génitales

genitive [ˈdʒenɪtɪv] **N** génitif *m*; **in the g.** au génitif
ADJ du génitif; **the g. case** le génitif

genito-urinary [ˌdʒenɪtəʊ-] **ADJ** génito-urinaire
▸▸ *genito-urinary tract* appareil *m* génito-urinaire

genius [ˈdʒiːnɪəs] (*pl senses* **1–3 geniuses**, *pl sense* **4 genii** [-nɪaɪ]) **N 1** *(person)* génie *m*; **she's a mathematical g.** c'est un génie en mathématiques
2 *(special ability)* génie *m*; **a work/writer of g.** une œuvre/un écrivain de génie; **to have a g. for sth** avoir le génie de qch; **she has a g. for remembering people's faces** elle a le génie *ou* le don de se souvenir des visages; **her g. lies in her power to evoke atmosphere** son génie, c'est de savoir recréer une atmosphère; **that goal was pure g.** ce but, c'était du génie pur et simple
3 *(special character ▸ of system, idea)* génie *m* (particulier), esprit *m*
4 *(spirit, demon)* génie *m*; **good/evil g.** bon/mauvais génie *m*

Genoa [ˈdʒenəʊə] **N** Gênes

genocidal [ˌdʒenəˈsaɪdəl] **ADJ** génocide

genocide [ˈdʒenəsaɪd] **N** génocide *m*

Genoese [ˌdʒenəʊˈiːz] (*pl* **inv**) **N** Génois(e) *m,f*
ADJ génois

genome [ˈdʒiːnəʊm] **N** *Biol* génome *m*

genotherapy [ˌdʒiːnəʊˈθerəpɪ] **N** *Med* génothérapie *f*

genotype [ˈdʒenəʊtaɪp] **N** génotype *m*

Genovese [ˌdʒenəˈviːz] = **Genoese**

genre [ˈʒɑ̃rə] **N** genre *m*
▸▸ *genre film, genre movie* film *m* de genre; ***genre painting*** peinture *f* de genre

gent [dʒent] **N** *Br Fam* **1** *(well-bred man)* gentleman[▫] *m*; **to behave like a (real) g.** agir en gentleman[▫] **2** *(man)* monsieur *m*; **gents' footwear** chaussures *fpl* pour hommes
• gents **N** *(toilets)* toilettes *fpl* (pour hommes); *(sign)* messieurs; **where's the gents?** où sont les toilettes?
▸▸ *gents' outfitters* magasin *m* de confection *ou* d'habillement pour hommes

genteel [dʒenˈtiːl] **ADJ 1** *(refined)* comme il faut, distingué; **to live in g. poverty** vivre dans une misère qui s'efforce de sauver les apparences; **g. society** la bonne société **2** *(affected ▸ speech)* maniéré, affecté; *(▸ manner)* affecté; *(▸ language)* précieux

> Note that the French word **gentil** is a false friend and is never a translation for the English word **genteel**. It means **kind**.

gentian [ˈdʒenʃən] **N** gentiane *f*
▸▸ *gentian blue* bleu *m* gentiane; ***gentian violet*** violet *m* gentiane

Gentile [ˈdʒentaɪl] *Hist* **N** gentil *m*
ADJ des gentils

gentility [dʒenˈtɪlətɪ] **N 1** *(good breeding)* distinction *f* **2** *(gentry)* petite noblesse *f* **3** *(UNCOUNT) (affected politeness)* manières *fpl* affectées

gentle [ˈdʒentəl] **ADJ 1** *(mild ▸ person, smile, voice)* doux (douce); *(▸ landscape)* agréable; **to be g. with sb** être doux avec qn; **the g. sex** le sexe faible; **as g. as a lamb** doux comme un agneau
2 *(light ▸ knock, push, breeze)* léger; *(▸ rain)* fin, léger; *(▸ exercise)* modéré; **a g. rain was falling** la pluie tombait doucement
3 *(discreet ▸ rebuke, reminder)* discret(ète); *Hum* **the g. art of persuasion** l'art subtil de la persuasion; **we gave him a g. hint** nous l'avons discrètement mis sur la voie
4 *(gradual ▸ slope, climb)* doux (douce); **a g. transition** une transition progressive *ou* sans heurts
5 *Arch (noble)* noble, de bonne naissance; **of g. birth** de bonne famille

> Note that the French word **gentil** is a false friend and is never a translation for the English word **gentle**. It means **kind**.

gentlefolk [ˈdʒentəlfəʊk] **NPL** *Arch* personnes *fpl* de bonne famille *ou* de la petite noblesse

gentleman [ˈdʒentəlmən] (*pl* **gentlemen** [-mən]) **N 1** *(man)* monsieur *m*; **there's a g. to see you** il y a un monsieur qui voudrait vous parler; **come in, gentlemen!** entrez, messieurs!; **he's no g.** il est mal élevé **2** *(well-bred man)* gentleman *m*; **he's a real g.** c'est un vrai gentleman; **to act like a g.** agir en gentleman; **that's not how a g. would behave** c'est (une conduite) indigne d'un gentleman **3** *(man of substance)* rentier *m*; *(at court)* gentilhomme *m*
▸▸ *gentleman's agreement* gentleman's agreement *m*, accord *m* reposant sur l'honneur; ***gentleman farmer*** gentleman-farmer *m*; *Br* ***gentleman's gentleman*** valet *m* de chambre

gentlemanly [ˈdʒentəlmənlɪ] **ADJ** *(person)* bien élevé; *(appearance, behaviour)* distingué; *(status)* noble; **it would have been more g. to say nothing** un homme bien élevé *ou* un gentleman n'aurait rien dit

gentlemen [ˈdʒentəlmən] *pl of* **gentleman**
▸▸ *gentlemen's club* = club dont l'accès est réservé aux hommes

gentleness [ˈdʒentəlnɪs] **N** douceur *f*, légèreté *f*

gently ['dʒentlɪ] ADV **1** *(mildly ▸ speak, smile)* avec douceur
2 *(discreetly ▸ remind, reprimand, suggest)* discrètement; **he broke the news to her as g. as possible** il fit de son mieux pour lui annoncer la nouvelle avec tact *ou* ménagement
3 *(lightly)* doucement
4 *(gradually)* doucement, progressivement; **the beach slopes g. down to the sea** la plage descend doucement *ou* en pente douce vers la mer; **g. rolling hills** des collines qui ondoient (doucement)
5 *(slowly ▸ move, heat)* doucement; **a g. flowing river** une rivière qui coule paisiblement; **g. does it!** doucement!

gentrification [ˌdʒentrɪfɪ'keɪʃən] N *Br* embourgeoisement *m*

gentrified ['dʒentrɪfaɪd] ADJ *Br (area, street)* qui s'est embourgeoisé

gentry ['dʒentrɪ] *(pl* **gentries***)* N petite noblesse *f*

genuflect ['dʒenju:flekt] VI faire une génuflexion

genuflection, genuflexion [ˌdʒenju:'flekʃən] N génuflexion *f*

genuine ['dʒenjʊɪn] ADJ **1** *(authentic ▸ antique)* authentique; *(▸ gold, mahogany)* véritable, vrai; **a g. Van Gogh** un Van Gogh authentique; *Fig* **he's the g. article** c'est un vrai de vrai
2 *(sincere ▸ person)* sincère, franc (franche); *(▸ emotion)* sincère, vrai; *(▸smile, laugh)* vrai, franc (franche); **I think he's being g.** je crois qu'il est sincère; **it is my g. belief that he is innocent** je suis intimement persuadé de son innocence; **her regret seemed g.** elle semblait sincèrement désolée
3 *(real ▸ mistake)* fait de bonne foi
4 *(not impersonated ▸ repairman, official)* vrai, véritable
5 *(serious ▸ buyer)* sérieux

genuinely ['dʒenjʊɪnlɪ] ADV *(truly)* authentiquement; *(sincerely)* sincèrement, véritablement; **g. surprised** vraiment *ou* véritablement surpris

genuineness ['dʒenjʊɪnnɪs] N **1** *(of manuscript etc)* authenticité *f* **2** *(sincerity)* sincérité *f*

genus ['dʒenəs] *(pl* **genera** [-ərə]*)* N *Biol* genre *m*

geo- ['dʒi:əʊ] PREF géo-

geode ['dʒi:əʊd] N géode *f*

geodemographic [ˌdʒi:əʊˌdeməʊ'græfɪk] ADJ *Mktg* géodémographique
▸▸ ***geodemographic profile*** profil *m* géodémographique; ***geodemographic segment*** segment *m* géodémographique

geodesic [ˌdʒi:əʊ'desɪk] ADJ géodésique
▸▸ ***geodesic dome*** dôme *m* géodésique; ***geodesic line*** (ligne *f*) géodésique *f*

geodesy [dʒi:'ɒdɪsɪ] N géodésie *f*

geodynamics [ˌdʒi:əʊˌdaɪ'næmɪks] N *(UNCOUNT)* géodynamique *f*

geographer [dʒɪ'ɒgrəfə(r)] N géographe *mf*

geographic [dʒɪə'græfɪk], **geographical** [dʒɪə'græfɪkəl] ADJ géographique

geographically [dʒɪə'græfɪkəlɪ] ADV géographiquement

geography [dʒɪ'ɒgrəfɪ] *(pl* **geographies***)* N **1** *(science)* géographie *f*; **physical/social g.** géographie *f* physique/humaine **2** *(layout)* **I don't know the g. of the building** je ne m'oriente pas très bien dans le bâtiment
COMP *(class, lesson)* de géographie

geolocation [ˌdʒi:əʊləʊ'keɪʃən] N géolocalisation *f*

geologically [dʒɪə'lɒdʒɪkəlɪ] ADV du point de vue géologique

geologist [dʒɪ'ɒlədʒɪst] N géologue *mf*

geology [dʒɪ'ɒlədʒɪ] N géologie *f*

geometer [dʒɪ'ɒmɪtə(r)] N *Math* géomètre *mf*

geometric [dʒɪə'metrɪk] ADJ géométrique
▸▸ ***geometric progression*** progression *f* géométrique; ***geometric series*** série *f* géométrique

geometrical [dʒɪə'metrɪkəl] ADJ géométrique

geometrically [dʒɪə'metrɪkəlɪ] ADV géométriquement

geometrician [ˌdʒɪəmə'trɪʃən] N géomètre *mf*

geometry [dʒɪ'ɒmətrɪ] N géométrie *f*

geomorphic [ˌdʒi:əʊ'mɔ:fɪk] ADJ géomorphologique

geomorphologic [ˌdʒi:əʊˌmɔ:fə'lɒdʒɪk], **geomorphological** [ˌdʒi:əʊˌmɔ:fə'lɒdʒɪkəl] ADJ géomorphologique

geomorphology [ˌdʒi:əʊˌmɔ:'fɒlədʒɪ] N géomorphologie *f*

geophysical [ˌdʒi:əʊ'fɪzɪkəl] ADJ géophysique

geophysicist [ˌdʒi:əʊ'fɪzɪsɪst] N géophysicien (enne) *m,f*

geophysics [ˌdʒi:əʊ'fɪzɪks] N *(UNCOUNT)* géophysique *f*

geopolitics [ˌdʒi:əʊ'pɒlɪtɪks] N *(UNCOUNT)* géopolitique *f*

Geordie ['dʒɔ:dɪ] *Br* N **1** *(person)* = surnom des habitants du Tyneside, dans le nord-est de l'Angleterre **2** *(dialect)* = dialecte parlé par les habitants du Tyneside
ADJ = caractéristique du Tyneside

George [dʒɔ:dʒ] PR N **1** *Fam Old-fashioned* **by G.!** sapristi! **2** *Br Fam Aviat* = le pilote automatique
▸▸ ***George Cross*** = décoration britannique décernée aux civils pour des actes de bravoure; ***George Medal*** = décoration britannique décernée aux civils ou aux militaires pour des actes de bravoure

georgette [dʒɔ:'dʒet] N crêpe *m* georgette

Georgia ['dʒɔ:dʒə] N *(in US, former USSR)* la Géorgie

Georgian ['dʒɔ:dʒən] N **1** *(inhabitant of Georgia)* Géorgien(enne) *m,f* **2** *(language)* géorgien *m*
ADJ **1** *(of Georgia)* géorgien **2** *Hist* géorgien *(du règne des rois George I–IV 1714–1830)*; **G. architecture** architecture *f* de style georgien; **a G. house** une maison datant de l'époque 1720–1830
COMP *(embassy)* de Géorgie; *(history, capital)* de la Géorgie; *(teacher)* de géorgien

geoscience [ˌdʒi:əʊ'saɪəns] N **1** *(particular)* science *f* de la terre **2** *(UNCOUNT) (collectively)* sciences *fpl* de la terre

geosphere ['dʒi:əʊˌsfɪə(r)] N géosphère *f*

geostationary [ˌdʒi:əʊ'steɪʃənərɪ] ADJ géostationnaire; **in g. orbit** en orbite géostationnaire
▸▸ ***geostationary satellite*** satellite *m* géostationnaire

geothermal [ˌdʒi:əʊ'θɜ:məl], **geothermic** [ˌdʒi:əʊ'θɜ:mɪk] ADJ géothermique

geotropism [ˌdʒi:əʊ'trəʊpɪzəm] N *Bot* géotropisme *m*

geranium [dʒɪ'reɪnɪəm] N géranium *m*
ADJ rouge géranium *(inv)*, incarnat

gerbil ['dʒɜ:bɪl] N gerbille *f*

geriatric [ˌdʒerɪ'ætrɪk] ADJ *Med* gériatrique
N **1** *(patient)* malade *mf* en gériatrie **2** *Pej (old person)* vieux (vieille) *m,f*
▸▸ ***geriatric hospital*** hospice *m*; ***geriatric medicine*** gériatrie *f*; ***geriatric nurse*** infirmier(ère) *m,f* (spécialisé(e)) en gériatrie; ***geriatric ward*** service *m* de gériatrie

geriatrician [ˌdʒerɪə'trɪʃən] N gériatre *mf*

geriatrics [ˌdʒerɪ'ætrɪks] N *(UNCOUNT)* gériatrie *f*

germ [dʒɜ:m] N **1** *(microbe)* microbe *m*, germe *m* **2** *Biol & Agr* germe *m*, *Belg* jet *m* **3** *Fig* germe *m*, ferment *m*; **the g. of an idea** le germe d'une idée
▸▸ ***germ cell*** cellule *f* germinale *ou* reproductrice; ***germ warfare*** guerre *f* bactériologique

German ['dʒɜ:mən] N **1** *(person)* Allemand(e) *m,f* **2** *(language)* allemand *m*
ADJ allemand
COMP *(embassy)* d'Allemagne; *(history)* de l'Allemagne; *(teacher)* d'allemand
▸▸ *Formerly* ***the German Democratic Republic*** la République démocratique allemande, la RDA; ***German measles*** *(UNCOUNT)* rubéole *f*; ***German shepherd*** berger *m* allemand

germander [dʒɜ:'mændə(r)] N *Bot* germandrée *f*

germane [dʒɜ:'meɪn] ADJ *Formal* pertinent; **g. to** en rapport avec; **it is not g. to my argument** cela n'a aucun rapport avec mon argument

Germanic [dʒɜ:'mænɪk] N *Ling* germanique *m*
ADJ germanique

Germanist ['dʒɜ:mənɪst] N *Ling* germaniste *mf*

germanize, -ise ['dʒɜ:mənaɪz] VT germaniser

Germanophile [dʒɜ:'mænəfaɪl] N germanophile *mf*

Germanophobe [dʒɜ:'mænəfəʊb] N germanophobe *mf*

Germany ['dʒɜ:mənɪ] N Allemagne *f*; *Formerly* **West/East G.** l'Allemagne de l'Ouest/de l'Est

germ-free ADJ stérilisé, aseptisé

germicidal [ˌdʒɜ:mɪ'saɪdəl] ADJ germicide, bactéricide

germicide ['dʒɜ:mɪsaɪd] N bactéricide *m*

germinate ['dʒɜ:mɪneɪt] VI **1** *Biol & Agr* germer, *Belg* jeter **2** *Fig (originate)* germer, prendre naissance
VT **1** *Biol* faire germer **2** *Fig* faire germer, donner naissance à

germination [ˌdʒɜ:mɪ'neɪʃən] N germination *f*

gerontocracy [ˌdʒerɒn'tɒkrəsɪ] *(pl* **gerontocracies***)* N gérontocratie *f*

gerontologist [ˌdʒerɒn'tɒlədʒɪst] N gérontologue *mf*

gerontology [ˌdʒerɒn'tɒlədʒɪ] N gérontologie *f*

gerrymander ['dʒerɪˌmændə(r)] *Pej* VI faire du charcutage électoral, redécouper des circonscriptions
VT redécouper (à des fins électorales)
N charcutage *m* électoral

gerrymandering ['dʒerɪˌmændərɪŋ] N *Pej* charcutage *m* électoral

gerund ['dʒerənd] N *Gram* gérondif *m*

gerundive [dʒɪ'rʌndɪv] *Gram* N adjectif *m* verbal
ADJ du gérondif

gesso ['dʒesəʊ] N *(for painting)* enduit *m* (au plâtre); *(for sculpture)* plâtre *m* (de Paris)

Gestalt [gə'ʃtælt] N *Psy* gestalt *f*
▸▸ ***Gestalt psychology*** gestaltisme *m*, théorie *f* de la forme; ***Gestalt therapy*** gestalt-thérapie *f*

Gestapo [ge'stɑ:pəʊ] N Gestapo *f*

gestate [dʒe'steɪt] VI être en gestation; *Fig* mûrir
VT **1** *Biol (young)* porter **2** *Fig (idea, plan)* laisser mûrir

gestation [dʒe'steɪʃən] N gestation *f*
▸▸ ***gestation period*** période *f* de gestation

gesticulate [dʒe'stɪkjʊleɪt] VI gesticuler
VT *(answer, meaning)* mimer

gesticulation [dʒeˌstɪkjʊ'leɪʃən] N gesticulation *f*

gesture ['dʒestʃə(r)] N **1** *(expressive movement)* geste *m*; **to make a g.** faire un geste; **a g. of acknowledgment** un signe de reconnaissance; **he made a g. of dismissal** il les a congédiés d'un geste **2** *(sign, token)* geste *m*; **as a g. of friendship** en signe *ou* en témoignage d'amitié; **it was a nice g.** c'était une gentille attention; **they offered him a salary rise as a g. of goodwill** ils lui ont offert une augmentation en gage de leur bonne volonté
VI **to g. with one's hands/head** faire un signe de la main/de la tête; **he gestured to me to stand up** il m'a fait signe de me lever; **she gestured towards the pile of books** elle désigna *ou* montra la pile de livres d'un geste
VT mimer

GET [get]

VT
- recevoir **A1, 4, 7, 9, B2, E10**
- avoir **A1, 2, B2, D3**
- toucher **A1, 9**
- trouver **A2, 8**
- obtenir **A2, 8**
- tenir **A3**
- offrir **A5**
- acheter **A6**
- prendre **A6, 11, 12**
- gagner **A9**
- chercher **A10**
- attraper **A11, 12, B1**
- réserver **A13**
- répondre à **A14**
- faire faire **C2–4**
- préparer **D1**
- entendre **D2**
- comprendre **D4**
- atteindre **E1**
- se venger de **E3**
- émouvoir **E5**
- énerver **E7**

VI
- devenir **A1**
- se faire **A2**
- commencer à **A3, B3**
- aller **B1**
- réussir à **B5**

(Br pt & pp **got** [gɒt], *cont* **getting** [getɪŋ], *Am pt* **got** [gɒt], *pp* **gotten** [gɒtən], *cont* **getting** [getɪŋ]*)*
VT **A. 1** *(receive ▸ gift, letter, phone call)* recevoir,

avoir; (▸ *benefits, pension)* recevoir, toucher; (▸ *medical treatment)* suivre; **I got a bike for my birthday** on m'a donné *ou* j'ai eu *ou* j'ai reçu un vélo pour mon anniversaire; **I g. 'The Times' at home** je reçois le 'Times' à la maison; **this part of the country doesn't g. much rain** cette région ne reçoit pas beaucoup de pluie, il ne pleut pas beaucoup dans cette région; **the living room gets a lot of sun** le salon est très ensoleillé; **I rang but I got no answer** *(at door)* j'ai sonné mais je n'ai pas obtenu *ou* eu de réponse; *(on phone)* j'ai appelé sans obtenir de réponse; **he got five years for smuggling** il a écopé de *ou* il a pris cinq ans (de prison) pour contrebande; **he got a bullet in his shoulder** il a reçu une balle dans l'épaule; *Fam* **you're really going to g. it!** qu'est-ce que tu vas prendre *ou* écoper!

2 *(obtain* ▸ *gen)* avoir, trouver, obtenir; (▸ *through effort)* se procurer, obtenir; (▸ *licence, loan, permission)* obtenir; (▸ *diploma, grades)* avoir, obtenir; **where did you g. that book?** où avez-vous trouvé ce livre?; **they got him a job** ils lui ont trouvé du travail; **I got the job!** ils m'ont embauché!; **can you g. them the report?** pouvez-vous leur procurer le rapport?; **I got the idea from a book** j'ai trouvé l'idée dans un livre; **I got a glimpse of her face** j'ai pu apercevoir son visage; **you g. a fine view from here** il y a une vue magnifique d'ici; **I've got six more to g.** *(in collection)* il m'en manque six; **the town gets its water from the reservoir** la ville reçoit son eau du réservoir; **they stopped in town to g. some lunch** *(had lunch there)* ils se sont arrêtés en ville pour déjeuner; *(bought something to eat)* ils se sont arrêtés en ville pour acheter de quoi déjeuner; **I'm going out to g. a breath of fresh air** je sors prendre l'air; **I'm going to g. something to drink/eat** *(fetch)* je vais chercher quelque chose à boire/manger; *(consume)* je vais boire/manger quelque chose; **g. yourself a good lawyer** trouvez-vous un bon avocat; **I need all the advice I can g.** j'ai besoin de tous les conseils qu'on peut me donner; **to g. sb to oneself** avoir qn pour soi tout seul; **to g. a divorce** obtenir le divorce; **g. plenty of exercise** faites beaucoup d'exercice; **g. plenty of sleep** dormez beaucoup; **try and g. a few days off work** essayez de prendre quelques jours de congé; **I'll do it if I g. the time/a moment** je le ferai si j'ai le temps/si je trouve un moment; **I got a lot from** *or* **out of my trip to China** mon voyage en Chine m'a beaucoup apporté; **he didn't g. a chance to introduce himself** il n'a pas eu l'occasion de se présenter

3 *(inherit* ▸ *characteristic)* tenir; **she gets her shyness from her father** elle tient sa timidité de son père

4 *(obtain in exchange)* recevoir; **they got a good price for the painting** le tableau s'est vendu à un bon prix; **what did you g. for your car?** combien est-ce que tu as vendu ta voiture?; **he got nothing for his trouble** il s'est donné de la peine pour rien

5 *(offer as gift)* offrir, donner; **what did she g. him for Christmas?** qu'est-ce qu'elle lui a offert *ou* donné pour Noël?; **I don't know what to g. Jill for her birthday** je ne sais pas quoi acheter à Jill pour son anniversaire

6 *(buy)* acheter, prendre; **g. your father a magazine when you go out** achète une revue à ton père quand tu sortiras; **g. the paper too** prends *ou* achète le journal aussi

7 *(learn* ▸ *information, news)* recevoir, apprendre; **she just got news** *or* **word of the accident** elle vient juste d'apprendre la nouvelle de l'accident

8 *(reach by calculation or experimentation* ▸ *answer, solution)* trouver; (▸ *result)* obtenir; **multiply 5 by 2 and you g. 10** multipliez 5 par 2 et vous obtenez 10

9 *(earn, win* ▸ *salary)* recevoir, gagner, toucher; (▸ *prize)* gagner; (▸ *reputation)* se faire; **someone's trying to g. your attention** *(calling)* quelqu'un vous appelle; *(waving)* quelqu'un vous fait signe

10 *(bring, fetch)* (aller) chercher; **go and g. a doctor** allez chercher un médecin; **g. me my coat** va me chercher *ou* apporte-moi mon manteau; **we had to g. a doctor** nous avons dû faire venir un médecin; **what can I g. you to drink?** qu'est-ce que je vous sers à boire?; **can I g. you anything?** *(to somebody ill etc)* est-ce que vous avez besoin de quelque chose?

11 *(catch* ▸ *ball)* attraper; (▸ *bus, train)* prendre, attraper; **did you g. your train?** est-ce que tu as eu ton train?

12 *(capture)* attraper, prendre; *(seize)* prendre, saisir; **the dog got him by the leg** le chien l'a attrapé à la jambe; **(I've) got you!** je te tiens!

13 *(book, reserve)* réserver, retenir; **we're trying to g. a flight to Budapest** nous essayons de réserver un vol pour Budapest

14 *(answer* ▸ *door, telephone)* répondre à; **the doorbell's ringing – I'll g. it!** quelqu'un sonne à la porte – j'y vais!; **will you g. the phone?** peux-tu répondre au téléphone?

B. 1 *(become ill with)* attraper; **he got a chill** il a pris *ou* attrapé froid; **I g. a headache when I drink red wine** le vin rouge me donne mal à la tête

2 *(experience, feel* ▸ *shock)* recevoir, ressentir, avoir; (▸ *fun, pain, surprise)* avoir; **I g. the impression he doesn't like me** j'ai l'impression que je ne lui plais pas; **to g. a thrill out of sth/doing sth** prendre plaisir à qch/faire qch; *Fam* **to g. religion** devenir croyant□

3 *(encounter)* **you g. some odd people on these tours** il y a de drôles de gens dans ces voyages organisés; **we don't g. many accidents here** nous n'avons pas beaucoup d'accidents par ici

C. 1 *(with adj or past participle) (cause to be)* **she managed to g. the window open** elle a réussi à ouvrir la fenêtre; **I got the car started** j'ai démarré la voiture; **don't g. your feet wet!** ne te mouille pas les pieds!; **g. the suitcases ready** préparez les bagages; **I finally got her on her own** *or* **alone** j'ai fini par réussir à la voir en tête à tête; **we managed to g. him in a good mood** nous avons réussi à le mettre de bonne humeur; **they've got me so I don't know whether I'm coming or going** c'en est à un tel point que je ne sais plus où j'en suis; **to g. people interested (in sth)** intéresser les gens (à qch); **to g. things under control** prendre les choses en main; **the flat is as clean as I'm going to g. it** j'ai nettoyé l'appartement le mieux que j'ai pu; **he got himself nominated president** il s'est fait nommer président

2 *(with infinitive) (cause to do or carry out)* **we couldn't g. her to leave** on n'a pas pu la faire partir; **g. him to move the car** demande-lui de déplacer la voiture; **I got it to work, I got it working** j'ai réussi à le faire marcher; **he got the other members to agree** il a réussi à obtenir l'accord des autres membres; **I can always g. someone else to do it** je peux toujours le faire faire par quelqu'un d'autre; **how do you g. jasmine to grow indoors?** comment peut-on faire pousser du jasmin à l'intérieur?

3 *(with past participle) (cause to be done or carried out)* **to g. sth done/repaired** faire faire/faire réparer qch; **to g. one's hair cut** se faire couper les cheveux; **it's impossible to g. anything done around here** *(by oneself)* il est impossible de faire quoi que ce soit ici; *(by someone else)* il est impossible d'obtenir quoi que ce soit ici

4 *(cause to come, go, move)* **they eventually got all the boxes downstairs/upstairs** ils ont fini par descendre/monter toutes leurs boîtes; **I managed to g. him away from the others** j'ai réussi à l'éloigner des autres; **they got her to the airport on time** ils l'ont amenée à l'aéroport à l'heure; **how are we going to g. the bike home?** comment est-ce qu'on va ramener le vélo à la maison?; **I got a message to them** je leur ai fait parvenir un message; **we couldn't g. the bed through the door** nous n'avons pas pu faire passer le lit par la porte; *Fig* **this is getting us nowhere** ça ne nous mène nulle part, ça ne nous mène à rien; **that won't g. you very far!** ça ne te servira pas à grand-chose!, tu ne seras pas beaucoup plus avancé!

D. 1 *(prepare* ▸ *meal, drink)* préparer; **he's in the kitchen getting dinner** il est à la cuisine en train de préparer le dîner; **who's going to g. the children breakfast?** qui va préparer le petit déjeuner pour les enfants?; **she got herself some breakfast** elle s'est préparé un petit déjeuner

2 *(hear correctly)* entendre, saisir; **I didn't g. his name** je n'ai pas saisi son nom

3 *(establish telephone contact with)* **I got her father on the phone** j'ai parlé à son père *ou* j'ai eu son père au téléphone; **I couldn't g. her at the office** je n'ai pas pu l'avoir au bureau; **did you g. the number you wanted?** avez-vous obtenu le numéro que vous vouliez?; **g. me extension 3500** passez-moi *ou* donnez-moi le poste 3500

4 *Fam (understand)* comprendre□, saisir□; **don't g. it, I don't g. the point** je ne comprends *ou* ne saisis pas, je n'y suis pas du tout; **I don't g. you** *or* **your meaning** je ne comprends pas ce que vous voulez dire; **if you g. my meaning** si tu vois ce que je veux dire□; **don't g. me wrong** comprenez-moi bien; **I think he's got the message now** je crois qu'il a compris maintenant; **I don't g. the joke** je ne vois pas ce qui est (si) drôle□; **g. it?, g. me?, g. my drift?** tu saisis?, tu piges?; **oh, I g. you!** ah! j'ai pigé!

5 *(take note of)* remarquer; **did you g. his address?** lui avez-vous demandé son adresse?

6 *Fam (look at)* viser; **g. him! who does he think he is?** vise un peu ce mec, mais pour qui il se prend?; **g. (a load of) that!** vise un peu ça!

7 *Fam (listen to)* écouter□; **g. a load of this** écoute un peu ça!; **g. him!** écoute-le, celui-là!

E. 1 *Fam (hit)* atteindre□; *(hit and kill)* tuer□; **she got him in the face with a custard pie** elle lui a jeté une tarte à la crème à la figure□; **the bullet got him in the back** il a pris la balle *ou* la balle l'a atteint dans le dos□

2 *Fam (harm, punish)* **everyone's out to g. me** tout le monde est après moi

3 *Fam (take vengeance on)* se venger de□; **we'll g. you for this!** on te revaudra ça!

4 *Fam (affect physically)* **the pain gets me in the back** j'ai des douleurs dans le dos□

5 *Fam (affect emotionally)* émouvoir□; **that song really gets me** cette chanson me fait vraiment quelque chose

6 *Fam (baffle, puzzle)* **you've got me there** alors là, aucune idée

7 *Fam (irritate)* énerver□, agacer□; **it really gets me when you're late!** qu'est-ce que ça peut m'énerver quand tu es en retard!

8 *Am (learn)* apprendre; **to g. sth by heart** apprendre qch par cœur

9 *Arch (beget)* engendrer; **to g. sb with child** faire un enfant à qn

10 *Rad & TV (signal, station)* capter, recevoir

VI A. 1 *(become)* devenir; **this is getting boring** ça devient ennuyeux; **I'm getting hungry/thirsty** je commence à avoir faim/soif; **g. dressed!** habille-toi!; **to g. married** se marier; **to g. divorced** divorcer; **don't g. lost!** ne vous perdez pas!; **how did that vase g. broken?** comment se fait-il que ce vase soit cassé?; **he got so he didn't want to go out any more** il en est arrivé à ne plus vouloir sortir; **to g. old** vieillir; **it's getting late** il se fait tard; **to g. used to sth/doing sth** s'habituer à qch/à faire qch

2 *(used to form passive)* **to g. elected** se faire élire être élu; **suppose he gets killed** et s'il se fait tuer?; **we got paid last week** on a été payés la semaine dernière; **I'm always getting invited to parties** on m'invite toujours à des soirées

3 *(with present participle) (start)* commencer à, se mettre à; **let's g. going** *or* **moving!** *(let's leave)* allons-y!; *(let's hurry)* dépêchons(-nous)!, grouillons-nous!; *(let's start to work)* au travail!; **I can't seem to g. going today** je n'arrive pas à m'activer aujourd'hui; **we got talking about racism** nous en sommes venus à parler de racisme

B. 1 *(go)* aller, se rendre; *(arrive)* arriver; **it's nice to g. home** ça fait du bien de rentrer chez soi; **how do you g. to the museum?** comment est-ce qu'on fait pour aller au musée?; **they should g. here today** ils devraient arriver ici aujourd'hui; **how did you g. here?** comment es-tu venu?; **how did that bicycle g. here?** comment se fait-il que ce vélo se trouve ici?; **he got as far as buying the tickets** il est allé jusqu'à acheter les billets; **I'd hoped things wouldn't g. this far** j'avais espéré qu'on n'en arriverait pas là; **are you getting anywhere with that report?** il avance, ce rapport?; **she won't g. anywhere** *or* **she'll g. nowhere if she's rude to people** elle n'arrivera à rien en étant grossière avec les gens; **where's your sister got to?** où est passée ta sœur?

2 *(move in specified direction)* **she got behind a tree** elle s'est mise derrière un arbre; **to g. into bed** se coucher; **g. in** *or* **into the car!** monte dans la voiture!; **g. over here!** viens ici!; **we couldn't g. past the truck** nous ne pouvions pas passer le camion

3 *(with infinitive) (start)* commencer à, se mettre à; **to g. to know sb** apprendre à connaître qn; **we got to like her husband** nous nous sommes mis à apprécier *ou* à aimer son mari; **you'll g. to like it in the end** ça finira par te plaire; **his father got to hear of the rumours** son père a fini par entendre les rumeurs; **they got to talking about the past** ils en sont venus *ou* ils se sont mis à parler du passé

4 *(become)* devenir; **it's getting to be impossible to find a flat** ça devient impossible de trouver un appartement; **she may g. to be president one day** elle pourrait devenir *ou* être président un jour

5 *(manage)* **to get to do sth** réussir à faire qch; **we never got to see that film** nous n'avons jamais réussi à *ou* nous ne sommes jamais arrivés à voir ce film; **I didn't g. to speak to him in person** je n'ai pas pu lui parler en personne

6 *Fam (be allowed)* **he never gets to stay up late** on ne le laisse jamais se coucher tard□

7 *Fam (leave)* se tirer; **g.!** fous le camp!, tire-toi!

N *Fam (in tennis)* beau retour□ *m*

▸**get about VI 1** *(be up and about, move around)* se déplacer; **she gets about on crutches/in a wheelchair** elle se déplace avec des béquilles/en chaise roulante

2 *(travel)* voyager; **I g. about quite a bit in my job** je suis assez souvent en déplacement pour mon travail

3 *(be socially active)* **she certainly gets about** elle connaît beaucoup de monde

4 *(story, rumour)* se répandre, circuler; **the news** *or* **it got about that they were splitting up** la nouvelle de leur séparation s'est répandue

▸**get across VI 1** *(succeed in crossing)* traverser, passer **2** *(be communicated)* **our message is not getting across** notre message ne passe pas

VT SEP 1 *(over water, street ▸ person)* faire traverser; **we couldn't g. the supplies across** *(across the river)* nous ne pouvions pas faire passer les vivres de l'autre côté; **it was easy to g. the people across** *(across the border)* il était facile de faire passer les gens **2** *(communicate)* communiquer; **I can't seem to g. the idea across to them** je n'arrive pas à leur faire comprendre ça; **he managed to g. his point across** il a réussi à faire passer son message

▸**get ahead VI 1** *(succeed)* réussir, arriver; **to g. ahead in life** *or* **in the world** réussir dans la vie; **if you want to g. ahead at the office, you have to work** si tu veux de l'avancement au bureau, il faut que tu travailles **2** *(move in front)* prendre la tête

▸**get along VI 1** *(fare, manage)* aller; **how are you getting along?** comment vas-tu?, comment ça va?; **she's getting along well in her new job** elle se débrouille bien dans son nouveau travail; **we can g. along without him** nous pouvons nous passer de lui *ou* nous débrouiller sans lui

2 *(advance, progress)* avancer, progresser

3 *(be on good terms)* s'entendre; **we g. along fine** nous nous entendons très bien, nous faisons bon ménage; **she's easy to g. along with** elle est facile à vivre

4 *(move away)* s'en aller, partir; *(go)* aller, se rendre; **it's time for me to be getting along, it's time I was getting along** il est temps que je parte; *Br* **g. along with you!** *(leave)* va-t'en!, fiche le camp!; *Fam (I don't believe you)* à d'autres!

▸**get around VT INSEP** *(obstacle, problem)* contourner; *(law, rule)* tourner; **there's no getting around it, we'll have to tell her** il n'y a pas d'autre moyen, il va falloir que nous le lui disions; **there's no getting around the fact that he lied to us** il reste qu'il nous a menti

VI = get about

▸**get around to VT INSEP she won't g. around to reading it before tomorrow** elle n'arrivera pas à (trouver le temps de) le lire avant demain; **he finally got around to fixing the radiator** il a fini par *ou* il est finalement arrivé à réparer le radiateur; **it was some time before I got around to writing to her** j'ai mis pas mal de temps avant de lui écrire

▸**get at VT INSEP 1** *(reach ▸ object, shelf)* atteindre; *(▸ place)* parvenir à, atteindre; **I've put the pills where the children can't g. at them** j'ai mis les pilules là où les enfants ne peuvent pas les prendre; *Fam* **just let me g. at him!** si jamais il me tombe sous la main!

2 *(discover)* trouver; **to g. at the truth** découvrir la vérité

3 *(mean, intend)* entendre; **what are you getting at?** qu'est-ce que vous entendez par là?, où voulez-vous en venir?; **what I'm getting at is why did she leave now?** ce que je veux dire, c'est pourquoi est-elle partie maintenant?

4 *Fam (criticize)* s'en prendre à□, s'attaquer à□; **you're always getting at me** tu t'en prends toujours à moi

5 *Fam (bribe, influence)* acheter, suborner□; **the witnesses had been got at** les témoins avaient été achetés

▸**get away VI 1** *(leave)* s'en aller, partir; **she has to g. away from home/her parents** il faut qu'elle parte de chez elle/s'éloigne de ses parents; **I was in a meeting and couldn't g. away** j'étais en réunion et je ne pouvais pas m'échapper *ou* m'en aller; **will you be able to g. away at Christmas?** allez-vous pouvoir partir (en vacances) à Noël?; **g. away from it all, come to Florida!** quittez tout, venez en Floride!

2 *(move away)* s'éloigner; **g. away from that door!** éloignez-vous *ou* écartez-vous de cette porte!; **g. away from me!** fichez-moi le camp!

3 *(escape)* s'échapper, se sauver; **there's no getting away from** *or* **you can't g. away from the fact that the other solution would have been cheaper** on ne peut pas nier (le fait) que l'autre solution aurait coûté moins cher

4 *Br Fam (idiom)* **g. away (with you)!** à d'autres!

VT SEP *(remove ▸ person)* emmener; **g. that child away from the road!** éloignez cet enfant de la route!; **g. me away from here!** fais-moi sortir d'ici!; **they managed to g. him away from the TV** ils ont fini par l'arracher de devant la télévision; **to g. sth away from sb** prendre qch à qn

▸**get away with VT INSEP he got away with cheating on his taxes** personne ne s'est aperçu qu'il avait fraudé le fisc; **I can't believe you got away with it!** je n'arrive pas à croire que personne ne t'ait rien dit!; **that child gets away with murder** on laisse tout faire à ce gamin; **her skirt is really tiny but she gets away with it** sa jupe est vraiment très courte mais elle peut se le permettre

▸**get back VI 1** *(move backwards)* reculer; **g. back!** éloignez-vous!, reculez! **2** *(return)* revenir, retourner; **I can't wait to g. back home** je suis impatient de rentrer (à la maison); **g. back into bed!** va te recoucher!, retourne au lit!; **to g. back to sleep** se rendormir; **to g. back to work** *(after break)* se remettre au travail; *(after holiday, illness)* reprendre le travail; **things eventually got back to normal** les choses ont peu à peu repris leur cours (normal); **getting** *or* **to g. back to the point** pour en revenir au sujet qui nous préoccupe; **I'll g. back to you on that** *(call back)* je vous rappelle pour vous dire ce qu'il en est; *(discuss again)* nous reparlerons de cela plus tard

VT SEP 1 *(recover ▸ something lost or lent)* récupérer; *(▸ force, strength)* reprendre, récupérer; *(▸ health, motivation)* retrouver; **he got his job back** il a été repris; **to g. one's money back** *(loan returned)* récupérer son argent; *(reimbursed)* se faire rembourser

2 *(return)* rendre; **we have to g. this book back to her** il faut que nous lui rendions ce livre

3 *(return to original place)* remettre, replacer; **I can't g. it back in the box** je n'arrive pas à le remettre *ou* le faire rentrer dans le carton

4 *Fam (idiom)* **to g. one's own back (on sb)** se venger (de qn)□

▸**get back at VT INSEP** *(have revenge on)* se venger de

▸**get behind VI** *(gen)* rester à l'arrière, se laisser distancer; *Sport* se laisser distancer; *Fig* prendre du retard; **he got behind with his work** il a pris du retard dans son travail; **we mustn't g. behind with the rent** il ne faut pas qu'on soit en retard pour le loyer

VT INSEP *(support, sympathize with)* appuyer

▸**get by VI 1** *(pass)* passer **2** *(manage, survive)* se débrouiller, s'en sortir; **how do you g. by on that salary?** comment tu te débrouilles *ou* tu t'en sors avec un salaire comme ça?; **we can g. by without him** nous pouvons nous passer de lui *ou* nous débrouiller sans lui

VT INSEP 1 *(move past)* **can you g. by the washing machine?** est-ce que vous avez assez de place pour passer à côté de la machine à laver? **2** *(escape attention of ▸ censor, editor)* échapper à

▸**get down VI** descendre; **g. down off that chair!** descends de cette chaise!; **may I g. down (from the table)?** *(leave the table)* puis-je sortir de table?; **they got down on their knees** ils se sont mis à genoux; **g. down!** *(hide)* couchez-vous!; *(to dog)* bas les pattes!

VT SEP 1 *(bring, fetch down ▸ book from shelf etc)* descendre

2 *(reduce ▸ temperature, inflation etc)* faire baisser; **to g. one's weight down** perdre du poids

3 *(write down)* noter

4 *(depress)* déprimer, démoraliser; **work is really getting me down at the moment** le travail me déprime vraiment en ce moment; **don't let it g. you down** ne te laisse pas abattre

5 *(swallow)* avaler, faire descendre

▸**get down to VT INSEP** se mettre à; **it's not so difficult once you g. down to it** ce n'est pas si difficile une fois qu'on s'y met; **to g. down to doing sth** se mettre à faire qch; **it's hard getting down to work after the weekend** c'est difficile de reprendre le travail après le week-end; **we eventually got down to details** nous avons fini par en arriver aux détails; **when you g. down to it, there's very little difference between them** en fin de compte, il y a très peu de différence entre eux

▸**get in VI 1** *(into building)* entrer; **the thief got in through the window** le cambrioleur est entré par la fenêtre; **a car pulled up and she got in** une voiture s'est arrêtée et elle est montée dedans; **water had got in everywhere** l'eau avait pénétré partout

2 *(return home)* rentrer

3 *(arrive)* arriver; **what time does your plane g. in?** à quelle heure ton avion arrive-t-il?

4 *(be admitted ▸ to club)* se faire admettre; *(▸ to school, university)* entrer, être admis *ou* reçu; **he applied to Oxford but he didn't g. in** il voulait entrer à Oxford mais il n'a pas pu

5 *(be elected ▸ person)* être élu; *(▸ party)* accéder au pouvoir

VT SEP 1 *(fit in)* **I hope to g. in a bit of reading on holiday** j'espère pouvoir lire *ou* que je trouverai le temps de lire pendant mes vacances; **she got in some last-minute revision before the exam** elle a réussi à faire des révisions de dernière minute avant l'examen

2 *(insert)* faire pénétrer; **I couldn't get a word in** je n'ai pas pu placer un mot, je n'ai pas pu en placer une

3 *(collect, gather ▸ crops)* rentrer, engranger; *(▸ debts)* recouvrer; *(▸ taxes)* percevoir

4 *(lay in)* **I must g. in some more coal** je dois faire une provision de charbon; **to g. in supplies** s'approvisionner

5 *(call in ▸ doctor, plumber)* faire venir; *(▸ dog, cat)* faire rentrer; **shouldn't Elaine be in on this meeting? – of course, could you g. her in?** on n'a pas besoin d'Elaine pour cette réunion? – si, bien sûr, tu peux lui demander de venir?

6 *(hand in, submit)* rendre, remettre; **did you g. your application in on time?** as-tu remis ton dossier de candidature à temps?

7 *(cause to be admitted ▸ to club, university)* faire admettre *ou* accepter

8 *(plant ▸ seeds)* planter, semer; *(▸ bulbs, plants)* planter

9 *Br Fam (pay for, stand)* payer□, offrir□; **he got the next round in** il a payé la tournée suivante

VT INSEP *(building)* entrer dans; *(vehicle)* monter dans; **he had just got in the door when the phone rang** il venait juste d'arriver *ou* d'entrer quand le téléphone a sonné

▸**get in with VT INSEP 1** *(ingratiate oneself with)* s'insinuer dans *ou* s'attirer les bonnes grâces de, se faire bien voir de; **they tried to g. in with the new director** ils ont essayé de se faire bien voir du nouveau directeur **2** *(associate with ▸ person, group etc)* fréquenter; **he has got in with a new gang** il n'est plus avec la même bande; **she got**

in with the wrong crowd at school elle avait de mauvaises fréquentations à l'école

▸ **get into** VT INSEP **1** *(building)* entrer dans; *(vehicle)* monter dans

2 *(arrive in)* arriver à; **we g. into Madrid at 3 o'clock** nous arrivons à Madrid à 3 heures

3 *(put on ▸ dress, shirt, shoes)* mettre; *(▸ trousers, stockings)* enfiler, mettre; *(▸ coat)* endosser; **she got into her clothes** elle a mis ses vêtements *ou* s'est habillée; **can you still g. into your jeans?** est-ce que tu rentres encore dans ton jean?

4 *(be admitted to ▸ club, school, university)* entrer dans; **her daughter got into medical school** sa fille a été admise dans *ou* est entrée dans une école de médecine; **to g. into office** être élu

5 *(become involved in)* **he wants to g. into politics** il veut se lancer dans la politique; **to g. into (a) conversation** entamer une conversation; **we got into a fight over who had to do the dishes** nous nous sommes disputés pour savoir qui devait faire la vaisselle

6 *Fam (take up)* s'intéresser à□; **he got into Eastern religions** il a commencé à s'intéresser aux religions orientales; **it's a hard book to g. into** c'est un livre dans lequel il est difficile de rentrer□

7 *(become accustomed to)* **he soon got into her way of doing things** il s'est vite fait *ou* s'est vite mis à sa façon de faire les choses

8 *(experience ▸ a specified condition or state)* **to g. into debt** s'endetter; **he got into a real mess** il s'est mis dans un vrai pétrin; **she got into trouble with the teacher** elle a eu des ennuis avec le professeur

9 *(cause to act strangely)* prendre; **what's got into you?** qu'est-ce qui te prend?, quelle mouche te pique?

VT SEP **1** *(insert into)* **to g. sth into sth** (faire) (r)entrer qch dans qch; **to g. the key into the lock** mettre *ou* introduire la clef dans la serrure; **to g. an idea into one's head** se mettre une idée en tête; *Fam* **when will you g. it into your thick head that I don't want to go?** quand est-ce que tu vas enfin comprendre que je ne veux pas y aller?□

2 *(cause to be admitted to ▸ club)* faire entrer à; *(▸ school, university)* faire entrer dans; **the president got his son into Harvard** le président a fait entrer *ou* accepter *ou* admettre son fils à Harvard

3 *(cause to be in a specified condition or state)* mettre; **she got herself into a terrible state** elle s'est mise dans tous ses états; **to g. sb into a good mood** mettre qn de bonne humeur; **he got them into a lot of trouble** il leur a attiré de gros ennuis

4 *(involve in)* impliquer dans, entraîner dans; **you're the one who got us into this** c'est toi qui nous as embarqués dans cette histoire

5 *Fam (make interested in)* faire découvrir□; *(accustom to)* habituer à□, faire prendre l'habitude de□; **he got me into jazz** il m'a initié au jazz□

▸ **get off** VI **1** *(leave bus, train etc)* descendre; **g. off at the next stop** descendez au prochain arrêt; *Fam* **I told him where to g. off!** je l'ai envoyé sur les roses!, je l'ai envoyé promener!; *Fam* **where do you g. off telling me what to do?** qu'est-ce qui te prend de me dicter ce que je dois faire?

2 *(depart ▸ person)* s'en aller, partir; *(▸ car)* démarrer; *(▸ plane)* décoller; *(▸ letter, parcel)* partir; *Fig* **the project got off to a bad/good start** le projet a pris un mauvais/bon départ

3 *(leave work)* finir, s'en aller; **can you g. off early tomorrow?** peux-tu quitter le travail de bonne heure demain?

4 *(escape punishment)* s'en sortir, s'en tirer, en être quitte; **she didn't think she'd g. off so lightly** elle n'espérait pas s'en tirer à si bon compte; **he got off with a small fine** il s'en est tiré avec une petite amende

5 *(let go of something)* lâcher; **hey! g. off! that's MY book!** hé! laisse ça! c'est à moi ce livre!

6 *(go to sleep)* s'endormir

VT INSEP **1** *(leave ▸ bus, train, plane etc)* descendre de

2 *(descend from ▸ bike, wall, chair etc)* descendre de; **he got off his horse** il est descendu de cheval; *Fig* **if only the boss would g. off my back** si seulement le patron me fichait la paix

3 *(depart from)* partir de, décamper de; **g. off my property** fichez le camp de chez moi; **g. off the grass!** ne marche pas sur la pelouse!

4 *(let go of)* **g. off me!** laisse-moi tranquille!, lâche-moi!

5 *(escape from)* se libérer de; *(avoid)* échapper à; **she managed to g. off work** elle a réussi à se libérer

VT SEP **1** *(cause to leave, climb down)* faire descendre; **g. the cat off the table** fais descendre le chat de (sur) la table; *Fig* **try to g. her mind off her troubles** essaie de lui changer les idées

2 *(send)* envoyer, faire partir; **I want to g. this letter off** je veux expédier cette lettre *ou* mettre cette lettre à la poste; **she got the boys off to school** elle a expédié *ou* envoyé les garçons à l'école

3 *(remove ▸ clothing, lid)* enlever, ôter; *(▸ stains)* faire partir *ou* disparaître, enlever; **I can't g. my boots off** je n'arrive pas à enlever mes bottes; **g. your hands off me!** ne me touche pas!; **g. your feet off the table!** enlève tes pieds de sur la table!; *Fig* **he'd like to g. that house off his hands** il aimerait bien se débarrasser de cette maison

4 *(free from punishment)* tirer d'affaire; *(in court)* faire acquitter; **he'll need a good lawyer to g. him off** il lui faudra un bon avocat pour se tirer d'affaire; **to g. sb off doing sth** dispenser qn de faire qch

5 *(put to sleep)* endormir; **I've just managed to g. the baby off (to sleep)** je viens de réussir à endormir le bébé

6 *(have as holiday)* **can you g. next week off?** est-ce que tu peux prendre un congé la semaine prochaine?

7 *(obtain)* **to g. sth off sb** obtenir qch de qn; **I got that story off Marie** je tiens cette histoire de Marie; **I got this cold off the woman next door** la voisine m'a passé son rhume

▸ **get off on** VT INSEP *Fam (sexually)* **he gets off on pornographic films** il prend son pied en regardant des films pornos; *Fig* **he gets off on teasing people** il adore taquiner les gens□

▸ **get off with** VT INSEP *Br Fam* **to g. off with sb** faire une touche avec qn

▸ **get on** VI **1** *(on bus, plane, train)* monter; *(on ship)* monter à bord

2 *(fare, manage)* **how's your husband getting on?** comment va votre mari?; **how did he g. on at the interview?** comment s'est passé son entretien?, comment ça a marché pour son entretien?

3 *(make progress)* avancer, progresser; **Jennifer is getting on very well in maths** Jennifer se débrouille très bien en maths; **how's your work getting on?** ça avance, ton travail?

4 *(succeed)* réussir, arriver; **to g. on in life** *or* **in the world** faire son chemin *ou* réussir dans la vie

5 *(continue)* continuer; **right, let's g. on, shall we?** bien, si on continuait?; **g. on with it!** *(continue speaking)* continuez!; *(hurry up)* mais dépêchez-vous enfin!; **g. on with your work!** allez! au travail!

6 *(be on good terms)* s'entendre; **she's never got on with him** elle ne s'est jamais entendue avec lui; **to be difficult/easy to g. on with** être difficile/facile à vivre

7 *(grow late ▸ time)* **time's getting on** il se fait tard

8 *(grow old ▸ person)* se faire vieux (vieille); **she's getting on (in years)** elle commence à se faire vieille

VT INSEP *(bus, train)* monter dans; *(plane)* monter dans, monter à bord de; *(ship)* monter à bord de; *(bed, horse, table, bike)* monter sur; **g. on your feet** levez-vous, mettez-vous debout; **how did these papers g. on my desk?** comment est-ce que ces papiers se sont retrouvés *ou* sont arrivés sur mon bureau?

VT SEP **1** *(help onto ▸ bus, train)* faire monter dans; *(▸ bed, bike, horse, table)* faire monter sur **2** *(coat, gloves, shoes)* mettre, enfiler; *(lid)* mettre; **I can't g. these trousers on any more** je n'entre plus dans ce pantalon **3** *Am Fam* **to g. it on (with sb)** *(have sex)* s'envoyer en l'air (avec qn); *(fight)* se friter (avec qn)

▸ **get on at** VT INSEP harceler; **he keeps getting on at me to have my hair cut** il est toujours après moi pour que je me fasse couper les cheveux

▸ **get on for** VT INSEP **the president is getting on for sixty** le président approche de la soixantaine *ou* a presque soixante ans; **it's getting on for midnight** il est presque minuit, il n'est pas loin de minuit; **there were getting on for 10,000 demonstrators** il n'y avait pas loin *ou* il y avait près de 10000 manifestants

▸ **get onto** VT INSEP **1** = **get on** *vt insep*

2 *(turn attention to)* **how did we g. onto reincarnation?** comment est-ce qu'on en est venus à parler de réincarnation?; **I'll g. right onto it!** je vais m'y mettre tout de suite!

3 *(contact)* prendre contact avec, se mettre en rapport avec; *(speak to)* parler à; *(call)* téléphoner à, donner un coup de fil à

4 *Fam (become aware of)* découvrir□

5 *(nag, rebuke)* harceler; **his father is always getting onto him to find a job** son père est toujours à le harceler pour qu'il trouve du travail

6 *(be elected to)* **he got onto the school board** il a été élu au conseil d'administration de l'école

VT SEP **1** = **get on** *vt sep* 1 **2** *(cause to talk about)* faire parler de, amener à parler de

▸ **get out** VI **1** *(leave building, room etc)* sortir; *(leave vehicle)* descendre; *(leave organization, town)* quitter; **g. out!** sortez!

2 *(go out)* sortir; **they don't g. out much** ils ne sortent pas beaucoup

3 *(be released from prison, hospital)* sortir

4 *(information, news)* se répandre, s'ébruiter; **the secret got out** le secret a été éventé

5 *(escape)* s'échapper; **he was lucky to g. out alive** il a eu de la chance de s'en sortir vivant

VT SEP **1** *(bring out ▸ champagne, furniture, books, car)* sortir; *(person)* (faire) sortir

2 *(produce, publish ▸ book)* publier, sortir; *(▸ list)* établir, dresser

3 *(speak with difficulty)* prononcer, sortir; **I could barely g. a word out** c'est à peine si je pouvais dire *ou* prononcer *ou* sortir un mot; **we have to g. this report out by Monday** nous devons sortir ce rapport pour lundi

4 *(free ▸ hostages etc)* libérer

5 *(remove)* enlever; *(nail etc)* arracher; *(cork)* retirer; *(stain)* faire disparaître

6 *Sport (in cricket ▸ batsman)* renverser le guichet à

▸ **get out of** VT INSEP **1** *(leave ▸ building)* sortir de; *(car, train)* descendre de; **let's g. out of here** partons d'ici; **he managed to g. out of the country** *(criminal, refugee)* il a réussi à quitter le pays; **to g. out of bed** se lever; **to g. out of prison** sortir de prison; **to g. out of the army** quitter l'armée; **to g. out of sb's way** s'écarter du chemin de qn, faire place à qn; **g. out of here!** *(leave)* sortez d'ici!; *Am Fam (I don't believe it)* mon œil! *very Fam* **g. the hell out of here!** fiche(-moi) le camp!

2 *(avoid)* éviter, échapper à; *(obligation)* se dérober *ou* se soustraire à; **how did you g. out of doing the dishes?** comment as-tu pu échapper à la vaisselle?; **he tried to g. out of helping me** il a essayé de se débrouiller pour ne pas devoir m'aider; **we have to go, there's no getting out of it** il faut qu'on y aille, il n'y a rien à faire *ou* il n'y a pas moyen d'y échapper

3 *(escape from)* **to g. out of trouble** se tirer d'affaire

4 *(become unaccustomed to)* **to g. out of the habit of doing sth** perdre l'habitude de faire qch

VT SEP **1** *(take out of)* sortir de; **she got a handkerchief out of her handbag** elle a sorti un mouchoir de son sac à main; **to g. a book out of the library** emprunter un livre à la bibliothèque

2 *(help to avoid)* **he'll never g. himself out of this one!** il ne s'en sortira jamais!; **my confession got him out of trouble** ma confession l'a tiré d'affaire

3 *(remove ▸ cork)* sortir de; *(▸ nail, splinter)* enlever de; *(▸ stain)* faire partir de, enlever de; **I can't g. the cork out of the bottle** je n'arrive pas à déboucher la bouteille; **the police got a confession/the truth out of him** la police lui a arraché une confession/la vérité; **we got the money out of him** nous avons réussi à obtenir l'argent de lui; **I can't g. anything out of him** je ne peux rien tirer de lui; **I can't g. the idea out of my mind** je ne peux pas chasser cette idée de mon esprit

4 *(gain from)* gagner, retirer; **to g. a lot out of sth** tirer (un) grand profit de qch; **I didn't g. much out of that class** ce cours ne m'a pas apporté grand-chose, je n'ai pas retiré grand-chose de ce cours

▸ **get over** VT INSEP **1** *(cross ▸ river, street)* traverser, franchir; *(▸ fence, wall)* franchir, passer par-dessus **2** *(recover from ▸ illness)* se remettre de, guérir de; *(▸ accident)* se remettre de; *(▸ loss)* se remettre de, se consoler de; **I'll never g. over her** je ne l'oublierai jamais; **he can't g. over her death** il n'arrive pas à se remettre de sa mort *ou* disparition; **I can't g. over how much he's grown!** qu'est-ce qu'il a grandi, je n'en reviens pas!; **he'll g. over it!** il n'en mourra pas! **3** *(master, overcome ▸ obstacle, fear, shyness)* surmonter; *(▸ difficulty)* surmonter, venir à bout de

VT SEP 1 *(cause to cross)* faire traverser **2** *(communicate ▸ idea, message)* faire passer

VI 1 *(cross)* traverser; **to g. over to France/America** aller en France/Amérique; **we'll try to g. over next weekend** *(to visit)* nous essayerons de venir vous voir le week-end prochain **2** *(idea, message)* passer

▸ **get over with VT INSEP** *(finish with)* en finir avec; **let's g. it over with** finissons-en; **I expect you'll be glad to g. it over with** j'imagine que vous serez soulagé quand ce sera terminé

▸ **get round VT INSEP 1 = get around 2** *(exhibition, museum)* faire le tour de; *(corner)* passer **3** *(circumvent ▸ difficulty, regulations etc)* contourner; *(persuade ▸ person)* embobiner; **will you be able to g. round your dad?** est-ce que tu réussiras à persuader ton père?

VT SEP *(bring, take)* **I'll g. the books round (to you) as soon as I can** je t'apporterai les livres dès que je le pourrai

VI 1 = get about 2 the doctor said she'd g. round as soon as she could le docteur a dit qu'elle viendrait *ou* passerait dès qu'elle pourrait

▸ **get round to VT INSEP = get around to**

▸ **get through VI 1** *(reach destination)* parvenir; **the road was blocked and no one could g. through** la route était bloquée et personne ne pouvait passer; **the letter got through to her** la lettre lui est parvenue; **the message didn't g. through** le message n'est pas arrivé

2 *(candidate, student ▸ succeed)* réussir; *(▸ in exam)* être reçu, réussir; **the team got through to the final** l'équipe s'est classée pour la finale

3 *(bill, motion)* passer, être adopté *ou* voté

4 *(make oneself understood)* se faire comprendre; **I can't seem to g. through to her** elle et moi ne sommes pas sur la même longueur d'onde

5 *(contact)* contacter; *Tel* obtenir la communication; **I can't g. through to his office** je n'arrive pas à avoir son bureau

6 *Am (finish)* finir, terminer

VT INSEP 1 *(come through ▸ hole, window)* passer par; *(▸ crowd)* se frayer un chemin à travers *ou* dans; *(▸ military lines)* percer, franchir

2 *(survive ▸ storm, winter)* survivre à; *(▸ difficulty)* se sortir de, se tirer de; *(endure, pass ▸ time)* faire passer; **he got through it alive** il s'en est sorti (vivant); **I thought I'd never g. through the day** j'ai cru que la journée n'en finirait jamais; **how will I g. through this without you?** comment pourrai-je vivre cette épreuve sans toi?; **they got through the day without a single argument** ils ne se sont pas disputés une seule fois de toute la journée

3 *(complete, finish ▸ book)* finir, terminer; *(▸ job, project)* achever, venir à bout de; **I got through an enormous amount of work** j'ai abattu beaucoup de travail; **it took us a week to g. through the play** il nous a fallu une semaine pour venir à bout de la pièce

4 *(consume, use up)* consommer, utiliser; **we g. through a litre of olive oil a week** nous utilisons un litre d'huile d'olive par semaine; **they got through their monthly salary in one week** en une semaine ils avaient dépensé tout leur salaire du mois; **he gets through eight shirts a week** il salit huit chemises par semaine

5 *(exam)* réussir, être reçu à

VT SEP 1 *(transport, send successfully)* faire parvenir; **they got the food supplies through** ils ont réussi à faire parvenir les provisions alimentaires (à destination); **to g. sth through customs** (faire) passer qch à la douane; **you'll never g. that desk through** tu n'arriveras jamais à faire passer ce bureau

2 *(transmit ▸ message)* faire passer, transmettre, faire parvenir

3 *(make understood) Fam* **when will you g. it through your thick head that I don't want to go?** quand est-ce que tu vas enfin comprendre que je ne veux pas y aller?□

4 *(bill, motion)* faire adopter, faire passer

5 *(cause to succeed)* **it was your essay that got you through (the exam)** c'est grâce à ta dissertation que tu as réussi l'examen

6 *(enable to endure)* **I need four cups of coffee to g. me through the day** il me faut mes quatre tasses de café par jour

▸ **get together VI 1** *(meet)* se réunir, se rassembler; **can we g. together after the meeting?** on peut se retrouver après la réunion? **2** *(reach an agreement)* se mettre d'accord; **you'd better g. together with him on the proposal** vous feriez bien de vous entendre avec lui au sujet de la proposition

VT SEP *(people)* réunir, rassembler; *(things)* rassembler, ramasser; *(thoughts)* rassembler; **to g. some money together** réunir une somme d'argent; **let me g. my thoughts together** laissez-moi rassembler mes idées; *Fam* **I never thought he would g. it together** je n'aurais jamais pensé qu'il y arriverait□

▸ **get up VI 1** *(arise from bed)* se lever; **I like to g. up late on Sundays** j'aime faire la grasse matinée le dimanche; **g. up!** sors du lit!, debout!, lève-toi!

2 *(rise to one's feet)* se lever, se mettre debout; **to g. up from the table** se lever *ou* sortir de table; **g. up off the floor!** relève-toi!; **please don't bother getting up** restez assis, je vous prie

3 *(climb up)* monter; **they got up on the roof** ils sont montés sur le toit

4 *(of wind)* se lever

VT INSEP *(stairs)* monter; *(ladder, tree)* monter à; *(hill)* gravir

VT SEP 1 *(cause to rise to feet)* faire lever; *(awaken)* réveiller

2 *(move up)* monter; **how are we going to g. this desk up to the fifth floor?** comment allons-nous monter ce bureau jusqu'au cinquième étage?; **to g. sb up the stairs** *(help climb)* aider qn à monter l'escalier

3 *(generate, work up)* **to g. up speed** gagner de la vitesse; **I can't g. up any enthusiasm for the job** je n'arrive pas à éprouver d'enthousiasme pour ce travail

4 *Fam (organize ▸ entertainment, party)* organiser□, monter□; *(▸ petition)* organiser

5 *(dress)* habiller; *(in costume)* déguiser; **to g. oneself up as sb/sth** *(dress up)* se déguiser en qn/qch

6 *Fam (study ▸ subject)* bûcher, travailler□; *(▸ notes, speech)* préparer□

7 *very Fam (idiom)* **to g. it up** *(achieve an erection)* bander

▸ **get up to VT INSEP 1** *(do)* faire; **he gets up to all kinds of mischief** il fait des tas de bêtises; **what have you been getting up to lately?** qu'est-ce que tu deviens? **2** *(reach)* **I've got up to chapter five** j'en suis au chapitre cinq; **where have you got up to?** *(in book, work)* où en êtes-vous?

---

getatable [get'ætəbəl] **ADJ** *Fam* accessible□, d'accès facile□

getaway ['getəweɪ] **N 1** *(escape)* fuite *f*; **to make one's g.** s'enfuir, filer; **they made a quick g.** ils ont vite filé **2** *Aut (start)* démarrage *m*; *(in racing)* départ *m*

▸▸ ***getaway car, getaway vehicle*** véhicule *m* de fuyard

get-go N *Am Fam* **from the g.** *(from the beginning)* dès le début□; **he's a crook from the g.** *(completely)* c'est un escroc total,□ c'est un véritable escroc□

Gethsemane [geθ'semənɪ] **N** *Bible* Gethsémani

get-rich-quick ADJ *Fam* **a g. scheme** un projet pour faire fortune rapidement□

get-together N *(meeting)* (petite) réunion *f*; *(party)* (petite) fête *f*; **I'm having a g. with some friends** nous faisons une petite soirée entre amis; **you and I must have a little g. one day** il faut qu'on se voie un de ces jours tous les deux

get-up N *Fam* **1** *(outfit)* accoutrement□ *m*; *(disguise)* déguisement□ *m*; **you're not going out in that g.!** tu ne vas pas sortir (habillé) comme ça *ou* dans cet accoutrement! **2** *(of book, product)* présentation□ *f*

get-up-and-go N *Fam* allant□ *m*, dynamisme□ *m*; **to have plenty of g.** avoir beaucoup d'allant, être très dynamique; *Hum* **my g. has got up and gone** je suis sur les rotules

gewgaw ['gju:gɔ:] **N** *Br* bibelot *m*, babiole *f*, colifichet *m*

geyser [*Br* 'gi:zə(r), *Am* 'gaɪzər] **N 1** *Geol* geyser *m* **2** *Br Old-fashioned (water heater)* chauffe-eau *m inv* (à gaz)

G-force N pesanteur *f*

Ghana ['gɑ:nə] **N** Ghana *m*

Ghanaian [gɑ:'neɪən], **Ghanian** ['gɑ:nɪən] **N** Ghanéen(enne) *m,f*

ADJ ghanéen

ghastliness ['gɑ:stlɪnɪs] **N 1** *(of crime)* horreur *f*, atrocité *f* **2** *(of place, building, sight)* aspect *m* sinistre *ou* épouvantable; *(of experience, situation)* caractère *m* horrible *ou* affreux

ghastly ['gɑ:stlɪ] *(compar* **ghastlier**, *superl* **ghastliest)** **ADJ 1** *Fam (very bad)* affreux□, épouvantable□, atroce□; **what g. weather!** quel temps épouvantable *ou* abominable!; **she wore the most g. outfit!** elle était accoutrée d'une façon indescriptible!; **there's been a g. mistake** une terrible erreur a été commise; **you look g.!** vous avez l'air d'un déterré! **2** *(frightening, unnatural)* horrible, effrayant **3** *(pale)* blême; *(pallor)* mortel; *(light)* blafard

GHB [ˌdʒi:eɪtʃ'bi:] **N** *Chem (abbr* **gamma hydroxybutyrate)** GHB *m*

ghee [gi:] **N** *Culin* beurre *m* clarifié

Ghent [gent] **N** Gand

gherkin ['gɜ:kɪn] **N** cornichon *m*

ghetto ['getəʊ] *(pl* **ghettos** *or* **ghettoes)** **N** ghetto *m*

▸▸ *Fam* ***ghetto blaster*** = grand radiocassette portatif

ghillie = gillie

ghost [gəʊst] **N 1** *(phantom)* fantôme *m*, revenant *m*; **to believe in ghosts** croire aux fantômes; **you look as if you've just seen a g.!** on dirait que vous venez de voir un fantôme!

2 *(shadow)* ombre *f*; **the g. of a smile** l'ombre d'un sourire, un vague sourire; **you don't have the g. of a chance** vous n'avez pas la moindre chance *ou* l'ombre d'une chance

3 *TV* image *f* secondaire *ou* résiduelle

4 *Rel* **the Holy G.** l'Esprit *m* saint, le Saint-Esprit

5 *(writer)* nègre *m*

6 *(idioms)* **to give up the g.** rendre l'âme; *Hum* **this typewriter has given up the g.** cette machine à écrire a rendu l'âme; **to lay any ghosts to rest about sth** dissiper le moindre doute quant à qch

VT to g. a book for an author servir de nègre à l'auteur d'un livre

ADJ *(story, film)* de revenants, de fantômes

▸▸ ***ghost ship*** vaisseau *m* fantôme; ***ghost story*** histoire *f* de revenants; ***ghost town*** ville *f* fantôme; ***ghost train*** train *m* fantôme

ghosting ['gəʊstɪŋ] **N** *TV* image *f* fantôme, fantôme *m*

ghostly ['gəʊstlɪ] *(compar* **ghostlier**, *superl* **ghostliest)** **ADJ** spectral, fantomatique; **a g. figure** une véritable apparition; **a g. silence** un silence de mort

ghostwrite ['gəʊstraɪt] *(pt* **ghostwrote** [-rəʊt], *pp* **ghostwritten** [-rɪtən]) **VT** écrire *ou* rédiger (comme nègre); **I'm sure his books are ghostwritten** je suis sûr qu'il n'a écrit aucun des livres publiés sous son nom

VI to g. for sb servir de nègre à qn

ghostwriter ['gəʊstˌraɪtə(r)] **N** nègre *m*

ghostwritten ['gəʊstrɪtən] *pp of* **ghostwrite**

ghostwrote ['gəʊstrəʊt] *pt of* **ghostwrite**

ghoul [gu:l] **N 1** *(evil spirit)* goule *f* **2** *(macabre person)* amateur *m* de macabre; **don't be such a g.!** tu es vraiment morbide! **3** *Old-fashioned (grave robber)* déterreur *m* de cadavres

ghoulish ['gu:lɪʃ] **ADJ 1** *(ghostly)* de goule, vampirique **2** *(person, humour)* morbide, macabre

GHQ [ˌdʒi:eɪtʃ'kju:] **N** *(abbr* **general headquarters)** GQG *m*

GHz *(written abbr* **gigahertz)** GHz

GI [ˌdʒiː'aɪ] **N 1** *Fam (abbr* **Government Issue**) *(soldier)* soldat *m* américain□, GI *m* **2** *Med (abbr* **Glycaemic Index**) IG *m*

▸▸ ***GI bride*** épouse *f* (étrangère) d'un GI; ***GI Joe*** = surnom collectif des soldats américains, notamment pendant la Seconde Guerre mondiale

giant ['dʒaɪənt] **N 1** *(in size)* géant(e) *m,f* **2** *Fig* **a literary g.** un géant de la littérature; **an industrial g.** un magnat de l'industrie

ADJ géant, gigantesque; **with g. strides** à pas de géant; **the company has taken g. strides towards modernizing its production techniques** la société a fait d'énormes efforts pour moderniser ses techniques de production

▸▸ ***the Giant's Causeway*** la Chaussée des Géants; *Zool* ***giant panda*** panda *m* géant, grand panda *m*; *Bot* ***giant redwood, giant sequoia*** séquoia *m* géant; ***giant slalom*** slalom *m* géant; *Zool* ***giant tortoise*** tortue *f* géante

giantess ['dʒaɪəntes] **N** géante *f*

Gib [dʒɪb] **N** *Fam* Gibraltar□

gibber ['dʒɪbə(r)] **VI 1** *(person)* bredouiller, bafouiller; **to g. with fear** bafouiller de peur; **it reduced him to a gibbering wreck** il en est devenu bègue; *Fam* **gibbering idiot** espèce de crétin **2** *(monkey)* crier, hurler

gibberish ['dʒɪbərɪʃ] **N** baragouin *m*, charabia *m*; **it's complete g. to me** je ne comprends absolument rien; **the man's talking g.** ce que dit cet homme est totalement incompréhensible *ou* n'a ni queue ni tête

gibbet ['dʒɪbɪt] **N** potence *f*, gibet *m*

gibbon ['gɪbən] **N** *Zool* gibbon *m*

gibbous ['gɪbəs] **ADJ 1** *Astron* gibbeux **2** *(humpbacked)* bossu

gibe [dʒaɪb] **N** *(remark)* raillerie *f*, moquerie *f*

VT *(taunt)* railler, se moquer de

VI to g. at sb railler qn, se moquer de qn

giblets ['dʒɪblɪts] **NPL** abats *mpl* de volaille

Gibraltar [dʒɪ'brɔːltə(r)] **N** Gibraltar

giddily ['gɪdɪlɪ] **ADV 1** *(dizzily)* vertigineusement **2** *(frivolously)* étourdiment, avec insouciance

giddiness ['gɪdɪnɪs] **N** *(UNCOUNT)* **1** *(dizziness)* vertiges *mpl*, étourdissements *mpl*; **fits of g.** des étourdissements, des vertiges **2** *(frivolousness)* frivolité *f*, étourderie *f*

giddy ['gɪdɪ] *(compar* **giddier**, *superl* **giddiest**) **ADJ 1** *(dizzy ▸ person)* **to be** *or* **to feel g.** *(afraid of height)* avoir le vertige, être pris de vertige; *(unwell)* avoir un étourdissement; **I feel g. just watching them** j'ai la tête qui tourne *ou* le vertige rien que de les regarder **2** *(lofty)* vertigineux, qui donne le vertige; **the g. heights of success** les hautes cimes de la réussite; *Ironic* **he had reached the g. heights of senior assistant** il avait atteint le grade prestigieux d'assistant en chef **3** *(frivolous ▸ person, behaviour)* frivole, écervelé; **a g. round of parties and social events** un tourbillon de soirées et de sorties mondaines

GIF [gɪf] **N** *Comput (abbr* **Graphics Interchange Format**) GIF *m*

gift [gɪft] **N 1** *(present ▸ personal)* cadeau *m*; *(▸ official)* don *m*; **to make sb a g. of sth** offrir qch à qn, faire cadeau de qch à qn; **I wouldn't have it as a g.!** je n'en voudrais pas même si on m'en faisait cadeau!; *Prov* **don't** *or* **never look a g. horse in the mouth** à cheval donné on ne regarde pas la bouche

2 *(talent)* don *m*; **he has a great g. for telling jokes** il n'a pas son pareil pour raconter des plaisanteries; **she has a g. for music** elle a un don *ou* elle est douée pour la musique; *Fam* **to have the g. of the gab** avoir la langue bien pendue, avoir du bagou (t)

3 *Com (on presentation of coupons)* prime *f*; **free g.** cadeau *m*

4 *Fam (bargain)* affaire□ *f*; **at £5, it's a g.** 5 livres, c'est donné

5 *Fam (easy thing)* **that exam question was a g.** ce sujet d'examen, c'était du gâteau

6 *(donation)* don *m*, donation *f*; *Law* **as a g.** à titre d'avantage *ou* gracieux; **the posts abroad are in the g. of the French department** l'attribution des postes à l'étranger relève du département de français

VT *Am Formal (present)* donner, faire don de; **gifted by Mr Evans** *(on plaque)* don de M. Evans

▸▸ ***gift shop*** boutique *f* de cadeaux; ***gift token*** bon *m* d'achat; *Br* ***gift voucher*** *(token)* bon *m* d'achat; *(coupon)* bon *m* de réduction, point-cadeau *m*; ***gift wrap, gift wrapping*** papier-cadeau *m*

gifted ['gɪftɪd] **ADJ** *(person)* doué; *(performance)* talentueux; **highly g. children** des enfants surdoués; **she's g. with a fantastic memory** elle a une mémoire fantastique

gift-wrap **VT do you want it gift-wrapped?** je vous fais un paquet-cadeau?

gift-wrapped [-ræpt] **ADJ** *(article)* sous paquet-cadeau

gig [gɪg] **N 1** *(carriage)* cabriolet *m*

2 *(boat)* yole *f*, guigue *f*

3 *Fam (concert)* concert□ *m (de rock, de jazz)*; *(show)* spectacle□ *m*

4 *Fam (job)* boulot *m*; **it's a good g.** c'est peinard comme boulot

giga- ['gɪgə] **PREF** giga-

gigabyte ['gɪgəbaɪt] **N** *Comput* gigaoctet *m*

gigahertz ['gɪgəhɜːts] **N** *Elec & Phys* gigahertz *m*

gigantic [dʒaɪ'gæntɪk] **ADJ** géant, gigantesque

gigantically [dʒaɪ'gæntɪkəlɪ] **ADV** de façon démesurée

giggle ['gɪgəl] **VI** *(stupidly)* rire bêtement, ricaner; *(nervously)* rire nerveusement; **they couldn't stop giggling** ils ne pouvaient pas se retenir de glousser *ou* de pouffer; **what are you giggling about?** qu'est-ce qui vous fait rire?

N *(uncontrollable)* fou rire *m*; *(nervous)* petit rire *m* nerveux; *(stupid)* ricanement *m*; **to have a fit of the giggles** avoir le fou rire; *Br Fam* **to do sth for a g.** faire qch pour rigoler; **the evening was a g. from start to finish** on s'est marré toute la soirée; **she was a real g. as usual** elle était tordante comme d'habitude

giggling ['gɪgəlɪŋ] **ADJ** qui rit bêtement

N *(UNCOUNT) (uncontrollable)* fou rire *m*; *(nervous)* petits rires *mpl* nerveux; *(of young girl)* rires *mpl* bébêtes, gloussements *mpl*

giggly ['gɪgəlɪ] *(compar* **gigglier**, *superl* **giggliest**) **ADJ** qui rit bêtement; **they're like g. schoolgirls** elles n'arrêtent pas de rire comme des gamines; **to get** *or* **go all g.** se mettre à rire bêtement

GIGO ['gaɪgəʊ, ˌdʒiːaɪdʒiː'əʊ] **N** *Comput (abbr* **garbage in, garbage out**) GIGO

gigolo ['ʒɪgələʊ] *(pl* **gigolos**) **N** gigolo *m*

gigot ['dʒɪgət] **N** gigot *m*

gild [gɪld] *(pt* **gilded**, *pp* **gilded** *or* **gilt** [gɪlt]) **VT** dorer; *Fig* **it would be gilding the lily** ce serait du peaufinage

gilding ['gɪldɪŋ] **N** dorure *f*

gill[1] [dʒɪl] **N** *(liquid measure)* = 0,142 l, quart *m* de pinte

gill[2] [gɪl] **N** *(of mushroom)* lamelle *f*

• **gills** **NPL** *(of fish)* ouïes *fpl*, branchies *fpl*; **to be green around the gills** *(from shock)* être vert (de peur); *(from illness)* avoir mauvaise mine

gillie ['gɪlɪ] **N** *Scot (for hunting)* guide *m*, accompagnateur *m*; *(for fishing)* accompagnateur *m*

gillyflower ['dʒɪlɪflaʊə(r)] **N** *Bot (stock)* giroflée *f*; *(wallflower)* giroflée *f* des murailles; **(clove) g.** œillet *m* giroflée

gilt [gɪlt] *pp of* **gild**

ADJ doré

N 1 *(gilding)* dorure *f*; *Br Fig* **to take the g. off the gingerbread** gâcher le plaisir **2** *St Exch* fonds *m* d'État, valeur *f* de premier ordre *ou* de père de famille

▸▸ ***gilts market*** marché *m* des valeurs de premier ordre

gilt-edged **ADJ 1** *St Exch (securities, stock)* de tout repos, de père de famille **2** *(page)* doré sur tranche **3** *Fig (opportunity)* en or

▸▸ *Am* ***gilt-edged bond*** valeur *f* du Trésor américain; ***gilt-edged market*** marché *m* des valeurs de premier ordre; ***gilt-edged stock(s)*** fonds *mpl* d'État

gimbals ['dʒɪmbəlz] **NPL** *Aviat & Naut* cardan *m*

gimcrack ['dʒɪmkræk] **ADJ** *Old-fashioned (jewellery)* en toc; *(ornament, car)* de pacotille; *(theory, idea)* bidon *(inv)*

gimlet ['gɪmlɪt] **N 1** *(tool)* vrille *f*; **his g. eyes** ses yeux perçants **2** *(drink)* = cocktail à base de vodka ou de gin et de jus de citron vert

gimme ['gɪmɪ] *Fam* = **give me**

• **gimmes** **NPL** *Am* **the gimmes** la cupidité□

gimmick ['gɪmɪk] **N 1** *(sales trick)* truc *m*, astuce *f*; *(in politics)* astuce *f*, gadget *m*; **advertising g.** trouvaille *f* publicitaire; **it's just a sales g.** c'est un truc pour faire vendre **2** *(gadget, device)* gadget *m*

gimmickry ['gɪmɪkrɪ] **N** *(UNCOUNT) Fam* truquage□ *m*, astuces□ *fpl*, gadgets□ *mpl*

gimmicky ['gɪmɪkɪ] **ADJ** *Fam* qui relève du procédé□; **the show was too g.** le spectacle relevait trop du procédé

gin [dʒɪn] *(pt & pp* **ginned**, *cont* **ginning**) **N 1** *(drink)* gin *m*; **g. and tonic** gin-tonic *m*; *Br* **g. and it** martini-gin *m* **2** *(trap)* **g. (trap)** piège *m* **3** *Ind (machine)* égreneuse *f* (de coton)

VT *(trap)* attraper, piéger

▸▸ *Am* ***gin mill***, *Br* ***gin palace*** tripot *m*; *Cards* ***gin rummy*** gin-rummy *m*, gin-rami *m*; ***gin sling*** gin sling *m*

ginger ['dʒɪndʒə(r)] **N 1** *(spice)* gingembre *m*; **crystallized g.** gingembre *m* confit; **ground g.** gingembre *m* en poudre; **root** *or* **fresh g.** gingembre *m* en racine *ou* frais

2 *Fam Fig* entrain□ *m*, allant□ *m*, dynamisme□ *m*

3 *(colour)* brun *m* roux

4 *Fam (redhead)* roux (rousse)□ *m,f*; **oi, g.!** ho poil de carotte!

5 *Scot Fam (fizzy drink)* boisson *f* gazeuse□

ADJ *(hair)* roux (rousse), rouquin; *(cat)* roux (rousse)

• **Ginger** **N** *Fam (nickname)* Poil de Carotte

▸▸ ***ginger ale*** = boisson gazeuse aux extraits de gingembre pouvant servir à couper un alcool; ***ginger beer*** *(drink)* = limonade au gingembre; *SEng Fam (homosexual)* pédale *f*; ***ginger biscuit*** biscuit *m* au gingembre; ***ginger group*** = dans une organisation politique ou autre, faction dynamique cherchant à faire bouger les choses en incitant à l'action; *Br* ***ginger nut*** biscuit *m* au gingembre; ***ginger snap*** biscuit *m* au gingembre; ***ginger wine*** = boisson alcoolisée à base de gingembre

▸ **ginger up** **VT SEP** *(activity, group, meeting)* animer; *(speech, story)* relever, pimenter, égayer; *(film, text, storyline etc)* donner du punch à; **we need something to g. up the party** il nous faut quelque chose pour mettre un peu d'animation dans la soirée

gingerbread ['dʒɪndʒəbred] **N** pain *m* d'épices

▸▸ ***gingerbread man*** = sujet en biscuit parfumé au gingembre

gingerly ['dʒɪndʒəlɪ] **ADV** *(cautiously)* avec circonspection, précautionneusement; *(delicately)* délicatement

ADJ *(cautious)* circonspect, prudent; *(delicate)* délicat

gingery ['dʒɪndʒərɪ] **ADJ 1** *(taste)* de gingembre **2** *(hair, colour)* qui tire sur le roux

gingham ['gɪŋəm] **N** (toile *f* de) vichy *m*

COMP en vichy

gingivitis [ˌdʒɪndʒɪ'vaɪtɪs] **N** *(UNCOUNT) Med* gingivite *f*

ginormous [ˌdʒaɪ'nɔːməs] **ADJ** *Fam* gigantesque□

ginseng ['dʒɪnseŋ] **N** ginseng *m*

gippo ['dʒɪpəʊ] *(pl* **gippoes**) **N** *Br Fam* = terme injurieux désignant un gitan

gippy ['dʒɪpɪ] **ADJ** *Br Fam* **to have a g. tummy** avoir la courante

gipsy ['dʒɪpsɪ] *(pl* **gipsies**) **N** gitan(e) *m,f*, bohémien(enne) *m,f*, *Pej* romanichel(elle) *m,f*; *Fig (wanderer)* vagabond(e) *m,f*

ADJ *(camp)* de gitans; *(dance, music)* gitan

▸▸ ***gipsy caravan*** roulotte *f*; ***gipsy moth*** zigzag *m*, bombyx *m* disparate

gipsyish ['dʒɪpsɪɪʃ], **gipsylike** ['dʒɪpsɪlaɪk] **ADJ** comme un bohémien, *Pej* comme un romanichel; *(dark-skinned)* brun de peau

giraffe [dʒɪ'rɑːf] **N** girafe *f*; **a baby g.** un girafeau, un girafon

gird [gɜːd] *(pt & pp* **girded** *or* **girt** [gɜːt]) **VT** *Literary* **1** *(waist)* ceindre; *Fig* **to g. (up) one's loins** se préparer à l'action **2** *(clothe)* **to g. with** revêtir de

girder ['gɜːdə(r)] **N** poutre *f* (métallique), fer *m* profilé; *(light)* poutrelle *f*

girdle ['gɜːdəl] **N 1** *(corset)* gaine *f* **2** *Literary (belt)* ceinture *f* **3** *Scot (iron plate)* plaque *f* en fonte; *(on top of stove)* plaque *f* chauffante

VT *Literary* **to g. sth with sth** ceindre qch de qch

▸▸ *Br* ***girdle cake, girdle scone*** = sorte de petite galette

girl [gɜːl] **N 1** *(child)* fille *f*; **a little g.** une fillette, une petite fille; **g.'s name** prénom *m* féminin *ou* de fille; **a girls' school** une école de filles; **I knew her when she was a g.** je l'ai connue toute petite; **poor little g.!** pauvre petite!; **a French/an Indian g.** une jeune Française/Indienne

2 *(daughter)* fille *f*; **the Murphy g.** la fille des Murphy

3 *(young woman)* (jeune) fille *f*; **come in, girls!** entrez, mesdemoiselles!; **she's having an evening with the girls** elle passe la soirée dehors avec les filles; **my dear g.** ma chère

4 *Fam (term of address)* **that's my g.!** je te reconnais bien là!; *Br* **how are you, old g.?** ça va, ma vieille?

5 *Fam (girlfriend)* (petite) amie▫ *f*, copine *f*

6 *Sch (pupil)* élève *f*

7 *(employee)* (jeune) employée *f*; *(maid)* bonne *f*; *(in shop)* vendeuse *f*; *(in factory)* ouvrière *f*

8 *(used to address dog, horse, ship)* ma belle; **come on, g.** allez, hue cocotte!

▸▸ ***girl band*** girls band *m*; ***girl Friday*** = employée de bureau affectée à des tâches diverses; ***Girl Guide*** éclaireuse *f*; ***Girl Scout*** éclaireuse *f*

girlfriend ['gɜːlfrend] **N 1** *(partner)* copine *f*, (petite) amie *f*; **g. trouble** problèmes *mpl* de cœur **2** *(platonic friend)* copine *f*, amie *f*

girlhood ['gɜːlhʊd] **N** *(as child)* enfance *f*; *(as adolescent)* adolescence *f*; **in my g.** dans ma jeunesse, quand j'étais jeune fille

girlie ['gɜːlɪ] **N** *Fam* **1** *(effeminate boy)* fillette *f* **2** *Br (young woman)* (jeune) fille▫ *f*; **to have a g. chat** bavarder entre filles

▸▸ ***girlie magazine*** magazine *m* de femmes à poil

girlish ['gɜːlɪʃ] **ADJ 1** *(appearance, smile, voice)* de fillette, de petite fille **2** *Pej (boy)* efféminé

girlishly ['gɜːlɪʃlɪ] **ADV** comme une petite fille

giro ['dʒaɪrəʊ] *(pl* **giros**) **N 1** *(system)* = système de virement interbancaire introduit par la Poste britannique; **(bank) g.** virement *m* bancaire; **National G.** Comptes *mpl* Chèques Postaux **2** *Fam (for unemployed)* chèque *m* d'allocation de chômage▫; **I haven't had my g. yet** mon allocation de chômage ne m'a pas encore été payée

▸▸ ***giro account*** compte *m* chèque postal, CCP *m*; ***giro cheque*** chèque *m* postal, chèque *m* de virement; ***giro transfer*** transfert *m* par CCP

Girobank ['dʒaɪrəʊbæŋk] **N** = service bancaire de la Poste britannique, service *m* de chèques postaux

girt [gɜːt] *pt & pp of* **gird**

-girt [gɜːt] **SUFF** *Literary* **a sea-g. country/isle** un pays/une île encerclé(e) par la mer

girth [gɜːθ] **N 1** *(circumference* ▸ *of tree etc)* circonférence *f*; *(*▸ *of chest, waist)* tour *m* **2** *(stoutness)* corpulence *f*, embonpoint *m* **3** *(of saddle)* sangle *f*

VT *(horse)* sangler

gismo = **gizmo**

gist [dʒɪst] **N** essentiel *m*; **give me the g. of the discussion** expliquez-moi les grandes lignes du débat; **could you just give me the g. (of it) now?** pourrais-tu m'en donner l'essentiel?; **I got the g. of what she was saying** j'ai compris l'essentiel de ce qu'elle disait; **the g. of what she was saying was…** elle a dit en substance…

git [gɪt] **N** *Br very Fam (man)* connard *m*; *(woman)* connasse *f*; **you stupid g.!** espèce de connard/connasse!

GIVE [gɪv]

VT
- donner **A1–3, B2–4, C1, 4, 5, D1, 3–6**
- imposer **C2**
- faire **D1–3, 6**
- offrir **A1, 3**
- conférer **B1**
- reconnaître **C6**

VI
- donner **1**
- s'affaisser **2**

N
- élasticité

(pt **gave** [geɪv], *pp* **given** ['gɪvən])

VT A. 1 *(hand over)* donner; *(as gift)* donner, offrir; **I gave him the book, I gave the book to him** je lui ai donné le livre; **we gave our host a gift** nous avons offert un cadeau à notre hôte; **the family gave the paintings to the museum** la famille a fait don des tableaux au musée; **he gave his daughter in marriage** il a donné sa fille en mariage; **she gave him her hand** *(to hold)* elle lui a donné *ou* tendu la main; *(in marriage)* elle lui a accordé sa main; *Literary* **to g. oneself to sb** se donner à qn; **I gave him my coat to hold** je lui ai confié mon manteau; **she gave them her trust** elle leur a fait confiance, elle leur a donné sa confiance; **I g. you our host** *(in proposing toast)* je bois à la santé de notre hôte; *Fam* **g. it all you've got!** mets-y le paquet!; *Fam* **to g. it to sb** *(beat up)* rosser qn; *(reprimand)* passer un savon à qn; **I gave him what for!** *(reprimanded him)* je lui ai passé un savon!

2 *(grant* ▸ *right, permission, approval, importance)* donner; **g. the matter your full attention** prêtez une attention toute particulière à cette affaire; **he gave your suggestion careful consideration** il a considéré votre suggestion avec beaucoup d'attention; *Law* **the court gave her custody of the child** la cour lui a accordé la garde de l'enfant

3 *(provide with* ▸ *drink, food)* donner, offrir; *(*▸ *lessons, classes, advice)* donner; *(*▸ *help)* prêter; **g. our guests something to eat/drink** donnez à manger/à boire à nos invités; **we gave them lunch** nous les avons invités *ou* nous leur avons fait à déjeuner; **an investment that gives 10 per cent** un placement qui rend *ou* rapporte 10 pour cent; **the children can wash up, it will g. them something to do** les enfants peuvent faire la vaisselle, ça les occupera; **to g. a child a name** donner un nom à un enfant; **to g. sb/sth one's support** soutenir qn/qch; **do you g. a discount?** faites-vous des tarifs préférentiels?; **this lamp gives a poor light** cette lampe éclaire mal; **g. me time to think** donnez-moi *ou* laissez-moi le temps de réfléchir; **just g. me time!** sois patient!; **we were given a choice** on nous a fait choisir; **g. me a chance!** donne-moi une chance!; *Fam* **g. me classical music any day!** à mon avis rien ne vaut la musique classique!▫

B. 1 *(confer* ▸ *award)* conférer; **they gave her an honorary degree** ils lui ont conféré un diplôme honorifique

2 *(dedicate)* donner, consacrer; **can you g. me a few minutes?** pouvez-vous m'accorder *ou* me consacrer quelques instants?; **he gave his life to save the child** il est mort *ou* il a donné sa vie pour sauver l'enfant

3 *(in exchange)* donner; *(pay)* payer; **I gave him my sweater in exchange for his gloves** je lui ai échangé mon pull contre ses gants; **I'll g. you a good price for the table** je vous donnerai *ou* payerai un bon prix pour la table; **I would g. a lot** *or* **a great deal to know…** je donnerais beaucoup pour savoir…

4 *(transmit)* donner, passer; **I hope I don't g. you my cold** j'espère que je ne vais pas te passer mon rhume

C. 1 *(cause)* donner, causer; *(headache)* donner; *(pleasure, surprise, shock)* faire; **the walk gave him an appetite** la promenade l'a mis en appétit *ou* lui a ouvert l'appétit; **the news gave me a shock** la nouvelle m'a fait un choc

2 *(impose* ▸ *task)* imposer; *(*▸ *punishment)* infliger; **to g. sb a black mark** infliger un blâme à qn; *Law* **he was given (a sentence of) 15 years** il a été condamné à 15 ans de prison

3 *(announce* ▸ *verdict, judgment)* **the court gives its decision today** la cour prononce *ou* rend l'arrêt aujourd'hui; *Sport* **the umpire gave the batsman out** l'arbitre a déclaré le joueur hors jeu

4 *(communicate* ▸ *impression, order, signal)* donner; *(*▸ *address, information)* donner, fournir; *(*▸ *news, decision)* annoncer; **to g. sb a message** communiquer un message à qn; **she gave her age as 45** elle a déclaré avoir 45 ans; **g. her my love** embrassе-la pour moi; **he is to g. his decision tomorrow** il devra faire connaître *ou* annoncer sa décision demain; **I was given to understand she was ill** on m'a donné à croire qu'elle était malade

5 *(suggest, propose* ▸ *explanation, reason)* donner, avancer; *(hint)* donner; **that's given me an idea** ça me donne une idée; **don't go giving him ideas!** ne va pas lui mettre des idées dans la tête!; *Fam* **don't g. me that (nonsense)!** ne me raconte pas d'histoires!; **don't g. me that stuff about how hard your life is** épargne-moi le récit de tous tes malheurs

6 *(admit, concede)* reconnaître, accorder; **he's keen, I'll g. you that** il est très enthousiaste, ça, je te l'accorde

D. 1 *(utter* ▸ *sound)* rendre, émettre; *(*▸ *answer)* donner, faire; *(*▸ *cry, sigh)* pousser; **he gave a laugh** il a laissé échapper un rire; **g. us a song** chantez-nous quelque chose

2 *(make* ▸ *action, gesture)* faire; **she gave them an odd look** elle leur a jeté *ou* lancé un regard curieux; **he gave her hand a squeeze** il lui a pressé la main; **she gave her hair a comb** elle s'est donné un coup de peigne; **he gave the table a wipe** il a essuyé la table; **g. me a kiss** *(gen)* fais-moi la bise; *(lover)* embrasse-moi; **she gave him a slap** elle lui a donné une claque

3 *(perform in public* ▸ *concert)* donner; *(*▸ *lecture, speech)* faire; *(*▸ *interview)* accorder; **that evening she gave the performance of a lifetime** ce soir-là elle était au sommet de son art

4 *(hold* ▸ *lunch, party, supper)* donner, organiser; **they gave a dinner for the professor** ils ont donné un dîner en l'honneur du professeur

5 *(estimate the duration of)* donner, estimer; **I'd g. their marriage about a year if that** je donne un an maximum à leur mariage

6 *Math (produce)* donner, faire; **17 minus 4 gives 13** 17 moins 4 font *ou* égalent 13; **that gives a total of 26** ça donne un total de 26

7 *(idioms)* **to g. way** *(ground)* s'affaisser; *(bridge, building, ceiling)* s'effondrer, s'affaisser; *(ladder, rope)* céder, (se) casser; **her legs gave way (beneath her)** ses jambes se sont dérobées sous elle; **don't g. way if he cries** ne cède pas s'il pleure; **I gave way to tears/to anger** je me suis laissé aller à pleurer/emporter par la colère; **he gave way to despair** il s'est abandonné au désespoir; **the fields gave way to factories** les champs ont fait place aux usines; **natural fibres have given way to synthetics** les fibres naturelles ont été remplacées par les synthétiques; **g. way to pedestrians** *(sign)* priorité aux piétons; **g. way** *(sign)* cédez le passage

VI 1 *(contribute)* donner; **please g. generously** nous nous en remettons à votre générosité; **to g. generously of one's time** donner beaucoup de son temps; *Prov* **it is better to g. than to receive** donner vaut mieux que recevoir; **in any relationship you have to learn to g. and take** dans toutes les relations, il faut apprendre à faire des concessions *ou* il faut que chacun y mette du sien; **to g. as good as one gets** rendre coup pour coup

2 *(collapse, yield* ▸ *ground, wall)* s'affaisser; *(*▸ *cloth, elastic)* se relâcher; *(*▸ *person)* céder; **the fence gave beneath** *or* **under my weight** la barrière a cédé *ou* s'est affaissée sous mon poids; **something's got to g.** quelque chose va lâcher

3 *Am Fam (talk)* **now g.!** accouche!, vide ton sac!

4 *Am Fam* **what gives?** qu'est-ce qui se passe?▫

N *(of metal, wood)* élasticité *f*, souplesse *f*; **there's not enough g. in this sweater** ce pull n'est pas assez ample

• **give or take PREP** à… près; **g. or take a few days** à quelques jours près

▸▸ ***give way sign*** signal *m* de priorité

▸ **give away VT SEP 1** *(hand over)* donner; *(as gift)* donner, faire cadeau de; *(prize)* distribuer; **it's so cheap they're practically giving it away** c'est tellement bon marché, c'est comme s'ils en faisaient

cadeau; **you couldn't g. them away** tu n'arriverais pas à t'en débarrasser (même si tu en faisais cadeau)
2 *(bride)* conduire à l'autel
3 *(throw away ▸ chance, opportunity)* gâcher, gaspiller
4 *(reveal ▸ information)* révéler; *(▸ secret)* révéler, trahir; **he didn't g. anything away** il n'a rien dit
5 *(betray)* trahir; **her accent gave her away** son accent l'a trahie; **no prisoner would g. another prisoner away** aucun prisonnier n'en trahirait un autre; **to g. oneself away** se trahir
6 *Austr (renounce ▸ habit)* renoncer à, abandonner; *(resign from ▸ job)* quitter; *(▸ position)* démissionner de

▸**give back** VT SEP **1** *(return)* rendre; *(property, stolen object)* restituer; **g. the book back to her** rendez-lui le livre; **the store gave him his money back** le magasin l'a remboursé **2** *(reflect ▸ image, light)* refléter, renvoyer; *(▸ sound)* renvoyer

▸**give in** VT SEP *(hand in ▸ book, exam paper)* rendre; *(▸ found object, parcel)* remettre; *(▸ application, name)* donner
VI *(relent, yield)* céder; **to g. in to sb/sth** céder à qn/qch; **the country refused to g. in to terrorist threats** le pays a refusé de céder aux menaces des terroristes; **you g. in too easily** tu abandonnes trop facilement

▸**give off** VT SEP *(emit, produce ▸ gas, smell)* émettre

▸**give onto** VT INSEP donner sur

▸**give out** VT SEP **1** *(hand out)* distribuer **2** *(emit ▸ smell)* dégager; *(▸ heat)* répandre; *(▸ sound)* émettre, faire entendre **3** *(make known)* annoncer, faire savoir; **it was given out that he was leaving** on a dit *ou* annoncé qu'il partait
VI **1** *(fail ▸ machine)* tomber en panne; *(▸ brakes)* lâcher; *(▸ heart)* flancher; **the old car finally gave out** la vieille voiture a fini par rendre l'âme **2** *(run out)* s'épuiser, manquer; **her strength was giving out** elle était à bout de forces, elle n'en pouvait plus; **my luck gave out** la chance m'a abandonné

▸**give over** VT SEP **1** *(entrust)* donner, confier; **2** *(set aside)* donner, consacrer; *Admin* affecter; **the land was given over to agriculture** la terre a été consacrée à l'agriculture
VT INSEP *Br Fam* cesser de␣, arrêter de␣; **g. over crying!** cesse de pleurer!
VI *Br Fam* cesser␣, arrêter␣; **g. over!** assez!, arrête!

▸**give up** VT SEP **1** *(renounce ▸ habit)* renoncer à, abandonner; *(▸ friend)* abandonner, délaisser; *(▸ chair, place)* céder; *(▸ activity)* cesser; **she'll never g. him up** elle ne renoncera jamais à lui; **he's given up smoking** il a arrêté de fumer, il a renoncé au tabac; **I haven't given up the idea of going to China** je n'ai pas renoncé à l'idée d'aller en Chine; **he gave up his seat to the old woman** il a cédé sa place à la vieille dame; **don't g. up hope** ne perdez pas espoir; **he was ready to g. up his life for his country** il était prêt à mourir pour la patrie; **they gave up the game** *or* **the struggle** ils ont abandonné la partie; **we gave her brother up for dead** nous avons conclu que son frère était mort; **to g. up the throne** renoncer au trône; **the doctors have given him up** les médecins disent qu'il est perdu **2** *(resign from ▸ job)* quitter; *(▸ position)* démissionner de; **they gave up the restaurant business** ils se sont retirés de la restauration **3** *(hand over ▸ keys)* rendre, remettre; *(▸ prisoner)* livrer; *(▸ responsibility)* se démettre de; **the murderer gave himself up (to the police)** le meurtrier s'est rendu *ou* livré (à la police); **he gave his accomplices up to the police** il a dénoncé *ou* livré ses complices à la police
VI **I g. up** *(in game, project)* je renonce; *(in guessing game)* je donne ma langue au chat; *(you're or it's etc hopeless)* j'abandonne; **we can't g. up now!** on ne va pas laisser tomber maintenant!

▸**give up on** VT INSEP **to g. up on sb** *(stop waiting for)* renoncer à attendre qn; *(stop expecting something from)* ne plus rien attendre de qn; **even his mother had given up on him** même sa mère avait perdu tout espoir à son sujet

give-and-take N *(compromise)* concessions *fpl* (mutuelles); **in a relationship there has to be some g.** pour fonder une relation, il faut que chacun fasse des concessions *ou* que chacun y mette du sien

giveaway ['gɪvəweɪ] N **1** *(free gift)* cadeau *m*; *Com* prime *f*, cadeau *m* publicitaire **2** *(revelation)* révélation *f* (involontaire); **her guilty expression was a dead g.** son air coupable l'a trahie; **the fact that he knew her name was a g.** le fait qu'il sache son nom était révélateur *ou* en disait long
ADJ **1** *(free)* gratuit; *(price)* dérisoire **2** *Fam (revealing)* révélateur␣

given ['gɪvən] *pp of* **give**
ADJ **1** *(specified)* donné; *(precise)* déterminé; **at a g. moment** à un moment donné; **at any g. time** à tout moment **2** *(prone)* **to be g. to sth** avoir une tendance à qch; **to be g. to doing sth** être enclin à faire qch; **he's g. to attacks of depression** il a des tendances dépressives; **I'm not g. to telling lies** je n'ai pas l'habitude de mentir **3** *(on official statement)* **g. in Melbourne on the sixth day of March** fait à Melbourne le six mars
PREP **1** *(considering)* étant donné; **g. her age** étant donné son âge **2** *Math* soit; **g. the rectangle ABCD** soit le rectangle ABCD **3** *(idioms)* **g. the chance** *or* **opportunity** si l'occasion se présentait; **she could be a good teacher, g. the opportunity** elle ferait un bon professeur si l'occasion se présentait
N *(sure fact)* fait *m*, acquis *m*, certitude *f*
• **given that** CONJ étant donné que + *indicative*
▸▸ *Am* ***given name*** prénom *m*

giver ['gɪvə(r)] N *(of blood, organ)* donneur(euse) *m,f*; *(of money)* donateur(trice) *m,f*

giving ['gɪvɪŋ] ADJ *(person)* généreux; **of a g. nature** d'une nature généreuse

gizmo ['gɪzməʊ] *(pl* **gizmos***)* N *Am* gadget *m*, truc *m*

gizzard ['gɪzəd] N gésier *m*; *Fig* **it sticks in my g.** ça me reste en travers de la gorge

glacé ['glæseɪ] ADJ **1** *(cherries)* glacé, confit **2** *(leather, silk)* glacé **3** *Am (frozen)* glacé, gelé
▸▸ ***glacé icing*** glaçage *m (d'un gâteau)*

glacial ['gleɪsɪəl] ADJ **1** *(weather, wind)* glacial **2** *(manner, atmosphere)* glacial **3** *Chem* cristallisé, en cristaux
▸▸ ***glacial period*** période *f* glaciaire

glaciation [ˌgleɪsɪ'eɪʃən] N glaciation *f*

glacier ['glæsɪə(r), *Am* 'gleɪʃər] N glacier *m*
▸▸ ***glacier climbing*** glaciérisme *m*

glad [glæd] ADJ **1** *(person)* heureux, content; **(I'm) g. you came** (je suis) heureux *ou* bien content que tu sois venu; **I'm g. you like him** je suis content que vous l'aimiez; **I'm feeling a lot better today – oh, I am g.!** je me sens beaucoup mieux aujourd'hui – j'en suis ravi!; **he's decided not to go – I'm g. about that** il a décidé de ne pas partir – tant mieux; **I was g. to hear the news** j'étais ravi d'apprendre la nouvelle; **I'd be only too g. to help** je ne demanderais pas mieux que d'aider; **could you do me a favour? – I'd be g. to** pourriez-vous me rendre service? – avec plaisir *ou* volontiers; **(I'm) g. to meet you!** enchanté!; **they were g. of the money** cet argent tombait à point nommé *ou* à pic; **we were g. of the opportunity to meet her** nous avons été heureux de pouvoir faire sa connaissance; **I was g. of your help** votre aide a été la bienvenue **2** *Literary (news, occasion)* joyeux, heureux; *(laughter)* de bonheur; *(shout)* joyeux; **it's a g. day for all of us** c'est un jour de fête pour nous tous **3** *Fam (idioms)* **to give sb the g. eye** faire les yeux doux à qn, faire de l'œil à qn; **to give sb the g. hand** serrer la main de qn avec de grands sourires *(souvent dans un but intéressé)*
▸▸ *Fam* ***glad rags*** vêtements *mpl* chics␣; **to put on one's g. rags** se mettre sur son trente et un, se saper

gladden ['glædən] VT *(person)* rendre heureux, réjouir; **it gladdens my heart to see them** cela me réjouit le cœur de les voir

glade [gleɪd] N *Literary* clairière *f*

glad-hand VT *Fam* **to g. sb** serrer la main de qn avec de grands sourires␣ *(souvent dans un but intéressé)*

gladiator ['glædɪeɪtə(r)] N gladiateur *m*

gladiatorial [ˌglædɪə'tɔːrɪəl] ADJ de gladiateurs; *Fig* **g. politics** = politique qui fait de la confrontation son moyen d'action

gladiolus [ˌglædɪ'əʊləs] *(pl* **gladioli** [-laɪ] *or* **gladioluses***)* N glaïeul *m*

gladly ['glædlɪ] ADV avec plaisir, avec joie, de bon cœur

gladness ['glædnɪs] N contentement *m*, joie *f*

Gladstone bag ['glædstən-] N = sacoche de voyage en cuir

glam [glæm] ADJ *Br Fam* glam *(inv)*, glamour *(inv)*
▸▸ ***glam rock*** glam rock *m*

glamor *Am* = **glamour**

glamorize, -ise ['glæməraɪz] VT idéaliser, montrer *ou* présenter sous un jour séduisant; **the film glamorizes peasant life** le film idéalise la vie des paysans; **to g. war** présenter la guerre sous un jour attrayant; **a TV programme that glamorizes violence** une émission de télé qui rend la violence attrayante; **an advertising campaign that seeks to g. smoking** une campagne publicitaire qui cherche à redorer l'image des fumeurs

glamorous ['glæmərəs] ADJ **1** *(alluring ▸ person)* séduisant, éblouissant; **a g. actress** une actrice éblouissante *ou* resplendissante; **a g. grandmother** une grand-mère sophistiquée **2** *(exciting, ▸ lifestyle)* brillant; *(▸ career)* brillant, prestigieux; *(▸ show)* splendide; *(▸ job, team)* prestigieux; *(▸ place)* chic; **working in the film industry is not always g.** il n'y a pas que des métiers de prestige dans le cinéma

glamour, *Am* **glamor** ['glæmə(r)] N **1** *(allure ▸ of person)* charme *m*, fascination *f*; *(▸ of appearance, dress)* élégance *f*, chic *m* **2** *(excitement ▸ of lifestyle, show)* éclat *m*, prestige *m*; **the novel captures all the g. of London in the 1920s** le roman dépeint tout l'éclat du Londres des années 20; **there isn't much g. in my job** mon travail n'a rien de bien excitant *ou* passionnant
COMP de charme
▸▸ *Fam* ***glamour boy*** beau gosse *m*; *Fam* ***glamour girl*** pin-up␣ *f inv*; *(model)* mannequin␣ *m*; *Fam* ***glamour puss*** pin-up␣ *f inv*

glance [glɑːns] VI **1** *(look)* **to g. at sb/sth** jeter un coup d'œil (rapide) à qn/sur qch **2** *(read quickly)* **she glanced through** *or* **over the letter** elle parcourut rapidement la lettre; **to g. through a book** feuilleter un livre **3** *(look in given direction)* **he glanced back** *or* **behind** il a jeté un coup d'œil en arrière; **he glanced up briefly when I came in** il a brièvement levé la tête quand je suis entré; **she opened the door and glanced round the room** elle ouvrit la porte et jeta un coup d'œil autour de la pièce; **they glanced towards the door** leurs regards se sont tournés vers la porte
N *(look)* coup *m* d'œil, regard *m*; **to have** *or* **to take a g. at sb/sth** jeter un coup d'œil à qn/sur qch; **at first g.** au premier coup d'œil, à première vue; **I could tell** *or* **see at a g.** je m'en suis aperçu tout de suite; **one g. was enough** il m'a suffi d'un regard; **I didn't give it a second g.** je n'y ai guère prêté attention; **she walked away without a backward g.** elle est partie sans se retourner; **to give sb a sidelong g.** lancer un regard oblique à qn

▸**glance off** VI *(arrow, bullet)* ricocher, faire ricochet; *(sword, spear)* être dévié, ricocher; **the arrow hit a tree and glanced off** la flèche a ricoché sur un arbre
VT INSEP **to g. off sth** *(of arrow, bullet)* ricocher sur qch; *(of sword, spear)* dévier sur qch

glancing ['glɑːnsɪŋ] ADJ *(blow)* **he struck me a g. blow** il m'asséna un coup oblique

gland [glænd] N **1** *Physiol* glande *f* **2** *Tech* presse-étoupe *m inv*

glanders ['glændəz] N *(UNCOUNT) Vet* morve *f*

glandes ['glændiːz] *pl of* **glans**

glandular ['glændjʊlə(r)] ADJ *Anat* glandulaire, glanduleux
▸▸ *Br Med* ***glandular fever*** *(UNCOUNT)* mononucléose *f* (infectieuse)

glans [glænz] *(pl* **glandes** ['glændiːz]*)* N *Anat* gland *m*
▸▸ ***glans penis*** gland *m*

glare [gleə(r)] VI **1** *(sun, light)* briller d'un éclat éblouissant; **the sun glared down from the cloud**

less sky il faisait un soleil éclatant *ou* éblouissant dans un ciel sans nuages **2** *(person)* **to g. at sb** regarder qn avec colère; **they glared at each other** ils échangèrent un regard menaçant; **he glared angrily at me** il m'a lancé un regard furieux
VT to g. hatred/defiance at sb lancer un regard plein de haine/de défi à qn
N 1 *(light)* lumière *f* éblouissante *ou* aveuglante; *(of sun)* éclat *m*; **he stood in the g. of the headlights** il était pris dans la lumière (aveuglante) des phares **2** *Fig* **politicians lead their lives in the (full) g. of publicity** la vie des hommes politiques est toujours sous les feux des projecteurs **3** *(of anger)* regard *m* furieux; *(of contempt)* regard *m* méprisant
▸▸ *Comput* ***glare filter*** filtre *m* antireflet; *Comput* ***glare screen*** écran *m* antireflet

glaring ['gleərɪŋ] **ADJ 1** *(dazzling ▸ light)* éblouissant, éclatant; *(▸ car headlights)* éblouissant; *(▸ sun)* aveuglant
2 *(bright ▸ colour)* vif; *Pej* criard, voyant
3 *(angry)* furieux
4 *(obvious ▸ error)* qui saute aux yeux, qui crève les yeux, patent; *(▸ injustice, lie, omission)* flagrant, criant

glaringly ['gleərɪŋlɪ] **ADV it's g. obvious** ça crève les yeux

glasnost ['glæznɒst] **N** glasnost *f*

glass [glɑːs] **N 1** *(substance)* verre *m*; **made of g.** en verre; **a pane of g.** un carreau, une vitre; **these plants are grown under g.** ces plantes sont cultivées en serre; *Prov* **people who live in g. houses shouldn't throw stones** = il faut être sans défauts pour critiquer autrui
2 *(single piece ▸ of window)* vitre *f*, carreau *m*; *(▸ of car)* glace *f*, vitre *f*; *(▸ of watch, lamp)* verre *m*
3 *(vessel, contents)* verre *m*; **a g. of water/beer** un verre d'eau/de bière; **a g. of champagne** une coupe de champagne; **to sell wine by the g.** vendre le vin au verre; **to raise one's g. to sb** *(in toast)* lever son verre à qn
4 *(in shop, museum)* vitrine *f*; **displayed under g.** exposé en vitrine
5 *(glassware)* verrerie *f*
6 *(telescope)* longue-vue *f*
7 *(mirror)* **(looking) g.** glace *f*, miroir *m*
8 *Opt (lens)* lentille *f*
9 *(barometer)* baromètre *m*; **the g. is falling** le baromètre baisse
COMP *(ornament, bottle)* en verre; *(door)* vitré; *(industry)* du verre
VT *(bookcase, porch)* vitrer; *(photograph)* mettre sous verre
• **glasses NPL 1** *(spectacles)* lunettes *fpl*; **to wear glasses** porter des lunettes **2** *(binoculars)* jumelles *fpl*
▸▸ ***glass case*** *(for display)* vitrine *f*; ***glasses case*** *(for spectacles)* étui *m* à lunettes; ***glass ceiling*** = plafond de verre qui désigne métaphoriquement l'ensemble des facteurs qui empêchent les femmes de parvenir aux postes les plus élevés dans le monde professionnel; ***glass cutting*** taille *f* du verre; ***glass eye*** œil *m* de verre; ***glass factory*** verrerie *f (usine)*; *Br* ***glass fibre***, *Am* ***glass fiber*** **N** fibre *f* de verre **ADJ** en fibre de verre; ***glass manufacturer*** verrier *m*; ***glass roof*** *(of station)* verrière *f*; ***glass wool*** laine *f* de verre

▸ **glass in VT SEP** *(bookcase, porch)* vitrer; *(photograph)* mettre sous verre

glassblower ['glɑːsbləʊə(r)] **N** souffleur *m (de verre)*

glassblowing ['glɑːsbləʊɪŋ] **N** soufflage *m (du verre)*

glassful ['glɑːsfʊl] **N** (plein) verre *m*

glasshouse ['glɑːshaʊs, *pl* -haʊzɪz] **N 1** *Br (greenhouse)* serre *f* **2** *Am (factory)* verrerie *f (usine)* **3** *Br Fam Mil slang (prison)* prison *f* militaire□, trou *m*

glasspaper ['glɑːspeɪpə(r)] **N** *Br* papier *m* de verre
VT poncer au papier de verre

glassware ['glɑːsweə(r)] **N** *(glass objects)* verrerie *f*; *(tumblers)* verrerie *f*, gobeleterie *f*

glassworks ['glɑːswɜːks] *(pl* **inv)** **N** verrerie *f (usine)*

glassy ['glɑːsɪ] *(compar* **glassier**, *superl* **glassiest)** **ADJ 1** *(eye, expression)* vitreux, terne **2** *(smooth ▸ surface)* uni, lisse; **a g. sea** une mer d'huile

Glastonbury ['glæstənbərɪ] **N**

> **THE GLASTONBURY FESTIVAL**
>
> Le festival de musique de Glastonbury a débuté en 1970 à l'initiative d'un fermier du coin du nom de Michael Eavis. Le festival a désormais lieu au moins une fois tous les deux ans, toujours dans le même champ, mais il attire aujourd'hui des centaines de milliers de personnes de tous milieux. Les gens viennent camper pour le week-end et assistent à toutes sortes de concerts rock; les plus grands noms partagent l'affiche avec des artistes beaucoup moins connus. Situé dans le sud-ouest de l'Angleterre, non loin de Stonehenge, Glastonbury est un lieu associé à la mythologie, au druidisme et au paganisme. C'est pourquoi ce festival attire de nombreux membres des communautés hippie et New Age.

Glaswegian [glæz'wiːdʒən] **N 1** *(inhabitant)* habitant(e) *m,f* de Glasgow; *(native)* originaire *mf* de Glasgow **2** *(dialect)* dialecte *m* de Glasgow
ADJ de Glasgow

glaucoma [glɔː'kəʊmə] **N** *(UNCOUNT) Med* glaucome *m*; **to have g.** avoir un glaucome

glaucous ['glɔːkəs] **ADJ** *Literary* glauque

glaze [gleɪz] **VT 1** *(floor, tiles)* vitrifier; *(pottery, china)* vernisser; *(leather, silk)* glacer
2 *(photo, painting)* glacer
3 *Culin* glacer
4 *(window)* vitrer
N 1 *(on pottery)* vernis *m*; *(on floor, tiles)* vernis *m*, enduit *m* vitrifié; *(on cotton, silk)* glacé *m*
2 *(on painting, paper, photo)* glacé *m*, glacis *m*
3 *Culin* glace *f*
4 *Am (ice)* verglas *m*
▸▸ *Br* ***glaze ice*** verglas *m*

▸ **glaze over VI his eyes glazed over** ses yeux sont devenus vitreux

glazed [gleɪzd] **ADJ 1** *(floor, tiles)* vitrifié; *(pottery)* vernissé, émaillé; *(leather, silk)* glacé
2 *(photo, painting)* glacé
3 *Culin* glacé
4 *(window)* vitré; *(picture)* sous verre
5 *(eyes)* vitreux, terne; **there was a g. look in her eyes** elle avait le regard vitreux *ou* absent

glazier ['gleɪzɪə(r)] **N** vitrier *m*

glazing ['gleɪzɪŋ] **N 1** *(of pottery)* vernissage *m*; *(of floor, tiles)* vitrification *f*; *(of leather, silk)* glaçage *m*
2 *Culin (process)* glaçage *m*; *(substance)* glace *f*
3 *(fitting of windows)* pose *f* des vitres
4 *(UNCOUNT) (windows)* vitrerie *f*

GLBT [ˌdʒiːel,biː'tiː] **ADJ** *(abbr* **gay, lesbian, bisexual and transgender)** allosexuel, = gay, lesbien, bisexuel et transsexuel

GLC [ˌdʒiːel'siː] **N** *Formerly (abbr* **Greater London Council)** = ancien organe administratif du grand Londres

gleam [gliːm] **VI 1** *(metal, polished surface)* luire, reluire; *(stronger)* briller; *(cat's eyes)* luire; *(water)* miroiter **2** *Fig* **her eyes gleamed with anticipation/mischief** ses yeux brillaient d'espoir/de malice
N 1 *(on surface)* lueur *f*, miroitement *m* **2** *Fig* lueur *f*; **a g. of hope** une lueur d'espoir; **she had a strange g. in her eye** il y avait une lueur étrange dans son regard; *Hum* **when you were just a g. in your father's eye** bien avant ta naissance

gleaming ['gliːmɪŋ] **ADJ** *(metal)* luisant, brillant; *(furniture)* reluisant; *(kitchen)* étincelant

glean [gliːn] **VT 1** *(collect ▸ information, news)* glaner, grappiller; **I couldn't g. much from the brochure** je n'ai pas pu tirer grand-chose de la brochure **2** *Agr* glaner

gleaner ['gliːnə(r)] **N** glaneur(euse) *m,f*

gleanings ['gliːnɪŋz] **NPL 1** *(information)* bribes *fpl* de renseignements (glanées çà et là) **2** *Agr* glanure *f*, glanures *fpl*

glebe [gliːb] **N 1** *Literary* glèbe *f*, terre *f* **2** *Br Rel* = terres faisant partie d'un bénéfice ecclésiastique

glee [gliː] **N 1** *(joy)* joie *f*, allégresse *f*; *(malicious pleasure)* jubilation *f*; **to jump up and down with g.** sauter de joie; **with great g.** avec allégresse; **she announced it with some g.** elle l'a annoncé avec un malin plaisir **2** *Mus* chant *m* a cappella *(à plusieurs voix)*
▸▸ *Am* ***glee club*** chorale *f*

gleeful ['gliːfʊl] **ADJ** joyeux, radieux; *(maliciously)* plein d'une joie malicieuse

gleefully ['gliːfʊlɪ] **ADV** joyeusement, avec allégresse *ou* joie; *(maliciously)* avec une joie malicieuse

glen [glen] **N** vallon *m*, = vallée étroite et encaissée en Écosse ou en Irlande

glib [glɪb] *(compar* **glibber**, *superl* **glibbest)** **ADJ** *(answer, excuse)* (trop) facile, désinvolte; *(lie)* éhonté, désinvolte; **he's rather too g.** il parle trop facilement, il est trop volubile; **he has a g. tongue** il a la langue bien pendue

glibly ['glɪblɪ] **ADV** *(talk, argue, reply)* avec aisance, facilement; *(lie)* avec désinvolture, sans sourciller

glibness ['glɪbnɪs] **N 1** *(of person)* facilité *f* de parole **2** *(of argument, excuse)* facilité *f*, désinvolture *f*

glide [glaɪd] **VI 1** *(gen)* glisser; *(person)* **to g. in/out** *(noiselessly)* entrer/sortir sans bruit; *(gracefully)* entrer/sortir avec grâce; *(stealthily)* entrer/sortir furtivement; **the swans glided across the lake** les cygnes traversaient le lac avec grâce *ou* glissaient sur le lac; **the clouds glided across the sky** les nuages passaient dans le ciel; **the actress glided majestically into the room** la comédienne entra dans la salle d'un pas majestueux
2 *Fig (time, weeks)* **to g. by** s'écouler
3 *Aviat* planer; *(in glider)* faire du vol à voile; **to go gliding** faire du vol à voile
4 *(in skating, skiing)* glisser
VT (faire) glisser
N 1 *(gen)* glissement *m*
2 *(in dance)* glissade *f*
3 *Mus* port *m* de voix; *(for trombone)* piston *m*
4 *(of glider)* vol *m* plané; *(of aircraft)* descente *f* en (vol) plané
5 *Ling (in diphthong)* glissement *m*; *(between two vowels)* semi-voyelle *f* de transition
▸▸ *Aviat* ***glide path, glide slope*** ligne *f* d'approche

glider ['glaɪdə(r)] **N 1** *Aviat* planeur *m* **2** *Am (swing)* balancelle *f*
▸▸ ***glider pilot*** pilote *m* de planeur

gliding ['glaɪdɪŋ] **N** *(sport)* vol *m* à voile
▸▸ ***gliding club*** club *m* de vol à voile

glimmer ['glɪmə(r)] **VI** *(moonlight, candle)* jeter une faible lueur, luire faiblement; *(water)* miroiter
N 1 *(of light)* (faible) lueur *f*; *(of water)* miroitement *m* **2** *Fig* **a g. of hope/interest** une (faible) lueur d'espoir/d'intérêt; **not a g. of interest** pas le moindre intérêt

glimmering ['glɪmərɪŋ] **N** *(of light)* (faible) lueur *f*; *(of water)* miroitement *m*
ADJ *(water)* miroitant; **a g. light** une faible lueur

glimpse [glɪmps] **VT** entrevoir, entrapercevoir
N to catch a g. of sth entrevoir *ou* entrapercevoir qch; **she had only caught a g. of her assailant** elle n'avait fait qu'entrevoir son assaillant; **a g. of the future** un aperçu de ce que sera le futur

glint [glɪnt] **VI 1** *(knife)* étinceler, miroiter; *(water)* miroiter; **the blade glinted in the sunlight** la lame miroita au soleil **2** *Fig (eyes)* étinceler
N 1 *(of light ▸ flash)* éclair *m*; *(▸ continuous)* scintillement *m*; *(of knife)* reflet *m* **2** *Fig* **"perhaps not," he said, with a g. in his eye** "peut-être que non", dit-il, une lueur dans le regard

glissando [glɪ'sændəʊ] *(pl* **glissandos** *or* **glissandi** [-diː]) **N** *Mus* glissando *m*

glisten ['glɪsən] **VI** luire, miroiter; **his eyes glistened with tears** des larmes brillaient dans ses yeux; **his forehead glistened with sweat** la sueur perlait sur son front

glistening ['glɪsənɪŋ] **ADJ** luisant

glitch [glɪtʃ] **N** *Fam (in plan)* pépin *m*; *(in machine)* = signal indiquant une baisse de tension du courant

glitter ['glɪtə(r)] **VI 1** *(bright object)* étinceler, scintiller, miroiter; *(jewel)* chatoyer, étinceler; *(metal)* reluire; **her eyes glittered with excitement** ses yeux brillaient *ou* scintillaient de joie; *Prov* **all that glitters is not gold** tout ce qui brille n'est pas or **2** *(eyes)* briller

N 1 *(of object)* scintillement *m* **2** *Fig (of occasion)* éclat *m*, splendeur *f* **3** *(UNCOUNT) (decoration, make-up)* paillettes *fpl*

glitterati [,glɪtə'rɑːtiː] **NPL** *Fam* **the g.** le beau monde

glittering ['glɪtərɪŋ] **ADJ 1** *(jewels)* scintillant, étincelant, brillant **2** *(glamorous)* éclatant, resplendissant; **the g. world of showbusiness** le monde fascinant du show-business

glitz [glɪts] **N** *Fam* tape-à-l'œil *m inv*, clinquant◻ *m*; **Hollywood g.** le clinquant d'Hollywood

glitzy ['glɪtsɪ] *(compar* **glitzier,** *superl* **glitziest)** **ADJ** *Fam* tape-à-l'œil *(inv)*; **the premiere was one of the year's glitziest occasions** la première fut l'un des événements les plus tape-à-l'œil de l'année

gloaming ['gləʊmɪŋ] **N** *Scot or Literary* crépuscule *m*; **in the g.** au crépuscule

gloat [gləʊt] **VI** exulter, se délecter, jubiler; **don't g.** ne te réjouis pas; **to g. over sth** se réjouir de qch; **he gloated over his success** son succès l'enivrait *ou* le faisait jubiler; **she gloated over the downfall of her enemy** elle se réjouissait de la chute de son ennemi

N exultation *f*, jubilation *f*; **to have a g.** exulter

gloating ['gləʊtɪŋ] **ADJ** *(smile, look)* triomphant

glob [glɒb] **N** globule *m*, (petite) boule *f*; **a g. of spittle** un crachat

global ['gləʊbəl] **ADJ 1** *(worldwide)* mondial, planétaire; **on a g. scale** à l'échelle mondiale **2** *(overall ▸ system, view)* global

▸▸ ***global economy*** économie *f* mondiale; *Com* ***global market, global marketplace*** marché *m* global *ou* international; *Mktg* ***global player*** acteur *m* international; *Comput* ***global search and replace*** recherche *f* et remplacement *m* global; ***global village*** village *m* planétaire; ***global warming*** réchauffement *m* planétaire *ou* de la planète

globalism ['gləʊbəlɪzəm] **N** mondialisme *m*

globalization [,gləʊbəlaɪ'zeɪʃən] **N 1** *(making worldwide)* mondialisation *f* **2** *(generalization)* globalisation *f*

globalize, -ise ['gləʊbəlaɪz] **VT 1** *(make worldwide)* rendre mondial, mondialiser; **a globalized conflict** un conflit mondial **2** *(generalize)* globaliser

globally ['gləʊbəlɪ] **ADV 1** *(worldwide)* mondialement, à l'échelle planétaire; **the problem of over-population must be dealt with g.** on doit résoudre le problème de la surpopulation à l'échelle planétaire **2** *(generally)* globalement

globe [gləʊb] **N 1** *Geog* globe *m* (terrestre), terre *f*; **all over the g.** *(surface)* sur toute la surface du globe; *(in all parts)* dans le monde entier **2** *(with map)* globe *m*, mappemonde *f* **3** *(spherical object)* globe *m*, sphère *f*; *(as lampshade)* globe *m*; *(as goldfish bowl)* bocal *m*; *(of eye)* globe *m*

• globes **NPL** *Fam (breasts)* nichons *mpl*

▸▸ ***globe artichoke*** artichaut *m*; ***globe lightning*** éclair *m* en boule

globetrotter ['gləʊbtrɒtə(r)] **N** globe-trotter *mf*

globetrotting ['gləʊbtrɒtɪŋ] **N** *(UNCOUNT)* voyages *mpl* aux quatre coins du monde

ADJ qui voyage beaucoup

globular ['glɒbjʊlə(r)] **ADJ** *(globe-shaped)* globulaire; *(composed of globules)* globuleux

globule ['glɒbjuːl] **N** *(of fat)* globule *m*; *(of wax, molten metal)* gouttelette *f*

globulin ['glɒbjʊlɪn] **N** globuline *f*

glockenspiel ['glɒkənʃpiːl] **N** glockenspiel *m*

glomerulus [glɒ'merʊləs] *(pl* **glomeruli** [-laɪ]) **N** *Anat* glomérule *m*

gloom [gluːm] **N** *(UNCOUNT)* **1** *(darkness)* obscurité *f*, ténèbres *fpl* **2** *(despondency)* tristesse *f*, mélancolie *f*; **the news filled me with g.** la nouvelle me plongea dans la consternation; **the announcement cast a g. over the meeting** l'annonce jeta un froid sur la réunion; **the news is all doom and g. these days** les nouvelles sont des plus sombres ces temps-ci

VI *(person)* être mélancolique, broyer du noir

gloomily ['gluːmɪlɪ] **ADV** sombrement, mélancoliquement, tristement; **he looked around him g.** il regarda autour de lui d'un air sombre *ou* morose

gloominess ['gluːmɪnɪs] **N 1** *(darkness)* obscurité *f*, ténèbres *fpl*; **the g. of the weather** ce temps maussade **2** *(despondency)* tristesse *f*, mélancolie *f*

gloomy ['gluːmɪ] *(compar* **gloomier,** *superl* **gloomiest)** **ADJ 1** *(person ▸ depressed)* triste, mélancolique; *(▸ morose)* sombre, lugubre; **don't look so g.** ne prends pas cet air malheureux

2 *(pessimistic ▸ prediction, outlook)* sombre; *(▸ news)* déprimant; **she always takes a g. view of things** elle voit toujours tout en noir; **g. thoughts** de noires pensées *fpl*; **the future looks g.** l'avenir se présente sous des couleurs sombres; **he paints a g. view of life** sa vision de la vie est assez noire

3 *(sky)* obscur, sombre; *(weather)* morne, triste; *(room)* lugubre; **to become g.** s'assombrir

4 *(place, landscape)* morne, lugubre

glorification [,glɔːrɪfɪ'keɪʃən] **N 1** *Rel* glorification *f* **2** *(of hero, writer)* exaltation *f* **3** *(of war, violence)* glorification *f*

glorified ['glɔːrɪfaɪd] **ADJ** **he's called an engineer but he's really just a g. mechanic** on a beau l'appeler ingénieur, il n'est que mécanicien, il n'a d'ingénieur que le nom, en réalité c'est un mécanicien; **it's just a g. motor scooter** ce n'est qu'un scooter amélioré

glorify ['glɔːrɪfaɪ] *(pt & pp* **glorified)** **VT 1** *Rel* glorifier, rendre gloire à **2** *(praise ▸ hero, writer)* exalter **3** *(war, violence)* glorifier, faire l'apologie de; **the film glorifies war** le film glorifie la guerre *ou* fait l'apologie de la guerre

glorious ['glɔːrɪəs] **ADJ 1** *(illustrious ▸ reign, saint, victory)* glorieux; *(▸ hero)* glorieux, illustre; *(▸ deed)* glorieux, éclatant **2** *(splendid, beautiful)* resplendissant, radieux; *(weather, day)* splendide, superbe, magnifique; *(colours)* superbe; **g. in her youth and beauty** resplendissante de jeunesse et de beauté **3** *(excellent)* magnifique, splendide; *(holiday, party)* merveilleux, sensationnel; **what g. weather!** quel temps superbe!

▸▸ *Br Hist* ***the Glorious Revolution*** la Glorieuse Révolution; ***the Glorious Twelfth*** *(celebration)* = célébration par les unionistes d'Irlande du Nord de la victoire des protestants sur les catholiques à la Boyne, le 12 juillet 1690; *Hunt* = date d'ouverture de la chasse à la grouse (le 12 août)

gloriously ['glɔːrɪəslɪ] **ADV** glorieusement

glory ['glɔːrɪ] *(pl* **glories,** *pt & pp* **gloried)** **N 1** *(honour, fame)* gloire *f*; *(magnificence)* magnificence *f*, éclat *m*; **to be covered in g.** être couvert de gloire; **the athletes get all the g.** ce sont les athlètes qui remportent toute la gloire; **a garden at the height of its g.** un jardin au plus beau moment; **to have one's hour of g.** avoir son heure de gloire

2 *(splendour)* gloire *f*, splendeur *f*; **the glories of the Irish countryside** les splendeurs de la campagne irlandaise; **in all her g.** dans toute sa splendeur *ou* gloire

3 *(masterpiece)* gloire *f*, joyau *m*; **the palace is one of the greatest glories of the age** le palais est un des joyaux *ou* des chefs-d'œuvre de cette époque

4 *Rel* **Christ in g.** le Christ en majesté *ou* en gloire; **to the greater g. of God** pour la plus grande gloire de Dieu; *Fam* **g. be!** mon Dieu!

5 *(halo ▸ of saint)* gloire *f*

▸▸ ***glory hole*** *Naut (locker)* petit placard *m*; *(storeroom)* soute *f*; *Br Fam (cupboard)* débarras◻ *m*; *(untidy place)* capharnaüm◻ *m*

▸ glory in **VT INSEP** **to g. in sth/doing sth** se glorifier de *ou* s'enorgueillir de qch/de faire qch; **she was glorying in her new-found freedom** elle jouissait de *ou* elle savourait sa nouvelle liberté; **he glories in the title of King of Hollywood** il se donne le titre ronflant de roi d'Hollywood

Glos *(written abbr* **Gloucestershire)** Gloucestershire *m*

gloss [glɒs] **N 1** *(sheen)* lustre *m*, brillant *m*, éclat *m*; *(on paper, photo)* glacé *m*, brillant *m*; *(on furniture)* vernis *m*

2 *(appearance)* apparence *f*, vernis *m*; **a g. of politeness/respectability** un vernis de politesse/de respectabilité

3 *(charm)* charme *m*, attrait *m*; **to take the g. off sth** gâcher *ou* gâter qch

4 *(annotation, paraphrase)* glose *f*, commentaire *m*

5 *(paint)* peinture *f* brillante

VT 1 *(paper)* satiner, glacer; *(metal)* faire briller, lustrer **2** *(paint)* laquer **3** *(explain, paraphrase)* gloser

▸▸ ***gloss finish*** *(painted)* brillant *m*; *Phot* glaçage *m*; ***gloss paint*** peinture *f* brillante

▸ gloss over **VT INSEP 1** *(minimize ▸ failure, shortcomings, mistake)* glisser sur, passer sur, atténuer **2** *(hide ▸ truth, facts)* dissimuler, passer sous silence

glossary ['glɒsərɪ] *(pl* **glossaries)** **N** glossaire *m*

glossiness ['glɒsɪnɪs] **N** lustre *m*, brillant *m*, éclat *m*

glossy ['glɒsɪ] *(compar* **glossier,** *superl* **glossiest,** *pl* **glossies)** **ADJ 1** *(shiny ▸ fur)* lustré, luisant; *(▸ hair)* brillant; *(▸ leather, satin)* lustré, luisant, glacé; *(▸ leaves)* luisant; *(surface ▸ polished)* brillant, poli; *(▸ painted)* brillant, laqué **2** *Fig (display, presentation, spectacle)* brillant, scintillant; *Pej* clinquant **3** *(photo)* glacé, sur papier glacé; *(paper)* glacé

N *Fam Journ* magazine◻ *m (sur papier glacé)*, *(women's magazine)* magazine *m* féminin de luxe◻; **the glossies** la presse féminine de luxe

▸▸ ***glossy magazine*** magazine *m (sur papier glacé)*

glottal ['glɒtəl] **ADJ 1** *Anat* glottique **2** *Ling* glottal

▸▸ *Ling* ***glottal stop*** coup *m* de glotte

glottis ['glɒtɪs] *(pl* **glottises** *or* **glottides** [-ɪdiːz]) **N** *Anat* glotte *f*

glove [glʌv] **N** gant *m*; **to put on one's gloves** mettre ses gants, se ganter; **it fits like a g.** ça me/te/lui/*etc* va comme un gant; **the gloves are off** plus la peine de prendre des gants

VT ganter

▸▸ *Aut* ***glove compartment*** boîte *f* à gants; ***glove factory*** ganterie *f (usine)*; ***glove maker*** gantier (ère) *m,f*; *Br* ***glove puppet*** marionnette *f (à gaine)*

glover ['glʌvə(r)] **N** gantier(ère) *m,f*

glow [gləʊ] **VI 1** *(embers, heated metal)* rougeoyer; *(sky, sunset)* s'embraser, flamboyer; la cigarette rougeoyait dans l'obscurité **2** *(person)* rayonner; *(eyes)* briller, flamboyer; **to g. with health** éclater *ou* rayonner de santé; **to g. with pleasure/pride** rayonner de plaisir/de fierté; **to be glowing with health** être rayonnant de santé; **his cheeks were glowing** il avait les joues en feu

N 1 *(of fire, embers)* rougeoiement *m*; *(of heated metal)* lueur *f*; *(of sky, sunset)* embrasement *m*, flamboiement *m*; *(of sun)* feux *mpl*; *(of colours, jewel)* éclat *m*; **it gives off a blue g.** cela émet une lumière bleue **2** *(of complexion)* **to have a healthy g. in one's cheeks** avoir les joues bien rouges; **g. of health** bonne mine *f*; **a g. of pleasure** une rougeur de plaisir **3** *Fig (warm feeling)* **it gave him a g. of pride** cela le faisait rayonner d'orgueil; **he felt a warm g. spread over him as the whisky went down** il sentit une sensation de chaleur dans tout le corps après avoir bu le whisky; **it gives you a warm g.** *(news, scene etc)* ça vous fait chaud au cœur

glower ['glaʊə(r)] **VI** avoir l'air furieux, lancer des regards furieux; **to g. at sb** *(angrily)* lancer à qn un regard noir; *(threateningly)* jeter à qn un regard menaçant; **she sat glowering in a corner** elle restait assise dans un coin, l'air furieux

glowering ['glaʊərɪŋ] **ADJ** *(expression)* mauvais, méchant, hostile; *(person)* à l'air mauvais *ou* méchant

glowing ['gləʊɪŋ] **ADJ 1** *(fire, embers)* rougeoyant; *(heated metal)* incandescent; *(sky, sunset)* radieux, flamboyant **2** *(complexion)* éclatant; *(eyes)* brillant, flamboyant; **g. with health** rayonnant *ou* florissant (de santé); **g. with happiness** rayonnant de joie **3** *(laudatory)* élogieux, dithyrambique; **I had read g. reports**

of the play j'avais lu des critiques dithyrambiques de la pièce; **he spoke of you in g. terms** il a chanté tes louanges; **to paint sth in g. colours** présenter qch sous un jour favorable

glow-worm N *Entom* ver *m* luisant

gloxinia [glɒk'sɪnɪə] N *Bot* gloxinia *m*

glucosamine [ˌgluː'kəʊsəmiːn] N *Pharm* glucosamine *f*

glucose ['gluːkəʊs] N glucose *m*
▸▸ ***glucose drink*** boisson *f* au glucose; ***glucose level*** glycémie *f*; ***glucose syrup*** sirop *m* de glucose

glue [gluː] VT **1** *(stick)* coller; **to g. sth to/onto sth** coller qch à/sur qch; **you'll have to g. it (back) together again** il faudra le recoller; **can't you g. it down?** vous ne pouvez pas le faire tenir avec de la colle? **2** *Fig* coller; **with her face glued to the window** le visage collé à la fenêtre; **to be glued to the spot** être *ou* rester cloué sur place; **they were glued to the television** ils étaient rivés à la télévision; **he's always glued to her side** il ne la quitte pas d'un pas *ou* d'une semelle
N colle *f*; *Fam* **he sticks to me like g.** il me suit partout comme un petit chien[a]
▸▸ *Med* ***glue ear*** otite *f* séreuse

gluepot ['gluːpɒt] N pot *m* de colle

glue-sniffer N **to be a g.** inhaler *ou* sniffer (de la colle)

glue-sniffing N inhalation *f* de colle

gluey ['gluːɪ] ADJ collant, gluant

glug [glʌg] *(pt & pp* **glugged**, *cont* **glugging**) *Fam* N **g. (g.)** glouglou *m*
VI faire glouglou

glum [glʌm] *(compar* **glummer**, *superl* **glummest**) ADJ triste, morose; **to be** *or* **to feel g.** avoir le cafard, broyer du noir; **to look g.** avoir l'air triste *ou* sombre; **don't look so g.!** ne fais pas cette tête-là!, ne sois pas si triste!

glumly ['glʌmlɪ] ADV tristement, avec morosité; **he watched them g.** il les regarda d'un œil triste *ou* morose

glumness ['glʌmnɪs] N tristesse *f*, morosité *f*

glut [glʌt] *(pt & pp* **glutted**, *cont* **glutting**) VT **1** *(with food)* **to g. oneself with** *or* **on sth** se gorger *ou* se gaver de qch; *Fig* **to be glutted with television** être saturé de télévision **2** *(market, economy)* encombrer, inonder; **the market is glutted with luxury goods** il y a surabondance d'objets de luxe sur le marché
N *(on market)* encombrement *m*; *(of commodity)* surabondance *f*; **there's a g. of apples this year** il y a surproduction de pommes cette année; **a g. of money** une pléthore de capitaux

glutamine ['gluːtəmiːn] N *Chem* glutamine *f*

gluten ['gluːtən] N gluten *m*

gluten-free ADJ sans gluten

glutes [gluːts] NPL *Fam (gluteal muscles)* muscles *mpl* fessiers[a]

glutinous ['gluːtɪnəs] ADJ glutineux

glutton ['glʌtən] N glouton(onne) *m,f*, goulu(e) *m,f*; *Fig* **to be a g. for punishment** être un peu masochiste; **he's a g. for work** c'est un bourreau *ou* un forcené de travail

gluttonous ['glʌtənəs] ADJ glouton, goulu

gluttonously ['glʌtənəslɪ] ADV gloutonnement, goulûment

gluttony ['glʌtənɪ] N gloutonnerie *f*, goinfrerie *f*

glycaemia, *Am* **glycemia** [glaɪ'siːmɪə] N *Med* glycémie *f*

glycaemic, *Am* **glycemic** [glaɪ'siːmɪk] ADJ glycémique
▸▸ ***glycaemic index*** index *m* glycémique

glycerin ['glɪsərɪn], **glycerine** ['glɪsəriːn] N glycérine *f*

glycerol ['glɪsərɒl] N *Chem* glycérol *m*

glycol ['glaɪkɒl] N glycol *m*

GM [ˌdʒiː'em] ADJ **1** *(abbr* **genetically modified**) génétiquement modifié **2** *(abbr* **grant maintained**) subventionné *(par l'État)*; **a GM school** une école privée subventionnée *(acceptant en échange un droit de regard de l'État sur la gestion de ses affaires)*
▸▸ ***GM food*** aliments *mpl* génétiquement modifiés

G-man N *Am* agent *m* du FBI

GMC [ˌdʒiːem'siː] N **1** *(abbr* **general management committee**) comité *m* de direction **2** *Br (abbr* **General Medical Council**) conseil *m* de l'ordre des médecins

GMO [ˌdʒiːem'əʊ] N *(abbr* **genetically modified organism**) OGM *m*

GMT [ˌdʒiːem'tiː] N *(abbr* **Greenwich Mean Time**) GMT *m*

gnarled [nɑːld] ADJ **1** *(tree, fingers)* noueux **2** *(character)* grincheux, hargneux

gnarly ['nɑːlɪ] ADJ *Am Fam (excellent, awful)* mortel

gnash [næʃ] VT **to g. one's teeth** grincer des dents

gnashing ['næʃɪŋ] N grincement *m*; *Literary or Hum* **there was much weeping and g. of teeth** il y eut moult pleurs et grincements de dents

gnat [næt] N moucheron *m*

gnaw [nɔː] VT ronger; **to g. a bone** *(dog)* ronger un os; *Fig* **gnawed by hunger** tenaillé par la faim; **gnawed by remorse** rongé par le remords
VI **to g. (away) at sth** ronger qch; **to g. through sth** ronger qch jusqu'à le percer; *Fig* **hunger gnawed at him** il était tenaillé par la faim

gnawing ['nɔːɪŋ] ADJ **1** *(pain)* lancinant, tenaillant; *(hunger)* tenaillant; **the g. pains of hunger** les affres *fpl ou* les tiraillements *mpl* de la faim **2** *(anxiety, doubt)* tenaillant, torturant

GNE [ˌdʒiːen'iː] N *Econ (abbr* **gross national expenditure**) DNB *f*

gneiss [naɪs] N *Geol* gneiss *m*

gnome [nəʊm] N *Myth* gnome *m*; **(garden) g.** nain *m* de jardin
▸▸ *Fam Banking* ***the gnomes of Zurich*** les grands banquiers *mpl* suisses[a]

gnomic ['nəʊmɪk] ADJ gnomique

gnosis ['nəʊsɪs] N gnose *f*

gnostic, Gnostic ['nɒstɪk] N gnostique *mf*
ADJ gnostique

gnosticism, Gnosticism ['nɒstɪsɪzəm] N gnosticisme *m*

GNP [ˌdʒiːen'piː] N *Econ (abbr* **gross national product**) PNB *m*
▸▸ ***GNP per capita*** PNB *m* par habitant

gnu [nuː] N *Zool* gnou *m*

go[1] [gəʊ] N *(game)* jeu *m* de go

GO[2] [gəʊ]

VI
- aller **A1–3, 5, 6, E1–3, G1**
- devenir **B2**
- se détériorer **B3**
- commencer **C1**
- marcher **C4**
- se passer **E4**
- s'appliquer **F2**
- contribuer **G3**
- tenir le coup **H3**
- s'en aller **A4**
- être **B1**
- tomber en panne **B3**
- s'user **B3**
- aller (+ infinitif) **C2, 3**
- disparaître **D1, 3**
- s'écouler **E5**
- se vendre **F4**
- aller ensemble **H1**

VT
- faire **1, 2**

N
- coup **1**
- tour **2**
- succès **4**
- essai **1**
- dynamisme **3**

(pl **goes** [gəʊz], *3rd pres sing* **goes** [gəʊz], *pt* **went** [went], *pp* **gone** [gɒn])

VI **A. 1** *(move, travel ▸ person)* aller; *(▸ vehicle)* aller, rouler; **we're going to Paris/Japan/Spain** nous allons à Paris/au Japon/en Espagne; **he went to the office/a friend's house** il est allé au bureau/chez un ami; **I want to go home** je veux rentrer; **we went by car/on foot** nous y sommes allés en voiture/à pied; **there goes the train!** voilà le train (qui passe)!; **the bus goes by way of** *or* **through Dover** le bus passe par Douvres; **does this train go to Glasgow?** ce train va-t-il à Glasgow?; **the truck was going at 150 kilometres an hour** le camion roulait à *ou* faisait du 150 kilomètres (à l')heure; **where do we go from here?** où va-t-on maintenant?; *Fig* qu'est-ce qu'on fait maintenant?; **to go to the doctor** aller voir *ou* aller chez le médecin; **to go to prison** aller en prison; **to go to the toilet** aller aux toilettes; **to go to sb for advice** aller demander conseil à qn; **let the children go first** laissez les enfants passer devant, laissez passer les enfants d'abord; **I'll go next** c'est à moi après; *Mil* **who goes there?** qui va là?, qui vive?; **here we go again!** ça y est, ça recommence!; **there he goes!** le voilà!; **there he goes again!** *(there he is again)* le revoilà!; *(he's doing it again)* ça y est, il est reparti!; *Fam Fig* **don't even go there!** ne m'en parle pas!

2 *(engage in a specified activity)* aller; **to go shopping** aller faire des courses; **to go fishing/hunting** aller à la pêche/à la chasse; **to go riding** aller faire du cheval; **let's go for a walk/bike ride/swim** allons nous promener/faire un tour à vélo/nous baigner; **they went on a trip** ils sont partis en voyage; **I'll go to see her** *or Am* **go see her tomorrow** j'irai la voir demain; **don't go and tell him!, don't go telling him!** ne va pas le lui dire!, ne le lui dis pas!; **you had to go and tell him!** il a fallu que tu le lui dises!; **he's gone and locked us out!** il est parti et nous a laissés à la porte!; **you've gone and done it now!** vraiment, tu as tout gâché!

3 *(proceed to specified limit)* aller; **he'll go as high as £300** il ira jusqu'à 300 livres; **now you've gone too far!** là tu as dépassé les bornes!; **the temperature sometimes goes below zero** la température descend *ou* tombe parfois au-dessous de zéro

4 *(depart, leave)* s'en aller, partir; **I must be going** il faut que je m'en aille *ou* que je parte; **what time does the train go?** à quelle heure part le train?; **either he goes or I go** l'un de nous deux doit partir

5 *(indicating regular attendance)* aller, assister; **to go to church/school** aller à l'église/l'école; **to go to a meeting** aller *ou* assister à une réunion; **to go to work** *(to one's place of work)* aller au travail

6 *(indicating direction or route)* aller, mener; **that road goes to the market square** cette route va *ou* mène à la place du marché

B. 1 *(be or remain in specified state)* être; **to go barefoot/naked** se promener pieds nus/tout nu; **to go armed** porter une arme; **the job went unfilled** le poste est resté vacant; **to go unnoticed** passer inaperçu; **such crimes must not go unpunished** de tels crimes ne doivent pas rester impunis

2 *(become)* devenir; **my father is going grey** mon père grisonne; **she went white with rage** elle a blêmi de colère; **my hands went clammy** mes mains sont devenues moites; **the tea's gone cold** le thé a refroidi; **have you gone mad?** tu es devenu fou?; **to go bankrupt** faire faillite; **the country has gone Republican** le pays est maintenant républicain

3 *(stop working, fail ▸ engine)* tomber en panne; *(▸ fuse)* sauter; *(▸ bulb, lamp)* sauter, griller; *(▸ health)* se détériorer; *(▸ hearing, sight)* baisser; **the battery's going** la pile commence à être usée; **his voice is going** il devient aphone; **her mind has started to go** elle n'a plus toute sa tête *ou* toutes ses facultés; **his trousers are going at the knees** son pantalon s'use aux genoux; **the jacket went at the seams** la veste a craqué aux coutures

C. 1 *(begin an activity)* commencer; **what are we waiting for? let's go!** qu'est-ce qu'on attend? allons-y!; *Fam* **here goes!, here we go!** allez!, on y va!; **go!** partez!; **you'd better get going on** *or* **with that report!** tu ferais bien de te mettre à *ou* de t'attaquer à ce rapport!; **it won't be so hard once you get going** ça ne sera pas si difficile une fois que tu seras lancé; *Fam* **go to it!** *(get to work)* au boulot!; *(in encouragement)* allez-y!

2 *(expressing intention)* **to be going to do sth** *(be about to)* aller faire qch, être sur le point de faire qch; *(intend to)* avoir l'intention de faire qch; **I was going to walk** *(intention)* j'avais l'intention d'y aller à pied

3 *(expressing future)* **are you going to be at home tonight?** est-ce que vous serez chez vous ce soir?; **we're going to do exactly as we please** nous ferons ce que nous voulons; **she's going to be a doctor** elle va être médecin; **there's going to be a storm** il va y avoir un orage; **he's going to have to work really hard** il va falloir qu'il travaille très dur

4 *(function ▸ clock, machine)* marcher, fonctionner; *(start functioning)* démarrer; **the car won't go** la voiture ne veut pas démarrer; **he had the tele-**

vision and the radio going il avait mis la télévision et la radio en marche; **the washing machine is still going** la machine à laver tourne encore, la lessive n'est pas terminée; **to get sth going** *(car, machine)* mettre qch en marche; *(business, project)* lancer qch; **her daughter kept the business going** sa fille a continué à faire marcher l'affaire; **to keep a conversation/fire going** entretenir une conversation/un feu

5 *(sound ▸ alarm clock, bell)* sonner; *(▸ alarm, siren)* retentir

6 *(make movement)* **she went like this with her eyebrows** elle a fait comme ça avec ses sourcils

7 *(appear)* **to go on radio/television** passer à la radio/à la télévision

D. 1 *(disappear)* disparaître; **the snow has gone** la neige a fondu *ou* disparu; **all the sugar's gone** il n'y a plus de sucre; **my coat has gone** mon manteau n'est plus là *ou* a disparu; **all our money has gone** *(spent)* nous avons dépensé tout notre argent; *(lost)* nous avons perdu tout notre argent; *(stolen)* on a volé tout notre argent; **I don't know where the money goes these days** l'argent disparaît à une vitesse incroyable ces temps-ci

2 *(be eliminated)* **the last paragraph must go** il faut supprimer le dernier paragraphe; **I've decided that car has to go** j'ai décidé de me débarrasser de cette voiture

3 *Euph (die)* disparaître, s'éteindre; **after I go...** quand je ne serai plus là...

E. 1 *(extend, reach)* aller, s'étendre; **our property goes as far as the forest** notre propriété va *ou* s'étend jusqu'au bois; **the path goes right down to the beach** le chemin descend jusqu'à la mer; **my salary doesn't go very far** je ne vais pas loin avec mon salaire; **money doesn't go very far these days** l'argent part vite à notre époque

2 *(belong)* aller, se mettre, se ranger; **the dictionaries go on that shelf** les dictionnaires se rangent *ou* vont sur cette étagère; **where do the towels go?** où est-ce qu'on met les serviettes?

3 *(be contained in, fit)* aller; **this last sweater won't go in the suitcase** ce dernier pull n'ira pas *ou* n'entrera pas dans la valise; **the piano barely goes through the door** le piano entre *ou* passe de justesse par la porte; **this belt just goes round my waist** cette ceinture est juste assez longue pour faire le tour de ma taille

4 *(develop, turn out)* se passer; **how did your interview go?** comment s'est passé ton entretien?; **I'll see how things go** je vais voir comment ça se passe; **everything went well** tout s'est bien passé; **if all goes well** si tout va bien; **the meeting went badly/well** la réunion s'est mal/bien passée; **the negotiations are going well** les négociations sont en bonne voie; **there's no doubt as to which way the decision will go** on sait ce qui sera décidé; *Fam* **how's it going?, how are things going?** (comment) ça va?; **the way things are going, we might both be out of a job soon** au train où vont *ou* vu comment vont les choses, nous allons bientôt nous retrouver tous les deux au chômage

5 *(time ▸ elapse)* s'écouler, passer; *(▸ last)* durer; **the journey went quickly** je n'ai pas vu le temps passer pendant le voyage; **time goes so slowly when you're not here** le temps me paraît tellement long quand tu n'es pas là; **how's the time going?** combien de temps reste-t-il?

F. 1 *(be accepted)* **whatever the boss says goes** c'est le patron qui fait la loi; **anything goes** on fait ce qu'on veut

2 *(be valid, hold true)* s'appliquer; **that rule goes for everyone** cette règle s'applique à tout le monde; **that goes for us too** *(that applies to us)* ça s'applique à nous aussi; *(we agree with that)* nous sommes aussi de cet avis

3 *(be expressed, run ▸ report, story)* **the story** *or* **rumour goes that she left him** le bruit court qu'elle l'a quitté; **so the story goes** du moins c'est ce que l'on dit *ou* d'après les on-dit; **how does the tune go?** c'est quoi *ou* c'est comment, l'air?; **her theory goes something like this** sa théorie est plus ou moins la suivante

4 *(be sold)* se vendre; **the necklace went for £350** le collier s'est vendu 350 livres; **going, going, gone!** *(at auction)* une fois, deux fois, adjugé!

G. 1 *(be given ▸ award, prize)* aller, être donné; *(▸ inheritance, property)* passer; **the contract is to go to a private firm** le contrat ira à une entreprise privée; **every penny will go to charity** tout l'argent va *ou* est destiné à une œuvre de bienfaisance

2 *(be spent)* **a small portion of the budget went on education** une petite part du budget a été consacrée *ou* est allée à l'éducation; **all his money goes on drink** tout son argent part dans la boisson

3 *(contribute)* contribuer, servir; **all that just goes to prove my point** tout ça confirme bien ce que j'ai dit; **it has all the qualities that go to make a good film** ça a toutes les qualités d'un bon film

4 *(have recourse)* avoir recours, recourir; **to go to arbitration** recourir à l'arbitrage

H. 1 *(be compatible ▸ colours, flavours)* aller ensemble; **orange and mauve don't really go** l'orange et le mauve ne vont pas vraiment ensemble

2 *(be available)* **let me know if you hear of any jobs going** faites-moi savoir si vous entendez parler d'un emploi; *Fam* **any whisky going?** tu as un whisky à m'offrir?□

3 *(endure)* tenir le coup; **we can't go much longer without water** nous ne pourrons pas tenir beaucoup plus longtemps sans eau

4 *Euph (go to the toilet)* **I went before I came** j'ai fait avant de venir

5 *Math* **5 into 60 goes 12** 60 divisé par 5 égale 12; **6 into 5 won't go** 5 n'est pas divisible par 6

6 *(idioms)* **she isn't bad, as teachers go** elle n'est pas mal comme enseignante; **as houses go, it's pretty cheap** ce n'est pas cher pour une maison; **as things go today** par les temps qui courent; **there goes my chance of winning a prize** je peux abandonner tout espoir de gagner un prix

VT 1 *(travel)* faire, voyager; **we've only gone five kilometres** nous n'avons fait que cinq kilomètres

2 *(say)* faire; *(make specified noise)* faire; **ducks go "quack"** les canards font "coin-coin"; **the gun went bang** et pan! le coup est parti; *Fam* **so she goes, "you're lying!" and I go, "no, I'm not!"** alors elle me fait "tu mens!", et je lui fais "non, je mens pas!"

3 *(in gambling)* **to go ten** risquer dix; *Cards* **to go no trumps/two trumps** annoncer sans atout/deux atouts; *Fig* **to go one better (than sb)** surenchérir (sur qn)

4 *Fam (do with)* **I could really go a beer** je me paierais bien une bière

5 *(idioms) Fam Old-fashioned* **to go it** *(go fast)* filer; *(behave wildly)* se défoncer; **to go it alone** agir tout seul; *(in business)* se lancer tout seul

N 1 *Br (attempt, try)* coup *m*, essai *m*; **to have a go at sth/doing sth** essayer qch/de faire qch; **he had another go** il a fait une nouvelle tentative, il a ressayé; **let's have a go!** essayons!; *Fam (let me try)* laisse-moi essayer!□; **have another go!** encore un coup!; **I've never tried it but I'll give it a go** je n'ai encore jamais fait l'expérience mais je vais essayer; **she passed her exams first go** elle a eu ses examens du premier coup; **he knocked down all the skittles at one go** il a renversé toutes les quilles d'un coup; **£1 a go** *(at fair etc)* 1 livre la partie *ou* le tour; **he wouldn't let me have** *or* **give me a go** *(on his bicycle etc)* il ne voulait pas me laisser l'essayer

2 *Br (in games ▸ turn)* tour *m*; **it's your go** c'est ton tour *ou* c'est à toi (de jouer); **whose go is it?** à qui de jouer?, à qui le tour?

3 *Fam (energy, vitality)* dynamisme□ *m*, entrain□ *m*; **to be full of go** avoir plein d'énergie, être très dynamique□; **she's got plenty of go** elle est pleine d'entrain□

4 *Fam (success)* succès□ *m*, réussite□ *f*; **he's made a go of the business** il a réussi à faire marcher l'affaire□; **I tried to persuade her but it was no go** j'ai essayé de la convaincre mais il n'y avait rien à faire

5 *Old-fashioned (fashion)* mode *f*; **short hair is all the go** les cheveux courts sont le dernier cri *ou* font fureur

6 *Fam (idioms)* **to have a go at sb** *(physically)* rentrer dans qn; *(verbally)* passer un savon à qn; **it's all go!** ça n'arrête pas!

• **going on** ADV **he must be going on 50** il doit approcher de la *ou* aller sur la 50; **it was going on (for) midnight by the time we finished** quand on a terminé, il était près de minuit

• **on the go** ADJ *Fam* **1** *(busy)* **I've been on the go all day** je n'ai pas arrêté de toute la journée□; **to be always on the go** être toujours à trotter *ou* à courir, avoir la bougeotte; **to keep sb on the go** faire trimer qn

2 *(in hand)* **I have several projects on the go at present** j'ai plusieurs projets en route en ce moment□

• **to go** ADV à faire; **there are only three weeks/five miles to go** il ne reste plus que trois semaines/cinq miles; **five done, three to go** cinq de faits, trois à faire ADJ *esp Am (to take out)* **two hamburgers to go** deux hamburgers à emporter

▸ **go about** VI **1** *(move)* circuler; *(rumour)* courir; **policemen usually go about in pairs** en général, les policiers circulent par deux; **you can't go about saying things like that!** il ne faut pas raconter des choses pareilles!; **she's been going about with that Smith boy** on l'a vue traîner avec le fils Smith **2** *Naut (change tack)* virer de bord

VT INSEP **1** *(get on with)* s'occuper de; **to go about one's business** vaquer à ses occupations **2** *(set about)* se mettre à; **she showed me how to go about it** elle m'a montré comment faire *ou* comment m'y prendre; **how do you go about applying for the job?** comment doit-on s'y prendre *ou* faire pour postuler l'emploi? **3** *(country)* parcourir

▸ **go across** VT INSEP traverser

VI traverser; **your brother has just gone across to the shop** ton frère est allé faire un saut au magasin en face

▸ **go after** VT INSEP **1** *(follow)* suivre **2** *(pursue, seek ▸ criminal)* poursuivre; *(▸ prey)* chasser; *(▸ job, prize)* essayer d'obtenir; **he goes after all the women** il court après toutes les femmes; **I'm going after that job** je vais essayer d'obtenir cet emploi

▸ **go against** VT INSEP **1** *(disregard)* aller contre, aller à l'encontre de; **he went against my advice** il n'a pas suivi mon conseil; **I went against my mother's wishes** je suis allé contre *ou* j'ai contrarié les désirs de ma mère **2** *(conflict with)* contredire; **it goes against my principles** c'est contre mes principes **3** *(be unfavourable to ▸ of luck, situation)* être contraire à; *(▸ of opinion)* être défavorable à; *(▸ of behaviour, evidence)* nuire à, être préjudiciable à; **the vote/verdict went against him** le vote/le verdict lui a été défavorable

▸ **go ahead** VI **1** *(precede)* passer devant; **he went ahead of us** il est parti avant nous; **I let him go ahead of me in the queue** je l'ai fait passer devant moi dans la queue **2** *(proceed)* aller de l'avant; **go ahead! tell me!** vas-y! dis-le-moi!; **the mayor allowed the demonstrations to go ahead** le maire a permis aux manifestations d'avoir lieu; **the move had gone ahead as planned** le déménagement s'était déroulé comme prévu; **to go ahead with sth** démarrer qch; **they're going ahead with the project after all** ils ont finalement décidé de mener le projet à bien; **he went ahead and did it** *(without hesitating)* il l'a fait sans l'ombre d'une hésitation; *(despite warnings)* rien ne l'a arrêté **3** *(advance, progress)* progresser, faire des progrès

▸ **go along** VI **1** *(move from one place to another)* aller, avancer; **she went along with them to the fair** elle les a accompagnés *ou* elle est allée avec eux à la foire; **we can talk it over as we go along** nous pouvons en discuter en chemin *ou* en cours de route; **I just make it up as I go along** j'invente au fur et à mesure **2** *(progress)* se dérouler, se passer; **things were going along nicely** tout allait *ou* se passait bien **3** *(go to meeting, party etc)* aller

▸ **go along with** VT INSEP *(decision, order)* accepter, s'incliner devant; *(rule)* observer, respecter; **that's what they decided and I went along with it** c'est la décision qu'ils ont prise et je l'ai acceptée; **she wouldn't go along with it** elle n'était pas d'accord

▸ **go around** VI **1** *(habitually)* **she just goes around annoying everyone** elle passe son temps à énerver tout le monde; **he goes around in black leather** il se promène toujours en *ou* il est toujours habillé en cuir noir **2** *(document, illness)* circuler; *(gossip, rumour)* courir, circuler; *Fig* **what goes around comes around** on récolte ce que l'on a semé

▸**go at** VT INSEP *Fam (attack ▸ food)* attaquer, se jeter sur; *(▸ job, task)* s'attaquer à□; *(▸ person)* attaquer□; **they were still going at it the next day** ils y étaient encore le lendemain; **she went at the cleaning with a will** elle s'est attaquée au nettoyage avec ardeur□

▸**go away** VI partir, s'en aller; **go away!** va-t'en!; **I'm going away for a few days** je pars pour quelques jours

▸**go back** VI **1** *(return)* revenir, retourner; **she went back to bed** elle est retournée au lit, elle s'est recouchée; **to go back to sleep** se rendormir; **they went back home** ils sont rentrés chez eux *ou* à la maison; **I went back downstairs/upstairs** je suis redescendu/remonté; **to go back to work** *(continue task)* se remettre au travail; *(return to place of work)* retourner travailler; *(return to employment)* reprendre le travail; **let's go back to chapter two** revenons *ou* retournons au deuxième chapitre; **we went back to the beginning** nous avons recommencé; **the clocks go back one hour today** on retarde les pendules d'une heure aujourd'hui

2 *(retreat)* reculer

3 *(revert)* revenir; **we went back to the old system** nous sommes revenus à l'ancien système; **he went back to his old habits** il a repris ses anciennes habitudes; **men are going back to wearing their hair long** les hommes reviennent aux cheveux longs *ou* se laissent à nouveau pousser les cheveux

4 *(in time)* remonter; **our records go back to 1850** nos archives remontent à 1850; **this building goes back to the Revolution** ce bâtiment date de *ou* remonte à la Révolution; *Fam* **we go back a long way, Brad and me** ça remonte à loin, Brad et moi

5 *(extend, reach)* s'étendre; **the garden goes back 150 metres** le jardin s'étend sur 150 mètres

▸**go back on** VT INSEP *(fail to keep ▸ agreement)* rompre, violer; *(▸ promise)* manquer à, revenir sur; **he won't go back on his word** il ne manquera pas à sa parole

▸**go before** VI *(precede)* passer devant; *(happen before)* précéder; **that question has nothing to do with what went before** cette question n'a rien à voir avec ce qui précède *ou* avec ce qui a été dit avant

VT INSEP **1** *(precede)* précéder **2** *(appear before)* **your suggestion will go before the committee** votre suggestion sera soumise au comité; **to go before a judge/jury** passer devant un juge/un jury

▸**go below** VI *Naut* descendre dans l'entrepont

▸**go by** VI *(pass ▸ car, person)* passer; *(▸ time)* passer, s'écouler; **half an hour went by** une demi-heure s'est écoulée; **as the years go by** avec les années, à mesure que les années passent; **in days** *or* **in times** *or* **in years gone by** autrefois, jadis; **to let an opportunity go by** laisser passer une occasion

VT INSEP **1** *(act in accordance with, be guided by)* suivre, se baser sur; **don't go by the map** ne vous fiez pas à la carte; **I'll go by what the boss says** je me baserai sur ce que dit le patron; **he goes by the rules** il suit le règlement **2** *(judge by)* juger d'après; **going by her accent, I'd say she's from New York** si j'en juge d'après son accent, je dirais qu'elle vient de New York; **you can't go by appearances** on ne peut pas juger d'après *ou* sur les apparences **3** *(be known by)* **to go by a different/false name** être connu sous un nom différent/un faux nom; **the product goes by the name of "Bango" in France** ce produit est vendu sous le nom de "Bango" en France

▸**go down** VI **1** *(descend, move to lower level)* descendre; **he went down on all fours** *or* **on his hands and knees** il s'est mis à quatre pattes; **going down!** *(in lift)* on descend!, pour descendre!

2 *(proceed, travel)* aller; **we're going down to Tours/the country/the shop** nous allons à Tours/à la campagne/au magasin; **go down to the end of the street** allez *ou* continuez jusqu'en bas de la rue

3 *(set ▸ moon, sun)* se coucher, tomber

4 *(sink ▸ ship)* couler, sombrer; *(▸ person)* couler, disparaître (sous l'eau)

5 *(decrease, decline ▸ level, price, quality)* baisser; *(▸ amount, numbers)* diminuer; *(▸ rate, temperature)* baisser, s'abaisser; *(▸ fever)* baisser, tomber; *(▸ tide)* descendre; **my weight has gone down** j'ai perdu du poids; **he's gone down in my estimation** il a baissé dans mon estime; **the neighbourhood's really gone down since then** le quartier ne s'est vraiment pas arrangé depuis; **to have gone down in the world** avoir connu des jours meilleurs

6 *(become less swollen ▸ swelling)* désenfler, dégonfler; *(▸ balloon, tyre)* se dégonfler

7 *(be received)* **to go down well** *(drink)* se laisser boire; *(food)* se laisser manger; *(entertainment, speech, suggestion)* plaire, être bien reçu; **a cup of coffee would go down nicely** une tasse de café serait la bienvenue

8 *(lose)* être battu; **Madrid went down to Milan by three points** Milan a battu Madrid de trois points; **I'm not going to go down without a fight** je me battrai jusqu'à la fin

9 *Sport (be relegated)* descendre

10 *(be noted, recorded)* être noté; *(in writing)* être pris *ou* couché par écrit; **this day will go down in history** ce jour restera une date historique; **she will go down in history as a woman of great courage** elle entrera dans l'histoire grâce à son grand courage

11 *(reach as far as)* descendre, s'étendre; **this path goes down to the beach** ce sentier va *ou* descend à la plage

12 *Br Univ* entrer dans la période des vacances

13 *Cards (in bridge)* chuter

14 *Comput* tomber en panne; *(computer network)* planter; **the server's gone down** le serveur est en panne

15 *Mus (lower pitch)* descendre

16 *Br Fam (be sent to prison)* **he went down for three years** il a écopé de trois ans

17 *Am Fam (happen)* se passer□

VT INSEP *(hill, stairs, ladder, street)* descendre; **my food went down the wrong way** j'ai avalé de travers; *Br Sch* **to go down a class** descendre d'une classe; *Fig* **I don't want to go down that road** je ne veux pas m'engager là-dedans

▸**go for** VT INSEP **1** *(fetch)* aller chercher

2 *(try to obtain)* essayer d'obtenir, viser; *Fam* **go for it!** vas-y!

3 *(attack ▸ physically)* tomber sur, s'élancer sur; *(▸ verbally)* s'en prendre à; **they went for each other** *(physically)* ils se sont jetés l'un sur l'autre; *(verbally)* ils s'en sont pris l'un à l'autre; **go for him!** *(to dog)* attaque!

4 *Fam (like)* aimer□, adorer□; **I don't really go for that idea** l'idée ne me dit pas grand-chose; **he really goes for her in a big way** il est vraiment fou d'elle

5 *(choose, prefer)* choisir, préférer

6 *(apply to, concern)* concerner, s'appliquer à; **what I said goes for both of you** ce que j'ai dit vaut pour *ou* s'applique à vous deux; **and the same goes for me** et moi aussi

7 *(have as result)* servir à; **his 20 years of service went for nothing** ses 20 ans de service n'ont servi à rien

8 *(be to the advantage of)* **she has a lot going for her** elle a beaucoup d'atouts; **that idea hasn't got much going for it frankly** cette idée n'est franchement pas très convaincante

▸**go forth** VI *Arch or Literary* **1** *(leave)* sortir; **the army went forth into battle** l'armée s'est mise en route pour la bataille; *Bible* **go forth and multiply** croissez et multipliez-vous **2** *(be pronounced)* être prononcé; *(be published)* paraître; **the command went forth that...** il fut décrété que... + *indicative*

▸**go forward** VI (s')avancer; **the clocks go forward tomorrow** on avance les pendules demain; **if this scheme goes forward...** si ce projet est accepté...

▸**go in** VI **1** *(enter)* entrer, rentrer; **it's cold, let's go in** il fait froid, entrons; **it's too big, it won't go in** c'est trop grand, ça ne rentrera pas

2 *(disappear ▸ moon, sun)* se cacher

3 *Sport (in cricket)* prendre son tour au guichet

4 *Mil (attack)* attaquer

▸**go in for** VT INSEP **1** *(engage in ▸ activity, hobby, sport)* pratiquer, faire; *(▸ occupation)* se consacrer à; *(▸ politics)* s'occuper de, faire; **she went in for company law** elle s'est lancée dans le droit commercial; **he thought about going in for teaching** il a pensé devenir enseignant

2 *Fam (be interested in)* s'intéresser à□; *(like)* aimer□; **I don't go in much for opera** je n'aime pas trop l'opéra, l'opéra ne me dit rien; **he goes in for special effects in a big way** il est très branché effets spéciaux; **we don't go in for that kind of film** nous n'aimons pas ce genre de film; **this publisher doesn't really go in for fiction** cet éditeur ne fait pas tellement dans le roman

3 *Fam (use)* **they don't go in for injections so much nowadays** ils ne sont pas tellement pour les piqûres de nos jours; **why do scientists go in for all that jargon?** pourquoi est-ce que les scientifiques utilisent tout ce jargon?

4 *(take part in ▸ competition, race)* prendre part à; *(▸ examination)* se présenter à

5 *(apply for ▸ job, position)* poser sa candidature à, postuler

▸**go into** VT INSEP **1** *(enter ▸ building, house)* entrer dans; *(▸ activity, profession)* entrer à *ou* dans; *(▸ politics, business)* se lancer dans; **she's gone into hospital** elle est (r)entrée à l'hôpital; **to go into the army** *(as profession)* devenir militaire de carrière; *(as conscript)* partir au service; **he went into medicine** il a choisi la médecine

2 *(be invested ▸ of effort, money, time)* **two months of research went into our report** nous avons mis *ou* investi deux mois de recherche dans notre rapport

3 *(embark on ▸ action)* commencer à; *(▸ explanation, speech)* se lancer *ou* s'embarquer dans, (se mettre à) donner; *(▸ problem)* aborder; **the car went into a skid** la voiture a commencé à déraper; **to go into fits of laughter** être pris d'un fou rire

4 *(examine, investigate)* examiner, étudier

5 *(explain in depth)* entrer dans; **I won't go into details** je ne vais pas entrer dans les détails; **let's not go into that** ne parlons pas de ça

6 *(hit, run into)* entrer dans; **a car went into him** une voiture lui est rentrée dedans

7 *Comput (file, program)* aller dans

▸**go off** VI **1** *(leave)* partir, s'en aller; **she went off to work** elle est partie travailler; **her husband has gone off and left her** son mari l'a quittée; *Theat* **the actors went off** les acteurs ont quitté la scène

2 *(stop operating ▸ light, radio)* s'éteindre; *(▸ heating)* s'éteindre, s'arrêter; *(▸ pain)* partir, s'arrêter; **the electricity went off** l'électricité a été coupée

3 *(become activated ▸ bomb, firework)* exploser; *(▸ gun)* partir; *(▸ alarm, alarm clock)* sonner; **the grenade went off in her hand** la grenade a explosé dans sa main; **the gun didn't go off** le coup n'est pas parti; *Fam* **to go off at the deep end** piquer une crise, péter les plombs

4 *(have specified outcome)* se passer; **the interview went off badly/well** l'entretien s'est mal/bien passé; **her speech went off well** son discours a été bien reçu

5 *(fall asleep)* s'endormir

6 *Br (deteriorate ▸ food)* s'avarier, se gâter; *(▸ milk)* tourner; *(▸ butter)* rancir; *(▸ athlete, sportsperson)* perdre sa forme; **the play goes off in the second half** la pièce se gâte pendant la seconde partie

VT INSEP *Br Fam (stop liking)* perdre le goût de□; **he's gone off classical music** il n'aime plus la musique classique□, la musique classique ne l'intéresse plus□; **I've gone off the idea** cette idée ne me dit plus rien; **funny how you can go off people** c'est drôle comme on se lasse des gens parfois

▸**go on** VI **1** *(move, proceed)* aller; *(without stopping)* poursuivre son chemin; *(after stopping)* repartir, se remettre en route; **you go on, I'll catch up** allez-y, je vous rattraperai (en chemin); **after dinner they went on to Susan's house** après le dîner, ils sont allés chez Susan

2 *(continue action)* continuer; **she went on (with her) reading** elle a continué à *ou* de lire; **"and that's not all," he went on** "et ce n'est pas tout", a-t-il poursuivi; **you can't go on being a student forever!** tu ne peux pas être étudiant toute ta vie!; **go on, ask her** vas-y, demande-lui; **go on, I'm listening** continuez, je vous écoute; **their affair has been going on for years** leur liaison dure depuis des années; **the party went on into the small hours** la soirée s'est prolongée jusqu'à très tôt le matin; **life goes on** la vie continue *ou* va son train; *Br Fam* **go on (with you)!** allons, arrête de me faire marcher!; **they have enough (work) to be going on with** ils ont du pain sur la planche *ou* de quoi faire pour le moment; **here's £25 to be going on with** voilà 25 livres pour te dépanner

3 *(proceed to another action)* **to go on to another question** passer à une autre question; **she went on to become a doctor** elle est ensuite devenue médecin

4 *(be placed, fit)* aller; **I can't get the lid to go on** je n'arrive pas à mettre le couvercle; **the cap goes on the other end** le bouchon se met *ou* va sur l'autre bout

5 *(happen, take place)* se passer; **what's going on here?** qu'est-ce qui se passe ici?; **several conversations were going on at once** il y avait plusieurs conversations à la fois

6 *(elapse)* passer, s'écouler; **as time goes on** avec le temps, à mesure que le temps passe

7 *Fam (chatter, talk)* parler[□], jacasser; **she does go on!** elle n'arrête pas de parler!, c'est un vrai moulin à paroles!; **he goes on and on about politics** il parle politique sans cesse; **don't go on about it!** ça va, on a compris!; **I don't want to go on about it, but...** je ne voudrais pas avoir l'air d'insister, mais...; **what are you going on about now?** qu'est-ce que vous racontez?

8 *Fam (act, behave)* se conduire[□], se comporter[□]; **what a way to go on!** en voilà des manières!

9 *(start operating ▸ light, radio, television)* s'allumer; *(▸ heating, motor, power)* s'allumer, se mettre en marche

10 *Sport (player)* prendre sa place, entrer en jeu

11 *Theat (actor)* entrer en scène

12 *(approach)* **he's going on for 40** il va sur ses 40 ans

VT INSEP 1 *(enter ▸ boat, train)* monter dans

2 *(embark on)* **to go on a journey/a holiday** partir en voyage/en vacances; **to go on a diet** se mettre au régime

3 *(be guided by)* se laisser guider par, se fonder *ou* se baser sur; **the detective didn't have much to go on** le détective n'avait pas grand-chose sur quoi s'appuyer *ou* qui puisse le guider; **she goes a lot on instinct** elle se fie beaucoup à *ou* se fonde beaucoup sur son instinct

4 *(approach) Hum* **she's 15 going on 45** *(wise)* elle a 15 ans mais elle est déjà très mûre; *(old beyond her years)* elle a 15 ans mais elle est vieille avant l'âge

▸**go out VI 1** *(leave)* sortir; **my parents made us go out of the room** mes parents nous ont fait sortir de la pièce *ou* quitter la pièce; **to go out for a meal** aller au restaurant; **to go out to dinner** sortir dîner; **to go out for a walk** aller se promener, aller faire une promenade; **she's gone out to get a paper** elle est sortie (pour) acheter un journal; **she goes out to work** elle travaille en dehors de la maison *ou* hors de chez elle; **she was dressed to go out** *(ready to leave)* elle était prête à sortir; *(dressed up)* elle était très habillée

2 *(travel)* partir; *(emigrate)* émigrer; **they went out to Africa** *(travelled)* ils sont partis en Afrique; *(emigrated)* ils sont partis vivre *ou* ils ont émigré en Afrique

3 *(date)* sortir; **to go out with sb** sortir avec qn; **we've been going out together for a month** ça fait un mois que nous sortons ensemble

4 *(fire, light)* s'éteindre

5 *(disappear)* disparaître; **the magic seemed to have gone out of their marriage** leur mariage semblait avoir perdu de son charme; **the joy went out of her eyes** la joie a disparu de son regard

6 *(tide)* descendre, se retirer

7 *(be sent ▸ letter)* être envoyé; *(be published ▸ brochure, pamphlet)* être distribué; *(be broadcast ▸ radio or television programme)* être diffusé; *Fig* **my heart goes out to her** je suis de tout cœur avec elle dans son chagrin

8 *Sport (be eliminated)* être éliminé; **Agassi went out to Henman** Agassi s'est fait sortir par Henman

9 *Cards* terminer

10 *Fam (idiom)* **she went all out to help us** elle a fait tout son possible pour nous aider[□]

▸**go over VI 1** *(move overhead ▸ plane etc)* passer

2 *(move in particular direction)* aller; *(cross)* traverser; **they went over to talk to her** ils sont allés lui parler; **to go over to Europe** aller en Europe

3 *(turn upside down)* se retourner; *(capsize ▸ boat)* chavirer, capoter

4 *(change, switch)* changer; **I've gone over to another brand of washing powder** je viens de changer de marque de lessive; **when will we go over to the metric system?** quand est-ce qu'on va passer au système métrique?

5 *(change allegiance)* passer, se joindre; **he's gone over to the Socialists** il est passé dans le camp des socialistes

6 *(be received)* passer; **the speech went over badly/well** le discours a mal/bien passé

VT INSEP 1 *(move, travel over)* passer par-dessus; **the horse went over the fence** le cheval a sauté (par-dessus) la barrière; **we went over a bump** on a pris une bosse

2 *(examine ▸ argument, problem)* examiner, considérer; *(▸ accounts, report)* examiner, vérifier; **would you go over my report?** voulez-vous regarder mon rapport?

3 *(repeat)* répéter; *(review ▸ notes, speech)* réviser, revoir; *(▸ facts)* récapituler, revoir; *Sch* réviser; **she went over the interview in her mind** elle a repassé l'entretien dans son esprit; **I kept going over everything leading up to the accident** je continuais de repenser à tous les détails qui avaient conduit à l'accident; **let's go over it again** reprenons, récapitulons

4 *(rehearse)* refaire; *(bars of music)* rejouer; *(sing)* rechanter

5 *TV & Rad* **let's go over now to our Birmingham studios** passons l'antenne à notre studio de Birmingham

▸**go round VI 1** *(be enough)* **is there enough cake to go round?** est-ce qu'il y a assez de gâteau pour tout le monde?; **to make the food go round** ménager la nourriture

2 *(visit)* aller; **we went round to his house** nous sommes allés chez lui; **I'm going round there later on** j'y vais plus tard

3 *(circulate ▸ rumour)* circuler, courir; *(▸ bottle, cold, flu)* circuler

4 *(be continuously present ▸ idea, tune)* **that song keeps going round in my head** j'ai cette chanson dans la tête

5 *(spin ▸ wheel)* tourner; *Fig* **my head's going round** j'ai la tête qui tourne

6 *(make a detour)* faire un détour; **to go round the long way** faire un long détour

VT INSEP *(tour ▸ museum)* faire le tour de; **I hate going round the shops** j'ai horreur de faire les boutiques

▸**go through VT INSEP 1** *(crowd, tunnel)* traverser

2 *(endure, experience)* subir, souffrir; **he's going through hell** c'est l'enfer pour lui; **I can't face going through all that again** je ne supporterais pas de passer par là une deuxième fois; **after everything she's gone through** après tout ce qu'elle a subi *ou* enduré

3 *(consume, use up ▸ supplies)* épuiser; *(▸ money)* dépenser; *(▸ food)* consommer; *(wear out)* user; **she goes through a pair of tights a week** elle use une paire de collants par semaine; **I've gone through the toes of my socks** j'ai usé *ou* troué mes chaussettes au bout

4 *(examine ▸ accounts, document)* examiner, vérifier; *(▸ list, proposal)* éplucher; *(▸ mail)* dépouiller; *(▸ drawer, pockets)* fouiller (dans); *(▸ files)* chercher dans; *(sort)* trier; **he went through her pockets** il a fouillé ses poches

5 *(carry out, perform ▸ movement, work)* faire; *(▸ formalities)* remplir, accomplir

6 *(participate in ▸ course of study)* étudier; *(▸ ceremony)* participer à

7 *(practise ▸ lesson, poem)* réciter; *(▸ role, scene)* répéter; **let's go through it again from the beginning** reprenons dès le début

VI 1 *(travel through, penetrate)* passer, traverser

2 *(offer, proposal)* être accepté; *(business deal)* être conclu, se faire; *(bill, law)* passer, être voté; *(divorce)* être prononcé; **the adoption finally went through** l'adoption s'est faite finalement

▸**go through with VT INSEP he'll never go through with it** il n'ira jamais jusqu'au bout; **she decided that she couldn't go through with the wedding** elle a décidé qu'elle ne pouvait pas se marier

▸**go together VI 1** *(colours, flavours)* aller bien ensemble; *(characteristics, ideas)* aller de pair; **the two things often go together** les deux choses vont souvent de pair **2** *Am (people)* sortir ensemble

▸**go under VI 1** *(go down ▸ ship)* couler, sombrer; *(▸ person)* couler, disparaître (sous l'eau) **2** *Fig (fail ▸ business)* couler, faire faillite; *(▸ project)* couler, échouer; *(▸ person)* échouer, sombrer **3** *(under anaesthetic)* s'endormir

VT INSEP 1 *(move, travel underneath)* passer par-dessous **2** *(be known)* **to go under a false/different name** utiliser *ou* prendre un faux nom/un nom différent; **a glue that goes under the name of Stikit** une colle qui s'appelle Stikit

▸**go up VI 1** *(ascend, climb ▸ person)* monter, aller en haut; *(▸ lift)* monter; **to go up to town** aller en ville; **I'm going up to bed** je monte me coucher; **going up!** *(in lift)* on monte!; **to go up in the world** faire son chemin

2 *(increase ▸ amount, numbers)* augmenter, croître; *(▸ price)* monter, augmenter; *(▸ temperature)* monter, s'élever; **rents are going up** les loyers sont en hausse; **to go up in sb's estimation** monter dans l'estime de qn

3 *(sudden noise)* s'élever; **a shout went up** un cri s'éleva

4 *(appear ▸ notices, posters)* apparaître; *(be built)* être construit; **new buildings are going up all over town** de nouveaux immeubles surgissent dans toute la ville

5 *(explode, be destroyed)* sauter, exploser

6 *Mus (raise pitch)* monter

7 *Theat (curtain)* se lever; **before the curtain goes up** avant le lever du rideau

8 *Br Univ* entrer à l'université; **she went up to Oxford in 1950** elle est entrée à Oxford en 1950

9 *Sport (be promoted)* **they look set to go up to the First Division** ils ont l'air prêts à entrer en première division

VT INSEP monter; **to go up a hill/ladder** monter une colline/sur une échelle; *Br Sch* **to go up a class** monter d'une classe

▸**go up to VT INSEP 1** *(approach)* **to go up to sb/sth** se diriger vers qn/qch **2** *(go as far as)* **the book only goes up to the end of the war** le livre ne va que jusqu'à la fin de la guerre; **I will go up to £100** je veux bien aller jusqu'à 100 livres

▸**go with VT INSEP 1** *(accompany, escort)* accompagner, aller avec

2 *(be compatible ▸ colours, flavours)* aller avec; **that hat doesn't go with your suit** ce chapeau ne va pas avec ton ensemble; **a white Burgundy goes well with snails** le bourgogne blanc se marie bien *ou* va bien avec les escargots

3 *(be part of)* aller avec; **the flat goes with the job** l'appartement va avec le poste; **the sense of satisfaction that goes with having done a good job** le sentiment de satisfaction qu'apporte le travail bien fait; **mathematical ability usually goes with skill at chess** des capacités en mathématiques vont souvent de pair avec un don pour les échecs

4 *Fam (spend time with)* sortir avec[□]; *Euph* **he's been going with other women** *(having sex)* il a été avec d'autres femmes

▸**go without VT INSEP** se passer de, se priver de; **he went without sleep** *or* **without sleeping for two days** il n'a pas dormi pendant deux jours

VI s'en passer; **we'll just have to go without** il faudra s'en passer, c'est tout; **they went without so that the children got enough to eat** ils ont dû se priver pour que les enfants aient assez à manger

goad [gəʊd] **N** aiguillon *m*

VT 1 *(cattle)* aiguillonner, piquer **2** *(person)* harceler, provoquer; **to g. sb into doing sth** pousser qn à faire qch, harceler qn jusqu'à ce qu'il fasse qch; **the threat of redundancy goaded the men into action** la peur d'un licenciement incita les hommes à l'action

▸**goad on VT SEP** aiguillonner; **she was goaded on by the prospect of wealth and power** elle était stimulée par la perspective des richesses et du pouvoir

go-ahead N feu *m* vert; **to give sb the g. to do sth** donner le feu vert à qn pour faire qch; **to give sth the g.** donner le feu vert pour qch
ADJ *(dynamic ▸ person)* dynamique, entreprenant, qui va de l'avant; *(▸ attitude, business)* dynamique

goal [gəʊl] N **1** *(aim)* but *m*, objectif *m*; **what's your g. in life?** quel est ton but *ou* quelle est ton ambition dans la vie?; **to set oneself a g.** se fixer un but *ou* objectif; **to achieve** *or* **attain one's g.** atteindre *ou* réaliser son but **2** *Sport* but *m*; **to score a g.** marquer un but; **they won by five goals to two** ils ont gagné par cinq buts à deux; **Macleod was in g. for Rangers** Macleod était dans les buts des Rangers; **the leading** *or* **top g. scorer** le meilleur buteur; **g.!** but!
▸▸ ***goal area*** (zone *f* des) six mètres *mpl*; ***goal average*** goal-average *m*; ***goal difference*** différence *f* de buts; ***goal kick*** coup *m* de pied au but, dégagement *m* aux six mètres; ***goal kicker*** *(in American football)* botteur *m*; ***goal line*** ligne *f* de but

goalkeeper ['gəʊlki:pə(r)] N gardien *m* (de but), goal *m*

goalless ['gəʊllɪs] ADJ **a g. draw** un match sans but marqué *ou* zéro à zéro

goalmouth ['gəʊlmaʊθ, *pl* -maʊðz] N entrée *f* de but; **in the g.** directement devant le but; **there was no shortage of g. incidents** il y avait beaucoup d'action devant les cages

goalpost ['gəʊlpəʊst] N poteau *m* (de but); *Fig* **to move the goalposts** changer les règles du jeu

goat [gəʊt] N **1** *Zool* chèvre *f*
2 *Fam* **old g.** *(lecherous man)* vieux cochon *m*; *Am (old woman)* vieille toupie *f*; *(old man)* vieux schnock *m*
3 *Fam Old-fashioned (foolish person)* andouille *f*; **to act** *or* **to play the (giddy) g.** faire l'andouille
4 *Fam (idiom)* **to get sb's g.** taper sur les nerfs *ou* le système à qn
▸▸ ***goat's cheese*** (fromage *m* de) chèvre *m*; ***goat's milk*** lait *m* de chèvre

goatee [gəʊ'ti:] N barbiche *f*, bouc *m*

goatherd ['gəʊthɜ:d] N chevrier(ère) *m,f*

goatskin ['gəʊtskɪn] N **1** *(hide)* peau *f* de chèvre **2** *(container)* outre *f* (en peau de chèvre)

goatsucker ['gəʊtsʌkə(r)] N *Orn* engoulevent *m*, tête-chèvre *m*

gob [gɒb] *(pt & pp* **gobbed**, *cont* **gobbing**) *Fam* N **1** *Br (mouth)* gueule *f*; **shut your g.!** ferme-la!, la ferme!; **he's got a bit of a g. on him** il est assez grande gueule **2** *(spittle)* crachat ◻ *m*, mollard *m*
VI *(spit)* cracher ◻, mollarder
• **gobs** NPL **gobs of** un tas de, des masses de

gobble ['gɒbəl] VI *(turkey)* glouglouter
VT *(eat greedily)* enfourner, engloutir; **don't g. your food!** ne mange pas si vite!
N *(of turkey)* glouglou *m*

▸ **gobble down** VT SEP *(eat quickly)* engloutir, engouffrer

▸ **gobble up** VT SEP *(eat quickly)* engloutir, engouffrer; *Fig (money, pay rise)* engloutir; *Fig* **the empire gobbled up these territories** l'empire a absorbé ces territoires

gobbledegook, gobbledygook ['gɒbəldɪgu:k] N *Fam* charabia *m*

go-between N intermédiaire *mf*; **to act** *or* **serve as a g.** servir d'intermédiaire

goblet ['gɒblɪt] N coupe *f*, verre *m* à pied; *Hist* gobelet *m*

goblin ['gɒblɪn] N esprit *m* maléfique, lutin *m*

gobo ['gəʊbəʊ] *(pl* **gobos** *or* **goboes**) N **1** *(on camera lens, spotlight etc)* volet *m* (coupe-flux), écran *m* (de protection) **2** *(on microphone)* bonnette *f* de micro

gobshite ['gɒbʃaɪt] N *Br very Fam (man)* trouduc *m*; *(woman)* connasse *f*

gobsmacked ['gɒbsmækt] ADJ *Br Fam* estomaqué; **I was absolutely g.** j'étais complètement estomaqué

gobstopper ['gɒbstɒpə(r)] N *Br* = gros bonbon rond qui change de couleur à mesure qu'on le suce

go-by N *Fam* **to give sb the g.** snober qn◻

GOC [ˌdʒi:əʊ'si:] N *Mil (abbr* **General Officer Commanding/Commanding-in-Chief**) = général commandant en chef

go-cart N **1** = **go-kart 2** *Br Old-fashioned or Am (babywalker)* trotteur *m*; *(toy wagon)* chariot *m*
▸▸ ***go-cart racing*** karting *m*

god [gɒd] N dieu *m*; **the g. of War** le dieu de la Guerre; **profit is their only g.** leur seul dieu, c'est le profit; *Arch or Hum* **ye gods!** grands dieux!
• **God** N **1** *Rel* Dieu *m*; **G. the Father, the Son and the Holy Ghost** Dieu le Père, le Fils, le Saint-Esprit; **a man of G.** un homme de Dieu; **to play G.** se prendre pour Dieu; *Fam* **he thinks he's G.'s gift (to mankind)** il ne se prend pas pour n'importe qui, il se croit sorti de la cuisse de Jupiter; *Fam* **he thinks he's G.'s gift to women** il croit que toutes les femmes vont tomber à ses pieds; *Fam* **he's not exactly G.'s gift to women** ce n'est pas vraiment l'homme dont rêvent toutes les femmes **2** *(in interjections and expressions) Fam* **oh G.!, my G.!** mon Dieu!; **G. bless you!** Dieu vous bénisse!; *Fam* **thank G.!** Dieu merci!; *Fam* **thank G. you didn't tell him** heureusement que tu ne lui as rien dit; **I wish to G. I'd never come here** je voudrais ne jamais être venu; *Fam* **what in G.'s name are you doing?** qu'est-ce que tu fais là, nom de Dieu?; *Fam* **for G.'s sake!, for the love of G.!** pour l'amour de Dieu!; *Fam* **for G.'s sake, don't tell him!** surtout ne lui dis rien!; *Fam* **G. knows why/how** Dieu sait pourquoi/comment; *Fam* **G. (only) knows** Dieu seul le sait; **G. willing** avec de la chance
• **gods** NPL *Br Fam* **the gods** *(in theatre)* le poulailler
▸▸ *Fam* ***God mode*** *(in computer games)* mode *m* dieu, god mode *m*; *Fam Pej* ***the God slot*** = expression humoristique désignant les émissions religieuses à la télévision; *Fam Pej* ***the God squad*** les bigots◻ *mpl*, les bondieusards *mpl*

godawful [gɒd'ɔ:fʊl] ADJ *Fam* minable, nul; **what g. weather!** quel sale temps!; **we ended up in some g. hotel** on a atterri dans un hôtel minable

god-botherer [-ˌbɒðərə(r)] N *Fam* cul-bénit *m*

godchild ['gɒdtʃaɪld] *(pl* **godchildren** [-tʃɪldrən]) N filleul(e) *m,f*

goddammit [ˌgɒd'dæmɪt] EXCLAM *very Fam* bordel!

goddamn ['gɒdæm] *Am very Fam* EXCLAM nom de Dieu!, merde!
ADJ sacré, fichu; **you g. fool!** pauvre imbécile!
ADV vachement; **it's g. hot** il fait vachement chaud

goddaughter ['gɒddɔ:tə(r)] N filleule *f*

goddess ['gɒdɪs] N déesse *f*; *Fig* **a g. of the screen, a screen g.** une idole du grand écran

godfather ['gɒdfɑ:ðə(r)] N parrain *m*

god-fearing [-fɪərɪŋ] ADJ croyant, pieux; **decent g. folk** les gens croyants bien comme il faut

godforsaken ['gɒdfəseɪkən] ADJ paumé; **what a g. place!** quel bled!

godhead ['gɒdhed] N divinité *f*; **the g.** Dieu

godless ['gɒdlɪs] ADJ irréligieux, impie

godlike ['gɒdlaɪk] ADJ divin, céleste

godliness ['gɒdlɪnɪs] N sainteté *f* (de l'âme), dévotion *f*

godly ['gɒdlɪ] *(compar* **godlier**, *superl* **godliest**) ADJ **1** *(pious)* pieux; **to lead a g. life** vivre pieusement **2** *(divine)* divin

godmother ['gɒdmʌðə(r)] N marraine *f*

godparent ['gɒdpeərənt] N *(woman)* marraine *f*; *(man)* parrain *m*; **my godparents** mon parrain et ma marraine

godsend ['gɒdsend] N aubaine *f*; **this money is a g. to him** cet argent est un don du ciel; **the president's gaffe was a g. to the opposition** la gaffe du président a été une aubaine pour l'opposition

godson ['gɒdsʌn] N filleul *m*

goer ['gəʊə(r)] N *Br Fam* **1** *(fast person)* fonceur (euse) *m,f*; *(vehicle)* bolide◻ *m*; **this horse is a real g.** il file *ou* il fonce, ce cheval **2 to be a g.** *(idea, plan)* être réalisable◻ **3 she's a real g.** *(promiscuous)* c'est une femme facile◻; *(good in bed)* c'est un bon coup

-goer ['gəʊə(r)] SUFF **church/cinema/theatre-g.** personne qui va souvent à l'église/au cinéma/au théâtre

gofer ['gəʊfə(r)] N **1** *esp Am Fam (menial assistant ▸ male)* homme *m* à tout faire; *(▸ female)* bonne *f* à tout faire **2** *Comput* (serveur *m*) gopher *m*

go-getter [-getə(r)] N *Fam* fonceur(euse) *m,f*, battant(e)◻ *m,f*

go-getting [-getɪŋ] ADJ *Fam (person)* plein d'allant◻, entreprenant◻; *(approach)* dynamique◻

goggle ['gɒgəl] VI ouvrir de grands yeux *ou* des yeux ronds; **to g. at sb/sth** regarder qn/qch avec des yeux ronds
• **goggles** NPL **1** *(protective)* lunettes *fpl* (de protection); *(for motorcyclist)* lunettes *fpl* (de motocycliste); *(for diver)* lunettes *fpl* de plongée; *(for swimmer, skier)* lunettes *fpl* **2** *Fam (glasses)* bésicles *fpl*
▸▸ *Br Fam Hum* ***goggle box*** télé *f*

goggle-eyed ADJ les yeux saillants *ou* exorbités *ou* globuleux; **to stare g.** regarder en écarquillant les yeux

go-go ADJ
▸▸ ***go-go dancer*** = homme ou femme légèrement vêtu(e) qui danse sur un podium de boîte de nuit

going ['gəʊɪŋ] N **1** *(leaving)* départ *m*
2 *(progress)* progrès *m*; **we made good g. on the return journey** on est allés vite pour le retour; **that's pretty good g.!** c'est plutôt rapide!; **it was slow g.** *(walking, climbing)* on progressait lentement; *(working, learning)* ça avançait lentement; **it was hard g.** *(walking, climbing)* on progressait difficilement; *(learning, working)* c'était dur
3 *(condition of ground)* état *m* du terrain; *Horse-racing* **good/heavy g.** bon terrain *m*/terrain *m* lourd; **it's rough** *or* **heavy g. on these mountain roads** c'est dur de rouler sur ces routes de montagne; *Fig* **this novel is heavy g.** ce roman ne se lit pas facilement; *Fig* **it's heavy g. getting him to talk** on a du mal à le faire parler; **to get out while the g.'s good** partir tant que les choses vont bien; *Prov* **when the g. gets tough, the tough get g.** = c'est dans les moments difficiles que les vrais hommes entrent en action;
4 g. back *(return)* retour *m*; *(retreat)* recul *m*; **g. back on one's word** manque *m* de parole; **there's no g. back now** il n'y a pas moyen de revenir en arrière
ADJ **1** *(functioning)* qui marche; **to start** *or* **to set sth g.** mettre qch en marche **2** *(profitable)* **the business is a g. concern** c'est une affaire qui marche; **for sale as a g. concern** *(sign, in property advertisement)* à vendre avec fonds **3** *(current)* actuel; **the g. price** le prix actuel, le prix sur le marché; **she's getting the g. rate for the job** elle touche le tarif en vigueur *ou* normal pour ce genre de travail; **the best computer/novelist g.** le meilleur ordinateur/romancier du moment

going-away ADJ *(party, present)* d'adieu

going-over *(pl* **goings-over**) N *Fam* **1** *(check-up)* révision◻ *f*, vérification◻ *f*; *(clean-up)* nettoyage◻ *m*; **the auditors gave the accounts a thorough g.** les experts ont soigneusement examiné les comptes◻ **2 to give sb a g.** *(beating)* tabasser qn; *(criticism)* sonner les cloches à qn; **the burglars had given the house a real g.** les cambrioleurs avaient laissé la maison sens dessus dessous◻

going-rate pricing N *Mktg* alignement *m* sur les prix du marché

goings-on NPL *Fam* **1** *Pej (behaviour)* conduite◻ *f*, activités◻ *fpl*; **there are some funny g. in that house** il s'en passe de drôles dans cette maison; **what extraordinary g.!** quelles histoires extraordinaires!◻ **2** *(events)* événements◻ *mpl*

goitre, *Am* **goiter** ['gɔɪtə(r)] N goitre *m*

goji berry ['gəʊdʒi:-] N baie *f* de goji

go-kart N kart *m*
▸▸ ***go-kart racing*** karting *m*

gold [gəʊld] N **1** *(metal, colour)* or *m*; **1,000 euros in g.** 1000 euros en or **2** *(gold medal)* médaille *f* d'or; **to win g.** gagner la médaille d'or; **to go for g.** viser la médaille d'or **3** *(colour)* or *m*; **the reds and golds of autumn** les rouges et les ors de l'automne

ADJ 1 *(made of gold ► necklace, ring)* en or **2** *(gold-coloured)* doré; **a g. dress** une robe couleur d'or *ou* dorée; **a g. lamé dress** une robe lamée d'or; **g. paint** peinture *f* dorée

ADV to go g. *(record)* devenir disque d'or

►► ***gold braid*** galon *m* d'or; ***gold bullion*** or *m* en barre *ou* en lingots, encaisse *f* or; ***gold card*** carte *f* de crédit illimité; ***the Gold Coast*** *(in Australia)* = suite de stations balnéaires sur la côte est de l'Australie; *Am (expensive area)* les beaux quartiers *mpl*; *Formerly (Ghana)* le Ghana; ***gold disc*** disque *m* d'or; ***gold dust*** poudre *f* d'or; *Fig* **tickets for the game are like g. dust** il est pratiquement impossible de se procurer des billets pour le match; ***gold fever*** fièvre *f* de l'or; ***gold filling*** *(in tooth)* obturation *f* à l'or *ou* en or; ***gold foil*** feuille *f* d'or, or *m* en feuille; ***gold leaf*** feuille *f* d'or, or *m* en feuille; ***gold market*** marché *m* de l'or; ***gold medal*** médaille *f* d'or; ***gold plate*** *(utensils)* orfèvrerie *f*, vaisselle *f* d'or; *(plating)* plaque *f* d'or; ***gold record*** disque *m* d'or; *Fin* ***gold reserve*** réserve *f* d'or; ***gold rush*** ruée *f* vers l'or; ***gold standard*** étalon-or *m*; ***gold star*** *(given to schoolchildren)* bon point *m*

goldbrick ['gəʊldbrɪk] **N** *Am Fam* **1 to sell sb a g.** rouler qn **2** *(malingerer)* tire-au-flanc *m inv*

VT *(swindle)* rouler

VI *(malinger)* tirer au flanc

goldcrest ['gəʊldkrest] **N** *Orn* roitelet *m* huppé

gold-digger **N** chercheur *m* d'or; *Fig (woman)* croqueuse *f* de diamants

golden ['gəʊldən] **ADJ 1** *also Fig (made of gold)* en or, d'or; *(opinion)* favorable **2** *(colour)* doré, (couleur) d'or; **g. brown** doré; **she has long g. hair** elle a de longs cheveux blonds; **g. yellow** jaune *m* d'or **3** *(excellent)* **g. boy/girl** enfant *mf* chéri(e); **a g. opportunity** une occasion en or

►► ***the Golden Age*** l'âge *m* d'or; ***golden calf*** veau *m* d'or; ***Golden Delicious*** *(apple)* golden *f*; *Orn* ***golden eagle*** aigle *m* royal; *Myth* ***the Golden Fleece*** la Toison d'or; ***the Golden Gate Bridge*** le Golden Gate; *Ftbl* ***golden goal*** but *m* en or; *Fam* ***golden handcuffs*** primes◻ *fpl (versées à un cadre à intervalles réguliers pour le dissuader de partir)*; *Fam* ***golden handshake*** gratification *f* de fin de service◻; *Fam* ***golden hello*** prime *f* d'embauche◻; ***golden jubilee*** (fête *f* du) cinquantième anniversaire *m*; ***golden labrador*** labrador *m* doré; ***the golden mean*** le juste milieu; *Fam* ***golden oldie*** vieux tube *m*; *Orn* ***golden oriole*** loriot *m* (jaune); *Fam* ***golden parachute*** prime *f* de licenciement◻ *(versée à certains cadres supérieurs en cas de rachat de l'entreprise)*; *Orn* ***golden pheasant*** faisan *m* doré; ***golden retriever*** golden retriever *m*; ***golden rule*** règle *f* d'or; ***the Golden State*** = surnom donné à la Californie; *Br* ***golden syrup*** mélasse *f* raffinée; ***golden triangle*** triangle *m* d'or; ***golden wedding*** noces *fpl* d'or

goldenrod ['gəʊldənrɒd] **N** *Bot* verge *f* d'or, solidage *f*

goldfield ['gəʊldfiːld] **N** terrain *m ou* région *f* aurifère

goldfinch ['gəʊldfɪntʃ] **N** *Orn* chardonneret *m*

goldfish ['gəʊldfɪʃ] **N 1** *(as pet)* poisson *m* rouge **2** *Ich* carassin *m* ou cyprin *m* doré

►► ***goldfish bowl*** bocal *m* (à poissons rouges); *Fig* **it's like living in a g. bowl** c'est comme si on était tout le temps dans une vitrine

Goldilocks ['gəʊldɪlɒks] **PR N** Boucles d'or

gold-plated **ADJ** *(jewellery, ornament)* plaqué or *(inv)*

gold-rimmed **ADJ** *(glasses)* à monture en or

goldsmith ['gəʊldsmɪθ] **N** orfèvre *m*

gold-tipped **ADJ** à bout doré

golf [gɒlf] **N** golf *m*

VI jouer au golf

►► ***golf bag*** sac *m* de golf; ***golf ball*** *(for golf)* balle *f* de golf; *(for typewriter)* boule *f*; ***golf ball typewriter*** machine *f* à écrire à boule; *Br* ***golf buggy*** voiture *f* de golf; ***golf cart*** *(trolley)* chariot *m* de golf; *(car)* voiturette *f*; ***golf club*** *(stick)* club *m ou* crosse *f ou* canne *f* de golf; *(building, association)* club *m* de golf; ***golf course*** (terrain *m* de) golf *m*; ***golf links*** links *mpl*; ***golf umbrella*** parapluie *m* de golf; *Fam Hum* ***golf widow*** = femme délaissée par un mari qui est toujours au golf

golfer ['gɒlfə(r)] **N** joueur(euse) *m,f* de golf, golfeur(euse) *m,f*

golfing ['gɒlfɪŋ] **N** golf *m (activité)*; **golfing holiday** vacances *fpl* de golf

Goliath [gə'laɪəθ] **PR N** *Bible* Goliath

golliwog ['gɒlɪwɒg] **N** = poupée de chiffon, au visage noir et aux cheveux hérissés

golly ['gɒlɪ] **EXCLAM** *Fam Old-fashioned* **(good) g.!** ciel!, mince (alors)!, flûte!

goloshes = **galoshes**

gonad ['gəʊnæd] **N** gonade *f*

gondola ['gɒndələ] **N 1** *(boat)* gondole *f*

2 *(on airship or balloon, for window cleaner)* nacelle *f*

3 *(in supermarket)* gondole *f*

4 *(cable car)* nacelle *f ou* cabine *f* de téléphérique

5 *Am Rail* **g. (car)** wagon *m* plat

►► *Mktg* ***gondola end*** tête *f* de gondole

gondolier [,gɒndə'lɪə(r)] **N** gondolier *m*

gone [gɒn] *pp of* **go**

ADJ 1 *(past)* passé, révolu; **those days are g. now** c'est bien fini tout ça; **g. is the time when…** le temps n'est plus où…

2 *(away)* **be g. (with you)!** disparaissez de ma vue!

3 *Fam (high, drunk)* parti; **to be well** *or* **far g.** être parti, planer

4 *Fam (pregnant)* **she is four months g.** elle est enceinte de quatre mois◻; **how far g. is she?** elle est enceinte de combien?◻

5 *Fam (infatuated)* **to be g. on sb/sth** être (complètement) toqué de qn/qch

6 *Euph (dead)* mort; **when I'm g.** quand je ne serai plus là

PREP *Br* **it's g. eleven** il est onze heures passées *ou* plus de onze heures

goner ['gɒnə(r)] **N** *Fam* **I thought she was a g.** je pensais qu'elle allait mourir◻; *Fig* **I'm a g. if she finds out where I've been** je suis fichu *ou* foutu si elle apprend où je suis allé

gong [gɒŋ] **N 1** *(instrument)* gong *m* **2** *Br Fam Hum (medal)* médaille◻ *f*

gonna ['gɒnə] *Fam* = **going to**

gonorrhoea, *Am* **gonorrhea** [,gɒnə'rɪə] **N** *(UNCOUNT) Med* blennorragie *f*; **to have g.** avoir *ou* faire une blennorragie

goo [guː] **N** *Fam* **1** *(sticky stuff)* matière *f* poisseuse◻ **2** *Fig Pej* sentimentalisme◻ *m*

goober ['guːbə(r)] **N** *Am Fam* crétin(e) *m,f*, andouille *f*

GOOD [gʊd]

ADJ	
• bon **A1–4, B1, C1–3, D1–4, E1–3**	• beau **A1, D2**
	• gentil **B1**
• sage **B2**	• favorable **C1**
ADV	
• bien **1, 2**	• bon **1**
N	
• bien **1, 3**	

(*compar* **better** ['betə(r)], *superl* **best** [best])

ADJ A. 1 *(enjoyable, pleasant ► book, feeling, holiday)* bon, agréable; *(► weather)* beau (belle); **we're g. friends** nous sommes très amis; **we're just g. friends** on est des amis, c'est tout; **they had a g. time** ils se sont bien amusés; **we had g. weather during the holidays** il faisait beau pendant nos vacances; **g. to eat/to hear** bon à manger/à entendre; **it's g. to be home** ça fait du bien *ou* ça fait plaisir de rentrer chez soi; **it's g. to be alive** il fait bon vivre; **wait until he's in a g. mood** attendez qu'il soit de bonne humeur; **to feel g.** être en forme; **he doesn't feel g. about leaving her alone** *(worried)* ça l'ennuie de la laisser seule; *(ashamed)* il a honte de la laisser seule; **it's too g. to be true** c'est trop beau pour être vrai *ou* pour y croire; **the g. life** la belle vie; **this is as g. as you can get** *or* **as it gets** c'est ce qui se fait de mieux; **she's never had it so g.!** elle n'a jamais eu la vie si belle!; **have a g. day!** bonne journée!; **it's g. to see you** je suis/nous sommes content(s) de te voir; **you can have too much of a g. thing** on se lasse de tout, même du meilleur

2 *(high quality ► clothing, dishes)* bon, de bonne qualité; *(► painting, film, food)* bon; **it's a g. school** c'est une bonne école; **he speaks g. English** il parle bien anglais; **she put her g. shoes on** elle a mis ses belles chaussures; **to protect their g. name** pour défendre leur réputation; **she's from a g. family** elle est de bonne famille; **this house is g. enough for me** cette maison me suffit; **this isn't g. enough** ça ne va pas; **this work isn't g. enough** ce travail laisse beaucoup à désirer; **nothing is too g. for her family** rien n'est trop beau pour sa famille; **it makes g. television** ça marche bien à la télévision

3 *(competent, skilful)* bon, compétent; **do you know a g. lawyer?** connaissez-vous un bon avocat?; **she's a very g. doctor** c'est un excellent médecin; **he's a g. swimmer** c'est un bon nageur; **she's a g. listener** c'est quelqu'un qui sait écouter; **to be g. in bed** être bien au lit; **to be g. at sth** être doué pour *ou* bon en qch; **he's g. with children** il sait s'y prendre avec les enfants; **to be g. with one's hands** être habile *ou* adroit de ses mains; **you're as g. as he is** tu le vaux bien, tu vaux autant que lui; **to be g. on French history/contract law** *(author)* être bon en histoire de France/sur le droit des contrats

4 *(useful)* bon; **to be g. for nothing** être bon à rien; **this product is also g. for cleaning windows** ce produit est bien aussi pour nettoyer les vitres

5 *(in greetings)* **g. afternoon!** *(hello)* bonjour!; *(goodbye)* bon après-midi!; *Old-fashioned* **g. day!** *(hello)* bonjour!; *Br (goodbye)* adieu!; **g. evening!** bonsoir!; **g. morning!** *(hello)* bonjour!; *(goodbye)* au revoir!, bonne journée!

B. 1 *(kind)* bon, gentil; *(loyal, true)* bon, véritable; *(moral, virtuous)* bon; **g. behaviour** *or* **conduct** bonne conduite *f*; **she's a g. person** c'est quelqu'un de bien; **he's a g. sort** c'est un brave type; **he's been a g. husband to her** il a été pour elle un bon mari; **you're too g. for him** tu mérites mieux que lui; **they took advantage of his g. nature** ils ont profité de son bon naturel *ou* caractère; **to lead a g. life** *(comfortable)* avoir une belle vie; *(moral)* mener une vie vertueuse *ou* exemplaire; **they've always been g. to me** ils ont toujours été gentils avec moi; **life has been g. to me** j'ai eu de la chance dans la vie; **that's very g. of you** c'est très aimable de votre part; **he was very g. about it** il s'est montré très compréhensif; **would you be g. enough to ask him?** auriez-vous la bonté de lui demander?, seriez-vous assez aimable pour lui demander?

2 *(well-behaved)* sage; **be g.!** sois sage!; **be a g. boy and fetch Mummy's bag** sois mignon, va chercher le sac de maman; **g. dog!** *(encouraging)* oh, le beau chien!; *(congratulating)* c'est bien, le chien!; **to be as g. as gold** être sage comme une image

C. 1 *(favourable ► contract, deal)* avantageux, favorable; *(► opportunity, sign)* bon, favorable; **to buy sth at a g. price** acheter qch bon marché *ou* à un prix avantageux; **you've got a g. chance** tu as toutes tes chances; **she's in a g. position to help us** elle est bien placée pour nous aider; **he put in a g. word for me with the boss** il a glissé un mot en ma faveur au patron; **we made the trip in g. time** le voyage n'a pas été trop long; **it's looking g.** *(is going well)* ça a l'air de bien se passer; *(is going to succeed)* ça se présente bien; **all g. wishes for the New Year** tous mes/nos meilleurs vœux pour le nouvel an

2 *(convenient, suitable ► place, time)* bon, propice; *(► choice)* bon, convenable; **it's a g. holiday spot for people with children** c'est un lieu de vacances idéal pour ceux qui ont des enfants; **is this a g. moment to ask him?** est-ce un bon moment pour lui demander?; **this is as g. a time as any** autant le faire maintenant; **it's as g. a place as any to stay** qu'on séjourne là ou ailleurs, ça ne fait pas de différence; **it's a g. job** *or* **g. thing he decided not to go** c'est une chance qu'il ait décidé de *ou* heureusement qu'il a décidé de ne pas y aller

3 *(beneficial)* bon, bienfaisant; **eat your spinach, it's g. for you** mange tes épinards, c'est bon pour toi; **to be g. for business** être bon pour les affaires; **he's not g. for her** il a une mauvaise influence sur elle; **this cold weather isn't g. for your health** ce froid n'est pas bon pour ta santé *ou* est mauvais pour toi; **it's g. for him to spend**

time outdoors ça lui fait du bien *ou* c'est bon pour lui de passer du temps dehors; *Fig* **he doesn't know what's g. for him** il ne sait pas ce qui est bon pour lui; *Fig* **if you know what's g. for you, you'll listen** si tu as le moindre bon sens, tu m'écouteras

D. 1 *(sound, strong)* bon, valide; **I can do a lot with my g. arm** je peux faire beaucoup de choses avec mon bras valide; **my eyesight/hearing is g.** j'ai une bonne vue/l'ouïe fine

2 *(attractive ▸ appearance)* bon, beau (belle); *(▸ features, legs)* beau (belle), joli; **you're looking g.!** *(healthy)* tu as bonne mine!; *(well-dressed)* tu es très bien!; **that colour looks g. on him** cette couleur lui va bien; **she has a g. figure** elle est bien faite; **the vase looks g. there** le vase rend très bien là

3 *(valid, well-founded)* bon, valable; **she had a g. excuse/reason for not going** elle avait une bonne excuse pour/une bonne raison de ne pas y aller; **they made out a g. case against drinking tap water** ils ont bien expliqué pourquoi il ne fallait pas boire l'eau du robinet

4 *(reliable, trustworthy ▸ brand, car)* bon, sûr; *Com & Fin (▸ cheque)* bon; *(▸ investment, securities)* sûr; *(▸ debt)* bon, certain; **my passport is g. for five years** mon passeport est bon *ou* valable pour cinq ans; **this coat is g. for another year** ce manteau fera encore un an; *Fam* **he's always g. for a laugh** il sait toujours faire rire□; **he should be g. for a couple of hundred pounds** on devrait pouvoir en tirer quelques centaines de livres

E. 1 *(ample, considerable)* bon, considérable; **we still have a g. way to go** nous avons encore un bon bout de chemin à faire; **a g. few people** pas mal de gens; **I make g. money** je gagne bien ma vie; **I was a g. way into the book when I realized that…** j'avais déjà bien avancé dans ma lecture quand je me suis rendu compte que… + *indicative*; **the trip will take you a g. two hours** il vous faudra deux bonnes heures pour faire le voyage; **she's been gone a g. while** ça fait un bon moment qu'elle est partie; **there's a g. risk of it happening** il y a de grands risques que ça arrive

2 *(proper, thorough)* bon, grand; **I gave the house a g. clean** j'ai fait le ménage à fond; **have a g. cry** pleure un bon coup; **we had a g. laugh** on a bien ri; **I managed to get a g. look at his face** j'ai pu bien regarder son visage; **he got a g. spanking** il a reçu une bonne fessée

3 *(indicating approval)* bon, très bien; **I'd like a new suit – very g., sir!** j'ai besoin d'un nouveau costume – (très) bien, monsieur!; **she left him – g.!** elle l'a quitté – tant mieux!; **g., that's settled** bon *ou* bien, voilà une affaire réglée; **(that) sounds g.!** *(good idea)* bonne idée!; *Fam* **that's a g. one!** *(joke)* elle est (bien) bonne, celle-là!; *Ironic (far-fetched story)* à d'autres!; *Fam* **g. for you!**, *Austr* **g. on you!** bravo!□, très bien!□; **g. old Eric, I knew he wouldn't let us down!** ce brave Eric, je savais qu'il ne nous laisserait pas tomber!; **the g. old days** le bon vieux temps

4 to make g. *(succeed)* réussir, faire son chemin; *(reform)* changer de conduite, se refaire une vie; **a local boy made g.** un garçon du pays *ou* du coin qui a fait son chemin; **the prisoner made g. his escape** le prisonnier est parvenu à s'échapper *ou* a réussi son évasion; **they made g. their promise** ils ont tenu parole *ou* ont respecté leur promesse; **to make sth g.** *(mistake)* remédier à qch; *(damages, injustice)* réparer qch; *(losses)* compenser qch; *(deficit)* combler qch; *(wall, surface)* apporter des finitions à qch

ADV 1 *(as intensifier)* bien, bon; **a g. hard bed** un lit bien dur; **I'd like a g. hot bath** j'ai envie de prendre un bon bain chaud; **the two friends had a g. long chat** les deux amis ont longuement bavardé

2 *Fam (well)* bien□; **she writes g.** elle écrit bien; **how are you? – g., thanks** comment allez-vous? – bien, merci□; **the boss gave it to them g. and proper** le patron leur a passé un de ces savons; **I'll do it when I'm g. and ready** je le ferai quand ça me chantera; **I like my coffee g. and strong** j'aime le café bien fort□

N 1 *(morality, virtue)* bien *m*; **to do g.** faire le bien; **that will do more harm than g.** ça fera plus de mal que de bien; **to return g. for evil** rendre le bien pour le mal; **she recognized the g. in him** elle a vu ce qu'il y avait de bon en lui; **there is g. and bad in everyone** il y a du bon et du mauvais en chacun de nous; **to be up to no g.** préparer un mauvais coup; **their daughter came to no g.** leur fille a mal tourné

2 *(use)* **this book isn't much g. to me** ce livre ne me sert pas à grand-chose; **I was never any g. at mathematics** je n'ai jamais été doué pour les maths, je n'ai jamais été bon *ou* fort en maths; **he's no g.** il est nul; **he'd be no g. as a teacher** il ne ferait pas un bon professeur; **what g. would it do to leave now?** à quoi bon partir maintenant?; *Fam* **a fat lot of g. that did you!** te voilà bien avancé maintenant!; **it's no g. worrying about it** ça ne sert à rien de *ou* ce n'est pas la peine de *ou* inutile de vous inquiéter; **I might as well talk to the wall for all the g. it does** je ferais aussi bien de parler au mur, pour tout l'effet que ça fait

3 *(benefit, welfare)* bien *m*; **I did it for your own g.** je l'ai fait pour ton (propre) bien; **a holiday will do her g.** des vacances lui feront du bien; **she resigned for the g. of her health** elle a démissionné pour des raisons de santé; **much g. may it do you!** grand bien vous fasse!; **the common g.** l'intérêt *m* commun

NPL *(people)* **the g.** les bons *mpl*, les gens *mpl* de bien; **the g. and the bad** les bons et les méchants

• **as good as** **ADV** pour ainsi dire, à peu de chose près; **I'm as g. as blind without my glasses** sans lunettes je suis pour ainsi dire aveugle; **he's as g. as dead** c'est comme s'il était mort; **the job is as g. as finished** la tâche est pour ainsi dire *ou* est pratiquement finie; **it's as g. as new** c'est comme neuf; **he as g. as admitted he was wrong** il a pour ainsi dire reconnu qu'il avait tort; **they as g. as called us liars** ils n'ont pas dit qu'on était des menteurs, mais c'était tout comme; **are you married? – as g. as** tu es marié? – non, mais c'est tout comme

• **for good** **ADV** pour de bon; **she's left for g.** elle est partie pour de bon; **they finally settled down for g.** ils se sont enfin fixés définitivement; **for g. and all** une (bonne) fois pour toutes, pour de bon

• **to the good** **ADV** **that's all to the g.** tant mieux; **he finished up the card game £15 to the g.** il a fait 15 livres de bénéfice *ou* il a gagné 15 livres aux cartes

▸▸ ***the Good Book*** la Bible; ***good cause*** juste titre *m*; **to do sth with g. cause** faire qch à juste titre; ***good faith*** bonne foi *f*; **to act in g. faith** agir en toute bonne foi; ***Good Friday*** le vendredi saint; ***good looks*** *(attractive appearance)* beauté *f*; *Bible* ***the Good Samaritan*** le bon Samaritain

GOOD FRIDAY

En Grande-Bretagne, il est traditionnel, le jour du vendredi saint, de manger des "hot cross buns" (petits pains ronds aux fruits secs, marqués d'une croix).

THE GOOD FRIDAY AGREEMENT

Le processus de paix en Irlande du Nord, qui a été amorcé par les cessez-le-feu des groupes paramilitaires républicains et unionistes en 1994, a abouti au "Good Friday Agreement", l'accord de paix signé à Belfast en avril 1998. Cet accord, parrainé par les Premiers ministres britannique et irlandais, et finalement approuvé par le Sinn Féin et par la plupart des partis unionistes, a mis en place la "Northern Ireland Assembly", un parlement en partie autonome avec un partage démocratique du pouvoir entre les communautés protestante et catholique. Depuis son instauration, cependant, le parlement a évolué dans un climat politique incertain et a été suspendu à plusieurs reprises, notamment à cause d'une polémique sur le désarmement de l'IRA et de dissensions continuelles entre unionistes et républicains. Cependant, la décision de l'IRA – rendue publique en juillet 2005 – de renoncer à la lutte armée de façon permanente puis l'annonce de la destruction de son arsenal laisse espérer une évolution vers des relations plus harmonieuses entre les deux communautés.

goodbye [gʊd'baɪ] **EXCLAM** au revoir!; **g. for now** à bientôt, à la prochaine

N adieu *m*, au revoir *m*; **I hate goodbyes** j'ai horreur des adieux; **we said our goodbyes and left** on a fait nos adieux et on est partis; **to say g. to sb** dire au revoir *ou* faire ses adieux à qn, prendre congé de qn; **to give sb a g. kiss/hug** embrasser qn/serrer qn dans ses bras pour lui dire au revoir; **g. present** cadeau *m* d'adieu

good-for-nothing **ADJ** bon *ou* propre à rien; **he's a g. layabout!** c'est un bon à rien et un fainéant!

N vaurien(enne) *m,f*, propre-à-rien *mf*

good-hearted [-'hɑːtɪd] **ADJ** *(person)* bon, généreux; *(action)* fait avec les meilleures intentions

good-humoured, *Am* **good-humored** **ADJ** *(person ▸ generally)* bon enfant *(inv)*; *(▸ on one occasion)* de bonne humeur; *(discussion)* amical; *(joke, remark)* sans malice; **he is always g.** il a bon caractère

good-humouredly, *Am* **good-humoredly** [-'hjuːmədlɪ] **ADV** avec bonne humeur

goodish ['gʊdɪʃ] **ADJ** *Fam* **1** *(quite good)* assez bon□, passable□ **2** *(number, quantity, amount)* assez grand□; **it's a g. step from here** c'est à un bon bout de chemin d'ici; **it's a g. size** c'est assez grand; **add a g. pinch of salt** ajoutez une bonne pincée de sel

good-looker **N** *Fam (man)* beau mec *m*; *(woman)* belle créature *f*; *(younger)* beau brin de fille *m*

good-looking **ADJ** *(person, car, shot)* beau (belle); **he's very g.** il est beau garçon; **she's quite g.** elle n'est pas mal; **hey, g.!** *(to woman)* eh, ma jolie!; *(to man)* eh, beau gosse!

goodly ['gʊdlɪ] *(compar* **goodlier**, *superl* **goodliest)** **ADJ** *Arch (amount, size)* considérable, important; **a g. sum of money** une belle somme d'argent

good-natured **ADJ** *(person)* facile à vivre, qui a un bon naturel; *(face, smile)* bon enfant *(inv)*; *(remark)* sans malice

good-naturedly [-'neɪtʃədlɪ] **ADV** avec bonne humeur, avec bonhomie

goodness ['gʊdnɪs] **N 1** *(of person)* bonté *f*, bienveillance *f*, bienfaisance *f*; *(of thing)* (bonne) qualité *f*, excellence *f*, perfection *f*; **out of the g. of my heart** par pure bonté **2** *(nourishment)* valeur *f* nutritive; **there's a lot of g. in fresh vegetables** les légumes frais sont pleins de bonnes choses **3** *Fam (in interjections)* **(my) g.!** mon Dieu!; **thank g.!** Dieu merci!; **g. gracious (me)!** Seigneur!, mon Dieu!; **for g. sake!** bon sang!; **g. knows!** Dieu seul le sait!; **g. knows why** Dieu sait pourquoi; **I wish to g. he would shut up!** si seulement il pouvait se taire!

goodnight [gʊd'naɪt] **EXCLAM** *(when leaving)* bonsoir!; *(when going to bed)* bonne nuit!

N **they said g. and left** ils ont dit bonsoir et sont partis; **she kissed her mother g. and went to bed** elle a dit bonsoir à sa mère et est allée se coucher; **give your mother a g. kiss** embrasse ta mère *(pour lui dire bonsoir)*

goods [gʊdz] **NPL 1** *(possessions)* biens *mpl*; **he gave up all his worldly g.** il a renoncé à tous ses biens *mpl* matériels; *Br* **g. and chattels** biens *mpl* et effets *mpl* **2** *Com* marchandises *fpl*, articles *mpl*; **send us the g. by rail** envoyez-nous la marchandise par chemin de fer; **leather g.** articles *mpl* de cuir, maroquinerie *f*; *Fam* **to deliver the g.** tenir parole□; *Fig* **a computer that can deliver the g.** un ordinateur qui tient ses promesses; *Fig* **to come up with the g.** faire le nécessaire; *Am Fam* **to have the g. on sb** avoir la preuve de la culpabilité de qn□

▸▸ *Br Rail* ***goods depot*** dépôt *m* de marchandises; *Br Rail* ***goods train*** train *m* de marchandises; *Br* ***goods vehicle*** poids *m* lourd, véhicule *m* utilitaire; *Br Rail* ***goods wagon*** wagon *m* de marchandises; *Br Rail* ***goods yard*** dépôt *m* de marchandises

good-tempered **ADJ** *(person)* qui a un bon caractère, d'humeur égale; *(reply, discussion)* aimable

good-till-cancelled order N *St Exch* ordre *m* à révocation

good-time girl N *Fam Pej* noceuse *f*

goodwill [ˌgʊd'wɪl] N *(UNCOUNT)* **1** *(benevolence)* bienveillance *f*; **to show g. towards sb** faire preuve de bienveillance à l'égard de qn; **to retain sb's g.** conserver les bonnes grâces de qn; **a gesture of g.** un geste de bonne volonté **2** *(willingness)* bonne volonté *f* **3** *Com* fonds *m* de commerce, (biens *mpl*) incorporels *mpl*

COMP *(gesture, visit)* d'amitié, de bienveillance

▸▸ ***goodwill ambassador*** ambassadeur(drice) *m,f* de bonne volonté; ***goodwill mission*** visite *f* d'amitié

goody ['gʊdɪ] *(pl* **goodies**) *Fam* EXCLAM génial!, chouette!, chic!

• **goodies** NPL **1** *(presents, prizes)* bonne choses□ *fpl*; *(sweets, treats)* bonbons□ *mpl*, friandises□ *fpl* **2 the goodies and the baddies** *(in film, game etc)* les bons *mpl* et les méchants *mpl*

goody-goody *(pl* **goody-goodies**) *Fam Pej* ADJ de petit saint; **she's awfully g.** elle prend toujours des airs de petite sainte

N petit(e) saint(e) *m,f*, *Hum* modèle *m* de vertu

goody-two-shoes N *Fam Pej* petit(e) saint(e) *m,f*, *Hum* modèle *m* de vertu

gooey ['gu:ɪ] *(compar* **gooier**, *superl* **gooiest**) ADJ *Fam* **1** *(substance)* gluant□, visqueux□, poisseux□; *(sweets)* qui colle aux dents□ **2** *(sentimental)* sentimental□; **she goes all g. over babies** elle devient gâteuse quand elle voit un bébé

goof [gu:f] *Fam* N **1** *(fool)* imbécile□ *mf*, andouille *f* **2** *(blunder)* gaffe *f*

VI **1** *(blunder)* faire une gaffe **2** *(joke)* rigoler; **to g. with sb** *(tease)* faire enrager qn□ **3** *(stare)* **to g. at sb/sth** regarder qn/qch bêtement□

▸**goof about, goof around** *Am Fam* VI **1** *(act foolishly)* faire le con, déconner **2** *(waste time)* glander, glandouiller

▸**goof off** *Am Fam* VT INSEP **to g. off school** sécher l'école; **to g. off work** ne pas aller bosser

VI *(waste time)* flemmarder; *(malinger)* tirer au flanc

▸**goof up** *Fam* VT SEP bousiller, saloper; **he goofed the job up** il a salopé le travail

VI merder

goofball ['gu:fbɔ:l] *Am Fam* N **1** *(drug)* barbiturique□ *m* **2** *(fool)* crétin(e) *m,f*, andouille *f*

goofy ['gu:fɪ] *(compar* **goofier**, *superl* **goofiest**) ADJ *Fam* **1** *(stupid)* dingo **2** *Br* **to have g. teeth** avoir les dents qui courent après le bifteck

google ['gu:gəl] *Fam* VT **to g. sb/sth** faire une recherche sur qn/qch sur Internet

VI **to g. (for sb/sth)** faire une recherche (sur qn/qch) sur Internet

googly ['gu:glɪ] *(pl* **googlies**) N *(in cricket)* = balle lancée avec de l'effet qui prend le batteur à contre-pied alors qu'il pensait l'avoir bien anticipée; *Fig* **to bowl sb a g.** essayer de tromper qn

gook [gu:k] N *Am Fam* **1** *(Oriental)* bridé(e) *m,f*, = terme injurieux désignant un Asiatique **2** *(muck)* saleté□ *f*, crasse *f*

goolies ['gu:lɪz] NPL *very Fam* couilles *fpl*

goon [gu:n] N *Fam* **1** *(fool)* abruti(e) *m,f* **2** *Am (hired thug)* casseur *m (au service de quelqu'un)*

goosander [gu:'sændə(r)] N *Orn* harle *m* bièvre

goose [gu:s] *(pl* **geese** [gi:s]) N **1** *(bird)* oie *f*; **g. egg** œuf *m* d'oie; *Am Fam* zéro□ *m*; *Fig* **to kill the g. that lays the golden egg** tuer la poule aux œufs d'or; *Fig* **your g. is cooked** tu es fichu; *Fig* **all his geese are swans** à l'entendre, tout ce qu'il fait tient du prodige **2** *Fam Old-fashioned (fool)* **don't be such a g.!** ne sois pas si bête!□

VT *Fam* **to g. sb** mettre la main au cul à qn

▸▸ *esp Am* ***goose bumps*** chair *f* de poule; ***goose fat*** graisse *f* d'oie; *Br* ***goose pimples*** chair *f* de poule; **to get** *or* **to come out in g. pimples** avoir la chair de poule; ***goose step*** pas *m* de l'oie

gooseberry ['gʊzbərɪ] *(pl* **gooseberries**) N **1** *Bot* groseille *f* à maquereau **2** *(unwanted person)* **to be** *or* **to play g.** tenir la chandelle

▸▸ ***gooseberry bush*** groseillier *m*; *Hum* **we found you under a g. bush** c'est la cigogne qui t'a apporté

goosegog ['gu:zgɒg] N *Br Fam* groseille *f* à maquereau□

goosestep ['gu:sstep] *(pt & pp* **goosestepped**, *cont* **goosestepping**) N pas *m* de l'oie

VI faire le pas de l'oie; **they goosestepped across the parade ground** ils ont traversé le terrain de manœuvres au pas de l'oie

GOP [ˌdʒi:əʊ'pi:] N *Am (abbr* **Grand Old Party**) = le parti républicain aux États-Unis

gopher[1] ['gəʊfə(r)] N **1** *(pouched rat)* gaufre *m* **2** *(ground squirrel)* spermophile *m* **3** *(tortoise)* = espèce de tortues qui s'enfouissent dans le sol

gopher[2] = **gofer**

gorblimey [gɔ:'blaɪmɪ] EXCLAM *Br Fam* mon Dieu!, mince!

gore [gɔ:(r)] N **1** *(blood)* sang *m* (coagulé); **blood and g.** du sang et encore du sang; **there's plenty of g. in this movie** ce film est sanglant à souhait **2** *Sewing* godet *m*; *Naut* pointe *f* (de voile); *(land)* langue *f* de terre

VT **1** *(wound)* blesser à coups de cornes, encorner; **he was gored to death** il a été tué d'un coup de corne **2** *Naut (sail)* mettre une pointe à

Gore-Tex® ['gɔ:teks] N Gore-Tex® *m*

gorge [gɔ:dʒ] N **1** *Geog* défilé *m*, gorge *f* **2** *Arch (throat)* gorge *f*, gosier *m*; *Fig* **it made my g. rise** cela m'a rendu malade *ou* m'a soulevé le cœur

VT **to g. oneself (on sth)** se gaver *ou* se gorger *ou* se bourrer (de qch)

VI **to g. (on sth)** se gaver *ou* se gorger *ou* se bourrer (de qch)

gorgeous ['gɔ:dʒəs] ADJ **1** *Fam (wonderful ▸ person, weather)* magnifique□, splendide□, superbe□; *(▸ flat, house)* magnifique□, très beau (belle)□; *(▸ food, meal)* délicieux□; *Fam* **hello g.!** bonjour, ma beauté! **2** *(magnificent ▸ fabric, clothing)* somptueux

gorgeously ['gɔ:dʒəslɪ] ADV **1** *Fam (wonderfully)* magnifiquement□ **2** *(magnificently)* somptueusement

Gorgon ['gɔ:gən] N *Myth* **the Gorgons** les Gorgones *fpl*

• **gorgon** N *(fierce woman)* harpie *f*, dragon *m*

gorilla [gə'rɪlə] N **1** *Zool* gorille *m* **2** *Fam (thug)* voyou□ *m*; *(bodyguard)* gorille *m*

gormless ['gɔ:mlɪs] ADJ *Br Fam (person, expression)* stupide□, abruti; **don't look so g.!** ne prends pas cet air d'abruti!

gorse [gɔ:s] N *(UNCOUNT)* ajoncs *mpl*

▸▸ ***gorse bush*** ajonc *m*

gory ['gɔ:rɪ] *(compar* **gorier**, *superl* **goriest**) ADJ *(battle, scene, sight, death)* sanglant; **in g. detail** avec les détails les plus sanglants; *Hum* **spare me all the g. details** épargne-moi les détails

gosh [gɒʃ] EXCLAM *Fam* oh dis donc!, ça alors!, hé ben!

goshawk ['gɒshɔ:k] N *Orn* autour *m*

gosling ['gɒzlɪŋ] N oison *m*

go-slow N *Br* grève *f* du zèle, grève *f* perlée

gospel ['gɒspəl] N **1** *Bible* évangile *m*; **St Mark's G., the G. according to St Mark** l'Évangile *m* selon saint Marc; **to preach the g.** prêcher l'évangile; *Fig* **to preach the g. of monetarism** prêcher le monétarisme; *Fig* **to take sth as g.** prendre qch pour parole d'évangile **2** *Mus* gospel *m*

▸▸ ***gospel music*** gospel *m*; ***gospel oath*** serment *m* prêté sur l'Évangile; ***gospel singer*** chanteur (euse) *m,f* de gospels; ***gospel song*** negro spiritual *m*; *Fig* ***the gospel truth*** la vérité vraie

gospeller, *Am* **gospeler** ['gɒspələ(r)] N évangéliste *mf*

gossamer ['gɒsəmə(r)] N *(UNCOUNT) (cobweb)* fils *mpl* de la Vierge, filandres *fpl*; *(gauze)* gaze *f*; *(light cloth)* étoffe *f* transparente; **like g.** avec une légèreté arachnéenne

COMP arachnéen, très léger, très fin

gossip ['gɒsɪp] N **1** *(UNCOUNT) (casual chat)* bavardage *m*, papotage *m*; *Pej (rumour)* commérage *m*, ragots *mpl*, racontars *mpl*; *(in newspaper)* potins *mpl*; **to have a good g.** bien papoter; **have you heard the latest (bit of) g.?** vous connaissez la dernière (nouvelle)?; **that's just (idle) g.** ce ne sont que des bavardages (futiles); **the paper gives all the local g.** il y a tous les petits potins du coin dans le journal **2** *Pej (person)* bavard(e) *m,f*, pie *f*, commère *f*; **he's such a g.** quelle commère!

VI bavarder, papoter; *(maliciously)* faire des commérages, dire du mal des gens; **people are always gossiping about their neighbours** les gens ont toujours des ragots à raconter sur leurs voisins

▸▸ ***gossip column*** échos *mpl*; ***gossip columnist***, ***gossip writer*** échotier(ère) *m,f*

gossiping ['gɒsɪpɪŋ] ADJ bavard; *Pej* cancanier

N bavardage *m*, papotage *m*; *Pej* commérage *m*

gossipmonger ['gɒsɪpˌmʌŋgə(r)] N commère *f*

gossipy ['gɒsɪpɪ] ADJ *Fam (person)* bavard; *Pej* cancanier; *(letter)* plein de bavardages; *(style)* de conversation mondaine

got [gɒt] *pt & pp of* **get**

gotcha ['gɒtʃə] EXCLAM *Fam* **1** *(I understand)* pigé! **2** *(when catching someone doing something)* je t'y prends!; *(when one has an advantage over someone)* je te tiens!; *(when hitting target)* je t'ai eu!

Goth [gɒθ] N **1** *Hist* Goth *m*; **the Goths** les Goths *mpl* **2** *(modern-day)* = amateur de musique "Gothic", aux vêtements généralement noirs et au maquillage blafard

Gothic ['gɒθɪk] ADJ *Art, Archit, Literature & Typ* gothique; *(music, style, clothes)* = relatif au mouvement "gothique"

N **1** *Art, Archit & Literature* gothique *m* **2** *Ling* gothique *m*, gothique *m*

▸▸ ***Gothic novel*** roman *m* gothique; ***Gothic rock*** = type de musique post-punk assez sombre, des années 80–90

gotta ['gɒtə] *Am Fam* = **have got a, have got to**

gotten ['gɒtən] *Am pp of* **get**

gouache [gʊ'a:ʃ] *Art* N *(paint, painting)* gouache *f*

ADJ à la gouache

gouge [gaʊdʒ] N gouge *f*

VT *(with gouge)* gouger; **to g. a hole in sth** *(intentionally)* creuser un trou dans qch; *(accidentally)* faire un trou dans qch;

▸**gouge out** VT SEP *(with gouge)* gouger, creuser (à la gouge); *(with thumb)* évider, creuser; *Fig* **to g. sb's eyes out** arracher les yeux à qn

goulash ['gu:læʃ] N goulache *m*, goulasch *m*

gourd [gʊəd] N **1** *(plant)* gourde *f*, cucurbitacée *f*; *(fruit)* gourde *f*, calebasse *f* **2** *(container)* gourde *f*, calebasse *f*

gourmand ['gʊəmənd] N *(glutton)* gourmand(e) *m,f*; *(gourmet)* gourmet *m*

gourmet ['gʊəmeɪ] N gourmet *m*, gastronome *mf*

COMP *(meal, restaurant, cooking)* gastronomique

▸▸ ***gourmet cook*** cordon-bleu *m*

gout [gaʊt] N **1** *(UNCOUNT) Med* goutte *f* **2** *Arch or Literary (blob)* goutte *f*

gouty ['gaʊtɪ] ADJ *(leg, person)* goutteux

Gov 1 *(written abbr* **government**) gouvernement *m* **2** *(written abbr* **governor**) gouverneur *m*

.gov [ˈdɒtˈgʌv] *Comput* = abréviation désignant les sites gouvernementaux dans les adresses électroniques

govern ['gʌvən] VT **1** *(country)* gouverner, régner sur; *(city, region, bank)* gouverner; *(affairs)* administrer, gérer; *(company, organization)* diriger, gérer; **when Louis XIV governed France** quand Louis XIV gouvernait la France *ou* régnait sur la France

2 *(determine ▸ behaviour, choice, events, speed)* déterminer; **laws that g. chemical reactions** lois qui régissent les réactions chimiques

3 *(restrain ▸ passions)* maîtriser, dominer

4 *Gram (case, mood)* régir

5 *Tech* régler

VI *Com & Pol* gouverner, commander, diriger

governance ['gʌvənəns] N **1** *(act, manner)* gouvernement *m*, régime *m* **2** *(control)* emprise *f*

governess ['gʌvənɪs] N gouvernante *f*

governing ['gʌvənɪŋ] ADJ **1** *Com & Pol* gouvernant, dirigeant; **the g. party** le parti au pouvoir **2** *(factor)* dominant; **the g. principle** le principe directeur

N gouvernement *m*

►► ***governing body*** conseil *m* d'administration

government ['gʌvənmənt] **N 1** *Pol (governing authority)* gouvernement *m*; *(type of authority)* gouvernement *m*, régime *m*; *(the State)* gouvernement *m*, État *m*; **to form a g.** constituer *ou* former un gouvernement; **the project is financed by the g.** le projet est financé par l'État *ou* le gouvernement **2** *(process of governing* ► *country)* gouvernement *m*, direction *f*; *(*► *company)* administration *f*, gestion *f*; *(*► *affairs)* conduite *f*; **democratic g.** la démocratie

COMP *(measure, policy)* gouvernemental, du gouvernement; *(expenditure)* de l'État, public; *(minister, department)* du gouvernement

►► ***government agency*** agence *f* gouvernementale; ***government bonds*** obligations *fpl* d'État, bons *mpl* du Trésor; ***government employee*** employé(e) *m,f* d'administration; ***government finance*** financement *m* par l'État; ***government grant*** subvention *f* de l'État; ***government health warning*** = avertissement officiel contre les dangers du tabac figurant sur les paquets de cigarettes et dans les publicités pour le tabac; *Br* ***Government House*** palais *m* du gouverneur; ***government issue*** émission *f* d'État *ou* par le gouvernement; ***government monopoly*** monopole *m* d'État; ***government offices*** bureaux *mpl* du gouvernement; ***government property*** propriété *f* de l'État; *Fin* ***government securities*** effets *mpl* publics, fonds *mpl* publics *ou* d'État; ***government spending*** dépenses *fpl* publiques; *Fin* ***government stock*** effets *mpl* publics, fonds *mpl* publics *ou* d'État

governmental [ˌgʌvən'mentəl] **ADJ** gouvernemental, du gouvernement; **a g. organization** une organisation gouvernementale

government-sponsored ADJ parrainé par le gouvernement; **g. terrorism** terrorisme *m* d'État

governor ['gʌvənə(r)] **N 1** *(of bank, country)* gouverneur *m*; *Br (of prison)* directeur(trice) *m,f*; *Br (of school)* membre *m* du conseil d'établissement; *Am* **State g.** gouverneur *m* d'État

2 *Br Fam (employer)* patron[□] *m*, boss *m*

3 *Br Fam (form of address)* **where to, g.?** on va où, patron?

4 *Tech* régulateur *m*

governorship ['gʌvənəʃɪp] **N** fonctions *fpl* de gouverneur

govt *(written abbr* **government)** gouv.

gown [gaʊn] **N 1** *(dress)* robe *f* **2** *(of magistrate, teacher, academic)* robe *f*, toge *f*; *(of surgeon)* blouse *f*

goy [gɔɪ] *(pl* **goys** *or* **goyim** ['gɔɪɪm]) **N** goy *mf*, goï *mf*

GP [ˌdʒiː'piː] **N** *(abbr* **general practitioner)** (médecin *m)* généraliste *mf*, *Can* omnipraticien(enne) *m,f*

GPA [ˌdʒiːpiː'eɪ] **N** *Am Sch (abbr* **grade point average)** moyenne *f*

GPO [ˌdʒiːpiː'əʊ] **N** *Br Formerly (abbr* **General Post Office) the G.** = titre officiel de la Poste britannique avant 1969

GPRS [ˌdʒiːpiːɑː'res] **N** *Tel (abbr* **General Packet Radio Service)** GPRS *m*

GPS [ˌdʒiːpiː'es] **N** *(abbr* **global positioning system)** GPS *m (système de navigation par satellite)*

gr 1 *(written abbr* **gramme(s))** g **2** *(written abbr* **gross)** brut

grab [græb] *(pt & pp* **grabbed**, *cont* **grabbing) VT 1** *(object)* saisir, empoigner; *(person)* attraper; **to g. hold of sth** saisir qch, empoigner qch; **to g. hold of sb** attraper qn; **he grabbed the book out of my hand** il m'a arraché le livre des mains; **he grabbed my purse and ran** il s'est emparé de mon porte-monnaie et est parti en courant; **she grabbed my arm** elle m'a attrapé par le bras **2** *Fig (opportunity)* saisir; *(attention)* retenir; *(power)* prendre; *(land)* s'emparer de; *(quick meal)* avaler, prendre (en vitesse); *(taxi)* prendre; **I'll g. a sandwich and work through the lunch hour** je vais me prendre un sandwich en vitesse et je travaillerai pendant l'heure du déjeuner **3** *Fam (idioms)* **how does that g. you?** qu'est-ce que tu en dis?[□]; **the film didn't really g. me** le film ne m'a pas vraiment emballé

VI to g. at sb/sth essayer d'agripper qn/qch; **don't g.!** pas touche!; *Fig* **I grabbed at the chance** j'ai sauté sur l'occasion

N 1 *(movement)* mouvement *m* vif; *(sudden theft)* vol *m* (à l'arraché); **to make a g. at** *or* **for sth** essayer de saisir *ou* faire un mouvement vif pour saisir qch; *Fam* **to be up for grabs** *(be available)* être à prendre[□]; *(be on market, for sale)* être à vendre[□]; **they're getting rid of all the furniture, so those chairs are up for grabs** ils se débarrassent de tous leurs meubles, alors ces chaises sont à qui veut les prendre; **is that last chocolate up for grabs?** est-ce que je peux prendre le chocolat qui reste? **2** *Br Tech* benne *f* preneuse **3** *Aut (of brakes)* blocage *m*

►► *Am* ***grab bag*** *(game)* = jeu consistant à chercher des cadeaux enfouis dans un grand sac; *(assortment)* fourre-tout *m inv*; *Tech* ***grab crane*** grue *f* à benne preneuse

grabby ['græbɪ] *(compar* **grabbier**, *superl* **grabbiest) ADJ** *Fam* **1 don't be so g.** *(don't grab things)* ne te jette pas sur les choses[□]; *(don't grab me)* ne t'agrippe pas à moi[□]; **he's very g.** *(of child picking things up)* il touche à tout[□] **2** *(miserly)* pingre, radin

grace [greɪs] **N 1** *(of movement, dancer, athlete)* grâce *f*; *(decency, politeness, tact)* tact *m*; **social graces** savoir-vivre *m*; **to do sth with good/bad g.** faire qch de bonne/mauvaise grâce; **at least he had the (good) g. to apologize** il a au moins eu la décence de s'excuser

2 *Rel* grâce *f*; **by the g. of God** par la grâce de Dieu; **in a state of g.** en état de grâce; **to fall from g.** perdre la grâce; *Fig* tomber en disgrâce; **there but for the g. of God (go I)** ça aurait très bien pu m'arriver aussi; *Arch or Literary* **in the year of g. 1066** en l'an de grâce 1066

3 *(amnesty)* grâce *f*; *(respite)* grâce *f*, répit *m*; *Law* **as an act of g., the King...** en exerçant son droit de grâce, le Roi...; **we have two days' g.** nous disposons de deux jours de répit; *Com* **days of g.** jours *mpl* de grâce

4 *(prayer* ► *before meal)* bénédicité *m*; *(*► *after meal)* grâces *fpl*; **to say g.** *(before meals)* dire le bénédicité; *(after meals)* dire les grâces

5 *Arch (pardon)* grâce *f*, pardon *m*

6 *(idiom)* **to be in sb's good/bad graces** être bien/mal vu par qn

VT 1 *(honour)* honorer; *Hum* **she graced us with her presence** elle nous a honorés de sa présence **2** *Formal or Literary (adorn)* orner, embellir; **some exquisite watercolours graced the walls** les murs étaient ornés de très jolies aquarelles

• **Grace N** *(term of address)* **Your G.** *(to Archbishop)* Monseigneur, (Votre) Excellence, votre Excellence l'Archevêque; *(to Duke)* Monsieur le duc; *(to Duchess)* Madame la duchesse; **His G. the Archbishop** Monseigneur *ou* Son Excellence l'Archevêque

• **Graces NPL** *Myth* **the three Graces** les trois Grâces *fpl*

►► ***grace note*** note *f* d'agrément, ornement *m*; ***grace period*** délai *m* de grâce

grace-and-favour ADJ *Br* **g. residence** = logement appartenant à la Couronne et prêté à une personne que le souverain souhaite honorer

graceful ['greɪsfʊl] **ADJ 1** *(person, movement)* gracieux; **a g. figure** une silhouette élégante; **she is a g. dancer** elle danse avec grâce **2** *(speech)* gracieux, poli, bien tourné

gracefully ['greɪsfʊlɪ] **ADV** *(dance, move)* avec grâce, gracieusement; *(apologize)* avec élégance

gracefulness ['greɪsfʊlnɪs] **N** grâce *f*, élégance *f*

graceless ['greɪslɪs] **ADJ** *(behaviour, person, movement)* gauche

gracious ['greɪʃəs] **ADJ 1** *(generous, kind* ► *gesture, smile)* gracieux, bienveillant; *(*► *action)* généreux; **to be g. to** *or* **towards sb** faire preuve de bienveillance envers qn; **to be g. in defeat** être bon perdant, accepter la défaite avec bonne grâce; **our g. King/Queen** notre gracieux souverain; **by the g. consent of...** par la grâce de... **2** *(luxurious)* **g. living** la vie facile

EXCLAM (good) g. (me)! mon Dieu!; **good g. no!** jamais de la vie!; *Old-fashioned* **goodness g.!** Seigneur Dieu!, bonté divine!

graciously ['greɪʃəslɪ] **ADV** *(smile)* gracieusement; *(accept, agree, allow)* avec bonne grâce, *Formal* gracieusement; *Rel* miséricordieusement

graciousness ['greɪʃəsnɪs] **N** *(of person)* bienveillance *f*, générosité *f*, gentillesse *f*; *(of action)* grâce *f*, élégance *f*; *(of lifestyle, surroundings)* élégance *f*, raffinement *m*; *Rel* miséricorde *f*, clémence *f*

gradate [grə'deɪt] **VT** *(colours)* fondre

VI se fondre **(into** en)

gradation [grə'deɪʃən] **N 1** *(gen)* gradation *f*; **gradations of meaning** nuances *fpl* de sens **2** *(of thermometer, scale)* gradation *f*, degré *m* **3** *Ling* alternance *f* (vocalique), apophonie *f*

grade [greɪd] **N 1** *(level)* degré *m*, niveau *m*; *(on scale)* échelon *m*, grade *m*; *(on salary scale)* indice *m*

2 *Mil* grade *m*, rang *m*, échelon *m*; *(in hierarchy)* échelon *m*, catégorie *f*

3 *(quality* ► *of product)* qualité *f*, catégorie *f*; *(*► *of petrol)* grade *m*; *(size of products)* calibre *m*; **g. A potatoes** pommes de terre de qualité A

4 *Am Sch (mark)* note *f*; *(year)* année *f*, classe *f*; **she gets good grades at school** elle a de bonnes notes à l'école

5 *Am (primary school)* école *f* primaire

6 *Math* grade *m*

7 *Am (gradient)* déclivité *f*, pente *f*; *Rail* rampe *f*

8 *Agr* **grades** bétail *m* amélioré par croisement

9 *(idiom)* **to make the g.** être à la hauteur

VT 1 *(classify* ► *by quality)* classer; *(*► *by size)* calibrer; *(arrange in order)* classer; **to g. questions** classer des questions par ordre de difficulté

2 *Am Sch (mark)* noter

3 *(cross* ► *livestock)* améliorer par sélection

4 *(level)* niveler

►► *Agr* ***grade cattle*** bétail *m* amélioré par croisement; *Am Rail* ***grade crossing*** passage *m* à niveau; *Am Sch* ***grade point average*** moyenne *f*; *Am* ***grade school*** école *f* primaire

► **grade down VT SEP** mettre dans une catégorie inférieure

► **grade up VT SEP 1** *(in rank, hierarchy)* mettre dans une catégorie supérieure **2** *(level)* niveler

graded ['greɪdɪd] **ADJ** *(by quality, arranged in order)* classé; *(by size)* calibré; **g. exercises** exercices *mpl* gradués; **g. tax** *(upwards)* impôt *m* progressif; *(downwards)* impôt *m* dégressif

gradient ['greɪdɪənt] **N 1** *Br (road)* déclivité *f*, pente *f*, inclinaison *f*; *Rail* rampe *f*, pente *f*, inclinaison *f*; **a steep g.** une ligne à forte pente; **a g. of three in ten** *or* **30 percent** une pente de 30 pour cent **2** *Met & Phys* gradient *m*; **pressure g.** gradient *m* de pression

grading ['greɪdɪŋ] **N 1** *(classification)* classification *f*; *(by size)* calibration *f* **2** *Am Sch* notation *f* **3** *Am Constr & Rail (of slope)* aménagement *m*

gradual ['grædʒʊəl] **ADJ** *(change, improvement)* graduel, progressif; *(slope)* doux (douce)

N *Rel* graduel *m*

gradualism ['grædʒʊəlɪzəm] **N** gradualisme *m*; *Pol* réformisme *m*

gradually ['grædʒʊəlɪ] **ADV** progressivement, petit à petit, peu à peu; **it happened very g.** ça s'est produit très progressivement; **g. you'll be able to type without looking at the keyboard** graduellement *ou* petit à petit *ou* progressivement, tu seras capable de taper sans regarder le clavier

graduate N ['grædʒʊət] **1** *Univ* licencié(e) *m,f*, diplômé(e) *m,f*; *Am Sch* bachelier(ère) *m,f*; **biology g.** licencié(e) *m,f* en biologie; **she's an Oxford g.** *or* **a g. of Oxford** elle a fait ses études à Oxford **2** *Am (container)* récipient *m* gradué

ADJ ['grædʒʊət] *Univ* diplômé, licencié

VI ['grædjʊeɪt] **1** *Univ* obtenir son diplôme/sa licence; *Am Sch* obtenir le *ou* être reçu au baccalauréat; **she graduated from the Sorbonne** elle a un diplôme de la Sorbonne; **he graduated in linguistics** il a une licence de linguistique; **I graduated in 1999** j'ai eu ma licence en 1999; *Am Sch* **to g. from high school** terminer ses études secondaires **2** *(gain promotion)* être promu, passer; **to g. from sth to sth** passer de qch à qch; *Fam Fig* **I've graduated from cheap plonk to fine wines** je suis passé du gros rouge aux bons vins

VT ['grædjʊeɪt] **1** *(calibrate)* graduer; **the ruler is graduated in millimetres** la règle est graduée en millimètres **2** *(change, improvement)* graduer **3** *Am Sch & Univ* conférer *ou* accorder un diplôme à

►► ***graduate entry*** échelon *m* d'entrée pour les diplômés; *Am Univ* ***graduate school*** = école où l'on poursuit ses études après la licence; *Univ* ***graduate student*** étudiant(e) *m,f* de deuxième/troisième cycle; *Am Univ* ***graduate studies*** études *fpl* de troisième cycle; ***graduate training scheme*** programme *m* de formation professionnelle pour les diplômés

graduated ['grædjʊ,eɪtɪd] ADJ *(tax, pay rise)* progressif; *(measuring container, exercise, thermometer)* gradué; *(colours)* dégradé

►► *Br* ***graduated pension scheme*** = système de retraite complémentaire géré par l'État et alimenté par les contributions des employés et des employeurs

graduation [,grædʒʊ'eɪʃən] N **1** *(gen)* graduation *f* **2** *Univ & Am Sch (ceremony)* (cérémonie *f* de) remise *f* des diplômes

►► ***graduation ceremony*** cérémonie *f* de remise des diplômes; ***graduation day*** jour *m* de la remise des diplômes

> **GRADUATION**
>
> Dans les pays anglo-saxons, la "graduation" est la cérémonie officielle au cours de laquelle les étudiants reçoivent leur diplôme des mains du président de l'université. La cérémonie de remise des diplômes est une occasion solennelle – dans certaines universités britanniques elle se fait en latin – et les étudiants doivent porter la toge traditionnelle avec capuchon et mortier. Le diplôme ainsi que la photo prise le jour de la cérémonie sont ensuite gardés précieusement par la famille. Aux États-Unis, le terme "graduation" désigne également la cérémonie organisée en l'honneur des élèves qui achèvent leurs études secondaires.

graffiti [grə'fiːtɪ] N *(UNCOUNT)* graffiti *mpl*; **a piece of g.** un graffiti; **there's some g. on the wall** il y a des graffitis sur le mur

►► ***graffiti artist*** tagueur(euse) *m,f*

graft [grɑːft] N **1** *Hort* greffe *f*, greffon *m*; *Med* greffe *f*; **bone/skin g.** greffe *f* osseuse/de peau; **I had to have a skin g.** on a dû me faire une greffe de peau **2** *(UNCOUNT) (corruption)* magouilles *fpl* **3** *(UNCOUNT) Br Fam (hard work)* travail *m* pénible❑; **to achieve sth by hard g.** réussir qch en bossant dur

VT **1** *Hort & Med* greffer; *Fig* **this piece was grafted onto the symphony later** ce morceau a été rajouté à la symphonie plus tard; **the tower was grafted onto the original edifice** la tour a été ajoutée à l'édifice d'origine **2** *(obtain by corruption)* obtenir par la corruption

VI **1** *(be involved in bribery)* donner *ou* recevoir des pots-de-vin **2** *Br Fam (work hard)* bosser dur

grafter ['grɑːftə(r)] N **1** *Fam (hard worker)* bourreau *m* de travail **2** *Fam (corrupt person)* corrupteur❑ *m*, escroc❑ *m*; *(corrupt official)* fonctionnaire *mf* corrompu(e)❑, concussionnaire❑ *mf*

grafting ['grɑːftɪŋ] N *Hort* greffe *f*, greffage *m*; *Med* greffe *f*; **skin g.** greffe *f* de peau

Grail [greɪl] N Graal *m*; **the (Holy) G.** le Saint-Graal; *Fig* **the G. of full employment/world peace** la croisade pour parvenir au plein emploi/instaurer la paix mondiale

grain [greɪn] N **1** *(UNCOUNT) (seeds of rice, wheat)* grain *m*; *(cereal)* céréales *fpl*; *Am* blé *m*; **a cargo of g.** une cargaison de céréales

2 *(single ► of wheat, rice, salt, sand)* grain *m*

3 *Fig (of madness, sense, truth etc)* grain *m*, brin *m*; **there's not a g. of truth in what he says** il n'y a pas un grain de vérité dans ce qu'il dit; **not a g. of common sense** pas un grain *ou* pas deux sous de bon sens, pas une once de bon sens

4 *(in leather, stone, wood etc)* grain *m*; *Phot* grain *m*; **against** *or* **across the g.** contre le fil, à contre-fil; **it goes against the g. for him to accept that they are right** ce n'est pas dans sa nature d'admettre qu'ils ont raison

5 *Br (unit of weight)* = 0,065 g, grain *m (poids)*

VT **1** *(salt)* cristalliser **2** *(leather, paper)* greneler; *(paint to imitate wood)* veiner

VI se cristalliser

COMP *(market)* céréalier

►► ***grain alcohol*** alcool *m* de grains; ***grain elevator*** silo *m* à céréales; ***grain mustard*** moutarde *f* à l'ancienne

grainy ['greɪnɪ] *(compar* **grainier**, *superl* **grainiest)** ADJ *(surface, texture ► of wood)* veineux; *(► of stone)* grenu, granuleux; *(► of leather, paper)* grenu, grené; *Phot* qui a du grain

gram [græm] N **1** *(metric unit)* gramme *m* **2** *Bot (plant)* pois *m*; *(seed)* pois *m*, graine *f* de pois

►► ***gram atom*** atome-gramme *m*; ***gram flour*** farine *f* de pois chiches

grammage ['græmɪdʒ] N *(of paper)* grammage *m*

grammar ['græmə(r)] N **1** *Ling* grammaire *f*; **that's not very good g.** ce n'est pas très correct du point de vue grammatical **2** *(book)* grammaire *f*; **a German g.** une grammaire *ou* un livre de grammaire allemande

►► ***grammar book*** grammaire *f*; *Comput* ***grammar checker*** correcteur *m* grammatical; ***grammar school*** *(in UK)* = type d'école secondaire; *(in US)* = école primaire

> **GRAMMAR SCHOOL**
>
> En Grande-Bretagne, ce terme désigne une école secondaire recevant une aide de l'État mais pouvant être privée, réputée dispenser un enseignement de qualité de type traditionnel et préparant aux études supérieures. L'admission se fait sur dossier. Moins de cinq pour cent des élèves britanniques fréquentent ce type d'école, qui existe en Angleterre, au pays de Galles et en Irlande du Nord.

grammarian [grə'meərɪən] N grammairien (enne) *m,f*

grammatical [grə'mætɪkəl] ADJ **1** *(relating to grammar)* grammatical; **g. error** faute *f* de grammaire **2** *(correct)* grammaticalement correct

grammatically [grə'mætɪkəlɪ] ADV grammaticalement, du point de vue grammatical

gramme [græm] N *(metric unit)* gramme *m*

Grammy ['græmɪ] *(pl* **Grammies** *or* **Grammys)** N **G. (award)** = distinction récompensant les meilleures œuvres musicales américaines de l'année (classique exclu)

gramophone ['græməfəʊn] N *Br Old-fashioned* gramophone *m*, phonographe *m*

►► ***gramophone needle*** aiguille *f* de phonographe *ou* de gramophone; ***gramophone record*** disque *m*

gramps [græmps] N *Fam (grandfather)* papy *m*, pépé *m*

grampus ['græmpəs] N *Zool* épaulard *m*, orque *f*

gran [græn] N *Br Fam (grandmother)* grand-mère *f*; *(term of address)* mamie *f*, mémé *f*

granary ['grænərɪ] *(pl* **granaries)** N grenier *m* à blé, silo *m* (à céréales)

COMP *(flour)* complet(ète)

►► ***granary bread, granary loaf*** pain *m* complet aux céréales

grand [grænd] ADJ **1** *(impressive ► house)* magnifique; *(► style)* grand, noble; *(► music, occasion)* grand; *(pretentious, self-important)* suffisant, prétentieux; *(dignified, majestic)* majestueux, digne; **to do sth in g. style** faire qch en grande pompe; **to live in g. style** mener la grande vie; **to make a g. entrance** faire une entrée en grande pompe; **she likes to do things on a g. scale** elle aime faire les choses en grand; **to entertain on a g. scale** recevoir des gens en grande pompe; **that dress is a bit too g. for me** cette robe est un peu trop chic pour moi; **it was all part of his g. design** tout cela faisait partie de son grand projet; **the g. old man of trade unionism/Scottish folk music** le patriarche du syndicalisme/de la musique folklorique écossaise **2** *Br Old-fashioned or Ir, NEng & Scot Fam (excellent ► food, accommodation)* excellent❑; *(► weather)* magnifique❑; **I'm not feeling too g.** je ne suis pas dans mon assiette; **to have a g. time** bien s'amuser❑; *Ironic* **we had a g. old time trying to find the house!** on s'est marré pour trouver la maison!

N **1** *Fam (money) Br* mille livres❑ *fpl*; *Am* mille dollars❑ *mpl*; **two g.** *Br* deux mille livres; *Am* deux mille dollars **2** *Mus* piano *m* à queue

EXCLAM *Ir, NEng & Scot Fam* impec!, très bien!❑

►► ***Grand Canary (Island)*** Grande Canarie *f*; **in G. Canary** à la Grande Canarie; ***the Grand Canyon*** le Grand Canyon; ***grand duchess*** grande-duchesse *f*; ***grand duchy*** grand-duché *m*; ***grand duke*** grand-duc *m*; ***grand finale*** apothéose *f*; *Am Law* ***grand jury*** jury *m* d'accusation; *Am* ***grand larceny*** vol *m* qualifié; ***Grand Master*** *(in chess)* grand maître *m*; *(of masonic lodge)* Grand Maître *m*; ***the Grand National*** = la plus importante course d'obstacles de Grande-Bretagne, qui se déroule à Aintree, dans la banlieue de Liverpool; ***grand opera*** grand opéra *m*; ***grand piano*** piano *m* à queue; *Sport & Cards* ***grand slam*** grand chelem *m*; ***grand total*** total *m*; **that comes to a g. total of £536** ça fait en tout 536 livres; ***the Grand Tour*** le tour d'Europe

grandad ['grændæd] N *Fam* grand-père❑ *m*; *(term of address)* pépé *m*, papy *m*; **a shirt with a g. collar** une chemise sans col

►► ***grandad shirt*** chemise *f* sans col

grandaddy ['grændædɪ] *(pl* **grandaddies)** N *Fam* **1** *(grandfather)* grand-père❑ *m*; *(term of address)* pépé *m*, papy *m* **2** *(most ancient)* ancêtre❑ *m*; **it's the g. of them all** c'est leur ancêtre à tous

grandchild ['grændtʃaɪld] *(pl* **grandchildren** [-tʃɪldrən]) N *(boy)* petit-fils *m*; *(girl)* petite-fille *f*; **is it your first g.?** vous étiez déjà grand-père/grand-mère?; **she has six grandchildren** elle a six petits-enfants

granddad ['grændæd], **granddaddy** ['grændædɪ] *(pl* **granddaddies)** N *Fam* grand-père❑ *m*; *(term of address)* pépé *m*, papy *m*

granddaughter ['grændɔːtə(r)] N petite-fille *f*

grandee [græn'diː] N grand *m* d'Espagne; *Fig* **Tory grandees** = personnes influentes du parti conservateur

grandeur ['grændjə(r)] N **1** *(of person)* grandeur *f*, noblesse *f*, éminence *f* **2** *(of building, surroundings etc)* splendeur *f*, magnificence *f*; **the g. of the landscape** la majesté du paysage; **an air of g.** quelque chose de grandiose; **faded g.** *(of house, furnishings etc)* splendeur *f* passée

grandfather ['grændfɑːðə(r)] N grand-père *m*

►► ***grandfather clock*** horloge *f* (de parquet)

grandfatherly ['grændfɑːðəlɪ] ADJ de grand-père

grandiloquence [græn'dɪləkwəns] N *Formal* grandiloquence *f*

grandiloquent [græn'dɪləkwənt] ADJ *Formal* grandiloquent

grandiose ['grændɪəʊz] ADJ *Pej (building)* prétentieux, massif; *(style, term, theory, title)* pompeux; *(plan)* ambitieux

grandly ['grændlɪ] ADV **1** *(impressively)* de façon grandiose *ou* impressionnante **2** *Pej (pompously)* pompeusement

grandma ['grænmɑː] N *Fam* grand-mère❑ *f*; *(term of address)* mémé *f*, mamie *f*

grandmother ['grænmʌðə(r)] N grand-mère *f*

grandnephew ['grænnefjuː] N petit-neveu *m*

grandness ['grændnɪs] N *(of behaviour)* grandeur *f*, noblesse *f*; *(of lifestyle)* faste *m*; *(of appearance)* panache *m*

grandniece ['grænniːs] N petite-nièce *f*

grandpa ['grænpɑː] N *Fam* grand-père❑ *m*; *(term of address)* pépé *m*, papy *m*

grandparent ['grænpeərənt] N **my grandparents** mes grands-parents *mpl*; **children are often looked after by a g.** les enfants sont souvent gardés par un de leurs grands-parents

grandson ['grænsʌn] N petit-fils *m*

grandstand ['grændstænd] N tribune *f*; **to have a g. view (of sth)** être aux premières loges (pour voir qch)

VI *Am* faire l'intéressant

►► ***grandstand finish*** *(of race)* arrivée *f* palpitante; *(of match)* fin *f* palpitante

grange [greɪndʒ] N 1 *Br (country house)* manoir *m*; *(farmhouse)* ferme *f* 2 *Am (farm)* ferme *f* 3 *Arch (granary)* grenier *m* à blé, grange *f*

granite ['grænɪt] N granit *m*, granite *m*
COMP de granit *ou* granite

granitic [græ'nɪtɪk] ADJ granitique, graniteux

granny, grannie ['grænɪ] *(pl* **grannies***)* N *Fam* grand-mère *f*; *(term of address)* mamie *f*, mémé *f*
▸▸ *Br Fam* ***granny flat*** appartement *m* indépendant *(dans une maison)*; ***granny knot*** nœud *m* de vache; ***Granny Smith*** *(apple)* granny-smith *f inv*

granola [grə'nəʊlə] N *Am* muesli *m*
▸▸ ***granola bar*** barre *f* aux céréales

grant [grɑːnt] VT 1 *(permission, wish)* accorder; *(request)* accorder, accéder à; *(goal, point, credit, loan, pension)* accorder; *(charter, favour, privilege, right)* accorder, octroyer, concéder; *(property)* céder; **to g. sb permission to do sth** accorder à qn l'autorisation de faire qch; **the countries that have been granted autonomy** les pays qui se sont vus accorder l'autonomie; **to g. sb their request** accéder à la requête de qn; *Literary* **God g. you good fortune** que Dieu vous protège 2 *(accept as true)* accorder, admettre, concéder; **I g. you I made an error of judgement** je vous accorde que j'ai fait une erreur de jugement; **I'll g. you that** je vous l'accorde; **granted, he's not very intelligent, but...** d'accord, il n'est pas très intelligent, mais... 3 *(idioms)* **to take sth for granted** considérer que qch va de soi, tenir qch pour certain *ou* établi; **you seem to take it for granted he'll agree/help you** vous semblez convaincu qu'il sera d'accord/vous aidera; **you take too much for granted** vous présumez trop; **he takes her for granted** il la traite comme si elle n'existait pas; **she felt that she was being taken for granted** elle avait le sentiment qu'elle ne comptait pas; **I'm tired of the way everybody just takes me for granted** j'en ai assez que personne ne fasse attention à moi
N 1 *(money given)* subvention *f*, allocation *f*; *(to student)* bourse *f* d'études; **to give sb a g.** accorder une subvention à qn; *(student)* accorder une bourse d'études à qn; **to receive a g.** être subventionné, recevoir une subvention; *(student)* recevoir *ou* se voir accorder une bourse d'études 2 *(transfer ▸ of property)* cession *f*; *(▸ of land)* concession *f*; *(permission)* octroi *m*; **g. of probate** validation *f ou* homologation *f* d'un testament

grant-aided ADJ subventionné par l'État

grant-in-aid N subvention *f (de l'État)*

grant-maintained ADJ *Br* subventionné *(par l'État)*; **g. school** école *f* privée subventionnée *(acceptant en échange un droit de regard de l'État sur la gestion de ses affaires)*

granular ['grænjʊlə(r)] ADJ *(surface)* granuleux, granulaire; *(structure)* grenu

granulate ['grænjʊleɪt] VT *(lead, powder, tin)* granuler; *(salt, sugar)* grener, grainer; *(surface)* grener, greneler, rendre grenu

granulated sugar [grænjʊleɪtɪd-] N sucre *m* en poudre, *Can* sucre *m* cristallisé

granulation [,grænjʊ'leɪʃən] N *(texture)* granulation *f*; *(action)* granulation *f*, grenage *m*

granule ['grænjuːl] N granule *m*; **coffee/tea granules** granules *mpl* de café/thé

granulocyte [grænjʊləʊsaɪt] N *Biol* granulocyte *m*

grape [greɪp] N 1 *(fruit)* grain *m* de raisin; **a (variety of) g.** un raisin; **to eat grapes** manger du raisin; **to pick grapes** faire les vendanges, cueillir le raisin; **black/white grapes** du raisin noir/blanc 2 *(grapeshot)* mitraille *f*
▸▸ ***grape harvest*** vendanges *fpl*; *Bot* ***grape hyacinth*** muscari *m*; ***grape juice*** jus *m* de raisin; ***grape picker*** vendangeur(euse) *m,f*; ***grape picking*** *(UNCOUNT)* vendanges *fpl*

> Note that the French word **grappe** is a false friend. It means **bunch** or **cluster**.

grapefruit ['greɪpfruːt] N pamplemousse *m*
▸▸ ***grapefruit juice*** jus *m* de pamplemousse; ***grapefruit segments*** quartiers *mpl* de pamplemousse; ***grapefruit tree*** pamplemoussier *m*

grapeshot ['greɪpʃɒt] N mitraille *f*

grapevine ['greɪpvaɪn] N 1 *Bot* vigne *f*, treille *f* 2 *Fig* téléphone *m* arabe; **I heard on the g. that...** j'ai entendu par le téléphone arabe que... + *indicative*

graph [grɑːf] N 1 *(diagram)* graphique *m*, courbe *f* 2 *Ling* graphie *f*
VT mettre en graphique, tracer
▸▸ ***graph paper*** papier *m* quadrillé; *(in millimetres)* papier *m* millimétré

graphic ['græfɪk] ADJ 1 *Math* graphique 2 *(vivid)* imagé; **in g. detail** dans tous les détails 3 *Art* graphique
• **graphics** N *(UNCOUNT) (drawing)* art *m* graphique NPL *Math* (utilisation *f* des) graphiques *mpl*; *(drawings)* représentations *fpl* graphiques; *Comput (images)* graphismes *mpl*, graphiques *mpl*
▸▸ *Comput* ***graphics accelerator*** accélérateur *m* graphique; *Comput* ***graphics accelerator card*** carte *f* accélérateur graphique; ***graphic artist*** graphiste *mf*; ***graphic arts*** arts *mpl* graphiques; *Comput* ***graphics card*** carte *f* graphique; ***graphic design*** conception *f* graphique; ***graphic designer*** graphiste *mf*, maquettiste *mf*; ***graphic display*** graphisme *m*; *Comput* ***graphics display*** affichage *m* graphique; ***graphic equalizer*** égaliseur *m* graphique; *Comput* ***Graphics Interchange Format*** GIF *m*; *Comput* ***graphic interface*** interface *f* graphique; ***graphic novel*** bande *f* dessinée

> Note that the French adjective **graphique** never means **vivid** or **shocking**.

graphical ['græfɪkəl] ADJ graphique
▸▸ *Comput* ***graphical user interface*** interface *f* utilisateur graphique

graphically ['græfɪkəlɪ] ADV 1 *Math* graphiquement 2 *(vividly)* de façon très imagée

graphite ['græfaɪt] N graphite *m*, plombagine *f*, mine *f* de plomb
ADJ en graphite

graphologist [græ'fɒlədʒɪst] N graphologue *mf*

graphology [græ'fɒlədʒɪ] N graphologie *f*

grapnel ['græpnəl] N *Naut* grappin *m*, crochet *m*; *(of balloon)* ancre *f*

grapple ['græpəl] N *Tech* grappin *m*
VT 1 *Tech* saisir avec un grappin 2 *Am (person)* **to g. sb** saisir qn contre soi; **to g. sb to the floor** mettre qn à terre
VI 1 *(physically)* **to g. with sb** en venir aux mains avec qn 2 *Fig* **to g. with sth** *(difficulty, problem, computer, machine)* se débattre avec qch; **to g. with inflation** être aux prises avec l'inflation

grappling hook, grappling iron ['græplɪŋ-] N *Naut* grappin *m*, crochet *m*; *(of balloon)* ancre *f*

grasp [grɑːsp] VT 1 *(physically)* saisir; *(opportunity)* saisir; *(power)* se saisir de, s'emparer de; **to g. (hold of) sth** saisir qch; **to g. (hold of) sb's hand** saisir la main de qn 2 *(understand)* saisir, comprendre; **I didn't quite g. what she meant** je n'ai pas bien compris *ou* saisi ce qu'elle a voulu dire; **to g. the importance of sth** saisir l'importance de qch
N 1 *(grip)* (forte) poigne *f*; *(action of holding)* prise *f*, étreinte *f*; **to have sth in one's g.** avoir prise sur qch; **to wrest sth from sb's g.** arracher qch des mains de qn; **to have a strong g.** *(handshake)* avoir de la poigne
2 *Fig (reach)* portée *f*; **within/beyond sb's g.** à la portée/hors de (la) portée de qn; **success is now within her g.** le succès est désormais à sa portée; **to let an opportunity slip from one's g.** rater une occasion
3 *(understanding)* compréhension *f*; **to have a good g. of modern history** avoir une bonne connaissance de l'histoire moderne; **his g. of the problem was poor** il dominait mal le problème
4 *(handle)* poignée *f*
▸ **grasp at** VT INSEP *(attempt to seize)* chercher à saisir, essayer de saisir; *(accept eagerly)* saisir; **to g. at an opportunity** sauter sur *ou* saisir l'occasion

grasping ['grɑːspɪŋ] ADJ avare, avide

grass [grɑːs] N 1 *(gen)* herbe *f*; *(lawn)* pelouse *f*, gazon *m*; **keep off the g.** *(sign)* défense de marcher sur la pelouse, pelouse interdite; **to cut** *or* **to mow the g.** tondre la pelouse; **she plays well on g.** *(in tennis)* elle joue bien sur gazon; *Fig* **he doesn't let the g. grow under his feet** il ne perd pas de temps; *Prov* **the g. is always greener (on the other side of the fence)** = c'est toujours mieux ailleurs
2 *(pasture)* herbage *m*; **to put** *or* **turn a horse out to g.** mettre un cheval au vert; *Fig* **to put sb out to g.** mettre qn à la retraite; **to be (out) at g.** *(animal)* être au vert; **to put land under g.** enherber une terre, mettre une terre en herbe
3 *Fam (marijuana)* herbe *f*
4 *Br Fam (informer)* mouchard *m*, indic *m*
VT 1 *(field)* enherber; *(garden)* gazonner, engazonner 2 *Am (animals)* mettre au vert
VI *Br Fam (inform)* cafarder; **to g. on sb** balancer qn, moucharder qn
• **grasses** NPL *Bot* graminées *fpl*
▸▸ ***grass court*** court *m* (en gazon); ***grass green*** vert *m* gazon; *Pol* ***the grass roots*** la base; **at (the) g. roots level** au niveau de la base; **g. roots support** soutien *m* de la base; ***grass seed*** *(for lawn)* graine *f* pour gazon; *(as feed)* graine *f* fourragère; ***grass skirt*** pagne *m (de feuilles)*; ***grass snake*** couleuvre *f* à collier; ***grass widow*** = femme dont le mari est toujours en déplacement; *Fig* **I'm a g. widow this weekend** je suis célibataire ce week-end; ***grass widower*** = homme dont la femme est toujours en déplacement
▸ **grass over** VT SEP *(field)* enherber; *(garden)* gazonner, engazonner
▸ **grass up** VT SEP *Br Fam* **to g. sb up** balancer qn, moucharder qn

grasshopper ['grɑːshɒpə(r)] N 1 *(insect)* sauterelle *f*, grillon *m*; *Fig* **he's got a g. mind** il papillonne constamment 2 *(cocktail)* grasshopper *m (cocktail à base de crème fraîche, de crème de menthe et de crème de cacao)*

grassland ['grɑːslænd] N prairie *f*, pré *m*

grassy ['grɑːsɪ] *(compar* **grassier**, *superl* **grassiest***)* ADJ herbu, herbeux; *(lane)* vert; *(plain)* verdoyant

grate [greɪt] N *(fireplace)* foyer *m*, âtre *m*; *(for holding coal)* grille *f* de foyer; **a fire in the g.** un feu dans la cheminée
VT 1 *Culin* râper 2 *(chalk, metal)* faire grincer; **to g. one's teeth** grincer des dents
VI 1 *(machine, metal)* grincer 2 *Fig* **his behaviour grates after a while** son comportement est agaçant au bout d'un moment; **to g. on the ear** *(music, particular accent)* écorcher les oreilles; *(noise)* faire mal aux oreilles

G-rated ADJ *Am (movie)* tous publics

grateful ['greɪtfʊl] ADJ *(person)* reconnaissant; **to be g. towards** *or* **to sb for sth** être reconnaissant envers qn de qch; **I am g. for your help** je vous suis reconnaissant de votre aide; **a g. letter** une lettre de remerciements; **I would be g. if you could let me know as soon as possible** je vous serais reconnaissant de m'informer dès que possible; **I was g. it wasn't me** j'étais bien content que ce ne soit pas moi; **with g. thanks** avec toute ma reconnaissance, avec mes sincères remerciements; **be g. for what you've got** estime-toi heureux avec ce que tu as; **I suppose we should be g. for that** on devrait s'en estimer heureux

gratefully ['greɪtfʊlɪ] ADV avec reconnaissance *ou* gratitude; **to smile g.** faire un sourire reconnaissant; **all contributions g. accepted** toutes les contributions sont les bienvenues

grater ['greɪtə(r)] N râpe *f*

gratification [,grætɪfɪ'keɪʃən] N *(state or action)* satisfaction *f*, plaisir *m*; *Psy* gratification *f*; **to do sth for one's own g.** faire qch pour sa propre satisfaction; **he has the g. of knowing that...** il a la satisfaction *ou* le plaisir de savoir que... + *indicative*

gratified ['grætɪfaɪd] ADJ satisfait, content (**with** de); *(smile)* de satisfaction

gratify ['grætɪfaɪ] *(pt & pp* **gratified***)* VT 1 *(person)* faire plaisir à, être agréable à; **it gratified him** *or* **he was gratified to learn that...** ça lui a fait plaisir *ou* lui a été agréable d'apprendre que... + *indicative* 2 *(whim, wish)* satisfaire

gratifying ['grætɪfaɪŋ] ADJ agréable, plaisant; *Psy* gratifiant; **it's g. to know that...** c'est agréable *ou* ça fait plaisir de savoir que... + *indicative*

grating ['greɪtɪŋ] N *(bars)* grille *f*, grillage *m*
ADJ *(irritating)* agaçant, irritant, énervant; *(sound)* grinçant, discordant; *(voice)* discordant

gratis ['grætɪs] ADJ gratuit
ADV gratuitement

gratitude ['grætɪtju:d] N gratitude *f*, reconnaissance *f*; **to show/to express one's g. (towards sb/ for sth)** témoigner/exprimer sa gratitude (envers qn/pour qch)

gratuitous [grə'tju:ɪtəs] ADJ *(unjustified)* gratuit, sans motif, injustifié; **g. violence** violence *f* gratuite

gratuitously [grə'tju:ɪtəslɪ] ADV *(without good reason)* gratuitement, sans motif

gratuity [grə'tju:ətɪ] *(pl* **gratuities***)* N 1 *Formal (tip)* gratification *f*, pourboire *m* 2 *Br (payment to employee)* prime *f*; *Mil* peine *f* de démobilisation

> Note that the French word **gratuité** is a false friend and is never a translation for the English word **gratuity**. It indicates that something is free of charge.

grave[1] [greɪv] N *(hole)* fosse *f*; *(burial place)* tombe *f*; **mass g.** fosse *f* commune; *(in wartime)* charnier *m*; **to be in one's g.** être dans la tombe; **she worked herself into an early g.** elle s'est tuée au travail; **he took his secret with him to the g.** il a emporté son secret dans la tombe; **he drank himself into an early g.** l'alcool l'a prématurément tué; *Fig* **he must have been turning in his g.** il a dû se retourner dans sa tombe; *Fig* **someone has just walked over my g.** j'ai eu un frisson; *Fig* **to be digging one's own g.** creuser sa propre tombe; *Fig* **to have one foot in the g.** avoir un pied dans la tombe; **from beyond the g.** d'outre-tombe
ADJ *(serious)* grave, sérieux; *(tone)* solennel; *(situation)* grave; *(error)* lourd; **to make a g. mistake** se tromper lourdement; **g. news** de graves nouvelles
▸▸ ***grave robber*** *(who robs valuables from graves)* = personne qui vole les objets de valeur laissés dans les tombes; *(body snatcher)* déterreur (euse) *m,f* de cadavres

grave[2] [grɑ:v] *Ling* N accent *m* grave
ADJ *(accent)* grave; **it's spelled with an "a" g.** ça s'écrit avec un "a" accent grave

gravedigger ['greɪvdɪgə(r)] N fossoyeur *m*

gravel ['grævəl] *(Br pt & pp* **gravelled**, *cont* **gravelling**, *Am pt & pp* **graveled**, *cont* **graveling***)* N gravier *m*; *(finer)* gravillon *m*; *Med* gravelle *f*
VT gravillonner, répandre du gravier sur
▸▸ ***gravel path*** chemin *m* de gravier; ***gravel pit*** gravière *f*, carrière *f* de gravier

gravelly ['grævəlɪ] ADJ 1 *(like or containing gravel)* graveleux; *(road)* de gravier; *(riverbed)* caillouteux 2 *(voice)* rauque, râpeux

gravely ['greɪvlɪ] ADV 1 *(speak)* gravement, sérieusement 2 *(as intensifier)* **g. ill** gravement malade; **to be g. mistaken** se tromper lourdement; **g. wounded** grièvement blessé

graven ['greɪvən] ADJ *Arch or Literary* **g. on my memory** gravé dans ma mémoire
▸▸ *Rel* ***graven image*** idole *f*, image *f*

graveness ['greɪvnɪs] N gravité *f*

Graves' disease [greɪvz-] N *Med* maladie *f* de Basedow

graveside ['greɪvsaɪd] N **at sb's g.** sur la tombe de qn; **his next of kin were there at the g.** ses proches étaient présents à l'enterrement

gravestone ['greɪvstəʊn] N pierre *f* tombale

graveyard ['greɪvjɑ:d] N *also Fig* cimetière *m*; *Fig* **this town is a g.** cette ville est mortelle; **this department has been the g. of more than one young hopeful's ambitions** ce service a mis fin aux ambitions de plus d'un jeune
▸▸ ***graveyard shift*** équipe *f* de nuit; *Rad & TV* ***graveyard slot*** tranche *f* nocturne

graving dock ['greɪvɪŋ-] N *Naut* bassin *m* de radoub

gravitate ['grævɪteɪt] VI graviter; **to g. towards sb/sth** graviter vers qn/qch; **many young people g. to the big cities** beaucoup de jeunes sont attirés par les grandes villes; **most of the guests had gravitated towards the bar/kitchen** la plupart des invités s'étaient rapprochés du bar/de la cuisine

gravitation [ˌgrævɪ'teɪʃən] N gravitation *f*; *Fig* **there was a general g. towards the bar** tout le monde s'est dirigé vers le bar; *Phys* **law of g.** loi *f* de la gravitation

gravitational [ˌgrævɪ'teɪʃənəl] ADJ gravitationnel, de gravitation
▸▸ ***gravitational field*** champ *m* de gravitation; ***gravitational force*** force *f* de gravitation *ou* gravitationnelle; ***gravitational pull*** gravitation *f*

gravity ['grævətɪ] N 1 *(of situation)* gravité *f*; *(of person)* gravité *f*, sérieux *m* 2 *Phys (force)* pesanteur *f*; *(phenomenon)* gravitation *f*; **the law of g.** la loi de la pesanteur
▸▸ ***gravity feed*** alimentation *f* par gravité

gravure [grə'vjʊə(r)] N *(process, impression)* gravure *f*; *(plate)* plaque *f* gravée

gravy ['greɪvɪ] N 1 *Culin* jus *m*; *(thickened)* sauce *f* (au jus) 2 *Am Fam (easy money)* bénef *m*; **it's g.** *(easy)* c'est du gâteau
▸▸ ***gravy boat*** saucière *f*; *Fam* ***gravy train*** assiette *f* au beurre; **to get on the g. train** être à la recherche d'un bon filon; **it's just a g. train for him and his friends** c'est une véritable mine d'or pour lui et ses amis

gray, graybeard *etc Am* = **grey, greybeard** *etc*

grayling ['greɪlɪŋ] N 1 *Ich* ombre *m* 2 *Entom* (papillon *m*) agreste *m*

graze [greɪz] VI *(animals)* brouter, paître, pâturer; *(humans)* grignoter
VT 1 *(touch lightly)* frôler, effleurer, raser; **the boat just grazed the bottom** le bateau a effleuré le fond 2 *(skin)* érafler, écorcher; **the bullet grazed his cheek** la balle lui a éraflé la joue; **she grazed her elbow on the wall** elle s'est écorché le coude sur le mur 3 *(animals)* faire paître; *(grass)* brouter, paître; *(field)* pâturer
N écorchure *f*, éraflure *f*; **it's just a g.** c'est juste un peu écorché

grazing ['greɪzɪŋ] N *(grass for animals)* pâturage *m*; *(land)* pâture *f*, pâturage *m*

grease [gri:s] N *(gen)* graisse *f*; *(lubricant) & Aut* graisse *f*, lubrifiant *m*; *(used lubricant)* cambouis *m*; *(dirt)* crasse *f*; **g. stain** *(on clothing, linen)* tache *f* de gras *ou* de graisse; **to remove g. from sth** dégraisser qch
VT *(gen)* graisser; *Aut* graisser, lubrifier; *Culin (cake tin)* beurrer; *Fam Fig* **to g. sb's palm** graisser la patte à qn
▸▸ ***grease gun*** (pistolet *m*) graisseur *m*, pompe *f* à graisse; *Am Fam (submachine gun)* mitraillette[□] *f*; *Fam* ***grease monkey*** mécano *m*; ***grease nipple*** graisseur *m*

▸**grease back** VT SEP **to g. back one's hair** se gominer les cheveux

greased lightning [gri:st-] N *Fam* **like g.** à tout berzingue, à fond la caisse

greasepaint ['gri:speɪnt] N *Theat* fard *m* (gras); **a stick of g.** un crayon gras; *Fig* **the smell of g.** le mirage du théâtre

greaseproof ['gri:spru:f] ADJ *Br* imperméable à la graisse
▸▸ *Culin* ***greaseproof paper*** papier *m* sulfurisé

greaser ['gri:sə(r)] N *Fam* 1 *(mechanic)* graisseur *m*, mécano *m* 2 *(biker)* motard *m* 3 *Am (offensive use)* = terme injurieux désignant une personne d'origine latino-américaine ou italienne

greasiness ['gri:sɪnɪs] N 1 *(gen)* état *m* graisseux, nature *f* graisseuse; *(of cosmetics)* onctuosité *f*; *(of hair, hands)* nature *f* grasse 2 *(of road)* surface *f* glissante

greasy ['gri:sɪ] *(compar* **greasier**, *superl* **greasiest***)* ADJ 1 *(food, substance)* graisseux, gras; *(tools)* graisseux; *(cosmetics, hair, hands)* gras
2 *(pavement, road)* gras, glissant
3 *(clothes ▸ dirty)* crasseux, poisseux; *(▸ covered in grease marks)* taché de graisse, plein de graisse; **you'll get your jacket all g.** tu vas mettre plein de graisse sur ta veste
4 *(obsequious)* obséquieux; **a g. manner** des manières obséquieuses
▸▸ *Sport & Fig* ***the greasy pole*** le mât de cocagne; *Fam* ***greasy spoon*** boui-boui *m*

GREAT [greɪt] *(compar* **greater**, *superl* **greatest***)*
ADJ 1 *(in size, scale, quantity)* grand; **a g. number of** un grand nombre de; **a g. crowd** une grande *ou* grosse foule, une foule nombreuse; **to a g. extent, in g. part** en grande partie; **the g. majority** la grande majorité; **the g. fire of London** le grand incendie de Londres *(qui, en 1666 détruisit les trois quarts de la ville, et notamment la cathédrale Saint-Paul)*; **he made a g. effort to be nice** il a fait un gros effort pour être agréable
2 *(in degree)* grand; **a g. friend** un grand ami; **they're g. friends** ce sont de grands amis; **there's g. ignorance about the problem** les gens ne sont pas conscients du problème; **g. willpower** une volonté de fer; **to my g. satisfaction** à ma grande satisfaction; **a g. surprise** une grande surprise; **with g. care** avec grand soin, avec beaucoup de soin; **with g. pleasure** avec grand plaisir; **to be in g. pain** souffrir (beaucoup); **to reach a g. age** parvenir à un âge avancé; **I have a g. liking for that country** j'aime beaucoup ce pays
3 *(important ▸ person, event)* grand; **a g. man** un grand homme; **Alfred the G.** Alfred le Grand; **France's greatest footballer** le plus grand footballeur français; **a g. occasion** une grande occasion; **a g. house** une grande demeure
4 *Fam (term of approval)* génial, super *(inv)*; **she has a g. voice** elle a une voix magnifique[□]; **he's a g. guy** c'est un type super *ou* génial; **she's g.!** *(nice person)* elle est super!; **to have a g. time** bien s'amuser[□]; **we had a g. holiday** nous avons passé des vacances merveilleuses[□]; **the g. thing is that...** le grand avantage *ou* ce qui est bien, c'est que...[□] + *indicative*; **I feel g.!** je me sens super bien!; **you look g. tonight!** *(in appearance)* tu es magnifique ce soir!; *Ironic* **he's coming too – oh, g.!** il vient aussi – oh génial *ou* super!
5 *(keen)* **she's a g. reader** elle adore lire, elle lit beaucoup; *Ironic* **she's a g. one for borrowing things without asking people** elle est spécialiste pour emprunter les choses sans demander l'autorisation
6 *Fam (good at or expert on)* **he's g. at languages** il est très doué pour les langues[□]; **she's g. on sculpture** elle s'y connaît vraiment en sculpture[□]
7 *Zool* **the g. apes** les grands singes *mpl*
N *(person)* **he's one of the greats of world cinema** c'est l'un des grands noms du cinéma mondial; **it's one of the all-time greats** c'est un des plus grands classiques; **the g. and the good** *(people)* les gens *mpl* influents
ADV 1 *(well)* très bien; **he's doing g.** *(in health)* il se porte à merveille; *(in career, life etc)* ça marche très bien pour lui; **we get on g.** on s'entend très bien
2 *(as intensifier)* **a g. big fish** un énorme poisson; **an enormous g. house** une maison immense; *Fam* **you g. fat slob!** espèce de gros lard!
▸▸ *Orn* ***great auk*** grand pingouin *m*; ***the Great Barrier Reef*** la Grande Barrière; *Astron* ***the Great Bear*** la Grande Ourse; ***Great Britain*** Grande Bretagne *f*; **in G. Britain** en Grande-Bretagne; ***Great Dane*** *(dog)* danois *m (chien)*; ***the Great Depression*** la grande dépression des années 30; ***the Great Divide*** = chaîne de montagnes dans le nord des États-Unis marquant la ligne de partage des eaux entre l'Atlantique et le Pacifique; *Hist* ***the Great Famine*** la Grande Famine *(en Irlande, de 1845 à 1849)*; ***the Great Lakes*** les Grands Lacs *mpl*; ***the Great Plains*** les Grandes Plaines *fpl*; *Geog* ***the Great Rift Valley*** la Rift Valley, la Great Rift Valley; *Orn* ***great tit*** mésange *f* charbonnière, charbonnier *m*; ***the Great Wall of China*** la Grande Muraille (de Chine); ***the Great War*** la Grande Guerre, la guerre de 14 *ou* de 14–18; *Zool* ***great white shark*** grand requin *m* blanc

great-aunt N grand-tante *f*

greatcoat ['greɪtkəʊt] N pardessus *m*, manteau *m*; *Mil* manteau *m*, capote *f*

greater ['greɪtə(r)] *compar of* **great**
▸▸ ***Greater London*** le Grand Londres, = zone du sud-est de l'Angleterre, comprenant Londres et son agglomération; ***Greater Manchester*** le Grand Manchester, = zone du nord-ouest de l'Angle-

terre, comprenant Manchester et son agglomération

greater-than sign N signe *m* "plus grand que", signe *m* "supérieur à"

greatest ['greɪtɪst] *superl of* **great** N **to be the g.** *(best)* être le meilleur/la meilleure
▸▸ ***greatest common denominator*** plus grand dénominateur *m* commun

great-grandchild N *(boy)* arrière-petit-fils *m*; *(girl)* arrière-petite-fille *f*; **great-grandchildren** arrière-petits-enfants *mpl*

great-granddaughter N arrière-petite-fille *f*

great-grandfather N arrière-grand-père *m*, *Can* bisaïeul *m*

great-grandmother N arrière-grand-mère *f*, *Can* bisaïeule *f*

great-grandparents NPL arrière-grands-parents *mpl*, *Can* bisaïeuls (bisaïeules) *mpl*, *fpl*

great-grandson N arrière-petit-fils *m*

great-great-grandfather N arrière-arrière-grand-père *m*

great-great-grandmother N arrière-arrière-grand-mère *f*

great-hearted ADJ *Literary* au grand cœur, magnanime

greatly ['greɪtlɪ] ADV très, beaucoup, fortement; **to be g. influenced/surprised/amused** être très influencé/surpris/amusé; **g. improved** beaucoup amélioré; **you'll be g. missed** vous nous manquerez beaucoup; **the difficulties have been g. exaggerated** on a beaucoup exagéré les difficultés; **g. surprised** très *ou* énormément surpris; **g. though I admired/respected him…** j'avais beau l'admirer/le respecter beaucoup…

great-nephew N petit-neveu *m*

greatness ['greɪtnɪs] N **1** *(size)* grandeur *f*, énormité *f*, immensité *f*; *(intensity)* intensité *f* **2** *(eminence)* grandeur *f*, importance *f*; **he never achieved g. as an artist** il n'est jamais devenu un grand artiste; *Prov* **some achieve g., some have g. thrust upon them** = c'est parfois dans l'adversité que se révèlent les grands hommes

great-niece N petite-nièce *f*

great-uncle N grand-oncle *m*

grebe [griːb] N *Orn* grèbe *m*

Grecian ['griːʃən] N Grec (Grecque) *m,f*
ADJ grec (grecque); **a G. profile** un profil grec

Greece [griːs] N Grèce *f*

greed [griːd] N **1** *(for material things)* avidité *f*, cupidité *f*; **g. for fame/power** la recherche avide de célébrité/pouvoir; **it's sheer g.** c'est de l'avidité pure et simple **2** *(gluttony)* gourmandise *f*

greedily ['griːdɪlɪ] ADV **1** *(hoard, keep for oneself etc)* avidement, cupidement **2** *(eat)* goulûment; *(look, say)* avec gourmandise

greediness ['griːdɪnɪs] = **greed**

greedy ['griːdɪ] *(compar* **greedier**, *superl* **greediest)** ADJ **1** *(for food)* glouton, gourmand; **don't be so g.!** ne sois pas si gourmand! **2** *(for fame, power, wealth)* avide (**for** de)
▸▸ ***greedy guts*** goinfre *mf*

Greek [griːk] N **1** *(person)* Grec (Grecque) *m,f*; *Prov* **beware of Greeks bearing gifts** = méfiez-vous des étrangers qui vous veulent du bien **2** *(language)* grec *m*; **ancient/modern G.** grec *m* ancien/moderne; *Fam* **it's all G. to me** tout ça, c'est du chinois *ou* de l'hébreu pour moi
ADJ grec (grecque); **the G. islands** les îles *fpl* grecques
COMP *(embassy)* de Grèce; *(history)* de la Grèce; *(teacher)* de grec
▸▸ ***the Greek Orthodox Church*** l'Église *f* orthodoxe grecque; ***Greek salad*** salade *f* grecque

green [griːn] ADJ **1** *(colour)* vert; *(field, valley)* vert, verdoyant; **the wall was painted g.** le mur était peint en vert; **to go** *or* **to turn g.** *(tree)* devenir vert, verdir; *(traffic light)* passer au vert; *(person)* devenir blême, blêmir; **to be** *or* **to go g. with envy** être vert de jalousie; *Fig* **to have** *Br* **g. fingers** *or Am* **a g. thumb** avoir la main verte
2 *(unripe fruit)* vert, pas mûr; *(undried timber)* vert; *(meat)* frais (fraîche); *(bacon)* non fumé
3 *(naive)* naïf; *(inexperienced)* inexpérimenté; **he's not as g. as he looks** il n'est pas aussi naïf qu'il en a l'air; **a g. reporter** un jeune reporter inexpérimenté
4 *(ecological)* écologique, vert; **to think g.** penser à l'environnement; **to go g.** virer écolo
5 *Literary (alive)* vivant, vivace; **to keep sb's memory g.** chérir la mémoire de qn
N **1** *(colour)* vert *m*; **g. suits you** le vert te va bien; **the girl in g.** la fille en vert; **dressed in g.** habillé de *ou* en vert
2 *(grassy patch)* pelouse *f*, gazon *m*; **village g.** place *f* du village, terrain *m* communal
3 *Golf* green *m*, *Can* vert *m*
4 *Am Fam (money)* fric *m*, flouze *m*, blé *m*
• **greens** NPL **1** *Br (vegetables)* légumes *mpl* verts **2** *Am (foliage)* feuillage *m (dans un bouquet)*
• **Green** *Br Pol*
N **the Greens** les Verts *mpl*, les écologistes *mpl*
ADJ vert
▸▸ ***green audit*** = rapport sur l'impact des activités d'une entreprise sur l'environnement; ***green bean*** haricot *m* vert; ***green belt*** ceinture *f* verte; ***the Green Berets*** les Bérets verts; ***green card*** *(for insurance)* carte *f* verte *(prouvant qu'un véhicule est assuré pour un voyage à l'étranger)*; *(work permit)* carte *f* de séjour *(temporaire, aux États-Unis)*; ***green channel*** *(at customs)* file *f* "rien à déclarer"; *Br* ***the green cross code*** le code de sécurité routière *(pour apprendre aux piétons à traverser la route avec moins de risques d'accident)*; *EU* ***green currency*** monnaie *f* verte; *EU* ***green dollar*** dollar *m* vert; *Br* ***green goddess*** = camion de pompiers de l'armée; *Sport* ***green jersey*** maillot *m* vert; *also Fig* ***green light*** feu *m* vert; *Fig* **to give sb/sth the g. light** donner le feu vert à qn/pour qch; ***green man*** *Br (at pedestrian crossing)* bonhomme *m* vert; *Hum (extraterrestrial)* petit homme *m* vert; **wait for the g. man before crossing** attends que le bonhomme passe au vert avant de traverser; **little g. men** petits hommes *mpl* verts; *Am* ***green onion*** ciboule *f*, cive *f*; *Br Pol* ***green paper*** = document formulant des propositions destinées à orienter la politique gouvernementale; ***the Green Party*** le Parti écologiste, les Verts *mpl*; ***green peas*** petits pois *mpl*; ***green pepper*** poivron *m* vert; ***green peppercorn*** grain *m* de poivre vert; *Br Econ* ***green pound*** livre *f* verte; ***green revolution*** révolution *f* verte; ***green salad*** salade *f* (verte); ***green tax*** écotaxe *f*; ***green tea*** thé *m* vert; ***green tourism*** tourisme *m* vert; ***green vegetables*** légumes *mpl* verts

greenback ['griːnbæk] N *Am Fam* billet *m* vert

greenery ['griːnərɪ] N verdure *f*

green-eyed ADJ aux yeux verts; *(jealous)* jaloux
▸▸ ***the green-eyed monster*** *(jealousy)* la jalousie

greenfield site ['griːnfiːld-] N = terrain non construit à l'extérieur d'une ville

greenfinch ['griːnfɪntʃ] N *Orn* verdier *m*

greenfly ['griːnflaɪ] *(pl* **inv** *or* **greenflies)** N *Entom* puceron *m* (vert); **to have g.** *(plant)* avoir des pucerons

greengage ['griːngeɪdʒ] N reine-claude *f*

greengrocer ['griːngrəʊsə(r)] N *Br* marchand *m* de fruits et légumes; **g.'s (shop)** magasin *m* de fruits et légumes

greenhorn ['griːnhɔːn] N *Fam* blanc-bec *m*

greenhouse ['griːnhaʊs, *pl* -haʊzɪz] N serre *f*
▸▸ *Ecol & Met* ***greenhouse effect*** effet *m* de serre; *Ecol* ***greenhouse gases*** gaz *mpl* à effet de serre

greening ['griːnɪŋ] N **the recent g. of the Labour Party** la récente conversion du Parti travailliste à l'écologie; **the g. of Great Britain** la sensibilisation des Britanniques aux problèmes écologiques

greenish ['griːnɪʃ] ADJ tirant sur le vert

Greenland ['griːnlənd] N Groenland *m*

Greenlander ['griːnləndə(r)] N Groenlandais(e) *m,f*

greenmail ['griːnmeɪl] N *Am* chantage *m* au dollar *ou* au billet vert, greenmail *m*

greenness ['griːnnɪs] N **1** *(colour)* couleur *f* verte, vert *m*; *(of field, valley)* verdure *f*; *(of fruit)* verdeur *f* **2** *(of person* ▸ *inexperience)* inexpérience *f*, manque *m* d'expérience; (▸ *naivety)* naïveté *f* **3** *Ecol & Pol* côté *m* écologique

greenroom ['griːnrʊm] N *TV* salle *f* de détente; *Theat* foyer *m* des artistes

greenstick fracture ['griːnstɪk-] N *Med* fracture *f* en bois vert

greenstuff ['griːnstʌf] N **1** *(UNCOUNT) (vegetables)* légumes *mpl* verts **2** *Am Fam (money)* fric *m*

greensward ['griːnswɔːd] N *Arch or Literary* pelouse *f*, gazon *m*, tapis *m* de verdure

Greenwich ['grenɪtʃ] N Greenwich
▸▸ ***Greenwich Mean Time*** heure *f* (du méridien) de Greenwich; ***Greenwich meridian*** méridien *m* de Greenwich

greenwood ['griːnwʊd] N *Arch* forêt *f* verdoyante

greet[1] [griːt] VT *(meet, welcome)* saluer, accueillir; **to g. sb with a wave of the hand** saluer qn de la main; **to g. sb/sth with open arms** accueillir qn/qch les bras ouverts; **the news was greeted with a sigh of relief** les nouvelles furent accueillies avec un soupir de soulagement; **a strange sound greeted our ears** un son étrange est parvenu à nos oreilles; **the sight that greeted her (eyes) defied description** la scène qui s'offrit à ses regards défiait toute description

greet[2] VI *Scot (cry)* pleurer; *(complain)* se plaindre

greeting ['griːtɪŋ] N salut *m*, salutation *f*; *(welcome)* accueil *m*
• **greetings** NPL *(good wishes)* compliments *mpl*, salutations *fpl*; **New Year/Christmas greetings** vœux *mpl* de bonne année/Noël; **birthday greetings** vœux *mpl* d'anniversaire; **to send (one's) greetings to sb** envoyer son bon souvenir *ou* le bonjour à qn
▸▸ *Br* ***greetings card***, *Am* ***greeting card*** carte *f* de vœux

GREETINGS CARDS

Le terme "greetings card" (ou "greeting card", sans "s", en anglais américain) s'emploie pour désigner toute carte pré-imprimée célébrant toute une gamme d'occasions telles qu'anniversaires, naissances, mariages, Noël, la Saint-Valentin, pour féliciter quelqu'un pour son nouveau travail, pour lui souhaiter un prompt rétablissement etc. La Grande-Bretagne et les États-Unis ont une industrie de la carte tout à fait florissante, avec des chaînes de magasins consacrés exclusivement à cette activité. Il faut noter que contrairement aux Français, qui envoient leurs cartes de vœux en janvier, les Britanniques envoient les leurs avant Noël. Le plus souvent, on donne les cartes aux gens que l'on côtoie quotidiennement en mains propres. Par ailleurs, on ne saurait se contenter de souhaiter "bon anniversaire!" à quelqu'un: la carte est de rigueur. Elle accompagne également tout cadeau.

gregarious [grɪ'geərɪəs] ADJ *(animal, bird)* grégaire; *(person)* sociable

> Note that the French adjective **grégaire** is a false friend. It never means **sociable**.

gregariously [grɪ'geərɪəslɪ] ADV *Zool (live)* en groupe; **she was not g. inclined** elle n'avait pas le tempérament grégaire

gregariousness [grɪ'geərɪəsnɪs] N *(of animal, bird)* grégarisme *m*; *(of person)* sociabilité *f*

Gregorian [grɪ'gɔːrɪən] ADJ grégorien
▸▸ ***the Gregorian calendar*** le calendrier grégorien; ***Gregorian chant*** chant *m* grégorien

gremlin ['gremlɪn] N *Fam Hum* = diablotin malfaisant que l'on dit responsable de défauts mécaniques ou d'erreurs typographiques

Grenada [grə'neɪdə] N Grenade *f (dans les Antilles)*

grenade [grə'neɪd] N *Mil* grenade *f*
▸▸ ***grenade attack*** attaque *f* à la grenade; ***grenade launcher*** lance-grenade *m*

grenadier [ˌgrenə'dɪə(r)] N *(soldier)* grenadier *m*

grenadine ['grenədiːn] N grenadine *f*

grew [gruː] *pt of* **grow**

grey, *Am* **gray** [greɪ] **ADJ 1** *(colour, weather)* gris; **to paint sth g.** peindre qch en gris; **g. skies** ciel *m* gris *ou* couvert; **a cold g. day** un jour de froid et de grisaille
2 *(hair)* blanc (blanche); **to be going g.** commencer à avoir des cheveux blancs
3 *(complexion)* gris, blême; **to turn g.** blêmir
4 *(life, situation)* morne; **Tracy leads a g. existence** Tracy mène une vie très morne
N 1 *(colour)* gris *m*; **hair touched with g.** cheveux grisonnants; *Comput* **shades of g.** niveaux *mpl* de gris **2** *(horse)* (cheval *m*) gris *m*
VI *(hair)* **his hair is greying** il commence à grisonner; **to be greying at the temples** avoir les tempes grisonnantes
►► ***grey area*** zone *f* d'incertitude *ou* de flou; **the g. area between right and wrong** la frontière indistincte qui sépare le bien du mal; ***Grey Friar*** franciscain *m*; *St Exch & Com* ***grey market*** marché *m* gris; *Anat* ***grey matter*** matière *f* grise; *Ich* ***grey mullet*** muge *m*; ***grey power*** = pouvoir économique, social etc des personnes âgées; *Zool* ***grey seal*** phoque *m* gris; *Zool* ***grey squirrel*** écureuil *m* gris, petit-gris *m*; *Zool* ***grey whale*** baleine *f* grise; *Zool* ***grey wolf*** loup *m* (gris)

greybeard, *Am* **graybeard** ['greɪbɪəd] **N** *Literary* vieil homme *m*

grey-eyed, *Am* **gray-eyed ADJ** aux yeux gris

grey-haired, *Am* **gray-haired ADJ** aux cheveux gris, grisonnant

greyhound ['greɪhaʊnd] **N** *(male)* lévrier *m*; *(female)* levrette *f*
►► ***greyhound racing*** course *f* de lévriers; ***greyhound stadium, greyhound track*** cynodrome *m*

greying, *Am* **graying** ['greɪɪŋ] **ADJ** grisonnant

greyish, *Am* **grayish** ['greɪɪʃ] **ADJ** tirant sur le gris; *(beard)* grisonnant

greylag, *Am* **graylag** ['greɪlæg] **N** *Orn* **g. (goose)** oie *f* cendrée

greyness, *Am* **grayness** ['greɪnɪs] **N 1** *(of paint, skin)* teinte *f* grise; *(of sky, weather)* grisaille *f*; **the g. of London** la grisaille de Londres **2** *(depressing quality)* caractère *m* morne *ou* sombre, tristesse *f*

greyout, *Am* **grayout** ['greɪaʊt] **N** voile *m* gris

greyscale, *Am* **grayscale** ['greɪskeɪl] **N** *Comput* niveau *m* de gris
►► ***greyscale monitor*** moniteur *m* de niveau de gris

grid [grɪd] **N 1** *(grating)* grille *f*, grillage *m*
2 *(electrode)* grille *f*; *Br Elec* réseau *m*
3 *(on chart, map)* grille *f*; *(lines on map)* quadrillage *m*; **the city was built on a g. pattern** la ville était construite en quadrillé
4 *Culin* gril *m*
5 *(on motor racing track)* grille *f* de départ; **he was second on the g.** il était deuxième sur la grille de départ
6 *Am (game)* football *m* américain; *(pitch)* terrain *m* de football
7 *Comput* grille *f*
►► ***grid layout*** *(of town)* quadrillage *m*, damier *m*; ***grid lines*** droites *fpl* du quadrillage; ***grid reference*** coordonnées *fpl* de la grille; ***grid system*** réseau *m* de quadrillage

griddle ['grɪdəl] **N** *(iron plate)* plaque *f* en fonte; *(on top of stove)* plaque *f* chauffante
VT cuire sur une plaque *(à galette)*
►► ***griddle cake*** = sorte de galette épaisse

gridiron ['grɪdaɪən] **N 1** *Culin* gril *m* **2** *Am (game)* football *m* américain; *(pitch)* terrain *m* de football

gridlock ['grɪdlɒk] **N 1** *(traffic jam)* embouteillage *m* **2** *Fig (situation)* impasse *f*; **to be in g. with sb** être dans une situation de conflit insoluble avec qn

grief [gri:f] **N** *(UNCOUNT)* **1** *(sorrow)* chagrin *m*, peine *f*, (grande) tristesse *f*; **to die of g.** mourir de chagrin
2 *Fam (trouble, inconvenience)* embêtements *mpl*; **to give sb g.** embêter qn; **I'm getting a lot of g. from my parents** mes parents n'arrêtent pas de m'embêter *ou* de me prendre la tête
3 *(as interjection)* **good g.!** mon Dieu!, ciel!
4 *(idiom)* **to come to g.** *(person ► in undertaking)* échouer; *(► have an accident)* avoir un accident; *(project, venture)* échouer, tomber à l'eau
►► *Am, Austr & NZ* ***grief counselling*** = service d'aide psychologique aux personnes frappées par un deuil

> Note that the French word **grief** is a false friend and is never a translation for the English word **grief**. It means **grievance**.

grief-stricken ADJ accablé de chagrin *ou* de douleur, affligé

grievance ['gri:vəns] **N 1** *(cause for complaint)* grief *m*, sujet *m* de plainte; *(complaint)* réclamation *f*, revendication *f*; **my only g. (against him) is...** le seul grief que j'aie (contre lui), c'est...
2 *(grudge)* **to nurse a g.** entretenir *ou* nourrir une rancune *ou* un ressentiment
3 *(injustice)* injustice *f*, tort *m*; **to redress a g.** redresser un tort *ou* une injustice
4 *(discontent)* mécontentement *m*; **they voiced** *or* **aired their grievances** ils ont exprimé leur mécontentement
►► ***grievance procedure*** = procédure permettant aux salariés de faire part de leurs revendications

grieve [gri:v] **VT** peiner, chagriner; **it grieved me to see him so ill/unhappy** ça m'a fait de la peine de le voir si malade/si malheureux; **I was grieved to discover that...** cela m'a fait beaucoup de peine d'apprendre que...
VI 1 *(feel grief)* avoir de la peine *ou* du chagrin, être peiné; **to g. at** *or* **over** *or* **about sth** avoir de la peine à cause de qch; **she is still grieving** elle a encore de la peine **2** *(express grief)* pleurer; **to g. for the dead** pleurer les morts

grieved [gri:vd] **ADJ** peiné, chagriné (**at** de); **to be deeply g. (at sth)** être navré (de qch)

grieving ['gri:vɪŋ] **ADJ** *(person)* en deuil; **the g. process** le (processus de) deuil
N *(UNCOUNT)* deuil *m*

grievous ['gri:vəs] **ADJ 1** *Formal (causing pain)* affreux, cruel, atroce; **a g. loss** une perte cruelle **2** *Literary (grave, serious)* grave, sérieux; **g. injury** des blessures *fpl* graves
►► *Law* ***grievous bodily harm*** coups *mpl* et blessures *fpl*

grievously ['gri:vəslɪ] **ADV** *Formal* gravement, sérieusement; **g. mistaken** tout à fait dans l'erreur; **g. wounded** grièvement blessé

griffin ['grɪfɪn] **N** *Myth* griffon *m*

griffon ['grɪfən] **N 1** *Zool (dog)* griffon *m* **2** *Myth* griffon *m* **3** *Orn* **g. (vulture)** vautour *m* griffon

grift [grɪft] *Am Fam* **N** *(graft)* corruption⁼ *f*; *(cunning trickery)* escroquerie⁼ *f*, filouterie⁼ *f*
VT escroquer⁼; **to g. sth out of sb** escroquer qch à qn
VI filouter⁼, vivre de l'arnaque

grifter ['grɪftə(r)] **N** *Am Fam* arnaqueur(euse) *m,f*, escroc⁼ *m*

grill [grɪl] **VT 1** *Br (food)* (faire) griller **2** *Fam (interrogate)* cuisiner
VI *Br (food)* griller
N 1 *Br (device)* gril *m*; *(dish)* grillade *f*; **to cook sth under the g.** faire cuire qch au gril
2 *(room in restaurant)* grill-room *m*; *(restaurant)* grill *m*
3 *(grating)* grille *f*, grillage *m*
4 *Aut* calandre *f*

grille [grɪl] **N 1** *(grating)* grille *f*, grillage *m* **2** *Aut* calandre *f*

grilled [grɪld] **ADJ** *Br* grillé; **g. meat** viande *f* grillée, grillade *f*

grilling ['grɪlɪŋ] **N 1** *Br (of food)* cuisson *f* sur le *ou* au gril **2** *Fam (interrogation)* **to give sb a g.** cuisiner qn

grillroom ['grɪlrʊm] **N** *(in restaurant)* grill-room *m*; *(restaurant)* grill *m*

grim [grɪm] *(compar* **grimmer**, *superl* **grimmest***)* **ADJ 1** *(hard, stern)* sévère; *(reality, necessity, truth)* dur; *(smile)* sardonique; *(humour)* macabre; **to look g.** avoir l'air sévère; **with g. determination** avec une volonté inflexible; **to hold on (to sb/sth) like g. death** se cramponner (à qn/qch)
2 *(gloomy)* sinistre, lugubre; *(news, report)* sombre; **g. prospects** de sombres perspectives; **it was a g. reminder of his years in prison** c'était un sinistre souvenir de ses années en prison; **the situation is looking pretty g.** la situation n'est pas très encourageante
3 *Fam (mediocre)* nul; **his new film is pretty g.** son nouveau film n'est vraiment pas terrible
4 *Fam (unwell)* patraque; *(depressed)* déprimé⁼, abattu⁼; **I felt pretty g. this morning** *(unwell)* je ne me sentais pas bien du tout ce matin; *(depressed)* je n'avais vraiment pas le moral ce matin

grimace ['grɪməs] **N** grimace *f*; **to make a g.** faire une grimace
VI *(in disgust, pain)* grimacer, faire la grimace; *(to amuse)* faire des grimaces

grime [graɪm] **N** crasse *f*, saleté *f*

griminess ['graɪmɪnɪs] **N** saleté *f*

grimly ['grɪmlɪ] **ADV 1** *(threateningly)* d'un air menaçant; *(unhappily)* d'un air mécontent **2** *(defend, struggle)* avec acharnement; *(hold on)* inflexiblement, fermement; *(with determination)* d'un air résolu, fermement

grimness ['grɪmnɪs] **N 1** *(sternness)* sévérité *f*, gravité *f* **2** *(gloominess)* caractère *m* sinistre *ou* macabre; *(of news, report)* caractère *m* sombre *(of situation)* difficulté *f*

grimy ['graɪmɪ] *(compar* **grimier**, *superl* **grimiest***)* **ADJ** sale, crasseux

grin [grɪn] *(pt & pp* **grinned**, *cont* **grinning***)* **N** grand sourire *m*; **a broad g.** un large sourire
VI sourire; **to g. at sb** faire *ou* adresser un grand sourire à qn; **what are you grinning at?** qu'est-ce que tu as à sourire comme ça?; *Fig* **we'll just have to g. and bear it** il faudra le prendre avec le sourire

grind [graɪnd] *(pt & pp* **ground** [graʊnd]*)* **N 1** *Fam (monotonous work)* corvée⁼ *f*; **the daily g.** le train-train quotidien; **what a g.!** quelle corvée!, quelle barbe!
2 *Fam (when dancing)* déhanchement *m*
3 *(sound)* grincement *m*, crissement *m*
4 *Am Fam (hard worker)* bûcheur(euse) *m,f*, bosseur(euse) *m,f*
VT 1 *(coffee, corn, pepper)* moudre; *(stones)* concasser; *Am (meat)* hacher; *(into powder)* pulvériser, réduire en poudre; *(crush)* broyer, écraser; **he ground his feet into the sand** il a enfoncé ses pieds dans le sable; **to g. sth under one's heel** écraser qch avec le talon; *Fig* **to g. the faces of the poor** opprimer les pauvres
2 *(rub together)* écraser l'un contre l'autre; **to g. one's teeth** grincer des dents; **to g. sth between one's teeth** broyer qch entre ses dents; *Aut* **to g. the gears** faire grincer les vitesses
3 *(polish ► lenses)* polir; *(► glass)* dépolir; *(► stones)* polir, égriser; *(sharpen ► knife)* aiguiser *ou* affûter (à la meule)
4 *(turn handle)* tourner; **to g. a pepper mill** tourner un moulin à poivre
5 *Am Fam (irritate)* taper sur les nerfs à
VI 1 *(crush)* **this pepper mill doesn't g. very well** ce moulin à poivre ne moud pas très bien **2** *(noisily)* grincer; *(wheels)* grincer, crisser; *(gears)* craquer; **to g. to a halt** *or* **to a standstill** *(machine, vehicle)* s'arrêter *ou* s'immobiliser en grinçant; *Fig (company, production)* s'arrêter net; *Fig (economy)* se retrouver paralysé; *Fig* **the whole country ground to a halt** *or* **standstill during the General Strike** le pays a été complètement paralysé pendant la grève générale **3** *Am Fam (work hard)* bûcher *ou* bosser (dur)

► **grind away VI** *Fam* progresser laborieusement⁼; **I've been grinding away at this essay all weekend** j'ai bûché sur cette dissertation tout le week-end

► **grind down VT SEP 1** *(pulverize)* pulvériser, réduire en poudre **2** *(lens)* meuler **3** *Fig (oppress)* opprimer, écraser; **don't let your job g. you down** ne te laisse pas abattre par ton boulot; **the people were ground down by years of poverty** la population était écrasée par des années de misère
VI *(substance)* **it grinds down easily** c'est facile à moudre

► **grind on VI** *Fam (speaker)* parler à n'en plus finir⁼; *(lecture, speech, week)* traîner en longueur⁼; **the accordion music ground on in the background** en fond sonore on entendait l'accordéon, interminable et monotone

► **grind out VT SEP 1** *(cigarette)* écraser **2** *Fig (produce mechanically)* **he was grinding out a tune on the barrel-organ** il jouait un air sur l'orgue de Barbarie; *Fam* **she's just ground out another blockbuster** elle vient de pondre un nouveau best-seller

grind up VT SEP pulvériser; **to g. sth up into powder** réduire qch en poudre

grinder ['graɪndə(r)] N **1** *(machine ▸ for crushing)* moulin *m*, broyeur *m*; *(▸ for sharpening)* affûteuse *f*, machine *f* à aiguiser **2** *(person ▸ of minerals)* broyeur(euse) *m,f*; *(▸ of knives, blades etc)* rémouleur *m* **3** *(tooth)* molaire *f*

grinding ['graɪndɪŋ] N *(sound)* grincement *m*
ADJ **1** *(sound)* **a g. noise** un bruit grinçant; **to come to a g. halt** *(vehicle)* s'immobiliser en grinçant; *(machine) & Fig (production)* stopper; *Fig* **to bring sth to a g. halt** *(production)* arrêter qch d'un seul coup; *(country, rail network)* paralyser qch **2** *(oppressive ▸ boredom, monotony)* mortel; *(▸ worry, insecurity)* accablant; **g. poverty** misère *f* noire

grindingly ['graɪndɪŋlɪ] ADV **g. boring/monotonous** ennuyeux/monotone à mourir; **g. poor** dans une misère noire

grindstone ['graɪndstəʊn] N meule *f*

gringo ['grɪŋgəʊ] *(pl* **gringos**) N *Fam* gringo *m*

grip [grɪp] *(pt & pp* **gripped**, *cont* **gripping**) N **1** *(strong hold)* prise *f*, étreinte *f*; *(on racket, club)* tenue *f*, grip *m*; *(of tyres on road)* adhérence *f*; **to lose one's g.** lâcher prise; **he tightened his g. on the rope** il a serré la corde plus fort; **to get a g. of** *or* **on sb/sth** empoigner qn/qch; **your g. is wrong** *(on tennis racket, golf club etc)* tu ne tiens pas ta raquette/ton club comme il faut; *Fig* **in the g. of despair/pessimism** en proie au désespoir/au pessimisme; *Fig* **the country was in the g. of the worst winter for years** le pays connaissait l'hiver le plus rigoureux qu'il ait connu depuis des années
2 *(handclasp)* poigne *f*; **a strong g.** une forte poigne
3 *Fam (control)* **he's losing his g.** il perd les pédales; **I must be losing my g.** je vieillis, je baisse; **to lose one's g. on reality** perdre le sens des réalités; **he was beginning to lose his g. on the situation** il commençait à perdre le contrôle de la situation; **get a g. (of** *or* **on yourself)!** *(control yourself)* reprends-toi!; *(behave normally, be realistic)* arrête de déconner!
4 *(understanding)* **he has a good g. of the subject** il connaît *ou* domine bien son sujet
5 *(handle ▸ of oar, handlebars)* poignée *f*; *(▸ of pistol)* poignée *f*, crosse *f*; *(▸ of racket, club)* manche *m*, grip *m*
6 (hair) g. pince *f* (à cheveux)
7 *Cin & Theat* machiniste *mf*
8 *Am Old-fashioned (bag)* sac *m* de voyage
9 *Tech (device)* pince *f*
10 *(idioms)* **to come** *or* **to get to grips with sb** *(physically)* s'en prendre à qn; **to come** *or* **to get to grips with a problem** s'attaquer à un problème; **I can't get to grips with Shakespeare** je n'arrive pas à comprendre Shakespeare
VT **1** *(grasp ▸ rope, rail)* empoigner, saisir; **he gripped my arm** il m'a saisi le bras
2 *(hold tightly)* serrer, tenir serré; **the region has been gripped by cold weather** la région a été saisie par une vague de froid
3 *(of tyres)* adhérer à; **to g. the road** *(car)* coller à la route
4 *(hold interest)* passionner; **the trial gripped the nation** le procès a passionné *ou* captivé le pays
VI *(tyres, shoes)* adhérer

gripe [graɪp] N **1** *Fam (complaint)* **what's your g.?** de quoi est-ce que tu te plains?ᵒ; **they've always got some g.** ils sont toujours en train de râler **2** *Med* coliques *fpl*
VI *Fam (complain)* ronchonner, rouspéter
• **gripes** NPL *Med* coliques *fpl*
▸▸ ***gripe water*** calmant *m (pour coliques)*

griping ['graɪpɪŋ] N *(UNCOUNT) Fam* ronchonnements *mpl*, rouspétance *f*
ADJ **g. pains** coliques *fpl*

gripping ['grɪpɪŋ] ADJ *(fascinating)* captivant, passionnant, palpitant

grisly ['grɪzlɪ] *(compar* **grislier**, *superl* **grisliest**) ADJ épouvantable, macabre, sinistre

grist [grɪst] N blé *m* (à moudre); **it's all g. to the mill** c'est toujours ça de pris

gristle ['grɪsəl] *(compar* **gristlier**, *superl* **gristliest**) N *(UNCOUNT) (cartilage)* cartilage *m*, tendons *mpl*; *(in meat)* nerfs *mpl*

gristly ['grɪslɪ] ADJ *(meat)* nerveux, tendineux

grit [grɪt] *(pt & pp* **gritted**, *cont* **gritting**) N **1** *(gravel)* gravillon *m*; **I have a piece of g. in my eye** j'ai un grain de poussière dans l'œil
2 *(sand)* sable *m*
3 *(for fowl)* gravier *m*
4 *(stone)* grès *m*
5 *Fam (courage)* cran *m*; **she's got real g.** elle a vraiment du cran
VT **1** *Br (road, steps)* sabler **2** *(idiom)* **to g. one's teeth** serrer les dents; *Fig* **you'll just have to g. your teeth** il va falloir que tu prennes ton mal en patience
• **grits** NPL *Am Culin* gruau *m* de maïs

gritstone ['grɪtstəʊn] N grès *m*

gritter ['grɪtə(r)] N camion *m* de sablage

gritting ['grɪtɪŋ] N *(of roads)* sablage *m*
▸▸ ***Br gritting lorry*** camion *m* de sablage

gritty ['grɪtɪ] *(compar* **grittier**, *superl* **grittiest**) ADJ **1** *(soil)* cendreux; *(texture, pear)* graveleux; *(coffee)* plein de marc; *(seafood)* sableux; *(leek)* terreux; *(road)* couvert de gravier
2 *Fam (courageous ▸ person)* qui a du cran; **g. determination** détermination farouche
3 *(incisive ▸ remark, comment)* incisif, mordant; **g. realism** *(of book, film etc)* réalisme cru
4 *(play, film)* réaliste et sans concessions

grizzle ['grɪzəl] VI *Br Fam* **1** *(cry fretfully)* pleurnicherᵒ, geindre **2** *(complain)* ronchonner

grizzled ['grɪzəld] ADJ *(person, hair, beard)* grisonnant

grizzling ['grɪzlɪŋ] N *Br Fam (whining)* pleurnicherieᵒ *f*, pleurnichementᵒ *m*

grizzly ['grɪzlɪ] *(compar* **grizzlier**, *superl* **grizzliest**, *pl* **grizzlies**) ADJ *(greyish)* grisâtre; *(hair)* grisonnant
N *(bear)* grizzli *m*, grizzly *m*
▸▸ ***grizzly bear*** grizzli *m*, grizzly *m*

groan [grəʊn] N **1** *(of pain)* gémissement *m*, plainte *f* **2** *(of disapproval, dismay)* grognement *m*; **he gave a g. of annoyance** il a poussé un grognement d'exaspération **3** *(of tree, timber, furniture)* grincement *m*
VI **1** *(in pain)* gémir
2 *(in disapproval, dismay)* grogner; **to g. inwardly** étouffer une plainte *ou* un gémissement; **everybody groaned at his corny jokes** tout le monde levait les yeux au ciel quand il sortait ses plaisanteries éculées
3 *(creak)* grincer
4 *Fig (be weighed down)* gémir; **the table groaned under the weight of the food** la table ployait sous le poids de la nourriture
5 *(complain)* ronchonner
VT *(say)* gémir

groats [grəʊts] NPL gruau *m* (d'avoine)

grobag® ['grəʊbæg] N **1** *(for plants)* = sac de terreau que l'on perfore et qui sert directement de pépinière **2** *(for baby)* gigoteuse *f*

grocer ['grəʊsə(r)] N épicier(ère) *m,f*; *Br* **at the g.'s (shop)** à l'épicerie, chez l'épicier

grocery ['grəʊsərɪ] *(pl* **groceries**) N *(shop)* épicerie *f*; **to be in the g. business** être dans l'épicerie
• **groceries** NPL *(provisions)* épicerie *f*, provisions *fpl*
▸▸ ***Am grocery store*** épicerie *f*

grog [grɒg] N **1** *(made with rum)* grog *m* **2** *Austr & NZ (any alcoholic drink)* boisson *f* alcoolisée

groggy ['grɒgɪ] *(compar* **groggier**, *superl* **groggiest**) ADJ *Fam* **1** *(weak)* faibleᵒ, affaibliᵒ; **to feel g.** avoir les jambes en coton **2** *(unsteady ▸ from exhaustion)* groggy *(inv)*; *(▸ from blows)* groggy *(inv)*, sonné

grogshop ['grɒgʃɒp] N *Austr & NZ Fam* = magasin où l'on vend des boissons alcoolisées

groin [grɔɪn] N **1** *Anat* aine *f*; **g. injury** blessure *f* à l'aine
2 *Br Euph (testicles)* bourses *fpl*; **she kneed him in the g.** elle lui a donné un coup de genou dans l'entrejambe
3 *Archit* arête *f*
4 *Am* = **groyne**

grommet ['grɒmɪt] N **1** *(metal eyelet)* œillet *m*
2 *Naut* erse *f*, estrope *f*, bague *f* en corde
3 *Med (in ear)* diabolo *m*
4 *Fam (novice surfer)* surfeur(euse) *m,f* débutant(e)ᵒ; *(novice skateboarder)* skateboardeur(euse) *m,f* débutant(e)ᵒ

groom [gruːm] N **1** *(for horses)* palefrenier(ère) *m,f*, valet *m* d'écurie **2** *(at wedding)* marié *m* **3** *(in royal household)* gentilhomme *m*, valet *m*
VT **1** *(clean ▸ horse)* panser; *(▸ dog)* toiletter **2** *(prepare ▸ candidate, successor)* préparer, former; **Heather is being groomed for an executive position** on prépare *ou* forme Heather pour un poste de cadre; **I'm grooming him to take over from me** c'est mon poulain, je prépare la relève
3 *Fig (of paedophile)* **to g. a child** = se lier d'amitié avec un enfant sur Internet dans le but d'organiser une rencontre

groomed [gruːmd] ADJ soigné; **to be well-g.** *(person)* être soigné (de sa personne); *(horse)* être bien entretenu

grooming ['gruːmɪŋ] N **1** *(of person)* toilette *f*; *(neat appearance)* présentation *f*; **good g. is very important** il est important d'avoir une bonne présentation
2 *(of horse)* pansage *m*; *(of dog)* toilettage *m*
3 *Fig (of candidate)* préparation *f*
4 *Fig (by paedophile)* = prise de contact avec un enfant sur Internet afin d'organiser une rencontre

groove [gruːv] N **1** *(in wood, metal, for sliding door)* rainure *f*; *(for pulley, in column)* cannelure *f*, gorge *f*; *(in folding knife)* onglet *m*
2 *(in piston)* gorge *f*
3 *(on record)* sillon *m*
4 *(notch)* encoche *f*
5 *Fam (rut)* **to get into** *or* **to be stuck in a g.** s'encroûter, être pris dans la routineᵒ
6 *Am Fam (idiom)* **to be in the g.** être branché, être dans le coup
VT *Tech (make a groove in)* canneler, rainurer, rainer
VI *Fam Old-fashioned (enjoy oneself)* s'éclater; *(dance)* danserᵒ; **to g. to the beat** danser en rythmeᵒ

groovy ['gruːvɪ] *(compar* **groovier**, *superl* **grooviest**) *Fam Old-fashioned or Hum* ADJ **1** *(excellent)* sensationnel, sensass *(inv)*, super *(inv)* **2** *(trendy)* dans le vent
EXCLAM chouette!, génial!, super!

grope [grəʊp] N *Fam (sexual)* pelotage *m*; **they were having a g.** ils se pelotaient
VT **1 to g. one's way in the dark** avancer à tâtons dans l'obscurité **2** *Fam (sexually)* tripoter, peloter
VI *(seek ▸ by touch)* tâtonner, aller à l'aveuglette; *(▸ for answer)* chercher; **to g. (about** *or* **around) for sth** chercher qch à tâtons *ou* à l'aveuglette; **to g. for a word/words** chercher un mot/ses mots

groper ['grəʊpə(r)] N *Ich* mérou *m*

groping ['grəʊpɪŋ] ADJ tâtonnant
N **1** *(in dark)* tâtonnement *m* **2** *Fam (sexual)* pelotage *m*

grosbeak ['grəʊsbiːk] N *Orn* gros-bec *m*, dur-bec *m*

grosgrain ['grəʊgreɪn] N gros-grain *m*

gross [grəʊs] *(pl sense* **1 grosses**, *pl sense* **2** *inv)* N **1** *(whole amount)* **the g.** la quantité totale **2** *(twelve dozen)* grosse *f*, douze douzaines *fpl*
ADJ **1** *(overall, total)* brut
2 *(flagrant ▸ inefficiency, injustice, carelessness)* flagrant; *(▸ error)* grossier, énorme; *(▸ ignorance)* crasse
3 *(vulgar, loutish ▸ person)* grossier, fruste; *(▸ joke)* cru, grossier
4 *(fat)* obèse, énorme
5 *Fam (disgusting)* dégueulasse
6 *Naut (displacement)* global, total
VT *Com (of company)* faire *ou* obtenir une recette brute de; *(of sale)* produire brut; *(of film)* rapporter une recette brute de
▸▸ ***gross amount*** montant *m* brut; ***gross assets*** actif *m* brut; *Fin* ***gross dividend*** dividende *m* brut; ***gross domestic product*** produit *m* intérieur brut; ***gross income*** *(in accounts)* produit *m* brut; *(of individual)* revenu *m* brut; *Law* ***gross indecency*** in-

décence *f* grave; *Fin* ***gross margin*** marge *f* brute; *Law* ***gross miscarriage of justice*** erreur *f* judiciaire grave; ***gross national product*** produit *m* national brut; *Law* ***gross negligence*** faute *f* lourde; *Acct* ***gross operating profit*** bénéfice *m ou* résultat *m* brut d'exploitation; ***gross profit*** bénéfice *m* brut; *Naut* ***gross ton*** tonne *f* de jauge; *Naut* ***gross tonnage*** (tonnage *m* de) jauge *f* brute, tonnage *m* brut; ***gross wage*** salaire *m* brut; ***gross weight*** poids *m* brut, brut *m*; *Fin* ***gross yield*** rendement *m* brut

▸ **gross out** VT SEP *Am Fam* dégoûter□, débecter; **it really grossed me out** ça m'a vraiment débecté

grossed-up price ['grəʊst-] N *Fin* prix *m* fort, plein tarif *m*

grossly ['grəʊslɪ] ADV **1** *(coarsely)* grossièrement **2** *(as intensifier)* outre mesure, excessivement; **g. unfair** extrêmement injuste; **his skills have been g. overrated** ses capacités ont été vraiment surestimées

grossness ['grəʊsnɪs] N **1** *(obesity)* obésité *f* **2** *(of abuse, stupidity, error etc)* énormité *f* **3** *(vulgarity)* grossièreté *f*

gross-out N *Am Fam* = chose ou situation répugnante; **what a g.!** c'est vraiment dégueulasse!

▸▸ *Fam Cin* ***gross-out movie*** comédie *f* lourde

grot [grɒt] N *Br Fam* crasse□ *f*, saleté□ *f*

grotesque [grəʊ'tesk] ADJ grotesque
N *Art* grotesque *m*

grotesquely [grəʊ'tesklɪ] ADV grotesquement, absurdement

grotto ['grɒtəʊ] *(pl* **grottos** *or* **grottoes**) N grotte *f*

grotty ['grɒtɪ] *(compar* **grottier**, *superl* **grottiest**) ADJ *Br Fam* **1** *(unattractive)* moche; *(unsatisfactory)* nul **2** *(unwell)* **to feel g.** ne pas se sentir bien□, être mal fichu

grouch [graʊtʃ] *Fam* VI rouspéter, ronchonner, grogner; **to g. about sth** rouspéter *ou* ronchonner après qch, grogner contre qch
N **1** *(person)* rouspéteur(euse) *m,f* **2** *(complaint)* rouspétance *f*; **to have a g. about sth** rouspéter contre qch

grouchy ['graʊtʃɪ] *(compar* **grouchier**, *superl* **grouchiest**) ADJ *Fam* grincheux□, ronchon, grognon

GROUND [graʊnd]

> **N**
> • terre **1, 10** • sol **1**
> • terrain **2–5, 8** • stade **3**
> • rez-de-chaussée **6** • domaine **7**
> • fond **9**
> **VT**
> • fonder **1** • former **2**
> • mettre à la terre **5** • priver de sortie **6**
> **VI**
> • échouer
> **ADJ**
> • moulu
> **NPL**
> • parc **1** • raison **2**
> • marc **3**

pt & pp of **grind**

N **1** *(earth)* terre *f*; *(surface)* sol *m*; **the g. is often frozen in winter** la terre est souvent gelée en hiver; **at g. level** au niveau du sol; **the children sat on the g.** les enfants se sont assis par terre; **to pick sth up off the g.** ramasser qch par terre; **drive the stakes firmly into the g.** enfoncez solidement les pieux dans le sol; **above g.** en surface; **below g.** sous terre; **to burn sth to the g.** réduire qch en cendres; **to fall to the g.** tomber par *ou* à terre; **to go to g.** se terrer; **to run a fox to g.** traquer un renard jusqu'à son terrier; **to run sb to g.** *(criminal, suspect etc)* traquer qn; *Fig* **to be on firm g.** être sûr de son fait; *Fig* **to change** *or* **to shift one's g.** changer de tactique; **to get off the g.** *(aeroplane)* décoller; *Fig (project)* démarrer; **it suits him down to the g.** ça lui va à merveille, ça lui convient parfaitement; **to run a car into the g.** utiliser une voiture jusqu'à ce qu'elle rende l'âme; **to work oneself into the g.** se tuer au travail; **to hit a g. stroke** *(in tennis)* frapper la balle au rebond

2 *(UNCOUNT) (land)* terrain *m*; *(region)* région *f*, coin *m*; **there's a lot of hilly g. in Scotland** il y a beaucoup de coins vallonnés en Écosse

3 *Br (piece of land)* terrain *m*; *(stadium)* stade *m*; **the crowds are leaving the g.** la foule des spectateurs sort du stade

4 *(area used for specific purpose)* **fishing grounds** zones *fpl* réservées à la pêche; **training g.** terrain *m* d'entraînement *ou* d'exercice

5 *Mil* terrain *m*; **to give/to lose g.** céder/perdre du terrain; **to stand** *or* **to hold one's g.** tenir bon; **to gain g.** *(in battle)* gagner du terrain; *(idea, concept)* faire son chemin, progresser; *(news)* se répandre

6 *(storey)* rez-de-chaussée *m inv*

7 *(UNCOUNT) (area of reference)* domaine *m*, champ *m*; **his article covers a lot of g.** dans son article, il aborde beaucoup de domaines; **this is new g. for me** pour moi, c'est un domaine nouveau

8 *(subject)* terrain *m*, sujet *m*; **you're on dangerous g.** vous êtes sur un terrain glissant; **for them, politics is forbidden g.** pour eux, la politique est un sujet tabou *ou* un domaine interdit; **a middle g.** un terrain d'entente, un compromis

9 *(background)* fond *m*; **on a green g.** *(painting)* sur fond vert

10 *Am Elec* terre *f*, masse *f*; **to connect to g.** mettre à la terre *ou* à la masse

11 *Mus* **g. (bass)** basse *f* contrainte

VT **1** *(base)* fonder, baser (**on** *or* **in** sur)

2 *(train)* former; **the students are well grounded in computer sciences** les étudiants ont une bonne formation *ou* de bonnes bases en informatique

3 *(plane, pilot)* **to be grounded** être interdit de vol; **the plane was grounded for mechanical reasons** l'avion a été interdit de vol à cause d'un incident mécanique

4 *(ship)* échouer

5 *Am Elec* mettre à la terre *ou* à la masse

6 *Fam (child)* priver de sortie□; **to be grounded** ne pas avoir le droit de sortir

7 *(in rugby)* **to g. the ball** aplatir (le ballon)

VI *(ship)* échouer; **the submarine had grounded on a sandbank** le sous-marin s'était échoué *ou* avait échoué sur un banc de sable

ADJ *(wheat, coffee)* moulu; *(pepper)* concassé; *(steel)* meulé; *Am (meat)* haché

• **grounds** NPL **1** *(around house)* parc *m*, domaine *m*; *(around block of flats, hospital)* terrain *m*; *(more extensive)* parc *m*; **the house has extensive grounds** la maison est entourée d'un grand parc; **the grounds are patrolled by dogs** le terrain est gardé par des chiens

2 *(reason)* motif *m*, raison *f*; *(cause)* cause *f*, raison *f*; *(basis)* base *f*, raison *f*; *(pretext)* raison *f*, prétexte *m*; **to have (good) grounds for doing sth** avoir de bonnes raisons de faire qch; **you have no grounds for believing that he's lying** vous n'avez aucune raison de croire qu'il ment; **there are grounds for suspecting arson** il y a lieu de penser qu'il s'agit d'un incendie criminel; **what grounds have you for saying that?** qu'est-ce qui vous permet d'affirmer cela?; **he was excused on the grounds of poor health** il a été exempté en raison de sa mauvaise santé; **on medical/moral grounds** pour (des) raisons médicales/morales; **on what grounds?** à quel titre?; *Law* **grounds for appeal** voies *fpl* de recours; **grounds for complaint** grief *m*; **grounds for divorce** motif *m* de divorce

3 *(of coffee)* marc *m*

▸▸ *Mil* ***ground attack*** offensive *f* terrestre; *Fishing* ***ground bait*** amorce *f* de fond, appât *m* de fond; *Am* ***ground beef*** steak *m* haché; *Aviat* ***ground control*** contrôle *m* au sol; ***ground cover*** végétation *f* basse; ***ground crew*** personnel *m* au sol, personnel *m* non-navigant; *Br* ***ground floor*** rez-de-chaussée *m inv*; *Fig* **to get in on the g. floor** *(at beginning of project)* participer dès le début; *(buy shares)* acheter des actions dès leur émission; *Mil* ***ground forces*** armée *f* de terre; ***ground frost*** gelée *f* blanche; ***ground glass*** *(glass)* verre *m* dépoli; *(as abrasive)* verre *m* pilé; ***ground level*** *(ground floor)* rez-de-chaussée *m inv*; *(lowest level in organization)* base *f*; **at g. level** au rez-de-chaussée; ***ground plan*** *(plan of ground floor)* plan *m* au sol; *(plan of action)* plan *m* préparatoire; ***ground rent*** redevance *f* foncière; ***ground rice*** farine *f* de riz; ***ground rule*** procédure *f*, règle *f*; **to lay down the g. rules** établir les règles du jeu; ***ground staff*** *Sport* personnel *m* responsable de l'entretien d'un terrain de sport; *Br (at airpor* personnel *m* au sol, personnel *m* non-navigan *Mil* ***ground war*** guerre *f* terrestre; *Geol* ***groun water*** nappe *f* phréatique; *Mil* ***ground zero*** hypc centre *m*, point *m* zéro; ***Ground Zero*** *(in New Yor* Ground Zero

groundbait ['graʊndbeɪt] N *Fishing* amorce *f* d fond

ground-breaking ADJ révolutionnaire; **this g. technology** c'est une véritable percée techno logique

grounded ['graʊndɪd] ADJ **1** *(based* ▸ *argumen belief etc)* fondé; **well/ill g.** *(belief)* bien/ma fondé **2** *Am Elec* (mis) à la masse, relié à la terr

groundhog ['graʊndhɒg] N marmotte *f* d'Amé rique

▸▸ *Am* ***Groundhog Day*** = le 2 février, jour où le marmottes sont censées avoir fini leur hiberna tion et sortir de leur terrier, annonçant l'arrivé prochaine du printemps si elles restent dehors et le prolongement de l'hiver si elles ne for qu'une brève apparition

grounding ['graʊndɪŋ] N **1** *(training)* formatio *f*, *(knowledge)* connaissances *fpl*, bases *fpl*; **t have a good g. in Latin** avoir de bonnes bases e latin

2 *(of argument)* assise *f*

3 *Am Elec* mise *f* à la terre *ou* à la masse

4 *(of ship)* échouage *m*; *(of plane)* interdiction de vol

5 *(of balloon)* atterrissage *m*

groundless ['graʊndlɪs] ADJ sans fondemen sans motif; **her fears proved g.** ses craintes s'avé rèrent sans fondement

groundnut ['graʊndnʌt] N *Br* arachide *f*

▸▸ ***groundnut oil*** huile *f* d'arachide

groundsel ['graʊndsəl] N séneçon *m*

groundsheet ['graʊndʃiːt] N tapis *m* de sol

groundsman ['graʊndzmən] *(pl* **groundsmen** mən]) N *Br* gardien *m*

groundspeed ['graʊndspiːd] N *Aviat* vitesse *f* a sol

groundswell ['graʊndswel] N lame *f* de fond *Fig* **there was a g. of public opinion in favour o the president** l'opinion publique a basculé mas sivement en faveur du président; **there has bee a g. of support for the proposal** il y a eu un raz-de marée en faveur de la proposition

ground-to-air ADJ *Mil (missile)* sol-air *(inv)*

ground-to-ground ADJ *Mil (missile)* sol-sc *(inv)*

groundwork ['graʊndwɜːk] N *(UNCOUNT)* tra vail *m* préparatoire, canevas *m*; *Fig* **to do** *or* **la the g. for a project/economic reform** jeter les fon dations d'un projet/de réformes économiques **I've done the g., the rest is up to you** j'ai préparé l terrain, le reste dépend de toi

group [gruːp] N **1** *(of people, companies)* group *m*; *Pol (party)* groupement *m*; *(literary)* groupe *m* cercle *m*

2 *(of objects)* groupe *m*, ensemble *m*; *(of moun tains)* massif *m*

3 *(in business)* groupe *m*; **they're in** *or* **part of th Thistle g.** ils font partie du groupe Thistle

4 *(blood type)* groupe *m*; **what (blood) g. are you – g. AB** quel est votre groupe sanguin? – l groupe AB

5 *Mus* groupe *m*; **a pop/rock g.** un groupe pop rock

6 *Ling* groupe *m*, syntagme *m*

7 *Mil* groupe *m*

COMP *(work)* de groupe; *(action, decision)* co lectif

VT **1** *(bring together)* grouper, réunir; *(put i groups)* disposer en groupes; **the teache grouped all the eight-year-olds together** l'institu trice a groupé *ou* regroupé tous les enfants d huit ans **2** *(combine)* combiner

VI se grouper, se regrouper; **they all groupe round their leader** ils se groupèrent tous autou de leur chef

▸▸ ***group booking*** réservation *f* de groupe; ***grou captain*** colonel *m* de l'armée de l'air; ***group decis ion*** décision *f* collective; ***group discount*** remise pour les groupes; *Psy* ***group dynamics*** dyna mique *f* de groupe; ***group leader*** *(on packag* *tour)* accompagnateur(trice) *m,f*; *(for group of children)* moniteur(trice) *m,f*; **group photograph** photographie *f* de groupe; *Med* **group practice** cabinet *m* médical; **group sex** sexe *m* de groupe; *Math* **group theory** théorie *f* des ensembles; **group therapy** thérapie *f* de groupe

groupage ['gru:pɪdʒ] **N** groupage *m*

grouped consignment [gru:pt-] **N** *Com* envoi *m* groupé

grouper ['gru:pə(r)] **N** *Ich* mérou *m*

groupie ['gru:pɪ] **N** *Fam* groupie *f*

grouping ['gru:pɪŋ] **N 1** *(putting together ▸ of packages, consignments)* groupage *m*; *(▸ of figures)* groupement *m*; *(▸ of people)* rassemblement *m* **2** *(group)* groupe *m*

groupware ['gru:pweə(r)] **N** *Comput* logiciel *m* de groupe, synergiciel *m*

grouse¹ [graʊs] *(pl* **inv** *or* **grouses)** **N** *(bird ▸ gen)* grouse *f*, tétras *m*; *(▸ red grouse)* lagopède *m* d'Écosse

▸▸ **grouse beating** rabattage *m*; **grouse moor** chasse *f* réservée (à la chasse à la grouse); **grouse shooting** chasse *f* à la grouse

grouse² *Fam* **N** *(grumble)* rouspétance *f*; *(complaint)* grief *m*; **to have a g. about sth** rouspéter contre qch

VI rouspéter, râler; **what are you grousing about?** pourquoi rouspètes-tu?

grouser ['graʊsə(r)] **N** *Fam (complainer)* grognon *m*, rouspéteur(euse) *m,f*

grousing ['graʊsɪŋ] **N** *(UNCOUNT) Fam* ronchonneries *fpl*; **I've had enough of your g.!** j'en ai assez de t'entendre ronchonner!

grout [graʊt] **N** coulis *m* au ciment

VT jointoyer

grove [grəʊv] **N** bosquet *m*; **beech g.** hêtraie *f*; **olive g.** oliveraie *f*; *Literary* **the groves of Academe** le milieu universitaire, l'Université *f*

grovel ['grɒvəl] *(Br pt & pp* **grovelled**, *cont* **grovelling**, *Am pt & pp* **groveled**, *cont* **groveling)** **VI 1** *(act humbly)* ramper, s'aplatir; **to g. to sb (for sth)** s'aplatir devant qn (pour obtenir qch); **to g. before sb** ramper devant qn **2** *(crawl on floor)* se vautrer par terre; **stop grovelling around on the floor** arrête de te traîner par terre

grovelling, *Am* **groveling** ['grɒvəlɪŋ] **ADJ** rampant, servile; **a g. letter** une lettre obséquieuse; **a g. apology** de viles excuses *fpl*

N flagornerie *f*

grow [grəʊ] *(pt* **grew** [gru:], *pp* **grown** [grəʊn]) **VI 1** *(plants)* croître, pousser; *(hair)* pousser; *(seeds)* germer; **orange trees g. best in a warm climate** les orangers poussent mieux en climat chaud; **she let her hair g. (long)** elle a laissé pousser ses cheveux, elle s'est laissé pousser les cheveux; **to g. back** *(plants, hair)* repousser; **money doesn't g. on trees** l'argent ne pousse pas sur les arbres

2 *(person ▸ in age, height)* grandir; **hasn't he grown!** qu'est-ce qu'il a grandi!; **she has grown two inches** elle a grandi de cinq centimètres

3 *(develop)* **to g. in wisdom/understanding** devenir plus sage/compréhensif

4 *(originate)* **this custom grew from** *or* **out of a pagan ceremony** cette coutume est née d'une *ou* a pour origine une cérémonie païenne

5 *(increase)* s'accroître, augmenter; **the crime rate in the big cities is growing** le taux de criminalité augmente dans les grandes villes; **the economy has grown by 5 percent in the last two years** la croissance de l'économie a été de 5 pour cent au cours des deux dernières années; **support for the strike is growing** la grève est de plus en plus soutenue; **our love/friendship grew over the years** notre amour/amitié a grandi au fil des ans; **he has grown in my esteem** il a grandi *ou* est monté dans mon estime; **the town grew in importance** la ville a gagné en importance

6 *(become)* devenir; **to g. angry** se mettre en colère; **to g. bigger** grandir, s'agrandir; **the noise grew louder** le bruit a augmenté *ou* s'est amplifié; **it's beginning to g. dark** il commence à faire nuit; **to g. old** devenir vieux, vieillir

7 *(with infinitive) (come gradually)* **I've grown to respect him** j'ai appris à le respecter; **to g. to like/to dislike sb/sth** finir par aimer/détester qn/qch

VT 1 *(crops, plants)* cultiver **2** *(beard, hair)* laisser pousser; **he's trying to g. a beard** il essaie de se laisser pousser la barbe; **she's growing her hair (long)** elle se laisse pousser les cheveux **3** *Fin (company)* agrandir; **to g. the business** augmenter le chiffre d'affaires

▸▸ **grow bag** = sac plastique rempli d'engrais dans lequel on fait pousser une plante

▸ **grow apart VI** *(people)* s'éloigner; **we gradually grew apart as we got older** nous nous sommes progressivement éloignés l'un de l'autre en vieillissant

▸ **grow in VI** *(hair)* repousser; *(nail)* s'incarner

▸ **grow into VT INSEP 1** *(become)* devenir (en grandissant); **both her sons grew into fine-looking men** ses deux fils sont devenus de beaux jeunes gens; **the company grew into a huge organization** l'entreprise est devenue une énorme société **2** *(clothes)* **the sweater's too big for him, but he'll g. into it** le pull est trop grand pour lui, mais il pourra le mettre un jour **3** *(become used to)* **to g. into a job** s'habituer à *ou* s'adapter à un travail

▸ **grow on VT INSEP** plaire de plus en plus à; **the song began to g. on him after a while** au bout d'un certain temps, la chanson commença à lui plaire de plus en plus; **it grows on you** on y prend goût; **the idea was beginning to g. on me** l'idée commençait à me séduire

▸ **grow out VI** *(hairstyle)* **her hair** *or* **hairstyle has grown out** ses cheveux sont maintenant trop longs pour son genre de coiffure; **she let the dye g. out** elle a laissé pousser ses cheveux jusqu'à ce que les traces de teinture aient disparu

▸ **grow out of VT INSEP 1** *(clothes)* **he's grown out of most of his clothes** la plupart de ses vêtements ne lui vont plus, il ne rentre plus dans la plupart de ses vêtements **2** *(become too old for)* **to g. out of doing sth** passer l'âge de faire qch; **she grew out of her dolls** elle a passé l'âge de jouer à la poupée; **it's just a phase, he'll g. out of it** ce n'est qu'une tocade, ça lui passera; **to g. out of one's friends** ne plus avoir grand-chose en commun avec ses amis; **he never grew out of (the habit of) biting his nails** il n'a jamais perdu cette habitude de se ronger les ongles

▸ **grow up VI 1** *(become adult)* grandir, devenir adulte; **what do you want to be when you g. up?** que veux-tu faire quand tu seras grand?; **we didn't have television when I was growing up** nous n'avions pas la télévision quand j'étais petit; **I hope he won't g. up to be a liar/thief** j'espère qu'il ne sera pas un menteur/voleur plus tard **2** *(behave like adult)* **g. up!** sois un peu adulte!; **I wish you'd g. up!** j'aimerais bien que tu cesses tes gamineries! **3** *(develop)* naître, se développer; **a strong feeling of hatred grew up between them** un puissant sentiment de haine est né entre eux; **a legend grew up around these events** une légende s'est développée autour de ces événements; **the town grew up around the castle** la ville s'est développée autour du château

grower ['grəʊə(r)] **N 1** *(producer)* producteur (trice) *m,f*; *(professional)* cultivateur(trice) *m,f*; *(amateur gardener)* amateur *m* de jardinage; **vegetable g.** maraîcher(ère) *m,f*; **rose g.** *(professional)* rosiériste *mf*; **he's a keen rose g.** *(amateur)* il se passionne pour la culture des roses **2** *(plant, tree)* **a slow/fast g.** une plante qui pousse lentement/vite

-growing ['grəʊɪŋ] **SUFF wine-g. region** région *f* vinicole; **wheat/potato-g. region** région *f* qui produit du blé/de la pomme de terre, région *f* à blé/pommes de terre; **fast/slow-g.** *(plant)* qui pousse vite/lentement

growing ['grəʊɪŋ] **ADJ 1** *(plant)* croissant, qui pousse; *(child)* grandissant, en cours de croissance; **a g. child needs a well balanced diet** un enfant en pleine croissance a besoin d'une alimentation bien équilibrée **2** *(increasing ▸ debt)* qui augmente; *(▸ amount, number)* grandissant, qui augmente; *(▸ friendship, impatience)* grandissant; *(▸ opinion, belief)* de plus en plus répandu; **g. numbers of people are out of work** de plus en plus de gens sont *ou* un nombre croissant de gens est au chômage; **a g. population** une population qui s'accroît; **there are g. fears of a nuclear war** on craint de plus en plus une guerre nucléaire

N *(of agricultural products)* culture *f*

▸▸ **growing pains** *(of children)* douleurs *fpl* de croissance; *(of business, project)* difficultés *fpl* de croissance, problèmes *mpl* de départ; **growing season** saison *f* nouvelle

growl [graʊl] **VI** *(animal)* grogner, gronder; *(person)* grogner, grommeler; *(thunder)* tonner, gronder; *(stomach)* gargouiller; **to g. at sb** grogner contre qn

VT *(answer, instructions)* grommeler, grogner

N grognement *m*, grondement *m*; *(in stomach)* gargouillement *m*

growling ['graʊlɪŋ] **N** *(of animal)* grognement *m*, grondement *m*; *(in stomach)* gargouillement *m*

grown [grəʊn] *pp of* **grow**

ADJ *(person)* adulte; **you don't expect g. adults to behave so stupidly** on ne s'attend pas à ce que des adultes se comportent de manière si stupide; **he's a g. man** il est adulte; **when fully g., these animals can...** lorsqu'ils ont atteint l'âge adulte, ces animaux peuvent...

grown-up N adulte *mf*, grande personne *f*

ADJ adulte; **our children are g. now** nos enfants sont grands maintenant; **he's very g. for his age** il est très mûr pour son âge

growth [grəʊθ] **N 1** *(development ▸ of child, plant)* croissance *f*; *(▸ of friendship)* développement *m*, croissance *f*; *(▸ of organization)* développement *m*; **intellectual/spiritual g.** développement *m* intellectuel/spirituel

2 *(increase ▸ in numbers, amount)* augmentation *f*, croissance *f*; *(▸ of market, industry)* croissance *f*, expansion *f*; *(▸ of influence, knowledge)* développement *m*, croissance *f*; **the experts predict a 2 percent g. in tourism/imports** les experts prédisent une croissance du tourisme/des importations de 2 pour cent; **economic g.** développement *m ou* croissance *f* économique; **population g.** croissance *f* de la population

3 *(of beard, hair, weeds)* pousse *f*; **the entrance was covered by a dense g. of weeds** l'entrée était envahie par les mauvaises herbes; **g. of hair** poussée *f* de cheveux; **two days' g. (of beard)** une barbe de deux jours

4 *Med (tumour)* excroissance *f*, tumeur *f*, grosseur *f*; **benign/malignant g.** tumeur *f* bénigne/maligne

▸▸ **growth area** secteur *m* en expansion; **alternative medicine has been a g. area in recent years** les médecines parallèles ont connu un boum ces dernières années; **growth hormone** hormone *f* de croissance; **growth industry** industrie *f* en plein essor *ou* de pointe; **growth market** marché *m* porteur; **growth rate** taux *m* de croissance; **growth ring** anneau *m* de croissance; *St Exch* **growth stock** actions *fpl* d'avenir *ou* de croissance

growth-share matrix N *Mktg* matrice *f* croissance-part de marché

groyne, *Am* **groin** [grɔɪn] **N** brise-lames *m inv*

grub [grʌb] *(pt & pp* **grubbed**, *cont* **grubbing)** **VI 1** *(animal)* fouir **2** *(rummage)* fouiller; **I was grubbing about in the dirt looking for my key** j'étais en train de farfouiller par terre dans les saletés pour trouver ma clef

N 1 *(larva)* larve *f*; *(maggot)* asticot *m* **2** *Fam (food)* bouffe *f*; **g.** *or* **g.'s up!** à la soupe!

▸▸ **Grub Street** le monde des plumitifs

▸ **grub out VT SEP** *(roots, stumps)* extirper

▸ **grub up VT SEP** *(bone)* déterrer; *(roots, stumps)* extirper; *(plant)* déraciner; *(insects)* déloger

grubbiness ['grʌbɪnɪs] **N** saleté *f*

grubby ['grʌbɪ] *(compar* **grubbier**, *superl* **grubbiest)** **ADJ** sale, crasseux, malpropre; *Fig (immoral)* sordide, sale; *Fig* **I felt g. when I found out he was married** je me suis méprisée quand j'ai appris qu'il était marié; **I don't want him getting his g. hands on these documents** je ne veux pas que cet animal mette la main sur ces documents

grubstake ['grʌbsteɪk] **N** *Am* = provisions données à un prospecteur contre un pourcentage de ses profits

grudge [grʌdʒ] N rancune f; **to bear** or **to hold a g. against sb** en vouloir à qn, avoir de la rancune contre qn; **she's not one to bear a g.** elle n'est pas du genre rancunier

VT **1** (give unwillingly) **to g. sb sth** donner qch à contrecœur à qn; **she grudged them every penny she gave them** elle leur donnait chaque penny à contrecœur; **to g. sb the food they eat** lésiner sur la nourriture de qn **2** (resent) **to g. sb their pleasures** mal supporter que qn passe du bon temps; **she grudges him his success** elle lui en veut à cause de son succès; **I don't g. spending money but...** je ne répugne pas à dépenser mais...; **I g. having to get up so early** je supporte très mal d'avoir à me lever si tôt

►► Sport **grudge match** règlement m de compte

grudging ['grʌdʒɪŋ] ADJ (compliment, praise) fait ou donné à contrecœur; (agreement) réticent

grudgingly ['grʌdʒɪŋlɪ] ADV à contrecœur, avec réticence

gruel [grʊəl] N bouillie f d'avoine, Can gruau m (d'avoine); (thin) brouet m

gruelling, Am **grueling** ['grʊəlɪŋ] ADJ (race, interview) éreintant, épuisant; (punishment) sévère; (experience) très difficile, très dur; **we had a g. time** ça a été très dur

gruesome ['gru:səm] ADJ (sight) horrible; (discovery) macabre; Hum **the g. twosome** les deux terreurs fpl

gruesomely ['gru:səmlɪ] ADV horriblement

gruff [grʌf] ADJ **1** (manner) brusque **2** (speech, tone) bourru; **a g. voice** (deep) une grosse voix; (brusque) une voix bourrue

gruffly ['grʌflɪ] ADV **1** (behave) avec brusquerie **2** (speak) d'un ton bourru

gruffness ['grʌfnɪs] N **1** (of manner) brusquerie f **2** (of speech, voice, tone) ton m bourru

grumble ['grʌmbəl] VI **1** (complain) grogner, grommeler; **he's always grumbling about something** il rouspète constamment contre quelque chose; **to g. at sb** grommeler ou rouspéter contre qn; **stop grumbling!** arrête de te plaindre!; Br **how are you? – oh, mustn't g.!** ça va? – on fait aller! **2** (thunder, artillery) gronder; **my stomach kept grumbling loudly** mon estomac n'arrêtait pas de gargouiller bruyamment

VT grommeler; **"I do all the work here," he grumbled** "c'est moi qui fais tout ici", a-t-il grommelé

N **1** (complaint) ronchonnement m, sujet m de plainte; **what's his latest g.?** pourquoi se plaint-il cette fois?; **his letter contained the usual grumbles** sa lettre contenait les plaintes habituelles; **to obey without a g.** obéir sans murmurer **2** (of thunder, artillery) grondement m

grumbler ['grʌmblə(r)] N grincheux(euse) m,f, mécontent(e) m,f

grumbling ['grʌmblɪŋ] ADJ grincheux, grognon; **g. noises** des ronchonnements mpl

N (UNCOUNT) plaintes fpl, protestations fpl

►► Med **grumbling appendix** appendicite f chronique

grummet ['grʌmɪt] = **grommet**

grump [grʌmp] N Fam bougon(onne) m,f, ronchon(onne) m,f; **you are an old g. this morning!** t'es qu'un vieux ronchon, ce matin!; **to have the grumps** être de mauvais poil

grumpily ['grʌmpɪlɪ] ADV Fam (say, speak etc) en ronchonnant, d'un ton ronchon; (look at) d'un air ronchon

grumpiness ['grʌmpɪnɪs] N Fam mauvaise humeur f, caractère m désagréable

grumpy ['grʌmpɪ] (compar **grumpier**, superl **grumpiest**) Fam ADJ ronchon, bougon; **a g. old woman** une vieille grincheuse

N (term of address) **what's wrong, g.?** qu'est-ce qui ne va pas, grincheux?

grundyism ['grʌndɪɪzəm] N pudibonderie f

grunge [grʌndʒ] N **1** Am (dirt) crasse f **2** (fashion, music) grunge m

grungy ['grʌndʒɪ] (compar **grungier**, superl **grungiest**) ADJ **1** Am (dirty) crasseux **2** (fashion, music) grunge (inv)

grunt [grʌnt] VI grogner, pousser un grognement

VT (reply) grommeler, grogner; **"what?" he grunted** "quoi?", grogna-t-il

N **1** (sound) grognement m; **to give a g.** pousser un grognement; **the pig gave a loud g.** le cochon grogna bruyamment **2** Am Fam Mil slang (soldier) troufion m

grunting ['grʌntɪŋ] ADJ grognant, qui grogne

gryphon ['grɪfən] N griffon m

GSM [ˌdʒi:es'em] N Tel (abbr **global system for mobile communication**) GSM m

GSP [ˌdʒi:es'pi:] N EU (abbr **Growth and Stability Pact**) PSC m

g-spot N point m G

GST [ˌdʒi:es'ti:] N Austr & Can Fin (abbr **goods and services tax**) TPS f

G-string N **1** Mus (corde f de) sol m **2** (item of clothing) cache-sexe m, string m

g-suit N combinaison f anti-G

gt (written abbr **great**) grand

Guadeloupe [ˌgwa:də'lu:p] N Guadeloupe f

guano ['gwa:nəʊ] N guano m

guarantee [ˌgærən'ti:] N **1** Com garantie f; **a g. against defective workmanship** une garantie contre les malfaçons; **money-back g.** remboursement m garanti; **to be under g.** être sous garantie; **this cooker has a five-year g.** cette cuisinière est garantie cinq ans; Comput **on-site/return-to-base g.** garantie f sur site/retour atelier

2 Law (pledge) caution f, garantie f, gage m, cautionnement m; **to give sth as a g.** donner qch en caution ou en gage

3 (person) garant(e) m,f, caution f; **to act as g. (for sb)** se porter garant (de qn)

4 (firm promise) garantie f; **what g. do I have that you'll bring it back?** comment puis-je être sûr que vous le rapporterez?; **there's no g. it will arrive today** il n'est pas garanti ou dit que ça arrivera aujourd'hui

VT **1** (goods) garantir; **the car is guaranteed against rust for ten years** la voiture est garantie contre la rouille pendant dix ans **2** (loan, cheque) garantir, cautionner; **to g. sb against loss** garantir des pertes de qn **3** (assure) certifier, assurer; **I can't g. that everything will go to plan** je ne peux pas vous certifier ou garantir que tout se passera comme prévu; **our success is guaranteed** notre succès est garanti

►► **guarantee certificate** certificat m de garantie; **guarantee company** société f de sécurité; **guarantee form** formulaire m ou fiche f de garantie

guaranteed [ˌgærən'ti:d] ADJ (success) garanti, assuré; **g. by** (on financial document) pour aval, bon pour aval

►► Fin **guaranteed bond** obligation f garantie; Fin **guaranteed loan** prêt m garanti; Am **guaranteed seat** réservation f ferme

guarantor [ˌgærən'tɔ:(r)] N garant(e) m,f, caution f; **to stand g. (for sb)** se porter garant (de qn)

guaranty ['gærəntɪ] (pl **guaranties**) N **1** (security) caution f, garantie f **2** (guarantor) garant(e) m,f **3** (written guarantee) garantie f

guard [ga:d] N **1** (person) gardien m, garde m; (group) garde f; **prison g.** gardien m de prison; **g. of honour** garde f d'honneur

2 (watch) garde f; **to be on g.** (duty) être de garde; **to mount (a) g.** monter la garde; **to mount g. on** or **over** veiller sur; **the military kept g. over the town** les militaires gardaient la ville; **to stand g.** monter la garde; **the changing of the g.** la relève de la garde; **there was a heavy police g. for the president's visit** il y avait d'importantes forces de police pour la visite du président

3 (supervision) garde f, surveillance f; **to keep a prisoner under g.** garder un prisonnier sous surveillance; **to put a g. on sb/sth** faire surveiller qn/qch; **the prisoners were taken under g. to the courthouse** les prisonniers furent emmenés sous escorte au palais de justice

4 (attention) garde f; **on g.!** (in fencing) en garde!; **to be on one's g.** être sur ses gardes; **we must warn him to be on his g. against robbers** nous devons lui dire de faire attention aux voleurs; **to put sb on his g.** mettre qn en garde; **to catch sb off g.** prendre qn au dépourvu; **his offer of help caught her off g.** elle ne s'attendait pas à ce qu'il lui propose son aide; **to drop** or **to lower one's g.** relâcher sa surveillance

5 Br Rail chef m de train

6 (protective device ► on machine) dispositif m de sûreté ou de protection; (► personal) protection f; **(fire) g.** garde-feu m inv

VT **1** (watch over ► prisoner) garder

2 (defend ► fort, town, entrance) garder, défendre; **the house was heavily guarded** la maison était étroitement surveillée

3 (protect ► life, reputation) protéger; **to g. sb against danger** protéger qn d'un danger; **g. this letter with your life** veille bien sur cette lettre

4 (in games) garder

• **Guards** NPL Mil (regiment) Garde f royale (britannique)

►► **guard dog** chien m de garde; Mil **Guards officer** officier m de la Garde royale; Br **guard's van** fourgon m du chef de train

► **guard against** VT INSEP se protéger contre ou de, se prémunir contre; **to g. against doing sth** se garder de faire qch; **plastic sheets help g. against frost** des housses en plastique aideront à protéger du gel; **how can we g. against such accidents (happening)?** comment éviter ou empêcher (que) de tels accidents (arrivent)?

guarded ['ga:dɪd] ADJ **1** (cautious) prudent, circonspect, réservé; **he was very g.** il est resté très prudent; **to give a g. reply** répondre avec réserve **2** (mechanism) protégé **3** (prisoner) gardé à vue (building) gardé, surveillé

guardedly ['ga:dɪdlɪ] ADV (cautiously) avec réserve, prudemment

guardhouse ['ga:dhaʊs, pl -haʊzɪz] N Mil (for guards) corps m de garde; (for prisoners) salle de garde

guardian ['ga:djən] N **1** (gen) gardien(enne) m,f (of museum) conservateur(trice) m,f **2** Law (of minor) tuteur(trice) m,f

►► **guardian angel** ange m gardien; **'Guardian' reader** = lecteur du 'Guardian' (représentatif de la gauche intellectuelle)

guardianship ['ga:djənʃɪp] N **1** (gen) garde f **2** Law tutelle f

guardrail ['ga:dreɪl] N **1** (on ship) bastingage m, garde-corps m inv **2** Rail contre-rail m **3** Am (on road) barrière f de sécurité

guardroom ['ga:drʊm] = **guardhouse**

guardsman ['ga:dzmən] (pl **guardsmen** [-mən]) N Mil Br soldat m de la Garde royale; Am soldat m de la garde nationale

Guatemala [ˌgwætə'ma:lə] N Guatemala m

Guatemalan [ˌgwætə'ma:lən] N Guatémaltèque mf

ADJ guatémaltèque

COMP (embassy, history) du Guatemala

guava ['gwa:və] N (tree) goyavier m; (fruit) goyave f

gubernatorial [ˌgu:bənə'tɔ:rɪəl] ADJ Am de ou du gouverneur; **g. elections** élections fpl des gouverneurs

gudgeon[1] ['gʌdʒən] N (socket) tourillon m

►► **gudgeon pin** axe m de piston

gudgeon[2] N Ich goujon m

guelder rose ['geldə-] N (shrub) boule-de-neige f, obier m

gueridon ['gerɪdən] N guéridon m

guerilla = **guerrilla**

Guernsey ['gɜ:nzɪ] N **1** (island) Guernesey f **2** (cow) vache f de Guernesey **3** (sweater) jersey m, tricot m

guerrilla [gə'rɪlə] N guérillero m

►► Mktg **guerrilla advertising** publicité f guérilla; **guerrilla band, guerrilla group** guérilla f, groupe m de guérilleros; Mktg **guerrilla marketing** guérilla marketing m; **guerrilla strike** grève f sauvage; **guerrilla warfare** guérilla f (combat)

> Note that the French word **guérilla** is a false friend and is never a translation for the English word **guerrilla**. It means **guerrilla warfare**.

guess [ges] N **1** (at facts, figures) estimation f; Br **to have** or Am **to take a g. at sth** (essayer de) deviner qch; **if you don't know, have a g.** si tu ne sais pas, essaie de deviner; **it was just a lucky g.** c'était un coup de chance; **at a (rough) g., I'd say 200** à vue de nez, je dirais 200; **he made a good/a wild g.** il a deviné juste/à tout hasard; **I'll give you three guesses** devine un peu **2** (hypothesis) supposition *f*, conjecture *f*; **it's anybody's g.** Dieu seul le sait, impossible de prévoir; **my g. is that he won't come** à mon avis il ne viendra pas, je pense qu'il ne viendra pas; **your g. is as good as mine** tu en sais autant que moi, je n'en sais pas plus que toi

VT 1 *(attempt to answer)* deviner; **g. what!** devine un peu!; **g. who!** devine qui c'est!; **g. who I saw in town** devine (un peu) qui j'ai vu en ville; **I guessed as much** je m'en doutais, c'est bien ce que je pensais; **you've guessed it!** tu l'as deviné!; **I guessed him to be 25** je lui ai donné 25 ans **2** *(imagine)* croire, penser, supposer; **I g. you're right** je suppose que vous avez raison; **I g. so** je pense que oui; **I g. not** non, effectivement

VI deviner; **to g. at sth** deviner qch; **how did you g.?** comment avez-vous deviné?; **g.!** devine un peu!; **the police guessed right** la police a deviné *ou* vu juste; **we guessed wrong** nous nous sommes trompés; **we could only g. at their plans** nous ne pouvions qu'essayer de deviner leurs intentions; **I couldn't begin to g.** je n'en ai pas la moindre idée; *Ironic* **I would never have guessed** je n'aurais jamais deviné; **to keep sb guessing** laisser qn dans le doute

guessing ['gesɪŋ] **N** estimation *f*

►► ***guessing game*** devinette *f*

guesstimate *Fam* **N** ['gestɪmət] calcul *m* au pifomètre

VT ['gestɪmeɪt] calculer au pifomètre

guesswork ['geswɜːk] **N** *(UNCOUNT)* conjecture *f*, hypothèse *f*; **to do sth by g.** faire qch au hasard; **it's pure** *or* **sheer g.** c'est une simple hypothèse *ou* supposition

guest [gest] **N 1** *(visitor ► at home)* invité(e) *m,f*, hôte *mf*; *(► at table)* invité(e) *m,f*, convive *mf*; *also Ironic* **be my g.!** fais donc!, je t'en prie!; *TV* **with a g. appearance from...** avec comme invité d'honneur...; *TV* **to make a g. appearance in a programme** être invité dans une émission **2** *(in hotel)* client(e) *m,f*; *(in boarding house)* pensionnaire *mf* **3** *Comput* invité(e) *m,f*

VI *TV & Rad* **to g. on sb's show** faire une apparition dans l'émission de qn; *Mus* **another guitarist guested on one of the tracks** un autre guitariste a participé à l'un des morceaux

►► ***guest artist*** invité-vedette (invitée-vedette) *m,f*; ***guest book*** *(in house, hotel) & Comput (of Web page)* livre *m* d'or; ***guest of honour*** invité(e) *m,f* d'honneur; ***guest list*** liste *f* des invités; ***guest night*** *(in club)* = soirée d'un club où les non-membres sont invités; ***guest room*** chambre *f* d'ami(s); ***guest speaker*** conférencier(ère) *m,f (invité à parler par une organisation, une association)*; ***guest star*** invité-vedette (invitée-vedette) *m,f*; **g. star Anthony Hopkins** *(in credits)* avec la participation d'Anthony Hopkins; ***guest worker*** travailleur(euse) *m,f* immigré(e)

guesthouse ['gesthaʊs, *pl* -haʊzɪz] **N** pension *f* de famille

guff [gʌf] **N** *(UNCOUNT) Fam* bêtises *fpl*, idioties *fpl*; **don't talk g.!** ne dis pas d'âneries!; **the film was a load of g.** le film était vraiment débile

guffaw [gʌ'fɔː] **N** gros éclat *m* de rire

VI rire bruyamment, s'esclaffer

VT "of course!" he guffawed "bien sûr!", s'esclaffa-t-il

GUI ['guːi:] **N** *Comput* (*abbr* **graphical user interface**) interface *f* utilisateur graphique

Guiana [gaɪ'ɑːnə] **N** Guyane *f*; **the Guianas** les Guyanes *fpl*; **French G.** Guyane *f* française; **Dutch G.** Guyane *f* hollandaise

guidance ['gaɪdəns] **N** *(UNCOUNT)* **1** *(advice)* conseils *mpl*

2 *(instruction)* direction *f*, conduite *f*; *(supervision)* direction *f*, supervision *f*; **to do sth under sb's g.** faire qch avec les conseils *ou* sous la direction de qn

3 *(information)* information *f*; **diagrams are given for your g.** les schémas sont donnés à titre d'information *ou* à titre indicatif

4 *Aviat (of missile)* guidage *m*

►► *Am* ***guidance counselor*** conseiller(ère) *m,f* d'orientation; *Aviat* ***guidance system*** système *m* de guidage

guide [gaɪd] **N 1** *(for tourists)* guide *mf*

2 *(influence, direction)* guide *m*, indication *f*; **let your conscience be your g.** laissez-vous guider par votre conscience; **to take sth as a g.** prendre qch comme règle de conduite

3 *(indication)* indication *f*, idée *f*; **as a rough g.** en gros, approximativement; **are these tests a good g. to intelligence?** ces tests fournissent-ils une bonne indication de l'intelligence?; **conversions are given as a g.** les conversions sont données à titre indicatif

4 *(manual)* guide *m*, manuel *m* pratique; **a g. to France** un guide de la France

5 *Br (girl scout)* **(Girl) G.** éclaireuse *f*

6 *(machine part)* guide *m*

VT 1 *(show the way)* guider, conduire; **to g. sb in/out** conduire qn jusqu'à l'entrée/la sortie; **the children guided us through the old city** les enfants nous ont guidés à travers la vieille ville

2 *(instruct)* diriger, conduire

3 *(advise)* conseiller, guider, orienter; **he guided the country through some difficult times** il a su conduire le pays durant des périodes difficiles; **I'll be guided by you** je me laisserai guider par vous

4 *Aviat* guider

►► ***guide dog*** chien *m* d'aveugle; ***Guide movement*** = mouvement féminin de scoutisme; ***guide rope*** *(for hoist)* corde *f* de guidage; *(for hot-air balloon)* guiderope *m*

guidebook ['gaɪdbʊk] **N** guide *m* touristique *(manuel)*

guided ['gaɪdɪd] **ADJ** guidé, sous la conduite d'un guide

►► ***guided missile*** missile *m* guidé *ou* téléguidé; ***guided tour*** visite *f* guidée

guideline ['gaɪdlaɪn] **N 1** *(for writing)* ligne *f* **2** *(hint, principle)* ligne *f* directrice, directives *fpl*; **as a general** *or* **rough g.** en règle générale

guidepost ['gaɪdpəʊst] **N** poteau *m* indicateur

guiding ['gaɪdɪŋ] **ADJ** *(principle)* directeur; *Fig* **she gave me a g. hand** elle m'a donné un coup de main

►► *Fig* ***guiding light, guiding star*** guide *m*

guild [gɪld] **N 1** *Hist (professional)* guilde *f*, corporation *f*; **the g. of goldsmiths** la guilde des orfèvres **2** *(association)* confrérie *f*, association *f*, club *m*; **women's/church g.** cercle *m* féminin/paroissial

guilder ['gɪldə(r)] **N** *Formerly (Dutch currency)* gulden *m*

guildhall ['gɪldhɔːl] **N** palais *m* des corporations; **The G.** = l'hôtel de ville de la City de Londres

guile [gaɪl] **N** *Formal (trickery)* fourberie *f*, tromperie *f*; *(cunning)* ruse *f*, astuce *f*

guileless ['gaɪllɪs] **ADJ** *Formal* candide, ingénu

guillemot ['gɪlɪmɒt] **N** *Orn* guillemot *m*

guillotine ['gɪləˌtiːn] **N 1** *(for executions)* guillotine *f*; **to be executed by g.** être guillotiné; **to go to the g.** aller à la guillotine, être mené à la guillotine

2 *(for paper)* massicot *m*

3 *Pol* = procédure parlementaire consistant à fixer des délais stricts pour l'examen de chaque partie d'un projet de loi

4 *Med (for performing tonsillectomy)* amygdalotome *m*, tonsillotome *m*

VT 1 *(person)* guillotiner **2** *(paper)* massicoter **3** *Pol* **to g. a debate** limiter la durée d'un débat

guilt [gɪlt] **N 1** *(responsibility)* culpabilité *f* (**for** pour); **the g. does not lie with him alone** il n'est pas le seul coupable **2** *(feeling)* culpabilité *f*; **a sense of g.** un sentiment de culpabilité; **g. drove him to suicide** un sentiment de culpabilité l'a poussé au suicide; **to be on a g. trip** culpabiliser

VT *Fam* **he guilted me into going with him** il a réussi à me faire culpabiliser si bien que finalement je l'ai accompagné

►► ***guilt complex*** complexe *m* de culpabilité

guiltily ['gɪltɪlɪ] **ADV** d'un air coupable

guiltless ['gɪltlɪs] **ADJ** innocent

guilty ['gɪltɪ] (*compar* **guiltier**, *superl* **guiltiest**) **ADJ 1** *Law* coupable; **g. of murder** coupable de meurtre; **to plead g./not g.** plaider coupable/non coupable; **the judge found her g./not g.** le juge l'a déclarée coupable/non coupable **2** *(responsible)* coupable; **they're g. of a terrible lack of sensitivity** ils font preuve d'un manque terrible de sensibilité; **to have a g. conscience** avoir mauvaise conscience; **I feel g. about not telling them** je me sens coupable *ou* je culpabilise de ne pas leur avoir dit; **you're making me feel g.** tu me culpabilises; **she gave me a g. look** elle me jeta un regard coupable

►► *Law* ***guilty party*** coupable *mf*

Guinea ['gɪnɪ] Guinée *f*

guinea ['gɪnɪ] **N 1** *(money)* guinée *f (ancienne monnaie britannique)* **2** *Am very Fam* Rital(e) *m,f*, = terme injurieux désignant un Italien

►► *Orn* ***guinea fowl*** pintade *f*; ***guinea pig*** cochon *m* d'Inde, cobaye *m*; *(used in experiments)* cobaye *m*; *Fig* **to use sb as a g. pig** se servir de qn comme d'un cobaye, prendre qn comme cobaye

Guinea-Bissau [-bɪ'saʊ] **N** Guinée-Bissau *f*; **in G.** en Guinée-Bissau

Guinean ['gɪnɪən] **N** Guinéen(enne) *m,f*

ADJ guinéen

guise [gaɪz] **N 1** *(appearance)* apparence *f*, aspect *m*; **the same old policies in a new g.** la même politique sous des dehors différents; **under** *or* **in the g. of** sous l'apparence de **2** *Arch (costume)* costume *m*

guitar [gɪ'tɑː(r)] **N** guitare *f*; **to play the g.** jouer de la guitare

►► ***guitar player*** guitariste *mf*

guitarist [gɪ'tɑːrɪst] **N** guitariste *mf*

gulch [gʌltʃ] **N** *Am* ravin *m*

gulf [gʌlf] **N 1** *(bay)* golfe *m* **2** *(chasm)* gouffre *m*, abîme *m*; *Fig* **a huge g. has opened up between the two parties** il y a désormais un énorme fossé entre les deux partis **3** *Geog* **the G.** le golfe (Persique)

COMP *(country, oil)* du Golfe

►► ***the Gulf of Alaska*** le golfe d'Alaska *ou* de l'Alaska; ***the Gulf of California*** le golfe de Californie; ***the Gulf of Mexico*** le golfe du Mexique; ***the Gulf States*** *(in US)* les États *mpl* du golfe du Mexique; *(round Persian Gulf)* les États *mpl* du Golfe; ***the Gulf Stream*** le Gulf Stream; ***the Gulf of Suez*** le golfe de Suez; ***the Gulf War*** la guerre du Golfe; ***Gulf War syndrome*** syndrome *m* de la guerre du Golfe

gull[1] [gʌl] **N** *(bird)* mouette *f*, goéland *m*

gull[2] *Arch* **N** *(dupe)* dupe *f*

VT duper

gullet ['gʌlɪt] **N** *(oesophagus)* œsophage *m*; *(throat)* gosier *m*; *Fam Fig* **it really sticks in my g.** ça me reste en travers du gosier

gulley (*pl* **gulleys**) = **gully**

gullibility [ˌgʌlə'bɪlətɪ] **N** crédulité *f*, naïveté *f*

gullible ['gʌləbəl] **ADJ** crédule, naïf

gully ['gʌlɪ] (*pl* **gullies**) **N 1** *(valley)* ravin *m* **2** *(drain)* caniveau *m*, rigole *f*

gulp [gʌlp] **VT** *(food)* engloutir; *(drink)* avaler à pleine gorge; *(air)* avaler

VI *(with emotion)* avoir un serrement de gorge; **he gulped in surprise** la surprise lui a serré la gorge

N 1 *(act of gulping)* **she swallowed it in one g.** elle l'a avalé d'un seul coup **2** *(with emotion)* serrement *m* de gorge; **"oh dear," he said with a g.** "mon Dieu", dit-il, la gorge serrée **3** *(mouthful)* grosse bouchée *f*; *(of drink)* goulée *f*; **he took a g. of water** il a avalé une goulée d'eau

► **gulp back VT SEP** avaler; **she gulped back her tears** elle a ravalé *ou* refoulé ses larmes

► **gulp down VT SEP** *(food)* engloutir; *(drink)* avaler à pleine gorge; *(air)* avaler

GUM [ˌdʒiːjuː'em] **N** (*abbr* **genito-urinary medicine**) médecine *f* génito-urinaire

►► ***GUM clinic*** = centre spécialisé dans le traitement des maladies sexuellement transmissibles

gum [gʌm] (*pt & pp* **gummed**, *cont* **gumming**) **N 1** *Anat* gencive *f*

2 *(chewing gum)* chewing-gum *m*; **to chew g.** mâcher du chewing-gum; **two sticks of g.** deux chewing-gums

3 *(adhesive)* gomme *f*, colle *f*

4 *Bot (substance)* gomme *f*

5 *Br (sweet)* boule *f* de gomme

VT 1 *(cover with gum)* gommer; **gummed paper**

papier *m* gommé **2** *(stick)* coller; **g. the two edges together** collez les deux bords ensemble

VI *Bot* exsuder de la gomme

EXCLAM *Br Fam Old-fashioned* **by g.!** nom d'un chien!, mince alors!

►► ***gum arabic*** gomme *f* arabique; ***gum disease*** gingivite *f*; ***gum tree*** gommier *m*; *Fam* **to be up a g. tree** être dans le pétrin

►**gum up** VT SEP *Fam (mechanism)* bousiller; *(plan)* ficher en l'air; *Fig* **that's gummed up the works!** ça a tout fichu en l'air!

gumboil [ˈgʌmbɔɪl] N parulie *f*, abcès *m* gingival

gumboot [ˈgʌmbuːt] N *Br* botte *f* de caoutchouc

gumdrop [ˈgʌmdrɒp] N boule *f* de gomme

gummed [gʌmd] ADJ *(label, envelope)* gommé

gummy [ˈgʌmɪ] *(compar* **gummier**, *superl* **gummiest)** ADJ **1** *(sticky)* collant, gluant **2** *(gum-like)* gommeux

gumption [ˈgʌmpʃən] N *Fam* **1** *Br (common sense)* jugeote *f*; **he didn't even have the g. to call the police** il n'a même pas eu la présence d'esprit d'appeler la police▫ **2** *(initiative)* initiative▫ *f*; **she's got plenty of g.** c'est une débrouillarde

gumshield [ˈgʌmʃiːld] N protège-dents *m inv*

gumshoe [ˈgʌmʃuː] N **1** *Am Fam Old-fashioned (detective)* privé *m* **2** *(rubber overshoe)* caoutchouc *m*

gun [gʌn] *(pt & pp* **gunned**, *cont* **gunning)** N **1** *(weapon)* arme *f* à feu; *(pistol)* pistolet *m*; *(revolver)* revolver *m*; *(rifle)* fusil *m*; *(cannon)* canon *m*; **the burglar had a g.** le cambrioleur était armé; **to draw a g. on sb** braquer une arme sur qn; **a 21-g. salute** une salve de 21 coups de canon; *Mil* **the guns** l'artillerie *f*; *Fam* **to be going great guns** *(enterprise)* marcher à merveille; *Fam* **to bring out one's big guns** mettre le paquet; **to jump the g.** *Sport (in race)* partir avant le signal; *Fig* brûler les étapes; **to stick to one's guns** tenir bon

2 *(hunter)* fusil *m*

3 *Fam (gunman)* gangster▫ *m*; **hired g.** tueur *m* à gages

4 *(dispenser)* pistolet *m*; **paint g.** pistolet *m* à peinture; **(grease) g.** seringue *f ou* injecteur *m* (à graisse)

5 *Electron* canon *m*

VT *Aut* **to g. the engine** accélérer

►► ***gun barrel*** *(of rifle)* canon *m* de fusil; *(of revolver)* canon *m* de revolver; ***gun carriage*** affût *m* de canon; *(at military funeral)* prolonge *f* d'artillerie; ***gun laws*** législation *f* réglementant le port d'armes; ***gun licence*** permis *m* de port d'armes; ***gun lobby*** lobby *m* favorable au port d'armes; ***gun room*** *(in house)* armurerie *f*; *(on warship)* poste *m* des aspirants; ***gun turret*** tourelle *f*

►**gun down** VT SEP abattre

►**gun for** VT INSEP **1** *(look for)* chercher; **the boss is gunning for you** le patron te cherche *ou* est après toi **2** *(try hard for)* faire des pieds et des mains pour obtenir

gunboat [ˈgʌnbəʊt] N canonnière *f*

►► ***gunboat diplomacy*** diplomatie *f* imposée par la force, politique *f* de la canonnière

gundeck [ˈgʌndek] N *Naut* batterie *f*

gunfight [ˈgʌnfaɪt] N fusillade *f*

gunfighter [ˈgʌnfaɪtə(r)] N *(in Western film, novel)* bandit *m* armé

gunfire [ˈgʌnfaɪə(r)] N *(UNCOUNT)* coups *mpl* de feu, fusillade *f*; *(of cannon)* tir *m* d'artillerie

gunge [gʌndʒ] N *(UNCOUNT) Fam* substance *f* visqueuse▫

gung-ho [ˌgʌŋˈhəʊ] ADJ *(enthusiastic)* tout feu tout flamme *(inv)*; *(ready to fight)* va-t-en-guerre *(inv)*

gunk [gʌŋk] N *(UNCOUNT) Fam* substance *f* visqueuse▫

gunmaker [ˈgʌnmeɪkə(r)] N armurier *m*

gunman [ˈgʌnmən] *(pl* **gunmen** [-mən]) N gangster *m* (armé); *(terrorist)* terroriste *m* (armé)

gunmetal [ˈgʌnmetəl] N **1** *(metal)* bronze *m* à canon **2** *(colour)* gris *m* foncé métallisé

►► ***gunmetal grey*** gris *m* foncé métallisé

gunnel = **gunwale**

gunner [ˈgʌnə(r)] N artilleur *m*, canonnier *m*

gunnery [ˈgʌnərɪ] N artillerie *f*

►► ***gunnery officer*** officier *m* d'artillerie

gunny [ˈgʌnɪ] N toile *f* de jute (grossière)

gunplay [ˈgʌnpleɪ] N *Am* échange *m* de coups de feu

gunpoint [ˈgʌnpɔɪnt] N **to have** *or* **to hold sb at g.** menacer qn d'une arme à feu; **a confession obtained at g.** une confession obtenue sous la menace d'un revolver

gunport [ˈgʌnpɔːt] N *Naut* sabord *m* de batterie

gunpowder [ˈgʌnpaʊdə(r)] N poudre *f* à canon

►► *Br Hist* ***the Gunpowder Plot*** la conspiration des poudres

THE GUNPOWDER PLOT

Les catholiques, menés par Guy Fawkes, organisèrent ce complot pour faire sauter le Parlement britannique et tuer le roi Jacques Ier et sa famille, le 5 novembre 1605, en réaction au refus royal d'instaurer la liberté de culte. Le complot fut déjoué. On commémore cet événement, appelé **Guy Fawkes' Night**, par des feux d'artifice et des feux de joie.

gunrunner [ˈgʌnrʌnə(r)] N trafiquant(e) *m,f* d'armes

gunrunning [ˈgʌnrʌnɪŋ] N trafic *m* d'armes

gunship [ˈgʌnʃɪp] N *(helicopter)* hélicoptère *m* armé

gunshot [ˈgʌnʃɒt] N **1** *(shot)* coup *m* de feu; **a g. wound** une blessure par balle **2** *(range)* **to be out of/within g.** être hors de portée de/à portée de fusil

gunshy [ˈgʌnʃaɪ] ADJ **to be g.** avoir peur des coups de feu

gunslinger [ˈgʌnslɪŋə(r)] N *Fam* bandit *m* armé▫

gunsmith [ˈgʌnsmɪθ] N armurier *m*; **g.'s (shop)** armurerie *f*

gunstock [ˈgʌnstɒk] N fût *m* (de fusil)

gunwale [ˈgʌnəl] N *Naut* plat-bord *m*; *Fig* **full to the gunwales** plein à ras bord

guppy [ˈgʌpɪ] *(pl* **guppies)** N **1** *Ich* guppy *m* **2** *Fam (gay yuppie)* homo *m* BCBG

gurgle [ˈgɜːgəl] N *(of liquid)* glouglou *m*, gargouillis *m*; *(of stream)* murmure *m*, gazouillement *m*; *(of pleasure, delight)* gloussement *m*, roucoulement *m*; *(of baby)* gazouillis *m*; **gurgles of laughter** des gloussements

VT **she gurgled her delight** elle roucoula de plaisir

VI *(liquid)* glouglouter, gargouiller; *(stream)* murmurer; *(person* ► *with pleasure, delight)* glousser, roucouler; *(baby)* gazouiller

gurgling [ˈgɜːgəlɪŋ] N *(of liquid)* glouglou *m*, gargouillis *m*; *(of stream)* murmure *m*, gazouillement *m*; *(of baby)* gazouillis *m*

ADJ *(liquid)* glougloutant, qui fait glouglou; *(stream)* murmurant; **a g. laugh** un rire perlé

Gurkha [ˈgɜːkə] N Gurkha *m*

gurn [gɜːn] VT *Br Fam* faire des grimaces▫

gurnard [ˈgɜːnəd] N *Ich* grondin *m*

gurner [ˈgɜːnə(r)] N *Br Fam* grimacier(ère)▫ *m,f*

gurnet [ˈgɜːnɪt] N *Ich* grondin *m*

gurney [ˈgɜːnɪ] N *Am* chariot *m* d'hôpital

guru [ˈguruː] N *Rel & Fig* gourou *m*

gush [gʌʃ] N **1** *(of liquid, gas)* jet *m*, flot *m*; *(of spring, fountain)* jaillissement *m*; *Fig* **a g. of words** un flot de paroles **2** *(of emotion)* vague *f*, effusion *f*; **a sudden g. of enthusiasm** une soudaine vague d'enthousiasme

VT **1** *(emit)* **to g. water/oil** lancer des jets d'eau/un jet de pétrole **2** *Pej (say effusively)* **"darling, you were wonderful!" he gushed** "chérie, tu as été formidable!", lança-t-il avec exubérance

VI **1** *(flow)* jaillir; **blood was gushing from his arm** le sang jaillissait de son bras; **water gushed forth** *or* **out** l'eau jaillissait **2** *Pej (talk effusively)* parler avec animation; **everyone was gushing over the baby** tout le monde se répandait en compliments sur le bébé

gusher [ˈgʌʃə(r)] N **1** *(oil well)* puits *m* jaillissant *ou* éruptif **2** *Fam Pej (person)* personne *f* trop exubérante▫

gushing [ˈgʌʃɪŋ] ADJ **1** *(liquid)* jaillissant, bouillonnant; **the car was swept away by a g. torrent of water** la voiture a été emportée par un véritable torrent d'eau **2** *Pej (person)* trop exubérant; **g. compliments/praise** compliments *mpl*/éloges *mpl* sans fin

gushy [ˈgʌʃɪ] *(compar* **gushier**, *superl* **gushiest)** ADJ *Fam Pej (person)* trop exubérant▫

gusset [ˈgʌsɪt] N **1** *Sewing* soufflet *m* **2** *Const* gousset *m*

gust [gʌst] N **a g. (of wind)** un coup de vent, une rafale; **a g. of hot air** une bouffée d'air chaud; **a g. of rain** une ondée, une giboulée; *Fig* **a g. of anger** un accès de colère

VI *(wind)* souffler en bourrasques; *(rain)* faire des bourrasques; **winds gusting up to 50 mph were recorded** on a enregistré des pointes de vent à 80 km/h

gustatory [ˈgʌstətərɪ] ADJ gustatif

gusto [ˈgʌstəʊ] N délectation *f*, enthousiasme *m*; **to do sth with (great) g.** faire qch avec (beaucoup d')enthousiasme

gusty [ˈgʌstɪ] *(compar* **gustier**, *superl* **gustiest)** ADJ *(weather)* venteux; *(day)* de grand vent; **it's a bit g. out** il y a des rafales (de vent) *ou* des bourrasques dehors; **a g. wind** un vent qui souffle en rafales, des rafales *fpl* de vent

gut [gʌt] *(pt & pp* **gutted**, *cont* **gutting)** N **1** *Ana* intestin *m*

2 *Fam (stomach)* bide *m*; **I've got a pain in the g.** j'ai mal au bide; **pull in your g.** rentre ton bide

3 *(UNCOUNT) (thread* ► *for violins)* corde *f* de boyau; *(*► *for rackets)* boyau *m*

4 *(in sea port)* goulet *m*, passage *m* étroit

VT **1** *(fish, poultry etc)* étriper, vider **2** *(building)* ne laisser que les quatre murs de; **the house had been gutted by the fire** la maison avait été ravagée par l'incendie; **she gutted the house and completely redecorated it** elle a cassé tout l'intérieur de la maison et a tout refait **3** *(book)* résumer, extraire l'essentiel de

• **guts** NPL **1** *(insides)* entrailles *fpl*

2 *Fam (courage)* cran *m*, courage▫ *m*; **to have guts** avoir du cran *ou* du cœur au ventre; **he's got no guts** il n'a rien dans le ventre; **I didn't have the guts to tell them** je n'ai pas eu le courage de le leur dire

3 *Fam (of machine)* intérieur▫ *m*

4 *Fam (idioms)* **to work** *or* **to sweat one's guts out** se casser les reins, se tuer au travail; **to hate sb's guts** ne pas pouvoir blairer qn; **I'll have your guts for garters** je vais faire de toi de la chair à pâté

►► ***gut feeling*** pressentiment *m*; ***gut reaction*** réaction *f* instinctive *ou* viscérale

gutless [ˈgʌtlɪs] ADJ *Fam (cowardly)* trouillard, dégonflé

gutsy [ˈgʌtsɪ] *(compar* **gutsier**, *superl* **gutsiest)** ADJ *Fam* **1** *(brave* ► *person)* qui a du cran **2** *(powerful* ► *film, language, novel)* qui a du punch, musclé; *(*► *performance)* plein de pêche; **she's a g. singer** elle chante avec ses tripes **3** *(greedy)* goinfre

gutted [ˈgʌtɪd] ADJ *Br Fam (disappointed)* dégoûté, hyper déçu

gutter [ˈgʌtə(r)] N **1** *(on roof)* gouttière *f*; *(in street)* caniveau *m*, ruisseau *m*; *Fig* **to end up in the g.** tomber *ou* rouler dans le ruisseau; *Fig* **to drag sb/oneself out of the g.** tirer qn/sortir du ruisseau; **to speak the language of the g.** parler le langage des rues

2 *(ditch)* rigole *f*, sillon *m (creusé par la pluie)*

3 *Typ (back margin)* (blanc *m* de) petit fond *m*; *(fore-edge)* (blanc *m* de) grand fond *m*; *(space between columns)* gouttière *f*

4 *(in ten-pin bowling)* rigole *f*

VI *(candle flame)* vaciller, trembler

►► *Typ* ***gutter margin*** marge *f* de gouttière; *Pej* ***gutter press*** presse *f* de bas étage, presse *f* à scandale

guttered [ˈgʌtəd] ADJ *Br Fam (drunk)* bourré, pété

guttering [ˈgʌtərɪŋ] N *(UNCOUNT) (of roof)* gouttières *fpl*

guttersnipe [ˈgʌtəsnaɪp] N *Pej* gosse *mf* des rues

guttural [ˈgʌtərəl] ADJ guttural

N *Ling* gutturale *f*

guv [gʌv], **guvnor** [ˈgʌvnə(r)] **N** *Br Fam* **the g.** *(boss)* le chef☐, le boss; *Old-fashioned (father)* le pater, le paternel; **got a fag, g.?** n'auriez pas un mégot, patron?

guy [gaɪ] **N 1** *Fam (man)* mec *m*, type *m*, gars *m*; **a good g.** un mec *ou* un type bien; **OK guys, let's go** allez les gars *ou* les mecs, on y va
2 *esp Am (to both men and women)* **what are you guys doing tonight?** vous faites quoi, vous, ce soir?; **OK guys, let's go** OK, les amis, on y va; **hi guys!** salut vous!; **are you guys ready?** tout le monde est prêt?
3 *Br (for bonfire)* = effigie de Guy Fawkes
4 *(for tent)* corde *f* de tente
VT *Old-fashioned* se moquer de
►► ***guy rope*** *(for tent)* corde *f* de tente

Guyana [gaɪˈænə] **N** Guyana *m*

Guyanese [ˌgaɪəˈniːz] *(pl* **inv***)* **N** Guyanais(e) *m,f*
ADJ guyanais

Guy Fawkes' Night [-ˈfɔːks-] **N** = fête célébrée le 5 novembre en commémoration de la conspiration des poudres

GUY FAWKES' NIGHT

Cette fête se déroule en plein air autour d'un grand feu de joie sur lequel on est censé brûler une effigie ("the Guy") de Guy Fawkes, l'instigateur de la conspiration des poudres. Des feux d'artifice sont également organisés.

guzzle [ˈgʌzəl] *Fam* **VT** *(food)* bouffer, bâfrer; *(drink)* siffler; **he's guzzled the whole lot!** *(food)* il a tout bouffé *ou* bâfré!; *(drink)* il a tout sifflé!; **to g. gas** *(of car)* bouffer de l'essence
VI *(eat)* s'empiffrer, se goinfrer; *(drink)* boire trop vite☐

guzzler [ˈgʌzlə(r)] **N** *Fam (person* ► *of food)* goinfre *mf*; *(*► *of drink)* soiffard(e) *m,f*

gym [dʒɪm] **N 1** *(hall, building)* gymnase *m*; *(fitness club)* club *m* de gym **2** *(activity, school subject)* gymnastique *f*, gym *f*
►► ***gym shoe*** chaussure *f* de gymnastique *ou* gym

gymkhana [dʒɪmˈkɑːnə] **N** concours *m* hippique

gymnasium [dʒɪmˈneɪzɪəm] *(pl* **gymnasiums** *or* **gymnasia** [-zɪə]*)* **N** gymnase *m*

gymnast [ˈdʒɪmnæst] **N** gymnaste *mf*; **I've never been much of a g.** je n'ai jamais été très fort en gymnastique

gymnastic [dʒɪmˈnæstɪk] **ADJ** *(exercises)* de gymnastique; *(ability)* de gymnaste

gymnastics [dʒɪmˈnæstɪks] **N** *(UNCOUNT)* gymnastique *f*; **to do g.** faire de la gymnastique; *Fig* **mental g.** gymnastique *f* cérébrale

gymnosperm [ˈdʒɪmnəʊspɜːm] **N** *Bot* gymnosperme *f*

gymslip [ˈdʒɪmslɪp] **N** *Br (part of uniform)* blouse *f* d'écolière

gynaecologic, *Am* **gynecologic** [ˌgaɪnɪkəˈlɒdʒɪk], **gynaecological,** *Am* **gynecological** [ˌgaɪnɪkəˈlɒdʒɪkəl] **ADJ** gynécologique

gynaecologist, *Am* **gynecologist** [ˌgaɪnɪˈkɒlədʒɪst] **N** gynécologue *mf*

gynaecology, *Am* **gynecology** [ˌgaɪnɪˈkɒlədʒɪ] **N** gynécologie *f*

gyp [dʒɪp] *(pt & pp* **gypped,** *cont* **gypping***)* *Fam* **N** *Br* **to give sb g.** *(cause pain)* dérouiller qn
VT *(cheat)* rouler; **you've been gypped** tu t'es fait rouler *ou* avoir

gypsum [ˈdʒɪpsəm] **N** gypse *m*

gypsy *(pl* **gypsies***)* = **gipsy**

gyrate [dʒaɪˈreɪt] **VI** tournoyer

gyration [dʒaɪˈreɪʃən] **N** giration *f*

gyratory [ˈdʒaɪrətərɪ] **ADJ** giratoire

gyrfalcon [ˈdʒɜːfɔːlkən] **N** *Orn* gerfaut *m*

gyro [ˈdʒaɪrəʊ] *(pl* **gyros***)* **ADJ** gyroscopique
N 1 *(gyroscope)* gyroscope *m* **2** *(gyrocompass)* gyrocompas *m*
►► ***gyro control*** commande *f* gyroscopique

gyrocompass [ˈdʒaɪrəʊˌkʌmpəs] **N** gyrocompas *m*

gyromagnetic [ˌdʒaɪrəʊˈmægˈnetɪk] **ADJ** gyromagnétique

gyropilot [ˈdʒaɪrəʊpaɪlət] **N** *Aviat* pilote *m* automatique, gyropilote *m*; *Naut (compass)* gyropilote *m*

gyroplane [ˈdʒaɪrəʊpleɪn] **N** *Aviat* autogyre *m*

gyroscope [ˈdʒaɪrəʊskəʊp] **N** gyroscope *m*

gyroscopic [ˌdʒaɪrəʊˈskɒpɪk] **ADJ** gyroscopique

gyrostat [ˈdʒaɪrəʊstæt] **N** gyrostat *m*

h

H, h [eɪtʃ] **N** *(letter)* H, h *m inv*; **two h's** deux h; **H for Harry** H comme Henri; **to drop one's h's** avaler ses h *(et révéler par là ses origines populaires)*

ha [hɑː] **EXCLAM** *(in triumph, sudden comprehension)* ha!, ah!; *(in contempt)* peuh!; *Ironic* **ha ha, very funny!** ha ha ha, très drôle!

habeas corpus [ˌheɪbɪəs'kɔːpəs] **N** *Law* habeas corpus *m*; **to issue a writ of h.** délivrer un (acte d')habeas corpus

haberdasher ['hæbədæʃə(r)] **N 1** *Br (draper)* mercier(ère) *m,f* **2** *Am (shirtmaker)* chemisier (ère) *m,f*

haberdashery [ˌhæbə'dæʃərɪ] *(pl* **haberdasheries***)* **N 1** *Br (draper's)* mercerie *f* **2** *Am (shirtmaker's)* marchand(e) *m,f* de vêtements d'hommes *(en particulier de gants et de chapeaux)*

habit ['hæbɪt] **N 1** *(custom)* habitude *f*; **to be in/to get into the h. of doing sth** avoir/prendre l'habitude de faire qch; **you'd better get into the h. of being more punctual** il vaudrait mieux que tu prennes l'habitude d'être plus ponctuel; **to get sb into the h. of doing sth** faire prendre à qn *ou* donner à qn l'habitude de faire qch, habituer qn à faire qch; **to make a h. of sth/of doing sth** prendre l'habitude de qch/de faire qch; **just don't make a h. of it!** ne recommence pas!, que cela ne se reproduise pas!; **to get out of a h.** perdre une habitude; **to get sb out of the h. of doing sth** faire perdre à qn l'habitude de faire qch **2** *Fam (drug dependency)* **to have a h.** être accro; **to have a heroin h.** être accro à l'héroïne **3** *(dress ▸ of monk, nun)* habit *m*; *(▸ for riding)* tenue *f* de cheval

habitable ['hæbɪtəbəl] **ADJ** habitable

habitat ['hæbɪtæt] **N** *Bot & Zool* habitat *m*

habitation [ˌhæbɪ'teɪʃən] **N 1** *(occupation)* habitation *f*; **there were signs of recent h.** l'endroit semblait avoir été habité dans un passé récent; **fit/unfit for h.** habitable/inhabitable; *(from sanitary point of view)* salubre/insalubre **2** *Formal (place)* habitation *f*, résidence *f*, demeure *f*

habit-forming [-'fɔːmɪŋ] **ADJ** *(drug)* qui crée une accoutumance *ou* une dépendance

habitual [hə'bɪtʃʊəl] **ADJ** *(customary ▸ generosity, lateness, good humour)* habituel, accoutumé; *(▸ liar, drinker)* invétéré

▸▸ *Mktg* ***habitual buying behaviour*** comportement *m* d'achat habituel; *Law* ***habitual offender*** récidiviste *mf*

habitually [hə'bɪtʃʊəlɪ] **ADV** habituellement, ordinairement

habituate [hə'bɪtʃʊeɪt] **VT** *Formal* **to h. oneself/sb to sth** s'habituer/habituer qn à qch; **to become habituated to sth** s'habituer à qch

Habsburg ['hæpsbɜːg] **PR N** *Hist* Habsbourg

hacienda [ˌhæsɪ'endə] **N** ranch *m*, hacienda *f*

hack [hæk] **N 1** *(sharp blow)* coup *m* violent; *(kick)* coup *m* de pied; **to take a h. at sb** *(kick)* donner un coup de pied à qn

2 *(cut)* entaille *f*

3 *Fam Pej (writer)* écrivaillon *m*; *(journalist)* journaleux(euse) *m,f*, tâcheron *m*; *(politician)* politicard *m*

4 *(horse for riding)* cheval *m* de selle; *(horse for hire)* cheval *m* de louage; *(old horse, nag)* rosse *f*, carne *f*

5 *Am Fam (taxi)* taxi[❑] *m*, tacot *m*; *(taxi driver)* chauffeur *m* de taxi[❑]

VT 1 *(cut)* taillader, tailler; **to h. sb/sth to pieces** tailler qn/qch en pièces; *Fig (opponent, manuscript)* mettre *ou* tailler qn/qch en pièces; **to h. sb to death** tuer qn à coups de couteau *ou* de hache; **he hacked his way through the jungle** il s'est taillé un passage à travers la jungle à coups de machette

2 *(kick ▸ ball)* donner un coup de pied sec dans; **to h. sb on the shins** donner un coup de pied dans les tibias à qn

3 *Comput* **to h. one's way into a system** entrer dans un système par effraction

4 *Fam (idiom)* **I can't h. it** *(cope)* je n'en peux plus[❑], je craque

VI 1 *(cut)* donner des coups de couteau/hache/*etc*; **to h. (away) at sth** taillader qch

2 *(kick)* **to h. at sb's shins** donner des coups de pied dans les tibias à qn

3 *Comput* **to h. into a system** entrer dans un système par effraction; **to h. into sth** *(system, file)* s'introduire en fraude dans qch

4 *(on horseback)* aller à cheval; **to go hacking** aller faire une promenade à cheval

▸▸ *Fam Pej* ***hack writer*** écrivaillon *m*; *Fam Pej* ***hack writing*** travail *m* d'écrivaillon

▸ hack down VT SEP *(tree)* abattre à coups de hache; *(person)* massacrer à coups de couteau/hache/*etc*

▸ hack into VT INSEP *(body, corpse)* taillader; *Fig (text, article)* massacrer

▸ hack off VT SEP 1 *(chop off)* trancher **2** *Fam (annoy)* **to h. sb off** prendre la tête à qn; **to be hacked off (with sb/sth)** en avoir marre (de qn/qch)

▸ hack up VT SEP *(meat, wood)* tailler *ou* couper en menus morceaux; *(body, victim)* mettre en pièces, découper en morceaux

hacker ['hækə(r)] **N** *Comput* **1** *(illegal user)* pirate *m* informatique, hacker *m*, *Offic* fouineur(euse) *m,f* **2** *(expert user)* bidouilleur(euse) *m,f*, hacker *m*

hacking ['hækɪŋ] **N** *(UNCOUNT)* **1** *(in football, rugby etc)* coups *mpl* de pied dans les tibias

2 *(coughing)* toux *f* sèche

3 *Comput* piratage *m (informatique)*

4 *Br (riding)* promenade(s) *f(pl)* à cheval

▸▸ ***hacking cough*** toux *f* sèche; ***hacking jacket*** veste *f* de cheval

hackle ['hækəl] **N** *(of bird)* plume *f* du cou

hackles ['hækəlz] **NPL** *(of dog)* poils *mpl* du cou; **the dog has its h. up** le chien a le poil hérissé; *Fig* **my h. rose** ça m'a hérissé le poil; **it gets my h. up, it makes my h. rise** ça me hérisse; **don't go getting your h. up** ne t'énerve pas

hackney ['hæknɪ] **N 1** *(taxi)* = taxi officiellement agréé

2 *(carriage for hire)* cabriolet *m* de louage

3 *(horse-drawn)* fiacre *m*

4 *(horse)* cheval *m* de selle; *(trotter)* trotteur *m*

▸▸ *Br* ***hackney cab, hackney carriage*** *(horse-drawn)* fiacre *m*; *(taxi)* = taxi officiellement agréé

hackneyed ['hæknɪd] **ADJ** *(subject)* réchauffé, rebattu; *(turn of phrase)* banal, commun; **h. expression** cliché *m*, lieu *m* commun

hacksaw ['hæksɔː] **N** scie *f* à métaux

hackwork ['hækwɜːk] **N** *Fam Pej* écrivaillerie *f*; **the report was a piece of shoddy h.** ce rapport c'était du travail d'écrivaillon

had [həd, *stressed* hæd] *pt & pp of* **have**

haddock ['hædək] **N** *Ich* aiglefin *m*, églefin *m*; **smoked h.** haddock *m*

Hades ['heɪdiːz] *Myth* **N** *(place)* les Enfers *mpl*

PR N *(god)* Hadès

hadn't ['hædənt] = **had not**

Hadrian ['heɪdrɪən] **PR N** *Hist* Hadrien

▸▸ ***Hadrian's Wall*** le mur d'Hadrien

haema-, *Am* **hema-** ['hiːmə] **PREF** *Med* héma-

haematite, *Am* **hematite** ['hiːmətaɪt] **N** *Chem & Miner* hématite *f*

haemato-, *Am* **hemato-** [ˌhiːmə'tɒ, ˌhiːmə'təʊ] **PREF** *Med* hémato-

haematology, *Am* **hematology** [ˌhiːmə'tɒlədʒɪ] **N** *Med* hématologie *f*

haematoma, *Am* **hematoma** [ˌhiːmə'təʊmə] *(Br pl* **haematomas** *or* **haematomata** [-mətə], *Am pl* **hematomas** *or* **hematomata** [-mətə]) **N** *Med* hématome *m*

haemo-, *Am* **hemo-** ['hiːməʊ, 'hiːmə] **PREF** *Med* hémo-

haemoglobin, *Am* **hemoglobin** [ˌhiːmə'gləʊbɪn] **N** *Physiol* hémoglobine *f*

haemophilia, *Am* **hemophilia** [ˌhiːmə'fɪlɪə] **N** *Med* hémophilie *f*

haemophiliac, *Am* **hemophiliac** [ˌhiːmə'fɪlɪæk] **N** *Med* hémophile *mf*

haemophilic, *Am* **hemophilic** [ˌhiːməʊ'fɪlɪk] **ADJ** *Med* hémophile

haemorrhage, *Am* **hemorrhage** ['hemərɪdʒ] **N** *Med* hémorragie *f*

VI 1 *Med* faire une hémorragie **2** *Fig (disappear, fade ▸ support etc)* s'évanouir, se dissiper; **party membership was haemorrhaging badly** les effectifs du parti diminuaient de façon spectaculaire

haemorrhoids, *Am* **hemorrhoids** ['hemərɔɪdz] **NPL** *Med* hémorroïdes *fpl*; **to have h.** avoir des hémorroïdes

haemostat, *Am* **hemostat** ['hiːməʊstæt] **N** *Med (instrument)* pince(s) *f(pl)* hémostatique(s)

haft [hæft] **N** *(of knife)* manche *m*; *(of sword)* poignée *f*

hag [hæg] **N** *(witch)* sorcière *f*; *Pej (old woman)* vieille sorcière *f*, vieille chouette *f*; *(unpleasant woman)* harpie *f*; **she's a real old h.** ce n'est qu'une vieille chouette

haggard ['hægəd] **ADJ 1** *(tired, drawn)* hâve; **he looked h.** il avait les traits tirés **2** *(wild ▸ face)* égaré, hagard

haggis ['hægɪs] **N** *Culin* = plat typique écossais fait d'une panse de brebis farcie (d'un hachis d'abats et de farine d'avoine très épicé)

haggle ['hægəl] **VI 1** *(bargain)* marchander; **to h. over the price** marchander sur le prix **2** *(argue over details)* chicaner, chipoter; **to h. over or about sth** chicaner *ou* chipoter sur qch

N **after a long h. over the price** après un long marchandage sur le prix

haggler ['hæglə(r)] **N 1** *(over price)* marchandeur (euse) *m,f* **2** *(over details, wording)* chicaneur (euse) *m,f*, chipoteur(euse) *m,f*

haggling ['hæglɪŋ] **N 1** *(over price)* marchandage *m* **2** *(about details, wording)* chicanerie *f*, chipotage *m*

hagiographer [,hægɪ'ɒgrəfə(r)] **N** hagiographe *mf*

hagiography [,hægɪ'ɒgrəfɪ] **N** hagiographie *f*

hag-ridden **ADJ** *Literary (tormented)* tourmenté, ravagé; *Hum (tormented by women)* persécuté par les femmes

Hague [heɪg] **N** *Geog* **The H.** La Haye

hah = **ha**

ha-ha[1] [hɑː'hɑː] **EXCLAM** *(mock amusement)* ha ha!; *(representing laughter ▸ in comic, novel)* ha ha ha!, hi hi hi!

ha-ha[2] ['hɑː,hɑː] **N** *(wall, fence)* = mur ou clôture installé dans un fossé

haiku ['haɪkuː] *(pl* **inv** *or* **haikus)** **N** *Literature* haïku *m*

hail [heɪl] **N 1** *Met* grêle *f*; *Fig (of stones)* grêle *f*, pluie *f*; *(of abuse)* avalanche *f*, déluge *m*; *(of blows)* grêle *f*; **he died in a h. of bullets** il est tombé sous une pluie de balles **2** *Literary (call)* appel *m*; **within h.** à portée de voix

VI *Met* grêler; **it's hailing** il grêle

VT 1 *(call ▸ taxi, ship, person)* héler; **within hailing distance** à portée de voix

2 *(greet ▸ person)* acclamer, saluer

3 *(acclaim ▸ person, new product, invention etc)* acclamer, saluer; **her book has been hailed as the most significant new novel this year** son livre a été acclamé comme le nouveau roman le plus marquant de cette année; **the plan was hailed as the solution to their problems** le projet a été salué comme la solution à tous leurs problèmes

4 *(idioms)* **to h. blows on sb** faire pleuvoir des coups sur qn; **to h. insults on sb** accabler qn d'injures

EXCLAM *Arch* salut à vous *ou* toi!; **h., Caesar!** Ave César!; **h., Mary, full of grace** je te salue, Marie, pleine de grâce

▸▸ *Rel* ***Hail Mary*** *(prayer)* Je vous salue Marie *m inv*, Ave (Maria) *m inv*; *Am Sport* ***Hail Mary pass*** = passe au petit bonheur; *Fig* **to throw a H. Mary pass** tenter sa chance

▸hail down **VI** *(blows, stones etc)* pleuvoir; **blows/rocks were hailing down on us** des coups/pierres nous pleuvaient dessus; **criticism hailed down on him** il a subi une avalanche *ou* un déluge de critiques

VT SEP they hailed insults down on the President ils ont déversé un flot d'insultes à l'intention du président; *Literary* **to h. down curses on sb** déverser un déluge de malédictions sur qn

hail-fellow-well-met **ADJ he's always very h.** il fait toujours montre d'une familiarité joviale

hailstone ['heɪlstəʊn] **N** *Met* grêlon *m*

hailstorm ['heɪlstɔːm] **N** *Met* averse *f* de grêle

hair [heə(r)] **N 1** *(UNCOUNT) (on person's head)* cheveux *mpl*; **to have long/short h.** avoir les cheveux longs/courts; **to get** *or* **to have one's h. cut** se faire couper les cheveux; **to get one's h. done** se faire coiffer; **who does your h.?** tu te fais coiffer où?, tu vas chez quel coiffeur?; **I like your h.** j'aime bien ta coiffure; **to wash one's h.** se laver les cheveux *ou* la tête; **to brush one's h.** se brosser (les cheveux); **to comb one's h.** se peigner (les cheveux); **she put her h. up** elle a relevé ses cheveux; **she let her h. down** elle a défait ses cheveux; **your h. looks nice** tu es bien coiffé; **my h.'s a mess** je suis vraiment mal coiffé

2 *(single hair ▸ on person's head)* cheveu *m*; *(▸ on person's or animal's face or body, on plant)* poil *m*; *Am Fam* **move it a h. over to the right** déplace-le un chouia vers la droite

3 *(UNCOUNT) (on body, face, animal)* poils *mpl*; *(on horse)* crin *m*; *(on pig)* soie *f*

4 *Opt (of gun sight etc)* cheveu *m*, fil *m*

5 *(idioms)* **it makes your h. stand on end** *(is frightening)* c'est à vous faire dresser les cheveux sur la tête; *Fam* **it would make your h. curl** *(ride, journey)* c'est à vous faire dresser les cheveux sur la tête; *(prices, bad language)* c'est à vous faire tomber à la renverse; *(drink)* ça arrache; *Br Fam* **keep your h. on!** ne t'excite pas!□; **to let one's h. down** se laisser aller□, se défouler□; *Fam* **to get in sb's h.** taper sur les nerfs de qn; *Fam* **keep him out of my h.** fais en sorte que je ne l'aie pas dans les jambes; *Fam* **I'll keep out of your h.** je ne vais pas t'embêter; *Hum* **to have a h. of the dog (that bit you)** reprendre un verre (pour faire passer sa gueule de bois); **to split hairs** couper les cheveux en quatre, chercher la petite bête; **if you harm one single h. of his head** si tu touches à un seul de ses cheveux; **she never has a h. out of place** *(is immaculate)* elle n'a jamais un cheveu de travers; **to win by a h.** gagner d'un cheveu *ou* à un quart de poil près; **to lose by a h.** perdre d'un cheveu *ou* à un quart de poil près; **she didn't turn a h.** elle n'a pas cillé; *Fam Hum* **this'll put hairs on your chest!** *(strong drink, good steak etc)* ça va te redonner du poil de la bête!; **the truck missed us by a h.'s breadth** le camion nous a manqués d'un cheveu *ou* de justesse; **we came within a h.'s breadth of going bankrupt/of winning first prize** nous avons été à deux doigts de la faillite/de gagner le premier prix

COMP 1 *(cream, lotion)* capillaire, pour les cheveux **2** *(colour)* de cheveux **3** *(mattress)* de crin

▸▸ ***hair appointment*** rendez-vous *m* chez le coiffeur; ***hair clippers*** tondeuse *f*; **a pair of h. clippers** une tondeuse; ***hair conditioner*** après-shampooing *m*; *Br* ***hair curlers*** bigoudis *mpl*; ***hair drier, hair dryer*** *(hand-held)* sèche-cheveux *m inv*, séchoir *m*; *(over the head)* casque *m*; ***hair extensions*** rajouts *mpl*; *Anat* ***hair follicle*** follicule *m* pileux; ***hair gel*** gel *m* pour les cheveux; *Bot* ***hair grass*** canche *f*; ***hair lacquer*** laque *f* (pour les cheveux); ***hair mousse*** mousse *f* coiffante; ***hair oil*** huile *f* capillaire; ***hair products*** produits *mpl* capillaires *ou* pour les cheveux; ***hair removal*** dépilation *f*; ***hair remover*** crème *f* dépilatoire; *Br* ***hair restorer*** produit *m* pour la repousse des cheveux; ***hair serum*** sérum *m* pour les cheveux; ***hair shirt*** haire *f*, cilice *m*; ***hair slide*** barrette *f*; *Typ* ***hair space*** espace *f* fine; ***hair straightener*** *(product)* produit *m* défrisant; ***hair straighteners*** *(appliance)* fer *m* à défriser, défriseur *m*; ***hair tonic*** lotion *f* capillaire; ***hair transplant*** implant *m* de cheveux; ***hair trigger*** *(in firearm)* détente *f ou* gâchette *f* sensible; ***hair weave*** toupet *m (intégré aux cheveux)*; ***hair wrap*** tresse *f* brésilienne

hairball ['heəbɔːl] **N** *(of cat's fur)* boule *f* de poils

hairband ['heəbænd] **N** bandeau *m*

hairbrush ['heəbrʌʃ] **N** brosse *f* à cheveux

haircut ['heəkʌt] **N** *(of person)* coupe *f* (de cheveux); **to have a h.** se faire couper les cheveux; **to give sb a h.** couper les cheveux à qn

hairdo ['heəduː] *(pl* **hairdos)** **N** *Fam* coiffure□ *f*

hairdresser ['heədresə(r)] **N** *(person)* coiffeur (euse) *m,f*; *(shop)* salon *m* de coiffure; **to go to the h.'s** aller chez le coiffeur

hairdressing ['heədresɪŋ] **N** *(skill)* coiffure *f*

▸▸ ***hairdressing salon*** salon *m* de coiffure; ***hairdressing school*** école *f* de coiffure

-haired [heəd] **SUFF long/short-h.** *(person)* aux cheveux longs/courts; *(animal)* à poil(s) long (s)/court(s); **wire-h.** *(dog)* à poil(s) dur(s)

hairgrip ['heəgrɪp] **N** *Br* pince *f* à cheveux

hairless ['heəlɪs] **ADJ** *(head)* chauve, sans cheveux; *(face, leaf)* glabre; *(body)* peu poilu; *(animal)* sans poils

hairline ['heəlaɪn] **N 1** *(of the hair)* naissance *f* des cheveux; **to have a receding h.** *(above forehead)* avoir le front qui se dégarnit; *(at temples)* avoir les tempes qui se dégarnissent **2** *(in telescope, gun sight)* fil *m* **3** *Typ* filet *m* ultra-fin; *(in calligraphy)* délié *m*

▸▸ ***hairline crack*** fêlure *f*; *Med* ***hairline fracture*** fêlure *f*; *Typ* ***hairline rule*** filet *m* maigre; *Typ* ***hairline space*** espace *f* fine

hairnet ['heənet] **N** résille *f*, filet *m* à cheveux

hairpiece ['heəpiːs] **N** *(toupee)* perruque *f (pour hommes)*; *(extra hair)* postiche *m*

hairpin ['heəpɪn] **N** *(for hair)* épingle *f* à cheveux; *(bend)* virage *m* en épingle à cheveux

▸▸ ***hairpin bend*** virage *m* en épingle à cheveux

hair-raising [-'reɪzɪŋ] **ADJ** *(adventure, experience, story, account)* à faire dresser les cheveux sur la tête, effrayant; *(prices, expenses)* affolant, exorbitant; **driving in London traffic can be a h. experience** conduire à Londres peut être une expérience terrifiante

hairsplitting ['heə,splɪtɪŋ] **ADJ that's a h. argument** *or* **distinction** c'est de la chicanerie, c'est couper les cheveux en quatre

N chicanerie *f*, pinaillage *m*; **that's just h.** tu es vraiment en train de couper les cheveux en quatre

hairspring ['heəsprɪŋ] **N** *(in clock)* spiral *m (de montre)*

hairstyle ['heəstaɪl] **N** coiffure *f*

hairstylist ['heəstaɪlɪst] **N** styliste *mf* en coiffure

hairy ['heərɪ] *(compar* **hairier**, *superl* **hairiest)** **ADJ 1** *(arms, chest)* poilu, velu; *(person, animal)* poilu; *(stalk of plant, leaf)* velu **2** *Fam (frightening)* à faire dresser les cheveux sur la tête□; *(difficult, daunting)* qui craint; **there were a few h. moments when the brakes seemed to be failing** il y a eu des moments craignos où les freins semblaient lâcher; **he gave a pretty h. description of his two hours at the dentist** il a fait une description assez horrible *ou* atroce des deux heures qu'il a passées chez le dentiste

Haiti ['heɪtɪ] **N** *Geog* Haïti

Haitian ['heɪʃən] **N** Haïtien(enne) *m,f*

ADJ haïtien

hake [heɪk] **N** *Ich* merlu *m*, colin *m*

halal [hə'lɑːl] *Rel* **N** *(meat)* viande *f* halal

ADJ halal *(inv)*

halation [hæ'leɪʃən] **N** *Phot* halo *m*, irradiation *f*

halberd ['hælbɜːd] **N** *Hist* hallebarde *f*

halcyon ['hælsɪən] **N** *Myth (kingfisher)* alcyon *m*

ADJ *Literary* **those h. days** ces temps heureux

hale [heɪl] **ADJ h. and hearty** en pleine santé

HALF [hɑːf]

N
- moitié **1**
- demi **1, 4, 5**
- mi-temps **2**
- camp **3**

PRON
- moitié

ADJ, PREDET
- demi

ADV
- à moitié **1**
- et demie **3**
- moitié **4**

(pl **halves** [hɑːvz])

N 1 *(gen)* moitié *f*; *(of standard measured amount)* demi(e) *m,f*; *(of ticket, coupon)* souche *f*; **h. an hour** une demi-heure; **h. a dozen** une demi-douzaine; **to cut/to break sth in h.** couper/casser qch en deux; **what's h. of 13.72?** quelle est la moitié de 13,72?; **two and two halves, please** *(on bus, train etc)* deux billets tarif normal et deux billets demi-tarif, s'il vous plaît; *Rail* **outward/return h.** *(of ticket)* coupon *m* d'aller/de retour; **you can have the smaller h.** la plus petite moitié est pour toi; **she gave each of us h.** elle nous en a donné la moitié à chacun; **it cuts the journey time in h.** cela réduit de moitié la durée du voyage; **three and a h.** trois et demi; **three and a h. pieces/years** trois morceaux/ans et demi; *Br* **bigger by h.** plus grand de moitié, moitié plus grand; **two halves make a whole** deux moitiés *ou* demis font un tout; **to go halves with sb** partager avec qn; **we'll go halves** on partage; **they don't do things by halves** ils ne font pas les choses à moitié; *Br Fam* **he always was too clever by h.** il a toujours été un peu trop malin; *Br Fam* **you're too cheeky by h.!** tu es bien trop effronté *ou* culotté!; *Fam* **a party/day/hangover and a h.** une sacrée nouba/journée/gueule de bois; *Fam* **and that's not the h. of it** et ce n'est que le début; *Fam* **you haven't heard the h. of it!** tu n'en sais pas encore le quart!; **it's sort of h. and h.** c'est un peu de chaque; *Hum* **my better** *or* **other h.** ma (chère) moitié; *Hum* **to see how the other h. lives** voir comment on vit de l'autre côté de la barrière, voir comment vivent les autres

2 *Sport (period of sports match)* mi-temps *f inv*; **France was in the lead in the first h.** la France menait pendant la première mi-temps

3 *Sport (area of football or rugby pitch)* camp *m*

4 *Sport (rugby or football player)* demi *m*

5 *Br (half pint of beer)* demi *m* (de bière)

PRON **leave h. of it for me** laisse-m'en la moitié; **h. of us were students** la moitié d'entre nous étions des étudiants

ADJ **a h. chicken** un demi-poulet; **oysters on the h.-shell** huîtres *fpl* servies dans leurs coquilles; **at h. speed** au ralenti; **at h. cock** *(gun)* à moitié armé, sur le cran de sûreté; *Fam* **to go off at h. cock** *(plan)* avorter❑

PREDET **h. the time he seems to be asleep** on a l'impression qu'il est endormi la moitié du temps; **he's h. a year older than me** il a six mois de plus que moi; *Fam* **h. a minute!** une (petite) minute!; *Fam* **I'll be down in h. a second** je descends tout de suite❑; **I'll be there in h. an hour** j'y serai dans une demi-heure; **just h. a cup for me** juste une demi-tasse pour moi; **he's not h. the man he used to be** il n'est plus que l'ombre de lui-même; *Fam* **to have h. a mind to do sth** avoir bien envie de faire qch❑; **that was h. the point of going there** c'était tout l'intérêt d'y aller

ADV **1** *(finished, asleep, dressed)* à moitié; *(full, empty, blind)* à moitié, à demi; **to be h. full of sth** être à moitié rempli de qch; **you're only h. right** tu n'as qu'à moitié raison; **h. done** *(work)* fait à moitié; *(cooked meat etc)* à moitié cuit; **a strange colour, h. green, h. blue** une couleur bizarre, entre le vert et le bleu; **to be h. English and h. French** être moitié anglais moitié français; **I h. think that...** je suis tenté de penser que... + *indicative*; **for a minute I h. thought that...** pendant une minute, j'ai presque pensé que... + *indicative*; **I was h. afraid you wouldn't understand** j'avais un peu peur que vous ne compreniez pas; **I was only h. joking** je ne plaisantais qu'à moitié; **h. laughing, h. crying** moitié riant, moitié pleurant

2 *Br Fam (as intensifier)* **they're not h. fit** ils sont en super-forme; **he's not h. lazy** il est drôlement *ou* rudement paresseux; **it's not h. cold today!** il fait rudement *ou* sacrément froid aujourd'hui!; **he didn't h. yell** il a hurlé comme un fou; **she can't h. run** elle court comme un lièvre; **you don't h. put your foot in it sometimes!** tu mets vraiment les pieds dans le plat parfois!; **they didn't h. complain** ils se sont plaints, et pas qu'un peu; **did you complain? – I didn't h.** *or* **not h.!** est-ce que vous vous êtes plaint? – et comment *ou* pas qu'un peu!; **he's/it's not h. bad** il est/c'est vraiment bon

3 *(time) Br* **it's h. past two, it's h. two** il est deux heures et demie; *Am* **h. after six** six heures et demie

4 *(idioms)* **to be h. as big/fast as sb/sth** être moitié moins grand/rapide que qn/qch; **to earn h. as much as sb** gagner moitié moins que qn; **to be h. as big again (as sb/sth)** être moitié plus grand (que qn/qch); **he earns h. as much again as you do** il gagne moitié plus que toi

▸▸ *Tech* ***half bearing*** demi-palier *m*; *Br* ***half board*** N demi-pension *f* ADV en demi-pension; *Am Fam* ***half buck*** 50 cents *mpl*; *Comput* ***half duplex*** semi-duplex *m*; **to send sth h. duplex** transmettre qch en semi-duplex; ***half fare*** demi-tarif *m*; **to travel h. fare** voyager à demi-tarif; *Am Mus* ***half step*** demi-ton *m*; *Br Sch* ***half term*** = congé scolaire en milieu de trimestre; *Archit & Constr* ***half timbering*** colombage *m*; ***half year*** semestre *m*

half-a-crown = **half-crown**

half-and-half N *Br (beer)* = mélange de deux bières; *Am (for coffee)* = mélange de crème et de lait

ADV moitié-moitié; **it's h.** c'est moitié-moitié; **how shall I mix them? – h.** comment faut-il les mélanger? – à doses égales

half-arsed [-'ɑːst], *Am* **half-assed** [-'æst] ADJ *very Fam (incompetent)* nul à chier; **he made a h. attempt at mending the fence** il a essayé de réparer la barrière mais il s'y est pris comme un manche

halfback ['hɑːfbæk] N **1** *Old-fashioned Ftbl* demi-arrière *m* **2** *Sport (in rugby)* demi *m*

half-baked ADJ *Fam Fig (scheme, idea, proposal)* qui ne tient pas debout; *(person)* niais❑

half-binding N demi-reliure *f*

half-blood N *Old-fashioned* métis(isse) *m,f*

half-breed N **1** *(animal)* hybride *m*; *(horse)* cheval *m* demi-sang *(inv)* **2** *Old-fashioned (person)* métis(isse) *m,f*

ADJ **1** *(animal)* hybride; *(horse)* demi-sang *(inv)* **2** *Old-fashioned (person)* métis

half-brother N demi-frère *m*

half-caste *Old-fashioned* N *(person)* métis(isse) *m,f*

ADJ métis

half-circle N demi-cercle *m*

half-cocked [-'kɒkt] ADJ *(gun, pistol)* à moitié armé

half-crown N *Br Hist* demi-couronne *f*

half-cut ADJ *Br Fam (drunk)* bourré, pété, fait

half-fare ticket N billet *m* demi-tarif

half-hearted [-'hɑːtɪd] ADJ *(attempt, attitude)* qui manque d'enthousiasme *ou* de conviction, hésitant; *(acceptance)* tiède, qui manque d'enthousiasme; **he was very h. about it** il était vraiment peu enthousiaste à ce propos; **they were a bit h. about accepting** ils ont accepté sans grand enthousiasme *ou* du bout des lèvres

half-heartedly [-'hɑːtɪdlɪ] ADV *(accept, agree, say)* sans enthousiasme *ou* conviction, du bout des lèvres

half-heartedness [-'hɑːtɪdnɪs] N manque *m* d'enthousiasme

half-hour N *(period)* demi-heure *f*; **on the h.** à la demie

half-hourly ADJ toutes les demi-heures; **there is a h. train service** il y a des trains toutes les trente minutes; **at h. intervals** toutes les demi-heures, toutes les trente minutes

ADV toutes les demi-heures

half-inch N *(unit of measurement)* = 1,27 cm, demi-pouce *m*

VT *Br Fam (rhyming slang* = **pinch**) piquer, faucher; **he got his wallet half-inched** il s'est fait piquer son portefeuille

half-length ADJ *(portrait)* en buste

half-life N **1** *Phys* demi-vie *f*, période *f* **2** *Med* demi-vie *f*

half-light N demi-jour *m*

half-mast N **at h.** *(flag)* en berne; *Hum (trousers)* arrivant à mi-mollet; *(socks)* en accordéon

half-measure N demi-mesure *f*

half-moon N demi-lune *f*; *(on fingernail)* lunule *f*

half-note N *Am Mus (minim)* blanche *f*

half-open ADJ *(eyes, door, window)* entrouvert

VT *(eyes, door, window)* entrouvrir

half-pay N demi-salaire *m*; *(in civil service)* demi-traitement *m*; *Mil* demi-solde *f*; **to be on h.** toucher un demi-salaire/un demi-traitement; *Mil* toucher une demi-solde

halfpenny ['heɪpnɪ] *(pl* **halfpennies***) Br Old-fashioned* N demi-penny *m*; **he's down to his last h.** il ne lui reste que quelques sous

COMP d'un demi-penny

half-price N demi-tarif *m*; **reduced to h.** réduit de moitié

ADJ *(goods)* à moitié prix; *(ticket)* (à) demi-tarif

ADV **children get in h.** les enfants payent demi-tarif; **I got it h.** *(purchase)* je l'ai eu à moitié prix

half-shaft N demi-arbre *m*

half-sister N demi-sœur *f*

half-size ADJ *(model)* réduit de moitié

N *(in shoes)* demi-pointure *f*; *(in clothing)* demi-taille *f*

half-staff N *Am* **at h.** *(flag)* en berne

half-term ADJ *Br Sch* **h. holiday** petites vacances *fpl*

half-timbered ADJ *Archit & Constr (house)* à colombages, à pans de bois

half-title N *Typ* faux-titre *m*

halftone ['hɑːftəʊn] N **1** *Phot (process)* similigravure *f* **2** *Art, Comput & Typ* demi-teinte *f* **3** *Am Mus* demi-ton *m*

▸▸ *Typ* ***halftone screen*** trame *f* optique

half-track N *(vehicle)* half-track *m*

half-truth N demi-vérité *f*

half-volley *Sport* N *(in tennis)* demi-volée *f*

VT *(in tennis)* **he half-volleyed the ball to the baseline** d'une demi-volée, il a envoyé la balle sur la ligne de fond

VI *(in tennis)* faire une demi-volée

halfway ['hɑːf'weɪ] ADV **1** *(between two places)* mi-chemin; **it's h. between Rennes and Cherbour** c'est à mi-chemin entre Rennes et Cherbour **we had got h. to Manchester** nous étions arrivé à mi-chemin de Manchester; **they have now trav elled h. to the moon** ils sont maintenant à m chemin de leur voyage vers la lune; **we ha climbed h. up the mountain** nous avions escalad la moitié de la montagne; **we had got h. down th mountain** nous avions descendu la moitié de l montagne; **the path stops h. up** le chemin s'arrêt à mi-côte; **there's a blockage h. up the pipe** il y a u bouchon à mi-hauteur du tuyau; **the ivy reache h. up the wall** le lierre monte jusqu'à la moitié d mur; **her hair hangs h. down her back** ses cheveu lui arrivent jusqu'au milieu du dos; **he kicked th ball h. into the French half** il a shooté dans le ba lon et l'a envoyé à la moitié du camp français **I've got h. through chapter six** je suis arrivé à l moitié du chapitre six; **h. through the pro gramme/film** à la moitié de l'émission/du film **to meet sb h.** retrouver qn à mi-chemin; *Fig* cou per la poire en deux, faire un compromis; **we'r almost h. there** *(in travelling, walking etc)* nou sommes presque à mi-chemin, nous avons fa presque la moitié du chemin; *(in work, negoti ations)* nous sommes presque à mi-chemin; **thi will go h. towards covering the costs** cela couvrir la moitié des dépenses; **it's h. between an alsa tian and a collie** c'est (à mi-chemin) entre le be ger allemand et le colley **2** *Fam (more or less)* **a h decent salary** un salaire à peu près décent❑ **don't you have something h. presentable to wear** tu n'as rien d'à peu près présentable à porter?❑

ADJ **work has reached the h. stage** le travail est mi-chemin; **at the h. point of his career** au milie de sa carrière; **they're at the h. mark** *(in race)* il sont à mi-course

▸▸ ***halfway house*** *(on journey)* (auberge *f*) relai *m*; *(for rehabilitation)* centre *m* de réadaptatio *(pour anciens détenus, malades mentaux, drogué etc)*; *Fig (halfway stage)* (stade *m* de) transition *f* *(compromise)* compromis *m*; *Sport* ***halfway lin*** ligne *f* médiane

halfwit ['hɑːfwɪt] N *Fam* imbécile❑ *mf*

halfwitted ['hɑːfwɪtɪd] ADJ *Fam (person)* faibl *ou* simple d'esprit❑; *(idea, suggestion, behaviour* idiot

half-yearly ADJ semestriel

ADV tous les six mois

halibut ['hælɪbət] N *Ich* flétan *m*

halitosis [,hælɪ'təʊsɪs] N mauvaise haleine *f* *Spec* halitose *f*

hall [hɔːl] N **1** *(of house)* entrée *f*, vestibule *m*; *(o hotel, very large house)* hall *m*; *Am (corridor)* cou loir *m*; **the h. carpet** le tapis dans l'entrée; **he lef the h. light on** il a laissé la lumière allumée dan l'entrée

2 *(large room)* salle *f*; **dining h.** *Sch & Univ* réfec toire *m*; *(of stately home)* salle *f* à manger; *Br Univ* **to eat in h.** manger à la cantine *ou* au restauran universitaire

3 *Br Univ* **I'm living in h.** je loge à l'université

4 *(mansion, large country house)* château *m*, ma noir *m*; **she works up at the h.** elle travaille au château *ou* au manoir; **Fotheringham H.** le châ teau *ou* le manoir de Fotheringham

▸▸ ***hall of fame*** *(group of famous people)* pan théon *m*; *(building)* musée *m*; **he's in the basebal h. of fame** il fait partie du panthéon de l'histoire du base-ball; *Am Fig* ***halls of ivy*** le monde uni versitaire; ***hall porter*** *(in hotel)* portier *m*; *Br Univ* ***hall of residence*** résidence *f* universitaire; *Am* ***hall tree*** portemanteau *m*

halleluiah, hallelujah [,hælɪ'luːjə] EXCLAM al léluia

N alléluia *m*

hallmark ['hɔːlmɑːk] N **1** *Metal (on precious metals)* poinçon *m* **2** *Fig* marque *f*; **it carries his h.** cela porte sa marque; **to have the h. of genius** porter la marque *ou* le sceau du génie

VT *(precious metals)* poinçonner

hallo = **hello**

hallow ['hæləʊ] VT *Formal* sanctifier, consacrer, **hallowed be Thy name** que Ton nom soit sanctifié

hallowed ['hæləʊd] ADJ saint, béni
▸▸ *Rel* **hallowed ground** terre *f* sainte *ou* bénie; *Fig* lieu *m* de culte

Hallowe'en [,hæləʊ'iːn] N = veille de la Toussaint

HALLOWE'EN

Il s'agit d'une fête d'origine païenne célébrée dans les pays anglo-saxons la veille de la Toussaint, à l'époque de l'année où les morts étaient censés rendre visite aux vivants. Aujourd'hui la tradition demeure: on évide des citrouilles pour les transformer en lanternes en forme de crâne, et les enfants déguisés vont de maison en maison. De nos jours, la coutume britannique a adopté la tradition américaine de "trick or treat" – une farce ou une friandise – consistant pour les enfants à demander un petit cadeau aux habitants des maisons visitées et à les menacer d'un mauvais tour s'ils refusent.

hallucinate [hə'luːsɪneɪt] VI avoir des hallucinations; **it made her h.** cela lui a donné des hallucinations

hallucination [hə,luːsɪ'neɪʃən] N hallucination *f*

hallucinatory [hə'luːsɪnətərɪ] ADJ hallucinatoire

hallucinogen [hə'luːsɪnə,dʒen] N hallucinogène *m*

hallucinogenic [hə,luːsɪnə'dʒenɪk] ADJ hallucinogène

hallway ['hɔːlweɪ] N *(of house)* vestibule *m*, entrée *f*; *(corridor)* couloir *m*

halo ['heɪləʊ] (*pl* **halos** *or* **haloes**) N **1** *(of saint, angel)* auréole *f*, nimbe *m*; *Hum* **her h. never slips** c'est un modèle de vertu **2** *Astron, Opt & Phot* halo *m*
▸▸ *Mktg* **halo effect** effet *m* de halo

halogen ['hælədʒen] N *Chem* (composé *m*) halogène *m*
COMP *(cooker, headlights, lamp)* (à) halogène

halt [hɔːlt] N **1** *(stop)* halte *f*; **to bring to a h.** *(vehicle)* arrêter, immobiliser; *(horse)* arrêter; *(production, project)* interrompre; **the strike has brought production to a complete h.** la grève a complètement interrompu la production; **to call a h. to sth** mettre fin à qch; **let's call a h. for today** arrêtons-nous pour aujourd'hui; **to come to a h.** *(vehicle, horse)* s'arrêter, s'immobiliser; *(in a speech)* rester sans rien dire; **the project has come to a h.** *(temporarily)* le projet s'est interrompu; *(for good)* le projet s'est définitivement arrêté **2** *Br (small railway station)* halte *f*
NPL *Bible* **the h. and the lame** les estropiés *mpl*
VI **1** *(stop)* s'arrêter; *Mil* **h.! (who goes there?)** halte! (qui va là?) **2** *Arch (limp)* boiter; *Fig (style, writing, verse)* être boiteux
VT arrêter; *(troops)* faire faire halte à, stopper; *(production ▸ temporarily)* interrompre, arrêter; *(▸ for good)* arrêter définitivement
▸▸ *Aut* **halt sign** stop *m*

halter¹ ['hɔːltə(r)] N **1** *(for horse)* licou *m*, collier *m* **2** *(on women's clothing)* bain *m* de soleil; **a dress with a h. neck** une robe dos nu *ou* bain de soleil **3** *Arch (noose)* corde *f* (de pendaison)
▸▸ **halter top** bain *m* de soleil

halter²['hæltə(r)], **haltere** ['hæltɪə(r)] (*pl* **halteres** [hæl'tɪəriːz]) N *Zool (balancer)* balancier *m*

halting ['hɔːltɪŋ] ADJ *(verse, style)* boiteux, heurté; *(voice, step, progress)* hésitant; *(growth)* discontinu

haltingly ['hɔːltɪŋlɪ] ADV *(say, speak)* de façon hésitante

halve [*Br* hɑːv, *Am* hæv] VT **1** *(separate in two)* couper *ou* diviser en deux **2** *(share)* partager en deux **3** *(reduce by half)* réduire *ou* diminuer de moitié

halves [*Br* hɑːvz, *Am* hævz] *pl of* **half**

halyard ['hæljəd] N *Naut* drisse *f*

ham [hæm] (*pt & pp* **hammed**, *cont* **hamming**) N **1** *Culin (meat)* jambon *m*; **a h.** un jambon; **h. and eggs** œufs *mpl* au jambon; **h. sandwich** sandwich *m* au jambon
2 *Fam (radio operator)* radioamateur□ *m*
3 *Fam (actor)* cabot□ *m*, cabotin(e)□ *m,f*
4 *(of leg)* cuisse *f*
VT *Fam* **he hams all his parts** il charge tous ses rôles
VI *Fam* en faire trop
▸▸ *Fam* **ham acting** cabotinage□ *m*; *Fam* **ham actor** cabot *m*, cabotin(e)□ *m,f*; *Fam* **ham licence** permis *m* de radioamateur□

▸**ham up** VT SEP *Fam* **to h. it up** en faire trop

Hamburg ['hæmbɜːg] N *Geog* Hambourg

hamburger ['hæmbɜːgə(r)] N *Culin (beefburger)* hamburger *m*; *Am (minced beef)* viande *f* hachée
▸▸ **hamburger relish** condiments *mpl* pour hamburgers

ham-fisted [-'fɪstɪd], **ham-handed** [-'hændɪd] ADJ *(person)* empoté, maladroit; *(behaviour)* maladroit

Hamitic [hæ'mɪtɪk] ADJ *Ling* chamitique

hamlet ['hæmlɪt] N *(small village)* hameau *m*

hammer ['hæmə(r)] N **1** *(tool)* marteau *m*; *Sport* **the h.** le marteau; **the h. and sickle** *(flag)* la faucille et le marteau; **to come** *or* **to go under the h.** *(at auction)* être mis aux enchères; **to be** *or* **to go at it h. and tongs** *(argue)* se disputer comme des chiffonniers; *(in work, match)* mettre le paquet, ne pas y aller de main morte; *Am Fam Aut* **to let the h. down** appuyer sur le champignon, mettre les gaz **2** *(of piano)* marteau *m*; *(of firearm)* chien *m* **3** *Anat (in ear)* marteau *m*
VT **1** *(nail, spike etc)* enfoncer au marteau; *(metal)* marteler; **to h. a nail into sth** enfoncer un clou dans qch; **to h. sth flat/straight** aplatir/redresser qch à coups de marteau; **to h. home** *(nail)* enfoncer à fond au marteau; *Fig (point of view)* insister lourdement sur; **she hammered it home with the heel of her shoe** elle l'a enfoncé avec le talon de sa chaussure; **I had it hammered into me that I mustn't do that type of thing** on m'a enfoncé dans la tête que je ne devais pas faire ce genre de choses
2 *Fam Fig (beat up)* tabasser
3 *Fam Fig (defeat)* battre à plate(s) couture(s), écraser
4 *Fam Fig (criticize)* descendre en flammes, massacrer
VI **1** *(hit with hammer)* frapper *ou* taper au marteau; *Fig (heart)* battre fort; **to h. on the table** *(with fist)* taper du poing sur la table; **to h. at the door** tambouriner à la porte; **the rain hammered at the window** la pluie tambourinait contre la fenêtre **2** *Fam (go fast, drive fast)* foncer, aller à fond de train; **he came hammering round the final bend** il a débouché à fond de train du dernier virage
▸▸ *Br* **hammer drill** perceuse *f* à percussion; **hammer thrower** lanceur(euse) *m,f* de marteau

▸**hammer away** VI *(with hammer)* donner des coups de marteau; **to h. away at sth** taper sur qch avec un marteau, donner des coups de marteau sur qch; *Fig (at agreement, contract)* travailler avec acharnement à la mise au point de qch; *(problem)* travailler avec acharnement à la solution de qch; **he hammered away at the door** *(with fists)* il a tambouriné à la porte; **to h. away at the piano/on the typewriter** marteler le piano/la machine à écrire

▸**hammer in** VT SEP *(nail, spike)* enfoncer (au marteau)

▸**hammer out** VT SEP *(dent)* aplatir au marteau; *Fig (solution, agreement)* mettre au point, élaborer; *(tune, rhythm)* marteler; **unions and management hammered out an agreement** les syndicats et le patronat sont finalement parvenus à un accord

hammered ['hæməd] ADJ *Fam (drunk)* bourré, beurré, pété

hammerhead ['hæməhed] N **1** *Ich* **h. (shark)** requin-marteau *m* **2** *Orn* ombrette *f* (du Sénégal)

hammering ['hæmərɪŋ] N **1** *(noise)* martèlement *m*; *Fig (of heart)* battement *m*; *(of rain)* tambourinement *m*
2 *Fam Fig (beating)* volée *f* de coups; **to give sb a h.** tabasser qn; **to get a h.** se faire tabasser
3 *Fam Fig (defeat)* branlée *f*, pâtée *f*; **to give sb a h.** battre qn à plates coutures; **to get a h.** être battu à plates coutures
4 *Fam Fig (criticism)* **to give sb/sth a h.** éreinter *ou* démolir qn/qch; **to get a h.** se faire éreinter *ou* démolir

hammertoe ['hæmətəʊ] N orteil *m* en marteau

hammock ['hæmək] N hamac *m*

hammy ['hæmɪ] (*compar* **hammier**, *superl* **hammiest**) ADJ *Fam (acting, performance)* de cabot□, exagéré□; **h. actor** cabot *m*, cabotin(e)□ *m,f*

hamper¹ ['hæmpə(r)] VT *(impede ▸ work, movements, person)* gêner; *(▸ project)* gêner la réalisation de, entraver; **high winds hampered the rescue work** les sauveteurs ont été gênés dans leur travail par la force des vents

hamper² N *(for picnic)* panier *m*; *(for laundry)* panier *m* à linge sale; **a Christmas h.** un panier de friandises de Noël

hamster ['hæmstə(r)] N hamster *m*

hamstring ['hæmstrɪŋ] (*pt & pp* **hamstrung** [-strʌŋ]) N tendon *m* du jarret; **to pull a h.** se claquer le tendon du jarret
VT *(cripple ▸ animal, person)* couper le(s) jarret(s) à; *Fig* handicaper; **the project is hamstrung** le projet est bloqué

hand- [hænd] PREF (à la) main; **h.-stitched** cousu main; **h.-knitted** tricoté à la main

HAND [hænd]

N
- main **1–3, 7**
- aiguille **8**
- paume **10**
- jeu **7**
- écriture **9**
- ouvrier **11**

VT
- passer, donner

N **1** *Anat (of person)* main *f*; **to hold sb's h.** tenir la main de qn; **I held her h.** je lui ai tenu la main; *Fig* **she's asked me to go along and hold her h.** elle m'a demandé de l'accompagner pour lui donner du courage; **to hold hands** se tenir par la main; **to take sb's h., to take sb by the h.** prendre qn par la main, prendre la main de qn; **to lead sb by the h.** conduire qn par la main; **he writes with his left h.** il écrit de la main gauche; **to be on one's hands and knees** être à quatre pattes; *Fig* **to go down on one's hands and knees** se mettre à genoux *ou* à plat ventre; **to be good with one's hands** être adroit de ses mains; **my hands are full** j'ai les mains occupées *ou* prises; *Fig* **to have one's hands full** avoir beaucoup à faire, avoir du pain sur la planche; **I've got my hands full trying to cope as it is** j'ai déjà assez à faire comme ça; **to lay one's hands on sth** *(find)* mettre la main sur qch; **to get** *or* **to lay one's hands on sth** *(obtain)* dénicher qch; **to lay hands on sb** faire violence à qn; *Fig* **just wait till I get** *or* **lay my hands on her!** attends un peu que je l'attrape!; **to lift** *or* **to raise a h. to sb** lever la main sur qn; *Fig* **he never lifts a h. to help** il ne lève jamais le petit doigt pour aider; **hands off!** bas les pattes!, pas touche!; **hands off the unions/education system!** pas touche aux syndicats/au système éducatif!; **he can't keep his hands to himself** il a la main baladeuse; **I only have one pair of hands!** je n'ai que deux mains!; **take your hands off me!** ne me touche pas!; **(put your) hands up!** les mains en l'air!, haut les mains!; *Sch* **hands up anyone who knows the answer** que ceux qui connaissent la réponse lèvent le doigt *ou* la main; **to tie sb's hands** attacher les mains de qn; **they tied my hands behind my back** ils m'ont lié *ou* attaché les mains dans le dos; **I could do it with one h. tied behind my back** je pourrais le faire sans aucun effort *ou* les doigts dans le nez; *Fig* **my hands are tied** j'ai les mains liées; *Fig* **to sit on one's hands** *(applaud half-heartedly)* applaudir sans enthousiasme; *(do nothing)* ne rien faire; **to ask for sb's h. in marriage** demander la main de qn, demander qn en mariage; **at h., near** *or* **close at h.** *(about to happen)* proche; *(nearby)* à proximité; **the hour is at h.** l'heure est proche; **to suffer at the hands of sb** souffrir aux mains *ou* dans les mains de qn; **to pass sth from h. to h.** faire passer qch de mains en mains; **h. in h.** la main dans la main; *Fig* **to go h. in h. (with sth)** aller de pair (avec qch); **to be h. in glove with sb** travailler en étroite collaboration avec qn; **to make money h. over fist** gagner un argent fou; *Br Fam* **she doesn't do a h.'s turn** elle n'en fiche pas une; **to live from h. to mouth** tirer le diable par la queue; *Fig* **to win hands down** gagner haut la main; **to beat sb hands down** battre qn à plate(s) couture(s); *Prov* **many hands make light work** = à beaucoup d'ouvriers la tâche devient aisée; **on the one h.... but on the other h....** *(used in the same sentence)* d'un côté... mais de l'autre...; **on the other h.** *(when beginning new sentence)* d'un autre côté

2 *(assistance)* **to give sb a h.** donner un coup de main à qn; **to lend a h.** mettre la main à la pâte; **do you need a h. (with that)?** as-tu besoin d'un coup de main?

3 *(control, management)* **to need a firm h.** avoir besoin d'être sérieusement pris en main; **to rule with a firm h.** diriger avec de la poigne; **to take sb/sth in h.** prendre qn/qch en main; **to be out of h.** *(dog, child)* ne rien écouter; **to get out of h.** *(dog, child)* devenir indocile; *(meeting, situation)* échapper à tout contrôle; **the garden is getting out of h.** le jardin à l'air d'une vraie jungle; **to change hands** *(company, restaurant etc)* changer de propriétaire; **it's out of my hands** cela ne m'appartient plus, ce n'est plus ma responsabilité *ou* de mon ressort; **the matter is in the hands of the headmaster** la question relève maintenant *ou* est maintenant du ressort du principal; **I have put the matter in the hands of a lawyer** j'ai confié l'affaire à un avocat; **to have too much time on one's hands** avoir trop de temps à soi; **to have sb/sth on one's hands** avoir qn/qch sur les bras; **now that that's off my hands** à présent que je suis débarrassé de cela; **it's out of my hands** je ne peux (plus) rien y faire; **to fall into the hands of the enemy** tomber entre les mains de l'ennemi; **to fall into the wrong hands** *(information, secret etc)* tomber en de mauvaises mains; **in the wrong hands this knowledge could be very dangerous** si elles tombaient aux mains de personnes malintentionnées, ces connaissances pourraient être très dangereuses; **in the right hands** en de bonnes mains; **to be in good** *or* **safe hands** être en de bonnes mains; **can I leave this in your hands?** puis-je te demander de t'en occuper?; **it leaves too much power in the hands of the police** cela laisse trop de pouvoir à la police; **to give sb a free h.** donner carte blanche à qn; **to take matters into one's own hands** prendre les choses en main

4 *(applause)* **to give sb a (big) h.** applaudir qn (bien fort)

5 *(influence, involvement)* **to have a h. in sth** avoir quelque chose à voir dans qch, être impliqué dans qch; **I had no h. in it** je n'avais rien à voir là-dedans, je n'y étais pour rien

6 *(skill, ability)* **to have a light h. with pastry** réussir une pâte légère; **she can turn her h. to anything** elle peut tout faire; **to keep one's h. in** garder la main; **to try one's h. at sth** s'essayer à qch

7 *(in cards ▸ cards held)* main *f*, jeu *m*; *(▸ round, game)* partie *f*; *(▸ player)* joueur(euse) *m,f*; **to have a good h.** avoir du jeu; **first/fourth h.** *(player)* premier(ère) *m,f*/dernier(ère) *m,f* en cartes; *Fig* **to show** *or* **to reveal one's h.** dévoiler son jeu; *Fig* **to throw in one's h.** jeter l'éponge

8 *(of clock, watch)* aiguille *f*; *(of signpost, barometer)* indicateur *m*; **the little h. is pointing to three** la petite aiguille est sur le trois

9 *(handwriting)* écriture *f*; **to have a good h.** avoir une belle écriture

10 *(measurement of horse)* paume *f*; **a horse 15 hands high** un cheval de 15 paumes

11 *(worker)* ouvrier(ère) *m,f*; *(on ship)* homme *m*, membre *m* de l'équipage; **the ship was lost with all hands** le navire a sombré corps et biens; **old h.** expert *m*, vieux *m* de la vieille; **to be an old h. at sth** avoir une vaste expérience de qch; *also Fig* **all hands to the pump** tout le monde à la rescousse

12 *(of bananas)* régime *m*; **h. of pork** jambonneau *m*

VT passer, donner; **to h. sth to sb, to h. sb sth** passer *ou* donner qch à qn; **to h. sb a letter/telegram** remettre une lettre/un télégramme à qn; *Fig* **to h. sth to sb on a plate** apporter à qn qch sur un plateau; **you've got to h. it to him** chapeau!; *Fig* **you have to h. it to her, she IS a good mother** c'est une bonne mère, il faut lui accorder cela

• **by hand** ADV *(written)* à la main; *(made, knitted, sewn)* (à la) main; **to wash sth by h.** laver qch à la main; **to send sth by h.** faire porter qch; **by h.** *(written on envelope)* en ville; **to rear an animal by h.** élever un animal au biberon

• **in hand** ADV **1** *(available ▸ money)* disponible; *(▸ time)* devant soi; *Br* **do we have any time in h.?** avons-nous du temps devant nous?

2 *(being dealt with)* en cours; **the matter is in h.** on s'occupe de l'affaire; **I have the situation well in h.** j'ai la situation bien en main; **to return to the matter in h.** revenir à ses moutons; **keep your mind on the job in h.** concentre-toi sur l'affaire en cours

• **on hand** ADJ *(person)* disponible

• **out of hand** ADV *(immediately)* sur-le-champ

• **to hand** ADV *(letter, information etc)* sous la main; **use what comes to h.** prends ce que tu as sous la main; **he took the first one that came to h.** il a pris le premier qui lui est tombé sous la main

▸▸ ***hand baggage*** *(UNCOUNT)* bagages *mpl* à main; ***hand blender*** mixeur *m*; ***hand controls*** commandes *fpl* manuelles; ***hand cream*** crème *f* pour les mains; *Mil* ***hand grenade*** grenade *f* à main; ***hand lotion*** lotion *f* pour les mains; ***hand luggage*** *(UNCOUNT)* bagages *mpl* à main; ***hand microphone*** micro *m* portatif; *Theat* ***hand puppet*** marionnette *f*; ***hand recognition*** reconnaissance *f* de la main; ***hand signal*** signal *m* de la main; **h. signals only** *(on vehicle)* = indique que les clignotants d'un véhicule ne fonctionnent pas; ***hand towel*** serviette *f*, essuie-mains *m inv*; ***hand wringer*** essoreuse *f* rouleaux

▸ **hand around** VT SEP *(distribute)* distribuer

▸ **hand back** VT SEP *(return)* rapporter, rendre; **she handed me back the bottle** elle m'a repassé la bouteille; *Rad & TV* **I now h. you back to the studio/Jon Snow** je rends maintenant l'antenne au studio/à Jon Snow

▸ **hand down** VT SEP **1** *(pass, give from high place)* passer, donner; **h. me down the hammer** passe-moi *ou* donne-moi le marteau (qui est là-haut) **2** *(heirloom, story)* transmettre; **all her clothes had been handed down from her older sisters** tous ses vêtements venaient de ses sœurs aînées **3** *Law (decision, sentence)* annoncer; *(judgment)* rendre; *Am* **to h. down the budget** annoncer le budget

▸ **hand in** VT SEP *(return, surrender ▸ book)* rendre; *(▸ ticket)* remettre; *(▸ exam paper)* rendre, remettre; *(something found ▸ to authorities, police etc)* déposer, remettre; **to h. in one's resignation** donner *ou* remettre sa démission, démissionner

▸ **hand off** VT SEP *Sport (in rugby)* raffûter

▸ **hand on** VT SEP **1** *(give to someone else)* passer; **to h. sth on to sb** passer qch à qn **2** = **hand down 2**

▸ **hand out** VT SEP *(distribute)* distribuer; **we h. out 200 free meals a day** nous servons 200 repas gratuits par jour; **he's very good at handing out advice** il est très fort pour ce qui est de distribuer des conseils; **he's fond of handing it out, but can't take it** *(criticism)* il se permet de critiquer les autres mais il déteste qu'on le critique; **the French boxer handed out a lot of punishment** le boxeur français a frappé à coups redoublés

▸ **hand over** VT SEP **1** *(pass, give ▸ object)* passer, donner; *Rad & TV* **we now h. you over to the weather man/Bill Smith in Moscow** nous passons maintenant l'antenne à notre météorologue/ Bill Smith à Moscou; *Tel* **I'm handing him over now** je te le passe tout de suite **2** *(surrender ▸ weapons, hostage)* remettre; *(▸ criminal)* livrer; *(▸ power, authority)* transmettre; *Law (▸ property)* céder; **he was handed over to the French police** il a été livré à la *ou* aux mains de la police française; **h. it over!** donne!

VI to h. over to *(government minister, chairman etc)* passer le pouvoir à; *(in meeting)* donner la parole à; *Tel* passer *ou* donner le combiné à

▸ **hand round** VT SEP *(distribute)* distribuer

handbag ['hændbæg] *(pt & pp* **handbagged**, *cont* **handbagging**) **N 1** *(bag)* sac *m* à main **2** *Mus (music)* = type de house influencée par la pop commerciale

VT *Br Fam (attack verbally)* **she handbagged him** elle l'a violemment attaqué▫

handball ['hændbɔːl] **N 1** *(team game)* handball *m* **2** *(pelota)* pelote *f* (basque) **3** *Ftbl (foul)* main *f*

handbell ['hændbel] **N** clochette *f*

handbill ['hændbɪl] **N** *Br* prospectus *m*

handbook ['hændbʊk] **N** *(for car, machine)* guide *m*, manuel *m*; *(for tourist's use)* guide *m*

handbrake ['hændbreɪk] **N** *Br Aut* frein *m* à main; **to put the h. on** mettre le frein à main

▸▸ ***handbrake turn*** demi-tour *m* au frein à main

h & c *(written abbr* **hot and cold**) eau *f* courante chaude et froide

handcart ['hændkɑːt] **N** charrette *f* à bras; *Fam* **the company is going to hell in a h.** l'entreprise est en train de sombrer▫

handclap ['hændklæp] **N** *Br* **to get the slow h.** *(performer)* se faire siffler; *Br* **to give sb the slow h.** siffler qn

handcuff ['hændkʌf] **VT** passer les menottes à; **to h. sb to sb/sth** attacher qn à qn/qch avec des menottes; **he was handcuffed** il avait les menottes aux poignets

• **handcuffs** NPL menottes *fpl*; **to be in handcuffs** avoir les menottes (aux mains)

hand-drill **N** perceuse *f* à main

handful ['hændfʊl] **N 1** *(amount)* poignée *f*; *Fig* **a h. of** *(a few)* quelques; **a h. of people** quelques personnes; **how many people were there? – only a h.** combien de personnes y avait-il? – seulement quelques-unes **2** *Fam (uncontrollable person)* **that child is a real h.** cet enfant-là me donne du fil à retordre

handgrip ['hændgrɪp] **N 1** *(on racket)* grip *m*; *(on bicycle)* poignée *f* **2** *(handshake)* poignée *f* de main **3** *(holdall)* fourre-tout *m inv*

handgun ['hændgʌn] **N** *Am* revolver *m*, pistolet *m*

hand-held ADJ *(appliance)* à main; *(camera)* portatif

N *(computer)* hand-held *m*

▸▸ *Comput* ***hand-held computer*** ordinateur *m* de poche; *Comput* ***hand-held scanner*** scanner *m ou* scanneur *m* à main

handhold ['hændhəʊld] **N** prise *f* (de main)

handicap ['hændɪkæp] *(pt & pp* **handicapped**, *cont* **handicapping**) **N 1** *(physical, mental)* handicap *m*; *Fig (disadvantage)* handicap *m*, désavantage *m*; **people with a (physical/mental) h.** les gens qui souffrent d'un handicap (physique/mental) **2** *Sport* handicap *m*; **time/distance h.** handicap *m* en temps/distance

VT 1 *Fig (disadvantage)* handicaper, désavantager; **they were always handicapped by a lack of money** ils ont toujours été handicapés par le manque d'argent **2** *Sport* handicaper

handicapped ['hændɪkæpt] ADJ handicapé; **to be mentally/physically h.** être handicapé(e) *m,f* mental(e)/physique; *Am* **h. parking** *(sign)* parking réservé aux handicapés

NPL **the h.** les handicapés *mpl*

handicraft ['hændɪkrɑːft] **N 1** *(UNCOUNT) (items)* objets *mpl* artisanaux, artisanat *m* **2** *(skill)* artisanat *m*

handily ['hændɪlɪ] ADV *(conveniently)* de façon commode *ou* pratique; **the shop is h. situated only 100 metres from the house** le magasin n'est qu'à 100 mètres de la maison, ce qui est pratique *ou* commode; **they h. left their fingerprints** ils ont laissé leurs empreintes, ce qui était bien pratique

handiness ['hændɪnɪs] **N 1** *(convenience, usefulness)* commodité *f*; **the h. of the house for the shops** l'emplacement très commode de la maison près des magasins **2** *(skill with hands)* adresse *f*, dextérité *f*

handing down **N** *(of tradition)* transmission *f*

handing over **N** *(of hostages, keys)* remise *f* (to aux mains de); *(of power)* transmission *f*; *Law (of property)* cession *f*

handiwork ['hændɪwɜːk] **N** *(UNCOUNT) (work)* travail *m* manuel; *(result)* œuvre *f*; **the graffiti is the h. of vandals** les graffiti sont l'œuvre de vandales; **this is YOUR h., is it?** c'est toi qui as fait ça?

hand-job **N** *Vulg* **to give sb a h.** branler qn

handkerchief ['hæŋkətʃɪf] (*pl* **handkerchiefs** *or* **handkerchieves** [-tʃi:vz]) **N** mouchoir *m*

hand-knit (*pt & pp* **hand-knitted**, *cont* **hand-knitting**) **N** pull *m*/etc tricoté à la main
VT tricoter à la main

hand-knitted **ADJ** tricoté main, tricoté à la main

HANDLE ['hændəl]

N
- manche **1**
- poignée **1, 3**
- anse **1**
- queue **1**

VT
- toucher à **1**
- manœuvrer **2**
- conduire **2**
- manier **2**
- traiter **3, 4**
- faire face à **3**
- supporter **3**
- s'occuper de **4**

VI
- répondre

N 1 *(of broom, knife, screwdriver)* manche *m*; *(of suitcase, box, drawer, door)* poignée *f*; *(of cup)* anse *f*; *(of saucepan)* queue *f*; *(of stretcher)* bras *m*; *Br Fam* **to fly off the h. (at sb)** piquer une colère (contre qn)
2 *Fam (name ▸ of citizens' band user)* nom *m* de code❑; *(▸ which sounds impressive)* titre *m* de noblesse❑
3 *Comput* poignée *f*
4 *Fam (idioms)* **to get a h. on sth** piger qch; **I'll get back to you once I've got a h. on the situation** je vous recontacterai quand j'aurai la situation en main❑
VT 1 *(touch)* toucher à, manipuler; **please do not h. the goods** *(sign)* ne pas toucher; **h. with care** *(on package)* fragile; **pesticides should be handled with caution** les pesticides doivent être manipulés avec précaution; **to h. the ball** *(in football)* faire une main
2 *(operate ▸ ship)* manœuvrer, gouverner; *(▸ car)* conduire; *(▸ gun)* se servir de, manier; *(work with ▸ words, numbers)* manier; **have you any experience of handling horses?** savez-vous vous y prendre avec les chevaux?
3 *(cope with ▸ crisis, problem)* traiter; *(▸ situation)* faire face à; *(▸ crowd, traffic, death)* supporter; **you handled that very well** tu as très bien réglé les choses; **I don't know how to h. her** je ne sais pas comment la prendre; **leave this to me, I'LL h. him** laisse-moi m'en occuper, je me charge de lui; **four babies are a lot for one person to h.** quatre bébés, cela fait beaucoup pour une seule personne; **do you think you can h. the job?** penses-tu être capable de faire le travail?; **I couldn't h. it if Dad died** si papa mourait, je ne le supporterais pas; **how is she handling it?** comment s'en sort-elle?; *Fam* **he can't h. his drink** il ne tient pas l'alcool; **it's nothing I can't h.** je me débrouille
4 *(manage, process)* s'occuper de; *(address ▸ topic, subject)* aborder, traiter; **she handles my tax for me** elle s'occupe de mes impôts; **we're too small to h. an order of that size** notre entreprise est trop petite pour traiter une commande de cette importance; **could you h. this task as well?** pourriez-vous également vous charger de ce travail?; **the airport handles 200 planes a day** chaque jour 200 avions passent par l'aéroport; **to h. stolen goods** receler des objets volés; **we don't h. chemical products** nous ne faisons pas de produits chimiques
VI *(car, ship)* répondre; **how does she h.?** *(car)* est-ce qu'elle répond bien?

handlebar ['hændəlbɑ:(r)] **ADJ**
▸▸ ***handlebar moustache*** moustache *f* en guidon de vélo

handlebars ['hændəlbɑ:z] **NPL** guidon *m*

handler ['hændlə(r)] **N** *(of dogs)* maître-chien *m*; *(of baggage)* bagagiste *mf*

handling ['hændlɪŋ] **N 1** *(touching, holding)* manipulation *f*, action *f* de toucher; *(of stolen goods)* recel *m*
2 *(of tool, weapon)* maniement *m*; *(of pesticides, chemicals, explosives)* manipulation *f*; *(of ship)* manœuvre *f*
3 *(of car)* maniabilité *f*, comportement *m* routier; **the size of the car makes for easy h.** la taille de la voiture permet une grande maniabilité
4 *(of person, situation, operation)* traitement *m*; **my h. of the problem** la façon dont j'ai traité le problème
5 *(of order, contract)* traitement *m*, exécution *f*; *(of goods, baggage)* manutention *f*
6 *(of funds)* maniement *m*
7 *Ftbl* (faute *f* de) main *f*; **a penalty was awarded for h.** un penalty a été accordé pour main
▸▸ ***handling capacity*** capacité *f* de traitement; ***handling charges*** *(administrative)* frais *mpl* de traitement; *(for physically shifting goods)* frais *mpl* de manutention

handmade [,hænd'meɪd] **ADJ** fabriqué *ou* fait (à la) main

handmaid ['hændmeɪd], **handmaiden** ['hændmeɪdən] **N** *Arch* servante *f*, bonne *f*; *Fig* bonne *f*

hand-me-down *Fam* **N** vêtement *m* de seconde main❑; **why do I always have to wear his hand-me-downs?** pourquoi dois-je toujours porter ses vieux vêtements?❑
ADJ *(clothes)* de seconde main❑; *Fig (ideas)* reçu❑

handout ['hændaut] **N 1** *(donation)* aide *f*, don *m*; **to live off handouts** vivre de dons; **government handouts** subventions *fpl* gouvernementales **2** *(printed sheet or sheets)* polycopié *m* **3** *(leaflet)* prospectus *m*; *(sample)* cadeau *m* publicitaire

handover ['hændəuvə(r)] **N** *(of power)* passation *f*, transmission *f*, transfert *m*; *(of territory)* transfert *m*; *(of hostage, prisoner)* remise *f*; *(of baton)* transmission *f*, passage *m*

handpick [,hænd'pɪk] **VT 1** *(fruit, vegetables)* cueillir à la main **2** *Fig (people)* sélectionner avec soin, trier sur le volet

handpicked [,hænd'pɪkt] **ADJ** *(people)* trié sur le volet

handrail ['hændreɪl] **N** *(on bridge)* rambarde *f*, garde-fou *m*; *Naut* rambarde *f*; *(of stairway ▸ gen)* rampe *f*; *(▸ against wall)* main *f* courante

handsaw ['hændsɔ:] **N** scie *f* à main; *(small)* (scie *f*) égoïne *f*

handset ['hændset] **N** *Tel (d'un téléphone fixe)* combiné *m*; *(mobile phone)* appareil *m*, téléphone *m*

hands-free [hænds-] **ADJ** *Tel* mains libres

handshake ['hændʃeɪk] **N 1** *(between people)* poignée *f* de main **2** *Comput* dialogue *m* d'établissement de liaison

handshaking ['hændʃeɪkɪŋ] **N** *Comput* établissement *m* d'une liaison

hands-off [hændz-] **ADJ** *(policy)* non interventionniste, de non-intervention; *(manager)* non interventionniste; **the director has a h. style of management** le directeur est partisan de laisser de l'autonomie à son personnel

handsome ['hænsəm] **ADJ 1** *(good-looking ▸ person, face, room)* beau (belle); *(▸ building, furniture)* élégant; **a h. man** un bel homme; **a h. woman** une belle femme **2** *(generous ▸ reward, compliment)* beau (belle); *(▸ conduct, treatment)* généreux; *(sincere ▸ praise, apology)* sincère; **he received very h. treatment** on l'a traité d'une façon très généreuse **3** *(substantial ▸ profit, price)* bon; *(▸ fortune)* joli; **a h. amount** une coquette *ou* jolie somme, une somme rondelette

handsomely ['hænsəmlɪ] **ADV 1** *(beautifully)* avec élégance, élégamment **2** *(generously ▸ reward, compliment, behave, treat)* généreusement, avec générosité; *(sincerely ▸ praise, apologize)* sincèrement **3** *(substantially)* **to win h.** gagner haut la main

handsomeness ['hænsəmnɪs] **N 1** *(beauty)* beauté *f* **2** *(generosity)* générosité *f*; *(sincerity)* sincérité *f*

hands-on ['hændz-] **ADJ** *(training, experience)* pratique; *(exhibition)* = où le public peut toucher les objets exposés; **I go for a h. style of management** je suis le genre de patron à contribuer concrètement au fonctionnement de mon entreprise *ou* à mettre la main à la pâte

handspring ['hændsprɪŋ] **N** *Gym* saut *m* de mains

handstand ['hændstænd] **N** *Gym* appui *m* renversé, équilibre *m* sur les mains

hand-to-hand **ADJ** *(fighting)* corps-à-corps *(inv)*
ADV to fight h. se battre au corps-à-corps

hand-to-mouth **ADJ to lead** *or* **to have a h. existence** tirer le diable par la queue
ADV to live h. tirer le diable par la queue

hand-tooling **N 1** *Tech (on a lathe etc)* travail *m* à la main **2** *(in bookbinding)* dorure *f* à froid faite à la main

handwork ['hændwɜ:k] **N** travail *m* à la main

handwriting ['hændraɪtɪŋ] **N** écriture *f*
▸▸ ***handwriting expert*** graphologue *mf*; *Comput* ***handwriting recognition*** reconnaissance *f* de l'écriture manuscrite

handwritten ['hændrɪtən] **ADJ** manuscrit, écrit à la main

handy ['hændɪ] (*compar* **handier**, *superl* **handiest**) **ADJ 1** *(near at hand)* proche; **I always keep my glasses h.** je range toujours mes lunettes à portée de main; **have you got a pen and paper h.?** as-tu un stylo et du papier sous la main? **2** *(person ▸ good with one's hands)* adroit de ses mains; **he's h. about the house** il est bricoleur; **he's not the handiest man in the world** ce n'est pas un très bon bricoleur; **to be h. at doing sth** être doué pour faire qch, bien savoir faire qch; **she's h. with a drill** elle sait se servir d'une perceuse; *Fam* **he's a bit h. with his fists** il sait se servir de ses poings **3** *(convenient, useful)* commode, pratique; **living in the centre is h. for work** pour le travail c'est pratique d'habiter en ville; **that's h.!** c'est pratique *ou* commode!; **he's a h. guy to have around in a crisis** c'est quelqu'un d'utile en cas de crise; **a h. piece of advice** un conseil utile; **to come in h.** être utile

handyman ['hændɪmæn] (*pl* **handymen** [-men]) **N** *(employee)* homme *m* à tout faire; *(DIY expert)* bricoleur *m*; *Am* **h.'s special** = maison qui a besoin de beaucoup de travaux

HANG [hæŋ]

VT
- accrocher **1**
- suspendre **1**
- fixer **1**
- coller **1**
- décorer **2**
- pendre **3**

VI
- être accroché **1**
- être suspendu **1, 3**
- être étendu **1**
- pendre **1**
- tomber **2**
- flotter **3**
- être pendu **4**
- traîner **5**

N
- coup **1**
- drapé **2**

(*pt & pp vt senses* **1, 2, 4** *& vi senses* **1–3, 5** **hung** [hʌŋ], *pt & pp vt* **3** *& vi* **4** **hanged**)
VT 1 *(suspend ▸ curtains, coat, decoration, picture)* accrocher, suspendre; *(▸ door)* fixer, monter; *(▸ art exhibition)* mettre en place; *(▸ wallpaper)* coller, poser; *Culin (▸ game, meat)* faire faisander; **to h. sth on the wall** accrocher qch au mur; **they hung banners from their windows** ils ont accroché des bannières à leurs fenêtres; **to h. a picture** suspendre un tableau; *Br* **to h. one's head (in shame)** baisser la tête (de honte); *Am Fam* **to h. one on sb** *(punch)* balancer un coup de poing à qn; **to h. fire** *(project)* être en suspens; *(decision)* traîner (en longueur); *(person)* mettre les choses en suspens
2 *(usu passive) (adorn)* décorer; **a tree hung with lights** un arbre décoré *ou* orné de lumières; **to h. a room with tapestries** tendre une salle de tapisseries
3 *(criminal)* pendre; **to be hanged for one's crime** être pendu pour son crime; **to h. oneself** se pendre; **hanged** *or* **hung, drawn and quartered** pendu, éviscéré et écartelé; *Fam* **h. him!** qu'il aille se faire voir!; *Br Fam* **I'll be hanged if I know** je veux bien être pendu si je le sais; *Br Fam* **I'll be hanged if I'm going out in that weather** il n'y a pas de danger que je sorte par ce temps❑; *Br Fam* **h. it (all)!** ras le bol!; *Br* **(you) might as well be hanged for a sheep as a lamb** quitte à être puni, autant l'être pour quelque chose qui en vaille la peine
4 *Am Fam (turn)* **to h. a left/right** prendre à gauche/droite❑
VI 1 *(be suspended ▸ rope, painting, light)* être accroché, être suspendu; *(▸ clothes on clothes line)* être étendu, pendre; *Culin (game)* se faisander; **to h. from sth** être accroché *ou* suspendu à qch;

to h. on sb's arm être accroché au bras de qn; **her pictures are now hanging in several art galleries** ses tableaux sont maintenant exposés dans plusieurs galeries d'art; **her hair hangs down her back** ses cheveux lui tombent le long du dos; **time hangs heavy (on) my/his hands** le temps me/lui semble long; *Fam* **how's it hanging?** ça gaze?; *Am Fam* **to h. loose** rester cool; *Am Fam* **to h. tough** s'accrocher

2 *(drapery, clothes etc)* tomber, se draper; **his suit hangs well** son costume tombe bien; **his clothes h. loosely on him** il flotte dans ses vêtements; **this door hangs badly** cette porte est mal suspendue (sur ses gonds)

3 *(float ▸ mist, smoke etc)* flotter, être suspendu; **the ball seemed to h. in the air** le ballon semblait suspendu en l'air

4 *(criminal)* être pendu; **you'll h. for your crime** vous serez pendu pour votre crime; *Br Fam* **she can go h.** elle peut aller se faire voir

5 *Am Fam (spend time)* traîner❑; **he's hanging with his friends** il traîne avec ses copains

N 1 *Fam (knack, idea)* **to get the h. of doing sth** prendre le coup pour faire qch; **I never did get the h. of skiing** je n'ai jamais réussi à prendre le coup pour skier; **to get the h. of sth** *(understand)* piger qch; **I can't get the h. of this computer** je n'arrive pas à piger comment marche cet ordinateur; **you'll soon get the h. of it** tu vas bientôt t'y faire❑

2 *(of clothing)* tombé *m*; *(of material)* drapé *m*

3 *(idiom) Br Fam* **he doesn't give a h.** *(couldn't care less)* il n'en a rien à taper *ou* à cirer

▸**hang about, hang around** *Fam* **VI 1** *(wait)* poireauter; **he kept me hanging about** *or* **around for half an hour** il m'a fait poireauter pendant une demi-heure; **I've been hanging about** *or* **around waiting for her to come** je tourne en rond à l'attendre; **I hate all this hanging about** *or* **around** je déteste toute cette attente❑, je déteste poireauter comme ça; *Br* **h. about (a bit)!** attends!❑; **h. about, that's not what I mean!** attends *ou* doucement, ce n'est pas ce que je veux dire!❑ **2** *(be idle, waste time)* traîner (à ne rien faire)❑; **to h. about** *or* **around on street corners** traîner dans les rues; **we can't afford to h. about if we want that contract** nous ne pouvons pas nous permettre de traîner si nous voulons obtenir ce contrat; **she doesn't h. about** *or* **around** *(soon gets what she wants)* elle ne perd pas de temps❑ **3** *(be an unwanted presence)* **Mum doesn't want me hanging around when the guests arrive** maman ne veut pas que je sois là quand les invités arriveront❑

VT INSEP to h. about *or* **around a place** traîner dans un endroit❑

▸**hang back VI** *(wait behind)* rester un peu plus longtemps; *(not go forward)* se tenir *ou* rester en arrière; **to h. back from doing sth** renâcler à faire qch; *Br Fig* **he hung back from saying what he really thought** il s'est retenu de dire ce qu'il pensait vraiment

▸**hang down VI** *(light)* pendre; *(hair)* descendre, tomber

▸**hang in VI** *Fam* **h. in there!** tiens bon!, accroche-toi!

▸**hang on VI 1** *(hold tight)* se tenir, s'accrocher; **h. on tight** tiens-toi *ou* accroche-toi bien **2** *Fam (wait)* attendre❑; **h. on!** *(wait)* attends!❑; *(indicating astonishment, disagreement etc)* une minute!❑; **h. on and I'll get him for you** *(on phone)* ne quitte pas, je te le passe❑; **do you mind hanging on for a minute or two?** ça ne te dérange pas de patienter quelques minutes?❑ **3** *(hold out, survive)* résister, tenir (bon); *Fam* **h. on in there!** *(don't give up)* tiens bon!, tiens le coup!

VT INSEP 1 *(listen to)* **she hung on his every word** elle buvait ses paroles, elle était suspendue à ses lèvres **2** *(depend on)* dépendre de; **it all hangs on whether we get the loan** pour nous, tout dépend de l'obtention ou non du prêt; **this is what it all hangs on** tout dépend de cela

VT SEP *Am Fam* **to h. one on** *(get drunk)* prendre une cuite

▸**hang onto VT INSEP 1** *(cling to)* s'accrocher à **2** *Fam (keep)* garder❑, conserver❑; **I'd h. onto those paintings if I were you** à ta place, je garderais précieusement ces tableaux; **he hung onto these outdated ideas** il se raccrochait à ces idées démodées❑

▸**hang out VI 1** *(protrude)* pendre; **his shirt tails were hanging out** sa chemise dépassait; **to h. out of the window** *(flags)* être déployé à la fenêtre; *(person)* se pencher par la fenêtre; *Fam* **to let it all h. out** *(person)* se relâcher complètement❑, se laisser aller❑; *(speak without restraint)* se défouler; *Hum (go naked)* se promener tout nu❑ **2** *Fam (spend time)* traîner❑; **he hangs out at the local bar** c'est un habitué du café du coin❑; **where does she h. out?** quels sont les endroits qu'elle fréquente?❑ **3** *(survive, not give in)* résister, tenir bon; **the strikers are hanging out in their demands** les grévistes tiennent bon dans leurs revendications; **they're hanging out for 10 percent** ils insistent pour obtenir 10 pour cent

VT SEP *(washing)* étendre; *(flags)* déployer

▸**hang over VT INSEP** être suspendu au-dessus de, planer sur; **(a) thick fog hung over the town** un brouillard épais flottait au-dessus de la ville; **a question mark hangs over his future** un point d'interrogation plane sur son avenir; **a heavy silence hung over the meeting** un lourd silence pesait sur l'assemblée; **she has got the threat of redundancy hanging over her head** *or* **her** une menace de licenciement plane sur elle; **I can't go out with exams hanging over me** avec les examens qui approchent, je ne peux pas sortir; **we've got the threat of eviction hanging over us** nous risquons d'être expulsés d'une minute à l'autre

▸**hang together VI 1** *(be united ▸ people)* se serrer les coudes **2** *(be consistent ▸ alibi, argument, plot etc)* (se) tenir; *(▸ different alibis, statements)* concorder

▸**hang up VT SEP** *(coat, hat etc)* accrocher; *Tel (receiver)* raccrocher; **to h. up one's boots/gloves/dancing shoes/***etc (retire)* raccrocher; *Am Fam* **to h. it up** *(stop)* laisser tomber

VI *Tel* raccrocher; **to h. up on sb** raccrocher au nez de qn

---

hangar ['hæŋə(r)] **N** *Aviat* hangar *m*

hangdog ['hæŋdɒg] **ADJ to have a h. look** *or* **expression** avoir un air penaud *ou* de chien battu

hanger ['hæŋə(r)] **N** *(hook)* portemanteau *m*; *(coat hanger)* portemanteau *m*, cintre *m*; *(loop on garment)* cordon *m ou* ganse *f* d'accrochage *(à l'intérieur d'un vêtement)*

hanger-on (*pl* **hangers-on**) **N** *Pej* parasite *m*

hang-glide VI *Sport* faire du deltaplane; **to h. down Mont Blanc** descendre le mont Blanc en deltaplane

hang-glider N *Sport (aircraft)* deltaplane *m*; *(person)* libériste *mf*, deltiste *mf*

hang-gliding N *Sport* deltaplane *m*; **to go h.** faire du deltaplane

hanging ['hæŋɪŋ] **ADJ** *(suspended)* suspendu

N 1 *(death penalty)* pendaison *f* **2** *(of wallpaper)* pose *f*; *(of decorations, pictures)* accrochage *m*, mise *f* en place; *(of door)* montage *m*, accrochage *m* **3** *(tapestry)* **(wall) h.** tenture *f* (murale)

▸▸ ***hanging basket*** panier *m* suspendu; *Art* ***hanging committee*** = comité de réception ou jury d'admission des tableaux; ***hanging cupboard*** armoire *f* murale; ***the Hanging Gardens of Babylon*** les jardins *mpl* suspendus de Babylone; *Comput* ***hanging indent*** présentation *f* en sommaire; *Law* ***hanging judge*** juge *m* à la main lourde; ***hanging offence*** crime *m* passible de pendaison; *Fig* **it's not a h. offence** ce n'est pas une affaire d'État; ***hanging paragraph*** paragraphe *m* en sommaire; *Geog* ***hanging valley*** vallée *f* suspendue; ***hanging wardrobe*** penderie *f*

hangman ['hæŋmən] (*pl* **hangmen** [-mən]) **N** *(executioner)* bourreau *m*; *(game)* le pendu; **to play h.** jouer au pendu

hangnail ['hæŋneɪl] **N** envie *f (peau)*

hang-out N *Fam* **this is one of my favourite hang-outs** j'adore traîner dans ce coin❑; **this is one of his hang-outs** c'est l'un des endroits où on le trouve le plus souvent❑; **it's a real student h.** c'est un endroit très fréquenté par les étudiants❑

hangover ['hæŋəʊvə(r)] **N 1** *(from alcohol)* gueule *f* de bois; **to have a h.** avoir la gueule de bois; **h. cure** remède *m* contre la gueule de bois **2** *(relic)* reste *m*, vestige *m*, survivance *f*; **a h. from the past** un reliquat du passé

hang-up N 1 *Fam (complex)* complexe❑ *m*, blocage❑ *m*; **she has a h. about her appearance/weight** elle est complexée par son allure/poids❑; **you've got a lot of hang-ups** tu es très complexé❑ **2** *Comput* blocage *m*, interruption *f*

hank [hæŋk] **N 1** *(of wool)* écheveau *m* **2** *Tex (measurement)* longueur *f* **3** *Naut* rocambeau *m*

hanker ['hæŋkə(r)] **VI to h. after** *or* **for sth** rêver de qch, avoir énormément envie de qch

hankering ['hæŋkərɪŋ] **N** rêve *m*, envie *f*; **to have a h. after** *or* **for sth** rêver de qch, avoir énormément envie de qch

hankie, hanky ['hæŋkɪ] (*pl* **hankies**) **N** *Fam (abbr* **handkerchief**) mouchoir❑ *m*

hanky-panky [-'pæŋkɪ] **N** *(UNCOUNT) Fam* **1** *(sexual activity)* galipettes *fpl*; **to have a bit of** *or* **a little h.** faire des galipettes **2** *(mischief)* entourloupettes *fpl*, blagues *fpl*; **to get up to (a bit of) h.** faire des entourloupettes *ou* des blagues

Hanoverian [ˌhænə'vɪərɪən] *Hist* **ADJ** hanovrien

N Hanovrien(enne) *m,f*

Hansard ['hænsɑːd] **N** *Br Pol* = compte rendu quotidien des débats de la Chambre des communes

Hanseatic League [ˌhænsɪ'ætɪk-] **N** *Hist* **the H.** la ligue hanséatique, la Hanse

hansom (cab) ['hænsəm-] **N** fiacre *m*

hantavirus ['hæntəvaɪrəs] **N** *Med* hantavirus *m*

Hants (*written abbr* **Hampshire**) Hampshire *m*

Hanukkah ['hɑːnəkə] **N** *Rel* Hanoukka *f*

ha'penny ['heɪpnɪ] (*pl* **ha'pence** [-pəns]) *Br Fam Old-fashioned* **N** demi-penny❑ *m*; **he's down to his last h.** il ne lui reste que quelques sous

COMP d'un demi-penny

haphazard [ˌhæp'hæzəd] **ADJ** mal organisé; **the whole thing was a bit h.** c'était un peu n'importe quoi; **the city grew in a h. fashion** la ville s'est agrandie au gré des circonstances

haphazardly [ˌhæp'hæzədlɪ] **ADV** sans organisation, n'importe comment; **to choose h.** choisir au petit bonheur la chance, choisir au hasard

hapless ['hæplɪs] **ADJ** *Literary* infortuné

HAPPEN ['hæpən] **VI 1** *(occur)* arriver, se passer, se produire; **what's happened?** qu'est-il arrivé?, que s'est-il passé?; **when did this h.?** quand cela s'est-il produit *ou* passé?, quand cela est-il arrivé?; **it happened ten years ago** cela s'est passé il y a dix ans; **did anyone see what happened?** quelqu'un a-t-il vu ce qui s'est passé *ou* est arrivé?; **don't let it h. again** faites en sorte que cela ne se reproduise pas; **as if nothing had happened** comme si de rien n'était; **I pulled the lever, but nothing happened** j'ai tiré sur le manche, mais il ne s'est rien passé *ou* ça n'a rien fait; **whatever happens** quoi qu'il arrive *ou* advienne; **as (so) often happens** comme c'est bien souvent le cas; **it all happened so quickly** tout s'est passé si vite; **these things h.** ce sont des choses qui arrivent; **what happened next?** que s'est-il passé ensuite?; **it's all been happening this morning** ça n'a pas arrêté ce matin; **it's all happening here** ça bouge ici; **I wonder what's happened to her** *(what has befallen her)* je me demande ce qui a bien pu lui arriver; *(what she is doing now)* je me demande ce qu'elle est devenue; **whatever happened to him?** qu'est-il devenu?; **if anything happens or should h. to me** s'il m'arrivait quelque chose; **it couldn't h. to a nicer person** il/elle le mérite bien; **a funny thing happened to me last night** il m'est arrivé une drôle d'aventure hier soir; **I don't like what's happening in this country** je n'aime pas ce qui se passe dans ce pays; **what's happened to my pen?** *(where is it?)* qu'est-ce qu'on a fait de mon stylo?; *(what's wrong with it?)* qu'est-il arrivé à mon stylo?; *Am Fam* **what's happening?** *(as greeting)* ça va?❑

2 *(chance)* **do you h. to have his address?** auriez-vous son adresse, par hasard?; **it just so happens that I do** eh bien justement, oui; **you wouldn't h. to know where I could find him, would you?** vous ne sauriez pas où je pourrais le trouver?; **as it happens** justement; **I h. to know her, it so**

happens that I know her, I know her, as it happens il se trouve que je la connais; **the man you're talking about happens to be my father** il se trouve que l'homme dont vous parlez est mon père; **if you h. to see him** si jamais tu le vois

happen along, happen by VI *Am Fam* passer par hasard□

happen on, happen upon VT INSEP tomber sur

---

happening ['hæpənɪŋ] N *(occurrence)* événement *m*; *Art & Theat* happening *m*

ADJ *Fam* **1** *(fashionable)* branché **2** *(interesting)* **he's a h. kind of guy** avec lui on ne s'ennuie pas une minute□; **this is a h. kind of place** il se passe toujours des tas de trucs ici

happenstance ['hæpənstæns] N *Am* hasard *m*; **we met by h.** nous nous sommes rencontrés par hasard

happily ['hæpɪlɪ] ADV **1** *(contentedly ▸ say, smile)* d'un air heureux; *(▸ play, chat)* tranquillement; **I could live here very h.** je serais très heureux ici; **we were sitting there quite h. watching television** nous étions installés tout tranquillement devant la télévision; **they lived h. ever after** *(at end of fairy tale)* ils vécurent heureux et eurent beaucoup d'enfants; **to be h. married** être heureux en ménage **2** *(gladly)* volontiers; **I could quite h. live here** je me verrais très bien vivre ici; **I could quite h. strangle him** j'ai bien envie de l'étrangler; **he'll quite h. say one thing and do the opposite** ça ne le gêne pas de dire une chose et de faire exactement le contraire **3** *(luckily)* heureusement; **h., no one was hurt** heureusement, il n'y a pas eu de blessés

happiness ['hæpɪnɪs] N bonheur *m*; *Prov* **money can't buy you h.** l'argent ne fait pas le bonheur

happy ['hæpɪ] *(compar* **happier**, *superl* **happiest)**

ADJ **1** *(content)* heureux; **to make sb h.** rendre qn heureux; **I want you to be h.** je veux que tu sois heureux, je veux ton bonheur; **I'm very h. for you** je suis très heureux pour toi; **would you be h. living here?** serais-tu heureux ici?; **in happier times** à une époque plus heureuse; **in happier circumstances** dans des circonstances plus heureuses; **those were h. days** c'était le bon temps; **I'm not at all h. about your decision** je ne suis pas du tout content de votre décision; **I'm still not h. about it** je n'en suis toujours pas content; **that should keep the kids h.** cela devrait occuper les enfants; **their h. smiling faces** leurs visages heureux et souriants; **h. ending** *(in book, film)* fin *f* heureuse, dénouement *m* heureux; **to have a h. ending** *(book, film)* bien finir; **h. birthday!** joyeux anniversaire!; **H. Christmas!** Joyeux Noël!; **H. New Year!** Bonne année!; *Fam* **he's not a h. camper** *or* *Br* **chappy** *or* **bunny** il est pas jouasse; **to be as h. as** *Br* **Larry** *or* **a lark** *or* **a sandboy** *or Am* **a clam** être heureux comme tout

2 *(willing)* **I'm only too h. to help** je suis ravi de rendre service; **I would be h. to do it** je le ferais volontiers; **h. to oblige** ravi de rendre service; **I'd be h. to live here/move to Scotland** j'aimerais bien habiter ici/aller habiter en Écosse

3 *(lucky, fortunate ▸ coincidence)* heureux; **the h. few** les privilégiés *mpl*

4 *(apt, appropriate ▸ turn of phrase, choice of words)* heureux

5 *Fam (drunk)* gris, pompette

▸▸ *Br* ***happy event*** *(birth)* heureux événement *m*; ***happy families*** *(card game)* jeu *m* des sept familles; ***happy hour*** *(in pub, bar)* happy hour *f (heure, généralement en début de soirée, pendant laquelle les boissons sont moins chères)*; ***happy hunting ground*** paradis *m* des Indiens; *Fig* mine *f* d'or; **the market is a h. hunting ground for collectors** le marché est une vraie mine d'or pour les collectionneurs; ***happy medium*** équilibre *m*, juste milieu *m*; **to strike a h. medium** trouver un équilibre *ou* un juste milieu; ***happy slapping*** happy slapping *m*, = pratique consistant à filmer une agression avec un téléphone portable puis à en diffuser les images

happy-clappy [-'klæpɪ] *(pl* **happy-clappies)** *Br Fam Pej* ADJ *(service, meeting, Christian)* agaçant de par sa joie exubérante□ *(appliqué aux chrétiens évangéliques)*

N chrétien(enne) *m,f* évangélique□ *(agaçant de par sa joie exubérante)*

happy-go-lucky ADJ décontracté; *Pej* insouciant

Hapsburg = **Habsburg**

harangue [hə'ræŋ] VT *(person)* sermonner; *(crowd)* haranguer; **to h. sb about sth** sermonner qn au sujet de qch; **to h. sb into doing sth** sermonner qn pour qu'il fasse qch

N harangue *f*

harass ['hærəs, hə'ræs] VT **1** *Mil (enemy forces)* harceler, tenir en alerte **2** *(person ▸ pester)* tracasser, tourmenter, harceler; *(▸ sexually)* harceler; **to h. sb to do sth** harceler qn pour qu'il fasse qch; **to h. sb into doing sth** harceler qn jusqu'à ce qu'il fasse qch; **he was harassing me for money** il me harcelait pour que je lui donne de l'argent; **he claimed that the police had harassed him** il a déclaré que la police l'avait harcelé; **to be sexually harassed** être victime de harcèlement sexuel

> Note that the French verb **harasser** is a false friend and is never a translation for the English verb **to harass**. It means **to exhaust**.

harassed ['hærəst, hə'ræst] ADJ stressé

harassment ['hærəsmənt, hə'ræsmənt] N *(pestering)* tracasserie *f*; *(with questions, demands)* harcèlement *m*; *(stress)* stress *m*; *Mil* harcèlement *m*; **police/sexual h.** harcèlement *m* policier/sexuel

harbinger ['hɑːbɪndʒə(r)] N *Literary* signe *m* avant-coureur; **swallows are a h. of spring** les hirondelles annoncent le printemps; **a h. of doom** *(event, incident etc)* un mauvais présage; *(person)* un oiseau de malheur

harbour, *Am* **harbor** ['hɑːbə(r)] N *(for boats)* port *m*; *Fig* havre *m*

VT **1** *(person)* abriter, héberger; *(criminal)* donner asile à, receler **2** *(grudge, suspicion)* nourrir, entretenir en soi; **to h. a grudge against sb** garder rancune à qn, nourrir de la rancune envers qn **3** *(conceal ▸ dirt, germs)* renfermer, receler

▸▸ ***harbour dues*** droits *mpl* de port; ***harbour lights*** lumières *fpl* du port; ***harbour master*** capitaine *m* de port; ***harbour terminal*** gare *f* maritime

---

HARD [hɑːd]

ADJ	
• dur **1–3, 8**	• difficile **2**
• froid **3**	• rude **3**
• concret **4**	
ADV	
• fort **1**	• dur **1**
• difficilement **2**	• durement **3**

ADJ **1** *(not soft ▸ substance, light, colour)* dur; **to get** *or* **to become h.** durcir; **rock h., (as) h. as rock** dur comme la pierre; **she is (as) h. as nails** *(emotionally)* elle est dure, elle n'a pas de cœur; *(physically)* c'est une dure à cuire

2 *(difficult ▸ question, problem etc)* difficile, dur; **the laws make it h. to leave the country** à cause des lois, il est difficile de quitter le pays; **to have a h. fight** *or* **struggle on one's hands** avoir une lourde tâche devant soi; **it's h. to explain** c'est difficile *ou* dur à expliquer; **I find it h. to understand why/believe that...** je n'arrive pas à comprendre pourquoi/croire que... + *indicative*; **it's h. to say** c'est difficile à dire; **he's h. to get on with** il n'est pas facile à vivre; **she is h. to please** *(never satisfied)* elle est difficile; *(difficult to buy gifts for etc)* c'est difficile de lui faire plaisir; **it's h. to beat** on trouve difficilement mieux; **it's h. to beat a good Bordeaux** il n'y a rien de meilleur qu'un bon bordeaux; **the hardest part of the job is done** le plus dur est fait; **life is h.** c'est dur, la vie; **times are h.** les temps sont durs *ou* difficiles; **to fall on h. times** *(financially)* connaître des temps difficiles *ou* une période de vaches maigres; *(have difficult times)* connaître des temps difficiles, en voir de dures; **to give sb a h. time** en faire voir de dures à qn; **come on, don't give me a h. time!** allez, laisse-moi tranquille!; **you'll have a h. time (of it) persuading him to do that** tu vas avoir du mal à le convaincre de faire cela; **she had a h. time of it after her mother's death** elle a traversé une période difficile après la mort de sa mère; **she had a h. time of it when she was a child** la vie n'était pas drôle pour elle quand elle était enfant; **she had a h. time of it** *(in childbirth, operation)* elle a souffert; **to learn sth the h. way** *(involving personal loss, suffering etc)* apprendre qch à ses dépens; *(in a difficult way)* faire le rude apprentissage de qch; **I learnt the h. way not to be under-insured** j'ai appris à mes dépens qu'il ne faut pas être sous-assuré; **I learnt skiing the h. way** j'ai appris à skier à la dure; **to do things the h. way** *(through choice)* se compliquer la vie; *(due to circumstances)* en baver; **some people always have to do things the h. way** il y a des gens qui choisissent toujours la difficulté; **to play h. to get** *(flirt)* jouer les insaisissables; *Hum* **their financial expert is playing h. to get** leur expert financier semble jouer à cache-cache; **the h. of hearing** les malentendants *mpl*; **to be h. of hearing** être dur d'oreille; **a glass of wine, or would you prefer a drop of the h. stuff?** un verre de vin, ou bien préféreriez-vous une goutte de quelque chose de plus fort?

3 *(severe ▸ voice, face, eyes)* dur, froid; *(▸ climate, winter)* rigoureux, rude; *(▸ frost)* fort, rude; **he's h.** *(tough)* c'est un dur; **to be h. on sb** être dur avec qn; **children are h. on their shoes** les enfants font subir de mauvais traitements à leurs chaussures; **it's h. on the nerves** c'est dur pour les nerfs; **it was h. on the others** ça a été dur pour les autres; **it's hardest on the children** le plus dur, c'est pour les enfants; **to be a h. taskmaster** être dur à la tâche; **to take a long h. look at sth** examiner qch de près; **you should take a long h. look at yourself** tu devrais bien te regarder; **it's a h. blow for him** c'est un coup terrible pour lui; **no h. feelings?** tu ne m'en veux pas?; *Fam* **h. luck!**, *Br* **h. cheese!**, **h. lines!** pas de chance!□, pas de veine!, pas de bol!; **it will be h. luck if he doesn't get the job** ça ne sera pas de veine *ou* de bol s'il n'obtient pas le travail; **don't give me any of your h. luck stories** ne me raconte pas tes malheurs; **he gave me some h. luck story about having lost his investments** il a essayé de m'apitoyer en me racontant qu'il avait perdu l'argent qu'il avait investi; *Fam* **a h. nut** *or* **man** un dur

4 *(concrete ▸ facts)* concret(ète), tangible; *(▸ evidence)* tangible; **the h. fact is that there isn't enough money** la vérité, c'est qu'il n'y a pas assez d'argent; **the argument was not backed up by any h. fact** l'argument ne s'appuyait sur rien de concret

5 *(strenuous)* **it's been a long h. day** la journée a été longue; **it's h. work** c'est dur; **it was h. work to convince him** j'ai eu fort à faire pour le convaincre; **she's h. work** *(difficult to get on with)* elle n'est pas facile à vivre; *(difficult to make conversation with)* elle n'est pas causante; **she's not afraid of h. work** le travail ne lui fait pas peur; **the climb was h. going** la montée était rude; **it's h. going making conversation with him** c'est difficile de discuter avec lui

6 *(intense)* **she's a h. worker** c'est un bourreau de travail; **he's a h. drinker** c'est un gros buveur, il boit beaucoup; **give it a good h. shove** pousse-le un bon coup, pousse-le fort

7 *Fin (stock, rates)* soutenu, ferme

8 *Ling (consonant)* dur

ADV **1** *(strenuously ▸ pull, push, hit, breathe)* fort; *(▸ work)* dur; *(▸ run)* à toutes jambes; *(▸ listen)* attentivement; **to work h. at sth** beaucoup travailler qch; **to work h. at improving one's service/French** beaucoup travailler pour améliorer son service/français; **to work sb h.** faire travailler qn dur; **he works h. and plays h.** il se dépense beaucoup dans son travail et dans ses loisirs; **you'll have to try harder** il faudra que tu fasses plus d'efforts; **to try h. to do sth** essayer de son mieux de faire qch; **try h.!** fais de ton mieux!; **to think h.** beaucoup réfléchir; **think h.!** réfléchis bien!; **think harder!** réfléchis un peu plus!; **we can't find it – well, look harder!** nous ne le trouvons pas – et bien cherchez mieux!; **you didn't look very h.!** tu n'as pas bien cherché!; **to look h. at sb** regarder qn bien en face; **to look h. at sth** examiner qch; **as h. as possible, as h. as one can** *(work, try)* le plus qu'on peut; *(push, hit, squeeze)* de toutes ses forces; *Naut* **h. astern!** arrière, toute!; *Aut* **to turn h. to the left** braquer à gauche, faire un virage très sec vers la gauche; **to swim h.**

for the shore nager de toutes ses forces vers le rivage; *Br* **they're h. at it** *(working)* ils sont plongés dans leur travail

2 *(with difficulty)* difficilement; **to be h. put** *or* **pushed** *or* **pressed to do sth** avoir du mal à faire qch; **you'll be h. put to find a shop open at this time** tu vas avoir du mal à trouver une boutique ouverte à cette heure-ci; **old habits die h.** les vieilles habitudes ont la vie dure

3 *(harshly, severely ▸ treat someone)* durement, sévèrement; *(▸ rain)* à verse; *(▸ freeze, snow)* fort; **he's feeling h. done by** il a l'impression d'avoir été injustement traité; **to be h. hit by sth** être durement touché par qch; **she took the news/his death pretty h.** la nouvelle/sa mort l'a beaucoup éprouvée; *Old-fashioned* **it'll go h. with him if he keeps telling lies** ça va aller mal pour lui s'il continue à raconter des mensonges

4 *(solid)* **the ground was frozen h.** le gel avait complètement durci la terre; **to set h.** *(concrete, mortar)* prendre

5 *(close)* **to follow h. on the heels of sb** être sur les talons de qn; **to follow** *or* **to come h. on the heels of sth** suivre qch de très près

6 *Fam (idioms)* **h. up** *(short of money)* fauché, à sec; **to be h. up for ideas** manquer d'idées□, être à court d'idées□; *Fig* **you must be h. up if you're going out with him!** il faut vraiment que tu n'aies rien à te mettre sous la dent pour sortir avec lui!

N to try one's hardest faire de son mieux

• **hard by** PREP *Old-fashioned* tout près de

▸▸ *Typ & Comput* ***hard carriage return*** retour *m* chariot obligatoire; *Fam* ***hard case*** *(person)* dur(e) *m,f* à cuire; ***hard cash*** (argent *m*) liquide *m*; *Am* ***hard cider*** cidre *m*; ***hard coal*** anthracite *m*; *Fin* ***hard commodities*** minerais *mpl*; *Ling* ***hard consonant*** consonne *f* dure; *Comput* ***hard copy*** copie *f* sur papier, sortie *f* papier; ***hard core*** *(nucleus)* noyau *m* dur; *Constr* empierrement *m*; *Mus* hard rock *m inv*, hard *m inv*; *(pornography)* porno *m* hard; *Br Sport* ***hard court*** *(for tennis)* court *m* en ciment; ***hard currency*** monnaie *f ou* devise *f* forte; **a h. currency shop** un magasin où on paye en devises; *Comput* ***hard disk*** disque *m* dur; *Com* ***hard discount*** maxidiscompte *m*; *Comput* ***hard disk drive*** unité *f* de disque dur; *Comput* ***hard drive*** unité *f* de disque dur; ***hard drug*** drogue *f* dure; *Horseriding* ***hard gallop*** galop *m* soutenu; ***hard hat*** *(of construction worker)* casque *m*; *Am Fam (construction worker)* ouvrier(ère) *m,f* du bâtiment; ***hard hat area*** = zone où le port du casque est obligatoire; **h. hat area** *(sign)* port du casque obligatoire; *Typ & Comput* ***hard hyphen*** césure *f* imposée, trait *m* d'union imposé; ***hard labour*** *(UNCOUNT)* travaux *mpl* forcés; ***hard landing*** *(by spacecraft)* atterrissage *m* avec impact; *Fig (during economic crisis)* atterrissage *m* brutal; *Metal* ***hard lead*** plomb *m* aigre; *Pol* ***the hard left*** l'extrême gauche; ***hard line*** ligne *f* de conduite dure; **to take a h. line on sb/sth** adopter une ligne de conduite dure avec qn/sur qch; ***hard liquor*** spiritueux *mpl*; *Fin* ***hard loan*** prêt *m* aux conditions du marché; ***hard money*** argent *m* liquide; *Press* ***hard news*** nouvelles *fpl* sûres *ou* vérifiées; *Vet* ***hard pad*** coussinet *m* dur; *Typ & Comput* ***hard page break*** fin *f* de page obligatoire; *Anat* ***hard palate*** voûte *f* du palais, palais *m* dur; ***hard porn*** porno *m* hard, hard *m inv*; *Comput* ***hard reset*** réinitialisation *f* totale de la machine; *Typ & Comput* ***hard return*** saut *m* de ligne manuel; *Pol* ***the hard right*** l'extrême droit; *Mus* ***hard rock*** hard rock *m inv*, hard *m inv*; *esp Am Culin* ***hard sauce*** = sauce au beurre, au sucre et au brandy ou au rhum servie avec le pudding; ***hard science*** science *f* dure; ***hard sell*** vente *f* agressive; **to give sth the h. sell** promouvoir qch de façon agressive; **the salesman gave us the h. sell** le vendeur a essayé de nous forcer la main; *Aut* ***hard shoulder*** bande *f* d'arrêt d'urgence; ***hard space*** espace *m* insécable; *Econ* ***hard terms*** conditions *fpl* du marché; ***hard water*** eau *f* calcaire *ou* dure

---

hard-and-fast ADJ *(rule)* strict, absolu; *(information)* correct, vrai; **there's no h. rule about it** il n'existe pas de règle absolue là-dessus

hardback ['hɑːdbæk] N *(book)* livre *m* cartonné; **available in h.** disponible en version cartonnée

ADJ cartonné

hard-bitten [-'bɪtən] ADJ *Fam* endurci□

hardboard ['hɑːdbɔːd] N Isorel® *m*; **a sheet of h.** un panneau dur

hardbody ['hɑːdbɒdɪ] *(pl* **hardbodies***)* N *Fam* = personne musclée

hard-boiled ADJ **1** *Culin (egg)* dur **2** *Fam (person)* dur à cuire

hard-core ADJ *(belief in political system)* dur; *(believer)* endurci; *(support)* ferme; *(pornography, music)* hard *(inv)*

▸▸ *Mktg* ***hard-core loyal*** fidèle *mf* absolu(e); *Mktg* ***hard-core loyalty*** fidélité *f* absolue

hardcover ['hɑːdˌkʌvə(r)] N *(book)* livre *m* cartonné; **available in h.** disponible en version cartonnée

ADJ cartonné

hard-earned [-'ɜːnd] ADJ *(money)* durement gagné; *(victory)* durement *ou* difficilement remporté; *(reputation)* durement acquis; *(holiday, reward)* bien mérité

harden ['hɑːdən] VT *(person ▸ physically, emotionally)* endurcir; *(steel)* tremper; *Ling (consonant)* durcir; *Med (arteries)* durcir, scléroser; **to h. oneself to sth** s'endurcir à qch; **to h. one's heart** endurcir son cœur; **she hardened her heart against him** elle lui a fermé son cœur

VI **1** *(snow, skin, steel)* durcir; *(concrete, mortar)* prendre; *Med (arteries)* durcir, se scléroser; *(person ▸ emotionally)* s'endurcir, se durcir; *(▸ physically)* s'endurcir; *(attitude)* se durcir **2** *Fin (prices, market)* s'affermir

▸ **harden off** VT SEP *(plant)* mettre en jauge, habituer à des conditions plus dures

VI *(plant)* s'habituer à des conditions plus dures

▸ **harden up** VT SEP *(toughen ▸ person)* endurcir

VI *Fin (shares)* se raffermir

hardened ['hɑːdənd] ADJ *(snow, skin, substance)* durci; *(steel)* trempé, durci; *Med (arteries)* sclérosé; **to become h. to sth** se blinder contre qch; **a h. criminal** un criminel endurci *ou* invétéré

hardener ['hɑːdənə(r)] N *(for glue, fingernails)* durcisseur *m*

hardening ['hɑːdənɪŋ] N *(of snow, skin, aititudes)* durcissement *m*; *(of steel)* trempe *f*; *(of person ▸ physical)* endurcissement *m*; *(▸ emotional)* durcissement *m*; *Fin (of prices)* affermissement *m*

▸▸ *Med* ***hardening of the arteries*** durcissement *m ou* sclérose *f* des artères

hard-faced [-'feɪst] ADJ au visage dur

hard-fought [-'fɔːt] ADJ *(game, battle)* rudement disputé

hard-hat ADJ *Am* = caractéristique des attitudes conservatrices des ouvriers du bâtiment

hard-headed [-'hedɪd] ADJ **1** *(tough, shrewd ▸ person)* à la tête froide; *(▸ realism)* froid, brut; *(▸ bargaining)* dur; *(▸ decision)* froid **2** *Am (stubborn ▸ person)* qui a la tête dure; *(▸ attitude)* entêté

hard-hearted [-'hɑːtɪd] ADJ *(person)* insensible, dur, au cœur de pierre; *(attitude)* dur; **to be h. towards sb** être dur avec *ou* envers qn

hard-hit ADJ gravement atteint *ou* touché; **one particularly h. village** un village touché de façon particulièrement dure

hard-hitting [-'hɪtɪŋ] ADJ **1** *(verbal attack)* rude; *(speech, report)* implacable, sans indulgence; **the speech was a h. attack on this policy** le discours était une attaque directe contre cette politique **2** *(boxer)* qui frappe dur

hardiness ['hɑːdɪnɪs] N *(of person)* résistance *f*, robustesse *f*; *(of plant, tree)* résistance *f*

hard-line ADJ *(policy, doctrine)* dur; *(politician)* intransigeant, endurci

hardliner [ˌhɑːd'laɪnə(r)] N partisan(e) *m,f* de la manière forte

hardly ['hɑːdlɪ] ADV **1** *(barely)* à peine, ne... guère; **he can h. read** il sait à peine *ou* tout juste lire; **I have h. started** je viens à peine *ou* tout juste de commencer; **I h. get a minute to myself these days** c'est tout juste si j'ai une minute à moi ces jours-ci; **I can h. believe it** j'ai du mal à le croire; **h. anyone/anywhere/anything** presque personne/nulle part/rien; **I h. ever see you these days** je ne te vois presque jamais ces temps-ci; **you've h. touched your food** tu n'as presque rien mangé; **I can h. wait to see her** je suis très impatient de la voir; *Ironic* **I can h. wait!** j'en frémis d'avance!; **she h. ever goes out** elle ne sort presque jamais; **need h. say that...** ai-je besoin de vous dire que...? + *indicative*, je n'ai pas besoin de vous dire que... + *indicative* **2** *(expressing negative opinion)* **this is h. the time to be selling your house** ce n'est vraiment pas le moment de vendre votre maison; **it's h. surprising that she left him** ce n'est pas surprenant qu'elle l'ait quitté, il n'est guère surprenant qu'elle l'ait quitté; **h.!** *(not in the slightest)* bien au contraire!, loin de là!; **she's h. likely to agree** elle ne risque pas d'accepter

hardness ['hɑːdnɪs] N **1** *(of snow, skin, water, substance)* dureté *f*; *(of steel)* trempe *f*, dureté *f*

2 *(difficulty)* difficulté *f*

3 *(severeness ▸ of personality)* dureté *f*; *(▸ of heart)* dureté *f*, froideur *f*

4 *(strenuousness)* difficulté *f*

5 *Fin (of prices)* affermissement *m*

▸▸ *Med* ***hardness of hearing*** surdité *f* partielle

hard-nosed [-'nəʊzd] ADJ *Fam (tough, shrewd ▸ person)* à la tête froide□; *(▸ realism)* froid□, brut□; *(▸ bargaining)* dur□; *(▸ decision)* froid□

hard-on N *Vulg* **to have a h.** bander; **to get a h.** se mettre à bander

hard-packed [-'pækt] ADJ *(snow, soil)* tassé

hard-pressed [-'prest], **hard-pushed** [-'pʊʃt] ADJ **to be h. for money/ideas/suggestions** être à court d'argent/d'idées/de suggestions; **to be h. for time** manquer de temps; **to be h. to do sth** avoir du mal à faire qch

hard-sectored [-'sektəd] ADJ *Comput (disk)* à secteurs pré-définis

hardship ['hɑːdʃɪp] N épreuves *fpl*; **to suffer great h.** *or* **hardships** subir *ou* traverser de rudes épreuves; **further h. is in store** d'autres épreuves nous attendent

▸▸ ***hardship allowance*** *(for student)* = aide accordée à un étudiant en cas de graves problèmes financiers; ***hardship fund*** = bourse accordée aux étudiants en difficulté financière

hardtack ['hɑːdtæk] N *Naut* biscuit *m* de marin

hardtop ['hɑːdtɒp] N **1** *Aut (of car)* hard-top *m*; *(car)* voiture *f* à hard-top **2** *Fam Cin* cinéma *m (bâtiment)*

hard-up ADJ *Fam* fauché, raide, sans un rond

hardware ['hɑːdweə(r)] N *(UNCOUNT)* **1** *(ironmongery)* quincaillerie *f*

2 *Comput* matériel *m*, hardware *m*; **h. problem** problème *m* de matériel

3 *Mil* matériel *m* de guerre, armement *m*

4 *Fam (guns)* armes□ *fpl*

COMP *Comput (company, manufacturer)* de matériel informatique; *(problem)* de matériel *ou* hardware

▸▸ ***hardware dealer*** quincaillier(ère) *m,f*; ***hardware shop, hardware store*** quincaillerie *f*

hardwearing [ˌhɑːd'weərɪŋ] ADJ robuste, résistant

hard-wired [-'waɪəd] ADJ **1** *Comput* câblé **2** *Fig* **to be h. to do sth** être programmé pour faire qch

hard-won [-'wʌn] ADJ *(victory, trophy, independence)* durement gagné; *(reputation)* durement acquis

hardwood ['hɑːdwʊd] N *(wood)* bois *m* dur; *(tree)* arbre *m* à feuilles caduques

COMP *(floor)* en bois dur

hardworking [ˌhɑːd'wɜːkɪŋ] ADJ *(person)* travailleur; *(engine, machine, printer)* robuste

hardy ['hɑːdɪ] *(compar* **hardier**, *superl* **hardiest***)* ADJ **1** *(strong ▸ person, animal)* robuste, résistant; *(▸ plant)* résistant **2** *(intrepid ▸ explorer, pioneer)* intrépide, courageux

▸▸ *Bot* ***hardy annual*** plante *f* annuelle; *Bot* ***hardy perennial*** plante *f* vivace; *Fig* serpent *m* de mer

hare [heə(r)] *(pl* **inv** *or* **hares***)* N **1** *Culin & Zool* lièvre *m*; *Br Fig* **to raise** *or* **to start a h.** mettre une question sur le tapis; *Fig* **to run with the hares and hunt with the hounds** jouer double jeu **2** *Sport (at dog race)* lièvre *m* **3** *Br (game)* **h. and hounds** jeu *m* de piste

VI *Fam* **to h. across/down/out** traverser/descendre/sortir à toutes jambes; **she came haring down the stairs** elle a dévalé les escaliers à fond de train

▸▸ *Sport* ***hare coursing*** chasse *f* à courre au lièvre

harebell ['heəbel] N *Bot* campanule *f* à feuilles rondes

harebrained ['heəbreɪnd] ADJ *(reckless, mad ▸ person)* écervelé; *(▸ scheme)* insensé, fou (folle)

harelip [ˌheə'lɪp] N *Med* bec-de-lièvre *m*

harem [*Br* hɑː'riːm, *Am* 'hærəm] N *also Fig* harem *m*

▸▸ ***harem pants*** pantalon *m* bouffant

haricot (bean) ['hærɪkəʊ-] N *Bot & Culin* haricot *m* blanc

hark [hɑːk] VI *Literary* prêter l'oreille, ouïr; **h., I hear voices!** écoutez *ou* chut, j'entends des voix!; *Br Fam* **h. at him!** écoutez-le donc!

▸ **hark back to** VT INSEP *(recall)* revenir à; **to h. back to sth** revenir (tout le temps) à qch; **the style harks back to the 1940s** le style rappelle celui des années 40

Harlequin ['hɑːlɪkwɪn] PR N Arlequin

• **harlequin** ADJ *(costume)* bigarré; *(dog's coat)* tacheté

harlot ['hɑːlət] N *Arch or Hum* prostituée *f*

harm [hɑːm] N *(physical)* mal *m*; *(psychological)* tort *m*, mal *m*; **to do sb h.** faire du mal à qn; **I hope Ed won't come to (any) h.** j'espère qu'il n'arrivera rien à Ed; **a bath wouldn't do him any h.** un bain ne lui ferait pas de mal; **they didn't mean any h.** ils ne voulaient pas (faire) de mal; **I know you didn't mean any h. when you said it** je sais que tu ne l'as pas dit méchamment; **the incident did a great deal of h. to his reputation** cet incident a beaucoup nui à sa réputation; **no h. done** il n'y a pas de mal; **there's no h. in trying** il n'y a pas de mal à essayer, on ne perd rien à essayer; **I see no h. in their going** je ne vois pas d'inconvénient à ce qu'ils y aillent; **what h. is there in it?** qu'est-ce qu'il y a de mal (à cela)?; **no h. will come of it** ça n'est pas grave; **to do more h. than good** faire plus de mal que de bien; **out of h.'s way** *(person)* en sûreté, en lieu sûr; *(things)* en lieu sûr

VT 1 *(person ▸ physically)* faire du mal à; *(▸ psychologically)* faire du tort à, nuire à; **Kyle wouldn't h. a hair on her head** Kyle ne lui ferait aucun mal; **he wasn't harmed by the experience** ça ne lui a pas fait de mal 2 *(surface)* abîmer, endommager; *(crops)* endommager; *(environment)* nuire à 3 *(cause, interests)* causer du tort à, être préjudiciable à; *(reputation)* salir

harmful ['hɑːmfʊl] ADJ 1 *(person, influence)* nuisible, malfaisant 2 *(chemicals)* nocif; *(effects)* nuisible; **h. to plants** nuisible pour les plantes; **in small doses the drug is not h.** à petites doses, ce médicament n'est pas dangereux

harmfully ['hɑːmfʊlɪ] ADV de façon nuisible

harmfulness ['hɑːmfʊlnɪs] N nature *f* nuisible; *(of chemicals)* nocivité *f*

harmless ['hɑːmlɪs] ADJ 1 *(person)* inoffensif, qui n'est pas méchant; *(animal)* inoffensif 2 *(joke)* sans malice, anodin; *(pastime)* innocent; **it was just a bit of h. fun** c'était pour rire; **h. gossip** propos *mpl* inoffensifs

harmlessly ['hɑːmlɪslɪ] ADV sans faire de mal, sans dommage *ou* dommages

harmonic [hɑː'mɒnɪk] N 1 *Mus (of root)* harmonique *m*; *(on stringed instrument)* harmonique *m*, son *m* flûté 2 *Math & Phys (of wave motion)* harmonique *m*

ADJ harmonique

▸▸ *Phys* ***harmonic motion*** mouvement *m* sinusoïdal; *Math* ***harmonic progression*** progression *f* harmonique; ***harmonic series*** *Mus* échelle *f* harmonique; *Math & Phys* série *f* harmonique

harmonica [hɑː'mɒnɪkə] N *Mus* harmonica *m*

harmonics [hɑː'mɒnɪks] N 1 *(UNCOUNT) (science)* harmonie *f* 2 *Mus (sounds)* sons *mpl* harmoniques

harmonious [hɑː'məʊnɪəs] ADJ harmonieux

harmoniously [hɑː'məʊnɪəslɪ] ADV harmonieusement; *(work, live)* en harmonie

harmonium [hɑː'məʊnɪəm] N *Mus* harmonium *m*

harmonization, -isation [ˌhɑːmənaɪ'zeɪʃən] N harmonisation *f*

harmonize, -ise ['hɑːmənaɪz] VT 1 *Mus (instrument, melody)* harmoniser 2 *(colours)* harmoniser, assortir 3 *(views, statements)* harmoniser, faire concorder; *(people)* concilier, amener à un accord

VI 1 *Mus (sing in harmony)* chanter en harmonie; *(be harmonious)* être harmonieux *ou* en harmonie; *(write harmony)* harmoniser, faire des harmonies 2 *(colours)* aller (bien) ensemble, se marier (bien); **choose colours that h. with the background** choisissez des couleurs qui soient assorties au décor 3 *(sounds)* s'harmoniser; *(temperaments, people, ideas etc)* se mettre en harmonie, s'accorder

harmony ['hɑːmənɪ] (*pl* **harmonies**) N 1 *Mus* harmonie *f*; **to study h.** étudier l'harmonie; **to sing in h.** chanter en harmonie; **a three-part h.** une harmonie en trois parties 2 *(agreement ▸ of colours)* harmonie *f*; *(▸ of temperaments, people, ideas etc)* harmonie *f*, accord *m*; **to live in h. with sb** vivre en harmonie avec qn; **the scene was one of perfect h.** une harmonie parfaite se dégageait de cette scène

harness ['hɑːnɪs] N 1 *(for horse, oxen)* harnais *m*, harnachement *m*

2 *(for parachute, car seat)* harnais *m*

3 *(for child)* harnais *m*

4 *Tex (of loom)* harnais *m*

5 *(idioms)* **to get back in h.** reprendre le collier; **to die in h.** mourir à la peine *ou* au travail *ou* à la tâche; **to work in h. (with sb)** travailler de concert (avec qn)

VT 1 *(horse)* harnacher, mettre le harnais à; *(oxen, dogs)* atteler; **the pony was harnessed to the cart** le poney était attelé à la charrette; *Fig* **to be harnessed to sth** être étroitement lié à qch 2 *(energy, resources)* exploiter, maîtriser

▸▸ ***harness horse*** cheval *m* d'attelage; *Sport* ***harness race*** course *f* attelée; ***harness room*** sellerie *f*

harnessing ['hɑːnɪsɪŋ] N 1 *(of horse)* harnachement *m*; *(of oxen, dogs)* attelage *m* 2 *(of energy, resources)* exploitation *f*

harp [hɑːp] *Mus* N harpe *f*

VI jouer de la harpe

▸ **harp on** *Fam* VI chanter (toujours) le même refrain *ou* la même rengaine; **to h. on about sth** rabâcher qch, revenir sans cesse sur qch□; **to h. on at sb about sth** rebattre les oreilles à qn au sujet de qch

VT INSEP **to h. on sth** revenir sans cesse sur qch□, rabâcher qch

harpist ['hɑːpɪst] N harpiste *mf*

harpoon [hɑː'puːn] N harpon *m*

VT harponner

harpsichord ['hɑːpsɪkɔːd] N *Mus* clavecin *m*

harpsichordist ['hɑːpsɪˌkɔːdɪst] N *Mus* claveciniste *mf*

harpy ['hɑːpɪ] (*pl* **harpies**) N *Fig* harpie *f*, mégère *f*

• **Harpy** N *Myth* Harpye *f*, Harpie *f*; **the Harpies** les Harpyes *fpl ou* Harpies *fpl*

▸▸ *Orn* ***harpy eagle*** harpie *f*

harridan ['hærɪdən] N harpie *f*, vieille sorcière *f*

harrier ['hærɪə(r)] N 1 *(dog)* harrier *m* 2 *Sport (runner)* coureur *m* (de cross); **Plymouth Harriers** l'équipe d'athlétisme de Plymouth 3 *Orn* busard *m*

harrow ['hærəʊ] N *Agr* herse *f*

VT 1 *Agr* labourer à la herse 2 *Fig (distress)* torturer, déchirer le cœur à

harrowed ['hærəʊd] ADJ *Fig (appearance)* meurtri

harrowing ['hærəʊɪŋ] ADJ *(story)* terrible; *(cry)* déchirant; *(experience)* pénible, traumatisant; **the report makes h. reading** le rapport raconte des faits pénibles à lire

Harry ['hærɪ] N *Br Fam Old-fashioned* **to play old H. with sb** en faire voir des vertes et des pas mûres à qn; **to play old H. with sb's health** ruiner la santé de qn□

harry ['hærɪ] (*pt & pp* **harried**) VT 1 *(harass ▸ person)* harceler, tourmenter; **he was harried by creditors** il était harcelé par ses créanciers 2 *(pillage ▸ village)* dévaster, mettre à sac 3 *Mil (enemy, troops)* harceler

harsh [hɑːʃ] ADJ 1 *(cruel, severe ▸ person)* dur, sévère, cruel; *(▸ punishment, treatment)* dur, sévère; *(▸ fate)* cruel; *(▸ criticism, judgement, words)* dur, sévère; **to be h. with sb** être dur envers *ou* avec qn 2 *(conditions, weather, climate)* rude, rigoureux 3 *(bitter ▸ struggle)* âpre, acharné 4 *(cry, voice)* criard, strident; *(tone)* dur 5 *(colour, contrast)* choquant; *(light)* cru 6 *(bleak ▸ landscape, desert)* dur, austère

harshly ['hɑːʃlɪ] ADV 1 *(treat, punish)* sévèrement, avec rigueur 2 *(answer, speak)* avec rudesse *ou* dureté; *(judge)* sévèrement, durement; **don't speak so h. of him** ne parlez pas de lui si durement 3 *(cry, shout)* d'un ton strident

harshness ['hɑːʃnɪs] N 1 *(of person, judgment)* dureté *f*, sévérité *f*; *(of punishment, treatment)* sévérité *f*; *(of statement, words, tone)* dureté *f*

2 *(of conditions, weather, climate)* rigueur *f*, rudesse *f*

3 *(of cry, voice)* discordance *f*

4 *(of light)* dureté *f*; *(of contrast)* caractère *m* choquant

hart [hɑːt] (*pl* **inv** *or* **harts**) N *Zool* cerf *m*

harum-scarum [ˌheərəm'skeərəm] *Fam* N casse-cou *mf inv*

ADJ *(wild, reckless)* casse-cou *(inv)*

ADV comme un fou (une folle)□

harvest ['hɑːvɪst] N 1 *(gathering ▸ of cereal, crops)* moisson *f*; *(▸ of fruit, mushrooms)* récolte *f*, cueillette *f*; *(▸ of grapes)* vendange *f*, vendanges *fpl*

2 *(yield)* récolte *f*; **a good/poor h.** une bonne/mauvaise récolte

3 *(time of year)* (temps *m ou* époque *f* de la) moisson; **at h. (time)** à l'époque de la moisson

4 *Fig (from experience, research)* moisson *f*; **it yielded a rich h. of information** on a récolté beaucoup d'informations; **a bitter h.** une moisson amère

VT 1 *Agr (cereal, crops)* moissonner; *(fruit, mushrooms)* cueillir, récolter; *(grapes)* vendanger 2 *Fig (benefits)* moissonner; *(consequences)* récolter 3 *Med (organ)* prélever

VI *(for cereal, crops)* moissonner, faire la moisson; *(for fruit)* faire les récoltes; *(for grapes)* vendanger

▸▸ *Br* ***harvest festival*** = action de grâce après la rentrée des récoltes; *Br* ***harvest home*** *(festival)* fête *f* de la moisson; *(harvesting)* moisson *f*; *Entom* ***harvest mite*** aoûtat *m*; ***harvest moon*** pleine lune *f* (de l'équinoxe d'automne); *Zool* ***harvest mouse*** rat *m* des moissons; *Entom* ***harvest spider*** faucheux *m*; *Am & Scot* ***Harvest Thanksgiving*** = action de grâce après la rentrée des récoltes; ***harvest time*** période *f* de la moisson; **at h. time** à la moisson

harvester ['hɑːvɪstə(r)] N 1 *(machine)* moissonneuse *f* 2 *(person)* moissonneur(euse) *m,f*

harvesting ['hɑːvɪstɪŋ] N *(UNCOUNT)* moisson *f*, moissons *fpl*

ADJ *(season)* des moissons

has-been ['hæzbiːn] N *Fam* has been *mf inv*

hash [hæʃ] N 1 *Br Fam (muddle, mix-up)* pagaille *f*, embrouillamini *m*; *(mess, botch)* gâchis□ *m*; **to make a h. of sth** bousiller qch, ficher qch en l'air; **I made a real h. of the interview** j'ai complètement foiré l'entretien

2 *Culin* hachis *m*

3 *Fam (marijuana)* hasch *m*

4 *(symbol)* dièse *m*

5 *Br Fam (idiom)* **to fix** *or* **to settle sb's h.** *(in revenge, punishment)* régler son compte à qn; *(reduce to silence)* clouer le bec à qn

VT *Culin* hacher

▸▸ *Culin* ***hash browns*** = pommes de terre rapées et sautées (présentées parfois sous forme de galette); *Fam* ***hash head*** = personne qui fume beaucoup de cannabis; *Am Fam* ***hash house*** *(restaurant)* gargote□ *f*; ***hash mark, hash sign*** *(symbol)* dièse *m*

▸ **hash over** VT SEP *esp Am Fam (discuss)* discuter□

▸ **hash up** VT SEP 1 *Br Fam (mess up)* bâcler, bousiller; **I'm afraid I completely hashed up the interview** j'ai bien peur d'avoir complètement foiré l'entretien 2 *Culin* hacher

hashed index [hæʃd-] N *Comput* index *m* de totalisation

hashish ['hæʃiːʃ] N haschisch *m*, hachisch *m*

hasn't ['hæzənt] = **has not**

hasp [hɑːsp] N *(for door)* loquet *m*, loqueteau *m*, moraillon *m*; *(for jewellery, lid, clothing, book)* fermoir *m*

VT *(door)* fermer au loquet; *(lid)* fermer; *(with padlock)* cadenasser

hassle [ˈhæsəl] *Fam* N **1** *(trouble, inconvenience)* embêtements *mpl*, emmerdements *mpl*; **it's too much h.** c'est trop galère; **it won't be any h.** ça ne posera pas de problèmes; **finding their house was quite a h.** trouver leur maison n'a pas été de la tarte, on a eu un mal fou à trouver leur maison; **all the h. of filling out the form** tous les embêtements pour remplir le formulaire **2** *(quarrel)* dispute *f*, chamaillerie *f*; **there was a big h. over who should drive** il y a eu une grosse dispute *ou* bagarre pour savoir qui allait conduire

VT *(annoy, nag)* embêter, harceler; **don't h. me about it** ne m'embête pas avec ça; **he keeps hassling me for money** il n'arrête pas de m'embêter pour que je lui donne de l'argent

VI *(argue)* se quereller, se chamailler

hassock [ˈhæsək] N **1** *Rel* coussin *m* d'agenouilloir **2** *(of grass)* touffe *f* d'herbe

haste [heɪst] N *(speed)* hâte *f*; *(rush)* précipitation *f*; **to do sth in h.** faire qch à la hâte, se dépêcher de faire qch; **to make h.** se hâter, se dépêcher; **in my h., I forgot my hat** dans ma hâte, j'ai oublié mon chapeau; *Prov* **more h. less speed** hâtez-vous lentement

hasten [ˈheɪsən] VT **1** *(speed up ▸ event, decline)* précipiter, hâter; **the accident hastened his death** l'accident précipita *ou* accéléra sa mort **2** *(urge on ▸ person)* presser; **we were hastened along a corridor** on nous a entraînés précipitamment dans un couloir **3** *(say quickly)* **she hastened to assure us that all would be well** elle s'empressa de nous assurer que tout irait bien; **it wasn't me, I h. to add** ce n'était pas moi, je vous assure

VI *Literary (verb of movement)* **to h. away/back** partir/revenir à la hâte, se hâter de partir/revenir

hastily [ˈheɪstɪlɪ] ADV **1** *(hurriedly)* précipitamment, avec précipitation, à la hâte **2** *(impetuously, rashly)* hâtivement, sans réfléchir

hastiness [ˈheɪstɪnɪs] N **1** *(speed)* précipitation *f*, hâte *f* **2** *(rashness)* irréflexion *f*

hasty [ˈheɪstɪ] ADJ **1** *(quick, hurried)* précipité, à la hâte; **I sent him a h. note** je lui ai envoyé un billet écrit à la hâte; **she beat a h. retreat** elle a rapidement battu en retraite **2** *(rash)* irréfléchi, hâtif; **a h. decision** une décision prise à la hâte *ou* à la légère; **let's not jump to any h. conclusions** ne concluons pas à la légère *ou* hâtivement **3** *(short-tempered)* vif; **to have a h. temper** s'emporter facilement

▸▸ *Culin* ***hasty pudding*** *Br* semoule *f* au lait; *Am* bouillie *f* de maïs *(servie avec de la mélasse)*

hat [hæt] N **1** *(for wearing)* chapeau *m*; **he always wears a h.** il porte toujours le *ou* un chapeau; *Fam* **keep this under your h.** gardez ceci pour vous, n'en soufflez mot à personne; *Fam* **my h.!** mon œil!; *Fam* **hats off!** chapeaux bas!; **I take my h. off to him!** chapeau! **2** *Fig (role)* rôle *m*, casquette *f*; **I'm wearing three different hats at the moment** je porte trois casquettes différentes *ou* j'ai trois rôles différents en ce moment; **I'm saying that with my lawyer's h. on** je dis ça en ma qualité de juriste **3** *(idioms)* **to hang up one's h.** raccrocher; **to pass the h. round** faire la quête; *Fam* **to talk through one's h.** parler à tort et à travers; *Pol* **to throw one's h. into the ring** se mettre sur les rangs; *Fam* **that's old h.** c'est dépassé

▸▸ ***hat rack*** porte-chapeaux *m inv*; *Br* ***hat trick*** *(three goals)* hat-trick *m*; *(three wins)* trois victoires *fpl* consécutives; *(in cricket)* = mise hors jeu de trois batteurs avec trois balles de suite

hatband [ˈhæt,bænd] N ruban *m* de chapeau

hatbox [ˈhæt,bɒks] N boîte *f* à chapeau

hatch[1] [hætʃ] N **1** *(hatching of egg)* éclosion *f* **2** *(brood)* couvée *f*

VT **1** *(chickens)* faire éclore; *(eggs)* incuber, (faire) couver; *(in fish farming ▸ eggs)* incuber **2** *Fig (plan, plot)* tramer, manigancer

VI *(eggs)* éclore; *(chicks)* sortir de l'œuf

▸**hatch out** VT *(chickens)* faire éclore; *(eggs)* incuber, (faire) couver; *(in fish farming ▸ eggs)* incuber

VI *(eggs)* éclore; *(chicks)* sortir de l'œuf

hatch[2] N **1** *Naut* écoutille *f*; **to batten down the hatches** fermer les descentes; *Fig* se préparer *(pour affronter une crise)*; *Fam* **down the h.!** *(when drinking)* à la vôtre!

2 *(trapdoor)* trappe *f*; *(for inspection, access)* trappe *f*, panneau *m*

3 *(in aircraft, spaceship)* sas *m*

4 *(in dam, dike)* vanne *f (d'écluse)*

5 *(for serving food)* passe-plat *m*

hatch[3] VT *Art* hachurer

hatchback [ˈhætʃ,bæk] N *Aut* **1** *(door)* hayon *m* **2** *(car)* voiture *f* à hayon, cinq portes *f inv*

hatchery [ˈhætʃərɪ] *(pl* **hatcheries***)* N **1** *(for chickens, turkeys)* couvoir *m* **2** *(for fish)* station *f* d'alevinage

hatchet [ˈhætʃɪt] N hachette *f*, hache *f* (à main)

▸▸ *Fam* ***hatchet job*** démolissage *m*; **to do a h. job on sb/sth** démolir qn/qch; *Fam* ***hatchet man*** *(killer)* tueur *m* à gages; *Ind & Pol* = personne dont le rôle est de restructurer une entreprise ou une organisation, le plus souvent à l'aide de mesures impopulaires

hatching[1] [ˈhætʃɪŋ] N **1** *(of eggs)* éclosion *f* **2** *(brood)* couvée *f*

hatching[2] N *(UNCOUNT) Art* hachures *fpl*

hatchway [ˈhætʃ,weɪ] N *Naut* écoutille *f*; *(gen)* trappe *f*

hate [heɪt] VT **1** *(dislike)* détester, avoir horreur de; *(intensely)* haïr, abhorrer; **I h. Sundays** je déteste les dimanches; **I h. getting up early** j'ai horreur de me lever tôt; **she hates having to wear school uniform** elle a horreur d'avoir à porter un uniforme scolaire; **she hates having her hair washed** elle déteste qu'on lui lave les cheveux; **he hates to be contradicted** il ne peut pas souffrir qu'on le contredise; **I h. it when he's in a bad mood** je déteste quand il est de mauvaise humeur; **I h. her for what she has done** je lui en veux vraiment pour ce qu'elle a fait; **I h. myself for letting them down** je m'en veux beaucoup de les avoir laissés tomber **2** *(regret)* **I would h. you to think I was avoiding you** je ne voudrais surtout pas vous donner l'impression que je cherchais à vous éviter; **I h. to mention it, but you still owe me £5** je suis désolé d'avoir à vous le faire remarquer, mais vous me devez toujours 5 livres; **I h. to bother you, but could I use your phone?** je ne voudrais surtout pas vous déranger, mais puis-je utiliser votre téléphone?; *Fam* **I h. to tell you, but I think you've missed your train** je regrette de devoir te le dire mais je pense que tu as raté ton train

N **1** *(emotion)* haine *f*; **I feel nothing but h. for him** je ne ressens que de la haine pour lui **2** *(person hated)* personne *f* que l'on déteste; *(thing hated)* chose *f* que l'on déteste

▸▸ *Am* ***hate crime*** = crime motivé par la haine; ***hate figure*** bête *f* noire; ***hate mail*** lettres *fpl* d'injures

hated [ˈheɪtɪd] ADJ détesté

hateful [ˈheɪtfʊl] ADJ odieux, détestable

hatefully [ˈheɪtfʊlɪ] ADV odieusement, détestablement

hater [ˈheɪtə(r)] N ennemi *m* (**of** de); **to be an animal-h.** détester les animaux

hatless [ˈhætlɪs] ADJ tête nue, sans chapeau

hatpeg [ˈhætpeg] N patère *f*

hatpin [ˈhæt,pɪn] N épingle *f* à chapeau

hatred [ˈheɪtrɪd] N haine *f*; **to feel h. for sb** avoir de la haine pour qn, haïr qn

hatshop [ˈhætʃɒp] N *(for men)* chapellerie *f*; *(for women)* boutique *f* de modiste

hatstand [ˈhætstænd] N portemanteau *m*

hatter [ˈhætə(r)] N chapelier(ère) *m,f*

haughtily [ˈhɔːtɪlɪ] ADV avec arrogance, de manière hautaine

haughtiness [ˈhɔːtɪnɪs] N arrogance *f*, caractère *m* hautain

haughty [ˈhɔːtɪ] *(compar* **haughtier**, *superl* **haughtiest***)* ADJ hautain, arrogant

haul [hɔːl] VT **1** *(pull)* tirer, traîner; *(tow)* tirer, remorquer; **they hauled the boat out of the water** ils ont tiré le bateau hors de l'eau; **they were hauled in front of** *or* **before a judge** on les traîna devant un tribunal; *Fig* **to h. sb over the coals** passer un savon à qn

2 *(transport)* transporter; *(by truck)* camionner transporter

3 *(move with effort)* hisser; **he hauled himself out of bed** il s'est péniblement sorti du lit

4 *Am very Fam (idiom)* **to h. ass** se magner

VI **1** *(pull)* tirer; **they hauled on the cable** ils ont tiré sur le câble **2** *Naut (boat)* lofer; **to h. alongside** accoster

N **1** *(catch, takings ▸ of fisherman, customs)* prise *f*, coup *m* de filet; *(▸ of robbers)* butin *m*; **the thieves have made a good h.** les voleurs ont rapporté un beau butin; *Fam* **you've got a good h.!** *(of presents)* c'est un joli tas de cadeaux que tu viens de recevoir!

2 *(pull)* **to give a h. on a rope/fishing net** tirer sur une corde/un filet de pêche

3 *(distance)* parcours *m*, trajet *m*; **it was a long h. from Madrid to Paris** la route fut longue de Madrid à Paris; **long-/short-h. flights** vols *mpl* long courrier/moyen courrier

4 *(in time)* **training to be a doctor is a long h.** les études de médecine sont très longues

▸**haul down** VT SEP **1** *(pull down)* descendre, faire descendre; **his parents had to h. him down from the tree** ses parents ont dû le faire descendre de l'arbre **2** *(lower ▸ flag, sail)* amener

▸**haul in** VT SEP *(catch, net, rope)* tirer, amener; *Fam (suspects, people for questioning)* emmener; **the ship was hauled in for repairs** le bateau a été mis en cale pour réparations; *Fam* **Tom was hauled in on a drink-driving charge** Tom a été épinglé pour conduite en état d'ivresse

▸**haul up** VT SEP **1** *(hoist)* monter; *Naut (flag)* hisser; **to h. up a boat** *(on ship)* rentrer une embarcation; *(on the beach)* haler un bateau à sec **2** *(call to account)* **to h. sb up (for sth)** demander des comptes à qn (de qch); **to be hauled up before the court** être traîné devant les tribunaux; **he was hauled up before the headmaster** il a dû se présenter devant le principal

haulage [ˈhɔːlɪdʒ] N *(UNCOUNT)* **1** *(as business)* transports *mpl*, transport *m* (routier); **she's in the h. business** elle travaille dans le transport routier **2** *(act)* transport *m* **3** *(cost)* (frais *mpl* de) transport *m*

COMP *(company)* de transport routier, de transports routiers

▸▸ ***haulage contractor*** entrepreneur *m* de transports routiers

haulier [ˈhɔːlɪə(r)], *Am* **hauler** [ˈhɔːlə(r)] N **1** *(business)* entreprise *f* de transports routiers **2** *(owner)* entrepreneur *m* de transports routiers **3** *(driver)* routier *m*, camionneur *m*

hauling [ˈhɔːlɪŋ] N *Naut* halage *m*

▸▸ ***hauling rope*** câble *m* de halage

haunch [hɔːntʃ] N **1** *Culin (of venison)* cuissot *m*; *(of beef)* quartier *m* **2** *(of human)* hanche *f*; **to squat down on one's haunches** s'accroupir

• **haunches** NPL *(of animal)* arrière-train *m*, derrière *m*

haunt [hɔːnt] VT **1** *(of ghost, spirit)* hanter **2** *(of problems)* hanter, tourmenter; **the memory still haunts me** le souvenir me hante encore; **his past continues to h. him** son passé ne cesse de le poursuivre *ou* hanter; **these problems have returned to h. us** ces problèmes nous minent une fois de plus **3** *Fam (frequent ▸ bar)* hanter, fréquenter; *(▸ streets)* hanter, traîner dans

N **1** *(place)* lieu *m* que l'on fréquente beaucoup, lieu *m* de prédilection; **it's one of his favourite haunts** c'est un des endroits qu'il préfère; **we couldn't find her in any of her usual haunts** nous ne l'avons pas trouvée dans les endroits qu'elle fréquente d'habitude **2** *(refuge ▸ for animals, criminals)* repaire *m*

haunted [ˈhɔːntɪd] ADJ **1** *(house, castle)* hanté **2** *(look)* hagard, égaré

haunting [ˈhɔːntɪŋ] ADJ *(memory, sound)* obsédant; *(tune)* qui vous trotte dans la tête; **she has a h. beauty** elle est d'une beauté obsédante

Havana [həˈvænə] **N** *Geog (city)* la Havane
N *(cigar, tobacco)* havane *m*
COMP *(cigar, tobacco)* de Havane

HAVE [hæv]

V AUX
- avoir **1**
- être **1**
- *usage elliptique* **2**
- *dans les question tags* **3**

VT
- avoir **A1–3, B2–5, C1, 2, F1, 4, 8, 9**
- posséder **A1**
- disposer de **A2**
- faire **B1**
- prendre **B3, F1**
- passer **B4**
- recevoir **C1, 2**
- vouloir **C3, F6**
- tenir **D1**
- faire faire **E2, 3**
- mettre **F2**
- maintenir **F5**
- dire **F5**
- devoir **G1, 2**
- concerner **G3**

NPL
- riches

Les formes négatives, **haven't** et **hasn't**, s'écrivent **have not** and **has not** dans un style plus soutenu.

Most French verbs will conjugate with **avoir** to form the perfect tense. However, all reflexive verbs and many intransitive verbs – mainly of motion – will conjugate with **être**.

(*3rd pers sing pres* **has** [hæz], *pt & pp* **had** [hæd]) **V AUX 1** *(used to form perfect tenses)* avoir, être; **to h. finished** avoir fini; **to h. left** être parti; **to h. sat down** s'être assis; **to h. been/had** avoir été/eu; **has she slept?** a-t-elle dormi?; **h. they arrived?** sont-ils arrivés?; **he has been ill** il a été malade; **when you've calmed down** quand vous vous serez calmé; **I will h. forgotten by next week** j'aurai oublié d'ici la semaine prochaine; **the children will h. gone to bed by the time we arrive** les enfants seront couchés quand nous arriverons; **you were silly not to h. accepted** tu es bête de ne pas avoir accepté; **after** *or* **when you h. finished, you may leave** quand vous aurez fini, vous pourrez partir; **she was ashamed of having lied** elle avait honte d'avoir menti; **she felt she couldn't change her mind, having already agreed to go** elle sentait qu'elle ne pouvait pas changer d'avis, étant donné qu'elle avait dit être d'accord pour y aller; **I h. been thinking** j'ai réfléchi; **he has been working here for two months** il travaille ici depuis deux mois, il y a deux mois qu'il travaille ici; **I h. known her for three years/since childhood** je la connais depuis trois ans/depuis mon enfance; **I had known her for years** cela faisait des années que je la connaissais, je la connaissais depuis des années; **she claimed she hadn't heard the news** elle a prétendu ne pas avoir entendu la nouvelle; **I had already gone to bed when he arrived** j'étais déjà couché quand il est arrivé; **we had gone to bed early** nous nous étions couchés de bonne heure; **when he had given his speech, I left** une fois qu'il eut terminé son discours, je partis; **had I known, I wouldn't h. insisted** si j'avais su, je n'aurais pas insisté; **if I had known, I wouldn't h. said anything** si j'avais su, je n'aurais rien dit; **they would h. been happy if it hadn't been for the war** ils auraient vécu heureux si la guerre n'était pas survenue; **why don't you just leave him and h. done with it?** pourquoi donc est-ce que vous ne le quittez pas, pour en finir?; *Fam* **he's had it** *(is in trouble)* il est fichu *ou* foutu; *(is worn out)* il est à bout; *Fam* **I've had it with all your complaining!** j'en ai jusque-là de tes jérémiades!; *Fam* **I've had it up to here with him** j'en ai jusque-là de ce type-là; *Fam* **the car has just about had it** la voiture va bientôt rendre l'âme; *Fam* **this plant has had it** cette plante est fichue

2 *(elliptical uses)* **h. you ever had the measles? – yes, I h./no, I haven't** avez-vous eu la rougeole? – oui/non; **she hasn't finished – yes, she has!** elle n'a pas fini – (mais) si!; **you've forgotten his birthday – no, I haven't!** tu as oublié son anniversaire – mais non!; **h. you ever considered going into politics? if you h..../if you haven't...** avez-vous déjà envisagé de rentrer dans la vie politique? si oui.../si non...; **you've forgotten your gloves – so I h.!** vous avez oublié vos gants – en effet! *ou* tiens, c'est vrai!

3 *(in tag questions)* **you've read 'Hamlet', haven't you?** vous avez lu 'Hamlet', n'est-ce pas?; **he hasn't arrived, has he?** il n'est pas arrivé, si?; **so she's got a new job, has she?** elle a changé de travail alors?

VT A. 1 *(be in possession of, own)* avoir, posséder; **do you h.** *or* **h. you got a car?** avez-vous une voiture?; **they h. (got) a lot of friends/money** ils ont beaucoup d'amis/d'argent; **they don't h.** *or* **they haven't got any more** ils n'en ont plus; **she shares everything she has (got) with them** elle partage tout ce qu'elle a avec eux; **he has (got) £10 left** il lui reste 10 livres; **we h. (got) six of them left** il nous en reste six; **do you h.** *or* **h. you got any children? if you h....** avez-vous des enfants? si vous en avez *ou* si oui...; **they h. (got) a 50 percent interest in the business** ils ont *ou* détiennent 50 pour cent des intérêts dans l'affaire; **I h. (got) a lot of work to finish** j'ai beaucoup de travail à finir; **do we h.** *or* **h. we got any milk in the house?** est-ce qu'on a du lait *ou* est-ce qu'il y a du lait à la maison?; **she has (got) a baker's shop/bookshop** elle tient une boulangerie/librairie; **do you h.** *or* **h. you got the time?** avez-vous l'heure?; **he doesn't h.** *or* **hasn't got a job** il n'a pas de travail, il est sans travail; **we h. (got) a deadline to meet** nous avons un délai à respecter; **I've got it!** ça y est, j'ai trouvé *ou* j'y suis!; **paper, envelopes and what h. you** du papier, des enveloppes et je ne sais quoi encore; *Prov* **you can't h. your cake and eat it** on ne peut pas avoir le beurre et l'argent du beurre; *Fam* **give it all you h.** *or* **all you've got!** mets-y le paquet!

2 *(enjoy the use of)* avoir, disposer de; **we had a couple of hours to do our errands** nous disposions de *ou* nous avions quelques heures pour faire nos courses; **I don't h. time** *or* **I haven't got time to stop for lunch** je n'ai pas le temps de m'arrêter pour déjeuner; **he has (got) a month to finish** il a un mois pour finir; **he hasn't (got) long to live** il ne lui reste pas longtemps à vivre; **do you h.** *or* **h. you (got) a minute (to spare)?** tu as une minute?; **she had the house to herself** elle avait la maison pour elle toute seule; **such questions h. an important place in our lives** ce genre de questions occupe une place importante dans notre vie; **he has (got) nothing to do/to read** il n'a rien à faire/à lire

3 *(possess as quality or attribute)* avoir; **she has (got) red hair** elle a les cheveux roux, elle est rousse; **you h. (got) beautiful eyes** tu as de beaux yeux; **the ticket has (got) a name on it** il y a un nom sur le billet; **to h. good taste** avoir bon goût; **to h. a bad temper** avoir mauvais caractère; **she has (got) a reputation for being difficult** elle a la réputation d'être difficile; **the house has (got) a beautiful view of the mountains** de la maison, on a une belle vue sur les montagnes; **she has (got) what it takes** *or* **she has it in her to succeed** elle a ce qu'il faut pour réussir; **you've never had it so good!** vous n'avez jamais eu la vie si belle!; *Fam* **he really has it bad for Emma** il a complètement craqué pour Emma

4 *(possess knowledge or understanding of)* **do you h.** *or* **h. you got any experience of teaching?** avez-vous déjà enseigné?; **she has (got) a clear sense of what matters** elle sait très bien ce qui est important; **he has some Greek and Latin** il connaît un peu le grec et le latin; **I h. a little Spanish** je parle un peu espagnol

B. 1 *(indicating experience of a specified situation)* **to h. a dream/nightmare** faire un rêve/cauchemar; **I h. no regrets** je n'ai aucun regret *ou* pas de regrets; **I didn't h. any trouble in finding it** je n'ai eu aucune peine à le trouver; **we h. (got) nothing** *or* **we don't h. anything against dogs** on n'a rien contre les chiens; **I've had my appendix out** je me suis fait opérer de l'appendicite; **he had all his money stolen** il s'est fait voler *ou* on lui a volé tout son argent; **I love having my back rubbed** j'adore qu'on me frotte le dos; **they had some strange things happen to them** il leur est arrivé de drôles de choses

2 *(be infected with, suffer from)* avoir; **to h. a cold** avoir un rhume, être enrhumé; **do you h.** *or* **h. you got a headache?** avez-vous mal à la tête?; **he has (got) problems with his back** il a des problèmes de dos

3 *(perform, take part in* ▸ *bath, lesson)* prendre; *(*▸ *meeting)* avoir; **we had our first argument last night** nous nous sommes disputés hier soir pour la première fois; **to h. a stroll** se promener, faire un tour; **I want to h. a think about it** je veux y réfléchir; **to h. a party** *(organize)* organiser une fête; *(celebrate)* faire la fête; **I'll h. no part in it** je refuse de m'en mêler

4 *(pass, spend)* passer, avoir; **I had a horrible day at work** j'ai passé une journée atroce au travail; **h. a nice day!** bonne journée!; **to h. a good time** s'amuser; **did you h. a good time?** c'était bien?, tu t'es bien amusé?; **a good time was had by all** tout le monde s'est bien amusé; **she's had a hard time of it lately** elle vient de traverser une mauvaise passe

5 *(exhibit, show)* avoir, montrer; **h. mercy on us!** ayez pitié de nous!; **he had the nerve to refuse** il a eu le culot de refuser; **he didn't even h. the decency to apologize** il n'a même pas eu la décence de s'excuser

C. 1 *(obtain, receive)* avoir, recevoir; **I'd like him to h. this picture** j'aimerais lui donner cette photo; **I'd like to h. your advice on something** j'aimerais que vous me donniez un conseil à propos de quelque chose; **we had a phone call from the mayor** nous avons reçu *ou* eu un coup de fil du maire; **they've still had no news of the lost plane** ils n'ont toujours pas de nouvelles de l'avion (qui a) disparu; **I h. it on good authority** je le tiens de bonne source; **I must h. your answer by tomorrow** il me faut votre réponse pour demain; **let me h. your answer by next week** donnez-moi votre réponse avant la semaine prochaine; **let me h. your keys** donne-moi tes clefs; **let me h. the book back when you've finished** rends-moi le livre quand tu auras fini; **she let them h. the wardrobe for £300** elle leur a laissé *ou* cédé l'armoire pour 300 livres; **there are plenty of flats to be had** il y a plein d'appartements; *Fam* **I let him h. it** *(attacked him)* je lui ai réglé son compte; *(told him off)* je lui ai passé un savon; *Fam* **you had it coming!** tu ne l'as pas volé!

2 *(invite)* recevoir, avoir; **she's having some people (over) for** *or* **to dinner** elle reçoit *ou* elle a du monde à dîner; **let's h. him round for a drink** et si on l'invitait à prendre un pot?; **did you h. any visitors?** avez-vous eu de la visite?; **after the movie we had them back for coffee** après le cinéma, nous les avons invités à venir prendre le café chez nous

3 *(accept, take)* vouloir; **he'd like to marry but nobody will h. him!** il aimerait se marier mais personne ne veut de lui!; **do what you want, I'm having nothing more to do with your schemes** fais ce que tu veux, je ne veux plus être mêlé à tes combines

D. 1 *(clutch)* tenir; **to h. sb in one's power** avoir qn en son pouvoir; **the teacher had (got) him by the arm/the ear** le maître le tenait par le bras/l'oreille; **he had (got) his assailant by the throat** il tenait son agresseur à la gorge

2 *Fig (gain control or advantage over)* **you h. me there!** là vous me tenez!; **I h. (got) you right where I want you now!** je vous tiens!; *Sport* **the Bears h. it!** les Bears ont gagné!

3 *(bewilder, perplex)* **who won? – you've got me there** qui a gagné? – là, tu me poses une colle

E. 1 *(cause to be)* **the news had me worried** la nouvelle m'a inquiété; **I'll h. this light fixed in a minute** j'en ai pour une minute à réparer cette lampe; **we'll h. everything ready** tout sera prêt

2 *(with past participle) (cause to be done)* **to h. sth done** faire faire qch; **I had my hair cut** je me suis fait couper les cheveux; **we must h. the curtains cleaned** nous devons faire nettoyer les rideaux *ou* donner les rideaux à nettoyer; **three houses had their windows shattered** trois maisons ont eu leurs fenêtres brisées; **she had coffee brought up to the room** elle a fait monter du café dans la chambre; **I had my watch stolen** je me suis fait voler ma montre

3 *(with infinitive) (cause to do)* **to h. sb do sth** faire faire qch à qn; **she had him invite all the neighbours round** elle lui a fait inviter tous les voisins; **h. them come in** faites-les entrer; **the boss had him up to his office** le patron l'a convoqué dans son bureau; **he soon had them all laughing** il eut tôt fait de les faire tous rire; **I had the children go to bed early** j'ai couché les enfants de bonne heure; **as he would h. us be-**

lieve comme il voudrait nous le faire croire

F. 1 *(consume ▸ food, meal)* avoir, prendre; **we were having lunch** nous étions en train de déjeuner; **we're having dinner out tonight** nous sortons dîner ce soir; **to h. breakfast in bed** prendre le petit déjeuner au lit; **would you like to h. coffee?** voulez-vous (prendre) un café?; **do you h. coffee or tea in the morning?** prenez-vous du café ou du thé le matin?; **I had tea with her** j'ai pris le thé avec elle; **we stopped and had a drink** nous nous sommes arrêtés pour boire quelque chose; **what will you h.? – I'll h. the lamb** *(in restaurant)* qu'est-ce que vous prenez? – je vais prendre de l'agneau; **we had fish for dinner** nous avons mangé *ou* eu du poisson au dîner; **he always has a cigarette after dinner** il fume toujours une cigarette après le dîner; **will you h. a cigarette?** voulez-vous une cigarette?

2 *(indicating location, position)* placer, mettre; **we'll h. the wardrobe here and the table in there** nous mettrons l'armoire ici et la table par là; **she had her arm around his shoulders** elle avait mis le bras autour de ses épaules; **I had my back to the window** je tournais le dos à la fenêtre; **he had his head down** il avait la tête baissée

3 *(be accompanied by)* **she had her mother with her** sa mère était avec elle; **I can't talk right now, I h. someone with me** je ne peux pas parler, je ne suis pas seul *ou* je suis avec quelqu'un

4 *(give birth to)* avoir; **she's had a baby** elle a eu un bébé; **she had her baby last week** elle a accouché la semaine dernière; **she's going to h. a baby** elle attend *ou* elle va avoir un bébé; **he's had three children by her** il a eu trois enfants d'elle; **our dog has just had puppies** notre chien vient d'avoir des petits

5 *(assert, claim)* soutenir, maintenir; **public opinion has it that he is not telling the truth** on pense généralement qu'il ne dit pas la vérité; **rumour has it that they're married** le bruit court qu'ils sont mariés; **as the government would h. it** comme dirait le gouvernement; **as Plato has it** comme dit Platon, comme l'a écrit Platon

6 *(with "will" or "would") (wish for)* vouloir; **what would you h. me do?** que voudriez-vous que je fasse?; **I'll h. you know I h. a degree in French** je vous fais remarquer que j'ai une licence de français

7 *(in negative) (allow, permit)* **I will not h. him in my house!** il ne mettra pas les pieds chez moi!; **I won't h. it!** ça ne va pas se passer comme ça!; **we can't h. you sleeping on the floor** nous ne pouvons pas vous laisser dormir par terre; *Fam* **we tried to give the dog a bath but he wasn't having any of it!** nous avons essayé de donner un bain au chien, mais rien n'y a fait!; *Fam* **I'm not having any of your nonsense** pas de bêtises

8 *(in passive) Fam (cheat, outwit)* avoir; **you've been had!** tu t'es fait avoir!

9 *very Fam (sleep with)* avoir

G. 1 *(with infinitive) (indicating obligation)* **to h. (got) to do sth** devoir faire qch, être obligé de faire qch; **do you h. to** *or* **h. you got to leave so soon?** êtes-vous obligé de partir *ou* faut-il que vous partiez si tôt?; **I h. (got) to go to the meeting** il faut que j'aille *ou* je dois aller *ou* je suis obligé d'aller à la réunion; **don't you h. to** *or* **haven't you got to phone the office?** est-ce que tu ne dois pas appeler le bureau?; **he'll do it if he's got to** il le fera s'il est obligé de le faire; **you don't h. to** *or* **you haven't got to go** tu n'es pas obligé d'y aller; **we had to take physics at school** nous étions obligés de suivre des cours de physique à l'école; **she had to take a blood test** elle a été obligée de *ou* elle a dû faire un examen sanguin; **I hate having to get up early** j'ai horreur de devoir me lever tôt; **I won't apologize – you h. to** je ne m'excuserai pas – il le faut; **you've got to be joking!** vous plaisantez!, c'est une plaisanterie!; **you didn't h. to tell your father what happened!** tu n'avais pas besoin d'aller dire à ton père ce qui s'est passé!; *Ironic* **the train WOULD h. to be late today of all days!** il fallait que le train soit en retard aujourd'hui!; *Fam* **that has (got) to be the stupidest idea I've ever heard!** ça doit être l'idée la plus idiote que j'aie jamais entendue!

2 *(with infinitive) (indicating necessity)* devoir; **you h. (got) to get some rest** il faut que vous vous reposiez, vous devez vous reposer; **I'll h. to think about it** il va falloir que j'y réfléchisse; **I h. (got) to know** il faut que je le sache; **we h. to be careful about what we say** on doit faire attention *ou* il faut qu'on fasse attention à ce qu'on dit; **some problems still h. to** *or* **h. still got to be worked out** il reste encore des problèmes à résoudre; **if you finish the report this evening you won't h. to come in to work tomorrow** si vous finissez le rapport ce soir, vous n'aurez pas besoin de venir travailler demain; **first the potatoes h. (got) to be washed** il faut d'abord laver les pommes de terre; **I don't like housework but it has (got) to be done** je n'aime pas faire le ménage mais il faut bien que quelqu'un le fasse; **the plumbing has (got) to be redone** la plomberie a besoin d'être refaite; **you'd h. to be deaf not to hear that noise** il faudrait être sourd pour ne pas entendre ce bruit; **do you h. to turn the music up so loud?** vous ne pourriez pas baisser un peu la musique?

3 *(with "to do") (idioms)* **the book has to do with archaeology** ce livre traite de l'archéologie; **their argument had to do with money** ils se disputaient à propos d'argent; **this has nothing to do with you** ça ne te concerne *ou* regarde pas; **I'll h. nothing more to do with her** je ne veux plus avoir affaire à elle; **they had nothing to do with her being fired** ils n'avaient rien à voir avec son licenciement

• **haves** NPL **the haves** les riches *mpl*, les nantis *mpl*; **the haves and the h.-nots** les riches *mpl* et les pauvres *mpl*, les nantis *mpl* et les démunis *mpl*

▸**have around** VT SEP *(keep available)* garder *ou* avoir sous la main; **I h. the documents around somewhere** les documents sont là quelque part, j'ai les documents quelque part; **she's a useful person to h. around in a crisis** c'est quelqu'un d'utile en cas de crise; **I don't like having children around** je n'aime pas la compagnie des enfants

▸**have away** VT SEP *Br very Fam* **to have it away (with sb)** s'envoyer en l'air (avec qn)

▸**have down** VT SEP *(invite from upstairs, the north)* inviter; **we're having his family down for the weekend** sa famille vient passer le week-end chez nous

▸**have in** VT SEP **1** *(cause to enter)* faire entrer; **she had him in for a chat** elle l'a fait entrer pour discuter

2 *(invite)* **to h. friends in for a drink** inviter des amis à prendre un pot

3 *(doctor, workman)* faire venir; **we had to h. the doctor in** nous avons dû faire venir le médecin; **they've got workmen in at the moment** ils ont des ouvriers en ce moment

4 *Fam (idiom)* **to h. it in for sb** avoir une dent contre qn; **they had it in for me from the day I arrived** ils en ont eu après moi dès mon arrivée

▸**have off** VT SEP **1** *(remove)* retirer; **the barber nearly had my ear off** le coiffeur a failli me couper l'oreille **2** *(have removed)* faire retirer; **she's having the plaster off next week** on lui retire son plâtre la semaine prochaine **3** *Br very Fam (have sexual intercourse)* **to h. it off (with sb)** s'envoyer en l'air (avec qn)

▸**have on** VT SEP **1** *(wear)* porter; **what does she h. on?** qu'est-ce qu'elle porte?, comment est-elle habillée?; **she had her black dress on** elle avait *ou* portait sa robe noire; **the child had nothing on** l'enfant était tout nu

2 *(radio, television)* **h. you got the radio on?** avez-vous allumé la radio?, est-ce que la radio est allumée?; **he has the radio/television on all night** sa radio/sa télévision est allumée toute la nuit

3 *(commitment, engagement)* **we h. a lot on today** nous avons beaucoup à faire aujourd'hui; **do you h. anything on for tonight?** avez-vous des projets pour *ou* êtes-vous pris ce soir?; **I h. nothing on for the weekend** je n'ai rien de prévu ce week-end

4 *Br Fam (tease, trick)* faire marcher; **you're having me on!** tu me fais marcher!; **I was only having you on** c'était juste pour te faire marcher

5 *(idiom)* **they h. nothing on me** ils n'ont aucune preuve contre moi; **the police h. nothing on him** la police n'a rien sur lui

▸**have out** VT SEP **1** *(tooth)* se faire arracher **2** *(settle)* **to h. it out with sb** s'expliquer avec qn; **she had it** *or* **the matter** *or* **the whole thing out with him** elle a eu une longue explication avec lui; **let's h. this out once and for all** mettons les choses au point une fois pour toutes

▸**have over** VT SEP *(invite)* inviter

▸**have up** VT SEP **1** *Fam (bring before the authorities)* **I'll h. you up for blackmail** je vais vous poursuivre (en justice) pour chantage; **he was had up (before the court) for breaking and entering** il a comparu (devant le tribunal) pour effraction **2** *(invite from downstairs, the south)* inviter; **he had them up (to his flat) for tea** il les a invités à venir prendre le thé

haven ['heɪvən] N **1** *(refuge)* abri *m*, refuge *m*; **a safe h.** un abri sûr; *Literary* **the garden is a h. of peace and tranquillity** le jardin est un havre de paix et de tranquillité **2** *Arch or Literary (harbour)* havre *m*

have-nots NPL **the h.** les démunis *mpl*, les défavorisés *mpl*

haven't ['hævənt] = **have not**

haversack ['hævəˌsæk] N havresac *m*

havoc ['hævək] N *(UNCOUNT)* ravages *mpl*, chaos *m*; **to wreak h. on sth** ravager qch; **the strike played h. with our plans** la grève a mis nos projets par terre

haw [hɔː] N *Bot (berry)* baie *f* d'aubépine, cenelle *f*; *(shrub)* aubépine *f*

VI *see* **hem²** VI, **hum** VI

Hawaii [hə'waɪɪ] N *Geog* Hawaii *f*, Hawaï *f*

Hawaiian [hə'waɪən] N **1** *(person)* Hawaiien(enne) *m,f*, Hawaïen(enne) *m,f* **2** *Ling* hawaiien *m*, hawaïen *m*

ADJ hawaiien, hawaïen

▸▸ ***Hawaiian guitar*** guitare *f* hawaiienne *ou* hawaïenne; ***Hawaiian shirt*** chemise *f* hawaiienne *ou* hawaïenne; ***Hawaiian Standard Time*** heure *f* de Hawaii *ou* de Hawaï

hawk [hɔːk] N **1** *Orn* faucon *m*; **to watch sb/sth like a h.** ne pas quitter qn/qch du regard; **he has eyes like a h.** *(sharp eyesight)* il a des yeux d'aigle *ou* de lynx; *(misses nothing)* rien ne lui échappe **2** *Pol* faucon *m* **3** *(cough)* raclement *m* de gorge

VI **1** *Hunt* chasser au faucon **2** *(clear throat)* se racler la gorge; *(spit)* cracher

VT **1** *(sell ▸ from door to door)* colporter; *(▸ in market, street)* vendre à la criée **2** *Fig (news, gossip)* colporter **3** *(cough up)* cracher

▸**hawk up** VT SEP expectorer

hawker ['hɔːkə(r)] N *(street vendor)* marchand(e) *m,f* ambulant(e); *(door-to-door)* démarcheur(euse) *m,f*, colporteur(euse) *m,f*; **no hawkers** *(sign)* démarchage interdit

hawk-eyed ADJ **1** *(keen-sighted)* au regard d'aigle **2** *Fig (vigilant)* qui a l'œil partout

hawking ['hɔːkɪŋ] N **1** *Hunt* chasse *f* au faucon **2** *(selling)* colportage *m*

hawkish ['hɔːkɪʃ] ADJ *Pol* belliciste

hawknosed ['hɔːknəʊzd] ADJ *(person)* au nez aquilin

hawser ['hɔːzə(r)] N *Naut* grelin *m*, aussière *f*; *(for mooring only)* amarre *f*

hawthorn ['hɔːθɔːn] N *Bot* aubépine *f*

COMP *(hedge, berry)* d'aubépine

hay [heɪ] N foin *m*; *Agr* **to make h.** faire les foins; *Prov* **to make h. while the sun shines** battre le fer pendant qu'il est chaud

▸▸ *Med* ***hay fever*** rhume *m* des foins; ***hay rake*** râteau *m*, fauchet *m*

haycart ['heɪkɑːt] N fourragère *f* de foin

haycock ['heɪkɒk] N tas *m* *ou* meulette *f* de foin

hayfork ['heɪfɔːk] N fourche *f* à foin

haying ['heɪɪŋ] N *Agr* fenaison *f*

hayloft ['heɪlɒft] N grenier *m* à foin

haymaker ['heɪˌmeɪkə(r)] N **1** *Agr (worker)* faneur(euse) *m,f*; *(machine)* faneuse *f* **2** *Fam (punch)* grand coup *m*

haymaking ['heɪˌmeɪkɪŋ] N *(UNCOUNT) Agr* fenaison *f*, foins *mpl*

hayrack ['heɪræk] N *(in barn)* râtelier *m*; *(on cart)* ridelle *f*

hayrick ['heɪrɪk] N *Agr* meule *f* de foin

hayride ['heɪraɪd] N *Am* = promenade dans un chariot rempli de paille; *Fig* **it was no h.** ça n'a pas été une partie de plaisir

hayseed ['heɪsiːd] N **1** *Bot* graine *f* de foin **2** *Am, Austr & NZ Fam Pej (yokel)* péquenaud(e) *m,f*

haystack ['heɪstæk] N *Agr* meule *f* de foin

haywire ['heɪwaɪə(r)] ADJ *Fam (system, person)* détraqué; **to go h.** *(machine)* débloquer, se détraquer; *(plans)* mal tourner

hazard ['hæzəd] N **1** *(danger, risk)* risque *m*, danger *m*; *Aut (place)* point *m* dangereux; **ice presents another h. for drivers** le verglas est un danger supplémentaire pour les automobilistes; **a health/fire h.** un risque pour la santé/d'incendie **2** *(in golf)* obstacle *m*

VT **1** *(risk ▸ life)* risquer, hasarder; *(▸ reputation)* risquer **2** *(venture ▸ statement, advice, suggestion)* hasarder, se risquer à faire; **to h. an opinion** risquer une opinion; **to h. a guess** essayer de deviner **3** *(stake, bet ▸ fortune)* risquer, miser

• **hazards** NPL *Aut (lights)* feux *mpl* de détresse

▸▸ *Mktg* ***hazard forecasting*** prévision *f* événementielle; *Aut* ***hazard lights*** feux *mpl* de détresse; *Am* ***hazard pay*** prime *f* de risque; *Aut* ***hazard warning*** signal *m* de danger; *Aut* ***hazard warning lights*** feux *mpl* de détresse

> Note that the French word **hasard** is a false friend and is never a translation for the English word **hazard**. It means **chance**.

hazardous ['hæzədəs] ADJ **1** *(dangerous)* dangereux, risqué; **a h. stretch of road** une partie de la route qui est dangereuse **2** *(uncertain)* hasardeux, incertain

▸▸ ***hazardous waste*** déchets *mpl* dangereux

Hazchem *Br (written abbr* **hazardous chemicals***)* *(sign)* produits dangereux

haze [heɪz] N **1** *Met (mist)* brume *f*; **a heat h.** une brume de chaleur **2** *(UNCOUNT) (steam)* vapeur *f*, vapeurs *fpl*; *(smoke)* nuage *m* **3** *(confusion)* brouillard *m*; **to be in a h.** être dans le brouillard; **a h. of uncertainty surrounded the affair** une atmosphère d'incertitude entourait l'affaire

VT *Am* **1** *Univ (play tricks on, bully)* brimer, bizuter **2** *Mil* faire subir des brimades à **3** *(harass)* harceler

hazel ['heɪzəl] N **1** *Bot (tree)* noisetier *m*, coudrier *m* **2** *(colour)* (couleur *f* de) noisette *f*

ADJ *(colour)* noisette *(inv)*; **h. eyes** yeux *mpl* (couleur) noisette

hazelnut ['heɪzəlnʌt] N *Bot (nut)* noisette *f*; *(tree)* noisetier *m*

COMP *(flavour)* de noisette; *(ice cream, yoghurt)* à la noisette

▸▸ ***hazelnut oil*** huile *f* de noisette

hazily ['heɪzɪlɪ] ADV vaguement

haziness ['heɪzɪnɪs] N **1** *(of sky, weather)* état *m* brumeux **2** *(of memory, thinking)* flou *m*, imprécision *f* **3** *Phot* flou *m*

hazing ['heɪzɪŋ] *Am* N *(UNCOUNT)* **1** *Univ* bizutage *m* **2** *Mil* brimades *fpl*

▸▸ *Univ* ***hazing week*** (semaine *f* du) bizutage *m*

hazy ['heɪzɪ] *(compar* **hazier**, *superl* **haziest***)* ADJ **1** *(weather, sky, air)* brumeux **2** *(memory, knowledge)* flou, vague; *(thinking, ideas)* flou, embrouillé; **she's rather h. about the details of what happened** elle n'a qu'un vague souvenir de ce qui s'est passé **3** *Phot* flou

HCI [ˌeɪtʃsiː'aɪ] N *Br Formerly (abbr* **Home Computing Initiative***)* = système permettant aux employés d'une société de bénéficier de remises sur l'achat des ordinateurs

HD [ˌeɪtʃ'diː] *Comput* **1** *(abbr* **hard disk***)* DD **2** *(abbr* **high density***)* HD

HDD [ˌeɪtʃdiː'diː] N *Comput (abbr* **hard disk drive***)* unité *f* de disque dur

HDTV [ˌeɪtʃdiːtiː'viː] N *TV (abbr* **high definition television***)* TVHD *f*

he- [hiː] PREF **he-bear** ours *m* mâle; **he-goat** bouc *m*

he [hiː] PRON il; **he works in London** il travaille à Londres; **he and I** lui et moi; **there he is!** le voilà!; *Formal* **she is older than he is** elle est plus âgée que lui; **every politician should do what he thinks best** chaque homme politique devrait faire ce qu'il pense être le mieux; **that's what HE thinks!** c'est ce qu'il croit!

N **1** *Fam (male)* mâle□ *m*; **it's a he** *(newborn child)* c'est un garçon□; *(animal)* c'est un mâle□ **2** *(children's game)* (jeu *m* de) chat *m*; **you're he!** c'est toi le chat!

HEAD [hed]

> **N**
> • tête **1, 2, 5, 9, 10, 12, 14, 16, 22**
> • côté face **11**
> • en-tête **17**
> • mal de tête **6**
> • chef **7**
> • personne **13**
>
> **VT**
> • être à la tête de **1**
> • diriger **3**
> • être en tête de **2, 4**
> • intituler **4**
>
> **VI**
> • aller
>
> **ADJ**
> • principal **1**
> • premier **2**

(pl sense **12** *inv)*

N **1** *(of human, animal)* tête *f*; **she has a fine h. of hair** elle a de très beaux cheveux *ou* une très belle chevelure; **he's already a h. taller than his mother** il dépasse déjà sa mère d'une tête; *Horseracing* **to win by a h.** gagner d'une tête; **from h. to toe** *or* **foot** de la tête aux pieds; **she was dressed in black from h. to toe** *or* **foot** elle était tout en noir *ou* entièrement vêtue de noir; **to fall h. over heels** tomber la tête la première; **to fall h. over heels in love with sb** tomber éperdument amoureux de qn; **to have one's h. in the clouds** avoir la tête dans les nuages; **wine always goes to my h.** le vin me monte toujours à la tête; **all this praise has gone to his h.** toutes ces louanges lui ont tourné la tête; **to give a horse its h.** lâcher la bride à un cheval; **to stand on one's h.** faire le poirier; *Fam* **I could do it standing on my h.** c'est simple comme bonjour; **that's the kind of thing he could do standing on his h.** c'est le genre de choses qu'il peut faire les yeux fermés; *Fam* **she's got her h. screwed on (the right way)** elle a la tête sur les épaules; **the girl's got a good h. on her shoulders** cette fille a la tête sur les épaules; **he's an old h. on young shoulders** il est très mûr pour son âge; *Fig* **she's h. and shoulders above the rest** les autres ne lui arrivent pas à la cheville; *Fam* **to laugh one's h. off** rire à gorge déployée; *Fam* **to shout** *or* **to scream one's h. off** crier à tue-tête; **they'll have your h. (on a plate) for this** ils auront ta tête pour ça; **heads will roll** des têtes tomberont; *Am* **heads up!** attention la tête!; *Am Fam* **to give sb a heads up** tuyauter qn

2 *(mind, thoughts)* tête *f*; **to do sums in one's h.** calculer de tête; **to take it into one's h. to do sth** se mettre en tête de faire qch; **the idea never entered my h.** ça ne m'est jamais venu à l'esprit; **don't put silly ideas into his h.** ne lui mettez pas des idées stupides en tête; **to get sth into one's h.** se mettre qch dans la tête; **I can't get these dates into my h.** je n'arrive pas à retenir ces dates; **she got it into her h. that she was being persecuted** elle s'est mis en tête *ou* dans l'idée qu'on la persécutait; **I can't get that into his h.** je n'arrive pas à le lui faire comprendre; **the answer has gone right out of my h.** j'ai complètement oublié la réponse; *Fam* **use your h.!** fais travailler tes méninges!; *Fam* **it's doing my h. in!** ça me tape sur le système!, ça me prend la tête!; *Fam* **I just can't get my h. round the idea that she's gone** je n'arrive vraiment pas à me faire à l'idée qu'elle est partie; *Fam* **to get one's h. straight** *or* **together** se ressaisir

3 *(aptitude)* **to have a good h. for business** avoir le sens des affaires, s'entendre aux affaires; **she has no h. for business** elle n'a pas le sens des affaires; **in my job, you need a good h. for figures** pour faire mon métier, il faut savoir manier les chiffres; **to have a (good) h. for heights** ne pas avoir le vertige; **I've no h. for heights** j'ai le vertige

4 *(clear thinking, common sense)* **keep your h.!** gardez votre calme!, ne perdez pas la tête!; **to keep a cool h.** garder la tête froide; **you'll need a clear h. in the morning** vous aurez besoin d'avoir l'esprit clair demain matin; **to let one's h. be ruled by one's heart** laisser son cœur gouverner sa raison; *Br Fam* **he's off his h.** il est malade, il n'est pas net; *Fam* **he's not quite right in the h., he's a bit soft in the h.** il est un peu timbré; *Fam* **to be out of one's h.** *(drunk)* être bourré; *(on drugs)* être défoncé

5 *(intelligence, ability)* tête *f*; **we'll have to put our heads together and find a solution** nous devrons nous y mettre ensemble pour trouver une solution; **off the top of my h., I'd say it would cost about £1,500** à vue de nez, je dirais que ça coûte dans les 1500 livres; **I don't know off the top of my h.** je ne sais pas, il faudrait que je vérifie; **she made some figures up off the top of her h.** elle a inventé des chiffres; **he's talking off the top of his h.** il raconte n'importe quoi; **her lecture was completely over my h.** sa conférence m'a complètement dépassé; **to talk over sb's h.** s'exprimer de manière trop compliquée pour qn; *Prov* **two heads are better than one** deux avis valent mieux qu'un

6 *Fam (headache)* mal *m* de tête□; **I've got a bit of a h. this morning** j'ai un peu mal à la tête ce matin

7 *(chief, boss ▸ of police, government, family)* chef *m*; *(▸ of school, company)* directeur(trice) *m,f*; **the European heads of government** les chefs *mpl* de gouvernement européens; **the crowned heads of Europe** les têtes *fpl* couronnées de l'Europe; **h. of department** *(in school)* chef *m* de département; *(in company)* chef *m* de service

8 *(authority, responsibility)* **she went over my h. to the president** elle est allée voir le président sans me consulter; **they were promoted over my h.** ils ont été promus avant moi; **on your (own) h. be it!** c'est toi qui en prends la responsabilité!, à tes risques et périls!; *Literary* **his blood will be upon your h.** la responsabilité de sa mort pèsera sur vos épaules

9 *(top ▸ of racquet, pin, hammer)* tête *f*; *(▸ of staircase)* haut *m*, tête *f*; *(▸ of bed)* chevet *m*, tête *f*; *(▸ of arrow)* pointe *f*; *(▸ of page)* tête *f*; *(▸ of letter)* en-tête *m*; *(▸ of cane)* pommeau *m*; *(▸ of valley)* tête *f*; *(▸ of river)* source *f*; *(▸ of mineshaft)* bouche *f*; *(▸ of column, rocket, still)* chapiteau *m*; *(▸ of torpedo)* cône *m*; *(▸ of cask)* fond *m*; **at the h. of the procession/queue** en tête de (la) procession/de (la) queue; **sitting at the h. of the table** assis au bout de la *ou* en tête de table; **to be at the h. of the list** venir en tête de liste

10 *Bot & Culin (of corn)* épi *m*; *(of garlic)* tête *f*, gousse *f*; *(of celery)* pied *m*; *(of asparagus)* pointe *f*; *(of flower)* tête *f*; **a h. of cauliflower** un chou-fleur

11 *(of coin)* côté *m* face; **heads or tails?** pile ou face?; **I can't make h. nor tail of this** pour moi ça n'a ni queue ni tête; *Fam Hum* **heads I win, tails you lose** pile je gagne, face tu perds; **it's a case of heads I win, tails you lose** de toutes les façons je suis gagnant

12 *(of livestock)* tête *f*; **50 h. of cattle** 50 têtes de bétail

13 *(in prices, donations)* **tickets cost £50 a h.** les billets valent 50 livres par personne

14 *Electron (of tape recorder, VCR, disk drive)* tête *f*

15 *(in rugby)* **to win the scrum against the h.** prendre le ballon à l'adversaire sur son introduction

16 *(title ▸ of chapter)* tête *f*; **under this h.** sous ce titre; **heads of agreement** *(draft)* protocole *m* d'accord

17 *Typ* en-tête *m*

18 *(on beer)* mousse *f*; *(on fermenting liquid)* chapeau *m*

19 *Phys (of fluid, gas)* charge *f*, pression *f*; **loss of h.** perte *f* de pression; **h. of water** charge *f ou* pression *f* d'eau; *Fig* **to get up** *or* **to work up a h. of steam** s'énerver

20 *(of drum)* peau *f*

21 *(of ship)* proue *f*

22 *Med (of abscess, spot)* tête *f*; **to come to a h.** *(abscess, spot)* mûrir; *Fig (problem)* arriver au point critique; **his resignation brought things to a h.** sa démission a précipité les choses

23 *Vulg (fellatio)* **to give sb h.** tailler une pipe à qn

24 *Am Fam or Naut (toilet)* toilettes□ *fpl*; **I'm going to the h.** je vais pisser

VT **1** *(command ▸ group, organization)* être à la tête de; *(▸ project, revolt)* diriger, être à la tête de; *(chair ▸ discussion)* mener; *(▸ commission)* présider; **she headed the attack on the Govern-**

ment's economic policy elle menait l'attaque contre la politique économique du gouvernement
2 *(be first in, on)* être *ou* venir en tête de; **Madrid heads the list of Europe's most interesting cities** Madrid vient *ou* s'inscrit en tête des villes les plus intéressantes d'Europe; *Sport* **she headed the pack from the start** elle était en tête du peloton dès le départ
3 *(steer ▸ vehicle)* diriger; *(▸ person)* guider, diriger; **we headed the sheep down the hill** nous avons fait descendre les moutons de la colline; **they are heading the country into chaos** ils conduisent le pays au chaos; **just h. me towards the nearest bar** dirigez-moi vers le bar le plus proche; **where are you headed?** où vas-tu?; *Naut* **to h. a ship westwards** mettre le cap à l'ouest
4 *(provide title for)* intituler; *(be title of)* être en tête de; **the essay is headed 'Democracy'** l'essai s'intitule *ou* est intitulé 'Démocratie'
5 *Ftbl (ball)* jouer de la tête; **he headed the ball into the goal** il a marqué de la tête
6 *Old-fashioned (skirt around ▸ lake)* contourner par l'amont; *(▸ river)* contourner par sa source
7 *(plant)* écimer, étêter
VI *(car, crowd, person)* aller, se diriger; *Naut* mettre le cap sur; **where are you heading?** où vas-tu?; **you're heading in the right direction** vous allez dans la bonne direction; **I'm going to h. home** je vais rentrer; **the train headed into/out of a tunnel** le train est entré dans un/sorti d'un tunnel
ADJ 1 *(main ▸ person)* principal
2 *(first in series)* premier
▸▸ ***head barman*** chef *m* barman; *Br Sch* ***head boy*** = élève chargé d'un certain nombre de responsabilités et qui représente son école aux cérémonies publiques; ***head cashier*** chef *m* caissier; ***head chef*** chef *m* de cuisine; *Com* ***head clerk*** premier commis *m*, chef *m* de bureau; ***head cold*** rhume *m* de cerveau; ***head count*** vérification *f* du nombre de personnes présentes; **the teacher did a h. count** la maîtresse a compté les élèves; ***head foreman*** chef *m* d'atelier; *Mining* ***head frame*** chevalement *m*; ***head gardener*** jardinier(ère) *m,f* en chef; *Aut* ***head gasket*** joint *m* de culasse; *Tech* ***head gate*** *(of lock)* porte *f* d'amont; *Br Sch* ***head girl*** = élève chargée d'un certain nombre de responsabilités et qui représente son école aux cérémonies publiques; ***head housekeeper*** *(in hotel)* gouvernante *f* générale; ***head louse*** pou *m*; ***head office*** siège *m* social, bureau *m* central; **it's** *Br* **h. office** *or Am* **the h. office on the phone** c'est le siège au téléphone; ***head porter*** *(in hotel)* chef-portier *m*; *(in university college)* appariteur *m* principal; ***head race 1*** *(in rowing)* tête-de-rivière *f* **2** *Tech* canal *m* de prise *ou* d'amenée; *(of water mill)* bief *m* d'amont; ***head receptionist*** chef *m* de réception; *Mus* ***head register*** voix *f* de tête; *Br Aut* ***head restraint*** appuie-tête *m*, repose-tête *m*; *TV & Cin* ***head shot*** gros plan *m* de tête; ***head start*** *(lead)* avance *f*; *(advantage)* avantage *m*; **he had a ten-minute h. start over the others** il a commencé dix minutes avant les autres; **being bilingual gives her a h. start over the others** étant bilingue, elle est avantagée par rapport aux autres; ***head of state*** chef *m* d'État; *Sch* ***head teacher*** *(man)* proviseur *m*, directeur *m*, chef *m* d'établissement; *(woman)* directrice *f*, chef *m* d'établissement; ***head torch*** lampe *f* frontale; *Mus* ***head voice*** voix *f* de tête; ***head waiter*** maître *m* d'hôtel; *Br Sch* ***head of year*** conseiller(ère) *m,f* (principal(e)) d'éducation

▸**head back** **VI** rentrer, retourner; **we headed back to the office** nous sommes retournés au bureau; **when are you heading back?** quand comptez-vous rentrer?

▸**head for** **VT INSEP** *(of car, person)* se diriger vers; *Naut* mettre le cap sur; **where are you headed for?** où vas-tu?; **she headed for home** elle rentra (à la maison); **the country is heading for civil war** le pays va droit à la guerre civile; **he's heading for trouble** il va s'attirer des ennuis; *Fig* **to be heading for a fall** courir à l'échec; *Fam* **to h. for the hills** filer

▸**head off** **VT SEP 1** *(divert ▸ animal, vehicle, person)* détourner de son chemin; *(▸ enemy)* forcer à reculer; *Fig* **she headed off all questions about her private life** elle a éludé toute question sur sa vie privée **2** *(crisis, disaster)* prévenir, éviter; *(rebellion, revolt, unrest)* éviter
VI partir; **the children headed off to school** les enfants sont partis pour *ou* à l'école

▸**head up** **VT SEP** *(be leader of)* diriger

headache ['hedeɪk] **N 1** *(pain)* mal *m* de tête; **to have a h.** *(gen)* avoir mal à la tête; **white wine gives me a h.** le vin blanc me donne mal à la tête; **he suffers a lot from headaches** il a souvent des maux de tête *ou* mal à la tête **2** *Fig (problem)* casse-tête *m inv*; **the trip was one big h.** le voyage a été un casse-tête du début à la fin; **it can be a h. finding somewhere to park** parfois c'est la croix et la bannière pour trouver à se garer; **convincing her is your h.** pour ce qui est de la convaincre, c'est ton problème

headband ['hedbænd] **N 1** *(worn around head)* bandeau *m* **2** *Typ* tranchefile *f*

headbanger ['hedbæŋə(r)] **N** *Fam* **1** *(heavy metal fan)* hardeux(euse) *m,f* **2** *Br (mad person)* cinglé(e) *m,f*, toqué(e) *m,f*

headboard ['hedbɔːd] **N** tête *f* de lit

headbutt ['hedbʌt] **N** coup *m* de tête, coup *m* de boule
VT donner un coup de tête *ou* de boule à

headcase ['hedkeɪs] **N** *Fam* dingue *mf*

headcheese ['hedˌtʃiːz] **N** *Am Culin* fromage *m* de tête

headdress ['hedˌdres] **N** *(gen)* coiffure *f*; *(belonging to regional costume)* coiffe *f*

-headed ['hedɪd] **SUFF** à tête…; **a silver-h. cane** une canne à pommeau d'argent; **a three-h. dragon** un dragon à trois têtes

headed notepaper ['hedɪd-] **N** *Br* papier *m* à en-tête

header ['hedə(r)] **N 1** *Fam (fall)* chute *f* (la tête la première)□; *(dive)* plongeon *m* (la tête la première)□; **he took a h. into the ditch** il est tombé la tête la première dans le fossé
2 *Ftbl* (coup *m* de) tête *f*; **he scored with a h.** il a marqué de la tête
3 *Comput & Typ* en-tête *m*
4 *Constr* (pierre *f* en) boutisse *f*
▸▸ *Br Aut* ***header tank*** collecteur *m* de tête

headfirst [ˌhed'fɜːst] **ADV 1** *(dive, fall, jump)* la tête la première; **he dived h. into the pool** il a piqué une tête dans la piscine **2** *(rashly)* sans réfléchir, imprudemment; **to jump h. into sth** se jeter tête baissée dans qch

headfuck ['hedfʌk] **N** *Vulg* **1** *(man)* mec *m* pas net; *(woman)* nana *f* pas nette **2** *(thing, experience)* épreuve□ *f*; **this movie is a bit of a h.** c'est un peu le bad trip, ce film

headgear ['hedˌgɪə(r)] **N** *(UNCOUNT)* couvre-chef *m*

headhunt ['hedˌhʌnt] **VT to be headhunted** être recruté par un chasseur de têtes
VI recruter des cadres (pour une entreprise)

headhunter ['hedˌhʌntə(r)] **N** *also Fig* chasseur *m* de têtes

headhunting ['hedˌhʌntɪŋ] **N** *(UNCOUNT) also Fig* chasse *f* aux têtes; *(recruiting)* chasse *f* aux têtes, recrutement *m* de cadres

headiness ['hedɪnɪs] **N 1** *(of wine)* bouquet *m* capiteux; **the h. of her perfume** son parfum capiteux; **the h. of sudden success** la griserie *ou* l'ivresse qu'apporte un succès imprévu **2** *(excitement)* exaltation *f*, excitation *f*; **the h. of the early 60s** l'euphorie du début des années 60

heading ['hedɪŋ] **N 1** *(title ▸ of article, book)* titre *m*; *(▸ of chapter)* titre *m*, intitulé *m*; *Comput* titre *m*; *(in bookkeeping)* poste *m*, rubrique *f*; **page h.** tête *f* de page
2 *(subject)* rubrique *f*; **this subject comes under the h. of rhetoric** cette discipline fait partie de la rhétorique
3 *(letterhead)* en-tête *m*
4 *Aviat & Naut (direction)* cap *m*
5 *Ftbl* jeu *m* de tête
6 *Mining (tunnel)* galerie *f* d'avancement; *(head of tunnel)* avancée *f*, avancement *m*
7 *Constr (course)* assise *f* de boutisses
▸▸ *Constr* ***heading course*** assise *f* de boutisses

headlamp ['hedlæmp] **N 1** *Br Aut (on car)* phare *m*; *(on train)* fanal *m*, feu *m* avant **2** *Mining* lampe-chapeau *f*

headland ['hedlənd] **N** promontoire *m*, cap *m*

headless ['hedlɪs] **ADJ 1** *(arrow, body, screw)* sans tête; *Hum* **he was running around like a headless chicken** il courait dans tous les sens **2** *(company, commission)* sans chef

headlight ['hedlaɪt] **N** *Aut (on car)* phare *m*; *(on train)* fanal *m*, feu *m* avant

headline ['hedlaɪn] **N 1** *Press (in newspaper)* (gros) titre *m*, manchette *f*; **the hijacking made the headlines** le détournement a fait la une des journaux; **I just glanced at the headlines** j'ai juste jeté un coup d'œil sur les gros titres; **pollution has been in the headlines a lot recently** la pollution a beaucoup fait la une récemment; **it made h. news** cela a fait la une des journaux; **to hit the headlines** faire les gros titres; **news of their marriage hit the headlines** l'annonce de leur mariage a fait les gros titres *ou* a défrayé la chronique **2** *Rad & TV (news summary)* grand titre *m*; **here are today's news headlines** voici les principaux titres de l'actualité
VT 1 *Press (place as headline ▸ news story)* mettre en manchette **2** *(provide heading for)* intituler; **the article was headlined 'The New Poor'** l'article avait pour titre 'Les Nouveaux Pauvres' **3** *TV, Cin & Theat (have top billing in)* avoir le rôle principal dans; **headlining the show is Eve Arden** Eve Arden est la vedette du spectacle
VI *TV, Cin & Theat (have top billing)* avoir le rôle principal
▸▸ *Typ* ***headline type*** gros corps *m*; *Press* ***headline writer*** titreur(euse) *m,f*

headlong ['hedlɒŋ] **ADV 1** *(dive)* la tête la première; *(fall)* de tout son long; **she dived h. into the lake** elle a piqué une tête dans le lac **2** *(rush ▸ head down)* tête baissée; *(▸ at great speed)* à toute allure *ou* vitesse; **he threw himself h. against the door** il s'est littéralement jeté contre la porte **3** *(rashly)* sans réfléchir, imprudemment; **she rushed h. to her downfall** elle courait tout droit à sa perte; **they rushed h. into the deal** ils se sont jetés à corps perdu dans l'affaire; **they rushed h. into marriage** ils se sont mariés trop vite et sans réfléchir
ADJ 1 *(dive)* la tête la première **2** *(impetuous ▸ action)* imprudent, impétueux; **h. flight** sauve-qui-peut *m inv*, débandade *f*; **the crowd made a h. dash for the exit** la foule s'est ruée vers la sortie; **there was a h. rush to buy the shares** tout le monde s'est précipité pour acheter les actions

headman ['hedmæn] *(pl* **headmen** [-men]) **N** chef *m*

headmaster [ˌhed'mɑːstə(r)] **N** *Br Sch* proviseur *m*, directeur *m*, chef *m* d'établissement

headmistress [ˌhed'mɪstrɪs] **N** *Br Sch* directrice *f*, chef *m* d'établissement

head-on **ADV 1** *(collide, hit)* de front, de plein fouet; **he ran h. into the tree** il a heurté l'arbre de plein fouet; **the ship ran h. into the wharf** le navire a heurté le quai par l'avant **2** *(confront, meet)* de front; **to meet a problem h.** aborder un problème de front; **management confronted the union h.** la direction a affronté le syndicat
ADJ 1 *(collision ▸ of car, plane)* de front, de plein fouet; *(▸ of ships)* par l'avant **2** *(confrontation, disagreement)* violent

headphones ['hedfəʊnz] **NPL** casque *m* *(à écouteurs)*

headquarter ['hedkwɔːtə(r)] *Am* **VI** *(company)* **to h. in Glasgow** établir son siège à Glasgow
VT to be headquartered in Glasgow avoir son siège à Glasgow

headquarters [ˌhed'kwɔːtəz] **NPL 1** *(of bank, company, office)* siège *m* social, bureau *m* central; *(of army, police)* quartier *m* général; *(of organization, government office)* bureau *m* principal; *(of UN etc)* siège *m*; **they have their h. in Geneva** leur siège est à Genève; **police h.** le quartier général de la police **2** *Mil (commanding officers)* quartier *m* général
▸▸ *Mil* ***headquarters staff*** état-major *m*

headrest ['hedrest] **N** appuie-tête *m*, repose-tête *m*

headroom ['hedrʊm] **N** hauteur *f*; **there's not much h. in the attic** le plafond du grenier n'est pas très haut, le grenier n'est pas très haut de plafond; **there wasn't enough h. for the bus** il n'y avait pas un dégagement suffisant au-dessus du bus

headscarf ['hedskɑ:f] (*pl* **headscarves** [-skɑ:vz]) **N** foulard *m*

headset ['hedset] **N** *(with microphone)* casque *m (à écouteurs et à micro); Am (headphones)* casque *m (à écouteurs)*

headship ['hedʃɪp] **N 1** *(leadership)* direction *f*; **under the h. of** sous la direction de **2** *Sch* poste *m* de directeur *ou* de directrice

headshrinker ['hedʃrɪŋkə(r)] **N 1** *(headhunter)* réducteur *m* de têtes **2** *Fam (psychiatrist)* psy *mf*

headstall ['hedstɔ:l] **N** *(for horse)* têtière *f*, licou *m*

headstand ['hedstænd] **N to do a h.** faire le poirier

headstone ['hedstəʊn] **N 1** *(of grave)* pierre *f* tombale **2** *Archit (keystone)* clef *f* de voûte

headstrong ['hedstrɒŋ] **ADJ 1** *(wilful)* têtu, entêté **2** *(rash)* impétueux, imprudent

head-up ADJ

▸▸ ***head-up display*** *(in aeroplane, car)* affichage *m* tête-haute

headway ['hedweɪ] **N 1** *(progress)* **to make h.** *(gen)* avancer, faire des progrès; *Naut* faire route; **they're making some/no h. in their plans** leurs projets avancent/n'avancent pas **2** *(headroom)* place *f*, hauteur *f*

headwind ['hedwɪnd] **N** *(gen) & Aviat* vent *m* contraire; *Naut* vent *m* debout

headword ['hedwɜ:d] **N** entrée *f*, adresse *f*

heady ['hedɪ] (*compar* **headier**, *superl* **headiest**) **ADJ 1** *(intoxicating ▸ wine)* capiteux, qui monte à la tête; *(▸ perfume)* capiteux; **she breathed in a h. draught of mountain air** elle respira l'air grisant *ou* enivrant des montagnes **2** *(intoxicated)* grisé, enivré; **he felt quite h. with success** il se sentait complètement grisé par le succès **3** *(exciting ▸ experience, time)* excitant, passionnant; *(▸ atmosphere)* excitant, enivrant; **she recalled her h. days as a young reporter** elle se rappelait l'époque excitante où elle était jeune reporter; **the h. heights of international finance** les sommets *mpl* de la finance internationale

heal [hi:l] **VT 1** *(make healthy ▸ person)* guérir; *(▸ wound)* guérir, cicatriser; **time heals all wounds** le temps guérit toutes les blessures **2** *(damage, division)* remédier à, réparer; *(disagreement)* régler; **I'd do anything to h. the breach between them** je ferais n'importe quoi pour les réconcilier *ou* pour les raccommoder

VI *(person)* guérir; *(wound)* se cicatriser, se refermer; *(fracture)* se consolider

▸ **heal over VI** se cicatriser

healer ['hi:lə(r)] **N** guérisseur(euse) *m,f*; **time is a great h.** le temps guérit toutes les blessures

healing ['hi:lɪŋ] **N** *(of person)* guérison *f*; *(of wound)* cicatrisation *f*, guérison *f*; *(of fracture)* consolidation *f*

ADJ 1 *(remedy, treatment)* curatif; *(ointment)* cicatrisant **2** *(wound)* qui se cicatrise, qui guérit; *(fracture)* qui se consolide, qui guérit **3** *(soothing ▸ influence)* apaisant

▸▸ ***healing hands*** mains *fpl* de guérisseur

health [helθ] **N 1** *(general condition)* santé *f*; **to be in good/poor h.** être en bonne/mauvaise santé; **his h. has never been good** il a toujours été fragile; **smoking is bad for your h.** le tabac est mauvais pour *ou* nuisible à ta santé; *Fig* **the economic h. of the nation** la (bonne) santé économique de la nation; **h. problems** problèmes *mpl* de santé **2** *(good condition)* (bonne) santé *f*; **has he regained his h.?** s'est-il remis?, a-t-il recouvré la santé?, a-t-il guéri?; **she's the picture of h.** elle respire la santé; *Hum* **I'm not doing this (just) for the good of my h.!** je ne fais pas ça pour le plaisir *ou* pour m'amuser! **3** *(in toast)* **(to your) good h.!** à votre santé!; **we drank (to) the h. of the bride and groom** nous avons porté un toast en l'honneur des mariés

▸▸ ***health centre*** centre *m* médico-social; ***health certificate*** certificat *m* sanitaire; ***health club*** club *m* de remise en forme; *Br Fin* ***health cover*** assurance *f* médicale; ***health expenditure*** dépenses *fpl* de santé; ***health farm*** centre *m* de remise en forme; ***health food*** aliments *mpl* diététiques *ou* biologiques; ***health food shop*** magasin *m* de produits diététiques; ***health hazard*** risque *m* pour la santé; ***health inspector*** inspecteur(trice) *m,f* sanitaire; ***health insurance*** assurance *f* maladie; ***health minister*** ministre *m* de la Santé; *Am Fin* ***health plan*** assurance *f* médicale; ***health resort*** station *f* climatique; *(by sea)* station *f* balnéaire; ***health risk*** risque *m* pour la santé; *Br* ***Health and Safety Executive*** inspection *f* du travail; *Br* ***health and safety inspector*** inspecteur (trice) *m,f* du travail; *Br* ***health and safety officer*** = membre du personnel d'une entreprise chargé de veiller à l'hygiène et à la sécurité; *Br* ***health and safety regulations*** réglementation *f* sur l'hygiène et la sécurité; *Br* ***Health Secretary*** ministre *m* de la Santé; ***health sector*** secteur *m* sanitaire; *Br* ***health service*** = système créé en 1946 en Grande-Bretagne et financé par l'État, assurant la gratuité des soins et des services médicaux, Sécurité *f* sociale; ***health services*** services *mpl* de santé; ***health tourism*** tourisme *m* de santé; *Br* ***health visitor*** = infirmière visiteuse qui s'occupe surtout des enfants en bas âge, des personnes âgées etc

healthcare ['helθ,keə(r)] **N** soins *mpl ou* services *mpl* médicaux

▸▸ *Br Admin* ***the Healthcare Commission*** = organisme non gouvernemental chargé de contrôler la qualité des soins de santé en Angleterre et au pays de Galles; ***healthcare professional*** professionnel(elle) *m,f* de (la) santé; *Am* ***healthcare provider*** professionnel(elle) *m,f* de (la) santé

health-giving ADJ *(effect etc)* bienfaisant, salutaire; *(air etc)* tonifiant, vivifiant

healthily ['helθɪlɪ] **ADV** *(eat, live)* sainement

healthiness ['helθɪnɪs] **N** *(of climate, place)* salubrité *f*; *(of person)* bonne santé *f*; *(of diet, relationship)* caractère *m* sain

healthy ['helθɪ] (*compar* **healthier**, *superl* **healthiest**) **ADJ 1** *(in good health ▸ person)* sain, en bonne santé; *(▸ animal, plant)* en bonne santé

2 *(showing good health ▸ colour, skin, lungs)* sain; *(▸ appetite)* robuste, bon

3 *(beneficial ▸ air, climate, place)* salubre; *(▸ diet, food, lifestyle)* sain; *(▸ exercise)* bon pour la santé, salutaire

4 *(thriving ▸ economy)* sain; *(▸ business)* prospère, bien assis; *(relationship)* sain; **the new measures are designed to make the economy healthier** les nouvelles lois sont destinées à assainir l'économie

5 *(substantial ▸ profits)* considérable; *(▸ sum)* considérable, important; *(▸ difference)* appréciable

6 *(sensible ▸ attitude)* sain; *(▸ respect)* salutaire; **he shows a h. disrespect for opinion polls** il fait montre d'un dédain salutaire pour les sondages; **to have a h. disregard for traditions** avoir un mépris louable des traditions

heap [hi:p] **N 1** *(pile)* tas *m*, amas *m*; **her things were piled in a h.** ses affaires étaient (mises) en tas; **he collapsed in a h. on the floor** il s'écroula *ou* tomba par terre comme une masse; *Br Fam Old-fashioned* **to be struck** *or* **knocked all of a h.** être soufflé, en rester comme deux ronds de flan **2** *Fam (large quantity)* tas *m*, masse *f*; **a h.** *or* **heaps of money** un paquet de fric; **I have a h.** *or* **heaps of work to do** j'ai un boulot monstre; **you've got heaps of time** tu as largement le temps *ou* tout ton temps; **he's helped us out heaps of times** il nous a rendu service mille fois *ou* des tas de fois; **they have heaps of room** ils ont de la place à ne plus savoir qu'en faire **3** *Fam (old car)* vieux clou *m*

VT 1 *(collect into a pile)* entasser, empiler; **she heaped roast beef onto his plate** elle l'a généreusement servi en (tranches de) rosbif; **the table was heaped with food** la table était couverte de victuailles; **the lorry was heaped with food supplies** le camion regorgeait de provisions **2** *Fig (lavish)* **to h. sth on sb** couvrir qn de qch; **to h. praise on** *or* **upon sb** couvrir *ou* combler qn d'éloges *ou* de compliments; **the teacher heaped homework on the students** le professeur a submergé ses élèves de devoirs

▸ **heap up VT SEP** *(pile ▸ books, furniture)* entasser, empiler; *(▸ money, riches)* amasser; **she heaped up our plates with food** elle a rempli nos assiettes

heaped [hi:pt], *Am* **heaping** ['hi:pɪŋ] **ADJ** gros (grosse); *(container, bowl)* entassé, amoncelé; **a h. teaspoonful** une bonne cuillère à café

heaps [hi:ps] **ADV** *Br Fam* drôlement; **I feel h. better** je me sens drôlement *ou* rudement mieux

HEAR [hɪə(r)]

VT
• entendre **1, 4** • écouter **2**
• apprendre **4**
VI
• entendre **1** • être au courant **2**

(*pt & pp* **heard** [hɜ:d])

VT 1 *(perceive with sense of hearing)* entendre; **can you h. me?** est-ce que vous m'entendez?; **he could h. someone crying** il entendait (quelqu'un) pleurer; **I can h. someone at the door** j'entends sonner à la porte; **a shout was heard** un cri se fit entendre; *Formal* **he was heard to observe** *or* **remark that he was against censorship** on l'a entendu dire qu'il était opposé à la censure; **I've heard it said that...** j'ai entendu dire que... + *indicative*; **I've heard tell of such things** j'ai entendu parler de choses de ce genre; **I couldn't make myself heard above the noise** je n'arrivais pas à me faire entendre dans le bruit; **to h. my sister talk you'd think we were poor** à entendre ma sœur, vous pourriez croire que nous sommes pauvres; **he went on and on about it – I can just h. him!** il n'a pas arrêté d'en parler – c'est comme si j'y étais *ou* pas la peine de me faire un dessin!; **don't believe everything you h.** n'écoutez pas tous les bruits qui courent, ne croyez pas tout ce qu'on raconte; **you're hearing things** tu t'imagines des choses; **I can hardly h. myself think** je n'arrive pas à me concentrer (tant il y a de bruit); *Ironic* **he hears what he wants to h.** il n'entend que ce qu'il veut; **let's h. it for the Johnson sisters!** un grand bravo pour les sœurs Johnson!, et on applaudit bien fort les sœurs Johnson!

2 *(listen to ▸ music, person)* écouter; *(▸ concert, lecture, mass)* assister à, écouter; **be quiet, d'you h.!** taisez-vous, vous entendez!; **let's h. what you think** dites voir *ou* un peu ce que vous pensez; **so let's h. it!** allez, dis ce que tu as à dire!; **I've never heard such nonsense!** qu'est-ce qu'il ne faut pas entendre!; **the Lord heard our prayers** le Seigneur a écouté *ou* exaucé nos prières

3 *(of authority, official)* **the priest hears confession on Saturdays** le prêtre confesse le samedi; *Law* **the court will h. the first witness today** la cour entendra le premier témoin aujourd'hui; **the case will be heard in March** l'affaire se plaidera au mois de mars

4 *(understand, be told)* entendre, apprendre; **I h. you're leaving** j'ai appris *ou* j'ai entendu (dire) que tu partais; **I h. you've lived in Thailand** il paraît que tu as vécu en Thaïlande; **have you heard the latest?** connaissez-vous la dernière?; **have you heard anything more about the accident?** avez-vous eu d'autres nouvelles de l'accident?; **for six months we heard nothing** *(received no news)* pendant six mois nous n'avons pas eu de nouvelles; **she was very famous for a while then we heard no more about her** elle a été célèbre pendant un moment puis on n'a plus entendu parler d'elle; **let me h. how you get on** donnez-moi de vos nouvelles; **from what I h.** à ce qu'on dit; **have you heard the one about the Scotsman and the Irishman?** connaissez-vous l'histoire de l'Écossais et de l'Irlandais?; **I've heard that one before!** on ne me la fait plus!; **she's heard it all before** elle connaît la musique; **I've heard good things about that school** j'ai eu des échos favorables de cette école; **you haven't heard the last of this!** *(gen)* vous n'avez pas fini d'en entendre parler!; *(threat)* vous aurez de mes nouvelles!; *Fam* **I h. you, I h. what you're saying** je comprends, j'ai compris; *Fam* **you heard!** tu m'as bien compris!

VI 1 *(able to perceive sound)* entendre; **she doesn't h. very well** elle n'entend pas très bien, elle est un peu dure d'oreille

2 *(be aware)* être au courant; **haven't you heard? he's dead** vous n'êtes pas au courant? il est mort

3 *(idiom)* **h., h.!** bravo!, tout à fait d'accord!

▸**hear of** VT INSEP **1** *(know of)* entendre parler de, connaître; **I've never heard of her** je ne la connais pas **2** *(receive news of)* entendre parler de; **the whole town had heard of his success** la ville entière était au courant de son succès *ou* sa réussite; **the director was never heard of again** on n'a plus jamais entendu parler du directeur; **have you ever heard of such a thing?** avez-vous déjà entendu parler d'une chose pareille?; **this is the first I've heard of it** c'est la première fois que j'en entends parler **3** *(usu neg) (accept, allow)* **her father won't h. of it** son père ne veut pas en entendre parler *ou* ne veut rien savoir; **I won't h. of you walking home** je ne veux absolument pas que tu rentres à pied

hearer ['hɪərə(r)] N auditeur(trice) *m,f*

hearing ['hɪərɪŋ] N **1** *(UNCOUNT) (sense)* ouïe *f*; **to have good/bad h.** entendre bien/mal; **a keen sense of h.** l'oreille *f ou* l'ouïe *f* fine; **he has very little h. left** son ouïe est défaillante, il n'entend presque plus; **his h. gradually deteriorated** petit à petit il est devenu dur d'oreille; **cats have better h. than humans** les chats entendent mieux *ou* ont l'ouïe plus fine que les humains

2 *(UNCOUNT) (earshot)* **within h.** à portée de voix; **in my h.** devant moi, en ma présence

3 *(act of listening)* audition *f*; **I didn't enjoy the symphony at (the) first h.** je n'ai pas aimé la symphonie à la première audition *ou* la première fois que je l'ai écoutée

4 *(chance to be heard)* audition *f*; **they were the only ones to get a h.** ils furent les seuls à être entendus; **at least give me a h.** laissez-moi au moins parler; **they judged the architect without a h.** ils ont jugé l'architecte sans l'entendre *ou* sans entendre sa défense; **to give sb a fair h.** laisser parler qn, écouter ce que qn a à dire

5 *Law* audition *f*; **the h. of witnesses** l'audition *f* des témoins; **the h. of a trial** l'audience *f*; **the case will come up for h. in March** l'affaire sera entendue *ou* plaidée en mars

6 *(official meeting)* séance *f*

▸▸ ***hearing aid*** appareil *m* acoustique, audiophone *m*; ***hearing dog*** *(for the deaf)* = chien entraîné à reconnaître certains bruits et aider ainsi une personne malentendante; ***the hearing impaired*** les malentendants *mpl*

hearken ['hɑːkən] VI *Arch or Literary* **to h. to sb/sth** écouter qn/qch

hearsay ['hɪəseɪ] N ouï-dire *m inv*, rumeurs *fpl*; **it's only h.** ce ne sont que des rumeurs; **I only know it by** *or* **from h.** je ne le sais que par ouï-dire

▸▸ *Law* ***hearsay evidence*** preuve *f* par ouï-dire

hearse [hɜːs] N corbillard *m*, fourgon *m* mortuaire

HEART [hɑːt]

• cœur **1, 2, 5, 7, 9–11**	• fond **3, 8, 9**
• courage **6**	• vif **8, 9**

N **1** *Anat (organ)* cœur *m*; **he has a weak h.** il est cardiaque, il a le cœur malade; **to have a h. condition** souffrir du cœur, être cardiaque; *Fig* **her h. leapt** son cœur bondit; *Fig* **her h. sank** elle eut un serrement de cœur; *Br* **he sat there, his h. in his boots** il était là, la mort dans l'âme; **her h. was in her mouth as she watched** elle regardait en retenant son souffle

2 *(seat of feelings, love)* cœur *m*; **to have a big h.** avoir très bon cœur; **he has a h. of gold/of stone** il a un cœur d'or/de pierre; **it does my h. good to see them together** cela me réchauffe le cœur de les voir ensemble; **to lose one's h. to sb** donner son cœur à qn, tomber amoureux de qn; **to win sb's h.** gagner le cœur de qn; **the letter was written straight from the h.** la lettre était écrite du fond du cœur; **to have one's h. set on sth** s'être mis qch dans la tête; **he has his h. set on winning** il veut à tout prix gagner; **they have your welfare at h.** ils ne pensent qu'à ton bien, c'est pour ton bien qu'ils font cela; **they have everything their hearts could desire** ils ont tout ce qu'ils peuvent désirer; *Literary* **my h.'s desire is to see Rome again** mon plus cher désir est *ou* ce que je désire le plus au monde c'est de revoir Rome; **she hardened** *or* **steeled her h. against him** elle s'est endurcie contre lui; **affairs** *or* **matters of the h.** affaires *fpl* de cœur; *Arch or Hum* **dear h.** mon cœur, mon (ma) chéri(e); **to wear one's h. on one's sleeve** montrer *ou* laisser paraître ses sentiments

3 *(innermost thoughts)* fond *m*; **in his h. of hearts** au fond de lui-même *ou* de son cœur, en son for intérieur; **in my h. I knew it was true** au fond de moi-même je savais que c'était la vérité; **there's a woman/a man after my own h.** voilà une femme/un homme selon mon cœur; **I thank you from the bottom of my h.** *or* **with all my h.** je vous remercie du fond du cœur *ou* de tout mon cœur; **to take sth to h.** prendre qch à cœur; **she opened** *or* **poured out her h. to me** elle m'a dévoilé son cœur

4 *(disposition, humour)* **to have a change of h.** changer d'avis

5 *(interest, enthusiasm)* **I worked hard but my h. wasn't in it** j'ai beaucoup travaillé mais je n'avais pas le cœur à l'ouvrage *ou* le cœur n'y était pas; **to eat/drink/read to one's h.'s content** manger/boire/lire tout son soûl; **a subject close to one's h.** un sujet qui tient à cœur; **she puts her h.** *or* **she throws herself h. and soul into her work** elle se donne à son travail corps et âme

6 *(courage)* **to lose h.** perdre courage, se décourager; **take h.!** courage!; **she took h. from the fact that others shared her experience** elle était encouragée par le fait que d'autres partageaient son expérience; **to be in good h.** *(person)* avoir bon moral; *Br (land)* être fécond *ou* productif

7 *(compassion)* cœur *m*; **he has no h.** il n'a pas de cœur, il manque de cœur; **she didn't have the h. to refuse, she couldn't find it in her h. to refuse** elle n'a pas eu le courage *ou* le cœur de refuser; **can you find it in your h. to forgive me?** est-ce que vous pourrez jamais me pardonner?; **her h.'s in the right place** elle a bon cœur; **have a h.!** pitié!; **to be all h.** être plein de bonne volonté; *Ironic* **you're all h.** tu es charmant!

8 *(core, vital part ▸ of matter, topic)* fond *m*, vif *m*; *(▸ of city, place)* centre *m*, cœur *m*; **the h. of the matter** le fond du problème; **the speaker went straight to the h. of the matter** le conférencier est allé droit au cœur du sujet *ou* du problème; **the law strikes at the h. of the democratic system** la loi porte atteinte aux fondements du régime démocratique; **in the h. of the financial district** au centre *ou* au cœur du quartier financier; **in the h. of winter** en plein hiver, au cœur de l'hiver; **in the h. of the forest** au cœur *ou* au beau milieu *ou* au fin fond de la forêt, en pleine forêt

9 *(of cabbage, celery, lettuce)* cœur *m*; *(of tree)* cœur *m*, vif *m*; *(of artichoke)* cœur *m*, fond *m*; *(of cable)* âme *f*, mèche *f*; *Br Literary* **hearts of oak** *(men)* hommes *mpl* courageux

10 *Cards* cœur *m*; **to play a h.** jouer un *ou* du cœur; **hearts are trumps** atout cœur; **have you got any hearts?** avez-vous du cœur?

11 *(shape)* cœur *m*; **a pattern of little red hearts** un motif de petits cœurs rouges

12 *(bosom)* poitrine *f*; **she clutched him to her h.** elle l'a serré contre sa poitrine *ou* sur son cœur

• **at heart** ADV au fond; **at h. she was a good person** elle avait un bon fond; **to be sick at h.** avoir la mort dans l'âme

• **by heart** ADV par cœur; **to learn/to know sth by h.** apprendre/savoir qch par cœur

• **hearts** NPL *Cards* = jeu de cartes dont l'objet est de faire des plis ne comprenant ni des cœurs ni la dame de pique

▸▸ *Med* ***heart attack*** crise *f* cardiaque; **to have a h. attack** avoir une crise cardiaque, faire un infarctus; *Fig* **she nearly had a h. attack when she heard about it** en apprenant la nouvelle, elle a failli avoir une attaque; *Med* ***heart disease*** maladie *f* de cœur, maladie *f* cardiaque; ***heart failure*** *(condition)* défaillance *f* cardiaque; *(cessation of heartbeat)* arrêt *m* du cœur; *Fig* **I nearly had h. failure when they told me I'd got the job** j'ai failli me trouver mal *ou* avoir une syncope quand ils m'ont dit que j'avais le poste; *Med* ***heart murmur*** souffle *m* au cœur; *Bot* ***heart of palm*** cœur *m* de palmier; ***heart patient*** cardiaque *mf*; *Mktg* ***heart share*** préférence *f*; *Med* ***heart sound*** bruit *m* cardiaque; ***heart surgeon*** chirurgien(enne) *m,f* cardiologue; *Med* ***heart surgery*** chirurgie *f* du cœur; *Med* ***heart trouble*** *(UNCOUNT)* maladie *f* du cœur, troubles *mpl* cardiaques; **to have** *or* **to suffer from h. trouble** souffrir du cœur, être cardiaque

heartache ['hɑːteɪk] N chagrin *m*, peine *f*

heartbeat ['hɑːtbiːt] N battement *m* de cœur pulsation *f*; **to be a h. away from sth** être à deux doigts de qch; *Am* **in a h.** sans hésiter

heartbreak ['hɑːtbreɪk] N *(grief ▸ gen)* (immense) chagrin *m*, déchirement *m*; *(▸ in love)* chagrin *m* d'amour; **I've had my share of h.** j'ai eu ma part de chagrins d'amour

heartbreaker ['hɑːtˌbreɪkə(r)] N *(man)* bourreau *m* des cœurs; *(woman)* femme *f* fatale

heartbreaking ['hɑːtˌbreɪkɪŋ] ADJ déchirant navrant; **it was h. to see children starving** c'était à vous fendre le cœur de voir des enfants mourir de faim; **h. scenes** des scènes *fpl* déchirantes *ou* navrantes

heartbroken ['hɑːtˌbrəʊkən] ADJ *(person ▸ gen)* qui a un immense chagrin; *(▸ stronger)* qui a le cœur brisé; *(sigh, sob)* à fendre le cœur; **she's h. over losing the job** elle n'arrive pas à se consoler *ou* à se remettre d'avoir perdu ce travail

heartburn ['hɑːtbɜːn] N *(UNCOUNT) Med* brûlures *fpl* d'estomac

hearten ['hɑːtən] VT encourager, donner du courage à; **we were heartened to learn of the drop in interest rates** nous avons été contents d'apprendre que les taux d'intérêt avaient baissé

heartening ['hɑːtənɪŋ] ADJ encourageant, réconfortant

heartfelt ['hɑːtfelt] ADJ *(apology, thanks)* sincère; **a h. wish** un souhait qui vient (du fond) du cœur

hearth [hɑːθ] N **1** *(of fireplace)* foyer *m*, âtre *m*; **a fire was burning in the h.** il y avait du feu dans la cheminée **2** *(home)* foyer *m*; **to leave h. and home** quitter le foyer

hearthstone ['hɑːθstəʊn] N foyer *m*, âtre *m*

heartily ['hɑːtɪlɪ] ADV **1** *(enthusiastically ▸ joke, laugh)* de tout son cœur; *(▸ say, thank, welcome)* chaleureusement, de tout cœur; *(▸ eat)* de bon appétit **2** *(thoroughly)* **I h. recommend it** je vous le conseille vivement; **she h. dislikes him** elle le déteste cordialement; **they were h. sick of the work** ils en avaient par-dessus la tête *ou* ils en avaient plus qu'assez du travail

heartiness ['hɑːtɪnɪs] N **1** *(of thanks, welcome)* cordialité *f*, chaleur *f*; *(of agreement)* sincérité *f*; *(of appetite)* vigueur *f*; *(of dislike)* ardeur *f*; *(of thanks)* sincérité *f* **2** *(cheerfulness)* bonne humeur *f*

heartland ['hɑːtlænd] N cœur *m*, centre *m*; **the h. of France** la France profonde; **the industrial h. of Europe** le principal centre industriel de l'Europe; **the Socialist h.** le fief des socialistes

heartless ['hɑːtlɪs] ADJ *(person)* sans cœur, impitoyable; *(laughter, treatment)* cruel

heartlessly ['hɑːtlɪslɪ] ADV sans pitié

heartlessness ['hɑːtlɪsnɪs] N *(of person)* manque *m* de cœur, caractère *m* impitoyable; *(of laughter, treatment)* cruauté *f*

heart-lung ADJ *Med*

▸▸ ***heart-lung machine*** cœur-poumon *m* artificiel; ***heart-lung transplant*** greffe *f* cœur-poumon

heartrending ['hɑːtˌrendɪŋ] ADJ déchirant, qui fend le cœur; **h. scenes of homeless refugees** des images navrantes *ou* déchirantes de réfugiés sans abri

heart-searching N examen *m* de conscience; **after much h. she decided to leave** après s'être longuement interrogée *ou* tâtée, elle décida de partir

heartsick ['hɑːtsɪk] ADJ découragé, démoralisé; **a h. lover** un amoureux transi; **to be h.** avoir la mort dans l'âme; **h. and disillusioned, he gave up his search** démoralisé *ou* abattu et désenchanté, il abandonna ses recherches

heartstrings ['hɑːtstrɪŋz] NPL **to play on** *or* **to pull on** *or* **to tug at sb's h.** faire vibrer *ou* toucher la corde sensible de qn

heart-throb N coqueluche *f*, idole *f*; **he's her h.** elle a le béguin pour lui; **he's the office h.** c'est la coqueluche du bureau

heart-to-heart N conversation *f* intime *ou* à cœur ouvert; **it's time we had a h.** il est temps qu'on se parle (à cœur ouvert)
ADJ à cœur ouvert
ADV à cœur ouvert

heartwarming ['hɑːtˌwɔːmɪŋ] ADJ réconfortant, qui réchauffe le cœur

hearty ['hɑːtɪ] (*compar* **heartier**, *superl* **heartiest**, *pl* **hearties**) ADJ **1** (*congratulations, welcome*) cordial, chaleureux; (*thanks*) sincère; (*approval, recommendation*) sans réserves; (*laugh*) gros (grosse), franc (franche); (*knock, slap*) vigoureux; **they're h. eaters** ils ont un bon coup de fourchette, ce sont de gros mangeurs
2 (*person* ▸ *robust*) vigoureux, robuste, solide; (▸ *cheerful*) jovial
3 (*meal*) copieux, abondant
4 (*thorough*) absolu; **I have a h. dislike of hypocrisy** j'ai horreur de l'hypocrisie
N **1** *Arch or Hum* **my hearties!** les gars! **2** *Fam* (*loud person*) chahuteur(euse) *m,f*

heat [hiːt] N **1** (*gen*) & *Physiol* chaleur *f*; (*of fire, sun*) ardeur *f*, chaleur *f*; **you should avoid excessive h. and cold** il faudrait que vous évitiez les trop grosses chaleurs et les trop grands froids; **the radiator gives off a lot of h.** le radiateur chauffe bien; **you shouldn't go out in this h.** tu ne devrais pas sortir par cette chaleur; **the h. of summer** le plus fort de l'été; **in the h. of the day** au (moment le) plus chaud de la journée; *Fig* **if you can't stand the h., get out of the kitchen** que ceux qui ne sont pas contents s'en aillent
2 (*temperature*) température *f*, chaleur *f*; **h. loss** perte *f ou* déperdition *f* de chaleur; *Culin* **turn up the h.** mettre le feu plus fort; **reduce the h.** réduire le feu *ou* la chaleur; **cook at a high/low h.** faire cuire à feu vif/doux
3 (*intensity of feeling, fervour*) feu *m*, passion *f*; **she replied with (some) h.** elle a répondu avec feu *ou* avec passion
4 (*high point of activity*) fièvre *f*, feu *m*; **in the h. of the argument** dans le feu de la discussion; **in the h. of the moment** dans l'agitation *ou* l'excitation du moment; **in the h. of battle** dans le feu du combat
5 *Fam* (*coercion, pressure*) **the h. is on** les choses sérieuses ont commencé; **to turn up the h.** faire pression, mettre la pression; **I'm lying low until the h. is off** je me tiens à carreau jusqu'à ce que les choses se calment; **the new deadline took the h. off him** le nouveau délai lui a permis de souffler un peu
6 *Sport* (*round of contest*) manche *f*; (*preliminary round*) (épreuve *f*) éliminatoire *f*
7 *Zool* chaleur *f*, rut *m*; *Br* **on h.**, *Am* **in h.** en chaleur, en rut
8 *Am Fam Crime slang* (*police*) **the h.** les flics *mpl*
9 *Am Fam Crime slang* (*guns*) **to be packing h.** être armé□
VT **1** (*gen*) & *Physiol* chauffer; (*overheat*) échauffer **2** *Fig* (*inflame*) échauffer, enflammer
VI (*food, liquid*) chauffer; (*air, house, room*) se réchauffer
▸▸ *Med* ***heat bump*** bouton *m* de chaleur; *Phys* ***heat constant*** constante *f* calorifique; *Tech* ***heat engine*** machine *f ou* moteur *m* thermique; *Tech* ***heat exchanger*** échangeur *m* de chaleur; *Med* ***heat exhaustion*** épuisement *m* dû à la chaleur; ***heat haze*** brume *f* de chaleur; ***heat loss*** perte *f ou* déperdition *f* de chaleur; *Med* ***heat prostration*** épuisement *m* dû à la chaleur; *Tech* ***heat pump*** pompe *f* à chaleur; *Med* ***heat rash*** irritation *f ou* inflammation *f* due à la chaleur; *Aviat* ***heat shield*** bouclier *m* thermique; *Med* ***heat treatment*** traitement *m* par la chaleur, *Spec* thermothérapie *f*; *Met* ***heat wave*** vague *f* de chaleur, canicule *f*
▸ **heat up** VT SEP réchauffer
VI (*food, liquid*) chauffer; (*air, house, room*) se réchauffer; *Fig* (*situation*) se dégrader, s'aggraver

heat-conducting ADJ *Phys* thermoconducteur

heated ['hiːtɪd] ADJ **1** (*room, swimming pool*) chauffé; (*towel rail*) chauffant **2** (*argument, discussion*) passionné; (*words*) vif; (*person*) échauffé; **he became quite h. about it** il s'est emporté *ou* échauffé à ce propos; **things got a bit h.** l'atmosphère a commencé à s'échauffer; **there were a few h. exchanges** ils échangèrent quelques propos vifs
▸▸ *Aut* ***heated rear window*** lunette *f* arrière chauffante

heatedly ['hiːtɪdlɪ] ADV (*debate, talk*) avec passion; (*argue, deny, refuse*) avec passion *ou* emportement, farouchement

heater ['hiːtə(r)] N **1** (*for room*) appareil *m* de chauffage; (*for water*) chauffe-eau *m inv*; (*for car*) (appareil *m* de) chauffage *m*; **I turned the h. on this morning** j'ai mis le chauffage ce matin **2** *Am Fam Crime slang* (*gun*) flingue *m* **3** *Electron* filament *m* incandescent

heath [hiːθ] N **1** (*moor*) lande *f* **2** *Bot* bruyère *f*

heathen ['hiːðən] (*pl* **inv** *or* **heathens**) N (*pagan*) païen(enne) *m,f*; (*barbaric person*) barbare *mf*
NPL *Literary* **the h.** (*pagans*) les païens *mpl*; (*barbarians*) les barbares *mpl*
ADJ (*pagan*) païen; (*barbaric*) barbare

heathenish ['hiːðənɪʃ] ADJ **1** (*pagan* ▸ *beliefs, rites*) païen **2** (*barbaric*) barbare

heathenism ['hiːðənɪzəm] N paganisme *m*

heather ['heðə(r)] N *Bot* bruyère *f*

Heath Robinson [ˌhiːθ'rɒbɪnsən] N = nom évoquant une machine d'une complexité absurde (d'après le nom d'un dessinateur qui imagina de nombreux dispositifs de ce genre)
ADJ d'une complexité absurde

heating ['hiːtɪŋ] N chauffage *m*; **there's no h. in the bathroom** il n'y a pas de chauffage dans la salle de bains; **to put the h. on** mettre le chauffage
COMP (*apparatus, appliance, bill, system*) de chauffage
▸▸ ***heating element*** (*burner on stove*) plaque *f* chauffante; (*in dishwasher, kettle*) élément *m* chauffant, résistance *f*; ***heating engineer*** chauffagiste *mf*

heatproof ['hiːtpruːf] ADJ (*gen*) résistant à la chaleur; (*dish*) qui va au four; (*asbestos*) incombustible

heat-resistant ADJ (*gen*) résistant à la chaleur, *Spec* thermorésistant; (*dish*) qui va au four

heat-seeking [-'siːkɪŋ] ADJ *Mil* (*missile*) à autodirecteur infrarouge

heatsink ['hiːtsɪŋk] N *Electron* dissipateur *m* thermique *ou* de chaleur

heatstroke ['hiːtstrəʊk] N (*UNCOUNT*) *Med* coup *m* de chaleur

heave [hiːv] (*pt & pp vt & vi senses* **1–3 heaved**, *pt & pp vi sense* **4 hove** [həʊv], *cont* **heaving**) VT **1** (*lift*) lever *ou* soulever avec effort; (*pull*) tirer fort; (*drag*) traîner avec effort; **he heaved the sacks of coal onto the truck** il a hissé les sacs de charbon dans le camion (à grand-peine); **I heaved myself out of the chair** je me suis arraché *ou* extirpé de ma chaise **2** (*throw*) jeter, lancer; **he heaved a rock at the bear** il a lancé une pierre sur l'ours **3** *Fig* **to h. a sigh of relief** pousser un soupir de soulagement
VI **1** (*rise and fall* ▸ *sea, waves, chest*) se soulever; (▸ *ship*) tanguer
2 (*lift*) lever, soulever; (*pull*) tirer; **h.!** ho! hisse!
3 (*retch*) avoir des haut-le-cœur; (*vomit*) vomir; **the sight made my stomach h.** le spectacle m'a soulevé le cœur *ou* m'a donné des nausées
4 *Naut* aller, se déplacer; **the ship hove alongside the quay** le navire a accosté le quai; *Naut & Fig* **to h. into sight** *or* **into view** paraître *ou Literary* poindre à l'horizon
N **1** (*attempt to move*) **I gave the rope one more h.** j'ai tiré une fois de plus sur la corde; **with a h. he dragged the table against the door** dans un effort il traîna la table jusqu'à la porte; *Fam* **to give sb the h.** (*employee*) virer qn; (*boyfriend, girlfriend*) plaquer qn **2** (*retching*) haut-le-cœur *m inv*, nausée *f*; (*vomiting*) vomissement *m*
• **heaves** NPL **1** *Vet* pousse *f*; **this horse has the heaves** ce cheval a la pousse *ou* est poussif **2** *Fam* **to have the heaves** (*retching*) avoir des haut-le-cœur□; (*vomiting*) vomir□
▸ **heave to** *Naut* VI se mettre en panne
VT SEP mettre en panne

heave-ho EXCLAM *Naut* oh hisse!
N *Fam* **to give sb the h.** (*of employer*) sacquer qn, virer qn; (*of boyfriend, girlfriend*) plaquer qn

heaven ['hevən] N **1** *Rel* ciel *m*, paradis *m*; **to go to h.** aller au ciel, aller au *ou* en paradis; **in h.** au ciel, au *ou* en paradis; **Our Father, who art in H.** notre Père qui êtes aux cieux
2 *Fig* (*place or state of happiness*) **the Caribbean was like h. on earth** les Caraïbes étaient un véritable paradis sur terre; **this is sheer h.!** c'est divin *ou* merveilleux!, c'est le paradis!
3 (*emphatic uses*) **h. forbid!** pourvu que non!, j'espère bien que non!; **h. forbid that I should see her** que Dieu me garde de la voir; **h. help us if they catch us** que le ciel nous vienne en aide s'ils nous attrapent; **h. knows I've tried!** Dieu sait si j'ai essayé!; **she bought books, magazines and h. knows what (else)** elle a acheté des livres, des revues et je ne sais *ou* Dieu sait quoi encore; *Fam* **what in h.'s name is that?** au nom du ciel, qu'est-ce que c'est que ça?; *Fam* **who in h.'s name told you that?** qui diable vous a dit ça?, mais qui a donc pu vous dire cela?; **thank h. (for that)!** Dieu merci!; *Fam* **good heavens!** ciel!, mon dieu!; *Fam* **(good) heavens, is that the time?** mon Dieu *ou* juste ciel, il est si tard que ça?; *Fam* **for h.'s sake!** (*in annoyance*) mince!; (*in pleading*) pour l'amour du ciel!; *Fam* **it smells** *or* **stinks to high h. in here!** qu'est-ce que ça peut puer ici!; **she's in h. when she's with him** elle est au septième ciel *ou* aux anges quand elle est avec lui; **to move h. and earth to do sth** remuer ciel et terre pour faire qch
• **heavens** NPL (*sky*) *Literary* **the heavens** le ciel, le firmament; **the heavens opened** il s'est mis à pleuvoir à torrents

heavenly ['hevənlɪ] ADJ **1** (*from heaven, the sky*) céleste, du ciel; (*holy*) divin; **H. Father** Père *m* céleste **2** *Fam* (*wonderful*) divin, merveilleux; **what h. peaches!** quelles pêches délicieuses!; **to have a h. evening** passer une soirée merveilleuse
▸▸ ***heavenly body*** corps *m* céleste

heaven-sent ADJ providentiel; **a h. opportunity** une occasion providentielle *ou* qui tombe à pic

heavily ['hevɪlɪ] ADV **1** (*fall, land*) lourdement, pesamment; (*walk*) d'un pas lourd *ou* pesant, lourdement; **she leaned h. on my arm** elle s'appuya de tout son poids sur mon bras; *Fig* **time hangs h. on her** elle trouve le temps long, le temps lui pèse; **it weighed h. on my conscience** cela me pesait sur la conscience
2 (*laboriously* ▸ *move*) avec difficulté, péniblement; (▸ *breathe*) péniblement, bruyamment
3 (*deeply* ▸ *sleep*) profondément; **she left the room, sighing h.** en poussant un énorme *ou* gros soupir, elle a quitté la pièce
4 (*as intensifier*) (*drink, smoke, gamble*) beaucoup; (*fine, load, tax*) lourdement; (*stress*) fortement, lourdement; **it was raining h.** il pleuvait des cordes; **it was snowing h.** il neigeait très fort *ou* dru *ou* à gros flocons; **they lost h.** (*team*) ils se sont fait écraser; (*gamblers*) ils ont perdu gros; *Fam* **they're h. into yoga** ils se donnent à fond dans le yoga; **the secret service was h. involved in training guerrillas** les services secrets étaient lourdement impliqués dans la formation des guérilleros; **they're h. dependent on foreign trade** ils sont fortement tributaires du commerce extérieur; **h. wooded** très boisé

heaviness ['hevɪnɪs] N **1** (*weight* ▸ *of object*) poids *m*; (▸ *of physique*) lourdeur *f*
2 (*of burden*) poids *m*
3 (*of movement, step*) lourdeur *f*, pesanteur *f*
4 (*depression*) abattement *m*, découragement *m*; (*sadness*) tristesse *f*; **h. of heart** tristesse *f*
5 (*of humour, irony*) manque *m* de subtilité; (*of style*) lourdeur *f*
6 (*of food, meal*) caractère *m* indigeste
7 (*of air, cloud, weather, silence*) lourdeur *f*

heaving ['hiːvɪŋ] ADJ *Br Fam* (*extremely busy*) hyper animé

HEAVY ['hevɪ]

ADJ
- lourd **1–3, 5, 6, 9, 11, 13–15, 18, 20**
- gros **3, 5–8**
- pénible **11**
- chargé **2, 11**
- important **3, 16**
- grave **9, 18**

ADV
- lourd **1**
- lourdement **1**

N
- rôle tragique **1**
- dur **2**

(*compar* **heavier**, *superl* **heaviest**, *pl* **heavies**)

ADJ 1 *(in weight)* lourd; *(object)* lourd, pesant; **how h. is he?** combien pèse-t-il?; **how h. is it?** est-ce que c'est lourd?; **it's too h. for me to lift** je ne peux pas le soulever, c'est *ou* ça pèse trop lourd

2 *(burdened, laden)* chargé, lourd; **the branches were h. with fruit** les branches étaient chargées *ou* lourdes de fruits; **her eyes were h. with sleep** elle avait les yeux lourds de sommeil; *Arch or Literary* **she was h. with child** elle était enceinte; *Zool* **h. with young** gravide, grosse

3 *(in quantity ▸ expenses, payments)* important, considérable; *(▸ fine, losses)* gros (grosse), lourd; *(▸ taxes)* lourd; *(▸ casualties, damages)* énorme, important; *(▸ crop)* abondant, gros (grosse); *(▸ dew)* abondant; *(▸ user)* gros (grosse); **she has a h. cold** elle a un gros rhume, elle est fortement enrhumée; **to have h. periods** avoir des règles abondantes; **there's a h. demand for teachers** il y a une forte *ou* grosse demande d'enseignants; **her students make h. demands on her** ses étudiants sont très exigeants avec elle *ou* exigent beaucoup d'elle; **h. rain** forte pluie *f*; **h. seas** grosse mer *f*; **h. showers** grosses *ou* fortes averses *fpl*; **h. sleep** sommeil *m* profond *ou* lourd; **to be a h. sleeper** avoir le sommeil profond *ou* lourd; **h. snow** neige *f* abondante, fortes chutes *fpl* de neige; **they expect h. trading on the Stock Exchange** ils s'attendent à ce que le marché soit très actif; **h. traffic** circulation *f* dense, grosse circulation *f*

4 *(using large quantities)* **he's a h. drinker/smoker** il boit/fume beaucoup, c'est un grand buveur/fumeur; **a h. gambler** un (une) flambeur(euse); *Br Fam* **the car's very h. on petrol** la voiture consomme énormément d'essence

5 *(laborious ▸ movement)* lourd; *(▸ step)* pesant, lourd; *(▸ sigh)* gros (grosse), profond; *(▸ thud)* gros (grosse); **he was dealt a h. blow** *(hit)* il a reçu un coup violent; *(from fate)* ça a été un rude coup *ou* un gros choc pour lui; **h. breathing** *(from effort, illness)* respiration *f* pénible; *(from excitement)* respiration *f* haletante; **h. fighting is reported in the Gulf** on signale des combats acharnés dans le Golfe; **to rule with a h. hand** gouverner de façon très autoritaire; **we could hear his h. tread on the stairs** nous l'entendions monter l'escalier d'un pas lourd; **a h. landing** un atterrissage brutal

6 *(thick ▸ coat, sweater, shoes)* gros (grosse); *(▸ soil)* lourd, gras

7 *(person ▸ fat)* gros (grosse), corpulent; *(▸ solid)* costaud, fortement charpenté; **a man of h. build** un homme solidement bâti

8 *(coarse, solid ▸ line, lips)* gros (grosse), épais (aisse); *(thick ▸ beard)* gros (grosse), fort; **h. features** gros traits *mpl*, traits *mpl* épais *ou* lourds

9 *(grave, serious ▸ news)* grave; *(▸ responsibility)* lourd; *(▸ defeat)* lourd, grave; *Fam* **things got a bit h.** les choses ont mal tourné

10 *(depressed ▸ mood, spirits)* abattu, déprimé; **with a h. heart, h. at heart** le cœur gros

11 *(tiring ▸ task)* lourd, pénible; *(▸ work)* pénible; *(▸ day, schedule, week)* chargé, difficile; **I've got a h. day ahead of me** j'ai une journée chargée devant moi; **h. going** *(in horseracing)* terrain *m* lourd; *Fig* **they found it h. going** ils ont trouvé cela pénible *ou* difficile; **I found his last novel very h. going** j'ai trouvé son dernier roman très indigeste

12 *(difficult to understand ▸ not superficial)* profond, compliqué, sérieux; *(▸ tedious)* indigeste; **the report makes for h. reading** le rapport n'est pas d'une lecture facile *ou* est ardu

13 *(clumsy ▸ humour, irony)* peu subtil, lourd; *(▸ style)* lourd

14 *(food, meal)* lourd, indigeste; *(wine)* corsé, lourd; **these scones are a bit on the h. side** ces scones sont un peu lourds *ou* indigestes

15 *(ominous, oppressive ▸ air, cloud, weather)* lourd; *(▸ sky)* couvert, chargé, lourd; *(▸ silence)* lourd, pesant, profond; *(▸ smell, perfume)* lourd, fort; *Fam (▸ situation)* difficile[□], menaçant[□]; **to make h. weather of doing sth** avoir du mal à faire qch; *Fam* **to get h. with sb** devenir agressif avec qn[□]

16 *Fam (important)* important[□]; **to have a h. date** avoir un rendez-vous galant

17 *(stress)* accentué; *(rhythm)* aux accents marqués

18 *Phys (body)* grave; *Nucl (atom)* lourd

19 *St Exch* **the market is h.** le marché est lourd *ou* orienté vers la baisse

20 *Theat (part ▸ difficult)* lourd, difficile; *(▸ dramatic)* tragique

ADV 1 *(lie, weigh)* lourd, lourdement; **the lie weighed h. on her conscience** le mensonge pesait lourd sur sa conscience; **time hangs h. on his hands** il trouve le temps long

2 *(harshly)* **to come on h. with sb** être dur avec qn

N 1 *Theat (serious part)* rôle *m* tragique; *(part of villain)* rôle *m* du traître; **he usually plays the h.** d'habitude il joue des rôles de traître

2 *Fam (tough guy)* dur *m*; **he sent round the heavies** il a envoyé les brutes *ou* les casseurs; **don't come the h. with me** ne joue pas au dur avec moi

3 *Fam (boxer, wrestler)* (poids *m*) lourd[□] *m*

4 *Mil* gros calibre *m*

5 *Scot (beer)* = bière relativement amère, à forte teneur en houblon

6 *Br Fam Press* **the heavies** = les quotidiens de qualité

▸▸ *Mil* ***heavy artillery*** artillerie *f* lourde *ou* de gros calibre; *Fam* ***heavy breather*** auteur *m* de coups de téléphone obscènes[□]; *Am Culin* ***heavy cream*** crème *f* fraîche épaisse; *Mil* ***heavy fire*** feu *m* nourri, feu *m* intense; *Br Transp* ***heavy goods vehicle*** poids *m* lourd; *Am* ***heavy hitter*** *(in baseball)* = joueur qui frappe fort et marque beaucoup de points; *Fig* homme *m* influent, gros bonnet *m*; *Chem* ***heavy hydrogen*** hydrogène *m* lourd, deutérium *m*; *Ind* ***heavy industry*** industrie *f* lourde; ***heavy machinery*** matériel *m* lourd; *St Exch* ***heavy market*** marché *m* lourd; ***heavy metal*** *Phys* métal *m* lourd; *Mus* heavy metal *m inv*; *Fam* ***the heavy mob*** les casseurs *mpl*, les durs *mpl*; ***heavy oil*** huile *f* lourde; ***heavy petting*** *(UNCOUNT)* caresses *fpl* très poussées; *Typ* ***heavy type*** caractères *mpl* gras; *Phys* ***heavy water*** eau *f* lourde

---

heavy-duty **ADJ 1** *(clothing, furniture)* résistant; *(boots)* solide, robuste; *(cleaning product, equipment)* à usage industriel; *(tyre)* tout-terrain *(inv)* **2** *Fam (meeting)* important[□]; *(activity, discussion)* intense[□]

heavy-eyed **ADJ** aux yeux battus

heavy-handed **ADJ 1** *(clumsy ▸ person)* maladroit; *(▸ style, writing)* lourd **2** *(harsh ▸ person)* dur, sévère; *(▸ action, policy)* arbitraire **3** *(tactless ▸ remark)* qui manque de tact; *(▸ joke)* lourd, qui manque de subtilité; *(▸ compliment)* lourd, (trop) appuyé

heavy-hearted [-'hɑ:tɪd] **ADJ** abattu, découragé; **she felt sad and h.** elle se sentait triste et avait le cœur gros

heavy-laden **ADJ** *(physically)* très chargé; *(emotionally)* accablé

heavyweight ['hevɪweɪt] **N 1** *(large person, thing)* colosse *m*; *Fam Fig (important person)* personne *f* de poids *ou* d'envergure, ponte *m*; **a literary h.** un écrivain profond *ou* sérieux, un grand écrivain **2** *Sport* poids *m* lourd

ADJ 1 *(cloth, wool)* lourd; *(coat, sweater)* gros (grosse) **2** *Fam Fig (important)* important[□]; **a h. industrialist** un grand *ou* gros industriel[□] **3** *Sport (championship, fight)* poids lourd *(inv)*; **he's a h. fighter** c'est un poids lourd

▸▸ *Sport* ***heavyweight champion*** champion *m* poids lourd *ou* dans la catégorie poids lourd; ***the heavyweight title*** le titre (des) poids lourds

hebe [hi:b] **N** *Am Fam* youpin(e) *m,f*, = terme injurieux désignant un Juif

Hebrew ['hi:bru:] **N 1** *(person ▸ man)* Hébreu *m*, Israélite *m*, Juif *m*; *(▸ woman)* Israélite *f*, Juive *f*; **the Hebrews** les Hébreux *mpl*; *Bible* **the Epistle of Paul to the Hebrews** l'Épître de saint Paul aux Hébreux **2** *(language)* hébreu *m*

ADJ *(person ▸ man)* hébreu, israélite, juif; *(▸ woman)* israélite, juive; *(object, art, etc)* hébraïque; **the H. state** l'état *m* hébreu

Hebridean [ˌhebrɪ'di:ən] **ADJ** des Hébrides

Hebrides ['hebrɪdi:z] **NPL** *Geog* **the H.** les (îles *fpl*) Hébrides *fpl*

heck [hek] *Fam* **N that's a h. of a lot of money!** c'est une sacrée somme d'argent!; **what the h. are you doing here?** qu'est-ce que tu fous là?; **where the h. did he go?** où diable est-il allé?; **who the h. said you could borrow my car?** bon sang! qui t'as dit que tu pouvais prendre ma voiture?; **why the h. didn't you tell me?** pourquoi est-ce que tu m'as pas prévenu, nom de nom!; **how the h. should I know?** mais enfin, comment veux-tu que je sache?; **he misses her a h. of a lot** elle lui manque vachement; **we saw a h. of a good film** on a vu un vachement bon film; **I went just for the h. of it** j'y suis allé, histoire de rire *ou* de rigoler; **oh, what the h.!** et puis flûte!

EXCLAM mince alors!

heckle ['hekəl] **VT** *(interrupt)* interrompre bruyamment; *(shout at)* interpeller, harceler

VI crier *(pour gêner un orateur)*

heckler ['heklə(r)] **N** chahuteur(euse) *m,f*

heckling ['heklɪŋ] **N** *(UNCOUNT)* harcèlement *m*, interpellations *fpl*

ADJ qui fait du harcèlement, qui interpelle

hectare ['hekteə(r)] **N** hectare *m*

hectic ['hektɪk] **ADJ 1** *(turbulent)* agité, bousculé; *(eventful)* mouvementé; **I've had a h. day** j'ai eu une journée mouvementée, j'ai été bousculé toute la journée; **we spent three h. weeks preparing the play** ça a été la course folle pendant les trois semaines où on préparait la pièce; **they lead a h. life** *(busy)* ils mènent une vie trépidante; *(eventful)* ils mènent une vie très mouvementée **2** *(flushed)* fiévreux; *Med (fever, flush)* hectique

hectically ['hektɪklɪ] **ADV** fiévreusement

hectolitre, *Am* **hectoliter** ['hektəˌli:tə(r)] **N** hectolitre *m*

hector ['hektə(r)] **VT** harceler, tyranniser

VI être tyrannique, être une brute

N brute *f*, tyran *m*

hectoring ['hektərɪŋ] **N** *(UNCOUNT)* harcèlement *m*, torture *f*

ADJ *(behaviour)* tyrannique; *(tone, voice)* impérieux, autoritaire

hectowatt ['hektəwɒt] **N** hectowatt *m*

he'd [hi:d] = **he had, he would**

hedge [hedʒ] **N 1** *(shrubs)* haie *f*; **hawthorn h.** haie *f* d'aubépine; *Hum* **he looks like he's been dragged through a h. backwards** il a l'air tout ébouriffé **2** *(protection)* sauvegarde *f*; **a h. against inflation** une sauvegarde *ou* une couverture contre l'inflation **3** *St Exch* couverture *f*

VT 1 *(enclose)* entourer d'une haie, enclore; **the field was hedged with beech** le champ était entouré d'une haie de hêtres **2** *(guard against losing)* couvrir; **to h. one's bets** *(in betting)* répartir les risques; *Fig (cover oneself)* se couvrir **3** *St Exch (position)* protéger, couvrir; *(shares)* arbitrer; *(transactions)* couvrir

VI 1 *(plant hedge)* planter une haie; *(trim hedge)* tailler une haie

2 *(in action, discussion)* essayer de gagner du temps, atermoyer; *(in answering)* éviter de répondre, répondre à côté; *(in explaining)* expliquer avec des détours; **they are hedging slightly on the trade agreement** ils essaient de gagner du temps avant de conclure l'accord commercial

3 *(protect)* se protéger; **it's a way of hedging against inflation** c'est un moyen de vous protéger *ou* vous couvrir contre l'inflation

4 *St Exch* se couvrir; **to h. against currency fluctuations** se couvrir contre les fluctuations monétaires

▸▸ ***hedge clippers*** cisaille *f* à haies; *St Exch* ***hedge fund*** société *f* d'investissement; *St Exch* ***hedge ratio*** ratio *m* de couverture; ***hedge trimmer*** taille-haie *m*

▸**hedge in** **VT SEP 1** *(surround with hedge)* entourer d'une haie, enclore **2** *(person)* **hedged in by restrictions** assorti de restrictions; **I'm feeling hedged in** je ne me sens pas libre

▸**hedge off** **VT SEP** *(area)* entourer d'une haie; *(part of area)* séparer par une haie

hedgehog ['hedʒhɒg] **N** *Zool* hérisson *m*; **to curl up like a h.** se pelotonner, se recroqueviller (sur soi-même)

hedgehop ['hedʒhɒp] *(pt & pp* **hedgehopped**, *cont* **hedgehopping)** **VI** *Aviat* voler en rase-mottes, faire du rase-mottes

hedgerow ['hedʒrəʊ] **N** haies *fpl*

hedging ['hedʒɪŋ] **N 1** *(care of hedges)* entretien *m* des haies; **h. and ditching** entretien *m* des haies et des fossés
2 *(hedges)* bordure *f*
3 *Horseracing* répartition *f* des risques
4 *St Exch* opérations *fpl* de couverture
5 *(in discussion etc)* faux-fuyants *mpl*

hedonism ['hi:dənɪzəm, 'hedənɪzəm] **N** hédonisme *m*

hedonist ['hi:dənɪst, 'hedənɪst] **N** hédoniste *mf*

hedonistic [ˌhi:də'nɪstɪk, 'hedənɪstɪk] **ADJ** hédoniste

heebie-jeebies [ˌhi:bɪ'dʒi:bɪz] **NPL** *Fam* **to have the h.** avoir la frousse *ou* les chocottes; **he gives me the h.** *(revolts me)* il me hérisse; *(scares me)* il me donne la chair de poule

heed [hi:d] **N to take h. of sth, to pay** *or* **to give h. to sth** tenir bien compte de qch; **I took no h. of her advice** je n'ai tenu aucun compte de ses conseils; **pay no h. to him** ne faites pas attention à lui
VT 1 *(warning, words)* faire bien attention à, tenir compte de, prendre garde à **2** *(person* ▸ *listen to)* bien écouter; *(*▸ *obey)* obéir à

heedful ['hi:dfʊl] **ADJ** *Formal* attentif; **they seemed h. of what they were doing** ils semblaient attentifs à ce qu'ils faisaient

heedless ['hi:dlɪs] **ADJ h. of the danger** sans se soucier du danger; **h. of my warning** sans tenir compte de mon avertissement

heedlessly ['hi:dlɪslɪ] **ADV 1** *(without thinking)* sans faire attention, à la légère **2** *(inconsiderately)* avec insouciance, négligemment

hee-haw [ˌhi:'hɔ:] **N 1** *(of donkey)* hi-han *m* **2** *(guffaw)* gros rire *m*
VI 1 *(donkey)* braire, faire hi-han **2** *(person)* rire bruyamment
EXCLAM hi-han!

heel [hi:l] **N 1** *(of foot)* talon *m*; **she spun** *or* **turned on her h. and walked away** elle a tourné les talons; **we followed hard on her heels** *(walked)* nous lui emboîtâmes le pas; *(tracked)* nous étions sur ses talons; **he brought the dog to h.** il a fait venir le chien à ses pieds; *Fig* **to bring sb to h.** mettre qn au pas; **to come to h.** *(dog)* venir au pied; *Fam Fig (person, state)* se soumettre❑; *Fam* **to take to one's heels, to show a clean pair of heels** se sauver à toutes jambes, prendre ses jambes à son cou
2 *(of boot, shoe)* talon *m*; **she was wearing heels** *(high-heeled shoes)* elle portait des talons; *Br* **to be down at h.**, *Am* **to be down at the heels** *(shoes)* être éculé; *Fig (person)* avoir l'air miteux
3 *(of glove, golf club, hand, knife, sock, tool)* talon *m*
4 *(of bread)* talon *m*, croûton *m*; *(of cheese)* talon *m*, croûte *f*
5 *Fam (contemptible person)* chameau *m*
6 *Naut (of keel)* talon *m*; *(of mast)* caisse *f*
7 *(of ship)* bande *f*, gîte *f*, inclinaison *f*
VT 1 *(boot, shoe)* refaire le talon de; **to get one's shoes heeled** (faire) refaire le talon de ses chaussures **2** *(in rugby)* talonner
VI 1 *(of ship)* avoir *ou* donner de la bande, prendre de la gîte **2** *(to dog)* **h.!** au pied!
▸▸ ***heel bar*** talon-minute *m*, réparations-minute *fpl*

▸**heel over VI** *(ship)* gîter, donner de la bande; *(vehicle, tower)* s'incliner, se pencher; *(cyclist)* se pencher

heelpiece ['hi:lpi:s] **N** *(of shoe)* contrefort *m* du talon

heeltap ['hi:ltæp] **N 1** *(in shoe)* rondelle *f* en cuir *(pour talon)* **2** *(in glass)* fond *m* de verre

Heely® ['hi:lɪ] **N** chaussure *f* à roulette

heft [heft] *Fam* **N 1** *(weight)* poids❑ *m* **2** *Am (main part)* gros❑ *m*
VT 1 *(lift)* soulever❑; *(hoist)* hisser❑ **2** *(test weight of)* soupeser❑

hefty ['heftɪ] *(compar* **heftier**, *superl* **heftiest)** **ADJ** *Fam* **1** *(package* ▸ *heavy)* lourd❑; *(*▸ *bulky)* encombrant❑, volumineux❑; *(book)* épais(aisse)❑, gros (grosse)❑; *(person)* costaud **2** *(part, profit)* gros (grosse)❑; **a h. sum** une jolie somme; **he paid a h. price for them** il les a payés drôlement cher; **she earns a h. salary** elle se fait une bonne *ou* sacrée paie **3** *(blow, slap)* puissant❑

Hegelian [her'gi:lɪən] **ADJ** *Phil* hégélien

hegemony [hɪ'gemənɪ] **N** hégémonie *f*

Hegira, Hejira ['hedʒɪrə] **N** *Rel* hégire *f*
▸▸ ***the Hegira calendar*** le calendrier musulman

heifer ['hefə(r)] **N 1** *(animal)* génisse *f* **2** *Fam (fat woman)* grosse dondon *f*; *Am (attractive woman)* canon *m*

heigh-ho ['her'həʊ] **EXCLAM 1** *(in weariness)* eh bien!; *(in resignation)* hélas! **2** *Old-fashioned or Literary (in surprise)* ça alors!, ça par exemple!; *(in happiness)* chouette alors!

height [haɪt] **N 1** *(tallness* ▸ *of person)* taille *f*, grandeur *f*; *(*▸ *of building, tree)* hauteur *f*; **what h. are you?** combien mesurez-vous?; **h.: 1 m 80** *(on form)* taille: 1 m 80; **I'm of average h.** je suis de taille moyenne; **redwoods grow to a h. of 100 metres** les séquoias peuvent atteindre 100 mètres (de haut)
2 *(distance above ground* ▸ *of mountain, plane)* altitude *f*; *(*▸ *of ceiling, river, stars)* hauteur *f*; **the plane was gaining/losing h.** l'avion prenait/perdait de l'altitude; **to be at a h. of 30 metres above the ground** être à 30 mètres au-dessus du sol
3 *(high position)* hauteur *f*; **to fall from a great h.** tomber de haut; **to have a good head for heights** ne pas avoir le vertige; **I'm afraid of heights** j'ai le vertige; *Fig* **to reach new heights** atteindre de nouveaux sommets
4 *Fig (peak* ▸ *of career, success)* point *m* culminant; *(*▸ *of fortune, fame)* apogée *m*; *(*▸ *of arrogance, stupidity)* comble *m*; **at the h. of her powers** en pleine possession de ses moyens; **at its h. the group had 300 members** à son apogée, le groupe comprenait 300 membres; **the tourist season is at its h.** la saison touristique bat son plein; **the h. of bad manners** le comble de l'impolitesse *ou* de la grossièreté; **at the h. of summer** en plein été, au plus chaud de l'été; **at the h. of the battle/storm** au plus fort de la bataille/de l'orage; **it's the h. of fashion** c'est le dernier cri
▸▸ ***height restriction*** limitation *f* de hauteur

height-adjustable ADJ réglable en hauteur

heighten ['haɪtən] **VT 1** *(make higher* ▸ *building, ceiling, shelf)* relever, rehausser **2** *(increase* ▸ *effect, fear, pleasure)* augmenter, intensifier; *(*▸ *flavour, colour)* relever; *(*▸ *contrast)* accentuer; *(*▸ *impression, speculation)* renforcer; *(*▸ *fever)* faire monter, aggraver; **the incident has heightened public awareness of environmental problems** l'incident a sensibilisé encore plus le public aux problèmes de l'environnement; **the riots have heightened racial tensions in the city** les émeutes ont accentué *ou* aggravé les tensions raciales dans la ville; **the colour heightened the deathly pallor of her skin** cette couleur faisait ressortir *ou* accentuait sa pâleur cadavérique
VI *(fear, pleasure)* augmenter, monter; *(speculation)* s'intensifier; *(tension)* monter

heightened ['haɪtənd] **ADJ 1** *(building, ceiling, shelf)* relevé, rehaussé **2** *(fear, pleasure)* intensifié; *(colour)* plus vif; **there is a h. awareness of the dangers of pollution** il y a une prise de conscience accrue des dangers de la pollution

heightening ['haɪtənɪŋ] **N 1** *(of building, ceiling, shelf)* rehaussement *m*, surélévation *f* **2** *(of fear, pleasure)* accroissement *m*, intensification *f*

Heimlich manoeuvre ['haɪmlɪk-] **N** *Med* méthode *f* d'Heimlich

heinous ['heɪnəs] **ADJ** *Literary or Formal* odieux, atroce; **a h. crime** un crime abominable *ou* odieux

> Note that the French word **haineux** is a false friend and is never a translation for the English word **heinous**. It means **full of hatred**.

Heinz [haɪnz] **N** *Fam Hum (dog)* bâtard❑ *m*

heir [eə(r)] **N** *(gen)* héritier *m*; *Law* héritier *m*, légataire *mf*; **he is h. to a vast fortune** il est l'héritier d'une immense fortune; **the h. to the throne** l'héritier du trône *ou* de la couronne
▸▸ ***heir apparent*** *Law* héritier *m* présomptif; *Fig (of political party, company)* dauphin *m*; *Law* ***heir presumptive*** héritier *m* présomptif *(sauf naissance d'un héritier en ligne directe)*

heiress ['eərɪs] **N** héritière *f*

heirloom ['eəlu:m] **N 1** *(family property)* **(family) h.** objet *m* de famille **2** *Law (legacy)* legs *m*

heist [haɪst] *Am Fam* **N** *(robbery)* vol❑ *m*; *(in bank)* braquage *m*; *(stolen objects)* butin❑ *m*
VT *(money)* voler❑; *(bank)* braquer

Helen ['helɪn] **PR N** *Myth* Hélène; **H. of Troy** Hélène de Troie

helianthus [ˌhi:lɪ'ænθəs] **N** *Bot* hélianthe *m*, tournesol *m*

helical ['helɪkəl, 'hi:lɪkəl] **ADJ** hélicoïdal

helicopter ['helɪkɒptə(r)] **N** *Aviat* hélicoptère *m*; **the wounded were transported by h.** les blessés ont été héliportés
COMP *(patrol, rescue)* en hélicoptère; *(pilot)* d'hélicoptère
VT transporter en hélicoptère
▸▸ ***helicopter carrier*** porte-hélicoptères *m inv*; ***helicopter gunship*** hélicoptère *m* de combat; ***helicopter ship*** porte-hélicoptères *m inv*; ***helicopter transfer, helicopter transport*** héliportage *m*

▸**helicopter in VT SEP** *(troops, supplies)* amener en hélicoptère, héliporter

▸**helicopter out VT SEP** *(people)* emmener en hélicoptère, héliporter

heliograph ['hi:lɪəʊgrɑ:f] **N 1** *(transmitter)* héliographe *m* **2** *Phot (camera)* photohéliographe *m*
VT transmettre par héliographe

heliotrope ['heliətrəʊp] **N 1** *Bot* héliotrope *m* **2** *(colour)* violet *m* clair
ADJ violet clair

helipad ['helɪpæd] **N** *Aviat* zone *f* d'atterrissage pour hélicoptère

heliport ['helɪpɔ:t] **N** *Aviat* héliport *m*

heliskiing ['helɪˌski:ɪŋ] **N** héliski *m*, ski *m* avec dépose en hélicoptère

helium ['hi:lɪəm] **N** *Chem* hélium *m*
▸▸ ***helium balloon*** ballon *m* gonflé à l'hélium

helix ['hi:lɪks] *(pl* **helices** ['helɪsi:z] *or* **helixes)** **N 1** *Archit & Geom (spiral)* hélice *f* **2** *Anat & Zool* hélix *m*

hell [hel] **N 1** *Rel* enfer *m*; *Myth (underworld)* les Enfers *mpl*; **to go to h.** *(Christianity)* aller en enfer; *Myth* descendre aux Enfers; **it's (as) hot as h. in there** il fait une chaleur de tous les diables *ou* infernale là-dedans; *Fam* **go to h.!** va te faire voir!; *Fam* **to h. with him!** qu'il aille au diable!; *Fam* **to h. with society!** au diable la société!; *Fam* **to h. with what they think!** leur avis, je m'assois dessus!; *Fam* **come h. or high water** contre vents et marées, envers et contre tout; *Fam* **when h. freezes over** à la saint-glinglin, la semaine des quatre jeudis; **that won't happen until h. freezes over** ça aura lieu la semaine des quatre jeudis; *Fam* **it'll be a cold day in h. before I apologize** je m'excuserai quand les poules auront des dents; *Fam* **the boyfriend/flatmate/neighbours from h.** un petit ami/un colocataire/des voisins *mpl* de cauchemar; *Fam* **it was a journey from h.!** ce voyage, c'était l'horreur!; *Fam* **all h. broke loose** ça a bardé; *Fam* **to give sb h.** passer un savon *ou* faire sa fête à qn; *Fam* **the damp weather plays h. with my arthritis** ce temps humide me fait rudement souffrir de mon arthrite!, par ces temps humides, qu'est-ce que je déguste avec mon arthrite!; *Fam* **there'll be h. to pay when he finds out** ça va barder *ou* chauffer quand il l'apprendra; *Fam* **they went into town to raise (a little) h.** ils sont allés faire la bringue en ville; *Fam* **the boss raised h. when he saw the report** le patron a fait une scène de tous les diables en voyant le rapport; *Fam* **I went along just for the h. of it** j'y suis allé histoire de rire *ou* de rigoler; *Fam* **he ran off h. for leather** il est parti ventre à terre; *Fam* **to ride h. for leather** aller au triple galop *ou* à bride abattue; *Am Fam* **the whole country's going to h. in a handcart** tout fout le camp dans ce pays; *Fam* **h.'s bells!, h.'s teeth!** mince alors!
2 *Fam (torture)* enfer *m*; **it's h. in here** c'est infernal ici; **it can be h. trying to park here** quelquefois, c'est la croix et la bannière pour se garer par ici; **working there was h. on earth** *or* **on wheels** c'était l'enfer de travailler là-bas; **he made her life h.** il lui a fait mener une vie infernale
3 *Fam (used as emphasis)* **it's colder/hotter than h.** il fait vachement froid/chaud; **he's as happy/tired as h.** il est vachement heureux/fatigué; **he's**

in a h. of a mess il est dans un sacré pétrin; *Br* **it's a h. of a cold outside** il fait un froid de canard dehors; **a h. of a wind** un vent du diable *ou* de tous les diables; **there was a** *or* **one h. of a fight** il y a eu une bagarre terrible; **you've got a h. of a nerve!** tu as un culot du diable!; **a h. of a lot of books** tout un tas *ou* un paquet de livres; **he likes her a h. of a lot** il est dingue d'elle; **we had a h. of a good time** nous nous sommes amusés comme des fous; **it was a h. of a good film** c'était un sacrément bon film; **they had a h. of a time getting the car started** ils en ont bavé pour faire démarrer la voiture; **my arm started to hurt like h.** mon bras a commencé à me faire vachement mal; **he worked like h.** il a travaillé comme une brute *ou* une bête; **to run/to shout like h.** courir/crier comme un fou; **will you lend me $50? – like h.** *or* **the h. I will!** peux-tu me prêter 50 dollars? – tu peux toujours courir!; **I'm leaving – like h.** *or* **the h. you are!** je pars – n'y compte pas!; **I wish to h. I could remember** si seulement je pouvais me souvenir□; **I just hope to h. he leaves** j'espère de tout mon cœur qu'il partira; **get the h. out of here!** fous *ou* fous-moi le camp!; **what the h.** *or* **in h.'s name are you doing?** qu'est-ce que tu fous?; **what the h.'s going on?** qu'est-ce qui se passe, nom de Dieu?; **why the h. did you go?** qu'est-ce qui t'a pris d'y aller?; **how the h. would I know?** comment veux-tu que je le sache?; *Am* **how the h. are you doing, my friend?** comment ça va, mon pote?; **where the h. are my keys?** où diable sont mes clefs?; **who the h. are you?** qui diable êtes-vous?; **oh well, what the h.!** oh qu'est-ce que ça peut bien faire?; **did you agree? – h., no!** as-tu accepté? – tu plaisantes!□

4 *Am Fam (high spirits)* **there's h. in that boy** ce garçon respire la joie de vivre□; **full of h.** plein d'entrain□ *ou* de vivacité□

EXCLAM (oh) h.! bon Dieu!

►► ***Hell's Angels*** = nom d'un groupe de motards au comportement violent; *Am Univ* ***hell week*** = semaine au cours de laquelle les étudiants qui souhaitent devenir membres d'une "fraternity" ou d'une "sorority" sont soumis à toutes sortes d'épreuves initiatiques

he'll [hi:l] = **he will**

hellacious [hel'eɪʃəs] **ADJ** *Am Fam* **1** *(bad, unpleasant)* infernal **2** *(excellent)* super, génial

hellbender ['hel,bendə(r)] **N** *Zool* = grande salamandre aquatique des États-Unis

hell-bent ADJ *Fam* **to be h. on doing sth** vouloir à tout prix faire qch□; **he's h. on going** il veut à tout prix y aller, il veut y aller coûte que coûte□; **society seems h. on self-destruction** la société semble décidée à aller tout droit à sa propre destruction□

hellcat ['helkæt] **N** harpie *f*, mégère *f*

hellebore ['helɪbɔ:(r)] **N** *Bot* hellébore *m*

Hellene ['heli:n] **N** Hellène *mf*

Hellenic [he'li:nɪk] **ADJ** *(people)* hellène; *(language, history)* hellénique

N *Ling* langue *f* hellénique

hellfire ['helfaɪə(r)] **N** feu *m* de l'enfer; *Fig (punishment)* châtiment *m* divin

EXCLAM *Fam* bon sang!, sacré nom de Dieu!

►► ***hellfire preacher*** prédicateur *m* fanatique *(qui est toujours en train de rappeler aux pécheurs qu'ils sont voués à la damnation éternelle)*

hellhole ['helhəʊl] **N** *Fam* trou *m* à rats

hellish ['helɪʃ] **ADJ 1** *(cruel ► action, person)* diabolique **2** *Fam (dreadful)* infernal; **she's had a pretty h. life** elle a eu une vie absolument infernale, sa vie a été un véritable enfer; **I feel h.** je ne me sens vraiment pas dans mon assiette

ADV *Fam* vachement

hellishly ['helɪʃlɪ] **ADV** *Fam* vachement

hello [hə'ləʊ] *(pl* **hellos) EXCLAM 1** *(greeting)* bonjour; *(in the evening)* bonsoir; *(on answering telephone)* allô

2 *(to attract attention)* hé!, ohé!; **h. there, wake up!** holà! réveille-toi!

3 *(in surprise)* tiens!; **h., what's this?** tiens!, qu'est-ce que c'est que ça?

4 *(expressing disbelief)* **no, he's not my boyfriend, I mean h., the guy's a total loser!** non, ce n'est pas mon petit ami, ne dis pas n'importe quoi, il est complètement nul, ce mec-là!

N *(greeting)* bonjour *m*, salutation *f*; **he gave me a cheery h.** il m'a salué joyeusement *ou* avec entrain; **say h. to the lady** dis bonjour à la dame; **say h. to him for me** dis-lui bonjour de ma part; **he asked me to say h. to you** il m'a demandé de vous donner le bonjour

hell-raiser N *Fam* fêtard(e) *m,f*

hell-raising N *Fam* vie *f* de patachon, vie *f* de bâton de chaise; **his h. days** sa vie de patachon

helluva ['heləvə] **ADJ** *Fam* **a h. noise** un sacré boucan; **a h. wind** un vent du diable *ou* de tous les diables; **a h. lot of money** un paquet de fric; **a h. lot of kids** des tas d'enfants; **he's a h. guy** c'est un type vachement bien; **I miss him a h. lot** il me manque vachement; **I had a h. time** *(awful)* je me suis emmerdé; *(wonderful)* je me suis vachement marré; **they had a h. time convincing her** ils ont eu vachement de mal à la convaincre

helm [helm] **N** *Naut* barre *f*, gouvernail *m*; **to be at the h.** tenir la barre *ou* le gouvernail; *Fig* tenir la barre *ou* les rênes; *also Fig* **to take the h.** prendre la barre, prendre la direction des opérations; **he's at the h. of the company now** c'est lui qui dirige la société maintenant

VT *Naut* gouverner, barrer; *Fig* diriger

helmet ['helmɪt] **N** *(gen)* casque *m*; *(medieval)* heaume *m*

helmsman ['helmzmən] *(pl* **helmsmen** [-mən]) **N** *Naut* timonier *m*, homme *m* de barre

HELP [help]

N
- aide **1, 2**
- secours **1, 2**
- personnel **3**
- femme de ménage **4**

VT
- aider **1**
- secourir **1**
- contribuer à **2**
- encourager **2**
- améliorer **3**
- servir **4**

VI
- être utile

EXCLAM
- au secours!

N 1 *(gen)* aide *f*, assistance *f*; *(to drowning or wounded person)* secours *m*, assistance *f*; **thank you for your h.** merci de votre aide; **can I be of any h.?** puis-je faire quelque chose pour vous?, puis-je vous rendre service?; **I had h.** *(I didn't do it on my own)* on m'a aidé; **he went to get h.** il est allé chercher du secours; **we yelled for h.** nous avons crié au secours; **with the h. of a neighbour** avec l'aide d'un voisin; **he opened the window with the h. of a crowbar** il a ouvert la fenêtre à l'aide d'un levier; **she did it without any h.** elle l'a fait toute seule; **the map wasn't much h.** la carte n'a pas servi à grand-chose; **some students need h. to decide which course to take** certains étudiants ont besoin qu'on les aide à choisir leur cursus; **she needs h. going upstairs** il faut qu'elle se fasse aider pour *ou* elle a besoin qu'on l'aide à monter l'escalier; *Fam* **she needs h.** il faut qu'elle voie un psychiatre, elle a des problèmes psychologiques; *Fam* **if you think that's funny, you need h.** si tu trouves ça drôle, c'est que tu dois avoir un problème; **the situation is now beyond h.** la situation est désespérée *ou* irrémédiable maintenant; **he's past h.** *(is dying)* il est perdu; *(is crazy, stupid)* on ne peut rien pour lui; **there's no h. for it** on n'y peut rien

2 *(something that assists)* aide *f*, secours *m*; **that was a big h. (to me)** ça m'a beaucoup aidé; **you've been a great h.** vous m'avez été d'un grand secours, vous m'avez beaucoup aidé; *Ironic* **he's a great h.!** il est d'un précieux secours!

3 *(UNCOUNT) (employees)* personnel *m*, employés *mpl*; **it's hard to get good h.** il est difficile de trouver des employés sérieux; **h. wanted** *(sign)* cherchons employés

4 *(domestic worker)* femme *f* de ménage

VT 1 *(assist, aid ► gen)* aider; *(► elderly, poor, wounded)* secourir, venir en aide à; **come and h. me** viens m'aider; **can I h. you with the dishes?** puis-je t'aider à faire la vaisselle?; **they got their neighbours to h. them move** ils se sont fait aider par leurs voisins pour le déménagement; **they h. one another take care of the children** ils s'entraident pour s'occuper des enfants; **we want to h. poorer countries to h. themselves** nous voulons aider les pays sous-développés à devenir autonomes *ou* à se prendre en main; **he helped me on/off with my coat** il m'a aidé à mettre/enlever mon manteau; *Euph* **a man is helping the police with their enquiries** la police est en train d'interroger un suspect; **she helped the old man to his feet/across the street** elle a aidé le vieux monsieur à se lever/à traverser la rue; **let me h. you up/down** laissez-moi vous aider à monter/descendre; **it helped me knowing that someone was waiting for me** ça m'a aidé de savoir que quelqu'un m'attendait; **can I h. you?** *(in shop)* vous désirez?; **Grant Publishing, how may I h. you?** *(on telephone)* les Éditions Grant, bonjour; *Law* **do you swear to tell the truth, so h. you God?** jurez-vous de dire la vérité, que Dieu vous vienne en aide?; **so h. me God!** je le jure devant Dieu!; *Fam* **I'll get you for this, so h. me** j'aurai ta peau, je le jure!; *Prov* **God helps those who h. themselves** aide-toi, le ciel t'aidera

2 *(contribute to)* contribuer à; *(encourage)* encourager, favoriser; **the rain helped firefighters to bring the flames under control** la pluie a permis aux pompiers de maîtriser l'incendie; **it helped to ease my headache** cela a soulagé mon mal de tête; **it helped to give the impression that…** cela a contribué à donner l'impression que…, à cause de cela, on avait l'impression que…

3 *(improve, remedy ► situation)* améliorer; *(► pain)* atténuer; **this cream should h. your back pain** cette crème devrait te soulager de ton mal de dos; **that doesn't h. the situation, that doesn't h. much** cela ne nous avance pas (beaucoup); **crying won't h. matters** cela ne sert à rien *ou* n'arrange rien de pleurer; *Ironic* **to h. matters, it started to pour with rain** pour tout arranger, il s'est mis à pleuvoir des cordes

4 *(serve)* servir; **she helped me to more rice** elle m'a servi du riz une deuxième fois; **I helped myself to the cheese** je me suis servi en fromage; **h. yourself!** servez-vous!; **they helped themselves to more meat** ils ont repris de la viande; *Euph* **he helped himself to the petty cash** il a pioché *ou* il s'est servi dans la caisse

5 *(with "can", usu negative) (avoid, refrain from)* **I can't h. thinking that we could have done more** je ne peux pas m'empêcher de penser qu'on aurait pu faire plus; **we couldn't h. laughing** *or* **but laugh** nous ne pouvions pas nous empêcher de rire; **she never writes any more than she can h.** elle ne se foule pas pour écrire, elle écrit un minimum de lettres *ou* le moins possible

6 *(with "can", usu negative) (control)* **she can't h. her temper** elle ne peut rien à ses colères; **I tried not to laugh but I couldn't h. myself** j'essayais de ne pas rire mais c'était plus fort que moi; **they can't h. being born there** ils n'ont pas demandé à naître là; **I'm not going back if I can h. it** si j'ai le choix, je n'y retournerai pas; **I can't h. it** je n'y peux rien, ce n'est pas de ma faute; **he can't h. it if she doesn't like it** il n'y est pour rien *ou* ce n'est pas de sa faute si cela ne lui plaît pas; **it can't be helped** tant pis! on n'y peut rien *ou* on ne peut pas faire autrement; **are they coming? – not if I can h. it!** est-ce qu'ils viennent? – pas si j'ai mon mot à dire!

VI être utile; **can I h.?** est-ce que je peux faire quelque chose?; **is there anything I can do to h.?** puis-je être utile?; **she helps a lot around the house** elle se rend très utile à la maison, elle rend souvent service à la maison; **he offered to h. with the clearing up** il a proposé de nous/les/*etc* aider à ranger; **I was only trying to h.!** je voulais seulement vous/les/*etc* aider!; **it might h. if you took more exercise** ça irait peut-être mieux si tu faisais un peu plus d'exercice; **it helps if you can speak the language** c'est plus facile si on parle la langue; **losing your temper isn't going to h.** ça ne sert à rien de perdre ton calme; **forgetting the map didn't h.** le fait d'avoir oublié la carte n'a pas arrangé les choses; **it's near the post office if that helps** c'est près du bureau de poste si ça peut vous aider; **every little helps** les petits ruisseaux font les grandes rivières; **every penny helps** il n'y a pas de petites économies

EXCLAM *(in distress)* au secours!, à l'aide!; *(in dismay)* zut!, mince!; **h.!, I'm late!** mince!, je suis en retard!

►► *Comput* ***help button*** case *f* d'aide; ***help desk*** service *m* d'assistance téléphonique; *Comput* for computing queries) service *m* d'assistance; Comput **help file** fichier *m* d'aide; *Comput* **help key** touche *f* d'aide; *Comput* **help menu** menu *m* d'aide; *Comput* **help screen** écran *m* d'aide

help out VT SEP *(gen)* aider, venir en aide à; *(with supplies, money)* dépanner; **the scholarship really helped her out** la bourse lui a été d'un grand secours; **she helps us out in the shop from time to time** elle vient nous donner un coup de main au magasin de temps en temps; **they h. each other out** ils s'entraident; **she helps him out with his homework** elle l'aide à faire ses devoirs
VI aider, donner un coup de main

helper ['helpə(r)] N **1** *(gen)* aide *mf*, assistant(e) *m,f*; *(professional)* auxiliaire *mf* **2** *Am (home help)* femme *f* de ménage

helpful ['helpfʊl] ADJ **1** *(person)* obligeant, serviable; **he always tries to be h.** il essaie toujours de rendre service; **his secretary was very h.** sa secrétaire nous a été très utile *ou* nous a été d'un grand secours **2** *(advice, suggestion)* utile; *(gadget, information, map)* utile; *(medication)* efficace, salutaire; **it's often h. to talk to your doctor about it** il peut s'avérer utile d'en parler à votre médecin; **this book isn't very h.** ce livre ne sert pas à grand-chose; **h. hints** conseils *mpl* utiles

helpfully ['helpfʊlɪ] ADV avec obligeance, obligeamment; **she very h. lent us her car** elle a eu la gentillesse *ou* l'amabilité de nous prêter sa voiture; *Ironic* **someone had very h. let the battery run down** quelqu'un a eu l'amabilité de décharger la pile

helpfulness ['helpfʊlnɪs] N **1** *(of person)* obligeance *f*, serviabilité *f* **2** *(of gadget, map etc)* utilité *f*

helping ['helpɪŋ] N *(of food)* portion *f*; **to ask for a second h.** demander à en reprendre; **he had four helpings** il en a repris trois fois
▸▸ ***helping hand*** main *f* secourable; **to give** *or* **to lend (sb) a h. hand** donner un coup de main *ou* prêter main-forte (à qn)

helpless ['helplɪs] ADJ **1** *(vulnerable)* désarmé, sans défense; **h. children** des enfants *mfpl* sans défense **2** *(physically)* faible, impotent; *(mentally)* impuissant; **he lay h. on the ground** il était allongé par terre sans pouvoir bouger **3** *(powerless* ▸ *person)* impuissant, sans ressource; *(*▸ *anger, feeling)* impuissant; *(*▸ *situation)* sans recours, désespéré; **he gave me a h. look** il m'a jeté un regard désespéré; **he was h. to stop her leaving** il était incapable de l'empêcher de partir; **I feel so h.** je ne sais vraiment pas quoi faire, je me sens vraiment désarmé; **I'm h. in the matter** je n'y peux rien; **they were h. with laughter** ils n'en pouvaient plus de rire, ils étaient morts de rire; **carry it yourself, you're not h.** débrouille-toi, tu peux très bien le porter tout seul

helplessly ['helplɪslɪ] ADV **1** *(without protection)* sans défense, sans ressource **2** *(unable to react)* sans pouvoir réagir; *(argue, struggle, try)* en vain; **to gesture h.** lever les mains en signe d'impuissance; **he looked on h.** il a regardé sans pouvoir intervenir; **she was lying h. on the floor** elle était allongée par terre sans pouvoir bouger; **she smiled h.** elle a eu un sourire où se lisait son impuissance

helplessness ['helplɪsnɪs] N **1** *(defencelessness)* incapacité *f* de se défendre, vulnérabilité *f* **2** *(physical)* incapacité *f*, impotence *f*; *(mental)* incapacité *f* **3** *(powerlessness* ▸ *of person)* impuissance *f*, manque *m* de moyens; *(*▸ *of anger, feeling)* impuissance *f*; **a feeling of h.** un sentiment d'impuissance

helpline ['helplam] N *Tel* service *m* d'assistance téléphonique; **Aids h.** SOS SIDA

Helsinki [hel'sɪŋkɪ] N Helsinki
▸▸ ***the Helsinki Accords, the Helsinki Agreement*** les accords *mpl* d'Helsinki

helter-skelter [ˌheltə'skeltə(r)] ADV *(run, rush)* en désordre, à la débandade; *(organize, throw)* pêle-mêle, en vrac
ADJ *(rush)* à la débandade; *(account, story)* désordonné
N *Br (at fairground)* toboggan *m*

hem[1] [hem] *(pt & pp* **hemmed**, *cont* **hemming)** N **1** *(of trousers, skirt)* ourlet *m*; *(of handkerchief, sheet)* bord *m*, ourlet *m*; **she let the h. down on her skirt** elle a défait l'ourlet pour rallonger sa jupe; **your h.'s coming down** ton ourlet s'est défait *ou* décousu **2** *(hemline)* (bas *m* de l')ourlet *m* **3** *Metal* ourlet *m*
VT ourler, faire l'ourlet de

▸ **hem in** VT SEP *(house, people)* entourer, encercler; *(enemy)* cerner; **he felt hemmed in** *(in room)* il faisait de la claustrophobie, il se sentait oppressé; *(in relationship)* il se sentait prisonnier *ou* pris au piège; *Fig* **hemmed in by rules** entravé par des règles *ou* règlements

hem[2] [həm] EXCLAM *(to call attention)* hem!; *(to indicate hesitation, pause)* euh!
VI faire hem; **to h. and haw** *(mumble)* bafouiller; *Fig (hesitate)* tergiverser, tourner autour du pot; **he hemmed and hawed before getting to the point** il a bafouillé *ou* hésité avant d'en venir au fait

hema-, hematite *etc Am* = **haema-, haematite** *etc*

he-man N *Fam* homme *m* viril[□]; **he thinks he's a real h.** il se croit viril

hemicycle ['hemɪˌsaɪkəl] N hémicycle *m*

hemiplegia [ˌhemɪ'pliːdʒɪə] N *Med* hémiplégie *f*

hemisphere ['hemɪˌsfɪə(r)] N hémisphère *m*

hemispheric [ˌhemɪ'sferɪk], **hemispherical** [ˌhemɪ'sferɪkəl] ADJ **1** *(in shape)* hémisphérique **2** *Am (pan-American)* panaméricain

hemline ['hemlaɪn] N (bas *m* de l')ourlet *m*; **hemlines are going up** les jupes vont raccourcir

hemlock ['hemlɒk] N **1** *Bot* grande ciguë *f* **2** *(poison)* ciguë *f* **3** *(tree)* sapin *m* du Canada, sapin-ciguë *m*

hemo-, hemoglobin *etc Am* = **haemo-, haemoglobin** *etc*

hemp [hemp] N **1** *Bot (fibre, plant)* chanvre *m* **2** *(marijuana)* marijuana *f*; *(hashish)* haschisch *m*, hachisch *m*

hemstitch ['hemstɪtʃ] *Sewing* N *(stitch)* jour *m*; **a row of h.** un jour
VT ourler à jour

hen [hen] N **1** *(chicken)* poule *f*
2 *(female bird)* femelle *f*
3 *Fam (woman)* mémère *f*; *Fam* **she's having her h. party** *or Br* **h. night** *(before wedding)* elle enterre sa vie de célibataire
4 *Scot Fam (term of address)* **hello, h.** bonjour, ma poule *ou* ma cocotte
▸▸ ***hen bird*** oiseau *m* femelle; ***hen coop*** mue *f*, cage *f* à poules; *Orn* ***hen harrier*** busard *m* Saint-Martin; ***hen house*** poulailler *m*; *Orn* ***hen pheasant*** poule *f* faisane

> **HEN NIGHT**
>
> En Grande-Bretagne, le phénomène des "hen nights" est une tradition bien établie. Il s'agit d'une sorte de rite de passage pour enterrer sa vie de jeune fille. La future mariée part en virée nocturne avec ses amies; souvent toutes portent des tee-shirts, des chapeaux ou des déguisements identiques. Généralement abondamment arrosées, ces soirées se prolongent jusqu'au petit matin dans une ambiance de fête et peuvent comporter des strip-teaseurs et d'autres divertissements. Dans la plupart des villes britanniques il est désormais courant de voir des groupes de jeunes femmes parcourir les rues en faisant la fête. Parfois les "hen nights" prennent la forme d'un week-end dépaysant passé entre copines dans une autre ville ou même à l'étranger. L'équivalent masculin de la "hen night" est la "stag party" (voir l'entrée **stag**).

henbane ['henbeɪn] N *Bot* jusquiame *f* noire

hence [hens] ADV **1** *(therefore)* donc, d'où; **he was born on Christmas Day, h. the name Noel** il est né le jour de Noël, d'où son nom **2** *Formal (from this time)* d'ici; **three days h.** dans *ou* d'ici trois jours **3** *Formal (from here)* d'ici **4 kilometres h.** à 5 kilomètres d'ici

henceforth [ˌhens'fɔːθ], **henceforward** [ˌhens'fɔːwəd] ADV dorénavant, désormais

henchman ['hentʃmən] *(pl* **henchmen** [-mən]) N **1** *(follower)* partisan *m*, *Pej* adepte *m*; *(right-hand man)* homme *m* de main, *Pej* suppôt *m* **2** *(squire, page)* écuyer *m*

henna ['henə] N *Bot* henné *m*
VT teindre au henné; **to h. one's hair** se faire un henné

henpecked ['henpekt] ADJ dominé; **a h. husband** un mari dominé par sa femme; **he's very h.** sa femme le mène par le bout du nez

henroost ['henruːst] N **1** *(perch)* juchoir *m*, perchoir *m* **2** *(hen house)* poulailler *m*

Henry ['henrɪ] PR N Henri; **H. the Eighth, H. VIII** Henri VIII

hep [hep] *(compar* **hepper**, *superl* **heppest)** ADJ *Fam Old-fashioned* dans le coup; **he's h. to your plan** il est au courant de tes projets

heparin ['hepərɪn] N *Pharm* héparine *f*

hepatic [hɪ'pætɪk] ADJ *Physiol* hépatique

hepatitis [ˌhepə'taɪtɪs] N *(UNCOUNT) Med* hépatite *f*; **h. A/B/C** hépatite *f* A/B/C; **serum h.** hépatite *f* B *ou* sérique

hepatology [hepə'tɒlədʒɪ] N *Med* hépatologie *f*

heptagon ['heptəgən] N *Geom* heptagone *m*

heptathlete [hep'tæθliːt] N heptathlète *m,f*

heptathlon [hep'tæθlɒn] N heptathlon *m*

her [hɜː(r)] ADJ **1** *(used of person, animal* ▸ *singular)* son (sa); *(*▸ *plural)* ses; **h. book** son livre; **h. secretary** sa secrétaire; **h. glasses** ses lunettes; **h. university** son université; **she has broken h. arm** elle s'est cassé le bras; **the dog's hurt h. paw** la chienne s'est fait mal à la patte **2** *(used of vehicle, ship, country)* **France reassured h. allies** la France rassura ses alliés; **the ship and h. crew** le navire et son équipage
PRON **1** *(direct object* ▸ *unstressed)* la; *(*▸ *stressed)* elle; **I recognize h.** je la reconnais; **I heard h.** je l'ai entendue
2 *(indirect object* ▸ *unstressed)* lui; *(*▸ *stressed)* à elle; **give h. the money** donne-lui l'argent; **he only told h., no one else** il ne l'a dit qu'à elle, c'est tout; **I am thinking of h.** je pense à elle; **why do they always give H. the interesting jobs?** pourquoi est-ce que c'est toujours à elle qu'on donne le travail intéressant?
3 *(after preposition)* elle; **I was in front of h.** j'étais devant elle; **as rich as/richer than h.** aussi riche/plus riche qu'elle; **she closed the door behind h.** elle a fermé la porte derrière elle
4 *(with "to be")* **it's h.** c'est elle; **if I were h.** si j'étais elle, si j'étais à sa place
5 *(used of vehicle, ship, country)* **Poland's friends deserted h.** la Pologne a été abandonnée par ses amis; **the enemy sank h.** il a été coulé par l'ennemi; *Fam* **I'll get h. started** *(car)* je vais la faire démarrer
6 *Formal (with relative pronoun)* celle; **(to) h. whom we adore** (à) celle que nous adorons
N *Fam* **it's a h. not a him** *(of baby)* c'est une fille, pas un garçon[□]; *(of animal)* c'est une femelle, pas un mâle[□]

herald ['herəld] VT **1** *(announce)* annoncer, proclamer; **his rise to power heralded a new era** son ascension au pouvoir a annoncé une nouvelle ère **2** *(hail)* acclamer
N **1** *(medieval messenger)* héraut *m*; *Literary* **the h. of morn** le messager de l'aube **2** *(forerunner)* héraut *m*, avant-coureur *m*; **a h. of spring** l'annonce *f* du printemps **3** *(record keeper)* généalogiste *mf* (chargé du registre des armoiries)

heraldic [he'rældɪk] ADJ *Her* héraldique

heraldry ['herəldrɪ] N *(UNCOUNT)* **1** *(system, study)* héraldique *f* **2** *(coat of arms)* blason *m* **3** *(pageantry)* faste *m*, pompe *f* (héraldique)

herb [*Br* hɜːb, *Am* ɜːrb] N **1** *Bot* herbe *f*; *Culin* **herbs** fines herbes *fpl*, herbes *fpl* aromatiques; **medicinal herbs** herbes *fpl* médicinales *ou* officinales, simples *mpl* **2** *Fam Drugs slang (marijuana)* herbe *f*
▸▸ *Hort* ***herb garden*** jardin *m* d'herbes aromatiques; *Bot* ***herb Paris*** parisette *f*; ***herb pillow*** oreiller *m* rempli d'herbes *(à effet soporifique)*; *Bot* ***herb Robert*** herbe *f* à Robert, géranium *m* robertin

herbaceous [*Br* hɜː'beɪʃəs, *Am* ɜːr'beɪʃəs] *Hort* ADJ *(plant, stem)* herbacé
▸▸ ***herbaceous border*** bordure *f* de plantes herbacées

herbage [*Br* 'hɜːbɪdʒ, *Am* 'ɜːrbɪdʒ] **N** *(UNCOUNT) Hort (herbaceous plants)* plantes *fpl* herbacées, herbages *mpl*; *(vegetation)* herbage *m*

herbal [*Br* 'hɜːbəl, *Am* 'ɜːrbəl] **ADJ** aux herbes
N traité *m* sur les plantes, herbier *m*
▸▸ ***herbal cigarette*** cigarette *f* aux plantes; ***herbal infusion*** infusion *f*, tisane *f*; ***herbal medicine*** *(practice)* phytothérapie *f*; *(medication)* médicament *m* à base de plantes; ***herbal pillow*** oreiller *m* rempli d'herbes *(à effet soporifique)*; ***herbal tea*** tisane *f*

herbalist [*Br* 'hɜːbəlɪst, *Am* 'ɜːrbəlɪst] **N** *Med & Pharm* herboriste *mf*

herbarium [*Br* hɜː'beərɪəm, *Am* ɜːr'beərɪəm] (*pl* **herbaria** [-rɪə]) **N** *Bot* herbier *m (collection)*

herbicide [*Br* 'hɜːbɪsaɪd, *Am* 'ɜːrbɪsaɪd] **N** *Agr* herbicide *m*

herbivore [*Br* 'hɜːbɪvɔː(r), *Am* 'ɜːrbɪvɔː(r)] **N** *Zool* herbivore *m*

herbivorous [*Br* hɜː'bɪvərəs, *Am* ɜːr'bɪvərəs] **ADJ** *Zool* herbivore

herculean, Herculean [ˌhɜːkjʊ'liːən] **ADJ** herculéen; **a h. task** un travail de Titan *ou* herculéen

Hercules ['hɜːkjʊliːz] **PR N** *Myth* Hercule; *Fig (strong man)* hercule *m*
N *Astron* Hercule
▸▸ *Comput* ***Hercules monitor*** moniteur *m* Hercules

herd [hɜːd] **N 1** *(of cattle, goats, sheep)* troupeau *m*; *(of wild animals)* troupe *f*; *(of horses)* troupe *f*, bande *f*; *(of deer)* harde *f* **2** *Fam (of people)* troupeau *m*, foule *f*; *Pej* **the h.** le peuple, la populace **3** *Arch (herdsman)* gardien *m* de troupeau, *Literary* pâtre *m*
VT 1 *(bring together)* rassembler (en troupeau); *(look after)* garder **2** *(drive)* mener, conduire; **the cattle were herded into the barn** on a fait entrer le bétail dans la grange; **he herded the students back into the classroom** il a reconduit les élèves dans la salle de cours; **the prisoners were herded onto trucks** on a entassé les prisonniers dans des camions
VI s'assembler en troupeau, s'attrouper
▸▸ ***herd instinct*** instinct *m* grégaire; *Pej* ***herd mentality*** panurgisme *m*

▸**herd together VI 1** *(animals* ▸ *live in herds)* vivre en troupeaux; *(*▸ *form a herd)* s'assembler en troupeau **2** *Fam (people)* se regrouper▫, s'assembler en troupeau▫, s'attrouper▫
VT SEP rassembler en troupeau

herder ['hɜːdə(r)] **N** *esp Am (gen)* gardien(enne) *m,f* de troupeau; *(of cattle)* vacher(ère) *m,f*, bouvier(ère) *m,f*; *(of sheep)* berger(ère) *m,f*

herdsman ['hɜːdzmən] (*pl* **herdsmen** [-mən]) **N** *(gen)* gardien *m* de troupeau; *(of cattle)* vacher *m*, bouvier *m*; *(of sheep)* berger *m*

HERE [hɪə(r)] **ADV 1** *(at, in this place)* **come h.!** (venez) ici!; **she left h. yesterday** elle est partie d'ici hier; **I've lived h. for two years** ça fait deux ans que j'habite ici, j'habite ici depuis deux ans; **is Susan h.?** est-ce que Susan est là?; **he won't be h. next week** il ne sera pas là la semaine prochaine; **they're h.** *(I've found them)* ils sont ici; *(they've arrived)* ils sont arrivés; **winter is h.** c'est l'hiver, l'hiver est arrivé; **where do I switch on the light? – h.** où est l'interrupteur? – ici; **sign h.** signez ici
2 *(after preposition)* **around h.** par ici; **it's 2 km from h.** c'est à 2 km d'ici; **from h. to h.** d'ici jusqu'ici; **bring them in h.** apportez-les (par) ici; **I'm in h.** je suis là *ou* ici; **they're over h.** ils sont ici; **where are you? – over h.!** où êtes-vous? – (par) ici!; **the water came up to h.** l'eau est montée jusqu'ici; *Fam* **I've had it up to h.** j'en ai jusque là; **h. today, gone tomorrow** tout passe
3 *(drawing attention to something)* voici, voilà; **h.'s the key!** voilà *ou* voici la clef!; **h. they come!** les voilà! *ou* voici!; **h. I am!** me voici!, me voilà!; **h. we are!** *(I've found it)* voilà! j'ai trouvé!, *(we've arrived)* nous y sommes!, nous voilà arrivés! *ou* rendus!; **h. we are in San Francisco** nous voici à San Francisco; **have you got the paper? – h. you are** vous avez le journal? – le voilà *ou* voici; *Fam Br* **h. goes,** *Am* **h. goes nothing** allons-y!; **h. we go!** *(excitedly)* c'est parti!; *(wearily)* et voilà, c'est reparti!; **h. we go again!** ça y est, c'est reparti pour un tour!
4 *(emphasizing specified object, person)* **ask the lady h.** demandez à cette dame ici; **it's this one h. that I want** c'est celui-ci que je veux; **my friend h. saw it** mon ami (que voici) l'a vu; *Fam* **this h. book** *(that I am pointing to)* ce livre-ci▫; *Fam* **this h. book you've all been talking about** ce bouquin dont vous n'arrêtez pas de parler tous
5 *(at this point)* maintenant; *(at that point)* alors, à ce moment-là; **h. I should like to remind you...** maintenant je voudrais vous rappeler...; **h. I am referring to taxation** c'est aux impôts que je fais allusion; **h. she paused** à ce moment-là, elle s'est arrêtée
6 *(idiom)* **h.'s to** *(in toasts)* à; **h.'s to the newlyweds!** aux nouveaux mariés!; **h.'s to your exams!** à tes examens!; **h.'s to us!** à nous!, à nos amours!
EXCLAM 1 *(present)* **Jessica Green? – h.!** Jessica Green? – présente!
2 *(giving, taking)* **h.!** tiens!, tenez!; **h., give me that!** tiens, donne-moi ça!
3 *(protesting)* **h.! what do you think you're doing?** hé! qu'est-ce que tu fais?; **h., I never said that!** mais dis donc, je n'ai jamais dit ça!; **h., stop that!** écoute, tu arrêtes un peu!
• **here and now ADV** sur-le-champ **N the h. and now** le présent
• **here and there ADV** ça et là; **the paintwork needs retouching h. and there** la peinture a besoin d'être refaite par endroits
• **here, there and everywhere ADV** *Fam* un peu partout; **her things were scattered h., there and everywhere** ses affaires étaient éparpillées un peu partout

hereabouts ['hɪərəˌbaʊts], *Am* **hereabout** ['hɪərəˌbaʊt] **ADV** par ici, près d'ici, dans les environs

hereafter [ˌhɪər'ɑːftə(r)] **N 1** *(life after death)* audelà *m inv*; **in the h.** dans l'autre monde **2** *Literary (future)* avenir *m*, futur *m*
ADV 1 *Formal (in document)* ci-après **2** *Literary (after death)* dans l'au-delà **3** *Literary (in the future)* désormais, dorénavant

hereby [ˌhɪə'baɪ] **ADV** *Formal (in statement)* par la présente (déclaration); *(in document)* par le présent (document); *(in letter)* par la présente; *(in act)* par le présent acte, par ce geste; *(in will)* par le présent testament; **I h. declare you man and wife** en vertu des pouvoirs qui me sont conférés, je vous déclare mari et femme

hereditary [hɪ'redɪtərɪ] **ADJ** héréditaire
▸▸ ***hereditary monarchy*** monarchie *f* héréditaire; *Br Parl* ***hereditary peer*** = membre de la Chambre des lords dont le titre est héréditaire

heredity [hɪ'redɪtɪ] **N** *Biol* hérédité *f*

herein [ˌhɪər'ɪn] **ADV** *Formal (in this respect)* en ceci, en cela; *Law (in this document)* ci-inclus; **the letter enclosed h.** la lettre ci-incluse

heresy ['herəsɪ] (*pl* **heresies**) **N** hérésie *f*; **an act of h.** une hérésie

heretic ['herətɪk] **N** hérétique *mf*

heretical [hɪ'retɪkəl] **ADJ** hérétique

hereto [ˌhɪə'tuː] **ADV** *Formal* à ceci, à cela; *Law* aux présentes

heretofore [ˌhɪətʊ'fɔː(r)] **ADV** *Formal* jusqu'ici, auparavant; *Law* ci-devant

hereunder [ˌhɪər'ʌndə(r)] **ADV** *Formal* **1** *(hereafter)* ci-après, ci-dessous **2** *(under the authority of this)* selon les modalités de ceci *ou* des présentes

hereupon [ˌhɪərə'pɒn] **ADV** *Formal* **1** *(immediately following)* sur ce, là-dessus **2** *(on this point)* sur ce point, là-dessus

herewith [ˌhɪə'wɪθ] **ADV** *Formal* **1** *(enclosed)* ci-joint, ci-inclus; **I enclose my curriculum vitae h.** veuillez trouver ci-joint mon curriculum vitae **2** *(in statement)* par la présente (déclaration); *(in document)* par le présent (document); *(in letter)* par la présente; *(in act)* par le présent acte, par ce geste; *(in will)* par le présent testament

heritable ['herɪtəbəl] **ADJ** *Law (property)* dont on peut hériter; *(person)* qui peut hériter

heritage ['herɪtɪdʒ] **N** héritage *m*, patrimoine *m*; **the national h.** le patrimoine national
▸▸ *Br* ***heritage centre*** = centre d'accueil et de documentation pour les visiteurs d'un site historique; ***heritage site*** site *m* patrimoine; ***heritage tourism*** tourisme *m* culturel; ***heritage trail*** = parcours touristique qui va d'un lieu historique un autre

hermaphrodite [hɜː'mæfrəˌdaɪt] *Biol & Bot* **N** hermaphrodite *m*
ADJ hermaphrodite

hermaphroditic [hɜːˌmæfrə'dɪtɪk] **ADJ** *Biol & Bot* hermaphrodite

hermetic [hɜː'metɪk] **ADJ** hermétique

hermetically [hɜː'metɪkəlɪ] **ADV** hermétiquement

hermit ['hɜːmɪt] **N** *(gen)* ermite *m*, solitaire *mf*; *Rel* ermite *m*; **to live like a h.** vivre en solitaire *ou* en ermite
▸▸ *Zool* ***hermit crab*** bernard-l'ermite *m inv*, pagure *m*

hermitage ['hɜːmɪtɪdʒ] **N** ermitage *m*

hernia ['hɜːnɪə] (*pl* **hernias** *or* **herniae** [-nɪiː]) **N** *Med* hernie *f*

hero ['hɪərəʊ] (*pl* **heroes**) **N 1** *(person)* héros *m*; **sporting h.** un champion sportif; **they gave him h.'s welcome** ils l'ont accueilli en héros; *Fam* **my h.!** mon héros! **2** *Am (sandwich)* = sorte de gros sandwich
▸▸ ***hero worship*** *(admiration)* adulation *f*, culte *m* (du héros); *Antiq* culte *m* des héros

Herod ['herəd] **PR N** *Bible* Hérode

heroic [hɪ'rəʊɪk] **ADJ 1** *(act, behaviour, person)* héroïque **2** *Literary* épique, héroïque
▸▸ *Literature* ***heroic couplet*** distique *m* héroïque; *Literature* ***heroic stanza*** quatrain *m* en vers croisés; *Literature* ***heroic verse*** *(UNCOUNT)* vers *mpl* héroïques

heroically [hɪ'rəʊɪklɪ] **ADV** héroïquement

heroics [hɪ'rəʊɪks] **NPL 1** *(language)* emphase *f*, déclamation *f*; *(behaviour)* affectation *f*, emphase *f*; **none of your h.** inutile de chercher à nous impressionner **2** *Literature (heroic verse)* vers *mpl* héroïques

heroin ['herəʊɪn] **N** héroïne *f*
▸▸ ***heroin addict*** héroïnomane *mf*; ***heroin addiction*** héroïnomanie *f*; ***heroin chic*** = apparence cultivée par certains mannequins, inspirée de celle des héroïnomanes (extrême maigreur, mauvaise mine etc); ***heroin user*** héroïnomane *mf*

> Attention: ne pas confondre avec **heroine**.

heroine ['herəʊɪn] **N** héroïne *f (femme)*

> Attention: ne pas confondre avec **heroin**.

heroism ['herəʊɪzəm] **N** héroïsme *m*

heron ['herən] (*pl* **inv** *or* **herons**) **N** *Orn* héron *m*

hero-worship VT aduler, idolâtrer

herpes ['hɜːpiːz] **N** *(UNCOUNT) Med* herpès *m*; **to have h.** avoir de l'herpès
▸▸ *Med* ***herpes simplex*** *(UNCOUNT)* herpès *m*; *Med* ***herpes zoster*** *(UNCOUNT)* zona *m*

herring ['herɪŋ] (*pl* **inv** *or* **herrings**) **N** *Ich* hareng *m*
▸▸ ***herring boat*** harenguier *m*; ***herring fleet*** flottille *f* de harenguiers

herringbone ['herɪŋbəʊn] **N 1** *(bone)* arête *f* de hareng
2 *Tex (pattern)* (dessin *m* à) chevrons *mpl*; *(fabric)* tissu *m* à chevrons
3 *Sewing (stitch)* point *m* croisé, point *m* de chausson
4 *(in skiing)* montée *f* en ciseaux *ou* en pas de canard
VI *Ski* monter en ciseaux *ou* en pas de canard
▸▸ *Sewing & Tex* ***herringbone stitch*** point *m* croisé, point de *m* chausson; *Tex* ***herringbone tweed*** tweed *m* à chevrons

hers [hɜːz] **PRON 1** *(gen* ▸ *singular)* le sien (la sienne) *m,f*; *(*▸ *plural)* les siens (les siennes) *mpl, fpl*; **this is my book, h. is over there** ça, c'est mon livre, le sien est là-bas; **this car is h.** cette voiture lui appartient *ou* est à elle; **h. was the best photograph** sa photographie était la meilleure; **most speeches lasted ten minutes, but h. lasted half an hour** la plupart des gens ont fait un discours de dix minutes, mais le sien a duré une demi-heure; **h. is not an easy task** elle n'a pas la tâche facile

2 *(after preposition)* **she took his hand in h.** elle a pris sa main dans la sienne; **he's an old friend of h.** c'est un de ses vieux amis; **when's that book of h. coming out?** quand est-ce qu'il sort, son livre?; **I blame that husband of h.** moi je dis que c'est de la faute de son sacré mari; **I can't stand that boyfriend/dog of h.** je ne supporte pas son copain/chien; **that (dreadful) voice of h.** sa voix (insupportable)

3 *(indicating authorship)* d'elle; **are these paintings h.?** ces tableaux sont-ils d'elle?

4 *Fam (her house, flat)* chez elle□

herself [hɜː'self] **PRON 1** *(reflexive form)* se, s' *(before vowel or silent "h")*; **she introduced h.** elle s'est présentée; **she bought h. a car** elle s'est acheté une voiture; **she considers h. lucky** elle considère qu'elle a de la chance

2 *(emphatic form)* elle-même; **she built the shelves h.** elle a monté les étagères elle-même; **I spoke with the teacher h.** j'ai parlé au professeur en personne

3 *(with preposition)* elle; **she took it upon h. to tell us** elle a pris sur elle de nous le dire; **she has a room to h.** elle a sa propre chambre *ou* sa chambre à elle; **the old woman was talking to h.** la vieille femme parlait toute seule; **"that's odd," she thought to h.** "c'est bizarre", se dit-elle; **she did it all by h.** elle l'a fait toute seule

4 *(her usual self)* **she isn't quite h.** elle n'est pas dans son état habituel; **she's feeling more h. now** elle va mieux maintenant

Herts *(written abbr* **Hertfordshire***)* Hertfordshire *m*

hertz [hɜːts] *(pl* **inv***)* **N** *Elec & Phys* hertz *m*

he's [hiːz] = **he is, he has**

hesitance ['hezɪtəns], **hesitancy** ['hezɪtənsɪ] **N** hésitation *f*, indécision *f*

hesitant ['hezɪtənt] **ADJ 1** *(person ▸ uncertain)* hésitant, indécis; *(▸ cautious)* réticent; **I'm h. about sending her to a new school** j'hésite à l'envoyer dans une nouvelle école **2** *(attempt, speech, voice)* hésitant

hesitantly ['hezɪtəntlɪ] **ADV** *(act, try)* avec hésitation, timidement; *(answer, speak)* d'une voix hésitante

hesitate ['hezɪˌteɪt] **VI** hésiter; **don't h. to call me** n'hésitez pas à m'appeler; **he will h. at nothing** il ne recule devant rien, rien ne l'arrête; *Prov* **he who hesitates is lost** = un moment d'hésitation peut coûter cher

hesitation [ˌhezɪ'teɪʃən] **N** hésitation *f*; **after much h.** après bien des hésitations, après avoir longuement hésité; **I would have no h. in recommending him** je n'hésiterais pas à le recommander; **without a moment's h.** sans la moindre hésitation

hessian ['hesɪən] *Tex* **N** (toile *f* de) jute *m*
COMP *(fabric, sack)* de jute

hetero ['hetərəʊ] *(pl* **heteros***)* *Fam* **N** hétéro *mf*
ADJ hétéro

heterodox ['hetərəʊdɒks] **ADJ** hétérodoxe

heterogeneous [ˌhetərəʊ'dʒiːnɪəs] **ADJ** hétérogène

heterosexism [ˌhetərəʊ'seksɪzəm] **N** hétérosexisme *m*

heterosexual [ˌhetərə'sekʃʊəl] **N** hétérosexuel (elle) *m,f*
ADJ hétérosexuel

het up ['het-] **ADJ** *Fam (angry)* énervé□; *(excited)* excité□, agité□; **to get all h. (about sth)** se mettre dans tous ses états (pour qch)

heuristic [hjʊə'rɪstɪk] **ADJ** *Math & Phil* heuristique
▸▸ ***heuristic model*** modèle *m* heuristique

hew [hjuː] *(pt* **hewed**, *pp* **hewed** *or* **hewn** [hjuːn]) **VT** *(wood)* couper; *(stone)* tailler; *(coal)* abattre; **they hewed a path through the undergrowth** ils se sont taillé *ou* frayé un chemin à travers les sous-bois (à coups de hache)

▸ **hew down VT SEP** *(tree)* abattre

▸ **hew off VT SEP** *(branch)* abattre

▸ **hew out VT SEP** creuser; **the cavern had been hewn out of the rock** la caverne a été creusée dans la pierre

hewer ['hjuːə(r)] **N** *(of tree)* abatteur *m*; *(of stone, wood)* tailleur *m*; *(of coal)* haveur *m*

hex [heks] *Am* **N 1** *(spell)* sort *m*, sortilège *m*; **to put a h. on sb** jeter un sort à qn **2** *(witch)* sorcière *f*
VT jeter un sort à

hexadecimal [ˌheksə'desɪməl] **ADJ** *Comput* hexadécimal
▸▸ ***hexadecimal notation*** codes *mpl* hexadécimaux, notation *f* hexadécimale

hexagon ['heksəgən] **N** *Geom* hexagone *m*

hexagonal [hek'sægənəl] **ADJ** *Geom* hexagonal

hexameter [hek'sæmɪtə(r)] **N** *Literature* hexamètre *m*

hey [heɪ] **EXCLAM** *(to draw attention)* hé!, ohé!; *(to show surprise)* tiens!; **h. ho!** *(in weariness)* eh bien!; *(in resignation)* hélas!; *Old-fashioned or Literary (in surprise)* ça alors!, ça par exemple!; *(in happiness)* chouette alors!; *Br* **h. presto!** passez muscade!, et hop!; *Am* **h. (there)!** *(as greeting)* salut!

heyday ['heɪdeɪ] **N** *(of cinema, movement)* âge *m* d'or, beaux jours *mpl*; *(of nation, organization)* zénith *m*, apogée *m*; **in her h.** *(youth)* quand elle était dans la force de l'âge; *(success)* à l'apogée de sa gloire, au temps de sa splendeur; **Hollywood in its h.** l'âge d'or d'Hollywood; **in its h. it was one of the busiest ports in the world** à son heure de gloire, c'était l'un des ports les plus importants du monde

HFEA [ˌeɪtʃefiː'eɪ] **N** *Br (abbr* **Human Fertilization and Embryology Authority***)* = organisme chargé de réglementer les traitements de la stérilité et la recherche en embryologie

HGH [ˌeɪtʃdʒiː'eɪtʃ] **N** *Biol (abbr* **human growth hormone***)* hormone *f* de croissance

HGV [ˌeɪtʃdʒiː'viː] **N** *Br Transp (abbr* **heavy goods vehicle***)* PL *m*
▸▸ ***HGV licence*** permis *m* PL

hi [haɪ] **EXCLAM** *Fam* **1** *(hello)* salut! **2** *(hey)* hé!, ohé!

hiatus [haɪ'eɪtəs] *(pl* **inv** *or* **hiatuses***)* **N 1** *Formal (gap in series, text etc)* lacune *f* **2** *Formal (break in conversation)* silence *m*; *(break in negotiations)* interruption *f*; **apart from a h. between 1923 and 1925** mis à part une interruption entre 1923 et 1925 **3** *Ling* hiatus *m*
▸▸ *Med* ***hiatus hernia*** hernie *f* hiatale

hibernate ['haɪbəneɪt] **VI** hiberner

hibernation [ˌhaɪbə'neɪʃən] **N** hibernation *f*; **to go into h.** hiberner

hibiscus [hɪ'bɪskəs] **N** *Bot* hibiscus *m*

hiccough ['hɪkʌp], **hiccup** ['hɪkʌp] **N 1** *(sound)* hoquet *m*; **to have (the) hiccoughs** avoir le hoquet; **it gave me the hiccoughs** cela m'a donné le hoquet **2** *Fam (problem)* anicroche *f*; **there's been some sort of h. with the delivery** il y a eu un hic à la livraison
VI hoqueter

hick [hɪk] *Am Fam Pej* **N** péquenaud(e) *m,f*, plouc *mf*
ADJ de péquenaud
▸▸ ***hick town*** bled *m*

hickey ['hɪkɪ] **N 1** *Am Fam (gadget)* bidule *m* **2** *Am Fam (lovebite)* suçon *m* **3** *Fam Typ* larron *m*, mouche *f*

hickory ['hɪkərɪ] *(pl* **hickories***)* **N** *(tree)* hickory *m*, noyer *m* blanc d'Amérique; *(wood)* (bois *m* de) hickory *m*
COMP *(table, chair)* en (bois de) hickory

hid [hɪd] *pt of* **hide**

hidden ['hɪdən] *pp of* **hide**
ADJ caché; **h. from sight** à l'abri des regards indiscrets, caché; **a village h. away in the mountains** un village caché *ou* niché dans les montagnes; **she has h. talents** elle a des talents cachés; **a h. meaning** un sens caché
▸▸ ***hidden agenda*** projets *mpl* tenus secrets; ***hidden camera*** caméra *f* cachée, caméra *f* invisible; *Fin* ***hidden cost*** coût caché; *Com* ***hidden defects*** défauts *mpl ou* vices *mpl* cachés; *Com* ***hidden extras*** dépenses *fpl* supplémentaires inattendues; **no h. extras** garanti tout compris; *Fig* ***hidden hand*** influence *f* occulte; *Fin* ***hidden reserves*** réserve *f* latente; **I have h. reserves** j'ai encore des réserves

hide [haɪd] *(pt* **hid** [hɪd], *pp* **hidden** ['hɪdən]) **VT 1** *(conceal ▸ person, thing)* cacher; *(▸ disappointment, dismay, fright)* dissimuler; **to h. sth from sb** *(ball, letter)* cacher qch à qn; *(emotion)* dissimuler qch à qn; **we have nothing to h.** nous n'avons rien à cacher *ou* à dissimuler; **the boy hid himself behind the door** le garçon s'est caché derrière la porte; **she hid her face** elle s'est caché le visage; **he hid it from sight** il l'a dissimulé *ou* l'a dérobé aux regards; **they hid him from the police** ils l'ont caché pour que la police ne le trouve pas; *Fig* **to h. one's light under a bushel** cacher ses talents; **she doesn't h. her light under a bushel** ce n'est pas la modestie qui l'étouffe; *Am* **to h. one's head (in shame)** baisser la tête (de honte) **2** *(keep secret)* taire, dissimuler; **to h. the truth (from sb)** taire *ou* dissimuler la vérité (à qn) **3** *Comput (files, records)* cacher
VI se cacher; **to h. from sb** se cacher de qn; **he's hiding from the police** il se cache de la police; *Fig* **to h. behind an excuse** prétexter une excuse; *Fig* **the ambassador hid behind his diplomatic immunity** l'ambassadeur s'est réfugié derrière son immunité diplomatique
N 1 *Br (place)* cachette *f*; *(in hunting)* affût *m* **2** *(animal skin ▸ raw)* peau *f*; *(▸ tanned)* cuir *m* **3** *Fam Fig (of person)* peau□ *f*; **to tan sb's h.** tanner le cuir à qn; **I'll have your h. for that** tu vas me le payer cher; **I haven't seen h. nor hair of them** je n'ai eu aucune nouvelle d'eux
COMP de *ou* en cuir

▸ **hide away VT SEP** cacher
VI se cacher; **to h. away (from sb/sth)** se cacher (de qn/ qch)

▸ **hide out VI** se tenir caché; **he's hiding out from the police** il se cache de la police

hide-and-seek, *Am* **hide-and-go-seek N** cache-cache *m*; **to play h.** jouer à cache-cache

hideaway ['haɪdəweɪ] **N** cachette *f*

hidebound ['haɪdbaʊnd] **ADJ** *(person)* obtus, borné; *(attitude, view)* borné, rigide

hideous ['hɪdɪəs] **ADJ 1** *(physically ugly)* hideux, affreux **2** *(ghastly ▸ conditions, situation)* atroce, abominable

hideously ['hɪdɪəslɪ] **ADV 1** *(deformed, wounded)* hideusement, atrocement, affreusement; **h. ugly** atrocement *ou* affreusement laid **2** *Fam Fig (as intensifier)* terriblement, horriblement; **h. expensive** horriblement cher

hideousness ['hɪdɪəsnɪs] **N 1** *(physical ugliness)* laideur *f* **2 the h. of his wounds/the crime** ses blessures *fpl* abominables/le crime abominable

hideout ['haɪdaʊt] **N** cachette *f*

hidey-hole ['haɪdɪ-] **N** *Fam* planque *f*

hiding ['haɪdɪŋ] **N 1** *(concealment)* **to be in h.** se tenir caché; **to go into h.** *(criminal)* se cacher, se planquer; *(spy, terrorist)* entrer dans la clandestinité

2 *Fam (thrashing)* rossée *f*; **to give sb a good h.** donner une bonne raclée à qn

3 *Fam (defeat)* raclée *f*, dérouillée *f*; **they got a good h. in the election** ils ont pris une raclée aux élections

4 *Br (idiom)* **to be on a h. to nothing** être voué à l'échec
▸▸ ***hiding place*** cachette *f*

hierarchic [ˌhaɪə'rɑːkɪk], **hierarchical** [ˌhaɪə'rɑːkɪkəl] **ADJ** hiérarchique; **in h. order** par ordre hiérarchique
▸▸ *Comput* ***hierarchical file system*** système *m* de fichiers hiérarchique; *Comput* ***hierarchical menu*** menu *m* hiérarchique

hierarchy ['haɪəˌrɑːkɪ] *(pl* **hierarchies***)* **N 1** *(organization into grades)* hiérarchie *f*; *(of animals, plants)* classification *f*, classement *m* **2** *(upper levels of authority)* dirigeants *mpl*, autorités *fpl*

hieroglyph ['haɪərəglɪf] **N** hiéroglyphe *m*

hieroglyphic [ˌhaɪərə'glɪfɪk] **N** hiéroglyphe *m*
ADJ hiéroglyphique

hieroglyphics [ˌhaɪərə'glɪfɪks] **NPL** hiéroglyphes *fpl*, écriture *f* hiéroglyphique; *Fam Fig (bad handwriting)* hiéroglyphes *mpl*

hifalutin, hifaluting = **highfalutin, highfaluting**

hi-fi ['haɪˌfaɪ] *(abbr* **high fidelity***)* **N 1** *(UNCOUNT)* hi-fi *f inv* **2** *(stereo system)* chaîne *f* (hi-fi); *(radio)* radio *f* (hi-fi)

COMP *(equipment, recording)* hi-fi *(inv)*

►► ***hi-fi system*** chaîne *f* (hi-fi)

higgledy-piggledy [ˌhɪgəldɪ'pɪgəldɪ] *Fam* **ADV** pêle-mêle, en désordre▫

ADJ pêle-mêle, en désordre▫

HIGH [haɪ]

ADJ
- haut **1, 2, 4, 6, 7, 13, 15, 16**
- noble **5**
- excité **19**
- élevé **2–5, 11**
- grand **3, 4**
- aigu **7**

ADV
- haut **1, 2**
- en haut **1**

N
- haut **1, 2**

ADJ 1 *(tall)* haut; **how h. is that building?** quelle est la hauteur de ce bâtiment?; **the walls are three metres h.** les murs ont *ou* font trois mètres de haut, les murs sont hauts de trois mètres; **the building is eight storeys h.** c'est un immeuble de *ou* à huit étages; **when I was only so h.** quand je n'étais pas plus grand que ça

2 *(above ground level* ► *river, tide)* haut; *(*► *altitude, shelf)* haut, élevé; **built on h. ground** construit sur un terrain élevé; **the sun was h. in the sky** le soleil était haut

3 *(above average* ► *number)* grand, élevé; *(*► *speed, value)* grand; *(*► *cost, price, rate)* élevé; *(*► *salary)* élevé, gros (grosse); *(*► *pressure)* élevé, haut; *(*► *polish)* brillant; **to the highest degree** au plus haut degré, à l'extrême; **of the highest importance** de première importance; **to pay a h. price** payer le prix fort; **built to withstand h. temperatures** conçu pour résister à des températures élevées; **he has a h. temperature** il a beaucoup de température *ou* fièvre; **areas of h. unemployment** des régions à fort taux de chômage; **milk is h. in calcium** le lait contient beaucoup de calcium; **h. winds** des vents *mpl* violents, de grands vents *mpl*; *Math* **the highest common factor** le plus grand commun diviseur

4 *(better than average* ► *quality)* grand, haut; *(*► *standard)* haut, élevé; *(*► *mark, score)* élevé, bon; *(*► *reputation)* bon; **to have a h. opinion of sb** avoir une bonne *ou* haute opinion de qn; **he has a h. opinion of himself** il a une haute idée de lui-même; **to have a h. profile** être très en vue; **she speaks of you in the highest terms** elle dit le plus grand bien de vous; *Com & Fin* **h. value added** à haute valeur ajoutée

5 *(honourable* ► *ideal, thought)* noble, élevé; *(*► *character)* noble; **he took a very h. moral tone** il prit un ton très moralisateur

6 *(of great importance or rank)* haut, important; **a h. official** un haut fonctionnaire; **to have friends in h. places** avoir des relations haut placées, avoir le bras long; **of h. rank** de haut rang

7 *(sound, voice)* aigu(ë); *Mus (note)* haut

8 *(at peak)* **h. summer** plein été *m*; **it was h. summer** c'était au cœur de l'été; **it's h. time we were leaving** il est grand temps qu'on parte

9 *(intensely emotional)* **moments of h. drama** des moments *mpl* extrêmement dramatiques; **h. adventure** grande aventure *f*; **to be h. farce** tourner à la farce

10 *Br (complexion)* rougeaud, rubicond; **to have a h. colour** avoir le visage congestionné

11 *(elaborate, formal* ► *language, style)* élevé, soutenu

12 *(prominent* ► *cheekbones)* saillant

13 *Cards* haut; **the highest card** la carte maîtresse

14 *Br (meat)* avancé, faisandé; *(butter, cheese)* rance

15 *(remote)* haut

16 *Geog (latitude)* haut

17 *(conservative)* **a h. Tory** un tory ultra-conservateur; **a h. Anglican** un(e) anglican(e) de tendance conservatrice

18 *Ling (vowel)* fermé

19 *(excited)* excité, énervé; *(cheerful)* plein d'entrain, enjoué; **to be in h. spirits** être plein d'entrain; **our spirits were h.** nous avions le moral

20 *Fam (person)* **to be h.** *(drugged)* planer; *Fig (euphoric)* être dans un état d'euphorie▫; **h. on cocaine** défoncé à la cocaïne; *Fig* **they were h. on success** ils ne se sentaient plus après ce succès; *Fig* **he gets h. on sailing** il prend son pied en faisant de la voile; **they were (as) h. as kites** *(drunk)* ils étaient bien partis; *(drugged)* ils planaient; *(happy)* ils avaient la pêche

ADV 1 *(at, to a height)* haut, en haut; *(at a great altitude)* à haute altitude, à une altitude élevée; **up h.** en haut; **higher up** plus haut; **higher and higher** de plus en plus haut; **the kite flew h. up in the sky** le cerf-volant est monté très haut dans le ciel; **she threw the ball h. into the air** elle a lancé le ballon très haut; **the shelf was h. above her head** l'étagère était bien au-dessus de sa tête; *Fig* **we looked h. and low for him** nous l'avons cherché partout; *Fig* **to set one's sights h., to aim h.** viser haut; *Fig* **they're flying h.** ils visent haut, ils voient grand; *also Fig* **to hold one's head h.** porter la tête haute; *Fig* **to leave sb h. and dry** laisser qn en plan

2 *(in intensity)* haut; **they set the price/standards too h.** ils ont fixé un prix/niveau trop élevé; **I turned the heating up h.** j'ai mis le chauffage à fond; **salaries can go as h. as £50,000** les salaires peuvent monter jusqu'à *ou* atteindre 50 000 livres; **I had to go as h. as £50** il a fallu que j'aille *ou* que je monte jusqu'à 50 livres; **the card players played h.** les joueurs de cartes ont joué gros (jeu); **to run h.** *(river)* être en crue; *(sea)* être houleuse *ou* grosse; **feelings were running h.** les esprits se sont échauffés

3 *(in tone)* haut; **I can't sing that h.** je ne peux pas chanter aussi haut

4 *Am Fam (idiom)* **to live h. off** *or* **on the hog** vivre comme un roi *ou* nabab

N 1 *(height)* haut *m*; **on h.** *(at a height)* en haut; *Fig (in heaven)* au ciel; *Hum* **the decision came from on h.** la décision fut prononcée en haut lieu

2 *(great degree or level)* haut *m*; **to reach a new h.** atteindre un nouveau record; **prices are at an all-time h.** les prix ont atteint leur maximum; **the Stock Market reached a new h.** la Bourse a atteint un nouveau record *ou* maximum; **the highs and lows** *(of share prices, career, life)* les hauts *mpl* et les bas *mpl*

3 *(setting* ► *on iron, stove)* **I put the oven on h.** j'ai mis le four sur très chaud

4 *Aut (fourth gear)* quatrième *f*; *(fifth gear)* cinquième *f*

5 *Met (anticyclone)* anticyclone *m*

6 *Fam (state of excitement)* **she's been on a permanent h. since he came back** elle voit tout en rose depuis son retour

• **High N** *Rel* **the Most H.** le Très-Haut

►► *Rel* ***high altar*** maître-autel *m*; *Hist* ***High Antiquity*** Haute Antiquité *f*; *Am Aut* ***high beam*** feux *mpl* de route; ***high camp*** *(affectation)* affectation *f*, cabotinage *m*; *(effeminate behaviour)* manières *fpl* efféminées; *(style)* kitsch *m*; ***high chair*** chaise *f* haute (pour enfants); *Br Rel* ***High Church*** **N** = fraction de l'Église d'Angleterre accordant une grande importance à l'autorité du prêtre, au rituel etc **ADJ** = de tendance conservatrice dans l'Église anglicane; *Mil* ***high command*** haut commandement *m*; *Admin* ***high commission*** haut-commissariat *m*; *Admin* ***high commissioner*** haut-commissaire *m*; *Law* **the High Court (of Justice)** le tribunal de grande instance *(principal tribunal civil en Angleterre et au pays de Galles)*; *Mil* ***high explosive*** explosif *m* puissant; ***high fashion*** haute couture *f*; ***high fidelity*** haute-fidélité *f*; ***high finance*** haute finance *f*; *Fam* ***high five*** = tape amicale donnée dans la paume de quelqu'un, bras levé, pour le saluer, le féliciter ou en signe de victoire; *Electron* ***high frequency*** haute fréquence *f*; ***high gear*** *Aut (fourth)* quatrième *f* (vitesse *f*); *(fifth)* cinquième *f* (vitesse *f*); *Fig* **they moved into h. gear** ils se sont dépêchés; ***High German*** haut allemand *m*; ***high heels*** hauts talons *mpl*; ***high jump*** *Sport* saut *m* en hauteur; *Br Fam Fig* **you're for the h. jump when he finds out!** qu'est-ce que tu vas prendre quand il l'apprendra!; *Sport* ***high jumper*** sauteur(euse) *m,f (qui fait du saut en hauteur)*; ***the high life*** la grande vie; *Rel* ***high mass, High Mass*** grand-messe *f*; *Comput* ***high memory*** mémoire *f* haute; *Comput* ***high memory area*** zone *f* de mémoire haute; ***high noon*** plein midi *m*; **at h. noon** à midi pile; ***high point*** *(major event* ► *of news)* événement *m* le plus marquant; *(*► *of evening, holiday)* point *m* culminant, grand moment *m*; *(*► *of film, novel)* point *m* culminant; ***high priest*** *Rel* grand prêtre *m*; *Fig* **the h. priests of fashion** les gourous *mpl* de la mode; ***high priestess*** *Rel* grande prêtresse *f*; *Fig* **the h. priestess of rock** la grande prêtresse du rock; *Art* ***high relief*** haut-relief *m*; ***high rise*** tour *f (immeuble)*; ***high road*** *(main road)* route *f* principale, grand-route *f*; *Fam* ***high roller*** richard(e) *m,f*; *Sch* ***high school*** *(in UK)* = établissement d'enseignement secondaire regroupant collège et lycée; *(in US)* lycée *m*; ***the high seas*** la haute mer; **on the h. seas** en haute *ou* pleine mer; ***high season*** haute *ou* pleine saison *f*; **during the h. season** en haute *ou* pleine saison; *Br Admin* ***High Sheriff*** = dans les comtés anglais et gallois, représentant officiel du monarque; ***high society*** haute société *f*, grand monde *m*; ***high spirits*** vitalité *f*, entrain *m*; **to be in h. spirits** avoir de l'entrain, être plein d'entrain; *Br* ***the high street*** *(street)* la grand-rue, la rue principale; *(shops)* les commerçants *mpl*, le commerce; *Com & Econ* **the h. street has been badly hit by the recession** les commerçants ont été durement touchés par la récession; *Br* ***high table*** *(for guests of honour)* table *f* d'honneur; *Sch & Univ* table *f* des professeurs; *Br* ***high tea*** = repas léger pris en début de soirée et accompagné de thé; ***high tech*** *(technology)* technologie *f* avancée *ou* de pointe; *(style)* hi-tech *m inv*; ***high tide*** *(of ocean, sea)* marée *f* haute; *Fig (of success)* point *m* culminant; **at h. tide** à marée haute; ***high treason*** haute trahison *f*; *Elec* ***high voltage*** haute tension *f*; ***high water*** *(of ocean, sea)* marée *f* haute; *(of river)* crue *f*; **the river is at h. water** le fleuve est en crue; ***high wire*** corde *f* raide *ou* de funambule; **to walk the h. wire** marcher sur la corde raide

high-angle shot N *Cin* plan *m* en plongée

highball ['haɪˌbɔːl] *Am* **N** = boisson à base d'un alcool avec de l'eau et des glaçons

highborn ['haɪbɔːn] **ADJ** bien né, de bonne *ou* haute naissance

highboy ['haɪbɔɪ] **N** *Am* commode *f* (haute)

highbrow ['haɪbraʊ] **ADJ** *(literature, film)* pour intellectuels; *(taste)* intellectuel

N intellectuel(elle) *m,f*, grosse tête *f*

high-class ADJ *(person)* de la haute société, du grand monde; *(flat, neighbourhood)* de grand standing; *(job, service)* de premier ordre; *(car, hotel, restaurant)* de luxe; **a h. prostitute** une prostituée de luxe

high-definition ADJ à haute définition

►► ***high-definition TV*** télévision *f* haute définition

high-density ADJ 1 *(housing)* à grande densité de population **2** *Comput (disk, graphics, printing)* (de) haute densité

high-diving N plongeon *m* de haut vol, haut vol *m*

high-end ADJ *(top-of-the-range)* haut de gamme

higher ['haɪə(r)] **ADJ 1** *(at greater height)* plus haut **2** *(advanced)* supérieur; **a sum h. than 50** une somme supérieure à 50; **people in the h. income brackets** *or* **groups** les gens appartenant aux tranches de revenus supérieurs; **institute of h. learning** institut *m* de hautes études

ADV plus haut

• **Higher N** *Scot Sch* = diplôme de fin d'études secondaires sanctionnant une matière déterminée

►► ***higher animals*** animaux *mpl* supérieurs; *Sch* ***the higher classes*** les grandes classes *fpl*, les classes *fpl* supérieures; *Law* ***higher court*** instance *f* supérieure; *Univ* ***higher degree*** diplôme *m* d'études supérieures; *Univ* ***higher education*** enseignement *m* supérieur; **to go on to h. education** faire des études supérieures; *Sch* ***the higher forms*** les grandes classes *fpl*, les classes *fpl* supérieures; *Scot Sch* ***Higher Grade*** = diplôme de fin d'études secondaires sanctionnant une matière déterminée; ***higher mathematics*** *(UNCOUNT)* mathématiques *fpl* supérieures

higher-income ADJ à revenu élevé
▸▸ ***higher-income group*** groupe *m* de contribuables à revenus élevés
higher-rate ADJ *Br (taxpayer)* situé dans la plus haute tranche d'imposition; **h. tax** tranche *f* d'imposition la plus haute
highest average system ['haɪɪst-] N *Pol* méthode *f* de la plus forte moyenne
highfalutin [,haɪfə'luːtɪn], **highfalting** [,haɪfə'luːtɪŋ] ADJ *Fam* affecté[□], prétentieux[□]
high-fibre, *Am* **high-fiber** ADJ *(food, diet)* riche en fibres
high-fidelity ADJ haute-fidélité *inv*
high-flier N *(ambitious person)* ambitieux (euse) *m,f*, jeune loup *m*; *(talented person)* crack *m*
high-flown ADJ **1** *(ideas, plans)* extravagant **2** *(language)* ampoulé, boursouflé; *(style)* ampoulé
high-flying ADJ **1** *(aircraft)* qui vole à haute altitude; *(bird)* qui vole haut **2** *(person)* ambitieux; *(behaviour, goal)* extravagant
high-frequency ADJ à ou de haute fréquence
high-grade ADJ de haute qualité, de premier ordre; **h. beef/fruit** bœuf *m*/fruits *mpl* de premier choix; **h. minerals** minéraux *mpl* à haute teneur; *Fig* **a h. idiot** un (une) imbécile de premier ordre
high-handed ADJ *(overbearing)* autoritaire, despotique; *(arbitrary)* arbitraire; *(inconsiderate)* cavalier
high-heeled [-'hiːld] ADJ à talons hauts, à hauts talons
high-income ADJ à haut revenu
▸▸ ***high-income group*** groupe *m* des gros salaires, groupe *m* des salaires élevés
high-involvement ADJ *Mktg (purchasing)* à forte participation des consommateurs
highjack, highjacker *etc* = **hijack, hijacker** *etc*
highland ['haɪlənd] N région *f* montagneuse
ADJ des montagnes
• **Highland** ADJ *(air, scenery)* des Highlands; *(holiday)* dans les Highlands
• **Highlands** NPL **the Highlands** *(of Scotland)* les Highlands *mpl*
▸▸ ***Highland cattle*** race *f* bovine des Highlands; *Hist* ***the Highland Clearances*** = aux XVIIIème et XIXème siècles, déplacement souvent forcé des populations d'une partie des Highlands d'Écosse dans le but d'affecter les terres à l'élevage de moutons

HIGHLAND GAMES

En Écosse, il s'agit d'une sorte de kermesse locale en plein air où se déroulent simultanément toutes sortes de concours (danse, cornemuse) et d'épreuves sportives (courses, lancer du marteau, mais aussi "tossing the caber", "tug o' war" etc).

highlander ['haɪləndə(r)] N *(mountain dweller)* montagnard(e) *m,f*
• **Highlander** N habitant(e) *m,f* des Highlands, Highlander *m*
high-level ADJ *(discussion, meeting)* à un haut niveau; *(diplomat, official)* de haut niveau, de rang élevé; *Mil* **h. officers** officiers *mpl* supérieurs
▸▸ *Comput* ***high-level language*** langage *m* évolué *ou* de haut niveau
highlight ['haɪlaɪt] VT **1** *(emphasize)* souligner, mettre en relief; **the report highlights the desperate plight of the refugees** le rapport fait ressortir *ou* souligne la situation désespérée des réfugiés
2 *(with pen)* surligner
3 *Comput (text block)* sélectionner; **to be highlighted** *(text)* apparaître en surimpression *ou* en surbrillance
4 *Art & Phot* rehausser
5 *(hair)* faire des mèches dans; **to have one's hair highlighted** se faire faire des mèches
N **1** *(important moment ▸ of news)* événement *m* le plus marquant; *(▸ of evening, holiday)* point *m* culminant, grand moment *m*; **the news highlights** les grands titres *mpl* de l'actualité; **the highlights of today's match will be shown later** les moments forts du match d'aujourd'hui seront diffusés ultérieurement; **the h. of the party** le clou de la soirée
2 *(in hair ▸ natural)* reflet *m*; *(▸ bleached)* mèche *f*; **she has had highlights (put in her hair)** elle s'est fait faire des mèches
3 *Comput* relief *m*
4 *Art & Phot* rehaut *m*
highlighter ['haɪlaɪtə(r)] N **1 h. (pen)** surligneur *m*, Stabilo® *m* **2** *(make-up)* enlumineur *m* de teint
highly ['haɪlɪ] ADV **1** *(very)* très, extrêmement; **it's h. improbable** c'est fort peu probable; **the dish was h. seasoned** le plat était fortement relevé *ou* épicé
2 *(very well)* très bien; **very h. paid** très bien payé
3 *(favourably)* **to speak/think h. of sb** dire/penser beaucoup de bien de qn; **he praised her work h.** il a chanté (haut) les louanges de son travail; **I h. recommend it** je vous le conseille vivement *ou* chaudement
4 *(at an important level)* haut; **a h. placed source** une source haut placée
highly-strung ADJ nerveux, tendu
high-margin product N *Com* produit *m* à forte marge
high-minded ADJ *(person)* de caractère noble, qui a des principes (élevés); *(action etc)* magnanime
high-mindedness [-'maɪndɪdnɪs] N noblesse *f* de sentiments, grandeur *f* d'âme; *(of action etc)* magnanimité *f*
highness ['haɪnɪs] N *(of building, wall)* hauteur *f*
• **Highness** N *(title)* **His/Her H.** son Altesse *f*
high-octane ADJ à haut degré d'octane; *Fig* explosif
▸▸ ***high-octane petrol*** supercarburant *m*, super *m*
high-performance ADJ performant
high-pitched ADJ **1** *(sound, voice)* aigu(ë); *Mus (note)* haut **2** *(argument, discussion)* passionné; *(style)* ampoulé; *(excitement)* intense **3** *(roof)* à forte pente
high-powered ADJ **1** *(engine, rifle)* puissant, de forte puissance; *(microscope)* à fort grossissement **2** *(dynamic ▸ person)* dynamique, entreprenant; *(▸ advertising, course, method)* dynamique **3** *(important)* très important
high-pressure ADJ **1** *(cylinder, gas, machine)* à haute pression **2** *Fig (methods, selling)* agressif; *(job, profession)* stressant; **a h. salesman** un vendeur de choc
▸▸ *Met* ***high-pressure area*** anticyclone *m*, zone *f* de hautes pressions (atmosphériques)
high-principled ADJ aux principes élevés
high-profile ADJ *(job, position)* qui est très en vue; *(campaign)* qui fait beaucoup de bruit
high-quality ADJ haut de gamme, de qualité supérieure
high-resolution ADJ *Comput (screen, graphics)* à haute résolution
high-rise ADJ *(flat)* qui est dans une tour; *(skyline)* composé de tours
high-risk ADJ à haut risque, à hauts risques
high-school ADJ *Am Sch*
▸▸ ***high-school diploma*** diplôme *m* de fin d'études secondaires; ***high-school teacher*** professeur *m* de lycée
high-season ADJ *(prices)* de haute saison
high-sounding ADJ *(ideas)* grandiloquent, extravagant; *(language, title)* grandiloquent, *Pej* ronflant
high-speed ADJ ultra-rapide; *Comput* à grande vitesse
▸▸ *Rail* ***high-speed train*** train *m* à grande vitesse
high-spirited ADJ **1** *(person)* plein d'entrain *ou* de vivacité; *(activity, fun)* plein d'entrain **2** *(horse)* fougueux, nerveux
high-street ADJ
▸▸ *Br* ***the high-street banks*** les grandes banques *fpl*; ***high-street fashion*** prêt-à-porter *m*; ***high-street shops*** commerces *mpl*
high-strung ADJ nerveux, tendu
hightail ['haɪteɪl] VT *esp Am Fam* **to h. it** filer; **I hightailed it out of there** j'ai foutu le camp
high-tech [-tek] ADJ **1** *(industry, sector, equipment)* de pointe **2** *(furniture, style)* hi-tech *(inv)*
high-tensile steel N *Constr & Tech* acier *m* à haute résistance élastique
high-tension ADJ *Elec* à haute tension
▸▸ ***high-tension cable*** câble *m* haute tension
high-up *Fam* N *(important person)* gros bonnet *m*, huile *f*; *(hierarchical superior)* supérieur(e)[□] *m,f*
ADJ haut placé[□]; **she is h. up in the government** elle est haut placée dans le gouvernement
high-viscosity ADJ *(oil)* à haute viscosité
highway ['haɪweɪ] N *(road)* route *f*, *Am (main road)* grande route *f*, route *f* nationale; *(public road)* voie *f* publique; *Am (interstate)* autoroute *f*; **all the highways and byways** tous les chemins
▸▸ *Br Aut* ***the Highway Code*** le code de la route; *Br* ***highway engineer*** ingénieur *m* des Ponts et Chaussées; *Am* ***highway patrol*** police *f* de la route; *Am* ***highway patrolman*** membre *m* de la police de la route; ***highway robbery*** banditisme *m* de grand chemin; *Fam Fig* **that's h. robbery!** c'est du vol!
highwayman ['haɪweɪmən] *(pl* **highwaymen** [-mən]) N bandit *m* de grand chemin
high-yield ADJ *Fin (bond, security)* à rendement élevé
hijab [hɪ'dʒæb] N hijab *m*, hidjab *m*
hijack ['haɪdʒæk] VT **1** *(plane)* détourner; *(car, train)* s'emparer de, détourner; *Fig* **the government hijacked the opposition's policy** le gouvernement s'est approprié la politique de l'opposition **2** *(rob)* voler
N détournement *m*
hijacker ['haɪdʒækə(r)] N **1** *(of plane)* pirate *m* (de l'air); *(of car, train)* gangster *m* **2** *(robber)* voleur (euse) *m,f*
hijacking ['haɪdʒækɪŋ] N **1** *(of car, plane, train)* détournement *m* **2** *(robbery)* vol *m*
hike [haɪk] VI faire de la marche à pied; **we went hiking in the mountains** nous avons fait des excursions *ou* des randonnées à pied dans les montagnes; **he hiked through Spain** il a parcouru l'Espagne à pied; **we hiked all the way home** on a dû faire le chemin du retour à pied
VT **1** *(walk)* faire à pied, marcher **2** *(increase ▸ price, interest rates, rent etc)* augmenter (brusquement)
N **1** *(gen) & Mil* marche *f* à pied; *(long walk)* randonnée *f* à pied, marche *f* à pied; *(short walk)* promenade *f*; *Fam* **it's a bit of a h. into town** ça fait une petite trotte pour aller en ville; *Fam* **take a h.!** dégage! **2** *(increase)* hausse *f*, augmentation *f*; **tax h.** augmentation *f* d'impôts
▸ **hike up** VT SEP **1** *(hitch up ▸ skirt)* relever; *(▸ trousers)* remonter; **she hiked herself up over the wall** elle s'est hissée au-dessus du mur **2** *(price, interest rates, rent etc)* augmenter (brusquement)
hiker ['haɪkə(r)] N *(gen) & Mil* marcheur(euse) *m, f*; *(in mountains, woods)* randonneur(euse) *m,f*, promeneur(euse) *m,f*
hiking ['haɪkɪŋ] N *(UNCOUNT) (gen) & Mil* marche *f* à pied; *(in mountains, woods)* randonnée *f*, trekking *m*
▸▸ ***hiking boots*** chaussures *fpl* de marche
hilarious [hɪ'leərɪəs] ADJ *(funny ▸ person, joke, story)* hilarant; **his stories are h.** ses histoires sont à se tordre de rire; **we had a h. time last night** nous nous sommes amusés comme des fous hier soir
hilariously [hɪ'leərɪəslɪ] ADV joyeusement, gaiement; **the film's h. funny** le film est à se tordre de rire
hilariousness [hɪ'leərɪəsnɪs] N *(of story, joke)* caractère *m* hilarant
hilarity [hɪ'lærətɪ] N hilarité *f*
hill [hɪl] N **1** *(small mountain)* colline *f*, coteau *m*; **up h. and down dale, over h. and dale** par monts et par vaux; **the soldiers fought up h. and down dale** les soldats ont mené le combat avec force et persévérance; **as old as the hills** vieux comme le monde *ou* Mathusalem; *Fam* **to be over the h.**

commencer à se faire vieux□ **2** *(slope)* côte *f*, pente *f*; **steep h.** *(sign)* *(up)* montée *ou* côte raide; *(down)* descente abrupte *ou* raide **3** *(mound ▸ of earth)* levée *f* de terre, remblai *m*; *(▸ of things)* tas *m*, monceau *m*; *Am Fam* **that car isn't worth a h. of beans** cette voiture ne vaut pas un clou; *Am* **on the H.** au parlement *(par allusion à Capitol Hill, siège du Congrès)*

▸▸ ***hill farm*** ferme *f* à flanc de coteau; ***hill farmer*** éleveur(euse) *m,f* de moutons dans les alpages

hillbilly [ˈhɪlˌbɪlɪ] *(pl* **hillbillies)** *Am* N montagnard(e) *m,f* des Appalaches; *Pej* péquenaud(e) *m,f*, plouc *mf*

ADJ des Appalaches

▸▸ ***hillbilly music*** folk *m* (des Appalaches)

hill-climbing N randonnée *f (en pays de collines)*

hilliness [ˈhɪlɪnɪs] N vallonnement *m*, caractère *m* accidenté

hillock [ˈhɪlək] N *(small hill)* mamelon *m*, butte *f*; *(artificial hill)* monticule *m*, amoncellement *m*

hillside [ˈhɪlˌsaɪd] N (flanc *m* de) coteau *m*; **on the h.** à flanc de coteau

hilltop [ˈhɪlˌtɒp] N sommet *m* de la colline; **on the h.** au sommet *ou* en haut de la colline

ADJ *(village)* au sommet *ou* en haut de la colline; *(view)* d'en haut de la colline

hillwalker [ˈhɪlˌwɔːkə(r)] N *Br* randonneur(euse) *m,f (en terrain vallonné)*

hillwalking [ˈhɪlˌwɔːkɪŋ] N *(UNCOUNT) Br* randonnée *f (en terrain vallonné)*

hilly [ˈhɪlɪ] *(compar* **hillier**, *superl* **hilliest)** ADJ *(country, land)* vallonné; *(road)* accidenté, à fortes côtes

hilt [hɪlt] N *(of dagger, knife)* manche *m*; *(of sword)* poignée *f*, garde *f*; *(of gun)* crosse *f*; *Fig* **(up) to the h.** au maximum; **to back sb up to the h.** soutenir qn à fond; **mortgaged up to the h.** *(person)* endetté jusqu'au cou, qui doit rembourser des emprunts énormes; *(property)* fortement hypothéqué

him [hɪm] PRON **1** *(direct object ▸ unstressed)* le, l' *(before vowel or silent "h")*; *(▸ stressed)* lui; **I recognize h.** je le reconnais; **I heard h.** je l'ai entendu; **why did you have to choose H.?** pourquoi l'as-tu choisi lui?

2 *(indirect object ▸ unstressed)* lui; *(▸ stressed)* à lui; **give h. the money** donne-lui l'argent; **we are thinking of h.** nous pensons à lui; **I object to h. borrowing the car** je m'oppose à ce qu'il emprunte la voiture

3 *(after preposition)* lui; **I was in front of h.** j'étais devant lui; **as rich as/richer than h.** aussi riche/plus riche que lui; **he closed the door behind h.** il a fermé la porte derrière lui

4 *(with "to be")* **it's h.** c'est lui; **if I were h.** si j'étais lui, si j'étais à sa place

5 *Formal (with relative pronoun)* celui; *Literary* **to h. who should take offence at this I would say…** à celui qui s'en offenserait, je dirais…

Himalayan [ˌhɪməˈleɪən] ADJ himalayen

Himalayas [ˌhɪməˈleɪəz] NPL *Geog* **the H.** l'Himalaya *m*

himself [hɪmˈself] PRON **1** *(reflexive form)* se, s' *(before vowel or silent "h")*; **he introduced h.** il s'est présenté; **he bought h. a car** il s'est acheté une voiture

2 *(emphatic form)* lui-même; **he built the shelves h.** il a monté les étagères lui-même; **I spoke with the teacher h.** j'ai parlé au professeur en personne

3 *(with preposition)* lui; **he has a room to h.** il a sa propre chambre *ou* sa chambre à lui; **the old man was talking to h.** le vieil homme parlait tout seul; **"that's odd," he thought to h.** "c'est bizarre", se dit-il; **he did it all by h.** il l'a fait tout seul

4 *(his usual self)* **he isn't quite h.** il n'est pas dans son état habituel; **he's feeling more h. now** il va mieux maintenant

hind [haɪnd] N *(deer)* biche *f*

ADJ de derrière; **h. leg** patte *f* de derrière; *Hum* **he could talk the h. legs off a donkey** il est bavard comme une pie; *Hum* **to get up on one's h. legs** se mettre debout

hinder[1] [ˈhɪndə(r)] VT *(person)* gêner; *(progress)* entraver, gêner; **to h. sb in his/her work** gêner qn dans son travail; **to h. sb from doing sth** empêcher qn de faire qch

hinder[2] [ˈhaɪndə(r)] ADJ *(at the back)* de derrière, postérieur

Hindi [ˈhɪndɪ] N *Ling* hindi *m*

ADJ hindi

hindmost [ˈhaɪndməʊst] ADJ dernier, du bout

hindquarters [ˈhaɪndkwɔːtəz] NPL arrière-train *m*

hindrance [ˈhɪndrəns] N **1** *(person, thing)* obstacle *m*, entrave *f*; **you'll be more of a h. than a help** tu vas gêner plus qu'autre chose **2** *(UNCOUNT) (action)* **without any h. from the authorities** *(referring to person)* sans être gêné par les autorités; *(referring to project)* sans être entravé par les autorités; **without any h. from the children/my husband** sans avoir les enfants/mon mari dans les jambes

hindsight [ˈhaɪndsaɪt] N **with the benefit** *or* **wisdom** *or* **gift of h.** avec du recul, après coup

Hindu [ˈhɪnduː] N Hindou(e) *m,f*

ADJ hindou

Hinduism [ˈhɪnduːɪzəm] N *Rel* hindouisme *m*

Hindustan [ˌhɪnduˈstɑːn] N *Geog* Hindoustan *m*

Hindustani [ˌhɪnduˈstɑːnɪ] N *Ling* hindoustani *m*

ADJ hindoustani

hinge [hɪndʒ] N *(of door)* gond *m*, charnière *f*; *(of box)* charnière *f*; **the door has come off its hinges** la porte est sortie de ses gonds; **(stamp) h.** charnière *f*

VT *(door)* munir de gonds *ou* charnières; *(box)* munir de charnières

▸▸ *Anat* ***hinge joint*** diarthrose *f*

▸**hinge on, hinge upon** VT INSEP *(depend on)* dépendre de; **the company's future hinges on whether we get the contract** l'avenir de l'entreprise dépend de *ou* tient à *ou* repose sur ce contrat

hinged [hɪndʒd] ADJ à charnière *ou* charnières

▸▸ ***hinged flap*** *(of counter)* abattant *m*

Hinglish [ˈhɪŋglɪʃ] N = mélange d'hindi et d'anglais utilisé par les Britanniques d'origine indienne ou pakistanaise

hinky [ˈhɪŋkɪ] ADJ *Am Fam* bizarre, louche; **it tastes h.** ça un drôle de goût; **his directions were a bit h.** ses indications étaient un peu douteuses

hint [hɪnt] N **1** *(indirect suggestion)* allusion *f*; *(clue)* indice *m*; **to drop a h. (about sth)** faire une allusion (à qch); **you could try dropping a h. that if his work doesn't improve…** tu pourrais essayer de lui faire comprendre que si son travail ne s'améliore pas…; **he can't take a h.** il ne comprend rien à demi-mot; **OK, I can take a h.** oh ça va, j'ai compris; **I took the h.** j'ai saisi ce qu'on essayait de me faire comprendre; **give me a h.** donne-moi un indice; **I just love plain chocolate, h., h.** j'adore le chocolat noir, si tu vois ce que je veux dire **2** *(helpful suggestion, tip)* conseil *m*, truc *m* **3** *(small amount, trace ▸ of emotion)* note *f*; *(▸ of colour)* touche *f*; *(▸ of flavouring)* soupçon *m*; **there's a h. of spring in the air** ça sent le printemps

VT insinuer; **that was what he hinted** c'est ce qu'il a insinué *ou* laissé entendre

VI **to h. at sth** faire allusion à qch; **what are you hinting at?** qu'est-ce que tu insinues?; *(in neutral sense)* à quoi fais-tu allusion?; **the speech seemed to h. at the possibility of agreement being reached soon** le discours semblait laisser entendre qu'un accord pourrait être conclu prochainement

hinterland [ˈhɪntəˌlænd] N arrière-pays *m inv*

HIP [hɪp] N *Br (abbr* **Home Information Pack)** = dossier contenant des informations détaillées sur une maison ou un appartement fourni aux acheteurs potentiels

hip[1] [hɪp] N **1** *Anat (part of body)* hanche *f*; **with one's hands on one's hips** les mains sur les hanches; **to be big/small around the hips** avoir les hanches larges/étroites; **to break one's h.** se casser le col du fémur; *Fig* **to shoot from the h.** réagir de façon impulsive **2** *Constr* **h. (piece** *or* **rafter)** *(of roof)* arêtier *m*, arête *f*

▸▸ *Br* ***hip bath*** bain *m* de siège; ***hip flask*** flasque *f*; ***hip measurement*** tour *m* de hanches; *Br* ***hip pocket*** poche *f* revolver; *Med* ***hip replacement*** *(operation)* remplacement *m* de la hanche par une prothèse; *(prosthesis)* prothèse *f* de la hanche; ***hip size*** tour *m* de hanches

hip[2] N *(berry)* cynorhodon *m*, gratte-cul *m inv*

hip[3] *Fam* ADJ *(fashionable)* branché; **to be h. to sth** être branché sur qch

VT *Am* **to h. sb to sth** mettre qn au courant de qch□; **I'll h. you to the latest** je vais te mettre au parfum

hip[4] EXCLAM **h. h., hooray!** hip hip hip, hourra!

hipbone [ˈhɪpbəʊn] N *Anat* os *m* iliaque

hiphuggers [ˈhɪpˌhʌgəz] NPL *Am* pantalon *m* à taille basse

-hipped [hɪpt] SUFF **broad-h.** aux hanches larges; **narrow-h.** aux hanches fines *ou* étroites

hippie [ˈhɪpɪ] N hippie *mf*, hippy *mf*

ADJ hippie, hippy

hippo [ˈhɪpəʊ] *(pl* **hippos)** N *Fam* hippopotame□ *m*

Hippocrates [hɪˈpɒkrətiːz] PR N Hippocrate

Hippocratic oath [ˌhɪpəˈkrætɪk-] N **the H.** le serment d'Hippocrate

hippodrome [ˈhɪpədrəʊm] N hippodrome *m*; *(not for racing)* arène *f*

hippopotamus [ˌhɪpəˈpɒtəməs] *(pl* **hippopotamuses** *or* **hippopotami** [-maɪ]) N *Zool* hippopotame *m*

hippy[1] [ˈhɪpɪ] *(pl* **hippies)** = **hippie**

hippy[2] ADJ *Fam (with large hips)* aux hanches larges□

hipster [ˈhɪpstə(r)] N *esp Am Old-fashioned* beatnick *mf (des années 40 et 50)*

• **hipsters** NPL *Br (trousers)* pantalon *m* (à) taille basse

hire [ˈhaɪə(r)] N **1** *Br (of car, room, suit etc)* location *f*; **for h.** *(sign)* à louer; *(taxi)* libre **2** *(cost ▸ of car, boat etc)* (prix *m* de) location *f*; *(▸ of worker)* paye *f* **3** *(of labour)* embauche *f*

VT **1** *Br (car, room, suit etc)* louer; **to h. sb's services** employer les services de qn; **to h. sth from sb** louer qch à qn **2** *(staff)* engager; *(labourer)* embaucher, engager; *(lawyer, private detective etc)* s'assurer les services de, engager; **hired killer** *or* **assassin** tueur *m* à gages

VI engager du personnel, embaucher (des ouvriers); **the personnel manager has the power to h. and fire** le chef du personnel s'occupe d'embaucher et de renvoyer les employés

▸▸ *Br* ***hire car*** voiture *f* de location; ***hire charges*** (frais *mpl ou* prix *m* de) location *f*; *Am* ***hired gun*** *(killer)* tueur *m* à gages; *(troubleshooter)* expert *m (appelé en cas de crise)*; ***hired hand*** *(on farm)* ouvrier(ère) *m,f* agricole; *(employee)* employé(e) *m,f*; *Br Com* ***hire purchase*** location-vente *f*, vente *f* à tempérament; **to buy** *or* **to get sth on h. purchase** acheter qch en location-vente; ***hire purchase agreement*** contrat *m* de location-vente

▸**hire out** VT SEP *Br (car, room, suit etc)* louer, donner en location; **to h. oneself out** se faire engager; *(labourer)* se faire engager *ou* embaucher

hireling [ˈhaɪəlɪŋ] N *Pej (menial)* larbin *m*; *(illegal or immoral)* mercenaire *m*

hi-res [ˈhaɪrez] ADJ *Fam Comput (abbr* **high-resolution)** (à) haute résolution□

hiring [ˈhaɪərɪŋ] N **1** *Br (of car, room, suit etc)* location *f* **2** *(of employee)* embauche *f*

hirsute [ˈhɜːsjuːt] ADJ *Formal* poilu, velu

his [hɪz] ADJ *(singular)* son (sa); *(plural)* ses; **h. table** sa table; **h. glasses** ses lunettes; **h. university** son université; **it's H. fault, not mine** c'est de sa faute à lui, pas de la mienne; **he has broken h. arm** il s'est cassé le bras; **with h. hands in h. pockets** les mains dans les poches; *Formal* **everyone must do h. best** chacun doit faire de son mieux; *Formal* **I object to h. borrowing the car** je m'oppose à ce qu'il emprunte la voiture

PRON **1** *(gen ▸ singular)* le sien (la sienne) *m,f*; *(▸ plural)* les siens (les siennes) *mpl, fpl*; **it's h.** c'est à lui, c'est le sien/la sienne; **the responsibility is h.** c'est lui qui est responsable; **is this coat h.?** ce manteau est-il à lui?, ce manteau est-il le sien?; **no, THIS one is h.** non, le sien c'est celui-ci; **the painting wasn't his to give away** il n'avait pas à donner ce tableau

2 *(after preposition)* **a friend of h.** un de ses amis;

that dog of h. is a nuisance son fichu chien est vraiment embêtant; it's always been a fault of h. ça a toujours été son défaut *ou* un de ses défauts
3 *(indicating authorship)* de lui; **are these paintings h.?** ces tableaux sont-ils de lui?
4 *Fam (his house, flat)* chez lui▫; **we're meeting at his** on se retrouve chez lui

Hispanic [hɪ'spænɪk] **N** Hispano-Américain(e) *m,f*
ADJ hispanique

Hispanic-American N Hispano-Américain(e) *m,f*
ADJ hispano-américain

Hispanicism [hɪ'spænɪ,sɪzəm] **N** *Ling* hispanisme *m*

Hispanicization, -isation [hɪ,spænɪsaɪ'zeɪʃən] **N** hispanisation *f*

Hispanicize, -ise [hɪ'spænɪ,saɪz] **VT** hispaniser

Hispano-American [hɪ'spænəʊ-] **N** Hispano-Américain(e) *m,f*
ADJ hispano-américain

hiss [hɪs] **N** *(of gas, steam)* sifflement *m*, chuintement *m*; *(of person, snake)* sifflement *m*; *(of cat)* crachement *m*; **"be quiet," she said in a h.** "tais-toi!", dit-elle nerveusement; **he was greeted with hisses** il est arrivé sous les sifflets (du public); **the cat backed away with a h.** le chat a reculé en crachant
VT *(say quietly)* souffler; *(bad performer, speaker etc)* siffler; **the audience hissed its disapproval** les spectateurs ont sifflé en signe de mécontentement; **the speaker was hissed off the platform** l'orateur quitta la tribune sous les sifflets (du public)
VI *(gas, steam)* siffler, chuinter; *(snake)* siffler; *(cat)* cracher; *(person ▸ in disapproval, anger)* siffler

hissing ['hɪsɪŋ] **N** *(of gas, steam)* sifflement *m*, chuintement *m*; *(of person, snake)* sifflement *m*

hissy fit ['hɪsɪ-] **N** *Br Fam* **to have a h.** faire une crise

histamine ['hɪstəmiːn] **N** *Biol & Chem* histamine *f*

histogram ['hɪstəgræm] **N** histogramme *m*

historian [hɪ'stɔːrɪən] **N** historien(enne) *m,f*

historic [hɪ'stɒrɪk] **ADJ 1** *(memorable ▸ day, occasion, meeting etc)* historique **2** *(of time past)* révolu, passé; *(fear)* ancestral; **in h. times** en des temps révolus
▸▸ ***historic building*** monument *m* historique

> Il faut noter que les adjectifs **historic** et **historical** ne sont pas interchangeables. **Historic** signifie **important d'un point de vue historique** alors que **historical** signifie **qui se rapporte à l'histoire.**

historical [hɪ'stɒrɪkəl] **ADJ** historique; **it's a h. fact** c'est un fait historique; **to be of h. interest** présenter un intérêt historique
▸▸ ***historical novel*** roman *m* historique

> Voir note ci-dessus.

historically [hɪ'stɒrɪkəlɪ] **ADV** historiquement; *(traditionally)* traditionnellement

historiography [,hɪstɔːrɪ'ɒgrəfɪ] **N** historiographie *f*

history ['hɪstərɪ] *(pl* **histories) N 1** *(UNCOUNT) (the past)* histoire *f*; **ancient/modern h.** histoire *f* ancienne/moderne; **the h. of France, French h.** l'histoire *f* de France; **to study h.** étudier l'histoire; **throughout h.** tout au long de l'histoire; **the h. plays of Shakespeare** les pièces *fpl* historiques de Shakespeare; **to make h.** entrer dans l'histoire; **a day that has gone down in h.** une journée qui est entrée dans l'histoire; **that's ancient h.** *(forgotten, in the past)* c'est de l'histoire ancienne; *(everyone knows that)* c'est bien connu; **the rest is h.** tout le monde connaît la suite; *Fam* **there's a lot of h. between them** il s'est passé beaucoup de choses entre eux▫; *Fam* **they used to go out with each other but they're h. now** ils sortaient ensemble mais maintenant c'est fini▫; *Fam* **he's h.!** *(in trouble)* il est fini!; *(no longer in my/her/etc life)* avec lui, c'est terminé
2 *(UNCOUNT) (development, lifespan)* histoire *f*; **the worst disaster in aviation h.** *or* **in the h. of aviation** le plus grand désastre de l'histoire de l'aviation
3 *(account)* histoire *f*; **Shakespeare's histories** les pièces *fpl* historiques de Shakespeare
4 *(UNCOUNT) (record)* **employment h.** expérience *f* professionnelle; **medical h.** antécédents *mpl* médicaux; **there is a h. of heart disease in my family** il y a des antécédents de maladie cardiaque dans ma famille; **there is a long h. of cultural links between these cities** il existe une longue tradition de liens culturels entre ces villes
COMP *(book, teacher, lesson)* d'histoire

histrionic [,hɪstrɪ'ɒnɪk] **ADJ 1** *Pej (melodramatic)* théâtral **2** *Literary Theat* théâtral

histrionics [,hɪstrɪ'ɒnɪks] **NPL** *Pej* comédie *f*, simagrées *fpl*; **I've had enough of his h.** j'en ai assez de ses simagrées

HIT [hɪt]

N
- coup **1, 2**
- hit **4**
- succès **3**
- occurrence **4**

VT
- frapper **1**
- attaquer **3**
- arriver à **5**
- marquer **7**
- heurter **2**
- toucher **4**
- buter sur **6**

VI
- frapper **1**
- se faire sentir **2**

(pt & pp **hit**, *cont* **hitting)**
N 1 *(blow)* coup *m*; *Fig* **that was a h. at me** ça m'était destiné, c'est moi qui étais visé
2 *Sport (in ball game)* coup *m*; *(in shooting)* tir *m* réussi; *(in fencing, billiards, snooker)* touche *f*; *(in baseball)* coup *m* de batte; *(in hockey)* coup *m* de crosse; **to score a h.** *(in shooting)* faire mouche, toucher la cible; *(in fencing)* faire *ou* marquer une touche; **he got three hits and one miss** il a réussi trois tirs et en a manqué un; **it only counts as a h. if the bullet goes inside the red line** le tir ne compte que si la balle se trouve à l'intérieur de la ligne rouge; **that was a h.** *(in fencing)* il y a eu touche
3 *(success ▸ record, play, book)* succès *m*; *(▸ song)* succès *m*, hit *m*, tube *m*; **Frank Sinatra's greatest hits** les plus grands succès de Frank Sinatra; **to be a big h.** *(record, play, book, song)* faire *ou* être un grand succès; **a h. with the public/the critics** un succès auprès du public/des critiques; **I think you've made a h. with him** je crois que tu l'as conquis; *(romantically)* je crois que tu as fait une touche
4 *Comput (visit to website)* hit *m*, accès *m*; *(in search)* occurrence *f*; **this website counted 20,000 hits last week** ce site Web a été consulté 20 000 fois la semaine dernière
5 *Fam Crime slang (murder)* liquidation *f*; **a Mafia h.** un meurtre perpétré par la Mafia
6 *Fam Drugs slang (of hard drugs)* fix *m*; *(of joint)* taffe *f*; *(effect of drugs)* effet▫ *m (procuré par une drogue)*; **you get a good h. off that grass** cette herbe fait rapidement de l'effet
VT 1 *(strike with hand, fist, stick etc ▸ person)* frapper; *(▸ ball)* frapper *ou* taper dans; *(▸ nail)* taper sur; *Comput (key)* appuyer sur; **to h. sb in the face/on the head** frapper qn au visage/sur la tête; **to h. a ball over the net** envoyer un ballon par-dessus le filet; *Fig* **to h. sb where it hurts (most)** toucher qn là où ça fait mal; *also Fig* **to h. a man when he's down** frapper un homme quand il est à terre; *Fig* **to h. the nail on the head** mettre le doigt dessus; *Fig* **he didn't know what had h. him** il se demandait ce qui lui était arrivé
2 *(come or bring forcefully into contact with ▸ of ball, stone)* heurter; *(▸ of bullet, arrow)* atteindre, toucher; **the bottle h. the wall and smashed** la bouteille a heurté le mur et s'est cassée; **the bullet h. him in the shoulder** la balle l'a atteint *ou* touché à l'épaule; **I've been h.!** j'ai été touché!; **he was h. by a stone** il a reçu une pierre; **to h. the target** *(with gun, missile etc)* toucher la cible; *Fig* **his comments really h. their target** ses remarques ont vraiment fait mouche, il a mis dans le mille avec ses remarques; **the car h. a tree** la voiture a heurté *ou* est rentrée dans un arbre; **to h. one's head/knee (against sth)** se cogner la tête/le genou (contre qch); **to h. sb's head against sth** frapper *ou* cogner la tête de qn contre qch; *Fig* **to h. the ground running** être opérationnel immédiatement; *Fig* **it suddenly h. me that...** il m'est soudain venu à l'esprit que...
3 *(attack ▸ enemy)* attaquer
4 *(affect)* toucher; **the company has been h. by the recession** l'entreprise a été touchée par la récession; **the region worst h. by the earthquake** la région la plus sévèrement touchée par le tremblement de terre; **to be hard h.** être durement touché; *Fam* **it hits everyone in the pocket** tout le monde en subit financièrement les conséquences▫, tout le monde le sent passer
5 *(reach)* arriver à; *Fam* **the new model can h. 130 mph on the straight** le nouveau modèle peut atteindre les 210 km/h en ligne droite; *Fam* **to h. a problem** se heurter à un problème *ou* une difficulté; *Mus* **to h. a note** *(singer)* chanter une note; *(instrumentalist)* jouer une note; **to h. the wrong note** *(singer)* chanter faux; *(instrumentalist) & Fig* faire une fausse note; *Fam* **we'll stop for dinner when we h. town** nous nous arrêterons pour dîner quand nous arriverons dans la ville; *Fam* **let's h. the beach!** allons à la plage!▫; *Fam* **when it hits the shops** *(product)* quand il sera mis en vente▫; **to h. an all-time high/low** *(unemployment, morale etc)* atteindre son plus haut/bas niveau▫; *Fam* **to h. rock-bottom** atteindre son point le plus bas▫
6 *(encounter ▸ problem, difficulty)* buter sur; **the tunnellers h. rock** les ouvriers qui creusaient le tunnel sont tombés sur de la roche; **you'll h. the rush hour traffic** tu vas te retrouver en plein dans la circulation de l'heure de pointe; **we h. a terrible snowstorm** nous nous sommes trouvés dans une tempête de neige terrible
7 *Sport (in cricket ▸ runs)* marquer; *Fencing* toucher; **to h. three runs** *(in cricket)* marquer trois points; **to h. a home run** *(in baseball)* faire un tour complet de circuit
8 *Fam Crime slang (kill)* descendre, liquider
9 *Am Fam (borrow money from)* taper; **to h. sb for $10** taper qn de 10 dollars; **to h. sb for a loan** emprunter de l'argent à qn▫
10 *(idioms) Am Fam* **to h. the books** se mettre à étudier▫; *Fam* **to h. the bottle** *(drink)* picoler; *(start to drink)* se mettre à picoler; *Fam* **to h. the ceiling** *or* **roof** sortir de ses gonds, piquer une colère folle; *Am Fam Aut* **to h. the gas** appuyer sur le champignon; *Fam* **to h. the hay** *or* **the sack** aller se pieuter; *Fam* **if ever this hits the headlines we're in trouble** si jamais cela paraît dans les journaux nous aurons des problèmes▫; **to h. home** *(remark, criticism)* faire mouche; **to h. the jackpot** gagner le gros lot; *Fam* **to h. the road** se mettre en route▫; *Fam* **h. the road!** *(go away)* fiche le camp!; *Fam* **that really hits the spot!** *(food, drink)* c'est juste ce dont j'avais besoin▫
VI 1 *(person, object)* frapper, taper; **the door was hitting against the wall** la porte cognait contre le mur; **the atoms h. against each other** les atomes entrent en collision
2 *(inflation, recession)* se faire sentir
▸▸ *Fam* **hit list** liste *f* noire; **to be on sb's h. list** être sur la liste noire de qn; *Fam* **hit man** tueur *m* à gages▫; *Old-fashioned* **hit parade** hit-parade *m*; *Fam* **hit squad** commando *m* de tueurs▫

▸**hit back VI** *(reply forcefully, retaliate)* riposter, rendre la pareille; **he h. back with accusations that they were giving bribes** il a riposté en les accusant de verser des pots-de-vin; **to h. back at sb/sth** *(in speech)* répondre à qn/qch; **our army h. back with a missile attack** notre armée a riposté en envoyant des missiles
VT SEP to h. the ball back renvoyer le ballon; **he h. me back** il m'a rendu mon coup

▸**hit off VT SEP** *Fam (idiom)* **to h. it off with sb** bien s'entendre avec qn▫; **we h. it off immediately** le courant est tout de suite passé entre nous

▸**hit on VT INSEP 1** *(find ▸ solution, plan etc)* trouver **2** *Am Fam (try to pick up)* draguer

▸**hit out VI 1** *(physically ▸ once)* envoyer un coup; *(▸ repeatedly)* envoyer des coups; **he started hitting out at me** il s'est mis à envoyer des coups dans ma direction **2** *(in speech, writing)* **to h. out at** *or* **against** s'en prendre à, attaquer; **he hits out in his new book** il lance l'offensive dans son nouveau livre

▸ **hit upon** VT INSEP *(find ▸ solution, plan etc)* trouver

hit-and-run N accident *m* avec délit de fuite; **he's confessed to the h.** il s'est reconnu coupable du délit de fuite
▸▸ ***hit-and-run accident*** accident *m* avec délit de fuite; *Mil* ***hit-and-run attack*** attaque *f* éclair; ***hit-and-run driver*** conducteur(trice) *m,f* coupable de délit de fuite

hitch [hɪtʃ] VT **1** *Fam (hitchhike)* **to h. a lift** *(gen)* se faire emmener en voiture❑; *(hitchhiker)* se faire prendre en stop; **I hitched a lift from the woman next door** je me suis fait emmener par la voisine; **she has hitched her way round Europe** elle a fait toute l'Europe en stop *ou* auto-stop **2** *(railway carriage)* attacher, atteler; *(horse ▸ to fence)* attacher; *(▸ to carriage, cart)* atteler; *(rope)* attacher, nouer **3** *Fam (idiom)* **to get hitched** *(one person)* se caser; *(couple)* passer devant Monsieur le Maire
VI faire du stop *ou* de l'auto-stop; **to h. to London** aller à Londres en stop; **I spent the summer hitching round the South of France** j'ai passé l'été à voyager dans le sud de la France en auto-stop
N **1** *(difficulty)* problème *m*, anicroche *f*; **there's been a h.** il y a eu un problème; **without a h.** *or* **any hitches** sans anicroche
2 *Am Fam (length of time)* **to do a three-year h. in prison** faire trois ans de prison❑; **he's doing a five-year h. in the navy** il s'est engagé pour cinq ans dans la marine❑
3 *(knot)* nœud *m*
4 *(pull)* **to give sth a h. (up)** remonter *ou* retrousser qch

▸ **hitch up** VT SEP **1** *(trousers, skirt etc)* remonter, retrousser **2** *(horse, oxen etc)* atteler

hitchhike [ˈhɪtʃhaɪk] VI faire du stop *ou* de l'auto-stop; **to h. to London** aller à Londres en stop; **I spent the summer hitchhiking round the South of France** j'ai passé l'été à voyager dans le sud de la France en auto-stop
VT **to h. one's way round Europe** faire l'Europe en auto-stop

hitchhiker [ˈhɪtʃhaɪkə(r)] N auto-stoppeur(euse) *m,f*, stoppeur(euse) *m,f*

hitchhiking [ˈhɪtʃhaɪkɪŋ], **hitching** [ˈhɪtʃɪŋ] N auto-stop *m*, stop *m*

hi-tech [ˈhaɪˌtek] N **1** *(in industry)* technologie *f* de pointe **2** *(style of interior design)* high-tech *m inv*
ADJ **1** *(equipment, industry)* de pointe; **they've adopted a h. approach** ils ont eu recours à la technologie de pointe **2** *(design, furniture)* high-tech *(inv)*

hither [ˈhɪðə(r)] ADV *Arch* ici; *Literary or Hum* **h. and thither** çà et là, de ci de là

hitherto [ˌhɪðəˈtuː] ADV *Formal* jusqu'ici, jusqu'à présent; **a h. incurable disease** une maladie jusqu'ici *ou* jusqu'à présent incurable

hit-or-miss ADJ *(method, approach)* basé sur le hasard; *(work)* fait n'importe comment *ou* à la va comme je te pousse; **the service here is a bit h.** le service ici est fait un peu n'importe comment

HIV [ˌeɪtʃaɪˈviː] N *Med (abbr* **human immunodeficiency virus***)* VIH *m*, HIV *m*; **to be H. negative** être séronégatif; **to be H. positive** être séropositif

hive [haɪv] N *(for bees)* ruche *f*; *(group of bees)* essaim *m*; *Fig* **a h. of industry** *or* **activity** une vraie *ou* véritable ruche
VT mettre en ruche
VI entrer dans une ruche

▸ **hive off** VT SEP **1** *(separate)* détacher *ou* séparer (d'un tout); **the subsidiary companies will be hived off** les filiales deviendront indépendantes **2** *(department, branch of industry)* se débarrasser de; **part of the industry was hived off to private ownership** une partie de cette industrie a été privatisée
VI *Fam (go away, slip off)* se tirer, se casser

hives [haɪvz] N *(UNCOUNT) Med* urticaire *f*; **to have h.** avoir de l'urticaire

hiya [ˈhaɪjə] EXCLAM *Fam* salut!

HM [ˌeɪtʃˈem] N *(abbr* **His/Her Majesty***)* SM, Sa Majesté

h'm [həm] EXCLAM hum, mmm

HMG [ˌeɪtʃemˈdʒiː] N *Br Admin (abbr* **His/Her Majesty's Government***)* = expression utilisée sur des documents officiels en Grande-Bretagne

HMI [ˌeɪtʃemˈaɪ] N *Br Sch (abbr* **His/Her Majesty's Inspector***)* = inspecteur de l'éducation nationale en Grande-Bretagne

HMS [ˌeɪtʃemˈes] N *Br Naut (abbr* **His/Her Majesty's Ship***)* = dénomination officielle précédant le nom de tous les bâtiments de guerre de la marine britannique

HMSO [ˌeɪtʃemˌesˈəʊ] N *Br Typ (abbr* **His/Her Majesty's Stationery Office***)* = maison d'édition publiant les ouvrages ou documents approuvés par le Parlement, les ministères et autres organismes officiels, ≃ l'Imprimerie *f* nationale

HNC [ˌeɪtʃenˈsiː] N *Br (abbr* **Higher National Certificate***)* = brevet de technicien en Grande-Bretagne, ≃ BTS *m*

HND [ˌeɪtʃenˈdiː] N *Br (abbr* **Higher National Diploma***)* = brevet de technicien supérieur en Grande-Bretagne, ≃ DUT *m*

ho[1] [həʊ] EXCLAM **1** *(attracting attention)* hé ho! **2** *(imitating laughter)* **ho ho!** ha ha ha! **3 ho hum!** *(expressing resignation)* bon!

ho[2] N *very Fam Black Am slang* pouffiasse *f*

hoar [hɔː(r)] N givre *m*

hoard [hɔːd] N *(of goods)* réserve *f*, provisions *fpl*; *(of money)* trésor *m*, magot *m*; **he has a whole h. of stories** il a une réserve d'histoires assez extraordinaire
VT *(goods)* faire provision *ou* des réserves de, stocker; *(money)* amasser, thésauriser
VI faire des réserves, stocker

> Attention: ne pas confondre avec le nom anglais **horde**.

hoarder [ˈhɔːdə] N *(gen)* = personne ou animal qui fait des réserves; *(of money)* thésauriseur (euse) *m,f*; **she's a real h.** elle garde tout, elle ne jette rien

hoarding[1] [ˈhɔːdɪŋ] N *(UNCOUNT) (of goods)* mise *f* en réserve *ou* en stock; *(of money)* thésaurisation *f*, accumulation *f*; **h. is forbidden** il est interdit de faire des réserves *ou* des stocks

hoarding[2] N *Br* **1** *(fence)* palissade *f* **2** *(billboard)* panneau *m* publicitaire *ou* d'affichage

hoarfrost [ˈhɔːˌfrɒst] N givre *m*

hoarse [hɔːs] ADJ *(person)* enroué; *(voice)* rauque, enroué; **to sound h.** être enroué, avoir la voix enrouée; **to shout oneself h.** s'enrouer à force de crier

hoarsely [ˈhɔːslɪ] ADV d'une voix rauque *ou* enrouée

hoarseness [ˈhɔːsnɪs] N enrouement *m*

hoary [ˈhɔːrɪ] *(compar* **hoarier**, *superl* **hoariest***)* ADJ **1** *(greyish white ▸ hair)* blanc (blanche); *(▸ person)* aux cheveux blancs, chenu **2** *(old ▸ problem, story)* vieux (vieille); **a h. old joke** une blague usée

hoax [həʊks] N canular *m*; **to play a h. on sb** jouer un tour à qn, monter un canular à qn; **bomb h.** fausse alerte *f* à la bombe
VT jouer un tour à, monter un canular à
▸▸ *Br* ***hoax call*** canular *m* téléphonique

hoaxer [ˈhəʊksə(r)] N mauvais plaisant *m*

hob [hɒb] N *(on stove top)* plaque *f* (chauffante); *(by open fire)* plaque *f*

hobble [ˈhɒbəl] VI boitiller; **she hobbled across the street** elle a traversé la rue en boitillant
VT *(horse)* entraver
N **1** *(limp)* boitillement *m*; **to walk with a h.** marcher en boitillant **2** *(for horse)* entrave *f*
▸▸ ***hobble skirt*** jupe *f* entravée

hobby [ˈhɒbɪ] *(pl* **hobbies***)* N *(pastime)* passe-temps *m inv*, hobby *m*

hobbyhorse [ˈhɒbɪhɔːs, *pl* -ˈhɔːsɪz] N **1** *(toy)* cheval *m* de bois *(composé d'une tête sur un manche)* **2** *(favourite topic)* sujet *m* favori, dada *m*; **she's off on her h. again** la voilà repartie sur son sujet favori *ou* son dada; **to get sb on his/her h.** brancher qn sur son sujet favori *ou* dada

hobgoblin [ˌhɒbˈgɒblɪn] N diablotin *m*

hobnail [ˈhɒbneɪl] N clou *m* à grosse tête, cabo che *f*
▸▸ ***hobnail boots*** chaussures *fpl* ferrées

hobnob [ˈhɒbnɒb] *(pt & pp* **hobnobbed**, *cont* **hob nobbing***)* VI **to h. with sb** frayer avec qn, fréquen ter qn

hobo [ˈhəʊbəʊ] *(pl* **hobos** *or* **hoboes***)* N *Am Fam (tramp)* clochard(e)❑ *m,f*, vagabond(e)❑ *m,f* *(itinerant labourer)* saisonnier(ère)❑ *m,f*

Hobson's choice [ˈhɒbsənz-] N **it's (a case of) H** il n'y a pas vraiment le choix *(se dit d'une situa tion où le choix n'est qu'apparent)*

hock [hɒk] N **1** *(joint, piece of meat)* jarret *m* *(wine)* vin *m* du Rhin **3** *Fam (idioms)* **in h.** *(i pawn)* au clou; *(in debt)* endetté❑; **how much ar you in h. for?** de combien es-tu endetté?; **I'm in h for $500** j'ai 500 dollars de dettes❑; **I'm in h. t him for $500** je lui dois 500 dollars❑; **to get st out of h.** retirer qch du clou
VT *(pawn)* mettre au clou

hockey [ˈhɒkɪ] *Sport* N **1** *Br (field hockey)* hocke *m* (sur gazon) **2** *Am (ice hockey)* hockey *m* su glace
COMP *(ball, match, pitch, team) Br* de hockey; *Am* de hockey sur glace
▸▸ ***hockey player*** *Br* joueur(euse) *m,f* de hocke hockeyeur(euse) *m,f*; *Am* joueur(euse) *m,f* d hockey sur glace; ***hockey stick*** *Br* crosse *f* d hockey; *Am* crosse *f* de hockey sur glace

hocus-pocus [ˌhəʊkəsˈpəʊkəs] N **1** *(of magicia ▸ tricks)* tours *mpl* de passe-passe; *(▸ chant* abracadabra *m* **2** *(trickery)* tricherie *f*, superche rie *f*; *(deceptive talk)* paroles *fpl* trompeuses; *(de ceptive action)* trucage *m*, supercherie *f*; **it's jus h.** ce n'est que de la supercherie

hod [hɒd] N *(for bricks)* = ustensile utilisé par le maçons pour porter les briques; *(for mortar* auge *f*, oiseau *m*; *(for coal)* seau *m* à charbon

hodgepodge [ˈhɒdʒpɒdʒ] *Am* = **hotchpotch**

Hodgkin's disease [ˈhɒdʒkɪnz-] N *Med* mala die *f* de Hodgkin

Hodgkin's lymphoma [ˈhɒdʒkɪnz-] N *Med* lymphome *m* hodgkinien

hoe [həʊ] *Agr & Hort* N houe *f*, binette *f*
VT biner, sarcler

hoedown [ˈhəʊdaʊn] N *Am* bal *m* populaire

hog [hɒg] *(pt & pp* **hogged**, *cont* **hogging***)* N **1** *(cas trated pig)* cochon *m ou* porc *m* châtré; *Am (pig* cochon *m*, porc *m*
2 *Fam Fig (greedy person)* goinfre *mf*; *(dirty per son)* porc *m*
3 *Am Fam (motorbike)* grosse bécane *f*, gros cube *m*
4 *Fam (idioms)* **to go the whole h.** ne pas faire les choses à moitié; **why don't we go the whole h and order champagne?** pourquoi ne pas faire les choses en grand et commander du cham pagne?; *Am* **to be in h. heaven** être comme un coq en pâte
VT *Fam* monopoliser❑; **to h. the television** monopoliser la télé; **to h. the limelight** accaparer *ou* monopoliser l'attention, se mettre en vedette; **to h. the middle of the road** prendre toute la route❑

Hogmanay [ˌhɒgməˈneɪ] N *Scot* la Saint-Sylvestre

> **HOGMANAY**
>
> Le mot "Hogmanay" vient soit de l'ancien français, soit du gaélique. Il désigne les fêtes de la veille du nouvel an célébrées en Écosse. Traditionnellement, les Écossais préféraient célébrer la nouvelle année plutôt que Noël et jusqu'au XVIIIème siècle, la tradition était d'offrir des cadeaux le jour de l'an. Les coutumes écossaises sont aussi anciennes que diverses: à minuit, les gens chantent la chanson **Auld Lang Syne** (voir ce mot), puis vont rendre visite à leurs voisins avec un morceau de charbon en guise de cadeau, et tout le monde boit une goutte de whisky pour fêter la nouvelle année.

hogshead [ˈhɒgzhed] N tonneau *m*, barrique *f*

ogtie ['hɒgtaɪ] VT *Am (animal)* lier les quatre)attes de; *Fig* **to be hogtied** être pieds et poings iés

ogwash ['hɒgwɒʃ] N *(UNCOUNT)* **1** *Fam (non-ense)* fadaises *fpl*, foutaises *fpl*; **to talk h.** racon-er des fadaises **2** *(pigswill)* eaux *fpl* grasses EXCLAM *Fam* n'importe quoi!

oi polloi [ˌhɔɪpə'lɔɪ] NPL *Pej* **the h.** la populace

oist [hɔɪst] VT *(sails, flag)* hisser; *(load, person)* ever, hisser; *Fig* **to be h. with one's own petard** être pris à son propre piège; **she hoisted herself on to the wall** elle s'est hissée sur le mur N **1** *(elevator)* monte-charge *m*; *(block and tackle)* palan *m* **2** *(upward push, pull)* **to give sb a h. up** *(lift)* soulever qn; *(pull)* tirer qn

oity-toity [ˌhɔɪtɪ'tɔɪtɪ] ADJ *Fam Pej* préten-ieux[□], péteux; **she's very h.** c'est une vraie bê-cheuse

okey ['həʊkɪ] ADJ *Am Fam (nonsensical)* ab-surde[□]; *(sentimental)* à l'eau de rose

▸▸ *Br* **hokey cokey** = danse et chanson tradition-nelles londoniennes

okum ['həʊkəm] N *(UNCOUNT) Am Fam (non-sense)* fadaises *fpl*, foutaises *fpl*; *(sentimentality)* guimauve *f*

HOLD [həʊld]

VT	
• tenir **A1, 6, 10, B1, 2, D2, 4**	• retenir **A2, 5, C2**
• avoir **A3**	• réserver **A5, 8**
• contenir **A6**	• exercer **A7**
• conserver **A9**	• détenir **A9, C1**
• stocker **A9**	• maintenir **B1, D1**
• croire **D1**	• considérer **D1–3**
• organiser **D4**	• continuer **D5**
VI	
• se tenir **1**	• tenir bon **2**
• durer **3**	• tenir **4**
• être valable **4**	• attendre **6**
N	
• prise **1–3**	• pause **4**
• prison **5**	• place forte **5**
• soute **6**	• cale **6**

(pt & pp **held** [held]*)*

VT **A. 1** *(clasp, grasp)* tenir; **to h. sth in one's hand** *(book, clothing, guitar)* avoir qch à la main; *(key, money)* tenir qch dans la main; **to h. sth with both hands** tenir qch à deux mains; **will you h. my coat a second?** peux-tu prendre *ou* tenir mon manteau un instant?; **to h. the door for sb** tenir la porte à *ou* pour qn; *also Fig* **to h. sb's hand** tenir la main à qn; **to h. hands** se donner la main, se tenir (par) la main; **h. my hand while we cross the street** donne-moi la main pour traverser la rue; **to h. sb close** *or* **tight** serrer qn contre soi; **h. it tight** tiens-le bien; **to h. one's nose** se boucher le nez; **to h. one's sides with laughter** se tenir les côtes de rire

2 *(keep, sustain)* **to h. sb's attention/interest** retenir l'attention de qn; **to h. an audience** tenir un auditoire; **to h. one's serve** *(in tennis)* défendre son service; *Pol* **to h. a seat** *(be an MP)* occuper un siège de député; *(be re-elected)* être réélu; **to h. one's own** se défendre, bien se débrouiller; **she is well able to h. her own** elle sait se défendre; **he can h. his own in chess** il se défend bien aux échecs; **to h. the floor** garder la parole; **the senator held the floor for an hour** le sénateur a gardé la parole pendant une heure

3 *(have, possess* ▸ *degree, permit, ticket)* avoir, posséder; *(*▸ *job, position)* avoir, occuper; **she holds the post of treasurer** elle occupe le poste de trésorière; **to h. office** *(chairperson, deputy)* être en fonction, remplir sa fonction; *(minister)* détenir *ou* avoir un portefeuille; *(political party, president)* être au pouvoir *ou* au gouvernement; *Fin* **to h. stock** *or* **shares** détenir *ou* avoir des actions; *also Fig* **to h. a record** détenir un record

4 *(keep control or authority over) Mil* **the guerrillas held the bridge for several hours** les guérilleros ont tenu le pont plusieurs heures durant; *Mil* **to h. the enemy** contenir l'ennemi; **h. it!, h. everything!** *(stop and wait)* attendez!; *(stay still)* arrêtez!, ne bougez plus!; *Fam Fig* **h. your horses!** pas si vite!

5 *(reserve, set aside)* retenir, réserver; **we'll h. the book for you until next week** nous vous réserverons le livre *ou* nous vous mettrons le livre de côté jusqu'à la semaine prochaine; **will the restaurant h. the table for us?** est-ce que le restaurant va nous garder la table?

6 *(contain)* contenir, tenir; **this bottle holds two litres** cette bouteille contient deux litres; **will this suitcase h. all our clothes?** est-ce que cette valise sera assez grande pour tous nos vêtements?; **the car is too small to h. us all** la voiture est trop petite pour nous tous; **the hall holds a maximum of 250 people** la salle peut accueillir *ou* recevoir 250 personnes au maximum, il y a de la place pour 250 personnes au maximum dans cette salle; **to h. one's drink** bien supporter l'alcool

7 *(have, exercise)* exercer; **the subject holds a huge fascination for some people** le sujet exerce une énorme fascination sur certaines personnes

8 *(have in store)* réserver; **who knows what the future may h.?** qui sait ce que nous réserve l'avenir?

9 *(conserve, store)* conserver, détenir; *Comput* stocker; **how much data will this disk h.?** quelle quantité de données cette disquette peut-elle stocker?; **the commands are held in the memory** les instructions sont gardées en mémoire; **my lawyer holds a copy of my will** mon avocat détient *ou* conserve un exemplaire de mon testament; **this photo holds fond memories for me** cette photo me rappelle de bons souvenirs

10 *Aut* **the new car holds the road well** la nouvelle voiture tient bien la route

B. 1 *(maintain in position)* tenir, maintenir; **her hair was held in place with hairpins** des épingles (à cheveux) retenaient *ou* maintenaient ses cheveux; **h. the picture a bit higher** tenez le tableau un peu plus haut

2 *(carry)* tenir; **to h. oneself upright** *or* **erect** se tenir droit; *also Fig* **to h. one's head high** garder la tête haute

C. 1 *(confine, detain)* détenir; **the police are holding him for questioning** la police l'a gardé à vue pour l'interroger; **they're holding him for murder** ils l'ont arrêté pour meurtre

2 *(keep back, retain)* retenir; **the post office will h. my mail for me while I'm away** la poste gardera mon courrier pendant mon absence; *Fig* **once she starts talking politics there's no holding her!** dès qu'elle commence à parler politique, rien ne peut l'arrêter!; *Am* **one burger, h. the mustard!** *(in restaurant)* un hamburger, sans moutarde!

3 *(delay)* **don't h. dinner for me** ne m'attendez pas pour dîner; **h. all decisions on the project until I get back** attendez mon retour pour prendre des décisions concernant le projet; **h. the lift!** retenez l'ascenseur!

4 *(keep in check)* **we have held costs to a minimum** nous avons limité nos frais au minimum; **inflation has been held at the same level for several months** le taux d'inflation est maintenu au même niveau depuis plusieurs mois

D. 1 *(assert, claim)* maintenir, soutenir; *(believe)* croire, considérer; *Formal* **I h. that teachers should be better paid** je considère *ou* j'estime que les enseignants devraient être mieux payés; **she holds strong views on the subject** elle a une opinion bien arrêtée sur le sujet; **her statement is held to be true** sa déclaration passe pour vraie

2 *(consider, regard)* tenir, considérer; **to h. sb responsible for sth** tenir qn pour responsable de qch; **to h. sb in contempt** mépriser *ou* avoir du mépris pour qn; **to h. sb in high esteem** avoir beaucoup d'estime pour qn, tenir qn en haute estime

3 *Law (judge)* juger; **the appeal court held the evidence to be insufficient** la cour d'appel a considéré que les preuves étaient insuffisantes

4 *(carry on, engage in* ▸ *conversation, meeting)* tenir; *(*▸ *party)* donner; *(organize)* organiser; **to h. an election/elections** procéder à une élection/à des élections; **the book fair is held in Frankfurt** la foire du livre se tient *ou* a lieu à Francfort; **interviews will be held in early May** les entretiens auront lieu au début du mois de mai *ou* début mai; **to h. talks** être en pourparlers; **mass is held at eleven o'clock** la messe est célébrée à onze heures

5 *(continue without deviation)* continuer; *Naut* **to h. course** tenir la route; **we held our southerly course** nous avons maintenu le cap au sud, nous avons continué notre route vers le sud; *Mus* **to h. a note** tenir une note

6 *Tel* **will you h. (the line)?** voulez-vous patienter?; **h. the line!** ne quittez pas!; **the line's busy just now – I'll h.** le poste est occupé pour le moment – je patiente *ou* je reste en ligne; **h. all my calls** ne me passez aucun appel

VI **1** *(cling* ▸ *person)* se tenir, s'accrocher; **she held tight to the railing** elle s'est cramponnée *ou* accrochée à la rampe; **h. fast!, h. tight!** accrochez-vous bien!; *Fig* **their resolve held fast** *or* **firm in the face of fierce opposition** ils ont tenu bon face à une opposition acharnée

2 *(remain in place* ▸ *nail, fastening)* tenir bon; **the rope won't h. for long** la corde ne tiendra pas longtemps

3 *(last* ▸ *luck)* durer; *(*▸ *weather)* durer, se maintenir; **the pound held firm against the dollar** la livre s'est maintenue par rapport au dollar; **we might buy him a guitar if his interest in music holds** nous lui achèterons peut-être une guitare s'il continue à s'intéresser à la musique

4 *(remain valid* ▸ *invitation, offer)* tenir; *(*▸ *argument, theory)* valoir, être valable; **to h. good** *(invitation, offer)* tenir; *(promises)* tenir, valoir; *(argument, theory)* rester valable; **that theory only holds if you consider...** cette théorie n'est valable que si vous prenez en compte...; **the same holds for Spain** il en est de même pour l'Espagne

5 *(stay, remain) Fam* **h. still!** ne bougez pas![□]

6 *(on telephone)* attendre; **the line's** *Br* **engaged** *or Am* **busy, will you h.?** la ligne est occupée, voulez-vous patienter?

N **1** *(grasp, grip)* prise *f*; *(in wrestling)* prise *f*; *Boxing* tenu *m*; **to catch** *or* **to grab** *or* **to seize** *or* **to take h. of sth** se saisir de *ou* saisir qch; **she caught h. of the rope** elle a saisi la corde; **grab (a) h. of that towel** tiens! prends cette serviette; **there was nothing for me to grab h. of** il n'y avait rien à quoi m'accrocher *ou* me cramponner; **get a good** *or* **take a firm h. on** *or* **of the railing** tenez-vous bien à la balustrade; **to get h. of sth** *(find)* se procurer *ou* trouver qch; **it's difficult to get h. of this book** ce livre est difficile à trouver; **where did you get h. of that idea?** où est-ce que tu es allé chercher cette idée?; **to get h. of sb** trouver qn; **I've been trying to get h. of you all week!** je t'ai cherché toute la semaine!; **just wait till the newspapers get h. of the story** attendez un peu que les journaux s'emparent de la nouvelle; **she kept h. of the rope** elle n'a pas lâché la corde; **you'd better keep h. of the tickets** tu ferais bien de garder les billets; **get a h. on yourself** ressaisis-toi, ne te laisse pas aller; **to take h.** *(fire)* prendre; *(idea)* se répandre; *Sport & Fig* **no holds barred** tous les coups sont permis

2 *(controlling force or influence)* prise *f*, influence *f*; **to have a h. over sb/sth** avoir de l'influence sur qn/qch; **I have no h. over him** je n'ai aucune prise *ou* influence sur lui; **the Mafia obviously has some kind of h. over him** de toute évidence, la Mafia le tient d'une manière ou d'une autre

3 *(in climbing)* prise *f*

4 *(delay, pause)* pause *f*, arrêt *m*; **the company has put a h. on all new orders** l'entreprise a suspendu *ou* gelé toutes les nouvelles commandes

5 *(prison)* prison *f*; *(cell)* cellule *f*; *(fortress)* place *f* forte

6 *(store* ▸ *in plane)* soute *f*; *(*▸ *in ship)* cale *f*

• **on hold** ADV *(gen) & Tel* en attente; **to put sb on h.** mettre qn en attente; **we've put the project on h.** nous avons mis le projet en attente

▸ **hold against** VT SEP **to h. sth against sb** en vouloir à qn de qch; **he lied to her and she still holds it against him** il lui a menti et elle lui en veut toujours; **I hope you won't h. it against me if I decide not to accept** j'espère que tu ne m'en voudras pas si je décide de ne pas accepter

▸ **hold back** VT SEP **1** *(control, restrain* ▸ *animal, person)* retenir, tenir; *(*▸ *crowd, enemy forces)* contenir; *(*▸ *anger, laughter, tears)* retenir, réprimer; *(*▸ *inflation)* contenir

2 *(keep* ▸ *money, supplies)* retenir; *Fig (*▸ *information, truth)* cacher, taire; **she's holding something back from me** elle me cache quelque chose

3 *Am Sch* **they held her back a year** ils lui ont fait redoubler une classe, ils l'ont fait redoubler

4 *(prevent progress of)* empêcher de progresser; **lack of investment is holding industry back** l'absence d'investissements freine l'industrie

VI *(stay back)* rester en arrière; *Fig (restrain oneself)* se retenir; **the president held back before sending in the army** le président a attendu avant d'envoyer l'armée; **don't h. back, tell me everything** vas-y, dis-moi tout

▸ **hold down VT SEP 1** *(keep in place* ▸ *paper, carpet)* maintenir en place; *(*▸ *person)* forcer à rester par terre, maintenir au sol; **it took four men to h. him down** il a fallu quatre hommes pour le maîtriser *ou* pour le maintenir au sol

2 *(keep to limit)* restreindre, limiter; **to h. prices down** empêcher les prix de monter, empêcher la montée des prix

3 *(of employee)* **to h. down a job** *(occupy)* avoir un emploi; *(keep)* garder un emploi; **he's never managed to h. down a job** il n'a jamais pu garder un emploi bien longtemps

4 *Comput (key, mouse button)* appuyer sur

▸ **hold forth VI** pérorer, disserter; **he held forth on the evils of drink** il a fait un long discours sur les conséquences néfastes de l'alcool

▸ **hold in VT SEP 1** *(stomach)* rentrer **2** *(emotion)* retenir; *(anger)* contenir

▸ **hold off VT SEP 1** *(keep at distance)* tenir à distance *ou* éloigné; **the troops held off the enemy** les troupes ont tenu l'ennemi à distance; **they managed to h. off the attack** ils ont réussi à repousser l'attaque; **I can't h. the reporters off any longer** je ne peux plus faire attendre *ou* patienter les journalistes **2** *(delay, put off)* remettre à plus tard; **he held off going to see the doctor until May** il a attendu le mois de mai pour aller voir le médecin; **I held off making a decision** j'ai remis la décision à plus tard

VI at least the rain held off au moins il n'a pas plu

▸ **hold on VI 1** *(grasp, grip)* tenir bien, s'accrocher; **to h. on to sth** bien tenir qch, s'accrocher à qch, se cramponner à qch; **h. on!** accrochez-vous!

2 *(keep possession of)* garder; **h. on to this contract for me** *(keep it)* garde-moi ce contrat; **all politicians try to h. on to power** tous les hommes politiques essaient de rester au pouvoir; **h. on to your dreams/ideals** accrochez-vous à vos rêves/idéaux

3 *(continue, persevere)* tenir, tenir le coup; **how long can you h. on?** combien de temps pouvez-vous tenir (le coup)?; **I can't h. on much longer** je ne vais pas pouvoir tenir (le coup) beaucoup plus longtemps

4 *(wait)* attendre; *(stop)* arrêter; **h. on just one minute!** *(stop)* arrêtez!; *(wait)* attendez!, pas si vite!; **h. on, how do I know I can trust you?** attends un peu! qu'est-ce qui me prouve que je peux te faire confiance?; *Tel* **h. on, please!** ne quittez pas!

VT SEP *(maintain in place)* tenir *ou* maintenir en place; **her hat is held on with pins** son chapeau est maintenu (en place) par des épingles

▸ **hold out VI 1** *(last* ▸ *supplies, stocks)* durer; **will the car h. out till we get home?** la voiture tiendra-t-elle (le coup) jusqu'à ce qu'on rentre? **2** *(refuse to yield)* tenir bon, tenir le coup; **the garrison held out for weeks** la garnison a tenu bon pendant des semaines; **the management held out against any suggested changes** la direction a refusé tous les changements proposés

VT SEP *(extend)* tendre; **she held out the book to him** elle lui a tendu le livre; *also Fig* **to h. out one's hand to sb** tendre la main à qn; **his mother held her arms out to him** sa mère lui a tendu les bras

VT INSEP *(offer)* offrir; **the doctors h. out little hope for him** les médecins ont peu d'espoir pour lui; **science holds out some hope for cancer patients** la science offre un espoir pour les malades du cancer

▸ **hold out on VT INSEP** *Fam* **you're holding out on me!** tu me caches quelque chose!□

▸ **hold over VT SEP 1** *(postpone)* remettre, reporter; **we'll h. these items over until the next meeting** on va remettre ces questions à la prochaine réunion; **payment was held over for six months** le paiement a été différé pendant six mois **2** *(retain)* retenir, garder; **they're holding the show over for another month** ils vont laisser le spectacle à l'affiche encore un mois

▸ **hold to VT INSEP** *(promise, tradition)* s'en tenir à, rester fidèle à; *(decision)* maintenir, s'en tenir à

VT SEP we held him to his promise nous lui avons fait tenir parole; **if I win, I'll buy you lunch – I'll h. you to that!** si je gagne, je t'invite à déjeuner – je te prends au mot!

▸ **hold together VT SEP** *(book, car)* maintenir; *(two objects)* maintenir ensemble; *(community, family)* maintenir l'union de; **the two pieces of wood are held together by nails** les deux morceaux de bois sont cloués ensemble; **we need a leader who can h. the workers together** il nous faut un chef qui puisse rallier les ouvriers

▸ **hold up VT SEP 1** *(lift, raise)* lever, élever; **I held up my hand** j'ai levé la main; **to h. up one's head** redresser la tête; *Fig* **she felt she would never be able to h. her head up again** elle pensait qu'elle ne pourrait plus jamais marcher la tête haute

2 *(support)* soutenir; **my trousers were held up with safety pins** mon pantalon était maintenu par des épingles de sûreté

3 *(present as example)* **they were held up as an example** on les présentai comme un exemple; **to h. sb up to ridicule** tourner qn en ridicule

4 *(delay)* retarder; *(stop)* arrêter; **the traffic held us up** la circulation nous a mis en retard; **the accident held up traffic for an hour** l'accident a bloqué la circulation pendant une heure; **our departure was held up by bad weather** notre départ a été retardé par le mauvais temps; **I was held up** j'ai été retenu; **the goods were held up at customs** les marchandises ont été immobilisées à la douane

5 *(rob)* faire une attaque à main armée; **to h. up a bank** faire un hold-up dans une banque

VI *(clothing, equipment)* tenir; *(supplies)* tenir, durer; *(weather)* se maintenir; **the car held up well during the trip** la voiture a bien tenu le coup pendant le voyage; **she's holding up well under the pressure** elle supporte bien la pression

▸ **hold with VT INSEP** *Br (agree with)* être d'accord avec; *(approve of)* approuver; **I don't h. with her ideas on socialism** je ne suis pas d'accord avec *ou* je ne partage pas ses idées concernant le socialisme

---

holdall ['həʊldɔːl] **N** *Br* (sac *m*) fourre-tout *m inv*

holder ['həʊldə(r)] **N 1** *(for lamp, plastic cup etc)* support *m* **2** *(person* ▸ *of ticket, permit)* détenteur(trice) *m,f*; *(*▸ *of passport, post, diploma, account)* titulaire *mf*; *(*▸ *of lease)* locataire *mf*; *(*▸ *of record, cup)* détenteur(trice) *m,f*; *(*▸ *of title)* détenteur(trice) *m,f*, tenant(e) *m,f*; *(*▸ *of opinion, belief)* tenant *m*; *Fin (*▸ *of stock, shares, bonds, bill)* porteur(euse) *m,f*, détenteur(trice) *m,f*; *(*▸ *of patent)* concessionnaire *mf*; *(*▸ *of insurance policy)* assuré(e) *m,f*

holding ['həʊldɪŋ] **N 1** *(of meeting)* tenue *f* **2** *(land)* propriété *f* **3** *Fin* participation *f*; **holdings** *(lands)* propriétés *fpl*, terres *fpl*; *(stocks)* participation *f*, portefeuille *m*; **he has holdings in several companies** il est actionnaire de plusieurs sociétés

▸▸ *Fin* ***holding company*** (société *f* en) holding *m*, société *f* à portefeuille

hold-up **N 1** *(robbery)* hold-up *m*, vol *m* à main armée **2** *(delay* ▸ *on road, railway track etc)* ralentissement *m*; *(*▸ *in production, departure etc)* retard *m*; **there's been a h. on the line** il y a eu des perturbations sur la ligne

hole [həʊl] **N 1** *(in the ground, in wall, roof etc)* trou *m*; *(in clouds)* éclaircie *f*; **to dig a h.** creuser un trou; **his socks were full of holes** ses chaussettes étaient pleines de trous; **to wear a h. in sth** faire un trou à qch; *Fig* **to make a h. in one's savings/a bottle of whisky** bien entamer ses économies/une bouteille de whisky; *Fig* **money burns a h. in my pocket** l'argent me file entre les doigts; **to try to pick holes in an argument** chercher des failles à une argumentation; **his argument's full of holes** son argumentation est pleine de défauts *ou* failles; *Fam* **a h. in the wall** *(restaurant)* un restaurant minuscule□; *(cash dispenser)* un distributeur (de billets)□; *Fam* **I need that like a h. in the head** c'est vraiment la dernière chose dont j'aie besoin□; *Fam* **you're talking through a h. in your head** tu racontes n'importe quoi□; *Fam* **that's filled a h.!** ça m'a bien calé!; *Med* **h. in the heart** malformation *f* du cœur; **to have a h. in the heart** avoir une malformation du cœur, avoir la maladie bleue

2 *Fam Pej (boring place)* trou *m*; **what a h.!** *(town)* quel trou!; **this is an awful h.!** *(house, pub, disco)* c'est mortel ici!

3 *Fam (tricky situation)* pétrin *m*; **to be in a h.** être dans le pétrin; **to get sb out of a h.** sortir qn du pétrin

4 *Golf* trou *m*; **to get a h. in one** faire un trou en un; **an 18-h. (golf) course** un parcours de 18 trous

VT 1 *(make hole in)* trouer **2** *Golf* **to h. a putt** faire le trou

VI 1 *(sock, stocking)* se trouer **2** *Golf* faire le trou; **to h. in four** faire le trou en quatre (coups)

▸▸ ***hole punch*** perforatrice *f*

▸ **hole out VI** *Golf* finir le trou

▸ **hole up VT SEP** *(usu passive)* **they're holed up in a hotel** ils se planquent *ou* ils sont planqués dans un hôtel

VI 1 *(animal)* se terrer **2** *Fam (hide)* se planquer

hole-and-corner **ADJ** *Fam (meeting, love affair etc)* clandestin□, secret(ète)□

hole-in-the-heart **ADJ** *Med (baby)* bleu; **a h. operation** une opération d'une malformation du cœur

hole-in-the-wall machine **N** *Fam Banking* distributeur *m* (de billets)

holey ['həʊlɪ] **ADJ** troué, plein de trous

holiday ['hɒlɪdeɪ] **N 1** *Br (period without work)* vacances *fpl*; **Christmas h.** vacances *fpl* de Noël; **summer h.** *or* **holidays** vacances *fpl* d'été; *Sch* grandes vacances *fpl*; **on h.** en vacances; **to go on h.** aller *ou* partir en vacances; **I'm going on h. in a week** je pars en vacances dans une semaine; **to take a h./two months' h.** prendre des vacances/deux mois de vacances; **how much** *or* **how long a h. do you get?** combien de vacances as-tu?; **h. with pay, paid holidays** congés *mpl* payés; **I need** *or* **could do with a h.** j'ai besoin de vacances; **take a h. from the housework** oublie un peu les travaux ménagers; **I wish I could take a h. from the children for a few days** si seulement je pouvais passer quelques jours sans les enfants

2 *(day off)* jour *m* de congé; **tomorrow is a h.** demain c'est férié

COMP *(mood, feeling, destination)* de vacances; *(pay)* versé pendant les vacances

VI *Br* passer les vacances

▸▸ *Br* ***holiday camp*** = centre de vacances familial (avec animations et activités diverses); *Br* ***holiday cottage*** gîte *m*; ***holiday entitlement*** droit *m* aux vacances; *Br* ***holiday home*** maison *f* de vacances, résidence *f* secondaire; *Br* ***holiday resort*** lieu *m* de vacances *ou* de séjour; *Br* ***holiday season*** saison *f* des vacances; ***the holiday traffic*** la circulation des départs en vacances

holidaymaker ['hɒlɪdeɪ,meɪkə(r)] **N** *Br* vacancier(ère) *m,f*

holier-than-thou ['həʊlɪə-] **ADJ** *Pej (attitude, tone, person)* moralisateur

holiness ['həʊlɪnɪs] **N** sainteté *f*; **His/Your H.** Sa/Votre Sainteté

holism ['həʊlɪzəm] **N** *Med & Phil* holisme *m*

holistic [həʊ'lɪstɪk] **ADJ** *Med & Phil* holistique

▸▸ ***holistic medicine*** médecine *f* holistique

Holland ['hɒlənd] **N** *Geog (country)* Hollande *f*, Pays-Bas *mpl*

holland ['hɒlənd] **N** *Tex* hollande *f*

holler ['hɒlə(r)] *esp Am Fam* **N** braillement *m*; **to give** *or* **to let out a h.** brailler

VT brailler

VI brailler, beugler

hollow ['hɒləʊ] **N 1** *(in tree)* creux *m*, cavité *f* **2** *(in ground, hand, back)* creux *m*

ADJ 1 *(not solid* ▸ *tree, container)* creux; **to have a h. feeling in one's stomach** avoir une sensation de vide dans l'estomac; **to feel h.** *(hungry)* avoir le ventre *ou* l'estomac creux; *Fam* **you must have h. legs!** *(able to eat a lot)* tu dois avoir le ver solitaire!; *(able to drink a lot)* qu'est-ce que tu peux boire!, tu as une sacrée descente!

2 *(sunken* ▸ *eyes, cheeks)* creux, cave

3 (empty ▸ sound) creux, caverneux; (▸ laugh, laughter) faux (fausse), forcé; **to feel h.** (emotionally) se sentir vide ou vidé; **in a h. voice** d'une voix éteinte; **she gave a h. laugh** elle a ri d'un air un peu faux ou forcé, elle a ri jaune

4 (worthless ▸ promise, words, excuse) vain; **it was a h. victory for her** cette victoire lui semblait dérisoire

ADV 1 **to sound h.** (tree, wall) sonner creux; (laughter, excuse, promise) sonner faux 2 Br Fam **to beat sb h.** battre qn à plate(s) couture(s)

VT creuser

▸ **hollow out** VT SEP creuser

hollow-cheeked ADJ aux joues creuses

hollow-eyed ADJ aux yeux caves ou enfoncés

hollowness ['hɒləʊnɪs] N 1 (of tree, container) creux m, cavité f 2 (of sound) timbre m caverneux; (of laugh, laughter) fausseté f 3 (of promise, words, excuse) fausseté f, manque m de sincérité

holly ['hɒlɪ] N Bot (tree, leaves) houx m

▸▸ **holly berry** baie f de houx, cenelle f

hollyhock ['hɒlɪhɒk] N Bot rose f trémière

Hollywood ['hɒlɪwʊd] N Hollywood

ADJ hollywoodien

holm [həʊm] N Bot chêne m vert, yeuse f

▸▸ **holm oak** chêne m vert, yeuse f

holocaust ['hɒləkɔːst] N holocauste m; Hist **the H.** l'Holocauste m

hologram ['hɒləgræm] N Phot hologramme m

holograph ['hɒləgrɑːf] N Phot document m olographe ou holographe

ADJ olographe, holographe

holographic [ˌhɒlə'græfɪk] ADJ Phot holographique

holography [hɒ'lɒgrəfɪ] N Phot holographie f

hols [hɒlz] NPL Br Fam vacances□ fpl

holster ['həʊlstə(r)] N (for gun ▸ on waist, shoulder) étui m de revolver; (▸ on saddle) fonte f; (for piece of equipment) étui m

holy ['həʊlɪ] (compar **holier**, superl **holiest**, pl **holies**) ADJ 1 (sacred ▸ bread, water) bénit; (▸ place, ground, day) saint 2 (devout) saint 3 Fam (as intensifier) **that child is a h. terror** (mischievous) cet enfant est un vrai démon; **the new headmaster is a h. terror** (intimidating) le nouveau principal est redoutable□; **to have a h. fear of sth** avoir une sainte peur de qch; Am Pej **he's a real h. roller** il est sans arrêt en train de faire des prêchi-prêcha; **h. smoke!, h. mackerel!, h. cow!** mince alors!, ça alors!, Seigneur!; Am Vulg **h. shit!** merde alors!

N **H. of Holies** Rel saint m des saints; Fig Hum (inner sanctum) sanctuaire m, antre m sacré; (special place) lieu m saint

▸▸ Rel **the Holy Bible** la Sainte Bible; **the Holy City** la Ville sainte; Rel **Holy Communion** la Sainte Communion; **to take H. Communion** communier, recevoir la Sainte Communion; Rel **the Holy Family** la Sainte Famille; Rel **the Holy Father** le Saint-Père; Rel **the Holy Ghost** le Saint-Esprit, l'Esprit m saint; **the Holy Grail** le (Saint) Graal; Rel **Holy Innocents' Day** la fête des saints Innocents; Fam **Holy Joe** (religious person) bigot m; Geog & Rel **the Holy Land** la Terre sainte; **holy matrimony** les liens mpl sacrés du mariage; **to be joined in h. matrimony** être unis par les liens mpl sacrés du mariage; **holy orders** ordres mpl; **to take h. orders** entrer dans les ordres; Hist **the Holy Roman Empire** le Saint-Empire romain; Rel **the Holy Rood** la Sainte Croix; Bible & Rel **Holy Scripture** l'Écriture f sainte, les Saintes Écritures fpl; Rel **the Holy See** le Saint-Siège; Bible **the Holy Sepulchre** le Saint-Sépulcre; **the Holy Spirit** le Saint-Esprit, l'Esprit m saint; Rel **the Holy Trinity** la Sainte Trinité; **holy war** guerre f sainte; Rel **Holy Week** la Semaine sainte; Bible & Rel **Holy Writ** l'Écriture f sainte, les Saintes Écritures fpl; Fig **it's not H. Writ!** ce n'est pas parole d'évangile!

homage ['hɒmɪdʒ] N hommage m; **to pay or to do h. to sb, to do sb h.** rendre hommage à qn

homburg ['hɒmbɜːg] N chapeau m mou, feutre m souple

HOME [həʊm]

N
- maison 1
- chez-soi 1
- foyer 2
- patrie 3
- habitat 4
- maison de repos 5
- maison de retraite 5
- arrivée 6
- début 7

ADV
- chez soi 1
- au pays natal 2
- à fond 3

ADJ
- familial 1
- pour la maison 2
- national 3, 4
- intérieur 3
- local 4

VI
- revenir chez soi

N 1 (one's house) maison f, (more subjectively) chez-soi m inv; **a h. from h.** un second chez-soi; **I left h. at 16** j'ai quitté la maison à 16 ans; **her h. is not far from mine** sa maison n'est pas loin de chez moi; **to have a h. of one's own** avoir un foyer ou un chez-soi; **to be away from h.** être parti ou absent ou en voyage; **he was found far away from h.** on l'a trouvé loin de chez lui; **his h. is in Nice** il habite Nice; **New York will always be h. for me!** c'est toujours à New York que je me sentirai chez moi!; **when did she make her h. in Hollywood?** quand s'est-elle installée à Hollywood?; **to give sb a h.** recueillir qn chez soi; **they sell lovely things for the h.** ils vendent toutes sortes de très jolis accessoires pour la maison; **they have a lovely h.!** c'est très agréable chez eux!; **at h.** chez soi, à la maison; **come and see me at h.** passez me voir à la maison; Formal **Mrs Carr is not at h. on Mondays** Mme Carr ne reçoit pas le lundi; **make yourself at h.** faites comme chez vous; **he made himself at h. in the chair** il s'est mis à l'aise dans le fauteuil; **I don't feel at h. here** je me sens dépaysé ici, je ne me sens pas chez moi ici; **he doesn't yet feel at h. with the machine** il n'est pas encore à l'aise avec la machine; **I work out of or at h.** je travaille à domicile ou chez moi; Fam **what's that when it's at h.?** qu'est-ce que c'est que ça?; Ironic **don't you have a h. to go to?** tu as l'intention de passer la nuit ici?; Prov **there's no place like h.** = on n'est vraiment bien que chez soi; Prov **h. is where the heart is** = où le cœur aime, là est le foyer; **h. sweet h.** foyer, doux foyer

2 (family unit) foyer m; Admin habitation f, logement m; **the father left h.** le père a abandonné le foyer; **to start or to set up a h.** fonder un foyer; **good h. wanted for three kittens** (advertisement) je donne trois chatons

3 (native land) patrie f, pays m natal; **at h. and abroad** dans notre pays et à l'étranger; Fig **this discussion is getting a bit close to h.!** on aborde un sujet dangereux!; **let's look at a situation closer to or nearer h.** examinons une situation qui nous concerne plus directement; **Kentucky, the h. of bourbon** Kentucky, le pays du bourbon; **the h. of jazz** le berceau du jazz

4 Bot & Zool habitat m

5 (mental hospital) maison f de repos; (old people's home) maison f de retraite; (children's home) foyer m pour enfants

6 Sport (finishing line) arrivée f; (on board game) case f départ; (goal) but m; **they play better at h.** ils jouent mieux sur leur terrain; **Arsenal are playing at h. on Saturday** Arsenal joue à domicile samedi; **to be at h. to** recevoir; **the Rams meet the Braves at h.** les Rams jouent à domicile contre les Braves

7 Comput (beginning of document) début m

ADV 1 (to or at one's house) chez soi, à la maison; **to go h.** rentrer (chez soi ou à la maison); **what time did you get h.?** à quelle heure est-ce que tu es rentré?; **I'd better be getting h.** il est temps que je rentre chez moi; **it's on my way h.** c'est sur mon chemin; Am **to be h. alone** être tout seul à la maison; **to see sb h.** raccompagner qn jusque chez lui/elle; **to take sb h.** ramener qn chez lui/elle; Fam **it's nothing to write h. about** ça ne casse rien; Fam Br **h. and dry**, Am **h. free** sauvé

2 (from abroad) au pays natal, au pays; **to send sb h.** rapatrier qn; **the grandparents want to go or to return h.** les grands-parents veulent rentrer dans leur pays

3 (all the way) à fond; **to drive a nail h.** enfoncer un clou jusqu'au bout; **the remark really went h.** le commentaire a fait mouche; **to push h. one's advantage** profiter au maximum d'un avantage; **to bring sth h. to sb** faire comprendre ou voir qch à qn

ADJ 1 (concerning family, household ▸ life) de famille, familial; (▸ for family consumption) familial, à usage familial

2 (to, for, at one's house) à ou pour la maison

3 (national ▸ gen) national, du pays; (▸ market, policy, sales) intérieur; **to be on h. ground** (near home) être en pays de connaissance; Fig (familiar subject) être en terrain connu

4 Sport (team ▸ national) national; (▸ local) local; **our h. ground** notre terrain; **when they play at their h. ground** quand ils jouent sur leur terrain, quand ils reçoivent

VI (person, animal) revenir ou rentrer chez soi; (pigeon) revenir au colombier

VT (person, pet) placer; **the orphans will be homed with local families** les orphelins seront placés dans des familles du coin

▸▸ **home address** (on form) domicile m (permanent); (not business address) adresse f personnelle; **home baking** (action) pâtisserie f, (cakes, biscuits) gâteaux mpl; Banking **home banking** banque f à domicile; Obst **home birth** accouchement m à la maison; **home brew** (beer) bière f faite maison; **home cinema** home cinéma m; Br **home comforts** confort m du foyer; Comput **home computer** ordinateur m familial; Br Formerly **Home Computing Initiative** = système permettant aux employés d'une société de bénéficier de remises sur l'achat des ordinateurs; **home cooking** cuisine f familiale; **the Home Counties** = l'ensemble des comtés limitrophes de Londres, à la population aisée et conservatrice; **home country** pays m natal; **home delivery** livraison f à domicile; **home economics**, Fam **home ec** (UNCOUNT) économie f domestique; **home front** (during war) arrière m; **on the h. front** à l'arrière; **what's the news on the h. front?** (in the home country) quelles sont les nouvelles du pays?; **how are things on the h. front?** (at home) comment ça va à la maison?; **home game** match m à domicile; Br Hist **the Home Guard** = section de volontaires de l'armée britannique restée sur le territoire pour le défendre en cas d'invasion; Br **home help** aide f ménagère; **home improvements** travaux mpl de rénovation; Fin **home improvement loan** prêt m pour travaux de rénovation; Br **Home Information Pack** = dossier contenant des informations détaillées sur une maison ou un appartement fourni aux acheteurs potentiels; Br Mil **home leave** permission f; **home life** vie f de famille; Fin **home loan** prêt m immobilier, prêt m d'épargne-logement; **home movie** film m d'amateur; **home news** nouvelles fpl nationales; Pol **the Home Office** = le ministère britannique de l'Intérieur; **home owner** propriétaire mf; **home ownership** = fait d'être propriétaire de son logement; **h. ownership is increasing** le nombre des personnes propriétaires de leur logement augmente; Comput **home page** (initial page, start page in browser) page f d'accueil; (personal page) page f personnelle; Naut **home port** port m d'attache; Hist **Home Rule** (in Ireland) = gouvernement autonome de l'Irlande; **home rule** (devolution) décentralisation f; **home run** Sport (in baseball) coup m de circuit (coup de batte qui permet au batteur de marquer un point en faisant un tour complet en une seule fois); Fig (last leg of trip) dernière étape f du circuit; Pol **Home Secretary** = ministre de l'Intérieur en Grande-Bretagne; Com **home shopping** téléachat m; Sport & Fig Br **home straight**, Am **home stretch** dernière ligne f droite; **they're on or in the h. straight** ils sont dans la dernière ligne droite; Sport **home team** l'équipe f qui reçoit; **home time** = heure où l'on rentre à la maison; **home town** (of birth) ville f natale; (of upbringing) = la ville où on a grandi; **home truth** vérité f désagréable; **to tell sb a few h. truths** dire ses (quatre) vérités à qn; **home video** = film vidéo réalisé par un particulier, généralement sur sa vie de famille; **home visit** (by doctor) visite f à domicile; **home waters** (territorial) eaux fpl territoriales; (near home port) eaux fpl voisines du port d'attache

▸**home in on, home on to** VT INSEP **1** *(of missile)* se diriger sur *ou* vers; *(proceed towards ▸ goal)* se diriger vers; *Fig* mettre le cap sur **2** *(direct attention to ▸ problem, solution)* mettre l'accent sur; *(▸ difficulty, question)* viser, cerner; **I made one mistake and he homed in on it** je n'ai fait qu'une seule faute mais il s'est fait un plaisir de me la faire remarquer

home-baked ADJ *Culin* maison *(inv)*, fait maison

homebird ['həʊmbɜːd] N *Fam (person)* casanier (ère) *m,f*

homebody ['həʊmˌbɒdɪ] *(pl* **homebodies***)* N *Fam* pantouflard(e) *m,f*

homeboy ['həʊmbɔɪ] N *Fam Black Am slang* **1** *(man from one's home town)* compatriote□ *m* **2** *(friend)* pote *m*

home-brewed ADJ *(beer)* fait maison

homecoming ['həʊmˌkʌmɪŋ] N *(to family)* retour *m* au foyer *ou* à la maison; *(to country)* retour *m* au pays

• **Homecoming** N *Am Sch & Univ* = fête donnée en l'honneur de l'équipe de football d'une université ou d'une école et à laquelle sont invités les anciens élèves

▸▸ *Am Sch & Univ* ***Homecoming Queen*** = élève élue "personne la plus appréciée de ses pairs", qui reçoit une couronne ainsi que le titre de reine lors du "Homecoming"

homegirl ['həʊmgɜːl] N *Fam Black Am slang* **1** *(woman from one's home town)* compatriote□ *f* **2** *(friend)* copine *f*

homegrown [ˌhəʊm'grəʊn] ADJ *(not foreign)* du pays; *(from own garden)* du jardin; *Br* **h. footballers** des footballeurs *mpl* du pays

N *Fam Drugs slang* = cannabis cultivé chez soi ou dans son jardin

homeland ['həʊmlænd] N **1** *(native country)* patrie *f* **2** *(South African political territory)* homeland *m*

homeless ['həʊmlɪs] ADJ sans foyer; **a h. person** un(e) sans-abri, un(e) SDF

NPL **the h., h. people** les sans-abri *mpl*, les SDF

homelessness ['həʊmlɪsnɪs] N **the problem of h.** le problème des sans-abri *ou* des SDF; **h. is an increasing problem** les sans-abri représentent un problème de plus en plus grave

home-lover N casanier(ère) *m,f*; *(woman)* femme *f* d'intérieur

home-loving ADJ casanier

homely ['həʊmlɪ] *(compar* **homelier**, *superl* **homeliest***)* ADJ **1** *(unpretentious)* simple, modeste; **they offer good but h. fare** on y mange bien mais sans façon; **they're h. folk** ce sont des gens sans prétention **2** *(kind)* aimable, plein de bonté; *(atmosphere)* accueillant **3** *Am (plain, unattractive ▸ person, features, face)* peu attrayant; **what a h. woman!** elle n'est vraiment pas belle cette femme!

home-made ADJ maison *(inv)*, fait maison; **a h. bomb** une bombe de fabrication artisanale; **h. apple pie** *(on menu)* tarte *f* aux pommes maison

homemaker ['həʊmˌmeɪkər] N femme *f* au foyer

homeopath ['həʊmɪəʊˌpæθ] N *Med* homéopathe *mf*

homeopathic [ˌhəʊmɪəʊ'pæθɪk] ADJ *Med* homéopathique

▸▸ ***homeopathic doctor*** (médecin *m*) homéopathe *mf*; ***homeopathic medecine*** médecine *f* homéopathique, homéopathie *f*

homeopathy [ˌhəʊmɪ'ɒpəθɪ] N homéopathie *f*

Homer ['həʊmə(r)] PR N Homère

homer ['həʊmə(r)] N *Fam* **1** *Am Sport (in baseball)* coup *m* de circuit□ **2** *(homing pigeon)* pigeon *m* voyageur□

Homeric [həʊ'merɪk] ADJ homérique

homesick ['həʊmsɪk] ADJ nostalgique; **to be h.** avoir le mal du pays; **to be h. for sb** s'ennuyer de qn

homesickness ['həʊmˌsɪknɪs] N mal *m* du pays

homespun ['həʊmspʌn] ADJ **1** *(wool)* filé à la maison; *(cloth)* de homespun **2** *(simple)* simple, sans recherche

N *(cloth)* homespun *m*

homestead ['həʊmsted] N **1** *Am Hist* = terre dont la propriété est attribuée à un colon sous réserve qu'il y réside et l'exploite **2** *(buildings and land)* propriété *f*; *(farm)* ferme *f*

▸▸ ***the Homestead Act*** = décret de 1862 par lequel le Congrès américain donnait 160 acres de terre à tout nouvel arrivant qui s'engageait à s'installer dans l'ouest

homeward ['həʊmwəd] ADJ du retour; **the h. trip** le (voyage de) retour

ADV = **homewards**

homeward-bound ADJ *(person)* qui rentre chez soi; *(ship)* sur le chemin du retour; **to be homeward bound** être sur le chemin du retour

homewards ['həʊmwədz] ADV **1** *(to house)* vers la maison; **to head h.** se diriger vers la maison **2** *(to homeland)* **to be h. bound** prendre le chemin du retour; **the ship sailed h.** le navire faisait route vers son port d'attache

homework ['həʊmwɜːk] N *(UNCOUNT) Sch* devoirs *mpl* (à la maison); *(research)* travail *m* préparatoire; **the minister hadn't done his h.** le ministre n'avait pas préparé son dossier

> Attention: ne pas confondre avec **housework**, qui signifie **travaux ménagers**.

homeworker ['həʊmˌwɜːkə(r)] N travailleur (euse) *m,f* à domicile

homeworking ['həʊmˌwɜːkɪŋ] N travail *m* à domicile

homey ['həʊmɪ] *(pl* **homies***)* N *Fam Black Am slang (fellow Black American ▸ from one's home town)* compatriote□ *mf*; *(▸ friend)* copain (copine) *m, f*; *(▸ gang member)* = membre de la même bande

homicidal [ˌhɒmɪ'saɪdəl] ADJ *Law* homicide; **a h. maniac** un(e) maniaque à tendances homicides *ou* meurtrières

homicide ['hɒmɪsaɪd] N *Law* **1** *(act)* homicide *m* **2** *(person)* homicide *mf*

homily ['hɒmɪlɪ] *(pl* **homilies***)* N **1** *Rel* homélie *f* **2** *Pej* sermon *m*, homélie *f*; **to read sb a h.** sermonner qn

homing ['həʊmɪŋ] ADJ *Mil (pre-programmed)* autoguidé; *(heat-seeking)* à tête chercheuse

▸▸ ***homing device*** mécanisme *m* d'autoguidage; ***homing instinct*** *(of animals)* instinct *m* d'orientation; ***homing missile*** missile *m* à tête chercheuse; ***homing pigeon*** pigeon *m* voyageur

hominy ['hɒmɪnɪ] N *Am Culin (grits)* bouillie *f* de semoule de maïs

▸▸ ***hominy grits*** bouillie *f* de semoule de maïs

homo ['həʊməʊ] *very Fam* N pédé *m*, homo *mf*, = terme injurieux désignant un homosexuel

ADJ pédé, homo

homoeopath, homoeopathic *etc* = **homeopath, homeopathic** *etc*

homoerotic [ˌhəʊməʊɪ'rɒtɪk] ADJ homoérotique

homogeneity [ˌhɒməʊdʒə'niːɪtɪ] N homogénéité *f*

homogeneous [ˌhɒmə'dʒiːnɪəs] ADJ homogène

homogenize, -ise [hə'mɒdʒənaɪz] VT homogénéiser, homogénéifier

▸▸ ***homogenized milk*** lait *m* homogénéisé

homograft ['hɒməˌgrɑːft] N *Med* allogreffe *f*, homogreffe *f*

homonym ['hɒmənɪm] N *Ling* homonyme *m*

homophobe ['həʊməʊˌfəʊb] N homophobe *mf*

homophobia [ˌhəʊməʊ'fəʊbjə] N homophobie *f*

homophobic [ˌhəʊməʊ'fəʊbɪk] ADJ homophobe

homophone ['hɒməfəʊn] N *Ling* homophone *m*

homosexual [ˌhɒmə'sekʃʊəl] N homosexuel (elle) *m,f*

ADJ homosexuel

homosexuality [ˌhɒməˌsekʃʊ'ælətɪ] N homosexualité *f*; **male/female h.** homosexualité *f* masculine/féminine

Hon. *Br (written abbr* **honourable***)* honorable

hon [hʌn] N *Am Fam (term of address)* chéri(e)□ *m,f*

hon. *Br (written abbr* **honorary***)* honoraire

honcho ['hɒntʃəʊ] N *Am Fam (boss)* chef□ *m*

Honduras [hɒn'djʊərəs] N *Geog* Honduras *m*

hone [həʊn] VT **1** *(sharpen)* aiguiser, affûter, affiler; *(re-sharpen)* repasser **2** *(refine ▸ analysis, thought)* affiner; **finely honed arguments** arguments *mpl* d'une grande finesse

N pierre *f* à aiguiser

honest ['ɒnɪst] ADJ **1** *(not deceitful)* honnête, probe; *(trustworthy)* intègre; **an h. answer** une réponse honnête; **the h. truth** la pure vérité; **he's (as) h. as the day is long** il n'y a pas plus honnête que lui

2 *(decent, upright)* droit; *(virtuous)* honnête; *Br Fam* **he's an h. bloke** c'est un brave type; *Hum* **he's decided to make an h. woman of her** il a décidé de régulariser sa situation

3 *(not fraudulent)* honnête; **he charges an h. price** ses prix ne sont pas excessifs; **an h. day's work** une bonne journée de travail; **an h. day's pay for an h. day's work** toute peine mérite salaire; **to earn an h. living** gagner honnêtement sa vie

4 *(frank ▸ face)* franc (franche), sincère; **let's be h. with each other** allons, soyons francs; **to be h., don't think it will work** à vrai dire, je ne crois pas que ça marchera; **give me your h. opinion** dites-moi sincèrement ce que vous en pensez

ADV *Fam* **I didn't mean it, h.!** je plaisantais, je te le jure!; **h. to goodness** *or* **to God!** parole d'honneur

▸▸ *Br* ***honest broker*** médiateur(trice) *m,f*

honestly ['ɒnɪstlɪ] ADV honnêtement; **it's not my fault, h.!** ce n'est pas ma faute, je te le jure!; **h. the way some people behave!** franchement *ou* vraiment, il y en a qui exagèrent!; **h.?** c'est vrai?

honesty ['ɒnɪstɪ] N **1** *(truthfulness ▸ of person)* honnêteté *f*; *(▸ of text, words)* véracité *f*, exactitude *f*; *Prov* **h. is the best policy** = l'honnêteté paie toujours

2 *(incorruptibility)* intégrité *f*; **we have never doubted his h.** nous n'avons jamais douté de son intégrité

3 *(sincerity)* sincérité *f*, franchise *f*; **the h. of his intentions is self-evident** la sincérité de ses intentions est évidente

4 *Bot* monnaie-du-pape *f*, lunaire *f*

• **in all honesty** ADV en toute sincérité

▸▸ ***honesty box*** = boîte où les usagers d'un service sont invités à déposer une somme d'argent en l'absence d'un préposé à l'encaissement

honey ['hʌnɪ] *(pl* **honies***)* N **1** *Culin (food)* miel *m*; **clear/thick h.** miel *m* liquide/solide

2 *Fig* miel *m*, douceur *f*; **he was all h.** il a été tout sucre et tout miel

3 *Fam (term of endearment)* chéri(e) *m,f*; **OK, h.** OK, chéri!

4 *esp Am Fam (nice person)* amour *m*; *(good-looking person ▸ woman)* belle nana *f*; *(▸ man)* beau mec *m*; *(excellent thing)* bijou *m*; **you're such a h.!** tu es un chou!

honeybee ['hʌnɪbiː] N *Entom* abeille *f*

honeybun ['hʌnɪbʌn], **honeybunch** ['hʌnɪbʌntʃ] N *Fam (person)* chou *m* (à la crème)

honeycomb ['hʌnɪkəʊm] N **1** *(in wax)* rayon *m* *ou* gâteau *m* de miel; *(for eating)* gâteau *m* de miel

2 *(material)* structure *f* alvéolaire

3 *Tex & (pattern)* nid *m* d'abeille

4 *Metal* soufflure *f*

VT **1** *(surface)* cribler **2** *(interior)* miner; **the hills are honeycombed with secret tunnels** les collines sont truffées de passages secrets

honeydew ['hʌnɪdjuː] N *(produced by insects)* miellat *m*; *(produced by plants)* miellée *f*

▸▸ *Bot* ***honeydew melon*** melon *m* d'hiver *ou* d'Espagne

honeyed ['hʌnɪd] ADJ *Fig* mielleux; **he spoke in h. tones** il parlait d'un ton mielleux

honeymoon ['hʌnɪmuːn] N **1** *(period)* lune *f* de miel; *(trip)* voyage *m* de noces; **they're on (their) h.** ils sont en voyage de noces **2** *Fig* état *m* de grâce; **the new Prime Minister's h. is over** l'état de grâce du nouveau Premier ministre est terminé

COMP *(couple)* en voyage de noces

VI passer sa lune de miel; *(go on trip)* aller en voyage de noces; **they're honeymooning in Jamaica** ils passent leur lune de miel en Jamaïque, ils sont en voyage de noces en Jamaïque

▸▸ *Fig* ***honeymoon period*** lune *f* de miel, état *m* de grâce; ***honeymoon suite*** *(in hotel)* suite *f* nuptiale

honeymooner ['hʌnɪmu:nə(r)] **N** nouveau(elle) marié(e) *m,f*

honeypot ['hʌnɪpɒt] **N 1** pot *m* à miel; *Fam Fig* **to have one's fingers in the h.** se sucrer; *Fig* **the actress's fans clustered around her like bees around a h.** les admirateurs de l'actrice s'agglutinaient autour d'elle **2** *Am very Fam (vagina)* chatte *f*, foufoune *f*

honeysuckle ['hʌnɪˌsʌkəl] **N** *Bot* chèvrefeuille *m*

Hong Kong [ˌhɒŋ'kɒŋ] **N** *Geog* Hong Kong, Hongkong

honk[1] [hɒŋk] **N 1** *(of car horn)* coup *m* de klaxon®; **h., h.!** tut-tut! **2** *(of geese)* cri *m*; **h., h.!** couin-couin!

VT to h. one's horn donner un coup de klaxon®; **h. your horn at him!** klaxonne-le!

VI 1 *(car)* klaxonner **2** *(goose)* cacarder

honk[2] **VI** *Br Fam (smell bad)* schlinguer, chlinguer

honker ['hɒŋkə(r)] **N** *Am Fam* **1** *(nose)* blaire *m*, tarin *m* **2** *(breast)* nichon *m* **3** *(device)* bécane *f*

honkie, honky ['hɒŋkɪ] *(pl* **honkies***)* **N** *very Fam Black Am slang* = terme injurieux désignant un Blanc

honky-tonk ['hɒŋkɪˌtɒŋk] **N 1** *Mus* musique *f* de bastringue **2** *Am Fam (brothel)* maison *f* close□; *Old-fashioned (nightclub)* bastringue *m*; *(gambling den)* tripot *m*

ADJ 1 *Mus* de bastringue **2** *Am Fam (unsavoury)* louche; **a h. bar** un bar louche; **a h. woman** une putain

honor, honorable *etc Am* = **honour, honourable** *etc*

honorarium [ˌɒnə'reərɪəm] *(pl* **honorariums** *or* **honoraria** [-rɪə]*)* **N** honoraires *mpl*

honorary [*Br* 'ɒnərərɪ, *Am* ɒnə'reərɪ] **ADJ** *(titular position)* honoraire; *(in name only)* à titre honorifique, honoraire; *(unpaid position)* à titre gracieux

►► *Univ* ***honorary degree*** diplôme *m* honoris causa; ***honorary secretary*** secrétaire *mf* honoraire

honorific [ˌɒnə'rɪfɪk] **N** *(gen)* témoignage *m* d'honneur; *(title)* titre *m* d'honneur

ADJ honorifique

honour, *Am* **honor** ['ɒnə(r)] **N 1** *(personal integrity)* honneur *m*; **on my h.!** parole d'honneur!; **it's a point of h. (with me) to pay my debts on time** je me fais un point d'honneur de *ou* je mets un *ou* mon point d'honneur à rembourser mes dettes; **the affair cost him his h.** l'affaire l'a déshonoré; *Prov* **(there is) h. amongst thieves** les loups ne se mangent pas entre eux

2 *(public, social regard)* honneur *m*; **they came to do her h.** ils sont venus pour lui faire *ou* rendre honneur

3 *Formal (pleasure)* **it is a great h. to introduce Mr Reed** c'est un grand honneur pour moi de vous présenter Monsieur Reed; **may I have the h. of your company/the next dance?** pouvez-vous me faire l'honneur de votre compagnie/de la prochaine danse?; **to do the honours** *(serve drinks, food)* faire le service; *(make introductions)* faire les présentations (entre invités)

4 *(credit)* honneur *m*, crédit *m*; **she's an h. to her profession** elle fait honneur à sa profession; **having him on the board will do h. to the company** ça fera honneur à la société de l'avoir comme membre du conseil d'administration

5 *(mark of respect)* honneur *m*; **military honours** honneurs *mpl* militaires; **to receive sb with full honours** recevoir qn avec tous les honneurs

6 *Law (in title)* **Your H.** Votre Honneur

7 *(award)* distinction *f* honorifique

8 *Cards (face card)* honneur *m*; **it's your h.** *(starter's right)* à vous l'honneur

VT 1 *(person)* honorer, faire honneur à; **my honoured colleague** mon (ma) cher (chère) collègue; *Formal* **I'm most honoured to be here tonight** je suis très honoré d'être parmi vous ce soir; *Ironic* **we're honoured!** quel honneur!

2 *(fulfil the terms of)* honorer; *(observe* ► *boycott, rule)* respecter; **he always honours his obligations** il honore toujours ses obligations

3 *(pay* ► *debt)* honorer; *Fin (cheque, bill of exchange)* honorer, payer

4 *(dance partner)* saluer

• **honours NPL** *Br Univ (degree)* = diplôme universitaire obtenu avec mention; **she got first-/second-class honours** elle a eu sa licence avec mention très bien/mention bien

• **in honour of PREP** en honneur de

►► *Br Univ* ***honours degree*** = diplôme universitaire obtenu avec mention; ***honour killing*** crime *m* d'honneur; *Br* ***honours list*** = liste de distinctions honorifiques conférées par le monarque deux fois par an; *Am* ***honor roll*** tableau *m* d'honneur

honourable, *Am* **honorable** ['ɒnərəbəl] **ADJ 1** *(worthy of honour)* honorable; *Old-fashioned or Hum* **are his intentions h.?** ses intentions sont-elles honorables?; **he got an h. discharge** il a été rendu à la vie civile **2** *(title)* **the (Right) H.** le (très) honorable; *Br Parl* **the H. Member for Suffolk South** le député de la circonscription Suffolk South; *Br Parl* **my H. Friend** *(to member of same party)* mon honorable collègue; *Br Parl* **the H. Lady will be aware that...** *(to member of another party)* mon honorable collègue n'est pas sans savoir que...; *Br Parl* **the H. Gentleman should know that...** *(to member of another party)* mon honorable collègue devrait savoir que...

honourably, *Am* **honorably** ['ɒnərəblɪ] **ADV** honorablement

Hons. *Br Univ (written abbr* **honours degree***)* = diplôme universitaire obtenu avec mention

hooch [hu:tʃ] **N** *Am very Fam* **1** *(drink)* gnôle *f* **2** *(marijuana)* herbe *f*

hood [hʊd] **N 1** *(of garment)* capuchon *m*; *(with collar)* capuche *f*; *(with eye-holes)* cagoule *f*; *Univ* épitoge *f*; **a rain h.** une capuche

2 *Br Aut (soft top)* capote *f*; *Am Aut (bonnet)* capot *m*

3 *(protective cover)* couvercle *m*; *(of pram)* capote *f*

4 *(of hairdryer)* casque *m*

5 *(for fumes, smoke)* hotte *f*

6 *(of animals, plants)* capuchon *m*; *(for falcons)* chaperon *m*, capuchon *m*

7 *Am Fam (delinquent)* voyou *m*; *(gangster)* gangster□ *m*, truand *m*

8 *Am Fam (neighbourhood)* **the h.** le quartier□

VT mettre le capuchon sur; *(falcon)* chaperonner, enchaperonner

> **-HOOD** SUFFIXE
>
> Le suffixe **-hood** sert à former des noms. Il a deux sens principaux:
>
> • Il désigne un ÉTAT:
> **childhood** enfance; **manhood** âge d'homme; **motherhood** maternité; **nationhood** statut de nation; **likelihood** probabilité
>
> • Il peut aussi désigner un GROUPE DE GENS, comme dans:
> **sisterhood** communauté de femmes; **manhood** hommes; **the priesthood** le clergé
>
> Dans les deux sens, **-hood** apparaît souvent dans des mots fantaisistes et humoristiques créés pour l'occasion: **the finest specimen in all doghood** le plus beau spécimen de la gent canine

hooded ['hʊdɪd] **ADJ** *(clothing)* à capuchon; *(person)* encapuchonné; *(executioner, thief)* au visage masqué; *Fig* **h. eyes** yeux *mpl* aux paupières tombantes

►► *Orn* ***hooded crow*** corneille *f* mantelée; *Zool* ***hooded seal*** phoque *m* à capuchon

hoodie ['hʊdɪ] **N** *Fam* **1** *(sweatshirt)* sweat-shirt *m* à capuche **2** *(person)* = jeune portant un sweat-shirt à capuche

> **HOODIE**
>
> Au cours de ces dernières années le **hoodie** est devenu l'archétype de l'adolescent associal et à tendance délinquante en Grande-Bretagne.

hoodlum ['hu:dləm] **N** *Fam (delinquent)* voyou *m*; *(gangster)* gangster□ *m*, truand *m*

hoodoo ['hu:du:] **N** *Am Fam (jinx)* porte-malheur□ *m inv*; *(bad luck)* poisse *f*, guigne *f*

VT porter la poisse *ou* la guigne à

hoodwink ['hʊdwɪŋk] **VT** tromper, avoir; **I was hoodwinked into signing** on m'a raconté des histoires pour me faire signer

hooey ['hu:ɪ] **N** *Fam* foutaises *fpl*; **that's h.** c'est des foutaises; **to talk a load of h.** raconter des foutaises

hoof [hu:f] *(pl* **hoofs** *or* **hooves** [hu:vz]*)* **N** *Zool* sabot *m (d'animal)*; **on the h.** *(alive)* sur pied; *Fig (on ad hoc basis)* au coup par coup; **I had lunch on the h.** à midi j'ai mangé sur le pouce

VT *Fam (idiom)* **to h. it** *(go on foot)* aller à pinces; *(dance)* guincher

►► *Am Vet* ***hoof and mouth disease*** fièvre *f* aphteuse

hoofed [hu:ft] **ADJ** à sabots; *Zool* ongulé

hoofer ['hu:fə(r)] **N** *Fam* danseur(euse)□ *m,f (de métier)*

hoo-ha ['hu:ˌhɑ:] **N** *Fam (noise)* boucan *m*, potin *m*; *(chaos)* pagaille *f*, tohu-bohu *m inv*; *(fuss)* bruit *m*, histoires *fpl*; **there was a lot of h. about it** ça en a fait des histoires

hook [hʊk] **N 1** *(gen)* crochet *m*; *(for coats)* patère *f*; *(on clothes)* agrafe *f*; *(for meat)* croc *m*; *Naut* gaffe *f*; **hooks and eyes** *(on clothes)* agrafes *fpl* (et œillets *mpl*); **your phone was off the h.** tu avais décroché ton téléphone; *(accidentally)* tu avais mal raccroché ton téléphone; **to put the phone back on the h.** reposer le combiné (sur son support); *Fam* **to get one's hooks into sb** mettre le grappin sur qn

2 *(on fishing line)* hameçon *m*; *Fam* **he swallowed the story, h., line and sinker** il a tout avalé

3 *(in advertising)* accroche *f*; *Mus (in song)* thème *m*

4 *Sport (in cricket)* coup *m* tourné; *Golf* hook *m*; *Boxing* **a right/left h.** un crochet (du) droit/gauche

5 *Fam (idioms)* **to get sb off the h.** tirer qn d'affaire; **to let sb off the h.** *(from obligation)* libérer qn de sa responsabilité□; **I'll let you off the h. this time** je laisse passer cette fois-ci; **we must do it by h. or by crook** nous devons le faire, coûte que coûte

VT 1 *(snag)* accrocher; *(seize* ► *person, prey)* attraper; *(*► *floating object)* gaffer, crocher; **he hooked his arm through hers** il lui a pris le bras

2 *(loop)* **she hooked one leg round the leg of the chair** elle passa *ou* enroula une jambe autour du pied de la chaise

3 *Fishing (fish)* prendre; *Tech* hameçonner

4 *Sport (in rugby)* talonner *(le ballon)*; *Golf* hooker; *Boxing* donner un crochet à

5 *Fam Hum (marry)* passer la corde au cou à; **she'll never manage to h. him** elle n'arrivera jamais à lui mettre le grappin dessus

VI 1 *(fasten)* s'agrafer **2** *Golf* hooker **3** *Am Fam (work as prostitute)* faire le trottoir

►► ***Hook of Holland*** Hoek *m* van Holland

▸**hook on VT SEP** accrocher

VI s'accrocher; **this strap hooks on at the back** cette bride s'accroche *ou* s'agrafe par derrière

▸**hook up VT SEP 1** *(trailer)* accrocher; *(dress)* agrafer; *(boat)* amarrer; **they hooked up an extra coach to the train** on a accroché un wagon supplémentaire au train

2 *Fam (install)* installer□; *(plug in)* brancher□

3 *Rad & TV* faire un duplex entre

4 *(horse, oxen etc)* atteler

VI 1 *(dress)* s'agrafer **2** *Am Fam (meet)* se donner rendez-vous□; *(work together)* faire équipe□; **to h. up with sb** *(get into relationship)* sortir avec qn **3** *Rad & TV* **to h. up with** faire une émission en duplex avec

hookah ['hʊkə] **N** narguilé *m*, houka *m*

hooked [hʊkt] **ADJ 1** *(hook-shaped)* recourbé; *(nose)* crochu **2** *(having hooks)* muni de crochets; *(fishing line)* muni d'un hameçon **3** *Fam Fig (addicted)* **he got h. on hard drugs** il est devenu accro aux drogues dures; **she's really h. on TV soaps** c'est une mordue *ou* une vraie addict des feuilletons télévisés

hooker ['hʊkə(r)] **N 1** *Sport (in rugby)* talonneur *m* **2** *very Fam (prostitute)* pute *f*

hookey ['hʊkɪ] **N** *Am, Austr & NZ Fam* **to play h.** sécher les cours, faire l'école buissonnière

hook-nosed **ADJ** au nez recourbé *ou* crochu

hook-up **N 1** *TV* relais *m* temporaire **2** *(for caravan, RV)* borne *f* de raccordement

hookworm ['hʊkwɜːm] **N** *Entom* ankylostome *m*

hooky = **hookey**

hooligan ['huːlɪgən] **N** hooligan *m*, vandale *m*

hooliganism ['huːlɪgənɪzəm] **N** vandalisme *m*

hoop [huːp] **N** *(ring)* cerceau *m*; *(on barrel)* cercle *m*; *(in croquet)* arceau *m*; *Fig* **I had to jump through hoops to get the job** j'ai dû faire des pieds et des mains pour obtenir ce travail; **to put sb through the hoops** *(interrogate)* mettre qn sur la sellette; *(test)* mettre qn à l'épreuve **2** *Am Fam (basketball)* **h., hoops** le basket; **to shoot hoops** jouer au basket

hoopla ['huːplɑː] **N 1** *Br (funfair game)* jeu *m* d'anneaux *(dans les foires)* **2** *Am Fam* = **hoo-ha**

hoopoe ['huːpuː] **N** *Orn* huppe *f*

hooray [hʊ'reɪ] **EXCLAM** hourra!, hurrah!

►► *Br Fam Pej* ***Hooray Henry*** = fils à papa exubérant et bruyant

hoosegow ['huːsgaʊ] **N** *Am Fam (prison)* taule *f*, bloc *m*; **in the h.** en taule, en bloc

hoot [huːt] **N 1** *(shout* ► *of delight, pain)* cri *m*; *(jeer)* huée *f*; **hoots of laughter** éclats *mpl* de rire

2 *(of owl)* hululement *m*

3 *Aut* coup *m* de klaxon®; *(of train)* sifflement *m*; *(of siren)* mugissement *m*

4 *Fam (least bit)* **I don't give** *or* **care a h.** *or* **two hoots** je m'en fiche, mais alors complètement, je m'en contrefiche; **it doesn't matter two hoots** ça n'a strictement aucune importance[□]

5 *Fam (amusing event)* **it was a h.!** *(hilarious)* c'était tordant!; **he's a real h.!** c'est un sacré rigolo!, il est tordant!

VT *(actor, speaker)* huer; *(play)* siffler

VI 1 *Fam (person)* **to h. with laughter** s'esclaffer **2** *(owl)* hululer **3** *Aut* klaxonner; *(train)* siffler; *(siren)* mugir

hootenanny ['huːtənænɪ] *(pl* **hootenannies***)* **N** *Am (party)* = fête populaire animée par des chanteurs de chansons folkloriques

hooter ['huːtə(r)] **N 1** *esp Br (car horn)* klaxon® *m*; *(in factory, ship)* sirène *f* **2** *Fam (nose)* pif *m* **3** *esp Am very Fam (breast)* nichon *m*

hooting ['huːtɪŋ] **N 1** *(of owl)* hululement *m* **2** *(of person* ► *jeering)* huées *fpl*; *(*► *laughter)* hurlements *mpl* de rire **3** *(of cars)* coups *mpl* de klaxon

hoover® ['huːvə(r)] *Br* **N** aspirateur *m*

VT *(carpet etc)* passer l'aspirateur sur; *(room)* passer l'aspirateur dans

VI passer l'aspirateur

►**hoover up** **VT SEP 1** *(with vacuum cleaner)* enlever avec l'aspirateur; **I'll just h. it up** je vais (y) donner un coup d'aspirateur **2** *Fam Hum (of person)* engloutir; **he hoovered up all the peanuts** il a englouti toutes les cacahuètes

hoovering ['huːvərɪŋ] **N** *Br* **to do the h.** passer l'aspirateur

hooves [huːvz] *pl of* **hoof**

hop[1] [hɒp] *(pt & pp* **hopped**, *cont* **hopping***)* **N 1** *(jump)* saut *m* à cloche-pied; *(in rapid series)* sautillement *m*; *Br* **to catch sb on the h.** prendre qn au dépourvu; *Br* **to keep sb on the h.** ne pas laisser chômer qn **2** *Aviat* étape *f*; **it's just a short h. from New York to Boston by plane** le trajet en avion de New York à Boston est très court **3** *Fam Old-fashioned (dance)* sauterie[□] *f*; *(for young people)* boum *f*

VT *Fam* **1** *Am (bus, subway etc* ► *legally)* sauter dans[□]; *(*► *illegally)* prendre en resquillant **2** *(idiom)* **to h. it** décamper, décaniller; **h. it!** allez, dégage!

VI 1 *(jump)* sauter; *(in rapid series)* sautiller; *Fam* **to h. on/off the bus** sauter dans le/du bus; **birds hopped about in the garden** les oiseaux sautillaient dans le jardin; *Fam* **to h. into bed with sb** coucher avec qn tout de suite; *Fam* **h. in!** *(into car etc)* montez! **2** *(jump on one leg)* sauter à cloche-pied **3** *Fam (travel)* **we hopped across to Paris for the weekend** nous avons fait un saut à Paris pour le week-end[□]

hop[2] **N** *Bot & Agr (plant)* houblon *m*; **to pick hops** cueillir le houblon

►► *Agr* ***hop picker*** cueilleur(euse) *m,f* de houblon; *Agr* ***hop picking*** cueillette *f* du houblon

►**hop off** **VI** *Fam (leave)* décamper

hope [həʊp] **N 1** *(desire, expectation)* espoir *m*; *Formal* espérance *f*; **in the h. of a reward** dans l'espoir d'une récompense; **I have every h. (that) he'll come** j'ai bon espoir qu'il viendra; **don't get your hopes up** ne comptez pas trop là-dessus; **don't raise his hopes too much** ne lui donne pas trop d'espoir; **to give up h. (of)** perdre l'espoir (de); **the situation is past** *or* **beyond h.** la situation est sans espoir; *Euph* **she is past** *or* **beyond all h.** *(is dying)* il n'y a plus aucun espoir; **to raise sb's hopes** faire naître l'espoir de qn *ou* chez qn; **they had high hopes for their daughter** ils avaient de grandes espérances pour leur fille; *Fam Ironic* **some h.!** tu parles!; **h. springs eternal (in the human breast)** l'espoir fait vivre **2** *(chance)* espoir *m*, chance *f*; **one's last/only h.** le dernier/l'unique espoir de quelqu'un **3** *Rel* espérance *f*

VI espérer; **to h. for sth** espérer qch; **to h. against h.** espérer contre toute attente; **we just have to h. for the best** espérons que tout finira *ou* se passera bien; **don't h. for too much** n'en attends pas trop; **you shouldn't h. for a high return** ne vous attendez pas à un rendement élevé

VT espérer; **he hopes** *or* **is hoping to go** il espère y aller; **he's hoping (that) she'll be there** il espère qu'elle sera là; **hoping** *or* **I h. to hear from you soon** *(in letter)* j'espère avoir de tes nouvelles bientôt; **I really h. so!** j'espère bien!; **I h. not** j'espère que non; **I should h. so!** j'espère bien!; **I should h. not!** j'espère bien que non!

►► *Am* ***hope chest*** coffre *m* à trousseau; *Fig* trousseau *m*

hopeful ['həʊpfʊl] **ADJ 1** *(full of hope)* plein d'espoir; **he's still h. that she'll come** il garde bon espoir qu'elle viendra; **he says he'll come, but I'm not that h.** il dit qu'il viendra mais je n'y compte pas trop; **I am h. about the outcome** je suis optimiste quant au résultat **2** *(inspiring hope)* encourageant, prometteur; **the news is h.** les nouvelles sont encourageantes; **the situation looks h.** la situation est encourageante

N aspirant(e) *m,f*, candidat(e) *m,f*; **a young h.** un jeune loup; **Davis Cup hopefuls** les prétendants à la coupe Davis

hopefully ['həʊpfəlɪ] **ADV 1** *(smile, speak, work)* avec espoir, avec optimisme **2** *(with luck)* on espère que…; **h., they'll leave tomorrow** on espère qu'ils partiront demain; **will you get it finished today? – h.!** est-ce que tu l'auras terminé pour aujourd'hui? – je l'espère *ou* oui, avec un peu de chance!

hopefulness ['həʊpfʊlnɪs] **N** *(of person)* confiance *f*, optimisme *m*

hopeless ['həʊplɪs] **ADJ 1** *(desperate* ► *person)* désespéré; *(*► *situation)* désespéré, sans espoir; **it's h.!** c'est sans espoir!

2 *(incurable* ► *addiction, ill person)* incurable; **a h. case** un cas désespéré; **to be in a h. condition** être dans un état désespéré

3 *(inveterate* ► *drunk, liar)* invétéré, incorrigible

4 *Fam (incompetent* ► *person)* nul; *(*► *at job)* incompétent[□]; **he's a h. dancer** il est nul comme danseur; **a h. case** un bon à rien; **I'm h. at this** je suis nul pour ce genre de chose; **he's h. at swimming** il est nul en natation

5 *(pointless)* inutile; **it's h. trying to explain to him** il est inutile d'essayer de lui expliquer

hopelessly ['həʊplɪslɪ] **ADV 1** *(speak, sigh, sob)* avec désespoir **2** *(irremediably)* **they are h. in debt/in love** ils sont complètement endettés/éperdument amoureux; **by this time we were h. lost** nous étions maintenant complètement perdus; **h. naive** d'une naïveté désespérante

hopelessness ['həʊplɪsnɪs] **N 1** *(despair)* désespoir *m* **2** *(of position, situation)* caractère *m* désespéré **3** *(pointlessness)* inutilité *f*

hophead ['hɒphed] **N** *Am Fam Drugs slang* défoncé(e) *m,f*

hopper ['hɒpə(r)] **N 1** *(jumper)* sauteur(euse) *m, f*; *Austr Fam* kangourou[□] *m* **2** *(feeder bin)* trémie *f*; *Agr (for sowing)* semoir *m*

►► *Naut* ***hopper barge*** marie-salope *f*; *Rail* ***hop[per] car*** wagon-trémie *m*

hopping ['hɒpɪŋ] **ADV** *Fam (as intensifier)* **he wa[s] h. mad** il était fou furieux

hopscotch ['hɒpskɒtʃ] **N** marelle *f*; **to play (at) h[opscotch]** jouer à la marelle

horde [hɔːd] **N** horde *f*; **hordes of tourists** des ho[rdes] des de touristes

> Attention: ne pas confondre avec **hoard**.

horizon [hə'raɪzən] **N** horizon *m*; *Fig* **a new sta[r] on the political h.** une nouvelle vedette sur l'ho[rizon] rizon politique

• **horizons** **NPL** *(perspectives)* horizons *mpl*; **t[o] broaden one's horizons** élargir ses horizons; **man of limited horizons** un homme aux vue[s] étroites *ou* à l'esprit étroit

horizontal [ˌhɒrɪ'zɒntəl] **ADJ** *(gen)* horizontal; **turn the lever to the h. position** mettez le levier [à] l'horizontale; *Fam* **I was h. for a few days with th[e] flu** je suis resté au lit pendant quelques jours [à] cause de la grippe[□]

N horizontale *f*

►► *Sport* ***horizontal bar*** barre *f* fixe; *Econ* ***horizon[tal] tal concentration*** concentration *f* horizontale; *Com* ***horizontal merger*** fusion *f* horizontale

horizontally [ˌhɒrɪ'zɒntəlɪ] **ADV** horizontale[ment]; **extend your arms h.** tendez vos bras à l'ho[rizontale]

hormonal [hɔː'məʊnəl] **ADJ** *Biol* hormonal

hormone ['hɔːməʊn] **N** *Biol* hormone *f*

►► *Med* ***hormone deficiency*** insuffisance *f* hor[monale] monale; *Med* ***hormone replacement therapy*** trai[tement] tement *m* hormonal substitutif

hormonotherapy [hɔːˌməʊnə'θerəpɪ] **N** *Me[d]* hormonothérapie *f*

horn [hɔːn] **N 1** *(gen)* corne *f*; *(pommel)* pom[meau] meau *m*; **horns** *(of deer)* bois *mpl*; **h. of plenty** corne *f* d'abondance; **the H. of Africa** la Corne de l'Afrique, la péninsule des Somalis; *Br Fig* **to draw** *or* **to pull in one's horns** *(back off)* se calmer; *(spend less)* restreindre son train de vie; *Br* **to be on the horns of a dilemma** être pris dans un di[lemme] lemme

2 *Mus* cor *m*; *Fam (trumpet)* trompette *f*; *Am Fig* **to blow one's own h.** se vanter

3 *Aut* klaxon® *m*; *(manual)* corne *f*; **to sound o[r] to blow the h.** klaxonner, corner

4 *Naut* sirène *f*; **to sound** *or* **to blow the h.** donne[r] un coup de sirène

5 *Br very Fam (erection)* érection[□] *f*; **to have the h.** avoir la trique *ou* le gourdin; **to give sb the h.** *(arouse)* exciter qn[□]

6 *Am Fam (telephone)* bigophone *m*; **to get on the h. to sb** passer un coup de fil *ou* de bigophone à qn

7 *Hunt* corne *f*, cor *m*, trompe *f*

COMP *(handle, comb)* en corne

►**horn in** **VI** *esp Am Fam (on conversation)* mettre son grain de sel; *(on a deal)* s'immiscer[□]

hornbeam ['hɔːnbiːm] **N** *Bot* charme *m*

hornbill ['hɔːnbɪl] **N** *Orn* calao *m*

horned ['hɔːnd] **ADJ** cornu; **a two-h. rhinoceros** un rhinocéros (d'Afrique) à deux cornes

►► *Orn* ***horned owl*** duc *m*; *Zool* ***horned toad*** crapaud *m* cornu; *Zool* ***horned viper*** vipère *f* cornue (d'Égypte), vipère *f* à cornes

hornet ['hɔːnɪt] **N** *Entom* frelon *m*; *Fig* **to stir up a h.'s nest** mettre le feu aux poudres

hornpipe ['hɔːnpaɪp] **N** *Mus* matelote *f (danse)*

horn-rimmed **ADJ** à monture d'écaille

horny ['hɔːnɪ] **ADJ 1** *(substance)* corné **2** *(calloused* ► *nail, skin)* calleux **3** *very Fam (sexually excited)* excité (sexuellement)[□]; *Br (sexually attractive)* sexy *(inv)*

horology [hɔː'rɒlədʒɪ] **N** horlogerie *f*

horoscope ['hɒrəskəʊp] **N** horoscope *m*

horrendous [hə'rendəs] **ADJ** affreux, horrible

horrendously [hə'rendəslɪ] **ADV** horriblement

horrible ['hɒrəbəl] **ADJ 1** *(horrific)* horrible, affreux; *(morally repulsive)* abominable; **a h. tragedy/scream** une tragédie/un cri horrible **2** *(dismaying)* horrible, effroyable; **in a h. mess** dans une effroyable *ou* horrible confusion; **I've a h. feeling that things are going to go wrong** j'ai 'horrible pressentiment que les choses vont nal se passer **3** *(very unpleasant)* horrible, atroce; *(food)* infect; **to be h. to sb** être méchant *ou* horrible avec qn; **to say h. things about sb** dire des horreurs *ou* des choses terribles sur qn

orribly ['hɒrəblɪ] ADV **1** *(nastily)* horriblement, atrocement, affreusement; **he treated her h.** il se conduisit d'une manière atroce *ou* atrocement mal envers elle; **the story of a woman who was h. murdered** l'histoire d'une femme qui fut assassinée de manière atroce **2** *(as intensifier)* affreusement, terriblement; **it's h. extravagant but...** c'est de la folie douce mais...; **things went h. wrong** les choses ont très mal tourné

orrid ['hɒrɪd] ADJ **1** *(dreadful)* horrible, affreux; *(weather)* abominable; **how h.!** quelle horreur!; **he's such a h. little man!** c'est un affreux petit bonhomme **2** *(unkind)* méchant; **he was h. to me** il a été méchant avec moi **3** *(ugly)* vilain, laid

orridly ['hɒrɪdlɪ] ADV *(as intensifier)* atrocement, affreusement

orrific [hɒ'rɪfɪk] ADJ **1** *(horrendous)* horrible, terrifiant **2** *Fig (very unpleasant)* horrible

orrify ['hɒrɪfaɪ] *(pt & pp* **horrified***)* VT **1** *(terrify)* horrifier **2** *(weaker use)* horrifier, scandaliser

orrifying ['hɒrɪfaɪɪŋ] ADJ **1** *(terrifying)* horrifiant, terrifiant **2** *(weaker use)* scandaleux

orror ['hɒrə(r)] N **1** *(feeling)* horreur *f*; **he has a h. of snakes** il a horreur des serpents; **to my h., I discovered...** c'est avec horreur que j'ai découvert... **2** *(unpleasantness)* horreur *f*; **I began to see the h. of it all** j'ai commencé à en mesurer toute l'horreur **3** *Fam (person, thing)* horreur *f*; **that child is a little h.** cet enfant est un petit monstre; **h. of horrors!** comble de l'horreur!

▸▸ ***horror film, horror movie*** film *m* d'épouvante; ***horror story*** histoire *f* d'épouvante; *Fam Fig* **they told some real h. stories about their holiday** ils ont raconté des trucs épouvantables qui leur sont arrivés pendant leurs vacances

horror-stricken, horror-struck ADJ glacé *ou* frappé d'horreur

horse [hɔːs, *pl* hɔːsɪz] N **1** *Zool (animal)* cheval *m*; **to ride a h.** monter à cheval; **to play the horses** jouer aux courses; *also Fig* **to back the wrong h.** miser sur le mauvais cheval; *Fam* **I could eat a h.!** j'ai une faim de loup!; **to eat like a h.** manger comme quatre; **(straight) from the h.'s mouth** de source sûre; *Br* **that's a h. of a different colour** c'est une autre paire de manches; **to get on one's high h.** monter sur ses grands chevaux; **wild horses couldn't drag it out of me** je serai muet comme une tombe

2 *(in breeding)* cheval *m* mâle, cheval *m* entier; **stud h.** étalon *m*

3 *(trestle)* tréteau *m*

4 *Mil & Hist (cavalry)* cavalerie *f*, troupes *fpl* montées; **regiment of h.** régiment *m* de cavalerie

5 *Sport (in gymnastics)* cheval *m* d'arçons

6 *Fam Drugs slang (heroin)* neige *f*, blanche *f*

NPL *Mil* cavalière *f*

▸▸ *Mil & Hist* ***horse artillery*** artillerie *f* montée; ***horse brass*** médaillon *m* de bronze *(fixé à une martingale)*; ***horse breeder*** éleveur(euse) *m,f* de chevaux; ***horse butcher*** boucher(ère) *m,f* hippophagique; *Bot* ***horse chestnut*** *(tree)* marronnier *m* (d'Inde); *(nut)* marron *m* (d'Inde); *Fam* ***horse doctor*** vétérinaire *mf*; *Br* ***the Horse Guards*** *(regiment)* = régiment de cavalerie attaché à la reine et remplissant certaines fonctions officielles; *(building)* = le bâtiment de Whitehall où se fait chaque jour la relève de la garde; ***Horse Guards Parade*** = grande place à Londres où ont lieu les défilés des "Horse Guards"; *Naut* ***horse latitudes*** pot *m* au noir; *Ich* ***horse mackerel*** chinchard *m*; ***horse manure*** crottin *m* de cheval; *(as fertilizer)* fumier *m* de cheval; *Cin Fam* ***horse opera*** western *m*; ***horse race*** course *f* de chevaux; ***horse racing*** *(UNCOUNT)* courses *fpl* (de chevaux); *Br* ***horse riding*** équitation *f*; *Fam* ***horse sense*** (gros) bon sens *m*; ***horse show*** concours *m* hippique; ***horse trader*** maquignon *m*; *Br Fam (hard bargainer)* négociateur(trice) *m,f* redoutable; ***horse trials*** concours *m* hippique

▸**horse about, horse around** VI *Fam (noisily)* chahuter

horseback ['hɔːsbæk] N **on h.** à cheval

▸▸ *Am* ***horseback riding*** équitation *f*

horsebox ['hɔːsbɒks] N *Br (trailer)* van *m*; *(stall)* box *m*

horsebreaker ['hɔːs,breɪkə(r)] N dresseur(euse) *m,f* de chevaux

horse-drawn ADJ tiré par des chevaux, à chevaux

horseflesh ['hɔːsfleʃ] N *(UNCOUNT)* **1** *(horses)* chevaux *mpl*; **he's a good judge of h.** il s'y connaît bien en chevaux **2** *(meat)* viande *f* de cheval

horsefly ['hɔːsflaɪ] *(pl* **horseflies***)* N *Entom* taon *m*

horsehair ['hɔːsheə(r)] N crin *m* (de cheval)

COMP *(mattress, sofa)* de crin (de cheval)

horseman ['hɔːsmən] *(pl* **horsemen** [-mən]*)* N **1** *Horseriding (rider)* cavalier *m*; **to be a good h.** bien monter à cheval, être bon cavalier; *Bible* **the four horsemen of the Apocalypse** les quatre cavaliers de l'Apocalypse **2** *(breeder)* éleveur (euse) *m,f* de chevaux

horsemanship ['hɔːsmənʃɪp] N **1** *(activity)* équitation *f* **2** *(skill)* talent *m* de cavalier

horseplay ['hɔːspleɪ] N *(UNCOUNT)* chahut *m* brutal, jeux *mpl* tapageurs *ou* brutaux; **they were having a bit of h. in the pool** ils faisaient les imbéciles dans la piscine; **it's just harmless h.** c'est une bagarre pour rire

horsepower ['hɔːs,paʊə(r)] N *Aut (unit)* cheval-vapeur *m*, cheval *m*; **a 10-h. motor** un moteur de 10 chevaux

horseradish ['hɔːs,rædɪʃ] N *Bot* raifort *m*

▸▸ *Culin* ***horseradish sauce*** sauce *f* au raifort

horseshoe ['hɔːsʃuː] N fer *m* à cheval

• **horseshoes** N *(game)* jeu *m* de fer à cheval

▸▸ *Zool* ***horseshoe crab*** crabe *m* des Moluques, limule *f*

horsewhip ['hɔːswɪp] *(pt & pp* **horsewhipped,** *cont* **horsewhipping***)* N cravache *f*

VT cravacher; **I'll have him horsewhipped** je le ferai fouetter

horsewoman ['hɔːs,wʊmən] *(pl* **horsewomen** [-'wɪmɪn]*)* N cavalière *f*; **she's a good h.** elle est bonne cavalière, elle monte bien

horsey, horsy ['hɔːsɪ] ADJ *Fam* **1** *(horse-like)* chevalin **2** *(fond of horses)* féru de cheval; **he mixes with a very h. crowd** il fréquente des (gens) passionnés de chevaux; **the h. set** le monde *ou* le milieu du cheval

horticultural [,hɔːtɪ'kʌltʃərəl] ADJ *Hort* horticole

▸▸ ***horticultural show*** exposition *f* horticole *ou* d'horticulture

horticulture ['hɔːtɪkʌltʃə(r)] N *Hort* horticulture *f*

horticulturist [,hɔːtɪ'kʌltʃərɪst] N *Hort* horticulteur(trice) *m,f*

hose [həʊz] N **1** *(tube)* tuyau *m*; *Aut* Durit® *f*; **turn off the h.** arrêtez le jet; **garden h.** tuyau *m* d'arrosage **2** *(UNCOUNT) (stockings)* bas *mpl*; *(tights)* collant *m*, collants *mpl*; *Hist* chausses *fpl*; *(knee breeches)* haut-de-chausse *m*, haut-de-chausses *m*, culotte *f* courte

VT *(lawn)* arroser au jet; *(fire)* arroser à la lance

▸**hose down** VT SEP **1** *(wash)* laver au jet **2** *(with fire hose)* arroser à la lance

▸**hose out** VT SEP *(wash out)* laver au jet

hosepipe ['həʊzpaɪp] N tuyau *m*; **a h. ban** une interdiction d'arroser

hosier ['həʊzɪə(r)] N bonnetier(ère) *m,f*

hosiery ['həʊzɪərɪ] N *(UNCOUNT)* **1** *(trade)* bonneterie *f* **2** *(stockings)* bas *mpl*; *(socks)* chaussettes *fpl*

hospice ['hɒspɪs] N **1** *(for travellers)* hospice *m* **2** *(for the terminally ill)* = hôpital pour malades en phase terminale

hospitable [hɒ'spɪtəbəl] ADJ hospitalier; *Fig* **a h. climate** un climat hospitalier

hospitably [hɒ'spɪtəblɪ] ADV avec hospitalité

hospital ['hɒspɪtəl] N hôpital *m*; **in h.** à l'hôpital; *Br* **to h.**, *Am* **to the h.** à l'hôpital; **to go into h.** aller à l'hôpital; **a children's h.** un hôpital pour enfants; **to do h. corners** *(on bed)* faire un lit au carré

COMP *(centre, service, staff, treatment)* hospitalier; *(bed, ward)* d'hôpital

▸▸ ***a hospital case*** un(e) patient(e) hospitalisé(e); ***hospital doctor*** médecin *m* hospitalier; ***hospital ship*** navire-hôpital *m*; ***hospital train*** train *m* sanitaire; *Br* ***hospital trolley*** chariot *m* d'hôpital

hospital-acquired ADJ *(infection, disease)* acquis à l'hôpital, *Spéc* nosocomial

hospitality [,hɒspɪ'tælətɪ] N hospitalité *f*; **thank you for your h.** merci pour votre hospitalité; *Old-fashioned Euph* **to enjoy His/Her Majesty's h.** faire de la prison

▸▸ ***hospitality industry*** industrie *f* hôtelière; ***hospitality room, hospitality suite*** salon *m* de réception *(où sont offerts des rafraîchissements lors d'une conférence, d'un événement sportif etc)*

hospitalization, -isation [,hɒspɪtəlaɪ'zeɪʃən] N hospitalisation *f*

▸▸ *Am* ***hospitalization insurance*** assurance *f* couvrant l'hospitalisation

hospitalize, -ise ['hɒspɪtəlaɪz] VT *(sick person)* hospitaliser; *Fam* **a couple of thugs hospitalized him** *(beat him up)* deux voyous l'ont envoyé à l'hôpital

host[1] [həʊst] N **1** *(person)* hôte *m (qui reçoit)*; *(on TV show)* animateur(trice) *m,f*; *(in hotel)* hôtelier(ère) *m,f*; *(innkeeper)* aubergiste *mf*; **he acted as our h. for the evening** il a été notre hôte pour la soirée; **Japan will be the next h. for the conference** c'est le Japon qui accueillera la prochaine conférence

2 *Biol & Zool* hôte *m*

3 *Literary (denizen)* hôte *m*

4 *Comput* ordinateur *m* principal; *(in network)* serveur *m*

ADJ *(cell)* hôte; *(team)* qui reçoit; **the h. city for the Olympic Games** la ville organisatrice des jeux Olympiques

VT **1** *(TV, radio programme)* présenter; *(game show)* animer; *(event)* organiser; *(party)* donner; **she adores hosting dinner parties** elle adore recevoir à dîner **2** *Comput (website)* héberger

▸▸ *Comput* ***host computer*** ordinateur *m* principal; *(in network)* serveur *m*; ***host country*** pays *m* d'accueil

host[2] N **1** *(large number)* foule *f*; **a h. of complaints** toute une série de plaintes **2** *Literary* armée *f*

host[3] N *Rel (consecrated bread)* hostie *f*

hostage ['hɒstɪdʒ] N otage *m*; **to take/to hold sb h.** prendre/garder qn en otage; *Fig* **the government doesn't want to give any hostages to fortune by promising tax cuts** le gouvernement ne veut pas prendre le risque de promettre des réductions d'impôts

▸▸ ***hostage taker*** preneur(euse) *m,f* d'otage

hostel ['hɒstəl] N **1** *(residence)* foyer *m* **2** *Arch (inn)* auberge *f*

hosteller, *Am* **hosteler** ['hɒstələ(r)] N **1** *(youth)* **h.** ajiste *mf* **2** *Arch (innkeeper)* aubergiste *mf*

hostelling, *Am* **hosteling** ['hɒstəlɪŋ] N *Br* **h. is popular with students** les étudiants aiment loger dans les auberges de jeunesse au cours de leurs voyages

hostelry ['hɒstəlrɪ] *(pl* **hostelries***)* N hôtellerie *f*; *Fam Hum* **the local h.** le bistrot du coin

hostess ['həʊstes] N **1** *(at home, on TV show)* hôtesse *f*; *(of inn)* aubergiste *f* **2** *(in nightclub)* entraîneuse *f* **3** **(air) h.** hôtesse *f* de l'air

▸▸ ***hostess agency*** agence *f* d'hôtesses; ***Hostess Trolley®*** = table roulante avec chauffe-plats

hostile [*Br* 'hɒstaɪl, *Am* 'hɒstəl] ADJ hostile; **to be h. to sb/sth** être hostile à qn/qch; **people who are h. to change** les gens qui n'aiment pas le changement

▸▸ *Mil* ***hostile forces*** forces *fpl* ennemies; *Com* ***hostile takeover bid*** OPA *f* hostile

hostility [hɒ'stɪlətɪ] *(pl* **hostilities***)* N **1** *(aggression)* hostilité *f*; **to show h. to** *or* **towards sb** manifester de l'hostilité *ou* faire preuve d'hostilité envers qn **2** **hostilities** *(fighting)* hostilités *fpl*

hosting ['həʊstɪŋ] N *Comput (of website)* hébergement *m*

HOT [hɒt]

- chaud **1, 2, 4, 11, 12, 20**
- épicé **5**
- tout frais **6**
- intense **9**
- sévère **13**
- recherché **15, 18**
- qui tient chaud **3**
- fort **5, 14**
- violent **8**
- enthousiaste **10**
- génial **14**
- sexy **16**

(*compar* **hotter**, *superl* **hottest**, *pt & pp* **hotted**, *cont* **hotting**)

ADJ **1** *(high in temperature)* chaud; **to be h.** *(person)* avoir (très *ou* trop) chaud; *(object)* être chaud; **I'm getting h.** je commence à avoir chaud; **how h. should the oven be?** le four doit être à quelle température?; **we sat in the h. sun** nous étions assis sous un soleil brûlant; **I'd like a h. bath** j'aimerais prendre un bain bien chaud; **the doctor said not to have any h. drinks** le médecin m'a conseillé de ne pas boire chaud *ou* m'a déconseillé les boissons chaudes; **a h. meal** un repas chaud; **keep the meat h.** tenez la viande au chaud; **the bread was h. from the oven** le pain sortait tout chaud du four; *Fig* **you're getting h.!** *(in guessing game)* tu brûles!; *Fam* **to be** *or* **to get (all) h. and bothered (about sth)** être dans tous ses états *ou* se faire du mauvais sang (au sujet de qch); *Fam* **to be** *or* **to get h. under the collar (about sth)** être en colère *ou* en rogne (au sujet de qch); **the books were selling like h. cakes** les livres se vendaient comme des petits pains; *Fam* **he's full of h. air** c'est une grande gueule; **all her promises are just a lot of h. air** toutes ses promesses ne sont que des paroles en l'air; **that's nothing but h. air!** tout ça n'est que du vent!

2 *(weather)* **it's h.** il fait très chaud; **one h. afternoon in August** (par) une chaude après-midi d'août; **we had a h. spell last week** c'était la canicule la semaine dernière

3 *(clothing)* qui tient chaud; **this jacket's too h.** cette veste tient trop chaud

4 *(colour)* chaud

5 *(pungent, spicy ▸ food)* épicé, piquant, relevé; *(▸ spice)* fort; **a h. curry** un curry relevé *ou* épicé

6 *(fresh, recent)* tout(e) frais (fraîche); **the news is h. off the presses** ce sont des informations de toute dernière minute; **this book is h. off the press** ce livre vient juste de paraître

7 *(close, following closely)* **to be h. on the trail** être sur la bonne piste; **the police were h. on their heels** *or* **on their trail** la police les talonnait *ou* était à leurs trousses; **he fled with the police in h. pursuit** il s'est enfui avec la police à ses trousses

8 *(fiery, vehement)* violent; **she has a h. temper** elle s'emporte facilement, elle est très soupe au lait

9 *(intense ▸ anger, shame)* intense, profond

10 *(keen)* enthousiaste, passionné; *Am Fam* **he's h. on my sister** il en pince pour ma sœur; **they're not very h. on hygiene** *(fussy about)* ils ne sont pas très portés sur l'hygiène

11 *Fam (exciting)* chaud; **the reporter was onto a h. story** le journaliste était sur un coup (fumant); **to have a h. date** avoir un rendez-vous galant❑; **this book is h. stuff** c'est un livre très audacieux❑; **this issue is h. stuff, I wouldn't touch it** c'est un sujet brûlant, je n'y toucherais pas

12 *Fam (difficult, unpleasant)* chaud, difficile❑; **we could make it** *or* **things very h. for you if you don't cooperate** nous pourrions vous mener la vie dure *ou* vous en faire voir de toutes les couleurs si vous ne vous montrez pas coopératif; **the situation was too h. to handle** la situation était trop délicate pour qu'on s'en mêle❑

13 *Br Fam (severe, stringent)* sévère❑, dur❑; **the police are really h. on drunk driving** la police ne badine vraiment pas avec la conduite en état d'ivresse

14 *Fam (very good)* génial; *(skilful)* fort❑, calé; **how is he? – not so h.** *(unwell)* comment va-t-il? – pas trop bien❑; **I don't feel so h.** je ne suis pas dans mon assiette; **I'm not so h. at maths** je ne suis pas très calé en maths; **his latest book isn't so h.** son dernier livre n'est pas terrible *ou* fameux; **that isn't such a h. idea** ce n'est pas terrible *ou* fameux comme idée; **a h. tip** un tuyau sûr *ou* increvable

15 *Fam (in demand, popular)* très recherché❑; **she's really h. just now** elle a vraiment beaucoup de succès en ce moment❑; **to be h. property** être très demandé❑; *Am Fam* **to be a h. ticket** faire fureur; **the play is the hottest ticket in town** c'est la pièce qui a le plus de succès actuellement❑

16 *Fam (sexually attractive)* **to be h. (stuff)** être sexy *(inv)*; **he's h.** *(sexually aroused)* il a le feu au derrière

17 *Fam (stolen)* volé❑

18 *Br Fam (sought by police)* recherché par la police❑

19 *Elec (wire)* sous tension

20 *Nucl (radioactive)* chaud, radioactif❑

21 *Am very Fam* **h. damn!** *(in excitement)* bon sang!, nom d'un chien!; *(in anger)* merde!

ADV **to go h. and cold at the thought of sth** avoir des sueurs froides à l'idée de qch

• **hots** NPL *Fam* **to have the hots for sb** craquer pour qn

▸▸ ***hot chocolate*** *(drink)* chocolat *m* chaud; ***hot desking*** = pratique qui consiste à ne pas assigner de bureaux individuels aux employés, ces derniers étant libres de s'installer à n'importe quel poste de travail inoccupé; ***hot dog*** N *(sausage)* hot-dog *m*; *Ski* ski *m* acrobatique; *(in surfing)* surf *m* acrobatique EXCLAM *Am Fam* génial!, super!; *Br Sport* ***hot favourite*** grand(e) favori(ite) *m,f*; *Med Am* ***hot flash,*** *Br* ***hot flush*** bouffée *f* de chaleur; ***hot gospeller*** = prêcheur évangéliste qui harangue les foules; *Fam* ***hot jazz*** (jazz *m*) hot *m inv*; *Comput* ***hot key*** touche *f* personnalisée; *Tel* ***hot line*** numéro *m* d'urgence; *Pol (between US and Kremlin)* téléphone *m* rouge; **he has a h. line to the president** il a une ligne directe avec le président; ***hot line support*** assistance *f* technique téléphonique, hot line *f*; *Comput* ***hot link*** lien *m* hypertexte; *Typ* ***hot metal*** hot metal *m*; *Fam* ***hot money*** *(UNCOUNT) (stolen)* argent *m* volé❑; *Fin* capitaux *mpl* flottants *ou* fébriles❑; *Am* ***hot pad*** dessous-de-plat *m inv*; ***hot pants*** mini-short *m (très court et moulant)*; *Bot & Culin* ***hot pepper*** piment *m*; *Fam Fig* ***hot potato*** sujet *m* brûlant et délicat; **to drop sb like a h. potato** laisser tomber qn comme une vieille chaussette *ou* savate; *Ir* ***hot press*** *(airing cupboard)* = placard chauffé où l'on fait sécher le linge; *Fam Aut* ***hot rod*** bagnole *f* trafiquée; *Am Fam* ***hot seat*** *(electric chair)* chaise *f* électrique❑; *Fig* **to be in the h. seat** *(difficult situation)* être sur la sellette; *Phot* ***hot shoe*** griffe *f* du flash, pied-sabot *m*; ***hot spot*** *Geog* point *m* chaud; *Comput* borne *f* Wi-Fi, point *m* d'accès Wi-Fi, hotspot *m*; *Fig (dangerous area)* point *m* chaud *ou* névralgique; *Fam (night club)* boîte *f* de nuit❑; ***hot spring*** source *f* chaude; ***hot stone grill*** pierrade® *f*, pierre *f* à griller; *Br Comput* ***hot swap*** *(of devices)* remplacement *m* à chaud; ***hot tub*** = sorte de Jacuzzi® qu'on installe dehors; ***hot water*** eau *f* chaude; *Fig* **their latest prank got them into** *or* **landed them in h. water** leur dernière farce leur a attiré des ennuis; **you'll be in h. water when she finds out** tu passeras un mauvais quart d'heure quand elle s'en apercevra; ***hot wire*** fil *m* sous tension

▸ **hot up** *Br Fam* VT SEP **1** *(intensify ▸ argument, contest)* échauffer❑; *(▸ bombing, fighting)* intensifier❑; *(▸ party)* mettre de l'animation dans❑; **they hotted up the pace** ils ont forcé l'allure **2** *Aut* **to h. up a car** gonfler le moteur d'une voiture

VI *(intensify ▸ discussion, campaign)* s'échauffer❑; *(▸ fighting, situation)* chauffer❑, s'intensifier❑; **things are beginning to h. up** ça se corse

---

hot-air balloon N montgolfière *f*

hotbed ['hɒtbed] N *Hort* couche *f* chaude, forcerie *f*; *Fig* pépinière *f*, foyer *m*; **a h. of crime/intrigue** un foyer de crime/d'intrigue

hot-blooded [-'blʌdɪd] ADJ *(person ▸ passionate)* fougueux, au sang chaud

hotchpotch ['hɒtʃpɒtʃ] N *Br* **1** *(jumble)* fatras *m*, salmigondis *m*; **a h. of ideas** un fatras d'idées **2** *Culin* hochepot *m*, salmigondis *m*

hot-dog VI **1** *Ski* faire du ski acrobatique; *(in surfing)* faire du surf acrobatique **2** *Am Fam (show off)* crâner, frimer, poser (pour la galerie)

hot-dogging [-dɒgɪŋ] N **1** *Ski* ski *m* acrobatique; *(in surfing)* surf *m* acrobatique **2** *Am Fam (showing off)* frime *f*

hotel [həʊ'tel] N **1** *(accommodation)* hôtel *m*; **to stay at a h.** descendre dans un hôtel; **a two-star h.** un hôtel deux étoiles; **a luxury h.** un hôtel de luxe **2** *Austr (pub)* pub *m*

COMP *(prices, reservation, room)* d'hôtel

▸▸ ***hotel desk*** réception *f (d'un hôtel)*; **leave a message at** *or* **with the h. desk** laissez un message à la réception; ***the hotel industry*** l'industrie *f* hôtelière, l'hôtellerie *f*; ***hotel manager*** gérant(e) *m,f* d'hôtel, directeur(trice) *m,f* d'hôtel; ***hotel receptionist*** réceptionniste *mf* d'hôtel; ***hotel staf***[f] personnel *m* hôtelier *ou* de l'hôtel

hotelier [həʊ'telɪə(r)] N hôtelier(ère) *m,f*

hotfoot ['hɒt,fʊt] *Fam* ADV à toute vitesse❑

VT **to h. it** galoper à toute vitesse

hothead ['hɒthed] N tête *f* brûlée, exalté(e) *m,f*

hotheaded [,hɒt'hedɪd] ADJ *(person)* impétueux, exalté; *(attitude)* impétueux; **she's very h[eaded]** c'est une exaltée *ou* une tête brûlée

hothouse ['hɒthaʊs, *pl* -haʊzɪz] N **1** *Hort* serre (chaude) **2** *Fig (hotbed)* foyer *m*; **a h. of creativity/of decadence** un foyer de création/de décadence

COMP de serre (chaude)

VT *(children)* stimuler

▸▸ *also Fig* ***hothouse plant*** plante *f* de serre (chaude); ***hothouse tomatoes*** tomates *fpl* de serre

hotlist ['hɒtlɪst] N *Comput* liste *f* de signets

hotly ['hɒtlɪ] ADV *(dispute)* vivement; *(deny)* vigoureusement; *(pursue)* avec acharnement *(say)* avec flamme; **it was a h. debated issue** c'étai[t] une question très controversée

hotplate ['hɒtpleɪt] N *(on stove)* plaque *f* chauffante; *(portable)* chauffe-plats *m inv*

hotpot ['hɒtpɒt] N *Br Culin* = ragoût de viande e[t] de pommes de terre

hotrod ['hɒtrɒd] N *Aut Fam* bolide *m*, voiture gonflée

hotshot ['hɒtʃɒt] *Fam* N *(expert)* as *m*, crack *m*; *B[r]* *(VIP)* gros bonnet *m*; *Am Pej (self-important person)* gros bonnet *m*

ADJ super; **they've hired some h. lawyer** ils on[t] pris un as du barreau

hotspot ['hɒtspɒt] N *Comput (for WiFi® access)* point *m* chaud

hot-tempered ADJ colérique, emporté; **he's very h.** il est très soupe au lait

Hottentot ['hɒtəntɒt] N **1** *(person)* Hottentot(e) *m,f* **2** *Ling* hottentot *m*

ADJ hottentot

hottie ['hɒtɪ] N *Am Fam (attractive woman)* canon *m*; *(attractive man)* beau mec *m*

hot-water ADJ

▸▸ ***hot-water bottle*** bouillotte *f*; ***hot-water tank*** ballon *m* d'eau chaude

hound [haʊnd] N **1** *(dog ▸ gen)* chien *m*; *(▸ for hunting)* chien *m* courant, chien *m* de meute; *Hunt* **the hounds, a pack of hounds** la meute; *Hunt* **to ride to** *or* **to follow the hounds** chasser à courre **2** *Pej Old-fashioned (person)* canaille *f*, crapule *f*

VT **1** *(give chase)* traquer, pourchasser **2** *(harass)* s'acharner sur, harceler; **she was hounded by reporters** elle était pourchassée *ou* harcelée par les journalistes

▸ **hound down** VT SEP prendre dans des rets, coincer; *Hunt* forcer

hour ['aʊə(r)] N **1** *(unit of time)* heure *f*; **a quarter of an h.** un quart d'heure; **half an h., a half h.** une demi-heure; **an h. and a half** une heure et demie; **at 60 km an** *or* **per h.** à 60 km à l'heure; **check it at least three times an h.** vérifie-le au moins trois fois par heure; **it's a two-h. drive/walk from here** c'est à deux heures de voiture/de marche d'ici; **the play is an h. long** la pièce dure une heure; **he gets £10 an h.** il touche 10 livres (de) l'heure; **are you paid by the h.?** êtes-vous payé à l'heure?; **a 35-h. week** une semaine de 35 heures; **the shop is open 24 hours a day** le magasin est ouvert 24 heures sur 24; **he was an h. late** il avait une heure de retard; **the situation is deteriorating by the h.** la situation s'aggrave d'heure en heure; **we waited for hours and hours** on a attendu des heures **2** *(time of day)* heure *f*; **it chimes on the h.** ça sonne à l'heure juste; **every h. on the h.** toutes les heures à l'heure pile; **in the early** *or* **small hours (of the morning)** au petit matin, au petit jour; **at this late h.** à cette heure avancée **3** *Fig (specific moment)* heure *f*, moment *m*; **the h. has come** l'heure est venue, c'est l'heure *ou* le moment; **the man of the h.** l'homme du moment; **in one's h. of need** quand on est dans le besoin; **the burning questions of the h.** l'actualité *f* du moment

• **hours** NPL heures *fpl*; *Ind* **flexible working**

hours des horaires *mpl* mobiles *ou* souples; **opening hours** heures *fpl* d'ouverture; **what hours do you work?** quels sont vos horaires de travail?; **do you work long hours?** as-tu de longues journées de travail?; **he keeps late hours** c'est un couche-tard, il veille tard; **to keep regular hours** avoir une vie réglée; **people come and go at all hours** les gens vont et viennent à toute heure; **he was out until all hours** il est rentré à une heure indue; **after hours** *(of office)* après les heures de travail; *Br (of pub)* après l'heure de la fermeture
▸▸ ***hour hand*** petite aiguille *f*

hourglass ['aʊəglɑːs] **N** sablier *m*
ADJ en forme d'amphore
▸▸ ***hourglass figure*** taille *f* mannequin

hour-long **ADJ** d'une heure

hourly ['aʊəlɪ] **ADJ 1** *(each hour ▸ flights, trains)* **h. departures** départs *mpl* toutes les heures **2** *Com & Tech (per hour ▸ earnings, rate)* horaire; **h. wage** salaire *m* horaire **3** *(continual ▸ anticipation)* constant, perpétuel
ADV 1 *(each hour)* une fois par heure, chaque heure, toutes les heures; **to be paid h.** être payé à l'heure **2** *(repeatedly)* sans cesse; *(at any time)* à tout moment; **we expect them h.** on les attend d'une minute à l'autre *ou* à tout moment

house **N** [haʊs, *pl* haʊzɪz] **1** *(for living in)* maison *f*; **at** *or* **to his h.** chez lui; **h. for sale** *(sign)* propriété à vendre; **to move h.** déménager; **to clean the h.**, *Am* **to clean h.** faire le ménage; **to keep h. (for sb)** tenir la maison *ou* le ménage (de qn); **to set up h.** monter son ménage, s'installer; **they set up h. together** ils se sont mis en ménage; **don't wake up the whole h.!** ne réveille pas toute la maison!; *Fam* **we got on** *or* **along like a h. on fire** nous nous entendions à merveille *ou* comme larrons en foire; *Fam* **it's coming on like a h. on fire** ça marche du feu de Dieu; *Fig* **to set** *or* **to put one's h. in order** mettre de l'ordre dans ses affaires; *Fig* **the government should set** *or* **put its own h. in order before criticizing others** le gouvernement devrait balayer devant sa porte avant de critiquer les autres; *Br Fam* **the bus goes all round the houses** le bus fait tout le tour de la ville; *Fam Fig* **to go all round the houses** *(not get to the point)* tourner autour du pot; *Fam Fig* **he was sent all round the houses when he tried to get a work permit** on l'a renvoyé de service en service quand il a essayé d'obtenir un permis de travail
2 *Com (company)* maison *f (de commerce)*; **publishing h.** maison *f* d'édition; **in h.** au sein de l'entreprise
3 *(restaurant, bar)* **to have a drink on the h.** prendre une consommation aux frais du patron *ou* de la maison; **a bottle of h. red** une bouteille de (vin) rouge de la maison
4 *Rel* maison *f* religieuse
5 *(household)* maison *f*; *(dynasty)* famille *f*, maison *f*; **the H. of York** la maison de York; **the whole h. was down with flu** toute la maisonnée avait la grippe
6 *Theat* salle *f*, auditoire *m*; **is there a good h. tonight?** est-ce qu'il y a beaucoup de monde ce soir?; **they played to an empty h.** ils ont joué devant les banquettes (vides); **to have a full h.** jouer à guichets fermés *ou* à bureaux fermés; **h. full** *(sign)* complet; **to bring the h. down** *(performer)* faire crouler la salle sous les applaudissements; *Fig* casser la baraque
7 *Br Sch* = groupe d'élèves qui rivalise avec un autre pour les activités sportives etc
8 *Mus* house *f*
9 *Astrol* maison *f*
10 *(of crane)* cabine *f*; *Naut (on deck)* rouf *m*; *(at helm)* kiosque *m*
11 *(in debate)* **this h. believes...** la motion à débattre est la suivante...
• **House** **N the H.** *Br Pol* la Chambre; *Am Pol* la Chambre des représentants; *St Exch* la Bourse (de Londres)
VT [haʊz] **1** *(provide with shelter ▸ person)* héberger, loger; **many families are still badly housed** de nombreuses familles sont encore mal logées **2** *(store ▸ of building)* recevoir; **this wing houses a laboratory** cette aile abrite un laboratoire; **his boat is housed in the garage during winter** son bateau est (remisé) au garage pendant l'hiver; **the archives are housed in the basement** on garde les archives dans les caves **3** *(protect by covering)* **the gears are housed in a steel case** l'engrenage est contenu dans un carter d'acier
EXCLAM [haʊs] *(in bingo)* carton!
▸▸ *Br* ***house agent*** agent *m* immobilier; ***house arrest*** assignation *f* à domicile *ou* à résidence; **to put sb under h. arrest** assigner qn à domicile *ou* à résidence; **he is under h. arrest** il est assigné à domicile, il est en résidence surveillée; *Fin* ***house bill*** double *m* de connaissement, lettre *f* de change creuse; *also Fig* ***house of cards*** château *m* de cartes; ***the House of Commons*** la Chambre des communes; ***house detective*** responsable *m* de la sécurité, détective *m* de l'hôtel; ***house dust mite*** acarien *m*; ***house of God*** *(church)* maison *f* de Dieu; *(Protestant)* temple *m*; ***house husband*** homme *m* au foyer; ***house journal*** journal *m* interne, bulletin *m*; ***the House of Lords*** la Chambre des lords; ***house magazine*** journal *m* interne, bulletin *m*; *Theat* ***house manager*** directeur(trice) *m,f* de théâtre; *Orn* ***house martin*** hirondelle *f* de fenêtre; *Zool* ***house mouse*** souris *f* commune; ***house music*** house *f* (music); ***house painter*** peintre *m* en bâtiment; *Parl* ***the Houses of Parliament*** le Parlement (britannique); ***house party*** *(social occasion)* fête *f* de plusieurs jours *(dans une maison de campagne)*; *(guests)* invités *mpl*; *Br* ***house physician*** *(in hospital)* interne *mf* (en médecine); *(in hotel)* médecin *m (attaché à un hôtel)*; *Parl* ***the House of Representatives*** la Chambre des représentants *(aux États-Unis)*; *Orn* ***house sparrow*** moineau *m* domestique; *Entom* ***house spider*** tégénaire *f*; *Br Typ & Press* ***house style*** style *m* maison; *Br* ***house surgeon*** interne *mf* (en chirurgie); ***the House Un-American Activities Committee*** = organisme maccarthyste de répression anticommuniste fondé en 1938 et dissous en 1975; *Br* ***house wine*** vin *m* de la maison; *f* ***house of worship*** église *f*; *(Protestant)* temple *m*

HOUSE OF COMMONS

La Chambre des communes britannique est composée de 659 députés ("MPs") élus pour cinq ans et qui siègent environ 175 jours par an. Les députés du parti majoritaire s'assoient d'un côté de la Chambre (les "government benches"), tandis que les députés de l'opposition s'assoient de l'autre côté (sur les "opposition benches"). Si un projet de loi n'obtient pas l'approbation de la majorité des députés dans la Chambre des communes, il est renvoyé à la Chambre des lords, et doit par ailleurs obtenir l'assentiment du souverain avant de devenir loi.

HOUSE OF LORDS

La Chambre des lords est composée de pairs et d'hommes d'Église. Il s'agit de la plus haute cour au Royaume-Uni (en excluant l'Écosse). Elle a le pouvoir d'amender certains projets de loi qui ont été votés par la Chambre des communes. Le gouvernement travailliste de Tony Blair entreprit des réformes visant à réduire les pouvoirs de la Chambre des lords de façon radicale.

HOUSE OF REPRESENTATIVES

La Chambre des représentants constitue, avec le Sénat, l'organe législatif américain; ses membres sont élus par le peuple, en proportion de la population de chaque État. Elle est composée d'un total de 435 membres représentant chacun une circonscription électorale. Tous les projets de loi concernant les dépenses du gouvernement doivent venir de la Chambre des représentants.

houseboat ['haʊsbəʊt] **N** house-boat *m*, péniche *f* (aménagée)

housebound ['haʊsbaʊnd] **ADJ** qui ne peut quitter la maison

housebreaker ['haʊs,breɪkə(r)] **N** cambrioleur (euse) *m,f*

housebreaking ['haʊs,breɪkɪŋ] **N** cambriolage *m*

housecoat ['haʊskəʊt] **N** robe *f* d'intérieur

housefly ['haʊsflaɪ] *(pl* **houseflies)** **N** *Entom* mouche *f* (commune *ou* domestique)

houseful ['haʊsfʊl] **N a h. of guests** une pleine maisonnée d'invités; **we've got a real h. this weekend** la maison est vraiment pleine (de monde) ce week-end

household ['haʊshəʊld] **N** *(people in house)* (membres *mpl* de la) maison *f*; *(economically, statistically)* ménage *m*; **she grew up as part of a large h.** elle a grandi au sein d'une famille nombreuse; **the head of the h.** le chef de famille; **households with more than two children** ménages *mpl ou* familles *fpl* de plus de deux enfants; **95 percent of households have a television set** 95 pour cent des ménages possèdent un poste de télévision; **the Royal H.** la maison royale
ADJ de ménage; *Admin & Econ* des ménages; **for h. use only** *(on packaging)* à usage domestique seulement
▸▸ ***household appliance*** appareil *m* ménager; ***Household Cavalry*** = division de cavalerie de la Garde royale britannique; *Hist* ***household gods*** dieux *mpl* du foyer; ***household goods*** articles *mpl* pour le ménage, produits *mpl* ménagers; ***household name*** *(brand, product)* nom *m* de marque connu; **we want to make our brand a h. name** nous voulons que notre marque soit connue de tous; **she's a h. name** tout le monde la connaît *ou* sait qui elle est; ***household troops*** garde *f* personnelle; *Hist* garde *f* du palais; *(in UK)* Garde *f* royale

householder ['haʊs,həʊldə(r)] **N** *(occupant)* occupant(e) *m,f*; *(owner)* propriétaire *mf*; *(tenant)* locataire *mf*

housekeeper ['haʊs,kiːpə(r)] **N** *(institutional)* économe *f*, intendante *f*; *(in a hotel)* gouvernante *f*; *(private)* gouvernante *f*; **she's a good/bad h.** c'est une bonne/mauvaise maîtresse de maison

housekeeping ['haʊs,kiːpɪŋ] **N** *(UNCOUNT)* **1** *(of household ▸ skill)* économie *f* domestique; *(▸ work)* ménage *m* **2** *(of organization)* services *mpl* généraux **3** *Comput* gestion *f* interne

housemaid ['haʊsmeɪd] **N** bonne *f*, femme *f* de chambre
▸▸ *Med* ***housemaid's knee*** inflammation *f* du genou

houseman ['haʊsmən] *(pl* **housemen** [-mən]) **N 1** *Br Med* interne *mf* **2** *(servant)* domestique *m*, valet *m*

housemaster ['haʊs,mɑːstə(r)] **N** *Br Sch* = professeur responsable d'une "house"

house-proud **ADJ he's very h.** il attache beaucoup d'importance à l'aspect intérieur de sa maison, tout est toujours impeccable chez lui

houseroom ['haʊsrʊm] **N** *Br* **I wouldn't give that table h.!** je ne voudrais pas de cette table chez moi!; **I wouldn't give her h.** je ne voudrais pas d'elle chez moi

house-sit **VI to h. for sb** = s'occuper de la maison de quelqu'un pendant son absence

house-sitter **N** = personne qui garde une maison en l'absence de ses occupants

house-to-house **ADJ** *(enquiry)* à domicile; **to make a h. search for sb/sth** fouiller chaque maison à la recherche de qn/qch
▸▸ *Mktg* ***house-to-house canvassing*** porte-à-porte *m inv*, démarchage *m*

housetop ['haʊstɒp] **N** toit *m*; *Fig* **to shout** *or* **to proclaim sth from the housetops** crier qch sur les toits

house-train **VT** *Br (pet)* dresser à la propreté; **has the dog been house-trained?** est-ce que le chien est propre?; *Fam Hum* **he used to be really untidy, but she soon got him house-trained!** avant, il était très brouillon, mais elle a eu tôt fait de le dresser!

housewarming ['haʊs,wɔːmɪŋ] **N** pendaison *f* de crémaillère
▸▸ ***housewarming party*** pendaison *f* de crémaillère; **to give** *or* **to have a h. (party)** pendre la crémaillère

housewife ['haʊswaɪf] *(pl* **housewives** [-waɪvz]) **N** ménagère *f*; *(not career woman)* femme *f* au foyer

housewifely ['haʊsˌwaɪflɪ] **ADJ** de ménagère

housewifery ['haʊswɪfərɪ] **N** économie *f* domestique

housework ['haʊswɜːk] **N** (travaux *mpl* de) ménage *m*; **to do the h.** faire le ménage

> Attention: ne pas confondre avec **homework**, qui signifie **devoirs à faire à la maison**.

housey-housey [ˌhaʊzɪ'haʊzɪ] **N** *Br* loto *m (joué pour de l'argent)*

housing ['haʊzɪŋ] **N 1** *(accommodation)* logement *m*; **low-cost h.** logements *mpl* à loyer modéré; **the budget allocation for h. has been cut** la part du budget réservée au logement a été réduite; **there's a lot of new h. going up in the area** il y a beaucoup de logements nouveaux en construction dans le quartier; **the government has no long-term h. strategy** le gouvernement n'a aucune stratégie à long terme en matière de logement **2** *Tech (of mechanism)* carter *m*; *Phot* boîtier *m*; **wheel h.** boîte *f* de roue; **watch h.** boîtier *m* de montre **3** *Constr* encastrement *m*

►► ***housing association*** = association britannique à but non lucratif qui construit ou rénove des logements pour les louer à ses membres; *Br Admin* ***housing benefit*** = allocation de logement versée par l'État aux individus justifiant de revenus faibles; ***housing development*** *(estate)* lotissement *m*; *(activity)* construction *f* de logements; *Br* ***housing estate*** *(privately owned houses)* lotissement *m*; *(council owned flats)* grand ensemble *m*; ***housing market*** marché *m* de l'immobilier; *Am* ***housing project*** grand ensemble *m*; *(plan)* plan *m* d'aménagement immobilier; ***housing scheme*** *(plan)* programme *m* municipal de logement; *(privately owned houses)* lotissement *m*; *(council owned flats)* grand ensemble *m*; ***housing shortage*** crise *f* du logement

hove [həʊv] *pt & pp of* **heave**

hovel ['hɒvəl] **N** taudis *m*, masure *f*

hover ['hɒvə(r)] **VI 1** *(in air* ► *smoke)* stagner; *(*► *balloon, scent)* flotter; *(*► *insects)* voltiger; *(*► *helicopter, hummingbird)* faire du surplace; **bees hovered around the roses** des abeilles voltigeaient autour des roses **2** *(linger* ► *person)* rôder; *(*► *smile)* flotter; *(*► *danger)* planer; **I don't like him hovering over me** je n'aime pas qu'il soit sur mon dos; **it's no use hovering over the phone like that** ça ne sert à rien de tourner autour du téléphone comme ça; **she was hovering between life and death** elle restait suspendue entre la vie et la mort; **don't just h. in the background** ne reste pas dans ton coin **3** *(hesitate)* hésiter; **his finger hovered over the button** son doigt hésita à appuyer sur le bouton; **I'm hovering between the two possible options** j'hésite entre les deux options possibles

N aéroglisseur *m*

►**hover around VT INSEP** *(move about near)* **to h. around sb** errer *ou* rôder autour de qn; **prices are hovering around the £3.50 mark** les prix oscillent autour de 3 livres 50

VI *(move about nearby)* tourner

hovercraft ['hɒvəkrɑːft] **N** aéroglisseur *m*

hoverport ['hɒvəpɔːt] **N** hoverport *m*

hovertrain ['hɒvətreɪn] **N** *Rail* train *m* à coussin d'air

HOW [haʊ]

ADV	
• comment **1, 2**	• comme **3**
• que **3**	• à quel point **4**
• combien **4**	
CONJ	
• comment **1, 2**	• que **2**
• comme **3**	
N	
• comment	

ADV 1 *(in what way)* comment; **h. do you spell it?** comment est-ce que ça s'écrit?; **h. was she dressed?** comment est-ce qu'elle était habillée?; **h. could you be so careless?** comment as-tu pu être aussi étourdi?; **h. could you!** tu n'as pas honte?; **h. is it that...?** comment se fait-il que... + *subjunctive*?; **h. so?, h. can that be?** comment cela (se fait-il)?; **h.'s that (again)?** comment?; **h.'s that for size?** ça va comme taille?; **suppose I offer you another £500, h.'s that?** et si je t'offre 500 livres en plus, qu'est-ce que tu en dis?; *Fam* **h. the heck should I know?** mais enfin, comment veux-tu que je sache?

2 *(in greetings, friendly enquiries etc)* comment; **h. are you?** comment allez-vous?; **h. are you doing?** comment ça va?; **h. do you do?** enchanté!; **h. are things?** ça va?; **h.'s business?** comment vont les affaires?; *Fam* **h.'s life?** comment ça va?; **h. did it go?** comment ça s'est passé?; **h. do you like this wine?** comment trouvez-vous ce vin?; **h. did you like** *or* **h. was the film?** comment as-tu trouvé le film?; **h. was your trip?** avez-vous fait bon voyage?; **h.'s the water?** l'eau est bonne?

3 *(in exclamations)* que, comme; **h. sad she is!** qu'elle est triste!, comme elle est triste!; **h. nice of you!** comme c'est aimable à vous!; **h. decadent!** quelle décadence!; **h. incredible!** c'est incroyable!; **h. I wish I could!** si seulement je pouvais!; *Fam* **h. stupid can you get!** est-il possible d'être bête à ce point-là!

4 *(with adj or adv) (to what extent)* **h. wide is the room?** quelle est la largeur de la pièce?; **h. tall are you?** combien mesures-tu?; **h. old is she?** quel âge a-t-elle?; **h. well can you see it?** est-ce que tu le vois bien?; **h. angry is he?** il est vraiment fâché?; **h. fast/slowly was he walking?** à quelle vitesse marchait-il?; **h. far is it from here to the sea?** combien y a-t-il d'ici à la mer?; **h. much does this bag cost?** combien coûte ce sac?; **h. much is it/do I owe you?** combien est-ce que ça coûte/vous dois-je?; **h. many are there of you?** vous êtes combien (de personnes)?; **h. often did she come?** combien de fois est-elle venue?; **h. often did he write?** est-ce qu'il écrivait souvent?; **h. long is the flight?** quelle est la durée du vol?; **h. soon can you deliver it?** à partir de quand pouvez-vous le livrer?; **h. late will you stay?** jusqu'à quelle heure resteras-tu?; **you know h. useful he is to me** vous savez à quel point il m'est utile; **you don't know h. right you are** vous ne savez pas combien vous dites vrai, vous ne savez pas à quel point vous avez raison

CONJ 1 *(in what way)* comment; **tell me h. you do it** dites-moi comment vous faites; **he's learning h. to read** il apprend à lire; **I need more information on h. the network functions** j'ai besoin de plus de renseignements sur le fonctionnement du réseau

2 *(the fact that)* **you know h. he always gets his own way** tu sais bien qu'il finit toujours par obtenir ce qu'il veut; **we all know h. smell can influence taste** tout le monde sait comment l'odorat a une influence sur le goût; **I remember h. he always used to turn up late** je me souviens qu'il était toujours en retard

3 *Fam (however)* comme□; **arrange the furniture h. you like** installe les meubles comme tu veux; **did you like it? – and h.!** ça t'a plu? – et comment!

N comment *m inv*; **the h. and the why of it don't interest me** le pourquoi et le comment ne m'intéressent pas

EXCLAM *Hum (greeting)* salut

• **how about ADV** *Fam* **h. about a beer?** et si on prenait une bière?; **h. about going out tonight?** si on sortait ce soir?; **h. about Friday?** vendredi, ça va?; **h. about you, what do you think?** et toi, qu'est-ce que tu en penses?; **h. about that!** c'est pas vrai!

• **how come ADV** *Fam* **h. come?** comment ça se fait?; **h. come you left?** comment ça se fait que tu sois parti?

howdy ['haʊdɪ] **EXCLAM** *Am Fam* salut!

however [haʊ'evə(r)] **ADV 1** *(indicating contrast or contradiction)* cependant, pourtant, toutefois; **I didn't see him, h.** cependant *ou* pourtant je ne l'ai pas vu; **if, h., you have a better suggestion...** si toutefois vous avez une meilleure suggestion (à faire)... **2** *(with adj or adv) (no matter how)* si... que + *subjunctive*, quelque... que + *subjunctive*; **all contributions will be welcome, h. small** si petites soient-elles, toutes les contributions seront les bienvenues; **he'll never do it, h. much** *or* **hard he tries** quelque effort qu'il fasse, il n'y arrivera jamais; **h. cold/hot the weather** même quand il fait très froid/chaud; **h. late/early you arrive, call me** quelle que soit l'heure à laquelle tu arrives, appelle-moi; **h. long it takes (you)** quel que soit le temps que cela (te) prend**; h. much he complains** même s'il se plaint beaucoup **3** *(in questions) (emphatic use)* comment **h. did he find it?** comment a-t-il bien pu le trouver?

CONJ *(in whatever way)* de quelque manière que + *subjunctive*, comme; **it'll be fine, h. you do it** quelle que soit la manière dont vous vous y prenez, ça ira; **we can present it h. you like** *or* **want** on peut le présenter comme vous voulez

howitzer ['haʊɪtsə(r)] **N** *Mil* obusier *m*

howl [haʊl] **N 1** *(of person, animal)* hurlement *m*; *(of child)* braillement *m*, hurlement *m*; *(of wind)* mugissement *m*; **to let out a h. of pain** pousser un hurlement de douleur; **the speech was greeted with howls of derision** le discours a été accueilli par des huées **2** *Electron* effet *m* Larsen

VI 1 *(person, animal)* hurler; *(child)* brailler; *(wind)* mugir; **to h. with laughter/with rage** hurler de rire/de rage **2** *Fam (cry)* chialer

VT crier, hurler; **they howled their defiance at the guards** ils ont hurlé leur colère aux gardes

►**howl down VT SEP** *(speaker)* **they howled him down** ils l'ont réduit au silence par leurs huées

howler ['haʊlə(r)] **N 1** *Fam (blunder)* gaffe *f*, bourde *f*; **schoolboy h.** perle *f (d'écolier)* **2** *Zool (monkey)* (singe *m*) hurleur *m*, alouate *m*

►► *Zool* ***howler monkey*** (singe *m*) hurleur *m*, alouate *m*

howling ['haʊlɪŋ] **N** *(of person, animal)* hurlement *m*, hurlements *mpl*; *(of child)* braillement *m*, braillements *mpl*; *(of wind)* mugissement *m*, mugissements *mpl*

ADJ 1 *(person, animal)* qui hurle; *(child)* qui braille; *(gale, wind)* furieux **2** *Fam (error)* énorme□; *(success)* fou (folle)□

►► *Naut* ***the Howling Fifties*** les cinquantièmes *mpl* hurlants

hoyden ['hɔɪdən] **N** garçon *m* manqué

hoydenish ['hɔɪdənɪʃ] **ADJ** qui fait garçon manqué

hp[1], **HP**[1] [ˌeɪtʃ'piː] **N** *Br (abbr* **hire purchase)** **to buy sth on hp** acheter qch à crédit

hp[2], **HP**[2] *Aut (written abbr* **horsepower)** CV

HQ [ˌeɪtʃ'kjuː] **N** *Mil (abbr* **headquarters)** QG *m*

HR [ˌeɪtʃ'ɑː(r)] **N** *Admin (abbr* **human resources)** RH *fpl*

hr *(written abbr* **hour)** h

HRH *(written abbr* **His/Her Royal Highness)** SAR

HRM [ˌeɪtʃɑː'rem] **N** *Admin (abbr* **human resource management)** GRH *f*

HRT [ˌeɪtʃɑː'tiː] **N** *Med (abbr* **hormone replacement therapy)** THS *m*

HT 1 *(written abbr* **high tension)** HT **2** *Sport (written abbr* **half-time)** mi-temps *f*

HTH *(written abbr* **hope this helps)** *(in e-mails, forums etc)* HTP, j'espère que ça te sera utile

HTML [ˌeɪtʃtiːˌem'el] **N** *Comput (abbr* **Hypertext Markup Language)** HTML *m*

►► ***HTML editor*** éditeur *m* HTML

HTTP [ˌeɪtʃtiːtiː'piː] **N** *Comput (abbr* **Hypertext Transfer Protocol)** protocole *m* HTTP

►► ***HTTP server*** serveur *m* Web

hub [hʌb] **N** *(of wheel)* moyeu *m*; *Fig* centre *m*; *Comput* hub *m*, concentrateur *m*

►► ***hub airport*** aéroport *m* important *(qui sert de plaque tournante)*

hubbub ['hʌbʌb] **N** *(of voices)* brouhaha *m*; *(uproar)* vacarme *m*, tapage *m*

hubby ['hʌbɪ] *(pl* **hubbies)** **N** *Fam* bonhomme *m*, petit mari *m*

hubcap ['hʌbkæp] **N** *Aut* enjoliveur *m* (de roue)

hubris ['hjuːbrɪs] **N** orgueil *m* démesuré, outrecuidance *f*

huckleberry ['hʌkəlbərɪ] *(pl* **huckleberries)** **N** *Bot* airelle *f*, myrtille *f*

huckster ['hʌkstə(r)] **N 1** *(pedlar)* colporteur (euse) *m,f* **2** *(profiteer)* profiteur(euse) *m,f*; **political h.** politicard(e) *m,f*

HUD [hʌd] **N** *Am Formerly (abbr* **Department of Housing and Urban Development)** = ancien ministère américain de l'Urbanisme et du Logement

huddle [ˈhʌdəl] **N 1** *(of people)* petit groupe *m* (serré); *(of objects)* tas *m*, amas *m*; *(of roofs)* enchevêtrement *m*; *Fam* **to go into a h.** se réunir en petit comité **2** *Sport* concentration *f* *(d'une équipe)*

VI 1 *(crowd together)* se blottir; **they huddled round the fire** ils se sont blottis autour du feu **2** *(crouch)* se recroqueviller, se blottir; **he huddled in a corner of his cell** il s'est recroquevillé dans un coin de sa cellule

▸ **huddle together VI** se serrer *ou* se blottir les uns contre les autres; *(for talk)* se mettre en petit groupe *ou* cercle serré; **they huddled together for warmth** ils se serraient *ou* se blottissaient les uns contre les autres pour se tenir chaud

▸ **huddle up VI** se blottir

hue [hjuː] **N 1** *(colour)* teinte *f*, nuance *f* **2** *(aspect)* nuance *f*; **that puts a different h. on the matter** cela fait voir l'affaire sous un autre jour **3** *Br (idiom)* **a h. and cry** une clameur; **to raise a h. and cry against sb/sth** crier haro sur qn/qch

huff [hʌf] **VI** *(idiom)* **to h. and puff** *(with exertion)* haleter; *(with annoyance)* maugréer; *Br Fig* **they'll h. and puff a bit but they won't stop us** ils protesteront, mais ils nous laisseront faire

VT 1 *(in draughts* ▸ *opponent's piece)* souffler **2** *Am Fam (glue, solvents)* sniffer

N *Fam* **to be in a h.** faire la tête, bouder□; *Br* **to take the h.** prendre la mouche; **it's no use getting into a h. about it** ça ne sert à rien de t'énerver□; **he went off in a h.** il est parti fâché□

huffily [ˈhʌfɪlɪ] **ADV** *Fam (reply)* d'un ton vexé *ou* fâché□; *(behave)* avec (mauvaise) humeur□

huffy [ˈhʌfɪ] *(compar* **huffier**, *superl* **huffiest)** **ADJ** *Fam* **to be h.** *(in bad mood)* faire la tête, bouder□; *(by nature)* être susceptible□, être chatouilleux□

hug [hʌg] *(pt & pp* **hugged**, *cont* **hugging)** **VT 1** *(in arms)* serrer dans ses bras, étreindre; *Fig* **to h. oneself with delight (over** *or* **about sth)** se réjouir vivement (de qch) **2** *Fig (idea)* tenir à, chérir; **she hugged the memory of that moment to herself** elle chérissait le souvenir de cet instant **3** *(keep close to)* serrer; *(boat)* **to h. the shore** serrer la côte; *Aut* **don't h. the kerb** ne serrez pas le trottoir; **this car hugs the corners well** cette voiture prend bien les virages; **clothes that h. the figure** vêtements *mpl* qui moulent la silhouette

N 1 *(gesture of affection)* étreinte *f*; **to give sb a h.** serrer qn dans ses bras; **give me a h.** prends-moi dans tes bras; **they greeted each other with hugs and kisses** ce furent de grandes embrassades quand ils se retrouvèrent **2** *(in wrestling)* prise *f*

huge [hjuːdʒ] **ADJ** *(in size, degree)* énorme, immense; *(in extent)* vaste, immense; *(in volume)* énorme, gigantesque

hugely [ˈhjuːdʒlɪ] **ADV** *(increase)* énormément; *(as intensifier)* énormément, extrêmement; **the project has been h. successful/expensive** le projet a été un succès complet/a coûté extrêmement cher

hugeness [ˈhjuːdʒnɪs] **N** immensité *f*; *(of error, demands)* énormité *f*

huggable [ˈhʌgəbəl] **ADJ** trognon

hugger-mugger [ˈhʌgə-] *Old-fashioned* **N 1** *(disorder)* fatras *m*, fouillis *m*, désordre *m* **2** *(secrecy)* secret *m*

ADJ désordonné

ADV en désordre

-hugging [ˈhʌgɪŋ] **SUFF hip/figure/***etc***-h.** *(clothes)* qui moule les hanches/la silhouette/*etc*

Huguenot [ˈhjuːgənəʊ] *Hist* **N** Huguenot(e) *m,f*

ADJ huguenot

Hula-Hoop® [ˈhuːləˌhuːp] **N** Hula-Hoop® *m*

hulk [hʌlk] **N 1** *(ship)* épave *f*; *Pej* vieux rafiot *m*; *Hist (used as prison, storehouse)* ponton *m* **2** *(person, thing)* mastodonte *m*; **a great h. of a man** un malabar

hulking [ˈhʌlkɪŋ] **ADJ 1** *(person)* balourd, massif; *(thing)* gros (grosse), imposant **2** *(as intensifier)* **you h. great oaf!** espèce de malotru!

hull [hʌl] **N 1** *Naut (of ship)* coque *f*; *Mil (of tank)* caisse *f* **2** *(of peas, beans)* cosse *f*, gousse *f*; *(of nut)* écale *f*; *(of strawberry)* calice *m*

VT 1 *(peas)* écosser; *(nuts)* écaler, décortiquer; *(grains)* décortiquer; *(strawberries)* équeuter **2** *(ship)* percer la coque de

hullabaloo [ˌhʌləbəˈluː] **N** *Fam* raffut *m*, chambard *m*, barouf *m*; **the press made a real h. about it** la presse en a fait tout un foin

hullo = **hello**

hum [hʌm] *(pt & pp* **hummed**, *cont* **humming)** **VI 1** *(audience, bee, wires)* bourdonner; *(person)* fredonner, chantonner; *Electron* ronfler; *(air conditioner)* ronronner; **the motors hummed into action** les moteurs se sont mis à ronfler *ou* vrombir; *Fig* **everything was humming along nicely** tout marchait comme sur des roulettes

2 *(be lively)* grouiller; **the airport/town was humming with activity** l'aéroport/la ville bourdonnait d'activité; **the party was just beginning to h. when the police arrived** la fête commençait à s'animer quand la police est arrivée

3 *Br Fam (stink)* cocotter

4 *(idiom)* **to h. and haw** *(mumble)* bafouiller; *Fig (hesitate)* tergiverser, tourner autour du pot; **he hummed and hawed before getting to the point** il a bafouillé *ou* hésité avant d'en venir au fait

VT *(tune)* fredonner, chantonner

N 1 *(of bees, voices)* bourdonnement *m*; *(of vehicle)* vrombissement *m*; *Electron* ronflement *m*; *(of machine)* ronronnement *m*; **the distant h. of traffic** le ronronnement lointain de la circulation **2** *Br Fam (stench)* puanteur□ *f*, mauvaise odeur□ *f*; **there's a bit of a h. in here!** ça cocotte là-dedans!

EXCLAM hem!, hum!

human [ˈhjuːmən] **ADJ** humain; **he's only h.** personne n'est parfait; **the accident was caused by h. error** l'accident était dû à une erreur *ou* défaillance humaine; **it's those little h. touches that make all the difference** ce sont les petites touches personnelles qui font toute la différence

N (être *m*) humain *m*

▸▸ ***human being*** être *m* humain; ***human cloning*** clonage *m* humain; *Ind* ***human engineering*** gestion *f* des relations humaines; *(ergonomics)* ergonomie *f*; *Med* ***human growth hormone*** hormone *f* somatotrope *ou* de croissance, somatotrophine *f*; *Med* ***human immunodeficiency virus*** virus *m* d'immunodéficience humaine; ***human nature*** nature *f* humaine; ***the human race*** la race *ou* l'espèce *f* humaine; *Admin* ***human resources*** ressources *fpl* humaines; ***human rights*** droits *mpl* de l'homme; **a h. rights organization** une organisation pour les droits de l'homme; ***human shield*** bouclier *m* humain; ***human trafficking*** trafic *m ou* traite *f* d'êtres humains

> Attention: ne pas confondre avec **humane**.

humane [hjuːˈmeɪn] **ADJ 1** *(compassionate* ▸ *action, person)* humain, plein d'humanité; *(▸ treatment)* humain; *(▸ killing)* qui évite de faire souffrir, humain; **a h. method of killing animals** une méthode pour abattre les animaux sans cruauté **2** *Formal Old-fashioned (education)* humaniste

▸▸ ***humane society*** *(for animals)* société *f* protectrice des animaux; *(for good works)* société *f ou* association *f* humanitaire

> Attention: ne pas confondre avec **human**.

humanely [hjuːˈmeɪnlɪ] **ADV** humainement

humanism [ˈhjuːmənɪzəm] **N** *Phil* humanisme *m*

humanist [ˈhjuːmənɪst] *Phil* **N** humaniste *mf*

ADJ humaniste

humanistic [ˌhjuːməˈnɪstɪk] **ADJ** humaniste

humanitarian [hjuːˌmænɪˈteərɪən] **N** humanitaire *mf*

ADJ humanitaire

▸▸ ***humanitarian aid*** aide *f* humanitaire; ***humanitarian sector*** secteur *m* humanitaire; ***humanitarian worker*** humanitaire *mf*

humanity [hjuːˈmænətɪ] **N 1** *(mankind)* humanité *f*; **for the good of h.** pour le bien de l'humanité **2** *(compassion)* humanité *f*; **to treat sb with h.** traiter qn avec humanité

• **humanities N** *Univ (arts)* lettres *fpl*; *(classical culture)* lettres *fpl* classiques

humanize, -ise [ˈhjuːmənaɪz] **VT** humaniser

humankind [ˌhjuːmənˈkaɪnd] **N** l'humanité *f*, le genre humain

humanly [ˈhjuːmənlɪ] **ADV** humainement; **I'll do all that is h. possible to help her** je ferai tout ce qui est humainement possible pour l'aider

humanoid [ˈhjuːmənɔɪd] **N** humanoïde *mf*

ADJ humanoïde

humble [ˈhʌmbəl] **ADJ 1** *(meek)* humble; **please accept my h. apologies** veuillez accepter mes humbles excuses; **in my h. opinion** à mon humble avis; *Fig* **to eat h. pie** faire de plates excuses, faire amende honorable **2** *(modest)* modeste; **she has h. origins** elle a des origines modestes; **to come from a h. background** venir d'un milieu modeste; *Hum* **welcome to my h. abode** bienvenue dans mon humble *ou* ma modeste demeure

VT humilier, mortifier; **to h. oneself before sb** s'humilier devant qn; **it was a humbling experience** c'était une expérience humiliante

humblebee [ˈhʌmbəlˌbiː] **N** *Entom (insect)* bourdon *m*

humbleness [ˈhʌmbəlnɪs] **N** humilité *f*

humbling [ˈhʌmbəlɪŋ] **ADJ** *(experience)* humiliant

N *(of person)* humiliation *f*

humbly [ˈhʌmbəlɪ] **ADV 1** *(speak, ask)* humblement, avec humilité **2** *(live)* modestement; **h. born** d'origine modeste *ou* humble

humbug [ˈhʌmbʌg] **N 1** *(person)* charlatan *m*, fumiste *mf*; *(UNCOUNT) (deception)* charlatanisme *m* **2** *(UNCOUNT) (nonsense)* balivernes *fpl* **3** *Br (sweet)* berlingot *m* à la menthe

humdinger [ˌhʌmˈdɪŋə(r)] **N** *Fam* **1** *(person)* **she's a real h.!** elle est vraiment extra *ou* sensass *ou* terrible! **2** *(thing)* **that was a h. of a game!** quel match extraordinaire!; **they had a real h. of a row!** ils se sont engueulés, quelque chose de bien!

humdrum [ˈhʌmdrʌm] **ADJ** *(person, story)* banal; *(task, life)* monotone, banal, routinier; **I'm sick of this h. routine** j'en ai marre de ce train-train

N monotonie *f*, banalité *f*

humerus [ˈhjuːmərəs] *(pl* **humeri** [-raɪ]) **N** *Anat* humérus *m*

humid [ˈhjuːmɪd] **ADJ** humide

humidifier [hjuːˈmɪdɪfaɪə(r)] **N** humidificateur *m*

humidify [hjuːˈmɪdɪfaɪ] *(pt & pp* **humidified)** **VT** humidifier

humidity [hjuːˈmɪdətɪ] **N** humidité *f*

humidor [ˈhjuːmɪdɔː(r)] **N** cave *f* à cigares

humiliate [hjuːˈmɪlɪeɪt] **VT** humilier; **he refused to h. himself by apologizing to them** il a refusé de s'humilier en leur présentant des excuses

humiliating [hjuːˈmɪlɪeɪtɪŋ] **ADJ** humiliant

humiliation [hjuːˌmɪlɪˈeɪʃən] **N** humiliation *f*

humility [hjuːˈmɪlətɪ] **N** humilité *f*

Hummer® [ˈhʌmə(r)] **N** *Aut* Hummer® *m* *(grosse voiture tout-terrain)*

humming [ˈhʌmɪŋ] **N** *(of bees, voices)* bourdonnement *m*; *(of air conditioner, traffic)* ronronnement *m*; *(of tune)* fredonnement *m*

▸▸ ***humming top*** toupie *f* ronflante

hummingbird [ˈhʌmɪŋbɜːd] **N** *Orn* oiseau-mouche *m*, colibri *m*

hummock [ˈhʌmək] **N 1** *(knoll)* monticule *m*, tertre *m*, mamelon *m* **2** *(in ice field)* hummock *m*

humor, -humored *etc Am* = **humour, -humoured** *etc*

humorist [ˈhjuːmərɪst] **N** humoriste *mf*

humorous [ˈhjuːmərəs] **ADJ** *(witty* ▸ *remark)* plein d'humour, amusant; *(▸ person)* plein d'humour, drôle; **he replied in (a) h. vein** il a répondu sur le mode humoristique

humorously [ˈhjuːmərəslɪ] **ADV** avec humour

humour, *Am* **humor** [ˈhjuːmə(r)] **N 1** *(wit, fun)* humour *m*; **the play is devoid of h.** la pièce est dénuée *ou* dépourvue d'humour; **the h. of the situation** le côté comique de la situation; **sense of h.** sens *m* de l'humour; **she has a sense of h.** elle a le sens de l'humour; **he has a very dry sense of h.** il est très pince-sans-rire **2** *Formal (mood)* humeur *f*, disposition *f*; **in a good/bad h.** de bonne/mauvaise humeur; *Literary* **to be out of h.** être de mauvaise humeur **3** *Arch (bodily fluid)* humeur *f*; **the four humours** les quatre humeurs *fpl*

VT *(person ▸ indulge, gratify)* faire plaisir à; *(▸ treat tactfully)* ménager; *(whim, fantasy)* se prêter à; **don't try to h. me** n'essaie pas de m'amadouer

> When translating the English word **humour**, note that the French words **humour** and **humeur** are not interchangeable. **Humour** is used as a translation when referring to somebody's sense of humour or to the humorous quality of something, while **humeur** is used when referring to somebody's mood or temperament.

humourless, *Am* **humorless** ['hju:məlɪs] **ADJ** *(person)* qui manque d'humour; *(book, situation, speech)* sans humour; **a h. smile** un sourire pincé

hump [hʌmp] **N 1** *(on flat surface, of hunchback, camel)* bosse *f*; *(hillock)* bosse *f*, mamelon *m*; *(bump)* tas *m*; *Fig* **we're over the h. now** on a fait le plus dur *ou* gros maintenant **2** *Br Fam* **to have the h.** être de mauvais poil; **to get** *or* **to take the h.** se mettre à faire la gueule

VT 1 *(back)* arrondir, arquer **2** *Fam (carry)* trimbaler, trimballer **3** *very Fam (have sex with)* baiser

VI *very Fam (have sex)* baiser, s'envoyer en l'air

humpback ['hʌmpbæk] **N 1** *(person)* bossu(e) *m,f* **2** *Zool (whale)* baleine *f* à bosse

▸▸ ***humpback bridge*** pont *m* en dos d'âne; *Zool* ***humpback whale*** baleine *f* à bosse, mégaptère *m*

humpbacked ['hʌmpbækt] **ADJ** bossu

▸▸ ***humpbacked bridge*** pont *m* en dos d'âne

humph [mm, hʌmf] **EXCLAM** hum!

humus ['hju:məs] **N** humus *m*

Humvee® ['hʌmvi:] **N** *Mil* Humvee® *m (véhicule militaire tout-terrain)*

Hun [hʌn] *(pl* **inv** *or* **Huns**) **N 1** *Antiq (from Asia)* Hun *m* **2** *Fam Old-fashioned Pej (German)* Boche *m*

hunch [hʌntʃ] **N 1** *(inkling)* pressentiment *m*, intuition *f*; **I have a h. we'll meet again** j'ai comme un pressentiment que nous nous reverrons; **to play** *or* **to follow one's h.** suivre son intuition; **to act on a h.** suivre son instinct; **it's only a h.** ce n'est qu'une idée **2** *(hump)* bosse *f*

VT to h. one's back arrondir le dos; **to h. one's shoulders** voûter les épaules; **don't h. (up) your shoulders like that!** ne rentre pas la tête dans les épaules comme ça!

hunchback ['hʌntʃbæk] **N** *(person)* bossu(e) *m,f*

hunchbacked ['hʌntʃbækt] **ADJ** bossu

hundred ['hʌndrəd] **N** cent *m*; **one h. and one** cent un; **two h.** deux cents; **two h. and one** deux cent un; **about a h., a h. odd** une centaine; **in nineteen h.** en dix-neuf cents; **in nineteen h. and ten** en dix-neuf cent dix; **I'll never forget him (even) if I live to be a h.** même si je deviens centenaire, je ne l'oublierai jamais; **give me $500 in hundreds** donnez-moi 500 dollars en billets de cent; **in the seventeen hundreds** au dix-huitième siècle; **hundreds of** des centaines de; **I've asked you hundreds of times!** je te l'ai demandé cent fois!; **hundreds and thousands of people** des milliers de gens; **they were dying in their hundreds** *or* **by the h.** ils mouraient par centaines

PRON cent; **about a h.** une centaine; **I need a h. (of them)** il m'en faut cent, j'en ai besoin de cent

ADJ cent; **a h. guests** cent invités; **six h. pages** six cents pages; **on page a h.** (à la) page cent; **about a h. metres** une centaine de mètres; **one** *or* **a h. percent** cent pour cent; **I'm a h. percent sure** j'en suis absolument certain; **to be a h. percent behind sb** soutenir qn à fond; **to give a** *or* **one h. percent** se donner à fond; **I'm not feeling a h. percent** je ne me sens pas dans mon assiette; *Fig* **I've got a h. and one things to do** j'ai mille choses à faire; **if I've told you once, I've told you a h. times!** je te l'ai dit cent fois!

▸▸ ***hundreds and thousands*** *(confectionery)* vermicelles *mpl* en sucre, nonpareilles *fpl*; *Hist* ***the Hundred Years' War*** la guerre de Cent Ans

hundredfold ['hʌndrədfəʊld] **ADJ** centuple

ADV he has increased his initial investment (by) a h. il a multiplié par cent son investissement initial, il a centuplé son investissement initial

hundredth ['hʌndrədθ] **N 1** *(fraction)* centième *m* **2** *(in series)* centième *mf*

ADJ centième

ADV *(in contest)* en centième position, à la centième place; *see also* **fifth**

hundredweight ['hʌndrədweɪt] **N** *Br* = 50,8 kg, (poids *m* de) 112 livres *fpl*; *Am* = 45,36 kg, (poids *m* de) 100 livres *fpl*

hung [hʌŋ] *pt & pp of* **hang**

ADJ *Fam* **h. up** coincé; **to be h. up on sb/sth** faire une fixation sur qn/qch; **to be h. up about sth** *(personal problem)* être complexé par qch; *(sexual matters)* être coincé quand il s'agit de qch

▸▸ *Pol & Law* ***hung jury*** jury *m* partagé; ***hung parliament*** parlement *m* sans majorité

Hungarian [hʌŋ'geərɪən] **N 1** *(person)* Hongrois (e) *m,f* **2** *(language)* hongrois *m*

ADJ hongrois

COMP *(embassy)* de Hongrie; *(history)* de la Hongrie; *(teacher)* de hongrois

Hungary ['hʌŋgərɪ] **N** *Geog* Hongrie *f*

hunger ['hʌŋgə(r)] **N** faim *f*; **a conference on world h.** une conférence sur la faim dans le monde; *Fig* **he was driven by a h. for truth/knowledge** il était poussé par une soif de vérité/de savoir

VI *Fig* **to h. after** *or* **for sth** avoir faim *ou* soif de qch; **he hungered for revenge** il avait faim *ou* soif de vengeance

▸▸ ***hunger strike*** grève *f* de la faim; **to go on (a) h. strike** faire la grève de la faim; ***hunger striker*** gréviste *mf* de la faim

hungover [hʌŋ'əʊvə(r)] **ADJ to be h.** avoir la gueule de bois

hungrily ['hʌŋgrəlɪ] **ADV** *(eat)* voracement, avidement; *Fig (read, listen)* avidement; **she eyed his lunch h.** elle jeta un regard de convoitise sur son déjeuner

hungry ['hʌŋgrɪ] *(compar* **hungrier**, *superl* **hungriest**) **ADJ 1** *(for food)* **to be h.** avoir faim; **we're very h.** nous avons très faim, nous sommes affamés; **he still felt h.** il avait encore faim; **she looked tired and h.** elle avait l'air fatiguée et affamée; **are you getting h.?** est-ce que tu commences à avoir faim?; **to go h.** souffrir de la faim; **he'd rather go h. than cook for himself** il se passerait de manger plutôt que de faire la cuisine; **that night he went h.** ce soir-là il ne mangea pas à sa faim; **this is h. work!** ce travail donne faim! **2** *Fig (desirous)* avide; **h. for affection** avide d'affection; **she was h. for news of her family** elle attendait avec impatience des nouvelles de sa famille; *Fig* **you have to be h. to make it to the top** ce sont les battants qui réussissent

hunk [hʌŋk] **N 1** *(piece)* gros morceau *m* **2** *Fam (man)* beau mec *m*; **he's a real h.** il est beau mec

hunky ['hʌŋkɪ] *(compar* **hunkier**, *superl* **hunkiest**) **ADJ** *Fam (man ▸ with good body)* bien foutu; *(▸ big and strong)* baraqué

hunky-dory [-'dɔ:rɪ] **ADJ** *Fam* **to be h.** être au poil; **everything's just h.!** tout baigne (dans l'huile)!

hunt [hʌnt] **VT 1** *(for food, sport ▸ of person)* chasser, faire la chasse à; *(▸ of animal)* chasser; **to h. whales** pêcher la baleine

2 *Br (area)* chasser dans; **to h. the pack** diriger la meute; **he hunts his horse all winter** il monte son cheval à la chasse tout l'hiver

3 *(pursue)* pourchasser, poursuivre; **he was being hunted by the police** il était pourchassé *ou* recherché par la police

4 *(drive out)* chasser; **people were hunted from their homes** des gens étaient chassés de leurs foyers

5 h. the slipper *or* **the thimble** *(game)* cache-tampon *m*

VI 1 *(for food, sport)* chasser; **to go hunting** aller à la chasse; **to h. for sth** *(person)* chasser *ou* faire la chasse à qch; *(animal)* chasser qch **2** *(search)* chercher (partout); **she hunted (around** *or* **about) in her bag for her keys** elle a fouillé dans son sac à la recherche de ses clefs; **you'll just have to h. until you find it** vous n'avez qu'à chercher jusqu'à ce que vous le trouviez; *Fig* **I've hunted high and low for it** j'ai remué ciel et terre pour le retrouver; **I've hunted all over town for a linen jacket** j'ai fait toute la ville pour trouver une veste en lin

Tech (gauge) osciller; *(engine)* pomper

N 1 *(sporting activity)* chasse *f*; *(hunters)* chasse *f*, chasseurs *mpl*; *(area)* chasse *f*; *(fox-hunt)* chasse *f* au renard; **a tiger/bear h.** une chasse au tigre/à l'ours **2** *(search)* chasse *f*, recherche *f*; **the h. is on for the terrorists** la chasse aux terroristes est en cours; **local people joined in the h. for the child** des gens de la région se sont joints aux recherches pour retrouver l'enfant; **I've had a h. for your scarf** j'ai cherché ton écharpe partout, j'ai tout retourné pour trouver ton écharpe

▸▸ *Br* ***hunt saboteur*** = personne qui intervient sur le terrain pour tenter d'arrêter une chasse à courre

▸ **hunt down VT SEP** *(animal)* forcer, traquer *(person)* traquer; *(thing, facts)* dénicher; *(abuses, errors)* faire la chasse à; *(truth)* débusquer

▸ **hunt out VT SEP** *Br* dénicher, découvrir; **I've hunted out that book you wanted to borrow** j'ai déniché le livre que vous vouliez emprunter

▸ **hunt up VT SEP** *Br (look up)* rechercher; **I'm going to the library to h. up that article she mentioned** je vais à la bibliothèque rechercher cet article dont elle parlait

hunted ['hʌntɪd] **ADJ** traqué; **he has a h. look about him** il a un air persécuté

hunter ['hʌntə(r)] **N 1** *(as sport ▸ person)* chasseur(euse) *m,f*; *(▸ horse)* cheval *m* de chasse; *(▸ dog)* chien *m* courant *ou* de chasse **2** *(who searches)* chasseur(euse) *m,f*; *(pursuer)* poursuivant(e) *m,f* **3** *(watch)* montre *f* à double boîtier

▸▸ ***hunter's moon*** = pleine lune qui suit celle de l'équinoxe d'automne

hunting ['hʌntɪŋ] **N 1** *(sporting activity)* chasse *f*; *Br (fox-hunting)* chasse *f* au renard; *Hist (mounted deer-hunt)* chasse *f* à courre; *Hist (as an art)* vénerie *f* **2** *(pursuit)* chasse *f*, poursuite *f*; **bargain h.** la chasse aux bonnes affaires

COMP *(boots, gun, knife, licence)* de chasse

▸▸ ***hunting dog*** chien *m* de chasse; *Sport & Fig* ***hunting ground*** terrain *m* de chasse; *Hunt* ***hunting horn*** cor *m ou* trompe *f* de chasse; *Hunt* ***hunting lodge*** pavillon *m* de chasse; ***hunting pink*** **N** *(UNCOUNT) Br* habit *m* rouge de chasse à courre **ADJ** rouge chasseur *(inv)*; *Hunt* ***hunting season*** saison *f* de la chasse

> **THE HUNTING DEBATE**
>
> Pendant de nombreuses années, la chasse à courre au renard a constitué pour le gouvernement britannique un dossier controversé. La majorité de la population était favorable à une interdiction pure et simple mais un groupe de pression pro-chasse très actif, la Countryside Alliance, s'opposait à toute réforme et mettait l'accent sur les conséquences néfastes qu'une telle mesure aurait sur le mode de vie rural et sur l'emploi dans les campagnes. En 2005 une loi fut finalement votée, interdisant ce type de chasse. Cependant certains irréductibles continuent à s'opposer à cette décision. Voir aussi l'encadré sur **The Countryside Debate**.

Huntington's chorea ['hʌntɪŋtənz-] **N** *Med* chorée *f* de Huntington

huntress ['hʌntrɪs] **N** chasseuse *f*; *Myth* **Diana the H.** Diane chasseresse

huntsman ['hʌntsmən] *(pl* **huntsmen** [-mən]) **N 1** *(hunter)* chasseur *m* **2** *(master of hounds)* veneur *m*

hurdle ['hɜ:dəl] **N 1** *Sport* haie *f*; **the 400-metre hurdles** le 400 mètres haies; **to run a h.** *or* **hurdles race** faire *ou* courir une course de haies; **she's the British hurdles champion** elle est la championne britannique de course de haies; **to take** *or* **to clear a h.** franchir une haie **2** *Fig* obstacle *m*; **she took that h. in her stride** elle a franchi cet obstacle sans le moindre effort; **the next h. will be getting funding for the project** la prochaine difficulté sera d'obtenir des fonds pour le projet **3** *(for fences)* claie *f*

VI *Sport* faire de la course de haies

hurdler ['hɜːdlə(r)] N *(person)* coureur(euse) *m,f (qui fait des courses de haies)*; *(horse)* sauteur *m*

hurdling ['hɜːdlɪŋ] N *Sport (in athletics) & Horse-racing* course *f* de haies; *(part of competition)* courses *fpl* de haies; **the world 400-metre h. champion** le champion du monde du 400 mètres haies

hurdy-gurdy ['hɜːdɪˌgɜːdɪ] *(pl* **hurdy-gurdies)** N *Mus* **1** *(barrel organ)* orgue *m* de Barbarie; **a h. man** un joueur d'orgue de Barbarie **2** *(medieval instrument)* vielle *f*

hurl [hɜːl] VT **1** *(throw)* lancer, jeter (avec violence); **to h. oneself at sb/sth** se ruer sur qn/qch; **he hurled a vase at him** il lui a lancé un vase à la figure; **they were hurled to the ground** ils ont été précipités *ou* jetés à terre; **she hurled herself off the top of the tower** elle s'est jetée du haut de la tour; **he hurled himself into the fight** il s'est jeté dans la bagarre; **the boat was hurled onto the rocks** le bateau a été projeté sur les rochers **2** *(yell)* lancer, jeter; **to h. abuse at sb** lancer des injures à qn, accabler qn d'injures

VI *Fam (vomit)* dégobiller, gerber

hurling ['hɜːlɪŋ] N *Sport* = jeu irlandais voisin du hockey sur gazon

hurly-burly [ˌhɜːlɪ'bɜːlɪ] *Br* N tohu-bohu *m inv*; **the h. of city life** le tourbillon de la vie urbaine

ADJ turbulent

hurrah [hʊ'rɑː], **hurray** [hʊ'reɪ] N hourra *m*

EXCLAM hourra!; **h. for the cook!** pour le chef, hip hip hip hourra!

hurricane ['hʌrɪkən] N *Met* ouragan *m*; **H. Mabel** l'ouragan *m* Mabel

▸▸ *Met* ***hurricane force*** force *f* douze (sur l'échelle Beaufort); ***hurricane lamp*** lampe-tempête *f*

hurried ['hʌrɪd] ADJ *(meeting, reply, gesture, trip)* rapide; *(departure, steps)* précipité; *(judgment, decision)* hâtif; *(work)* fait à la hâte; **to have a h. meal** manger à la hâte; **I wrote a h. note to reassure her** j'ai écrit un mot à la hâte *ou* un mot bref pour la rassurer; **they only had time for a few h. words** ils ont juste eu le temps d'échanger quelques mots rapides

hurriedly ['hʌrɪdlɪ] ADV *(examine)* à la hâte; *(leave)* précipitamment; **she passed h. over the unpleasant details** elle passa en vitesse sur les détails désagréables

hurry ['hʌrɪ] *(pl* **hurries,** *pt & pp* **hurried)** N **1** *(rush)* hâte *f*, précipitation *f*; **to be in a h.** être pressé; **not now, I'm in too much of a h.** pas maintenant, je suis trop pressé; **to be in a h. to do sth** avoir hâte de faire qch; **to do sth in a h.** faire qch à la hâte; **to leave in a h.** sortir à la hâte *ou* en courant; **there's no big** *or* **great h.** rien ne presse; **are you in a h. for it?** c'est urgent?; **there's no h.** cela ne presse pas; **what's the** *or* **your h.?** qu'est-ce qui (vous) presse?; **you won't see her again in a h.** vous ne la reverrez pas de sitôt; *Br Fam* **he won't try that again in a h.!** il ne ressayera pas de sitôt!, il n'est pas près de ressayer!

2 *(eagerness)* empressement *m*; **he's in no h. to see her again** il n'est pas pressé *ou* il n'a aucune hâte de la revoir

VI se dépêcher, se presser, se hâter; **I must** *or* **I'd better h.** il faut que je me dépêche; **you don't have to h. over that report** vous pouvez prendre votre temps pour faire ce rapport; **he hurried into/out of the room** il est entré dans/sorti de la pièce en toute hâte *ou* précipitamment; **he hurried down the stairs** il a descendu l'escalier en toute hâte *ou* précipitamment; **he hurried (over) to the bank** il s'est précipité à la banque, il s'est rendu à la banque en toute hâte; **to h. after sb** courir après qn; **h.! it's already started** dépêche-toi! c'est déjà commencé

VT **1** *(chivvy along)* faire se dépêcher, presser, bousculer; **don't h. him** ne le bouscule pas; **she won't be hurried, you can't h. her** vous ne la ferez pas se dépêcher; **they hurried him through customs** ils lui ont fait passer la douane à la hâte

2 *(preparations, work)* activer, presser, hâter; **this decision can't be hurried** cette décision exige d'être prise sans hâte

3 *(transport hastily)* emmener d'urgence; **she was hurried to hospital** elle a été transportée à l'hôpital en (toute) hâte

▸ **hurry along** VT SEP *(person)* faire presser le pas à, faire se dépêcher *ou* s'activer; *(work)* activer, accélérer

VI marcher d'un pas pressé; **h. along now!** pressons, pressons!; **we'd better be hurrying along** on ferait mieux de se presser

▸ **hurry away** VT SEP **he hurried the children away from the scene of the accident** il a vite éloigné les enfants du lieu de l'accident

VI partir précipitamment

▸ **hurry back** VI revenir *ou* retourner à la hâte; **she'll soon come hurrying back** elle reviendra vite; **don't h. back, I'll take care of everything** ne te presse pas de revenir, je me chargerai de tout

▸ **hurry off** VT SEP **they hurried her off to hospital** ils l'ont emmenée à l'hôpital en (toute) hâte

VI partir précipitamment, se sauver

▸ **hurry on** VT SEP *(person)* faire hâter le pas à; *(work)* activer

VI se dépêcher, continuer à la hâte *ou* en hâte; **can we h. on to the next item on the agenda?** peut-on vite passer *ou* passer sans tarder à la prochaine question inscrite à l'ordre du jour?

▸ **hurry up** VT SEP *(person)* faire se dépêcher; *(production, work)* activer; **I'll go and h. them up** je vais leur dire de se dépêcher

VI se dépêcher, se presser; **h. up!** dépêche-toi!; **h. up and get dressed** dépêche-toi de t'habiller; **h. up with that packing** dépêche-toi de faire ces bagages

hurt [hɜːt] *(pt & pp* **hurt)** VT **1** *(cause physical pain to)* faire mal à; **to h. oneself** se faire mal; **mind you don't h. yourself** faites attention de ne pas vous faire mal *ou* vous blesser; **I h. my elbow on the door** je me suis fait mal au coude contre la porte; **is your back hurting (you) today?** est-ce que tu as mal au dos aujourd'hui?; **where does it h. (you)?** où est-ce que vous avez mal?, où cela vous fait-il mal?; **the fall didn't h. him** il ne s'est pas fait mal en tombant

2 *(injure)* blesser; **two people were h. in the crash** deux personnes ont été blessées dans la collision; *Fam* **do as I say and no one gets h.!** faites ce que je dis et il n'y aura pas de casse!

3 *(upset)* blesser, faire de la peine à; **he was very h. by your criticism** il a été très blessé par vos critiques; **to h. sb's feelings** blesser *ou* froisser qn

4 *(disadvantage)* nuire à; **the new tax will h. the middle classes most** ce sont les classes moyennes qui seront les plus touchées par le nouvel impôt; **a bit of fresh air won't h. you** un peu d'air frais *ou* de grand air ne te fera pas de mal

5 *(damage ▸ crops, machine)* abîmer, endommager; *(▸ eyesight)* abîmer

VI faire mal; **it hurts** ça fait mal; **my head hurts** ma tête me fait mal; **where does it h.?** où est-ce que vous avez mal?; **I h. all over** j'ai mal partout; *Am* **he's hurting** il a mal; **nothing hurts like the truth** il n'y a que la vérité qui blesse

N **1** *(physical pain)* mal *m*; *(wound)* blessure *f* **2** *(mental pain)* peine *f*; **he wanted to make up for the h. he had caused them** il voulait réparer la peine qu'il leur avait faite **3** *(damage)* tort *m*

ADJ **1** *(physically)* blessé; **are you h.?** êtes-vous blessé?; **he was more frightened than h.** il a eu plus de peur que de mal **2** *(offended)* froissé, blessé; **a h. expression** un regard meurtri *ou* blessé; **don't feel h.** ne le prends pas mal

hurtful ['hɜːtfʊl] ADJ **1** *(remark)* blessant, offensant; *(memory)* pénible; **they ended up saying h. things to each other** ils ont fini par se dire des méchancetés; **what a h. thing to say!** comme c'est méchant *ou* cruel de dire cela! **2** *(detrimental)* préjudiciable, nuisible

hurtle ['hɜːtəl] VT *(throw violently)* lancer de toutes ses forces

VI **to h. along** avancer à toute vitesse *ou* allure; **he went hurtling down the stairs** il dévala les escaliers; **the motorbike came hurtling towards him** la moto fonça sur lui; **a rock hurtled through the air** une pierre a fendu l'air

husband ['hʌzbənd] N mari *m*, époux *m*; **are they h. and wife?** sont-ils mari et femme?; **they lived (together) as h. and wife** ils vivaient maritalement *ou* comme mari et femme

VT *(resources, strength)* ménager, économiser

husband-and-wife ADJ **h. business** entreprise *f* appartenant à deux époux *ou* à un couple marié; **h. team** équipe *f* formée par deux époux

husbandry ['hʌzbəndrɪ] N **1** *Agr* agriculture *f*; *(as science)* agronomie *f* **2** *Formal (thrift)* économie *f*; **good h.** bonne gestion *f*

hush [hʌʃ] N silence *m*, calme *m*; **a h. fell over the room** un silence s'est installé *ou* s'est fait dans la salle

EXCLAM *(gen)* silence!; *(stop talking)* chut!

VT **1** *(silence)* faire taire; **she hushed the murmurs/the crowd with a gesture** elle a fait taire les murmures/la foule d'un geste **2** *(appease)* apaiser, calmer

VI se taire

▸▸ *Fam* ***hush money*** *(UNCOUNT)* pot-de-vin◻ *m (pour acheter le silence)*; **to pay sb h. money** acheter le silence de qn◻; *Am Culin* ***hush puppy*** = sorte de beignet à base de farine de maïs

▸ **hush up** VT SEP **1** *(affair)* étouffer; *(witness)* faire taire, empêcher de parler **2** *(noisy person)* faire taire

hushed [hʌʃt] ADJ *(whisper, voice)* étouffé; *(conversation)* étouffé, discret(ète); *(silence)* profond, grand; **to speak in h. tones** parler à voix basse

hush-hush ADJ *Fam* archi-secret(ète); **it's all very h.** tout cela c'est archi-secret *ou* top secret

husk [hʌsk] N *(of wheat, oats)* balle *f*; *(of maize, rice)* enveloppe *f*; *(of nut)* écale *f*

VT *(oats, barley)* monder; *(maize)* éplucher; *(rice)* décortiquer; *(wheat)* vanner; *(nuts)* écaler

huskily ['hʌskɪlɪ] ADV *(speak ▸ naturally)* d'une voix rauque; *(▸ because of sore throat)* d'une voix enrouée; *(sing)* d'une voix voilée

huskiness ['hʌskɪnɪs] N enrouement *m*

husky ['hʌskɪ] *(compar* **huskier,** *superl* **huskiest,** *pl* **huskies)** ADJ **1** *(voice ▸ naturally)* rauque; *(▸ because of sore throat)* enroué **2** *Fam (burly)* costaud

N *(dog)* chien *m* esquimau *ou* de traîneau, husky *m*

hussar [hʊ'zɑː(r)] N *Mil* hussard *m*

hussy ['hʌsɪ] *(pl* **hussies)** N *Arch or Hum (shameless woman)* gourgandine *f*; **you shameless** *or* **brazen h.!** espèce de gourgandine!

hustings ['hʌstɪŋz] NPL *Br* **1** *(campaign)* campagne *f* électorale; **to go/to be out on the h.** partir/être en campagne électorale **2** *(occasion for speeches)* débat *m* public *(pendant la campagne électorale)*; **at the h.** au cours du débat public

hustle ['hʌsəl] VT **1** *(cause to move ▸ quickly)* presser; *(▸ roughly)* bousculer, pousser; **to h. sb in/out** faire entrer/sortir qn énergiquement; **after that, I was hustled off to boarding school** après cela, j'ai été expédié au pensionnat; **the doctor was hustled through the crowd** on a frayé un chemin au médecin dans la foule; **he was hustled away** *or* **off by two men** il a été emmené de force par deux hommes

2 *Fam (obtain ▸ resourcefully)* faire tout pour avoir◻; *(▸ underhandedly)* magouiller pour avoir; **they hustled that building permit** ils ont magouillé pour obtenir ce permis de construire

3 *Am Fam (swindle)* rouler, arnaquer; *(pressure)* **to h. sb into doing sth** forcer la main à qn pour qu'il fasse qch; **he hustled me out of $100** il m'a roulé *ou* arnaqué de 100 dollars

4 *Am Fam (steal)* piquer

5 *Am very Fam (of prostitute)* racoler; **she hustles the bars** elle racole dans les bars

VI **1** *Br (shove)* bousculer; **don't h. in the back!** ne bousculez pas derrière!

2 *(hurry)* se dépêcher, se presser; **we'd better h.!** on ferait mieux de se dépêcher *ou* presser!

3 *Am Fam (work hard)* se bagarrer (pour réussir)◻; **they want that market and they're ready to h. for it** ils veulent ce marché et ils sont prêts à tout (faire) *ou* à se bagarrer pour l'avoir

4 *Am very Fam (of prostitute)* faire le tapin, tapiner

N **1** *(crush)* bousculade *f* **2** *(bustle)* grande activité *f*; **the h. and bustle of the big city** le tourbillon d'activité des grandes villes **3** *Am Fam (swindle)* arnaque *f*

hustler ['hʌslə(r)] N **1** *Fam (dynamic person)* battant(e) *m,f* **2** *Fam (swindler)* arnaqueur(euse) *m,f* **3** *Am very Fam (prostitute)* putain *f*

hut [hʌt] N *(primitive dwelling)* hutte *f*; *(shed)* cabane *f*, baraque *f*; *(alpine)* refuge *m*, chalet-refuge *m*; *Mil* baraquement *m*

hutch [hʌtʃ] N **1** *(cage)* cage *f*; *(for rabbits)* clapier *m*
2 *(chest)* coffre *m*
3 *Am (Welsh dresser)* vaisselier *m*
4 *Tech (kneading trough)* pétrin *m*, huche *f*

hutment ['hʌtmənt] N *Mil* baraquements *mpl*

hyacinth ['haɪəsɪnθ] N **1** *Bot* jacinthe *f*; **wood** *or* **wild h.** jacinthe *f* des bois **2** *(gem)* hyacinthe *f* **3** *(colour)* bleu *m* jacinthe, bleu *m* violet
ADJ *(colour)* bleu jacinthe *(inv)*, bleu violet *(inv)*

hyaena = **hyena**

hybrid ['haɪbrɪd] N **1** *Biol & Fig* hybride *m* **2** *(bicycle)* vélo *m* tout chemin, VTC *m*
ADJ hybride
▸▸ ***hybrid car*** voiture *f* hybride

hybridism ['haɪbrɪˌdɪzəm] N *Biol* hybridisme *m*

hybridization, -isation [ˌhaɪbrɪdaɪ'zeɪʃən] N *Biol* hybridation *f*

hybridize, -ise ['haɪbrɪˌdaɪz] *Biol* VT hybrider
VI s'hybrider

hydra ['haɪdrə] *(pl* **hydras** *or* **hydrae** [-driː]) N *Zool & Fig* hydre *f*
• **Hydra** N *Myth* Hydre *f* (de Lerne)

hydrangea [haɪ'dreɪndʒə] N *Bot* hortensia *m*

hydrant ['haɪdrənt] N prise *f* d'eau

hydrate N ['haɪdreɪt] *Chem* hydrate *m*
VT [haɪ'dreɪt] hydrater
VI [haɪ'dreɪt] s'hydrater

hydration [haɪ'dreɪʃən] N hydratation *f*

hydraulic [haɪ'drɔːlɪk] ADJ *Tech* hydraulique
▸▸ *Aut & Tech* ***hydraulic brake*** frein *m* hydraulique; *Aut & Tech* ***hydraulic suspension*** suspension *f* hydraulique

hydraulics [haɪ'drɔːlɪks] N *(UNCOUNT) Tech* hydraulique *f*

hydro ['haɪdrəʊ] N **1** *Br (spa)* établissement *m* thermal *(hôtel)* **2** *Can (power)* énergie *f* hydroélectrique; *(plant)* centrale *f* hydroélectrique
ADJ hydroélectrique; *Can* **my h. bill has gone up** ma facture d'électricité a augmenté

hydrocarbon [ˌhaɪdrə'kɑːbən] N *Chem* hydrocarbure *m*

hydrochloric [ˌhaɪdrə'klɒrɪk] ADJ *Chem* chlorhydrique
▸▸ ***hydrochloric acid*** acide *m* chlorhydrique

hydrochloride [ˌhaɪdrə'klɔːraɪd] N *Chem* chlorhydrate *m*

hydrodynamics [ˌhaɪdrədaɪ'næmɪks] N *(UNCOUNT) Phys* hydrodynamique *f*

hydroelectric [ˌhaɪdrəʊɪ'lektrɪk] ADJ *Elec & Ind* hydroélectrique
▸▸ ***hydroelectric dam*** barrage *m* hydroélectrique; ***hydroelectric power*** énergie *f* hydroélectrique

hydroelectricity [ˌhaɪdrəʊɪlek'trɪsətɪ] N *Elec & Ind* hydroélectricité *f*

hydrofoil ['haɪdrəfɔɪl] N *Naut* hydrofoil *m*, hydroptère *m*

hydrogen ['haɪdrədʒən] N *Chem* hydrogène *m*
▸▸ *Mil & Nucl* ***hydrogen bomb*** bombe *f* à hydrogène; *Chem* ***hydrogen peroxide*** eau *f* oxygénée

hydrography [haɪ'drɒgrəfɪ] N hydrographie *f*

hydrolysis [haɪ'drɒlɪsɪs] N *Chem* hydrolyse *f*

hydromassage [*Br* ˌhaɪdrə'mæsɑːʒ, *Am* ˌhaɪdrəmə'sɑːʒ] N hydromassage *m*

hydrometer [haɪ'drɒmɪtə(r)] N *Phys* hydromètre *m*

hydrometry [haɪ'drɒmɪtrɪ] N *Phys* hydrométrie *f*

hydrophobia [ˌhaɪdrə'fəʊbjə] N *Med* hydrophobie *f*

hydrophobic [ˌhaɪdrə'fəʊbɪk] ADJ *Med* hydrophobe

hydroplane ['haɪdrəˌpleɪn] N **1** *(boat)* hydroglisseur *m* **2** *(seaplane)* hydravion *m* **3** *(on submarine)* stabilisateur *m* d'assiette *(d'un sous-marin)*

hydroponics [ˌhaɪdrəʊ'pɒnɪks] N *(UNCOUNT) Hort* culture *f* hydroponique

hydrostatics [ˌhaɪdrə'stætɪks] N *(UNCOUNT) Phys* hydrostatique *f*

hydrotherapy [ˌhaɪdrə'θerəpɪ] N *Med* hydrothérapie *f*

hydroxide [haɪ'drɒksaɪd] N *Chem* hydroxyde *m*

hyena [haɪ'iːnə] N *Zool* hyène *f*; **brown/spotted h.** hyène *f* brune/tachetée; *Fig* **to laugh like a h.** rire comme un bossu

hygiene ['haɪdʒiːn] N hygiène *f*; **personal h.** hygiène *f* personnelle *ou* corporelle

hygienic [haɪ'dʒiːnɪk] ADJ hygiénique

hygienically [haɪ'dʒiːnɪkəlɪ] ADV de façon hygiénique

hymen ['haɪmen] N *Anat* hymen *m*
• **Hymen** PR N *Myth* Hymen

hymn [hɪm] N **1** *Rel* hymne *f*, cantique *m* **2** *(gen ▸ song of praise)* hymne *m*; **a h. to nature** un hymne à la nature
VT *Literary* chanter un hymne à la gloire de
▸▸ ***hymn book*** livre *m* de cantiques; ***hymn sheet*** = feuille volante où figurent les paroles d'un cantique; *Fig* **to sing from the same h. sheet** parler d'une seule voix

hymnal ['hɪmnəl] N *Rel* livre *m* de cantiques

hype [haɪp] *Fam* N **1** *(UNCOUNT) (publicity)* battage *m* publicitaire; **the film got a lot of h.** il y a eu une publicité monstre autour de ce film; **it's all h.** ce n'est que du bla-bla **2** *Am (put-on)* baratin *m*; **don't give me any h.** ne me baratine pas, ne me fais pas d'esbroufe **3** *Am Drugs slang (hypodermic)* shooteuse *f*; *(addict)* camé(e) *m,f*
VT **1** *(falsify)* baratiner **2** *(publicize)* monter un gros coup de pub autour de; **her latest novel has been heavily hyped** son dernier roman a été lancé à grand renfort de publicité ▫

▸**hype up** VT SEP *Fam (publicize)* **to h. sb/sth up** faire du battage autour de qn/qch; **to h. up a new film/rock group** lancer un nouveau film/groupe de rock à grand renfort de publicité ▫

hyped up [haɪpt-] ADJ *Fam* **1** *(heavily publicized)* lancé à grand renfort de publicité ▫ **2** *(excited)* tout excité ▫

hyper ['haɪpə(r)] ADJ *Fam* **1** *(over-excited)* tout excité ▫ **2** *(angry)* furax *(inv)*; **he got** *or* **went really h. about it** ça l'a mis dans une colère noire

hyper- ['haɪpə(r)-] PREF hyper-

hyperacidity [ˌhaɪpərə'sɪdətɪ] N *Méd* hyperacidité *f*

hyperactive [ˌhaɪpər'æktɪv] ADJ hyperactif

hyperbola [haɪ'pɜːbələ] *(pl* **hyperbolas** *or* **hyperbole** [-liː]) N *Math* hyperbole *f*

hyperbole [haɪ'pɜːbəlɪ] N *Ling* hyperbole *f*

hyperbolic [ˌhaɪpə'bɒlɪk], **hyperbolical** [ˌhaɪpə'bɒlɪkə] ADJ *Math & Ling* hyperbolique
▸▸ *Math* ***hyperbolic function*** fonction *f* hyperbolique

hypercritical [ˌhaɪpə'krɪtɪkəl] ADJ hypercritique

hyperglycaemia, *Am* **hyperglycemia** [ˌhaɪpəglaɪ'siːmɪə] N *Med* hyperglycémie *f*

hyperglycaemic, *Am* **hyperglycemic** [ˌhaɪpəglaɪ'siːmɪk] ADJ *Med* hyperglycémiant; **to be h.** *(permanently)* faire de l'hyperglycémie; *(temporarily)* avoir une crise d'hyperglycémie

hyperinflation [ˌhaɪpərɪn'fleɪʃən] N *Econ* hyperinflation *f*

hyperlink ['haɪpəˌlɪŋk] N *Comput* hyperlien *m*

hypermarket [ˌhaɪpə'mɑːkɪt] N *Br Com* hypermarché *m*

hypernova ['haɪpənəʊvə] *(pl* **hypernovas** *or* **hypernovae** [-viː]) N *Astron* hypernova *m*

hyperpower ['haɪpəpaʊə(r)] N *Pol* hyperpuissance *f*

hypersensitive [ˌhaɪpə'sensɪtɪv] ADJ hypersensible

hypersensitivity ['haɪpəˌsensɪ'tɪvətɪ] N hypersensibilité *f*

hypertension [ˌhaɪpə'tenʃən] N *Med* hypertension *f*

hypertext ['haɪpətekst] N *Comput & Literature* hypertexte *m*
▸▸ *Comput* ***hypertext link*** lien *m* hypertexte

hyperthyroidism [ˌhaɪpə'θaɪrɔɪˌdɪzəm] N *Med* hyperthyroïdie *f*

hyphen ['haɪfən] *Ling* N trait *m* d'union
VT mettre un trait d'union à

hyphenate ['haɪfəneɪt] VT *Ling* mettre un trait d'union à; **a hyphenated word** un mot à trait d'union; **is that hyphenated?** est-ce que ça prend un trait d'union?

hyphenation [haɪfə'neɪʃən] N *(in printing)* césure *f*, coupure *f* des mots
▸▸ *Comput* ***hyphenation program*** programme *m* de césure, logiciel *m* de syllabation

hypnosis [hɪp'nəʊsɪs] N *Psy* hypnose *f*; **to be under h.** être en état d'hypnose; **to put sb under h.** mettre qn sous hypnose

hypnotic [hɪp'nɒtɪk] ADJ hypnotique; **h. state** état *m* d'hypnose; **in a h. trance** en état d'hypnose; *Fig* **to have a h. effect on sb** hypnotiser qn
N *(drug)* hypnotique *m*; *(person)* hypnotique *mf*

hypnotism ['hɪpnətɪzəm] N *Psy* hypnotisme *m*

hypnotist ['hɪpnətɪst] N *Psy* hypnotiseur(euse) *m,f*

hypnotize, -ise ['hɪpnətaɪz] VT *Psy* hypnotiser

hypo- ['haɪpəʊ] PREF hypo-

hypoallergenic ['haɪpəʊˌælə'dʒenɪk] ADJ hypoallergique, hypoallergénique

hypochondria [ˌhaɪpə'kɒndrɪə] N *Psy* hypocondrie *f*

hypochondriac [ˌhaɪpə'kɒndrɪæk] *Psy* ADJ hypocondriaque
N hypocondriaque *mf*, malade *mf* imaginaire; **she's such a h.** c'est une véritable malade imaginaire

hypocrisy [hɪ'pɒkrəsɪ] *(pl* **hypocrisies**) N hypocrisie *f*

hypocrite ['hɪpəkrɪt] N hypocrite *mf*

hypocritical [ˌhɪpə'krɪtɪkəl] ADJ hypocrite; **a h. remark** une remarque hypocrite; **it would be h. of me** ce serait hypocrite de ma part

hypocritically [ˌhɪpə'krɪtɪkəlɪ] ADV hypocritement

hypodermic [ˌhaɪpə'dɜːmɪk] *Med* ADJ hypodermique
N **1** *(syringe)* seringue *f* hypodermique **2** *(injection)* injection *f* hypodermique
▸▸ *Med* ***hypodermic needle*** aiguille *f* hypodermique; ***hypodermic syringe*** seringue *f* hypodermique

hypoglycaemia, *Am* **hypoglycemia** [ˌhaɪpəʊglaɪ'siːmɪə] N *Med* hypoglycémie *f*

hypoglycaemic, *Am* **hypoglycemic** [ˌhaɪpəʊglaɪ'siːmɪk] ADJ *Med* hypoglycémiant; **to be h.** *(permanently)* faire de l'hypoglycémie; *(temporarily)* avoir une crise d'hypoglycémie

hyponym ['haɪpənɪm] N *Ling* hyponyme *m*

hypotenuse [haɪ'pɒtənjuːz] N *Geom* hypoténuse *f*

hypothalamus [ˌhaɪpəʊ'θæləməs] N *Anat* hypothalamus *m*

hypothermia [ˌhaɪpəʊ'θɜːmɪə] N *Med* hypothermie *f*

hypothesis [haɪ'pɒθɪsɪs] *(pl* **hypotheses** [-siːz]) N hypothèse *f*; **according to your h.** selon *ou* suivant votre hypothèse; **to put forward** *or* **to advance a h.** émettre *ou* énoncer une hypothèse

hypothesize, -ise [haɪ'pɒθɪsaɪz] VT supposer; **let's h. the following** faisons les hypothèses suivantes; **he hypothesized that she was not in fact the killer** il a formulé l'hypothèse selon laquelle ce ne serait pas elle l'assassin
VI faire des hypothèses *ou* des suppositions

hypothetical [ˌhaɪpə'θetɪkəl] ADJ hypothétique; **it's purely h.** c'est purement hypothétique

hypothetically [ˌhaɪpə'θetɪkəlɪ] ADV hypothétiquement

hypothyroidism [ˌhaɪpəʊ'θaɪrɔɪdɪzəm] N *Med* hypothyroïdie *f*

hysterectomy [ˌhɪstə'rektəmɪ] *(pl* **hysterectomies**) N *Med* hystérectomie *f*; **to have a h.** subir une hystérectomie

hysteria [hɪs'tɪərɪə] N **1** *Psy* hystérie *f* **2** *(hysterical behaviour)* crise *f* de nerfs; **an atmosphere of**

barely controlled h. reigned in the office** une atmosphère de folie à peine contenue régnait dans le bureau; *Fig* **a country in the grip of war h.** un pays en proie à une hystérie guerrière

hysteric [hɪs'terɪk] **N** *Psy* hystérique *mf*

hysterical [hɪs'terɪkəl] **ADJ 1** *Psy* hystérique
2 *(sobs, voice, reaction)* hystérique; *(laugh)* hystérique, nerveux; **h. passengers fought to reach the emergency exits** des passagers hystériques se battaient pour atteindre la sortie de secours; **he's the h. type** c'est un grand nerveux; **he was h. with grief** il était fou de chagrin
3 *(overexcited)* **it's nothing to get h. about!** ce n'est pas la peine de faire une crise (de nerfs)!
4 *Fam (very funny)* écroulant, tordant
►► *Am Psy* **hysterical pregnancy** grossesse *f* nerveuse

hysterically [hɪs'terɪkəlɪ] **ADV 1** *(very emotionally)* sans pouvoir maîtriser ses émotions; **he was waving his arms h.** il agitait ses bras de façon incontrôlée; **to weep h.** avoir une crise de larmes; **to laugh h.** être pris d'un rire nerveux **2** *Fam* **h. funny** écroulant, tordant **3** *Fam* **to laugh h.** *(with great amusement)* avoir le fou rire

hysterics [hɪs'terɪks] **NPL 1** *(hysterical behaviour)* crise *f* de nerfs; **to go into** *or* **to have h.** avoir une (violente) crise de nerfs **2** *Fam (laughter)* crise *f* de rire; **to go into** *or* **to have h.** attraper un *ou* avoir le fou rire; **we were in h. about** *or* **over it** on était pliés en deux de rire; **he had me in h.** il m'a fait mourir de rire

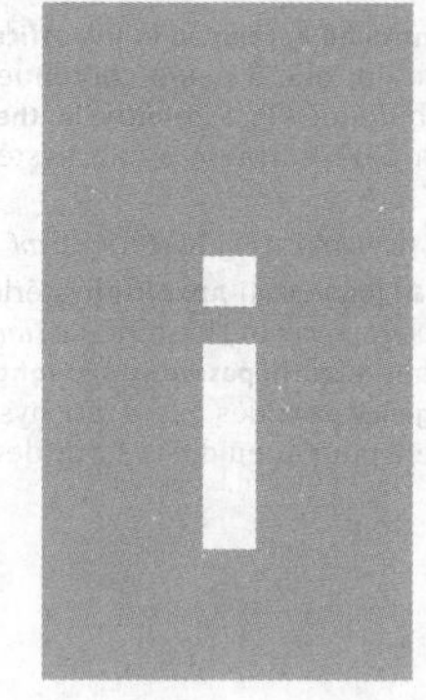

I¹, i [aɪ] **N** *(letter)* I, i *m inv*; **two i's** deux i; **I for Ivor** I comme Irma

►► ***I beam*** *Constr* fer *m* en I *ou* en double T; *Comput* pointeur *m* en I

I² **PRON** *(gen)* je; *(emphatic)* moi; **I like skiing** j'aime skier; **Rosie and I have known each other for years** Rosie et moi nous connaissons depuis des années; **I found it, not you** c'est moi qui l'ai trouvé, pas vous; **I too have a twin sister** moi aussi, j'ai une jumelle; **here I am** me voici; *Formal* **it is I who should be apologizing** c'est moi qui devrais m'excuser

IAEA [ˌaɪeɪˌiːˈaɪ] **N** *Nucl* (*abbr* **International Atomic Energy Agency**) AIEA *f*

iambic [aɪˈæmbɪk] *Literature* **N** *(line, poem)* iambe *m*

ADJ iambique

►► ***iambic foot*** iambe *m*; ***iambic pentameter*** pentamètre *m* iambique

IAP [ˌaɪeɪˈpiː] **N** *Comput* (*abbr* **Internet Access Provider**) fournisseur *m* d'accès à l'Internet

IASC [ˌaɪeɪˌesˈsiː] **N** *Fin* (*abbr* **International Accounting Standards Committee**) comité *m* international des normes comptables

IATA [aɪˈɑːtə, iːˈɑːtə] **N** *Aviat* (*abbr* **International Air Transport Association**) IATA *f*

IBAS [ˈaɪbæs] **N** *Br Fin* (*abbr* **Independent Banking Advisory Service**) = service de conseil bancaire aux PME et aux entreprises nouvellement créées

IBC [ˌaɪbiːˈsiː] **N** *Press* (*abbr* **inside back cover**) troisième *f* de couverture

Iberia [aɪˈbɪərɪə] **N** Ibérie *f*

Iberian [aɪˈbɪərɪən] *Geog* **N 1** *(person)* Ibère *mf* **2** *Ling* ibère *m*

ADJ ibérique

►► ***the Iberian Peninsula*** la péninsule Ibérique

ibex [ˈaɪbeks] (*pl* **inv** *or* **ibexes**) **N** *Zool* bouquetin *m*

ibid (*written abbr* **ibidem**) ibid

ibis [ˈaɪbɪs] (*pl* **inv** *or* **ibises**) **N** *Orn* ibis *m*

IBM-compatible [ˌaɪbiːˈem-] **ADJ** *Comput* compatible IBM

IBOR [ˈaɪbɔː(r)] **N** *Fin* (*abbr* **interbank offered rate**) taux *m* interbancaire offert

IBRD [ˌaɪbiːˌɑːˈdiː] **N** *Banking* (*abbr* **International Bank for Reconstruction and Development**) BIRD *f*

IBS [ˌaɪbiːˈes] **N** *Med* (*abbr* **irritable bowel syndrome**) syndrôme *m* du côlon irritable

IC [ˌaɪˈsiː] **N** *Comput* (*abbr* **integrated circuit**) circuit *m* intégré

►► ***IC card*** carte *f* à circuits intégrés

ICAO [ˌaɪsiːˌeɪˈəʊ] **N** *Aviat* (*abbr* **International Civil Aviation Organization**) OACI *f*

ICC [ˌaɪsiːˈsiː] **N** *Com* (*abbr* **International Chamber of Commerce**) CCI *f*

ice [aɪs] **N 1** *(UNCOUNT) (frozen water)* glace *f*; *(ice cubes)* glaçons *mpl*; **her feet were like i.** elle avait les pieds gelés; **the reforms have been put on i.** les réformes ont été gelées; *Fig* **to walk** *or* **to be on thin i.** avancer en terrain miné

2 *(on road)* verglas *m*

3 *(in ice rink)* glace *f*

4 *Br Old-fashioned (ice-cream)* glace *f*

5 *(UNCOUNT) Fam (diamonds)* diams *mpl*, cailloux *mpl*

6 *Fam Drugs slang* ice *f*

VT 1 *(chill ▸ drink)* rafraîchir; (▸ *with ice cubes)* mettre des glaçons dans **2** *(cake)* glacer **3** *Fam Crime slang (kill)* liquider

VI (se) givrer

►► ***ice age*** période *f* glaciaire; *Br* ***ice axe***, *Am* ***ice ax*** piolet *m*; ***ice bag*** sac *m* à glaçons; ***ice blue*** bleu *m* très pâle; ***ice bucket*** seau *m* à glace; ***ice cap*** calotte *f* glaciaire; ***ice cube*** glaçon *m*; *Sport* ***ice dancer*** danseur(euse) *m,f* sur glace; *Sport* ***ice dancing*** danse *f* sur glace; ***ice floe*** glace *f* flottante; *Br Sport* ***ice hockey*** hockey *m* sur glace; ***ice jam*** embâcle *m*; *Br* ***ice lolly*** glace *f* à l'eau; ***ice machine, ice maker*** machine *f* à glace; *Fam Pej* ***ice maiden*** glaçon *m (femme distante)*; ***ice pack*** *(pack ice)* banquise *f*; *(ice bag)* sac *m* à glaçons; *Med* poche *f* à glace; ***ice pick*** pic *m* à glace; ***ice point*** point *m* de congélation; *Fam Pej* ***ice queen*** glaçon *m (femme distante)*; *Sport* ***ice rink*** patinoire *f*; ***ice scraper*** *(for car window)* raclette *f* (antigivre); ***ice screw*** *(for mountaineering)* broche *f* à glace; ***ice sculpture*** sculpture *f* de glace; ***ice sheet*** nappe *f* de glace; ***ice show*** spectacle *m* sur glace; ***ice skate*** patin *m* (à glace); ***ice storm*** chutes *fpl* de pluie verglaçante, tempête *f* de verglas; ***ice track*** piste *f* de patinage de vitesse; *Am* ***ice water*** eau *f* glacée; *Br* ***ice yacht*** char *m* à voile (sur patins)

▸**ice over** **VT SEP** **to be iced over** *(lake, river etc)* être gelé; *(window, propellers)* être givré

VI *(lake, river etc)* geler; *(window, propellers)* (se) givrer

▸**ice up** **VT SEP** **to be iced up** *(lock, windscreen, propellers)* être givré; *(road)* être verglacé

VI 1 *(lock, windscreen, propellers)* (se) givrer, se couvrir de givre **2** *(road)* se couvrir de verglas

iceberg [ˈaɪsbɜːg] **N 1** *(in sea)* iceberg *m* **2** *Fam (cold person)* glaçon *m*

►► ***iceberg lettuce*** = salade aux feuilles serrées et croquantes

icebound [ˈaɪsbaʊnd] **ADJ** bloqué par les glaces

icebox [ˈaɪsbɒks] **N 1** *Br (freezer compartment)* freezer *m*

2 *Am Old-fashioned (refrigerator)* réfrigérateur *m*, frigo *m*

3 *(coolbox)* glacière *f*

4 *Fig* glacière *f*; **their house is like an i.** c'est une vraie glacière *ou* on gèle chez eux

icebreaker [ˈaɪsˌbreɪkə(r)] **N 1** *(vessel)* brise-glace *m inv* **2** *(at party)* **if you're looking for an i.** si tu veux briser la glace

ice-cold **ADJ** *(hands, drink)* glacé; *(house, manners)* glacial

ice-cream **N** glace *f*; **chocolate/strawberry i.** glace *f* au chocolat/à la fraise

►► ***ice-cream bar*** barre *f* glacée; ***ice-cream cone, ice-cream cornet*** cornet *m* de glace; ***ice-cream maker*** sorbetière *f*; ***ice-cream man*** marchand *m* de glaces; ***ice-cream parlour*** salon *m* de dégustation de glaces; ***ice-cream soda*** soda *m* avec de la glace; ***ice-cream van*** camionnette *f* de vendeur de glaces

iced [aɪst] **ADJ 1** *(chilled ▸ drink)* glacé **2** *(decorated ▸ cake, biscuit)* glacé

►► ***iced water*** eau *f* avec glaçons

Iceland [ˈaɪslənd] **N** *Geog* Islande *f*

Icelander [ˈaɪsləndə(r)] **N** Islandais(e) *m,f*

Icelandic [aɪsˈlændɪk] **N** *(language)* islandais *m*

ADJ islandais

COMP *(embassy)* d'Islande; *(history)* de l'Islande; *(teacher)* d'islandais

ice-skate **VI** *Sport* patiner; *(professionally)* faire du patinage (sur glace); *(for pleasure)* faire du patin (à glace)

ichthyology [ˌɪkθɪˈɒlədʒɪ] **N** ichtyologie *f*

ichthyosaurus [ˌɪkθɪəˈsɔːrəs] (*pl* **inv** *or* **ichthyosauri** [-raɪ]) **N** ichtyosaure *m*

icicle [ˈaɪsɪkəl] **N** glaçon *m (qui pend d'une gouttière etc)*

icily [ˈaɪsɪlɪ] **ADV** d'une manière glaciale; **to answer i.** répondre sur un ton glacial

iciness [ˈaɪsɪnɪs] **N** *(of wind, water)* température *f* glaciale; **because of the i. of the steps** parce que les marches étaient verglacées; *Fig* **the i. of her voice** son ton glacial

icing [ˈaɪsɪŋ] **N 1** *esp Br Culin* glaçage *m*; *Fig* **it's the i. on the cake** c'est la cerise sur le gâteau **2** *(on aeroplane ▸ process)* givrage *m*; (▸ *ice)* givre *m*

►► *Br Culin* ***icing sugar*** sucre *m* glace

ICJ [ˌaɪsiːˈdʒeɪ] **N** *Law* (*abbr* **International Court of Justice**) CIJ *f*

ickle [ˈɪkəl] **ADJ** *(in children's language) & Fam* petit□; **what a cute i. puppy!** quel mignon petit chien!

icky [ˈɪkɪ] (*compar* **ickier**, *superl* **ickiest**) **ADJ** *Fam (repulsive)* dégueulasse; *(sticky)* poisseux□; *(sentimental)* mièvre□, à la guimauve

icon [ˈaɪkɒn] **N 1** *Rel* icône *f*; *Fig* **a 60s i.** un symbole des années 60; **a gay i.** une idole gay **2** *Comput* icône *f*

►► *Comput* ***icon bar*** barre *f* d'icônes; *Comput* ***icon editor*** éditeur *m* d'icônes

iconize, -ise [ˈaɪkənaɪz] **VT** *Comput* représenter en icône

iconoclast [aɪˈkɒnəklæst] **N** iconoclaste *mf*

iconoclastic [aɪˌkɒnəˈklæstɪk] **ADJ** iconoclaste

iconography [ˌaɪkɒˈnɒgrəfɪ] **N** iconographie *f*

ICT [ˌaɪsiːˈtiː] **N** (*abbr* **information and communications technology**) informatique *f*

ICTR [aɪˌsiːtiːˈɑː(r)] **N** (*abbr* **International Criminal Tribunal for Rwanda**) TPIR *m*

ICTY [aɪˌsiːtiːˈwaɪ] **N** (*abbr* **International Criminal Tribunal for the former Yugoslavia**) TPIY *m*

ICU [ˌaɪsiːˈjuː] **N** *Med* (*abbr* **intensive care unit**) unité *f* de soins intensifs

icy [ˈaɪsɪ] (*compar* **icier**, *superl* **iciest**) **ADJ 1** *(weather, water, wind)* glacial; *(hands)* glacé; *(ground)* gelé **2** *(covered in ice ▸ road)* verglacé; (▸ *window, propeller)* givré, couvert de givre; *Rail* (▸ *points)* gelé **3** *Fig (reception, stare)* glacial; **his i. manner** sa froideur

ID¹ [ˌaɪˈdiː] (*pl* **ID's**, *pt & pp* **ID'd**, *cont* **ID'ing**) **N** *(UNCOUNT)* (*abbr* **identification**) **1** *(documents)* papiers *mpl*; **do you have any ID?** vous avez une pièce d'identité? **2** *Comput* numéro *m* d'identification

VT (*abbr* **identify**) **to ID sb** identifier qn; **to be** *or* **to get ID'd** subir un contrôle d'identité

►► ***ID card*** carte *f* d'identité

ID² (*written abbr* **Idaho**) Idaho

I'd [aɪd] = I had, I would

IDE [ˌaɪdiːˈiː] N *Comput (abbr* integrated drive electronics) IDE *m*

idea [aɪˈdɪə] N 1 *(plan, suggestion, inspiration)* idée *f*; I've had an i. j'ai une idée; it wasn't MY i.! l'idée n'était pas de moi!; the i. of leaving you never entered my head l'idée de te quitter ne m'a jamais effleuré; where did you get the i. for your book? d'où vous est venue l'idée de votre livre?; I thought the i. was for them to come here il n'était pas prévu que ce serait eux qui viendraient ici?; that's an i.! ça, c'est une bonne idée!; that's the i.! c'est ça!; what's the i.? *(showing disapproval)* qu'est-ce que ça veut dire *ou* signifie?; the very i.! en voilà une idée!
2 *(notion)* idée *f*; our ideas about the universe notre conception de l'univers; if this is your i. of a joke si tu trouves que c'est drôle; you've got a funny i. of loyalty tu as une conception bizarre de la loyauté; don't put ideas into his head ne va pas lui mettre des idées dans la tête; she hasn't an i. in her head elle n'a pas un grain de jugeote; it was a nice i. to phone c'est gentil d'avoir pensé à téléphoner; you've no i. how difficult it was tu n'imagines pas à quel point c'était difficile; has anyone any i. how the accident occurred? est-ce qu'on a une idée de la façon dont l'accident est arrivé?; I have a rough i. of what happened je m'imagine assez bien ce qui est arrivé; no i.! aucune idée!; I haven't the slightest i. je n'en ai pas la moindre idée; what gave him the i. that it would be easy? qu'est-ce qui lui a laissé croire que ce serait facile?
3 *(estimate)* indication *f*, idée *f*; can you give me an i. of how much it will cost? est-ce que vous pouvez m'indiquer à peu près combien ça va coûter?
4 *(suspicion)* soupçon *m*, idée *f*; she had an i. that something was going to happen elle se doutait que quelque chose allait arriver; I've an i. that he'll succeed j'ai dans l'idée qu'il finira par réussir
5 *(objective, intention)* but *m*; the i. of the game le but du jeu; the i. is to provide help for people in need il s'agit d'aider ceux qui sont dans le besoin
►► ***ideas man*** concepteur *m*

ideal [aɪˈdɪəl] N 1 *(perfect example)* idéal *m*; the i. of beauty l'idéal *m* de la beauté 2 *(principle)* idéal *m*; a man with no ideals un homme sans idéaux; with such high ideals you'll never be satisfied si tu es aussi idéaliste, tu ne seras jamais satisfait
ADJ idéal; an i. couple un couple idéal; that's i.! c'est parfait! in an i. world dans l'idéal
►► ***the Ideal Home Exhibition*** le Salon de l'habitat

idealism [aɪˈdɪəlɪzəm] N idéalisme *m*

idealist [aɪˈdɪəlɪst] N idéaliste *mf*
ADJ idéaliste

idealistic [ˌaɪdɪəˈlɪstɪk] ADJ idéaliste

idealize, -ise [aɪˈdɪəlaɪz] VT idéaliser

ideally [aɪˈdɪəlɪ] ADV 1 *(perfectly)* parfaitement; they're i. suited c'est un couple parfaitement assorti; the shop is i. situated l'emplacement du magasin est idéal 2 *(in a perfect world)* dans l'idéal; i., this wine should be served at room temperature normalement *ou* pour bien faire, ce vin doit être servi chambré; i., I would like to work in advertising dans l'idéal, je voudrais travailler dans la publicité

ident [ˈaɪdent] N *TV & Rad* indicatif *m*, identification *f*

identical [aɪˈdentɪkəl] ADJ identique; i. to *or* with identique à; your hairstyle is i. to *or* with Lauren's tu as exactement la même coiffure que Lauren; they were wearing i. dresses elles portaient la même robe
►► ***identical twins*** *(boys)* vrais jumeaux *mpl*; *(girls)* vraies jumelles *fpl*

identically [aɪˈdentɪkəlɪ] ADV identiquement; to be i. dressed être habillé exactement de la même façon

identifiable [aɪˈdentɪˌfaɪəbəl] ADJ identifiable

identification [aɪˌdentɪfɪˈkeɪʃən] N 1 *(of body, criminal)* identification *f* 2 (UNCOUNT) *(identity papers)* papiers *mpl*; the police asked me for i. la police m'a demandé mes papiers *ou* une pièce d'identité 3 *(association)* identification *f*
►► ***identification card*** carte *f* d'identité; *Aviat & Naut* ***identification marks*** (lettres *fpl* et numéros *mpl* d')immatriculation *f*; ***identification papers*** papiers *mpl* d'identité; *Br* ***identification parade*** séance *f* d'identification *(au cours de laquelle on demande à un témoin de reconnaître une personne)*

identifier [aɪˈdentɪfaɪə(r)] N *Comput* identificateur *m*, identifieur *m*

identify [aɪˈdentɪfaɪ] *(pt & pp* identified) VT 1 *(recognize, name)* identifier; he was identified as one of the ringleaders il fut identifié comme étant l'un des meneurs; the winner has asked not to be identified le gagnant a tenu à garder l'anonymat
2 *(distinguish ► of physical feature, badge etc)* she wore a red rose to i. herself elle portait une rose rouge pour se faire reconnaître *ou* pour qu'on la reconnaisse; his accent immediately identified him to the others les autres l'ont immédiatement reconnu à son accent
3 *(acknowledge ► difficulty, issue etc)* définir; the report identifies two major problems le rapport met en lumière deux problèmes principaux
4 *(associate ► people, ideas etc)* he has long been identified with right-wing groups il y a longtemps qu'il est assimilé *ou* identifié aux groupuscules de droite; she identifies herself with the activists elle s'identifie avec les militants
VI to i. with s'identifier à *ou* avec; I can't i. with his problems/with the way she feels j'ai du mal à comprendre ses problèmes/ce qu'elle ressent

identifying marks [aɪˈdentɪfaɪɪŋ-] N signes *mpl* particuliers

Identikit® [aɪˈdentɪkɪt] N *(picture)* portrait-robot *m*
►► ***Identikit® picture*** portrait-robot *m*

identikit [aɪˈdentɪkɪt] ADJ *Fam* our cities are full of i. coffee chains these days nos villes sont remplies de chaînes de cafés qui se ressemblent toutes

identity [aɪˈdentətɪ] *(pl* identities) N 1 *(name, set of characteristics)* identité *f*; it was a case of mistaken i. il y a eu erreur sur la personne 2 *(sense of belonging)* identité *f*
►► ***identity bracelet*** bracelet *m* d'identité; ***identity card*** carte *f* d'identité; *Psy* ***identity crisis*** crise *f* d'identité; *Mil* ***identity disc*** plaque *f* d'identité; ***identity papers*** papiers *mpl* d'identité; *Br* ***identity parade*** séance *f* d'identification *(au cours de laquelle on demande à un témoin de reconnaître une personne)*; ***identity theft*** vol *m* d'identité

ideogram [ˈɪdɪəʊgræm], **ideograph** [ˈɪdɪəʊgrɑːf] N idéogramme *m*

ideological [ˌaɪdɪəˈlɒdʒɪkəl] ADJ idéologique

ideologically [ˌaɪdɪəˈlɒdʒɪkəlɪ] ADV du point de vue idéologique, idéologiquement

ideologist [ˌaɪdɪˈɒlədʒɪst] N idéologue *mf*

ideologue [ˈaɪdɪəlɒg] N idéologue *mf*

ideology [ˌaɪdɪˈɒlədʒɪ] *(pl* ideologies) N idéologie *f*

ides [aɪdz] N *Antiq* ides *fpl*
►► ***the Ides of March*** les ides *fpl* de mars

idiocy [ˈɪdɪəsɪ] N 1 *(stupidity)* stupidité *f*, idiotie *f* 2 *Arch Med (mental retardation)* idiotie *f*

idiolect [ˈɪdɪəlekt] N *Ling* idiolecte *m*

idiom [ˈɪdɪəm] N 1 *Ling (expression)* locution *f*, expression *f* idiomatique 2 *(language)* idiome *m* 3 *(style ► of music, writing etc)* style *m*

idiomatic [ˌɪdɪəˈmætɪk] ADJ idiomatique
►► ***idiomatic expression*** expression *f* idiomatique

idiomatically [ˌɪdɪəˈmætɪkəlɪ] ADV de manière idiomatique

idiosyncrasy [ˌɪdɪəˈsɪŋkrəsɪ] *(pl* idiosyncrasies) N *(peculiarity)* particularité *f*, *(foible)* manie *f*

idiosyncratic [ˌɪdɪəsɪŋˈkrætɪk] ADJ *(style, behaviour)* caractéristique

idiot [ˈɪdɪət] N 1 *(fool)* idiot(e) *m,f*, imbécile *mf*; (you) stupid i.! espèce d'idiot!; don't be an i.! ne sois pas idiot!; that i. Peter cet imbécile de Peter 2 *Arch Med* idiot(e) *m,f*
►► *Fam TV* ***idiot board*** téléprompteur□ *m*; *Fam Pej* ***idiot box*** télé *f*, téloche *f*; *Aut* ***idiot light*** *(on dashboard)* voyant *m* lumineux; *Psy* ***idiot savant*** autiste *mf (à la mémoire particulièrement développée)*

idiotic [ˌɪdɪˈɒtɪk] ADJ idiot

idiotically [ˌɪdɪˈɒtɪkəlɪ] ADV stupidement, bêtement; he behaved i. il s'est comporté comme un imbécile; he smiled i. il a souri bêtement

idiotism [ˈɪdɪəˌtɪzəm] N *Am (of language)* idiotisme *m*

idle [ˈaɪdəl] ADJ 1 *(person ► inactive)* inoccupé, désœuvré; *(► lazy)* paresseux; in her i. moments à ses moments perdus; 1,500 men have been made i. 1500 hommes ont été mis au chômage
2 *(factory, equipment)* arrêté, à l'arrêt; *St Exch (markets)* improductif, dormant; to stand i. *(machine)* être arrêté *ou* au repos; to lie i. *(factory)* chômer; *(money)* dormir, être improductif; to let one's money lie i. laisser dormir son argent
3 *(futile, pointless)* inutile, vain; *(empty ► threat, promise etc)* vain, en l'air; *(► rumour)* sans fondement; *(► boast)* mal placé; it would be i. to speculate il ne servirait à rien de se livrer à de vaines conjectures
4 *(casual)* an i. glance un regard distrait; out of i. curiosity par pure curiosité
VI *(engine)* tourner au ralenti
VT *Am (make unemployed ► permanently)* mettre au chômage; *(► temporarily)* mettre en chômage technique
►► ***idle gossip*** ragots *mpl*; ***idle pleasure*** plaisir *m* futile; ***the idle rich*** les riches *mpl* désœuvrés *ou* oisifs
► **idle away** VT SEP to i. away one's time tuer le temps

idleness [ˈaɪdəlnɪs] N 1 *(laziness)* oisiveté *f*, paresse *f*; *(inactivity)* désœuvrement *m* 2 *(futility)* futilité *f*

idler [ˈaɪdlə(r)] N 1 *(lazy person)* paresseux(euse) *m,f*, fainéant(e) *m,f* 2 *Tech (pulley)* poulie *f* folle; *(wheel)* roue *f* folle

idling [ˈaɪdəlɪŋ] N 1 *(time-wasting)* fainéantise *f*; that's more than enough i. for one day assez fainéanté pour aujourd'hui 2 *(of engine)* (marche *f* au) ralenti *m*
►► ***idling speed*** *(of engine)* ralenti *m*

idly [ˈaɪdəlɪ] ADV 1 *(lazily)* paresseusement 2 *(casually)* négligemment 3 *(unresponsively)* sans réagir; we will not stand i. by nous n'allons pas rester sans rien faire

idol [ˈaɪdəl] N idole *f*; a 70s pop i. une idole (pop) des années 70

idolater [aɪˈdɒlətə(r)] N 1 *Rel* idolâtre *m* 2 *Fig* adorateur *m* (of de)

idolatrous [aɪˈdɒlətrəs] ADJ idolâtre

idolatry [aɪˈdɒlətrɪ] N idolâtrie *f*

idolize, -ise [ˈaɪdəlaɪz] VT idolâtrer

idolizing, -ising [ˈaɪdəˌlaɪzɪŋ] N idolâtrie *f*
ADJ plein d'adoration

idyll [ˈɪdɪl] N 1 *(scene)* scène *f* bucolique 2 *(poem)* idylle *f*

> Note that the French word **idylle** is rarely a translation for the English word **idyll**. Its most common meaning is **romance**.

idyllic [ɪˈdɪlɪk, aɪˈdɪlɪk] ADJ idyllique

ie [ˌaɪˈiː] ADV *(abbr* id est) c'est-à-dire, à savoir

IF [ɪf] CONJ 1 *(supposing that)* si; if he comes, we'll ask him s'il vient, on lui demandera; if possible si (c'est) possible; if necessary si (c'est) nécessaire, le cas échéant; if so si c'est le cas; if so, when? si oui, quand?; if all goes well si tout va bien; if I'd known you were coming, I'd have bought some wine si j'avais su que tu venais, j'aurais acheté du vin; if I were a millionaire, I'd buy a yacht si j'étais millionnaire, j'achèterais un yacht; would you mind if I invited Angie too? ça te dérangerait si j'invitais aussi Angie?; if he agrees and (if) we have time s'il est d'accord et que nous avons le temps
2 *(whenever)* si; if you mix blue and yellow you get green si on mélange du bleu et du jaune, on obtient du vert; if you ever come *or* if ever you come to London, do visit us si jamais tu passes à Londres, viens nous voir; if you are "gratified" by something, you are pleased by it si (on dit que) quelque chose nous "satisfait", cela veut dire que ça nous fait plaisir; he gets angry if I so much as open my mouth si j'ai seulement le malheur d'ouvrir la bouche, il se fâche

3 *(given that)* si; **if Paul was the brains in the family, then Julia was the organizer** si Paul était le cerveau de la famille, Julia en était l'organisatrice

4 *(whether)* si; **to ask/to know/to wonder if** demander/savoir/se demander si; **it doesn't matter if he comes or not** peu importe qu'il vienne ou (qu'il ne vienne) pas

5 *(with verbs or adjectives expressing emotion)* si; **I'm sorry if I upset you** je suis désolé si je t'ai fait de la peine; **if I gave you that impression, I apologize** je m'excuse si c'est l'impression que je vous ai donnée

6 *(used to qualify a statement)* **few, if any, readers will have heard of him** peu de lecteurs auront entendu parler de lui, ou même aucun; **modifications, if any, will have to be made later** les modifications éventuelles devront être apportées plus tard; **he was intelligent if a little arrogant** il était intelligent, mais quelque peu arrogant; **pleasant weather, if rather cold** temps agréable, bien qu'un peu froid

7 *(introducing comments or opinions)* **if I could just come in here...** si je puis me permettre d'intervenir...; **it's rather good, if I say so myself** c'est assez bon, sans fausse modestie; **I'll leave it there, if I may, and go on to my next point** j'en resterai là, si vous voulez bien et passerai au point suivant; **I thought you were rather rude, if you don't mind my saying so** je vous ai trouvé assez grossier, si je peux me permettre; **well, if you want my opinion** *or* **if you ask me, I thought it was dreadful** eh bien, si vous voulez mon avis, c'était affreux; **if you think about it, it is rather odd** si vous y réfléchissez, c'est plutôt bizarre; **if I remember rightly, she was married to a politician** si j'ai bonne mémoire, elle était mariée à un homme politique; **if I know Sophie, she won't have done it!** comme *ou* telle que je connais Sophie, elle ne l'aura pas fait!

8 *(in polite requests)* si; **if you could just write your name here...** si vous voulez bien inscrire votre nom ici...; **would you like me to wrap it for you? – if you would, please** vous voulez que je vous l'emballe? – oui, s'il vous plaît

9 *(expressing surprise, indignation)* tiens, ça alors; **well, if it isn't my old mate Jim!** tiens *ou* ça alors, c'est ce vieux Jim!

N si *m inv*; **if you get the job – and it's a big if – you'll have to move to London** si tu obtiens cet emploi, et je dis bien si, tu devras aller t'installer à Londres; **no ifs and buts, we're going** il n'y a pas de "mais" qui tienne *ou* pas de discussions, on y va; **the agreement is full of ifs and buts** l'accord n'est qu'une suite de conditions

• **if and when** CONJ au cas où; **if and when he phones, I'll simply tell him to leave me alone** au cas où il appellerait, je lui dirais tout simplement de me laisser tranquille

• **if anything** ADV plutôt; **he doesn't look any slimmer, if anything, he's put on weight** il n'a pas l'air plus mince, il a même plutôt grossi; **I am, if anything, even keener to be involved** j'ai peut-être encore plus envie d'y participer

• **if ever** CONJ **there's a hopeless case if ever I saw one!** voilà un cas désespéré s'il en est!; **if ever I saw a man driven by ambition, it's him** si quelqu'un est poussé par l'ambition, c'est bien lui

• **if I were you** ADV à ta place; **if I were you I'd accept the offer** si j'étais toi *ou* à ta place, j'accepterais la proposition

• **if not** CONJ sinon; **I'm happy to eat out if you want to, if not, I'll just rustle something up here** on peut aller manger quelque part si tu veux, sinon je préparerai quelque chose ici; **did you finish on time? and if not, why not?** avez-vous terminé à temps? sinon, pourquoi?; **hundreds, if not thousands** des centaines, voire des milliers

• **if only** CONJ **1** *(providing a reason)* au moins; **I think I should come along too, if only to make sure you don't get into mischief** je crois que je devrais venir aussi, ne serait-ce que pour m'assurer que vous ne faites pas de bêtises; **all right, I'll let you go to the party, if only to keep you quiet** bon d'accord, tu peux aller à la fête, comme ça au moins, j'aurai la paix

2 *(expressing a wish)* si seulement; **if only!** si seulement!; **if only I could drive** si seulement je savais conduire; **if only someone would tell us what has happened** si seulement quelqu'un nous disait ce qui s'est passé; **if only we'd known** si seulement nous avions su

IFA [ˌaɪef'eɪ] N *Br Fin* (*abbr* **independent financial adviser**) conseiller(ère) *m,f* financier(ère) indépendant(e)

IFC [ˌaɪef'siː] N *Typ* (*abbr* **inside front cover**) deuxième *f* de couverture

iffy ['ɪfɪ] *(compar* **iffier**, *superl* **iffiest**) ADJ *Fam* **1** *(uncertain ▸ situation)* aléatoire; **the picnic/project is looking very i.** le pique-nique/projet semble très compromis; **the car's a bit i. these days** la voiture n'est pas très fiable ces jours-ci; **I'm still a bit i. about the whole thing** *(haven't made my mind up)* j'hésite encore; *Br* **my stomach's been a bit i. lately** je me sens un peu barbouillé ces temps-ci; **that sky looks a bit i.** le ciel est un peu menaçant; **the ice looks a bit i.** *(on pond)* la glace n'a pas l'air très sûre; **it's still a bit i. but I think I WILL be going to the conference** je ne suis pas complètement sûr mais je pense que j'irai à la conférence **2** *(suspect ▸ person, appearance)* louche; **it all sounded rather i.** tout ça m'avait l'air plutôt louche

if-then operation N *Comput* inclusion *f*

IGC [ˌaɪdʒiː'siː] N (*abbr* **Intergovernmental Conference**) CIG *f*

igloo ['ɪgluː] N igloo *m*, iglou *m*

igneous ['ɪgnɪəs] ADJ *Geol* igné

ignite [ɪg'naɪt] VT *(set fire to)* mettre le feu à, enflammer; *(light)* allumer; *Fig (situation, conflict)* enflammer

VI *(catch fire)* prendre feu, s'enflammer; *(be lit)* s'allumer; *Fig (situation, conflict)* s'enflammer

ignition [ɪg'nɪʃən] N **1** *Aut* allumage *m*; **to turn on/off the i.** mettre/couper le contact; **the key was still in the i.** la clé était encore sur le contact **2** *Phys & Chem* ignition *f*

▸▸ *Aut* ***ignition coil*** bobine *f* d'allumage; *Aut* ***ignition cycle*** cycle *m* d'allumage; *Aut* ***ignition key*** clef *f* de contact; *Aut* ***ignition lock*** antivol-contact *m*; *Aut* ***ignition switch*** contact *m*; *Aut* ***ignition system*** circuit *m* d'allumage

ignoble [ɪg'nəʊbəl] ADJ infâme

ignominious [ˌɪgnə'mɪnɪəs] ADJ ignominieux

ignominiously [ˌɪgnə'mɪnɪəslɪ] ADV ignominieusement

ignominy ['ɪgnəmɪnɪ] N ignominie *f*

ignoramus [ˌɪgnə'reɪməs] *(pl* **ignoramuses**) N ignare *mf*

ignorance ['ɪgnərəns] N **1** *(lack of knowledge, awareness)* ignorance *f*; **out of** *or* **through sheer i.** par pure ignorance; **they kept him in i. of his sister's existence** ils lui ont caché l'existence de sa sœur; **forgive my i., but...** excuse mon ignorance, mais...; **i. of the law is no excuse** nul n'est censé ignorer la loi; **in a situation like this, i. is bliss** dans ce genre de situation, il vaut mieux ne pas savoir **2** *Pej (bad manners)* grossièreté *f*

ignorant ['ɪgnərənt] ADJ **1** *(uneducated)* ignorant; **I'm really i. about classical music/politics** je ne connais absolument rien à la musique classique/la politique **2** *(lacking knowledge ▸ person)* ignorant; *(▸ question, remark)* qui trahit l'ignorance; **I was i. as to his whereabouts** j'ignorais où il se trouvait; **he was i. of the facts** il ignorait les faits **3** *Pej (bad-mannered)* mal élevé, grossier

> Note that the French word **ignorant** never means **bad-mannered**.

ignorantly ['ɪgnərəntlɪ] ADV *(behave)* d'une manière grossière

ignore [ɪg'nɔː(r)] VT **1** *(pay no attention to ▸ person, remark)* ne pas prêter attention à, ignorer; *(▸ letter, invitation)* ne pas répondre à; *(▸ signal, red light)* ne pas respecter; **she completely ignored me** elle a fait semblant de ne pas me voir; **i. him and he'll go away** fais comme s'il n'était pas là et il te laissera tranquille; **we can't continue to i. these objections** on ne peut pas continuer à ne tenir aucun compte de ces objections; **I'll i. that!** *(what you said)* je ferai comme si je n'avais rien entendu! **2** *(take no account of ▸ warning, request, order)* ne pas tenir compte de; **he ignored the doctor's advice and continued smoking** il n'a pas suivi les conseils de son médecin et a continué de fumer **3** *(overlook)* **they can no longer i. what is going on here** il ne leur est plus possible d'ignorer *ou* de fermer les yeux sur ce qui se passe ici; **the report ignores certain crucial facts** le rapport passe sous silence des faits cruciaux

▸▸ *Comput* ***ignore character*** caractère *m* de suppression

> Note that the French verb **ignorer** also means **not to know**.

IGO [ˌaɪdʒiː'əʊ] N (*abbr* **Intergovernmental Organization**) OIG *f*

iguana [ɪ'gwɑːnə] N *Zool* iguane *m*

ikon = **icon**

IL *(written abbr* **Illinois**) Illinois *m*

ilex ['aɪleks] *(pl* **ilexes**) N *Bot* yeuse *f*, chêne *m* vert

ilium ['ɪlɪəm] N *Anat* ilion *m*

ilk [ɪlk] N *(type)* **people of that i.** ce genre de personnes; **books of that i.** des livres de ce genre

I'll [aɪl] = **I shall, I will**

ill [ɪl] ADJ **1** *(sick, unwell)* malade; **to fall** *or* **to be taken i.** tomber malade; **the smell makes me i.** l'odeur me rend malade; **I feel i. just thinking about it** rien que d'y penser, j'en suis malade **2** *Br (injured)* **he is critically i. with stab wounds** il est dans un état critique après avoir reçu de nombreux coups de couteau **3** *Literary (bad)* mauvais, néfaste; **i. fortune, i. luck** malheur *m*, malchance *f*; **the i. effects of alcohol** les effets *mpl* néfastes de l'alcool; **i. deeds** méfaits *mpl*; **house of i. repute** une maison mal famée; *Prov* **it's an i. wind that blows nobody any good** à quelque chose malheur est bon

N **1** *Literary (evil)* mal *m*; **to think/speak i. of sb** penser/dire du mal de qn; **for good or i.** *(whatever happens)* quoi qu'il arrive **2** *(difficulty, trouble)* malheur *m*; **the nation's ills** les malheurs *mpl* du pays **3** *(wrong)* dommage *m*, tort *m*; **I have suffered no i. at his hands** il ne m'a fait aucun tort

ADV **1** *(hardly)* difficilement; **we can i. afford these luxuries** ce sont des luxes que nous pouvons difficilement nous permettre; **we can i. afford to wait** nous ne pouvons vraiment pas nous permettre d'attendre **2** *Formal (badly)* mal; **it i. becomes** *or* **befits you to criticize** il vous sied mal de critiquer; **to augur** *or* **to bode i.** être de mauvais augure

▸▸ ***ill feeling*** ressentiment *m*, animosité *f*; ***ill health*** mauvaise santé *f*; **to suffer from i. health** *or* **to be in i. health** avoir des problèmes de santé; **because of i. health** pour des raisons de santé; ***ill humour*** mauvaise humeur *f*; **to be in an i. humour** être de mauvaise humeur; ***ill will*** malveillance *f*; **I bear them no i. will** je ne leur garde pas rancune, je ne leur en veux pas

ill-advised ADJ *(remark, comment)* peu judicieux, hors de propos, déplacé; *(action)* peu judicieux, déplacé; **he was i. to go away** il a eu tort *ou* il a été mal avisé de partir

ill-assorted ADJ mal assorti, disparate

ill-behaved ADJ qui se conduit *ou* se tient mal

ill-bred ADJ mal élevé

ill-concealed ADJ mal dissimulé

ill-considered ADJ *(hasty)* hâtif; *(thoughtless)* irréfléchi

ill-defined [-dɪ'faɪnd] ADJ mal défini

ill-disposed ADJ **1** *(unfriendly, unhelpful)* **to be i. towards sb** être mal disposé envers qn; **to be i. towards an idea/a proposal** ne pas être favorable à une idée/une proposition **2** *(disinclined)* **to be i. to do sth** être peu disposé à faire qch

illegal [ɪ'liːgəl] ADJ **1** *Law* illégal; *(parking)* interdit **2** *Comput (character, file name, instruction)* non autorisé

▸▸ *Med* ***illegal abortion*** interruption *f* illégale de grossesse; ***illegal confinement*** séquestration *f*; ***illegal entry*** violation *f* de domicile; ***illegal immigrant*** immigré(e) *m,f* clandestin(e)

illegality [ˌɪliː'gælətɪ] *(pl* **illegalities**) N illégalité *f*

illegally [ɪ'liːgəlɪ] ADV illégalement, d'une manière illégale; **to be i. parked** être en stationnement interdit

illegible [ɪ'ledʒɪbəl] ADJ illisible

illegibly [ɪ'ledʒɪblɪ] ADV illisiblement

illegitimacy [ˌɪlɪ'dʒɪtɪməsɪ] N illégitimité *f*

illegitimate [ˌɪlɪ'dʒɪtɪmət] ADJ **1** *(child)* naturel, illégitime **2** *(activity)* illégitime, interdit **3** *(argument)* illogique

N enfant *mf* naturel(elle)

illegitimately [ˌɪlɪ'dʒɪtɪmətlɪ] ADV **1** *(outside marriage)* hors du mariage **2** *(illegally)* illégitimement

ill-equipped ADJ **1** *(lacking equipment)* mal équipé, mal préparé **2** *(lacking qualities ▸ for job, situation)* **to be i. (for)** ne pas être à la hauteur (de), être mal armé (pour); **he felt i. to cope with the pressures of the job** il ne se sentait pas capable d'affronter les problèmes posés par son travail

ill-fated ADJ *(action)* malheureux, funeste; *(person)* qui joue de malheur, malheureux; *(day)* néfaste, de malchance; *(journey)* funeste, fatal

ill-favoured, *Am* **ill-favored** ADJ **1** *(ugly)* laid **2** *(unpleasant)* désagréable

ill-fitting ADJ *(garment, lid, window)* mal ajusté

ill-founded [-'faʊndɪd] ADJ *(hopes, confidence)* mal fondé; *(suspicions)* sans fondement

ill-gotten gains NPL biens *mpl* mal acquis

ill-humoured, *Am* **ill-humored** ADJ de mauvaise humeur

illiberal [ɪ'lɪbərəl] ADJ **1** *(bigoted, intolerant)* intolérant; *Pol (regime)* intolérant; *(legislation)* restrictif **2** *(ungenerous)* avare

illiberality [ɪˌlɪbə'rælɪtɪ] N **1** *(intolerance)* intolérance *f*, étroitesse *f* d'esprit; *Pol (of regime)* intolérance *f*; *(of legislation)* caractère *m* restrictif **2** *(lack of generosity)* avarice *f*

illicit [ɪ'lɪsɪt] ADJ illicite

illicitly [ɪ'lɪsɪtlɪ] ADV illicitement

illimitable [ɪ'lɪmɪtəbəl] ADJ illimité, infini

ill-informed ADJ **1** *(having the wrong information ▸ person)* mal renseigné **2** *(having insufficient information)* peu informé; **we continue to be i. about their intentions** nous ne sommes toujours pas sûrs de savoir quelles sont leurs intentions; **he made an i. attack on the government** il a attaqué le gouvernement en utilisant des arguments sans fondement

ill-intentioned [-ɪn'tenʃənd] ADJ malintentionné (**towards** envers)

illiquid [ɪ'lɪkwɪd] ADJ *Fin* non liquide

▸▸ ***illiquid assets*** actif *m* non-disponible *ou* immobilisé

illiquidity [ɪlɪ'kwɪdɪtɪ] N *Fin* illiquidité *f*

illiteracy [ɪ'lɪtərəsɪ] N analphabétisme *m*; **functional i.** illettrisme *m*

illiterate [ɪ'lɪtərət] ADJ **1** *(unable to read or write)* analphabète; **functionally i.** illettré **2** *(uneducated)* ignorant, sans éducation; **many young people are scientifically i.** de nombreux jeunes gens n'ont aucune formation *ou* connaissance scientifique; *Fig* **to be emotionally i.** ne pas savoir exprimer ses émotions **3** *(lacking culture ▸ person)* qui n'a aucune culture; (▸ *usage, style)* incorrect

N analphabète *mf*; **functional i.** illettré(e) *m,f*

ill-judged [-dʒʌdʒd] ADJ *(remark, attempt)* peu judicieux

ill-mannered ADJ *(person)* mal élevé, impoli; *(behaviour)* grossier, impoli

ill-matched ADJ mal assorti

ill-natured ADJ *(person)* d'un mauvais caractère, désagréable; *(remark, criticism etc)* désagréable; **to be i.** avoir mauvais caractère

illness ['ɪlnɪs] N maladie *f*

illogical [ɪ'lɒdʒɪkəl] ADJ illogique; **that's i.** ce n'est pas logique; **she knew it was i., but she felt very bitter** elle savait que c'était absurde, mais elle éprouvait une vive amertume

illogicality [ɪˌlɒdʒɪ'kælətɪ] *(pl* **illogicalities)** N illogisme *m*

illogically [ɪ'lɒdʒɪkəlɪ] ADV d'une manière illogique; **he assumed, i., that he meant nothing to her** il supposait, sans raison, qu'il n'était rien pour elle

ill-prepared ADJ mal préparé

ill-starred [-stɑːd] ADJ *Literary (person)* né sous une mauvaise étoile; *(day)* néfaste, funeste

ill-suited ADJ *(couple)* mal assorti; **to be i. for sth** être inapte à qch; **such clothes were i. to a hot climate** ces vêtements n'étaient pas adaptés à un climat chaud; **arts graduates are i. to this job** les diplômés en lettres ne sont pas aptes à ce travail

ill-tempered ADJ *(by nature)* grincheux, qui a mauvais caractère; *(temporarily)* de mauvaise humeur; *(remark, outburst etc)* plein de mauvaise humeur

ill-timed [-taɪmd] ADJ *(arrival, visit)* inopportun, intempestif, qui tombe mal; *(remark, question)* déplacé, mal à propos *(inv)*; **the meeting was very i.** cette réunion ne pouvait plus mal tomber

ill-treat VT maltraiter

ill-treatment N mauvais traitement *m*

illuminate [ɪ'luːmɪneɪt] VT **1** *(light up)* illuminer, éclairer **2** *(make clearer)* éclairer **3** *(manuscript)* enluminer

VI s'illuminer

illuminated [ɪ'luːmɪneɪtɪd] ADJ **1** *(lit up ▸ sign, notice)* lumineux **2** *(decorated ▸ manuscript)* enluminé

illuminating [ɪ'luːmɪneɪtɪŋ] ADJ *(speech, interview)* qui éclaire la situation/le sujet/*etc*; *(comparison, remark, example)* éclairant; **the programme was very i.** l'émission m'a appris beaucoup de choses

N **1** *(of building)* illumination *f* **2** *(of manuscript)* enluminure *f*

illumination [ɪˌluːmɪ'neɪʃən] N **1** *(light)* éclairage *m*; *(of building)* illumination *f*; **a candle was the only means of i.** il n'y avait pour tout éclairage qu'une bougie

2 *Art (of manuscript)* enluminure *f*

3 *Opt (of lens etc)* éclat *m*; *Phys* **(degree of) i.** éclairement *m*

4 *Rel (enlightenment)* illumination *f*

• **illuminations** NPL *(coloured lights)* illuminations *fpl*

illuminator [ɪ'luːmɪneɪtə(r)] N **1** *Elec* source *f* lumineuse **2** *Art (artist)* enlumineur(euse) *m,f*

illumine [ɪ'luːmɪn] VT *Literary* illuminer

ill-use *Literary* N [ˌɪl'juːs] *(cruel treatment)* mauvais traitement *m*

VT [ˌɪl'juːz] **1** *(physically)* maltraiter **2** *(behave badly towards)* ne pas bien traiter; **he feels he's been ill-used** il a le sentiment qu'il n'a pas été bien traité

illusion [ɪ'luːʒən] N **1** *(false impression)* illusion *f*; **mirrors give an i. of space** les miroirs donnent une illusion d'espace **2** *(false belief)* illusion *f*; **to be under an i.** se faire une illusion; **I have no illusions** *or* **am under no i. on that score** je ne me fais aucune illusion à ce sujet **3** *(magic trick)* illusion *f*

illusionist [ɪ'luːʒənɪst] N *(conjurer, magician)* illusionniste *mf*

illusive, illusory [ɪ'luːsərɪ] ADJ illusoire

illustrate ['ɪləstreɪt] VT **1** *(with pictures)* illustrer **2** *(demonstrate)* illustrer; **it clearly illustrates the need for improvement** cela montre bien que des améliorations sont nécessaires; **to i. my point** pour illustrer ce que je veux dire; **the lecture will be illustrated by slides** la conférence sera accompagnée de diapositives

illustrated ['ɪləstreɪtɪd] ADJ illustré

illustration [ˌɪlə'streɪʃən] N **1** *(picture)* illustration *f*; **illustrations** *(in book)* iconographie *f* **2** *(publishing process)* illustration *f*; **she works in i.** elle est illustratrice **3** *(demonstration)* illustration *f*; **it's a clear i. of a lack of government interest** cela illustre bien un manque d'intérêt de la part du gouvernement; **by way of i.** à titre d'exemple

▸▸ *Comput* ***illustration software*** logiciel *m* graphique

illustrative ['ɪləstrətɪv] ADJ *(picture, diagram)* qui illustre, explicatif; *(action, event, fact)* qui démontre, qui illustre; **the demonstrations are i. of the need for reform** les manifestations montrent que des réformes sont nécessaires

▸▸ ***illustrative example*** exemple *m* illustratif

illustrator ['ɪləstreɪtə(r)] N illustrateur(trice) *m,f*

illustrious [ɪ'lʌstrɪəs] ADJ illustre

illustriously [ɪ'lʌstrɪəslɪ] ADV de façon illustre

ILO [ˌaɪel'əʊ] N *Ind (abbr* **International Labour Organization)** OIT *f*

IM [ˌaɪ'em] *Comput (abbr* **instant messaging)** N messagerie *f* instantanée

VI communiquer par messagerie instantanée

I'm [aɪm] = **I am**

image ['ɪmɪdʒ] N **1** *(mental picture)* image *f*; **I still have an i. of her as a child** je la vois encore enfant; **many people have the wrong i. of her/of life in New York** beaucoup de gens se font une fausse idée d'elle/de la vie à New York

2 *(public appearance)* **(public) i.** image *f* de marque; **its i. is that of a dirty industrial city** cette ville a la réputation d'être une ville industrielle sale; **she's tired of her hippy i.** elle en a assez de son image baba cool; **their brief is to update the product's i.** ils ont pour mission de moderniser l'image du produit

3 *(likeness)* image *f*; **man was made in God's i.** l'homme a été créé à l'image de Dieu; **you are the (very** *or* **living) i. of your mother** tu es tout le portrait *ou* le portrait craché de ta mère

4 *(representation)* portrait *m*; *(sculpture)* image *f* (sculptée); *(of god etc)* représentation *f*, statue *f*; *(for worship)* idole *f*

5 *(in art)* image *f*; *(in literature)* image *f*, métaphore *f*; **I tried to create an i. of wartime Britain** j'ai essayé de brosser un tableau de la vie en Grande-Bretagne pendant la guerre

6 *Opt, Phot & Comput* image *f*

▸▸ *Comput* ***image bank*** banque *f* d'images; *Phys* ***image converter*** convertisseur *m* d'image(s); *Comput* ***image digitizer*** numériseur *m* d'image; *TV* ***image distortion*** distorsion *f* de l'image; *Opt & Phot* ***image enhancement*** correction *f* de l'image, retouche *f* d'images; *Opt & Phot* ***image enhancer*** correcteur *m* d'images; *Comput* ***image file*** fichier *m* vidéo *or* image; *Opt & Phot* ***image filtering*** filtrage *m* des images; ***image format*** format *m* graphique; *Opt* ***image intensifier*** intensificateur *m* d'image, amplificateur *m* de luminance; *Mktg* ***image pricing*** fixation *f* de prix en fonction de l'image; *Comput* ***image processing*** traitement *m* des images; *Comput* ***image processor*** unité *f* de traitement d'images

image-conscious ADJ conscient *ou* soucieux de son image

image-maker N conseiller(ère) *m,f* en image

imager ['ɪmɪdʒə(r)] N *Comput* imageur *m*

imagery ['ɪmɪdʒərɪ] N *(UNCOUNT)* **1** *(in literature)* images *fpl* **2** *(visual images)* imagerie *f*

imagesetter ['ɪmɪdʒˌsetə(r)] N *Comput & Typ* photocomposeuse *f*

imagesetting ['ɪmɪdʒˌsetɪŋ] N *Comput & Typ* photocomposition *f*

imaginable [ɪ'mædʒɪnəbəl] ADJ imaginable; **the worst thing i. happened** ce qu'on pouvait imaginer de pire est arrivé

imaginary [ɪ'mædʒɪnərɪ] ADJ **1** *(in one's imagination ▸ sickness, danger)* imaginaire **2** *(fictional ▸ character)* fictif

imagination [ɪˌmædʒɪ'neɪʃən] N imagination *f*; **to have no i.** n'avoir aucune imagination; **use your i.!** fais preuve d'un peu d'imagination!; **it's all in her i.** elle se fait des idées; **it was only my i.** c'est mon imagination qui me jouait des tours

imaginative [ɪ'mædʒɪnətɪv] ADJ *(person)* imaginatif; *(writing, idea, plan)* original

imaginativeness [ɪ'mædʒɪnətɪvnɪs] N *(of person)* imagination *f*; *(of story, idea, solution)* inventivité *f*

imagine [ɪ'mædʒɪn] VT **1** *(picture ▸ scene, person)* imaginer, s'imaginer, se représenter; **I can just i. her saying/doing that** je la vois très bien dire/faire ça; **I'd imagined him to be a much smaller man** je l'imaginais plus petit; **i. yourself in his situation** imaginez-vous dans sa situation, mettez-vous à sa place; **i. (that) you're on a beach** imagine-toi sur une plage; **you can't i. how awful it was** vous ne pouvez pas (vous) imaginer combien c'était horrible; **(you can) i. his delight!** vous pensez s'il était ravi!; **i. meeting you here!** ça alors, toi ici!; **you're imagining things** tu te fais des idées; **I was beginning to i. all sorts of things!** je commençais à m'imaginer des tas de choses **2** *(suppose, think)* supposer, imaginer; **I i. you're tired** je suppose *ou* j'imagine que vous êtes fatigué; **I i. them to be fairly rich** j'imagine qu'ils sont assez riches; **an intelligent child, I'd i.** un enfant intelligent, j'imagine; **i. (that) you've won** imagine que tu as gagné, suppose que tu aies gagné; **don't i. I'll help you again** ne t'imagine pas que je t'aiderai encore

VI **he ate all of it, can you i.?** il a tout mangé, tu t'imagines?; **I can i.** je veux bien le croire, j'imagine; **just i.!** tu t'imagines!

imagined [ɪ'mædʒɪnd] ADJ imaginé, imaginaire

imaging device ['ɪmɪdʒɪŋ-] N *Comput* imageur *m*

imaginings [ɪ'mædʒɪnɪŋz] NPL *(fears, dreams)* **never in my worst i. did I think it would come to this** je n'aurais jamais pensé que les choses en arriveraient là

imam [ɪ'mɑːm] N *Rel* imam *m*

IMAX® ['aɪmæks] N (procédé *m*) Imax® *m*

►► ***IMAX® cinema*** cinéma *m* Imax®

imbalance [ˌɪm'bæləns] N déséquilibre *m*

VT déséquilibrer

imbecile ['ɪmbɪsiːl] N **1** *(idiot)* imbécile *mf*, idiot (e) *m,f*; **to act the i.** faire l'imbécile; **you i.!** espèce d'imbécile *ou* d'idiot! **2** *Med* imbécile *mf*

ADJ imbécile, idiot

imbecilic [ˌɪmbɪ'sɪlɪk] ADJ imbécile, idiot

imbecility [ˌɪmbɪ'sɪlətɪ] *(pl* **imbecilities)** N **1** *(stupidity)* idiotie *f*, imbécillité *f* **2** *(stupid action)* idiotie *f*, imbécillité *f* **3** *Med* imbécillité *f*

imbibe [ɪm'baɪb] VT **1** *Formal or Hum (drink)* absorber **2** *Literary (knowledge, ideas, culture)* assimiler

VI *Formal or Hum* boire

imbroglio [ɪm'brəʊlɪəʊ] N imbroglio *m*

imbue [ɪm'bjuː] VT imprégner; **her parents had imbued her with high ideals** ses parents lui avaient inculqué de nobles idéaux; **his words were imbued with resentment** ses paroles étaient pleines de ressentiment

IMF [ˌaɪem'ef] N *Fin (abbr* **International Monetary Fund)** FMI *m*

imitable ['ɪmɪtəbəl] ADJ imitable

imitate ['ɪmɪteɪt] VT **1** *(copy ▸ person)* imiter, copier **2** *(mimic ▸ person)* singer, mimer; *(▸ call of bird etc)* imiter; **to i. its surroundings** *(insect etc)* prendre l'aspect de son milieu

imitation [ˌɪmɪ'teɪʃən] N **1** *(copy)* imitation *f*; **it's a cheap i.** c'est du toc; **a poor i. of the real thing** une pâle imitation de l'original; **beware of imitations** *(in advertisement)* méfiez-vous des contrefaçons; **an i. diamond necklace** un collier en faux diamants **2** *(action)* imitation *f*; **to learn by i.** apprendre par mimétisme; **he does everything in i. of his brother** il imite *ou* copie son frère en tout; *Prov* **i. is the sincerest form of flattery** = l'imitation est la flatterie la plus sincère qui soit

COMP faux (fausse)

►► ***imitation fur*** fourrure *f* synthétique; ***imitation jewellery*** bijoux *mpl* (de) fantaisie; ***imitation leather*** imitation *f* cuir, similicuir *m*; ***imitation pearls*** fausses perles *fpl*

imitative ['ɪmɪtətɪv] ADJ *(behaviour, sound)* imitatif; *(person, style)* imitateur; *Mktg (product)* d'imitation

imitator ['ɪmɪteɪtə(r)] N imitateur(trice) *m,f*

immaculate [ɪ'mækjʊlət] ADJ **1** *(clean ▸ house, clothes, room)* impeccable, d'une propreté irréprochable **2** *(faultless ▸ work, behaviour, performance etc)* parfait, impeccable **3** *(morally pure)* irréprochable

►► ***the Immaculate Conception*** l'Immaculée Conception *f*

immaculately [ɪ'mækjʊlətlɪ] ADV **1** *(spotlessly ▸ clean, tidy)* impeccablement; **i. dressed** tiré à quatre épingles; **i. white** d'une blancheur éclatante **2** *(faultlessly ▸ behave, perform etc)* d'une manière irréprochable, impeccablement, parfaitement

immanent ['ɪmənənt] ADJ immanent

immaterial [ˌɪmə'tɪərɪəl] ADJ **1** *(unimportant)* sans importance; **that point is i. to what we are discussing** cela n'a rien à voir avec ce dont nous sommes en train de parler **2** *Phil* immatériel

immature [ˌɪmə'tjʊə(r)] ADJ **1** *(childish)* immature; **she's very i.** elle manque vraiment de maturité; **stop being so i.!** arrête de te comporter comme un gamin! **2** *Bot & Zool* immature, jeune

immaturity [ˌɪmə'tjʊərətɪ] N **1** *(childishness)* manque *m* de maturité, immaturité *f* **2** *Bot & Zool* immaturité *f* **3** *Psy* immaturation *f*

immeasurable [ɪ'meʒərəbəl] ADJ **1** *(very large)* incommensurable **2** *Fig (as intensifier)* illimité, incommensurable; **to have an i. influence on sth** avoir une influence énorme sur qch

immeasurably [ɪ'meʒərəblɪ] ADV **1** *(long, high)* incommensurablement **2** *Fig (as intensifier)* infiniment

immediacy [ɪ'miːdjəsɪ] N impact *m* immédiat; **the i. of the crisis** les effets immédiats de la crise

immediate [ɪ'miːdjət] ADJ **1** *(instant)* immédiat, urgent; **the problem needs i. attention** il est urgent de régler le problème; **we need an i. answer** il nous faut une réponse immédiate

2 *(close in time)* immédiat; **in the i. future** dans les heures *ou* les jours qui viennent; **my i. objective** mon objectif premier; **I have no i. plans to retire** je n'ai pas l'intention de prendre ma retraite dans un futur proche

3 *(nearest)* immédiat, proche; **my i. relatives** mes parents les plus proches

4 *(direct ▸ cause, influence)* immédiat, direct

►► *Comput* ***immediate access*** accès *m* direct

immediately [ɪ'miːdjətlɪ] ADV **1** *(at once)* tout de suite, immédiatement; **I left i. after** je suis parti tout de suite après **2** *(directly)* directement; **it does not affect me i.** cela ne me touche pas directement **3** *(just)* juste; **i. above the window** juste au-dessus de la fenêtre

CONJ *Br* dès que; **let me know i. he arrives** dès qu'il sera là, prévenez-moi

immemorial [ˌɪmə'mɔːrɪəl] ADJ immémorial; **since** *or* **from time i.** de temps immémorial

immense [ɪ'mens] ADJ immense, considérable

immensely [ɪ'menslɪ] ADV immensément, extrêmement; **I'm i. grateful to you** je vous suis extrêmement reconnaissant; **she is i. fat** elle est absolument énorme

immensity [ɪ'mensətɪ] N **1** *(of universe, fortune etc)* immensité *f* **2** *(of problem, task)* énormité *f*

immerse [ɪ'mɜːs] VT **1** *(in liquid)* immerger, plonger; **I'm going to i. myself in a hot bath** je vais me plonger dans un bain chaud **2** *Fig* **I immersed myself in my work** je me suis plongé dans mon travail; **she went to London to i. herself in the English language** elle est allée à Londres en séjour linguistique **3** *Rel* baptiser par immersion

immersion [ɪ'mɜːʃən] N **1** *(in liquid)* immersion *f* **2** *Fig (in reading, work)* absorption *f* **3** *Astron & Rel* immersion *f*

►► ***immersion course*** cours *m* de langue intensif *(dans lequel seule la langue apprise est utilisée)*; ***immersion heater*** chauffe-eau *m inv* électrique

immigrant ['ɪmɪgrənt] N immigré(e) *m,f*

ADJ immigré

►► ***immigrant worker*** travailleur(euse) *m,f* immigré(e)

immigrate ['ɪmɪgreɪt] VI immigrer

immigration [ˌɪmɪ'greɪʃən] N **1** *(act of immigrating)* immigration *f* **2** *(control section)* services *mpl* de l'immigration; **to go through i.** passer l'immigration

COMP de l'immigration

►► ***immigration authorities, immigration control*** services *mpl* de l'immigration; ***immigration laws*** lois *fpl* sur l'immigration; ***immigration officer*** agent *m* du service de l'immigration; ***immigration quotas*** quotas *mpl* d'immigration; ***immigration regulations*** réglementation *f* relative à l'immigration

imminence ['ɪmɪnəns] N imminence *f*

imminent ['ɪmɪnənt] ADJ imminent

immobile [*Br* ɪ'məʊbaɪl, *Am* ɪ'məʊbəl] ADJ immobile

immobility [ˌɪmə'bɪlətɪ] N immobilité *f*

immobilize, -ise [ɪ'məʊbɪlaɪz] VT *(gen) & Fin* immobiliser

immobilizer, -iser [ɪ'məʊbɪlaɪzə(r)] N *Aut* (système *m*) antidémarrage *m*

immoderate [ɪ'mɒdərət] ADJ immodéré, excessif

immoderately [ɪ'mɒdərətlɪ] ADV immodérément

immodest [ɪ'mɒdɪst] ADJ **1** *(indecent)* impudique **2** *(vain)* prétentieux

immodestly [ɪ'mɒdɪstlɪ] ADV **1** *(indecently)* impudiquement, de façon indécente **2** *(vainly)* sans modestie; **he rather i. claims to be the best** il déclare non sans prétention qu'il est le meilleur

immolate ['ɪməleɪt] VT *Literary* immoler

immoral [ɪ'mɒrəl] ADJ immoral; *Law* **for i. purposes** aux fins de débauche

►► *Law* ***immoral earnings*** gains *mpl* immoraux; **to live off i. earnings** gagner sa vie par des procédés immoraux

immorality [ˌɪmə'rælətɪ] N immoralité *f*

immorally [ɪ'mɒrəlɪ] ADV immoralement

immortal [ɪ'mɔːtəl] N immortel(elle) *m,f*

ADJ immortel

immortality [ˌɪmɔː'tælətɪ] N immortalité *f*

immortalize, -ise [ɪ'mɔːtəˌlaɪz] VT immortaliser

immovable, immoveable [ɪ'muːvəbəl] ADJ **1** *(fixed)* fixe; *(impossible to move)* impossible à déplacer **2** *(determined ▸ person, opposition)* inébranlable

• **immovables** NPL *Law* biens *mpl* immobiliers

►► *Rel* ***immovable feast*** fête *f* fixe; *Law* ***immovable property*** biens *mpl* immeubles *ou* immobiliers

immune [ɪ'mjuːn] ADJ **1** *Biol & Med* immunisé (**to** contre) **2** *Fig* **to be i. to temptation/flattery** être immunisé contre les tentations/la flatterie **3** *(exempt)* **i. from** exempt de, exonéré de; **i. from taxation** exonéré d'impôts; **i. from prosecution** inviolable

►► *Med* ***immune deficiency*** déficience *f* immunitaire; *Med* ***immune reaction, immune response*** réaction *f* immunitaire; *Med* ***immune serum*** immunsérum *m*, antisérum *m*; *Biol* ***immune system*** système *m* immunitaire

immunity [ɪ'mjuːnətɪ] N **1** *Biol & Med* immunité *f* (**to** contre) **2** *(exemption)* **i. from** exonération *f* de, exemption *f* de; **i. from taxation** exonération *f* d'impôts **3** *Pol (diplomatic, parliamentary)* immunité *f*; **i. from prosecution** immunité *f*, inviolabilité *f*

immunization, -isation [ˌɪmjuːnaɪ'zeɪʃən] N *Med* immunisation *f* (**to** contre)

immunize, -ise ['ɪmjuːnaɪz] VT *Med* immuniser, vacciner (**to** contre)

immunodeficiency [ˌɪmjuːnəʊdɪ'fɪʃənsɪ] *(pl* **immunodeficiencies)** N *Med* immunodéficience *f*

immunoglobulin [ˌɪmjuːnəʊ'glɒbjʊlɪn] N *Med* immunoglobuline *f*

immunological [ˌɪmjuːnəʊ'lɒdʒɪkəl] ADJ *Med* immunologique

immunology [ˌɪmjuːn'ɒlədʒɪ] N *Med* immunologie *f*

immunosuppressant [ˌɪmjuːnəʊsə'presənt] *Med* ADJ immunosuppresseur

N immunosuppresseur *m*

immunosuppression [ˌɪmjuːnəʊsə'preʃən] N *Med* immunosuppression *f*

immunosuppressive [ˌɪmjuːnəʊsə'presɪv] ADJ *Med* immunosuppresseur

immunotherapy [ˌɪmjuːnəʊ'θerəpɪ] N *Med* immunothérapie *f*

immure [ɪ'mjʊə(r)] VT *Arch or Literary* **1** *(shut away ▸ person)* enfermer, cloîtrer; **he had immured himself in the library** il s'était enfermé dans la bibliothèque; **immured in silence** cloîtré dans le silence **2** *(wall up ▸ victim)* emmurer

immutability [ɪˌmjuːtə'bɪlətɪ] N immuabilité *f*

immutable [ɪ'mjuːtəbəl] ADJ immuable

immutably [ɪ'mjuːtəblɪ] ADV immuablement

imp [ɪmp] N *(devil)* lutin *m*; *(child)* coquin(e) *m,f*; **she's a little i.!** c'est une petite coquine!

impact N [ˈɪmpækt] **1** *(force)* impact *m*; **on i.** au moment de l'impact **2** *Fig (of speech, play, advertising campaign etc)* impact *m*, impression *f*; **the scandal had little i. on the election results** le scandale a eu peu de répercussions *ou* d'incidence sur les résultats de l'élection; **you made** *or* **had quite an i. on him** vous avez fait une forte impression sur lui **3** *Mktg* impact *m*
VT [ɪmˈpækt] **1** *(collide with)* entrer en collision avec **2** *(influence)* avoir un impact sur
VI [ɪmˈpækt] **1** *(affect)* **to i. on** produire un effet sur, impacter **2** *Comput* frapper
▸▸ *Br* **impact adhesive** colle *f* instantanée; *Aut* **impact bar** barre *f* de renfort; *St Exch* **impact day** = jour où l'on annonce une nouvelle émission d'actions; *Comput* **impact printer** imprimante *f* à impact; *Mktg* **impact study** étude *f* d'impact

impacted [ɪmˈpæktɪd] ADJ *(tooth)* inclus; *(fracture)* avec impaction

impair [ɪmˈpeə(r)] VT *(sight, hearing, mental faculties)* diminuer, affaiblir; *(strength)* diminuer; *(authority)* saper; *(relationship, chances, ability)* compromettre

impairment [ɪmˈpeəmənt] N *(of sight, hearing, mental faculties, chances)* affaiblissement *m*, diminution *f*; *(of relationship)* détérioration *f*

impala [ɪmˈpɑːlə] N *Zool* impala *m*

impale [ɪmˈpeɪl] VT empaler; **to i. oneself on sth** s'empaler sur qch

impalpable [ɪmˈpælpəbəl] ADJ impalpable; *(ideas)* insaisissable

impanel [ɪmˈpænəl] *(pt & pp* **impaneled**, *cont* **impaneling)** VT *Am (jury)* constituer; *(juror)* inscrire sur la liste *ou* le tableau du jury

impart [ɪmˈpɑːt] VT **1** *(communicate ▸ news, truth)* apprendre **2** *(transmit ▸ knowledge, wisdom)* transmettre **3** *(give ▸ quality, flavour)* donner

impartial [ɪmˈpɑːʃəl] ADJ impartial

impartiality [ɪmˌpɑːʃɪˈælətɪ] N impartialité *f*

impartially [ɪmˈpɑːʃəlɪ] ADV impartialement

impassable [ɪmˈpɑːsəbəl] ADJ *(river, frontier)* infranchissable; *(road)* impraticable

impasse [æmˈpɑːs] N impasse *f*; **the talks have reached an i.** les pourparlers sont dans une impasse

impassioned [ɪmˈpæʃənd] ADJ passionné; *(plea)* fervent

impassive [ɪmˈpæsɪv] ADJ impassible

impassively [ɪmˈpæsɪvlɪ] ADV impassiblement; **to look at sb/sth i.** regarder qn/qch d'un air impassible

impatience [ɪmˈpeɪʃəns] N **1** *(lack of patience)* impatience *f* **2** *(irritation)* irritation *f*; **I fully understand your i. at the delay** je comprends parfaitement que ce retard vous irrite **3** *(intolerance)* intolérance *f*; *Formal* **he was known for his i. of sloppy work** il avait la réputation de mal supporter le travail brouillon

impatient [ɪmˈpeɪʃənt] ADJ **1** *(eager, anxious)* impatient; **I'm i. to see her again** je suis impatient de la revoir; **they were i. for the results** ils attendaient les résultats avec impatience **2** *(irritated)* **she's i. with her children** elle n'a aucune patience avec ses enfants; **I'm getting i.** je commence à m'impatienter *ou* à perdre patience **3** *(intolerant)* intolérant; **he's i. with people who always ask the same questions** il ne supporte pas les gens qui lui posent toujours les mêmes questions

impatiently [ɪmˈpeɪʃəntlɪ] ADV impatiemment, avec impatience

impeach [ɪmˈpiːtʃ] VT **1** *Br Law (accuse)* accuser, inculper
2 *Am Law & Pol* entamer une procédure d'"impeachment" contre
3 *Br Formal (doubt ▸ motives, honesty)* mettre en doute; *(▸ character)* attaquer
4 *Law* **to i. a witness** récuser un témoin

impeachable [ɪmˈpiːtʃəbəl] ADJ *Am Law & Pol* = qui peut donner lieu à une procédure d'impeachment

impeachment [ɪmˈpiːtʃmənt] N **1** *Br Law (accusation)* mise *f* en accusation **2** *Am Law & Pol* = mise en accusation d'un élu devant le Congrès

impeccable [ɪmˈpekəbəl] ADJ *(house, room)* impeccable; *(conduct, management)* irréprochable; *(manners)* impeccable, irréprochable; **he speaks i. English** son anglais est impeccable

impeccably [ɪmˈpekəblɪ] ADV impeccablement

impecunious [ˌɪmpɪˈkjuːnɪəs] ADJ *Formal* impécunieux

impedance [ɪmˈpiːdəns] N *Elec* impédance *f*

impede [ɪmˈpiːd] VT **1** *(obstruct ▸ traffic, player)* gêner **2** *(hinder ▸ progress)* ralentir, entraver; *(▸ plan)* faire obstacle à, entraver; *(▸ person)* gêner

impediment [ɪmˈpedɪmənt] N **1** *(obstacle)* obstacle *m* **2** *(handicap)* défaut *m* (physique) **3** *Law* empêchement *m*

impedimenta [ɪmˌpedɪˈmentə] NPL *Fig* impedimenta *mpl*

impel [ɪmˈpel] *(pt & pp* **impelled**, *cont* **impelling)** VT **1** *(urge, incite)* inciter; *(compel)* obliger, contraindre; **I felt impelled to intervene** je me suis senti obligé d'intervenir **2** *(propel)* pousser

impeller [ɪmˈpelə(r)] N *Tech* rotor *m*; *(of water pump)* turbine *f*; *(of converter)* roue *f* pompe

impending [ɪmˈpendɪŋ] ADJ imminent

impenetrability [ɪmˌpenɪtrəˈbɪlɪtɪ] N **1** *(of wall, forest, fog, defences)* impénétrabilité *f*; *Fig (of mystery)* caractère *m* inexplicable **2** *(incomprehensibility ▸ of jargon, system etc)* caractère *m* incompréhensible

impenetrable [ɪmˈpenɪtrəbəl] ADJ **1** *(wall, forest, fog, defences)* impénétrable; *Fig (mystery)* insondable, impénétrable **2** *(incomprehensible ▸ jargon, system etc)* incompréhensible

impenitence [ɪmˈpenɪtəns] N impénitence *f*

impenitent [ɪmˈpenɪtənt] ADJ impénitent; **he is still utterly i.** il n'a toujours pas le moindre remords

impenitently [ɪmˈpenɪtəntlɪ] ADV avec impénitence

imperative [ɪmˈperətɪv] ADJ **1** *(essential)* (absolument) essentiel, impératif; **it's i. that you reply immediately** il faut absolument que vous répondiez tout de suite; **it was i. to finalize the deal** il fallait impérativement conclure l'affaire **2** *(categorical ▸ orders, voice, tone)* impérieux, impératif **3** *Gram* impératif
N *Gram* impératif *m*; **in the i.** à l'impératif

imperceptible [ˌɪmpəˈseptəbəl] ADJ imperceptible; **i. to the human eye/ear** invisible/inaudible (pour l'homme)

imperceptibly [ˌɪmpəˈseptəblɪ] ADV imperceptiblement

imperfect [ɪmˈpɜːfɪkt] ADJ **1** *(flawed ▸ work, argument)* imparfait
2 *(faulty ▸ machine)* défectueux; *(▸ goods)* de second choix; **it's slightly i.** *(item for sale)* il a un léger défaut
3 *(incomplete)* incomplet(ète), inachevé
4 *Gram* imparfait
N *Gram* imparfait *m*; **in the i.** à l'imparfait

imperfection [ˌɪmpəˈfekʃən] N **1** *(imperfect state)* imperfection *f* **2** *(fault)* imperfection *f*, défaut *m*

imperfectly [ɪmˈpɜːfɪktlɪ] ADV imparfaitement

imperial [ɪmˈpɪərɪəl] ADJ **1** *(in titles)* impérial; **His I. Majesty** Sa Majesté Impériale
2 *(majestic)* majestueux, auguste
3 *(imperious)* impérieux
4 *Br (weights and measures)* = relatif au système de mesure anglo-saxon utilisant les miles, les pintes etc
N *(beard)* impériale *f*, barbe *f* à l'impériale
▸▸ *Br* **imperial gallon** gallon *m* (britannique); **imperial pint** pinte *f* (britannique)

imperialism [ɪmˈpɪərɪəlɪzəm] N impérialisme *m*

imperialist [ɪmˈpɪərɪəlɪst] N impérialiste *mf*
ADJ impérialiste

imperialistic [ɪmˌpɪərɪəˈlɪstɪk] ADJ impérialiste

imperially [ɪmˈpɪərɪəlɪ] ADV **1** *(majestically)* majestueusement **2** *(authoritatively)* impérieusement

imperil [ɪmˈperɪl] *(Br pt & pp* **imperilled**, *cont* **imperilling**, *Am pt & pp* **imperiled**, *cont* **imperiling)** VT mettre en péril

imperious [ɪmˈpɪərɪəs] ADJ *(authoritative)* impérieux, autoritaire

imperiously [ɪmˈpɪərɪəslɪ] ADV *(authoritatively)* impérieusement, autoritairement

imperishable [ɪmˈperɪʃəbəl] ADJ *(quality, truth)* impérissable; *(goods)* non périssable

impermanent [ɪmˈpɜːmənənt] ADJ fugace

impermeable [ɪmˈpɜːmɪəbəl] ADJ *(soil, cell, wall etc)* imperméable; *(container)* étanche

impersonal [ɪmˈpɜːsənəl] ADJ **1** *(objective)* impartial **2** *(cold)* froid, impersonnel **3** *Gram* impersonnel
▸▸ *Fin* **impersonal accounts** comptes *mpl* impersonnels

impersonally [ɪmˈpɜːsənəlɪ] ADV **1** *(objectively)* impartialement **2** *(coldly)* avec froideur

impersonate [ɪmˈpɜːsəneɪt] VT **1** *(imitate)* imiter **2** *(pretend to be)* se faire passer pour

impersonation [ɪmˌpɜːsəˈneɪʃən] N **1** *(imitation)* imitation *f*; **to do an i. of sb** imiter qn **2** *(pretence of being)* imposture *f*

impersonator [ɪmˈpɜːsəneɪtə(r)] N **1** *(mimic)* imitateur(trice) *m,f* **2** *(impostor)* imposteur *m*

impertinence [ɪmˈpɜːtɪnəns] N impertinence *f*

impertinent [ɪmˈpɜːtɪnənt] ADJ **1** *(rude)* impertinent, insolent (**to** envers) **2** *(irrelevant)* hors de propos, non pertinent

impertinently [ɪmˈpɜːtɪnəntlɪ] ADV avec impertinence

imperturbable [ˌɪmpəˈtɜːbəbəl] ADJ imperturbable

impervious [ɪmˈpɜːvɪəs] ADJ **1** *(unreceptive, untouched ▸ person)* imperméable, fermé; **i. to criticism** imperméable à la critique; **he was i. to her charm** il était insensible à son charme **2** *(resistant ▸ material)* **i. to heat** résistant à la chaleur; **i. to damp/water** imperméable

impetigo [ˌɪmpɪˈtaɪgəʊ] N *(UNCOUNT) Med* impétigo *m*

impetuosity [ɪmˌpetjʊˈɒsətɪ] N impétuosité *f*

impetuous [ɪmˈpetʃʊəs] ADJ impétueux; *(decision)* hâtif

impetuously [ɪmˈpetʃʊəslɪ] ADV avec impétuosité

impetuousness [ɪmˈpetʃʊəsnɪs] N impétuosité *f*

impetus [ˈɪmpɪtəs] N **1** *(force)* force *f* d'impulsion; *(speed)* élan *m*; *(weight)* poids *m*; **to gain i.** prendre *ou* gagner de l'importance; **to lose i.** perdre de son élan **2** *Fig (incentive, drive)* impulsion *f*, élan *m*; **to give new i. to sth** donner un nouvel élan à qch, relancer qch

impiety [ɪmˈpaɪətɪ] *(pl* **impieties)** N **1** *Rel* impiété *f* **2** *Formal (disrespect)* irrévérence *f*

▸ **impinge on, impinge upon** [ɪmˈpɪndʒ] VT INSEP **1** *(affect)* affecter; **it impinges in a big way on all our lives** ça affecte énormément notre vie à tous; **to i. sb's conscious mind** venir à la conscience de qn; **it didn't even i. his consciousness** il ne s'en est même pas rendu compte **2** *(infringe on ▸ rights)* empiéter sur

impingement [ɪmˈpɪndʒmənt] N empiètement *m*

impious [ˈɪmpɪəs] ADJ **1** *Rel* impie **2** *Formal (disrespectful)* irrévérent

impiously [ˈɪmpɪəslɪ] ADV **1** *Rel* avec impiété **2** *Formal (disrespectfully)* avec irrévérence

impish [ˈɪmpɪʃ] ADJ *(laughter, face)* de petit diable, d'espiègle; *(child, remark)* espiègle, malicieux

impishly [ˈɪmpɪʃlɪ] ADV de façon espiègle

impishness [ˈɪmpɪʃnɪs] N espièglerie *f*

implacable [ɪmˈplækəbəl] ADJ implacable

implacably [ɪmˈplækəblɪ] ADV implacablement

implant N [ˈɪmplɑːnt] *Med (under skin)* implant *m*; *(graft)* greffe *f*
VT [ɪmˈplɑːnt] **1** *(instil ▸ idea, feeling)* inculquer (**in sb** à qn) **2** *Med (graft)* greffer; *(place under skin)* implanter

implantable [ɪmˈplɑːntəbəl] ADJ *Med* implantable

implausible [ɪmˈplɔːzəbəl] ADJ invraisemblable

implausibly [ɪmˈplɔːzəblɪ] ADV invraisemblablement; **to end i.** *(book, film etc)* se terminer de façon peu vraisemblable

implement N [ˈɪmplɪmənt] **1** *(tool)* outil *m*; **agricultural implements** matériel *m* agricole; **gardening implements** outils *mpl* de jardinage; **kitchen implements** ustensiles *mpl* de cuisine **2** *Fig (means)* instrument *m*

VT [ˈɪmplɪment] *(plan, orders)* exécuter; *(ideas, policies)* appliquer, mettre en œuvre; *(product, campaign)* mettre en œuvre

implementation [ˌɪmplɪmenˈteɪʃən] N *(of plan, orders)* exécution *f*; *(of ideas, policies)* application *f*, mise *f* en œuvre; *(of product, campaign)* mise *f* en œuvre

implicate [ˈɪmplɪkeɪt] VT **1** *(show involvement of)* impliquer **2** *Formal (imply)* impliquer, renfermer

implication [ˌɪmplɪˈkeɪʃən] N **1** *(possible repercussion)* implication *f*; **the full implications of the report are not yet clear** il est encore trop tôt pour mesurer pleinement les implications de ce rapport **2** *(suggestion)* suggestion *f*; *(insinuation)* insinuation *f*; *(hidden meaning)* sous-entendu *m*; **by i.** par voie de conséquence; **the i. was that we would be punished** tout portait à croire que nous serions punis **3** *(involvement)* implication *f*

implicit [ɪmˈplɪsɪt] ADJ **1** *(implied)* implicite; **his feelings were i. in his words** ses paroles laissaient deviner ses sentiments **2** *(absolute ▸ confidence, obedience)* total, absolu; **i. faith** confiance *f* aveugle

implicitly [ɪmˈplɪsɪtlɪ] ADV **1** *(by implication)* implicitement **2** *(absolutely)* absolument

implied [ɪmˈplaɪd] ADJ implicite, sous-entendu

implode [ɪmˈpləʊd] VI imploser

implore [ɪmˈplɔː(r)] VT supplier, implorer; **I i. you!** je vous en supplie!

imploring [ɪmˈplɔːrɪŋ] ADJ suppliant, implorant

imploringly [ɪmˈplɔːrɪŋlɪ] ADV *(say)* d'un ton suppliant *ou* implorant; *(look at)* d'un air suppliant *ou* implorant

implosion [ɪmˈpləʊʒən] N implosion *f*

imply [ɪmˈplaɪ] *(pt & pp* **implied***)* VT **1** *(insinuate)* insinuer; *(give impression)* laisser entendre *ou* supposer; **are you implying that I'm mistaken?** voulez-vous insinuer que je me trompe?; **she implied that it wouldn't take long** elle a laissé entendre que cela ne prendrait pas longtemps; **your silence implies that you are guilty** votre silence laisse à penser que vous êtes coupable **2** *(presuppose)* impliquer; *(involve)* comporter; **it implies a lot of hard work** cela implique beaucoup de travail

impolite [ˌɪmpəˈlaɪt] ADJ impoli (**to** envers)

impolitely [ˌɪmpəˈlaɪtlɪ] ADV impoliment

impoliteness [ˌɪmpəˈlaɪtnɪs] N impolitesse *f*

impolitic [ɪmˈpɒlətɪk] ADJ peu *ou* mal avisé, maladroit

imponderability [ɪmˌpɒndərəˈbɪlɪtɪ] N impondérabilité *f*

imponderable [ɪmˈpɒndrəbəl] N impondérable *m*

ADJ impondérable

import N [ˈɪmpɔːt] **1** *Com (activity)* importation *f*; *(imported article)* importation *f*, article *m* importé; **the government has put a tax on imports** le gouvernement a instauré une taxe sur les produits d'importation *ou* les produits importés **2** *Formal (meaning)* signification *f*; *(content)* teneur *f* **3** *Formal (importance)* importance *f*; *(of remark)* portée *f*

COMP [ˈɪmpɔːt] *(company, licence, surcharge)* d'importation; *(duty)* de douane, sur les importations; *(trade)* des importations

VT [ɪmˈpɔːt] **1** *Com* importer; **lamb imported from New Zealand into Britain** agneau de Nouvelle-Zélande importé en Grande-Bretagne

2 *(imply)* signifier

3 *Comput* importer (**from** depuis)

4 *Arch or Literary (be important)* **these questions i. us nearly** ces questions nous importent fort; **it imports us to know whether...** il nous importe de savoir si..., il est important que nous sachions si...

►► ***import agent*** commissionnaire *mf* importateur(trice), agent *m* importateur; ***import ban*** interdiction *f* d'importation; **to impose an i. ban on sth** interdire qch d'importation; ***import controls*** contrôles *mpl* à l'importation; ***import goods*** marchandises *fpl* à l'import; ***import list*** liste *f* des importations; *(of prices)* tarif *m* d'entrée; ***import permit*** permis *m* d'importer *ou* d'importation; ***import potential*** capacité *f* d'importation; ***import price*** prix *m* à l'importation, prix *m* (à l')import; ***import quotas*** contingents *mpl* d'importation; ***import restrictions*** restrictions *fpl* à l'importation; ***import substitution*** substitution *f* d'importation; ***import tariff*** tarif *m* import; ***import tax*** taxe *f* à l'importation

importable [ɪmˈpɔːtəbəl] ADJ importable

importance [ɪmˈpɔːtəns] N importance *f*; **to be of i.** avoir de l'importance; **it is of great i. to act now** il est très important d'agir maintenant; **it's of no i. whatsoever** cela n'a aucune espèce d'importance; **to give** *or* **to attach i. to sth** attacher de l'importance à qch; **a position of i.** un poste important; *Pej* **to be full of one's own i.** être imbu de sa personne

important [ɪmˈpɔːtənt] ADJ **1** *(gen)* important; **it's not i.** ça n'a pas d'importance; **it is i. that you (should) get the job** il est important que vous obteniez cet emploi; **my job is i. to me** mon travail compte beaucoup pour moi; **stop trying to look i.** cesse de te donner des airs importants **2** *(influential)* **an i. book/writer** un livre-clef/grand écrivain

importantly [ɪmˈpɔːtəntlɪ] ADV *(look at)* d'un air important; *(say)* d'un ton important; **and, more i.... et**, ce qui est plus important...

importation [ˌɪmpɔːˈteɪʃən] N **1** *Com (of goods)* importation *f*; *Am (imported article)* importation *f*, article *m* d'importation **2** *Comput* importation *f*

importer [ɪmˈpɔːtə(r)] N *Com* **1** *(person)* importateur(trice) *m,f* **2** *(country)* pays *m* importateur; **an oil i.** un pays importateur de pétrole

import-export *Com* N import-export *m*

COMP *(company)* d'import-export

importing [ɪmˈpɔːtɪŋ] N **1** *Com (of goods)* importation *f* **2** *Comput* importation *f*

ADJ *Com (country)* importateur(trice)

importunate [ɪmˈpɔːtjʊnət] ADJ *Formal (visitor, beggar)* importun; *(demands, questions)* incessant

importune [ɪmˈpɔːtjuːn] *Formal* VT importuner, harceler; **to i. sb with questions** harceler *ou* presser qn de questions

importunity [ˌɪmpɔːˈtjuːnətɪ] N *(harassment)* sollicitation *f*

impose [ɪmˈpəʊz] VT *(price, tax, attitude, belief, restrictions)* imposer; *(fine, penalty)* infliger; **to i. a ban on sth** interdire qch; **to i. a task on sb** imposer une tâche à qn

VI s'imposer; **I'm sorry to i.** je suis désolé de vous déranger; **to i. on sb** abuser de la gentillesse de qn; **they i. upon his hospitality** ils abusent de son hospitalité

imposing [ɪmˈpəʊzɪŋ] ADJ *(person, building)* impressionnant; *(air, tone)* imposant

imposition [ˌɪmpəˈzɪʃən] N **1** *(of tax, sanction)* imposition *f* **2** *(burden)* charge *f*, fardeau *m*; *(unfair demand)* abus *m*; **I don't want to be an i. (on you)** je ne veux pas abuser de votre gentillesse *ou* de votre bonté; **her asking me to do that was a bit of an i.** elle abuse un peu de m'avoir demandé de faire ça **3** *Typ* imposition *f*

impossibility [ɪmˌpɒsəˈbɪlətɪ] *(pl* **impossibilities***)* N impossibilité *f*; **it's a physical i. for us to arrive on time** nous sommes dans l'impossibilité matérielle d'arriver à l'heure; **it's a total i.** c'est totalement impossible

impossible [ɪmˈpɒsəbəl] ADJ **1** *(not possible)* impossible; **it's i. for me to leave work before 6 p.m.** il m'est impossible de quitter mon travail avant 18 heures **2** *(difficult to believe)* impossible, invraisemblable; **it is i. that he should be lying** il est impossible qu'il mente **3** *(unbearable)* impossible, insupportable; **he made their lives i.** il leur a rendu la vie insupportable *ou* impossible

N impossible *m*; **to attempt/to ask the i.** tenter/demander l'impossible

impossibly [ɪmˈpɒsəblɪ] ADV **1** *(extremely)* extrêmement; **i. difficult** extrêmement difficile; **the film is i. long** le film n'en finit pas **2** *(unbearably)* insupportablement; **they were behaving i.** ils sont totalement insupportables

impostor, imposter [ɪmˈpɒstə(r)] N imposteur *m*

imposture [ɪmˈpɒstʃə(r)] N *Formal* imposture *f*

impotence [ˈɪmpətəns] N **1** *Med & Physiol (sexual)* impuissance *f* **2** *(powerlessness)* impuissance *f*; *(weakness)* faiblesse *f*, impotence *f*

impotent [ˈɪmpətənt] ADJ **1** *Med & Physiol (sexually)* impuissant **2** *(powerless)* impuissant; *(weak)* faible

> Note that the French word **impotent** is a false friend. It means **infirm**.

impound [ɪmˈpaʊnd] VT **1** *Law (goods)* confisquer, saisir **2** *(put in pound ▸ animal, car)* mettre en fourrière

impounding [ɪmˈpaʊndɪŋ] N **1** *Law (of goods)* confiscation *f*, saisie *f* **2** *(putting in pound ▸ of animal, car)* mise *f* en fourrière

impoverish [ɪmˈpɒvərɪʃ] VT appauvrir

impoverished [ɪmˈpɒvərɪʃt] ADJ appauvri, très pauvre

impoverishment [ɪmˈpɒvərɪʃmənt] N appauvrissement *m*

impracticability [ɪmˌpræktɪkəˈbɪlɪtɪ] N impraticabilité *f*

impracticable [ɪmˈpræktɪkəbəl] ADJ *(not feasible)* irréalisable, impraticable

> Attention: ne pas confondre avec **impractical**.

impractical [ɪmˈpræktɪkəl] ADJ *(plan, suggestion)* irréaliste; *(person)* qui manque d'esprit pratique; **he's completely i.** il n'a aucun sens pratique

> Attention: ne pas confondre avec **impracticable**.

imprecation [ˌɪmprɪˈkeɪʃən] N *Formal* imprécation *f*

imprecise [ˌɪmprɪˈsaɪs] ADJ imprécis

imprecision [ˌɪmprɪˈsɪʒən] N imprécision *f*

impregnable [ɪmˈpregnəbəl] ADJ **1** *(fortress)* imprenable **2** *Fig (argument)* irréfutable; **his position is i.** sa position est inattaquable

impregnate [ˈɪmpregneɪt] VT **1** *(saturate)* imprégner (**with** de); **allow the oil to i. the wood** laissez le bois s'imprégner d'huile **2** *Formal (make pregnant)* féconder

impregnation [ˌɪmpregˈneɪʃən] N **1** *(saturation)* imprégnation *f* **2** *Formal (fertilization)* fécondation *f*

impresario [ˌɪmprɪˈsɑːrɪəʊ] *(pl* **impresarios***)* N impresario *m*

impress VT [ɪmˈpres] **1** *(create impression on)* faire impression sur, impressionner; **I was favourably impressed by her appearance** son apparence m'a fait bonne impression; **I'm not in the least impressed** ça ne m'impressionne pas du tout; **he impressed the jury** il a fait une forte impression sur le jury; **I wasn't impressed by her friend** son ami ne m'a pas fait grande impression **2 to i. sth on sb** *(make understand)* faire comprendre qch à qn **3** *(print)* imprimer, marquer; **the clay was impressed with a design** un motif était imprimé dans l'argile; *Fig* **her words are impressed on my memory** ses paroles sont gravées dans ma mémoire

N [ˈɪmpres] empreinte *f*

impression [ɪmˈpreʃən] N **1** *(impact ▸ on person, mind, feelings)* impression *f*; **to make a good/bad i. (on)** faire bonne/mauvaise impression (sur); **he made a strong i. on them** il leur a fait une forte impression; **he always tries to make an i.** il essaie toujours d'impressionner les gens; **my words made no i. on him whatsoever** mes paroles n'ont eu absolument aucun effet sur lui; **they got a good i. of my brother** mon frère leur a fait bonne impression

2 *(idea, thought)* impression *f*; **to create** *or* **give the i. that...** donner *ou* produire l'impression que...; **I don't know where she got that i. from** je

ne sais pas où elle est allée chercher ça; **you should never trust first impressions** il ne faut pas se fier aux premières impressions; **it's my i.** *or* **I have the i. that she's rather annoyed with us** j'ai l'impression qu'elle est en colère contre nous; **I was under the i. that you were unable to come** j'étais persuadé que vous ne pouviez pas venir
3 *(mark, imprint)* marque *f*, empreinte *f*; **to take an i. of sth** prendre l'empreinte *ou* l'impression de qch; **i. cylinder** cylindre *m* de rotative
4 *(printing)* impression *f*; *(edition)* tirage *m*
5 *(impersonation)* imitation *f*; **to do impressions** faire des imitations; **she does a very good i. of the Queen** elle imite très bien la reine

impressionable [ɪmˈpreʃənəbəl] **ADJ** influençable; **he is at a very i. age** il est à l'âge où on se laisse facilement influencer

> Note that the French word **impressionnable** is a false friend. It means **easily upset**.

impressionism, Impressionism [ɪmˈpreʃənɪzəm] **N** *Art & Literature* impressionnisme *m*

impressionist [ɪmˈpreʃənɪst] **N 1** *(entertainer)* imitateur(trice) *m,f* **2** *Art & Literature* impressionniste *mf*
ADJ *Art & Literature* impressionniste
• **Impressionist** *Art & Literature* **N** impressionniste *mf* **ADJ** impressionniste

impressionistic [ɪm,preʃəˈnɪstɪk] **ADJ** *(vague)* vague, imprécis

impressive [ɪmˈpresɪv] **ADJ** impressionnant

impressively [ɪmˈpresɪvlɪ] **ADV** remarquablement

imprest [ˈɪmprest] **N** *Formerly Fin* avance *f*
▸▸ *impress account* compte *m* d'avances (à montant fixe); *imprest fund* fonds *m* de caisse à montant fixe; *imprest system* comptabilité *f* de prévision

imprimatur [,ɪmprɪˈmeɪtə(r)] **N** *Rel & Typ* imprimatur *m inv*

imprint N [ˈɪmprɪnt] **1** *(mark)* empreinte *f*, marque *f*; **the i. of a hand** l'empreinte *f* d'une main; *Fig* **the i. of suffering on her face** les marques de la souffrance sur son visage; *Fig* **the war had left its i. on all of us** la guerre nous avait tous marqués **2** *Typ* adresse *f* bibliographique; **published under the Pentagon i.** édité chez Pentagon **3** *(design)* logo *m*
VT [ɪmˈprɪnt] **1** *(print)* imprimer **2** *(in sand, clay, mud)* imprimer **3** *Fig (fix)* implanter, graver; **her face was imprinted on my mind** son visage est resté gravé dans mon esprit
▸▸ *Typ* ***imprint page*** page *f* portant l'adresse bibliographique

imprinting [ɪmˈprɪntɪŋ] **N** *Zool* empreinte *f*, imprégnation *f*

imprison [ɪmˈprɪzən] **VT 1** *(put in prison)* mettre en prison, incarcérer; **he has been imprisoned several times** il a fait plusieurs séjours en prison **2** *Fig (confine, restrain)* enfermer

imprisonment [ɪmˈprɪzənmənt] **N** emprisonnement *m*; **to be sentenced to six months' i.** être condamné à six mois de prison

improbability [ɪm,prɒbəˈbɪlətɪ] *(pl* **improbabilities) N 1** *(of event)* improbabilité *f* **2** *(of story)* invraisemblance *f*

improbable [ɪmˈprɒbəbəl] **ADJ 1** *(unlikely)* improbable; **I think it highly i. that he ever came here** il me paraît fort peu probable qu'il soit jamais venu ici **2** *(hard to believe)* invraisemblable

improbably [ɪmˈprɒbəblɪ] **ADV** invraisemblablement; **he was wearing an i. large hat** il portait un chapeau d'une grandeur invraisemblable

impromptu [ɪmˈprɒmptju:] **ADJ** impromptu, improvisé; **an i. speech** un discours improvisé
ADV impromptu; **to speak i.** parler impromptu
N impromptu *m*

improper [ɪmˈprɒpə(r)] **ADJ 1** *(rude, shocking* ▸ *words, action)* déplacé
2 *(unsuitable)* peu convenable
3 *(dishonest)* malhonnête
4 *(incorrect* ▸ *method, equipment)* inadapté, inadéquat
▸▸ *Math* ***improper fraction*** expression *f* fractionnaire; ***improper practices*** pratiques *fpl* irrégulières

improperly [ɪmˈprɒpəlɪ] **ADV 1** *(indecently)* de manière déplacée; **he behaved most i.** il s'est comporté d'une manière tout à fait déplacée
2 *(unsuitably)* d'une façon peu convenable; **he was i. dressed** il n'était pas habillé d'une façon convenable
3 *(dishonestly)* malhonnêtement
4 *(incorrectly)* incorrectement, de manière incorrecte

impropriety [ɪmprəˈpraɪətɪ] *(pl* **improprieties) N 1** *(of behaviour)* inconvenance *f*; *(of language)* impropriété *f* **2** *(act, expression, gesture)* inconvenance *f*

improv [ˈɪmprɒv] **N** *Fam Theat (abbr* **improvisation)** impro *m*

improve [ɪmˈpru:v] **VT 1** *(make better* ▸ *work, facilities, result)* améliorer; *(*▸ *system, device)* perfectionner; *(*▸ *wine, soil)* bonifier; **to i. one's chances** augmenter ses chances; **if you cut your hair it would i. your looks** tu serais mieux avec les cheveux plus courts **2** *(increase* ▸ *knowledge, productivity)* accroître, augmenter **3** *(cultivate)* **to i. one's mind** se cultiver l'esprit; **reading improves the mind** on se cultive en lisant
VI *(get better)* s'améliorer; *(increase)* augmenter; *(make progress)* s'améliorer, faire des progrès; *(wine)* se bonifier; **her health is improving** son état (de santé) s'améliore; **business is improving** les affaires reprennent; **your maths has improved** vous avez fait des progrès en maths; **to i. with age** s'améliorer en vieillissant; *Formal* **he improves on acquaintance** il gagne à être connu
▸ **improve on, improve upon VT INSEP 1** *(result, work)* améliorer **2** *(offer)* **to i. on sb's offer** enchérir sur qn

improved [ɪmˈpru:vd] **ADJ** *(gen)* amélioré; *(services)* amélioré, meilleur; *(offer, performance)* meilleur

improvement [ɪmˈpru:vmənt] **N 1** *(gen)* amélioration *f*; *(in person's work, performance)* progrès *m*; **what an i.!** c'est nettement mieux!; **this is a great i. on her previous work** c'est bien mieux que ce qu'elle faisait jusqu'à présent; **there has been some i.** il y a un léger mieux; **there has been a slight i. in his work** son travail s'est légèrement amélioré; **there is no i. in the weather** le temps ne s'est pas arrangé; **her new boyfriend's a bit of an i.** son nouveau petit ami est un peu mieux que le précédent/les précédents; **to show some i.** *(in condition)* aller un peu mieux; *(in work)* faire quelques progrès; **there's room for i.** ça pourrait être mieux **2** *(in building, road etc)* rénovation *f*, aménagement *m*; **to carry out improvements** effectuer des travaux de rénovation; **motorway improvements** travaux *mpl* de réfection des autoroutes
▸▸ *Br* ***improvement grant*** subvention *f* pour la rénovation d'une maison

improvidence [ɪmˈprɒvɪdəns] **N** *Formal* **1** *(rashness)* imprévoyance *f* **2** *(carelessness with money)* prodigalité *f*

improvident [ɪmˈprɒvɪdənt] **ADJ** *Formal* **1** *(rash* ▸ *person)* imprévoyant; *(*▸ *life)* insouciant **2** *(careless with money)* dépensier

improvidently [ɪmˈprɒvɪdəntlɪ] **ADV** *Formal* **1** *(rashly)* avec imprévoyance **2** *(with careless use of money)* dispendieusement

improving [ɪmˈpru:vɪŋ] **ADJ** *(instructive* ▸ *book)* édifiant; *(*▸ *influence, environment)* bénéfique

improvisation [,ɪmprəvaɪˈzeɪʃən] **N** improvisation *f*

improvise [ˈɪmprə,vaɪz] **VT** improviser; **hastily improvised** sommairement organisé; **an improvised raft** un radeau de fortune; **they improvised bandages from bedsheets** ils ont fait des bandages de fortune avec des draps
VI improviser; **to i. on the piano** improviser au piano; **you will have to i.** *(make do)* il faudra que vous vous débrouilliez avec ce qu'il y a

improviser [ˈɪmprə,vaɪzə(r)] **N** improvisateur(trice) *m,f*

imprudence [ɪmˈpru:dəns] **N** imprudence *f*

imprudent [ɪmˈpru:dənt] **ADJ** imprudent; **i. with money** imprudent dans ses dépenses; **she's rather i. in her choice of friends** elle choisit mal ses amis

imprudently [ɪmˈpru:dəntlɪ] **ADV** imprudemment

impudence [ˈɪmpjʊdəns] **N** effronterie *f*, impudence *f*

impudent [ˈɪmpjʊdənt] **ADJ** effronté, impudent; **he is i. to his teachers** il est effronté avec ses professeurs

impudently [ˈɪmpjʊdəntlɪ] **ADV** effrontément, impudemment

impugn [ɪmˈpju:n] **VT** *Formal (declaration)* contester; *(testimony)* récuser

impulse [ˈɪmpʌls] **N 1** *(desire, instinct)* impulsion *f*, besoin *m*, envie *f*; **I felt an irresistible i. to hit him** j'ai éprouvé une irrésistible envie de le frapper; **a sudden i. made me start running** instinctivement, j'ai commencé à courir; **to act on i.** agir par impulsion; **I bought it on i.** je l'ai acheté sur un coup de tête; **I'm sorry, I did it on i.** je m'excuse, j'ai fait ça sans réfléchir
2 *Formal (impetus)* impulsion *f*, poussée *f*; **government grants have given an i. to trade** les subventions gouvernementales ont relancé les affaires
3 *Elec & Physiol* impulsion *f*
4 *Phys* impulsion *f*
▸▸ *Mktg* ***impulse buy*** achat *m* d'impulsion; *Mktg* ***impulse buyer*** acheteur(euse) *m,f* impulsif(ive); *Mktg* ***impulse buying*** *(UNCOUNT)* achats *mpl* d'impulsion; *Mktg* ***impulse purchase*** achat *m* d'impulsion; *Mktg* ***impulse purchaser*** acheteur (euse) *m,f* impulsif(ive); *Mktg* ***impulse purchasing*** *(UNCOUNT)* achats *mpl* d'impulsion

impulsion [ɪmˈpʌlʃən] **N** impulsion *f*

impulsive [ɪmˈpʌlsɪv] **ADJ 1** *(instinctive, spontaneous)* impulsif; *(thoughtless)* irréfléchi **2** *(force)* impulsif

impulsively [ɪmˈpʌlsɪvlɪ] **ADV** par *ou* sur impulsion, impulsivement; **he kissed her i.** pris d'une envie irrésistible, il l'embrassa; **I acted i.** j'ai agi par impulsion

impulsiveness [ɪmˈpʌlsɪvnɪs] **N** caractère *m* impulsif

impunity [ɪmˈpju:nətɪ] **N** *Formal* impunité *f*; **to act with i.** agir en toute impunité *ou* impunément

impure [ɪmˈpjʊə(r)] **ADJ 1** *(unclean* ▸ *air, milk)* impur **2** *Literary (sinful* ▸ *thought)* impur, mauvais; *(*▸ *motive)* bas

impurity [ɪmˈpjʊərətɪ] *(pl* **impurities) N** impureté *f*

imputation [,ɪmpju:ˈteɪʃən] **N** *Formal* **1** *(attribution)* attribution *f* **2** *(accusation)* imputation *f*

impute [ɪmˈpju:t] **VT** *Formal* **1** *(attribute)* attribuer; **the blame must be imputed to them** la responsabilité leur en revient **2** *(accuse)* imputer

IMS [,aɪemˈes] **N** *Econ (abbr* **International Monetary System)** SMI *m*

IN [ɪn]

> **PREP**
> • dans **A1–5, B3, C4, D1, F1**
> • chez **G2**
> • sur **G2**
> • à **A6, 7, F2**
> • en **A6–8, B1, 2, C1, 2, 4, 5, E2**
>
> **ADV**
> • à l'intérieur **A1**
> • à la mode **E2**
>
> **ADJ**
> • à la mode **1**
>
> **N**
> • influence
>
> **NPL**
> • tenants

PREP A. 1 *(within a defined area or space)* dans; **in a box** dans une boîte; **she was sitting in an armchair** elle était assise dans un fauteuil; **in the house** dans la maison; **in Catherine's house** chez Catherine; **they're playing in the garden/street** ils jouent dans le jardin/la rue; **he's still in bed/in the bath** il est encore au lit/dans son bain; **she shut herself up in her bedroom** elle s'est enfermée dans sa chambre; *Law* **in camera** à huis clos
2 *(within an undefined area or space)* dans; **she trailed her hand in the water** elle laissait traîner sa main dans l'eau; **there's a smell of spring in the air** ça sent le printemps

3 *(indicating movement)* dans; **put it in your pocket** mets-le dans ta poche; **throw the letter in the bin** jette la lettre à la poubelle; **we headed in the direction of the port** nous nous sommes dirigés vers le port

4 *(contained by a part of the body)* dans; **he had a knife in his hand** il avait un couteau dans *ou* à la main; **she held me tight in her arms** elle me serrait dans ses bras; **with tears in his eyes** les larmes aux yeux

5 *(on or behind a surface)* dans; **a hole in the wall** un trou dans le mur; **a reflection in the mirror** un reflet dans la glace; **how much is that jumper in the window?** combien coûte ce pull en vitrine?; **who's that man in the photo?** qui est cet homme sur la photo?

6 *(in a specified institution)* **she's in hospital/in prison** elle est à l'hôpital/en prison; **he teaches in a language school** il enseigne dans une école de langues

7 *(with geographical names)* **in Paris** à Paris; **in France** en France; **in the States** aux États-Unis; **in Portugal** au Portugal; **in the Pacific** dans l'océan Pacifique; **in the Third World** dans les pays du tiers-monde

8 *(wearing)* en; **he was in uniform/in a suit** il était en uniforme/en costume; **she was still in her dressing gown** elle était encore en robe de chambre; **he always dresses in green** il s'habille toujours en vert; **who's that woman in the hat?** qui est la femme avec le *ou* au chapeau?

9 *(covered by)* **sardines in tomato sauce** des sardines à la sauce tomate; **beef in a red wine sauce** bœuf mijoté dans une sauce au vin rouge; **fish in breadcrumbs** poisson pané

B. 1 *(during a specified period of time)* en; **in 1992** en 1992; **in March** en mars, au mois de mars; **in the thirties** dans les années trente; **in (the) summer/autumn/winter** en été/automne/hiver; **in (the) spring** au printemps; **he doesn't work in the afternoon/morning** il ne travaille pas l'après-midi/le matin; **I'll come sometime in the morning** je viendrai dans la matinée; **at 5 o'clock in the afternoon/morning** à 5 heures de l'après-midi/du matin; **in the future** à l'avenir; **in the past** autrefois

2 *(within a specified period of time)* en; **he cooked the meal in ten minutes** il prépara le repas en dix minutes

3 *(after a specified period of time)* dans; **I'll be back in five minutes** je reviens dans cinq minutes, j'en ai pour cinq minutes

4 *(indicating a long period of time)* **we haven't had a proper talk in ages** nous n'avons pas eu de véritable conversation depuis très longtemps; **I hadn't seen her in years** ça faisait des années que je ne l'avais pas vue

5 *(during a specified temporary situation)* **in my absence** en *ou* pendant mon absence; **in the ensuing chaos** dans la confusion qui s'ensuivit

C. 1 *(indicating arrangement, shape)* en; **in five rows/parts** en cinq rangées/parties; **stand in a circle** mettez-vous en cercle; **line up in twos** mettez-vous par deux; **cut the cake in half** coupe le gâteau en deux

2 *(indicating form, method)* **in cash** en liquide; **in writing** par écrit; **in English/French** en anglais/français; **written in ink** écrit à l'encre; **do you have these shoes in a 5?** est-ce que vous auriez ces chaussures en 38?; **have you got this jacket in a large?** est-ce que vous auriez cette veste dans une taille plus grande?; **does it come in red?** est-ce que ça se fait en rouge?

3 *(indicating state of mind)* **she's in a bit of a state** elle est dans tous ses états; **to be in love** être amoureux; **don't keep us in suspense** ne nous tiens pas en haleine plus longtemps; **he watched in wonderment** il regardait avec émerveillement

4 *(indicating state, situation)* dans, en; **in the present circumstances** dans les circonstances actuelles; **in the dark** dans l'obscurité; **in this weather** par *ou* avec ce temps; **in the sun** au soleil; **in the rain/snow** sous la pluie/neige; **in danger/silence** en danger/silence; **in my presence** en ma présence; **she's got her leg in plaster** elle a une jambe dans le plâtre

5 *(referring to plants and animals)* **in blossom** en fleur *ou* fleurs; **in pup/calf/cub** plein; *Am* **in heat** en chaleur

6 *(among)* chez; **a disease common in young children** une maladie très répandue chez les enfants en bas âge; **the sense of smell is more developed in dogs** l'odorat est plus développé chez les chiens

D. 1 *(forming part of)* dans; **in chapter six** dans le chapitre six; **we were standing in a queue** nous faisions la queue; **she's appearing in his new film** elle joue dans son nouveau film; **the best player in the team** le meilleur joueur de l'équipe; **service is included in the price** le service est inclus dans le prix

2 *(indicating a personality trait)* **she hasn't got it in her to be nasty** elle est bien incapable de méchanceté; **I didn't think she had it in her** je ne l'en croyais pas capable; **it's the Irish in me** c'est mon côté irlandais

3 *(indicating feelings about a person or thing)* **she has no confidence in him** elle n'a aucune confiance en lui; **they showed no interest in my work** mon travail n'a pas eu l'air de les intéresser le moins du monde

4 *(according to)* **in my opinion** *or* **view** à mon avis

E. 1 *(indicating purpose, cause)* **he charged the door in an effort to get free** dans un effort pour se libérer, il donna un grand coup dans la porte; **in reply** *or* **response to your letter...** en réponse à votre lettre...; **there's no point in complaining** il est inutile de *ou* ça ne sert à rien de se plaindre

2 *(as a result of)* en; **in doing so, you only encourage him** en faisant cela, vous ne faites que l'encourager; **in attempting to save her son's life, she almost died** en essayant de sauver son fils, elle a failli mourir

3 *(as regards)* **it's five feet in length** ça fait cinq pieds de long; **the town has grown considerably in size** la ville s'est beaucoup agrandie; **a change in direction** un changement de direction; **he's behind in maths** il ne suit pas en maths; **spinach is rich in iron** les épinards sont riches en fer; **we've found the ideal candidate in Richard** nous avons trouvé en Richard le candidat idéal

4 *(indicating source of discomfort)* **I've got a pain in my arm** j'ai une douleur au *ou* dans le bras

F. 1 *(indicating specified field, sphere of activity)* dans; **to be in the army** être dans l'armée; **she's in advertising** elle est dans la publicité; **an expert in economics** un expert en économie politique; **he's in business with his sister** il dirige une entreprise avec sa sœur; **a degree in Italian** une licence d'italien

2 *(indicating activity engaged in)* **our days were spent in swimming and sailing** nous passions nos journées à nager et à faire de la voile; **they spent hours (engaged) in complex negotiations** ils ont passé des heures en négociations difficiles; **you took your time in getting here!** tu en as mis du temps à venir!

G. 1 *(indicating approximate number, amount)* **people arrived in droves/in dribs and drabs** les gens sont arrivés en foule/par petits groupes; **they came in their thousands** ils sont venus par milliers; **he's in his forties** il a la quarantaine

2 *(in ratios)* sur; **one child in three** un enfant sur trois; **a one-in-five hill** une pente de 20 pour cent; **once in ten years** une fois tous les dix ans

ADV A. 1 *(into an enclosed space)* à l'intérieur, dedans; **she opened the door and looked in** elle ouvrit la porte et regarda à l'intérieur; **he jumped in** il sauta dedans

2 *(indicating movement from outside to inside)* **breathe in then out** inspirez puis expirez; **we can't take in any more refugees** nous ne pouvons pas accueillir plus de réfugiés; **she's been in and out of mental hospitals all her life** elle a passé presque toute sa vie dans des hôpitaux psychiatriques; **she and I were always in and out of each other's houses** nous étions tout le temps fourrées l'une chez l'autre

3 *(at home or place of work)* **is the boss in?** est-ce que le patron est là?; **it's nice to spend an evening in** c'est agréable de passer une soirée chez soi; **to eat/to stay in** manger/rester à la maison; **we've got the builders in** nous avons des ouvriers à la maison; **he usually comes in about 10 o'clock** en général, il est là vers 10 heures; *Fam* **what's he in for?** *(in prison)* pourquoi est-ce qu'il fait de la tôle?; *(in hospital)* pourquoi est-ce qu'il est à l'hôpital?▫

B. 1 *(indicating entry)* **to go in** entrer; **come in!** entrez!; **to saunter/to run in** entrer d'un pas nonchalant/en courant; **in we go!** on y va!

2 *(indicating arrival)* **the bus isn't in yet** le bus n'est pas encore arrivé; **what time does your train get in?** quand est-ce que votre train arrive?

3 *(towards the centre)* **the walls fell in** les murs se sont écroulés; **the edges bend in** le bord est recourbé

4 *(towards the shore)* **the tide is in** la marée est haute

C. 1 *(indicating transmission)* **write in for further information** écrivez-nous pour plus de renseignements; **entries must be in by 1 May** les bulletins doivent nous parvenir avant le 1 mai

2 *(indicating participation, addition)* **to be in at the start/finish of sth** assister au début/à la fin de qch; **we asked if we could join in** nous avons demandé si nous pouvions participer; **stir in the sliced onions** ajouter les oignons en lamelles; **fill in the blanks** remplissez les espaces vides

D. 1 *Sport (within area of court)* **the ball was in** la balle était bonne

2 *(in cricket)* à l'attaque; **the other side went in first** c'est l'autre équipe qui était d'abord à l'attaque

E. 1 *Pol (elected)* **he failed to get in at the last election** il n'a pas été élu aux dernières élections

2 *(in fashion)* à la mode; **short skirts are coming back in** les jupes courtes reviennent à la mode

F. *(idioms)* **you're in for a bit of a disappointment** tu vas être déçu; **he's in for a surprise/shock** il va avoir une surprise/un choc; **we're in for a storm** nous aurons sûrement de l'orage; **they don't know what they're in for** ils ne savent pas ce qui les attend; **now he's really in for it** cette fois-ci, il va y avoir droit; **he's in on the secret** il est dans le secret; **he's in on it** il est dans le coup; **we were all in on the plot** on était tous au courant; *Fam* **to be in with sb** être en bons termes avec qn; **he's trying to get in with the boss** il essaie de se faire bien voir du patron

ADJ *Fam* **1** *(fashionable)* à la mode▫, branché; **it's the in place to go** c'est l'endroit branché du moment; **to be the in thing** être à la mode; **the in crowd** les gens dans le coup

2 *(for a select few)* **it's an in joke** c'est une plaisanterie entre nous/elles/*etc*▫

N *Am Fam (influence)* **to have an in** avoir de l'influence; **he has an in with the senator** il a ses entrées chez le sénateur

• **ins NPL the ins and outs (of a situation)** les tenants et les aboutissants (d'une situation)

• **in all ADV** en tout; **there are 30 in all** il y en a 30 en tout

• **in between ADV 1** *(in intermediate position)* **a row of bushes with little clumps of flowers in between** une rangée d'arbustes séparés par des petites touffes de fleurs; **he's neither right nor left but somewhere in between** il n'est ni de droite ni de gauche mais quelque part entre les deux; **she either plays very well or very badly, never in between** elle joue très bien ou très mal, jamais entre les deux

2 *(in time)* entretemps, dans l'intervalle **PREP** entre

• **in itself ADV** en soi; **this was in itself an achievement** c'était déjà un exploit en soi

• **in that CONJ** puisque; **I'm not badly off in that I have a job and a flat but...** je ne peux pas me plaindre puisque j'ai un emploi et un appartement mais...; **we are lucky in that there are only a few of us** nous avons de la chance d'être si peu nombreux

PRÉFIXE

IN-, IL-, IM-, IR-

Ces préfixes sont fréquemment employés pour exprimer de façon générale la NÉGATION, l'OPPOSITION ou le MANQUE. Ils sont le plus souvent associés à des adjectifs, des adverbes et des noms, et plus rarement à des verbes.

La forme **il-** se place devant des mots commençant par *l*; **im-** devant des mots commençant par *b*, *m* et *p*; **ir-** devant des mots commençant par *r*.

Bien qu'on utilise souvent les mêmes préfixes en français, il faut parfois trouver une

traduction différente, par exemple avec le préfixe **dé(s)-** ou bien un mot comme **manque** ou **sans**:
insensitive insensible; **illogical** illogique; **impossible** impossible; **immaterial** sans importance; **irregular** irrégulier; **illegally** illégalement; **immobilize** immobiliser; **irrelevance** manque de rapport; **inadvisable** déconseillé; **inadvertently** par mégarde

nability [ˌɪnəˈbɪlətɪ] (*pl* **inabilities**) **N** incapacité *f*; **our i. to help them** notre incapacité à les aider

naccessibility [ˌɪnəkˌsesɪˈbɪlətɪ] **N** inaccessibilité *f*

naccessible [ˌɪnəkˈsesəbəl] **ADJ 1** *(impossible to reach)* inaccessible **2** *(unavailable ▸ person)* inaccessible, inabordable; *(▸ information)* inaccessible **3** *(obscure ▸ film, book, music)* inaccessible, incompréhensible

naccuracy [ɪnˈækjʊrəsɪ] (*pl* **inaccuracies**) **N** *(of calculation, information, figures)* inexactitude *f*; *(of word, expression, term)* inexactitude *f*, impropriété *f*; *(of description)* inexactitude *f*; *(of report, account, result)* inexactitude *f*, manque *m* de précision

naccurate [ɪnˈækjʊrət] **ADJ** *(incorrect ▸ calculation, information, figures)* inexact; *(▸ word, expression, term)* impropre; *(▸ description)* inexact; *(▸ report, account, result)* erroné

naccurately [ɪnˈækjʊrətlɪ] **ADV** inexactement; **the events have been i. reported** les événements ont été présentés de façon inexacte

naction [ɪnˈækʃən] **N** inaction *f*

nactive [ɪnˈæktɪv] **ADJ 1** *(person, animal ▸ resting)* inactif, peu actif; *(▸ not working)* inactif
2 *(lazy)* paresseux, oisif
3 *(inoperative ▸ machine)* au repos, à l'arrêt
4 *(dormant ▸ volcano)* qui n'est pas en activité; *(▸ disease, virus)* inactif
5 *Fin (money, bank account)* inactif
6 *Chem & Phys* inerte

nactivity [ˌɪnækˈtɪvətɪ] **N** inactivité *f*, inaction *f*

nadequacy [ɪnˈædɪkwəsɪ] (*pl* **inadequacies**) **N 1** *(insufficiency ▸ of resources, facilities)* insuffisance *f* **2** *(social)* incapacité *f*, inadaptation *f*; *(sexual)* impuissance *f*, incapacité *f*; **feelings of i.** un sentiment d'impuissance **3** *(failing)* défaut *m*, faiblesse *f*

nadequate [ɪnˈædɪkwət] **ADJ 1** *(insufficient)* insuffisant; **our resources are i. to meet our needs** nos ressources ne correspondent pas à nos besoins
2 *(unsatisfactory)* médiocre; **his performance in the test was i.** il n'a pas bien réussi son examen; **their response to the problem was i.** ils n'ont pas su trouver de réponse satisfaisante au problème; **that is an i. explanation of his behaviour** cela ne suffit pas à justifier son comportement
3 *(unsuitable ▸ equipment)* inadéquat; **our machinery is i. for this type of work** notre outillage n'est pas adapté à ce genre de travail
4 *(incapable)* incapable; *(sexually)* impuissant; **he's hopelessly i. for the job** il n'est vraiment pas fait pour ce travail; **being unemployed often makes people feel i.** les gens au chômage se sentent souvent inutiles; **he's socially i.** c'est un inadapté

nadequately [ɪnˈædɪkwətlɪ] **ADV** de manière inadéquate; *(fund, invest)* insuffisamment; **they were i. equipped for climbing a mountain** ils n'avaient pas l'équipement adéquat pour faire une ascension

inadmissible [ˌɪnədˈmɪsɪbəl] **ADJ** inadmissible, inacceptable; *Law (evidence)* inadmissible

inadvertence [ˌɪnədˈvɜːtəns] **N** manque *m* d'attention, étourderie *f*, inadvertance *f*; **by i.** par mégarde *ou* inadvertance

inadvertent [ˌɪnədˈvɜːtənt] **ADJ** accidentel, involontaire

inadvertently [ˌɪnədˈvɜːtəntlɪ] **ADV** par mégarde *ou* inadvertance

inadvisability [ˈɪnədˌvaɪzəˈbɪlətɪ] **N** inopportunité *f*

inadvisable [ˌɪnədˈvaɪzəbəl] **ADJ** déconseillé; **this plan is i.** ce projet est à déconseiller

inalienable [ɪnˈeɪljənəbəl] **ADJ** *Law (right)* inaliénable

inane [ɪˈneɪn] **ADJ** *(person)* idiot, imbécile; *(behaviour)* stupide, inepte; *(remark)* idiot, stupide, inepte

inanely [ɪˈneɪnlɪ] **ADV** de façon idiote *ou* stupide *ou* inepte

inanimate [ɪnˈænɪmət] **ADJ** inanimé

inanition [ˌɪnəˈnɪʃən] **N** *Med* **1** *(debility)* = faiblesse due à une alimentation insuffisante **2** *(lethargy)* léthargie *f*, torpeur *f*

inanity [ɪˈnænətɪ] (*pl* **inanities**) **N 1** *(stupidity)* stupidité *f* **2** *(stupid remark)* ineptie *f*, bêtise *f*

inapplicable [ˌɪnəˈplɪkəbəl] **ADJ** inapplicable (**to** à); **the rule is i. to this case** dans ce cas, la règle ne s'applique pas

inappropriate [ˌɪnəˈprəʊprɪət] **ADJ** *(action, remark)* inopportun, mal à propos; *(behaviour, joke)* déplacé; *(time, moment)* inopportun; *(clothing, equipment)* peu approprié, inadéquat; *(name)* mal choisi; **you've come at an i. time** vous arrivez au mauvais moment, vous tombez mal; **principles which are i. to modern life** des principes qui ne sont pas adaptés à la vie moderne

inappropriately [ˌɪnəˈprəʊprɪətlɪ] **ADV** de manière peu convenable *ou* appropriée; **she was i. dressed** elle n'était pas vêtue pour la circonstance

inapt [ɪnˈæpt] **ADJ 1** *(unsuitable ▸ remark)* mal choisi; *(▸ behaviour)* peu convenable **2** *(incapable)* inapte, incapable

inaptitude [ɪnˈæptɪtjuːd] **N 1** *(unsuitability ▸ of remark)* manque *m* d'à-propos; *(▸ of behaviour)* inconvenance *f* **2** *(incapability)* incapacité *f*, inaptitude *f*

inarticulate [ˌɪnɑːˈtɪkjʊlət] **ADJ 1** *(person)* qui bredouille; **an i. old man** un vieil homme qui a du mal à s'exprimer; **to be i. with rage** bégayer de rage; **his i. suffering** la souffrance qu'il ne pouvait exprimer **2** *(words, sounds)* indistinct; **i. expressions of love** des mots d'amour bredouillés **3** *Anat & Biol* inarticulé

inartistic [ˌɪnɑːˈtɪstɪk] **ADJ 1** *(painting, drawing etc)* dénué de toute valeur artistique **2** *(person ▸ lacking artistic taste)* sans goût artistique; *(▸ unskilled)* sans talent

inasmuch as [ˌɪnəzˈmʌtʃ-] **CONJ** *Formal (given that)* étant donné que, vu que; *(insofar as)* dans la mesure où

inattention [ˌɪnəˈtenʃən] **N** manque *m* d'attention, inattention *f*; **your essay shows i. to detail** il y a beaucoup d'erreurs de détail dans votre travail

inattentive [ˌɪnəˈtentɪv] **ADJ 1** *(paying no attention)* inattentif **2** *(neglectful)* peu attentionné, négligent; **to be i. towards sb** être peu attentionné envers qn, négliger qn

inattentively [ˌɪnəˈtentɪvlɪ] **ADV 1** *(without paying attention)* sans prêter *ou* faire attention **2** *(neglectfully)* négligemment

inaudible [ɪˈnɔːdɪbəl] **ADJ** inaudible

inaudibly [ɪˈnɔːdɪblɪ] **ADV** indistinctement; **"yes," she answered i.** "oui", répondit-elle d'une voix inaudible

inaugural [ɪˈnɔːgjʊrəl] **ADJ** inaugural, d'inauguration
N *Am* discours *m* inaugural *(d'un président des États-Unis)*
▸▸ ***inaugural address*** discours *m* inaugural; *Aviat* ***inaugural flight*** vol *m* inaugural; ***inaugural speech*** discours *m* inaugural

inaugurate [ɪˈnɔːgjʊreɪt] **VT 1** *(open ceremoniously ▸ building)* inaugurer; *(▸ conference, exhibition)* ouvrir
2 *(commence formally)* inaugurer; **to i. a new policy** instaurer *ou* inaugurer une nouvelle politique
3 *(herald ▸ new era)* inaugurer; *(▸ new system, tradition etc)* instaurer
4 *(instate ▸ official)* installer (dans ses fonctions), investir; *(▸ king, bishop)* introniser

inauguration [ɪˌnɔːgjʊˈreɪʃən] **N 1** *(of building)* inauguration *f*, cérémonie *f* d'ouverture **2** *(of policy, new era etc)* inauguration *f* **3** *(of official)* investiture *f*
▸▸ ***Inauguration Day*** = jour de l'investiture du président des États-Unis (le 20 janvier)

inauspicious [ˌɪnɔːˈspɪʃəs] **ADJ** défavorable, peu propice; **things got off to an i. start** les choses ont pris un mauvais départ; **an i. event** un événement de mauvais augure *ou* de sinistre présage

inauspiciously [ˌɪnɔːˈspɪʃəslɪ] **ADV** défavorablement; **to start i.** prendre un mauvais départ

inauthentic [ɪnɔːˈθentɪk] **ADJ** inauthentique

in-between N it's hard to find shoes to fit if you're an i. c'est difficile de trouver des chaussures quand on est entre deux pointures
ADJ intermédiaire

inborn [ˌɪnˈbɔːn] **ADJ** *(characteristic, quality)* inné; *Med* congénital, héréditaire

inbound [ˈɪnbaʊnd] **ADJ** *(flight, passenger etc)* à l'arrivée

inbox [ˈɪnbɒks] **N** *Comput (for e-mail)* boîte *f* de réception, corbeille *f* d'arrivée

inbred [ˌɪnˈbred] **ADJ 1** *(characteristic, quality)* inné **2** *Biol (trait)* acquis par sélection génétique; *(strain)* produit par le croisement d'individus consanguins; *(person)* de parents consanguins; *(family, group)* consanguin

inbreed [ˈɪnˈbriːd] *(pt & pp* **inbred** [-bred]) **VI** se reproduire entre eux

inbreeding [ˈɪnˈbriːdɪŋ] **N** *(UNCOUNT) (of animals)* croisement *m*; **generations of i.** *(of people)* des générations d'alliances consanguines

inbuilt [ˈɪnbɪlt] **ADJ 1** *(device)* incorporé, intégré **2** *(quality, defect)* inhérent

INC [ˌaɪenˈsiː] **N** *Pol (abbr* **Iraqi National Congress**) CNI *m*

Inc. *Am (written abbr* **incorporated**) SARL

inc. *(written abbr* **inclusive**) **12–15 April i.** du 12 au 15 avril inclus

Inca [ˈɪŋkə] (*pl* **inv** *or* **Incas**) **N** *Hist* Inca *mf*

incalculable [ɪnˈkælkjʊləbəl] **ADJ** incalculable; *(loss, help)* inestimable

incalculably [ɪnˈkælkjʊləblɪ] **ADV** de façon inestimable

incandescence [ˌɪnkænˈdesəns] **N** incandescence *f*

incandescent [ˌɪnkænˈdesənt] **ADJ** incandescent
▸▸ ***incandescent lamp*** lampe *f* à incandescence

incantation [ˌɪnkænˈteɪʃən] **N** incantation *f*

incapability [ɪnˌkeɪpəˈbɪlətɪ] **N** incapacité *f*

incapable [ɪnˈkeɪpəbəl] **ADJ 1** *(unable)* incapable; **to be i. of doing sth** être incapable de faire qch; **she's i. of such an act** elle est incapable de faire une chose pareille; **he's i. of speech** il ne peut pas parler; *Literary* **feelings i. of expression** des sentiments impossibles à exprimer **2** *(incompetent)* incapable; *Law* **to be declared i.** être déclaré incapable, être frappé d'incapacité juridique

incapacitate [ˌɪnkəˈpæsɪteɪt] **VT 1** *(cripple)* rendre infirme *ou* invalide; **he was temporarily incapacitated by the accident** à la suite de l'accident, il a été temporairement immobilisé **2** *Law* frapper d'incapacité légale

incapacity [ˌɪnkəˈpæsətɪ] (*pl* **incapacities**) **N 1** *(lack of power, ability)* incapacité *f*; **his i. for work/to adapt** son incapacité à travailler/à s'adapter **2** *Law* incapacité *f*
▸▸ *Br Admin* ***incapacity benefit*** prestation *f* d'invalidité

in-car ADJ *Aut*
▸▸ ***in-car information*** information *f* embarquée; ***in-car listening*** écoute *f* de la radio en voiture; *Br* ***in-car stereo*** autoradio *f* (à cassette)

incarcerate [ɪnˈkɑːsəreɪt] **VT** incarcérer

incarceration [ɪnˌkɑːsəˈreɪʃən] **N** incarcération *f*

incarnate [ɪnˈkɑːneɪt] *Literary* **ADJ 1** *(personified)* incarné; **the devil i.** le diable incarné **2** *(colour)* incarnat
VT incarner

incarnation [ˌɪnkɑːˈneɪʃən] **N** incarnation *f*; **in a previous i.** dans une vie antérieure
• **Incarnation N** *Rel* **the I.** l'Incarnation *f*

incautious [ɪnˈkɔːʃəs] **ADJ** imprudent

incautiously [ɪnˈkɔːʃəslɪ] ADV imprudemment

incendiary [ɪnˈsendjərɪ] (*pl* **incendiaries**) N **1** *(arsonist)* incendiaire *mf* **2** *(bomb)* bombe *f* incendiaire **3** *Fig (agitator)* fauteur *m* de troubles

ADJ **1** *(causing fires)* incendiaire **2** *(combustible)* inflammable **3** *Fig (speech, statement)* incendiaire, séditieux

▸▸ ***incendiary bomb*** bombe *f* incendiaire; ***incendiary device*** dispositif *m* incendiaire

incense[1] [ˈɪnsens] N encens *m*

VT *(perfume)* encenser

▸▸ ***incense bearer*** thuriféraire *m*; ***incense burner*** encensoir *m*; ***incense stick*** bâtonnet *m* d'encens

incense[2] [ɪnˈsens] VT *(anger)* rendre furieux, excéder; **he was incensed by** *or* **at her indifference** son indifférence l'a rendu furieux; **I was absolutely incensed** j'étais hors de moi

> Note that the French verb **encenser** is a false friend and is never a translation for the English verb **to incense**. It means **to praise lavishly**.

incent [ɪnˈsent] VT *Am* motiver, encourager

incentive [ɪnˈsentɪv] N **1** *(motivation)* motivation *f*; **they have lost their i.** ils ne sont plus très motivés; **to give sb the i. to do sth** motiver qn à faire qch **2** *Fin & Ind* incitation *f*, encouragement *m*; *(payment)* prime *f*; *Mktg* stimulation *f*; *(reduction, free gift)* stimulant *m*; **the firm offers various incentives** la société offre diverses primes; **tax incentives** avantages *mpl* fiscaux

COMP incitateur, incitatif

▸▸ *Com Br* ***incentive bonus*** prime *f* de rendement *ou* d'encouragement; *Com & Mktg* ***incentive marketing*** marketing *m* de stimulation; *Com & Mktg Am* ***incentive plan****, Br* ***incentive scheme*** *(for buyers)* programme *m* de stimulation; *(for workers)* système *m* de primes; ***incentive travel*** voyage *m* de récompense

inception [ɪnˈsepʃən] N création *f*

incessant [ɪnˈsesənt] ADJ incessant

incessantly [ɪnˈsesəntlɪ] ADV continuellement, sans cesse

> Note that the French word **incessamment** is a false friend. It means **very shortly**.

incest [ˈɪnsest] N inceste *m*

incestuous [ɪnˈsestjʊəs] ADJ incestueux; *Fig* **publishing is a very i. business** le monde de l'édition est très fermé

inch [ɪntʃ] N inch *m*, pouce *m*; **it's about 6 inches wide** cela fait à peu près 15 centimètres de large; **it's a few inches shorter** c'est plus court de quelques centimètres; **the car missed me by inches** la voiture m'a manqué de peu; **give him an i. and he'll take a yard** *or* **a mile** on lui donne le doigt et il vous prend le bras; **i. by i.** petit à petit, peu à peu; *Fig* **we'll have to fight every i. of the way** nous ne sommes pas au bout de nos peines; **he's every i. a Frenchman** il est français jusqu'au bout des ongles; **the unions won't budge** *or* **give an i.** les syndicats ne céderont pas d'un pouce; **to beat sb to within an i. of their life** laisser qn pour mort; **to be within an i. of doing sth** être à deux doigts de faire qch

VT **to i. one's way in/out** entrer/sortir petit à petit; **he inched his way to the door** petit à petit, il s'approcha de la porte; **she inched the car forward slowly** elle fit avancer la voiture très lentement

VI **to i. in/out** entrer/sortir petit à petit; **he inched along the ledge** il avançait petit à petit le long du rebord

incidence [ˈɪnsɪdəns] N **1** *(rate)* taux *m*; **there is a higher/lower i. of crime** le taux de criminalité est plus élevé/plus faible; **the i. of the disease in adults** la fréquence de la maladie chez les adultes **2** *Geom, Phys & Opt* incidence *f*; **angle/point of i.** angle *m*/point *m* d'incidence

incident [ˈɪnsɪdənt] N incident *m*

ADJ **1** *Formal* lié, attaché (**to** à); **2** *Phys* incident

▸▸ *Br* ***incident room*** *(in police station)* salle *f* des opérations

incidental [ˌɪnsɪˈdentəl] ADJ **1** *(minor)* secondaire, accessoire; *(additional)* accessoire, supplémentaire; **the project will have other i. benefits** ce projet aura encore d'autres avantages **2** *(related)* **i. to** en rapport avec, occasionné par; **the fatigue i. to such work** la fatigue occasionnée par un tel travail

N *(chance happening)* événement *m* fortuit; *(minor detail)* détail *m* secondaire

• **incidentals** NPL *(expenses)* faux frais *mpl*

▸▸ ***incidental costs, incidental expenses*** faux frais *mpl*; ***incidental music*** *(for film)* musique *f* de film; *(for play)* musique *f* de scène

incidentally [ˌɪnsɪˈdentəlɪ] ADV **1** *(by chance)* incidemment, accessoirement **2** *(by the way)* à propos, au fait; **i., I really need that money I lent you** à propos *ou* au fait, j'aurais vraiment besoin de l'argent que je t'ai prêté **3** *(additionally)* accessoirement

> Note that the French word **incidemment** only means **accidentally**.

incinerate [ɪnˈsɪnəreɪt] VT incinérer

incineration [ɪnˌsɪnəˈreɪʃən] N incinération *f*

incinerator [ɪnˈsɪnəreɪtə(r)] N incinérateur *m*; *(in crematorium)* four *m* crématoire

incipient [ɪnˈsɪpɪənt] ADJ naissant

incise [ɪnˈsaɪz] VT **1** *Art* graver **2** *Med* inciser

incision [ɪnˈsɪʒən] N *Med* incision *f*; **to make an i. in sth** inciser qch, pratiquer une incision dans qch

incisive [ɪnˈsaɪsɪv] ADJ *(mind)* perspicace, pénétrant; *(wit, remark)* incisif

incisively [ɪnˈsaɪsɪvlɪ] ADV *(think)* de façon incisive; *(ask, remark)* de manière perspicace *ou* pénétrante

incisor [ɪnˈsaɪzə(r)] N *Anat* incisive *f*

incite [ɪnˈsaɪt] VT **to i. sb to do sth** inciter qn à faire qch; **to i. sb to violence** inciter qn à la violence

incitement [ɪnˈsaɪtmənt] N incitation *f*; **i. to riot/violence** incitation *f* à la révolte/à la violence; *Law* **i. to racial hatred** incitation *f* à la haine raciale

incivility [ˌɪnsɪˈvɪlətɪ] (*pl* **incivilities**) N *Formal* **1** *(rudeness)* impolitesse *f*, manque *m* de savoir-vivre, *Literary* incivilité *f* **2** *(act, remark)* impolitesse *f*, indélicatesse *f*

incl. **1** *(written abbr* **inclusive***)* inclus; **from 14 to 23 November i.** du 14 au 23 novembre inclus; **i. of gas and electricity** gaz et électricité compris **2** *(written abbr* **including***)* avec; **i. VAT** TVA comprise; **200 euros i. VAT** 200 euros TTC

inclemency [ɪnˈklemənsɪ] N *Literary* rigueur *f*, inclémence *f*

inclement [ɪnˈklemənt] ADJ *Literary (weather)* inclément

inclination [ˌɪnklɪˈneɪʃən] N **1** *(tendency)* disposition *f*, prédisposition *f*, tendance *f*; **a decided i. towards laziness** une nette prédisposition à la paresse; **my i. would be to say yes** je serais enclin à dire oui

2 *(liking)* penchant *m*, inclination *f*; **she had no i. to help him** elle n'avait pas du tout envie de l'aider; **to have lost all i. for sth** n'avoir plus envie de qch; **to show little i. to do sth** se montrer peu enclin à faire qch

3 *(slant, lean)* inclinaison *f*; *(of body, head)* inclination *f*

4 *Astron & Math* inclinaison *f*

incline VT [ɪnˈklaɪn] **1** *(dispose)* disposer, pousser; **it's unlikely to i. them to work harder** il est peu probable que cela les pousse *ou* incite à travailler davantage **2** *(lean, bend)* incliner; **to i. one's head** incliner la tête; *Literary* **to i. one's ear to sb** prêter l'oreille à qn

VI [ɪnˈklaɪn] **1** *(tend)* tendre, avoir tendance; **to i. to do sth** avoir tendance à faire qch; **he inclines towards exaggeration** il a tendance à exagérer, il exagère facilement **2** *(lean, bend)* s'incliner

N [ˈɪnklaɪn] inclinaison *f*; *(slope)* pente *f*, déclivité *f*; *Rail* rampe *f*

inclined [ɪnˈklaɪnd] ADJ **1** *(tending, disposed* ▸ *temporarily)* disposé (**to** à); *(*▸ *permanently)* enclin (**to** à); **to feel** *or* **to be i. to do sth** *(tend to)* avoir tendance à faire qch; *(have desire to)* avoir envie de faire qch; **he's i. to exaggeration** il a tendance à exagérer, il exagère facilement; **he's i. to put on weight** il a tendance à grossir; **to be well i. towards sb** être bien disposé envers qn; **i. you are so i.** si ça vous dit, si le cœur vous en dit; **I'm not musically i.** *(don't like music)* je ne suis pa[s] très porté sur la musique; *(have no talent)* je n'a[i] pas de talent musical; **if you're that way i.** *(if yo[u] want to)* si cela vous dit; *Fam* **he's the other way i.** *(in his sexual orientation)* il est de l'autre bord **2** *(slanting, leaning)* incliné

▸▸ ***inclined plane*** plan *m* incliné; *Am* ***inclined rai[l]road****, Br* ***inclined railway*** (chemin *m* de fer) funiculaire *m*

include [ɪnˈkluːd] VT comprendre, inclure; **each team includes eight forwards** chaque équipe comprend huit avants; **the price includes VAT** la TVA est comprise (dans le prix); **does that re[mark] mark i. me?** cette remarque vaut-elle aussi pour moi?; **don't forget to i. the cheque** n'oubliez pas de joindre le chèque; **if you i. Christmas Day** en comptant le jour de Noël; **to i. sb among one's friends** compter qn parmi *ou* au nombre de ses amis; **my duties i. sorting the mail** trier le courrier entre dans mes attributions *ou* fait partie de mon travail

▸ **include out** VT SEP *Br Fam* **you can i. me out** ne comptez pas sur moi□

included [ɪnˈkluːdɪd] ADJ **all his property was sold, his house i.** tous ses biens furent vendus, y compris sa maison; **i. in the price are two excur[sions]** deux excursions sont comprises dans le prix; **myself i.** y compris moi; **service not i.** *(on bill, menu)* service non compris; **batteries not i.** *(on packaging)* piles non fournies

including [ɪnˈkluːdɪŋ] PREP (y) compris; **14 guests i. the children** 14 invités y compris les enfants; **14 guests not i. the children** 14 invités sans compter les enfants; **up to and i. page 40** jusqu'à la page 40 incluse

inclusion [ɪnˈkluːʒən] N inclusion *f*

inclusive [ɪnˈkluːsɪv] ADJ **1** *(including everything)* inclus, compris; *Fin* net; **from July to September i.** de juillet à septembre inclus; **i. prices** prix nets; **i. of VAT** TVA comprise; **£200 i. of VAT** 200 livres TTC **2** *(list)* exhaustif; *(survey)* complet(ète), poussé

inclusively [ɪnˈkluːsɪvlɪ] ADV inclusivement

incognito [ˌɪnkɒgˈniːtəʊ] (*pl* **incognitos**) N incognito *m*; **to travel under an i.** voyager incognito

ADV incognito; **to remain i.** *(witness)* garder l'anonymat; *(star, politician)* garder l'incognito

incoherence [ˌɪnkəʊˈhɪərəns] N incohérence *f*

incoherent [ˌɪnkəʊˈhɪərənt] ADJ *(person, argument)* incohérent; *(thought)* incohérent, décousu

incoherently [ˌɪnkəʊˈhɪərəntlɪ] ADV de manière incohérente; **to mutter i.** marmonner des paroles incohérentes

incombustible [ˌɪnkəmˈbʌstəbəl] ADJ incombustible

income [ˈɪŋkʌm] N **1** *Com & Fin (of person)* revenu *m*; **a high/low i.** un revenu élevé/faible; **to declare one's i.** déclarer ses revenus; **their combined i.** leurs revenus additionnés; **the i. from her shares/investments** les revenus de ses actions/placements **2** *(of company)* recettes *fpl*, revenus *mpl*, rentrées *fpl*; *Fin* **i. and expenditure account** compte *m* de dépenses et recettes; *Acct* **i. from operations** produits *mpl* de gestion courante, produits *mpl* d'exploitation

▸▸ *Acct* ***income account*** compte *m* de produits; *Fin* ***income bond*** obligation *f* à intérêt conditionnel; ***income bracket*** tranche *f* de salaire *ou* de revenu; **most people in this area belong to the lower/higher i. bracket** la plupart des habitants de ce quartier sont des économiquement faibles/ont des revenus élevés; *Econ* ***income distribution*** répartition *f* des revenus; *Econ* ***income elasticity*** élasticité *f* par rapport au revenu; *Econ* ***income group*** tranche *f* de salaire *ou* de revenu; *Br Pol* ***incomes policy*** politique *f* des revenus; ***income redistribution*** redistribution *f* des revenus; ***income smoothing*** manipulations *fpl* de revenu; *Am Acct* ***income statement*** compte *m* de résultat; *Am St Exch* ***income stocks*** valeurs *fpl* de rendement; *Fin* ***income stream*** flux *m* de revenus; *Br Admin* ***income support*** = prestation complémentaire en faveur des personnes justifiant de faibles revenus, revenu *m* minimum d'insertion;

Fin **income tax** impôt *m* sur le revenu (des personnes physiques); ***income tax allowance*** déduction *f* avant impôt, déduction *f* fiscale; **i. tax is deducted at source** les impôts sont prélevés à la source; ***income tax inspector*** inspecteur *m* des contributions directes *ou* des impôts; ***income tax return*** déclaration *f* de revenus, feuille *f* d'impôt; *Fin* ***income velocity of capital*** vitesse *f* de circulation du capital en revenus; *Fin* ***income velocity of circulation*** vitesse *f* de circulation de la monnaie en revenus

incomer ['ɪn,kʌmə(r)] **N** nouveau (nouvelle) venu(e) *m,f*

incoming ['ɪn,kʌmɪŋ] **ADJ 1** *(in direction ▸ flight, train, passengers)* à l'arrivée; *(▸ tide)* montant
2 *(telephone call)* de l'extérieur; *(fax)* en entrée; *(e-mail)* à l'arrivée; **this telephone takes i. calls only** ce téléphone ne permet que de recevoir des appels; **please make a note of any i. calls** veuillez noter tous les appels que vous recevez
3 *(cash, interest)* qui rentre
4 *(official, administration, tenant)* nouveau (nouvelle)
• **incomings NPL** *(revenue)* recettes *fpl*, revenus *mpl*; **incomings and outgoings** dépenses *fpl* et recettes *fpl*
▸▸ ***incoming mail*** courrier *m* (du jour)

incommensurable [,ɪnkə'menʃərəbəl] **N** *Math* quantité *f* incommensurable
ADJ *(gen) & Math* incommensurable

incommensurate [,ɪnkə'menʃərət] **ADJ** *Formal* **1** *(disproportionate)* disproportionné, inadéquat; **it is i. with our needs** cela ne correspond pas à nos besoins **2** *(incommensurable)* incommensurable

incommode [,ɪnkə'məʊd] **VT** *Formal* incommoder, indisposer

incommodious [,ɪnkə'məʊdjəs] **ADJ** *Formal* **1** *(cramped)* exigu, étriqué **2** *(troublesome)* ennuyeux, fâcheux

incommunicado [,ɪnkəmju:nɪ'kɑ:dəʊ] **ADJ & ADV** sans communication avec le monde extérieur; **the prisoners are being kept** *or* **held i.** les prisonniers sont (gardés) au secret; *Fig* **I'll be i. for a month while I'm on holiday** je serai injoignable pendant un mois quand je partirai en vacances

in-company ADJ *Br* **i. training** formation *f* sur le lieu de travail; **i. training scheme** stage *m* organisé par la société; **i. cafeteria** cantine *f* de la société

incomparable [ɪn'kɒmpərəbəl] **ADJ** incomparable

incomparably [ɪn'kɒmpərəblɪ] **ADV** incomparablement, infiniment

incompatibility ['ɪnkəm,pætə'bɪlətɪ] **N** incompatibilité *f*; *(grounds for divorce)* incompatibilité *f* d'humeur

incompatible [,ɪnkəm'pætɪbəl] **ADJ** incompatible

incompetence [ɪn'kɒmpɪtəns], **incompetency** [ɪn'kɒmpɪtənsɪ] **N** incompétence *f*

incompetent [ɪn'kɒmpɪtənt] **ADJ 1** *(lacking skill, ability)* incompétent **2** *Law (judge, court)* incompétent
N incompétent(e) *m,f*, incapable *mf*

incomplete [,ɪnkəm'pli:t] **ADJ 1** *(unfinished)* inachevé **2** *(lacking something)* incomplet(ète) **3** *(in logic)* incomplet(ète)

incompletely [,ɪnkəm'pli:tlɪ] **ADV** incomplètement

incompleteness [,ɪnkəm'pli:tnɪs], **incompletion** [,ɪnkəm'pli:ʃən] **N 1** *(unfinished nature)* inachèvement *m*; **there's a feeling of i. about his paintings** ses tableaux donnent l'impression de ne pas être finis *ou* achevés **2** *(lacking something)* caractère *m* incomplet **3** *(in logic)* incomplétude *f*

incomprehensible [,ɪnkɒmprɪ'hensəbəl] **ADJ** incompréhensible

incomprehensibly [,ɪnkɒmprɪ'hensəblɪ] **ADV** incompréhensiblement, de manière incompréhensible; **they were i. absent** chose incompréhensible, ils étaient absents

incomprehension [,ɪnkɒmprɪ'henʃən] **N** incompréhension *f*

inconceivable [,ɪnkən'si:vəbəl] **ADJ** inconcevable, inimaginable

inconceivably [,ɪnkən'si:vəblɪ] **ADV** incroyablement; **i. rich** incroyablement riche

inconclusive [,ɪnkən'klu:sɪv] **ADJ** peu concluant; **the results are i.** les résultats sont peu concluants; **the talks have been i.** les pourparlers n'ont pas abouti

inconclusively [,ɪnkən'klu:sɪvlɪ] **ADV** de manière peu concluante; **the meeting ended i.** la réunion n'a abouti à aucune conclusion

incongruity [,ɪnkɒŋ'gru:ətɪ] *(pl* **incongruities) N 1** *(strangeness, discordancy)* incongruité *f* **2** *(disparity)* disparité *f*; **their statements were full of incongruities** leurs témoignages contenaient un grand nombre d'incohérences

incongruous [ɪn'kɒŋgrʊəs] **ADJ** *(strange, discordant)* incongru; *(disparate)* incohérent; **he was an i. figure among the factory workers** on le remarquait tout de suite au milieu des ouvriers de l'usine; **they are such an i. couple** ils sont tellement bizarrement assortis

incongruously [ɪn'kɒŋgrʊəslɪ] **ADV** de manière incongrue, incongrûment

inconsequence [ɪn'kɒnsɪkwəns] **N** inconséquence *f*

inconsequential [,ɪnkɒnsɪ'kwenʃəl] **ADJ 1** *(unimportant ▸ matter, remarks)* sans importance; **an i. detail** un détail insignifiant **2** *(not following logically ▸ reasoning, ideas)* décousu

inconsiderate [,ɪnkən'sɪdərət] **ADJ** *(person)* qui manque de prévenance; *(action, remark)* irréfléchi; **he's i. of other people's feelings** peu lui importe ce que pensent les autres; **that was very i. of you** vous avez agi sans aucun égard pour les autres; **to be i. towards sb** manquer d'égards envers qn; **don't be so i.** pense un peu aux autres

inconsiderately [,ɪnkən'sɪdərətlɪ] **ADV** sans aucune considération

inconsistency [,ɪnkən'sɪstənsɪ] *(pl* **inconsistencies) N 1** *(incoherence)* manque *m* de cohérence, incohérence *f* **2** *(contradiction)* contradiction *f*

inconsistent [,ɪnkən'sɪstənt] **ADJ 1** *(person)* incohérent *(dans ses comportements)*; **you're being i.** *(in saying that)* tu te contredis; *(in doing that)* tu n'es pas cohérent; **they're i. in what they say** leurs dires sont contradictoires
2 *(performance)* inégal; *(work)* irrégulier; **his films are very i. in quality** la qualité de ses films est très irrégulière
3 *(reasoning, argument)* incohérent
4 *(incompatible)* incompatible (**with** avec)

> Note that the French word **inconsistant** is a false friend. It means **thin, runny** or **vacuous**, depending on the context.

inconsistently [,ɪnkən'sɪstəntlɪ] **ADV** *(behave)* de façon incohérente; *(perform)* de façon irrégulière *ou* inégale; *(assert)* de façon contradictoire; *(argue)* de façon incohérente

inconsolable [,ɪnkən'səʊləbəl] **ADJ** inconsolable

inconspicuous [,ɪnkən'spɪkjʊəs] **ADJ** *(difficult to see)* à peine visible, qui passe inaperçu; *(discreet)* peu voyant, discret(ète); **she tried to make herself as i. as possible** elle fit tout son possible pour passer inaperçue

inconspicuously [,ɪnkən'spɪkjʊəslɪ] **ADV** discrètement

inconstancy [ɪn'kɒnstənsɪ] **N 1** *(of phenomenon)* variabilité *f*, instabilité *f*; *(of weather)* instabilité *f*, caractère *m* changeant **2** *(of person)* versatilité *f*, inconstance *f*

inconstant [ɪn'kɒnstənt] **ADJ 1** *(weather)* variable **2** *(person)* inconstant, volage

incontestable [,ɪnkən'testəbəl] **ADJ** incontestable

incontestably [,ɪnkən'testəblɪ] **ADV** incontestablement, sans conteste

incontinence [ɪn'kɒntɪnəns] **N** *Med* incontinence *f*
▸▸ ***incontinence pads*** couches *fpl* pour adultes

incontinent [ɪn'kɒntɪnənt] **ADJ** *Med* incontinent

incontrovertible [,ɪnkɒntrə'vɜ:təbəl] **ADJ** *(fact, proof)* irréfutable; *(truth)* indiscutable; **i. evidence** une preuve irréfutable

inconvenience [,ɪnkən'vi:njəns] **N 1** *(disadvantage)* inconvénient *m*; **the language barrier was a major i. to the participants** la barrière de la langue a beaucoup gêné les participants **2** *(trouble)* **to cause i.** déranger, gêner; **I hope it's not putting you to too much i.** j'espère que cela ne vous dérange pas trop; **we apologize for any i.** nous vous prions de nous excuser pour tout désagrément éventuel **3** *(disadvantages)* incommodité *f*, inconvénients *mpl*; **the i. of a small flat** les désagréments d'un petit appartement; **we apologize to our customers for any i. caused** nous prions notre aimable clientèle de nous excuser pour la gêne occasionnée
VT déranger, incommoder

inconvenient [,ɪnkən'vi:njənt] **ADJ 1** *(inopportune, awkward)* inopportun; **at an i. time** au mauvais moment; **if it's not i.** si cela ne vous dérange pas; **he has chosen to ignore any i. facts** il a choisi d'ignorer tout ce qui pouvait poser problème; **Friday's a bit i.** vendredi ne me convient pas tellement **2** *(impractical ▸ tool, kitchen)* peu pratique; **the house is very i. for the shops** la maison est mal située par rapport aux commerces

inconveniently [,ɪnkən'vi:njəntlɪ] **ADV 1** *(happen, arrive)* au mauvais moment, inopportunément; **the announcement was i. timed** le moment de l'annonce a été mal choisi **2** *(be situated)* de façon malcommode, mal; **the switch was i. placed above the door** l'interrupteur était placé à un endroit très peu pratique au-dessus de la porte

inconvertible [,ɪnkən'vɜ:təbəl] **ADJ** inconvertible, non convertible

incorporate [ɪn'kɔ:pəreɪt] **VT 1** *(include, add)* incorporer; **the territory was incorporated into Poland** le territoire fut incorporé *ou* annexé à la Pologne; **i. the butter into the flour** incorporez le beurre à la farine; **to i. amendments into a text** apporter des modifications à un texte **2** *Com (company)* constituer en société commerciale; *(banks)* réunir en société **3** *(merge)* **these organizations were incorporated into a national fire brigade** ces organismes ont été regroupés pour constituer une brigade nationale de pompiers
VI *Com (form a corporation)* se constituer en société commerciale; *(merge)* fusionner

incorporated [ɪn'kɔ:pəreɪtɪd] **ADJ** *Am Com* constitué en société commerciale; **Bradley & Jones I.** Bradley & Jones SARL
▸▸ ***incorporated company*** société *f* à responsabilité limitée; ***incorporated sector*** sociétés *fpl* à responsabilité limitée

incorporation [ɪn,kɔ:pə'reɪʃən] **N 1** *(inclusion)* incorporation *f*, intégration *f* **2** *Com* constitution *f* en société commerciale

incorrect [,ɪnkə'rekt] **ADJ 1** *(wrong ▸ answer, result)* erroné, faux (fausse); *(▸ sum, statement)* inexact, incorrect; **i. use of a word** usage *m* impropre d'un mot **2** *(improper)* incorrect; *(behaviour)* déplacé

incorrectly [,ɪnkə'rektlɪ] **ADV 1** *(wrongly)* **she answered i.** elle a mal répondu; **I was i. quoted** j'ai été cité de façon incorrecte; **the illness was i. diagnosed** il y a eu erreur de diagnostic; **you're using that tool i.** vous utilisez mal cet outil **2** *(improperly)* incorrectement; **he behaved most i.** il s'est conduit de façon déplacée

incorrigible [ɪn'kɒrɪdʒəbəl] **ADJ** incorrigible

incorruptible [,ɪnkə'rʌptəbəl] **ADJ** incorruptible

incoterms ['ɪnkəʊtɜ:mz] **NPL** *Com* termes *mpl* commerciaux, incoterms *mpl*

increase VI [ɪn'kri:s] *(price, takings, salary, speed etc)* augmenter; *(noise, dissatisfaction)* augmenter, croître; *(pain, population)* s'accroître, augmenter; **to i. by 10 percent** augmenter de 10 pour cent; **production has increased** la production a augmenté; **the attacks have increased in frequency** la fréquence des attaques a augmenté; **to i. in size** grandir; **to i. in intensity** s'intensifier; **to i. in price** augmenter; **to i. in value** prendre de la valeur
VT [ɪn'kri:s] augmenter; **to i. output to 500 units a week** augmenter *ou* faire passer la production à

500 unités par semaine; **recent events have increased speculation** des événements récents ont renforcé les rumeurs

N ['ɪnkri:s] *(in price, takings, salary, speed etc)* augmentation *f*; *(of noise, dissatisfaction)* augmentation *f*; *(in pain, population)* accroissement *m*, augmentation *f*; **the i. in productivity/in the cost of living** l'augmentation de la productivité/du coût de la vie; **a 10 percent pay i.** une augmentation de salaire de 10 pour cent; **an i. in population** un accroissement de la population; **an i. in the number of patients** une augmentation *ou* un accroissement du nombre des malades

• **on the increase** **ADJ** **crime is on the i.** la criminalité est en hausse; **shoplifting is on the i.** les vols à l'étalage sont de plus en plus nombreux

increasing [ɪn'kri:sɪŋ] **ADJ** croissant, grandissant; **there has been an i. number of complaints** les réclamations sont de plus en plus nombreuses; **they make i. use of computer technology** ils ont de plus en plus souvent recours à l'informatique

▸▸ *Econ* ***increasing returns*** rendements *mpl* croissants

increasingly [ɪn'kri:sɪŋlɪ] **ADV** de plus en plus; **i., people are saying that…** de plus en plus, les gens disent que…

incredible [ɪn'kredəbəl] **ADJ 1** *(unbelievable)* incroyable, invraisemblable; **I find it i. that she didn't know** je n'arrive pas à croire qu'elle n'était pas au courant **2** *Fam (excellent)* fantastique, incroyable

incredibly [ɪn'kredəblɪ] **ADV 1** *(unbelievably)* **i., we were on time** aussi incroyable que cela puisse paraître, nous étions à l'heure **2** *Fam (extremely)* incroyablement

incredulity [ˌɪnkrɪ'dju:lətɪ] **N** incrédulité *f*

incredulous [ɪn'kredjʊləs] **ADJ** incrédule

incredulously [ɪn'kredjʊləslɪ] **ADV** avec incrédulité

increment ['ɪnkrɪmənt] **N 1** *(increase)* augmentation *f*; **the scale goes up in increments of 0.25** le barème augmente par paliers de 0,25 **2** *Comput* incrément *m* **3** *Math* accroissement *m*

VT *Comput* incrémenter

incremental [ˌɪnkrɪ'mentəl] **ADJ 1** *(increasing)* croissant; **i. increases** augmentations *fpl* régulières **2** *Comput* incrémentiel, incrémental

▸▸ *Fin* ***incremental cash flow*** cashflow *m* marginal; *Comput* ***incremental compiler*** compilateur *m* incrémentiel; *Fin* ***incremental cost*** coût *m* marginal

incriminate [ɪn'krɪmɪneɪt] **VT** incriminer, mettre en cause; **to i. oneself** se compromettre; **all the evidence seems to i. the maid** tous les indices semblent accuser la bonne

incriminating [ɪn'krɪmɪneɪtɪŋ] **ADJ** accusateur, compromettant; *Law* **i. evidence** pièces *fpl* à conviction

incrimination [ɪnˌkrɪmɪ'neɪʃən] **N** mise *f* en cause, incrimination *f*

incriminatory [ɪn'krɪmɪnətrɪ] **ADJ** accusateur, compromettant

incrustation [ˌɪnkrʌs'teɪʃən] **N** incrustation *f*

incubate ['ɪnkjʊbeɪt] **VT 1** *Biol (eggs ▸ of bird)* couver; *(▸ of fish)* incuber; *(▸ in incubator)* incuber **2** *Fig (plot, idea)* couver

VI 1 *Biol (egg)* être en incubation **2** *Med (virus)* incuber; **the disease incubates for several days** la maladie a une période d'incubation de plusieurs jours **3** *Fig (plan, idea)* couver

incubation [ˌɪnkjʊ'beɪʃən] **N** *Biol & Med (of egg, virus, disease)* incubation *f*

▸▸ ***incubation period*** (période *f* d')incubation *f*

incubator ['ɪnkjʊbeɪtə(r)] **N** *Med (for premature baby)* couveuse *f*, incubateur *m*; *(for eggs, bacteria)* incubateur *m*

incubus ['ɪnkjʊbəs] *(pl* **incubuses** *or* **incubi** [-baɪ]) **N 1** *(demon)* incube *m* **2** *Literary (nightmare)* cauchemar *m*

in-cue **N** *Rad & TV* signal *m* de départ

inculcate ['ɪnkʌlkeɪt] **VT** inculquer; **to i. sb with sth, to i. sth in sb** *(idea, principle, habit etc)* inculquer qch à qn

inculcation [ˌɪnkʌl'keɪʃən] **N** inculcation *f*

incumbent [ɪn'kʌmbənt] *Formal* **ADJ 1** *(imposed)* **it is i. on** *or* **upon the manager to check the takings** il incombe *ou* il appartient au directeur de vérifier la recette **2** *(in office)* en fonction, en exercice; **the i. mayor** *(current)* le maire en exercice; *(during election campaign)* le maire sortant

N 1 *(office holder)* titulaire *mf* **2** *Rel* bénéficiaire *m*, titulaire *m (d'une charge)*

incunabulum [ˌɪnkju:'næbjʊləm] *(pl* **incunabula** [-jʊlə]) **N** incunable *m*

incur [ɪn'kɜ:(r)] *(pt & pp* **incurred**, *cont* **incurring)** **VT** *(blame, loss, penalty)* s'exposer à, encourir; *(debt)* contracter; *(losses)* subir; *(expenses)* engager; **the expenses incurred** les dépenses encourues; **to i. sb's wrath** s'attirer les foudres de qn

▸▸ *Acct* ***incurred expenditure, incurred expenses*** dépenses *fpl* engagées

incurable [ɪn'kjʊərəbəl] **ADJ 1** *(illness)* incurable, inguérissable **2** *Fig (optimist, romantic)* incorrigible

N incurable *mf*

incurably [ɪn'kjʊərəblɪ] **ADV 1 to be i. ill** avoir une maladie incurable **2** *Fig* **to be i. lazy/optimistic/romantic** être un incorrigible paresseux/optimiste/romantique

incurious [ɪn'kjʊərɪəs] **ADJ** *Literary* incurieux, sans curiosité

incursion [*Br* ɪn'kɜ:ʃən, *Am* ɪn'kɜ:ʒən] **N** incursion *f*; **an i. into enemy territory** une incursion en territoire ennemi

Ind 1 *(written abbr* **Independent)** indépendant **2** *(written abbr* **Indiana)** Indiana *m*

indebted [ɪn'detɪd] **ADJ 1** *(for help)* redevable; **I am greatly i. to you for doing me this favour** je vous suis extrêmement reconnaissant de m'avoir rendu ce service **2** *Fin (owing money)* endetté

indebtedness [ɪn'detɪdnɪs] **N 1** *(for help)* dette *f*, obligation *f*; **my i. to her** ma dette envers elle **2** *(financial)* endettement *m* **3** *Fin (amount owed)* dette *f*, dettes *fpl*

indecency [ɪn'di:snsɪ] *(pl* **indecencies**) **N** indécence *f*; **he was brought in on an i. charge** il a été mis en examen pour attentat à la pudeur; *Law* **an act of gross i.** un grave outrage à la pudeur

indecent [ɪn'di:sənt] **ADJ 1** *(obscene)* indécent; **an i. proposition** une proposition indécente **2** *(unseemly)* indécent, inconvenant, déplacé; **an i. display of wealth** un étalage indécent de richesse; **with i. haste** avec une précipitation déplacée

▸▸ *Law* ***indecent assault*** attentat *m* à la pudeur; *Law* ***indecent exposure*** outrage *m* public à la pudeur

indecently [ɪn'di:səntlɪ] **ADV** indécemment

indecipherable [ˌɪndɪ'saɪfərəbəl] **ADJ** indéchiffrable

indecision [ˌɪndɪ'sɪʒən] **N** indécision *f*

indecisive [ˌɪndɪ'saɪsɪv] **ADJ 1** *(hesitating ▸ person)* indécis, irrésolu; **she was i. about whether to go or stay** elle ne savait pas si elle devait partir ou rester **2** *(inconclusive)* peu concluant

indecisiveness [ˌɪndɪ'saɪsɪvnɪs] **N** indécision *f*

indeclinable [ˌɪndɪ'klaɪnəbəl] **ADJ** indéclinable

indecorous [ɪn'dekərəs] **ADJ** inconvenant, malséant

indecorously [ɪn'dekərəslɪ] **ADV** de manière inconvenante

indecorum [ˌɪndɪ'kɔ:rəm] **N** inconvenance *f*

indeed [ɪn'di:d] **ADV 1** *(used to confirm)* effectivement, en effet; **there was i. a problem** il y avait effectivement *ou* bien un problème; **we are aware of the problem; i., we are already investigating it** nous sommes conscients du problème; en fait, nous sommes déjà en train de l'étudier

2 *(used to qualify)* **the problem, if i. there is one, is theirs** c'est leur problème, si problème il y a; **it is difficult, i. virtually impossible, to get in** il est difficile, pour ne pas dire *ou* voire impossible, d'entrer

3 *(used as intensifier)* vraiment; **I'm very tired i.** je suis vraiment très fatigué; **thank you very much i.** merci beaucoup

4 *(in replies)* en effet; **I believe you support their policy – I do i.** je crois que vous soutenez leur politique – en effet; **you've been to Venice haven't you? – i. I have!** tu es allé à Venise, n'est-ce pas? – oui, j'y suis allé; **you haven't been to Venice – i. have!** tu n'es jamais allé à Venise – si, j'y suis déjà allé!; **yes i.!** mais certainement!, pour sûr!

5 *(as surprised, ironic response)* **he asked us for a pay rise – i.?** il nous a demandé une augmentation – eh bien! *ou* vraiment?; **I've bought a new car – have you i.?** j'ai acheté une nouvelle voiture – vraiment?

indefatigable [ˌɪndɪ'fætɪgəbəl] **ADJ** infatigable

indefatigably [ˌɪndɪ'fætɪgəblɪ] **ADV** infatigablement, sans se fatiguer, inlassablement

indefensible [ˌɪndɪ'fensəbəl] **ADJ 1** *(conduct)* injustifiable, inexcusable; *(argument, theory)* insoutenable, indéfendable **2** *Mil* indéfendable

indefinable [ˌɪndɪ'faɪnəbəl] **ADJ** indéfinissable

indefinite [ɪn'defɪnɪt] **ADJ 1** *(indeterminate)* indéterminé, illimité; **for an i. period** pour une période indéterminée; **an i. strike** une grève illimitée; **of i. origin** d'origine incertaine **2** *(vague, imprecise)* flou, peu précis **3** *Gram* indéfini

▸▸ *Gram* ***indefinite article*** article *m* indéfini; *Gram* ***indefinite pronoun*** pronom *m* indéfini

indefinitely [ɪn'defɪnətlɪ] **ADV 1** *(without limit)* indéfiniment; **we can't go on i.** on ne peut pas continuer indéfiniment; **I could go on i.** *(continue speaking)* je pourrais continuer à l'infini; **closed i.** *(sign)* fermé jusqu'à nouvel avis *ou* ordre **2** *(imprecisely)* vaguement

indelible [ɪn'deləbəl] **ADJ** *(ink, stain)* indélébile; *(memory)* impérissable

▸▸ *Br* ***indelible marker (pen)*** marqueur *m* indélébile

indelibly [ɪn'deləblɪ] **ADV** de manière indélébile *Fig* **her face remained i. fixed in his memory** son visage resta à jamais gravé dans sa mémoire

indelicacy [ɪn'delɪkəsɪ] *(pl* **indelicacies**) **N 1** *(of behaviour, remark)* indélicatesse *f* **2** *(tactless remark, action)* manque *m* de tact

indelicate [ɪn'delɪkət] **ADJ** *(action)* déplacé, indélicat; *(person, remark)* indélicat, qui manque de tact

indemnification [ɪnˌdemnɪfɪ'keɪʃən] **N 1** *(act of compensation)* indemnisation *f*, dédommagement *m* **2** *(sum reimbursed)* indemnité *f*

indemnify [ɪn'demnɪfaɪ] *(pt & pp* **indemnified**) **VT 1** *(compensate)* indemniser, dédommager; **to be indemnified for sth** être indemnisé *ou* dédommagé de qch **2** *(insure)* assurer, garantir; **to be indemnified for** *or* **against sth** être assuré contre qch

indemnity [ɪn'demnətɪ] *(pl* **indemnities**) **N 1** *(compensation)* indemnité *f*, dédommagement *m*; **war indemnities** réparations *fpl* de guerre **2** *Ins (insurance)* assurance *f* **3** *(exemption ▸ from prosecution)* immunité *f*

indent **N** ['ɪndent] **1** *Br Com (order)* commande *f*; *(order form)* bordereau *m* de commande **2** *Typ (in line of text)* renfoncement *m*, alinéa *m* **3** *(notch)* entaille *f*; *(in metal)* bosselure *f*

VT [ɪn'dent] **1** *(line of text)* mettre en retrait

2 *(edge)* denteler, découper; *(more deeply)* échancrer

3 *(surface)* marquer, faire une empreinte dans

4 *Br Com (goods)* commander

5 *(contract)* contrat *m*; *(of apprentice)* contrat *m* d'apprentissage

VI [ɪn'dent] **1** *(at start of paragraph)* faire un alinéa **2** *Br Com* passer commande; **to i. on sb for sth** commander qch à qn

indentation [ˌɪnden'teɪʃən] **N 1** *Typ (in line of text)* renfoncement *m*, alinéa *m*

2 *(in edge)* dentelure *f*; *(deeper)* échancrure *f*; *(in coastline)* découpure *f*

3 *(on surface)* empreinte *f*

4 *(contract)* contrat *m* synallagmatique; *(of apprentice)* contrat *m* d'apprentissage

indenture [ɪn'dentʃə(r)] **N** *(often pl)* contrat *m* synallagmatique; *(of apprentice)* contrat *m* d'apprentissage

VT 1 *(bind by contract)* engager par contrat **2** *Arch (of parent or guardian)* mettre en apprentissage (**to sb** chez qn); *(of employer)* prendre en apprentissage

▸▸ *Br* ***indentured labour*** *(workers)* main-d'œuvre

f sous contrat; *(work)* travail *m* sous contrat; *Br* **indentured labourer** ouvrier *m* sous contrat

ndependence [ˌɪndɪ'pendəns] **N** *(gen) & Pol* indépendance *f*; **the country has recently gained its i.** le pays vient d'accéder à l'indépendance; **the (American) War of I.** la guerre d'Indépendance (américaine)
▸▸ ***Independence Day*** fête *f* nationale de l'Indépendance *(aux États-Unis)*; ***independence movement*** mouvement *m* indépendantiste

ndependent [ˌɪndɪ'pendənt] **ADJ 1** *(person, country etc)* indépendant; **to become i.** *(country)* accéder à l'indépendance; **she is i. of her parents** elle ne dépend plus de ses parents; **he is incapable of i. thought** il est incapable de penser par lui-même; **a man of i. means** un rentier **2** *Gram, Phil & Math* indépendant
N 1 *(gen)* indépendant(e) *m,f* **2** *Pol* indépendant (e) *m,f*, non-inscrit(e) *m,f*
▸▸ ***independent cinema*** cinéma *m* indépendant; *Gram* ***independent clause*** proposition *f* indépendante; ***independent film-maker*** cinéaste *mf* indépendant(e); ***independent film-making*** cinéma *m* d'auteur; *Br Fin* ***independent financial adviser*** conseiller(ère) *m,f* financier(ère) indépendant (e); ***independent income*** revenus *mpl* indépendants, rentes *fpl*; ***independent inquiry*** enquête *f* indépendante; **an i. inquiry has been set up** une enquête indépendante a été ouverte; ***independent radio*** radio *f* privée; ***independent retailer*** détaillant(e) *m,f* indépendant(e); *Br* ***independent school*** école *f* privée; *Br* ***the Independent Television Commission*** = commission de surveillance des télévisions britanniques privées

ndependently [ˌɪndɪ'pendəntlɪ] **ADV** de manière indépendante, de manière autonome; **i. of** indépendamment de; **to be i. wealthy** vivre de sa fortune personnelle

n-depth ADJ en profondeur

ndescribable [ˌɪndɪ'skraɪbəbəl] **ADJ** indescriptible

ndescribably [ˌɪndɪ'skraɪbəblɪ] **ADV** incroyablement

ndestructible [ˌɪndɪ'strʌktəbəl] **ADJ** indestructible

ndeterminable [ˌɪndɪ'tɜːmɪnəbəl] **ADJ 1** *(fact, amount, distance)* indéterminable **2** *(controversy, problem)* insoluble

ndeterminate [ˌɪndɪ'tɜːmɪnət] **ADJ 1** *(undetermined, indefinite)* indéterminé; **for an i. period** pour une période indéterminée; **i. sentence** peine *f* (de prison) de durée indéterminée **2** *(vague, imprecise)* flou, vague **3** *Ling, Math & Phil* indéterminé

ndeterminately [ˌɪndɪ'tɜːmɪnətlɪ] **ADV 1** *(indefinitely)* de façon indéterminée **2** *(vaguely)* de manière floue, imprécisément

ndex ['ɪndeks] *(pl senses* **1–3, 8 indexes,** *pl senses* **4–7 indices** [-dɪsiːz]) **N 1** *(in book, database)* index *m*
2 *(in library)* catalogue *m*, répertoire *m*; *(on index cards)* fichier *m*
3 *Anat (finger)* index *m*
4 *Econ & St Exch* indice *m*
5 *Phys* indice *m*
6 *(pointer on scale)* aiguille *f*, indicateur *m*; *Fig (sign)* indice *m*, indicateur *m*; **it is a good i. of the current political mood** c'est un bon indicateur du climat politique actuel
7 *Math (subscript)* indice *m*; *(superscript)* exposant *m*
8 *Typ (pointing fist)* renvoi *m*
VT 1 *(word, book, database)* indexer; **all geographical names are indexed** tous les noms géographiques sont indexés; **you'll find it indexed under "science"** vous trouverez ça indexé à "science" ou dans l'index sous (l'entrée) "science" **2** *Fin (salary, pension)* indexer; **indexed to inflation** indexé sur l'inflation **3** *Tech* indexer
▸▸ *Am St Exch* ***index arbitrage*** arbitrage *m* sur indice; ***index box*** boîte *f* à fiches; ***index card*** fiche *f*; *Anat* ***index finger*** index *m*; *St Exch* ***index fund*** fonds *m* à gestion indicielle, fonds *m* indiciel; *Econ* ***index of growth*** indice *m* de croissance; ***index number*** *(in statistics)* indice *m*; *St Exch* ***index option*** option *f* sur indice; *Opt* ***index of refraction*** indice *m* de réfraction; ***index register*** registre *m* d'index

indexation [ˌɪndek'seɪʃən] **N** indexation *f*
▸▸ *Fin* ***indexation clause*** clause *f* d'indexation

index-based ADJ *Econ* indiciaire

indexing ['ɪndeksɪŋ] **N** *Comput* indexation *f*

index-link VT *Fin* indexer (**to** sur)

index-linked ADJ *Fin* indexé (**to** sur)
▸▸ ***index-linked fund*** fonds *m* à gestion indicielle, fonds *m* indiciel

index-linking N *Fin* indexation *f*

India ['ɪndɪə] **N** *Geog* Inde *f*
▸▸ *Am* ***India ink*** encre *f* de Chine; ***India paper*** papier *m* bible; *Br* ***India rubber*** *(substance)* caoutchouc *m*; *(eraser)* gomme *f*

Indian ['ɪndɪən] **N 1** *(Asian person)* Indien(enne) *m,f*
2 *(Native American)* Indien(enne) *m,f* (d'Amérique)
3 *(language* ▸ *in America)* langue *f* amérindienne
4 *Fam (restaurant)* restau *m* indien; *(meal)* repas *m* indien[□]; **we went out for an I.** on est allés dans un restau indien
ADJ *(American or Asian)* indien; **in I. file** en file *f* indienne; *Pej* **to be an I. giver** = demander la restitution de quelque chose qu'on a donné
COMP *(of India* ▸ *embassy)* d'Inde; *(*▸ *history)* de l'Inde
▸▸ *Am & Can* ***Indian agent*** délégué(e) *m,f* aux affaires indiennes; ***Indian buffalo*** buffle *m* d'Asie; ***Indian club*** massue *f (pour la gymnastique)*; *Am Agr* ***Indian corn*** maïs *m*; *Zool* ***Indian elephant*** éléphant *m* d'Asie; ***Indian head massage*** massage *m* indien du crâne; *Br* ***Indian hemp*** chanvre *m* indien, cannabis *m*; *Br* ***Indian ink*** encre *f* de Chine; *Hist* ***the Indian Mutiny*** = grande révolte indienne contre les Britanniques en 1857; *Geog* ***the Indian Ocean*** l'océan *m* Indien; ***Indian reserve*** réserve *f* indienne; ***Indian summer*** *Met* été *m* de la Saint-Martin, été *m* indien; *Fig* vieillesse *f* heureuse; ***Indian Territory*** = région à l'ouest du Mississippi où les Indiens furent contraints d'immigrer à la fin du XIXème siècle; ***Indian Wars*** = guerres entre les Indiens d'amérique et les colons aux XVIIIème et XIXème siècles

indicate ['ɪndɪkeɪt] **VT 1** *(show, point to)* indiquer; **to i. the way** indiquer *ou* montrer le chemin
2 *(make clear)* signaler; **as I have already indicated** comme je l'ai déjà signalé *ou* fait remarquer; **she indicated that the interview was over** elle a fait comprendre que l'entretien était terminé
3 *Br Aut* **to i. (that one is turning) left/right** mettre son clignotant à gauche/à droite (pour tourner)
4 *(recommend, require)* indiquer; **surgery is indicated** l'opération semble tout indiquée; **strong measures were clearly indicated** il était évident que la situation exigeait des mesures rigoureuses
VI *Br Aut* mettre son clignotant

indication [ˌɪndɪ'keɪʃən] **N 1** *(sign)* indication *f*; **she gave no i. that she had seen me** rien ne pouvait laisser supposer qu'elle m'avait vu; **he gave early indications of his talent** son talent se révéla de bonne heure; **he gave us a clear i. of his intentions** il nous a clairement fait comprendre *ou* clairement indiqué ses intentions; **all the indications are that…, there is every i. that…** tout porte à croire que… **2** *(act of indicating)* indication *f*
• **indications NPL** *Med & Pharm (for taking medicines)* indications *fpl* (thérapeutiques)

indicative [ɪn'dɪkətɪv] **ADJ 1** *(symptomatic)* indicatif; **his handwriting is i. of his mental state** son écriture est révélatrice de son état mental; **it is i. of a strong personality** cela témoigne d'une forte personnalité **2** *Gram* indicatif
N *Gram* indicatif *m*; **in the i.** à l'indicatif
▸▸ *Gram* ***indicative mood*** mode *m* indicatif, indicatif *m*

indicator ['ɪndɪkeɪtə(r)] **N 1** *(instrument)* indicateur *m*; *(warning lamp)* voyant *m*; *(needle, pointer)* index *m*, aiguille *f*; **temperature i.** indicateur *m* de température
2 *Aut* clignotant *m*, *Belg* clignoteur *m*, *Suisse* signofil(e) *m*
3 *(at station, in airport)* **arrivals/departures i.** panneau *m* des arrivées/des départs
4 *Fig* indicateur *m*; **economic indicators** indicateurs *mpl* économiques
5 *Chem* indicateur *m*
6 *Ling* indicateur *m*
▸▸ ***indicator light*** signal *m* lumineux; *(on monitor)* voyant *m*

indict [ɪn'daɪt] **VT** *Law* inculper, *Spec* mettre en examen

indictable [ɪn'daɪtəbəl] **ADJ** *Law* **1** *(person)* passible de poursuites **2** *(crime)* passible des tribunaux
▸▸ ***indictable offence*** infraction *f* majeure

indictment [ɪn'daɪtmənt] **N 1** *Law (act)* inculpation *f*, mise *f* en examen; *(document)* acte *m* d'accusation **2** *Fig* **a damning i. of government policy** un témoignage accablant contre la politique gouvernementale

indie ['ɪndɪ] *Fam* **N** *(music)* indie-rock *m*
ADJ *(band, charts)* indépendant[□] *(dont les disques sont produits par des maisons indépendantes)*
▸▸ ***indie music*** indie-rock *m*

Indies ['ɪndɪz] **NPL** *Geog* **the I.** les Indes *fpl*

indifference [ɪn'dɪfərəns] **N 1** *(unconcern)* indifférence *f* (**to** *or* **towards sb/sth** à l'égard de qn/pour qch); **with total i.** avec une indifférence totale **2** *(mediocrity)* médiocrité *f* **3** *(unimportance)* insignifiance *f*; **it is a matter of great i. to me** c'est une question qui me laisse totalement indifférent

indifferent [ɪn'dɪfərənt] **ADJ 1** *(unconcerned, cold)* indifférent; **she was i. to the beauty of the landscape** elle était indifférente à la beauté du paysage; **he was i. to her pleas** il est resté sourd à ses suppliques; **i. to the danger** insouciant du danger
2 *(unimportant)* indifférent; **it's i. to me whether they go or stay** qu'ils partent ou qu'ils restent, cela m'est égal *ou* indifférent
3 *(mediocre)* médiocre, quelconque; **good, bad or i.** bon, mauvais ou ni l'un ni l'autre
4 *Biol (cell, tissue)* indifférencié

indifferently [ɪn'dɪfərəntlɪ] **ADV 1** *(unconcernedly)* indifféremment, avec indifférence **2** *(in mediocre manner)* médiocrement

indigence ['ɪndɪdʒəns] **N** *Formal* indigence *f*

indigenous [ɪn'dɪdʒɪnəs] **ADJ 1** *(animal, plant, custom)* indigène; *(population)* autochtone; **rabbits are not i. to Australia** à l'origine, il n'y avait pas de lapins en Australie **2** *(innate)* inné, natif
▸▸ *Com* ***indigenous company*** *(local)* entreprise *f* locale; *(national)* entreprise nationale

indigent ['ɪndɪdʒənt] *Formal* **N** indigent(e) *m,f*
ADJ indigent, nécessiteux

indigestible [ˌɪndɪ'dʒestəbəl] **ADJ** indigeste

indigestion [ˌɪndɪ'dʒestʃən] **N** *(UNCOUNT) Med* indigestion *f*; **to have i.** avoir une indigestion

indignant [ɪn'dɪgnənt] **ADJ** indigné, outré; **he was i. at her attitude** il était indigné par son attitude

indignantly [ɪn'dɪgnəntlɪ] **ADV** avec indignation

indignation [ˌɪndɪg'neɪʃən] **N** indignation *f*; **public i.** indignation *f* générale

indignity [ɪn'dɪgnətɪ] *(pl* **indignities) N** indignité *f*; **he suffered the i. of having to ask for a loan** il a dû s'abaisser à solliciter un prêt; **the i. of it!** quelle honte!

indigo ['ɪndɪgəʊ] *(pl* **indigos** *or* **indigoes) N 1** *(dye, colour)* indigo *m* **2** *(plant)* indigotier *m*
ADJ indigo *(inv)*
▸▸ ***indigo blue*** indigo *m*

indirect [ˌɪndɪ'rekt] **ADJ** indirect; **by an i. route** par un chemin indirect *ou* détourné; **the i. effects of radioactivity** les effets indirects *ou* secondaires de la radioactivité; **an i. reference** une allusion voilée
▸▸ *Com* ***indirect costs*** coûts *mpl* indirects; *Pol* ***indirect election*** élection *f* indirecte; *Fin* ***indirect investment*** investissement *m* indirect; *Gram* ***indirect object*** objet *m* indirect; *Mktg* ***indirect promotional costs*** coûts *mpl* de promotion indirects; ***indirect question*** question *f* indirecte; *Mktg* ***indirect selling*** vente *f* indirecte; *Gram* ***indirect speech*** discours *m* indirect; *Pol* ***indirect suffrage*** suffrage *m* indirect; *Com & Fin* ***indirect tax*** impôt *m*

indirect; *Com & Fin* ***indirect taxation*** contributions *fpl* indirectes, impôts *mpl* indirects; *Pol* ***indirect universal suffrage*** suffrage *m* universel indirect; *Pol* ***indirect vote*** vote *m* indirect

indirectly [ˌɪndɪˈrektlɪ] ADV indirectement; **I heard about it i.** je l'ai appris indirectement *ou* par personnes interposées

indiscernible [ˌɪndɪˈsɜːnəbəl] ADJ indiscernable, imperceptible

indiscipline [ɪnˈdɪsɪplɪn] N indiscipline *f*

indiscreet [ˌɪndɪˈskriːt] ADJ indiscret(ète)

indiscreetly [ˌɪndɪˈskriːtlɪ] ADV indiscrètement

indiscretion [ˌɪndɪˈskreʃən] N **1** *(lack of discretion)* manque *m* de discrétion, indiscrétion *f* **2** *(unwise act)* écart *m* de conduite; *(unwise remark)* indiscrétion *f*; **to be guilty of an i.** *(blunder)* commettre une inconséquence; *(sexual)* se compromettre

indiscriminate [ˌɪndɪˈskrɪmɪnət] ADJ **it was i. slaughter** ce fut un massacre aveugle; **to distribute i. punishment** distribuer des punitions à tort et à travers; **children are i. in their television viewing** les enfants regardent la télévision sans discernement; **i. admiration** admiration *f* inconditionnelle

indiscriminately [ˌɪndɪˈskrɪmɪnətlɪ] ADV **he reads i.** il lit tout ce qui lui tombe sous la main; **he fired i. into the crowd** il a tiré dans la foule sans faire de distinction; **the plague struck rich and poor i.** la peste a frappé indifféremment les riches et les pauvres

indispensable [ˌɪndɪˈspensəbəl] ADJ indispensable (**to** à *or* pour)

indisposed [ˌɪndɪˈspəʊzd] ADJ *Formal* **1** *Euph (sick)* indisposé, souffrant **2** *(unwilling)* peu enclin, peu disposé; **to be i. to do sth** être peu enclin *ou* peu disposé à faire qch

indisposition [ˌɪndɪspəˈzɪʃən] N *Formal* **1** *Euph (illness)* indisposition *f* **2** *(unwillingness)* dispositions *fpl* peu favorables, manque *m* d'empressement

indisputable [ˌɪndɪˈspjuːtəbəl] ADJ incontestable, indiscutable

indisputably [ˌɪndɪˈspjuːtəblɪ] ADV incontestablement, indiscutablement

indissoluble [ˌɪndɪˈsɒljʊbəl] ADJ indissoluble

indistinct [ˌɪndɪˈstɪŋkt] ADJ indistinct

indistinctly [ˌɪndɪˈstɪŋktlɪ] ADV indistinctement

indistinguishable [ˌɪndɪˈstɪŋgwɪʃəbəl] ADJ **1** *(alike)* impossible à distinguer; **his handwriting is i. from his brother's** son écriture est impossible à distinguer de celle de son frère; **the twins are i.** les jumeaux se ressemblent à s'y méprendre **2** *(imperceptible)* imperceptible

individual [ˌɪndɪˈvɪdʒʊəl] ADJ **1** *(for one person)* individuel; **his pupils get i. attention** il s'occupe de ses élèves individuellement; **she has i. tuition** elle prend des cours particuliers **2** *(single, separate)* particulier; **we cannot consider each i. case** nous ne pouvons pas considérer tous les cas particuliers; **it's impossible to investigate each i. complaint** il est impossible d'étudier séparément chaque réclamation; **each i. case is different** chaque cas est différent **3** *(distinctive)* personnel, particulier; **she has a very i. way of working** elle a une façon très particulière *ou* personnelle de travailler

N individu *m*; **who's that strange i.?** qui est cet individu bizarre?; **as a private i.** comme simple particulier

▸▸ *Fin* ***individual company accounts*** comptes *mpl* sociaux, comptes *mpl* d'entreprise individuelle; *Am Fin* ***individual retirement account*** plan *m* d'epargne retraite personnel; ***individual rights*** droits *mpl* de l'individu *ou* de la personne; *Fin* ***individual savings account*** plan *m* d'epargne en actions; *Law* ***Individual Voluntary Arrangement*** = accord légal établi par un administrateur judiciaire qui permet à un débiteur de trouver un compromis avec ses créanciers, lui évitant ainsi les conséquences d'une faillite

individualism [ˌɪndɪˈvɪdʒʊəlɪzəm] N *(gen)* & *Phil & Pol* individualisme *m*

individualist [ˌɪndɪˈvɪdʒʊəlɪst] N individualiste *mf*

individualistic [ˌɪndɪˌvɪdʒʊəˈlɪstɪk] ADJ individualiste

individuality [ˈɪndɪˌvɪdʒʊˈælətɪ] *(pl* **individualities)** N individualité *f*

individualize, -ise [ˌɪndɪˈvɪdʒʊəlaɪz] VT individualiser

individually [ˌɪndɪˈvɪdʒʊəlɪ] ADV **1** *(separately)* individuellement; **he spoke to us all i.** il nous a parlé à tous un par un **2** *(distinctively)* de façon distinctive; **he dresses very i.** il s'habille de façon très originale, il a une façon très personnelle de s'habiller

indivisible [ˌɪndɪˈvɪzəbəl] ADJ indivisible; **17 is i. by 3** 17 n'est pas divisible par 3

Indochina [ˌɪndəʊˈtʃaɪnə] N *Geog* Indochine *f*

indoctrinate [ɪnˈdɒktrɪneɪt] VT endoctriner; **they were indoctrinated with revolutionary ideas** on leur a inculqué des idées révolutionnaires

indoctrination [ɪnˌdɒktrɪˈneɪʃən] N endoctrinement *m*

Indo-European *Ling* N indo-européen *m*

ADJ indo-européen

indolence [ˈɪndələns] N **1** *(laziness)* paresse *f*, indolence *f* **2** *Med* indolence *f*

indolent [ˈɪndələnt] ADJ **1** *(lazy)* paresseux, indolent **2** *Med* indolent

indolently [ˈɪndələntlɪ] ADV paresseusement, indolemment

indomitable [ɪnˈdɒmɪtəbəl] ADJ indomptable, irréductible

Indonesia [ˌɪndəˈniːzjə] N *Geog* Indonésie *f*

Indonesian [ˌɪndəˈniːzjən] N **1** *(person)* Indonésien(enne) *m,f* **2** *(language)* indonésien *m*

ADJ indonésien

COMP *(embassy)* d'Indonésie; *(history)* de l'Indonésie; *(teacher)* d'indonésien

indoor [ˈɪndɔː(r)] ADJ *(toilet)* à l'intérieur; *(clothing)* d'intérieur; *(swimming pool, tennis court)* couvert; *(sport)* pratiqué en salle

▸▸ *Br* ***indoor aerial***, *Am* ***indoor antenna*** antenne *f* intérieure; ***indoor athletics*** athlétisme *m* en salle; ***indoor games*** *(sports)* jeux *mpl* pratiqués en salle; *(board games, charades etc)* jeux *mpl* d'intérieur; ***indoor plants*** plantes *fpl* d'intérieur *ou* d'appartement; *Cin & TV* ***indoor scene*** scène *f* tournée en intérieur; *Cin & TV* ***indoor set*** decor *m* en intérieur

> Attention: ne pas confondre avec l'adverbe **indoors**.

indoors [ˌɪnˈdɔːz] ADV à l'intérieur; **let's go i.** rentrons (à l'intérieur); **I don't like being i. all day** je n'aime pas rester enfermée toute la journée

> Attention: ne pas confondre avec l'adjectif **indoor**.

indorse, indorsee *etc* = **endorse, endorsee** *etc*

indrawn [ˌɪnˈdrɔːn] ADJ **1** *(air)* aspiré; **i. breath** aspiration *f*, inspiration *f* **2** *(person)* replié sur soi-même, renfermé

indubitable [ɪnˈdjuːbɪtəbəl] ADJ indubitable

indubitably [ɪnˈdjuːbɪtəblɪ] ADV assurément, indubitablement

induce [ɪnˈdjuːs] VT **1** *(cause)* entraîner, provoquer; **this drug sometimes induces sleepiness** ce médicament peut provoquer la somnolence

2 *(persuade)* persuader, décider; **nothing will i. me to change my mind** rien ne me fera changer d'avis

3 *Med (labour)* déclencher (artificiellement); **she's had to be induced** on a dû lui faire une piqûre pour provoquer l'accouchement *ou* déclencher le travail

4 *Phil (infer)* induire

5 *Elec* induire

inducement [ɪnˈdjuːsmənt] N **1** *(encouragement)* persuasion *f*; **fears for his daughter's safety will be enough of an i.** le fait qu'il craint pour la sécurité de sa fille sera une motivation suffisante **2** *(reward)* incitation *f*, récompense *f*; *(bribe)* pot-de-vin *m*; **he was offered considerable financial inducements to leave his company** on lui a offert des sommes considérables pour l'inciter à quitter son entreprise

induct [ɪnˈdʌkt] VT **1** *(into office, post)* installer

2 *(into mystery, unknown field)* initier (**into** à)

3 *Am Mil* appeler (sous les drapeaux)

4 *Elec* induire

▸▸ *Aut* ***inducted gas*** gaz *m* aspiré

induction [ɪnˈdʌkʃən] N **1** *(into office, post)* ins tallation *f*

2 *(into mystery, new field)* initiation *f*

3 *(causing)* provocation *f*, déclenchement *m*; **of sleep by drugs** sommeil *m* provoqué par de médicaments

4 *Med (of labour)* déclenchement *m* (artificiel)

5 *Phil* induction *f*

6 *Am Mil* conscription *f*, appel *m* sous les dra peaux

7 *Biol, Elec & Tech* induction *f*

▸▸ *Elec* ***induction coil*** bobine *f* d'inductance; *B* ***induction course*** stage *m* préparatoire *ou* de fo mation; *Phys* ***induction heating*** chauffage *m* pa induction; ***induction loop*** circuit *m* d'inductior *Elec* ***induction motor*** moteur *m* à induction

inductive [ɪnˈdʌktɪv] ADJ **1** *(reasoning)* inducti par induction **2** *Elec (current etc)* inducteur

indulge [ɪnˈdʌldʒ] VT **1** *(person)* gâter; **she in dulges her children** elle gâte ses enfants, ell passe tout à ses enfants; **to i. oneself** se fair plaisir **2** *(desire, vice)* assouvir; *(hope)* nourri *(passion)* se livrer à, donner libre cours à; **she in dulged her passion for skiing** elle a satisfait s passion pour le ski; **he indulges her every whir** il se prête à *ou* il lui passe tous ses caprices *Com (debtor)* accorder un délai de paiement à

VI **to i. in sth** se livrer à qch; **let us i. in a littl speculation** livrons-nous à quelques suppos tions; **I occasionally i. in a cigar** je me permets u cigare de temps en temps; **no thank you, I don't** *(drink)* non merci, je ne bois pas; *(smoke)* no merci, je ne fume pas

indulgence [ɪnˈdʌldʒəns] N **1** *(tolerance, kind ness)* indulgence *f*

2 *(gratification)* assouvissement *m*; **the i. of hi every desire** l'assouvissement *m* de tous ses dé sirs; **i. in bad habits** fait *m* de se complaire dan de mauvaises habitudes

3 *(privilege)* privilège *m*; *(treat)* gâterie *f*; **smok ing is my only i.** mon seul vice, c'est le tabac

4 *Rel* indulgence *f*

indulgent [ɪnˈdʌldʒənt] ADJ *(liberal, kind)* indul gent, complaisant; **you shouldn't be so i. wit your children** vous ne devriez pas vous montre aussi indulgent envers vos enfants

indulgently [ɪnˈdʌldʒəntlɪ] ADV avec indul gence

industrial [ɪnˈdʌstrɪəl] ADJ *(gen)* industriel; **an i city** une ville industrielle

• **industrials** NPL *St Exch* valeurs *fpl* industriel les

▸▸ ***industrial accident*** accident *m* du travail; ***in dustrial accident insurance*** assurance *f* contre le accidents du travail; *Br* ***industrial action*** *(UN COUNT)* grève *f*, grèves *fpl*; **they threatened (t take) i. action** ils ont menacé de faire grève; ***in dustrial activity*** activité *f* industrielle; *Am Sch* ***in dustrial art*** = cours technique où l'on apprend l maniement des machines propres à une indus trie particulière; *Fin* ***industrial bank*** banque *f* in dustrielle; ***industrial centre*** centre *m* industriel ***industrial complex*** complexe *m* industriel; ***indus trial democracy*** démocratie *f* industrielle; ***indus trial design*** dessin *m* industriel; ***industria diamond*** diamant *m* industriel *ou* de nature; ***in dustrial disease*** maladie *f* professionnelle *ou* d travail; *Br* ***industrial dispute*** conflit *m* social; ***in dustrial earnings*** produit *m* industriel; ***industria economics*** économie *f* industrielle; ***industria espionage*** espionnage *m* industriel; *Br* ***industria estate*** zone *f* industrielle; ***industrial grou*** groupe *m* industriel; ***industrial injury*** accident *n* du travail; ***industrial injuries benefit*** indemnité pour accidents du travail; *Med* ***industrial medi cine*** médecine *f* du travail; *Fin* ***industrial mon opoly*** trust *m* industriel; ***industrial organizatio*** économie *f* industrielle; *Am* ***industrial park*** zon *f* industrielle; ***industrial power*** puissance *f* in dustrielle; ***industrial production*** production *f* in dustrielle; ***industrial redeployment*** reconversio *f* industrielle; ***industrial relations*** relations *fpl* en tre le patronat et les travailleurs; **i. relations hav**

deteriorated le climat social s'est dégradé; *Hist* ***the Industrial Revolution*** la révolution industrielle; *Am* ***industrial school*** école *f* technique; *St Exch* ***industrial shares*** valeurs *mpl* industrielles; ***industrial trade*** échanges *mpl* industriels; *Br & Austr Law* ***industrial tribunal*** conseil *m* de prud'hommes; ***industrial union*** syndicat *m* d'industrie; ***industrial unit*** atelier *m*; ***industrial unrest*** agitation *f* syndicale; ***industrial workers*** travailleurs *mpl* de l'industrie

> Note that the French adjective **industriel** never refers to the relationship between employers and employees.

ndustrialism [ɪnˈdʌstrɪəlɪzəm] **N** industrialisme *m*

ndustrialist [ɪnˈdʌstrɪəlɪst] **N** industriel *m*

ndustrialization, -isation [ɪnˌdʌstrɪəlaɪˈzeɪʃən] **N** industrialisation *f*

ndustrialize, -ise [ɪnˈdʌstrɪəlaɪz] **VT** industrialiser
VI s'industrialiser

ndustrialized, -ised [ɪnˈdʌstrɪəlaɪzd] **ADJ** industrialisé
►► ***the industrialized countries*** les pays *mpl* industrialisés

ndustrial-strength **ADJ** *(adhesive, bleach etc)* à usage industriel; *Hum (coffee)* hyper-costaud

ndustrious [ɪnˈdʌstrɪəs] **ADJ** travailleur

ndustriously [ɪnˈdʌstrɪəslɪ] **ADV** avec application

ndustriousness [ɪnˈdʌstrɪəsnɪs] **N** application *f*, diligence *f*

ndustry [ˈɪndʌstrɪ] *(pl* **industries) N 1** *(business)* industrie *f*; **both sides of i.** syndicats *mpl* et patronat *m*, les partenaires *mpl* sociaux; **the oil/film i.** l'industrie *f* pétrolière/cinématographique **2** *(diligence)* application *f*, diligence *f*
►► ***industry expert*** expert *m* de l'industrie; ***industry forecast*** prévision *f* de l'industrie; ***industry sector*** secteur *m* industriel *ou* secondaire

ndustry-standard **ADJ** normalisé

ndy [ˈɪndɪ] **N** *Fam (abbr* **Indianapolis)** Indianapolis
►► ***Indy car*** = type de voiture de course, aux États-Unis; ***the Indy 500*** = course automobile qui se déroule à Indianapolis, aux États-Unis

nebriate *Formal* **N** [ɪˈniːbrɪət] ivrogne *mf*, alcoolique *mf*
ADJ [ɪˈniːbrɪət] ivre
VT [ɪˈniːbrɪeɪt] enivrer, griser

nebriated [ɪˈniːbrɪeɪtɪd] **ADJ** ivre; *Fig* **i. by his success** grisé par son succès

nebriation [ɪˌniːbrɪˈeɪʃən] **N** *Formal* **1** *(act of making drunk)* enivrement *m* **2** *(drunkenness)* ivresse *f*, ébriété *f*

nedible [ɪnˈedɪbəl] **ADJ 1** *(unsafe to eat)* non comestible **2** *(unpleasant to eat)* immangeable

neducable [ɪnˈedjʊkəbəl] **ADJ** inéducable

neffable [ɪnˈefəbəl] **ADJ** *Literary* ineffable, indicible

neffective [ˌɪnɪˈfektɪv] **ADJ 1** *(person)* inefficace, incapable, incompétent; **an i. leader** un dirigeant incompétent **2** *(action)* inefficace, sans effet; **the drug is i. against the new virus** le médicament est inefficace *ou* n'a aucun effet contre le nouveau virus

neffectively [ˌɪnɪˈfektɪvlɪ] **ADV** sans résultat

neffectual [ˌɪnɪˈfektʃʊəl] **ADJ** inefficace

nefficacious [ˌɪnefɪˈkeɪʃəs] **ADJ** inefficace, sans effet

nefficacity [ˌɪnefɪˈkæsətɪ], **inefficacy** [ɪnˈefɪkəsɪ] **N** inefficacité *f*

nefficiency [ˌɪnɪˈfɪʃənsɪ] *(pl* **inefficiencies) N** inefficacité *f*, manque *m* d'efficacité; **the i. of the old machines** le manque de rendement *ou* le faible rendement des anciennes machines

nefficient [ˌɪnɪˈfɪʃənt] **ADJ** inefficace; **an i. use of resources** une mauvaise utilisation des ressources; **these old machines are too i.** le rendement de ces vieilles machines est vraiment insuffisant

nefficiently [ˌɪnɪˈfɪʃəntlɪ] **ADV** inefficacement

inelastic [ˌɪnɪˈlæstɪk] **ADJ 1** *(material)* rigide, inélastique; *(schedule)* rigide, inflexible **2** *Phys (collision)* inélastique

inelegant [ɪnˈelɪgənt] **ADJ** inélégant

inelegantly [ɪnˈelɪgəntlɪ] **ADV** de façon peu élégante

ineligible [ɪnˈelɪdʒəbəl] **ADJ 1** *(unqualified)* non qualifié; **he is i. for the post** il n'est pas qualifié pour le poste; **to be i. for military service** être inapte au service militaire; **they are i. for unemployment benefit** ils n'ont pas droit aux allocations de chômage; **they are i. to vote** ils n'ont pas le droit de voter **2** *(for election)* inéligible

ineluctable [ˌɪnɪˈlʌktəbəl] **ADJ** *Formal* inéluctable

inept [ɪˈnept] **ADJ** inepte

ineptitude [ɪˈneptɪtjuːd] **N** ineptie *f*

ineptly [ɪˈneptlɪ] **ADV** absurdement, stupidement

inequality [ˌɪnɪˈkwɒlətɪ] *(pl* **inequalities) N** inégalité *f*

inequitable [ɪnˈekwɪtəbəl] **ADJ** inéquitable

ineradicable [ˌɪnɪˈrædɪkəbəl] **ADJ** indéracinable

inert [ɪˈnɜːt] **ADJ 1** *(lethargic, lifeless)* inerte **2** *Chem & Phys* inerte
►► *Chem* ***inert gas*** gaz *m* inerte

inertia [ɪˈnɜːʃə] **N** inertie *f*

inertia-reel seat belt **N** *Br Aut* ceinture *f* de sécurité à enrouleur

inescapable [ˌɪnɪˈskeɪpəbəl] **ADJ** *(outcome)* inévitable, inéluctable; *(fact)* indéniable

inessential [ˌɪnɪˈsenʃəl] **ADJ** non essentiel
• **inessentials NPL** superflu *m*

inestimable [ɪnˈestɪməbəl] **ADJ** inestimable, incalculable

inevitability [ɪnˌevɪtəˈbɪlətɪ] **N** inévitabilité *f*

inevitable [ɪnˈevɪtəbəl] **ADJ** *(outcome, consequence)* inévitable, inéluctable; *(end)* inévitable, fatal; **it's i. that someone will feel left out** il est inévitable *ou* on ne pourra empêcher que quelqu'un se sente exclu
N inévitable *m*; **we had to resign ourselves to the i.** il fallut nous résoudre à accepter l'inévitable

inevitably [ɪnˈevɪtəblɪ] **ADV** inévitablement, fatalement

inexact [ˌɪnɪgˈzækt] **ADJ** *(imprecise)* imprécis; *(wrong)* inexact, erroné; **it's an i. science** ce n'est pas une science exacte

inexactitude [ˌɪnɪgˈzæktɪtjuːd] **N 1** *(imprecision)* imprécision *f*; *(incorrectness)* inexactitude *f* **2** *(mistake)* inexactitude *f*

inexactly [ˌɪnɪgˈzæktlɪ] **ADV** *(imprecisely)* de façon imprécise; *(incorrectly)* inexactement, incorrectement

inexactness [ˌɪnɪgˈzæktnɪs] **N** *(imprecision)* imprécision *f*; *(incorrectness)* inexactitude *f*

inexcusable [ˌɪnɪkˈskjuːzəbəl] **ADJ** inexcusable, impardonnable

inexcusably [ˌɪnɪkˈskjuːzəblɪ] **ADV** inexcusablement, impardonnablement; **i. rude** d'une grossièreté impardonnable; **he behaved quite i. at the party** la façon dont il s'est comporté à la soirée est inexcusable

inexhaustible [ˌɪnɪgˈzɔːstəbəl] **ADJ 1** *(source, energy, patience)* inépuisable, illimité; **she had an i. supply of jokes** elle avait un stock de blagues inépuisable **2** *(person)* infatigable

inexorable [ɪnˈeksərəbəl] **ADJ** inexorable

inexorably [ɪnˈeksərəblɪ] **ADV** inexorablement

inexpedient [ˌɪnɪkˈspiːdjənt] **ADJ** peu judicieux, malavisé

inexpensive [ˌɪnɪkˈspensɪv] **ADJ** bon marché *(inv)*, peu cher

inexpensively [ˌɪnɪkˈspensɪvlɪ] **ADV** *(sell)* (à) bon marché, à bas prix; *(live)* à peu de frais

inexperience [ˌɪnɪkˈspɪərɪəns] **N** inexpérience *f*, manque *m* d'expérience

inexperienced [ˌɪnɪkˈspɪərɪənst] **ADJ 1** *(person)* inexpérimenté, sans expérience; **she is still i.** elle manque encore d'expérience; **he's i. in handling staff** il n'a pas l'habitude de diriger le personnel **2** *(eye, ear)* inexercé

inexpert [ɪnˈekspɜːt] **ADJ** inexpérimenté, inexpert; **he was i. in such matters** il ne connaissait pas grand-chose à ces choses; **her i. handling of the situation** la façon maladroite dont elle a géré l'affaire

inexpertly [ɪnˈekspɜːtlɪ] **ADV** maladroitement

inexpiable [ɪnˈekspɪəbəl] **ADJ** *Formal* inexpiable

inexplicable [ˌɪnɪkˈsplɪkəbəl] **ADJ** inexplicable

inexplicably [ˌɪnɪkˈsplɪkəblɪ] **ADV** inexplicablement

inexpressible [ˌɪnɪkˈspresəbəl] **ADJ** inexprimable, indicible

inexpressive [ˌɪnɪkˈspresɪv] **ADJ** inexpressif

inextinguishable [ˌɪnɪkˈstɪŋgwɪʃəbəl] **ADJ** *(fire)* impossible à éteindre; *(need, desire)* insatiable; *(thirst)* inextinguible; *(passion)* irrépressible, incontrôlable

in extremis [ɪnɪkˈstriːmɪs] **ADV** à l'extrême rigueur, à la limite
ADJ to be i. être à l'article de la mort

inextricable [ˌɪnɪkˈstrɪkəbəl] **ADJ** inextricable

inextricably [ˌɪnɪkˈstrɪkəblɪ] **ADV** inextricablement

infallibility [ɪnˌfæləˈbɪlətɪ] **N** infaillibilité *f*

infallible [ɪnˈfæləbəl] **ADJ** infaillible

infallibly [ɪnˈfæləblɪ] **ADV** infailliblement, immanquablement

infamous [ˈɪnfəməs] **ADJ 1** *(notorious)* tristement célèbre, notoire **2** *(shocking ▸ conduct)* infâme

infamously [ˈɪnfəməslɪ] **ADV** *(behave)* de manière infâme

infamy [ˈɪnfəmɪ] *(pl* **infamies) N 1** *(notoriety)* triste notoriété *f* **2** *(notorious act, event)* infamie *f*

infancy [ˈɪnfənsɪ] *(pl* **infancies) N 1** *(early childhood)* petite enfance *f*; **a child in its i.** un enfant en bas âge **2** *Fig* débuts *mpl*, enfance *f*; **when electronics was still in its i.** quand l'électronique n'en était qu'à ses balbutiements **3** *Law* minorité *f* (légale)

infant [ˈɪnfənt] **N 1** *(young child)* petit(e) enfant *mf*, enfant *mf* en bas âge; *(baby)* bébé *m*; *(newborn)* nouveau-né(e) *m,f* **2** *Br Sch* = élève dans les premières années d'école primaire **3** *Law* mineur(e) *m,f*
COMP 1 *(food)* pour bébés; *(disease)* infantile **2** *Br (teacher, teaching)* des premières années d'école primaire
ADJ *(organization)* naissant
►► *Econ* ***infant industry*** industrie *f* naissante; ***infant mortality*** mortalité *f* infantile; ***infant mortality rate*** taux *m* de mortalité infantile; *Br Sch* ***infant school*** école *f* maternelle *(5–7 ans)*

infanticide [ɪnˈfæntɪsaɪd] **N** *Law* **1** *(act)* infanticide *m* **2** *(person)* infanticide *mf*

infantile [ˈɪnfəntaɪl] **ADJ 1** *Pej (childish)* infantile, puéril **2** *(of, for infants)* infantile **3** *Med & Psy* infantile

infantilism [ɪnˈfæntɪlɪzəm] **N** *Med & Psy* infantilisme *m*

infantry [ˈɪnfəntrɪ] *Mil* **N** infanterie *f*
ADJ de l'infanterie

infantryman [ˈɪnfəntrɪmən] *(pl* **infantrymen** [-mən]) **N** *Mil* soldat *m* d'infanterie, fantassin *m*

infarct [ɪnˈfɑːkt] **N** *Med* infarctus *m (du myocarde)*

infarction [ɪnˈfɑːkʃən] **N** *Med* infarctus *m (du myocarde)*

infatuated [ɪnˈfætjʊeɪtɪd] **ADJ** entiché (**with** de); **to become i. with sb/sth** s'enticher de qn/qch

infatuation [ɪnˌfætjʊˈeɪʃən] **N** engouement *m* (**for** *or* **with** pour)

infect [ɪnˈfekt] **VT 1** *Med (wound, organ, person, animal)* infecter; **is the liver infected?** est-ce que le foie est infecté *ou* atteint?; **I hope that cut won't get infected** j'espère que cette coupure ne s'infectera pas; **to i. sb with sth** transmettre qch à qn; **he infected all his friends with the flu** il a transmis *ou* donné sa grippe à tous ses amis
2 *(food, water, area, clothing)* contaminer
3 *Comput (file, disk)* infecter
4 *Fig (of vice)* corrompre, contaminer; *(of emotion)* se communiquer à; **they infected us with their enthusiasm** ils nous ont communiqué leur enthousiasme

infected [ɪnˈfektɪd] ADJ **1** *(wound, organ, person, animal)* infecté **2** *(food, water, area, clothing)* contaminé **3** *Comput* infecté

infectiology [ˌɪnfektɪˈɒlədʒɪ] N *Med* infectiologie *f*

infection [ɪnˈfekʃən] N **1** *Med* infection *f*; **a throat i.** une infection de la gorge, une angine **2** *Fig* contagion *f*, contamination *f*

infectious [ɪnˈfekʃəs] ADJ **1** *Med (disease)* infectieux, infectant; *(person)* contagieux **2** *Fig (laughter, enthusiasm etc)* contagieux, communicatif

▸▸ *Med* ***infectious hepatitis*** *(UNCOUNT)* hépatite *f* infectieuse, hépatite *f* virale A; *Med* ***infectious mononucleosis*** *(UNCOUNT)* mononucléose *f* infectieuse

infectiousness [ɪnˈfekʃəsnɪs] N **1** *Med* caractère *m* infectieux **2** *Fig* caractère *m* contagieux *ou* communicatif

infective [ɪnˈfektɪv] ADJ *Med (disease)* infectieux, infectant; *(person)* contagieux

infectiveness [ɪnˈfektɪvnɪs], **infectivity** [ˌɪnfekˈtɪvɪtɪ] N *Med* infectiosité *f*

infelicitous [ˌɪnfɪˈlɪsɪtəs] ADJ *Literary* malheureux, malchanceux

infelicity [ˌɪnfɪˈlɪsɪtɪ] *(pl* **infelicities***)* N *Literary* **1** *(state of misfortune)* malchance *f*, infortune *f* **2** *(piece of bad luck)* malchance *f* **3** *(remark)* parole *f* malheureuse, maladresse *f*

infer [ɪnˈfɜː(r)] *(pt & pp* **inferred**, *cont* **inferring***)* VT **1** *(deduce)* conclure, inférer, déduire; **what are we to i. from their absence?** que devons-nous conclure de leur absence?; **I inferred from his look that I had done something wrong** à son regard, j'ai compris que j'avais fait quelque chose de mal **2** *Fam (imply)* suggérer[□], laisser supposer[□]; **what are you inferring by that?** qu'insinuez-vous par là?[□]

inference [ˈɪnfərəns] N déduction *f*; *(in logic)* inférence *f*; **what inferences can we draw from it?** quelles conclusions pouvons-nous en tirer?, que pouvons-nous en déduire?

inferior [ɪnˈfɪərɪə(r)] N *(in social status)* inférieur (e) *m,f*; *(in rank, hierarchy)* subalterne *mf*, subordonné(e) *m,f*

ADJ **1** *(quality, worth, social status)* inférieur; **he always felt i. to his brother** il a toujours éprouvé un sentiment d'infériorité par rapport à son frère; **to make sb feel i.** donner un sentiment d'infériorité à qn; **i. imported goods** marchandises *fpl* importées de qualité inférieure **2** *(in rank)* subalterne; **she holds an i. position in the company** elle a un poste subalterne dans la société **3** *(in space, position)* inférieur

▸▸ *Typ* ***inferior character*** (caractère *m* en) indice *m*; *Law* ***inferior court*** cour *f* de juridiction inférieure; ***inferior planet*** planète *f* inférieure

inferiority [ɪnˌfɪərɪˈɒrətɪ] *(pl* **inferiorities***)* N infériorité *f*

▸▸ *Psy* ***inferiority complex*** complexe *m* d'infériorité

infernal [ɪnˈfɜːnəl] ADJ **1** *Fam (awful)* infernal; **stop that i. racket** *or* **din!** arrêtez ce raffut *ou* boucan infernal!; **that i. fuse has blown again!** ce satané fusible a encore sauté! **2** *(of hell)* infernal; *(diabolical)* infernal, diabolique; **the i. regions** l'enfer *m*

infernally [ɪnˈfɜːnəlɪ] ADV *Fam* terriblement, épouvantablement; **it's i. hot** il fait une chaleur d'enfer

inferno [ɪnˈfɜːnəʊ] *(pl* **infernos***)* N **1** *(fire)* brasier *m*; **the hotel was a blazing i.** l'hôtel n'était qu'un gigantesque brasier **2** *(hell)* enfer *m*

infertile [ɪnˈfɜːtaɪl] ADJ *(person, animal)* stérile; *(land, soil)* stérile, infertile

infertility [ˌɪnfəˈtɪlətɪ] N *Med (of person)* stérilité *f*; *(of soil)* stérilité, infertilité *f*

▸▸ *Med* ***infertility clinic*** = service qui s'occupe des problèmes de stérilité dans un établissement hospitalier

infest [ɪnˈfest] VT infester (**with** de); **shark-infested waters** eaux *fpl* infestées de requins

infestation [ˌɪnfeˈsteɪʃən] N *Med* infestation *f*; *Bot (of plants by parasites etc)* invasion *f*

infidel [ˈɪnfɪdəl] N infidèle *mf*

ADJ infidèle, incroyant

infidelity [ˌɪnfɪˈdelətɪ] *(pl* **infidelities***)* N **1** *(betrayal)* infidélité *f* **2** *(lack of faith)* incroyance *f*, irréligion *f*

infighting [ˈɪnˌfaɪtɪŋ] N *(UNCOUNT)* **1** *Br (within group)* conflits *mpl* internes, luttes *fpl* intestines **2** *(in boxing)* corps à corps *m*

infill [ˈɪnfɪl] N matériau *m* de remplissage

VT remplir, combler

infiltrate [ˈɪnfɪltreɪt] VT **1** *(organization)* infiltrer, noyauter; **the police had infiltrated the terrorist group** la police avait infiltré *ou* noyauté le groupe terroriste; **they infiltrated spies into the organization** ils ont envoyé des espions pour infiltrer l'organisation **2** *(of liquid ▸ substance)* s'infiltrer dans **3** *(cause to enter ▸ liquid)* faire pénétrer (**into** dans)

VI s'infiltrer

N *Chem & Med* infiltrat *m*

infiltration [ˌɪnfɪlˈtreɪʃən] N **1** *(of group)* infiltration *f*, noyautage *m* **2** *(by liquid)* infiltration *f* (**into/through** dans/à travers)

infiltrator [ˈɪnfɪltreɪtə(r)] N agent *m* infiltré; **there are infiltrators in the party** le parti a été infiltré *ou* noyauté

infinite [ˈɪnfɪnət] ADJ **1** *(not finite)* infini **2** *Fig (very great)* infini, incalculable; **he showed i. patience** il a fait preuve d'une patience infinie; *Ironic* **the government, in its i. wisdom, has decided to close the factory** le gouvernement, dans son infinie sagesse, a décidé de fermer l'usine

N infini *m*

▸▸ *Math* ***infinite set*** ensemble *m* infini

infinitely [ˈɪnfɪnətlɪ] ADV infiniment

infinitesimal [ˌɪnfɪnɪˈtesɪməl] ADJ **1** *Math* infinitésimal **2** *(tiny)* infinitésimal, infime

infinitive [ɪnˈfɪnɪtɪv] *Gram* N infinitif *m*; **in the i.** à l'infinitif

ADJ infinitif

infinity [ɪnˈfɪnətɪ] *(pl* **infinities***)* N **1** *(of space, time, quantity etc)* infinité *f*, infini *m*; *Fig* **there is an i. of names to choose from** on peut choisir parmi une infinité de noms; **it stretches to i.** cela s'étend jusqu'à l'infini **2** *Math & Phot* infini *m*; **to focus on** *or* **for i.** mettre au point sur l'infini

▸▸ ***infinity pool*** piscine *f* à débordement

infirm [ɪnˈfɜːm] ADJ **1** *(in health, body)* invalide, infirme **2** *Literary (in moral resolution)* indécis, irrésolu; **to be i. of purpose** manquer de détermination **3** *Law* invalide

NPL **the i.** les infirmes *mpl*

infirmary [ɪnˈfɜːmərɪ] *(pl* **infirmaries***)* N *(hospital)* hôpital *m*; *(sickroom)* infirmerie *f*

infirmity [ɪnˈfɜːmətɪ] *(pl* **infirmities***)* N **1** *(physical)* infirmité *f* **2** *(moral)* défaut *m*, faiblesse *f*

inflame [ɪnˈfleɪm] VT **1** *(rouse ▸ person, crowd)* exciter, enflammer; *(▸ anger, hatred, passion)* attiser, exacerber; **the argument became inflamed** la discussion s'est enflammée; **she was inflamed with anger/passion** elle brûlait de colère/de passion

2 *Med (wound, infection)* enflammer; *(organ, tissue)* irriter, infecter

3 *(set fire to)* enflammer, mettre le feu à

4 *Literary (redden)* enflammer

VI **1** *(person, heart, passion)* s'enflammer **2** *Med (wound, infection)* s'enflammer; *(organ, tissue)* s'irriter, s'infecter **3** *(catch fire)* s'enflammer, s'embraser

inflamed [ɪnˈfleɪmd] ADJ **1** *Med (eyes, throat, tendon, wound)* enflammé, irrité **2** *Fig (passion, hatred)* enflammé, ardent (**with** de); **i. with passion** brûlant d'amour

inflammable [ɪnˈflæməbəl] N matière *f* inflammable

ADJ *(substance, material)* inflammable; *Fig (person, crowd)* prompt à s'échauffer; *Fig* **an i. situation** une situation explosive

inflammation [ˌɪnfləˈmeɪʃən] N inflammation *f*

inflammatory [ɪnˈflæmətərɪ] ADJ **1** *(speech, propaganda)* incendiaire **2** *Med* inflammatoire

inflatable [ɪnˈfleɪtəbəl] ADJ *(toy)* gonflable; *(mattress, boat)* pneumatique

N structure *f* gonflable

inflate [ɪnˈfleɪt] VT **1** *(tyre, balloon, boat)* gonfler; *(lungs)* emplir d'air; *(chest)* gonfler, bomber

2 *(opinion, importance)* gonfler, exagérer; **to i. the importance of an event** exagérer *ou* grossir l'importance d'un événement

3 *Econ (prices)* faire monter, augmenter; *(economy)* provoquer l'inflation de; **to i. the currency** accroître la circulation monétaire

4 *Com (account)* grossir, charger; *(expense account, figures)* gonfler

VI **1** *(tyre)* se gonfler; *(lungs)* s'emplir d'air; *(chest)* se gonfler, se bomber **2** *Econ (prices, money)* subir une inflation; **the government decided to i.** le gouvernement a décidé d'avoir recours à des mesures inflationnistes

inflated [ɪnˈfleɪtɪd] ADJ **1** *(balloon, tyre)* gonflé **2** *(opinion, importance)* exagéré; *(style)* emphatique, pompier; **i. with pride** bouffi d'orgueil **3** *Econ (price)* exagéré

▸▸ ***inflated currency*** inflation *f* monétaire

inflation [ɪnˈfleɪʃən] N **1** *Econ* inflation *f*; **i. is down/up on last year** l'inflation est en baisse/en hausse par rapport à l'année dernière **2** *(of tyre, balloon, boat)* gonflement *m* **3** *(of idea, importance)* grossissement *m*, exagération *f*

▸▸ *Econ* ***inflation accounting*** comptabilité *f* d'inflation; *Fin* ***inflation tax*** impôt *m* à la production

inflationary [ɪnˈfleɪʃənrɪ] ADJ *Econ* inflationniste, *Belg* inflatoire

▸▸ ***inflationary policy*** politique *f* inflationniste; ***inflationary pressure*** pression *f* inflationniste; ***inflationary spiral*** spirale *f* inflationniste; ***inflationary trend*** tendance *f* inflationniste

inflect [ɪnˈflekt] VT **1** *Ling (verb)* conjuguer; *(noun, pronoun, adjective)* décliner **2** *(tone, voice)* moduler; *Mus (note)* altérer **3** *(curve, light beam)* infléchir

VI *Ling* se décliner; *(verb)* se conjuguer

inflected [ɪnˈflektɪd] ADJ *Ling (language)* à flexions, flexionnel; *(vowel)* infléchi

▸▸ ***inflected form*** forme *f* fléchie

inflection [ɪnˈflekʃən] N **1** *(of tone, voice)* inflexion *f*, modulation *f*

2 *Ling* désinence *f*, flexion *f*

3 *(curve)* flexion *f*, inflexion *f*, courbure *f*

4 *Math* inflexion *f*; **point of i.** point *m* d'inflexion

inflexibility [ɪnˌfleksəˈbɪlətɪ] N inflexibilité *f*, rigidité *f*

inflexible [ɪnˈfleksəbəl] ADJ inflexible, rigide

inflexion *Br* = **inflection**

inflict [ɪnˈflɪkt] VT infliger; **to i. pain/suffering on sb** faire mal à/faire souffrir qn; **to i. a defeat on sb** infliger une défaite à qn; **I don't want to i. myself** *or* **my company on you** je ne veux pas m'imposer

infliction [ɪnˈflɪkʃən] N *(action)* action *f* d'infliger; **to take pleasure in the i. of pain** prendre du plaisir à infliger de la douleur

in-flight ADJ *Aviat* en vol

▸▸ ***in-flight magazine*** magazine *m* de bord; ***in-flight meal*** plateau-repas *m*; ***in-flight refuelling*** ravitaillement *m* en vol; ***in-flight video*** vidéo *f* projetée en vol

inflorescence [ˌɪnfləˈresəns] N *Bot* **1** *(part of plant)* inflorescence *f* **2** *(blossoming)* floraison *f*

inflow [ˈɪnfləʊ] N *(of water, gas)* arrivée *f*; *(of people, goods)* afflux *m*; **the i. of capital** l'afflux *m* de capitaux

influence [ˈɪnflʊəns] N influence *f*; **to have i.** avoir de l'influence; **to bring one's i. to bear on sth** exercer son influence sur qch; **he is a man of i.** c'est un homme influent; **I have no i. over them** je n'ai aucune influence sur eux; **he is a bad i. on them** il a une mauvaise influence sur eux; **she is a disruptive i.** c'est un élément perturbateur; **his music has a strong reggae i.** sa musique est fortement influencée par le reggae; **they acted under his i.** ils ont agi sous son influence; **she was under the i. of drink/drugs** elle était sous l'emprise de l'alcool/de la drogue; **driving under the i. of alcohol** conduite *f* en état d'ivresse; *Fam* **to be under the i.** *(drunk)* être soûl[□]

VT influencer, influer sur; **influenced by cubism** influencé par le cubisme; **don't let yourself be influenced by them** ne te laisse pas influencer par eux; **to i. sb to the good** exercer une bonne in-

fluence sur qn; **he is easily influenced** il se laisse facilement influencer, il est très influençable; **how can the stars i. our lives?** comment les étoiles peuvent-elles influer sur notre vie?
►► *Pol* ***influence peddling*** trafic *m* d'influence

influencer ['ɪnfluənsə(r)] **N** *Mktg* préconisateur *m*, influenceur *m*

influential [ˌɪnflu'enʃəl] **ADJ** influent, puissant; *(newspaper, TV programme)* influent, qui a de l'influence; **she's an i. woman** c'est une femme qui a de l'influence; **he was i. in getting her a job** il a fait jouer son influence pour l'aider à obtenir du travail

influenza [ˌɪnflu'enzə] **N** *(UNCOUNT) Formal* grippe *f*; **to have i.** avoir la grippe

influx ['ɪnflʌks] **N 1** *(of water, gas)* arrivée *f*; *(of people, goods, cash)* afflux *m*; **an i. of capital** un afflux de capitaux **2** *(of river)* embouchure *f*

info ['ɪnfəʊ] **N** *(UNCOUNT) Fam* informations *fpl*, renseignements *mpl*; *(brochure, leaflet)* doc *f*, documentation *f*; **a piece of i.** une information, un renseignement

infobahn ['ɪnfəʊbɑːn] **N** *Br Comput* autoroute *f* de l'information, *Can* inforoute *f*

infohighway [ˌɪnfəʊ'haɪweɪ] **N** *Comput* autoroute *f* de l'information, *Can* inforoute *f*

infomercial [ˌɪnfəʊ'mɜːʃəl] **N** infomercial *m*

inform [ɪn'fɔːm] **VT 1** *(tell)* informer; **will you i. him of your decision?** allez-vous l'informer de votre décision?; **I have been informed that the funds have arrived** on m'a informé que les fonds sont arrivés; **I'll keep you informed** je vous tiendrai au courant; **why was I not informed (of this)?** pourquoi est-ce que je n'en ai pas été informé?; **I regret to have to i. you that...** j'ai le regret de vous annoncer que...; **we are writing to i. you of the dispatch of...** nous vous avisons de l'envoi de...
2 *Literary (pervade* ► *literary work etc)* imprégner
VI to i. on *or* **against sb** dénoncer qn

informal [ɪn'fɔːməl] **ADJ 1** *(discussion, meeting)* informel; *(dinner)* décontracté; **he's very i. for a prime minister** il est très décontracté pour un premier ministre; **British offices tend to be more i. than German ones** en Grande-Bretagne l'ambiance dans les bureaux tend à être plus décontractée qu'en Allemagne
2 *(clothes)* **his dress was i.** il était habillé simplement; **i. or evening dress?** tenue de ville ou tenue de soirée?
3 *(unofficial* ► *arrangement, agreement)* officieux; *(*► *visit, talks)* non officiel; **I had an i. chat with the boss** j'ai discuté un peu avec le patron
4 *(colloquial* ► *speech, language, words)* familier
►► *Art* ***informal art*** art *m* informel; *Econ* ***informal economy*** travail *m* au noir; *Austr* ***informal vote*** bulletin *m* nul

informality [ˌɪnfɔː'mælətɪ] *(pl* **informalities) N 1** *(of gathering, meal)* simplicité *f*; *(of discussion, interview)* absence *f* de formalité; *(of manners)* naturel *m* **2** *(of speech, language, words)* familiarité *f*, liberté *f*

informally [ɪn'fɔːməlɪ] **ADV 1** *(casually* ► *entertain, discuss)* sans cérémonie; *(*► *behave)* simplement, avec naturel; *(*► *dress)* simplement **2** *(unofficially)* officieusement **3** *(colloquially)* familièrement, avec familiarité

informant [ɪn'fɔːmənt] **N** informateur(trice) *m,f*; **I have it from a reliable i.** je le tiens de source sûre

informatics [ˌɪnfə'mætɪks] **N** *(UNCOUNT)* sciences *fpl* de l'information

information [ˌɪnfə'meɪʃən] **N 1** *(UNCOUNT) (facts)* renseignements *mpl*, informations *fpl*; **a piece** *or* **bit of i.** un renseignement, une information; **if my i. is correct** si mes informations sont exactes; **do you have any i. on** *or* **about the new model?** avez-vous des renseignements concernant *ou* sur le nouveau modèle?; **I'd like some i. about train times** je voudrais des renseignements sur les horaires des trains; **for more i., call this number** pour plus de renseignements *ou* de précisions, appelez ce numéro; **I am sending you this brochure for your i.** je vous envoie cette brochure à titre d'information; **for your i., I'm not stupid** sachez que je ne suis pas complètement idiot; **for your i., I've done the dishes for the past week!** je t'apprendrai *ou* je te signale que j'ai fait la vaisselle toute cette semaine!; **his head is full of useless i.** il encombre sa mémoire de choses inutiles; **the government is operating an i. blackout** le gouvernement fait de la rétention d'information
2 *(communication)* information *f*; **they discussed the importance of i. in our time** ils ont parlé de l'importance de l'information à notre époque; **i. overload** surinformation *f*
3 *(UNCOUNT) (knowledge)* connaissances *fpl*; **her i. on the subject is unequalled** elle connaît ce sujet mieux que personne
4 *Comput (data)* information *f*; **the transmission of genetic i.** la transmission de l'information génétique
5 *(UNCOUNT) (service, department)* (service *m* des) renseignements *mpl*; **ask at the i. desk** adressez-vous aux renseignements
6 *Am Tel* renseignements *mpl*; **to call i.** appeler les renseignements
7 *Law* acte *m* d'accusation; **to lay an i. against sb** déposer une plainte contre qn
►► *Br* ***information bureau*** bureau *m or* service *m* des renseignements; ***information carrier*** support *m* d'information; ***information copy*** *(of document)* copie *f* pour information; ***information desk*** *(in hotel etc)* bureau *m* des renseignements; *Mil* ***information dominance*** infodominance *f*; ***information gathering*** collecte *f* d'informations; *Comput* ***information highway*** autoroute *f* de l'information, *Can* inforoute *f*; ***information market*** marché *m* des informations; ***information office*** bureau *m ou* service *m* des renseignements; ***information officer*** *(press officer)* responsable *mf* de la communication; *(archivist)* documentaliste *mf*; ***information pack*** dossier *m* d'information; *Comput* ***information processing*** *(action)* traitement *m* de l'information; *(domain)* informatique *f*; ***information processing error*** erreur *f* dans le traitement de l'information; ***information retrieval*** recherche *f* documentaire; *Comput* recherche *f* d'information; *Comput* ***information science*** science *f* de l'information; *Comput* ***information scientist*** informaticien(enne) *m,f*; ***information sheet*** fiche *f* explicative; *Comput* ***information society*** société *f* de l'information; ***information storage*** mémorisation *f* des informations; ***information system*** système *m* informatique; *Comput* ***information superhighway*** autoroute *f* de l'information, *Can* inforoute *f*; *Comput* ***information technology*** technologie *f* de l'information, informatique *f*; ***information theory*** théorie *f* de l'information

informative [ɪn'fɔːmətɪv] **ADJ** *(lecture, book, TV programme)* instructif; **he wasn't very i. about his future plans** il ne nous a pas dit grand-chose de ses projets
►► *Mktg* ***informative advertising*** publicité *f* informative

informed [ɪn'fɔːmd] **ADJ 1** *(having information)* informé, renseigné; **i. opinion has it that...** on sait de source sûre *ou* dans les milieux renseignés que...; **he made an i. guess** il a essayé de deviner en s'aidant de ce qu'il sait; **according to i. sources** selon des sources bien informées **2** *(based on information)* **an i. choice** un choix fait en toute connaissance de cause; **it will allow us to make i. decisions** cela nous permettra de prendre des décisions en toute connaissance de cause **3** *(learned, cultured)* cultivé
►► *Med* ***informed consent*** consentement *m* éclairé; ***the informed consumer*** le consommateur averti

informer [ɪn'fɔːmə(r)] **N 1** *(denouncer)* informateur *m*; **police i.** indicateur *m* (de police) **2** *(information source)* informateur(trice) *m,f*

infosphere ['ɪnfəʊsfɪə(r)] **N** infosphère *f*

infotainment ['ɪnfəʊˌteɪnmənt] **N** *(UNCOUNT)* infotainment *m*, infospectacle *m*

infowar ['ɪnfəʊˌwɔː(r)] **N** *Comput* cyberguerre *f*

infraction [ɪn'frækʃən] **N** infraction *f*; **i. of the code/regulations** infraction *f* au code/règlement

infra dig [ˌɪnfrə'dɪg] **ADJ** *Br Fam* dégradant

infrared [ˌɪnfrə'red] **N** infrarouge *m*
ADJ infrarouge
►► *Astron* ***infrared astronomy*** astronomie *f* infrarouge; ***infrared camera*** caméra *f* infrarouge; ***infrared imaging*** imagerie *f* infrarouge; ***infrared keyboard*** clavier *m* à infrarouge; *Med* ***infrared lamp*** lampe *f* à rayons infrarouges; *Comput* ***infrared mouse*** souris *f* à infrarouge; *Phot* ***infrared photography*** photographie *f* (à l')infrarouge; *Phys* ***infrared radiation, infrared rays*** radiation *f* infrarouge, infrarouge *m*; ***infrared remote control*** télécommande *f* (à) infrarouge

infrastructure ['ɪnfrəˌstrʌktʃə(r)] **N** infrastructure *f*

infrequency [ɪn'friːkwənsɪ] **N** rareté *f*

infrequent [ɪn'friːkwənt] **ADJ** *(event)* peu fréquent, rare; *(visitor)* épisodique

infrequently [ɪn'friːkwəntlɪ] **ADV** rarement, peu souvent

infringe [ɪn'frɪndʒ] **VT** *(agreement, rights)* violer, enfreindre; *(law)* enfreindre, contrevenir à; *(patent)* contrefaire; **to i. copyright** enfreindre les lois de copyright
VI to i. on *or* **upon** empiéter sur

infringement [ɪn'frɪndʒmənt] **N** *(violation)* infraction *f*, atteinte *f*; *(encroachment)* empiètement *m*; **an i. of the treaty conditions** une violation des termes du traité; **an i. on freedom of speech** une atteinte à la liberté d'expression; **that's an i. of my rights** c'est une atteinte à mes droits; **i. of copyright** non-respect *m* des droits d'auteur

infuriate [ɪn'fjʊərɪeɪt] **VT** *(enrage)* rendre furieux; *(exasperate)* exaspérer

infuriated [ɪn'fjʊərɪeɪtɪd] **ADJ** furieux

infuriating [ɪn'fjʊərɪeɪtɪŋ] **ADJ** agaçant, exaspérant; **it's i. the way she's always right** ça me met hors de moi qu'elle ait toujours raison

infuriatingly [ɪn'fjʊərɪeɪtɪŋlɪ] **ADV i. stubborn** d'un entêtement exaspérant; **she remained i. polite** elle restait d'une politesse exaspérante

infuse [ɪn'fjuːz] **VT 1** *(inspire)* inspirer, insuffler, *Literary* infuser; **to i. sb with sth, to i. sth into sb** inspirer *ou* insuffler qch à qn **2** *Culin* (faire) infuser **3** *(blood)* faire une perfusion de
VI *Culin* infuser

infuser [ɪn'fjuːzə(r)] **N (tea) i.** boule *f* à thé

infusion [ɪn'fjuːʒən] **N 1** *(drink, process)* infusion *f* **2** *(of blood)* perfusion *f* **3** *(injection)* **an i. of new blood into the company** un apport de sang neuf dans la société; **the news gave her a big i. of energy** la nouvelle lui a redonné beaucoup d'énergie

ingenious [ɪn'dʒiːnjəs] **ADJ** *(person, idea, device)* ingénieux, astucieux

> Attention: ne pas confondre avec **ingenuous.**

ingeniously [ɪn'dʒiːnjəslɪ] **ADV** ingénieusement

ingenuity [ˌɪndʒɪ'njuːətɪ] *(pl* **ingenuities) N** ingéniosité *f*

> Attention: ne pas confondre avec **ingenuousness.**

ingenuous [ɪn'dʒenjʊəs] **ADJ 1** *(naive)* ingénu **2** *(frank)* candide

> Attention: ne pas confondre avec **ingenious.**

ingenuously [ɪn'dʒenjʊəslɪ] **ADV 1** *(naively)* ingénument **2** *(frankly)* franchement

ingenuousness [ɪn'dʒenjʊəsnɪs] **N 1** *(naivety)* ingénuité *f*, naïveté *f* **2** *(frankness)* franchise *f*, candeur *f*

> Attention: ne pas confondre avec **ingenuity.**

ingest [ɪn'dʒest] **VT** *Physiol (food, liquid)* ingérer

ingestion [ɪn'dʒestʃən] **N** *Physiol* ingestion *f*

inglenook ['ɪŋgəlnʊk] **N** coin *m* du feu
►► ***inglenook fireplace*** vaste cheminée *f* à l'ancienne

inglorious [ɪn'glɔːrɪəs] **ADJ** *(shameful)* déshonorant

ingloriously [ɪn'glɔːrɪəslɪ] **ADV** sans gloire

ingot ['ɪŋgət] **N** lingot *m*; **a gold i.** un lingot d'or

ingrained [ˌɪn'greɪnd] **ADJ 1 i. with dirt** encrassé; **i. dirt** crasse *f* **2** *(deep-seated* ► *attitude, fear, prejudice)* enraciné, inébranlable; *(*► *habit)* invétéré, tenace; *(*► *belief)* inébranlable

ingratiate [ɪnˈɡreɪʃɪeɪt] VT **to i. oneself with sb** s'insinuer dans les bonnes grâces de qn; **I'll try to i. myself** je vais essayer de me faire bien voir

ingratiating [ɪnˈɡreɪʃɪeɪtɪŋ] ADJ *(manners, person)* insinuant; *(smile)* mielleux

ingratiatingly [ɪnˈɡreɪʃɪeɪtɪŋlɪ] ADV mielleusement

ingratitude [ɪnˈɡrætɪtjuːd] N ingratitude *f*

ingredient [ɪnˈɡriːdjənt] N **1** *Culin* ingrédient *m*; **ingredients: fruit juice, water** *(on packaging)* composition: jus de fruit, eau **2** *(element)* élément *m*, ingrédient *m*; *Literary* **what are the ingredients of her success?** qu'est-ce qui fait son succès?

ingress [ˈɪnɡres] N **1** *Formal or Literary (entry, right to enter)* entrée *f*; **to have free i.** avoir accès libre **2** *Astron* immersion *f*

ingrowing toenail [ˈɪn,ɡrəʊɪŋ-] N *Br* ongle *m* incarné

inhabit [ɪnˈhæbɪt] VT habiter; **the island is no longer inhabited** l'île n'est plus habitée *ou* est maintenant inhabitée

inhabitable [ɪnˈhæbɪtəbəl] ADJ habitable

> Note that the French word **inhabitable** is a false friend and is never a translation for the English word **inhabitable**. It means **uninhabitable**.

inhabitant [ɪnˈhæbɪtənt] N habitant(e) *m,f*

inhabited [ɪnˈhæbɪtɪd] ADJ habité, peuplé

> Note that the French word **inhabité** is a false friend and is never a translation for the English word **inhabited**. It means **uninhabited**.

inhalant [ɪnˈheɪlənt] N inhalation *f*

inhalation [,ɪnhəˈleɪʃən] N **1** *(of air)* inspiration *f* **2** *(of gas, glue)* inhalation *f*

inhale [ɪnˈheɪl] VT **1** *(fumes, gas)* inhaler; *(fresh air, scent)* respirer; *(smoke)* avaler **2** *Am Fam (eat quickly)* engouffrer; *(drink quickly)* descendre

VI *(breathe in)* inspirer; *(smoker)* avaler la fumée

inhaler [ɪnˈheɪlə(r)] N inhalateur *m*

inhaling [ɪnˈheɪlɪŋ] N inhalation *f*

inherent [ɪnˈhɪərənt, ɪnˈherənt] ADJ inhérent (**in** *or* **to** à)

►► ***inherent stability*** *(of plane, ship etc)* stabilité *f* propre; *Com* ***inherent vice*** vice *m* inhérent

inherently [ɪnˈhɪərəntlɪ, ɪnˈherəntlɪ] ADV intrinsèquement, par nature; **the system is i. inefficient** le système est inefficace par nature

inherit [ɪnˈherɪt] VT **1** *Law (property, right)* hériter (de); *(title, peerage)* accéder à; **she inherited a million dollars** elle a hérité d'un million de dollars; **they inherited the house from their parents** ils ont hérité la maison de leurs parents **2** *(situation, tradition, attitude)* hériter; **the problems inherited from the previous government** les problèmes hérités du gouvernement précédent **3** *Biol (characteristic, feature)* hériter (de)

VI hériter; **she stands to i. when her aunt dies** elle doit hériter à la mort de sa tante

inheritance [ɪnˈherɪtəns] N **1** *Law (legacy)* héritage *m*; **to come into an i.** faire *ou* toucher un héritage

2 *(succession)* succession *f*; **to claim sth by right of i.** revendiquer qch en faisant valoir son droit à la succession

3 *Biol (of characteristic, feature)* hérédité *f*; **genetic i.** patrimoine *m* génétique

4 *(heritage)* héritage *m*, patrimoine *m*; **our cultural i.** notre héritage culturel

►► *Fin* ***inheritance tax*** droits *mpl* de succession

inherited [ɪnˈherɪtɪd] ADJ hérité

inhibit [ɪnˈhɪbɪt] VT **1** *(hinder ► person, freedom)* gêner, entraver; **were you inhibited by him being there?** est-ce que sa présence vous a gêné?; **a law which inhibits free speech** une loi qui constitue une entrave à la liberté d'expression

2 *(check ► growth, development)* freiner, entraver; **to i. progress** entraver la marche du progrès

3 *(suppress ► desires, emotions)* inhiber, refouler; *Psy* inhiber

4 *(forbid)* interdire

5 *Chem* inhiber

►► *Comput* ***inhibit code*** code *m* inhibiteur

inhibited [ɪnˈhɪbɪtɪd] ADJ *Psy* inhibé; **to be sexually i.** souffrir d'inhibition sexuelle

inhibiting [ɪnˈhɪbɪtɪŋ] ADJ inhibant

inhibition [,ɪnhɪˈbɪʃən] N **1** *Psy* inhibition *f*; **to have no inhibitions** ne pas avoir de complexes; **he had no inhibitions about lying to her face** ça ne le gênait pas de la regarder dans les yeux et de lui raconter des mensonges **2** *Physiol* inhibition *f* **3** *Law* prohibition *f*

inhibitive [ɪnˈhɪbɪtɪv] ADJ *Physiol & Psy* inhibiteur

inhibitor [ɪnˈhɪbɪtə(r)] N *Physiol & Pharm* inhibiteur *m*

inhibitory [ɪnˈhɪbɪtərɪ] ADJ **1** *Physiol & Psy* inhibiteur **2** *(prohibitory)* prohibitif

inhospitable [,ɪnhɒˈspɪtəbəl] ADJ **1** *(person)* peu accueillant, inhospitalier; **I don't wish to appear i., but...** je ne voudrais pas vous mettre à la porte, mais... **2** *(area, climate)* inhospitalier

inhospitably [,ɪnhɒˈspɪtəblɪ] ADV d'une manière peu accueillante

in-house ADJ interne *(à une entreprise)*

ADV sur place; **we prefer to train our staff i.** nous préférons former notre personnel au sein de l'entreprise

►► ***in-house journal, in-house magazine*** journal *m* interne; ***in-house staff*** personnel *m* permanent; **a very small i. staff** un personnel permanent très peu nombreux; ***in-house training*** formation *f* interne

inhuman [,ɪnˈhjuːmən] ADJ *(behaviour)* inhumain, barbare; *(person, place, process)* inhumain

inhumane [,ɪnhjuːˈmeɪn] ADJ cruel, inhumain

►► *Law* ***inhumane treatment*** traitement *m* inhumain

inhumanity [,ɪnhjuːˈmænətɪ] (*pl* **inhumanities**) N **1** *(quality)* inhumanité *f*, barbarie *f*, cruauté *f*; **man's i. to man** la cruauté de l'homme pour l'homme **2** *(act)* atrocité *f*, brutalité *f*

inimical [ɪˈnɪmɪkəl] ADJ **1** *(unfavourable)* hostile; **i. to** peu favorable à **2** *(unfriendly)* inamical

inimitable [ɪˈnɪmɪtəbəl] ADJ inimitable

inimitably [ɪˈnɪmɪtəblɪ] ADV d'une façon inimitable

iniquitous [ɪˈnɪkwɪtəs] ADJ inique

iniquitously [ɪˈnɪkwɪtəslɪ] ADV iniquement

iniquity [ɪˈnɪkwətɪ] N iniquité *f*

initial [ɪˈnɪʃəl] (*Br pt & pp* **initialled**, *cont* **initialling**, *Am pt & pp* **initialed**, *cont* **initialing**) ADJ initial; **my i. reaction** ma première réaction; **the project is still in its i. stages** le projet en est encore à ses débuts; *Ling* **in i. position** en position initiale

N **1** *(letter)* initiale *f*; **initials** initiales *fpl*; *(to alteration of cheque etc)* paraphe *m*; *(of supervisor etc)* visa *m*; *(on garment)* monogramme *m* **2** *Typ (of chapter)* lettrine *f*

VT *Br (memo, page, correction)* parapher, parafer, signer de ses initiales

►► *Fin* ***initial capital*** capital *m* initial *ou* d'apport; *Fin* ***initial cost*** coût *m* inital; *(of manufactured product)* prix *m* de revient; *Fin* ***initial expenditure*** frais *mpl* de premier établissement; *Fin* ***initial investment*** investissements *mpl* initiaux; ***initial letter*** initiale *f*; *St Exch* ***initial margin*** dépôt *m* initial *ou* de marge; *Am St Exch* ***initial public offering*** introduction *f* en Bourse; *Com* ***initial stock*** stock *m* de départ; *Fin* ***initial value*** valeur *f* de départ

initialization, -isation [ɪ,nɪʃəlaɪˈzeɪʃən] N *Comput (of computer, modem, printer)* initialisation *f*

initialize, -ise [ɪˈnɪʃəlaɪz] VT **1** *Comput (computer, modem, printer)* initialiser **2** *Am (memo, page, correction)* parapher, parafer, signer de ses initiales

initially [ɪˈnɪʃəlɪ] ADV au départ, à l'origine; **she was i. against the idea** au départ, elle était contre

initiate VT [ɪˈnɪʃɪeɪt] **1** *(talks, debate, conversation)* engager; *(policy)* lancer; *(measures)* instaurer; *(quarrel, reaction)* provoquer, déclencher; **the pilot has initiated landing procedures** le pilote a entamé *ou* amorcé les procédures d'atterrissage; *Law* **to i. proceedings against sb** entamer des poursuites contre qn **2** *(person)* initier; **to i. sb into sth** initier qn à qch

N [ɪˈnɪʃɪət] initié(e) *m,f*

initiated [ɪˈnɪʃɪeɪtɪd] ADJ initié

NPL **the i.** les initiés *mpl*

initiation [ɪ,nɪʃɪˈeɪʃən] N **1** *(start)* commencement *m*, début *m*; **he fought for the i. of new policies** il s'est battu pour la mise en œuvre de politiques différentes **2** *(of person)* initiation *f*; **her i. into politics** son initiation à la politique

►► ***initiation ceremony*** cérémonie *f* d'initiation

initiative [ɪˈnɪʃətɪv] N **1** *(drive)* initiative *f*; **she's certainly got i.** elle a de l'initiative, il n'y a pas de doute; **to act on one's own i.** agir de sa propre initiative; **you'll have to use your i.** vous devrez prendre des initiatives; *Am Pol* **citizen's i.** initiative *f* populaire **2** *(first step)* initiative *f*; **to take the i.** prendre l'initiative **3** *(lead)* initiative *f*; **to have the i.** avoir l'initiative; **they lost the i. to foreign competition** ils ont été dépassés par la concurrence étrangère

ADJ **1** *(preliminary)* préliminaire **2** *(ritual)* initiatique

initiator [ɪˈnɪʃɪeɪtə(r)] N initiateur(trice) *m,f*, instigateur(trice) *m,f*

inject [ɪnˈdʒekt] VT **1** *Med (drug)* faire une piqûre de, injecter; **to i. sb with penicillin** faire une piqûre de pénicilline à qn; **have you been injected against tetanus?** êtes-vous vacciné contre le tétanos? **2** *Fig (money)* injecter; **they've injected billions of dollars into the economy** ils ont injecté des milliards de dollars dans l'économie; **to i. new life into sth** donner un nouvel essor à qch; **he tried to i. some humour into the situation** il a tenté d'introduire un peu d'humour dans la situation

injectable [ɪnˈdʒektəbəl] ADJ *(drug)* injectable

injection [ɪnˈdʒekʃən] N *Med & Fig* injection *f*; *Med* **to give sb an i.** faire une injection *ou* une piqûre à qn; *Fig* **an i. of capital** une injection de capitaux

►► *Tech* ***injection moulding*** moulage *m* par injection; ***injection pump*** *Constr* pompe *f* à injection; *Aut* pompe *f* d'injection (de carburant)

injector [ɪnˈdʒektə(r)] N injecteur *m*

injudicious [,ɪndʒuːˈdɪʃəs] ADJ peu judicieux, imprudent

injudiciously [,ɪndʒuːˈdɪʃəslɪ] ADV peu judicieusement

Injun [ˈɪndʒən] N *Am Fam* Peau-Rouge *mf*, = terme injurieux désignant un Amérindien

injunction [ɪnˈdʒʌŋkʃən] N **1** *Law* injonction *f*; **to take out an i. against sb** mettre qn en demeure; **he has been served with an i. banning him from contacting his ex-wife** une injonction lui interdit d'entrer en contact avec son ex-femme **2** *(warning)* injonction *f*, recommandation *f* formelle

injure [ˈɪndʒə(r)] VT **1** *(physically)* blesser; **he injured his knee skiing** il s'est blessé au genou en faisant du ski; **ten people were injured in the accident** l'accident a fait dix blessés; **you could i. yourself lifting that box** vous pourriez vous faire mal en soulevant cette caisse

2 *(damage ► relationship, interests)* nuire à

3 *(offend)* blesser, offenser; **to i. sb's pride** blesser qn dans son amour-propre; **try not to i. her feelings** faites en sorte de ne pas l'offenser *ou* la blesser

4 *(wrong)* faire du tort à

> Note that the French verb **injurier** is a false friend and is never a translation for the verb **to injure**. It means **to insult, to abuse**.

injured [ˈɪndʒəd] ADJ **1** *(physically)* blessé; **her head is badly i.** elle est grièvement blessée à la tête **2** *(offended ► person)* offensé; **to feel i.** être offensé; **it's just his i. pride** il est blessé dans son amour-propre, c'est tout

NPL **the i.** les blessés *mpl*

►► ***the injured party*** l'offensé(e) *m,f*, *Law* la partie lésée

injurious [ɪnˈdʒʊərɪəs] ADJ *Formal* **1** *(detrimental)* nuisible, préjudiciable (**to** à) **2** *(insulting)* offensant, injurieux

injury [ˈɪndʒərɪ] (*pl* **injuries**) N **1** *(physical)* blessure *f*; **the explosion caused serious injuries** l'explosion a fait des blessés graves; **he escaped without i.** il s'en est sorti indemne; *Br* **be careful, you'll do yourself an i.!** fais attention, tu vas te blesser!

2 *Formal or Literary (wrong)* tort *m*, préjudice *m*; **you do him i.** vous lui faites du tort
3 *(offence)* offense *f*
4 *Law* préjudice *m*
▸▸ *Sport* ***injury time*** *(UNCOUNT)* arrêts *mpl* de jeu; **to play i. time** jouer les arrêts de jeu; **they scored during i. time** ils ont marqué un but pendant les arrêts de jeu

> Note that the French word **injure** is a false friend. It means **insult**.

injustice [ɪnˈdʒʌstɪs] **N 1** *(of law, system etc)* injustice *f* **2** *(unjust act, remark)* injustice *f*; **to do sb an i.** être injuste envers qn

ink [ɪŋk] **N 1** *(for writing, printing)* encre *f*; **in i.** à l'encre **2** *Zool (of squid, octopus etc)* encre *f*, noir *m*
VT 1 *(surface)* encrer **2** *Am (document, name)* signer; **the bill was inked this morning by the President** le président a signé le projet de loi ce matin; *Fig* **she inked her name in the record books** elle a établi un nouveau record
▸▸ *Zool* ***ink bag*** poche *f* à encre; ***ink bottle*** bouteille *f* d'encre; ***ink cartridge*** cartouche *f* d'encre; *Comput* ***ink channel*** *(in printer)* canal *m* encreur; ***ink drawing*** dessin *m* à l'encre; ***ink eraser*** gomme *f* à encre; ***ink pen*** stylo *m* à encre; *Br* ***ink rubber*** gomme *f* à encre; *Zool* ***ink sac*** sac *m ou* poche *f* à encre

▸**ink in VT SEP** *(drawing)* repasser à l'encre; *(lines)* retracer à l'encre; *(writing)* réécrire à l'encre

▸**ink out VT SEP** *(word)* oblitérer *ou* rayer *ou* biffer à l'encre

inkblot [ˈɪŋkblɒt] **N** tache *f* d'encre, pâté *m*; *Psy (in Rorschach test)* tache *f* d'encre
▸▸ ***inkblot test*** test *m* de Rorschach *ou* des taches d'encre

inking [ˈɪŋkɪŋ] **N** *Typ (of rollers)* encrage *m*

inkjet printer [ˈɪŋkdʒet-] **N** *Comput* imprimante *f* à jet d'encre

inkling [ˈɪŋklɪŋ] **N** vague *ou* petite idée *f*; **I had some i. of the** *or* **as to the real reason** j'avais bien une petite idée de la véritable raison; **you must have an i.** tu dois bien avoir une petite idée; **I had no i.** je ne m'en doutais pas du tout; **she didn't have the slightest i. that her husband had been unfaithful** elle était à cent lieues de se douter que son mari l'avait trompée

inkstand [ˈɪŋkstænd] **N** encrier *m*

inkwell [ˈɪŋkwel] **N** encrier *m* (encastré)

inky [ˈɪŋkɪ] *(compar* **inkier**, *superl* **inkiest)** **ADJ 1** *(inkstained)* taché d'encre **2** *(dark)* noir comme l'encre
▸▸ ***inky black*** noir d'encre; ***inky blue*** bleu-noir

inlaid [ˌɪnˈleɪd] *pt & pp of* **inlay**
ADJ incrusté; *(wood)* marqueté, incrusté; *(floor)* parqueté; **an i. table** une table en marqueterie

inland ADJ [ˈɪnlənd] **1** *(not coastal ▸ town, sea)* intérieur **2** *Br (not foreign)* intérieur
ADV [ɪnˈlænd] *(travelling)* vers l'intérieur; *(located)* à l'intérieur; **to go i.** pénétrer vers l'intérieur *ou* dans les terres; **the town is situated a few miles i.** la ville est située à quelques kilomètres dans les terres
▸▸ ***inland clearance depot*** dépôt *m* de dédouanement intérieur; ***inland freight*** fret *m* intérieur; ***inland haulage*** transport *m* routier; ***inland mail*** courrier *m* intérieur; ***inland navigation*** navigation *f* fluviale; *Br* ***the Inland Revenue*** le fisc, la Direction Générale des Impôts; ***the Inland Sea*** la mer Intérieure; ***inland waterways*** voies *fpl* navigables; ***inland waterway transport*** transport *m* fluvial

in-laws NPL *Fam (gen)* belle-famille◻ *f*; *(parents-in-law)* beaux-parents◻ *mpl*

inlay *(pt & pp* **inlaid)** **N** [ˈɪnleɪ] **1** *(gen)* incrustation *f*; *(in woodwork)* marqueterie *f*; *(in metalwork)* damasquinage *m*; **the brooch has very fine i. work** la broche a de très belles incrustations; **with ivory i.** incrusté d'ivoire **2** *(in dentistry)* incrustation *f*
VT [ˈɪnleɪ] incruster; **the table was inlaid with ivory** la table avait des incrustations *ou* était incrustée d'ivoire

inlet [ˈɪnlet] **N 1** *(in coastline)* anse *f*, crique *f*; *(between offshore islands)* bras *m* de mer **2** *Tech (intake)* arrivée *f*, admission *f*; *(opening)* (orifice *m* d')entrée *f*; *(for air)* prise *f* (d'air)
COMP *Tech* d'arrivée
▸▸ ***inlet manifold*** conduits *mpl* d'admission, collecteur *m* d'admission; ***inlet pipe*** tuyau *m* d'arrivée; ***inlet valve*** soupape *f* d'admission; *(of fuel pump)* soupape *f* d'alimentation

in-line ADJ
▸▸ *Aut* ***in-line engine*** moteur *m* en ligne; *Sport* ***in-line skates*** rollers *mpl* in-line; *Sport* ***in-line skating*** roller *m* in-line; **to do** *or* **to go i. skating** faire du roller in-line

inmate [ˈɪnmeɪt] **N** *(of prison)* détenu(e) *m,f*; *(of mental institution)* interné(e) *m,f*; *(of hospital)* malade *mf*; *(of house)* occupant(e) *m,f*, résident (e) *m,f*

in memoriam [ˌɪnmɪˈmɔːrɪəm] **PREP** à la mémoire de; *(on gravestone)* in memoriam

inmost [ˈɪnməʊst] = **innermost**

inn [ɪn] **N** *(pub, small hotel)* auberge *f*
▸▸ *Eng Law* ***the Inns of Court*** = associations auxquelles appartiennent les avocats et les juges et dont le siège se trouve dans le quartier historique du même nom à Londres

innards [ˈɪnədz] **NPL** *Fam* entrailles◻ *fpl*

innate [ɪˈneɪt] **ADJ** *(inborn)* inné, naturel; **her i. gift for music** son don inné pour la musique

inner [ˈɪnə(r)] **ADJ 1** *(interior ▸ courtyard, pocket, walls, lane)* intérieur; *(▸ structure, workings)* interne; **I. London** Londres intra-muros; **in the i. circles of power** dans les milieux proches du pouvoir; **her i. circle of advisers/friends** le cercle de ses conseillers/amis les plus proches **2** *(inward ▸ feeling, conviction)* intime; *(▸ life, voice, struggle, warmth)* intérieur; **i. calm** paix *f* intérieure; **the i. meaning** le sens profond; **the i. man/woman** *(spiritual self)* l'être *m* intérieur; *Hum (stomach)* l'estomac *m*
N *(in archery, darts)* = zone rouge entourant le centre de la cible; **he got three inners** il a mis trois fois dans le rouge
▸▸ *Psy* ***the inner child*** l'enfant *mf* qui est en nous; ***inner city*** = quartier défavorisé dans le centre d'une grande ville; *Anat* ***inner ear*** oreille *f* interne; *Geog* ***the Inner Hebrides*** les Hébrides *fpl* intérieures; *Comput & Typ* ***inner margin*** marge *f* intérieure; *Geog* ***Inner Mongolia*** Mongolie-Intérieure *f*; ***inner tube*** *(of tyre)* chambre *f* à air

inner-city ADJ i. areas = quartiers défavorisés du centre des grandes villes; **i. crime** = crimes se produisant dans les quartiers défavorisés du centre des grandes villes; **i. children** = enfants des quartiers défavorisés du centre des grandes villes

innermost [ˈɪnəməʊst] **ADJ 1** *(feeling, belief)* intime; **my i. thoughts** mes pensées les plus secrètes; **in her i. being** au plus profond d'elle-même **2** *(central ▸ place, room)* le plus au centre; **in the i. depths of the cave** au plus profond de la grotte

inning [ˈɪnɪŋ] **N** *Sport (in baseball)* tour *m* de batte

innings [ˈɪnɪŋz] *(pl inv)* **N** *Sport (in cricket)* tour *m* de batte; *Br Fig* **he's had a good i.** il a vécu longtemps
NPL *(reclaimed land)* polders *mpl*

innit [ˈɪnɪt] **ADV** *Br Fam* **1** *(isn't it)* hein?; **it's great, i.?** c'est super, hein? **2** *(general question tag)* hein?; **that was a kicking night out, i.?** on a passé une super soirée, hein?; **you fancy her, i.?** elle te plaît, hein?

innkeeper [ˈɪnˌkiːpə(r)] **N** aubergiste *mf*

innocence [ˈɪnəsəns] **N** innocence *f*; **to take advantage of sb's i.** abuser de l'innocence de qn; **in all i.** en toute innocence

innocent [ˈɪnəsənt] **ADJ 1** *(not guilty)* innocent; **to be i. of a crime** être innocent d'un crime; **to be proven i. of sth** être reconnu innocent de qch; **he was proven i.** il a été innocenté; **an i. person** un(e) innocent(e); *Fam* **to act all i.** faire l'innocent **2** *(naïve)* innocent, naïf; **an i. remark** une remarque innocente **3** *Formal (devoid)* **i. of** dépourvu de, sans
N innocent(e) *m,f*; **don't play the i.!** ne fais pas l'innocent!

innocently [ˈɪnəsəntlɪ] **ADV** innocemment

innocuous [ɪˈnɒkjʊəs] **ADJ** inoffensif, anodin

innocuously [ɪˈnɒkjʊəslɪ] **ADV** de façon inoffensive *ou* anodine

innocuousness [ɪˈnɒkjʊəsnɪs] **N** *(of remark, joke etc)* caractère *m* anodin; *Med* innocuité *f*

innovate [ˈɪnəveɪt] **VT** innover
VI innover

innovating company [ˈɪnəveɪtɪŋ-] **N** *Mktg* entreprise *f* innovatrice

innovation [ˌɪnəˈveɪʃən] **N** innovation *f*; **innovations in management techniques** des innovations en matière de gestion

innovative [ˈɪnəvətɪv] **ADJ** innovateur, novateur
▸▸ *Mktg* ***innovative product*** produit *m* novateur, produit *m* innovateur

innovator [ˈɪnəveɪtə(r)] **N** innovateur(trice) *m,f*, novateur(trice) *m,f*

innuendo [ˌɪnjuːˈendəʊ] *(pl* **innuendos** *or* **innuendoes)** **N 1** *(insinuation)* insinuation *f*; **to discredit sb by i.** discréditer qn par sous-entendus **2** *(in jokes)* allusion *f* grivoise; **the play is full of innuendos** la pièce est pleine de sous-entendus **3** *Law* insinuation *f*, mot *m* couvert *(destiné à atteindre quelqu'un dans son honneur)*

innumerable [ɪˈnjuːmərəbəl] **ADJ** innombrable; **i. times** un nombre incalculable de fois

innumeracy [ɪˈnjuːmərəsɪ] **N** incapacité *f* à compter

innumerate [ɪˈnjuːmərət] **N** personne *f* qui ne sait pas compter
ADJ qui ne sait pas compter; **he's completely i.** il est incapable d'additionner deux et deux

inoculate [ɪˈnɒkjʊleɪt] **VT** *Med (person, animal)* vacciner; **to i. sb against sth** vacciner qn contre qch; **they inoculated guinea pigs with the virus** ils ont inoculé le virus à des cobayes

inoculation [ɪˌnɒkjʊˈleɪʃən] **N** *Med* inoculation *f*

inoffensive [ˌɪnəˈfensɪv] **ADJ** inoffensif; *(smell)* pas désagréable

inoperable [ɪnˈɒprəbəl] **ADJ 1** *Med* inopérable **2** *(unworkable)* impraticable

inoperative [ɪnˈɒprətɪv] **ADJ** inopérant

inopportune [ɪnˈɒpətjuːn] **ADJ** *(remark)* déplacé, mal à propos; *(time)* mal choisi, inopportun; *(behaviour)* inconvenant, déplacé

inopportunely [ɪnˈɒpətjuːnlɪ] **ADV** *Formal* inopportunément, mal à propos

inordinate [ɪnˈɔːdɪnət] **ADJ** *(immense ▸ size)* démesuré; *(▸ pleasure, relief)* incroyable; *(▸ amount of money)* exorbitant; **they spent an i. amount of time on it** ils y ont consacré énormément de temps

inordinately [ɪnˈɔːdɪnətlɪ] **ADV** démesurément, excessivement

inorganic [ˌɪnɔːˈgænɪk] **ADJ** inorganique
▸▸ *Chem* ***inorganic chemistry*** chimie *f* inorganique *ou* minérale

in-patient N *Med* hospitalisé(e) *m,f*, malade *mf*

inpoint [ˈɪnpɔɪnt] **N** *(on tape, film)* point *m* d'entrée

input [ˈɪnpʊt] *(pt & pp* **input**, *cont* **inputting)** **N** *(UNCOUNT)* **1** *(during meeting, discussion)* contribution *f*; **we'd like some i. from marketing before committing ourselves** nous aimerions consulter le service marketing avant de nous engager plus avant
2 *Comput (data)* données *fpl* (en entrée); *(action)* entrée *f*, introduction *f*; **the program requires i. from the user** ce programme exige que l'utilisateur entre des données
3 *Elec* énergie *f*, puissance *f*; **to reduce the voltage i. to a circuit** réduire la tension d'un circuit
4 *Econ* input *m*, intrant *m*
COMP *Comput (file, program)* d'entrée
VT 1 *(gen)* (faire) entrer, introduire **2** *Comput* entrer
▸▸ *Comput* ***input device*** périphérique *m* d'entrée; *Fin* ***input tax*** TVA *f* récupérée; *Elec* ***input transformer*** courant *m ou* transformateur *m* d'entrée

input/output N *Comput* entrée/sortie *f*
▸▸ ***input/output device*** périphérique *m* d'entrée/sortie

input-output analysis N *Econ* analyse *f* d'entrée-sortie

inquest ['ɪnkwest] N *Law* enquête *f*; *(into death)* = enquête menée pour établir les causes des morts violentes, non naturelles ou mystérieuses

inquire [ɪn'kwaɪə(r)] VT *(ask)* demander; **to i. sth of sb** s'enquérir de qch auprès de qn; **she inquired how to get to the park** elle a demandé qu'on lui indique le chemin du parc; **may I i. what brings you here?** puis-je vous demander l'objet de votre visite?

VI *(seek information)* se renseigner, demander; **i. within** *(sign)* s'adresser ici; **to i. about sth** demander des renseignements *ou* se renseigner sur qch

▸**inquire after** VT INSEP *Br* demander des nouvelles de; **she inquired after you** elle a demandé de vos nouvelles

▸**inquire into** VT INSEP se renseigner sur; *(investigate)* faire des recherches sur; *Admin & Law* enquêter sur

inquiring [ɪn'kwaɪərɪŋ] ADJ *(voice, look)* interrogateur; *(mind)* curieux

inquiringly [ɪn'kwaɪərɪŋlɪ] ADV d'un air interrogateur

inquiry [*Br* ɪn'kwaɪərɪ, *Am* 'ɪnkwərɪ] *(pl* **inquiries***)* N **1** *(request for information)* demande *f* (de renseignements); **to make inquiries** se renseigner; **to make inquiries about sb** prendre des renseignements sur qn; **to make inquiries into sth** faire des recherches sur qch; **with reference to your i. of 5 May,...** *(in letter)* en réponse à votre demande du 5 mai,...; **we have received hundreds of inquiries** nous avons reçu des centaines de demandes de renseignements **2** *(investigation)* enquête *f*; **to hold** *or* **to conduct an i. into sth** faire une enquête sur qch; **the police are making inquiries** la police enquête, une enquête (policière) est en cours; *Euph* **he is helping police with their inquiries** la police est en train de l'interroger; **upon further i.** après vérification; **commission of i.** commission *f* d'enquête **3** *(questioning)* **a look/tone of i.** un regard/ton interrogateur

▸▸ *Br* **inquiry agent** détective *m* (privé)

inquisition [ˌɪnkwɪ'zɪʃən] N **1** *(gen)* inquisition *f*; **the interview turned into an i.** l'entrevue s'est transformée en inquisition **2** *Law* enquête *f*

• **Inquisition** N *Hist* **the I.** l'Inquisition *f*

inquisitive [ɪn'kwɪzətɪv] ADJ **1** *(curious)* curieux; *(look)* plein de curiosité **2** *Pej (nosy)* indiscret (ète)

inquisitively [ɪn'kwɪzətɪvlɪ] ADV **1** *(curiously)* avec curiosité **2** *Pej (nosily)* de manière indiscrète; **he stared i. into the room** il jeta dans la pièce un regard inquisiteur

inquisitiveness [ɪn'kwɪzətɪvnɪs] N **1** *(curiosity)* curiosité *f* **2** *Pej (nosiness)* indiscrétion *f*

inquisitor [ɪn'kwɪzɪtə(r)] N **1** *(investigator)* enquêteur(euse) *m,f*; *(interrogator)* interrogateur (trice) *m,f* **2** *Hist* inquisiteur *m*

inquisitorial [ɪnˌkwɪzɪ'tɔːrɪəl] ADJ inquisitorial

inroad ['ɪnrəʊd] N *(raid)* incursion *f*; *(advance)* avance *f*

• **inroads** NPL **1** *Mil* **to make inroads into enemy territory** avancer en territoire ennemi **2** *Fig* **to make inroads in** *or* **into** *or* **on** *(supplies, funds)* entamer; *(spare time, someone's rights)* empiéter sur; **they have made significant inroads into our market share** ils ont considérablement mordu sur notre part du marché; **they've made great inroads on the work** ils ont bien avancé le travail

inrush ['ɪnrʌʃ] N afflux *m*

ins 1 *(written abbr* **insurance***)* asse. **2** *(written abbr* **inches***)* pouces

insalubrious [ˌɪnsə'luːbrɪəs] ADJ *Formal (district, climate)* insalubre, malsain

insane [ɪn'seɪn] ADJ **1** *(mentally disordered)* fou (folle); **temporarily i.** en état de démence temporaire; **to go i.** perdre la raison; **to be i. with grief/jealousy** être fou de douleur/jalousie **2** *Fig (person)* fou (folle); *(scheme, price)* démentiel; **it's driving me i.!** ça me rend fou!

NPL **the i.** les malades *mpl* mentaux

▸▸ *Am* **insane asylum** hospice *m ou* asile *m* d'aliénés

insanely [ɪn'seɪnlɪ] ADV **1** *(crazily* ▸ *laugh, behave, talk)* comme un fou (une folle); **they clapped i.** ils applaudissaient comme des fous **2** *Fig (as intensifier* ▸ *funny, rich)* follement; **he was i. jealous** il était fou de jalousie

insanitary [ɪn'sænɪtrɪ] ADJ insalubre, malsain

insanity [ɪn'sænətɪ] N **1** *(mental disorder)* folie *f*, démence *f* **2** *Fig (of scheme, plan etc)* folie *f*; **it's sheer i. doing that** c'est de la folie pure et simple (que) de faire cela

insatiable [ɪn'seɪʃəbəl] ADJ insatiable

insatiably [ɪn'seɪʃəblɪ] ADV insatiablement

inscribe [ɪn'skraɪb] VT **1** *(on list)* inscrire; *(on plaque, tomb etc)* graver, inscrire; **he had the ring inscribed with her name** il a fait graver son nom sur la bague; *Fig* **it's inscribed on my memory** c'est inscrit *ou* gravé dans ma mémoire **2** *(dedicate)* dédicacer; **an inscribed copy of the book** un exemplaire dédicacé du livre **3** *Geom* inscrire

inscription [ɪn'skrɪpʃən] N *(on plaque, tomb)* inscription *f*; *(on coin)* inscription *f*, légende *f*; *(in book)* dédicace *f*

inscrutability [ɪnˌskruːtə'bɪlɪtɪ] N impénétrabilité *f*

inscrutable [ɪn'skruːtəbəl] ADJ *(person, face)* énigmatique, impénétrable; *(remark)* énigmatique

insect ['ɪnsekt] N **1** *(animal)* insecte *m* **2** *Fam Pej (person)* vermisseau *m*

▸▸ ***insect bite*** piqûre *f* d'insecte; ***insect repellent*** produit *m* insectifuge

insecticide [ɪn'sektɪsaɪd] N insecticide *m*

insectivore [ɪn'sektɪvɔː(r)] N *Zool* insectivore *m*

insectivorous [ˌɪnsek'tɪvərəs] ADJ *Zool* insectivore

insecure [ˌɪnsɪ'kjʊə(r)] ADJ **1** *(person* ▸ *temporarily)* inquiet(ète); *(*▸ *generally)* pas sûr de soi, qui manque d'assurance; **he's so i.** il est vraiment mal dans sa peau

2 *(chair, nail, scaffolding etc)* peu solide

3 *(place)* peu sûr

4 *(future, market)* incertain; *(peace, job, relationship)* précaire

insecurity [ˌɪnsɪ'kjʊərətɪ] *(pl* **insecurities***)* N **1** *(lack of confidence)* manque *m* d'assurance; *(uncertainty)* incertitude *f*; **job i.** précarité *f* de l'emploi **2** *(lack of safety)* insécurité *f*

inseminate [ɪn'semɪneɪt] VT *Physiol* inséminer

insemination [ɪnˌsemɪ'neɪʃən] N *Physiol* insémination *f*

insensate [ɪn'senseɪt] ADJ *Formal* **1** *(unfeeling)* insensible **2** *(foolish)* insensé

insensibility [ɪnˌsensə'bɪlɪtɪ] *(pl* **insensibilities***)* N *Formal* **1** *(unconsciousness)* inconscience *f* **2** *(indifference)* insensibilité *f*; **his i. to music** son manque de sensibilité pour la musique

insensible [ɪn'sensəbəl] ADJ *Formal* **1** *(unconscious)* inconscient, sans connaissance; *(numb)* insensible; **she was knocked i. by her fall** sa chute lui a fait perdre connaissance; **her body was i. to any pain** son corps était insensible à toute douleur

2 *(cold, indifferent)* **i. to the suffering of others** insensible *ou* indifférent à la souffrance d'autrui

3 *(unaware)* inconscient; **i. of the risks** inconscient des risques

4 *(imperceptible)* insensible, imperceptible

insensitive [ɪn'sensətɪv] ADJ **1** *(cold-hearted)* insensible, dur; **they are i. brutes** ce sont des brutes épaisses; **the government's reaction was highly i.** le gouvernement a fait preuve d'une indifférence extrême **2** *(physically)* insensible (**to** à)

insensitivity [ɪnˌsensə'tɪvətɪ], **insensitiveness** [ɪn'sensətɪvnɪs] N insensibilité *f*

inseparable [ɪn'sepərəbəl] ADJ inséparable

inseparably [ɪn'sepərəblɪ] ADV inséparablement

insert VT [ɪn'sɜːt] **1** *(put, put in)* introduire, insérer; **i. your coin/card into the machine** introduisez votre pièce/carte dans la machine; **she inserted a small ad in the local paper** elle a mis une petite annonce dans le journal local; **to i. a name on a list** ajouter un nom à une liste **2** *Typ (line)* intercaler **3** *Comput* insérer

N ['ɪnsɜːt] **1** *(gen)* insertion *f*; *(in book, magazine)* encart *m*

2 *Sewing* pièce *f* rapportée; *(decorative)* incrustation *f*

3 *Cin* scène-raccord *f*

4 *Typ (in proofs)* insertion *f*

5 *Comput* insertion *f*

▸▸ *Comput* ***insert key*** touche *f* d'insertion; *Typ* ***insert mark*** signe *m* d'insertion; *Comput* ***insert mode*** mode *m* (d')insertion; *Comput* ***insert point*** point *m* d'insertion

insertion [ɪn'sɜːʃən] N **1** *(act)* insertion *f* **2** *(thing inserted)* insertion *f* **3** *Anat & Bot* insertion *f*; **point of i.** point *m* d'insertion

▸▸ *Typ* ***insertion point*** point *m* d'insertion

inset ['ɪnset] *(pt & pp* **inset**, *cont* **insetting***)* VT **1** *(detail, map, diagram)* insérer en encadré; **town plans are i. in the main map** des plans de ville figurent en encadrés sur la carte principale

2 *Sewing (extra material)* rapporter

3 *Typ* rentrer

4 *(jewel)* incruster (**with** de)

N **1** *(in map, text)* encadré *m*; *(on video, TV screen)* incrustation *f* **2** *Press (in newspaper, magazine)* encart *m* **3** *Sewing* panneau *m* rapporté; **lace i.** incrustation *f* de dentelle

▸▸ *Sewing* ***inset pocket*** poche *f* couture

inshore ADJ ['ɪnʃɔː(r)] côtier

ADV [ɪn'ʃɔː(r)] *(near shore)* près de la côte; *(towards shore)* vers la côte; **the boat was keeping close i.** le bateau longeait la côte

▸▸ ***inshore current*** courant *m* qui porte vers la côte; ***inshore fishing*** pêche *f* côtière; ***inshore waters*** eaux *fpl* près de la côte; ***inshore wind*** vent *m* de mer

INSIDE

ADV
• dedans **1** • à l'intérieur **1, 2**
• au fond **4**

PREP
• à l'intérieur de **1** • dans **1**
• en moins de **2**

N
• intérieur **1**

ADJ
• intérieur **1**

NPL
• estomac • intestins

ADV [ɪn'saɪd] **1** *(within enclosed space)* dedans, à l'intérieur; **there's nothing i.** il n'y a rien dedans *ou* à l'intérieur; **it's hollow i.** c'est creux à l'intérieur, l'intérieur est creux; **i. and out** au dedans et au dehors, à l'intérieur et à l'extérieur

2 *(indoors)* à l'intérieur; **bring the chairs i.** rentre les chaises; **she opened the door and went i.** elle ouvrit la porte et entra; **go and play i.** va jouer à l'intérieur; **come i.!** entrez!

3 *Fam (in prison)* en taule; **he's been i.** il a fait de la taule

4 *(in one's heart)* au fond (de soi-même); **i. I was furious** au fond de moi-même, j'étais furieux

PREP [ɪn'saɪd] **1** *(within)* à l'intérieur de, dans; **i. the house** à l'intérieur de la maison; *Fig* **what goes on i. his head?** qu'est-ce qui se passe dans sa tête?; *Fam* **get this i. you** avale ça; **a little voice i. me kept saying "no"** une petite voix intérieure n'arrêtait pas de me dire "non"; **it's just i. the limit** c'est juste (dans) la limite; **the attack took place i. Turkey itself** l'assaut a eu lieu sur le propre territoire turc; **someone i. the company must have told them** quelqu'un de l'entreprise a dû le leur dire

2 *(in less than)* en moins de; **I'll have it finished i. 6 days** je l'aurai terminé en moins de 6 jours

N [ɪn'saɪd] **1** *(inner part)* intérieur *m*; **the i. of the box** l'intérieur de la boîte; **the door doesn't open from the i.** la porte ne s'ouvre pas de l'intérieur

2 *(of pavement, road)* **walk on the i.** marchez loin du bord; *Aut* **to overtake on the i.** *(driving on left)* doubler à gauche; *(driving on right)* doubler à droite; *Horseracing* **coming up on the i. is Golden Boy** Golden Boy remonte à la corde

3 *Fig* **only someone on the i. would know that** seul quelqu'un de la maison saurait ça

ADJ ['ɪnsaɪd] **1** *(door, wall)* intérieur; *Constr (measurement, stair etc)* dans œuvre; *(diameter)* interne;
2 *Fig* **he has i. information** il a quelqu'un dans la place qui le renseigne; **it looks like an i. job** on dirait que c'est quelqu'un de la maison qui a fait le coup; **I speak with i. knowledge** ce que je dis je le sais de bonne source; **find out the i. story** essaie de découvrir les dessous de l'histoire
3 *Ftbl* **i. left/right** inter *m* gauche/droite
• **insides** [ɪn'saɪdz] **NPL** *Fam (stomach)* estomac *m*; *(intestines)* intestins *mpl*, tripes *fpl*; **to have pains in one's insides** avoir mal au ventre
• **inside of PREP** *Fam* **1** *(in less than)* en moins de
2 *Am (within)* à l'intérieur de, dans
• **inside out ADV 1** *(with inner part outwards)* **your socks are on i. out** tu as mis tes chaussettes à l'envers; **he turned his pockets i. out** il a retourné ses poches; *Fig* **they turned the room i. out** ils ont mis la pièce sens dessus dessous
2 *(thoroughly)* **he knows this town i. out** il connaît cette ville comme sa poche; **she knows her job i. out** elle connaît parfaitement son travail
►► *Typ* ***inside back cover*** troisième *f* de couverture; ***inside centre*** *(in rugby)* premier centre *m*; *Aut* ***inside door*** portière *f* côté trottoir; *Ftbl* ***inside forward*** inter *m*, intérieur *m*; *Typ* ***inside front cover*** deuxième *f* de couverture; ***the inside lane*** *(in athletics)* la corde, le couloir intérieur; *(of road ► driving on left)* la voie de gauche; *(► driving on right)* la voie de droite; ***inside leg (measurement)*** hauteur *f* de l'entrejambe; *Typ* ***inside margin*** marge *f* de reliure, (blanc *m* de) petit fond *m*; *Am Sport* ***inside track*** corde *f*, couloir *m* intérieur; *Fig* **to be on** *or* **to have the i. track** être en position de force; *Aut* ***inside wheel*** roue *f* côté trottoir

---

insider [ˌɪn'saɪdə(r)] **N** initié(e) *m,f*; **according to an i.** selon une source bien informée; **I got a hot tip from an i.** quelqu'un dans la place m'a donné un bon tuyau; *St Exch* **the insiders** les initiés *mpl*
►► *St Exch* ***insider dealing, insider trading*** *(UNCOUNT)* délit *m* d'initié; **to be accused of i. dealing** être accusé de délit d'initié

insidious [ɪn'sɪdɪəs] **ADJ** insidieux

insidiously [ɪn'sɪdɪəslɪ] **ADV** insidieusement

insight ['ɪnsaɪt] **N 1** *(perspicacity)* perspicacité *f*; **she has great i.** elle est très fine; **his book shows remarkable i. into the problem** son livre témoigne d'une compréhension très fine du problème **2** *(idea, glimpse)* aperçu *m*, idée *f*; **I managed to get** *or* **gain an i. into her real character** j'ai pu me faire une idée de sa véritable personnalité; **his book offers us new insights into human behaviour** son livre nous propose un nouveau regard sur le comportement humain

insightful ['ɪnsaɪtfʊl] **ADJ** pénétrant, perspicace

insignia [ɪn'sɪgnɪə] *(pl* **inv** *or* **insignias) N** insigne *m*, insignes *mpl*

insignificance [ˌɪnsɪg'nɪfɪkəns] **N** insignifiance *f*; **my problems fade into i. beside yours** mes problèmes semblent totalement insignifiants à côté des tiens

insignificant [ˌɪnsɪg'nɪfɪkənt] **ADJ** insignifiant

insincere [ˌɪnsɪn'sɪə(r)] **ADJ** peu sincère; **his grief turned out to be i.** il s'avéra que son chagrin était feint; **did you think I was being i.?** croyais-tu que je n'étais pas sincère?

insincerity [ˌɪnsɪn'serətɪ] **N** manque *m* de sincérité

insinuate [ɪn'sɪnjʊeɪt] **VT 1** *(imply)* insinuer, laisser entendre **2** *Formal (introduce)* insinuer; **he insinuated himself into their favour** il s'est insinué dans leurs bonnes grâces

insinuation [ɪnˌsɪnjʊ'eɪʃən] **N 1** *(hint)* insinuation *f*, allusion *f* **2** *(act, practice)* insinuation *f*

insipid [ɪn'sɪpɪd] **ADJ** insipide, fade

insipidity [ˌɪnsɪ'pɪdətɪ], **insipidness** [ɪn'sɪpɪdnɪs] **N** insipidité *f*, fadeur *f*

insist [ɪn'sɪst] **VI 1** *(demand)* insister; **if you i.** si tu insistes; **he insisted on a new contract** il a exigé un nouveau contrat; **I i. on seeing the manager** j'exige de voir le directeur; **she insists on doing it her way** elle tient à le faire à sa façon; **he insisted on my taking the money** il a tenu à ce que je prenne l'argent **2** *(maintain)* **to i. on** maintenir; **she insists on her innocence** elle maintient qu'elle est innocente **3** *(stress)* **to i. on** insister sur; **I must i. on this point** je dois insister sur ce point
VT 1 *(demand)* insister; **I i. that you tell no one** j'insiste pour que vous ne le disiez à personne; **you should i. that you be paid** vous devriez exiger qu'on vous paye **2** *(maintain)* maintenir, soutenir; **she insists that she locked the door** elle maintient qu'elle a fermé la porte à clef

insistence [ɪn'sɪstəns] **N** insistance *f*; **their i. on secrecy has hindered negotiations** en exigeant le secret, ils ont entravé les négociations; **her i. on her innocence** ses protestations d'innocence; **because of his i. on paying** parce qu'il tenait à payer; **at** *or* **on my i.** sur mon insistance; **I came here at her i.** je suis venu ici parce qu'elle a insisté

insistent [ɪn'sɪstənt] **ADJ** *(person)* insistant; *(demand)* pressant; *(denial, refusal)* obstiné; **to be i. about sth** insister sur qch; **she was most i.** elle a beaucoup insisté; **the child's i. cries** les pleurs incessants de l'enfant

insistently [ɪn'sɪstəntlɪ] **ADV** *(stare, knock)* avec insistance; *(ask, urge)* avec insistance, instamment

in situ [ˌɪn'sɪtjuː] **ADV** sur place, in situ

insofar as [ˌɪnsəʊ'fɑːr-] **CONJ** dans la mesure où; **I'll help her i. I can** je l'aiderai dans la mesure de mes capacités; **i. it's possible** dans la limite *ou* mesure du possible

insole ['ɪnsəʊl] **N** *(inner sole)* première semelle *f*; *(separate piece ► of cork, felt etc)* semelle *f* intérieure

insolence ['ɪnsələns] **N** insolence *f* (**to** envers)

insolent ['ɪnsələnt] **ADJ** insolent (**to** envers)

insolently ['ɪnsələntlɪ] **ADV** insolemment, avec insolence

insolubility [ɪnˌsɒljʊ'bɪlətɪ] **N** insolubilité *f*

insoluble [ɪn'sɒljʊbəl] **ADJ** *(problem, substance)* insoluble

insolvency [ɪn'sɒlvənsɪ] **N** *Fin (of person)* insolvabilité *f*; *(of company)* faillite *f*; **they're going to declare i.** *(people)* ils vont se déclarer insolvables; *(company)* ils vont déposer leur bilan

insolvent [ɪn'sɒlvənt] **ADJ** *Fin (person)* insolvable; *(company)* en faillite; **he was i. by 2 million dollars** il laissait une dette de 2 millions de dollars; **to declare oneself i.** *(person)* se déclarer insolvable; *(company)* déposer son bilan
N insolvable *mf*

insomnia [ɪn'sɒmnɪə] **N** *(UNCOUNT) Med* insomnie *f*

insomniac [ɪn'sɒmnɪæk] *Med* **N** insomniaque *mf*
ADJ insomniaque

insomuch as [ˌɪnsəʊ'mʌtʃ-] **CONJ** *Formal (given that)* étant donné que, vu que; *(insofar as)* dans la mesure où

inspect [ɪn'spekt] **VT 1** *(scrutinize)* examiner, inspecter **2** *(check officially ► school, product, prison)* inspecter; *(► ticket)* contrôler; *(► accounts)* contrôler; *(► machinery, vehicle)* contrôler, vérifier **3** *Mil (troops)* passer en revue
VI faire une inspection

inspecting officer [ɪn'spektɪŋ-] **N** inspecteur(trice) *m,f*

inspection [ɪn'spekʃən] **N 1** *(of object)* examen *m* (minutieux); *(of place)* inspection *f*; **on closer i.** en regardant de plus près; **to buy goods on i.** acheter des marchandises sur examen **2** *(official check)* inspection *f*; *(of ticket, passport)* contrôle *m*; *(of school, prison)* (visite *f* d')inspection *f*; *(of machinery, vehicle)* contrôle *m*, vérification *f*; **customs i.** contrôle *m* douanier; **product quality i.** contrôle *m* de qualité des produits **3** *Mil (of troops)* revue *f*, inspection *f*
►► ***inspection chamber*** bouche *f* d'égout; ***inspection copy*** *(in publishing)* spécimen *m*; *Tech* ***inspection hole*** orifice *m ou* trou *m ou* regard *m* de visite; *Tech* ***inspection panel*** panneau *m* de visite; *Aut* ***inspection pit*** fosse *f* (de réparations); *Tech* ***inspection port*** orifice *m ou* trou *m ou* regard *m* de visite

inspector [ɪn'spektə(r)] **N 1** *(gen)* inspecteur(trice) *m,f*; *(on public transport)* contrôleur(euse) *m,f* **2** *Br Sch* inspecteur(trice) *m,f* **3** *(in police force)* **(police) i.** inspecteur *m* (de police)
►► ***inspector general*** *(gen)* inspecteur *m* général; *Mil* général *m* inspecteur; *Br* ***inspector of taxes*** inspecteur(trice) *m,f* des impôts

inspectorate [ɪn'spektərət] **N** *(body of inspectors)* inspection *f*; *(duties, term of office)* inspection *f*, inspectorat *m*

inspiration [ˌɪnspə'reɪʃən] **N 1** *(source of ideas)* inspiration *f*; **to draw one's i. from** s'inspirer de; **to be an i. to sb** être une source d'inspiration pour qn; **your generosity has been an i. to us all** votre générosité nous a tous inspirés; **the i. for her screenplay** l'idée de son scénario **2** *(bright idea)* inspiration *f*; **hey, I've had an i.!** hé! j'ai une idée géniale! **3** *Formal (inhalation)* inspiration *f*

inspirational [ˌɪnspə'reɪʃənəl] **ADJ 1** *(inspiring)* inspirant **2** *(inspired)* inspiré

inspire [ɪn'spaɪə(r)] **VT 1** *(person, work of art)* inspirer; **to i. sb to do sth** inciter *ou* pousser qn à faire qch; **he inspired her to become a doctor** il suscita en elle une vocation de médecin **2** *(arouse ► feeling)* inspirer; **whatever inspired you to do that?** qu'est-ce qui a bien pu te donner l'idée de faire ça?; **the decision was inspired by the urgent need for funds** la décision a dû être prise pour répondre à un besoin urgent de fonds; **to i. confidence/respect** inspirer (la) confiance/le respect; **his success inspired me with confidence** sa réussite m'a donné confiance en moi; **to i. courage in sb** insuffler du courage à qn **3** *Formal (inhale)* inspirer
VI *Formal (inhale)* inspirer

inspired [ɪn'spaɪəd] **ADJ** *(artist, poem)* inspiré; *(moment)* d'inspiration; *(performance)* extraordinaire; *(choice, decision)* bien inspiré, heureux; **I'm not feeling very i. today** je n'ai pas vraiment l'inspiration aujourd'hui; **an i. idea** une inspiration; **to make an i. guess** deviner *ou* tomber juste

inspiring [ɪn'spaɪərɪŋ] **ADJ** *(speech, book)* stimulant; *(music)* exaltant; **it wasn't a very i. debate** ce débat n'avait rien de bien passionnant; **the menu wasn't very i.** le menu n'avait rien de bien tentant

instability [ˌɪnstə'bɪlətɪ] *(pl* **instabilities) N** instabilité *f*

install, *Am* **instal** [ɪn'stɔːl] **VT 1** *(machinery, equipment, software)* installer; **we're having central heating installed** nous faisons installer le chauffage central **2** *(settle ► person)* installer; **she installed herself in an armchair** elle s'installa dans un fauteuil **3** *(appoint ► manager, president)* nommer; **the Tories were installed with a huge majority** les conservateurs ont été élus avec une écrasante majorité

installation [ˌɪnstə'leɪʃən] **N 1** *(of machinery, equipment, software)* installation *f*
2 *(thing installed)* installation *f*
3 *Art* installation *f*
4 *Mil (base)* base *f*
►► *Comput* ***installation CD*** CD *m* d'installation; *Comput* ***installation disk*** *(floppy)* disquette *f* d'installation; *(CD-ROM)* CD *m* d'installation; *Comput* ***installation manual*** manuel *m* d'installation; *Comput* ***installation program*** programme *m* d'installation

installer [ɪn'stɔːlə(r)] **N** *Comput (program)* programme *m* d'installation

instalment, *Am* **installment** [ɪn'stɔːlmənt] **N 1** *(payment)* acompte *m*, versement *m* partiel; **monthly instalments** mensualités *fpl*; **to pay in** *or* **by instalments** payer par versements échelonnés **2** *(of serial, story)* épisode *m*; *(of book)* fascicule *m*; *(of TV documentary)* volet *m*, partie *f* **3** *(installation ► of machinery, equipment, software)* installation *f*
►► *Fin* ***instalment loan*** prêt *m* à tempérament *ou* à remboursements échelonnés; *Am* ***installment plan*** système *m* de paiements échelonnés; **to buy sth on the i. plan** acheter qch à crédit *(avec remboursement par paiements échelonnés)*

instance ['ɪnstəns] **N 1** *(example)* exemple *m*; *(case)* occasion *f*, circonstance *f*; **as an i. of** comme exemple de; **he agrees with me in most instances** la plupart du temps *ou* dans la plupart des cas il est d'accord avec moi; **our policy, in that i., was to raise interest rates** notre politique en la circonstance *ou* l'occurrence a consisté à augmenter les taux d'intérêt; **what would you have decided in that i.?** qu'auriez-vous décidé en pareil cas? **2** *(stage)* **in the first/second i.** en premier/second lieu; *Law* **court of first i.** tribunal *m* de première instance **3** *Formal (request)* demande *f*, instances *fpl*; **at the i. of** à la demande de

VT donner *ou* citer en exemple

• **for instance** **ADV** par exemple

> Note that the French noun **instance** is a false friend: it never means **example**.

instant ['ɪnstənt] **ADJ 1** *(immediate)* immédiat; **this wound needs i. attention** cette blessure doit être soignée immédiatement; **for i. weight loss** pour perdre du poids rapidement

2 *Culin (coffee)* instantané, soluble; *(soup, sauce)* instantané, en sachet; *(milk)* en poudre; *(mashed potato)* en flocons; *(dessert)* à préparation rapide

3 *Literary (urgent)* pressant, urgent

4 *Old-fashioned Com (in letter* ▸ *of current month)* courant

N 1 *(moment)* instant *m*, moment *m*; **at that i.** à ce moment-là; **the next i. he'd disappeared** l'instant d'après, il avait disparu; **do it this i.** fais-le tout de suite *ou* immédiatement *ou* à l'instant; **she read it in an i.** elle l'a lu en un rien de temps; **I'll be with you in an i.** je serai à vous dans un instant; **call me the i. you arrive** appelle-moi dès que *ou* aussitôt que tu seras arrivé; **I didn't believe it for one i.** je ne l'ai pas cru un seul instant; **he left on the i.** il est parti immédiatement *ou* sur-le-champ **2** *Fam (instant coffee)* café *m* instantané; **I've only got i., I'm afraid** je suis désolé mais je n'ai que de l'instantané

▸▸ *Comput* ***instant message*** message *m* instantané; *Comput* ***instant messaging*** messagerie *f* instantanée; *TV* ***instant replay*** = répétition immédiate d'une séquence; *Pol* ***instant runoff voting*** = mode de scrutin par élimination

instant-access **ADJ** *Fin (bank account)* à accès immédiat

instantaneous [ˌɪnstən'teɪmjəs] **ADJ** instantané

instantaneously [ˌɪnstən'teɪnjəslɪ] **ADV** instantanément

instantly ['ɪnstəntlɪ] **ADV** *(immediately)* immédiatement, instantanément; **he was killed i.** il a été tué sur le coup

instead [ɪn'sted] **ADV** **he didn't go to the office, he went home i.** au lieu d'aller au bureau, il est rentré chez lui; **I don't like sweet things, I'll have cheese i.** je n'aime pas les sucreries, je prendrai plutôt du fromage; **since I'll be away, why not send Eva i.?** puisque je ne serai pas là, pourquoi ne pas envoyer Eva à ma place?

• **instead of** **PREP** au lieu de, à la place de; **i. of reading a book** au lieu de lire un livre; **her son came i. of her** son fils est venu à sa place

instep ['ɪnstep] **N 1** *Anat* cou-de-pied *m*; **to have a high i.** avoir le pied très cambré **2** *(of shoe)* cambrure *f*

instigate ['ɪnstɪgeɪt] **VT 1** *(initiate* ▸ *gen)* être à l'origine de; *(*▸ *project)* promouvoir; *(*▸ *strike, revolt, change)* provoquer; *(*▸ *plot)* ourdir **2** *(urge)* inciter, pousser; **to i. sb to do sth** pousser *ou* inciter qn à faire qch

instigation [ˌɪnstɪ'geɪʃən] **N** *(urging)* instigation *f*, incitation *f*; **at her i.** à son instigation

instigator ['ɪnstɪgeɪtə(r)] **N** instigateur(trice) *m,f*

instil, *Am* **instill** [ɪn'stɪl] **VT** *(principles, ideals)* inculquer **(in** à); *(loyalty, courage, fear)* insuffler **(in** à)

instinct ['ɪnstɪŋkt] **N** instinct *m*; **by i.** d'instinct; **she has an i. for business** elle a le sens des affaires; **he has an i. for the right word** il a le don pour trouver le mot juste; **her first i. was to run away** sa première réaction a été de s'enfuir

instinctive [ɪn'stɪŋktɪv] **ADJ** instinctif

instinctively [ɪn'stɪŋktɪvlɪ] **ADV** instinctivement; **animals are i. afraid of fire** les animaux ont une peur instinctive du feu

institute ['ɪnstɪtju:t] **VT 1** *(establish* ▸ *system, guidelines)* instituer, établir; *(*▸ *change)* introduire, apporter; *(*▸ *committee)* créer, constituer; *(*▸ *award, organization)* fonder, créer **2** *(take up* ▸ *proceedings)* engager, entamer; *(*▸ *inquiry)* ouvrir; **he threatened to i. legal action against them** il a menacé de leur intenter un procès **3** *(induct)* installer; *Rel* instituer

N institut *m*; **i. for the blind** institut *m* pour aveugles; **research i.** institut *m* de recherche

▸▸ *Br* ***institute of education*** = école formant des enseignants, IUFM *m*

institution [ˌɪnstɪ'tju:ʃən] **N 1** *(of rules)* institution *f*, établissement *m*; *(of committee)* création *f*, constitution *f*; *(of change)* introduction *f*; *Law (of action)* début *m*; *(of official)* installation *f*

2 *(organization)* organisme *m*, établissement *m*; *(governmental)* institution *f*; *(financial, educational, penal, religious)* établissement *m*; *(private school)* institution *f*; *(hospital)* hôpital *m*, établissement *m* hospitalier; *Euph (mental hospital)* établissement *m* psychiatrique

3 *(custom, political or social structure)* institution *f*; **the i. of marriage** l'institution du mariage

4 *Hum (person)* institution *f*; **she's a national i.** elle est devenue une véritable institution nationale

institutional [ˌɪnstɪ'tju:ʃənəl] **ADJ 1** *(hospital, prison, school etc)* institutionnel; **after years of i. life** après des années d'internement **2** *(belief, values)* séculaire **3** *Com* institutionnel

▸▸ *Com* ***institutional advertising*** publicité *f* institutionnelle; *Com* ***institutional buying*** achats *mpl* institutionnels; ***institutional care*** soins *mpl* hospitaliers; **he'd be better off in i. care** il serait mieux dans un établissement *ou* centre spécialisé; *Com* ***institutional investment*** investissement *m* institutionnel; *Com* ***institutional investors*** investisseurs *mpl* institutionnels; *Com* ***institutional savings*** épargne *f* institutionnelle

institutionalize, -ise [ˌɪnstɪ'tju:ʃənəˌlaɪz] **VT 1** *(establish)* institutionnaliser **2** *(place in a hospital, home)* placer dans un établissement *(médical ou médico-social)*

institutionalized, -ised [ˌɪnstɪ'tju:ʃənəˌlaɪzd] **ADJ 1** *(person)* marqué par la vie en collectivité; **after years in a psychiatric hospital, she had become completely i.** après des années en hôpital psychiatrique, elle était devenue complètement dépendante; **things are less i. in this establishment** cet établissement a un caractère moins institutionnel **2** *(practice)* établi

in-store **ADJ** *(bakery, childcare facilities etc)* dans le magasin, sur place

▸▸ *Mktg* ***in-store advertising*** PLV *f*, publicité *f* sur le lieu de vente; *Mktg* ***in-store advertising space*** espace *m* de PLV, espace *m* de publicité sur le lieu de vente; ***in-store demonstration*** démonstration *f* sur le lieu de vente; ***in-store promotion*** promotion *f* sur le lieu de vente

instruct [ɪn'strʌkt] **VT 1** *(command, direct)* charger; **we have been instructed to accompany you** nous sommes chargés de *ou* nous avons mission de vous accompagner

2 *(teach)* former; **to i. sb in sth** enseigner *ou* apprendre qch à qn

3 *(inform)* informer; **I have been instructed that the meeting has been cancelled** on m'a informé *ou* avisé que la réunion a été annulée

4 *Law (jury, solicitor)* donner des instructions à; *Br* **to i. counsel** constituer avocat

instruction [ɪn'strʌkʃən] **N 1** *(order)* instruction *f*; **to give sb instructions to do sth** ordonner à qn de faire qch; **to carry out instructions** exécuter des ordres; **our instructions were to arrest him** nous avions reçu l'ordre de l'arrêter; **she gave instructions for the papers to be destroyed** elle a donné des instructions pour qu'on détruise les documents; **they were given instructions not to let him out of their sight** ils avaient reçu l'ordre de ne pas le perdre de vue; **instructions (for use)** mode *m* d'emploi **2** *(UNCOUNT) (teaching)* leçons *fpl*; *Mil* instruction *f* **3** *Comput* **instructions** *(in program)* instructions *fpl*

▸▸ ***instruction book*** livret *m* d'instruction(s); *Comput* ***instruction code*** code *m* d'instruction; ***instruction manual*** manuel *m* (d'utilisation et d'entretien); *Comput* guide *m* de l'utilisateur; *Comput* ***instruction set*** jeu *m* d'instructions

instructive [ɪn'strʌktɪv] **ADJ** instructif

instructor [ɪn'strʌktə(r)] **N 1** *(gen)* professeur *m*; *Mil* instructeur *m*; **music i.** professeur *m* de musique; **sailing i.** moniteur(trice) *m,f* de voile **2** *Am Univ* assistant(e) *m,f*

instructress [ɪn'strʌktrɪs] **N** professeur *m*; *Mil* instructrice *f*; **music i.** professeur *m* de musique; **sailing i.** monitrice *f* de voile

instrument ['ɪnstrʊmənt] **N 1** *Med, Mus & Tech* instrument *m*; **to fly by** *or* **on instruments** naviguer à l'aide d'instruments **2** *Fig (means)* instrument *m*, outil *m*; **to serve as the i. of sb's vengeance** servir d'instrument à la vengeance de qn **3** *Fin* effet *m*, titre *m*; *Law* instrument *m*, acte *m* juridique; **i. of incorporation** statut *m*, acte *m* de constitution; **an i. of payment** un moyen de paiement; **i. to order** papier *m* à ordre

COMP *Aviat (flying, landing)* aux instruments (de bord)

VT 1 *Mus* orchestrer **2** *Tech* munir *ou* équiper d'instruments

VI *Law* instrumenter

▸▸ *Aviat & Aut* ***instrument board*** tableau *m* de bord; *Tech* tableau *m* de contrôle; *Tech* ***instrument error*** erreur *f* due aux instruments; ***instrument panel*** *Aviat & Aut* tableau *m* de bord; *Tech* tableau *m* de contrôle

instrumental [ˌɪnstrʊ'mentəl] **ADJ 1** *(significant)* **to be i. in doing sth** contribuer à faire qch, jouer un rôle décisif dans qch; **an i. role** un rôle déterminant **2** *Mus* instrumental **3** *Tech* d'instruments

N 1 *Mus* morceau *m* instrumental **2** *Ling* instrumental *m*

▸▸ *Ling* ***instrumental case*** (cas *m*) instrumental *m*; *Tech* ***instrumental error*** erreur *f* due aux instruments

instrumentalist [ˌɪnstrʊ'mentəlɪst] **N** *Mus* instrumentiste *mf*

instrumentation [ˌɪnstrʊmen'teɪʃən] **N 1** *Mus (musical arrangement)* orchestration *f*, instrumentation *f*; *(musical instruments)* instruments *mpl* **2** *Tech* instrumentation *f*

insubordinate [ˌɪnsə'bɔ:dɪnət] **ADJ** insubordonné

▸▸ ***insubordinate behaviour*** conduite *f* insubordonnée *ou* rebelle

insubordination ['ɪnsəˌbɔ:dɪ'neɪʃən] **N** insubordination *f*

insubstantial [ˌɪnsəb'stænʃəl] **ADJ 1** *(structure)* peu solide; *(book)* facile, peu substantiel; *(garment, snack, mist)* léger; *(claim)* sans fondement; *(reasoning)* faible, sans substance **2** *(imaginary)* imaginaire, chimérique

insufferable [ɪn'sʌfərəbəl] **ADJ** insupportable, intolérable

insufferably [ɪn'sʌfərəblɪ] **ADV** insupportablement, intolérablement; **he's i. arrogant** il est d'une arrogance insupportable

insufficiency [ˌɪnsə'fɪʃənsɪ] *(pl* **insufficiencies)** **N** insuffisance *f*

insufficient [ˌɪnsə'fɪʃənt] **ADJ** insuffisant; **there is i. evidence** les preuves sont insuffisantes

▸▸ *Fin* ***insufficient capital*** insuffisance *f* de capitaux; *Fin* ***insufficient funds*** provision *f* insuffisante, insuffisance *f* de provision

insufficiently [ˌɪnsə'fɪʃəntlɪ] **ADV** insuffisamment

insular ['ɪnsjʊlə(r)] **ADJ 1** *(island* ▸ *tradition, authorities)* insulaire; *(isolated)* isolé; **he leads a very i. existence** il vit comme un ermite **2** *Fig Pej (mentality)* limité, borné; **she's very i.** elle est très bornée *ou* a l'esprit très étroit

> Note that the French word **insulaire** only means **pertaining to an island**.

insularity [ˌɪnsjʊ'lærətɪ] **N 1** *(of tradition, authorities)* insularité *f*; *(isolation)* isolement *m* **2** *Fig Pej (of mentality)* caractère *m* borné; *(of person)* étroitesse *f* d'esprit

insulate ['ɪnsjʊleɪt] **VT 1** *(against cold, heat, radiation)* isoler; *(hot water pipes, tank)* calorifuger; *(soundproof)* insonoriser **2** *Elec* isoler **3** *Fig (protect)* protéger; **they are no longer insulated from the effects of inflation** ils ne sont plus à l'abri des effets de l'inflation

▸▸ ***insulated screwdriver*** tournevis *m* isolant; ***insulated sleeping bag*** sac *m* de couchage isolant

insulating ['ɪnsjʊleɪtɪŋ] ADJ isolant; *(against loss of heat)* calorifuge; *(soundproofing)* insonore
▸▸ *Elec* ***insulating material*** isolant *m*; ***insulating tape*** ruban *m* isolant, chatterton *m*

insulation [ˌɪnsjʊ'leɪʃən] N 1 *(against cold)* isolation *f* (calorifuge), calorifugeage *m*; *Constr (sound-proofing)* insonorisation *f*, isolation *f*; **loft i.** isolation *f* thermique du toit
2 *Elec* isolation *f*
3 *(feathers, foam etc)* isolant *m*
4 *Fig (protection)* protection *f*

> Attention: ne pas confondre avec le terme anglais **isolation**, qui signifie **isolement**.

insulator ['ɪnsjʊleɪtə(r)] N *(material)* isolant *m*; *(device)* isolateur *m*

insulin ['ɪnsjʊlɪn] N *Med & Physiol* insuline *f*
▸▸ ***insulin reaction, insulation shock*** choc *m* insulinique

insulin-dependent ADJ *Med* insulinodépendant

insult VT [ɪn'sʌlt] *(abuse)* insulter, injurier; *(offend)* faire (un) affront à, offenser; **don't be insulted if I don't tell you everything** ne le prends pas mal *ou* ne t'offense pas si je ne te dis pas tout
N ['ɪnsʌlt] insulte *f*, injure *f*, affront *m*; **they were hurling insults at each other** ils se lançaient des insultes à la figure; **his remarks were an i. to their intelligence** ses commentaires étaient une insulte à leur intelligence; **their ads are an i. to women** leurs pubs sont insultantes *ou* une insulte pour les femmes; **to add i. to injury** pour couronner le tout

insulting [ɪn'sʌltɪŋ] ADJ *(language)* insultant, injurieux; *(attitude)* insultant, offensant; *(behaviour)* grossier; **it is i. to suggest that…** il est insultant de suggérer que…

insultingly [ɪn'sʌltɪŋlɪ] ADV *(speak)* d'un ton insultant *ou* injurieux; *(act)* d'une manière insultante; **he behaved most i. towards her** son comportement a été très injurieux à son égard

insuperable [ɪn'suːprəbəl] ADJ insurmontable

insuperably [ɪn'suːprəblɪ] ADV de façon insurmontable; **i. difficult** d'une difficulté insurmontable

insupportable [ˌɪnsə'pɔːtəbəl] ADJ 1 *(unbearable)* insupportable, intolérable 2 *(indefensible)* insoutenable

insurable [ɪn'ʃɔːrəbəl] ADJ assurable
▸▸ ***insurable interest*** intérêt *m* pécuniaire

insurance [ɪn'ʃɔːrəns] N 1 *(UNCOUNT) Ins (against fire, theft, accident)* assurance *f*; *(cover)* garantie *f* (d'assurance), couverture *f*; *(premium)* prime *f* (d'assurance); **to take out i. (against sth)** prendre *ou* contracter une assurance (contre qch), s'assurer (contre qch); **to have i. against sth** être assuré pour *ou* contre qch; **he's in i.** il est dans les assurances; **he bought himself a stereo out of the i.** il s'est acheté une chaîne stéréo avec (une partie de) l'argent de l'assurance; **she got £2,000 in i.** elle a reçu 2000 livres de l'assurance; **how much do you pay in i.?** combien payez-vous (de prime) d'assurance? 2 *Fig (means of protection)* garantie *f*, moyen *m* de protection; **take Sam with you, just as an i.** emmenez Sam avec vous, on ne sait jamais *ou* au cas où
COMP *Ins (scheme)* d'assurance; *(company)* d'assurances
▸▸ ***insurance adviser*** assureur-conseil *m*; ***insurance agent*** agent *m* d'assurance(s); ***insurance banker*** bancassureur *m*; ***insurance broker*** courtier(ère) *m,f* d'assurances; *Ins* ***insurance certificate*** certificat *m* d'assurance; ***insurance claim*** demande *f* d'indemnité; *(for more serious damage)* déclaration *f* de sinistre; **to make an i. claim** faire une demande d'indemnité; *(for more serious damage)* faire une déclaration de sinistre; ***insurance cover*** couverture *f* d'assurance; ***insurance group*** groupe *m* d'assurance; ***insurance inspector*** inspecteur *m* d'une société d'assurances; ***insurance policy*** police *f* d'assurance, contrat *m* d'assurance; **to take out an i. policy** contracter une assurance; ***insurance portfolio*** portefeuille *m* d'assurances; ***insurance premium*** prime *f* d'assurance; ***insurance value*** valeur *f* d'assurance

insure [ɪn'ʃɔː(r)] VT 1 *Ins (car, building, person)* assurer; **he insured himself** *or* **his life** il a pris *ou* contracté une assurance-vie 2 *Fig (protect)* **what strategy can i. (us) against failure?** quelle stratégie peut nous prévenir contre l'échec *ou* nous garantir que nous n'échouerons pas?
VI *Ins* **to i. against sth** s'assurer *ou* se faire assurer contre qch

insured [ɪn'ʃɔːd] *(pl* **inv***) Ins* N assuré(e) *m,f*
ADJ assuré; **i. against** assuré contre
▸▸ ***insured risk*** risque *m* couvert

insurer [ɪn'ʃɔːrə(r)] N *Ins* assureur *m*

insurgent [ɪn'sɜːdʒənt] N insurgé(e) *m,f*
ADJ insurgé

insurmountable [ˌɪnsə'maʊntəbəl] ADJ insurmontable

insurrection [ˌɪnsə'rekʃən] N insurrection *f*; **armed i.** soulèvement *m* armé, insurrection *f* armée

insurrectionary [ˌɪnsə'rekʃənərɪ] *(pl* **insurrectionaries***)* N insurgé(e) *m,f*
ADJ insurrectionnel

insurrectionist [ˌɪnsə'rekʃənɪst] N insurgé(e) *m,f*
ADJ insurrectionnel

intact [ɪn'tækt] ADJ intact

intaglio [ɪn'tɑːlɪəʊ] *(pl* **intaglios** *or* **intagli** [-ljiː]) N *(gem)* intaille *f*; *(design)* dessin *m* en intaille; *(technique)* gravure *f* en creux
▸▸ ***intaglio printing*** impression *f* en taille-douce

intake ['ɪnteɪk] N 1 *Sch & Univ* admission *f*, inscription *f*; *Mil* recrutement *m*; **the i. of refugees** l'accueil *m* des réfugiés; **they've increased their i. of medical students** ils ont décidé d'admettre davantage d'étudiants en médecine; **this year's i. of pupils is** *or* **are of a higher standard than usual** cette année, les nouveaux élèves sont d'un niveau plus élevé que d'habitude 2 *Tech (of water)* prise *f*, arrivée *f*; *(of gas, steam)* admission *f*; **an i. rate of 10 litres per second** un débit d'admission de 10 litres par seconde; **a high energy i.** une consommation importante d'énergie; **air i.** admission *f* d'air 3 *Physiol (of food, alcohol)* consommation *f*; **a daily i. of 2,000 calories** une ration quotidienne de 2000 calories; **there was a sharp i. of breath** tout le monde/il/elle/*etc* retint son souffle; **oxygen i.** absorption *f* d'oxygène
▸▸ *Br* ***intake class*** cours *m* préparatoire; *Tech* ***intake manifold*** conduits *mpl* d'admission, collecteur *m* d'admission; *Tech* ***intake valve*** soupape *f* d'admission

intangible [ɪn'tændʒɪbəl] ADJ *(quality, reality)* intangible, impalpable; *(idea, difficulty)* indéfinissable, difficile à cerner
N impondérable *m*
• **intangibles** NPL *Fin* valeurs *fpl* immatérielles, actif *m* incorporel
▸▸ *Fin* ***intangible asset*** valeur *f* immatérielle, actif *m* incorporel; *Law* ***intangible property*** biens *mpl* incorporels

integer ['ɪntɪdʒə(r)] N *Math* (nombre *m*) entier *m*; *(whole unit)* entier *m*

integral ['ɪntɪgrəl] ADJ 1 *(essential ▸ part, element)* intégrant, constitutif; **it's an i. part of your job** cela fait partie intégrante de votre travail
2 *(entire)* intégral, complet(ète)
3 *Math* intégral
4 *Tech (forming a part)* incorporé (**with** à); **to be i. with** faire partie intégrante de
N *Math* intégrale *f*
▸▸ *Math* ***integral calculus*** calcul *m* intégral; *Math* ***integral number*** nombre *m* entier; ***integral power supply*** accumulateur *m* incorporé

integrate ['ɪntɪgreɪt] VT 1 *(combine)* combiner; **the two systems have been integrated** on a combiné les deux systèmes
2 *(include in a larger unit)* intégrer; **to i. sb in a group** intégrer qn dans un groupe; **his brief was to i. the new building into the historic old quarter** il avait pour mission de concevoir un bâtiment qui soit en harmonie avec la vieille ville
3 *(end segregation of)* **the law was intended to i. racial minorities** cette loi visait à l'intégration des minorités raciales; **to i. a school** mettre fin à la ségrégation raciale dans une école
4 *Math* intégrer
VI 1 *(fit in)* s'intégrer (**into** *or* **with** dans) 2 *(desegregate)* ne plus pratiquer la ségrégation raciale

integrated ['ɪntɪgreɪtɪd] ADJ 1 *(gen)* intégré 2 *(fax, modem)* intégré; **vertically i. company** société *f* à intégration verticale
▸▸ *Electron* ***integrated circuit*** circuit *m* intégré; *Electron* ***integrated circuit card*** carte *f* à circuit intégré; *Agr* ***integrated farming*** agriculture *f* raisonnée; *Am* ***integrated neighborhood*** quartier *m* multiracial; *Comput* ***integrated package*** logiciel *m ou* progiciel *m* intégré, intégré *m*; *Am* ***integrated school*** = école où se pratique l'intégration (raciale); *Comput* ***integrated software*** logiciel *m* intégré; *Sch* ***integrated studies*** études *fpl* interdisciplinaires

integration [ˌɪntɪ'greɪʃən] N 1 *(process of integrating)* intégration *f*; **racial i.** déségrégation *f*; *Am* **school i.** déségrégation *f* des établissements scolaires; *Econ* **vertical/horizontal i.** intégration *f* verticale/horizontale 2 *Math* intégration *f*

integrative ['ɪntɪgreɪtɪv] ADJ intégratif
▸▸ *Econ* ***integrative growth*** croissance *f* par intégration

integrator ['ɪntɪgreɪtə(r)] N *(device)* intégrateur *m*

integrity [ɪn'tegrətɪ] N 1 *(uprightness)* intégrité *f*, probité *f*; **she's a woman of great i.** c'est une femme d'une grande intégrité 2 *(wholeness)* intégrité *f*; **cultural i.** identité *f* culturelle

integument [ɪn'tegjʊmənt] N *Biol* tégument *m*

intellect ['ɪntəlekt] N 1 *(intelligence)* intelligence *f*; **a man of i.** un homme intelligent 2 *(mind, person)* esprit *m*

intellectual [ˌɪntə'lektjʊəl] N intellectuel(elle) *m,f*
ADJ *(mental)* intellectuel; *(attitude, image)* d'intellectuel; **an i. set** un petit groupe d'intellectuels
▸▸ *Law* ***intellectual property*** propriété *f* intellectuelle

intellectually [ˌɪntə'lektjʊəlɪ] ADV intellectuellement

intelligence [ɪn'telɪdʒəns] N *(UNCOUNT)* 1 *(mental ability)* intelligence *f*; **to have the i. to do sth** avoir l'intelligence de faire qch; **use your i.!** réfléchis un peu! 2 *(information)* renseignements *mpl*, information *f*, informations *fpl*; *(department)* services *mpl* de renseignements; **he used to work in i.** il travaillait pour les services de renseignements; **army i.** service *m* de renseignements de l'armée 3 *(intelligent being)* intelligence *f*
▸▸ *Am Pol* ***intelligence agency*** services *mpl* de renseignements; ***intelligence gathering*** renseignement *m*, espionnage *m*; ***intelligence officer*** officier *m* de renseignements; ***intelligence quotient*** quotient *m* intellectuel; *Br Pol* ***intelligence service, intelligence services*** services *mpl* de renseignements; *Psy* ***intelligence test*** test *m* d'aptitude intellectuelle

intelligent [ɪn'telɪdʒənt] ADJ 1 *(clever)* intelligent
2 *Mil (weapon, bomb)* intelligent
▸▸ *Br* ***intelligent card*** carte *f* à mémoire *ou* à puce; ***intelligent design*** dessein *m* intelligent; *Rad* ***intelligent speech*** émissions *fpl* culturelles; *Comput* ***intelligent terminal*** terminal *m* intelligent

intelligently [ɪn'telɪdʒəntlɪ] ADV intelligemment

intelligentsia [ɪnˌtelɪ'dʒentsɪə] N intelligentsia *f*

intelligibility [ɪnˌtelɪdʒə'bɪlətɪ] N intelligibilité *f*

intelligible [ɪn'telɪdʒəbəl] ADJ intelligible

intelligibly [ɪn'telɪdʒəblɪ] ADJ intelligiblement

intemperance [ɪn'tempərəns] N *Formal* 1 *(overindulgence)* intempérance *f*, manque *m* de modération 2 *(of behaviour, remark)* caractère *m* outrancier

intemperate [ɪn'tempərət] ADJ *Formal* 1 *(overindulgent)* intempérant; **i. drinking** consommation *f* excessive d'alcool 2 *(uncontrolled ▸ behaviour, remark)* excessif, outrancier; **her i. refusal** la violence de son refus 3 *(harsh ▸ climate)* rigoureux, rude

intend [ɪn'tend] VT 1 *(plan, have in mind)* **to i. to do sth, to i. doing** *or Am* **on doing sth** avoir l'intention de *ou* projeter de faire qch; **how do you i. to do it?** comment avez-vous l'intention de vous y prendre?; **we arrived later than (we had) intended** nous sommes arrivés plus tard que prévu; **his statement was intended to mislead** sa déclaration visait à induire en erreur; **I had intended staying** *or* **to stay longer** j'avais l'intention *ou* prévu de rester plus longtemps; **he didn't i. her to see the letter** il n'avait pas l'intention de lui laisser voir la lettre; **we i. to increase our sales** nous entendons développer nos ventes; *Literary* **to i. marriage** avoir l'intention de se marier; **no harm was intended** c'était sans mauvaise intention; **I'm sorry, no criticism/insult was intended** je suis désolé, je ne voulais pas vous critiquer/offenser; **no pun intended!** sans jeu de mots! **2** *(destine)* destiner; **a book intended for the general public** un livre destiné *ou* qui s'adresse au grand public; **the funds were intended for disabled children** les fonds étaient destinés à l'enfance handicapée; **the device is intended to reduce pollution** ce dispositif a pour but *ou* fonction de réduire la pollution; **the reform is intended to limit the dumping of toxic waste** cette réforme vise à limiter le déversement de déchets toxiques

intended [ɪn'tendɪd] **ADJ 1** *(planned ▸ event, trip)* prévu; *(▸ result, reaction)* voulu; *(▸ market, public)* visé **2** *(deliberate)* intentionnel, délibéré
N *Arch or Hum* **his i.** sa future, sa promise; **her i.** son futur, son promis

intense [ɪn'tens] **ADJ 1** *(gen)* intense; *(battle, debate)* acharné; *(hatred)* violent, profond; *(pleasure)* vif; **a period of i. activity** une période d'activité intense; **to my i. satisfaction/annoyance** à ma très grande satisfaction/mon grand déplaisir **2** *(person)* **he's so i.** *(serious)* il prend tout très au sérieux; *(emotional)* il prend tout très à cœur **3** *Am Fam (very good)* génial

intensely [ɪn'tenslɪ] **ADV 1** *(with intensity ▸ work, stare)* intensément, avec intensité; *(▸ love)* profondément, passionnément **2** *(extremely ▸ hot, painful, curious)* extrêmement; *(▸ moving, affected, bored)* profondément

intensification [ɪn,tensɪfɪ'keɪʃən] **N** intensification *f*

intensifier [ɪn'tensɪfaɪə(r)] **N 1** *Ling* intensif *m* **2** *Phot* renforçateur *m*

intensify [ɪn'tensɪfaɪ] *(pt & pp* **intensified)** **VT** *(feeling, impression, colour)* renforcer; *(sound)* intensifier; **the police have intensified their search for the child** la police redouble d'efforts pour retrouver l'enfant
VI s'intensifier, devenir plus intense

intensity [ɪn'tensətɪ] *(pl* **intensities)** **N 1** *(of emotion, colour etc)* intensité *f*; **the emotional i. of his paintings** la force des sentiments exprimés dans ses tableaux; **the i. of the debate** la véhémence du débat **2** *Phys (of sound, current etc)* intensité *f*; *Chem (of reaction)* énergie *f* **3** *Phot (of negative)* densité *f*

intensive [ɪn'tensɪv] **ADJ** intensif; **an i. course in English** un cours *ou* stage intensif d'anglais; **i. security measures** mesures *fpl* de sécurité draconiennes
▸▸ *Med* ***intensive care*** *(UNCOUNT)* soins *mpl* intensifs; **in i. care** en réanimation; *Med* ***intensive care unit*** unité *f* de soins intensifs; *Mktg* ***intensive distribution*** distribution *f* intensive; ***intensive farming*** culture *f* intensive; *Am* ***intensive security prison*** prison *f* où la surveillance est renforcée

intensively [ɪn'tensɪvlɪ] **ADV** intensivement

intent [ɪn'tent] **N** intention *f*, but *m*; **with good/evil i.** dans une bonne/mauvaise intention; *Law* **with criminal i.** dans un but délictueux; **declaration of i.** déclaration *f* d'intention
ADJ 1 *(concentrated)* attentif, absorbé; **with i. application** avec une concentration extrême; **he was silent, i. on the meal** il était silencieux, tout à son repas **2** *(determined)* résolu, déterminé; **to be i. on doing sth** être déterminé *ou* résolu à faire qch; **they left i. on murder** ils sont partis, déterminés à commettre un meurtre; **a woman i. on success** une femme déterminée à réussir
• **to all intents and purposes ADV** pratiquement, quasiment; **to all intents and purposes, it was a failure** tout bien considéré, ce fut un échec

intention [ɪn'tenʃən] **N** intention *f*; **I have absolutely no i. of spending my life here** je n'ai aucune intention de passer ma vie ici; **I have every i. of calling her!** j'ai bien l'intention de l'appeler; **he went to Australia with the i. of making his fortune** il est parti en Australie dans l'intention de *ou* dans le but de faire fortune; *Old-fashioned or Hum* **his intentions are honourable** *(towards her)* il a l'intention de l'épouser; *Mktg* **i. to buy** intention *f* d'achat

intentional [ɪn'tenʃənəl] **ADJ** intentionnel, voulu

intentionally [ɪn'tenʃənəlɪ] **ADV** intentionnellement; **he didn't do it i.** il ne l'a pas fait exprès *ou* intentionnellement; **I i. didn't invite her** c'est intentionnellement que je ne l'ai pas invitée

intently [ɪn'tentlɪ] **ADV** *(alertly ▸ listen, watch)* attentivement; *(thoroughly ▸ question, examine)* minutieusement

inter [ɪn'tɜː(r)] *(pt & pp* **interred**, *cont* **interring)** **VT** *Formal* enterrer, inhumer

interact [,ɪntər'ækt] **VI 1** *(person)* **they i. very well together** ils ont de très bons rapports, ils s'entendent très bien; **a person who doesn't i. well with others** une personne qui a du mal dans ses rapports avec les autres; **the way the two characters in the novel i.** l'interaction entre les deux personnages dans le roman **2** *(forces)* interagir; *(substances)* avoir une action réciproque; **the cold air interacts with the warm** il se produit une réaction entre l'air chaud et l'air froid **3** *Comput* dialoguer

interaction [,ɪntər'ækʃən] **N** *Phys* interaction *f*

interactive [,ɪntər'æktɪv] **ADJ** interactif
▸▸ *Comput* ***interactive CD*** CD-I *m*, disque *m* compact interactif; ***interactive digital media*** médias *mpl* numériques interactifs; ***interactive learning*** apprentissage *m* interactif; ***interactive marketing*** marketing *m* interactif; *Comput* ***interactive mode*** mode *m* conversationnel *ou* interactif; ***interactive television*** télévision *f* interactive; *Comput* ***interactive terminal*** terminal *m* (informatique) interactif

interactiveness [,ɪntər'æktɪvnɪs], **interactivity** [,ɪntəræk'tɪvɪtɪ] **N** interactivité *f*

inter alia [,ɪntər'eɪlɪə] **ADV** *Formal* entre autres

interbank ['ɪntəbæŋk] **ADJ** *Banking* interbancaire
▸▸ ***interbank deposit*** dépôt *m* interbancaire; ***interbank loan*** prêt *m* de banque à banque *ou* entre banques; ***interbank money*** argent *m* de gré à gré entre banques; ***interbank offered rate*** taux *m* interbancaire offert; ***interbank transfer*** virement *m* interbancaire

interbreed [,ɪntə'briːd] *(pt & pp* **interbred** [-bred]) *Biol* **VT 1** *(crossbreed ▸ animals)* croiser; *(▸ races)* métisser **2** *(breed from same stock)* croiser *(des animaux consanguins)*
VI 1 *(crossbreed ▸ animals)* se croiser; *(▸ races)* se métisser **2** *(within family, community)* contracter des mariages consanguins

interbreeding [,ɪntə'briːdɪŋ] **N** *Biol* **1** *(crossbreeding ▸ of animals)* croisement *m*; *(▸ of races)* métissage *m* **2** *(within breed)* croisement *m* d'animaux de même souche; *(within family, community)* union *f* consanguine, unions *fpl* consanguines

intercede [,ɪntə'siːd] **VI** intercéder; **she interceded with the boss on my behalf** elle a intercédé en ma faveur auprès du patron

intercept VT [,ɪntə'sept] intercepter; **to i. a blow** parer un coup
VI [,ɪntə'sept] *(in football)* intercepter une passe
N ['ɪntəsept] interception *f*

interception [,ɪntə'sepʃən] **N** interception *f*

interceptor [,ɪntə'septə(r)] **N 1** *(person ▸ of message)* personne *f* qui intercepte **2** *Aviat & Mil (aircraft)* avion *m* d'interception, intercepteur *m*
▸▸ *Aviat & Mil* ***interceptor aircraft*** avion *m* d'interception, intercepteur *m*

intercession [,ɪntə'seʃən] **N** intercession *f*

interchange N ['ɪntətʃeɪndʒ] **1** *(exchange)* échange *m* **2** *(road junction)* échangeur *m*
VT [,ɪntə'tʃeɪndʒ] **1** *(exchange ▸ opinions, information)* échanger **2** *(switch round)* intervertir, permuter; **these tyres can be interchanged** ces pneus sont interchangeables

interchangeable [,ɪntə'tʃeɪndʒəbəl] **ADJ** interchangeable

interchangeably [,ɪntə'tʃeɪndʒəblɪ] **ADV** indifféremment

intercharacter spacing [ɪntə'kærəktə-] **N** *Typ* espacement *m* entre les caractères

intercity [,ɪntə'sɪtɪ] *(pl* **intercities)** *Br Transp* **N** *(train)* (train *m*) rapide *m*, train *m* grandes lignes
ADJ *(travel)* d'une ville à l'autre, interurbain
▸▸ ***intercity train*** (train *m*) rapide *m*, train *m* grandes lignes

intercom ['ɪntəkɒm] **N** *Tel* Interphone® *m*; **to call sb on** *or* **over the i.** appeler qn à *ou* par l'Interphone®; **to speak over the i.** parler dans l'Interphone®

intercommunicate [,ɪntəkə'mjuːnɪkeɪt] **VI** communiquer

intercommunion [,ɪntəkə'mjuːnjən] **N** *Rel* intercommunion *f*

intercompany [,ɪntə'kʌmpənɪ] **ADJ** interentreprises, intersociétés

interconnect [,ɪntəkə'nekt] **VT** *(gen)* connecter; **the buildings are interconnected by underground walkways** les immeubles sont reliés par des passages souterrains; **interconnected corridors** couloirs *mpl* communicants; *Fig* **interconnected ideas** idées *fpl* étroitement reliées
VI *(rooms, buildings)* communiquer; *(circuits)* être connecté

interconnecting [,ɪntəkə'nektɪŋ] **ADJ** *(wall, room)* mitoyen; **i. doors** portes *fpl* de chambres communiquantes

interconnection [,ɪntəkə'nekʃən] **N** connexion *f*, lien *m*; *Elec* interconnexion *f*

interconnectivity [,ɪntəkənek'tɪvɪtɪ] **N** *(of networks, systems)* interconnexion *f*

intercontinental ['ɪntə,kɒntɪ'nentəl] **ADJ** intercontinental
▸▸ *Mil* ***intercontinental ballistic missile*** missile *m* balistique intercontinental

intercooled ['ɪntə,kuːld] **ADJ** *Aut (engine)* refroidi

intercooler ['ɪntə,kuːlə(r)] **N** *Aut* intercooler *m*, refroidisseur *m* intermédiaire

intercostal [,ɪntə'kɒstəl] **ADJ** *Anat* intercostal
▸▸ ***intercostal muscles*** muscles *mpl* intercostaux

intercourse ['ɪntəkɔːs] **N 1** *(sexual)* rapports *mpl* (sexuels); **to have i. (with sb)** avoir des rapports sexuels (avec qn) **2** *Formal (communication)* relations *fpl*, rapports *mpl*; **social i.** communication *f*

intercut [,ɪntə'kʌt] **VT** *Cin & TV* insérer

intercutting [,ɪntə'kʌtɪŋ] **N** *Cin & TV* plans *mpl* insérés

interdenominational ['ɪntədɪ,nɒmɪ'neɪʃənəl] **ADJ** interconfessionnel

interdepartmental ['ɪntə,diːpɑːt'mentəl] **ADJ** *(in company, hospital)* entre services; *(in university, ministry)* interdépartemental

interdependence [,ɪntədɪ'pendəns] **N** interdépendance *f*

interdependent [,ɪntədɪ'pendənt] **ADJ** interdépendant

interdict N ['ɪntədɪkt] **1** *Law* interdiction *f* **2** *Rel* interdit *m*
VT [,ɪntə'dɪkt] **1** *Law* interdire **2** *Rel* jeter l'interdit sur

interdiction [,ɪntə'dɪkʃən] **N** *Law & Rel* interdiction *f*

interdisciplinary [,ɪntə,dɪsɪ'plɪnərɪ] **ADJ** *Univ* interdisciplinaire

interest ['ɪntrəst] **N 1** *(curiosity, attention)* intérêt *m*; **centre of i.** centre *m* d'intérêt; **to take/have an i. in sb/sth** s'intéresser à qn/qch; **to show (an) i. in sth** manifester de l'intérêt pour qch; **two people have shown an i. in (buying) the house** deux personnes sont intéressées par la maison; **she takes a great/an active i. in politics** elle s'intéresse beaucoup/activement à la politique; **he has** *or* **takes no i. whatsoever in music** il ne s'intéresse absolument pas à la musique; **he lost all i. in his work** il a perdu tout intérêt pour son travail;

pupils can often lose i. il arrive souvent que les élèves décrochent; **to hold sb's i.** retenir l'attention de qn; **the book created** *or* **aroused a great deal of i.** le livre a suscité un intérêt considérable; **there's little i. in these old chairs nowadays** on ne s'intéresse pas beaucoup à ces vieilles chaises de nos jours
2 *(appeal)* intérêt *m*; **there was little of i. on television** il n'y avait pas grand-chose d'intéressant à la télévision; **of no i.** sans intérêt; **politics has** *or* **holds no i. for me** la politique ne présente aucun intérêt pour moi; **to be of i. to sb** intéresser qn; **what he does is of no i. to me** ça ne m'intéresse pas de savoir ce qu'il fait
3 *(pursuit, hobby)* centre *m* d'intérêt; **we share the same interests** nous avons les mêmes centres d'intérêt; **her interests include skiing and photography** le ski et la photographie font partie de ses centres d'intérêt; **his only interests are television and comic books** la télévision et les bandes dessinées sont les seules choses qui l'intéressent
4 *(advantage, benefit)* intérêt *m*; **it's in your own i.** *or* **interests** c'est dans votre propre intérêt; **it's in my i. to do it** c'est dans mon intérêt de le faire; **it's not in their i. to offend her** ce n'est pas dans leur intérêt de l'offenser, ils n'ont pas intérêt à l'offenser; **to act in/against one's own interests** agir dans son intérêt (propre)/à l'encontre de ses propres intérêts; **to act in sb's best i.** *or* **interests** agir dans l'intérêt de qn; **we look after British interests** nous défendons les intérêts britanniques; **I have your interests at heart** tes intérêts me tiennent à cœur; **a conflict of interests** un conflit d'intérêts; **of public i.** d'intérêt public; **it would not be in the public i.** ça ne serait pas dans l'intérêt public; **in the interests of justice/peace** dans l'intérêt de la justice/paix; **in the interests of hygiene** par mesure d'hygiène; **in the interests of accuracy** par souci d'exactitude
5 *(group with common aim)* intérêt *m*; **the oil/steel interests in the country** l'industrie pétrolière/sidérurgique du pays; **big business interests** de gros intérêts commerciaux
6 *(share, stake)* intérêts *mpl*; **he has an i. in a sawmill** il a des intérêts dans une scierie; **I have no financial i. in the business** je ne suis pas intéressé dans cette entreprise; **his i. in the company is £10,000** il a une commandite de 10 000 livres
7 *Fin* intérêts *mpl*; **to pay i. on a loan** payer des intérêts sur un prêt; **to bear** *or* **yield i.** porter intérêt, rapporter (des intérêts); **the investment will bear 6 percent i.** le placement rapportera 6 pour cent; **i. accrued** fraction *f* d'intérêt; **i. on arrears** intérêt *m* de retard; **i. on capital** rémunération *f* de capital; **i. due** intérêts *mpl* dus *ou* exigibles; **i. due and payable** intérêts *mpl* exigibles; **i. paid** intérêts *mpl* versés; **i. payable** intérêt *m* exigible; **i. received** produits *mpl* financiers, intérêts *mpl* perçus; *Fig* **he'll get it back with i.!** il va le payer cher!
VT intéresser; **can I i. you in our new model?** puis-je attirer votre attention sur notre nouveau modèle?; **we couldn't i. her in the idea** nous ne sommes pas parvenus à susciter son intérêt pour cette idée; **can I i. you in a drink?** puis-je vous proposer un verre?; **it might i. you to learn** *or* **know that...** ça t'intéressera peut-être d'apprendre *ou* de savoir que...
►► *Fin* ***interest and dividend income*** produits *mpl* financiers; *Fin* ***interest charges*** intérêts *mpl* (à payer); *Banking (on overdraft)* agios *mpl*; *Fin* ***interest days*** jours *mpl* d'intérêt; ***interest group*** groupe *m* d'intérêt; *Fin* ***interest payment date*** date *f* d'échéance des intérêts; *Fin* ***interest rate*** taux *m* d'intérêt; **the i. rate is 4 percent** le taux d'intérêt est de 4 pour cent; *St Exch* ***interest rate differential*** differentiel *m* de taux; *St Exch* ***interest rate swap*** échange *m* de taux d'intérêt; *Fin* ***interest relief*** bonification *f* d'intérêts

interest-bearing **ADJ** *Fin* productif d'intérêts
►► *Banking* ***interest-bearing account*** compte *m* rémunéré; ***interest-bearing capital*** capital *m* productif d'intérêts; ***interest-bearing loan*** prêt *m* à intérêt; *St Exch* ***interest-bearing securities*** titres *mpl* qui produisent des intérêts

interested [ˈɪntrestɪd] **ADJ 1** *(showing interest)* intéressé; **to be i. in sth** s'intéresser à qch; **she is i. in fashion** elle s'intéresse à la mode, la mode l'intéresse; **would you be i. in meeting him?** ça t'intéresserait de le rencontrer?; **anyone i.?** il y en a que ça intéresse?, est-ce que quelqu'un est intéressé?; **we'd be i. to know** nous aimerions *ou* voudrions savoir; **I'm i. to see how they do it** je suis curieux de voir comment c'est fait; **she seems i. in the offer** elle semble intéressée par la proposition **2** *(involved, concerned)* intéressé; **i. party** partie *f* intéressée

interest-free **ADJ** *Fin (loan)* sans intérêt; *(credit)* gratuit

interesting [ˈɪntrəstɪŋ] **ADJ** intéressant

interestingly [ˈɪntrəstɪŋlɪ] **ADV** de façon intéressante; **i., a number of her supporters voted against her** il est intéressant de noter qu'un certain nombre de ses partisans ont voté contre elle; **i. enough, they were out** chose intéressante, ils étaient sortis

interface **N** [ˈɪntəfeɪs] *(gen) & Comput* interface *f*; **the patient-doctor i.** les relations médecin-patient
VT [ˌɪntəˈfeɪs] *(connect)* connecter; *(two computers)* mettre en interface, interfacer
VI [ˌɪntəˈfeɪs] avoir une interface (**with** avec); **this device interfaces with most PC's** ce dispositif permet une interface avec la plupart des ordinateurs individuels

interfacing [ˌɪntəˈfeɪsɪŋ] **N** *Sewing* entoilage *m*

interfere [ˌɪntəˈfɪə(r)] **VI 1** *(intrude)* s'immiscer, s'ingérer; **to i. in sb's life** s'immiscer *ou* s'ingérer dans la vie de qn; **I warned him not to i.** je l'ai prévenu de ne pas s'en mêler *ou* de rester à l'écart; **don't i. between them** ne vous mêlez pas de leurs affaires
2 *(clash, conflict)* **to i. with** entraver; **to i. with the course of justice** entraver le cours de la justice; **it interferes with my work** cela me gêne dans mon travail; **he lets his pride i. with his judgment** il laisse son orgueil troubler son jugement
3 *(meddle)* **to i. with** toucher (à); **don't i. with those wires!** laisse ces fils tranquilles!; *Euph* **to i. with a child** se livrer à des attouchements sur un enfant
4 *Phys* interférer; *Chem* perturber
5 *Rad* **local radio sometimes interferes with police transmissions** la radio locale brouille *ou* perturbe parfois les transmissions de la police

interference [ˌɪntəˈfɪərəns] **N 1** *(gen)* ingérence *f*, intervention *f*; *Sport (from opponent)* obstruction *f*; **she won't tolerate i. in** *or* **with her plans** elle ne supporte pas qu'on s'immisce dans ses projets **2** *Phys* interférence *f*; *Chem* perturbation *f* **3** *(UNCOUNT) Rad* parasites *mpl*, interférence *f*
►► *Opt* ***interference figure*** figure *f* d'interférence; *Rad* ***interference filter*** filtre *m* anti-parasites; *Opt* ***interference pattern*** figure *f* d'interférence; *Rad* ***interference suppressor*** filtre *m* antiparasites

interfering [ˌɪntəˈfɪərɪŋ] **ADJ** *(person)* importun

interferon [ˌɪntəˈfɪərɒn] **N** *Med & Physiol* interféron *m*

interhuman [ˌɪntəˈhjuːmən] **ADJ** *Med* interhumain

interim [ˈɪntərɪm] **N** intérim *m*
ADJ *(government, measure, report)* provisoire; *(post, function)* intérimaire; **the i. minister** le ministre par intérim *ou* intérimaire
• **in the interim** **ADV** entretemps
►► *Acct* ***interim accounts*** comptes *mpl* semestriels; *Fin* ***interim dividend*** dividende *m* intérimaire; *Law* ***interim order*** avant faire-droit *m*; ***interim payment*** paiement *m* provisoire; ***the interim period*** l'intérim *m*; *Acct* ***interim profit and loss statement*** compte *m* de résultat prévisionnel; *Acct* ***interim statement*** bilan *m* intérimaire

interior [ɪnˈtɪərɪə(r)] **N 1** *(gen)* intérieur *m*; *Pol* **the French Minister of the I.** le ministre français de l'Intérieur; *Pol* **Secretary/Department of the I.** = ministre/ministère chargé de l'administration des domaines et des parcs nationaux aux États-Unis **2** *Art* (tableau *m* d')intérieur *m*
ADJ intérieur
►► *Math* ***interior angle*** angle *m* interne; ***interior decoration*** décoration *f* (d'intérieurs); ***interior decorator*** décorateur(trice) *m,f* (d'intérieurs); ***interior design*** architecture *f* d'intérieurs; ***interior designer*** architecte *mf* d'intérieurs; *Literature* ***interior monologue*** monologue *m* intérieur; *TV & Cin* ***interior shot*** intérieur *m*, scène *f* d'intérieur; *Aut* ***interior trim*** habillage *m* intérieur

interior-sprung mattress **N** *Br* matelas *m* à ressorts

interject [ˌɪntəˈdʒekt] **VT** *(question, comment)* placer; **"not like that," he interjected** "pas comme ça", coupa-t-il

interjection [ˌɪntəˈdʒekʃən] **N 1** *Ling* interjection *f* **2** *(interruption)* interruption *f*

interlace [ˌɪntəˈleɪs] **VT 1** *(entwine)* entrelacer **2** *(intersperse)* entremêler
VI s'entrelacer, s'entrecroiser

interlaced [ˌɪntəˈleɪst] **ADJ** *Comput (display, monitor)* entrelacé

interlard [ˌɪntəˈlɑːd] **VT** entrelarder (**with** de)

interleave [ˌɪntəˈliːv] **VT** *(book)* interfolier; *(sheet)* intercaler

interletter spacing [ˈɪntəˌletə-] **N** *Typ* interlettrage *m*

interlibrary [ˌɪntəˈlaɪbrərɪ] **ADJ** inter-bibliothèques

interline [ˌɪntəˈlaɪn] **VT 1** *(text)* interligner **2** *Sewing* poser une doublure intermédiaire à
►► *Typ* ***interline spacing*** interligne *m*

interlinear [ˌɪntəˈlɪnɪə(r)] **ADJ** *Typ (text)* interlinéaire

interlining [ˌɪntəˈlaɪnɪŋ] **N** *Sewing* doublure *f* intermédiaire

interlock [ˌɪntəˈlɒk] **VT 1** *Tech* enclencher **2** *(entwine)* entrelacer
VI 1 *Tech (mechanism)* s'enclencher; *(cogwheels)* s'engrener **2** *(groups, issues)* s'imbriquer

interlocking [ˌɪntəˈlɒkɪŋ] **ADJ** *(parts)* emboîtable; *Tech (gears)* qui s'engrènent *ou* s'enclenchent; **i. chairs** chaises *fpl* empilables

interlocutor [ˌɪntəˈlɒkjʊtə(r)] **N** interlocuteur (trice) *m,f*

interloper [ˈɪntələʊpə(r)] **N** intrus(e) *m,f*

interlude [ˈɪntəluːd] **N 1** *(period of time)* intervalle *m*; **a pleasant i. in her troubled life** un moment de répit dans sa vie mouvementée **2** *Theat* intermède *m*; *Mus & TV* interlude *m*

intermarriage [ˌɪntəˈmærɪdʒ] **N 1** *(within family)* mariage *m* consanguin; *(within tribe)* endogamie *f* **2** *(between different races, religions, nationalities)* mariage *m* mixte

intermarry [ˌɪntəˈmærɪ] *(pt & pp* **intermarried***)* **VI 1** *(within family)* se marier entre membres d'une même famille; *(within family)* pratiquer l'endogamie **2** *(between different groups)* **members of different religions intermarried freely** les mariages mixtes se pratiquaient librement

intermediary [ˌɪntəˈmiːdjərɪ] *(pl* **intermediaries***)*
N intermédiaire *mf*
ADJ intermédiaire

intermediate [ˌɪntəˈmiːdjət] **ADJ 1** *(gen)* intermédiaire **2** *Sch (class)* moyen; **an i. English course** un cours d'anglais de niveau moyen *ou* intermédiaire
N 1 *Am (car)* voiture *f* de taille moyenne **2** *Chem* produit *m* intermédiaire
►► *Fin* ***intermediate broker*** intermédiaire *mf*, remisier *m* (en Bourse); *Fin* ***intermediate credit*** crédit *m* à moyen terme; *Elec* ***intermediate frequency*** fréquence *f* moyenne; ***intermediate goods*** biens *mpl* intermédiaires; *Mil* ***intermediate range missile*** missile *m* de moyenne portée *ou* de portée intermédiaire; *Mil* ***intermediate range nuclear forces*** forces *fpl* nucléaires intermédiaires; *NZ* ***intermediate school*** = école qui ne comprend que les classes de sixième et de cinquième; ***intermediate students*** étudiants *mpl* de niveau moyen *ou* intermédiaire; ***intermediate technology*** technologie *f* intermédiaire

interment [ɪnˈtɜːmənt] **N** *Formal* enterrement *m*, inhumation *f*

intermezzo [ˌɪntəˈmetsəʊ] *(pl* **intermezzos** *or* **intermezzi** [-ˈmetsiː]*)* **N** *Theat* intermède *m*; *Mus* intermezzo *m*

interminable [ɪnˈtɜːmɪnəbəl] **ADJ** interminable

interminably [ɪnˈtɜːmɪnəblɪ] **ADV** interminablement; **the play seemed i. long** la pièce semblait interminable; **the discussions dragged on i.** les discussions s'éternisaient

intermingle [ˌɪntəˈmɪŋgəl] **VI** se mêler

intermission [ˌɪntəˈmɪʃən] **N 1** *(break)* pause *f*, trêve *f*; *(in illness, fever)* intermission *f*, intermittence *f*; **without i.** sans relâche **2** *Am Cin & Theat* entracte *m*

intermittent [ˌɪntəˈmɪtənt] **ADJ** intermittent; **i. rain** pluies *fpl* intermittentes, averses *fpl*

intermittently [ˌɪntəˈmɪtəntlɪ] **ADV** par intervalles, par intermittence; **the journal has been published only i.** la revue n'a connu qu'une parution irrégulière

intermodal [ˌɪntəˈməʊdəl] **ADJ 1** *(container)* intermodal **2** *Psy* intermodal

▸▸ ***intermodal transport system*** réseau *m* de transport intermodal

intern N [ˈɪntɜːn] **1** *Med* interne *mf*; *Am Sch* (professeur *m*) stagiaire *mf*; *Am (in firm)* stagiaire *mf* **2** *(internee)* interné(e) *m,f* (politique)

VT [ɪnˈtɜːn] *Pol* interner

VI [ɪnˈtɜːn] *Am Med* faire son internat; *Sch* faire son stage pédagogique; *(with firm)* faire un stage en entreprise

internal [ɪnˈtɜːnəl] **ADJ 1** *(gen)* interne, intérieur; **the i. workings of the mind** les opérations *fpl* secrètes de l'esprit

2 *(inside country)* intérieur

3 *(inside organization, institution)* interne; **i. disputes are crippling the party** des luttes intestines paralysent le parti

4 *Med* interne

N *Med* examen *m* gynécologique

▸▸ ***internal affairs*** affaires *fpl* intérieures; *Fin* ***internal audit*** audit *m* interne; *Fin* ***internal auditor*** audit *m* interne, auditeur(trice) *m,f* interne; ***internal bleeding*** hémorragie *f* interne; *Tel* ***internal cable*** câble *m* d'immeuble; *Comput* ***internal command*** commande *f* interne; ***internal company document*** document *m* interne à l'entreprise; ***internal debt*** endettement *m* intérieur; *Comput* ***internal drive*** unité *f* (de disque) interne; *Med* ***internal examination*** examen *m* interne; *Sch* ***internal examiner*** examinateur(trice) *m,f (faisant passer un examen dans son propre établissement)*; ***internal flight*** vol *m* intérieur; *Econ* ***internal growth*** croissance *f* interne; *Med* ***internal haemorrhage*** hémorragie *f* interne; ***internal injuries*** lésions *fpl* internes; ***internal labour market*** marché *m* interne du travail; ***internal mail*** courrier *m* interne; ***internal marketing*** marketing *m* interne; *Am* ***internal medicine*** médecine *f* générale; ***internal memo*** note *f* à circulation interne; ***internal modem*** modem *m* interne; ***internal rate of return*** taux *m* de rentabilité interne; ***internal revenue*** recettes *fpl* fiscales; *Am Fin* ***the Internal Revenue Service*** le fisc, la Direction Générale des Impôts; ***internal rhyme*** rime *f* intérieure; ***internal telephone*** téléphone *m* intérieur; ***internal travel*** voyages *mpl* à l'intérieur d'un même pays

internalize, -ise [ɪnˈtɜːnəlaɪz] **VT 1** *(values, behaviour, feeling, emotion)* intérioriser **2** *Ind & Fin* internaliser

internally [ɪnˈtɜːnəlɪ] **ADV 1** *(within body, object)* intérieurement; *Pharm* **not to be taken i.** *(on packaging)* à usage externe, ne pas avaler **2** *(within a company, organization)* en interne

international [ˌɪntəˈnæʃənəl] **ADJ** international

N 1 *Sport (match)* match *m* international; *(player)* international(e) *m,f* **2** *Pol* **the I.** l'Internationale *f*; **the First I.** la Première Internationale

▸▸ ***the International Air Transport Association*** l'Association *f* internationale de transport aérien; *Nucl* ***the International Atomic Energy Agency*** l'Agence *f* internationale de l'énergie atomique; *Banking* ***the International Bank for Reconstruction and Development*** la Banque internationale pour la reconstruction et le développement; ***international call*** appel *m* international, communication *f* internationale; *Law* ***the International Chamber of Commerce*** la chambre de commerce internationale; ***the International Court of Justice*** la Cour internationale de justice; ***the International Criminal Court*** la Cour internationale pénale; *Fin* ***international currency*** devise *f* internationale; ***the International Date Line*** la ligne de changement de date; *Tel Br* ***international direct dialling code***, *Am* ***international dial code*** indicatif *m* du pays; *Ind* ***the International Labour Organization*** l'Organisation *f* internationale du travail; *Law* ***international law*** droit *m* international; *Fin* ***the International Monetary Fund*** le Fonds monétaire international; *Fin* ***international monetary reserves*** réserves *fpl* monétaires internationales; *Fin* ***international money market*** marché *m* monétaire international; *Fin* ***international money order*** mandat *m* international; *Sport* ***the International Olympic Committee*** le comité international olympique; *Ling* ***the International Phonetic Alphabet*** l'alphabet *m* phonétique international; *Pol* ***international relations*** relations *fpl* internationales; ***international relief agency*** organisation *f* humanitaire internationale; ***international reply coupon*** coupon-réponse *m* international; ***International Standard Book Number*** ISBN *m*; ***the International Standards Organization*** l'organisation *f* internationale de normalisation; *Com* ***international trading corporation*** société *f* de commerce international, SCI *f*; ***international waters*** eaux *fpl* internationales

internationalism [ˌɪntəˈnæʃənəlɪzəm] **N** internationalisme *m*

internationalize, -ise [ˌɪntəˈnæʃənəlaɪz] **VT** internationaliser

internationally [ˌɪntəˈnæʃənəlɪ] **ADV** internationalement; **i. (speaking), the situation is improving** sur le *ou* au plan international, la situation s'améliore

interne [ˈɪntɜːn] **N** *Am Med* interne *mf*

internecine [*Br* ˌɪntəˈniːsaɪn, *Am* ˌɪntərˈniːsən] **ADJ** *Formal* **1** *(within a group)* intestin; **i. struggles** luttes *fpl* intestines **2** *(mutually destructive)* **i. warfare** guerre *f* qui ravage les deux camps

interned [ɪnˈtɜːnd] **ADJ** *Pol* interné

internee [ˌɪntɜːˈniː] **N** interné(e) *m,f* (politique)

Internet [ˈɪntənet] **N** *Comput* **the I.** l'Internet, l'internet *m*; **to surf the I.** naviguer sur l'Internet *ou* sur Internet

▸▸ ***Internet access*** accès *m* (à l')Internet; ***Internet access provider*** fournisseur *m* d'accès à l'Internet; ***Internet account*** compte *m* Internet; ***Internet address*** adresse *f* Internet; ***Internet bank*** banque *f* en ligne, cyberbanque *f*; ***Internet banking*** opérations *fpl* bancaires par l'Internet; ***Internet café*** cybercafé *m*; ***Internet chatroom*** site *m*, café *m* Internet *ou* salon *m* de bavardage; ***Internet connection*** connexion *f* à l'Internet; ***Internet dating*** rencontres *fpl* sur Internet; ***Internet dating agency*** agence *f* de rencontres sur Internet; ***Internet number*** numéro *m* Internet; ***Internet phone*** téléphone *m* Internet; ***Internet presence provider*** = fournisseur d'accès à l'Internet proposant l'hébergement de sites Web; ***Internet protocol*** protocole *m* Internet; ***Internet relay chat*** service *m* de bavardage Internet, canal *m* de dialogue en direct; ***Internet service provider*** fournisseur *m* d'accès à l'Internet; ***Internet surfer*** internaute *mf*; ***Internet surfing*** navigation *f* sur l'Internet; ***Internet telephone*** téléphone *m* Internet; ***Internet telephony*** téléphonie *f* sur l'Internet; ***Internet user*** internaute *mf*

internist [ɪnˈtɜːnɪst] **N** *Am Med* interniste *mf*, spécialiste *mf* de médecine interne

internment [ɪnˈtɜːnmənt] **N 1** *(gen)* internement *m* (politique); **i. without trial** internement *m* sans jugement **2** *(in Ireland)* = système de détention des personnes suspectées de terrorisme en Irlande du Nord

▸▸ ***internment camp*** camp *m* d'internement

internship [ˈɪntɜːnʃɪp] **N** *Am Med* internat *m*; *(with firm)* stage *m* en entreprise

interoperability [ˌɪntərˌɒpərəˈbɪlətɪ] **N** interopérabilité *f*

interpenetrate [ˌɪntəˈpenɪtreɪt] **VT** *(permeate)* imprégner, pénétrer

interpenetration [ˈɪntəˌpenɪˈtreɪʃən] **N** *(permeation)* imprégnation *f*, pénétration *f*

interpersonal [ˌɪntəˈpɜːsənəl] **ADJ** interpersonnel

▸▸ ***interpersonal relationships*** relations *fpl* interpersonnelles; ***interpersonal skills*** qualités *fpl* relationnelles

interplanetary [ˌɪntəˈplænɪtrɪ] **ADJ** *Astron* interplanétaire

▸▸ ***interplanetary matter*** matière *f* interplanétaire

interplay [ˈɪntəpleɪ] **N** *(between forces, events, people)* interaction *f*; **the i. of colours** le jeu des couleurs

Interpol [ˈɪntəpɒl] **N** Interpol

interpolate [ɪnˈtɜːpəleɪt] **VT 1** *Formal (passage or text)* interpoler **2** *Formal (interrupt)* interrompre **"that's utter nonsense," she interpolated** "c'est complètement absurde", interrompit-elle **3** *Math* interpoler

interpolation [ɪnˌtɜːpəˈleɪʃən] **N 1** *Formal (gen)* interpolation *f* **2** *Math & Comput* interpolation *f*

interpose [ˌɪntəˈpəʊz] **VT 1** *(between objects)* interposer, intercaler **2** *(interject)* lancer; **"that simply isn't true!" he interposed** "c'est tout simplement faux!" lança-t-il

interpret [ɪnˈtɜːprɪt] **VT** interpréter

VI servir d'interprète, faire l'interprète; **can you i. for me?** est-ce que vous pouvez me servir d'interprète?

interpretation [ɪnˌtɜːprɪˈteɪʃən] **N** interprétation *f*; **she puts quite a different i. on the facts** l'interprétation qu'elle donne des faits est assez différente; **she wasn't sure what i. to put on the remarks** elle ne savait pas trop comment elle devait interpréter ces remarques; **to be open to i.** donner lieu à interprétation

▸▸ *Can* ***interpretation centre*** = centre d'accueil et de documentation pour les visiteurs d'un site touristique

interpretative [ɪnˈtɜːprɪtətɪv] **ADJ** interprétatif

interpreter [ɪnˈtɜːprɪtə(r)] **N 1** *(person)* interprète *mf* **2** *Comput (software)* interpréteur *m*

interpreting [ɪnˈtɜːprɪtɪŋ] **N** *(occupation)* interprétariat *m*, interprétation *f*

interpretive [ɪnˈtɜːprɪtɪv] **ADJ** interprétatif

▸▸ ***interpretive centre*** = centre d'accueil et de documentation pour les visiteurs d'un site touristique

interracial [ˌɪntəˈreɪʃəl] **ADJ** *(relations, harmony)* interracial

interregnum [ˌɪntəˈregnəm] (*pl* **interregnums** *or* **interregna** [-ˈregnə]) **N** interrègne *m*

interrelation [ˌɪntərɪˈleɪʃən], **interrelationship** [ˌɪntərɪˈleɪʃənʃɪp] **N** corrélation *f*

interrogate [ɪnˈterəgeɪt] **VT** *(gen) & Comput* interroger

interrogation [ɪnˌterəˈgeɪʃən] **N** *(gen) & Ling & Comput* interrogation *f*; *(by police)* interrogatoire *m*; **to undergo (an) i.** subir un interrogatoire **she's been under i.** elle a subi un interrogatoire

▸▸ *Mil* ***interrogation centre*** *(for prisoners of war)* centre *m* d'interrogatoires; *Br* ***interrogation mark***, *Am* ***interrogation point*** point *m* d'interrogation

> Note that the primary sense of **interrogation** in English, as in a police interrogation, is translated by **interrogatoire** and not **interrogation**.

interrogative [ˌɪntəˈrɒgətɪv] **N** *Gram (word)* interrogatif *m*; *(grammatical form)* interrogative *f*; **in the i.** à la forme interrogative

ADJ 1 *(inquiring)* interrogateur **2** *Gram* interrogatif

interrogatively [ˌɪntəˈrɒgətɪvlɪ] **ADV 1** *(look)* interrogativement, d'un air interrogateur; *(remark)* d'un *ou* sur un ton interrogateur **2** *Gram* interrogativement

interrogator [ɪnˈterəgeɪtə(r)] **N** *(questioner)* interrogateur(trice) *m,f*

interrogatory [ˌɪntəˈrɒgətrɪ] **ADJ** interrogateur

interrupt [ˌɪntəˈrʌpt] **VT 1** *(lecture, conversation)* interrompre; *(person talking)* interrompre, couper la parole à; **am I interrupting something?** est-ce que je vous dérange? **2** *(process, activity)* interrompre; **we i. this programme for a news flash** nous interrompons notre émission pour un flash d'information **3** *(uniformity)* rompre; **only an occasional tree interrupted the monotony of the landscape** seul un arbre ici et là venait rompre la monotonie du paysage

VI interrompre; **he tried to explain but you kept interrupting** il a essayé de s'expliquer mais vous n'avez cessé de l'interrompre *ou* de lui couper la parole; **sorry to i. but...** désolé de vous interrompre mais...

N *Comput* interruption *f*

nterruption [ˌɪntəˈrʌpʃən] **N** interruption *f*; **without i.** sans interruption, sans arrêt; **he hates interruptions** il a horreur d'être interrompu

nterscholastic [ˌɪntəskəˈlæstɪk] **ADJ** interscolaire, inter-écoles

ntersect [ˌɪntəˈsekt] **VI** se couper, se croiser; *Math* **intersecting lines** lignes *fpl* intersectées

VT couper, croiser; **the valley is intersected by a network of small roads** la vallée est quadrillée d'innombrables petites routes; **the two lines i. each other** les deux lignes se coupent *ou* se croisent

ntersection [ˌɪntəˈsekʃən] **N 1** *esp Am (road junction)* carrefour *m*, croisement *m* **2** *Math* intersection *f*; **point of i.** point *m* d'intersection

nterspace [ˌɪntəˈspeɪs] **VT** *Typ* espacer

ntersperse [ˌɪntəˈspɜːs] **VT** parsemer, semer; **our conversation was interspersed with long silences** notre conversation était ponctuée de longs silences; **there were small blue flowers interspersed amongst the daisies** les marguerites étaient parsemées de petites fleurs bleues; **sunny weather interspersed with the odd shower** temps ensoleillé entrecoupé de quelques averses

nterstate [ˈɪntəsteɪt] *Am* **N** autoroute *f*

ADJ *(commerce, highway)* entre États

▸▸ ***interstate carrier*** transporteur *m* inter-États

nterstellar [ˌɪntəˈstelə(r)] **ADJ** *Astron* interstellaire

▸▸ ***interstellar space*** espace *m* interstellaire

nterstice [ɪnˈtɜːstɪs] **N** interstice *m*

ntertextual [ˌɪntəˈtekstjʊəl] **ADJ** *Literature* intertextuel

ntertextuality [ˌɪntəˈtekstjʊˈælətɪ] **N** *Literature* intertextualité *f*

ntertitle [ˈɪntəˌtaɪtəl] **N** *Cin* intertitre *m*

ntertribal [ˌɪntəˈtraɪbəl] **ADJ** entre tribus

ntertwine [ˌɪntəˈtwaɪn] **VT** entrelacer; **their lives are inextricably intertwined** leurs vies sont inextricablement liées

VI s'entrelacer; **intertwining branches** branches *fpl* entrelacées

nterurban [ˌɪntəˈɜːbən] **ADJ** interurbain

nterval [ˈɪntəvəl] **N 1** *(period of time)* intervalle *m*; **there was an i. of three months between applying for the job and being accepted** trois mois se sont écoulés entre la candidature et l'embauche; **I saw him again after an i. of six months** je l'ai revu après un intervalle de six mois; **at intervals** par intervalles, de temps en temps; **at regular intervals** à intervalles réguliers; **at short intervals** à intervalles rapprochés; **at weekly intervals** toutes les semaines, chaque semaine

2 *(interlude)* pause *f*; *Br Cin & Theat* entracte *m*; *Sport* mi-temps *f*

3 *(distance)* intervalle *m*, distance *f*; **at two-metre intervals** à deux mètres d'écart, à un intervalle de deux mètres; **trees planted at regular intervals** des arbres plantés à intervalles réguliers

4 *Met* **sunny intervals** éclaircies *fpl*

5 *Math & Mus* intervalle *m*

▸▸ *Med* ***interval surgery*** opération *f* à froid; *Sport* ***interval training*** entraînement *m* par intervalles, interval training *m*

intervene [ˌɪntəˈviːn] **VI 1** *(person, government)* intervenir; **I warned him not to i.** *(in fight)* je lui avais bien dit de ne pas intervenir *ou* s'interposer; *(in argument)* je lui avais bien dit de ne pas s'en mêler; **the government intervened to save the dollar from falling** le gouvernement est intervenu pour arrêter la chute du dollar

2 *(event)* survenir; **he was about to go to college when war intervened** il allait entrer à l'université lorsque la guerre a éclaté

3 *(time)* s'écouler

4 *(interrupt)* intervenir; **if I might just i. here...** si je peux me permettre d'intervenir sur ce point...

intervening [ˌɪntəˈviːnɪŋ] **ADJ** *(period of time)* intermédiaire; **during the i. period** dans l'intervalle, entre-temps

intervention [ˌɪntəˈvenʃən] **N** intervention *f*; **armed i.** intervention *f* armée

▸▸ *Mil* ***intervention forces*** forces *fpl* d'intervention; *Econ* ***intervention price*** prix *m* d'intervention; *Fin* ***intervention rate*** taux *m* d'intervention

interventional [ˌɪntəˈvenʃənəl] **ADJ** *Med (radiology)* interventionnel

interventionism [ˌɪntəˈvenʃənɪzəm] **N** *Econ* interventionnisme *m*

interventionist [ˌɪntəˈvenʃənɪst] *Econ* **N** interventionniste *mf*

ADJ interventionniste

interview [ˈɪntəvjuː] **N 1** *(for job, university place etc)* entrevue *f*, entretien *m*; **interviews will be held at our London offices** les entretiens se dérouleront dans nos bureaux de Londres; **he's already had several interviews** il a déjà eu plusieurs entretiens; **to invite** *or* **to call sb for i.** convoquer qn pour une entrevue *ou* un entretien **2** *Press, Rad & TV* interview *f*; **she gave him an exclusive i.** elle lui a accordé une interview en exclusivité **3** *(in survey, for research)* entretien *m*

VT 1 *(for job, university place etc)* avoir une entrevue *ou* un entretien avec; **shortlisted applicants will be interviewed in March** les candidats sélectionnés seront convoqués pour un entretien en mars; **we have interviewed ten people for the post** nous avons déjà vu dix personnes pour ce poste

2 *Press, Rad & TV* interviewer; **she's being interviewed by their top reporter** leur meilleur journaliste l'interviewe *ou* l'interroge en ce moment

3 *(in survey, for research)* interroger, sonder; **900 voters were interviewed** 900 électeurs ont été interrogés, l'enquête a été effectuée auprès de 900 électeurs

4 *(of police)* interroger, questionner; **he is being interviewed in connection with a series of thefts** on l'interroge pour une série de vols

VI *(job interviewer)* faire passer un entretien; **I'm interviewing all day** je fais passer des entretiens toute la journée; **he interviews well/badly** *(candidate)* il s'en sort/ne s'en sort pas bien aux entretiens; *(celebrity)* il passe/ne passe pas bien dans les interviews

▸▸ ***interview room*** salle *f* d'entretien

interviewee [ˌɪntəvjuːˈiː] **N** personne *f* interviewée

interviewer [ˈɪntəvjuːə(r)] **N 1** *(for job, university place etc)* **the i. asked me what my present salary was** la personne qui m'a fait passer l'entretien *ou* l'entrevue m'a demandé quel était mon salaire actuel **2** *Press, Rad & TV* interviewer *m*, intervieweur(euse) *m,f* **3** *(in survey, for research)* enquêteur(euse) *m,f*

interwar [ˌɪntəˈwɔː(r)] **ADJ** *Hist* **the i. period, the i. years** l'entre-deux-guerres *m inv*

interweave [ˌɪntəˈwiːv] *(pt* **interwove** [-ˈwəʊv] *or* **interweaved**, *pp* **interwoven** [-ˈwəʊvən] *or* **interweaved)** **VT** entrelacer; **interwoven with** entrelacé de; *Fig* **our lives have become closely interwoven** nos deux vies sont devenues intimement liées

VI s'entrelacer, s'entremêler

interword spacing [ˈɪntəˈwɜːd-] **N** *Typ* espacement *m* entre les mots

intestate [ɪnˈtesteɪt] *Law* **ADJ** intestat *(inv)*; **to die i.** décéder intestat

N intestat *mf*

▸▸ ***intestate estate, intestate succession*** succession *f* ab intestat

intestinal [ɪnˈtestɪnəl] **ADJ** *Anat* intestinal

▸▸ *Am* ***intestinal fortitude*** cran *m*; *Biol & Med* ***intestinal flora*** flore *f* intestinale

intestine [ɪnˈtestɪn] **N** *(usu pl) Anat* intestin *m*; **large i.** gros intestin *m*; **small i.** intestin *m* grêle

intifada [ˌɪntɪˈfɑːdə] **N** intifada *f*

intimacy [ˈɪntɪməsɪ] *(pl* **intimacies)** **N 1** *(closeness, warmth)* intimité *f*

2 *(privacy)* intimité *f*; **in the i. of one's own home** dans l'intimité du foyer

3 *(intimate remark etc)* familiarité *f*; **they never really exchanged intimacies** ils ont toujours gardé une certaine réserve l'un envers l'autre

4 *(UNCOUNT) Euph Formal (sexual relations)* relations *fpl* sexuelles, rapports *mpl*; **i. took place on more than one occasion** ils ont eu des rapports à plusieurs reprises

intimate **ADJ** [ˈɪntɪmət] **1** *(friend, relationship)* intime; **we were never very i.** nous n'avons jamais été (des amis) intimes; **we're on i. terms with them** nous sommes très amis, ils font partie de nos amis intimes

2 *(small and cosy)* intime; **an i. dinner for two** un dîner en amoureux; **an i. (little) dinner party** un dîner en tête-à-tête, un petit dîner à deux

3 *Euph Formal (sexually)* **they were i. on more than one occasion** ils ont eu des rapports (intimes) à plusieurs reprises; **he admitted to having had i. relations with her** il a reconnu avoir eu des rapports avec elle

4 *(personal, private)* intime; *Hum* **spare me the i. details!** fais-moi grâce de tous ces détails!

5 *(thorough)* profond, approfondi; **she has an i. knowledge of the field** elle connaît le sujet à fond

6 *(close, direct)* étroit; **an i. link** un lien étroit

N [ˈɪntɪmət] intime *mf*

VT [ˈɪntɪmeɪt] **1** *(hint, imply)* laisser entendre, insinuer; **he intimated that he had had an affair with her** il a laissé entendre qu'il avait eu une liaison avec elle; **her speech intimated strong disapproval** son discours laissait paraître son profond désaccord **2** *Formal (make known* ▸ *order)* intimer; *(*▸ *one's intentions)* signifier

intimately [ˈɪntɪmətlɪ] **ADV 1** *(talk, behave* ▸ *in a friendly way)* intimement; **to know sb i.** connaître qn intimement **2** *(know* ▸ *thoroughly)* à fond; *(*▸ *closely, directly)* étroitement; **the two questions are i. related** les deux questions sont intimement liées; **I am i. acquainted with the details of the matter** je connais l'affaire dans ses moindres détails

intimation [ˌɪntɪˈmeɪʃən] **N** *Formal (suggestion)* suggestion *f*; *(sign)* indice *m*, indication *f*; *(premonition)* pressentiment *m*; **we had no i. that disaster was imminent** rien ne laissait pressentir l'imminence d'une catastrophe; **her letter was the first i. we had that she was in any danger** sa lettre a été pour nous le premier indice du danger qu'elle courait

intimidate [ɪnˈtɪmɪdeɪt] **VT** intimider; **to i. sb into doing sth** intimider qn pour qu'il fasse qch

intimidating [ɪnˈtɪmɪdeɪtɪŋ] **ADJ** intimidant

intimidation [ɪnˌtɪmɪˈdeɪʃən] **N** *(UNCOUNT)* intimidation *f*, menaces *fpl*

into [ˈɪntʊ] **PREP 1** *(indicating direction, movement etc)* dans; **come i. my office** venez dans mon bureau; **to run/stroll i. a room** entrer dans une pièce en courant/d'un pas nonchalant; **they sank deeper i. debt** ils se sont endettés de plus en plus; **to feed data i. a computer** entrer des données dans un ordinateur; **planes take off i. the wind** les avions décollent face au vent

2 *(indicating collision)* dans; **the truck ran** *or* **crashed i. the wall** le camion est rentré dans *ou* s'est écrasé contre le mur

3 *(indicating transformation)* en; **the frog changed i. a prince** la grenouille s'est transformée en prince; **he's grown i. a man** c'est un homme maintenant; **mix the ingredients i. a paste** mélangez les ingrédients jusqu'à ce qu'ils forment une pâte

4 *(indicating result)* **to frighten sb i. confessing** faire avouer qn en lui faisant peur; **they were shocked i. silence** le choc leur a fait perdre la parole

5 *(indicating division)* en; **cut it i. three** coupe-le en trois; **7 i. 63 goes 9** 63 divisé par 7 donne 9; **6 i. 10 won't go** on ne peut pas diviser 10 par 6

6 *(indicating elapsed time)* **we worked well i. the night** nous avons travaillé (jusque) tard dans la nuit; **he must be well i. his forties** il doit avoir largement dépassé la quarantaine; **a week i. her holiday and she's bored already** il y a à peine une semaine qu'elle est en vacances et elle s'ennuie déjà

7 *Fam (fond of)* **to be i. sb/sth** *(like)* bien aimer qn/qch[□]; **I was never really i. pop music** je n'ai jamais été un fana de musique pop; **is he i. drugs?** est-ce qu'il se drogue?[□]; **he's i. leather** il est cuir; **we're not i. cheating people** *(that's not our style)* nous ne cherchons pas à rouler les gens

8 *(curious about)* **the baby's i. everything** le bébé est curieux de tout

9 *Am (in debt to)* **he's i. them for $5,000** il leur doit 5000 dollars

intolerable [ɪnˈtɒlərəbəl] ADJ intolérable, insupportable; **I find it i. that...** je trouve intolérable que...

intolerably [ɪnˈtɒlərəblɪ] ADV intolérablement, insupportablement; **he had been i. rude** il avait été d'une grossièreté intolérable

intolerance [ɪnˈtɒlərəns] N *(gen) & Med* intolérance *f*

intolerant [ɪnˈtɒlərənt] ADJ intolérant; **she is very i. of noisy children** elle ne supporte absolument pas les enfants bruyants; *Med* **to be i. of a drug** ne pas tolérer *ou* supporter un médicament

intolerantly [ɪnˈtɒlərəntlɪ] ADV avec intolérance

intonation [ˌɪntəˈneɪʃən] N intonation *f*

▸▸ *Ling* ***intonation pattern*** intonation *f*

intone [ɪnˈtəʊn] VT psalmodier

intoxicate [ɪnˈtɒksɪkeɪt] VT **1** *also Fig (make drunk)* enivrer, griser **2** *Med (poison)* intoxiquer

intoxicated [ɪnˈtɒksɪkeɪtɪd] ADJ **1** *(drunk)* ivre, *Formal* en état d'ébriété **2** *Fig* ivre; **she was i. by success** son succès l'avait grisée *ou* lui avait fait tourner la tête

intoxicating [ɪnˈtɒksɪkeɪtɪŋ] ADJ enivrant; *Fig* grisant, enivrant, excitant; **an i. perfume** un parfum enivrant *ou* capiteux

▸▸ ***intoxicating liquor*** boisson *f* alcoolisée

intoxication [ɪnˌtɒksɪˈkeɪʃən] N **1** *also Fig* ivresse *f* **2** *Med (poisoning)* intoxication *f*

intra-Community [ˌɪntrəkəˈmjuːnɪtɪ] ADJ *EU* intracommunautaire

intra-company [ˌɪntrəˈkʌmpənɪ] ADJ *Com* intra-entreprise *(inv)*

intractability [ɪnˌtræktəˈbɪlətɪ] N **1** *(of person)* intransigeance *f*, fermeté *f*, opiniâtreté *f* **2** *(of problem)* caractère *m* insoluble, insolubilité *f*; *(of situation)* caractère *m* inextricable

intractable [ɪnˈtræktəbəl] ADJ **1** *(person)* intraitable, intransigeant **2** *(problem)* insoluble; *(situation)* inextricable, sans issue

intraday [ˌɪntrəˈdeɪ] ADJ *St Exch* intrajournalier

intramural [ˌɪntrəˈmjʊərəl] ADJ *Sch & Univ (courses, sports)* interne (à l'établissement); **i. teams** = équipes sportives d'un même établissement jouant les unes contre les autres

intramuscular [ˌɪntrəˈmʌskjʊlə(r)] ADJ *Med* intramusculaire

Intranet [ˈɪntrənet] N *Comput* Intranet *m*

intransigence [ɪnˈtrænzɪdʒəns] N intransigeance *f*

intransigent [ɪnˈtrænzɪdʒənt] N intransigeant (e) *m,f*

ADJ intransigeant

intransitive [ɪnˈtrænsətɪv] *Gram* N intransitif *m*

ADJ intransitif

intransitively [ɪnˈtrænsətɪvlɪ] ADV *Gram* intransitivement

intransmissibility [ˌɪntrænsmɪsɪˈbɪlɪtɪ] N intransmissibilité *f*

intransmissible [ˌɪntrænsˈmɪsɪbəl] ADJ intransmissible

intrastate [ˌɪntrəˈsteɪt] ADJ à l'intérieur d'un même État

intrauterine [ˌɪntrəˈjuːtəraɪn] ADJ *Med* intra-utérin

▸▸ *Med* ***intrauterine contraceptive device*** stérilet *m*

intravenous [ˌɪntrəˈviːnəs] ADJ *Med* intraveineux

▸▸ ***intravenous drip*** perfusion *f* intraveineuse; ***intravenous drugs user*** = toxicomane qui s'injecte sa drogue; ***intravenous injection*** (injection *f*) intraveineuse *f*

intravenously [ˌɪntrəˈviːnəslɪ] ADV *Med* par voie intraveineuse; **he's being fed i.** on l'alimente par perfusion; **to take drugs i.** s'injecter de la drogue

in-tray N *Br* corbeille *f* de courrier à traiter *ou* "arrivée"; **put it in my i.** posez ça sur le courrier à traiter

intrepid [ɪnˈtrepɪd] ADJ intrépide

intrepidity [ˌɪntrɪˈpɪdɪtɪ] N intrépidité *f*

intrepidly [ɪnˈtrepɪdlɪ] ADV intrépidement

intricacy [ˈɪntrɪkəsɪ] *(pl* **intricacies***)* N **1** *(complicated detail)* complexité *f*; **he knows all the legal intricacies** il connaît toutes les subtilités du droit; **I couldn't follow all the intricacies of her argument** je n'ai pas suivi toutes les subtilités de son raisonnement **2** *(complexity)* complexité *f*

intricate [ˈɪntrɪkət] ADJ *(mechanism, drawing, design)* compliqué; *(question, argument, plot)* complexe

intricately [ˈɪntrɪkətlɪ] ADV de façon complexe *ou* compliquée; **an i. carved chair** une chaise aux sculptures complexes *ou* très travaillées

intrigue N [ˈɪntriːg] **1** *(plotting)* intrigue *f* **2** *(plot, treason)* complot *m* **3** *(love affair)* intrigue *f*

VT [ɪnˈtriːg] intriguer; **I'd be intrigued to know where they met** je serais curieux de savoir où ils se sont rencontrés

VI [ɪnˈtriːg] intriguer, comploter; **they intrigued with republicans against the throne** ils ont comploté avec des Républicains contre le roi

intriguing [ɪnˈtriːgɪŋ] ADJ curieux; **I find the whole thing most i.** tout cela me paraît très curieux

intrinsic [ɪnˈtrɪnsɪk] ADJ intrinsèque; **the picture has little i. value** ce tableau a peu de valeur en soi; **such ideas are i. to my argument** de telles idées sont essentielles *ou* inhérentes à mon raisonnement

▸▸ *St Exch* ***intrinsic value*** valeur *f* intrinsèque

intrinsically [ɪnˈtrɪnsɪklɪ] ADV intrinsèquement

intro [ˈɪntrəʊ] *(pl* **intros***)* N *Fam (introduction)* intro *f*

introduce [ˌɪntrəˈdjuːs] VT **1** *(present ▸ one person to another)* présenter; **she introduced me to her sister** elle m'a présenté à sa sœur; **may I i. you?** permettez-moi de *ou* laissez-moi vous présenter; **let me i. myself, I'm John** je me présente? John; **I don't think we've been introduced, have we?** nous n'avons pas été présentés, je crois; **to i. a speaker** présenter un conférencier; **the main character is introduced in chapter 2** le personnage principal fait son apparition au chapitre 2; *Cin* **introducing Simon McLean** et pour la première fois à l'écran, Simon McLean; **to be introduced to society** *(débutante)* faire son entrée dans le monde

2 *(radio or TV programme)* présenter

3 *(bring in)* introduire; **when were rabbits introduced into Australia?** quand a-t-on introduit les lapins en Australie?; **I'd like to i. a new topic into the debate, if I may** si vous le permettez, j'aimerais introduire dans le débat un nouveau sujet; *Mus* **the arpeggio introduces the final movement** l'arpège marque le début du dernier mouvement

4 *(laws, legislation)* déposer, présenter; *(reform, fashion, new methods)* introduire; **the government hopes to i. the new bill next week** le gouvernement espère déposer son nouveau projet de loi la semaine prochaine

5 *(initiate)* initier; **to i. sb to sth** initier qn à qch, faire découvrir qch à qn; **she introduced me to the pleasures of French cooking** elle m'a initié aux *ou* révélé les délices de la cuisine française

6 *(start)* ouvrir, donner le départ de; **a fanfare introduced the start of the ceremony** une fanfare a ouvert la cérémonie

7 *Formal (insert)* introduire

8 *Gram (phrase)* introduire

9 *Com (product)* lancer; *St Exch (shares)* introduire

introduction [ˌɪntrəˈdʌkʃən] N **1** *(of one person to another)* présentation *f*; *Fam* **would you do** *or* **make the introductions?** peux-tu faire les présentations?; **our next guest needs no i.** inutile de vous présenter l'invité suivant

2 *(first part ▸ of speech, piece of music)* introduction *f*; *(▸ of book)* introduction *f*, avant-propos *m inv*

3 *(basic textbook, course)* introduction *f*, initiation *f*; **an i. to linguistics** une introduction à la linguistique

4 *(bringing in)* introduction *f*; **the i. of computer technology into schools** l'introduction de l'informatique à l'école

5 *(of bill, law)* introduction *f*, présentation *f*; *(of reform, fashion, new methods)* introduction *f*

6 *(initiation)* introduction *f*, premier contact *m*; **this was my i. to Shakespeare** ça a été mon premier contact avec Shakespeare; **this record is a good i. to her work** cet album constitue une bonne introduction à son œuvre

7 *Formal (insertion)* introduction *f*

8 *Com (of product)* lancement *m*; *St Exch (of shares)* introduction *f* au marché hors cote

introductory [ˌɪntrəˈdʌktrɪ] ADJ *(remarks)* préliminaire; *(chapter, course)* d'introduction; **after a few i. words** après quelques mots d'introduction

▸▸ *Com* ***introductory offer*** offre *f* de lancement; *Com* ***introductory price*** prix *m* de lancement

intro-ident N *TV & Rad* identification *f* d'intro

introit [ˈɪntrɔɪt] N *Mus & Rel* introït *m*

introspection [ˌɪntrəˈspekʃən] N introspection *f*

introspective [ˌɪntrəˈspektɪv] ADJ introspectif

introversion [ˌɪntrəˈvɜːʃən] N *Psy* introversion *f*

introvert [ˈɪntrəvɜːt] *Psy* N introverti(e) *m,f*

VT introvertir

introverted [ˈɪntrəvɜːtɪd] ADJ introverti; **she's become very i. since the accident** elle est devenue très renfermée depuis l'accident

intrude [ɪnˈtruːd] VI **1** *(disturb)* déranger, s'imposer; **disturbing memories kept intruding** de douloureux souvenirs continuaient à le/me/*etc* hanter; **I hope I'm not intruding** j'espère que je ne vous dérange pas **2** *(interfere)* **I don't let my work i. on my private life** je ne laisse pas mon travail empiéter sur ma vie privée; **they're intruding on our private lives** ils se mêlent de *ou* ils s'immiscent dans notre vie privée; **I felt I was intruding on their grief** j'ai eu l'impression de les déranger dans leur chagrin; **a supermarket would i. on the character of the village** un supermarché gâcherait le caractère pittoresque du village **3** *Geol* pénétrer par intrusion

VT *Formal* imposer; **a doubt intruded itself into my mind** un doute m'est venu à l'esprit

intruder [ɪnˈtruːdə(r)] N *(criminal)* intrus *m*; *(outsider)* intrus(e) *m,f*, importun(e) *m,f*; **they made us feel like intruders** nous avons eu l'impression de déranger *ou* d'être de trop

intrusion [ɪnˈtruːʒən] N **1** *(gen)* intrusion *f*, ingérence *f*; **it's an i. into our privacy** c'est une intrusion dans notre vie privée **2** *Geol* intrusion *f*

intrusive [ɪnˈtruːsɪv] ADJ **1** *(person)* importun; **he was an i. presence in the house** sa présence dans la maison était importune; **far away from the i. sounds of the city** loin de la rumeur importune de la ville **2** *Geol* intrusif

▸▸ *Ling* ***intrusive consonant*** consonne *f* d'appui

intubate [ˈɪntjʊbeɪt] VT *Med* intuber

intuit [ɪnˈtjuːɪt] VT *Formal* savoir *ou* connaître intuitivement; **I could only i. what had happened between them** je n'ai pu que deviner ce qui s'était passé entre eux

intuition [ˌɪntjuːˈɪʃən] N intuition *f*; **I had an i. something was wrong** j'avais le sentiment que quelque chose n'allait pas

intuitive [ɪnˈtjuːɪtɪv] ADJ intuitif; **an i. understanding** une connaissance intuitive; **he's very i.** c'est un intuitif

intuitively [ɪnˈtjuːɪtɪvlɪ] ADV intuitivement; **knew i. that she was lying** je savais intuitivement qu'elle mentait, je sentais bien qu'elle ne disait pas la vérité

Inuit [ˈɪnʊɪt] *(pl* **inv** *or* **Inuits***)* N Inuit *mf*

ADJ inuit

inundate [ˈɪnʌndeɪt] VT *also Fig* inonder; **we've been inundated with phone calls/letters** nous avons été submergés de coups de fil/courrier; **I'm inundated with work just now** pour l'instant je suis débordé (de travail) *ou* je croule sous le travail

inundation [ˌɪnʌnˈdeɪʃən] N inondation *f*

inure [ɪˈnjʊə(r)] VT aguerrir; **to become inured to sth** s'habituer à qch

invade [ɪnˈveɪd] VT **1** *Mil* envahir **2** *Fig* envahir; **the village was invaded by reporters** les journalistes ont envahi le village; **her mind was invaded by sudden doubts** le doute s'empara soudain de son esprit; **to i. sb's privacy** s'immiscer dans la vie privée de qn

invader [ɪn'veɪdə(r)] **N** envahisseur(euse) *m,f*; **to repel invaders** repousser l'envahisseur

invading [ɪn'veɪdɪŋ] **ADJ 1** *(army)* d'invasion; **the i. barbarians** l'envahisseur barbare **2** *(plants, insects)* envahissant

invalid¹ ['ɪnvəlɪd] **N** *(disabled person)* infirme *mf*, invalide *mf*; *(ill person)* malade *mf*; **I'm not an i.!** je ne suis pas infirme!

ADJ *(disabled)* infirme, invalide; *(ill)* malade; **he has to look after his i. mother** il doit s'occuper de sa mère infirme

VT 1 *(disable)* rendre infirme **2** *Br Mil* **he was invalided home** il a été rapatrié pour raisons médicales

▸▸ *Br* ***invalid car, invalid carriage*** voiture *f* d'infirme; ***invalid chair*** fauteuil *m* roulant

invalid² [ɪn'vælɪd] **ADJ 1** *(passport, ticket)* non valide, non valable; **your passport will soon be i.** votre passeport sera bientôt périmé

2 *(law, marriage, election)* nul

3 *(argument)* non valable; **your reasoning is i.** votre raisonnement n'est pas valable *ou* ne tient pas

4 *Comput* invalide

▸▸ *Comput* ***invalid file name*** nom *m* de fichier invalide

▸ **invalid out VT SEP** *Mil* **to i. sb out of the army** réformer qn pour raisons médicales

invalidate [ɪn'vælɪdeɪt] **VT 1** *(contract, agreement)* invalider, annuler; *(verdict)* casser, infirmer **2** *(argument)* infirmer

invalidation [ɪnˌvælɪ'deɪʃən] **N 1** *(of contract, agreement)* invalidation *f*, annulation *f*; *(of verdict)* infirmation *f*, cassation *f* **2** *(of argument)* infirmation *f*

invalidity [ˌɪnvə'lɪdətɪ] **N 1** *Med* invalidité *f* **2** *(of contract, agreement etc)* manque *m* de validité, nullité *f* **3** *(of argument)* manque *m* de fondement; **to demonstrate the i. of an argument** prouver qu'un argument n'est pas valable

▸▸ *Br* ***invalidity benefit*** prestation *f* d'invalidité *(aujourd'hui remplacée par l'"incapacity benefit")*; *Br* ***invalidity pension*** pension *f* d'invalidité

invaluable [ɪn'væljʊəbəl] **ADJ** inestimable, très précieux; **your help has been i. (to me)** votre aide m'a été très précieuse; **she's an i. asset (to the company)** elle représente un atout inestimable (pour l'entreprise)

> Attention: ne pas confondre avec l'adjectif **valueless**, qui signifie **sans valeur.**

invariability [ɪnˌveərɪə'bɪlɪtɪ] **N** constance *f*

invariable [ɪn'veərɪəbəl] **N** *Math* constante *f*

ADJ invariable

invariably [ɪn'veərɪəblɪ] **ADV** invariablement; **almost i.** presque toujours

invariant [ɪn'veərɪənt] *Math* **N** invariant *m*

ADJ invariant

invasion [ɪn'veɪʒən] **N 1** *Mil* invasion *f*, envahissement *m*; **the Roman i. of England** l'invasion de l'Angleterre par les Romains **2** *Fig* invasion *f*, intrusion *f*; **a pitch i.** une intrusion des supporters sur le terrain; **we expect the usual i. of tourists this summer** nous nous attendons à l'habituelle invasion de touristes cet été

▸▸ *Law* ***invasion of privacy*** atteinte *f* à la vie privée; **he considered it an i. of (his) privacy** il l'a ressenti comme une intrusion dans sa vie privée

invasive [ɪn'veɪsɪv] **ADJ** *Med (treatment)* invasif

▸▸ *Med* ***invasive surgery*** chirurgie *f* invasive *ou* effractoire

invective [ɪn'vektɪv] **N** *(UNCOUNT)* invective *f*, invectives *fpl*; **a stream of i.** un torrent d'invectives

inveigh [ɪn'veɪ] **VI** *Formal* **to i. against sb/sth** invectiver qn/qch

inveigle [ɪn'veɪgəl] **VT** entortiller; **he had been inveigled into letting them in** on l'avait adroitement manipulé pour qu'il les laisse entrer; **she inveigled him into giving her a lift** elle a réussi à l'entortiller pour qu'il la conduise en voiture

inveiglement [ɪn'veɪgəlmənt] **N** captation *f*

inveigler [ɪn'veɪglə(r)] **N** captateur(trice) *m,f*

invent [ɪn'vent] **VT 1** *(new machine, process)* inventer **2** *(lie, excuse)* inventer; **he invented a movie-star mother** il s'est inventé une mère star de cinéma

invention [ɪn'venʃən] **N 1** *(discovery, creation)* invention *f*; **television is a wonderful i.** la télévision est une invention merveilleuse; **a story of his own i.** une histoire de son cru **2** *(untruth)* invention *f*, fabrication *f*; **the whole thing was an i. of the press** la presse a inventé *ou* monté cette histoire de bout en bout; **it was pure i.** ce n'était que pure invention, c'était complètement faux

inventive [ɪn'ventɪv] **ADJ** *(person, mind)* inventif; *(plan, solution)* ingénieux

inventiveness [ɪn'ventɪvnɪs] **N** esprit *m* d'invention, inventivité *f*

inventor [ɪn'ventə(r)] **N** inventeur(trice) *m,f*

inventory [*Br* 'ɪnvəntərɪ, *Am* 'ɪnvən'tɔːrɪ] *(pl* **inventories,** *pt & pp* **inventoried) N** *Com* **1** *(list)* inventaire *m*; **to draw up** *or* **to make an i.** dresser un inventaire; **to take the i.** faire l'inventaire **2** *(UNCOUNT) Am (stock)* stock *m*, stocks *mpl*; **our i. is low** nos stocks sont bas

VT inventorier

▸▸ *Fin* ***inventory account*** compte *m* de stock; ***inventory control*** contrôle *m* des stocks; ***inventory level*** niveau *m* des stocks; ***inventory management*** gestion *f* des stocks; ***inventory turnaround*** rotation *f* des stocks; ***inventory turnover*** rotation *f* des stocks; ***inventory valuation*** valorisation *f* des stocks; ***inventory value*** valeur *f* d'inventaire

inverse [ɪn'vɜːs] **N** inverse *m*, contraire *m*; *Math* inverse *m*

ADJ inverse; **to be in i. proportion to** être inversement proportionnel à; *Comput* **in i. video** en vidéo inverse

inversely [ɪn'vɜːslɪ] **ADV** inversement; **to be i. proportional to** être inversement proportionnel à

inversion [ɪn'vɜːʃən] **N 1** *(gen)* inversion *f*; *(of roles, relations)* renversement *m*

2 *Mus (of chord)* renversement *m*; *(in counterpoint)* inversion *f*

3 *Chem* inversion *f*

4 *Anat* inversion *f*

5 *Elec & Math* inversion *f*

6 *Psy* **(sexual) i.** inversion *f* sexuelle

invert VT [ɪn'vɜːt] **1** *(turn upside down or inside out)* inverser, retourner; *(switch around)* intervertir; *(roles)* intervertir, renverser **2** *Mus (chord)* renverser; *(interval)* inverser **3** *Chem (sugar)* invertir

N ['ɪnvɜːt] *Psy* inverti(e) *m,f*

ADJ ['ɪnvɜːt] *(sugar)* inverti

invertebrate [ɪn'vɜːtɪbreɪt] *Zool* **ADJ** invertébré

N invertébré *m*

inverted [ɪn'vɜːtɪd] **ADJ 1** *(upside down)* renversé; *Mus (chord)* renversé **2** *(reversed* ▸ *word order etc)* renversé; *Opt (image)* renversé **3** *Psy (instinct)* inverti

▸▸ *Br* ***inverted commas*** guillemets *mpl*; **in i. commas** entre guillemets; **her "best friend", in i. commas, ran off with her husband** sa "meilleure amie", entre guillemets, est partie avec son mari; *Sewing* ***inverted pleat*** pli *m* inverti *ou* creux

invest [ɪn'vest] **VI** *Fin* investir, faire des placements; **to i. in shares/in the oil industry/on the Stock Market** investir en actions/dans l'industrie pétrolière/en Bourse; **to i. in property** faire des placements dans l'immobilier; **they decided to i. in an automated system** ils ont décidé d'investir dans un système automatisé; *Fam* **you ought to i. in a new coat** tu devrais t'offrir *ou* te payer un nouveau manteau ▫

VT 1 *Fin (money)* investir, placer; *(capital)* investir; **to i. money in a business** mettre de l'argent *ou* placer des fonds dans un commerce; **they invested $5 million dollars in new machinery** ils ont investi 5 millions de dollars dans de nouveaux équipements

2 *(time, effort)* investir

3 *Formal (confer on)* investir; **invested with the highest authority** investi de la plus haute autorité; **by the power invested in me** par les pouvoirs qui me sont conférés

4 *Mil (besiege, surround)* investir

5 *(install* ▸ *bishop, pope)* introniser; *(*▸ *president)* installer

6 *Literary (provide* ▸ *person)* investir (**with** de); **to i. a subject with interest** rendre un sujet intéressant

investigate [ɪn'vestɪˌgeɪt] **VT** *(allegation, crime, accident)* enquêter sur; *(problem, situation)* examiner, étudier

VI enquêter, mener une enquête; **I'll go and i.** je vais voir ce qui se passe

investigating [ɪn'vestɪˌgeɪtɪŋ] **ADJ**

▸▸ ***investigating committee*** commission *f* d'enquête; *Law* ***investigating magistrate*** juge *m* d'instruction; ***investigating officer*** officier *m* chargé de l'enquête

investigation [ɪnˌvestɪ'geɪʃən] **N** *(into crime, accident)* enquête *f*; *(of problem, situation)* examen *m*, étude *f*; **his activities are under i.** une enquête a été ouverte sur ses activités; **your case is currently under i.** nous étudions actuellement votre cas; **on further i.** en poursuivant les recherches; **on further i., the ruins turned out to be...** des recherches plus approfondies ont révélé que les ruines étaient...; **to make investigations** faire des investigations; *(police)* procéder à une enquête

investigative [ɪn'vestɪgətɪv] **ADJ** *Press, Rad & TV* d'investigation

▸▸ ***investigative journalism*** journalisme *m* d'investigation *ou* d'enquête; ***investigative journalist*** journaliste *mf* d'investigation *ou* d'enquête; ***investigative report*** reportage *m* d'investigation; ***investigative reporter*** journaliste *mf* *ou* reporter *m* d'investigation; ***investigative team*** équipe *f* d'investigation

investigator [ɪn'vestɪˌgeɪtə(r)] **N** enquêteur(euse) *m,f*, enquêteur(trice) *m,f*

investiture [ɪn'vestɪtʃə(r)] **N** investiture *f*; *(of bishop, pope)* intronisation *f*

investment [ɪn'vestmənt] **N 1** *Fin (of money, capital)* investissement *m*, placement *m*; *(money invested)* investissement *m*, mise *f* de fonds; **are these shares a good i.?** ces actions sont-elles un bon placement?; **property is no longer such a safe i.** l'immobilier n'est plus un placement aussi sûr; **the company has investments all over the world** la société a des capitaux investis dans le monde entier; **i. in industry/real estate** investissement *m* industriel/immobilier **2** *(of time, effort)* investissement *m*

▸▸ *Banking* ***investment account*** compte *m* d'investissement; ***investment advice*** conseil *m* en placements; ***investment adviser*** conseiller(ère) *m,f* en placements; ***investment analyst*** analyste *mf* en placements; *Am* ***investment bank*** banque *f* d'affaires; *Am* ***investment banker*** banquier(ère) *m,f* d'affaires; *Am* ***investment banking*** banque *f* d'affaires; ***investment borrowing*** = emprunts destinés à l'investissement; ***investment capital*** capital-investissement *m*; ***investment company*** société *f* de portefeuille *ou* d'investissement; ***investment consultancy*** société *f* de conseil en investissement; ***investment curve*** courbe *f* d'investissement; ***investment fund*** fonds *m* commun de placement, fonds *m* d'investissement; ***investment grant*** subvention *f* d'investissement; ***investment house*** société *f* financière; ***investment incentives*** encouragements *mpl* à l'investissement; ***investment income*** revenu *m* provenant d'investissements; ***investment institution*** société *f* d'investissements; ***investment instrument*** instrument *m* de placement; ***investment management*** gestion *f* des investissements; ***investment market*** marché *m* des capitaux; ***investment officer*** responsable *mf* des investissements; ***investment performance*** performance *f* des investissements; ***investment plan*** plan *m* d'investissement; ***investment policy*** politique *f* d'investissement; ***investment portfolio*** portefeuille *m* d'investissements; ***investment programme*** programme *m* d'investissement; ***investment return*** retour *m* sur investissements; ***investment securities*** valeurs *fpl* en portefeuille *ou* de placement; ***investment services*** services *mpl* d'investissement; ***investment spending*** dépenses *fpl* d'investissement; ***investment stock*** valeurs *fpl* en portefeuille *ou* de placement; ***investment subsidy*** prime *f* à l'investissement; ***investment trust*** société *f* de placement, trust *m* de placement

investor [ɪnˈvestə(r)] N *Fin* investisseur *m*; *(shareholder)* actionnaire *mf*

inveterate [ɪnˈvetərət] ADJ **1** *(habit, dislike)* invétéré; *(hatred)* tenace **2** *(drinker, gambler, liar, smoker)* invétéré; *(bachelor)* endurci

invidious [ɪnˈvɪdɪəs] ADJ **1** *(unfair)* injuste; **i. comparisons** des comparaisons injustes **2** *(unpleasant)* ingrat, pénible; **an i. task** une tâche pénible; **to be in an i. position** être dans une position peu enviable

invigilate [ɪnˈvɪdʒɪˌleɪt] *Br Sch & Univ* VT *(exam)* surveiller
VI surveiller les candidats *(à un examen)*

invigilator [ɪnˈvɪdʒɪˌleɪtə(r)] N *Br Sch & Univ* surveillant(e) *m,f (d'un examen)*

invigorate [ɪnˈvɪgəˌreɪt] VT revigorer, vivifier; **she felt invigorated by the cold wind** le vent frais la revigorait

invigorating [ɪnˈvɪgəˌreɪtɪŋ] ADJ *(air, climate)* tonique, tonifiant, vivifiant; *(walk)* revigorant; *(bath)* tonifiant; *(discussion)* enrichissant

invincibility [ɪnˌvɪnsɪˈbɪlətɪ] N invincibilité *f*; *(of belief, faith)* caractère *m* inébranlable

invincible [ɪnˈvɪnsɪbəl] ADJ *(army, troops)* invincible; *(belief)* inébranlable

inviolability [ɪnˌvaɪələˈbɪlətɪ] N inviolabilité *f*

inviolable [ɪnˈvaɪələbəl] ADJ inviolable

inviolably [ɪnˈvaɪələblɪ] ADV inviolablement

inviolate [ɪnˈvaɪələt] ADJ *Literary* inviolé; **to remain i.** demeurer inviolé

invisibility [ɪnˌvɪzɪˈbɪlətɪ] N invisibilité *f*

invisible [ɪnˈvɪzɪbəl] ADJ invisible; **i. to the naked eye** invisible à l'œil nu; *Fig* **I felt like the i. man** c'était comme si j'étais invisible; **he's been the i. man recently** il se fait rare ces temps-ci
• **invisibles** NPL *Fin* invisibles *mpl*
▸▸ *Com & Fin* ***invisible assets*** biens *mpl* incorporels; *Fin* ***invisible balance*** balance *f* des invisibles; *Fin* ***invisible earnings*** gains *mpl* invisibles; *Com & Fin* ***invisible exports*** exportations *fpl* invisibles; *Com & Fin* ***invisible imports*** importations *fpl* invisibles; ***invisible ink*** encre *f* invisible *ou* sympathique; *Sewing* ***invisible mending*** stoppage *m*; ***invisible trade*** commerce *m* de services

invisibly [ɪnˈvɪzɪblɪ] ADV invisiblement

invitation [ˌɪnvɪˈteɪʃən] N invitation *f*; *(card)* carte *f* d'invitation; **have you sent out the wedding invitations?** as-tu envoyé les invitations au mariage?; **she's here at my i.** c'est moi qui l'ai invitée; **we went to the congress at the i. of the President himself** nous sommes allés au congrès sur l'invitation du président en personne; **by i. only** sur invitation seulement; **a standing i.** une invitation permanente; *Fig* **prison conditions are an (open) i. to violence** les conditions de détention sont une véritable incitation à la violence
▸▸ ***invitation card*** carte *f* d'invitation

invite VT [ɪnˈvaɪt] **1** *(ask to come)* inviter; **to i. sb for lunch** inviter qn à déjeuner; **the Thomsons have invited us over** *or* **round** les Thomson nous ont invités chez eux; **I invited him up for a coffee** je l'ai invité à monter prendre un café
2 *(ask to do something)* demander, solliciter; **they invited her to become president** ils lui ont demandé de devenir présidente; **I've been invited for interview** j'ai été convoqué à un entretien
3 *(solicit)* **to i. bids** *or* **tenders** faire un appel d'offres; **applications are invited for the position** toute personne intéressée est invitée à déposer un dossier de candidature; **we i. suggestions from readers** toute suggestion de la part de nos lecteurs est la bienvenue
4 *(trouble, defeat, disaster)* aller au-devant de; *(criticism)* s'exposer à; *(doubt, sympathy)* appeler, attirer; **you're just inviting failure** tu vas au-devant d'un échec
N [ˈɪnvaɪt] *Fam* invitation▫ *f*, invit *f*

inviting [ɪnˈvaɪtɪŋ] ADJ *(gesture)* d'invitation; *(eyes, smile)* engageant; *(display)* attirant, attrayant; *(idea)* tentant, séduisant; *(place, fire)* accueillant; **not very i.** peu attrayant; **the water looks i.** l'eau donne envie de se baigner

invitingly [ɪnˈvaɪtɪŋlɪ] ADV d'une manière attrayante; **she smiled at him i.** elle lui adressa un sourire engageant; **the box lay open i. on the desk** la boîte était ouverte sur la table, tentante

in vitro [ˌɪnˈviːtrəʊ] *Med* ADJ in vitro
ADV in vitro
▸▸ ***in vitro fertilization*** fécondation *f* in vitro

invocation [ˌɪnvəˈkeɪʃən] N **1** *Law & Pol* invocation *f* **2** *Rel* invocation *f*; **invocations to the gods** l'invocation des dieux

invoice [ˈɪnvɔɪs] N *Com* facture *f*; **to make out an i.** établir *ou* faire une facture; **invoices should be settled within 30 days** les factures doivent être réglées sous 30 jours; **as per i.** conformément à la facture; **payable against i.** à payer à réception de la facture; **i. of origin** facture *f* originale
VT *(goods)* facturer, porter sur une facture; *(person, company)* envoyer la facture à; **who do I i.?** à qui dois-je adresser la facture?; **to i. sb for sth** facturer qch à qn
▸▸ *Com* ***invoice clerk*** facturier(ère) *m,f*; ***invoice date*** date *f* de facturation; ***invoice price*** prix *m* facturé; ***invoice value*** valeur *f* de facture

invoiceable [ˈɪnvɔɪsəb(ə)l] ADJ facturable

invoicing [ˈɪnvɔɪsɪŋ] N *Com (of goods etc)* facturation *f*
▸▸ ***invoicing address*** adresse *f* de facturation; ***invoicing instructions*** instructions *fpl* de facturation; ***invoicing software*** logiciel *m* de facturation

invoke [ɪnˈvəʊk] VT **1** *(cite)* invoquer; **she invoked the principle of free speech** elle a invoqué le principe de la liberté d'expression **2** *(call upon)* en appeler à, faire appel à; **to i. sb's help** requérir l'aide de qn **3** *(summon up)* invoquer; **to i. evil spirits** invoquer les mauvais esprits

involuntarily [ɪnˈvɒləntrəlɪ] ADV involontairement; **she smiled i.** elle ne put réprimer un sourire *ou* s'empêcher de sourire

involuntary [ɪnˈvɒləntərɪ] ADJ involontaire
▸▸ ***involuntary memory*** mémoire *f* involontaire; *Anat & Physiol* ***involuntary muscle*** muscle *m* lisse *ou* viscéral; *Econ* ***involuntary unemployment*** chômage *m* involontaire

involve [ɪnˈvɒlv] VT **1** *(entail)* impliquer, comporter; **it involves a lot of work** cela implique *ou* nécessite *ou* veut dire beaucoup de travail; **what does the job i.?** en quoi consiste le travail?; **my job involves a lot of travel** je dois beaucoup voyager dans mon travail; **it won't i. you in much expense** cela ne t'entraînera pas dans de grosses dépenses
2 *(concern, affect)* concerner, toucher; **this discussion doesn't i. you** cette discussion ne vous concerne pas; **there are too many accidents involving children** il y a trop d'accidents dont les enfants sont les victimes
3 *(bring in, implicate)* impliquer; **over 200 people were involved in planning the event** plus de 200 personnes ont participé à la préparation de l'événement; **several vehicles were involved in the accident** plusieurs véhicules étaient impliqués dans cet accident; **we try to i. the parents in the running of the school** nous essayons de faire participer les parents à la vie de l'école; **I'm not going to i. myself in their private affairs** je ne vais pas me mêler de leur vie privée *ou* de leurs affaires
4 *(absorb, engage)* absorber; **the novel doesn't really i. the reader** le lecteur ne se sent pas impliqué dans le roman

involved [ɪnˈvɒlvd] ADJ **1** *(complicated)* compliqué, complexe
2 *(implicated)* impliqué; **were the CIA i.?** est-ce que la CIA était impliquée?; **I don't want to get i.** je ne veux pas être impliqué, je ne veux rien avoir à faire avec cela; **they became i. in a long war** ils se sont trouvés entraînés dans une longue guerre; **the amount of work i. is enormous** la quantité de travail à fournir est énorme; **there are important principles i.** les principes en cause *ou* en jeu sont importants; **he had no idea of the problems i.** il n'avait aucune idée des problèmes en jeu *ou* en cause; **I think he's i. in advertising** je crois qu'il est dans la publicité; **to be i. in politics** prendre part à la vie politique; **he's getting i. with the school orchestra** il commence à prendre part aux activités de l'orchestre de l'école
3 *(absorbed)* absorbé; **she's too i. in her work to notice** elle est trop absorbée par son travail pour remarquer quoi que ce soit
4 *(emotionally)* **to be i. with sb** avoir une liaison avec qn; **he doesn't want to get i.** il ne veut pas s'engager

involvement [ɪnˈvɒlvmənt] N **1** *(participation)* participation *f*; *(in crime)* implication *f*; **my i. in the project is strictly limited** ma participation au projet est strictement limitée; **they were against American i. in the war** ils étaient opposés à toute participation américaine au conflit
2 *(commitment)* investissement *m*, engagement *m*; **she's looking for work that requires total i.** elle cherche un emploi qui demanderait un investissement total
3 *(relationship)* liaison *f*; **I've had no further i. with him since** je n'ai plus jamais eu affaire à lui depuis; **he's frightened of emotional i.** il a peur de s'engager sentimentalement, il redoute tout engagement affectif
4 *(complexity)* complexité *f*, complication *f*

invulnerability [ɪnˌvʌlnərəˈbɪlətɪ] N invulnérabilité *f*

invulnerable [ɪnˈvʌlnərəbəl] ADJ invulnérable; *(position)* inattaquable

inward [ˈɪnwəd] ADJ **1** *(thoughts, satisfaction)* intime, secret(ète) **2** *(movement)* vers l'intérieur
ADV *Am* = **inwards**
▸▸ ***inward charges*** *(of ship)* frais *mpl* à l'entrée; *Customs* ***inward customs clearance*** entrée *f* en douane; *Fin* ***inward investment*** investissements *mpl* étrangers; *Acct* ***inward payment*** paiement *m* reçu

inward-looking ADJ *Br (person)* introverti, replié sur soi; *(group)* replié sur soi, fermé; *(philosophy)* introspectif, *Pej* nombriliste; **he's become very i. lately** il s'est beaucoup refermé *ou* replié sur lui-même ces derniers temps

inwardly [ˈɪnwədlɪ] ADV *(pleased, disgusted)* secrètement; **he smiled i.** il sourit intérieurement; **i. I was still convinced that I was right** en mon for intérieur, j'étais toujours convaincu d'avoir raison; **we all groaned i. at the thought** à cette idée nous avons tous réprimé un mouvement d'humeur

inwards [ˈɪnwədz], *Am* **inward** [ˈɪnwərd] ADV **1** *(turn, face)* vers l'intérieur; **the doors open i.** les portes s'ouvrent vers l'intérieur **2** *(into one's own heart, soul etc)* **my thoughts turned i.** je me suis replié sur moi-même

in-your-face ADJ *Fam* **1** *(uncompromising ▸ documentary, film)* cru▫ **2** *(aggressive ▸ attitude, personality)* agressif▫

I/O *Comput (written abbr* **input/output***)* E/S *f*

IOC [ˌaɪəʊˈsiː] N *Sport (abbr* **International Olympic Committee***)* CIO *m*

iodine [*Br* ˈaɪədiːn, *Am* ˈaɪədaɪn] N *Chem* iode *m*
Pharm teinture *f* d'iode

iodize, -ise [ˈaɪədaɪz] VT ioder

iodoform [aɪˈɒdəfɔːm] N *Med & Pharm* iodoforme *m*

ion [ˈaɪən] N *Chem* ion *m*
▸▸ ***ion beam*** faisceau *m* ionique; ***ion engine*** moteur *m* ionique; *Tech* ***ion implantation*** implantation *f* d'ions

Ionian [aɪˈəʊnɪən] N *(person)* Ionien(enne) *m,f*
ADJ ionien
▸▸ *Geog* ***the Ionian Islands*** les îles *fpl* Ioniennes; *Mus* ***Ionian mode*** mode *m* ionien; *Geog* ***the Ionian Sea*** la mer Ionienne

Ionic [aɪˈɒnɪk] ADJ *Archit* ionique

ionic [aɪˈɒnɪk] ADJ *Chem & Phys* ionique
▸▸ ***ionic bond*** lien *m* ionique

ionization, -isation [ˌaɪənaɪˈzeɪʃən] N **1** *Chem, Phys & Elec* ionisation *f* **2** *Med* (traitement *m* par) ionisation *f*
▸▸ ***ionization chamber*** chambre *f* d'ionisation; ***ionization potential*** potentiel *m* d'ionisation

ionize, -ise [ˈaɪəˌnaɪz] *Chem & Phys* VT ioniser
VI *(acid etc)* s'ioniser

ionosphere [aɪˈɒnəˌsfɪə(r)] N *Phys* ionosphère *f*

iota [aɪˈəʊtə] N **1** *(Greek letter)* iota *m inv* **2** *(tiny bit)* brin *m*, grain *m*, iota *m inv*; **there's not one i. of truth in the letter** il n'y a pas un brin *ou* un grain de vrai dans cette lettre; **I don't care one i.** cela m'est complètement égal, je m'en fiche complètement; **they haven't changed one i.** ils n'ont absolument pas changé

OU [ˌaɪəʊ'juː] N (*abbr* **I owe you**) reconnaissance *f* de dette

P [ˌaɪ'piː] N *Comput* (*abbr* **Internet Protocol**)
▸▸ ***IP address*** adresse *f* IP; ***IP number*** numéro *m* IP

PA [aɪpiː'eɪ] N (*abbr* **International Phonetic Alphabet**) API *m*

PO [ˌaɪpiː'əʊ] N *Am St Exch* (*abbr* **initial public offering**) introduction *f* en Bourse

Pod® ['aɪpɒd] N iPod® *m*

PP [ˌaɪpiː'piː] N *Comptr* (*abbr* **Internet Presence Provider**) = fournisseur d'accès à l'Internet proposant l'hébergement de sites Web

PPR [aɪˌpiːpiː'ɑː(r)] N *Br* (*abbr* **Institute for Public Policy Research**) = groupe d'experts de centre gauche à l'origine de plusieurs grandes politiques du gouvernement travailliste britannique

pso facto [ˌɪpsəʊ'fæktəʊ] ADV ipso facto

Q [ˌaɪ'kjuː] N *Psy* (*abbr* **intelligence quotient**) QI *m*

RA ['aɪɑː'reɪ] N **1** *Pol* (*abbr* **Irish Republican Army**) IRA *f* **2** *Am Fin* (*abbr* **individual retirement account**) plan *m* d'épargne retraite personnel

> **IRA**
>
> L'IRA est une organisation qui lutte pour la réunification de l'Irlande. En 1969, elle s'est scindée en deux factions: la "Provisional IRA", qui a recours à la violence, et la "Official IRA", qui privilégiait un réglement politique du conflit en Irlande du Nord. La "Provisional IRA" s'est longtemps opposée militairement aux forces armées britanniques présentes en Irlande du Nord ainsi qu'aux groupes paramilitaires protestants. En 1995, au début du processus de paix qui a abouti à l'accord de 1998 (le **Good Friday Agreement**, voir cet encadré) la "Provisional IRA" a déclaré un cessez-le-feu. Le processus de paix a néanmoins longtemps buté sur la question du refus de l'IRA de renoncer à son arsenal. Finalement, en juillet 2005, l'IRA a rendu publique sa décision de renoncer définitivement à la lutte armée dans son combat pour la réunification de l'Irlande. En septembre 2005, la destruction des stocks d'armes de l'IRA fut annoncée.

ran [ɪ'rɑːn] N *Geog* Iran *m*

ranian [ɪ'reɪnjən] N **1** (*person*) Iranien(enne) *m,f* **2** (*language*) iranien *m*
ADJ iranien
COMP (*embassy*) d'Iran; (*history*) de l'Iran; (*teacher*) d'iranien

raq [ɪ'rɑːk] N *Geog* Iraq *m*, Irak *m*

raqi [ɪ'rɑːkɪ] N Irakien(enne) *m,f*, Iraquien(enne) *m,f*
ADJ irakien, Iraquien
COMP (*embassy*) d'Irak, d'Iraq; (*history*) de l'Irak *ou* l'Iraq
▸▸ ***Iraqi National Congress*** Congrès *m* national irakien

rascibility [ɪˌræsə'bɪlətɪ] N irascibilité *f*

rascible [ɪ'ræsəbəl] ADJ irascible, coléreux

rascibly [ɪ'ræsəblɪ] ADV (*say etc*) sur un ton irrité

rate [aɪ'reɪt] ADJ furieux; **an i. letter** une lettre courroucée

RC [ˌaɪɑː'siː] N *Comput* (*abbr* **Internet Relay Chat**) IRC *m*, service *m* de bavardage Internet, dialogue *m* en direct
▸▸ ***IRC channel*** canal *m* IRC, canal *m* de dialogue en direct

re ['aɪə(r)] N *Literary* ire *f*, courroux *m*

reland ['aɪələnd] N *Geog* Irlande *f*; **Northern I.** l'Irlande *f* du Nord; **the Republic of I.** la République d'Irlande

ridescence [ˌɪrɪ'desəns] N irisation *f*

ridescent [ˌɪrɪ'desənt] ADJ irisé, *Literary* iridescent

ris ['aɪrɪs] (*pl sense* **1 irises** *or* **irides** ['ɪrɪdiːz], *pl senses* 2 and 3 **irises**) N **1** *Anat* iris *m* **2** *Bot* iris *m* **3** *Phot* (*diaphragm*) iris *m*
▸▸ *Phot* ***iris diaphragm*** iris *m*; ***iris recognition*** reconnaissance *f* de l'iris

rish ['aɪrɪʃ] (*pl* **inv**) NPL **the I.** les Irlandais *mpl*
N (*language*) irlandais *m*
ADJ **1** (*from or relating to Ireland*) irlandais **2** *Fam* (*illogical*) loufoque; **that's a bit I.** c'est un peu loufoque
COMP (*embassy*) de la République d'Irlande; (*history*) de l'Irlande; (*teacher*) d'irlandais
▸▸ ***Irish American*** Américain(e) *m,f* d'origine irlandaise; *Culin* ***Irish coffee*** irish-coffee *m*, = café noir au whiskey irlandais couronné de crème fraîche; ***the Irish Free State*** l'État *m* libre d'Irlande; ***Irish joke*** = histoire drôle aux dépens des Irlandais, ≃ histoire *f* belge; *Formerly* ***Irish pound*** livre *f* irlandaise; ***Irish pub*** pub *m* irlandais; ***the Irish Republic*** la République d'Irlande; ***the Irish Republican Army*** l'IRA *f*; *see also* **IRA**; *Geog* ***the Irish Sea*** la mer d'Irlande; ***Irish setter*** setter *m* irlandais; *Culin* ***Irish stew*** ragoût *m* de mouton; ***Irish wolfhound*** lévrier *m* irlandais

Irishism ['aɪrɪʃɪzəm] N (*idiom*) locution *f* irlandaise; (*custom*) coutume *f* irlandaise

Irishman ['aɪrɪʃmən] (*pl* **Irishmen** [-mən]) N Irlandais *m*

Irishwoman ['aɪrɪʃˌwʊmən] (*pl* **Irishwomen** [-ˈwɪmɪn]) N Irlandaise *f*

irk [ɜːk] VT irriter, agacer; **it really irks me that he won't do the washing-up** cela m'agace vraiment qu'il ne fasse jamais la vaisselle

irksome ['ɜːksəm] ADJ irritant, agaçant

iron ['aɪən] ADJ **1** (*made of, containing iron*) de fer, en fer **2** *Fig* (*strong*) de fer, d'acier; **i. discipline** une discipline de fer; **an i. hand** *or* **fist in a velvet glove** une main de fer dans un gant de velours
VT (*laundry*) repasser
VI (*person*) repasser; (*laundry*) se repasser
N **1** (*metal*) fer *m*; **made of i.** de *ou* en fer; **she has a will of i.** elle a une volonté de fer; **the i. and steel industry** la sidérurgie; **(as) hard as i.** dur comme *ou* aussi dur que le fer
2 (*in diet*) fer *m*; **spinach has a high i. content** les épinards contiennent beaucoup de fer
3 (*for laundry*) fer *m* (à repasser); **your shirt needs an i.** ta chemise a besoin d'un coup de fer *ou* d'être repassée
4 (*tool, appliance*) fer *m*; **to have many irons in the fire** avoir plusieurs fers au feu
5 *Golf* (*golf club*) fer *m*; **a five i.** un fer cinq
6 *Horseriding* (*of stirrup*) étrier *m*
• **irons** NPL (*chains*) fers *mpl*; **clap them in irons!** mettez-les aux fers!
▸▸ ***the Iron Age*** l'âge *m* du fer; **an I. Age tool** un outil de l'âge du fer; *Chem & Metal* ***iron alloy*** alliage *m* ferreux; ***iron bar*** barre *f* de fer; ***iron bridge*** pont *m* en fer; *Hist* ***Iron Chancellor*** chancelier *m* de fer; *Hist* ***the Iron Curtain*** le rideau de fer; **the I. Curtain countries** les pays *mpl* de l'Est; *Med* ***iron deficiency*** carence *f* en fer; ***iron filings*** limaille *f* de fer; ***iron foundry*** fonderie *f* (*de fonte*); ***an iron grating*** une grille en fer; *Am Hist* ***the iron horse*** = la locomotive; *Br Pol* ***the Iron Lady*** la Dame de Fer (*surnom donné à Margaret Thatcher*); *Med* ***iron lung*** poumon *m* d'acier; ***iron maiden*** = instrument de torture consistant en un coffre à l'intérieur parsemé de pointes, dans lequel on place la victime; *Miner* ***iron ore*** minerai *m* de fer; *Miner* ***iron oxide*** oxyde *m* de fer; *Miner* ***iron pyrites*** pyrite *f* (de fer); *Golf* ***iron shot*** coup *m* de fer; ***an iron will*** une volonté de fer

▸ **iron out** VT SEP **1** (*crease*) enlever au fer **2** *Fig* (*problem, difficulty*) aplanir; **have you ironed out your differences?** est-ce que vous avez résolu vos différends?

ironclad ['aɪənklæd] ADJ **1** (*ship*) cuirassé **2** (*argument*) inattaquable **3** (*rule*) inflexible
N cuirassé *m*

iron-grey ADJ gris acier

ironic [aɪ'rɒnɪk], **ironical** [aɪ'rɒnɪkəl] ADJ ironique

ironically [aɪ'rɒnɪkəlɪ] ADV **1** (*smile, laugh*) ironiquement **2** (*paradoxically*) **i. enough, he was the only one to remember** paradoxalement, il était le seul à s'en souvenir; **i., the box was empty** comble d'ironie, la boîte était vide

ironing ['aɪənɪŋ] N repassage *m*; **to do the i.** faire le repassage, repasser; **I've got a lot of i. to do** j'ai beaucoup de repassage à faire
▸▸ ***ironing board*** planche *f ou* table *f* à repasser; ***ironing board cover*** housse *f* de table à repasser

ironmonger ['aɪənˌmʌŋgə(r)] N *Br* quincaillier(ère) *m,f*; **i.'s (shop)** quincaillerie *f*

ironmongery ['aɪənˌmʌŋgərɪ] N *Br* quincaillerie *f*

iron-on transfer N transfert *m* (*appliqué au fer à repasser*)

ironstone ['aɪənstəʊn] N minerai *m* de fer

ironware ['aɪənˌweə(r)] N ferronnerie *f*

ironwork ['aɪənwɜːk] N *Metal* ferronnerie *f*

ironworks ['aɪənwɜːks] (*pl* **inv**) N *Metal* (*for smelting*) fonderie *f* de fonte; (*for casting*) usine *f* sidérurgique

irony ['aɪrənɪ] (*pl* **ironies**) N (*gen*) & *Literature* ironie *f*; **the i. is that it might be true** ce qui est ironique *ou* ce qu'il y a d'ironique, c'est que cela pourrait être vrai; **in one of life's little ironies** par une ironie du sort; **and, i. of ironies,...** et, comble de l'ironie,...

IRR [ˌaɪɑː'rɑː(r)] N *Fin* (*abbr* **internal rate of return**) taux *m* de rentabilité interne

irradiate [ɪ'reɪdɪeɪt] VT **1** *Med & Phys* (*expose to radiation*) irradier; (*food*) irradier **2** (*light up*) illuminer, éclairer

irradiation [ɪˌreɪdɪ'eɪʃən] N **1** *Med & Phys* (*exposure to radiation*) irradiation *f*; (*X-ray therapy*) radiothérapie *f*; (*of food*) irradiation *f* **2** *Opt* irradiation *f* **3** (*by light*) illumination *f*

irrational [ɪ'ræʃənəl] ADJ **1** (*person, behaviour, feeling*) irrationnel; (*fear*) irraisonné; (*creature, being*) incapable de raisonner; **don't be so i.!** sois raisonnable! **2** *Math* irrationnel
N **the i.** l'irrationnel *m*
▸▸ *Math* ***irrational number*** nombre *m* irrationnel

irrationally [ɪ'ræʃənəlɪ] ADV irrationnellement

irreconcilable [ɪ'rekənˌsaɪləbəl] ADJ **1** (*aims, views, beliefs*) inconciliable, incompatible; **his beliefs are i. with his work** ses convictions sont incompatibles avec son travail **2** (*conflict, disagreement*) insoluble; **to be i. enemies** être ennemis jurés

irrecoverable [ˌɪrɪ'kʌvərəbəl] ADJ **1** (*thing lost*) irrécupérable; (*debt*) irrécouvrable **2** (*loss, damage, wrong*) irréparable

irrecoverably [ˌɪrɪ'kʌvərəblɪ] ADV (*lost*) pour toujours; (*damaged*) irrémédiablement

irredeemable [ˌɪrɪ'diːməbəl] ADJ **1** *Fin* (*share*) non remboursable; (*bond*) non amortissable; (*paper money, bill*) non convertible **2** (*person*) incorrigible, impénitent **3** (*loss, damage, wrong*) irréparable

irredeemably [ˌɪrɪ'diːməblɪ] ADV irrémédiablement; **to be i. wicked** être foncièrement méchant

irreducible [ˌɪrɪ'djuːsɪbəl] ADJ irréductible

irrefutable [ˌɪrɪ'fjuːtəbəl] ADJ (*argument, proof, fact*) irréfutable; (*testimony*) irrécusable

irregular [ɪ'regjʊlə(r)] ADJ **1** (*object, shape etc*) irrégulier; (*surface*) inégal; **an i. polygon** un polygone irrégulier
2 (*intermittent, spasmodic*) irrégulier; **she works i. hours** elle a des horaires de travail irréguliers; **i. breathing** respiration *f* irrégulière *ou* saccadée
3 *Formal* (*unorthodox*) irrégulier; **your request is highly i.** votre demande n'est absolument pas régulière
4 *Gram & Math* irrégulier
N **1** *Mil* (*soldier*) irrégulier *m* **2** *Am Com* article *m* de second choix
▸▸ ***irregular conduct*** conduite *f* irrégulière; ***irregular migrant*** migrant(e) *m,f* irrégulier(ère), migrant(e) *m,f* en situation irrégulière; *Mil* ***irregular troops*** troupes *fpl* irrégulières, irréguliers *mpl*; *Gram* ***irregular verb*** verbe *m* irrégulier

irregularity [ɪˌregjʊ'lærətɪ] (*pl* **irregularities**) N (*of surface, work, breathing*) irrégularité *f*; **there was an i. to do with his passport** il y avait quelque chose qui n'était pas en règle dans son passeport
• **irregularities** NPL *Law* irrégularités *fpl*; **there were some irregularities in the paperwork** il y avait quelques irrégularités dans les écritures

irregularly [ɪ'regjʊləlɪ] ADV **1** (*spasmodically*) irrégulièrement **2** (*unevenly*) inégalement; **i. shaped triangles** des triangles aux formes irrégulières

irrelevance [ɪ'reləvəns], **irrelevancy** [ɪ'reləvənsɪ] (*pl* **irrelevancies**) N **1** (*of fact, comment*) manque *m* de rapport, non-pertinence *f* **2**

(pointless fact or matter) inutilité *f*; **don't waste your time on irrelevances** ne perdez pas votre temps avec des choses sans importance; **the monarchy has become an i.** la monarchie n'a plus de raison d'être, la monarchie a perdu sa raison d'être

irrelevant [ɪ'reləvənt] **ADJ** sans rapport, hors de propos; **your question is totally i. to the subject in hand** votre question n'a aucun rapport *ou* n'a rien à voir avec le sujet qui nous intéresse; **that is i.** cela n'a aucun rapport *ou* n'a rien à voir avec la question; **the monarchy has become i.** la monarchie n'a plus de raison d'être, la monarchie a perdu sa raison d'être; **i. information** information *f* non pertinente; **our personal feelings on the matter are i.** nos sentiments personnels n'ont rien à voir ici; **age is i.** l'âge est sans importance *ou* n'est pas un critère

irreligious [ˌɪrɪ'lɪdʒəs] **ADJ** irréligieux

irremediable [ˌɪrɪ'miːdɪəbəl] **ADJ** irrémédiable
▸▸ ***irremediable damage*** dégâts *mpl* irrémédiables

irremediably [ˌɪrɪ'miːdɪəblɪ] **ADV** irrémédiablement

irremovable [ˌɪrɪ'muːvəbəl] **ADJ** *(stain)* indélébile; *(official)* inamovible

irreparable [ɪ'repərəbəl] **ADJ** *(damage)* irréparable; *(loss)* irrémédiable, irrécupérable; **he's done i. harm to his career** il a compromis sa carrière de façon irréparable

irreparably [ɪ'repərəblɪ] **ADV** *(damaged)* irréparablement; *(lost)* irrémédiablement

irreplaceable [ˌɪrɪ'pleɪsəbəl] **ADJ** irremplaçable

irrepressible [ˌɪrɪ'presəbəl] **ADJ 1** *(need, desire, urge)* irrépressible; *(good humour)* à toute épreuve **2** *(person)* que rien n'abat; **he's i.** rien ne l'abat

irrepressibly [ˌɪrɪ'presɪblɪ] **ADV i. optimistic/enthusiastic/good-humoured** d'un optimisme/d'un enthousiasme/d'une bonne humeur à toute épreuve

irreproachable [ˌɪrɪ'prəʊtʃəbəl] **ADJ** irréprochable

irreproachably [ˌɪrɪ'prəʊtʃəblɪ] **ADV** irréprochablement, de façon irréprochable

irresistible [ˌɪrɪ'zɪstəbəl] **ADJ** irrésistible; **when they argue, it's a case of an i. force meeting an immovable object** quand ils se disputent, chacun campe sur ses positions

irresistibly [ˌɪrɪ'zɪstəblɪ] **ADV** irrésistiblement; **i. delicious cakes** des gâteaux irrésistibles

irresolute [ɪ'rezəluːt] **ADJ** irrésolu, indécis

irresolutely [ɪ'rezəluːtlɪ] **ADV** d'un air irrésolu

irresoluteness [ɪ'rezəluːtnɪs], **irresolution** [ɪˌrezə'luːʃən] **N** indécision *f*, irrésolution *f*

irrespective [ˌɪrɪ'spektɪv] **irrespective of PREP** sans tenir compte de, indépendamment de; **i. of race or religion** sans discrimination de race ou de religion; **i. of what has been said before** indépendamment de ce qui a été dit auparavant

irresponsibility [ˌɪrɪˌspɒnsə'bɪlətɪ] **N** irresponsabilité *f*

irresponsible [ˌɪrɪ'spɒnsəbəl] **ADJ** *(person, parent, driver)* irresponsable; *(act)* irréfléchi; **you're so i.!** tu n'as aucun sens des responsabilités!

irresponsibly [ˌɪrɪ'spɒnsəblɪ] **ADV 1** *(act, behave, drive)* de manière irresponsable **2** *Law* irresponsablement

irretrievable [ˌɪrɪ'triːvəbəl] **ADJ** *(object)* impossible à récupérer; *(loss, harm, damage)* irréparable; *Comput (file)* irrécupérable; **the situation is i.** la situation est irrémédiable
▸▸ *Law* ***irretrievable breakdown*** *(of marriage)* non-conciliation *f*

irretrievably [ˌɪrɪ'triːvəblɪ] **ADV** *(lost)* irrémédiablement, à tout jamais; **to break down i.** *(of marriage)* se briser irrémédiablement

irreverence [ɪ'revərəns] **N** irrévérence *f*

irreverent [ɪ'revərənt] **ADJ** irrévérencieux; **i. remarks** remarques irrévérencieuses *ou* insolentes; **an i. sense of humour** un sens de l'humour insolent *ou* impertinent

irreverently [ɪ'revərəntlɪ] **ADV** irrévérencieusement

irreversible [ˌɪrɪ'vɜːsɪbəl] **ADJ 1** *(decision, step)* irrévocable **2** *(process)* irréversible

irrevocable [ɪ'revəkəbəl] **ADJ** *(gen) & Fin (letter of credit)* irrévocable

irrevocably [ɪ'revəkəblɪ] **ADV** irrévocablement

irrigable ['ɪrɪgəbəl] **ADJ** irrigable

irrigate ['ɪrɪgeɪt] **VT** *(gen) & Med* irriguer

irrigation [ˌɪrɪ'geɪʃən] **N** *(gen) & Med* irrigation *f*
▸▸ ***irrigation canal*** canal *m* d'irrigation; ***irrigation channel*** fossé *m ou* rigole *f* d'irrigation

irritability [ˌɪrɪtə'bɪlətɪ] **N** *(gen) & Med* irritabilité *f*

irritable ['ɪrɪtəbəl] **ADJ** *(gen) & Med* irritable
▸▸ *Med* ***irritable bowel syndrome*** syndrome *m* du côlon irritable

irritably ['ɪrɪtəblɪ] **ADV** avec irritation

irritant ['ɪrɪtənt] *Med & Fig* **N** irritant *m*; **at least we can be an i.** au moins nous pouvons jouer les empêcheurs de tourner en rond
ADJ irritant

irritate ['ɪrɪteɪt] **VT 1** *(annoy)* irriter, contrarier, énerver **2** *Med* irriter

irritating ['ɪrɪteɪtɪŋ] **ADJ 1** *(annoying)* irritant, contrariant, énervant **2** *Med* irritant, irritatif

irritatingly ['ɪrɪteɪtɪŋlɪ] **ADV** de façon agaçante *ou* irritante; **he's i. slow** il est d'une lenteur irritante

irritation [ɪrɪ'teɪʃən] **N 1** *(annoyance)* irritation *f*, agacement *m*; **she tried to hide her i.** elle tenta de cacher son agacement; **it's just one of life's little irritations** ce n'est qu'une de ces petites choses énervantes de la vie **2** *Med* irritation *f*

IRS [ˌaɪɑː'res] **N** *Am Fin (abbr* **Internal Revenue Service***)* **the I.** le fisc

IS [ˌaɪ'es] **N** *(abbr* **information system***)* système *m* informatique

is [ɪz] *see* **be**

ISA ['aɪsə] **N** *Br Fin (abbr* **individual savings account***)* PEA *m*

ISBN [ˌaɪesˌbiː'en] **N** *(abbr* **International Standard Book Number***)* ISBN *m*

ISDN [ˌaɪesˌdiː'en] *(abbr* **integrated services digital network***)* **N** *Comput* RNIS *m*
VT *Fam* **to I. sth** envoyer qch par RNIS▫
▸▸ ***ISDN card*** carte *f* RNIS; ***ISDN line*** ligne *f* RNIS; ***ISDN modem*** modem *m* RNIS *ou* Numéris

SUFFIXE

-ISH

• Le suffixe **-ish** sert à produire des adjectifs à partir de noms et d'adjectifs. Certains d'entre eux, notamment les adjectifs de nationalité, sont fixes et n'ont aucune connotation particulière:

English anglais; **Swedish** suédois; **Turkish** turc; **foolish** idiot; **childish** puéril; **feverish** fiévreux

• Mais dans de nombreux cas, ce suffixe exprime un caractère d'APPROXIMATION:

blueish bleuâtre; **reddish** rougeâtre; **whitish** blanchâtre, etc.

• On peut ajouter **-ish** à de très nombreux adjectifs; il se traduit alors le plus souvent en employant les adverbes **plutôt** ou **assez**:

a biggish house une maison plutôt grande; **a prettyish girl** une fille assez jolie; **a longish film** un film plutôt long; **shall we meet round eightish?** on se retrouve vers huit heures?

C'est un suffixe très productif: par exemple, à partir du pronom **more**, on a créé l'adjectif **moreish**, qui désigne quelque chose qui a un goût de revenez-y, comme dans la phrase **this cake is very moreish**.

Il est même possible d'utiliser **-ish** tout seul pour nuancer un jugement comme dans l'exemple suivant:

was the film funny ? – ish... est-ce que le film était amusant? – assez amusant...

ISIC card [ˌaɪesˌaɪ'siː-] **N** *(abbr* **International Student Identity Card***)* carte *f* ISIC

isinglass ['aɪzɪŋglɑːs] **N 1** *(glue)* ichtyocolle *f* **2** *Miner (mica)* mica *m*

Islam ['ɪzlɑːm] **N** *Rel* Islam *m*

Islamic [ɪz'læmɪk] **ADJ** islamique

Islamism ['ɪzləmɪzəm] **N** islamisme *m*; *(Islamic identity)* islamité *f*

Islamist ['ɪzləmɪst] **N** islamiste *mf*

Islamization, -isation [ˌɪzləmaɪ'zeɪʃən] **N** islamisation *f*

Islamize, -ise ['ɪzləˌmaɪz] **VT** islamiser

Islamophobe [ɪz'læməˌfəʊb] **N** islamophobe *mf*

Islamophobia [ɪzˌlæmə'fəʊbɪə] **N** islamophobie *f*

Islamophobic [ɪzˌlæmə'fəʊbɪk] **ADJ** islamophobe

island ['aɪlənd] **N 1** *Geog* île *f*; *Am Fam* **the I.** *(Long Island)* Long Island▫; **they are an i. race** c'est une race insulaire; **we didn't stay in one place, we went i.-hopping** nous ne sommes pas toujours restés au même endroit, nous sommes allés d'île en île; **the i. of Ireland** l'Irlande; *Fig* **an i. of calm** une oasis de tranquillité **2** *(in road)* îlot *m*; *(for pedestrians)* refuge *m*; *(of houses etc)* groupe *m* **3** *(for displaying goods)* îlot *m*
▸▸ *Geol* ***island arc*** arc *m* insulaire

islander ['aɪləndə(r)] **N** insulaire *mf*
• **Islander N** *NZ* habitant(e) *m,f* des îles du Pacifique

isle [aɪl] **N** île *f*
▸▸ ***the Isle of Dogs*** = quartier de l'est de Londres faisant partie des Docklands; ***the Isle of Man*** l'île *f* de Man; ***the Isle of Wight*** l'île *f* de Wight, = comté au sud de l'Angleterre

islet ['aɪlɪt] **N 1** *(small island)* îlot *m* **2** *Med (cluster of cells)* îlot *m*

ism ['ɪzəm] **N** *Fam Pej* doctrine▫ *f*, idéologie▫ *f*

SUFFIXE

-ISM, -IST

Ces suffixes ont diverses fonctions; ils se traduisent le plus souvent en français par **-isme** et **-iste**.

• On peut ajouter **-ism** à des noms pour former des termes se rapportant à une CROYANCE, une DOCTRINE ou un MOUVEMENT. Les noms et adjectifs se rapportant à un adepte de ceux-ci se forment grâce au suffixe **-ist**.

Ces suffixes se traduisent respectivement par **-isme** et **-iste**:

Impressionism impressionnisme; **the Impressionists/Impressionist paintings** les Impressionnistes/des peintures impressionnistes; **Communism/Communist views** communisme/des opinions communistes; **realism/he's a realist** réalisme/c'est un réaliste; **feminism/feminist literature** féminisme/la littérature féministe. (On notera la présence de capitales lorsqu'il est question de mouvements politiques, religieux ou artistiques.)

Dans le sens politique, **-ism** peut s'employer seul, sans trait d'union, comme dans **Fascism, Communism and all the other isms** le fascisme, le communisme et tous les autres "ismes". Il prend alors une nuance péjorative.

Accolé au nom de politiciens, le suffixe **-ism** sert aussi à créer des noms décrivant le style de politique menée par ces derniers, tout comme **-isme** en français:

Gaullism Gaullisme; **Thatcherism** Thatchérisme; **Blairism** Blairisme.

• **-ism** peut s'employer pour parler d'un TRAIT CARACTÉRISTIQUE D'UNE LANGUE ou d'un type de langage:

an Americanism un américanisme; **regionalisms** des régionalismes; **an article full of colloquialisms** un article plein d'expressions familières.

On citera le néologisme **Bushism**, qui désigne les impropriétés de langage du président George W. Bush.

• Ces suffixes servent également à construire des termes ayant trait à la DISCRIMINATION et aux PRÉJUGÉS. Là encore, on emploie les suffixes **-isme** et **-iste** en français:

sexism/sexist sexisme/sexiste; **racism/racist** racisme/raciste.

Il existe de nombreux néologismes formés sur ce modèle; on citera:
ageism âgisme; **sizeism** discrimination anti-gros; **ableism** discrimination contre les handicapés; **classism** discrimination sociale.
• Le suffixe **-ist** s'emploie également pour désigner des personnes pratiquant un MÉTIER, un ART ou une ACTIVITÉ donnée:
cyclist cycliste; **dentist** dentiste; **novelist** romancier(ère); **typist** dactylo; **guitarist** guitariste.
On notera que les noms désignant les activités correspondantes ne se terminent pas nécessairement en **-ism**: ainsi, les activités correspondant aux termes ci-dessus sont respectivement **cycling**, **dentistry**, **novel-writing**, **typing**, **guitar-playing**.

sn't [ˈɪzənt] = **is not**

SO [ˌaɪesˈəʊ] **N** *(abbr* **International Standards Organization***)* ISO *f*

sobar [ˈaɪsəbɑː(r)] **N** *Met & Phys* isobare *f*

SOC [ˌaɪes,əʊˈsiː] **N** *Comput (abbr* **Internet Society***)* = organisation non gouvernementale chargée de veiller à l'évolution de l'Internet

solate [ˈaɪsəleɪt] **VT** *(gen) & Med, Biol & Elec* isoler (**from** de *ou* d'avec); **she isolated herself from other people** elle s'est isolée des autres

solated [ˈaɪsəleɪtɪd] **ADJ 1** *(alone, remote)* isolé **2** *(single)* unique, isolé; **an i. incident** un incident isolé; **i. case** cas *m* isolé; **i. instance** cas *m* isolé

solation [ˌaɪsəˈleɪʃən] **N** *(gen) & Med, Biol & Elec* isolement *m*; **in i.** en soi, isolément; **you cannot consider the problem in i.** on ne peut pas considérer le problème isolément
►► *Med* ***isolation hospital*** hôpital *m* d'isolement; *Med* ***isolation ward*** service *m* des contagieux

Attention: ne pas confondre avec le nom anglais **insulation**, qui signifie **isolation**.

solationism [ˌaɪsəˈleɪʃəˌnɪzəm] **N** *Pol* isolationnisme *m*

solationist [ˌaɪsəˈleɪʃənɪst] **ADJ** *Pol* isolationniste

sosceles [aɪˈsɒsɪliːz] **ADJ** *Geom* isocèle
►► ***isosceles triangle*** triangle *m* isocèle

sotherapy [ˌaɪsəʊˈθerəpɪ] **N** *Med* isothérapie *f*

sotherm [ˈaɪsəʊθɜːm] **N** *Met & Phys* isotherme *f*

sotonic [ˌaɪsəʊˈtɒnɪk] **ADJ** *Phys, Mus & Med* isotonique

sotope [ˈaɪsətəʊp] **N** *Chem & Phys* isotope *m*

SP [ˌaɪesˈpiː] **N** *Comput (abbr* **Internet Service Provider***)* fournisseur *m* d'accès à l'Internet

-spy **N** *Br* = jeu d'enfant où l'un des joueurs donne la première lettre d'un objet qu'il voit et les autres doivent deviner de quoi il s'agit

srael [ˈɪzreɪəl] **N** *Geog* Israël

sraeli [ɪzˈreɪlɪ] *(pl* **inv** *or* **Israelis***)* **N** Israélien (enne) *m,f*
ADJ israélien
COMP *(embassy, history)* d'Israël

sraelite [ˈɪzrəlaɪt] **N** Israélite *mf*

SSN [ˌaɪesesˈen] **N** *(abbr* **International Standard Serial Number***)* ISSN *m*

SSUE [ˈɪʃuː]

N
- question **1**
- différend **2**
- numéro **3**
- distribution **4**
- délivrance **4**
- émission **4**
- prêt **4**
- issue **5**

VT
- publier **1, 3**
- sortir **1**
- délivrer **2**
- prêter **2**
- émettre **4**
- distribuer **5**

VI
- sortir **1**
- provenir **1, 2**

N 1 *(matter, topic)* question *f*, problème *m*; **where do you stand on the abortion i.?** quel est votre point de vue sur (la question de) l'avortement?; **the i. was raised at the meeting** le problème a été soulevé à la réunion; **that's not the i.** ce n'est pas la question; **it's become an international i.** le problème a pris une dimension internationale; **at i.** en question; **the point at i. is not the coming election** le problème n'est pas l'élection à venir; **her competence is not at i.** sa compétence n'est pas en cause; **to join i. with sb (about sth)** discuter l'opinion de qn (au sujet de qch); **to cloud** *or* **confuse the i.** brouiller les cartes; **to avoid** *or* **to duck** *or* **to evade the i.** esquiver la question; **to force the i.** forcer la décision; *Law* **i. (of fact/of law)** question *f ou* point *m* de fait/de droit
2 *(cause of disagreement)* différend *m*; **the subject has now become a real i. between us** ce sujet est maintenant source de désaccord entre nous; **to be at i. with sb over sth** être en désaccord avec qn au sujet de qch; **to make an i. of sth** monter qch en épingle; **don't make such an i. of it!** inutile d'en faire toute une histoire!; **to take i. with sb/sth** être en désaccord avec qn/qch; **I would take i. with that** je ne suis pas d'accord là-dessus
3 *(edition ► of newspaper, magazine etc)* numéro *m*; **the latest i. of the magazine** le dernier numéro du magazine
4 *(distribution ► of supplies, equipment)* distribution *f*; *(► of official document, passport)* délivrance *f*; *(► of shares, money, stamps)* émission *f*; *(► of library book)* prêt *m*; **date of i.** date *f* de délivrance; **standard i.** modèle *m* standard; **army i.** modèle *m* de l'armée
5 *Formal (result, outcome)* issue *f*, résultat *m*; **I hope your request has a favourable i.** j'espère que votre demande connaîtra une issue *ou* recevra une réponse favorable
6 *Arch or Law (progeny)* descendance *f*, progéniture *f*; **he died without i.** il est mort sans héritiers
7 *Med (of blood, pus)* décharge *f*
VT 1 *(book, newspaper)* publier, sortir; *(record)* sortir; **the magazine is issued on Wednesdays** le magazine sort *ou* paraît le mercredi
2 *(official document, passport)* délivrer; *Law (warrant, writ, summons)* lancer; *(library book)* prêter; **where was the passport issued?** où le passeport a-t-il été délivré?; **no books will be issued after eight p.m.** le service de prêt ferme à vingt heures
3 *(statement, proclamation)* publier; **the government has issued a denial** le gouvernement a publié un démenti
4 *(shares, money, stamps)* émettre; *(letter of credit)* fournir; **to i. a draft on sb** fournir une traite sur qn
5 *(distribute ► supplies, tickets etc)* distribuer; **the magazine is issued free to every household** le magazine est distribué gratuitement à *ou* dans tous les foyers; **we were all issued with rations** on nous a distribué à tous des rations; **each man will be issued with two uniforms** chaque homme recevra deux uniformes
VI *Formal* **1** *(come or go out)* sortir (**from** de); *(blood, water)* s'écouler (**from** de); *(smoke)* s'échapper (**from** de); **delicious smells issued from the kitchen** des odeurs délicieuses provenaient de la cuisine
2 *(result, originate)* **to i. from** provenir de; **all our difficulties i. from that first mistake** c'est de cette première erreur que proviennent tous nos ennuis; **the children issuing from this marriage** les enfants issus de ce mariage
►► *Admin* ***issue card*** carte *f* (de) sortie de stock; *Fin* ***issue premium*** prime *f* d'émission; *Fin* ***issue price*** prix *m* d'émission, valeur *f* d'émission; *Pol* ***issue voting*** = notion selon laquelle les électeurs se prononcent en fonction des enjeux en présence, plus que par loyauté envers tel ou tel parti

Note that the French word **issue** is a false friend and is seldom a translation for the English word **issue**. It means **exit**.

issued [ˈɪʃuːd] **ADJ**
►► *St Exch* ***issued capital*** capital *m* émis; ***issued securities*** titres *mpl* émis; *St Exch* ***issued share capital*** capital-action *m* émis

issueless [ˈɪʃuːlɪs] **ADV** *Formal* **to die i.** mourir sans laisser de descendance

issuer [ˈɪʃuːə(r)] **N** *(of shares, money, stamps)* émetteur *m*

issuing [ˈɪʃuːɪŋ] **N** *(of loan, banknotes)* émission *f*; *(of provisions)* distribution *f*; *(of library books)* prêt *m*; *(of passport)* délivrance *f*; *(of arrest warrant)* lancement *m*
►► *Br* ***issuing bank*** banque *f* d'émission *ou* émettrice; ***issuing company*** société *f* émettrice; ***issuing house*** banque *f* émettrice *ou* d'émission

Istanbul [ˌɪstænˈbʊl] **N** *Geog* Istanbul

isthmus [ˈɪsməs] *(pl* **isthmuses** *or* **isthmi** [-maɪ]*)* **N** *Geog & Anat* isthme *m*

IT [ˌaɪˈtiː] **N** *Comput (abbr* **information technology***)* technologie *f* de l'information; **she's our IT expert** c'est notre spécialiste en informatique; **IT has revolutionized the way we do business** l'informatique a complètement transformé le monde du commerce

IT [ɪt]

PRON
- il/elle **1**
- le/la **1**
- lui **1**
- en **2**
- il *(impersonnel)* **3**
- ça **3**
- ce **3, 5**

PRON 1 *(referring to specific thing, animal etc ► as subject)* il (elle); *(► as direct object)* le (la); *(► as indirect object)* lui; **is it a boy or a girl?** c'est un garçon ou une fille?; **the building's dangerous, it should be pulled down** le bâtiment est dangereux, il devrait être démoli; **I'd lend you my computer but it's broken** je te prêterais bien mon ordinateur mais elle est cassée; **I took my hat off and now I can't find it** j'ai enlevé mon chapeau et je ne le trouve plus; **take this plate and put it on the table** prends cette assiette et mets-la sur la table; **give it a tap with a hammer** donnez un coup de marteau dessus; **fetch the dog and give it something to eat** va chercher le chien et donne-lui à manger
2 *(after preposition)* **he told me all about it** il m'a tout raconté; **as we walked away from it** tandis que nous nous en éloignions; **he's not bad, far from it** il n'est pas méchant, loin de là; **give me half of it** donnez-m'en la moitié; **there was nothing inside it** il n'y avait rien dedans *ou* à l'intérieur; **don't tread on it** ne marchez pas dessus; **I went over to it** je m'en suis approché; **did he consent to it?** est-ce qu'il y a consenti?; **I left the bag under it** j'ai laissé le sac dessous; **I cracked his head with it** je lui ai fendu la tête avec
3 *(as unspecified subject)* **it's me!** c'est moi!; **it's raining/snowing** il pleut/neige; **it's cold/dark today** il fait froid/sombre aujourd'hui; **it's Friday today** nous sommes *ou* c'est vendredi aujourd'hui; **it seemed like a good idea** cela *ou* ça semblait être une bonne idée; **it's 500 miles from here to Vancouver** Vancouver est à 800 km d'ici; **it's not easy for me to say this, but...** je n'aime pas dire ce genre de chose, mais...; **it'll take us hours to get there** on va mettre des heures pour y arriver; **it'll cost (us) a fortune to have it repaired** ça va (nous) coûter une fortune pour le faire réparer; **it was agreed that we should move out** il a été convenu que nous déménagerions; **it's impossible to work in this heat** c'est impossible de travailler par cette chaleur; **it might look rude if I don't go** si je n'y vais pas, cela pourrait être considéré comme une impolitesse; **it seems** *or* **appears** *or* **would appear that there's been some trouble** il semble qu'il y ait eu des problèmes; **it says on the box/in the instructions that...** c'est écrit sur la boîte/dans les instructions que...; **it's the Johnny Carson Show!** voici le Johnny Carson Show!; **it's a goal!** but!; **it's his constant complaining I can't stand** ce que je ne supporte pas, c'est sa façon de se plaindre constamment
4 *(as unspecified object)* **I like it here** je me plais beaucoup ici; **I love it when we go on a picnic** j'adore quand on va pique-niquer; **I couldn't bear it if she left** je ne supporterais pas qu'elle parte; **she found it easy to make new friends** ça lui a été facile de se faire de nouveaux amis; *Fam* **blast it!** zut!
5 *(as complement)* **who is it?** qui est-ce?
N *Fam* **1** *(in games)* **you're it!** c'est toi le chat!, c'est toi qui y es!
2 *(most important person)* **he thinks he's it** il s'y croit

3 *Fam (Italian vermouth)* **gin and it** gin *m* avec du vermouth italien□
▸▸ *Br Fam* ***it girl*** jeune mondaine□ *f*

Italian [ɪ'tæljən] **N 1** *(person)* Italien(enne) *m,f* **2** *(language)* italien *m* **3** *Fam (restaurant)* restau *m* italien; *(meal)* repas *m* italien□; **we went out for an I.** on est allés dans un restau italien
ADJ italien
COMP *(embassy)* d'Italie; *(history)* de l'Italie; *(teacher)* d'italien
▸▸ *Culin* ***Italian dressing*** vinaigrette *f* aux fines herbes; ***Italian Switzerland*** Suisse *f* italienne; ***Italian vermouth*** vermouth *m* italien

Italianate [ɪ'tæljəneɪt] **ADJ** *Archit* italianisant

Italianism [ɪ'tæljəˌnɪzəm] **N 1** *Ling* italianisme *m* **2** *(custom)* italianisme *m*

Italianist [ɪ'tæljənɪst] **N 1** *(specialist)* italianisant (e) *m,f* **2** *(devotee)* amateur(trice) *m,f* de l'Italie

Italianize, -ise [ɪ'tæljəˌnaɪz] **VT** italianiser

italic [ɪ'tælɪk] *Typ*
ADJ italique; **i.** *or* **italics face** *or* **type** caractères *mpl* italiques; **in i. face** en italique
N italique *m*; **in italics** en italique; **the italics are mine** les italiques sont de moi
▸▸ ***italic character*** caractère *m* italique; ***italic print*** caractères *mpl* italiques

italicization, -isation [ɪˌtælɪsaɪ'zeɪʃən] **N** *Typ* mise *f* en italique

italicize, -ise [ɪ'tælɪˌsaɪz] **VT** *Typ* mettre en italique; **the italicized words** les mots en italique

Italo- [ɪ'tæləʊ] **PREF** italo-; **Italo-American** italo-américain

Italy ['ɪtəlɪ] **N** *Geog* Italie *f*

ITC [ˌaɪtiː'siː] **N** *Br* (*abbr* **Independent Television Commission**) = commission de surveillance des télévisions britanniques privées

itch [ɪtʃ] **N 1** *(physical)* démangeaison *f*; **I've got an i.** ça me démange *ou* me gratte **2** *Fam Fig (desire)* envie□ *f*; **I've got the i. to work abroad** ça me démange d'aller travailler à l'étranger; *Fam Fig* **if you've got an i., scratch it** si ça te dit, vas-y
VI 1 *(physically)* avoir des démangeaisons; **I'm itching all over** j'ai des démangeaisons partout, je suis couvert de démangeaisons; **does it i.?** est-ce que cela te démange?; **my back itches** mon dos me démange *ou* me gratte; **that sweater itches** ce pull me gratte; *Fig* **to have an itching palm** être cupide **2** *Fam Fig (desire)* **I was itching to tell her** ça me démangeait de lui dire; **we're itching to go** nous ne tenons plus en place

itching ['ɪtʃɪŋ] **N** démangeaison *f*
▸▸ ***itching powder*** poil *m* à gratter

itchy ['ɪtʃɪ] *(compar* **itchier**, *superl* **itchiest)** **ADJ** qui gratte, qui démange; **an i. pullover** un pull qui gratte; **I've got an i. leg** ma jambe me démange; *Fam Fig* **to have i. feet** avoir la bougeotte

it'd ['ɪtəd] = **it would, it had**

> **-ITE** — SUFFIXE
>
> Dans son sens moderne le plus courant, **-ite** sert à former des noms et des adjectifs désignant les PARTISANS d'une personne, notamment d'un homme politique:
>
> **a Trotskyite** un(e) trotskiste; **she's a Blairite** c'est une fidèle de Blair; **Reaganite policies** une politique reaganienne; **Darwinites** les darwiniens; **Pre-Raphaelite paintings** des peintures préraphaélites.
>
> Bien que ces mots aient parfois une connotation péjorative, **-ite** est aujourd'hui le suffixe neutre le plus couramment employé dans le domaine politique.

item ['aɪtəm] **N 1** *(object)* article *m*; **the items in the shop window** les articles en vitrine; **the only i. he bought was a lighter** la seule chose qu'il ait achetée, c'est un briquet; **an i. of clothing** un vêtement **2** *(point, issue)* point *m*, question *f*; **there are two important items on the agenda** il y a deux points importants à l'ordre du jour; **I've several items of business to attend to** j'ai plusieurs affaires à régler
3 *(in newspaper)* article *m*; *(very brief)* entrefilet *m*; *(on TV or radio)* point *m ou* sujet *m* d'actualité; **there was an i. on the news about it yesterday** ils en ont parlé aux informations hier; **and here are today's main news items** et voici les principaux points de l'actualité
4 *(performance in show)* numéro *m*
5 *Comput (on menu)* élément *m*
6 *Ling* item *m*; **lexical i.** item *m* lexical
7 *Acct* écriture *f*, article *m*; **i. of expenditure** article *m* de dépense
8 *Fam (couple)* **are they an i.?** est-ce qu'ils sortent ensemble?□; **they're no longer an i.** ils ne sortent plus ensemble□
ADV *Old-fashioned (when listing)* item
▸▸ *Am Pol* ***item veto*** veto *m* partiel

itemize, -ise ['aɪtəmaɪz] **VT** détailler
▸▸ ***itemized bill*** facture *f* détaillée; ***itemized billing, itemized invoicing*** facturation *f* détaillée; ***itemized list*** liste *f* détaillée

iterate ['ɪtəreɪt] **VT** *Formal (say again)* réitérer; *(do again)* refaire, répéter; *Comput & Math* itérer

iteration [ˌɪtə'reɪʃən] **N** *Formal & Comput & Math* itération *f*

iterative ['ɪtərətɪv] **ADJ** *(gen) & Ling & Math* itératif

itinerant [ɪ'tɪnərənt] **ADJ** itinérant; *(actors)* ambulant, itinérant; **i. preacher** prédicateur *m* itinérant; *Am* **i. teacher** professeur *m* remplaçant
N nomade *mf*

itinerary [aɪ'tɪnərərɪ] *(pl* **itineraries)** **N** itinéraire *m*

it'll [ɪtəl] = **it will**

ITN [ˌaɪtiː'en] **N** *Br* (*abbr* **Independent Television News**) = service d'actualités télévisées pour les chaînes relevant de l'"ITC"

ITO [ˌaɪtiː'əʊ] **N** (*abbr* **International Trade Organization**) OMC *f*

it's [ɪts] = **it is, it has**

> Attention: ne pas confondre avec l'adjectif et le pronom possessifs **its**.

its [ɪts] **ADJ** *(singular)* son (sa); *(plural)* ses; **the committee has i. first meeting on Friday** le comité se réunit pour la première fois vendredi; **the dog wagged i. tail** le chien a remué la queue; **the jug's lost i. handle** le pichet n'a plus de poignée
PRON *(singular)* le sien (la sienne); *(plural)* les siens (les siennes)

> Attention: ne pas confondre avec **it's**, qui est la forme abrégée de **it is** ou **it has**.

itself [ɪt'self] **PRON 1** *(reflexive use)* se; **the cat was licking i. clean** le chat faisait sa toilette; **the dog hurt i.** le chien s'est blessé **2** *(emphatic use)* lui même (elle-même); **the town i. is quite small** la ville elle-même est assez petite; **she's kindness i** c'est la gentillesse même **3** *(after preposition)* **it switches off by i.** ça s'éteint tout seul; **it's not dangerous in i.** ce n'est pas dangereux en soi; **working with her was in i. fascinating** le seul fait de travailler avec elle était fascinant

ITV [ˌaɪtiː'viː] **N** *Br* (*abbr* **Independent Television**) = sigle désignant les programmes diffusés par les chaînes relevant de l'"ITC"

iTV [ˌaɪtiː'viː] **N** *Br* (*abbr* **interactive television**) télévision *f* interactive

IUD [ˌaɪjuː'diː] **N** *Med* (*abbr* **intrauterine device**) stérilet *m*

IV [ˌaɪ'viː] *Med* (*abbr* **intravenous**) **N** perfusion *f* intraveineuse
ADJ intraveineux
ADV par voie intraveineuse
▸▸ ***IV drip*** perfusion *f* intraveineuse; ***IV pump*** pompe *f* de perfusion sous pression

IVA [ˌaɪviː'eɪ] **N** *Law* (*abbr* **Individual Voluntary Arrangement**) = accord légal établi par un administrateur judiciaire qui permet à un débiteur de trouver un compromis avec ses créanciers lui évitant ainsi les conséquences d'une faillite

I've [aɪv] = **I have**

IVF [ˌaɪviː'ef] **N** *Med* (*abbr* **in vitro fertilization**) FIV

ivory ['aɪvərɪ] *(pl* **ivories)** **N 1** *(substance)* ivoire *m* **2** *(object)* ivoire *m*
ADJ 1 *(made of ivory)* d'ivoire, en ivoire; **an i. carving** une sculpture d'ivoire **2** *(ivory-coloured)* (couleur) ivoire *(inv)*
• **ivories** **NPL** *Fam* **1** *(piano keys)* touches□ *fpl Hum* **to tickle the ivories** toucher du piano□ **2** *(teeth)* ratiches *fpl*
▸▸ ***ivory tower*** tour *f* d'ivoire

ivory-white **ADJ** *(teeth)* d'une blancheur d'ivoire

ivy ['aɪvɪ] *(pl* **ivies)** **N** *Bot* lierre *m*
▸▸ ***the Ivy League*** = groupe des huit universités les plus prestigieuses du nord-est des États Unis

> **THE IVY LEAGUE**
>
> Ce terme désignait à l'origine un groupe de huit universités de l'est des États-Unis: Brown, Columbia, Cornell, Dartmouth, Harvard, l'Université de Pennsylvanie, Princeton et Yale. Ces universités se caractérisent par une forte proportion d'étudiants de troisième cycle, des moyens financiers importants et la réputation d'excellence de leurs universitaires. De nos jours le terme "Ivy League", ou plus familièrement "the Ivies", a une signification moins précise que par le passé et il s'applique souvent à n'importe laquelle des plus prestigieuses universités privées. Le terme "second-tier Ivies" s'applique quant à lui à un groupe d'établissements un peu moins prestigieux.

IYHF [ˌaɪwaɪˌeɪtʃ'ef] **N** (*abbr* **International Youth Hostel Federation**) FIAJ *f*

[1], j [dʒeɪ] **N** *(letter)* J, j *m inv*; **two j's** deux j

[2] **N** *Fam Drugs slang (joint)* joint *m*

ab [dʒæb] *(pt & pp* **jabbed**, *cont* **jabbing)** **N 1** *(poke)* coup *m (donné avec un objet pointu)*; **she gave him a sharp j. in the ribs (with her elbow)** elle lui a mis un coup de coude dans les côtes **2** *Fam (injection)* piqûre*f*; **to give sb a j.** faire une injection ou une piqûre à qn; *(for TB, malaria etc)* vacciner qn; **I've got to get a tetanus j.** je dois me faire vacciner contre le tétanos **3** *Boxing* coup *m* droit, direct *m*

VT 1 *(poke, prick)* **to j. sb/sth (with sth)** piquer qn/qch (avec qch *ou* du bout de qch); **to j. sb with one's elbow/a knife** donner un coup de coude/de couteau à qn **2** *(thrust)* enfoncer, planter (d'un coup sec) **(into dans)**; **she jabbed a finger at him to emphasize her point** elle a pointé le doigt dans sa direction pour appuyer ses propos

VI 1 *(poke, prick)* **to j. at sb/sth (with sth)** piquer qn/qch (avec qch *ou* du bout de qch); **to j. at sb with a knife/an umbrella** donner un coup de couteau/de parapluie à qn **2** *Boxing* envoyer un coup droit *ou* un direct **(at à)**

abber ['dʒæbə(r)] *Fam* **VI** *(idly)* jacasser, *Pej* caqueter; *(inarticulately)* bredouiller, bafouiller; *(in foreign language)* baragouiner; **they j. (away) for hours on the phone** ils passent des heures à jacasser au téléphone; **they were all jabbering away in different languages** chacun baragouinait dans sa langue

VT to j. (out) bredouiller, bafouiller

N *(UNCOUNT)* **1** *(noise)* brouhaha *m* **2** *(chat)* conversation *f*, *Pej* jacasseries *fpl*; **to have a j.** bavarder

abbering ['dʒæbərɪŋ] **N** *(UNCOUNT)* **1** *(incomprehensible)* baragouinage *m* **2** *(chattering)* bavardage *m*, *Pej* jacasseries *fpl*

acaranda [ˌdʒækə'rændə] **N** *Bot* jacaranda *m*

ack [dʒæk] **VT** *Tech* soulever avec un vérin; *Aut* mettre sur cric

N 1 *Tech (tool)* vérin *m*; *Aut* cric *m*

2 *(playing card)* valet *m*

3 *(in bowls)* cochonnet *m*

4 *Tel* prise *f*; *Elec (socket)* prise *f ou* fiche *f* femelle; *(plug, connector)* prise *f ou* fiche *f* mâle; **microphone/headphone j.** prise *f* de microphone/de casque

5 *Am Fam (money)* blé *m*, fric *m*

6 (roasting) j. tournebroche *m*

7 *Naut (flag)* pavillon *m* beaupré

8 *Ich* brocheton *m*

9 *Br Fam* **every man j. (of them)** tous autant qu'ils sont

• **Jack PR N** *Br Fam* **I'm all right, J.** moi ça va; *Fam* **an "I'm all right, J." attitude** une attitude égoïste; *Am* **hey, J.!** *(to stranger)* hé, vous là-bas!; *Br Fam* **before you could say J. Robinson** avant d'avoir pu dire ouf

• **jacks N** *(UNCOUNT) (game)* osselets *mpl*

►► ***Jack Frost*** le Bonhomme Hiver; *Tech* ***jack plug*** prise *f ou* fiche *f* mâle, jack *m*; *Zool* ***jack rabbit*** = gros lièvre d'Amérique; ***Jack Russell*** Jack Russell (terrier) *m*; *Elec* ***jack socket*** prise *f ou* fiche *f* femelle; *Fam Old-fashioned* ***jack tar*** marin *m*, matelot *m*

►**jack around** *Am Fam* **VT SEP to j. sb around** *(treat badly)* se ficher de qn; *(waste time of)* faire perdre son temps à qn

VI *(waste time)* glander, glandouiller

►**jack in VT SEP** *Br Fam* plaquer; **I've jacked my job in** j'ai plaqué mon boulot; **oh, j. it in, will you!** oh, ferme-la, tu veux!

►**jack off** *Vulg* **VT SEP to j. sb off** branler qn

VI se branler, se palucher

►**jack up VT SEP 1** *(car)* lever avec un cric **2** *Fam (price, wage)* augmenter, monter **3** *Br Fam Drugs slang (inject oneself with)* se piquer à

VI *Br Fam Drugs slang (inject oneself)* se piquer

jackal ['dʒækəl] **N** *also Fig* chacal *m*

jackaroo [ˌdʒækəˌruː] *(pl* **jackaroos)** **N** *Austr Fam* bleu *m (dans une ferme)*

jackass ['dʒækæs] **N 1** *(donkey)* âne *m*, baudet *m* **2** *Fam (imbecile)* imbécile *mf*

jackboot ['dʒækbuːt] **N** botte *f* (de militaire); *Fig* **life under the j.** la vie sous la botte de l'ennemi

jackdaw ['dʒækdɔː] **N** *Orn* choucas *m*

jacket ['dʒækɪt] **N 1** *(garment)* veste *f*; *(shorter)* blouson *m*; *(of man's suit)* veston *m*; *(of woman's suit)* jaquette *f*; **leather j.** blouson *m* de cuir; *(longer)* veste *f* de cuir

2 *(of book)* jaquette *f*; *Am (of record)* pochette *f*

3 *(of baked potato)* peau *f*; **potato (cooked) in its j.** pomme *f* de terre en robe des champs *ou* en robe de chambre

4 *Tech (of boiler, bullet)* chemise *f*

VT *Tech (boiler etc)* garnir *ou* envelopper d'une chemise, chemiser

►► ***jacket potato*** pomme *f* de terre en robe des champs *ou* en robe de chambre

jackhammer ['dʒækˌhæmə(r)] **N** marteau *m* piqueur

jacking point ['dʒækɪŋ-] **N** point *m* de levage, emplacement *m* prévu pour le cric

jack-in-the-box *(pl* **jack-in-the-boxes** *or* **jacks-in-the-box)** **N** diable *m* (à ressort); *Fam* **to jump up and down like a j.** ne pas tenir en place

jackknife ['dʒæknaɪf] *(pl* **jackknives** [-naɪvz]**)** **N** couteau *m* de poche

VI the truck jackknifed le camion s'est mis en portefeuille

►► *Sport* ***jackknife dive*** saut *m* de carpe

jack-of-all-trades *(pl* **jacks-of-all-trades)** **N** *Pej* homme *m* à tout faire; *Prov* **j. and master of none** propre à tout et bon à rien

jack-o'-lantern N 1 *(Hallowe'en lantern)* = lanterne faite dans une citrouille sur laquelle on a creusé un visage **2** *(will-o'-the-wisp)* feu *m* follet

jackpot ['dʒækpɒt] **N 1** *Cards (in poker etc)* pot *m* **2** *(in competition, of lottery)* gros lot *m*; **to hit** *or* **win the j.** gagner le gros lot; *Fig* **to hit the j.** *(be successful ► person)* gagner le gros lot, décrocher la timbale; **she's hit the j. with her latest book** elle a fait un malheur avec son dernier livre

jacksie ['dʒæksɪ] **N** *Br very Fam (buttocks)* popotin *m*

Jack-the-Lad N *Fam* jeune frimeur *m*

Jacobean [ˌdʒækə'bɪən] **ADJ** *Hist & Archit* jacobéen, de l'époque de Jacques Ier (d'Angleterre)

Jacobite ['dʒækəbaɪt] *Hist* **N** Jacobite *mf*

ADJ jacobite

►► ***the Jacobite Rising*** = nom donné aux deux tentatives conduites par les Stuarts pour s'emparer du trône d'Angleterre en 1715 et 1745

Jacuzzi® [dʒə'kuːzɪ] *(pl* **Jacuzzis)** **N** Jacuzzi® *m*, bain *m* à remous

jade [dʒeɪd] **N 1** *Miner (stone)* jade *m*

2 *(colour)* vert jade *m inv*

3 *Arch (horse)* rosse *f*, haridelle *f*

4 *Arch (woman ► shrewish)* mégère *f*; *(► disreputable)* friponne *f*

ADJ 1 *(made of jade)* de *ou* en jade **2** *(colour)* vert jade *(inv)*

jaded ['dʒeɪdɪd] **ADJ** *(person ► tired)* las, fatigué; *(► unenthusiastic)* blasé; *(performance, piece of writing, cliché)* faiblard; **I'm feeling a bit j. today** je ne suis pas très en forme aujourd'hui

►► ***jaded palate*** palais *m* blasé; *Fig* appétit *m* fatigué

Jag [dʒæg] **N** *Fam (Jaguar® car)* Jaguar® *f*

jag [dʒæg] *(pt & pp* **jagged**, *cont* **jagging)** **N 1** *(jagged projection)* pointe *f*, aspérité *f*; *(of saw)* dent *f* **2** *Am Fam (drinking bout)* soûlerie *f*; **to go on a (drinking) j.** se soûler, prendre une cuite; **a crying j.** une crise de larmes **3** *Scot Fam (injection)* piquouse *f*

VT déchiqueter; *(fabric)* taillader

jagged ['dʒægɪd] **ADJ** *(coastline, mountain top)* découpé; *(edge)* découpé, dentelé; *(line, tear)* irrégulier; *(rock)* pointu, dentelé; **the j. outline of the coast** les dentelures *fpl ou* découpures *fpl* de la côte

jaggy ['dʒægɪ] **ADJ 1** *(coastline, mountain top)* déchiqueté, découpé; *(edge)* déchiqueté, découpé, dentelé **2** *Scot (prickly)* plein de piquants

jaguar ['dʒægjʊə(r)] **N** *Zool* jaguar *m*

jail [dʒeɪl] **N** prison *f*; **to be in j.** être en prison; **to be sent to j.** être incarcéré *ou* emprisonné; **to go to j.** aller en prison, faire de la prison; **he was sent to j.** *or* **he went to j. for ten years** il a été condamné à dix ans de prison; **she was in j. for ten years, she went to j. for ten years** elle a fait dix ans de prison; **to break out of j.** s'évader de prison

VT emprisonner, mettre en prison, incarcérer; **to be jailed for life** être condamné à perpétuité *ou* à vie

jailbait ['dʒeɪlbeɪt] **N** *(UNCOUNT) Am Fam* mineur(e) *m,f*; **she's j.** c'est un coup à se retrouver en taule *(pour détournement de mineue)*

jailbird ['dʒeɪlbɜːd] **N** *Fam (actually in prison)* taulard(e) *m,f*; *(constantly going to prison)* cheval *m* de retour

jailbreak ['dʒeɪlbreɪk] **N** évasion *f*; **to carry out a j.** s'évader

jailbreaker ['dʒeɪlˌbreɪkə(r)] **N** évadé(e) *m,f*

jailer ['dʒeɪlə(r)] **N** geôlier(ère) *m,f*

jailhouse ['dʒeɪlhaus, *pl* -hauzɪz] **N** *Am* prison *f*

jailor = **jailer**

Jakarta [dʒə'kɑːtə] **N** *Geog* Djakarta, Jakarta

jake [dʒeɪk] **N** *Br Fam Drugs slang* joint *m*

jalapeño [hɑːlə'peɪnjəʊ] *(pl* **jalapeños)** **N** *Bot & Culin* petit piment *m* vert

jalopy, jaloppy [dʒə'lɒpɪ] *(pl* **jalopies** *or* **jaloppies)** **N** *Fam* (vieille) bagnole *f*, (vieux) tacot *m*

jam [dʒæm] (*pt & pp* **jammed,** *cont* **jamming**) **N 1** *Culin (preserve)* confiture *f*; **strawberry j.** confiture *f* de fraises; *Br Fam* **he wants j. on it!** et avec ça, on est difficile!; *Br Fam* **it's a case of j. tomorrow** ce sont des promesses en l'air

2 *(traffic jam)* bouchon *m*, embouteillage *m*, encombrement *m*

3 *(crowd)* **there was a great j. of people outside the theatre** il y avait une foule énorme devant le théâtre

4 *Fam (predicament)* pétrin *m*; **I'm in a bit of a j.** je suis plutôt dans le pétrin

5 *Fam (by musicians)* bœuf *m*, jam-session *f*

COMP *(tart, pudding, sandwich)* à la confiture

VT 1 *(crowd, cram)* entasser, tasser; *(push roughly, ram)* fourrer; **we were jammed in like sardines** on était entassés *ou* serrés comme des sardines; **all my clothes are jammed into one drawer** tous mes vêtements sont entassés dans un seul tiroir; **I was jammed (up) against the wall** j'étais coincé contre le mur; **he jammed the gun into his pocket** il fourra le pistolet dans sa poche; **she jammed her hat on** elle enfonça *ou* vissa son chapeau sur sa tête; **to j. one's foot on the brake(s)** écraser le frein *ou* la pédale de frein

2 *(make stick)* coincer, bloquer; *(weapon, mechanism)* enrayer, bloquer; *(pipe)* boucher; **she jammed the window shut with a wedge** elle coinça *ou* bloqua la fenêtre avec une cale; **to j. a door open with a book** maintenir une porte ouverte à l'aide d'un livre

3 *(congest)* encombrer, bloquer, boucher; **a crowd of late arrivals jammed the entrance** une foule de retardataires bloquait l'entrée; **the streets were jammed with cars** les rues étaient embouteillées

4 *Rad* brouiller

5 *Tel (lines)* encombrer; *(switchboard)* faire sauter; **the switchboard was jammed** le standard était saturé

VI 1 *(crowd)* se tasser, s'entasser

2 *(drawer, window, lift etc)* se coincer, se bloquer; *(gun, machine)* s'enrayer, se bloquer; *(brakes, wheel, paper in printer)* se bloquer

3 *Fam (play in a jam session)* faire un bœuf; *(play on one's own)* improviser[◻]; **I was just jamming** c'était juste de l'impro

4 *(in mountaineering)* faire un verrou, coincer

▸▸ *Br Fam Hum* ***jam sandwich*** *(police car)* voiture *f* de police[◻]; *Fam* ***jam session*** bœuf *m*, jam-session *f*

▸**jam in VT SEP 1** *(wedge in)* coincer; **the crowd were jamming him in** il était coincé par la foule; **her car was being jammed in by a large truck** un gros camion était en train de la coincer **2** *(pack or press tightly in ▸ passengers etc)* (en)tasser; *(▸ objects)* bourrer; **he had jammed as many quotations as he could find into the essay** il avait farci sa dissertation de toutes les citations qu'il avait trouvées

VI *(crowd in)* s'entasser; **they all jammed in** *(into train)* ils s'y entassèrent tous; **thousands of people jammed in for the concert** des milliers de personnes se sont entassées pour assister au concert

▸**jam on VT SEP 1** *Aut* **to j. on the brakes** écraser le frein *ou* la pédale de frein **2** *(lid, hat etc)* enfoncer

Jamaica [dʒə'meɪkə] **N** *Geog* Jamaïque *f*

▸▸ ***Jamaica pepper*** poivre *m* de la Jamaïque, toute-épice *m*; ***Jamaica rum*** rhum *m* jamaïquain *ou* jamaïcain *ou* de la Jamaïque

Jamaican [dʒə'meɪkən] **N** Jamaïcain(e) *m,f*, Jamaïquain(e) *m,f*

ADJ jamaïcain, jamaïquain

jamb [dʒæm] **N** chambranle *m*, jambage *m*, montant *m*

jamboree [ˌdʒæmbə'riː] **N 1** *(scouts' meeting)* jamboree *m* **2** *Fam (celebration, party)* fête[◻] *f*, réunion[◻] *f*; *(festivities)* réjouissances[◻] *fpl* (tapageuses); **village j.** fête *f* de village

jammies ['dʒæmɪz] **NPL** *(in children's language)* pyjama *m*

jamming ['dʒæmɪŋ] **N 1** *(sticking)* coincement *m*; *(of brakes)* blocage *m*

2 *Rad* brouillage *m*; **electronic j.** brouillage *m* électronique

3 *Tel (of lines)* encombrement *m*

4 *(in mountaineering)* coincement *m*

jammy ['dʒæmɪ] (*compar* **jammier,** *superl* **jammiest**) **ADJ 1** *(covered with jam)* plein de confiture **2** *Br Fam (lucky)* veinard, verni; **he's a j. devil!** quel veinard, celui-là!, il est verni, celui-là! **3** *Br Fam (easy)* facile[◻]; **j. job** filon *m*, bonne planque *f*

jam-packed ADJ *(suitcase, bag etc)* plein à craquer, bourré (**with** de); **j. (with people)** *(hall, bus)* plein à craquer, bondé; *(street)* noir de monde, bondé; **this magazine is j. with interesting articles** ce magazine est truffé *ou* regorge d'articles intéressants

jams [dʒæmz] **NPL** *Am (shorts)* bermuda *m*

Jan. *(written abbr* **January***)* janv

Jane [dʒeɪn] **N** *Am Fam (woman)* nana *f*

▸▸ *Am* ***Jane Doe*** *(average person)* l'Américaine *f* moyenne, Madame Dupont; *(unidentified woman ▸ under arrest)* inconnue *f*; *(▸ corpse)* morte *f* non identifiée

jangle ['dʒæŋgəl] **N** *(of bells)* tintamarre *m*; *(of money)* bruit *m*, cliquetis *m*; **the j. of keys** le cliquetis des clés

VT faire retentir; *(more quietly)* faire cliqueter; *Fig* **my nerves are all jangled** j'ai les nerfs en boule *ou* en pelote

VI retentir (avec un bruit métallique *ou* avec fracas); *(more quietly)* cliqueter; **his keys jangled in his pocket** ses clés cliquetaient dans sa poche; **it jangled on my nerves** cela me mettait les nerfs en pelote

jangling ['dʒæŋglɪŋ] **N** bruit *m* métallique; **a j. of keys** un bruit de clés

ADJ *(bells)* retentissant; *(keys)* qui tintent; **a j. noise** un bruit métallique

janitor ['dʒænɪtə(r)] **N** *Am & Scot (caretaker)* gardien *m*, concierge *m*

January ['dʒænjʊərɪ] **N** janvier *m*; *see also* **February**

Jap [dʒæp] *very Fam* **N** Jap *mf*, = terme injurieux désignant un Japonais

ADJ jap, japonais[◻]

Japan [dʒə'pæn] **N** *Geog* Japon *m*

Japanese [ˌdʒæpə'niːz] (*pl* **inv**) **NPL the J.** les Japonais *mpl*

N 1 *(person)* Japonais(e) *m,f* **2** *(language)* japonais *m*

ADJ japonais

COMP *(embassy, history)* du Japon; *(teacher)* de japonais

▸▸ *Bot* ***Japanese cherry*** *(tree)* cerisier *m* (à fleurs) du Japon; ***Japanese lantern*** lanterne *f* vénitienne; *Bot* ***Japanese red cedar*** cryptoméria *m* du Japon

jape [dʒeɪp] **N** *Fam Old-fashioned* farce[◻] *f*, blague *f*

japonica [dʒə'pɒnɪkə] **N** *Bot* cognassier *m* du Japon

jar [dʒɑː(r)] (*pt & pp* **jarred,** *cont* **jarring**) **N 1** *(container ▸ glass)* bocal *m*; *(▸ for jam)* pot *m*; *(▸ earthenware)* pot *m*, jarre *f* **2** *Br Fam (drink)* pot *m*; **he's having a few jars with the lads** il prend un pot *ou* un verre avec les copains **3** *(jolt)* secousse *f*, choc *m*

VI 1 *(make harsh noise)* grincer, crisser; **there's something about her voice which really jars** sa voix a quelque chose qui vous écorche les oreilles **2** *(clash ▸ note)* détonner; *(▸ colour)* jurer (**with** avec); *(▸ ideas, styles, remarks)* détonner, être incompatible, ne pas s'accorder (**with** avec); **it jars with your red dress** cela jure avec ta robe rouge; **his constant complaining jars on my nerves** ses lamentations continuelles me hérissent

VT 1 *(shake ▸ structure)* secouer, ébranler; **I've jarred my wrist** je me suis fait mal au poignet **2** *(of news)* ébranler, secouer

• **on the jar ADJ** *(door)* entrouvert

jargon ['dʒɑːgən] **N** jargon *m*; **legal j.** jargon *m* juridique, langage *m* du Palais; **to talk (in) j.** parler en jargon, jargonner

jarhead ['dʒɑːhed] **N** *Am Fam (US marine)* marine[◻] *m*

jarring ['dʒɑːrɪŋ] **ADJ** *(sound)* discordant; *(colour)* criard; **a loud j. noise** un bruit discordant

jasmine ['dʒæzmɪn] **N** *Bot* jasmin *m*

▸▸ ***jasmine tea*** thé *m* au jasmin

jaundice ['dʒɔːndɪs] **N 1** *(UNCOUNT) Med* jaunisse *f* **2** *Fig (bitterness)* amertume *f*

jaundiced ['dʒɔːndɪst] **ADJ 1** *Med* ictérique, bilieux **2** *Fig (bitter)* aigri, amer; *(jealous)* jaloux; **to look on the world** *or* **on things with a j. eye** *(bitterly)* voir tout en noir; *(jealously)* tout regarder d'un œil jaloux; **to take a j. view of a situation** voir une situation d'un mauvais œil

jaunt [dʒɔːnt] **N** balade *f*; **to go on** *or* **for a j.** faire une (petite) excursion *ou* une balade

VI she's always jaunting off to Paris elle est toujours en balade entre ici et Paris

jauntily ['dʒɔːntɪlɪ] **ADV** *(remark ▸ casually)* d'une manière désinvolte, avec désinvolture; *(▸ cheerfully)* gaiement, avec entrain, d'un air enjoué; *(walk)* d'un pas guilleret; *(wear one's hat)* d'une façon désinvolte

jauntiness ['dʒɔːntɪnɪs] **N** *(carefreeness)* désinvolture *f*, insouciance *f*; *(cheerfulness)* enjouement *m*, vivacité *f*; **the j. of his step** son pas guilleret

jaunty ['dʒɔːntɪ] **ADJ** *(carefree)* désinvolte, insouciant, dégagé; *(cheerful, lively)* enjoué; **with a j. air** d'un air dégagé; **j. step** pas *m* guilleret; **he wore his cap at a j. angle** sa casquette était négligemment posée sur sa tête

Java[1] ['dʒɑːvə] **N** *Geog* (île *f* de) Java *f*

▸▸ ***Java Man*** homme *m* de Java

Java[2]® ['dʒɑːvə] **N** *Comput* Java® *m*

▸▸ ***Java® script*** (langage *m*) Javascript® *m*

java ['dʒɑːvə] **N** *Am Fam (coffee)* caoua *m*, kawa *m*

Javanese [ˌdʒɑːvə'niːz] (*pl* **inv**) **NPL the J.** les Javanais *mpl*

N 1 *(person)* Javanais(e) *m,f* **2** *(language)* javanais *m*

ADJ javanais

javelin ['dʒævəlɪn] **N** *(weapon)* javelot *m*, javeline *f*; *Sport* javelot *m*; *Sport* **the j.** *(event)* l'épreuve *f* de javelot

▸▸ ***javelin thrower*** lanceur(euse) *m,f* de javelot

jaw [dʒɔː] **N 1** *Anat* mâchoire *f*; *(of insect)* mandibule *f*; **his j. dropped in astonishment** il en est resté bouche bée; **upper/lower j.** mâchoire *f* supérieure/inférieure; *Fig* **snatched from the jaws of death** arraché aux griffes de la mort; *Fig* **to set one's j.** *(show determination)* décider de s'accrocher; *Am Fam* **to flap one's j.** gueuler

2 *(of valley, cave)* entrée *f*; *(of volcano)* bouche *f*; *Fig* **the jaws of hell** les portes *fpl* de l'enfer

3 *(of tool)* mâchoire *f*

4 *Fam (chat)* **to have a good old j.** tailler une petite bavette, papoter

5 *Fam (moralizing speech)* sermon[◻] *m*

VI *Fam* **1** *(chat)* papoter, tailler une bavette; **she's been jawing away on the phone all morning** elle n'a pas arrêté de toute la matinée de papoter au téléphone **2** *(moralize)* prêcher, moraliser[◻]

VT *Fam (remonstrate with)* sermonner[◻]

jawbone ['dʒɔːbəʊn] **N** *Anat* maxillaire *m*

jawbreaker ['dʒɔːˌbreɪkə(r)] **N** *Fam* **1** *(word)* mot *m* difficile à prononcer[◻]; *(name)* nom *m* à coucher dehors **2** *Am (sweet)* = sorte de bonbon dur

-jawed [dʒɔːd] **SUFF round/long/***etc***-j.** à la mâchoire ronde/allongée/*etc*; *Fam Boxing* **glass-j.** à la mâchoire fragile[◻]

jay [dʒeɪ] **N** *Orn* geai *m*

jaywalk ['dʒeɪwɔːk] **VI** *Am* = marcher en dehors des passages pour piétons

jaywalker ['dʒeɪwɔːkə(r)] **N** *Am* = piéton qui traverse en dehors des passages pour piétons

jaywalking ['dʒeɪwɔːkɪŋ] **N** *Am* = délit mineur qui consiste à traverser une rue en dehors des clous ou au feu vert

jazz [dʒæz] **N 1** *(music)* jazz *m*; **they've done a j. version of her song** ils ont fait une version jazz de sa chanson **2** *Fam (rigmarole)* baratin *m*, bla bla *m*; **don't give me that j.!** ne me raconte pas de salades!; **what's (all) this j. about your leaving?** qu'est-ce que c'est que cette histoire comme quoi tu t'en vas?; **and all that j.** et tout le bataclan

COMP *(club, record, singer)* de jazz

VT *very Fam Black Am slang (have sex with)* baiser avec

▸▸ ***the Jazz Age*** = l'âge d'or du jazz américain; ***jazz band*** jazz-band *m*; ***jazz pants*** pantalon *m* jazz; ***jazz poetry*** = poésie récitée sur fond sonore de jazz; ***jazz rock*** jazz-rock *m*

jazz up VT SEP **1** *(song)* mettre sur un rythme (de) jazz; **it's jazzed up Beethoven** c'est du Beethoven sur un rythme de jazz **2** *Fam (enliven)* égayer▫; **they've jazzed the hotel up** ils ont refait la déco de l'hôtel

azzy ['dʒæzɪ] *(compar* **jazzier**, *superl* **jazziest**) ADJ **1** *(music)* (de) jazz *(inv)*, sur un rythme de jazz; **a j. version of 'Carmen'** une version jazz de 'Carmen' **2** *Fam (gaudy)* tapageur, voyant; *(smart)* chic *(inv)*

CB® [,dʒeɪsiː'biː] N *Br* tractopelle *f*

ealous ['dʒeləs] ADJ **1** *(fearful of rivals)* jaloux; **a j. lover** un amant jaloux; **he gets terribly j.** il a des crises de jalousie terribles **2** *(envious)* jaloux; **to be j. of sb** être jaloux de qn; **he became very j. of her sudden success** sa réussite soudaine l'a rendu très jaloux **3** *(possessive)* jaloux, possessif; **to be j. of one's reputation** être jaloux de *ou* veiller à sa réputation

ealously ['dʒeləslɪ] ADV **1** *(enviously)* jalousement, avec jalousie **2** *(possessively)* avec un soin jaloux; **a j. guarded secret** un secret jalousement gardé

ealousy ['dʒeləsɪ] *(pl* **jealousies**) N jalousie *f*

eans [dʒiːnz] NPL jean *m*, blue-jean *m*; **a pair of j.** un jean

▸▸ *Am **jeans jacket*** veste *f* en jean

eep® [dʒiːp] N Jeep® *f*

eepers ['dʒiːpəz] EXCLAM *Am Fam* **j. (creepers)!** oh là là!

eer [dʒɪə(r)] N *(scoffing)* raillerie *f*; *(boo, hiss)* huée *f*

VT *(scoff at)* railler; *(boo, hiss at)* huer, conspuer

VI *(scoff)* railler, se moquer; *(boo, hiss)* pousser des cris hostiles *ou* de dérision; **everybody jeered at me** ils se sont tous moqués de moi

eering ['dʒɪərɪŋ] N *(UNCOUNT) (scoffing)* railleries *fpl*; *(boos, hisses)* huées *fpl*

ADJ railleur, moqueur

eez [dʒiːz] EXCLAM *Fam* purée!

ehovah [dʒɪ'həʊvə] PR N *Bible* Jéhovah

▸▸ *Rel **Jehovah's Witness*** témoin *m* de Jéhovah

ejune [dʒɪ'dʒuːn] ADJ *Literary* **1** *(puerile)* naïf, puéril **2** *(dull)* ennuyeux, morne; *(unrewarding)* ingrat

ejunum [dʒɪ'dʒuːnəm] N *Anat* jéjunum *m*

ekyll and Hyde [,dʒekələnd'haɪd] N **he's a real J.** c'est un véritable docteur Jekyll; **to have a J. personality** faire un dédoublement de la personnalité

ell [dʒel] VI **1** *(idea, plan ▸ take shape)* prendre forme *ou* tournure, se cristalliser; *(team)* se souder **2** *(jellify)* se gélifier

N *Am Fam* = **jelly**

ellied ['dʒelɪd] ADJ *Culin* en gelée

ell-o® ['dʒeləʊ] N *Am Culin (dessert)* gelée *f*

elly ['dʒelɪ] *(pl* **jellies**, *pt & pp* **jellied**) N **1** *(gen)* gelée *f*; **my legs feel like j.** j'ai les jambes en coton *ou* comme du coton; **my legs just turned to j.** j'en ai eu les jambes coupées, je n'avais plus de jambes; **it's like trying to nail j. to a tree** c'est comme essayer de faire passer un chameau dans le chas d'une aiguille

2 *Br Culin (dessert)* gelée *f*

3 *Am Culin (jam)* confiture *f*

4 *Fam Mil slang (gelignite)* gélignite▫ *f*

5 *Br Fam Drugs slang* gélule *f* de Temazepam▫

VT gélifier

▸▸ *Br **jelly baby*** bonbon *m* gélifié *(en forme de bébé)*; ***jelly bag*** poche *f* à gelée *(dans laquelle on presse les fruits)*; ***jelly bean*** dragée *f* à la gelée de sucre *(en forme de haricot)*; *Am **jelly roll*** (gâteau *m*) roulé *m*; ***jelly shoes*** sandalettes *fpl* en plastique

ellyfish ['dʒelɪfɪʃ] *(pl* **inv** *or* **jellyfishes**) N méduse *f*

emmy ['dʒemɪ] *(pl* **jemmies**, *pt & pp* **jemmied**) *Br* N pince-monseigneur *f*

VT **to j. a door (open)** forcer une porte avec une pince-monseigneur

enny ['dʒenɪ] *(pl* **jennies**) N **1** *(female of bird or animal)* **j. wren** roitelet *m* femelle; **j. (ass)** ânesse *f* **2** *(machine)* jenny *f*

jeopardize, -ise ['dʒepədaɪz] VT *(health, future, life)* compromettre, mettre en danger *ou* en péril; *(chances, career)* compromettre; *(one's business)* laisser péricliter

jeopardy ['dʒepədɪ] N danger *m*, péril *m*; **our future is in j.** notre avenir est en péril *ou* menacé *ou* compromis; **his business is in j.** son affaire périclite; **to put sb in j.** mettre qn en danger *ou* en péril

jerbil = **gerbil**

jerk¹ [dʒɜːk] VT **1** *(pull)* tirer d'un coup sec, tirer brusquement; **the door was jerked open** la porte s'ouvrit brusquement *ou* d'un coup sec **2** *(shake)* secouer

VI **1** *(jolt)* cahoter, tressauter; **the train began to j. violently** le train se mit à cahoter *ou* brinquebaler dans tous les sens; **to j. to a halt** s'arrêter en cahotant **2** *(person ▸ jump)* sursauter; **to j. awake** se réveiller en sursaut **3** *(person, muscle ▸ twitch)* se contracter; **her hand jerked up instinctively** instinctivement, elle leva la main

N **1** *(bump)* secousse *f*, saccade *f*; **the train came to a halt with a j.** le train s'arrêta brutalement; **she gave the rope a j.** elle a donné une secousse à la corde, elle a tiré d'un coup sec sur la corde

2 *(wrench)* coup *m* sec; **she gave the handle a j.** elle a tiré d'un coup sec sur la poignée

3 *(brusque movement)* mouvement *m* brusque; **with a j. of his head he indicated that I should leave** d'un brusque signe de la tête, il me fit comprendre qu'il me fallait partir; **to wake up with a j.** se réveiller en sursaut

4 *very Fam (person)* abruti(e) *m,f*, crétin(e) *m,f*

5 *(in weightlifting)* jeté *m*

jerk² *Culin* N viande *f* séchée; **beef j.** bœuf *m* séché

ADJ **j. chicken/pork** = poulet/porc roulé dans des épices puis cuit au four, spécialité des Caraïbes

▸**jerk off** *Vulg* VT SEP **to j. sb off** branler qn

VI se branler, se palucher

jerkily ['dʒɜːkɪlɪ] ADV *(move)* par saccades, par à-coups; *(walk)* d'un pas saccadé; *(write, speak)* d'une manière saccadée *ou* hachée

jerky ['dʒɜːkɪ] *(compar* **jerkier**, *superl* **jerkiest**) N viande *f* séchée; **beef j.** bœuf *m* séché

ADJ **1** *(movement)* saccadé; *(voice, style, speech)* saccadé, heurté, haché; **a j. ride** un trajet cahotant; **in j. French** dans un français heurté *ou* haché; *Fig* **we got off to a j. start** nos débuts ont été houleux **2** *Am very Fam (stupid)* débile

Jerry ['dʒerɪ] *(pl* **Jerries**) N *Fam Old-fashioned Pej (German)* Fritz *m*, Boche *m*; *(the Germans)* les Boches *mpl*

jerry-built ADJ *Pej (house, building)* construit en carton-pâte, peu solide

Jersey ['dʒɜːzɪ] N **1** *Geog* Jersey *f* **2** *Am Fam (New Jersey)* New Jersey▫ *m* **3** *(cow)* vache *f* de Jersey *ou* jersiaise

jersey ['dʒɜːzɪ] N **1** *(pullover)* pull-over *m*, tricot *m*; *Sport* maillot *m* **2** *(fabric)* jersey *m*

Jerusalem [dʒə'ruːsələm] N *Geog* Jérusalem

▸▸ *Bot & Culin **Jerusalem artichoke*** topinambour *m*

jessie ['dʒesɪ] N *Scot Fam* femmelette *f*

jest [dʒest] N plaisanterie *f*, *(witty remark)* mot *m* d'esprit; **to say sth in j.** dire qch pour rire *ou* pour plaisanter; **(only) half in j.** en ne plaisantant qu'à moitié; **to act in j.** plaisanter; *Prov* **there's many a true word spoken in j.** = on dit souvent la vérité sous le couvert d'une plaisanterie

VI plaisanter

jester ['dʒestə(r)] N *Hist* bouffon *m*, fou *m* (du roi); *(joker)* farceur(euse) *m,f*

jesting ['dʒestɪŋ] N *(jokes)* plaisanteries *fpl*; *(witty remarks)* mots *mpl* d'esprit

ADJ *(remark)* fait pour plaisanter *ou* pour rire

jestingly ['dʒestɪŋlɪ] ADV en plaisantant; **j. known as…** désigné par le terme farceur de…

Jesuit ['dʒezjʊɪt] *Cathol* N jésuite *m*

ADJ jésuite; *(college, seminary)* de jésuites

▸▸ ***Jesuit priest*** prêtre *m* jésuite

jesuitical [,dʒezjʊ'ɪtɪkəl] ADJ jésuitique

jesuitism ['dʒezjʊɪ,tɪzəm] N *Cathol* jésuitisme *m*

Jesus ['dʒiːzəs] PR N Jésus; **J. Christ** Jésus-Christ

EXCLAM *Fam* **J. (Christ)!** nom de Dieu!; *Br* **J. wept!** bon sang!; *Am* **J. Holy Christ!, J. H. Christ!** nom de Dieu!

▸▸ *Br Fam **Jesus creepers*** sandales▫ *fpl*; *Fam **Jesus freak*** chrétien(enne) *m,f* hippie; ***the Jesus movement*** = mouvement chrétien pratiquant le prosélytisme

jet¹ [dʒet] *(pt & pp* **jetted**, *cont* **jetting**) N **1** *Aviat (aircraft)* avion *m* à réaction, jet *m*; **to travel by j.** voyager en jet *ou* en avion à réaction; *Am Fam* **cool your jets!** du calme! **2** *(stream ▸ of liquid)* jet *m*, giclée *f*; (▸ *of gas, steam)* jet *m* **3** *(nozzle)* jet *m*, ajutage *m*, buse *f*; *(on printer)* buse *f*; *(of stove)* brûleur *m*; *Aut* gicleur *m*; **(water) j.** *(in whirlpool, bath etc)* gicleur *m*

COMP *(fighter, bomber)* à réaction; *(transport, travel)* en avion (à réaction)

VI **1** *Fam (travel by jet)* voyager en avion (à réaction)▫; **they jetted (over) to Paris for the weekend** ils ont pris l'avion pour passer le week-end à Paris▫ **2** *(liquid)* gicler, jaillir

VT **1** *(transport by jet)* transporter par avion (à réaction); **supplies are being jetted into** *or* **to the disaster area** des avions apportent des vivres à la zone sinistrée **2** *(direct ▸ liquid)* faire gicler

▸▸ *Aviat **jet-assisted take-off*** décollage *m* (avec fusées) JATO; ***jet engine*** moteur *m* à réaction; ***jet fuel*** kérosène *m*; *Aviat **jet plane*** avion *m* à réaction; ***jet propulsion*** propulsion *f* par réaction; *Fam **jet set*** jet-set *m ou f*; ***jet stream*** jet-stream *m*, courant-jet *m*; ***jet trail*** traînée *f* de condensation

jet² N **1** *Miner* jais *m* **2** *(colour)* noir *m* de jais

COMP *(necklace, earrings)* de *ou* en jais

ADJ *(colour)* noir comme (du) jais, (noir) de jais

▸▸ ***jet black*** noir *m* de jais

▸**jet in** VI arriver par avion

▸**jet off** VI s'envoler (**to** pour)

jetfoil ['dʒetfɔɪl] N hydroglisseur *m*

jetlag ['dʒetlæg] N fatigue *f* due au décalage horaire; **I'm still suffering from j.** je suis encore sous le coup du décalage horaire

jetlagged ['dʒetlægd] ADJ fatigué par le décalage horaire; **I'm still a bit j.** je ne suis pas complètement remis du décalage horaire

jet-powered [-paʊəd], **jet-propelled** [-prə'peld] ADJ *Aviat (engine, aircraft)* à réaction

jetsam ['dʒetsəm] N *(UNCOUNT)* objets *mpl* jetés à la mer

jet-setter N *Fam* membre *m* du *ou* de la jet-set

jet-skiing N *Sport* scooter *m* des mers, jet-ski *m*

jettison ['dʒetɪsən] VT **1** *Naut* jeter à la mer, jeter par-dessus bord; *Aviat (bombs, cargo)* larguer **2** *Fig (unwanted possession)* se débarrasser de; *(theory, hope)* abandonner

jetty ['dʒetɪ] *(pl* **jetties**) N *(landing stage)* embarcadère *m*, débarcadère *m*; *(breakwater)* jetée *f*, môle *m*

Jew [dʒuː] N **1** *Rel* Juif(ive) *m,f* **2** *Fam Old-fashioned Pej (miser)* Juif *m*

Jew-baiting [-'beɪtɪŋ] N persécution *f* des Juifs

jewel ['dʒuːəl] N **1** *(precious stone)* bijou *m*, joyau *m*, pierre *f* précieuse; *(in watch)* rubis *m*; **a three-j. wristwatch** une montre trois rubis; **the village is the j. in the crown of the south coast** ce village est la perle de la côte sud **2** *Fig (person, thing)* bijou *m*, perle *f*; **the new receptionist is an absolute j.** la nouvelle réceptionniste est une vraie perle

▸▸ ***jewel box*** coffret *m* à bijoux; ***jewel case*** *(for gems)* coffret *m* à bijoux; *(for compact disc)* coffret *m*

jewelled, *Am* **jeweled** ['dʒuːəld] ADJ orné de bijoux; *(watch)* monté sur rubis

jeweller, *Am* **jeweler** ['dʒuːələ(r)] N *(person)* bijoutier(ère) *m,f*, joaillier(ère) *m,f*; **j.'s (shop)** bijouterie *f*

jewellery, *Am* **jewelry** ['dʒuːəlrɪ] N *(UNCOUNT)* bijoux *mpl*; **a piece of j.** un bijou

▸▸ ***jewellery box*** coffret *m* à bijoux

Jewess ['dʒuːɪs] N Juive *f*

Jewish ['dʒuːɪʃ] ADJ *Rel* juif

▸▸ ***the Jewish calendar*** le calendrier juif; ***Jewish New Year*** nouvel an *m* juif

Jewry ['dʒʊərɪ] N *(Jews collectively)* la communauté juive

jew's-harp N guimbarde *f*

JFK [,dʒeɪef'keɪ] *(abbr* **John Fitzgerald Kennedy)**
PR N *(person)* John Kennedy
N *(airport)* aéroport *m* JFK *(de New York)*

jib [dʒɪb] *(pt & pp* **jibbed,** *cont* **jibbing)** N **1** *Naut* foc *m*; *Fig* **I don't like the cut of his j.** *(look)* je n'aime pas son allure; *(manner, behaviour)* je n'aime pas ses façons de faire **2** *(of crane)* flèche *f*, bras *m*
VI *Br (horse)* regimber; *(person)* regimber (**at sth** devant qch), rechigner (**at sth** devant qch); **to j. at doing sth** rechigner à faire qch
▸▸ *Naut* ***jib boom*** bâton *m* de foc

jibe [dʒaɪb] N *(remark)* raillerie *f*, moquerie *f*
VT *(taunt)* railler, se moquer de
VI **1** *Am Fam (agree)* s'accorder□, coller **2 to j. at sb** *(taunt)* railler qn, se moquer de qn

jiff [dʒɪf], **jiffy** ['dʒɪfɪ] *(pl* **jiffies)** N *Fam* **to do sth in a j.** faire qch en un rien de temps *ou* en moins de deux; **I'll be back/there in a j.!** je reviens/j'arrive tout de suite *ou* dans un instant!□; **half a j.** une petite minute

Jiffy bag® ['dʒɪfɪ-] N *Br* enveloppe *f* matelassée

jig [dʒɪg] *(pt & pp* **jigged,** *cont* **jigging)** N **1** *(dance, music)* gigue *f*
2 *Tech* gabarit *m*
3 *Fishing* leurre *m*
4 *Am very Fam (black person)* nègre (négresse) *m,f*, = terme raciste désignant un Noir
5 *Am Fam (idiom)* **the j. is up** c'est cuit
VT *(shake)* secouer (légèrement)
VI **1** *(dance)* danser allègrement **2** *Br* **to j. (around** *or* **about)** sautiller, se trémousser

jigger ['dʒɪgə(r)] N **1** *(spirits measure)* mesure *f (42 ml)*; **a j. of gin/whisky** un petit verre de gin/whisky
2 *(golf club)* fer *m* quatre
3 *(in billiards)* chevalet *m*, appui-queue *m inv*
4 *Naut* tapecul *m*
5 *Am Fam (thing)* machin *m*, truc *m*
6 *Br (flea)* chique *f*, puce-chique *f*
7 *Mining* crible *m* (pour minerai), classeur-pulsateur *m*
VT *Fam (break* ▸ *TV, machine etc)* bousiller

jiggered ['dʒɪgəd] ADJ *Fam* **1** *Br (exhausted)* crevé, vidé **2** *Br (as expletive)* **well, I'll be j.!** mince alors!; **I'm j. if I'll do it!** pas question que je le fasse! **3** *Fam (broken* ▸ *TV, machine etc)* nase, déglingué, foutu; **my ankle/back is j.** je me suis foutu en l'air la cheville/le dos

jiggery-pokery [,dʒɪgərɪ'pəʊkərɪ] N *(UNCOUNT) Br Fam* micmacs *mpl*; **there's some j. going on** il se passe des choses pas très catholiques

jiggle ['dʒɪgəl] N secousse *f*; **give it a j.** secoue-le un peu
VT secouer (légèrement); **you have to j. the key a bit to get it in** il faut tourner et retourner un peu la clef pour la faire entrer dans la serrure
VI **to j. (about** *or* **around)** être légèrement secoué; *(earrings)* se balancer; **try not to let it j. about** fais en sorte qu'il ne soit pas trop secoué; **I can feel something jiggling about** je sens quelque chose qui remue; **her breasts j. when she runs** ses seins ballottent quand elle court; **stop jiggling about!** arrête de gigoter!

jiggy ['dʒɪgɪ] ADJ *Am Fam* **to get j. (with it)** s'envoyer en l'air

jigsaw ['dʒɪgsɔː] N **1** *(game)* puzzle *m*; *Fig* **the pieces of the j. were beginning to fall into place** peu à peu tout devenait clair **2** *(tool)* scie *f* sauteuse
▸▸ ***jigsaw puzzle*** puzzle *m*

jihad [dʒɪ'hɑːd] N djihad *m*

jihadi [dʒɪ'hɑːdɪ] N djihadiste *m*, jihadiste *m*

jilt [dʒɪlt] VT *(lover)* laisser tomber

jimjams ['dʒɪmdʒæmz] NPL *Fam* **1 to have the j.** *(fear)* avoir les chocottes; *(revulsion)* avoir la chair de poule□; *(anxiety)* avoir les nerfs en pelote **2** *Br (pyjamas)* pyjama□ *m*

jimmy ['dʒɪmɪ] *(pl* **jimmies,** *pt & pp* **jimmied)** *Am* N pince-monseigneur *f*
VT **to j. a door (open)** forcer une porte avec une pince-monseigneur

jingle ['dʒɪŋgəl] N **1** *(of bells)* tintement *m*; *(of keys etc)* tintement *m*, cliquetis *m*; *(of spurs)* cliquetis *m* **2** *(catchy tune)* ritournelle *f*; *(for children)* comptine *f*; *Rad & TV (in advertisement)* jingle *m*, *Offic* sonal *m*
VT *(coins, keys etc)* faire tinter *ou* cliqueter; *(bells)* faire tinter
VI *(bells)* tinter; *(keys, coins etc)* tinter, cliqueter

jingling ['dʒɪŋglɪŋ] N = **jingle 1**
ADJ **j. sound** *(of bells)* tintement *m*; *(of keys)* cliquetis *m*

jingo ['dʒɪŋgəʊ] N *Fam Old-fashioned* **by j.!** crénom de nom!

jingoism ['dʒɪŋgəʊ,ɪzəm] N *Pej* chauvinisme *m*

jingoistic [,dʒɪŋgəʊ'ɪstɪk] ADJ *Pej* chauvin, cocardier

jinks [dʒɪŋks] NPL *Fam* **high j.** la rigolade; **we had high j.** on a eu une séance de rigolade, on s'est bien marrés; **that's enough high j. for today** assez rigolé pour aujourd'hui; *Ironic* **there'll be high j. when my parents find out** ça va barder *ou* chauffer quand mes parents l'apprendront

jinx [dʒɪŋks] *Fam* N *(person, object)* porte-malheur□ *m inv*, porte-guigne *m inv*; *(spell, curse)* maléfice□ *m*, (mauvais) sort□ *m*; *(bad luck)* guigne *f*; **to have a j.** avoir la guigne; **to put a j. on sb** jeter un sort à qn; **to put a j. on sth** porter la guigne à qch; **there's a j. on this car** cette voiture porte malheur□ *ou* la guigne
VT porter la guigne à; **to be jinxed** avoir la guigne

JIT [,dʒeɪaɪ'tiː] ADJ *Com & Mktg (abbr* **just-in-time)** juste à temps, JAT
▸▸ ***JIT distribution*** distribution *f* JAT; ***JIT production*** production *f* JAT; ***JIT purchasing*** achat *m* JAT

jitterbug ['dʒɪtəbʌg] *(pt & pp* **jitterbugged,** *cont* **jitterbugging)** N **1** *(dance)* jitterbug *m* **2** *Fam (nervous person)* nerveux(euse)□ *m,f*
VI *(dance)* danser le jitterbug

jitters ['dʒɪtəz] NPL *Fam* frousse *f*; **to have the j.** avoir la frousse *ou* le trac; **to give sb the j.** flanquer la frousse à qn

jittery ['dʒɪtərɪ] ADJ *Fam (person)* nerveux□; *(situation)* tendu□, délicat□; **he's always j. before exams** il a toujours le trac avant un examen

jiu-jitsu [dʒuː'dʒɪtsuː] N jiu-jitsu *m inv*

jive [dʒaɪv] N **1** *(dance)* swing *m* **2** *(slang)* **j. (talk)** argot *m (employé par les Noirs américains, surtout les musiciens de jazz)* **3** *Fam Black Am slang (lies, nonsense)* baratin *m*, bla-bla *m inv*; **don't give me all that j.** arrête ton char
VI **1** *(dance)* danser le swing **2** *Fam Black Am slang (fool around)* déconner; **stop jiving and get to work!** assez déconné, au boulot!

jive-ass ADJ *very Fam Black Am slang* à la noix

Jnr *(written abbr* **Junior)** junior, fils

Joan of Arc [,dʒəʊnəv'ɑːk] PR N Jeanne d'Arc

Job [dʒəʊb] PR N *Bible* Job; **to have the patience of J.** avoir la patience d'un ange; **he's a real J.'s comforter** *(adds to distress)* pour remonter le moral, tu peux lui faire confiance

JOB [dʒɒb]

N	
• travail **1–3, 6**	• tâche **1**
• emploi **3**	• mal **4**
• coup **5**	
VI	
• faire des petits travaux **1**	• travailler à la tâche **2**
VT	
• négocier **1**	• arnaquer **2**

(pt & pp **jobbed,** *cont* **jobbing)**
N **1** *(piece of work, task)* travail *m*, tâche *f*; **the j. took longer than expected** le travail a pris plus longtemps qu'on ne pensait; **to do its j.** *(medicine, alcohol)* faire son effet; **to do the j.** faire l'affaire; *Fig* **it's not perfect, but it does the j.** ce n'est pas parfait, mais ça fait l'affaire; **if that ointment doesn't do the j.** si cette pommade n'a pas d'effet; **to make a good j. of sth** bien réussir qch; **she made a good j. of fixing the car** elle s'en est bien sortie pour réparer la voiture; **it's quite a difficult j. (to do sth)** c'est tout un travail (que de faire qch); *Fig* **to lie down** *or* **fall down on the j.** *(avoid working)* tirer au flanc; **on a j.** en déplacement; *Fam* **to** **on the j.** *(be having sex)* faire une partie de jar bes en l'air; **this shelf isn't strong** *or* **good enoug for the j.** cette étagère ne tiendra pas le coup; **do odd jobs** faire des petits travaux, bricoler droite et à gauche; *Ind* **it's a precision j.** c'est u travail de précision; *Fam* **the car has had a pai j.** la bagnole a été repeinte; **he's done a good j. work** il a fait du bon boulot
2 *(responsibility, duty)* travail *m*; **they are on doing their j.** ils ne font que leur travail; **I w given the j. of breaking the bad news** c'est à m que la tâche est revenue *ou* c'est moi qui ai é chargé d'annoncer la mauvaise nouvelle; **it's n j. to...** je suis chargé de..., c'est mon trava de...; **it's my j. to remind her** c'est à moi de le l rappeler; **that's not your j.** ce n'est pas votre tr vail, ce n'est pas à vous de faire ça; **I make it my to...** je me charge de...; **I'll have the j. of clearin it all up later** c'est moi qui serai obligé de rang *ou* qui devrai ranger tout ça plus tard; **th muscle has the j. of...** le rôle de ce muscle e de...; **that's not part of his j.** ça n'entre pas dar ses fonctions, ça ne fait pas partie de son trava *ou* de ses attributions
3 *(employment, post)* emploi *m*, travail *m*; **to fin a j.** trouver un emploi *ou* du travail; **to look for a** chercher un emploi *ou* du travail; **to be out of a** être sans emploi *ou* sans travail; **what kind of does she do?** qu'est-ce qu'elle fait comme tr vail?; **to create (new) jobs** créer des emploi créer de nouveaux emplois; **she knows her j.** el connaît son travail *ou* son affaire *ou* son métie **to give up one's j., to resign from one's j.** démi sionner; *Ind* **500 jobs were lost** *or* **axed** il y a e 500 suppressions d'emplois, 500 emplois c postes ont été supprimés; **it's more than my j. worth** ça serait risquer de perdre mon emplo ça ne vaut pas la peine de perdre mon empl pour ça; *Br Fam* **to give jobs to the boys** place ses copains; *Br Fam* **it's jobs for the boys** les bo lots vont directement aux copains
4 *(difficulty, trouble)* **to have (quite) a j. doing** *or* **t do sth** avoir du mal à faire qch; **it was quite a getting her to come at all** ça a déjà été diffici de la convaincre de venir; *Fam* **she had the dev of a j. doing it** elle a eu tout le mal du monde o un mal de tous les diables *ou* un mal fou à l faire; *Fam* **they've got a real j. on their hands wit that baby** ils ont du pain sur la planche avec c bébé; **it's a j. and a half** c'est un sacré boulot
5 *Fam Crime slang (robbery)* coup *m*; **to do a** monter un coup; **they did that bank j.** ils or monté le coup de la banque
6 *Comput* travail *m*; **j. control** gestion *f* des travau
7 *Fam (thing)* **that TV is a really nice j.** cette télé c'est du beau travail; **his car is the red j. parked o the corner** sa voiture, c'est le bel engin rouge qu est garé au coin
8 *Br Fam (excrement)* caca *m*; **the baby has done big j.** le bébé a fait un gros caca
9 *Fig (phrases) Br* **it's a good j. (that)...** heureuse ment que... + *indicative*, c'est heureux que... *subjunctive*; *Br Fam* **he got what he deserved (and) a good j. too!** il a eu ce qu'il méritait, et c'es tant mieux *ou* c'est bien fait pour lui *ou* j'en sui très heureux!; **the make-up department did good j. (on him)** les maquilleurs se sont surpas sés; **you've done a really good j.** tu as vraimen fait du bon travail; **that's just the j.** c'est exacte ment ce qu'il faut; **to give sb/sth up as a bad j** laisser tomber qn/qch qui n'en vaut pas l peine; **we decided to make the best of a bad j** nous avons décidé de faire avec ce que nou avions; *Fam* **to do a j. on a car** *(wreck)* bousille une voiture; *Fam* **to do a j. on sb** *(beat up)* tabas ser qn; **that journalist did a real j. on him** ce jour naliste l'a descendu en flammes *ou* l'a vraimen soigné
VI **1** *(do small jobs)* faire des petits travaux, bri coler
2 *(do piecework)* travailler à la tâche *ou* à l pièce
3 *Br Com* **he jobs in used cars** il revend des voitu res d'occasion
VT **1** *Br St Exch* négocier; **she jobs government se curities** elle négocie des fonds d'État
2 *Am Fam (swindle)* arnaquer, truander; *(betray* vendre

▸▸ ***job analysis*** analyse *f* des tâches *ou* du travail; ***job application*** demande *f* d'emploi; ***job assignment*** assignation *f* des tâches; *Br* ***job club*** = association d'aide aux personnes sans emploi; ***job creation*** création *f* d'emplois; ***job creation scheme*** programme *m* de création d'emplois; ***job description*** description *f* de poste; **that's not in my j. description** ça ne fait pas partie de mon travail; *Admin* ***job evaluation*** analyse *f* des postes; ***job hunter*** demandeur(euse) *m,f* d'emploi; ***job hunting*** recherche *f* d'un emploi; **to go/to be j. hunting** aller/être à la recherche d'un emploi; ***job losses*** suppressions *fpl* d'emplois; *Br Com* ***job lot*** lot *m*; **a j. lot of books** des livres en vrac, un lot de livres; **to buy/sell sth as a j. lot** acheter/vendre qch en lot *ou* en vrac; ***job offer*** offre *f* d'emploi; ***job opportunities*** perspectives *fpl* d'emploi, débouchés *mpl*; ***job prospects*** perspectives *fpl* de carrière; ***job protection*** protection *f* de l'emploi; *Br Comput* ***job queue*** file *f* d'attente des tâches; ***job rotation*** rotation *f* des postes; ***job satisfaction*** satisfaction *f* professionnelle; ***job security*** sécurité *f* de l'emploi; ***job seeker*** demandeur(euse) *m,f* d'emploi; ***job seeking*** recherche *f* d'un emploi; ***job sharing*** partage *m* d'emploi; ***job specification***, *Fam* ***job spec*** description *f* d'emploi; ***job title*** titre *m* (de fonction); ***job vacancy*** poste *m* à pourvoir

jobbery ['dʒɒbərɪ] **N** *(UNCOUNT) Br* **1** *Fam (intrigue)* micmacs *mpl*, trafics *mpl* **2** *St Exch* agiotage *m*, tripotage *m*

jobbing ['dʒɒbɪŋ] *Br* **ADJ j. gardener** jardinier (ère) *m,f* à la journée; **j. tailor** tailleur *m* à façon; **j. workman** ouvrier *m* à la tâche

N 1 *(piecework)* travail *m* à la tâche **2** *(odd jobs)* bricolage *m*

Jobcentre Plus ['dʒɒbˌsentə-] **N** *Br* = agence locale pour l'emploi, ANPE *f*

jobless ['dʒɒblɪs] **ADJ** au chômage, sans emploi

NPL the j. les chômeurs *mpl*, les sans-emploi *mpl*

job-share N partage *m* du travail; **we could do it as a j.** nous pourrions nous partager le travail; **they applied for the post as a j.** ils se sont présentés pour le poste en proposant de se partager le travail

VI partager le travail; **we could apply to j.** nous pourrions nous présenter en proposant de nous partager le travail

jobsworth ['dʒɒbzwəθ] **N** *Br Fam* petit employé *m (qui invoque le règlement pour éviter toute initiative)*

Jock [dʒɒk] **N** *Fam* **1** *(Scotsman)* = terme injurieux ou humoristique désignant un Écossais **2** *(Scottish soldier)* soldat *m* écossais^Ⓓ

jock [dʒɒk] **N** *Fam* **1** *Am (athlete)* sportif^Ⓓ *m* **2** *Horseracing (jockey)* jockey^Ⓓ *m* **3** *(disc jockey)* disc-jockey^Ⓓ *m*, animateur(trice)^Ⓓ *m,f*

jockey ['dʒɒkɪ] **N 1** *Horseracing* jockey *m*; **(woman) j.** femme *f* jockey **2** *Am Fam (driver)* conducteur(trice)^Ⓓ *m,f*; *(operator)* opérateur (trice)^Ⓓ *m,f*; *Hum* **desk j.** rond-de-cuir *m*; **elevator j.** liftier^Ⓓ *m*; **truck j.** routier^Ⓓ *m*

VT 1 *(horse)* monter **2** *(trick)* manipuler, manœuvrer; **they jockeyed him into lending them money** ils l'ont adroitement *ou* habilement amené à leur prêter de l'argent; **to j. sb out of a job** évincer *ou* chasser qn d'un poste

VI *also Fig* **to j. for position** essayer de se placer avantageusement; *Fig* **the companies were all jockeying for position** toutes les entreprises essayaient de se placer

▸▸ ***jockey cap*** casquette *f* de jockey; ***the Jockey Club*** = organisme chargé de l'organisation des courses hippiques en Grande-Bretagne

Jockey shorts® ['dʒɒkɪ-] **NPL** *Am* slip *m* kangourou

jockstrap ['dʒɒkstræp] **N** suspensoir *m*

jocose [dʒə'kəʊs] **ADJ** *Literary* facétieux

jocular ['dʒɒkjʊlə(r)] **ADJ 1** *(jovial)* gai, jovial, enjoué **2** *(facetious)* facétieux, badin; **a j. remark** une remarque facétieuse

jocularity [ˌdʒɒkjʊ'lærɪtɪ] **N** *(humour)* humour *m*; *(jollity)* jovialité *f*

jocularly ['dʒɒkjʊləlɪ] **ADV** *(humorously)* facétieusement; *(with jollity)* jovialement; **he was j. known as "the Walrus" by his pupils** ses élèves lui donnaient le surnom facétieux du "Morse"

jocund ['dʒɒkənd] **ADJ** *Literary* gai, jovial

jodhpurs ['dʒɒdpəz] **NPL** jodhpurs *mpl*

Joe [dʒəʊ] **N** *Fam* **1** *Am (man)* type *m*, gars *m*; **he's an ordinary J.** c'est un mec comme les autres **2** *Am (GI)* soldat^Ⓓ *m*, GI^Ⓓ *m inv*

▸▸ *Br* ***Joe Bloggs***, *Am & Austr* ***Joe Blow*** Monsieur Tout-le-monde; *Am* ***Joe College*** l'étudiant *m* type^Ⓓ; ***Joe Public***, *Am* ***Joe Schmo***, *Am* ***Joe Six-pack***, *Br* ***Joe Soap*** Monsieur Tout-le-monde

joey ['dʒəʊɪ] **N** *Austr Fam* **1** *(kangaroo)* jeune kangourou^Ⓓ *m* **2** *(child)* môme *mf*, marmot *m*

jog [dʒɒg] *(pt & pp* **jogged**, *cont* **jogging) N 1** *(slow run)* jogging *m*; *Horseriding* petit trot *m*; **at a j. (trot)** au petit trot; **to break into a j.** *(person, horse)* se mettre à trotter; **to go for a j.** aller faire un jogging **2** *(push)* légère poussée *f*; *(nudge)* coup *m* de coude

VI 1 *(run)* courir à petites foulées; *(for fitness)* faire du jogging; **she jogs to work every morning** tous les matins, elle va travailler en joggant **2** *(bump)* se balancer; **his rifle jogged against his back** son fusil se balançait dans son dos

VT *(nudge)* donner un léger coup à; **she jogged my elbow** elle m'a poussé le coude; *Fig* **to j. sb's memory** rafraîchir la mémoire de *ou* à qn; *Fig* **to j. sb into action** inciter qn à l'action; **to j. sb out of it** secouer qn; **to j. sb out of their complacency** tirer qn de sa complaisance

▸▸ ***jog pants*** pantalon *m* de jogging; ***jog top*** *(sweatshirt)* sweat *m*; ***jog trot*** petit trot *m*

▸**jog along VI 1** *Horseriding* trottiner, aller au petit trot **2** *Fig (person, factory, country etc)* aller tant bien que mal; *Fig* **I'm jogging along quite happily** je vais mon petit bonhomme de chemin; **my work is jogging along pretty steadily** mon travail avance assez bien

jogger ['dʒɒgə(r)] **N** jogger *mf*, joggeur(euse) *m,f*

▸▸ *Fam* ***jogger's nipple*** = irritation des tétons due au frottement contre les vêtements

jogging ['dʒɒgɪŋ] **N** jogging *m*; **to go j.** faire du jogging; **to like j.** aimer faire du jogging, aimer le jogging

▸▸ *Br* ***jogging bottoms***, *Am* ***jogging pants*** pantalon *m* de jogging; ***jogging suit*** jogging *m* *(vêtement)*

joggle ['dʒɒgəl] **N** *(shake, jolt)* secousse *f*

VT *(shake)* secouer (légèrement)

VI cahoter, ballotter; **the truck joggled along the track** le camion cahotait sur la piste; **they joggled up and down in the back** ils étaient secoués *ou* bringuebalés à l'arrière

jog-trot *(pt & pp* **jog-trotted**, *cont* **jog-trotting) VI** trottiner, aller au petit trot

Johannesburg [dʒə'hænɪsˌbɜːg] **N** *Geog* Johannesburg

John [dʒɒn] **PR N** *Bible* Jean; **the Gospel According to (Saint) J.** l'Évangile *m* selon saint Jean; **(Saint) J. the Baptist** (saint) Jean-Baptiste

▸▸ *Hum* ***John Barleycorn*** = personnage symbolisant l'alcool, notamment le whisky; ***John Bull*** John Bull *(personnification de la nation anglaise, du peuple anglais)*; *Am* ***John Doe*** *(average person)* l'Américain *m* moyen, Monsieur Dupont; *Fam (unidentified man* ▸ *under arrest)* inconnu^Ⓓ *m*; *(corpse)* mort *m* non identifié^Ⓓ; *Ich* ***John Dory*** saint-pierre *m inv*; *Am Fam* ***John Hancock***, ***John Henry*** signature^Ⓓ *f*, gribouillis *m*; **to lay one's J. Hancock** = apposer sa signature au bas d'un document; ***John o'Groats*** = village d'Écosse qui marque le point le plus septentrional de la Grande-Bretagne continentale; *Am Fam* ***John Q. Public*** Monsieur *m* Tout-le-monde; *Fam* ***John Thomas*** *(penis)* zizi *m*, zob *m*

john [dʒɒn] **N** *Fam* **1** *Am (lavatory)* waters^Ⓓ *mpl*, W-C^Ⓓ *mpl* **2** *(prostitute's client)* micheton *m*

johnny ['dʒɒnɪ] *(pl* **johnnies) N 1** *Br Fam Old-fashioned (man)* type *m*, gars *m*; **what does that inspector j. want?** ce type-là, l'inspecteur, qu'est-ce qu'il veut? **2** *Br Fam (condom)* **(rubber) j.** capote *f*

▸▸ *Am & Austr* ***johnny cake*** crêpe *f*

Johnny-come-lately ['dʒɒnɪ-] *(pl* **Johnny-come-latelies** *or* **Johnnies-come-lately) N** *Fam (newcomer)* nouveau(elle) venu(e) *m,f*; *Pej (upstart)* parvenu(e) *m,f*

JOIN [dʒɔɪn]

VT
- adhérer à **1**
- entrer dans **1**
- rejoindre **2, 5**
- joindre **3**
- raccorder **3**
- s'engager dans **1**
- s'inscrire à **1**
- se joindre à **2**
- unir **3, 4**
- relier **4**

VI
- devenir membre **1**
- se raccorder **2**
- se joindre **2, 3**
- s'unir **3**

N
- raccord
- joint
- couture

VT 1 *(political party, club)* adhérer à; *(armed forces, police)* s'engager dans; *(company, group, religious order)* entrer dans; *(class, course)* s'inscrire à; **j. the army!** engagez-vous!; *Fig* **so you've been burgled too? j. the club!** alors, toi aussi tu as été cambriolé? bienvenue au club!

2 *(join company with, meet)* rejoindre; *(in activity or common purpose)* se joindre à; **I'll j. you later** je vous rejoindrai *ou* retrouverai plus tard; **she joined the procession** elle se joignit au cortège; **I joined the queue at the ticket office** j'ai fait la queue au guichet; **to j. one's ship** rallier son navire; **to j. one's regiment** rejoindre son régiment; **will you j. us?** voulez-vous vous joindre à nous?; **may I j. you?** puis-je me joindre à vous?; **they joined us for lunch** ils nous ont retrouvés pour déjeuner; **will you j. me for** *or* **in a drink?** vous prendrez bien un verre avec moi?; **why don't you j. (us at) our table?** venez donc vous asseoir à notre table!; **we are joined in the studio by Bruce Johnson** Bruce Johnson vient nous rejoindre *ou* vient se joindre à nous dans notre studio; **he didn't want to j. the dancing** il n'a pas voulu se joindre *ou* se mêler aux danseurs; **my wife joins me in offering our sincere condolences** ma femme se joint à moi pour vous adresser nos sincères condoléances

3 *(attach, fasten* ▸ *planks, pieces of material)* joindre, unir; *(*▸ *pipes, electric wires)* raccorder; *(*▸ *edges of a wound)* rapprocher, réunir; **to j. (up) the two ends of a rope** nouer les deux bouts d'une corde; **you have to j. these two electric wires** il faut raccorder ces deux fils électriques; **the workmen joined the pipes (together)** les ouvriers ont raccordé les tuyaux; **the Siamese twins are joined at the thigh** les frères siamois sont rattachés (l'un à l'autre) par la cuisse

4 *(unite)* relier, unir; **to be joined in marriage** *or* **matrimony** être unis par les liens du mariage; **to j. hands** *(in prayer)* joindre les mains; *(link hands)* se donner la main; **we must j. forces (against the enemy)** nous devons unir nos forces (contre l'ennemi); **she joined forces with her brother** elle s'est alliée à son frère; **to j. battle (with)** entrer en lutte (avec), engager le combat (avec)

5 *(intersect with)* rejoindre; **does this path j. the main road?** est-ce que ce chemin rejoint la route?; **we camped where the stream joins the river** nous avons campé là où le ruisseau rejoint la rivière

VI 1 *(become a member)* devenir membre

2 *(planks, pieces of material)* se joindre; *(pipes, electric wires)* se raccorder

3 *(form an alliance)* s'unir, se joindre; **they joined together to fight drug trafficking** ils se sont unis pour lutter contre le trafic de drogue; **we all j. with you in your sorrow** *(sympathize)* nous nous associons tous à votre douleur

N *(in broken china, wallpaper, carpet)* (ligne *f* de) raccord *m*; *Sewing (in fabric)* couture *f*; *Tech (junction between elements)* joint *m*

▸**join in VI** se mettre de la partie, participer, prendre part; **she started singing and the others joined in** elle a commencé à chanter et les autres se sont mis à chanter avec elle

VT INSEP participer à, prendre part à; **she never joins in the conversation** elle ne participe jamais à la conversation; **he joined in the protest** il s'associa aux protestations; **all j. in the chorus!** reprenez tous le refrain en chœur!

▸**join on VI** s'attacher; **where does this part j. on?** où cette pièce vient-elle se rattacher?; **they**

joined on at the end of the parade ils se sont mis à la queue du défilé

VT SEP attacher, ajouter; **we got off the train while they were joining on more coaches** nous sommes descendus du train pendant que l'on accrochait de nouveaux wagons

▸**join up VI 1** *(for armed forces)* s'engager; *(for class, course)* s'inscrire **2** *(planks, pieces of material)* se toucher, se joindre; *(pipes, electric wires)* se raccorder **3** *(meet)* **to j. up with sb** rejoindre qn

VT SEP *(planks, pieces of material)* joindre, assembler; *(pipes, electric wires)* raccorder; *(two machines)* accoupler

joined-up [dʒɔɪnd-] **ADJ can you do j. writing yet?** tu sais lier les lettres?; *Fig* **j. thinking** vision *f* d'ensemble

joiner ['dʒɔɪnə(r)] **N 1** *(carpenter)* menuisier *m* **2** *Fam (member of many clubs)* **he's a real j.** il est de toutes les bonnes causes; **he's not really a j.** il n'est pas très sociable

joinery ['dʒɔɪnərɪ] **N** menuiserie *f*; **piece of j.** article *m ou* pièce *f* de menuiserie

joint [dʒɔɪnt] **N 1** *Tech* joint *m*, jointure *f*; *Carp* assemblage *m*; **(soldered** *or* **welded) j.** soudure *f*

2 *Anat* articulation *f*, jointure *f*; **out of j.** déboîté; **to put one's shoulder out of j.** se démettre *ou* se déboîter l'épaule; *Fig* **the change in schedule has put everything out of j.** le changement de programme a tout chamboulé

3 *Br Culin* rôti *m*; **j. of beef** rôti *m* de bœuf; **j. of lamb** *(leg)* gigot *m* d'agneau; *(shoulder)* épaule *f* d'agneau

4 *Fam (cannabis cigarette)* joint *m*

5 *Fam (night club)* boîte *f*; *(bar)* troquet *m*, bouiboui *m*; *(gambling house)* tripot *m*; **strip j.** club *m* de strip-tease

6 *Am Fam (house)* baraque *f*; **nice j. you have here!** c'est pas mal chez toi!

7 *Am Fam (prison)* taule *f*, placard *m*; **in the j.** en taule, à l'ombres

8 *Geol* diaclase *f*

9 *Am very Fam (penis)* pine *f*, bite *f*

ADJ 1 *(united, combined)* conjugué, commun; **to take j. action** mener une action commune; **thanks to their j. efforts...** grâce à leurs efforts conjugués... **2** *(shared, collective)* joint, commun; *(contract* ▸ *between two parties)* bilatéral; *(*▸ *between more than two parties)* collectif

VT 1 *Tech* assembler, emboîter

2 *Br Culin* découper aux jointures

3 *Constr* jointoyer

4 *Carp* varloper

▸▸ *Comput* ***the Joint Academic Network*** = réseau Internet composé d'universités et d'organismes de recherche britanniques; *Banking* ***joint account*** compte *m* joint *ou* conjoint; ***joint agreement*** *(gen)* accord *m* commun; *Ind* convention *f* collective; ***joint author*** coauteur *m*; *Fin* ***joint beneficiary*** bénéficiaire *mf* conjoint(e); *Mil* ***the Joint Chiefs of Staff*** = organe consultatif du ministère américain de la Défense, composé des chefs d'état-major des trois armées; ***joint commission*** commission *f* mixte; ***joint committee*** *(gen)* commission *f* mixte; *Ind* comité *m* paritaire; *Fin* ***joint creditor*** cocréancier(ère) *m,f*; *Law* ***joint custody*** garde *f* conjointe; *Fin* ***joint debtor*** codébiteur(trice) *m,f*; *Law* ***joint donor*** codonataire(trice) *m,f*; ***joint enterprise*** entreprise *f* en participation; *Law* ***joint estate*** communauté *f* de biens; *Law* ***joint guardian*** cotuteur(trice) *m,f*; *Law* ***joint guardianship*** cotutelle *f*; ***joint heir*** cohéritier *m*; ***joint holder*** *(of record, trophy etc)* codétenteur(trice) *m,f*; *Br Univ* ***joint honours*** = licence portant sur deux matières; ***joint liability*** responsabilité *f* conjointe; ***joint management*** cogestion *f*; ***joint occupancy*** colocation *f*; *Br* ***joint owner*** *(of property)* copropriétaire *mf*; **to be j. owners of sth** *(car, shares etc)* posséder *ou* détenir qch en commun; *Br* ***joint ownership*** copropriété *f*; ***joint partnership*** coassociation *f*; ***joint passport*** passeport *m* conjoint; **we have a j. passport** nous sommes sur le même passeport; *Law* ***joint plaintiff*** codemandeur(eresse) *m,f*; *Ins* ***joint policy*** police *f* conjointe; ***joint production*** coproduction *f*; ***joint property*** biens *mpl* communs; ***joint purchase*** coacquisition *f*; ***joint report*** rapport *m* collectif; *Am Pol* ***joint resolution*** projet *m* de loi; ***joint responsibility*** responsabilité *f* conjointe; **the project is their j. responsibility** le projet relève de leur responsabilité à tous les deux; ***joint statement*** déclaration *f* commune; *Fin* ***joint stock*** capital *m* social; ***joint tenancy*** location *f* commune; ***joint tenant*** colocataire *mf*; ***joint venture*** *(undertaking)* entreprise *f* commune; *Com (agreement)* coentreprise *f*, joint-venture *m*; *(company)* société *f* commune, société *f* en participation; ***joint venture agreement*** accord *m* de partenariat; ***joint venture company*** société *f* d'exploitation en commun

jointed ['dʒɔɪntɪd] **ADJ 1** *Tech* articulé **2** *Culin (poultry)* découpé

jointing ['dʒɔɪntɪŋ] **N 1** *Tech (joining* ▸ *of boards)* assemblage *m*; *(*▸ *of pipes)* emmanchage *m*

2 *Culin* découpage *m*

3 *Constr (of brickwork)* jointoiement *m*

4 *Carp* varlopage *m*

▸▸ *Carp* ***jointing plane*** varlope *f*; *Tech* ***jointing tape*** bande *f* de collure

jointly ['dʒɔɪntlɪ] **ADV** conjointement; **to own/manage j.** coposséder/cogérer; **the house is j. owned** la maison est en copropriété; *Law* **j. liable** coresponsable, conjointement responsable; *Fin* **j. and severally** conjointement et solidairement

joint-stock ADJ *Br Fin*

▸▸ ***joint-stock bank*** banque *f* de dépôt; ***joint-stock company*** société *f* (anonyme) par actions

joist [dʒɔɪst] **N** *Constr* solive *f*

jojoba [həʊ'həʊbə] **N** *Bot* jojoba *m*

joke [dʒəʊk] **N 1** *(verbal)* plaisanterie *f*, blague *f*; **to tell a j.** raconter une histoire drôle *ou* une blague; **to make a j.** faire une plaisanterie *ou* une blague; **to make a j. of** *or* **about sth** plaisanter sur *ou* à propos de qch; **he tried to make a j. of it** il a essayé d'en rire; **we did it for a j.** nous l'avons fait pour rire *ou* pour rigoler; **he didn't see** *or* **get the j.** *(didn't appreciate something funny)* il n'a pas trouvé ça drôle; *(didn't understand somebody's joke)* il n'a pas compris la plaisanterie; **he can't take a j.** il n'a pas le sens de l'humour; **it's gone beyond a j.** la plaisanterie a assez duré; **it's a private j.** c'est une plaisanterie entre nous/eux/elles; **what a j.!** *(how ridiculous)* quelle blague!; **the j. is that...** le comique de l'histoire, c'est que...; **the test was a j.!** *(easy)* ce test, c'était de la rigolade!; **that's** *or* **it's no j.!** *(not easy)* ce n'est pas de la tarte!; *(serious)* ce n'est pas de la blague!; **it was no j. climbing that cliff!** escalader cette falaise, ce n'était pas de la tarte *ou* de la rigolade! **2** *(prank)* plaisanterie *f*, farce *f*, blague *f*; **to play a j. on sb** jouer un tour à qn, faire une farce à qn; **the j. is on you** la plaisanterie s'est retournée contre toi; **the j. is on me** je suis le dindon de la farce **3** *(object of derision)* risée *f*; **their so-called planning is a j.** leur soi-disant planification est risible; **his staff just regard him as a j.** il est la risée de tous ses employés; **the new legislation is just a j.** la nouvelle législation est une plaisanterie; **this is turning into a j.** *(is getting annoying)* c'est en train de tourner à la farce

VI plaisanter, blaguer (**about** sur); **I was only joking** je ne faisais que plaisanter; **I'm not joking!** je ne plaisante pas!; **you must be joking!, you have (got) to be joking!** vous plaisantez!, vous n'êtes pas sérieux!; **Nicola's passed her driving test – you're joking!** Nicola a eu son permis de conduire – sans blague! *ou* tu veux rire?

joker ['dʒəʊkə(r)] **N 1** *(funny person)* farceur (euse) *m,f*, blagueur(euse) *m,f*; *Pej (frivolous person)* plaisantin *m*

2 *(in cards)* joker *m*

3 *Fam (man)* type *m*, mec *m*; *(stupid person)* abruti *m*; **some j. has stolen my umbrella** il y a un abruti qui m'a piqué mon parapluie

4 *(clause)* clause *f* ambiguë; **the contract contained a j.** le contrat contenait une clause piège

jokey ['dʒəʊkɪ] *(compar* **jokier**, *superl* **jokiest) ADJ** *(person)* blagueur; *(mood, conversation etc)* jovial; *(remark)* moqueur; *(gift, novelty)* farfelu

jokily ['dʒəʊkɪlɪ] **ADV** en plaisantant

joking ['dʒəʊkɪŋ] **ADJ** *(tone)* moqueur, de plaisanterie; *(comment, response)* moqueur

N *(UNCOUNT)* plaisanterie *f*, plaisanteries *fpl*, blagues *fpl*; **the j. must stop** assez plaisanté *ou* blagué; **j. apart** *or* **aside** plaisanterie mise à part, blague à part

jokingly ['dʒəʊkɪŋlɪ] **ADV** en plaisantant, pour plaisanter

joky = **jokey**

jollies ['dʒɒlɪz] **NPL** *Am Fam* **to get one's j. (doing sth)** prendre son pied (à faire qch)

jollification [ˌdʒɒlɪfɪ'keɪʃən] **N** *(UNCOUNT) Fam (merrymaking)* réjouissances *fpl*

jolliness ['dʒɒlɪnɪs], **jollity** ['dʒɒlɪtɪ] **N** *(UNCOUNT) (cheerfulness)* jovialité *f*, gaieté *f*; *(merrymaking)* réjouissances *fpl*

jolly ['dʒɒlɪ] *(compar* **jollier**, *superl* **jolliest**, *pt & pp* **jollied**, *pl* **jollies) ADJ 1** *(person)* gai, joyeux, jovial; **what are you so j. about?** qu'est-ce qui te met de si bonne humeur? **2** *Br (enjoyable)* agréable, plaisant; **we had a very j. time** nous nous sommes bien amusés; **j. hockey sticks** = expression parodique utilisée en parlant d'une femme bourgeoise, éduquée dans une "public school", caractérisée par un enthousiasme débordant et une certaine naïveté

ADV *Br* rudement, drôlement; **it's a j. good thing he came** c'est rudement bien qu'il soit venu; **j. good!** formidable!; **and a j. good job too!** et c'est tant mieux!; **a j. good fellow** un chic type; **you'll j. well do what you're told!** tu feras ce qu'on te dit de faire, un point c'est tout!; **it j. well serves them right!** c'est vraiment bien fait pour eux!

VT *Br (coax)* enjôler, entortiller; **she jollied me into going** avec ses paroles enjôleuses, elle a fini par me convaincre d'y aller; **he'll come if you j. him along a bit** il viendra si tu le pousses un peu

N *Fam Pej* voyage *m* aux frais de la princesse

▸▸ ***Jolly Roger*** pavillon *m* noir, drapeau *m* de pirate

> Note that the French word **joli** is a false friend and is never a translation for the English word **jolly**. It means **pretty**.

jolt [dʒəʊlt] **VT 1** *(physically)* secouer; **the passengers were jolted about in the bus** les passagers étaient secoués dans le bus **2** *(mentally)* secouer, choquer; **to j. sb into action** secouer (les puces à) qn; *Fig* **the nation was jolted into action by the news** cette nouvelle a poussé le pays à entrer en action; *Fig* **to j. sb out of a depression** faire sortir qn de son état dépressif d'un seul coup; *Fig* **that jolted him out of his smugness!** ça lui a fait perdre sa belle suffisance d'un seul coup!

VI cahoter; *(plane)* être secoué; **the Jeep® jolted along the track** la Jeep® avançait en cahotant sur la piste; **to j. forward** *(vehicle, train)* s'ébranler avec une secousse; **his head jolted forward/back** *(on impact)* sa tête a été rejetée en avant/en arrière; **to j. to a stop** *(vehicle, train)* s'arrêter en cahotant *ou* avec des à-coups

N 1 *(jar)* secousse *f*, coup *m*; *(of vehicle)* cahot *m*, secousse *f*, à-coup *m*; *(of plane)* secousse *f*; *(of engine)* à-coup *m*, secousse *f*; **the fall gave his spine a j.** dans sa chute, il a reçu un choc à la colonne vertébrale **2** *(start)* sursaut *m*, choc *m*; **to wake up with a j.** se réveiller en sursaut; **it gave me a bit of a j.** ça m'a fait un choc *ou* un coup

jolting ['dʒəʊltɪŋ] **N** *(UNCOUNT) (of vehicle)* cahots *mpl*; *(of plane)* secousses *fpl*

Jonah ['dʒəʊnə] **PR N** *Bible* Jonas

N *Fig (jinx)* porte-malheur *m inv*

jones [dʒəʊnz] **N** *Am Fam* **to have a j. for sth** adorer qch; **I've always had a j. for a challenge** j'ai toujours adoré les défis

Joneses ['dʒəʊnzɪz] **NPL** *Fam* **to keep up with the J.** vouloir faire aussi bien que le voisin, ne pas vouloir être en reste

jonquil ['dʒɒŋkwɪl] **N** *Bot* (petite) jonquille *f*

Jordan ['dʒɔːdən] **N** *Geog* Jordanie *f*; **the (River) J.** le Jourdain

Jordanian [ˌdʒɔː'deɪnɪən] **N** Jordanien(enne) *m,f*

ADJ jordanien

COMP *(embassy)* de Jordanie; *(history)* de la Jordanie

josh [dʒɒʃ] *Fam* **VI** blaguer; **I'm only joshing** je plaisante

VT chambrer, vanner (**about** sur), mettre en boîte (**about** à cause de)

N quolibet *m*, moquerie *f*

oss stick [dʒɒs-] N bâtonnet *m* d'encens

ostle ['dʒɒsəl] VI se bousculer; **they were jostling for seats** ils se bousculaient pour avoir des places; *Fig* **to j. for position** essayer de bien se placer

VT bousculer, heurter; **she was jostled by the demonstrators** elle a été bousculée par les manifestants; **to j. sb out of the way** écarter qn à coups de coudes *ou* en jouant des coudes; **to j. one's way (through)** se frayer un chemin à coups de coude

N bousculade *f*

ostling ['dʒɒsəlɪŋ] N *(UNCOUNT) (of crowd)* bousculade(s) *f(pl)*

ot [dʒɒt] *(pt & pp* **jotted**, *cont* **jotting**) N **it won't change his mind one j.** ça ne le fera absolument pas changer d'avis; **there isn't a j. of truth in what he says** il n'y a pas un brin de vérité dans ce qu'il raconte; **it doesn't matter a j.** cela n'a pas la moindre importance; **not one j. or tittle** pas un iota

·jot down VT SEP noter, prendre note de; **she jotted a few ideas down before the meeting** elle a rapidement noté quelques idées avant la réunion

otter ['dʒɒtə(r)] N *Br (exercise book)* cahier *m*, carnet *m*; *(pad)* bloc-notes *m*

ottings ['dʒɒtɪŋz] NPL notes *fpl*

oule [dʒu:l] N *Phys* joule *m*

▸▸ ***Joule effect*** effet *m* Joule; ***Joule's law*** loi *f* de Joule

ournal ['dʒɜ:nəl] N **1** *(publication)* revue *f*

2 *(diary)* journal *m* intime

3 *Naut (logbook)* journal *m* de bord

4 *Acct (for transactions)* livre *m* de comptes, (livre *m*) journal *m*

5 *Law* procès-verbal *m*

6 *Tech* tourillon *m*

▸▸ *Tech* ***journal bearing*** palier *m* (de tourillon); ***journal entry*** écriture *f* comptable, contre-passation *f*

> Note that the most common meaning of the French word **journal** is **newspaper**.

ournalese [ˌdʒɜ:nə'li:z] N *Pej* jargon *m* journalistique

ournalism ['dʒɜ:nəlɪzəm] N journalisme *m*
COMP *(college, diploma)* de journalisme

ournalist ['dʒɜ:nəlɪst] N journaliste *mf*

ournalistic [dʒɜ:nə'lɪstɪk] ADJ journalistique

ourney ['dʒɜ:nɪ] N **1** *(gen)* voyage *m*; **have a good j.!** bon voyage!; **it was quite a j. to get here** ça a été toute une épopée pour arriver jusqu'ici; **it is a two-day j. by car** c'est à deux journées de route en voiture; **to set out on a j.** partir en voyage; **to go (away) on a j.** partir en voyage; **she went on a j. to Europe** elle a fait un voyage en Europe; **to go on a train j.** prendre le train, voyager par le train; **the j. back** *or* **home** le (voyage du) retour; **to break one's j.** *(in plane, bus)* faire escale; *(in car)* faire une halte, s'arrêter; **to reach (one's) j.'s end** *(arrive)* arriver à destination; *Fig (die)* arriver au bout du voyage; *Fig* **the j. into adulthood** le passage à l'âge adulte **2** *(shorter distance)* trajet *m*; **a short tube j.** un court trajet en métro; **the j. to work takes me ten minutes** je mets dix minutes pour aller à mon travail

VI *Formal* voyager

▸▸ ***journey time*** *(gen)* durée *f* du voyage; *(shorter distance)* durée *f* du trajet

> Note that the French word **journée** is a false friend and is never a translation for the English word **journey**. It means **day**.

journeyman ['dʒɜ:nɪmən] *(pl* **journeymen** [-mən]) N *(qualified apprentice)* compagnon *m*; **j. carpenter** compagnon *m* charpentier

journo ['dʒɜ:nəʊ] *(pl* **journos**) N *Fam* journaleux (euse) *m,f*

joust [dʒaʊst] N *Hist* joute *f*
VI *Hist* jouter (**with** contre); *Fig* batailler

jousting ['dʒaʊstɪŋ] N *(UNCOUNT) Hist* joutes *fpl*; *Fig (verbal)* joutes *fpl* oratoires

▸▸ *Fig* ***jousting match*** joutes *fpl* oratoires

jovial ['dʒəʊvɪəl] ADJ jovial, enjoué; **she's in a j. mood** elle est d'humeur joviale; **to feel j.** être enjoué

joviality [ˌdʒəʊvɪ'ælətɪ] N jovialité *f*, entrain *m*

jovially ['dʒəʊvɪəlɪ] ADV jovialement

jowl [dʒaʊl] N **1** *(jaw)* mâchoire *f* **2** *(hanging flesh on cheek)* bajoue *f*; **he had heavy jowls** il avait de grosses bajoues

-jowled [dʒaʊld] SUFF **a heavy-j. man** un homme aux joues flasques

joy [dʒɔɪ] N **1** *(pleasure)* joie *f*, plaisir *m*; **to shout with** *or* **for j.** crier de joie; **she moved out, to the great j. of her neighbours** elle a déménagé, à la grande joie de ses voisins; **her grandchildren are a great j. to her** ses petits-enfants sont une source de joie pour elle *ou* sa grande joie; **it was a j. to see him laughing again** c'était un plaisir de le voir rire à nouveau; **the joys of gardening** les plaisirs *ou* les charmes du jardinage; **full of the joys of spring** au comble du bonheur; **the joys of having children** les joies qu'apportent les enfants; **the joys of having a car** les joies d'avoir une voiture; **her style is a j. to watch** son style est un plaisir pour les yeux; **he's a j. to work for** c'est un plaisir de travailler pour lui; **our new car is a j. to drive** avec notre nouveau modèle, la conduite est un plaisir; **she's a j. to be with, it's a j. to be with her** c'est un plaisir que d'être à ses côtés; *Ironic* **oh j.!** ô joie! **2** *Br Fam (success)* **they had no j. at the casino** ils n'ont pas eu de chance au casino; **any j. at the job centre?** tu as trouvé quelque chose à l'agence pour l'emploi?; **(did you have** *or* **get) any j.?** ça a marché?, tu as réussi?; **no j.!** ça n'a rien donné!, ça n'a pas marché!; **you won't get any j. from him** tu n'arriveras à rien avec lui

joyful ['dʒɔɪfʊl] ADJ joyeux, enjoué

joyfully ['dʒɔɪfʊlɪ] ADV joyeusement

joyfulness ['dʒɔɪfʊlnɪs] N joie *f*, allégresse *f*

joyless ['dʒɔɪlɪs] ADJ *(unhappy)* triste, sans joie; *(dull)* morne, maussade

joylessly ['dʒɔɪlɪslɪ] ADV *(unhappily)* tristement, sans joie; *(dully)* de façon morne

joyous ['dʒɔɪəs] ADJ *Literary* joyeux; *(news)* heureux

joyously ['dʒɔɪəslɪ] ADV *Literary* joyeusement

joypad ['dʒɔɪpæd] N *Comput* joypad *m*

joyride ['dʒɔɪraɪd] *(pt* **joyrode** [-rəʊd], *pp* **joyridden** [-rɪdən]) N virée *f* (dans une voiture volée); **to go for a** *or* **on a j.** faire une virée (dans une voiture volée); *Fig* **it's no j. working with him** travailler avec lui, ce n'est pas une partie de plaisir

VI **to go joyriding** faire une virée dans une voiture volée; **they were had up for joyriding** ils ont été convoqués devant les tribunaux pour vol de voiture

joyrider ['dʒɔɪraɪdə(r)] N = personne qui vole une voiture pour faire un tour

joystick ['dʒɔɪstɪk] N **1** *Aviat* manche *m* à balai **2** *Comput* manette *f* de jeu, manche *m* à balai

JP [ˌdʒeɪ'pi:] N *Br Law (abbr* **Justice of the Peace**) juge *m* d'instance

JPEG ['dʒeɪpeg] N *Comput (abbr* **Joint Photographic Experts Group**) (format *m*) JPEG *m*

Jr. *(written abbr* **Junior**) junior, fils

jubilant ['dʒu:bɪlənt] ADJ *(shouts)* de joie; *(expression)* épanoui, radieux; *(crowd)* exultant; *(party, celebration)* joyeux; **the Prime Minister was j. at the election results** le Premier ministre fut transporté de joie à la vue des résultats du scrutin; **the j. champion** le champion radieux

jubilantly ['dʒu:bɪləntlɪ] ADV avec jubilation

jubilation [ˌdʒu:bɪ'leɪʃən] N *(UNCOUNT) (rejoicing)* joie *f*, jubilation *f*; *(celebration)* réjouissances *fpl*; **to be a cause for (great) j.** être l'occasion de (grandes) réjouissances; **scenes of j.** scènes de réjouissance

jubilee ['dʒu:bɪli:] N jubilé *m*; **silver/diamond j.** (fête *f* du) vingt-cinquième/soixantième anniversaire *m*

Judaea [dʒu:'dɪə] N *Bible & Hist* Judée *f*

Judaic [dʒu:'deɪɪk] ADJ *Rel* judaïque

Judaism ['dʒu:deɪˌɪzəm] N *Rel* judaïsme *m*

Judas ['dʒu:dəs] PR N *Bible* Judas; **J. Iscariot** Judas Iscariote

N *(traitor)* judas *m*

▸▸ ***Judas kiss*** baiser *m* de Judas; ***Judas tree*** arbre *m* de Judée, gainier *m*

judas ['dʒu:dəs] N *(peephole)* judas *m*

judder ['dʒʌdə(r)] N trépidation *f*; *(of vehicle, machine)* broutement *m*

VI *Br* vibrer; *(brakes, clutch)* brouter; **the bus juddered to a halt** le bus s'est arrêté en cahotant

judge [dʒʌdʒ] N **1** *Law* juge *m*; **J. Jeffries** le juge Jeffries; **presiding j.** président *m* du tribunal; *Fig* **you can't just appoint yourself j. and jury** tu n'as pas le droit de décider sans consulter personne **2** *(in a competition)* membre *m* du jury; *Sport* juge *m*; **the judges were divided** le jury était partagé **3** *Fig* juge *m*; **a good j. (of)** *(of cars, horses, wine)* un/une spécialiste (en); **she fancies herself as a good j. of men** elle croit savoir juger les hommes; **I'm not sure he's the best j. of such things** je ne suis pas sûr qu'il soit très bon juge en la matière; **to be a good** *or* **keen j. of character** être bon *ou* fin psychologue; **I'll let you be the j. of that** je vous en fais juge, je vous laisse juge; **I will be the j. of that** c'est moi qui jugerai de cela

VT **1** *(pass judgment on, adjudicate)* juger; **the case will be judged tomorrow** l'affaire sera jugée demain; **a panel of critics judged the competition** le concours a été jugé par un panel de critiques; **the assistant referee judged him offside** le juge de touche a estimé qu'il était hors jeu; **don't j. him too harshly** ne le juge pas trop sévèrement **2** *(consider)* juger, considérer; **she judged it her duty to protest** elle a considéré qu'il était de son devoir de protester; **her latest novel has been judged a failure by the critics** les critiques ont estimé que son dernier roman était mauvais **3** *(estimate)* juger de, estimer; **can you j. the distance?** peux-tu évaluer la distance?; **I'd j. him to be about thirty** je lui donnerais la trentaine

VI juger; **who will be judging?** *(in competition)* qui va faire fonction de juge?; **if you don't believe me, j. for yourself** si vous ne me croyez pas, jugez-en par vous-même; **it isn't for me to j.** ce n'est pas à moi d'en juger; **you're in no position to j.** vous n'êtes pas en mesure d'en juger; **as far as I can j.** pour autant que je puisse en juger; **judging from** *or* **by what he said** si j'en juge par ce qu'il a dit; **to j. from** *or* **by her accent** à en juger par son accent, d'après son accent

• **Judges** N *Bible* **(the book of) Judges** (le livre des) Juges

▸▸ *Mil* ***judge advocate*** assesseur *m (d'un tribunal militaire)*; *Mil* ***judge advocate general*** assesseur *m* général

judgeship ['dʒʌdʒʃɪp] N *Law* fonction *f* de juge

judgment, judgement ['dʒʌdʒmənt] N **1** *Law & Rel* jugement *m*; **to pass j. on sb** prononcer *ou* rendre un jugement sur qn; *Fig* **to pass j. on sb/sth** porter un jugement sur qn/qch; **to sit in j.** *(court)* siéger; *Fig* **to sit in j. on** juger; *Fig* **they have no right to sit in j. over us!** ils n'ont pas le droit de nous juger! **2** *(opinion)* jugement *m*, opinion *f*, avis *m*; **to give one's j. on** donner *ou* exprimer son avis sur; **to form a j.** se faire une opinion; **in my j.** à mon sens, à mon avis; **to reserve j. on sth** réserver son jugement *ou* opinion sur qch; *Fig* **we will have to reserve j. on the new arrangements** nous devrons attendre avant de nous prononcer sur les nouvelles dispositions; **against my better j. we decided to go** je pensais que c'était une erreur, mais nous avons quand même décidé d'y aller **3** *(discernment)* jugement *m*; **he is a man of j.** c'est un homme perspicace; **political/financial j.** discernement *m* en matière de politique/finances; **to have/lack (good** *or* **sound) j.** avoir du/manquer de jugement; **this decision shows good j.** cette décision montre du discernement; **to trust sb's j.** s'en remettre au jugement de qn

▸▸ *Rel* ***Judgment Day*** (jour *m* du) Jugement *m* dernier; *Mktg* ***judgment sample*** échantillon *m* discrétionnaire; *Mktg* ***judgment sampling*** échantillonnage *m* discrétionnaire

judgmental, judgemental [dʒʌdʒ'mentəl] ADJ *(person, book etc)* critique; **I don't want to seem j., but...** je ne veux pas avoir l'air de critiquer, mais...

▸▸ *Mktg* ***judgmental forecasting*** prévision *f* par estimation; *Mktg* ***judgmental method*** méthode *f* estimative

judicature [ˈdʒuːdɪkətʃə(r)] **N** *Law* **1** *(judge's authority)* administration *f* de la justice **2** *(court's jurisdiction)* juridiction *f*; **court of j.** cour *f* de justice **3** *(position of judge)* fonction *f* de juge; *(judges collectively)* magistrature *f*

judicial [dʒuːˈdɪʃəl] **ADJ 1** *Law* judiciaire; **to take** *or* **to bring j. proceedings against sb** attaquer qn en justice **2** *(impartial)* impartial, critique; **a j. mind** un esprit critique

▸▸ ***judicial inquiry*** enquête *f* judiciaire; *Am* ***judicial review*** *(of ruling)* examen *m* d'une décision de justice *(par une juridiction supérieure)*; *(of law)* examen *m* de la constitutionnalité d'une loi; *Br* ***judicial separation*** séparation *f* de corps

judicially [dʒuːˈdɪʃəlɪ] **ADV** judiciairement

judiciary [dʒuːˈdɪʃərɪ] *Law* **N 1** *(judicial authority)* pouvoir *m* judiciaire **2** *(judges collectively)* magistrature *f*

ADJ judiciaire

judicious [dʒuːˈdɪʃəs] **ADJ** judicieux

judiciously [dʒuːˈdɪʃəslɪ] **ADV** judicieusement

judiciousness [dʒuːˈdɪʃəsnɪs] **N** *(of person, mind)* discernement *m*, bon sens *m*; *(of thought, remark)* caractère *m* judicieux

judo [ˈdʒuːdəʊ] **N** *Sport* judo *m*

jug [dʒʌg] *(pt & pp* **jugged**, *cont* **jugging) N 1** *Br (small ▸ for milk)* pot *m*; *(▸ for water)* carafe *f*; *(▸ for wine)* pichet *m*, carafe *f*; *(large ▸ earthenware)* cruche *f*; *(▸ metal, plastic)* broc *m*; **a j. of wine** une carafe de vin; **wine j.** carafe *f* à vin; *Fam* **his ears are like j. handles** il a les oreilles en contrevent *ou* comme des esgourdes

2 *Br (beer glass)* chope *f (contenant une pinte)*

3 *Fam (jail)* tôle *f*, cabane *f*; **five years in (the) j.** cinq ans en tôle

4 *Am (narrow-necked)* bonbonne *f*

5 *very Fam* **jugs** *(breasts)* nichons *mpl*, roberts *mpl*

VT 1 *Culin* cuire à l'étouffée *ou* à l'étuvée **2** *Fam (imprison)* mettre en tôle *ou* en cabane

▸▸ *Am Mus* ***jug band*** orchestre *m* de folk/jazz *(jouant avec des instruments de fortune)*; ***jug kettle*** = bouilloire électrique haute; *Am* ***jug wine*** vin *m* ordinaire

jugful [ˈdʒʌgfʊl] **N** *(of milk)* (contenu *m* d'un) pot *m*; *(of water, wine)* (contenu *m* d'une) carafe *f*; **he drank a whole j. of water** il a bu toute une carafe d'eau

jugged hare [dʒʌgd-] **N** *Culin* civet *m* de lièvre

juggernaut [ˈdʒʌgənɔːt] **N 1** *Br (large lorry)* gros poids *m* lourd **2** *(force)* force *f* fatale; **the j. of history** la force aveugle de l'histoire; **the j. of war** le pouvoir destructeur de la guerre

juggins [ˈdʒʌgɪnz] **N** *Br Fam Old-fashioned (simpleton)* nigaud(e) *m,f*, cruche *f*

juggle [ˈdʒʌgəl] **VI** *(as entertainment)* jongler; *Fig* **to j. with sth** *(figures, dates)* jongler avec qch

VT *also Fig* jongler avec; *Fig* **he juggled all the different possibilities** il envisagea toutes les possibilités

N jonglerie *f*

juggler [ˈdʒʌglə(r)] **N 1** *(entertainer)* jongleur (euse) *m,f* **2** *(deceitful person)* tricheur(euse) *m,f*

juggling [ˈdʒʌglɪŋ], **jugglery** [ˈdʒʌglərɪ] **N** *also Fig* jonglerie *f*

Jugoslav, Jugoslavia *etc* = **Yugoslav, Yugoslavia** *etc*

jugular [ˈdʒʌgjʊlə(r)] *Anat* **N** jugulaire *f*; *Fam* **to go for the j.** attaquer qn sur ses points faibles□

ADJ jugulaire

▸▸ ***jugular vein*** jugulaire *f*

juice [dʒuːs] **N 1** *Culin (of fruit, vegetables, meat)* jus *m*; **grapefruit j.** jus *m* de pamplemousse; **meat j.** jus *m* de viande

2 *Biol* suc *m*

3 *Fam (electricity)* jus *m*; *(petrol)* essence□ *f*; *Br (gas)* gaz□ *m*

4 *Am Fam (spirits)* tord-boyaux *m inv*; *(wine)* pinard *m*

5 *Am Fam (popularity, recognition)* succès□ *m*; **to have a lot of j.** faire un tabac

VT *(fruit)* presser

▸▸ ***juice bar*** = bar où l'on sert des jus de fruit; *Br* ***juice extractor*** centrifugeuse *f (pour faire des jus de fruit)*

▸ **juice up VT SEP** *Am Fam* **1** *(battery)* recharger□ **2** *(enliven)* égayer□, animer□ **3** *(intoxicate)* soûler; **he got juiced up on whisky** il s'est soûlé au whisky

juiced [dʒuːst] **ADJ** *Am Fam (drunk)* pété, bourré, beurré

juicer [ˈdʒuːsə(r)] **N 1** *(machine)* presse-fruits *m inv* **2** *Am Fam (alcoholic)* alco(o)lo *mf*, poivrot(e) *m,f*

juiciness [ˈdʒuːsɪnɪs] **N 1** *(of fruit)* **I chose these oranges for their j.** j'ai choisi ces oranges parce qu'elles sont juteuses **2** *Fam (of story)* piquant *m*

juicy [ˈdʒuːsɪ] *(compar* **juicier**, *superl* **juiciest) ADJ 1** *(fruit)* juteux; *(meat)* plein de jus, qui rend du jus; **a big j. steak** un bon steak bien tendre **2** *Fam (profitable)* juteux; **a j. deal** une affaire juteuse **3** *Fam (racy)* savoureux; **a j. story** une histoire osée *ou* piquante; **let's hear all the j. details** racontenous les détails croustillants

ju-jitsu = **jiu-jitsu**

juju [ˈdʒuːdʒuː] **N** *(charm)* amulette *f*

jujube [ˈdʒuːdʒuːb] **N** *(fruit)* jujube *m*

jukebox [ˈdʒuːkbɒks] **N** juke-box *m*

Jul. *(written abbr* **July)** juil

julep [ˈdʒuːlɪp] **N 1** *(soft drink)* boisson *f* sucrée **2** *(alcoholic drink)* **(mint) j.** = cocktail au bourbon et à la menthe **3** *Pharm* julep *m*

Julian [ˈdʒuːlɪən] **ADJ** *(relating to Julius Caesar)* julien, de Jules César

▸▸ ***Julian calendar*** calendrier *m* julien; ***Julian year*** année *f* julienne

Julius Caesar [ˌdʒuːlɪəsˈsiːzə(r)] **PR N** Jules César

July [dʒuːˈlaɪ] **N** juillet *m*; *see also* **February**

jumble [ˈdʒʌmbəl] **N 1** *(confusion, disorder)* fouillis *m*, désordre *m*; **my things are all in a j.** mes affaires sont tout en désordre; **a j. of colours** un kaléidoscope de couleurs

2 *(of thoughts, ideas)* méli-mélo *m*, fouillis *m*, fatras *m*; *(of words)* fatras *m*

3 *Br (articles for jumble sale)* bric-à-brac *m*

4 *Am Culin* = petit gâteau en forme d'anneau

VT 1 *(objects, belongings)* mélanger; **the pages got all jumbled** les pages se sont complètement mélangées; **her clothes were all jumbled (up** *or* **together) in a suitcase** ses vêtements étaient fourrés pêle-mêle dans une valise **2** *(thoughts, ideas)* embrouiller; **his essay was just a collection of jumbled ideas** sa dissertation n'était qu'un fourre-tout d'idées confuses

▸▸ *Br* ***jumble sale*** = vente de charité où sont vendus des articles d'occasion et des produits faits maison

jumbo [ˈdʒʌmbəʊ] *(pl* **jumbos)** *Fam* **N 1** *(elephant)* éléphant□ *m*, pachyderme□ *m* **2** *(aircraft)* avion *m* gros porteur□, gros-porteur□ *m*

ADJ 1 *(giant-sized)* énorme□, géant□ **2** *Am Fin (loan)* géant□

▸▸ *Aviat* ***jumbo jet*** avion *m* gros porteur□, gros-porteur□ *m*; *Am Fam Fin* ***jumbo loan*** prêt *m* géant; *Fam St Exch* ***jumbo trade*** opération *f* jumbo

JUMP [dʒʌmp]

N	
• saut **1, 4**	• bond **1, 2**
• hausse **2**	• obstacle **3**
• prise **5**	
VT	
• sauter **1, 3**	• faire sauter **2**
VI	
• sauter **1, 2, 4**	• bondir **1**
• sursauter **2**	• monter en flèche **3**

N 1 *(leap, bound)* saut *m*, bond *m*; **she got up with a j.** elle se leva d'un bond; *Fig* **we need to keep one j. ahead of the competition** nous devons garder une longueur d'avance sur nos concurrents; *Fam* **to have the j. on sb** avoir pris une longueur d'avance sur qn dès le départ; *Fam* **to get the j. on sb** devancer qn□; *Am Fam* **to be on the j.** être pressé *ou* débordé; *Fam* **go take a j.!** va te faire voir (ailleurs)!, va te faire cuire un œuf!

2 *(sharp rise)* bond *m*, hausse *f*; **there has been a sudden j. in house prices** il y a eu une flambée des prix de l'immobilier; **inflation took a sudden j. last month** l'inflation a subitement augmenté l[...] mois dernier

3 *Horseriding (fence, obstacle)* obstacle *m*

4 *Comput* saut *m*

5 *(in board games)* prise *f* (de pion)

VT 1 *(leap over)* sauter; **to j. a fence** sauter o[...] franchir un obstacle; *Am* **to j. rope** sauter à l[...] corde; **to j. a piece** *(in draughts)* prendre un pio[...]

2 *(horse)* faire sauter; **she jumped her horse ove[...] the stream** elle a fait sauter *ou* franchir le ruis[...] seau à son cheval

3 *(omit, skip)* sauter; **to j. a line** sauter une ligne

4 *Fam (attack)* sauter sur□, agresser□; **two me[...] jumped him in the park** deux hommes lui on[...] sauté dessus dans le parc

5 *Fam (leave, abscond from)* **to j. bail** ne pas com[...] paraître au tribunal□ *(après avoir été libéré sou[...] caution)*; *also Fig* **to j. ship** quitter le navire□; *A[...]* **the fugitive jumped town** le fugitif a réussi à qui[...] ter la ville□

6 *(not wait one's turn at)* **to j. the queue** ne pa[...] attendre son tour, resquiller; **she jumped th[...] lights** elle a grillé *ou* brûlé le feu (rouge)

7 *esp Am Fam* **to j. a train** *(not buy ticket for)* voya[...] ger sans billet□

8 *Am Fam* **he jumped a (mining) claim** *(took i[...] legally)* il s'est approprié une concession (mi[...] nière)□

VI 1 *(leap)* sauter, bondir; **they jumped across th[...] crevasse** ils ont traversé la crevasse d'un bond; **to j. back** faire un bond en arrière; **can you j. ove[...] the hedge?** peux-tu sauter par-dessus la haie? **he jumped up, he jumped to his feet** il se leva d'u[...] bond; **to j. to the ground** sauter à terre; **the fro[...] jumped from stone to stone** la grenouille bondis[...] sait de pierre en pierre; **to j. for joy** sauter de joie; **she was jumping up and down with rage** elle trépi[...] gnait de rage; *Fam* **j. to it!** grouille!; *Fam* **to j[...] down sb's throat** *(reply sharply to)* rabrouer qn[...] rembarrer qn; *(criticize)* engueuler qn; *Am Fa[...]* **to j. all over sb** passer un savon à qn, engueule[...] qn; **let's wait and see which way she jumps** atten[...] dons de voir sa réaction, attendons de voir com[...] ment elle va réagir

2 *(make a sudden movement ▸ person)* sursauter[...] tressauter; *(▸ record player needle, chisel, drill[...]* sauter; **the noise made her j.** le bruit l'a fait sur[...] sauter; **this record jumps** ce disque saute; **w[...] nearly jumped out of our skins** *(from surprise[...]* nous avons failli sauter au plafond; *(from fea[...] shock)* ça nous a fait un de ces coups

3 *(rise sharply)* monter *ou* grimper en flèche; **prices jumped dramatically in 1974** les prix on[...] grimpé de façon spectaculaire en 1974

4 *(go directly)* sauter; **he jumped from one topic t[...] another** il passait rapidement d'un sujet à un au[...] tre; **to j. to conclusions** tirer des conclusions hâti[...] ves; **she immediately jumped to the conclusio[...] that he was being unfaithful** elle en a immédiate[...] ment conclu qu'il la trompait; **I jumped to th[...] third chapter** je suis passé directement au troi[...] sième chapitre; **the film then jumps to the presen[...]** puis le film fait un saut jusqu'au présent; *Compu[...]* **to j. from one Web page to another** passer d'un[...] page Web à une autre

5 *Fam (be lively)* être très animé□; **by midnigh[...] the joint was jumping** à minuit, ça chauffait dan[...] la boîte

▸▸ *Sport* ***jump ball*** *(in basketball)* entre-deux *m[...] inv*; *Am* ***jump cables*** câbles *mpl* de démarrage; *Cin* ***jump cut*** faux *m* raccord, saut *m* de montage; *Br Aviat* ***jump jet*** avion *m* à décollage vertical; *B[...]* ***jump leads*** câbles *mpl* de démarrage; *Am* ***jum[...] rope*** corde *f* à sauter; *Br* ***jump seat*** strapontin *m*; ***jump shot*** *(in basketball)* tir *m* en suspension

▸ **jump about, jump around VI** sautiller; *Fi[...] (story, film)* partir dans toutes les directions

▸ **jump in VI 1** *(into vehicle)* monter; *(into water, hole, ditch)* sauter; **if you want a lift, j. in!** si tu veux que je te dépose, monte!; *Fig* **to j. in at the deep end** se jeter tête baissée dans les problèmes **2** *Fam Fig (intervene)* intervenir□; **he jumpe[...] in to defend her** il est intervenu pour la défendre, il est venu à sa rescousse□

▸ **jump into VT INSEP** sauter dans; **she jumpe[...] into her car** elle a sauté dans sa voiture; **to j. into bed with sb** coucher avec qn tout de suite

jump off VI **1** *(leap* ▸ *from wall)* sauter (**from** de); *(get off* ▸ *from bicycle, bus, train, horse)* descendre **2** *Horseriding* faire un barrage
VT INSEP *(leap from* ▸ *wall)* sauter de; *(get off from* ▸ *bicycle, bus, train, horse)* descendre de; **he jumped off the train** *(leapt from)* il a sauté du train; *(got off from)* il est descendu du train; **he jumped off the bridge** il s'est jeté du haut du pont

jump on VT INSEP **1** *(bicycle, horse)* sauter sur; *(bus, train)* monter dans; *(person)* sauter sur **2** *Fig (mistake)* repérer; **the boss jumps on every little mistake** aucune faute n'échappe au patron; *Fam* **to j. on sb** *(reprimand)* passer un savon à qn
VI *(on to bicycle, horse)* sauter dessus; *(on to bus, train)* monter

jump out VI *(from hiding place)* sortir d'un bond (**from** de); *(from high place)* sauter; *(from vehicle)* descendre (**of** *or* **from** de); **I'll j. out at the traffic lights** je vais descendre au feu rouge; **to j. out of bed** sauter (à bas) du lit; **to j. out of the window** sauter par la fenêtre; **to j. out of the bushes/one's hiding place** bondir d'entre les buissons/de sa cachette; *Fig* **the answer suddenly jumped out at me** la réponse m'a subitement sauté aux yeux

umped-up [dʒʌmpt-] ADJ *Br Fam Pej* parvenu; **she's just a j. shop assistant** ce n'est qu'une petite vendeuse qui se donne de grands airs *ou* qui se prend au sérieux

umper ['dʒʌmpə(r)] N **1** *Br (sweater)* pull(over) *m*
2 *Am (dress)* robe-chasuble *f*
3 *(person)* sauteur(euse) *m,f*
4 *Comput (pin)* cavalier *m*
▸▸ *Am* ***jumper cables*** câbles *mpl* de démarrage

umpily ['dʒʌmpɪlɪ] ADV *(nervously)* nerveusement

umpiness ['dʒʌmpɪnɪs] N *(of person)* nervosité *f*; *St Exch (of markets)* instabilité *f*

umping ['dʒʌmpɪŋ] N *Horseriding* jumping *m*
ADJ *Fam (party, nightclub)* hyper animé
▸▸ *Bot* ***jumping bean*** pois *m* sauteur; ***jumping jack*** *(firework)* pétard *m* mitrailette; *(puppet)* pantin *m*; *(exercise)* = saut avec extension latérale des membres; *Am* ***jumping rope*** corde *f* à sauter

umping-off point, jumping-off place N point *m* de départ, tremplin *m*; *Fig* **his success could be a j. for a new career** sa réussite pourrait être le point de départ d'une nouvelle carrière

umpmaster ['dʒʌmp,mæstə(r)] N *Am Mil* moniteur(trice) *m,f* de parachutisme

ump-off N *Horseriding* barrage *m*

ump-start N **to give sb a j.** *(by pushing or rolling car)* faire démarrer la voiture de qn en la poussant/en la mettant dans une pente; *(with jump leads)* faire démarrer la voiture de qn avec des câbles *(branchés sur la batterie d'une autre voiture)*; *Fig* **to give a j. to the economy** relancer l'économie
VT **to j. a car** *(by pushing or rolling)* faire démarrer une voiture en la poussant/en la mettant dans une pente; *(with jump leads)* faire démarrer une voiture avec des câbles *(branchés sur la batterie d'une autre voiture)*; *Fig* **to j. the economy** relancer l'économie

umpy ['dʒʌmpɪ] *(compar* **jumpier**, *superl* **jumpiest**) ADJ **1** *Fam (edgy)* nerveux▫ **2** *St Exch* instable, fluctuant **3** *(fitful, jerky* ▸ *style, gestures etc)* saccadé

un. **1** *(written abbr* **June**) juin **2** *(written abbr* **Junior**) junior, fils

unction ['dʒʌŋkʃən] N **1** *(of roads)* carrefour *m*, croisement *m*; *(of railway lines, traffic lanes)* embranchement *m*; *(of rivers, canals)* confluent *m*; *(in pipes)* embranchement *m*, jonction *f*, raccordement *m*; *Br* **j. 5** *(on motorway* ▸ *exit)* la sortie 5; *(*▸ *entrance)* l'entrée *f* 5 **2** *Elec (of wires)* raccordement *m*; *(between semiconductors)* jonction *f* **3** *Formal (joining)* jonction *f*
▸▸ *Br Elec* ***junction box*** boîte *f* de dérivation

> Attention: ne pas confondre avec **juncture**.

uncture ['dʒʌŋktʃə(r)] N **1** *Formal (moment)* conjoncture *f*; **at this j.** dans la conjoncture actuelle, dans les circonstances actuelles; **at a crucial j.** à un moment critique **2** *Ling* joncture *f*, jointure *f*, frontière *f* **3** *Tech* jointure *f*

> Attention: ne pas confondre avec **junction**.

June [dʒuːn] N juin *m*; *see also* **February**
▸▸ *Entom* ***June beetle, June bug*** hanneton *m*

jungle ['dʒʌŋgəl] N **1** *(tropical forest)* jungle *f* **2** *Fig* jungle *f*; **the world of business is a real j.** le monde des affaires est une véritable jungle; **it's a j. out there** c'est la jungle là-bas; **the j. of tax laws** le labyrinthe du droit fiscal
COMP *(animal)* de la jungle
▸▸ *very Fam* ***jungle bunny*** nègre (négresse) *m,f*, = terme injurieux désignant un Noir/Une Noire; ***jungle fever*** *(UNCOUNT)* paludisme *m*; ***jungle fowl*** coq *m* sauvage; *Am* ***jungle gym*** cage *f* à poules *(jeu)*; *Br Fam* ***jungle juice*** gnôle *f*; ***jungle warfare*** combat *m* de jungle

junior ['dʒuːnjə(r)] N **1** *(younger person)* cadet (ette) *m,f*; **he is five years her j.** il est de cinq ans son cadet, il a cinq ans de moins qu'elle
2 *(subordinate)* subordonné(e) *m,f*, subalterne *mf*
3 *Br (pupil)* écolier(ère) *m,f (entre 7 et 11 ans)*; **she teaches juniors** elle est institutrice
4 *Am Sch* élève *mf* de troisième année; *Am Univ* étudiant(e) *m,f* de troisième année
COMP *Br (teaching, teacher)* dans le primaire; *Sport (event, team)* junior
ADJ **1** *(younger)* cadet, plus jeune; **to be j. to sb** être plus jeune que qn
2 *(lower in rank)* subordonné, subalterne; **a j. member of staff** un employé subalterne; **he's j. to her in the department** il est son subalterne dans le service
3 *(juvenile)* jeune
4 *(small)* petit
• **Junior** N **1** **Hudson J.** *(the son)* Hudson fils *ou* junior; *(one of two or more brothers)* Hudson junior **2** *Am Fam (term of address)* fiston *m*; **bring J. with you next time** amène ton fiston la prochaine fois
▸▸ ***Junior College*** *(in US)* = établissement d'enseignement supérieur où l'on obtient un diplôme en deux ans; *Br Univ* ***junior common room*** salle *f* des étudiants; ***junior doctor*** interne *mf*; ***junior executive*** cadre *m* débutant, jeune cadre *m*; *Am Univ* ***the junior faculty*** les enseignants *mpl* non titulaires; *Am* ***junior high school*** collège *m* d'enseignement secondaire; *Br* ***junior hospital doctor*** interne *mf*; ***junior minister*** sous-secrétaire *m* d'État; ***junior miss*** *(clothes size)* fillette *f*; ***junior partner*** associé(e) *m,f* adjoint(e); ***junior portion*** *(in restaurant)* portion *f* enfants; *Br* ***junior school*** école *f* élémentaire *(pour les enfants de 7 à 11 ans)*; *Com* ***junior sizes*** petites tailles *fpl*; *Am Sch & Univ* ***junior year*** avant-dernière année *f*

juniper ['dʒuːnɪpə(r)] N *Bot* genévrier *m*
▸▸ ***juniper berry*** baie *f* de genièvre; ***juniper oil*** essence *f* de genièvre

junk [dʒʌŋk] N **1** *(UNCOUNT) Fam (poor-quality, worthless things)* pacotille *f*, camelote *f*; **this watch is a real piece of j.** cette montre, c'est vraiment de la camelote *ou* c'est de la vraie camelote; **all his so-called antiques were just a pile of j.** ses prétendues antiquités n'étaient en fait qu'un ramassis de vieilleries; **his latest film is utter j.** son dernier film est absolument nul *ou* un vrai navet; **she eats nothing but j.** elle ne mange que des cochonneries
2 *(UNCOUNT) (second-hand or unwanted goods)* bric-à-brac *m*
3 *(UNCOUNT) Fam (stuff)* trucs *mpl*, machins *mpl*; **can you get your j. off the table?** tu peux enlever tes trucs *ou* ton bazar de la table?; **what's all that j. in the hall?** qu'est-ce que c'est que ce bric-à-brac *ou* ce bazar dans l'entrée?
4 *(boat)* jonque *f*
5 *(UNCOUNT) Fam Drugs slang* came *f*
VT *Fam* jeter (à la poubelle)▫, balancer
▸▸ *St Exch* ***junk bond*** junk bond *m (obligation à haut rendement mais à haut risque)*; *Biol* ***junk DNA*** ADN *m* non génique; *Comput* ***junk e-mail*** messages *mpl* publicitaires; *Fam* ***junk food*** nourriture *f* de mauvaise qualité▫; **their kids eat nothing but j. food** leurs gosses ne mangent que des cochonneries; ***junk heap*** dépotoir *m*; ***junk jewellery*** *(UNCOUNT)* bijoux *mpl* fantaisie; ***junk mail*** *(UNCOUNT)* courrier *m* publicitaire; ***junk room*** pièce *f* de débarras; ***junk shop*** magasin *m* de brocante; **at the j. shop** chez le brocanteur

junker ['dʒʌŋkə(r)] N *Am Fam (old car)* vieille bagnole *f*

junket ['dʒʌŋkɪt] N **1** *Fam Pej (trip)* voyage *m* aux frais de la princesse **2** *Fam (festive occasion)* banquet▫ *m*, festin▫ *m* **3** *Culin* lait *m* caillé (sucré et parfumé)
VI **1** *Fam (feast)* banqueter▫, festoyer▫ **2** *Fam Pej (go on trip)* voyager aux frais de la princesse

junketing ['dʒʌŋkɪtɪŋ] N *(UNCOUNT) Fam Pej* voyages *mpl* aux frais de la princesse

junkie ['dʒʌŋkɪ] N *Fam* **1** *(drug addict)* drogué(e)▫ *m,f*, junkie *mf* **2** *Fig* dingue *mf*, accro *mf*; **a television/football j.** un(e) dingue de la télé/du football

junkman ['dʒʌŋkmæn] *(pl* **junkmen** [-men]) N *Am (dealer in old furniture)* brocanteur *m*; *(ragman)* chiffonnier *m*; *(scrap metal dealer)* ferrailleur *m*, marchand *m* de ferraille

junky *(pl* **junkies**) = **junkie**

junkyard ['dʒʌŋk,jɑːd] N **1** *(for scrap metal)* entrepôt *m* de ferraille; **at the j.** chez le ferrailleur **2** *(for discarded objects)* dépotoir *m*; *Fig* **their garden is a real j.** leur jardin est un véritable dépotoir

Juno ['dʒuːnəʊ] PR N *Myth* Junon

Junoesque [,dʒuːnəʊ'esk] ADJ *(woman)* imposant

junta [*Br* 'dʒʌntə, *Am* 'hʊntə] N junte *f*

Jupiter ['dʒuːpɪtə(r)] PR N *Myth* Jupiter
N *Astron* Jupiter *f*

Jurassic [dʒʊ'ræsɪk] ADJ jurassique
N jurassique *m*

juridical [dʒʊ'rɪdɪkəl] ADJ juridique
▸▸ ***juridical day*** jour *m* d'audience

jurisdiction [,dʒʊərɪs'dɪkʃən] N **1** *Law & Admin* compétence *f*; **the federal government has no j. over such cases** de tels cas ne relèvent pas de la compétence *ou* des attributions du gouvernement fédéral; **to come** *or* **to fall within the j. of** relever de la juridiction de; **this territory is within the j. of the United States** ce territoire est soumis à l'autorité judiciaire des États-Unis **2** *(general authority)* autorité *f*; **to have j. over sb** avoir autorité sur qn; **he has no j. over his brother's activities** il n'a aucune emprise *ou* aucun pouvoir sur ce que fait son frère **3** *Fig (field of activity)* compétence *f*, ressort *m*; **this matter does not come within** *or* **is not in** *or* **falls outside our j.** cette affaire ne relève pas de notre compétence, cette affaire n'est pas de notre compétence *ou* de notre ressort

jurisprudence [,dʒʊərɪs'pruːdəns] N *Law* philosophie *f* du droit

jurist ['dʒʊərɪst] N *Formal (expert)* juriste *mf*, légiste *m*; *(writer)* juriste *mf*; *Am (lawyer)* avocat (e) *m,f*; *(judge)* juge *mf*

juristic [dʒʊ'rɪstɪk] ADJ juridique

juror ['dʒʊərə(r)] N *Law* juré *m*

jury ['dʒʊərɪ] *(pl* **juries**) N **1** *Law* jury *m*; **to serve on a j.** faire partie d'un jury; **ladies and gentlemen of the j., members of the j.** *(term of address)* Mesdames et Messieurs les jurés; **the j. is out** le jury est en délibération; *Fig* **the j. is still out on that one** ça reste à voir **2** *(in contest)* jury *m*
ADJ *Naut* de fortune, improvisé
▸▸ *Law* ***jury box*** banc *m ou* box *m* des jurés; **she was in the j. box** elle faisait partie des jurés; ***jury charge*** directives *fpl* au jury; ***jury duty*** participation *f* à un jury; **to do (one's) j. duty** s'acquitter de son devoir de participation au jury; **to be called (up) for j. duty** être convoqué comme juré; *Fam* ***jury nobbling*** subornation *f* des jurés; *Br* ***jury service*** participation *f* à un jury; **to do (one's) j. service** s'acquitter de son devoir de participation au jury; **to be called (up) for j. service** être convoqué comme juré; *Am* ***jury shopping*** choix *m* vétilleux des jurés *(par les avocats de la défense)*; ***jury tampering*** subornation *f* des jurés; ***jury trial*** procès *m* devant jury

juryman ['dʒʊərɪmən] *(pl* **jurymen** [-mən]) **N** *Law* juré *m*

jurywoman ['dʒʊərɪ,wʊmən] *(pl* **jurywomen** [-'wɪmɪn]) **N** *Law* jurée *f*

JUST¹ [dʒʌst]

- juste **1–6**
- exactement **4**
- absolument **9**
- seulement **3**
- à peine **5**

ADV 1 *(indicating immediate past)* juste; **j. the other day** pas plus tard que l'autre jour; **j. last week** pas plus tard que la semaine dernière; **she has j. gone out** elle vient juste de sortir; **they had (only) j. arrived** ils venaient (tout) juste d'arriver; **I've (only) j. seen him going downstairs** je viens de le voir à l'instant qui descendait; **I've j. been speaking to him on the phone** je viens juste de lui parler au téléphone, je lui parlais au téléphone à l'instant; **she's j. this moment** *or* **minute left the office** elle vient de sortir du bureau à l'instant; **he's j. been to Mexico** il revient *ou* rentre du Mexique; **I saw him j. yesterday, I j. saw him yesterday** je l'ai vu pas plus tard qu'hier; **he has j. left school** il sort du lycée; *Scot & Ir Fam* **I'm j. after seeing him** je viens de le voir❑

2 *(indicating present or immediate future)* juste; **I was j. going to phone you** j'allais juste *ou* justement te téléphoner, j'étais sur le point de te téléphoner; **my hair is j. turning grey** *or* **is j. beginning to turn grey** mes cheveux commencent juste à grisonner; *Fam* **I'm j. off** je m'en vais❑; *Fam* **j. coming!** j'arrive tout de suite!❑; **to be j. about to do sth** être sur le point de faire qch; **I was j. about to tell you** j'allais justement te le dire; **I'm j. making tea, do you want some?** je suis en train de faire du thé, tu en veux?

3 *(only, merely)* juste, seulement; **j. a few** quelques-uns/quelques-unes seulement; **j. a little** juste un peu; **j. a minute** *or* **a moment** *or* **a second, please** une (petite) minute *ou* un (petit) instant, s'il vous plaît; **j. a minute, aren't you supposed to be somewhere else?** une seconde, tu n'es pas censé être ailleurs?; **tell him j. to wait** dites-lui qu'il n'a qu'à attendre; *Fam* **I'll j. pop in** je ne ferai qu'entrer et sortir; **j. ask if you need money** vous n'avez qu'à demander si vous avez besoin d'argent; **do you want some whisky? – j. a drop** est-ce que tu veux du whisky? – juste une goutte; **it costs j. $10** ça ne coûte que 10 dollars, ça coûte 10 dollars seulement; **we have j. a few copies left** il nous (en) reste quelques exemplaires seulement *ou* juste quelques exemplaires; **it was j. a dream** ce n'était qu'un rêve; **he's j. a clerk** ce n'est qu'un simple employé; **she's j. a baby** ce n'est qu'un bébé; **we're j. friends** nous sommes amis, c'est tout; **I have come j. to see you** je viens seulement *ou* juste *ou* uniquement pour vous voir; **he was j. trying to help** il voulait juste *ou* simplement rendre service; **if he could j. work a little harder!** si seulement il pouvait travailler un peu plus!; **if the job is so unpleasant you should j. leave** si le travail est désagréable à ce point, tu n'as qu'à démissionner; **don't argue, j. do it!** ne discute pas, fais-le, c'est tout!; **if you can j. sign here, please** juste une petite signature ici, s'il vous plaît; **you can't ask j. anybody to present the prizes** tu ne peux pas demander au premier venu de présenter les prix; **this is not j. any horse race, this is the Derby!** ça n'est pas n'importe quelle course de chevaux, c'est le Derby!

4 *(exactly, precisely)* exactement, juste; **j. here/there** juste ici/là; **j. at that moment** juste à ce moment-là; **that's j. what I needed** c'est exactement *ou* juste ce qu'il me fallait; *Ironic* il ne me manquait plus que ça; **j. what are you getting at?** où veux-tu en venir exactement?; **he's j. like his father** c'est son père tout craché; **she's j. the person for the job** elle a exactement le profil requis pour ce poste; **that dress is j. the same as yours** cette robe est exactement la même que la tienne; **oh, I can j. picture it!** oh, je vois tout à fait!; **that hat is j. you** ce chapeau te va à merveille; **you speak French j. as well as I do** ton français est tout aussi bon que le mien; **I'd j. as soon go tomorrow** j'aimerais autant y aller demain; **it's j. ten o'clock** il est dix heures juste(s) *ou* pile, il est tout juste dix heures; *Ironic* **(it's) j. my luck!** c'est bien ma chance!; **don't come in j. yet** n'entre pas tout de suite; **that's j. it** *or* **j. the point!** précisément!, justement!, voilà!

5 *(barely)* (tout) juste, à peine; **I could j. make out what they were saying** je parvenais tout juste à entendre ce qu'ils disaient; **you came j. in time!** tu es arrivé juste à temps!; **she's j. in time for a drink** elle arrive pile pour *ou* elle arrive juste à temps pour prendre un verre; **he (only) j. managed to catch the train** il a eu le train de justesse, c'est tout juste s'il a eu le train; **she caught the train but (only) j.** elle a eu le train mais c'était juste *ou* c'était de justesse; **they (only) j. missed the train** ils ont manqué le train de peu; **I j. missed a lorry** j'ai failli heurter un camion; **the trousers j. fit me** je rentre tout juste dans le pantalon

6 *(a little)* **it costs j. over/under £50** ça coûte un tout petit peu plus de/moins de 50 livres; **it's j. after/before two o'clock** il est un peu plus/moins de deux heures; **j. after my birthday** juste après *ou* peu après mon anniversaire; **j. afterwards** juste après; **j. in front/behind/above/below** juste devant/derrière/au-dessus/au-dessous; **it's j. to the right of the painting** c'est juste à droite du tableau

7 *(possibly)* **I may** *or* **might j. be able to do it** il n'est pas impossible que je puisse le faire; **his story might** *or* **could j. be true** son histoire pourrait être vraie, il est possible que son histoire soit vraie

8 *(emphatic use)* **j. think what might have happened!** imagine un peu ce qui aurait pu arriver!; **we j. can't understand it** nous n'arrivons vraiment pas à comprendre; **j. wait till I find the culprit!** attends un peu que je trouve le coupable!; **j. be quiet, will you!** veux-tu bien te taire!; **now j. you wait a minute, Kate!** hé, une petite minute, Kate!; **j. (you) try!** essaie donc un peu!; **I j. won't do it** il n'est pas question que je le fasse; **it j. isn't good enough** c'est loin d'être satisfaisant, c'est tout; *Br* **he looks terrible in that suit – doesn't he j.!** ce costume ne lui va pas du tout – je ne te le fais pas dire!; *Br* **do you remember? – don't I j.!** tu t'en souviens? – et comment (que je m'en souviens)!; **why don't you want to go? – I j. don't** pourquoi est-ce que tu ne veux pas y aller? – je ne veux pas, c'est tout!

9 *(utterly, completely)* absolument; **the meal was j. delicious** le repas était tout simplement *ou* vraiment délicieux; **everything is j. fine** tout est parfait; **this is j. ridiculous!** c'est vraiment ridicule!; **don't you j. love that hat?** adorable, ce chapeau, non?; **I j. loved Barcelona** j'ai vraiment adoré Barcelone

10 *(on signs)* **j. picked** cueilli du jour; **j. cooked** cuit du jour; **j. arrived** fraîchement arrivé

• **just about ADV 1** *(very nearly)* presque, quasiment; **it's j. about ten o'clock** il est plus ou moins *ou* à peu près dix heures; **dinner is j. about ready** le dîner est presque prêt; **she's j. about as tall as you** elle est presque aussi grande que toi; *Fam* **that j. about does it!** ça suffit comme ça!; **I've j. about had enough of your sarcasm!** j'en ai franchement assez de tes sarcasmes!; **have you finished? – j. about** est-ce que vous avez terminé? – presque

2 *(barely)* (tout) juste; **can you reach the shelf? – j. about!** est-ce que tu peux atteindre l'étagère? – (tout) juste!; **his handwriting is j. about legible** son écriture est tout juste *ou* à peine lisible

3 *(approximately)* **their plane should be taking off j. about now** leur avion devrait être sur le point de décoller

• **just as CONJ 1** *(at the same time as)* juste au moment où; **they arrived j. as we were leaving** ils sont arrivés juste au moment où nous partions; **j. as the door was opening** au moment même où la porte s'ouvrait

2 *(exactly as)* **j. as I thought/predicted** comme je le pensais/prévoyais; **j. as you like** *or* **wish** comme vous voulez *ou* voudrez; **why not come j. as you are?** pourquoi ne viens-tu pas comme tu es?

• **just in case CONJ** juste au cas où; **j. in case we don't see each other** juste au cas où nous ne nous verrions pas **ADV** au cas où; **take a coat, j. in case** prends un manteau, on ne sait jamais *ou* au cas où

• **just like that ADV** *Fam* comme ça; **he told me to clear off, j. like that!** il m'a dit de me tirer, carrément!; **I can't do it j. like that, I need some notice** je ne peux pas le faire comme ça, sans être prévenu à l'avance

• **just now ADV 1** *(at this moment)* **I'm busy j. now** je suis occupé pour le moment; **not j. now** pas en ce moment; **she's not leaving j. now** elle ne part pas encore, elle ne part pas tout de suite

2 *(a short time ago)* **I heard a noise j. now** je viens juste d'entendre un bruit; **I've j. now come from there** j'en viens à l'instant; **when did this happen? – j. now** quand cela s'est-il passé? – à l'instant

• **just on ADV** *Br* exactement; **they've been married j. on 30 years** ça fait exactement 30 ans qu'ils sont mariés; **the fish weighed j. on three kilos** le poisson pesait exactement trois kilos; **it's j. on ten o'clock** il est dix heures juste(s) *ou* pile, il est tout juste dix heures

• **just so ADV** *Formal (expressing agreement)* c'est exact; **are you a magistrate? – j. so** vous êtes magistrat? – c'est exact **ADJ** *Br (properly arranged)* parfait; **she likes everything (to be) j. so** elle aime que tout soit parfait

• **just then ADV** à ce moment-là; **I was j. then getting ready to go out** je me préparais justement à sortir; **j. then, a strange figure appeared** à ce moment-là, une silhouette étrange apparut

• **just the same ADV** *(nonetheless)* quand même; **j. the same, it's as well to check** il vaut quand même mieux vérifier

just² **ADJ 1** *(fair, impartial)* juste, équitable; **a j. law** une loi juste *ou* équitable; **a ruler who was j. to** *or* **towards all men** un souverain qui a su faire preuve d'équité (envers tous)

2 *(reasonable, moral)* juste, légitime; **a j. war** une guerre juste; **a j. cause** une juste cause; **he has j. cause for complaint** il a de bonnes raisons pour se plaindre; **to show j. cause for concern, to have j. cause to be concerned** avoir de bonnes raisons de s'inquiéter

3 *(deserved)* juste, mérité; **a j. reward** une juste récompense, une récompense bien méritée; **he got his j. deserts** il n'a eu que ce qu'il méritait, ce n'est que justice

4 *(accurate)* juste, exact; **a j. account of the facts** un compte rendu exact des faits

5 *Rel (righteous)* juste

NPL the j. les justes *mpl*; **to sleep the sleep of the j.** dormir du sommeil du juste

justice ['dʒʌstɪs] **N 1** *Law (power of law)* justice *f*; **a court of j.** une cour de justice; **to dispense j.** rendre la justice; **to bring sb to j.** traduire qn en justice; *Am* **the Department of J.** le ministère de la Justice

2 *(fairness)* justice *f*, équité *f*; **where's your sense of j.?** qu'est-il advenu de ton sens de la justice?; **they believe in the j. of their cause** ils croient à la justesse de leur cause; **there's no j. in their claim** leur demande est dénuée de fondement; **to do sb/sth j.** *(represent fairly)* rendre justice à qn, qch; **the portrait didn't do her j.** son portrait ne lui rendait pas justice; **to do oneself j.** se mettre en valeur, se montrer sous son meilleur jour; **to do him j., he wasn't informed of the decision** il faut lui rendre cette justice que *ou* il faut reconnaître que l'on ne l'avait pas mis au courant de la décision; **to do j. to a meal** faire honneur à un repas

3 *(punishment, vengeance)* justice *f*; **the whole town called for j.** la ville entière réclamait vengeance

4 *(judge)* juge *mf*; **Mr J. Long** *(title)* Monsieur le juge Long; **Mrs J. Long** Madame le *ou* la juge Long

▸▸ *Am* ***the Justice Department*** le ministère de la Justice; ***Justice of the Peace*** juge *m* d'instance

justifiable ['dʒʌstɪ,faɪəbəl] **ADJ** justifiable; *Law* légitime

▸▸ *Law* ***justifiable homicide*** *(killing in self defence)* homicide *m* justifiable; *(state execution)* application *f* de la peine de mort

justifiably ['dʒʌstɪ,faɪəblɪ] **ADV** légitimement, à juste titre; **she was j. angry** elle était fâchée, et à juste titre

justification [,dʒʌstɪfɪ'keɪʃən] **N 1** *(gen)* justification; **what j. do you have for such a statement?** comment justifiez-vous une telle affirmation?; **poverty is no j. for theft** la pauvreté ne saurait justifier le vol; **he was accused of cheating, with some j.** il fut accusé d'avoir triché, non sans rai ɔon; **he spoke out in j. of his actions** il a parlé pour ustifier ses actes; **that's no j.!** ce n'est pas une raison! **2** *Comput & Typ* justification *f*; **left/right** j. justification *f* à gauche/à droite; **vertical j.** justification *f* verticale

ustify ['dʒʌstɪfaɪ] *(pt & pp* **justified)** **VT 1** *(gen)* justifier; **nothing can j. such cruelty** rien ne saurait excuser *ou* justifier une telle cruauté; **she tried to j. her behaviour to her parents** elle a essayé de justifier son comportement auprès de ses parents **2** *Comput & Typ (text)* justifier **3** *Law* **to j. a lawsuit** justifier une action en justice

ust-in-time **ADJ** *Com & Mktg* juste à temps *(inv)*

▸▸ ***just-in-time distribution*** distribution *f* juste à temps; ***just-in-time production*** production *f* juste à temps; ***just-in-time purchasing*** achat *m* juste à temps

ustly ['dʒʌstlɪ] **ADV 1** *(fairly)* justement, avec justice **2** *(accurately, deservedly)* à juste titre; **a j. unpopular decision** une décision impopulaire à juste titre

justness ['dʒʌstnɪs] **N** *(of claim, demand)* bien-fondé *m*, légitimité *f*; *(of idea, reasoning)* justesse *f*

jut [dʒʌt] *(pt & pp* **jutted,** *cont* **jutting)** **VI to j. out** dépasser, faire saillie; **a rocky peninsula juts (out) into the sea** une péninsule rocheuse avance dans la mer; **a large rock jutted out over the path** un gros rocher surplombait le sentier; **his chin juts out** il a un menton en galoche

jute [dʒu:t] **N** *Tex (textile)* jute *m*

juvenile ['dʒu:vənaɪl, *Am* 'dʒu:vənəl] **ADJ 1** *(young, for young people)* jeune, *Formal* juvénile **2** *(immature)* puéril, enfantin; **don't be so j.!** ne sois pas si puéril!

N 1 *Formal* mineur(e) *m,f* **2** *Theat* jeune acteur (trice) *m,f*

▸▸ *Law* ***juvenile court*** tribunal *m* pour enfants *(10–16 ans)*; *Law* ***juvenile delinquency*** délinquance *f* juvénile; *Law* ***juvenile delinquent*** jeune délinquant(e) *m,f*, mineur(e) *m,f* délinquant(e); ***juvenile detention centre*** centre *m* pour mineurs délinquants; ***juvenile lead*** jeune premier *m*; ***juvenile literature*** *(UNCOUNT)* livres *mpl* pour enfants *ou* pour la jeunesse; ***juvenile offender*** accusé(e) *m,f* mineur(e)

juvenilia [ˌdʒu:və'nɪlɪə] **NPL** œuvres *fpl* de jeunesse

juvie ['dʒu:vɪ] *Am & Austr Fam* **N** centre *m* pour mineurs délinquants[□]

ADJ pour mineurs délinquants[□]

juxtapose [ˌdʒʌkstə'pəʊz] **VT** juxtaposer

juxtaposition [ˌdʒʌkstəpə'zɪʃən] **N** juxtaposition *f*; **to be in j.** se juxtaposer

K[1], **k** [keɪ] **N 1** *(letter)* K, k *m inv*; **two k's** deux k
2 *Comput (abbr* **kilobyte***)* K *m*, Ko *m*; **how many K are left?** combien de Ko reste-t-il?; **720K diskette** disquette *f* de 720 Ko
3 *(abbr* **thousand***)* K
4 *Fam (abbr* **thousand pounds***)* **he earns 30K** il gagne 30 000 livres◻
5 *Fam (abbr* **kilometre(s)***)* kilomètre(s)◻ *m(pl)*; **a 10K race** une course de 10 kilomètres

K[2] *(written abbr* **Knight***)* chevalier *m*

kabuki [kə'bu:kɪ] **N** *Theat* kabuki *m*

Kabul ['kɑ:bəl] **N** *Geog* Kaboul, Kabul

kaffeeklatsch ['kæfeɪˌklætʃ] **N** *Am* = réunion de femmes qui bavardent en prenant le café

Kaffir, Kafir ['kæfə(r)] **N 1** *SAfr very Fam* nègre (négresse) *m,f*, = terme raciste désignant un Noir **2** *(member of ethnic group)* Cafre *mf*
• **kaffir N** *Fam St Exch* valeur-or *f* sud-africaine◻

Kafkaesque [ˌkæfkə'esk] **ADJ** kafkaïen

kaftan ['kæftæn] **N** caftan *m*, cafetan *m*

kalashnikov [kə'læʃnɪkɒv] **N** kalachnikov *m ou f*

kale [keɪl] **N** *Bot* chou *m* frisé

kaleidoscope [kə'laɪdəskəʊp] **N** *also Fig* kaléidoscope *m*

kaleidoscopic [kəˌlaɪdə'skɒpɪk] **ADJ** kaléidoscopique

Kama Sutra [ˌkɑ:mə'su:trə] **N the K.** le Kamasutra

kamikaze [ˌkæmɪ'kɑ:zɪ] **N** kamikaze *m*
ADJ *Fig* suicidaire
►► ***kamikaze pilot*** kamikaze *m*; ***kamikaze plane*** kamikaze *m*, avion-suicide *m*

Kampuchea [ˌkæmpʊ'tʃɪə] **N** *Formerly* Kampuchéa *m*

kangaroo [ˌkæŋgə'ru:] *(pl* **kangaroos**, *pt & pp* **kangarooed***)* **N 1** *Zool (animal)* kangourou *m* **2** *Fam St Exch* valeur *f* australienne◻
VI *Fam (car)* avoir des à-coups
►► *Aut* ***kangaroo bars*** pare-buffles *m inv*; ***kangaroo court*** tribunal *m* illégal; *(held by strikers, prisoners etc)* tribunal *m* populaire; *Zool* ***kangaroo rat*** rat-kangourou *m*, potoroo *m*, potorou *m*

kaolin ['keɪəlɪn] **N** kaolin *m*

kapok ['keɪpɒk] *Bot & Tex* **N** kapok *m*
COMP de kapok
►► ***kapok tree*** kapokier *m*

Kaposi's sarcoma [kæ'pəʊsɪz-] **N** *Med* sarcome *m* de Kaposi

kaput, kaputt [kə'pʊt] **ADJ** *Fam* fichu, foutu

karakul ['kærəkʊl] **N** *(sheep, fur)* karakul *m*, caracul *m*

karaoke [ˌkærɪ'əʊkɪ] **N** karaoké *m*
►► ***karaoke machine*** karaoké *m*

karate [kə'rɑ:tɪ] **N** *Sport* karaté *m*
►► ***karate chop*** coup *m* de karaté *(donné avec le tranchant de la main)*

karma ['kɑ:mə] **N** karma *m*, karman *m*

kart [kɑ:t] **N** kart *m*

karting ['kɑ:tɪŋ] **N** *Sport* karting *m*; **to go k.** faire du karting

kasbah ['kæzbɑ:] **N** casbah *f*

Kashmir [kæʃ'mɪə(r)] **N** *Geog* Cachemire *m*, Kashmir *m*

Kashmiri [kæʃ'mɪərɪ] **N 1** *(person)* Cachemirien(enne) *m,f* **2** *(language)* kashmiri *m*
ADJ cachemirien

Kathmandu, Katmandu [ˌkætmæn'du:] **N** Katmandou

kayak ['kaɪæk] **N** kayak *m*

Kazakhstan [ˌkæzæk'stɑ:n] **N** *Geog* Kazakhstan *m*

kazoo [kə'zu:] *(pl* **kazoos***)* **N 1** *(instrument)* mirliton *m* **2** *Am Fam (buttocks)* derrière *m*, arrière-train *m*; **to have problems/debts up the k.** avoir des problèmes/des dettes jusqu'au cou

KB [ˌkeɪ'bi:] **N** *Comput (abbr* **kilobyte***)* Ko *m*

KBE [ˌkeɪbi:'i:] **N** *Br (abbr* **Knight (Commander of the Order) of the British Empire***)* Chevalier *m* de l'Ordre de l'Empire britannique

Kbps [ˌkeɪbi:ˌpi:'es] **N** *Comput (abbr* **kilobits per second***)* Kb/s

KCB [ˌkeɪsi:'bi:] **N** *Br (abbr* **Knight Commander (of the Order) of the Bath***)* Chevalier Commandeur de l'Ordre du Bain

kebab [kɪ'bæb] **N** *Culin* brochette *f*; **shish k.** chiche-kebab *m*; **doner k.** sandwich *m* grec
►► ***kebab house*** = restaurant grec ou turc

kecks [keks] **NPL** *Br Fam (trousers)* fute *m*, falzar *m*

kedge [kedʒ] **N** ancre *f* à jet
VT haler, touer
VI se haler, se touer

kedgeree ['kedʒəri:] **N** *Br Culin* = riz pilaf au poisson fumé et aux œufs durs

keel [ki:l] **N** *Naut* quille *f*; **on an even k.** à tirant d'eau égal; *Fig* en équilibre; **to be back on an even k.** *(situation)* être de nouveau stable, s'être stabilisé; *(person)* avoir retrouvé son équilibre; **to put a company/the economy back on an even k.** remettre une entreprise/l'économie d'aplomb
VT faire chavirer, cabaner
VI chavirer

►**keel over VT SEP** *Naut* faire chavirer, cabaner
VI 1 *Naut* chavirer **2** *(fall)* s'effondrer; *(faint)* s'évanouir; *(drop dead)* tomber raide mort

keelhaul ['ki:lhɔ:l] **VT 1** *Naut* faire passer sous la quille **2** *Fam Fig (rebuke)* houspiller, enguirlander

keen [ki:n] **ADJ 1** *(eager, enthusiastic)* passionné, enthousiaste; **she's a k. gardener** c'est une passionnée de jardinage; **he was k. to talk to her** il tenait à *ou* voulait absolument lui parler; **I'm k. that they should get a second chance** je tiens à ce qu'ils aient une deuxième chance; **I'm not so k. on the idea** l'idée ne m'enchante *ou* ne m'emballe pas vraiment; **they aren't so k. on going out tonight** ils n'ont pas (très) envie *ou* ça ne leur dit pas tellement de sortir ce soir; **Suzanne is really k. on Stuart** Suzanne a vraiment le béguin pour Stuart; *Fam* **to be as k. as mustard** *(enthusiastic)* être très enthousiaste; *(clever)* avoir l'esprit vif
2 *(senses, mind, wit)* fin, vif; **to have a k. sense of smell** avoir un odorat subtil; **to have a k. eye** avoir le coup d'œil
3 *(fierce ► competition, rivalry)* acharné
4 *Br (cold ► wind)* glacial
5 *Br (sharp ► blade, knife)* affilé
6 *(intense)* intense, profond; **she felt a k. desire to break free** elle ressentit une profonde envie de partir; **k. appetite** rude appétit *m*; **to have a k. appetite for success** avoir un solide appétit de succès
7 *Br (competitive ► price)* imbattable
8 *Am Fam (very good)* génial
VT *(mourn)* pleurer
VI *(mourn)* pleurer
N *(dirge)* mélopée *f* funèbre

keenly ['ki:nlɪ] **ADV 1** *(deeply, intensely)* vivement, profondément; **she's k. interested in the project** elle s'intéresse vivement *ou* elle porte un vif intérêt au projet; **he felt her death k.** sa mort l'a profondément affecté **2** *(fiercely)* âprement; **a k. contested game** un match âprement disputé **3** *(eagerly)* ardemment, avec enthousiasme; *(attentively)* attentivement

keenness ['ki:nnɪs] **N 1** *(enthusiasm)* enthousiasme *m*, empressement *m*, ardeur *f*; **there's no doubting her k. to help** son empressement à rendre service ne fait aucun doute
2 *(of senses)* acuité *f*, finesse *f*; **k. of eye** acuité visuelle; **k. of mind** perspicacité *f*, finesse *f*
3 *(intensity, fierceness)* intensité *f*, âpreté *f*
4 *(of blade, knife)* tranchant *m*

KEEP [ki:p]

VT	
• garder **A1–3, B5, D4**	• mettre **A3**
• faire **B3**	• retenir **B4**
• avoir **C2**	• tenir **C3, 6, D1**
• vendre **C4**	• élever **C5**
• observer **D2**	• respecter **D2**
• maintenir **D3**	• empêcher **E1**
• cacher **E2**	
VI	
• continuer **1**	• rester **2**
• se tenir **2**	• se conserver **3**
• aller **4**	
N	
• pension **1**	• donjon **2**

(pt & pp **kept** [kept]*)*
VT A. 1 *(retain ► receipt, change)* garder; **you can k. the book I lent you** vous pouvez garder le livre que je vous ai prêté; **she's kept her English accent** elle a gardé son accent anglais; **please k. your seats** veuillez rester assis; **he's never kept a job for more than a year** il n'a jamais gardé *ou* conservé le même emploi plus d'un an; **to k. a secret** garder un secret; **to k. one's temper/composure** garder son calme/son sang-froid; **to k. one's figure** garder la ligne; **to k. its shape/colour** *(garment)* conserver sa forme/couleur; **to k. sth to oneself** garder qch pour soi; **k. it to yourself!** garde ça pour toi!; **k. your hands to yourself!** bas les mains!; **to k. oneself to oneself** rester dans son coin; **they k. themselves very much to themselves** ils ne se mêlent pas du tout aux autres; *Fam* **if that's your idea of a holiday, you can k. it!** si c'est ça ton idée des vacances, tu peux te la garder!; *Fam* **tell him he can k. his rotten job!** dis-lui qu'il peut se le garder, son sale boulot!
2 *(save)* garder; **to k. sth for sb** garder qch pour qn; **we've kept some cake for you** on t'a gardé du gâteau; **can you k. my seat?** pouvez-vous (me) garder ma place?; **we'll k. the tickets for you until Wednesday** nous vous garderons les tickets jus-

qu'à mercredi; **I'm keeping this cigar for later** je garde ce cigare pour plus tard

3 *(store, put)* mettre, garder; **she keeps her money in the bank** elle met son argent à la banque; **I k. my comb in my pocket** je mets toujours mon peigne dans ma poche; **how long can you k. fish in the freezer?** combien de temps peut-on garder *ou* conserver du poisson au congélateur?; **where do you k. the playing cards?** où est-ce que vous rangez les cartes à jouer?; **I've got nowhere to k. my books** je n'ai nulle part où mettre mes livres; **k. out of the reach of children** *(on medicine, harmful products)* ne pas laisser à la portée des enfants

B. 1 *(with adj complement) (maintain in the specified state)* **to k. sth clean/secret** tenir qch propre/ secret; **to k. sb quiet** faire tenir qn tranquille; **to k. oneself warm** *(by staying in the warmth)* se tenir au chaud; *(by dressing warmly)* s'habiller chaudement; **to k. sth warm** garder qch au chaud; **the noise kept me awake** le bruit m'a empêché de dormir, le bruit m'a tenu éveillé; **to k. the door open/shut** garder *ou* laisser la porte ouverte/fermée; **the doors are kept locked** les portes sont toujours fermées à clef; **to k. sth up to date** tenir qch à jour

2 *(with adv complement) (maintain in the specified manner or place)* **a well-kept/badly-kept office** un bureau bien/mal tenu; **the weather kept us indoors** le temps nous a empêchés de sortir; **troops were kept on the alert** les soldats ont été maintenus en état d'alerte; **he kept his hands in his pockets** il a gardé les mains dans les poches; **k. your eyes on the red dot** ne quittez pas le point rouge des yeux; **k. the noise to a minimum** essayez de ne pas faire trop de bruit

3 *(with present participle)* **to k. sb waiting** faire attendre qn; **k. the engine running** n'arrêtez pas le moteur; **we kept the fire burning all night** nous avons laissé le feu allumé toute la nuit; **to k. sth going** *(organization, business)* faire marcher qch; *(music, conversation)* ne pas laisser qch s'arrêter; **alcohol is the only thing that keeps me going** l'alcool est la seule chose qui me permette de tenir le coup

4 *(delay)* retenir; **I hope I've not kept you** j'espère que je ne vous ai pas retenu; **what kept you?** qu'est-ce qui t'a retenu?

5 *(detain)* garder; **to k. sb in hospital/prison** garder qn à l'hôpital/en prison; **the doctor kept him in bed** le médecin l'a obligé à garder le lit; **I don't want to k. you from your work** je ne veux pas vous empêcher de travailler; **there was nothing to k. me in England/with that company** rien ne me retenait en Angleterre/dans cette entreprise

C. 1 *(support)* **he hardly earns enough to k. himself** il gagne à peine de quoi vivre; **she has a husband and six children to k.** elle a un mari et six enfants à nourrir; **it keeps me in cigarettes** ça paie mes cigarettes; **the grant barely keeps me in food** ma bourse me permet tout juste de me payer de quoi manger

2 *(have as dependant or employee)* avoir; **he keeps a mistress** il a une maîtresse; **they k. a maid and a gardener** ils ont une bonne et un jardinier

3 *(run ▸ shop, business)* tenir

4 *Com (have in stock)* vendre; **I'm afraid we don't k. that article** je regrette, nous ne vendons pas *ou* nous ne faisons pas cet article

5 *(farm animals)* élever; **they k. pigs/bees** ils élèvent des porcs/des abeilles

6 *(diary, list etc)* tenir; **my secretary keeps my accounts** ma secrétaire tient *ou* s'occupe de ma comptabilité; **to k. a record of events** prendre les événements en note; **to k. a note of sth** noter qch

D. 1 *(fulfil ▸ a promise)* tenir; **to k. one's word** tenir sa parole

2 *(observe ▸ silence)* observer; *(▸ the Sabbath)* respecter; *(▸ law)* respecter, observer; *(▸ vow)* rester fidèle à; *(▸ treaty)* tenir, respecter, observer; *(▸ date, appointment)* ne pas manquer; *Rel* **to k. the commandments** observer les commandements

3 *(uphold)* maintenir; **to k. order/the peace** maintenir l'ordre/la paix; **to k. a lookout** faire le guet

4 *(guard)* garder; **to k. goal** être gardien de but; **to k. wicket** *(in cricket)* garder le guichet; *Arch* **God k. you!** Dieu vous garde!

E. 1 *(prevent)* **to k. sb from doing sth** empêcher qn de faire qch; **nothing will k. me from going** rien ne m'empêchera d'y aller

2 *(withhold)* **to k. sth from sb** cacher qch à qn; **to k. information from sb** dissimuler des informations à qn; **I can't k. anything from her** je ne peux rien lui cacher; **they deliberately kept the news from his family** ils ont fait exprès de cacher les nouvelles à sa famille

VI 1 *(with present participle) (continue)* continuer; **letters k. pouring in** les lettres continuent d'affluer; **don't k. apologizing** arrête de t'excuser; **they k. teasing him** ils n'arrêtent pas de le taquiner; **to k. smiling** garder le sourire; **don't k. asking questions** ne posez pas tout le temps des questions; **I wish you wouldn't k. saying that** j'aimerais bien que tu arrêtes de répéter cela; **she had several failures but kept trying** elle a essuyé plusieurs échecs mais elle a persévéré; **to k. going** *(not give up)* continuer; **k. going till you get to the crossroads** allez jusqu'au croisement; **with so few customers, it's a wonder the shop keeps going** avec si peu de clients, c'est un miracle que le magasin ne ferme pas

2 *(stay, remain)* rester, se tenir; **to k. quiet** se tenir *ou* rester tranquille; **k. calm!** restez calmes!, du calme!; **she kept warm by jumping up and down** elle se tenait chaud en sautillant sur place; **k. to the path** ne vous écartez pas du chemin; **to k. in touch with sb** rester en contact avec qn; **to k. to oneself** se tenir à l'écart

3 *(last, stay fresh)* se conserver, se garder; **it will k. for a week in the refrigerator** vous pouvez le garder *ou* conserver au réfrigérateur pendant une semaine; **what I've got to tell you won't k. till tomorrow** ce que j'ai à te dire n'attendra pas jusqu'à demain; **will it k. till later?** *(news)* est-ce que ça peut attendre?

4 *(in health)* aller; **how are you keeping?** comment allez-vous?, comment ça va?; **I'm keeping well** je vais bien, ça va (bien)

N 1 *(board and lodging)* **the grant is supposed to be enough to pay your k.** la bourse est censée vous permettre de payer la nourriture et le logement; **he gives his mother £50 a week for his k.** il donne 50 livres par semaine à sa mère pour sa pension; **to earn one's k.** = payer ou travailler pour être nourri et logé; **our cat certainly earns his k.** notre chat vaut bien ce qu'il nous coûte

2 *Archit & Hist (in castle)* donjon *m*

3 *(idiom) Fam* **for keeps** pour de bon❑

▸**keep at VT SEP the sergeant kept us hard at it all morning** le sergent nous a fait travailler toute la matinée

VT INSEP 1 *(pester)* harceler; **she kept at him until he agreed** elle l'a harcelé jusqu'à ce qu'il accepte

2 *(idiom)* **to k. at it** persévérer; **he kept at it until he found a solution** il a persévéré jusqu'à trouver une solution

▸**keep away VT SEP** tenir éloigné, empêcher d'approcher; **k. the baby away from the fire** empêche le bébé d'approcher du feu; **the rain kept a lot of spectators away** la pluie a dissuadé bien des spectateurs de venir; **k. that dog away (from me)!** tenez ce chien loin de moi!; **the wind will k. the rain away** le vent empêchera la pluie

VI ne pas s'approcher; **k. away (from me)!** n'approchez pas!; **k. away from the cooker** ne t'approche pas de la cuisinière; **k. away from those people** évitez ces gens-là; **I felt my visits were unwelcome and so I kept away** je n'avais pas l'impression que mes visites étaient bienvenues, alors je n'y suis plus allé; **I can't k. away from chocolates** je ne peux pas résister quand je vois des chocolats

▸**keep back VT SEP 1** *(keep at a distance ▸ crowd, spectators)* tenir éloigné, empêcher de s'approcher

2 *(not reveal ▸ names, facts)* cacher; **I'm sure he's keeping something back (from us)** je suis sûr qu'il (nous) cache quelque chose

3 *(retain)* retenir; **part of our salary is kept back every month** une partie de notre salaire est retenue tous les mois

4 *(detain)* retenir; **to be kept back after school** être en retenue; *Sch* **to be kept back a year** redoubler

5 *(restrain)* retenir; **he struggled to k. back the tears** il s'est efforcé de retenir ses larmes

VI rester en arrière, ne pas s'approcher; **k. back!** restez où vous êtes!, n'approchez pas!

▸**keep down VT SEP 1** *(not raise)* ne pas lever; **k. your head down!** ne lève pas la tête!, garde la tête baissée!; **k. your voices down!** parlez moins fort *ou* plus bas

2 *(prevent from increasing)* limiter; **we must k. our expenses down** il faut que nous limitions nos dépenses; **our aim is to k. prices down** notre but est d'empêcher les prix d'augmenter; **to k. one's weight down** garder la ligne

3 *(repress)* réprimer; *(control ▸ vermin, weeds)* empêcher de proliférer; **the army kept the population/the revolt down** l'armée a tenu la population en respect/a maté la révolte; **you can't k. a good man down** rien n'arrête un homme de mérite

4 *(food)* garder; **she can't k. solid foods down** son estomac ne garde aucun aliment solide

5 *Sch* faire redoubler; **to be kept down a year** redoubler une année

VI ne pas se relever; **k. down!** ne vous relevez pas!

▸**keep from VT INSEP** s'empêcher de, se retenir de; **I couldn't k. from laughing** je n'ai pas pu m'empêcher de rire

▸**keep in VT SEP 1** *(not allow out)* empêcher de sortir; *Sch* donner une consigne à, garder en retenue; **the bad weather kept us in** le mauvais temps nous a empêchés de sortir; **they're keeping him in overnight** *(in hospital)* ils le gardent pour la nuit

2 *(fire)* entretenir

3 *(stomach)* rentrer

4 *(idiom)* **to k. one's hand in** garder la main

VI *(not go out)* ne pas sortir, rester chez soi

▸**keep in with VT INSEP to k. in with sb** ne pas se mettre mal avec qn

▸**keep off VT SEP 1** *(dogs, birds, trespassers)* éloigner; *(rain, sun)* protéger de; **this cream will k. the mosquitoes off** cette crème vous/le/te/*etc* protégera contre les moustiques; **k. your hands off!** pas touche!, bas les pattes! **2** *(coat, hat)* ne pas remettre

VT INSEP 1 *(avoid)* éviter; **k. off drink and tobacco** évitez l'alcool et le tabac; **we tried to k. off the topic** on a essayé d'éviter le sujet **2** *(keep at a distance from)* ne pas s'approcher de; **k. off the grass** *(sign)* pelouse interdite

VI 1 *(keep at a distance)* ne pas s'approcher; **that's mine, k. off!** c'est à moi, n'y touchez pas! **2** *(weather)* **the rain/snow kept off** il n'a pas plu/neigé; **if the storm keeps off** si l'orage n'éclate pas

▸**keep on VT SEP 1** *(coat, hat)* garder **2** *(employee)* garder **3** *(not turn off)* **to k. the central heating on** laisser le chauffage central en marche; **don't k. the lights on all day** ne laissez pas la lumière allumée toute la journée

VI 1 *(continue)* continuer; **k. on until you come to a crossroads** continuez jusqu'à ce que vous arriviez à un carrefour; **they kept on talking** ils ont continué à parler; **don't k. on asking questions** ne posez pas tout le temps des questions; **I k. on making the same mistakes** je fais toujours les mêmes erreurs **2** *Fam (talk continually)* parler sans cesse; **he keeps on about his kids** il n'arrête pas de parler de ses gosses; **don't k. on about it!** ça suffit, j'ai compris!; **he just keeps on and on about it** il n'arrête pas d'en parler

▸**keep on at VT INSEP** *Fam (pester)* **to k. on at sb (to do sth)** harceler qn (pour qu'il fasse qch)❑

▸**keep out VT SEP** empêcher d'entrer; **a guard dog to k. intruders out** un chien de garde pour décourager les intrus; **a scarf to k. the cold out** une écharpe pour vous protéger du froid

VI ne pas entrer; **k. out** *(sign)* défense d'entrer, entrée interdite; **to k. out of an argument** ne pas intervenir dans une discussion; **to k. out of danger** rester à l'abri du danger; **try to k. out of trouble** essaie de ne pas t'attirer d'ennuis

▸**keep to VT INSEP 1** *(observe, respect)* respecter; **you must k. to the deadlines** vous devez respecter les délais **2** *(not deviate from)* ne pas s'écarter de; **to k. to the script** *(actors)* s'en tenir au script; **k. to the point** *or* **the subject!** ne vous écartez pas du sujet!; **k. to the main roads when it's icy** restez sur les grandes routes quand il y a du verglas **3** *(stay in)* garder; **to k. to one's room/bed** garder la chambre/le lit

▸**keep up** VT SEP **1** *(prevent from falling ▸ shelf, roof)* maintenir; **I need a belt to k. my trousers up** j'ai besoin d'une ceinture pour empêcher mon pantalon de tomber; *Fig* **it will k. prices up** ça empêchera les prix de baisser; **it's to k. the troops' morale up** c'est pour maintenir le moral des troupes; **k. your spirits up!** ne te laisse pas abattre!

2 *(maintain ▸ attack, bombardment)* poursuivre; *(▸ correspondence, contacts, conversation)* entretenir; **you have to k. up the payments** on ne peut pas interrompre les versements; **she kept up a constant flow of questions** elle ne cessait de poser des questions; **it's a tradition which hasn't been kept up** c'est une tradition qui s'est perdue; **k. up the good work!** c'est du bon travail, continuez!; **you're doing well, k. it up!** c'est bien, continuez!; **once they start talking politics, they can k. it up all night** une fois lancés sur la politique, ils sont capables d'y passer la nuit

3 *(prevent from going to bed)* empêcher de dormir; **the baby kept us up all night** nous n'avons pas pu fermer l'œil de la nuit à cause du bébé

4 *(not allow to deteriorate ▸ house, garden)* entretenir; **the lawns haven't been kept up** les pelouses n'ont pas été entretenues; **she goes to evening classes to k. up her French** elle suit des cours du soir pour entretenir son français

VI **1** *(continue)* continuer; **if this noise keeps up much longer, I'm going to scream!** si ce bruit continue, je crois que je vais hurler! **2** *(not fall)* se maintenir; **if prices k. up** si les prix se maintiennent; **how are their spirits keeping up?** est-ce qu'ils gardent le moral? **3** *(not fall behind)* suivre; **he's finding it hard to k. up in his new class** il a du mal à suivre dans sa nouvelle classe; **things change so quickly I can't k. up** les choses bougent si vite que j'ai du mal à suivre

▸**keep up with** VT INSEP **1** *(stay abreast of)* **to k. up with the news** se tenir au courant de l'actualité; **I can barely k. up with her** *(she changes so much)* ça change tellement vite avec elle que j'ai du mal à suivre; **to k. up with the times** être à la page **2** *(keep in touch with)* rester en contact avec; **have you kept up with your cousin in Australia?** est-ce que tu es resté en contact avec ton cousin d'Australie? **3** *(remain level with)* **to k. up with sb** aller à la même allure que qn; **I can't k. up with you** vous marchez/parlez/*etc* trop vite pour moi; **he couldn't k. up with the rest of the children in his class** il n'arrivait pas à suivre dans sa classe

keeper ['ki:pə(r)] N **1** *(gen)* gardien(enne) *m,f*; *(in museum)* conservateur(trice) *m,f*; *Bible* **am I my brother's k.?** suis-je le gardien de mon frère?; *Fig* **I'm not his k.!** je ne suis pas responsable de ses actions

2 *Fam (goalkeeper)* goal *m*, gardien *m* de but[❑]

3 *Tech (safety catch)* cran *m* de sûreté

4 *Fam (thing or person to be kept)* **this photo's a k.** il faut garder cette photo[❑]; **good-looking, intelligent and a great cook? this guy's a k.!** il est beau, intelligent et il fait très bien la cuisine? Il ne faut pas le laisser filer, ce mec!

keep-fit N culture *f* physique, gymnastique *f* (d'entretien); **she goes to k. (classes) every week** toutes les semaines elle va à son cours de gymnastique

keeping ['ki:pɪŋ] N **1** *(care, charge)* garde *f*; **he left the manuscript in his wife's k.** il a confié le manuscrit à son épouse; **in safe k.** en sécurité, sous bonne garde **2** *(observing ▸ of rule, custom etc)* observation *f*

• **in keeping** ADJ conforme

• **in keeping with** PREP conformément à; **in k. with government policy** conformément à la politique du gouvernement; **it's in k. with everything I have been told about her** cela concorde avec tout ce qu'on m'a dit sur elle; **their dress was not at all in k. with the seriousness of the occasion** leur tenue ne convenait pas du tout à la gravité de la circonstance

• **out of keeping with** PREP **to be out of k. with** être en désaccord avec; **it was rather out of k. with the spirit of the occasion** cela détonnait avec l'esprit de l'occasion

keepsake ['ki:pseɪk] N souvenir *m (objet)*; **he gave it to her as a k.** il le lui a donné en souvenir

keg [keg] N **1** *(barrel)* tonnelet *m*, baril *m*; *(of fish)* baril *m*; *(of beer)* tonnelet *m*; *(of herring)* caque *f* **2** *(beer)* bière *f* (à la) pression

▸▸ ***keg beer*** bière *f* pression

keister ['ki:stə(r)] N *Am Fam (buttocks)* derrière *m*, derche *m*

kelp [kelp] N *Bot* varech *m*

ken [ken] *(pt & pp* **kenned**, *cont* **kenning**) N *Old-fashioned or Hum* **it is beyond my k.** cela dépasse mon entendement

VT *Scot* savoir; *(person, place)* connaître

VI *Scot* savoir

kennel ['kenəl] *(Br pt & pp* **kennelled**, *cont* **kennelling**, *Am pt & pp* **kenneled**, *cont* **kenneling**) N **1** *Br (doghouse)* niche *f* **2** *Am (for boarding or breeding)* chenil *m* **3** *Hunt* **the k.** *(hounds)* la meute

VT mettre dans un chenil

• **kennels** NPL *Br (for boarding or breeding)* chenil *m*

kennelmaid ['kenəlˌmeɪd] N employée *f* d'éleveur de chiens *ou* de chenil

Kenya ['kenjə] N *Geog* Kenya *m*

Kenyan ['kenjən] N Kenyan(e) *m,f*

ADJ kenyan

COMP *(embassy, history)* du Kenya

kept [kept] *pt & pp of* **keep**

ADJ *Hum or Pej* **a k. man** un homme entretenu; **a k. woman** une femme entretenue

keratosis [ˌkerə'təʊsɪs] N *Med & Physiol* kératose *f*

kerb, *Am* **curb** [kɜ:b] N **1** *(on road)* bord *m* du trottoir; **he stepped off the k.** il est descendu du trottoir; **the bus pulled into the k.** l'autobus s'est arrêté le long du trottoir **2** *Fam St Exch* **to buy/sell on the k.** acheter/vendre après la clôture officielle de la Bourse[❑]; **business done on the k.** opérations *fpl* effectuées en coulisse *ou* après clôture de Bourse[❑]

▸▸ *Fam St Exch* ***kerb broker*** coulissier[❑] *m*, courtier(ère) *m,f* hors Bourse[❑]; ***kerb crawler*** = personne qui longe le trottoir en voiture à la recherche d'une prostituée; ***kerb crawling*** = recherche d'une prostituée en voiture; ***kerb drill*** précautions *fpl* pour traverser la rue; *Fam St Exch* ***kerb market*** marché *m* hors cote[❑], coulisse[❑] *f*; ***kerb weight*** poids *m* à vide

kerbstone, *Am* **curbstone** ['kɜ:bstəʊn] N pierre *f* de bordure *(d'un trottoir)*

▸▸ *Fam St Exch* ***kerbstone market*** marché *m* hors cote[❑], coulisse[❑] *f*

kerchief ['kɜ:tʃɪf] N *Old-fashioned* foulard *m*, fichu *m*

ker-ching [kɜ:'tʃɪŋ] EXCLAM *Fam* = exclamation imitant le bruit d'une caisse enregistreuse, pour parler de quelqu'un qui est sur le point de s'enrichir, d'une idée lucrative, etc; **I hear she's marrying a professional footballer – k.!** il paraît qu'elle va épouser un footballeur professionnel – ouah, par ici les picaillons!

kerfuffle [kə'fʌfəl] N *Br Fam (fuss)* histoire *f*, histoires *fpl*; *(disorder)* désordre[❑] *m*, chahut *m*; *(fight)* bagarre[❑] *f*; **trying to get tickets was a right k.** ça a été tout une histoire pour avoir des billets; **there was a k. at the exit** il y a eu des remous à la sortie

kern [kɜ:n] *Typ & Comput* N approche *f*

VT créner, rapprocher

kernel ['kɜ:nəl] N **1** *(fruit stone)* amande *f*; *(of nut)* intérieur *m*; *(of cereal)* graine *f* **2** *Fig (heart, core)* cœur *m*, noyau *m*; **the k. of the problem** le fond du problème; **a k. of truth** un fond de vérité

kerning ['kɜ:nɪŋ] N *Typ & Comput* crénage *m*, rapprochement *m* de caractères

kerosene, kerosine ['kerəsi:n] N *Am (for aircraft)* kérosène *m*; *(for lamps, stoves)* pétrole *m*

COMP *(lamp, stove)* à pétrole

kestrel ['kestrəl] N *Orn* crécerelle *f*

ketch [ketʃ] N *Naut* ketch *m*

ketchup ['ketʃəp] N *Culin* ketchup *m*

kettle ['ketəl] N **1** *(for water)* bouilloire *f*; **to put the k. on** mettre de l'eau à chauffer; **the k.'s boiling** l'eau bout **2** *(for fish)* poissonnière *f*; *Fam* **that's another** *or* **a different k. of fish** c'est une autre paire de manches; *Br Fam* **this is a fine** *or* **pretty k. of fish!** quelle salade!, quel sac de nœuds!

kettledrum ['ketəldrʌm] N timbale *f*

key [ki:] N **1** *(for lock)* clé *f*, clef *f*; *(for clock mechanism etc)* clé *f*, remontoir *m*; **the k. to the drawer** la clé du tiroir; **where are the car keys?** où sont les clés de la voiture?; **he was given the keys to the city** on lui a remis les clés de la ville; *Br Old-fashioned* **to get the k. of the door** atteindre sa majorité; *esp Am Hum* **to get the k. to the executive washroom** obtenir une promotion importante; **the (House of) Keys** = une des deux chambres du parlement de l'île de Man

2 *Fig (means)* clé *f*, clef *f*; **the k. to happiness** la clé du bonheur; **communication is the k. to a good partnership** la communication est la clé d'une bonne association

3 *(on typewriter, computer, piano, organ)* touche *f*; *(on wind instrument)* clé *f*, clef *f*

4 *Mus* ton *m*; **in the k. of B minor** en si mineur; **to play in/off k.** jouer dans le ton/dans le mauvais ton; **to sing in/off k.** chanter juste/faux

5 *(on map, diagram)* légende *f*

6 *(answers)* corrigé *m*, réponses *fpl*; *Comput (of sort, identification etc)* indicatif *m*, critère *m*; **the k. to the exercises is on page 155** le corrigé des exercices se trouve page 155

7 *Tech* clé *f ou* clef *f* (de serrage)

8 *(island)* îlot *m*; *(reef)* (petit) récif *m (qui s'étend au sud de la Floride)*

9 *Constr (roughness of surface)* rappointis *m*

10 *Fam Drugs slang* kilo[❑] *m (de marijuana)*

ADJ clé, clef; **the k. conspirator** la cheville ouvrière du complot; **one of the k. issues in the election** un des enjeux fondamentaux de ces élections; **she was appointed to a k. post** elle a été nommée à un poste clé

VT **1** *(data, text)* taper, saisir **2** *(adjust, adapt)* adapter; **his remarks were keyed to the occasion** ses commentaires étaient adaptés aux circonstances

▸▸ *Com & Mktg* ***key account*** compte-clé *m*; ***key bar*** *(in shop)* stand *m* de clé-minute; *Mktg* ***key brand*** marque *f* clé; ***key case*** porte-clés *m inv*; *Mus* ***key change*** changement *m* de ton; *Am* ***key club*** = club privé dont les membres possèdent chacun une clé; *Comput* ***key combination*** combinaison *f* de touches; ***key factor*** facteur *m* clé; *Cin* ***key grip*** technicien(enne) *m,f* en chef *(chargé(e) de l'installation des décors et des rails de caméra au cinéma)*; *Econ* ***key indicator*** clignotant *m*; *Econ* ***key industry*** industrie *f* clé; ***Key Lime pie*** tarte *f* au citron vert; ***key man*** homme *m* clé; ***key money*** pas *m* de porte; ***key numbers*** *(on squared map)* numéros *mpl* de repérage; ***key position*** position *f* clé; ***key rack*** *(in hotel etc)* tableau *m* (des clés); ***key ring*** porte-clés *m inv*; *Mus* ***key signature*** armature *f*, armure *f*; *Br Sch* ***key stage*** étape *f* clé de la scolarité; ***key worker*** = personne qui travaille dans un secteur clé de la société tel que la santé, l'enseignement, la police, les services sociaux etc

▸**key in, key up** VT SEP *Comput (word, number)* entrer; *(data, text)* taper, saisir

key-account ADJ *Com & Mktg*

▸▸ ***key-account management*** gestion *f* de comptes-clés; ***key-account sales*** ventes *fpl* aux comptes-clés

keyboard ['ki:bɔ:d] N *(of musical instrument, typewriter, computer)* clavier *m*; **who's on keyboards?** qui est aux claviers?

VT taper, saisir

VI introduire des données par clavier

▸▸ ***keyboard instrument*** instrument *m* à clavier; ***keyboard layout*** disposition *f* de clavier; ***keyboard map*** schéma *m* de clavier; ***keyboard operator*** claviste *mf*; ***keyboard shortcut*** raccourci *m* clavier; ***keyboard skills*** compétences *fpl* de claviste

keyboarder ['ki:bɔ:də(r)] N *Comput* claviste *mf* opérateur(trice) *m,f* de saisie

keyboarding ['ki:bɔ:dɪŋ] N *Comput (of data)* frappe *f*, saisie *f*

▸▸ ***keyboarding accuracy*** précision *f* de frappe; ***keyboarding error*** faute *f* de frappe; ***keyboarding skills*** compétences *fpl* de claviste; ***keyboarding speed*** vitesse *f* de frappe

keyhole [ˈkiːhəʊl] **N** trou *m* de serrure; **he looked through the k.** il regarda par le trou de la serrure
▸▸ *Med* ***keyhole surgery*** chirurgie *f* endoscopique

keying [ˈkiːɪŋ] **N** *Comput (of data, text)* frappe *f*, saisie *f*
▸▸ ***keying error*** faute *f* de frappe; ***keying speed*** vitesse *f* de frappe

keyless entry [ˈkiːlɪs-] **N** *(to room)* ouverture *f* sans clé

keyline [ˈkiːlaɪn] **N** *Comput* tracé *m* de contour

keylogger [ˈkiːˌlɒgə(r)] **N** *Comput* logiciel *m* de keylogging

keylogging [ˈkiːˌlɒgɪŋ] **N** *Comput* keylogging *m*, = technique de piratage consistant à enregistrer tout ce qu'un utilisateur d'ordinateur saisit sur son clavier, pour obtenir des informations telles que mots de passe, numéros de cartes de crédit, etc

Keynesian [ˈkeɪnzɪən] **ADJ** *Econ* keynésien
▸▸ ***Keynesian economics*** économie *f* keynésienne; ***Keynesian unemployment*** chômage *m* keynésien

keynote [ˈkiːnəʊt] **N 1** *(main point)* point *m* capital; **industrial recovery is the k. of government policy** le redressement industriel constitue l'axe central de la politique gouvernementale **2** *Mus* tonique *f*
COMP *(address, speech)* introductif; *(speaker)* principal
VT insister sur, mettre en relief; **she keynoted the need for party unity** elle a insisté sur la nécessité de cohésion au sein du parti

keynoter [ˈkiːnəʊtə(r)] **N** *Am* = orateur qui prononce le discours d'ouverture

keypad [ˈkiːpæd] **N** *Comput* pavé *m*

keystone [ˈkiːstəʊn] **N** *Constr & Fig* clé *f ou* clef *f* de voûte

keystroke [ˈkiːstrəʊk] **N** frappe *f* (de touche); **codes are entered with a single k.** une seule touche suffit pour entrer les codes; **keystrokes per minute/hour** vitesse *f* de frappe à la minute/à l'heure

keyword [ˈkiːwɜːd] **N** mot-clé *m*
▸▸ *Mktg* ***keyword advertising*** publicité *f* par mots-clés

kg *(written abbr* **kilogram(me)***)* kg

KGB [ˌkeɪdʒiːˈbiː] **N** *Formerly (abbr* **Komitet Gosudarstvennoi Bezopasnosti***)* KGB *m*
▸▸ ***KGB agent*** agent *m* du KGB; ***KGB officer*** officier *m* du KGB

khaki [ˈkɑːkɪ] **N** *(colour)* kaki *m*; *(material)* treillis *m*
ADJ kaki *(inv)*
• **khakis NPL** *Am (khaki trousers)* pantalon *m* de treillis

Khartoum [kɑːˈtuːm] **N** *Geog* Khartoum

kHz *(written abbr* **kilohertz***)* kHz

kibbutz [kɪˈbʊts] *(pl* **kibbutzes** *or* **kibbutzim** [-bʊtˈsiːm]*)* **N** kibboutz *m*

kibitz [ˈkɪbɪts] **VI** *Am Fam (gen)* mettre son grain de sel; *(during card game)* = commenter une partie sans y avoir été invité

kibitzer [ˈkɪbɪtsə(r)] **N** *Am Fam (meddler)* mouche *f* du coche; *(at card game)* donneur(euse) *m,f* de conseils□; *(joker)* plaisantin *m*; **he's a real k.** il fourre son nez partout

kibosh [ˈkaɪbɒʃ] **N** *Fam* **to put the k. on sth** ficher qch en l'air

KICK [kɪk]

N	
• coup de pied **1**	• plaisir **2**
• entrain **4**	• engouement **5**
• recul **6**	• retour en arrière **7**
VT	
• donner un/des coup(s) de pied à **1**	
VI	
• donner un/des coup(s) de pied **1**	• lancer les jambes en l'air **2**
• reculer **3**	

N 1 *(with foot)* coup *m* de pied; **to give sb/sth a k.** donner un coup de pied à qn/qch; **to aim a k. at sb/sth** lancer *ou* donner un coup de pied en direction de qn/qch; **a long k. upfield** un long coup de pied en avant; **to have a powerful k.** *(footballer, horse)* avoir un coup de pied puissant; *(swimmer)* avoir un battement de pied puissant; *Fam* **it was a real k. in the teeth for him** ça lui a fait un sacré coup; *Fam* **she needs a k. up the backside** *or* **in the pants** elle a besoin d'un coup de pied aux fesses
2 *Fam (thrill)* plaisir□*m*; **to get a k. from** *or* **out of doing sth** prendre son pied à faire qch; **to do sth for kicks** faire qch pour rigoler *ou* pour s'amuser
3 *Fam (strength* ▸ *of drink)* **his cocktail had quite a k.** son cocktail était costaud; **this beer's got no k. in it** cette bière est un peu plate *ou* manque de vigueur□
4 *Fam (vitality, force)* entrain□*m*, allant□*m*; **she's still got plenty of k. in her** elle a encore du ressort
5 *Fam (fad)* engouement□*m*; **she's on a yoga k. at the moment** elle est emballée *ou* elle ne jure que par le yoga en ce moment
6 *(recoil* ▸ *of gun)* recul *m*; *(of mechanism)* cahot *m*, secousse *f*
7 *(of engine)* retour *m* en arrière
VT 1 *(once)* donner un coup de pied à; *(several times)* donner des coups de pied à; **she kicked the ball over the wall** elle a envoyé la balle par-dessus le mur (d'un coup de pied); **I kicked the door open** j'ai ouvert la porte d'un coup de pied; *Fam* **to k. sb's behind** flanquer à qn un coup de pied au derrière; **he had been kicked to death** il avait été tué à coups de pied; **the dancers kicked their legs in the air** les danseurs lançaient les jambes en l'air; **to k. a penalty** *(in rugby)* marquer *ou* réussir une pénalité; *(in football)* tirer un penalty; **to k. the ball into touch** mettre la balle en touche, botter (la balle) en touche; *Fam Fig* **she got sick of her boyfriend lying to her and kicked him into touch** elle en a eu marre que son petit ami lui mente alors elle l'a larguée; *Fam Fig* **we need to k. racism into touch** il faut éliminer le racisme□; *Fam* **to k. the bucket** *(die)* passer l'arme à gauche, casser sa pipe; *Fam Fig* **to get kicked in the teeth** recevoir un coup en vache; *Fig* **you shouldn't k. a man when he's down** il ne faut pas s'acharner sur quelqu'un qui a déjà été fortement éprouvé; **I could have kicked myself!** je me serais donné des gifles!; **I could k. myself!** quel imbécile je fais!; **they must be kicking themselves** ils doivent s'en mordre les doigts; *Br Fam* **he was kicked upstairs** *(promoted)* on l'a promu pour se débarrasser de lui□; *Pol* on s'est débarrassé de lui en l'envoyant siéger à la chambre des Lords□; *Fam* **to k. one's heels** faire le pied de grue, poireauter
2 *Fam* **to k. a habit** se défaire d'une mauvaise habitude□; **I used to smoke but I've managed to k. the habit** je fumais, mais j'ai réussi à m'arrêter□
VI 1 *(once)* donner un coup de pied; *(several times)* donner des coups de pied; **I told you not to k.!** je t'ai dit de ne pas donner de coups de pied!; **they dragged him away kicking and screaming** il se débattait comme un beau diable quand ils l'ont emmené; **the baby lay on its back kicking** le bébé gigotait, allongé sur le dos; *Sport* **to k. for touch** *(in rugby)* chercher une touche; *Br* **to k. over the traces** ruer dans les brancards
2 *(in dance)* lancer les jambes en l'air
3 *(gun)* reculer
4 *Am Fam (die)* calancher, passer l'arme à gauche
▸▸ ***kick boxer*** tireur(euse) *m,f*, personne *f* pratiquant la boxe française; ***kick boxing*** boxe *f* française, kickboxing *m*; ***kick turn*** *(in skiing, skateboarding)* conversion *f*

▸ **kick about, kick around VT SEP 1 to k. a ball about** jouer au ballon; **they were kicking a tin can about** ils jouaient au foot avec une boîte de conserve **2** *Fam Fig (idea)* débattre; **we kicked a few ideas about** on a discuté à bâtons rompus **3** *Fam Fig (mistreat)* malmener, maltraiter; **I'm not going to let her k. me about any more** je ne vais plus me laisser faire par elle
VT INSEP *Fam (spend time in)* **to k. about the world/Africa** rouler sa bosse *ou* traîner ses guêtres autour du monde/en Afrique; *Br* **is my purse kicking about the kitchen somewhere?** est-ce que mon porte-monnaie traîne quelque part dans la cuisine?
VI *Fam* traîner; **I know my old overalls are kicking about here somewhere** je suis sûr que mon vieux bleu de travail traîne quelque part par là

▸ **kick against VT INSEP** *Fam* regimber contre; **he was always trying to k. against the system** il n'arrêtait pas de regimber contre le système; *Br* **to k. against the pricks** se rebeller en pure perte

▸ **kick back VT SEP 1** *(ball)* renvoyer du pied **2** *(person)* rendre un coup de pied à; **I immediately kicked him back** je lui ai tout de suite rendu son coup de pied **3** *Am (money)* verser; **he got 10 per cent kicked back on the contract** il a touché 10 pour cent du contrat en dessous-de-table
VI *Am Fam (relax)* se détendre□; **they kicked back after the midterm exams** ils se sont détendus après les partiels

▸ **kick in VT SEP** défoncer à coups de pied; *Fam* **I'll k. his teeth in!** je vais lui casser la figure!
VI *Fam* entrer en action□; **the painkillers haven't kicked in yet** les analgésiques n'ont pas encore fait effet□

▸ **kick off VT SEP 1** *(shoes)* enlever d'un coup de pied **2** *Fam Fig (start)* démarrer□ **3** *Sport* donner le coup d'envoi à
VI 1 *Sport* donner le coup d'envoi; **they kicked off an hour late** le match a commencé avec une heure de retard **2** *Fam Fig (start)* démarrer□, commencer□ **3** *Am Fam (die)* calancher, passer l'arme à gauche

▸ **kick out VT SEP** *Fam (person)* chasser à coups de pied□; *Fig* foutre dehors; *Fam Hum* **I wouldn't k. her out of bed!** si elle me faisait des avances, je ne dirais pas non!
VI 1 *(person)* lancer des coups de pied; *(horse, donkey)* ruer; **she would k. out at anyone who came near** elle donnait des coups de pied à tous ceux qui s'approchaient **2** *Fam (complain)* râler, rouspéter; *(revolt)* se révolter□

▸ **kick over VT SEP** renverser du pied *ou* d'un coup de pied

▸ **kick up VT SEP 1** *(dust, sand)* faire voler (du pied) **2** *Fam Fig* **to k. up a fuss** *or* **a row (about sth)** faire toute une histoire *ou* tout un plat (au sujet de qch); **to k. up a din** *or* **a racket** faire un boucan d'enfer

kick-ass ADJ *Fam* super; **he's got this new stereo with these big k. speakers** il a une nouvelle chaîne avec de grosses enceintes super-puissantes; **the DJ played some real k. tunes last night** le DJ a passé de la musique trop cool hier soir

kickback [ˈkɪkbæk] **N 1** *Fam (bribe)* dessous-de-table□ *m inv*, pot-de-vin□ *m* **2** *Tech* recul *m* **3** *(backlash)* contrecoup *m*

kicker [ˈkɪkə(r)] **N 1** *Sport (in rugby)* buteur *m*; *(in American football)* botteur *m*
2 *(horse)* cheval *m* qui rue; *(mule)* mulet *m* qui rue
3 *TV (light)* projecteur *m* de décrochement, contre-jour *m*
4 *Am Fam (hidden drawback)* os *m*, hic *m*
5 *Am Fam (worst part of situation)* **the work's tough and the k. is the pay's lousy** le travail est dur, et en plus de ça, c'est payé avec un lance-pierres
▸▸ *TV* ***kicker light*** projecteur *m* de décrochement, contre-jour *m*

kicking [ˈkɪkɪŋ] *Fam* **N** *Br* **to give sb a k.** tabasser qn à coups de latte; **to get a k.** se faire tabasser à coups de latte
ADJ *(party, nightclub)* hyper animé

kickoff [ˈkɪkɒf] **N 1** *Sport* coup *m* d'envoi; **the k. is at three o'clock** le coup d'envoi sera donné à trois heures **2** *Br Fam Fig* **for a k.** pour commencer□

kickstand [ˈkɪkstænd] **N** béquille *f (de moto)*

kick-start N kick *m*
VT démarrer (au kick); *Fig* **measures to k. the economy** des mesures pour faire repartir l'économie

kick-starter N kick *m*

kid [kɪd] *(pt & pp* **kidded**, *cont* **kidding***)* **N 1** *Fam (child, young person)* gosse *mf*, môme *mf*, gamin(e) *m,f*; **she's just a k.** ce n'est qu'une gamine; **listen to me, k.!** écoute-moi bien, petit!; **that's kids' stuff** c'est pour les bébés; *Am* **college kids** étudiants□*mpl*; *NEng Fam* **our k.** *(brother)* le petit frère□, le frérot; *(sister)* la petite sœur□, la sœurette **2** *(young goat)* chevreau(ette) *m,f* **3** *(hide)* chevreau *m*
ADJ 1 *Fam (young)* **k. brother** petit frère□*m*, frérot

m; **k. sister** petite sœur[□]*f*, sœurette *f* **2** *(coat, jacket)* en chevreau

VI *Fam (joke)* blaguer; **I won it in a raffle – no kidding!** *or* **you're kidding!** je l'ai gagné dans une tombola – sans blague! *ou* tu rigoles!; **don't get upset, I was just kidding** ne te fâche pas, je plaisantais *ou* c'était une blague; **you're not kidding!** je ne te le fais pas dire!

VT *Fam* **1** *(tease)* taquiner[□], se moquer de[□]; **they kidded him about his accent** ils se moquaient de lui à cause de son accent **2** *(deceive, mislead)* charrier, faire marcher; **don't k. yourself!** il ne faut pas te leurrer *ou* te faire d'illusions!; **who do you think you're kidding?** tu te fous de moi?; **I k. you not** sans blague, sans rigoler

►► ***kids' club*** *(at holiday resort etc)* club *m* pour enfants, garderie *f*; ***kid gloves*** gants *mpl* de chevreau; *Fig* **to handle** *or* **to treat sb with k. gloves** prendre des gants avec qn

▸**kid on** *Br Fam* **VT SEP** charrier, faire marcher

VI faire semblant; **they were kidding on that I'd won** ils voulaient me faire croire que j'avais gagné

kiddie = **kiddy**

kiddo ['kɪdəʊ] *(pl* **kiddos***)* **N** *Fam (addressing boy or young man)* mon grand; *(addressing girl or young woman)* ma grande

kiddy ['kɪdɪ] *(pl* **kiddies***)* **N** *Fam* gosse *mf*, gamin(e) *m,f*

kiddy-fiddler **N** *Br very Fam* pédophile[□] *mf*

kid-glove **ADJ to give sb the k. treatment** prendre des gants avec qn

kidnap ['kɪdnæp] *(Br pt & pp* **kidnapped,** *cont* **kidnapping,** *Am pt & pp* **kidnaped,** *cont* **kidnaping***)* **N** enlèvement *m*, rapt *m*, kidnapping *m*

VT enlever, kidnapper

kidnapper, *Am* **kidnaper** ['kɪdnæpə(r)] **N** ravisseur(euse) *m,f*, kidnappeur(euse) *m,f*

kidnapping, *Am* **kidnaping** ['kɪdnæpɪŋ] **N** enlèvement *m*, rapt *m*, kidnapping *m*

kidney ['kɪdnɪ] **N 1** *Anat* rein *m* **2** *Culin* rognon *m*; **pork kidneys** rognons *mpl* de porc **3** *Br Literary (temperament)* nature *f*, caractère *m*; **a man of (quite) a different k.** un homme d'un (tout) autre caractère

COMP *Anat (ailment, trouble)* des reins, rénal

►► *Bot & Culin* ***kidney bean*** *(red)* haricot *m* rouge; *(white)* haricot *m* de Soissons; *Med* ***kidney donor*** donneur(euse) *m,f* de rein; ***kidney failure*** insuffisance *f* rénale; ***kidney machine*** rein *m* artificiel; **he's on a k. machine** il est sous rein artificiel *ou* en dialyse *ou* en hémodialyse; ***kidney specialist*** néphrologue *mf*; ***kidney stone*** calcul *m* rénal; *Med* ***kidney tray*** cuvette *f* à pansements réniforme; *Bot* ***kidney vetch*** (anthyllide *f*) vulnéraire *f*

kidney-shaped **ADJ** en forme de haricot, réniforme

kidology [kɪ'dɒlədʒɪ] **N** *Br Fam* esbroufe *f*, bluff *m*

kill [kɪl] **VT 1** *(person, animal)* tuer; **to k. oneself** se tuer, *Formal* se donner la mort; **the frost killed the flowers** le gel a tué les fleurs; **I'll finish it even if it kills me** j'en viendrai à bout même si je dois me tuer à la tâche; **don't k. yourself working** ne te tue pas au travail; *Hum* **he didn't exactly k. himself to find a job** il ne s'est pas trop fatigué pour trouver du travail; *Hum* **don't k. yourself!** ne te fatigue pas trop!, ne te tue pas à la tâche!; **if you tell them, I'll k. you!** si tu leur dis, je te tue!; **this joke will k. you** cette plaisanterie va te faire mourir de rire; **they were killing themselves (laughing** *or* **with laughter)** ils étaient morts de rire; *Prov* **to k. two birds with one stone** faire d'une pierre deux coups; **to k. sb with kindness** trop gâter qn; **to k. time** tuer le temps

2 *Fam Fig (cause pain to)* faire très mal à[□]; **these shoes are killing me** ces chaussures me font un mal de chien; **my back's killing me** j'ai très *ou* horriblement mal au dos[□]; **the heat will k. you** tu vas crever de chaleur

3 *(put an end to)* tuer, mettre fin à; **the accident killed all his hopes of becoming a dancer** avec son accident, ses espoirs de devenir danseur se sont évanouis *ou* envolés

4 *(alleviate, deaden)* atténuer, soulager; *(smell)* neutraliser; **this injection should k. the pain** cette piqûre devrait atténuer la douleur; **to k. the sound** étouffer *ou* amortir le son

5 *Fam (defeat)* rejeter[□], faire échouer[□]; **the Senate killed the appropriations bill** le Sénat a fait échouer le projet de loi de finances

6 *Fam (cancel, remove)* supprimer[□], enlever[□]; *(computer file)* effacer[□]; *Press* **the editor had to k. the story** le rédacteur en chef a dû supprimer l'article

7 *Fam (switch off)* arrêter[□], couper[□]; **to k. the engine** arrêter le moteur; **to k. the lights** éteindre les lumières[□]

VI tuer; **to shoot to k.** tirer dans l'intention de tuer; *Bible* **thou shalt not k.** tu ne tueras point; **it's a case of k. or cure** c'est un remède de cheval; *Fam* **I'd k. for a beer** je me damnerais pour une bière

N 1 *(act of killing* ▸ *animal)* mise *f* à mort; **the tiger had made three kills that week** le tigre avait tué à trois reprises *ou* avait fait trois victimes cette semaine-là; **to be in at the k.** assister au coup de grâce; **to move in for the k.** donner *ou* porter le coup de grâce **2** *(prey* ▸ *killed by animal)* proie *f*; *(*▸ *killed by hunter)* chasse *f*; **the k. was plentiful** la chasse a été bonne **3** *Mil (destruction* ▸ *of enemy aircraft)* descente *f*; *(*▸ *of enemy warship)* coulée *f*

▸**kill off** **VT SEP 1** *(gen)* exterminer; *Fig* **high prices could k. off the tourist trade** des prix élevés pourraient porter un coup fatal au tourisme **2** *(fictional character)* faire mourir

killer ['kɪlə(r)] **N 1** *(murderer)* tueur(euse) *m,f*; **a convicted k.** une personne reconnue coupable d'homicide; **tuberculosis was once a major k.** jadis, la tuberculose faisait de nombreuses victimes *ou* des ravages **2** *Fam (thing)* **the exam was a real k.** l'examen était vraiment coton; **their new album's a k.** *(excellent)* leur dernier album est vraiment génial *ou* mortel; **that walk was a k.!** cette promenade était vraiment crevante!; **this one's a k.** *(joke)* celle-là est à mourir de rire

COMP *(disease)* meurtrier

ADJ *Am very Fam (excellent)* d'enfer

►► *Comput Fam* ***killer app*** application *f* phare, killer app *f*; *Fam* ***killer heels*** talons *mpl* vertigineux; *Fig* ***killer instinct*** agressivité *f*; **he's got the k. instinct** c'est un battant; **he lacks the k. instinct** il manque d'agressivité *ou* de combativité, il a trop de scrupules; *Zool* ***killer shark*** requin *m* tueur; *Zool* ***killer whale*** épaulard *m*, orque *f*

killing ['kɪlɪŋ] **N 1** *(of person)* assassinat *m*, meurtre *m*; **a wave of killings** une vague d'assassinats; **the k. of endangered species is forbidden** il est interdit de tuer un animal appartenant à une espèce en voie de disparition **2** *Fam (profit)* **to make a k.** se remplir les poches, s'en mettre plein les poches

ADJ *Br Fam* **1** *(tiring)* crevant, tuant **2** *Old-fashioned (hilarious)* tordant, bidonnant; **it was absolutely k.** c'était à se tordre *ou* à mourir de rire

killingly ['kɪlɪŋlɪ] **ADV** *Br Fam* **it was k. funny** c'était à se tordre *ou* à mourir de rire

killjoy ['kɪldʒɔɪ] **N** trouble-fête *mf inv*; **don't be such a k.!** ne sois pas rabat-joie!

kiln [kɪln] **N** four *m (à céramique, à briques etc)*

►► ***kiln drying*** séchage *m* au four

kilo ['kiːləʊ] *(pl* **kilos***)* **N** *(abbr* **kilogram(me)***)* kilo *m*

kilobaud ['kɪləbɔːd] **N** *Comput* kilobaud *m*

kilobit ['kɪləbɪt] **N** *Comput* kilobit *m*

kilobyte ['kɪləbaɪt] **N** *Comput* kilo-octet *m*

kilocalorie ['kɪlə,kælərɪ] **N** kilocalorie *f*, grande calorie *f*

kilocycle ['kɪlə,saɪkəl] **N** kilocycle *m*, kilohertz *m*

kilogram, kilogramme ['kɪlə,græm] **N** kilogramme *m*

kilohertz ['kɪlə,hɜːts] **N** kilohertz *m*

kilometre, *Am* **kilometer** ['kɪlə,miːtə(r), kɪ'lɒmɪtə(r)] **N** kilomètre *m*

kilometric [,kɪlə'metrɪk] **ADJ** kilométrique

kilovolt ['kɪlə,vəʊlt] **N** *Elec* kilovolt *m*

kilowatt ['kɪlə,wɒt] **N** *Elec* kilowatt *m*

kilowatt-hour **N** kilowattheure *m*

kilt [kɪlt] **N** kilt *m*

kilted ['kɪltɪd] **ADJ 1** *(person)* en kilt **2** *(pleated)* **k. skirt** kilt *m*

kilter ['kɪltə(r)] **out of kilter** **ADJ** en dérangement, en panne

kimono [kɪ'məʊnəʊ] *(pl* **kimonos***)* **N** kimono *m*

kin [kɪn] **NPL** parents *mpl*, famille *f*

KIND[1] [kaɪnd] **N 1** *(sort, type)* sorte *f*, type *m*, genre *m*; **hundreds of different kinds of book** des centaines de livres de toutes sortes; **they have every k. of bird imaginable** ils ont tous les oiseaux possibles et imaginables; **it's a k. o[f] fish** c'est une espèce de poisson; **what k. of fis[h] is this?** quel type *ou* quelle sorte de poisson est ce?; **what k. of computer have you got?** qu'est-c[e] que vous avez comme (marque d')ordinateur?; **have you got any other k.?** en avez-vou[s] d'autres?; **they did have some flour, but it wasn'[t] the right k.** ils avaient bien de la farine, mais c[e] n'était pas la bonne; **all kinds of people** toute[s] sortes de gens; **what k. of people go there? – oh all kinds** quel type de gens y va? – oh, des gen[s] très différents; **the worst k. of people** des gens d[e] la pire espèce; **the place was packed wit[h] paintings of all kinds** il y avait là toutes sortes d[e] tableaux; **it's a different k. of problem** c'est u[n] tout autre problème, c'est un problème d'u[n] autre ordre; **I think he's some k. of specialist** *or* **a specialist of some k.** je crois que c'est une sort[e] de spécialiste; **he's that k. of person** il es[t] comme ça; *Fam* **are you some k. of nut?** tu e[s] malade ou quoi?; **what k. of person do you thin[k] I am?** pour qui me prenez-vous?; **it's all right, i[f] you like that k. of thing** c'est bien si vous aime[z] ce genre de choses; **is this the k. of thing you'r[e] looking for?** est-ce que c'est quelque chose d[e] ce genre que vous cherchez?; **this is not the k. of thing you can do overnight** ce n'est pas l[e] genre de chose qu'on fait du jour a[u] lendemain; **his books are not the k. to becom[e] best-sellers** ses livres ne sont pas du genre [à] devenir des best-sellers; **he's not the k. tha[t] would betray his friends** il n'est pas du genre [à] trahir ses amis; **they're not our k. of people** *(no[t] the sort we mix with)* nous ne sommes pas d[u] même monde; **Las Vegas is my k. of town** La Vegas est le genre de ville que j'aime; **you're m[y] k. of girl** tu es mon type de femme, tu es le type de femme que j'aime; **I'm not that k. of girl** ce n'es[t] pas mon genre; **he's not the understanding k.** i[l] n'est pas du genre compréhensif; **she's not th[e] marrying k.** elle n'est pas du genre à se marier; **she's more the stay-at-home k.** elle est plus d[u] genre à rester à la maison; **I know your k.!** j[e] connais les gens de ton espèce!; **I said nothin[g] of the k.!** je n'ai rien dit de pareil *ou* de tel!; **yo[u] were drunk last night – I was nothing of the k.!** t[u] étais ivre hier soir – absolument pas *ou* mai[s] pas du tout!

2 *(class of person, thing)* **he's a traitor to his k.** il [a] trahi les siens; **it's one of the finest of its k.** *(animal)* c'est l'un des plus beaux spécimens d[e] son espèce; *(object)* c'est l'un des plus beau[x] dans son genre

3 *(idioms)* **a k. of** une sorte de, une espèce de; **a hat with a k. of (a) veil** un chapeau avec un[e] espèce de voilette; **it was a k. of saucer-shape[d] thing** c'était une espèce de truc en forme d[e] soucoupe; **she had a k. of fit** elle a eu une sort[e] d'attaque; **I had a k. of (a) feeling you'd com[e]** j'avais comme l'impression que tu viendrais; **[I] heard a k. of thump** j'ai entendu une espèce d[e] cognement *ou* comme un cognement; *Fam* **k. of** plutôt[□]; **it's k. of big and round** c'est plutôt *o[u]* dans le genre grand et rond; **I'm k. of sad about i[t]** ça me rend un peu triste[□]; **did you hit him? – well, k. of** tu l'as frappé? – oui, si on veut; **d[o] you agree? – k. of** tu es d'accord? – plus o[u] moins[□]; **we just k. of wandered about** on s'es[t] un peu baladés[□]; **they're two of a k.** ils sont d[e] la même espèce; **one of a k.** unique (en so[n] genre); **did he give you any tips? – of a k.** vous a-t-il donné des conseils? – si on peut appeler ça des conseils; **well, it's beer of a k., I suppose** ou[i] on peut appeler ça de la bière, je suppose; **h[e] speaks French – of a k.** il parle français – plu[s] ou moins; **it's work of a k., but only as a stopga[p]** c'est un emploi, d'accord, mais pas pour trè[s] longtemps

• **in kind** **ADV 1** *(with goods, services)* en nature **to pay sb in k.** payer qn en nature

2 *(in similar fashion)* de même; **he insulted me, and I replied in k.** il m'a insulté, et je lui ai rendu la monnaie de sa pièce

kind[2] **ADJ 1** *(good-natured, considerate)* gentil, aimable; **she's a very k. woman** c'est une femme très gentille *ou* une femme d'une grande bonté; **to be k. to sb** être gentil avec qn; **it's very k. of you to take an interest** c'est très gentil à vous de vous y intéresser; **how k.!** comme c'est gentil!; **you are really too k.** vous êtes vraiment trop aimable; **she was k. enough to say nothing** elle a eu la gentillesse de ne rien dire; **would you be so k. as to post this for me?** auriez-vous l'amabilité de mettre ceci à la poste pour moi?; **by k. permission of...** avec l'aimable autorisation de...; **give him my k. regards** faites-lui mes amitiés **2** *(favourable)* favorable; **most of the reviews were k. to the actors** la plupart des critiques étaient favorables aux acteurs **3** *(delicate, not harmful)* doux (douce); **a detergent that is k. to your hands** une lessive qui n'abîme pas les mains

kinda ['kaɪndə] *Am Fam* = **kind of**

kindergarten ['kɪndəˌgɑːtən] **N** jardin *m* d'enfants, (école *f*) maternelle *f*, *Suisse* école *f* enfantine, *Belg* gardienne *f*

kind-hearted **ADJ** bon, généreux; **she's very k.** elle a bon cœur, elle est d'une grande générosité

kindle ['kɪndəl] **VT 1** *(wood)* allumer, faire brûler; *(flame, fire)* allumer **2** *Fig (interest)* susciter; *(passion, desire)* embraser, enflammer; *(hatred, jealousy)* attiser, susciter

VI 1 *(wood)* s'enflammer, brûler **2** *Fig (interest)* s'éveiller; *(passion, desire)* s'embraser, s'enflammer; *(hatred, jealousy)* s'éveiller

kindliness ['kaɪndlɪnɪs] **N** gentillesse *f*, amabilité *f*, bonté *f*

kindling ['kɪndlɪŋ] **N** petit bois *m*, bois *m* d'allumage

kindly ['kaɪndlɪ] *(compar* **kindlier**, *superl* **kindliest)**

ADV 1 *(affably, warmly)* chaleureusement, affablement; **he has always treated me k.** il a toujours été gentil avec moi

2 *(obligingly)* gentiment, obligeamment; **she k. offered to help us** elle a gentiment offert de nous aider

3 *(favourably)* **to look k. on sth** voir qch d'un bon œil; **they don't take k. to people arriving late** ils n'apprécient pas beaucoup *ou* tellement qu'on arrive en retard; **I have always thought k. of him** j'ai toujours eu une bonne opinion de lui; **she spoke very k. of you** elle a dit des choses très aimables *ou* gentilles à votre égard; **to be k. disposed towards sb/sth** être bien disposé envers qn/qch

4 *(in polite requests)* **would** *or* **will you k. pass the salt?** auriez-vous la gentillesse *ou* l'amabilité de me passer le sel?; **k. reply by return of post** prière de répondre par retour du courrier; **k. refrain from smoking** prière de ne pas fumer

5 *(in anger or annoyance)* **will you k. sit down!** asseyez-vous, je vous prie!

ADJ *(person, attitude)* gentil; *(smile)* bienveillant

kindness ['kaɪndnɪs] **N 1** *(thoughtfulness)* bonté *f*, gentillesse *f*; **an act of k.** un acte de bonté; **she did it out of the k. of her heart** elle l'a fait par bonté d'âme; *Ironic* **and I suppose it was out of the k. of your heart that you did that?** et je suppose que c'est ton bon cœur qui t'a poussé à faire ça? **2** *Br (considerate act)* service *m*; **to do sb a k.** rendre service à qn; *Formal* **please do me the k. of replying** pourriez-vous être assez gentil pour *ou* pourriez-vous avoir l'amabilité de me donner une réponse?

kindred ['kɪndrɪd] **N** *Arch or Literary (relationship)* parenté *f*; *(family)* famille *f*, parents *mpl*

ADJ *(related)* apparenté; *(similar)* similaire, analogue

►► ***kindred spirits*** âmes *fpl* sœurs

kinematic [ˌkɪnə'mætɪk, ˌkaɪnə'mætɪk] **ADJ** *Phys* cinématique

kinematics [ˌkɪnɪ'mætɪks] **N** *(UNCOUNT) Phys* cinématique *f*

kinetic [kɪ'netɪk, kaɪ'netɪk] **ADJ** *Phys* cinétique

►► *Art* ***kinetic art*** art *m* cinétique; *Phys* ***kinetic energy*** énergie *f* cinétique

kinetics [kɪ'netɪks] **N** *(UNCOUNT) Phys* cinétique *f*

kinfolk ['kɪnfəʊk] **NPL** *Am* parents *mpl*, famille *f*

king [kɪŋ] **N 1** *(person)* roi *m*; **K. Henry the Eighth** le roi Henri VIII; **the K. of Spain/Belgium** le roi d'Espagne/des Belges; **the Three Kings** les trois Mages, les Rois mages; *Fig* **the k. of (the) beasts** le roi des animaux; *Fig* **the fast-food k.** le roi *ou* le magnat de la restauration rapide; **to live like a k.** vivre en grand seigneur; *Fam* **I'm the k. of the castle!** *(in children's games)* c'est moi le plus fort!; *Br Law* **to turn K.'s evidence** témoigner contre ses complices; **to pay a k.'s ransom (for sth)** payer une fortune *ou* un prix fou (pour qch) **2** *(in cards, chess)* roi *m*; *(in draughts)* dame *f*; **the k. of hearts** le roi de cœur

• **Kings** **N** *Bible* **(the book of) Kings** (le livre des) Rois *mpl*

►► *Law* ***King's Bench*** = en Angleterre et au Pays de Galles, l'une des trois divisions de la "High Court", tribunal *m* de grande instance; *Law* ***King's Bench Division*** cour *f* d'assises *(en Grande-Bretagne et au Canada)*; ***King Charles spaniel*** king-charles *m inv*, épagneul *m* du roi Charles; *Zool* ***king cobra*** cobra *m* royal, hamadryade *f*; ***King's Counsel*** avocat(e) *m,f* de la Couronne *(en Grande-Bretagne)*, *Can* conseil *m* du roi; *Zool* ***king crab*** limule *f*, crabe *m* des Moluques; *Bot & Culin* ***King Edward*** *(potato)* (pomme *f* de terre) King Edward *f*; *Br* ***the King's English*** le bon anglais; *Br* ***the King's highway*** la voie publique; ***King James Bible, King James Version*** = version anglaise de la Bible publiée en 1611, "autorisée" par le roi Jacques Ier d'Angleterre; *Orn* ***king penguin*** manchot *m* royal; *Br* ***king prawn*** (grosse) crevette *f*

kingcup ['kɪŋkʌp] **N** *Br Bot* populage *m*, souci *m* d'eau

kingdom ['kɪŋdəm] **N 1** *(realm)* royaume *m*; *Bible* **the k. of God/Heaven** le royaume de Dieu/des cieux; **Thy k. come** que Ton règne vienne; **till k. come** jusqu'à la fin des temps; **they were blown to k. come** ils ont été expédiés dans l'autre monde *ou* dans l'au-delà **2** *(division)* règne *m*; **the animal/vegetable/mineral k.** le règne animal/végétal/minéral

kingfisher ['kɪŋˌfɪʃə(r)] **N** *Orn* martin-pêcheur *m*

kingly ['kɪŋlɪ] *(compar* **kinglier**, *superl* **kingliest)**

ADJ royal, majestueux; **to behave in a k. manner** *(be like a king)* se conduire en roi; *(be generous)* se conduire comme un prince

kingpin ['kɪŋˌpɪn] **N 1** *Tech* pivot *m* **2** *Fig (of organization, company)* pivot *m*, cheville *f* ouvrière **3** *(in tenpin bowling)* quille *f* du milieu

kingship ['kɪŋʃɪp] **N** royauté *f*

king-size, king-sized **ADJ** *(bed, mattress)* (très) grand format *(de 2 mètres sur 1,95 mètre)*; *(cigarette)* long (longue); *(packet, container)* géant; *Fam Fig* **I've got a k. hangover** j'ai une gueule de bois carabinée

kink [kɪŋk] **N 1** *(in hair)* ondulation *f*; **the rope has got a k. in it** la corde fait une boucle; **the hose has got a k. in it** le tuyau est tordu **2** *Fam Fig (sexual deviation)* perversion *f*, aberration *f*; *(quirk)* bizarrerie *f*, excentricité *f* **3** *Am Fam (flaw)* problème *m*

VT *(cable, hose)* tordre

VI *(rope)* faire une boucle; *(cable, hose)* être tordu

kinkiness ['kɪŋkɪnɪs] **N** *Fam (of sexual tastes)* bizarrerie *f*

kinky ['kɪŋkɪ] *(compar* **kinkier**, *superl* **kinkiest) ADJ 1** *Fam (behaviour)* farfelu, loufoque; *(sexually ► person)* qui a des goûts spéciaux; *(► tastes)* bizarre, spécial; **he likes k. sex** il a des goûts sexuels un peu spéciaux; **she wears k. clothes** elle a une façon très spéciale de s'habiller **2** *(rope)* qui fait des boucles; *(cable, hose)* tordu; *(hair)* ondulé

kinsfolk ['kɪnzfəʊk] **NPL** parents *mpl*, famille *f*

kinship ['kɪnʃɪp] **N** *(relationship)* parenté *f*; *Fig (closeness)* intimité *f*; **I feel no real k. with my colleagues** je ne me sens pas du tout proche de mes collègues

kinsman ['kɪnzmən] *(pl* **kinsmen** [-mən]) **N** parent *m*

kinswoman ['kɪnzˌwʊmən] *(pl* **kinswomen** [-'wɪmɪn]) **N** parente *f*

kiosk ['kiːɒsk] **N** *(for newspapers, magazines)* kiosque *m*; *Am (for advertisements)* colonne *f* Morris; *Comput* borne *f* interactive

kip [kɪp] *(pt & pp* **kipped**, *cont* **kipping)** *Br Fam* **N 1** *(sleep)* roupillon *m*; **to have a** *or* **to get some k.** faire *ou* piquer un roupillon; **I got no k. last night** je n'ai pas fermé l'œil de la nuit **2** *(bed)* pieu *m*, plumard *m*; **to be still in one's k.** être encore au plumard

VI roupiller

►**kip down** **VI** *Br Fam* se pieuter

kipper ['kɪpə(r)] **N** hareng *m* fumé, kipper *m*

VT *(fish)* fumer; **kippered herring** hareng *m* fumé, kipper *m*

►► ***kipper tie*** large cravate *f*

kir [kɪə(r)] **N** *(drink)* kir *m*, blanc *m* cassis

►► ***kir royale*** kir *m* royal

kirby-grip ['kɜːbɪ-] **N** *Br* pince *f* à cheveux

kirk [kɜːk] **N** *Scot* église *f*; **the K.** l'Église *f* (presbytérienne) d'Écosse

kiss [kɪs] **N 1** *(with lips)* baiser *m*; **they gave her a k.** ils l'ont embrassée; *Fam* **give us a k.!** fais-moi un (gros) bisou!; **she gave him a goodnight k.** elle lui a souhaité une bonne nuit en l'embrassant, elle l'a embrassé pour lui souhaiter (une) bonne nuit; **to give sb the k. of life** faire du bouche-à-bouche à qn; *Fig* **it could be the k. of life for the building trade** cela pourrait permettre à l'industrie du bâtiment de retrouver un *ou* son second souffle; **k. of death** coup *m* fatal; **the new supermarket was the k. of death for local shopkeepers** l'ouverture du supermarché a entraîné la ruine des petits commerçants **2** *(sweet)* **chocolate k.** (petit) bonbon *m* au chocolat **3** *(in snooker, pool)* touche *f*, contre *m*

VT 1 *(with lips)* embrasser; **he kissed her on the lips/forehead** il l'embrassa sur la bouche/le front; **he kissed her hand** il lui a baisé la main, il lui a fait le baisemain; **I kissed her goodnight** je l'ai embrassée *ou* je lui ai fait une bise pour lui souhaiter (une) bonne nuit; **k. your dad goodnight!** embrasse ton père *ou* fais une bise à ton père avant d'aller te coucher!; **mummy will k. it better** maman va te faire un bisou et tu n'auras plus mal; *Fam* **you can k. your money goodbye!** tu peux faire ton deuil de *ou* tu peux faire une croix sur ton fric! **2** *Literary (touch lightly)* caresser; **the sunlight kissed her hair** le soleil lui caressait les cheveux **3** *(in snooker, pool)* toucher

VI 1 *(people)* s'embrasser; **they kissed goodbye** ils se sont dit au revoir en s'embrassant; **to k. and make up** s'embrasser et faire la paix; **to k. and tell** = dévoiler les détails de sa liaison avec une personne connue **2** *(in snooker, pool)* se toucher

►► ***kiss chase*** = jeu enfantin qui consiste à attraper un ou une camarade pour lui donner un baiser; *Br* ***kiss curl*** accroche-cœur *m*

►**kiss away** **VT SEP** **she kissed away my tears** ses baisers ont séché mes larmes

►**kiss off** *Am Fam* **VT SEP 1** *(dismiss)* envoyer promener **2** *(kill)* descendre, buter **3** *(give up hope of)* faire une croix sur, dire adieu à; **you can k. off your promotion!** tu peux faire une croix sur *ou* dire adieu à ta promotion!

VI aller se faire voir; **k. off!** va te faire voir!

kisser ['kɪsə(r)] **N 1** *(person)* **to be a great k.** bien embrasser **2** *Fam (face, mouth)* tronche *f*

kiss-off **N** *Am Fam* **to give sb the k.** envoyer promener qn

kissogram ['kɪsəgræm] **N** *Br* = message délivré par une personne déguisée et accompagné d'un baiser

►► ***kissogram girl*** = fille qui délivre des messages et est chargée d'embrasser le destinataire

kit [kɪt] *(pt & pp* **kitted**, *cont* **kitting)** **N 1** *(set)* trousse *f*; **tool/sewing k.** trousse *f* à outils/à couture

2 *(equipment, clothing)* affaires *fpl*, matériel *m*; **have you got your squash k.?** as-tu tes affaires de squash?; *Fam* **to get one's k. off** se désaper, se mettre à poil; *Fam* **get your k. off!** à poil!; *Fam* **the whole k. and caboodle** tout le bazar *ou* bataclan

3 *(soldier's gear)* fourniment *m*; **in full battle k.** en tenue de combat

4 *(parts to be assembled)* kit *m*; **it's sold in k. form** c'est vendu en kit; **model aircraft k.** maquette *f* d'avion

►► *Br* ***kit bag*** musette *f*, sac *m* de toile; ***kit inspection*** revue *f* de détail

►**kit out, kit up** VT SEP *Br Fam* équiper[□]; **we kitted ourselves out for a long trip** nous nous sommes équipés pour un long voyage; **he was kitted out for golf** il était en tenue de golf

kitchen ['kɪtʃɪn] N cuisine *f*

COMP *(salt, scissors, table, utensil)* de cuisine

►► ***kitchen cabinet*** *(furniture)* buffet *m* (de cuisine); *Br Pol* = conseillers proches du chef du gouvernement; ***kitchen floor*** sol *m* de la cuisine; ***kitchen foil*** aluminium *m* ménager, papier *m* d'aluminium; *Br* ***kitchen garden*** (jardin *m*) potager *m*; ***kitchen hand*** aide *mf* de cuisine; *Br* ***kitchen paper, kitchen roll*** essuie-tout *m*, Sopalin® *m*; ***kitchen shop*** magasin *m* d'articles de cuisine; ***kitchen sink*** évier *m*; *Fam Fig* **to take everything but the k. sink** *(on holiday)* emporter toute la maison; *(thief, person moving out etc)* ne laisser que les murs; ***kitchen sink drama*** = théâtre réaliste britannique des années 50–60 dépeignant la vie des gens ordinaires; ***kitchen stove*** cuisinière *f*, *(fourneau)* ***kitchen unit*** élément *m* (de cuisine)

KITCHEN SINK DRAMA

Kitchen sink drama est le nom qui fut donné à un style d'écriture théâtrale qui se développa en Angleterre dans les années 50 et 60. Jusqu'alors le théâtre s'était intéressé presque exclusivement à la bonne société. Une nouvelle génération d'écrivains et de dramaturges (notamment les **angry young men**, voir cet encadré) révolutionna la scène théâtrale en adoptant un style plus réaliste qui mettait en scène la vie de gens de la classe ouvrière avec leurs problèmes et leur difficultés. Sur les scènes des théâtres, les salons cossus firent place aux intérieurs modestes et aux cuisines. Bien que le terme kitchen sink drama ne concerne que le théâtre, le terme "kitchen sink realism", lui, est employé pour parler de ce style réaliste en littérature et dans les arts en général.

kitchenette [ˌkɪtʃɪ'net] N kitchenette *f*, *Offic* cuisinette *f*

kitchenware ['kɪtʃɪnˌweə(r)] N *(UNCOUNT)* vaisselle *f* et ustensiles *mpl* de cuisine

kite [kaɪt] N **1** *(toy)* cerf-volant *m*; **to fly a k.** faire voler un cerf-volant; *Fig* lancer un ballon d'essai; **go fly a k.!** va voir là-bas si j'y suis!

2 *Orn* milan *m*

3 *Fam Fin* traite *f* en l'air[□], billet *m* de complaisance[□]; **to fly** *or* **to send up a k.** tirer en l'air *ou* à découvert

4 *Br Fam Old-fashioned (aeroplane)* zinc *m*

VT *Fam Fin* **to k. a cheque** faire un chèque en bois

►► ***kite balloon*** ballon *m* observateur; ***kite flyer*** cerf-voliste *mf*, lucanophile *mf*; *Fam Fin* tireur *m* en l'air *ou* à découvert; ***kite flying*** le cerf-volant; *Fam Fin* tirage *m* en l'air *ou* à découvert; **he enjoys k. flying** il aime faire du cerf-volant; ***Kite mark*** = label représentant un petit cerf-volant, apposé sur les produits conformes aux normes officielles britanniques

kiteboarding ['kaɪtˌbɔ:dɪŋ] N kiteboarding *m*, = surf tracté par cerf-volant; **to go k.** faire du kiteboarding

kitesurfing ['kaɪtˌsɜ:fɪŋ] N kitesurf *m*, = surf tracté par cerf-volant; **to go k.** faire du kitesurf

kith [kɪθ] NPL **k. and kin** amis *mpl* et parents *mpl*; **he's one of our own k. and kin** il est l'un des nôtres

kiting ['kaɪtɪŋ] N *Fam Fin* tirage *m* en l'air[□], tirage *m* à découvert[□]

kitsch [kɪtʃ] N kitsch *m inv*

ADJ kitsch *(inv)*

kitschy ['kɪtʃɪ] ADJ *(compar* **kitschier**, *superl* **kitschiest)** kitsch *(inv)*

kitten ['kɪtən] N **1** *(animal)* chaton *m*; **our cat has had kittens** notre chatte a eu des petits; *Br Fam* **he was having kittens** il était dans tous ses états *ou* aux cent coups **2** *(term of endearment)* ma petite, ma mignonne

►► ***kitten heels*** talons *mpl* bobine

kittenish ['kɪtənɪʃ] ADJ *(playful)* joueur, espiègle; *(flirtatious)* coquet

kittiwake ['kɪtɪweɪk] N *Orn* mouette *f* tridactyle

kitty ['kɪtɪ] *(pl* **kitties)** N **1** *Fam (kitten)* chaton[□] *m*; **here, k. k.** viens, mon minou *ou* minet **2** *(funds held in common)* cagnotte *f*, caisse *f* (commune); *(in gambling)* cagnotte *f* **3** *(in bowls)* cochonnet *m*

kiwi ['ki:wi:] N **1** *Orn* kiwi *m*, aptéryx *m* **2** *(fruit)* kiwi *m*

• **Kiwi** N *Fam (New Zealander)* Néo-Zélandais (e)[□] *m,f*

►► ***kiwi fruit*** kiwi *m*

KKK [ˌkeɪkeɪ'keɪ] N *Am (abbr* **Ku Klux Klan)** Ku Klux Klan *m*

Klaxon® ['klæksən] N *Br Aut* Klaxon® *m*

Kleenex® ['kli:neks] N Kleenex® *m inv*, mouchoir *m* en papier

kleptomania [ˌkleptə'meɪnɪə] N kleptomanie *f*, cleptomanie *f*

kleptomaniac [ˌkleptə'meɪnɪæk] ADJ kleptomane, cleptomane

N kleptomane *mf*, cleptomane *mf*

klieg light [kli:g-] N *Am* lampe *f* à arc

klutz [klʌts] N *Am Fam* balourd(e) *m,f*, godiche *f*

km *(written abbr* **kilometre)** km

km/h *(written abbr* **kilometres per hour)** km/h

knack [næk] N tour *m* de main, truc *m*; **there's a k. to it** il y a un truc; **it's easy once you get the k. (of it)** c'est facile une fois qu'on a compris le truc; **she's got a k. of finding the right word** elle sait toujours trouver le mot juste; *Hum* **he's got a k. of turning up at meal-times** il a le chic pour arriver à l'heure du repas

knacker ['nækə(r)] *Br* VT *Fam* **1** *(exhaust)* crever; **that run completely knackered me** cette course m'a mis sur les genoux **2** *(break, wear out)* bousiller; **I've knackered my hi-fi** j'ai bousillé ma chaîne stéréo

N **1** *(slaughterer)* équarrisseur *m* **2** *(of buildings, ships)* démolisseur *m*

• **knackers** NPL *Br Vulg (testicles)* couilles *fpl*

►► ***knacker's yard*** équarrissoir *m*, abattoir *m*

knackered ['nækəd] ADJ *Br Fam* **1** *(exhausted)* crevé, lessivé, naze **2** *(broken, worn out)* bousillé

knackering ['nækərɪŋ] ADJ *Br Fam* crevant

knapsack ['næpsæk] N havresac *m*, sac *m* à dos

knave [neɪv] N **1** *Arch (rogue)* fripon *m*, canaille *f* **2** *Cards* valet *m*; **k. of clubs** valet *m* de trèfle

knavery ['neɪvərɪ] *(pl* **knaveries)** N *Arch* friponnerie *f*, canaillerie *f*

knead [ni:d] VT *(dough, clay, muscles)* pétrir, malaxer

knee [ni:] N **1** *(part of body)* genou *m*; **the snow was up to our knees, we were up to our knees in snow** on avait de la neige jusqu'aux genoux; **at k. level** à hauteur du genou; **to go down on one's knees, to fall to one's knees** se mettre à genoux; *also Fig* **to be on one's knees** être à genoux; *Literary* **to bend** *or* **to bow the k. to** *or* **before sb** fléchir le genou devant qn, s'incliner devant qn; **to bring sb to his/her knees** faire capituler qn; **the war nearly brought the country to its knees** la guerre a failli entraîner la ruine du pays

2 *(of trousers)* genou *m*; **worn at the knees** usé aux genoux

3 *(lap)* genoux *mpl*; **come and sit on my k.** viens t'asseoir sur mes genoux; **to put sb over one's k.** donner la fessée à *ou* corriger qn; **I learnt it at my mother's k.** j'ai appris cela dès ma plus tendre enfance; **on bended k.** à genoux; **to go down on bended k.** se mettre à genoux

4 *Tech (in pipe)* genou *m*, coude *m*; *(device)* rotule *f*

VT donner un coup de genou à; **he kneed me in the groin** il m'a donné un coup de genou dans l'aine; **she kneed the door open** elle poussa la porte du genou

►► *Tech* ***knee bracket*** console-équerre *f*; *Br* ***knee breeches*** knickers *mpl*; ***knee drop*** *(in wrestling)* projection *f* sur le genou; ***knee jerk*** réflexe *m* rotulien; ***knee joint*** articulation *f* du genou; ***knee pad*** genouillère *f*; ***knee plate*** gousset *m* (de charpente); ***knee reflex*** réflexe *m* rotulien; *Carp* ***knee timber*** bois *m* courbant *ou* coudé

kneecap ['ni:kæp] *(pt & pp* **kneecapped**, *cont* **kneecapping)** N *Anat* rotule *f*

VT **to k. sb** punir qn en lui brisant les rotules *(pratique terroriste)*

kneecapping ['ni:kæpɪŋ] N mutilation *f* des rotules

knee-deep ADJ **the snow was k.** on avait de la neige jusqu'aux genoux; **the water was only k.** l'eau ne nous arrivait qu'aux genoux; **we were k. in water** l'eau nous arrivait *ou* nous étions dans l'eau jusqu'aux genoux; *Fig* **he was k. in trouble** il était dans les ennuis jusqu'au cou

knee-high ADJ *(grass)* à hauteur de genou; **the grass was k.** l'herbe nous arrivait (jusqu')aux genoux; *Fam Hum* **k. to a grasshopper** haut comme trois pommes

►► ***knee-high boots*** chaussures *fpl* montantes; ***knee-high socks*** chaussettes *fpl* montantes

knee-jerk ADJ *(reflex)* automatique

►► *Fig Pej* ***knee-jerk reaction*** réflexe *m*, automatisme *m*

kneel [ni:l] *(pt & pp* **knelt** [nelt] *or* **kneeled)** VI s'agenouiller, se mettre à genoux; **she was kneeling on the floor** elle était agenouillée *ou* à genoux par terre; **to k. in prayer** s'agenouiller pour prier; **to k. before sb** se mettre à genoux devant qn

knee-length ADJ *(dress)* qui descend jusqu'aux genoux; *(boot, socks)* qui monte jusqu'aux genoux

►► *Cin & TV* ***knee-length shot*** plan *m* genoux

kneeler ['ni:lə(r)] N *(cushion in church)* agenouilloir *m*

kneeling ['ni:lɪŋ] ADJ agenouillé, à genoux; **in a k. position** à genoux

kneeroom ['ni:rum] N **have you got enough k.?** avez-vous assez de place pour vos genoux *ou* vos jambes?

knees-up [ni:z-] N *Br Fam* java *f*; **to have a k.** faire la java; **there was a bit of a k. in the pub** on a un peu fait la java au pub

knee-trembler [-tremblə(r)] N *Br Fam Hum* **to have a k.** faire l'amour debout[□]

knell [nel] N *Literary* glas *m*; **to toll the k.** sonner le glas

knelt [nelt] *pt & pp of* **kneel**

knew [nju:] *pt of* **know**

knickerbocker glory ['nɪkəˌbɒkə-] N = coupe de glace avec fruits et crème Chantilly

knickerbockers ['nɪkəˌbɒkəz] NPL knickers *mpl*; *(for golf)* culotte *f* de golf

knickers ['nɪkəz] NPL **1** *Br (underwear)* **(pair of) k.** culotte *f*, slip *m (de femme)*; *Fam* **don't get your k. in a twist!** *(don't panic)* ne t'affole pas![□]; *(don't get angry)* du calme!, calme-toi!; *Vulg* **to get into sb's k.** s'envoyer qn, culbuter qn **2** *Am (knickerbockers)* knickers *mpl*; *(for golf)* culotte *f* de golf

EXCLAM *Br Fam Old-fashioned* mon œil!

knick-knack ['nɪknæk] N *(trinket)* bibelot *m*; *(brooch)* colifichet *m*

knife [naɪf] *(pl* **knives** [naɪvz]) N **1** *(for eating)* couteau *m*; **a k. and fork** une fourchette et un couteau; **her words cut me like a k.** ses paroles m'ont piqué au vif *ou* m'ont profondément blessé; **fish k.** couteau *m* à poisson; **like a k. through butter** comme dans du beurre; **this k. wouldn't cut butter** ce couteau ne coupe que ce qu'il voit *ou* ne coupe rien; *Fam* **to be** *or* **to go under the k.** passer sur le billard; *Fam Old-fashioned* **before you could say k.** en un rien de temps, en moins de rien **2** *(as a weapon)* couteau *m*; **to carry a k.** porter un couteau sur soi; *Fig* **she really got her k. into them** elle en avait drôlement après eux, elle leur en voulait drôlement; *Fig* **the knives are out** ils sont à couteaux tirés *ou* en guerre ouverte; *Fam* **you really stuck the k. in!** tu ne l'as pas loupé!; *Fig* **to turn** *or* **to twist the k. (in the wound)** retourner le couteau dans la plaie

VT donner un coup/des coups de couteau à; **to k. sb to death** tuer qn à coups de couteau; **he's been knifed** il a reçu un coup/des coups de cou

:au; **he was knifed in the back** il a reçu un coup/ es coups de couteau *ou* on lui a planté un cou- au dans le dos; *Fig* on lui a tiré dans le dos *ou* ans les pattes

▸ ***knife attack*** attaque *f* à coups de couteau; ***nife pleat*** pli *m* plat; *Elec* ***knife switch*** interrup- ur *m* à lame; ***knife wound*** blessure *f* à coups de outeau

ife-edge **N 1** *(blade)* fil *m* du couteau; *Fig* **we ere on a k.** on était sur des charbons ardents; **s decision was (balanced) on a k.** sa décision ne nait qu'à un fil **2** *(of scales)* couteau *m*

ife-point **N at k.** sous la menace du couteau

ife-rest **N** porte-couteau *m*

ifing ['naɪfɪŋ] **N** agression *f* à coups de cou- au

ight [naɪt] **N 1** *Hist* chevalier *m*; **a k. in shining rmour** *(romantic hero)* un prince charmant; *(sa- our)* un sauveur, un redresseur de torts **2** *Br onorary title)* chevalier *m*; **Laurence Olivier was ade a k.** Laurence Olivier a été anobli *ou* fait hevalier **3** *(chess piece)* cavalier *m*

VT faire chevalier

▸ *Br* ***knight bachelor*** chevalier *m (n'appartenant aucun ordre)*; *Br* ***Knight Commander (of the rder) of the Bath*** Chevalier *m* Commandeur de Ordre du Bain; ***Knight of (the Order of) the Gar- er*** Chevalier *m* de l'Ordre de la Jarretière; ***the nights of the Round Table*** les Chevaliers *mpl* de Table ronde; ***Knight Templar*** Templier *m*

ighthood ['naɪthʊd] **N 1** *Br (title)* titre *m* de hevalier; **to receive a k.** être fait chevalier, être nobli **2** *Hist* chevalerie *f*

ightly ['naɪtlɪ] **ADJ** chevaleresque

it [nɪt] *(pt & pp* **knit** *or* **knitted**, *cont* **knitting**) **VT** *(garment)* tricoter; **he knitted himself a scarf** il est tricoté une écharpe

2 *(in instructions)* **k. 2 purl 2** (tricoter) 2 mailles à endroit, 2 mailles à l'envers; **k. 2 together** trico- er 2 mailles ensemble

3 *(unite)* unir

4 *(idiom)* **to k. one's brows** froncer les sourcils

VI 1 *(make garment)* tricoter; **I like to k. in the venings** j'aime bien tricoter *ou* faire du tricot le oir **2** *(as opposed to purl)* tricoter à l'endroit **3** *bones)* se souder

knit together **VT SEP** *(unite)* unir; *Med (bones)* ouder

VI *(heal ▸ bones)* se souder

knit up **VT SEP** *(garment)* tricoter; **she knitted up scarf from the spare wool** elle a fait une écharpe vec la laine qui restait

VI *(yarn)* **this wool knits up easily** cette laine se icote facilement

nitted ['nɪtɪd] **ADJ** tricoté, en tricot

▸ ***knitted fabric*** tricot *m*; ***knitted goods*** tricots *pl*, articles *mpl* en tricot

nitter ['nɪtə(r)] **N** tricoteur(euse) *m,f*; **she's a ood/a quick k.** elle tricote bien/vite

nitting ['nɪtɪŋ] **N 1** *(garment)* tricot *m*; **have you een my k.?** avez-vous vu mon tricot? **2** *(activity)* ricot *m*; *(on industrial scale)* tricotage *m*; **to do ome k.** faire du tricot; **k. helps me relax** le tricot aide à me détendre; **machine k.** tricots *mpl* faits la machine; *Am & Scot Fam* **to stick to one's k.** occuper de ses oignons **3** *(of bones)* soudure *f*

COMP *(wool)* à tricoter; *(pattern)* de tricot; *(fac- ry)* de tricotage

▸ ***knitting machine*** machine *f* à tricoter; ***knit- ng needle, knitting pin*** aiguille *f* à tricoter

nitwear ['nɪtweə(r)] **N** *(UNCOUNT) (garments)* ainages *mpl*; *(in department store)* rayon *m* lai- ages

▸ ***knitwear manufacturer*** fabricant *m* de laina- es

nob [nɒb] **N 1** *(handle ▸ of door, drawer)* poi- née *f*, bouton *m*; *Br Fam* **the same to you with nobs on!** toi-même!

2 *(control ▸ on appliance)* bouton *m*

3 *(ball-shaped end ▸ of walking stick)* pommeau ; *(▸ on furniture)* bouton *m*

4 *(of butter)* noix *f*

5 *Br Vulg (penis)* queue *f*, bite *f*

6 *Br Vulg (man)* trou *m* du cul

nobbed [nɒbd] **ADJ** *(stick)* à pommeau

knobbly ['nɒblɪ] *(compar* **knobblier**, *superl* **knob- bliest**) **ADJ** *Br* noueux; **k. knees** genoux *mpl* cou- verts de bosses

KNOCK [nɒk]

N	
• coup **1–3**	• critique **4**
• cognement **5**	
VT	
• heurter **2**	• cogner **2**
• éreinter **3**	• critiquer **3**
VI	
• frapper **1**	• heurter **2**
• cogner **2, 3**	

N 1 *(blow)* coup *m*; **give it a k. with a hammer** donne un coup de marteau dessus; **there was a k. at the door/window** on a frappé à la porte/fe- nêtre; **she gave three knocks on the door** elle a frappé trois fois *ou* coups à la porte; **to hear a k.** entendre frapper; **no one answered my k.** per- sonne n'a répondu quand j'ai frappé; **k.! k.!** toc! toc!; **can you give me a k. tomorrow morning?** est- ce que vous pouvez (venir) frapper à ma porte demain matin pour me réveiller?

2 *(bump)* coup *m*; **to give sb a k. on the head** por- ter à qn un coup à la tête; **I got a nasty k. on the elbow** *(in fight, accident)* j'ai reçu un sacré coup au coude; *(by one's own clumsiness)* je me suis bien cogné le coude; **the car's had a few knocks, but nothing serious** la voiture est un peu cabos- sée mais rien de grave

3 *(setback)* coup *m*; **his reputation has taken a hard k.** sa réputation en a pris un sérieux coup; **I've taken a few knocks in my time** j'ai encaissé des coups moi aussi

4 *Fam (criticism)* critique[□] *f*; **she's taken a few knocks from the press** la presse n'a pas toujours été très tendre avec elle

5 *Aut (in engine)* cognement *m*

VT 1 *(hit)* **to k. a nail in** enfoncer un clou; **she knocked a nail into the wall** elle a planté un clou dans le mur; **she knocked a hole in the wall** elle a fait un trou dans le mur; **he was knocked into the ditch** il a été projeté dans le fossé; **the boy was knocking the ball against the wall** le garçon lan- çait *ou* envoyait la balle contre le mur; **the force of the explosion knocked us to the floor** la force de l'explosion nous a projetés à terre; *Fam* **to k. sb unconscious** *or* **cold** assommer qn; **the boom knocked him off balance** la bôme, en le heurtant, l'a déséquilibré *ou* lui a fait perdre l'équilibre; *Fig* **the news knocked me off balance** la nouvelle m'a sidéré *ou* coupé le souffle

2 *(bump)* heurter, cogner; **I knocked my head on** *or* **against the low ceiling** je me suis cogné la tête contre le *ou* au plafond

3 *Fam (criticize ▸ author, film)* éreinter; *(▸ driv- ing, cooking)* critiquer[□]; **knocking your col- leagues isn't going to help** ce n'est pas en débinant vos collègues *ou* en cassant du sucre sur le dos de vos collègues que vous changerez quoi que ce soit; **they're always knocking the trade unions** ils n'arrêtent pas de taper sur les syndicats; **don't k. it till you've tried it!** n'en dis pas de mal avant d'avoir essayé[□]

4 *Br very Fam (have sex with)* se faire, se taper

5 *(idioms)* **to k. holes in a plan/an argument** dé- molir un projet/un argument; **maybe it will k. some sense into him** cela lui mettra peut-être du plomb dans la cervelle, cela le ramènera peut- être à la raison; **to k. sb into shape** mettre qn au pas; *Br Fam* **to k. sth on the head** *(put a stop to)* faire cesser qch[□]; *Br Fam* **our plans have been knocked on the head** nos projets sont tombés à l'eau; *Br Fam* **k. it on the head, will you!** c'est pas bientôt fini?; *Br Fam* **he can k. spots off me at chess/tennis** il me bat à plate couture aux échecs/au tennis; *Am Fam* **it really knocked me for a loop** ça m'a vraiment scié; **to k. sb dead** *(im- press)* en mettre plein la vue à qn; **Eminem knocked them dead last night** hier soir, Eminem a fait un tabac

VI 1 *(hit)* frapper; **to k. on** *or* **at the door** frapper (à la porte); **she came in without knocking** elle est entrée sans frapper; **they k. on the wall when we're too noisy** ils tapent *ou* cognent contre le mur quand on fait trop de bruit; **it was a branch knocking against the window** c'était une branche qui cognait contre la fenêtre

2 *(bump)* **to k. against** *or* **into** heurter, cogner; **she knocked into the desk** elle s'est heurtée *ou* co- gnée contre le bureau; **my elbow knocked against the door frame** je me suis cogné *ou* heurté le coude contre le chambranle de la porte

3 *(make sound)* cogner; **my heart was knocking** je sentais mon cœur cogner dans ma poitrine, j'avais le cœur qui cognait; **the car engine is knocking** le moteur cogne; *Hum* **his knees were knocking** ses genoux jouaient des castagnettes; **the pipes k. when you run the taps** les tuyaux co- gnent quand on ouvre les robinets

▸**knock about, knock around** **VI** *Fam (loiter)* traîner; **Vicky must be knocking about here some- where** Vicky doit traîner quelque part dans le coin; **I knocked about in Australia for a while** j'ai bourlingué *ou* roulé ma bosse en Australie pen- dant quelque temps; *Br* **are my fags knocking about?** est-ce que mes clopes sont dans le coin?; **that's what I wear to k. about in** ce sont mes vêtements d'intérieur[□]

VT INSEP *Fam* traîner dans; **I knocked about town all day** j'ai traîné en ville toute la journée; **she spent a year knocking about Europe** elle a passé une année à se balader en Europe; **these clothes are OK for knocking about the house in** ces vête- ments, ça va pour traîner à la maison; **your keys are knocking about the kitchen somewhere** tes clés traînent dans un coin de la cuisine

VT SEP 1 *(beat)* battre; *(ill-treat)* malmener; **he used to k. his wife about a lot** il tapait sur *ou* il battait sa femme; **the old car's been knocked about a bit** la vieille voiture a pris quelques coups ici et là; **the furniture has been badly knocked about** les meubles ont été fort maltrai- tés **2** *(jolt, shake)* ballotter; **we were really knocked about in the back of the truck** nous étions ballottés à l'arrière du camion **3** *Fam (discuss)* débattre[□]; **we knocked the idea about for a while** nous en avons vaguement discuté pendant un certain temps

▸**knock back** **VT SEP** *Fam* **1** *(drink)* descendre; **she could k. back ten vodkas in an hour** elle pou- vait s'envoyer dix vodkas en une heure; **he cer- tainly knocks it back!** qu'est-ce qu'il descend!

2 *(cost)* coûter à[□]; **that car must have knocked him back a few thousand pounds** cette voiture a bien dû lui coûter quelques milliers de livres

3 *(surprise, shock)* secouer, bouleverser; **the news really knocked me back** la nouvelle m'a vrai- ment abasourdi *ou* m'a laissé pantois

4 *Br (reject)* **to k. sb back** rejeter qn[□]; **to k. sth back** *(offer, invitation)* refuser qch[□]; **she knocked him back** il s'est pris une veste

▸**knock down** **VT SEP 1** *(person)* renverser; *(in fight)* envoyer par terre, étendre; **she was knocked down by a bus** elle a été renversée par un bus; **he knocked the champion down in the first round** il a envoyé le champion au tapis *ou* il a mis le champion knock-down dans la première re- prise

2 *(hurdle, vase, pile of books)* faire tomber, ren- verser

3 *(demolish ▸ building)* démolir; *(▸ wall)* démo- lir, abattre; *(▸ argument)* démolir

4 *(price)* baisser; *(salesman)* faire baisser; **I man- aged to k. him down to $500** j'ai réussi à le faire baisser jusqu'à 500 dollars

5 *Br (at auction)* adjuger; **it was knocked down to her for £300** on le lui a adjugé pour 300 livres

▸**knock off** **VT SEP 1** *(from shelf, wall etc)* faire tomber; **the statue's arm had been knocked off** la statue avait perdu un bras; **he knocked the earth off the spade** il fit tomber la terre qui était restée collée à la bêche; **he was knocked off his bicycle by a car** il s'est fait renverser à vélo par une voi- ture; *Fig* **to k. sb off their pedestal** *or* **perch** faire tomber qn de son piédestal; *Fam* **to k. sb's block off** casser la figure à qn

2 *(reduce by)* faire une réduction de; **the sales- man knocked 10 percent off (for us)** le vendeur nous a fait un rabais *ou* une remise de 10 pour cent; **I managed to get something knocked off the price** j'ai réussi à faire baisser un peu le prix

3 *Fam (write rapidly)* torcher; **she can k. off an art- icle in half an hour** elle peut pondre un article en une demi-heure

4 *very Fam (kill)* descendre, buter
5 *Br very Fam (steal)* piquer, faucher; *(rob)* braquer; **they knocked off a bank** ils ont braqué une banque
6 *Br Vulg (have sex with)* baiser
7 *Fam (idiom)* **k. it off!** *(stop it)* arrête ton char!
VI *Fam (stop work)* cesser le travail□; **we k. off at five o'clock** on finit à cinq heures
▸ **knock out** **VT SEP 1** *(nail)* faire sortir; *(wall)* abattre; **one of his teeth was knocked out** il a perdu une dent
2 *(make unconscious)* assommer; *(in boxing)* mettre K-O; *Fam* **the sleeping pill knocked her out for ten hours** le somnifère l'a assommée *ou* mise K-O pendant dix heures
3 *Fam (astound)* épater; **her performance really knocked me out!** son interprétation m'a vraiment épaté!
4 *(eliminate)* éliminer; **our team was knocked out in the first round** notre équipe a été éliminée au premier tour
5 *(put out of action)* mettre hors service; **it can k. out a tank at 2,000 metres** cela peut mettre un tank hors de combat à 2000 mètres
6 *Fam (exhaust)* crever; **I'm not going to k. myself out working for him** je ne vais pas m'esquinter à travailler pour lui
7 *Am Fam* **to k. oneself out** *(indulge oneself)* se faire plaisir□; **there's plenty of food left, k. yourself out!** il reste plein de nourriture, sers-toi autant que tu veux!□
8 *(pipe)* débourrer
▸ **knock over** **VT SEP 1** *(capsize)* renverser, faire tomber; **I knocked a pile of plates over** j'ai renversé *ou* fait tomber une pile d'assiettes; **she was knocked over by a bus** elle a été renversée par un bus **2** *Am Fam (rob)* braquer
▸ **knock together** **VT SEP 1** *(hit together)* cogner l'un contre l'autre; **they make music by knocking bamboo sticks together** ils font de la musique en frappant des bambous l'un contre l'autre; *Fam* **they need their heads knocking together, those two** ces deux-là auraient bien besoin qu'on leur secoue les puces **2** *Fam (make quickly)* faire à la hâte□; **we knocked together a rough shelter** on s'est fabriqué une espèce d'abri□
VI s'entrechoquer
▸ **knock up** **VT SEP 1** *Fam (make quickly)* faire à la hâte□; **these buildings were knocked up after the war** ces bâtiments ont été construits à la hâte après la guerre; **he knocked up a delicious meal in no time** en un rien de temps, il a réussi à préparer quelque chose de délicieux□
2 *Br (waken)* réveiller (en frappant à la porte)
3 *Am Fam (damage)* esquinter; **the furniture is pretty knocked up** les meubles sont plutôt esquintés *ou* amochés
4 *very Fam (make pregnant)* mettre en cloque; **she got knocked up** elle s'est fait mettre en cloque
5 *(in cricket)* marquer; **he knocked up 50 runs before rain stopped play** il a marqué 50 points avant que la pluie n'interrompe la partie
VI *Br (in ball games)* faire des balles

knockabout ['nɒkəbaʊt] **N 1** *(game)* partie *f* pour rire **2** *Naut* dériveur *m*
ADJ *(game)* pour rire; **a k. comedy** *or* **farce** une grosse farce; **a k. comedian** un clown

knockback ['nɒkbæk] **N** *Br Fam (rejection)* veste *f*; **to get a k.** prendre une veste

knockdown ['nɒk,daʊn] **ADJ 1** *(forceful)* **a k. blow** un coup à assommer un bœuf; **a k. argument** un argument massue **2** *(easy to dismantle)* démontable; **sold in k. form** vendu en kit **3** *Br (reduced)* **for sale at k. prices** en vente à des prix imbattables *ou* défiant toute concurrence; **I got it for a k. price** je l'ai eu pour trois fois rien
N 1 *(in boxing)* knock-down *m inv* **2** *Am Fam Old-fashioned (introduction)* présentation□ *f*; **I'll give you a k. to him** je te le présenterai□

knocker ['nɒkə(r)] **N 1** *(on door)* heurtoir *m*, marteau *m* (de porte) **2** *Fam (critic)* débineur(euse) *m,f*
• **knockers** **NPL** *very Fam (breasts)* nichons *mpl*

knocking ['nɒkɪŋ] **N 1** *(noise)* bruit *m* de coups, cognement *m* **2** *(in engine)* cognement *m*, cliquetis *m* **3** *Br Fam (injury, defeat)* **to take a k.** *(in fight)* se faire rouer de coups; *(in match)* se faire battre à plate couture; **their prestige took a k.** leur prestige en a pris un coup
▸▸ ***knocking copy*** *(UNCOUNT)* publicité *f* comparative; ***knocking sheet*** = feuille sur laquelle sont inscrits les points faibles de ses principaux concurrents commerciaux; *Br Fam* ***knocking shop*** bordel *m*

knocking-off time **N** *Br Fam* **it's k.** c'est l'heure de se tirer

knock-kneed [-'ni:d] **ADJ** cagneux

knock-on **N** *(in rugby)* en-avant *m inv*
▸▸ ***knock-on effect*** répercussion *f*; **to have a k. effect** déclencher une réaction en chaîne; **businesses are feeling the k. effect of a strong pound** les entreprises subissent le contrecoup d'une livre forte

knockout ['nɒkaʊt] **N 1** *Boxing* knock-out *m inv*, K-O *m*; **to win by a k.** gagner par K-O
2 *Fam (sensation)* **to be a k.** être sensationnel *ou* génial; **she's a k.!** *(beautiful)* elle est canon!
3 *Sport* tournoi *m* (par élimination directe)
4 *(at auction)* entente *f (entre concurrents pour baisser les prix)*
▸▸ ***knockout blow*** *Boxing* coup *m* qui met K-O; *Fig* coup *m* de grâce; **to deliver the k. blow** *Boxing* mettre K-O; *Fig* donner le coup de grâce; *Sport* ***knockout competition*** tournoi *m* par élimination; *Fam* ***knockout drops*** soporifique□ *m*, somnifère□ *m*; ***knockout stages*** *(of competition)* (épreuves *fpl*) éliminatoires *fpl*

knock-up **N** *Br Sport (in ball games)* échauffement *m*; **to have a k.** faire des balles

knoll [nəʊl] **N** monticule *m*, tertre *m*

knot [nɒt] (*pt & pp* **knotted**, *cont* **knotting**) **N 1** *(fastening)* nœud *m*; *Fig (bond)* lien *m*; **to tie sth in a k., to tie a k. in sth** nouer qch, faire un nœud à qch; **to tie/to untie a k.** faire/défaire un nœud; *Fam Fig* **to tie the k.** se maquer; *Br Fam* **tie a k. in it!** ferme-la!
2 *(tangle)* nœud *m*; **the wool is full of knots** la laine est toute emmêlée; *Fig* **my stomach was in knots** j'avais l'estomac noué; *Fam* **to get tied up in knots, to tie oneself (up) in knots** s'emmêler les pinceaux
3 *(in wood)* nœud *m*
4 *Anat & Med* nœud *m*, nodule *m*; *(in muscle)* raideur *f*
5 *(cluster of people)* petit groupe *m*
6 *Naut* nœud *m*; **we are doing 15 knots** nous filons 15 nœuds; *Fig* **at a rate of knots** à toute allure, à un train d'enfer; *Fam* **she was spending her money at a rate of knots** elle jetait l'argent par les fenêtres
VT *(string)* nouer, faire un nœud dans; *(tie)* nouer; **he knotted the rope around his waist** il s'est attaché *ou* noué la corde autour de la taille; **k. the ropes together** noue les cordes ensemble
VI *(stomach)* se nouer; *(muscles)* se contracter, se raidir; **my stomach knotted up with fear** j'avais l'estomac noué par la peur

knotty ['nɒtɪ] (*compar* **knottier**, *superl* **knottiest**) **ADJ 1** *(wood, hands)* noueux **2** *(wool, hair, rope)* plein de nœuds **3** *(question, problem)* épineux

KNOW [nəʊ]

VT
- connaître **1–4, 7, 8, 10**
- savoir **3, 4**
- reconnaître **5**
- distinguer **6**
- discerner **6**
- considérer **9**

VI
- savoir

(*pt* **knew** [nju:], *pp* **known** [nəʊn])
VT 1 *(person)* connaître; **to k. sb by sight/by reputation** connaître qn de vue/de réputation; **we've known each other for years** ça fait des années que nous nous connaissons; **I don't k. him to speak to** je ne le connais pas assez pour lui parler; **I k. him to say hello to** nous nous saluons; **when I first knew her** quand j'ai fait sa connaissance; **knowing him, he'll still be in bed** tel que je le connais, il sera encore au lit; **I'd like to get to k. him better** j'aimerais bien le connaître mieux
2 *(place)* connaître; **I k. Budapest well** je connais bien Budapest
3 *(fact, information)* **do you k. her phone number?** vous connaissez son numéro de téléphone?; **it'll be easier once you get to k. the system** ce sera
plus facile une fois que tu te seras familiari
avec le système; **civilization as we k. it** la civilis
tion telle que nous la connaissons; **how was I**
k. she wouldn't come? comment aurais-je pu s
voir *ou* deviner qu'elle ne viendrait pas?; **I k. fo**
fact that he's lying je sais pertinemment qu
ment; **she is known to be a keen photographer**
sait qu'elle aime beaucoup la photographie;
let it be known that he was available il a fait sav
qu'il était disponible; **I don't k. that it's the b**
solution je ne suis pas certain *ou* sûr que ce s
la meilleure solution; **you don't k.** *or* **you'll nev**
k. how glad I am that it's over tu ne peux pas s
voir combien *ou* à quel point je suis content q
ce soit terminé; **she thinks she knows all the a**
swers elle croit tout savoir; **she didn't quite**
what to say elle ne savait trop que dire; **I k. wh**
I'm talking about je sais de quoi je parle; **I'll**
you k. how it turns out je te dirai comment
s'est passé; **any problems, let me k.** au moinc
problème, n'hésitez pas; **do you k. anythi**
about him that could help us? est-ce que vous s
vez quelque chose à son sujet qui pourrait no
aider?; **do you k. anything about physics?** est-
que tu connais quelque chose en physique
she knows a lot about politics elle s'y connaît
politique; **she doesn't k. what fear is** elle ne s
pas ce que c'est que d'avoir peur; **there's**
knowing how he'll react on ne peut pas sav
comment il réagira; *Fam* **she knows a thing**
two about business elle s'y connaît en affaires
she knows her own mind elle sait ce qu'elle ve
Fam **it's not an easy job – don't I k. it!** ce n'est p
un travail facile – à qui le dis-tu!; *Fam* **would**
you k. it! comme par hasard!; **you k. what I me**
tu vois ce que je veux dire; *Fam* **he was just sort**
lying there, k. what I mean? il était allongé là,
vois; *Fam* **well, what do you k.!** ça alors!, ça p
exemple!; **what do YOU k.?** qu'est-ce que tu
sais?; *very Fam* **you k. what you can do with it!**
sais où tu peux te le mettre!; *Fam* **God** *or* **Heav**
knows why! Dieu sait pourquoi!
4 *(language, skill)* **he knows French** il compre
le français; **I k. a few words of Welsh** je conna
quelques mots de gallois; **she really knows h**
job/subject elle connaît son boulot/sujet; **to**
how to do sth savoir faire qch; **they knew how**
make cars in those days! en ce temps-là, les v
tures, c'était du solide!
5 *(recognize)* reconnaître; **I knew her the m**
ment I saw her je l'ai reconnue dès que je
vue; **I'd k. him anywhere** je le reconnaîtrais n'i
porte où; **I knew her by her walk** je l'ai reconnu
son allure *ou* à sa démarche; **the town centre h**
changed so much you wouldn't k. it le centre-vi
a tellement changé que vous auriez du mal à
reconnaître; **she knows a bargain when she se**
one elle sait reconnaître une bonne affaire;
wouldn't k. a good novel if it hit him il est tout
fait incapable de reconnaître un bon roman
6 *(distinguish)* distinguer, discerner; **she does**
k. right from wrong elle ne sait pas discerner
bien du mal *ou* faire la différence entre le bien
le mal; *Fam* **he doesn't k. one end of a car from a**
other il n'y connaît absolument rien en voit
res□
7 *(experience)* connaître; **I've known povert**
failure j'ai connu la pauvreté/l'échec; **I've nev**
known anything like it je n'ai jamais rien vu
semblable; **I have never known him tell a lie** à
que je sache, il n'a jamais menti; **I've nev**
known him (to) be this late je ne l'ai jamais vu ê
aussi en retard; **it has been known (to happe**
c'est une chose qu'on a vue se produire, ça s'e
vu; **such coincidences have been known** de tell
coïncidences se sont déjà vues
8 *(nickname, call)* **Ian White, known as "Chalk**
Ian White, connu sous le nom de "Chalky
they're known as June bugs in America on les a
pelle des "June bugs" en Amérique
9 *(regard)* considérer; **she's known as one of o**
finest singers elle est considérée comme l'u
de nos meilleures chanteuses
10 *Arch or Bible (have sex with)* connaître
VI savoir; **who knows?** qui sait?; *Fam* **I wouldn't**
je ne saurais dire□; **I don't want to k.** je ne ve
pas le savoir; **when I mentioned that he just did**
want to k. quand j'ai mentionné ça, il n'a rie
voulu savoir; **you never k.** on ne sait jamais;

might *or* **should have known better** ce n'était pas très sage de sa part; **he's old enough to k. better** à son âge, il devrait être plus raisonnable; **you can't blame him, he doesn't k. any better** on ne peut pas lui en vouloir, il ne se rend pas compte; **he always thinks he knows best** il croit toujours avoir raison; **Mother knows best** maman sait de quoi elle parle; **to k. about sth** être au courant de qch; **I've known about it for a week** je le sais *ou* je suis au courant depuis une semaine; **do you k. about the new arrangements?** est-ce que vous êtes au courant *ou* avez-vous entendu parler des nouvelles dispositions?; **he knows about cars** il s'y connaît en voitures; **I don't k. about that** *(I'm not certain)* je n'en suis pas sûr; **I don't k. about you, but I'm exhausted** toi, je ne sais pas, mais moi, je suis épuisé; **to k. of sb/sth** avoir entendu parler de qn/qch; **do you k. her? – well, I k. of her** est-ce que tu la connais? – non, mais j'ai entendu parler d'elle; **do you k. of a good bookshop?** vous connaissez une bonne librairie?; **not that I k. (of)** pas que je sache; **have they got much money? – not that I k. of** ont-ils beaucoup d'argent? – pas que je sache; **it's just so difficult – oh, I k.** c'est tellement difficile – oh, je sais; **it's difficult, I k., but not impossible** c'est difficile, je sais, mais pas impossible; **what's his name? – I don't k.** comment s'appelle-t-il? – je ne sais pas; **are you going to accept? – I don't k.** tu vas accepter? – je ne sais pas

N *(idiom) Fam* **to be in the k.** être au courant□

• **as far as I know ADV** (pour) autant que je sache; **not as far as I k.** pas que je sache; **as far as I k., he lives in London** autant que je sache, il vit à Londres

• **you know ADV 1** *(for emphasis)* **I was right, you k.** j'avais raison, tu sais

2 *(indicating hesitancy)* **he was just, you k., a bit boring** il était juste un peu ennuyeux, si tu vois ce que je veux dire

3 *(to add information)* **it was that blonde woman, you k., the one with the dog** c'était la femme blonde, tu sais, celle avec le chien

4 *(to introduce a statement)* **you k., sometimes I wonder why I do this** tu sais, parfois je me demande pourquoi je fais ça

know-all, *Am* **know-it-all N** *Fam Pej* je-sais-tout *mf*, monsieur *m*/madame *f*/mademoiselle *f* je-sais-tout; **she's a real k.** c'est une vraie (madame) je-sais-tout

know-how N savoir-faire *m inv*, know-how *m inv*; *(technical)* connaissances *fpl* techniques

knowing ['nəʊɪŋ] **ADJ 1** *(look, laugh)* entendu, complice; **she gave him a k. look** elle l'a regardé d'un air entendu **2** *(intelligent, educated)* intelligent, instruit **3** *(cunning)* fin, malin(igne), rusé

knowingly ['nəʊɪŋlɪ] **ADV 1** *(act)* sciemment, consciemment **2** *(look, laugh)* d'un air entendu

know-it-all *Am* = **know-all**

knowledge ['nɒlɪdʒ] **N 1** *(learning)* connaissance *f*, savoir *m*; *(total learning)* connaissances *fpl*; **she has a good k. of English** elle a une bonne connaissance de l'anglais; **he has a basic k. of computing** il a un minimum de connaissances en informatique; **to have a thorough k. of sth** connaître qch à fond; *Prov* **k. is power** savoir c'est pouvoir **2** *(awareness)* connaissance *f*; **I have no k. of what happened** je ne sais absolument rien de *ou* j'ignore totalement ce qui s'est passé; **it has come to my k. that...** j'ai appris que...; **he brought the theft to my k.** il a porté le vol à ma connaissance, il m'a fait part du vol; **to (the best of) my k.** (pour) autant que je sache, à ma connaissance; **not to my k.** pas que je sache; **without my k.** à mon insu, sans que je le sache; **it's (a matter of) common k.** c'est de notoriété publique, personne ne l'ignore

►► *Comput* ***knowledge base*** base *f* de connaissances; ***knowledge economy*** économie *f* de la connaissance; *Comput* ***knowledge engineer*** cogniticien(enne) *m,f*; ***knowledge management*** gestion *f* des connaissances

knowledgeable ['nɒlɪdʒəbəl] **ADJ 1** *(well researched)* bien documenté **2** *(expert)* bien informé; **he's very k. about computing** il connaît bien l'informatique, il s'y connaît en informatique

knowledge-based system N *Comput* système *m* basé sur les connaissances

known [nəʊn] *pp of* **know**

ADJ 1 *(notorious)* connu, notoire; **he's a k. drugs dealer** c'est un revendeur de drogue notoire **2** *(recognized)* reconnu; **she's a k. expert in the field** c'est un expert reconnu *ou* qui fait autorité dans ce domaine; **it's a k. fact** c'est un fait établi; **to make oneself k.** se faire connaître; **to let it be k.** faire savoir

►► ***known reserves*** *(of oil)* réserves *fpl* prouvées

knuckle ['nʌkəl] **N 1** *(of human)* articulation *f ou* jointure *f* (du doigt); *(of animal)* première phalange *f*; **I grazed my knuckles on the wall** je me suis écorché les doigts contre le mur; **near the k.** *(joke, remark)* limite **2** *(joint of meat)* jarret *m*

• **knuckles NPL** *Am* coup-de-poing *m* américain

►► *Fam* ***knuckle sandwich*** coup *m* de poing□; **I gave him a k. sandwich** je lui ai mis mon poing sur la gueule

►**knuckle down VI** *Br* s'y mettre; **we'd better k. down to some work** il vaudrait mieux se mettre *ou* s'atteler au travail

►**knuckle under VI** céder, se soumettre; **don't k. under to the pressure/management** ne cédez pas à la pression/la direction

knuckle-duster N coup-de-poing *m* américain

knurl [nɜːl] **N 1** *(in wood)* nœud *m* **2** *(on screw)* moletage *m*

VT *Tech* moleter

►► *Tech* ***knurled ring*** bague *f* moletée

KO [ˌkeɪ'əʊ] *(pl* **KO's**, *pt & pp* **KO'd**, *cont* **KO'ing**) *Fam (abbr* **knockout**) **N** K-O *m*

VT mettre K-O; *(in boxing)* battre par K-O

koala [kəʊ'ɑːlə] **N** *Zool* koala *m*

►► ***koala bear*** koala *m*

Koch's bacillus [kɒxs-] **N** *Med* bacille *m* de Koch

kohlrabi [kəʊl'rɑːbɪ] **N** chou-rave *m*

kola = **cola**

Komodo dragon, Komodo lizard [kə'məʊdəʊ-] **N** *Zool* dragon *m* de Komodo, varan *m* géant

kook [kuːk] **N** *Am Fam* dingo *m*, cinglé(e) *m,f*

kookaburra ['kʊkəˌbʌrə] **N** *Orn* martin-chasseur *m* (australien), kookaburra *m*

kookie, kooky ['kuːkɪ] *(compar* **kookier**, *superl* **kookiest**) **ADJ** *Am Fam* loufoque, loufedingue

kopeck, kopek ['kəʊpek] **N** kopeck *m*

Koran [kə'rɑːn] **N the K.** le Coran

Koranic [kə'rænɪk] **ADJ** coranique

Korea [kə'rɪə] **N** Corée *f*

Korean [kə'rɪən] **N 1** *(person)* Coréen(enne) *m,f* **2** *(language)* coréen *m*

ADJ coréen

COMP *(embassy)* de Corée; *(history)* de la Corée; *(teacher)* de coréen

►► ***the Korean War*** la guerre de Corée

korma ['kɔːmə] **N** *Culin* **chicken/prawn k.** poulet *m*/crevettes *fpl* korma

kosher ['kəʊʃə(r)] **ADJ 1** *Rel* kasher *(inv)*, cacher *(inv)* **2** *Fam (honest)* honnête□, régulier; **it's not k.** c'est louche, c'est pas catholique

N nourriture *f* kasher

kowtow [ˌkaʊ'taʊ] **VI to k. to sb** faire des courbettes à qn

KP [ˌkeɪ'piː] **N** *Am Fam Mil slang (abbr* **kitchen police**) **looks like we're on KP tonight** on dirait qu'on est de corvée de cuisine ce soir

kph *(written abbr* **kilometres per hour**) km/h

kraft [krɑːft] **N** papier *m* kraft

Krakow ['krækaʊ] **N** Cracovie *f*

Kraut [kraʊt] *Fam Pej* **N** Boche *mf*

ADJ boche

Kremlin ['kremlɪn] **N the K.** le Kremlin

Kremlinologist [ˌkremlɪ'nɒlədʒɪst] **N** kremlinologiste *mf*

krill [krɪl] **N** krill *m*

krona ['krəʊnə] **N** *(in Sweden)* couronne *f* suédoise; *(in Iceland)* couronne *f* islandaise

krone ['krəʊnə] **N** *(in Norway)* couronne *f* norvégienne; *(in Denmark)* couronne *f* danoise

kudos ['kjuːdɒs] **N** gloire *f*, prestige *m*

Ku Klux Klan [ˌkuːklʌks'klæn] **N** Ku Klux Klan *m*

kumquat ['kʌmkwɒt] **N** kumquat *m*

kung fu [ˌkʌŋ'fuː] **N** kung-fu *m inv*

Kurd [kɜːd] **N** Kurde *mf*

Kurdish ['kɜːdɪʃ] **N** *(language)* kurde *m*

ADJ kurde

Kurdistan [ˌkɜːdɪ'stɑːn] **N** Kurdistan *m*

Kuwait [kʊ'weɪt] **N 1** *(country)* Koweït *m* **2** *(city)* **K. (City)** Koweït, Koweit City

Kuwaiti [kʊ'weɪtɪ] **N** Koweïtien(enne) *m,f*

ADJ koweïtien

COMP *(embassy, history)* du Koweït

kV *(written abbr* **kilovolt**) kV

kvetch [kvetʃ] **VI** *Fam* rouspéter

kW *(written abbr* **kilowatt**) kW

kWh *(written abbr* **kilowatt-hour**) kWh

KY jelly® ['keɪwaɪ-] **N** gel *m* intime

Kyoto ['kjəʊtəʊ] **N** Kyoto

►► ***the Kyoto Protocol*** le Protocole de Kyoto

Kyrie ['kɪrɪeɪ] **N** *Rel* **K. (eleison)** Kyrie (eleison) *m inv*

L[1], **l**[1] [el] **N** *(letter)* L, l *m inv*; **two l's** deux l

L[2] **1** (*written abbr* **lake**) lac *m*
2 (*written abbr* **large**) L
3 (*written abbr* **left**) g
4 (*written abbr* **learner**) = lettre apposée sur une voiture et signalant un apprenti conducteur (en Grande-Bretagne), A

l[2] (*written abbr* **litre**) l

LA[1] [ˌelˈeɪ] **N** *(abbr* **Los Angeles***)* Los Angeles

LA[2] (*written abbr* **Louisiana**) Louisiane *f*

la [lɑː] **N** *Mus* la *m*

laager [ˈlɑːgə(r)] **N** *Mil* camp *m*

Lab (*written abbr* **Labour, Labour Party**) parti *m* travailliste

lab [læb] **N 1** *(abbr* **laboratory***)* labo *m* **2** *Fam (abbr* **labrador***)* labrador[□] *m*
COMP *(assistant, equipment, experiment)* de laboratoire
▸▸ ***lab coat*** blouse *f*

label [ˈleɪbəl] (*Br pt & pp* **labelled**, *cont* **labelling**, *Am pt & pp* **labeled**, *cont* **labeling**) **N 1** *also Fig* étiquette *f*; **they brought out the record on the Mega l.** ils ont sorti le disque chez Mega; **it's a good l.** c'est une bonne marque **2** *Comput (of tape, file)* label *m* **3** *Chem* marque *f*
VT 1 *(suitcase, jar)* étiqueter; **you must l. your clothes clearly** tous vos vêtements doivent être clairement marqués à votre nom; **the bottle was labelled "shake before use"** la bouteille portait l'étiquette "agiter avant emploi" **2** *Fig (person)* étiqueter, cataloguer; **he's been labelled (as) a troublemaker** on l'a étiqueté *ou* catalogué comme fauteur de troubles **3** *Chem* marquer

labelling, *Am* **labeling** [ˈleɪbəlɪŋ] **N** étiquetage *m*

labellum [ləˈbeləm] (*pl* **labella** [-lə]) **N** *Bot* labelle *m*

labia [ˈleɪbɪə] **NPL** *Anat* lèvres *fpl*
▸▸ ***labia majora*** grandes lèvres *fpl*; ***labia minora*** petites lèvres *fpl*

labial [ˈleɪbɪəl] *Ling* **N** labiale *f*
ADJ labial
▸▸ ***labial consonant*** consonne *f* labiale

labialize, -ise [ˈleɪbɪəlaɪz] **VT** *Ling* labialiser

labiate [ˈleɪbɪeɪt] *Bot* **N** labiée *f*
ADJ labié

labiodental [ˌleɪbɪəʊˈdentəl] *Ling* **N** labiodentale *f*
ADJ labiodental

labor *Am* = **labour**

laboratory [*Br* ləˈbɒrətrɪ, *Am* ˈlæbrəˌtɔːrɪ] (*pl* **laboratories**) **N** laboratoire *m*; **tested under l. conditions** testé en laboratoire
COMP *(assistant, equipment, experiment)* de laboratoire

laboratory-tested **ADJ** testé en laboratoire

laborious [ləˈbɔːrɪəs] **ADJ** laborieux

laboriously [ləˈbɔːrɪəslɪ] **ADV** laborieusement

laboriousness [ləˈbɔːrɪəsnɪs] **N** caractère *m* laborieux

labour, *Am* **labor** [ˈleɪbə(r)] **N 1** *(work, task)* travail *m*; *(hard effort)* labeur *m*; **a l. of love** un travail fait pour le plaisir **2** *Ind (manpower)* main-d'œuvre *f*; *(workers)* ouvriers *mpl*, travailleurs *mpl*; **cost of l.** prix *m* de la main-d'œuvre; **capital and l.** le capital et la main-d'œuvre **3** *Obst* travail *m*; **to be in l.** être en travail; **to go into l.** commencer le travail
COMP *(shortage)* de main-d'œuvre
VI 1 *(work)* travailler dur **2** *(struggle* ▸ *person)* **he laboured up the stairs** il monta péniblement l'escalier; *Fig* **to l. under a misapprehension** *or* **a delusion** se méprendre, être dans l'erreur **3** *(move with difficulty* ▸ *vehicle)* peiner; **the car laboured up the slope** la voiture peinait dans la montée; **the ship was labouring through heavy seas** le bateau avançait péniblement dans la mer démontée
VT *(stress)* insister sur; **there's no need to l. the point** ce n'est pas la peine de t'étendre *ou* d'insister là-dessus
• **Labour** *Pol* **N** = le parti travailliste britannique; **to vote L.** voter travailliste **ADJ** *(policy, government, MP, victory)* travailliste
▸▸ ***labour camp*** camp *m* de travail; *Am* ***labor contract*** contrat *m* de travail; *Ind* ***labour costs*** coûts *mpl* de la main-d'œuvre; *Am* ***Labor Day*** fête *f* du travail *(aux États-Unis et au Canada, célébrée le premier lundi de septembre)*; ***labour dispute*** conflit *m* du travail; *Br & Can Formerly* ***labour exchange*** agence *f* pour l'emploi; ***labour force*** *(in country)* population *f* active; *(in company)* main-d'œuvre *f*; ***labour law*** droit *m* du travail; ***labour laws*** législation *f* du travail; *Pol* ***Labour leader*** dirigeant(e) *m,f* (du parti) travailliste; ***labour market*** marché *m* du travail; *Pol* ***Labour Member (of Parliament)*** député *m* travailliste; *Ind* ***labour movement*** mouvement *m* ouvrier; *Obst* ***labour pains*** douleurs *fpl* de l'accouchement; *Pol* ***the Labour Party*** le parti travailliste; *Ind* ***labour relations*** relations *fpl* sociales; *Ind* ***labour turnover*** rotation *f* du personnel; *Am* ***labor union*** syndicat *m*; *Pol* ***Labour voter*** = personne qui vote travailliste; *Obst* ***labour ward*** salle *f* d'accouchement

laboured, *Am* **labored** [ˈleɪbəd] **ADJ 1** *(breathing)* pénible, difficile **2** *(style, joke)* lourd, laborieux

labourer, *Am* **laborer** [ˈleɪbərə(r)] **N** *(gen)* ouvrier(ère) *m,f*; *(on building site)* manœuvre *m*

labouring, *Am* **laboring** [ˈleɪbərɪŋ] **ADJ the l. class** la classe ouvrière; **a l. job** un travail manuel

labour-intensive, *Am* **labor-intensive** **ADJ** **craftwork is very l.** le travail artisanal nécessite un travail considérable; **a l. industry** une industrie à forte main-d'œuvre

Labourite [ˈleɪbəraɪt] *Pol* **N** travailliste *mf*
ADJ travailliste

labour-saving device, *Am* **labor-saving device** **N** *(in home)* appareil *m* ménager; *(at work)* = appareil permettant un gain de temps

Labrador [ˈlæbrədɔː(r)] **N** *Geog* Labrador *m*
• **labrador** **N** *(dog)* labrador *m*

laburnum [ləˈbɜːnəm] **N** *Bot* cytise *m*, faux ébénier *m*

labyrinth [ˈlæbərɪnθ] **N** labyrinthe *m*, dédale *m*

labyrinthine [ˌlæbəˈrɪnθaɪn] **ADJ** labyrinthique

lac [læk] **N** gomme *f* laque, laque *f*

lace [leɪs] **N 1** *Tex* dentelle *f* **2** *(in shoe, boot, corset)* lacet *m*
COMP *(handkerchief, tablecloth etc)* en dentelle
VT 1 *(tie)* lacer; *(put laces in)* mettre des lacets **2** *(add alcohol to)* ajouter de l'alcool à; **he lace my orange juice with gin** il a mis du gin dan mon jus d'orange; *Fig* **he laced his story with sal acious details** il ajoutait des détails salaces à so histoire
VI *(shoes, boots)* se lacer

▸ **lace into** **VT INSEP** *Br Fam (physically)* rosser; *(i criticism)* attaquer violemment[□]

▸ **lace up** *Br* **VT SEP** *(shoes, boots)* lacer
VI *(shoes, boots)* se lacer; **they l. up at the side** elles se lacent *ou* s'attachent sur le côté

lacemaker [ˈleɪsˌmeɪkə(r)] **N** dentellier(ère) *m,f*

lacemaking [ˈleɪsˌmeɪkɪŋ] **N** industrie *f* dente lière

lacerate [ˈlæsəreɪt] **VT** lacérer; **his hands were la cerated by the broken glass** il avait les mains lacé rées par le verre brisé; *Fig* **the encounter left he emotions lacerated** la rencontre lui avait déchir le cœur *ou* l'avait meurtrie
▸▸ *Bot* ***lacerate leaves*** feuilles *fpl* dentées *ou* den telées

laceration [ˌlæsəˈreɪʃən] **N 1** *(action)* lacération **2** *(gash)* entaille *f*; **he had deep lacerations on hi back** il avait le dos profondément lacéré *ou* en taillé

lace-up **ADJ** *(shoe, boot)* à lacets
• **lace-ups** **NPL** *Br* chaussures *fpl* à lacets

lacewing [ˈleɪswɪŋ] **N** *Entom* hémérobe *m*

lacework [ˈleɪswɜːk] **N** *(art)* dentellerie *f*
▸▸ ***lacework objects*** objets *mpl* en dentelle

lachrymal [ˈlækrɪməl] **ADJ** lacrymal
▸▸ ***lachrymal duct*** conduit *m* lacrymal; ***lachryma gland*** glande *f* lacrymale

lachrymose [ˈlækrɪməʊs] **ADJ** *Literary* lar moyant

lacing [ˈleɪsɪŋ] **N 1** *(on shoe, garment)* laçage *m* **2** *(of food, drink)* adjonction *f* d'alcool

lack [læk] **N** manque *m*; **through** *or* **for l. of** pa manque de, faute de; **there's no l. of volunteer** ce ne sont pas les volontaires qui manquent
VT manquer de; **they certainly don't l. confidenc** ils ne manquent certes pas de confiance e eux; **we l. the necessary resources** nous n'avon pas les ressources nécessaires; **what the cour try lacks in modern tourist amenities, it more tha makes up for in natural beauty** la beauté naturell du paysage compense largement le manqu d'infrastructures touristiques

lackadaisical [ˌlækəˈdeɪzɪkəl] **ADJ** *(person* ▸ *apathetic)* apathique; *(*▸ *lazy)* indolent

lackey [ˈlækɪ] **N** laquais *m*; *Pej* larbin *m*

lacklustre, *Am* **lackluster** [ˈlækˌlʌstə(r)] **AD** terne

laconic [ləˈkɒnɪk] **ADJ** laconique

laconically [ləˈkɒnɪkəlɪ] **ADV** laconiquement

lacquer [ˈlækə(r)] **N** *(varnish, hairspray)* laque *f*
VT *(wood)* laquer; *(hair)* mettre de la laque sur; **to l. one's hair** se mettre de la laque (sur les che veux)

lacquerwork [ˈlækəwɜːk] **N** *(objects)* laques *mp*

lacrimal = **lachrymal**

acrosse [lə'krɒs] N lacrosse *f*, crosse *f*
COMP *(match, player)* de crosse
▸▸ ***lacrosse stick*** crosse *f*

acrymal = **lachrymal**

actate [læk'teɪt] VI sécréter du lait

actation [,læk'teɪʃən] N lactation *f*

acteal ['læktɪəl] ADJ *Anat & Med* lacté

actic ['læktɪk] ADJ *Chem* lactique
▸▸ ***lactic acid*** acide *m* lactique

actose ['læktəʊs] N lactose *m*

acuna [lə'kjuːnə] (*pl* **lacunas** *or* **lacunae** [-niː]) N lacune *f*

acustrine [lə'kʌstraɪn] ADJ *Biol* lacustre

acy ['leɪsɪ] (*compar* **lacier**, *superl* **laciest**) ADJ *(lace-like)* fin comme de la dentelle; *(made of lace)* en dentelle

ad [læd] N **1** *(young boy)* garçon *m*; *(son)* fils *m*; **he's only a l.** c'est seulement un gamin; **when I was a l.** quand j'étais jeune; **come here, l.** viens ici, mon gars *ou* mon garçon
2 *Br Fam (friend)* copain *m*; *(colleague)* collègue[□] *m*, gars *m*; **he went out for a drink with the lads** il est allé boire un coup avec des copains; **morning, lads!** salut, les gars!; **to be one of the lads** aimer sortir en bande
3 *Br Fam (rake)* noceur *m*; **he was a bit of a l. when he was young** il a eu une jeunesse assez tumultueuse
4 *Br Horseracing* **(stable) l.** lad *m*
▸▸ *Br Fam* ***lad mag*** = magazine destiné à un public d'hommes jeunes

adder ['lædə(r)] N **1** *also Fig* échelle *f*; *also Fig* **to be at the top of the l.** être arrivé au sommet *ou* en haut de l'échelle; *Fig* **to get one's foot on the l.** mettre un pied dans le circuit; **fish** *or* **salmon l.** échelle *f* à saumons **2** *Br (in stocking, tights)* maille *f* filée; **you've got a l. in your stocking** ton bas a filé, tu as filé ton bas
VT *Br (stocking, tights)* filer
VI *Br (stocking, tights)* filer

adderproof ['lædəpruːf] ADJ *Br (stockings, tights)* indémaillable

addie ['lædɪ] N *Scot Fam* gars *m*; **come here, l.** viens là, mon petit gars

addish ['lædɪʃ] ADJ *Br Fam* = typique d'un style de vie caractérisé par de fréquentes sorties entre copains, généralement copieusement arrosées, un comportement arrogant et macho, et un goût prononcé pour le sport et les activités de groupe

aden ['leɪdən] ADJ chargé (**with** de); **I was l. with shopping** j'avais les bras chargés de commissions; **apple-l. trees** arbres *mpl* couverts de pommes; **a heavily l. ship** un navire à forte charge

adette [læ'det] N *Br Fam* = jeune femme se revendiquant l'égale des hommes pour ce qui est des sorties, de la vulgarité etc

a-di-da [,lɑːdɪ'dɑː] *Fam Pej* ADJ *(manner)* snob[□], prétentieux[□]; *(voice)* maniéré[□]; **she speaks in a very l. way** elle est assez pimbêche
ADV d'une façon prétentieuse[□]

adies ['leɪdɪz] *pl of* **lady** N *Br* toilettes *fpl* pour dames; *(sign)* dames; **can you tell me where the l. is?** pouvez-vous m'indiquer où sont les toilettes?
▸▸ *Culin* ***ladies' fingers*** gombo *m*; ***ladies' man*** don Juan *m*, homme *m* à femmes; ***ladies' night*** *(in bar)* = soirée où les femmes ont droit à des réductions; *(in gym)* = soir réservé aux femmes; *Am* ***ladies room*** toilettes *fpl* pour dames

ading ['leɪdɪŋ] N **1** *(action ▸ of ship)* chargement *m*; *(of merchandise)* mise *f* à bord **2** *(cargo)* cargaison *f*, chargement *m*

adle ['leɪdəl] N **1** *(for soup)* louche *f* **2** *Ind* puisoir *m*; *Metal* **foundry l.** poche *f* de fonderie
VT servir (à la louche)

adleful ['leɪdəlfʊl] N pleine louche *f* (**of** de)

ady ['leɪdɪ] (*pl* **ladies**) N **1** *(woman)* dame *f*; **Ladies and Gentlemen** Mesdames et Messieurs; **the l. of the house** la maîtresse de maison; **young l.** *(girl)* jeune fille *f*; *(young woman)* jeune femme *f*; **ask the young l. over there** *(in shop)* demandez à la demoiselle que vous voyez là-bas; **well, young l., what have you got to say for yourself?** eh bien, ma fille, qu'avez-vous à répondre?; *Hum* **ladies who lunch** = femmes de la bourgeoisie qui passent leur temps à faire les magasins et à déjeuner entre amies
2 *(refined woman)* dame *f*; **she's a real l.** c'est une vraie dame; **she's no l.** elle n'a aucune classe
3 *(term of address)* **my L.** Madame
4 *(as title)* **L. Browne** Lady Browne *(titre de noblesse féminin)*; **to act like L. Muck** jouer à la grande dame
5 *Am Fam (term of address)* madame[□] *f*; **hey l.!** eh, ma petite dame!
6 *Old-fashioned (wife)* femme *f*, épouse *f*; **how's your good l.?** comment va votre dame?; **my young l.** *(fiancée)* ma fiancée, ma future
7 *Rel* **Our L.** Notre-Dame *f*
COMP *Old-fashioned* **l. doctor** femme *f* médecin; **l. novelist** romancière *f*; **l. teacher** institutrice *f*
▸▸ *Pej or Hum* ***lady bountiful*** généreuse bienfaitrice *f*; ***Lady Chapel*** chapelle *f* de la Sainte Vierge; ***Lady Day*** (fête *f* de) l'Annonciation *f*; *Culin Br* ***lady's finger***, *Am* ***lady finger*** *(biscuit)* boudoir *m*; ***Lady Luck*** la chance; ***lady's maid*** femme *f* de chambre; ***lady's man*** don Juan *m*, homme *m* à femmes; *Br* ***Lady Mayoress*** femme *f* du maire; *Bot* ***lady's slipper*** sabot-de-Vénus *m*

ladybird ['leɪdɪbɜːd] N *Br* coccinelle *f*

ladyboy ['leɪdɪ,bɔɪ] N = jeune transsexuel asiatique

lady-in-waiting N dame *f* d'honneur

ladykiller ['leɪdɪ,kɪlə(r)] N *Fam* bourreau *m* des cœurs

ladylike ['leɪdɪlaɪk] ADJ *(person)* distingué, bien élevé; *(manners)* raffiné, élégant; **it's not very l. to smoke in the street!** une fille comme il faut ne fume pas dans la rue!

ladyship ['leɪdɪʃɪp] N **Your/Her L.** Madame (la baronne/la vicomtesse/la comtesse); *Fig or Hum* Madame

lag [læg] (*pt & pp* **lagged**, *cont* **lagging**) N **1** *(gap)* décalage *m* **2** *Br very Fam (convict)* **an old l.** un cheval de retour
VT *(pipe)* calorifuger
VI rester en arrière, traîner

▸ **lag behind** VT INSEP *(competitor)* traîner derrière, avoir du retard sur
VI **1** *(dawdle)* traîner, lambiner; *(be at the back)* rester derrière; **the youngest children were lagging behind** les enfants les plus jeunes restaient en arrière **2** *(be outdistanced)* se laisser distancer; **our country is lagging behind in medical research** notre pays a du retard en matière de recherche médicale; **salaries are still lagging behind** les salaires sont restés à un niveau inférieur

lager ['lɑːgə(r)] N *Br (beer)* bière *f* blonde
▸▸ *Br Fam* ***lager lout*** = jeune qui, sous l'influence de l'alcool, cherche la bagarre ou commet des actes de vandalisme

lagered (up) ['lɑːgəd-] ADJ *Br Fam* bourré à la bière; **he gets l. up with his mates every Friday night** tous les vendredi soir, il se bourre la gueule à la bière avec ses potes

laggard ['lægəd] N *(person)* traînard(e) *m,f*

lagging ['lægɪŋ] N **1** *(action)* calorifugeage *m* **2** *(material)* isolant *m*, calorifuge *m*

lagoon [lə'guːn] N *(gen)* lagune *f*; *(in coral reef)* lagon *m*

lah = **la**

lah-di-dah = **la-di-da**

laid [leɪd] *pt & pp of* **lay**

laid-back ADJ *Fam* décontracté[□], cool

lain [leɪn] *pp of* **lie**

lair [leə(r)] N *(for animals)* tanière *f*; *Fig* repaire *m*, tanière *f*

laird [leəd] N laird *m*, propriétaire *m* foncier *(en Écosse)*

lairy ['leərɪ] ADJ *Br & Austr Fam* **they get a bit loud and l. after a few pints** ils deviennent assez lourds et bruyants après quelques pintes

laisser-faire, laissez-faire [,leseɪ'feə] N non-interventionnisme *m*
▸▸ ***laisser-faire economy*** économie *f* basée sur le non-interventionnisme; ***laisser-faire policy*** politique *f* du laisser-faire

laity ['leɪətɪ] N *(UNCOUNT)* **1** *Rel* laïcs *mpl* **2** *(non-specialists)* profanes *mpl*

lake [leɪk] N **1** *Geog* lac *m*; *Fig* **a wine l.** des excédents *mpl* de vin; *Fam* **go jump in a l.!** va te faire cuire un œuf! **2** *(pigment)* laque *f*
• **Lakes** NPL *Br* **the Lakes** le Lake District, la région des lacs *(dans le nord-ouest de l'Angleterre)*
▸▸ ***Lake Baikal*** le lac Baïkal; ***Lake Como*** le lac de Côme; ***Lake Constance*** le lac de Constance; ***the Lake District*** le Lake District, la région des lacs *(dans le nord-ouest de l'Angleterre)*; ***lake dwelling*** habitation *f* lacustre; ***Lake Erie*** le lac Érié; ***Lake Garda*** le lac de Garde; ***Lake Geneva*** le lac Léman, le lac de Genève; ***Lake Huron*** le lac Huron; ***Lake Maggiore*** le lac Majeur; ***Lake Michigan*** le lac Michigan; ***Lake Ontario*** le lac Ontario; ***the Lake Poets*** les lakistes *mpl (poètes anglais du début du XIXème siècle, dont Wordsworth et Coleridge)*; ***Lake Superior*** le lac Supérieur; ***Lake Victoria*** le lac Victoria

Lakeland ['leɪklənd] ADJ *(of or in the Lake District)* de la région des lacs

lakeshore ['leɪkʃɔː(r)], **lakeside** ['leɪksaɪd] N rive *f* d'un lac
ADJ au bord du lac

lam [læm] (*pt & pp* **lammed**, *cont* **lamming**) *Fam* VT *(beat)* rosser
N *Am (escape)* cavale *f*; **on the l.** en cavale; **to take it on the l.** faire la belle

lama ['lɑːmə] N *Rel* lama *m*

lamb [læm] N **1** *(animal)* agneau *m*; **like lambs to the slaughter** comme des veaux que l'on mène à l'abattoir **2** *(meat)* agneau *m* **3** *Fig (innocent person)* agneau *m*; *(lovable person)* **be a l. and fetch my glasses** sois un ange *ou* sois gentil, va me chercher mes lunettes; **you poor l.!** mon pauvre chou!
COMP *(chop, cutlet)* d'agneau
VI agneler, mettre bas
▸▸ *Rel* ***the Lamb of God*** l'Agneau *m* de Dieu; ***lamb's lettuce*** mâche *f*; *Fam* ***lamb's tails*** *(of hazel tree)* chatons *mpl*

lambada [,læm'bɑːdə] N lambada *f*

lambast [læm'bæst], **lambaste** [læm'beɪst] VT *(scold)* réprimander; *(thrash)* battre, rosser

lambing ['læmɪŋ] N agnelage *m*; **at l. time** au moment de l'agnelage

lambskin ['læmskɪn] N (peau *f* d')agneau *m*
COMP *(coat, gloves)* en agneau

lambswool ['læmzwʊl] COMP *(scarf, sweater etc)* en laine d'agneau, en lambswool

lame [leɪm] ADJ **1** *(person, horse)* boiteux; **to be l.** boiter; **to go l.** se mettre à boiter; **his left leg is l., he's l. in his left leg** il boite de la jambe gauche **2** *(weak ▸ excuse)* piètre, bancal; *(▸ argument, reasoning)* boiteux; *(▸ plot)* boiteux, bancal; **what a l. joke!** quelle blague idiote! **3** *Am Fam (conventional)* vieux jeu[□] *(inv)*; *(stupid)* cloche, nouille
VT estropier
N *Am Fam (stupid person)* andouille *f*, cruche *f*
NPL **the l.** les boiteux *mpl*
▸▸ *Fig* ***lame duck*** *(gen) & Ind* canard *m* boiteux; *Am Pol* = candidat sortant non réélu qui attend l'arrivée de son successeur

lamé ['lɑːmeɪ] N lamé *m*; **a gold l. dress** une robe en lamé d'or

lamebrain ['leɪmbreɪn] N *Fam* crétin(e) *m,f*, andouille *f*

lamely ['leɪmlɪ] ADV de façon peu convaincante, maladroitement

lameness ['leɪmnɪs] N **1** *(limping)* boiterie *f*, *Spec* claudication *f*; **his l. is the result of a childhood accident** il boite à la suite d'un accident qu'il a eu dans son enfance **2** *(weakness ▸ of excuse, argument etc)* faiblesse *f*

lament [lə'ment] VT *(feel sorrow for)* regretter, pleurer; *(complain about)* se lamenter sur, se plaindre de; **she lamented the passing of her youth** elle pleurait sa jeunesse perdue; **"I'll never finish in time!" she lamented** "je n'aurai jamais fini à temps!" gémit-elle
VI se lamenter; **she was lamenting loudly over the loss of her jewels** elle se lamentait bruyamment *ou* à grands cris d'avoir perdu ses bijoux
N **1** *(lamentation, complaint)* lamentation *f* **2** *(poem)* élégie *f*; *(song)* complainte *f*

lamentable ['læməntəbəl] ADJ *(regrettable)* regrettable; *(poor)* lamentable

lamentably ['læməntəblı] ADV lamentablement

lamentation [ˌlæmən'teıʃən] N lamentation *f*

• **Lamentations** NPL *Bible* **the Lamentations (of Jeremiah)** les Lamentations *fpl* (de Jérémie)

lamented [lə'mentıd] ADJ **the late l. Mr Jones** le regretté M. Jones

laminate ['læmıneıt] *Tech* VT **1** *(bond in layers)* laminer; *(glass)* feuilleter; *(plastic)* stratifier; *(wood)* contreplaquer
2 *(split)* diviser en lamelles
3 *(veneer)* plaquer
4 *(document, card)* plastifier
VI **1** *(bond)* se laminer **2** *(split)* se diviser en lamelles
N stratifié *m*

laminated ['læmıneıtıd] ADJ **1** *(glass)* feuilleté; *(plastic)* stratifié; *(wood)* contreplaqué **2** *(document, card)* plastifié
►► ***laminated spring*** ressort *m* à lames (superposées); ***laminated windscreen*** pare-brise *m inv* (en verre) feuilleté

lamination [ˌlæmı'neıʃən] N *Typ* pelliculage *m*

Lammas ['læməs] N **L. (Day)** le premier août

lammergeier ['læməˌgaıə(r)] N *Orn* gypaète *m* barbu

lamp [læmp] N **1** *(gen)* lampe *f*; *(street lamp)* réverbère *m*; *(on car, train)* lumière *f*, feu *m* **2** *Med* lampe *f*
VT *Scot Fam (hit) (once)* filer un gnon à; *(more than once)* dérouiller, filer une raclée à
►► ***lamp bracket*** applique *f*; ***lamp standard*** lampadaire *m*

lampblack ['læmpblæk] N noir *m* de carbone *ou* de fumée

lamplight ['læmplaıt] N **her hair shone in the l.** la lumière de la lampe faisait briller ses cheveux; **to read/work by l.** lire/travailler à la lumière d'une lampe

lamplit ['læmplıt] ADJ éclairé par une lampe

lampoon [læm'pu:n] N *(satire)* satire *f*; *(written)* pamphlet *m*
VT ridiculiser, tourner en dérision

lampoonist [læm'pu:nıst] N *(satirist)* satiriste *mf*; *(in writings)* pamphlétaire *mf*

lamppost ['læmppəust] N réverbère *m*

lamprey ['læmprı] N *Ich* lamproie *f*

lampshade ['læmpʃeıd] N abat-jour *m inv*

lampstand ['læmpstænd] N pied *m* de lampe

LAN [læn] N *Comput (abbr* **local area network**) réseau *m* local

lance [lɑ:ns] N *(weapon)* lance *f*; *Br Fig* **to break a l. with sb** se disputer avec qn
VT *Med* percer, inciser
►► *Br* ***lance corporal*** caporal *m*, *Suisse* appointé *m*

lanceolate ['lɑ:nsıəˌleıt], **lanceolated** ['lɑ:nsıəˌleıtıd] ADJ lancéolé

lancer ['lɑ:nsə(r)] N *Hist & Mil* lancier *m*
• **lancers** NPL *(dance)* (quadrille *m* des) lanciers *mpl*

lancet ['lɑ:nsıt] N *Med* lancette *f*, bistouri *m*
►► *Archit* ***lancet arch*** arc *m* lancéolé *ou* en lancette; *Archit* ***lancet window*** fenêtre *f* en ogive

Lancs *(written abbr* **Lancashire**) Lancashire *m*

LAND [lænd]

N
• terre **1, 2, 4**
• terres **2**
• région **3**
• pays **5, 6**
• royaume **6**

VT
• poser **1**
• débarquer **1**
• hisser **2**
• décrocher **3**
• ficher **4**
• flanquer **5**

VI
• atterrir **1, 4**
• arriver à quai **2**
• débarquer **2**
• tomber **3**
• se réceptionner **3**
• se poser **3**
• finir **4**

N **1** *(for farming, building etc)* terre *f*; **he works on the l.** il travaille la terre; **this is good farming l.** c'est de la bonne terre; **building l.** terrain *m* constructible; **l. for sale** *(sign)* terrain à vendre; **a piece of l.** *(for farming)* un lopin de terre; *(for building)* un terrain (à bâtir); **to live off the l.** vivre des ressources naturelles de la terre; *Fig* **to see how the l. lies, to find out the lie** *or* **lay of the l.** tâter le terrain
2 *(property)* terre *f*, terres *fpl*; **their lands were confiscated** leurs terres ont été confisquées; **get off my l.!** sortez de mes terres!
3 *(area, region)* région *f*; **the desert lands of Northern Australia** les régions *fpl* désertiques du nord de l'Australie
4 *(not sea)* terre *f*; *Naut* **to make l.** reconnaître la terre; *Naut* **they sighted l.** ils aperçurent la terre; **we travelled by l. to Cairo** nous sommes allés au Caire par la route; **over l. and sea** sur terre et sur mer
5 *Literary or Formal (nation, country)* pays *m*; **to travel in distant lands** voyager dans des pays lointains; **the victory was celebrated throughout the l.** le pays tout entier a fêté la victoire; **a l. of opportunity** un pays où tout est possible
6 *Fig (realm)* royaume *m*, pays *m*; **he is no longer in the l. of the living** il n'est plus de ce monde; **she lives in a l. of make-believe** elle vit dans un monde de chimères
VT **1** *(plane)* poser; *(cargo, passengers)* débarquer; **they landed him on the deck of the ferry** ils l'ont fait atterrir sur le pont du ferry; **they have succeeded in landing men on the moon** ils ont réussi à envoyer des hommes sur la Lune
2 *(fish* ► *onto bank)* hisser sur la rive; *(*► *onto boat)* hisser dans le bateau
3 *Fam (job, contract)* décrocher
4 *Fam (put, place)* ficher; **he caught me a blow that nearly landed me in the water** il m'a flanqué un tel coup que j'ai bien failli me retrouver dans l'eau; **this could l. us in real trouble** ça pourrait nous attirer de gros ennuis *ou* nous mettre dans le pétrin; **you've landed us in a nice mess!** tu nous as mis dans de beaux draps!; **it'll l. you in prison!** tu finiras en prison!
5 *Fam (blow)* flanquer; **I landed him a blow** *or* **landed him one on the nose** je lui ai flanqué *ou* collé mon poing dans la figure
6 *Fam (encumber)* **I got landed with the job of organizing the party** c'est moi qui me suis retrouvé avec la fête à organiser□, c'est moi qui me suis tapé l'organisation de la fête; **I've been landed with the job of telling him** c'est à moi qu'il est revenu de le lui dire; **we got landed with their children for the weekend** ils nous ont refilé leurs gosses *ou* il a fallu se farcir leurs gosses tout le week-end; **as usual, I got landed with all the work** comme d'habitude, c'est moi qui me suis tapé tout le travail; **they landed me with the bill** c'est moi qui ai écopé de l'addition
VI **1** *Aviat & Astron* atterrir; **they l. at 7 p.m.** ils atterrissent *ou* leur avion arrive à 19 heures; **to l. on the moon** atterrir sur la Lune, alunir; **to l. in the sea** amerrir
2 *Naut (boat)* arriver à quai; *(passengers)* débarquer
3 *(ball)* tomber, retomber; *(gymnast, ski-jumper, horse, high jumper)* se réceptionner; *(falling object, bomb, parachutist)* tomber; *(bird)* se poser; **an apple/the ball landed on her head** elle a reçu une pomme/le ballon sur la tête; **to l. on one's feet** retomber sur ses pieds; *(of cat)* retomber sur ses pattes; *Fam Fig* **he always manages to l. on his feet** il arrive toujours à retomber sur ses pattes
4 *Fam (finish up)* finir□, atterrir; **he slipped and landed in a puddle** il a glissé et a atterri dans une flaque d'eau; **I hope that problem doesn't l. on my desk** j'espère que ce problème ne va pas atterrir sur mon bureau; **the car landed in the ditch** la voiture a terminé sa course dans le fossé□; **he landed in jail** il s'est retrouvé en prison□
COMP *(prices* ► *in town)* du terrain; *(*► *in country)* de la terre; *(ownership)* foncier; *Br Hist (army)* de terre; *(worker)* agricole
►► ***land agent*** *(administrator)* régisseur *m*, intendant(e) *m,f*; *Br (estate agent)* agent *m* immobilier; ***land bank*** crédit *m* foncier; ***land breeze*** brise *f* de terre; ***land bridge*** isthme *m*; *Acct* ***land charge*** dette *f* foncière; *Zool* ***land crab*** crabe *m* terrestre; ***Land's End*** = pointe de la Cornouailles; ***the Lan[d] of the Midnight Sun*** la terre du soleil de minui[t]; ***land reform*** réforme *f* agraire; ***land register, lan[d] registry*** cadastre *m*; ***land registry office*** burea[u] *m* du cadastre; ***land route*** voie *f* de terre; ***lan[d] tax*** impôt *m* foncier, contribution *f* foncière

► **land up** VI *Fam (finish up)* finir□, atterrir; **the le[t]ter landed up in Finland** la lettre a atterri en Fi[n]lande; **you'll l. up in jail!** tu finiras en prison!; **landed up at a friend's house** j'ai atterri *ou* échou[é] chez un ami; **I landed up having to dance with hi[m]** il a fallu que je danse avec lui□; **I always lande[d] up with the worst jobs** je me tapais toujours le[s] tâches les plus ingrates

landau ['lændɔ:] N landau *m*

landed ['lændıd] ADJ *Br* foncier
►► *Com* ***landed cost*** *(of goods)* prix *m* à quai; *Fi[n]* ***landed costs*** coûts *mpl* fonciers; ***the landed ge[n]try*** la noblesse terrienne; ***landed immigrant*** résident(e) *m,f* permanent(e); ***landed propert[y]*** propriété *f* foncière *ou* territoriale; ***landed pr[o]prietor*** propriétaire *mf* terrien(enne)

landfall ['lændfɔ:l] N *Naut (arrival)* atterrissag[e] *m*; *(sight of land)* arrivée *f* en vue de terre; **to mak[e] l.** apercevoir la terre, arriver en vue d'une côte

landfill ['lændfıl] N ensevelissement *m* de dé[] chets; **to use sth as l.** utiliser qch pour remblaye[r] *ou* comme remblai
►► ***landfill site*** décharge *f* publique

landing ['lændıŋ] N **1** *(of plane, spacecraft)* atte[r]rissage *m*; *(on moon)* alunissage *m*; *(on sea)* amerrissage *m*; *(on deck of ship)* appontage *m* *(of passengers, foods)* débarquement *m*; *Hist* **th[e] Normandy landings** le débarquement (en No[r]mandie)
2 *Sport (of skier, high jumper, gymnast)* réceptio[n] *f*; **he made a bad l.** il s'est mal reçu
3 *(in staircase)* palier *m*; *(floor)* étage *m*
4 *(jetty)* débarcadère *m*, embarcadère *m*
►► *Aviat* ***landing beacon*** balise *f* d'atterrissage; ***landing card*** carte *f* de débarquement; ***landin[g] certificate*** certificat *m* de déchargement; ***landin[g] charges*** frais *mpl* de déchargement; ***landing cra[ft]*** navire *m* de débarquement; ***landing field*** terrai[n] *m* d'atterrissage; ***landing flap*** volet *m* d'atterris[]sage; *Mil & Naut* ***landing force*** troupes *fpl* de dé[]barquement; *Aviat* ***landing gear*** train [*m*] d'atterrissage; ***landing lights*** *(on plane)* phare[s] *mpl* d'atterrissage; *(at airport)* balises *fpl* (d'atte[r]rissage); ***landing net*** épuisette *f* *(filet)*; ***landin[g] operation*** opération *f* de débarquement; ***landin[g] order*** permis *m* de débarquement; *Mil & Na[ut]* ***landing party*** compagnie *f* de débarquemen[t]; *Com* ***landing and port charges*** frais *mpl* de déba[r]quement et de port; ***landing stage*** débarcadè[re] *m*; ***landing strip*** piste *f* d'atterrissage; ***landin[g] wheels*** train *m* d'atterrissage; *Mil & Aviat* ***landin[g] zone*** zone *f* d'atterrissage *(des troupes aéropo[r]tées)*

landlady ['lændˌleıdı] *(pl* **landladies**) N **1** *(fro[m] whom one rents accommodation* ► *owner)* pro[]priétaire *f*; *(*► *living on premises)* logeuse *f* **2** *B[r] (of pub* ► *owner)* propriétaire *f*; *(*► *manager)* gé[]rante *f* **3** *(of small hotel)* aubergiste *f*, hôtelière *f* *(of guesthouse)* patronne *f*

landlegs ['lændlegz] NPL *Fam* **to get one's l.** *(sai[l]or)* se familiariser de nouveau avec la terre□

landless ['lændlıs] ADJ sans terre

landlocked ['lændlɒkt] ADJ *(country)* enclavé sans accès à la mer; *(sea)* intérieur

landlord ['lændlɔ:d] N **1** *(of property)* bailleur *m* *(from whom one rents accommodation* ► *owne[r])* propriétaire *m*; *(*► *living on premises)* logeur *m* [**2**] *Br (of pub* ► *owner)* propriétaire *m*; *(*► *manage[r])* gérant *m*; *(form of address)* patron *m* **3** *(lan[d] owner)* propriétaire *m* (foncier)

landlubber ['lændˌlʌbə(r)] N *Fam Hum* terrien *m*, éléphant *m*

landmark ['lændmɑ:k] N **1** *(building, statue et[c])* point *m* de repère; **the major Paris landmarks** le[s] principaux monuments de Paris **2** *Fig* étape décisive, jalon *m*; *Fig* **the trial was a l. in legal hi[s]tory** le procès a fait date dans les annales juridi[]ques
COMP *(decision, book)* qui fait date; *(case, victory)* décisif

▸▸ **landmark building** bâtiment *m* reconnaissable

andmass ['lændmæs] **N** étendue *f* de terre; **the American l.** le continent américain

andowner ['lænd,əʊnə(r)] **N** propriétaire *mf* foncier(ère)

andowning ['lænd,əʊnɪŋ] **ADJ**
▸▸ ***the landowning classes*** la classe des propriétaires fonciers

andscape ['lændskeɪp] **N 1** *(gen)* paysage *m*; *Fig* **the political l.** le paysage politique **2** *Comput & Typ (paper format)* (format *m*) paysage *m*; **to print sth in l.** *Comput* imprimer qch en (mode) paysage; *Typ* imprimer qch à l'italienne
ADJ *Comput* paysage *(inv)*; *Typ* à l'italienne
VT *(garden)* dessiner; *(waste land)* aménager; **they had their garden landscaped** ils ont fait dessiner leur jardin par un paysagiste
▸▸ ***landscape architect*** architecte *mf* paysagiste; ***landscape architecture*** architecture *f* de paysage; ***landscape design*** architecture *f* de paysage; ***landscape designer*** paysagiste *mf*; *Hort* ***landscape gardener*** jardinier(ère) *m,f* paysagiste; *Hort* ***landscape gardening*** paysagisme *m*; *Comput* ***landscape mode*** mode *m* paysage; *Art* ***landscape painter*** (peintre *m*) paysagiste *mf*; ***landscape painting*** le paysage

andscaping ['lænd,skeɪpɪŋ] **N** aménagement *m* paysager

andslide ['lændslaɪd] **N 1** *(of earth, rocks)* glissement *m* de terrain **2** *(victory)* victoire *f* écrasante; **to win the elections by a l.** gagner les élections avec une majorité écrasante
COMP *(majority, victory)* écrasant

andslip ['lændslɪp] **N** *Br* éboulement *m*

andward ['lændwəd] *Naut* **ADJ** du côté de la terre; **l. breeze** vent *m* marin *ou* qui souffle de la mer; **on the l. side** du côté terre
ADV en direction de la terre; *(on land)* vers l'intérieur (des terres)

ane [leɪn] **N 1** *(road ▸ in country)* chemin *m* **2** *(for traffic)* voie *f*; *(line of vehicles)* file *f*; *(for shipping, aircraft)* couloir *m*; **get into the right-hand l.** mettez-vous dans la file *ou* sur la voie de droite; **keep in l.** *(sign)* ne changez pas de file; **get in l.** *(sign)* mettez-vous sur la bonne file; **a 4-l. road** une route à 4 voies; **to be in the wrong l.** être dans la mauvaise file; **traffic is reduced to two lanes** la circulation ne se fait plus que sur deux voies **3** *(in athletics, swimming)* couloir *m*
▸▸ ***lane closure*** fermeture *f* de voies; **the traffic was held up by l. closures** la circulation a été ralentie par des rétrécissements de voie (dus à des travaux); ***lane markings*** *(on road)* signalisation *f* au sol *ou* horizontale des voies; *Sport (on track)* lignes *fpl* de marquage des couloirs; *(in swimming pool)* lignes *fpl* d'eau

anglauf ['lænlaʊf] **N** ski *m* de fond
▸▸ ***langlauf skier*** skieur(euse) *m,f* de fond

anguage ['læŋgwɪdʒ] **N 1** *(concept, vocabulary)* langage *m*; **the child's acquisition of l.** l'acquisition du langage par l'enfant
2 *(specific tongue)* langue *f*; *Sch & Univ (area of study)* langue *f*; **the French l.** la langue française; **to study languages** faire des études de langue; **to speak the same l.** parler le même langage; *Fig* **you speak my l.** nous parlons le même langage; *Fig* **we don't talk the same l.** nous ne parlons pas le même langage
3 *(code)* langage *m*; **a computer l.** un langage machine; **the l. of love/flowers** le langage de l'amour/des fleurs
4 *(terminology)* langue *f*, langage *m*; **medical/legal l.** langage *m* médical/juridique; **the l. of diplomacy** *(jargon)* le langage diplomatique
5 *(manner of expression)* expression *f*, langue *f*; **I find his l. very pompous** je trouve qu'il s'exprime avec emphase *ou* de façon très pompeuse
6 *(rude words)* gros mots *mpl*, grossièretés *fpl*; **(mind your) l.!** surveille ton langage!
COMP *(acquisition)* du langage; *(teaching, learning)* des langues; *(course)* de langues; *(barrier)* linguistique; *(student)* en langues
▸▸ ***language laboratory***, *Fam* ***language lab*** labo *m* de langues; ***language studies*** études *fpl* de langues

> When translating **language**, note that **langue** and **langage** are not interchangeable. **Langue** is used when talking about a specific language used in a country or region, while **langage** refers to the concept of language in general or to a set of vocabulary or terminology.

languid ['læŋgwɪd] **ADJ** langoureux, alangui

languidly ['læŋgwɪdlɪ] **ADV** langoureusement

languidness ['læŋgwɪdnɪs] **N** langueur *f*

languish ['læŋgwɪʃ] **VI 1** *(suffer)* languir; **to l. in prison** croupir en prison **2** *(become weak)* dépérir; **to l. in the heat** *(plant)* dépérir à la chaleur; *(person)* souffrir de la chaleur; **the project was languishing for lack of funds** le projet traînait, faute d'argent **3** *Literary (pine)* languir

languishing ['læŋgwɪʃɪŋ] **ADJ** langoureux, alangui

languor ['læŋgə(r)] **N** langueur *f*

languorous ['læŋgərəs] **ADJ** langoureux

languorously ['læŋgərəslɪ] **ADV** langoureusement

lank [læŋk] **ADJ** *(hair)* terne; *(plant)* étiolé, grêle

lankness ['læŋknɪs] **N** *(of hair)* aspect *m* terne

lanky ['læŋkɪ] *(compar* **lankier**, *superl* **lankiest)** **ADJ** grand et maigre, efflanqué

lanolin, lanoline ['lænəlɪn] **N** lanoline *f*

lantana [læn'tænə] **N** *Bot* lantana *m*

lantern ['læntən] **N** *(lamp)* lanterne *f*; *Naut (of lighthouse)* fanal *m*
▸▸ ***lantern slide*** plaque *f* de lanterne magique

lantern-jawed [-dʒɔːd] **ADJ** aux joues creuses

lanyard ['lænjəd] **N** corde *f*, cordon *m*; *Naut* ride *f*

Laos [laʊs] **N** Laos *m*

Laotian ['laʊʃən] **N 1** *(person)* Laotien(enne) *m,f* **2** *(language)* laotien *m*
ADJ laotien
COMP *(embassy, history)* du Laos; *(teacher)* de laotien

lap [læp] *(pt & pp* **lapped**, *cont* **lapping)** **N 1** *(knees)* genoux *mpl*; **come and sit on my l.** viens t'asseoir sur mes genoux; *Fam* **don't think it's just going to fall into your l.!** ne t'imagine pas que ça va te tomber tout cuit dans le bec!; *Fig* **to drop sth in sb's l.** coller qch à qn; **it's in the l. of the gods** c'est entre les mains des dieux; **to live in the l. of luxury** vivre dans le plus grand luxe
2 *Sport* tour *m* de piste; **we ran two laps** nous avons fait deux tours de piste; **a 30-l. race** une course sur 30 tours; **the last l.** le tour de l'arrivée, le dernier tour (avant l'arrivée); *Fig* **we're on the last l.** on arrive au bout de nos peines; **l. of honour** tour *m* d'honneur
3 *(of journey)* étape *f*
4 *Tech (overlap)* recouvrement *m*; *Constr (of tiles, slates)* chevauchement *m*, recouvrement *m*
5 *(of wire around cylinder etc)* tour *m*
VT 1 *Sport (competitor, car)* dépasser, prendre un tour d'avance sur; **the slower drivers were soon lapped by the leaders** les pilotes les plus rapides n'ont pas tardé à prendre un tour d'avance sur les autres concurrents
2 *(time)* chronométrer; **Kelly was lapped at over 200 mph** Kelly a été chronométré sur un tour à plus de 300 km/h
3 *(milk)* laper
4 *(of waves)* clapoter contre
5 *(wrap)* **to l. sth round sth** enrouler qch autour de qch
6 *Constr (planks)* enchevaucher, poser à recouvrement; *(tiles)* donner du recouvrement à; **to l. a joint with sheet metal** chaperonner un assemblage
VI 1 *Sport* tourner, faire un tour de circuit; **Kelly was lapping at over 200 mph** Kelly tournait à plus de 300 km/h de moyenne **2** *(waves)* clapoter; **the waves lapped against the boat** les vagues clapotaient contre le bateau
▸▸ *Aut* ***lap belt*** ceinture *f* ventrale; ***lap dancer*** = entraîneuse qui danse nue pour un client; ***lap dancing*** = type de danse exécutée pour un client par une entraîneuse nue; *Cin & TV* ***lap dissolve*** fondu *m* enchaîné; *Tech* ***lap joint*** enchevauchure *f*, assemblage *m* par recouvrement; *Am* ***lap robe*** plaid *m*; *Aut* ***lap and shoulder belt*** ceinture *f* trois points; *Metal* ***lap weld*** soudure *f* à recouvrement; *Metal* ***lap welding*** soudage *m* à recouvrement

▸**lap up VT SEP 1** *(milk)* laper **2** *Fam Fig (praise)* boire; *(information)* avaler, gober; **he laps up every word she says** il gobe tout ce qu'elle dit; **they were all paying her compliments and she was just lapping it up** tous lui faisaient des compliments et elle s'en délectait

laparoscope ['læpərəskəʊp] **N** laparoscope *m*

laparoscopy [,læpə'rɒskəpɪ] **N** laparoscopie *f*

laparotomy [,læpə'rɒtəmɪ] *(pl* **laparotomies)** **N** *Med* laparotomie *f*

lapdog ['læpdɒg] **N** petit chien *m* d'appartement; *Fig Pej (person)* toutou *m*, caniche *m*

lapel [lə'pel] **N** revers *m*; **he grabbed me by the lapels** il m'a saisi par le revers de ma veste

lapidary ['læpɪdərɪ] *(pl* **lapidaries)** **N** lapidaire *m*
ADJ *(cut in stone)* lapidaire

lapis lazuli [,læpɪs'læzjʊlaɪ] **N** lapis *m*, lapis-lazuli *m inv*

Lapland ['læplænd] **N** Laponie *f*

Laplander ['læplændə(r)] **N** Lapon(one) *m,f*

Lapp [læp] **N 1** *(person)* Lapon(one) *m,f* **2** *(language)* lapon *m*
ADJ lapon

lapping ['læpɪŋ] **N** *(of waves)* clapotis *m*

lapse [læps] **N 1** *(failure)* **l. of memory** trou *m* de mémoire; **l. in concentration** moment *m* d'inattention
2 *(in behaviour)* écart *m* (de conduite); *(in standards)* baisse *f*; **she has occasional lapses** elle fait des bêtises de temps en temps; **the slightest l. was punished harshly** la moindre faute était sévèrement punie
3 *(interval)* laps *m* de temps, intervalle *m*; **after a l. of six months** au bout de six mois
4 *(of contract)* expiration *f*; *(of custom)* disparition *f*; *(of legal right)* déchéance *f*
VI 1 *(decline)* baisser, chuter; *Rel* **to l. from grace** pécher; **he only lapsed once** il n'a fait qu'une seule erreur; **his concentration lapsed for a split second** il a relâché sa concentration pendant une fraction de seconde; **if standards of education are allowed to l.** si on laisse baisser les niveaux scolaires
2 *(drift)* tomber; **she lapsed into a coma** elle est tombée dans le coma; **to l. into bad habits** prendre de mauvaises habitudes; **to l. into silence** garder le silence, s'enfermer dans le silence; **she kept lapsing into Russian** elle repassait sans cesse au russe
3 *(pass ▸ time)* passer
4 *(law, custom)* tomber en désuétude; *(licence, passport)* se périmer; *(subscription)* prendre fin, expirer; *(estate)* devenir disponible; *(legacy)* devenir caduc; **he let his insurance l.** il a laissé périmer son assurance
5 *Rel (cease practising one's faith)* cesser de pratiquer

lapsed [læpst] **ADJ** *(law)* caduc; *(passport)* périmé; *Fin (fund)* périmé
▸▸ ***lapsed Catholic*** catholique *mf* qui ne pratique plus; *St Exch* ***lapsed option*** option *f* expirée

laptop ['læptɒp] **N** ordinateur *m* portable, *Can* ordinateur *m* portatif
▸▸ ***laptop computer*** ordinateur *m* portable, *Can* ordinateur *m* portatif

lapwing ['læpwɪŋ] **N** *Orn* vanneau *m*

larceny ['lɑːsənɪ] *(pl* **larcenies)** **N** *Law* vol *m* simple, larcin *m*

larch [lɑːtʃ] **N** *Bot* mélèze *m*

lard [lɑːd] **N** saindoux *m*; *Fam* **he's a tub of l.** c'est un sac de graisse
VT larder; *Fig* **an essay larded with quotations** une rédaction truffée de citations

> Note that the French word **lard** is a false friend. Its most common meaning is **bacon**.

lardarse ['lɑːdɑːs], *Am* **lardass** ['lɑːdæs] **N** *very Fam (man)* gros *m* plein de soupe; *(woman)* grosse vache *f*

larder ['lɑːdə(r)] N *(room)* cellier *m*; *(cupboard)* garde-manger *m inv*; *Fam* **to raid the l.** faire une razzia dans le garde-manger

lardy ['lɑːdɪ] ADJ *Fam* gros

large [lɑːdʒ] ADJ **1** *(in size)* grand; *(family)* grand, nombreux; *(person ▸ fat)* gros (grosse); *(▸ tall)* grand; *(organization)* gros (grosse), grand; **l. size** *(clothes)* grande taille *f*; *(of product)* grand modèle *m*; **on a l. scale** à grande échelle; **to a l. extent** dans une large mesure; **she's a l. woman** c'est une femme plutôt grosse *ou* forte

2 *(in number, amount)* grand, important; **a l. proportion** une grande proportion, une part importante; **she wrote him a l. cheque** elle lui a fait un chèque pour une somme importante *ou* une grosse somme; **a l. helping of potatoes/apple pie** une grosse portion de pommes de terre/part de tarte aux pommes; **a l. number of** beaucoup de; **to grow** *or* **get larger** *(town, deficit)* s'agrandir; *(person, amount)* grossir; **he was standing there as l. as life** il était là, en chair et en os; **larger than life** exagéré, outrancier

3 *(extensive, significant ▸ changes)* considérable, important; **a l. part of my time/job/day** une grande partie de mon temps/mon travail/la journée

4 *(liberal ▸ views, ideas)* libéral, large

5 *(generous ▸ heart)* grand, généreux

ADV **1 to loom l.** menacer, sembler imminent; **to be writ l.** être évident **2** *Br Fam (to a large extent)* **Arsenal got thrashed l.** Arsenal s'est fait ratatiner *ou* s'est fait battre à plate(s) couture(s); **we got ratted l. last night** on s'est pris une cuite maison hier soir

N *(size)* **I take a l.** je prends une grande taille; **this T-shirt's a l.** ce tee-shirt est une grande taille

• **at large** ADJ *(at liberty)* en liberté; *(prisoner)* en fuite; **the rapist is at l. somewhere in the city** le violeur se promène en (toute) liberté quelque part dans cette ville; **he was acting as the UN's ambassador at l.** il a été ambassadeur itinérant des Nations unies ADV **1** *(as a whole)* dans son ensemble; **the country at l.** le pays dans son ensemble; **people at l.** le grand public, la grande masse du public; **teachers at l.** la masse des professeurs **2** *(in detail)* tout au long, en détail; **to talk at l.** parler au hasard

• **by and large** ADV de manière générale, dans l'ensemble; **by and l. they vote Conservative** ils votent conservateur pour la plupart

• **in large** ADV *Am* en profondeur

▸▸ *Fin* ***large denominations*** grosses coupures *fpl*; *Anat* ***the large intestine*** le gros intestin; *Entom* ***large white*** piéride *f* (du chou)

> Note that the most common meaning of the French adjective **large** is **wide**, **broad**.

large-hearted [-'hɑːtɪd] ADJ au grand cœur

largely ['lɑːdʒlɪ] ADV *(mainly)* en grande partie, pour la plupart; *(in general)* en général, en gros

> Note that the French word **largement** is a false friend. It means **widely** or **generously**, depending on the context.

large-minded ADJ large d'esprit, ouvert

largeness ['lɑːdʒnɪs] N *(in size)* grandeur *f*, (grande) taille *f*; *(of sum)* importance *f*; *(of number)* grandeur *f*, importance *f*

large-print ADJ en gros caractères

large-scale ADJ à grande échelle; **l. disaster** grande catastrophe *f*

▸▸ *Comput* ***large-scale integration*** intégration *f* à grande échelle

large-size, large-sized ADJ *(clothes)* grande taille *(inv)*; *(product)* grand modèle *(inv)*; *(envelope)* grand format *(inv)*

largesse [lɑː'dʒes] N *(UNCOUNT)* largesse *f*, largesses *fpl*

largish ['lɑːdʒɪʃ] ADJ *(in size)* assez grand; *(in amount)* assez grand, assez gros; *(in number)* assez nombreux

largo ['lɑːgəʊ] N largo *m*

ADJ largo

ADV largo

lariat ['lærɪət] N **1** *Am (lasso)* lasso *m* **2** *(for tethering animals)* corde *f* à piquet

lark [lɑːk] N **1** *Orn* alouette *f*; **to rise** *or* **to be up with the l.** se lever avec les poules *ou* au chant du coq; *Br* **as happy as a l.** gai comme un pinson **2** *Fam (joke)* rigolade *f*; *(prank)* blague *f*, farce *f*; **for a l.** pour blaguer, pour rigoler; **what a l.!** quelle rigolade!, quelle bonne blague! **3** *Fam (rigmarole, business)* histoire *f*; **I don't like the sound of this fancy dress l.** je n'aime pas beaucoup cette histoire de déguisement, cette idée de déguisement ne me dit rien qui vaille; **are you still at the teaching l.?** tu fais toujours ce sacré métier de prof?

▸ **lark about, lark around** VI *Br Fam* faire le fou (la folle); **stop larking about!** arrêtez de faire les fous *ou* les imbéciles!; **some children were larking around with an old tyre** des enfants s'amusaient avec un vieux pneu

larkspur ['lɑːkspɜː(r)] N *Bot* pied-d'alouette *m*

larva ['lɑːvə] *(pl* **larvae** [-viː]) N *Zool* larve *f*

larval ['lɑːvəl] ADJ *Zool* larvaire

laryngitis [ˌlærɪn'dʒaɪtɪs] N *(UNCOUNT)* laryngite *f*; **to have l.** avoir une laryngite

laryngoscope [lə'rɪŋgəskəʊp] N laryngoscope *m*

larynx ['lærɪŋks] N larynx *m*

lasagne, lasagna [lə'zænjə] N *(UNCOUNT)* lasagnes *fpl*

lascivious [lə'sɪvɪəs] ADJ lascif, lubrique

lasciviously [lə'sɪvɪəslɪ] ADV lascivement

lasciviousness [lə'sɪvɪəsnɪs] N lascivité *f*

laser ['leɪzə(r)] N laser *m*

▸▸ ***laser beam*** rayon *m ou* faisceau *m* laser; ***laser card*** carte *f* à puce; ***laser checkout*** *(in supermarket)* caisse *f* munie de lecteurs laser; ***laser disc*** disque *m* laser; ***laser engraving*** gravure *f* au laser; ***laser hair removal*** épilation *f* au laser; ***laser pen*** pointeur *m* laser; ***laser pointer*** pointeur *m* laser; ***laser printer*** imprimante *f* (à) laser; ***laser printing*** impression *f* au laser; *Comput* ***laser quality*** qualité *f* laser; ***laser recording*** enregistrement *m* laser; ***laser show*** spectacle *m* laser; ***laser surgery*** chirurgie *f* (au) laser

laser-guided ADJ *(missile, bomb)* guidé au laser

lash [læʃ] N **1** *(whip)* lanière *f*; *(blow from whip)* coup *m* de fouet; **he was given 60 lashes** on lui a donné *ou* il a reçu 60 coups de fouet; **the l.** *(punishment)* le (supplice du) fouet **2** *Fig (of scorn, criticism)* **he'd often felt the l. of her tongue** il avait souvent été la cible de ses propos virulents **3** *(eyelash)* cil *m*

VT **1** *(with whip)* fouetter

2 *(of rain, waves)* battre, fouetter; **the waves lashed the shore** les vagues venaient se fracasser sur la grève; **the cold rain lashed my face** la pluie froide me cinglait *ou* me fouettait le visage; *Fig* **he lashed them with his tongue** il leur adressa quelques remarques cinglantes

3 *(move)* **the tiger lashed its tail** le tigre fouettait l'air de sa queue

4 *(tie)* attacher; **they lashed him to the chair** ils l'ont attaché solidement à la chaise; **they lashed the cargo to the deck** ils arrimèrent la cargaison sur le pont

VI **its tail lashed wildly** il fouettait l'air furieusement de sa queue; **the hail lashed against the window** la grêle cinglait la vitre

▸ **lash out** VT SEP *Br Fam (spend)* **I lashed out £10 on a bottle of wine/on sweets** j'ai claqué 10 livres pour une bouteille de vin/en bonbons

VI **1** *(struggle ▸ with fists)* donner des coups de poing; *(▸ with feet)* donner des coups de pied; **she lashed out in all directions** elle se débattit de toutes ses forces **2** *Fig (verbally)* **he lashed out at his critics** il a fustigé ses détracteurs **3** *Br Fam (spend)* **to l. out (on sth)** dépenser un fric monstre (pour/en qch); **he lashed out and bought himself a new suit** il a claqué son fric pour s'acheter un nouveau costume

lashed [læʃt] ADJ *Br Fam* bourré, pété; **to get l.** se bourrer la gueule, prendre une cuite

lashing ['læʃɪŋ] N **1** *(with whip)* flagellation *f*, fouet *m*; **to give sb a l.** donner des coups de fouet à qn **2** *Fig (scolding)* réprimandes *fpl*, correction *f* **3** *(rope)* corde *f*; *Naut* amarre *f*

ADJ *(rain)* cinglant

• **lashings** NPL *Br (in amount)* des montagne **with lashings of chocolate sauce** couvert de sauc au chocolat

lass [læs] N *Scot & NEng (girl)* fille *f*

Lassa ['lɑːsə] N Lhassa

▸▸ ***Lassa fever*** fièvre *f* de Lhassa

lassie ['læsɪ] N *Scot & Ir* fillette *f*, gamine *f*

lassitude ['læsɪtjuːd] N lassitude *f*

lasso [læ'suː] *(pl* **lassos** *or* **lassoes**, *pp & pt* **lassoe** *cont* **lassoing**) N lasso *m*

VT prendre au lasso

LAST[1] [lɑːst] ADJ **1** *(with dates, times of da* dernier; **l. Monday** lundi dernier; **l. week/year** l semaine/l'année dernière; **l. July** en juille dernier, l'année dernière au mois de juillet; **night** *(at night)* cette nuit, la nuit dernière; *(i the evening)* hier soir

2 *(final)* dernier; **the l. train** le dernier train; **the guest to arrive** le dernier des invités à arriver; **th l. syllable but one** l'avant-dernière syllabe; **tha was the l. time I saw him** c'était la dernière foi que je le voyais; **it's your l. chance** c'est votr dernière chance; **at the l. minute** *or* **moment** à l dernière minute, au dernier moment; **it's our day here** c'est notre dernière journée ici; **I'r down to my l. cigarette** il ne me reste plu qu'une seule cigarette; **one of the l. fe survivors** un des tout derniers survivants; **the two pages** les deux dernières pages; **I'll sac every l. one of them!** je vais tous les virer!; **sh used up every l. ounce of energy** elle a utilis tout ce qui lui restait d'énergie; **to the l. deta** dans les moindres détails; *Am* **the concert wa her l. hurrah** c'est avec ce concert qu'elle a fa ses adieux au public; **they were prepared t fight to the l. man** ils étaient prêts à se battr jusqu'au dernier; **she was on her l. legs** elle éta au bout du rouleau; **your car is on its l. legs** votr voiture ne va pas tarder à vous lâcher; **th regime is on its l. legs** le régime vit ses dernier jours *ou* est au bord de l'effondrement; **I'll ge my money back if it's the l. thing I do** j récupérerai mon argent coûte que coûte; **always clean my teeth l. thing at night** je m brosse toujours les dents juste avant de m coucher; **we finished the work l. thing on Tuesda afternoon** on a terminé le travail juste avant d partir mardi après-midi

3 *(most recent)* dernier; **you said that l. time** c'es ce que tu as dit la dernière fois; **I've been here fo the l. five years** je suis ici depuis cinq ans, cel fait cinq ans que je suis ici; **I haven't been t church for the l. few weeks** je ne suis pas allé l'église ces dernières semaines; **I didn't like he l. film** je n'ai pas aimé son dernier film

4 *(least likely)* **he's the l. person I expected to se** c'est bien la dernière personne que j m'attendais à voir; **that's the l. thing that worrying me** ça c'est le cadet de mes soucis **that's the l. place I'd have looked** c'est bien l dernier endroit où j'aurais cherché; **that's the thing I wanted** je n'avais vraiment pas besoin d ça

ADV **1** *(finally)* **she arrived l.** elle est arrivée l dernière *ou* en dernier; **she came** *or* **finished** *(in race)* elle est arrivée dernière; **and l. but no least...** et en dernier, mais non par ordr d'importance,...

2 *(most recently)* **when did you l. see him?** quan l'avez-vous vu la dernière fois?; **they l. came t see us in 1989** leur dernière visite remonte 1989; **I can't remember when I l. ate** je ne sai plus quand j'ai pris mon dernier repas; *Com Fin* **l. in, first out** dernier entré, premier sorti

3 *(lastly)* enfin, en dernier lieu; **l., I would like t say...** et pour finir, je voudrais dire...

N **1** *(final one)* dernier(ère) *m,f*; **am I the l.?** *(t arrive)* suis-je le dernier?; **she was the l. to arriv** elle est arrivée la dernière; **the l. of the Romanov** le dernier des Romanov; **the next to l., the l. bu one** l'avant-dernier

2 *(previous one)* **each more handsome than the** tous plus beaux les uns que les autres; **the da before l.** avant-hier; **the night before l.** *(at night)* l nuit d'avant-hier; *(in the evening)* avant-hier soir **the winter before l.** l'hiver d'il y a deux ans; **th Prime Minister before l.** l'avant-dernier Premie ministre

3 *(end)* **that was the l. I saw of her** c'est la dernière fois que je l'ai vue, je ne l'ai pas revue depuis; **I hope that's the l. we see of them** j'espère qu'on ne les reverra plus; **I think we've heard the l. of him** je pense qu'on n'en entendra plus parler; **we'll never hear the l. of it** on n'a pas fini d'en entendre parler; **you haven't heard the l. of this!** *(as threat)* vous aurez de mes nouvelles!; **leave the pans till l.** gardez les casseroles pour la fin, lavez les casseroles en dernier; *Literary* **to look one's l. on sth** voir qch pour la dernière fois; *Literary* **to breathe one's l.** rendre le dernier soupir

4 *(remainder)* reste *m*; **we drank the l. of the wine** on a bu ce qui restait de vin

• **at last** ADV enfin; **free at l.** enfin libre; **at long l. she's found a job she enjoys** elle a enfin trouvé un emploi qui lui plaît; **at l.! where on earth have you been?** (te voilà) enfin! mais où étais-tu donc?

• **at the last** ADV *Formal* **at the l. the judges came out in her favour** à la dernière minute, les juges ont décidé en sa faveur; **she was there at the l.** elle est restée jusqu'au bout

• **to the last** ADV jusqu'au bout; **faithful to the l.** fidèle jusqu'au bout

►► *Am* **last call** = dans un bar, moment où le barman annonce que l'heure de la fermeture approche et qu'il s'apprête à servir les dernières consommations; **the Last Judgment** le Jugement dernier; **last name** nom *m* de famille; *Tel* **last number redial** touche *f* bis; *Br* **last orders** = dans un pub, moment où le barman annonce que l'heure de la fermeture approche et qu'il s'apprête à servir les dernières consommations; *Br Mil* **last post** *(at night)* extinction *f* des feux; *(at funeral)* sonnerie *f* aux morts; **to sound the l. post (over the grave)** jouer la sonnerie aux morts; **last rites** derniers sacrements *mpl*; **the Last Supper** la (sainte) Cène; *St Exch* **last trading day** dernier jour *m* de cotation; **last word** *(final decision)* dernier mot *m*; *(latest style)* dernier cri *m*; **the Treasury has the l. word on defence spending** le ministère des Finances a le dernier mot en matière de dépenses militaires; **she was wearing the very l. word in hats** elle portait un chapeau du dernier cri

---

LAST² [lɑːst] VI **1** *(continue to exist or function)* durer; **it's too good to l.** c'est trop beau pour durer; **if the good weather lasts** si le beau temps se maintient; **it lasted (for) ten days** cela a duré dix jours; **how long did the film l.?** combien de temps le film a-t-il duré?, quelle était la durée du film?; **how long can we l. without water?** combien de temps tiendrons-nous sans eau?; **the supplies will not l. two months** les vivres ne feront pas deux mois; **he didn't l. more than a year as a singer** il n'a pas tenu plus d'un an dans la chanson; **he won't l. long** *(in job)* il ne tiendra pas longtemps; *(will soon die)* il n'en a plus pour longtemps; **the batteries didn't l. (for) long** les piles n'ont pas duré longtemps; **built/made to l.** construit/fait pour durer

2 *(be enough)* **we've got enough food to l. another week** nous avons assez à manger pour une semaine encore

3 *(keep fresh* ► *food)* se conserver; **these flowers don't l. (long)** ces fleurs ne tiennent *ou* ne durent pas (longtemps)

VT **this money didn't l. him to the end of the holiday** il n'a pas eu assez d'argent pour tenir jusqu'à la fin des vacances; **have we got enough to l. us until tomorrow?** en avons-nous assez pour tenir *ou* aller jusqu'à demain?; **my camera's lasted me ten years** mon appareil photo a duré dix ans; **it has lasted him well** ça lui a fait de l'usage

► **last out** VI **1** *(survive)* tenir; **I'm not sure I'll l. out at this job** je ne sais pas si je pourrai faire ce travail longtemps; **how long will he l. out?** combien de temps peut-il tenir? **2** *(be enough)* suffire; **will our supplies l. out till the end of the month?** les provisions suffiront-elles jusqu'à la fin du mois?

VT SEP **he didn't l. the night out** il n'a pas passé la nuit, il est mort pendant la nuit; **will the play l. out the month?** est-ce que la pièce tiendra le mois?; **to l. the year out** *(person)* survivre jusqu'à la fin de l'année; *(supplies)* suffire pour l'année; **my overcoat will l. the winter out** mon pardessus fera encore l'hiver; **I don't know if I'll be able to l. out the afternoon without any coffee** je ne sais pas si j'arriverai à tenir tout l'après-midi sans café

---

last³ N *(for shoes)* forme *f*

last-ditch ADJ *(ultimate)* ultime; *(desperate)* désespéré; **a l. attempt** *or* **effort** un ultime effort

lasting ['lɑːstɪŋ] ADJ durable; **to their l. regret/shame** à leur plus grand regret/plus grande honte

lastly ['lɑːstlɪ] ADV enfin, en dernier lieu

last-minute ADJ de dernière minute

lat *(written abbr* **latitude***)* lat.

latch [lætʃ] N loquet *m*; **leave the door on the l.** ne fermez pas la porte à clé; **the door was on the l.** la porte n'était pas fermée à clé

VT fermer au loquet

VI se fermer

► **latch on** VI *Fam* piger

latchkey ['lætʃkiː] N clef *f ou* clé *f (de la porte d'entrée)*

►► **latchkey child** = enfant dont les parents travaillent et ne sont pas là quand il rentre de l'école

---

LATE [leɪt]

> ADJ
> • en retard **1, 6** • tardif **2**
> • dernier **2, 5** • tard **2, 3**
> • défunt **4** • feu **4**
> • récent **5**
>
> ADV
> • tard **1** • récemment **2**
> • autrefois **3**

ADJ **1** *(behind schedule)* en retard; **to be l. (for sth)** être en retard (pour qch); **the train is l.** le train a du retard; **to be ten minutes l.** avoir dix minutes de retard; **to make sb l.** retarder qn, mettre qn en retard; **we apologize for the l. arrival of flight 906** nous vous prions d'excuser le retard du vol 906; **it was too l. to do anything about it** il était trop tard pour faire quoi que ce soit; **her baby was five days l.** son bébé est né avec cinq jours de retard

2 *(in time)* tardif; *(news, edition)* dernier; **at a l. hour** à une heure tardive; **to keep l. hours** veiller, se coucher tard; **in the l. afternoon** tard dans l'après-midi, en fin d'après-midi; **she's in her l. fifties** elle approche de la soixantaine; **in the l. seventies** à la fin des années soixante-dix; **in l. 1970** fin 1970; **at this l. date** à cette date avancée; **at this l. stage** à ce stade avancé; **to have a l. lunch** déjeuner tard; **there have been some l. developments in the talks** il y a du nouveau dans les discussions; **he was a l. developer** *(physically)* il a eu une croissance tardive; *(intellectually)* son développement intellectuel fut un peu tardif

3 *(far on in the day)* tard; **it's l.** il est tard; **it's getting l.** il se fait tard; **it is too l.** il est trop tard; **I was l. going to bed** je me suis couché tard

4 *(deceased)* **the l. Mr Fox** le défunt M. Fox, *Formal* feu M. Fox; **her l. husband** son défunt mari, *Formal* feu son mari; **his l. wife** sa défunte femme, *Formal* feu sa femme

5 *(recent)* récent, dernier

6 to be l. *(with one's period)* avoir un retard de règles; **I'm two days l.** je suis en retard de deux jours

ADV **1** *(in time)* tard; **to arrive/to go to bed l.** arriver/se coucher tard; **to arrive ten minutes l.** arriver avec dix minutes de retard; **l. in the afternoon** tard dans l'après-midi; **she came to poetry l. in life** elle est venue à la poésie sur le tard; **l. in the day** vers la fin de la journée; *Fig* **it's rather l. in the day to be thinking about that** c'est un peu tard pour penser à ça

2 *(recently)* récemment; **even as l. as last year he was still painting** pas plus tard que l'année dernière, il peignait encore

3 *Formal (formerly)* autrefois, anciennement; **Mr Fox, l. of Delhi** M. Fox, anciennement domicilié à Delhi

• **of late** ADV récemment; **I haven't seen him of l.** je ne l'ai pas vu récemment *ou* ces derniers temps

►► **late arrival** *(at hotel)* arrivée *f* tardive; **he will be a l. arrival** il arrivera tard; **late booking** réservation *f* de dernière minute; *Fin* **late payment** retard *m* de paiement; *Fin* **late payment penalty** pénalité *f* de retard; **late tackle** *(in rugby)* plaquage *m* à retardement; *(in football)* tacle *m* à retardement; *St Exch* **late trading** opérations *fpl* de clôture

---

latecomer ['leɪt,kʌmə(r)] N retardataire *mf*; **latecomers will not be admitted** *(sign)* les retardataires ne sont pas admis après la fermeture des portes; **he was a l. to football** il est venu au football sur le tard

lately ['leɪtlɪ] ADV récemment, ces derniers temps, dernièrement; **I haven't been feeling well l.** je ne me sens pas bien ces temps-ci; **until l.** jusqu'à ces derniers temps, jusqu'à récemment

latency ['leɪtənsɪ] N latence *f*

lateness ['leɪtnɪs] N **1** *(of bus, train, person)* retard *m*; **I find persistent l. infuriating** les gens qui sont toujours en retard m'exaspèrent **2** *(late time)* heure *f* tardive; **given the l. of the hour** étant donné *ou* vu l'heure tardive

late-night ADJ *(play, show, film)* de minuit; **what's tonight's l. movie?** *(on TV)* qu'est-ce qu'il y a au ciné-club ce soir?; **a l. film** *(in cinema)* une séance de minuit; **a l. bus service** un bus de nuit

►► **late-night opening** nocturne *f*; **late-night shopping** courses *fpl* en nocturne; **l. opening is on Thursdays** le magasin reste ouvert tard le jeudi

latent ['leɪtənt] ADJ latent

►► **latent defect** vice *m* caché; **latent heat** chaleur *f* latente; **latent image** image *f* latente; **latent period** *Med* incubation *f*; *Psy* latence *f*, état *m* latent, temps *m* de latence; *Psy* **latent time** latence *f*, état *m* latent, temps *m* de latence

later ['leɪtə(r)] *(compar of* **late***)* ADJ ultérieur; **we can always catch a l. train** on peut toujours prendre un autre train, plus tard; **a collection of her l. poems** un recueil de ses derniers poèmes; **l. events proved that...** la suite des événements a démontré que...; **at a l. date** à une date ultérieure; **at a l. stage** à un stade plus avancé; **in l. life** plus tard dans la vie

ADV plus tard; **l. that day** plus tard dans la journée; **l. on** plus tard; **see you l.!** à plus tard!; **no l. than tomorrow** demain dernier délai, demain au plus tard

lateral ['lætərəl] ADJ latéral

►► *Econ* **lateral integration** intégration *f* latérale; **lateral thinking** approche *f* originale; **we need a bit of l. thinking on this problem** il nous faut adopter une approche du problème plus originale

laterally ['lætərəlɪ] ADV latéralement

latest ['leɪtɪst] *(superl of* **late***)* ADJ dernier; **the l. date/time** la date/l'heure *f* limite; **the l. news** les dernières nouvelles *fpl*; **the l. fashions** la dernière mode; **let's hope her l. novel won't be her last** espérons que le roman qu'elle vient de publier ne sera pas le dernier

N **1** *(most recent* ► *news)* **have you heard the l.?** vous connaissez la dernière?; **what's the l. on the trial?** qu'y a-t-il de nouveau sur le procès?; **tune in at 7 p.m. for the l. on the elections** soyez à l'écoute à 19 heures pour les dernières informations sur les élections; *Fam* **have you met his/her l.?** *(boyfriend, girlfriend)* avez-vous fait la connaissance de sa dernière conquête? **2** *(in time)* **at the l.** au plus tard; **when is the l. you can come?** jusqu'à quelle heure pouvez-vous venir?

latex ['leɪteks] N latex *m*

lath [lɑːθ] N *(wooden)* latte *f*; *(in venetian blind)* lame *f*

lathe [leɪð] N tour *m (à bois ou à métal)*; **precision l.** tour *m* de précision; **capstan** *or* **turret l.** tour *m* (à) revolver; **polishing l.** touret *m* à polir *ou* de polisseur

►► **lathe bed** banc *m ou* bâti *m* de tour; **lathe operator** tourneur(euse) *m,f*

lather ['lɑːðə(r)] N **1** *(from soap)* mousse *f* **2** *(foam* ► *on horse, seawater)* écume *f*; *Br* **to get into a l. (about** *or* **over sth)** s'énerver *ou* se mettre dans tous ses états (à propos de qch); **he got into a real l. over the unpaid bills** les factures impayées l'ont mis dans tous ses états

VT *(clean)* savonner; **to l. one's face** se savonner le visage

VI 1 *(soap)* mousser **2** *(horse)* écumer

lathe-turned ADJ fait au tour, tourné

Latin ['lætɪn] **N 1** *(person)* Latin(e) *m,f*; **the Latins** *(in Europe)* les Latins *mpl*; *(in US)* les Latino-Américains *mpl* **2** *(language)* latin *m*

ADJ latin

►► ***Latin America*** Amérique *f* latine; ***Latin American*** **N** Latino-Américain(e) *m,f* ADJ latino-américain; ***Latin cross*** croix *f* latine; ***the Latin Quarter*** le Quartier latin

Latinate ['lætɪneɪt] ADJ *(vocabulary)* d'origine latine; *(style)* empreint de latinismes

Latinism ['lætɪˌnɪzəm] **N 1** *Ling* latinisme *m*, tournure *f* latine **2** *Rel* influence *f* de l'Église latine

Latinist ['lætɪnɪst] **N** latiniste *mf*

Latinization, -isation [ˌlætɪnaɪ'zeɪʃən] **N** latinisation *f*

Latinize, -ise ['lætɪnaɪz] **VT** latiniser

Latino [læ'tiːnəʊ] (*pl* **Latinos**) **N** latino *mf*

latish ['leɪtɪʃ] **ADJ 1** *(after the appointed time)* un peu en retard **2** *(far on in the day)* un peu tardif; **at a l. hour** à une heure assez avancée; **it was getting l.** il commençait à se faire tard

latitude ['lætɪtjuːd] **N 1** *Astron & Geog* latitude *f*; **at a l. of 50° south** à 50° de latitude sud; **in northern/southern latitudes** dans les latitudes boréales/australes; **few animals live in these latitudes** rares sont les animaux qui vivent sous ces latitudes; *Literary* **in other latitudes** sous d'autres cieux **2** *(freedom)* latitude *f*; **they don't allow** *or* **give the children much l. for creativity** ils n'encouragent guère les enfants à être créatifs

latrine [lə'triːn] **N** latrines *fpl*

latte ['læteɪ] **N** café *m* au lait

latter ['lætə(r)] **ADJ 1** *(in relation to former)* dernier, second; **the l. proposal is unrealistic** la seconde *ou* cette dernière proposition est irréaliste; **the l. half of the book was better** la seconde moitié du livre était meilleure **2** *(later)* dernier, second; **in the l. years of her life** au cours des dernières années de sa vie; **the l. part of the holiday** la seconde partie des vacances

N the former... the l.... le premier... le second..., celui-là... celui-ci...; **the l. is definitely the better book** le second livre est sans aucun doute le meilleur; **of tigers and cheetahs, the l. are by far the faster runners** des tigres et des guépards, ces derniers sont de loin les plus rapides

latter-day ADJ d'aujourd'hui; **a l. St Francis** un saint François moderne; **Church of the L. Saints** Église *f* de Jésus-Christ des saints des derniers jours

latterly ['lætəlɪ] **ADV 1** *(recently)* récemment, dernièrement **2** *(towards the end)* vers la fin

lattice ['lætɪs] **N** *(fence, frame)* treillage *m*; *(design)* treillis *m*; *(pastry)* en croisillons

►► ***lattice beam, lattice girder*** poutre *f* en treillis *ou* à croisillons; ***lattice window*** fenêtre *f* à croisillons

latticed ['lætɪst] ADJ *(fence)* à claire-voie; *(ceramics)* treillissé; *(pastry)* en croisillons; *(dress)* ajouré

latticework ['lætɪswɜːk] **N** *(UNCOUNT)* treillis *m*

Latvia ['lætvɪə] **N** Lettonie *f*

Latvian ['lætvɪən] **N 1** *(person)* Letton(onne) *m,f* **2** *(language)* letton *m*

ADJ letton

COMP *(embassy)* de Lettonie; *(history)* de la Lettonie; *(teacher)* de letton

laud [lɔːd] **VT** *Formal or Literary* louer, chanter les louanges de, glorifier

laudable ['lɔːdəbəl] ADJ louable, digne de louanges

laudably ['lɔːdəblɪ] ADV de manière louable; **you behaved l.** votre comportement a été admirable

laudanum ['lɔːdənəm] **N** *(UNCOUNT) Pharm* laudanum *m*

laudatory ['lɔːdətrɪ] ADJ *Formal* laudatif, élogieux

laugh [lɑːf] **VI 1** *(in amusement)* rire; **we all laughed at the joke/the film** la blague/le film nous a tous fait rire; **she was laughing about his gaffe all day** sa gaffe l'a fait rire toute la journée; **you have to l.** mieux vaut en rire; **to burst out laughing** éclater de rire; **we laughed until we cried** on a ri aux larmes, on a pleuré de rire; **we laughed about it afterwards** après coup, cela nous a fait bien rire, on en a ri après coup; **to l. aloud** *or* **out loud** rire aux éclats; **he was laughing to himself** il riait dans sa barbe; **they didn't know whether to l. or cry** ils ne savaient pas s'ils devaient en rire ou en pleurer; *Br* **to l. up one's sleeve** rire dans sa barbe; *Br* **I'll make him l. on the other side of his face** je lui ferai passer l'envie de rire, moi; *Br* **you'll l. on the other side of your face one of these days** un de ces jours tu vas rire jaune; *Prov* **he who laughs last laughs** *Br* **longest** *or Am* **best** rira bien qui rira le dernier

2 *(in contempt, ridicule)* rire; **to l. at sb/sth** se moquer de qn/qch, rire de qn/qch; **they laughed at the dangers** ils (se) riaient des dangers; **they laughed in my face** ils m'ont ri au nez; **he laughed about his mistakes** il a ri de ses erreurs; *Fam Ironic* **don't make me l.!** laisse-moi rire!

3 *Br Fam Fig (be in comfortable situation)* **once we get the contract, we're laughing** une fois qu'on aura empoché le contrat, on sera tranquilles; **if we win this match, we'll be laughing** si on gagne ce match, on n'a plus de souci à se faire□; **if your offer's accepted, you'll be laughing** s'ils acceptent ta proposition, ce sera super pour toi; **she's laughing all the way to the bank** elle s'en met plein les poches

VT 1 *(in amusement)* **to l. oneself silly** se tordre de rire, être plié en deux de rire **2** *(in contempt, ridicule)* **he was laughed off the stage/out of the room** il a quitté la scène/la pièce sous les rires moqueurs; *Br* **they laughed him to scorn** ils se sont moqués de lui; *Fig* **to l. sth out of court** tourner qch en dérision **3** *Br (express)* **she laughed her scorn** elle eut un petit rire méprisant

N 1 *(of amusement)* rire *m*; *(burst of laughter)* éclat *m* de rire; **to give a l.** rire; **we had a good l. about it** ça nous a bien fait rire; **she left the room with a l.** elle sortit en riant *ou* dans un éclat de rire; **look outside if you want a l.** regarde dehors si tu veux rigoler

2 *(of contempt, ridicule)* rire *m*; **we all had a good l. at his expense** nous nous sommes bien moqués de lui; **to have the last l.** avoir le dernier mot

3 *Br Fam (fun)* rigolade *f*; **to have a l.** rigoler *ou* se marrer un peu; **he's always good for a l.** avec lui, on se marre bien; **these old horror films are usually good for a l.** ces vieux films d'horreur sont souvent marrants

4 *Fam (joke)* **we did it for a l.** *or* **just for laughs** on l'a fait pour rigoler; **what a l.!** qu'est-ce qu'on s'est marré!; *Ironic* **home-made cakes? that's a l.!** gâteaux faits maison? c'est une blague *ou* ils plaisantent!

►**laugh down** **VT SEP** *(objection, proposal)* ridiculiser

►**laugh off** **VT SEP** *(difficulty)* rire de, se moquer de; *(difficult situation)* désamorcer; **I managed to l. off an awkward situation** j'ai réussi à éviter une situation fâcheuse en plaisantant; **he tried to l. off the defeat** il s'efforça de ne pas prendre sa défaite trop au sérieux

laughable ['lɑːfəbəl] ADJ ridicule, risible; **he made a l. attempt at reconciliation** il fit une tentative de réconciliation pitoyable

laughably ['lɑːfəblɪ] ADV ridiculement

laughing ['lɑːfɪŋ] **N** *(UNCOUNT)* rires *mpl*; **we could hear the sound of l.** nous entendions des rires

ADJ riant; **I'm in no l. mood** je n'ai pas envie de rire; **this is no l. matter** il n'y a pas de quoi rire

►► ***laughing gas*** gaz *m* hilarant; *Br Fam* ***laughing gear*** bouche□*f*, clapet *m*; **get your l. gear round that!** mets-toi ça dans le cornet!; ***laughing hyena*** hyène *f* tachetée; ***laughing jackass*** martin-chasseur *m (d'Australie)*, kookaburra *m*; ***laughing stock*** risée *f*; **they were the l. stock of the whole neighbourhood** ils étaient la risée de tout le quartier; **they made l. stocks of themselves** ils se sont couverts de ridicule

laughingly ['lɑːfɪŋlɪ] **ADV 1** *(cheerfully)* en riant **2** *(inappropriately)* **this noise is l. called folk music** c'est ce bruit qu'on appelle le plus sérieusement du monde de la musique folk

laughter ['lɑːftə(r)] **N** *(UNCOUNT)* rire *m*, rires *mpl*; **to cause l.** provoquer les rires *ou* l'hilarité; **there was much l. over the misunderstanding** le malentendu provoqua des éclats de rire; **she continued to speak amid loud l.** elle a continué à parler au milieu des éclats de rire

launch [lɔːntʃ] **N 1** *(boat)* vedette *f*; *(long boat)* chaloupe *f*; **(pleasure) l.** bateau *m* de plaisance **2** *(of ship, spacecraft, new product, new scheme)* lancement *m*; **a book l.** le lancement d'un livre

VT 1 *(boat ► from ship)* mettre à la mer; *(► from harbour)* faire sortir; *(► for first time)* lancer

2 *Com* lancer; **our firm has launched a new perfume on** *or* **onto the market** notre société a lancé un nouveau parfum; **to l. a £3 million cash bid** lancer une offre au comptant de 3 millions de livres

3 *St Exch (company)* introduire en Bourse; *(shares)* émettre

4 *(start)* **that was the audition that launched my career** cette audition a donné le coup d'envoi de ma carrière; **to l. a military offensive** déclencher *ou* lancer une attaque

5 *Comput* lancer

►► *Astron* ***launch pad*** rampe *f ou* plate-forme *f* de lancement; ***launch party*** réception *f* *(pour le lancement d'un produit)*; *Astron* ***launch site*** base de lancement; *Astron* ***launch vehicle*** fusée *f* de lancement

►**launch into** **VT INSEP** *(start)* se lancer dans; **she launched into her work with vigour** elle s'est lancée dans son travail avec énergie

►**launch out** **VI** se lancer; **Blakes have launched out into distilling** Blakes s'est lancé dans la distillation; **she's just launched out on her own** elle vient de se mettre à son compte

launcher ['lɔːntʃə(r)] **N** *(vehicle)* lanceur *m*; *(launching pad)* rampe *f ou* plate-forme *f* de lancement; *(for planes)* catapulte *f* de lancement

launching ['lɔːntʃɪŋ] **N 1** *(of ship, spacecraft)* lancement *m*; *(of lifeboat ► from ship)* mise *f* à la mer; *(► from shore)* sortie *f* **2** *(of new product)* lancement *m*

►► *Aviat* ***launching catapult*** catapulte *f* de lancement; ***launching ceremony*** cérémonie *f* de lancement; ***launching pad, launching platform*** rampe *ou* plate-forme *f* de lancement; ***launching ramp*** rampe *f* de lancement; ***launching site*** aire *f* de lancement; ***launching vehicle*** fusée *f* de lancement

launder ['lɔːndə(r)] **VT 1** *(clothes)* laver; *(at laundry)* blanchir; **the sheets have been freshly laundered** *(at home)* les draps viennent d'être lavés; *(at laundry)* les draps reviennent de chez le blanchisseur *ou* le teinturier **2** *Fig (money)* blanchir

launderette [ˌlɔːndə'ret] **N** *Br* laverie *f* automatique

laundering ['lɔːndrɪŋ] **N 1** *(of clothes)* blanchissage *m* **2** *Fig (of money)* blanchiment *m*

laundress ['lɔːndrɪs] **N** blanchisseuse *f*

laundrette [lɔːn'dret] **N** *Br* laverie *f* automatique

Laundromat® ['lɔːndrəmæt] **N** *Am* laverie *f* automatique

laundry ['lɔːndrɪ] (*pl* **laundries**) **N 1** *(shop)* blanchisserie *f*; *(in house)* buanderie *f*; **to send sth to the l.** envoyer qch à la blanchisserie **2** *(washing)* linge *m*; **to do the l.** faire la lessive

►► ***laundry bag*** sac *m* de blanchisserie; ***laundry basket*** panier *m* à linge; ***laundry list*** liste *f* de blanchissage; ***laundry mark*** étiquette *f* de la blanchisserie; ***laundry room*** buanderie *f*; ***laundry service*** service *m* de blanchissage; ***laundry van*** camionnette *f* du blanchisseur

laureate ['lɔːrɪət] **N 1** *(prize winner)* lauréat *m*; **a Nobel l.** un prix Nobel **2** *(poet)* poète *m* lauréat

laurel ['lɒrəl] **N** *Bot* laurier *m*

COMP *(crown, wreath)* de laurier

• **laurels** **NPL** *(honours)* lauriers *mpl*; **to look to one's laurels** ne pas s'endormir sur ses lauriers; **to rest on one's laurels** se reposer sur ses lauriers

LAUTRO ['lautrəʊ] **N** *Br* (*abbr* **Life Assurance and Unit Trust Regulatory Organization**) = organisme britannique contrôlant les activités de compagnies d'assurance-vie et de SICAV

lav [læv] **N** *Br Fam* cabinets□ *mpl*, W-C□ *mpl*

ava ['lɑːvə] N lave *f*
▸▸ ***lava bed*** champ *m* de lave; ***lava flow*** coulée *f* de lave; ***lava lamp*** lampe *f* magma; ***lava stream*** coulée *f* de lave

avabo [lə'veɪbəʊ] (*pl* **lavabos**) N *Rel* lavabo *m*

avalier, lavaliere [læ,vælɪ'eə(r)] N *Am* pendentif *m*

avatorial [,lævə'tɔːrɪəl] ADJ *(style, humour)* scatologique

avatory ['lævətrɪ] (*pl* **lavatories**) *Br* N toilettes *fpl*, cabinets *mpl*; *(bowl)* cuvette *f*; **to go to the l.** aller aux toilettes
ADJ des W-C; *(humour)* scatologique
▸▸ ***lavatory bowl, lavatory pan*** cuvette *f* (de W-C); ***lavatory paper*** papier *m* hygiénique

avender ['lævəndə(r)] N lavande *f*
ADJ *(colour)* lavande *(inv)*
▸▸ ***lavender bag*** sachet *m* de lavande; ***lavender blue*** bleu *m* lavande; ***lavender water*** eau *f* de lavande

avish ['lævɪʃ] ADJ **1** *(abundant)* copieux, abondant; *(luxurious)* somptueux, luxueux **2** *(generous)* généreux; **to be l. with one's money** dépenser sans compter; **he was l. in his praise** il ne tarissait pas d'éloges
VT prodiguer; **to l. money on sb** dépenser des fortunes pour qn; **they l. all their attention on their son** ils sont aux petits soins pour leur fils; **he lavished praise on the book** il ne tarissait pas d'éloges sur le livre

avishly ['lævɪʃlɪ] ADV **1** *(generously, extravagantly)* généreusement, sans compter; **she spends l.** elle dépense sans compter, elle ne regarde pas à la dépense; **he praised us l.** il n'a pas tari d'éloges à notre égard **2** *(luxuriously)* luxueusement, somptueusement; **l. decorated/furnished** somptueusement décoré/meublé

avishness ['lævɪʃnɪs] N **1** *(generosity)* générosité *f*; *(extravagance)* extravagance *f* **2** *(luxuriousness)* luxe *m*, somptuosité *f*

aw [lɔː] N **1** *(legal provision)* loi *f*; **a l. against gambling** une loi qui interdit les jeux d'argent; **there's no l. against it!** il n'y a pas de mal à cela!; *Hum* **there ought to be a l. against it** ça devrait être interdit par la loi; **to be a l. unto oneself** ne connaître ni foi ni loi
2 *(legislation)* loi *f*; **it's against the l. to sell alcohol** la vente d'alcool est illégale; **by l.** selon la loi; **in** *or* **under British l.** selon la loi britannique; **to break/to uphold the l.** enfreindre/respecter la loi; **the bill became l.** le projet de loi a été voté *ou* adopté; **the l. of the land** la loi, les lois *fpl*; **the l. of the jungle** la loi de la jungle; *Fig* **to lay down the l.** imposer sa loi, faire la loi; *Fig* **her word is l.** ses décisions sont sans appel
3 *(legal system)* droit *m*; **a student of l.** un(e) étudiant(e) en droit
4 *(justice)* justice *f*, système *m* juridique; *Br* **to go to l.** aller en justice; *Br* **to take a case to l.** porter une affaire en justice *ou* devant les tribunaux; **to take the l. into one's own hands** (se) faire justice soi-même; **l. and order** l'ordre *m* public
5 *Fam* **the l.** *(police)* les flics *mpl*; **I'll have the l. on you!** je vais appeler les flics!
6 *(rule ▸ of club, sport)* règle *f*; **the laws of rugby** les règles *fpl* du rugby
7 *(principle)* loi *f*; *Phys* **the laws of gravity** les lois *fpl* de la pesanteur; *Econ* **the l. of supply and demand** la loi de l'offre et de la demande
COMP *(book, faculty, school)* de droit
▸▸ *Br* ***law centre*** bureau *m* d'aide judiciaire; ***law court*** tribunal *m*, cour *f* de justice; ***law enforcement*** application *f* de la loi; ***law enforcement agency*** organisme *m* chargé de faire respecter la loi; ***law enforcement officer*** agent *m* de police; ***law firm*** cabinet *m* d'avocats *ou* juridique; *Br* ***Law Lords*** = membres de la Chambre des lords siégeant en tant que cour d'appel de dernière instance; ***law officer*** conseiller(ère) *m,f* juridique; ***law reports*** recueil *m* de jurisprudence; ***law school*** faculté *f* de droit; ***law student*** étudiant(e) *m,f* en droit

aw-abiding ADJ respectueux de la loi; **a l. citizen** un honnête citoyen

aw-and-order ADJ **l. issues** questions *fpl* d'ordre public; **he presents himself as the l. candidate** il se présente comme le candidat de l'ordre (public)

law-breaker N personne *f* qui transgresse la loi

law-breaking N infraction *f* à la loi

lawful ['lɔːfʊl] ADJ *(legal)* légal; *(legitimate)* légitime; *(valid)* valide; **to go about one's l. business** vaquer à ses occupations; **by all l. means** par tous les moyens légaux; **my l. wedded wife** mon épouse légitime

lawfully ['lɔːfʊlɪ] ADV légalement, de manière légale; **did you come by that money l.?** est-ce que vous avez gagné cet argent par des moyens légaux?

lawgiver ['lɔː,gɪvə(r)] N législateur(trice) *m,f*

lawless ['lɔːlɪs] ADJ *(person)* sans foi ni loi; *(activity)* illégal; *(country)* livré à l'anarchie

lawlessness ['lɔːlɪsnɪs] N non-respect *m* de la loi; *(anarchy)* anarchie *f*; *(illegality)* illégalité *f*; **the town was in a state of utter l.** la ville était plongée dans l'anarchie la plus totale

lawmaker ['lɔː,meɪkə(r)] N législateur(trice) *m,f*

lawmaking ['lɔː,meɪkɪŋ] ADJ législateur(trice)

lawn [lɔːn] N **1** *(grass)* pelouse *f*, gazon *m*; **to mow** *or* **cut the l.** tondre le gazon **2** *Tex* linon *m*
▸▸ *Am* ***lawn bowling*** boules *fpl*; *Am* ***lawn chair*** chaise *f* de jardin; ***lawn fertilizer, lawn food*** engrais *m* à gazon; *Am* ***lawn party*** garden-party *f*; ***lawn sprinkler*** arrosoir *m* de pelouse; *(spinning)* tourniquet *m* arroseur; ***lawn tennis*** tennis *m* sur gazon

lawnmower ['lɔːn,məʊə(r)] N tondeuse *f* à gazon

Lawrence ['lɒrəns] PR N **L. of Arabia** Lawrence d'Arabie

lawsuit ['lɔːsuːt] N action *f* en justice; **to bring a l. against sb** intenter une action (en justice) contre qn

lawyer ['lɔːjə(r)] N **1** *(barrister)* avocat(e) *m,f* **2** *(solicitor ▸ for wills, conveyancing etc)* notaire *m* **3** *(legal expert)* juriste *mf*; *(adviser)* conseil *m* juridique

lax [læks] ADJ **1** *(person)* négligent; *(behaviour, discipline)* relâché; *(justice)* laxiste; **to be l. about sth** négliger qch **2** *(not tense ▸ string)* lâche, relâché; *Med (bowels)* relâché **3** *(imprecise ▸ definition, usage)* imprécis, vague

laxative ['læksətɪv] N laxatif *m*
ADJ laxatif

laxity ['læksətɪ] N **1** *(negligence)* négligence *f*; **moral l.** relâchement *m* moral **2** *(lack of tension)* relâchement *m* **3** *(imprecision)* imprécision *f*

LAY [leɪ]

VT	
• poser **1, 2**	• mettre **1, 3**
• étendre **1**	• préparer **4**
• pondre **5**	• imposer **6**
• porter **7**	• soumettre **8**
• dissiper **9**	
VI	
• pondre **1**	
ADJ	
• laïque **1**	• profane **2**
N	
• coup **1**	• lai **2**

(*pt & pp* **laid** [leɪd]) *pt of* **lie**
VT **1** *(in specified position)* poser, mettre; *(spread out)* étendre; **to l. sb/sth flat** coucher *ou* étendre qn/qch (par terre); **l. the cards face upwards** posez les cartes face en l'air; **he laid the baby on the bed** il a couché l'enfant sur le lit; **she laid her head on my shoulder** elle a posé sa tête sur mon épaule; *Euph* **to l. sb to rest** enterrer qn; **she laid the blanket on the ground** elle a étendu la couverture par terre; *Fam* **to l. eyes on sb/sth** voir qn/qch[□]; **to l. it on the line** ne pas y aller par quatre chemins
2 *(tiles, bricks, pipes, cable, carpet, foundations)* poser; *(wreath)* déposer; *(mine)* poser, mouiller; *(concrete)* couler; **to l. lino on the floor, to l. the floor with lino** poser du linoléum; *Fig* **the plan lays the basis** *or* **the foundation for economic development** le projet jette les bases du développement économique
3 *(set ▸ table)* mettre; **l. the table for six** mettez la table pour six (personnes), mettez six couverts; **they hadn't laid enough places** ils n'avaient pas mis assez de couverts, il manquait des couverts
4 *(prepare, arrange ▸ fire)* préparer; **to l. a trail** tracer un chemin; **they laid a trap for him** ils lui ont tendu un piège
5 *(egg)* pondre; *Am Fam Fig* **to l. an egg** faire une gaffe
6 *(impose ▸ burden, duty, penalty)* imposer; *(▸ fine)* infliger; **to l. emphasis** *or* **stress on sth** mettre l'accent sur qch; **to l. the blame (for sth) on sb** faire porter la responsabilité (de qch) à qn; **to l. a curse on sb/sth** jeter un sort à qn/qch
7 *Law (lodge)* porter; **to l. a complaint** déposer une plainte, porter plainte; **to l. a matter before the court** saisir le tribunal d'une affaire; **to l. an accusation against sb** porter une accusation contre qn; **charges have been laid against five men** cinq hommes ont été inculpés
8 *(present, put forward ▸ question, request)* soumettre (**before sb** devant qn); **he laid all the facts before me** il me présenta tous les faits; **she laid the scheme before him** elle lui soumit le projet
9 *(allay ▸ fears)* dissiper; *(exorcize ▸ ghost)* exorciser; *(refute ▸ rumour)* démentir
10 *(bet)* faire; **I'll l. you ten to one that she won't come** je te parie à dix contre un qu'elle ne viendra pas
11 *very Fam (have sex with)* s'envoyer; **to get laid** s'envoyer en l'air
12 *Literary (strike)* **to l. a whip across sb's back** fouetter qn
13 *(with adjective complements)* **to l. oneself open to criticism** s'exposer à la critique
VI **1** *(bird, fish)* pondre
2 = *vi*
ADJ **1** *(non-clerical)* laïque; **in l. dress** en habit laïque
2 *(not professional)* profane, non spécialiste; **the book is intended for a l. audience** le livre est destiné à un public de profanes
N **1** *very Fam (person)* **he's/she's a good l.** c'est un bon coup
2 *(poem, song)* lai *m*
▸▸ *Rel* ***lay brother*** frère *m* lai; ***lay days*** starie *f*, jours *mpl* de planche; *Art* ***lay figure*** mannequin *m*; ***lay person*** profane *mf*, non-initié(e) *m,f*; ***lay preacher*** prédicateur(trice) *m,f* laïque; ***lay reader*** prédicateur(trice) *m,f* laïque; ***lay sister*** sœur *f* converse

> Attention: ne pas confondre avec le verbe **to lie**, qui signifie **être couché** ou **être posé à plat**.

▸**lay aside** VT SEP **1** *(put down)* mettre de côté; **she laid her knitting aside to watch the news** elle posa son tricot pour regarder les informations; *Fig* **you should l. aside any personal opinions you might have** vous devez faire abstraction de toute opinion personnelle **2** *(save)* mettre de côté; **we have some money laid aside** nous avons de l'argent de côté

▸**lay back** VT SEP *(of horse ▸ ears)* rabattre, coucher

▸**lay by** VT SEP *Br (provisions)* mettre de côté

▸**lay down** VT SEP **1** *(put down)* poser; **to l. down one's arms** déposer *ou* rendre les armes
2 *(renounce, relinquish)* renoncer à; **to l. down one's life** se sacrifier
3 *(formulate, set out ▸ plan, rule)* formuler, établir; *(▸ condition)* imposer; *(▸ duties)* spécifier; **as laid down in the contract, the buyer keeps exclusive rights** il est stipulé *ou* il est bien précisé dans le contrat que l'acheteur garde l'exclusivité
4 *Naut (ship)* mettre en chantier *ou* sur cale
5 *(store ▸ wine)* mettre en cave
6 *Mus (record ▸ song, track)* enregistrer

▸**lay in** VT SEP *(stores)* faire provision de; **to l. in provisions** faire des provisions; **we've laid in plenty of food for the weekend** nous avons prévu beaucoup de nourriture pour le week-end; *Com* **to l. in goods** *or* **stock** faire provision de marchandises

▸**lay into** VT INSEP **1** *(attack ▸ physically)* tomber (à bras raccourcis) sur; *(▸ verbally)* prendre à partie, passer un savon à; **he really laid into his opponent** il est tombé à bras raccourcis sur son adversaire; **she laid into the government for their**

hard-line attitude elle a pris le gouvernement à partie pour son attitude intransigeante **2** *(eat greedily)* se jeter sur

▸ **lay off** VT SEP **1** *(employees)* licencier; *(temporarily)* mettre en chômage technique

2 *(in gambling ▸ bet)* couvrir

3 *Ins* **to l. off a risk** effectuer une réassurance

4 *Ftbl* **to l. the ball off for sb** placer le ballon en bonne position pour qn

VT INSEP *Fam* **1 to l. off sb** *(stop annoying, nagging)* ficher la paix à qn; **just l. off me!** fiche-moi la paix!; **I told her to l. off my husband** je lui ai dit de laisser mon mari tranquille□ **2** *(abstain from)* **to l. off the chocolate** ne plus manger de chocolat□; **to l. off the cigarettes** s'arrêter de fumer□; **you'd better l. off the booze for a while** tu devrais t'arrêter de boire pendant quelque temps□; *Fam* **l. off it, will you!** laisse tomber, tu veux!

VI *Fam (drop the subject)* laisser tomber; **l. off!** *(leave me alone)* fiche-moi la paix!

▸ **lay on** VT SEP **1** *(provide)* fournir; **drinks will be laid on** les boissons seront fournies; **the meal was laid on by our hosts** le repas nous fut offert par nos hôtes; **they had transport laid on for us** ils s'étaient occupés de nous procurer un moyen de transport

2 *Br (install)* installer, mettre; **the caravan has electricity laid on** la caravane a l'électricité

3 *(spread ▸ paint, plaster)* étaler; *Fam Fig* **to l. it on thick** *or* **with a trowel** en rajouter

4 *Am Fam* **to l. sth on sb** *(give)* filer qch à qn; *(tell)* raconter qch à qn□; **let me l. some advice on you** je vais te filer un bon conseil; **did she l. a heavy one on me!** elle n'a pas mâché ses mots!

5 *Fam (idiom)* **if you're not careful, I'll l. one on you!** *(hit)* fais gaffe ou je t'en mets une!

▸ **lay out** VT SEP **1** *(arrange, spread out)* étaler; **he laid his wares out on the ground** il a étalé *ou* déballé sa marchandise sur le sol

2 *(present, put forward)* exposer, présenter; **her ideas are clearly laid out in her book** ses idées sont clairement exposées dans son livre

3 *(design)* concevoir; **the house is badly laid out** la maison est mal agencée

4 *(corpse)* faire la toilette de

5 *(spend)* mettre; **we've already laid out a fortune on the project** nous avons déjà mis une fortune dans ce projet

6 *(knock out)* assommer, mettre K-O; **he was laid out cold** il a été mis K-O

7 *Typ* faire la maquette de, monter

▸ **lay over** VI *Am (stop off)* faire une halte, faire escale

▸ **lay up** VT SEP *Br* **1** *(store, save)* mettre de côté; *Fig* **you're just laying up trouble for yourself** tu te prépares des ennuis **2** *(confine to bed)* aliter; **she's laid up with mumps** elle est au lit avec les oreillons **3** *(ship)* désarmer; *(car)* mettre au garage; **my car is laid up** ma voiture est au garage

---

layabout ['leɪəbaʊt] N *Br Fam* paresseux(euse)□ *m,f,* fainéant(e) *m,f*

lay-away plan N *Am Com* vente *f* réservée *ou* à terme

lay-by *(pl* **lay-bys)** N **1** *Br Aut* aire *f* de stationnement **2** *Austr & NZ (deposit)* arrhes *fpl*; **to buy sth on l.** retenir qch en versant des arrhes

layer ['leɪə(r)] N **1** *(of skin, paint, wood)* couche *f*; *(of fabric, clothes)* épaisseur *f*; *Fig* **the poem has many layers of meaning** le poème peut être lu de différentes façons

2 *Geol* strate *f*, couche *f*

3 *Hort* marcotte *f*

4 *(hen)* pondeuse *f*

5 *Comput* couche *f*

VT **1** *(arrange in layers)* poser *ou* disposer en couches **2** *(hair)* couper en dégradé; **I'd like my hair layered** j'aimerais un dégradé; **a layered cut** une coupe en dégradé **3** *Hort* marcotter

▸▸ ***layer cake*** génoise *f*; **chocolate l. cake** génoise *f* au chocolat

layette [leɪ'et] N layette *f*

laying ['leɪɪŋ] N **1** *(of egg)* ponte *f* **2** *(of cables, carpets, rails, pipes)* pose *f*; *(of mine)* pose *f*, mouillage *m*; *(of wreath)* dépôt *m*; **a wreath-l. ceremony** un dépôt de gerbe; *Rel* **l. on of hands** imposition *f* des mains

▸▸ ***laying down*** *(of principle, rule etc)* établissement *m*; *(of sewage system, cable)* pose *f*; *(of ship)* mise *f* en chantier *ou* sur cale; *(of arms)* dépôt *m*; ***laying hen*** poule *f* pondeuse; ***laying out*** *(of dead body)* toilette *f*

layman ['leɪmən] *(pl* **laymen** [-mən]) N **1** *(non-specialist)* non-initié(e) *m,f*, profane *mf*; **the book is incomprehensible to the l.** le livre est incompréhensible pour le profane; **a l.'s guide to the stock market** un manuel d'initiation au système boursier **2** *(non-clerical)* laïc (laïque) *m,f*

lay-off N **1** *(sacking)* licenciement *m* **2** *(inactivity)* chômage *m* technique

▸▸ *Am* ***lay-off pay*** indemnité *f* de licenciement

layout ['leɪaʊt] N **1** *(gen)* disposition *f*; *(of building, park)* agencement *m*; *(of essay)* plan *m*; **the l. of the controls is very straightforward** la disposition des commandes est très simple **2** *Typ* maquette *f*, mise *f* en page **3** *(diagram)* schéma *m*

▸▸ *Typ* ***layout artist*** maquettiste *mf*

layover ['leɪəʊvə(r)] N *Am* escale *f*, halte *f*; **we had a three-hour l. in Miami** nous avons eu *ou* fait une escale de trois heures à Miami

laywoman ['leɪˌwʊmən] *(pl* **laywomen** [-ˌwɪmɪn]) N **1** *(non-specialist) f* non-initiée *f*, profane *f* **2** *(non-clerical)* laïque *f*

Lazarus ['læzərəs] PR N *Bible* Lazare

laze [leɪz] VI *(relax)* se reposer; *(idle)* paresser; **to l. in bed** traîner au lit; **we spent the holidays lazing on the beach** nous avons passé nos vacances à paresser sur la plage

N farniente *m*; **to have a l. in bed** traîner au lit

lazily ['leɪzɪlɪ] ADV paresseusement, avec paresse

laziness ['leɪzɪnɪs] N paresse *f*, fainéantise *f*

lazy ['leɪzɪ] *(compar* **lazier**, *superl* **laziest)** ADJ **1** *(idle)* paresseux, fainéant; *(relaxed)* indolent, nonchalant; **we spent a l. afternoon on the beach** on a passé l'après-midi à paresser sur la plage; **I feel too l. to do it** je n'ai pas l'énergie de le faire **2** *(movement)* paresseux, lent

▸▸ ***lazy eye*** amblyopie *f*; **to have a l. eye** être amblyope; ***lazy Susan*** *(on table)* plateau *m* tournant

lazybones ['leɪzɪbəʊnz] N *Fam* fainéant(e)□ *m,f*; **come on, l.!** allez, secoue-toi *ou* remue-toi un peu!

lb *(written abbr* **pound)** **3 lb** *or* **lbs** 3 livres

LBD [ˌelbiː'diː] N *(abbr* **little black dress)** petite robe *f* noire

LBO [ˌelbiː'əʊ] N *Fin (abbr* **leveraged buy-out)** rachat *m* d'entreprise financé par l'endettement

L/C *Com (written abbr* **letter of credit)** lettre *f* de crédit

LCD [ˌelsiː'diː] N *Comput (abbr* **liquid crystal display)** affichage *m* à cristaux liquides, LCD *m*

▸▸ ***LCD screen*** écran *m* LCD

LCL *Com (written abbr* **less than container load)** conteneur *m* chargé en partie

LDL-cholesterol [ˌeldiː'el-] N *Med* LDL-cholestérol *m*

LEA [ˌeliː'eɪ] N *Br Admin & Sch (abbr* **local education authority)** = organisme chargé de l'enseignement au niveau régional

lea [liː] N *Literary* pré *m*

leach [liːtʃ] VT **1** *Tech* lessiver, extraire par lessivage **2** *Chem & Pharm* lixivier

VI *(liquid)* filtrer (**through** à travers); **fertilizers have been leaching into the water supply** des engrais ont infiltré la réserve d'eau

lead[1] [led] N **1** *(metal)* plomb *m*; **it's made of l.** c'est en plomb

2 *Fam (bullets)* plomb *m*; **they pumped him full of l.** ils l'ont plombé

3 *(in pencil)* mine *f*

4 *(piece of lead ▸ for sounding)* plomb *m* (de sonde); *(▸ on car wheel, fishing line)* plomb *m*; *Typ* interligne *m*

5 *(idioms) Am Fam* **to get the l. out (of one's pants)** se magner (le train); *very Fam* **that'll put some l. in your pencil!** *(invigorate)* ça te requinquera!

VT **1** *(seal)* plomber **2** *Typ* interligner

ADJ *(made of lead)* de *ou* en plomb; *(containing lead)* plombifère; *Fam* **to go down like a l. balloon** tomber à plat□

• **leads** NPL *Br Constr (on roof)* plombs *mpl* (de couverture); *(on window)* plombures *fp*

plombs *mpl*

▸▸ ***lead crystal*** *(UNCOUNT)* verre *m* de *ou* a plomb; ***lead glass*** verre *m* de *ou* au plomb; ***lea ore*** minerai *m* de plomb; ***lead paint*** peinture *f* base de plomb; ***lead pencil*** crayon *m* noir *ou* à papier *ou* à mine de plomb; ***lead poisoning*** *Me* intoxication *f* par le plomb, saturnisme *m*; *Am Fam (death)* mort *f* par balle(s); *(injury)* blessure *f* par balle(s); *Am Fam* **to get l. poisoning** être tué, blessé par balle(s); ***lead pipe*** tuyau *m* de plomb ***lead shot*** grenaille *f* de plomb

LEAD[2] [liːd]

N
- tête **1**
- indice **3**
- rôle principal **5**
- fil **8**
- initiative **2**
- gros titre **4**
- laisse **7**

VT
- mener **1, 3, 5**
- diriger **2**
- demander **6**
- être à la tête de **2**
- amener **4**

VI
- mener **1, 2**
- aller devant **4**
- être en tête **2**
- conduire **7**

ADJ
- principal

(pt & pp **led** [led])

N **1** *Sport* tête *f*; **to be in the l.** être en tête, mener **to go into** *or* **to take the l.** *(in race)* prendre la tête *(in match)* mener; **to have a 10-point/10-length l** avoir 10 points/10 longueurs d'avance; **to have a good l. over the rest of the field** avoir une bonne avance sur les autres concurrents; **he's opened up a tremendous l.** il a pris une avance considérable

2 *(initiative)* initiative *f*; **he took the l. in asking questions** il fut le premier à poser des questions **take your l. from me** prenez exemple sur moi; **to follow sb's l.** suivre l'exemple de qn; **it's up to the government to give a l. on housing policy** c'est au gouvernement (qu'il revient) de donner l'exemple en matière de politique du logement

3 *(indication, clue)* indice *m*, piste *f*; **to give sb a l.** mettre qn sur la voie; **the police have several leads** la police tient plusieurs pistes; **we're currently following up an important l.** nous sommes actuellement sur une piste prometteuse

4 *Br Press* gros titre *m*; **the news made the l. in all the papers** la nouvelle était à la une de tous les journaux

5 *Cin & Theat (role)* rôle *m* principal; *(actor)* premier rôle *m* masculin; *(actress)* premier rôle *m* féminin; **Jude Law plays the male l.** Jude Law tient le premier rôle masculin

6 *Cards* **to have the l.** jouer le premier; **your l.!** à vous de jouer!; **whose l. is it?** c'est à qui de jouer?; **you must follow the l.** il faut fournir à la couleur demandée; **a heart l.** une ouverture à cœur

7 *(for dog)* laisse *f*; **dogs must be kept on a l.** *(sign)* les chiens doivent être tenus en laisse

8 *Elec* fil *m*

VT **1** *(take, guide)* mener, emmener, conduire; **was led into the garden** on m'a emmené *ou* conduit dans le jardin; **he led them across the lawn** il leur fit traverser la pelouse; **she led him down the stairs** elle lui fit descendre l'escalier; **she led them to safety** elle les a conduits en lieu sûr; **to l. an army into battle** mener une armée au combat; **to l. a team to victory** mener une équipe à la victoire; **the captain led the team onto the field** le capitaine a conduit son équipe sur le terrain; **she led them through the garden** *(to get out)* elle les fit passer par le jardin; *(to visit)* elle leur fit visiter le jardin; *Literary* **he led her to the altar** il la prit pour épouse; **to l. the way** montrer le chemin; **police motorcyclists led the way** des motards de la police ouvraient la route; **they led the cable along the edge of the floor** ils ont fait passé le câble par terre, le long du mur; *Bible* **l. us not into temptation** ne nous soumets pas à la tentation; *Prov* **you can l. a horse to water but you cannot make him drink** on ne saurait faire boire un âne qui n'a pas soif; *Fig* **to l. sb up the garden path** mener qn en bateau

2 *(be leader of)* être à la tête de, diriger; *(orchestra)* diriger; **to l. the prayers/singing** diriger la prière/les chants

3 *Sport (be in front of)* mener; **Stardust is leading Black Beauty by 10 lengths** Stardust a pris 10 longueurs d'avance sur Black Beauty; **to l. the field** mener; **to l. sb by 8 points** avoir une avance sur qn de 8 points; *Fig* **Great Britain leads the field in heart transplant technology** la Grande-Bretagne est le pays le plus avancé dans le domaine des greffes cardiaques

4 *(induce)* amener; **to l. sb to do sth** amener qn à faire qch; **despair led him to commit suicide** le désespoir l'a poussé au suicide; **he led me to believe (that) he was innocent** il m'a amené à croire qu'il était innocent; **everything leads us to believe (that) she is still alive** tout porte à croire *ou* nous avons toutes les raisons de croire qu'elle est encore en vie; **I was led to the conclusion that he had been lying all along** je suis arrivé à la conclusion qu'il mentait depuis le début; **what led you to apply for this job?** qu'est-ce qui vous a conduit *ou* amené à postuler?; **he is easily led** il se laisse facilement influencer; *Fig* **subsequent events led the country into war** des événements ultérieurs ont entraîné le pays dans la guerre; **this leads me to my second point** ceci m'amène à ma seconde remarque

5 *(life)* mener; **he has led a life of debauchery** il a mené une vie de débauche; **she has led a full and happy life** elle a eu une vie heureuse et bien remplie

6 *Cards* demander, jouer; **to l. trumps** demander *ou* jouer atout

7 *Law* **to l. a witness** poser des questions tendancieuses à un témoin

VI 1 *(go)* mener; **this path leads to the village** ce chemin mène au village; **where does this door l. to?** sur quoi ouvre cette porte?; **take the street that leads away from the station** prenez la rue qui part de la gare; **that road leads nowhere** cette route ne mène nulle part; *Fig* **this is leading nowhere!** cela ne rime à rien!

2 *Sport* mener, être en tête; **to l. by 2 metres** avoir 2 mètres d'avance; **to l. by 3 points to 1** mener par 3 points à 1; **Black Beauty is leading** Black Beauty est en tête

3 *Cards* **hearts led** cœur (a été) demandé; **Joanne to l.** c'est à Joanne de jouer

4 *(go in front)* aller devant; *(in mountaineering)* grimper en tête; **if you l., I'll follow** allez-y, je vous suis

5 *Br Press* **to l. with sth** mettre qch à la une; **the 'Times' led with news of the plane hijack** le détournement d'avion faisait la une *ou* était en première page du 'Times'

6 *Boxing* **he leads with his right** il attaque toujours du droit *ou* de la droite

7 *(in dancing)* conduire

8 *Law* être l'avocat principal; **he led for the prosecution** il dirigea l'accusation en tant qu'avocat principal

ADJ *(actor, singer)* principal, premier; *Press (article)* de tête

▸▸ *Law* ***lead counsel*** avocat(e) *m,f* principal(e); *Banking & St Exch* ***lead manager*** (banque *f*) chef *m* de file; ***lead time*** *Ind* délai *m* de préparation; *Com* délai *m* de livraison

▸**lead away VT SEP** emmener; **he led her away from the scene of the accident** il l'éloigna du lieu de l'accident

▸**lead back VT SEP** ramener, reconduire; **they led him back to his room** ils l'ont ramené *ou* reconduit à sa chambre

VI this path leads back to the beach ce chemin ramène à la plage

▸**lead off VI** *(in conversation)* commencer, débuter; *(in debate)* entamer les débats; *(in game)* jouer le (la) premier(ère); *(at dance)* ouvrir le bal; *(in relay race)* être le premier relayeur

VT INSEP 1 *(begin)* commencer, entamer **2** *(go from)* partir de; **several avenues l. off the square** plusieurs avenues partent de la place

VT SEP *(person)* conduire; **they were led off to jail** ils ont été conduits *ou* emmenés en prison

▸**lead on VI** aller *ou* marcher devant; **l. on!** allez-y!

VT SEP 1 *(trick)* **to l. sb on** faire marcher qn **2** *(bring on)* faire entrer; **l. on the horses!** faites entrer les chevaux! **3** *(in progression)* amener; **this leads me on to my second point** ceci m'amène à mon deuxième point

▸**lead out VT SEP** *Typ (lines of text)* augmenter l'interlignage de

▸**lead up to VT INSEP 1** *(path, road)* conduire à, mener à; **a narrow path led up to the house** un étroit sentier menait jusqu'à la maison; **those stairs l. up to the attic** cet escalier mène au grenier **2** *(in reasoning)* **she's leading up to something** je me demande où elle veut en venir; **what are you leading up to?** où voulez-vous en venir?; **I was just leading up to that** j'allais justement y venir **3** *(precede, cause)* **the events leading up to the war** les événements qui devaient déclencher la guerre; **the months leading up to her death** les mois qui précédèrent sa mort; *Mus* **the chords that l. up to the final movement** les accords qui introduisent le dernier mouvement

---

leaded ['ledɪd] **ADJ 1** *(door, box, billiard cue)* plombé **2** *(petrol)* au plomb **3** *Typ* interligné

▸▸ ***leaded window*** fenêtre *f* avec verre cathédrale

leaden ['ledən] **ADJ 1** *(made of lead)* de *ou* en plomb **2** *(dull ▸ sky)* de plomb, plombé; *(heavy ▸ sleep)* de plomb; *(▸ heart)* lourd; **he walked with l. steps** il marchait d'un pas lourd **3** *(oppressive ▸ atmosphere)* lourd, pesant; *(▸ silence)* de mort

leader ['li:də(r)] **N 1** *(head)* chef *m*; *Pol* chef *m*, leader *m*, dirigeant(e) *m,f*; *(of association)* dirigeant(e) *m,f*; *(of strike, protest, riot)* meneur (euse) *m,f*; **to be a born l.** être fait pour donner des ordres *ou* commander; **the leaders of the march were arrested** les organisateurs de la manifestation ont été arrêtés

2 *Sport (horse)* cheval *m* de tête; *(athlete)* coureur *m* de tête; *(in championship)* leader *m*; **she was up with the leaders** elle était parmi les premiers *ou* dans le peloton de tête

3 *(main body or driving force)* **the institute is a world l. in cancer research** l'institut occupe une des premières places mondiales en matière de recherche contre le cancer; **the leaders of fashion** ceux qui font la mode

4 *Mus (of orchestra) Br* premier violon *m*; *Am* chef *m* d'orchestre

5 *Br Journ* éditorial *m*

6 *Br Law* avocat(e) *m,f* principal(e)

7 *Mktg (product)* leader *m*; *(company)* chef *m* de file, leader *m*; *Am (loss leader)* produit *m* d'appel

8 *(for film, tape)* amorce *f*

9 *(in mountaineering)* premier *m* de cordée

▸▸ *Pol* ***the Leader of the House*** *(in the Commons)* = parlementaire de la majorité chargé de certaines fonctions dans la mise en place du programme gouvernemental; *(in the Lords)* = porte-parole du gouvernement; ***the Leader of the Opposition*** le chef de l'opposition; *Br Journ* ***leader writer*** éditorialiste *mf*

leaderboard ['li:dəbɔ:d] **N** tableau *m* de classement; *(in golf)* leaderboard *m*; *Fig* **to be top of the l.** être en tête du classement

leadership ['li:dəʃɪp] **N 1** *(direction)* direction *f*; **during** *or* **under her l.** sous sa direction; **he was offered the party l.** on lui a offert la direction du parti; **no one showed any l.** personne n'a montré des qualités de chef; **he has great l. qualities** c'est un excellent meneur d'hommes; **they looked to us for l.** ils comptaient sur nous pour leur montrer le chemin **2** *(leaders)* direction *f*, dirigeants *mpl*; **the l. of the movement is divided on this issue** les chefs *ou* les dirigeants du mouvement sont divisés sur cette question

▸▸ ***leadership battle, leadership contest*** bataille *f* pour la direction; ***leadership election*** élections *fpl* pour la position de leader; ***leadership potential*** qualités *fpl* de chef

lead-free [led-] **ADJ** *(paint, petrol)* sans plomb; *(toy)* (garanti) sans plomb

lead-in [li:d-] **N** *Br* **1** *(introductory remarks)* introduction *f*, remarques *fpl* préliminaires; *(introductory music)* introduction *f* **2** *Elec & Tel (of cable)* entrée *f*; *(to aerial)* descente *f* d'antenne

▸▸ ***lead-in groove*** *(on record)* sillon *m* initial

leading[1] ['li:dɪŋ] **ADJ 1** *(prominent)* premier, de premier plan; *(major)* majeur, principal, dominant; **l. figure** figure *f* de premier plan; **he is the l. actor in the company** c'est le meilleur acteur de la troupe **2** *Sport (in race)* de tête; *(in championship)* premier; **to be in the l. position** être en tête; **the l. runners/riders** les coureurs/cavaliers de tête **3** *(in front ▸ car)* de tête

N *(of horses)* conduite *f*, manège *m*

▸▸ ***leading article*** *Br* éditorial *m*; *Am* article *m* leader *ou* de tête; ***leading axle*** *(of vehicle)* essieu *m* porteur d'avant; *Cards* ***leading card*** première carte *f*; *Br Law* ***leading counsel*** avocat(e) *m,f* principal(e); *Elec* ***leading current*** courant *m* déphasé en avant; *Aviat* ***leading edge*** *(of wing)* bord *m* d'attaque; *Fig* **to be at the l. edge of technology** être à la pointe de la technologie; ***leading edge technology*** technologie *f* de pointe; *Econ* ***leading indicators*** principaux indicateurs *mpl* économiques; *Cin & Theat* ***leading lady*** premier rôle *m* (féminin); **Vivien Leigh was the l. lady** Vivien Leigh tenait le premier rôle féminin; ***leading light*** personnage *m* (de marque); **she's a l. light in the environmental lobby** c'est une personnalité très influente du mouvement écologiste; *Cin & Theat* ***leading man*** premier rôle *m* (masculin); **he was the l. man** il tenait le premier rôle masculin; *Mus* ***leading note*** sensible *f*; *Cin & Theat* ***leading part*** premier rôle *m*; **they played a l. part in the discussions** ils ont joué un rôle prépondérant dans le débat; *Mil* ***leading patrol*** patrouille *f* de tête; *Am* ***leading price indicator*** indice *m* composite des principaux indicateurs; ***leading question*** question *f* orientée; *Law* question *f* tendancieuse; ***leading rein*** *(for horse)* longe *f*; *Br* ***leading reins*** *(for child)* harnais *m*; *Cin & Theat* ***leading role*** rôle *m* principal, premier rôle *m*; **to play the l. role in a film** tenir le rôle principal d'un film; *St Exch* ***leading shares*** valeurs *fpl* vedettes; *St Exch* **a *leading shareholder*** un des principaux actionnaires; *Am* ***leading strings*** harnais *m (pour enfant)*; ***leading technology*** technologie *f* de pointe; ***leading wheels*** *(of vehicle)* essieu *m* porteur d'avant

leading[2] ['ledɪŋ] **N** *Typ & Comput (process)* interlignage *m*; *(space)* interligne *m*

lead-out [li:d-] **N** *Elec & Tel (of wire etc)* sortie *f*

▸▸ ***lead-out groove*** *(of record)* sillon *m* de sortie

lead-up [li:d-] **N** veille *f*; **in the l. to independence** dans la période qui a précédé l'indépendance

leadwork ['ledwɜ:k] **N** *Archit (of window)* plombs *mpl*

leaf [li:f] *(pl* **leaves** [li:vz]) **N 1** *(on plant, tree)* feuille *f*; **to come into l.** se couvrir de feuilles; **the tree has lost its leaves** l'arbre a perdu son feuillage *ou* ses feuilles; **the trees are in l.** les arbres sont en feuilles

2 *(page)* feuillet *m*, page *f*; **to take a l. out of sb's book** prendre exemple *ou* modèle sur qn

3 *(on table ▸ hinged)* abattant *m*; *(▸ inserted board)* allonge *f*, rallonge *f*

4 *(of door)* battant *m*, vantail *m*; *(of shutter)* battant *m*; *(of spring)* lame *f*

5 *(of metal)* feuille *f*

6 *Fam Drugs slang (marijuana)* marie-jeanne *f inv*, herbe *f*

▸▸ *Entom* ***leaf beetle*** chrysomèle *f*; ***leaf bud*** bourgeon *m* à feuille; ***leaf curl*** frisolée *f*; ***leaf green*** vert prairie *m inv*; *Entom* ***leaf insect*** phyllie *f*; ***leaf mould*** terreau *m* de feuilles; *Am* ***leaf peeping*** = activité consistant à admirer les feuillages d'automne; ***leaf spot*** *(UNCOUNT)* (maladie *f* des) taches *fpl* noires; *Tech* ***leaf spring*** ressort *m* à lames; ***leaf tobacco*** tabac *m* en feuilles

▸**leaf through VT INSEP** *(book, magazine)* feuilleter, parcourir

leaflet ['li:flɪt] **N 1** *(brochure)* prospectus *m*, dépliant *m*; *(political)* tract *m* **2** *(instruction sheet)* notice *f* (explicative), mode *m* d'emploi

VT distribuer des prospectus *ou* des tracts à; **has the area been leafleted?** est-ce qu'on a distribué des tracts dans le quartier?

VI distribuer des prospectus *ou* des tracts

▸▸ ***leaflet drop*** distribution *f* de prospectus

leafleter ['li:flɪtə(r)] **N** distributeur(trice) *m,f* de prospectus *ou* de tracts

leafstalk ['li:fstɔ:k] **N** *Bot* pétiole *f*

leafy ['li:fɪ] *(compar* **leafier**, *superl* **leafiest**) **ADJ** *(tree)* feuillu; *(woodland)* boisé, vert; **a l. avenue** une avenue bordée d'arbres; **a l. suburb** une banlieue verte

league [liːg] **N 1** *(alliance)* ligue *f*; **to be in l. (with sb)** être de mèche *ou* de connivence (avec qn); **they're all in l. against me** ils se sont tous ligués contre moi

2 *Sport (competition)* championnat *m*; *(division)* division *f*; **United are l. leaders at the moment** United est en tête du championnat en ce moment

3 *Fig (class)* **I'm not in your l., I'm not in the same l. as you** je ne suis pas de votre niveau; **I thought I was good but he's in another l.** je pensais que j'étais bon mais il est bien meilleur que moi; **to be in the big l.** être parmi les meilleurs; **that's way out of our l.** ce n'est pas du tout dans nos possibilités

4 *Arch (distance)* lieue *f*

►► *Ftbl* ***league champions*** champion *m*; **to become l. champions** remporter le championnat; *Ftbl* ***league championship*** championnat *m*; *Ftbl* ***league match*** match *m* de championnat; *Hist* ***the League of Nations*** la Société des Nations; *Br Ftbl* ***league table*** (classement *m* du) championnat *m*; *Fig* **a l. table of statistics** un classement statistique

leak [liːk] **N 1** *(in pipe, tank, roof)* fuite *f*; *(in boat)* voie *f* d'eau **2** *(disclosure* ► *of information, secret)* fuite *f* **3** *very Fam (idioms)* **to go for** *or* **to take a l.** *(urinate)* pisser un coup

VI 1 *(pen, roof, bucket, pipe)* fuir; *(boat, shoe)* prendre l'eau; **the roof leaks** il y a une fuite dans le toit **2** *(gas, liquid)* fuir, s'échapper; **the rain leaks through the ceiling** la pluie s'infiltre par le plafond

VT 1 *(liquid)* répandre, faire couler; **the can leaked oil onto my trousers** de l'huile du bidon s'est répandue sur mon pantalon; **the radiator had been leaking water everywhere** le radiateur avait fui et il y avait de l'eau partout **2** *(information)* divulguer; **to l. sth to the press** divulguer qch à la presse; **the budget details were leaked** il y a eu des fuites sur le budget

►**leak out VI 1** *(liquid, gas)* fuir, s'échapper **2** *(news, secret)* filtrer, transpirer; **the truth finally leaked out** la vérité a fini par se savoir

leakage ['liːkɪdʒ] **N** *(UNCOUNT)* fuite *f*; **damage caused by l.** des dégâts dus à des fuites

leaky ['liːkɪ] *(compar* **leakier**, *superl* **leakiest) ADJ** *(pen, roof, bucket, pipe)* qui fuit; *(boat, shoes)* qui prend l'eau

lean¹ [liːn] *(Br pt & pp* **leaned** *or* **leant** [lent], *Am pt & pp* **leaned) VT 1** *(prop* ► *ladder, bicycle)* appuyer; **he leant the ladder/bike (up) against the tree** il appuya l'échelle/le vélo contre l'arbre **2** *(rest* ► *head, elbows)* appuyer; **to l. one's elbows on sth** s'accouder à qch; **she leant her head on his shoulder** elle posa sa tête sur son épaule **3** *(incline)* pencher; **to l. one's head to one side** pencher *ou* incliner la tête

VI *(be on incline)* pencher, s'incliner; **she/a ladder was leaning (up) against the wall** elle/une échelle était appuyée contre le mur; **he was leaning with his back to** *or* **against the wall** il était adossé au mur; **she leant down to speak to me** elle s'est penchée pour me parler; **to l. in through the window** pencher la tête par la fenêtre; **l. on my arm** appuyez-vous *ou* prenez appui sur mon bras

lean² [liːn] **N 1** *(slope)* inclinaison *f* **2** *(meat)* maigre *m*

ADJ 1 *(animal, meat)* maigre; *(person* ► *thin)* maigre; *(*► *slim)* mince; *Fig* **the company is now fitter and leaner than it was before** l'entreprise se porte mieux depuis que sa structure a été allégée **2** *(poor* ► *harvest)* maigre, pauvre; *(*► *period of time)* difficile; **we had a l. time** nous avons eu une période de vaches maigres **3** *(deficient* ► *ore, mixture)* pauvre

lean-burn ADJ *(engine)* à mélange pauvre

leaning ['liːnɪŋ] **N** *(tendency)* inclination *f* (**towards** pour), penchant *m* (**towards** pour *ou* vers), tendance *f* (**towards** à); **she has communist leanings** elle a des penchants communistes; **she has literary leanings** elle aimerait être écrivain

ADJ *(tree, wall)* penché

►► ***the Leaning Tower of Pisa*** la tour de Pise

leanness ['liːnnɪs] **N** maigreur *f*

leant [lent] *Br pt & pp of* **lean**

lean-to N *Br* appentis *m*

►► ***lean-to garage*** = garage attenant à la maison, avec un toit incliné; ***lean-to roof*** comble *m* en appentis

leap [liːp] *(Br pt & pp* **leaped** *or* **leapt** [lept], *Am pt & pp* **leaped) N 1** *(jump)* saut *m*, bond *m*; **with one l. she cleared the ditch** d'un saut *ou* d'un bond elle franchit le fossé; *also Fig* **to take a l. forward** faire un bond en avant, sauter en avant; **it's a great l. forward in medical research** c'est un grand bond en avant pour la recherche médicale; **his heart gave a l.** son cœur bondit, son cœur fit un bond; **by leaps and bounds** à pas de géant; **his French had improved by leaps and bounds** il avait fait des progrès phénoménaux en français; *Fig* **to take a l. in the dark** faire un saut dans l'inconnu **2** *(in prices)* bond *m*

VT 1 *(fence, stream)* sauter (par-dessus), franchir d'un bond **2** *(horse)* faire sauter

VI 1 *(person, animal)* bondir, sauter; *(flame)* jaillir; **to l. to one's feet** se lever d'un bond; **to l. for joy** *(person)* sauter de joie; *(heart)* faire un bond; **we leapt back in fright** de frayeur, nous fîmes un bond en arrière; **to l. into the air** sauter en l'air; **we had to l. over the stream** nous avons dû sauter par-dessus le ruisseau **2** *Fig* faire un bond; **the price of petrol leapt by 10 percent** le prix du pétrole a fait un bond de 10 pour cent; **the answer almost leapt off the page at me** la réponse m'a pour ainsi dire sauté aux yeux; **she leapt to the wrong conclusion** elle a conclu trop hâtivement

►► ***leap day*** jour *m* intercalaire; ***leap second*** seconde *f* intercalaire; ***leap year*** année *f* bissextile

►**leap up VI** *(into the air)* sauter (en l'air); *(to one's feet)* se lever d'un bond; **to l. up in surprise** sauter au plafond, sursauter; **to l. up in indignation** bondir d'indignation; **the dog leapt up at him** le chien lui a sauté dessus

leapfrog ['liːpfrɒg] *(pt & pp* **leapfrogged**, *cont* **leapfrogging) N** saute-mouton *m*; **to play l.** jouer à saute-mouton

VT to l. sb/sth sauter par-dessus qn/qch à saute-mouton; *Br Fig* dépasser qn/qch; **he leapfrogged several of his more senior colleagues to get the post** il a obtenu le poste en passant devant plusieurs de ses collègues d'un échelon supérieur

VI *Br* **to l. over sb** sauter par-dessus qn; *Fig* **to l. into the computer age** se trouver propulsé à l'ère de l'informatique

leapt [lept] *Br pt & pp of* **leap**

learn [lɜːn] *(Br pt & pp* **learned** *or* **learnt** [lɜːnt], *Am pt & pp* **learned) VT 1** *(by instruction)* apprendre; **to l. (how) to do sth** apprendre à faire qch; **she's learning the violin** elle apprend à jouer du violon, elle étudie le violon; **to l. sth by heart** apprendre qch par cœur; *Fig* **he's learnt his lesson now** cela lui a servi de leçon **2** *(discover, hear)* apprendre; **I subsequently learnt that he wouldn't be coming** j'ai appris par la suite qu'il ne viendrait pas **3** *Fam (teach)* apprendre[□]; **that'll l. you!** ça t'apprendra!

VI 1 *(by instruction, experience)* apprendre; **to l. about sth** apprendre qch; **to l. by** *or* **from one's mistakes** tirer la leçon de ses erreurs; **they learnt the hard way** ils ont été à dure école; **it's never too late to l.** il n'est jamais trop tard pour apprendre **2** *(be informed)* **to l. of sth** apprendre qch

►**learn off VT SEP** *Br* apprendre par cœur

►**learn up VT SEP** *Br Fam* bûcher, potasser; **I've been learning up all about the town's history** j'ai potassé tout ce qui a trait à l'histoire de la ville

learned *[senses* **1**, **2** 'lɜːnɪd, *sense* **3** lɜːnd] **ADJ 1** *(erudite* ► *person)* savant, érudit; *(*► *subject, book, society)* savant **2** *Law (lawyer)* **my l. friend** mon éminent confrère **3** *Psy (behaviour)* acquis

►► ***learned profession*** profession *f* intellectuelle

learner ['lɜːnə(r)] **N** apprenant(e) *m,f*; *Br (driver)* = personne qui apprend à conduire; **to be a quick l.** apprendre vite; **learners of English** les apprenants d'anglais, les gens qui apprennent l'anglais

►► *Br* ***learner driver*** = personne qui apprend à conduire; *Am* ***learner's permit*** permis *m* de conduire provisoire *(autorisation que l'on doit obtenir avant de prendre des leçons)*

learning ['lɜːnɪŋ] **N 1** *(erudition)* érudition *f*, savoir *m*; **a man of great l.** *(in sciences)* un grand savant; *(in arts)* un homme d'une grande érudition ou culture **2** *(acquisition of knowledge)* étude *f*; *Mktg* apprentissage *m*; **language l.** l'étude *f* ou l'apprentissage *m* des langues; **adults/children with l. difficulties** *or* **disabilities** adultes *mpl*/enfants *mpl* atteints d'un handicap mental

►► ***learning capacity*** capacités *fpl* d'apprentissage; ***learning curve*** courbe *f* d'assimilation; **it was a steep l. curve** l'apprentissage a été difficile; ***learning support*** = soutien scolaire pour les enfants ayant des difficultés d'apprentissage

learnt [lɜːnt] *Br pt & pp of* **learn**

ADJ *Psy* acquis

lease [liːs] **N 1** *Law* bail *m*; *(of equipment)* location *f*; *(of house to let)* bail *m* (à loyer); *(of farming land)* bail *m* à ferme; *(document)* (contrat *m* de) bail *m*; **a 99-year l.** un bail de 99 ans; **to take (out) a l. on a house, to take a house on l.** prendre une maison à bail; **to sign a l.** signer un bail **2** *(idioms)* **to take on a new l. of life** *(person)* renaître à la vie; *(industry, town, football club)* retrouver un nouveau souffle; **the trip has given her a new l.** *Br* **o** *orAm* **on life** le voyage l'a remise en forme *ou* lui a redonné du tonus; **cleaning the engine will give the car a new l. of life** ça va retaper la voiture de nettoyer le moteur

VT 1 *(of owner* ► *house)* louer *ou* céder à bail; *(*► *equipment, vehicle)* louer; *(*► *land)* affermer **2** *(of tenant* ► *house)* louer, prendre à bail; *(of person* ► *equipment, vehicle)* louer; *(*► *land)* prendre en fermage

►► ***lease contract*** *(for property)* contrat *m* de bail *(for equipment)* contrat *m* en location; *Fin* ***lease financing*** leasing *m*, location *f* avec option d'achat; *Comput* ***leased line*** ligne *f* louée

►**lease back VT SEP** *Fin* = louer dans le cadre d'une cession-bail

leaseback ['liːsbæk] **N** cession-bail *f*

leasehold ['liːshəʊld] **N** *(lease)* bail *m*; *(property)* location *f* à bail

ADJ loué à bail

leaseholder ['liːs,həʊldə(r)] **N** *(tenant)* locataire *mf*

lease-purchase N crédit-bail *m*

►► ***lease-purchase contract*** contrat *m* de crédit-bail

leash [liːʃ] **N** *(for dog)* laisse *f*; **to put a dog on the l.** mettre une laisse à un chien; **dogs must be kept on a l.** *(sign)* les chiens doivent être tenus en laisse; *Fig* **to keep sb on a tight l.** tenir la bride haute à qn; **to keep one's emotions on a tight l.** avoir étroitement en mains les rênes de ses émotions

leasing ['liːsɪŋ] **N** *(of house)* location *f* à bail; *(of equipment, vehicle)* location *f*; *(of land)* affermage *m*; *(on lease-purchase)* location-bail *f*; *(system)* location *f* avec option d'achat, crédit-bail *m*, leasing *m*

►► ***leasing company*** société *f* de leasing

LEAST [liːst]

PRON
• le moins **1** • le/la moindre **2**

ADJ
• le moins de **1** • le/la moindre **2**

ADV
• le moins

PRON 1 *(in quantity, size)* **he's the one who drank the l.** c'est lui qui a bu le moins; **he's got the l.** c'est lui qui en a le moins

2 *(slightest)* **it was the l. we could do** c'était la moindre des choses; **that's the l. of our worries** c'est le moindre *ou* c'est le cadet de nos soucis; *Prov* **l. said, soonest mended** moins on en dit, mieux on se porte

ADJ *(superl of* **little) 1** *(in quantity, size)* **I ate the l. chocolate** c'est moi qui ai mangé le moins de chocolat; **she has the l. money out of all of us** c'est elle qui a le moins d'argent d'entre nous tous

2 *(slightest)* **I haven't the l. idea** je n'en ai pas la moindre idée; **the l. thing upsets her** un rien la contrarie; **I'm not the l. bit musical** je ne suis pas musicien pour un sou; **I'm not the l. bit interested** cela ne m'intéresse pas le moins du monde

ADV (le) moins; **which do you find (the) l. useful?** à votre avis, lequel est le moins utile?; **the l. interesting film I've ever seen** le film le moins intéressant que j'aie jamais vu; **it's what we l. expected** c'est ce à quoi nous nous attendions le moins

• **at least** ADV **1** *(not less than)* au moins; **at l. $500** au moins 500 dollars; **she's at l. 70** elle a au moins 70 ans; **she's at l. as tall as you** elle est au moins aussi grande que toi

2 *(as a minimum)* au moins; **I can at l. try** je peux toujours essayer; **you could at l. have phoned** vous auriez pu au moins téléphoner; **at the very l. he might have warned us** la moindre des choses aurait été de nous avertir

3 *(indicating an advantage)* au moins, du moins; **at l. we've got an umbrella** au moins *ou* du moins on a un parapluie

4 *(used to qualify)* du moins; **I didn't like him, at l. not at first** il ne m'a pas plu, en tout cas *ou* du moins pas au début

• **in the least** ADV *(with negative)* **not in the l.** pas du tout, pas le moins du monde; **am I boring you? – not in the l.** je t'ennuie? – pas du tout; **she's not in the l. angry** elle n'est pas du tout fâchée; **she didn't seem to mind in the l.** ça ne semblait pas la déranger le moins du monde

• **least of all** ADV surtout pas, encore moins; **nobody could understand it, Liz l. of all** *or* **l. of all Liz** personne ne comprenait, surtout pas Liz *ou* Liz encore moins que les autres; **we didn't expect to win any prizes, l. of all this one** nous ne nous attendions pas à gagner un prix, et en tout cas, certainement pas celui-là

• **not least** ADV **many politicians, not l. the Foreign Secretary, are in favour** de nombreux hommes politiques y sont favorables, notamment le ministre des Affaires étrangères

►► *Br* ***least common denominator*** plus petit dénominateur *m* commun

least-developed country N pays *m* parmi les moins avancés

leastways ['li:stweɪz], *Am* **leastwise** ['li:stwaɪz] ADV *Fam* du moins[□]

leather ['leðə(r)] N **1** *(material)* cuir *m*; **real l.** cuir *m* véritable; **made of l.** de *ou* en cuir; *Br Fam* **leathers** *(clothes)* cuir *m* **2** *(for polishing)* **(wash** *or* **window) l.** peau *f* de chamois **3** *(of pump, valve etc)* cuir *m*; **stirrup l.** étrivière *f*

COMP *(jacket, shoes, sofa, bag)* de *ou* en cuir

VT *Fam (punish)* tanner le cuir à

►► ***leather goods*** *(ordinary)* articles *mpl* en cuir; *(finer)* maroquinerie *f*

leatherbound ['leðəbaʊnd] ADJ relié (en) cuir

leathercloth ['leðəklɒθ] N toile *f* cuir

leatherette [ˌleðə'ret] N similicuir *m*

COMP *(purse, bag, clothing)* en similicuir

leathering ['leðərɪŋ] N *Br Fam* raclée *f*; **to give sb a l.** tanner le cuir à qn

leatherjacket ['leðəˌdʒækɪt] N *Entom* larve *f* de la tipule

leatherneck ['leðənek] N *Am Fam* marine[□] *m*, marsouin *m*

leatherwork ['leðəwɜ:k] N *(activity, products)* maroquinerie *f*

leathery ['leðərɪ] ADJ *(meat)* coriace; *(skin)* parcheminé, tanné

LEAVE [li:v]

VI
• partir **1, 2**

VT
• quitter **1, 2, 4**
• laisser **3–8, 10–12, 15**
• oublier **7**
• rester **9**
• confier **12**
• léguer **14**

N
• congé **1, 3**
• permission **1, 2**

(pt & pp **left** [left])

VI **1** *(depart)* partir; **my flight leaves at ten** mon avion part à dix heures; **we're leaving for Mexico tomorrow** nous partons pour le Mexique demain; **which station do you l. from?** vous partez de quelle gare?; **he's just left for lunch** il vient de partir déjeuner; **if you'd rather I left...** si vous voulez que je vous laisse...

2 *(quit)* partir; **half of the staff have left** la moitié du personnel est partie; **fewer schoolchildren are now leaving at 16** les élèves sont aujourd'hui moins nombreux à quitter l'école à 16 ans

3 *(end relationship)* **Charles, I'm leaving!** Charles, je te quitte!

VT **1** *(depart from* ► *place)* quitter; **she left London yesterday** elle est partie de *ou* elle a quitté Londres hier; **he left the room** il est sorti de *ou* il a quitté la pièce; **I l. home at 8 o'clock every morning** je pars *ou* je sors de chez moi tous les matins à 8 heures; **she never leaves the house** elle ne sort jamais de la maison; **to l. the table** se lever de table; **may I l. the table?** est-ce que je peux sortir de table?; **his brakes failed and the car left the road** ses freins ont lâché et la voiture a quitté la route; **the train left the rails** le train a déraillé; **his eyes never left her** il ne la quittait pas des yeux

2 *(quit* ► *job, institution)* quitter; **I left home at 18** je suis parti de chez moi *ou* de chez mes parents à 18 ans; **to l. school** quitter l'école; *Mil* **to l. the service** quitter le service

3 *(in specified place or state)* laisser; **you can't l. them alone for a minute** on ne peut pas les laisser seuls une minute; **he left her asleep on the sofa** elle était endormie sur le canapé lorsqu'il la quitta; **I left him to his reading** je l'ai laissé à sa lecture; **I left him to himself** je l'ai laissé seul; **left to himself, who knows what he'd do?** qui sait ce qu'il ferait s'il était livré à lui-même?; **just l. me alone!** laissez-moi tranquille!; **let's l. it at that, we'll l. it at that** *(not do any more work)* arrêtons-nous là; *(not argue any more)* n'en parlons plus

4 *(abandon* ► *person)* quitter; *(take leave of* ► *person)* laisser; **she left him for another man** elle l'a quitté pour un autre; **the prisoners were left to die** les prisonniers furent abandonnés à une mort certaine; **you may l. us now** vous pouvez disposer maintenant

5 *(deposit, set down)* laisser; **it's no trouble to l. you at the station** ça ne me dérange pas de vous laisser *ou* déposer à la gare

6 *(for someone's use, information etc)* laisser; **I've left your dinner in the oven for you** je t'ai laissé de quoi dîner dans le four; **he's out, do you want to l. (him) a message?** il n'est pas là, voulez-vous (lui) laisser un message?; **she left word for you to call her back** elle a demandé que vous la rappeliez

7 *(forget)* laisser, oublier; **I must have left my gloves at the café** j'ai dû oublier mes gants au café

8 *(allow or cause to remain)* laisser; **l. some cake for your brother** laisse du gâteau pour ton frère; **if you don't like your dinner, then l. it** si tu n'aimes pas ton dîner, laisse-le; **l. the stew to cook for two hours** laissez mijoter le ragoût pendant deux heures; **l. yourself an hour to get to the airport** prévoyez une heure pour aller à l'aéroport; **I only left myself £20 a week to live on** je n'avais plus que 20 livres par semaine pour me nourrir; **don't l. things to the last minute** n'attendez pas la dernière minute (pour faire ce que vous avez à faire); **he left his work unfinished** il n'a pas terminé son travail; **he left his dinner untouched** il ne toucha pas à son dîner; **to l. sth unsaid** passer qch sous silence; **their behaviour leaves a lot to be desired** leur conduite laisse beaucoup à désirer; **her words left me curious to know more** le peu qu'elle a dit m'a donné l'envie d'en savoir plus; **the decision leaves me in a bit of a quandary** cette décision me place devant un dilemme; **I want to be left on/off the list** je veux que mon nom reste/ je ne veux pas que mon nom figure sur la liste; **I was left with the bill** c'est moi qui ai dû payer l'addition; **she had been left a widow at 30** elle s'était retrouvée veuve à l'âge de 30 ans; **the flood has left thousands homeless** les inondations ont fait des milliers de sans-abri

9 *(passive use)* **to be left** *(remain)* rester; **we finished what was left of the cake** on a fini ce qui restait du gâteau; **there's nothing left** il ne reste (plus) rien; **there wasn't enough left to go round** il n'en restait pas assez pour tout le monde; **I've got £10/10 minutes left** il me reste 10 livres/10 minutes; **there's no doubt left in my mind** il n'y a plus le moindre doute dans mon esprit; **he had nothing left to do but lock up the house** il ne lui restait (plus) qu'à fermer la maison

10 *(mark, trace)* laisser; **the wine left a stain** le vin a fait une tache

11 *(allow)* **can I l. you to deal with it, then?** vous vous en chargez, alors?; **she leaves me to get on with things** elle me laisse faire; **to l. sb in charge of sth** confier la responsabilité de qch à qn; **right then, I'll l. you to it** bon, eh bien, je te laisse

12 *(entrust)* laisser, confier; **can I l. my suitcase with you for a few minutes?** puis-je vous confier ma valise quelques instants?; **she left the detailed arrangements to her secretary** elle a laissé à sa secrétaire le soin de régler les détails; **nothing was left to chance** on avait paré à toutes les éventualités; **I'll l. it to you to finish it off** je vous laisse (le soin de) finir; **l. it to me!** je m'en occupe!, je m'en charge!; **l. it with me** laissez-moi faire, je m'en charge

13 *Br Math* **9 from 16 leaves 7** 16 moins 9 égale 7

14 *(bequeath)* léguer; **she left all her money to charity** elle légua toute sa fortune à des œuvres de charité

15 *(be survived by)* **he leaves a wife and two children** il laisse une femme et deux enfants

N **1** *(from work)* congé *m*; *Mil* permission *f*; **to be/ to go on l.** *(gen)* être/partir en congé; *Mil* être/ partir en permission

2 *(permission)* permission *f*, autorisation *f*; **he asked l. to address the meeting** il a demandé la permission de prendre la parole devant l'assemblée; **by** *or* **with your l.** avec votre permission; **without so much as a by your l.** sans même en demander la permission

3 *(farewell)* congé *m*; **to take one's l. (of sb)** prendre congé (de qn); **to take l. of sb** prendre congé de qn; *Fig* **to take l. of one's senses** perdre la tête *ou* la raison

►► ***leave of absence*** congé *m* (exceptionnel); *(without pay)* congé *m* sans solde; *Mil* permission *f* exceptionnelle

►**leave behind** VT SEP **1** *(not take)* laisser; **it's hard to l. all your friends and relations behind** c'est dur de laisser tous ses amis et sa famille derrière soi; **they left me behind** ils sont partis sans moi

2 *(forget)* laisser, oublier; **somebody left their watch behind** quelqu'un a laissé *ou* oublié sa montre

3 *(leave as trace)* laisser; **the cyclone left behind a trail of destruction** le cyclone a tout détruit sur son passage

4 *(outstrip)* distancer, devancer; **she soon left the other runners behind** elle a vite distancé tous les autres coureurs; **if you don't work harder you'll soon get left behind** si tu ne travailles pas plus, tu vas vite te retrouver loin derrière les autres

►**leave in** VT SEP *(word, paragraph)* garder, laisser

►**leave off** VI *(stop)* s'arrêter; **we'll carry on from where we left off** nous allons reprendre là où nous nous étions arrêtés; *Br Fam* **l. off, will you!** arrête, tu veux!

VT INSEP *Br Fam (stop)* **to l. off doing sth** arrêter de faire qch[□]; **if it leaves off raining, we'll go for a walk** s'il s'arrête de pleuvoir *ou* si la pluie cesse, nous irons nous promener

VT SEP **1** *(not put on)* ne pas remettre; **who left the top of the toothpaste off?** qui a laissé le tube de dentifrice débouché?; **you can l. your jacket off** ce n'est pas la peine de remettre ta veste **2** *(not switch or turn on* ► *tap, gas)* laisser fermé; *(*► *light)* laisser éteint; *(not plug in* ► *appliance)* laisser débranché; **we left the heating off while we were away** nous avons arrêté *ou* coupé le chauffage pendant notre absence

►**leave on** VT SEP **1** *(not take off* ► *garment)* garder; *(*► *top, cover)* laisser; **don't l. the price tag on** enlève l'étiquette **2** *(not switch or turn off* ► *tap, gas)* laisser ouvert; *(*► *light)* laisser allumé; *(not unplug* ► *appliance)* laisser branché; **I hope I didn't l. the gas on** j'espère que j'ai éteint le gaz

►**leave out** VT SEP **1** *(omit)* omettre; **l. out any reference to her husband in your article** dans votre article, évitez toute allusion à son mari

2 *(exclude)* exclure; **I felt completely left out at the party** j'ai eu le sentiment d'être totalement tenu à l'écart *ou* exclu de leur petite fête; **l. her out of this!** laissez-la en dehors de ça!, ne la mêlez pas à ça!

3 *(not put away* ► *by accident)* ne pas ranger; *(*► *on purpose)* laisser sorti, ne pas ranger; **he left a meal out for the children** il a laissé un repas tout prêt pour les enfants; **l. the disks out where I can see them** laisse les disquettes en évidence; **who left the milk out overnight?** qui a oublié de mettre le lait au frigo hier soir?

4 *(leave outdoors)* laisser dehors; **to l. the washing out to dry** mettre le linge à sécher (dehors)

5 *Br Fam (idiom)* **l. it out!** arrête!

▸**leave over** VT SEP *(allow or cause to remain)* laisser; **to be left over** rester; **there are still one or two left over** il en reste encore un ou deux

---

-leaved [li:vd] SUFF **three-l.** *(screen)* à trois panneaux; **broad-l.** feuillu; **ivy-l.** à feuilles de lierre

leaven ['levən] N *(yeast)* levain *m*; *Fig* **he brought a l. of humour to the dullest occasion** il apportait une touche *ou* pointe d'humour dans les occasions les plus sinistres

VT **1** *Culin* faire lever **2** *Fig (occasion, atmosphere)* égayer

▸▸ ***leavened bread*** pain *m* au levain

leavening ['levənɪŋ] N *also Fig* levain *m*

leaver ['li:və(r)] N *Br* **(school) leavers** élèves *mpl* sortants

▸▸ ***leavers' ball*** bal *m* (de lycéens)

leave-taking N *(UNCOUNT)* adieux *mpl*

leaving ['li:vɪŋ] N départ *m*

▸▸ *Ir Sch* ***Leaving Certificate*** baccalauréat *m*

leavings ['li:vɪŋz] NPL *(from meal)* restes *mpl*

Lebanese [ˌlebə'ni:z] *(pl* **inv**) N Libanais(e) *m,f*

ADJ libanais

COMP *(embassy, history)* du Liban

Lebanon ['lebənən] N Liban *m*; **in (the) L.** au Liban

lech [letʃ] *Fam* N obsédé▫ *m*

VI **stop leching!** ne prends pas ce regard lubrique!▫; **he's always leching after my secretary** il n'arrête pas de reluquer ma secrétaire

lecher ['letʃə(r)] N débauché *m*, obsédé *m* (sexuel)

lecherous ['letʃərəs] ADJ lubrique

lecherously ['letʃərəslɪ] ADV lubriquement, avec lubricité; **to look at sb l.** regarder qn d'un œil lubrique

lechery ['letʃərɪ] N lubricité *f*

lecithin ['lesɪθɪn] N *Chem* lécithine *f*

lectern ['lektən] N lutrin *m*; *(in library)* pupitre *m*, lutrin *m*

lector ['lektə(r)] N *Rel & Univ* lecteur(trice) *m,f*

lecture ['lektʃə(r)] N **1** *(talk)* conférence *f*, exposé *m*; *Univ (as part of course)* cours *m* (magistral); **she gave a very good l. on Yeats** elle a fait un très bon cours sur Yeats; **have you been to his linguistics lectures?** avez-vous suivi ses cours de linguistique? **2** *Fig (sermon)* sermon *m*, discours *m*; **to give sb a l.** sermonner qn, faire des remontrances à qn; **she gave the children a l. on how to behave** elle a donné aux enfants une leçon de bonne conduite

COMP *(notes)* de cours

VI *(talk)* faire *ou* donner une conférence; *(teach)* faire (un) cours; **he lectures twice a week** il fait cours deux fois par semaine; **she lectures in linguistics** elle enseigne la *ou* donne des cours de linguistique; **she lectures on Dante** elle donne des cours sur Dante; **he lectures at Stirling** il enseigne à l'université de Stirling

VT *(reprimand)* réprimander, sermonner

▸▸ ***lecture hall*** salle *f* de cours, amphithéâtre *m*; ***lecture room*** salle *f* de cours *ou* de conférences; ***lecture theatre*** salle *f* de cours, amphithéâtre *m*

> Note that the French word **lecture** is a false friend and is never a translation for the English word **lecture**. It means **reading**.

lecturer ['lektʃərə(r)] N *(speaker)* conférencier (ère) *m,f*; *Univ (teacher)* enseignant(e) *m,f* du supérieur; **she's a l. in English at the University of Dublin** elle enseigne l'anglais à l'université de Dublin; **assistant l.** assistant(e) *m,f*; **is she a good l.?** est-ce que c'est un bon professeur?; **senior l.** maître *m* de conférences

lectureship ['lektʃəʃɪp] N *Univ* poste *m* d'enseignant dans le supérieur; **he got a l. at the University of Oxford** il a obtenu un poste à l'université d'Oxford; **senior l.** poste *m* de maître de conférences

LED [ˌeli:'di:] N *Comput (abbr* **light-emitting diode**) DEL *f*, LED *f*

▸▸ ***LED display*** affichage *m* (par) LED

led [led] *pt & pp of* **lead²**

> **-LED** SUFFIXE
>
> Le suffixe **-led** s'associe à des substantifs pour former des adjectifs auxquels il donne le sens de QUI EST LE FACTEUR LE PLUS IMPORTANT dans l'activité en question:
>
> **export-led growth** une croissance fondée sur les exportations; **design-led products** des produits qui privilégient le design; **trade-led recovery** une reprise dans laquelle le commerce joue un rôle essentiel.
>
> Il s'agit d'un suffixe assez productif, notamment dans le domaine des affaires et de la politique.

ledge [ledʒ] N **1** *(shelf)* rebord *m* **2** *Geog (on mountain)* saillie *f*; *(on rock or cliff face)* corniche *f*; *(on seabed)* haut-fond *m* **3** *Geol (vein)* filon *m*

ledger ['ledʒə(r)] N **1** *Com & Fin* grand-livre *m*, livre *m* de comptabilité *ou* de comptes **2** *Tech* longrine *f*

▸▸ *Mus* ***ledger line*** ligne *f* supplémentaire

lee [li:] N **1** *Naut* bord *m* sous le vent **2** *(shelter)* abri *m*; **in the l. of a rock** à l'abri d'un rocher

ADJ sous le vent

▸▸ ***lee shore*** terre *f* sous le vent

leeboard ['li:bɔ:d] N *Naut* aile *f ou* semelle *f* de dérive

leech [li:tʃ] N *also Fig* sangsue *f*; **to cling to sb like a l.** s'accrocher *ou* coller à qn comme une sangsue

VI *Fam* **to l. onto sb** s'accrocher *ou* coller à qn comme une sangsue

leek [li:k] N poireau *m*

COMP *(soup, tart)* aux poireaux

leer [lɪə(r)] N *(malevolent)* regard *m* méchant; *(lecherous)* regard *m* concupiscent *ou* lubrique

VI **to l. at sb** *(malevolently)* regarder qn méchamment; *(lecherously)* lorgner qn

leering ['lɪərɪŋ] ADJ *(malevolent)* méchant; *(lecherous)* concupiscent, lubrique

leery ['lɪərɪ] *(compar* **leerier**, *superl* **leeriest**) ADJ *Fam* méfiant▫; **to be l. of sth** se méfier de qch

lees [li:z] NPL *(sediment)* lie *f*

leet speak [li:t-] N *Comput* = écriture codée, utilisée sur Internet, consistant à remplacer les mots par une combinaison de lettres, chiffres, symboles et autres caractères présents sur un clavier d'ordinateur

leeward ['li:wəd] N bord *m* sous le vent; *Naut* **to l.** sous le vent

ADJ sous le vent

leeway ['li:weɪ] N *(UNCOUNT)* **1** *(margin)* marge *f* (de manœuvre); **it doesn't give us much l.** cela ne nous laisse pas une grande marge de manœuvre; **a quarter of an hour should be enough l.** une marge de sécurité d'un quart d'heure devrait suffire **2** *(lost time)* retard *m*; **he has a lot of l. to make up** il a un fort retard à rattraper **3** *Aviat & Naut (drift)* dérive *f*; **to make l.** dériver (à la voile)

left¹ [left] *pt & pp of* **leave**

▸▸ *Br* ***left luggage*** *(UNCOUNT) (cases)* bagages *mpl* en consigne; *(office)* consigne *f*

left² [left] N **1** *(gen)* gauche *f*; **on the l.** sur la gauche, à gauche; **to drive on the l.** rouler à gauche; **the building on the l.** le bâtiment de gauche; **on your l.** à *ou* sur votre gauche; **it's to the l. of the fireplace** c'est à gauche de la cheminée; **it's to** *or* **on the l. of the picture** *(in the picture)* c'est sur la gauche du tableau; *(next to the picture)* c'est à gauche du tableau; **move a bit to the l.** déplacez-vous un peu vers la gauche; **to keep to the l.** tenir sa gauche; **the second figure from the l.** le deuxième chiffre en partant de la gauche; **he doesn't know his l. from his right** il ne reconnaît pas sa droite de sa gauche **2** *Pol* gauche *f*; **the far** *or* **extreme l.** l'extrême gauche; **she is further to the l. than her husband** elle est (politiquement) plus à gauche que son mari; **the party has moved** *or* **shifted to the l.** le parti s'est gauchisé **3** *(in boxing)* gauche *m*; **he knocked him out with a l. to the chin** il l'a étendu d'un gauch au menton

ADJ *(foot, eye)* gauche; **on the l. side** sur la gau che, du côté gauche; **I always sleep on my l. side** j dors toujours sur le côté gauche; **with her l. han** de la main gauche; **to make a l. turn** tourner gauche; **take the l. fork** prenez à gauche à l'em branchement; *Fam* **to be way out in l. field** êtr complètement excentrique▫; *Fam* **it came ou of l. field** *(comment, question)* c'est tombé comm un cheveu sur la soupe

ADV **1** *(gen)* à gauche; **turn l. at the junction** tour nez *ou* prenez à gauche au croisement; *Mil* **eye l.!** tête à gauche!; *Mil* **l. turn!** à gauche! gauche **l., right and centre** *(in, from all directions)* de tou les côtés; *Typ* **l. justified** justifié à gauche **2** *Pol* gauche; **to vote l.** voter à gauche

▸▸ *Comput* ***left arrow*** flèche *f* vers la gauche *Comput* ***left arrow key*** touche *f* de déplacemen vers la gauche; *Sport* ***left back*** arrière *m* gauche ***the Left Bank*** *(in Paris)* la rive gauche; *Sport* ***le half*** demi *m* gauche; *Comput & Typ* ***left indent*** in dentation *f* à gauche; *Comput & Typ* ***left justifica tion*** justification *f* à gauche; ***left margin*** marge de gauche; ***left wing*** *Pol* gauche *f*; *Sport (pos ition)* aile *f* gauche; *(player)* ailier *m* gauche; **th l. wing of the party** l'aile *f* gauche du parti

left-click *Comput* VT cliquer avec le bouton gau che de la souris sur

VI cliquer avec le bouton gauche de la souris (**on** sur)

left-hand ADJ **1** *(gen)* gauche; **a l. bend** un virage à gauche; **on the l. side** à gauche, sur la gauche **on my l. side, the Grand Palace** à *ou* sur ma gauche le Grand Palais **2** *Tech (lock, screw, drill)* à gau che

▸▸ ***left-hand drive*** conduite *f* à gauche; **my car is a l. drive** ma voiture a le volant à gauche; *Compu & Typ* ***left-hand margin*** marge *f* de gauche; *Tech* ***left-hand thread*** filetage *m* à gauche

left-handed ADJ **1** *(person)* gaucher; **she's l.** elle est gauchère **2** *(scissors, instrument, golf club* pour gauchers **3** *(blow, punch, shot)* de la mai gauche

ADV de la main gauche

▸▸ *Am* ***a left-handed compliment*** un faux compli ment

left-hander N *(person)* gaucher(ère) *m,f* *(blow)* coup *m* (donné de la main gauche)

leftie = **lefty**

leftist ['leftɪst] N *(gen* ▸ *man)* homme *m* de gau che; (▸*woman)* femme *f* de gauche; *(extreme left winger)* gauchiste *mf*

ADJ *(gen)* de gauche; *(extremely left-wing)* gau chiste

left-leaning ADJ *Pol* gauchisant

leftover ['leftəʊvə(r)] ADJ *(food, material)* qu reste; *(stock)* en surplus; **she used the l. wool to knit a scarf** elle a tricoté une écharpe avec la laine qui restait; **there was some l. chicken** il res tait du poulet

N *(throwback, vestige)* vestige *m*; **the gun is a l. from the war** le fusil est un souvenir de la guerre

leftovers ['leftəʊvəz] NPL *(food)* restes *mpl*

left-wing ADJ *Pol* de gauche; **she's very l.** elle est très à gauche; **he has slightly l. ideas** il a des idées gauchisantes

left-winger N **1** *Pol (man)* homme *m* de gauche; *(woman)* femme *f* de gauche **2** *Sport* ailier *m* gau che

lefty ['leftɪ] *(pl* **lefties**) N *Fam* **1** *Pej Pol (man)* homme *m* de gauche▫; *(woman)* femme *f* de gauche▫ **2** *Am (left-handed person)* gaucher (ère)▫ *m,f*

leg [leg] *(pt & pp* **legged**, *cont* **legging**) N **1** *Anat (o human, horse)* jambe *f*; *(of smaller animals and birds)* patte *f*; *Fig* **you don't have a l. to stand on** vos arguments ne tiennent pas debout; **you won't have a l. to stand on if they find this letter** s'ils trouvent cette lettre, vous êtes fichu; *very Fam* **to get one's l. over** s'envoyer en l'air; *Fam* **to pull sb's l.** faire marcher qn; *Fam* **to have legs** *(film)* faire recette au box-office

2 *Culin (of lamb)* gigot *m*; *(of pork)* jambon *m*; *(o chicken)* cuisse *f*; **frog's legs** cuisses *fpl* de gre nouille

3 *(of chair, table)* pied *m*; *(of compasses)* branche f; *(of tripod)* jambe f; *(of trestle)* montant m

4 *(of trousers, pyjamas, stockings)* jambe f; **these trousers are a bit short in the l.** ce pantalon est un peu court au niveau des jambes

5 *(stage ▸ of journey)* étape f; *(▸ of competition)* manche f; *(▸ in relay race)* relais m; *Sport* **they won the first/second l.** ils ont gagné le match aller/retour

6 *Sport* **l. (side)** *(when the batsman is right-handed)* côté m gauche du terrain; *(when the batsman is left-handed)* côté m droit du terrain; **l. before wicket** = au cricket, faute d'un joueur qui intercepte avec sa jambe une balle qui allait frapper le guichet

VT *Fam* **to l. it** *(run)* courir□; *(walk)* aller à pied□; *(flee)* se sauver, se tirer

▸▸ *Med* ***leg iron*** appareil m orthopédique; ***leg rest*** appui-jambes m inv; *Med* étrier m; *Fam* ***leg show*** revue f légère□

legacy ['legəsɪ] *(pl* **legacies***)* **N 1** *Law* legs m; **to leave sb a l.** faire un legs *ou* laisser un héritage à qn; **to come into a l.** faire un héritage; **the money is a l. from my aunt** j'ai hérité cet argent de ma tante, ma tante m'a légué cet argent **2** *Fig* héritage m; **this desk is a l. from my predecessor** j'ai hérité ce bureau de mon prédécesseur; **the crisis left a l. of bitterness** la crise a créé un climat d'amertume

legal ['li:gəl] **ADJ 1** *(lawful)* légal; *(legitimate)* légal, légitime; **to make sth l.** légaliser qch; **to have a l. claim to sth** avoir légalement droit à qch; **to be above the l. limit** *(for drinking)* dépasser le taux légal (d'alcoolémie)

2 *(judicial ▸ mind, matter, question)* juridique; *(▸ power, investigation, error)* judiciaire; **to take l. advice** consulter un juriste *ou* un avocat; **by l. process** par voies légales, par voies de droit; **he's a member of the l. profession** c'est un homme de loi

3 *Comput (character, symbol)* autorisé

4 *Am (paper format)* légal *(216 mm œ 356 mm)*

N *Am (paper size)* légal m *(216 mm œ 356 mm)*

▸▸ ***legal action*** action f en justice; **to take l. action (against sb)** intenter une action (en justice) (contre qn); ***legal adviser*** conseil m juridique; ***legal age*** âge m légal; **they're below the l. age** ils n'ont pas atteint l'âge légal; ***legal aid*** aide f juridique; ***legal assistant*** auditeur(trice) m,f; *Fin* ***legal currency*** monnaie f courante; ***legal department*** *(in bank, company)* (service m du) contentieux m; ***legal dispute*** litige m; ***legal document*** acte m authentique; *Fam Hum* ***legal eagle*** jeune avocat(e) m,f dynamique□; ***legal entity*** personne f morale; ***legal executive*** assistant(e) m,f *(d'un avocat)*; ***legal fiction*** fiction f juridique; *Am* ***legal holiday*** jour m férié, fête f légale; ***legal malpractice*** faute f ou négligence f professionnelle; ***legal manager*** responsable mf juridique; ***legal medicine*** médecine f légale; ***legal notice*** annonce f judiciaire; ***legal obstacle*** difficulté f d'exécution; ***legal owner*** propriétaire mf légitime; *Am* ***legal pad*** bloc-notes m; ***legal proceedings*** poursuites fpl judiciaires; **to initiate l. proceedings (against sb)** engager des poursuites judiciaires (contre qn); ***legal representation*** représentation f en justice; ***legal representative*** représentant(e) m,f légal(e); ***legal secretary*** secrétaire mf juridique; *Law* ***legal separation*** séparation f de corps; ***legal share*** *(of inheritance)* réserve f légale; ***legal status*** statut m légal *ou* juridique; ***legal system*** système m juridique; ***legal technicality*** vice m de forme; ***legal tender*** cours m légal; **to be l. tender** avoir cours (légal); **these coins are no longer l. tender** ces pièces n'ont plus cours *ou* ont été démonétisées

legalese [ˌli:gə'li:z] **N** *Pej* jargon m juridique

legalism ['li:gəˌlɪzəm] **N 1** *(strict respect of law)* légalisme m **2** *(technicality)* argutie f juridique

legalistic [ˌli:gə'lɪstɪk] **ADJ** légaliste, formaliste

legality [li:'gælətɪ] **N** légalité f

legalization, -isation [ˌli:gəlaɪ'zeɪʃən] **N** légalisation f

legalize, -ise ['li:gəlaɪz] **VT** légaliser, rendre légal

legally ['li:gəlɪ] **ADV** légalement; **to act l.** agir légalement *ou* dans la légalité; **to be l. binding** avoir force de loi, être juridiquement contraignant; **to be held l. responsible for sth** être tenu légalement *ou* juridiquement responsable de qch; **they were not l. married** ils vivaient maritalement

legate ['legɪt] **N** *Rel* légat m; *(gen)* messager(ère) m,f

legatee [ˌlegə'ti:] **N** légataire mf

legation [lɪ'geɪʃən] **N** légation f

legato [lɪ'gɑ:təʊ] *Mus* **N** legato m

ADV legato

legend ['ledʒənd] **N 1** *(myth)* légende f; **she became a l. in her own lifetime** elle est entrée dans la légende de son vivant **2** *(inscription)* légende f

legendary ['ledʒəndərɪ] **ADJ** légendaire

legerdemain [ˌledʒədə'meɪn] **N** *(UNCOUNT) (conjuring)* (tours *mpl* de) prestidigitation f; *(cunning)* tours *mpl* de passe-passe

-legged ['legɪd, legd] **SUFF short/bare-l.** aux jambes courtes/nues

leggings ['legɪŋz] **NPL** caleçon m long

leggy ['legɪ] *(compar* **leggier**, *superl* **leggiest***)* **ADJ** *(person)* tout en jambes; *(colt, young animal)* haut sur pattes

Leghorn [ˌleg'hɔ:n] **N** Livourne

legibility [ˌledʒɪ'bɪlətɪ] **N** lisibilité f

legible ['ledʒəbəl] **ADJ** lisible

legibly ['ledʒəblɪ] **ADV** lisiblement

legion ['li:dʒən] **N** *Mil & Fig* légion f

ADJ *Formal* légion *(inv)*; **their name is l.** ils sont légion; **the difficulties were l.** les difficultés étaient innombrables

legionary ['li:dʒənərɪ] *(pl* **legionaries***)* **N** légionnaire m

ADJ de la légion

legionnaire [ˌli:dʒə'neə(r)] **N** légionnaire m

▸▸ *Med* ***legionnaire's disease*** maladie f du légionnaire

legislate ['ledʒɪsleɪt] **VI** légiférer; **to l. in favour of/against sth** légiférer en faveur de/contre qch; **we can't l. for all possible situations** nous ne pouvons pas prévoir des lois pour tous les cas de figure possibles

legislation [ˌledʒɪs'leɪʃən] **N** législation f; **the l. on immigration** la législation sur l'immigration; **a piece of l.** une loi; **to bring in l. in favour of/against sth** légiférer en faveur de/contre qch

legislative ['ledʒɪslətɪv] **ADJ** législatif

▸▸ ***legislative assembly*** assemblée f législative; ***the Legislative Assembly*** *(in Ireland, Australia, India, Canada)* l'Assemblée f législative; ***legislative body*** corps m législatif; ***legislative council*** conseil m législatif; ***the Legislative Council*** *(in Australia, India)* le Conseil législatif; ***legislative power*** pouvoir m législatif

legislatively ['ledʒɪslətɪvlɪ] **ADJ** législativement

legislator ['ledʒɪsˌleɪtə(r)] **N** législateur(trice) m, f

legislature ['ledʒɪsˌleɪtʃə(r)] **N** (corps m) législatif m

legit [lə'dʒɪt] **ADJ** *Fam* réglo

legitimacy [lɪ'dʒɪtɪməsɪ] **N** légitimité f

legitimate **ADJ** [lɪ'dʒɪtɪmət] **1** *(legal, lawful)* légitime; **l. child** enfant mf légitime **2** *(valid)* légitime, valable; **his criticisms are perfectly l.** ses critiques sont parfaitement légitimes *ou* fondées; **it would be perfectly l. to ask them to pay** on serait tout à fait en droit d'exiger qu'ils paient **3** *(theatre)* sérieux

VT [lɪ'dʒɪtɪmeɪt] légitimer

▸▸ ***legitimate government*** gouvernement m légitime; ***legitimate state*** État m légitime

legitimately [lɪ'dʒɪtɪmətlɪ] **ADV 1** *(legally, lawfully)* légitimement; **both l. and effectively** de droit comme de fait **2** *(justifiably)* légitimement, avec raison; **it could l. be argued that...** on peut soutenir, non sans raison, que...

legitimatize, -ise [lɪ'dʒɪtɪməˌtaɪz] **VT** légitimer

legitimization, -isation [lɪˌdʒɪtɪmaɪ'zeɪʃən] **N** légitimisation f

legless ['leglɪs] **ADJ 1** *(without legs)* cul-de-jatte **2** *Br Fam (drunk)* bourré, pété

legman ['legmæn] *(pl* **legmen** [-mən]*)* **N** *Am* **1** *Journ* = reporter qui fait la chronique des chiens écrasés **2** *(errand boy etc)* factotum m

leg-of-mutton **ADJ**

▸▸ ***leg-of-mutton sleeves*** manches fpl gigot

leg-pull **N** *Fam* canular□ m, farce□ f; **it was only a l.!** on te faisait marcher!

leg-puller [-'pʊlə(r)] **N** *Fam* blagueur(euse)□ m, f, farceur(euse)□ m,f

legroom ['legrʊm] **N** place f pour les jambes; **these little cars don't give you any l.** dans ces petites voitures, on n'a aucune place pour les jambes

legume [le'gju:m] **N** légumineuse f

leguminous [le'gju:mɪnəs] **ADJ** légumineux

legwarmers ['legˌwɔ:məz] **NPL** jambières fpl

legwork ['legwɜ:k] **N** *Fam* **who's going to do the l.?** qui va se taper la marche?; **there's a lot of l. in this job** c'est un travail où l'on marche beaucoup

Leics *(written abbr* **Leicestershire***)* Leicestershire m

leisure [*Br* 'leʒə(r), *Am* 'li:ʒər] **N** *(UNCOUNT)* **1** *(spare time)* loisir m, loisirs mpl, temps m libre; **during my l. (time)** pendant mes loisirs, à mes heures perdues; **to be at l. to do sth** avoir (tout) le loisir de faire qch; **to do sth at one's l.** faire qch à loisir *ou* dans ses moments de loisir; **I'll read it at (my) l.** je le lirai à tête reposée **2** *(relaxation)* loisir m; **to lead a life of l.** mener une vie oisive; **he's a man of l.** il mène une vie de rentier

COMP *(activity, clothes)* de loisir *ou* loisirs

▸▸ ***leisure break*** court séjour m de détente; ***leisure centre*** centre m de loisirs; ***leisure club*** club m de loisirs; ***leisure hours*** heures fpl de loisir; ***leisure industry*** industrie f des loisirs; ***leisure market*** marché m des loisirs; ***leisure time*** temps m libre; ***leisure tourism*** tourisme m de loisir, tourisme m ludique

leisured [*Br* 'leʒəd, *Am* 'li:ʒərd] **ADJ** oisif, qui mène une vie oisive

leisureliness [*Br* 'leʒəlɪnɪs, *Am* 'li:ʒərlɪnɪs] **N** *(of pace)* caractère m mesuré; *(of weekend)* caractère m détendu; **the l. of sea travel** la détente apportée par une croisière

leisurely [*Br* 'leʒəlɪ, *Am* 'li:ʒərlɪ] **ADJ** *(gesture)* mesuré, nonchalant; *(lifestyle)* paisible, indolent; **to do sth in a l. fashion** faire qch sans se presser; **we went for a l. stroll through the park** nous sommes allés faire une petite balade dans le parc; **at a l. pace** sans se presser

ADV *(calmly)* paisiblement, tranquillement; *(unhurriedly)* sans se presser

lemming ['lemɪŋ] **N** *Zool* lemming m; *Fig* mouton m

lemon ['lemən] **N 1** *(fruit)* citron m; *(tree)* citronnier m

2 *(colour)* jaune citron m inv

3 *Br Fam (awkward person)* idiot(e) m,f; **I'm going to look a right l.** je vais avoir l'air plutôt débile; **everyone was chatting away in French and I was just standing there like a l.** tout le monde parlait français et moi j'étais là, comme un idiot

4 *Fam (useless object)* **it's a l.** c'est de la camelote; **she got sold a l.** elle s'est fait rouler

5 *Am Fam (useless car)* = voiture de mauvaise qualité

ADJ *(colour)* (jaune) citron *(inv)*; *(flavour)* citron *(inv)*

COMP *(ice-cream, tart)* au citron

▸▸ *Bot* ***lemon balm*** mélisse f, citronnelle f; ***lemon cheese, lemon curd*** lemon curd m, crème f au citron; ***lemon drop*** bonbon m au citron; ***lemon juice*** jus m de citron; *(lemon squash)* citronnade f; *(freshly squeezed)* citron m pressé; *Am* ***lemon juicer*** presse-citron m inv; ***lemon meringue pie*** tarte f au citron meringuée; ***lemon oil*** essence f de citron; ***lemon sole*** limande-sole f; ***lemon squash*** citronnade f, sirop m de citron; *Br* ***lemon squeezer*** presse-citron m inv; ***lemon tea*** thé m au citron; ***lemon verbena*** verveine f citronnelle; ***lemon zest*** zeste m de citron; ***lemon zester*** zesteur m

lemonade [ˌlemə'neɪd] **N** *(freshly squeezed)* citron m pressé; *Br (carbonated)* limonade f

lemongrass ['leməŋˌgrɑ:s] **N** citronnelle f, lemon-grass m

lemony ['lemənɪ] **ADJ** *(smell, taste)* citronné

lemur ['liːmə(r)] N *Zool* lémur *m*; *(ring-tailed)* lémur *m* catta, maki *m*

lend [lend] *(pt & pp* **lent** [lent]) **VT 1** *(money, object)* prêter; **to l. sth to sb, to l. sb sth** prêter qch à qn; **to l. money at interest** prêter de l'argent à intérêt; **to l. money against security** prêter de l'argent sur titres

2 *(contribute)* apporter, conférer; **to l. credibility/drama to a story** rendre une histoire crédible/dramatique; **her presence lent glamour to the occasion** sa présence a conféré un certain éclat à l'événement; **the bright uniforms lent colour to the ceremony** les uniformes éclatants apportaient une touche de couleur à la cérémonie

3 *(give ▸ support)* apporter; *(▸ name)* prêter; **to l. sb a hand** donner un coup de main à qn; **you can't expect me to l. my name to such an enterprise** ne comptez pas sur moi pour prêter mon nom à *ou* cautionner cette affaire; *Fig* **to l. an ear** prêter l'oreille

4 *(adapt ▸ to circumstances, interpretation)* **the novel doesn't l. itself to being filmed** le roman ne se prête pas à une adaptation cinématographique; **his voice really lends itself to reading aloud** sa voix se prête très bien à la lecture à voix haute

N *Br Fam* **can I have a l. of your book?** tu peux me prêter ton livre?

VI *Fin* prêter; **to l. at 12 percent** prêter à 12 pour cent

lender ['lendə(r)] N prêteur(euse) *m,f*; *Fin (institution)* organisme *m* de crédit

lending ['lendɪŋ] N prêt *m*; **bank l. has increased** le volume des prêts bancaires a augmenté
▸▸ *Fin* ***lending bank*** banque *f* de crédit; ***lending country*** pays *m* créancier; ***lending library*** bibliothèque *f* de prêt; *Fin* ***lending limit*** plafond *m* de crédit; ***lending policy*** *(of bank, country)* politique *f* de prêt; *Fin* ***lending rate*** taux *m* de prêt

lend-lease N *(UNCOUNT) Econ & Hist* prêt-bail *m*

length [leŋθ] **N 1** *(measurement, distance)* longueur *f*; **what l. is the room?** quelle est la longueur de la pièce?; **the room is 20 metres in l.** la pièce fait 20 mètres de long *ou* de longueur; **we walked the l. of the garden** nous sommes allés jusqu'au bout du jardin; **flower beds ran the l. of the street** il y avait des massifs de fleurs tout le long de la rue; **throughout the l. and breadth of the continent** partout sur le continent; **what l. skirts are in this year?** *(in fashion)* quelle est la longueur des jupes cette année?

2 *(effort)* **to go to considerable** *or* **great lengths to do sth** se donner beaucoup de mal pour faire qch; **he would go to any lengths to meet her** il ferait n'importe quoi pour la rencontrer; **I never dreamed that they would go to such lengths** je n'aurais jamais imaginé qu'ils iraient si loin

3 *(duration)* durée *f*, longueur *f*; **the l. of time required to do sth** le temps qu'il faut pour faire qch; **the wine is kept in casks for a great l. of time** le vin séjourne très longtemps dans des fûts; **bonuses are given for l. of service** les primes sont accordées selon l'ancienneté

4 *(of text)* longueur *f*; **articles must be less than 5,000 words in l.** les articles doivent faire moins de 5000 mots; **his essay was a bit over/under l.** sa dissertation était un peu trop longue/courte

5 *Sport (in racing, rowing)* longueur *f*; *(in swimming)* longueur *f* (de bassin); **to win by a l./by half a l.** gagner d'une longueur/d'une demi-longueur; **to have a three-l. lead** avoir trois longueurs d'avance; **I swam ten lengths** j'ai fait dix longueurs

6 *(piece ▸ of string, tubing)* morceau *m*, bout *m*; *(▸ of wood)* morceau *m*; *(▸ of wallpaper)* lé *m*; *(▸ of fabric)* pièce *f*; **what l. of material do I need to make these curtains?** quel métrage faut-il pour faire ces rideaux?

7 *Ling (of syllable, vowel)* longueur *f*

8 *Sport (in tennis, cricket)* longueur *f* de balle

• **at length** ADV *(finally)* finalement, enfin; *(in detail, for a long time)* longuement; **she went on** *or* **spoke at some l. about her experience** elle a parlé assez longuement de son expérience

lengthen ['leŋθən] **VT** *(garment)* allonger, rallonger; *(holiday, visit)* prolonger; *Ling (vowel)* allonger

VI *(shadow)* s'allonger; *(day)* rallonger; *(holiday, visit)* se prolonger

lengthening ['leŋθənɪŋ] N *(of garment, vowel)* allongement *m*; *(of holiday, visit)* prolongement *m*

lengthily ['leŋθɪlɪ] ADV longuement

lengthways ['leŋθweɪz], **lengthwise** ['leŋθwaɪz] ADJ en longueur, longitudinal
ADV dans le sens de la longueur, longitudinalement

lengthy ['leŋθɪ] *(compar* **lengthier**, *superl* **lengthiest**) ADJ (très) long (longue); **after a l. wait** après avoir attendu très longtemps, après une attente interminable; **his speech was a bit l.** son discours n'en finissait plus

leniency ['liːnjənsɪ] N clémence *f*, indulgence *f*

lenient ['liːnjənt] ADJ *(jury, sentence)* clément; *(attitude, parent)* indulgent; **his parents are too l. with him** ses parents sont trop indulgents avec lui

leniently ['liːnjəntlɪ] ADV avec clémence *ou* indulgence; **the magistrate had treated him l.** le magistrat s'était montré indulgent *ou* avait fait preuve d'indulgence à son égard

Lenin ['lenɪn] PR N Lénine

Leningrad ['lenɪngræd] N *Formerly* Leningrad

Leninism ['lenɪnɪzəm] N léninisme *m*

Leninist ['lenɪnɪst] N léniniste *mf*
ADJ léniniste

lenitive ['lenɪtɪv] N lénitif *m*
ADJ lénitif

lens [lenz] **N 1** *Opt (in microscope, telescope)* lentille *f*; *(in spectacles)* verre *m*; *(in camera)* objectif *m*; *(contact lens)* lentille *f ou* verre *m* (de contact)
2 *Anat (in eye)* cristallin *m*
▸▸ ***lens attachment*** accessoire *m* d'objectif; ***lens cap*** bouchon *m* d'objectif; ***lens cleaning fluid*** produit *m* de nettoyage pour lentilles; ***lens holder*** étui *m* à objectif; ***lens hood*** pare-soleil *m inv*; *Cin & TV* ***lens turret*** tourelle *f*

Lent [lent] N *Rel* le carême; **to keep L.** faire carême, observer le carême; **I've given up chocolate for L.** j'ai renoncé au chocolat pour le carême
▸▸ *Br Univ* ***Lent term*** deuxième trimestre *m (de janvier à Pâques)*

lent [lent] *pt & pp of* **lend**

lentil ['lentɪl] *Bot & Culin* N lentille *f*
COMP *(soup)* aux lentilles

Leo ['liːəʊ] **N 1** *Astron* Lion *m* **2** *Astrol* Lion *m*; **he's a L.** il est (du signe du) Lion
ADJ *Astrol* du Lion; **he's L.** il est (du signe du) Lion

leonine ['liːənaɪn] ADJ *Literary* de lion, léonin

leopard ['lepəd] N léopard *m*; *Prov* **a l. can't change its spots** chassez le naturel, il revient au galop
▸▸ *Entom* ***leopard moth*** zeuzère *f*; ***leopard skin*** N peau *f* de léopard COMP *(coat, rug)* en (peau de) léopard

leotard ['liːətɑːd] N body *m (pour le sport)*

leper ['lepə(r)] N lépreux(euse) *m,f*, *Fig* pestiféré(e) *m,f*
▸▸ ***leper colony*** léproserie *f*

lepidopteran [ˌlepɪ'dɒptərən] *(pl* **lepidopterans** *or* **lepidoptera** [-rə]) *Entom* N lépidoptère *m*
ADJ lépidoptère

leprechaun ['leprəkɔːn] N lutin *m*

leprosy ['leprəsɪ] N lèpre *f*; **to have l.** avoir la lèpre

leprous ['leprəs] ADJ lépreux

lesbian ['lezbɪən] N lesbienne *f*
ADJ lesbien

lesbianism ['lezbɪənɪzəm] N lesbianisme *m*

lesbo ['lezbəʊ] N *very Fam* gouine *f*, = terme injurieux désignant une lesbienne

lesion ['liːʒən] N lésion *f*

Lesotho [lə'suːtuː] N Lesotho *m*

LESS [les] ADJ *(compar of* **little**) moins de; **l. money/time/bread** moins d'argent/de temps/de pain; **we have l. time than we thought** nous avons moins de temps que nous ne pensions; **of l. importance/value** de moindre importance/valeur

PRON *(compar of* **little**) moins; **a bit l.** un peu moins; **the evening was l. of a success than she had hoped** la soirée était moins réussie qu'elle ne l'avait espéré; **let's hope we see l. of them in future** espérons que nous les verrons moins souvent à l'avenir; **l. of your noise!** faites moins de bruit!; *Fam* **l. of that!, l. of it!** ça suffit!

ADV **1** *(forming comparatives)* moins; **they couldn't be l. friendly if they tried** il leur serait difficile d'être plus désagréables; **she is l. musical than her sister** elle est moins musicienne que sa sœur; **he was l. amusing than I remembered** il était moins drôle que dans mes souvenirs

2 *(to a lesser extent or degree)* **the blue dress costs l.** la robe bleue coûte moins cher; **not a penny l.** pas un sou de moins; **we saw his books l. as literature than as propaganda** nous considérions ses livres moins comme de la littérature que comme de la propagande; **I don't think any (the) l. of her** *or* **I think no l. of her because of what happened** ce qui s'est passé ne l'a pas fait baisser dans mon estime; **we don't like her any the l. for all her faults** nous ne l'aimons pas moins à cause de ses défauts; **the more I see of her the l. I like her** plus je la vois, moins elle me plaît; **the l. you know the better** moins tu en sais mieux c'est; **there's nothing I want l. than to hurt him** je ne veux surtout pas le blesser

PREP **that's £300 l. ten percent for store card holders** ça fait 300 livres moins dix pour cent avec la carte du magasin; **8 l. 3 is 5** 8 moins 3 *ou* 3 ôté de 8 égale 5

• **less and less** ADJ de moins en moins; **I seem to have l. and l. energy** on dirait que j'ai de moins en moins d'énergie ADV de moins en moins; **l. and l. interesting** de moins en moins intéressant; **we found we had l. and l. to say to each other** nous nous sommes rendu compte que nous avions de moins en moins de choses à nous dire; **I see him l. and l. these days** je le vois de moins en moins ces temps-ci

• **much less, still less** CONJ encore moins; **they don't own a fridge, much l. a freezer** ils n'ont pas de réfrigérateur, et encore moins de congélateur; **he wouldn't even phone her, much l. visit her** il ne voulait même pas l'appeler, encore moins aller la voir

• **less than** PREP *(with numbers, measurements etc)* moins de; **it took me l. than five minutes** ça m'a pris moins de cinq minutes; **you won't get another one like it for l. than $1,000** vous n'en retrouverez pas un comme ça à moins de 1000 dollars; **nothing l. than a four-star hotel is good enough for them** il leur faut au moins un quatre étoiles; **in l. than no time** en un rien de temps, en moins de deux ADV moins que; **there was l. than I expected** il y en avait moins que je m'y attendais; **he eats l. than he used to** il mange moins qu'avant; **the weather was rather l. than ideal** le temps était vraiment loin d'être idéal

• **no less** ADV **1** *(in size, amount, degree)* **I expected no l. from you** je n'en attendais pas moins de vous; **the news of his death came as no l. of a shock for being expected** on avait beau s'y attendre, la nouvelle de sa mort n'en fut pas moins un choc

2 *(for emphasis)* **he won the Booker prize, no l.!** il a gagné le prix Booker, rien que ça!; **she married a duke, no l.!** elle a épousé un duc, s'il vous plaît!; **she had invited no l. a person than the President himself** elle avait invité rien moins que le président lui-même

• **no less than** ADV pas moins de; **this wall is no l. than a metre thick** ce mur n'a pas moins d'un mètre d'épaisseur; **taxes rose by no l. than 15 percent** les impôts ont augmenté de 15 pour cent, ni plus ni moins

SUFFIXE

-LESS

• Ce suffixe peut venir s'ajouter à un grand nombre de noms pour former des adjectifs où il véhicule la notion d'ABSENCE. Il se traduit souvent à l'aide de la préposition **sans**. Parmi les termes courants construits avec ce suffixe, citons:

penniless sans le sou; **hatless** tête nue, sans chapeau; **childless** sans enfants; **speechless**

muet; **endless** interminable, sans fin; **harmless** inoffensif; **a hopeless situation** une situation désespérée, une situation sans espoir.

Il s'agit d'un suffixe très productif qui permet la création de nombreux néologismes; ainsi l'on pourra dire:

we're garageless at the moment nous ne disposons pas de garage en ce moment; **somebody stole my handbag, so I'm phoneless** on m'a volé mon sac à main, alors je suis sans téléphone

• Ajouté à des verbes, **-less** peut également servir à former quelques adjectifs où il véhicule la notion d'IMPOSSIBILITÉ. Citons **countless** incalculable; **tireless** infatigable; **dauntless** déterminé

ess-developed country N pays *m* moins avancé

essee [le'siː] N preneur(euse) *m,f* (à bail)

essen ['lesən] VT *(cost, importance)* diminuer, réduire; *(impact, effect)* atténuer, amoindrir; *shock)* amortir; *(noise)* atténuer; *(activity)* ralentir; *(fervour, enthusiasm)* calmer
VI s'atténuer, s'amoindrir

essening ['lesənɪŋ] N *(UNCOUNT) (of cost, importance)* diminution *f*; *(of value, rate)* réduction *f*, diminution *f*, baisse *f*; *(of powers)* réduction *f*, baisse *f*; *(of impact, effect)* amoindrissement *m*; *of shock)* amortissement *m*

esser ['lesə(r)] ADJ **1** *(gen)* moindre; **to be of l. intelligence** être moins intelligent; **Wordsworth, Coleridge and their l. contemporaries** Wordsworth, Coleridge et leurs contemporains de moindre envergure; **to a l. extent** dans une moindre mesure; **it's the l. evil** *or* **of two evils** c'est le moindre mal; *Hum* **l. mortals like me** les simples mortels comme moi **2** *Bot, Geog, Orn & Zool* petit
►► *Orn* ***lesser black-backed gull*** goéland *m* brun; *Br Zool* ***the lesser panda*** le petit panda; *Orn* ***lesser spotted woodpecker*** (pic *m*) épeichette *f*

esson ['lesən] N **1** *(gen)* leçon *f*; *Sch* leçon *f*, cours *m*; **an English l.** une leçon *ou* un cours d'anglais; **a dancing/driving l.** une leçon de danse/de conduite; **to give a l.** donner un cours *ou* une leçon; **lessons start at half past eight** les cours commencent à huit heures et demie; **private lessons** cours *mpl* particuliers **2** *(example)* leçon *f*; **her downfall was a l. to us all** sa chute nous a servi de leçon à tous; **to teach sb a l.** donner une (bonne) leçon à qn; **that'll teach him a l.!** cela lui servira de leçon!; **let that be a l. to you!** que cela vous serve de leçon! **3** *Rel* leçon *f*, lecture *f*
►► ***lesson plan*** plan *m* de cours

essor [le'sɔː(r)] N bailleur(eresse) *m,f*

est [lest] CONJ **1** *Literary (in case)* de peur que + *subjunctive*, de crainte que + *subjunctive*; **they whispered l. the children should hear** ils parlèrent à voix basse de peur *ou* de crainte que les enfants ne les entendent; **she wrote it down, l. she forget** *or* **l. she might forget** elle l'a noté, de peur d'oublier; **l. we forget** *(on memorial)* in memoriam **2** *Arch (after verbs of fearing)* **I feared l. he should fall** je craignais qu'il (ne) tombât

et[1] [let] *(pt & pp* **let**, *cont* **letting)** N **1** *(rental)* location *f*; **she took a six-month l. on a house** elle a loué une maison pour six mois; **a short/long l.** une location de courte/longue durée **2** *Sport (in tennis, squash)* balle *f* let; **l.!** let!; **to play a l.** jouer une balle let **3** *Law (hindrance)* **without l. or hindrance** librement, sans entrave
VT **1** *(rent)* louer; **to l.** *(sign)* à louer **2** *Arch or Literary* **to l. (sb's) blood** faire une saignée (à qn)
►► *Sport* ***let ball*** balle *f* let

ET[2] [let] *(pt & pp* **let**, *cont* **letting)** VT **1** *(permit)* laisser, permettre; *(allow)* laisser; **to l. sb do sth** laisser qn faire qch, permettre à qn de faire qch; **she l. them watch the programme** elle les a laissés regarder l'émission; **I couldn't come because my parents wouldn't l. me** je ne suis pas venu parce que mes parents ne me l'ont pas permis; **I l. the cakes burn** j'ai laissé brûler les gâteaux; **l. me buy you all a drink** laissez-moi vous offrir un verre; **don't l. me stop you going** je ne veux pas t'empêcher d'y aller; **l. me see the newspaper** fais-moi voir le journal; **to l. sb past** laisser passer qn; **they don't l. anyone near the reactor** ils ne laissent personne approcher du réacteur; **l. me tell you that…** permettez-moi de vous dire que…; **it wasn't easy, l. me tell you!** ça n'a pas été facile, crois-moi!; *Fam* **don't l. it get you down!** ne te laisse pas abattre pour ça!; **don't l. him get to you** ne te soucie pas de lui; **to l. sb have sth** donner qch à qn; **I'll l. you have a copy of the report** je vous ferai parvenir une copie du rapport; **she l. him know what she thought of him** elle lui a fait savoir ce qu'elle pensait de lui; **l. me know when he wakes up** prévenez-moi quand il se réveillera; **I'll l. him know you're here** je vais le prévenir que vous êtes arrivé; **please God don't l. anything happen to her!** faites qu'il ne lui arrive rien!; **to l. sth pass** laisser passer qch; *Fam* **to l. sb have it** *(physically)* casser la figure à qn; *(verbally)* dire ses quatre vérités à qn

2 *(followed by "go")* **to l. sb go** *(allow to leave)* laisser partir qn; *(release)* relâcher qn; *(allow to escape)* laisser échapper qn; *Euph (dismiss, fire)* licencier qn; **to l. sb go, to l. go of sb** *(stop holding)* lâcher qn; **to l. sth go** *(allow to escape)* laisser échapper qch; **to l. sth go, to l. go of sth** *(stop holding)* lâcher qch; **hold the rope and don't l. go (of it)!** tiens la corde et ne la lâche pas!; **to l. oneself go** *(neglect oneself, relax)* se laisser aller; **that remark was uncalled-for but I'll l. it go** cette réflexion était déplacée mais restons-en là; **give me £5 and we'll l. it go at that** donne-moi 5 livres et on n'en parle plus

3 *(in making suggestions)* **l.'s hurry!** dépêchons-nous!; **l.'s go to bed** allons nous coucher; **l.'s go!** allons-y!; **don't l.'s go out** *or* **l.'s not go out tonight** ne sortons pas ce soir; **l.'s not have an argument about it!** on ne va pas se disputer pour ça!; **now, l.'s not have any nonsense!** allons, pas de bêtises!; **shall we have a picnic? – yes, l.'s!** si on faisait un pique-nique? – d'accord!; *Formal* **l. us pray** prions ensemble

4 *(to focus attention)* **l. me start by saying how pleased I am to be here** laissez-moi d'abord vous dire combien je suis ravi d'être ici; **l. me put it another way** je vais tâcher d'être plus clair; **l. me try and explain** je vais essayer de vous expliquer

5 *(in hesitation)* **l. me think** attends, voyons voir; **l. me see, l.'s see** voyons

6 *(to express criticism or defiance)* **if she doesn't want my help, l. her do it herself!** si elle ne veut pas de mon aide, qu'elle le fasse toute seule!; **l. them talk!** laisse-les dire!

7 *(in threats)* **don't l. me catch you at it again!** que je ne t'y reprenne plus!

8 *(in commands) Bible* **l. there be light** que la lumière soit; **l. the festivities begin!** que la fête commence!; **l. them be!** laisse-les tranquilles!, fiche-leur la paix!

9 *(in making assumptions)* **l. us suppose that…** supposons que…; *Math* **l. x equal 17** soit x égal à 17; *Math* **l. ABC be a right-angled triangle** soit un triangle rectangle ABC

• **let alone** CONJ **I wouldn't go out with him, l. alone marry him** je ne sortirais même pas avec lui, alors pour ce qui est de l'épouser…; **he's never even used a computer, l. alone surfed the Internet** il ne s'est jamais servi d'un ordinateur et encore moins de l'Internet

► **let by** VT SEP **to l. sb by** laisser passer qn

► **let down** VT SEP **1** *(disappoint)* laisser tomber, faire faux bond à; **to l. sb down gently** ménager qn; **I felt really l. down** j'ai eu l'impression qu'on me laissait tomber; **our old car has never l. us down** notre vieille voiture ne nous a jamais lâchés; **he has been badly l. down by his colleagues** ses collègues lui ont vraiment fait faux bond

2 *(lower, let fall* ► *object)* baisser, (faire) descendre; *(*► *hair)* dénouer

3 *(garment)* rallonger; **to l. the hem of a dress down** rallonger une robe

4 *(deflate)* dégonfler

► **let in** VT SEP **1** *(person, animal)* laisser entrer; **his mother l. me in** sa mère m'a fait entrer *ou* m'a ouvert (la porte); **she l. herself in with a pass key** elle est entrée avec un passe **2** *(air, water)* laisser passer; **the roof lets the rain in** le toit laisse entrer *ou* passer la pluie; **my shoes l. in water** mes chaussures prennent l'eau **3** *Aut* **to l. in the clutch** embrayer

► **let into** VT SEP **1** *(allow to enter)* **my mother l. her into the flat** ma mère l'a laissée entrer dans l'appartement **2** *(allow to know)* **I'll l. you into a secret** je vais te confier un secret **3** *(insert)* encastrer dans; **the pipes are l. into the wall** les tuyaux sont encastrés dans le mur; **to l. a door/window into a wall** percer une porte/fenêtre dans un mur

► **let off** VT SEP **1** *(excuse)* dispenser; **to l. sb off doing sth** dispenser qn de faire qch; **I've been l. off work** je suis dispensé de travailler

2 *(allow to leave)* laisser partir; *(allow to disembark)* laisser descendre; **we were l. off an hour early** on nous a laissés partir une heure plus tôt; **they l. us off the bus** on nous a laissés descendre du bus

3 *(criminal, pupil, child)* ne pas punir; **the judge l. him off lightly** le juge a fait preuve d'indulgence à son égard; **she was l. off with a fine** elle s'en est tirée avec une amende; **I'll l. you off this time** pour cette fois, je passe

4 *(bomb, explosive)* faire exploser; *(firework)* faire partir; *(gun)* laisser partir

5 *(release* ► *steam, liquid)* laisser échapper; *Fig* **to l. off steam** se défouler

6 *(rent)* louer; **the whole building is l. off as offices** tout l'immeuble est loué en bureaux
VI *Fam (break wind)* péter

► **let on** VT SEP *(allow to embark)* laisser monter; **they l. us on the train** on nous a laissés monter dans le train
VI *Fam* parler❑; **she never l. on** elle ne l'a jamais dit❑; **somebody l. on about the wedding to the press** quelqu'un a parlé du mariage à *ou* a révélé le mariage à la presse❑; **he didn't l. on that he saw her** *(didn't tell anyone)* il n'a pas dit qu'il l'avait vue❑; *(didn't acknowledge her)* il a fait semblant de ne pas la voir❑; **don't l. on!** pas un mot!❑

► **let out** VT SEP **1** *(allow to leave)* laisser sortir; *(bird)* laisser échapper; *(prisoner)* libérer; **my secretary will l. you out** ma secrétaire va vous reconduire; **don't get up, I'll l. myself out** ne vous levez pas, je connais le chemin

2 *(water, air)* laisser échapper; **someone's l. the air out of the tyres** quelqu'un a dégonflé les pneus

3 *(shout, oath, whistle)* laisser échapper

4 *(secret)* révéler; **who l. it out that they're getting married?** qui est allé raconter qu'ils allaient se marier?

5 *(garment)* élargir

6 *Aut* **to l. out the clutch** débrayer

7 *Br (rent)* louer
VI *Am (end)* finir

► **let through** VT SEP *(person, water, light)* laisser passer

► **let up** VI **1** *(stop)* arrêter; *(diminish)* diminuer; **the rain didn't l. up all day** il n'a pas cessé *ou* arrêté de pleuvoir de toute la journée; **once he's started he never lets up** une fois lancé, il ne s'arrête plus **2** *(relax)* **he never lets up** il ne s'accorde aucun répit; **don't l. up now, you're in the lead** ce n'est pas le moment de faiblir, tu es en tête

letdown ['letdaʊn] N *Fam* déception❑ *f*; **the party was a bit of a l.** la fête a été plutôt décevante

lethal ['liːθəl] ADJ fatal, mortel; *Med* létal; **in the hands of a child, a plastic bag can be l.** dans les mains d'un enfant, un sac en plastique peut être dangereux; **this substance is l. to rats** c'est une substance mortelle pour les rats; *Fam Fig* **this vodka's l.!** cette vodka est mortelle!
►► ***lethal dose*** dose *f* mortelle *ou* létale; ***lethal weapon*** arme *f* meurtrière

lethally ['liːθəlɪ] ADV mortellement

lethargic [lə'θɑːdʒɪk] ADJ *(person, sleep)* léthargique; *(atmosphere)* soporifique; **I feel really l. today** je me sens complètement à plat aujourd'hui

lethargically [lɪ'θɑːdʒɪklɪ] ADV d'une manière léthargique; **to move l.** se déplacer mollement

lethargy ['leθədʒɪ] N léthargie *f*; **to fall into a state of l.** tomber en léthargie

let-out N *Br (excuse)* prétexte *m*; *(way out)* échappatoire *f*; **I've been invited but I'm looking for a l.** j'ai été invité, mais je cherche un prétexte pour ne pas y aller
►► ***let-out clause*** échappatoire *f*

letter ['letə(r)] N **1** *(of alphabet)* lettre *f*; **the l. B** la lettre B; **a six-l. word** un mot de six lettres; **to have letters after one's name** *(have academic qualifications)* être diplômé; *(have official title)* avoir un titre
2 *(communication)* lettre *f*; **I've had a l. from him** j'ai reçu une lettre de lui; **by l.** par lettre *ou* courrier; **he's a good l. writer** *(writes regularly)* il écrit régulièrement; *(writes well)* il écrit de belles lettres; **I'm a bad l. writer** *(don't write regularly)* je n'écris pas souvent; *(don't write good letters)* je ne suis pas très doué pour écrire; *Br* **to post letters** poster des lettres *ou* du courrier; **letters to the editor** *(in newspapers, magazines)* courrier *m* des lecteurs; **the letters of DH Lawrence** la correspondance de DH Lawrence
3 *Fig (exact meaning)* lettre *f*; **to keep** *or* **to stick to the l. of the law** respecter la loi au pied de la lettre *ou* à la lettre; **she obeyed the instructions to the l.** elle a suivi les instructions à la lettre *ou* au pied de la lettre
4 *Am (paper size)* lettre *f (216 mm œ279 mm)*
5 *Am Univ* = écusson à l'initiale du nom de l'université décerné à un étudiant qui s'est distingué en sport
ADJ *Am (paper)* lettre *(216 mm œ 279 mm)*
VT *(write)* inscrire des lettres sur; *(engrave)* graver (des lettres sur); *(manuscript)* enluminer
VI *Am Univ* se voir décerner un écusson pour s'être distingué en sport; **she lettered on the soccer team** on lui a décerné un écusson pour sa prestation dans l'équipe de foot
• **letters** NPL *Formal (learning)* belles-lettres *fpl*; **a man of letters** *(scholar)* un lettré; *(writer)* un homme de lettres; *Br* **English letters** littérature *f* anglaise
▸▸ ***letter of acknowledgement*** accusé *m* de réception; ***letter of advice*** lettre *f* d'avis; *St Exch* ***letter of allotment*** avis *m* d'attribution *ou* de répartition, lettre *f* d'allocation; ***letter of apology*** lettre *f* d'excuse; ***letter of application*** *(for job)* lettre *f* de candidature; *St Exch (for shares)* lettre *f* de souscription; ***letter of appointment*** lettre *f* de nomination *ou* d'affectation; ***letter bomb*** lettre *f* piégée; ***letter card*** carte-lettre *f*; ***letter of complaint*** lettre *f* de réclamation; ***letter of confirmation*** lettre *f* de confirmation; *Admin* ***letters of credence*** lettres *fpl* de créance; *Com* ***letter of credit*** lettre *f* de crédit *ou* de créance; ***letter of dismissal*** lettre *f* de licenciement; *Com* ***letter of exchange*** lettre *f* de change; ***letter of guarantee*** lettre *f* de garantie; *Fin* ***letter of guaranty*** lettre *f* d'aval; *Fin* ***letter of indemnity*** cautionnement *m*, lettre *f* de garantie (d'indemnité); *Fin* ***letter of intent*** lettre *f* d'intention; ***letter of introduction*** lettre *f* de recommandation; ***letter opener*** coupe-papier *m inv*; ***the letters page*** le courrier des lecteurs; ***letters patent*** lettres *fpl* patentes; *Comput* ***letter quality*** qualité *f* courrier; **near l. quality** qualité *f* quasi-courrier *(pour une imprimante)*; ***letter rack*** porte-lettres *m inv*; ***letter rate*** tarif *m* lettres; ***letter of reference*** lettre *f* de recommandation; ***letter scales*** pèse-lettre *m*; ***letter tray*** corbeille *f ou* panier *m* à courrier

lettered ['letəd] ADJ **1** *Formal (person)* lettré **2** *(inscribed)* **the title was l. in gilt** le titre était inscrit en lettres dorées; **the rooms are l. from A to K** les salles portent des lettres de A à K

letterhead ['letəhed] N en-tête *m (de lettre)*; *(paper)* papier *m* à en-tête

lettering ['letərɪŋ] N *(UNCOUNT)* **1** *(action)* lettrage *m* **2** *(inscription)* inscription *f* **3** *(characters)* caractères *mpl*; **gold l.** lettres *fpl* en or

letterpress ['letəpres] N *(technique)* typographie *f*; *(text)* texte *m* (imprimé)

letter-quality ADJ qualité courrier *(inv)*

letterspace ['letə,speɪs] VI *Comput & Typ* interlettrer

letterspacing ['letə,speɪsɪŋ] N *Comput & Typ* interlettrage *m*

letting ['letɪŋ] N *(of house, property)* location *f*
▸▸ ***letting agency*** agence *f* de location

lettuce ['letɪs] N *Culin* salade *f*; *Bot* laitue *f*
▸▸ ***lettuce leaf*** feuille *f* de salade *ou* de laitue

let-up N *(stop)* arrêt *m*, pause *f*; *(abatement)* répit *m*; **it's been raining for days without l.** ça fait des jours qu'il n'arrête pas de pleuvoir *ou* qu'il pleut sans arrêt

leucocyte ['lu:kə,saɪt] N *Anat* leucocyte *m*

leucocytosis [,lu:kəsaɪ'təʊsɪs] N *Med* leucocytose *f*

leucosis [,lu:'kəʊsɪs] N *Med* leucose *f*

leukaemia, *Am* **leukemia** [lu:'ki:mɪə] N *(UNCOUNT)* leucémie *f*; **he has l.** il a une leucémie, il est atteint de leucémie

leukaemic, *Am* **leukemic** [lu:'ki:mɪk] ADJ *Med* leucémique

Levant [lɪ'vænt] N **the L.** le Levant

Levantine ['levəntaɪn] N Levantin(e) *m,f*
ADJ levantin

levee[1] ['levɪ] N *Am* **1** *(embankment)* levée *f*; *(surrounding field)* digue *f* **2** *(landing place)* quai *m*

levee[2] N *Hist (in royal chamber)* lever *m* (du roi); *Br (at court)* réception *f* à la cour

LEVEL ['levəl]

N
- niveau **1–4, 6, 8**
- hauteur **1**
- taux **2**
- échelon **3**
- étage **6**
- plat **7**

ADJ
- plat **1**
- au même niveau **2**
- à la même hauteur **2**
- horizontal **3**
- de/à niveau **3**
- à égalité **4**
- calme **5**
- réglo **6**

ADV
- à l'horizontale

VT
- aplanir **1**
- niveler **1, 3**
- braquer **2**

(*Br pt & pp* **levelled**, *cont* **levelling**, *Am pt & pp* **leveled**, *cont* **leveling**)
N **1** *(height ▸ in a horizontal plane)* niveau *m*; (▸ *in a vertical plane)* hauteur *f*; **at ground l.** au niveau du sol; **the l. of the river has risen overnight** le niveau de la rivière a monté pendant la nuit; **the flood waters have reached the l. of the bridge** la crue a atteint le niveau du pont; **the sink is on a l. with the work surface** l'évier est au niveau du *ou* de niveau avec le plan de travail; **on the same l.** au même niveau
2 *(amount)* niveau *m*; *(percentage)* taux *m*; **noise levels are far too high** le niveau sonore est bien trop élevé; **a low l. of sugar in the bloodstream** un faible taux de sucre dans le sang; **inflation has reached new levels** l'inflation a atteint de nouveaux sommets; **check the oil l.** *(in car)* vérifiez le niveau d'huile; **her ambition is on a l. with mine** son ambition est du même ordre que la mienne; *Comput & Typ* **levels of grey** échelle *f* des gris
3 *(rank)* niveau *m*, échelon *m*; **at cabinet/national l.** à l'échelon ministériel/national; **at a regional l.** au niveau régional; **talks are being held at the highest l.** on négocie au plus haut niveau
4 *(standard)* niveau *m*; **her l. of English is poor** elle n'a pas un très bon niveau en anglais; **students at beginners' l.** étudiants *mpl* au niveau débutant; **a high l. of competence/intelligence** un haut niveau de compétence/d'intelligence; **she's on a different l. from the others** elle n'est pas au même niveau que les autres; **to come down to sb's l.** se mettre au niveau de qn; **don't descend** *or* **sink to their l.** ne t'abaisse pas à leur niveau
5 *(point of view)* **on a personal l., I really like him** sur le plan personnel, je l'aime beaucoup; **on a practical l.** du point de vue pratique
6 *(storey)* niveau *m*, étage *m*; **the library is on l. three** la bibliothèque est au niveau trois *ou* au troisième étage
7 *(flat land)* plat *m*; **100 km/h on the l.** 100 km/h sur le plat
8 *(for woodwork, building etc)* **(spirit) l.** niveau *m* (à bulle)
9 *Fam (idiom)* **on the l.** *(honest)* honnête□, réglo; **do you think he's on the l.?** tu crois qu'il est réglo *ou* que c'est un type réglo?; **I'm giving it to you on the l.** je te dis ça franchement *ou* sans détour; **this deal is definitely on the l.** cette affaire est tout ce qu'il y a de plus réglo
ADJ **1** *(flat)* plat; **a l. spoonful** une cuillerée rase; **to make sth l.** aplanir qch
2 *(at the same height)* au même niveau, à la même hauteur; *(at the same standard)* au même niveau; **the terrace is l. with the pool** la terras est au même niveau que *ou* de plain-pied ave la piscine; **his head is just l. with my shoulder** tête m'arrive exactement à l'épaule
3 *(horizontal)* horizontal; *(ground)* de niveau, niveau
4 *(equal)* à égalité; **the leading cars are almost** les voitures de tête sont presque à la mêm hauteur; **to draw l.** se trouver à égalité; **the oth runners drew l. with me** les autres coureurs m'o rattrapé
5 *(calm, steady)* calme, mesuré; **to speak in a voice** parler d'une voix calme *ou* posée; **to kee a l. head** garder la tête froide
6 *Fam (honest)* honnête□, réglo; **you're n being l. with me** tu ne joues pas franc jeu ave moi□
7 *(idioms)* **to do one's l. best** faire de son mieu **she did her l. best to irritate me** elle a tout fait po me mettre en colère; *Br* **it's l. pegging** *(betwee the two)* il y a égalité; **they're l. pegging** ils sont égalité
ADV à l'horizontale; **hold the tray l.** tenez le pl teau à l'horizontale *ou* bien à plat; *Aviat* **to fly** voler en palier
VT **1** *(flatten)* aplanir, niveler; **to l. a town (to th ground)** raser une ville
2 *(aim)* **to l. a gun at sb** braquer une arme sur q **to l. accusations at sb** lancer des accusatio contre qn; **a lot of criticism has been levelled me** on m'a beaucoup critiqué
3 *(in surveying)* effectuer des opérations de n vellement dans, niveler
VI *Fam* **to l. with sb** être franc avec qn□, jou franc jeu avec qn□
▸▸ *Br & Can* ***level crossing*** passage *m* à nivea *Aviat* ***level flight*** vol *m* horizontal; *Cin & TV* ***lev shot*** plan *m* à niveau
▸**level down** VT SEP *(surface)* aplanir, nivele *(standard)* niveler par le bas
▸**level off** VI **1** *(production, rise, developmen* s'équilibrer, se stabiliser; **the curve on the grap levels off at this point** la courbe du graphique s stabilise à partir d'ici; **the team's performance ha levelled off this season** les résultats de l'équipe s sont stabilisés cette saison **2** *Aviat* amorcer u palier
VT SEP *(flatten)* aplatir, niveler
▸**level up** VT SEP niveler (par le haut)

level-headed ADJ équilibré, pondéré, réfl chi; **he's a l. boy** c'est un garçon qui a la tête s les épaules

leveller, *Am* **leveler** ['levələ(r)] N *Pol* égalitarist *mf*, niveleur(euse) *m,f*; **death is a great l.** nou sommes tous égaux devant la mort

THE LEVELLERS

Ce mouvement de républicains apparut en 1647 pendant la guerre civile en Angleterre. Les "niveleurs" réclamaient un renforcement des pouvoirs du Parlement ainsi qu'une plus large représentation populaire, mais furent durement réprimés par Cromwell.

lever [*Br* 'li:və(r), *Am* 'levər] N *also Fig* levier *n*; *(smaller)* manette *f*
VT manœuvrer à l'aide d'un levier; **he levere the box open with a piece of wood** il a forcé l caisse à l'aide d'un morceau de bois; **the levered the engine into position** ils installèrent l moteur à l'aide d'un levier; *Fig* **he has levere himself into a very strong position** il s'est hissé un poste très important
▸▸ *Tech* ***lever arm*** bras *m* de levier; *Tech & F* ***lever effect*** effet *m* de levier
▸**lever off** VT SEP *(lid, top, tyre)* enlever (avec u levier); *(padlock)* faire sauter
▸**lever out** VT SEP extraire *ou* extirper (à l'aid d'un levier); *Fig* **he levered himself out of bed** s'extirpa du lit; **they levered the president out o office** ils ont délogé le président de son poste
▸**lever up** VT SEP soulever (au moyen d'un le vier); *Fig* **she levered herself up onto the rock** ell se hissa sur le rocher

leverage [*Br* 'li:vərɪdʒ, *Am* 'levərɪdʒ] N **1** *Tech* forc *f* (de levier); **I can't get enough l.** je n'ai pas asse de prise **2** *(influence)* influence *f*; **to exert some l. on sb** exercer de l'influence sur qn; **he has no l. with the management** il n'a aucun moyen de pression sur la direction **3** *Am Econ (gearing)* effet *m* de levier; *(as percentage)* ratio *m* d'endettement *ou* de levier

VT *(make use of)* mettre à profit; **the company leveraged their local knowledge to launch their product in Japan** la société a mis à profit sa bonne connaissance du terrain pour lancer son produit au Japon

everaged [*Br* 'li:vərɪdʒd, *Am* 'levərɪdʒd] **ADJ**

▸▸ *Fin* ***leveraged buyout*** rachat *m* d'entreprise financé par l'endettement; *Fin* ***leveraged management buyout*** rachat *m* d'entreprise par les salariés

ever-arch file **N** classeur *m* à levier

everet ['levərɪt] **N** levraut *m*

eviathan [lɪ'vaɪəθən] **N** *(ship)* navire *m* géant; *(institution, organization)* institution *f ou* organisation *f* géante

• **Leviathan** **PR N** *Bible* Léviathan

.evis® ['li:vaɪz] **NPL** jean *m ou* jeans *mpl* (Levi's®)

evitate ['levɪteɪt] **VT** faire léviter, soulever par lévitation

VI léviter

evitation [,levɪ'teɪʃən] **N** lévitation *f*

evity ['levətɪ] (*pl* **levities**) **N** légèreté *f*, manque *m* de sérieux

evy ['levɪ] (*pl* **levies**, *pt & pp* **levied**) **N 1** *(action)* prélèvement *m*; **tax l.** prélèvement *m* fiscal; **a capital l. of 10 percent** un prélèvement de 10 pour cent sur le capital **2** *(tax, duty)* impôt *m*, taxe *f*, droit *m*; **to impose a l. on sugar imports** taxer les importations de sucre; **special l.** taxe *f* exceptionnelle **3** *Mil* levée *f*

VT 1 *(impose ▸ tax)* prélever; *(▸ fine)* imposer, infliger; **to l. a duty on imports** prélever une taxe sur les importations **2** *(collect ▸ taxes, fine)* lever, percevoir **3** *Mil (troops)* lever

ewd [lju:d] **ADJ** *(behaviour)* lubrique; *(speech)* obscène

ewdly ['lju:dlɪ] **ADV** *(behave)* lubriquement; *(speak)* de façon obscène

ewdness ['lju:dnɪs] **N** *(of behaviour)* lubricité *f*; *(of speech)* obscénité *f*

exical ['leksɪkəl] **ADJ** lexical

exicalize, -ise ['leksɪkəlaɪz] **VT** lexicaliser

exicographer [,leksɪ'kɒgrəfə(r)] **N** lexicographe *mf*

exicographical [,leksɪkə'græfɪkəl] **ADJ** lexicographique

exicography [,leksɪ'kɒgrəfɪ] **N** lexicographie *f*

exicology [,leksɪ'kɒlədʒɪ] **N** lexicologie *f*

exicon ['leksɪkən] **N** lexique *m*

exis ['leksɪs] **N** lexique *m*

ez [lez], **lezzy** ['lezɪ] **N** *very Fam* gouine *f*, = terme injurieux désignant une lesbienne

LGBT [,eldʒi:,bi:'ti:] **ADJ** (*abbr* **lesbian, gay, bisexual and transgender**) allosexuel, = lesbien, gay, bisexuel et transsexuel

lh [,el'eɪtʃ] *Mus* (*abbr* **left hand**) main *f* gauche

iability [,laɪə'bɪlətɪ] (*pl* **liabilities**) **N 1** *(UNCOUNT) Law (responsibility)* responsabilité *f* (légale); **he refused to admit l. for the damage** il refusa d'endosser la responsabilité des dégâts

2 *(UNCOUNT) (eligibility)* assujettissement *m*; **l. for tax** assujettissement *m* à l'impôt; **l. for military service** obligations *fpl* militaires

3 *(hindrance)* gêne *f*, handicap *m*; **the house he had inherited was a real l.** la maison dont il avait hérité lui coûtait une petite fortune *ou* lui revenait cher; **that man is a (total) l.** ce type est un vrai poids mort *ou* un véritable boulet

4 *Acct & Fin* dette *f*

5 *Com (on bills of exchange)* encours *m*

• **liabilities** **NPL** *Acct & Fin (debts)* passif *m*, dettes *fpl*; **to meet one's liabilities** rembourser ses dettes; **assets and liabilities** actif *m* et passif *m*

▸▸ *Am Law* ***liability suit*** procès *m* en responsabilité civile

iable ['laɪəbəl] **ADJ 1** *Law (responsible)* responsable; **to be held l. for sth** être tenu (pour) responsable de qch; **employers are l. for their staff's mistakes** les employeurs sont (civilement) responsables des erreurs de leur personnel; **to be l. for sb's debts** répondre des dettes de qn; **you'll be l. for damages** on sera en droit de vous demander *ou* réclamer des dommages et intérêts **2** *(likely)* **to be l. to do sth** *(person, thing)* risquer de faire qch; **the programme is l. to change** le programme est susceptible d'être modifié, il se peut que le programme subisse des modifications; **he's l. to arrive at any moment** il peut arriver d'une minute à l'autre; **we are all l. to make mistakes** tout le monde peut se tromper; **if you don't remind him, he's l. to forget** si on ne lui rappelle pas, il risque d'oublier **3** *Admin* **to be l. for tax** *(person)* être assujetti à *ou* redevable de l'impôt; *(goods)* être assujetti à une taxe; **offenders are l. to a fine** les contrevenants sont passibles d'une amende; **he is l. to be prosecuted** il s'expose à des poursuites judiciaires; *Mil* **to be l. for military service** être astreint au service militaire

liaise [lɪ'eɪz] **VI to l. with sb** *(be in contact with)* être en contact avec qn; *(work together with)* collaborer avec qn; **the two parties have agreed to l.** les deux parties ont accepté de collaborer; **her role is to l. with the accounts department** son rôle est d'assurer la liaison avec le service de la comptabilité

liaison [lɪ'eɪzɒn] **N** liaison *f*

▸▸ ***liaison officer*** *(between services, companies)* agent *m* de liaison; *Mil* officier *m* de liaison

liana [lɪ'ɑ:nə] **N** liane *f*

liar ['laɪə(r)] **N** menteur(euse) *m,f*; **you l.!** espèce de menteur!

Lib [lɪb] **N** *Formerly Pol* (*abbr* **Liberal**) libéral(e) *m,f*

▸▸ ***Lib Dem*** **N** = membre du parti libéral démocrate **ADJ** libéral démocrate

lib [lɪb] **N** *Fam* (*abbr* **liberation**) libération *f*

libation [laɪ'beɪʃən] **N** *Literary (offering)* libation *f*; *Hum* **can I offer you a small l.?** puis-je vous offrir un petit quelque chose?

libel ['laɪbəl] (*Br pt & pp* **libelled**, *cont* **libelling**, *Am pt & pp* **libeled**, *cont* **libeling**) **N** *Law (act of publishing)* diffamation *f*; *(publication)* écrit *m* diffamatoire; *Fig (calumny)* calomnie *f*, mensonge *m*; **to sue sb for l.** poursuivre qn en justice pour diffamation; **that's l.!** c'est une calomnie *ou* de la diffamation!

VT *Law* diffamer; *Fig* calomnier

▸▸ ***libel case*** procès *m* en diffamation; ***libel laws*** législation *f* en matière de diffamation; ***libel suit*** procès *m* en diffamation

libellant, *Am* **libelant** ['laɪbələnt] **N** diffamateur(trice) *m,f*

libellee, *Am* **libelee** [,laɪbə'li:] **N** personne *f* poursuivie pour diffamation

libeller, *Am* **libeler** ['laɪbələ(r)] **N** diffamateur(trice) *m,f*

libellous, *Am* **libelous** ['laɪbələs] **ADJ** diffamatoire

liberal ['lɪbərəl] **ADJ 1** *(tolerant ▸ person)* libéral, large d'esprit; *(▸ ideas, mind)* libéral, large; *(▸ education)* libéral **2** *(generous)* libéral, généreux; **the cook was a bit too l. with the salt** le cuisinier a eu la main un peu lourde avec le sel; **he was always very l. with his praise** il n'était jamais avare de compliments **3** *(copious ▸ helping, portion)* abondant, copieux

N *(moderate)* **she's a l.** elle est de centre gauche

• **Liberal** *Formerly Pol* **ADJ** libéral **N** *(party member)* libéral(e) *m,f*; *(voter, supporter)* partisan *m* du parti libéral; **to vote L.** voter pour le parti libéral

▸▸ ***the liberal arts*** les sciences *fpl* humaines; ***Liberal Democrat*** **N** = membre du parti libéral démocrate **ADJ** libéral démocrate; ***the Liberal Democrats*** parti *m* libéral démocrate *(parti politique britannique de tendance centriste)*; *Br Formerly* ***the Liberal Party*** le parti libéral; ***liberal studies*** programme *m* de culture générale

liberalism ['lɪbərəlɪzəm] **N** libéralisme *m*

liberality [,lɪbə'rælətɪ] (*pl* **liberalities**) **N 1** *(tolerance)* libéralisme *m* **2** *(generosity)* libéralité *f*, largesse *f*

liberalize, -ise ['lɪbərəlaɪz] **VT** libéraliser

liberally ['lɪbərəlɪ] **ADV** libéralement; **a l. spiced dish** un plat généreusement épicé

liberal-minded **ADJ** large d'esprit

liberate ['lɪbəreɪt] **VT 1** *(gen)* libérer; *Fin* **to l. capital** libérer des capitaux **2** *Chem & Phys (gas, heat)* libérer, dégager **3** *Hum (steal)* piquer

liberated ['lɪbəreɪtɪd] **ADJ** *(person)* libéré; *(ideas, views)* progressiste; **these are l. times** on vit une époque libérée

liberating ['lɪbəreɪtɪŋ] **ADJ** libérateur

liberation [,lɪbə'reɪʃən] **N 1** *(gen)* libération *f*; **she doesn't believe in women's l.** elle ne croit pas à la libération de la femme **2** *Chem & Phys (of gas, heat)* dégagement *m*

▸▸ ***liberation movement*** mouvement *m* de libération; ***liberation theology*** théologie *f* de la libération

liberator ['lɪbəreɪtə(r)] **N** libérateur(trice) *m,f*

Liberia [laɪ'bɪərɪə] **N** Liberia *m*

Liberian [laɪ'bɪərɪən] **N** Libérien(enne) *m,f*

ADJ libérien

COMP *(embassy, history)* du Liberia

libertarian [,lɪbə'teərɪən] **N** libertaire *mf*

ADJ libertaire

libertine ['lɪbəti:n] **N** libertin(e) *m,f*

ADJ libertin

liberty ['lɪbətɪ] (*pl* **liberties**) **N** *(in behaviour)* liberté *f*; **to take liberties with sb** prendre *ou* se permettre des libertés avec qn; **the government is taking liberties** le gouvernement se fiche du monde; **to take liberties with the truth** prendre des libertés avec la vérité; **I took the l. of inviting them** j'ai pris la liberté *ou* je me suis permis de les inviter; **what a l.!** *(cheek)* quel toupet!; *Fam Pej* **it's l. hall in this house** chacun fait ce qui lui plaît *ou* c'est la pétaudière dans cette maison

• **at liberty** **ADJ the criminals are still at l.** les criminels sont toujours en liberté *ou* courent toujours; **you are at l. to leave** vous êtes libre de partir; **I'm not at l. to say** il ne m'est pas possible *ou* permis de le dire

▸▸ ***liberty bodice*** chemise *f* américaine; ***liberty cap*** bonnet *m* phrygien *ou* d'affranchi; ***Liberty Island*** île *f* de la Liberté; ***liberty ship*** = navire de marchandises préfabriqué construit par les États-Unis pendant la Seconde Guerre mondiale; *Naut* ***liberty ticket*** permission *f* de terre *ou* d'aller à terre

libidinous [lɪ'bɪdɪnəs] **ADJ** libidineux

libido [lɪ'bi:dəʊ] (*pl* **libidos**) **N** libido *f*

LIBOR ['laɪbɔ:(r)] **N** *Br Fin* (*abbr* **London Inter-Bank Offer Rate**) TIOP *m*

Libra ['li:brə] **N 1** *Astron* Balance *f* **2** *Astrol* Balance *f*; **he's a L.** il est (du signe de la) Balance

ADJ *Astrol* de la Balance; **he's L.** il est (du signe de la) Balance

librarian [laɪ'breərɪən] **N** bibliothécaire *mf*

> Note that the French word **libraire** is a false friend and is never a translation for the English word **librarian**. It means **bookseller**.

librarianship [laɪ'breərɪənʃɪp] **N** *(science)* bibliothéconomie *f*; **to study l.** faire des études de bibliothécaire *ou* de bibliothéconomie

library ['laɪbrərɪ] (*pl* **libraries**) **N 1** *(gen)* bibliothèque *f* **2** *(series ▸ of books)* bibliothèque *f*, collection *f*; *(▸ of records, tapes, CDs)* discothèque *f*; *(▸ of films, videos)* collection *f* **3** *Comput (of programs)* bibliothèque *f*

COMP *(book, card)* de bibliothèque

▸▸ ***the Library of Congress*** la bibliothèque du Congrès *(équivalent américain de la Bibliothèque nationale)*; ***library document*** document *m* d'archives; ***library edition*** édition *f* de luxe; ***library film*** film *m* d'archives; *Br* ***library footage*** images *fpl* d'archives; ***library music*** musique *f* d'archives; ***library pictures*** images *fpl* d'archives; ***library science*** bibliothéconomie *f*; **she's studying l. science** elle fait des études de bibliothécaire; ***library steps*** escabeau *m* de bibliothèque

> Note that the French word **librairie** is a false friend and is never a translation for the English word **library**. It means **bookshop**.

librettist [lɪ'bretɪst] **N** librettiste *mf*

libretto [lɪ'bretəʊ] *(pl* **librettos** *or* **libretti** [-tɪ]*)* **N** *Mus* livret *m*, libretto *m*

Libya ['lɪbɪə] **N** Libye *f*

Libyan ['lɪbɪən] **N** Libyen(enne) *m,f*
ADJ libyen
COMP *(embassy)* de Libye; *(history)* de la Libye
►► ***the Libyan Desert*** le désert de Libye

lice [laɪs] *pl of* **louse**

licence, *Am* **license**[1] ['laɪsəns] **N 1** *(permit)* permis *m*; *(for marriage)* certificat *m* de publication des bans; *(for trade, bar)* licence *f*; *(for TV, radio)* redevance *f*; *(for pilot)* brevet *m*; *(for driver)* permis *m* (de conduire); **do you have a TV l.?** avez-vous payé la redevance (télé)?; **a l. to sell alcoholic drinks** une licence de débit de boissons
2 *Admin & Com (permission)* licence *f*, autorisation *f*; **to manufacture sth under l.** fabriquer qch sous licence; **to marry by special l.** se marier sans publication de bans; *Fig* **that job's a l. to print money!** ce travail est une sinécure!
3 *(liberty)* licence *f*, liberté *f*; **the biographer has allowed himself a certain l. in his interpretation** le biographe s'est permis certaines libertés d'interprétation; **artistic l.** licence *f* artistique
4 *(immoral behaviour)* licence *f*, débordements *mpl*; **sexual l.** débordements *mpl* sexuels
►► *Comput* ***licence agreement*** licence *f*; *Br* ***licence fee*** redevance *f* télévisuelle; ***licence number*** *(on vehicle)* numéro *m* d'immatriculation; *(on driving licence)* numéro *m* de permis de conduire; ***licence plate*** plaque *f* minéralogique *ou* d'immatriculation

> Note that the French noun **licence** also means **bachelor's degree**.

license[2] **VT 1** *Admin & Com (premises, trader)* accorder une licence *ou* une autorisation à; **licensed to practise medicine** habilité à exercer la médecine; **to l. a car** immatriculer une voiture **2** *(allow)* **to l. sb to do sth** autoriser qn à faire qch, permettre à qn de faire qch

licensed ['laɪsənst] **ADJ 1** *Com (product)* fabriqué sous licence; **these premises are l. to sell alcoholic drinks** cet établissement est autorisé à vendre des boissons alcoolisées **2** *(pilot)* breveté; *(driver)* qui a son permis (de conduire); *Br* **is this vehicle l.?** ce véhicule est-il immatriculé?
►► ***licensed brand name*** nom *m* de marque sous licence; *Am* ***licensed practical nurse*** infirmier (ère) *m,f*; ***licensed premises*** *(bar, pub)* débit *m* de boissons; *(restaurant, cafeteria)* établissement *m* autorisé à vendre des boissons alcoolisées; *Formal* ***licensed victualler*** débitant *m* de boissons

licensee [,laɪsən'siː] **N** *(gen)* titulaire *mf* d'une licence *ou* d'un permis; *(pub-owner, landlord)* débitant *m* de boissons

licensing ['laɪsənsɪŋ] **N** *(of car)* immatriculation *f*; *(of activity)* autorisation *f*
►► ***licensing agreement*** accord *m* de licence; ***licensing authority*** = organisme chargé de la délivrance des licences; *Br* ***licensing hours*** = heures d'ouverture des pubs; *Br* ***licensing laws*** = lois réglementant la vente d'alcools

> **LICENSING HOURS**
>
> Traditionnellement, les heures d'ouverture des pubs répondent à une réglementation stricte (liée à la législation sur la vente des boissons alcoolisées), mais celle-ci a été assouplie en 1988. Les pubs d'Angleterre et du pays de Galles peuvent désormais rester ouverts de 11h à 23h. En Écosse, en revanche, la réglementation est moins stricte et les pubs qui en font la demande peuvent rester ouverts beaucoup plus tard certains soirs. Depuis 2005, les pubs d'Angleterre et du pays de Galles ont également la possibilité de faire une demande de licence spéciale les autorisant à ouvrir 24 heures sur 24 mais peu d'établissements se sont montrés intéressés.

licensor ['laɪsənsə(r)] **N** concédant *m*

licentiate [laɪ'senʃɪət] **N** diplômé(e) *m,f*

licentious [laɪ'senʃəs] **ADJ** licencieux

licentiousness [laɪ'senʃəsnɪs] **N** licence *f*

lichen ['laɪkən, 'lɪtʃən] **N** lichen *m*

licit ['lɪsɪt] **ADJ** licite

licitly ['lɪsɪtlɪ] **ADV** licitement

licitness ['lɪsɪtnɪs] **N** licéité *f*

lick [lɪk] **N 1** *(with tongue)* coup *m* de langue; **to give sth a l.** lécher qch; **can I have a l. of your ice-cream?** je peux goûter ta glace?; **a l. of paint** un (petit) coup de peinture
2 *Br Fam (speed)* **at a tremendous l.** à fond la caisse, à fond de train
3 l. (of hair) mèche *f*
4 *Agr* pierre *f* à lécher
5 *Am Fam* **we got our last licks on the beach before the weather changed** on est allé à la plage une dernière fois avant que le temps ne se gâte; **he started the debate so you get last licks** c'est lui qui a entamé le débat, ce sera donc à toi de le clore
VT 1 *(gen)* lécher; *(stamp)* humecter; **the dog licked its bowl clean** le chien a nettoyé sa gamelle à coups de langue; **the dog licked her hand** le chien lui a léché la main; **the cat licked (up) the milk from the plate** le chat a lapé le lait qui était dans l'assiette; **he licked the jam off the bread** il lécha la confiture de la tartine; *Fam* **to l. one's chops** se lécher les babines; *Fig* **the flames licked the walls of the house** les flammes léchaient les murs de la maison; *Fam* **to l. sb's boots** lécher les bottes à qn; *Br Vulg* **to l. sb's arse** lécher le cul de qn; **to l. one's lips** se lécher les lèvres; *Fig (with satisfaction, lust)* se frotter les mains; *(with eager anticipation)* se lécher les babines; **to l. one's wounds** *(of animal)* lécher ses plaies; *Fig* panser ses blessures; *Br* **how long did it take to l. the garden into shape?** combien de temps vous a-t-il fallu pour que le jardin prenne forme?; **a spell in the army will soon l. him into shape** un séjour à l'armée lui fera le plus grand bien **2** *Fam (defeat)* battre à plate couture; *(in fight)* donner une raclée à; **this crossword has got me licked** ces mots croisés sont trop durs pour moi; **we've finally got the problem licked** nous sommes enfin venus à bout du problème; **when it comes to marketing, they've got us licked** pour ce qui est du marketing, on ne leur arrive pas à la cheville

lickety-split [,lɪkətɪ-] **ADV** *Am Fam* à toute(s) pompe(s)

licking ['lɪkɪŋ] **N** *Fam (thrashing)* raclée *f*, dégelée *f*; *(defeat)* raclée *f*, déculottée *f*; **to get a good l.** prendre une raclée

lickspittle ['lɪk,spɪtəl] **N** *Fam* lèche-bottes *mf inv*

licorice *Am* = **liquorice**

lid [lɪd] **N 1** *(gen)* couvercle *m*
2 *Anat (eyelid)* paupière *f*
3 *Fam (hat)* galure *m*, galurin *m*; *(helmet)* casque *m*
4 *Fam (idioms)* **the scandal put the l. on the Chicago operation** le scandale mit fin à l'opération de Chicago; **the firm is keeping a l. on expenses** l'entreprise met un frein aux dépenses; *Br* **that puts the (tin) l. on it!** ça, c'est le bouquet!; **to take** *or* **to lift the l. off sth** percer *ou* mettre qch à jour; *Am Fam* **keep a l. on it!** la ferme!

lidar ['laɪdɑː(r)] **N** *Tech (abbr* **light detection and ranging***)* lidar *m*

lidded ['lɪdɪd] **ADJ** *(container)* à couvercle

lidless ['lɪdlɪs] **ADJ 1** *(container)* sans couvercle **2** *(eyes)* sans paupières

lido ['liːdəʊ] *(pl* **lidos***)* **N** *(pool)* piscine *f* découverte; *(resort)* station *f* balnéaire

LIE [laɪ]

> **VI**
> - mentir **1**
> - être couché **2**
> - être classé **4**
> - se trouver **5, 7**
> - s'étendre **7**
> - se coucher **2**
> - reposer **3**
> - être **5, 7**
> - rester **6**
>
> **N**
> - mensonge **1**
> - position **3**
> - configuration **2**

(cont **lying**, *pt & pp sense* **1 lied**, *pt senses* **2–10 lay** [leɪ], *pp senses* **2–10 lain** [leɪn]*)*
VI 1 *(tell untruth)* mentir; **he lied about his age** il a menti sur son âge; **"it wasn't me," she lied** "ce n'était pas moi", dit-elle en mentant; **to l. through one's teeth** mentir effrontément; *Fig* **the camera never lies** une photo ne ment pas
2 *(person, animal* ► *recline)* se coucher, s'allonger, s'étendre; *(*► *be in lying position)* être couch(à plat); **to l. on one's back/side** être couché sur ldos/côté; **to be lying ill in bed** être (malade et alité; **she lay on the beach all day** elle est restéallongée sur la plage toute la journée; **she walying on the couch** elle était couchée *ou* allongésur le divan; **we found him lying dead** nous l'avons trouvé mort; **he lay helpless on the floo** il gisait là sans pouvoir bouger; **l. still!** ne bougpas!; **I like lying in bed on Sunday mornings** j'aimrester au lit *ou* faire la grasse matinée le dimanche matin; **they lay sound asleep** ils dormaienprofondément, ils étaient profondément endormis; **she lay awake for hours** elle resta plusieurs heures sans pouvoir s'endormir; **to l. iwait for sb** guetter l'arrivée de qn
3 *(corpse)* reposer; **he will l. in state at Westminster Abbey** son corps sera exposé solennellement à l'abbaye de Westminster; **here lies JohSmith** *(on gravestone)* ci-gît John Smith
4 *(team, competitor* ► *rank)* être classé, se classer; **France lies second, after Italy** la France esclassée deuxième, après l'Italie; **she was lyinfourth** *(in race)* elle était en quatrième position
5 *(thing* ► *be, be placed)* être, se trouver; **thpapers lay on the table** les papiers étaient sur ltable; **a folder lay open on the desk before her** udossier était ouvert devant elle sur le bureau; **pile of ammunition lay ready** des munitionétaient là, prêtes à servir; **I found your watclying on the floor** j'ai trouvé ta montre qui traînait par terre; **several boats lay in the harbour** plusieurs bateaux étaient mouillés dans le port **snow lay (thick) on the ground** il y avait un(épaisse) couche de neige; **the castle now lies iruins** le château est aujourd'hui en ruines; *Fig* **aher hopes and dreams lay in ruins** tous ses espoiret ses rêves étaient anéantis *ou* réduits à néant **the obstacles that l. in our way** les obstacles qubloquent notre chemin
6 *(thing* ► *remain, stay)* rester; **the jewel lay hidden for many years** le bijou est resté caché pendant de nombreuses années; **our machines arlying idle** nos machines sont arrêtées *ou* ne tournent pas; **the money is just lying in the bank doinnothing** l'argent dort à la banque; **the snow didn'l.** la neige n'a pas tenu
7 *(place* ► *be situated)* se trouver, être; *(land* ► *stretch, extend)* s'étendre; **Texas lies to the south oOklahoma** le Texas se trouve *ou* s'étend au sud dl'Oklahoma; **these hills l. between us and the se** ces collines sont entre nous et la mer; **a vast desert lay before us** un immense désert s'étendaidevant nous
8 *(future event)* **they didn't know what lay aheaof them** ils ne savaient pas ce qui les attendait **who knows what may l. in store for us** qui sait cqui nous attend *ou* ce que l'avenir nous réserve
9 *(answer, explanation, duty etc)* **the problem liein getting them motivated** le problème, c'est dréussir à les motiver; **where do our real interestl.?** qu'est-ce qui compte vraiment pour nous? **the fault lies with you** c'est de votre faute; **responsibility for the strike lies with the management** lresponsabilité de la grève incombe à la direction; **the onus of proof lies with them** c'est à euqu'il incombe de fournir la preuve; **my talents dnot l. in that direction** je n'ai pas de disposition*ou* de talent pour cela
10 *Law (appeal, claim)* être recevable
VT she lied her way into the building elle a pénétré dans l'immeuble grâce à quelques mensonges; **he always lies his way out of difficulties** il ssort toujours des difficultés en mentant
N 1 *(untruth)* mensonge *m*; **to tell lies** dire demensonges, mentir; *Literary* **to give the l. to st** démentir qch; **it was in June, no, I tell a l., in Jul** c'était en juin, non, je me trompe, en juillet **there are lies, damned lies and statistics** on faidire ce que l'on veut aux chiffres
2 *(of land)* configuration *f*, disposition *f*
3 *Golf (of golf ball)* position *f*; **he's got a bad l** c'est une balle difficile
►► ***lie detector*** détecteur *m* de mensonges; **ttake a l. detector test** passer au détecteur dmensonges

►**lie about, lie around VI 1** *(person)* traîner; **lay about all weekend doing nothing** j'ai traîné tout le week-end à ne rien faire **2** *(thing)* traîner; **don't leave your things lying about** ne laisse pas traîner tes affaires

▸ **lie back** VI **he lay back in his armchair** il s'est renversé dans son fauteuil; *Fig* **when you've finished you'll be able to l. back and take things easy** quand tu auras fini tu pourras te reposer

▸ **lie down** VI se coucher, s'allonger, s'étendre; **go and l. down for an hour** va t'allonger une heure; **to l. down on the ground** se coucher *ou* s'allonger par terre; *Fig* **I won't take this lying down!** je ne vais pas me laisser faire comme ça!

▸ **lie in** VI *(stay in bed)* faire la grasse matinée

▸ **lie off** VI *Naut* rester au large

▸ **lie to** VI *Naut* se tenir *ou* (se) mettre à la cape

▸ **lie up** VI *(person)* rester au lit, garder le lit; *(machine)* ne pas tourner, être arrêté; *(car)* rester au garage

> Attention: ne pas confondre avec le verbe **to lay**, qui signifie **poser à plat**.

Liechtenstein ['lɪktənstaɪn] N Liechtenstein *m*

lie-down N *Br Fam* **to have a l.** se coucher□, s'allonger□; **I think I'll go for a little l.** je crois que je vais aller m'allonger un peu

lief [li:f] ADV *Arch or Literary* **I'd as l. die as marry him** plutôt mourir que de l'épouser

liege [li:dʒ] N *Arch* seigneur *m*, suzerain *m*

▸▸ ***liege lord*** seigneur *m*, suzerain *m*; ***liege man*** homme *m* lige

lie-in N *Br Fam* **to have a l.** faire la grasse matinée

lien ['lɪən] N *Law (on property)* privilège *m*, droit *m* de rétention; **to have a l. on a cargo** avoir un recours sur un chargement; *Fin* **l. on shares** nantissement *m* d'actions

lieu [lju:, lu:] **in lieu** ADV **take Monday off in l.** prends ton lundi pour compenser

• **in lieu of** PREP au lieu de, à la place de; **two weeks salary in l. of notice** deux semaines de salaire en guise de préavis

Lieut *Mil (written abbr* **lieutenant***)* Lieut.

Lieut-Col *Mil (written abbr* **Lieutenant-Colonel***)* Lieut.-Col.

lieutenant [lu:'tenənt, *Br* lef'tenənt] N **1** *Mil (in army)* lieutenant *m*; *(in navy)* lieutenant *m* de vaisseau

2 *(in US and Canadian police)* inspecteur *m* (de police)

3 *Fig* lieutenant *m*, second *m*; **the marketing director and his lieutenants** le directeur du marketing et ses lieutenants

4 *Hist* lieutenant *m*

▸▸ ***lieutenant colonel*** lieutenant-colonel *m*; ***lieutenant commander*** capitaine *m* de corvette; ***lieutenant general*** *(in army)* général *m* de corps d'armée; *(in US airforce)* général *m* de corps aérien; ***lieutenant governor*** *(in Canada)* lieutenant (e) *m,f* gouverneur(e); *(in US)* gouverneur(e) *m, f* adjoint(e)

LIFE [laɪf]

> • vie **1–4, 6–9, 11** • sensation **5**
> • nature **10** • réalité **10**
> • prison à vie **12** • durée **13**
> COMP
> • à vie

(pl **lives** [laɪvz]*)*

N **1** *(existence)* vie *f*; **to give l. to sb** donner la vie à qn; **they believe in l. after death** ils croient à la vie après la mort; **it's a matter of l. and death** c'est une question de vie ou de mort; **l. is hard** la vie est dure; **he hasn't seen much of l.** il ne connaît pas grand-chose de la vie; **you really see l. as a cop** quand on est flic, on en voit de toutes les couleurs; **there have been several attempts on her l.** elle a été victime de plusieurs attentats; **he's in hospital fighting for his l.** il lutte contre la mort à l'hôpital; *Fam* **how's l.?** comment ça va?; **what a l.!** quelle vie!; **just relax and enjoy l.!** profite donc un peu de la vie!; **I want to live my own l.** je veux vivre ma vie; **l. is worth living when I'm with her** avec elle, la vie vaut la peine d'être vécue; **meeting him has made my l. worth living** le rencontrer *ou* notre rencontre a donné un sens à ma vie; **he makes her l. a misery** il lui rend la vie impossible; **to live l. to the** *Br* **full** *or Am* **fullest** croquer la vie à belles dents; **hundreds lost their lives** des centaines de personnes ont trouvé la mort; **he emigrated in order to make a new l. for himself** il a émigré pour commencer une nouvelle vie *ou* pour repartir à zéro; **to depart this l.** quitter ce monde; **to save sb's l.** sauver la vie à qn; **to risk one's l. (to do sth)** risquer sa vie (pour faire qch); **to risk l. and limb** risquer sa peau; **a cat has nine lives** un chat a neuf vies; **to have nine lives** *(person)* avoir l'âme chevillée au corps; **to take sb's l.** tuer qn; **she took her own l.** elle s'est donné la mort; **she's the only woman in his l.** c'est la seule femme dans sa vie; **to run for one's l.** *or* **for dear l.** s'enfuir à toutes jambes; **run for your lives!** sauve qui peut!; **she was hanging on for dear l.** elle s'accrochait de toutes ses forces; **for the l. of me I can't remember where we met** rien à faire, je n'arrive pas à me rappeler où nous nous sommes rencontrés; *Fam* **get a l.!** t'as rien de mieux à faire de ton temps?; *Br Fam* **my l.!** c'est pas vrai!; *Fam* **he can't sing to save his l.** il chante comme un pied; **not on your l.!** jamais de la vie!; **you take your l. in your hands when cycling in London** on risque sa vie quand on fait du vélo à Londres; **that's l.!, such is l.!** c'est la vie!; **this is the l.!** (ça, c'est) la belle vie!; **I had the time of my l.** je ne me suis jamais autant amusé; *Arch* **upon my l.** seigneur!, mon Dieu!

2 *(period of existence)* vie *f*; **I've worked hard all my l.** j'ai travaillé dur toute ma vie; **in his early l.** quand il était jeune; **I began l. as a labourer** j'ai débuté dans la vie comme ouvrier; **it began l. as a car chassis** à l'origine c'était un châssis de voiture; **we don't want to spend the rest of our lives here** on ne veut pas finir nos jours ici; **I've never eaten snails in my l.** je n'ai jamais mangé d'escargots de ma vie; **I ran the race of my l.!** j'ai fait la course de ma vie!; **it gave me the fright of my l.** je n'ai jamais eu aussi peur de ma vie; **my/his/her/***etc* **l.'s work** l'œuvre *f* de toute ma/sa/*etc* vie; **the fire destroyed his l.'s work** l'incendie a détruit l'œuvre de toute sa vie; **to mate for l.** *(animal, bird)* s'unir pour la vie

3 *(mode of existence)* vie *f*; **they lead a strange l.** ils mènent une drôle de vie; **school l.** la vie scolaire; **she's not used to city l.** elle n'a pas l'habitude de vivre en ville; **married l.** la vie conjugale; *Fam* **to live the l. of Riley** mener une vie de pacha

4 *(living things collectively)* vie *f*; **is there l. on Mars?** y a-t-il de la vie sur Mars?

5 *(UNCOUNT) (physical feeling)* sensation *f*; **l. began to return to her frozen fingers** le sang se remit peu à peu à circuler dans ses doigts gelés

6 *(liveliness)* vie *f*; **she's still young and full of l.** elle est encore jeune et pleine de vie; **there's no l. in this place** ça manque d'entrain ici; **there's a lot more l. in Sydney than in Wellington** Sydney est nettement plus animé que Wellington; **to come to l.** s'animer; **to bring sb to l.** *(play, book etc)* faire vivre qn; **his arrival put new l. into the firm** son arrivée a donné un coup de fouet à l'entreprise; **there's l. in the old dog yet!** il est encore vert, le bonhomme!; **she was the l. and soul of the party** c'est elle qui a mis de l'ambiance dans la soirée, elle fut le boute-en-train de la soirée

7 *(living person)* vie *f*; **a phone call can save a l.** un coup de fil peut sauver une vie; **200 lives were lost in the disaster** 200 personnes ont perdu la vie dans la catastrophe, la catastrophe a fait 200 morts; **no lives were lost** il n'y a eu aucune victime, on ne déplore aucune victime

8 *(durability)* (durée *f* de) vie *f*; **double the l. of your batteries** multipliez par deux la durée de vos piles; **the average l. of an isotope** la durée de vie moyenne d'un isotope; **during the l. of the previous government** sous le gouvernement précédent

9 *(biography)* vie *f*; **she's writing a l. of James Joyce** elle écrit une biographie de James Joyce

10 *Art* nature *f*; *Literature* réalité *f*; **to draw from l.** dessiner d'après nature; **his novels are very true to l.** ses romans sont très réalistes; **that's her to the l.** c'est elle tout craché

11 *(in games)* vie *f*; **when you lose three lives you're out** quand on perd trois vies, on est éliminé

12 *Fam (imprisonment)* prison *f* à vie□; **the kidnappers got l.** les ravisseurs ont été condamnés à perpétuité *ou* à la prison à vie□; **he's doing l.** il purge une peine à perpétuité□

13 *Fin (of loan)* durée *f*

COMP *(post, president)* à vie

• **for life** ADV **he was crippled for l.** il a été estropié à vie; **sent to prison for l.** condamné à perpétuité; **if you help me, I'll be your friend for l.** si tu m'aides, je serai ton ami pour la vie; **a job for l.** un emploi à vie

▸▸ *Fin* ***life annuity*** rente *f* viagère; *Br* ***life assurance*** assurance-vie *f*; ***life belt*** bouée *f* de sauvetage; ***life buoy*** bouée *f* de sauvetage; *Fin* ***life capitalization*** capitalisation *f* viagère; ***life class*** cours *m* de dessin avec modèle nu; ***life coach*** coach *m* personnel; ***life coaching*** coaching *m* personnel; ***life cycle*** cycle *m* de vie; ***life drawing*** dessin *m* d'après modèle; ***life expectancy*** *(of human, animal)* espérance *f* de vie; *(of machine, product)* durée *f* (utile) de vie; ***the Life Guards*** = régiment de cavalerie de la garde royale britannique; ***life history*** vie *f*; **the organism takes on many different forms during its l. history** l'organisme prend de nombreuses formes au cours de sa vie *ou* de son existence; **she told me her whole l. history** elle m'a raconté l'histoire de sa vie; ***life imprisonment*** prison *f* à vie; ***life insurance*** assurance-vie *f*; **to take out l. insurance** contracter une assurance-vie; ***life jacket*** gilet *m* de sauvetage; ***life member*** membre *m* à vie; ***life membership*** adhésion *f* à vie; *Br* ***life peer*** pair *m* à vie; *Br* ***life peerage*** pairie *f* à vie; *Fin* ***life pension*** pension *f* à vie; *Am* ***life preserver*** *(life belt)* bouée *f* de sauvetage; *(life jacket)* gilet *m* de sauvetage; ***life raft*** radeau *m* de sauvetage; ***the life sciences*** les sciences *fpl* de la vie; **anthropology is a l. science** l'anthropologie fait partie des sciences de la vie; ***life sentence*** condamnation *f* à vie *ou* à perpétuité; ***life skills*** = aptitude à fonctionner efficacement en société; ***life span*** *(of human, animal)* espérance *f* de vie; *(of machine, product)* durée *f* de vie; ***life story*** biographie *f*; **she told me her whole l. story** elle m'a raconté l'histoire de sa vie; ***life subscription*** abonnement *m* à vie; ***life tenant*** usufruitier(ère) *m,f*; ***life vest*** gilet *m* de sauvetage

life-affirming [-ə'fɜ:mɪŋ] ADJ euphorisant, jubilatoire

life-and-death ADJ **a l. matter** une question de vie ou de mort; **this is a l. decision** c'est une décision vitale; **a l. struggle** un combat à mort, une lutte désespérée

lifeblood ['laɪfblʌd] N *(of company etc)* âme *f*; *Literary (of person)* sang *m*; **the government are draining the l. from small businesses** le gouvernement est en train de saigner les petites entreprises; **the l. of the economy** le pivot de l'économie

lifeboat ['laɪfbəʊt] N **1** *(launched from coast)* canot *m* de sauvetage **2** *(ship's)* **l.** chaloupe *f* de sauvetage

▸▸ ***lifeboat station*** poste *m* de sauvetage

lifeboatman ['laɪfbəʊtmən] *(pl* **lifeboatmen** [-mən]*)* N sauveteur *m* (en mer)

life-cycle chart N *Mktg (of product)* courbe *f* du cycle de vie

life-cycle hypothesis N *Econ* hypothèse *f* du cycle de vie

life-giving ADJ qui insuffle la vie, vivifiant

lifeguard ['laɪfgɑ:d] N *(at seaside)* surveillant *m* de baignade; *(at swimming pool)* maître *m* nageur; **to be on l. duty** surveiller la baignade

lifeless ['laɪflɪs] ADJ **1** *(dead body)* sans vie; **his l. form** son corps sans vie; **she fell l. to the floor** elle est tombée raide sur le sol **2** *(where no life exists)* sans vie; **a l. desert** un désert sans vie **3** *(dull ▸ eyes)* éteint; *(▸ hair)* terne; *(▸ town)* mort; *(▸ style, performance)* plat

lifelessly ['laɪflɪslɪ] ADV **1** *(inanimately)* sans vie **2** *(dully ▸ perform, write, speak)* platement

lifelessness ['laɪflɪsnɪs] N **1** *(of body)* absence *f* de vie **2** *(dullness ▸ of town)* manque *m* d'animation; *(▸ of style, performance)* platitude *f*

lifelike ['laɪflaɪk] ADJ **1** *(portrait)* ressemblant **2** *(seeming alive)* **the new robots are extremely l.** ces nouveaux robots ont l'air *ou* paraissent vraiment vivants

lifeline ['laɪflaɪn] **N 1** *Naut (thrown to boat)* remorque *f*; *(stretched across deck)* sauvegarde *f*, filière *f* de mauvais temps *ou* de sécurité; **they threw the drowning man a l.** ils ont lancé un filin à l'homme qui se noyait

2 *(for diver)* corde *f* de sécurité

3 *Fig* **it's his l. to the outside world** c'est son lien avec le monde extérieur; **to cut off sb's l.** couper les vivres à qn; **to throw sb a l.** venir à l'aide de qn; *Fig* **for us it was a financial l.** cet argent a permis notre survie

4 *(in palmistry)* ligne *f* de vie

lifelong ['laɪflɒŋ] **ADJ** de toute une vie; **a l. friend** un ami de toujours; **it's been my l. ambition to meet her** toute ma vie, j'ai espéré la rencontrer

►► ***lifelong learning*** éducation *f* permanente

lifer ['laɪfə(r)] **N** *Fam* condamné(e) *m,f* à perpète

lifesaver ['laɪfˌseɪvə(r)] **N 1** *(lifeguard)* maître *m* nageur **2** *Fam Fig* **thank you, you're a l.!** merci, tu m'as sauvé la vie!; **that money was a l.** cet argent m'a sauvé la vie; **that cup of tea was a l.!** cette tasse de thé m'a redonné vie!

life-saving **ADJ l. apparatus** appareils *mpl ou* engins *mpl* de sauvetage; **l. vaccine** vaccin *m* qui sauve la vie

life-size, life-sized **ADJ** grandeur nature *(inv)*

lifestyle ['laɪfstaɪl] **N** style *m ou* mode *m* de vie

►► *Mktg* ***lifestyle analysis*** analyse *f* du style de vie; *Mktg* ***lifestyle data*** données *fpl* de style de vie; *Mktg* ***lifestyle group*** sociostyle *m*

life-support **ADJ**

►► *Med* ***life-support machine*** respirateur *m* artificiel; **he's on a l. machine** il est sous assistance respiratoire; **to turn off sb's l. machine** arrêter le respirateur de qn; ***life-support system*** *Med* respirateur *m* artificiel; *Aviat & Astron* équipement *m* de vie; **he's on a l. system** il est sous assistance respiratoire; **to turn off sb's l. system** arrêter le respirateur de qn

life-threatening **ADJ** *(illness)* qui peut être mortel; **it's not l.** ce n'est pas mortel

lifetime ['laɪftaɪm] **N** *(of person)* vie *f*; *(of lamp, machine) & Fin (of option)* durée *f*, vie *f*; *Nucl (of atom, isotope)* durée *f* de vie, longévité *f*; *St Exch (of an option)* durée *f* de vie; **in** *or* **during one's l.** de son vivant; **such a bill is unlikely within the l. of this parliament** un tel projet de loi est peu probable tant que ce parlement est en place; **a l. of happiness** toute une vie de bonheur; **it's the chance** *or* **opportunity of a l.** cette chance n'arrive qu'une fois dans la vie; **the holiday of a l.** des vacances sensationnelles; **a l. supply** une réserve pour la vie; **he's bought enough envelopes to last him a l.** il a acheté suffisamment d'enveloppes pour tenir jusqu'à la fin de ses jours

LIFFE [laɪf, 'lɪfɪ] **N** *Fin (abbr* **London International Financial Futures Exchange***)* = marché à terme britannique d'instruments financiers, MATIF *m*

LIFO ['laɪfəʊ] **N** *Com & Fin (abbr* **last in, first out***)* DEPS *m*

lift [lɪft] **VT 1** *(object)* soulever, lever; *(one's head, eyes, arm)* lever; **she lifted the washing basket off** *or* **from the table** elle a soulevé le panier à linge de la table; **I lifted the books out of the crate** j'ai sorti les livres de la caisse; **she lifted her eyes from her magazine** elle leva les yeux de sa revue; **she lifted the suitcase down from the top of the wardrobe** elle a descendu la valise de dessus l'armoire; **to l. weights** *(as exercise)* faire des haltères; **I feel as if a burden has been lifted from my shoulders** j'ai l'impression qu'on m'a enlevé un poids des épaules; **the forward lifted the ball over the goalkeeper** l'avant a lobé le gardien de but

2 *Formal (voice)* élever

3 *(spirits, heart)* remonter; **his music never fails to l. my spirits** sa musique me remonte toujours le moral

4 *(end* ► *blockade, embargo etc)* lever; *(*► *control, restriction)* supprimer

5 *Fam (steal)* piquer, faucher; *(plagiarize)* plagier[❑], piquer; **he had his wallet lifted** il s'est fait piquer son portefeuille; **to l. a passage from an author/a book** piquer un passage chez un auteur/dans un livre

6 *Br Fam (arrest)* agrafer, alpaguer; **he got lifted for stealing cars** il s'est fait agrafer *ou* alpaguer pour vol de voitures

7 *(bulbs, potatoes, turnips)* arracher

8 *Am (debt)* rembourser

9 *(face)* **she's had her face lifted** elle s'est fait faire un lifting

VI 1 *(rise)* se lever, se soulever; **our spirits lifted at the news** la nouvelle nous a remonté le moral **2** *(fog, mist)* se lever, se dissiper; *(cloud)* se dissiper; **his bad mood didn't l. all day** sa mauvaise humeur ne s'est pas dissipée de la journée

N 1 *(act of lifting)* **to give sth a l.** soulever qch

2 *(in morale, energy)* **to give sb a l.** remonter le moral à qn; **glucose tablets are good if you need a quick l.** les comprimés de glucose sont bons si vous avez besoin d'un coup de fouet

3 *Br (elevator)* ascenseur *m*; **goods l.** monte-charge *m inv*

4 *Br (car ride)* **to give sb a l.** prendre *ou* emmener qn en voiture; **could you give me a l. to the station?** *(it's on your way)* est-ce que tu peux me déposer à la gare?; *(make special trip)* est-ce que tu peux m'emmener à la gare?; **can I give you a l.?** est-ce que je peux vous conduire *ou* déposer quelque part?; **we've been waiting over two hours for a l.** cela fait deux heures que nous attendons que quelqu'un veuille bien nous prendre

5 *(extent of rise* ► *of crane etc)* hauteur *f* de levage; *(*► *of pump)* hauteur *f* d'élévation; *Tech (*► *of valve, cam)* levée *f*; *(*► *of millrace)* (hauteur *f* de) chute *f*; *(between bearings)* différence *f* de niveau

6 *(raising power* ► *of balloon, gas)* force *f* ascensionnelle; *Aviat* portance *f*, poussée *f* (aérodynamique), sustentation *f*

7 *(in shoe)* talonnette *f*

►► *Br* ***lift attendant*** liftier(ère) *m,f*; *Br* ***lift engineer*** ascensoriste *mf*; *Br* ***lift operator*** liftier(ère) *m,f*; *Br* ***lift shaft*** cage *f* d'ascenseur

►**lift off** **VT SEP** *(hat, lid)* enlever, ôter

VI *(plane, rocket)* décoller

►**lift out** **VT SEP** *(from box etc)* sortir (**from** de); *Mil (troops)* évacuer (par avion *ou* hélicoptère)

►**lift up** **VT SEP 1** *(object)* soulever, lever; *(part of body)* lever; **to l. sb up** *(who has fallen)* aider qn à se relever; **l. me up so I can see the parade** soulève-moi pour que je puisse voir le défilé; **she lifted up the mat and found a key** elle souleva le paillasson et trouva une clé; **to l. up one's head** lever la tête **2** *Formal (voice, heart)* élever; **the choir lifted up their voices in song** le chœur s'est mis à chanter; **l. up your hearts in prayer** élevez vos âmes *ou* cœurs dans la prière

liftboy ['lɪftbɔɪ] **N** *Br* liftier *m*

liftgate ['lɪftgeɪt] **N** *Am Aut* hayon *m*

lifting ['lɪftɪŋ] **N 1** *(of weight)* levage *m* **2** *(of blockade, embargo etc)* levée *f*; *(of control, restriction)* suppression *f* **3** *(of bulbs, potatoes, turnips)* arrachage *m*, récolte *f*

►► ***lifting gear*** appareil *m* de levage; ***lifting jack*** cric *m* (de levage)

lift-off **N** décollage *m*; **we have l.!** lancement réussi!

ligament ['lɪgəmənt] **N** *Anat* ligament *m*; **to tear a l.** se déchirer un ligament

ligature ['lɪgətjə(r)] **N 1** *Med* ligature *f* **2** *Typ* ligature *f* **3** *Mus* liaison *f*

VT 1 *Med (vein)* ligaturer, barrer **2** *Typ (two vowels)* ligaturer; **o e ligatured** e dans l'o

LIGHT [laɪt]

N
- lumière **1, 2**
- lueur **3**
- phare **4, 10**
- fenêtre **8**
- lampe **2**
- feu **4, 5, 7**
- jour **6, 8**
- solution **9**

ADJ
- clair **1, 2**
- léger **4–6**
- atone **3**

ADV
- léger

VT
- éclairer **1**
- allumer **2**

VI
- s'allumer **1**
- s'enflammer **1**

(pt & pp **lit** [lɪt] *or* **lighted***)*

N 1 *(luminosity, brightness)* lumière *f*; **there's not enough l. to read by** il n'y a pas assez de lumière pour lire; **it looks brown in this l.** on dirait que c'est marron avec cette lumière; **by the l. of our flashlamps** à la lumière de nos lampes de poche; **by the l. of the moon** au clair *ou* à la clarté de la lune; **the l. was beginning to fail** le jour commençait à baisser; **she took the picture against the l.** elle a pris la photo à contre-jour; *Literary* **at first l.** au point *ou* au lever du jour; **you're (standing) in my l.** tu me fais de l'ombre; **in the cold l. of the morning** dans la lueur pâle du matin; *Fig* **to bring sth to l.** révéler qch; **to be brought** *or* **to come to l.** être découvert *ou* révélé; **the trial will throw** *or* **cast l. on their real motives** le procès permettra d'en savoir plus sur *ou* de percer à jour leurs véritables mobiles; **can you throw any l. on this problem?** peux-tu apporter tes lumières sur ce problème?, peux-tu éclaircir cette question?; **at last we can see (some** *or* **the) l. at the end of the tunnel** enfin on voit le bout du tunnel; **to see the l.** *(understand)* comprendre; *(be converted)* trouver le chemin de la vérité; **to see the l. of day** voir le jour

2 *(light source)* lumière *f*; *(lamp)* lampe *f*; **the lights of the city** les lumières de la ville; **a l. went on in the window** une lumière s'est allumée à la fenêtre; **turn the l. on/off** allume/éteins (la lumière); **during the storm the lights went out** il y a eu une panne d'électricité *ou* de lumière pendant l'orage; **to go out like a l.** *(fall asleep)* s'endormir tout de suite; *(faint)* tomber dans les pommes; *Fam Hum* **the lights are on but there's nobody home** c'est pas une lumière

3 *Fig (in someone's eyes)* lueur *f*

4 *Aut (gen)* feu *m*; *(headlamp)* phare *m*; **dip your lights** roulez en code

5 *(traffic light)* feu *m* (rouge); **turn left at the lights** tournez à gauche au feu rouge; **she jumped the lights** elle a brûlé le feu rouge; **the lights were (on) amber** le feu était à l'orange

6 *(aspect, viewpoint)* jour *m*; **I see the problem in a different l.** je vois le problème sous un autre jour; **in a good/bad/new l.** sous un jour favorable/défavorable/nouveau; *Literary* **to act according to one's lights** agir selon ses principes

7 *(flame)* feu *m*; **could you give me a l.?** pouvez-vous me donner du feu?; **have you got a l.?** vous avez du feu?; **to set l. to sth** mettre le feu à qch

8 *(window)* fenêtre *f*; *(small round)* lucarne *f*; *(of mullioned window)* jour *m*; *(of greenhouse)* carreau *m*

9 *(in crossword)* solution *f*

10 *(lighthouse)* phare *m*

ADJ 1 *(bright, well-lit)* clair; **a large, l. room** une grande pièce claire; **it isn't l. enough to read** il n'y a pas assez de lumière pour lire; **it's getting l. already** il commence déjà à faire jour; **it stays l. until 10** il fait jour jusqu'à 10 heures du soir

2 *(pale)* clair; **she has l. hair** elle a des cheveux clairs; **l. yellow/brown** jaune/marron clair *(inv)*

3 *Ling (in phonetics)* atone

4 *(in weight)* léger; **as l. as a feather** léger comme une plume; **l. clothes** vêtements *mpl* légers; **to be l. on one's feet** être leste; **l. touch** *(of painter, author, film director)* finesse *f*

5 *(comedy, music etc)* léger, facile; **l. conversation** conversation *f* peu sérieuse, propos *mpl* anodins

6 *(not intense, strong etc)* léger; **there was a l. tap at the door** on frappa tout doucement à la porte; **the traffic was l.** la circulation était fluide; **I had a l. lunch** j'ai mangé légèrement à midi, j'ai déjeuné léger; **a l. rain was falling** il tombait une pluie fine; **take some l. reading** prends quelque chose de facile à lire; **I'm a l. sleeper** j'ai le sommeil léger; **a l. wine** un vin léger; **he can only do l. work** il ne peut faire que des travaux peu fatigants; **to make l. of sth** prendre qch à la légère

ADV to travel l. voyager léger

VT 1 *(illuminate)* éclairer; **the room was lit by a single bare bulb** la pièce n'était éclairée que par une ampoule nue; **I'll l. the way for you** je vais t'éclairer le chemin

2 *(lamp, candle, cigarette)* allumer; *(match)* craquer; **to l. a fire** allumer un feu, faire du feu

VI *(lamp)* s'allumer; *(match)* s'enflammer; *(fire, coal)* prendre

• **lights** **NPL** *(lungs)* mou *m*

• **in (the) light of** **PREP** **in (the) l. of these new facts** à la lumière de ces faits nouveaux

►► ***light aircraft*** avion *m* de tourisme; *Br* ***light ale*** = bière brune légère; *Mil* ***light artillery*** artillerie *f* légère *ou* de petit calibre; ***light beam*** faisceau *m* lumineux; ***light box*** table *f* lumineuse; ***light breeze*** *(gen)* petite brise *f*, brise *f* légère; *(on Beaufort scale)* légère brise *f*; ***light bulb*** ampoule *f* (électrique); *Am* ***light cream*** crème *f* liquide; *TV* ***light cue*** signal *m* lumineux; ***light entertainment*** variétés *fpl*; ***light fitting*** applique *f* (électrique); ***light flare*** fusée *f* éclairante; ***light industry*** industrie *f* légère; ***light infantry*** infanterie *f* légère; ***light meter*** posemètre *m*; ***light opera*** opéra *m* comique, opérette *f*; *Comput* ***light pen*** crayon *m* optique; ***light pollution*** excès *m* de lumière artificielle; ***light ray*** rayon *m* lumineux; ***light show*** spectacle *m* de lumière; **a laser l. show** un spectacle laser; ***light switch*** interrupteur *m*; ***light table*** table *f* lumineuse; *Mktg* ***light user*** faible utilisateur(trice) *m,f*; ***light vehicle*** véhicule *m* léger; ***light wave*** onde *f* lumineuse; ***light weapons*** armes *fpl* légères

▸ **light into** VT INSEP *Fam* **to l. into sb** *(attack)* rentrer dans le lard à qn

▸ **light on** VT INSEP tomber (par hasard) sur, trouver par hasard

▸ **light out** VI *Am Fam* se tirer; **they lit out for Mexico** ils se sont tirés au Mexique

▸ **light up** VT SEP éclairer; **the house was all lit up** la maison était tout *ou* toute éclairée; **joy lit up her face** son visage rayonnait de bonheur

VI **1** *(lamp)* s'allumer; **the whole sky lit up** le ciel entier s'illumina **2** *(face, eyes)* s'éclairer, s'illuminer **3** *Fam (light cigarette)* allumer une cigarette▫

light-coloured, *Am* **light-colored** ADJ clair, de couleur claire

light-emitting diode [-ɪ'mɪtɪŋ-] N diode *f* électroluminescente

lighten ['laɪtən] VT **1** *(make brighter)* éclairer, illuminer; **a single candle lightened the darkness** seule une bougie trouait l'obscurité **2** *(make paler)* éclaircir; **l. the blue with a little white** éclaircissez le bleu avec un peu de blanc; **to have one's hair lightened** se faire éclaircir les cheveux **3** *(make less heavy)* alléger; **having an assistant will l. my workload** avec un assistant ma charge de travail sera moins lourde

VI **1** *(become light)* s'éclairer, s'éclaircir; **the sky has lightened a little** le ciel s'est légèrement éclairci; **her mood lightened** sa mauvaise humeur se dissipa **2** *(load, burden)* s'alléger; **my heart lightened** j'ai été soulagé

▸ **lighten up** VI *Fam* se remettre▫; **oh come on, l. up!** allez, remets-toi *ou* ne fais pas cette tête!

lighter ['laɪtə(r)] N **1** *(for cigarettes)* briquet *m*; *(in car)* allume-cigare *m*; *(for gas)* allume-gaz *m inv* **2** *Naut* allège *f*, chaland *m*, gabare *f*

COMP *(flint, fluid, fuel)* à briquet

lighterage ['laɪtərɪdʒ] N *Naut (unloading)* déchargement *m* par allèges *ou* par gabares, gabarage *m*; *(fee)* droits *mpl ou* frais *mpl* d'allège *ou* de gabarage

lighter-than-air N appareil *m* plus léger que l'air

ADJ *(aircraft)* plus léger que l'air

lightface ['laɪtfeɪs] *Typ* N (caractère *m*) maigre *m*

ADJ maigre

light-fingered ADJ chapardeur

light-footed [-'fʊtɪd] ADJ au pied léger, à la démarche légère

light-headed ADJ *(dizzy)* étourdi; *(tipsy)* ivre, enivré; **to feel l.** avoir des vertiges *ou* la tête qui tourne; **the wine had made me l.** le vin m'était monté à la tête; **the realization that she had won made her feel quite l.** elle était tout excitée de réaliser qu'elle avait gagné

light-hearted [-'hɑːtɪd] ADJ *(person, atmosphere)* enjoué, gai; *(poem, irony)* léger; **a l. remark** une remarque bon enfant; **this programme takes a l. look at politics** cette émission pose un regard amusé sur la politique

lighthouse ['laɪthaʊs, *pl* -haʊzɪz] N phare *m*

▸▸ ***lighthouse keeper*** gardien *m* de phare

lighting ['laɪtɪŋ] N **1** *(gen)* éclairage *m*; **artificial/neon l.** éclairage *m* artificiel/au néon **2** *(UNCOUNT) Theat & Cin* éclairages *mpl*

▸▸ *Theat & Cin* ***lighting cameraman*** directeur *m* de la photographie, chef opérateur *m* cadreur; ***lighting crew*** équipe *f* des éclairagistes; ***lighting effects*** effets *mpl* d'éclairage *ou* de lumière; ***lighting engineer*** éclairagiste *mf*; ***lighting technician*** éclairagiste *mf*

lightly ['laɪtlɪ] ADV **1** *(not heavily)* légèrement; **l. dressed** légèrement vêtu; **it was raining l.** il tombait une pluie fine; **she stepped l. onto the dance floor** elle entra sur la piste de danse d'un pas léger; **l. fry the onions** faites légèrement dorer les oignons; **to sleep l.** *(generally)* avoir le sommeil léger; *(on one occasion)* dormir d'un sommeil léger **2** *(casually)* légèrement, à la légère; **to take sth l.** prendre qch à la légère; **"I'm getting married tomorrow," he said l.** "je me marie demain", annonça-t-il d'un air détaché; **this is not a decision that we took l.** ce n'est pas une décision que nous avons prise à la légère **3** *(idiom)* **to get off l.** s'en tirer à bon compte

lightness ['laɪtnɪs] N **1** *(brightness, light)* clarté *f* **2** *(of object, tone, step)* légèreté *f*; **l. of heart** gaieté *f* de cœur; **l. of touch** *(of pianist, tennis player)* légèreté *f*; *(of artist)* légèreté *f* de pinceau; *(of writer)* légèreté *f* de style

lightning ['laɪtnɪŋ] N *(UNCOUNT)* éclairs *mpl*, foudre *f*; **l. frightens me** les éclairs me font peur; **a flash of l.** un éclair; **to be struck by l.** être frappé par la foudre *ou* foudroyé; *Fam* **as quick as l., with l. speed, like greased l.** rapide comme l'éclair▫; *Prov* **l. never strikes twice in the same place** la foudre ne frappe jamais deux fois au même endroit

ADJ *(raid, visit)* éclair *(inv)*

▸▸ ***lightning arrester*** parafoudre *m* (de surtension); *Am* ***lightning bug*** luciole *f*; *Br* ***lightning chess*** échecs *mpl* rapides; ***lightning conductor, lightning rod*** paratonnerre *m*; ***lightning strike*** grève *f* surprise *(inv)*

lightproof ['laɪtpruːf] ADJ opaque

light-sensitive ADJ *Phys* photosensible

lightship ['laɪtʃɪp] N *Naut* bateau-feu *m*, bateau-phare *m*

lights-out N extinction *f* des feux

lightweight ['laɪtweɪt] N **1** *Boxing* poids *m* léger; **the world l. championship** le championnat du monde des poids légers **2** *(insignificant person)* personne *f* sans envergure; **he's a literary l.** c'est un écrivain sans envergure **3** *Br Fam* = personne qui ne tient pas l'alcool

ADJ **1** *(clothes, equipment)* léger **2** *Boxing* léger

light-year N année-lumière *f*; **it seems light-years away** ça paraît si loin

lignite ['lɪgnaɪt] N *Geol* lignite *m*

likable = **likeable**

LIKE[1] [laɪk] VT **1** *(find pleasant)* aimer (bien); **I l. him** je l'aime bien, il me plaît bien; **I l. her, but I don't love her** je l'aime bien, mais je ne suis pas amoureux d'elle; **I don't l. him** je ne l'aime pas beaucoup, il ne me plaît pas; **I l. Elaine better than Simon** j'aime mieux Elaine que Simon; **I l. Sally best** c'est Sally que je préfère; **what do you l. about him?** qu'est-ce qui te plaît chez lui?; **do you l. coffee?** est-ce que tu aimes le café?; **these plants don't l. direct sunlight** ces plantes ne supportent pas l'exposition directe à la lumière du soleil; *Hum* **I l. curry but it doesn't l. me!** j'aime le curry mais ça ne me réussit pas tellement!

2 *(enjoy)* aimer; **he likes school** il aime l'école; **to l. doing** *or* **to do sth** aimer faire qch; **I l. dancing** *or* **to dance** j'aime danser; **I don't l. being shouted at** je n'aime pas qu'on me crie dessus; **he doesn't l. people talking about it** il n'aime pas qu'on en parle; **how would HE l. being kept waiting in the rain?** ça lui plairait, à lui, qu'on le fasse attendre sous la pluie?

3 *(approve of)* aimer; **I l. people to be frank with me** j'aime qu'on soit franc avec moi; **if he doesn't l. it he can go elsewhere** si ça ne lui plaît pas il peut aller ailleurs; **I don't l. you swearing, I don't l. it when you swear** je n'aime pas que tu dises des gros mots; **they're not going to l. it!** ça ne va pas leur plaire!; **whether you l. it or not!** que ça te plaise ou non!; *Ironic* **well, I l. that!** ça, c'est le bouquet!

4 *(want, wish)* aimer, vouloir; **I'd l. some tea** je prendrais bien une tasse de thé; **take any dress you l.** prends la robe que tu veux *ou* qui te plaît; **as much as you l.** tant que vous voudrez; **do what you l.** fais ce que tu veux *ou* ce qui te plaît; **he thinks he can do anything he likes** il se croit tout permis; **she is free to do as she likes** elle est libre d'agir à sa guise *ou* de faire comme il lui plaira; **as you l.** comme vous voudrez; **what I'd l. to know is where he got the money from** ce que je voudrais savoir, c'est où il a obtenu cet argent; **come whenever you l.** venez quand vous voulez; **I didn't l. to say anything, but...** je ne voulais rien dire mais...; **I'd l. nothing better than a hot bath** il n'y a rien qui me ferait autant plaisir qu'un bon bain chaud; **I'd l. your opinion on this wine** j'aimerais savoir ce que tu penses de ce vin; **I would** *or* **I'd l. to go out tonight** j'aimerais (bien) sortir ce soir

5 *(in polite offers, requests)* **would you l. to go out tonight?** ça te dirait de *ou* tu as envie de sortir ce soir?; **would you l. tea or coffee?** voulez-vous du thé ou du café?; **would you l. to leave a message?** voulez-vous laisser un message?; **would you l. me to do it for you?** veux-tu que je le fasse à ta place?; **I'd l. to speak to Mr Smith, please** je voudrais parler à M. Smith, s'il vous plaît; **I'd l. the soup followed by a salad** je prendrai la soupe puis une salade; **I'd l. my steak rare, please** je voudrais mon steak saignant, s'il vous plaît

6 *(asking opinion)* **how do you l. my jacket?** comment trouves-tu ma veste?; **how would you l. a trip to Paris?** ça te dirait d'aller à Paris?

7 *(asking preference)* **how do you l. your coffee, black or white?** vous prenez votre café noir ou avec du lait?

8 *(in generalizations)* **I l. to be in bed by 10 p.m.** j'aime être couché pour 10 heures; **one doesn't l. to interrupt** c'est toujours délicat d'interrompre quelqu'un

• **likes** NPL *(preferences)* goûts *mpl*; **try to discover their likes and dislikes** essayez de découvrir ce qu'ils aiment et ce qu'ils n'aiment pas

• **if you like** ADV **1** *(expressing willingness)* si tu veux; **I can do it, if you l.** je peux le faire, si tu veux; **I'll get lunch, shall I? – if you l.** je vais chercher de quoi manger, d'accord? – si tu veux

2 *(as it were)* si tu veux; **it was a surprise, a shock, if you l.** ça m'a surpris, choqué si tu veux

• **like it or not** ADV **l. it or not, we're heading for a confrontation** qu'on le veuille ou non, nous ne pouvons éviter une confrontation

LIKE[2] [laɪk] PREP **1** *(similar to)* comme; **to be l. sb/sth** être semblable à qn/à qch, ressembler à qn/à qch; **their house is a bit l. ours** leur maison est un peu comme la nôtre; **there's no place l. home** rien ne vaut son chez-soi; **we're l. sisters** nous sommes comme des sœurs; **she's nothing l. her sister** elle ne ressemble pas du tout à sa sœur; **he was l. a father to me** il a été comme un père pour moi; **he talks l. his father** il parle comme son père; **it's shaped l. an egg** ça a la forme d'un œuf; **it tastes a bit l. celery** ça a un peu le goût de céleri; **do you have any more l. this?** en avez-vous d'autres?; **I want to find one just l. it** je veux trouver le/la même; **there's nothing l. it** il n'y a rien de mieux; **it seemed l. hours** c'était comme si des heures entières s'étaient écoulées; **it looks l. rain** on dirait qu'il va pleuvoir

2 *(asking for opinion or description)* **what's your new boss l.?** comment est ton nouveau patron?; **what's the weather l.?** quel temps fait-il?; **what does it taste l.?** quel goût ça a?; **what was it l.?** c'était comment?

3 *(such as)* comme; **in a family l. ours** dans une famille comme la nôtre; **it makes me angry to hear things l. that** ça me met en colère d'entendre des choses pareilles; **cities l. Toronto and Ottawa** des villes comme Toronto et Ottawa; **I'm useless at things l. sewing** je ne suis bon à rien quand il s'agit de couture et de choses comme ça

4 *(indicating typical behaviour)* **you know what she's l.** vous savez comme elle est; **kids are l. that, what do you expect?** les gosses sont comme ça, qu'est-ce que tu veux!; **it's not l. him to be rude** ça ne lui ressemble pas *ou* ce n'est pas son genre d'être impoli; **it's just l. him not to show up!** c'est bien son style *ou* c'est bien de lui de ne pas venir!; *Fam* **be l. that then!** tant pis pour toi!; *Fam* **don't be l. that, he didn't mean what he said** ne le prends pas mal, ce n'est pas ce qu'il voulait dire▫; **that's just l. a man!** c'est typiquement

masculin!; **l. father l. son** tel père, tel fils
5 *(in the same manner as)* comme; **I think l. you** je pense comme vous; **you're acting l. a fool** tu te comportes comme un imbécile; **to speak French l. a native** parler français comme un natif; **we, l. everyone else, were forced to queue all night** nous avons dû faire la queue toute la nuit, comme tout le monde; **do it l. this/that** voici/voilà comment il faut faire; **l. so** comme ça; **sorry to interrupt you l. this** désolé de t'interrompre comme ça; **don't talk to me l. that!** ne me parle pas sur ce ton!
6 *(in approximations)* **it cost something l. £200** ça a coûté dans les 200 livres; **we don't have anything l. as many people as we need** on est loin d'avoir tout le monde qu'il nous faut; **it was more l. midnight when we got home** il était plus près de minuit quand nous sommes arrivés à la maison; **that's more l. it!** voilà qui est mieux!; **she is nothing l. as intelligent as you** elle est loin d'être aussi intelligente que vous; *Fam* **he ran l. anything** *or* **l. hell** *or* **l. blazes** il a couru comme un dératé *ou* comme s'il avait le feu aux fesses
ADJ we were treated in l. manner on nous a traités de la même façon; **they are of l. temperament** ils ont le même tempérament; *Math* **l. terms/quantities** termes *mpl*/quantités *fpl* semblables
CONJ *Fam* **1** *(as)* comme[□]; **l. I was saying** comme je disais; **they don't make them l. they used to!** ils/elles ne sont plus ce qu'ils/elles étaient!; **it was just l. in the films** c'était exactement comme au cinéma; **tell it l. it is** dis les choses comme elles sont
2 *(as if)* comme si[□]; **he acted l. he was in charge** il se comportait comme si c'était lui le chef; **she felt l. she wanted to cry** elle avait l'impression qu'elle allait pleurer; **he looked l. he'd seen a ghost** on aurait dit qu'il avait vu un fantôme
ADV *Fam (in conversation, reported speech)* **I was hungry, l., so I went into this café** j'avais faim, tu vois, alors je suis entré dans un café; **there were l. three thousand people there** il devait y avoir environ trois mille personnes[□]; **he just came up behind me, l.** il s'est approché de moi par derrière[□]; **I was l. "no way"** alors je lui ai fait "pas question"
N he and his l. lui et ses semblables; **l. attracts l.** qui se ressemble s'assemble; **you can only compare l. with l.** on ne peut comparer que ce qui est comparable; **to give** *or* **to return l. for l.** rendre la pareille; **she goes in for shiatzu, yoga and the l.** elle fait du shiatsu, du yoga et d'autres choses comme ça; **I've never seen the l. of it!** je n'ai jamais rien vu de pareil!; **he was a president the l.** *or* **likes of which we will probably never see again** c'était un président comme on n'en verra probablement plus jamais
• **likes NPL the likes of us/them/***etc* les gens comme nous/eux/*etc*; **it's not for the likes of us** ça n'est pas pour les gens comme nous
• **like enough, like as not ADV** *Br Fam* probablement[□]; **he's still at the office, l. enough** il y a des chances qu'il soit encore au bureau; **l. enough, she hasn't even read it yet** elle ne l'a probablement même pas encore lu

likeable ['laɪkəbəl] **ADJ** sympathique, agréable; **he's a l. person** c'est un type sympathique

likeableness ['laɪkəbəlnɪs] **N** caractère *m* sympathique *ou* agréable

likelihood ['laɪklɪhʊd] **N** probabilité *f*; **there's not much l. of us moving** il est peu probable que nous déménagions; **there is little l. of us still being here** *or* **that we'll still be here in August** il y a peu de chances (pour) que nous soyons encore là en août; **there is every l. of an agreement** tout porte à croire qu'un accord sera conclu
• **in all likelihood ADV** vraisemblablement, selon toute vraisemblance

likely ['laɪklɪ] *(compar* **likelier**, *superl* **likeliest) ADJ 1** *(probable)* vraisemblable, probable; **it's not a very l. scenario** ce scénario n'est pas très vraisemblable; **the pub is a l. place to find him** le pub est probablement l'endroit où le trouver; *Fam Ironic* **that's a l. story!** la belle histoire!, en voilà une bonne!; **it's more than l.** c'est plus que probable; **it's not very l.** c'est peu probable; **it's not** *or* **hardly l. to happen** il est peu probable *ou* il y a peu de chances que cela se produise; **it's l. to rain** il y a des chances pour qu'il pleuve; **she is quite l. to do it** il y a des chances qu'elle le fasse; **books l. to interest young people** ouvrages susceptibles d'intéresser les jeunes; **this plan is most l. to succeed** ce projet a beaucoup de chances de réussir; **are the neighbours l. to object?** y a-t-il des chances que les voisins s'y opposent?; **rain is l. in the east** il risque de pleuvoir dans l'Est
2 *(promising)* prometteur; **we found a l.** *or* **l.-looking spot for a picnic** on a trouvé un endroit qui a l'air idéal pour pique-niquer
ADV probablement, sans doute; **they'll very l.** *or* **most l. forget** ils vont très probablement oublier; **as l. as not she's already home** elle est sûrement déjà rentrée; *Fam* **would you do it again? – not l.!** tu recommencerais? – ça risque pas *ou* y a pas de risque!

like-minded ADJ du même avis; *(having same tastes)* qui ont les mêmes goûts

liken ['laɪkən] **VT** comparer; **his style has been likened to that of Peter Wolfe** on a comparé son style à celui de Peter Wolfe

likeness ['laɪknɪs] **N 1** *(resemblance)* ressemblance *f*; **a family l.** un air de famille; **she bears a strong l. to her mother** elle ressemble beaucoup à sa mère; **God created man in his own l.** Dieu a créé l'homme à son image **2** *(portrait)* portrait *m*; **to paint sb's l.** faire le portrait de qn; **it's a very good l. of him** c'est tout à fait lui; **it isn't a very good l. of him** ça ne lui ressemble pas beaucoup

likewise ['laɪkwaɪz] **ADV 1** *(similarly)* de même; **l. in Israel, talks are in progress** en Israël aussi, des pourparlers ont été entamés; **he worked hard and expected his daughters to do l.** il travaillait beaucoup et attendait de ses filles qu'elles fassent de même; **and I suggest you do l.** et je suggère que tu en fasses autant; **pleased to meet you – l.** ravi de vous rencontrer – moi de même
2 *(by the same token)* de même, de plus, en outre

liking ['laɪkɪŋ] **N 1** *(affection)* sympathie *f*, affection *f*; **I have a great l. for Alan** j'ai beaucoup de sympathie pour Alan; **to take a l. to sb** se prendre d'amitié pour qn; **I took an instant l. to Rome** j'ai tout de suite aimé Rome **2** *(taste)* goût *m*, penchant *m*; **to have a l. for sth** avoir du goût pour qch, aimer qch; **she has a l. for expensive jewellery** elle a un faible pour les bijoux de prix; **the decor is not really to my l.** le décor n'est pas tout à fait à mon goût; **is everything to your l.?** est-ce que tout est à votre convenance?; **it's too small for my l.** c'est trop petit à mon goût

lilac ['laɪlək] **N** *(colour, flower)* lilas *m*
ADJ *(colour)* lilas *(inv)*

Lilliputian [ˌlɪlɪ'pjuːʃən] **N** lilliputien(enne) *m,f*
ADJ lilliputien

Lilo® ['laɪləʊ] *(pl* **Lilos) N** *Br* matelas *m* pneumatique

lilt [lɪlt] **N 1** *(in voice)* modulation *f*; **her voice has a l. to it** sa voix a des inflexions mélodieuses; **to speak with a Welsh l.** parler avec des intonations galloises
2 *(in music)* rythme *m*, cadence *f*
3 *(in movement)* balancement *m* harmonieux
4 *Scot (tune)* chant *m*, air *m*

lilting ['lɪltɪŋ] **ADJ 1** *(voice, accent)* mélodieux **2** *(music, tune)* chantant, mélodieux **3** *(movement)* souple, harmonieux

lily ['lɪlɪ] *(pl* **lilies) N** *Bot* lis *m*, lys *m*; **l. of the valley** muguet *m*
▸▸ ***lily pad*** feuille *f* de nénuphar

lily-livered [-'lɪvəd] **ADJ** froussard

lily-white ADJ d'une blancheur de lis, d'un blanc immaculé; *Fam (character)* blanc (blanche) comme neige

lima bean ['laɪmə-] **N** haricot *m* de Lima *ou* du Cap, pois *m* de sept ans

limb [lɪm] **N 1** *(of body)* membre *m*; *Hum* **let's rest our weary limbs!** si on soufflait un peu!; **I'll tear him l. from l.!** je le taillerai en pièces! **2** *(of tree)* (grosse) branche *f*; *Fam* **to be out on a l.** *(be alone)* être en plan[□]; *(be in dangerous position)* être dans une situation délicate[□]; *Fam* **his refusal to compromise left him out on a l.** son refus d'accepter un compromis l'a mis dans une situation délicate; *Fam* **to go out on a l.** prendre des risques[□] **3** *Astron, Bot & Math* limbe *m*

-limbed [lɪmd] **SUFF to be long-l.** avoir les membres longs, être élancé; **to be loose-l.** être délié *ou* souple

limber ['lɪmbə(r)] **N** *Mil (of gun carriage)* avant-train *m*
ADJ souple, agile
VT *Mil* **to l. a gun** attacher une pièce de canon à l'avant-train
▸ **limber up VT SEP** *(muscles)* se chauffer
VI s'échauffer, faire des assouplissements; **do some limbering-up exercises first** commence par des exercices d'assouplissement; *Fig* **they're limbering up for a fight with the unions** ils se préparent à une bataille *ou* ils fourbissent leurs armes en vue d'une bataille avec les syndicats

limbless ['lɪmlɪs] **ADJ** *(person)* = à qui il manque un ou plusieurs membres; *(with no arms or legs)* sans membres; **l. ex-servicemen** grands mutilés *mpl* de guerre

limbo ['lɪmbəʊ] *(pl sense* **3 limbos) N 1** *(UNCOUNT) Rel* limbes *mpl* **2** *(dance)* limbo *m* **3** *Fig* **to be in (a state of) l.** être dans l'incertitude; **they kept us in l. for weeks** ils nous ont laissés dans l'incertitude pendant des semaines
▸▸ ***limbo dancer*** danseur(euse) *m,f* de limbo

lime [laɪm] **N 1** *(substance)* chaux *f*; **caustic/slaked l.** chaux *f* vive/éteinte; **burnt l.** chaux *f* vive
2 *(fruit)* citron *m* vert, lime *f*; **lager and l.** bière blonde au sirop de citron vert
3 *(citrus tree)* limettier *m*
4 *(linden)* tilleul *m*
5 *(for catching birds)* glu *f*
VT 1 *Agr (soil)* chauler **2** *(with birdlime* ▸ **branch, bird)** engluer
▸▸ ***lime cordial*** sirop *m* de citron vert; ***lime green*** vert *m* jaune *(inv)*; ***lime juice*** jus *m* de citron vert; ***lime kiln*** four *m* à chaux; ***lime pit*** *(quarry)* fosse *f* à chaux; *(in tanning)* pelain *m*; ***lime tree*** tilleul *m*; ***lime twig*** gluau *m*

limeade [laɪ'meɪd] **N** boisson *f* au citron vert

limelight ['laɪmlaɪt] **N in the l.** sous les feux de la rampe, très en vue; **she doesn't like the l.** elle n'aime pas sentir les projecteurs braqués sur elle; **an actor who's never out of the l.** un acteur très en vue; **to seek the l.** rechercher la vedette; **to steal the l.** voler la vedette

limerick ['lɪmərɪk] **N** limerick *m (poème absurde ou indécent en cinq vers, dont les rimes doivent suivre un ordre précis)*

limestone ['laɪmstəʊn] *Geol* **N** calcaire *m*, roche *f* calcaire
COMP *(cave, rock formation)* calcaire; *(quarry)* de calcaire
▸▸ ***limestone landscape*** relief *m* calcaire; ***limestone pavement*** lapiaz *m*

limey ['laɪmɪ] *Am Fam Pej* **N 1** *(English person)* Angliche *mf* **2** *(English sailor)* matelot *m* anglais[□]
ADJ angliche

limit ['lɪmɪt] **N 1** *(boundary, greatest extent, maximum)* limite *f*; **I know my limits** je connais mes limites, je sais ce dont je suis capable; **his arrogance knows no limits** son arrogance ne connaît pas de limites; **there is no l. to his powers** ses pouvoirs sont illimités; **our resources are stretched to the l.** nous sommes au bout de nos ressources; **there's a l. to my patience** ma patience a des limites; **within limits** dans une certaine mesure; **within the limits of the present regulations** dans le cadre délimité par le présent règlement; **I'd like to help but there are limits** je veux bien aider mais il y a des limites; **off limits** interdit d'accès; **the bar's off limits to servicemen** le bar est interdit aux militaires; **that's the (absolute) l.!** c'est le comble!; **she really is the l.!** elle dépasse vraiment les bornes!; **what is the l. on this road?** *(speed)* quelle est la limitation *ou* *Can* limite de vitesse sur cette route?; **to fix a l.** *(in insurance)* fixer les pleins **2** *(restriction)* limitation *f*; **the l. on Japanese imports** la limitation des importations japonaises; **to put** *or* **to set a l. on sth** limiter qch; **weight l.** limitation *f* de poids; *Br* **to be over the l.** *(driver)* dépasser le taux d'alcoolémie autorisé
VT limiter; **they are limiting their research to one**

kind of virus ils limitent leurs recherches à un seul type de virus; **to l. oneself to two whiskies** se limiter à deux whiskies; **she limits herself to one visit a week** elle se contente d'une visite par semaine; **I will l. myself to observing that...** je me bornerai à observer que...

limitation [,lɪmɪ'teɪʃən] **N 1** *(restriction, control)* limitation *f*, restriction *f*; **we will accept no l. on our freedom** nous n'accepterons aucune entrave à notre liberté; **arms l. talks** négociations *fpl* sur la limitation des armements **2** *(shortcoming)* limite *f*; **we all have our limitations** nous avons tous nos limites; **to know one's limitations** connaître ses limites **3** *Law* prescription *f*

limited ['lɪmɪtɪd] **ADJ 1** *(restricted)* limité, restreint; **the choice was rather l.** le choix était plutôt limité; **only a l. number of players will be successful** seul un nombre limité *ou* un petit nombre de participants gagneront; **the play met with only l. success** la pièce n'a connu qu'un succès relatif; **to a l. extent** jusqu'à un certain point; **they are of l. intelligence** ils ont une intelligence limitée **2** *Am (train, bus)* semi-direct

▸▸ ***limited circulation*** circulation *f* restreinte; ***limited company*** société *f* à responsabilité limitée, SARL *f*; ***limited edition*** édition *f* à tirage limité; ***limited liability*** responsabilité *f* limitée; ***limited liability company*** société *f* à responsabilité limitée, SARL *f*; *Fin* ***limited partner*** commanditaire *m*; *Fin* ***limited partnership*** société *f* en commandite (simple); ***limited stop bus*** bus *m* à nombre d'arrêts limité; ***limited stop train*** train *m* à nombre d'arrêts limité

limiter ['lɪmɪtə(r)] **N** *Electron* limiteur *m*

limitless ['lɪmɪtlɪs] **ADJ** illimité

limousine ['lɪməzi:n] **N** limousine *f*

limp [lɪmp] **N to walk with a l., to have a l.** boiter; **a man with a l.** un boiteux

ADJ 1 *(cloth, lettuce, handshake)* mou (molle); *(skin)* flasque; **the plants had gone l. through lack of water** les plantes s'étaient étiolées faute d'être arrosées; **his body went completely l.** il s'affaissa; **to feel l.** *(person)* se sentir mou *ou* sans énergie **2** *(book ▸ cover, binding)* souple

VI boiter; *(slightly)* clopiner; **he limped into the room** il entra dans la pièce en boitant; **she was limping badly** elle boitait beaucoup; *Fig* **the ship limped into harbour** le navire gagna le port tant bien que mal

limpet ['lɪmpɪt] **N** *Zool* patelle *f*, bernique *f*, chapeau *m* chinois; *Fig (person)* sangsue *f*; **to cling to sth like a l.** se cramponner à qch de toutes ses forces

▸▸ ***limpet mine*** mine-ventouse *f*

limpid ['lɪmpɪd] **ADJ** limpide, clair

limply ['lɪmplɪ] **ADV** mollement, flasquement; *(without energy)* mollement, sans énergie

limpness ['lɪmpnɪs] **N** *(of handshake, bearing)* mollesse *f*; *(of temperament)* manque *m* de vigueur; *(of attitude)* manque *m* de fermeté

limp-wristed [-'rɪstɪd] **ADJ** *Fam Pej* efféminé

linage = **lineage**[2]

linchpin ['lɪntʃpɪn] **N 1** *Tech* esse *f* (d'essieu), cheville *f* d'essieu **2** *Fig (person)* pivot *m*, cheville *f* ouvrière; **it's the l. of government policy** c'est l'axe central de la politique du gouvernement

Lincs *(written abbr* **Lincolnshire***)* Lincolnshire *m*

linctus ['lɪŋktəs] **N** sirop *m* (pour la toux)

linden ['lɪndən] **N** *(tree)* tilleul *m*

▸▸ ***linden tree*** tilleul *m*

LINE [laɪn]

N
- ligne **1–3, 5, 7, 10–15, 18, 22**
- trait **1**
- ride **1**
- rang **3**
- queue **3**
- vers **5**
- réplique **5**
- mot **6**
- corde **7**
- tuyau **8**
- voie **9**
- frontière **16**
- branche **17**
- domaine **17**
- chaîne **19**
- lignée **20**

VT
- border **1**
- régler **2**
- doubler **3**
- garnir **3, 4**

N 1 *(mark, stroke)* ligne *f*, trait *m*; *(wrinkle)* ride *f*; *Math, Mus, Sport & TV* ligne *f*; **to draw a l.** tracer *ou* tirer une ligne; *Sport* **to beat sb on the l.** *(at the finishing line)* coiffer qn au poteau; **to score 50 points above/below the l.** *(in bridge)* marquer 50 points d'honneur/de marche; **his face was covered with lines** son visage était plein de rides

2 *(path)* ligne *f*; **light travels in a straight l.** la lumière se propage en ligne droite; **it's on a l. between Houston and Dallas** c'est sur la ligne qui va de Houston à Dallas; **the two grooves must be exactly in l.** les deux rainures doivent être parfaitement alignées; **I don't follow your l. of thinking** je ne suis pas ton raisonnement; **to be in the l. of fire** être dans la ligne de tir; **l. of sight** *or* **of vision** ligne *f* de visée; **let's try a different l. of attack** essayons une approche différente; **it's all in the l. of duty** cela fait partie de mes fonctions; **to be killed in the l. of duty** *(policeman)* mourir dans l'exercice de ses fonctions; *(soldier)* mourir au champ d'honneur; *Br* **to take the l. of least resistance** choisir la solution de facilité; **there's been a terrible mistake somewhere along the l.** il s'est produit une erreur grave quelque part; **I'll support them all along** *or* **right down the l.** je les soutiendrai jusqu'au bout *ou* sur toute la ligne; **the population is split along religious lines** la population est divisée selon des critères religieux; **he reorganized the company along more rational lines** il a réorganisé l'entreprise sur une base plus rationnelle; **we shall take action along the lines suggested** nous agirons dans le sens de ce qui a été proposé; **another idea along the same lines** une autre idée dans le même genre; **we seem to be thinking along the same lines** il semble que nous voyions les choses de la même façon; **to be on the right lines** être sur la bonne voie

3 *(row ▸ side by side)* ligne *f*, rang *m*, rangée *f*; *(▸ one behind another)* rang *m*, file *f*; *Am (queue)* file *f* (d'attente), queue *f*; **a l. of traffic** une colonne de véhicules; **to fall** *or* **get into l., to form a l.** *(people)* se mettre en ligne; *(children)* se mettre en rang; *(soldiers)* former les rangs; **stand in l., children** mettez-vous en rang, les enfants; **to step into l.** se mettre en rang; **a l. of trees** une rangée d'arbres; **we joined the l. at the bus stop** nous avons fait la queue à l'arrêt de bus; **they wanted to be first in l.** ils voulaient être les premiers dans la file d'attente; *Fig* **he's in l. for promotion** il est sur les rangs pour une promotion; **he's first in l. for the throne** c'est l'héritier du trône; **to be on the l.** *(job, reputation)* être en jeu; **to put one's job/reputation on the l.** mettre son travail/sa réputation en jeu; **to lay one's reputation/life on the l. (for sb/sth)** mettre sa réputation/vie en jeu (pour qn/qch)

4 *Fig (conformity)* **it's in/out of l. with company policy** c'est conforme/ce n'est pas conforme à la politique de la société; **it's more or less in l. with what we'd expected** cela correspond plus ou moins à nos prévisions; **to bring wages into l. with inflation** actualiser les salaires en fonction de l'inflation; **the rebels have been brought into l.** les rebelles ont été mis au pas; **to fall into l. with government policy** accepter la politique gouvernementale; **to step out of l.** s'écarter du droit chemin

5 *(of writing, text)* ligne *f*; *(of poem, song)* vers *m*; *(of play)* réplique *f*; **new l.** *(in dictation)* à la ligne; *Comput* **a 20-l. program** un programme de 20 lignes; *Sch* **she gave me 100 lines** elle m'a donné 100 lignes (à faire); **he forgot his lines** il a oublié son texte; **he gave me the usual l. about his wife not understanding him** il m'a fait son numéro habituel comme quoi sa femme ne le comprend pas; *Fam* **to shoot a l.** *(boast)* frimer; *(smooth talk)* baratiner; *Am Fam* **to hand** *or* **give** *or* **pass sb a l.** *(chat up)* draguer qn

6 *Fam (letter)* mot *m*; **to drop sb a l.** envoyer un mot à qn

7 *(rope)* corde *f*, *Naut* bout *m*; *Fishing* ligne *f*; *(in surveying) & Constr* cordeau *m*; **to hang the washing on the l.** mettre le linge à sécher, étendre le linge; **your clothes are out on the l.** tes vêtements sont sur la corde à linge

8 *(pipe)* tuyau *m*; *(pipeline)* pipeline *m*

9 *Br Rail (track)* voie *f*, *(single rail)* rail *m*; **the train left the l.** le train a déraillé

10 *(travel route)* ligne *f*; **underground l.** ligne *f* de métro; **to keep the lines of communication open** maintenir ouvertes les lignes de communication; **shipping l.** compagnie *f* de navigation

11 *Elec* ligne *f*; **the power lines have been cut** les lignes électriques ont été coupées; **the power station comes on l. in June** la centrale entre en service en juin

12 *Tel* ligne *f*; **the l. went dead** la communication a été coupée; **I was on the l. to Paris** je téléphonais à Paris; **all the lines to London are busy** toutes les lignes pour Londres sont occupées; **I have Laura on the l.** j'ai Laura en ligne; **a direct l. to Washington** une ligne directe avec Washington; **hold the l.** ne quittez pas; **the l. is** *Br* **engaged** *or Am* **busy** la ligne est occupée; **there's someone on the l.** il y a quelqu'un sur la ligne; **the l.'s very bad** la communication est mauvaise; **she's on the other l.** elle est sur l'autre ligne; *Comput* **on l.** en ligne

13 *(outline)* ligne *f*; **the graceful l.** *or* **lines of the new model** la ligne harmonieuse du nouveau modèle; **can you explain the main** *or* **broad lines of the project to me?** pouvez-vous m'expliquer les grandes lignes du projet?

14 *(policy)* ligne *f*; **they took a hard** *or* **tough l. on terrorism** ils ont adopté une politique de fermeté envers le terrorisme; **to follow** *or* **to toe the party l.** suivre la ligne du parti; **what l. are you going to take?** quel parti allez-vous prendre?; **we must take a firm l. with such people** il nous faut être ferme avec des gens comme ça

15 *Mil* ligne *f*; **they struggled vainly to hold the l.** ils ont vainement tenté de maintenir leur position; **battle lines** lignes *fpl* de bataille; **to infiltrate enemy lines** infiltrer les lignes ennemies; **regiment/ship of the l.** régiment *m*/navire *m* de ligne

16 *(boundary)* frontière *f*, limite *f*; **the distant l. of the horizon** la ligne lointaine de l'horizon; **the (dividing) l. between frankness and rudeness** la limite entre la franchise et l'impolitesse; **to overstep the l.** dépasser la mesure; **they crossed the state l. into Nevada** ils ont franchi la frontière du Nevada; **to cross the L.** *(equator)* traverser l'équateur

17 *(field of activity)* branche *f*; *(job)* métier *m*; *(field of interest)* domaine *m*; **she's in the same l. (of work) as you** elle travaille dans la même branche que toi; **what l. (of business) are you in?, what's your l. (of business)?** qu'est-ce que vous faites dans la vie?; **if you need anything doing in the plumbing l.** si vous avez besoin de faire faire des travaux de plomberie; **that's not my l.** ce n'est pas mon rayon; **that's more in Katy's l.** c'est plus du domaine de Katy

18 *(range ▸ of products)* ligne *f*; **a new l. of office furniture** une nouvelle ligne de meubles de bureau; **they produce** *or* **do an interesting l. in chairs** ils produisent une gamme intéressante de chaises; *Fam* **a rice pudding or something in that l.** un gâteau de riz ou quelque chose dans ce genre(-là)

19 *(production line)* chaîne *f*; **the new model will be coming off the l. in May** le nouveau modèle sortira de l'usine en mai

20 *(lineage, ancestry)* lignée *f*; **l. of descent** filiation *f*; **to be descended in (a) direct l. from sb** descendre en droite ligne de qn; **the Windsor l.** la lignée des Windsor; **the title is transmitted by the male l.** le titre se transmet par les hommes; **he comes from a long l. of doctors** il est issu d'une longue lignée de médecins

21 *Fam (information)* **I'll try and get a l. on what actually happened** j'essaierai d'avoir des tuyaux sur ce qui s'est réellement passé; **the police have got a l. on him** la police sait des choses sur lui

22 *Fam Drugs slang (of powdered drugs)* ligne *f*

VT 1 *(road, river)* border; **the avenue is lined with trees** l'avenue est bordée d'arbres; **crowds lined the streets** la foule était *ou* s'était massée sur les trottoirs

2 *(paper)* régler, ligner

3 *Sewing (clothes, curtains)* doubler; *(container, drawer, cupboard)* tapisser, garnir; **lined with silk** doublé de soie; **the tissue that lines the digestive tract** la paroi interne de l'appareil digestif; *Culin* **l. the baking tin with pastry** disposez la pâte dans le moule; **walls lined with books** des murs tapissés de livres; *Fam* **to l. one's (own) pockets** s'en mettre plein les poches

4 *Tech (bearing)* garnir, recouvrir; *(brakes)* garnir; *(wall, furnace)* revêtir, incruster; *(well)* cuveler; **to l. a shaft with metal** blinder un puits; **the tubes are lined with plastic** l'intérieur des tubes est revêtu d'une couche de plastique

►► *Comput* ***line break*** saut *m* de ligne; ***line call*** *(in tennis)* décision *f* du juge de ligne; *Comput* ***line command*** ligne *f* de commande; *Fin* ***line of credit*** ligne *f* de crédit *ou* de découvert; ***line dancing*** = danse de style country effectuée en rangs; ***line drawing*** dessin *m* au trait; *Sport* ***line drive*** *(in baseball)* flèche *f*; *Typ & Comput* ***line end*** fin *f* de ligne; *Typ & Comput* ***line end hyphen*** tiret *m* de fin de ligne; ***line engraving*** gravure *f* au trait; *Comput* ***line feed*** changement *m* de ligne; *Am* ***line fence*** clôture *f*; ***line fishing*** pêche *f* à la ligne; *Sport* ***line judge*** juge *m* de ligne; *Com* ***line management*** organisation *f* hiérarchique; *Com* ***line manager*** chef *m* hiérarchique; ***line noise*** parasites *mpl*; ***line organization*** organisation *f* hiérarchique; *Comput* ***line printer*** imprimante *f* ligne à ligne; *Comput* ***line printout*** imprimé *m* ligne à ligne; *Cin & TV* ***line producer*** producteur(trice) *m,f* délégué(e); *Theat* ***line rehearsal*** lecture *f* collective; *Tel* ***line rental*** abonnement *m*; *Typ & Comput* ***line space*** interligne *m*; **three l. spaces** un triple interligne; *Typ & Comput* ***line spacing*** interlignage *m*, espacement *m* de lignes; *TV* ***line system*** linéature *f*; *Typ & Comput* ***line width*** longueur *f* de ligne

▸**line up** VT SEP **1** *(put in line* ▸ *objects)* aligner, mettre en ligne; *(*▸ *people)* faire aligner; **he lined up the troops for inspection** il fit aligner les hommes pour passer l'inspection **2** *(bring into alignment)* aligner; **the two grooves must be lined up exactly** les deux rainures doivent être parfaitement alignées; **he had the pheasant lined up in his sights** il avait le faisan dans sa ligne de mire **3** *Fam (plan)* préparer□, prévoir□; **he's lined up an all-star cast for his new film** la distribution de son nouveau film ne comprend que des stars; **have you got anyone lined up for the job?** avez-vous quelqu'un en vue pour le poste?; **what have you got lined up for us?** qu'est-ce que vous nous préparez?

VI *(stand in line)* s'aligner, se mettre en ligne; *Am (queue up)* faire la queue; *Fig* **the Liberals lined up behind the government** les libéraux ont apporté leur soutien au gouvernement

lineage[1] [ˈlɪnɪɪdʒ] N *(ancestry)* ascendance *f*, famille *f*; *(descendants)* lignée *f*, descendance *f*; **of noble l.** de famille *ou* d'ascendance noble; **to trace one's l.** retracer sa généalogie

lineage[2] [ˈlaɪnɪdʒ] N *(for newspaper advertisement)* lignage *m*

lineal [ˈlɪnɪəl] ADJ en ligne directe

lineament [ˈlɪnɪəmənt] N *Literary* linéament *m*

linear [ˈlɪnɪə(r)] ADJ linéaire

►► *Phys* ***linear accelerator*** accélérateur *m* linéaire; ***linear equation*** équation *f* linéaire; *Phys* ***linear expansion*** dilatation *f* linéaire; ***linear measure*** mesure *f* linéaire *ou* de longueur; *Mktg* ***linear metre*** mètre *m* linéaire; *Phys* ***linear momentum*** moment *m* linéaire; ***linear motor*** moteur *m* linéaire; *Art* ***linear perspective*** perspective *f* linéaire; *Comput* ***linear programming*** programmation *f* linéaire

lined [laɪnd] ADJ **1** *(paper)* réglé
2 *(face, skin)* ridé
3 *(jacket)* doublé; *(box)* tapissé
4 *Aut (brake)* garni

linen [ˈlɪnɪn] N **1** *(fabric)* (toile *f* de) lin *m* **2** *(sheets, tablecloths, towels etc)* linge *m* (de maison); *Old-fashioned (underclothes)* linge *m* (de corps); **dirty l.** linge *m* sale; *Br Fig* **to wash one's dirty l. in public** laver son linge sale en public

COMP *(garment, sheet)* en lin; *(thread)* de lin

►► ***linen basket*** corbeille *f* à linge; ***linen cupboard***, *Am* ***linen closet*** armoire *f ou* placard *m* à linge; ***linen paper*** papier *m* toilé; ***linen room*** *(in hospital, hotel)* lingerie *f*

line-out N *Sport* touche *f*, remise *f* en jeu

liner [ˈlaɪnə(r)] N **1** *(ship)* paquebot *m* (de grande ligne)
2 *(eyeliner)* eye-liner *m*
3 *(for clothing)* doublure *f*
4 *Tech* chemise *f*

►► ***liner notes*** = texte figurant au dos des pochettes de disques, des boîtiers de CD et de cassettes

linesman [ˈlaɪnzmən] (*pl* **linesmen** [-mən]) N *Sport (in rugby, football)* juge *m ou* arbitre *m* de touche; *(in tennis)* juge *m* de ligne

line-up N **1** *(queue)* queue *f* (de personnes); *(identity parade)* séance *f* d'identification; *(line of suspects)* rangée *f* de suspects **2** *(composition)* **a jazz band with a traditional l.** une formation de jazz traditionnelle; **the England l. for tonight's match** la composition de l'équipe anglaise pour le match de ce soir; **we have an all-star l. for tonight's programme** nous avons un plateau de vedettes pour l'émission de ce soir

linework [ˈlaɪnwɜːk] N *Art* dessin *m* au trait

ling [lɪŋ] N **1** *(sea fish)* lingue *f*, julienne *f*; *(freshwater fish)* lotte *f* **2** *(heather)* bruyère *f*

linger [ˈlɪŋgə(r)] VI **1** *(memory, custom)* persister, subsister; *(smell, taste, sound)* persister; **a doubt lingered (on) in my mind** il subsistait un doute dans mon esprit **2** *(person)* s'attarder, traîner; **we lingered over lunch** nous nous sommes attardés à table; **a few students lingered outside the classroom** quelques étudiants s'attardaient devant la salle de cours; **the camera lingered on the scene** la caméra s'est attardée sur cette scène **3** *(stay alive)* **she might l. on for years yet** il se pourrait qu'elle tienne encore des années; **those attitudes still l. on today** ces attitudes survivent *ou* perdurent encore aujourd'hui

lingerie [ˈlænʒərɪ] N lingerie *f*

lingering [ˈlɪŋgrɪŋ] ADJ **1** *(long)* long (longue); **he gave her a long l. look** il lui lança un long regard langoureux **2** *(persistent)* persistant; **a l. feeling of dissatisfaction** un irréductible sentiment d'insatisfaction **3** *(illness)* qui traîne, chronique; *(death)* lent; **she died a l. death** la mort l'a emportée lentement

lingo [ˈlɪŋgəʊ] (*pl* **lingoes**) N *Fam* **I don't speak the l.** je ne parle pas la langue du pays□; **technical/scientific l.** jargon *m* technique/scientifique□

lingua franca [ˌlɪŋgwəˈfræŋkə] (*pl* **lingua francas** *or* **linguae francae** [ˌlɪŋgwiːˈfræŋkiː]) N lingua franca *f inv*, langue *f* véhiculaire

linguist [ˈlɪŋgwɪst] N **1** *Br (in foreign languages* ▸ *student)* étudiant(e) *m,f* en langues étrangères; *(*▸ *specialist)* spécialiste *mf* en langues étrangères; **to be a good l.** être doué pour les langues **2** *(in linguistics)* linguiste *mf*

linguistic [lɪŋˈgwɪstɪk] ADJ linguistique; **he had no l. ability** il n'avait aucune aptitude pour les langues

►► ***linguistic atlas*** atlas *m* linguistique

linguistically [lɪŋˈgwɪstɪklɪ] ADV linguistiquement

linguistics [lɪŋˈgwɪstɪks] N *(UNCOUNT)* linguistique *f*

COMP *(textbook, professor, degree)* de linguistique

liniment [ˈlɪnɪmənt] N pommade *f*

lining [ˈlaɪnɪŋ] N **1** *(of clothes, curtains)* doublure *f*; *(of hat)* coiffe *f* **2** *Tech (of container, bearing)* revêtement *m*; *(of brake, clutch)* garniture *f* **3** *Anat* paroi *f* interne; **the stomach l.** la paroi de l'estomac

►► ***lining paper*** *(for drawer)* papier *m* pour tiroirs; *(for shelves)* papier *m* pour recouvrir les étagères

link [lɪŋk] N **1** *(of chain)* chaînon *m*, maillon *m*; *Fig* **the weak l.** le maillon faible

2 *(bond, relationship)* lien *m*; **she's severed all links with her family** elle a coupé les ponts avec sa famille; **Britain's trade links with Spain** les relations commerciales entre la Grande-Bretagne et l'Espagne; **he is a l. between the old world and the new** il sert de trait d'union entre le vieux monde et le nouveau; **the l. between inflation and unemployment** le lien *ou* rapport entre l'inflation et le chômage

3 *(physical connection)* liaison *f*; **a road/rail/radio l.** une liaison routière/ferroviaire/radio

4 *Comput (hyperlink)* lien *m* (**to** avec)

5 *Tech* pièce *f* de liaison, tige *f* d'assemblage

6 *(unit of measurement)* = 7,92 pouces, centième partie *f* de la chaîne (d'arpenteur)

VT **1** *(relate)* lier; **the two crimes are linked** les deux crimes sont liés; **the two companies are in no way linked** il n'y a aucun lien entre les deux sociétés; **his name has been linked with several well-known actresses** son nom a été associé à plusieurs actrices bien connues; **wages linked to the cost of living** salaires indexés sur le coût de la vie **2** *(connect physically)* relier; *Comput* lier, relier (**to** à); **it can be linked (up) to a computer** on peut le relier *ou* connecter à un ordinateur; **to l. hands/arms** se donner la main/le bras; **a tunnel linking Britain and France** un tunnel reliant la Grande-Bretagne à la France

VI *Comput* **to l. to** être relié à

►► ***link road*** route *f* de jonction; ***link sausage*** saucisse *f (vendue en chapelet)*

▸**link up** VI **1** *(meet* ▸ *people, roads, paths)* se rejoindre; *(*▸ *troops)* effectuer une jonction; *(*▸ *spacecraft)* s'arrimer; **the space rocket will l. up with the orbiting satellite** la navette spatiale rencontrera le satellite en orbite **2** *(form a partnership)* s'associer; **we'll be linking up with a French company for this project** nous serons associés à une entreprise française pour ce projet **3** *(be connected)* se relier; **it can l. up to a computer** on peut le relier *ou* connecter à un ordinateur

VT SEP relier (**to** à); **the computers are all linked up** les ordinateurs sont tous reliés les uns aux autres

linkage [ˈlɪŋkɪdʒ] N **1** *(connection)* lien *m*, rapport *m*; **they deny any l. between the two issues** ils nient l'existence d'un lien *ou* rapport quelconque entre les deux problèmes **2** *Tech* transmission *f* par tringles, tringlerie *f*; *Aut* timonerie *f*

links [lɪŋks] NPL *(golf course* ▸ *any)* terrain *m* de golf; *(*▸ *beside the sea)* links *mpl*

linnet [ˈlɪnɪt] N *Orn* linotte *f*

linoleum [lɪˈnəʊljəm] N linoléum *m*

Linotype® [ˈlaɪnəʊˌtaɪp] N *Typ* Linotype® *f*

linseed [ˈlɪnsiːd] N graine *f* de lin

►► ***linseed oil*** huile *f* de lin

lint [lɪnt] N *(UNCOUNT)* **1** *Med* pansement *m* ouatiné **2** *(fluff)* peluches *fpl*

lintel [ˈlɪntəl] N linteau *m*

lint-free ADJ *(cloth)* sans peluches

lion [ˈlaɪən] N **1** *(animal)* lion *m*; **to put one's head in the l.'s mouth** se jeter dans la gueule du loup; **the l.'s share** la part du lion **2** *Fig (courageous person)* lion(onne) *m,f*; *(celebrity)* célébrité *f*; **a literary l.** un grand nom de la littérature

►► ***lion cub*** lionceau *m*; ***the lion's den*** l'antre *m* du lion; ***lion house*** *(at zoo)* fauverie *f*; ***lion hunter*** chasseur *m* de lions; ***lion tamer*** dompteur(euse) *m,f* (de lions)

lioness [ˈlaɪənes] N lionne *f*

lionheart [ˈlaɪənˌhɑːt] N *Hist* **(Richard) the L.** Richard Cœur de Lion

lionize, -ise [ˈlaɪənaɪz] VT *Br (make a celebrity)* célébrer; *(treat like a celebrity)* porter aux nues

lip [lɪp] N **1** *(of person)* lèvre *f*; *(of animal)* lèvre *f*, babine *f*; **my lips are sealed** je ne dirai rien; **her name is on everyone's lips** son nom est sur toutes les lèvres; **to read sb's lips** lire sur les lèvres de qn; *Fam* **read my lips** *(believe what I say)* écoutez-moi bien□; **to do** *or* **pay l. service to sth** faire semblant de s'intéresser à qch **2** *(of jug)* bec *m*; *(of cup, bowl)* rebord *m*; *(of wound)* lèvre *f*, bord *m*; *(of well)* margelle *f*; *(of crater, golf hole)* bord *m* **3** *Fam (impertinence)* culot *m*; **enough of your l.!** ne sois pas insolent!; **don't give me any of your l.!** ne te fiche pas de moi!

►► ***lip balm*** baume *m* pour les lèvres; ***lip gloss*** brillant *m* à lèvres; ***lip pencil*** crayon *m* à lèvres; ***lip salve*** pommade *f ou* baume *m* pour les lèvres

lip-flap N *(in dubbing)* lèvres *fpl* non synchro

lipid [ˈlɪpɪd] N *Biol & Chem* lipide *m*

lipo [ˈlɪpəʊ] N *Fam (abbr* **liposuction***)* lipo *f*

lipoma [lɪˈpəʊmə] N *Med* lipome *m*

lipoprotein [ˌlɪpəʊˈprəʊtiːn] N *Biol* lipoprotéine *f*

liposuction [ˈlɪpəʊˌsʌkʃən] N liposuccion *f*

-lipped [lɪpt] SUFF **thin-l.** aux lèvres minces

lippy [ˈlɪpɪ] (*compar* **lippier**, *superl* **lippiest**, *pl* **lippies**) *Fam* N *Br (lipstick)* rouge *m* à lèvres□

ADJ insolent□, culotté

lip-read (*pt & pp* **lip-read** [-red]) VT lire sur les lèvres de; **she can l. what you're saying** elle peut lire sur vos lèvres
VI lire sur les lèvres

lip-reader N **to be a good l.** bien savoir lire sur les lèvres

lip-reading N lecture *f* sur les lèvres

lipstick ['lɪpstɪk] N **1** *(substance)* rouge *m* à lèvres **2** *(stick)* (tube *m* de) rouge *m* à lèvres

lip-sync, lip-synch *Cin & TV* N play-back *m*
VT *(song)* chanter en play-back
VI *(of singer)* chanter en play-back

liquefaction [,lɪkwɪ'fækʃən] N liquéfaction *f*

liquefied ['lɪkwɪ,faɪd] ADJ **l. natural/petroleum gas** gaz *m* naturel/de pétrole liquéfié

liquefy ['lɪkwɪ,faɪ] (*pt & pp* **liquefied**) VT liquéfier
VI se liquéfier

liqueur [lɪ'kjʊə(r)] N **1** *(drink)* liqueur *f*; **cherry l.** liqueur *f* aux cerises **2** *(sweet)* chocolat *m* à la liqueur
►► ***liqueur chocolate*** chocolat *m* à la liqueur; ***liqueur glass*** verre *m* à liqueur

liquid ['lɪkwɪd] ADJ **1** *(fluid)* liquide; *Hum* **to have a l. lunch** boire de l'alcool en guise de déjeuner; *Hum* **how about some l. refreshment?** et si nous prenions un petit quelque chose?
2 *Fin* liquide
3 *(clear* ► *eyes, sound)* limpide
4 *Ling (consonant)* liquide
N **1** *(fluid)* liquide *m* **2** *Ling (consonant)* liquide *f*
►► ***liquid air*** air *m* liquide; ***liquid assets, liquid capital*** actif *m* liquide, liquidités *fpl*; ***liquid crystal*** cristal *m* liquide; ***liquid crystal display*** affichage *m* à cristaux liquides; ***liquid diet*** régime *m* ne comprenant que des liquides, *Spec* diète *f* hydrique; *Chem* ***liquid fuel*** combustible *m* liquide; *Fig* ***liquid gold*** *(oil)* or *m* noir; ***liquid measure*** mesure *f* de capacité pour les liquides; ***liquid nitrogen*** azote *m* liquide; ***liquid oxygen*** oxygène *m* liquide; ***Liquid paper®*** correcteur *m* liquide; ***liquid paraffin*** huile *f* de paraffine; ***liquid securities*** valeurs *fpl* liquides

liquidate ['lɪkwɪdeɪt] VT **1** *Fam Crime slang (kill, eliminate)* liquider, éliminer **2** *Fin & Law (debt, company, estate)* liquider; *(capital)* mobiliser; *St Exch* **to l. a position** liquider une position

liquidation [,lɪkwɪ'deɪʃən] N **1** *Fam Crime slang (killing, elimination)* liquidation *f* **2** *Fin & Law (of debt, company, estate)* liquidation *f*; *(of capital)* mobilisation *f*; **to go into l.** entrer en liquidation, déposer son bilan

liquidator ['lɪkwɪdeɪtə(r)] N *Fin & Law* liquidateur(trice) *m,f*

liquidity [lɪ'kwɪdɪtɪ] N **1** *(of substance)* liquidité *f* **2** *Fin* liquidité *f*
►► *Fin* ***liquidity ratio*** ratio *m* ou coefficient *m* de liquidité

liquidize, -ise ['lɪkwɪdaɪz] VT **1** *Culin* passer au mixeur **2** *Phys* liquéfier

liquidizer, -iser ['lɪkwɪdaɪzə(r)] N mixer *m*, mixeur *m*

liquor ['lɪkə(r)] N **1** *Am (alcohol)* alcool *m*, boissons *fpl* alcoolisées; **he can't hold** *or* **take his l.** il ne supporte pas l'alcool; **to be the worse for l.** être ivre
2 *Culin* jus *m*, bouillon *m*
3 *Pharm* solution *f* aqueuse
4 *(in brewing)* = eau chaude que l'on mélange au malt pour obtenir le moût
►► ***liquor cabinet, liquor case*** bar *m (meuble)*; *Am* ***liquor store*** magasin *m* de vins et spiritueux

►**liquor up** *Am Fam* VT SEP soûler[□], saouler[□]; **to get liquored up** se pinter *ou* se beurrer (la gueule)
VI se pinter *ou* se beurrer (la gueule)

liquorice, *Am* **licorice** ['lɪkərɪs] N *(plant, root, sweet)* réglisse *f*
►► ***liquorice allsorts*** = bonbons à la réglisse de différentes couleurs; ***liquorice root*** racine *f* de réglisse; ***liquorice stick*** bâton *m* de réglisse

lira ['lɪərə] (*pl* **lire** [-rɪ] *or* **liras**) N lire *f*

LISA [,elaɪ,es'eɪ] N *Br Fin (abbr* **long-term individual savings account***)* plan *m* de retraite en actions

Lisbon ['lɪzbən] N Lisbonne

lisle [laɪl] N *(thread)* fil *m* d'Écosse
►► ***lisle thread*** fil *m* d'Écosse

lisp [lɪsp] N zézaiement *m*; **to speak with** *or* **to have a l.** avoir un cheveu sur la langue, zézayer
VT dire en zézayant
VI parler avec un cheveu sur la langue, zézayer

lissom, lissome ['lɪsəm] ADJ *Literary* souple, agile

list [lɪst] N **1** *(record)* liste *f*, *Admin* bordereau *m*; **l. of names** liste *f* nominative; *Fig* **it's (at the) top of my l.** *(I'll do it first)* c'est la première chose que je doive faire; **a fridge is top of my l.** *(to buy)* la première chose que je doive acheter, c'est un réfrigérateur; **top of the l. for the government is the appointment of…** ce qui figure en tête des priorités du gouvernement c'est de nommer…; *Fig* **it's (at the) bottom of the l.** *(least important)* ce n'est pas à faire en priorité; **you're/your name's not on the l.** vous ne figurez pas sur la liste; **to make out** *or* **draw up a l.** établir *ou* dresser une liste; **to enter sth on a l.** porter qch sur une liste; *St Exch* **l. of applicants** *or* **applications** *(for loan, shares)* liste *f* des souscripteurs **2** *(lean)* inclinaison *f*; *Naut* gîte *f*, bande *f*; **to have a l.** donner de la bande, prendre de la gîte
VT **1** *(make list of)* dresser la liste de; *(enumerate)* énumérer; *(enter in a list)* inscrire (sur une liste); **I've listed the things to be done** j'ai dressé une liste de choses à faire; **she listed the reasons for her decision** elle a énuméré les raisons pour lesquelles elle avait pris cette décision; **my name isn't listed** mon nom ne figure pas sur la liste; **his phone number isn't listed (in the directory)** son numéro de téléphone ne figure pas dans l'annuaire
2 *(classify)* classer; **they are listed by family name** ils sont classés par nom de famille; **it was officially listed as suicide** ce fut officiellement classé comme un suicide
3 *(price)* **what are the new laptops listed at?** les nouveaux portables sont vendus combien?
4 *Comput* lister
5 *St Exch (shares)* coter
VI **1** *(lean)* pencher, être incliné; *Naut* gîter, donner de la bande **2** *Am* **this car lists (at** *or* **for) $10,000** cette voiture se vend *ou* s'est vendue 10 000 dollars
►► *Fin* ***list of investments*** (bordereau *m* de) portefeuille *m*; ***list price*** prix *m* du catalogue; **I can get 20 percent off (the) l. price** je peux avoir un rabais de 20 pour cent sur le prix de vente; *St Exch* ***list of quotations*** bulletin *m* des cours; *Pol* ***list system*** scrutin *m* de liste

listed ['lɪstɪd] ADJ *Fin* **to be l. on the Stock Exchange** être coté en Bourse
►► *Br* ***listed building*** bâtiment *m* classé; *Br St Exch* ***listed company*** société *f* cotée en Bourse; *St Exch* ***listed securities, listed stock*** valeurs *fpl* admises *ou* inscrites à la cote officielle

listen ['lɪsən] VI **1** *(gen)* écouter; **to l. to sb/sth** écouter qn/qch; **to l. with half an ear** n'écouter que d'une oreille; **we listened to their daughter singing** nous avons écouté chanter leur fille **2** *(pay attention)* faire attention, écouter; **he wouldn't l.** il n'a rien voulu savoir; **to l. to reason** écouter la voix de la raison; **don't l. to him, make up your own mind** n'écoute pas ce qu'il te dit, prends la décision toi-même; **l.! I've got an idea** écoutez, j'ai une idée; **if only I'd listened to my mother!** si seulement j'avais écouté ma mère *ou* suivi les conseils de ma mère!
N *Fam* **have a l. to their latest record** écoute un peu leur dernier disque; **give it another l.** écoute-le encore une fois[□]

►**listen in** VI **1** *(to radio)* écouter, être à l'écoute; **l. in tomorrow at the same time** soyez à l'écoute demain à la même heure **2** *(eavesdrop)* écouter; **it's rude to l. in on other people's conversations** c'est impoli d'écouter les conversations; **I'd like to l. in on the discussion** j'aimerais assister à cette discussion

listener ['lɪsənə(r)] N **1** *(gen)* personne *f* qui écoute; **he's a good/bad l.** il sait/il ne sait pas écouter (les autres) **2** *Rad* auditeur(trice) *m,f*

listening ['lɪsənɪŋ] N écoute *f*; *(in language learning)* compréhension *f* orale
►► ***listening device*** écoute *f*; ***listening post*** poste *m* d'écoute

listeriosis [lɪ,stɪərɪ'əʊsɪs] N *Med* listériose *f*

listing ['lɪstɪŋ] N **1** *(gen* ► *list)* liste *f*; (►*entry*) entrée *f*; **I found no l. for the company in the directory** je n'ai pas trouvé la société dans l'annuaire; **do you have a l. for Jacqui Dunn?** est-ce que vous avez une Jacqui Dunn dans vos fichiers? **2** *Comput* listing *m*, listage *m* **3** *St Exch* admission *f* à la cote officielle; **to have a l.** être coté en Bourse
• **listings** NPL **cinéma/TV listings** programme *m* des films/émissions de la semaine
►► ***listings magazine*** magazine *m* de spectacles; ***listing paper*** papier *m* continu, papier *m* listing

listless ['lɪstlɪs] ADJ *(torpid, unenergetic)* apathique, endormi, avachi; *(weak)* mou (molle), inerte; *(bored)* indolent, alangui; *(indifferent)* indifférent, insensible

listlessly ['lɪstlɪslɪ] ADV *(without energy)* sans énergie *ou* vigueur, avec apathie; *(weakly)* mollement; *(without interest)* d'un air absent

listlessness ['lɪstlɪsnɪs] N *(lack of energy)* manque *m* d'énergie *ou* de vigueur, apathie *f*; *(weakness)* mollesse *f*; *(boredom)* langueur *f*, indolence *f*; *(indifference)* indifférence *f*

lit[1] [lɪt] *pt & pp of* **light**
ADJ **1** *(illuminated)* éclairé; **the room is well/badly l.** la pièce est bien/mal éclairée **2** *Am Fam (drunk)* allumé

lit[2] N *Fam (abbr* **literature***)* **she teaches English l.** elle enseigne la littérature anglaise[□]
►► ***lit crit*** critique *f* littéraire[□]

litany ['lɪtənɪ] (*pl* **litanies**) N *Rel* litanies *fpl*; *Fig* **a l. of complaints** des jérémiades *fpl*

litchi = **lychee**

liter *Am* = **litre**

literacy ['lɪtərəsɪ] N *(of individual)* capacité *f* de lire et d'écrire; *(of population)* alphabétisation *f*; **a l. campaign** une campagne d'alphabétisation *ou* contre l'illettrisme; **the work requires a high degree of l.** le poste exige une solide culture générale; **l. level** degré *m* d'instruction *ou* d'alphabétisation; **adult l.** l'alphabétisation *f* des adultes
►► ***literacy test*** test *m* pour mesurer le niveau d'alphabétisation

literal ['lɪtərəl] ADJ **1** *(translation)* littéral, mot à mot; **in the l. sense of the word** au sens propre du mot; **to take sth in a l. sense** prendre qch au pied de la lettre; **it meant l. starvation for thousands of farmers** cela signifiait que des milliers de fermiers allaient littéralement mourir de faim **2** *Math (coefficient)* littéral
N *Typ* coquille *f*
►► *Typ* ***literal error*** coquille *f*

literally ['lɪtərəlɪ] ADV **1** *(not figuratively)* littéralement, au sens propre; *(word for word)* littéralement; **to take sth l.** prendre qch au pied de la lettre *ou* à la lettre; **to translate l.** faire une traduction littérale; **l. speaking** à proprement parler; **he was l. bleeding to death** il se vidait de son sang **2** *(in exaggeration)* littéralement; **we've had l. hundreds of letters** nous avons reçu littéralement des centaines de lettres

literary ['lɪtərərɪ] ADJ **1** *(style, work etc)* littéraire; **a l. man** un homme de lettres **2** *(formal, written* ► *language)* littéraire
►► ***literary agent*** agent *m* littéraire; ***literary critic*** critique *mf* littéraire; ***literary criticism*** critique *f* littéraire; ***literary journal*** revue *f* littéraire; ***literary prize*** prix *m* littéraire

literate ['lɪtərət] ADJ **1** *(able to read and write)* qui sait lire et écrire; **only 20 percent of the population is l.** 20 pour cent seulement de la population sait lire et écrire **2** *(educated)* instruit, cultivé

literature ['lɪtrətʃə(r)] N *(UNCOUNT)* **1** *(written works)* littérature *f*; **French l.** la littérature française **2** *(printed material)* documentation *f*; **scientific/medical l.** documentation *f* scientifique/médicale; **can you give me some l.?** pouvez-vous me donner de la documentation?; **sales l.** documentation *f*, brochures *fpl* de vente

lithe [laɪð] ADJ *(movement, person)* agile; *(body)* souple

lithium ['lɪθɪəm] N *Chem* lithium *m*

lithograph ['lɪθəgrɑːf] N lithographie *f (estampe)*
VT lithographier
lithographer [lɪ'θɒgrəfə(r)] N lithographe *mf*
lithographic [ˌlɪθə'græfɪk] ADJ lithographique
lithography [lɪ'θɒgrəfɪ] N lithographie *f (procédé)*
Lithuania [ˌlɪθjʊ'emjə] N Lituanie *f*
Lithuanian [ˌlɪθjʊ'emjən] N 1 *(person)* Lituanien(enne) *m,f* 2 *(language)* lituanien *m*
ADJ lituanien
COMP *(embassy)* de Lituanie; *(history)* de la Lituanie; *(teacher)* de lituanien
litigant ['lɪtɪgənt] *Law* N plaideur(euse) *m,f*, partie *f*
ADJ en litige; **the l. parties** les parties *fpl* plaidantes *ou* en litige
litigate ['lɪtɪgeɪt] *Law* VT contester (en justice)
VI plaider, intenter une action en justice
litigation [ˌlɪtɪ'geɪʃən] N *Law* litige *m*; **the case went to l.** le cas est passé en justice; **they are in l.** ils sont en procès
litigious [lɪ'tɪdʒəs] ADJ 1 *Formal Pej (fond of lawsuits)* procédurier 2 *Formal Pej (argumentative)* chicaneur, chicanier 3 *Law* litigieux, contentieux
litmus ['lɪtməs] N *Chem* tournesol *m*
▸▸ ***litmus paper*** papier *m* de tournesol; ***litmus test*** réaction *f* au tournesol; *Fig* test *m* décisif; **this will be a l. test of the government's will** ce sera un test décisif pour juger de la détermination du gouvernement
litre, *Am* **liter** ['liːtə(r)] N litre *m*
litter ['lɪtə(r)] N 1 *(UNCOUNT) (rubbish)* détritus *mpl*, ordures *fpl*; *(dropped in street)* papiers *mpl* (gras); **no l.** *(sign)* respectez la propreté des lieux
2 *(clutter)* fouillis *m*; **his desk was covered in a l. of papers** son bureau était envahi par les papiers
3 *(of animal)* portée *f*; **five young at a l.** *or* **in one l.** cinq petits d'une portée
4 *(for carrying wounded)* civière *f*; *Hist (conveyance)* litière *f*
5 *Agr (of straw, hay ▸ to bed animals)* litière *f*; *(▸ to protect plants)* paille *f*, paillis *m*
6 *(for cat)* litière *f*
VT 1 *(make untidy ▸ public place)* laisser des détritus dans; *(▸ house, room)* mettre du désordre dans; *(▸ desk)* encombrer; **don't l. the table (up) with your tools** n'encombre pas la table avec tes outils 2 *(usu passive) (cover, strew)* joncher, couvrir; *Fig* parsemer; **beer cans littered the dance floor** la piste de danse était jonchée de cannettes de bière; **his life is littered with failed love affairs** sa vie est jalonnée d'échecs amoureux; **her works are littered with allusions to the classics** ses écrits sont encombrés d'allusions aux auteurs classiques 3 *(horse)* faire la litière à; *(plants)* empailler; **to l. (down) a stable** étendre de la paille dans une écurie
VI 1 *Zool* mettre bas 2 *Am* **no littering** *(sign)* respectez la propreté des lieux
▸▸ ***litter basket*** *(in street)* poubelle *f*, boîte *f* à ordures; *Br* ***litter bin*** poubelle *f*, boîte *f* à ordures; *Br Fam* ***litter lout*** = personne qui jette des papiers ou des détritus par terre; ***litter tray*** caisse *f* (pour litière)
litterbug ['lɪtəbʌg] N *Fam* = personne qui jette des papiers ou des détritus par terre
little- [lɪtəl] PREF **a l.-understood phenomenon** un phénomène (encore) mal compris; **a l.-explored area** une zone presque inexplorée *ou* (encore) peu explorée

LITTLE¹ ['lɪtəl] ADJ 1 *(in size, quantity)* petit; **would you like a l. drop of gin?** tu veux un peu de gin?; **a l. smile/sob/cry** un petit sourire/sanglot/cri; **here's a l. something for your new house** voilà un petit quelque chose pour ta nouvelle maison; **would you like a l. something to eat?** voudriez-vous manger un petit quelque chose?; **the l. hand** *(of clock)* la petite aiguille
2 *(young, younger ▸ child, animal)* petit; **a l. boy** un petit garçon; **a l. girl** une petite fille, une fillette; **when I was l.** quand j'étais petit; **my l. sister** ma petite sœur
3 *(short ▸ time, distance)* **we spent a l. time in France** nous avons passé quelque temps en France; **a l. while ago** *(moments ago)* il y a quelques instants; *(days, months ago)* il y a quelque temps; **she only stayed (for) a l. while** elle n'est pas restée très longtemps; **the shop is a l. way along the street** le magasin se trouve un peu plus loin dans la rue
4 *(unimportant)* petit; **they had a l. argument** ils se sont un peu disputés
5 *(expressing affection, pleasure, irritation)* petit; **I've got my own l. house in Oxford now** j'ai maintenant ma petite maison à moi à Oxford; **a l. old lady** une petite vieille; **poor l. thing!** pauvre petit!; **she's a l. horror!** c'est une petite peste!; *Fam* **you're a filthy l. pig!** espèce de petit cochon!; **I'm used to his l. ways** je connais ses petites habitudes; *Fam* **I've worked out his l. game!** j'ai compris son petit jeu!
• **a little bit** ADV *Fam* = **a little**
▸▸ *Astron* ***the Little Bear*** la Petite Ourse; ***little black dress*** petite robe *f* noire; *Euph* ***the little boys' room*** le petit coin *(toilettes des hommes)*; *Am Astron* ***the Little Dipper*** la Petite Ourse; *Br Aut* ***little end*** pied *m* de bielle; ***little Englander*** *Hist* isolationniste *mf (hostile à l'expansion de l'empire britannique)*; *(chauvinistic)* = anglais chauvin et xénophobe; ***little finger*** auriculaire *m*, petit doigt *m*; **to twist sb round one's l. finger** faire ce qu'on veut de qn; *Euph* ***the little girls' room*** le petit coin *(toilettes des femmes)*; *Orn* ***little grebe*** petit grèbe *m*; *Fam Hum* ***little green men*** petits hommes verts *mpl*, extraterrestres▫ *mpl*; *Orn* ***little owl*** chevêche *f*; *Ir* ***the little people*** les lutins *mpl*; *Cards* ***little slam*** *(in bridge)* petit chelem *m*; ***little toe*** petit orteil *m*; *Old-fashioned* ***the little woman*** *(wife)* ma/ta/sa tendre moitié *f*; *Pej* **she plays the l. woman** *(helpless)* elle joue les faibles femmes

LITTLE² *(compar* **less** [les], *superl* **least** [liːst]) ADJ *(opposite of "much")* peu de; **very l. time/money** très peu de temps/d'argent; **I had l. time to relax** je n'ai guère eu le temps de me détendre; **I watch very l. television** je regarde très peu la télévision; **I'm afraid there's l. hope left** je crains qu'il n'y ait plus beaucoup d'espoir; **to have l. chance of doing sth** avoir peu de chances de faire qch; **there is l. point in complaining** ça ne vaut pas vraiment la peine de porter plainte; **it makes l. sense** ça n'a pas beaucoup de sens; **there was too l. money** il y avait trop peu d'argent; **with what l. French I knew** avec le peu de français que je connaissais; *Formal* **with no l. difficulty** non sans peine
PRON 1 *(small amount)* pas grand-chose; **there's l. one can say** il n'y a pas grand-chose à dire; **I see very l. of him now** je ne le vois plus que très rarement; **he has done l. for us** il n'a pas fait grand-chose pour nous; **very l. is known about his childhood** on ne sait pas grand-chose *ou* on ne sait que très peu de choses sur son enfance; **I gave her as l. as possible** je lui ai donné le minimum; **you may be paid as l. as £3 an hour** tu ne seras peut-être payé que 3 livres de l'heure; **so l.** si peu; **you know so l. about me** tu ne sais presque rien de moi; **too l.** trop peu; **to make l. of sth** *(fail to understand)* ne pas comprendre grand-chose à qch; *(not emphasize)* minimiser qch; *(scorn)* faire peu de cas de qch
2 *(certain amount)* **a l. of everything** un peu de tout; **the l. I saw looked excellent** le peu que j'en ai vu paraissait excellent; *Prov* **a l. of what you fancy does you good** il n'y a pas de mal à se faire du bien
ADV 1 *(to a limited extent)* **it's l. short of madness** ça frise la folie; **he's l. more than a waiter** il n'est rien de plus qu'un simple serveur; **he's l. known outside Birmingham** il n'est pas très connu en dehors de Birmingham; **I realized how l. I knew him** je me suis rendu compte à quel point je le connaissais peu; **l. more than an hour ago** il y a à peine une heure
2 *(rarely)* peu; **we go there as l. as possible** nous y allons le moins possible; **we talk very l. now** nous ne nous parlons presque plus
3 *Formal (never)* **I l. thought** *or* **l. did I think we would be friends one day** jamais je n'aurais cru que nous serions amis un jour; **l. did he suspect that his wife was the culprit** il ne se doutait pas que c'était sa femme qui était coupable
• **a little** ADJ un peu de; **there's still a l. time/bread left** il reste encore un peu de temps/pain; **I speak a l. French** je parle quelques mots de français; *Prov* **a l. knowledge** *or* **learning is a dangerous thing** = il est moins dangereux de ne rien savoir que d'en savoir trop peu PRON un peu
ADV 1 *(slightly)* un peu; **I'm a l. tired** je suis un peu fatigué; **a l. less/more sugar** un (petit) peu moins/plus de sucre; **not even a l. interested** pas le moins du monde intéressé; **I was not a l. afraid** j'avais très peur
2 *(for a short time or distance)* un peu; **I walked on a l.** j'ai marché encore un peu; **I paused there (for a l.) and then said...** j'ai marqué un petit temps d'arrêt, puis j'ai dit...
• **little by little** ADV peu à peu, petit à petit; **he pieced the story together l. by l.** il reconstitua l'histoire peu à peu

little-boy ADJ de petit garçon, de garçonnet *(haircut)* à la garçonne
little-girl ADJ de petite fille, de fillette
little-known ADJ peu connu
littoral ['lɪtərəl] N littoral *m*
ADJ littoral
liturgical [lɪ'tɜːdʒɪkəl] ADJ liturgique
liturgy ['lɪtədʒɪ] (*pl* **liturgies**) N liturgie *f*
livable ['lɪvəbəl] ADJ *Fam* 1 *(inhabitable)* habitable▫; **we're trying to make the house l. (in)** nous essayons de rendre la maison habitable 2 *(bearable)* supportable▫; **his visits made her life l.** ses visites lui ont rendu la vie supportable; **she's not l. with** elle est invivable

LIVE¹ [lɪv]

VI	
• vivre **1, 2, 4, 6**	• habiter **3**
• se nourrir **5**	
VT	
• vivre	

VI 1 *(be or stay alive)* vivre; **as long as I l.** tant que je vivrai, de mon vivant; **was she still living when her grandson was born?** est-ce qu'elle était encore en vie quand son petit-fils est né?; **he hasn't long to l.** il ne lui reste pas beaucoup de temps à vivre; **she didn't l. long after her son died** elle n'a pas survécu longtemps à son fils; **the doctors think she'll l.** les médecins pensent qu'elle vivra; *Ironic* **you'll l.!** tu n'en mourras pas!; **she'll l. to be 100** elle vivra jusqu'à 100 ans, elle sera centenaire; **to l. on borrowed time** être en sursis; **to l. to a ripe old age** vivre vieux *ou* jusqu'à un âge avancé; *Fig* **the dialogue is what makes the characters l.** ce sont les dialogues qui donnent de la vie aux personnages; **your words will l. in our hearts/memories** vos paroles resteront à jamais dans nos cœurs/notre mémoire
2 *(have a specified way of life)* vivre; **to l. dangerously** vivre dangereusement; *Fam* **go on, l. dangerously!** allez, vas-y, on n'a qu'une vie!; **they lived happily ever after** ils vécurent heureux jusqu'à la fin de leurs jours; **he lives by the rules** il mène une vie bien rangée; **she lives for her children/for skiing** elle ne vit que pour ses enfants/que pour le ski; **we're living for the day we emigrate** nous vivons dans l'attente du jour où nous émigrerons; **to l. in poverty/luxury** vivre dans la pauvreté/le luxe; **to l. in fear** vivre dans la peur; **he lives in the past** il vit dans le passé; **we l. in uncertain times** nous vivons une époque incertaine; *Prov* **l. and let l.!** = il faut savoir faire preuve de tolérance!; **well, you l. and learn!** on en apprend tous les jours!
3 *(reside)* habiter; **where does she l.?** où habite-t-elle?; **they have nowhere to l.** ils sont à la rue; **the giant tortoise lives mainly in the Galapagos** la tortue géante vit surtout aux Galapagos; **they l. in Rome** ils habitent (à) Rome, ils vivent à Rome; **I lived in France for a year** j'ai vécu en France pendant un an; **to l. in a flat/a castle** habiter (dans) un appartement/un château; **she lives in a fifth-floor flat** elle vit dans un appartement au cinquième étage; **to l. at number 10** habiter au numéro 10; **to l. in the town/country** habiter *ou* vivre en ville/à la campagne; **I l. in** *or* **on Bank Street** j'habite Bank Street; **they l. in** *or* **on my street** ils habitent (dans) ma rue; **to l. on the**

street être à la rue; **he practically lives in** *or* **at the library** il passe sa vie à la bibliothèque; **do you l. with your parents?** habitez-vous chez vos parents?; *Old-fashioned or Hum* **to l. in sin (with sb)** vivre dans le péché (avec qn)

4 *(support oneself)* vivre; **they don't earn enough to l.** ils ne gagnent pas de quoi vivre; **he lives by teaching** il gagne sa vie en enseignant; **the tribe lives by hunting** la tribu vit de la chasse

5 *(obtain food)* se nourrir; **we've been living out of cans** *or* **tins lately** on se nourrit de conserves depuis quelque temps; **he was reduced to living out of rubbish bins** il en était réduit à fouiller les poubelles pour se nourrir

6 *(exist fully, intensely)* vivre; **she really knows how to l.** elle sait vraiment profiter de la vie; **let's l. for the moment** *or* **for today!** vivons l'instant présent!; **I want to l. a little** je veux profiter de la vie; **if you haven't been to New York, you haven't lived!** si tu n'es jamais allé à New York, tu n'as rien vu!

VT vivre; **to l. a life of poverty** vivre dans la pauvreté; **to l. a life of luxury** mener la grande vie; **to l. a solitary life** mener une vie solitaire; **to l. a lie** être dans une situation fausse; **she lived the life of a film star for six years** elle a vécu comme une star de cinéma pendant six ans; *Fam* **to l. it up** faire la fête; **my father lives and breathes golf** mon père ne vit que pour le golf

live[2] [laɪv] **ADJ 1** *(alive ▸ animal, person)* vivant; *Fam* **a real l. cowboy** un cow-boy, un vrai de vrai

2 *Mus, Rad & TV (programme, interview, concert)* en direct; **l. pictures from Mars** des images en direct de Mars; **Sinatra l. at the Palladium** Sinatra en concert au Palladium; **recorded before a l. audience** enregistré en public

3 *Elec (connected)* sous tension

4 *Tech (load)* roulant, mobile

5 *(unexploded)* non explosé

6 *(still burning ▸ coals, embers)* ardent

7 *(not extinct ▸ volcano)* actif

8 *(controversial)* controversé; **a l. issue** un sujet controversé

ADV 1 *Mus, Rad & TV* en direct; **to perform l.** *(singer)* chanter en direct; *(group)* jouer en direct; **they've never performed l.** ils n'ont jamais fait de scène; **the match can be seen/is going out l. at 3.30 p.m.** on peut suivre le match/le match est diffusé en direct à 15 heures 30; **the show comes l. from New York City** le spectacle nous arrive en direct de New York **2** *St Exch* **to go l.** *(of company)* entrer en Bourse

▸▸ ***live ammunition*** balles *fpl* réelles; *Art* ***live art*** performance *f*; *Tech* ***live axle*** essieu *m* moteur, pont *m*; ***live births*** naissances *fpl* viables; *Rad & TV* ***live broadcast*** émission *f* en direct; *Comput* ***live cam*** caméra *f* Internet; *Elec* ***live circuit*** circuit *m* alimenté *ou* sous tension; *Rad & TV* ***live commentary*** commentaire *m* en direct; *Rad & TV* ***live coverage*** reportage *m* en direct; ***live entertainment*** spectacle *m*; *(broadcast)* spectacles *mpl* en direct; **the theatre and other forms of l. entertainment** le théâtre et autres formes de divertissement; ***live music*** musique *f* live; ***live oak*** chêne *m* vert; *Am Fam* ***live one*** *(dupe)* poire *f*, pigeon *m*; ***live recording*** enregistrement *m* live *ou* public; *Elec* ***live wire*** fil *m* sous tension; *Fam Fig* **she's a real l. wire** elle déborde d'énergie□; *Culin* ***live yoghurt*** yaourt *m* actif

▸**live down VT SEP** *(recover from ▸ error, disgrace, ridicule)* **if I forget her birthday, I'll never l. it down!** si j'oublie son anniversaire, elle ne me le pardonnera jamais!; **you'll never l. this down!** tu n'as pas fini d'en entendre parler!

▸**live in VI 1** *(servant)* être logé et nourri; *(worker, nurse)* être logé *ou* habiter sur place **2** *(pupil)* être interne

▸**live off VT INSEP 1** *(sponge off)* vivre aux crochets de; **he lives off his parents** il vit aux crochets de ses parents **2** *(savings)* vivre de; *(nuts, berries)* se nourrir de; **to l. off the land** vivre de la terre

▸**live on VI** *(person)* continuer à vivre; *(custom, ideal)* persister; **she lived on to the end in the same house** elle a vécu dans la même maison jusqu'à sa mort; **his memory lives on** son souvenir est encore vivant

VT INSEP 1 *(food)* vivre de, se nourrir de; **to l. on fruit and vegetables** vivre de fruits et de légumes **2** *(salary)* vivre de; **it's not enough to l. on** ce n'est pas suffisant pour vivre; **to earn enough to l. on** gagner de quoi vivre; **how does she l. on that salary?** comment s'en sort-elle avec ce salaire?; **to l. on $800 a month** vivre avec 800 dollars par mois **3** *Fig* **to l. on one's wits** vivre d'expédients; **to l. on one's name** vivre sur sa réputation

▸**live out VT SEP 1** *(spend)* passer; **she lived out the rest of her life in Spain** elle a passé le reste de sa vie en Espagne **2** *(fulfil)* vivre; **to l. out one's fantasies** réaliser ses rêves

VI the maid lives out la bonne ne loge pas sur place; **he studies here but lives out** il est étudiant ici mais il n'habite pas sur le campus

▸**live through VT INSEP** *(experience ▸ war, hard times etc)* vivre, connaître; *(survive ▸ war, drought)* survivre à; **they've lived through war and famine** ils ont connu la guerre et la famine; **he's unlikely to l. through the winter** il est peu vraisemblable qu'il passe l'hiver

▸**live together VI** *(as a couple)* vivre ensemble, cohabiter

▸**live up to VT INSEP** *(name, reputation)* se montrer à la hauteur de; *(expectation)* être *ou* se montrer à la hauteur de, répondre à; **we have a reputation to l. up to!** nous avons une réputation à défendre!; **the holiday didn't l. up to our expectations** les vacances n'étaient pas à la hauteur de nos espérances

liveable = **livable**

lived-in ['lɪvd-] **ADJ** *(house, flat)* accueillant; *Fig (face)* marqué; **the cottage has a l. feel (to it)** la maison est accueillante et confortable

live-in ['lɪv-] **ADJ** *(maid)* logé et nourri; *(nurse, governess)* à demeure; **his l. girlfriend** sa compagne, la femme avec qui il vit

▸▸ ***live-in accommodation*** *(for staff)* logement *m* à demeure; *Hum* ***live-in lover*** compagnon *(compagne) m,f* (avec qui l'on vit)

livelihood ['laɪvlɪhʊd] **N** *(UNCOUNT)* moyens *mpl* d'existence, gagne-pain *m inv*; **to earn** *or* **gain one's l.** gagner sa vie *ou* son pain; **tourism is our l.** le tourisme est notre gagne-pain; **writing isn't a hobby, it's my l.** écrire n'est pas un passe-temps, c'est mon gagne-pain *ou* mon métier

liveliness ['laɪvlɪnɪs] **N** *(of person)* vivacité *f*; *(of conversation, party)* animation *f*; *(of debate, style)* vigueur *f*; *(of music, dance)* gaieté *f*, allégresse *f*; *(of colours)* éclat *m*, gaieté *f*

livelong ['lɪvlɒŋ] **ADJ** *Literary* **all the l. day** toute la journée, tout au long du jour; **the l. night** toute la nuit

lively ['laɪvlɪ] *(compar* **livelier**, *superl* **liveliest)** **ADJ 1** *(full of life ▸ person)* vif, plein d'entrain; *(▸ kitten, puppy)* plein de vie, espiègle; *(▸ horse)* fringant; *(▸ car, engine)* nerveux; *(▸ music)* gai, entraînant; **she's l. company** on ne s'ennuie pas avec elle

2 *(keen ▸ mind, curiosity)* vif; *(▸ imagination)* fertile; **to take a l. interest in sth** s'intéresser vivement à qch

3 *(exciting ▸ place, description, party, conversation)* animé; **a very l. debate** un débat très animé; **the town gets a bit livelier in summer** la ville s'anime un peu en été; **a l. performance** une interprétation très enlevée

4 *(eventful ▸ day, time)* mouvementé, agité; **things got l. when the police arrived** il y a eu de l'animation quand la police est arrivée; *Fam* **to make it** *or* **things l. for sb** rendre la vie dure à qn; *Br Fam* **look l.!** grouille-toi!

5 *(brisk ▸ pace)* vif

6 *(vivid ▸ colour)* vif, éclatant

liven ['laɪvən]

▸**liven up VT SEP** *(person, meeting, party)* animer, égayer; *(proceedings)* activer; **to l. up the conversation** ranimer la conversation; **you need to l. up your style** vous devriez mettre plus de mouvement dans votre style; **some pictures would l. up the text a bit** quelques photos égaieraient un peu le texte

VI s'animer, s'activer

liver[1] ['lɪvə(r)] **N 1** *Anat* foie *m* **2** *Culin* foie *m* **3** *(colour)* rouge brun *m inv*, brun roux *m inv*

▸▸ *Anat* ***liver complaint*** maladie *f* du foie; *Vet* ***liver fluke*** grande douve *f*; *Culin* ***liver pâté*** pâté *m* de foie; *Br* ***liver salts*** lithiné *m*; ***liver sausage*** pâté *m* de foie; ***liver spot*** tache *f* de vieillesse

liver[2] **N** *(person) Fam* **fast** *or* **high l.** fêtard(e) *m,f*, noceur(euse) *m,f*

liveried ['lɪvərɪd] **ADJ** en livrée

liverish ['lɪvərɪʃ] **ADJ** *Fam* **1** *(ill)* **to be** *or* **to feel l.** avoir mal au foie□ **2** *(peevish)* irritable□, bilieux□

Liverpudlian [ˌlɪvə'pʌdlɪən] **N** *(inhabitant)* habitant(e) *m,f* de Liverpool; *(native)* originaire *mf* de Liverpool

ADJ de Liverpool

liverwurst ['lɪvəwɜːst] **N** *Am* pâté *m* de foie

livery ['lɪvərɪ] *(pl* **liveries) N 1** *(uniform)* livrée *f*; **full l.** grande livrée *f*; **in l.** en livrée **2** *(of company)* couleurs *fpl*; **the cars have been painted in the new company l.** les voitures ont été peintes aux nouvelles couleurs de la maison

▸▸ *Br* ***livery company*** confrérie *f (de la cité de Londres)*; ***livery horse*** cheval *m* de louage; ***livery stable*** *(for boarding)* écurie *f* prenant des chevaux en pension; *(for hiring)* écurie *f* de chevaux de louage

livestock ['laɪvstɒk] **N** bétail *m*, cheptel *m*

livid ['lɪvɪd] **ADJ 1** *(blue-grey)* livide; **a l. sky** un ciel de plomb **2** *Fam (angry)* furax; *Fam* **to be l. with anger, to be absolutely l.** être fou de rage; **it makes me l.!** ça me met en rage!

living ['lɪvɪŋ] **N 1** *(livelihood)* vie *f*; **I have to work for a l.** je suis obligé de travailler pour vivre; **what do you do for a l.?** qu'est-ce que vous faites dans la vie?; **to write for a l.** vivre de sa plume; **she made a (good) l. as a pianist** elle gagnait (bien) sa vie comme pianiste; **you can't make a decent l. in this business** on gagne mal sa vie *ou* on a du mal à gagner sa vie dans ce métier **2** *(life, lifestyle)* vie *f*; **come to California where the l. is easy** venez en Californie, la vie y est facile; **plain l.** la vie simple **3** *Br Rel* bénéfice *m*

ADJ *(alive)* vivant; **the study of l. organisms** l'étude des organismes vivants; **he has no l. relatives** il n'a plus de famille; **who's the greatest l. boxer?** quel est le plus grand boxeur vivant?; **while she was l.** de son vivant; **it was the worst storm in l. memory** de mémoire d'homme on n'avait jamais vu une tempête aussi violente; **I didn't see a l. soul** je n'ai pas vu âme qui vive; **she's l. proof that the treatment works** elle est la preuve vivante que le traitement est efficace; **they made her life a l. hell** ils lui ont rendu la vie infernale; **the l. dead** les morts *mpl* vivants; **his life became a l. death** sa vie ne fut plus qu'une longue souffrance

NPL the l. les vivants *mpl*

COMP *(conditions)* de vie

▸▸ ***living allowance*** indemnité *f* de séjour; ***living area*** aire *f* de séjour; **the l. area is separated from the bedrooms** la partie séjour est séparée des chambres; *Fin* ***living expenses*** indemnité *f* de séjour; ***living quarters*** *(for servants)* logements *mpl*; *(on ship)* partie *f* habitée; **these are the crew's l. quarters** ce sont les quartiers de l'équipage; *Geol* ***the living rock*** la roche non exploitée; **sculpted from the l. rock** taillé à même le roc; ***living room*** **N** (salle *f* de) séjour *m* **COMP** du salon; ***living space*** espace *m* vital; ***living standards*** niveau *m* de vie; ***living thing*** être *m* vivant; ***a living wage*** le minimum vital; **£400 a month isn't a l. wage** on ne peut pas vivre avec 400 livres par mois; ***living will*** testament *m* de vie

Livy ['lɪvɪ] **PR N** Tite-Live

lizard ['lɪzəd] **N** *(reptile)* lézard *m*

COMP *(belt, shoes)* en lézard

llama ['lɑːmə] **N** *Zool* lama *m*

LLB [ˌelel'biː] **N** *Univ (abbr* **Bachelor of Laws)** *(person)* = titulaire d'une licence de droit; *(qualification)* licence *f* de droit

LLD [ˌelel'diː] **N** *Univ (abbr* **Doctor of Laws)** *(person)* docteur *m* en droit; *(qualification)* doctorat *m* en droit

LMBO [ˌelem,biː'əʊ] **N** *Fin (abbr* **leveraged management buy-out)** = rachat d'entreprise par les salariés

LNG [ˌelen'dʒiː] **N** *(abbr* **liquefied natural gas)** GNL *m*

lo [ləʊ] EXCLAM **1** *Arch or Literary* regardez!, voyez! **2** *(idiom)* **and lo and behold there he was!** et voilà, il était là!

loach [ləʊtʃ] N *Ich* loche *f*

load [ləʊd] N **1** *(of lorry, ship etc)* charge *f*, chargement *m*; *(carrying capacity)* charge *f*; **she was carrying a l. of books/washing** elle portait des livres/du linge; **to be carrying a heavy l.** être lourdement chargé; **a l. of gravel** un chargement de gravier; **we moved all the stuff in ten loads** nous avons tout transporté en dix voyages

2 *Fig (burden)* fardeau *m*, charge *f*; **the reforms should lighten the l. of classroom teachers** les réformes devraient faciliter la tâche des enseignants; **hire somebody to share the l.** embauchez quelqu'un pour vous faciliter la tâche; **that's a l. off my mind!** me voilà soulagé d'un poids!

3 *(batch of laundry)* machine *f*; **I've two more loads to do** j'ai encore deux machines à faire

4 *Elec, Constr & Tech* charge *f*; **safe l.** charge *f* de sécurité; **the machine is working at full l.** la machine fonctionne *ou* travaille à pleine charge; **under l.** en charge; *Elec* **to shed the l.** délester

5 *(idioms) Fam* **get a l. of this** *(look)* vise un peu ça; *(listen)* écoute-moi ça; *Am Fam* **he has a l. on, he's carrying a l.** il est complètement bourré; *Vulg* **to shoot one's l.** *(ejaculate)* décharger

VT **1** *(person, animal, vehicle)* charger; **to l. sth with sth** charger qch sur qch; **we loaded the trolley with food** on a rempli le chariot de nourriture; **l. the bags into the car** chargez *ou* mettez les sacs dans la voiture; **he was loaded with shopping** il avait les bras chargés de courses; **I'm going to l. some more work onto you** je vais vous confier encore un peu de travail; **I don't think it's fair to l. all the work onto one person** je trouve que ce n'est pas juste de donner tout le travail à une seule personne

2 *(camera, gun, machine)* charger; **l.! take aim! fire!** chargez! en joue! feu!; **to l. a film/tape** mettre une pellicule/une cassette; **l. the cassette into the recorder** introduisez la cassette dans le magnétophone

3 *Comput* charger; **to l. a program into the memory** charger un programme en mémoire

4 *(insurance premium)* majorer, augmenter

5 *Tech (spring)* serrer, bander

6 *(idioms)* **to l. the dice** piper les dés; *Fig* **the dice are loaded against us** nous n'aurons pas la partie facile

VI **1** *(receive freight)* faire le chargement; **the ship is loading** le navire est en cours de chargement; *Aut* **no loading or unloading between 9 a.m. and 4 p.m.** *(sign)* chargement ou déchargement interdits entre 9h et 16h **2** *(camera, gun)* se recharger **3** *Comput (computer program)* se charger

COMP *Comput (program)* de chargement; *(module)* chargeable

• **a load of** ADJ *Br Fam* **what a l. of rubbish!** c'est vraiment n'importe quoi!

►► ***load bed*** *(of truck)* plateau *m* de chargement; ***load box*** *(on vehicle)* soute *f*; ***load carrying capacity*** charge *f* utile; ***load factor*** *(of plane)* coefficient *m* de remplissage; *Elec* facteur *m ou* coefficient *m* de charge; *Tech* facteur *m* de charge; *Naut* ***load line*** ligne *f* de charge; *Comput* ***load mode*** mode *m* chargement; *Elec* ***load shedding*** délestage *m*

▸**load down** VT SEP charger (lourdement); **he was loaded down with packages** il avait des paquets plein les bras; **I'm loaded down with work** je suis surchargé de travail

▸**load up** VT SEP **1** *(truck, ship etc)* charger; **load the wheelbarrow up with bricks** remplissez la brouette de briques **2** *Comput (disk, program)* charger

VI charger

loadable [ˈləʊdəbəl] ADJ *Comput (software)* qui peut se charger, chargeable

loaded [ˈləʊdɪd] ADJ **1** *(vehicle)* chargé; **is the lorry fully l.?** le camion est-il vraiment plein?

2 *Fig* **to be l. with** être chargé de *ou* plein de; **his writing is l. with metaphors** ses textes sont pleins de métaphores; **the word is l. with meaning** c'est un mot lourd de sens

3 *(gun, camera)* chargé

4 *(dice)* pipé

5 *(statement, comment, question)* insidieux

6 *Fam (rich)* plein aux as

7 *Fam (drunk)* plein, bourré; *(on drugs)* défoncé

►► ***loaded question*** question *f* insidieuse

loader [ˈləʊdə(r)] N **1** *(person)* chargeur(euse) *m,f*

2 *Elec, Mil & Phot (device)* chargeur *m*

3 *Constr (machine)* chargeuse *f*, loader *m*

4 *Comput* (programme *m*) chargeur *m*

loading [ˈləʊdɪŋ] N **1** *(of vehicle, machine, gun, computer program)* chargement *m* **2** *Austr (payment)* indemnité *f*, allocation *f*

►► ***loading bay*** aire *f* de chargement; ***loading dock*** embarcadère *m*; ***loading point*** point *m* de chargement; ***loading ramp*** rampe *f* de chargement; ***loading time*** délai *m* de chargement; *(on ship)* délai *m* d'embarquement

loaf [ləʊf] *(pl* **loaves** [ləʊvz]*)* N **1** *(of bread)* pain *m*; *(large, round)* miche *f*; **two loaves (of bread) please** deux pains, s'il vous plaît; *Prov* **half a l. is better than none** faute de grives, on mange des merles **2** *Br Fam (rhyming slang* **loaf of bread** = **head)** **to use one's l.** faire marcher son ciboulot

VI *Fam* fainéanter☐, traîner; **I spent the day loafing about** *or* **around the house** j'ai passé la journée à traîner chez moi

►► ***loaf sugar*** sucre *m* en pains; ***loaf tin*** *(for bread)* moule *m* à pain; *(for cake)* moule *m* à cake

loafer [ˈləʊfə(r)] N **1** *Fam (person)* fainéant(e)☐ *m,f* **2** *(shoe)* mocassin *m*

loam [ləʊm] N **1** *Agr & Hort* terreau *m* **2** *Constr* pisé *m*

loamy [ˈləʊmɪ] *(compar* **loamier**, *superl* **loamiest)** ADJ *(soil)* riche en terreau

loan [ləʊn] N **1** *(money* ▸ *from borrower's point of view)* emprunt *m*; *(*▸ *from lender's point of view)* prêt *m*; **a £500 l.** un prêt de 500 livres; **to take out a l.** faire un emprunt; **to apply for a l.** demander un prêt; **to repay a l.** rembourser un emprunt; **he asked me for a l.** il m'a demandé de lui prêter de l'argent; **it's a l., you can have it as a l.** je vous le prête; **long/short-term l.** prêt *m*/emprunt *m* à long/court terme; **secured l.** prêt *m*/emprunt *m* gagé *ou* garanti; **unsecured l., l. without security** prêt *m*/emprunt *m* à découvert; **l. on** *or* **against securities** emprunt *m* sur titre; **l. against security** prêt *m* sur gage; **l. at interest** prêt *m* à intérêts; **l. to value** = rapport entre le capital restant dû et la valeur du bien financé; *Acct* **loans and advances to customers** créances *fpl* clients; *Acct* **loans outstanding** encours *m*; *Fin* **l. at call, l. repayable on demand** prêt *m* remboursable sur demande; *Fin* **l. at notice** prêt *m* à terme; *Fin* **l. on collateral** prêt *m* sur gage *ou* sur nantissement; *Fin* **l. on mortgage** prêt *m* hypothécaire *ou* sur hypothèque; *Fin* **l. on overdraft** prêt *m* à découvert; *Fin* **l. on trust** prêt *m* d'honneur **2** *(act of lending)* **to give sb a l. of sth** prêter qch à qn; *Br* **may I have the l. of your typewriter?** peux-tu me prêter ta machine à écrire?; **I have three books on l. from the library** j'ai emprunté trois livres à la bibliothèque; **the book you want is out on l.** le livre que vous voulez est sorti; **the picture is on l. to an American museum** le tableau a été prêté à un musée américain **3** *Ling* (mot *m* d') emprunt *m*

VT prêter; **to l. sb sth, to l. sth to sb** prêter qch à qn; **he asked me to l. him £20/my car** il m'a demandé de lui prêter 20 livres/ma voiture

►► *Banking* ***loan account*** compte *m* de prêt; ***loan agreement*** contrat *m* de prêt; *Fin* ***loan capital*** capital *m* sur prêt *ou* d'emprunt; *Fin* ***loan certificate*** titre *m* de prêt; *Fin* ***loan charges*** frais *mpl* financiers; ***loan collection*** collection *f* en prêt; *Fin* ***loan company*** société *f* de crédit, maison *f* de prêt; *Fin* ***loan department*** service *m* des crédits; ***loan insurance*** assurance *f* crédit; ***loan maturity*** échéance *f* emprunt; *Fin* ***loan note*** titre *m* d'obligation *ou* de créance; *Fin* ***loan office*** organisme *m* de crédit, maison *f* de prêt; ***loan repayment insurance*** assurance *f* crédit; ***loan risk cover*** couverture *f* du risque de crédit; *Fam Pej* ***loan shark*** usurier(ère)☐ *m,f*; ***loan stock*** emprunt *m* obligataire

loath [ləʊθ] ADJ **to be l. to do sth** n'avoir pas du tout envie de faire qch, répugner à faire qch; **I'm very l. to admit it** j'ai beaucoup de mal à l'admettre; **they were l. to leave** ils étaient peu disposés à partir; **nothing l.** avec plaisir, très volontiers

loathe [ləʊð] VT détester; **I l. having to get up in the mornings** j'ai horreur d'être obligé de me lever le matin; **I l. milk** j'ai horreur du lait, je déteste le lait; **I l. being mistaken for a tourist** je déteste qu'on me prenne pour un touriste

loathing [ˈləʊðɪŋ] N aversion *f*, répugnance *f*; **have an absolute l. for people like them** j'ai horreur des gens comme eux; **it fills me with l.** ça me révolte

loathsome [ˈləʊðsəm] ADJ *(person)* répugnant; *(habit)* détestable; *(smell)* nauséabond; **that was a l. thing to do/say!** c'était vraiment dégoûtant de faire/dire ça!

loathsomeness [ˈləʊðsəmnɪs] N nature *f* répugnante *ou* dégoûtante

lob [lɒb] *(pt & pp* **lobbed**, *cont* **lobbing)** N *Sport* lob *m*

VT **1** *(throw)* lancer; **he lobbed the stone into the air** il envoya la pierre en l'air; *Fam* **l. me those cigarettes** balance-moi ces cigarettes **2** *Sport (ball)* envoyer haut; *(opponent)* lober; **she lobbed the ball over my head** elle m'a lobé

VI *Sport (player)* faire un lob

lobby [ˈlɒbɪ] *(pl* **lobbies**, *pt & pp* **lobbied)** N **1** *(in hotel)* hall *m*; *Theat* foyer *m*; *(in large house, apartment block)* entrée *f* **2** *Pol (pressure group)* groupe *m* de pression, lobby *m*; *(action)* pression *f*; **the ecology l.** le lobby écologiste; **the nurses' l. for increased pay** la pression exercée par les infirmières pour obtenir une augmentation de salaire **3** *Br Pol (hall)* salle *f* des pas perdus; **division lobbies** = vestibules où passent les députés lors qu'ils se divisent pour voter

VI faire campagne; **ecologists are lobbying for the closure of the plant** les écologistes font pression pour obtenir la fermeture de la centrale; **he's being paid to l. on behalf of the dairy farmers** il est payé par les producteurs laitiers pour défendre leurs intérêts

VT *(person, parliament)* faire pression sur

►► *Br Pol* ***lobby correspondent*** journaliste *mf* parlementaire

lobbying [ˈlɒbɪɪŋ] N *(UNCOUNT) Pol* pressions *fpl*; **there has been intense l. against the bill** il y a eu de fortes pressions pour que le projet de loi soit retiré

lobbyist [ˈlɒbɪɪst] N lobbyiste *mf*, membre *m* d'un groupe de pression

lobe [ləʊb] N *Anat, Bot & Rad* lobe *m*

lobelia [ləˈbiːljə] N *Bot* lobélie *f*

lobotomize, -ise [ləˈbɒtəmaɪz] VT lobotomiser

lobotomy [ləˈbɒtəmɪ] *(pl* **lobotomies)** N lobotomie *f*, leucotomie *f*

lobster [ˈlɒbstə(r)] *(pl inv or* **lobsters)** N homard *m*; *(spiny lobster)* langouste *f*

►► ***lobster boat*** homardier *m*; *(for spiny lobster)* langoustier *m*; ***lobster thermidor*** homard *m* thermidor

local [ˈləʊkəl] ADJ **1** *(gen)* local; *(hospital, shop)* de quartier; *(inhabitants)* du quartier, du coin; **a l. woman** une femme du quartier *ou* du coin; **the l. doctor** le médecin du quartier; **l. traders** les commerces *mpl* de proximité **2** *Admin & Pol* local, communal, municipal **3** *Med (infection, pain)* localisé

N **1** *(person)* habitant(e) *m,f* (du lieu); **the locals** les gens *mpl* du pays *ou* du coin; **ask one of the locals** demande à quelqu'un du coin

2 *Br Fam (pub)* troquet *m* du coin; **it used to be our l.** c'est là qu'on allait boire un pot

3 *Am (train)* omnibus *m*; *(bus)* bus *m* local

4 *Am (union branch)* section *f* syndicale

5 *Fam (anaesthetic)* anesthésie *f* locale☐

6 *Can Tel* poste *m*; **l. 476, please** le poste 476, s'il vous plaît

7 *Am Press (item)* nouvelle *f* locale

►► *Med* ***local anaesthetic*** anesthésie *f* locale; **to give sb a l. anaesthetic** faire une anesthésie locale à qn; *Comput* ***local area network*** réseau *m* local; *Pol* ***local authorities*** autorités *fpl* locales *ou* régionales; ***local authority*** administration *f* locale; *(in town)* municipalité *f*; *Comput* ***local bus*** bus *m* local; ***local bus card*** carte *f* de bus local; *Tel* ***local call*** appel *m* local, communication *f* locale; ***local colour*** couleur *f* locale; ***local currency*** monnaie *f* locale; ***local edition*** édition *f* locale; ***local education authority*** direction *f* régionale de l'enseignement *(en Angleterre et au pays de Galles)*; ***local government*** administration *f* municipale; ***local government elections*** élections *fpl* municipales; ***local government finance*** finances *fpl* des collectivités locales; ***local government minister*** = ministre responsable des collectivités locales; ***local health authority*** services *mpl* municipaux de la santé; ***local housing department*** antenne *f* logement (de la commune); ***local labour market*** marché *m* du travail régional; ***local news*** informations *fpl* régionales; ***local paper*** journal *m* local; ***local politics*** politique *f* locale; ***local radio*** radio *f* locale; ***local radio station*** station *f* de radio locale; *Br Tel* ***local rate number*** numéro *m* à tarification locale; ***local showers*** averses *fpl* éparses; *Am Fin* ***local taxes*** impôt *m* local; ***local taxation*** impôts *mpl* locaux; ***local television*** télévision *f* locale; ***local time*** heure *f* locale; **6 a.m. l. time** 6 heures du matin heure locale; ***local train*** (train *m*) omnibus *m*

locale [ləʊ'kɑːl] **N** *(place)* endroit *m*, lieu *m*; *(scene, setting)* cadre *m*; **a rural l.** un cadre champêtre

locality [lə'kælətɪ] *(pl* **localities***)* **N 1** *(neighbourhood)* voisinage *m*, environs *mpl*; *(general area)* région *f*; **a man was seen in the l. at around 8 o'clock** un homme a été vu dans les environs vers 8 heures; **he was seen in the (general) l. of the station** on l'a vu dans le quartier de la gare **2** *(location ▸ of building, place)* lieu *m*, site *m*; *(▸ of species)* localité *f*

localize, -ise ['ləʊkəlaɪz] **VT 1** *(locate)* localiser, situer; **the source of the problem has been localized** on a réussi à localiser l'origine du problème **2** *(confine)* localiser, limiter; **they have tried to l. the effect of the strike** ils ont essayé de limiter l'effet de la grève; **to become localized** *(disease, pain)* se localiser
3 *(concentrate ▸ power, money)* concentrer
4 *(acclimatize ▸ species, plant)* acclimater
5 *(adapt ▸ software, product)* localiser

localized, -ised ['ləʊkəlaɪzd] **ADJ** localisé; **l. flooding** des inondations par endroits

locally ['ləʊkəlɪ] **ADV** localement; **she is well known l.** *(in region)* elle est très connue dans la région; *(in neighbourhood)* elle est très connue dans le quartier; **he lives l.** il vit par ici; **we shop l.** nous faisons nos courses dans le quartier; **many issues have to be decided l., not nationally** de nombreux problèmes doivent être résolus au niveau local, et non au niveau national; **l. grown potatoes/carrots** *(sign)* pommes de terre/carottes du pays; **l. manufactured goods** articles *mpl* de fabrication locale

locate [*Br* ləʊ'keɪt, *Am* 'ləʊkeɪt] **VT 1** *(find ▸ lost object, person)* retrouver; *(▸ fault, technical problem)* localiser; *(on a map ▸ place)* repérer; **the police are trying to l. possible witnesses** la police recherche des témoins éventuels; **we are trying to l. his sister** nous essayons de savoir où se trouve sa sœur; **to l. a ship** déterminer la position d'un navire (en mer); **he had hoped to l. precisely the site of Troy** il avait espéré trouver l'emplacement exact de Troie **2** *(usu passive) (situate)* situer; **to be located** se situer, être situé; **the house is conveniently located for shops and public transport** la maison est située à proximité des magasins et des transports en commun
VI 1 *Com (company, factory)* s'établir, s'implanter **2** *Am (settle)* s'installer, s'établir

location [ləʊ'keɪʃən] **N 1** *(place, site)* emplacement *m*, site *m*; **what a beautiful l. for a campus!** quel site magnifique pour un campus universitaire!; **the firm has moved to a new l.** la société a déménagé; **what is your present l.?** *(whereabouts)* où te trouves-tu en ce moment?
2 *Cin* **to be on l.** tourner en extérieur; **filmed on l.** filmé en extérieur
3 *(finding ▸ on map)* repérage *m*; *(▸ of fault, technical problem)* localisation *f*; **l. of the wreckage is proving difficult** l'endroit exact du naufrage s'avère difficile à déterminer
4 *Comput (of data)* position *f*; **memory l.** position *f* (en) mémoire
5 *Comput (of website)* adresse *f* URL
6 *SAfr (township)* township *m*; *(reservation)* réserve *f* (noire)
▸▸ *Cin* ***location filming*** tournage *m* en extérieur; *Cin* ***location manager*** régisseur *m* d'extérieurs; *Cin* ***location marks*** *(in studio)* points *mpl* de repère au sol; *Cin* ***location scout*** = personne chargée des repérages; *Cin* ***location shot*** plan *m* en extérieur

> Note that the French word **location** is a false friend and is never a translation for the English word **location**. It means **renting**.

locative ['lɒkətɪv] *Gram* **N** locatif *m*
ADJ locatif

loch [lɒχ] **N** *Scot* loch *m*, lac *m*; **sea l.** bras *m* de mer, fjord *m*
▸▸ ***Loch Lomond*** le loch Lomond; ***Loch Ness*** le loch Ness; ***the Loch Ness monster*** le monstre du loch Ness

LOCK [lɒk]

> **N**
> • serrure **1** • écluse **2**
> • prise **3** • braquage **4**
> • verrou **5** • verrouillage **6**
> • boucle **8** • mèche **8**
> **VT**
> • fermer à clé **1** • verrouiller **1, 5**
> • enfermer **2** • serrer **3**
> • bloquer **4**
> **VI**
> • (se) fermer à clef **1** • se joindre **2**
> • se bloquer **3**

N 1 *(on door, drawer etc)* serrure *f*; **under l. and key** *(object)* sous clé; *(person)* sous les verrous
2 *(on canal)* écluse *f*
3 *(grip ▸ gen)* prise *f*; *(▸ in wrestling)* clé *f*, prise *f*
4 *Br Aut* (rayon *m* de) braquage *m*; **on full l.** braqué à fond
5 *Tech (device ▸ gen)* verrou *m*; *(▸ on gun)* percuteur *m*
6 *Comput* verrouillage *m*; **shift** *or* **caps l.** touche *f* de verrouillage majuscule
7 *Sport (in rugby)* **l. (forward)** deuxième ligne *m*
8 *(curl)* boucle *f*; *(stray strand)* mèche *f*
9 *(idioms)* **l., stock and barrel** en entier; **she bought the company l., stock and barrel** elle a acheté la société en bloc; **his essay was lifted l., stock and barrel from a textbook** il a copié sa rédaction telle quelle *ou* mot pour mot dans un manuel scolaire; **the family has moved l., stock and barrel to Canada** la famille est partie avec armes et bagages s'installer au Canada
VT 1 *(door, drawer, room etc ▸ with key)* fermer à clé; *(▸ with bolt)* verrouiller; **check that all the doors and windows are locked** vérifiez que toutes les portes et les fenêtres sont bien fermées
2 *(valuables, person)* enfermer; **l. all these papers in the safe** enfermez tous ces papiers dans le coffre-fort; *Fig* **they were locked into the agreement** ils étaient tenus par l'accord
3 *(hold tightly)* serrer; **they were locked in a passionate embrace** ils étaient unis *ou* enlacés dans une étreinte passionnée; **the unions were locked in a dispute with the management** les syndicats étaient aux prises avec la direction; **to be locked in combat** être engagé dans un combat; *Fig* être aux prises; **to l. horns** *(stags)* s'entremêler les bois; *Fig* avoir une prise de bec
4 *(device, wheels, brakes)* bloquer
5 *Comput (file, disk, keyboard)* verrouiller
VI 1 *(door, drawer, car etc)* (se) fermer à clé; **the door locks on the inside** la porte se ferme de l'intérieur; **the safe locks automatically** le coffre-fort se verrouille automatiquement
2 *(engage)* se joindre; **push the lever back until it locks into place** pousse le levier jusqu'à ce qu'il s'enclenche
3 *(wheels, brakes, nut)* se bloquer
• **locks NPL** *Literary* chevelure *f*
▸▸ ***lock chamber*** *(on canal)* sas *m* (d'écluse); ***lock gate*** porte *f* d'écluse; ***lock keeper*** éclusier(ère) *m,f*; *Br Aut* ***lock ring*** jonc *m* d'arrêt; ***lock turns*** tours *mpl* de volant
▸ **lock in VT SEP 1** *(in building, room)* enfermer; **he locked himself in** il s'est enfermé (à l'intérieur) **2 to be locked in** *(to pension scheme)* ne pas avoir la possibilité de changer; *(to contract)* être lié
▸ **lock off VT SEP** *Typ & Comptr* débloquer; *(bad sector)* interdire l'accès à; **this key locks the caps on and off** cette touche bloque et débloque les majuscules
▸ **lock on VT SEP** *Typ & Comptr* bloquer, verrouiller; **l. the caps on before you start typing** bloque les majuscules avant de commencer à taper
▸ **lock out VT SEP 1** *(accidentally)* enfermer dehors; *(deliberately)* laisser dehors; **her father threatened to l. her out if she was late home** son père a menacé de la laisser à la porte *ou* dehors si elle rentrait en retard; **I've locked myself out** j'ai fermé la porte en laissant les clés à l'intérieur, je me suis enfermé dehors **2** *Ind (workers)* lock-outer
▸ **lock up VT SEP 1** *(house, shop)* fermer à clef
2 *(valuables)* mettre sous clef; *(criminal)* incarcérer, mettre sous les verrous; **he should be locked up!** il faudrait l'enfermer!
3 *Fin (capital)* immobiliser
4 *Typ (type)* caler; *(forme)* serrer
VI fermer à clef; **it's time to l. up** c'est l'heure de fermer

locked-in syndrome [lɒkt-] **N** *Med* locked-in syndrome *m*, syndrome *m* d'enfermement

locker ['lɒkə(r)] **N 1** *(for luggage, in school)* casier *m*; *Naut* coffre *m*; *Aviat* **overhead l.** coffre *m* à bagages **2** *Am (freezer)* congélateur *m*
▸▸ *Am* ***locker room*** vestiaire *m (avec casiers)*

locket ['lɒkɪt] **N** médaillon *m*

lock-in N *Br* **there was a l. at the pub last night** hier soir, le patron du pub nous a laissés boire après l'heure normale de fermeture

locking ['lɒkɪŋ] **ADJ** *(door, briefcase)* à serrure, qui ferme à clef
▸▸ ***locking mechanism*** mécanisme *m* de verrouillage; ***locking up*** mise *f* sous clef; *(of house, room)* fermeture *f*; *Fin (of capital)* immobilisation *f*

lockjaw ['lɒkdʒɔː] **N** tétanos *m*; **to have l.** avoir le tétanos

locknut ['lɒknʌt] **N** *(supplementary nut)* contre-écrou *m*; *(self-locking)* écrou *m* autobloquant

lockout ['lɒkaʊt] **N** *(of workers)* lock-out *m inv*

locksmith ['lɒksmɪθ] **N** serrurier *m*

lock-to-lock ADV *Aut* de butée à butée

lockup ['lɒkʌp] **N 1** *Am (jail)* prison *f*, *(cell)* cellule *f* **2** *Br (for storage)* remise *f*, *(garage)* garage *m* **3** *(act of locking up)* fermeture *f*

loco ['ləʊkəʊ] *(pl* **locos***)* **N** *(train)* loco *f*
ADJ 1 *Am Fam (crazy)* dingue, cinglé **2** *Com* loco *(inv)*
ADV *Com* loco; **the prices are l. Hull** les prix incluent le transport jusqu'à Hull

locomotion [ˌləʊkə'məʊʃən] **N** locomotion *f*

locomotive [ˌləʊkə'məʊtɪv] **N** locomotive *f*
ADJ locomotif; *Anat* locomoteur
▸▸ ***locomotive works*** usine *f* de construction de machines

locum ['ləʊkəm] **N** *Br* remplaçant(e) *m,f (de prêtre, de médecin)*; **to take a l. job** faire un remplacement, prendre un emploi de remplaçant; **she's working as a l. in a hospital in London** elle fait un remplacement dans un hôpital de Londres
▸▸ *Br Formal* ***locum tenens*** remplaçant(e) *m,f (de prêtre, de médecin)*

locus ['ləʊkəs] *(pl* **loci** [-saɪ, -kaɪ]*)* **N 1** *Formal (place)* lieu *m*; *Law* lieux *mpl* **2** *Math* lieu *m* (géométrique) **3** *Biol (of gene)* locus *m*

locust ['ləʊkəst] **N 1** *(insect)* locuste *f*, criquet *m* migrateur **2** *Bot (false acacia)* robinier *m*, faux acacia *m*; *(carob tree)* caroubier *m*
▸▸ ***locust bean*** caroube *f*; *Bot* ***locust tree*** *(false acacia)* robinier *m*, faux acacia *m*; *(carob tree)* caroubier *m*

locution [lə'kjuːʃən] **N** *Formal Ling* **1** *(phrase)* locution *f* **2** *(style)* style *m*, phraséologie *f*, *(manner of speech)* élocution *f*

lode [ləʊd] **N** *(vein ▸ of metallic ore)* veine *f*; *(▸ of gold, copper, silver)* filon *m*

lodestar ['ləʊdstɑː(r)] **N** (étoile *f*) Polaire *f*; *Fig* guide *m*, point *m* de repère

lodestone ['ləʊdstəʊn] N *Miner* pierre *f* à aimant, magnétite *f*; *Fig* aimant *m*

lodge [lɒdʒ] N **1** *(cabin ▸ for hunters)* pavillon *m*; *(▸ for skiers)* chalet *m*
2 *Br (on country estate)* maison *f* du gardien; *(of porter)* loge *f*; **shooting l.** pavillon *m* de chasse
3 *Am (in park, resort)* bâtiment *m* central
4 *(Masonic)* loge *f*
5 *(hotel)* hôtel *m*, relais *m*
6 *(of beavers)* hutte *f*
7 *(of Native Americans)* hutte *f*, wigwam *m*
VT **1** *(house)* héberger, loger; **the hotel can l. 65 people** l'hôtel peut accueillir 65 personnes
2 *(stick, embed)* mettre, placer; **a fish bone had lodged itself in his throat** il s'était coincé une arête dans le gosier
3 *Br (make, file ▸ claim)* déposer; **to l. a complaint** porter plainte; *Law* **to l. an accusation against sb** porter plainte contre qn; **to l. an appeal** interjeter appel, faire appel
4 *(deposit for safekeeping)* consigner, déposer, mettre en sûreté; **to l. securities with a bank** déposer des titres dans une banque
VI **1** *(stay)* loger, être logé; **he is lodging at Mrs Smith's** *or* **with Mrs Smith** il loge chez Mme Smith; *(with board)* il est en pension chez Mme Smith **2** *(stick, become embedded)* se loger; **a fishbone lodged in his throat** il s'est coincé une arête dans le gosier; **a bullet lodged close to his spine** il a reçu une balle qui est allée se loger près de la colonne vertébrale
▸▸ ***lodge keeper*** portier *m*; ***lodge meeting*** *(Masonic)* tenue *f*

lodger ['lɒdʒə(r)] N locataire *mf*; *(with board)* pensionnaire *mf*; **to take (in) lodgers** louer des chambres; *(provide meals too)* prendre des pensionnaires

lodging ['lɒdʒɪŋ] N logement *m*; **they offered the family free l.** ils ont offert d'héberger gratuitement la famille; **full board and l.** pension *f* complète
• **lodgings** NPL *Br* chambre *f* meublée *(chez un particulier)*; **most of the students live in lodgings** la plupart des étudiants habitent dans des chambres meublées
▸▸ ***lodging house*** garni *m*

loft [lɒft] N **1** *(attic)* grenier *m*
2 *(elevated space ▸ in church)* tribune *f*, galerie *f*
3 *(warehouse apartment)* loft *m*
4 *(for pigeons)* pigeonnier *m*
5 *(of golf club)* angle *m* de la face, ouverture *m*
VT *Sport (hit)* envoyer très haut
▸▸ ***loft conversion*** combles *mpl* aménagés, loft *m*; **they spent a lot of money on the l. conversion** ils ont dépensé beaucoup d'argent pour aménager les combles; ***loft ladder*** échelle *f* escamotable *(permettant d'accéder au grenier)*

loftily ['lɒftɪlɪ] ADV avec mépris, dédaigneusement

loftiness ['lɒftɪnɪs] N **1** *(of mountain, tree, building)* hauteur *f* **2** *Pej (of person, manner)* arrogance *f*, hauteur *f*

lofty ['lɒftɪ] *(compar* **loftier**, *superl* **loftiest)** ADJ **1** *(mountain, tree, building)* haut, élevé; **the l. peaks of the Alps** les hauts sommets des Alpes; **a l. interior** des pièces hautes (de plafond)
2 *Pej (person, manner)* hautain, arrogant
3 *(exalted ▸ in spirit)* noble, élevé; *(▸ in rank, position)* éminent
4 *(elevated ▸ style, prose)* relevé, soutenu

log¹ [lɒg] *(pt & pp* **logged**, *cont* **logging)** N **1** *(for firewood)* bûche *f*; *(for building)* rondin *m*
2 *(record)* journal *m*, registre *m*; *Comput (file)* fichier *m* compte-rendu; *Naut* journal *m*, livre *m* de bord; *Aviat* carnet *m* de vol; *(lorry driver's)* carnet *m* de route; **keep a l. of all phone calls** notez tous les appels téléphoniques
3 *Naut (apparatus)* loch *m*
4 *(cake)* **Yuletide** *or* **Christmas l.** bûche *f* de Noël
VT **1** *(information ▸ on paper)* consigner, inscrire; *(▸ in computer memory)* entrer **2** *(speed, distance, time)* **he has logged 2,000 hours' flying time** il a 2000 heures de vol à son actif, il totalise 2000 heures de vol; **the ship logged 15 knots** le navire filait 15 nœuds **3** *(tree)* tronçonner; *(forest)* mettre en coupe
VI *Am (company)* exploiter une forêt; *(person)* travailler comme bûcheron
▸▸ ***log cabin*** cabane *f* en rondins; *Comput* ***log file*** fichier *m* compte-rendu; ***log fire*** feu *m* de bois; ***log running*** flottage *m* du bois; *Math* ***log tables*** tables *fpl* de logarithmes; ***log transporter*** fardier *m*

log² [lɒg] N *Math (abbr* **logarithm)** log *m*

▸**log in** *Comput* VT SEP *(user name, password)* entrer, introduire
VI *(user)* entrer, ouvrir une session

▸**log off** *Comput* VT SEP faire sortir
VI *(user)* sortir, terminer *ou* clore une session

▸**log on** *Comput* VT SEP faire entrer
VI *(user)* entrer, ouvrir une session; *(to remote system)* entrer en communication; **to l. on to a system** se connecter à un système; **to l. on to a database** entrer dans une base de données

▸**log out** VI *Comput (user)* sortir, se déconnecter

loganberry ['ləʊgənbərɪ] *(pl* **loganberries)** N *(plant)* framboisier *m* (hybride); *(fruit)* ronce-framboise *f*, mûre-framboise *f*

logarithm ['lɒgərɪðəm] N logarithme *m*

logarithmic [ˌlɒgə'rɪðmɪk] ADJ logarithmique
▸▸ ***logarithmic table*** table *f* des logarithmes

logbook ['lɒgbʊk] N **1** *(record)* journal *m*, registre *m*; *Naut* journal *m ou* livre *m* de bord; *Aviat* carnet *m* de vol; *(of machine)* journal *m* de travail **2** *Br Aut* carte *f* grise

logger ['lɒgə(r)] N **1** *Am (lumberjack)* bûcheron *m* **2** *Br (tractor)* tracteur *m* forestier

loggerheads ['lɒgəhedz] NPL **to be at l. with sb (about sth)** avoir un différend avec qn (au sujet de qch); **they were constantly at l.** ils se disputaient tout le temps; **his views were at l. with...** ses opinions étaient en contradiction avec…

loggia ['ləʊdʒə] *(pl* **loggias** *or* **loggie** [-dʒe]) N loggia *f*; *Theat* galerie *f*

logging ['lɒgɪŋ] N **1** *(of details, events)* inscription *f* dans un journal; *(of order) & Comput* enregistrement *m* **2** *(felling timber etc)* exploitation *f* forestière; **the l. of mahogany** l'abattage *m* de l'acajou
▸▸ ***logging camp*** camp *m* forestier; ***logging company*** société *f* d'exploitation forestière

logic ['lɒdʒɪk] N *(gen) & Comput* logique *f*; *(reasoning)* raisonnement *m*; **I don't see the l. of it** je ne vois pas la logique (dans tout cela); **if you follow my l.** si tu suis mon raisonnement
▸▸ *Comput* ***logic bomb*** bombe *f* logique *ou* à retardement; ***logic card*** carte *f* logique; ***logic chip*** puce *f* logique; ***logic circuit*** circuit *m* logique; ***logic gate*** porte *f* logique; ***logic operator*** opérateur *m* logique

logical ['lɒdʒɪkəl] ADJ logique; **it's a l. impossibility** c'est logiquement impossible; **he is incapable of l. argument** il est incapable d'avoir un raisonnement logique
▸▸ *Comput* ***logical file*** fichier *m* logique; *Comput* ***logical operator*** opérateur *m* logique; *Phil* ***logical positivism*** positivisme *m* logique, néopositivisme *m*; ***logical positivist*** logicopositiviste *mf*

logically ['lɒdʒɪkəlɪ] ADV logiquement; **if you think about it l.** si on y réfléchit bien

logic-chopper N ergoteur(euse) *m,f*

logic-chopping N ergotage *m*

login ['lɒgɪn] N *Comput* ouverture *f* de session
▸▸ ***login name*** nom *m* d'utilisateur *ou* de login

logistic [lɒ'dʒɪstɪk], **logistical** [lɒ'dʒɪstɪkəl] ADJ logistique; **a l. problem** un problème de logistique; **it's a l. nightmare** c'est un casse-tête du point de vue de la logistique
▸▸ ***logistic support*** soutien *m* logistique

logistics [lə'dʒɪstɪks] NPL logistique *f*; **the l. of the situation** les données logistiques de la situation

logo ['ləʊgəʊ] *(pl* **logos)** N logo *m*

logoff ['lɒgɒf] N *Comput* fin *f* de session

logon ['lɒgɒn] N *Comput* ouverture *f* de session

logroll ['lɒgrəʊl] *Am Pej Pol* VT *(bill, legislation)* = faire voter grâce à des échanges de faveurs
VI user d'échanges de faveurs

logrolling ['lɒgrəʊlɪŋ] N **1** *(sport)* = sport pratiqué par les bûcherons, qui consiste à se maintenir debout sur un tronc d'arbre flottant que l'on fait tourner sous ses pieds, *Can* concours *m* de draveurs **2** *Am Pej Pol* échange *m* de faveurs *(accord entre hommes politiques selon lequel on se rend mutuellement des services)*

logwood ['lɒgwʊd] N *(wood)* campêche *m*, bois *m* de campêche; *(tree)* campêche *m*

loin [lɔɪn] N *Culin (of pork)* longe *f*, échine *f*, filet *m*; *(of beef)* aloyau *m*; *(of veal)* longe *f*; *(of lamb)* carré *m*
• **loins** NPL *Anat* reins *mpl*; *Euph (genitals)* parties *fpl*
▸▸ ***loin chop*** côtes *fpl* premières

loincloth ['lɔɪnklɒθ] N pagne *m*

loiter ['lɔɪtə(r)] VI **1** *(hang about)* traîner; *(lurk)* rôder; **there was someone loitering in the car park** il y avait quelqu'un qui rôdait dans le parking; **no loitering** *(sign)* zone sous surveillance *(où il est interdit de s'attarder)*; **to l. with intent** *Law* rôder d'une manière suspecte; *Fig Hum* rôder **2** *(dawdle)* traîner; *(lag behind)* traîner (en route)

loitering ['lɔɪtərɪŋ] N *Law* **l. with intent** = délit qui consiste à rôder dans le but de commettre un méfait

LOL *Comput & Tel (written abbr* **laughing out loud)** MDR

loll [lɒl] VI **1** *(lounge)* se prélasser; **he was lolling against the wall** il était nonchalamment appuyé contre le mur **2** *(head)* tomber en avant; *(tongue)* pendre

▸**loll about, loll around** VI *(in grass, armchair etc)* se prélasser; **I just lolled about** *or* **around all day** j'ai paressé toute la journée

lollipop ['lɒlɪpɒp] N **1** *(sweet)* sucette *f* **2** *Br (ice lolly)* Esquimau® *m*, sucette *f* glacée
▸▸ *Br Fam* ***lollipop lady*** = femme chargée d'aider les enfants à traverser la rue; *Br Fam* ***lollipop man*** = homme chargé d'aider les enfants à traverser la rue

lollop ['lɒləp] VI *(person)* marcher lourdement; *(animal)* galoper; **the rabbit lolloped off** le lapin s'éloigna en bondissant

lolly ['lɒlɪ] *(pl* **lollies)** N **1** *Br Fam (on stick)* sucette *f* **2** *Br Fam (money)* fric *m*, pognon *m* **3** *Austr & NZ Fam (sweet)* bonbon *m*

London ['lʌndən] N Londres
COMP *(museums, bus, taxi)* londonien; *(life)* à Londres; *(street)* de Londres
▸▸ ***London Bridge*** = pont construit sur la Tamise en 1968 pour remplacer l'ancien pont, qui fut vendu et remonté dans l'Arizona; ***the London Eye*** = la grande roue construite à Londres pour le nouveau millénaire; *Fin* ***London Inter-Bank Offer Rate*** = taux interbancaire offert à Londres; *Fin* ***the London International Financial Futures Exchange*** = marché à terme britannique d'instruments financiers, MATIF *m*; *Bot* ***London pride*** saxifrage *f* à feuilles en coin, mignonnette *f*; *Univ* ***London School of Economics*** = grande école de sciences économiques et politiques à Londres; *St Exch* ***the London Stock Exchange*** = la Bourse de Londres; *Br* ***London weighting*** = indemnité de vie chère venant compléter certains salaires londoniens

> **THE LONDON EYE**
> Le London Eye est une grande roue (135 m de haut) équipée de cabines d'où les passagers peuvent observer tout Londres. Il fut achevé à la fin de 1999 pour fêter le nouveau millénaire et se trouve près de Westminster sur la rive Sud de la Tamise, qui est une zone qui a fait l'objet d'importantes rénovations au cours de ces dernières années. Le London Eye est devenu un des symboles du Londres moderne.

Londoner ['lʌndənə(r)] N Londonien(enne) *m,f*

lone [ləʊn] ADJ *(gunman, rider, stag)* solitaire; *(isolated ▸ house)* isolé; *(single, unique)* unique, seul; **a l. fishing boat on the horizon** un seul bateau de pêche à l'horizon
▸▸ ***lone parent*** parent *m* unique; *Fig* ***lone wolf*** solitaire *mf*; **to be a bit of a l. wolf** être un peu solitaire

loneliness ['ləʊnlɪnɪs] N *(of person)* solitude *f*, isolement *m*; *(of place)* isolement *m*

lonely ['ləʊnlɪ] *(compar* **lonelier**, *superl* **loneliest)** ADJ **1** *(sad ▸ person)* seul; *(▸ life)* solitaire; **to be**

or **to feel l.** se sentir seul; **a l. figure** une silhouette; *Fig (politician etc)* une figure isolée; **the house seems l. without you** la maison paraît vide sans toi; **the loneliest hour of the day** l'heure de la journée où l'on se sent le plus seul **2** *(unfrequented ▸ spot, farmhouse)* isolé; *(▸ street)* peu fréquenté, vide

▸▸ ***lonely hearts club*** club *m* de rencontres; ***lonely hearts column*** rubrique *f* rencontres *(des petites annonces)*

loner ['ləʊnə(r)] **N** *Fam (person)* solitaire□ *mf*; **he's a bit of a l.** il est un peu sauvage *ou* farouche□

lonesome ['ləʊnsəm] **ADJ** *Am* solitaire, seul; **to feel l.** se sentir seul

N on one's l. tout seul

LONG [lɒŋ] *(compar* **longer** ['lɒŋgə(r)], *superl* **longest** ['lɒŋgɪst]) **ADJ 1** *(in size)* long (longue); **how l. is the pool?** quelle est la longueur de la piscine?, la piscine fait combien de long?; **the pool's 33 metres l.** la piscine fait 33 mètres de long; **the article is 80 pages l.** l'article fait 80 pages; **is it a l. way (away)?** est-ce loin (d'ici)?; **it's a l. way to the beach** la plage est loin; **to take the l. way round** prendre le chemin le plus long; **the best by a l. way** de loin le meilleur; **to get** *or* **grow longer** *(shadows)* s'allonger; *(hair, beard)* pousser; **l. in the leg** aux longues jambes; **a l. face** un visage allongé; *Fig* **to have** *or* **pull a l. face** faire la tête, faire une tête de six pieds de long

2 *(in time ▸ pause, speech, separation)* long (longue); **how l. will the flight be/was the meeting?** combien de temps durera le vol/a duré la réunion?; **the film is three hours l.** le film dure trois heures; **her five-year-l. battle with the authorities** sa lutte de cinq années contre les autorités; **to have a l. memory** avoir une bonne mémoire; **to have a l. talk with sb** parler longuement avec qn; **to get longer** *(days, intervals)* devenir plus long; **they want longer holidays** ils veulent des vacances plus longues; **they took a l. look at the view** ils restèrent longtemps à regarder la vue qui s'offrait à eux; **it was a l. two months** ces deux mois ont été longs; **I've had a l. day** j'ai eu une journée bien remplie; **in the l. term** à long terme; **it will take a l. time** cela prendra longtemps, ce sera long; **a l. time ago** il y a (bien) longtemps; **it's a l. time since I was (last) in Paris** ça fait longtemps que je ne suis pas allé à Paris; **I've been wanting to go for a l. time** ça fait longtemps que j'ai envie d'y aller; **I've known her (for) a l. time** *or* **while** je la connais depuis longtemps, cela fait longtemps que je la connais; **it was a l. haul** *(journey)* le voyage a été long; *(task, recovery)* c'était un travail de longue haleine; **at l. last!** enfin!

3 *Gram (vowel, syllable)* long (longue)

4 *St Exch* **they're l. on copper, they've taken a l. position on copper** ils ont investi dans le cuivre

5 *Fam (in tennis)* **that serve was l.** ce service était trop long

6 *(idiom)* **his speeches are l. on rhetoric but short on substance** ce n'est pas la rhétorique qui manque dans ses discours, c'est la substance

N 1 *Gram (vowel, syllable)* longue *f*

2 *Fin (bill)* effet *m* à longue échéance

3 *(idioms) Fam* **the l. and the short of it is that I got fired** enfin bref, j'ai été viré; **that's the l. and the short of it!** un point c'est tout!

ADV 1 *(a long time)* longtemps; **they live longer than humans** ils vivent plus longtemps que les êtres humains; **he won't keep you l./much longer** il ne vous gardera pas longtemps/beaucoup plus longtemps; **I haven't been here l.** ça ne fait pas longtemps que je suis là; **how l. will he be/was he in jail?** (pendant) combien de temps restera-t-il/est-il resté en prison?; **how l. has he been in jail?** ça fait combien de temps qu'il est en prison?, depuis combien de temps est-il en prison?; **how l. is it since we last visited them?** quand sommes-nous allés les voir pour la dernière fois?; **it happened l. ago/not l. ago** cela s'est passé il y a longtemps/il n'y a pas longtemps; **as l. ago as 1937** déjà en 1937; **l. before you were born** bien avant que tu sois né; **not l. before/after their divorce** peu avant/après leur divorce; **l. after** *or* **afterwards, when these events were mostly forgotten...** bien après, alors que ces évènements étaient presque complètement oubliés...; **a law which had come into force not l. since** une loi qui était entrée en vigueur depuis peu; **to look at sb/sth l. and hard** fixer qn/qch longuement; *Fig* **to look at sth l. and hard** se pencher longuement sur qch; **I've thought l. and hard about this** j'y ai longuement réfléchi; **we talked l. into the night** nous avons parlé jusque tard dans la nuit

2 *(with "be", "take")* **will you be l.?** tu en as pour longtemps?; **I won't be l.** je n'en ai pas pour longtemps; **please wait, she won't be l.** attendez, s'il vous plaît, elle ne va pas tarder; **are you going to be much longer?** tu en as encore pour longtemps?; **how much longer will he be?** *(when will he be ready?)* il en a encore pour longtemps?; *(when will he arrive?)* dans combien de temps sera-t-il là?; **don't be** *or* **take too l.** fais vite; **it wasn't l. before he realized, it didn't take l. for him to realize** il n'a pas mis longtemps à s'en rendre compte, il s'en est vite rendu compte; **he took** *or* **it took him so l. to make up his mind...** il a mis si longtemps à se décider..., il lui a fallu tellement de temps pour se décider...; **how l. does it take to get there?** combien de temps faut-il pour y aller?; **this won't take l.** ça va être vite fait; **this won't take longer than five minutes** ça sera fait en moins de cinq minutes

3 *(in wishes, toasts)* **l. may our partnership continue!** à notre collaboration!; **l. live the Queen!** vive la reine!

4 *(for a long time)* depuis longtemps; **it has l. been known that...** on sait depuis longtemps que...; **the longest-running TV series** le feuilleton télévisé qui existe depuis le plus longtemps

5 *(throughout)* **all day/week l.** toute la journée/la semaine

6 *St Exch* **to go l.** acheter à la hausse, prendre une position longue; **to buy l.** acheter à long terme

7 *Fam (idiom)* **so l.!** salut!, à bientôt!□

VI l. for him il me manque énormément; **she was longing for a letter from you** elle attendait impatiemment que vous lui écriviez; **we were longing for a cup of tea** nous avions très envie d'une tasse de thé; **to l.** *or* **to be longing to do sth** être impatient *ou* avoir hâte de faire qch; **he's longing to go back to Italy** il meurt d'envie de retourner en Italie; **I've been longing to meet you for years** cela fait des années que je souhaite faire votre connaissance

• **longs NPL** *St Exch* titres *mpl* longs, obligations *fpl* longues

• **as long as, so long as CONJ 1** *(during the time that)* aussi longtemps que, tant que; **as l. as he's in power, there will be no hope** tant qu'il sera au pouvoir, il n'y aura aucun espoir; **I'll never forget that day for as l. as I live** jamais de ma vie je n'oublierai ce jour

2 *(providing)* à condition que, pourvu que; **you can have it as l. as you give me it back** vous pouvez le prendre à condition que *ou* pourvu que vous me le rendiez; **I'll do it as l. as I get paid for it** je le ferai à condition d'être payé; **as l. as you're happy** du moment que tu es heureux

3 *Am Fam (seeing that)* puisque□; **as l. as you're going to the post office get me some stamps** puisque tu vas à la poste, achète-moi des timbres

• **before long ADV** *(soon)* dans peu de temps, sous peu; *(soon afterwards)* peu (de temps) après; **she'll be back before l.** elle sera de retour dans peu de temps *ou* sous peu; **before l., everything had returned to normal** tout était rapidement rentré dans l'ordre

• **for long ADV** longtemps; **he's still in charge here, but not for l.** c'est encore lui qui s'en occupe, mais plus pour longtemps

• **no longer ADV** ne... plus; **not any longer** plus maintenant; **I can't wait any longer** je ne peux pas attendre plus longtemps, je ne peux plus attendre; **they used to live there, but not any longer** ils habitaient là autrefois, mais plus maintenant

▸▸ ***long black*** grand café *m* noir; *Fin* ***long credit*** crédit *m* à long terme; *Math* ***long division*** division *f* posée; **to do long division/a long division** faire des divisions/une division *(à la main)*; ***long dress*** *(for evening wear)* robe *f* longue; ***long drink*** long drink *m*; *(non-alcoholic)* = grand verre de jus de fruits, de limonade etc; ***Long Island*** Long Island; **on L. Island** à Long Island; *Fam* ***long johns*** caleçon *m* long□, caleçons *mpl* longs□; *Sport* ***long jump*** saut *m* en longueur; *Sport* ***long jumper*** sauteur(euse) *m,f* en longueur; *Phot* ***long lens*** téléobjectif *m*; *Hist* ***the Long March*** la Longue Marche; *Am* ***long pants*** pantalon *m* long; ***the Long Parliament*** le Long Parlement, = Parlement convoqué par Charles Ier en 1640, renvoyé par Cromwell en 1653 et dissous en 1660; *St Exch* ***long position*** position *f* acheteur *ou* longue; **to take a l. position** acheter à la hausse, prendre une position longue; ***long shot*** *(competitor, racehorse etc)* outsider *m*; *(bet)* pari *m* risqué; *Cin* plan *m* éloigné; *Fig* entreprise *f* hasardeuse; **it's a bit of a l. shot** il y a peu de chances pour que cela réussisse; **I haven't finished, not by a l. shot** je n'ai pas fini, loin de là; *Mktg* ***long tail*** longue traîne *f*; *Cin & TV* ***long take*** prise *f* longue; *Tech* ***long ton*** tonne *f* anglaise; ***long trousers*** pantalon *m* long; *Univ* ***long vacation*** grandes vacances *fpl*, vacances *fpl* d'été; ***long view*** prévisions *fpl* à long terme; **to take the l. view** envisager les choses à long terme; *Rad* ***long wave*** grandes ondes *fpl*; **on l. wave** sur les grandes ondes; ***long weekend*** week-end *m* prolongé; **to take a l. weekend** prendre un week-end prolongé

long-awaited [-ə'weɪtɪd] **ADJ** très attendu

longboard ['lɒŋbɔːd] **N** *(surfboard)* longboard *m*; *(skateboard)* longskate *m*

longboarding ['lɒŋbɔːdɪŋ] **N** *(surfboarding)* longboard *m*; *(skateboarding)* longskate *m*

longboat ['lɒŋbəʊt] **N** *Naut* chaloupe *f*; *(of Vikings)* drakkar *m*

longbow ['lɒŋbəʊ] **N** arc *m*

long-dated ADJ *St Exch* à longue échéance

▸▸ ***long-dated securities*** titres *mpl* longs, obligations *fpl* longues

long-distance ADJ *Tel* longue distance *(inv)*; **is it l.?** est-ce que c'est un appel longue distance?

ADV to telephone l. faire un appel longue distance; **I'm phoning l. from Aberdeen** c'est un appel interurbain, j'appelle d'Aberdeen

▸▸ ***long-distance call*** communication *f* hors circonscription; ***long-distance footpath*** sentier *m* de grande randonnée; *Br* ***long-distance lorry driver*** conducteur(trice) *m,f* de poids lourd, *Fam* routier *m*; *Sport* ***long-distance race*** course *f* de fond; *Sport* ***long-distance runner*** coureur (euse) *m,f* de fond

long-drawn-out ADJ *(sigh)* prolongé; *(story, explanation)* interminable

long-established ADJ *(tradition)* qui existe depuis longtemps

longevity [lɒn'dʒevətɪ] **N** longévité *f*

long-forgotten ADJ oublié depuis longtemps; **a l. tradition** une tradition tombée en désuétude

longhair ['lɒŋheə(r)] *Am* **N** *Fam* **1** *Old-fashioned (intellectual)* intello *mf* **2** *(hippie)* chevelu *m*

ADJ 1 *(cat, dog)* à poil(s) long(s) **2** *Fam Old-fashioned (for intellectuals)* pour les intellos

▸▸ *Fam* ***longhair music*** musique *f* classique□

longhaired ['lɒŋheəd] **ADJ 1** *(cat, dog)* à poil(s) long(s); *(person)* aux cheveux longs **2** *Am Fam Old-fashioned (for intellectuals)* pour les intellos

longhand ['lɒŋhænd] **N** écriture *f* courante; **in l.** *(not on a typewriter)* à la main; *(not in shorthand)* en entier

long-haul ADJ *(aircraft, flight)* long-courrier

▸▸ ***long-haul carrier*** long-courrier *m*

longing ['lɒŋɪŋ] **N** envie *f*, désir *m*; **I had a l. to see the sea** j'avais très envie de voir la mer; **the sight of her filled him with l.** en la voyant le désir s'empara de lui

ADJ d'envie, de désir; **a l. look** un regard plein d'envie

longingly ['lɒŋɪŋlɪ] **ADV** *(with desire)* avec désir *ou* envie; *(with regret)* avec regret; **to look l. at sth** couver qch des yeux; **to think l. of the past** penser au passé avec nostalgie

longish ['lɒŋɪʃ] ADJ assez long (longue)

longitude ['lɒndʒɪtju:d] N longitude *f*; **at a l. of 60° east** par 60° de longitude est

longitudinal [ˌlɒndʒɪ'tju:dɪnəl] ADJ longitudinal
▸▸ ***longitudinal section*** coupe *f* longitudinale; *Phys* ***longitudinal wave*** onde *f* longitudinale

longitudinally [ˌlɒndʒɪ'tju:dɪnəlɪ] ADV longitudinalement

long-legged ADJ *(person)* aux jambes longues; *(animal)* aux pattes longues

long-life ADJ *(milk, juice)* longue conservation *(inv)*; *(lightbulb, battery)* longue durée *(inv)*

long-lived [-lɪvd] ADJ *(person, animal, plant)* qui vit longtemps; *(family, species)* d'une grande longévité; *(friendship, theory)* durable; *(prejudice)* tenace, qui a la vie dure

long-lost ADJ *(manuscript, painting etc)* perdu depuis longtemps; **she has been reunited with her l. brother** elle a retrouvé son frère dont elle avait été séparée depuis très longtemps; **he welcomed me like a l. friend** il m'a accueilli comme si on était des amis qui ne s'étaient pas vus depuis des années

long-playing record N 33 tours *m inv*, microsillon *m*

long-range ADJ **1** *(weapon)* à longue portée; *(vehicle, aircraft)* à long rayon d'action **2** *(plan)* à long terme
▸▸ *Met* ***long-range forecast*** prévisions *fpl* météorologiques à long terme

long-running ADJ *(film, play)* qui tient l'affiche; *(TV or radio programme)* qui est diffusé depuis longtemps

long-service man N *Mil* engagé *m* à long terme

longship ['lɒŋʃɪp] N drakkar *m*

longshoreman ['lɒŋʃɔ:mən] (*pl* **longshoremen** [-mən]) N *Am* docker *m*

longsighted [ˌlɒŋ'saɪtɪd] ADJ **1** *Opt* hypermétrope; *(in old age)* presbyte **2** *Fig (policy, decision)* prévoyant

longsightedness [ˌlɒŋ'saɪtɪdnɪs] N **1** *Opt* hypermétropie *f*; *(in old age)* presbytie *f* **2** *Fig (of policy, decision)* prévoyance *f*, discernement *m*

long-sleeved ADJ à manches longues

long-standing ADJ de longue date
▸▸ *Fin* ***long-standing accounts*** vieux comptes *mpl*

long-stay ADJ
▸▸ *Med* ***long-stay bed*** lit *m* (de) long séjour; *Br* ***long-stay car park*** parking *m* longue durée; ***long-stay hospital*** unité *f ou* centre *m* de soins de longue durée

long-suffering ADJ (extrêmement) patient, d'une patience à toute épreuve; *(resigned)* résigné

long-term ADJ **1** *(detainee, prisoner)* qui subit un emprisonnement de longue durée; *(impact, effect)* à long terme; **the l. unemployed** les chômeurs de longue durée **2** *Fin (loan, policy etc)* à long terme
▸▸ *Fin* ***long-term bond*** obligation *f* à long terme; *Acct* ***long-term borrowings*** emprunts *mpl* à long terme; *Acct* ***long-term capital*** capitaux *mpl* permanents; *Fin* ***long-term credit*** crédit *m* (à) long terme; *Fin* ***long-term debt*** dette *f* à long terme; *Br Fin* ***long-term individual savings account*** plan *m* de retraite en actions; *Fin* ***long-term financing*** financement *m* à long terme; *Fin* ***long-term interest rate*** taux *m* d'intérêt à long terme; *Fin* ***long-term investments*** placements *mpl* à long terme; *(on balance sheet)* immobilisations *fpl* financières; *Fin* ***long-term liabilities*** dettes *fpl ou* passif *m* à long terme; *Fin* ***long-term loan*** prêt *m* à long terme; ***long-term memory*** mémoire *f* à long terme; ***long-term planning*** planification *f* à long terme; ***long-term unemployment*** chômage *m* de longue durée

longways ['lɒŋweɪz] ADV longitudinalement, dans le sens de la longueur

long-winded [-'wɪndɪd] ADJ *(person)* prolixe, bavard; *(article, essay, lecture)* interminable; *(style)* verbeux, diffus

loo [lu:] N *Br Fam* cabinets *mpl*, petit coin *m*; **to go to the l.** aller aux toilettes; **in the l.** aux toilettes, aux cabinets
▸▸ *Br Fam* ***loo paper*** papier *m* toilette; *Br Fam* ***loo roll*** rouleau *m* de papier toilette; *(paper)* papier *m* toilette; *Br Fam* ***loo seat*** siège *m* des toilettes *ou* des WC

loofa, loofah ['lu:fə] N luffa *m*, loofa *m*

LOOK [lʊk]

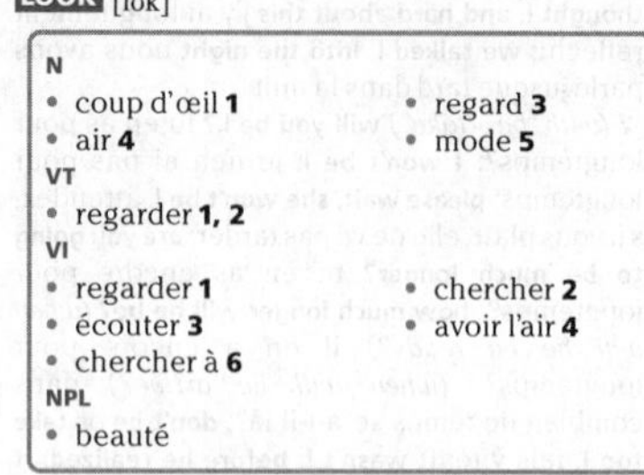

N	
• coup d'œil **1**	• regard **3**
• air **4**	• mode **5**
VT	
• regarder **1, 2**	
VI	
• regarder **1**	• chercher **2**
• écouter **3**	• avoir l'air **4**
• chercher à **6**	
NPL	
• beauté	

N **1** *(gen)* coup *m* d'œil; **to have** *or* **to take a l. (at sth)** jeter un coup d'œil (sur *ou* à qch), regarder (qch); *Fam* **let's have a l.** *(show me)* fais voir; **would you like a l. through my binoculars?** voulez-vous regarder avec mes jumelles?; **it's worth a quick l.** ça vaut le coup d'œil; **we need to take a long hard l. at our image abroad** il est temps que nous examinions de près notre image de marque à l'étranger; **did you get a good l. at him?** vous l'avez vu clairement?; **do you mind if I take a l. around?** ça vous gêne si je jette un coup d'œil?; **we'll just have a quick l. round the garden** nous allons jeter un coup d'œil dans le jardin; **we had a l. round the town** nous avons fait un tour dans la ville; **I took a quick l. through the drawers** j'ai jeté un rapide coup d'œil dans les tiroirs

2 *(search)* **to have a l. for sth** chercher qch; **have another l.** cherche encore

3 *(glance)* regard *m*; **a suspicious/nasty/angry l.** un regard soupçonneux/mauvais/méchant; **she gave me a dirty l.** elle m'a jeté un regard mauvais; **we were getting some very odd looks** on nous regardait d'un drôle d'air; **he didn't say anything, but if looks could kill!** il n'a pas dit un mot, mais il y a des regards qui tuent!

4 *(appearance, air)* air *m*; **he had a strange l. in his eyes** *(expression)* il avait un drôle de regard; **the old house has a neglected l.** la vieille maison a l'air négligé; **she has the l. of someone who's going places** elle a l'air de quelqu'un qui réussira dans la vie; **by the l.** *or* **looks of her, I'd say she failed the exam** à la voir *ou* rien qu'en la voyant, je dirais qu'elle a raté son examen; **there's trouble brewing by the l. of it** *or* **things** on dirait que quelque chose se trame; **I quite like the l. of the next candidate** j'aime assez le profil du prochain candidat; **I don't like the l. of it** ça ne me dit rien de bon *ou* rien qui vaille; **I didn't like the l. of her at all** son allure ne m'a pas du tout plu

5 *(fashion)* mode *f*, look *m*; **the sporty/punk l.** le look sportif/punk

VT **1** *(in imperative)* **l. who's coming!** regarde qui arrive!; **l. who's talking!** tu peux parler, toi!; **l. what you've done/where you're going!** regarde un peu ce que tu as fait/où tu vas!

2 *(idioms)* **to l. sb up and down** regarder qn de haut en bas, toiser qn du regard; **to l. sb (full** *or* **straight) in the face** regarder qn (bien) en face *ou* dans les yeux; **I can never l. her in the face again** je ne pourrai plus jamais la regarder en face

VI **1** *(gen)* regarder; **l., there's Brian!** regarde, voilà Brian!; **what's happening outside? let me l.** qu'est-ce qui se passe dehors? laissez-moi voir; **have you cut yourself? let me l.** tu t'es coupé? montre-moi *ou* laisse-moi voir; **they crept up on me while I wasn't looking** ils se sont approchés de moi pendant que j'avais le dos tourné; **I'm just looking** *(in shop)* je regarde; **l. and see if there's anyone there** regarde voir s'il y a quelqu'un; **if you l. very carefully you can see a tiny crack in it** si tu regardes bien, tu verras une toute petite fissure; **l. this way** regardez par ici; **to l. into sb's eyes** regarder qn dans les yeux; **she looked along the row/down the list** elle a parcouru la rangée/la liste du regard; **he was looking out of the window/over the wall/up the chimney** il regardait par la fenêtre/par-dessus le mur/dans la cheminée; **to l. on the bright side** voir les choses du bon côté; **to l. over sb's shoulder** regarder par-dessus l'épaule de qn; *Fig* surveiller ce que fai[t] qn; **to l. the other way** détourner les yeux; *Fig* fer[mer] les yeux; *Prov* **l. before you leap** = il faut ré[fléchir] deux fois avant d'agir

2 *(search)* chercher

3 *(in imperative ▸ listen, pay attention)* écouter **l., I can't pay you back just yet** écoute, je ne peu[x] pas te rembourser tout de suite; **l. here!** dite[s] donc!

4 *(seem, appear)* avoir l'air; **to l. old** avoir l'air *o[u]* faire vieux; **to l. ill** avoir l'air malade, avoir mau[-]vaise mine; **to l. well** *(person)* avoir bonne mine **that looks delicious!** ça a l'air délicieux!; **you l. o[r] are looking better today** tu as l'air (d'aller) mieux aujourd'hui; **how do I l.?** comment tu me trou[-]ves?; **you l. absolutely stunning in that dress** tu es vraiment ravissante dans cette robe; **it makes him l. ten years older/younger** ça le vieillit/rajeu[-]nit de dix ans; **he's 70, but he doesn't l. it** il a 70 ans mais il n'en a pas l'air *ou* mais il ne les fait pas; **I can't hang the picture there, it just doesn't l. righ[t]** je ne peux pas mettre le tableau là, ça ne va pas **it looks all right to me** moi, je trouve ça bien; **how does the situation l. to you?** que pensez-vous de la situation?; **things will l. very different when you leave school** les choses te sembleront très diffé[-]rentes quand tu quitteras l'école; **it'll l. bad if I don't contribute** ça fera mauvaise impression si je ne contribue pas; **things are looking black for the economy** les perspectives économiques sont assez sombres; **she's not as stupid as she looks** elle est moins bête qu'elle n'en a l'air; **I must have looked a fool** j'ai dû passer pour un imbé[-]cile; **to make sb l. a fool** *or* **an idiot** tourner qn en ridicule; **he makes the rest of the cast l. very ordin[-]ary** à côté de lui, les autres acteurs ont l'air vrai[-]ment quelconques; **to l. like sb/sth** *(resemble)* ressembler à qn/qch; **she looks like her mother** elle ressemble à sa mère; **what does she l. like?** *(describe her)* comment est-elle?; *(she looks a mess)* non mais, à quoi elle ressemble!; **it looks like an oil refinery** ça ressemble à une raffinerie de pétrole, on dirait une raffinerie de pétrole; **it looks like rain** on dirait qu'il va pleuvoir; **it looks (to me) like he was lying** j'ai l'impression qu'il mentait; **is this our room? – it looks like it** c'est notre chambre? – ça m'en a tout l'air; **the meeting looked like going on all day** la réunion avait l'air d'être partie pour durer toute la journée; **you l. as if you've seen a ghost** on dirait que tu as vu un revenant; **it looks as if Natalie's going to resign** Natalie a l'air de vouloir démissionner; **it looks as if he didn't want to go** il semble qu'il ne veuille pas y aller; **it doesn't l. as if they're coming** on dirait qu'ils ne vont pas venir; **you're looking good** tu as l'air en forme; **he looks good in jeans** les jeans lui vont bien; **that hat looks very good on you** ce chapeau te va très bien; **it'll l. good on your CV** ça fera bien sur ton curriculum *ou* CV; **things are looking pretty good here** les choses ont l'air de se présenter plutôt bien ici

5 *(face ▸ house, window)* **to l. (out) onto a park** donner sur un parc; **to l. north/west** être exposé au nord/à l'ouest

6 *(intend)* **to be looking to do sth** chercher à faire qch; **we're looking to expand our export business** nous cherchons à développer nos exportations; **I'm not looking to cause any trouble** je ne veux pas causer de problèmes

• **looks** NPL *(beauty)* **she's got everything – looks, intelligence, youth...** elle a tout pour elle, elle est belle, intelligente, jeune...; **he's kept his looks** il est resté beau; **looks don't matter** l'apparence ne compte pas; **she's got her mother's looks** elle a la beauté de sa mère; **he's lost his looks** il n'est plus aussi beau qu'avant

▸ **look after** VT INSEP **1** *(take care of)* s'occuper de; **my mother's looking after the kids/the cat this weekend** ma mère va s'occuper des enfants/du chat ce week-end; **she has a sick mother to l. after** elle a une mère malade à charge; **you should l. after your clothes more carefully** tu devrais prendre plus grand soin de tes vêtements; *Fig* **l. after yourself!** fais bien attention à toi!; **the car has been well looked after** la voiture est bien entretenue; **don't worry, he can l. after himself** ne t'inquiète pas, il est capable de se débrouiller tout seul **2** *(be responsible for)* s'occuper de; **they l. after our interests in Europe** ils s'occupent de nos affaires en Europe **3** *(watch over)* surveiller; **can you l. after my bag for a couple of minutes?** tu peux surveiller mon sac deux minutes?

▸ **look around** = **look round**

▸ **look at** VT INSEP **1** *(gen)* regarder; **she looked at herself in the mirror** elle se regarda dans la glace; **they looked at each other** ils ont échangé un regard; **oh dear, l. at the time!** oh là là, regardez l'heure!; **just l. at you!** *(you look awful)* mais regarde-toi donc!; **it's not much to l. at** ça ne paie pas de mine; **she's not much to l. at** ce n'est pas une beauté; **he's not much to l. at** il n'est pas très beau; **you wouldn't think, to l. at him, that he's a multi-millionaire** à le voir on ne croirait pas avoir affaire à un multi-millionnaire; **just l. at the mess we're in!** regarde les ennuis qu'on a! **2** *(consider)* considérer; **l. at the problem from my point of view** considérez le problème de mon point de vue; **that's not the way I l. at it** ce n'est pas comme ça que je vois les choses; **they won't even l. at the idea** ils refusent même de prendre cette idée en considération **3** *(check)* vérifier, regarder; **could you l. at the tyres?** pouvez-vous regarder les pneus?; **to have one's teeth looked at** se faire examiner les dents; *Fam* **you need your head looking at!** ça va pas, la tête?

▸ **look away** VI détourner les yeux

▸ **look back** VI **1** *(in space)* regarder derrière soi; **she walked away without looking back** elle est partie sans se retourner **2** *(in time)* regarder en arrière; **there's no point in looking back** ça ne sert à rien de regarder en arrière; **the author looks back on the war years** l'auteur revient sur les années de guerre; **it seems funny now we l. back on it** ça semble drôle quand on y pense aujourd'hui; **we can l. back on some happy times** nous avons connu de bons moments; *Fig* **after she got her first job she never looked back** à partir du moment où elle a trouvé son premier emploi, tout lui a réussi

▸ **look down** VI regarder en bas; *(in embarrassment)* baisser les yeux; **we looked down on** *or* **at the valley** nous regardions la vallée en dessous

▸ **look down on** VT INSEP *(despise)* mépriser

▸ **look for** VT INSEP **1** *(seek)* chercher; **go and l. for him** allez le chercher; **she's still looking for a job** elle est toujours à la recherche d'un emploi; **are you looking for a fight?** tu cherches la bagarre? **2** *(expect)* attendre

▸ **look forward** VI *(to the future)* regarder vers l'avenir

▸ **look forward to** VT INSEP attendre avec impatience; **we're looking forward to the end of term** nous attendons la fin du trimestre avec impatience; **I'm looking forward to the weekend** vivement le week-end!; **to l. forward to doing sth** être impatient de faire qch; **I'm looking forward to seeing her again** *(eager)* il me tarde de la revoir; *(polite formula)* je serai heureux de la revoir; **see you on Saturday – right, I'll l. forward it** à samedi alors – oui, c'est entendu; **I'm not exactly looking forward to going** je n'ai pas vraiment envie d'y aller; **I l. forward to hearing from you soon** *(in letter)* dans l'attente de votre réponse; **I'm not looking forward to the operation** la perspective de cette opération ne m'enchante guère

▸ **look in** VI **1** *(inside)* regarder à l'intérieur **2** *(pay a visit)* passer; **to l. in on sb** rendre visite à *ou* passer voir qn; **I'll l. in again tomorrow** je repasserai demain; **he looked in at the pub on the way home** il s'est arrêté au pub en rentrant chez lui **3** *(watch TV)* regarder la télévision

▸ **look into** VT INSEP examiner, étudier; **it's a problem that needs looking into** c'est un problème qu'il faut examiner *ou* sur lequel il faut se pencher

▸ **look on** VT INSEP considérer; **I l. on him as my brother** je le considère comme mon frère; **to l. on sb/sth favourably/unfavourably** voir qn/qch d'un œil favorable/défavorable

VI regarder; **the passers-by just looked on** les passants se sont contentés de regarder

▸ **look out** VT SEP *Br* **I'll l. that book out for you** je te chercherai ce livre; **have you looked out those photos to give me?** est-ce que tu as trouvé les photos que tu devais me donner?

VI **1** *(person)* regarder dehors **2** *(room, window)* **the bedroom looks out on** *or* **over the garden** la chambre donne sur le jardin **3** *(be careful)* faire attention; **l. out, it's hot!** attention, c'est chaud!; **you'll be in trouble if you don't l. out** tu vas t'attirer des ennuis si tu ne fais pas attention

▸ **look out for** VT INSEP **1** *(be on watch for)* guetter; **I'll l. out for you at the station** je te guetterai à la gare; **l. out for the sign to Dover** guettez le panneau pour Douvres; **she's always looking out for bargains** elle est toujours à la recherche *ou* à l'affût d'une bonne affaire; **you have to l. out for snakes** il faut faire attention *ou* se méfier, il y a des serpents **2** *Fam (idiom)* **to l. out for oneself** penser à soi

▸ **look over** VT INSEP *(glance over)* jeter un coup d'œil sur; *(examine)* examiner, étudier

▸ **look round** VT INSEP *(museum, cathedral, factory)* visiter; *(shop, room)* jeter un coup d'œil dans

VI **1** *(look at surroundings)* regarder (autour de soi); **I'm just looking round** *(in shop)* je regarde; **I'd rather l. round on my own than take the guided tour** je préférerais faire le tour moi-même plutôt que de suivre la visite guidée; **I looked round for an exit** j'ai cherché une sortie **2** *(look back)* regarder derrière soi, se retourner

▸ **look through** VT INSEP **1** *(window, screen)* regarder à travers **2** *(book, report)* jeter un coup d'œil sur *ou* à, regarder **3** *Fig (person)* **he looked straight through me** il m'a regardé comme si je n'étais pas là

▸ **look to** VT INSEP **1** *(turn to)* se tourner vers; **don't l. to her for help** ne compte pas sur elle pour t'aider; **they are looking to us to find a solution to this problem** ils comptent sur nous pour trouver une solution à ce problème **2** *Formal (attend to)* veiller à; **he should l. to his reputation** il devrait veiller à sa réputation; **l. to it that discipline is properly maintained** veillez à ce que la discipline soit maintenue

▸ **look up** VT SEP **1** *(in reference work, directory etc)* chercher **2** *(visit)* passer voir, rendre visite à; **l. us up when you're in New York** passe nous voir quand tu seras à New York

VI **1** *(raise one's eyes)* lever les yeux **2** *(improve)* s'améliorer; **things are looking up for the economy** les perspectives économiques semblent meilleures

▸ **look up to** VT INSEP respecter, avoir du respect pour

▸ **look upon** VT INSEP considérer

lookalike [ˈlʊkəˌlaɪk] N *(double)* sosie *m*; **a Brad Pitt l.** un sosie de Brad Pitt; **it's just another Renault l.** c'est la copie conforme de la Renault

looker [ˈlʊkə(r)] N *Fam* **she's a real l.** elle est vraiment canon; **she's not much of a l.** ce n'est pas une beauté

looker-on *(pl* **lookers-on***)* N *(spectator)* spectateur(trice) *m,f*, *Pej* badaud(e) *m,f*

look-in N *Br Fam (chance)* **she talked so much that I didn't get a l.** elle ne m'a pas laissé le temps de placer un mot *ou* d'en placer une; **the other people applying for the job don't have a l.** les autres candidats n'ont aucune chance◻

looking-glass N *Old-fashioned* miroir *m*, glace *f*

looking room N *TV* salle *f* de visionnage

lookout [ˈlʊkaʊt] N **1** *(post)* poste *m* d'observation *ou* de vigie

2 *(person)* & *Mil* guetteur *m*; *Naut* homme *m* de veille *ou* de vigie

3 *(action)* surveillance *f*, observation *f*; *Naut* veille *f*; **to keep a l.** être aux aguets; *Naut* veiller, être en *ou* de vigie; **to be on the l. for** *(person)* guetter; *(thing)* être à la recherche de

4 *Fam* **it's a poor l. when even doctors are on the dole** il y a de quoi s'inquiéter quand même les médecins sont au chômage; **that's your l.!** ça c'est tes oignons!

▸▸ ***lookout post*** poste *m* d'observation *ou* de vigie

look-over N *Fam* coup *m* d'œil◻; **I've given the report a l.** j'ai jeté un coup d'œil sur le rapport

look-see N *Fam* **to have** *or* **to take a l.** jeter un petit coup d'œil

look-up N *Comput* recherche *f*, consultation *f*

▸▸ ***look-up table*** table *f* de recherche *ou* de référence

loom [luːm] VI **1** *(appear)* surgir; **an iceberg loomed out of** *or* **through the fog** un iceberg a soudain surgi du brouillard; **a figure loomed in the doorway** une silhouette est apparue dans l'encadrement de la porte; **above us loomed a high cliff** une falaise se dressait au-dessus de nos têtes **2** *(approach)* être imminent; **the deadline was looming nearer and nearer** la date fatidique approchait **3 to l. large** *(threaten)* menacer; **the idea of eviction loomed large in their minds** l'idée d'être expulsés ne les quittait pas

N *Tex* métier *m* à tisser; **hand/power l.** métier *m* manuel/mécanique

▸ **loom up** VI apparaître indistinctement, surgir

loon [luːn] N **1** *Fam (lunatic)* dingue *mf*; *(fool)* imbécile *mf* **2** *Am Orn* plongeon *m*, *Can* huart *m*

• **loons** NPL = pantalon taille basse à pattes d'éléphant

▸▸ ***loon pants*** = pantalon taille basse à pattes d'éléphant

looney [ˈluːnɪ] = **loony**

loonie [ˈluːnɪ] N *Can Fam* pièce *f* d'un dollar

loony [ˈluːnɪ] *(pl* **loonies**, *compar* **loonier**, *superl* **looniest***)* *Fam* N dingue *mf*, malade *mf*

ADJ dingue, loufoque; *Am Fam* **loony tunes** *(crazy)* barjo, foldingue

▸▸ *Fam Hum* ***loony bin*** maison *f* de fous; **he's ready for the loony bin** il est bon pour l'asile; *Pej* ***the loony left*** = l'aile gauche extrémiste du parti travailliste

loop [luːp] N **1** *(of ribbon, film etc)* boucle *f*; *(of fingerprint)* anse *f*; *(of river)* méandre *m*, boucle *f*; *(in skating)* croisé *m*; *(of spiral, spool)* tour *m*; **a l. of string served as a handle** une ficelle servait de poignée; **the film/the tape runs in a l.** le film/la bande défile en continu; *Am Fam* **to be out of the l.** ne pas être dans le coup; *Am Fam* **to cut sb out of the l.** mettre qn aux oubliettes

2 *Comput* boucle *f*

3 *Elec* boucle *f*, bouclage *m*; *Nucl (of reactor)* boucle *f*, circuit *m*

4 *(contraceptive device)* stérilet *m*

5 *Aviat* boucle *f*, looping *m*

6 *Rail (line)* voie *f* d'évitement *ou* de raccordement; *(at terminus)* boucle *f* d'évitement

VT **1** *(in string, rope etc)* faire une boucle à; **l. the rope around your waist/through the ring** passez la corde autour de votre taille/dans l'anneau **2** *Aviat* **to l. the l.** faire un looping, boucler la boucle

VI *(road)* faire des lacets; *(river)* faire des méandres *ou* des boucles

▸▸ *Rad* ***loop aerial***, *Am* ***loop antenna*** (antenne *f*) cadre *m*; *Elec* ***loop circuit*** circuit *m* bouclé; *Rail* ***loop line*** voie *f* d'évitement *ou* de raccordement; *(at terminus)* boucle *f* d'évitement; ***loop stitch*** point *m* de bouclette

▸ **loop back** VT SEP *(curtain)* retenir avec une embrasse

VI *(river etc)* faire une boucle; *Comput (program)* faire une boucle pour retourner (**to** à)

loophole [ˈluːphəʊl] N **1** *(in law, regulations etc)* point *m* faible; **to find a l.** trouver une échappatoire; **a legal l.** un vide juridique **2** *(gap)* trou *m*, ouverture *f*; *(in fortified wall)* meurtrière *f*

looping [ˈluːpɪŋ] N *Cin, Tel & TV* bouclage *m*

loopy [ˈluːpɪ] *(compar* **loopier**, *superl* **loopiest***)* ADJ *Fam (crazy)* dingue, cinglé

LOOSE [luːs] ADJ **1** *(not tightly fixed* ▸ *nail)* mal enfoncé; *(*▸ *screw, bolt)* desserré; *(*▸ *button)* qui pend, mal cousu; *(*▸ *knot)* qui se défait; *(*▸ *floor tile)* décollé; *(*▸ *shelf)* mal fixé; *(*▸ *handle, brick)* branlant; *(*▸ *floorboard)* disjoint; *(*▸ *slate)* mal fixé; *(*▸ *tooth)* qui bouge; **your button's l.** ton bouton est décousu; **he prised a brick l.** il a réussi à faire bouger une brique; **remove all the l. plaster** enlève tout le plâtre qui se détache; **the steering seems l.** il y a du jeu dans la direction; **to work l.** *(nail)* sortir; *(screw, bolt)* se desserrer; *(knot)* se défaire; *(tooth, slate)* bouger; *(button)* se détacher; *Br* **to have a l. cough** avoir une toux grasse

2 *(free, unattached)* libre; **tie the l. end of the rope to the post** attache le bout libre de la corde au poteau; **a l. sheet of paper** une feuille volante; **her hair hung l. about her shoulders** ses cheveux flottaient librement sur ses épaules; **several pages have come l.** plusieurs pages se sont détachées; **I got one hand l.** j'ai réussi à dégager une de mes mains; **if I manage to tear myself l.** si je réussis à me libérer *ou* à me dégager; **he decided to cut l. from his family** il a décidé de couper les ponts avec sa famille; **a lion got l. from the zoo** un lion s'est échappé du zoo; **he set** *or* **let** *or* **turned a mouse l. in the kitchen** il a lâché une souris dans la cuisine; *Fig* **he let l. a torrent of abuse** il a lâché un torrent d'injures

3 *Com (not packaged)* en vrac; **l. coal** charbon *m* en vrac; **l. cheese** fromage *m* à la coupe; **I always buy vegetables l.** j'achète mes légumes au poids

4 *(slack ▸ grip, hold)* mou (molle); *(▸ skin, flesh)* flasque; *(▸ bowstring, rope, knot)* lâche; *Fig (▸ discipline)* relâché; **she tied the ribbon in a l. bow** elle noua le ruban sans le serrer; **his arms hung l. at his sides** il avait les bras ballants; **to have a l. tongue** ne pas savoir tenir sa langue

5 *(not tight-fitting ▸ dress, jacket)* ample, flottant; **this skirt is much too l. at the waist** cette jupe est bien trop large à la taille

6 *(weak ▸ connection, link)* vague; **they have l. ties with other political groups** ils sont vaguement liés à d'autres groupes politiques

7 *(informal ▸ organization)* peu structuré; *(▸ agreement)* officieux

8 *(imprecise, broad ▸ thinking, application)* peu rigoureux; *(▸ translation, terminology)* approximatif; **we can make a l. distinction between the two phenomena** nous pouvons faire une vague distinction entre les deux phénomènes

9 *Pej (woman)* facile; *(morals)* léger

10 *(not dense or compact ▸ earth)* meuble; *(▸ knit, weave)* lâche

11 *(relaxed ▸ muscles)* détendu, relâché, au repos; *(▸ athlete, sportsman)* échauffé; **to have l. bowels** avoir la diarrhée

12 *Fin* disponible

13 *Am Fam* **to keep** *or* **to stay l.** rester cool; *Fam* **hang** *or* **stay l.!** relax!, du calme!

14 *(idiom)* **I have a few l. ends to tie up** j'ai encore quelques petits détails à régler; **to be** *Br* **at a l. end** *or Am* **at l. ends** être dans un moment creux

N *(in rugby)* **in the l.** dans la mêlée ouverte

VT *Literary* **1** *(unleash ▸ dogs)* lâcher; *(▸ panic, chaos)* semer; **she loosed her tongue** *or* **fury upon me** elle s'est déchaînée contre moi

2 *(let fly ▸ bullet)* tirer; *(▸ arrow)* décocher; *Fig* **he loosed a volley of threats/abuse at her** il s'est répandu en menaces/invectives contre elle

3 *(undo ▸ knot)* défaire; *(▸ hair)* détacher; *(unfasten ▸ boat, raft)* démarrer, détacher; *(▸ sail)* déferler

• **on the loose** **ADJ** **to be on the l.** *(gen)* être en liberté; *(on the run)* être en fuite; **a gang of hooligans on the l.** une bande de jeunes voyous qui rôdent; **there was a gunman on the l. in the neighbourhood** il y avait un homme armé qui rôdait dans le quartier

▸▸ ***loose change*** petite monnaie *f*; *Elec* ***loose connection*** mauvais contact *m*; *Br* ***loose cover*** *(for armchair, sofa)* housse *f*; ***loose insert*** *(in newspaper, magazine)* encart *m* libre; ***loose living*** débauche *f*, vie *f* dissolue; *Fin* ***loose money*** argent *m* disponible, liquidités *fpl*; ***loose talk*** des propos *mpl* lestes

▸ **loose off** **VT SEP** *(bullet)* tirer; *(arrow)* décocher; *(gun)* décharger; *(curses)* lâcher

VI *(with gun)* tirer; **he loosed off into the crowd** il tira au hasard dans la foule; *Am Fig* **to l. off at sb** *(with insults, criticism etc)* se déchaîner contre qn, s'en prendre violemment à qn

---

loose-fitting **ADJ** *(garment)* ample, large, flottant

loose-leaf(ed) **ADJ** à feuilles mobiles *ou* volantes

▸▸ ***loose-leaf binder*** classeur *m* (à feuilles mobiles); ***loose-leaf paper*** feuillets *mpl* mobiles

loose-limbed **ADJ** souple, agile

loosely ['lu:slɪ] **ADV 1** *(not firmly ▸ pack, fit, hold, wrap)* sans serrer; *(not closely ▸ knit, weave)* lâchement; **the dress was l. gathered at the waist** la robe était peu ajustée à la taille; **the rope hung l.** *(unattached)* la corde pendait; *(slackly)* la corde était lâche **2** *(apply, interpret)* mollement; **l. translated** *(freely)* traduit librement; *(inaccurately)* mal traduit; **the word is often used l.** le mot est souvent employé de façon imprécise **3** *(vaguely ▸ connect, relate)* vaguement; **the book is only l. based on my research** le livre n'a qu'un rapport lointain avec mes recherches

loosen ['lu:sən] **VT 1** *(knot, screw, lid)* desserrer; *(rope, cable)* détendre; *(grip, reins)* relâcher; *Agr (soil)* ameublir; **this mixture helps l. the cough** ce sirop aide à dégager les bronches; **he loosened his grip** il relâcha *ou* desserra son étreinte; **I loosened my belt a notch** j'ai desserré ma ceinture d'un cran; **he loosened his tie** il a desserré son nœud de cravate; **the punch has loosened several of his teeth** le coup lui a déchaussé plusieurs dents; **l. the cake from the sides of the tin** détachez le gâteau des bords du moule; **it loosens the bowels** c'est un laxatif; **the wine soon loosened his tongue** le vin eut vite fait de lui délier la langue **2** *(rules, restrictions)* assouplir

VI *(knot, screw, lid)* se desserrer; *(rope, cable)* se détendre; *(grip)* se relâcher

▸ **loosen up** **VT SEP** *(muscles)* assouplir

VI 1 *(become less severe)* se montrer moins sévère; **to l. up on discipline** relâcher la discipline; **will they l. up on immigration?** vont-ils adopter une position plus souple vis-à-vis de l'immigration? **2** *(relax socially)* se détendre; **l. up a bit!** détends-toi un peu!

looseness ['lu:snɪs] **N 1** *(of screw, nail, lever)* jeu *m*; *(of rope)* relâchement *m*, mou *m*

2 *(of clothing)* ampleur *f*

3 *(of thinking, interpretation)* manque *m* de rigueur; *(of translation, terminology)* manque *m* de précision

4 *Pej (of way of life)* débauche *f*, licence *f*

loosestrife ['lu:sstraɪf] **N** *Bot* **(yellow) l.** lysimachie *f*, lysimaque *f*; **(purple) l.** salicaire *f* commune

loot [lu:t] **N 1** *(stolen goods)* butin *m* **2** *Fam (money)* pognon *m*, fric *m*; **he's got plenty of l.** il est plein aux as

VT *(town, goods, tomb)* piller; *Fig* **state coffers were looted to finance the war** les coffres de l'État ont été pillés pour financer la guerre

VI piller, se livrer au pillage

looter ['lu:tə(r)] **N** *(in war, riot)* pillard(e) *m,f*, pilleur(euse) *m,f*; *(of tombs, churches)* pilleur(euse) *m,f*

looting ['lu:tɪŋ] **N** pillage *m*

lop [lɒp] *(pt & pp* **lopped**, *cont* **lopping) VT 1** *(tree)* élaguer, tailler; *(branch)* couper **2** *Fig (budget)* élaguer, faire des coupes sombres dans; *(sum of money, item of expenditure)* retrancher, supprimer

▸ **lop off** **VT SEP 1** *(branch)* couper, tailler **2** *Fig (price, time)* réduire; **they could easily l. another 10 percent off fares** ils pourraient facilement baisser le prix des billets de 10 pour cent

▸ **lope along** **VI** *(person)* avancer à grandes enjambées; *(leopard)* courir tout en puissance; *(hare)* avancer en bondissant

▸ **lope off** **VI** *(person)* partir d'une démarche élastique; **the tiger loped off into the jungle** le tigre pénétra dans la jungle de sa démarche souple

lop-eared **ADJ** *Br* aux oreilles tombantes *ou* pendantes

lopsided [,lɒp'saɪdɪd] **ADJ** qui manque de symétrie, asymétrique; *(picture, roof)* de guingois, de travers; **a l. grin** un sourire en coin; **a l. group with twice as many women as men** un groupe déséquilibré comptant deux fois plus de femmes que d'hommes; **her handwriting is all l.** son écriture part dans tous les sens; **the article presents a rather l. picture of events** l'article présente les événements de façon plutôt partiale

loquacious [lə'kweɪʃəs] **ADJ** *Formal* loquace, volubile

lord [lɔ:d] **N 1** *(master)* seigneur *m*; *(nobleman)* noble *m*; **l. of the manor** châtelain *m*; **to live like a l.** mener grand train, vivre en grand seigneur; *Hum* **her l. and master** son seigneur et maître **2** *Astrol* maître *m*

• **Lord** **N** *Br* **1** *(title)* lord *m*; **L. (Peter) Snow** lord (Peter) Snow **2** *(term of address)* **my L.** *(to noble)* monsieur le marquis/monsieur le baron; *(to judge)* monsieur le juge; *(to bishop)* monseigneur, Excellence **PR N 1** *Rel* **the L.** le Seigneur; **in the year of our L. 1897** en l'an de grâce 1897 **2** *Fam (in interjections and expressions)* **Good L.!** Seigneur!; **oh L.!** mon Dieu!; **L. (only) knows!** Dieu seul le sait!; **L. knows where he's put it** Dieu sait où il l'a mis **VT to l. it** mener la grande vie; *Br* **to l. it over sb** prendre des airs supérieurs avec qn

▸▸ *Law* ***Lord Advocate*** procureur *m* de la République, procureur *m* général *(en Écosse)*; ***Lord Chamberlain*** grand chambellan *m (en Grande Bretagne)*; ***Lord Chancellor*** lord *m* Chancelier, ministre *m* de la Justice *(en Grande-Bretagne)*; ***Lord Chief Justice*** président *m* de la Haute Cour *(en Grande-Bretagne)*; *Rel* ***the Lord's day*** le jour du Seigneur; ***Lord God Almighty*** Seigneur Dieu Tout-puissant; ***Lord Justice of Appeal*** président *m* de la cour d'appel; *Bot* ***lords and ladies*** arum *m* maculé, pied-de-veau *m*; ***Lord Lieutenant*** lord-lieutenant *m (en Grande-Bretagne)*; ***Lord Mayor*** lord-maire *m*; ***the Lord's Prayer*** le Notre Père; ***the Lord Privy Seal*** = titre du doyen du gouvernement britannique; ***Lord Provost*** maire *m (dans les villes d'Aberdeen, Dundee, Édimbourg, Glasgow et Perth)*; ***Lords Spiritual*** = membres ecclésiastiques de la Chambre des lords; ***the Lord's Supper*** l'eucharistie *f*; ***Lords Temporal*** = membres laïques de la Chambre des lords

lordly ['lɔ:dlɪ] **ADJ 1** *(arrogant)* arrogant, hautain; **with l. indifference** avec une indifférence souveraine **2** *(noble ▸ gesture)* noble, auguste; *(splendid ▸ feast, occasion, lifestyle)* somptueux

lordship ['lɔ:dʃɪp] **N 1** *(form of address)* **Your/His L.** *(to noble)* monsieur le marquis/monsieur le baron; *Br (to judge)* monsieur le juge; *(to bishop)* Excellence/Son Excellence; *Hum* **if His L. would care to sit down** si Votre Altesse daigne s'asseoir **2** *(lands, rights)* seigneurie *f*; *(power)* autorité *f*

lordy ['lɔ:dɪ] **EXCLAM** *Fam* Seigneur!

lore [lɔ:(r)] **N 1** *(folk legend)* tradition *f*, traditions *fpl*, coutume *f*, coutumes *fpl*; **according to Celtic l., it was built by fairies** la tradition celtique veut qu'il ait été construit par des fées **2** *(traditional knowledge)* science *f*, savoir *m*

lorgnette [lɔ:'njet] **N 1** *(spectacles)* lorgnon *m*, face-à-main *m* **2** *(opera glasses)* jumelles *fpl* de théâtre, lorgnette *f*

lorry ['lɒrɪ] *(pl* **lorries) N** *Br* camion *m*, poids *m* lourd; *Fam Euph* **it fell off the back of a l.** c'est de la marchandise volée

▸▸ ***lorry driver*** chauffeur *m* de camion, routier (ère) *m,f*; ***lorry park*** aire *f* de stationnement pour poids lourds

---

LOSE [lu:z]

VT	
• perdre **1–3**	• semer **4**
• coûter à **5**	
VI	
• perdre **1**	• retarder **2**

(pt & pp **lost** [lɒst])

VT 1 *(gen ▸ limb, job, money, patience etc)* perdre; **I've lost my umbrella again** j'ai encore perdu mon parapluie; **to l. one's way** se perdre, s'égarer; **what have you got to l.?** qu'est-ce que tu as à perdre?; **you've got nothing to l.** tu n'as rien à perdre; **we haven't got a moment to l.** il n'y a pas une seconde à perdre; **he lost no time in telling her she was wrong** il ne s'est pas gêné pour lui dire qu'elle avait tort; **his shop is losing money** son magasin perd de l'argent; **we lost 80 days in strikes last year** l'année dernière, nous avons perdu 80 journées de travail à cause des grèves; **you lost me when you started using technical terms** j'ai perdu le fil quand tu as commencé à employer des termes techniques; **at what age did he l. his mother?** à quel âge a-t-il perdu sa mère?; **they lost their homes in the flood** ils ont perdu leur maison dans l'inondation; **30 lives were lost in the fire** 30 personnes ont péri dans l'incendie, l'incendie a fait 30 morts; **she lost a leg/her eyesight in an accident** elle a perdu une jambe/la vue dans un accident; **to l. one's voice** avoir une extinction de voix; **his work loses a lot in translation** son œuvre se prête très mal à la traduction; **to l. one's appetite** perdre l'appétit; **the plane is losing altitude** *or* **height** l'avion perd de l'altitude; **to l. one's balance** perdre l'équilibre; **to l. consciousness** perdre connaissance; **to l. face** perdre la face; **to l. ground** perdre du terrain; **I've lost interest in it** ça ne m'intéresse plus; **he lost his nerve at the last minute** le courage lui a manqué au dernier moment; *Fam* **to l. one's head** perdre la tête; *Fam* **to l. it** *(go mad)* perdre la boule; *(lose one's temper)* piquer une crise, péter les plombs; *Br Fam* **to l. the plot** perdre la boule

2 *(not win)* perdre; **he lost four games to Karpov** il a perdu quatre parties contre Karpov

3 *(shed, get rid of)* perdre; **to l. weight** perdre du poids; **I've lost several pounds** j'ai perdu plusieurs kilos; **the trees l. their leaves in winter** les arbres perdent leurs feuilles en hiver

4 *(elude, shake off)* semer

5 *(cause to lose)* coûter à, faire perdre à; **it lost him his job** ça lui a fait perdre son emploi; **it lost us the contract** cela nous a fait perdre le contrat; **that mistake lost him the match** cette faute lui coûta la partie

6 *(of clock, watch)* **my watch loses five minutes a day** ma montre prend cinq minutes de retard par jour

VI 1 *(gen)* perdre; **they lost by one goal** ils ont perdu d'un but; **either way, I can't l.** je suis gagnant à tous les coups; **the dollar is losing in value (against the euro)** le dollar baisse (par rapport à l'euro); **I lost on the deal** j'ai été perdant dans l'affaire

2 *(clock, watch)* retarder

▸ **lose out** VI perdre, être perdant; **to l. out on a deal** être perdant dans une affaire; **will the Americans l. out to the Japanese in computers?** les Américains vont-ils perdre le marché de l'informatique au profit des Japonais?

loser ['lu:zə(r)] **N 1** *(gen) & Sport* perdant(e) *m,f*; **to be a good/bad l.** être bon/mauvais joueur; **you'll be the l.** c'est toi qui y perdras; *Br Fig* **they're the losers by it** ce sont eux les perdants dans cette affaire **2** *Fam (failure ▸ man)* raté *m*, loser *m*; *(▸ woman)* ratée *f*; **he's a born l.** c'est un vrai raté

ADJ *Am Fam* **a real l. guy** un vrai raté

losing ['lu:zɪŋ] **ADJ 1** *(gen) & Sport* perdant; **to fight a l. battle** engager une bataille perdue d'avance **2** *(unprofitable)* **the business was a l. concern** cette entreprise n'était pas viable; **it's a l. proposition** ce n'est pas rentable

▸▸ ***the losing side*** les vaincus *mpl*; *Sport* l'équipe *f* perdante

loss [lɒs] **N 1** *(gen)* perte *f*; **have you reported the l. to the police?** avez-vous signalé cette perte à la police?; **it's your l.!** tant pis pour vous!; **her retirement will be a great l. to us all** son départ à la retraite sera une grande perte pour nous tous; **it's no great l. to me** ce n'est pas une grosse perte pour moi; **it can cause temporary l. of vision** cela peut provoquer *ou* entraîner une perte momentanée de la vue; **the l. of a close relative** la perte *ou* la mort d'un parent proche; **the party suffered heavy losses in the last elections** le parti a subi de lourdes pertes *ou* a perdu de nombreux sièges lors des dernières élections; **the closure will cause the l. of hundreds of jobs** la fermeture provoquera la disparition de centaines d'emplois; **fortunately there was little l. of life** heureusement, il n'y eut que peu de victimes; **there was terrible l. of life in the last war** la dernière guerre a coûté beaucoup de vies humaines; **to sustain** *or* **suffer heavy losses** subir de grosses pertes; **to cut one's losses** faire la part du feu

2 *(financial)* déficit *m*; **to make a l.** perdre de l'argent; **the company announced losses of** *or* **a l. of a million pounds** la société a annoncé un déficit d'un million de livres; **we made a l. of 10 percent on the deal** nous avons perdu 10 pour cent dans l'affaire; **to sell at a l.** vendre à perte; **to run at a l.** *(business)* tourner à perte; *Fin* **l. carry back** report *m* déficitaire sur les exercices précédents; *Fin* **l. carry forward** déficit *m* reportable, report *m* déficitaire sur les exercices ultérieurs

3 *(feeling of pain, unhappiness)* malheur *m*, chagrin *m*; **his family rallied round him in his l.** sa famille l'a beaucoup entouré dans son chagrin; **to feel a sense of l.** ressentir un vide

4 *Ins* sinistre *m*

5 *Com (of product being manufactured or transported)* freinte *f*; **l. in transit** freinte *f* de route

6 *(idioms)* **to be at a l.** ne savoir que faire; *(not know what to say)* ne savoir que dire; *(not know what to answer)* ne savoir que répondre; **to be at a (total) l. to explain...** être (totalement) incapable d'expliquer...; **to be at a l. (to know) what to do/say** ne savoir que faire/dire; **she's never at a l. for an answer** elle a *ou* trouve toujours réponse à tout

▸▸ *Br* ***loss adjuster*** *Ins* expert *m*; *Naut* dispatcheur *m*; ***loss assessment*** fixation *f* des dommages; ***loss of earnings*** manque *m* à gagner; **to sue for l. of earnings** intenter une action en justice pour recouvrement d'un manque à gagner; *Mktg* ***loss leader*** produit *m* d'appel

loss-making **ADJ** *Br Com* qui tourne à perte, déficitaire

lost [lɒst] *pt & pp of* **lose**

ADJ 1 *(mislaid, not found)* perdu; **all is not yet l.** tout n'est pas perdu; **they have discovered a l. masterpiece** ils ont découvert un chef-d'œuvre disparu; **to give sth up for l.** abandonner tout espoir de retrouver qch; **the l. city of Atlantis** Atlantide, la ville engloutie

2 *(person ▸ in direction)* perdu, égaré; **can you help me, I'm l.** pouvez-vous m'aider, je me suis perdu *ou* égaré; **to get l.** se perdre; *Mil* **l. in action** mort au combat; **30 people were reported l. at sea** 30 personnes auraient péri en mer; *also Fig* **a l. sheep** une brebis égarée; **a l. soul** une âme en peine; *Fam* **get l.!** va te faire voir!

3 *Fig (engrossed)* perdu, plongé, absorbé; **she was l. in her book** elle était plongée dans son livre; **to be l. in thought** être perdu dans ses pensées

4 *(wasted ▸ time)* perdu; *(▸ opportunity)* perdu, manqué; *(▸ youth)* gâché; **the allusion was l. on me** je n'ai pas compris *ou* saisi l'allusion; **your advice would be l. on them** leur donner un conseil serait peine perdue; **the hint/the suggestion was not l. on him** l'allusion/la suggestion ne lui a pas échappé; **your compliment was l. on her** elle ne s'est pas rendu compte que tu lui faisais un compliment; **French humour is l. on us** nous ne comprenons rien à l'humour français

5 *(confused, bewildered)* perdu; **I'm l., start again!** je suis perdu *ou* je ne vous suis plus, recommencez!; **I'm l. for words** je ne sais pas quoi dire

6 *(oblivious)* insensible; **he was l. to the world** il avait l'esprit ailleurs

▸▸ ***lost cause*** cause *f* perdue; *Am* ***lost and found*** objets *mpl* trouvés; ***the Lost Generation*** la génération perdue; *Br* ***lost property*** objets *mpl* trouvés; *Br* ***lost property office*** bureau *m* des objets trouvés; *Am* ***lost river*** rivière *f* souterraine

LOT [lɒt]

- groupe **1**
- sort **4**
- terrain **6**
- paquet **8**
- lot **2, 3**
- tirage au sort **5**
- studio **7**

N 1 *(group of people)* **this l. are leaving today and another l. are arriving tomorrow** ce groupe part aujourd'hui et un autre (groupe) arrive demain; **the new recruits are quite an interesting l.** les nouveaux sont tous assez intéressants; **I don't want you getting mixed up with that l.** je ne veux pas que tu traînes avec cette bande; *Pej* **that l. next door** la bande d'à côté; **come here, you l.!** venez ici, vous autres!; **you rotten l.!** bande de vauriens!; **he's a bad l.** c'est un sale type

2 *(group of things)* **most of the last l. of fans we had in were defective** presque tous les ventilateurs du dernier lot étaient défectueux; **take all this l. and dump it in my office** prends tout ça et mets-le dans mon bureau;

3 *(item in auction, in lottery)* lot *m*; **l. 49 is a set of five paintings** le lot 49 est un ensemble de cinq tableaux

4 *(destiny, fortune)* sort *m*, destin *m*; **to be content with one's l.** être content de son sort; **it was his l. in life to be the underdog** il était destiné à rester un sous-fifre; **it fell to my l. to be the first to try** le sort a voulu que je sois le premier à essayer; **to throw in one's l. with sb** se mettre du côté de qn

5 *(random choice)* **the winners are chosen by l.** les gagnants sont choisis par tirage au sort; **to draw** *or* **cast lots** tirer au sort

6 *Am (plot of land)* terrain *m*; **a vacant l.** un terrain vague; **a used car l.** un parking de voitures d'occasion

7 *Am Cin* studio *m* (de cinéma)

8 *Fin & St Exch (of bonds, shares)* paquet *m*; **in lots** par lots; **to buy/sell in one l.** acheter/vendre en bloc

• **lots** *Fam* **PRON** beaucoup☐; **do you need any paper/envelopes? I've got lots** est-ce que tu as besoin de papier/d'enveloppes? j'en ai plein; **there are lots to choose from** il y a du choix **ADV** beaucoup☐; **are you feeling better now? – oh, lots, thank you** vous vous sentez mieux maintenant? – oh, beaucoup mieux, merci; **this is lots easier than the last exam** c'est vachement plus facile que le dernier exam

• **a lot** **PRON** beaucoup; **there's a l. still to be done** il y a encore beaucoup à faire; **there's an awful l. wrong with the plan** il y a beaucoup de choses qui ne vont pas dans ce projet; **there's not a l. you can do about it** tu n'y peux pas grand-chose; **what did you think of his speech? – not a l.!** qu'as-tu pensé de son discours? – pas grand-chose!; **it did me a l. of good** ça m'a fait beaucoup de bien; **a l. of people think it's true** beaucoup de gens pensent que c'est vrai; **what a l. of people!** quelle foule!, que de monde!; **there's a l. of work still to be done** il reste encore beaucoup de travail à faire; **you have a l. of explaining to do** tu me dois des explications; **I've had such a l. of cards from well-wishers** j'ai vraiment reçu beaucoup de cartes de sympathie; **she takes a l. of care over her appearance** elle fait très attention à son apparence; **the party was a l. of fun** la soirée était vraiment bien; **we see a l. of them** nous les voyons beaucoup *ou* souvent; *Ironic* **a (fat) l. of help you were!, you were a (fat) l. of help!** ça, pour être utile, tu as été utile! **ADV** beaucoup; **a l. better/more** beaucoup mieux/plus; **their house is a l. bigger** leur maison est beaucoup plus grande; **she travels a l. on business** elle voyage beaucoup pour ses affaires; **thanks a l.!** merci beaucoup!; *Ironic* **a (fat) l. she cares!** elle s'en fiche pas mal!

• **lots of** **ADJ** *Fam* plein de☐; **we had lots of fun** on s'est bien marrés; **I've been there lots of times** j'y suis allé plein de fois; **lots of love** *(at end of letter)* je t'embrasse, grosses bises; **they've got money and lots of it!** ils ont de l'argent, et pas qu'un peu!

• **the lot** **PRON** le tout; **there isn't much, take the l.** il n'y en a pas beaucoup, prenez tout; **there aren't many, take the l.** il n'y en a pas beaucoup, prenez-les tous; **she ate the (whole) l.** elle a tout mangé; **the (whole) l. of them came** ils sont tous venus; **clear off, the l. of you** débarrassez-moi tous le plancher; **it only cost me a pound for the l.** le tout ne m'a coûté qu'une livre; **that's the l.** tout est là

▸▸ *Fin & St Exch* ***lot size*** unité *f* de transaction

loth = **loath**

lotion ['ləʊʃən] **N** lotion *f*

lottery ['lɒtərɪ] *(pl* **lotteries**) **N** loterie *f*; *Fig* **it's a bit of a l.** c'est une loterie

▸▸ *Br* ***lottery funding*** = fonds provenant de la loterie nationale; *Fin* ***lottery loan*** emprunt *m* à lots; *Fin* ***lottery loan bond*** titre *m* à lots; ***lottery ticket*** billet *m* de loterie

lotto ['lɒtəʊ] **N** loto *m* *(jeu de société)*

lotus ['ləʊtəs] **N** lotus *m*

▸▸ ***lotus position*** position *f* du lotus

lotus-eater **N** *Myth* lotophage *m*; *Fig* doux rêveur *m*

loud [laʊd] **ADJ 1** *(noise, shout)* grand, puissant; *(voice, music)* fort; *(explosion)* fort, violent; *(protest, applause)* vif; **the television is too l.** la télévision est trop forte, le son de la télévision est trop fort; **in a l. voice** à haute voix; **the door slammed with a l. bang** la porte a claqué très fort; **a l. argu-**

ment was going on in the next room on se disputait bruyamment dans la pièce voisine; **they were l. in their support/condemnation of the project** ils ont vigoureusement soutenu/condamné le projet **2** *Pej (loudmouthed, brash)* bruyant, tapageur; **he's a bit l., isn't he?** ce n'est pas le genre discret! **3** *(garish ▸ colour)* criard, voyant; *(▸ pattern, clothes)* voyant; **he wore a suit with a l. check** il portait un costume à carreaux très voyant

ADV fort; **can you speak a little louder?** pouvez-vous parler un peu plus fort?; **the music was turned up l.** on avait mis la musique à fond; **to read out l.** lire à haute voix; **I was thinking out l.** je pensais tout haut; **I hear you l. and clear** je te reçois cinq sur cinq; *Fam (I understand)* j'ai compris□

▸▸ *Mus* ***loud pedal*** pédale *f* forte

loudhailer [ˌlaʊd'heɪlə(r)] **N** *Br* porte-voix *m inv*, mégaphone *m*

loudly ['laʊdlɪ] **ADV 1** *(noisily ▸ speak)* d'une voix forte; *(▸ laugh)* bruyamment; *(vigorously)* avec force *ou* vigueur; **our neighbour banged l. on the wall** notre voisin a donné de grands coups contre le mur; **the supporters cheered l.** les supporters ont applaudi bruyamment; **we protested l.** nous avons protesté vigoureusement **2** *(garishly)* de façon tapageuse *ou* voyante

loudmouth ['laʊdmaʊθ, *pl* -maʊðz] **N** *Fam Pej* **to be a l.** *(noisy)* être *ou* avoir une grande gueule; *(indiscreet)* ne pas savoir tenir sa langue

loudmouthed ['laʊdmaʊðd] **ADJ** *Fam Pej (noisy)* fort en gueule, gueulard; *(indiscreet)* bavard, frimeur

loudness ['laʊdnɪs] **N 1** *(of sound)* intensité *f*, force *f*; *(of voice)* intensité *f*; *(of cheers)* vigueur *f*; **the l. of the music makes conversation impossible** la musique est tellement forte qu'on ne s'entend pas **2** *(of colours)* éclat *m*; **the l. of his ties** ses cravates voyantes

loudspeaker [ˌlaʊd'spiːkə(r)] **N** haut-parleur *m*; *(on stereo)* enceinte *f*, baffle *m*

lough [lɒk] **N** *Ir (lake)* lac *m*; *(inlet)* lagune *f*

Louisiana [luːˌiːzɪ'ænə] **N** *Geog* la Louisiane

lounge [laʊndʒ] **N 1** *(in house, on ship, in hotel)* salon *m*; *(at airport)* salle *f* d'attente **2** *(bar)* (salle *f* de) bar *m* **3** *(rest)* **to have a l. in the sun** paresser *ou* se prélasser au soleil

VI 1 *(recline)* s'allonger, se prélasser; *(sprawl)* être allongé; **he spent the afternoon lounging on the sofa reading** il a passé l'après-midi à lire allongé sur le canapé; **he lounged against the counter** il était appuyé nonchalamment contre le comptoir **2** *(laze)* paresser; *(hang about)* traîner

▸▸ *Br* ***lounge bar*** = salon dans un pub (plus confortable et plus cher que le "public bar"); ***lounge chair*** fauteuil *m*; *Fam Old-fashioned* ***lounge lizard*** salonnard *m*; *Br* ***lounge suit*** costume *m* de ville; *(on invitation)* tenue *f* de ville

▸**lounge about, lounge around VI** *(laze)* paresser; *(hang about)* traîner

lounger ['laʊndʒə(r)] **N 1** *(sunbed)* lit *m* bain de soleil **2** *(person)* paresseux(euse) *m,f*

louse [laʊs] *(pl sense* **1 lice** [laɪs], *pl sense* **2 louses)** **N 1** *Entom* pou *m* **2** *Fam (person)* peau *f* de vache

VT *(remove lice from)* épouiller

▸**louse up VT SEP** *Fam (spoil)* foutre en l'air

lousewort ['laʊswɜːt] **N** *Bot* pédiculaire *f* des forêts

lousiness ['laʊzɪnɪs] **N** *Fam (poor quality ▸ of performance, weather, service, salary)* nullité *f*

lousy ['laʊzɪ] *(compar* **lousier**, *superl* **lousiest)** **ADJ 1** *Fam (appalling ▸ film, singer)* nul; *(▸ weather)* pourri; **we had a l. holiday** on a passé des vacances nulles; **they made a l. job of it** ils ont fait ça n'importe comment; **I feel l. this morning** je suis mal fichu ce matin; **I'm l. at tennis, I'm a l. tennis player** je suis nul au tennis, je joue au tennis comme un pied; **it's in l. condition** il est en très mauvais état□; **you're a l. liar** *(lie badly)* tu ne sais pas mentir□; *(as intensifier)* tu n'es qu'un sale menteur

2 *Fam (annoying)* fichu, sacré; **I've got these l. letters to write!** j'ai ces fichues lettres à écrire!; **all for a l. £5** tout ça à cause de 5 malheureuses livres

3 *Fam (mean)* vache; **that's a l. thing to do/say** c'est dégueulasse *ou* moche de faire/dire une chose pareille; **he's l. to his wife** il est dégueulasse avec sa femme; **a l. trick** un sale tour

4 *Fam (guilty)* **I feel l. about what happened** je culpabilise à cause de ce qui est arrivé

5 *Fam (full)* **the town was l. with police** la ville grouillait de flics; **they're l. with money** ils sont bourrés de fric *ou* pleins aux as

6 *(lice-infested)* pouilleux

lout [laʊt] **N** *(bumpkin)* rustre *m*; *(hooligan)* voyou *m*; **you ignorant l.!** espèce de brute épaisse!

loutish ['laʊtɪʃ] **ADJ** *(behaviour)* grossier; *(manners)* de rustre, mal dégrossi

louvre, *Am* **louver** ['luːvə(r)] **N 1** *Archit (board)* abat-vent *m inv*, abat-son *m* **2** *(in door, window)* persienne *f*; *Naut* louvre *m*; *Aut & Aviat (of ventilation inlet, car bonnet)* persienne *f*, volet *m*; *Tech (of air intake)* ouïe *f*

▸▸ *Archit* ***louvre board*** abat-vent *m inv*, abat-son *m*; ***louvre door*** porte *f* à persiennes

louvred, *Am* **louvered** ['luːvəd] **ADJ** à claire-voie

lovable ['lʌvəbəl] **ADJ** charmant, attachant; **l. rogue** petit coquin *m*

lovage ['lʌvɪdʒ] **N** *Bot* livèche *f*

LOVE [lʌv]

> **N**
> • amour **1–3** • passion **4**
> • zéro **6**
> **VT**
> • aimer **1–3**

N 1 *(for person)* amour *m*; **we didn't marry for l.** nous n'avons pas fait un mariage d'amour; **he did it out of l. for her** il l'a fait par amour pour elle; **it was l. at first sight** ce fut le coup de foudre; **to be in l. (with sb)** être amoureux (de qn), *Can* être en amour (avec qn); **they were deeply in l.** ils s'aimaient profondément; **to fall in l. (with sb)** tomber amoureux (de qn), *Can* tomber en amour (avec qn); **to make l.** *(have sex)* faire l'amour; *Literary (flirt)* se faire la cour; **to make l. to sb** *(have sex with)* faire l'amour à qn; *Literary (court)* faire la cour à qn; **make l. not war!** faites l'amour, pas la guerre!; *Fam* **for the l. of God** *or Br* **Mike!** pour l'amour du ciel!; **Mark sends** *or* **gives you his l.** Mark t'embrasse; **give my l. to Gordon** embrasse Gordon de ma part *ou* pour moi; **(lots of) l. from Jayne, all my l., Jayne** *(in letter)* affectueusement, Jayne; *Fam* **you can't get a taxi for l. nor money round here** pas moyen de trouver un taxi par ici; **there's no l. lost between them** ils se détestent cordialement

2 *(for object, hobby, one's country etc)* amour *m*; **his l. of good food** sa passion pour la bonne chère; **he has a great l. of Scotland** il aime beaucoup l'Écosse; **she fell in l. with the house immediately** elle a eu le coup de foudre pour la maison; **I don't do this job for the l. of it** je ne fais pas ce travail pour le *ou* par plaisir

3 *(beloved person)* amour *m*; **he's one of her many loves** c'est un des nombreux hommes qu'elle a aimés; **she's the l. of his life** c'est la femme de sa vie; *Br Fam* **isn't he a l.!** ce qu'il est mignon *ou* chou!

4 *(favourite activity)* passion *f*; **music is his great l.** la musique est sa grande passion

5 *(term of endearment)* **(my) l.** mon amour; *Br Fam* **more coffee, l.?** tu prends encore du café, mon petit/ma petite?; *Br Fam* **there you are, l.!** *(speaking to customer)* voilà madame/mademoiselle/monsieur!

6 *Sport (in tennis)* zéro *m*; **40 l.** 40 zéro; **two sets to l.** deux sets à rien *ou* à zéro

VT 1 *(partner, spouse)* aimer; *(friends, relatives)* aimer beaucoup *ou* bien; **I like you but I don't l. you** je t'aime bien mais je ne suis pas amoureux de toi; *Fam* **I'll have to l. you and leave you** ce n'est pas le tout mais il faut que j'y aille

2 *(enjoy)* aimer, adorer; **don't you just l. that little dress?** cette petite robe est vraiment adorable, tu ne trouves pas?; **I l. lying** *or* **to lie in bed on Sunday mornings** j'adore faire la grasse matinée le dimanche; **she loves to hear you sing** elle adore vous entendre chanter; **I'd l. to come** j'aimerais beaucoup venir; **I'd l. you to come** j'aimerais beaucoup que *ou* cela me ferait très plaisir que tu viennes; **she'd l. to see you again** elle serait enchantée *ou* ravie de vous revoir; **would you like to come too? – I'd l. to** voudriez-vous venir aussi? – avec grand plaisir

3 *(prize ▸ one's country, freedom etc)* aimer

▸▸ ***love affair*** liaison *f* (amoureuse); *Fig* passion *f*; **his l. affair with Paris** sa passion pour Paris; ***love child*** enfant *mf* de l'amour; *Fam Hum* ***love handles*** poignées *fpl* d'amour; ***love knot*** lacs *m* d'amour; ***love letter*** lettre *f* d'amour, billet *m* doux; ***love life*** vie *f* sentimentale; *Fam* **how's your l. life?** comment vont tes amours?; ***love match*** mariage *m* d'amour; ***love nest*** nid *m* d'amour; ***love potion*** philtre *m*; ***love scene*** scène *f* d'amour; ***love song*** chanson *f* d'amour; ***love story*** histoire *f* d'amour; ***love token*** gage *m* d'amour; ***love triangle*** ménage *m* à trois

lovebird ['lʌvbɜːd] **N 1** *Orn* perruche *f*; **lovebirds** inséparables *mpl* **2** *Hum (lover)* amoureux(euse) *m,f*

lovebite ['lʌvbaɪt] **N** *Br* suçon *m*

loved-up [lʌvd-] **ADJ** *Br Fam (in love)* amoureux; *Drugs slang* tout gentil *(sous l'effet de l'ecstasy)*; **she's all l. with her new boyfriend** elle file le parfait amour avec son nouveau copain

love-hate ADJ

▸▸ ***a love-hate relationship*** une relation d'amour-haine

love-in-a-mist N *(UNCOUNT) Bot* cheveux *mpl* de Vénus, nigelle *f* de Damas

loveless ['lʌvlɪs] **ADJ** *(marriage)* sans amour; *(person ▸ unloved)* mal aimé; *(▸ unloving)* sans cœur, incapable d'aimer

love-lies-bleeding N *(UNCOUNT) Bot* queue-de-renard *f*, amarante *f*

loveliness ['lʌvlɪnɪs] **N** beauté *f*

lovelorn ['lʌvlɔːn] **ADJ** qui a des peines d'amour; **to be l.** avoir le mal d'amour

lovely ['lʌvlɪ] *(compar* **lovelier**, *superl* **loveliest)** **ADJ 1** *(in appearance ▸ person)* beau (belle), joli; *(▸ child)* joli, mignon; *(▸ home, scenery, dress)* joli **2** *(view, evening, weather)* beau (belle); *(holiday)* (très) agréable; *(meal)* excellent; **what a l. day!** quelle belle journée!; **we had a l. day at the beach** nous avons passé une très agréable journée à la plage; **have a l. time!** amusez-vous bien!; **it's a l. idea** c'est une très bonne idée; **it's l. to see you** je suis enchanté *ou* ravi de vous voir; *Br* **this wool is l. and soft** cette laine est très douce au toucher; *Br* **it's l. and warm by the fire** il fait bon près de la cheminée; **it sounds l.** cela a l'air très bien; **would you like to come to dinner next week? – that'd be l.** tu veux venir dîner la semaine prochaine? – ça serait vraiment bien *ou* avec plaisir **3** *(in character)* charmant, très aimable; **what a l. woman!** quelle femme charmante!

N *Fam (girl)* mignonne *f*; **come on, my l.** *(said to a horse)* allez, hue cocotte

lovemaking ['lʌvˌmeɪkɪŋ] **N 1** *(sexual intercourse)* ébats *mpl* (amoureux); **during their l.** pendant qu'ils faisaient l'amour **2** *Arch (courtship)* cour *f*

lover ['lʌvə(r)] **N 1** *(sexual partner)* amant(e) *m,f*; **he fancies himself as a great l.** il se considère comme un merveilleux amant **2** *Old-fashioned (suitor)* amoureux *m*, soupirant *m*; **the young lovers** les jeunes amoureux *mpl* **3** *(enthusiast)* amateur(trice) *m,f*; **he's a real music l.** c'est un mélomane; **I'm not a dog l. myself** moi-même je n'aime pas beaucoup les chiens; **for all lovers of good food** pour tous les amateurs de bonne cuisine; **she's a great l. of the cinema** elle adore le cinéma, c'est une grande cinéphile

lover-boy N *Fam Ironic (womanizer)* don Juan□ *m*, tombeur *m*, séducteur□ *m*; **morning, l.!** bonjour, chéri!; **she's gone out with l.** elle est sortie avec son jules; **when's l. coming round to see you?** quand est-ce qu'il vient te voir, ton jules?

lovesick ['lʌvsɪk] **ADJ to be l.** se languir d'amour

lovesickness ['lʌvsɪknɪs] **N** mal *m* d'amour

lovey-dovey ['lʌvɪˌdʌvɪ] **ADJ** *Fam Pej* doucereux

-loving [ˈlʌvɪŋ] SUFF **wine-l.** qui aime le vin, amateur de vin; **music-l.** amateur de musique, mélomane; **home-l.** casanier

loving [ˈlʌvɪŋ] ADJ *(affectionate)* affectueux; *(tender)* tendre; **l. kindness** bonté *f*; **your l. mother** *(at end of letter)* ta mère qui t'aime

►► ***loving cup*** coupe *f* de l'amitié

lovingly [ˈlʌvɪŋlɪ] ADV *(affectionately)* affectueusement; *(tenderly)* tendrement; *(passionately)* avec amour, amoureusement; *(with great care)* soigneusement, avec soin

LOW [ləʊ]

ADJ
- bas **1–4, 6, 9, 10**
- faible **2–5, 9**
- mauvais **5**
- grossier **7**

ADV
- bas **1–3**
- à bas prix **4**

N
- bas **1**
- niveau bas **2**
- minimum **3**
- dépression **4**

VI
- beugler

ADJ **1** *(in height)* bas; **this room has a l. ceiling** cette pièce est basse de plafond; **l. hills** collines peu élevées; **a l. neckline** un décolleté; **the sun was already l. in the sky** le soleil était déjà bas dans le ciel; **the houses are built on l. ground** les maisons sont bâties dans une cuvette; **l. bridge** *(sign)* hauteur limitée

2 *(in scale ► temperature)* bas; *(► level)* faible; **the temperature is in the l. twenties** il fait un peu plus de vingt degrés; **old people are given very l. priority** les personnes âgées ne sont absolument pas considérées comme prioritaires; **I've reached a l. point in my career** j'ai atteint un creux dans ma carrière; **a l. blood count** une numération globulaire basse

3 *(in degree, intensity ► probability, visibility)* faible; *(► fire)* bas; *(► lighting)* faible, tamisé; **cook on a l. heat** faire cuire à feu doux

4 *(below average ► number, cost, price, rate)* bas, faible; *(► profit)* faible, maigre; *(► salary)* peu élevé; **attendance was l.** il y avait peu de monde; **we're only playing for l. stakes** nous ne jouons que de petites mises, nous ne jouons pas de grosses sommes; **we're rather l. on whisky** on n'a plus beaucoup de whisky; **we're getting l. on kerosene** nous allons bientôt être à court de kérosène; **our water supply is getting l.** notre réserve d'eau baisse; **the ammunition is getting l.** nous aurons bientôt épuisé les munitions; **l. in calories** pauvre en calories

5 *(poor ► intelligence, standard)* faible; *(► opinion)* faible, piètre; *(► in health)* mauvais, médiocre; *(► in quality)* mauvais; **he's very l. at the moment** il est bien bas *ou* bien affaibli en ce moment; **I'm in rather l. spirits, I feel rather l.** je n'ai pas le moral, je suis assez déprimé; **a l. quality carpet** une moquette de mauvaise qualité

6 *(in rank)* bas, inférieur; **to be of l. birth** être de basse extraction *ou* d'origine modeste; **l. ranking officials** petits fonctionnaires *mpl*, fonctionnaires *mpl* subalternes

7 *(vulgar ► behaviour)* grossier; *(► tastes)* vulgaire; **that was a l. trick** c'était un sale tour; **a man of l. cunning** un homme d'une ruse ignoble

8 *(primitive)* **l. forms of life** des formes de vie inférieures *ou* peu évoluées

9 *(soft ► voice, music)* bas, faible; *(► light)* faible; **keep your voice l.** ne parlez pas trop fort; **in a l. voice** à voix basse, à mi-voix; **turn the radio down l.** mettez la radio moins fort; **turn the lights down l.** baissez les lumières; **she gave a l. groan** elle poussa un faible gémissement

10 *(deep ► note, voice)* bas

11 *Cards* **to play a l. trump** jouer un petit atout

ADV **1** *(in height)* bas; **lower down** plus bas; **aim l.** visez bas; **I can't bend down that l.** je ne peux pas me pencher si bas; **a helicopter flew l. over the town** un hélicoptère a survolé la ville à basse altitude; **he bowed l.** il s'inclina profondément; **to lie l.** *(hide)* se cacher; *(keep low profile)* adopter un profil bas; **to be laid l.** *(ill)* être immobilisé

2 *(in intensity)* bas; **the fire had burnt l.** le feu avait baissé; **stocks are running l.** les réserves baissent; **the batteries are running l.** les piles sont usées; **turn the music down l.** baisse la musique

3 *(in tone)* bas; **I can't sing that l.** je ne peux pas chanter aussi bas

4 *(in price)* **to buy l.** acheter à bas prix; *St Exch* acheter quand les cours sont bas

5 *(morally)* **I wouldn't stoop** *or* **sink so l. as to tell lies** je ne m'abaisserais pas à mentir

N **1** *(in height)* bas *m*

2 *(degree, level)* niveau *m* bas, point *m* bas; **the dollar has reached a record l.** le dollar a atteint son niveau le plus bas; **the share price has reached a new l.** l'indice des actions est descendu à son plus bas niveau; **inflation is at an all-time l.** l'inflation est à son niveau le plus bas; **relations between them are at an all-time l.** leurs relations n'ont jamais été si mauvaises; *St Exch* **the highs and lows** les hauts *mpl* et les bas *mpl*

3 *(setting)* minimum *m*; **the heating is on l.** le chauffage est au minimum

4 *Met* dépression *f*

5 *Am Aut* **in l.** en première/seconde

VI meugler, beugler

►► ***Cards the low cards*** les basses cartes *fpl*; ***Low Church*** N = section de l'Église anglicane qui se distingue par la simplicité du rituel ADJ = de tendance conservatrice, dans l'Église anglicane; *Theat* ***low comedy*** farce *f*; ***the Low Countries*** les Pays-Bas *mpl*; **in the L. Countries** aux Pays-Bas; *Am* ***low gear*** première (vitesse) *f*; *Aut* **engage l. gear** *(sign)* utilisez le frein moteur; ***Low German*** bas allemand *m*; ***Low Latin*** bas latin *m*; ***low life*** pègre *f*; *(individual ► disreputable)* voyou *m*, crapule *f*; *(► criminal)* membre *m* du milieu *ou* de la pègre; *Rel* ***Low Mass*** messe *f* basse; ***low pressure*** basse pression *f*; *Met* **a l. pressure area, an area of l. pressure** une zone de basse pression; ***the low season*** la basse saison; ***low technology*** technologie *f* de base; ***low tide*** marée *f* basse; **at l. tide** à marée basse; ***low water*** *(UNCOUNT)* basses eaux *fpl*

low-alcohol ADJ à faible teneur en alcool

low-angle shot N *TV & Cin* contre-plongée *f*

lowboy [ˈləʊbɔɪ] N commode *f* (basse)

lowbrow [ˈləʊbraʊ] *Pej* N personne *f* sans prétentions intellectuelles *ou* terre à terre

ADJ *(person)* peu intellectuel, terre à terre *(inv)*; *(book, film)* sans prétentions intellectuelles; *(literature)* de hall de gare

low-budget ADJ économique

low-calorie, low-cal [-kæl] ADJ (à) basses calories

low-carb ADJ *(food, diet)* à faible teneur en glucides

low-class ADJ *(lower-class)* populaire

low-cost ADJ à bas prix; *(housing, accommodation)* à loyer modéré

►► *Aviat* ***low-cost airline*** low-cost *m ou f*

low-cut ADJ décolleté

low-density housing N zones *fpl* d'habitation peu peuplées

low-down ADJ **1** *(shameful)* honteux, bas; *(mean)* mesquin; **that was a dirty l. trick** c'était un sale tour **2** *Am (depressed)* cafardeux; **I'm feeling l.** j'ai le cafard

low-end ADJ *Mktg* bas de gamme

lower[1] [ˈləʊə(r)] ADJ *(compar of* **low**) inférieur, plus bas; **people in the l. income brackets** *or* **groups** les gens appartenant aux tranches de revenus inférieures

ADV *(compar of* **low**) **the l. paid** la tranche inférieure du salariat

VT **1** *(eyes, blind, head, window)* baisser; *(sails)* abaisser, amener; *(lifeboat)* mettre à la mer; **l. your aim a bit** visez un peu plus bas; **supplies were lowered down to us on a rope** on nous a descendu des provisions au bout d'une corde; *Theat* **to l. the curtain** baisser le rideau; **she lowered herself into the water** elle se laissa glisser dans l'eau; **to l. one's guard** *Boxing* baisser sa garde; *Fig* prêter le flanc **2** *(reduce ► price, interest rate, pressure, standard)* baisser, diminuer; *(► temperature)* abaisser; **l. your voice** parlez moins fort, baissez la voix **3** *(morally)* **she wouldn't l. herself to talk to them** elle ne s'abaisserait pas au point de leur adresser la parole

VI *(diminish ► pressure)* diminuer; *(► price)* baisser

►► ***Lower Austria*** la Basse-Autriche; *Anat* ***lower back*** reins *mpl*; **to have l. back pain** avoir mal aux reins; ***Lower California*** la Basse-Californie; *Br Pol* ***the lower Chamber*** la Chambre basse *ou* des communes; ***the lower classes*** les classes *fpl* inférieures; ***the lower deck*** *(of ship)* le pont inférieur; *Br Pol* ***the Lower House*** la Chambre basse *ou* des communes; *Anat* ***lower jaw*** mâchoire *f* inférieure; ***the lower middle class*** la petite bourgeoisie; ***the lower ranks*** *(in army)* les rangs *mpl* inférieurs; ***Lower Saxony*** la Basse-Saxe; ***the lower school*** les petites classes *fpl*; ***lower vertebrates*** vertébrés *mpl* inférieurs

lower[2] [ˈlaʊə(r)] VI **1** *(sky, weather)* se couvrir **2** *(person)* regarder d'un air menaçant; **he sat in the corner and lowered at me** il s'assit dans un coin et il me regarda d'un œil *ou* d'un air menaçant

lower-case [ˈləʊə-] *Typ* N bas *m* de casse, minuscule *f*; **in l.** en bas de casse, minuscule

ADJ en bas de casse, minuscule

lower-class [ˈləʊə-] ADJ populaire

lower-income [ˈləʊər-] ADJ à revenu moyens

►► ***lower-income group*** groupe *m* de contribuables à revenus moyens

lowering[1] [ˈləʊərɪŋ] N **1** *(of flag)* abaissement *m*; *(of boat)* mise *f* à la mer; **the l. of the coffin into the grave** la descente du cercueil dans la tombe **2** *(reduction ► of temperature, standards, prices)* baisse *f*

ADJ humiliant

lowering[2] [ˈlaʊərɪŋ] ADJ *(sky)* sombre, couvert; *(clouds, look)* menaçant

lowest [ˈləʊɪst] ADJ *(superl of* **low**) le plus bas; **the sun was at its l.** le soleil était très bas sur l'horizon; **the l. of the low** le dernier des derniers

►► ***lowest bidder*** moins-disant *m*; *Math & Fig* ***the lowest common denominator*** le plus petit dénominateur commun; *Fig Pej* **TV is dumbing down to appeal to the l. common denominator** la télévision vise le niveau le plus bas pour plaire au plus grand nombre; *Math* ***the lowest common multiple*** le plus petit commun multiple

low-flying ADJ qui vole à basse altitude

low-grade ADJ *(in quality)* de qualité inférieure; *(in rank)* (de rang) inférieur, subalterne

low-hanging fruit N *Am Fam Fig* = tâche la plus facile à réaliser ou objectif le plus facile à atteindre

low-heeled [-hiːld] ADJ à talons plats

low-income ADJ à faible revenu

►► ***low-income group*** groupe *m* de contribuables à faibles revenus

lowing [ˈləʊɪŋ] N *(UNCOUNT) Literary* meuglement *m*, beuglement *m*, mugissement *m*

low-interest ADJ *Fin (credit, loan)* à taux réduit

low-key ADJ *(style)* discret(ète); *(person)* réservé; **the meeting was a very l. affair** la réunion s'est tenue dans la plus grande discrétion; **a l. approach** une approche discrète

lowland [ˈləʊlənd] N plaine *f*, basse terre *f*

• **Lowlands** NPL **the Lowlands** *(in Scotland)* les Lowlands *fpl*

►► ***Lowland Scots*** écossais *m* *(parlé dans les Lowlands)*

low-level ADJ *(talks)* à bas niveau; *(operation)* de faible envergure

►► *Aviat* ***low-level flying*** vol *m* à basse altitude; *Med* ***low-level infection*** infection *f* bénigne; *Comput* ***low-level language*** langage *m* non évolué *ou* de bas niveau; *Nucl* ***low-level radiation*** irradiation *f* de faible intensité

low-life ADJ *(criminal)* du milieu; *(disreputable)* louche

lowlights [ˈləʊlaɪts] NPL **1** *(in hair)* mèches *fpl* **2** *Fam (worst points)* points *mpl* noirs

lowliness [ˈləʊlɪnɪs] N humilité *f*

low-loader N *Rail* wagon *m* à plate-forme surbaissée; *Aut* camion *m* à plate-forme surbaissée

lowly [ˈləʊlɪ] *(compar* **lowlier**, *superl* **lowliest**) ADJ *(modest)* modeste; *(meek)* humble; *(simple)* sans prétention *ou* prétentions; **of l. birth** issu d'un milieu humble

low-lying ADJ *(land ▸ gen)* bas; *(▸ below sea level)* au-dessous du niveau de la mer; *(cloud)* bas

low-maintenance ADJ *(pet)* qui ne demande pas beaucoup de soins; *(garden, hairstyle)* qui ne demande pas beaucoup d'entretien; *Hum (girlfriend, boyfriend)* peu exigeant
▸▸ ***low-maintenance battery*** batterie *f* à entretien réduit

low-necked ADJ décolleté

lowness [ˈləʊnɪs] N **1** *(of wall, building)* faible hauteur *f*; *(of land)* faible élévation *f*
2 *(of wages, prices)* modicité *f*
3 *(of temperature)* faible élévation *f*
4 *(of voice ▸ softness)* douceur *f*; *(▸ in pitch)* profondeur *f*

low-octane fuel N carburant *m* à faible indice d'octane

low-pitched ADJ **1** *(voice, note)* bas, grave **2** *(roof)* à faible pente

low-pressure ADJ **1** *(gas)* sous faible pression, de basse pression; *(tyre)* à basse pression **2** *(job)* peu stressant

low-profile ADJ *(talks, visit)* discret(ète)
▸▸ *Aut* ***low-profile tyre*** pneu *m* à profil bas

low-rent ADJ **1** *(housing)* à loyer modéré **2** *Pej (low-quality)* bas de gamme

low-resolution ADJ à basse résolution

low-rise N immeuble *m* bas
ADJ **1** *(building)* de faible hauteur, bas **2** *(jeans, trousers)* taille basse *(inv)*

low-salt ADJ à faible teneur en sel

low-speed ADJ *(engine)* à petite vitesse, à vitesse réduite

low-spirited ADJ déprimé, démoralisé

low-tar ADJ *(cigarettes)* à faible teneur en goudron

low-tech ADJ rudimentaire

low-tension ADJ *Elec* (de) basse tension *(inv)*
▸▸ ***low-tension circuit*** circuit *m* basse tension

low-voltage ADJ à faible voltage, à faible tension

low-wage ADJ
▸▸ ***low-wage economy*** économie *f* où les salaires sont bas

loyal [ˈlɔɪəl] ADJ loyal, fidèle; *Mktg (customer)* fidèle; **to be l. to sb** être loyal envers qn, faire preuve de loyauté envers qn; **a l. friend** un ami fidèle; **l. supporters** partisans *mpl* fidèles

loyalist [ˈlɔɪəlɪst] N loyaliste *mf*
ADJ loyaliste
• **Loyalist** N loyaliste *mf*

> **LOYALIST**
> Dans le contexte britannique, le mot "Loyalist" désigne un protestant d'Irlande du Nord souhaitant rester au sein du Royaume-Uni.

loyally [ˈlɔɪəlɪ] ADV loyalement, fidèlement

loyalty [ˈlɔɪəltɪ] *(pl* **loyalties**) N **1** *(faithfulness)* loyauté *f*, fidélité *f*; **the party demands l. to the principles of democracy** le parti exige le respect des principes de la démocratie; **her l. to the cause is not in doubt** son dévouement à la cause n'est pas mis en doute **2** *(tie)* **tribal loyalties** liens *mpl* tribaux; **my loyalties are divided** je suis déchiré (entre les deux), entre les deux mon cœur balance
▸▸ *Mktg* ***loyalty card*** carte *f* de fidélité; *Mktg* ***loyalty discount*** remise *f* de fidélité; *Mktg* ***loyalty magazine*** = magazine publié par une chaîne de magasins, une banque etc, pour ses clients

lozenge [ˈlɒzɪndʒ] N **1** *(sweet)* pastille *f*; **throat l.** pastille *f* pour la gorge **2** *(rhombus)* losange *m*

> Note that the French word **losange** never refers to a medicated tablet.

LP [ˌelˈpiː] N *(abbr* **long-player**) 33 tours *m*

L-plate N *Br* = plaque apposée sur une voiture et signalant un apprenti conducteur, A

LQ [ˌelˈkjuː] *Comput (abbr* **letter quality**) qualité *f* courrier
▸▸ ***LQ printer*** imprimante *f* de qualité courrier

LSD[1] [ˌelesˈdiː] N *(abbr* **lysergic acid diethylamide**) LSD *m*

LSD[2], **lsd** N *Formerly (abbr* **librae, solidi, denarii**) = symboles représentant les "pounds", les "shillings" et les "pence" de l'ancienne monnaie britannique avant l'adoption du système décimal en 1971

LSE [ˌelesˈiː] N **1** *Univ (abbr* **London School of Economics**) = grande école de sciences économiques et politiques à Londres **2** *St Exch (abbr* **London Stock Exchange**) = la Bourse de Londres

L-shaped ADJ en (forme de) L

LSI [ˌelesˈaɪ] N *Comput (abbr* **large scale integration**) intégration *f* à grande échelle

LT *(written abbr* **low tension**) BT

Lt. *Mil (written abbr* **lieutenant**) Lieut.

LTA [ˌeltiːˈeɪ] N *(abbr* **Lawn Tennis Association**) = la Fédération britannique de tennis

Ltd, **ltd** *(written abbr* **limited**) SARL, *Can* limité; **Smith and Sons L.** Smith & Fils, SARL

lube [luːb] *Fam* N *(lubricant)* lubrifiant[□] *m*
VT lubrifier[□]

lubricant [ˈluːbrɪkənt] N lubrifiant *m*
ADJ lubrifiant

lubricate [ˈluːbrɪkeɪt] VT *(gen)* lubrifier; *(mechanism)* lubrifier, graisser, huiler

lubricating [ˈluːbrɪkeɪtɪŋ] N lubrification *f*
▸▸ ***lubricating oil*** huile *f* de graissage

lubrication [ˌluːbrɪˈkeɪʃən] N *(gen)* lubrification *f*; *(of mechanism)* lubrification *f*, graissage *m*, huilage *m*; *Fam Hum (alcohol)* gnôle *f*
▸▸ ***lubrication nipple*** graisseur *m*; ***lubrication oil*** huile *f* de lubrification; ***lubrication system*** circuit *m* de lubrification

lubricator [ˈluːbrɪkeɪtə(r)] N graisseur *m*

lubricity [luːˈbrɪsətɪ] N *Literary (lewdness)* lubricité *f*

Lucerne [luːˈsɜːn] N Lucerne

lucerne [luːˈsɜːn] N *Br Bot* luzerne *f*

lucid [ˈluːsɪd] ADJ **1** *(clear-headed)* lucide; **he has his l. moments** il a des moments de lucidité **2** *(clear)* clair, limpide; **a l. narrative style** un style d'une grande clarté; **she gave a l. account of events** elle donna un compte rendu net et précis des événements
▸▸ ***lucid interval*** intervalle *f* de lucidité

lucidity [luːˈsɪdətɪ] N **1** *(of mind)* lucidité *f* **2** *(of style, account)* clarté *f*, limpidité *f*

lucidly [ˈluːsɪdlɪ] ADV lucidement, avec lucidité

Lucifer [ˈluːsɪfə(r)] PR N Lucifer

luck [lʌk] N **1** *(fortune)* chance *f*; **to have good l.** avoir de la chance; **good l.!** bonne chance!; *Ironic* **good l. to you!** je vous souhaite bien du plaisir!; **good l. in your new job!** bonne chance pour ton nouveau travail!; **we had a bit of bad l. with the car** on a eu un pépin avec la voiture; **you've brought me nothing but bad l.** tu ne m'as causé que des malheurs; **it's bad l. to spill salt** renverser du sel porte malheur; **bad** *or* **hard** *or* **tough l.!** pas de chance!; **we thought the exam was cancelled – no such l.** nous croyions que l'examen était annulé – ç'aurait été trop beau; **to be down on one's l.** avoir la poisse *ou* la guigne; **to push one's l.** jouer avec le feu; **with (any) l.** avec un peu de chance; **no, he hasn't asked me out, worse l.!** non, il ne m'a pas invitée à sortir, tant pis! **2** *(good fortune)* **that's a bit of l.!** c'est de la chance!; **you're in l., your l.'s in** vous avez de la chance; **we're out of l.** on n'a pas de chance; **better l. next time** vous aurez plus de chance la prochaine fois; **any l.?** alors, ça a marché?; **some people have all the l.!** il y en a qui ont vraiment de la chance!; *Ironic* **it would be just my l. to bump into my boss** ce serait bien ma veine de tomber sur mon patron **3** *(chance, opportunity)* hasard *m*; **it's the l. of the draw** c'est une question de chance; **to try one's l.** tenter sa chance; **as l. would have it** *(by chance)* par hasard; *(by good luck)* par bonheur; *(by bad luck)* par malheur

▸ **luck into** VT INSEP *Fam* **to l. into sth** dégoter qch

▸ **luck out** VI *Fam (succeed)* avoir de la veine

luckily [ˈlʌkɪlɪ] ADV heureusement, par chance; **l. for him, he escaped** heureusement pour lui, il s'est échappé

luckless [ˈlʌklɪs] ADJ *(person)* malchanceux; *(escapade, attempt)* malheureux

lucky [ˈlʌkɪ] *(compar* **luckier**, *superl* **luckiest**) ADJ *(fortunate ▸ person)* chanceux; *(▸ encounter, winner)* heureux; **to be l.** *(person)* avoir de la chance *(thing)* porter bonheur; *Fam* **to get l.** avoir un coup de bol; *(sexually)* faire une touche; **you're l. to have escaped with your life** vous avez eu de la chance de vous en tirer vivant; **what a l. escape!** on l'a échappé belle!; **it was l. for them that we were there** heureusement pour eux que nous étions là; **it's my l. day** c'est mon jour de chance; **to be born l.** être né coiffé; **who's the l. man?** *(she's going to marry)* qui est l'heureux élu?; *Fam* **you l. devil** *or* **thing!** sacré veinard!; **I'd like a pay rise – you'll be l.** *or* **you should be so l.!** j'aimerais une augmentation – tu peux toujours courir!; **you!** vous en avez de la chance! **2** *(token, number)* porte-bonheur *(inv)* **3** *(guess)* heureux
▸▸ *Fam* ***lucky break*** coup *m* de pot *ou* de bol; ***lucky charm*** porte-bonheur *m inv*; *Br* ***lucky dip*** = jeu consistant à chercher des cadeaux enfouis dans une caisse remplie de sciure ou dans un sac; *Fig* **the job market is a real l. dip at the moment** de nos jours, trouver un emploi, c'est vraiment une question de chance

Lucozade® [ˈluːkəzeɪd] N = boisson gazeuse à base de glucose

lucrative [ˈluːkrətɪv] ADJ *(job)* bien rémunéré, lucratif; *(activity, deal)* lucratif, rentable

lucre [ˈluːkə(r)] N *Hum Pej* **(filthy) l.** lucre *m*

Luddite [ˈlʌdaɪt] N luddite *m*; *Fig* personne *f* opposée au progrès
ADJ luddite

ludicrous [ˈluːdɪkrəs] ADJ ridicule, absurde

ludicrously [ˈluːdɪkrəslɪ] ADV ridiculement

ludo [ˈluːdəʊ] N *Br* (jeu *m* des) petits chevaux *mpl*

luff [lʌf] *Naut* N guindant *m*
VI lofer, aller au lof

lug [lʌg] *(pt & pp* **lugged**, *cont* **lugging**) N **1** *(for fixing)* ergot *m*, (petite) patte *f*; *(handle)* anse *f*, poignée *f* **2** *Br Fam (ear)* esgourde *f* **3** *Am (fool)* niais *m*; **of course I love you, you big l.!** bien sûr que je t'aime, gros bêta!
VT *Fam (carry, pull)* trimbaler; **he lugged his bicycle up the stairs** il s'est trimbalé sa bicyclette jusqu'en haut des escaliers
▸▸ ***lug screw*** vis *f* sans tête

luge [luːʒ] N *Sport* luge *f*

luggage [ˈlʌgɪdʒ] N *(UNCOUNT)* bagages *mpl*; **a piece of l.** un bagage
▸▸ ***luggage carrier*** porte-bagages *m inv*; ***luggage compartment*** compartiment *m* à bagages; *Br* ***luggage handler*** bagagiste *m*; *Naut* ***luggage hold*** soute *f* à bagages; ***luggage label*** étiquette *f* à bagages; ***luggage locker*** consigne *f* automatique; *Br* ***luggage rack*** *Rail (shelf)* porte-bagages *m inv (net)* filet *m* (à bagages); *Aut* galerie *f* (de toit); *Naut* ***luggage room*** soute *f* à bagages; ***luggage trolley*** chariot *m* à bagages; *Br Rail* ***luggage van*** fourgon *m* (à bagages)

lugger [ˈlʌgə(r)] N lougre *m*

lughole [ˈlʌghəʊl] N *Br Fam (ear)* esgourde *f*

lugsail [ˈlʌgseɪl] N *Naut* voile *f* à bourcet

lugubrious [lʊˈguːbrɪəs] ADJ lugubre

lugubriously [lʊˈguːbrɪəslɪ] ADV lugubrement, de façon lugubre

lugworm [ˈlʌgwɜːm] N *Zool* arénicole *f*

Luke [luːk] PR N *Bible* Luc; **the Gospel According to (Saint) L.** l'Évangile selon saint Luc

lukewarm [ˈluːkwɔːm] ADJ *(water, soup)* tiède *Fig* **a l. reception** *(of person)* un accueil peu chaleureux; *(of book, film)* un accueil mitigé

lull [lʌl] N *(in weather)* accalmie *f*; *(in fighting)* accalmie *f*, pause *f*; *(in conversation)* pause *f*; **the l. before the storm** le calme avant la tempête
VT *(calm ▸ anxiety, person)* calmer, apaiser; **she lulled the child to sleep** elle berça l'enfant jusqu'à ce qu'il s'endorme; **the sound of the engine lulled me to sleep** le ronronnement du moteur m'a endormi; **they were lulled into a false sense of security** ils ont fait l'erreur de se laisser rassurer par des propos lénifiants

lullaby [ˈlʌləbaɪ] *(pl* **lullabies**) N berceuse *f*

lumbago [lʌmˈbeɪgəʊ] N *Med (UNCOUNT)* lumbago *m*, lombalgie *f*

lumbar ['lʌmbə(r)] ADJ *Anat* lombaire
▸▸ ***lumbar adjustable seat*** siège *m* à réglage lombaire; *Med* ***lumbar puncture*** ponction *f* lombaire, rachicentèse *f*; ***lumbar vertebra*** lombaire *f*

lumber ['lʌmbə(r)] N **1** *Am (cut wood)* bois *m* (d'œuvre); *(ready for use)* bois *m* de construction *ou* de charpente **2** *Br (junk)* bric-à-brac *m inv*
VT *Am (logs)* débiter; *(tree)* abattre, couper
VI **1** *(large person, animal)* marcher pesamment; **I could hear him lumbering down the stairs** je l'entendais descendre l'escalier d'un pas pesant; **the tanks lumbered into the centre of the town** la lourde colonne de chars avançait vers le centre de la ville **2** *Am (fell trees)* abattre des arbres *(pour le bois)*
▸▸ ***lumber jacket*** grosse veste *f* de bûcheron; *Br* ***lumber room*** débarras *m*

lumbering ['lʌmbərɪŋ] N *Am* exploitation *f* forestière
ADJ *(heavy ▸ step)* pesant, lourd; (▸ *person)* lourd, maladroit

lumberjack ['lʌmbədʒæk] N bûcheron(onne) *m,f*
▸▸ ***lumberjack shirt*** chemise *f* de bûcheron *(chemise épaisse à grands carreaux)*

lumberman ['lʌmbəmən] *(pl* **lumbermen** [-mən]) N *Am* bûcheron *m*

lumberyard ['lʌmbəjɑːd] N *Am* dépôt *m* de bois

luminary ['luːmɪnərɪ] *(pl* **luminaries**) N *(celebrity)* lumière *f*, sommité *f*

luminescence [ˌluːmɪ'nesəns] N luminescence *f*

luminescent [ˌluːmɪ'nesənt] ADJ luminescent

luminosity [ˌluːmɪ'nɒsətɪ] N luminosité *f*

luminous ['luːmɪnəs] ADJ *(paint, colour, sky, watch face)* lumineux; *Fig (explanation, argument)* lumineux, limpide; *(clothing)* fluorescent
▸▸ *Phys* ***luminous flux*** flux *m* lumineux; *Phys* ***luminous intensity*** intensité *f* lumineuse

lumme ['lʌmɪ] EXCLAM *Br Fam Old-fashioned* ben mon vieux!

lummox ['lʌməks] N *Fam* empoté(e) *m,f*

lump [lʌmp] N **1** *(of sugar)* morceau *m*; **one l. or two?** un ou deux sucres?
2 *(of solid matter ▸ small)* morceau *m*; (▸ *large)* masse *f*; *(in food)* grumeau *m*; *(of stone, marble)* bloc *m*; *(of earth, clay)* motte *f*; **to have a l. in one's throat** avoir une boule dans la gorge, avoir la gorge serrée
3 *(bump)* bosse *f*; **I've got a l. on my forehead** j'ai une bosse au front; **there are lots of lumps in this mattress** ce matelas est plein de bosses *ou* est complètement défoncé
4 *Med (swelling)* grosseur *f*, protubérance *f*; **she has a l. in her breast** elle a une grosseur au sein
5 *(of money)* **you don't have to pay it all in one l.** vous n'êtes pas obligé de tout payer en une seule fois
6 *Fam Pej (clumsy person)* empoté(e) *m,f*
7 *Br Constr* **the l.** *(casual workers)* ouvriers *mpl* indépendants (non déclarés); *Fam* **to work on the l.** travailler au noir *(avec rémunération au forfait)*
VT *Fam (put up with)* **if that's her final decision, we'll just have to l. it!** puisque c'est sa décision définitive, on n'a plus qu'à s'écraser!; **if you don't like it you can l. it!** si ça ne te plaît pas, tant pis pour toi!
▸▸ ***lump sugar*** sucre *m* en morceaux; ***lump sum*** somme *f* forfaitaire, montant *m* forfaitaire; **to work for a l. sum** travailler à forfait; **to be paid in a l. sum** être payé en une seule fois

▸**lump together** VT SEP **1** *(gather together)* réunir, rassembler **2** *(consider the same)* mettre dans la même catégorie

lumpectomy [ˌlʌm'pektəmɪ] *(pl* **lumpectomies**) N *Med* ablation *f* d'une tumeur au sein

lumpen ['lʌmpən] ADJ grossier

lumpfish ['lʌmpfɪʃ] *(pl* **inv** *or* **lumpfishes**) N *Ich* lump *m*, lompe *m*
▸▸ ***lumpfish roe*** œufs *mpl* de lump

lumpish ['lʌmpɪʃ] ADJ *(clumsy)* maladroit; *(dull-witted)* idiot, abruti

lumpy ['lʌmpɪ] *(compar* **lumpier**, *superl* **lumpiest**) ADJ *(sauce)* plein de grumeaux; *(mattress)* plein de bosses, défoncé

lunacy ['luːnəsɪ] *(pl* **lunacies**) N **1** *(madness)* démence *f*, folie *f* **2** *(folly)* folie *f*; **it would be l. to accept such a proposal** ce serait de la folie d'accepter pareille proposition

lunar ['luːnə(r)] ADJ *(rock, month, cycle)* lunaire; *(eclipse)* de Lune
▸▸ *Astron* ***lunar landing*** alunissage *m*

lunaria [luː'neərɪə] N *Bot* lunaire *f*

lunatic ['luːnətɪk] N **1** *(madman)* aliéné(e) *m,f*, dément(e) *m,f* **2** *Fam (fool)* cinglé(e) *m,f*; **he's a complete l.!** il est fou à lier!, il est complètement cinglé!
ADJ **1** *(insane)* fou (folle), dément **2** *Fam (crazy ▸ person)* cinglé, dingue; (▸ *idea)* dément, démentiel
▸▸ ***lunatic asylum*** asile *m* d'aliénés; *Pej* ***lunatic fringe*** extrémistes *mpl* fanatiques

> Note that the French adjective **lunatique** is a false friend and is never a translation for the English word **lunatic**. It means **moody**.

lunch [lʌntʃ] N déjeuner *m*, *Can & Belg* dîner *m*; **to have l.** déjeuner; **after l.** après le déjeuner; **she's gone out for l.** elle est partie déjeuner; **what's for l.?** qu'y a-t-il pour le déjeuner?; **we're having trout for l.** il y a de la truite au déjeuner; **I've invited him for l. on Tuesday** je l'ai invité à déjeuner mardi prochain; **I have a l. date** je déjeune avec quelqu'un, je suis pris pour le déjeuner; *(for business)* j'ai un déjeuner d'affaires; **what did you have for l.?** qu'est-ce que tu as mangé à midi?; **he's out to l.** il est parti déjeuner; *Fam Fig* il débloque
VI *Formal* déjeuner, *Can & Belg* dîner; **we lunched on sandwiches** nous avons déjeuné de sandwichs
▸▸ ***lunch break*** *(in course of working day)* pause *f* du déjeuner; *Am* ***lunch counter*** *(in store)* bar *m* de restauration rapide; ***lunch hour*** heure *f* du déjeuner; **she's not here, it's her l. hour** elle n'est pas là, c'est l'heure à laquelle elle déjeune; ***lunch menu*** menu *m* déjeuner

lunchbox ['lʌntʃbɒks] N **1** *(for carrying lunch ▸ gen)* = boîte dans laquelle on transporte son déjeuner; (▸ *for workmen)* gamelle *f* **2** *Br Fam Hum (man's genitals)* service *m* trois pièces, bijoux *mpl* de famille

lunchbucket ['lʌntʃbʌkɪt] N *Am (for carrying lunch ▸ gen)* = boîte dans laquelle on transporte son déjeuner; (▸ *for workmen)* gamelle *f*

luncheon ['lʌntʃən] N *Formal* déjeuner *m*; **a literary l.** un déjeuner littéraire
▸▸ ***luncheon meat*** = bloc de viande de porc en conserve; *Br* ***luncheon voucher*** Ticket-Restaurant® *m inv*

luncheonette [ˌlʌntʃə'net] N *Am* snack *m*, snack-bar *m*

lunchpail ['lʌntʃpeɪl] N *Am (for carrying lunch ▸ gen)* = boîte dans laquelle on transporte son déjeuner; (▸ *for workmen)* gamelle *f*

lunchroom ['lʌntʃrʊm] N *Am* = pièce où l'on peut manger ses sandwichs etc à l'heure du déjeuner

lung [lʌŋ] N poumon *m*; **to shout at the top of one's lungs** crier à tue-tête
COMP *(artery, congestion, disease)* pulmonaire; *(transplant)* du poumon
▸▸ ***lung cancer*** cancer *m* du poumon; ***lung specialist*** pneumologue *mf*

lunge [lʌndʒ] N **1** *(sudden movement)* **to make a l. for sth** se précipiter vers qch **2** *Fencing & (in aerobics)* fente *f* (avant) **3** *Horseriding* longe *f*
VI **1** *(move suddenly)* faire un mouvement brusque en avant; **she lunged at him with a knife** elle se précipita sur lui avec un couteau **2** *Fencing* **he lunged at his opponent** il allongea une botte à son adversaire

▸**lunge forward** VI **1** se jeter en avant **2** *Fencing* se fendre

lupin ['luːpɪn] N *Bot* lupin *m*

lupine ['luːpaɪn] N *Am Bot* lupin *m*
ADJ de loup

lupus ['luːpəs] N *Med* lupus *m*; **l. vulgaris** lupus *m* vulgaire

lurch [lɜːtʃ] VI *(person)* tituber, chanceler; *(car ▸ swerve)* faire une embardée; (▸ *jerk forwards)* avancer par à-coups; *(ship)* tanguer; **she was lurching along** elle marchait en titubant; **he lurched into the room** il entra dans la pièce en titubant; **the car lurched out of control** la voiture livrée à elle-même fit une embardée
N *(of ship)* embardée *f*, coup *m* de roulis; *(of car)* embardée *f*; **the car gave a sudden l. and left the road** la voiture fit une embardée et quitta la route; **with a l., the train was off again** le train est reparti avec un à-coup; **to leave sb in the l.** laisser qn en plan

lurcher ['lɜːtʃə(r)] N = chien bâtard, croisement de lévrier et de colley

lure [ljʊə(r)] N **1** *(attraction)* attrait *m*; *(charm)* charme *m*; *(temptation)* tentation *f* **2** *Fishing & Hunt* leurre *m*
VT **1** *(person)* attirer (sous un faux prétexte); **he lured them into a trap** il les a attirés dans un piège **2** *Fishing & Hunt* leurrer

Lurex® ['lʊəreks] N *(thread)* Lurex® *m*; *(cloth)* tissu *m* en Lurex®

lurgy ['lɜːgɪ] N *Br Fam Hum* crève f; **I've got the dreaded l.** j'ai attrapé quelque chose

lurid ['ljʊərɪd] ADJ **1** *(sensational ▸ account, story)* macabre, atroce, horrible; *(salacious)* salace, malsain; **many newspapers go in for l. sensationalism** de nombreux journaux exploitent le goût du public pour le sensationnel; **their affair was described in l. detail** leur liaison était décrite avec force détails scabreux **2** *(glaring ▸ sky, sunset)* sanglant, rougeoyant; (▸ *wallpaper, shirt)* criard, voyant; **a l. green dress** une robe d'un vert criard

luridly ['ljʊərɪdlɪ] ADV *(garishly)* violemment, tapageusement

lurk [lɜːk] VI **1** *(person, animal)* se tapir; *(danger)* se cacher, menacer; *(doubt, worry)* persister; **the burglar was lurking behind the trees** le cambrioleur était tapi derrière les arbres **2** *Comput* rôder

lurking ['lɜːkɪŋ] ADJ *(suspicion)* vague; *(danger)* menaçant

luscious ['lʌʃəs] ADJ **1** *(fruit)* succulent; *(colour)* riche **2** *(woman)* séduisant; *(lips)* pulpeux

lush [lʌʃ] ADJ **1** *(vegetation)* riche, luxuriant; *(fruit)* succulent; *Fig (description)* riche **2** *(luxurious)* luxueux
N *Fam* poivrot(e) *m,f*

lushness ['lʌʃnɪs] N **1** *(of vegetation)* richesse *f*, luxuriance *f*; *(of fruit)* succulence *f*, *Fig (of description)* richesse *f* **2** *(luxuriousness)* luxe *m*

lust [lʌst] N **1** *(sexual desire)* désir *m* sexuel, concupiscence *f*; *(as sin)* luxure *f* **2** *(greed)* soif *f*, convoitise *f*; **l. for power** soif *f* de pouvoir

▸**lust after** VT INSEP *(person)* désirer, avoir envie de, convoiter; *(money, property)* convoiter

▸**lust for** VT INSEP *(money)* convoiter; *(revenge, power)* avoir soif de

luster *Am* = **lustre**

lustful ['lʌstfʊl] ADJ **1** *(lecherous)* lascif, sensuel **2** *(greedy)* avide

lustfully ['lʌstfʊlɪ] ADV **1** *(lecherously)* lascivement **2** *(greedily)* avidement

lustily ['lʌstɪlɪ] ADV *(sing, shout)* à pleine gorge, à pleins poumons

lustre, *Am* luster ['lʌstə(r)] N **1** *(sheen)* lustre *m*, brillant *m* **2** *Fig (glory)* éclat *m* **3** *Cer (glaze)* lustre *m*

lustreless, *Am* lusterless ['lʌstəlɪs] ADJ terne, sans éclat

lustreware, *Am* lusterware ['lʌstəweə(r)] N *(UNCOUNT) Cer* poterie *f* à reflets métalliques, poterie *f* lustrée

lustrous ['lʌstrəs] ADJ *(shiny ▸ pearls, stones)* lustré, chatoyant; (▸ *eyes)* brillant; (▸ *cloth)* lustré; **l. black hair** cheveux *mpl* d'un noir de jais

lusty ['lʌstɪ] *(compar* **lustier**, *superl* **lustiest**) ADJ *(strong ▸ person, baby)* vigoureux, robuste; (▸ *voice, manner)* vigoureux

lute [luːt] N **1** *Mus* luth *m* **2** *Tech* lut *m*
▸▸ *Mus* ***lute stop*** jeu *m* de luth

Lutheran ['luːθərən] N Luthérien(enne) *m,f*
ADJ luthérien

luv *Br Fam* = **love**

luvvie [ˈlʌvɪ] **N** *Fam Hum* acteur(trice) *m,f* prétentieux(euse)

luxation [lʌkˈseɪʃən] **N** *Med* luxation *f*

Luxembourg [ˈlʌksəmbɜːg] **N 1** *(country)* Luxembourg *m* **2** *(town)* Luxembourg
▸▸ *Formerly* **Luxembourg franc** franc *m* luxembourgeois

Luxembourger [ˈlʌksəmbɜːgə(r)] **N** Luxembourgeois(e) *m,f*

luxuriance [lʌgˈʒʊərɪəns] **N 1** *(luxury)* luxe *m*, somptuosité *f* **2** *(of vegetation)* luxuriance *f*, richesse *f*; *(of plants)* exubérance *f*, abondance *f*; *(of hair)* abondance *f*

luxuriant [lʌgˈʒʊərɪənt] **ADJ 1** *(luxurious ▸ surroundings)* luxueux, somptueux **2** *(vegetation)* luxuriant; *(crops, undergrowth)* abondant, riche; *(countryside)* couvert de végétation, luxuriant; *Fig (style)* luxuriant, riche **3** *(flowing ▸ hair, beard)* abondant

Attention: ne pas confondre avec **luxurious**.

luxuriantly [lʌgˈʒʊərɪəntlɪ] **ADV** *(grow)* en abondance, de façon luxuriante

luxuriate [lʌgˈʒʊərɪeɪt] **VI** *(take pleasure)* **to l. in sth** se délecter de qch; **to l. in the sun/in a hot bath** se prélasser au soleil/dans un bain chaud

luxurious [lʌgˈʒʊərɪəs] **ADJ** *(opulent ▸ house, decor, clothes)* luxueux, somptueux; *(▸ car)* luxueux; **to have l. tastes** avoir des goûts de luxe

Attention: ne pas confondre avec **luxuriant**.

luxuriously [lʌgˈʒʊərɪəslɪ] **ADV** *(with, in luxury)* luxueusement; **l. furnished** luxueusement *ou* richement meublé; **to live l.** vivre dans le luxe *ou* dans l'opulence

luxuriousness [lʌgˈʒʊərɪəsnɪs] **N** luxe *m*

luxury [ˈlʌkʃərɪ] *(pl* **luxuries***)* **N 1** *(comfort)* luxe *m*; **to live in l., to lead a life of l.** vivre dans le luxe **2** *(treat)* luxe *m*; **whisky is the one l. I still allow myself** le whisky est le seul luxe que je me permette encore; **one of life's little luxuries** un des petits plaisirs de la vie
COMP *(car, restaurant, kitchen)* de luxe; *(apartment)* de luxe, de standing
▸▸ ***luxury brand*** marque *f* de luxe; ***luxury goods*** articles *mpl* de luxe; *Fin* ***luxury tax*** taxe *f* (sur les produits) de luxe

Note that the French word **luxure** is a false friend and is never a translation for the English word **luxury**. It means **lust**.

LV *Br (written abbr* **luncheon voucher***)* Ticket-Restaurant® *m inv*

LW *Rad (written abbr* **long wave***)* GO

-LY SUFFIXE

• La plupart des adjectifs peuvent être transformés en adverbes de MANIÈRE par l'adjonction du suffixe **-ly**. **Quick** devient ainsi **quickly** (rapidement, vite); **intense** devient **intensely** (intensément, avec intensité), etc. La terminaison de l'adjectif doit parfois être modifiée avant la suffixation: **gay** devient **gaily** (gaiement); **whole** devient **wholly** (entièrement); **magnetic** devient **magnetically** (magnétiquement).

Les adverbes en **-ly** se traduisent souvent par un adverbe en **-ment** ou bien à l'aide d'une périphrase du type d'une "manière + adjectif". La forme "avec + nom" est également possible dans de nombreux cas:
completely complètement; **comparatively** relativement; **skilfully** habilement, d'une manière habile, avec habileté; **financially sound** solvable; **legally (speaking)** légalement, du point de vue légal.

Il existe quelques verbes dont le prétérit peut servir de radical dans la formation d'adverbes en **-ly**, p. ex.:
ashamedly d'une façon honteuse; **markedly better** nettement meilleur; **I feel decidedly unwell today** je ne me sens vraiment pas bien aujourd'hui.

Dans ce cas, le **-ed** de la terminaison se prononce comme une syllabe à part entière.

• Lorsqu'il vient s'ajouter à un substantif correspondant à une durée, **-ly** prend le sens de QUI SE PRODUIT À INTERVALLES RÉGULIERS, comme dans **his weekly visits** ses visites hebdomadaires; **she has a daily bath** elle prend un bain tous les jours.

Les mots formés de cette façon peuvent également s'utiliser comme adverbes: **he's paid hourly** il est payé à l'heure; **it is checked monthly** il est contrôlé une fois par mois.

• Le suffixe **-ly** peut aussi se combiner avec un nom pour former un adjectif. Il signifie alors COMME la chose ou la personne désignée par le nom:
friendly aimable, amical; **cowardly** lâche; **ghostly** spectral; **brotherly love** amour fraternel; **deathly pale** pâle comme la mort; **a princely sum** une somme princière.

lychee [ˌlaɪˈtʃiː] **N** litchi *m*, lychee *m*

lycopene [ˈlaɪkəpiːn] **N** *Chem* lycopène *m*

Lycra® [ˈlaɪkrə] **N** Lycra® *m*

lye [laɪ] **N** *Chem* lessive *f*

lying [ˈlaɪɪŋ] **ADJ 1** *(reclining)* couché, étendu, allongé **2** *(dishonest ▸ person)* menteur; *(▸ story)* mensonger, faux (fausse); *very Fam* **you l. bastard!** sale menteur!
N 1 *(of corpse)* **l. in state** exposition *f* du corps **2** *(UNCOUNT) (dishonesty)* mensonges *mpl*

lying-in **N** *Med* couches *fpl*

Lyme disease [laɪm-] **N** *Med* maladie *f* de Lyme

lymph [lɪmf] **N** lymphe *f*
▸▸ ***lymph gland, lymph node*** ganglion *m* lymphatique

lymphangitis [ˌlɪmfænˈdʒaɪtɪs] **N** *Med* lymphangite *f*

lymphatic [lɪmˈfætɪk] **ADJ** lymphatique
▸▸ ***lymphatic system*** système *m* lymphatique
lymphatic vessels vaisseaux *mpl* lymphatiques

lymphocyte [ˈlɪmfəʊsaɪt] **N** *Biol* lymphocyte *m*

lymphoma [lɪmˈfəʊmə] **N** *Med* lymphome *m*

lynch [lɪntʃ] **VT** lyncher
▸▸ ***Lynch law*** loi *f* de Lynch; ***lynch mob*** lyncheurs *mpl*

lynching [ˈlɪntʃɪŋ] **N** lynchage *m*

lynx [lɪŋks] *(pl* **inv** *or* **lynxes***)* **N** *Zool* lynx *m inv* *(European)* loup-cervier *m*

lynx-eyed **ADJ** aux yeux de lynx

Lyon, Lyons [liːɔ̃] **N** Lyon

lyre [ˈlaɪə(r)] **N** lyre *f*

lyrebird [ˈlaɪəbɜːd] **N** *Orn* oiseau-lyre *m*

lyric [ˈlɪrɪk] **ADJ** lyrique
N *(poem)* poème *m* lyrique
• **lyrics** **NPL** *(of song)* paroles *fpl*
▸▸ ***lyrics writer*** parolier(ère) *m,f*

lyrical [ˈlɪrɪkəl] **ADJ 1** *(poetic)* lyrique **2** *Fig (enthusiastic)* passionné; **he was positively l. about his visit to China** son séjour en Chine l'a véritablement enthousiasmé

lyrically [ˈlɪrɪkəlɪ] **ADV 1** *(poetically)* avec lyrisme **2** *(enthusiastically)* avec enthousiasme

lyricism [ˈlɪrɪsɪzəm] **N** lyrisme *m*

lyricist [ˈlɪrɪsɪst] **N** *(of poems)* poète *m* lyrique; *(of song, opera)* parolier(ère) *m,f*

lysergic [laɪˈsɜːdʒɪk] **ADJ** lysergique
▸▸ ***lysergic acid*** acide *m* lysergique

m

M[1], **m**[1] [em] **N** *(letter)* M, m *m inv*; **two m's** deux m; **M for mother** ≃ M comme Marcel; *Br* **the M5** *(road)* l'autoroute *f* M5

M[2] *(written abbr* **medium)** M

m[2] **1** *(written abbr* **metre)** m **2** *(written abbr* **million)** M **3** *(written abbr* **mile)** mile *m*

MA[1] ['em'eɪ] **N 1** *Univ (abbr* **Master of Arts)** *(in England, Wales and US ▸ person)* = titulaire d'une maîtrise de lettres; *(▸ qualification)* maîtrise *f* de lettres; *(in Scotland ▸ person)* = titulaire du premier examen universitaire, équivalent de la licence; *(▸ qualification)* = premier examen universitaire, équivalent de la licence; **to have an MA in Russian** avoir une maîtrise/licence de russe; **Susan Long, MA** Susan Long, licenciée ès lettres **2** *(abbr* **military academy)** école *f* militaire

MA[2] *(written abbr* **Massachusetts)** Massachusetts *m*

ma [mɑː] **N** *Fam* maman *f*; *Hum* **Ma Baker** la mère Baker

ma'am [mæm] **N** madame *f*

Mac [mæk] **N** *Comput* Mac *m*; **available for the M.** disponible en version Mac

▸▸ ***Mac disk*** disquette *f* pour Mac; ***Mac OS*** Mac-OS *m*

mac[1] [mæk] *Am Fam* **N 1** *(term of address)* chef *m* **2** *(abbr* **macaroni)** macaronis *mpl*; **m. and cheese** gratin *m* de macaronis

mac[2] **N** *Br Fam (abbr* **mackintosh)** imper *m*

macabre [mə'kɑːbrə] **ADJ** macabre

macadam [mə'kædəm] **N** macadam *m*

COMP *(road)* macadamisé, en macadam

macadamize, -ise [mə'kædəmaɪz] **VT** macadamiser

macaque [mə'kɑːk] **N** *Zool* macaque *m*

macaroni [ˌmækə'rəʊnɪ] **N** *(UNCOUNT)* macaronis *mpl*; **a piece of m.** un macaroni

▸▸ *Br* ***macaroni cheese***, *Am* ***macaroni and cheese*** gratin *m* de macaronis

macaroon [ˌmækə'ruːn] **N** *Culin* macaron *m*

macaw [mə'kɔː] **N** *Orn* ara *m*

Mac-compatible ADJ *Comput* compatible Mac

Mace® [meɪs] **N** *(spray)* gaz *m* lacrymogène

VT *Am Fam* bombarder au gaz lacrymogène

mace [meɪs] **N 1** *(spice)* macis *m* **2** *(club)* massue *f*, masse *f* d'armes; *(ceremonial)* masse *f*

▸▸ ***mace bearer*** massier *m*

Macedonia [ˌmæsɪ'dəʊnɪə] **N** Macédoine *f*

Macedonian [ˌmæsɪ'dəʊnɪən] **N 1** *(person)* Macédonien(enne) *m,f* **2** *(language)* macédonien *m*

ADJ macédonien

COMP *(embassy)* de Macédoine; *(history)* de la Macédoine; *(teacher)* de macédonien

macerate ['mæsəreɪt] **VT** macérer

VI macérer

Mach [mæk] **N** Mach; **to fly at M. 3** voler à Mach 3

▸▸ ***Mach number*** nombre *m* de Mach

machete [mə'ʃetɪ] **N** machette *f*

Machiavellian [ˌmækɪə'velɪən] **ADJ** machiavélique

machinations [ˌmæʃkɪ'neɪʃənz] **NPL** machinations *fpl*

machine [mə'ʃiːn] **N 1** *(mechanical device)* machine *f*; **to do sth by m.** *or* **on a m.** faire qch à la machine

2 *Fig Pej (person)* machine *f*, automate *m*; **he thinks she's just a m. for doing housework** il la considère comme une machine à faire le ménage; **a thinking m.** une machine à penser

3 *Fig (organization)* machine *f*, appareil *m*; **the party m.** l'appareil *m* du parti

4 *(car, motorbike)* machine *f*; *(plane)* appareil *m*

5 *(computer)* ordinateur *m*

VT *Sewing* coudre à la machine; *Ind (manufacture)* fabriquer à la machine; *(work on machine)* usiner

▸▸ ***the machine age*** l'ère *f* de la machine; *Comput* ***machine code*** code *m* machine; ***machine gun*** mitrailleuse *f*; *Comput* ***machine language*** langage *m* machine; ***machine operator*** opérateur(trice) *m,f* (sur machine); ***machine pistol*** mitraillette *f*, pistolet *m* mitrailleur; ***machine shop*** atelier *m* d'usinage; ***machine time*** temps-machine *m*; ***machine tool*** machine-outil *f*; ***machine tool operator*** machiniste *mf*; *Comput* ***machine translation*** traduction *f* assistée par ordinateur

▸ **machine down VT SEP** *Ind (metal)* amincir

machine-finished ADJ *(paper)* apprêté, calandré; *(clothes)* fini à la machine

machine-gun VT mitrailler

machine-gunning [-'gʌnɪŋ] **N** mitraillage *m*

machine-hour N heure-machine *f*

machine-made ADJ fait à la machine

machine-readable ADJ *Comput* lisible par ordinateur

machinery [mə'ʃiːnərɪ] *(pl* **machineries) N 1** *(UNCOUNT) (machines)* machines *fpl*, machinerie *f*; *(mechanism)* mécanisme *m* **2** *Fig* rouages *mpl*; **the m. of state/of government** les rouages *mpl* de l'État/du gouvernement

machinist [mə'ʃiːnɪst] **N 1** *Ind* opérateur(trice) *m,f* (sur machine) **2** *Sewing* mécanicien(enne) *m,f*

machismo [mə'tʃɪzməʊ, mə'kɪzməʊ] **N** machisme *m*

macho ['mætʃəʊ] **N** macho *m*

ADJ macho; **m. type** macho *m*

macintosh = **mackintosh**

mack [mæk] **N** *Am Fam* **1** *(pimp)* maquereau *m*, mac *m* **2** *(seducer)* tombeur *m*

▸ **mack on VT INSEP** *Am Fam* **to m. on sb** draguer qn

mackerel ['mækərəl] *(pl inv or* **mackerels) N** *Ich* maquereau *m*

▸▸ ***mackerel sky*** ciel *m* pommelé

mackintosh ['mækɪntɒʃ] **N** *Br* imperméable *m*

mackle ['mækəl] *Typ* **N** maculage *m*

VT mâchurer

mackled ['mækəld] **ADJ** *Typ* bavocheux

macramé [mə'krɑːmɪ] **N** macramé *m*

COMP en macramé

macro ['mækrəʊ] *(pl* **macros) N** *Comput* macro-instruction *f*, macro *f*, macrocommande *f*

▸▸ ***macro language*** macrolangage *m*; ***macro virus*** virus *m* de macro

macrobiotic [ˌmækrəʊbaɪ'ɒtɪk] **ADJ** macrobiotique

• **macrobiotics N** *(UNCOUNT)* macrobiotique *f*

macrocomputing [ˌmækrəʊkəm'pjuːtɪŋ] **N** *Comput* macroinformatique *f*

macrocosm ['mækrəʊˌkɒzəm] **N** macrocosme *m*

macroeconomic ['mækrəʊˌiːkə'nɒmɪk] **ADJ** macroéconomique

• **macroeconomics N** *(UNCOUNT)* macroéconomie *f*

macroeconomy [ˌmækrəʊɪ'kɒnəmɪ] **N** macroéconomie *f*

macromarketing [ˌmækrəʊ'mɑːkɪtɪŋ] **N** macromarketing *m*

macron ['mækrɒn] **N** *Typ* macron *m*

macroscopic [ˌmækrəʊ'skɒpɪk] **ADJ** macroscopique

MACRS [ˌemeɪˌsiːɑː'res] **N** *Am Acct (abbr* **modified accelerated cost recovery system)** = méthode d'amortissement accéléré

mad [mæd] *(compar* **madder**, *superl* **maddest) ADJ 1** *esp Br (crazy)* fou (folle); **to go m.** devenir fou; **to be m. with joy/grief** être fou de joie/douleur; **it's a case of patriotism gone m.** c'est du patriotisme poussé à l'extrême *ou* qui frise la folie; **to drive sb m.** rendre qn fou; **it's enough to drive you m.** il y a de quoi devenir fou, c'est à vous rendre fou; **to be as m. as a hatter** *or* **a March hare** être fou à lier

2 *(absurd ▸ ambition, plan)* fou (folle), insensé; **he's always full of m. schemes for making money** il a toujours des plans insensés pour se faire de l'argent

3 *(angry)* en colère, furieux; **he went m. when he saw them** il s'est mis dans une colère noire en les voyant; **to be m. at** *or* **with sb** être en colère *ou* fâché contre qn; **she makes me m.** elle m'énerve; **don't get m.** ne vous fâchez pas

4 *(frantic)* **there was a m. rush for the door** tous les gens se sont rués vers la porte comme des fous; **there was a m. panic to sell** les gens n'avaient plus qu'une idée en tête, vendre; *Fig* **don't go m. and try to do it all yourself** tu ne vas pas te tuer à essayer de tout faire toi-même?; *Fam* **to run like m.** courir comme un fou *ou* un dératé

5 *Fam (enthusiastic, keen)* **to be m. about** *or* **on sth** être fou (folle) *ou* dingue de qch; **she's m. about cats** elle adore les chats; **he's m. about her** il est fou d'elle; **I can't say I'm m. about going** je ne peux pas dire que ça m'emballe *ou* que je meure d'envie d'y aller; *Br* **to be m. for it** *(raring to go)* être prêt à s'éclater

6 *(dog)* enragé; *(bull)* furieux

ADV *Br Fam* **to be m. keen on** *or* **about sth** être dingue *ou* un(e) mordu(e) de qch

▸▸ *Vet* ***mad cow disease*** maladie *f* de la vache folle; *Fam Fin* ***mad dog*** *(company)* société *f* en pleine expansion

Madagascan [ˌmædə'gæskən] **N** Malgache *mf*

ADJ malgache

Madagascar [ˌmædə'gæskə(r)] **N** Madagascar *f*

madam ['mædəm] **N 1** *Formal (form of address)* madame *f*; **Dear M.** (Chère) Madame; **m. Chairman** Madame la Présidente; *Br Fam* **that's enough of your cheek, m.!** ça suffit comme ça, petite insolente! **2** *Br Fam Pej (arrogant girl)* **she's a little m.** c'est une petite pimbêche **3** *Fam (of brothel)* (mère *f*) maquerelle *f*

madcap [ˈmædˌkæp] **N** fou (folle) *m,f*, hurluberlu(e) *m,f*
ADJ fou (folle), insensé; **a m. scheme** un projet insensé

madden [ˈmædən] **VT** *(drive insane)* rendre fou (folle); *(exasperate)* exaspérer, rendre fou (folle)

maddening [ˈmædənɪŋ] **ADJ** exaspérant; **the really m. thing is that we could so easily have won** ce qui est rageant c'est qu'on aurait facilement pu gagner

maddeningly [ˈmædənɪŋlɪ] **ADV** de façon exaspérante; **a m. long wait** une attente interminable; **m. slow** d'une lenteur exaspérante

madder [ˈmædə(r)] **N** *Bot & Tex* garance *f*
▸▸ *Bot* ***madder root*** alizari *m*

madding [ˈmædɪŋ] **ADJ** *Arch or Literary* effréné, frénétique

made [meɪd] *pt & pp of* **make**

made-for-TV movie **N** téléfilm *m*

Madeira [məˈdɪərə] **N 1** *(island)* Madère *m* **2** *(wine)* vin *m* de Madère, madère *m*
▸▸ ***Madeira cake*** ≃ quatre-quarts *m inv*

made-to-measure **ADJ** (fait) sur mesure

made-to-order **ADJ** (fait) sur commande

made-up **ADJ 1** *(wearing make-up)* maquillé; **a heavily m. face** un visage très maquillé **2** *(invented ▸ story)* fabriqué; *(▸ evidence)* faux (fausse) **3** *NEng Fam (very pleased)* vachement content

madhouse [ˈmædhaʊs, *pl* -haʊzɪz] **N** *Fam also Fig* maison *f* de fous; **the place was a complete m. when we arrived** lorsque nous sommes arrivés, on se serait crus dans une maison de fous

madly [ˈmædlɪ] **ADV 1** *(passionately)* follement; **m. in love** éperdument *ou* follement amoureux; **m. jealous** fou (folle) de jalousie; **I can't say I'm m. interested in it** je ne peux pas dire que ça m'intéresse follement **2** *(frantically)* comme un fou (une folle), frénétiquement; *(wildly)* comme un fou (une folle), follement; **the dog was barking m.** le chien aboyait frénétiquement **3** *(desperately)* désespérément

madman [ˈmædmən] *(pl* **madmen** [-mən]*)* **N** fou *m*, aliéné *m*; **he's a complete m.!** il est complètement fou!

madness [ˈmædnɪs] **N 1** *(insanity)* folie *f*, démence *f*; **in a fit of m.** dans un accès *ou* dans un moment de folie **2** *(folly)* folie *f*; **it's sheer m.** c'est insensé, c'est de la folie; **it's m. even to think of going away now** il faut être fou pour songer à partir maintenant

Madonna [məˈdɒnə] **PR N** *Rel* Madone *f*; *(image)* madone *f*

madras [məˈdrɑːs] **N** madras *m*
▸▸ ***madras curry*** curry *m* de Madras

madrigal [ˈmædrɪgəl] **N** *Mus* madrigal *m*

madwoman [ˈmædˌwʊmən] *(pl* **madwomen** [-ˌwɪmɪn]*)* **N** folle *f*, aliénée *f*

maelstrom [ˈmeɪlˌstrɒm] **N** maelström *m*, malstrom *m*; *Fig* **the m. of modern life** le tourbillon de la vie moderne

maestro [ˈmaɪstrəʊ] *(pl* **maestros***)* **N** maestro *m*

MAFF [mæf] **N** *Br Formerly (abbr* **Ministry of Agriculture, Fisheries and Food***)* ≃ ministère *m* de l'Agriculture

mafia [ˈmæfɪə] **N** *Fig* mafia *f*, maffia *f*
• **Mafia** **N the M.** la Mafia, la Maffia

mafioso [ˌmæfɪˈəʊsəʊ] *(pl* **mafiosi** [-siː]*)* **N** mafioso *m*, maffioso *m*

mag[1] [mæg] **N** *Fam (magazine)* revue▫*f*, magazine▫*m*

mag[2] **ADJ** *(abbr* **magnetic***)*
▸▸ ***mag tape*** bande *f* magnétique; ***mag tape cassette*** cassette *f* à bande magnétique; ***mag tape reader*** lecteur *m* de bandes magnétiques

magalogue, *Am* **magalog** [ˈmægəlɒg] **N** magalogue *m*

magazine [ˌmægəˈziːn] **N 1** *(publication)* magazine *m*, revue *f*; *Rad & TV (programme)* magazine *m* (télévisé), émission *f* magazine **2** *(in gun)* magasin *m*; *(cartridges)* chargeur *m* **3** *Mil (store)* magasin *m*; *(for weapons)* dépôt *m* d'armes; *(munitions)* munitions *fpl*
4 *Phot* magasin *m*; *(for slides)* panier *m*, magasin *m*
▸▸ *Rad & TV* ***magazine programme*** magazine *m* (télévisé), émission *f* magazine; ***magazine rack*** porte-revues *m*; ***magazine rifle*** fusil *m* à répétition *ou* à chargeur

magenta [məˈdʒentə] **N** magenta *m*
ADJ magenta *(inv)*

maggot [ˈmægət] **N** asticot *m*

maggoty [ˈmægətɪ] **ADJ** *(food)* véreux

Magi [ˈmeɪdʒaɪ] **NPL** *Bible* **the M.** les Rois *mpl* mages

magic [ˈmædʒɪk] **N 1** *(enchantment)* magie *f*; **black/white m.** magie noire/blanche; *Fig* **like** *or* **as if by m.** comme par enchantement *ou* magie; **the medicine worked like m.** le remède a fait merveille **2** *(conjuring)* magie *f*, prestidigitation *f* **3** *(special quality)* magie *f*; **discover the m. of Greece** découvrez les merveilles de la Grèce; **the m. had gone out of their marriage** leur vie conjugale n'avait plus rien de magique
ADJ 1 *(supernatural)* magique; **just say the m. words** il suffit de dire la formule magique; *Fam* **say the m. word!** *(say please)* qu'est-ce qu'on dit? **2** *(special ▸ formula, moment)* magique **3** *Br Fam (excellent)* super, génial
▸▸ ***magic carpet*** tapis *m* volant; ***magic lantern*** lanterne *f* magique; *Fam* ***magic mushroom*** champignons *mpl* (hallucinogènes); ***magic spell*** sortilège *m*; ***magic square*** carré *m* magique; ***magic wand*** baguette *f* magique
▸ **magic away** **VT SEP** faire disparaître comme par enchantement

magical [ˈmædʒɪkəl] **ADJ** magique; **her songs had a m. quality** ses chansons avaient quelque chose de magique
▸▸ *Literature* ***Magical Realism*** réalisme *m* magique

magically [ˈmædʒɪkəlɪ] **ADV** magiquement; *Fig (to disappear)* (comme) par magie *ou* par enchantement

magician [məˈdʒɪʃən] **N** magicien(enne) *m,f*

magisterial [ˌmædʒɪˈstɪərɪəl] **ADJ 1** *Law* de magistrat **2** *Fig* magistral

magistrate [ˈmædʒɪstreɪt] **N** juge *mf* de tribunal inférieur
▸▸ *Eng Law* ***magistrates' court*** = tribunal de première instance compétent en matière civile et pénale

magma [ˈmægmə] **N** *Chem & Geol* magma *m*

Magna Carta, Magna Charta [ˌmægnəˈkɑːtə] **N** *Br Hist* la Grande Charte

> MAGNA CARTA
>
> Souvent prise pour le symbole de la lutte contre l'oppression, cette charte, imposée en 1215 au roi Jean sans Terre par les barons anglais, énonce les droits et privilèges des nobles, de l'Église et des hommes libres ("freemen") face à l'arbitraire royal.

magnanimity [ˌmægnəˈnɪmətɪ] **N** magnanimité *f*

magnanimous [ˌmægˈnænɪməs] **ADJ** magnanime

magnanimously [ˌmægˈnænɪməslɪ] **ADV** avec magnanimité, magnanimement

magnate [ˈmægneɪt] **N** magnat *m*; **a press m.** un magnat de la presse

magnesia [mægˈniːʃə] **N** *Chem* magnésie *f*

magnesium [mægˈniːzɪəm] **N** *Chem* magnésium *m*
▸▸ ***magnesium oxide*** magnésie *f*, oxyde *m* de magnésium

magnet [ˈmægnɪt] **N 1** *Phys* aimant *m* **2** *Fig (for tourists etc)* pôle *m* d'attraction; *Fam* **his new car's a babe** *or* **chick m.** sa nouvelle voiture est super pour emballer les gonzesses

magnetic [mægˈnetɪk] **ADJ** magnétique; *Fig* **a m. personality** une personnalité magnétique *ou* charismatique
▸▸ *Comput* ***magnetic card*** carte *f* magnétique; *Comput* ***magnetic card reader*** lecteur *m* de cartes magnétiques; *Comput* ***magnetic character reader*** lecteur *m* de cartes; *Comput* ***magnetic disk*** disque *m* magnétique; *(floppy)* disquette *f* magnétique; *Comput* ***magnetic drive*** dérouleur *m* *ou* unité *f* de bande magnétique; ***magnetic field*** champ *m* magnétique; ***magnetic lock*** serrure *f* magnétique; ***magnetic media*** supports *mpl* magnétiques; ***magnetic needle*** aiguille *f* aimantée; ***magnetic north*** nord *m* magnétique; ***magnetic pole*** pôle *m* magnétique; *Med* ***magnetic resonance imaging*** imagerie *f* par résonance magnétique; ***magnetic soundtrack*** bande *f* son magnétique; ***magnetic storm*** orage *m* magnétique; ***magnetic strip, magnetic stripe*** piste *f* magnétique; ***magnetic stripe card*** carte *f* à piste magnétique; ***magnetic stripe reader*** lecteur *m* de pistes magnétiques; ***magnetic tape*** bande *f* magnétique; *Comput* ***magnetic tape unit*** dérouleur *m ou* unité *f* de bande magnétique

magnetically [mægˈnetɪkəlɪ] **ADV** magnétiquement

magnetism [ˈmægnɪtɪzəm] **N** magnétisme *m*

magnetization, -isation [ˌmægnɪtaɪˈzeɪʃən] **N** *Phys* aimantation *f*, magnétisation *f*

magnetize, -ise [ˈmægnɪtaɪz] **VT 1** *Phys* aimanter, magnétiser **2** *Fig (charm)* magnétiser; **he was magnetized by her good looks** il était fasciné par sa beauté

magnetizing, -ising [ˈmægnɪtaɪzɪŋ] **ADJ** *Phys (current, field etc)* magnétisant

magneto [mægˈniːtəʊ] **N** *Elec* magnéto *f*

magnetoelectric [mægˌniːtəʊəˈlektrɪk] **ADJ** *Phys* magnétoélectrique

magneto-optical **ADJ** *Comput* magnéto-optique

magnificat [mægˈnɪfɪkæt] **N** *Rel* magnificat *m inv*; **the M.** le Magnificat

magnification [ˌmægnɪfɪˈkeɪʃən] **N 1** *Opt* grossissement *m*; *(acoustics)* amplification *f* **2** *Rel* glorification *f*

magnificence [mægˈnɪfɪsəns] **N** magnificence *f*, splendeur *f*

magnificent [mægˈnɪfɪsənt] **ADJ** magnifique, splendide

magnificently [mægˈnɪfɪsəntlɪ] **ADV** magnifiquement

magnifier [ˈmægnɪfaɪə(r)] **N** *Opt* verre *m* grossissant

magnify [ˈmægnɪfaɪ] *(pt & pp* **magnified***)* **VT 1** *Opt* grossir; *(acoustics)* amplifier; *Comput* agrandir **2** *(exaggerate)* exagérer, grossir; **the incident was magnified out of all proportion** on a terriblement exagéré l'importance de cet incident **3** *Literary (exalt)* exalter, magnifier; *Rel* glorifier

magnifying [ˈmægnɪfaɪɪŋ] **ADJ**
▸▸ ***magnifying glass*** loupe *f*; *Opt* ***magnifying power*** *(of lens, microscope)* grossissement *m*

magnitude [ˈmægnɪtjuːd] **N 1** *(scale)* ampleur *f*, étendue *f*; *Astron & Geol* magnitude *f*; *Math* grandeur *f*, valeur *f*; *Astron* **star of the first m.** étoile *f* de première magnitude **2** *(of problem ▸ importance)* importance *f*; *(▸ size)* ampleur *f*; *Fig* **of the first m.** de premier ordre

magnolia [mægˈnəʊlɪə] **N** *Bot* magnolia *m*
ADJ couleur magnolia *(inv)*, blanc rosé *(inv)*
▸▸ ***magnolia tree*** magnolia *m*, magnolier *m*

magnum [ˈmægnəm] **N** *(wine bottle, gun)* magnum *m*

magnum opus **N** œuvre *f* maîtresse, chef-d'œuvre *m*

magpie [ˈmægpaɪ] **N 1** *Orn* pie *f* **2** *Fam Fig (chatterbox)* pie *f*, moulin *m* à paroles; *Br (hoarder)* chiffonnier(ère) *m,f*

Magyar [ˈmægjɑː(r)] **N 1** *(person)* Magyar(e) *m,f* **2** *Ling* magyar *m*
ADJ magyar

maharaja, maharajah [ˌmɑːhəˈrɑːdʒə] **N** maharaja *m*, maharadjah *m*

maharani [ˌmɑːhəˈrɑːniː] **N** maharani *f*

maharishi [ˌmɑːhəˈriːʃɪ] **N** maharishi *m*

mahogany [məˈhɒgənɪ] *(pl* **mahoganies***)* **N** *(wood, colour)* acajou *m*
ADJ 1 *(colour)* acajou *(inv)* **2** *(furniture)* en acajou

►► **mahogany brown** brun acajou *(inv)*; **mahogany tree** acajou *m*

Mahometan [mə'hɒmɪtən] *Old-fashioned Rel* **N** Mahométan(e) *m,f*

ADJ mahométan

MAI [ˌemeɪ'aɪ] **N** *Fin (abbr* **multilateral agreement on investment)** AMI *m*

maid [meɪd] **N 1** *(servant)* bonne *f*, domestique *f*; *(in hotel)* femme *f* de chambre; **m. of all work** bonne *f* à tout faire; **lady's m.** femme *f* de chambre **2** *Literary* jeune fille *f*, demoiselle *f*

►► **maid of honour** *(to queen)* demoiselle *f* d'honneur; *Am (at wedding)* première demoiselle *f* d'honneur; *Br Culin (cake)* petit gâteau *m* aux amandes; **the Maid of Orléans** la Pucelle d'Orléans; **maid service** *(at self-catering apartment)* service *m* de femme de ménage

maiden ['meɪdən] **N 1** *Literary (young girl)* jeune fille *f*; *(virgin)* vierge *f* **2** *Sport* **m. (over)** *(in cricket)* = série de six balles pendant laquelle aucun point n'est marqué

►► **maiden aunt** tante *f* célibataire; **maiden flight** premier vol *m*, vol *m* inaugural; **maiden name** nom *m* de jeune fille; *Br* **maiden speech** = premier discours prononcé par un parlementaire nouvellement élu; **maiden voyage** voyage *m* inaugural

maidenhair ['meɪdənheə(r)] **N** *Bot (fern)* capillaire *m*, cheveu-de-Vénus *m*

►► **maidenhair fern** capillaire *m*, cheveu-de-Vénus *m*

maidenly ['meɪdənlɪ] **ADJ** virginal

maidservant ['meɪdˌsɜːvənt] **N** servante *f*

mail [meɪl] **N 1** *(postal service)* poste *f*; **to send sth by m.** envoyer une lettre par la poste

2 *(letters, parcels)* courrier *m*; **was there any m. for me?** est-ce qu'il y avait du courrier pour moi?; **the m. is only collected twice a week** il n'y a que deux levées par semaine

3 *Comput* courrier *m* électronique, *Offic* mél *m*, *Can* courriel *m*

4 *Arch (coach)* malle *f*, malle-poste *f*

5 *(UNCOUNT) (armour)* mailles *fpl*

VT *(parcel, goods, cheque)* envoyer *ou* expédier (par la poste); *(letter)* poster

►► *Comput* **mail address** adresse *f* électronique; **mail bomb 1** *Am (letter)* lettre *f* piégée; *(parcel)* colis *m* piégé **2** *Comput* = messages envoyés en masse pour bloquer une boîte aux lettres, *Can* message *m* piégé, bombard *m*; *Am* **mail carrier** facteur(trice) *m,f*; *Comput* **mail forwarding** réexpédition *f* du courrier électronique; *Comput* **mail gateway** passerelle *f* (de courrier électronique); **mail order** vente *f* par correspondance; **to buy sth by m. order** acheter qch par correspondance *ou* sur catalogue; *Comput* **mail server** serveur *m* de courrier; **mail train** train *m* postal; *Am* **mail truck** camionnette *f ou* fourgonnette *f* des postes; *Br* **mail van** camionnette *f ou* fourgonnette *f* des postes; *Rail* voiture-poste *f*

mailbag ['meɪlbæg] **N** sac *m* postal

mailbot ['meɪlbɒt] **N** *Comptr* fonction *f* de réponse automatique

mailbox ['meɪlbɒks] **N 1** *esp Am (postbox)* boîte *f* à *ou* aux lettres **2** *Am (letterbox)* boîte *f* à *ou* aux lettres **3** *Comput* boîte *f* à lettres

mailing ['meɪlɪŋ] **N 1** *(posting)* expédition *f*, envoi *m* par la poste **2** *Com, Mktg & Comput* mailing *m*, publipostage *m*

►► **mailing address** adresse *f* postale; **mailing list** *Mktg* liste *f* de publipostage; *Comput* liste *f* de diffusion; **are you on our m. list?** est-ce que vous êtes sur notre fichier?; *Mktg* **mailing shot** mailing *m*, publipostage *m*

mailman ['meɪlmən] *(pl* **mailmen** [-mən]) **N** *Am* facteur *m*

mailmerge ['meɪlmɜːdʒ] **N** *Comput* publipostage *m*

►► **mailmerge letter** lettre *f* envoyée par publipostage; **mailmerge program** programme *m* de publipostage

mail-order ADJ

►► **mail-order bride** = nom donné aux jeunes femmes originaires de pays pauvres cherchant à épouser des occidentaux par le biais d'agences matrimoniales spécialisées; **mail-order catalogue** catalogue *m* de vente par correspondance; **mail-order company, mail-order firm** maison *f* de vente par correspondance; **mail-order retailing** vente *f* par correspondance

mailroom ['meɪlruːm] **N** service *m* du courrier

mailshot ['meɪlʃɒt] *Br* **N** mailing *m*, publipostage *m*; **to do** *or* **to send a m.** faire un mailing

maim [meɪm] **VT 1** *(disable)* mutiler, estropier; *(injure)* blesser **2** *(psychologically)* marquer, perturber; **the experience maimed her for life** l'expérience l'a marquée pour la vie

main [meɪn] **ADJ 1** *(principal)* principal; *(largest)* principal, plus important; *(essential* ► *idea, theme, reason)* principal, essentiel; **the m. body of public opinion** le gros de l'opinion publique; **the m. points** les points *mpl* principaux; **you're safe, that's the m. thing** tu es sain et sauf, c'est le principal; **that's the m. thing to remember** c'est ce dont il faut se souvenir avant tout; *Fam* **he always has an eye to the m. chance** il ne perd jamais de vue ses propres intérêts[□]; *Fam* **m. man** *(friend)* pote *m*; *Br Fam* **when it comes to scoring goals, Wayne Rooney's the m. man** pour ce qui est de marquer des buts, Wayne Rooney est champion **2** *Literary (sheer)* **to do sth by m. force** employer la force pour faire qch

N 1 *(for gas, water* ► *public)* canalisation *f* principale; *(for electricity)* conducteur *m* principal **2** *Arch* **the m.** *(ocean)* le grand large, l'océan *m*; **the Spanish M.** la mer des Antilles

• **in the main ADV** en gros, dans l'ensemble

►► **main beam** *Aut* feux *mpl* de route; *Constr* poutre *f* maîtresse; *Aut* **to be on m. beam** rouler pleins phares; **main branch** *(of bank)* établissement *m* principal; *Gram* **main clause** proposition *f* principale; **main course** plat *m* principal; *(on menu)* plat *m*; *Naut* **main deck** pont *m* principal; *Am Fam* **main drag** rue *f* principale[□], grande rue[□] *f*; **main entrance** entrée *f* principale; **main line 1** *Rail* grande ligne *f*; *Am (road)* grande route *f* **2** *Fam Drugs slang (vein)* veine *f* apparente *(choisie pour s'injecter de la drogue)*; *Br* **main road** grande route *f*, route *f* à grande circulation, ≃ nationale *f*; **main street** rue *f* principale, grand-rue *f*; *Am Fig* **Main Street** *(shops)* les commerçants *mpl*, le commerce

mainbrace ['meɪnbreɪs] **N** *Naut* grand bras *m* de vergue

maincrop ['meɪnkrɒp] **ADJ m. vegetables** légumes *mpl* de saison

mainframe ['meɪnfreɪm] **N** *(computer)* ordinateur *m* central

►► **mainframe computer** ordinateur *m* central

mainland ['meɪnlənd] **N** continent *m*; **we live on the m.** *(not on island)* nous n'habitons pas dans les îles; **you can see the Scottish m.** on voit la côte écossaise; **the Danish m.** le Danemark continental; **the British m.** la Grande-Bretagne *(le Royaume-Uni sans l'Irlande du Nord)*

ADJ continental; **in m. Europe** en Europe continentale; **in m. Britain** en Grande-Bretagne proprement dite *(par opposition aux îles qui l'entourent)*

mainline ['meɪnlaɪn] *Fam Drugs slang* **VT** se faire un shoot de; *(habitually)* se shooter à

VI se piquer, se shooter

mainliner ['meɪnˌlaɪnə(r)] **N** *Fam Drugs slang* junkie *mf*, shooté(e) *m,f*

mainly ['meɪnlɪ] **ADV** *(chiefly)* principalement, surtout; *(in the majority)* pour la plupart, dans l'ensemble; **the passengers were m. old men** la plupart des passagers étaient des vieux messieurs; **a m. Spanish-speaking population** une population à majorité *ou* principalement *ou* surtout hispanophone; **their diet consists m. of insects** ils se nourrissent essentiellement *ou* principalement *ou* surtout d'insectes; **she was m. to blame** c'est elle la principale responsable, c'est surtout de sa faute

mains [meɪnz] **N 1** *(main supply)* réseau *m*; **where's the m.?** où est la conduite principale?; **did you turn the gas/electricity off at the m.?** as-tu fermé l'arrivée de gaz/d'électricité?; **the village doesn't have m. electricity** le village n'est pas raccordé au réseau électrique **2** *Elec* secteur *m*; **my shaver works on battery or m.** mon rasoir marche sur piles ou sur (le) secteur

►► **mains adaptor** adaptateur *m* secteur; **mains set** poste *m* secteur; **mains supply** réseau *m* de distribution de gaz/d'eau/d'électricité; **mains water** eau *f* courante

mainsail ['meɪnseɪl, 'meɪnsəl] **N** *Naut* grand-voile *f*

mainsheet ['meɪnshiːt] **N** *Naut* écoute *f* de (la) grand-voile

mains-operated [-'ɒpəreɪtɪd], **mains-powered ADJ** fonctionnant sur secteur

mainspring ['meɪnsprɪŋ] **N 1** *Tech* ressort *m* moteur **2** *Fig* moteur *m*

mainstay ['meɪnsteɪ] **N 1** *Naut* étai *m* (de grand mât) **2** *Fig* soutien *m*, point *m* d'appui; *(of economy, philosophy, policy)* base *f*, pilier *m*; **maize is the m. of their diet** le maïs constitue la base de leur alimentation

mainstream ['meɪnstriːm] **N** courant *m*; **he is in the m. of politics** en politique, il suit la tendance générale; **to live outside the m. of society** vivre en marge de la société

ADJ m. French politics le courant dominant de la politique française; **m. Hollywood movies** films *mpl* dans la grande tradition hollywoodienne; **their music is hardly what you'd call m.!** leur musique se démarque nettement de ce qu'on entend habituellement!

maintain [meɪn'teɪn] **VT 1** *(retain* ► *institution, tradition)* conserver, préserver

2 *(preserve* ► *peace, standard)* maintenir; **to m. law and order** maintenir l'ordre; *Mil & Fig* **to m. a position** tenir une position

3 *(look after* ► *roads, machinery)* entretenir; **the grounds are well maintained** les jardins sont bien entretenus *ou* tenus

4 *(uphold, keep* ► *correspondence, friendship)* entretenir; *(*► *silence, advantage, composure)* garder; *(*► *reputation)* défendre

5 *(financially* ► *dependants)* entretenir; **they have two children at university to m.** ils ont deux enfants à charge à l'université

6 *(assert* ► *opinion)* soutenir, défendre; *(*► *innocence)* affirmer; **I still m. she's innocent** je soutiens *ou* je maintiens toujours qu'elle est innocente

maintenance ['meɪntənəns] **N 1** *(of roads, building)* entretien *m*; *(of machinery, computer)* maintenance *f*

2 *(financial support)* entretien *m*

3 *Law (alimony)* pension *f* alimentaire

4 *(of order)* maintien *m*; *(of regulations)* application *f*; *(of situation)* maintien *m*; **m. of a reasonable standard of living** le maintien d'un niveau de vie correct

COMP *(crew)* d'entretien

►► **maintenance allowance** *(to student)* bourse *f* d'études; *(to businessman)* indemnité *f* pour frais de déplacement; **maintenance contract** contrat *m* de maintenance *ou* d'entretien; **maintenance costs** frais *mpl* d'entretien; **maintenance department** service *m* de maintenance *ou* d'entretien; **maintenance engineer** technicien(enne) *m,f* de maintenance; **maintenance grant** *(to student)* bourse *f* d'études; **maintenance kit** trousse *f* d'entretien; *Law* **maintenance order** obligation *f* alimentaire; **she got a m. order against him** elle a obtenu du tribunal qu'il lui verse une pension alimentaire; **maintenance vehicle** camion-atelier *m*

maintenance-free ADJ sans entretien, sans maintenance

maisonette [ˌmeɪzə'net] **N** *Br (small house)* maisonnette *f*; *(flat)* duplex *m*

maître d' [ˌmetrə'diː], **maître d'hôtel** [ˌmetrədəʊ'tel] **N** maître *m* d'hôtel

maize [meɪz] **N** maïs *m*

Maj. *Mil (written abbr* **Major)** ≃ Cdt, *Can & Belg* Maj.

majestic [mə'dʒestɪk] **ADJ** majestueux

majestically [mə'dʒestɪkəlɪ] **ADV** majestueusement

majesty ['mædʒəstɪ] *(pl* **majesties) N 1** *(impressiveness)* majesté *f* **2** *(sovereign)* majesté *f*; **yes, your m.** oui, Votre Majesté; *Hum* à vos ordres!; **His M. the King** Sa Majesté le Roi; **Her M. the Queen** Sa Majesté la Reine; *Br* **on His/Her M.'s Service** (pour le) service de Sa Majesté (≃ service de l'État); *(on envelope)* ≃ en franchise

►► *Br Admin* **His/Her Majesty's Government** = expression utilisée sur des documents officiels en Grande-Bretagne; *Br* ***His/Her Majesty's Prison Service*** = système pénitentiaire britannique; *Br* ***His/Her Majesty's Stationery Office*** = maison d'édition publiant les ouvrages ou documents approuvés par le Parlement, les ministères et autres organismes officiels, ≃ l'Imprimerie *f* nationale

Maj. Gen. *Mil (written abbr* **Major General***)* ≃ général *m* de division, *Belg* ≃ général-major *m*, *Suisse* ≃ divisionnaire *m*, *Can* ≃ major-géneral *m*

major [ˈmeɪdʒə(r)] **ADJ 1** *(main)* **the m. part of our research** l'essentiel de nos recherches; **the m. portion of my time is devoted to politics** la majeure partie *ou* la plus grande partie de mon temps est consacrée à la politique

2 *(significant* ▸ *decision, change, factor, event)* majeur; *(company)* de première importance, de premier ordre; **we shouldn't have any m. problems** nous ne devrions pas rencontrer de problèmes majeurs; **don't worry, it's not a m. problem** ne t'inquiète pas, ce n'est pas très grave; **any problems? – nothing m.** des problèmes? – rien d'important; **of m. importance** d'une grande importance, d'une importance capitale; **a m. role** *(in play, film)* un grand rôle; *(in negotiations, reform)* un rôle capital *ou* essentiel; **he's taken up Spanish in a m. way** il s'est mis à fond à l'espagnol

3 *(serious* ▸ *obstacle, difficulty)* majeur; **the roof is in need of m. repair work** la toiture a grand besoin d'être remise en état; **she underwent m. surgery** elle a subi une grosse opération

4 *Mus* majeur; **a sonata in E m.** une sonate en mi majeur; **in a m. key** en (mode) majeur

5 *Br Old-fashioned Sch (elder)* **Smith m.** Smith aîné

6 *Cards* majeur; **m. suit** majeure *f*

N 1 *Mil (in airforce)* ≃ commandant *m*; *Can & Belg* ≃ major *m*; *(in infantry)* ≃ chef *m* de bataillon, *Belg, Can & Suisse* ≃ major *m*; *(in cavalry)* ≃ commandant *m*, *Belg, Can & Suisse* ≃ major *m*

2 *Formal (person over 18)* personne *f* majeure

3 *Am Univ (subject)* matière *f* principale; **Tina is a physics m.** Tina fait des études de physique

4 *Mus* (mode *m*) majeur *m*

5 *Am (big company)* **the oil majors** les grandes compagnies *fpl* pétrolières; **the Majors** *(film companies)* = les cinq compagnies de production les plus importantes à Hollywood

6 *Golf* tournoi *m* du grand chelem

VI *Am Univ* **1** *(specialize)* se spécialiser; **Joe majors in chemistry** Joe se spécialise en chimie **2** *(be a student)* **she majored in sociology** elle a fait des études de sociologie

▸▸ *Mil* ***major general*** ≃ général *m* de division, *Belg* ≃ général-major *m*, *Suisse* ≃ divisionnaire *m*, *Can* ≃ major-général *m*; *Am Sport* ***major league*** *(in baseball)* = une des deux principales divisions de base-ball professionnel aux États-Unis et au Canada; *(gen)* première division *f*; *Mil* ***major offensive*** vaste offensive *f*; *Phil* ***major premise*** majeure *f*; ***major road*** route *f* principale *ou* à grande circulation, ≃ nationale *f*; *Fin* ***major shareholder*** actionnaire *mf* de référence

Majorca [məˈjɔːkə] **N** Majorque *f*

Majorcan [məˈjɔːkən] **N** Majorquin(e) *m,f*

ADJ majorquin

majordomo [ˌmeɪdʒəˈdəʊməʊ] *(pl* **majordomos***)* **N** majordome *m*

majorette [ˌmeɪdʒəˈret] **N** majorette *f*

majority [məˈdʒɒrətɪ] *(pl* **majorities***)* **N 1** *(of a group)* majorité *f*, plupart *f*; **the m. of people** la plupart des gens; **in the m. of cases** dans la plupart des cas; **the m. was** *or* **were in favour** la majorité *ou* la plupart d'entre eux était pour; **the vast m. of the tourists were Japanese** les touristes, dans leur très grande majorité, étaient des Japonais **2** *(in voting, opinions)* majorité *f*; **to be in a m.** être majoritaire; **a two-thirds m.** une majorité des deux tiers; **she was elected by a m. of 6** elle a été élue avec une majorité de 6 voix *ou* par 6 voix de majorité **3** *Law (voting age)* majorité *f*; **to attain** *or* **reach one's m.** atteindre sa majorité, devenir majeur

COMP majoritaire

▸▸ ***majority decision*** décision *f* prise à la majorité; ***majority government*** gouvernement *m* majoritaire; ***majority holding, majority interest*** participation *f* majoritaire; ***majority party*** parti *m* majoritaire; ***majority rule*** gouvernement *m* à la majorité absolue, système *m* majoritaire; *Br* ***majority shareholder***, *Am* ***majority stockholder*** actionnaire *mf* majoritaire; ***majority verdict*** verdict *m* majoritaire; ***majority vote*** vote *m* majoritaire, majorité *f*; ***majority world*** tiers-monde *m*

MAKE [meɪk]

VT
- faire **A1–3, 5, 6, B2–4, C4, D1–3**
- former **A4**
- atteindre **C1, 2**
- marquer **D4**
- fabriquer **A1**
- établir **A3**
- rendre **B1**
- gagner **C4**
- faire le succès de **E1**

N
- marque **1**

(pt & pp **made** [meɪd]*)*

VT A. 1 *(construct, create, manufacture)* faire, fabriquer; **to m. one's own clothes** faire ses vêtements soi-même; **to m. a meal** préparer un repas; **they m. computers** ils fabriquent des ordinateurs; **made in Japan** *(on packaging)* fabriqué au Japon; **a vase made of** *or* **from clay** un vase en *ou* de terre cuite; **what's it made (out) of?** en quoi est-ce que c'est fait?; **he makes models out of matchsticks** il fait des maquettes avec des allumettes; *Knitting* **to m. one/two** faire un jeté simple/double; **they're made for each other** ils sont faits l'un pour l'autre; *Fam* **we're not made of money!** on n'a pas d'argent à jeter par les fenêtres!; *Fam* **I'll show them what I'm made of!** je leur montrerai de quel bois je me chauffe *ou* qui je suis!

2 *(cause to appear or happen* ▸ *hole, tear, mess, mistake, noise)* faire; **it made a dent in the bumper** ça a cabossé le pare-chocs; **he's always making trouble** il faut toujours qu'il fasse des histoires

3 *(establish* ▸ *law, rule)* établir, faire; **I don't m. the rules** ce n'est pas moi qui fais les règlements

4 *(form* ▸ *circle, line)* former

5 *Cin & TV (direct, act in)* faire; **he's made several films with Ridley Scott** il a fait plusieurs films avec Ridley Scott

6 *(indicating action performed)* **to m. an offer/a request** faire une offre/une demande; **to m. a note of sth** prendre note de qch; **to m. a speech** faire un discours; **to m. one's bed** faire son lit; **to m. a phone call** passer un coup de fil; **we've made a few changes** nous avons fait *ou* apporté quelques modifications; **I have no further comments to m.** je n'ai rien à ajouter

B. 1 *(with adj or pp complement) (cause to be)* rendre; **to m. sb happy/mad** rendre qn heureux/fou (folle); **to m. oneself useful** se rendre utile; **this will m. things easier** cela facilitera les choses; **it makes her tired** ça la fatigue; **what makes the sky blue?** qu'est-ce qui fait que le ciel est bleu?; **m. yourselves comfortable** mettez-vous à l'aise; **it was hard to m. myself heard/understood** j'ai eu du mal à me faire entendre/comprendre

2 *(with noun complement or with "into") (change into)* faire; **the film made her (into) a star** le film a fait d'elle une vedette; **to m. a success of sth** réussir qch; **he was made president for life** il a été nommé président à vie; **they made Bonn the capital** ils ont choisi Bonn pour capitale; **the building has been made into offices** l'immeuble a été réaménagé *ou* converti en bureaux; **the latest cheque makes the total £10,000** le dernier chèque porte la somme totale à 10 000 livres; **I can't come in the morning, shall we m. it 2 p.m.?** je ne peux pas venir le matin, est-ce que 14 heures vous conviendrait?; **if we made it a Wednesday...** si on faisait ça un mercredi...; **can we m. it your place?** est-ce qu'on peut faire ça chez toi?; **better m. it** *or* **that TWO whiskies** mettez-moi un deuxième whisky

3 *(with verb complement) (cause)* faire; **what makes you think they're wrong?** qu'est-ce qui te fait penser qu'ils ont tort?; **peeling onions makes my eyes water** les oignons me font pleurer; **I can't m. the coffee machine work** je n'arrive pas à faire marcher la machine à café; **you m. it look easy** à vous voir, on croirait que c'est facile; **the hat/photo makes you look ridiculous** tu as l'air ridicule avec ce chapeau/sur cette photo; **don't m. me laugh!** ne me fais pas rire!

4 *(force, oblige)* **to m. sb do sth** faire faire qch à qn; *(stronger)* forcer *ou* obliger *ou* contraindre qn à faire qch; **they made me wait** ils m'ont fait attendre; **if he doesn't want to do it you can't m. him** s'il ne veut pas le faire, tu ne peux pas l'y obliger *ou* forcer; **she made herself keep running** elle s'est forcée à continuer à courir

C. 1 *(attain, achieve* ▸ *goal)* atteindre; **we made all our production targets** nous avons atteint tous nos objectifs de production; **their first record made the top ten** leur premier disque est rentré au top ten; **you won't m. the team if you don't train** tu n'entreras jamais dans l'équipe si tu ne t'entraînes pas; **the story made the front page** l'histoire a fait la une des journaux

2 *(arrive at, get to* ▸ *place)* atteindre; **we should m. Houston/port by evening** nous devrions arriver à Houston/atteindre le port d'ici ce soir; **did you m. your train?** as-tu réussi à avoir ton train?

3 *(be available for)* **I won't be able to m. lunch** je ne pourrai pas déjeuner avec toi/elle/vous/*etc*; **can you m. Friday afternoon?** vendredi après-midi, ça vous convient?; **I can m. two o'clock** je peux être là à deux heures

4 *(earn, win)* faire, gagner; **how much do you m. a month?** combien gagnes-tu par mois?; **she made her first million selling beauty products** elle a gagné son premier million en vendant des produits de beauté

D. 1 *(amount to, add up to)* faire; **17 and 19 m.** *or* **makes 36** 17 plus 19 font *ou* égalent 36; **if Kay comes, that will m. eight** si Kay vient, ça fera huit; **that makes the third time you've been late this week** c'est la troisième fois que vous êtes en retard cette semaine; **how old does that m. him?** quel âge ça lui fait?

2 *(reckon to be)* **I m. the answer 257** d'après moi, ça fait 257; **I m. it $14 each** si je compte bien, ça fait 14 dollars par personne; **what time do you m. it?** quelle heure as-tu?

3 *(with noun complement) (fulfil specified role, function etc)* faire; **he'll m. somebody a good husband** ce sera un excellent mari; **he'd m. a good teacher** il ferait un bon enseignant; **they m. a handsome couple** ils forment un beau couple; **her reminiscences m. interesting reading** ses souvenirs sont intéressants à lire

4 *(score)* marquer; **Smith made his second century** Smith a marqué deux cents points

E. 1 *(make successful)* faire le succès de; **it's her performance that makes the film** tout le film repose sur son interprétation; **if this deal comes off we're made!** si ça marche, on touche le gros lot!; **you've got it made!** tu n'as plus de souci à te faire!; **what happens today will m. us or break us** notre avenir dépend entièrement de ce qui va se passer aujourd'hui

2 *Am (in directions)* **m. a right/left** tournez à droite/à gauche

3 *(idioms)* **to m. it** *(arrive)* arriver; *(be successful)* réussir; *(be able to attend)* être là; **I'll never m. it for ten o'clock** je ne pourrai jamais y être pour dix heures; **we made it to the airport with an hour to spare** nous sommes arrivés à l'aéroport avec une heure d'avance; **I hope she makes it through the winter** j'espère qu'elle passera l'hiver; **he'll never m. it as a businessman** il ne réussira jamais dans les affaires; **I can't m. it for supper tomorrow** je ne peux pas dîner avec eux/toi/*etc* demain; *Am Fam* **to m. sb, to m. it with sb** *(have sex with)* coucher avec qn

VI *(act)* **to m. (as if) to** faire mine de; **she made (as if) to stand up** elle fit mine de se lever; **he made towards the door** il s'est dirigé vers la porte; *Fam* **I walked in trying to m. like a businessman** je suis entré en essayant d'avoir l'air d'un homme d'affaires[□]; *Fam* **m. like you don't know anything** fais comme si tu ne savais pas; *Fam* **m. like you're asleep!** fais semblant de dormir![□]; **to m. believe** imaginer; **m. believe you're a bird** imagine que tu es un oiseau; **to m. do (with)** *(manage)* se débrouiller (avec); *(be satisfied)* se contenter (de); **it's broken but we'll just have to m. do** c'est cassé mais il faudra faire avec *ou* nous débrouiller avec; **we could m. do with ten** nous pourrions nous débrouiller avec dix

N 1 *(brand)* marque *f*; **what m. of washing ma-**

chine have you got? quelle est la marque de votre machine à laver?, qu'est-ce que vous avez comme machine à laver?

2 *(in bridge)* contrat *m*

3 *Fam (idiom)* **to be on the m.** *(financially)* chercher à se faire du fric, chercher à s'en mettre plein les poches; *(looking for sexual partner)* chasser, draguer

▸ **make after** VT INSEP se lancer à la poursuite de

▸ **make away with** VT INSEP **1** *(steal)* partir avec, voler **2** *(kill)* tuer, supprimer; **to m. away with oneself** se suicider

▸ **make for** VT INSEP **1** *(head towards)* se diriger vers; *(hastily)* se précipiter vers; **he made straight for the fridge** il se dirigea tout droit vers le frigo; **when it started to rain everyone made for the trees** quand il s'est mis à pleuvoir, tout le monde s'est précipité vers les arbres; **he made for his gun** il fit un geste pour saisir son pistolet **2** *(contribute to)* mener à; **the treaty should m. for a more lasting peace** le traité devrait mener *ou* aboutir à une paix plus durable; **this typeface makes for easier reading** cette police permet une lecture plus facile; **a good diet makes for healthier babies** un bon régime alimentaire donne des bébés en meilleure santé

▸ **make of** VT SEP **1** *(understand)* comprendre à; **I don't know what to m. of that remark** je ne sais pas comment interpréter cette remarque; **can you make anything of these instructions?** est-ce que tu comprends quelque chose à ce mode d'emploi? **2** *(attach importance to)* **I think you're making too much of a very minor problem** je pense que tu exagères l'importance de ce petit problème; **you're making too much of this** tu y attaches trop d'importance; **the press has made a lot of this visit** la presse a fait beaucoup de bruit autour de cette visite; *Fam* **do you want to make something of it, then?** *(threat)* tu cherches des histoires ou quoi?

VT INSEP *(think of)* penser de; **what do you m. of the Caines?** qu'est-ce que tu penses des Caine?

▸ **make off** VI partir

▸ **make off with** VT INSEP partir avec; **he made off with the cash** il est parti avec l'argent

▸ **make out** VT SEP **1** *(see)* distinguer; *(hear)* entendre, comprendre; *(read)* déchiffrer; **I could just m. out the outline of the castle** je distinguais juste la silhouette du château; **I couldn't m. out what he said** je ne comprenais pas ce qu'il disait; **I can't m. out the address** je n'arrive pas à déchiffrer l'adresse

2 *(understand)* comprendre; **I couldn't m. out how to fit it together** je ne comprenais pas comment l'assembler; **I can't m. her out at all** je ne la comprends pas du tout

3 *(claim)* prétendre; **she made out that she was busy** elle a fait semblant d'être occupée; **don't m. yourself out to be something you're not** ne prétends pas être ce que tu n'es pas; **it's not as bad as everyone makes out** ce n'est pas aussi mauvais qu'on le prétend

4 *(fill out ▸ form)* remplir; **to m. out a cheque (to sb)** faire un chèque (à l'ordre de qn); **who shall I m. the cheque out to?** je fais le chèque à quel ordre?

5 *(draw up ▸ list)* dresser, faire; *(▸ will, contract)* faire, rédiger, établir; *(▸ receipt)* faire

VI **1** *Fam (manage)* se débrouiller; **how did you m. out at work today?** comment ça s'est passé au boulot aujourd'hui? **2** *very Fam (sexually)* se peloter; **to m. out with sb** peloter qn

▸ **make over** VT SEP **1** *(transfer)* transférer, céder; **she has made the estate over to her granddaughter** elle a cédé la propriété à sa petite-fille **2** *Am (convert ▸ room, house)* réaménager; **the garage had been made over into a workshop** le garage a été transformé en atelier **3** *(change the appearance of)* transformer

▸ **make up** VT SEP **1** *(put make-up on)* maquiller; **to m. oneself up** se maquiller; **he was heavily made up** il était très maquillé *ou* fardé

2 *(prepare)* faire, préparer; **we can m. up a bed for you in the living room** nous pouvons vous faire un lit dans le salon; **the chemist made up the prescription** le pharmacien a préparé l'ordonnance; **the fire needs making up** il faut remettre du charbon/du bois sur le feu

3 *(invent)* inventer; **I'm sure he made the story up** je suis sûr qu'il a inventé cette histoire (de toutes pièces); **I'm making it up as I go along** j'improvise au fur et à mesure

4 *Typ* mettre en pages

5 *(idioms)* **to m. up with sb**, *Br* **to m. it up with sb** se réconcilier avec qn; **have you made up** *or Br* **made it up with him?** est-ce que vous vous êtes réconciliés?; **I'll m. it up to you** *(for forgetting your birthday etc)* je me rattraperai, je me ferai pardonner; *(for helping me)* je te rendrai ça

VT INSEP **1** *(constitute)* composer, constituer; **the different ethnic groups that m. up our organization** les différents groupes ethniques qui constituent notre organisation; **the cabinet is made up of eleven ministers** le cabinet est composé de onze ministres **2** *(compensate for ▸ losses)* compenser; **to m. up lost ground** regagner le terrain perdu; **we made up the time** nous avons rattrapé notre retard **3** *(complete)* **we need two more players to m. up the team** nous avons besoin de deux joueurs de plus pour que l'équipe soit au complet; **I was only invited to m. up the numbers** *(in team, for meal etc)* je n'ai été invité que pour compléter l'équipe/la table/*etc*; **I'll m. up the difference** je mettrai la différence

VI **1** *(put on make-up)* se maquiller **2** *(become reconciled)* se réconcilier

▸ **make up for** VT INSEP compenser; **the pay doesn't m. up for the poor conditions** le salaire ne compense pas les piètres conditions de travail; **how can I m. up for all the trouble I've caused you?** que puis-je faire pour me faire pardonner tous les ennuis que je vous ai causés?; *also Fig* **she's making up for lost time now!** elle est en train de rattraper le temps perdu!

▸ **make up to** VT INSEP **to m. up to sb** *(try to win favour)* essayer de se faire bien voir par qn; *(make advances)* faire du plat à qn

▸ **make with** VT INSEP *Am Fam* **m. with the drinks!** à boire!; **m. with the music!** musique!

---

make-believe N **it's only m.** ce n'est qu'illusion; **a world of m.** un monde d'illusions; **to play at m.** jouer à faire semblant; **to live in the land of m.** vivre dans un monde de chimères

ADJ imaginaire; **they turned the bed into a m. raft** ils imaginèrent que le lit était un radeau

make-or-break ADJ **it's m. time!** maintenant, ça passe ou ça casse!; **it was one of those m. moments** c'était un moment décisif

makeover ['meɪk,əʊvə(r)] N **1** *(of building, room)* transformation *f* **2** *(of person)* changement *m* de look, avant-après *m*; *(at cosmetics counter)* séance *f* de maquillage

maker ['meɪkə(r)] N **1** *(craftsman)* fabricant(e) *m,f* **2** *(manufacturer)* fabricant(e) *m,f*; *(of machinery, planes, cars etc)* constructeur *m*

• **Maker** N *Rel* Créateur *m*; *Euph or Hum* **to go to meet one's M.** passer de vie à trépas

make-ready N *Typ* mise *f* en train

makeshift ['meɪkʃɪft] N *(solution)* pis-aller *m inv*, expédient *m*; *(object)* moyen *m* de fortune

ADJ de fortune; **a m. shelter** un abri de fortune; **the accommodation was very m.** le logement était plutôt improvisé

make-up N **1** *(cosmetics)* maquillage *m*; **to put (one's) m. on** se maquiller; **she had a lot of m. on** elle était très maquillée; **she doesn't wear m.** elle ne se maquille pas; **eye m.** fard *m* pour les yeux

2 *(constitution)* constitution *f*

3 *(nature, character)* nature *f*, caractère *m*; **spontaneous generosity is not really in her m.** elle n'est pas généreuse de nature

4 *Typ* mise *f* en pages

5 *Am (test, exam)* examen *m* de rattrapage

▸▸ ***make-up artist*** maquilleur(euse) *m,f*; ***make-up bag*** trousse *f* de maquillage; ***make-up box*** boîte *f* à maquillage; *Am Sch* ***make-up classes*** cours *mpl* de rattrapage; ***make-up remover*** démaquillant *m*; *TV* ***make-up room*** salle *f* de maquillage

makeweight ['meɪkweɪt] N *(on scales)* complément *m* de poids; *Fig* **I'm only here as a m.** je ne suis là que pour faire nombre

-making ['meɪkɪŋ] SUFF **cake-m.** fabrication *f* de gâteaux; **decision-m.** prise *f* de décisions; *Br Fam* **it's absolutely sick-m.** c'est à vous donner la nausée

making ['meɪkɪŋ] N **1** *(manufacture, creation)* fabrication *f*; **the situation is entirely of his own m.** il est entièrement responsable de la situation dans laquelle il se trouve; **this ordeal was the m. of him** cette épreuve lui a forgé le caractère; *Elec* **m. and breaking** *(of circuit)* fermeture *f* et ouverture *f* **2** *(preparation ▸ of cake)* confection *f*, préparation *f*; *(▸ of film)* tournage *m*

• **in the making** ADJ *(idea)* en gestation; *(plan)* à l'étude; *(building)* en construction; **it's history in the m.** c'est une page d'histoire qui s'écrit sous nos yeux; **the film was three years in the m.** le tournage du film a duré trois ans

• **makings** NPL **1** *(essential elements)* ingrédients *mpl*; **his war stories have the makings of a good film** il y a de quoi faire un bon film avec ses récits de guerre; **the affair has all the makings of a national scandal** il y a dans cette affaire largement de quoi déclencher un scandale national **2** *(potential)* **that child has the makings of a genius** cet enfant présente toutes les caractéristiques du génie

malachite ['mæləkaɪt] N *Miner* malachite *f*

maladjusted [,mælə'dʒʌstɪd] ADJ **1** *Psy (person)* inadapté; **m. children** l'enfance *f* inadaptée **2** *(engine, TV picture)* mal réglé; *(mechanism)* mal ajusté

maladjustment [,mælə'dʒʌstmənt] N **1** *(psychological or social)* inadaptation *f*; *(emotional)* déséquilibre *m* **2** *(of engine, TV)* mauvais réglage *m*; *(of mechanism)* mauvais réglage *m*, mauvais ajustement *m*

maladministration ['mæləd,mɪnɪs'treɪʃən] N *(of country, economy)* mauvaise administration *f*; *(of business)* mauvaise gestion *f*

maladroit [,mælə'drɔɪt] ADJ maladroit, gauche, malhabile

maladroitly [,mælə'drɔɪtlɪ] ADV maladroitement, gauchement

malady ['mælədɪ] *(pl* **maladies**) N *Literary* maladie *f*, affection *f*, mal *m*

Malagasy [,mælə'gæsɪ] N **1** *(person)* Malgache *mf* **2** *(language)* malgache *m*

ADJ malgache

COMP *(embassy, history)* de Madagascar; *(teacher)* de malgache

malaise [mæ'leɪz] N malaise *m*

malapropism ['mæləprɒpɪzəm] N lapsus *m*

malaria [mə'leərɪə] N *Med* malaria *f*, paludisme *m*; **to have m.** avoir la malaria *ou* le paludisme

malarial [mə'leərɪəl] ADJ *(disease, fever)* paludéen, paludique, palustre

malarkey [mə'lɑːkɪ] N *(UNCOUNT) Fam* bêtises *fpl*, sottises *fpl*; **I don't believe in ghosts or any of that m.** je ne crois pas aux fantômes et à toutes ces sottises; **he can't be bothered with that fancy-dress m.** il n'aime pas du tout les soirées où les gens doivent se déguiser

Malawi [mə'lɑːwɪ] N Malawi *m*

Malay [mə'leɪ] N **1** *(person)* Malais(e) *m,f* **2** *(language)* malais *m*

ADJ malais

COMP *(embassy)* de Malaisie; *(history)* de la Malaisie; *(teacher)* de malais

▸▸ ***the Malay Peninsula*** (la presqu'île de) Malacca *f*, la presqu'île Malaise

Malaya [mə'leɪə] N Malaisie *f*, Malaysia *f* occidentale

Malayan [mə'leɪən] N Malais(e) *m,f*

ADJ malais

Malaysia [mə'leɪzɪə] N Malaysia *f*

Malaysian [mə'leɪzɪən] N Malais(e) *m,f*

ADJ malais

malcontent ['mælkən,tent] N *Formal* mécontent(e) *m,f*

male [meɪl] ADJ **1** *Biol, Zool & Bot* mâle; **m. attitudes** l'attitude *f* des hommes; **a m. friend** un ami; **when I phoned her, a m. voice answered** quand je l'ai appelée, c'est une voix d'homme qui a répondu **2** *(virile)* mâle, viril **3** *Tech (plug)* mâle; **m. to female adaptor** adaptateur *m* mâle/femelle

N *Zool* mâle *m*; *(man)* homme *m*; **the average French m.** le Français moyen

▸▸ ***male bonding*** amitié *f* virile; *Fam Hum* **they're** doing some m. bonding in the pub ils sont au pub, entre hommes; ***male chauvinism*** phallocratie *f*; ***male chauvinist*** phallocrate *m*; ***male chauvinist pig*** sale phallocrate *m*; *Anat* ***male member*** membre *m* viril; *Hum* ***male menopause*** andropause *f*; ***male nurse*** infirmier *m*; ***the male sex*** le sexe masculin; ***male voice choir*** chœur *m* d'hommes

> Note that the French word **mâle** is not always a translation for the English word **male**.

malediction [ˌmælɪˈdɪkʃən] **N** *Literary* malédiction *f*

malefactor [ˈmælɪˌfæktə(r)] **N** *Literary* malfaiteur *m*

malevolence [məˈlevələns] **N** malveillance *f*

malevolent [məˈlevələnt] **ADJ** malveillant

malevolently [məˈlevələntlɪ] **ADV** avec malveillance

malformation [ˌmælfɔːˈmeɪʃən] **N** malformation *f*

malformed [ˌmælˈfɔːmd] **ADJ** difforme

malfunction [ˌmælˈfʌŋkʃən] **N** *(fault)* fonctionnement *m* défectueux; *(breakdown)* panne *f*, défaillance *f*

VI *(go wrong)* mal fonctionner; *(break down)* tomber en panne

Mali [ˈmɑːlɪ] **N** Mali *m*

Malian [ˈmɑːlɪən] **N** Malien(enne) *m,f*

ADJ malien

COMP *(embassy, history)* du Mali

malice [ˈmælɪs] **N** méchanceté *f*, malveillance *f*; **I don't bear any m. towards them, I don't bear them any m.** je ne leur en veux pas, je ne leur veux aucun mal; **out of** *or* **through m.** par méchanceté, par malveillance; *Law* **with m. aforethought** avec préméditation

> Note that the French word **malice** is a false friend and is never a translation for the English word **malice**. Its most common meaning is **mischief**.

malicious [məˈlɪʃəs] **ADJ 1** *(gen)* méchant, malveillant; **m. gossip** médisances *fpl* **2** *Law* criminel

▸▸ *Br Law* ***malicious damage*** ≃ dommage *m* causé avec intention de nuire; ***malicious intent*** intention *f* de nuire *ou* criminelle

> Note that the French word **malicieux** is a false friend and is never a translation for the English word **malicious**. It means **mischievous**.

maliciously [məˈlɪʃəslɪ] **ADV 1** *(gen)* méchamment, avec malveillance **2** *Law* avec préméditation, avec intention de nuire

malign [məˈlaɪn] **VT** *(slander)* calomnier; *(criticize)* critiquer, dire du mal de; **the much-maligned government** le gouvernement, dont on dit beaucoup de mal *ou* que l'on a souvent critiqué

ADJ 1 *(evil)* pernicieux, nocif **2** *Med* malin(igne)

malignancy [məˈlɪgnənsɪ] *(pl* **malignancies)** **N 1** *(ill will)* malignité *f*, malveillance *f*, méchanceté *f* **2** *Med* malignité *f*

malignant [məˈlɪgnənt] **ADJ 1** *(person, behaviour, intentions)* malveillant, malfaisant, méchant **2** *Med* malin(igne)

▸▸ *Med* ***malignant melanoma*** nævo-carcinome *m*

malignantly [məˈlɪgnəntlɪ] **ADV** avec malveillance, méchamment

malinger [məˈlɪŋgə(r)] **VI** simuler la maladie, faire semblant d'être malade

malingerer [məˈlɪŋgərə(r)] **N** faux (fausse) malade *mf*, personne *f* qui fait semblant d'être malade

malingering [məˈlɪŋgərɪŋ] **N** simulation *f* (de maladie)

mall [mɔːl] **N 1** *(avenue)* mail *m*, avenue *f* **2 (shopping) m.** galerie *f* marchande, centre *m* commercial

mallard [ˈmælɑːd] **N** *Orn* colvert *m*

▸▸ ***mallard duck*** colvert *m*

malleability [ˌmælɪəˈbɪlətɪ] **N** malléabilité *f*

malleable [ˈmælɪəbəl] **ADJ** *(substance)* malléable; *(person)* influençable, malléable

mallet [ˈmælɪt] **N** maillet *m*

mallow [ˈmæləʊ] **N** *Bot* mauve *f*

malnourished [ˌmælˈnʌrɪʃt] **ADJ** sous-alimenté

malnutrition [ˌmælnjuːˈtrɪʃən] **N** malnutrition *f*

malodorous [ˌmælˈəʊdərəs] **ADJ** malodorant, nauséabond

malpractice [ˌmælˈpræktɪs] **N** *(UNCOUNT) (professional)* faute *f* professionnelle; *(financial)* malversation *f*, malversations *fpl*; *(political)* fraude *f*

▸▸ *Am Law* ***malpractice suit*** = procès pour faute ou négligence professionnelle

malt [mɔːlt] **N 1** *(substance)* malt *m* **2** *(whisky)* whisky *m* de malt **3** *Am (milk shake)* milk-shake *m* au malt, *Can* lait *m* frappé au malt

COMP *(extract, sugar, vinegar)* de malt

VT malter

▸▸ *Am* ***malt liquor*** = boisson alcoolisée tirée du malt; ***malt whisky*** whisky *m* au malt

Malta [ˈmɔːltə] **N** Malte *f*

Maltese [ˌmɔːlˈtiːz] *(pl* **inv)** **N 1** *(person)* Maltais(e) *m,f* **2** *(language)* maltais *m* **3** *(dog)* bichon *m* (maltais)

ADJ maltais

COMP *(embassy, history)* de Malte; *(teacher)* de maltais

▸▸ ***the Maltese Cross*** la croix de Malte

maltreat [ˌmælˈtriːt] **VT** maltraiter

maltreatment [ˌmælˈtriːtmənt] **N** *(UNCOUNT)* mauvais traitement *m ou* traitements *mpl*, sévices *mpl*

malware [ˈmælˌweə(r)] **N** *Comput* code *m* malicieux, malware *m*

mam [mæm] **N** *NEng Fam* maman *f*

mama [*Br* məˈmɑː, *Am* ˈmɑːmə] **N** *Br Old-fashioned or Hum or Am* maman *f*; *Am Fam* ***mama's boy*** fils *m* à sa maman

mamma [ˈmæmə] **N** *esp Am Fam* **1** *(mother)* maman *f* **2** *(woman)* môme *f*, nana *f* **3 big m.** *(object)* mastodonte *m*

mammal [ˈmæməl] **N** mammifère *m*

mammalian [məˈmeɪlɪən] **ADJ** mammalien

mammary [ˈmæmərɪ] **ADJ** *Anat* mammaire

▸▸ ***mammary gland*** glande *f* mammaire

mammogram [ˈmæməgræm], **mammograph** [ˈmæməgrɑːf] **N** *Med* mammographie *f*

mammography [mæˈmɒgrəfɪ] **N** *Med* mammographie *f*

Mammon [ˈmæmən] **PR N** Mammon *m*

mammoth [ˈmæməθ] **N** mammouth *m*

ADJ immense, colossal, gigantesque; **a m. task** un travail de Titan

mammy [ˈmæmɪ] *(pl* **mammies)** **N** *Fam* **1** *(mother)* maman *f* **2** *Pej Old-fashioned (black nanny)* = bonne d'enfants noire

Man *(written abbr* **Manitoba)** Manitoba *m*

MAN [mæn]

N	
• homme **1–6, 9, 11**	• valet **7**
• ouvrier **8**	• soldat **9**
• matelot **9**	• joueur **10**
• pièce **13**	• pion **13**
VT	
• armer **1**	• s'occuper de **2**
• assurer le service de **2**	

(pl **men** [men], *pt & pp* **manned**, *cont* **manning)**

N 1 *(adult male)* homme *m*; **a young m.** un jeune homme; **an old m.** un vieux monsieur; **a blind m.** un aveugle; **he seems a nice m.** il a l'air gentil; **he's lived here, m. and boy, for 40 years** c'est ici qu'il a grandi et vécu pendant 40 ans; **one move and you're a dead m.!** un (seul) geste et tu es un homme mort!; **he's a m.'s m.** il aime bien être avec ses copains; **he's a m. of the world** c'est un homme d'expérience; **the m. in the moon** le visage de la lune; **men's clothes/trousers** vêtements *mpl*/pantalon *m* pour homme; **men's department** *(in shop)* rayon *m* hommes; *Fam* **a m.'s gotta do what a m.'s gotta do** quand il faut y aller, il faut y aller

2 *(of the specified type)* homme *m*; **he's not a betting/drinking m.** ce n'est pas un homme qui parie/boit; **he was never a m. for taking risks** il n'a jamais été homme à *ou* ce n'est pas le genre d'homme à prendre des risques; **I'm a whisky m[an] myself** moi, c'est le whisky que je préfère; **he['s] the m. for the job** c'est l'homme qu'il faut pou[r] faire ce travail; **I'm your m.** je suis votre homm[e]; **a medical m.** un médecin; **a m. of God** un homm[e] d'église; **a m. of learning** un savant; **a m. of lette[rs]** un homme de lettres; **I'm a Dublin m.** je suis d[e] Dublin; **he's a local m.** c'est un homme du pays; **he['s] a Harvard m.** *(at present)* il fait ses études à Ha[r]vard; *(in the past)* il a fait ses études à Harvard

3 *(with manly qualities)* homme *m*; **to act like a m[an]** se comporter en homme; **he took the news like [a] m.** il a pris la nouvelle avec courage; **he's not m[an] enough to own up** il n'aura pas le courag[e] d'avouer; **the army will make a m. of him!** l'armé[e] en fera un homme!; *Fig* **this will separate or so[rt] the men from the boys** c'est là qu'on verra le[s] vrais hommes

4 *(person, individual)* homme *m*, individu *m*; **an[y] m.** n'importe qui; **few men** peu de gens; **wha[t] more can a m. do?** qu'est-ce qu'on peut faire d[e] plus?; **all men are born equal** tous les homme[s] naissent égaux; **the m. must be mad!** il doit êt[re] fou!; **I've never met the m.** je n'ai jamais rencontr[é] l'individu en question; **to be one's own m.** êtr[e] indépendant *ou* son propre maître; **to the las[t] m.** *(without exception)* sans exception; *(until d[e]feat)* jusqu'au dernier; **it's every m. for himse[lf]** c'est chacun pour soi; **the m. in the stree[t]** l'homme *m* de la rue; *Br Fam* **every m. jack of ther[m]** chacun d'eux sans exception▫

5 *(as husband, father)* homme *m*; **m. and wife** ma[ri] *m* et femme *f*; **to live as m. and wife** vivre mar[i]talement *ou* en concubinage; **he's a real famil[y] m.** c'est un vrai père de famille; **the m. of th[e] house** l'homme *m* de la maison; *Hum* le pater fa[]milias; *Fam* **my old m.** *(husband)* mon homme *(father)* mon vieux

6 *Br Fam (boyfriend, lover)* homme *m*, mec *m*; **she's got a new m.** elle a un nouveau mec; **hav[e] you met her young m.?** *(boyfriend)* avez-vous ren[]contré son petit ami?; *(fiancé)* avez-vous ren[]contré son fiancé?

7 *(servant)* valet *m*, domestique *m*

8 *(employee ▸ in industry, on farm)* ouvrier *m*; *(▸ in business, shop)* employé *m*; **the men have gon[e] on strike** les hommes se sont mis en grève; **the[y] took on 200 men** ils ont embauché 200 ouvriers; **a TV repair m.** un réparateur télé; **our m. in Par[is]** *(representative)* notre représentant à Paris; *(jour[]nalist)* notre correspondant à Paris; *(diploma[t])* notre envoyé diplomatique à Paris; *(spy)* notr[e] agent à Paris

9 *(in armed forces ▸ soldier)* soldat *m*, homme *m* (de troupe); *(▸ sailor)* matelot *m*, homme *m* (d'équipage); **officers and men** *(in army)* officier[s] *mpl* et hommes *mpl* de troupe; *(in navy)* officier[s] *mpl* et matelots *mpl*

10 *(player)* joueur *m*, équipier *m*; **a three-m. tea[m]** une équipe de trois joueurs; **the m. of the matc[h]** le héros du match

11 *(mankind)* homme *m*; **primitive/modern m[an]** l'homme *m* primitif/moderne; **one of the mos[t] deadly poisons known to m.** un des plus dange[]reux poisons connus de l'homme; *Prov* **m. can[not] live by bread alone** l'homme ne vit pas qu[e] de pain; *Fig* **this is no use to m. nor beast** cela n'es[t] d'aucune utilité à personne

12 *Fam (as term of address)* **come on, m.!** allez viens!; **hey, m.!** *(as greeting)* salut vieux!

13 *(in chess)* pièce *f*, *(in draughts)* pion *m*

VT 1 *Mil (ship)* armer, équiper; *(cannon)* servir; **t[o] m. the barricades** défendre les barricades; **th[e] tanker was manned by Greek seamen** le pétrolie[r] avait un équipage grec; **m. the pumps!** armez le[s] pompes!; **m. the lifeboats!** mettez les canots à l[a] mer!; **the fort was manned by 20 soldiers** le fo[rt] était tenu par une garnison de 20 soldats

2 *(staff ▸ machine)* faire tourner, s'occuper de *(▸ switchboard)* assurer le service *ou* la perma[]nence de; **reception wasn't manned at the tim[e]** personne n'assurait *ou* n'était à la réception [à] ce moment-là; **someone has to be there to m. th[e] phone** quelqu'un doit être là pour répondre a[u] téléphone; **the campaign office was manned b[y] volunteers** la permanence de la campagne éta[it] assurée par des volontaires; **the office is manne[d] by a skeleton staff** le bureau tourne à effectif ré[]duit

EXCLAM *Fam* la vache!; **m., was it big!** bon sang, qu'est-ce que c'était grand!; **you should have seen it, m.!** bon sang, tu aurais dû voir ça!

• **as one man ADV** comme un seul homme; **they replied as one m.** ils répondirent d'une seule voix

• **to a man ADV** sans exception; **they agreed to a m.** ils ont accepté à l'unanimité; **they were patriots/communists to a m.** ils étaient tous patriotes/communistes

▸▸ ***man bag*** petit sac *m* pour homme; *Fam Hum* ***man flu*** rhume *m (lorsque la personne affectée est un homme qui exagère les symptômes de son mal)*; *Literature* **Man Friday** Vendredi; ***man Friday*** *(servant)* fidèle serviteur *m*; *(office worker)* = employé de bureau affecté à des tâches diverses; *Br* ***man management*** gestion *f* des ressources humaines; *Am* ***man purse*** petit sac *m* pour homme

> Note that the French expression **homme du monde** doesn't mean **man of the world**; it means a man who belongs to high society.

man-about-town *(pl* **men-about-town)** **N** *Br* homme *m* du monde, mondain *m*

manacle ['mænəkəl] **VT** *(shackle)* enchaîner; *(handcuff)* mettre *ou* passer les menottes à; **his wrists were manacled** il portait des menottes

• **manacles NPL** *(shackles)* fers *mpl*, chaînes *fpl*; *(handcuffs)* menottes *fpl*

manage ['mænɪdʒ] **VT 1** *(business, hotel, shop)* gérer, diriger; *(property, estate, economy, money, resources)* gérer; *(crisis, illness)* gérer; *(team)* être le manager de, diriger; **she manages a shoe shop** elle est gérante d'une boutique de chaussures; **he manages Melchester United** c'est le manager de *ou* il manage Melchester United; **to m. sb's affairs** gérer les affaires de qn; **I'm very bad at managing money** je suis incapable de gérer un budget

2 *(accomplish)* réussir; **she managed a smile** elle trouva la force de sourire; **to m. to do sth** réussir *ou* parvenir *ou* arriver à faire qch; **he managed to keep a straight face** il est parvenu à garder son sérieux; **did you m. to get anything to eat?** as-tu finalement trouvé quelque chose à manger?; **he always manages to arrive at meal times** il se débrouille toujours pour arriver *ou* il trouve toujours le moyen d'arriver à l'heure des repas

3 *(handle* ▸ *person, animal)* savoir s'y prendre avec; *(manipulate* ▸ *machine, tool)* manier, se servir de; **he doesn't know how to m. people** il ne sait pas s'y prendre avec les gens; **she finds it difficult to m. her pupils** elle a du mal à tenir ses élèves

4 *(be available for)* **can you m. nine o'clock/next Saturday?** pouvez-vous venir à neuf heures/samedi prochain?; **can you m. lunch tomorrow?** pouvez-vous déjeuner avec moi demain?

5 *(cope with)* **I can't m. all this extra work** je ne peux pas faire face à ce surcroît de travail; **can you m. that rucksack?** pouvez-vous porter ce sac à dos?; **he can't m. the stairs any more** il n'arrive plus à monter l'escalier; **I think I could m. another slice** j'en reprendrais volontiers une tranche; **can you m. £10?** pouvez-vous aller jusqu'à 10 livres?

VI *(cope)* se débrouiller, y arriver; *(financially)* se débrouiller, s'en sortir; **we'll have to m. on our own** nous devrons nous débrouiller tout seuls; **can you m.?** ça ira?; **give me a fork, I can't m. with chopsticks** donne-moi une fourchette, je ne m'en sors pas avec des baguettes; **we had to m. without heating** nous avons dû nous passer de chauffage; **they just about m. on her salary** ils arrivent tout juste à s'en sortir avec son salaire; **I don't know how I would have managed without you** je ne sais pas comment j'aurais fait sans toi

manageable ['mænɪdʒəbəl] **ADJ** *(size, amount)* raisonnable; *(tool, car, boat)* maniable; *(undertaking, task)* faisable; *(hair)* facile à coiffer; **cut the wood into m. pieces** coupez le bois en morceaux faciles à manipuler; **the smaller suitcase is a more m. size** la plus petite valise est plus maniable

managed ['mænɪdʒd] **ADJ** *(farmland, woodland, estate)* exploité

▸▸ *Fin* ***managed currency*** devise *f* contrôlée, monnaie *f* dirigée; *Fin* ***managed fund*** *(in insurance)* fonds *m* géré

management ['mænɪdʒmənt] **N 1** *(control* ▸ *of firm, finances, property)* gestion *f*, direction *f*; *(of economy, money, resources)* gestion *f*; **all their problems are due to bad m.** tous leurs problèmes sont dus à une mauvaise gestion; **under Gordon's m. sales have increased significantly** depuis que c'est Gordon qui s'en occupe, les ventes ont considérablement augmenté; **who looks after the m. of the farm?** qui s'occupe de l'exploitation de la ferme?; **m. by exception** direction *f* par exceptions; **m. by objectives** gestion *f* par objectifs

2 *(handling* ▸ *of crisis, illness etc)* gestion *f*; **she was praised for her m. of the situation** on a applaudi la façon dont elle s'est comportée dans cette situation

3 *(of shop, hotel etc)* direction *f*; **the m. cannot accept responsibility for any loss or damage** *(sign)* la direction décline toute responsabilité en cas de perte ou de dommage; **under new m.** *(sign)* changement de direction *ou* de propriétaire

4 *Ind (managers, employers)* administration *f*, direction *f*; **senior m.** les cadres *mpl* supérieurs, la Direction; **negotiations between m. and unions have broken down** les négociations entre le patronat et les syndicats ont échoué

▸▸ ***management accountant*** contrôleur(euse) *m*, *f* de gestion; ***management accounting*** comptabilité *f* de gestion; *Br* ***management buy-out*** rachat *m* d'une société par la direction; ***management committee*** comité *m* de direction; ***management consultancy*** *(activity)* conseil *m* en gestion (d'entreprise); *(firm)* cabinet *m* (de) conseil; ***management consultant*** conseiller(ère) *m,f* en *ou* de gestion (d'entreprise); ***management information system*** système *m* intégré de gestion; ***management skills*** qualités *fpl* de gestionnaire; ***management style*** mode *m* de gestion; ***management team*** équipe *f* dirigeante

manager ['mænɪdʒə(r)] **N 1** *(of company, bank)* directeur(trice) *m,f*; *(of shop)* directeur(trice) *m, f*, gérant(e) *m,f*; *(of bar, restaurant)* gérant(e) *m,f*; *(of pop star, celebrity)* manager *m*; *(of sports team)* manager *m*, entraîneur(euse) *m,f*; *Fin (of funds, money)* gestionnaire *mf*; *(of assets)* administrateur(trice) *m,f*; *(of estate)* régisseur *m*; **he's been made m.** il est passé cadre **2** *(organizer)* **she's a good home m.** elle sait tenir une maison **3** *Comput (of disk etc)* gestionnaire *m*

manageress [ˌmænɪdʒə'res] **N** *(of company, bank)* directrice *f*, *(of shop)* directrice *f*, gérante *f*; *(of bar, restaurant)* gérante *f*

managerial [ˌmænɪ'dʒɪərɪəl] **ADJ** gestionnaire, directorial; *(position)* de commande; **at m. level** au niveau de la direction; **m. experience** expérience *f* de la direction

▸▸ ***managerial skills*** qualités *fpl* de gestionnaire; ***managerial staff*** cadres *mpl*, encadrement *m*

managing ['mænɪdʒɪŋ] **N** *(handling)* gestion *f*

▸▸ ***managing director*** directeur(trice) *m,f* général(e), P-DG *m*; ***managing editor*** rédacteur(trice) *m,f* en chef

manatee [ˌmænə'tiː] **N** *Zool* lamantin *m*

Manc [mæŋk] **N** *Br Fam (abbr* **Mancunian)** *(inhabitant)* habitant(e) *m,f* de Manchester; *(native)* personne *f* originaire de Manchester

manchego [mæn'tʃegəʊ] **N** *(cheese)* manchego *m*

Manchuria [mæn'tʃʊərɪə] **N** Mandchourie *f*

Manchurian [mæn'tʃʊərɪən] **N 1** *(person)* Mandchou(e) *m,f* **2** *(langue)* mandchou *m*

ADJ mandchou

Mancunian [mæŋ'kjuːnjən] **N** *(inhabitant)* habitant(e) *m,f* de Manchester; *(native)* personne *f* originaire de Manchester

ADJ de Manchester

M&A [ˌemən'eɪ] **N** *Fin (abbr* **mergers and acquisitions)** fusions et acquisitions *fpl*

mandarin ['mændərɪn] **N 1** *Hist & Fig* mandarin *m*

2 *Bot (tree)* mandarinier *m*

3 *(fruit)* mandarine *f*

4 *(colour)* mandarine *f*

• **Mandarin N** *Ling* mandarin *m*

▸▸ *Ling* ***Mandarin Chinese*** mandarin *m*; ***mandarin collar*** col *m* Mao; *Orn* ***mandarin duck*** (canard *m*) mandarin *m*; ***mandarin orange*** mandarine *m*

mandate N ['mændeɪt] **1** *Pol* mandat *m*; **the government receives its m. from the electorate** c'est l'électorat qui mandate les membres du gouvernement; **the government has no m. to introduce the new tax** le gouvernement n'a pas été mandaté pour mettre en place ce nouvel impôt **2** *(country)* (territoire *m* sous) mandat *m* **3** *(task)* tâche *f*, mission *f*

VT [ˌmæn'deɪt] **1** *(give authority)* mandater; **to m. sb to do sth** donner mandat à qn de faire qch **2** *(country)* mettre sous mandat, administrer par mandat

▸▸ *Fin* ***mandate form*** lettre *f* de signatures autorisées

mandatory ['mændətərɪ] *(pl* **mandatories) ADJ 1** *(obligatory)* obligatoire; **participation is m.** la participation est obligatoire **2** *(relating to a mandate)* relatif à un mandat

N mandataire *mf*

▸▸ ***mandatory powers*** pouvoirs *mpl* donnés par mandat; *Law* ***mandatory sentence*** peine *f* obligatoire

mandible ['mændɪbəl] **N 1** *(of insect)* mandibule *f* **2** *(of vertebrate)* mâchoire *f* inférieure

mandolin(e) ['mændəlɪn] **N** mandoline *f*

mandrake ['mændreɪk] **N** *Bot* mandragore *f*

mandrel, mandril ['mændrəl] **N** *Tech* mandrin *m*, arbre *m* (de tour)

mandrill ['mændrɪl] **N** *Zool* mandrill *m*

mane [meɪn] **N** *(of horse, lion)* crinière *f*; *Fig* **a m. of golden hair** une crinière blonde

man-eater N 1 *(animal)* mangeur *m* d'hommes; *(cannibal)* cannibale *m*, anthropophage *m* **2** *Fam Hum (woman)* dévoreuse *f* *ou* mangeuse *f* d'hommes

man-eating ADJ *(animal)* mangeur d'hommes, anthropophage; *(people)* cannibale, anthropophage

▸▸ ***man-eating shark*** requin *m* mangeur d'hommes

maneuver, maneuverable *etc Am* = **manoeuvre, manoeuvrable** *etc*

manful ['mænfʊl] **ADJ** *(courageous)* vaillant, ardent

manfully ['mænfʊlɪ] **ADV** *(courageously)* vaillamment, courageusement; **he was struggling m. with the suitcases/his second steak** il se démenait vaillamment avec les valises/son deuxième steak

manganese ['mæŋgəniːz] **N** *Chem* manganèse *m*

▸▸ ***manganese steel*** acier *m* au manganèse

mange [meɪndʒ] **N** *Vet* gale *f*

mangel-wurzel ['mæŋgəlˌwɜːzəl] **N** betterave *f* fourragère

manger ['meɪndʒə(r)] **N 1** *(trough)* mangeoire *f* **2** *Bible* crèche *f*

mangle ['mæŋgəl] **N** *(for clothes)* essoreuse *f* (à rouleaux)

VT 1 *(body)* mutiler, déchiqueter; *(vehicle)* rendre méconnaissable; **their bodies were horribly mangled** leurs corps ont été atrocement mutilés; **the mangled wreckage of the two cars** les carcasses en accordéon des deux voitures **2** *(quotation, text)* estropier, mutiler **3** *(laundry, linen)* essorer *(dans une essoreuse à rouleaux)*

mango ['mæŋgəʊ] *(pl* **mangos** *or* **mangoes) N 1** *(fruit)* mangue *f* **2** *(tree)* manguier *m*

▸▸ ***mango chutney*** = condiment à la mangue

mangrove ['mæŋgrəʊv] **N** manglier *m*, palétuvier *m*

▸▸ ***mangrove swamp*** mangrove *f*

mangy ['meɪndʒɪ] *(compar* **mangier**, *superl* **mangiest) ADJ 1** *(having mange* ▸ *animal)* galeux **2** *Fam (shabby* ▸ *coat, carpet)* miteux, pelé

manhandle ['mænˌhændəl] **VT 1** *(treat roughly)* maltraiter, malmener **2** *(move)* porter *ou* transporter (à bras d'homme); **they manhandled the piano into position** ils ont poussé le piano pour le mettre à sa place

manhole ['mænhəʊl] **N** bouche *f* d'égout, regard *m*

▸▸ ***manhole cover*** plaque *f* d'égout

manhood ['mænhʊd] **N 1** *(age)* âge *m* d'homme; **he has reached m.** c'est un homme maintenant

2 *(virility)* virilité *f*
3 *(men collectively)* hommes *mpl*, population *f* masculine; **British m.** les hommes *mpl* britanniques
4 *Fam Hum (genitals)* bijoux *mpl* de famille

man-hour **N** *Br Ind etc* heure *f* de travail, *Spec* heure-homme *f*; **300 man-hours** 300 heures *fpl* de travail

manhunt ['mæn,hʌnt] **N** chasse *f* à l'homme

SUFFIXE

-MANIA, -MANIAC

Ajoutés à des racines d'origine latine ou grecque, ces suffixes servent à former des noms, **-mania** signalant un état pathologique et **-maniac** la personne affectée. Dans un contexte médical ils se traduisent le plus souvent par **-manie** et **-mane**, respectivement. Le suffixe **-maniac** sert aussi parfois à former des adjectifs:
(a) dans le contexte de la psychiatrie, ces suffixes, tout comme leurs équivalents français, véhiculent une notion de compulsion pathologique:
kleptomania la kleptomanie; **megalomania** la mégalomanie; **he is a pyromaniac** c'est un pyromane; **nymphomaniac tendencies** des tendances nymphomanes
(b) dans un sens plus large et non technique, ils indiquent une notion d'ENTHOUSIASME débridé, voire d'OBSESSION pour quelque chose ou quelqu'un:
bibliomania la bibliomanie; **anglomania** l'anglomanie
Ces suffixes sont très générateurs. On peut les accoler à n'importe quel mot pour suggérer l'adulation ou l'obsession à l'égard de la chose ou de la personne désignée:
textmania la folie des SMS; **Potter-mania is sweeping the nation's bookshops** les librairies du pays sont en proie à la folie Harry Potter; **celeb-mania has boosted magazine sales** l'enthousiasme débridé du public pour les célébrités a fait décoller les ventes des magazines; **he's a complete Beckham-maniac** c'est un fanatique de David Beckham

mania ['meɪnjə] **N 1** *Psy* manie *f*; *(obsession)* obsession *f* **2** *(zeal)* passion *f*, *Pej* manie *f*; **he has a m. for collecting old photographs** il a la manie de collectionner les vieilles photos; **he's got football m.** c'est un passionné de football

maniac ['meɪnɪæk] **N 1** *(dangerous person)* fou (folle) *m,f*; *(sexual)* obsédé(e) *m,f*; **I've been working like a m. for the past two months** ça fait deux mois que je travaille comme un fou; **to drive like a m.** conduire comme un fou **2** *(fan)* fou (folle) *m,f*; **he's a football m.** c'est un fan *ou* un mordu de football **3** *Psy* maniaque *mf*
ADJ 1 *(gen)* fou (folle) **2** *Psy* maniaque

Note that the French word **maniaque** is most commonly used to describe someone who is obsessive about order and tidiness.

maniacal [mə'naɪəkəl] **ADJ 1** *(crazy)* fou (folle); **m. laughter** rire *m* hystérique **2** *Psy* maniaque

manic ['mænɪk] **N** maniaque *mf*
ADJ 1 *(crazy)* fou (folle) **2** *Psy* maniaque
►► ***manic depression*** psychose *f* maniaco-dépressive

manic-depressive **N** maniaco-dépressif (ive) *m,f*
ADJ maniaco-dépressif

manicure ['mænɪ,kjʊə(r)] **N** manucure *f*; **to have a m.** se faire faire les mains; **to give sb a m.** faire les mains à qn, manucurer qn
COMP *(case, scissors)* de manucure, à ongles
VT faire les mains à, manucurer; **she was manicuring her nails** elle était en train de se faire les ongles; **a manicured lawn** une pelouse impeccable
►► ***manicure set*** trousse *f* de manucure

manicurist ['mænɪ,kjʊərɪst] **N** manucure *mf*

manifest ['mænɪfest] **N** *(of ship, plane)* manifeste *m*
ADJ *Formal* manifeste, évident; **to make sth m.** rendre qch évident
VT manifester; **how did this mania m. itself?** comment cette obsession s'est-elle manifestée?
VI *(ghost, spirit)* se manifester
►► *Am Hist* ***Manifest Destiny*** = au XIXème siècle, idée selon laquelle l'établissement des colons en Amérique du Nord relevait de la volonté divine

manifestation [,mænɪfes'teɪʃən] **N** manifestation *f*

Note that the French word **manifestation** also means **demonstration**.

manifestly ['mænɪfestlɪ] **ADV** manifestement, à l'évidence

manifesto [,mænɪ'festəʊ] *(pl* **manifestos** *or* **manifestoes***)* **N** manifeste *m*

manifold ['mænɪfəʊld] **N** *Tech* **(exhaust) m.** collecteur *m* d'échappement; **(inlet** *or* **intake) m.** conduits *mpl* d'admission, collecteur *m* d'admission
ADJ *Formal (numerous)* multiple, nombreux; *(varied)* varié, divers

manikin = **mannikin**

Manila [mə'nɪlə] **N** Manille

manila, manilla [mə'nɪlə] **ADJ** en chanvre de Manille
►► ***manila envelope*** enveloppe *f* en papier kraft; ***manila paper*** papier *m* kraft; ***manila rope*** (cordage *m* en) manille *f*

manioc ['mænɪɒk] **N** manioc *m*

manipulate [mə'nɪpjʊleɪt] **VT 1** *(equipment)* manœuvrer, manipuler; *(tool)* manier; *(vehicle)* manœuvrer **2** *Pej (person)* manipuler, manœuvrer; *(facts, figures)* manipuler; **he skilfully manipulates situations to his own advantage** il a l'art de tirer profit de toutes les situations; *Fin* **to m. the accounts** trafiquer les comptes **3** *Med* **to m. bones** pratiquer des manipulations

manipulation [mə,nɪpjʊ'leɪʃən] **N 1** *(of equipment)* manœuvre *f*, manipulation *f* **2** *Pej (of people, facts, situation)* manipulation *f* **3** *Med* manipulation *f*

manipulative [mə'nɪpjʊlətɪv] **ADJ** *Pej* manipulateur; **he can be very m.** il n'hésite pas à manipuler les gens

manipulator [mə'nɪpjʊleɪtə(r)] **N** manipulateur (trice) *m,f*

Manitoba [,mænɪ'təʊbə] **N** le Manitoba

mankind [mæn'kaɪnd] **N 1** *(species)* l'humanité *f*, l'espèce *f* humaine **2** *(men in general)* les hommes *mpl*

manky ['mæŋkɪ] *(compar* **mankier**, *superl* **mankiest***)* **ADJ** *Br Fam (worthless)* nul; *(dirty)* miteux, pourri

manlike ['mænlaɪk] **ADJ 1** *(virile)* viril, masculin **2** *(woman)* masculin

manliness ['mænlɪnɪs] **N** virilité *f*

manly ['mænlɪ] *(compar* **manlier**, *superl* **manliest***)* **ADJ** *(sport, activity)* d'homme, masculin; *(behaviour, character, voice)* mâle, viril

man-made **ADJ** *(fibre, fabric, product)* synthétique; *(construction, lake, beach)* artificiel; *(landscape)* modelé *ou* façonné par l'homme

manna ['mænə] **N 1** *Bible & Fig* manne *f*; *Fig* **m. from heaven** manne *f* céleste **2** *Bot* manne *f*

manned [mænd] **ADJ** *(ship, machine)* ayant un équipage
►► ***manned spacecraft*** vaisseau *m* spatial habité

mannequin ['mænɪkɪn] **N** mannequin *m*

manner ['mænə(r)] **N 1** *(way)* manière *f*, façon *f*; **in the same m.** de la même manière *ou* façon; **it's just a m. of speaking** c'est juste une façon de parler; **in a m. of speaking** en quelque sorte, dans un certain sens; **not by any m. of means** en aucune manière, aucunement; **it was the m. in which he did it that upset me** c'est la manière *ou* la façon dont il s'y est pris qui m'a blessé; **he does it (as if** *or* **as) to the m. born** il le fait comme s'il avait fait ça toute sa vie; *Gram* **adverb of m.** adverbe *m* de manière
2 *(attitude)* attitude *f*, manière *f*; *(behaviour)* comportement *m*, manière *f* de se conduire; **to have a pleasant m.** avoir des manières agréables; **I don't like his m.** je n'aime pas ses façons; **he has a good telephone m.** il fait bonne impression au téléphone
3 *(style)* manière *f*; **in the m. of Rembrandt** dans le style ou à la manière de Rembrandt
4 *(kind)* sorte *f*, genre *m*; **all m. of rare books** toutes sortes de livres rares; *Arch* **what m. of man is he?** quel genre d'homme est-ce?
• **manners** **NPL 1** *(social etiquette)* manières *fpl*; **(good) manners** bonnes manières *fpl*; **bad manners** mauvaises manières *fpl*; **to have good/bad table manners** savoir/ne pas savoir se tenir à table; **it's bad manners to talk with your mouth full** c'est mal élevé *ou* ce n'est pas poli de parler la bouche pleine; **she has no manners** elle n'a aucune éducation, elle est mal élevée; **where are your manners?** *(say thank you)* qu'est-ce qu'on dit quand on est bien élevé?; *(behave properly)* est-ce que c'est une façon de se tenir?; **I'm forgetting my manners, would you like some tea?** je manque à tous mes devoirs, je ne vous ai pas proposé de thé; *Prov* **manners maketh the man** = un homme n'est rien sans les manières **2** *Literary (social customs)* mœurs *fpl*, usages *mpl*

mannered ['mænəd] **ADJ** maniéré, affecté, précieux

mannerism ['mænərɪzəm] **N** tic *m*, manie *f*
• **Mannerism** **N** *Art* maniérisme *m*

mannerly ['mænəlɪ] **ADJ** bien élevé, courtois

mannikin ['mænɪkɪn] **N 1** *(dwarf)* nain(e) *m,f* **2** *(model)* mannequin *m*

mannish ['mænɪʃ] **ADJ** *(woman)* masculin; **she has a m. voice** elle a une voix d'homme

manny ['mænɪ] *(pl* **mannies***)* **N** garde *m* d'enfants *(homme)*

manoeuvrability, *Am* **maneuverability** [mə,nuːvrə'bɪlətɪ] **N** manœuvrabilité *f*, maniabilité *f*

manoeuvrable, *Am* **maneuverable** [mə'nuːvrəbəl] **ADJ** manœuvrable, maniable

manoeuvre, *Am* **maneuver** [mə'nuːvə(r)] **N 1** *Mil & Naut (action)* manœuvre *f*; **to be on manoeuvres** être en manœuvres **2** *(action, remark)* manœuvre *f*; **it was only a m. to get him to resign** ce n'était qu'une manœuvre pour l'amener à démissionner; **there wasn't much room for m.** *(physically)* il n'y avait pas beaucoup de place pour manœuvrer; *Fig* il y avait peu de marge de manœuvre
VT 1 manœuvrer; **he manoeuvred the ladder through the window** il a manœuvré pour faire passer l'échelle par la fenêtre; **she manoeuvred her car into the space** elle a garé sa voiture dans l'emplacement (en manœuvrant); *Fig* **they manoeuvred him into resigning** ils l'ont poussé à démissionner
VI manœuvrer; *Naut (ship)* évoluer

manoeuvring, *Am* **maneuvering** [mə'nuːvərɪŋ] **N 1** *Mil & Naut* manœuvres *fpl* **2** *Pej (plotting)* menées *fpl*, intrigues *fpl*

man-of-war [,mænə'wɔː(r)] *(pl* **men-of-war** [,men-]*)* **N** *Naut* bâtiment *m* de guerre

manometer [mə'nɒmɪtə(r)] **N** manomètre *m*

manor ['mænə(r)] **N 1** *(house)* manoir *m*, château *m* **2** *Hist* seigneurie *f*, domaine *m* seigneurial; **the lord/lady of the m.** le châtelain/la châtelaine **3** *Br Fam Crime slang (police district)* îlot *m*
►► ***manor house*** manoir *m*, château *m*

manorial [mə'nɔːrɪəl] **ADJ** *Hist* seigneurial

manpower ['mæn,paʊə(r)] **N** *(UNCOUNT) (personnel)* main-d'œuvre *f*, *Mil* effectifs *mpl*
►► ***manpower planning*** planification *f* de la main-d'œuvre; ***manpower shortage*** manque *m* de main-d'œuvre

manqué ['mɒŋkeɪ] **ADJ** manqué

mansard ['mænsɑːd] **N** *(roof)* toit *m* mansardé; *(attic)* mansarde *f*

manse [mæns] **N** presbytère *m*

manservant ['mæn,sɜːvənt] **N** *(gen)* domestique *m*; *(valet)* valet *m* (de chambre)

mansion ['mænʃən] **N** *(in town)* hôtel *m* particulier; *(in country)* château *m*, manoir *m*
►► ***mansion block*** résidence *f* de standing; ***the Mansion House*** = la résidence officielle du maire de Londres

man-size, man-sized ADJ *(job, task)* ardu, difficile; *(meal)* copieux
►► ***man-sized tissues*** grands mouchoirs *mpl* (en papier)

manslaughter ['mænˌslɔːtə(r)] N *Law* homicide *m* involontaire

mantel ['mæntəl] N *(shelf)* (tablette *f* de) cheminée *f*; *(frame)* manteau *m*

mantelpiece ['mæntəlˌpiːs] N 1 *(surround)* (manteau *m* de) cheminée *f* 2 *(shelf)* (tablette *f* de) cheminée *f*

mantilla [mæn'tɪlə] N mantille *f*

mantis ['mæntɪs] N *Entom* mante *f*

mantle ['mæntəl] N 1 *(cloak)* cape *f*; *Fig (covering)* manteau *m*; **a m. of fog** un manteau de brume; *Fig* **to take on the m. of office** assumer les responsabilités qui incombent au poste
2 *Zool & Geol* manteau *m*
3 *(of gas lamp)* manchon *m*
4 *(shelf)* (tablette *f* de) cheminée *f*; *(frame)* manteau *m*
VT *Arch or Literary* 1 *(cover with cloak)* envelopper d'une cape 2 *(obscure)* cacher, voiler 3 *(cover)* couvrir, envelopper (**with** de)
VI *Arch or Literary* 1 *(liquid* ► *froth)* écumer, mousser 2 *(blood, blush)* se répandre; *(face, cheeks)* rougir; *Fig* **the dawn mantled in the sky** l'aurore envahit le ciel

man-to-man ADJ & ADV entre hommes, d'homme à homme
►► ***man-to-man marking*** marquage *m* individuel

mantrap ['mæntræp] N piège *m* à hommes

manual ['mænjʊəl] N 1 *(handbook)* manuel *m*
2 *(of organ)* clavier *m*
3 *(car)* voiture *f* à embrayage manuel
4 *(mode of operation)* **to be on m.** être sur commande manuelle
ADJ *(work, labour, worker)* manuel
►► ***manual dexterity*** dextérité *f*, habileté *f* manuelle; *Aut* ***manual gearbox, manual gears*** boîte *f* de vitesses mécanique, boîte *f* manuelle *ou* mécanique; *Aut* ***manual transmission*** transmission *f* mécanique; ***manual typewriter*** machine *f* à écrire mécanique

manually ['mænjʊəlɪ] ADV manuellement, à la main

manufacture [ˌmænjʊ'fæktʃə(r)] N 1 *(making)* fabrication *f*; *(of cars, aircraft)* construction *f*; *(of clothes)* confection *f* 2 *Tech (product)* produit *m* manufacturé
VT 1 *(produce)* fabriquer, produire; *(car, aircraft)* construire; *(clothes)* confectionner 2 *(invent* ► *news, story)* inventer; *(*► *evidence)* fabriquer; **to m. an opportunity to do sth** inventer une occasion de faire qch
►► ***manufactured goods*** biens *mpl* manufacturés; ***manufactured products*** produits *mpl* manufacturés

manufacturer [ˌmænjʊ'fæktʃərə(r)] N fabricant(e) *m,f*; *(of cars, aircraft)* constructeur(trice) *m,f*; **send it back to the manufacturers** renvoyez-le au fabricant
►► ***manufacturer's agent*** agent *m* exclusif; ***manufacturer's brand*** marque *f* de fabricant; ***manufacturer's liability*** responsabilité *f* du fabricant; ***manufacturer's recommended price*** prix *m* conseillé par le fabricant

manufacturing [ˌmænjʊ'fæktʃərɪŋ] N fabrication *f*; **the decline of m.** le déclin de l'industrie manufacturière
ADJ *(city, area)* industriel
►► ***manufacturing company*** entreprise *f* industrielle; ***manufacturing costs*** frais *mpl* de fabrication; ***manufacturing defect*** vice *m ou* défaut *m* de fabrication; ***manufacturing industry*** les industries *fpl* manufacturières *ou* de transformation; ***manufacturing licence*** licence *f* de fabrication; ***manufacturing plant*** usine *f* de fabrication

manure [mə'njʊə(r)] N *(farmyard)* fumier *m*; *(fertilizer)* engrais *m*; **liquid m.** purin *m*, lisier *m*; **m. heap** tas *m* de fumier
VT *(with dung)* fumer; *(with fertilizer)* répandre de l'engrais sur

manuscript ['mænjʊskrɪpt] N manuscrit *m*; **m. (paper)** *(for music)* papier *m* à musique; **I read the book in m.** j'ai lu le manuscrit du livre
ADJ manuscrit, (écrit) à la main

Manx [mæŋks] NPL **the M.** les habitants *mpl* de l'île de Man
N *(language)* mannois *m*
ADJ de l'île de Man
►► ***Manx cat*** chat *m* (sans queue) de l'île de Man

many ['menɪ] *(compar* **more** [mɔː], *superl* **most** [məʊst]) ADJ beaucoup de, de nombreux; **m. people** beaucoup de *ou* bien des gens; **m. years** bien des années, de nombreuses années; **m. times** souvent, bien des fois; **she had cards from all her m. admirers** elle a reçu des cartes de ses nombreux admirateurs; **take as m. books as you like** prenez autant de livres *ou* tous les livres que vous voudrez; **they admitted as m. people as they could** ils ont laissé entrer autant de gens que possible; **we visited six cities in as m. days** nous avons visité six villes en autant de jours; **how m....?** combien de...?; **how m. students came?** combien d'étudiants sont venus?; **so m. people** tant de gens; **there are only so m. ways you can cook chicken** il n'y a pas une infinité de façons de préparer le poulet; **too m. people** trop de gens; **I've received a great m. applications** j'ai reçu de très nombreuses *ou* un grand nombre de candidatures
PRON beaucoup; **m. of the audience were children** il y avait de nombreux enfants *ou* beaucoup d'enfants dans l'assistance; **m. of them** beaucoup d'entre eux; **m.'s the time** bien des fois; **m.'s the holiday I spent there** j'y ai passé bien des vacances; **they admitted as m. as they could** ils ont laissé entrer autant de gens que possible; **as m. again** encore autant; **twice/three times as m.** deux/trois fois plus; **as m. as 8,000 students enrolled** jusqu'à *ou* près de 8000 étudiants se sont inscrits; **how m.?** combien?; **how m. were there?** combien étaient-ils?; **we can only fit in so m.** nous n'avons de place que pour un certain nombre de personnes; **don't give me too m.** ne m'en donne pas trop; **a good/great m.** un bon/grand nombre
PREDET **m. a time** bien des fois; **m. a child would be glad of it** bien des enfants s'en contenteraient
NPL *(masses)* **the m.** la majorité; **the m. who loved her** tous ceux qui l'aimaient; **the sacrifices made by the few for the m.** les sacrifices faits par la minorité pour la masse

many-coloured, *Am* **many-colored** ADJ multicolore

man-year N *Br* année-personne *f*

many-sided ADJ 1 *(figure, shape)* qui a de nombreux côtés 2 *(problem)* aux aspects multiples, multiforme 3 *(personality)* qui a de nombreuses facettes; *(individual)* aux talents multiples

Maoist ['maʊɪst] N maoïste *mf*
ADJ maoïste

Maori ['maʊrɪ] *(pl inv or* **Maoris**) N 1 *(person)* Maori(e) *m,f* 2 *Ling* maori *m*
ADJ maori

map [mæp] *(pt & pp* **mapped**, *cont* **mapping**) N 1 *(of country)* carte *f*; *(of town, network)* plan *m*; **a m. of India** une carte de l'Inde; *Fig* **it's off the m.** c'est à l'autre bout du monde; *Fig* **the city was wiped off the m.** la ville a été rayée de la carte; *Fig* **to put sth on the m.** faire connaître qch; **the election results put them firmly on the political m.** le résultat des élections leur assure une place sur l'échiquier politique 2 *Am Fam (face)* tronche *f*, trombine *f*
VT 1 *(country, region)* faire *ou* dresser la carte de; *(town)* faire *ou* dresser le plan de 2 *Math* faire un graphique de; **to m. sth onto sth** représenter qch sur qch 3 *Fig (plot* ► *progress etc)* consigner
►► ***map reading*** lecture *f* de carte; ***map reference*** référence *f* topographique, coordonnées *fpl*

► **map out** VT SEP *(itinerary)* tracer; *(essay)* faire le plan de; *(plan)* établir les grandes lignes de; *(career, future)* organiser, prévoir; **they have Laura's future all mapped out for her** ils ont déjà planifié l'avenir de Laura

maple ['meɪpəl] N érable *m*
►► ***maple leaf*** feuille *f* d'érable; ***maple sugar*** sucre *m* d'érable; ***maple syrup*** sirop *m* d'érable; ***maple tree*** érable *m*

mapping ['mæpɪŋ] N 1 *(of region)* établissement *m* d'une carte
2 *Math* application *f*, fonction *f*
3 *Comput (in network)* unité *f* logique
4 *Mktg* mapping *m*
►► ***mapping pen*** plume *f* à dessin

maquette [mæ'ket] N *Art* maquette *f*

Mar. *(written abbr* **March**) mars *m*

mar [mɑː(r)] *(pt & pp* **marred**, *cont* **marring**) VT gâter, gâcher; **to make or m. sb** faire la fortune ou la ruine de qn; **today will make or m. their future** c'est aujourd'hui que se décide *ou* se joue leur avenir

marabou ['mærəbuː] N *Orn* marabout *m*

maraca [mə'rækə] N *Mus* maraca *f*

maraschino [ˌmærə'skiːnəʊ] *(pl* **maraschinos**) N marasquin *m*
►► ***maraschino cherry*** cerise *f* au marasquin

marathon ['mærəθən] N *Sport* marathon *m*; *Fig* **dance m.** marathon *m* de danse
ADJ marathon *(inv)*
►► ***marathon race*** marathon *m*; ***marathon runner*** coureur(euse) *m,f* de marathon, marathonien(enne) *m,f*

marathoner ['mærəθənə(r)] N coureur(euse) *m,f* de marathon, marathonien(enne) *m,f*

maraud [mə'rɔːd] VI marauder, être en maraude; **to go marauding** partir en maraude

marauder [mə'rɔːdə(r)] N *(person)* maraudeur(euse) *m,f*; *(animal, bird)* maraudeur *m*, prédateur *m*

marauding [mə'rɔːdɪŋ] N maraude *f*
ADJ maraudeur, en maraude; **m. soldiers** des soldats en maraude

marble ['mɑːbəl] N 1 *(stone, sculpture)* marbre *m*
2 *(for game)* bille *f*; **to play marbles** jouer aux billes; *Fam Fig* **to lose one's marbles** perdre la boule; *Fam Fig* **she's still got all her marbles** elle a encore toute sa tête
COMP *(fireplace, staircase, statue)* de *ou* en marbre; *(industry)* marbrier
VT marbrer
►► ***marble cake*** gâteau *m* marbré; ***marble cutter*** *(person)* marbrier *m*; ***marble quarry*** marbrière *f*, carrière *f* de marbre

marbled ['mɑːbəld] ADJ marbré; *(meat)* persillé

marbling ['mɑːbəlɪŋ] N *(gen)* marbrure *f*; *(in meat)* marbré *m*

March [mɑːtʃ] N mars *m*; *see also* **February**

march [mɑːtʃ] N 1 *Mil* marche *f*; **troops on the m.** des troupes en marche; *Fig* **the middle classes are on the m.** la classe moyenne s'est mobilisée; **their camp was a day's m. away** leur camp était à une journée de marche; *Fig* **the m. of time/events** la marche du temps/des événements; **quick m.!** en avant, marche!
2 *(demonstration)* manifestation *f*, marche *f*; **to go on a m.** manifester, descendre dans la rue; **peace m.** marche *f* pour la paix
3 *(music)* marche *f*; **slow/quick m.** marche *f* lente/rapide
4 *(usu pl) (frontier)* frontière *f*; **the Welsh Marches** les marches *fpl* galloises
VT 1 *Mil* faire marcher au pas 2 *(lead forcibly)* **the prisoner was marched away/back to his cell** on conduisit/ramena le prisonnier dans sa cellule; **the children were marched off to bed** les enfants ont été expédiés au lit (au pas de gymnastique)
VI 1 *Mil* marcher (au pas); *(at a ceremony, on parade)* défiler; **the regiment marched past the President** le régiment défila devant le Président; **to m. off to war/into battle** partir à la guerre/au combat; **to m. on a city** marcher sur une ville
2 *(walk briskly)* avancer d'un pas ferme *ou* résolu; **to m. down the street/into a room** descendre la rue/entrer dans une pièce d'un pas résolu; **they marched off in a huff** ils partirent furieux; **she marched up to him and slapped him across the face** elle se dirigea droit sur lui et le gifla
3 *(in demonstration)* manifester
4 *Fig (time, seasons)* avancer, s'écouler; **time marches on** le temps s'écoule inexorablement

marcher ['mɑːtʃə(r)] N *(in demonstration)* manifestant(e) *m,f*

marching ['mɑːtʃɪŋ] N *(gen) & Mil* marche *f*
ADJ cadencé; **the sound of m. feet** le bruit de pas cadencés
►► ***marching band*** fanfare *f*; *Mil* ***marching orders*** feuille *f* de route; *Br Fam Fig* **to give sb his/her m.**

orders flanquer qn à la porte; *Br Fam Fig* **she got her m. orders** elle a été virée

marchioness [ˌmɑːʃəˈnes] **N** *(aristocrat)* marquise *f*

Mardi Gras [ˌmɑːdiˈgrɑː] **N** mardi *m* gras, carnaval *m*

mardy [ˈmɑːdi] **ADJ** *NEng Fam* grincheux; **she's a right m. cow!** elle a un caractère de cochon!

mare[1] [meə(r)] **N 1** *(animal)* jument *f* **2** *Br Fam Pej (woman)* grognasse *f*; **you silly m.!** espèce d'andouille!

▸▸ ***mare's nest*** *(illusion)* illusion *f*; *(disappointment)* déception *f*

mare[2] **N** *Br Fam (nightmare)* cauchemar *m*

margarine [ˌmɑːdʒəˈriːn, ˌmɑːgəˈriːn] **N** margarine *f*

margarita [ˌmɑːgəˈriːtə] **N** margarita *f*

marge [mɑːdʒ] **N** *Br Fam* margarine *f*

margin [ˈmɑːdʒɪn] **N 1** *(on page)* marge *f*; **written in the m.** écrit dans la *ou* en marge

2 *(leeway)* marge *f*; **a m. of error/of safety** une marge d'erreur/de sécurité

3 *(distance, gap)* marge *f*; **the opposition candidate won by a 10 percent m.** le candidat de l'opposition a gagné avec une marge de 10 pour cent; **to beat sb by a m. of 20 seconds** battre qn de 20 secondes; **they won by a narrow/wide m.** ils ont gagné de justesse/avec une marge confortable

4 *Com, Fin & Mktg (profit)* marge *f*; *St Exch* acompte *m (versé à un courtier)*, marge *f* de garantie; **to have a low/high m.** avoir une faible/forte marge; **we make a 10 percent m.** nous faisons 10 pour cent de marge; **the margins are very tight** les marges sont très réduites

5 *(periphery ▸ of field, lake)* bord *m*; *(▸ of wood)* lisière *f*, orée *f*; *(▸ of society)* marge *f*; **on the margin(s) of society** en marge de la société

▸▸ *Typ* ***margin release*** déclenche-marge *m inv*; *Typ* ***margin setting*** marge *f*; *(action)* pose *f* de marges; *Typ* ***margin stop*** margeur *m*

marginal [ˈmɑːdʒɪnəl] **ADJ 1** *(slight ▸ improvement)* léger; *(▸ effect)* minime, insignifiant; *(▸ importance)* mineur, secondaire; *(▸ problem)* d'ordre secondaire; **a m. case** un cas limite **2** *Com (business, profit)* marginal **3** *(in margin ▸ notes)* marginal, en marge

N *Pol* **m. (seat)** = en Grande-Bretagne, circonscription dont le député ne dispose que d'une majorité très faible

▸▸ *Com* ***marginal cost*** coût *m* marginal; *Agr* ***marginal land*** terre *f* de faible rendement; *Econ* ***marginal productivity*** productivité *f* marginale; *Econ* ***marginal utility*** utilité *f* marginale

marginalist [ˈmɑːdʒɪnəlɪst] *Econ* **N** marginaliste *mf*

ADJ marginaliste

marginalization, -isation [ˌmɑːdʒɪnəlaɪˈzeɪʃən] **N** marginalisation *f*

marginalize, -ise [ˈmɑːdʒɪnəlaɪz] **VT** marginaliser

marginally [ˈmɑːdʒɪnəlɪ] **ADV** à peine, légèrement; **his health is only m. improved** son état ne s'est guère amélioré

marguerite [ˌmɑːgəˈriːt] **N** *Bot* marguerite *f*

marigold [ˈmærɪgəʊld] **N** *Bot (African)* rose *f* d'Inde; *(French)* œillet *m* d'Inde; **(pot) m.** souci *m* (des jardins)

marihuana, marijuana [ˌmærɪˈwɑːnə] **N** marihuana *f*, marijuana *f*

marina [məˈriːnə] **N** port *m* de plaisance, marina *f*

marinade [ˌmærɪˈneɪd] *Culin* **N** marinade *f*

VT mariner

marine [məˈriːn] **N 1** *(ships collectively)* marine *f* **2** *(soldier)* fusilier *m* marin; *(British or American)* marine *m*; *Am Fam* **go tell it to the marines!** mon œil!, à d'autres!

ADJ 1 *(underwater)* marin **2** *(naval)* maritime

▸▸ ***marine architect*** ingénieur *m* des constructions navales; ***marine artist*** peintre *m* de marines; ***marine biologist*** biologiste *m* marin; ***marine biology*** biologie *f* marine; *Am Mil* ***Marine Corps*** Marines *mpl*; ***marine engineer*** mécanicien *m* de bord; ***marine engineering*** génie *m* maritime; ***marine insurance*** assurance *f* maritime; ***marine life*** vie *f* marine

mariner [ˈmærɪnə(r)] **N** *Formal or Literary* marin *m*

marionette [ˌmærɪəˈnet] **N** marionnette *f*

marital [ˈmærɪtəl] **ADJ** *(vows, relations, duty, rights)* conjugal; *(problem)* conjugal, matrimonial

▸▸ ***marital aid*** gadget *m* érotique; ***marital bliss*** bonheur *m* conjugal; ***marital home*** foyer *m* conjugal; ***marital rape*** viol *m* conjugal; ***marital status*** situation *f* de famille

maritime [ˈmærɪtaɪm] **ADJ** maritime

▸▸ ***maritime climate*** climat *m* maritime; ***maritime law*** droit *m* maritime; ***the Maritime Provinces*** les Provinces *fpl* Maritimes

marjoram [ˈmɑːdʒərəm] **N** *Bot* marjolaine *f*

Mark [mɑːk] **PR N** *Bible* Marc; **M. Antony** Marc Antoine; **the Gospel According to (Saint) M.** l'Évangile selon saint Marc

MARK [mɑːk]

N
- marque **1, 2, 4–6, 8**
- modèle **3**
- note **7**
- but **10**
- mark **13**
- niveau **2**
- trace **6**
- empreinte **8**
- cible **10**

VT
- marquer **1, 2, 4–6, 9**
- tacheter **3**
- corriger **7**
- tacher **2**
- célébrer **5**

VI
- être salissant

N 1 *(symbol, sign)* marque *f*, signe *m*; **to make a m. on sth** faire une marque sur qch, marquer qch

2 *(on scale, in number, level)* marque *f*, niveau *m*; **sales topped the 5 million m.** les ventes ont dépassé la barre des 5 millions; **to reach the halfway m.** arriver à mi-course; **don't go beyond the 50-metre m.** ne dépassez pas les 50 mètres; *Br Culin* **gas m. 6** thermostat 6

3 *Com (model)* **m. 3** modèle *m ou* série *f* 3

4 *(feature)* marque *f*; **the town bears the m. of Greek classicism** la ville porte la marque du classicisme grec

5 *(token)* marque *f*, signe *m*; **a m. of affection** une marque d'affection; **as a m. of respect** en signe de respect

6 *(trace, stain, blemish)* trace *f*, marque *f*; **there are finger marks on the mirror** il y a des traces *ou* des marques de doigts sur la glace; **the years she spent in prison have left their m. (on her)** ses années en prison l'ont marquée; **there wasn't a m. on the body** le corps ne portait aucune trace de coups

7 *Br Sch (grade)* note *f*; *(point)* point *m*; **to give sb/sth marks out of ten/twenty** noter qn/qch sur dix/vingt; **to get good marks** avoir de bonnes notes; **to get full marks** obtenir la meilleure note (possible); **she deserves full marks for imagination** il faut saluer son imagination; **no marks for guessing the answer!** il ne faut pas être sorcier pour deviner la réponse!

8 *(impact)* empreinte *f*, impression *f*; *(distinction)* marque *f*; **to make one's m.** s'imposer, se faire un nom; **she made her m. as a singer** elle s'est imposée *ou* elle s'est fait un nom dans la chanson

9 *Br (standard)* **he's not up to the m.** il n'est pas à la hauteur; **I'm afraid the work just isn't up to the m.** malheureusement le travail laisse à désirer; **I still don't feel quite up to the m.** je ne suis pas encore en pleine forme

10 *Br (target)* but *m*, cible *f*; **to hit the m.** atteindre la cible; *Fig* faire mouche; **to miss the m.** rater la cible; *Fig* mettre à côté de la plaque

11 *Sport* **on your marks, (get) set, go!** à vos marques, prêts, partez!; *Br Fig* **she's quick/slow off the m.** *(clever)* elle est/n'est pas très maligne, elle a/n'a pas l'esprit très vif; *(in reactions)* elle est/n'est pas très rapide; **you have to be quick off the m.** il faut réagir tout de suite *ou* immédiatement; **you were too slow off the m.** tu as mis trop de temps

12 *Sport (in rugby)* arrêt *m* de volée; **to call for the m.** crier "marque" (en faisant un arrêt de volée)

13 *Formerly (currency)* mark *m*, Deutschmark *m*

VT 1 *(put mark on)* marquer; **the towels were marked with his name** les serviettes étaient à son nom, son nom était marqué sur les serviettes; **shall I m. her absent?** est-ce que je la marque absente?; **the table was marked "sold"** la table portait l'étiquette "vendue"; *Fig* **his face was marked by suffering** son visage était marqué par la souffrance; *Fig* **the scandal marked him for life** *(mentally)* le scandale l'a marqué pour la vie

2 *(stain)* tacher, marquer

3 *Zool* tacheter; **brown wings marked with blue** des ailes *fpl* brunes tachetées de bleu

4 *(indicate)* indiquer, marquer; **the stream marks the boundary of the estate** le ruisseau marque la limite de la propriété; **X marks the spot** l'endroit est marqué d'un X; **this decision marks a change in policy** cette décision marque un changement de politique

5 *(celebrate ▸ anniversary, event)* célébrer, marquer; **let's have some champagne to m. the occasion** ouvrons une bouteille de champagne pour fêter l'événement

6 *(distinguish)* marquer; **the period was marked by religious persecution** cette époque fut marquée par des persécutions religieuses

7 *Br Sch (essay, homework)* corriger; *(student)* noter; **the exam was marked out of 100** l'examen a été noté sur 100; **to m. sth wrong/right** marquer qch comme étant faux/juste

8 *(pay attention to)* **(you) m. my words!** souvenez-vous de ce que je vous dis!; *Br* **m. you, I didn't believe him** remarquez, je ne l'ai pas cru

9 *Sport (opponent)* marquer

10 *(idiom)* **to m. time** *Mil* marquer le pas; *Fig* attendre son heure *ou* le moment propice; **the government is just marking time until the elections** le gouvernement fait traîner les choses en attendant les élections

VI *(garment)* être salissant, se tacher facilement; **this material marks easily** ce tissu est salissant

▸**mark down VT SEP 1** *(write)* noter, prendre note de, inscrire

2 *(reduce ▸ price)* baisser; *(▸ article)* baisser le prix de, démarquer; **everything has been marked down to half price** tout a été réduit à moitié prix

3 *Sch (essay, student)* baisser la note de; **he was marked down for bad grammar** il a perdu des points à cause de la grammaire

4 *(single out)* désigner; **my brother was marked down for the managership** mon frère a été désigné pour le poste de directeur; **I marked him down as a troublemaker** j'avais remarqué qu'il n'était bon qu'à créer des ennuis

▸**mark in VT SEP** *(event in diary etc)* noter; *(area on map etc)* hachurer

▸**mark off VT SEP 1** *(divide, isolate ▸ area, period of time)* délimiter; **one corner of the field had been marked off by a fence** un coin du champ avait été isolé par une barrière

2 *(measure ▸ distance)* mesurer; **the route was marked off in 1 km sections** le trajet était divisé en tronçons d'un kilomètre

3 *Br (distinguish)* distinguer; **his intelligence marked him off from his school friends** il se distinguait de ses camarades d'école par son intelligence

4 *(on list)* cocher

▸**mark out VT SEP 1** *(with chalk, paint ▸ court, pitch)* tracer les lignes de; *(with stakes)* jalonner; *(with lights, flags)* baliser **2** *(designate)* désigner; **Steven was marked out for promotion** Steven était désigné pour obtenir une promotion; **they were marked out for special treatment** ils ont bénéficié d'un régime particulier **3** *Br (distinguish)* distinguer

▸**mark up VT SEP 1** *(on notice)* marquer; **the menu is marked up on the blackboard** le menu est sur le tableau

2 *(increase ▸ price)* augmenter, majorer; *(▸ goods)* augmenter le prix de, majorer

3 *Sch (essay)* majorer la note de

4 *(proofs, manuscript ▸ correct)* corriger; *(▸ annotate)* annoter

markdown [ˈmɑːkdaʊn] **N** *(article)* article *m* démarqué; *(action)* démarque *f*

marked [mɑːkt] **ADJ 1** *(noticeable)* marqué, sensible; *(accent)* prononcé **2** *(bearing a mark* ▸ *gen)* marqué; *(*▸ *path)* balisé; *Fig* **he's a m. man** c'est l'homme à abattre **3** *Ling* marqué
▸▸ *Mktg* ***marked price*** prix *m* marqué

marked-down **ADJ** *Com* démarqué, soldé

markedly ['mɑːkɪdlɪ] **ADV** nettement, sensiblement; **m. better** nettement meilleur; **m. different** nettement *ou* sensiblement différent

marked-up **ADJ** *Com* majoré

marker ['mɑːkə(r)] **N 1** *(pen)* feutre *m*, marqueur *m*
2 *(indicator, landmark)* jalon *m*, balise *f*; *(flag)* fanion *m*; *(stick)* piquet *m* d'alignement *ou* de jalonnement
3 *(scorekeeper)* marqueur(euse) *m,f*
4 *Br Sch* correcteur(trice) *m,f*; **to be a hard m.** noter sévèrement
5 *(page marker)* marque-page *m*, signet *m*
6 *Sport* marqueur(euse) *m,f*; **to lose one's m.** se démarquer (d'un adversaire)
7 *Ling* marque *f*
8 *Am Fam (gambling debt)* dette *f* de jeu▫; *(note)* reconnaissance *f* de dette de jeu▫
▸▸ *Aviat* ***marker beacon*** radiobalise *f*; *Naut* ***marker buoy*** bouée *f* de balisage; ***marker pen*** feutre *m*, marqueur *m*

market ['mɑːkɪt] **N 1** *(gen)* marché *m*; **to go to (the) m.** aller au marché, aller faire son marché
2 *Econ* marché *m*; *(demand)* demande *f*, marché *m*; *(outlet)* débouché *m*, marché *m*; **to be on the m.** être en vente; **to come onto the m.** arriver sur le marché; **the job m.** le marché de l'emploi; **to put sth on the m.** mettre qch en vente *ou* sur le marché; **the most economical car on the m.** la voiture la plus économique du marché; **to take sth off the m.** retirer qch du marché; **she's in the m. for Persian rugs** elle cherche à acheter des tapis persans, elle est acheteuse de tapis persans; **there's always a (ready) m. for computer software** il y a toujours une forte demande pour les logiciels; **this ad should appeal to the teenage m.** cette pub devrait séduire les jeunes; **to find a m. for sth** trouver un débouché *ou* des acheteurs pour qch; **to find a ready m.** trouver à vendre facilement; **the bottom has fallen out of the m.** le marché s'est effondré
3 *St Exch* marché *m*; *(index)* indice *m*; *(prices)* cours *mpl*; **the m. has risen 10 points** l'indice est en hausse de 10 points; **to play the m.** jouer en bourse, spéculer
VT *(sell)* vendre, commercialiser; *(launch)* lancer *ou* mettre sur le marché
VI *Am (go shopping)* faire le marché; **to go marketing** aller faire ses courses
▸▸ ***market analysis*** analyse *f* de marché; ***market day*** jour *m* de marché; ***market economy*** économie *f* de marché *ou* libérale; ***market forces*** les forces *fpl* du marché; *Br* ***market garden*** jardin *m* maraîcher; *Br* ***market gardener*** maraîcher(ère) *m,f*; *Br* ***market gardening*** culture *f* maraîchère; ***market leader*** *(product)* premier produit *m* sur le marché; *(firm)* leader *m* du marché; ***market price*** *Com* prix *m* courant; *St Exch* cours *m* de (la) Bourse; *St Exch* ***market rate*** taux *m* du marché; ***market research*** recherche *f* commerciale, étude *f ou* études *fpl* de marché; **he works in m. research** il travaille dans le marketing; ***market researcher*** chargé(e) *m,f* d'étude de marché; ***market share*** part *f* de marché; *Br* ***market square*** place *f* du marché; ***market survey*** enquête *f* de marché; ***market town*** bourg *m*; *Br* ***market trader*** vendeur (euse) *m,f* qui fait les marchés; ***market value*** *Com (of object, product)* valeur *f* marchande; *St Exch (of share)* valeur *f* boursière *ou* en bourse

marketability [ˌmɑːkɪtə'bɪlətɪ] **N** possibilité *f* de commercialisation; **we are doubtful about the m. of these machines** nous doutons que ces machines soient commercialisables

marketable ['mɑːkɪtəbəl] **ADJ** vendable, commercialisable; *St Exch (shares, securities)* négociable

market-driven **ADJ** déterminé par les contraintes du marché
▸▸ ***market-driven economy*** économie *f* de marché

marketeer [ˌmɑːkə'tɪə(r)] **N 1 black m.** trafiquant (e) *m,f* (au marché noir) **2** *Br Pol* **pro-/anti-m.** partisan(e) *m,f*/adversaire *mf* du Marché commun

marketer ['mɑːkɪtə(r)] **N** *Mktg* mercaticien (enne) *m,f*, spécialiste *mf* en marketing

marketing ['mɑːkɪtɪŋ] **N** *(selling)* commercialisation *f*, distribution *f*; *(promotion, study, theory, field)* marketing *m*, commercialisation *f*; **to work in m.** travailler dans le marketing
▸▸ ***marketing campaign*** campagne *f* de marketing; ***marketing department*** service *m* du marketing; ***marketing executive*** responsable *mf* du marketing, cadre *m* en marketing; ***marketing intelligence*** intelligence *f* marketing; ***marketing manager*** directeur(trice) *m,f* du marketing, responsable *mf* du marketing; ***marketing mix*** marchéage *m*, marketing mix *m*, logistique *f* commerciale; ***marketing strategy*** stratégie *f* marketing

marketization, -isation [ˌmɑːkɪtaɪ'zeɪʃən] **N** *Econ* marchéisation *f*

marketize, -ise ['mɑːkɪtaɪz] **VT** *Econ* convertir à l'économie de marché

market-led **ADJ** généré par le marché

market-orientated economy **N** économie *f* de marché

marking ['mɑːkɪŋ] **N 1** *(gen)* marquage *m*
2 *Br Sch (of homework)* correction *f*; *(work to be marked)* copies *fpl* (à corriger)
3 *Sport* marquage *m*
4 *St Exch (of shares)* cotation *f*; **m. to market** comptabilisation *f* au prix de marché
• **markings** **NPL** *(distinctive marks)* marques *fpl*; *(on animal* ▸ *spots)* taches *fpl*; *(*▸ *stripes)* rayures *fpl*; *Aviat* insignes *mpl*
▸▸ ***marking ink*** encre *f* à marquer; ***marking scheme*** barème *m*

markka ['mɑːkə] **N** *Formerly* mark *m* finlandais

marksman ['mɑːksmən] *(pl* **marksmen** [-mən]) **N** tireur *m* d'élite

marksmanship ['mɑːksmənʃɪp] **N** habileté *f* au tir

markswoman ['mɑːksˌwʊmən] *(pl* **markswomen** [-ˌwɪmɪn]) **N** tireuse *f* d'élite

mark-up **N** *Com* majoration *f*; **we operate a 2.5 times m.** nous appliquons une marge de 2,5

marl [mɑːl] *Agr* **N** marne *f*
VT marner
▸▸ *Naut* ***marl pit*** marnière *f*

marlin[1] ['mɑːlɪn] **N** *Ich* makaire *m*

marlin[2], **marline** ['mɑːlɪn] **N** *Naut* merlin *m*

marly ['mɑːlɪ] **ADJ** marneux

marmalade ['mɑːməleɪd] **N** *(gen)* confiture *f* d'agrumes; *(orange)* marmelade *f* d'orange
ADJ *(cat)* roux (rousse)

marmoset ['mɑːməzet] **N** *Zool* ouistiti *m*

marmot ['mɑːmət] **N** *Zool & (fur)* marmotte *f*

maroon [mə'ruːn] **N 1** *(colour)* bordeaux *m* **2** *Br (rocket)* fusée *f* de détresse
ADJ *(colour)* bordeaux *(inv)*
VT *(abandon)* abandonner *(sur une île ou une côte déserte)*; **to be marooned** *(shipwrecked)* faire naufrage; *Fig* **he felt marooned in his suburban flat** il se sentait abandonné dans son appartement de banlieue

> Note that the French word **marron** is a false friend. When referring to a colour, it means **brown**.

marquee [mɑː'kiː] **N 1** *Br (tent)* grande tente *f*; *(for circus)* chapiteau *m* **2** *Am (canopy at hotel, theatre)* marquise *f*

marquess ['mɑːkwɪs] **N** marquis *m*

marquetry ['mɑːkɪtrɪ] **N** marqueterie *f*
COMP *(table)* en marqueterie

marram ['mærəm] **N** *Bot* gourbet *m*
▸▸ ***marram grass*** gourbet *m*

marriage ['mærɪdʒ] **N 1** *(state, relationship)* mariage *m*; *(ceremony)* mariage *m*, noces *fpl*; **to give sb in m.** donner qn en mariage; **to take sb in m.** prendre qn pour époux (épouse), épouser qn; **he's my uncle by m.** c'est mon oncle par alliance **2** *Fig (union)* mariage *m*, alliance *f*; **a m. of minds** une union des esprits; **a m. made in heaven** un mélange exquis
COMP conjugal, matrimonial
▸▸ ***marriage bed*** lit *m* conjugal; ***marriage broker*** agent *m* matrimonial; *Br* ***marriage bureau*** agence *f* matrimoniale; ***marriage ceremony*** cérémonie *f* de mariage; ***marriage certificate*** extrait *m* d'acte de mariage; ***marriage contract*** contrat *m* de mariage; ***marriage of convenience*** mariage *m* de raison; ***marriage guidance*** conseil *m* conjugal; ***marriage guidance counsellor*** conseiller(ère) *m,f* conjugal(e); ***marriage licence*** ≃ certificat *m* de non-opposition au mariage; *Br Fam Old-fashioned* ***marriage lines*** extrait *m* d'acte de mariage▫; ***marriage settlement*** *(dowry)* dot *f*; *(between couple)* ≃ contrat *m* de mariage, ≃ régime *m* matrimonial; ***marriage vows*** vœux *mpl* de mariage

marriageable ['mærɪdʒəbəl] **ADJ** mariable; **to be of m. age** être en âge de se marier

married ['mærɪd] **ADJ** *(man, woman)* marié; *(life)* conjugal; **just m.** *(on car)* jeunes mariés; *Fig* **he's m. to his job** il ne vit que pour son travail
NPL marrieds *(married couples)* couples *mpl* mariés
▸▸ ***married couple*** couple *m* marié; ***married name*** nom *m* de femme mariée; *Br* ***married quarters*** logements *mpl* pour familles

marrow ['mærəʊ] **N 1** *Anat & Fig* moelle *f*; **frozen** *or* **chilled to the m.** gelé jusqu'à la moelle des os **2** *(vegetable)* courge *f*

marrowbone ['mærəʊbəʊn] **N** os *m* à moelle

marrowfat ['mærəʊfæt] **N** pois *m* carré
▸▸ ***marrowfat pea*** pois *m* carré

marry ['mærɪ] *(pt & pp* **married**) **VT 1** *(of fiancé)* épouser, se marier avec; **to get married** se marier; **to be married (to sb)** être marié (avec qn); **they're happily married** ils forment un ménage heureux; **will you m. me?** veux-tu m'épouser?; **to m. money** faire un mariage d'argent **2** *(of priest, minister, official)* marier **3** *Fig (combine)* marier, allier
VI 1 *(person, couple)* se marier; **she never married** elle ne s'est jamais mariée; **he's not the marrying type** ce n'est pas le genre à se marier; **she married beneath herself** elle s'est mésalliée; **to m. again** *or* **a second time** se remarier; **to m. for money** faire un mariage d'argent; **to m. into money** épouser quelqu'un issu d'une famille riche; *Prov* **m. in haste, repent at leisure** tel se marie à la hâte qui s'en repent à loisir **2** *Fig (combine)* se marier, s'allier; **the flavours m. well** les saveurs se marient bien
▸ **marry off** **VT SEP** marier; **she married off her daughter to an aristocrat** elle a marié sa fille à un aristocrate
▸ **marry up** **VT SEP** *(bring together* ▸ *two parts)* joindre; *(*▸ *colours)* marier
VI *(line up, fit)* coïncider, concorder; *(colours)* aller bien ensemble, se marier; **check that the two parts m. up** vérifier que les deux parties coïncident

Mars [mɑːz] **PR N** *Myth* Mars
N *Astron* Mars *f*

marsh [mɑːʃ] **N** marais *m*, marécage *m*
▸▸ ***marsh fever*** fièvre *f* des marais, paludisme *m*; ***marsh gas*** gaz *m* des marais, méthane *m*; *Bot* ***marsh marigold*** souci *m* d'eau, populage *m*; *Orn* ***marsh warbler*** rousserolle *f* verderolle

marshal ['mɑːʃəl] *(Br pt & pp* **marshalled,** *cont* **marshalling,** *Am pt & pp* **marshaled,** *cont* **marshaling**) **N 1** *Mil* maréchal *m* **2** *(at public event)* membre *m* du service d'ordre; *(in law court)* huissier *m*; *(at race-track)* commissaire *m* **3** *Am (police chief)* commissaire *m* de police; *(fire chief)* capitaine *m* des pompiers; *(district police officer)* commissaire *m*
VT 1 *Mil (troops)* masser, rassembler; *(people, group)* canaliser, diriger; **the troops were marshalled into the square** on rassembla les troupes sur la place; **she marshalled the children out of the room** elle dirigea les enfants vers la porte **2** *(organize* ▸ *arguments, thoughts)* rassembler; **to m. facts** rassembler des faits et les mettre en ordre; **he's trying to m. support for his project** il essaie d'obtenir du soutien pour son projet **3** *Rail (trucks, wagons)* trier, manœuvrer
▸▸ *Br Mil* ***marshal of the Royal Air Force*** ≃ chef *m* d'état-major de l'armée de l'air, *Can* ≃ maréchal *m* de l'ARC

marshalling yard ['mɑːʃəlɪŋ-] **N** *Br Rail* centre *m ou* gare *f* de triage

marshland ['mɑːʃlænd] **N** marais *m*, terrain *m* marécageux

marshmallow [*Br* ˌmɑːʃ'mæləʊ, *Am* 'mɑːrʃˌmeləʊ] **N 1** *Bot* guimauve *f* **2** *Culin (sweet)* guimauve *f*

marshy ['mɑːʃɪ] *(compar* **marshier**, *superl* **marshiest**) **ADJ** marécageux

marsupial [mɑː'suːpɪəl] *Zool* **N** marsupial *m*
ADJ marsupial

mart [mɑːt] **N 1** *(market)* marché *m*; **second-hand car m.** magasin *m* de voitures d'occasion **2** *Am (shop)* magasin *m* **3** *(auction room)* salle *f* des ventes

marten ['mɑːtɪn] **N** *Zool* marte *f*, martre *f*

martial ['mɑːʃəl] **ADJ** *(military)* martial; *(warlike)* martial, guerrier
▸▸ ***martial art*** art *m* martial; ***martial law*** loi *f* martiale; **to declare m. law** proclamer l'état de siège

Martian ['mɑːʃən] **N** Martien(enne) *m,f*
ADJ martien

martin ['mɑːtɪn] **N** *Orn* hirondelle *f*

martinet [ˌmɑːtɪ'net] **N** tyran *m*

martingale ['mɑːtɪŋgeɪl] **N 1** *(of horse)* martingale *f* **2** *Naut* **m. (guy** *or* **stay)** martingale *f* du beaupré

Martini® [mɑː'tiːnɪ] **N** Martini® *m*

Martinican [ˌmɑːtɪ'niːkən] **N** Martiniquais(e) *m,f*
ADJ martiniquais

Martinmas ['mɑːtɪnməs] **N** la Saint-Martin *f*; **at M.** à la Saint-Martin

martyr ['mɑːtə(r)] **N** martyr(e) *m,f*; **to die a m.** mourir en martyr; *Fig* **she's always making a m. of herself** elle joue toujours les martyres; **he's a m. to rheumatism** ses rhumatismes lui font souffrir le martyre
VT martyriser

martyrdom ['mɑːtədəm] **N** *Rel* martyre *m*; *Fig* martyre *m*, calvaire *m*

martyrize, -ise ['mɑːtəraɪz] **VT** martyriser

marvel ['mɑːvəl] (*Br pt & pp* **marvelled**, *cont* **marvelling**, *Am pt & pp* **marveled**, *cont* **marveling**) **N 1** *(miracle)* merveille *f*, miracle *m*, prodige *m*; **the marvels of science/the world** les merveilles *fpl* de la science/du monde; **to do** *or* **to work marvels** faire des merveilles; **it's a m. to me that she managed to survive** pour moi, c'est un miracle qu'elle ait survécu **2** *(marvellous person)* **you're a m.!** tu es une vraie petite merveille!
VT he marvelled that she had kept so calm il n'en revenait pas qu'elle ait pu rester si calme
VI to m. at sth s'émerveiller de qch; **I m. at the speed they get things done** je suis émerveillé par la vitesse à laquelle ils font les choses

marvellous, *Am* **marvelous** ['mɑːvələs] **ADJ** *(amazing)* merveilleux, extraordinaire; *(miraculous)* miraculeux

marvellously, *Am* **marvelously** ['mɑːvələslɪ] **ADV** merveilleusement, à merveille

Marxian ['mɑːksɪən] **ADJ** marxien

Marxism ['mɑːksɪzəm] **N** marxisme *m*

Marxism-Leninism **N** marxisme-léninisme *m*

Marxist ['mɑːksɪst] **N** marxiste *mf*
ADJ marxiste

Marxist-Leninist **N** marxiste-léniniste *mf*
ADJ marxiste-léniniste

Mary ['meərɪ] **PR N** *Bible* Marie; **M. Magdalene** Marie Madeleine; **the Virgin M.** la Vierge Marie; **M., Queen of Scots** Marie Stuart

marzipan ['mɑːzɪpæn] **N** pâte *f* d'amandes
COMP *(cake, sweet etc)* à la pâte d'amandes
▸▸ *Fam Com* ***marzipan fruits*** fruits *mpl* en pâte d'amandes

mascara [mæs'kɑːrə] **N** mascara *m*
VT she had heavily mascara'd eyes elle avait les cils très maquillés

mascot ['mæskət] **N** mascotte *f*

masculine ['mæskjʊlɪn] **N** *Gram* masculin *m*; **in the m.** au masculin
ADJ masculin

masculinity [ˌmæskjʊ'lɪnətɪ] **N** masculinité *f*

maser ['meɪzə(r)] **N** *Phys* maser *m*

MASH [mæʃ] **N** *Am (abbr* **mobile army surgical hospital)** = hôpital militaire de campagne

mash [mæʃ] **N 1** *Br Fam (mashed potatoes)* purée *f* (de pommes de terre)[□]
2 *(for horses)* mash *m*; *(for pigs, poultry)* pâtée *f*
3 *(in brewing)* empâtage *m*
4 *Fam (pulp)* pulpe[□] *f*, bouillie[□] *f*
VT 1 *(crush)* écraser, broyer; **m. it all together** écraser le tout; **m. it (up) well** bien écraser **2** *Culin (potatoes etc)* faire une purée de **3** *(in brewing)* empâter

mashed [mæʃt] **ADJ 1** *Culin* **m. potato** *or* **potatoes** purée *f* (de pommes de terre) **2** *Br Fam (drunk)* bourré, pété; *(on drugs)* défoncé, raide

masher ['mæʃə(r)] **N** broyeur *m*; *(for potatoes)* presse-purée *m inv*

mashie ['mæʃɪ] **N** *Golf* mashie *m*

mask [mɑːsk] **N 1** *also Fig* masque *m*; **to put on a m.** mettre un masque, se masquer; *Fig* **a m. of happiness/confidence** une apparence de bonheur/confiance trompeuse; *Fig* **the m. had slipped** le masque était tombé **2** *(in photography)* cache *m* **3** *Comput* masque *m*
VT 1 *(face)* masquer
2 *(truth, feelings)* masquer, cacher, dissimuler
3 *(view)* boucher, masquer; *(flavour, smell)* masquer, recouvrir
4 *(in painting, photography)* masquer, cacher

masked [mɑːskt] **ADJ** *(face, man)* masqué
▸▸ ***masked ball*** bal *m* masqué; *Mil* ***masked battery*** batterie *f* masquée; *Comput* ***masked ROM*** mémoire *f* morte masquée

masking ['mɑːskɪŋ] **N** masquage *m*
▸▸ ***masking tape*** ruban *m* adhésif *(utilisé pour masquer une surface que l'on ne veut pas peindre)*

masochism ['mæsəkɪzəm] **N** masochisme *m*

masochist ['mæsəkɪst] **N** masochiste *mf*
ADJ masochiste

masochistic [ˌmæsə'kɪstɪk] **ADJ** masochiste

mason ['meɪsən] **N** *(stoneworker)* maçon(onne) *m,f*
• **Mason** **N** *(Freemason)* Maçon *m*, franc-maçon *m*
▸▸ ***Mason jar*** bocal *m* à conserves

Masonic [mə'sɒnɪk] **ADJ** maçonnique, franc-maçonnique
▸▸ ***Masonic lodge*** loge *f* maçonnique

masonry ['meɪsənrɪ] **N** *(stonework, skill)* maçonnerie *f*; **a large piece of m.** un gros bloc de pierre; **beware of falling m.** *(sign)* attention, chute de matériaux
• **Masonry** **N** *(Freemasonry)* Maçonnerie *f*, franc-maçonnerie *f*
▸▸ ***masonry bit, masonry drill*** foret *m* de maçonnerie

masquerade [ˌmæskə'reɪd] **N** *also Fig* mascarade *f*
VI to m. as *(pretend to be)* se faire passer pour; *(disguise oneself as)* se déguiser en

Mass [mæs] **N** *Rel* **1** *(music)* messe *f*; **M. in B minor** messe *f* en si mineur **2** *(ceremony)* messe *f*; **to go to M.** aller à la messe; **to celebrate/say M.** célébrer/dire la messe

mass [mæs] **N 1** *Phys* masse *f*
2 *(large quantity or amount)* masse *f*, quantité *f*; **he was a m. of bruises** il était entièrement couvert de bleus; **the streets were a solid m. of people/traffic** les rues regorgeaient de monde/de voitures
3 *(bulk)* masse *f*
4 *(majority)* majorité *f*; **the m. of the people are in favour of this policy** la majorité des gens est favorable à cette politique; **in the m.** dans l'ensemble
5 *Geog* **land m.** masse *f* continentale
ADJ *(for all* ▸ *communication, education)* de masse; *(large-scale* ▸ *starvation, unemployment)* à *ou* sur une grande échelle; *(involving many* ▸ *resignation)* massif, en masse; *(collective* ▸ *funeral)* collectif; **this product will appeal to a m. audience** ce produit plaira à un large public
VI *(people)* se masser; *(clouds)* s'amonceler
VT *(troops)* masser
• **masses** **NPL 1 the masses** les masses *fpl*; **culture for the masses** la culture à la portée de tous **2** *Fam (large amount)* **we've got masses** on en a plein; **masses of** des masses de, plein de; **I've masses (of things) to do** j'ai un tas *ou* des masses de choses à faire
▸▸ ***mass circulation*** grande diffusion *f*, diffusion de masse; ***mass execution*** exécution *f* en masse; ***mass grave*** charnier *m*; ***mass hysteria*** hystérie collective; ***mass market*** marché *m* de masse; ***mass marketing*** marketing *m* de grande consommation, marketing *m* de masse; ***mass media*** mass media *mpl*; ***mass meeting*** grand rassemblement *m*; ***mass murder*** tuerie *f*; ***mass murderer*** *(serial killer)* tueur(euse) *m,f* en série; *(tyrant dictator)* boucher *m*; *Gram* ***mass noun*** nom *m* non comptable; *Chem* ***mass number*** nombre *m* de masse; ***mass production*** fabrication *f ou* production *f* en série; *Chem & Phys* ***mass spectrograph*** spectrographe *m* de masse; *Comput* ***mass storage*** mémoire *f* de masse; ***mass suicide*** suicide *m* collectif; *Am* ***mass transit*** *(public transport)* transports *mpl* publics, transports *mpl* en commun; ***mass unemployment*** chômage *m* sur une grande échelle

massacre ['mæsəkə(r)] **N** massacre *m*; *Sport Fam* **it was a m.** cela a été un massacre *ou* une hécatombe
VT 1 *(kill)* massacrer **2** *Sport* écraser

massage [*Br* 'mæsɑːʒ, *Am* mə'sɑːʒ] **N** massage *m* *(of scalp)* friction *f*
VT masser; *Fig (statistics, facts)* manipuler
▸▸ ***massage parlour*** salon *m* de massage

masseur [*Br* mæ'sɜː(r), *Am* mæ'sʊər] **N** masseur *m*

masseuse [*Br* mæ'sɜːz, *Am* mæ'suːz] **N** masseuse *f*

massif [mæ'siːf] **N** massif *m* (montagneux)

massive ['mæsɪv] **ADJ** *(in size)* massif, énorme *(dose, increase)* massif; *(majority)* écrasant *(change, explosion)* énorme; *(sound)* retentissant; *(heart attack, stroke)* foudroyant

massively ['mæsɪvlɪ] **ADV** *(increase, reduce)* considérablement; *(invest, fund)* massivement; *(popular, successful)* extrêmement; **he's m. built** il est solidement bâti

mass-market **ADJ** *(products)* de grande consommation

mass-produce **VT** fabriquer en série

mass-produced **ADJ** fabriqué en série

mast [mɑːst] **N 1** *(on ship, for flag)* mât *m*; *(for radio or TV aerial)* pylône *m*; **the masts** *(of a ship)* les mâts *mpl*, la mâture; **to sail before the m.** servir comme simple matelot **2** *(animal food)* faine *f* *(destinée à l'alimentation animale)*

mastectomy [mæs'tektəmɪ] *(pl* **mastectomies) N** *Med* mastectomie *f*, mammectomie *f*

-masted ['mɑːstɪd] **SUFF** *Naut* **three/four/***etc***-m.** à trois/quatre/*etc* mâts

master ['mɑːstə(r)] **N 1** *(of household, dog, servant, situation)* maître *m*; **the m. of the house** le maître de maison; **to be m. in one's own house** être maître chez soi; **to be one's own m.** être son propre maître; **he's m. of the situation** il est maître de la situation; *Prov* **like m. like man** tel maître, tel valet
2 *(expert)* maître *m*; **chess m.** maître *m*; **he's a m. at the art of ducking questions** il est maître dans l'art d'éluder les questions
3 *Sch (in primary school)* instituteur *m*, maître *m* d'école; *(in secondary school)* professeur *m*; *(private tutor)* maître *m*; **history m.** professeur *m* d'histoire
4 *Univ* **M. of Arts/Science** *(person)* titulaire *mf* d'une maîtrise de lettres/de sciences; *(qualification)* maîtrise *f* ès lettres/ès sciences; **she's doing a m.'s (degree) in philosophy** elle prépare une maîtrise de philosophie
5 *Old-fashioned Formal (boy's title)* **M. David Thomas** Monsieur David Thomas; **M. David** *(said by servant)* Monsieur David
6 *Art* maître *m*
7 *Naut (of ship)* capitaine *m*; *(of fishing boat)* patron *m*; *Naut* **m.'s certificate** brevet *m* de capitaine
8 *Univ (head of college)* principal *m*
9 *(original copy)* original *m*; *(standard)* étalon *m*; *Comput* **m. (disk)** disque *m* maître
ADJ 1 *(overall)* directeur, maître
2 *(in trade)* maître; **m. chef/craftsman** maître chef *m*/artisan *m*; **a m. thief** un(e) voleur(euse) de génie

3 *(controlling)* principal; **m. switch** interrupteur *m* général
4 *(original)* original
VT 1 *(person, animal)* maîtriser, dompter; *(problem, difficulty)* surmonter, venir à bout de; *(emotions)* maîtriser, surmonter; *(situation)* maîtriser, se rendre maître de; **to m. oneself** se maîtriser, se dominer **2** *(subject, technique)* maîtriser; **she mastered Portuguese in only six months** six mois lui ont suffi pour maîtriser le portugais; **I never really mastered the language** je n'ai jamais eu une bonne maîtrise de la langue
▸▸ ***master bedroom*** chambre *f* principale; ***master builder*** maître *m* bâtisseur; ***master card*** carte *f* maîtresse; ***master of ceremonies*** *(at reception)* maître *m* des cérémonies; *(on TV show)* présentateur *m*; ***master class*** cours *m* de maître; *Mus* master class *m*; ***master copy*** original *m*; *Comput* ***master disk*** disque *m* maître; *Comput* ***master file*** fichier *m* principal *ou* maître; *Hunt* ***master of hounds, master of foxhounds*** maître *m* d'équipage; ***master key*** passe-partout *m inv*; ***master plan*** stratégie *f* globale; ***master race*** race *f* supérieure; *Mus* ***master record*** disque *m* original; *Br Law* ***Master of the Rolls*** ≃ président *m* de la cour d'appel *(en Grande-Bretagne)*; ***master switch*** commutateur *m ou* disjoncteur *m* principal; ***master tape*** bande *f* originale

masterbrand ['mɑːstəˌbrænd] **N** *Mktg* marque *f* vedette

Mastercard® ['mɑːstəkɑːd] **N** carte *f* Mastercard®

masterful ['mɑːstəfʊl] **ADJ 1** *(dominant* ▸ *person)* qui sait se faire obéir; **you're so m.!** quel homme/quelle femme! **2** *(tone, voice, performance)* magistral; **the race was another m. display of Formula 1 driving by the world champion** le Grand Prix de formule 1 fut une nouvelle démonstration magistrale du champion du monde

masterfully ['mɑːstəfʊlɪ] **ADV 1** *(dominantly)* fermement, autoritairement; **to speak m.** parler sur un ton autoritaire **2** *(skilfully)* magistralement

masterly ['mɑːstəlɪ] **ADJ** magistral; **a m. performance** une performance magistrale; **in a m. fashion** magistralement, avec maestria

mastermind ['mɑːstəmaɪnd] **N** *(genius)* cerveau *m*, génie *m*; *(of crime, operation)* cerveau *m*
VT diriger, organiser; **she masterminded the whole operation** c'est elle qui a dirigé toute l'opération, c'est elle le cerveau de toute l'opération

masterpiece ['mɑːstəpiːs] **N** *also Fig* chef-d'œuvre *m*

masterstroke ['mɑːstəstrəʊk] **N** coup *m* de maître

mastery ['mɑːstərɪ] *(pl* **masteries) N 1** *(domination, control* ▸ *gen)* maîtrise *f*, domination *f*; *(*▸ *of situation)* maîtrise *f* (**of** *ou* **over** sur); *(*▸ *of opponent)* supériorité *f* (**of** *ou* **over** sur); **to gain m. over sth/sb** se rendre maître de qch/soumettre qn **2** *(of art, subject, language)* maîtrise *f*, connaissance *f* **3** *(masterly skill)* maestria *f*, brio *m*

masthead ['mɑːsthed] **N 1** *Naut* tête *f* de mât **2** *Press* cartouche *f* de titre

mastic ['mæstɪk] **N** mastic *m*

masticate ['mæstɪkeɪt] **VT 1** *(food)* mâcher, mastiquer **2** *Ind (rubber etc)* triturer, malaxer
VI mastiquer, mâcher

mastiff ['mæstɪf] **N** mastiff *m*

mastitis [mæs'taɪtɪs] **N** *Med & Vet* mastite *f*

mastodon ['mæstədɒn] **N** *Zool* mastodonte *m*

mastoid ['mæstɔɪd] **N 1** *Anat (bone)* mastoïde *f* **2** *Fam Med (mastoiditis)* mastoïdite *f*
ADJ *Anat* mastoïdien, mastoïde

masturbate ['mæstəbeɪt] **VT** masturber
VI se masturber

masturbation [ˌmæstə'beɪʃən] **N** masturbation *f*, *Fig Pej* **mental m.** masturbation *f* intellectuelle

masturbatory [ˌmæstə'beɪtərɪ] **ADJ** masturbatoire

mat [mæt] *(pt & pp* **matted**, *cont* **matting) N 1** *(floor covering* ▸ *of wool etc)* (petit) tapis *m*, carpette *f*; *(*▸ *of straw, rushes)* natte *f*; *(*▸ *doormat)* paillasson *m*; *(*▸ *in gym)* tapis *m*; *Fam* **to be on the m.** *(be in trouble)* être sur la sellette; *Fam* **to have sb on the m.** faire passer un mauvais quart d'heure à qn; *Am Fam* **to go to the m.** se démener **2** *(on table)* set *m* de table; *(for hot dishes)* dessous-de-plat *m inv*; *(for vase, ornament)* napperon *m*
ADJ mat
VT *(hair etc)* emmêler
VI 1 *(hair)* s'emmêler **2** *(material)* (se) feutrer

matador ['mætədɔː(r)] **N** matador *m*

MATCH [mætʃ]

N	
• match **1**	• égal **2**
• coupie **3**	• allumette **5**
• mèche **6**	
VT	
• égaler **1, 5**	• s'assortir à **2**
• aller (bien) avec **2**	• opposer **4**
VI	
• aller (bien) ensemble	• correspondre

N 1 *Sport (of football, rugby, baseball, cricket)* match *m*; *(of tennis)* match *m*, partie *f*; *(of golf)* partie *f*; *(swimming)* compétition *f*; **a rugby/boxing m.** un match de rugby/de boxe
2 *(equal)* égal(e) *m,f*; **he's found** *or* **met his m. (in Heather)** il a trouvé à qui parler (avec Heather); **he's a m. for her any day** il est de taille à lui faire face; **David is no m. for Andrew** David ne fait pas le poids contre Andrew; **they were more than a m. for us** nous ne faisions pas le poids contre eux
3 *(couple)* couple *m*; *(marriage)* mariage *m*; **to make a good m.** faire un bon mariage; **he's a good m.** c'est un bon *ou* un excellent parti
4 *(combination)* **these colours are a good m.** ces couleurs se marient bien *ou* vont bien ensemble; **to find a m. for a wallpaper** *(find curtains etc in suitable colour)* assortir un papier peint; *(find the same)* réassortir un papier peint
5 *(for lighting)* allumette *f*; **to light** *or* **to strike a m.** frotter *ou* craquer une allumette; **to put** *or* **to set a m. to sth** mettre le feu à qch; **a box/book of matches** une boîte/une pochette d'allumettes
6 *(fuse)* mèche *f*
VT 1 *(be equal to)* être l'égal de, égaler; **his arrogance is matched only by that of his father** son arrogance n'a d'égale que celle de son père; **there's nobody to m. him** il n'a pas son pareil
2 *(go with* ▸ *of clothes, colour)* s'assortir à, aller (bien) avec, se marier (harmonieusement) avec; **the gloves m. the scarf** les gants sont assortis à l'écharpe; **his jacket doesn't m. his trousers** sa veste ne va pas avec son pantalon; **the music didn't m. her mood** la musique ne correspondait pas à son humeur
3 *(coordinate)* **I'm trying to m. this paint** je cherche une peinture identique à celle-ci; **can you m. the names with the photographs?** pouvez-vous attribuer à chaque photo le nom qui lui correspond?; **he and his wife are well matched** lui et sa femme vont bien ensemble
4 *(oppose)* **to m. sb against sb** opposer qn à qn; **he matched his skill against the champion's** il mesura son habileté à celle du champion; **the two teams are well** *or* **evenly matched** les deux équipes sont de force égale
5 *(find equal to)* égaler; **to m. an offer** égaler une offre; **we can't m. their prices** nous ne pouvons pas rivaliser avec leurs prix
VI *(colours etc)* aller (bien) ensemble, être bien assorti; *(fingerprints, descriptions etc)* correspondre; **these colours don't m.** ces couleurs ne vont pas très bien ensemble; **a red hat with a scarf to m.** un chapeau rouge avec un foulard assorti; **I can't find two socks that m.** je ne parviens pas à trouver deux chaussettes identiques
▸▸ *Golf* ***match play*** match-play *m*, partie *f* par trous; *Sport* ***match point*** *(in tennis)* balle *f* de match

▸**match up VT SEP** faire correspondre; **to m. up the names with the faces** faire correspondre les noms et les visages; **to m. up two colours** harmoniser *ou* assortir deux couleurs
VI *(dates, figures)* correspondre; *(clothes, colours)* aller (bien) ensemble, être bien assorti; **the descriptions didn't m. up** les descriptions ne correspondaient pas

▸**match up to VT INSEP** valoir; **his jokes don't m. up to Mark's** ses plaisanteries ne valent pas celles de Mark; **the hotel didn't m. up to our expectations** l'hôtel nous a déçus *ou* ne répondait pas à notre attente

matchbox ['mætʃbɒks] **N** boîte *f* d'allumettes

matched bargain [mætʃt-] **N** *St Exch* mariage *m*

matching ['mætʃɪŋ] **ADJ** assorti; **a blue suit with a m. tie** un costume bleu avec une cravate assortie; **a m. pair** une paire assortie

matchless ['mætʃlɪs] **ADJ** *Literary* sans égal, sans pareil

matchmaker ['mætʃˌmeɪkə(r)] **N 1** *(gen)* entremetteur(euse) *m,f*; *(for marriage)* marieur(euse) *m,f* **2** *(manufacturer)* fabricant *m* d'allumettes

matchmaking ['mætʃˌmeɪkɪŋ] **N he loves m.** *(gen)* il adore jouer les entremetteurs; *(for marriage)* il adore jouer les marieurs

matchstick ['mætʃstɪk] **N** *Br* allumette *f*; **to have m. legs** avoir des jambes comme des allumettes
▸▸ ***matchstick men*** personnages *mpl* stylisés *(dessinés de simples traits)*

matchwood ['mætʃwʊd] **N** bois *m* d'allumettes; *Br* **smashed** *or* **reduced to m.** réduit en miettes

mate[1] [meɪt] **N 1** *Br & Austr Fam (friend)* pote *m*; **listen, m.!** écoute, mon vieux!; **thanks, m.** *(to friend)* merci vieux; *(to stranger)* merci chef; **watch where you're going, m.!** hé, regarde devant toi!
2 *(colleague)* camarade *mf* (de travail)
3 *(workman's helper)* aide *mf*; **plumber's m.** aide-plombier *m*
4 *Naut (in navy)* second maître *m*; *(on merchant vessel)* **(first) m.** second *m*; **second m.** lieutenant *m*
5 *(sexual partner* ▸ *animal)* mâle *m*/femelle *f*; *Hum (*▸ *husband)* époux *m*; *(*▸ *wife)* épouse *f*; *(*▸ *lover)* partenaire *mf*
6 *(in chess)* mat *m*
VT 1 *Zool* accoupler; **to m. a cow with a bull** accoupler une vache à un taureau **2** *(in chess)* mettre échec et mat, mater
VI s'accoupler

mate[2], **maté** ['mæteɪ] **N** *(drink)* maté *m*

mater ['meɪtə(r)] **N** *Br Old-fashioned or Hum* **(the) m.** ma mère, maman *f*

material [mə'tɪərɪəl] **N 1** *(wood, plastic, stone etc)* matière *f*, substance *f*; *Constr & Ind* matériau *m*; **building materials** matériaux *mpl* de construction
2 *(cloth)* tissu *m*, étoffe *f*; **curtain m.** tissu *m* pour faire des rideaux
3 *(UNCOUNT) (ideas, data)* matériaux *mpl*, documentation *f*; **I'm collecting m. for a novel** je rassemble des matériaux pour un roman; **background m.** documentation *f* de base
4 *(finished work)* **written m.** des textes *mpl*; **published m.** des publications *fpl*; **a comic who writes his own m.** un comique qui écrit ses propres textes *ou* sketches; **publicity m.** publicité *f*; **reading m.** lecture *f*
5 *(necessary equipment)* matériel *m*; **writing m.** matériel *m* pour écrire; *Sch* **teaching materials** supports *mpl* pédagogiques
6 *(suitable person or persons)* **is he officer m.?** a-t-il l'étoffe d'un officier?; **he's not university m.** il n'est pas au niveau pour aller en fac
ADJ 1 *(concrete)* matériel; **the m. world** le monde matériel; **of m. benefit** d'un apport capital **2** *Formal (relevant)* pertinent; **that is not m. to the present discussion** cela n'a aucun rapport *ou* n'a rien à voir avec ce dont nous discutons; **the facts m. to the investigation** les faits qui présentent un intérêt pour l'enquête
▸▸ ***material comforts*** confort *m* matériel; *Law* ***material evidence*** preuve *f* matérielle *ou* substantielle; *Law* ***material facts*** faits *mpl* matériels; ***material possessions*** biens *mpl* matériels; *Law* ***material witness*** témoin *m* important

materialism [mə'tɪərɪəlɪzəm] **N** matérialisme *m*

materialist [mə'tɪərɪəlɪst] **N** matérialiste *mf*
ADJ matérialiste

materialistic [məˌtɪərɪə'lɪstɪk] **ADJ** matérialiste

materialize, -ise [mə'tɪərɪəlaɪz] **VI 1** *(become fact)* se matérialiser, se réaliser; *(take shape)* prendre forme; **the promised pay rise never materialized** l'augmentation promise ne s'est jamais matérialisée *ou* concrétisée; **she promised to lend me £1,000 but the money never materialized** elle avait promis de me prêter 1000 livres mais je n'en ai jamais vu la couleur **2** *Fam (arrive)* se pointer **3** *(ghost, apparition)* se matérialiser

VT matérialiser

materially [məˈtɪərɪəlɪ] **ADV 1** *Phil, Phys & Rel* matériellement **2** *(appreciably* ▸ *affect, alter)* sensiblement

materiel, matériel [mə,tɪərɪˈel] **N** *Mil* matériel *m*

maternal [məˈtɜːnəl] **ADJ 1** *(motherly* ▸ *love, instinct)* maternel **2** *(related through mother)* maternel; **m. grandfather** grand-père *m* maternel

maternally [məˈtɜːnəlɪ] **ADV** maternellement

maternity [məˈtɜːnətɪ] **N** maternité *f*

COMP *(clothes, dress)* de grossesse

▸▸ ***maternity allowance*** = allocation de maternité versée par l'État à une femme n'ayant pas droit à la "maternity pay"; ***maternity benefit*** ≃ allocations *fpl* de maternité; ***maternity hospital*** maternité *f*; ***maternity leave*** congé *m* (de) maternité; ***maternity pay*** = allocation de maternité versée par l'employeur; ***maternity ward*** maternité *f*

matey [ˈmeɪtɪ] *Br Fam* **N** *(term of address)* **all right, m.?** ça va, mon vieux?; **just watch it, m.!** fais gaffe!

ADJ *(pally)* copain, copain-copain; **they're very m. all of a sudden** ils sont très copains tout d'un coup

math [mæθ] **N** *(UNCOUNT) Am* maths *fpl*

mathematical [,mæθəˈmætɪkəl] **ADJ** mathématique; **a m. genius** un génie en mathématiques; **I haven't got a m. mind, I'm not very m.** je ne suis pas matheux; **victory for the party is now a m. impossibility** mathématiquement, le parti ne peut pas gagner

mathematically [,mæθəˈmætɪkəlɪ] **ADV** mathématiquement; **I'm not very m. minded** je ne suis pas très matheux

mathematician [,mæθəməˈtɪʃən] **N** mathématicien(enne) *m,f*

mathematics [,mæθəˈmætɪks] **N** *(UNCOUNT) (science, subject)* mathématiques *fpl*

NPL *(calculations involved)* **can you explain the m. of it to me?** pouvez-vous m'expliquer comment on parvient à ce résultat *ou* ce chiffre?

maths [mæθs] **N** *(UNCOUNT) Br* maths *fpl*

▸▸ *Comput* ***maths coprocessor*** coprocesseur *m* mathématique

matinee, matinée [ˈmætɪneɪ] **N** *Cin & Theat* matinée *f*

▸▸ *Old-fashioned or Hum* ***matinee idol*** = acteur idolâtré par les femmes surtout dans les années 30 ou 40; *Br Cin & Theat* ***matinee performance*** matinée *f*

matiness [ˈmeɪtɪnɪs] **N** *Br Fam* camaraderie*f*

mating [ˈmeɪtɪŋ] **N** accouplement *m*

▸▸ ***mating call*** appel *m* du mâle/de la femelle; ***mating instinct*** instinct *m* sexuel; ***mating ritual*** parade *f* nuptiale; ***mating season*** saison *f* des amours

matins [ˈmætɪnz] **N** *Rel (in Roman Catholic church)* matines *fpl*; *(in Church of England)* office *m* du matin

matriarch [ˈmeɪtrɪɑːk] **N** *(ruler, head of family)* femme *f* chef de famille; *(old woman)* matrone *f*

matriarchal [,meɪtrɪˈɑːkəl] **ADJ** matriarcal

matriarchy [ˈmeɪtrɪɑːkɪ] *(pl* **matriarchies***)* **N** matriarcat *m*

matric [məˈtrɪk] **N** *Br Fam Univ (abbr* **matriculation***)* inscription*f*

matricide [ˈmætrɪsaɪd] **N 1** *(act)* matricide *m* **2** *(person)* matricide *mf*

matriculate [məˈtrɪkjʊleɪt] **VI 1** *(register)* s'inscrire, se faire immatriculer; *(at university)* s'inscrire **2** *Br Formerly Sch* ≃ obtenir son baccalauréat

matriculation [mə,trɪkjʊˈleɪʃən] **N 1** *(registration)* inscription *f*, immatriculation *f*; *(at university)* inscription *f* **2** *Br Formerly Sch* = ancien examen équivalent au baccalauréat

COMP *(exam)* d'inscription; *(card)* d'étudiant

▸▸ ***matriculation fees*** droits *mpl* d'inscription

matrimonial [,mætrɪˈməʊnjəl] **ADJ** matrimonial, conjugal

▸▸ ***matrimonial home*** foyer *m ou* domicile *m* conjugal; ***matrimonial law*** droit *m* matrimonial

matrimony [ˈmætrɪmənɪ, *Am* ˈmætrɪməʊnɪ] *(pl* **matrimonies***)* **N** *Formal* mariage *m*; *Rel* **joined in holy m.** unis par les liens sacrés du mariage

matrix [ˈmeɪtrɪks] *(pl* **matrixes** *or* **matrices** [-trɪsiːz]*)* **N** matrice *f*; *Miner* gangue *f*

▸▸ *Comput* ***matrix printer*** imprimante *f* matricielle

matron [ˈmeɪtrən] **N 1** *Br (in hospital)* infirmière *f* en chef; *(in school)* = personne assumant le rôle d'infirmière ainsi que certaines tâches matérielles

2 *(in retirement home, orphanage)* directrice *f*

3 *Literary (married woman)* matrone *f*, mère *f* de famille

4 *Am (in prison)* gardienne *f*, surveillante *f*

▸▸ ***matron of honour*** *(at wedding)* dame *f* d'honneur

matronly [ˈmeɪtrənlɪ] **ADJ** *(figure, stature, appearance)* de matrone; **she looks very m.** elle fait très matrone

matt [mæt] **ADJ** mat

▸▸ ***matt paint*** peinture *f* mate

matte [mæt] **N** *Metal* matte *f*, maton *m*

ADJ mat

▸▸ *Cin & TV* ***matte artist*** peintre *m* de caches; *Cin & TV* ***matte shot*** cache *m* contre-cache

matted [ˈmætɪd] **ADJ** *(material)* feutré; *(hair)* emmêlé; *(vegetation, roots)* enchevêtré; **to become m.** *(hair, wool)* s'emmêler; **his hair was m. with blood** il avait du sang séché dans les cheveux

MATTER [ˈmætə(r)]

N	
• affaire **1**	• sujet **1**
• question **2**	• matière **3, 4**
• imprimés **4**	• pus **5**
VI	
• importer	

N 1 *(affair)* affaire *f*; *(subject)* sujet *m*; **I reported the m. to the police** j'ai rapporté les faits à la police; **business matters** affaires *fpl*; **money matters** questions *fpl* d'argent; **the m. in hand** les faits *mpl* qui nous préoccupent; **I consider the m. closed** pour moi, c'est une affaire classée; **it is a m. for regret** c'est regrettable; **this is no laughing m.** il n'y a pas de quoi rire; **it's no easy m.** c'est une question difficile *ou* un sujet délicat; **that is a m. for the courts to decide** sur ce point, c'est à la justice de trancher; **I will give the m. my immediate attention** j'accorderai toute mon attention à ce problème; **you're not going out, and that's the end of** *or* **there's an end to the m.!** tu ne sortiras pas, un point c'est tout!

2 *(question)* question *f*; **there's the small m. of the £100 you owe me** il y a ce petit problème des 100 livres que tu me dois; **a m. of life and death** une question de vie ou de mort; **that's quite another m., that's a different m. altogether** ça c'est une (tout) autre affaire; **a m. of taste** une question de goût; **that's a m. of opinion** ça c'est une question d'opinion; **as a m. of course** automatiquement; **as a m. of principle** par principe; **as a m. of urgency** d'urgence; **within a m. of minutes** en quelques minutes; **it'll be a m. of days rather than weeks before we get a result** obtenir le résultat sera une question de jours plutôt que de semaines; **it's only a m. of time** ce n'est qu'une question de temps; **it's just a m. of knowing which button to press** il s'agit juste de savoir sur quel bouton appuyer

3 *(physical substance)* matière *f*; **organic/inorganic m.** matière *f* organique/inorganique

4 *(written material)* matière *f*, copie *f*; *(sent by post)* imprimés *mpl*; **advertising m.** matériel *m* publicitaire; **printed m.** texte *m* imprimé

5 *Med (pus)* pus *m*

6 *(idioms)* **what's the m.?** qu'est-ce qu'il y a?, qu'est-ce qui ne va pas?; **what's the m. with you?** qu'est-ce que tu as?, qu'est-ce qui ne va pas?; **what's the m. with Susan?** qu'est-ce qu'elle a, Susan?; **what's the m. with the way I dress?** qu'est-ce que vous reprochez à ma façon de m'habiller?; **what's the m. with telling him the truth?** quel ma[l] y a-t-il à lui dire la vérité?; **I don't know what's th[e] m. with me** je ne sais pas ce que j'ai; **there's something the m.** il y a quelque chose (qui ne va pas), il se passe quelque chose; **there's something th[e] m. with my leg** j'ai quelque chose à la jambe; **there's something the m. with the aerial** il y a u[n] problème avec l'antenne; **is there something** *o[r]* **is anything the m.?** il y a quelque chose qui n[e] va pas?, il y a un problème?; **nothing's the** *o[r]* **there's nothing the m.** il n'y a rien, tout va bien; **nothing's the m. with me** je vais parfaitement bien; **no m.!** peu importe!; **no m. what I do** quo[i] que je fasse; **no m. what the boss thinks** peu importe ce qu'en pense le patron; **don't go back, n[o] m. how much he begs you** même s'il te le demande à genoux, n'y retourne pas; **I'll be ther[e] tomorrow no m. what** j'y serai demain quoi qu'i[l] arrive; **no m. how** par n'importe quel moyen; **n[o] m. how hard I try** quels que soient les efforts qu[e] je fais; **no m. when** à n'importe quel moment; **n[o] m. when it happens** peu importe quand ça arrivera; **no m. who** qui que ce soit; **no m. who gav[e] it to you** peu importe qui te l'a donné; **no m[.] where** où que ce soit

VI importer, avoir de l'importance; **nothing matters to him any more since his wife died** plus rie[n] n'a d'importance pour lui depuis la mort de s[a] femme; **nothing else matters** tout le reste es[t] sans importance; **what does it m.?** quelle importance est-ce que ça a?, qu'importe?; **it doesn't m[.]** cela n'a pas d'importance, ça ne fait rien; **[it] doesn't m. how much it costs** peu importe le prix; **it doesn't m. to me what you do with your mone[y]** ce que tu fais de ton argent m'est égal; **it doesn['t] m. to her what people think** elle se moque de c[e] que pensent les gens; **money is all that matters t[o] him** il n'y a que l'argent qui l'intéresse; **she matters a lot to him** il tient beaucoup à elle, ell[e] compte beaucoup pour lui; **that's what matter[s] most** c'est le plus important; **she knows all th[e] people who m.** elle connaît tous les gens qu[i] comptent

• **matters NPL as matters stand** les choses étan[t] ce qu'elles sont; **getting angry won't help matter[s]** se mettre en colère n'arrangera pas les choses; **her remarks made matters worse** ses remarque[s] n'ont fait qu'aggraver les choses; **to make matter[s] worse, it had started to rain** pour tout arranger, i[l] s'était mis à pleuvoir

• **as a matter of fact ADV** en fait, à vrai dire, e[n] réalité

• **for that matter ADV** d'ailleurs; **and so am I fo[r] that m.** moi aussi d'ailleurs; **he isn't very wel[l] known in London, or anywhere else for that m.** i[l] n'est pas très connu à Londres, et nulle pa[rt] ailleurs en fait

Matterhorn [ˈmætəhɔːn] **N the M.** le mont Cervin

matter-of-fact ADJ *(down-to-earth)* terre-àterre *(inv)*; *(prosaic)* prosaïque; *(unemotional)* neutre; **in a m. voice** d'une voix neutre; **she too[k] the news in a very m. way** elle a pris les nouvelle[s] avec beaucoup de sang-froid

Matthew [ˈmæθjuː] **PR N** *Bible* Matthieu; **the Gospel According to (Saint) M.** l'Évangile selon sain[t] Matthieu

mattify [ˈmætɪfaɪ] *(pt & pp* **mattified***)* **VT** matifie[r]

matting [ˈmætɪŋ] **N** *(UNCOUNT) (used as mat)* natte *f*, tapis *m*

mattins = **matins**

mattock [ˈmætək] **N** *Agr* pioche *f*

mattress [ˈmætrɪs] **N** matelas *m*; **inflatable** *or* **ai[r] m.** matelas *m* pneumatique

maturation [,mætjʊˈreɪʃən] **N** *(of fruit, abscess)* maturation *f*; *(of wine, whisky)* vieillissement *m*; *(of cheese)* maturation *f*, affinage *m*

mature [məˈtjʊə(r)] **ADJ 1** *(person* ▸ *physically)* mûr; *(*▸ *mentally)* mûr, mature; *(animal)* adulte; **to be m. for one's age** *or* **years** être mûr pour so[n] âge; **a man of m. years** un homme d'âge mûr; **he[r] style is not yet m.** son style n'est pas encore arrivé à maturité

2 *(fruit)* mûr; *(plant)* adulte; *(garden)* planté depuis plusieurs années

3 *(cheese)* fait; *(wine, spirits)* arrivé à maturité

4 *Fin (bill, bond, insurance policy)* échu

VI 1 *(person, attitude)* & *Fig (plan)* mûrir; **she had matured into a sophisticated young woman** elle était devenue une jeune femme sophistiquée 2 *(wine)* vieillir; *(cheese)* se faire 3 *Fin* arriver à échéance, échoir

VT *(cheese)* faire mûrir, affiner; *(wine, spirits)* faire vieillir

▸▸ *Br Univ* ***mature student*** = étudiant plus âgé que la moyenne ou qui entreprend des études sur le tard, *Can* étudiant(e) *m,f* adulte

naturely [mə'tjʊəlɪ] ADV *(decide)* de façon raisonnable; **to behave m.** se comporter en adulte

maturity [mə'tjʊərətɪ] N 1 *(of person, fruit, wine, cheese etc)* maturité *f*; **to reach m.** *(person)* devenir majeur; **she lacks m.** elle n'est pas très mûre 2 *Fin* **(date of) m.** échéance *f* 3 *Mktg (of market)* maturité *f*

▸▸ *Fin* ***maturity date*** date *f* d'échéance; *Fin* ***maturity value*** valeur *f* à l'échéance

maudlin ['mɔːdlɪn] ADJ larmoyant; **he gets m. when he drinks** il a le vin triste

maul [mɔːl] VT 1 *(attack* ▸ *of animal)* déchiqueter; *(*▸ *of person, crowd)* malmener; **he was mauled to death by a lion** il a été déchiqueté par un lion 2 *Fam (sexually* ▸ *grope)* tripoter 3 *(criticize)* démolir, mettre en pièces, éreinter

VI 1 *(fight)* se battre 2 *(in rugby)* faire un maul

N *Sport (in rugby)* maul *m*

mauling ['mɔːlɪŋ] N 1 *(attack)* **to get a m.** *(from animal)* être blessé; *(more seriously)* être mutilé; *(from person, crowd)* être malmené 2 *Fam* **to get a m.** *(get defeated)* être battu à plates coutures, recevoir une raclée; *(get criticized)* se faire éreinter *ou* démolir

maunder ['mɔːndə(r)] VI *Br* 1 *(talk)* divaguer, parler à tort et à travers; **what's he maundering on about?** qu'est-ce qu'il raconte? 2 *(walk)* errer

Maundy ['mɔːndɪ] N

▸▸ *Br* ***Maundy money*** *(UNCOUNT)* = pièces de monnaie spéciales offertes par le souverain britannique à certaines personnes âgées le jour du jeudi saint; *Rel* ***Maundy Thursday*** jeudi *m* saint

Mauritania [,mɒrɪ'teɪnjə] N Mauritanie *f*

Mauritanian [,mɒrɪ'teɪnjən] N Mauritanien(enne) *m,f*

ADJ mauritanien

Mauritian [mə'rɪʃən] N Mauricien(enne) *m,f*

ADJ mauricien

Mauritius [mə'rɪʃəs] N l'île *f* Maurice

mausoleum [,mɔːzə'lɪəm] N mausolée *m*

mauve [məʊv] N mauve *m*

ADJ mauve

maverick ['mævərɪk] N 1 *(person)* franc-tireur *m*, indépendant(e) *m,f* 2 *(calf)* veau *m* non marqué

ADJ non conformiste, indépendant; **a m. Marxist** un franc-tireur du marxisme; **a m. MP** un député non conformiste

maw [mɔː] N *Zool* 1 *(stomach* ▸ *of cow)* caillette *f*; *(of bird)* jabot *m* 2 *(mouth)* gueule *f*; *Fig* gouffre *m*

mawkish ['mɔːkɪʃ] ADJ *(sentimental)* mièvre; *(nauseating)* écœurant

mawkishness ['mɔːkɪʃnɪs] N *(sentimentality)* mièvrerie *f*

max [mæks] *(abbr* **maximum)** N max *m*; *Am Fam* **to the m.** *(totally)* un max; **did you have a good time? – to the m.!** tu t'es bien amusé? – vachement!, un max!

ADV *Fam (at the most)* maxi; **it'll take three days m.** ça prendra trois jours maxi

VT *Am Fam* **to m. an exam** = obtenir le maximum de points à un examen

▸ **max out** *Am Fam* VT SEP **to m. out one's credit card** = dépenser le maximum autorisé avec sa carte de crédit

VI **to m. out on chocolate** se gaver de chocolat; **to m. out on booze** picoler un max

maxed [mækst] ADJ *Am Fam* 1 *(extremely drunk)* bourré comme un coing, pété à mort 2 **to be m. out on one's credit card** = avoir dépensé le maximum autorisé avec sa carte de crédit; **to be m. out on chocolate/sci-fi movies** avoir fait une overdose de chocolat/de films de science-fiction

maxi ['mæksɪ] N *(skirt)* jupe *f* maxi

ADJ *(skirt, dress etc)* maxi *(inv)*

maxillofacial [mæk,sɪləʊ'feɪʃəl] ADJ *Med* maxillofacial

maxim ['mæksɪm] N maxime *f*

maximal ['mæksɪməl] ADJ maximal

maximization, -isation [,mæksɪmaɪ'zeɪʃən] N maximalisation *f*, maximisation *f*

maximize, -ise ['mæksɪmaɪz] VT maximiser, maximaliser; *Comput (window)* agrandir

maximum ['mæksɪməm] *(pl* **maximums** *or* **maxima** [-mə]) N 1 *(gen)* maximum *m*; **a m. of 40 people** un maximum de 40 personnes, 40 personnes au maximum; **at the m.** au (grand) maximum; **to the m.** au maximum 2 *(in snooker, darts)* maximum *m*

ADJ maximum, maximal; **m. temperatures** températures *fpl* maximales

ADV au maximum; **it happens twice a year m.** ça se produit deux fois par an au maximum; **you can stay for two hours m.** vous ne pouvez pas rester plus de deux heures

▸▸ ***maximum efficiency*** rendement *m* maximum; ***maximum load*** charge *f* maximale *ou* limite; ***maximum security prison*** prison *f* de haute sécurité; ***maximum speed*** *(highest possible)* vitesse *f* maximale *ou* maximum; *(highest permitted)* vitesse *f* limite

May [meɪ] N mai *m*; *see also* **February**

▸▸ *Entom* ***May beetle*** hanneton *m*; *Entom* ***May bug*** hanneton *m*; ***May Day*** le Premier mai; ***May queen*** = reine des festivités du Premier mai

MAY¹ [meɪ]

> **May** et **might** peuvent s'utiliser indifféremment ou presque dans les expressions de la catégorie **1**.

V AUX 1 *(expressing possibility)* **this m. take some time** ça prendra peut-être *ou* il se peut que ça prenne du temps; **symptoms m. disappear after a few days** les symptômes peuvent disparaître après quelques jours; **you m. be right** vous avez peut-être raison, il se peut que vous ayez raison; **it m. well be that he misunderstood** il est fort possible *ou* il se peut bien qu'il ait mal compris; **she m. not have arrived yet** il se peut *ou* il se pourrait qu'elle ne soit pas encore arrivée; **he m. have been right** il avait peut-être raison; **I fear you m. be right** j'ai bien peur que tu aies raison; **you m. be wondering why I'm doing that** vous vous demandez peut-être pourquoi je fais cela

2 *(expressing permission)* **you m. go** vous pouvez partir; **m. I write to you? – of course you m.** pourrais-je vous écrire? – je vous en prie; **passengers m. take only one item of hand luggage** les passagers ne peuvent prendre *ou* ne sont autorisés à prendre qu'un bagage à main; **I will go home now, if I m.** je vais rentrer chez moi, si vous me le permettez; **if I m. be allowed to express an opinion** si je puis me permettre; **if I m. say so** si je peux *ou* puis me permettre cette remarque; **you m. well ask!** bonne question!

3 *(in polite questions, suggestions)* **m. I make a suggestion?** puis-je me permettre de faire une suggestion?; **m. I help you?** puis-je vous aider?; **and how, m. I ask, did you find out?** et comment vous en êtes-vous rendu compte, s'il vous plaît?; **m. I?** vous permettez?; **m. I say how pleased we are that you could come** permettez-moi de vous dire à quel point nous sommes ravis que vous ayez pu venir; **we m. remind ourselves at this point that…** il n'est pas inutile de rappeler ici que…; **can I go home now? – you m. as well** est-ce que je peux rentrer chez moi maintenant? – tu ferais aussi bien; **we m. as well stay where we are** autant rester où nous sommes

4 *(contradicting a point of view)* **you m. think I'm imagining things, but…** tu vas croire que je divague mais…; **whatever faults he m. have he's never dull** quels que soient ses défauts, il n'est jamais ennuyeux; **he m. not be very bright, but he's got a heart of gold** il n'est peut-être pas très brillant mais il a un cœur d'or; **be that as it m.** quoi qu'il en soit; **that's as m. be** c'est possible; **that's as m. be, but we can't afford it** peut-être, mais nous ne pouvons pas nous le permettre

5 *Formal (expressing purpose)* **they work hard so that their children m. have a better life** ils travaillent dur pour que leurs enfants aient une vie meilleure; **so that others m. sleep in peace** pour que les autres puissent dormir en paix

6 *(expressing wishes, hopes)* **m. she rest in peace** qu'elle repose en paix; **m. the best man win!** que le meilleur gagne!; **much good m. it do you!** grand bien vous fasse!

may² N *Br Bot (hawthorn)* aubépine *f*, épine *f* de mai

▸▸ ***may blossom*** *(UNCOUNT)* fleurs *fpl* d'aubépine; ***may tree*** aubépine *f*

Maya ['maɪə] *(pl sense* **1** *inv or* **Mayas)** N 1 *(person)* Indien(enne) *m,f* maya; **the M.** *or* **Mayas** les Mayas *mpl* 2 *Ling* maya *m*

Mayan ['maɪən] N 1 *(person)* Indien(enne) *m,f* maya 2 *Ling* maya *m*

ADJ maya

maybe ['meɪbiː] ADV peut-être; **m. she won't accept** peut-être qu'elle n'acceptera pas, elle n'acceptera peut-être pas; **m. so** peut-être bien que oui; **m. not** peut-être bien que non; **m. so, but…** peut-être bien, mais…

N *Fam* **I don't want any maybes** c'est oui ou non!

Mayday ['meɪdeɪ] N *(emergency call)* SOS *m*; **to send out a M. (signal)** envoyer un signal de détresse *ou* un SOS

mayfly ['meɪflaɪ] *(pl* **mayflies)** N *Entom* éphémère *m*

mayhem ['meɪhem] N 1 *(disorder)* désordre *m*; **it was absolute m. in that office** c'était le désordre le plus complet dans ce bureau; **to create** *or* **to cause m.** semer la panique 2 *Law* mutilation *f* du corps humain

mayn't [meɪnt] *Br* = **may not**

mayo ['meɪəʊ] N *Fam* mayonnaise *f*

mayonnaise [,meɪə'neɪz] N mayonnaise *f*

mayor [meə(r)] N *(man)* maire *m*; *(woman)* maire *m ou f*, mairesse *f*

mayoress ['meərɪs] N 1 *(woman mayor)* maire *m ou f*, mairesse *f* 2 *(wife of mayor)* femme *f* du maire, mairesse *f*

maypole ['meɪpəʊl] N ≃ arbre *m* de mai *(mât autour duquel on danse le Premier mai)*

may've ['meɪəv] *Fam* = **may have**

maze [meɪz] N *also Fig* labyrinthe *m*, dédale *m*; **the hospital is a m. of corridors** cet hôpital est un vrai labyrinthe; **a m. of streets/lanes** un dédale de rues/ruelles

MB 1 *Comput (written abbr* **megabyte)** Mo 2 *(written abbr* **Manitoba)** Manitoba *m*

Mb *Comput (written abbr* **megabit)** Mb

MBA [,embiː'eɪ] N *Univ (abbr* **Master of Business Administration)** *(person)* = titulaire d'une maîtrise de gestion; *(qualification)* maîtrise *f* de gestion, MBA *m*

MBE [,embiː'iː] N *(abbr* **Member of the Order of the British Empire)** *(award)* ordre *m* de l'Empire britannique; *(person)* = membre de l'ordre de l'Empire britannique

MBI [,embiː'aɪ] N *Fin (abbr* **management buy-in)** apport *m* de gestion

MBO [,embiː'əʊ] N *Br Fin* 1 *(abbr* **management buy-out)** rachat *m* d'une société par la direction 2 *(abbr* **management by objectives)** gestion *f* par objectifs

MBS [,embiː'es] N *Fin (abbr* **mortgage-backed security)** titre *m* garanti par des créances hypothécaires

MC [,em'siː] N 1 *(abbr* **master of ceremonies)** *(at reception)* maître *m* de cérémonie; *(on TV show)* présentateur(trice) *m,f*; *(rap artist)* rappeur (euse) *m,f* 2 *Br Mil (abbr* **Military Cross)** = distinction militaire britannique 3 *Am (abbr* **Member of Congress)** membre *m* du Congrès

VI *(at reception)* être le maître de cérémonie; *(on TV show)* être le (la) présentateur(trice); *(of rap artist)* rapper

Mcjob [mək'dʒɒb] N *Fam* boulot *m* à la con *(ennuyeux et mal payé)*

McMansion [mək'mænʃən] N *Fam* = grande maison de parvenus, neuve et souvent de mauvais goût

m-commerce N commerce *m* mobile

MCP [ˌemsiːˈpiː] **N** *Fam* (*abbr* **male chauvinist pig**) phallo *m*, macho *m*

MD¹ [ˌemˈdiː] **N 1** (*abbr* **Doctor of Medicine**) docteur *m* en médecine **2** (*abbr* **managing director**) P-DG *m*

MD² (*written abbr* **Maryland**) Maryland *m*

MDF [ˌemdiːˈef] **N** (*abbr* **medium-density fibreboard**) MDF *m*, panneaux *mpl* de fibres de moyenne densité

MDT [ˌemdiːˈtiː] **N** (*abbr* **Mountain Daylight Time**) heure *f* d'été des montagnes Rocheuses

ME [ˌemˈiː] **N** *(UNCOUNT) Med* (*abbr* **myalgic encephalomyelitis**) encéphalomyélite *f* myalgique

Me (*written abbr* **Maine**) Maine *m*

me¹ [miː] **PRON 1** (*direct or indirect object* ▸ *unstressed*) me; (▸ *stressed*) moi; **do you love me?** tu m'aimes?; **give me a light** donne-moi du feu; **lend it (to) me** prêtez-le-moi; **what, me, tell a lie?** moi, mentir?

2 (*after preposition*) moi; **they're talking about me** ils parlent de moi; **come with me** viens avec moi

3 (*as complement of verb "to be"*) moi; **it's me** c'est moi; **it's always me who pays** c'est toujours moi qui paie; **is it just me or is it cold in here?** c'est moi, ou bien il fait froid ici?; **she's bigger than me** elle est plus grande que moi; *Fig* **this hairstyle isn't really me** cette coiffure, ce n'est pas vraiment mon style

4 (*in interjections*) **poor me!** pauvre de moi!; **silly me!** que je suis bête!

N moi *m*; **now I'm going to show you the real me** maintenant je vais te montrer qui je suis

ADJ *Br Fam* (*my* ▸ *singular*) mon (ma)ᵔ; (▸ *plural*) mesᵔ; **where's me specs?** où sont mes binocles?

me² = **mi**

mead [miːd] **N 1** *Literary* (*meadow*) pré *m*, prairie *f* **2** (*drink*) hydromel *m*

meadow [ˈmedəʊ] **N** pré *m*, prairie *f*

▸▸ *Bot* **meadow grass** pâturin *m*; *Orn* **meadow pipit** pipit *m* des prés, farlouse *f*; *Br Bot* **meadow saffron** safran *m* des prés, colchique *m* d'automne

meadowland [ˈmedəʊlænd] **N** prairie *f*, pâturages *mpl*

meadowsweet [ˈmedəʊswiːt] **N** *Bot* **1** (*Filipendula ulmaria*) reine-des-prés *f* **2** (*Spiraea*) spirée *f*

meagre, *Am* **meager** [ˈmiːgə(r)] **ADJ** maigre; **I can't live on such a m. salary** je ne peux pas vivre avec un salaire aussi maigre

meagrely, *Am* **meagerly** [ˈmiːgəlɪ] **ADV** maigrement, piètrement

meal [miːl] **N 1** (*breakfast, lunch etc*) repas *m*; **to have a m.** prendre un repas; **I've had a huge m.** j'ai mangé comme quatre; **go to bed as soon as you've finished your m.** va te coucher dès que tu as fini de manger; **have a nice m.!, enjoy your m.!** bon appétit!; **they've invited us round for a m.** ils nous ont invités à manger; **evening m.** dîner *m*; **we have our evening m. early** nous dînons tôt; *Fam Fig* **to make a m. of sth** faire tout un plat de qch **2** (*flour*) farine *f* **3** *(UNCOUNT) Scot* (*oatmeal*) flocons *mpl* d'avoine

▸▸ **meal ticket** *Am* (*for meal*) ticket-restaurant *m*; *Fam Fig* (*source of income*) gagne-pain *m inv*; *Fam Fig* **he's just a m. ticket to her** elle n'est avec lui que pour son argent; *Br* **meals on wheels** = service de repas à domicile à l'intention des invalides et des personnes âgées

mealtime [ˈmiːltaɪm] **N** (*lunch*) heure *f* du déjeuner; (*dinner*) heure *f* du dîner; **at mealtimes** aux heures des repas

mealworm [ˈmiːlwɜːm] **N** *Zool* ver *m* de farine

mealy [ˈmiːlɪ] (*compar* **mealier**, *superl* **mealiest**) **ADJ 1** (*floury*) farineux; **m. potatoes** des pommes *f* de terre farineuses **2** (*pale*) pâle

mealy-mouthed [-ˈmaʊðd] **ADJ** *Pej* doucereux, patelin; **don't be so m.!** arrête de tourner autour du pot!

MEAN [miːn]

ADJ
- avare **1**
- méchant **2**
- moyen **4**
- super **5**
- miteux **6**

N
- milieu **1**
- moyenne **2**

VT
- vouloir dire **1, 2, 5**
- signifier **3**
- compter **4**
- avoir l'intention **6**
- être censé **7**

(*pt & pp* **meant** [ment])

ADJ 1 (*miserly*) avare, mesquin; **he's m. with his money** il est près de ses sous; **to be m. with one's praise** être avare de compliments

2 (*nasty, unkind*) méchant; **don't be m. to your sister!** ne sois pas méchant avec ta sœur!; **go on, don't be m.!** allez, ne sois pas vache!; **he has a m. streak** il peut être méchant quand il veut; **to play a m. trick on sb** jouer un sale tour à qn; **I feel m. about not inviting her** j'ai un peu honte de ne pas l'avoir invitée; **that's m. of her** ce n'est pas chic de sa part

3 (*inferior*) **the meanest intelligence** l'esprit *m* le plus borné; **he's no m. architect/guitarist** c'est un architecte/guitariste de talent; **it was no m. feat** ce n'était pas un mince exploit

4 (*average*) moyen

5 *Fam* (*excellent*) super (*inv*), génial; **she's a m. chess player** elle joue super bien aux échecs, elle touche sa bille aux échecs; **he makes a m. curry** il fait super bien le curry

6 (*shabby*) miteux, misérable; **m. slums** taudis *mpl* misérables

7 *Literary* (*of lower rank or class*) **of m. birth** de basse extraction

N 1 (*middle point*) milieu *m*, moyen terme *m*; **the golden** *or* **happy m.** le juste milieu

2 *Math* moyenne *f*

VT 1 (*signify* ▸ *of word, gesture*) vouloir dire, signifier; (▸ *of person*) vouloir dire; **what is meant by...?** que veut dire...?; **what does this term m.?** que signifie *ou* que veut dire ce terme?; **what do you m.?** qu'est-ce que tu veux dire?; **how do you m.?** qu'entendez-vous par là?; **what do you m. by that?** qu'entendez-vous par là?; **what do you m. you don't like the cinema?** comment ça, vous n'aimez pas le cinéma?; **she knew what it meant to be hungry** elle savait ce que c'était que d'avoir faim; **the name means nothing to me** ce nom ne me dit rien; **that was when the word "friendship" still meant something** c'était à l'époque où le mot "amitié" avait encore un sens; **that doesn't m. a thing!** ça ne veut (strictement) rien dire!

2 (*giving clarification, speaking sincerely*) **do you m. it?** tu es sérieux?; **do you m. him?** c'est de lui que tu parles?; **I didn't m. that** ce n'est pas ce que je voulais dire; **you don't m. it!** vous voulez rire!, vous plaisantez!; **I m. it** je parle sérieusement; **she always says what she means** elle dit toujours ce qu'elle pense; **I'll never speak to you again, I m. it** *or* **I m. what I say** je ne t'adresserai plus jamais la parole, je suis sérieux; **I want to see him now, and I m. now!** je veux le voir tout de suite, et quand je dis tout de suite, c'est tout de suite!; **I was with Barry, I m. Harry** j'étais avec Barry, je veux dire Harry; **why diet? I m., you're not exactly fat** pourquoi te mettre au régime? on ne peut pas dire que tu sois grosse; **I know what you m.!** (*I quite agree*) et comment!; **I m. to say...** ce que je veux dire c'est...; **do you m. to tell me...?** est-ce que tu es en train de me dire que...?

3 (*imply, entail* ▸ *of event, change*) signifier; **this means war/the end of our relationship** c'est la guerre/la fin de notre amitié; **going to see a film means driving into town** pour voir un film, nous sommes obligés de prendre la voiture et d'aller en ville; **it would m. the children having to change school again** cela signifierait que les enfants devraient changer d'école une fois de plus; **just because you've been to university doesn't m. you know everything** ce n'est pas parce que tu es allé à l'université que tu sais tout; **it doesn't m. we have to stop seeing each other** ça ne veut pas dire que nous devons cesser de nous voir; **she's never known what it means to be loved** elle n'a jamais su ce que c'est que d'être aimée

4 (*matter, be of value*) compter; **this watch means a lot to me** je suis très attaché à cette montre; **your friendship means a lot to her** votre amitié compte beaucoup pour elle; **doesn't your daughter's education m. anything to you?** est-ce que l'éducation de ta fille ne t'intéresse pas?; **you m. everything to me** tu es tout pour moi; **he means nothing to me** il n'est rien pour moi; **I can't tell you what this means to me** je ne peux pas te dire ce que ça représente pour moi; **my independence means a lot to me** mon indépendance est sacrée pour moi

5 (*refer to*) **do you m. us?** tu veux dire nous?; **it was you she meant when she said that** c'était à vous qu'elle pensait *ou* qu'elle faisait allusion quand elle a dit ça

6 (*intend*) **to m. to do sth** avoir (bien) l'intention de faire qch, (bien) compter faire qch, vouloir faire qch; **we m. to win** nous avons (bien) l'intention de gagner, nous comptons (bien) gagner; *Formal* **I m. to be obeyed** j'entends qu'on m'obéisse; **I meant to phone you last night** je voulais *ou* j'avais l'intention de vous téléphoner hier soir; **I didn't m. to hurt you** je ne voulais pas te faire de mal; **I only meant to help** je voulais seulement me rendre utile; **I didn't m. it!** (*action*) je ne l'ai pas fait exprès!; (*words*) je n'étais pas sérieux!; **you annoyed him when you said that – I meant to!** il n'a pas apprécié que tu dises ça – c'était bien mon intention!; **without meaning to** involontairement; **I m. him no harm** je ne lui veux pas de mal; **I meant it as a joke** c'était une plaisanterie; **it was meant as a compliment/an insult** c'était censé être un compliment/une insulte; **that remark was meant for you** cette remarque s'adressait à vous; **the present was meant for your brother** le cadeau était destiné à ton frère; **they're meant for each other** ils sont faits l'un pour l'autre; **it's meant to be a horse** c'est censé représenter un cheval; **perhaps I was meant to be a doctor** peut-être que j'étais fait pour être médecin; **you're meant to bow when she comes in** tu dois faire la révérence quand elle entre; **you weren't meant to open the presents until tomorrow** tu n'étais pas censé ouvrir les cadeaux avant demain; **it was meant to be** c'était écrit; **he means well** il a de bonnes intentions; **he meant well** il croyait bien faire

7 (*consider, believe*) **it's meant to be good for arthritis** il paraît que c'est bon pour l'arthrite

meander [mɪˈændə(r)] **N** méandre *m*

VI 1 (*river*) serpenter, faire des méandres **2** (*person*) errer (sans but), se promener au hasard; (*in speaking*) divaguer

meandering [mɪˈændərɪŋ] **ADJ 1** (*river*) qui serpente *ou* fait des méandres **2** (*speech*) sans plan sans suite

meanie [ˈmiːnɪ] **N** *Fam* **1** *Br* (*miser*) radin(e) *m,f*, pingre *mf* méchant(e); **you old m.!** vieux radin **2** (*unpleasant person*) méchant(e)ᵔ *m,f*

meaning [ˈmiːnɪŋ] **N** sens *m*, signification *f*; **what is the m. of this word?** que signifie *ou* que veut dire ce mot?; **loyalty? you don't know the m. of the word!** tu ne sais pas ce que c'est que la loyauté!; **...if you get my m.** ...si vous voyez ce que je veux dire; **what's the m. of this?** (*in anger*) qu'est-ce que ça veut dire?; **the m. of life** le sens de la vie; **a building that has given new m. to the term "skyscraper"** un bâtiment qui redéfinit le concept de "gratte-ciel"; **a look full of m.** un regard lourd de sens

ADJ (*look, smile*) significatif, éloquent

meaningful [ˈmiːnɪŋfʊl] **ADJ 1** (*expressive* ▸ *gesture*) significatif, éloquent; **she gave him a m. look** elle lui adressa un regard qui en disait long

2 (*significant*) significatif; **m. talks** conversations *fpl* constructives

3 (*comprehensible* ▸ *explanation*) compréhensible

4 (*profound* ▸ *experience, relationship*) profond; **wouldn't say we had a very m. relationship** je ne qualifierais pas notre relation de profonde

meaningfully [ˈmiːnɪŋfʊlɪ] **ADV** de façon significative; **he smiled m. at her** le sourire qu'il lui fit en disait long; **"they left together," she said m.** "ils sont partis ensemble", dit-elle d'un ton lourd de sous-entendus

meaningless [ˈmiːnɪŋlɪs] **ADJ 1** (*devoid of sense* ▸ *act, word, question, world*) dénué de sens; **the lyrics of this song are completely m.** les paroles de cette chanson n'ont absolument aucun sens **2** (*futile* ▸ *life*) futile, vain; (▸ *violence*) gratuit; **a m. task** une tâche inutile

meanly ['miːnlɪ] ADV **1** *esp Br (in miserly fashion)* en lésinant, chichement **2** *(ignobly ▸ act, behave)* méchamment **3** *(wretchedly)* misérablement, pauvrement

meanness ['miːnnɪs] N **1** *esp Br (with money)* avarice *f* **2** *(nastiness, unkindness)* méchanceté *f*, mesquinerie *f* **3** *Literary (wretchedness)* pauvreté *f*

means [miːnz] *(pl inv)* N **1** *(way, method)* moyen *m*; **a m. of doing sth** un moyen de faire qch; **is there no m. of doing it any faster?** n'y a-t-il pas moyen de le faire plus vite?; **he has no m. of support** il est sans ressources; **there is no m. of escape** il n'y a pas d'issue; **it's just a m. to an end** ce n'est qu'un moyen d'arriver au but; *Prov* **the end justifies the m.** la fin justifie les moyens; **by some m. or other** *or* **another** d'une façon ou d'une autre; **m. of transport** moyen *m* de transport; **m. of production** moyens *mpl* de production **2** *(idiom)* **she's not his friend by any (manner of) m.** elle est loin d'être son amie
NPL *(money, resources)* moyens *mpl*, ressources *fpl*; **to have the m. to do sth** avoir les moyens de faire qch; **to live within/beyond one's m.** vivre selon/au-dessus de ses moyens; **the m. at our disposal** les moyens *mpl* dont nous disposons; **her family obviously has m.** il est évident qu'elle vient d'une famille aisée; **a man of m.** un homme riche
• **by means of** PREP au moyen de; **by m. of a screwdriver** à l'aide d'un tournevis; **they communicate by m. of signs** ils communiquent par signes
• **by all means** ADV *(of course)* bien sûr; **may I leave? – by all m.!** puis-je partir? – je vous en prie *ou* mais bien sûr!; **by all m. go if you really want to** surtout, si tu veux y aller, vas-y
• **by no means** ADV pas du tout; **it's by no m. easy** c'est loin d'être facile; **he's by no m. the worst in the class** il est loin d'être le plus mauvais de la classe
▸▸ ***means test*** enquête *f* sur les revenus *(d'une personne désirant bénéficier d'une allocation d'État)*

means-test VT **is unemployment benefit means-tested?** les allocations de chômage sont-elles attribuées en fonction des ressources *ou* des revenus du bénéficiaire?; **all applicants are means-tested** tous les candidats font l'objet d'une enquête sur leurs revenus

meant [ment] *pt & pp of* **mean**

meantime ['miːn,taɪm] ADV pendant ce temps
• **in the meantime** ADV entre-temps
• **for the meantime** ADV pour l'instant

measles ['miːzəlz] N *Med* rougeole *f*; **to have (the) m.** avoir la rougeole

measly ['miːzlɪ] *(compar* **measlier**, *superl* **measliest**) ADJ *Fam* minable, misérable⁼; **all I got was one m. bar of chocolate!** je n'ai eu qu'une misérable tablette de chocolat!; **all that for a m. £5!** tout ça pour cinq malheureuses livres!

measurable ['meʒərəbəl] ADJ **1** *(rate, change, amount)* mesurable **2** *(noticeable, significant)* sensible, perceptible; **we've made m. progress** nous avons sensiblement progressé

measure ['meʒə(r)] N **1** *(measurement)* mesure *f*; **to give good** *or* **full m.** *(in length, quantity)* faire bonne mesure; *(in weight)* faire bon poids; **to give short m.** *(in quantity)* tricher sur la quantité; *(in weight)* tricher sur le poids; *Fig* **then she insulted the other man for good m.** elle a aussi insulté l'autre pour ne pas faire de jaloux; *Fig* **he gave him a couple of kicks for good m.** il lui a donné quelques coups de pied en prime; *Fig* **to take** *or* **to get the m. of sb** jauger qn, se faire une opinion de qn; **this award is a m. of their success** ce prix ne fait que refléter leur succès; **her joy was beyond m.** sa joie était incommensurable; **irritated/shocked beyond m.** extrêmement irrité/choqué
2 *(degree)* mesure *f*; **the country has gained a m. of independence** le pays a acquis une certaine indépendance; **in some m.** dans une certaine mesure, jusqu'à un certain point; **in large m.** dans une large mesure, en grande partie; **she inspired fear and respect in equal m.** elle inspirait autant de crainte que de respect
3 *(instrument ▸ ruler)* mètre *m*, règle *f*; *(▸ container)* mesure *f*
4 *(portion)* portion *f*, dose *f*; **she poured me a generous m. of gin** elle m'a servi une bonne dose de gin
5 *(step, legislation)* mesure *f*; **we have taken measures to correct the fault** nous avons pris des mesures pour rectifier l'erreur; **as a precautionary m.** par mesure de précaution
6 *Mus & Literature* mesure *f*
VT **1** *(take measurement of)* mesurer; **he measured me for a suit** il a pris mes mesures pour me faire un costume; *Fam Fig* **to m. one's length (on the floor** *or* **ground)** s'étaler de tout son long **2** *(judge)* jauger, mesurer, évaluer; **to m. oneself** *or* **one's strength against sb** se mesurer à qn; *Fig* **to m. one's words** mesurer *ou* peser ses paroles
VI **the room measures 18 feet by 12** la pièce mesure 18 pieds sur 12; **an earthquake measuring 6.2 on the Richter scale** un tremblement de terre d'une magnitude de 6,2 sur l'échelle de Richter

▸ **measure off** VT SEP mesurer

▸ **measure out** VT SEP mesurer; **m. out a pound of flour** mesurez une livre de farine; **he measured out a double gin** il versa un double gin

▸ **measure up** VT SEP *(wood)* mesurer; **to m. sb up for a suit** prendre les mesures de qn pour un costume; **to get measured up for a new suit** se faire prendre ses mesures pour un nouveau costume; *Fig* **to m. sb up** jauger qn, prendre la mesure de qn
VI être *ou* se montrer à la hauteur; **to m. up to sb's expectations** être à la mesure des espérances de qn; **the hotel didn't m. up** l'hôtel nous a déçus

measured ['meʒəd] ADJ **1** *(distance, length etc)* mesuré; *Sport* **the record over a m. mile** le record officiel sur un mile **2** *(careful, deliberate)* mesuré; **with m. steps** à pas mesurés *ou* comptés; **to speak in m. tones** parler sur un ton modéré

measurement ['meʒəmənt] N **1** *(dimension)* mesure *f*; **to take (down) the measurements of a piece of furniture** prendre les dimensions d'un meuble; **he took my measurements** il a pris mes mesures; **waist/hip m.** tour *m* de taille/de hanches; **what are her measurements?** quelles sont ses mensurations? **2** *(of freight)* cubage *m*, encombrement *m* **3** *(action)* mesurage *m*
▸▸ ***measurement ton*** tonne *f* d'encombrement

measuring ['meʒərɪŋ] N mesurage *m*
▸▸ ***measuring chain*** *(in surveying)* chaîne *f* d'arpenteur *ou* d'arpentage; ***measuring cup*** gobelet *m* doseur, *Can* tasse *f* à mesurer; ***measuring jug*** verre *m* gradué *ou* doseur; ***measuring spoon*** cuillère *f* à doser; ***measuring tape*** mètre *m* (à) ruban

meat [miːt] N **1** *(from animal)* viande *f*; *(from crab, lobster etc)* chair *f*; **red/white m.** viande *f* rouge/blanche; **cooked** *or* **cold meats** viande *f* froide; *Br* **m. and two veg** *Fam (stereotypical British meal)* = plat comportant de la viande et deux légumes *(typique de la gastronomie britannique traditionnelle)*; *very Fam Hum (male genitals)* service *m* trois pièces; *Fam* **there isn't much m. on him** il n'est pas très gras⁼; *Fam* **you're dead m.!** t'es mort!; *Prov* **one m.'s meat is another m.'s poison** le malheur des uns fait le bonheur des autres **2** *Literary (food)* nourriture *f*; **m. and drink** de quoi manger et boire; *Fig* **such incidents are m. and drink to novelists** les romanciers se repaissent de ce genre d'incidents **3** *(substance, core)* substance *f*; **there's not much m. in his report** il n'y a pas grand-chose dans son rapport
▸▸ ***meat cleaver*** hachoir *m*, couperet *m*; ***meat diet*** régime *m* carné; ***meat hook*** crochet *m* de boucherie; ***meat loaf*** pain *m* de viande; *Br Fam Pej* ***meat market*** *(nightclub)* = boîte de nuit réputée pour être un lieu de drague; ***meat pie*** pâté *m* de viande en croûte; ***meat products*** produits *mpl* à base de viande; ***meat safe*** garde-manger *m inv*; *Am Fam* ***meat wagon*** *(ambulance)* ambulance⁼ *f*

meatball ['miːtbɔːl] N **1** *Culin* boulette *f* (de viande) **2** *Am Fam (person)* crétin(e) *m,f*, andouille *f*

meathead ['miːt,hed] N *Am Fam* crétin(e) *m,f*, andouille *f*

meatpacking ['miːt,pækɪŋ] N *Am* abattage *m* et boucherie *f*

meaty ['miːtɪ] *(compar* **meatier**, *superl* **meatiest**) ADJ **1** *(taste, smell)* de viande; *(food)* riche en viande **2** *(fleshy ▸ hands, limbs)* épais **3** *(substantial ▸ role)* substantiel; *(▸ topic, story)* riche; *(▸ wine)* qui a du corps; **a m. novel** un roman riche

Mecca ['mekə] N La Mecque; *Fig* **it's a M. for book lovers** c'est la Mecque des bibliophiles; **the M. of country music** le haut lieu de la country

mechanic [mɪ'kænɪk] N mécanicien(enne) *m,f*
• **mechanics** N *(UNCOUNT) (study)* mécanique *f* NPL *(functioning)* mécanisme *m*; **the mechanics of government** les mécanismes *mpl* gouvernementaux, les rouages *mpl* du gouvernement

> Note that the French word **mécanique** is a false friend and is never a translation for the English word **mechanic**. It means **mechanics**.

mechanical [mɪ'kænɪkəl] ADJ **1** *(device, process)* mécanique **2** *(machine-like)* machinal, mécanique; **a m. gesture** un geste machinal; **her playing is very m.** *(of musician)* elle joue d'une façon très mécanique
▸▸ ***mechanical digger*** pelleteuse *f* mécanique; ***mechanical drawing*** dessin *m* aux instruments; ***mechanical engineer*** ingénieur *m* mécanicien; ***mechanical engineering*** génie *m* mécanique; ***mechanical failure*** défaillance *f ou* mécanique; ***mechanical fault*** défaut *m* mécanique; ***mechanical shovel*** pelle *f* mécanique, pelleteuse *f*

mechanically [mɪ'kænɪkəlɪ] ADV **1** *(operated)* mécaniquement; **I'm not m. minded** je ne suis pas très doué pour tout ce qui est mécanique; **m. recovered meat** viande *f* séparée mécaniquement **2** *Fig (like a machine)* machinalement, mécaniquement; **he answered m.** il a répondu machinalement

mechanism ['mekənɪzəm] N *also Fig* mécanisme *m*

mechanistic [,mekə'nɪstɪk] ADJ mécaniste

mechanization, -isation [,mekənaɪ'zeɪʃən] N mécanisation *f*

mechanize, -ise ['mekənaɪz] VT **1** *(equip with machinery)* mécaniser; **a highly mechanized industry** une industrie fortement mécanisée **2** *Mil (motorize)* motoriser

MEd [,em'ed] N *Univ (abbr* **Master of Education**) *(person)* = titulaire d'une maîtrise en sciences de l'éducation; *(qualification)* maîtrise *f* en sciences de l'éducation

Med [med] N *Br Fam* **the M.** la Méditerranée⁼

medal ['medəl] N médaille *f*; **to be awarded a m. for bravery** être décoré pour sa bravoure; *Fam* **you deserve a m.!** tu mérites une médaille!
▸▸ ***medal holder*** médaillé(e) *m,f*; *Am Mil* ***Medal of Honor*** = la plus haute distinction américaine donnée en récompense à un soldat

medallion [mɪ'dæljən] N médaillon *m*

medallist, *Am* **medalist** ['medəlɪst] N *(winner of medal)* médaillé(e) *m,f*; **the bronze m.** le (la) détenteur(trice) de la médaille de bronze

meddle ['medəl] VI **1** *(interfere)* **to m. in sth** se mêler de qch; **stop meddling in my affairs!** cessez de vous mêler de mes affaires!; **he can't resist the temptation to m.** il ne peut pas s'empêcher de se mêler de tout *ou* de ce qui ne le regarde pas **2** *(tamper)* **to m. with sth** toucher à qch, tripoter qch

meddler ['medələ(r)] N *(busybody)* **she's such a m.** il faut toujours qu'elle fourre son nez partout

meddlesome ['medəlsəm] ADJ indiscret(ète), qui se mêle de tout

meddling ['medəlɪŋ] N *(action)* ingérence *f* (in dans)
ADJ indiscret(ète), qui se mêle de tout

media ['miːdɪə] *pl of* **medium**
NPL **1** *(often sg)* **the m.** les médias *mpl*; **he works in the m.** il travaille dans les médias; **the news m.** la presse; **he knows how to handle the m.** il sait s'y prendre avec les journalistes; **the m. follow** *or* **follows her everywhere** les journalistes la suivent partout **2** *Comput (hardware)* support *m*
COMP des médias; *(interest, event, hype)* médiatique
▸▸ ***media circus*** cirque *m* médiatique; ***media coverage*** couverture *f* médiatique, médiatisation *f*; **to get too much m. coverage** être surmédiatisé;

media exposure *(coverage)* couverture *f* médiatique, médiatisation *f*; *(of product)* exposition *f* dans les médias; ***media group*** groupe *m* de médias; ***media mogul*** magnat *m* des médias; ***media overkill*** surmédiatisation *f*, médiatisation *f* excessive; ***media person*** homme *m*/femme *f* de communication; ***media studies*** = études en communication et journalisme

media-conscious ADJ *(politician etc)* médiatique

mediaeval, mediaevalism *etc* = **medieval, medievalism** *etc*

media-friendly ADJ médiatique

mediagenic [ˈmiːdɪəˌdʒenɪk] ADJ *(person)* médiatique

medial [ˈmiːdɪəl] N *Ling* médiale *f*
ADJ **1** *(average)* moyen **2** *(middle)* médian **3** *Ling* médial, médian

median [ˈmiːdjən] N **1** *Math* médiane *f* **2** *Am Aut* terre-plein *m* central, *Belg & Suisse* berme *f* centrale
ADJ médian
▸▸ *Am* ***median strip*** terre-plein *m* central, *Belg & Suisse* berme *f* centrale

mediant [ˈmiːdɪənt] N *Mus* médiante *f*

media-shy ADJ qui fuit les médias

mediate [ˈmiːdɪeɪt] VT **1** *(agreement, peace)* obtenir par médiation; *(dispute)* servir de médiateur dans, se faire le médiateur de; **the United States mediated an agreement between the two countries** les États-Unis ont servi de médiateur pour qu'un accord soit conclu entre les deux pays **2** *(moderate)* modérer
VI *(act as a peacemaker)* servir de médiateur; **to m. between** servir d'intermédiaire entre

mediation [ˌmiːdɪˈeɪʃən] N médiation *f*; **to go to m.** recourir à une médiation

mediator [ˈmiːdɪeɪtə(r)] N médiateur(trice) *m,f*

medic [ˈmedɪk] N *Fam* **1** *(doctor)* toubib *m* **2** *Br (medical student)* étudiant(e) *m,f* en médecine[□]

Medicaid [ˈmedɪkeɪd] N = aux États-Unis, programme fédéral d'assistance médicale pour les personnes défavorisées de moins de 65 ans

medical [ˈmedɪkəl] ADJ médical
N visite *f* médicale; **to have a m.** passer une visite médicale; **to pass/fail a m.** être déclaré apte/inapte à un travail après un bilan de santé
▸▸ ***medical attention*** soins *mpl* médicaux; ***medical care*** soins *mpl* médicaux; ***medical certificate*** certificat *m* médical; ***medical examination*** visite *f* médicale; *Am* ***medical examiner*** médecin *m* légiste; ***medical history*** *(of patient* ▸ *file)* dossier *m* médical; *(*▸ *previous problems)* antécédents *mpl* médicaux; ***medical insurance*** assurance *f* maladie; *Br* ***medical officer*** *Ind* médecin *m* du travail; *Mil* médecin *m* militaire; ***Medical Officer of Health*** directeur(trice) *m,f* de la santé publique; ***medical practitioner*** (médecin *m*) généraliste *mf*; ***the medical profession*** *(people)* le corps médical; *(activity)* la profession médicale; ***medical record*** dossier *m* médical; ***Medical Research Council*** = organisme public de financement des centres de recherche médicale et des hôpitaux en Grande-Bretagne; ***medical school*** faculté *f* de médecine; ***medical student*** étudiant(e) *m,f* en médecine

medically [ˈmedɪkəlɪ] ADV médicalement; **m. speaking** d'un point de vue médical; **m. approved** approuvé par les autorités médicales; **to be m. examined** passer une visite médicale

medicament [mɪˈdɪkəmənt] N médicament *m*

Medicare [ˈmedɪkeə(r)] N = aux États-Unis, programme fédéral d'assistance médicale pour les personnes âgées qui a largement contribué à réhabiliter socialement le troisième âge

medicate [ˈmedɪkeɪt] VT *(patient)* faire suivre un traitement à

medicated [ˈmedɪkeɪtɪd] ADJ *(shampoo, soap)* traitant

medication [ˌmedɪˈkeɪʃən] N médication *f*; **to be on m.** être sous traitement

medicinal [məˈdɪsɪnəl] ADJ médicinal; *Hum* **it's just for m. purposes** *(when having a drink)* c'est mon médicament
▸▸ ***medicinal plants*** plantes *fpl* médicinales; ***medicinal properties*** vertus *fpl* curatives

medicinally [məˈdɪsɪnəlɪ] ADV *(use a herb, substance)* médicalement, comme médicament; *(treat)* médicalement

medicine [ˈmedsɪn] N **1** *(practice, science)* médecine *f*; **to practise m.** exercer la médecine; **he studies m.** il est étudiant en médecine; **she studied m.** elle a fait des études de médecine **2** *(substance)* médicament *m*, remède *m*; *Br Fig* **to take one's m.** avaler la pilule; **to give sb a dose** *or* **taste of his/her own m.** rendre à qn la monnaie de sa pièce
▸▸ ***medicine ball*** medicine-ball *m*, médecine-ball *m*; ***medicine bottle*** flacon *m* de pharmacie; *Br* ***medicine cabinet, medicine chest*** (armoire *f* à) pharmacie *f*; ***medicine man*** sorcier *m*, medicine-man *m*

> Note that the French word **médecine** never means **remedy**.

medico [ˈmedɪkəʊ] *(pl* **medicos***)* *Br Fam* **1** *(doctor)* toubib *m* **2** *(medical student)* étudiant(e) *m,f* en médecine[□]

medieval [ˌmedɪˈiːvəl] ADJ **1** *Hist (art, literature, city)* médiéval; *(castle, church)* médiéval, du Moyen Âge; *(poet, lord)* du Moyen Âge; **in m. times** au Moyen Âge **2** *Fig Pej (primitive* ▸ *attitudes, facilities, person)* moyenâgeux
▸▸ ***Medieval Latin*** latin *m* médiéval

medievalist [ˌmedɪˈiːvəlɪst] N médiéviste *mf*

mediocre [ˌmiːdɪˈəʊkə(r)] ADJ médiocre

mediocrity [ˌmiːdɪˈɒkrətɪ] *(pl* **mediocrities***)* N **1** *(gen)* médiocrité *f* **2** *(mediocre person)* médiocre *mf*, incapable *mf*

meditate [ˈmedɪteɪt] VI **1** *(practise meditation)* méditer **2** *(reflect, ponder)* réfléchir, songer; **to m. on** *or* **upon sth** réfléchir *ou* songer à qch
VT songer à

meditation [ˌmedɪˈteɪʃən] N **1** *(thinking)* méditation *f*, réflexion *f* **2** *(state)* recueillement *m* **3** *Literature* **meditations** méditations *fpl* (**on** sur)

meditative [ˈmedɪtətɪv] ADJ méditatif; **m. atmosphere** atmosphère *f* de recueillement; **m. exercise** exercice *m* de méditation

meditatively [ˈmedɪtətɪvlɪ] ADV d'un air méditatif *ou* songeur

Mediterranean [ˌmedɪtəˈreɪnɪən] N **1 the M.** la Méditerranée **2** *(person)* Méditerranéen(enne) *m,f*
ADJ méditerranéen; **the M. sea** la mer Méditerranée

medium [ˈmiːdɪəm] *(pl sense* **1 media** [-dɪə], *pl senses* **2** *and* **3 media** [-dɪə] *or* **mediums**, *pl senses* **4, 5** *and* **6 mediums***)* N **1** *(means of communication)* moyen *m* (de communication), médium *m*, support *m*; *Art (for working in)* matériau *m*; **through the m. of the press** par voie de presse, par l'intermédiaire des journaux; **television is a powerful m. in education** la télévision est un très bon instrument éducatif; **his favourite m. is watercolour** son moyen d'expression favori est l'aquarelle
2 *Phys (means of transmission)* véhicule *m*, milieu *m*
3 *Biol (environment)* milieu *m*
4 *(spiritualist)* médium *m*
5 *(middle course)* milieu *m*; **the happy m.** le juste milieu
6 *(size)* taille *f* moyenne; **this T-shirt's a m.** ce tee-shirt est une taille moyenne *ou* un deux; **available in small, m. and large** disponible en petit, moyen et grand
ADJ **1** *(gen)* moyen; **in the m. term** à moyen terme; **she's of m. height** elle est de taille moyenne; **m. dry wine** vin *m* demi-sec **2** *Culin (meat)* à point
▸▸ *Cin* ***medium close-up*** plan *m* rapproché; *Am Rad* ***medium frequency*** *(UNCOUNT)* ondes *fpl* moyennes; *Cin & TV* ***medium shot*** plan *m* moyen; *Br Rad* ***medium wave*** *(UNCOUNT)* ondes *fpl* moyennes; **on m. wave** sur (les) ondes moyennes

medium-dry ADJ *(wine)* demi-sec

medium-haul ADJ *(flight, route)* moyen-courrier

medium-range ADJ *(missile)* à moyenne portée

medium-rare ADJ *Culin (meat)* entre saignant et à point

medium-size, medium-sized ADJ moyen, de taille moyenne

medium-term ADJ à moyen terme
▸▸ *Fin* ***medium-term credit*** crédit *m* (à) moyen terme; *EU* ***medium-term financial assistance*** aide *f* financière à moyen terme; *Fin* ***medium-term liabilities*** dettes *fpl* à moyen terme; *Fin* ***medium-term note*** billet *m* à moyen terme (négociable)

medlar [ˈmedlə(r)] N *Bot (fruit)* nèfle *f*; *(tree)* néflier *m*

medley [ˈmedlɪ] N **1** *(mixture)* mélange *m* **2** *Mus* pot-pourri *m* **3** *(in swimming)* quatre nages *m inv*; **400 metres m. (race)** 4 x 100 mètres quatre nages

medulla [mɪˈdʌlə] N **1** *Anat (part of organ, structure)* moelle *f* **2** *Bot* moelle *f*
▸▸ *Anat* ***medulla oblongata*** *(of brain)* bulbe *m* rachidien

meek [miːk] ADJ doux (douce), docile; **m. and mild** doux comme un agneau

meekly [ˈmiːklɪ] ADV doucement, docilement

meekness [ˈmiːknɪs] N douceur *f*, docilité *f*

meerschaum [ˈmɪəʃəm] N **1** *(pipe)* pipe *f* en écume **2** *(mineral)* écume *f* de mer, magnésite *f*

MEET [miːt]

> **VT**
> - rencontrer **1, 5, 8, 9**
> - rejoindre **2**
> - aller/venir chercher **3**
> - satisfaire **6**
> - accueillir **10**
> - retrouver **2**
> - attendre **3**
> - faire la connaissance de **5**
> - régler **7**
>
> **VI**
> - se rencontrer **1, 3, 5–7**
> - faire connaissance **3**
> - se retrouver **2**
> - se rejoindre **2**
> - se réunir **4**

(pt & pp **met** [met]*)*
VT **1** *(by chance)* rencontrer; **guess who I met this morning** devine qui j'ai rencontré ce matin; **to m. sb on the stairs** croiser qn dans l'escalier; *Fam* **fancy meeting you here!** je ne m'attendais pas à te trouver ici![□]
2 *(by arrangement)* retrouver, rejoindre; **I'll m. you after work** je te retrouverai après le travail; **I'm meeting Gregory this afternoon** j'ai rendez-vous avec Gregory cet après-midi
3 *(wait for, collect)* attendre, aller *ou* venir chercher; **nobody was at the station to m. me** personne ne m'attendait à la gare; **I'll be there to m. the bus** je serai là à l'arrivée du car; **he'll m. us at the station** il viendra nous chercher à la gare
4 *(greet)* **she came to m. us** elle est venue à notre rencontre
5 *(make acquaintance of)* rencontrer, faire la connaissance de; **I met him last year** je l'ai rencontré *ou* j'ai fait sa connaissance l'année dernière; **have you met my husband?** vous connaissez mon mari?; **I'd like you to m. Mr Jones** j'aimerais vous présenter M. Jones; **m. Mrs Dickens** je vous présente Mme Dickens; **(I'm very) glad** *or* **pleased to m. you** enchanté (de faire votre connaissance); **nice meeting you** *or* **to have met you** enchanté d'avoir fait votre connaissance; **she's the nicest person I've ever met** c'est la personne la plus gentille que j'ai jamais rencontrée; **I like meeting people** j'aime rencontrer des gens
6 *(satisfy* ▸ *a need)* satisfaire, répondre à; **to m. sb's requirements** satisfaire aux besoins de qn; **supply isn't meeting demand** l'offre est inférieure à la demande; **it didn't m. my expectations** ce n'était pas aussi bien que je l'espérais; *Fig* **to m. sb halfway** trouver un compromis avec qn
7 *(settle* ▸ *payment)* régler; **to m. sb's expenses** subvenir aux frais de qn; **the cost will be met by the company** les frais seront pris en charge par la compagnie
8 *(face* ▸ *opponent)* rencontrer; *(enemy)* affronter; *(difficulty, obstacle)* se heurter à, rencontrer; **he meets the champion on Saturday** il rencontre le champion samedi; **how are we going to m. the**

challenge? comment allons-nous relever le défi?; **to m. one's death** trouver la mort
9 *(come in contact with)* rencontrer; **his hand/mouth met hers** leurs mains/bouches se rencontrèrent; **my eyes met his** nos regards se croisèrent *ou* se rencontrèrent; **he couldn't m. her eye** il ne pouvait pas la regarder dans les yeux; **a remarkable sight met our eyes** nous avons été témoins d'un spectacle incroyable; **there's more to this than meets the eye** on ne connaît pas les dessous de cette affaire
10 *(treat)* accueillir; **his suggestion was met with howls of laughter** sa proposition a été accueillie par des éclats de rire
11 *(join)* **the stream meets the river** le ruisseau se jette dans la rivière; **where East meets West** où l'est et l'ouest se rencontrent; **here the road meets the railway** c'est ici que la route rejoint *ou* croise le chemin de fer
VI 1 *(by chance)* se rencontrer
2 *(by arrangement)* se retrouver, se rejoindre, se donner rendez-vous; **let's m. for lunch** on déjeune ensemble?; **shall we m. at the station?** on se retrouve *ou* on se donne rendez-vous à la gare?; **we arranged to m. at the station** nous nous sommes donné rendez-vous à la gare; **we should m. more often** on devrait se voir plus souvent; **they weren't to m. again for a long time** ils ne devaient pas se revoir avant longtemps
3 *(become acquainted)* se rencontrer, faire connaissance; **we met in 1989** nous nous sommes rencontrés en 1989; **have you two met?** est-ce que vous vous connaissez déjà?, vous vous êtes déjà rencontrés?
4 *(assemble)* se réunir; **the committee meets once a month** le comité se réunit une fois par mois
5 *(join ▸ lines, wires)* se rencontrer, se joindre; **the cross stands where four roads m.** la croix se trouve à la jonction de quatre routes; **their eyes met** leurs regards se rencontrèrent *ou* se croisèrent; **his eyebrows m. in the middle** ses sourcils se touchent
6 *(teams, opponents)* se rencontrer, s'affronter; *(armies)* s'affronter, se heurter
7 *(come into contact)* se rencontrer; **the two cars met head on** les deux voitures se sont heurtées de plein fouet
N 1 *Br (in hunting)* rendez-vous *m* (de chasse)
2 *esp Am Sport* rencontre *f*, **athletics m.** rencontre *f ou* meeting *m* d'athlétisme
ADJ *Arch or Formal (suitable)* séant, convenable; *(right)* juste; **it is only m. that...** ce n'est que justice que...
▸ **meet up VI** *(by chance)* se rencontrer; *(by arrangement)* se retrouver, se donner rendez-vous; **we'll have to m. up next time I'm in Paris** il faudra qu'on se voie la prochaine fois que je passerai à Paris; **we met up with an Australian** nous avons rencontré un Australien
▸ **meet with VT INSEP 1** *(encounter ▸ difficulty)* rencontrer; **they met with considerable difficulties** ils ont rencontré d'énormes difficultés; **the agreement met with general approval** l'accord a reçu l'approbation générale; **to m. with a refusal** se heurter à *ou* essuyer un refus; **to m. with failure** échouer; **the proposal has met with fierce opposition** la proposition s'est heurtée à une opposition très vive; **the expedition met with disaster** l'expédition a tourné au désastre; **I'm afraid your dog has met with an accident** j'ai bien peur que votre chien n'ait eu un (petit) accident **2** *esp Am (person ▸ by chance)* rencontrer; *(▸ by arrangement)* rejoindre, retrouver; **the Governor met with Church dignitaries** le Gouverneur s'est entretenu avec *ou* a rencontré les dignitaires de l'Église

meet-and-greet N rencontre *f*
VT *(guests)* accueillir

meeting ['mi:tɪŋ] **N 1** *(assembly)* réunion *f*; *Pol* assemblée *f*, meeting *m*; *Br Sport* rencontre *f*, meeting *m*; **to hold a m.** tenir une réunion; **he's in a m.** il est en réunion; **to call a m. of the committee/the workforce** convoquer les membres du comité/le personnel; **to open the m.** déclarer la séance ouverte; **to address the m.** prendre la parole; **the m. voted in favour of the measure** l'assemblée a voté la proposition; **the (general) m. of shareholders** l'assemblée (générale) des actionnaires
2 *(encounter)* rencontre *f*; **a chance m. in the street** une rencontre fortuite dans la rue; *Fig* **m. of minds** accord *m* possible
3 *(arranged)* rendez-vous *m*; **I have a m. with the boss this morning** j'ai rendez-vous avec le patron ce matin
4 *(junction ▸ of roads)* jonction *f*, rencontre *f*; *(▸ of rivers)* confluent *m*
5 *Rel (for Quakers)* culte *m*; **to go to m.** aller au culte
▸▸ ***meeting place*** *(for gatherings)* lieu *m* de réunion; *(for rendez-vous)* (lieu *m* de) rendez-vous *m*

meet-up N *Comput* rencontre *f* organisée sur Internet

meg [meg] **N** *Fam Comput* méga *m*

> **MEGA-** PRÉFIXE
>
> • Dans un contexte scientifique, le préfixe **mega-**, qui signifie 'million', sert à former des termes tels que:
> **megabyte** méga-octet; **megawatt** mégawatt; **megadeath** million de morts; **a five-megaton bomb** une bombe de cinq mégatonnes.
>
> • Dans un contexte plus familier, **mega-** peut véhiculer deux notions distinctes:
> (a) la notion de TRÈS GRANDE TAILLE. Dans ce sens il s'emploie avec des noms pour former de nouveaux termes tels que:
> **megastore** très grand magasin; **megamerger** mégafusion; **she's a megastar** c'est une superstar; **her job pays megabucks** elle gagne une fortune dans son travail.
> (b) la notion d'INTENSITÉ. Dans ce sens on l'emploie avec des adjectifs pour former de nouveaux termes, et il se traduit le plus souvent par le préfixe **hyper-**:
> **mega-famous** hyper célèbre; **mega-stupid** hyper débile; **she's mega-rich** elle est hyper riche; **it's mega-difficult** c'est hyper difficile.

mega ['megə] *Fam* **ADJ** *(excellent)* génial, super *(inv)*, géant; *(enormous)* énorme[□]; **all their records have been m. hits** tous leurs disques ont eu un succès énorme
ADV *(very)* hyper, méga

mega- ['megə] **PREF** *Fam* hyper; **m.-rich** hyper riche; **m.-famous** hyper célèbre; **m.-angry** hyper en colère

megabit ['megəbɪt] **N** *Comput* mégabit *m*

megabucks ['megəbʌks] **N** *Fam* un fric fou, une fortune

megabyte ['megəbaɪt] **N** *Comput* méga-octet *m*; **512 megabytes of RAM** capacité *f* mémoire de 512 méga-octets

megacycle ['megəˌsaɪkəl] **N** mégacycle *m*

megadeath ['megədeθ] **N** million *m* de morts; **weapons capable of causing 100 megadeaths** des armes capables de faire des centaines de millions de morts

megahertz ['megəhɜ:ts] *(pl* **inv***)* **N** *Comput* mégahertz *m*

megalith ['megəlɪθ] **N** mégalithe *m*

megalithic [ˌmegə'lɪθɪk] **ADJ** mégalithique

megalomania [ˌmegələ'meɪnjə] **N** mégalomanie *f*

megalomaniac [ˌmegələ'meɪnɪæk] **N** mégalomane *mf*
ADJ mégalomane

megamerger ['megəˌmɜ:dʒə(r)] **N** *Fin* mégafusion *f*

megaphone ['megəfəʊn] **N** porte-voix *m inv*, mégaphone *m*

megapixel ['megəpɪksəl] **N** mégapixel *m*

megaplex ['megəpleks] **N** *Am Cin* complexe *m ou* cinéma *m* multisalle(s)

megastar ['megəstɑ:(r)] **N** *Fam* superstar *f*

megastore ['megəstɔ:(r)] **N** mégastore *f*

megaton ['megətʌn] **N** mégatonne *f*; **a five m. bomb** une bombe de cinq mégatonnes

megavolt ['megəvɒlt] **N** mégavolt *m*

megawatt ['megəwɒt] **N** mégawatt *m*

megilla [mə'gɪlə] **N** *Am Fam* **the whole m.** tout le tremblement

meiosis [maɪ'əʊsɪs] *(pl* **meioses** [-si:z]*)* **N 1** *Biol* méiose *f* **2** *(in rhetoric)* litote *f*

melaena [me'li:nə] **N** *Med* melæna *m*, méléna *m*

melancholia [ˌmelən'kəʊlɪə] **N** *Old-fashioned Psy* mélancolie *f*

melancholic [ˌmelən'kɒlɪk] **N** mélancolique *mf*
ADJ mélancolique

melancholy ['melənkəlɪ] **N** *Literary* mélancolie *f*
ADJ *(person, mood)* mélancolique; *(news, sight, thought)* sombre, triste

melee, mêlée ['meleɪ] **N** mêlée *f*

mellifluous [me'lɪfluəs], **mellifluent** [me'lɪfluənt] **ADJ** *Literary* mélodieux, doux (douce); **m. prose** un style fluide

mellow ['meləʊ] **ADJ 1** *(fruit)* mûr; *(wine)* velouté **2** *(bricks)* patiné; *(light)* doux (douce), tamisé; *(colour)* doux (douce); *(voice, music)* doux (douce), mélodieux
3 *(person, mood)* serein, tranquille; **to become** *or* **to grow m.** s'adoucir; *(with age)* mûrir
4 *Fam (tipsy)* éméché
5 *Fam (on drugs)* **to be m.** être parti, planer
VT *(of age, experience)* adoucir, faire mûrir; *(of food, alcohol)* détendre, décontracter
VI 1 *(fruit)* mûrir; *(wine)* devenir moelleux, se velouter **2** *(light, colour)* s'adoucir; *(stone, brick, building)* se patiner; *(sound, music)* s'adoucir, devenir plus mélodieux; **her voice has mellowed** sa voix s'est adoucie **3** *(person ▸ with age)* s'adoucir; *(▸ with food, alcohol)* se décontracter; **he's mellowed a lot since those days** il s'est beaucoup adouci depuis cette époque; **after the second whisky he began to m.** après le deuxième whisky, il a commencé à se décontracter
▸ **mellow out VI** *Fam (relax)* se relaxer

mellowing ['meləʊɪŋ] **N 1** *(of fruit, wine)* maturation *f* **2** *(of person, mood, light)* adoucissement *m*
ADJ adoucissant; **the alcohol had a m. effect on them** l'alcool les a détendus

mellowness ['meləʊnɪs] **N 1** *(of fruit)* douceur *f*; *(of wine)* moelleux *m*, velouté *m* **2** *(of light, colour)* douceur *f*; *(of voice, music)* douceur *f*, mélodie *f* **3** *(of person, mood)* douceur *f*, sérénité *f*

melodic [mɪ'lɒdɪk] **ADJ** mélodique

melodious [mɪ'ləʊdjəs] **ADJ** mélodieux

melodiously [mɪ'ləʊdjəslɪ] **ADV** mélodieusement

melodrama ['meləˌdrɑ:mə] **N** mélodrame *m*

melodramatic [ˌmelədrə'mætɪk] **ADJ** mélodramatique; **don't be so m.!** n'en fais pas tout un drame!
• **melodramatics NPL** goût *m* du mélodrame; **I'm fed up with his melodramatics** j'en ai assez de son cinéma

melodramatically [ˌmelədrə'mætɪkəlɪ] **ADV** de façon mélodramatique; *(say, speak)* d'un air mélodramatique

melody ['melədɪ] *(pl* **melodies***)* **N** mélodie *f*

melon ['melən] **N 1** *(fruit)* melon *m* **2** *Am Fam (profits, money)* gros bénéfices *mpl* (à distribuer)[□]; **to carve** *or* **to cut up the m.** distribuer les bénéfices **3** *Fam* **melons** *(breasts)* nichons *mpl*, roberts *mpl*

melt [melt] **VI 1** *(become liquid)* fondre; **that chocolate melts in your mouth** ce chocolat fond dans la bouche; *Fig* **his heart melted** ça l'a attendri **2** *(disappear)* **to m. (away), to m. into thin air** disparaître, s'évaporer **3** *(blend)* se fondre; **he tried to m. into the crowd** il a essayé de se fondre *ou* de disparaître dans la foule; **the images melted into one another** les images se fondaient les unes dans les autres
VT *(gen)* (faire) fondre; *(metal)* fondre; **the sun will m. the ice** le soleil fera fondre la glace; **m. the butter in a pan** faire fondre le beurre dans une poêle; *Fig* **to m. sb's heart** attendrir (le cœur de) qn

N *(sandwich)* **bacon/tuna m.** sandwich *m* au bacon/au thon recouvert de fromage fondu

▸ **melt away** **VI 1** *(snow)* fondre complètement **2** *(clouds, vapour)* se dissiper; *(crowd)* se disperser; *(anger, objections, resistance etc)* se dissiper, s'évanouir

▸ **melt down** **VT SEP** (faire) fondre
VI fondre

meltdown ['meltdaʊn] **N 1** *Nucl* fusion *f* (du cœur) **2** *Fig* désintégration *f*; *(of Stock Exchange)* dégringolade *f*

melting ['meltɪŋ] **ADJ 1** *(becoming liquid)* fondant; **m. ice/snow** de la glace/neige qui fond **2** *Fig* attendrissant
N *(of ice, snow)* fonte *f*; *(of metal)* fusion *f*, fonte *f*
▸▸ ***melting point*** point *m* de fusion; ***melting pot*** creuset *m*; *Fig* melting-pot *m*; *Fig* **everything's in the m. pot** tout est à refaire; *Fig* **a m. pot of several cultures** un mélange de plusieurs cultures

member ['membə(r)] **N 1** *(of club, union, political party etc)* membre *m*, adhérent(e) *m,f*; **to become a m. of a club/of a political party** devenir membre d'un club/d'un parti politique, adhérer à un club/à un parti politique
2 *(of group, family, class)* membre *m*; **to be a m. of the family** faire partie de la famille; **it's a m. of the cat family** il fait partie de *ou* il appartient à la famille des félins; **a m. of the opposite sex** une personne du sexe opposé; **a m. of the audience** un spectateur; **a m. of the public** un membre du public
3 *Archit* membre *m*
4 *Math* membre *m*
5 *Anat* membre *m*; **(male) m.** membre *m* (viril)
• **Member** **N** *(of legislative body)* **the M. (of Parliament) for Oxford** le député d'Oxford
▸▸ ***Member of Congress*** membre *m* du Congrès; ***member country*** pays *m* membre; ***Member of the European Parliament*** député(e) *m,f* européen (enne), membre *m* du Parlement européen; *St Exch* ***member firm*** société *f* membre; ***Member of the House of Representatives*** membre *m* de la Chambre des représentants; *Br* ***Members' Lobby*** = salle adjacente à la salle des débats de la Chambre des communes, où se retrouvent les députés; ***Member of Parliament*** membre *m* de la Chambre des communes, ≃ député(e) *m,f*; ***member state*** État *m* membre

membership ['membəʃɪp] **N 1** *(condition)* adhésion *f*; **m. of the union will entitle you to vote in meetings** l'adhésion au syndicat vous donne le droit de voter lors des réunions; **to apply for m.** faire une demande d'adhésion; **they have applied for m. of the EU** ils ont demandé à entrer dans *ou* à faire partie de l'UE; **she resigned her m. of the party** elle a rendu sa carte du parti **2** *(body of members)* **our club has a large m.** notre club compte de nombreux adhérents *ou* membres; **m. increased last year** le nombre d'adhérents a augmenté l'année dernière; **we have a m. of about 20** nous avons environ 20 adhérents
▸▸ ***membership card*** carte *f* d'adhérent *ou* de membre; ***membership fee*** cotisation *f*; ***membership list*** liste *f* des membres

membrane ['membreɪn] **N** *(gen)* & *Biol* membrane *f*

membranous ['membrənəs] **ADJ** membraneux

memento [mɪ'mentəʊ] *(pl* **mementos** *or* **mementoes)** **N** souvenir *m*

memo ['meməʊ] *(pl* **memos)** **N** note *f* de service
▸▸ ***memo pad*** bloc-notes *m*

memoir ['memwɑː(r)] **N 1** *(biography)* biographie *f* **2** *(essay, monograph)* mémoire *m*
• **memoirs** **NPL** *(autobiography)* mémoires *mpl*

> Attention: ne pas confondre avec le nom anglais **memory**.

memorable ['memərəbəl] **ADJ** mémorable, inoubliable; **one of the more m. scenes in the film** l'une des scènes les plus mémorables du film

memorably ['memərəblɪ] **ADV as Racine so m. puts it…** comme l'a si bien dit Racine…

memorandum [ˌmemə'rændəm] *(pl* **memoranda** [-də]) **N 1** *Com* note *f* (de service)
2 *Law* sommaire *m*
3 *(diplomatic communication)* mémorandum *m*
4 *(of contract, sale)* mémoire *m*
▸▸ *Br* ***memorandum and articles of association*** statuts *mpl* de société; *Br* ***memorandum of association*** charte *f* constitutive d'une société à responsabilité limitée, acte *m* de société; ***memorandum book*** carnet *m*, calepin *m*, agenda *m*

memorial [mɪ'mɔːrɪəl] **N 1** *(monument)* monument *m* (commémoratif), mémorial *m* **2** *(diplomatic memorandum)* mémorandum *m*; *(petition)* pétition *f*; *(official request)* requête *f*, mémoire *m*
ADJ 1 *(commemorative* ▸ *statue, festival, tablet, plaque etc)* commémoratif; **the Marcel Proust m. prize** le prix Marcel Proust **2** *(of memory)* mémoriel
▸▸ *Am* ***Memorial Day*** = dernier lundi du mois de mai *(férié aux États-Unis en l'honneur des soldats américains morts pour la patrie)*; ***memorial service*** commémoration *f*

memorize, -ise ['meməraɪz] **VT** mémoriser

memory ['memərɪ] *(pl* **memories)** **N 1** *(faculty)* mémoire *f*; **to have a good/bad m.** avoir (une) bonne/mauvaise mémoire; **to have a short m.** avoir la mémoire courte; **I've got a very good/bad m. for names** j'ai/je n'ai pas une très bonne mémoire des noms; **to quote a figure from m.** citer un chiffre de mémoire *ou* de tête; **to commit sth to m.** apprendre qch par cœur; **to lose one's m.** perdre la mémoire; **m. loss, loss of m.** perte *f* de mémoire; **it will long remain in our memories** nous nous en souviendrons longtemps; **if (my) m. serves me well** *or* **right, to the best of my m.** si j'ai bonne mémoire, autant que je m'en souvienne; **within living m.** de mémoire d'homme
2 *(recollection)* souvenir *m*; **childhood memories** des souvenirs *mpl* d'enfance; **to have good/bad memories of sth** garder un bon/mauvais souvenir de qch; **I have very bad memories of that evening** j'ai de très mauvais souvenirs *ou* j'ai (gardé) un très mauvais souvenir de cette soirée; **to have no m. of sb/sth** n'avoir aucun souvenir de qn/qch; **her earliest memories are of music** ses plus anciens souvenirs sont des airs de musique; **to the m. of** à la mémoire de; **to keep the m. of sb/sth alive** *or* **green** garder vivant *ou* entretenir le souvenir de qn/qch; **to take a trip down m. lane** *(visit place)* aller sur les lieux de son passé; **this television programme will take viewers on a trip down m. lane** cette émission rappellera de vieux souvenirs aux téléspectateurs
3 *Comput* mémoire *f*; **how much m. does this computer have?** cet ordinateur a combien de mémoire?
• **in memory of** **PREP** en souvenir de
▸▸ *Comput* ***memory address*** adresse *f* de mémoire; ***memory bank*** bloc *m* de mémoire; ***memory card*** carte *f* mémoire; ***memory chip*** puce *f* mémoire; ***memory dump*** vidage *m* de mémoire; ***memory expansion card*** carte *f* d'extension de mémoire; ***memory management*** gestion *f* de mémoire; ***memory manager*** gestionnaire *m* de mémoire; ***memory mapping*** adresses *fpl* mémoire; ***memory stick*** clé *f* USB; ***memory upgrade*** ajout *m* de mémoire

> Attention: ne pas confondre avec le nom anglais **memoir**.

memory-intensive **ADJ** *Comput (application)* qui prend beaucoup de place en mémoire

memory-loadable **ADJ** *Comput* chargeable en résident

memory-resident **ADJ** *Comput* résident en mémoire

men [men] *pl of* **man**
▸▸ *Am* ***men's room*** toilettes *fpl (pour hommes)*

menace ['menəs] **N 1** *(threat)* menace *f*; **there was m. in his voice** il parlait d'un ton menaçant; *Br Law* **to demand money with menaces** = exiger de l'argent sous la menace **2** *(source of danger)* danger *m*; **these steps are a real m. at night** ces escaliers sont vraiment dangereux la nuit; **some drivers are a public m.** certains conducteurs constituent un véritable danger public *ou* sont de véritables dangers publics **3** *Fam (annoying person or thing)* plaie *f*; **that kid's a m.** cet enfant est une véritable plaie
VT menacer

menacing ['menəsɪŋ] **ADJ** menaçant

menacingly ['menəsɪŋlɪ] **ADV** *(act)* de manière menaçante; *(speak, look)* d'un air menaçant *(say)* d'un ton menaçant

menagerie [mɪ'nædʒərɪ] **N** ménagerie *f*

mend [mend] **N 1** *(darn)* reprise *f*; *(patch)* pièce **2** *Fam (idiom)* **to be on the m.** *(economy, situation* s'améliorer[□]; *(ill person)* se remettre[□], être e voie de guérison[□]
VT 1 *(repair* ▸ *machine, television, broken vase* réparer; *(*▸ *clothes)* raccommoder; *(*▸ *fishin net)* rem(m)ailler; *(*▸ *tool, road, shoes etc)* répa rer; *(darn* ▸ *socks)* repriser, ravauder; **to get o to have sth mended** faire réparer qch **2** *(rectif* rectifier, réparer; **to m. matters** arranger les cho ses; **to m. one's manners, to mend one's way** s'amender
VI *(improve* ▸ *patient)* se remettre, être en voi de guérison; *(*▸ *weather)* s'améliorer; *(*▸ *fracture broken bones)* se ressouder; *Fam* **you'll soon m.** t t'en remettras[□]

mendacious [men'deɪʃəs] **ADJ** *Formal (state ment, remark)* mensonger, fallacieux; *(person* menteur

mendacity [men'dæsətɪ] *(pl* **mendacities)** **N** *(UN COUNT) Formal* **1** *(characteristic)* propension *f* a mensonge **2** *(of account, report)* caractère *n* mensonger **3** *(lie)* mensonge *m*, mensonges *mp*

Mendelian [ˌmen'diːljən] **ADJ** mendélien

mendicant ['mendɪkənt] **N** mendiant(e) *m,f*
ADJ mendiant
▸▸ *Rel* ***mendicant order*** ordre *m* mendiant

mending ['mendɪŋ] **N 2** *(of clothes)* raccommo dage *m*; **I was doing some m.** je raccommodai des vêtements **2** *(clothes)* vêtements *mpl* à rac commoder; **I've got a whole pile of m. to do** j'a toute une pile de vêtements à raccommoder

menfolk ['menfəʊk] **NPL** hommes *mpl*; **all the m of the village** tous les hommes du village

menial ['miːnjəl] **ADJ** *(task)* ingrat; *(job, position* subalterne
N *(subordinate)* subalterne *mf*; *(servant)* domes tique *mf*, *Pej* laquais *m*

meningitis [ˌmenɪn'dʒaɪtɪs] **N** *Med* méningite *f* **to have m.** avoir la méningite

meniscus [mə'nɪskəs] *(pl* **meniscuses** *or* **menisc** [-'nɪsaɪ]) **N** ménisque *m*

menopausal [ˌmenə'pɔːzəl] **ADJ** ménopau sique; *(woman)* à la ménopause

menopause ['menəpɔːz] **N** ménopause *f*; **to be going through the m.** être en ménopause

mensch [menʃ] **N** *Am Fam (man)* chic type *m (woman)* brave femme *f*

menses ['mensiːz] **NPL** *Physiol* menstruations *fpl* règles *fpl*

menstrual ['menstrʊəl] **ADJ** menstruel
▸▸ ***menstrual cycle*** cycle *m* menstruel

menstruate ['menstrʊeɪt] **VI** avoir ses règles

menstruation [ˌmenstrʊ'eɪʃən] **N** menstruation *f*, règles *fpl*

mensuration [ˌmenʃə'reɪʃən] **N** mesurage *m*, mensuration *f*

menswear ['menzˌweə(r)] **N** *(UNCOUNT)* vête ments *mpl* pour hommes; **m. (department)** rayon *m* hommes

mental ['mentəl] **ADJ 1** *(intellectual)* mental
2 *(in the mind)* mental; **to make a m. note of st** prendre note de qch; **she made a m. note to speak to him about the matter** elle se promit de lui en parler
3 *(psychiatric)* mental; **it can cause great m. strain** cela peut provoquer une grande tension ner veuse; **he had a m. breakdown** il a fait une dé pression nerveuse
4 *Fam (mad)* dingue, cinglé; **to go m.** *(go mad)* devenir dingue *ou* cinglé, perdre la boule; *(lose one's temper)* péter les plombs, péter une durite, piquer une crise; *Br* **you should have seen the way they were shouting at each other, it was m.!** t'aurais vu comme ils se criaient dessus, c'était dingue!
▸▸ ***mental age*** âge *m* mental; ***mental arithmetic*** calcul *m* mental; ***mental block*** blocage *m* psychologique; **to have a m. block about sth** faire un blocage à propos de qch; ***mental cruelty*** cruauté

f mentale; ***mental defective*** handicapé(e) *m,f* mental(e); ***mental deficiency*** déficience *f ou* débilité *f* mentale; ***mental handicap*** handicap *m* mental; ***mental health*** santé *f* mentale; ***mental home, mental hospital*** hôpital *m* psychiatrique; ***mental illness*** maladie *f* mentale; ***mental image*** image *f*; ***mental patient*** malade *mf* mental(e); ***mental reservation*** doute *m*; ***mental retardation*** déficience *f* mentale *ou* intellectuelle

mentalist ['mentəlɪst] **N** *Fam* dingue *mf*

mentality [men'tælətɪ] (*pl* **mentalities**) **N** mentalité *f*

mentally ['mentəlɪ] **ADV** mentalement; **she's m. and physically exhausted** elle est épuisée mentalement et physiquement; **to be m. handicapped** être un(e) handicapé(e) mental(e); **the m. handicapped** les handicapés mentaux; **m. ill** malade *(mentalement)*; **the m. ill** les malades *mpl* mentaux; **m. defective** *or* **deficient** mentalement déficient; **m. disturbed** déséquilibré (mental); **m. retarded** (mentalement) arriéré

menthol ['menθɒl] **N** menthol *m*

▸▸ ***menthol cigarette*** cigarette *f* au menthol *ou* mentholée

mentholated ['menθəleɪtɪd] **ADJ** au menthol, mentholé

mention ['menʃən] **VT 1** *(talk about)* mentionner, faire mention de, parler de; **the newspapers didn't m. it** les journaux n'en ont pas fait mention *ou* n'en ont pas parlé; **she never mentions her past** elle ne parle jamais de son passé; **I'll m. it to him sometime** je lui en parlerai *ou* toucherai un mot à l'occasion; **I heard my name mentioned** j'ai entendu prononcer mon nom; **thank you very much – don't m. it!** merci beaucoup – il n'y a pas de quoi! *ou* je vous en prie!; **it's not worth mentioning** ça ne vaut pas la peine d'en parler; **I have no money worth mentioning** je n'ai pour ainsi dire pas d'argent

2 *(remark, point out)* signaler; **I should m. that it was dark at the time** il faut signaler *ou* je tiens à faire remarquer qu'il faisait nuit; **she mentioned that she had lived in Bristol** elle mentionna qu'elle avait vécu à Bristol

3 *(name, cite)* mentionner, citer, nommer; **don't m. any names** ne citez aucun nom; **someone, without mentioning any names, has broken my hairdryer** je ne citerai personne, mais quelqu'un a cassé mon sèche-cheveux; **just m. my name to her** dites-lui que c'est de ma part; **to m. sb in one's will** coucher qn sur son testament; **a range of subjects too numerous to m.** des sujets trop nombreux pour être tous cités

N mention *f*; **there's no m. of it in the papers** les journaux n'en parlent pas; **to make no m. of sth** passer qch sous silence, ne pas faire mention de qch; **there is no m. of this extra charge in the brochure** la brochure ne mentionne pas ce supplément; **he gets a brief m. in her autobiography** elle le mentionne brièvement dans son autobiographie; **at the m. of her name he turned white** quand il entendit son nom il pâlit; **special m. should be made of all the people behind the scenes** n'oublions pas tous ceux qui ont travaillé dans l'ombre *ou* en coulisse; **honourable m.** mention *f*

• **not to mention** **PREP** sans parler de; **not to m. the children** sans parler des enfants

mentor **N** ['mentɔː(r)] mentor *m*

VT ['mentə(r)] jouer les mentors auprès de

mentoring ['mentərɪŋ] **N** mentoring *m (relation de conseil et de soutien entre une personne expérimentée et un débutant)*

▸▸ ***mentoring scheme*** programme *m* de mentoring

menu ['menjuː] **N 1** *(in restaurant)* menu *m*; *(written)* menu *m*, carte *f*; **on the m.** au menu; **they have a very varied m.** ils ont une carte très variée *ou* des menus très variés **2** *Comput* menu *m*

▸▸ *Comput* ***menu bar*** barre *f* de menu; ***menu item*** élément *m* de menu; ***menu option*** option *f* de menu

menu-controlled **ADJ** *Comput* contrôlé par menu

menu-driven **ADJ** *Comput* commandé par menu

MEP [ˌemiː'piː] **N** *EU (abbr* **Member of the European Parliament)** député(e) *m,f* européen(enne), membre *m* du Parlement européen

Merc [mɜːk] **N** *Fam (abbr* **Mercedes®)** Mercedes®*f*

mercantile ['mɜːkəntaɪl] **ADJ 1** *Com & Fin* commercial **2** *Econ (concerning mercantilism)* mercantiliste

▸▸ ***mercantile bank*** banque *f* de commerce; ***mercantile law*** droit *m* commercial; ***mercantile nation*** nation *f* commerçante

mercantilism ['mɜːkəntɪlɪzəm] **N** mercantilisme *m*

mercantilist ['mɜːkəntɪlɪst] **N** mercantiliste *mf*

ADJ mercantiliste

mercenary ['mɜːsɪnərɪ] (*pl* **mercenaries**) **N** *Mil* mercenaire *m*

ADJ 1 *Pej* intéressé; **for purely m. reasons** uniquement pour l'argent; **must you be so m.?** tu ne penses qu'à l'argent! **2** *Mil* **m. soldier** mercenaire *m*

mercerized, -ised ['mɜːsəraɪzd] **ADJ** *(cotton)* mercerisé

merchandise ['mɜːtʃəndaɪz] **N** *(UNCOUNT)* marchandises *fpl*

VT commercialiser, marchandiser

merchandiser ['mɜːtʃəndaɪzə(r)] **N** *(object)* présentoir *m*; *(person)* marchandiseur *m*

merchandising ['mɜːtʃəndaɪzɪŋ] **N** merchandising *m*, marchandisage *m*, commercialisation *f*; **m. techniques** techniques *fpl* marchandes

merchant ['mɜːtʃənt] **N 1** *(trader)* négociant(e) *m,f*; *(shopkeeper)* marchand(e) *m,f*; **wool m.** lainier(ère) *m,f*, négociant(e) *m,f* en laines; **wine m.** marchand(e) *m,f* de vin **2** *Fig* **a doom m.** un prophète de malheur; *Fam* **speed m.** *Br (fast driver)* chauffard *m*; *Br Fam* **rip-off** *or* **con m.** arnaqueur(euse) *m,f*

ADJ marchand

▸▸ ***merchant bank*** banque *f* d'affaires *ou* d'investissement; ***merchant banker*** banquier(ère) *m,f* d'affaires; *Am* ***merchant marine*** marine *f* marchande; *Br* ***merchant navy*** marine *f* marchande; ***merchant seaman*** marin *m* de la marine marchande; ***merchant ship, merchant vessel*** navire *m* de commerce

merchantman ['mɜːtʃəntmən] (*pl* **merchantmen** [-mən]) **N** *Naut* navire *m* de commerce

merciful ['mɜːsɪfʊl] **ADJ** clément, miséricordieux; **to be m. to** *or* **towards sb** faire preuve de clémence *ou* de miséricorde envers qn; **her death was a m. release** sa mort a été une délivrance

mercifully ['mɜːsɪfʊlɪ] **ADV 1** *(luckily)* heureusement, par bonheur; **m., nobody was hurt** par bonheur il n'y a pas eu de blessés **2** *(with clemency)* avec clémence

merciless ['mɜːsɪlɪs] **ADJ** impitoyable, implacable

mercilessly ['mɜːsɪlɪslɪ] **ADV** sans merci, impitoyablement, implacablement; **the rain beat down m.** la pluie tombait sans répit

Mercosur ['mɜːkəʊsʊə(r)] **N** *(abbr* **Southern Common Market)** Mercosur *m*

mercurial [mɜː'kjʊərɪəl] **ADJ 1** *(changeable ▸ temperament, character, person)* versatile, changeant **2** *(lively)* vif, plein de vie, gai **3** *Chem* mercuriel

mercury ['mɜːkjʊrɪ] **N** *Chem* mercure *m*

• **Mercury** **PR N** *Myth* Mercure **N** *Astron* Mercure *f*

▸▸ ***mercury poisoning*** empoisonnement *m* au mercure

mercy ['mɜːsɪ] (*pl* **mercies**) **N 1** *(clemency)* clémence *f*, pitié *f*, indulgence *f*; *Rel* miséricorde *f*; **without m.** sans pitié, sans merci; **she had** *or* **showed no m.** elle n'a eu aucune pitié, elle a été sans pitié; **to have m. on sb** avoir pitié de qn; **(have) m.!** (ayez) pitié!; **to beg for m.** demander grâce; **to throw oneself on sb's m.** s'abandonner à la merci de qn **2** *(blessing)* chance *f*, bonheur *m*; **it's a m. that he doesn't know** heureusement qu'il ne sait pas, c'est une chance qu'il ne sache pas; **we must be thankful** *or* **grateful for small mercies** il faut savoir apprécier les moindres bienfaits **3** *(power)* merci *f*; **to be at sb's/sth's m.** être à la merci de qn/qch; **the ship was at the m. of the storm** le navire était à la merci de la tempête; *Ironic* **to leave sb to the tender mercies of sb** abandonner qn aux bons soins de qn

COMP *(flight)* de secours, humanitaire

EXCLAM *Old-fashioned* grâce!

▸▸ ***mercy killing*** *(euthanasia)* euthanasie *f*; *(individual death)* acte *m* d'euthanasie; ***mercy mission*** mission *f* humanitaire

mere¹ [mɪə(r)] **ADJ** seul, simple, pur; **it's a m. formality** ce n'est qu'une simple formalité; **a m. coincidence** une coïncidence pure et simple; **he's a m. child** ce n'est qu'un enfant; **the m. thought of it disgusts her** rien que d'y penser ça lui répugne; **the m. sight of fish makes me queasy** la seule vue du poisson me donne la nausée; **a m. 5 percent of the population** 5 pour cent seulement de la population; **his eyes light up at the m. mention of money** son regard s'allume dès qu'on commence à parler d'argent; **a m. assistant like me** un simple assistant comme moi; *Hum* **us m. mortals** nous autres, simples mortels

mere² **N** *Arch or Literary (lake)* (petit) lac *m*, étang *m*

merely ['mɪəlɪ] **ADV** seulement, (tout) simplement; **I was m. wondering if this is the best solution** je me demandais seulement *ou* simplement si c'était la meilleure solution; **she m. glanced at it** elle n'a fait qu'y jeter *ou* elle s'est contentée d'y jeter un coup d'œil; **I mention this m. to draw attention to...** je n'ai dit cela que pour attirer l'attention sur...

merengue [mə'reŋgeɪ] **N** *(dance, music)* merengué *m*

meretricious [ˌmerɪ'trɪʃəs] **ADJ** *Formal (glamour, excitement)* factice; *(impression)* faux (fausse); *(style)* ampoulé, pompier

merge [mɜːdʒ] **VI 1** *(join ▸ rivers)* se rejoindre, confluer; *(▸ roads)* se rejoindre; *(▸ colours, voices)* se confondre; *(▸ cultures)* se mélanger; *Pol* s'unir; **the sea and sky merged** le ciel et la mer se confondaient; **to m. into the background** *(building, person)* se fondre dans le décor **2** *(vanish)* **the thief merged into the crowd** le voleur s'est fondu dans la foule **3** *Fin (banks, companies)* fusionner

VT joindre, fusionner; *(banks, companies) & Comput* fusionner; *Pol* unifier; **the two regiments were merged (into one)** les deux régiments ont été regroupés

merger ['mɜːdʒə(r)] **N** *Fin (of banks, companies)* fusion *f*; *(takeover)* absorption *f*; **mergers and acquisitions** fusions *fpl* et acquisitions *fpl*

▸▸ ***merger talks*** discussions *fpl* en vue d'une fusion

meridian [mə'rɪdɪən] **N 1** *Astron, Geog & Med* méridien *m* **2** *Math* méridienne *f* **3** *Fig (zenith)* zénith *m*, sommet *m*, apogée *m*

ADJ *Astron & Geog (angle, latitude)* méridien

▸▸ ***meridian line*** (ligne *f*) méridienne *f*

meridional [mə'rɪdɪənəl] **N** méridional(e) *m,f*

ADJ 1 *(relating to a meridian)* méridien **2** *(southern)* méridional

meringue [mə'ræŋ] **N** meringue *f*

merino [mə'riːnəʊ] (*pl* **merinos**) **N** *(sheep, wool)* mérinos *m*

ADJ en mérinos

merit ['merɪt] **N** mérite *m*; **in order of m.** par ordre de mérite; **its great m. is its simplicity** ça a le grand mérite d'être simple; **promotion is on m. alone** l'avancement se fait uniquement au mérite; **according to one's merits** *(to be rewarded)* selon ses mérites; **a work of great m.** une œuvre remarquable; **to judge a proposal on its merits** juger une proposition pour ce qu'elle vaut; **the relative merits of theatre and cinema** les avantages *mpl* respectifs du théâtre et du cinéma

VT mériter; **the case merits closer examination** le cas mérite d'être examiné de plus près

▸▸ ***merit rating*** notation *f* du personnel; *Am Admin* ***merit system*** système *m* d'avancement fondé sur le mérite

meritocracy [ˌmerɪ'tɒkrəsɪ] (*pl* **meritocracies**) **N** méritocratie *f*

meritocratic [ˌmerɪtə'krætɪk] **ADJ** méritocratique

meritorious [ˌmerɪˈtɔːrɪəs] ADJ *(person)* méritant; *(act)* méritoire, louable

merlin [ˈmɜːlɪn] N*Orn* émerillon *m*

mermaid [ˈmɜːmeɪd] N*Myth* sirène *f*

merman [ˈmɜːmæn] *(pl* **mermen** [-men]*)* N *Myth* triton *m*

Merovingian [ˌmerəˈvɪndʒɪən] N Mérovingien (enne) *m,f*
ADJ mérovingien

merrily [ˈmerɪlɪ] ADV *(happily)* joyeusement, gaiement; *(blithely)* allègrement

merriment [ˈmerɪmənt] N *(joy)* joie *f*, gaieté *f*; *(laughter)* rire *m*, rires *mpl*, hilarité *f*; **there was much m. at the thought of this** l'idée fit beaucoup rire; **sounds of m. came from the garden** on entendait des éclats de rire venant du jardin

merry [ˈmerɪ] *(compar* **merrier**, *superl* **merriest)** ADJ **1** *(happy)* joyeux, gai; **M. Christmas!** Joyeux Noël!; **to make m.** s'amuser; *Prov* **the more the merrier** plus on est de fous, plus on rit **2** *Fam (tipsy)* éméché, pompette **3** *(good)* **the m. month of May** le joli mois de mai; *Literature* **Robin Hood and his m. men** Robin des Bois et ses joyeux compères; *Fam* **the weather is playing m. hell with the rail timetables** le mauvais temps a complètement chamboulé l'horaire des trains; *Fam* **my back is giving me m. hell** mon dos me fait souffrir le martyre; *Br* **to lead sb a m. dance** *(exasperate)* donner du fil à retordre à qn; *(deceive)* faire marcher qn; *(in romantic context)* mener qn en bateau
►► ***Merry England*** l'Angleterre *f* du bon vieux temps

merry-go-round N manège *m*, *Can, Belg & Suisse* carrousel *m*; *Fig (whirl)* tourbillon *m*

merrymaking [ˈmerɪˌmeɪkɪŋ] N*(UNCOUNT)* réjouissances *fpl*, festivités *fpl*

mescaline [ˈmeskəliːn], **mescalin** [ˈmeskəlɪn] N mescaline *f*

mesh [meʃ] N **1** *(of net)* mailles *fpl*; *(of sieve)* grille *f*; **fine-m. stockings** des bas *mpl* à mailles fines; **3 cm m. netting** du filet *m* à mailles de 3 cm; **a m. shopping bag** un filet à provisions
2 *(fabric)* tissu *m* à mailles; **nylon m.** tulle *m* de nylon
3 *Fig (trap)* rets *mpl*, piège *m*; **caught in a m. of lies** enfermé dans *ou* prisonnier de ses propres mensonges
4 *Fig (network)* réseau *m*; **a m. of intrigue** un réseau d'intrigues
5 *Tech (of gears)* engrenage *m*; **in m.** en prise
VI **1** *(be in harmony) (characters, temperaments)* s'harmoniser, s'accorder **2** *(tally, coincide)* cadrer, concorder (**with** avec) **3** *Tech (gears)* s'engrener

mesmeric [mezˈmerɪk] ADJ *Formal* magnétique, hypnotique

mesmerize, -ise [ˈmezməraɪz] VT **1** *(hypnotise)* hypnotiser **2** *(entrance)* ensorceler, envoûter

mesmerizing, -ising [ˈmezməraɪzɪŋ] ADJ fascinant

meson [ˈmiːzɒn] N *Phys* méson *m*

Mesopotamia [ˌmesəpəˈteɪmjə] N Mésopotamie *f*

MESS [mes]

> **N**
> • désordre **1** • saleté **2**
> • gâchis **3** • pétrin **4**
> • mess **5**
> **VT**
> • salir
> **VI**
> • embêter **1**

N **1** *(untidiness)* désordre *m*, fouillis *m*; **what a m.!** quel désordre!, quelle pagaille!; **Fiona's room is (in) a real m.!** il y a une de ces pagailles *ou* un de ces fouillis dans la chambre de Fiona!; **my papers are in a m.** mes papiers sont en désordre; **clear up this m.!** mets un peu d'ordre là-dedans!, range un peu tout ce fouillis!; *Fam* **your essay is a real m.!** ta rédaction est un vrai torchon!; **my hair's a m.!** je suis coiffé n'importe comment!; **you're a m., go and clean up** tu n'es pas présentable, va t'arranger
2 *(dirtiness)* saleté *f*, saletés *fpl*; **the cooker is (in) a horrible m.** la cuisinière est vraiment sale *ou* dégoûtante; **the dog has made a m. on the carpet** le chien a fait des saletés sur le tapis
3 *(muddle)* gâchis *m*; **to make a m. of sth** gâcher qch; **she's made a real m. of her life** elle a vraiment gâché sa vie; **to make a m. of things** tout gâcher; **this country is in a m.!** la situation dans ce pays n'est pas vraiment réjouissante!
4 *Fam (predicament)* pétrin *m*; **he's got himself into a bit of a m.** il s'est fourré dans de beaux draps *ou* dans le pétrin; **thanks for getting me out of that m.** merci de m'avoir tiré de ce pétrin
5 *Mil (canteen)* mess *m*
6 *Mil (food)* ordinaire *m*, gamelle *f*
7 *Arch (dish)* plat *m*; *Bible* **a m. of pottage** un plat de lentilles
VT *(dirty)* salir, souiller
VI **1** *Fam (meddle)* **to m. with sb** embêter qn; **don't m. with me!** ne me cherche pas!; **you shouldn't m. with people like that** *(get involved with)* tu ne devrais pas fréquenter des gens comme ça[a]; *(get on wrong side of)* tu ne devrais pas mécontenter ces gens-là[a]; **that's what happens when you m. with drugs!** voilà ce qui arrive quand on touche à la drogue!
2 *Br Fam (joke)* **it's true, no messing!** c'est vrai, sans blague!
3 *Mil* manger *ou* prendre ses repas au mess
►► *Naut* ***mess deck*** poste *m* d'équipage; *Mil* ***mess hall*** cantine *f*; *Br* ***mess tin*** gamelle *f*

►**mess about, mess around** *Fam* VT SEP *(person)* **to m. sb about** se moquer de qn, faire tourner qn en bourrique; **I'm fed up with being messed about by men** j'en ai marre des hommes qui me font tourner en bourrique
VI *Br* **1** *(waste time)* glander, glandouiller; *(dawdle, hang around)* traîner
2 *(potter)* bricoler; **he likes messing about in the garden** il aime s'occuper dans le jardin[a]
3 *(play the fool)* faire l'imbécile; **stop messing about and listen to me!** arrête de faire l'imbécile et écoute-moi!
4 *(meddle, fiddle)* tripoter, tripatouiller; **don't m. about with my computer** ne tripote pas mon ordinateur; *Fig* **to m. about with sb** *(annoy)* embêter qn; *(have an affair)* fricoter avec qn; **if I catch her messing about with my husband I'll kill her!** si je l'attrape à faire du gringue à mon mari, je la tue!

►**mess up** VT SEP **1** *(make disorderly* ► *room, papers)* mettre en désordre; **stop it, you'll m. up my hair!** arrête, tu vas me décoiffer! **2** *Fam (spoil)* ficher en l'air; **that's really messed up our plans!** ça a vraiment fichu nos projets en l'air! **3** *(dirty)* salir, souiller
VI *esp Am Fam (make a mistake)* tout rater; **to m. up on an exam** merdouiller dans *ou* à un examen

message [ˈmesɪdʒ] N **1** *(communication)* message *m*, commission *f*; *(written)* message *m*, mot *m*; *(e-mail, on answering machine)* message *m*; **to take/to leave a m.** prendre/laisser un message; **can you give her a m.?** pouvez-vous lui transmettre un message?
2 *(theme* ► *of book, advert)* message *m*; *(teaching* ► *of prophet)* message *m*, enseignement *m*; **a book/film with a m.** un livre/film qui fait passer un message; **to get one's m. across** se faire comprendre; *Fam* **(do you) get the m.?** tu piges?
3 *Scot* commission *f*, course *f*; **to go a m. for sb** faire une commission pour qn
4 *Ling* message *m*
• **messages** NPL *Ir & Scot (shopping)* courses *fpl*
►► *Comput* ***message board*** boîte *f* à messages; *Br Comput* ***message body*** corps *m* du message; *Comput* ***message box*** boîte *f* de dialogue; *Comput* ***message handling*** messagerie *f* (électronique); *Comput* ***message header*** en-tête *m* de message; *Comput* ***message switching*** commutation *f* de messages

messenger [ˈmesɪndʒə(r)] N *(gen)* messager (ère) *m,f*; *(errand boy* ► *in office)* coursier *m*; *(in hotel)* chasseur *m*, coursier *m*; *(in post office)* télégraphiste *mf*; *Br* **King's/Queen's m.** ≃ courrier *m* d'État; **by special m.** par porteur spécial
►► ***messenger boy*** coursier *m*, garçon *m* de courses; ***messenger service*** service *m* de messagerie

messiah [mɪˈsaɪə] N messie *m*
• **Messiah** N *Rel* Messie *m*

messianic [ˌmesɪˈænɪk] ADJ messianique

messily [ˈmesɪlɪ] ADV **1** *(untidily)* mal, de façon peu soignée; *(in a disorganized way)* n'importe comment; **she did it really m.** elle l'a vraiment fait n'importe comment; *Fig* **the affair ended m.** l'affaire s'est mal terminée **2** *(dirtily)* comme un cochon

messmate [ˈmesˌmeɪt] N = personne qui mange à la même table

Messrs, Messrs. [ˈmesəz] NPL *(abbr* **Messieurs)** MM *mpl*

mess-up N *Fam* confusion[a] *f*; **there was a m. over the dates** on s'est embrouillé dans les dates

messy [ˈmesɪ] *(compar* **messier**, *superl* **messiest)** ADJ **1** *(dirty* ► *hands, clothes)* sale, malpropre; **he's a m. eater** il mange salement; **don't get all m.** ne te salis pas; **it's a m. job** c'est salissant
2 *(untidy* ► *place)* en désordre, désordonné, mal tenu; *(*► *person)* peu soigné, négligé, débraillé; *(*► *hair)* ébouriffé, en désordre, en bataille
3 *(badly done)* bâclé; **a m. piece of homework** un devoir bâclé
4 *Fig (complicated)* compliqué, embrouillé, délicat; **a very m. business** une affaire très embrouillée; **a m. divorce** un divorce difficile *ou* compliqué

mestiza [meˈstiːzə] N = métisse d'Hispano-Américain et d'Indien d'Amérique

mestizo [meˈstiːzəʊ] *(pl* **mestizos)** N = métis d'Hispano-Américain et d'Indien d'Amérique

met [met] *pt & pp of* **meet**

metabolic [ˌmetəˈbɒlɪk] ADJ *Physiol* métabolique
►► ***metabolic rate*** taux *m* métabolique

metabolism [mɪˈtæbəlɪzəm] N *Physiol* métabolisme *m*; **to have a fast m.** avoir un métabolisme rapide

metabolize, -ise [mɪˈtæbəlaɪz] VT *Physiol* métaboliser

metacarpal [ˌmetəˈkɑːpəl] *Anat* N métacarpien *m*
ADJ métacarpien

metacarpus [ˌmetəˈkɑːpəs] *(pl* **metacarpi** [-paɪ]*)* N *Anat* métacarpe *m*

metal [ˈmetəl] *(Br pt & pp* **metalled**, *cont* **metalling**, *Am pt & pp* **metaled**, *cont* **metaling)** N **1** *(gen) & Chem* métal *m*; **made of m.** en métal
2 *Typ* plomb *m*
3 *(for road-building)* cailloutis *m*, empierrement *m*
4 *(in glassmaking)* pâte *f* de verre
COMP en métal
VT **1** *(cover with metal)* couvrir de métal **2** *(road)* empierrer
• **metals** NPL *Br Rail* voie *f* ferrée, rails *mpl*
►► ***metal detector*** détecteur *m* de métaux; ***metal engraver*** graveur(euse) *m,f* sur métaux; ***metal fatigue*** fatigue *f* du métal; ***metal polish*** produit *m* pour faire briller les métaux; ***metal wood*** *(golf club)* bois-métal *m*

metalanguage [ˈmetəˌlæŋgwɪdʒ] N métalangue *f*, métalangage *m*

metallic [mɪˈtælɪk] ADJ **1** *Chem* métallique **2** *(voice)* métallique; *(sound)* métallique, grinçant; *(taste)* de métal; **m. blue/grey** bleu *m*/gris *m* métallisé
►► ***metallic paint*** peinture *f* métallisée

metallurgic [ˌmetəˈlɜːdʒɪk], **metallurgical** [ˌmetəˈlɜːdʒɪkəl] ADJ métallurgique

metallurgy [meˈtælədʒɪ] N métallurgie *f*

metalorganic [ˌmetəlɔːˈgænɪk] ADJ *Chem* organométallique
►► ***metalorganic compound*** organométallique *f*

metalwork [ˈmetəlwɜːk] N **1** *(objects)* ferronnerie *f* **2** *(activity)* travail *m* des métaux **3** *(metal framework)* tôle *f*, métal *m*; *(of crashed car, plane)* carcasse *f*

metalworker [ˈmetəlˌwɜːkə(r)] N **1** *(in factory)* métallurgiste *mf* **2** *(craftsman)* ferronnier(ère) *m,f*

metamorphic [ˌmetəˈmɔːfɪk] ADJ métamorphique

metamorphose [ˌmetəˈmɔːfəʊz] VT métamorphoser

VI se métamorphoser; **to m. into sth** se métamorphoser en qch

metamorphosis [ˌmetəˈmɔːfəsɪs, ˌmetəmɔːˈfəʊsɪs] (*pl* **metamorphoses** [-siːz]) **N** métamorphose *f*

metaphor [ˈmetəfə(r)] **N** métaphore *f*; **it's a m. for loneliness** c'est une métaphore de la solitude

metaphoric [ˌmetəˈfɒrɪk], **metaphorical** [ˌmetəˈfɒrɪkəl] **ADJ** métaphorique

metaphorically [ˌmetəˈfɒrɪkəlɪ] **ADV** métaphoriquement; **m. speaking** métaphoriquement

metaphysical [ˌmetəˈfɪzɪkəl] **ADJ** métaphysique; *Fig (abstract)* métaphysique, abstrait

metaphysics [ˌmetəˈfɪzɪks] **N** *(UNCOUNT)* métaphysique *f*

metasearch [ˈmetəˌsɜːtʃ] **N** *Comput* métarecherche *f*

▸▸ ***metasearch engine*** métamoteur *m* (de recherche)

metatarsal [ˌmetəˈtɑːsəl] *Anat* **N** métatarsien *m*
ADJ métatarsien

metatarsus [ˌmetəˈtɑːsəs] (*pl* **metatarsi** [-saɪ]) **N** *Anat* métatarse *m*

▸ **mete out** [miːt-] **VT SEP** *(punishment)* infliger; *(judgment, justice)* rendre; *(reward)* décerner

metempsychosis [ˌmetəmsaɪˈkəʊsɪs] **N** métempsychose *f*

meteor [ˈmiːtɪə(r)] **N** *Astron* météore *m*

▸▸ ***meteor shower*** pluie *f* d'étoiles filantes, averse *f* météorique

meteoric [ˌmiːtɪˈɒrɪk] **ADJ 1** *Astron* météorique **2** *Fig* fulgurant, très rapide; **Hitler's m. rise to power** l'ascension fulgurante d'Hitler au pouvoir

meteorite [ˈmiːtjəraɪt] **N** *Astron* météorite *f*

meteorological [ˌmiːtjərəˈlɒdʒɪkəl] **ADJ** météorologique

▸▸ ***meteorological office*** office *m* météorologique

meteorologist [ˌmiːtjəˈrɒlədʒɪst] **N** météorologue *mf*, météorologiste *mf*

meteorology [ˌmiːtjəˈrɒlədʒɪ] **N** météorologie *f*

meter [ˈmiːtə(r)] **N 1** *(for water, gas, electricity)* compteur *m*; **to read the m.** relever le compteur; **to feed the m.** mettre des pièces dans le compteur **2** *(parking)* **m.** parcmètre *m*, parcomètre *m*; *(taxi)* **m.** taximètre *m*, compteur *m*; *Fam* **I'm on a m.** je suis garé à un parcmètre[a] **3** *Am* = **metre**

VT 1 *(electricity, water, gas)* mesurer à l'aide d'un compteur **2** *(mail)* affranchir *(avec une machine)*

▸▸ *Am Fam* ***meter maid*** contractuelle[a] *f*, pervenche *f*, *Can* préposée *f* au stationnement; ***meter reader*** *(person)* releveur(euse) *m,f* de(s) compteur(s); ***meter reading*** relevé *m* (de(s) compteur(s))

methadone [ˈmeθəˌdəʊn] **N** *Pharm* méthadone *f*; **to be on m.** *(drug addict)* prendre de la méthadone

methane [ˈmiːθeɪn] **N** *Chem* méthane *m*

methinks [mɪˈθɪŋks] (*pt* **methought** [-ˈθɔːt]) **VT** *Arch or Hum* ce me semble

method [ˈmeθəd] **N 1** *(means)* méthode *f*, moyen *m*; *(manner)* manière *f*; *(instruction)* méthode *f*, mode *m* d'emploi; **m. of doing sth** manière *f* de faire qch, méthode *f* (employée) pour faire qch; *Fin* **m. of payment** mode *m* ou modalité *f* de paiement, mode *m* ou modalité *f* de règlement; **their methods of investigation have come under fire** la façon dont ils mènent leurs enquêtes a été critiquée, on a critiqué leur façon d'enquêter **2** *(organization)* méthode *f*, organisation *f*; **his work lacks m.** son travail manque de méthode; **there's m. in her madness** elle n'est pas aussi folle qu'elle en a l'air

• **Method N** *Cin & Theat* **the M.** la méthode Stanislavski

▸▸ *Cin & Theat* ***Method acting*** la méthode Stanislavski; *Cin & Theat* ***Method actor*** acteur *m* adepte de la méthode de Stanislavski

methodical [məˈθɒdɪkəl] **ADJ** méthodique

methodically [məˈθɒdɪkəlɪ] **ADV** méthodiquement, de façon méthodique, avec méthode

Methodism [ˈmeθədɪzəm] **N** méthodisme *m*

Methodist [ˈmeθədɪst] **N** méthodiste *mf*
ADJ méthodiste

methodology [ˌmeθəˈdɒlədʒɪ] (*pl* **methodologies**) **N** méthodologie *f*

meths [meθs] **N** *Br Fam (abbr* **methylated spirits**) alcool *m* à brûler[a]

▸▸ ***meths drinker*** = alcoolique qui boit de l'alcool à brûler

Methuselah [ˌmɪˈθjuːzələ] **PR N** *Bible* Mathusalem; **as old as M.** vieux comme Mathusalem *ou* Hérode

methyl [ˈmeθɪl] **N** *Chem* méthyle *m*

▸▸ ***methyl acetate*** acétate *m* de méthyle; ***methyl alcohol*** méthanol *m*, alcool *m* méthylique

methylated spirits [ˈmeθɪˌleɪtɪd-] **N** *Chem* alcool *m* à brûler

methylene [ˈmeθəliːn] **N** *Chem* méthylène *m*

▸▸ ***methylene blue*** bleu *m* de méthylène

meticulous [mɪˈtɪkjʊləs] **ADJ** méticuleux, minutieux; **with m. attention to detail** avec une attention méticuleuse *ou* minutieuse pour les détails

meticulously [mɪˈtɪkjʊləslɪ] **ADV** méticuleusement; **m. honest** d'une honnêteté scrupuleuse

meticulousness [mɪˈtɪkjʊləsnɪs] **N** minutie *f*, *Literary* méticulosité *f*; **with great m.** avec un soin tout particulier

metonymic [ˌmetəˈnɪmɪk] **ADJ** *Ling* métonymique

metonymy [mɪˈtɒnɪmɪ] **N** *Ling* métonymie *f*

me-too ADJ

▸▸ *Mktg* ***me-too product*** produit *m* tactique; *Mktg* ***me-too strategy*** stratégie *f* d'imitation

metre, *Am* **meter** [ˈmiːtə(r)] **N 1** *(measurement)* mètre *m* **2** *Literature* mètre *m*; **in iambic m.** en vers *mpl* iambiques **3** *Mus* mesure *f*

metric [ˈmetrɪk] **ADJ** *Math* métrique; **to go m.** adopter le système métrique

▸▸ ***the metric system*** le système métrique; ***metric ton*** tonne *f*

metrical [ˈmetrɪkəl] **ADJ** *Literature* métrique

metrication [ˌmetrɪˈkeɪʃən] **N** conversion *f* au système métrique, métrisation *f*

metrics [ˈmetrɪks] **N** *(UNCOUNT) (in poetry)* métrique *f*

metro [ˈmetrəʊ] (*pl* **metros**) **N** métro *m*

metronome [ˈmetrənəʊm] **N** métronome *m*

metropolis [mɪˈtrɒpəlɪs] (*pl* **metropolises** [-ɪz]) **N** métropole *f*, grande ville *f*, grand centre *m* urbain

metropolitan [ˌmetrəˈpɒlɪtən] **N** *Rel* métropolitain *m*; *(in orthodox church)* métropolite *m*
ADJ 1 *Geog* métropolitain; **m. France/Spain** la France/l'Espagne *f* métropolitaine; **m. Milan/Glasgow** l'agglomération *f* de Milan/Glasgow **2** *Rel* métropolitain

▸▸ ***metropolitan district*** *(in UK)* circonscription *f* administrative; ***Metropolitan Police*** *Br* police *f* londonienne; *Am* police *f* urbaine

metrosexual [ˌmetrəʊˈsekʃuːəl] **N** métrosexuel *m*
ADJ métrosexuel

mettle [ˈmetəl] **N** courage *m*; **to show** *or* **to prove one's m.** montrer ce dont on est capable; **to be on one's m.** être prêt à donner le meilleur de soi-même

mettlesome [ˈmetəlsəm] **ADJ** *Literary* courageux; *(horse)* fougueux

mew [mjuː] **N** *(of cat)* miaulement *m*; *(of gull)* cri *m*
VI *(cat)* miauler; *(gull)* crier

mewing [ˈmjuːɪŋ] **N** *(of cat)* miaulement *m*; *(of gull)* cris *mpl*

mews [mjuːz] **N** *Br* **1** *(flat)* = appartement chic aménagé dans une écurie rénovée **2** *(street)* ruelle *f (sur laquelle donnaient des écuries)*
NPL *Arch* écurie *f*, écuries *fpl*

▸▸ *Br* ***mews flat*** = appartement chic aménagé dans une écurie rénovée

Mex [meks] *Am Fam (abbr* **Mexican**) **N** = terme injurieux désignant un Mexicain
ADJ mexicain[a]

Mexican [ˈmeksɪkən] **N** Mexicain(e) *m,f*
ADJ mexicain
COMP *(embassy, history)* du Mexique

▸▸ ***Mexican American*** **N** Américain(e) *m,f* d'origine mexicaine **ADJ** *(history, culture)* de la population américaine d'origine mexicaine; *(population)* américaine d'origine mexicaine; ***Mexican jumping bean*** pois *m* sauteur; ***Mexican wave*** ola *f*

Mexico [ˈmeksɪkəʊ] **N** Mexique *m*

▸▸ ***Mexico City*** Mexico

mezzanine [ˈmetsəniːn] **N 1** *(floor)* mezzanine *f*, entresol *m* **2** *Am Theat (first balcony)* corbeille *f* **3** *Br Theat (beneath stage)* premier dessous *m (de la scène)*

▸▸ *Fin* ***mezzanine debt*** dette *f* subordonnée *ou* mezzanine; ***mezzanine finance*** = méthode de financement d'une partie du capital nécessaire pour acheter une entreprise *(utilisée principalement par ses employés)*; ***mezzanine floor*** mezzanine *f*, entresol *m*

mezzo [ˈmetsəʊ] *Mus* **N** *Fam* **1** *(singer)* mezzo-soprano[a] *f* **2** *(voice)* mezzo-soprano[a] *m*
ADV mezzo

mezzo-soprano (*pl* **mezzo-sopranos**) **N** *Mus* **1** *(singer)* mezzo-soprano *f* **2** *(voice)* mezzo-soprano *m*

mezzotint [ˈmedzəʊˌtɪnt] **N** mezzotinto *m inv*

mfd *Com (written abbr* **manufactured**) fabriqué

mg *(written abbr* **milligram**) mg

Mgr 1 *Rel (written abbr* **Monseigneur, Monsignor**) Mgr **2** *(written abbr* **manager**) directeur(trice) *m,f*

MHz *Elec (written abbr* **megahertz**) MHz

MI[1] **1** *(written abbr* **Michigan**) Michigan *m* **2** *Comput (written abbr* **machine intelligence**) IA *f*

MI[2] [ˌemˈaɪ] **N** *Med (abbr* **myocardial infarction**) infarctus *m* du myocarde

mi [miː] **N** *Mus* mi *m inv*

MI5 [ˌemaɪˈfaɪv] **N** *Br (abbr* **Military Intelligence 5**) = service de contre-espionnage britannique

MI6 [ˌemaɪˈsɪks] **N** *Br (abbr* **Military Intelligence 6**) = service de renseignements britannique

MIA [ˌemaɪˈeɪ] *Mil (abbr* **missing in action**) **N** soldat *m* porté disparu
ADJ porté disparu au combat

miaow [miːˈaʊ] *Br* **N** miaulement *m*
EXCLAM miaou!
VI miauler

mic [maɪk] **N** *TV & Rad* micro *m*

mica [ˈmaɪkə] **N** *Miner* mica *m*

mice [maɪs] *pl of* **mouse**

Mich. *(written abbr* **Michigan**) Michigan *m*

Michael [ˈmaɪkəl] **PR N** *Br Fam Hum* **are you taking the M.?** tu me fais marcher ou quoi?

Michaelmas [ˈmɪkəlməs] **N** *Rel* la Saint-Michel; **at M.** à la Saint-Michel

▸▸ *Bot* ***Michaelmas daisy*** aster *m* (d'automne); *Br Univ* ***Michaelmas term*** premier trimestre *m*

Michelangelo [ˌmaɪkəlˈændʒɪləʊ] **PR N** Michel-Ange

Michelin [ˈmɪtʃəlɪn] **N**

▸▸ ***Michelin Guide*** Guide *m* Michelin; ***the Michelin man*** le bonhomme Michelin, Bibendum *m*; *Fam Hum* **he looked like a M. man** on aurait dit le bonhomme Michelin *ou* Bibendum

Michigan [ˈmɪʃɪgən] **N** le Michigan

Michigander [ˈmɪʃɪˌgændə(r)] **N** *(native)* personne *f* originaire du Michigan; *(inhabitant)* habitant(e) *m,f* du Michigan

Mick [mɪk] **N** *Fam (Irishman)* = terme injurieux désignant un Irlandais

mick [mɪk], **mickey** [ˈmɪkɪ] **N** *Br Fam* **to take the m. out of sb/sth** se ficher de qn/qch; **are you taking the m.?** tu te fiches de moi?

Mickey (Finn) [ˌmɪkɪ(ˌfɪn)] **N** *Fam* = boisson alcoolisée dans laquelle on a versé un sédatif

Mickey Mouse PR N Mickey
ADJ *Fam Pej* à la gomme, à la noix; *(job, course, firm)* bidon *(inv)*, pas sérieux; *(degree)* bidon *(inv)*, sans aucune valeur[a]

micro [ˈmaɪkrəʊ] (*pl* **micros**) **N** *(microcomputer)* micro-ordinateur *m*, micro *m*
ADJ très petit, microscopique

micro- [ˈmaɪkrəʊ] **PREF** micro-

microanalysis [ˌmaɪkrəʊəˈnæləsɪs] (*pl* **microanalyses** [-siːz]) **N** microanalyse *f*

microbe [ˈmaɪkrəʊb] **N** *Biol* microbe *m*

microbial [maɪˈkrəʊbɪəl], **microbic** [maɪˈkrəʊbɪk] **ADJ** *Biol* microbien

microbicide [maɪˈkrəʊbɪsaɪd] **N** *Pharm* microbicide *m*

microbiology [ˌmaɪkrəʊbaɪˈɒlədʒɪ] **N** microbiologie *f*

microbrewery [ˈmaɪkrəʊˌbruːərɪ] **N** microbrasserie *f*

microbusiness [ˈmaɪkrəʊˌbɪznɪs] **N** *Com* microentreprise *f*

microcamera [ˌmaɪkrəʊˈkæmərə] **N** appareil *m* de microphotographie

microchip [ˈmaɪkrəʊtʃɪp] **N** puce *f*

microcircuit [ˈmaɪkrəʊˌsɜːkɪt] **N** microcircuit *m*

microcircuitry [ˌmaɪkrəʊˈsɜːkɪtrɪ] **N** *(UNCOUNT)* microcircuits *mpl*

microclimate [ˈmaɪkrəʊˌklaɪmət] **N** microclimat *m*

micrococcus [ˌmaɪkrəʊˈkɒkəs] (*pl* **micrococci** [-kaɪ]) **N** *Biol* microcoque *m*, micrococcus *m*

microcode [ˈmaɪkrəʊkəʊd] **N** microcode *m*

microcomputer [ˌmaɪkrəʊkəmˈpjuːtə(r)] **N** micro-ordinateur *m*

microcosm [ˈmaɪkrəʊˌkɒzəm] **N** microcosme *m*

microdermabrasion [ˌmaɪkrəʊˌdɜːməˈbreɪʒən] **N** microdermabrasion *f*

microdot [ˈmaɪkrəʊdɒt] **N** micropoint *m*, micro-image *f*

microeconomic [ˈmaɪkrəʊˌiːkəˈnɒmɪk] **ADJ** microéconomique

microeconomics [ˈmaɪkrəʊˌiːkəˈnɒmɪks] **N** *(UNCOUNT)* microéconomie *f*

microeconomy [ˌmaɪkrəʊɪˈkɒnəmɪ] **N** microéconomie *f*

microelectronics [ˈmaɪkrəʊɪˌlekˈtrɒnɪks] **N** *(UNCOUNT)* microélectronique *f*

microenterprise [ˌmaɪkrəʊˈentəpraɪz] **N** microentreprise *f*

microfibre, *Am* **microfiber** [ˈmaɪkrəʊˌfaɪbə(r)] **N** *Tex* microfibre *f*

microfiche [ˈmaɪkrəʊfiːʃ] **N** microfiche *f*

microfilm [ˈmaɪkrəʊfɪlm] **N** microfilm *m*
VT microfilmer, mettre sur microfilm
►► ***microfilm reader*** micro-lecteur *m*, lecteur *m* de microfilms

microfloppy [ˈmaɪkrəʊˌflɒpɪ] **N** *Comput* microdisquette *f*

microgroove [ˈmaɪkrəˌɡruːv] **N** microsillon *m*

microlight [ˈmaɪkrəʊlaɪt] **N** *Aviat* ultraléger *m* motorisé, ULM *m*

micromanage [ˈmaɪkrəʊˌmænɪdʒ] **VT he was criticized for micromanaging the department** on l'accuse d'être trop interventionniste dans sa gestion du service
VI = être trop interventionniste dans son style de gestion

micromanagement [ˌmaɪkrəʊˈmænɪdʒmənt] **N** style *m* de gestion trop interventionniste

micromarketing [ˌmaɪkrəʊˈmɑːkɪtɪŋ] **N** micromarketing *m*

micromesh [ˈmaɪkrəʊmeʃ] **N** micromesh *m*
ADJ *(tights)* surfin

micrometer [maɪˈkrɒmɪtə(r)] **N** *Tech (device)* micromètre *m (instrument)*

micron [ˈmaɪkrɒn] (*pl* **microns** *or* **micra** [-krə]) **N** micron *m*

Micronesia [ˌmaɪkrəˈniːzjə] **N** Micronésie *f*

microorganism [ˌmaɪkrəʊˈɔːɡənɪzəm] **N** *Biol* micro-organisme *m*

micropayment [ˈmaɪkrəʊˌpeɪmənt] **N** *Comput* micro-paiement *m*

microphone [ˈmaɪkrəfəʊn] **N** microphone *m*; **to talk into a m.** parler dans un micro

microphysics [ˌmaɪkrəʊˈfɪzɪks] **N** *(UNCOUNT)* microphysique *f*

microprocessor [ˈmaɪkrəʊˌprəʊsesə(r)] **N** *Comput* microprocesseur *m*

microreader [ˈmaɪkrəʊˌriːdə(r)] **N** micro-lecteur *m*, lecteur *m* de microformes

microscooter [ˈmaɪkrəʊˌskuːtə(r)] **N** trottinette *f*

microscope [ˈmaɪkrəskəʊp] **N** microscope *m*; **to look at sth under the m.** observer *ou* examiner qch au microscope; *Fig* examiner qch à la loupe

microscopic [ˌmaɪkrəˈskɒpɪk] **ADJ 1** *(tiny)* microscopique **2** *(using a microscope)* au microscope, microscopique

microscopy [maɪˈkrɒskəpɪ] **N** microscopie *f*

microsecond [ˈmaɪkrəʊˌsekənd] **N** microseconde *f*

microsite [ˈmaɪkrəʊsaɪt] **N** *Comput* microsite *m*

microstate [ˈmaɪkrəʊsteɪt] **N** *Pol* micro-État *m*

microsurgery [ˌmaɪkrəʊˈsɜːdʒərɪ] **N** microchirurgie *f*

microtechnology [ˌmaɪkrəʊtekˈnɒlədʒɪ] **N** microtechnologie *f*, microtechnique *f*

microwave [ˈmaɪkrəweɪv] **N 1** *Phys* micro-onde *f* **2** *(oven)* (four *m* à) micro-ondes *m inv*
VT faire cuire au micro-ondes
►► ***microwave oven*** (four *m* à) micro-ondes *m inv*

micturition [ˌmɪktjʊəˈrɪʃən] **N** *Formal* miction *f*

> **MID-** PRÉFIXE
>
> Le préfixe **mid-** s'emploie dans un grand nombre de contextes pour former noms et adjectifs, et il véhicule l'idée de MILIEU, de point intermédiaire. Citons les exemples suivants:
>
> **midsummer** le milieu de l'été; **the mid-sixties** le milieu des années soixante; **in midstream** au milieu du cours d'eau; **we had a mid-afternoon break** on a fait une pause en milieu d'après-midi; **a midair collision** une collision en plein ciel; **in the mid-Victorian period** au milieu de l'époque victorienne; **a mid-Atlantic accent** un accent mi-américain mi-britannique
>
> Notons qu'il n'existe pas véritablement de règle régissant l'usage du trait d'union.

mid [mɪd] **ADJ 1** *(middle)* **in m. October** à la mi-octobre, au milieu du mois d'octobre; **in m. ocean** en plein océan, en pleine mer; **m. season** demi-saison *f*; **he's in his m. fifties** il a environ cinquante-cinq ans; **she stopped in m. sentence** elle s'est arrêtée au milieu de sa phrase, sa phrase est restée en suspens **2** *(central)* central, du milieu; **m. Wales** le centre *ou* la région centrale du pays de Galles

mid-afternoon **N** milieu *m* de l'après-midi; **we had a m. break** on a fait une pause en milieu d'après-midi

midair [ˌmɪdˈeə(r)] **N in m.** en plein ciel
ADJ *(collision)* en plein ciel

Midas [ˈmaɪdəs] **PR N** *Myth* Midas; **to have the M. touch** transformer tout ce que l'on touche en or

mid-Atlantic **N in (the) m.** au milieu de l'Atlantique
ADJ *(accent)* mi-américain mi-britannique

midband [ˈmɪdbænd] *Tel & Comput* **N** connexion *f* RNIS
ADJ RNIS

midday [ˈmɪddeɪ] **N** midi *m*; **at m.** à midi; **the m. heat** la chaleur de midi
►► ***midday meal*** repas *m* de midi

midden [ˈmɪdən] **N 1** *Fam (dung heap)* (tas *m* de) fumier *m*; *Scot* **this room is like a m.!** cette pièce est une vraie porcherie! **2** *Archeol* ordures *fpl* ménagères, rejets *mpl* domestiques

middle [ˈmɪdəl] **N 1** *(in space)* milieu *m*, centre *m*; **in the m. (of)** au milieu (de), au centre (de); **in the m. of the road** au milieu de la route; **two seats in the m. of the row** deux places en milieu de rangée; **in the m. of London** en plein Londres; **they live in the m. of nowhere** ils habitent dans un coin perdu *ou* loin de tout, *Pej* ils habitent dans un trou perdu; *Fam* **they split the money down the m.** ils ont partagé l'argent en deux parties égales **2** *(in time)* milieu *m*; **in the m. of the week** au milieu de la semaine; **in the m. of October** à la mi-octobre, au milieu (du mois) d'octobre; **in the m. of the night** en pleine nuit, en plein milieu de la nuit; **in the m. of winter** en plein hiver **3** *(in activity)* **to be in the m. of doing sth** être en train de faire qch; **I'm in the m. of something, can you call back?** là je suis occupé mais est-ce qu tu peux me rappeler plus tard? **4** *(stomach)* ventre *m*; *(waist)* taille *f*; **round one's m.** autour de sa taille; **he's got rather fat around the m.** il a pris du ventre
ADJ 1 *(in the centre)* du milieu; **the m. shelf** l'étagère *f* du milieu; **she was the m. child of three** elle était la deuxième de trois enfants; *Fig* **to steer a m. course** adopter une position intermédiaire; **in the m. distance** à mi-distance; *(in picture)* au second plan **2** *(average)* moyen; *(intermediate)* moyen, intermédiaire; *Br* **of m. height** de taille moyenne; **this car is in the m. price range** cette voiture se situe dans un ordre de prix moyen
VT *Sport (ball)* frapper franchement
►► ***middle age*** la cinquantaine; **a man in m. age** un homme d'un certain âge; ***the Middle Ages*** le Moyen Âge *m*; **in the M. Ages** au Moyen Âge; **the early/late M. Ages** le haut/bas Moyen Âge; ***Middle America*** *Geog* Amérique *f* centrale; *Fig (American middle class)* l'Amérique *f* moyenne *Pej* l'Amérique *f* bien pensante; ***Middle American*** **N** Américain(e) *m,f* du Middle-West *ou* du Midwest; *Fig* Américain(e) *m,f* moyen(enne) **ADJ** *Geog* du Middle-West *ou* du Midwest; *Fig* de l'américain moyen; *Mus* **middle C** do *m inv* du milieu du clavier; ***the middle class, the middle classes*** les classes *fpl* moyennes; *Pej* la bourgeoisie *Anat* ***middle ear*** oreille *f* moyenne; ***the Middle East*** le Moyen-Orient; **in the M. East** au Moyen Orient; ***Middle Eastern*** moyen-oriental; ***Middle England*** l'Angleterre *f* moyenne *(aux tendances conservatrices)*; *Ling* ***Middle English*** le moyen anglais; ***middle finger*** majeur *m*, médius *m*; *Br Fam* ***middle finger salute*** doigt *m* d'honneur; **to give sb the m. finger salute** faire un doigt d'honneur à qn ***Middle French*** le moyen français; ***middle ground*** *(in picture)* second plan *m*; *Fig* terrain *m* neutre *Fig* **to occupy the m. ground** adopter une position de compromis; *Ling* ***Middle High German*** le moyen haut-allemand; ***middle management*** *(UNCOUNT)* cadres *mpl* moyens; ***middle manager*** cadre *m* moyen; ***middle name*** deuxième prénom *m*; **honesty is her m. name** c'est l'honnêteté même; **laziness is his m. name** c'est un incorrigible paresseux; **generosity isn't exactly his m. name!** on ne peut pas dire qu'il soit particulièrement généreux; ***middle school*** *Br* = école pour enfants de 8 ou 9 ans à 13 ans; *Am* = école pour enfants de 10 à 13 ans, ≃ collège *m*; *Am Geog* ***the Middle West*** le Middle West, le Midwest; ***middle youth*** = tranche d'âge allant de la trentaine à la cinquantaine

middle-aged **ADJ** d'une cinquantaine d'années
►► ***middle-aged spread*** bourrelets *mpl* (qui viennent avec l'âge)

middlebrow [ˈmɪdəlbraʊ] *Pej* **N** personne *f* aux activités intellectuelles limitées; *(reader)* lecteur(trice) *m,f* moyen(enne); *(audience)* spectateur(trice) *m,f* moyen(enne)
ADJ *(reader, audience)* moyen; **their music's very m.** leur musique s'adresse à un public moyen; **m. books** livres *mpl* sans prétentions intellectuelles

middle-class **ADJ** des classes moyennes; *Pej* bourgeois

middle-income group **N** *Mktg* groupe *m* de contribuables à revenus moyens

middleman [ˈmɪdəlmæn] (*pl* **middlemen** [-men]) **N** intermédiaire *mf*; **to cut out the m.** éliminer les intermédiaires

middlemost [ˈmɪdəlməʊst] **ADJ** le plus proche du centre

middle-of-the-road **ADJ** *(opinions, policies)* modéré; *Pej* timide, circonspect; **m. music** musique *f* grand public; *Pej* musique *f* passe-partout

middle-roader [-ˈrəʊdə(r)] **N** *Am Pol* modéré(e) *m,f*

middle-sized **ADJ** de taille moyenne

middleweight [ˈmɪdəlweɪt] **N** poids *m* moyen
ADJ *(championship)* de poids moyen; **he's the world m. champion** c'est le champion du monde des poids moyens

middling ['mɪdlɪŋ] **ADJ** *Fam (average)* moyen◻; *(mediocre)* médiocre◻; **how are you? – (fair to) m.** ça va? – on fait aller *ou* comme ci comme ça

middy ['mɪdɪ] **N** *Fam Naut* midship◻*m*

Mideast [,mɪd'iːst] **N** *Am* **the M.** le Moyen-Orient

mid-engined **ADJ** *Aut* à moteur central

midfield [,mɪd'fiːld] **N** *Sport* milieu *m* du terrain; **in m.** au milieu du terrain

►► ***midfield player*** (joueur *m* du) milieu *m* de terrain

midfielder [,mɪd'fiːldə(r)] **N** *Ftbl* milieu *m* de terrain

midge [mɪdʒ] **N** *Entom* moucheron *m*

midget ['mɪdʒɪt] **N** *(dwarf)* nain(e) *m,f*

ADJ *(gen)* minuscule; *(by design)* miniature

MIDI ['mɪdɪ] **N** *Comput* (*abbr* **musical instrument digital interface**) MIDI *m*

midi ['mɪdɪ] **N** *(coat)* manteau *m* à mi-mollet; *(skirt)* jupe *f* à mi-mollet

►► ***midi system*** *(stereo)* chaîne *f* midi

midland ['mɪdlənd] **ADJ** au centre du pays

Midlands ['mɪdləndz] **NPL** **the M.** les Midlands *mpl*, = comtés du centre de l'Angleterre

midlife ['mɪdlaɪf] **N** la cinquantaine; **in m., it's hard to find a new job** la cinquantaine passée, il est difficile de retrouver un emploi; **he's having** *or* **going through a m. crisis** il a du mal à passer le cap de la cinquantaine

mid-morning **N** milieu *m* de la matinée; **we had a m. snack** nous avons mangé quelque chose vers onze heures

midnight ['mɪdnaɪt] **N** minuit *m*; **at m.** à minuit

ADJ *(swim)* de minuit; *Fig* **to burn the m. oil** travailler tard dans la nuit

►► ***midnight blue*** bleu nuit *m inv*; ***midnight feast*** = petit repas pris en cachette la nuit par des enfants, à l'insu de leurs parents; ***midnight Mass*** messe *f* de minuit; ***midnight sun*** soleil *m* de minuit

mid-range **ADJ** *Com (computer, car)* de milieu de gamme

midriff ['mɪdrɪf] **N 1** *(stomach)* ventre *m*; **there's a fashion for bare midriffs at the moment** les vêtements qui laissent le ventre à l'air sont à la mode en ce moment **2** *Anat* diaphragme *m*

midshipman ['mɪd,ʃɪpmən] *(pl* **midshipmen** [-mən]) **N** *Naut* ≃ aspirant *m*, *Can* ≃ cadet *m*

midships ['mɪdʃɪps] **ADV** *Naut* au milieu du navire, par le travers

midst [mɪdst] **N** **in the m. of sth** au milieu de qch; **in the m. of all this** *(these events)* sur ces entrefaites; **in the m. of the celebration** en plein milieu de la fête; **in our/your/their m.** parmi nous/vous/eux; **there are traitors in our m.** il y a des traîtres parmi nous

midstream [,mɪd'striːm] **N** **in m.** au milieu du courant; *Fig* **he stopped talking in m.** il s'arrêta au beau milieu d'une phrase; *Fig* **to change horses in midstream** se raviser en cours de route

midsummer ['mɪd,sʌmə(r)] **N** *(middle of summer)* milieu *m ou* cœur *m* de l'été; *(solstice)* solstice *m* d'été; **in m.** au milieu de l'été, en été; **a m. night** une nuit d'été

►► ***Midsummer Day, Midsummer's Day*** la Saint-Jean; ***midsummer madness*** folie *f* estivale

midterm [,mɪd'tɜːm] **N 1** *Pol Am* milieu *m* du mandat présidentiel, *Br* milieu du mandat du Premier Ministre **2** *Sch & Univ* milieu *m* du trimestre **3** *Med (of pregnancy)* milieu *m*

►► *Sch & Univ* ***midterm break*** vacances *fpl* de milieu de trimestre; *Pol* ***midterm elections*** = aux États-Unis, élections législatives qui ont lieu au milieu du mandat présidentiel; *Sch & Univ* ***midterm exams*** examens *mpl* du milieu du trimestre

midway **ADV** [,mɪd'weɪ] à mi-chemin; **she was m. through writing the first chapter** elle avait déjà écrit la moitié du premier chapitre; **m. between... and...** à mi-distance *ou* à mi-chemin entre... et...; **a style m. between Craig's and Andrew's** un style intermédiaire entre celui de Craig et celui d'Andrew

N ['mɪdweɪ] *Am (in fairground)* allée *f* centrale

►► ***midway point*** *(in time, space)* milieu *m*

midweek **ADJ** ['mɪdwiːk] *(travel)* en milieu de semaine; *(prices, performance)* de milieu de semaine; *Rail* ≃ (en) période bleue

ADV [,mɪd'wiːk] *(travel, arrive, meet)* au milieu de la semaine; *Rail* ≃ en période bleue

Midwest [,mɪd'west] **N** **the M.** le Midwest; **in the M.** dans le Midwest

Midwestern [,mɪd'westən] **ADJ** du Midwest

midwife ['mɪdwaɪf] *(pl* **midwives** [-waɪvz]) **N** sage-femme *f*

midwifery ['mɪd,wɪfərɪ] **N 1** *(profession)* profession *f* de sage-femme **2** *(obstetrics)* obstétrique *f*

midwinter [,mɪd'wɪntə(r)] **N** *(middle of winter)* milieu *m ou* cœur *m* de l'hiver; *(solstice)* solstice *m* d'hiver; **in m.** au milieu de l'hiver; **a m.** *or* **m.'s day** un jour d'hiver

mien [miːn] **N** *Literary* mine *f*, air *m*

miffed [mɪft] **ADJ** *Fam (person, expression)* froissé◻; **to be m. at sb** être fâché contre qn◻

MIG [mɪg] **N** *Br Fin* (*abbr* **minimum income guarantee**) ≃ minimum *m* vieillesse

MIGHT[1] [maɪt]

> La forme négative **mightn't** s'écrit **might not** dans un style plus soutenu. **Might** et **may** peuvent s'utiliser indifféremment ou presque dans les expressions de la catégorie **1**.

V AUX 1 *(expressing possibility)* **you m. well be right** il se pourrait bien que vous ayez raison; **I m. be home late tonight** je rentrerai peut-être tard ce soir; **why not come with us? – I m.** pourquoi ne viens-tu pas avec nous? – peut-être; **don't eat it, it m. be poisonous** n'en mange pas, tu pourrais t'empoisonner; **she m. have decided not to go** il se peut qu'elle ait décidé de ne pas y aller

2 *(past form of "may")* **I never considered that she m. want to come** je n'avais jamais pensé qu'elle pouvait avoir envie de venir; **we feared you m. be dead** nous avons eu peur que vous ne soyez mort

3 *(in polite questions, suggestions)* **m. I interrupt?** puis-je me permettre de vous interrompre?; **and what, m. I ask, was the reason?** et puis-je savoir quelle en était la raison?; **m. I** *or* **if I m. make a suggestion?** puis-je me permettre de suggérer quelque chose?; **you m. try using a different approach** vous pourriez adopter une approche différente; **I thought we m. have tea together somewhere** je m'étais dit que nous pourrions aller prendre un thé ensemble quelque part; **you m. want to ask the managing director first** ce serait une bonne idée de demander au directeur avant

4 *(commenting on a statement made)* **that, I m. add, was not my idea** cela n'était pas mon idée, soit dit en passant; **this, as one m. expect, did not go down well with the government** le gouvernement, est-il nécessaire de le préciser, n'a guère apprécié

5 *(ought to)* **you m. at least tidy up your room!** tu pourrais au moins ranger ta chambre!; **you m. have warned me!** tu aurais pu me prévenir!

6 *(used to contradict or challenge)* **they m. say they support women, but they do nothing practical to help them** ils ont beau dire qu'ils soutiennent les femmes, concrètement ils ne font rien pour les aider; **he m. not be the best-looking man in the world but he's very kind** ce n'est peut-être pas un apollon mais il est très gentil

7 *Formal or Hum (in questions)* **and who m. you be?** et qui êtes-vous donc?; **and what m. you be up to?** et que faites-vous donc?

8 *(idioms)* **we m. as well go home (as stay here)** nous ferions aussi bien de rentrer chez nous (plutôt que de rester ici); **I m. as well have stayed in bed** j'aurais aussi bien fait de rester au lit; **he's regretting it now, as well he m.!** il le regrette maintenant, et pour cause!

might[2] **N 1** *(power ► of nation)* pouvoir *m*, puissance *f*; (► *of army*) puissance *f* **2** *(physical strength)* force *f*; **with all one's m.**, *Literary* **with m. and main** de toutes ses forces; *Prov* **m. is right** la raison du plus fort est toujours la meilleure

might-have-been **N 1** *(opportunity)* occasion *f* manquée; *(hope)* espoir *m* déçu **2** *Fam (person)* raté(e) *m,f*

mightily ['maɪtɪlɪ] **ADV 1** *(with vigour)* avec vigueur, vigoureusement **2** *(extremely)* extrêmement; **to be m. relieved** être vraiment soulagé

mightn't ['maɪtənt] = **might not**

might've ['maɪtəv] = **might have**

mighty ['maɪtɪ] *(compar* **mightier**, *superl* **mightiest**) **ADJ 1** *(powerful)* puissant **2** *(impressive)* imposant; *(enormous)* énorme **3** *Am Fam (considerable)* grand◻

ADV *Am Fam* rudement, vachement; **that's m. kind of you** c'est rudement gentil de votre part; **she looked m. pleased with herself** elle avait l'air sacrément contente d'elle

mignonette [,mɪnjə'net] **N** *Bot* réséda *m*, mignonnette *f*

migraine ['miːgreɪn, 'maɪgreɪn] **N** migraine *f*; **to suffer from migraines** avoir des migraines; **I've got a m.** j'ai la migraine

►► ***migraine sufferer*** migraineux(euse) *m,f*

migrant ['maɪgrənt] **N 1** *(bird, animal)* migrateur *m* **2** *(worker* ► *in agriculture)* saisonnier(ère) *m,f*, travailleur(euse) *m,f* saisonnier(ère); (► *foreign)* travailleur(euse) *m,f* immigré(e)

ADJ *(bird, animal)* migrateur

►► ***migrant worker*** *(seasonal)* (travailleur(euse) *m,f*) saisonnier(ère) *m,f*; *(foreign)* travailleur (euse) *m,f* immigré(e)

migrate [*Br* maɪ'greɪt, *Am* 'maɪgreɪt] **VI 1** *(bird, animal)* migrer; **to m. south** migrer vers le sud **2** *(person, family* ► *from region)* migrer, se déplacer; (► *from country)* émigrer; **the people migrated to the cities** les gens ont migré vers les villes

migration [maɪ'greɪʃən] **N** *(of birds, animals)* migration *f*; *(of people)* émigration *f*

migratory ['maɪgrətərɪ] **ADJ 1** *(bird, fish)* migrateur **2** *(habit, movement)* migratoire

Mike [maɪk] **PR N** *Fam* **for the love of M.!** pour l'amour du ciel!, c'est pas vrai!

mike [maɪk] **N** *Fam* (*abbr* **microphone**) micro *m*

milch [mɪltʃ] **ADJ** laitier

►► ***milch cow*** vache *f* laitière; *Fig* vache *f* à lait

mild [maɪld] **ADJ 1** *(person, remark)* doux (douce); *(answer)* conciliant; *(criticism)* léger (ère), anodin

2 *(punishment)* peu sévère, léger(ère)

3 *(climate)* doux (douce), tempéré; *(winter)* doux (douce), clément; **the weather is getting milder** le temps s'adoucit

4 *(dish)* peu épicé; *(cigar, tobacco, soap)* doux (douce); *(sedative, medicine)* léger(ère); **a m. curry** un curry peu épicé

5 *Med (illness, infection)* bénin(igne); **a m. form of measles** une forme bénigne de rougeole

6 *(slight* ► *astonishment)* léger(ère); **the joke caused some m. amusement** la plaisanterie a fait sourire; **the play caused a m. sensation** la pièce a fait un peu de bruit

N *Br* = bière moins riche en houblon et plus foncée que la "bitter"

►► ***mild cheddar*** cheddar *m* doux; ***mild steel*** acier *m* doux

mildew ['mɪldjuː] **N 1** *(on cereals, flowers)* rouille *f*; *(on vines, potatoes, tomatoes)* mildiou *m* **2** *(on paper, leather, food)* moisissure *f*

VI 1 *(cereals, flowers)* se rouiller; *(vines, potatoes, tomatoes)* être atteint par le mildiou **2** *(paper, leather, food)* moisir

mildewy ['mɪldjuːɪ] **ADJ** *(food, wallpaper, leather)* moisi; **a m. smell** une odeur de moisi; **to go m.** *(plant)* se rouiller; *(bread, paper)* moisir; *(vine)* être atteint par le mildiou

mildly ['maɪldlɪ] **ADV 1** *(say, act)* doucement, avec douceur **2** *(slightly)* modérément, légèrement; **it has a m. laxative effect** ça a un léger effet laxatif; **to be m. successful** *(play)* obtenir un succès modéré; **it was rather silly, to put it m.** c'était plutôt idiot, c'est le moins qu'on puisse dire; **he's a bastard, and that's putting it m.!** c'est un salaud, et c'est peu dire!

mild-mannered **ADJ** doux (douce)

mildness ['maɪldnɪs] **N 1** *(of person, weather)* douceur *f*; *(of criticism)* caractère *m* anodin; *(of punishment)* légèreté *f* **2** *(of disease)* bénignité *f*

mile [maɪl] **N 1** *(measurement)* = 1609 m, mile *m*; **it's 10 miles away** ≃ c'est à une quinzaine de kilomètres d'ici; **miles per hour** milles par heure; **smaller cars do more miles to the** *or* **per gallon** les petites voitures consomment moins; **a 100-m. journey** ≃ un voyage de 160 kilomètres; **m. after m. of sandy beaches** ≃ des plages de sable sur des kilomètres et des kilomètres

2 *(long distance)* **you can see it a m. off** ça se voit de loin; **you can smell the factory a m. off** on sent les fumées de l'usine à des kilomètres; **the best doctor for miles around** le meilleur médecin à des kilomètres à la ronde; **we're miles from the nearest town** on est à des kilomètres de la ville la plus proche; **it's miles from anywhere** c'est un endroit complètement isolé; **you can see for miles and miles** on voit à des kilomètres à la ronde; **we walked (for) miles** on a fait des kilomètres (à pied)

3 *Fig* **they're miles ahead of their competitors** ils ont une avance considérable sur leurs concurrents; **he was miles away** *(daydreaming)* il était dans la lune; **you could see what was going to happen a m. off** on voyait d'ici ce qui allait arriver; *Fam* **it sticks out a m.** ça vous crève les yeux, ça se voit comme le nez au milieu de la figure; **your calculations are miles out** vous vous êtes complètement trompé dans vos calculs; **I feel miles better** je me sens vachement mieux; **you're miles too slow** t'es vachement trop lent, t'es mille fois trop lent; **she's miles better than me at languages** elle est vachement plus forte que moi en langues; **someone not a million miles from us** une certaine personne qui ne se trouve pas très loin de nous; **to go the extra m.** faire un petit effort supplémentaire

mileage [ˈmaɪlɪdʒ] **N 1** *Aut (distance)* distance *f* en milles, ≃ kilométrage *m*; **the car's got a very low m.** la voiture a très peu roulé *ou* a un kilométrage bas; *Fig* **the papers got tremendous m. out of the scandal** les journaux ont exploité le scandale au maximum; *Fam Fig* **there's no m. in it** *(in idea etc)* ça ne nous mènera nulle part□, on ne peut rien en tirer□ **2** *(consumption)* consommation *f* (d'essence); **you get better m. with a small car** on consomme moins avec une petite voiture; **what m. do you get?** combien est-ce que la voiture consomme aux cent?

▸▸ ***mileage allowance*** ≃ indemnité *f* kilométrique

mileometer [maɪˈlɒmɪtə(r)] **N** compteur *m* (kilométrique)

milestone [ˈmaɪlstəʊn] **N 1** *(on road)* ≃ borne *f* (kilométrique) **2** *Fig (important event)* jalon *m*, étape *f* importante; **a m. in the history of aviation** une étape importante dans l'histoire de l'aviation

MILF [mɪlf] **N** *very Fam (abbr* **mother I'd like to fuck***)* mère *f* baisable

milieu [*Br* ˈmiːljɜː, *Am* miːlˈjuː] **N** environnement *m*, milieu *m*

militancy [ˈmɪlɪtənsɪ] **N** militantisme *m*

militant [ˈmɪlɪtənt] **N** militant(e) *m,f*

ADJ militant

• **Militant (Tendency)** **N** *Br Pol* = groupe d'extrême gauche à l'intérieur du Parti travailliste britannique

militarily [*Br* ˈmɪlɪtərɪlɪ, *Am* ˌmɪləˈterəlɪ] **ADV** militairement

militarism [ˈmɪlɪtərɪzəm] **N** militarisme *m*

militarist [ˈmɪlɪtərɪst] **N** militariste *mf*

militaristic [ˌmɪlɪtəˈrɪstɪk] **ADJ** militariste

militarize, -ise [ˈmɪlɪtəraɪz] **VT** militariser

▸▸ ***militarized zone*** zone *f* militarisée

military [ˈmɪlɪtərɪ] **ADJ** *(aircraft, base etc)* militaire; **a strong m. presence** une forte présence militaire

NPL the m. les militaires *mpl*, l'armée *f*; **the m. were called in** on a fait venir l'armée

▸▸ ***military academy*** école *f* militaire; ***military attaché*** attaché(e) *m,f* militaire; *Br* ***military man*** militaire *m*; ***military police*** police *f* militaire; ***military policeman*** = membre de la police militaire; ***military service*** service *m* militaire

▸ **militate against** [ˈmɪlɪteɪt] **VT INSEP** *(facts, actions)* militer contre; **her temperament militates against her** son tempérament joue contre elle

militia [mɪˈlɪʃə] **N 1** *(body of citizens)* milice *f* **2** *Am (reserve army)* réserve *f*

militiaman [mɪˈlɪʃəmən] *(pl* **militiamen** [-mən]*)* **N** milicien *m*

milk [mɪlk] **N** lait *m*; **mother's m.** lait *m* maternel; **cow's/goat's m.** lait *m* de vache/de chèvre; **a land flowing with m. and honey** un pays de cocagne; *Fig* **the m. of human kindness** le lait de la tendresse humaine

COMP *(bottle, churn, jug etc* ▸ *empty)* à lait; *(*▸ *full)* de lait

VT 1 *(cow, goat)* traire **2** *(snake)* extraire le venin de **3** *Fig* **to m. a country of its resources** dépouiller un pays de ses ressources; **the newspapers milked the story for all it was worth** les journaux ont tiré tout ce qu'ils ont pu de l'histoire; **they just milked all his ideas** ils se sont approprié toutes ses idées

VI the cow milks well la vache donne beaucoup de lait

▸▸ ***milk bar*** milk-bar *m*; ***milk chocolate*** chocolat *m* au lait; ***milk duct*** canal *m* galactophore; *Vet* ***milk fever*** fièvre *f* lactée; *Br* ***milk float*** camionnette *f* du laitier; ***milk gland*** glande *f* lactéale *ou* galactophore; ***milk loaf*** pain *m* brioché; ***Milk of Magnesia*** lait *m* de magnésie; ***milk powder*** lait *m* en poudre; *Br* ***milk pudding*** entremets *m* au lait; *Br* ***milk round*** *(for milk delivery)* tournée *f* du laitier; *Univ* = tournée des universités par les employeurs pour recruter des étudiants en fin d'études; *Fam* ***milk run*** *Aviat* vol *m* sans histoire, partie *f* de rigolade; *(regular journey)* trajet *m* habituel□, tournée *f* habituelle□; *Br* ***milk stout*** bière *f* brune; ***milk tooth*** dent *f* de lait; ***milk train*** premier train *m* (du matin)

milk-and-water **ADJ** *Br Old-fashioned* insipide

milker [ˈmɪlkə(r)] **N 1** *(cow)* **a good m.** une bonne laitière **2** *(dairy hand)* trayeur(euse) *m,f* **3** *(machine)* trayeuse *f*

milkiness [ˈmɪlkɪnɪs] **N** *(of liquid etc)* couleur *f* laiteuse, aspect *m* laiteux

milking [ˈmɪlkɪŋ] **N** traite *f*; **to do the m.** traire les vaches

▸▸ ***milking machine*** machine *f* à traire, trayeuse *f*; ***milking pail*** seau *m* à traire; ***milking parlour*** salle *f* de traite; ***milking stool*** tabouret *m* à traire; ***milking time*** l'heure *f* de la traite

milkmaid [ˈmɪlkmeɪd] **N** vachère *f*, trayeuse *f*

milkman [ˈmɪlkmən] *(pl* **milkmen** [-mən]*)* **N** *(who delivers milk)* laitier *m*

milkshake [ˈmɪlkʃeɪk] **N** milk shake *m*; *Can* lait *m* frappé

milksop [ˈmɪlksɒp] **N** chiffe *f* molle

milkweed [ˈmɪlkwiːd] **N** *Bot (gen)* plante *f* à suc laiteux; *(sow thistle)* laiteron *m*, lait *m* d'âne

milk-white **ADJ** d'un blanc laiteux

milky [ˈmɪlkɪ] *(compar* **milkier**, *superl* **milkiest***)* **ADJ 1** *(taste)* laiteux, de lait; *(drink, dessert)* lacté, à base de lait; *(tea, coffee)* avec du lait; **I like my tea m.** *(with lots of milk)* j'aime mon thé avec beaucoup de lait **2** *(colour)* laiteux; *(skin)* d'un blanc laiteux **3** *(cloudy* ▸ *liquid)* laiteux, lactescent

▸▸ *Astron* ***the Milky Way*** la Voie lactée

mill [mɪl] **N 1** *(for flour)* moulin *m*; *(on industrial scale)* meunerie *f*, minoterie *f*; *Fig* **she's been through the m.** elle a souffert; *Fig* **she put him through the m.** elle lui en a fait voir

2 *(factory)* usine *f*; **steel m.** aciérie *f*

3 *(domestic* ▸ *for coffee, pepper)* moulin *m*; **coffee/pepper m.** moulin *m* à café/à poivre

4 *Tech (for coins)* machine *f* à créneler; *(for metal)* fraiseuse *f*; *(for rolling)* laminoir *m*

VT 1 *(grain)* moudre; *(ore)* broyer **2** *(mark* ▸ *coin)* créneler; *(*▸ *screw)* moleter; *(*▸ *surface)* strier, rainer; **a coin with a milled edge** une pièce crénelée

▸▸ *Old-fashioned* ***mill hand*** ouvrier(ère) *m,f*; ***mill owner*** industriel *m*

▸ **mill about, mill around** **VI** *(crowd, people)* grouiller

millboard [ˈmɪlbɔːd] **N** carton *m* gris

milled [mɪld] **ADJ** *(grain etc)* moulu

▸▸ ***milled edge*** *(on coin)* crénelage *m*, grènetis *m*

millennial [mɪˈlenɪəl] **ADJ** du millénaire; **the m. celebrations** les festivités *fpl* organisées pour le passage à l'an 2000

millennium [mɪˈlenɪəm] *(pl* **millenniums** *or* **millennia** [-nɪə]*)* **N 1** *(thousand years)* millénaire *m* **2** *Rel & Fig* **the m.** le millénium

▸▸ *Comput* ***the millennium bug*** le bogue de l'an 2000; ***the Millennium Dome*** = centre d'expositions en forme de dôme construit à Londres à l'occasion de l'an 2000

millepede = **millipede**

miller [ˈmɪlə(r)] **N** meunier(ère) *m,f*; *(on large scale)* minotier *m*

millet [ˈmɪlɪt] **N** millet *m*

millibar [ˈmɪlɪbɑː(r)] **N** *Met* millibar *m*

milligram, milligramme [ˈmɪlɪgræm] **N** milligramme *m*

millilitre, *Am* **milliliter** [ˈmɪlɪˌliːtə(r)] **N** millilitre *m*

millimetre, *Am* **millimeter** [ˈmɪlɪˌmiːtə(r)] **N** millimètre *m*

milliner [ˈmɪlɪnə(r)] **N** modiste *mf*

millinery [ˈmɪlɪnrɪ] **N** *(hat-making)* fabrication *f* de chapeaux de femmes; *(hat-selling)* vente *f* de chapeaux de femmes

milling [ˈmɪlɪŋ] **N 1** *(of grain)* mouture *f*, moulage *m* **2** *Metal* fraisage *m*; *(of screw etc)* moletage *m*; *(of coin)* cordonnage *m* **3** *(on coin)* cordon *m*, grènetis *m*, tranche *f* cannelée

▸▸ ***milling cutter*** fraise *f*, fraiseuse *f*; ***milling machine*** fraiseuse *f*

million [ˈmɪljən] **N 1** *(a thousand thousand)* million *m*; **two m. dollars** deux millions *mpl* de dollars; **half a m.** un demi-million; **millions of pounds** des millions *mpl* de livres; **her secretary is one in a m.** sa secrétaire est une perle rare; **he's worth millions** il est plusieurs fois milliardaire; *Fam* **I feel like a m. dollars** je me sens en pleine forme; *Fam* **to look like a m. dollars** être superbe **2** *(enormous number)* **an actor who gave pleasure to millions** un acteur qui a diverti des millions de gens; **I've told you a m. times not to do that** je t'ai dit cent fois de ne pas faire ça; *Fam* **thanks a m.!** merci mille fois!; *Ironic* eh bien, merci!

millionaire [ˌmɪljəˈneə(r)] **N** millionnaire *mf*; *(multi-millionaire)* milliardaire *mf*; **he's a dollar m.** il possède des millions de dollars; **to be a m. twice/three times over** être deux/trois fois millionnaire

▸▸ *Fam Fig* ***millionaire's row*** = rue où l'immobilier est particulièrement cher

millionairess [ˌmɪljəˈneərɪs] **N** millionnaire *f*; *(multi-millionairess)* milliardaire *f*

millionth [ˈmɪljənθ] **N 1** *(ordinal)* millionième *mf* **2** *(fraction)* millionième *m*

ADJ millionième

millipede [ˈmɪlɪpiːd] **N** *Entom* mille-pattes *m inv*

millisecond [ˈmɪlɪˌsekənd] **N** milliseconde *f*, millième *m* de seconde

millpond [ˈmɪlpɒnd] **N** retenue *f* de moulin; *Fig* **the sea was like a m.** la mer était d'huile

millrace [ˈmɪlreɪs] **N** *(channel)* bief *m* (de moulin); *(water)* courant *m* du bief

millstone [ˈmɪlstəʊn] **N 1** *(stone)* meule *f* **2** *Fig* fardeau *m*; **a m. round my neck** un boulet que je traîne

millstream [ˈmɪlstriːm] **N** courant *m* du bief

millwheel [ˈmɪlwiːl] **N** roue *f* (de moulin)

millwright [ˈmɪlraɪt] **N** constructeur *m* de moulins

milt [mɪlt] **N** *(of fish* ▸ *fluid)* laitance *f*; *(*▸ *organ)* testicule *m*

MIME [maɪm] **N** *Comput (abbr* **Multipurpose Internet Mail Extensions***)* (protocole *m*) MIME *m*

mime [maɪm] **N** *(performance)* mime *m*; *(actor)* mime *mf*; **to explain something in m.** expliquer quelque chose par gestes

VT mimer; *(derisively)* singer

VI 1 *Theat* faire du mime **2** *(pop singer)* chanter en play-back; **to m. to a song** chanter en play-back

▸▸ ***mime artist*** mime *mf*

mimeograph [ˈmɪmɪəˌgrɑːf] **N 1** *(machine)* Ronéo® *f*, duplicateur *m* (à stencil) **2** *(text)* polycopié *m*, texte *m* ronéotypé

VT ronéotyper, ronéoter

mimic ['mɪmɪk] *(pt & pp* **mimicked,** *cont* **mimicking)** **VT 1** *(person)* mimer; *(satirically)* parodier, singer; *(voice, walk, behaviour, nature etc)* imiter **2** *Biol* imiter (par mimétisme)
N imitateur(trice) *m,f*

mimicry ['mɪmɪkrɪ] **N 1** *(imitation)* imitation *f* **2** *Biol* mimétisme *m*

miming ['maɪmɪŋ] **N** *(to a song)* play-back *m*

mimosa [mɪ'məʊzə] **N 1** *Bot* mimosa *m* **2** *Am (drink)* = cocktail composé de champagne et de jus d'orange

min. 1 *(written abbr* **minute)** min **2** *(written abbr* **minimum)** min

minaret [mɪnə'ret] **N** minaret *m*

mince [mɪns] **VT 1** *Culin* hacher; **minced meat** viande *f* hachée **2** *(idiom)* **he doesn't m. his words** il ne mâche pas ses mots
VI 1 *(speak)* parler avec affectation **2** *(move)* marcher en se trémoussant; **he minced into the room** il est entré dans la salle en se trémoussant
N *Br (meat)* viande *f* hachée
▸▸ ***mince pie*** = tartelette fourrée avec un mélange de fruits secs et d'épices que l'on sert à Noël en Grande-Bretagne

mincemeat ['mɪnsmiːt] **N 1** *(meat)* viande *f* hachée **2** *(sweet filling)* = mélange de fruits secs et d'épices qui sert de garniture à des tartelettes **3** *Fam (idiom)* **to make m. of sb** *(in fight, boxing match)* réduire qn en bouillie, démolir qn; *(in football, tennis match)* écraser qn; *(in debate, argument)* démolir qn

mincer ['mɪnsə(r)] **N** hachoir *m*, hache-viande *m inv*

mincing ['mɪnsɪŋ] **ADJ** *(manner, tone)* affecté, minaudier; *(steps, gait)* efféminé
▸▸ ***mincing machine*** hachoir *m*, hache-viande *m inv*

MIND [maɪnd]

N
- esprit **1, 4, 5, 8**
- attention **2**
- avis **7**
- envie **9**

VT
- faire attention à **1–3**
- déranger **4**
- garder **5**

VI
- déranger **1**
- faire attention **3**

N 1 *(thoughts)* esprit *m*; **the power of m. over matter** le pouvoir de l'esprit sur la matière; **such a thought had never entered his m.** une telle pensée ne lui était jamais venue à l'esprit; **nothing was further from my m.** je n'en avais nullement l'intention; **to be strong in m. and body** être physiquement et mentalement solide; **there's something on her m.** il y a quelque chose qui la tracasse; **I have a lot on my m.** j'ai beaucoup de soucis; **at the back of one's m.** au fond de soi-même; **I just can't get him out of my m.** je n'arrive absolument pas à l'oublier; **to have sb/sth in m.** penser à qn/qch de précis; **who do you have in m. for the role?** à qui songez-vous pour le rôle?, qui avez-vous en vue pour le rôle?; **I had something smaller in m.** je pensais à quelque chose de plus petit; **put it out of your m.** n'y pensez plus; **to set one's m. on doing sth** se mettre en tête de faire qch; **to have one's m. set on sth** vouloir qch à tout prix; **a drink will take your m. off the accident** bois un verre, ça te fera oublier l'accident; **to put** *or* **set sb's m. at rest** rassurer qn; **in her m.'s eye she could see them staring at her** elle se les imaginait la fixant; **it's all in your m.!** tu te fais des idées!; **it's all in the m.** tout ça, c'est dans la tête

2 *(attention)* **to give one's whole m. to sth** accorder toute son attention à qch; **to keep one's m. on sth** se concentrer sur qch; **I'm sure if you put your m. to it you could do it** je suis sûr que si tu essayais vraiment, tu pourrais le faire; **your m. is not on the job** tu n'as pas la tête à ce que tu fais; *Am* **don't pay him any m.** ne fais pas attention à lui

3 *(memory)* **my m. has gone blank** j'ai un trou de mémoire; **Churchill's words come to m.** on pense aux paroles de Churchill; **it went clean** *or* **right out of my m.** cela m'est complètement sorti de l'esprit *ou* de la tête; **to put sb in m. of sb/sth** rappeler qn/qch à qn; **it puts me in m. of Japan** cela me fait penser au *ou* me rappelle le Japon; **to bear** *or* **keep sth in m.** *(think about)* songer à qch; *(take into account)* tenir compte de qch; *(not forget)* ne pas oublier qch, garder qch à l'esprit; **we must bear in m. that she is only a child** il ne faut pas oublier que ce n'est qu'une enfant; **I'll bear it in m.** *(what you suggested)* je prends note; **it must have slipped my m.** j'ai dû oublier

4 *(intellect)* esprit *m*; **she has an outstanding m.** elle est d'une très grande intelligence; **he has the m. of a child** il a l'esprit d'un enfant

5 *(intelligent person, thinker)* esprit *m*, cerveau *m*; **the great minds of our century** les grands esprits *ou* cerveaux de notre siècle; *Prov* **great minds think alike(, fools seldom differ)** les grands esprits se rencontrent

6 *(way of thinking)* **the Western m.** la pensée occidentale; **I haven't got a scientific m.** je n'ai pas l'esprit scientifique; **you've got a dirty m.!** tu as l'esprit mal placé!; **she has a nasty m.** elle voit le mal partout; **he has a suspicious m.** il est soupçonneux de nature

7 *(opinion)* **to be of the same** *or* **of like** *or* **of one m.** être du même avis; **to know one's own m.** savoir ce qu'on veut; **you've got a m. of your own** tu peux décider toi-même; **the car seemed to have a m. of its own** la voiture semblait faire ce que bon lui semblait; **to my m.,...** à mon avis,..., selon moi,...; **I'm in two minds about going** je ne sais pas si je vais y aller; **to make up one's m.** se décider, prendre une décision; **make up your m.!** décidez-vous!; **I can't make up your m. for you** je ne peux pas décider à ta place; **my m. is made up** ma décision est prise; **to make up one's m. to do sth** se décider à faire qch; **to speak one's m.** dire ce qu'on pense; **to keep an open m. about sth** réserver son opinion sur qch; *Fam* **I gave him a piece of my m.** je lui ai dit son fait *ou* ses quatre vérités

8 *(reason)* esprit *m*, raison *f*; **to be of sound m.** être sain d'esprit; **to be/to go out of one's m.** être/devenir fou (folle); **are you out of your m.?, you must be out of your m.!** est-ce que tu as perdu la tête?; **he was out of his m. with worry** il était fou d'inquiétude; **to be bored out of one's m.** mourir d'ennui; **he's not in his right m.** il n'a plus toute sa raison; **no one in their right m. would do such a thing** aucune personne sensée n'agirait ainsi

9 *(desire)* **I've half a m. to give up** j'ai presque envie de renoncer; **I've a good m. to tell him what I think** j'ai bien envie de lui dire ce que je pense

VT 1 *(pay attention to)* faire attention à; **would you m. where you're putting your feet, please?** est-ce que tu peux faire attention où tu mets les pieds, s'il te plaît?; *Br Fam* **m. how you go!** fais attention à toi!; **m. your own business!** occupe-toi de ce qui te regarde!, mêle-toi de tes oignons!; **m. your language!** surveille ton langage!; **to m. one's manners** se surveiller; **m. the step** *(sign)* attention à la marche; **m. what you say** *(pay attention)* réfléchissez à *ou* faites attention à ce que vous dites; *(don't be rude)* mesurez vos paroles; **m. what you're doing!** regarde ce que tu fais!

2 *(take care, be sure that)* faire attention à; **m. you write to him!** n'oubliez pas de lui écrire!; **m. you don't fall!** faites attention de ne pas tomber!; **m. you don't forget** n'oubliez surtout pas; **m. you're not late!** faites en sorte de ne pas être en retard!

3 *(concern oneself with)* faire attention à, s'inquiéter de *ou* pour; **don't m. me, I'll just sit here quietly** ne vous inquiétez pas pour moi, je vais m'asseoir ici et je ne dérangerai personne; **don't m. him, he's always like that** ne fais pas attention à lui, il est toujours comme ça; *Ironic* **don't m. me, I only live here!** je t'en prie, fais comme chez toi!; **I really don't m. what he says/thinks** je me fiche de ce qu'il peut dire/penser

4 *(object to)* **I don't m. the cold** le froid ne me gêne pas; **I don't m. trying** je veux bien essayer; **you don't m. me using the car, do you? – I m. very much** cela ne te dérange pas que je prenne la voiture? – cela me dérange beaucoup; **do you m. me smoking?** cela ne vous ennuie *ou* dérange pas que je fume?; **would you m. turning out the light, please?** est-ce que tu peux éteindre la lumière, s'il te plaît?; **how much do you earn, if you don't m. my** *or* **me asking?** combien est-ce que vous gagnez, sans indiscrétion?; **I wouldn't m. having his salary** ça ne me dérangerait pas de gagner autant que lui; **I wouldn't m. a cup of tea** je prendrais bien *ou* volontiers une tasse de thé

5 *(look after* ▸ *children)* garder; *(*▸ *bags, possessions)* garder, surveiller; *(*▸ *shop, business)* garder, tenir; *(*▸ *plants, garden)* s'occuper de, prendre soin de; **can you m. the house for us while we're away?** *(watch)* pouvez-vous surveiller la maison pendant notre absence?; *(look after)* pouvez-vous vous occuper de la maison pendant notre absence?

6 *Scot (remember)* se rappeler, se souvenir de

7 *(idioms)* **m. (you), I'm not surprised** remarque *ou* tu sais, cela ne m'étonne pas; **m. you, he's a bit young** ceci dit, il est un peu jeune; **never m. that now** *(leave it)* ne vous occupez pas de cela tout de suite; *(forget it)* ce n'est plus la peine de s'en occuper; **never m. what people say/think** peu importe ce que disent/pensent les gens; **never m. his feelings, I've got a business to run!** je me moque de ses états d'âme, j'ai une entreprise à diriger!

VI 1 *(object* ▸ *in requests)* **would you m. if I opened the window?** est-ce que cela vous dérangerait si j'ouvrais la fenêtre?; **do you m. if I smoke?** est-ce que cela vous gêne *ou* dérange que je fume?; **I don't m.** *(it doesn't matter to me)* cela m'est égal; *(go ahead)* je veux bien; **if you don't m.** si vous voulez bien, si vous n'y voyez pas d'inconvénient; *Fam* **I don't m. if I do** *(in reply to offer)* je ne dis pas non, ce n'est pas de refus

2 *(care, worry)* **if you don't m., I haven't finished** si cela ne vous fait rien, je n'ai pas terminé; **do you m.?** *(politely)* vous permettez?; *Ironic* **do you m.!** *(indignantly)* non mais!; **never m.** *(it doesn't matter)* cela ne fait rien, tant pis; *(don't worry)* ne vous en faites pas; **never you m.!** *(don't worry)* ne vous en faites pas!; *(mind your own business)* ce n'est pas votre affaire!; **never m. about the money now** ne t'en fais pas pour l'argent, on verra plus tard

3 *Br (be careful)* faire attention; **m.!** attention!
▸▸ ***mind reader*** voyant(e) *m,f*; **he must be a m. reader** il lit dans les pensées comme dans un livre; **I'm not a m. reader** je ne suis pas devin

▸ **mind out VI** *Br* faire attention (**for** à); **m. out!** attention!

mind-blowing **ADJ** *Fam (drug)* hallucinant; *(experience)* époustouflant

mind-boggling **ADJ** *Fam* extraordinaire[□], stupéfiant[□]; **he earns a m. £72,000 a month** il gagne la somme astronomique de 72 000 livres par mois

minded ['maɪndɪd] **ADJ** *Formal* disposé (**to do sth** à faire qch); **if you were so m.** si vous le vouliez; **she could easily lend us the money, if she were m. to do so** elle pourrait facilement nous prêter l'argent, si elle y était disposée *ou* le voulait

-minded ['maɪndɪd] **SUFF 1** *(with adjective)* **simple-m.** simple d'esprit; **they're so narrow-m.** ils sont tellement étroits d'esprit **2** *(with adverb)* **to be politically-m.** s'intéresser beaucoup à la politique; **many young people are scientifically-m.** beaucoup de jeunes ont l'esprit scientifique **3** *(with noun)* **she isn't very money-m.** *(money isn't important to her)* elle n'est pas très préoccupée par les questions d'argent; **he's very sports-m.** c'est un passionné de sports

minder ['maɪndə(r)] **N 1** *Fam (bodyguard)* garde *m* du corps[□], gorille *m* **2** *(gen)* gardien(enne) *m,f*, surveillant(e) *m,f* **3** **(child** *or* **baby) m.** nourrice *f*

mindful ['maɪndfʊl] **ADJ** *Formal* **to be m. of sth** *(remember)* se souvenir de qch, ne pas oublier qch; **m. of her feelings on the subject, he fell silent** attentif à ce qu'elle ressentait à ce sujet, il se tut; **he was always m. of his children's future** il a toujours été soucieux *ou* il s'est toujours préoccupé de l'avenir de ses enfants

mindless ['maɪndlɪs] **ADJ 1** *(stupid* ▸ *film, book)* idiot, stupide; *(senseless* ▸ *cruelty, violence)* gratuit **2** *(boring)* bête, ennuyeux; **a m. job** un travail ingrat *ou* stupide

mind-numbing [-nʌmɪŋ] **ADJ** abêtissant

mindset ['maɪndset] **N** façon *f* de voir les choses

mine[1] [maɪn] **PRON 1** *(gen ▸ singular)* le mien (la mienne) *m,f*; *(▸ plural)* les miens (les miennes) *mpl,fpl*; **is this pen m.? – no, it's m.!** il est à moi ce stylo? – non, c'est le mien!; **this bag is m.** ce sac m'appartient *ou* est à moi; **this signature is not m.** cette signature n'est pas de moi; **he's an old friend of m.** c'est un vieil ami à moi; **where did that brother of m. get to?** mais où est-ce que mon frère est encore passé?; **I took her hands in m.** j'ai pris ses mains dans les miennes; **m. is an exceptional situation** je me trouve dans une situation exceptionnelle; **what's m. is yours** ce qui est à moi est à toi; *Br Fam* **m.'s a beer** *(in pub)* pour moi, ce sera une bière ◻ **2** *Fam (my house, flat)* chez moi ◻

ADJ *Arch (singular)* mon (ma); *(plural)* mes; *Hum* **m. host** l'aubergiste *m*

mine[2] **N 1** *(for coal, gold, salt etc)* mine *f*; **he went down the m.** *or* **mines at 16** il est descendu à la mine à 16 ans **2** *Fig (valuable source)* mine *f*; **she's a m. of information** c'est une véritable mine de renseignements **3** *(explosive)* mine *f*; **to clear a road of mines** déminer une route; **to lay a m.** *(on land)* poser une mine; *(at sea)* mouiller une mine

VT 1 *Geol (coal, gold etc)* extraire; *(coal seam)* exploiter; **they m. coal in the area** il y a des mines de charbon dans la région **2** *Mil (road, sea)* miner **3** *(undermine ▸ fortification)* saper

VI exploiter une mine; **to m. for uranium** *(prospect)* chercher de l'uranium, prospecter pour trouver de l'uranium; *(extract)* exploiter une mine d'uranium

▸▸ ***mine detector*** détecteur *m* de mines; ***mine shaft*** puits *m* de mine; ***mine workings*** chantiers *mpl* d'exploitation minière

minefield ['maɪnfi:ld] **N 1** *(containing mines)* champ *m* de mines **2** *Fig* **a political m.** une situation épineuse du point de vue politique

minehunter ['maɪn,hʌntə(r)] **N** *Naut* chasseur *m* de mines

minelayer ['maɪn,leɪə(r)] **N** *Mil* poseur *m* de mines; *Naut* mouilleur *m* de mines

minelaying ['maɪn,leɪɪŋ] **N** *Mil* pose *f* de mines; *Naut* mouillage *m* de mines

miner ['maɪnə(r)] **N** *Mining* mineur *m*

▸▸ ***miner's lamp*** lampe *f* de mineur; *Med* ***miner's lung*** anthracose *f*; ***miners' strike*** grève *f* des mineurs

mineral ['mɪnərəl] **N 1** *Geol* minéral *m*; **the m. resources of a country** les ressources *fpl* minières d'un pays **2** *Br (soft drink)* boisson *f* gazeuse (non alcoolique), soda *m*

ADJ minéral

▸▸ ***mineral deficiency*** déminéralisation *f*; ***mineral deposits*** gisements *mpl* miniers *ou* minéraux; ***the mineral kingdom*** le monde minéral; ***mineral oil*** *Br* huile *f* minérale; *Am* huile *f* de paraffine; ***mineral ore*** minerai *m*; ***mineral water*** eau *f* minérale

mineralogist [,mɪnə'rælədʒɪst] **N** minéralogiste *mf*

mineralogy [,mɪnə'rælədʒɪ] **N** minéralogie *f*

minestrone (soup) [,mɪnɪ'strəʊnɪ-] **N** minestrone *m*

minesweeper ['maɪn,swi:pə(r)] **N** dragueur *m* de mines

minesweeping ['maɪn,swi:pɪŋ] **N** dragage *m* des mines

ming [mɪŋ] *Br Fam* **VI** coincer, schlinguer; **it mings in here!** ça schlingue ici!

minger ['mɪŋə(r)] **N** *Br Fam (unattractive person)* mocheté *f*

minging ['mɪŋɪŋ] **ADJ** *Br Fam* **1** *(having a bad smell)* qui coince, qui schlingue **2** *(disgusting)* dégueulasse **3** *(ugly)* moche comme un pou

mingle ['mɪŋgəl] **VT** mélanger, mêler; **he mingled truth with lies** il mélangeait le vrai et le faux; **joy mingled with sadness** joie *f* mêlée de tristesse

VI *(of things)* se mélanger; *(of person) (at party)* se mêler aux gens; **to m. with the crowd** se mêler à la foule; **excuse me, I must m.** excusez-moi, il faut que je salue d'autres invités

mingy ['mɪndʒɪ] *(compar* **mingier**, *superl* **mingiest)** **ADJ** *Br Fam (mean ▸ person)* radin, pingre; *(▸ salary, gift, amount of money)* minable; **a m. helping** une portion minuscule; **a m. five pounds** cinq malheureuses livres

mini ['mɪnɪ] **N** *Fam* **1** *(skirt)* minijupe ◻ *f* **2** *Comput* mini-ordinateur ◻ *m*, mini *m*

ADJ mini *(inv)*

▸▸ ***mini system*** *(hi-fi)* mini-chaîne *f*; *Comput* ***mini tower*** mini-tour *f*

mini- ['mɪnɪ] **PREF** mini(-); **minibiography** minibiographie *f*; **minirecording studio** mini-studio *m* d'enregistrement

miniature ['mɪnətʃə(r)] **N** *(gen) & Art* miniature *f*; **in m.** en miniature

ADJ *(in miniature)* en miniature; *(model)* miniature; *(tiny)* minuscule; **a m. Eiffel Tower** une tour Eiffel miniature

▸▸ ***miniature golf*** golf *m* miniature, minigolf *m*; ***miniature poodle*** caniche *m* nain; ***miniature railway*** chemin *m* de fer miniature

miniaturist ['mɪnətʃərɪst] **N** *Art* miniaturiste *mf*

miniaturize, -ise ['mɪnətʃəraɪz] **VT** miniaturiser

minibar ['mɪnɪbɑ:(r)] **N** minibar *m*

mini-break **N** *(holiday)* mini-séjour *m*

minibudget ['mɪnɪ,bʌdʒɪt] **N** *Br Pol* budget *m* auxiliaire

minibus ['mɪnɪbʌs] *(pl* **minibuses)** **N** minibus *m*

minicab ['mɪnɪkæb] **N** *Br* = voiture de série convertie en taxi, radio-taxi *m*

minicomputer [,mɪnɪkəm'pju:tə(r)] **N** mini-ordinateur *m*

mini-cruise **N** mini-croisière *f*

MiniDisc® ['mɪnɪdɪsk] **N** MiniDisc® *m*

▸▸ ***MiniDisc® player*** lecteur *m* de MiniDiscs®

minidish ['mɪnɪdɪʃ] **N** mini antenne *f* parabolique

minidisk ['mɪnɪdɪsk] **N** mini-disquette *f*

minigolf ['mɪnɪgɒlf] **N** minigolf *m*

minim ['mɪnɪm] **N 1** *Br Mus* blanche *f* **2** *(measure)* 0,5 ml, ≃ goutte *f*

▸▸ *Br Mus* ***minim rest*** demi-pause *f*

minimal ['mɪnɪməl] **ADJ 1** *(very small)* minime; **there has been only a m. improvement** il n'y a eu qu'une infime amélioration; **there was m. interest** cela n'a suscité qu'un intérêt minime *ou* que peu d'intérêt **2** *(minimum)* minimal, minimum

▸▸ *Med* ***minimal invasive therapy*** chirurgie *f* à invasion minimale; *Ling* ***minimal pair*** paire *f* minimale; ***minimal value*** valeur *f* minimale

minimalism ['mɪnɪməlɪzəm] **N** minimalisme *m*

minimalist ['mɪnɪməlɪst] **N** minimaliste *mf*

ADJ minimaliste

minimization [,mɪnɪmaɪ'zeɪʃən] **N** minimisation *f*

minimize, -ise ['mɪnɪmaɪz] **VT 1** *(reduce ▸ size, amount, impact)* réduire au minimum, diminuer le plus possible **2** *(diminish ▸ importance, achievement)* minimiser **3** *Comput (window)* réduire

minimum ['mɪnɪməm] *(pl* **minimums** *or* **minima** [-mə]) **N** minimum *m*; **a m. of two years' experience** un minimum de deux ans d'expérience; **as a m.** au minimum; **to reduce sth to a m.** réduire qch au minimum; **keep the questions to a m.** essayez de poser le moins de questions possible; **in order to reduce delays to a m.** de façon à réduire l'attente au maximum; **we will need £50 each m.** *or* **a m. of £50 each** il nous faudra 50 livres chacun (au) minimum

ADJ minimum, minimal

▸▸ ***minimum charge*** charge *f ou* tarif *m* minimum; *Br Fin* ***minimum income guarantee*** ≃ minimum *m* vieillesse; *Br Formerly Fin* ***minimum lending rate*** taux *m* de base, taux *m* officiel d'escompte; ***minimum rate*** taux *m* minimum; ***minimum wage*** salaire *m* minimum *(légal)*, ≃ SMIC *m*

mining ['maɪnɪŋ] **N 1** *Mining* exploitation *f* minière, extraction *f*; **the m. industry** l'industrie *f* minière **2** *Mil (on land)* pose *f* de mines; *(at sea)* mouillage *m* de mines

ADJ *(town, area, company)* minier; *(family)* de mineurs

▸▸ ***mining engineer*** ingénieur *m* des mines

minion ['mɪnjən] **N** *Pej* laquais *m*; *Fam Ironic (subordinate)* sous-fifre *m*

minipill ['mɪnɪpɪl] **N** minipilule *f*

mini-roundabout **N** *Br* mini rond-point *m*

mini-series **N** *TV* mini-feuilleton *m*

miniskirt ['mɪnɪskɜ:t] **N** minijupe *f*

minister ['mɪnɪstə(r)] **N 1** *Pol* ministre *m*; **the M. of Education/Defence/Finance** le ministre de l'Éducation/de la Défense/des Finances; **M. for Agriculture** ministre *m* de l'Agriculture; **M. of State** secrétaire *mf* d'État; **M. without Portfolio** ministre *m* sans portefeuille **2** *(diplomat)* ministre *m* **3** *Rel* pasteur *m*, ministre *m*; **m. of God** ministre *m* du culte

VI 1 *(provide care)* **to m. to sb** prodiguer des soins à qn; **to m. to sb's needs** pourvoir aux besoins de qn; **he ministered to the sick** il secourait les malades **2** *Rel* **to m. to a parish** desservir une paroisse

▸▸ ***Minister Plenipotentiary*** ministre *m* plénipotentiaire

ministerial [,mɪnɪ'stɪərɪəl] **ADJ 1** *Pol (project, crisis, responsibility)* ministériel; *(post)* de ministre; **to hold m. office** être ministre; **m. functions** fonctions *fpl* exécutives **2** *Rel* pastoral, sacerdotal **3** *Law* exécutif

▸▸ *Pol* ***ministerial adviser*** conseiller(ère) *m,f* ministériel(elle)

ministering angel ['mɪnɪstərɪŋ-] **N** *Fig* ange *m* de bonté

ministration [,mɪnɪ'streɪʃən] **N** *Rel* ministère *m*, sacerdoce *m*

• **ministrations** **NPL** *Formal* soins *mpl*; **despite her ministrations the animal died** malgré les soins qu'elle lui a prodigués, l'animal est mort

ministry ['mɪnɪstrɪ] *(pl* **ministries)** **N 1** *Pol (department)* ministère *m*; *(government)* gouvernement *m*; *Br* **the M. of Defence** le ministère de la Défense; **the M. of Transport** le ministère des Transports **2** *Rel (collective body)* sacerdoce *m*, saint ministère *m*; *(period of office)* ministère *m*; **to go into** *or* **join the m.** *(Roman Catholic)* se faire ordonner prêtre; *(Protestant)* devenir pasteur; **at the end of his m. in London he moved away** il quitta Londres au terme de son ministère dans cette ville

mink [mɪŋk] **N 1** *Zool* **(American) m.** vison *m*, martre *f* du Canada **2** *(fur)* vison *m*; **a m. (coat)** un manteau de vison, un vison

▸▸ ***mink farm*** visonnière *f*; ***mink oil*** huile *f* de vison; ***mink ranch*** visonnière *f*

Minn *(written abbr* **Minnesota)** Minnesota *m*

minnow ['mɪnəʊ] *(pl inv or* **minnows)** **N 1** *Ich (specific fish)* vairon *m*; *(any small fish)* fretin *m* **2** *Br Fig (insignificant person)* (menu) fretin *m*

Minoan [mɪ'nəʊən] **N** minoen(enne) *m,f*

ADJ minoen

minor ['maɪnə(r)] **ADJ 1** *(secondary ▸ road, position)* secondaire; *(▸ writer)* mineur; *(▸ importance, interest)* secondaire, mineur; *(▸ share)* petit, mineur; **to play a m. part** *or* **role** *Cin & Theat* avoir un petit rôle; *Fig* jouer un rôle mineur *ou* accessoire

2 *(unimportant ▸ problem, worry)* mineur, peu important

3 *(small ▸ alteration, disagreement)* mineur, petit; *(▸ detail, expense)* mineur, petit, menu

4 *(not serious ▸ accident)* mineur, petit; *(▸ illness, injury)* bénin(igne); *Med* **to have a m. operation** subir une petite intervention chirurgicale *ou* une intervention chirurgicale bénigne

5 *(for emphasis)* **the film is a m. classic** le film est un petit chef-d'œuvre

6 *Mus* mineur; **in A m.** en la mineur; **in a m. key** en mode mineur; **a m. third/seventh** una tierce/une septième mineure

7 *Br Old-fashioned Sch* **Jones m.** Jones junior

8 *Am Univ (subject)* facultatif

N 1 *(in age)* mineur(e) *m,f* **2** *Am Univ* matière *f* secondaire

VI *Am Univ* **she minored in French** elle a pris le français comme matière secondaire

▸▸ ***minor league*** **N** *Am Sport* ≃ division *f* d'honneur, *Can* ligue *f* mineure **ADJ** *Fig* secondaire, de peu d'importance; **they're m. league compared with some American corporations** ils sont loin d'avoir l'envergure de certaines grandes sociétés américaines; *Law* ***minor offence*** délit *m* mineur; *Rel* ***minor orders*** ordres *mpl* mineurs; *Astron* ***minor planet*** astéroïde *m*; ***minor road*** route *f* secondaire

Minorca [mɪ'nɔːkə] N Minorque

Minorcan [mɪ'nɔːkən] N Minorquin(e) *m,f*
ADJ minorquin

minority [maɪ'nɒrətɪ] *(pl* **minorities)** N **1** *(small group)* minorité *f*; **to be in a** *or* **the m.** être en minorité; *Hum* **I'm afraid you're in a m. of one** j'ai bien peur que vous ne soyez le seul de cet avis; **the vocal m.** la minorité qui se fait entendre **2** *Law (age)* minorité *f*
COMP *(government, party, tastes)* minoritaire
▸▸ *Fin* ***minority holding, minority interest*** participation *f* minoritaire; ***minority opinion*** opinion *f* d'une minorité; **m. opinion must be respected** on doit respecter l'opinion de la minorité; ***minority report*** contre-rapport *m (soumis par une minorité)*; *Fin Br* ***minority shareholder,*** *Am* ***minority stockholder*** actionnaire *mf* minoritaire; *Law* ***minority verdict*** verdict *m* de la minorité

Minotaur ['maɪnətɔː(r)] N **the M.** le Minotaure

minster ['mɪnstə(r)] N *(abbey church)* (église *f*) abbatiale *f*; *(cathedral)* cathédrale *f*

minstrel ['mɪnstrəl] N **1** *(in Middle Ages)* ménestrel *m* **2** *Literary (poet)* poète *m*; *(musician)* musicien *m*; *(singer)* chanteur *m* **3** *(actor, singer with blackened face)* = acteur/musicien blanc maquillé en noir
▸▸ *Theat* ***minstrel show*** = spectacle de music-hall avec des acteurs blancs déguisés en Noirs

mint[1] [mɪnt] N **1** *(plant)* menthe *f* **2** *(sweet)* bonbon *m* à la menthe
COMP *(chocolate, sauce, tea)* à la menthe
▸▸ ***mint julep*** cocktail *m* au bourbon et à la menthe

mint[2] N **1** *(for coins)* **the (Royal) M.** l'Hôtel *m* de la Monnaie, la Monnaie **2** *Fam (fortune)* fortune▫*f*; **to make a m.** faire fortune; **it's worth a m.** cela vaut une fortune
ADJ *(stamps, coins)* (tout) neuf; *Fig* **in m. condition** en parfait état, à l'état neuf
VT **1** *(coins)* frapper; *Fam Fig* **he must be minting it** il doit rouler sur l'or **2** *(invent ▸ word)* inventer, créer; *(▸ expression)* forger

minted ['mɪntɪd] ADJ *Br Fam* plein aux as, bourré de fric

minuet [ˌmɪnjʊ'et] N *Mus* menuet *m*

minus ['maɪnəs] *(pl* **minuses** *or* **minusses)** PREP **1** *Math* moins; **seven m. two leaves** *or* **equals five** sept moins deux font cinq **2** *(in temperature)* **it's m. five outside** il fait moins cinq dehors **3** *Fam (without)* sans▫; **he came home m. his shopping** il est rentré sans ses achats
N **1** *(sign)* moins *m* **2** *(drawback)* inconvénient *m*
ADJ **1** *(number)* négatif; *Sch* **B m.** B moins **2** *Fig* négatif; **but, on the m. side, the pay is low** mais le revers de la médaille, c'est que c'est mal payé
▸▸ ***minus sign*** signe *m* moins, moins *m*

minuscule ['mɪnəskjuːl] ADJ *(tiny)* minuscule

minute[1] ['mɪnɪt] N **1** *(period of sixty seconds)* minute *f*; **for ten minutes** pendant dix minutes; **I'll be ready in ten minutes** je serai prêt dans dix minutes; **it's only a few minutes' walk (from here)** c'est seulement à quelques minutes (d'ici) à pied; **to observe a m.'s silence** observer une minute de silence; **two minutes past/to ten** dix heures deux/moins deux
2 *(moment)* instant *m*, minute *f*; **I'll be back in a m.** je reviens dans une minute *ou* dans un instant *ou* tout de suite; **I won't be a m.** *(I'll be right back)* je reviens dans une minute *ou* dans un instant *ou* tout de suite; *(I've nearly finished)* j'en ai pour une minute; **it only took him a m.** il en a eu pour une minute; **a m.'s rest** un moment de repos; **wait a m., please** attendez un instant, s'il vous plaît; **just a m.!** un instant!, une minute!; *(aggressively)* une minute!; **come here this m.!** viens ici tout de suite!; **I think of you every m. of the day** je pense à vous à chaque instant de la journée; **I'll talk to him the m. he arrives** je lui parlerai dès qu'il arrivera; **the m. my back was turned she…** j'avais à peine le dos tourné qu'elle…; **any m. now** d'un instant à l'autre; **at the m.** en ce moment; **right up till the last m.** jusqu'à la toute dernière minute; **at the last m.** à la dernière minute; **she left the house within minutes of his arrival** elle a quitté la maison dans les minutes qui ont suivi son arrivée; **the flight took two hours to the m.** le vol a duré deux heures à la minute près *ou* exactement
3 *Geom (of degree)* minute *f*
4 *(note)* note *f* (de service)
VT **1** *(facts, comments)* prendre note de; *(meeting)* dresser le procès-verbal *ou* le compte rendu de **2** *(time)* minuter, chronométrer
• **minutes** NPL **1** *(of meeting)* procès-verbal *m*, compte rendu *m*; **to take the minutes of a meeting** faire le compte rendu d'une réunion **2** *(report)* note *f*
▸▸ ***minute book*** registre *m* des délibérations *ou* des procès-verbaux; ***minute hand*** grande aiguille *f*, aiguille *f* des minutes; ***minute steak*** entrecôte *f* minute; ***minute timer*** minuterie *f*

minute[2] [maɪ'njuːt] ADJ **1** *(tiny)* minuscule, infime; *(very slight ▸ difference, improvement)* infime, minime **2** *(precise)* minutieux, détaillé; **with m. care** avec un soin minutieux; **in m. detail** par le menu; **in the minutest detail** dans les moindres détails

minutely [maɪ'njuːtlɪ] ADV **1** *(carefully)* minutieusement, avec un soin minutieux; *(in detail)* en détail, par le menu **2** *(fold)* tout petit; *(move)* imperceptiblement, très légèrement

minutiae [maɪ'njuːʃɪaɪ] NPL menus détails *mpl*, petits détails *mpl*; *Pej (trivialities)* vétilles *fpl*, riens *mpl*

minx [mɪŋks] N *Fam* coquine *f*, friponne *f*; **you little m.!** petite espiègle!, petite polissonne!

mips [mɪps] N *Comput (abbr* **million instructions per second)** MIPS *m*

miracle ['mɪrəkəl] N **1** *Rel & Fig* miracle *m*; **to work** *or* **perform miracles** faire *ou* accomplir des miracles; **I can't perform miracles!** je ne peux pas faire de miracles!; **by a m., disaster was averted** la catastrophe a été évitée par miracle; **it was a m. (that) she survived** c'est un miracle qu'elle ait survécu; **a m. of modern science** un prodige *ou* miracle de la science moderne **2** *(play)* miracle *m (drame)*
▸▸ *Fig* ***miracle cure, miracle drug*** remède *m* miracle; ***miracle play*** miracle *m (drame)*; ***miracle worker*** faiseur(euse) *m,f* de miracles

miraculous [mɪ'rækjʊləs] ADJ miraculeux; **they had a m. escape** c'est un miracle qu'ils s'en soient tirés (vivants); *Ironic* **she made a m. recovery as soon as the weekend arrived** comme par miracle, son état de santé s'est amélioré juste avant le week-end

miraculously [mɪ'rækjʊləslɪ] ADV **1** *(by a miracle)* miraculeusement, par miracle; **m., no one was hurt** tout le monde s'en est sorti miraculeusement indemne **2** *(extremely)* merveilleusement, prodigieusement; **m. low prices** des prix *mpl* incroyablement bas

mirage [mɪ'rɑːʒ] N mirage *m*

MIRAS ['maɪræs] N *Br Formerly Fin (abbr* **Mortgage Interest Relief at Source)** = système par lequel les intérêts dus à une société de crédit immobilier sont déductibles des impôts

mire [maɪə(r)] *Literary* N boue *f*, bourbe *f*, fange *f*; *(deep)* bourbier *m*; *Fig* **to drag sb's name through the m.** traîner le nom de qn dans la boue
VT *(usu passive)* **1** *(in debt, difficulty)* empêtrer; **the project was mired in controversy from the start** dès le début, le projet a été freiné par toutes sortes de controverses **2** *(in mud)* embourber

mirror ['mɪrə(r)] N *(looking glass)* miroir *m*, glace *f*; *Aut (rearview mirror, side mirror)* rétroviseur *m*; **when I look at my face in the m.** quand je me regarde dans le miroir *ou* la glace; *Fig* **it's all done with mirrors** c'est de la magie; *Fig* **to hold a m. (up) to sth** refléter qch; **the tabloid press is not necessarily a m. of national opinion** la presse à sensation ne reflète pas nécessairement l'opinion du pays
VT **1** *(reflect)* réfléchir, refléter; **the steeple is mirrored in the lake** le clocher se reflète *ou* se mire dans le lac **2** *(imitate)* imiter; **his experience exactly mirrors my own** nous avons eu des expériences identiques
▸▸ ***mirror finish*** fini *m* spéculaire; ***mirror image*** image *f* en miroir, image *f* spéculaire; *Fig* copie *f* conforme; *Comput* ***mirror site*** *(on Internet)* site *m* miroir; ***mirror writing*** écriture *f* spéculaire *ou* en miroir

mirrorball ['mɪrəbɔːl] N sphère *f* à facettes de verre

mirth [mɜːθ] N *(UNCOUNT)* **1** *(laughter)* rires *mpl*, hilarité *f*; **he could barely control his m.** il avait du mal à se retenir de rire **2** *(gaiety)* allégresse *f*, joie *f*

mirthful ['mɜːθfʊl] ADJ *Literary (laughing)* rieur; *(merry)* joyeux

mirthless ['mɜːθlɪs] ADJ *Literary* triste, sombre, morne; *(laugh)* faux (fausse), forcé

MIRV [mɜːv] N *Mil (abbr* **multiple independently targeted re-entry vehicle)** MIRV *m*

miry ['maɪərɪ] *(compar* **mirier,** *superl* **miriest)** ADJ *Literary* boueux, fangeux

> **PRÉFIXE**
> **MIS-**
> Le préfixe **mis-** se combine avec de très nombreux noms, verbes et leurs dérivés. Il véhicule la notion d'ERREUR ou d'ÉCHEC, et se traduit le plus souvent en employant l'adverbe **mal** ou l'adjectif **mauvais** ou bien encore par une périphrase:
> **to misbehave** se conduire mal; **to miscalculate an amount** mal calculer une somme; **a misunderstanding** un malentendu; **misfortune** malchance, infortune; **mismanagement** mauvaise gestion; **a misprint** une faute d'impression, une coquille; **misleadingly** de façon trompeuse; **he was miscast in the part** ce n'était pas un rôle qui lui convenait; **the joke misfired** la plaisanterie a manqué son effet.

MIS [ˌemaɪ'es] N **1** *Comput (abbr* **management information system)** système *m* intégré de gestion **2** *Mktg (abbr* **marketing information system)** système *m* d'information marketing

misadventure [ˌmɪsəd'ventʃə(r)] N *(accident)* mésaventure *f*; *(misfortune)* malheur *m*; *Law* **a verdict of death by m.** un verdict de mort accidentelle

misalliance [ˌmɪsə'laɪəns] N mésalliance *f*

misanthrope ['mɪsənθrəʊp] N misanthrope *mf*

misanthropic [ˌmɪsən'θrɒpɪk] ADJ *(person)* misanthrope; *(thoughts, mood)* misanthropique

misanthropist [mɪ'sænθrəpɪst] N misanthrope *mf*

misanthropy [mɪ'sænθrəpɪ] N misanthropie *f*

misapply [ˌmɪsə'plaɪ] *(pt & pp* **misapplied)** VT mal utiliser, mal exploiter; *(law)* mal appliquer, appliquer à tort; *(money)* détourner

misapprehend ['mɪsˌæprɪ'hend] VT *Formal* mal comprendre; *(person's words)* mal comprendre, se méprendre sur

misapprehension ['mɪsˌæprɪ'henʃən] N *Formal* malentendu *m*, méprise *f*; **to be** *or* **to labour under a m.** se méprendre, se tromper; **the Government appears to be (labouring) under the m. that…** le gouvernement semble s'imaginer que…

misappropriate [ˌmɪsə'prəʊprɪeɪt] VT *Formal (money, funds)* détourner; *(property)* voler

misappropriation ['mɪsəˌprəʊprɪ'eɪʃən] N *Formal* détournement *m*
▸▸ *Fin* ***misappropriation of funds*** détournement *m* de fonds, abus *m* de biens sociaux

misbegotten [ˌmɪsbɪ'gɒtən] ADJ *Formal* **1** *(plan)* mal conçu, bâtard **2** *(child)* bâtard, illégitime **3** *(illegally obtained)* d'origine douteuse

misbehave [ˌmɪsbɪ'heɪv] VI **to m. (oneself)** se conduire mal; *(child)* se tenir mal; **he has been misbehaving at school** il n'a pas été sage à l'école; *Fig* **the VCR has been misbehaving again** le magnétoscope fait encore des siennes

misbehaviour, *Am* **misbehavior** [ˌmɪsbɪ'heɪvjə(r)] N *(bad behaviour)* mauvaise conduite *f*, *(more serious)* inconduite *f*

misc *(written abbr* **miscellaneous)** divers

miscalculate [ˌmɪs'kælkjʊleɪt] VT *(amount, distance)* mal calculer; *Fig* mal évaluer
VI *Math* se tromper dans ses calculs; *Fig (judge wrongly)* se tromper

miscalculation [ˌmɪskælkjʊ'leɪʃən] **N** *Math* erreur *f* de calcul; *Fig* mauvais calcul *m*

miscarriage [ˌmɪs'kærɪdʒ] **N 1** *Med* fausse couche *f*, *Spec* avortement *m* spontané; **to have a m.** faire une fausse couche **2** *(failure)* échec *m* **3** *Br (in post ▸ of letter, package)* égarement *m*, perte *f*

▸▸ *Law* ***miscarriage of justice*** erreur *f* judiciaire

miscarry [ˌmɪs'kærɪ] *(pt & pp* **miscarried***)* **VI 1** *Med* faire une fausse couche **2** *(fail ▸ plan, hopes)* échouer, avorter, mal tourner **3** *Br (letter, parcel)* s'égarer, se perdre; *(reach wrong address)* parvenir à une fausse adresse

miscast [ˌmɪs'kɑːst] *(pt & pp* **miscast***)* **VT** *Cin & Theat (play)* se tromper dans la distribution de; *(actor)* mal choisir le rôle de; **to m. sb** donner à qn un rôle qui ne lui convient pas; **he was m. in the part** ce n'était pas un rôle qui lui convenait; **Ralph was hopelessly m. as Romeo** Ralph n'était vraiment pas fait pour jouer le rôle de Roméo

miscegenation [ˌmɪsɪdʒɪ'neɪʃən] **N** *Biol* métissage *m (de races humaines)*

miscellaneous [ˌmɪsə'leɪnɪəs] **ADJ** *(assorted)* divers, varié; *(jumbled)* hétérogène, hétéroclite, disparate; **the file marked "m."** le dossier "divers"

▸▸ ***miscellaneous expenses*** frais *mpl* divers; *Journ* ***miscellaneous news*** faits *mpl* divers

miscellany [*Br* mɪ'selənɪ, *Am* 'mɪsəleɪnɪ] *(pl* **miscellanies***)* **N 1** *(mixture, assortment)* amalgame *m*, mélange *m* **2** *(anthology)* recueil *m*, anthologie *f*

mischance [ˌmɪs'tʃɑːns] **N** *Formal (bad luck)* malheur *m*, malchance *f*; *(stroke of bad luck)* mésaventure *f*; **by m.** par malchance; *(stronger)* par malheur

mischief ['mɪstʃɪf] **N 1** *(UNCOUNT) (naughtiness)* espièglerie *f*, malice *f*; **to get up to m.** faire des bêtises *ou* sottises; **to keep sb out of m.** *(prevent from being naughty)* empêcher qn de faire des sottises *ou* des bêtises; *(keep busy)* occuper qn; **to do sth out of sheer m.** faire qch par pure espièglerie *ou* par pure malice; **he's full of m.** il est très espiègle; **they're always up to (some) m.** ils trouvent toujours des bêtises à faire; **she looked at me with m. in her eyes** elle me regardait d'un air taquin *ou* malicieux

2 *(UNCOUNT) (trouble)* **to make m. (for sb)** créer des problèmes (à qn); **to make m. between people** semer la zizanie entre les gens

3 *(UNCOUNT) Formal (damage)* dommages *mpl*, dégâts *mpl*

4 *Br (injury)* **to do oneself a m.** se blesser, se faire mal

5 *Fam Hum (child)* polisson(onne) *m,f*, (petite) canaille *f*; **little m.** petit(e) espiègle *mf*, petit(e) coquin(e) *m,f*

mischief-maker **N** faiseur(euse) *m,f* d'histoires *ou* d'embarras; **she's a terrible m.** *(naughty)* elle est très espiègle; *(nasty)* elle est toujours en train d'intriguer *ou* de semer la zizanie

mischief-making **N 1** *(naughtiness)* espièglerie *f* **2** *(trouble-making)* intrigues *fpl*

mischievous ['mɪstʃɪvəs] **ADJ 1** *(child)* espiègle, malicieux; *(look)* taquin, narquois; *(thought)* malicieux; **m. trick** *or* **prank** espièglerie *f*; **to play a m. trick on sb** jouer un tour *ou* faire une farce à qn; **a m. grin/wink** un sourire/clin d'œil malicieux **2** *(harmful)* méchant, malveillant; **m. gossip** médisances *fpl*

mischievously ['mɪstʃɪvəslɪ] **ADV 1** *(naughtily, teasingly)* malicieusement **2** *(nastily)* méchamment, avec malveillance

mischievousness ['mɪstʃɪvəsnɪs] **N 1** *(naughtiness)* espièglerie *f*, malice *f* **2** *(nastiness)* malveillance *f*, méchanceté *f*

misconceive [ˌmɪskən'siːv] **VT** *(misunderstand)* mal comprendre, mal interpréter; *(have wrong idea of)* se faire une idée fausse de

misconceived [ˌmɪskən'siːvd] **ADJ** *(plan)* mal conçu; *(idea)* faux (fausse), erroné

misconception [ˌmɪskən'sepʃən] **N** *(poor understanding)* mauvaise compréhension *f*; *(complete misunderstanding)* idée *f* fausse, méprise *f*; **a popular m.** une idée fausse couramment répandue

misconduct **N** [ˌmɪs'kɒndʌkt] **1** *(bad behaviour)* mauvaise conduite *f*; *(immoral behaviour)* inconduite *f*; *(adultery)* adultère *m*; **(professional) m.** faute *f* professionnelle **2** *(bad management)* mauvaise gestion *f*; **they accused her of m. of the company's affairs** ils l'ont accusée d'avoir mal géré la société

VT [ˌmɪskən'dʌkt] *(mismanage ▸ business)* mal gérer; *(▸ affair)* mal conduire

misconstruction [ˌmɪskən'strʌkʃən] **N 1** *(gen)* fausse interprétation *f*; **the law is open to m.** la loi peut prêter à des interprétations erronées **2** *Gram* mauvaise construction *f*

misconstrue [ˌmɪskən'struː] **VT** mal interpréter

miscount **N** ['mɪskaʊnt] *(miscalculation)* erreur *f* de calcul; *(mistake in addition)* erreur *f* d'addition; *Pol (of votes)* erreur *f* dans le dépouillement du scrutin

VT [ˌmɪs'kaʊnt] mal compter, faire une erreur en comptant

VI [ˌmɪs'kaʊnt] se tromper dans le compte

miscreant ['mɪskrɪənt] **N** *Literary (villain)* scélérat(e) *m,f*, vaurien(enne) *m,f*

> Note that the French word **mécréant** is a false friend and is never a translation for the English word **miscreant**. It means **unbeliever**.

misdeal [ˌmɪs'diːl] *(pt & pp* **misdealt** [-'delt]*)* *Cards* **N** maldonne *f*

VT to m. the cards faire (une) maldonne

VI faire (une) maldonne

misdeed [ˌmɪs'diːd] **N** *Formal* méfait *m*; *Law* délit *m*

misdemeanour, *Am* **misdemeanor** [ˌmɪsdɪ'miːnə(r)] **N 1** *Law* délit *m* **2** *(minor act of misbehaviour)* écart *m* de conduite; *(more serious)* méfait *m*

misdiagnose [ˌmɪs'daɪəgnəʊz] **VT** *Med* **to m. the symptoms/illness/***etc* faire une erreur de diagnostic; **she was misdiagnosed as having cancer** les médecins ont diagnostiqué un cancer mais ils se sont trompés; *Fig* **to m. the situation** faire une mauvaise analyse de la situation

misdiagnosis [ˌmɪsdaɪəg'nəʊsɪs] *(pl* **misdiagnoses** [-siːz]*)* **N** *Med & Fig* erreur *f* de diagnostic, mauvais diagnostic *m*

misdirect [ˌmɪsdɪ'rekt] **VT 1** *(to destination ▸ traveller)* mal orienter, mal renseigner; *(▸ letter, parcel)* mal adresser

2 *(misuse ▸ efforts, talents)* mal employer, mal orienter; **misdirected energy** énergie *f* mal utilisée

3 *(blow)* mal diriger

4 *Law (jury)* mal renseigner

misdirected [ˌmɪsdɪ'rektɪd] **ADJ 1** *(letter, parcel)* envoyé à la mauvaise adresse **2** *(efforts, talents)* mal employé **3** *(blow)* frappé à faux, mal dirigé

misdirection [ˌmɪsdɪ'rekʃən] **N 1** *(on letter)* erreur *f* d'adresse **2** *(of efforts, talents)* mauvais emploi *m*, mauvais usage *m*

miser ['maɪzə(r)] **N** avare *mf*; **he's a real m.** c'est un vrai grippe-sou

miserable ['mɪzərəbəl] **ADJ 1** *(unhappy)* malheureux, triste; **to look m.** avoir l'air déprimé *ou* malheureux; **I feel really m. today** je n'ai vraiment pas le moral aujourd'hui; **to make sb m.** rendre qn malheureux, faire de la peine à qn; **don't be so m.!** allez! ne fais pas cette tête!

2 *(unpleasant ▸ evening, sight)* pénible; *(▸ weather, summer)* épouvantable, pourri; *(▸ conditions, holiday)* déplorable, lamentable; **if only I didn't have this m. cold!** si je n'avais pas cet affreux rhume!; **what m. weather!** quel temps épouvantable!; **we had a m. time on holiday** nous avons passé des vacances atroces *ou* détestables

3 *(poor ▸ hotel)* miteux; *(▸ tenement)* misérable; *(▸ meal)* maigre; **a m. failure** *(plan etc)* un ratage complet *ou* lamentable; *(person)* un(e) raté(e)

4 *(mean ▸ reward)* minable, misérable; *(▸ salary)* de misère, minable; *(▸ donation, amount)* dérisoire; **I've only got a m. £70** je n'ai que 70 malheureuses livres

5 *Scot & Austr (stingy)* avare

> Note that the French adjective **misérable** never means **unhappy**.

miserably ['mɪzərəblɪ] **ADV 1** *(unhappily)* malheureusement, d'un air malheureux; *(say)* d'un ton malheureux; **she sat m. at the back of the class** elle était assise, l'air malheureux *ou* pitoyable, au fond de la classe

2 *(unpleasantly ▸ unhappy, cold)* extrêmement

3 *(poorly ▸ perform, play)* de façon lamentable *ou* déplorable; **to fail m.** échouer lamentablement; **to be m. paid** avoir un salaire de misère

4 *(in poverty)* misérablement, dans la misère

Miserere [mɪzə'rɪərɪ] **N** *Rel* **1** *(psalm)* miséréré *m* miserere *m inv* **2** *(seat)* miséricorde *f*, patience *f* (de stalle)

▸▸ ***miserere seat*** miséricorde *f*, patience *f* de stalle

misericord [mɪ'zerɪkɔːd] **N** *Rel* **1** *(in monastery)* miséricorde *f* **2** *(seat)* miséricorde *f*, patience *f* (de stalle)

miserliness ['maɪzəlɪnɪs] **N** avarice *f*

miserly ['maɪzəlɪ] **ADJ** avare

misery ['mɪzərɪ] *(pl* **miseries***)* **N 1** *(unhappiness)* malheur *m*, tristesse *f*; **to make sb's life a m.** rendre la vie insupportable à qn

2 *(suffering)* souffrance(s) *f(pl)*; *Hum* **to put sb out of their m.** mettre fin aux souffrances *ou* au supplice de qn; **go on, put me out of my m. and tell me the worst** continue, mets fin à mon supplice dis-moi tout; *Euph* **to put an animal out of its m.** achever un animal

3 *(poverty)* misère *f*

4 *Br Fam (gloomy person)* rabat-joie *m inv*, grincheux(euse) *m,f*; **don't be such an old m.!** cesse de jouer les rabat-joie!

▸▸ ***misery memoir*** = ouvrage dans lequel l'auteur se concentre sur un ou plusieurs épisodes traumatisants de son existence

> Note that the French word **misère** is a false friend and is rarely a translation for the English word **misery**. Its most common meaning is **extreme poverty**.

misery-guts **N** *Fam* rabat-joie *m inv*, grincheux(euse) *m,f*

misfire **N** ['mɪsfaɪə(r)] *Mil & Aut* raté *m*

VI [ˌmɪs'faɪə(r)] **1** *(gun)* faire long feu; *(joke)* manquer son effet; *(plan)* rater **2** *(engine)* avoir des problèmes d'allumage *ou* des ratés

misfit ['mɪsfɪt] **N** inadapté(e) *m,f*, marginal(e) *m,f*; **she was always a m. at school** à l'école, elle n'a jamais été acceptée par les autres; **a social m.** un(e) inadapté(e) social(e)

misfortune [ˌmɪs'fɔːtʃuːn] **N 1** *(bad luck)* malchance *f*, infortune *f*; **allies** *or* **companions in m.** compagnons *mpl* d'infortune; **I had the m. to meet him in Paris** j'ai eu la malchance de le rencontrer à Paris **2** *(unfortunate event)* malheur *m*; **to be plagued by misfortunes** jouer de malchance

misgiving [ˌmɪs'gɪvɪŋ] **N** doute *m*, appréhension *f*; **not without m.** *or* **misgivings** non sans hésitation; **to have misgivings about sth** avoir des doutes quant à qch, douter de qch; **she had misgivings about allowing them to go** elle hésitait à les laisser y aller; **to be filled with m.** être en proie au doute

misgovern [ˌmɪs'gʌvən] **VT** mal gouverner

VI mal gouverner

misgovernment [ˌmɪs'gʌvənmənt] **N** *(of country)* mauvais gouvernement *m*; *(of affairs)* mauvaise gestion *f*

misguided [ˌmɪs'gaɪdɪd] **ADJ** *(person)* malavisé, mal inspiré; *(attempt)* malencontreux; *(decision)* peu judicieux *ou* pertinent; *(energy, idealism)* mal placé; *(idealist)* égaré; **a m. genius** un génie dévoyé; **it was very m. of him to try to intervene** il a commis une grosse bévue en essayant d'intervenir; **in the m. belief that...** croyant à tort que...

misguidedly [ˌmɪs'gaɪdɪdlɪ] **ADV** malencontreusement

mishandle [ˌmɪs'hændəl] **VT 1** *(equipment)* mal utiliser, mal se servir de; *(substance, product)* manipuler sans prendre les précautions nécessaires **2** *(affair, situation)* mal gérer; **the case was mishandled from the outset** l'affaire a été mal menée depuis le début **3** *(treat insensitively ▸ customer)* malmener, traiter avec rudesse

mishandling [mɪs'hændəlɪŋ] **N** *(of situation, staff etc)* mauvaise gestion *f*

mishap ['mɪshæp] **N** *(misadventure)* mésaventure *f*, accident *m*; **he arrived without m.** il est arrivé sans encombre

mishear [ˌmɪs'hɪə(r)] *(pt & pp* **misheard** [-'hɜːd]) **VT** mal entendre, mal comprendre
VI mal entendre, mal comprendre

mishmash ['mɪʃmæʃ] **N** *Fam* méli-mélo *m*, micmac *m*

misinform [ˌmɪsɪn'fɔːm] **VT** *(unintentionally)* mal renseigner; *(intentionally)* donner de faux renseignements à, tromper; **I think you have been misinformed** je pense qu'on vous a mal renseigné

misinformation [ˌmɪsɪnfə'meɪʃən] **N** *(UNCOUNT)* fausse information *f*

misinterpret [ˌmɪsɪn'tɜːprɪt] **VT** mal comprendre, mal interpréter; **this decision should not be misinterpreted as…** cette décision ne doit pas être interprétée comme…; **she misinterpreted his silence as contempt** elle a pris à tort son silence pour du mépris

misinterpretation ['mɪsɪnˌtɜːprɪ'teɪʃən] **N** mauvaise interprétation; **the rules are open to m.** l'interprétation du règlement prête à confusion

misjudge [ˌmɪs'dʒʌdʒ] **VT** *(distance, reaction)* mal juger, mal évaluer; *(person)* mal juger; **it appears I misjudged you** il semblerait que je vous ai mal jugé

misjudgement, misjudgment [ˌmɪs'dʒʌdʒmənt] **N** erreur *f* de jugement; *(of distance)* mauvaise évaluation *f* ou estimation *f*

miskey ['mɪskiː] **N** faute *f* de frappe
VT [ˌmɪs'kiː] ne pas taper correctement

mislay [ˌmɪs'leɪ] *(pt & pp* **mislaid** [-'leɪd]) **VT** égarer

mislead [ˌmɪs'liːd] *(pt & pp* **misled** [-'led]) **VT** tromper, induire en erreur; **we were misled into believing he was dead** on nous a fait croire qu'il était mort; **her behaviour misled him into thinking her feelings were stronger** sa conduite lui a laissé croire que ses sentiments étaient plus profonds, mais il n'en était rien

misleading [ˌmɪs'liːdɪŋ] **ADJ** *(false)* trompeur, fallacieux; *(confusing)* équivoque; **the map is very m.** cette carte n'est pas claire du tout; **the description she gave was deliberately m.** elle a fait exprès de donner une fausse description
▸▸ ***misleading advertising*** publicité *f* mensongère

misled [mɪs'led] *pt & pp of* **mislead**

mismanage [ˌmɪs'mænɪdʒ] **VT** mal gérer, mal diriger

mismanagement [ˌmɪs'mænɪdʒmənt] **N** mauvaise gestion *f*, mauvaise administration *f*

mismatch **N** ['mɪsmætʃ] **1** *(clash)* **there is a m. between the skills graduates have and the jobs available** il y a une disparité entre les compétences des étudiants diplômés et les emplois disponibles
2 *(in a relationship)* mésalliance *f*
3 *Sport* match *m* inégal
4 *Comput* incohérence *f*
VT [ˌmɪs'mætʃ] **1** *(colours, clothes)* mal assortir **2** *(in a relationship)* **they were totally mismatched** *(socially)* ils étaient vraiment mal assortis; *(by temperament)* ils n'étaient absolument pas faits pour s'entendre

misnomer [ˌmɪs'nəʊmə(r)] **N** nom *m* inapproprié; **to call it a democratic country is a complete m.** ce pays ne mérite vraiment pas le nom de démocratie

misogynist [mɪ'sɒdʒɪnɪst] **N** misogyne *mf*

misogynistic [mɪˌsɒdʒɪ'nɪstɪk], **misogynous** [mɪ'sɒdʒɪnəs] **ADJ** misogyne

misogyny [mɪ'sɒdʒɪnɪ] **N** misogynie *f*

misplace [ˌmɪs'pleɪs] **VT 1** *(put in wrong place)* **to m. sth** ne pas mettre qch à sa place ou au bon endroit **2** *(mislay)* égarer **3** *(trust, confidence)* mal placer

misprint **N** ['mɪsprɪnt] faute *f* d'impression, coquille *f*
VT [ˌmɪs'prɪnt] imprimer incorrectement

mispronounce [ˌmɪsprə'naʊns] **VT** *(word)* mal prononcer, prononcer incorrectement; *(name)* estropier, écorcher

mispronunciation ['mɪsprəˌnʌnsɪ'eɪʃən] **N** *(act)* prononciation *f* incorrecte; *(instance)* faute *f* de prononciation

misquotation [ˌmɪskwəʊ'teɪʃən] **N** citation *f* inexacte

misquote **N** ['mɪskwəʊt] *Fam* citation *f* inexacte[□]
VT [ˌmɪs'kwəʊt] *(author, text)* citer inexactement; *(speaker)* déformer les propos de; **I've been misquoted** *(by the press etc)* on a déformé mes propos

misread *(pt & pp* **misread** [-'red]) **N** ['mɪsriːd] *Comput* erreur *f* de lecture
VT [ˌmɪs'riːd] *(word, text)* mal lire; *Fig (actions, motives, situation)* mal interpréter, mal comprendre

misrepresent ['mɪsˌreprɪ'zent] **VT** *(facts, events)* déformer, dénaturer; *(person)* donner une image fausse de; **I have been grossly misrepresented by my opponents** mes adversaires donnent de moi une image entièrement fausse

misrepresentation ['mɪsˌreprɪzen'teɪʃən] **N** *(of truth)* déformation *f*; **what they say is a complete m. of the facts** ils déforment complètement la réalité

misrule [ˌmɪs'ruːl] **N 1** *(misgovernment)* mauvais gouvernement *m* **2** *(anarchy)* désordre *m*, anarchie *f*
VT mal gouverner

Miss[1] *(written abbr* **Mississippi**) Mississippi *m*

Miss[2] [mɪs] **N** mademoiselle *f*; **M. Brett** Mademoiselle *f* Brett; **Dear M. Brett** Chère Mademoiselle Brett, Chère Mlle Brett; *Formal* **the Misses Brett** Mesdemoiselles Brett
▸▸ ***Miss World*** Miss *f* Monde

MISS[1] [mɪs]

VT
• manquer **1, 2, 4** • rater **1**
• faillir **3** • manquer de **5**
VI
• manquer son coup **1** • manquer **3**
N
• coup manqué **1**

VT 1 *(bus, film, target)* manquer, rater; *(opportunity, turn)* manquer, laisser passer; **a life of missed opportunities** une vie d'occasions manquées; **we missed the train by five minutes** on a manqué le train de cinq minutes; **I missed him (by two minutes)** je l'ai manqué ou raté (de deux minutes); **this film is not to be missed** c'est un film à ne pas manquer ou à ne manquer sous aucun prétexte; **I missed the first five minutes of the programme** j'ai raté les cinq premières minutes de l'émission; **he never misses a chance to put other people down** il ne manque jamais une occasion de rabaisser les autres; **you didn't m. much** vous n'avez pas raté grand-chose; *Fam* **you don't know what you're missing** tu ne sais pas ce que tu rates; *Fig* **to m. the boat** rater une occasion, manquer le coche; *Theat* **to m. one's cue** manquer sa réplique
2 *(fail to do, find, see, attend)* manquer; *(fail to hear) (question, remark etc)* ne pas entendre; *(omit) (word, line)* omettre, sauter; **to m. school** manquer l'école; **it's at the end of the street, you can't m. it** c'est au bout de la rue, vous ne pouvez pas le manquer; **to m. one's stop** *(of passenger)* rater son arrêt; **to m. a turning** rater un tournant; **he missed breakfast** *(was too late)* il a manqué le petit déjeuner; *(didn't go)* il a sauté le petit déjeuner; **I missed seeing them in Australia** *(for lack of time)* je n'ai pas eu le temps de les voir en Australie; *(for lack of opportunity)* je n'ai pas eu l'occasion ou la possibilité de les voir en Australie; **they've missed my name off the list** ils ont oublié mon nom sur la liste; **you m. a lot if you read this novel in translation** on perd beaucoup à ne pas lire ce roman dans le texte; **you've missed** or **you're missing the point!** vous n'avez rien compris!; **you don't m. much!** rien ne t'échappe!
3 *(escape, manage to avoid)* **I narrowly** or **just missed being killed** j'ai bien failli me faire tuer
4 *(regret the absence of)* **I m. her** elle me manque; **don't you m. your family?** est-ce que ta famille ne te manque pas?; **you'll be missed when you retire** on vous regrettera ou vous nous manquerez quand vous serez à la retraite; **I m. the warm weather/the sea** la chaleur/la mer me manque; **I m. being able to do what I like** ça me manque de ne pas pouvoir faire ce que je veux; **I missed my umbrella** mon parapluie m'aurait été bien utile; **you can't m. what you've never had** ce que l'on n'a jamais eu ne nous manque pas
5 *(be short of, lack)* manquer de; **I'm missing two books from my collection** il me manque deux livres dans ma collection, deux livres de ma collection ont disparu; **the table's missing one of its legs** il manque un pied à la table
6 *(notice absence or disappearance of)* **he disappeared for a week and no one ever missed him** il a disparu pendant une semaine et personne ne s'en est aperçu; **I missed him at the meeting** j'ai remarqué qu'il n'était pas à la réunion; **we're sure to be missed** on va sûrement remarquer notre absence; **he's got so many records he won't m. one** il a tellement de disques qu'il ne s'apercevra pas qu'il lui en manque un
VI 1 *(fail to hit target)* manquer ou rater son coup; **missed!** raté!
2 *(engine)* avoir des ratés
3 to be missing manquer; **there's a piece missing** il manque une pièce
N 1 *(gen) & Sport* coup *m* raté ou manqué; *Br Prov* **a m. is as good as a mile** = rater de peu ou de beaucoup, c'est toujours rater
2 *(idiom) Br* **to give sth a m.** se passer de qch; **why don't you give the TV a m. tonight?** pourquoi ne pas te passer de (la) télé ce soir?; **I think I'll give that film/the party a m.** je ne pense pas que j'irai voir ce film/que j'irai à cette soirée

▸ **miss out** **VT SEP** *(omit)* omettre, sauter; *(forget)* oublier; *(in distribution)* oublier, sauter; **they missed out my first name** on a oublié mon prénom; **you've missed out one important fact** vous avez omis ou oublié un fait important
VI he missed out because he couldn't afford to go to college il a été désavantagé parce qu'il n'avait pas les moyens de poursuivre ses études; **you missed out there** vous avez raté quelque chose

▸ **miss out on** **VT INSEP** *(advantage, opportunity)* manquer, rater; **you're missing out on all the fun** tu rates une occasion de bien t'amuser; **he missed out on a proper education** il n'a pas eu la possibilité de faire de vraies études; **a lot of people are missing out on state benefits they are entitled to** bien des gens ne profitent pas des allocations auxquelles ils ont droit

miss[2] **N 1** *Fam (girl)* jeune fille *f*; **everything for the modern m.** tout ce qu'il faut pour la jeune fille moderne[□]; **(young) m.** jeune demoiselle[□]*f*; **m.!** *(to waitress etc)* Mademoiselle!, s'il vous plaît!; **impudent little m.!** petite effrontée! **2** *Br Sch* la maîtresse; *(in secondary school)* la prof; **yes, m.** oui, madame; **(please) m.!** Madame!

missal ['mɪsəl] **N** *Rel* missel *m*

misshapen [ˌmɪs'ʃeɪpən] **ADJ** difforme, tordu, déformé

missile [*Br* 'mɪsaɪl, *Am* 'mɪsəl] **N 1** *Mil* missile *m* **2** *(object thrown)* projectile *m*
▸▸ ***missile base*** base *f* de missiles; ***missile launcher*** lance-missiles *m inv*

missing ['mɪsɪŋ] **ADJ 1** *(lacking)* manquant; **there are two cups m.** il manque deux tasses, il y a deux tasses qui manquent; **the table had one leg m.** il manquait un pied à la table; **fill in the m. words** complétez avec les mots manquants **2** *(lost ▸ person)* disparu; *(▸ object)* manquant, égaré, perdu; **to go m.** disparaître; *(in war)* être porté disparu; **the m. diamonds were found in her suitcase** les diamants qui avaient disparu ont été retrouvés dans sa valise; **one climber is m.** on est sans nouvelles d'un des alpinistes; *Mil* **m. in action** porté disparu au combat; *Mil* **m. presumed dead** porté disparu, présumé mort
▸▸ *also Fig Hum* ***missing link*** chaînon *m* manquant; ***missing person*** personne *f* disparue; *Mil* disparu(e) *m,f*; ***missing persons*** *(department)* service *m* des personnes disparues

mission [ˈmɪʃən] **N 1** *(task)* mission *f*; **m. of inquiry** mission *f* d'enquête; **he was sent on a rescue m.** il fut envoyé en mission de sauvetage; **his m. in life is to raise awareness of the environment** il tient absolument à sensibiliser l'opinion publique aux problèmes d'environnement
2 *(delegation)* mission *f*; *Am (permanent)* représentation *f* diplomatique; **a Chinese trade m.** une mission commerciale chinoise
3 *(organization, charity)* mission *f*; **M. to Seamen** Mission *f* aux Marins
4 *Rel (campaign, building)* mission *f*
5 *Mil, Com & Astron* mission *f*; **he had flown 20 missions** il avait effectué 20 missions; **m. accomplished** mission accomplie
▸▸ ***mission control*** centre *m* de contrôle; ***mission statement*** ordre *m* de mission; ***mission station*** mission *f*

missionary [ˈmɪʃənrɪ] *(pl* **missionaries***)* **N** missionnaire *mf*
ADJ *(work)* missionnaire
▸▸ ***missionary position*** position *f* du missionnaire; ***missionary society*** société *f* de missionnaires; *also Fig* ***missionary zeal*** fanatisme *m*

mission-critical **ADJ** *Fam* indispensable

missis = **missus**

missive [ˈmɪsɪv] **N** *Formal* missive *f*

misspell [ˌmɪsˈspel] *(pt & pp* **misspelt** [-ˈspelt] *or* **misspelled***)* **VT** *(in writing)* mal écrire, mal orthographier; *(in speaking)* mal épeler

misspelling [ˌmɪsˈspelɪŋ] **N** faute *f* d'orthographe

misspelt [ˌmɪsˈspelt] *pt & pp of* **misspell**

misspend [ˌmɪsˈspend] *(pt & pp* **misspent** [-ˈspent]*)* **VT** *(money, talents)* gaspiller, gâcher; **my misspent youth** ma folle jeunesse

missus [ˈmɪsɪz] **N** *Br Fam* **1** *(wife)* **the m.** la patronne, ma bourgeoise **2** *(woman)* **eh, m.!** dites, m'dame *ou* ma p'tite dame!

mist [mɪst] **N 1** *(fog)* brume *f*; **the morning m. will clear** les brumes matinales se dissiperont; *Fig* **lost in the mists of time** perdu dans la nuit des temps **2** *(on window, glasses)* buée *f*; *(from spray)* brouillard *m*, nuage *m*
VT to m. (over *or* **up)** embuer; **tears misted his eyes** ses yeux étaient brouillés par les larmes; **the windscreen is all misted up** le pare-brise est tout couvert de buée
VI to m. (over *or* **up)** *(landscape)* disparaître dans la brume; *(mirror)* se couvrir de buée, s'embuer; *(eyes)* se voiler, s'embuer

mistakable [mɪˈsteɪkəbəl] **ADJ easily m. (for)** facile à confondre (avec)

mistake [mɪˈsteɪk] *(pt* **mistook** [-ˈstʊk], *pp* **mistaken** [-ˈsteɪkən]*)* **N 1** *(error)* erreur *f*; *(in grammar, spelling)* faute *f*; **to make a m.** *(gen)* se tromper; *(in grammar, spelling)* faire une faute; *(in sums, calculations)* faire une faute *ou* une erreur; **to make the m. of doing sth** faire *ou* commettre l'erreur de faire qch; **I made the m. of losing my temper** j'ai commis l'erreur de *ou* j'ai eu le tort de me fâcher; **you're making a big m.** vous faites une grave erreur; **it would be a m. to make promises that we can't keep** ce serait une erreur de faire des promesses que nous ne pouvons pas tenir; **make no m. (about it)** ne vous y trompez pas; **there must be some m.** il doit y avoir erreur *ou* un malentendu; **it's an easy m. to make** c'est une erreur qu'il est facile de faire; **she knew it was a m. ever to have married him** elle savait bien qu'elle n'aurait pas dû commettre l'erreur de l'épouser; **sorry, my m.** *(my fault)* excusez-moi, c'est (de) ma faute; *(I got it wrong)* excusez-moi, c'est moi qui me trompe
2 *(inadvertence)* **by m.** par mégarde *ou* erreur; **I went into the wrong room by m.** je suis entré par erreur dans la mauvaise pièce; **I took her scarf in m. for mine** en croyant prendre mon écharpe, j'ai pris la sienne
3 *Br (idiom)* **he's a big man and no m.!** pour être costaud, il est costaud!
VT 1 *(misunderstand ▸ meaning, intention)* se méprendre sur; **there's no mistaking what she said** on ne peut pas se méprendre sur le sens de ses propos
2 *(fail to distinguish)* se tromper sur; **you can't m. our house, it's got green shutters** vous ne pouvez pas vous tromper *ou* il n'y a pas de confusion possible, notre maison a des volets verts
3 *(confuse)* **I'm often mistaken for my sister** on me prend souvent pour ma sœur; **I mistook him for someone else** je l'ai pris pour quelqu'un d'autre, je l'ai confondu avec quelqu'un d'autre; **I mistook his shyness for arrogance** j'ai pris sa timidité pour de l'arrogance

mistaken [mɪˈsteɪkən] *pp of* **mistake**
ADJ *(opinion)* erroné; *(idea)* faux (fausse); **to be m.** se tromper, être dans l'erreur; **I was m. about the date** je faisais erreur en ce qui concerne la date; **it was a case of m. identity** il y avait erreur sur la personne; **unless I'm very much m.,…, if I'm not m.,…** si je ne me trompe,…, si je ne m'abuse,…; **he proposed to her in the m. belief that she loved him** il la demanda en mariage, croyant à tort qu'elle l'aimait

mistakenly [mɪˈsteɪkənlɪ] **ADV** *(in error)* par erreur; *(wrongly)* à tort; **they m. believed that it would be easy** ils croyaient, à tort, que ce serait facile

mister [ˈmɪstə(r)] **N** *Fam* monsieur *m*; **hey m.!** dites, m'sieur!

mistime [ˌmɪsˈtaɪm] **VT** *(announcement)* faire au mauvais moment; *(entrance on stage)* rater; *(counterattack, shot, tackle)* mal calculer; **the launch of the new product had been badly mistimed** le nouveau produit n'avait pas été lancé au moment propice; **she mistimed her volley** elle a mal calculé sa volée, le timing de sa volée était mauvais; **he badly mistimed it** il a vraiment choisi le mauvais moment

mistiness [ˈmɪstɪnɪs] **N 1** *(mist)* brume *f*; *(drizzle)* bruine *f* **2** *(condensation)* condensation *f*, buée *f*

mistletoe [ˈmɪsəltəʊ] **N** *Bot* gui *m*

mistook [mɪˈstʊk] *pt of* **mistake**

mistranslate [ˌmɪstrænsˈleɪt] **VT** mal traduire
VI faire des contresens

mistranslation [ˌmɪstrænsˈleɪʃən] **N 1** *(mistake)* contresens *m*, faute *f ou* erreur *f* de traduction **2** *(faulty text)* traduction *f* inexacte, mauvaise traduction *f*

mistreat [ˌmɪsˈtriːt] **VT** maltraiter

mistreatment [ˌmɪsˈtriːtmənt] **N** mauvais traitement *m*

mistress [ˈmɪstrɪs] **N 1** *(woman in control)* maîtresse *f*; **she's her own m.** elle est sa propre maîtresse; **she was m. of the situation** elle était maîtresse de la situation, elle maîtrisait la situation; **the m. of the house** la maîtresse de maison
2 *(lover)* maîtresse *f*
3 *Br Sch (in primary school)* maîtresse *f*; *(in secondary school)* professeur *m (femme)*; **the PE m.** le professeur de gymnastique
4 *Br (of servants)* maîtresse *f*; **the m. wouldn't like it** cela déplairait à Madame
5 *Arch (title)* **M. Bacon** Madame *ou* Mme Bacon
6 *(of pet)* maîtresse *f*

mistrial [ˈmɪstraɪəl] **N** *Law* jugement *m* entaché d'un vice de procédure; *Am (because jury cannot agree)* procès *m* ajourné *(l'unanimité n'ayant pas été atteinte parmi le jury)*

mistrust [ˌmɪsˈtrʌst] **N** méfiance *f*, défiance *f*; **she has an instinctive m. of doctors** elle éprouve une méfiance instinctive à l'égard des médecins
VT *(be suspicious, wary of)* se méfier de; *(doubt)* douter de, ne pas avoir confiance en; **he mistrusts his own abilities** il doute de ses propres capacités

mistrustful [ˌmɪsˈtrʌstfʊl] **ADJ** méfiant, défiant; **to be m. of sb** se méfier de qn

mistrustfully [ˌmɪsˈtrʌstfʊlɪ] **ADV** avec méfiance, avec défiance

misty [ˈmɪstɪ] *(compar* **mistier**, *superl* **mistiest***)* **ADJ 1** *(weather, morning)* brumeux; **it's m.** le temps est brumeux
2 *(window, eyes)* embué; *(horizon, mountain)* embrumé; **her eyes were m. with tears** ses yeux étaient embués *ou* voilés de larmes
3 *(vague ▸ idea, memory)* flou, nébuleux
4 *(like mist)* vaporeux; **m. blue** bleu *m* pâle

misunderstand [ˌmɪsʌndəˈstænd] *(pt & pp* **misunderstood** [-ˈstʊd]*)* **VT 1** *(misinterpret)* mal comprendre, comprendre de travers; **we misunderstood each other** il y a eu un malenten du entre nous; **don't m. me** comprenez-moi bien **2** *(usu passive) (misjudge)* méconnaître; **he feels misunderstood** il se sent incompris
VI mal comprendre; **if I have not misunderstood** si j'ai bien compris

misunderstanding [ˌmɪsʌndəˈstændɪŋ] **N** *(misapprehension)* méprise *f*, quiproquo *m*, malentendu *m*; **there seems to have been some m.** il semble qu'il y ait eu méprise *ou* une erreur; **the whole dispute hinges on a m.** cette discussion repose toute entière sur un malentendu; **to clear up a m.** dissiper un malentendu **2** *(disagreement)* malentendu *m*, désaccord *m*, différend *m*

misuse **VT** [ˌmɪsˈjuːz] **1** *(privilege, position etc)* abuser de; *(word, phrase)* employer abusivement; *(equipment, gun)* mal employer, mal utiliser; *(money, time)* mal employer **2** *(funds)* détourner **3** *(ill-treat)* maltraiter, malmener
N [ˌmɪsˈjuːs] *(of privilege, one's position)* abus *m*; *(of word, phrase)* emploi *m* abusif; *(of equipment, gun)* mauvais usage *m*, mauvaise utilisation *f*; *(of money, time)* mauvais emploi *m*; **m. of funds** détournement *m* de fonds

mite [maɪt] **N 1** *Entom* acarien *m*
2 *(little bit)* grain *m*, brin *m*, tantinet *m*; **it's a m. expensive** c'est un peu cher
3 *Fam (child)* mioche *mf*; *(animal)* petite bête *f*; **poor little m.!** pauvre petit!
4 *Arch or Literary (coin)* denier *m*; *(donation)* obole *f*; **the widow's m.** le denier de la veuve

miter *Am* = **mitre**

mitigate [ˈmɪtɪgeɪt] **VT** *(anger, grief, pain)* adoucir, apaiser, alléger; *(conditions, consequences, harm)* atténuer

mitigating [ˈmɪtɪgeɪtɪŋ] **ADJ**
▸▸ *Law* ***mitigating circumstances*** circonstances *fpl* atténuantes

mitigation [ˌmɪtɪˈgeɪʃən] **N** *Formal (of anger, grief, pain)* adoucissement *m*, allègement *m*; *(of conditions, consequences, harm)* atténuation *f*, mitigation *f*; **in m., it is obvious that she was provoked** il est évident qu'elle a été provoquée, ce qui constitue une circonstance atténuante

mitral valve [ˈmaɪtrəl-] **N** *Anat* valvule *f* mitrale

mitre, *Am* **miter** [ˈmaɪtə(r)] **N 1** *Rel* mitre *f* **2** *(in carpentry)* onglet *m*
VT *(in carpentry ▸ cut)* tailler en onglet; *(join)* assembler en onglet
▸▸ ***mitre block, mitre box*** boîte *f* à onglet; ***mitre joint*** (assemblage *m* à *ou* en) onglet *m*; ***mitre square*** équerre *f* à onglet

mitt [mɪt] **N 1** *(with fingers joined)* moufle *f*; *(fingerless)* mitaine *f*; *(glove)* gant *m*; *(boxing glove)* gant *m* (de boxe), mitaine *f*; **oven/baseball m.** gant *m* isolant/de base-ball **2** *Fam (hand)* patte *f*, pogne *f*; **keep your mitts off my lunch!** touche pas à mon déjeuner!

mitten [ˈmɪtən] **N** *(with fingers joined)* moufle *f*; *(fingerless)* mitaine *f*; *(boxing glove)* gant *m* (de boxe), mitaine *f*

MIX [mɪks]

N	
• mélange **1**	• préparation **3**
• mixage **4**	
VT	
• mélanger **1**	• préparer **2**
• tourner **3**	• mixer **4**
VI	
• se mélanger **1**	• aller ensemble **2**

N 1 *(combination, blend)* mélange *m*; **a fascinating m. of cultures** un mélange de cultures fascinant; **there's not enough cement in the m.** le mélange ne contient pas assez de ciment; **there was a good m. of people at the party** il y avait un mélange intéressant de personnes à la soirée
2 *Br (act of mixing)* **give the paint a (good) m.** mélangez (bien) la peinture
3 *Culin (in package)* préparation *f*; *(batter)* pâte *f*; **a packet of cake m.** un paquet de préparation pour gâteau
4 *Cin, Electron & Mus* mixage *m*; **the record has**

been released as a dance m. ils ont sorti une version dance du disque

VT 1 *(combine, blend)* mélanger; **m. the sugar and** *or* **with the flour** mélangez le sucre et *ou* avec la farine; **m. the sugar into the batter** incorporez le sucre à la pâte; **the screws and nails were all mixed together** les vis et les clous étaient tous mélangés; **I never m. business and pleasure** je ne mélange jamais les affaires et le plaisir; **never m. your drinks** ne faites jamais de mélanges (d'alcools); **to m. metaphors** faire des amalgames de métaphores; *Br Fam* **to m. it** *(fight)* chercher la bagarre, être bagarreur

2 *(prepare ▸ cocktail, medicine)* préparer; *(▸ cement, plaster)* malaxer; **sit down and I'll m. you a drink** assieds-toi, je te sers un verre

3 *(stir ▸ salad)* tourner, retourner, fatiguer

4 *Cin, Electron & Mus* mixer

VI 1 *(combine, blend)* se mélanger; **oil and water don't m.** l'huile et l'eau ne se mélangent pas

2 *(go together)* aller ensemble, faire bon ménage; **drinking and driving don't m.** l'alcool et le volant ne font pas bon ménage

3 *(socialize)* **he mixes with a strange crowd** il fréquente de drôles de gens; **I don't m. much** je ne fréquente pas beaucoup de gens; **my friends and his just don't m.** mes amis et les siens ne sympathisent pas

▸ **mix up VT SEP 1** *(mistake)* confondre; **I always mix her up with her sister** je la confonds toujours avec sa sœur

2 *(confuse)* embrouiller; **I'm mixed up about my feelings for him** mes sentiments pour lui sont très confus; **I was getting all mixed up** je ne savais plus où j'en étais; **you've got the story completely mixed up** tu t'es complètement embrouillé dans cette histoire

3 *(usu passive) (involve)* impliquer; **he was mixed up in a burglary** il a été impliqué *ou* mêlé à une affaire de cambriolage; **she got mixed up with some awful people** elle s'est mise à fréquenter des gens épouvantables; **I got mixed up in their quarrel** je me suis trouvé mêlé à leur querelle

4 *(disorder)* mélanger; **you've mixed all my papers up** tu as mélangé tous mes papiers

5 *(combine, blend)* mélanger

6 *Am Fam* **to mix it up** *(fight)* se castagner, se bastonner

mixed [mɪkst] **ADJ 1** *(assorted)* mélangé; **there was a very m. crowd at the party** il y avait toutes sortes de gens à la fête; **a bag of m. sweets** un sachet de bonbons assortis; **we had rather m. weather** nous avons eu un temps assez variable **2** *(not wholly positive)* mitigé; **to meet with a m. reception** recevoir un accueil mitigé; **I have m. feelings about it** je ne sais pas très bien ce que j'en pense, je suis partagé à ce sujet; *Fam* **it's a bit of a m. bag** il y a un peu de tout; **her resignation was a m. blessing** sa démission avait du bon et du mauvais **3** *(sexually, racially)* mixte; **it's not a proper topic for m. company** ce n'est pas un sujet à aborder devant les dames; **man/woman of m. race** métis *m*/métisse *f*

▸▸ *Sport* ***mixed doubles*** double *m* mixte; ***mixed economy*** économie *f* mixte; *Agr* ***mixed farming*** agriculture *f* mixte; *Culin* ***mixed grill*** assortiment *m* de grillades, mixed grill *m*; *Culin* ***mixed herbs*** herbes *fpl* de Provence; ***mixed marriage*** mariage *m* mixte; ***mixed metaphor*** mélange *m* de métaphores; *Br* ***mixed school*** école *f* mixte; *Pol* ***mixed system*** *(of voting)* scrutin *m* mixte; ***mixed vegetables*** jardinière *f* de légumes

mixed-ability ADJ *(class, teaching)* sans niveaux

mixed-media ADJ multimédia

mixed-up ADJ *(confused)* désorienté, déboussolé; *Fam* **she's a crazy m. kid** elle est un peu paumée, cette gamine

mixer ['mɪksə(r)] **N 1** *(device ▸ gen)* mélangeur *m*; *Culin* (▸ *mechanical)* batteur *m*; (▸ *electric)* mixeur *m*, mixer *m*

2 *Cin, Electron & Mus* mixeur *m*, mélangeur *m* de signaux

3 *(sociable person)* **to be a good/poor m.** être sociable/peu sociable

4 *Fam (troublemaker)* provocateur(trice)ᵖ *m,f*

5 *(soft drink)* boisson *f* gazeuse *(que l'on ajoute à une boisson alcoolisée)*

6 *Am Fam Univ (party)* = soirée pour permettre aux étudiants de faire connaissance

▸▸ ***mixer tap*** (robinet *m*) mélangeur *m*; *(with single control)* mitigeur *m*

mixing ['mɪksɪŋ] **N 1** *(gen)* mélange *m* **2** *Cin, Electron & Mus* mixage *m*

▸▸ ***mixing bowl*** *(big)* saladier *m*; *(smaller)* bol *m*; ***mixing console, mixing desk*** table *f* de mixage; *Rad & TV* ***mixing room*** régie *f*

mixologist [mɪk'sɒlədʒɪst] **N** spécialiste *mf* en cocktails

mixture ['mɪkstʃə(r)] **N 1** *(gen)* mélange *m*; **they speak a m. of French and English** ils parlent un mélange de français et d'anglais; **(cake) m.** préparation *f* pour gâteaux **2** *Chem & Pharm* mixture *f*, mixtion *f*

mix-up N *(confusion)* confusion *f*; *(misunderstanding)* malentendu *m*; *Fam (mess)* pagaïe *f*, pagaille *f*; **there's been a m. with the reservations** ils se sont embrouillés dans les réservations

mizzen ['mɪzən] **N** *Naut* artimon *m*

mizzenmast ['mɪzənmɑːst] **N** *Naut* artimon *m*, mât *m* d'artimon

MJPEG ['emdʒeɪ,peg] **N** *Comput (abbr* **Moving Joint Photographic Expert Group**) (format *m*) MJPEG *m*

ml *(written abbr* **millilitre**) ml

MLM [,eme'lem] **N** *Mktg (abbr* **multi-level marketing**) VRC *f*

MLR [,emel'ɑː(r)] **N** *Br Formerly Fin (abbr* **minimum lending rate**) taux *m* de base

mm *(written abbr* **millimetre**) mm

MMC [,emem'siː] **N** *Formerly Com (abbr* **Monopolies and Mergers Commission**) = commission britannique veillant au respect de la législation antitrust

MMF [,emem'ef] **N** *St Exch (abbr* **money market fund**) ≃ SICAV *f* monétaire

MMS [,emem'es] **N** *Tel (abbr* **multimedia message service**) MMS *m*

MNA [,emen'eɪ] **N** *Can (abbr* **Member of the National Assembly**) *(in Quebec)* MAN *m*

mnemonic [nɪ'mɒnɪk] **N** formule *f* mnémotechnique, aide *f* à la mémoire; *Comput* mnémonique *m*

ADJ 1 *(aiding memory)* mnémonique, mnémotechnique **2** *(relating to memory)* mnémonique

MO[1] [,em'əʊ] **N 1** *(abbr* **medical officer**) *Ind* médecin *m* du travail; *Mil* médecin *m* militaire **2** *(abbr* **modus operandi**) *(of criminal)* façon *f* d'agir **3** *(abbr* **money order**) mandat-poste *m*

MO[2] *(written abbr* **Missouri**) Missouri *m*

mo, mo' [məʊ] **N** *Br Fam* momentᵖ *m*, instantᵖ *m*; **half a mo!, wait a mo!** une seconde!, une minute!

moan [məʊn] **N 1** *(sound)* gémissement *m*, plainte *f* **2** *Fam (complaint)* plainteᵖ *f*, jérémiadesᵖ *fpl*; **to have a (good) m.** râler un bon coup

VT dire en gémissant

VI 1 *(make sound)* gémir, pousser des gémissements; *(of wind)* mugir, gémir **2** *Fam (complain)* râler, ronchonner; **to m. about sth** râler contre qch; **he's always moaning** il est toujours à râler; **what are they moaning about now?** de quoi se plaignent-ils maintenant?

moaner ['məʊnə(r)] **N** *Fam* râleur(euse) *m,f*, ronchonneur(euse) *m,f*

moaning ['məʊnɪŋ] **N** *(UNCOUNT)* **1** *(sound)* gémissement *m*, gémissements *mpl*; *(of wind)* mugissement *m*, gémissement *m* **2** *Fam (complaining)* plaintes *fpl*, jérémiades *fpl*; **stop your m.!** arrête de ronchonner!

ADJ 1 *(groaning)* gémissant; **a m. sound** un gémissement **2** *(complaining)* grognon, râleur; *Br Fam* **she's a real m. Minnie** quelle râleuse, celle-là!

moat [məʊt] **N** douves *fpl*, fossé *m*, fossés *mpl*

mob [mɒb] *(pt & pp* **mobbed**, *cont* **mobbing**) **N 1** *(crowd)* foule *f*, cohue *f*; **we were surrounded by an angry m.** nous étions cernés par une foule en colère; **mobs of drunken hooligans** des hordes *fpl* de hooligans ivres

2 *Pej (common people)* **the m.** la populace

3 *Fam (of criminals)* gangᵖ *m*

4 *Fam (bunch, clique)* bandeᵖ *f*, *Pej* cliqueᵖ *f*

VT *(person)* assiéger, assaillir; *(place)* assiéger; **the crowds mobbing the entrance** la foule qui se pressait à l'entrée

• **Mob N** *Fam* **the M.** la Mafiaᵖ

▸▸ ***mob cap*** charlotte *f (bonnet)*; ***mob hysteria*** hystérie *f* collective; ***mob rule*** règne *m* de la populace

mobbed [mɒbd] **ADJ** *Fam (crowded)* bondé

mobile ['məʊbaɪl] **ADJ 1** *(capable of moving, being moved)* mobile; **she's no longer m.** elle ne peut plus se déplacer seule

2 *(features, face)* mobile, expressif

3 *(socially)* **the middle classes tend to be particularly m.** les classes moyennes se déplacent plus facilement que les autres

4 *Fam (having transport)* **are you m.?** tu es motorisé?

N 1 *(hanging decoration)* mobile *m* **2** *(phone)* (téléphone *m*) portable *m*, *Belg* GSM *m*, G *m*, *Suisse* Natel® *m inv*, *Can* cellulaire *m*

▸▸ ***mobile home*** *(caravan)* camping-car *m*; *(house)* = maison sans fondations qui peut être déplacée; ***mobile library*** bibliobus *m*; ***mobile phone*** (téléphone *m*) portable *m*, *Belg* GSM *m*, *Suisse* Natel® *m inv*, *Can* cellulaire *m*; ***mobile shop*** commerce *m* ambulant; ***mobile studio*** studio *m* mobile; ***mobile telephony*** téléphonie *f* mobile *ou* portable; *Rad & TV* ***mobile unit*** car *m* régie, car *m* de reportage

mobility [mə'bɪlɪtɪ] **N** *(gen)* mobilité *f*; **she has very little m. in her right arm** elle peut à peine bouger son bras droit

▸▸ ***mobility allowance*** indemnité *f* de déplacement *(versée aux personnes handicapées)*

mobilization [,məʊbɪlaɪ'zeɪʃən] **N** mobilisation *f*; *Fin* **m. of capital** mobilisation *f* des capitaux *ou* des fonds

mobilize, -ise ['məʊbɪlaɪz] **VT** mobiliser

VI mobiliser

mobster ['mɒbstə(r)] **N** *Fam* gangsterᵖ *m (particulièrement de la Mafia)*

moby ['məʊbɪ] **N** *Br Fam (mobile phone)* mobile *m*

moccasin ['mɒkəsɪn] **N** *(shoe)* mocassin *m*

mocha ['mɒkə] **N 1** *(coffee)* (café *m*) moka *m* **2** *(coffee and chocolate flavour)* parfum *m* café-chocolat **3** *(colour)* couleur *f* chocolat

ADJ *(colour)* (couleur) chocolat *(inv)*

COMP *(ice cream, icing)* café-chocolat *(inv)*

mock [mɒk] **N 1** *Br Fam Sch & Univ (examination)* examen *m* blancᵖ **2** *(idiom) Literary* **to make a m. of sb/sth** tourner qn/qch en dérision

ADJ 1 *(imitation)* faux (fausse), factice; **m. tortoiseshell** *(rims, frame)* en imitation écaille **2** *(feigned)* feint; **m. horror/surprise** horreur *f*/surprise *f* feinte; **m. trial/fight/elections** simulacre *m* de procès/de combat/d'élections

VT 1 *(deride)* se moquer de, tourner en dérision; **don't m. the afflicted!** ne te moque pas des malheureux! **2** *(imitate)* singer, parodier **3** *Literary (thwart)* déjouer

VI se moquer; **you shouldn't m.** tu ne devrais pas te moquer

▸▸ ***mock battle*** exercice *m* de combat; *Sch & Univ* ***mock examination*** examen *m* blanc; *Bot* ***mock orange*** seringa *m*; ***mock turtle soup*** consommé *m* à la tête de veau

▸ **mock up VT SEP** *Br* faire une maquette de

mocker ['mɒkə(r)] **N** moqueur(euse) *m,f*

mockery ['mɒkərɪ] *(pl* **mockeries**) **N 1** *(derision)* moquerie *f*, raillerie *f*; **to hold sth up to m.** tourner qch en ridicule *ou* en dérision **2** *(person, thing)* **to make a m. of sb** ridiculiser qn; **to make a m. of sth** faire perdre toute crédibilité à qch **3** *(pretence)* parodie *f*, simulacre *m* (**of** de); **the trial was a m.** le procès n'a été qu'un simulacre

mocking ['mɒkɪŋ] **N** moquerie *f*, raillerie *f*

ADJ moqueur, railleur

mockingbird ['mɒkɪŋbɜːd] **N** *Orn* moqueur *m* (polyglotte)

mockingly ['mɒkɪŋlɪ] **ADV** de façon moqueuse

Mockney ['mɒknɪ] *Br Fam* **N** = personne issue d'un milieu aisé qui affecte l'accent cockney

ADJ = caractéristique des personnes issues d'un milieu aisé qui affectent l'accent cockney

mock-up N maquette *f*

MOD [,eməʊ'diː] **N** *Br (abbr* **Ministry of Defence**) ministère *m* de la Défense

mod [mɒd] **N 1** *(person)* = en Grande-Bretagne, dans les années 60–70, membre d'un groupe de

jeunes au code vestimentaire particulier (parkas, pantalons étroits, socquettes blanches) qui s'opposait aux rockers **2** *(festival)* = festival de littérature et de musique gaélique en Écosse
3 *Comput* mod *m*
▸▸ ***mod cons*** confort *m* moderne; **with all m. cons** avec tout le confort moderne

modal ['məʊdəl] **N** *Gram* verbe *m* modal
ADJ *Gram, Phil & Math* modal
▸▸ *Gram* ***modal verb*** verbe *m* modal

modality [mə'dæləti] *(pl* **modalities***)* **N** modalité *f*

modder ['mɒdə] **N** *Comput* moddeur *m*

modding ['mɒdɪŋ] **N** *Comput* modding *m*

mode [məʊd] **N 1** *(manner)* mode *m*, manière *f*; **m. of life** mode *m* de vie; **mode of transport** moyen *m* de transport
2 *Gram, Phil & Math* mode *m*
3 *Comput* mode *m*; **access/control m.** mode *m* d'accès/de contrôle
4 *(fashion)* mode *f*; **the current m. is for sixties fashion** le dernier cri, c'est la mode des années soixante

model ['mɒdəl] *(Br pt & pp* **modelled**, *cont* **modelling**, *Am pt & pp* **modeled**, *cont* **modeling***)* **N 1** *(copy, representation)* modèle *m*, maquette *f*; *(built as hobby)* modèle *m* réduit; *(theoretical pattern)* modèle *m*
2 *(perfect example)* modèle *m*; **to take sb as one's m.** prendre modèle sur qn; **they always hold my brother up as a m. of intelligence** ils citent toujours mon frère comme un modèle d'intelligence
3 *Art & Phot (sitter)* modèle *m*
4 *(in fashion show)* mannequin *m*; **male m.** mannequin *m* (homme)
5 *Com* modèle *m*; **it's the latest m.** c'est le dernier modèle; **demonstration m.** modèle *m* de démonstration
VT 1 *(shape)* modeler; **to m. figures out of clay** modeler des figures en argile; *Fig* **to m. oneself on sb** prendre modèle sur qn **2** *(in fashion show)* **she models clothes** elle est mannequin; **Jacqueline is modelling a grey chinchilla coat** Jacqueline porte un manteau de chinchilla gris
VI *(for artist, photographer)* poser; *(in fashion show)* être mannequin
ADJ 1 *(miniature)* (en) miniature **2** *(exemplary)* modèle; **he's a m. pupil/husband** c'est un élève/mari modèle
▸▸ ***model aeroplane*** maquette *f* d'avion; ***model car*** *(toy)* petite voiture *f*; *(for collectors)* modèle *m* réduit; ***model kit*** modèle *m* en pièces détachées; ***model making*** *(as hobby)* modélisme *m*

modeller, *Am* **modeler** ['mɒdələ(r)] **N** *(of clay etc)* modeleur(euse) *m,f*

modelling, *Am* **modeling** ['mɒdəlɪŋ] **N 1** *(building models)* modelage *m*; *(as a hobby)* construction *f* de maquettes **2** *(in fashion shows)* travail *m ou* métier *m* de mannequin, mannequinat *m*; **to make a career in m.** faire une carrière de mannequin **3** *Math* modélisation *f*
▸▸ ***modelling clay*** pâte *f* à modeler

modem ['məʊdem] **N** modem *m*
VT envoyer par modem
▸▸ ***modem cable*** câble *m* modem; ***modem card*** carte *f* modem; ***modem port*** port *m* de modem

moderate ADJ ['mɒdərət] **1** *(restrained, modest)* modéré; *(language)* mesuré; **he's a m. drinker** il boit avec modération **2** *(average)* moyen; **pupils of m. ability** élèves *mfpl* moyens(ennes); **bake the cake for 20 minutes in a m. oven** faire cuire le gâteau à four moyen pendant 20 minutes **3** *Met* modéré
N ['mɒdərət] *Pol* modéré(e) *m,f*
VT ['mɒdəreɪt] **1** *(make less extreme)* modérer; **they have since moderated their demands** depuis, ils ont modéré leurs exigences **2** *(meeting, debate)* présider **3** *Nucl (neutrons)* modérer, ralentir
VI ['mɒdəreɪt] **1** *(storm)* s'apaiser, se calmer **2** *(at meeting)* présider
▸▸ ***moderate breeze*** *(on Beaufort scale)* jolie brise *f*

moderately ['mɒdərətlɪ] **ADV 1** *(with moderation)* modérément, avec modération; **m. priced** d'un prix raisonnable *ou* abordable **2** *(slightly)* moyennement; **she was only m. pleased with her new job** elle n'était que moyennement satisfaite de son nouvel emploi

moderating ['mɒdəreɪtɪŋ] **ADJ** modérateur; **to be a m. influence on sb** exercer une influence modératrice sur qn

moderation [mɒdə'reɪʃən] **N** *(restraint)* modération *f*, mesure *f*; *(of language)* sobriété *f*; **in m.** avec modération, modérément; **taken in m. alcohol is not harmful** consommé avec modération, l'alcool n'est pas nocif

moderator ['mɒdəreɪtə(r)] **N 1** *(at meeting)* président(e) *m,f*; *(mediator)* médiateur(trice) *m,f*; *Mktg (of group meeting)* animateur(trice) *m,f*; *Rel* modérateur *m* **2** *Nucl* modérateur *m*, ralentisseur *m* **3** *Comput & Phys* modérateur *m*

modern ['mɒdən] **N 1** *(person)* moderne *mf* **2** *Typ* didot *m*
ADJ moderne; **in m. times** à l'époque moderne; **m. English/French/Greek** anglais *m*/français *m*/grec *m* moderne
▸▸ ***modern art*** art *m* moderne; ***modern languages*** langues *fpl* vivantes

modernism ['mɒdənɪzəm] **N 1** *(in art, literature etc)* modernisme *m* **2** *(expression, word)* néologisme *m*

modernist ['mɒdənɪst] **N** moderniste *mf*
ADJ moderniste

modernity [mɒ'dɜːnətɪ] **N** modernité *f*

modernization [,mɒdənaɪ'zeɪʃən] **N** modernisation *f*

modernize, -ise ['mɒdənaɪz] **VT** moderniser
VI se moderniser

modernizer, -iser ['mɒdənaɪzə(r)] **N** *Pol* modernisateur(trice) *m,f*

modest ['mɒdɪst] **ADJ 1** *(unassuming)* modeste; **she's very m. about her success** son succès ne lui est pas monté à la tête **2** *(moderate, simple)* modeste; *(meagre)* modique; **a m. salary** un salaire modique; **a m. house** une maison sans prétentions *ou* à l'aspect modeste; **we are very m. in our needs** nous avons besoin de très peu **3** *(decent)* pudique

modestly ['mɒdɪstlɪ] **ADV 1** *(unassumingly)* modestement, avec modestie **2** *(simply)* modestement, simplement; **they live very m.** ils vivent très simplement, ils mènent une vie très simple **3** *(in sexual sense)* avec pudeur, pudiquement; **to dress m.** s'habiller avec pudeur

modesty ['mɒdɪstɪ] **N 1** *(lack of conceit)* modestie *f*; **in all m.** en toute modestie **2** *(moderation)* modestie *f*; *(meagreness)* modicité *f* **3** *(decency)* pudeur *f*; **she lowered her gaze out of m.** la pudeur lui a fait baisser les yeux

modicum ['mɒdɪkəm] **N a m. of...** un petit peu de..., un brin de...; **a m. of truth** une petite part de vérité; **she doesn't have even a m. of taste** elle n'a aucun goût

modification [,mɒdɪfɪ'keɪʃən] **N** modification *f*; **he made several modifications in** *or* **to the text** il apporta plusieurs modifications au texte

modifier ['mɒdɪfaɪə(r)] **N** *Gram* modificateur *m*
▸▸ *Comput* ***modifier key*** touche *f* de modification

modify ['mɒdɪfaɪ] *(pt & pp* **modified***)* **VT 1** *(alter)* modifier; **she modified her opinion of him in the light of this information** elle a changé d'avis à son égard lorsqu'elle a appris cela **2** *(reduce ▸ punishment, demands)* modérer **3** *Gram* modifier; **the adjective agrees with the noun it modifies** l'adjectif s'accorde avec le nom auquel il se rapporte

modish ['məʊdɪʃ] **ADJ** à la mode

modishly ['məʊdɪʃlɪ] **ADV** selon la mode

modiste [məʊ'diːst] **N** modiste *mf*

modular ['mɒdjʊlə(r)] **ADJ** modulaire
▸▸ *Electron* ***modular construction*** construction *f* modulaire; *Br Univ* ***modular degree*** ≃ licence *f* à UV; ***modular furniture*** mobilier *m* modulaire *ou* à éléments

modulate ['mɒdjʊleɪt] **VT 1** *(voice)* moduler **2** *Electron & Mus* moduler **3** *(moderate)* adapter, ajuster
VI *Mus* moduler

modulation [,mɒdjʊ'leɪʃən] **N 1** *(of voice)* modulation *f*, inflexion *f* **2** *Mus, Elec & Electron* modulation *f*

modulator ['mɒdjʊleɪtə(r)] **N** *Elec & Electron* modulateur *m*

module ['mɒdjuːl] **N 1** *(gen)* module *m* **2** *Br Univ* ≃ unité *f* de valeur, UV *f*

modulus ['mɒdjʊləs] **N** *Phys & Math* module *m*; *Phys* **m. of elasticity/rupture** module *m ou* coefficient *m* d'élasticité/de rupture

modus operandi ['məʊdəs,ɒpə'rændiː] **N** *Formal or Literary* méthode *f* (de travail), procédé *m*

modus vivendi ['məʊdəsvɪ'vendiː] **N** *Formal or Literary* modus vivendi *m*

mofo ['məʊ,fəʊ] **N** *Vulg Black Am slang* enfoiré(e) *m,f*

mog [mɒg], **moggie, moggy** ['mɒgɪ] *(pl* **moggies***)* **N** *Br Fam* minou *m*

mogul ['məʊgəl] **N 1** *(magnate)* magnat *m*; **movie m.** grand manitou *m* du cinéma **2** *(on ski slope)* bosse *f*; **moguls** *(event)* bosses *fpl*
• **Mogul N** Moghol(e) *m,f* **ADJ** moghol

mohair ['məʊheə(r)] **N** mohair *m*
COMP *(sweater, blanket)* en *ou* de mohair

Mohammed [mə'hæmɪd] **PR N** *Rel* Mahomet

Mohammedan [mə'hæmɪdən] *Rel* **N** mahométan(e) *m,f*
ADJ mahométan

Mohawk ['məʊhɔːk] *(pl* **inv** *or* **Mohawks***)* **N** Mohawk *mf*
• **mohawk N 1** *(in ice-skating)* mohawk *m* **2** *Am (hairstyle)* iroquoise *f*

Mohican [məʊ'hiːkən, 'məʊɪkən] *(pl* **inv** *or* **Mohicans***)* **N 1** *(person)* Mohican(e) *m,f* **2** *Ling* mohican *m*
ADJ mohican
• **mohican N** *Br (hairstyle)* iroquoise *f*

moiré ['mwɑːreɪ] *Tex*
N moiré *m*
ADJ moiré
▸▸ *Typ* ***moiré pattern*** moirage *m*; ***moiré silk*** moire *f* de soie

moist [mɔɪst] **ADJ** *(climate, soil, surface)* humide; *(skin, air, heat)* moite; *(cake)* moelleux; **her eyes were m. with tears** ses yeux étaient mouillés de larmes, ses yeux étaient embués; **to grow m.** se mouiller, s'humecter

moisten ['mɔɪsən] **VT** humecter, mouiller; **she moistened her lips** elle s'humecta les lèvres
VI *(eyes)* se mouiller; *(palms)* devenir moite

moistness ['mɔɪstnɪs] **N** *(of climate, soil, surface)* humidité *f*; *(of skin, air, heat)* moiteur *f*; *(of cake)* moelleux *m*

moisture ['mɔɪstʃə(r)] **N** humidité *f*; *(on mirror, window etc)* buée *f*
▸▸ ***moisture content*** teneur *f* en humidité *ou* en eau

moisturize, -ise ['mɔɪstʃəraɪz] **VT** *(skin)* hydrater; *(air)* humidifier
VI appliquer une crème hydratante; **it is important to m. twice daily** il est important d'utiliser une crème hydratante deux fois par jour

moisturizer, -iser ['mɔɪstʃəraɪzə(r)] **N** *(cream)* crème *f* hydratante; *(lotion)* lait *m* hydratant

mojito [məʊ'hiːtəʊ] **N** *(cocktail)* mojito *m*

molar ['məʊlə(r)] **N** *(tooth)* molaire *f*
ADJ 1 *Chem (quantity, solution)* molaire **2** *Med* môlaire

molasses [mə'læsɪz] **N** *(UNCOUNT)* mélasse *f*; *Am Fam* **to be as slow as m. (in winter)** être d'une lenteur de limace *ou* d'escargot *ou* de tortue

mold, molder *etc Am* = **mould, moulder** *etc*

Moldavia [mɒl'deɪvɪə] **N** Moldavie *f*

Moldavian [mɒl'deɪvɪən] **N 1** *(person)* Moldave *mf* **2** *(language)* moldave *m*
ADJ moldave
COMP *(embassy)* de Moldavie; *(history)* de la Moldavie; *(teacher)* de moldave

mole [məʊl] **N 1** *(on skin)* grain *m* de beauté
2 *(animal)* taupe *f*
3 *Fig (spy)* taupe *f*
4 *(breakwater)* môle *m*, digue *f*
5 *Chem* mole *f*

6 *Med* môle *m*
▸▸ *Entom* **mole catcher** taupier *m*

molecular [mə'lekjʊlə(r)] ADJ *Phys* moléculaire
▸▸ ***molecular biology*** biologie *f* moléculaire; ***molecular genetics*** génétique *f* moléculaire; ***molecular weight*** poids *m* moléculaire

molecule ['mɒlɪkju:l] N molécule *f*

molehill ['məʊlhɪl] N taupinière *f*

moleskin ['məʊlskɪn] N 1 *(fur)* (peau *f* de) taupe *f* 2 *(cotton)* coton *m* sergé
COMP 1 *(fur)* en (peau *f* de) taupe *f* 2 *(cotton)* en coton sergé

molest [mə'lest] VT *(bother)* importuner, tracasser; *(more violently)* molester, malmener; *(sexually)* agresser (sexuellement)

> Note that the French verb **molester** only means **to rough up**.

molestation [,məʊle'steɪʃən] N *(UNCOUNT)* brutalité *f*, violences *fpl*; *(sexual)* attentat *m* à la pudeur

molester [mə'lestə(r)] N agresseur *m*; **child m.** pédophile *mf*

moll [mɒl] N *Fam* **(gangster's) m.** poule *f*, môme *f* *(d'un gangster)*

mollify ['mɒlɪfaɪ] VT *(pt & pp* **mollified***)* apaiser, amadouer

mollusc, *Am* **mollusk** ['mɒləsk] N *Zool* mollusque *m*

mollycoddle ['mɒlɪ,kɒdəl] VT *Fam* dorloter, materner

Molotov cocktail ['mɒlətɒf-] N cocktail *m* Molotov

molt, molting *Am* = **moult, moulting**

molten ['məʊltən] ADJ *(metal, lava)* en fusion

molybdenum [mə'lɪbdənəm] N *Chem* molybdène *m*

mom [mɒm] N *Am Fam* maman *f*

moment ['məʊmənt] N 1 *(period of time)* moment *m*, instant *m*; **at the m.** en ce moment; **at that m.** à ce moment-là; **at this m.** *(now)* en ce moment; **at this m. in time** à l'heure qu'il est; **from that m. on** désormais; **the man of the m.** l'homme *m* du jour *ou* du moment; **for the m.** pour le moment; **I'll do it in a m.** je le ferai dans un instant; **I didn't believe them for a** *or* **for one m.** je ne les ai pas crus un seul instant; **wait a m.!, just a m.!, one m.!** une seconde!, une minute!, un instant!; **one m., please** *(on telephone)* ne quittez pas; **she's just this m. gone out** elle vient de sortir; **I have just** *or* **only this m. heard about it** je viens de l'apprendre, je l'apprends à l'instant; **at the last m.** à la dernière minute, au dernier moment; **the next m. the phone rang** l'instant d'après, le téléphone a sonné; **he may return at any m.** il peut revenir d'un instant à l'autre; **I saw her a m. ago** je l'ai vue il y a un instant *ou* une seconde; **without a m.'s hesitation** sans la moindre hésitation; **the m. he arrives** dès qu'il arrivera, dès son arrivée; **the m. she saw him** dès l'instant où elle le vit; **it was one of the worst moments of my life** ce fut un des pires moments de ma vie; **her m. of glory** son heure de gloire; **to live for the m.** profiter du moment présent; **the m. of truth** l'heure de vérité; **the film has its moments** le film est parfois intéressant *ou* a de bons passages; **I have my moments, you know** ça m'arrive, des fois!
2 *Formal (importance)* **of great m.** d'une importance considérable, de grande *ou* haute importance; **of little m.** de peu d'importance
3 *Phys* moment *m*
▸▸ *Phys* ***moment of inertia*** moment *m* d'inertie

momentarily [*Br* 'məʊməntərɪlɪ, *Am* ,məʊmen'terɪlɪ] ADV 1 *(briefly, temporarily)* momentanément 2 *Am (immediately)* immédiatement, tout de suite; **I'll be with you m.** je suis à vous dans une seconde

momentary ['məʊməntərɪ] ADJ *(brief, temporary)* momentané; **I had a m. lapse of concentration** pendant un instant ma concentration s'est relâchée

momentous [mə'mentəs] ADJ capital, d'une importance capitale; **on this m. occasion** en cette occasion mémorable

momentousness [mə'mentəsnɪs] N importance *f* capitale

momentum [mə'mentəm] N 1 *(impetus)* vitesse *f*, élan *m*; **to gain** *or* **gather m.** *(of moving object)* prendre de la vitesse; *(of political movement etc)* prendre de l'ampleur, s'amplifier; **to lose m.** *(vehicle)* perdre de la vitesse, être en perte de vitesse; *(campaign)* s'essouffler 2 *Tech & Phys* moment *m*

Mon. *(written abbr* **Monday***)* Lu

Monaco ['mɒnəkəʊ] N **(principality of) M.** (principauté *f* de) Monaco

monad ['məʊnæd] *(pl* **monads** *or* **monades** [-di:z]*)* N 1 *Phil* monade *f* 2 *Biol* organisme *m* unicellulaire

monadic [mɒ'nædɪk] ADJ 1 *Phil* monadiste, monadaire 2 *Biol* unicellulaire 3 *Chem* univalent, monoatomique

Mona Lisa [,məʊnə'li:zə] N **the M.** la Joconde; **she had a M. smile** elle avait un sourire énigmatique

monarch ['mɒnək] N *(ruler)* monarque *m*

monarchical [mə'nɑ:kɪkəl] ADJ monarchique

monarchist ['mɒnəkɪst] N monarchiste *mf*
ADJ monarchiste

monarchy ['mɒnəkɪ] *(pl* **monarchies***)* N monarchie *f*

monastery ['mɒnəstərɪ] *(pl* **monasteries***)* N monastère *m*

monastic [mə'næstɪk] ADJ monastique

monasticism [mə'næstɪsɪzəm] N 1 *(way of life)* vie *f* monastique 2 *(system)* système *m* monastique, monachisme *m*

monaural [mɒ'nɔ:rəl] ADJ monaural

Monday ['mʌndɪ] N lundi *m*; **I've got that M. morning feeling** je me sens comme on peut se sentir un lundi matin; *see also* **Friday**
▸▸ *Am Fam* ***Monday morning quarterback*** stratège *m* en chambre *(qui commente notamment les résultats sportifs)*

mondo ['mɒndəʊ] ADV *Am Fam* vachement

monetarism ['mʌnɪtərɪzəm] N monétarisme *m*

monetarist ['mʌnɪtərɪst] N monétariste *mf*
ADJ monétariste

monetary ['mʌnɪtərɪ] ADJ *Econ & Fin* monétaire
▸▸ ***monetary policy*** politique *f* monétaire; ***monetary reserves*** réserves *fpl* de change; ***monetary unit*** unité *f* monétaire

money ['mʌnɪ] *(pl* **moneys** *or* **monies***)* N 1 *(gen)* argent *m*; **have you got any m. on you?** est-ce que tu as de l'argent *ou* du liquide sur toi?; **they don't accept foreign m.** ils n'acceptent pas l'argent étranger *ou* les devises étrangères; **your m. or your life!** la bourse ou la vie!; **to get one's m.'s worth** en avoir pour son argent; **to put m. into sth** investir dans qch; **to put up the m. for sth** fournir les fonds pour qch, financer qch; **it's m. well spent** c'est une bonne affaire; **the best dictionary that m. can buy** le meilleur dictionnaire qui existe *ou* qui soit; **to make m.** *(person)* gagner de l'argent; *(business, investment)* rapporter de l'argent; **to be worth a lot of m.** *(thing)* valoir cher, avoir beaucoup de valeur; *(person)* être riche; **the deal is worth a lot of m.** c'est un contrat qui porte sur de très grosses sommes; **to get one's m. back** *(get reimbursed)* se faire rembourser; *(recover one's expenses)* rentrer dans ses fonds; **m. is no object** peu importe le prix, l'argent n'entre pas en ligne de compte; **I'm no good with m.** je n'ai pas la notion de l'argent; **there's no m. in translating** la traduction ne rapporte pas *ou* ne paie pas; **toys cost m., you know** les jouets, ce n'est pas gratuit, tu sais; **the job's boring but the m.'s good** le travail est ennuyeux mais ça paye bien *ou* c'est bien payé; **we paid good m. for it** cela nous a coûté cher; **you can earn big m. selling carpets** on peut gagner beaucoup d'argent en vendant des tapis; **I'm not made of m., you know** tu as l'air de croire que je roule sur l'or; **to put m. on a horse** miser sur un cheval; *Fam* **to be in the m.** être plein aux as; *Sport* **to finish out of/in the m.** remporter/ne pas remporter un prix en argent; *Fig* **put your m. where your mouth is** il est temps de joindre le geste à la parole; *Fig* **to have m. to burn** avoir de l'argent à jeter par les fenêtres; *Fig* **to throw good m. after bad** s'enfoncer davantage dans une mauvaise affaire; *Fig* **it's throwing m. away, it's m. down the drain** c'est de l'argent gaspillé *ou* jeté par la fenêtre; *Br Fam Fig* **it's m. for old rope** *or* **for jam** c'est de l'argent vite gagné *ou* du fric vite fait; **for my m., he's the best candidate** à mon avis, c'est le meilleur candidat; **m. talks** l'argent peut tout; **m. doesn't grow on trees** l'argent ne tombe pas du ciel; *Prov* **m. is the root of all evil** l'argent est la source de tous les maux; *Fam* **on the m.** *(correct* ▸ *guess, answer)* correct, exact; *(on time)* à l'heure 2 *Fin (currency)* monnaie *f*
COMP *(problems, matters)* d'argent, financier
• **moneys, monies** NPL *Law (sums)* sommes *fpl* (d'argent); **public moneys** deniers *mpl* publics
▸▸ ***money-back guarantee*** garantie *f* de remboursement intégral; ***money belt*** ceinture *f* portefeuille; *Fin* ***money broker*** prêteur(euse) *m,f* sur titre; ***money laundering*** blanchiment *m* d'argent; *Fin* ***money market*** marché *m* monétaire *ou* financier; *Fin* ***money order*** mandat *m* (postal); *Br* ***money spider*** = petite araignée censée apporter bonheur et richesse à ceux qu'elle touche; *Fin* ***money supply*** masse *f* monétaire

> Note that the French word **monnaie** is a false friend and is very rarely a translation for the English word **money**. It means **change** or **currency**, depending on the context.

moneybag ['mʌnɪbæg] N *(bag)* sac *m* à argent; *(of bus conductor etc)* sacoche *f*
• **moneybags** NPL *Fam (person)* richard(e) *m,f*, rupin(e) *m,f*

moneybox ['mʌnɪbɒks] N *Br* tirelire *f*

moneychanger ['mʌnɪ,tʃeɪndʒə(r)] N 1 *(person)* cambiste *mf*, courtier(ère) *m,f* de change 2 *Am (machine)* changeur *m ou* distributeur *m* de monnaie

moneyed ['mʌnɪd] ADJ riche, nanti; **the m. classes** les classes *fpl* possédantes

money-grubber [-'grʌbə(r)] N *Fam* rapace *m*, requin *m*

money-grubbing [-'grʌbɪŋ] *Fam* N radinerie *f*
ADJ radin

moneylender ['mʌnɪ,lendə(r)] N *Fin* prêteur(euse) *m,f*; *(usurer)* usurier(ère) *m,f*; *(pawnbroker)* prêteur(euse) *m,f* sur gages

moneymaker ['mʌnɪ,meɪkə(r)] N affaire *f* qui rapporte, mine *f* d'or; **to be a m.** *(shop, business, product)* rapporter

moneymaking ['mʌnɪ,meɪkɪŋ] ADJ lucratif; **it's another of her m. schemes** c'est encore une de ses idées pour faire fortune

> **-MONGER** SUFFIXE
>
> • A l'origine le terme **monger** signifiait VENDEUR; en anglais moderne ce suffixe conserve son sens premier dans les termes **fishmonger** poissonnier(ère), **ironmonger** quincaillier(ère) et **cheesemonger** fromager (ère).
>
> • Au sens figuré ce suffixe prend une connotation péjorative et sert à désigner une PERSONNE À L'INFLUENCE NÉFASTE, comme dans les exemples suivants: **warmonger** belliciste; **rumourmonger, gossipmonger** commère; **scandalmonger** mauvaise langue.
> Il est possible de former de nouveaux termes tels que **fearmonger** alarmiste, **hatemonger** personne qui incite à la haine.
> Il n'existe pas de traduction particulière pour ce sens du suffixe **monger**.

Mongol ['mɒŋgəl] *Hist* N 1 *(person)* Mongol(e) *m,f* 2 *(language)* mongol *m*
ADJ mongol

mongol ['mɒŋgəl] *Old-fashioned* N mongolien (enne) *m,f*, = terme injurieux désignant un trisomique
ADJ mongolien, = terme injurieux désignant un trisomique

Mongolia [mɒŋ'gəʊlɪə] N Mongolie *f*, **Inner M.** Mongolie-Intérieure *f*; *Formerly* **Outer M.** Mongolie-Extérieure *f*

Mongolian [mɒŋ'gəʊlɪən] N 1 *(person)* Mongol(e) *m,f* 2 *(language)* mongol *m*
ADJ mongol

COMP *(embassy)* de Mongolie; *(history)* de la Mongolie; *(teacher)* de mongol

mongolism ['mɒŋgəlɪzəm] N *Old-fashioned* mongolisme *m*, trisomie *f*, = terme injurieux désignant la trisomie 21

mongoloid ['mɒŋgəlɔɪd] *Old-fashioned* N mongolien(enne) *m,f*, = terme injurieux désignant un trisomique

ADJ mongolien, = terme injurieux se rapportant à la trisomie 21

mongoose ['mɒŋguːs] N *Zool* mangouste *f*

mongrel ['mʌŋgrəl] N *(dog)* bâtard(e) *m,f*; *(other animal)* hybride *m*

ADJ *(dog)* bâtard; *(other animal)* hybride

monies ['mʌnɪz] *pl of* **money**

moniker ['mɒnɪkə(r)] N *Fam (name)* blase *m*; *(nickname)* surnom□*m*

monitor ['mɒnɪtə(r)] N **1** *Med & Tech (checking device)* moniteur *m*

2 *Comput & TV (screen)* moniteur *m*

3 *Sch* ≃ chef *m* de classe; **dinner m.** = élève chargé de veiller au bon déroulement des repas à la cantine

4 *Rad* employé(e) *m,f* d'un service d'écoute

VT **1** *(check)* suivre, surveiller; *Mktg (market)* surveiller, contrôler; **their progress is carefully monitored** leurs progrès sont suivis de près; **this instrument monitors the pulse rate** cet instrument surveille le pouls du patient **2** *(broadcasts, telephone conversation)* écouter

►► *Zool* ***monitor lizard*** varan *m*

monitoring ['mɒnɪtərɪŋ] N **1** *(of progress)* suivi *m*; *(of patient)* surveillance *f* continue, monitorage *m*; *Mktg (of market)* surveillance *f*, contrôle *m* continu **2** *(of broadcasts, phone calls)* écoute *f*; *(of conversation)* surveillance *f*

►► *Rad* ***monitoring service*** = service d'écoute des émissions de radio étrangères; *Rad* ***monitoring station*** station *f ou* centre *m* d'écoute

monk [mʌŋk] N moine *m*, religieux *m*

monkey ['mʌŋkɪ] N **1** *(animal)* singe *m*; **female m.** guenon *f*; *Fam* **to make a m. out of sb** se payer la tête de qn; *Br Fam* **I don't give a m.'s** je m'en fiche pas mal, j'en ai rien à battre; *Am Fam Drugs slang* **to have a m. on one's back** *(be addicted to drugs)* être accro **2** *Fam (scamp)* polisson(onne) *m,f*, galopin *m*; **you little m.!** petit polisson!, petit espiègle! **3** *Br Fam (£500)* 500 livres□*fpl*

►► *Am* ***monkey bars*** cage *f* d'écureuil; *Fam* ***monkey business*** *(UNCOUNT) (suspect activity)* combines *fpl*; *(mischief)* bêtises□*fpl*; **they're up to some m. business** ils sont en train de combiner quelque chose; ***monkey jacket*** spencer *m (de garçon de café etc)*; *Br* ***monkey nut*** cacahouète *f*, cacahuète *f*; *Bot* ***monkey puzzle tree*** désespoir *m* des singes, *Spec* araucaria *m* du Chili; *Am* ***monkey shine*** farce *f*; *Fam* ***monkey suit*** *(formal suit)* costard *m* chic *m*; *Am (uniform)* uniforme□*m*; ***monkey wrench*** clef *f* anglaise *ou* à molette

►**monkey about, monkey around** VI *Fam* **1** *(play the fool)* faire l'imbécile **2** *(tamper)* **to m. about** *or* **around with sth** tripoter qch

monkfish ['mʌŋkfɪʃ] *(pl* **inv** *or* **monkfishes)** N *Ich (angler fish)* baudroie *f*, lotte *f*; *(angel shark)* ange *m* de mer

monkish ['mʌŋkɪʃ] ADJ monacal, de moine

mono ['mɒnəʊ] *(pl* **monos)** N **1** *(abbr* **monophony)** monophonie *f*; **in m.** en mono **2** *Am Fam (abbr* **mononucleosis)** mononucléose *f* (infectieuse)□

ADJ *(abbr* **monophonic)** mono *(inv)*, monophonique

monobrow ['mɒnəʊbraʊ] N *Fam Hum* **to have a m.** avoir les sourcils qui se rejoignent au milieu

monochrome ['mɒnəkrəʊm] N **1** *(technique)* monochromie *f*; *Phot & TV* noir et blanc *m*; *Art* camaïeu *m* **2** *(photograph)* photographie *f* en noir et blanc; *(painting)* camaïeu *m*; *(in modern art)* monochrome *m*

ADJ *(photograph, television set)* en noir et blanc *(inv)*; *(computer screen)* monochrome; *(painting)* en camaïeu; *Fig* **he leads a very m. existence** il mène une existence très terne

monocle ['mɒnəkəl] N monocle *m*

monoclonal [ˌmɒnə'kləʊnəl] ADJ *Biol* monoclonal

►► ***monoclonal antibody*** anticorps *m* monoclonal

monocoque ['mɒnəkɒk] N *Aviat* construction *f* monocoque; *Aut* monocoque *f*

monoculture ['mɒnəˌkʌltʃə(r)] N monoculture *f*

monogamous [mɒ'nɒgəməs] ADJ *(person, animal)* monogame; *(relationship)* monogamique

monogamy [mɒ'nɒgəmɪ] N monogamie *f*

monogram ['mɒnəgræm] *(pt & pp* **monogrammed,** *cont* **monogramming)** N monogramme *m*

VT marquer d'un monogramme

monogrammed, *Am* **monogramed** ['mɒnəgræmd] ADJ qui porte un monogramme; **m. handkerchiefs** mouchoirs *mpl* avec un monogramme brodé

monograph ['mɒnəgrɑːf] N monographie *f*

monokini ['mɒnəkiːnɪ] N monokini *m*

monolingual [ˌmɒnə'lɪŋgwəl] ADJ monolingue

monolith ['mɒnəlɪθ] N *Geol & Fig* monolithe *m*

monolithic [ˌmɒnə'lɪθɪk] ADJ *Geol* monolithe, monolithique; *Fig (government, state)* monolithique

monologue, *Am* **monolog** ['mɒnəlɒg] N *Theat & Fig* monologue *m*

monomania [ˌmɒnə'meɪnjə] N *Psy* monomanie *f*

mononucleosis ['mɒnəʊˌnjuːklɪ'əʊsɪs] N *(UNCOUNT) Med* mononucléose *f* (infectieuse)

monophonic [ˌmɒnə'fɒnɪk] ADJ monophonique, monaural

monoplane ['mɒnəpleɪn] N monoplan *m*

monopolist [mə'nɒpəlɪst] N monopoleur(euse) *m,f*

monopolistic [məˌnɒpə'lɪstɪk] ADJ monopoliste, monopolistique; *Econ* **m. competition** concurrence *f* monopolistique

monopolization, -isation [məˌnɒpəlaɪ'zeɪʃən] N monopolisation *f*

monopolize, -ise [mə'nɒpəlaɪz] VT **1** *(power, access, use)* monopoliser; **he always monopolizes the conversation** il monopolise systématiquement la conversation; **she monopolized him the whole evening** elle l'a monopolisé toute la soirée **2** *Com & Mktg (market, trade)* monopoliser

monopoly [mə'nɒpəlɪ] *(pl* **monopolies)** N *also Fig* monopole *m*; **to have a m. of sth** *or* **on sth** avoir *ou* détenir le monopole de qch, monopoliser qch; *Fig* **no political party has a m. on morality** aucun parti politique ne détient le monopole de la moralité; **state m.** monopole *m* d'État; *Formerly* **the Monopolies and Mergers Commission** = commission veillant au respect de la législation antitrust en Grande-Bretagne

• **Monopoly®** N *(game)* Monopoly® *m*

►► ***monopoly control*** contrôle *m* monopolistique; ***monopoly market*** marché *m* monopolistique; *Fig* ***Monopoly® money*** des sommes *fpl* astronomiques

monopsonist [mə'nɒpsənɪst] N *Econ* = partisan du monopsone

monopsonistic [məˌnɒpsə'nɪstɪk] ADJ *Econ* monopsoniste

monopsony [mə'nɒpsənɪ] *(pl* **monopsonies)** N *Econ* monopsone *m*

monorail ['mɒnəreɪl] N monorail *m*

monoski ['mɒnəʊskɪ] N monoski *m*

VI faire du monoski

monosodium glutamate [ˌmɒnə'səʊdjəm'gluːtəmeɪt] N *Culin* glutamate *m* de sodium

monospaced ['mɒnəʊspeɪst] ADJ *Comput & Typ* non proportionnel

monosyllabic [ˌmɒnəsɪ'læbɪk] ADJ **1** *Ling* monosyllabe, monosyllabique **2** *(person)* qui s'exprime par monosyllabes; **he's very m.** il ne parle que par monosyllabes

monosyllable ['mɒnəˌsɪləbəl] N monosyllabe *m*; **he replied in monosyllables** il a répondu par monosyllabes

monotheism ['mɒnəθiːˌɪzəm] N *Rel* monothéisme *m*

monotheistic [ˌmɒnəθiː'ɪstɪk] ADJ *Rel* monothéiste

monotone ['mɒnətəʊn] N ton *m* monocorde *ou* monotone; **to speak in a m.** parler d'un ton monocorde *ou* monotone

ADJ monocorde

monotonous [mə'nɒtənəs] ADJ *(gen)* monotone; *(voice)* monotone, monocorde

monotonously [mə'nɒtənəslɪ] ADV de façon monotone; **he droned m. on** il ânonnait d'un ton monotone

monotony [mə'nɒtənɪ] *(pl* **monotonies)** N monotonie *f*; **to relieve** *or* **break the m.** rompre la monotonie; **the m. of the landscape** l'uniformité *f ou* la monotonie du paysage

monotype ['mɒnətaɪp] N *Art & Biol* monotype *m*

• **Monotype®** N *Typ (machine)* Monotype® *f*

monounsaturated [ˌmɒnəʊʌn'sætʃəreɪtɪd] ADJ *(fat)* mono-insaturé

monoxide [mɒ'nɒksaɪd] N *Chem* monoxyde *m*

monozygote [ˌmɒnəʊ'zaɪgəʊt] N *Biol* jumeau (elle) *m,f* monozygote

monozygotic [ˌmɒnəʊzaɪ'gɒtɪk], **monozygous** [ˌmɒnəʊ'zaɪgəs] ADJ *Biol* monozygote, univitellin

Monsignor [mɒn'siːnjə(r)] *(pl* **Monsignors** *or* **Monsignori** [-siː'njɔːrɪ]) N *Rel* monseigneur *m*

monsoon [mɒn'suːn] N mousson *f*; **the m. season** la mousson

monster ['mɒnstə(r)] N **1** *(beast, cruel person)* monstre *m* **2** *Fam (large person, thing)* colosse□*m*, géant(e)□*m,f*; **his last novel was a m.** son dernier roman est un pavé; **it's a m. of a machine** c'est un vrai monstre, cette machine

ADJ *Fam* colossal□, monstre

monstrance ['mɒnstrəns] N *Rel* ostensoir *m*

monstrosity [mɒn'strɒsətɪ] *(pl* **monstrosities)** N **1** *(monstrous nature)* monstruosité *f* **2** *(ugly person, thing)* horreur *f*; **the town hall is a huge Victorian m.** la mairie est une horreur de l'époque victorienne

monstrous ['mɒnstrəs] ADJ **1** *(appalling)* monstrueux, atroce **2** *(enormous)* colossal, énorme **3** *(abnormal)* monstrueux

monstrously ['mɒnstrəslɪ] ADV affreusement

mons veneris [mɒnz'venərɪs] N *Anat* mont *m* de Vénus

Mont *(written abbr* **Montana)** Montana *m*

montage ['mɒntɑːʒ] N *Art, Cin & Phot* montage *m*

Monte Carlo [ˌmɒntɪ'kɑːləʊ] N Monte-Carlo

Montezuma [mɒntɪ'zuːmə] PR N Moctezuma, Montezuma

►► *Fam Hum* ***Montezuma's revenge*** la turista *f*

month [mʌnθ] N mois *m*; **in the m. of August** au mois d'août; **in the summer/winter months** pendant les mois d'été/d'hiver; **how much does she earn a m.?** combien gagne-t-elle par mois?; **a ten-m.-old baby** un bébé de dix mois; *Fam* **he got six months** il a été condamné à six mois de prison□; **once a m.** une fois par mois; **every m.** tous les mois; **a m. ago today** il y a aujourd'hui un mois; **in a m.'s time** dans un mois; **by the m.** au mois; *Fam* **never in a m. of Sundays** jamais de la vie; *Euph* **is it that** *or* **your time of the m.?** *(are you menstruating?)* tu es indisposée?

monthly ['mʌnθlɪ] *(pl* **monthlies)** N *(periodical)* mensuel *m*

ADJ mensuel

ADV tous les mois, mensuellement; **it happens twice m.** ça arrive deux fois par mois; **to be paid m.** être payé au mois *ou* mensuellement

• **monthlies** NPL *Fam Old-fashioned (menstrual period)* règles□*fpl*

►► ***monthly instalment, monthly payment*** mensualité *f*; *Med* ***monthly period*** règles *fpl*; ***monthly season ticket*** (billet *m* d')abonnement *m* mensuel

Montreal [ˌmɒntrɪ'ɔːl] N Montréal

monument ['mɒnjʊmənt] N **1** *(memorial)* monument *m*; **it is a m. to man's stupidity** c'est un monument à la bêtise humaine **2** *(historic building)* monument *m* historique; **a national m.** un monument national

monumental [ˌmɒnjʊ'mentəl] ADJ *(statue, literary work, error, stupidity)* monumental; *(ignorance)* prodigieux; **the film is a m. failure** le film est un échec monumental *ou* complet; **he's a m. bore** il est prodigieusement ennuyeux

►► ***monumental mason*** marbrier *m*

monumentally [ˌmɒnjʊˈmentəlɪ] **ADV 1** *(build)* de façon monumentale **2** *(extremely)* extrêmement

moo [muː] **N 1** *(sound)* meuglement *m*, beuglement *m*, mugissement *m* **2** *Br Fam (woman)* vieille bique *f*, vieille toupie *f*; **you silly m.!** espèce d'andouille!

VI meugler, beugler, mugir

ONOMAT meuh

mooch [muːtʃ] *Fam* **VI 1** *Br (wander aimlessly)* traîner, flemmarder **2** *(cadge)* taxer; **he's always mooching off** *or* **on people** il passe son temps à quémander, il est toujours en train de taper quelqu'un

VT 1 *(cadge)* taper; **to m. $10 off** *or* **from sb** taper qn de 10 dollars **2** *(steal)* chiper, piquer

N *Br* **I had a m. round the shops** je suis allé traîner dans les boutiques

mooch about, mooch around *Br Fam* **VT INSEP to m. about the house** traîner dans la maison

VI *(loaf)* glander, glandouiller; **I was just mooching about at home** je traînais *ou* flemmardais à la maison

moocher [ˈmuːtʃə(r)] **N** *Am Fam* tapeur(euse) *m,f*

moocow [ˈmuːˌkaʊ] **N** *Fam (in children's language)* vache*ᵅ* *f*, meu-meu *f*

mood [muːd] **N 1** *(humour)* humeur *f*, disposition *f*; **to be in a good/bad m.** être de bonne/mauvaise humeur; **to be in a generous m.** être en veine de générosité; **it's hard to predict the m. of the electorate** il est difficile de prédire l'état d'esprit *ou* l'humeur des électeurs; **she can be quite funny when the m. takes her** elle peut être plutôt drôle quand l'envie lui en prend; **to be in the m. for reading/dancing** avoir envie de lire/danser; **he's in no m. for jokes** il n'est pas d'humeur à rire; **I'm not in the m.** ça ne me dit rien

2 *(bad temper, sulk)* mauvaise humeur *f*, bouderie *f*; **to be in a m.** être de mauvaise humeur; **she's in one of her moods** elle est de mauvaise humeur, elle fait la tête

3 *(atmosphere)* ambiance *f*, atmosphère *f*; **the m. is one of cautious optimism** l'ambiance est à l'optimisme prudent

4 *Gram* mode *m*; **imperative m.** impératif *m*

►► ***mood music*** musique *f* d'ambiance; ***mood swing*** saute *f* d'humeur

moodily [ˈmuːdɪlɪ] **ADV** *(behave)* maussadement, d'un air morose; *(talk, reply)* d'un ton maussade

moodiness [ˈmuːdɪnɪs] **N 1** *(sullenness)* humeur *f* maussade, maussaderie *f* **2** *(volatility)* humeur *f* changeante

moody [ˈmuːdɪ] *(compar* **moodier,** *superl* **moodiest) ADJ 1** *(sullen)* de mauvaise humeur, maussade, grincheux **2** *(temperamental)* versatile, d'humeur changeante, lunatique

moola, moolah [ˈmuːlə] **N** *Fam* flouze *m*, fric *m*

moon [muːn] **N 1** *(of planet)* lune *f*; **there's a m. tonight** on voit la lune ce soir; **by the light of the m.** au clair de (la) lune; *Hum* **many moons ago** il y a bien des lunes; *Fam* **to be over the m.** être aux anges; *Fig* **to ask for the moon** demander la lune; *Fig* **he promised her the m. (and the stars)** il lui promit la lune *ou* monts et merveilles **2** *Am Fam (bare buttocks)* lune *f*

COMP *(base, flight, rocket)* lunaire

VT *Fam (show one's buttocks to)* montrer ses fesses à*ᵅ*

VI *Fam (bare one's buttocks)* montrer ses fesses*ᵅ*

►► ***moon buggy*** Jeep® *f* lunaire; ***moon landing*** atterrissage *m* sur la lune, alunissage *m*; *Astron* ***moon shot*** lancement *m* d'un vaisseau lunaire; *Astron* ***moon walk*** marche *f* sur la lune

▸**moon about, moon around VI** *Fam (idly)* paresser, traîner, flemmarder; *(dreamily)* rêvasser; *(gloomily)* se morfondre*ᵅ*

▸**moon over VT INSEP** *Fam (person)* soupirer après; *(photograph)* regarder amoureusement

moonbeam [ˈmuːnbiːm] **N** rayon *m* de lune

moon-faced ADJ joufflu, aux joues rebondies

moonless [ˈmuːnlɪs] **ADJ** sans lune

moonlight [ˈmuːnlaɪt] **N** clair *m* de lune; **by m., in the m.** au clair de (la) lune

ADJ *(walk)* au clair de (la) lune; *Br Fam* **to do a m. flit** déménager à la cloche de bois

VI *Fam (have second job)* avoir un deuxième emploi*ᵅ*; *(illegally)* travailler au noir

moonlighter [ˈmuːnˌlaɪtə(r)] **N** travailleur(euse) *m,f* non déclaré(e)

moonlighting [ˈmuːnˌlaɪtɪŋ] **N** *(UNCOUNT) (illegal work)* travail *m* au noir

moonlit [ˈmuːnlɪt] **ADJ** éclairé par la lune; **a m. night** une nuit de lune

moonrise [ˈmuːnraɪz] **N** lever *m* de la lune

moonshine [ˈmuːnʃaɪn] **N** *(UNCOUNT)* **1** *Am Fam (illegally made spirits)* alcool *m* de contrebande*ᵅ* **2** *Fam (foolishness)* sornettes *fpl*, sottises *fpl*

moonstone [ˈmuːnstəʊn] **N** pierre *f* de lune, adulaire *f*

moonstruck [ˈmuːnstrʌk] **ADJ** *Fam (dreamy)* dans la lune; *(mad)* détraqué, toqué

moony [ˈmuːnɪ] *(compar* **moonier,** *superl* **mooniest) ADJ** *Fam* **1** *(dreamy)* dans la lune **2** *Br (crazy)* dingue, timbré

Moor [mɔː(r)] **N** Maure *m*, Mauresque *f*

moor [mɔː(r)] **N** lande *f*

VT *(boat)* amarrer; *(buoy)* mouiller

VI mouiller

moorcock [ˈmɔːkɒk] **N** *Br Orn* lagopède *m* d'Écosse mâle

moorhen [ˈmɔːhen] **N** *Orn* **1** *(waterfowl)* poule *f* d'eau **2** *(female grouse)* lagopède *m* d'Écosse femelle

mooring [ˈmɔːrɪŋ] **N 1** *(act)* amarrage *m*, mouillage *m* **2** *(place)* mouillage *m*

• **moorings NPL** *(cables, ropes etc)* amarres *fpl*; **the boat was (riding) at her moorings** le bateau tirait sur ses amarres; *Fig* **he's lost his moorings** il est à la dérive

►► ***mooring buoy*** corps-mort *m*; ***mooring line*** câble *m* d'amarrage

Moorish [ˈmɔːrɪʃ] **ADJ** maure; *(art, architecture)* mauresque

moorland [ˈmɔːlənd] **N** lande *f*

moose [muːs] *(pl inv)* **N** *Zool (in North America)* orignal *m*, élan *m* du Canada; *(in Europe)* élan *m*, orignal *m*

moot [muːt] **VT** *(question, topic)* soulever; **it has been mooted that…** on a suggéré que…

N 1 *Hist* assemblée *f* **2** *Univ (in law faculties)* tribunal *m* fictif

ADJ that's a m. point c'est discutable, ce n'est pas sûr

►► *Law* ***moot court*** tribunal-école *m*, tribunal *m* fictif

mop [mɒp] *(pt & pp* **mopped,** *cont* **mopping) N 1** *(for floor* ▸ *string, cloth)* balai *m* (à franges), balai *m* espagnol; *(*▸ *sponge)* balai-éponge *m*; *Naut* vadrouille *f*; *(for dishes)* lavette *f* (à vaisselle) **2** *(of hair)* tignasse *f*; **a m. of blond hair** une tignasse blonde

VT *(floor)* laver; *(table, face, spilt liquid)* essuyer, éponger; **he mopped the sweat from his brow** il s'épongea le front

▸**mop up VT SEP 1** *(floor, table, spilt liquid)* essuyer, éponger; **have some bread to m. up the sauce** prenez un morceau de pain pour saucer votre assiette **2** *Fam (win, make off with)* rafler; **they mopped up all the gold medals** ils ont raflé toutes les médailles d'or **3** *Mil (resistance)* liquider

mope [məʊp] **VI** broyer du noir; **he's been moping around** *or* **about all week** il a passé la semaine à broyer du noir; **there's no use moping about** *or* **over it** ça ne sert à rien de passer ton temps à ressasser ce qui s'est passé

moped [ˈməʊped] **N** Mobylette® *f*, vélomoteur *m*

moppet [ˈmɒpɪt] **N** *Fam (term of affection)* chou *m*

mopping-up operation [ˈmɒpɪŋ-] **N** opération *f* de nettoyage

moquette [mɒˈket] **N** *Tex* moquette *f (étoffe)*

MOR [ˌeməʊˈɑː(r)] **ADJ** *(abbr* **middle-of-the-road)** *(music)* grand public *(inv)*; *Pej* passe-partout *(inv)*

moraine [mɒˈreɪn] **N** *Geol* moraine *f*

moral [ˈmɒrəl] **ADJ** moral; **the decline in m. standards** le déclin des valeurs morales, le relâchement des mœurs; **we have a m. duty to help them** nous sommes moralement obligés de les aider; **young people today have no m. fibre** les jeunes d'aujourd'hui n'ont ni caractère ni moralité; **to give sb m. support** soutenir qn moralement

N *(lesson)* morale *f*; **there's a m. to that story** cette histoire a une morale; **story with a m.** conte *f* moral

• **morals NPL** *(standards)* sens *m* moral, moralité *f*; **he has no morals** il n'a aucun sens moral; **man of loose morals** homme *m* de mœurs relâchées

►► ***the moral majority*** les néo-conservateurs *mpl (surtout aux États-Unis)*; ***moral philosophy*** morale *f*, éthique *f*; ***moral rights*** *(of author)* droit *m* moral; ***moral values*** valeurs *fpl* morales; ***moral victory*** victoire *f* morale

> Attention: ne pas confondre avec le nom anglais **morale**.

morale [məˈrɑːl] **N** moral *m*; **m. is high/low among the troops** les troupes ont bon/mauvais moral, les troupes ont/n'ont pas le moral; **she tried to raise their m.** elle a essayé de leur remonter le moral *ou* de leur redonner (du) courage; **to sap** *or* **to undermine sb's m.** saper le moral à qn, démoraliser qn

> Attention: ne pas confondre avec le nom anglais **moral**.

moralist [ˈmɒrəlɪst] **N** moraliste *mf*

moralistic [ˌmɒrəˈlɪstɪk] **ADJ** moraliste

morality [məˈrælətɪ] *(pl* **moralities) N** *(of person, decision, principles)* moralité *f*

►► *Theat* ***morality play*** moralité *f*

moralize, -ise [ˈmɒrəlaɪz] **VI** moraliser; **to m. about sth** moraliser sur qch

VT moraliser

moralizing, -ising [ˈmɒrəlaɪzɪŋ] **ADJ** moralisateur, moralisant

N *(UNCOUNT)* leçons *fpl* de morale, *Pej* prêches *mpl*

morally [ˈmɒrəlɪ] **ADV** moralement; **to be m. bound to do sth** être moralement obligé de faire qch; **the parents are m. responsible** les parents sont moralement responsables; **m. wrong** contraire à la morale

morass [məˈræs] **N 1** *(disordered situation)* bourbier *m*; *(of paperwork, information)* fouillis *m*, fatras *m*; **bogged down in a m. of rules and regulations** empêtré dans un fatras de règles et de règlements **2** *(marsh)* marais *m*, bourbier *m*

moratorium [ˌmɒrəˈtɔːrɪəm] *(pl* **moratoriums** *or* **moratoria** [-rɪə]**) N 1** *(suspension of activity)* moratoire *m*; **they are calling for a m. on arms sales** ils appellent à un moratoire sur les ventes d'armes **2** *Econ, Law & Fin* moratoire *m*; *(of debt)* moratoire *m*, suspension *f*; **to declare a m.** décréter un moratoire

morbid [ˈmɔːbɪd] **ADJ 1** *(gen)* morbide; *(curiosity)* malsain; **he has a m. outlook on life** il voit les choses en noir; **don't be so m.!** ne sois pas si morbide! **2** *Med (state, growth, symptom)* morbide

►► *Med* ***morbid anatomy*** anatomie *f* pathologique; ***morbid obesity*** obésité *f* morbide

morbidity [mɔːˈbɪdətɪ] **N 1** *(gen)* morbidité *f* **2** *Med* morbidité *f* (relative)

►► *Med* ***morbidity rate*** morbidité *f* (relative)

morbidly [ˈmɔːbɪdlɪ] **ADV** maladivement; **m. obese** d'une obésité morbide

morbidness [ˈmɔːbɪdnɪs] **N** morbidité *f*

mordant [ˈmɔːdənt] **ADJ** mordant, caustique

MORE [mɔː(r)]

ADJ
- plus de **1, 2**
- autre **2**
- davantage de **1**

PRON
- plus **1, 2**
- encore **2**
- davantage **1**

ADV
- plus **1, 2**
- plutôt **3**
- davantage **2**
- encore **4**

ADJ **1** *(compar of* **many, much***)* plus de, davantage de; **there were m. boys than girls** il y avait plus de garçons que de filles; **there's much** *or* **a lot** *or* **far m. room in the other building** il y a beaucoup plus de place dans l'autre bâtiment

2 *(additional quantity or number of)* **three m. people arrived** trois autres personnes sont arrivées; **you should eat m. fish** tu devrais manger davantage de *ou* plus de poisson; **I need m. time** j'ai besoin de plus de temps; **there's only one m. problem to solve** il n'y a plus qu'un problème à résoudre; **do you have any m. questions?** avez-vous d'autres questions?; **I have no m. money** je n'ai plus d'argent; **is there any m. butter?** est-ce qu'il reste du beurre?; **have some m. wine** reprends du vin; **no m. talking** maintenant, taisez-vous *ou* silence!; **there'll be no m. skiing this winter** le ski est fini pour cet hiver; **there's some m. paper in that drawer** il y a encore du papier dans ce tiroir; **would you like some m. soup?** voulez-vous un peu plus de soupe?

PRON **1** *(compar of* **many, much***)* *(larger amount)* plus, davantage; *(greater number)* plus; **he earns m. than I do** *or* **than me** il gagne plus que moi; **m. than 500 people** plus de 500 personnes; **I wish I could do m. for her** j'aimerais pouvoir l'aider plus *ou* davantage; **there are m. of them than there are of us** ils sont plus nombreux que nous; **I won't be m. than two hours** je n'en ai pas pour plus de deux heures, j'en ai pour deux heures au maximum; **she's m. of a singer than a dancer** c'est une chanteuse plus qu'une danseuse

2 *(additional amount)* plus, encore; **there's m. if you want it** il y en a encore si tu veux; **she just can't take any m.** elle n'en peut vraiment plus; **please can I have some m.?** *(food)* puis-je en reprendre, s'il vous plaît?; **we should see m. of each other** nous devrions nous voir plus *ou* davantage; **there are some m. here that you haven't washed** il en reste ici que tu n'as pas lavés; **I have something/nothing m. to say** j'ai encore quelque chose/je n'ai plus rien à dire; **he's just a good friend, nothing m.** c'est un bon ami, rien de plus; **the latest budget is just m. of the same** il n'y a rien de nouveau dans le dernier budget; **what m. can I say?** que puis-je dire de plus?; **what is m., what's m.** qui plus est; **but m. of that later...** mais nous reparlerons de ça plus tard...; **that's m. like it!** voilà, c'est mieux!; **no m. no less** ni plus ni moins; **any m. for the ferry?** qui d'autre prend le ferry?[□]; **need I say m.?** si tu vois ce que je veux dire; *Fam* **say no m.!** cela suffit!, n'en dis pas plus!

ADV **1** *(forming comparatives)* plus; **m. intelligent** plus intelligent; **m. comfortably** plus confortablement

2 *(to a greater extent or degree)* plus, davantage; **you should read m.** tu devrais lire plus *ou* davantage; **I like wine m. than beer** je préfère le vin à la bière, j'aime mieux le vin que la bière; **he's intelligent but his sister is m. so** il est intelligent mais sa sœur l'est davantage; **I'll give you £20, not a penny m.** je te donnerai 20 livres, pas un sou de plus; **the m. so because...** d'autant plus que...

3 *(rather)* plutôt; **it's m. a question of who foots the bill** il s'agit plutôt de savoir qui paiera la facture

4 *(again)* **once/twice m.** encore une/deux fois

• **more and more** ADJ de plus en plus; **m. and m. people are using it** de plus en plus de gens l'utilisent ADV de plus en plus; **I was growing m. and m. tired** j'étais de plus en plus fatigué

• **more or less** ADV **1** *(roughly)* plus ou moins; **that's m. or less what I expected** c'est plus ou moins ce à quoi je m'attendais **2** *(almost)* presque; **we've m. or less finished** nous avons presque terminé

• **more than** ADV plus que; **this m. than makes up for it** ça fait plus que compenser; **I'd be m. than happy to do it** je serais ravi de le faire; **that's m. than enough** c'est plus qu'il n'en faut; **we were m. than a little shocked** nous étions vraiment choqués

• **no more** ADV **1** *(neither)* non plus; **he doesn't believe the rumours and no m. do I** il ne croit pas les rumeurs et moi non plus **2** *(as little)* pas plus; **she's no m. a spy than I am!** elle n'est pas plus espionne que moi!; *Fam* **they can no m. act than fly in the air** ils jouent comme des pieds **3** *Literary (no longer)* **the Empire is no m.** l'Empire n'est plus

• **not... any more** ADV **we don't go there any m.** nous n'y allons plus; **he still works here, doesn't he? – not any m. (he doesn't)** il travaille encore ici, n'est-ce pas? – non, plus maintenant

• **the more... the more** CONJ plus... plus; **the m. they have, the m. they want** plus ils en ont, plus ils en veulent

moreish [ˈmɔːrɪʃ] ADJ *Br Fam* appétissant[□]; **these peanuts are very m.** on en mangerait de ces cacahuètes, ces cacahuètes ont un petit goût de revenez-y

morel [məˈrel] N morille *f*

morello [məˈreləʊ] *(pl* **morellos***)* N griotte *f*

▸▸ ***morello cherry*** *(fruit)* griotte *f*; *(tree)* griottier

moreover [mɔːˈrəʊvə(r)] ADV de plus

mores [ˈmɔːreɪz] NPL *Formal* mœurs *fpl*

morganatic [ˌmɔːgəˈnætɪk] ADJ morganatique

morgue [mɔːg] N **1** *(mortuary)* morgue *f*; *Fam* **it's like a m. here** c'est complètement mort ici **2** *Fam Journ* archives[□] *fpl*

MORI [ˈmɒrɪ] N *Br (abbr* **Market & Opinion Research Institute***)* = institut britannique de sondage

moribund [ˈmɒrɪbʌnd] ADJ moribond

morish = **moreish**

Mormon [ˈmɔːmən] *Rel* N mormon(e) *m,f*

ADJ mormon

morn [mɔːn] N **1** *Literary (morning)* matin *m* **2** *Scot* **the m.** *(tomorrow)* demain

morning [ˈmɔːnɪŋ] N **1** *(gen)* matin *m*; *(referring to duration)* matinée *f*; **at three/ten o'clock in the m.** à trois/dix heures du matin; **this m.** ce matin; **that m.** ce matin-là; **the previous m., the m. before** la veille au matin; **the next m., the m. after** le lendemain matin; **I worked all m.** j'ai travaillé toute la matinée; **one summer m.** un matin d'été; **when I awoke it was m.** quand je me suis réveillé il faisait jour; **every Saturday/Sunday m.** tous les samedis/dimanches matin; **from m. till night, m., noon and night** du matin jusqu'au soir; **there's a flight in the m.** *(before noon)* il y a un vol le matin; *(sometime during)* il y a un vol dans la matinée; *(tomorrow)* il y a un vol demain matin; **see you in the m.!** à demain matin!; **in the early/late m.** en début/fin de matinée; **on Monday m.** lundi matin; **the cleaning lady comes on Monday mornings** la femme de ménage vient le lundi matin; **on the m. of the twelfth** le matin du douze, le douze au matin; **I'm on mornings this week** je travaille le matin cette semaine; **could I have the m. off?** puis-je avoir la matinée de libre?; **(good) m.!** *(hello)* bonjour!; *(goodbye)* au revoir!; *Fam* **the m. after the night before** un lendemain de cuite; **the m. rush hour** les heures *fpl* de pointe du matin **2** *Literary (beginning)* matin *m*, aube *f*; **in the m. of one's life** à l'aube de sa vie

COMP *(dew, sun, bath)* matinal, du matin; *(newspaper, broadcast)* du matin

• **mornings** ADV *esp Am* le matin

▸▸ ***morning coat*** queue-de-pie *f*; ***morning coffee*** pause-café *f* (dans la matinée); *Br* ***morning dress*** = habit porté lors des occasions importantes et comportant queue-de-pie, pantalon gris et haut-de-forme gris; *Bot* ***morning glory*** ipomée *f*, volubilis *m*; *Rel* ***Morning Prayer*** office *m* du matin *(Église anglicane)*; ***morning room*** petit salon *m*; ***morning sickness*** nausées *fpl* matinales *ou* du matin; ***morning star*** étoile *f* du matin

> When translating **morning**, note that **matin** and **matinée** are not interchangeable. **Matin** is used to refer to the morning as part of the day, as opposed to the evening or the afternoon. For **matinée**, the emphasis is on duration.

morning-after pill N pilule *f* du lendemain

Moroccan [məˈrɒkən] N Marocain(e) *m,f*

ADJ marocain

COMP *(embassy, history)* du Maroc

Morocco [məˈrɒkəʊ] N Maroc *m*

• **morocco** N maroquin *m*; **m.-bound** relié en maroquin

▸▸ ***morocco leather*** maroquin *m*

moron [ˈmɔːrɒn] N **1** *Fam (stupid person)* imbécile *mf*, crétin(e) *m,f*; **you m.!** pauvre imbécile! **2** *Old-fashioned (mentally retarded person)* débile *mf* léger(ère)

moronic [məˈrɒnɪk] ADJ imbécile, débile

morose [məˈrəʊs] ADJ morose

morosely [məˈrəʊslɪ] ADV avec morosité

moroseness [məˈrəʊsnɪs] N morosité *f*, humeur *f* morose

morph [mɔːf] N *Ling* morphe *f*

VT *Comput (image)* transformer par morphing

VI *Comput* **to m. into sth** se transformer en qch

morpheme [ˈmɔːfiːm] N *Ling* morphème *m*

Morpheus [ˈmɔːfjuːs] PR N *Myth* Morphée; **in the arms of M.** dans les bras de Morphée

morphine [ˈmɔːfiːn], **morphia** [ˈmɔːfjə] N morphine *f*

▸▸ ***morphine addict*** morphinomane *mf*; ***morphine addiction*** morphinomanie *f*

morphing [ˈmɔːfɪŋ] N *Comput* morphing *m*

morphological [ˌmɔːfəˈlɒdʒɪkəl] ADJ *Biol & Ling* morphologique

morphology [mɔːˈfɒlədʒɪ] N *Biol & Ling* morphologie *f*

morris [ˈmɒrɪs] N

▸▸ ***morris dance*** = danse folklorique anglaise; ***morris dancer*** = danseur folklorique anglais; ***morris dancing*** = danses folkloriques anglaises

morrow [ˈmɒrəʊ] N **1** *Literary (next day)* lendemain *m*; **on the m.** le lendemain **2** *Arch or Literary (morning)* matin *m*

Morse [mɔːs] N *(code)* morse *m*

▸▸ ***Morse alphabet*** alphabet *m* morse; ***Morse code*** morse *m*; ***Morse signals*** signaux *mpl* en morse

morsel [ˈmɔːsəl] N *(gen)* morceau *m*; *(mouthful)* bouchée *f*; **a choice m.** un morceau de choix

mortadella [ˌmɔːtəˈdelə] N mortadelle *f*

mortal [ˈmɔːtəl] ADJ **1** *(not immortal)* mortel; **all men are m.** tous les hommes sont mortels

2 *(fatal ▸ blow, disease, injury)* mortel, fatal *(deadly ▸ enemy, danger)* mortel

3 *Fam Old-fashioned (as intensifier)* sacré, satané; **I've tried every m. thing!** j'ai absolument tout essayé!

4 *(very great)* **he lived in m. fear of being found out** il vivait dans une peur mortelle d'être découvert

N mortel(elle) *m,f*; **a mere m.** un simple mortel

▸▸ ***mortal combat*** combat *m* à mort; ***mortal remains*** dépouille *f* mortelle; ***mortal sin*** péché *m* mortel

mortality [mɔːˈtælətɪ] *(pl* **mortalities***)* N **1** *(loss of life)* mortalité *f*; **infant m.** la mortalité infantile **2** *(of mortal)* mortalité *f*

▸▸ ***mortality rate*** taux *m* de mortalité; ***mortality tables*** tables *fpl* de mortalité *ou* de létalité

mortally [ˈmɔːtəlɪ] ADV mortellement; **m. offended** mortellement offensé; **m. wounded** blessé à mort; **to be m. afraid (of sb)** être mort de peur (devant qn)

mortar [ˈmɔːtə(r)] N **1** *Constr* mortier *m* **2** *Pharm & Culin* mortier *m*; **m. and pestle** pilon *m* et mortier *m* **3** *Mil* mortier *m*

VT *Constr* cimenter

▸▸ ***mortar attack*** attaque *f* au mortier; ***mortar shell*** obus *m* de mortier

mortarboard [ˈmɔːtəbɔːd] N **1** *Sch & Univ* ≃ mortier *m (couvre-chef de professeur, d'universitaire)* **2** *Constr* taloche *f*

mortgage [ˈmɔːgɪdʒ] N **1** *(to buy house)* prêt *m* (immobilier), crédit *m* immobilier; **a 25-year m at 13 percent** un emprunt sur 25 ans à 13 pour cent; **to take out a m.** prendre un crédit *ou* un prêt immobilier; **to pay off** *or* **to clear one's m** rembourser l'emprunt sur sa maison; **second m** hypothèque *f* **2** *(raised on property)* hypothèque *f*; **to take out** *or* **to raise a m.** lever une hypothèque; **to pay off a m.** purger une hypothèque

VT *(land, house)* hypothéquer, prendre une hypothèque sur; *(title deeds)* engager, mettre en gage; **to be mortgaged to the hilt** *(person)* croule sous les remboursements; **to m. one's happiness** engager son bonheur

▸▸ ***mortgage broker*** courtier(ère) *m,f* en prêts hypothécaires; ***mortgage market*** marché *m* hypothécaire; ***mortgage payment*** remboursement *m* d'un emprunt-logement; **we can't meet our m. payments** nous ne pouvons pas payer les mensualités de notre emprunt; ***mortgage rate*** taux *m* de crédit immobilier; ***mortgage repayment*** remboursement *m* d'un emprunt-logement

mortgagee [ˌmɔːgɪ'dʒiː] **N** créancier(ère) *m,f* hypothécaire, prêteur(euse) *m,f (sur une hypothèque)*

mortgagor ['mɔːgɪdʒə(r)] **N** débiteur(trice) *m,f* hypothécaire, emprunteur(euse) *m,f (sur une hypothèque)*

mortice = **mortise**

mortician [mɔː'tɪʃən] **N** *Am* entrepreneur(euse) *m,f* de pompes funèbres

mortification [ˌmɔːtɪfɪ'keɪʃən] **N 1** *(humiliation)* humiliation *f*; **to my (eternal) m.** à ma (grande) honte **2** *Rel (of the flesh)* mortification *f* **3** *Med* nécrose *f*

mortify ['mɔːtɪfaɪ] *(pt & pp* **mortified***)* **VT 1** *(humiliate)* humilier, *Literary* mortifier; **I was mortified** j'étais mort de honte **2** *Rel (the flesh)* mortifier

VI *Med (become gangrenous)* se gangrener; *(undergo tissue death)* se nécroser, se mortifier

mortifying ['mɔːtɪfaɪɪŋ] **ADJ** *(experience etc)* humiliant

mortise ['mɔːtɪs] **N** mortaise *f*

VT mortaiser; **to m. two beams together** emmortaiser *ou* emboîter deux poutres

▸▸ ***mortise lock*** serrure *f* encastrée

mortuary ['mɔːtʃʊərɪ] *(pl* **mortuaries***)* **N** morgue *f*

ADJ mortuaire

Mosaic [məʊ'zeɪɪk] **ADJ** *Bible* mosaïque, de Moïse

mosaic [məʊ'zeɪɪk] **N** mosaïque *f*

ADJ en mosaïque; **m. floor** dallage *m* en mosaïque

Moscow ['mɒskəʊ] **N** Moscou

Moses ['məʊzɪz] **PR N** *Bible* Moïse; *Fam* **Holy M.!** Seigneur!

▸▸ ***Moses basket*** couffin *m*

mosey ['məʊzɪ] **VI** *Am Fam (amble)* marcher d'un pas tranquille[□]; **I'll just m. down to the bar** je vais faire un tour au bar; **to m. along** aller *ou* se promener sans se presser[□]; **I'll be moseying along now** *(leaving)* je vais y aller[□]

Moslem ['mɒzləm] *Rel* **N** musulman(e) *m,f*

ADJ musulman

mosque [mɒsk] **N** *Rel* mosquée *f*

mosquito [mə'skiːtəʊ] *(pl* **mosquitos** *or* **mosquitoes***)* **N** *Entom* moustique *m*

▸▸ ***mosquito bite*** piqûre *f* de moustique; ***mosquito net*** moustiquaire *f*; ***mosquito repellent*** produit *m* antimoustique

moss [mɒs] **N** *Bot* mousse *f*

▸▸ *Mining* ***moss agate*** agate *f* mousseuse; ***moss green*** vert *m* mousse *(inv)*; *Bot* ***moss rose*** rose *f* moussue *ou* mousseuse; *Sewing* ***moss stitch*** point *m* de riz

mossy ['mɒsɪ] *(compar* **mossier**, *superl* **mossiest***)* **ADJ** moussu, couvert de mousse

SUFFIXE

-MOST

Le suffixe **-most** s'emploie pour former des adjectifs qui véhiculent la notion d'ÉLOIGNEMENT dans une direction donnée, et n'a pas d'équivalent en français:

the southernmost town in England la ville la plus au sud de l'Angleterre; **the topmost sail** la voile la plus haute; **the uppermost drawer** le tiroir du haut.

MOST [məʊst]

ADJ
- le plus de **1**
- la plupart de **2**

PRON
- le plus **1**
- la plus grande partie **2**
- la plupart **2**

ADV
- le plus **1, 2**
- bien **3**
- presque **4**

ADJ *(superl of* **many, much***)* **1** *(largest quantity or number of)* **(the) m.** le plus de; **the candidate who gets (the) m. votes** le candidat qui obtient le plus de voix *ou* le plus grand nombre de voix; **which of your inventions gave you (the) m. satisfaction?** laquelle de vos inventions vous a procuré la plus grande satisfaction?; **for the m. part** *(in largest number of cases)* pour la plupart; *(most often)* le plus souvent, la plupart du temps

2 *(the majority of)* la plupart de, la majorité de; **m. Europeans** la plupart *ou* la majorité des Européens; **I go out m. evenings** je sors presque tous les soirs; **I don't like m. modern art** en général, je n'aime pas l'art moderne

PRON *(superl of* **many, much***)* **1** *(the largest amount)* **(the) m.** le plus; **he is more reliable than m.** on peut compter sur lui plus que sur bien des gens; **Diana earns (the) m.** c'est Diana qui gagne le plus; **that is the m. one can say in his defence** c'est tout ce qu'on peut dire en sa faveur; *Am Fam Old-fashioned* **her latest album is the m.!** son dernier album est vraiment génial!; **to make the m. of sth** *(advantage, chance, good weather)* profiter de qch; *(bad situation, ill-luck)* tirer le meilleur parti de qch; *(resources, skills)* employer *ou* utiliser qch au mieux; **she made the m. of her time in Mexico** elle a profité au maximum du temps qu'elle a passé au Mexique; **the opposition made the m. of the scandal** l'opposition a tiré tout ce qu'elle pouvait du scandale

2 *(the larger part)* la plus grande *ou* la majeure partie; *(the larger number)* la plupart *ou* majorité; **m. of my salary** la majeure partie de mon salaire; **m. of the snow has melted** presque toute la neige a fondu; **m. of the time** la plupart du temps; **m. of us/them** la plupart d'entre nous/eux

ADV 1 *(forming superlatives)* **it's the m. beautiful house I've ever seen** c'est la plus belle maison que j'aie jamais vue; **she was the one who explained things m. clearly** c'est elle qui expliquait les choses le plus clairement

2 *(to the greatest extent or degree)* **(the) m.** le plus; **what worries you (the) m.?, what m. worries you?** qu'est-ce qui vous inquiète le plus?; **it's the one I like m. of all** de tous, c'est celui que je préfère

3 *(as intensifier)* bien, fort; **a m. interesting theory** une théorie fort intéressante; **m. likely** *or* **probably** très probablement; **we had the m. awful weather** nous avons eu un temps détestable; **it's m. kind of you to say so** c'est extrêmement *ou* bien gentil à vous de dire ça; **m. certainly you may!** mais bien entendu!

4 *Am Fam (almost)* presque[□]; **m. everybody had heard of it** presque *ou* pratiquement tout le monde était au courant

• **at (the) most** **ADV** au plus, au maximum; **at the very m.** tout au plus, au grand maximum

mostly ['məʊstlɪ] **ADV 1** *(mainly)* principalement, surtout; **it's m. sugar** c'est surtout du sucre; **the soldiers were m. young men** il s'agissait pour la plupart *ou* surtout *ou* principalement de jeunes soldats; **I've travelled a lot, m. in Europe** j'ai beaucoup voyagé, en Europe surtout **2** *(usually)* le plus souvent, la plupart du temps

MOT [ˌeməʊ'tiː] *(pt & pp* **MOT'd** [-'tiːd], *cont* **MOT'ing** [-'tiːɪŋ]) *Br (abbr* **Ministry of Transport***)* **N 1** *Formerly (ministry)* ministère *m* des Transports **2** *(certificate)* = certificat de contrôle technique annuel obligatoire pour les véhicules de plus de trois ans; **six months' M.** *(in advertisement)* = certificat de contrôle technique valable pendant six mois **3** *(test)* = contrôle technique; **that car of yours will never pass its M.** ta voiture n'obtiendra jamais son certificat de contrôle technique

VT **to have one's car M.'d** soumettre sa voiture au contrôle technique

mote [məʊt] **N** *Literary* atome *m*, grain *m*, particule *f*; *Bible* **the m. in thy brother's eye** la paille dans l'œil de ton frère

motel [məʊ'tel] **N** motel *m*

motet [məʊ'tet] **N** *Mus* motet *m*

moth [mɒθ] **N 1** *Zool* papillon *m* (nocturne) **2** *(in clothes)* mite *f*

mothball ['mɒθbɔːl] **N** boule *f* de naphtaline; **it smells of mothballs in here** ça sent la naphtaline ici; *Fig* **to put sth in mothballs** mettre qch au placard *ou* en sommeil

VT *(project)* mettre en suspens

moth-eaten **ADJ 1** *(clothing)* mité **2** *Fam Fig (shabby)* miteux

mother ['mʌðə(r)] **N 1** *(parent)* mère *f*; **m. of three** mère *f* de trois enfants; **yes, M.** oui, mère, oui, maman; *Br* **shall I be m.?** c'est moi qui fais le service?; **every m.'s son** tous sans exception; **m.'s little helper** *(helpful child)* = enfant qui aide sa mère dans les tâches ménagères; *Fig Hum* = alcool ou médicament consommé pour oublier ses soucis; **m. and toddler group** réunion *f* de mamans

2 *(original cause, source)* mère *f*; **the M. of parliaments** le Parlement britannique *(qui a servi de modèle à d'autres parlements)*

3 *Fam (large person, thing)* **I've got a m. of a hangover** j'ai une vache de gueule de bois; **we had the m. and father of a row** nous avons eu une de ces empoignades!

4 *Am very Fam* enfoiré(e) *m,f*, enculé(e) *m,f*; **some m.'s stolen my drink** il y a un enfoiré qui m'a pris mon verre

VT 1 *(take care of)* servir de mère à; *(coddle)* dorloter, materner; **she mothers him too much** elle le dorlote trop **2** *(give birth to)* donner naissance à

• **Mother** **N** *Rel* mère *f*; **M. superior** Mère *f* supérieure; **M. of God** *(Virgin Mary)* Mère *f* de Dieu

▸▸ ***mother's boy*** fils *m* à sa maman; ***mother church*** église *f* mère; ***mother country*** (mère) patrie *f*; ***Mother's Day*** la fête des Mères; ***Mother Earth*** la Terre; ***mother figure*** figure *f* maternelle; *also Fig* ***mother hen*** mère *f* poule; ***mother love*** amour *m* maternel; ***Mother Nature*** la Nature; *Br Hum* ***mother's ruin*** gin *m*; *Mil* ***mother ship*** ravitailleur *m*; ***mother tongue*** langue *f* maternelle; ***mother wit*** bon sens *m*

motherboard ['mʌðəbɔːd] **N** *Comput* carte *f* mère

motherfucker ['mʌðəˌfʌkə(r)] **N** *Am Vulg* **1** *(person)* enfoiré(e) *m,f*, enculé(e) *m,f*; **he's a stupid m.** c'est un pauvre con **2** *(thing)* saloperie *f*; **the m. won't start** cette saloperie ne veut pas démarrer

motherfucking ['mʌðəˌfʌkɪŋ] **ADJ** *Am Vulg* foutu; **open up or I'll kick the m. door in!** ouvre ou j'enfonce cette putain de porte!

motherhood ['mʌðəhʊd] **N** maternité *f*

mothering ['mʌðərɪŋ] **N** soins *mpl* maternels

▸▸ ***mothering skills*** capacité *f* à s'occuper d'un petit; *Br* ***Mothering Sunday*** la fête des Mères

mother-in-law *(pl* **mothers-in-law***)* **N** belle-mère *f*

▸▸ *Bot* ***mother-in-law's tongue*** sansevière *f*

motherland ['mʌðəlænd] **N** (mère) patrie *f*, pays *m* natal

motherless ['mʌðəlɪs] **ADJ** sans mère

motherly ['mʌðəlɪ] **ADJ** maternel

mother-of-pearl **N** nacre *f*

COMP en *ou* de nacre

mothproof ['mɒθpruːf] **ADJ** traité à l'antimite

VT traiter à l'antimite

motif [məʊ'tiːf] **N** *Art, Literature & Mus* motif *m*

motion ['məʊʃən] **N 1** *(movement)* mouvement *m*; **the gentle m. of the boat** le mouvement léger du bateau

2 *(gesture)* geste *m*, mouvement *m*; **he made a m. as if to step back** il esquissa un geste de recul; **with a swaying m. of the hips** en ondulant des hanches; **to go through the motions of doing sth** faire qch machinalement; **he's just going through the motions** il fait juste semblant

3 *(proposal)* motion *f*, résolution *f*; **to propose** *or* **to bring a m.** présenter une motion, soumettre une proposition; **the m. was carried/defeated** la motion fut adoptée/rejetée; **to table a m. of no confidence** déposer une motion de censure

4 *Law (application)* requête *f*

5 *Med (faeces)* selles *fpl*; **to have** *or* **to pass a m.** aller à la selle

VI **to m. to sb (to do sth)** faire signe à qn (de faire qch)

VT **to m. sb to do sth** faire signe à qn de faire qch; **to m. sb in/away/out** faire signe à qn d'entrer/de s'éloigner/de sortir

• **in motion** **ADJ** *(moving)* en mouvement; *(working)* en marche; **do not alight while the train is in m.** il est interdit de descendre du train avant l'arrêt complet **ADV** **he set the machine in m.** il mit la machine en marche; *Fig* **to put** *or* **set a process in m.** mettre un processus en branle; *Fig* **to set the wheels in m.** mettre les choses en route *ou* en branle

►► *Am Cin* ***motion picture*** film *m*; **the m. picture industry** l'industrie *f* du cinéma; *Am* ***motion sickness*** mal *m* des transports; ***motion study*** analyse *f* du mouvement, chronophotographie *f*

motionless ['məʊʃənlɪs] **ADJ** immobile

motivate ['məʊtɪveɪt] **VT** motiver; **how can I m. my pupils?** comment puis-je motiver mes élèves?; **to m. sb to do sth** pousser *ou* inciter qn à faire qch; **they were motivated by a desire to help others** ils étaient poussés par un désir d'aider les autres

motivated ['məʊtɪveɪtɪd] **ADJ** motivé; **a highly m. young woman** une jeune femme extrêmement motivée *ou* débordant d'ardeur

motivating ['məʊtɪveɪtɪŋ] **ADJ** motivant

motivation [ˌməʊtɪ'veɪʃən] **N** motivation *f* (**to do sth** pour faire qch); **the pupils lack m.** les élèves sont peu motivés, les élèves ne sont pas assez motivés

►► *Mktg* ***motivation research*** recherche *f* de motivation

motivational [ˌməʊtɪ'veɪʃənəl] **ADJ** motivationnel

►► *Mktg* ***motivational research*** recherche *f* de motivation

motivator ['məʊtɪveɪtə(r)] **N he's a good m.** il sait motiver les gens

motive ['məʊtɪv] **N 1** *(reason)* motif *m*, raison *f*; **the motives for her behaviour** ce qui explique sa conduite, les raisons *fpl* de sa conduite; **my m. for asking is simple** la raison pour laquelle je pose cette question est simple **2** *Law* mobile *m*; **what could have been his m. for committing the crime?** quelles sont les raisons qui ont pu le pousser à commettre ce crime? **3** *Art (of painting)* motif *m*

ADJ moteur

►► ***motive energy*** énergie *f* motrice; ***motive power*** force *f* motrice

motley ['mɒtlɪ] **ADJ 1** *(diverse, assorted)* hétéroclite, composite, disparate; **a m. crew** une foule bigarrée **2** *(multicoloured)* multicolore, bariolé

N *Arch (jester's dress)* livrée *f* de bouffon

motocross ['məʊtəkrɒs] **N** motocross *m*

motor ['məʊtə(r)] **N 1** *(engine)* moteur *m* **2** *Br Fam (car)* bagnole *f*

ADJ *Anat (nerve, muscle)* moteur

VI *Br* **1** *Old-fashioned (go by car)* aller en voiture; **we motored up to London/across Europe** nous sommes allés à Londres/nous avons traversé l'Europe en voiture **2** *Fam* **to be motoring** *(going fast)* foncer; *Fig* **now we're motoring!** cette fois on y vient!

►► *Formal* ***motor car*** automobile *f*, voiture *f*; ***motor caravan*** camping-car *m*; ***motor coach*** autocar *m*; *Physiol* ***motor functions*** motricité *f*; *Am* ***motor home*** camping-car *m*; ***motor industry*** industrie *f* automobile; *Am* ***motor inn*** motel *m*; ***motor insurance*** assurance *f* automobile; ***motor launch*** vedette *f*; *Am* ***motor lodge*** motel *m*; ***motor mechanic*** mécanicien(enne) *m,f*; ***motor mower*** tondeuse *f* à moteur; *Med* ***motor neurone disease*** maladie *f* de Charcot; ***motor race*** course *f* automobile; ***motor racing*** courses *fpl* automobiles; ***motor rally*** rallye *m* automobile; ***motor scooter*** scooter *m*; ***motor show*** salon *m* de l'auto(mobile); ***motor sport*** sport *m* automobile; ***motor vehicle*** véhicule *m* automobile; *Naut* ***motor vessel*** bateau *m* à moteur

Motorail® ['məʊtəreɪl] **N** *Br* train *m* autocouchette *ou* autos-couchettes

motor-assisted ADJ

►► ***motor-assisted bicycle*** cyclomoteur *m*

motorbike ['məʊtəbaɪk] **N** moto *f*

motorboat ['məʊtəbəʊt] **N** canot *m* automobile *ou* à moteur

motorcade ['məʊtəkeɪd] **N** cortège *m* (de voitures)

motorcycle ['məʊtəˌsaɪkəl] **N** motocyclette *f*, moto *f*

VI aller en moto

►► ***motorcycle combination*** moto *f* et sidecar; *Am Fam* ***motorcycle cop*** motard *m (de la police)*; ***motorcycle courier*** coursier(ère) *m,f*, porteur(euse) *m,f*; ***motorcycle racing*** motocyclisme *m*; ***motorcycle rider*** motocycliste *mf*, motard(e) *m,f*

motorcycling ['məʊtəˌsaɪklɪŋ] **N** motocyclisme *m*

motorcyclist ['məʊtəˌsaɪklɪst] **N** motocycliste *mf*

motor-driven ADJ à moteur; *(device)* actionné *ou* commandé par un moteur

motoring ['məʊtərɪŋ] **N** *(UNCOUNT)* l'automobile *f*

►► *Journ* ***motoring correspondent*** chroniqueur (euse) *m,f* automobile; ***motoring holiday*** virée *f* en voiture; ***motoring offence*** infraction *f* au code de la route; ***motoring organization*** association *f* d'automobilistes

motorist ['məʊtərɪst] **N** automobiliste *mf*

motorization, -isation [ˌməʊtəraɪ'zeɪʃən] **N** motorisation *f*

motorize, -ise ['məʊtəraɪz] **VT** motoriser; **motorized bicycle** vélomoteur *m*; **motorized wheelchair** fauteuil *m* roulant à moteur

►► ***motorized troops*** troupes *fpl* motorisées

motorman ['məʊtəmən] *(pl* **motormen** [-mən]*)* **N** mécanicien *m*, conducteur *m*

motormouth ['məʊtəˌmaʊθ, *pl* -maʊðz] **N** *Fam Pej* **he's a bit of a m.** c'est un véritable moulin à paroles

motorway ['məʊtəˌweɪ] **N** *Br* autoroute *f*

►► ***motorway accident*** accident *m* sur autoroute; ***motorway driving*** conduite *f* sur autoroute; ***motorway exit*** sortie *f* d'autoroute; ***motorway network*** réseau *m* autoroutier; ***motorway police*** police *f* de l'autoroute; ***motorway restaurant*** restauroute *m*, restoroute *m*; ***motorway services*** services *mpl* autoroutiers

Motown ['məʊtaʊn] **N 1** *Am Fam* = surnom de la ville de Détroit **2** *Mus* style *m* Motown

mottled ['mɒtəld] **ADJ** tacheté, moucheté; *(skin)* marbré

motto ['mɒtəʊ] *(pl* **mottos** *or* **mottoes)** **N 1** *(maxim)* devise *f*; **the college m.** la devise du collège **2** *(in Christmas cracker ▸ joke)* blague *f*; *(▸ riddle)* devinette *f*

3 *Typ (in book)* épigraphe *f*

4 *Mus* motif *m*

mould, *Am* **mold** [məʊld] **VT 1** *(fashion ▸ statue, vase)* façonner, modeler; **to m. sth in** *or* **from** *or* **out of clay** sculpter qch dans de l'argile; *Fig* **to m. sb's character** façonner *ou* former le caractère de qn; *Fig* **she moulded them into a team** elle a fait d'eux une équipe; *Fig* **they're trying to m. public opinion** ils essaient de façonner l'opinion publique **2** *Art & Metal (make in a mould)* mouler; **moulded plastic chairs** chaises *fpl* en plastique moulé **3** *(cling to ▸ body, figure)* mouler

N 1 *Art & Metal (hollow form)* moule *m*; *(prototype)* modèle *m*, gabarit *m*

2 *(moulded article)* pièce *f* moulée; **rice m.** gâteau *m* de riz

3 *Fig (pattern)* moule *m*; **they're all cast in the same m.** ils sortent tous du *ou* ils ont tous été coulés dans le même moule; **cast in a heroic m.** fait de l'étoffe des héros; **a star in the John Wayne m.** une star du style John Wayne; **to break the m.** sortir des sentiers battus; **when they made him they broke the m.** il n'y en a pas deux comme lui

4 *Archit* moulure *f*

5 *(mildew)* moisissure *f*

6 *(soil)* humus *m*, terreau *m*

moulder, *Am* **molder** ['məʊldə(r)] **VI 1** *(decay ▸ corpse, compost)* se décomposer; *(▸ house, beams)* se délabrer; *(▸ bread)* moisir **2** *(languish ▸ person, article)* moisir; *(▸ economy, institution)* dépérir; **he's mouldering away in prison** il moisit *ou* croupit en prison

moulding, *Am* **molding** ['məʊldɪŋ] **N 1** *Archit (decorative)* moulure *f*, *(at join of wall and floor)* baguette *f*, plinthe *f* **2** *(moulded article)* objet *m* moulé, pièce *f* moulée **3** *(act of shaping)* moulage *m*; *Fig (of character, public opinion)* formation *f*, façonnement *m*

mouldy, *Am* **moldy** ['məʊldɪ] *(Br compar* **mouldier,** *superl* **mouldiest,** *Am compar* **moldier,** *superl* **moldiest)** **ADJ 1** *(covered with mould)* moisi; **it smells m.** ça sent le moisi **2** *Fam (measly)* minable; *(nasty)* vache, rosse

Mouli® ['muːlɪ] *Br* **N** moulin *m* à légumes

VT passer à la Moulinette®

moult, *Am* **molt** [məʊlt] **VI** muer; *(cat, dog)* perdre ses poils

VT *(hair, feathers)* perdre

N mue *f*

moulting, *Am* **molting** ['məʊltɪŋ] **N** mue *f*

ADJ en mue

mound [maʊnd] **N 1** *(of earth, stones)* butte *f*, monticule *m*, tertre *m*; **burial m.** tertre *m* funéraire, tumulus *m* **2** *(heap)* tas *m*; *Fam* **he ate mounds of rice** il a mangé une montagne de riz **3** *(in palmistry)* mont *m*

mount [maʊnt] **N 1** *(mountain)* mont *m*, montagne *f* **2** *(horse)* monture *f*; *Horseracing (ride)* monte *f* **3** *(support ▸ of photo)* carton *m*, support *m*; *(▸ of gem, lens, tool)* monture *f*; *(▸ of machine)* support *m*; *(▸ for stamp in collection)* charnière *f*; *(▸ for object under microscope)* lame *f*

VT 1 *(climb ▸ slope, steps)* monter

2 *(climb onto ▸ horse, bicycle)* monter sur, enfourcher; *(▸ stage, throne etc)* monter sur; **a truck mounted the pavement** un camion monta sur le trottoir

3 *(organize, put on ▸ exhibition, campaign etc)* monter, organiser; *Com (bid)* lancer; *Mil* **to m. an offensive** lancer une offensive; *Mil* **to m. guard** monter la garde; **they mounted an attack on the party leadership** ils montèrent une attaque contre la direction du parti

4 *(fix, support)* monter; **to m. a gem** monter une pierre; **to m. photographs/stamps** coller des photos/timbres (dans un album); **they mounted machine guns on the roofs** ils installèrent des mitrailleuses sur les toits; **an old sword mounted in a glass case** une épée de collection exposée dans une vitrine

5 *(mate with)* monter, saillir, couvrir

VI 1 *(onto horse)* monter (à cheval), se mettre en selle **2** *(rise, increase)* monter, augmenter, croître; **her anger mounted** sa colère montait; **the cost was mounting** le coût augmentait

►► ***Mount Everest*** le mont Everest, l'Everest *m*; ***Mount Fuji*** le (mont) Fuji-Yama; ***the Mount of Olives*** le mont des Oliviers; ***Mount Olympus*** le mont Olympe, l'Olympe *m*; ***Mount Sinaï*** le (mont) Sinaï

▸**mount up VI 1** *(increase)* monter, augmenter, s'accroître; **the bill was mounting up** la facture augmentait **2** *(accumulate)* s'accumuler, s'amonceler; **you'll be amazed how quickly the money mounts up** vous serez stupéfait de voir la somme qu'on peut atteindre en si peu de temps; **it all mounts up** ça finit par chiffrer

mountain ['maʊntɪn] **N 1** *(geographical feature)* montagne *f*; **we spent a week in the mountains** on a passé une semaine à la montagne; *Fig* **to make a m. out of a molehill** se faire une montagne d'un rien; *Fig* **to move mountains** déplacer des montagnes, faire l'impossible; *Fig* **if the m. won't go to Mohammed, Mohammed will have to go to the m.** si la montagne ne vient pas à Mahomet, Mahomet ira à la montagne; *Fig* **they've got a (huge) m. to climb** ils ont du pain sur la planche **2** *(heap, accumulation)* montagne *f*, tas *m*; **a m. of papers** une énorme pile de papiers; **a m. of evidence** des quantités *fpl* de preuves; **I've got mountains of work to get through** j'ai un travail fou *ou* monstre à terminer; *Econ* **the butter/beef m.** la montagne de beurre/bœuf

COMP *(people)* montagnard; *(resort, stream, scenery, guide)* de montagne; *(air)* de la montagne; *(life)* en *ou* à la montagne; *(flora, fauna)* de montagne, des montagnes

►► *Bot* ***mountain ash*** *(rowan)* sorbier *m*; *(eucalyptus)* eucalyptus *m*; ***mountain bike*** VTT *m*, vélo *m* tout-terrain; ***mountain biking*** VTT *m*, vélo *m* tout-terrain; **to go m. biking** faire du VTT; *Zool* ***mountain cat*** *(lynx)* lynx *m*; *(puma)* puma *m*, cougouar *m*; ***mountain climber*** alpiniste *mf*; ***mountain climbing*** alpinisme *m*; **to go m. climbing** faire de l'alpinisme; ***Mountain Daylight Time*** heure *f* d'été des montagnes Rocheuses; *Zool* ***mountain goat*** chamois *m*; *Zool* ***mountain lion*** puma *m*, cougouar *m*; ***mountain pass*** col *m*, défilé *m*; *Bot* ***mountain pine*** pin *m* de montagne; ***mountain range*** chaîne *f* de montagnes; ***mountain rescue*** secours *m* en montagne; ***mountain rescue service*** service *m* de secours en montagne; ***mountain sickness*** mal *m* des montagnes; ***Mountain (Standard) Time*** heure *f* d'hiver des montagnes Rocheuses; ***mountain top*** sommet *m*, cime *f*; ***mountain troops*** chasseurs *mpl* alpins

mountaineer [ˌmaʊntɪˈnɪə(r)] **N** alpiniste *mf*

mountaineering [ˌmaʊntɪˈnɪərɪŋ] **N** alpinisme *m*; **to go m.** faire de l'alpinisme

COMP *(club, equipment)* d'alpinisme

mountainous [ˈmaʊntɪnəs] **ADJ 1** *(region)* montagneux **2** *Fig (huge)* énorme, colossal; **m. seas** vagues *fpl* énormes

mountebank [ˈmaʊntɪbæŋk] **N** charlatan *m*

mounted [ˈmaʊntɪd] **ADJ** *(troops)* monté, à cheval

►► ***the mounted police*** la police montée; ***mounted policeman*** policier *m* à cheval

Mountie [ˈmaʊntɪ] **N** *Fam* membre *m* de la police montée□ *(au Canada)*; **the Mounties** la police montée *(au Canada)*

mounting [ˈmaʊntɪŋ] **N 1** *(act of fixing)* installation *f* **2** *(support ► of photo)* carton *m*, support *m*; *(► of gem, lens, tool)* monture *f*; *(► of machine)* support *m*; *(► for stamp in collection)* charnière *f*; *(► for object under microscope)* lame *f*; **engine mountings** pièces *fpl* d'assemblage de moteur

ADJ *(pressure, anxiety)* croissant; **there is m. evidence against her** il y a de plus en plus de preuves contre elle; **m. costs/death toll** coût/nombre de morts qui continue de grimper; **he felt a m. sense of panic** il sentait la panique le gagner

►► ***mounting board*** carton *m* pour montage

mounting-block **N** *Horseriding* montoir *m*

mourn [mɔːn] **VT** *(person)* pleurer, porter le deuil de; *(death, loss)* pleurer; **there's no point mourning what might have been** cela ne sert à rien de se lamenter sur ce qui aurait pu se passer

VI *(feel grief)* pleurer; *(be in mourning)* être en deuil, porter le deuil; **to m. for sb, to m. over the loss of sb** pleurer (la mort de) qn; **we m. with you** nous partageons votre douleur; **he mourns for** *or* **over his lost youth** il se lamente sur *ou* il pleure sa jeunesse perdue

mourner [ˈmɔːnə(r)] **N** *(friend, relative)* proche *mf* du défunt; **the mourners followed the hearse** le cortège funèbre suivait le corbillard; **the streets were lined with mourners** la foule en deuil s'était massée sur les trottoirs

mournful [ˈmɔːnfʊl] **ADJ** *(person, eyes, mood)* triste, mélancolique; *(tone, voice)* lugubre; *(place)* lugubre, sinistre; **a m. occasion** de tristes *ou* douloureuses circonstances *fpl*

mournfully [ˈmɔːnfʊlɪ] **ADV** mélancoliquement, tristement

mourning [ˈmɔːnɪŋ] **N** *(UNCOUNT)* **1** *(period)* deuil *m*; *(clothes)* (vêtements *mpl* de) deuil *m*; **to be in m.** être en deuil, porter le deuil; **to be in m. for sb** porter le deuil de qn; **in deep m.** en grand deuil; **to go into/come out of m.** prendre/quitter le deuil; **a day of m. was declared** une journée de deuil a été décrétée **2** *(cries)* lamentations *fpl*

COMP *(dress, suit)* de deuil

mouse [maʊs] *(pl* **mice** [maɪs]) **N 1** *(animal)* souris *f* **2** *(shy person)* timide *mf*, timoré(e) *m,f* **3** *Comput* souris *f*

VI *(cat)* chasser les souris

►► *Comput* ***mouse button*** bouton *m* de souris; *Comput* ***mouse click*** clic *m* de souris; *Comput* ***mouse driver*** programme *m* de commande de la souris; *Comput* ***mouse mat, mouse pad*** tapis *m* de souris; *Comput* ***mouse port*** port *m* souris

mouser [ˈmaʊsə(r)] **N** *(cat)* chasseur(euse) *m,f* de souris; **she's a good m.** elle attrape bien les souris

mousetrap [ˈmaʊstræp] **N** souricière *f*

►► *Br* ***mousetrap cheese*** fromage *m* ordinaire

moussaka [muːˈsɑːkə] **N** moussaka *f*

mousse [muːs] **N** mousse *f*; **chocolate m.** mousse *f* au chocolat

moustache [məˈstɑːʃ], *Am* **mustache** [ˈmʌstæʃ] **N** moustache *f*, moustaches *fpl*; **he's growing a m.** il se fait pousser la moustache

mousy [ˈmaʊsɪ] *(compar* **mousier**, *superl* **mousiest**) **ADJ 1** *Pej (shy)* timide, effacé **2** *Pej (hair)* châtain terne **3** *(colour)* gris sale

mouth **N** [maʊθ, *pl* maʊðz] **1** *(of person, horse)* bouche *f*; *(of other animal)* gueule *f*; **don't talk with your m. full!** ne parle pas la bouche pleine!; **breathe through your m.** respirez par la bouche; **I have five mouths to feed** j'ai cinq bouches à nourrir; *Pharm* **to be taken by m.** *(on packaging)* à prendre par voie orale; **he didn't open his m. once during the meeting** il n'a pas ouvert la bouche *ou* il n'a pas dit un mot pendant toute la réunion; **keep your m. shut about this** n'en parlez à personne, gardez-le pour vous; **he's incapable of keeping his m. shut** il ne sait pas tenir sa langue; *Fam* **he's all m. (and no trousers)** parler, c'est tout ce qu'il sait faire; *Fam* **he's got a big m.** c'est une grande gueule *ou* un fort en gueule; *Fam* **you had to open your big m., didn't you!** il a fallu que tu ouvres ta grande gueule!; *Fam* **me and my big m.!** j'ai encore perdu une occasion de me taire!; **to be down in the m.** avoir le cafard; **to put words into sb's m.** *(misquote)* faire dire à qn ce qu'il ne dit pas **2** *(of river)* embouchure *f*, bouche *f*, bouches *fpl* **3** *(opening ► gen)* ouverture *f*, orifice *m*, bouche *f*; *(► of bottle)* goulot *m*; *(► of cave)* entrée *f*

VT [maʊð] **1** *(silently ► insults, obscenities)* dire à voix basse, marmonner; **she mouthed something to me** elle a essayé de me dire quelque chose en remuant les lèvres silencieusement; **don't talk/sing, just m. the words** ne parle/chante pas, fais seulement semblant **2** *(pompously)* déclamer; *(mechanically)* débiter; *(insincerely ► excuses)* dire du bout des lèvres; *(► regrets)* formuler sans conviction

VI [maʊð] *esp Am (grimace)* grimacer, faire des grimaces

►► ***mouth organ*** harmonica *m*; ***mouth ulcer*** aphte *m*

► **mouth off** **VI** *Fam* **1** *(brag)* se vanter□, crâner **2** *(be insolent)* se montrer insolent□; *(talk indiscreetly)* parler à tort et à travers

mouthful [ˈmaʊθfʊl] **N 1** *(of food)* bouchée *f*; *(of liquid)* gorgée *f*; **to swallow sth in one m.** *(food)* ne faire qu'une bouchée de qch; *(soup, wine)* avaler qch d'une seule gorgée; **I swallowed** *or* **got a m. (of water)** *(when swimming etc)* j'ai bu la *ou* une tasse; **I couldn't eat another m.!** je ne pourrais rien avaler de plus!

2 *Fam (word ► hard to pronounce)* mot *m* difficile à prononcer□; *(► complicated)* mot *m* compliqué□; **his name's a bit of a m.** il a un nom à coucher dehors; **"myalgic encephalomyelitis" is quite a m.** "myalgic encephalomyelitis" est vraiment difficile à prononcer

3 *Am Fam (important remark)* **you said a m.!** ça, tu peux le dire!, tu l'as dit, bouffi!

4 *Br Fam (abusive language)* **to give sb a m.** traiter qn de tous les noms

mouthpiece [ˈmaʊθpiːs] **N 1** *(of clarinet, oboe)* bec *m*, embouchure *f*; *(of flute, recorder)* bec *m*; *(of trumpet, trombone)* embouchure *f*; *(of pipe)* tuyau *m*; *(of telephone)* microphone *m* **2** *(spokesperson)* porte-parole *m inv*; *(newspaper, magazine)* organe *m*, porte-parole *m inv* **3** *Am Fam (lawyer)* avocat(e) *m,f* (au criminel)□

mouth-to-mouth **N** bouche-à-bouche *m inv*

►► ***mouth-to-mouth resuscitation*** bouche-à-bouche *m inv*; **to give sb m. resuscitation** faire du bouche-à-bouche à qn

mouthwash [ˈmaʊθwɒʃ] **N** *(for cleansing)* bain *m* de bouche; *(for gargling)* gargarisme *m*

mouthwatering [ˈmaʊθˌwɔːtərɪŋ] **ADJ** appétissant, alléchant; **a m. display of pastries** un appétissant étalage de pâtisseries, un étalage de pâtisseries qui vous mettent l'eau à la bouche

mouthy [ˈmaʊðɪ] *(compar* **mouthier**, *superl* **mouthiest**) **ADJ** *Fam* grande gueule

movable [ˈmuːvəbəl] **ADJ** mobile

N *Law* **movables** effets *mpl* mobiliers, biens *mpl* meubles

►► *Law* ***movable assets*** valeurs *fpl* mobilieres; *Rel* ***movable feast*** fête *f* mobile; *Law* ***movable property*** biens *mpl* meubles

MOVE [muːv]

N	
• mouvement **1**	• déménagement **2**
• changement d'emploi **3**	• pas **4**
	• tour **5**
VT	
• déplacer **1, 3**	• bouger **1**
• transférer **2**	• émouvoir **4**
• pousser **5**	• céder **6**
• proposer **7**	• vendre **8**
VI	
• bouger **1**	• avancer **2, 7**
• partir **4**	• jouer **5**
• se déplacer **5**	• déménager **6**
• agir **9**	• céder **10**
• se vendre **11**	

N 1 *(movement)* mouvement *m*; **one m. out of you and you're dead!** un seul geste et tu es mort!; **he made a m. to take out his wallet** il s'apprêta à sortir son portefeuille; **the police were watching her every m.** la police surveillait ses moindres gestes; **to make a m.** *(leave)* y aller, bouger; **it's late, I ought to be making a m.** il se fait tard, il faut que j'y aille *ou* que je parte; **she made a m. to leave** elle se leva pour partir; **to be always on the m.** ne jamais rester en place; **he's a travelling salesman, so he's always on the m.** c'est un représentant de commerce, c'est pourquoi il est toujours en déplacement *ou* il est toujours par monts et par vaux; *Fam* **to get a m. on** se grouiller; *Fam* **get a m. on!** grouille-toi!, active!

2 *(change of home, premises)* déménagement *m*; **how did the m. go?** comment s'est passé le déménagement?; **we're considering a m. to bigger premises** nous envisageons d'emménager dans des locaux plus spacieux

3 *(change of job)* changement *m* d'emploi; **after ten years in the same firm she felt it was time for a m.** après dix ans dans la même société elle avait le sentiment qu'il était temps de changer d'air *ou* d'horizon

4 *(step, measure)* pas *m*, démarche *f*; **she made the first m.** elle a fait le premier pas; **she wondered when he would make his m.** elle se demandait quand il allait se décider; **don't make a m. without contacting me** ne fais rien sans me contacter; *Fam* **to make a m. on sb** faire des avances à qn; **the new management's first m. was to increase all salaries** la première mesure de la nouvelle direction a été de relever tous les salaires; **at one time there was a m. to expand** à un moment, on avait envisagé de s'agrandir; **what do you think their next m. will be?** selon vous, que vont-ils faire maintenant?

5 *(in games ► turn to move)* tour *m*; *(► act of moving)* coup *m*; *(► way piece moves)* marche *f*; **it's my m.** c'est à moi (de jouer); **to make a m.** jouer; *Chess* **white always has first m.** c'est toujours les blancs qui commencent

VT 1 *(put elsewhere ► object)* déplacer; *(► part of body)* bouger, remuer; *(in games ► piece)* jouer; **we moved all the chairs indoors/outdoors** nous avons rentré/sorti toutes les chaises; **m. your chair closer to the table** rapproche ta chaise de la table; **we've moved the couch into the spare room** nous avons mis le canapé dans la chambre d'amis; **don't m. anything on my desk** ne touche à rien sur mon bureau; **I can't m. my leg** je n'arrive pas à bouger la jambe; **can you m. your bag (out of the way), please?** est-ce que tu peux pousser ton sac, s'il te plaît?; **m. your head to the left** inclinez la tête vers la gauche; **he moves his lips when he reads** il remue les lèvres en lisant; **to m. house** déménager; *Fam* **m. it!** grouille-toi!

2 *(send elsewhere ► prisoner, troops etc)* transférer; **she's been moved to the New York office/to accounts** elle a été mutée au bureau de New York/affectée à la comptabilité; **he asked to be moved to a room with a sea view** il a demandé qu'on lui donne une chambre avec vue sur la mer; **troops are being moved into the area** des troupes sont envoyées dans la région

3 *(change time or date of)* déplacer; **the meeting has been moved to Friday** *(postponed)* la réunion a été remise à vendredi; *(brought forward)* la réunion a été avancée à vendredi

4 *(affect, touch)* émouvoir; **I was deeply moved**

j'ai été profondément ému *ou* touché; **to m. sb to anger** provoquer la colère de qn; **to m. sb to tears** émouvoir qn (jusqu')aux larmes

5 *(motivate, prompt)* pousser, inciter; **to m. sb to do sth** pousser *ou* inciter qn à faire qch; **what moved you to change your mind?** qu'est-ce qui vous a fait changer d'avis?

6 *(usu negative) (cause to yield)* **you won't m. me** tu ne me feras pas changer d'avis; **nothing will m. him** il est inflexible; **we shall not be moved!** nous ne céderons pas!

7 *(propose)* proposer; **I m. that we vote on it** je propose que nous procédions au vote

8 *Com (sell)* écouler, vendre

9 *Med* **to m. one's bowels** aller à la selle

VI 1 *(shift, change position)* bouger; **don't m.!** ne bougez pas!; **I'm sure the curtains moved** je suis sûr d'avoir vu les rideaux bouger; **something moved in the bushes** quelque chose a bougé dans les buissons; **to m. to another seat** changer de place; **you can't m. for furniture in their flat** il y a tellement de meubles dans leur appartement qu'il n'y a pas la place de se retourner; **the handle won't m.** la poignée ne bouge pas; **she wouldn't m. out of my way** elle ne voulait pas s'écarter de mon chemin; **could you m. so that we can get in?** pourriez-vous vous pousser pour que nous puissions entrer?; **the dancers m. so elegantly** les danceurs évoluent avec beaucoup de grâce

2 *(be in motion ▸ vehicle)* **the traffic was only just moving** les voitures avançaient à peine; **wait till the car stops moving** attends que la voiture soit arrêtée; **I jumped off while the train was still moving** j'ai sauté avant l'arrêt du train

3 *(travel in specified direction)* **the guests moved into/out of the dining room** les invités passèrent dans/sortirent de la salle à manger; **the depression is moving westwards** la dépression se déplace vers l'ouest; **the earth moves round the sun** la Terre tourne autour du Soleil; *Fig* **public opinion is moving to the left/right** l'opinion publique évolue vers la gauche/droite; **to m. in high circles** fréquenter la haute société

4 *(leave)* partir; **it's getting late, I ought to be** *or* **get moving** il se fait tard, il faut que j'y aille *ou* que je parte

5 *(in games ▸ player)* jouer; *(▸ piece)* se déplacer; **you can't m. until you've thrown a six** on ne peut pas jouer avant d'avoir fait sortir *ou* d'avoir amené un six; *Chess* **pawns can't m. backwards** les pions ne peuvent pas reculer

6 *(to new premises, location)* déménager; **when are you moving to your new apartment?** quand est-ce que vous emménagez dans votre nouvel appartement?; **she's moving to San Francisco** elle va habiter (à) San Francisco; **the company has moved to more modern premises** la société s'est installée dans des locaux plus modernes

7 *(develop, progress)* avancer, progresser; **things have started moving now** les choses ont commencé à avancer; **to get things moving** faire avancer les choses

8 *Fam (travel fast)* filer, foncer; **that car can really m.!** cette voiture a quelque chose dans le ventre!

9 *(take action)* agir; **if you want to succeed now is the time to m.** si vous voulez réussir, il vous faut agir maintenant *ou* dès à présent; **I'll get moving on it first thing tomorrow** je m'en occuperai demain à la première heure

10 *(yield)* céder; **they won't m. on the question of compensation** ils ne céderont *ou* ne fléchiront pas sur la question des compensations

11 *Com (sell)* se vendre, s'écouler

▸ **move about, move around** *Br* **VI** se déplacer, bouger; **I can hear somebody moving about upstairs** j'entends des bruits de pas là-haut; **it's hard to m. about on crutches** c'est dur de se déplacer avec des béquilles; **he moves around a lot** *(in job etc)* il est toujours en déplacement

VT SEP déplacer; **they keep moving her around from one department to another** ils n'arrêtent pas de la faire passer d'un service à l'autre

▸ **move along VI 1** *(to make room)* se déplacer, se pousser

2 *(leave)* partir, s'en aller; **I ought to be moving along** il faut que je m'en aille; **m. along, please!** circulez, s'il vous plaît!

3 *(continue)* **moving along to my next question** pour passer à ma question suivante

4 *(advance)* avancer, progresser

VT SEP *(bystanders, busker)* faire circuler

▸ **move away VI 1** *(go in opposite direction)* s'éloigner, partir **2** *(change address)* déménager; **her best friend moved away** sa meilleure amie a déménagé

VT SEP éloigner

▸ **move back VI 1** *(back away)* reculer **2** *(return to original position)* retourner; **they've moved back to the States** ils sont retournés habiter *ou* ils sont rentrés aux États-Unis

VT SEP 1 *(push back ▸ person, crowd)* repousser; *(▸ chair)* reculer **2** *(return to original position)* remettre; **you can change the furniture around as long as you m. it back afterwards** vous pouvez déplacer les meubles à condition de les remettre ensuite à leur place *ou* là où ils étaient

▸ **move down VI 1** *(from higher level, floor, position)* descendre; **the team moved down to the fourth division** l'équipe est descendue en quatrième division **2** *(make room)* se pousser

VT INSEP m. down the bus, please avancez jusqu'au fond de l'autobus, s'il vous plaît

VT SEP *(from higher level, floor, position)* descendre; *Sch* **he was moved down a class** on l'a fait descendre d'une classe; **move this section down** mettez cette section plus bas

▸ **move forward VI** avancer

VT SEP avancer; *(troops)* faire avancer; **the meeting has been moved forward to the 28th** la réunion a été avancée au 28

▸ **move in VI 1** *(into new home, premises)* emménager; **his mother-in-law has moved in with them** sa belle-mère s'est installée *ou* est venue habiter chez eux **2** *(close in, approach)* avancer, s'approcher; **troops moved in to quell the riots** les troupes sont intervenues pour réprimer les émeutes; **the camera then moves in on the bed** la caméra s'approche ensuite du lit **3** *(intervene)* intervenir; **the unions moved in and stopped the strike** les syndicats prirent les choses en main et mirent un terme à la grève

VT SEP 1 *(install ▸ furniture)* installer **2** *(send ▸ troops)* envoyer; **troops were moved in by helicopter** les troupes ont été transportées par hélicoptère

▸ **move off VI** s'éloigner, partir; *(of car etc)* démarrer; **the train finally moved off** le train partit *ou* s'ébranla enfin

▸ **move on VI 1** *(proceed on one's way)* poursuivre son chemin; **we spent a week in Athens, then we moved on to Crete** on a passé une semaine à Athènes avant de partir pour la Crète **2** *(progress ▸ to new job, new subject etc)* **she's moved on to better things** elle a trouvé une meilleure situation; **after five years in the same job I feel like moving on** après avoir occupé le même emploi pendant cinq ans, j'ai envie de changer d'air; **technology has moved on since then** la technologie a évolué depuis; **can we m. on to the second point?** pouvons-nous passer au deuxième point?

VT SEP *(bystanders, busker)* faire circuler

▸ **move out VI 1** *(of home, premises)* déménager; **when are you moving out of your room?** quand est-ce que tu déménages de *ou* tu quittes ta chambre?; **his girlfriend has moved out** sa petite amie ne vit plus avec lui **2** *Mil (troops)* se retirer

VT SEP *Mil (troops)* retirer; **the troops will be moved out** les troupes se retireront; **people were moved out of their homes to make way for the new road** les gens ont dû quitter leur maison pour permettre la construction de la nouvelle route

▸ **move over VI 1** *(to make room)* se pousser **2** *(stand down ▸ politician)* se désister; **it's time he moved over to make way for a younger man** il serait temps qu'il laisse la place à un homme plus jeune **3** *(change over)* **we're moving over to mass production** nous passons à la fabrication en série

▸ **move up VI 1** *(to make room)* se pousser **2** *(to higher level, floor, position)* monter; *(in company)* avoir de l'avancement; **he has moved up in my estimation** il est monté dans mon estime; **you've moved up in the world!** tu en as fait du chemin!; **shares moved up three points today** les actions ont gagné trois points aujourd'hui

VT SEP 1 *(to make room)* pousser, écarter **2** *(to higher level, floor, position)* faire monter; *Sch* **he's been moved up a class** on l'a fait passer dans la classe supérieure; **move this section up** mettez cette section plus haut **3** *Mil (troops)* faire avancer

moveable = **movable**

movement ['mu:vmənt] **N 1** *(change of position)* mouvement *m*; **population/troop movements** mouvements *mpl* de populations/de troupes; **the m. of goods** le transport des marchandises; **there was a general m. towards the bar** tout le monde se dirigea vers le bar; **she heard m. in the next room** elle a entendu des bruits dans la pièce voisine; **his movements are being watched** ses faits et gestes sont surveillés; **I'm not sure what my movements are going to be over the next few weeks** je ne sais pas exactement ce que je vais faire *ou* quel sera mon emploi du temps dans les quelques semaines à venir; **freedom of m.** la liberté de circulation

2 *(gesture)* mouvement *m*, geste *m*; **all her movements were rapid and precise** tous ses gestes étaient rapides et précis

3 *(change, tendency)* mouvement *m*, tendance *f*; **there's a growing m. towards privatization** la tendance à la privatisation s'accentue; **the upward/downward m. of interest rates** la hausse/baisse des taux d'intérêts; **there has been no further m. on the issue of introducing a smoking ban** il n'y pas eu de progrès en ce qui concerne les projets d'interdiction de fumer

4 *Fin (of capital)* circulation *f*; *(of share prices)* mouvement *m*; *(of market)* activité *f*

5 *(group)* mouvement *m*; **liberation m.** mouvement *m* de libération

6 *Tech (mechanism ▸ of clock etc)* mouvement *m*

7 *Mus (of symphony, sonata etc)* mouvement *m*

8 *Med (faeces)* selles *fpl*; **to have a (bowel) m.** aller à la selle

mover ['mu:və(r)] **N 1** *(physical)* **sloths are extraordinarily slow movers** les paresseux sont des animaux à mouvements extrêmement lents; *Fam* **she's a lovely m.** elle bouge bien; *Fam* **he's a fast m.** c'est un tombeur; **the movers and the shakers** *(key people)* les acteurs *mpl* **2** *(of a proposal, motion)* motionnaire *mf* **3** *Am (removal company)* déménageur *m*

movie ['mu:vɪ] **N** film *m*; **the m. of the book** le film tiré du livre; **full-length/short-length m.** (film *m*) long/court métrage *m*; **to shoot** *or* **to make a m. (about sth)** tourner *ou* faire un film (sur qch)

COMP *(sequence)* de film; *(archives, award, rights)* cinématographique

• **movies NPL to go to the movies** aller au cinéma; **she's in the movies** elle travaille dans le cinéma

▸▸ ***movie actor*** acteur *m* de cinéma; ***movie actress*** actrice *f* de cinéma; ***movie camera*** caméra *f*; ***movie channel*** chaîne *f* de cinéma; ***movie clip*** extrait *m* de film; ***movie critic*** critique *mf* de cinéma; ***movie director*** metteur *m* en scène; *Am* ***movie house*** (salle *f* de) cinéma *m*; ***the movie industry*** l'industrie *f* cinématographique *ou* du cinéma; ***movie maker*** cinéaste *mf*; ***movie premiere*** première *f*; ***movie producer*** producteur (trice) *m,f* de cinéma; ***movie star*** vedette *f* de cinéma; *Am* ***movie theater*** cinéma *m (lieu)*

moviegoer ['mu:vɪˌgəʊə(r)] **N** cinéphile *mf*; **she is a regular m.** elle va régulièrement au cinéma

moving ['mu:vɪŋ] **N** mouvement *m*; *(being moved)* déplacement *m*; *(leaving house, premises)* déménagement *m*

ADJ 1 *(in motion)* en mouvement; *(vehicle)* en marche; *(target)* mouvant; **slow-/fast-m.** qui se déplace lentement/rapidement

2 *(not fixed)* mobile

3 *(touching)* émouvant, touchant

4 *(motivating)* **she's the m. force** *or* **spirit behind the project** c'est elle l'instigatrice *ou* le moteur du projet

▸▸ ***moving in*** *(into house, premises)* emménagement *m*; ***moving out*** *(from house, premises)* déménagement *m*; *Tech* ***moving parts*** pièces *fpl* mobiles; *Br* ***moving pavement*** trottoir *m* roulant;

Old-fashioned ***moving picture*** film *m*; ***moving staircase*** escalier *m* roulant, escalator *m*; *Am* ***moving van*** camion *m* de déménagement; ***moving walkway*** tapis *m* ou trottoir *m* roulant

movingly [ˈmuːvɪŋlɪ] **ADV** de façon émouvante *ou* touchante

mow [məʊ] (*pt* **mowed**, *pp* **mowed** *or* **mown** [məʊn]) **VT** *(lawn)* tondre; *(hay, corn, field)* faucher

▸ **mow down VT SEP** faucher, abattre

mower [ˈməʊə(r)] **N 1** *(person)* faucheur(euse) *m,f* **2** *(machine ▸ for lawn)* tondeuse *f*; *(▸ for hay)* faucheuse *f*

mowing [ˈməʊɪŋ] **N** *(of lawn)* tonte *f*; *Agr* fauchage *m*

▸▸ ***mowing machine*** faucheuse *f*

mown [məʊn] *pp of* **mow**

MOX [mɒks] **ADJ** *(abbr* **mixed oxide**) MOX

▸▸ ***MOX fuel*** combustible *m* MOX

Mozambican [ˌməʊzæmˈbiːkən] **N** Mozambicain(e) *m,f*

ADJ mozambicain

Mozambique [ˌməʊzæmˈbiːk] **N** Mozambique *m*

MP [ˌemˈpiː] **N 1** *(abbr* **Military Police**) PM *f* **2** *Br & Can (abbr* **Member of Parliament**) ≃ député *m*; **the MP for Finchley** le député de Finchley **3** *Can (abbr* **Mounted Policeman**) policier *m*

MP3 [ˌempiːˈθriː] **N** *Comput* (format *m*) MP3 *m*

▸▸ ***MP3 player*** lecteur *m* MP3

MPEG [ˈemˌpeg] **N** *Comput (abbr* **Moving Pictures Expert Group**) (format *m*) MPEG *m*

mpg [ˌempiːˈdʒiː] **N** *(abbr* **miles per gallon**) consommation *f* d'essence; **my old car did 20 m.** ≃ mon ancienne voiture faisait *ou* consommait 3,5 litres au cent

mph [ˌempiːˈeɪtʃ] **N** *(abbr* **miles per hour**) miles *mpl* à l'heure; **100 m.** ≃ 160 km/h

MPhil [ˌemˈfɪl] **N** *Univ (abbr* **Master of Philosophy**) *(person)* = titulaire d'une maîtrise de lettres; *(qualification)* maîtrise *f* de lettres

MPV [ˌempiːˈviː] **N** *Aut (abbr* **multi-purpose vehicle**) monospace *m*

Mr [ˈmɪstə(r)] **N** *(abbr* **mister**) M., Monsieur; **Mr Brown** M. Brown; **Mr President** Monsieur le Président; *Fam* **no more Mr Nice Guy!** j'en ai assez d'être la bonne pâte!; *Fam Fig* **he's a regular Mr Fixit** on peut toujours compter sur lui pour trouver une solution

▸▸ *Fam* ***Mr Big*** le chef, le patron[▫]; *Fam* ***Mr Right*** l'homme *m* idéal[▫], le prince charmant

MRAM [ˈemˌræm] **N** *Comput (abbr* **magnetic random access memory**) MRAM *f*

MRC [ˌemɑːˈsiː] **N** *Br (abbr* **Medical Research Council**) = institut de recherche médicale situé à Londres

MRI [ˌemɑːˈraɪ] **N** *(abbr* **magnetic resonance imaging**) IRM *f*

mrp [ˌemɑːˈpiː] **N** *Mktg (abbr* **manufacturer's recommended price**) prix *m* conseillé par le fabricant

Mrs [ˈmɪsɪz] **N** *(abbr* **mistress**) Mme, Madame; **M. Brown** Mme Brown

MRSA [emˌɑːresˈeɪ] **N** *Med (abbr* **methicillin-resistant Staphylococcus aureus**) SAMR *m*

MS[1] [ˌemˈes] **N 1** *Med (abbr* **multiple sclerosis**) SEP *f* **2** *Am Univ (abbr* **Master of Science**) *(person)* = titulaire d'une maîtrise de sciences; *(qualification)* maîtrise *f* de sciences

MS[2] **1** *(written abbr* **Mississippi**) Mississippi *m* **2** *(written abbr* **manuscript**) ms

Ms [mɪz, məz] **N** = titre que les femmes peuvent utiliser au lieu de "Mrs" ou "Miss" pour éviter la distinction entre les femmes mariées et les célibataires

MSc [ˌemesˈsiː] **N** *Br Univ (abbr* **Master of Science**) *(person)* = titulaire d'une maîtrise de sciences; *(qualification)* maîtrise *f* de sciences

MS-DOS [ˌemesˈdɒs] **N** *Comput (abbr* **Microsoft Disk Operating System**) MS-DOS *m*

MSG [ˌemesˈdʒiː] **N** *(abbr* **monosodium glutamate**) glutamate *m* de sodium

MSP [ˌemesˈpiː] **N** *(abbr* **Member of the Scottish Parliament**) député *m* du parlement écossais

MST [ˌemesˈtiː] **N** *(abbr* **Mountain Standard Time**) heure *f* d'hiver des montagnes Rocheuses

Mt *(written abbr* **mount**) Mt

MTBF [ˌemtiːbiːˈef] **N** *Comput (abbr* **mean time between failures**) moyenne *f* de temps entre deux pannes

MUCH [mʌtʃ] **ADJ**

> Hormis dans la langue soutenue et dans certaines expressions, ne s'utilise que dans des structures négatives ou interrogatives.

beaucoup de; **we don't have m. time** on n'a pas beaucoup de temps; **the tablets didn't do m. good** les comprimés n'ont pas servi à grand-chose *ou* n'ont pas fait beaucoup d'effet; *Ironic* **m. good may it do you!** grand bien vous fasse!

PRON 1 *(gen)* beaucoup; **is there m. left?** est-ce qu'il en reste beaucoup?; **is there any left? – not m.** est-ce qu'il en reste? – pas beaucoup; **m. remains to be done** il reste encore beaucoup à faire; **there's not m. anyone can do about it** personne n'y peut grand-chose; **we have m. to be thankful for** nous avons beaucoup de raisons d'être reconnaissants; **m. of the time** *(long period)* la majeure partie du temps; *(very often)* la plupart du temps; **I agreed with m. of what she said** j'étais d'accord avec presque tout ce qu'elle a dit

2 *(as intensifier)* **I'm not m. of a hiker** je ne suis pas un très bon marcheur; **it hasn't been m. of a holiday** ce n'était pas vraiment des vacances; **it wasn't m. of a surprise** ce n'était pas une grande surprise; **what he said didn't amount to m.** il n'avait pas grand-chose d'important à dire; **the defence made m. of the witness's criminal record** la défense a beaucoup insisté sur le casier judiciaire du témoin; **I don't think m. of him/of his technique** je n'ai pas une très haute opinion de lui/de sa technique; **there's m. to be said for the old-fashioned method** la vieille méthode a beaucoup d'avantages; **it's not up to m.** ça ne vaut pas grand-chose; **there's not m. in it** il n'y a pas une grande différence; *Fam Ironic* **he doesn't want** *or* **ask** *or* **expect m., does he?** il n'est pas difficile, lui, au moins!; *Fam* **that's a bit m.!** c'est un peu fort!

ADV beaucoup; **I don't like them m., I don't m. like them** je ne les aime pas beaucoup; **I feel very m. better** je me sens beaucoup mieux; **thank you very m. (for)** merci beaucoup (de *ou* pour); **m. admired/appreciated** très admiré/apprécié; **m. happier/more slowly** beaucoup plus heureux/plus lentement; **m. worse** bien pire; *Formal* **it is m. to be regretted that...** il est fort regrettable que...; **m. to my surprise** à mon grand étonnement; **we are m. obliged to you for...** nous vous sommes très obligés de *ou* pour...; **it's m. the best/the fastest** c'est le meilleur/le plus rapide de beaucoup; **it's (pretty** *or* **very) m. the same thing** c'est à peu près la même chose; **she's still m. the same as yesterday** son état n'a pas changé depuis hier; *Fam Ironic* **he doesn't like beer, does he? – not m. he doesn't!** il n'aime pas la bière, non? – et comment, il aime ça!

• **as much PRON** *(that, the same)* **I thought/suspected as m.** c'est bien ce que je pensais/soupçonnais; **I expected as m.** je m'y attendais; **I said as m. to him yesterday** c'est ce que je lui ai dit hier; **would you do as m. for me?** en ferais-tu autant pour moi? **ADV** *(with multiples, fractions)* **twice/three times as m.** deux/trois fois plus; **half as m.** la moitié (de ça); **as m. again** encore autant

• **as much... as ADJ** *(the same amount as)* autant de... que; **I've got as m. money as you** j'ai autant d'argent que vous **CONJ** autant... que; **he's as m. to blame as her** elle n'est pas plus responsable que lui, il est responsable autant qu'elle

• **as much as PRON 1** *(the same as)* **it costs as m. as the Japanese model** ça coûte le même prix que le modèle japonais; **he looked at me as m. as to say...** il me regarda avec l'air de (vouloir) dire...

2 *(all)* **it was as m. as I could do to keep a straight face** j'ai failli éclater de rire; **it was as m. as we could do to stand upright** nous avions le plus grand mal à nous tenir debout **CONJ** autant que; **I hate it as m. as you do** ça me déplaît autant qu'à vous; **as m. as ever** toujours autant; **not quite as m. as...** pas tout à fait autant que...

• **however much ADV however m. you dislike the idea...** quelle que soit votre aversion pour cette idée...; **however m. I try, it doesn't work** j'ai beau essayer, ça ne marche pas

• **how much ADJ** combien de; **how m. flour have we got left?** combien de farine nous reste-t-il? **PRON** combien; **how m. do you want?** *(gen)* combien en voulez-vous?; *(money)* combien voulez-vous?

• **much as CONJ m. as I admire him, I have to admit that...** malgré toute mon admiration pour lui, je dois admettre que...; **m. as I would like to, I can't come** à mon grand regret, il m'est véritablement impossible de venir; **the result was m. as I expected** le résultat correspondait bien à ce que j'attendais

• **so much ADJ** tant de, tellement de; **it takes up so m. time** ça prend tellement de temps **PRON 1** *(such a lot)* tant; **there's still so m. to do** il y a encore tant à faire; **he has drunk so m. that...** il a tellement bu que...

2 *(this amount)* **there's only so m. one can do** il y a une limite à ce qu'on peut faire; **how m. water shall I put in? – about so m.** combien d'eau est-ce que je dois mettre? – à peu près ça; **so m. a kilo** tant le kilo **ADV** tellement; **I miss you so m.** tu me manques tellement; **so m. the better** tant mieux; **so m. so that...** au point que..., à tel point que...; **not so m. a..., more a...** pas vraiment un..., mais plutôt un...

• **so much as ADV** même; **if you so m. as breathe a word of this...** si seulement tu répètes un mot de tout ça...; **without so m. as saying goodbye** sans même dire au revoir

• **so much for PREP so m. for that idea!** on peut oublier cette idée!; **so m. for his friendship!** et voilà ce qu'il appelle l'amitié!

• **this/that much ADJ there was that m. food, we thought we'd never finish it** il y avait tellement à manger qu'on pensait ne jamais arriver à finir **PRON was there m. damage? – not that m.** y a-t-il eu beaucoup de dégâts? – pas tant que ça; **how m. do you want? – about this m.** combien en veux-tu? – à peu près ça; **this m. is true...** une chose au moins est vraie...; **I'll say this m. for her, she's got guts** il faut reconnaître une chose, c'est qu'elle a du cran **ADV not that m. better** pas beaucoup mieux; **she's that m. taller than me** elle est plus grande que moi de ça

• **too much ADJ** trop de **PRON** trop; **there's too m. to do** il y a trop à faire; **to cost too m.** coûter trop cher; **£10 too m.** 10 livres de trop; *Fam* **she's too m.!** elle est trop!; *Fam* **that's too m.!** ça, c'est trop! **ADV** *(work, speak)* trop

muchness [ˈmʌtʃnɪs] **N** *Br Fam (idiom)* **they're all much of a m.** *(objects)* c'est du pareil au même[▫]; *(people)* ils se valent[▫]

muck [mʌk] *(UNCOUNT) Fam* **N 1** *(mud)* boue[▫]*f*, gadoue[▫]*f*; *(dirt)* saletés[▫]*fpl*; *(manure)* fumier[▫]*m*; *(dung ▸ of horse)* crottin[▫]*m*; *(▸ of dog)* crotte[▫]*f*; *Br Prov* **where there's m., there's brass** = c'est peut-être sale, mais ça rapporte! *(fait référence aux travaux salissants mais rentables)* **2** *Fig (inferior literature, films etc)* idioties *fpl*; *(bad food)* cochonneries *fpl*; *(worthless objects)* camelote *f* **3** *Br Fam* **to make a m. of sth** *(bungle)* bousiller qch

▸▸ ***muck spreader*** épandeur *m*

▸ **muck about, muck around** *Fam* **VI 1** *(waste time)* traîner, perdre son temps[▫] **2** *(act foolishly)* faire l'imbécile; **stop mucking about!** arrête de faire l'imbécile! **3** *(interfere)* **to m. about with sth** *(equipment)* toucher à qch, tripoter qch; *(belongings)* déranger qch, mettre la pagaille dans qch

VT SEP 1 *(person ▸ waste time of)* faire perdre son temps à; *(▸ be inconsiderate to)* malmener **2** *(belongings, papers)* déranger, toucher à

▸ **muck in VI** *Br Fam (share task)* mettre la main à la pâte, donner un coup de main[▫]; *(share costs)* participer aux frais[▫]

▸ **muck out** *Br* **VT SEP** *(horse, stable)* nettoyer, curer

VI nettoyer l'écurie/les écuries

▸ **muck up VT SEP** *Fam* **1** *(dirty)* cochonner **2** *(ruin)* bousiller, foutre en l'air

mucker [ˈmʌkə(r)] **N** *Br Fam* **1** *(friend)* pote *m* **2** *(term of address)* vieux *m*

muckheap [ˈmʌkhiːp] **N** *Br Fam* tas *m* de fumier[▫]

muckraker ['mʌkˌreɪkə(r)] N *Pej (journalist)* fouineur(euse) *m,f*
muckraking ['mʌkˌreɪkɪŋ] N *(UNCOUNT) Pej* **it's the kind of paper that specializes in m.** c'est le type de journal spécialisé dans les scandales
mucky ['mʌkɪ] *(compar* **muckier**, *superl* **muckiest)** ADJ *Fam* **1** *(dirty, muddy ▸ hands)* sale[□], crasseux; *(▸ shoes)* sale[□], crotté[□]; *(▸ water, road)* sale[□], boueux[□]; **you're a m. pup!** que tu es sale!; *Br* **the weather was m.** il faisait un sale temps **2** *Br (obscene ▸ book, film)* obscène
mucous ['mju:kəs] ADJ muqueux
▸▸ *Anat* ***mucous membrane*** muqueuse *f*
mucus ['mju:kəs] N mucus *m*, mucosité *f*; *(from nose)* morve *f*
mud [mʌd] N *(gen)* boue *f*; *(in river, lake)* vase *f*; *(in swamp)* bourbe *f*; **my car got stuck in the m.** ma voiture s'est embourbée; *Fam Old-fashioned* **here's m. in your eye!** à la tienne!; **to drag sb** *or* **sb's name through the m.** traîner qn dans la boue; *Fam* **my name is m. in certain circles** je suis en disgrâce *ou* persona non grata dans certains milieux; **to throw** *or* **to sling m. at sb** couvrir qn de boue; *Fam* **as clear as m.** clair comme du jus de boudin
▸▸ ***mud bath*** bain *m* de boue; ***mud hut*** case *f* en pisé *ou* en terre; ***mud pie*** *(made of mud)* pâté *m* (de sable); *(cake)* = sorte de gâteau au chocolat; ***mud wrestling*** catch *m* dans la boue
mudbank ['mʌdbæŋk] N banc *m* de vase
muddle ['mʌdəl] N *(confusion)* confusion *f*; *(mess)* désordre *m*, fouillis *m*; **all her belongings were in a m.** toutes ses affaires étaient en désordre *ou* sens dessus dessous; **my finances are in an awful m.** ma situation financière est complètement embrouillée; **Holly was in a real m. over the holiday plans** Holly ne savait plus où elle en était dans ses projets de vacances; **to get into a m. (about sth)** s'embrouiller (au sujet de qch); **there must have been a m. over the train times** quelqu'un a dû se tromper dans les horaires de train
VT **1** *(mix up ▸ dates)* confondre, mélanger; *(▸ facts)* embrouiller, mélanger; **the dates got muddled** il y a eu une confusion dans les dates **2** *(confuse ▸ person)* embrouiller (l'esprit *ou* les idées de); **to get muddled** s'embrouiller; **now you've got me muddled** maintenant, je ne sais plus où j'en suis **3** *(stir ▸ cocktail)* remuer
▸ **muddle along** VI se débrouiller tant bien que mal
▸ **muddle through** VT INSEP se tirer de
VI se tirer d'affaire, s'en tirer tant bien que mal
▸ **muddle up** VT SEP **1** *(mix up ▸ dates)* confondre, mélanger; *(▸ facts)* embrouiller **2** *(confuse ▸ person)* embrouiller
muddled ['mʌdəld] ADJ **1** *(objects)* en désordre **2** *(person, ideas)* confus, embrouillé
muddleheaded [ˌmʌdəl'hedɪd] ADJ *(person)* désordonné, brouillon, écervelé; *(idea, speech, essay)* confus
muddler ['mʌdələ(r)] N *(person)* brouillon (onne) *m,f*, esprit *m* brouillon
muddy ['mʌdɪ] *(compar* **muddier**, *superl* **muddiest)** ADJ **1** *(hands, car)* plein *ou* couvert de boue; *(shoes)* plein de boue, crotté; *(road, path, stream)* boueux **2** *Fig (complexion)* terreux; *(colour)* terne, sale; *(liquid)* boueux, trouble; **m. brown** couleur (de) terre **3** *(indistinct ▸ thinking, ideas)* confus, embrouillé, peu clair; *(out of focus ▸ image)* brouillé, trouble, flou
VT **1** *(hands, shoes)* salir, couvrir de boue; *(road, stream)* rendre boueux; *Fig* **to m. the waters** semer la confusion **2** *(situation)* compliquer, embrouiller
mudflap ['mʌdflæp] N *(on car)* bavette *f*; *(on truck)* pare-boue *m inv*
mudflat ['mʌdflæt] N laisse *f ou* banc *m* de boue
mudguard ['mʌdgɑ:d] N garde-boue *m inv*
mudlark ['mʌdlɑ:k] N *Literary (person)* gamin(e) *m,f* des rues, gavroche *m*
mudpack ['mʌdpæk] N masque *m* à l'argile
mudskipper ['mʌdˌskɪpə(r)] N *Ich* gobie *m* marcheur *ou* des marais
mudslinger ['mʌdˌslɪŋə(r)] N fauteur(trice) *m,f* de scandales
mudslinging ['mʌdˌslɪŋɪŋ] N *(UNCOUNT)* calomnie *f*; **a lot of m. went on during the elections** ils ont passé leur temps à se traîner les uns les autres dans la boue pendant les élections
mud-stained ADJ taché de boue
muesli ['mju:zlɪ] N muesli *m*, *Suisse* bircher *m*
muezzin [mu:'ezɪn] N muezzin *m*
muff [mʌf] N **1** *(for hands)* manchon *m*; *(for ears)* oreillette *f* **2** *Vulg (woman's genitals)* chatte *f*, con *m*
VT *(bungle)* rater, manquer; **to m. a catch** rater une prise
muffin ['mʌfɪn] N **1** *(sponge cake)* muffin *m*, = petit gâteau **2** *Br (served warm)* muffin *m*, = petit pain rond servi chaud et beurré
▸▸ *Fam Hum* ***muffin top*** = bourrelet de graisse qui dépasse du pantalon
muffle ['mʌfəl] VT **1** *(quieten ▸ sound)* étouffer, assourdir; *(▸ engine)* étouffer le bruit de; *(drum)* assourdir **2** *(wrap)* emmitoufler; **to m. oneself up** s'emmitoufler
muffled ['mʌfəld] ADJ **1** *(sound, voice)* sourd, étouffé; *(drums)* assourdi; **we could hear m. cries coming from the next room** on entendait des cris étouffés *ou* sourds qui venaient de la pièce voisine **2** *(wrapped)* **m. (up)** emmitouflé
muffler ['mʌflə(r)] N **1** *Old-fashioned (scarf)* écharpe *f*, cache-nez *m inv* **2** *Am Aut* silencieux *m* **3** *Mus (on piano)* étouffoir *m*
Mufti ['mʌftɪ] N *Rel* mufti *m*, muphti *m*
mufti ['mʌftɪ] N *Old-fashioned* tenue *f* civile; **wearing m., in m.** en civil
mug [mʌg] *(pt & pp* **mugged**, *cont* **mugging)** N **1** *(beer glass)* chope *f*; *(for tea, coffee)* grande tasse *f*, mug *f*; *(made of metal)* quart *m* **2** *Fam (face)* gueule *f*, tronche *f*, trombine *f*; **shut your ugly m.!** ferme ta sale gueule! **3** *Br Fam (dupe)* poire *f*; *(fool)* nigaud(e) *m,f*; **it's a m.'s game** c'est bon pour les poires; **the lottery's a m.'s game** le loto, c'est un attrape-couillon
VT *Fam (attack)* agresser[□]
▸▸ *Fam* ***mug shot*** *(of criminal)* photo *f* d'identité judiciaire[□]; *Pej Hum (passport-sized photo)* photo *f* d'identité[□]
▸ **mug up** *Br Fam* VT SEP potasser, bosser
VI bûcher, boulonner; **I'd better m. up on my French** je ferais mieux de potasser mon français
mugful ['mʌgfʊl] N *(of tea, coffee)* tasse *f* (pleine); *(of beer)* chope *f* (pleine)
mugger ['mʌgə(r)] N agresseur *m*
mugging ['mʌgɪŋ] N agression *f*; **m. is on the increase** il y a une augmentation des agressions
muggins ['mʌgɪnz] *(pl* **inv** *or* **mugginses)** N *Br Fam* mézigue; **I suppose m. will have to go** je suppose que c'est bibi *ou* ma pomme qui devra y aller; **m. (here) paid the bill as usual** comme d'habitude c'est mézigue qui a payé l'addition
muggy ['mʌgɪ] *(compar* **muggier**, *superl* **muggiest)** ADJ *Met* lourd et humide
mugwump ['mʌgwʌmp] N *Am Pej Pol* indépendant(e) *m,f*
mukhabarat [mʊ'khæbəˌræt] N Moukhabarat *f*
mulatto [mju:'lætəʊ] *(pl* **mulattos** *or* **mulattoes)** *Old-fashioned* N mulâtre(esse) *m,f*
ADJ mulâtre
mulberry ['mʌlbərɪ] N **1** *(fruit)* mûre *f*; *(tree)* mûrier *m*; **m. (bush/tree)** mûrier *m* **2** *(colour)* violet *m* foncé
ADJ violet foncé *(inv)*
mulch [mʌltʃ] *Hort* N paillis *m*
VT pailler, couvrir de paillis
mulct [mʌlkt] *Formal* N amende *f*
VT **1** *(fine)* infliger une amende à **2** *(defraud)* escroquer; *(overcharge)* escroquer
mule [mju:l] N **1** *(animal ▸ male)* mulet *m*; *(▸ female)* mule *f*; **(as) stubborn as a m.** têtu comme une mule *ou* un mulet **2** *(slipper)* mule *f* **3** *Fam Drugs slang (drug smuggler)* mule *f*
▸▸ ***mule driver*** muletier[□]*m*; *Am Fam* ***mule skinner*** muletier[□]*m*; ***mule train*** caravane *f* de mules
muleteer [ˌmju:lɪ'tɪə(r)] N muletier(ère) *m,f*
mulish ['mju:lɪʃ] ADJ têtu, entêté
mulishness ['mju:lɪʃnɪs] N entêtement *m*, obstination *f*
mull [mʌl] VT *(wine, beer)* chauffer et épicer
▸ **mull over** VT SEP réfléchir (longuement) à; **I've been mulling it over and…** j'y ai réfléchi et…
mulled [mʌld] ADJ
▸▸ ***mulled wine*** vin *m* chaud épicé
mullered ['mʊləd] ADJ *Br Fam (drunk)* bourré, beurré, pété
mullet ['mʌlɪt] *(pl sense* **1 inv** *or* **mullets**, *pl sense* **2 mullets)** N **1** *Ich* mulet *m*; *(grey)* muge *m*, mulet *m* gris; *(red)* rouget *m*, mulet *m* rouge **2** *Fam (hair style)* = coupe de cheveux longue sur la nuque, courte sur les côtés et en brosse longue sur le dessus
mulligatawny [ˌmʌlɪgə'tɔ:nɪ] N *Br* mulligatawny *m*, soupe *f* au curry
mullion ['mʌlɪən] N *Archit* meneau *m*
mullioned ['mʌlɪənd] ADJ *Archit (window)* à meneaux
multi- ['mʌltɪ] PREF multi-
multiaccess [ˌmʌltɪ'ækses] ADJ *Comput* à accès multiple
multiangle [ˌmʌltɪ'æŋgəl] ADJ *Cin (shot, scene)* multiangle
multibrand ['mʌltɪbrænd] N *Mktg* marque *f* multiple, multimarque *f*
▸▸ ***multibrand store*** point *m* de vente multimarque
multicamera unit ['mʌltɪˌkæmərə-] N *TV* car *m* multicaméra
multicast ['mʌltɪkɑ:st] N *Comput* multidiffusion *f*, multicast *m*
multichannel [ˌmʌltɪ'tʃænəl] ADJ multicanal
multicoloured, *Am* **multicolored** ['mʌltɪˌkʌləd] ADJ multicolore
multicultural [ˌmʌltɪ'kʌltʃərəl] ADJ multiculturel
multicurrency [ˌmʌltɪ'kʌrənsɪ] ADJ multidevise
multidirectional [ˌmʌltɪdɪ'rekʃənəl, ˌmʌltɪdaɪ'rekʃənəl] ADJ multidirectionnel
multifaceted [ˌmʌltɪ'fæsɪtɪd] ADJ présentant de multiples facettes
multifarious [ˌmʌltɪ'feərɪəs] ADJ *(varied)* (très) divers *ou* varié; *(numerous)* (très) nombreux
multiform ['mʌltɪfɔ:m] ADJ multiforme
multi-fuel engine N moteur *m* polycarburant
multifunction [ˌmʌltɪ'fʌŋkʃən] ADJ multifonction(s)
multifunctional [ˌmʌltɪ'fʌŋkʃənəl] ADJ multifonction(s)
▸▸ ***multifunctional keyboard*** clavier *m* multifonction(s); ***multifunctional key*** touche *f* multifonction(s)
multigrade ['mʌltɪgreɪd] ADJ multigrade
multigrain ['mʌltɪgreɪn] ADJ multicéréale
multilateral [ˌmʌltɪ'lætərəl] ADJ multilatéral
▸▸ ***multilateral diplomacy*** diplomatie *f* multilatérale; ***multilateral trade agreement*** accord *m* commercial multilatéral
multilateralism [ˌmʌltɪ'lætərəlɪzəm] N multilatéralisme *m*
multilevel [ˌmʌltɪ'levəl] ADJ *Comput* multiniveaux
▸▸ *Mktg* ***multilevel marketing*** marketing *m* de réseau, vente *f* par réseau coopté
multilingual [ˌmʌltɪ'lɪŋgwəl] ADJ multilingue
multimedia [ˌmʌltɪ'mi:dɪə] N multimédia *m*
ADJ multimédia
▸▸ ***multimedia computer*** ordinateur *m* multimédia
multimillionaire ['mʌltɪˌmɪlɪə'neə(r)] N multimillionnaire *mf*
multimodal operator [ˌmʌltɪ'məʊdəl-] N opérateur *m* de transport multimodal, OTM *m*
multinational [ˌmʌltɪ'næʃənəl] N multinationale *f*
ADJ multinational
▸▸ ***multinational company*** entreprise *f* multinationale; ***multinational corporation*** société *f* multinationale
multi-ownership N multipropriété *f*

ıultiparty ['mʌltɪ,pɑːtɪ] ADJ multipartite, pluri-ɔartite; **the m. system** le multipartisme, le pluri-ɔartisme

ıulti-plate clutch N embrayage *m* à disques multiples

ıultiple ['mʌltɪpəl] N **1** *Math* multiple *m*; **in mul-ːiples of 100** en *ou* par multiples de 100 **2** *Br (store)* chaîne *f* de magasins **3** *Tel* multiplage *m*
ADJ **1** *(gén)* multiple; **he died of m. stab wounds** il a été tué de plusieurs coups de couteau **2** *Elec* en parallèle
▸▸ ***multiple birth*** naissance *f* multiple; ***multiple collision*** collision *f* multiple; *Comput* ***multiple mailboxes*** = possibilité d'avoir plusieurs boîtes aux lettres auprès d'un fournisseur d'accès à l'Internet; ***multiple occupancy*** *(by tenants)* colo-cation *f*; *(by owners)* copropriété *f*; ***multiple own-ership*** multipropriété *f*; *Psy* ***multiple personality*** personnalité *f* multiple; *Med* ***multiple sclerosis*** sclérose *f* en plaques; *Br* ***multiple shop****, Am* ***multi-ple store*** grand magasin *m* à succursales, chaîne *f* de magasins

ıultiple-choice ADJ à choix multiples

ıultiplex ['mʌltɪpleks] N **1** *Tel* multiplex *m* **2** *Cin* complexe *m ou* cinéma *m* multisalle(s)
COMP *Tel* multiplex
VT *Tel* multiplexer
▸▸ *Tel* ***multiplex broadcast*** transmission *m* en multiplex; *Cin* ***multiplex cinema*** complexe *m ou* cinéma *m* multisalle(s)

ıultiplexer ['mʌltɪ,pleksə(r)] N *Tel* multiplexeur *m*

ıultiplexing ['mʌltɪ,pleksɪŋ] N *Tel* multi-plexage *m*

ıultiplication [,mʌltɪplɪ'keɪʃən] N *(gen) & Math* multiplication *f*
▸▸ ***multiplication sign*** signe *m* de multiplication; ***multiplication table*** table *f* de multiplication

ıultiplicity [,mʌltɪ'plɪsətɪ] N multiplicité *f*

ıultiplier ['mʌltɪplaɪə(r)] N **1** *Econ, Electron & Math* multiplicateur *m* **2** *Comput* multiplieur *m*

ıultiply[1] ['mʌltɪplaɪ] *(pt & pp* **multiplied***)* VT multiplier; **to m. 2 by 6** multiplier 2 par 6
VI **1** *Math* faire des multiplications **2** *(reproduce, increase)* se multiplier

ıultiply[2] ['mʌltɪplɪ] ADV *Med* **m. disabled** poly-handicapé

ıultiprocessing [,mʌltɪ'prəʊsesɪŋ] N *Comput* multitraitement *m*

ıultiprocessor [,mʌltɪ'prəʊsesə(r)] N *Comput* multiprocesseur *m*

ıultipurpose [,mʌltɪ'pɜːpəs] ADJ à usages mul-tiples, polyvalent
▸▸ *Aut* ***multipurpose vehicle*** monospace *m*

ıultiracial [,mʌltɪ'reɪʃəl] ADJ multiracial

ıultirole ['mʌltɪrəʊl] ADJ multirôle

ıultiscan monitor ['mʌltɪskæn-] N moniteur *m* à balayage multiple

ıultiscreen ['mʌltɪskriːn] N **1** *Cin* complexe *m ou* cinéma *m* multisalle(s) **2** *TV* écran-mosaïque *m*, multi-écran *m*
▸▸ *TV* ***multiscreen channel*** canal *m* mosaïque; *Cin* ***multiscreen cinema*** complexe *m ou* cinéma *m* multisalle(s)

ıultisector ['mʌltɪ,sektə(r)] ADJ multisectoriel
▸▸ ***multisector journey*** voyage *m* multi-secteur; ***multisector ticketing*** délivrance *f* de billets multi-secteurs

ıulti-spreadsheet N multifeuille *f*

ıultistage ['mʌltɪsteɪdʒ] ADJ **1** *(procedure)* à plusieurs étapes **2** *(rocket)* à plusieurs étages
▸▸ ***multistage synthesis*** synthèse *f* multistades

ıulti-station ADJ *Comput* multipostes

ıultistorey [,mʌltɪ'stɔːrɪ], *Am* **multistoried** [,mʌltɪ'stɔːrɪd] ADJ
▸▸ ***multistorey building*** grand immeuble *m*; *Br* ***multistorey car park*** parking *m* à plusieurs ni-veaux

ıultisyllabic [,mʌltɪsɪ'læbɪk] ADJ polysylla-bique

ıulti-talented ADJ aux talents multiples

ıultitasker ['mʌltɪ,tɑːskə(r)] N = personne ca-pable de mener plusieurs tâches de front

multitasking ['mʌltɪ,tɑːskɪŋ] N **1** = capacité à mener plusieurs tâches de front **2** *Comput* mul-titâche *m*

multitrack [mʌltɪtræk] ADJ *(recording)* multipis-tes

multitracking [,mʌltɪ'trækɪŋ] N *(in recording)* enregistrement *m* multipistes

multitude ['mʌltɪtjuːd] N **1** *(large number* ▸ *of people, animals)* multitude *f*; *(*▸ *of details, rea-sons)* multitude *f*, foule *f*; *Fig* **it covers a m. of sins** *(job title, definition)* ça peut vouloir dire n'im-porte quoi; **my new dress covers a m. of sins!** j'ai pris une robe ample exprès pour cacher mes formes! **2** *(ordinary people)* **the m.** la multitude, la foule

multitudinous [,mʌltɪ'tjuːdɪnəs] ADJ innom-brable

multiuser [,mʌltɪ'juːzə(r)] ADJ *Comput* multi-utilisateur, pour utilisateurs multiples
▸▸ ***multiuser software*** logiciel *m* multi-utilisateur; ***multiuser system*** système *m* multi-utilisateur

multi-valve ADJ multisoupapes

multivision ['mʌltɪvɪʒən] N multivision *f*

multivitamin [*Br* 'mʌltɪ,vɪtəmɪn, *Am* 'mʌltɪ-,vaɪtəmɪn] N *Pharm* multivitamine *f*, polyvita-mine *f*

multiway bra ['mʌltɪweɪ-] N soutien-gorge *m* multipositions

mum [mʌm] ADJ **to keep m. (about sth)** ne pas souffler mot (de qch); *Fam* **m.'s the word!** motus et bouche cousue!
N *Br (mother)* maman *f*

mumble ['mʌmbəl] VI marmonner; **what are you mumbling about?** qu'est-ce que tu as à marmon-ner comme ça?; **to m. to oneself** marmonner tout seul
VT marmonner; **to m. an apology** marmonner des excuses
N paroles *fpl* indistinctes, marmonnement *m*, marmonnements *mpl*; **he replied in a m.** il mar-monna une réponse

mumbo jumbo [,mʌmbəʊ'dʒʌmbəʊ] N *Pej (non-sense)* âneries *fpl*; *(words)* charabia *m*; *(ritual phrases)* bla-bla *m inv*; **as far as I'm concerned as-trology is just a load of m.** pour moi, l'astrologie n'est que de la superstition ridicule

mummer ['mʌmə(r)] N *Theat* mime *mf*

mummery ['mʌmərɪ] *(pl* **mummeries***)* N **1** *Pej (ceremony)* cérémonie *f* pompeuse **2** *Theat (show)* momerie *f*, = spectacle de danses folklo-riques dans lequel les danseurs sont masqués

mummification [,mʌmɪfɪ'keɪʃən] N momifica-tion *f*

mummify ['mʌmɪfaɪ] *(pt & pp* **mummified***)* VT momifier
VI se momifier

mummy ['mʌmɪ] *(pl* **mummies***)* N **1** *(body)* mo-mie *f* **2** *Br (mother)* maman *f*
▸▸ *Br Pej* ***mummy's boy*** fils *m* à maman

mumps [mʌmps] N *(UNCOUNT)* oreillons *mpl*; **to have (the) m.** avoir les oreillons

munch [mʌntʃ] VT *(crunchy food)* croquer; *(food in general)* mâcher
VI **to m. on an apple** croquer une pomme; **she was munching away at some toast** elle mâchon-nait un toast
▸ **munch out** VI *Am Fam* se goinfrer, s'empiffrer

Munchausen ['mʌntʃaʊzən] N *Med* **M. by proxy** syndrome *m* de Münchhausen par procuration
▸▸ ***Munchausen('s) syndrome*** syndrome *m* de Münchhausen; ***Munchausen('s) syndrome by proxy*** syndrome *m* de Münchhausen par procu-ration

munchies ['mʌntʃɪz] NPL *Fam* **1** *(desire to eat)* fringale *f*; **to have the m.** avoir la dalle **2** *(snacks)* petites choses *fpl* à grignoter, amuse-gueule(s) *mpl*

mundane [mʌn'deɪn] ADJ *(gen)* banal, ordi-naire; *(task)* prosaïque

> Note that the French adjective **mondain** is a false friend and is never a translation for the English word **mundane**. It refers to people or events in high society.

municipal [mjuː'nɪsɪpəl] ADJ municipal, de la ville
▸▸ *Am Fin* ***municipal bond*** obligation *f* de collec-tivité locale; ***municipal buildings*** ≃ mairie *f*; *(in large town)* hôtel *m* de ville; *Am Law* ***municipal court*** = tribunal local de première instance; *Can & Austr* ***municipal district*** ≃ municipalité *f*

municipality [mjuː,nɪsɪ'pælətɪ] *(pl* **municipali-ties***)* N municipalité *f*

munificence [mjuː'nɪfɪsəns] N munificence *f*

munificent [mjuː'nɪfɪsənt] ADJ munificent

munitions [mjuː'nɪʃənz] NPL munitions *fpl*; **she was a m. worker** elle travaillait dans une fa-brique de munitions
▸▸ ***munitions dump*** dépôt *m* de munitions; ***muni-tions factory*** fabrique *f* de munitions

munter ['mʌntə(r)] N *Br Fam (ugly woman)* laide-ron *f*, mocheté *f*, cageot *m*

muppet ['mʌpɪt] N *Br Fam (idiot)* andouille *f*

mural ['mjuːərəl] N *(painting)* mural *m*, peinture *f* murale
ADJ mural

muralist ['mjuːərəlɪst] N muraliste *mf*

murder ['mɜːdə(r)] N **1** *(killing)* meurtre *m*, as-sassinat *m*; **to commit (a) m.** commettre un meurtre/assassinat; **he's up on a m. charge** il est accusé de meurtre; *Fig* **he gets away with m.** il peut tout se permettre, personne ne lui dit quoi que ce soit; **their kids get away with m.** leurs gos-ses font absolument tout ce qu'ils veulent **2** *Fam Fig (difficult task, experience)* calvaire *m*, enfer *m*; **the traffic is m. on Fridays** il y a une circulation épouvantable le vendredi; **it's m. trying to park in the town centre** c'est l'enfer pour trouver à se garer dans le centre-ville; **standing all day is m. on your feet** ça fait vachement mal aux pieds de rester debout toute la journée
VT **1** *(kill)* tuer, assassiner; *(slaughter)* tuer, mas-sacrer; *Fam Fig* **I'll m. you (for that)!** je vais te tuer!; *Br Fam Fig* **I could m. a fag/a beer** je me ta-perais bien une clope/une bière **2** *Fam Fig (lan-guage, play, song)* massacrer **3** *Fam Fig (defeat)* ratatiner, écraser
▸▸ ***murder case*** affaire *f* de meurtre; ***murder hunt*** chasse *f* à l'homme *(pour retrouver l'auteur d'un meurtre)*; ***murder mystery*** *(film)* ≃ film *m* policier; *(book)* ≃ roman *m* policier; ***murder trial*** procès *m* pour meurtre; ***murder weapon*** arme *f* du crime

murderer ['mɜːdərə(r)] N meurtrier(ère) *m,f*, as-sassin *m*

murderess ['mɜːdərɪs] N meurtrière *f*

murderous ['mɜːdərəs] ADJ **1** *(deadly* ▸ *regime, attack, intention)* meurtrier
2 *(hateful* ▸ *look, expression)* meurtrier, assas-sin, de haine; **to give sb a m. look** lancer un re-gard meurtrier à qn; **with m. intent** dans une intention homicide; **a m.-looking knife** un cou-teau à l'apparence particulièrement mena-çante
3 *(dangerous* ▸ *road, bend)* meurtrier, redou-table
4 *(hellish)* infernal, épouvantable

murk [mɜːk] N *(UNCOUNT)* obscurité *f*, ténèbres *fpl*

murky ['mɜːkɪ] *(compar* **murkier***, superl* **murkiest***)*
ADJ **1** *(dark* ▸ *sky, night)* noir, sombre; *(muddy* ▸ *water)* boueux, trouble; *(dirty* ▸ *windows, weath-er)* sale **2** *Fig (shameful)* **a m. episode** une histoire sombre *ou* trouble; **to have a m. past** avoir un passé trouble

murmur ['mɜːmə(r)] N **1** *(sound)* murmure *m*; *(of conversation)* bruit *m*, bourdonnement *m*; **there wasn't a m.** on aurait pu entendre une mouche voler; **without a m.** sans broncher **2** *Med (of heart)* murmure *m*, souffle *m*
VT murmurer, dire à voix basse; **to m. excuses** murmurer des excuses
VI murmurer; **to m. at** *or* **against sth** murmurer contre qch

murmuring ['mɜːmərɪŋ] N murmure *m*
ADJ murmurant
• **murmurings** NPL murmures *mpl*

Murphy's law ['mɜːfɪz-] N loi *f* de l'emmerde-ment maximum; **that's M.!** c'est la poisse!

muscatel [,mʌskə'tel] N muscat *m*

muscle [ˈmʌsəl] **N 1** *Anat & Zool* muscle *m*; *(strength)* muscle *m*, force *f*; **he has plenty of m.** il est bien musclé; **she didn't move a m.** elle est restée parfaitement immobile **2** *(UNCOUNT) Fam (strong men)* costauds *mpl*; **we need some m. to help lift these shelves** on a besoin d'hommes forts pour soulever ces étagères **3** *(influence, power)* puissance *f*, poids *m*; **it would give our campaign more m.** cela donnerait plus de force à notre campagne
▸▸ ***muscle fibre*** fibres *fpl* musculaires; *Med* ***muscle strain*** élongation *f*; ***muscle tone*** tonus *m* musculaire

▸**muscle in VI** *Fam* intervenir▫; **to m. in on sth** intervenir autoritairement dans qch▫; **to m. in on sb's territory** marcher sur les plates-bandes de qn; **a lot of big companies are muscling in** de nombreuses grosses sociétés arrivent en force▫

muscle-bound ADJ 1 *(muscular)* extrêmement musclé **2** *(rigid)* inflexible, rigide

muscleman [ˈmʌsəlmæn] *(pl* **musclemen** [-men]*)* **N** *(strongman)* hercule *m*; *(bodyguard)* garde *m* du corps, homme *m* de main

muscovado (sugar) [ˌmʌskəˈvɑːdəʊ-] **N** cassonade *f*

Muscovite [ˈmʌskəvaɪt] **N** Moscovite *mf*
ADJ moscovite

muscular [ˈmʌskjʊlə(r)] **ADJ 1** *(body, person)* musclé **2** *(pain, tissue)* musculaire
▸▸ *Med* ***muscular dystrophy*** *(UNCOUNT)* dystrophie *f* musculaire progressive, myopathie *f*

musculature [ˈmʌskjʊlətʃə(r)] **N** musculature *f*

Muse [mjuːz] **N** *Myth* Muse *f*; **the (nine) Muses** les (neuf) Muses *fpl*; *Literary* **the M.** *(poetry)* la Muse *f*, les Muses *fpl*; *(of poet)* la muse *f*

muse [mjuːz] **VI** rêvasser, songer; **to m. on** *or* **upon** *or* **over sth** songer à qch
VT "I wonder what happened to him," she mused "je me demande bien ce qu'il est devenu", dit-elle d'un air songeur

museum [mjuːˈziːəm] **N** musée *m*
▸▸ *also Fig* ***museum piece*** pièce *f* de musée

mush¹ [mʌʃ] **N 1** *(food)* bouillie *f*; *Am (porridge)* bouillie *f* de maïs **2** *Fam Fig (sentimentality)* mièvrerie *f*
VT réduire en purée

mush² [mʊʃ] **N** *Br Fam* **1** *(face)* poire *f*, trombine *f* **2** *(term of address)* **oi, m.!** eh, machin!

mush³ [mʌʃ] **N** *(journey)* trajet *m* en traîneau à chiens
EXCLAM allez, hue!, *Can* marche!

mushroom [ˈmʌʃrʊm] **N 1** *(fungus, nuclear cloud)* champignon *m* **2** *Sewing* boule *f* à repriser **3** *(colour)* beige *m* rosé
ADJ *(colour)* beige rosé *(inv)*
COMP *(soup, omelette)* aux champignons
VI 1 *(gather mushrooms)* **to go mushrooming** aller aux champignons **2** *(spring up)* pousser comme des champignons; **video shops mushroomed in almost every town** les magasins de vidéo se sont multipliés dans presque toutes les villes **3** *(grow quickly)* s'étendre, prendre de l'ampleur; **the conflict mushroomed into full-scale war** le conflit a vite dégénéré en véritable guerre; **a mushrooming estate** un lotissement qui s'étend rapidement
▸▸ ***mushroom cloud*** champignon *m* atomique; ***mushroom farm*** champignonnière *f*; ***mushroom grower*** champignonniste *mf*; *Fig* ***mushroom growth*** poussée *f ou* croissance *f* rapide; ***mushroom town*** ville *f* champignon

mushrooming [ˈmʌʃruːmɪŋ] **N 1** *(mushroom picking)* cueillette *f* des champignons **2** *(rapid growth)* croissance *f* exponentielle

mushy [ˈmʌʃɪ] *(compar* **mushier**, *superl* **mushiest)** **ADJ 1** *(vegetables)* en bouillie; *(fruit)* trop mûr, blet; *(ground)* détrempé **2** *Fam Fig (sentimental)* à l'eau de rose, mièvre
▸▸ ***mushy peas*** purée *f* de petits pois

music [ˈmjuːzɪk] **N** musique *f*; *(score)* partition *f*, musique *f*; **to set to m.** mettre en musique; **to read m.** lire une partition; **the news was m. to my ears** la nouvelle m'a fait très plaisir *ou* m'a ravi
COMP *(teacher, lesson, festival)* de musique
▸▸ ***music box*** boîte *f* à musique; ***music case*** porte-musique *m inv*; *Old-fashioned* ***music centre*** chaîne *f* (midi); *TV* ***music channel*** chaîne *f* musicale; ***music critic*** critique *mf* musical(e); ***music director*** directeur(trice) *m,f* musical(e); ***music hall*** **N** *(theatre)* théâtre *m* de variétés; *(entertainment)* music-hall *m* **COMP** *(song, artist)* de music-hall; ***music lover*** mélomane *mf*; ***music paper*** papier *m* à musique; ***music piracy*** piratage *m* musical; ***music press*** presse *f* musicale; ***music publishing*** édition *f* musicale; ***music stand*** pupitre *m* (à musique); ***music station*** station *f* musicale; ***music video*** clip *m* (vidéo)

musical [ˈmjuːzɪkəl] **ADJ 1** *(evening, taste, composition)* musical **2** *(person)* musicien; **they are a m. family** *(liking music)* c'est une famille de mélomanes; *(including musicians)* c'est une famille de musiciens; **I'm not very m.** je n'ai pas tellement l'oreille musicale **3** *(pleasant ▸ voice, chimes)* musical
N comédie *f* musicale, musical *m*
▸▸ *Br* ***musical box*** boîte *f* à musique; *also Fig* ***musical chairs*** jeu *m* des chaises musicales; **to play m. chairs** jouer aux chaises musicales; ***musical comedy*** comédie *f* musicale, musical *m*; ***musical instrument*** instrument *m* de musique

musician [mjuːˈzɪʃən] **N** musicien(enne) *m,f*

musicianship [mjuːˈzɪʃənʃɪp] **N** don *m* pour la musique

musicologist [ˌmjuːzɪˈkɒlədʒɪst] **N** musicologue *mf*

musicology [ˌmjuːzɪˈkɒlədʒɪ] **N** musicologie *f*

musing [ˈmjuːzɪŋ] **N** *(UNCOUNT)* songes *mpl*, rêverie *f*
ADJ songeur, rêveur
• **musings NPL** songeries *fpl*

musk [mʌsk] **N 1** *(smell)* musc *m* **2** *Bot* mimule *m* musqué
▸▸ *Zool* ***musk cat*** civette *f*; *Zool* ***musk deer*** porte-musc *m*; *Zool* ***musk ox*** bœuf *m* musqué, ovibos *m*; *Bot* ***musk rose*** *(flower)* rose *f* musquée; *(bush)* rosier *m* musqué

musket [ˈmʌskɪt] **N** mousquet *m*

musketeer [ˌmʌskɪˈtɪə(r)] **N** mousquetaire *m*

musketry [ˈmʌskɪtrɪ] **N** *(UNCOUNT)* **1** *(technique)* tir *m* au fusil **2** *(muskets)* mousquets *mpl* **3** *(musketeers)* mousquetaires *mpl*

muskrat [ˈmʌskræt] *(pl* **inv** *or* **muskrats)** **N 1** *Zool* rat *m* musqué, ondatra *m* **2** *(fur)* rat *m* d'Amérique, loutre *f* d'Hudson

musky¹ [ˈmʌskɪ] *(compar* **muskier**, *superl* **muskiest)** **ADJ** musqué

musky² [ˈmʌskɪ] *(pl* **muskies)** **N** *Fam (poisson)* maskinongé *m*

Muslim [ˈmʊzlɪm] **N** musulman(e) *m,f*
ADJ musulman

Muslim-Croat Federation [ˌmʊzlɪmˈkrəʊæt-] **N** Fédération *f* croato-musulmane

muslin [ˈmʌzlɪn] *Tex* **N** mousseline *f*
COMP de *ou* en mousseline
▸▸ *Culin* ***muslin bag*** nouet *m*

muso [ˈmjuːzəʊ] **N** *Br Fam (abbr* **musician)** musico *m*

musquash [ˈmʌskwɒʃ] **N 1** *Zool* rat *m* musqué, ondatra *m* **2** *(fur)* rat *m* d'Amérique, loutre *f* d'Hudson

muss [mʌs] **VT** *Fam (rumple)* friper▫, froisser▫; *(dirty)* salir▫; **don't m. my hair** ne me décoiffe pas▫

▸**muss up VT SEP** *Am Fam* **1** *(rumple)* friper▫, froisser▫; *(dirty)* salir▫ **2** *(upset ▸ plans)* ficher par terre

mussel [ˈmʌsəl] **N** moule *f*
▸▸ ***mussel bed*** parc *m* à moules; ***mussel farm*** moulière *f*

MUST¹ [məs, məst, *stressed* mʌst] **V AUX 1** *(expressing necessity, obligation)* devoir; **you m. lock the door** vous devez fermer *ou* il faut que vous fermiez la porte à clé; **I m. go now** il faut que je parte (maintenant); **I m. admit the idea intrigues me** je dois avouer que l'idée m'intrigue; *Ironic* **very clever, I m. say!** je dois dire que c'est très astucieux!; **if I/you/***etc* **m.** s'il le faut; **I can't! – you m.!** je ne peux pas! – mais il le faut!; **if you m. know, he's asked me out to dinner** si tu veux tout savoir, il m'a invitée à dîner; **you really m. see h[is] latest film** il faut vraiment que tu voies son de[r]nier film; **m. you be so rude?** es-tu obligé d'êt[re] aussi grossier?; **they told us we m. leave** ils no[us] ont dit qu'il fallait que nous partions, ils no[us] ont dit que nous devions partir; **you mustn't te[ll] anyone** vous ne devez le dire à personne, il n[e] faut le dire à personne; **I mustn't say any more** j[e] n'ai pas le droit d'en dire plus; **we mustn't be late** [il] ne faut pas que nous soyons en retard; **they to[ld] us we mustn't come before 10 o'clock** ils nous o[nt] dit de ne pas arriver avant 10 heures; **you mustn['t] forget to press this button** n'oubliez (surtout) pa[s] d'appuyer sur ce bouton; **if you m. drink so much what do you expect?** si tu t'entêtes à boire autan[t] il ne faut pas t'étonner!
2 *(suggesting, inviting)* **you m. meet my wife** faut que vous rencontriez *ou* fassiez la connais[]sance de ma femme; **we m. go out for a drink** faut que nous allions boire un verre
3 *(expressing likelihood)* devoir; **you m. be Aliso[n]** vous devez être Alison; **you m. be famished** vou[s] devez être morts de faim; **it m. be very hard f[or] you** ça doit être très dur pour toi; **you m. be jo[k]ing!** tu plaisantes!; **if he says so it m. be true** s'il l[e] dit, c'est que c'est vrai
4 *(with "have" + past participle) (making assump[]tions, stating requirements)* **she m. have forgotte[n]** elle a dû oublier, elle a sans doute oublié; **ha[s] she forgotten? – she m. have** elle a oublié? – san[s] doute *ou* certainement; **you m. have known** vous le saviez sûrement!; **was it her? – it m. hav[e] been** est-ce que c'était elle? – oui, je pense **there m. have been at least a thousand people** [il] devait y avoir au moins un millier de personnes **I saw that he m. have suspected something** j'ai bie[n] vu qu'il avait dû se douter de quelque chose
N *Fam* **sunglasses are a m.** les lunettes de sole[il] sont absolument indispensables▫; **this film/h[is] new album is a m.** il faut absolument avoir vu c[e] film/acheter son dernier album▫; **fake fur is a m[ust] this year** la fausse fourrure est un must cette an[]née

must² [mʌst] **N 1** *(mould)* moisissure *f* **2** *(f[ruit] wine)* moût *m*

mustache [ˈmʌstæʃ] *Am* = **moustache**

mustang [ˈmʌstæŋ] **N** mustang *m*

mustard [ˈmʌstəd] **N** moutarde *f*; *Fam Fig* **to cu[t] the m.** se montrer à la hauteur; **m. and cress** = mélange de cresson alénois et de pousses d[e] moutarde blanche utilisé en salade
ADJ *(colour)* moutarde *(inv)*
▸▸ ***mustard bath*** bain *m* sinapisé; ***mustard ga[s]*** gaz *m* moutarde, ypérite *f*; *Pharm* ***mustard pla[s]ter*** sinapisme *m*; ***mustard pot*** moutardier *m*, po[t] *m* à moutarde; ***mustard powder*** farine *f* de mou[]tarde; ***mustard seed*** graine *f* de moutarde

must-do N must *m*; **going on safari is a m. in Ken[]ya** quand on va au Kenya, il faut absolumen[t] faire un safari
ADJ wine-tasting is a m. activity in Californi[a] quand on va en Californie, il faut absolumen[t] faire des dégustations de vins

muster [ˈmʌstə(r)] **VT 1** *(gather ▸ troops)* rassem[]bler, réunir; *(▸ courage, strength, energy)* rassem[]bler; *(▸ finance, cash)* réunir; **they were unable t[o] m. enough support** ils n'ont pas pu trouver suffi[]samment de gens pour soutenir leur initiative **to m. one's courage to do sth** prendre son courag[e] à deux mains pour faire qch **2** *(take roll-call o[f])* faire l'appel de
VI se rassembler
N 1 *Mil* revue *f*, inspection *f*; *Br Fig* **to pass m.** *(i[n] dress, appearance)* être présentable; *(in conten[t])* être acceptable **2** *(assembly)* rassemblement *m*
▸▸ ***muster roll*** feuille *f* d'appel; ***muster statio[n]*** point *m* de ralliement

▸**muster up VT INSEP** *(courage)* rassembler; **can't m. up much enthusiasm for a family caravan[]ning holiday** j'ai du mal à m'enthousiasmer [à] l'idée de partir en vacances en caravane ave[c] ma famille

must-have N must *m*
ADJ the latest m. accessory le must en matièr[e] d'accessoires

mustn't [ˈmʌsənt] = **must not**

nust-see **N that film/TV programme is a m.** il ne 'aut surtout pas manquer ce film/cette émission de télévision, ce film/cette émission de télévision est à voir absolument
ADJ the latest m. film/TV series le dernier film/la dernière série télévisée à voir absolument *ou* à ne pas manquer

nust've ['mʌstəv] = **must have**

nusty ['mʌstɪ] (*compar* **mustier**, *superl* **mustiest**) **ADJ 1** *(smell)* de moisi; *(books)* qui sent le moisi; *(room)* qui sent le renfermé; **to smell m.** sentir le moisi; *(of room etc)* sentir le renfermé **2** *Fig (old-fashioned)* suranné, vieux jeu *(inv)*

nutability [ˌmju:tə'bɪlɪtɪ] **N** mutabilité *f*

nutable ['mju:təbəl] **ADJ** *(gen)* mutable; *Astrol* mutable, commun

nutant ['mju:tənt] **N** mutant(e) *m,f*
ADJ mutant

nutate [mju:'teɪt] **VT** faire subir une mutation à
VI 1 *(gen)* subir une mutation; **to m. into sth** se transformer en qch **2** *Biol* muter

nutation [mju:'teɪʃən] **N** mutation *f*

nute [mju:t] **ADJ 1** *Med* muet **2** *Ling (vowel, letter)* muet **3** *(silent ▸ person)* muet, silencieux; *(unspoken ▸ feeling)* muet; **to stand m.** rester muet *ou* silencieux
VT *(sound)* amortir, atténuer; *(feelings, colour)* atténuer; **to m. the sound** *(on TV)* mettre en sourdine
N 1 *Med* muet(ette) *m,f* **2** *Mus* sourdine *f*
▸▸ *Orn* **mute swan** cygne *m* muet *ou* tuberculé

nuted ['mju:tɪd] **ADJ 1** *(sound)* assourdi, amorti, atténué; *(voice)* feutré, sourd; *(colour)* sourd; *(criticism, protest)* voilé; *(applause)* faible; **to discuss sth in m. tones** discuter qch à voix basse **2** *Mus* en sourdine

nutely ['mju:tlɪ] **ADV** *(stare, gaze)* en silence

nutilate ['mju:tɪleɪt] **VT 1** *(maim ▸ body, face)* mutiler **2** *(damage ▸ property, object)* dégrader, détériorer **3** *(adulterate ▸ text)* mutiler

nutilation [ˌmju:tɪ'leɪʃən] **N 1** *(of body, face)* mutilation *f* **2** *(of property, object)* détérioration *f*, dégradation *f* **3** *(of text)* mutilation *f*

nutineer [ˌmju:tɪ'nɪə(r)] **N** mutin *m*, mutiné(e) *m,f*

nutinous ['mju:tɪnəs] **ADJ 1** *(rebellious ▸ crew, soldiers)* mutiné, rebelle; **the inmates of the prison were m.** les détenus étaient au bord de la rébellion **2** *(unruly ▸ child)* indiscipliné, rebelle

nutiny ['mju:tɪnɪ] (*pl* **mutinies**) **N** *(on ship)* mutinerie *f*; *(in prison, barracks)* rébellion *f*, mutinerie *f*; *(in city)* soulèvement *m*, révolte *f*
VI se mutiner, se rebeller

nutism ['mju:tɪzəm] **N** *(gen) & Psy* mutisme *m*; *Med* mutité *f*

nutt [mʌt] **N** *Fam* **1** *(dog)* clébard *m* **2** *(fool)* crétin(e) *m,f*, andouille *f*

nutter ['mʌtə(r)] **VT** *(mumble)* marmonner, grommeler; **he muttered a threat** il grommela *ou* marmonna une menace; **he muttered something to himself** il marmonna quelque chose entre ses dents
VI 1 *(mumble)* marmonner, parler dans sa barbe *ou* entre ses dents; **what are you muttering about?** qu'est-ce que tu as à marmonner?; **to m. to oneself** marmonner tout seul **2** *(grumble)* grommeler, grogner
N murmure *m*, murmures *mpl*, marmonnement *m*; **this provoked mutters of discontent** cela a provoqué un murmure de mécontentement; **to speak in a m.** marmonner dans sa barbe

nuttering ['mʌtərɪŋ] **N** marmottement *m*

nutton ['mʌtən] **N** *(meat)* mouton *m*; **she's m. dressed as lamb** elle joue les jeunesses
COMP *(chop, stew)* de mouton

nuttonchops [ˌmʌtən'tʃɒps], **muttonchop whiskers** **NPL** favoris *mpl (bien fournis)*

muttonhead ['mʌtənhed] **N** *Fam* crétin(e) *m,f*

mutual ['mju:tʃʊəl] **ADJ 1** *(reciprocal ▸ admiration, help)* mutuel, réciproque; **the feeling is m.** c'est réciproque **2** *(shared ▸ friend, interest)* commun; **by m. consent** à l'amiable, par consentement mutuel
▸▸ *Fin* ***mutual benefit society*** société *f* de secours mutuel; *Am Fin* ***mutual fund*** *(unit trust)* fonds *m* commun de placement; *Fin* ***mutual insurance company*** société *f* de crédit mutuel, société *f* de mutualité; *Fin* ***mutual status*** statut *m* de mutuelle

mutually ['mju:tʃʊəlɪ] **ADV** mutuellement, réciproquement; **m. exclusive** qui s'excluent l'un l'autre

Muzak® ['mju:zæk] **N** musique *f* de fond, fond *m* sonore

muzzle ['mʌzəl] **N 1** *(for dog, horse)* muselière *f*
2 *Fig (censorship)* bâillon *m*, censure *f*
3 *(of gun)* canon *m*
4 *(of animal)* museau *m*
VT 1 *(animal)* museler, mettre une muselière à **2** *Fig (speaker)* museler, empêcher de s'exprimer librement; *(press)* bâillonner, museler
▸▸ ***muzzle velocity*** vitesse *f* initiale

muzzle-loader **N** = arme à feu dont le chargement s'opère par la bouche

muzzy ['mʌzɪ] (*compar* **muzzier**, *superl* **muzziest**) **ADJ** *Br* **1** *(person)* aux idées embrouillées; *(mind)* confus; *(ideas)* embrouillé, flou; **my head feels a bit m.** j'ai la tête qui tourne **2** *(picture)* flou, indistinct

MV [ˌem'vi:] **N 1** *Elec (abbr* **megavolt(s)***)* MV **2** *Naut (abbr* **motor vessel***)* bateau *m* à moteur

MVP [ˌemvi:'pi:] **N** *Am Sport (abbr* **most valuable player***)* = titre décerné au meilleur joueur d'une équipe

MW [ˌem'dʌbəlju:] **N 1** *Elec (abbr* **megawatt(s)***)* MW **2** *Rad (abbr* **Medium Wave***)* PO *fpl*

my [maɪ] **ADJ 1** *(belonging to me ▸ singular)* mon (ma); *(▸ plural)* mes; **my dog/car/ear** mon chien/ma voiture/mon oreille; **my dogs/cars/ears** mes chiens/voitures/oreilles; **my hat and gloves** mon chapeau et mes gants; **I have a car of my own** j'ai une voiture (à moi); **this is MY chair** cette chaise est à moi; **one of my friends** un de mes amis, un ami à moi; **my hair is grey** j'ai les cheveux gris; **I've broken my glasses** j'ai cassé mes lunettes; **I've broken my arm** je me suis cassé le bras; **she looked into my eyes** elle m'a regardé dans les yeux; **if you don't mind my asking** si je peux me permettre de vous le demander **2** *(in titles)* **my Lord** *(to judge)* Monsieur le juge; *(to nobleman)* Monsieur le Comte/le Duc; *(to bishop)* Monseigneur
EXCLAM oh là là!; **my, but you've grown!** oh là là! *ou* dis donc, qu'est-ce que tu as poussé!; **(oh) my!** ça par exemple!; **my, my! aren't we touchy!** oh là là! que vous êtes susceptible!

myalgic encephalomyelitis [maɪ'ældʒɪkenˌsefələʊˌmaɪə'laɪtɪs] **N** *Med* encéphalomyélite *f* myalgique

mycology [maɪ'kɒlədʒɪ] **N** *Bot* mycologie *f*

myelin ['maɪəlɪn] **N** *Physiol* myéline *f*

myelitis [ˌmaɪə'laɪtɪs] **N** *Med* myélite *f*

myeloma [ˌmaɪə'ləʊmə] **N** *Med* myélome *m*

myna(h) (bird) ['maɪnə-] **N** *Orn* martin *m*; *(Gracula religiosa)* mainate *m*

myocardial [ˌmaɪəʊ'kɑ:dɪəl] **ADJ**
▸▸ *Med* ***myocardial infarction*** infarctus *m* du myocarde

myopia [maɪ'əʊpjə] **N** *Opt* myopie *f*

myopic [maɪ'ɒpɪk] **ADJ** *Opt* myope; *Fig* **they have a m. view of things** ils ne voient pas plus loin que le bout de leur nez

myriad ['mɪrɪəd] **N** myriade *f*
ADJ *Literary* innombrable

myriapod ['mɪrɪəpɒd] *Entom* **N** myriapode *m*
ADJ = relatif aux myriapodes

Myrmidon ['mɜ:mɪdən] **N 1** *Myth* Myrmidon *m* **2** *Fig (follower)* acolyte *m*

myrrh [mɜ:(r)] **N** myrrhe *f*

myrtle ['mɜ:təl] **N** myrte *m*

myself [maɪ'self] **PRON 1** *(reflexive use)* **may I help m.?** puis-je me servir?; **I knitted m. a cardigan** je me suis tricoté un gilet; **I can see m. reflected in the water** je vois mon reflet dans l'eau; **I can't see m. going on holiday this year** je ne crois pas que je pourrai partir en vacances cette année
2 *(after preposition)* **I live by m.** je vis tout seul; **I was laughing to m.** je riais tout seul; **it is meant for people like m.** c'est fait pour les gens comme moi; **I'll keep it for m.** je le garderai pour moi
3 *(emphatic use)* **I'm not a great fan of opera m.** personnellement, je ne suis pas un passionné d'opéra; **I'm a stranger here m.** je ne suis pas d'ici non plus; **I m. saw him leave** je l'ai vu partir de mes propres yeux; **m., I don't believe him, I m. don't believe him** pour ma part, je ne le crois pas; *Hum* **it doesn't taste bad, though I say so** *or* **it m.** sans fausse modestie, ça n'est pas mauvais
4 *(replacing "me")* **the group included m. and Liz** Liz et moi faisions partie du groupe; **I'm not (feeling) m. today** je ne me sens pas très bien *ou* je ne suis pas dans mon assiette aujourd'hui
5 *(unaided, alone)* moi-même; **I can do it m.** je peux le faire moi-même *ou* tout seul

mysterious [mɪ'stɪərɪəs] **ADJ** mystérieux

mysteriously [mɪ'stɪərɪəslɪ] **ADV** mystérieusement

mysteriousness [mɪ'stɪərɪəsnɪs] **N** caractère *m* mystérieux, mystère *m*

mystery ['mɪstərɪ] (*pl* **mysteries**) **N 1** *(strange or unexplained event)* mystère *m*; **it's a m. to me why she came** la raison de sa venue est un mystère pour moi, je n'ai aucune idée de la raison pour laquelle elle est venue; **his past is a m.** son passé est bien mystérieux; **there's no m. about that** ça n'a rien de mystérieux, cela n'est un mystère pour personne; **why make such a m. out of it?** pourquoi (faire) tant de mystères?
2 *(strangeness)* mystère *m*; **she has a certain m. about her** il se dégage de sa personne une impression de mystère
3 *(story)* histoire *f* policière
4 *Theat & Rel* mystère *m*
COMP *(man, voice)* mystérieux; *(guest, prize)* surprise
▸▸ *Theat* ***mystery play*** mystère *m*; ***mystery shopper*** client(e) *m,f* mystère; ***mystery story*** histoire *f* policière; ***mystery tour*** = excursion dont la destination est inconnue des participants

mystic ['mɪstɪk] **N** mystique *mf*
ADJ mystique

mystical ['mɪstɪkəl] **ADJ 1** *Phil & Rel* mystique **2** *(occult)* occulte

mysticism ['mɪstɪsɪzəm] **N** mysticisme *m*

mystification [ˌmɪstɪfɪ'keɪʃən] **N** mystification *f*

mystify ['mɪstɪfaɪ] (*pt & pp* **mystified**) **VT** *(puzzle)* déconcerter, laisser *ou* rendre perplexe; **I was mystified** j'étais perplexe

> Note that the French verb **mystifier** is a false friend. It means **to fool, to take in.**

mystique [mɪ'sti:k] **N** mystique *f*, côté *m* mystique

myth [mɪθ] **N** mythe *m*

mythical ['mɪθɪkəl] **ADJ** mythique

mythological [ˌmɪθə'lɒdʒɪkəl] **ADJ** mythologique

mythology [mɪ'θɒlədʒɪ] (*pl* **mythologies**) **N** mythologie *f*

myxomatosis [ˌmɪksəmə'təʊsɪs] **N** *Vet* myxomatose *f*

N[1], **n** [en] **N** *(letter)* N, n *m inv*; **two n's** deux n; **N for Norman** ≃ N comme Nicolas

N[2] *(written abbr* **North***)* N

n/a, N/A *(written abbr* **not applicable***)* s.o.

NAACP [ˌenerˌeisiːˈpiː] **N** *Am (abbr* **National Association for the Advancement of Colored People***)* = ligue américaine pour la défense des droits de la population noire

Naafi [ˈnæfɪ] **N** *Br Mil (abbr* **Navy, Army, and Air Force Institutes***)* *(organization)* = organisme approvisionnant les forces armées britanniques en biens de consommation; *(canteen)* cantine *f* militaire; *(shop)* magasin *m* réservé aux militaires

naan [nɑːn] **N n. (bread)** naan *m*

nab [næb] *(pt & pp* **nabbed,** *cont* **nabbing***)* **VT** *Fam* **1** *(catch, arrest)* pincer, alpaguer; **to get nabbed** se faire pincer **2** *(catch ▸ to speak to)* coincer, agrafer **3** *(steal, take)* piquer, faucher; *(▸ seat)* prendre◻, accaparer◻; *(▸ parking place)* piquer

nabob [ˈneɪbɒb] **N** nabab *m*

nacelle [næˈsel] **N 1** *(of aircraft)* carlingue *f*, habitacle *m* **2** *(of airship, balloon)* nacelle *f*

nacre [ˈneɪkə(r)] **N** nacre *f*

nadir [ˈneɪdɪə(r)] **N 1** *Astron* nadir *m* **2** *Fig (lowest point)* point *m* le plus bas *ou* profond; **to reach a n.** être au plus bas, toucher le fond, atteindre le niveau le plus bas

nads [nædz] **NPL** *Br very Fam (testicles)* couilles *fpl*

naevus, *Am* **nevus** [ˈniːvəs] *(Br pl* **naevi,** *Am pl* **nevi** [-vaɪ]*)* **N** *Med* nævus *m*

naff [næf] *Br Fam* **ADJ** *(clothes, place, person)* ringard; *(comment, behaviour)* débile

• **naff all ADJ** que dalle; **I've got n. all money** j'ai que dalle comme argent

▸ **naff off VI** *Br Fam* s'arracher, se casser; **n. off!** *(go away)* tire-toi!, casse-toi!; *(as refusal)* arrête ton char!; *(expressing contempt, disagreement)* va te faire voir!

naffing [ˈnæfɪŋ] *Br Fam* **ADJ** *(for emphasis)* foutu, sacré; **shut your n. mouth!** ferme-la!, ferme ton clapet!

ADV *(for emphasis)* vachement; **you're so n. stupid!** t'es vraiment débile!

NAFTA [ˈnæftə] **N** *(abbr* **North American Free Trade Agreement***)* ALENA *m*

nag [næg] *(pt & pp* **nagged,** *cont* **nagging***)* **VT 1** *(pester)* houspiller, harceler; **she's always nagging him** elle est toujours après lui; **he nagged me into buying him a hi-fi** il m'a harcelé jusqu'à ce que je lui achète une chaîne stéréo **2** *(of pain, sorrow)* ronger, travailler; *(of doubt)* tourmenter, ronger

VI trouver à redire, maugréer; **to n. at sb** harceler qn; **she's always nagging at him to get it fixed** elle n'arrête pas de lui casser les pieds *ou Fam* de l'asticoter pour qu'il le fasse réparer

N *Fam* **1** *(person)* enquiquineur(euse) *m,f*; **his wife's a real n.** sa femme est toujours sur son dos *ou* ne lui laisse pas une seconde de répit **2** *(horse)* rosse *f*

nagger [ˈnægə(r)] **N** enquiquineur(euse) *m,f*

nagging [ˈnægɪŋ] **ADJ 1** *(wife, husband)* grincheux, acariâtre **2** *(doubt, feeling)* tenace, harcelant; *(pain)* tenace; **I have a n. suspicion he won't come** je reste persuadé qu'il ne viendra pas; **I've still got this n. doubt about him** je n'arrête pas de me poser des questions à son sujet

N *(UNCOUNT)* plaintes *fpl* continuelles; **I've had enough of your n.!** j'en ai assez que tu me harcèles!

naiad [ˈnaɪæd] **N** naïade *f*

nail [neɪl] **N 1** *(pin)* clou *m*; *Fig* **to hit the n. (right) on the head** mettre le doigt dessus; *Fig* **to pay on the n.** payer rubis sur l'ongle; *Fig* **it's another n. in his coffin** *(ruin)* pour lui, c'est un pas de plus vers la ruine; *(death)* pour lui, c'est un pas de plus vers la tombe **2** *(on finger)* ongle *m*; **to do one's nails** se faire les ongles

VT 1 *(attach)* clouer; **she nailed the plank into place** elle a fixé la planche à l'aide de clous; **nailed to the door** cloué sur la porte; **to n. sth shut** clouer qch; *Fig* **he stood nailed to the spot** il est resté cloué sur place; *Fig* **to n. one's colours to the mast** exprimer clairement son opinion

2 *Fam (catch, trap ▸ person)* pincer, coincer

3 *Fam (expose ▸ rumour)* démentir◻; *(▸ lie)* dénoncer◻, révéler◻; **we should n. the lie that unemployment is falling** nous devrions démontrer que la soi-disant baisse du chômage n'est qu'un tissu de mensonges

4 *Fam (shoot)* descendre

▸▸ ***nail bar*** salon *m* de manucure; ***nail bomb*** bombe *f* à fragmentation *(bourrée de clous)*; ***nail clippers*** coupe-ongles *m inv*, pince *f* à ongles; *Am* ***nail enamel*** vernis *m* à ongles; ***nail file*** lime *f* à ongles; ***nail polish*** vernis *m* à ongles; ***nail polish remover*** dissolvant *m*; ***nail punch*** chasse-clou *m*; ***nail scissors*** ciseaux *mpl* à ongles; *Tech* ***nail set*** chasse-clou *m*, chasse-pointe *m*; *Br* ***nail varnish*** vernis *m* à ongles; *Br* ***nail varnish remover*** dissolvant *m* (pour vernis à ongles)

▸ **nail down VT SEP 1** *(fasten)* clouer, fixer avec des clous **2** *(make definite ▸ details, date)* fixer (définitivement); *(▸ agreement)* parvenir à, arriver à; *(▸ person)* amener à se décider; **try to n. her down to a definite date** essayez de faire en sorte qu'elle vous fixe une date précise; **he's difficult to n. down** il est difficile d'obtenir une réponse précise de sa part

▸ **nail up VT SEP 1** *(shut ▸ door, window)* condamner *(en fixant avec des clous)*; *(▸ box)* clouer **2** *(fix to wall, door ▸ picture, photo etc)* fixer (avec un clou); *(▸ notice)* clouer, afficher

nail-biter N 1 *(person)* personne *f* qui se ronge les ongles **2** *Fig (situation)* situation *f* au suspense insoutenable

nail-biting N *(habit)* manie *f* de se ronger les ongles

ADJ *(situation)* angoissant, stressant; *(finish)* haletant

nailbrush [ˈneɪlbrʌʃ] **N** brosse *f* à ongles

naive, naïve [naɪˈiːv] **ADJ** naïf

▸▸ *Art* ***naive art*** l'art *m* naïf

naively, naïvely [naɪˈiːvlɪ] **ADV** naïvement, avec naïveté

naivety, naïveté [naɪˈiːvtɪ] **N** naïveté *f*

naked [ˈneɪkɪd] **ADJ 1** *(unclothed ▸ person, body, leg)* nu; *Fig* **the n. ape** l'homme *m*, l'espèce *f* humaine

2 *(bare ▸ tree)* nu, dénudé, sans feuilles; *(▸ landscape)* nu, dénudé; *(▸ wall, room)* nu

3 *(unprotected ▸ flame, light, sword)* nu; *(▸ wir*[e]*)* nu, dénudé; **a n. lightbulb lit the room** une simpl[e] ampoule électrique éclairait la pièce

4 *(undisguised ▸ reality, truth)* tout nu, tout cr[u]; *(▸ facts)* brut; *(▸ fear)* pur et simple; *(▸ aggre*[s]*sion)* délibéré; **an expression of n. terror** une expression de pure terreur

5 *(eye)* nu; **visible to the n. eye** visible à l'œil nu

nakedness [ˈneɪkɪdnɪs] **N** nudité *f*

NALGO [ˈnælgəʊ] **N** *Br Formerly (abbr* **National a**[nd] **Local Government Officers' Association***)* = ancie[n] syndicat de la fonction publique en Grande-Bretagne

Nam [næm] **N** *Am Fam Mil slang (Vietnam)* le Viê[t]nam◻

namby-pamby [ˌnæmbɪˈpæmbɪ] *Fam* **ADJ** *(pe*[r]*son)* gnangnan *(inv)*, cucul *(inv)*; *(remark, att*[i]*tude)* faiblard; *(style)* à l'eau de rose, fadasse

N lavette *f*, gnangnan *mf*

NAME [neɪm]

N	
• nom **1–4**	• titre **1**
• réputation **3**	• personnage **4**
VT	
• nommer **1–3**	• appeler **1**
• baptiser **1**	• désigner **2, 3**
• citer **2**	

N 1 *(of person, animal)* nom *m*; *(of company)* ra[i]son *f* sociale; *Fin (of account)* intitulé *m*; *(of ship)* devise *f*, nom *m*; *(of play, novel etc)* titre *m*; **full** [n.] nom et prénoms *mpl*; **what's your n.?** quel est vo[]tre nom?, comment vous appelez-vous?; **my n.** [is] **Richard** je m'appelle Richard; **what n. shall I say** *(to caller)* qui dois-je annoncer?; **the house is i**[n] **his wife's n.** la maison est au nom de sa femme; **I know her only by n.** je ne la connais que de nom; **she knows all the children by n.** elle connaît l[e] nom de tous les enfants; **to mention sb/sth by n.** nommer qn/qch; **he is known** *or* **he goes by the n. of Penn** il est connu sous le nom de Penn, il s[e] fait appeler Penn; **someone by** *or* **of the n. of Pen**[n] quelqu'un du nom de *ou* qui s'appelle Penn; *Am Fam* **a guy n. of Jones** un type du nom de Jones; [I] **know it by** *or* **under a different n.** je le connai[s] sous un autre nom; **he writes novels under the n. of A.B. Alderman** il écrit des romans sous l[e] pseudonyme de A.B. Alderman; **our dog answers to the n. of Oscar** notre chien répond a[u] nom d'Oscar; **to put a n. to a face** mettre u[n] nom sur un visage; **you were mentioned by n.** o[n] a cité votre nom, on vous a nommé; **have you pu**[t] **your n. down for evening classes?** est-ce que vou[s] vous êtes inscrit aux cours du soir?; **she was hi**[s] **wife in all but n.** ils n'étaient pas mariés, mai[s] c'était tout comme; **to take sb's n.** *(of police offic*[er]*)* prendre le nom de qn; *Ftbl* donner un carto[n] jaune à qn; *Ftbl* **he had his n. taken** il a eu un ca[r]ton jaune; **he is president in n. only** il n'a de prés[i]dent que le nom, c'est un président san[s] pouvoir; **what's in a n.?** on n'a pas toujours l[e] nom que l'on mérite; **to call sb names** injurier o[u] insulter qn; **she called me a rude n.** elle m'a in[]sulté; **money is the n. of the game** c'est une affair[e] d'argent; **not to have a penny/a decent pair o**[f] **shoes to one's n.** ne pas avoir un centime/un paire de chaussures convenable à soi; **to have several books to one's n.** être l'auteur de plusieurs livres; **the company trades under the n. of Scandia** la société a pour dénomination Scandia

2 *(sake, authority)* nom *m*; **in the n. of freedom** au nom de la liberté; **in God's n.!, in the n. of God!** pour l'amour de Dieu!; *Fam* **what in the n. of God** *or* **Heaven are you doing?** que diable faites-vous là?; **in the n. of the law** au nom de la loi; **halt in the n. of the King!** halte-là, au nom du Roi!

3 *(reputation ▸ professional or business)* nom *m*, réputation *f*; **to make** *or* **to win a n. for oneself** se faire un nom *ou* une réputation; **we have the company's (good) n. to think of** il faut penser au renom de la société; **they have a n. for efficiency** ils ont la réputation d'être efficaces; **to have a good/bad n.** avoir (une) bonne/mauvaise réputation; **to get a bad n.** se faire une mauvaise réputation

4 *(famous person)* nom *m*, personnage *m*; **he's a big n. in the art world** c'est une figure de proue du monde des arts; **all the great political names were there** tous les ténors de la scène politique étaient présents; **famous n.** *(person)* célébrité *f*

VT 1 *(give name to ▸ person, animal)* nommer, appeler, donner un nom à; *(▸ ship, discovery)* baptiser; **they named the baby Felix** ils ont appelé *ou* prénommé le bébé Felix; **to n. sb after sb** *or Am* **for sb** donner à qn le nom de qn; **someone named Thompson** un nommé Thompson

2 *(give name of)* désigner, nommer; *(cite)* citer, mentionner; **the journalist refused to n. his source** le journaliste a refusé de révéler *ou* de donner le nom de son informateur; **you n. it, we've got it** demandez-nous n'importe quoi, nous l'avons; **n. the books of the Old Testament** citez les livres de l'Ancien Testament; **to n. names** donner des noms; **naming no names** sans nommer personne; **he is named as one of the consultants** son nom est cité *ou* mentionné en tant que consultant; *Law* **to n. sb as a beneficiary** *(in one's will)* désigner qn comme bénéficiaire; *Law* **to n. sb as a witness** citer qn comme témoin; **to n. and shame** dénoncer publiquement les responsables

3 *(appoint)* nommer, désigner; *(day, date)* fixer; **she has been named as president** elle a été nommée présidente; **22 June has been named as the date for the elections** la date du 22 juin a été retenue *ou* choisie pour les élections; **n. your price** votre prix sera le mien, dites votre prix

▸▸ *Mktg* ***name brand*** marque *f*; ***name day*** *(of person)* fête *f*; *Br Cin & Theat* ***name part*** vrai rôle *m*; *(title role)* = rôle qui donne son titre à la pièce ou au film; *Mktg* ***name product*** marque *f*

name-calling **N** *(UNCOUNT)* insultes *fpl*, injures *fpl*

name-dropper **N she's an awful n.** à la croire, elle connaît tout le monde

name-dropping **N** = allusion fréquente à des personnes connues dans le but d'impressionner

nameless ['neɪmlɪs] **ADJ 1** *(anonymous, unmentioned)* sans nom, anonyme; *(unknown ▸ grave, writer)* anonyme, inconnu; **someone who shall remain n.** quelqu'un que je ne nommerai pas; **to remain n.** garder l'anonymat **2** *(indefinable ▸ fear, regret)* indéfinissable, indicible **3** *(atrocious ▸ crime)* innommable, sans nom, inouï

namely ['neɪmlɪ] **ADV** c'est-à-dire, à savoir

nameplate ['neɪmpleɪt] **N** plaque *f*; **manufacturer's n.** plaque *f* du fabricant *ou* du constructeur

namesake ['neɪmseɪk] **N** homonyme *m*; **she's my n.** nous portons toutes les deux le même nom

nametape ['neɪmteɪp] **N** nom *m (du propriétaire, sur ses vêtements)*

Namibia [nə'mɪbɪə] **N** Namibie *f*

Namibian [nə'mɪbɪən] **N** Namibien(enne) *m,f*

ADJ namibien

COMP *(embassy)* de Namibie; *(history)* de la Namibie

naming ['neɪmɪŋ] **N 1** *(gen)* attribution *f* d'un nom; *(of ship)* baptême *m* **2** *(citing)* mention *f*, citation *f* **3** *(appointment)* nomination *f*

nan [næn] **N** *Br Fam (grandmother)* grand-mère *f*; *(term of address)* mémé *f*, mamie *f*

nancy (boy) ['nænsɪ-] *Fam* **N** *(effeminate man)* chochotte *f*; *(homosexual man)* homo *m*

ADJ *(effeminate)* de chochotte, de tapette

nandrolone ['nændrɪləʊn] **N** *Pharm* nandrolone *f*

nang [næŋ] **ADJ** *Br Fam* super, génial

nanny ['nænɪ] *(pl* **nannies) N 1** *(child carer ▸ nowadays)* garde *mf* d'enfants; *(▸ formerly)* nurse *f*, bonne *f* d'enfants **2** *Br Fam (grandmother)* grand-mère *f*; *(term of address)* mémé *f*, mamie *f*

▸▸ ***nanny goat*** chèvre *f*; ***the nanny state*** l'État *m* paternaliste

nanoengineering [ˌnænəʊendʒɪ'nɪərɪŋ] **N** nano-ingénierie *f*

nanosecond ['nænəʊˌsekənd] **N** nanoseconde *f*

nanotechnology ['nænəʊˌteknɒlədʒɪ] **N** nanotechnologie *f*

nap [næp] *(pt & pp* **napped**, *cont* **napping) N 1** *(sleep)* somme *m*; **afternoon n.** sieste *f*; **to take** *or* **to have a n.** faire un petit somme; *(after lunch)* faire la sieste

2 *Tex* poil *m*; **cloth with raised n.** étoffe *f* molletonnée *ou* tirée à poil *ou* garnie; **against the n.** à rebrousse-poil, à rebours

3 *(card game)* = jeu de cartes ressemblant au whist

4 *(in horseracing)* tuyau *m* sûr

VI *(sleep ▸ gen)* faire un (petit) somme; *(▸ in afternoon)* faire la sieste; *Fig* **to be caught napping** *(off guard)* être pris au dépourvu

VT 1 *Tex (cloth)* lainer, gratter; *(velvet)* brosser **2** *(in horseracing)* désigner comme favori, donner gagnant; **to n. a winner** donner un tuyau sûr

napalm ['neɪpɑːm] **N** napalm *m*

VT bombarder au napalm

▸▸ ***napalm bomb*** bombe *f* au napalm

nape [neɪp] **N n. (of the neck)** nuque *f*

naphtha ['næfθə] **N** *Chem* naphta *m*

naphthalene, naphthaline ['næfθəliːn] **N** *Chem* naphtalène *m*; *(for mothballs)* naphtaline *f*

napkin ['næpkɪn] **N 1** *(on table)* serviette *f* (de table) **2** *Br Formal (for baby)* couche *f* **3** *Am* **(sanitary) n.** serviette *f* hygiénique

▸▸ ***napkin ring*** rond *m* de serviette

Napoleon [nə'pəʊlɪən] **PR N** Napoléon; **N. Bonaparte** Napoléon Bonaparte

Napoleonic [nəˌpəʊlɪ'ɒnɪk] **ADJ** napoléonien

▸▸ ***the Napoleonic Code*** le Code Napoléon; ***the Napoleonic Wars*** les guerres *fpl* napoléoniennes

nappy ['næpɪ] *(pl* **nappies) N** *Br* couche *f* (pour bébé)

ADJ *Am (fabric)* feutré

▸▸ *Br* ***nappy liner*** change *m* (jetable); *Br* ***nappy rash*** érythème *m* fessier; **babies often get n. rash** les bébés ont souvent les fesses rouges et irritées

narc [nɑːk] **N** *Am Fam (narcotics agent)* agent *m* de la brigade des stups

narcissism ['nɑːsɪsɪzəm] **N** narcissisme *m*

narcissistic [ˌnɑːsɪ'sɪstɪk] **ADJ** narcissique

narcissus [nɑː'sɪsəs] *(pl* **inv** *or* **narcissuses** *or* **narcissi** [-aɪ]) **N** narcisse *m*

narcosis [nɑː'kəʊsɪs] **N** narcose *f*

narcotic [nɑː'kɒtɪk] **ADJ** narcotique

N 1 *Pharm* narcotique *m* **2** *Am (illegal drug)* stupéfiant *m*; **narcotics** *(department)* brigade *f* des stupéfiants

▸▸ ***narcotics agent*** agent *m* de la brigade des stupéfiants; ***narcotics squad*** brigade *f* des stupéfiants

nark [nɑːk] *Fam* **N 1** *Crime slang (informer)* mouchard(e) *m,f* **2** *Am (narcotics agent)* agent *m* de la brigade des stups

VT *Br (annoy)* foutre en rogne *ou* en boule; **to get narked** s'énerver, s'exciter; **she's really narked about it** ça l'énerve vraiment

VI *Crime slang (inform)* moucharder; **to n. on sb** balancer qn

narky ['nɑːkɪ] *(compar* **narkier**, *superl* **narkiest) ADJ** *Br Fam* ronchon

narrate [*Br* nə'reɪt, *Am* 'næreɪt] **VT 1** *(relate ▸ story)* raconter, *Literary* narrer; *(▸ event)* faire le récit de, relater **2** *(read commentary for)* lire *ou* dire le commentaire de; **the film was narrated by an American actor** le commentaire du film a été lu *ou* dit par un acteur américain

narration [*Br* nə'reɪʃən, *Am* næ'reɪʃən] **N 1** *(narrative)* narration *f* **2** *(commentary)* commentaire *m*

narrative ['nærətɪv] **ADJ** narratif

N 1 *Literature* narration *f* **2** *(story)* histoire *f*, récit *m*

▸▸ ***narrative writer*** narrateur(trice) *m,f*

narrator [*Br* nə'reɪtə(r), *Am* 'næreɪtə(r)] **N** narrateur(trice) *m,f*

narrow ['nærəʊ] **ADJ 1** *(not wide ▸ street, passage, valley)* étroit; *(tight ▸ skirt, shoe)* étroit, serré; *(long ▸ nose)* mince; *(▸ face)* allongé; **to grow** *or* **to become narrow(er)** se rétrécir; **to have n. shoulders** être petit de carrure, ne pas être large d'épaules; **to have a n. face** être mince de visage; **to have a n. waist** avoir la taille fine

2 *(scant, small ▸ advantage, budget, majority)* petit, faible; *(close ▸ result)* serré; **it was another n. victory/defeat for the French side** l'équipe française l'a encore emporté de justesse/a encore perdu de peu; **we had a n. escape** on l'a échappé belle; **by a n. margin** de peu; **to win/lose by the narrowest of margins** gagner/perdre de très peu

3 *(restricted ▸ scope, field, research)* restreint, limité; *(strict ▸ sense, interpretation)* restreint, strict; **in the narrowest sense of the word** au sens le plus strict du mot

4 *(bigoted, illiberal ▸ mind, attitude)* borné, étroit; *(▸ person)* borné; **to take a n. view of sth** adopter un point de vue étroit sur qch

5 *Formal (detailed ▸ search)* minutieux, détaillé; **we were subjected to n. scrutiny** nous avons été soumis à un examen minutieux

6 *Ling (vowel)* tendu

VT 1 *(make narrow ▸ road)* rétrécir; **to n. one's eyes** plisser les yeux **2** *(reduce ▸ difference, gap)* réduire, restreindre; *(limit ▸ search)* limiter, restreindre; **the police have narrowed their search to a few streets in central Leeds** la police concentre ses recherches sur quelques rues du centre de Leeds

VI 1 *(become narrow ▸ road, space)* se rétrécir, se resserrer; **the old man's eyes narrowed** le vieil homme plissa les yeux **2** *(be reduced ▸ difference, choice)* se réduire, se limiter; *(▸ number, majority)* s'amenuiser, se réduire; **the gap between rich and poor has narrowed** l'écart entre les riches et les pauvres s'est resserré

• **narrows NPL** *(gen)* passage *m* étroit; *(of river)* étranglement *m*

▸▸ ***narrow boat*** péniche *f* (étroite); ***narrow gauge*** voie *f* étroite; *Fin* ***narrow money*** = ensemble des billets et pièces de monnaie en circulation

▸ **narrow down VT SEP** *(limit ▸ choice, search)* limiter, restreindre; *(reduce ▸ majority, difference)* réduire; **that narrows it down to two suspects** cela nous laisse avec *ou* nous ramène à deux suspects

VI *(search)* se limiter, se restreindre; **the choice narrowed down to just two people** il ne restait que deux personnes en lice

narrowcast ['nærəʊkɑːst] **VT** diffuser localement

VI diffuser des émissions destinées à un public spécialisé

narrowing ['nærəʊɪŋ] **N** *Med (of artery etc)* rétrécissement *m*; *Fig (of choice)* réduction *f*

narrowly ['nærəʊlɪ] **ADV 1** *(barely)* de justesse, de peu; **he n. avoided capture** il s'en est fallu de peu qu'il (ne) soit capturé; **she n. missed being run over** elle a failli se faire écraser **2** *(closely)* de près, étroitement **3** *Formal (strictly)* de manière stricte, rigoureusement

narrow-minded **ADJ** *(person)* étroit d'esprit, borné; *(attitude, opinions)* borné

narrow-mindedness [-'maɪndɪdnɪs] **N** *(of person)* étroitesse *f* d'esprit; *(of attitude, opinions)* caractère *m* borné

narrowness ['nærəʊnɪs] **N 1** *(of path, shoulders, passage etc)* étroitesse *f*, *(of someone's nose, waist)* minceur *f*; *(of space)* exiguïté *f* **2** *(of majority, advantage)* faiblesse *f* **3** *(of intelligence)* faiblesse *f*; **n. of mind** étroitesse *f* d'esprit

narwal, narwhal, narwhale ['nɑːwəl] **N** *Zool* narval *m*

NASA ['næsə] **N** *Am (abbr* **National Aeronautics and Space Administration***)* NASA *f*

nasal ['neɪzəl] **ADJ 1** *Anat & Ling* nasal; **the n. cavities** les fosses *fpl* nasales; **to have a n. voice** parler du nez **2** *(voice, sound)* nasillard

N *Ling* nasale *f*

nasalize, -ise ['neɪzəlaɪz] **VT** *Ling* nasaliser

nasally ['neɪzəlɪ] **ADV** *Ling* de manière nasale; *(speak)* d'une voix nasillarde

nascent ['neɪsənt] **ADJ 1** *(in early stages)* naissant; **a n. rebellion** un début de rébellion **2** *Chem* naissant

Nasdaq® ['næzdæk] **N** *St Exch (abbr* **National Association of Securities Dealers Automated Quotation***)* le Nasdaq® *(Bourse américaine des valeurs technologiques)*

nastily ['nɑːstɪlɪ] **ADV 1** *(unpleasantly ▸ answer, remark)* méchamment, avec méchanceté **2** *(seriously ▸ burnt, bitten)* gravement

nastiness ['nɑːstɪnɪs] **N 1** *(of person)* méchanceté *f*; *(of remark, behaviour)* méchanceté *f*, malveillance *f* **2** *(unpleasantness)* caractère *m* très désagréable; **the n. of the weather** le mauvais temps **3** *(of injury)* gravité *f*

nasturtium [nəs'tɜːʃəm] **N** capucine *f*

nasty ['nɑːstɪ] *(compar* **nastier**, *superl* **nastiest**, *pl* **nasties***)* **ADJ 1** *(mean, spiteful ▸ person)* mauvais, méchant; *(▸ remark, rumour)* désagréable, désobligeant; **to be n. to sb** être méchant avec qn; **to turn n.** devenir méchant; **that was a n. thing to do** c'était vraiment méchant de faire ça; **he's got a n. temper** il a un sale caractère; **what a n. man!** quel homme désagréable *ou* déplaisant!; **n. trick** vilain tour, *Fam* sale tour; *Fam* **he's a n. piece of work** c'est un sale individu *ou* un sale type

2 *(unpleasant ▸ smell, taste, impression, surprise)* mauvais, désagréable; *(▸ weather, job)* sale; *(▸ crime)* atroce; **a n. war** une sale guerre; **to give sb a n. fright** faire une peur bleue à qn; **it was a very n. moment!** on a passé un mauvais moment!; **things started to turn n.** la situation a pris une vilaine tournure; **the weather turned n.** le temps s'est dégradé

3 *(in children's language) (dragon, giant, wolf)* vilain, méchant

4 *(ugly, in bad taste)* vilain, laid; **n. plastic flowers** d'horribles fleurs artificielles

5 *(serious ▸ sprain, burn, disease)* grave; **a n. cold** un gros rhume; **she had a n. accident** elle a eu un grave accident; **she's had a n. attack of bronchitis** elle a fait une mauvaise bronchite; **he's had quite a n. blow to the head** il a pris un mauvais coup sur la tête

6 *(dangerous ▸ bend, junction)* dangereux

7 *(difficult ▸ problem, question)* difficile, épineux

8 *(book, film, scene ▸ violent)* violent, dur; *(▸ obscene)* obscène, indécent

9 *Am Fam (excellent)* super *(inv)*, génial; **she makes a n. pizza** elle fait super bien la pizza

N 1 *(person)* méchant(e) *m,f*; **protect your computer from viruses and other nasties** protégez votre ordinateur contre les virus et autres programmes nuisibles **2** *Fam (obscene film)* film *m* porno; *(violent film)* film *m* violent□

natal ['neɪtəl] **ADJ** natal

natality [neɪ'tælətɪ] *(pl* **natalities***)* **N** (taux *m* de) natalité *f*

natch [nætʃ] *Fam* **EXCLAM** bien sûr!□

nation ['neɪʃən] **N 1** *(country)* pays *m*, nation *f*; **the British n.** la nation britannique **2** *(people)* nation *f*; **to address the n.** s'adresser à la nation; **the whole n. mourned** la nation tout entière était en deuil

▸▸ ***nation state*** État-nation *m*

national ['næʃənəl] **ADJ** national; **the n. newspapers** la presse nationale; **he became a n. hero** il est devenu un héros national; **a source of n. pride** une source de fierté nationale; **the killings caused a n. outcry** les assassinats ont scandalisé le pays; **on a n. scale** à l'échelle nationale; **it's not in the n. interest** ce n'est pas dans l'intérêt du pays

N 1 *(person)* ressortissant(e) *m,f*; **all EU nationals** tous les ressortissants des pays de l'Union européenne; **a French n.** un(e) Français(e) **2** *(newspaper)* journal *m* national

▸▸ ***national anthem*** hymne *m* national; ***National Assembly*** *(in Quebec, France)* Assemblée *f* nationale; *Br Old-fashioned* ***national assistance*** assistance *f* publique; *Br* ***the National Audit Office*** ≃ la Cour des comptes; *Am* ***national bank*** = banque agréée par le gouvernement américain et qui doit faire partie du système bancaire fédéral; *Tel* ***national call*** appel *m* national; ***national costume*** costume *m* national; ***the National Curriculum*** = programme introduit en 1988 définissant au niveau national (Angleterre et pays de Galles) le contenu de l'enseignement primaire et secondaire; *Fin* ***national debt*** dette *f* publique, dette *f* de l'État; ***national dress*** costume *m* national; *Br Pol* ***the National Executive Committee*** = comité chargé de définir la ligne d'action du parti travailliste; *Br* ***National Extension College*** centre *m* d'enseignement à distance; ***the National Front*** = parti d'extrême droite britannique; ***national government*** *(central)* gouvernement *m* central; *(coalition)* gouvernement *m* de coalition; ***national grid*** *Br Elec* réseau *m* national d'électricité; *Geog* réseau *m*; ***the National Guard*** *(in the US)* la Garde nationale *(armée nationale américaine composée de volontaires)*; ***the National Health (Service)*** = système créé en 1946 en Grande-Bretagne et financé par l'État, assurant la gratuité des soins et des services médicaux, ≃ la Sécurité sociale; **to get treatment on the N. Health (Service)** se faire soigner sous le régime de la Sécurité sociale; ***national hunt (racing)*** courses *fpl* d'obstacles; ***national income*** revenu *m* national; *Br* ***National Insurance*** = système britannique de sécurité sociale (maladie, retraite) et d'assurance chômage; ***National Insurance contributions*** cotisations *fpl* à la Sécurité sociale; ***National Insurance number*** numéro *m* de Sécurité sociale; ***National League*** = l'une des deux ligues professionnelles de base-ball aux États-Unis; ***the National Lottery*** = loterie nationale britannique; ***the National Liberation Front*** le Front de libération nationale; ***national park*** parc *m* national; *Fin* ***national product*** produit *m* national; ***National Public Radio*** = réseau américain de stations de radio libres; ***national readership survey*** étude *f* nationale sur le lectorat; ***the National Rifle Association*** = association américaine défendant le droit au port d'armes; *Br* ***National Savings Bank*** ≃ Caisse *f* nationale d'épargne; ***National Savings certificate*** bon *m* de caisse d'épargne; *Pol* ***the National Security Council*** le Conseil de sécurité nationale; *Br* ***national service*** service *m* militaire; *Br* ***national serviceman*** appelé *m*, militaire *m* du contingent; *Pol* ***national socialism*** national-socialisme *m*; *Br* ***the National Trust*** = organisme non gouvernemental britannique assurant la conservation de certains paysages et monuments historiques; ***National Vocational Qualification*** = diplôme britannique professionnel national

> **NATIONAL HEALTH SERVICE**
>
> Le "National Health Service" ou "NHS" fut créé par le gouvernement travailliste en 1948, donnant accès à chacun aux soins médicaux gratuits. Cependant, suite notamment aux coupes budgétaires réalisées dans les années 80, le système de santé britannique entra dans une période de crise, peinant à faire face aux besoins de la population. Au cours des dernières années la polémique autour du NHS s'est intensifiée et à chaque élection l'avenir des services de santé est un enjeu majeur.

nationalism ['næʃənəlɪzəm] **N** nationalisme *m*

nationalist ['næʃənəlɪst] **N** nationaliste *mf*

ADJ nationaliste; **N. China** la Chine nationaliste

nationalistic [ˌnæʃənə'lɪstɪk] **ADJ** nationaliste

nationality [ˌnæʃə'nælətɪ] *(pl* **nationalities***)* **N** nationalité *f*; **what n. are you?** de quelle nationalité êtes-vous?, quelle est votre nationalité?; **to take** *or* **to adopt British n.** se faire naturaliser britannique

nationalization, -isation [ˌnæʃənəlaɪ'zeɪʃən] **N** nationalisation *f*

nationalize, -ise ['næʃənəlaɪz] **VT** nationaliser

nationalized, -ised ['næʃənəlaɪzd] **ADJ** nationalisé

▸▸ ***nationalized industry*** industrie *f* nationalisée

nationally ['næʃənəlɪ] **ADV** nationalement; **n. recognized qualification** un diplôme reconnu dans tout le pays; **a n. televised speech** un discours retransmis sur les chaînes nationales; **n., men still outnumber women in these sectors** sur l'ensemble du pays, les hommes sont toujours plus nombreux que les femmes dans ces secteurs

nationwide ['neɪʃənwaɪd] **ADJ** national; **a n. strike** une grève nationale; **n. survey** une enquête à l'échelle nationale

ADV à l'échelle nationale, dans tout le pays; **the speech was broadcast n.** le discours a été diffusé dans tout le pays

native ['neɪtɪv] **N 1** *(of country)* natif(ive) *m,f*, autochtone *mf*; *(of town)* natif(ive) *m,f*; **I'm a n. of Portland** je suis originaire de Portland, je suis né à Portland; **she's a n. of Belgium** elle est belge de naissance, elle est née en Belgique; **she speaks English like a n.** elle parle anglais comme si c'était sa langue maternelle *ou* comme les Anglais; *Hum Pej* **the natives** les autochtones *mpl* **2** *Pej (of colony)* indigène *mf* **3** *Bot (plant)* plante *f* indigène; *Zool (animal)* animal *m* indigène; *(species)* espèce *f* indigène; **this plant/animal is a n. of southern Europe** c'est une plante/un animal indigène au sud de l'Europe

ADJ 1 *(of birth ▸ country)* natal; *(▸ language)* maternel; **his n. London** Londres, sa ville natale; **he always writes in his n. Russian** il écrit toujours en russe, sa langue maternelle

2 *(by birth)* natif

3 *(indigenous ▸ resources)* du pays; *(▸ tribe, customs, labour)* indigène; *(▸ costume)* du pays, national; **to go n.** adopter les us et coutumes locaux

4 *(innate ▸ ability, attraction)* inné, naturel

5 *Bot & Zool* indigène, originaire; **n. to India** originaire de l'Inde

6 *Miner (ore, silver)* natif

▸▸ ***Native American*** Indien(enne) *m,f* d'Amérique, Amérindien(enne) *m,f*; ***Native Australian*** aborigène *mf* (d'Australia); ***native land*** pays *m* natal; *Ling* ***native speaker*** locuteur(trice) *m,f* natif(ive); **a n. speaker of French/German, a French/German n. speaker** une personne de langue maternelle française/allemande, un francophone/germanophone; **I'm not a n. speaker** ce n'est pas ma langue maternelle; ***native wit*** esprit *m* naturel

native-born **ADJ** indigène, natif; **a n. German** un(e) Allemand(e) de naissance

nativism ['neɪtɪvɪzəm] **N 1** *esp Am Pol* exclusivisme *m* en faveur des natifs **2** *Phil* innéisme *m* **3** *Psy* nativisme *m*

nativist ['neɪtɪvɪst] **N 1** *esp Am Pol* partisan(e) *m,f* de l'exclusivisme en faveur des natifs **2** *Phil* nativiste *mf*

nativity [nə'tɪvətɪ] *(pl* **nativities***)* **N** *Rel* **the N.** la Nativité

▸▸ ***Nativity play*** = pièce jouée par des enfants et représentant l'histoire de la Nativité; ***Nativity scene*** crèche *f*

NATO ['neɪtəʊ] **N** *(abbr* **North Atlantic Treaty Organization***)* l'OTAN *f*

natter ['nætə(r)] *Fam* **N** *Br* causerie *f*, causette *f*; **to have a n.** tailler une bavette, faire la causette

VI papoter; **what were you two nattering about?** de quoi étiez-vous en train de parler, tous les deux?□

natty ['nætɪ] *(compar* **nattier**, *superl* **nattiest***)* **ADJ** *Fam* **1** *(smart, neat ▸ person)* bien sapé; *(▸ dress)* chic□, qui a de l'allure□; **he's a n. dresser** il est toujours très bien sapé **2** *(clever ▸ device)* astucieux□

natural ['nætʃərəl] **ADJ 1** *(created by or existing in nature ▸ scenery, environment, light, resources, process)* naturel; **a n. harbour** un port naturel; **in a n. state** à l'état naturel; **the n. world** la nature

2 *(not artificial ▸ wood, finish)* naturel; **she's a n. redhead** c'est une vraie rousse

3 *(normal ▸ explanation, desire, wish)* naturel, normal; **it's only n. for her to be worried** *or* **that she should be worried** il est tout à fait normal *ou*

il est tout naturel qu'elle se fasse du souci; **I'm sure there's a perfectly n. explanation for it** je suis sûr qu'on peut l'expliquer de façon tout à fait naturelle; **death from n. causes** mort *f* naturelle; **in the n. course of events** dans le cours normal des choses; **my n. inclination would be to…** j'inclinerais naturellement à…; **one's** *or* **the n. reaction is to…** la réaction instinctive est de…; **as is (only) n.** comme de juste
4 *(unaffected ▸ person, manner)* naturel, simple
5 *(innate ▸ talent)* inné, naturel; **she's a n. organizer** c'est une organisatrice-née, elle a un sens inné de l'organisation
6 *(free of additives)* naturel
7 *(child)* naturel
8 *(real ▸ parents)* naturel
9 *Mus* naturel; *(after accidental)* bécarre *(inv)*; **G n.** sol *m* bécarre
10 *Math* naturel
ADV *Fam* **try to act n.!** soyez naturel!
N **1** *Fam (gifted person)* **she's a n.** elle a ça dans le sang; **as an actor, he's a n.** c'est un acteur-né; **she's a n. for the part** elle est faite pour ce rôle **2** *Mus* bécarre *m*
▸▸ ***natural break*** *(in film, text)* coupure *f* qui va de soi; **they reached a n. break in the meeting** ils arrivèrent à une étape de la réunion où il était naturel de faire une pause; ***natural childbirth*** accouchement *m* naturel; ***natural disaster*** catastrophe *f* naturelle; *Phys & Elec* ***natural frequency*** fréquence *f* propre; ***natural gas*** gaz *m* naturel; ***natural historian*** naturaliste *mf*; ***natural history*** histoire *f* naturelle; ***natural justice*** droits *mpl* naturels; ***natural language*** langage *m* naturel, langue *f* naturelle; ***natural law*** loi *f* naturelle; ***natural life*** *(of person, animal, company)* durée *f* de vie; *(of product)* durée *f* utile; **for the rest of his/her n. life** *(sentenced)* à perpétuité; ***natural medicine*** médecine *f* douce *ou* naturelle, physiothérapie *f*; *Math* ***natural number*** nombre *m* naturel; *Old-fashioned Phys* ***natural philosophy*** physique *f*; ***natural resources*** ressources *fpl* naturelles; ***natural science(s)*** *(UNCOUNT)* sciences *fpl* naturelles; ***natural selection*** sélection *f* naturelle; *Econ & Ind* ***natural wastage*** départs *mpl* volontaires et en retraite; ***natural yoghurt*** yaourt *m* nature

natural-born ADJ *(singer, leader etc)* -né; **n. Frenchwoman** Française *f* de naissance

naturalism ['nætʃərəlɪzəm] N naturalisme *m*

naturalist ['nætʃərəlɪst] N naturaliste *mf*

naturalistic [ˌnætʃərə'lɪstɪk] ADJ naturaliste

naturalization, -isation [ˌnætʃərəlaɪ'zeɪʃən] N **1** *(of alien, foreign word)* naturalisation *f* **2** *(of plant, animal)* acclimatation *f*

naturalize, -ise ['nætʃərəlaɪz] VT **1** *(person, expression, custom)* naturaliser; **to become naturalized** *(person)* se faire naturaliser **2** *(plant, animal)* acclimater
VI *Biol* s'acclimater

naturally ['nætʃərəlɪ] ADV **1** *(of course)* naturellement, bien sûr, bien entendu; **you have got the money? – n.!** tu as l'argent? – bien sûr!; **I was n. surprised** évidemment, cela m'a surpris; **she n. assumed that he was joking** naturellement, elle a cru qu'il plaisantait; **these questions were n. somewhat embarrassing for me** ces questions, comme vous le pensez bien, n'étaient pas sans m'embarrasser
2 *(by nature ▸ lazy)* de nature, par tempérament; *(▸ difficult)* naturellement, par sa nature; **n. curly hair** cheveux *mpl* qui frisent naturellement; **skiing comes n. to her** on dirait qu'elle a fait du ski toute sa vie; **it comes n. to him** c'est un don chez lui; **although it didn't come n., he forced himself to ask questions** bien que cela ne lui vienne pas naturellement, il se forçait à poser des questions
3 *(unaffectedly)* naturellement, de manière naturelle
4 *(in natural state ▸ occur)* naturellement, à l'état naturel; **n. occurring** présent à l'état naturel

naturalness ['nætʃərəlnɪs] N **1** *(unaffectedness)* naturel *m*, simplicité *f*; **his acting was impressive for its n.** le naturel de cet acteur était remarquable **2** *(natural appearance)* naturel *m*

nature ['neɪtʃə(r)] N **1** *(the natural world)* nature *f*; **N. can be cruel** la nature peut être cruelle; **to go back** *or* **to return to n.** retourner à la nature; **in a state of n.** à l'état de nature; *Hum (naked ▸ man)* en costume d'Adam; *(▸ woman)* en costume d'Ève; **the n.-nurture debate** le débat sur l'inné et l'acquis; **to let n. take its course** laisser faire la nature; **to draw/paint from n.** dessiner/peindre d'après nature; **to go against n.** aller contre la nature
2 *(character)* nature *f*, caractère *m*; **he has such a kind n.** il a une si bonne nature *ou* un si bon caractère; **it's not in her n. to struggle** ce n'est pas dans sa nature de lutter; **lazy by n.** paresseux de nature; **to appeal to sb's better n.** faire appel aux bons sentiments de qn; **human beings are by n. gregarious** l'homme est, par nature, un être sociable; **in the n. of things** dans la nature des choses
3 *(type)* nature *f*, type *m*, genre *m*; **an incident of a serious n.** un incident grave; **questions of a personal n.** des questions à caractère personnel; **do you sell chocolates or anything of that n.?** est-ce que vous vendez des chocolats ou ce genre de choses?; **something in the n. of a…** une espèce *ou* une sorte de…; *Formal* **what is the n. of your complaint?** quelle est la nature de votre réclamation?; *Admin* **n. of contents** *(on parcel)* désignation du contenu
▸▸ ***nature cure*** naturopathie *f*, naturothérapie *f*; ***nature lover*** amoureux(euse) *m,f* de la nature; *Br* ***nature reserve***, *Am* ***nature preserve*** réserve *f* naturelle; *Sch* ***nature study*** sciences *fpl* naturelles, histoire *f* naturelle; ***nature trail*** sentier *m* écologique

naturism ['neɪtʃərɪzəm] N *Br* naturisme *m*

naturist ['neɪtʃərɪst] *Br* N naturiste *mf*
ADJ naturiste

naught [nɔːt] N **1** *esp Am* = **nought 2** *Arch or Literary (nothing)* **their plans came to n.** leurs projets ont échoué *ou* n'ont pas abouti
ADV *Arch or Literary* nullement; **it matters n.** cela n'a aucune importance

naughtily ['nɔːtɪlɪ] ADV **1** *(mischievously)* avec malice, malicieusement; **to behave n.** se conduire mal, ne pas être sage, être vilain **2** *(suggestively)* avec grivoiserie

naughtiness ['nɔːtɪnɪs] N **1** *(disobedience)* désobéissance *f*, *(mischievousness)* malice *f*; **she will be punished for her n.** elle sera punie pour avoir désobéi **2** *(indecency)* grivoiserie *f*, gaillardise *f*

naughty ['nɔːtɪ] *(compar* **naughtier**, *superl* **naughtiest)** ADJ **1** *(child ▸ badly behaved)* méchant, désobéissant, vilain; *(▸ mischievous)* coquin, malicieux; **that was very n. of you** ce que tu as fait était très vilain; **you n. boy!** petit vilain! **2** *(indecent ▸ joke, story, postcard)* paillard, osé; *(▸ word)* vilain, gros (grosse) **3** *(sexy)* coquin; **n. underwear** dessous *mpl* coquins
▸▸ *Br Euph* ***naughty bits*** parties *fpl* honteuses; ***the naughty nineties*** ≃ la Belle Époque *(1890–1900)*

nausea ['nɔːzɪə] N **1** *(sickness)* nausée *f*; **to be overcome with n.** avoir mal au cœur, avoir des nausées **2** *Fig (disgust)* dégoût *m*, nausée *f*, écœurement *m*

nauseate ['nɔːzɪeɪt] VT *also Fig* donner la nausée à, écœurer; **the sight of blood nauseated him** en voyant le sang, il eut un haut-le-cœur

nauseating ['nɔːzɪeɪtɪŋ] ADJ *(food, sight, idea)* écœurant, qui donne la nausée; *(smell)* écœurant, nauséabond; *(person, behaviour)* écœurant, dégoûtant, répugnant; **the stench was n.** la puanteur vous levait *ou* soulevait le cœur; **in n. detail** avec des détails écœurants *ou* à donner la nausée

nauseatingly ['nɔːzɪeɪtɪŋlɪ] ADV à vous donner la nausée, à vous écœurer; **she was n. smug** elle prenait des airs écœurants de supériorité, elle était d'une supériorité écœurante

nauseous [*Br* 'nɔːzɪəs, *Am* 'nɔːʃəs] ADJ **1** *(revolting ▸ smell)* nauséabond, qui donne la nausée, écœurant **2** *(queasy ▸ person)* **to feel n.** avoir mal au cœur, avoir des nausées; **it made me feel n.** cela m'a levé *ou* soulevé le cœur **3** *Am Fam (disgusting)* dégueulasse

nautical ['nɔːtɪkəl] ADJ nautique, marin; *(term, expression)* de navigation, de marine; **he comes from a n. background** il vient d'une famille de marins
▸▸ ***nautical almanac*** éphémérides *fpl* nautiques; ***nautical club*** club *m* nautique; ***nautical mile*** mille *m* marin

nautilus ['nɔːtɪləs] N *Zool* nautile *m*

NAV [ˌeneɪ'viː] N *Fin (abbr* **net asset value)** valeur *f* d'actif net

naval ['neɪvəl] ADJ *(gen)* naval; *(power)* maritime
▸▸ ***naval architect*** architecte *mf* naval(e); *(for warships)* ingénieur *m* du génie maritime *ou* en construction navale; ***naval architecture*** construction *f* navale; ***naval base*** base *f* navale; ***naval college*** école *f* navale; ***naval dockyard*** arsenal *m* maritime; ***naval hospital*** hôpital *m* naval; ***naval officer*** officier *m* de marine; ***naval station*** base *f* navale; ***naval stores*** *(depot)* entrepôts *mpl* maritimes; *(supplies)* approvisionnements *mpl ou* matériel *m ou* fournitures *fpl* de navires; ***naval warfare*** guerre *f* navale

nave [neɪv] N **1** *(of church)* nef *f* **2** *(hub)* moyeu *m*

navel ['neɪvəl] N nombril *m*; *Fig* **to contemplate one's n.** se regarder le nombril, faire du nombrilisme
▸▸ ***navel orange*** navel *f*

navel-gazing [-'geɪzɪŋ] N nombrilisme *m*

navigability [nævɪgə'bɪlɪtɪ] N *(of water)* navigabilité *f*, *(of craft, balloon)* dirigeabilité *f*

navigable ['nævɪgəbəl] ADJ *(water)* navigable; *(craft, balloon)* dirigeable

navigate ['nævɪgeɪt] VT **1** *(seas)* naviguer dans *ou* sur; **to n. a ship** *(steer)* gouverner *ou* diriger un navire; *(plot path of)* calculer le parcours d'un navire; **to n. the Atlantic** traverser l'Atlantique (en bateau); **this river is difficult to n.** la navigation est difficile sur ce fleuve; **she navigated us successfully through Bombay** *(in car)* elle nous a fait traverser Bombay sans problèmes **2** *Fig* **she navigated her way across the crowded room** elle se fraya un chemin à travers la salle bondée **3** *Comput (Web site)* naviguer sur; **to n. the Net** naviguer sur l'Internet
VI **1** *(gen)* naviguer; **to n. by the stars** naviguer aux étoiles; **you drive and I'll n.** toi tu conduis et moi je prends la carte routière **2** *Comput (around Web site)* naviguer

navigating officer ['nævɪgeɪtɪŋ-] N officier *m* de navigation, officier *m* navigateur

navigation [ˌnævɪ'geɪʃən] N **1** *(act, skill of navigating)* navigation *f* **2** *Am (shipping)* navigation *f*, trafic *m* (maritime) **3** *Comput (around Web site)* navigation *f*
▸▸ ***navigation aids*** aides *fpl* à la navigation; ***navigation bar*** barre *f* de navigation; ***navigation lights*** *Aviat* feux *mpl* de position; *Naut* fanaux *mpl*, feux *mpl* de bord *ou* de route; ***navigation officer*** officier *m* de navigation, officier *m* navigateur

navigational [ˌnævɪ'geɪʃənəl] ADJ de (la) navigation; **his n. skills** ses talents de navigateur
▸▸ ***navigational aid*** aide *f* à la navigation

navigator ['nævɪgeɪtə(r)] N navigateur(trice) *m,f*; *(in a car)* copilote *mf*

navvy ['nævɪ] *(pl* **navvies)** N *Br Fam* terrassier *m*

navy ['neɪvɪ] *(pl* **navies)** N **1** *(service)* marine *f* (nationale); **to be** *or* **to serve in the n.** être dans la marine **2** *(warships collectively)* marine *f* de guerre; *(fleet)* flotte *f* **3** *(colour)* bleu *m* marine *(inv)*
ADJ **1** *(gen)* de la marine **2** *(colour)* (bleu) marine *(inv)*
▸▸ ***navy blue*** bleu *m* marine *(inv)*; *Br* ***Navy List*** ≃ liste *f* navale; ***navy patrol*** patrouille *f* navale; ***navy yard*** arsenal *m* maritime

nay [neɪ] ADV *Arch or Hum* voire, que dis-je; **I am astounded, n., disgusted** j'en suis ahuri, voire révolté; **I was asked, n. ordered to come** on m'a demandé, ou plutôt donné l'ordre, de venir
N vote *m* défavorable; **the nays have it** les non l'emportent

Nazarene [ˌnæzə'riːn] N Nazaréen(enne) *m,f*
ADJ nazaréen

Nazi ['nɑːtsɪ] N nazi(e) *m,f*
ADJ nazi

Nazification [ˌnɑːtsɪfɪˈkeɪʃən] **N** nazification *f*

Nazism [ˈnɑːtsɪzəm], **Naziism** [ˈnɑːtsɪˌɪzəm] **N** nazisme *m*

NB **1** (*written abbr* **nota bene**) NB **2** (*written abbr* **New Brunswick**) Nouveau-Brunswick *m*

NBC [ˌenbiːˈsiː] **N** *TV* (*abbr* **National Broadcasting Company**) = chaîne de télévision américaine
ADJ (*abbr* **nuclear, biological and chemical**) NBC
▸▸ ***NBC suit*** survêtement *m* de protection NBC; ***NBC weapons*** armes *fpl* NBC

NBV [ˌenbiːˈviː] **N** *Fin* (*abbr* **net book value**) valeur *f* comptable nette

NC **1** (*written abbr* **no charge**) gratuit **2** (*written abbr* **North Carolina**) Caroline *f* du Nord

NC-17 [ˌensiːˌsevənˈtiːn] **N** *Am Cin* = indique qu'un film est interdit aux moins de 17 ans

NCB [ˌensiːˈbiː] **N** *Br Formerly* (*abbr* **National Coal Board**) = ancien nom des charbonnages britanniques

NCO [ˌensiːˈəʊ] **N** *Mil* (*abbr* **non-commissioned officer**) sous-officier *m*

ND (*written abbr* **North Dakota**) Dakota *m* du Nord

NDP [ˌendiːˈpiː] **N** *Fin* (*abbr* **net domestic product**) produit *m* intérieur net

NE **1** (*written abbr* **Nebraska**) Nebraska *m* **2** (*written abbr* **New England**) Nouvelle-Angleterre *f* **3** (*written abbr* **north-east**) NE

Neanderthal, neanderthal [nɪˈændətɑːl] **N** **1** (*during Stone Age*) néandertalien *m* **2** *Fig Pej* (*uncouth man*) primate *m*
ADJ **1** (*during Stone Age*) néandertalien **2** *Fig Pej* (*primitive* ▸ *man*) fruste, primaire; (▸ *method, system*) primitif; (▸ *attitude*) primaire
▸▸ ***Neanderthal man*** l'homme *m* de Neandertal

neap [niːp] **N** morte-eau *f*
ADJ faible
▸▸ ***neap tide*** marée *f* de morte-eau

Neapolitan [ˌnɪəˈpɒlɪtən] **N** Napolitain(e) *m,f*
ADJ napolitain
▸▸ ***Neapolitan ice cream*** tranche *f* napolitaine

near- [nɪə(r)] **PREF** **n.-perfect** pratiquement *ou* quasi parfait; **a n.-disaster** un désastre évité de peu

NEAR [nɪə(r)]

> **PREP**
> • près de **1–3, 5** • proche de **2**
> • au bord de **5**
> **ADV**
> • près **1, 2** • proche **2**
> • quasi **3**
> **ADJ**
> • proche **1, 2, 5**
> **VT**
> • approcher de
> **VI**
> • approcher

(*compar* **nearer**, *superl* **nearest**)
PREP **1** (*in space*) près de; **n. Paris** près de Paris; **don't go n. the fire** ne t'approche pas du feu; **is there a chemist's n. here?** est-ce qu'il y a un pharmacien près d'ici *ou* dans le coin?; **she likes to have her family n. her** elle aime avoir sa famille près d'elle *ou* auprès d'elle; **n. the end of the book** vers la fin du livre; **I haven't been n. a horse since the accident** je n'ai pas approché un cheval depuis l'accident; **you can't trust him n. a gun** il est dangereux avec une arme à feu; **she wouldn't let anyone n. her** (*physically*) elle ne voulait pas qu'on l'approche; (*emotionally*) elle ne voulait être proche de personne
2 (*in time*) près de, proche de; **ask me nearer the time** repose-moi la question quand l'heure viendra; **n. the end of the film** vers la fin du film
3 (*similar to*) près de; **language that is nearer Latin than Italian** langue qui est plus près *ou* proche du latin que de l'italien; **that would be nearer the truth** ce serait plus près de la vérité; **nobody comes anywhere n. her** il n'y a personne à son niveau; **he's nowhere n. it!** (*with guess, calculation*) il n'y est pas du tout!
4 (*in amount or number*) **profits were n. the 30 percent mark** les bénéfices approchaient la barre des 30 pour cent; **it will cost nearer £5,000** ça coûtera plutôt dans les 5000 livres
5 (*on the point of*) près de, au bord de; **to be n. tears** être au bord des larmes; **n. death** sur le point de mourir
ADV **1** (*in space*) près, à côté, à proximité; **she lives quite n.** elle habite tout près; **to draw n.** s'approcher; **come nearer** venez plus près, approchez-vous; **to bring sth nearer (to)** rapprocher qch (de); **nearer and nearer** de plus en plus près; **so n. and yet so far!** c'est dommage, si près du but!; **n. at hand** tout près, à proximité
2 (*in time*) proche, près; **as the time drew n.** à mesure que le moment approchait; **it's getting n. to Christmas** Noël approche, c'est bientôt Noël
3 (*almost, bordering on*) **a n. impossible task** une tâche quasi *ou* quasiment *ou* pratiquement impossible; **it's n. freezing** il ne fait pas loin de zéro, la température avoisine zéro degré; **I came n. to leaving several times** j'ai failli partir plusieurs fois; **to be n. to death** être sur le point de mourir; **to be n. to tears** être au bord des larmes
4 (*idioms*) **those n. and dear to him** ceux qui le touchent de près, ses proches; **as n. as makes no difference** à peu de chose près, à quelque chose près; **as n. as I can remember** autant que je puisse m'en souvenir; **it's n. enough** ça va comme ça; **it's n. enough 50 lbs** ça pèse dans les 50 livres; **it's nowhere n. good enough** c'est loin d'être suffisant; **she's nowhere n. finished** elle est loin d'avoir fini; **there weren't anywhere n. enough people** il y avait bien trop peu de gens
ADJ **1** (*in space*) proche; **the n. edge** le bord le plus proche; **our n. neighbours** nos proches voisins; **the nearest post office** le bureau de poste le plus proche; **the n. front wheel** (*driving on left*) la roue avant gauche; (*driving on right*) la roue avant droite
2 (*in time*) proche; **when the time is n.** quand le moment approchera; **in the n. future** dans un proche avenir
3 (*virtual*) **it was a n. disaster** on a frôlé la catastrophe; **he found himself in n. darkness** il s'est retrouvé dans une obscurité quasi totale; **it was a n. thing** (*we only just escaped*) on l'a échappé belle, il était moins une; **I caught the train, but it was a n. thing** j'ai eu mon train de justesse; **it's the nearest you'll get to a bookshop in these parts** c'est ce que vous trouverez de mieux en matière de librairie par ici
4 (*in amount, number*) **to the nearest £10** à 10 livres près; **round it up/down to the nearest euro** arrondissez à l'euro supérieur/inférieur
5 (*closely related*) proche; **her nearest relatives** ses parents les plus proches; *Hum* **your nearest and dearest** vos proches
VT (*approach* ▸ *place, date, event*) approcher de; (▸ *state*) être au bord de; **the train was nearing the station** le train approchait de la gare; **he was nearing 70 when he got married** il allait sur ses 70 ans quand il s'est marié; **the book is nearing completion** le livre est sur le point d'être terminé; **we are nearing our goal** nous touchons au but; **we're nearing the point of no return** il sera bientôt trop tard pour faire marche arrière, on atteindra bientôt le point de non-retour
VI (*date, place*) approcher
▸▸ ***the Near East*** le Proche-Orient; **in the N. East** au Proche-Orient; ***near gale*** (*on Beaufort scale*) grand frais *m*; *Comput* ***near letter quality*** qualité *f* quasi-courrier; ***near letter quality printer*** imprimante *f* de qualité courrier; ***near miss*** (*gen*) & *Sport* coup *m* qui a raté de peu; (*between planes, vehicles etc*) collision *f* évitée de justesse; **it was a n. miss** (*accident*) on a frôlé l'accident; **that was a n. miss!** (*escape*) on l'a échappé belle!; **the two cars had a n. miss** les deux voitures ont bien failli se rentrer dedans; *Fin* ***near money*** quasi-monnaie *f*

nearby **ADV** [ˌnɪəˈbaɪ] (*near here*) près d'ici; (*near there*) près de là; **I live just n.** j'habite tout près d'ici; **is there a station n.?** est-ce qu'il y a une gare près d'ici *ou* à proximité?; **in a house n.** dans une maison voisine
ADJ [ˈnɪəbaɪ] **we stopped at a n. post office** nous nous sommes arrêtés dans un bureau de poste situé non loin de là

near-death experience **N** expérience *f* aux frontières de la mort

nearly [ˈnɪəlɪ] **ADV** **1** (*almost*) presque, à peu près; **I'm n. ready** je suis presque prêt; **we're n. there** on y est presque; **he's n. 80** il a près de *ou* presque 80 ans; **I n. fell** j'ai failli tomber; **I very n. didn't come** j'ai bien failli ne pas venir; **he very n. died** il a frôlé la mort; **he was n. crying** *or* **in tears** il était au bord des larmes; **n. new** (*clothes etc*) d'occasion **2** (*with negative*) **he's not n. as important as he likes to think** il est loin d'être aussi important qu'il le croit; **it's not n. as difficult as I thought** c'est bien moins difficile que je ne l'imaginais
▸▸ *Fam* ***nearly man*** espoir *m* raté

nearness [ˈnɪənɪs] **N** proximité *f*

nearside [ˈnɪəsaɪd] *Br* **N** (*when driving on right*) côté *m* droit; (*when driving on left*) côté *m* gauche
ADJ (*when driving on right*) (du côté) droit, du côté trottoir; (*when driving on left*) (du côté) gauche, du côté trottoir; **keep to the n. lane** serrez (*in Britain*) à gauche *ou* (*in France etc*) à droite

nearsighted [ˌnɪəˈsaɪtɪd] **ADJ** *Am* myope

nearsightedness [ˌnɪəˈsaɪtɪdnɪs] **N** *Am* myopie *f*

neat [niːt] **ADJ** **1** (*tidy* ▸ *person*) ordonné, qui a de l'ordre; (▸ *in one's appearance*) net, soigné; (▸ *work, handwriting*) soigné; (▸ *exercise book*) bien tenu, propre; (▸ *desk, room*) net, bien rangé; (▸ *garden*) bien tenu *ou* entretenu, soigné; **her clothes are always n.** ses vêtements sont toujours impeccables; **he's a n. worker** son travail est très soigné; **she made a n. job of it** elle a fait du bon travail; **the surgeon made a n. job of those stitches** le chirurgien a très bien fait ces points de suture; **as n. as a new pin** tiré à quatre épingles; **n. and tidy** propre et net; **her room is always n. and tidy** sa chambre est toujours impeccable
2 (*trim* ▸ *waist, figure*) mince
3 (*skilful, clever* ▸ *turn of phrase, answer etc*) bien tourné, adroit; (▸ *solution*) ingénieux; **that's a n. trick** c'est malin
4 (*effective* ▸ *organization*) net, efficace; (▸ *system, plan*) bien conçu; **a n. little gadget** un petit gadget bien conçu;
5 *Am Fam* (*great*) chouette; **that's really n.** c'est vraiment chouette, c'est super
6 (*undiluted* ▸ *spirits*) sec (sèche), sans eau; **to take** *or* **drink one's whisky n.** boire son whisky sec
EXCLAM *Am Fam* super!, chouette!

neaten [ˈniːtən] **VT** (*room, house*) remettre en ordre, ranger; (*garden*) ranger; (*clothing*) arranger, ajuster; (*hair*) arranger, mettre en ordre; (*presentation*) fignoler, peaufiner; **you ought to n. (up) the place before they arrive** tu devrais mettre un peu d'ordre dans la maison avant qu'ils arrivent; **go and n. yourself up a bit** va t'arranger un peu

neatly [ˈniːtlɪ] **ADV** **1** (*tidily*) avec soin *ou* ordre; (*carefully* ▸ *write, work*) avec soin, soigneusement; **put the papers n. on the desk** posez les papiers soigneusement sur le bureau; **to dress n.** s'habiller avec soin; **the desk fits n. into the corner of the room** le bureau rentre pile dans le coin de la pièce **2** (*skilfully*) habilement, adroitement; **n. phrased** bien tourné; **you put that very n.** vous l'avez très bien dit *ou* exprimé; **he n. avoided the issue** il a habilement évité le sujet

neatness [ˈniːtnɪs] **N** **1** (*tidiness* ▸ *of dress*) aspect *m* soigné, netteté *f*; (▸ *of room*) ordre *m*; (▸ *of work*) aspect *m* soigné; (▸ *of exercise book*) propreté *f*; **a passion for n.** la passion de l'ordre; **the n. of her writing** l'élégance *f* de son écriture **2** (*skilfulness* ▸ *of phrase*) tournure *f* adroite; (▸ *of solution, idea*) ingéniosité *f*; (▸ *of scheme*) habileté *f* **3** (*prettiness* ▸ *of figure, legs*) finesse *f*

nebula [ˈnebjʊlə] (*pl* **nebulas** *or* **nebulae** [-liː]) **N** *Astron* nébuleuse *f*

nebulous [ˈnebjʊləs] **ADJ** **1** (*vague*) vague, flou, nébuleux **2** *Astron* nébulaire

NEC [ˌeniːˈsiː] **N** *Br* (*abbr* **National Exhibition Centre**) = parc d'expositions près de Birmingham en Angleterre

necessarily [ˌnesəˈserɪlɪ] **ADV** **1** (*gen*) nécessairement, forcément; **we don't n. have to go** rien ne nous oblige à partir, nous ne sommes pas forcés de partir; **not n.** pas forcément **2** (*inevitably*) inévitablement, forcément

necessary [ˈnesəsrɪ] (*pl* **necessaries**) **ADJ** **1** (*essential*) nécessaire, essentiel; (*indispensable*) indispensable; *(compulsory)* obligatoire; **water is n. to or for life** l'eau est indispensable à la vie; **is this visit really n.?** est-ce que cette visite est vraiment indispensable?; **it is n. for him to come** il est nécessaire qu'il vienne, il faut qu'il vienne; **circumstances made it n. to delay our departure** les circonstances nous ont obligés à retarder notre départ; **I'll do everything n. to make her agree** je ferai tout pour qu'elle accepte; **he did no more than was (absolutely) n.** il n'a fait que le strict nécessaire; **if n.** *(if forced)* s'il le faut; *(if need arises)* le cas échéant, si besoin est; **will you make the n. arrangements?** pouvez-vous prendre les dispositions nécessaires? **2** *(inevitable)* nécessaire, inéluctable; **a n. evil** un mal nécessaire

N 1 *Br Fam* **to do the n.** faire le nécessaire[a] **2** *Br Fam (cash)* **have you got the n.?** tu as de quoi payer?[a] **3 the necessaries** *(food, money etc)* ce qu'il faut pour vivre; *Law (means to live)* le nécessaire

necessitate [nɪ'sesɪteɪt] **VT** *Formal* nécessiter, rendre nécessaire; **family problems have necessitated his resignation** des problèmes familiaux l'ont obligé *ou* contraint à démissionner

necessitous [nɪ'sesɪtəs] **ADJ** *Formal* nécessiteux, démuni, pauvre

necessity [nɪ'sesətɪ] *(pl* **necessities***)* **N 1** *(need)* nécessité *f*, besoin *m*; **there is no n. for drastic measures** il n'y a pas lieu de prendre des mesures draconiennes; **there's no real n. for us to go** nous n'avons pas vraiment besoin d'y aller, il n'est pas indispensable que nous y allions; **the n. for** *or* **of keeping careful records** la nécessité de prendre des notes détaillées; **if the n. should arise** si le besoin se faisait sentir; **in case of absolute n.** en cas de force majeure; **out of** *or* **by** *or* **through n.** par nécessité, par la force des choses; *Prov* **n. has no law** nécessité fait loi; *Prov* **n. is the mother of invention** = en cas de besoin on trouve toujours une solution **2** *Formal (poverty)* besoin *m*, nécessité *f* **3** *(essential)* chose *f* nécessaire *ou* essentielle; **the basic** *or* **bare necessities of life** les choses qui sont absolument essentielles *ou* indispensables à la vie; **a car is not one of life's necessities** une voiture n'est pas indispensable; **it's one of life's necessities** c'est un élément vital

• **of necessity ADV** nécessairement

neck [nek] **N 1** *(part of body)* cou *m*; **he threw his arms round her n.** il s'est jeté à son cou, il lui a sauté au cou; **water was dripping down my n.** l'eau me coulait dans le cou; **to get a stiff n.** attraper le torticolis; *Fig* **he's always breathing down my n.** il est tout le temps sur mon dos; **to be up to one's n. in work** avoir du travail par-dessus la tête, être débordé de travail; **they were up to their necks in debt** ils étaient endettés jusqu'au cou; **I'm up to my n. in trouble** j'ai des ennuis par-dessus la tête; **the problem is still hanging round my n.** je n'ai toujours pas résolu ce problème; **to risk one's n.** risquer sa peau; *Br Fam* **she'll get it in the n.** ça va chauffer pour son matricule; *Br Fam* **it's n. or nothing** ça passe ou ça casse; *Fig* **to stick one's n. out** prendre des risques; *(commit oneself)* s'engager

2 *Culin (of lamb)* collet *m*; *(of beef)* collier *m*

3 *Sport* **to win by a n.** gagner d'une encolure; **to be n. and n.** être à égalité; **the two candidates are n. and n.** les deux candidats sont au coude à coude

4 *(narrow part or extremity ▸ of bottle, flask)* goulot *m*, col *m*; *(▸ of pipe)* tuyau *m*; *(▸ of womb, femur)* col *m*; *(▸ of violin)* manche *m*; *(▸ of bolt, tooth)* collet *m*

5 *Geog (peninsula)* péninsule *f*, presqu'île *f*; *(strait)* détroit *m*; **a n. of land** une langue de terre; **in our n. of the woods** par chez nous; **what are you doing in this n. of the woods?** qu'est-ce que tu fais dans le coin?

6 *(of dress, pullover)* col *m*, encolure *f*; **a low n.** un décolleté; **a dress with a low n.** une robe décolletée; **high n.** col *m* montant; **square/round n.** encolure *f* carrée/ronde; **what n. size** *or* **what size n. do you take?** combien faites-vous de tour de cou?

7 *Br Fam (cheek)* toupet *m*, culot *m*; **you've got a n.!** tu ne manques pas de culot!; **she's got some n.!** elle a un sacré culot!

VI *Fam (couple)* se peloter

▸▸ ***neck brace*** minerve *f*

neckband ['nekbænd] **N** *(ribbon, piece of jewellery)* tour *m* de cou; *(on garment)* col *m*, bande *f* d'encolure

neckerchief ['nekətʃɪf] **N** foulard *m*

necklace ['neklɪs] **N** collier *m*

necklet ['neklɪt] **N** collier *m*

neckline ['neklaɪn] **N** col *m*, encolure *f*; **her dress had a low/plunging n.** elle avait une robe décolletée/très décolletée

necktie ['nektaɪ] **N** *Am* cravate *f*

neckwear ['nekweə(r)] **N** *Com* = cravates et foulards

necrology [ne'krɒlədʒɪ] **N** nécrologie *f*

necromancer ['nekrəˌmænsə(r)] **N** nécromancien(enne) *m,f*

necromancy ['nekrəˌmænsɪ] **N** nécromancie *f*

necrophilia [ˌnekrə'fɪlɪə] **N** nécrophilie *f*

necrophobia [ˌnekrə'fəʊbɪə] **N** nécrophobie *f*

necropolis [ne'krɒpəlɪs] **N** nécropole *f*

necrosis [ne'krəʊsɪs] *(pl* **necroses** [-siːz]*)* **N** *Med* nécrose *f*

nectar ['nektə(r)] **N** *Bot & Fig* nectar *m*

nectarine ['nektərɪn] **N** nectarine *f*

ned [ned] **N** *esp Scot Fam* lascar *m*

NEDC [ˌeniːˌdiː'siː] **N** *Br Formerly (abbr* **National Economic Development Council***)* = agence nationale britannique de développement économique supprimée en 1992

neddy ['nedɪ] *(pl* **neddies***)* *Fam* **N 1** *Br (donkey)* baudet *m* **2** *Austr (horse)* canasson *m*; **to go to the neddies** aller aux courses

née, nee [neɪ] **ADJ** *Formal* **Evelyn Mulwray, n. Cross** Evelyn Mulwray, née Cross

NEED [niːd] **VT 1** *(as basic requirement)* avoir besoin de; **she needs rest** elle a besoin de repos *ou* de se reposer; **I n. more money/time** j'ai besoin de plus d'argent/de temps; **have you got everything you n.?** est-ce que tu as tout ce qu'il te faut?; **he likes to feel needed** il aime se sentir indispensable; **you only n. to ask** vous n'avez qu'à demander; **you don't n. me to tell you that** vous devez le savoir mieux que moi; **these facts n. no (further) comment** ces faits se passent de commentaire; **it needs a great deal of skill to do it properly** il faut beaucoup d'habileté pour le faire correctement; **it needs more patience than I have** cela exige *ou* requiert plus de patience que je n'en ai

2 *(would benefit from)* **I n. a drink/a shower** j'ai besoin de boire quelque chose/de prendre une douche; **what he needs is a good hiding** ce qu'il lui faut, c'est une bonne correction; **this soup needs more salt** cette soupe manque de sel; **it's just what I n.** c'est exactement ce qu'il me faut; *Ironic* **that's all we n.!** il ne nous manquait plus que ça!; **the last thing we n. is someone like him snooping about the place** la dernière chose qu'il nous faut c'est bien que quelqu'un comme lui vienne fouiner par ici; **who needs money anyway?** de toute façon, l'argent n'a aucune importance; **your hair needs combing** vos cheveux ont besoin d'un coup de peigne; **I gave the car a much-needed wash** j'ai lavé la voiture, elle en avait bien besoin; **liquid nitrogen needs careful handling** *or* **to be handled with care** l'azote liquide demande à être manié avec précaution; **there are still a few points that n. to be made** il reste encore quelques questions à soulever

3 *(expressing obligation)* **to n. to do sth** avoir besoin de *ou* être obligé de faire qch; **I n. to be home by ten** il faut que je sois rentré *ou* je dois être rentré pour dix heures; **you n. to try harder** tu vas devoir faire *ou* il va falloir que tu fasses un effort supplémentaire; **he didn't n. to be told twice** il ne se l'est pas fait dire deux fois; **I'll help you – you don't n. to** je vais t'aider – tu n'es pas obligé

MODAL AUX V

> La forme modale de **need** est la même à toutes les personnes, et s'utilise sans **do/does**. (**he need only worry about himself**; **need she go?**; **it needn't matter.**)

you needn't come if you don't want to vous n'avez pas besoin de *ou* vous n'êtes pas obligé de venir si vous n'en avez pas envie; **you needn't wait** il est inutile que vous attendiez, inutile (pour vous) d'attendre; **I needn't tell you how important it is** je n'ai pas besoin de vous dire *ou* vous savez à quel point c'est important; **I needn't have bothered** je me suis donné bien du mal pour rien, ce n'était pas la peine que je me donne autant de mal; **the accident n. never have happened** cet accident aurait pu être évité; **no-one else n. ever know** ça reste entre nous; **n. I say more?** ai-je besoin d'en dire davantage *ou* plus?; **n. that be the case?** est-ce nécessairement *ou* forcément le cas?; **adults only n. apply** les adultes seuls peuvent postuler

N 1 *(necessity)* besoin *m*; **I feel the n. of some fresh air** *or* **to get some fresh air** j'ai besoin d'air; **phone me if you feel the n. for a chat** appelle-moi si tu as besoin de parler; **I have no n. of your sympathy** je n'ai que faire de votre sympathie; **there's no n. to adopt that tone** inutile d'employer ce ton; **there's no n. to hurry** rien ne presse, inutile de se presser; **I'll help with the dishes – no n., I've done them already** je vais vous aider à faire la vaisselle – inutile, c'est terminé; **without the n. for sth** sans nécessiter qch; **to be in n. of sth, to have n. of sth** avoir besoin de qch; **I'm in n. of help** j'ai besoin d'aide *ou* qu'on m'aide; **the ceiling is badly in n. of repair** le plafond a bien *ou* grand besoin d'être réparé; **should the n. arise** si cela s'avérait nécessaire, si le besoin s'en faisait sentir; *Hum* **your n. is greater than mine** vous en avez plus besoin que moi

2 *(requirement)* besoin *m*; **he saw to her every n.** il subvenait à ses moindres besoins; **that will meet my needs** cela fera mon affaire; **£1,000 should be enough for our immediate needs** 1000 livres devraient suffire pour répondre à nos besoins immédiats

3 *(poverty)* besoin *m*, nécessité *f*; *(adversity)* adversité *f*, besoin *m*; **to be in n.** être dans le besoin; **in my hour of n.** au moment où j'en ai eu besoin

• **needs ADV** *Prov* **needs must when the devil drives** nécessité fait loi; **if needs must, I'll go** s'il le faut absolument *ou* si c'est indispensable, j'irai

• **if need be, if needs be ADV** si besoin est, le cas échéant

▸▸ *Mktg* ***needs analysis*** analyse *f* des besoins; *Mktg* ***needs assessment*** estimation *f* des besoins; *Mktg* ***need set*** ensemble *m* de besoins; *Mktg* ***needs study*** étude *f* des besoins; *Mktg* ***needs and wants exploration*** exploration *f* des besoins et des désirs

needful ['niːdfʊl] **ADJ** *Formal* nécessaire, requis

N *Br Fam (what is necessary)* **to do the n.** faire le nécessaire[a]; **to find the n.** *(money)* trouver le fric

neediness ['niːdɪnɪs] **N** indigence *f*

needle ['niːdəl] **N 1** *Med & Sewing* aiguille *f*; *(for record player)* pointe *f* de lecture, saphir *m*; *(of pine tree)* aiguille *f*; *(spine ▸ of hedgehog)* piquant *m*; **it's like looking for a n. in a haystack** autant chercher une aiguille dans une botte de foin; *Fam* **I hate needles** j'ai horreur des piqûres![a]; *Fam Drugs slang* **to be on the n.** *(take drugs)* se piquer

2 *(as indicator ▸ in compass, on dial)* aiguille *f*

3 *Art* **engraving n.** pointe *f* pour taille douce, pointe *f* sèche

4 *Geol (rocky outcrop)* aiguille *f*, pic *m*

5 *(monument)* obélisque *m*; *(on top of building)* aiguille *f*, flèche *f*

6 *Fam* **to get the n.** *(become annoyed)* se foutre en boule *ou* en rogne; **to give sb the n.** foutre qn en boule *ou* rogne; *Br* **a bit of n. has crept into the match** les joueurs commencent à s'énerver *ou* disputent le match avec plus d'âpreté

VT *(irritate)* foutre en boule *ou* en rogne; **he's always needling her about her weight** il passe son temps à la charrier à propos de son poids; **they needled him into retaliating** à force d'être asticoté, il a fini par riposter

VI *Fam Drugs slang (inject drugs)* se shooter, se piquer

▸▸ *Br* ***needle bank, needle exchange*** distributeur-échangeur *m* de seringues; *Br* ***needle exchange scheme*** programme *m* d'échange de seringues;

Br Fam ***needle match*** match *m* âprement disputé; ***needle valve*** soupape *f* à pointeau

needlecord ['ni:dəlkɔ:d] **N** velours *m* mille-raies
COMP *(trousers, skirt)* en velours mille-raies

needlecraft ['ni:dəlkrɑ:ft] **N** travaux *mpl* d'aiguille

needle-nosed pliers **N** pince *f* à bec fin

needlepoint ['ni:dəlpɔɪnt] **N** *(embroidery)* broderie *f*, tapisserie *f*; *(lace)* dentelle *f* à l'aiguille

needless ['ni:dlɪs] **ADJ** *(unnecessary ▸ expense, effort, fuss)* superflu, inutile; *(▸ remark)* inopportun, déplacé; **n. to say I won't go** il va sans dire que je n'irai pas

needlessly ['ni:dlɪslɪ] **ADV** *(be rude, pedantic, worry)* inutilement; *(die, suffer, work)* pour rien

needletime ['ni:dəltaɪm] **N** *(for broadcasting records)* durée *f* de passage à l'antenne

needlewoman ['ni:dəl,wʊmən] *(pl* **needlewomen** [-,wɪmɪn]) **N** couturière *f*; **I'm no n.** je ne sais pas coudre

needlework ['ni:dəlwɜ:k] **N** *(UNCOUNT)* travaux *mpl* d'aiguille

needn't ['ni:dənt] = **need not**

need-to-know **ADJ information is given on a n. basis** les renseignements ne sont donnés qu'aux personnes concernées

needy ['ni:dɪ] *(compar* **needier**, *superl* **neediest)**
ADJ *(financially)* nécessiteux, indigent; *(emotionally)* en manque d'affection; **to be emotionally n.** manquer d'affection
NPL the n. les nécessiteux *mpl*

ne'er [neə(r)] *Literary* = **never ADV**

ne'er-do-well **N** bon (bonne) *m,f* à rien
ADJ bon à rien; **my n. cousins** mes bons à rien de cousins

nefarious [nɪ'feərɪəs] **ADJ** infâme, vil

nefariously [nɪ'feərɪəslɪ] **ADV** d'une manière infâme

nefariousness [nɪ'feərɪəsnɪs] **N** *(of deed, crime, behaviour)* infamie *f*; *(of person)* scélératesse *f*

neg *(written abbr* **negotiable)** négociable, à débattre

negate [nɪ'geɪt] **VT 1** *(deny)* réfuter, nier **2** *(nullify ▸ law)* abroger; *(▸ order)* annuler; *(▸ efforts)* réduire à néant; *(▸ argument, theory)* invalider, rendre non valide **3** *Gram* mettre au négatif

negation [nɪ'geɪʃən] **N 1** *(denial ▸ of fact, proposition)* négation *f* **2** *(nullification ▸ of someone's work, efforts)* anéantissement *m*

negative ['negətɪv] **ADJ** négatif; **don't be so n.** ne sois pas aussi négatif; **he's a very n. sort of person** c'est quelqu'un de très négatif; **she's always so n. about my plans** elle trouve toujours quelque chose à redire à mes projets; **the test was n.** le résultat de l'examen était négatif
N 1 *Gram* négation *f*; **in the n.** à la forme négative; **double n.** double négation *f*
2 *(answer)* réponse *f* négative, non *m inv*; **to reply in the n.** répondre négativement *ou* par la négative
3 *Phot* négatif *m*
4 *Elec & Phys* (pôle *m*) négatif *m*
VT 1 *(cancel ▸ instruction)* annuler; *(nullify ▸ effect)* neutraliser, réduire à néant **2** *(reject ▸ proposition, evidence)* rejeter, repousser **3** *(deny)* nier, réfuter
▸▸ *Fin* ***negative equity*** *(UNCOUNT)* plus-value *f* immobilière négative, = situation où l'acquéreur d'un bien immobilier reste redevable de l'emprunt contracté alors que son logement enregistre une moins-value; ***negative feedback*** *(in electronic circuit)* contre-réaction *f*, réaction *f* négative; *(in mechanical or cybernetic system)* feed-back *m* négatif, rétroaction *f* négative; *Fig* **we got a lot of n. feedback from the questionnaire** ce questionnaire a révélé de nombreuses réactions négatives; *Br Fin* ***negative income tax*** impôt *m* négatif sur le revenu; ***negative pole*** *(of magnet)* pôle *m* sud; *Psy* ***negative reinforcement*** renforcement *m* négatif; ***negative sign*** signe *m* moins *ou* négatif

negatively ['negətɪvlɪ] **ADV 1** *(in the negative)* négativement **2** *Elec & Phys* **n. charged** chargé négativement

negativism ['negətɪvɪzəm] **N** négativisme *m*

negativity [,negə'tɪvɪtɪ] **N** négativité *f*; **because of the n. of his attitude** à cause de son attitude négative; **to feel a lot of n. towards sb** avoir beaucoup de sentiments négatifs contre qn

neglect [nɪ'glekt] **N 1** *(lack of attention, care ▸ of building, garden)* abandon *m*, manque *m* de soins *ou* d'entretien; *(▸ of child, invalid)* manque *m* de soins *ou* d'attention; *(▸ of people's demands, needs)* manque *m* d'égards; **out of** *or* **from** *or* **through n.** par négligence; **the roof fell in through n.** le toit s'est effondré faute d'entretien; **his n. of his children led to a court case** le fait qu'il néglige ses enfants a donné lieu à un procès; **to suffer from n.** *(person)* souffrir d'un manque de soins; *(building, garden)* être laissé à l'abandon; **his n. of his appearance** le peu d'intérêt qu'il accorde à son apparence **2** *(bad condition ▸ of building, garden)* délabrement *m*; **to be in a state of n.** être à l'abandon; **the buildings fell into n.** les bâtiments sont tombés en ruine **3** *(disregard ▸ of duty, promise, rules)* manquement *m*; **he was reprimanded for n. of duty** il a été réprimandé pour avoir manqué à ses devoirs
VT 1 *(fail to attend to, to care for ▸ building, garden)* négliger, laisser à l'abandon; *(▸ work)* négliger; *(▸ child, invalid, friend)* délaisser, négliger; **he neglects himself/his appearance** il se néglige, il se laisse aller; **you shouldn't n. your health** vous devriez vous soucier un peu plus de votre santé; **the garden looks neglected** le jardin est mal tenu *ou* à l'abandon; **he neglected his wife all evening** il n'a pas prêté la moindre attention à sa femme de toute la soirée; **are you feeling neglected?** est-ce que vous avez l'impression qu'on vous néglige? **2** *(disregard ▸ duty, promise)* manquer à; *(▸ advice)* ignorer **3** *Formal (omit, overlook)* omettre, oublier; **to n. to do sth** oublier *ou* omettre de faire qch; **they neglected to lock the door when they went out** ils ont oublié de fermer la porte à clé en sortant

neglectful [nɪ'glektfʊl] **ADJ** *(person, attitude)* négligent; **to be n. of sb/sth** négliger qn/qch; **to be n. of one's duty** manquer à ses devoirs; **to be n. of one's responsibilities/obligations** manquer à ses responsabilités/obligations; **he's very n. of his appearance** il ne prend aucun soin de sa tenue

negligee, negligée, negligé ['neglɪʒeɪ] **N** négligé *m*, déshabillé *m*

negligence ['neglɪdʒəns] **N** *(inattention)* négligence *f*; *(of duties, rules)* négligence *f*, manquement *m*; **due to** *or* **through n.** par négligence; **n. of basic precautions can be fatal** le non-respect des précautions élémentaires peut se révéler fatal

negligent ['neglɪdʒənt] **ADJ 1** *(neglectful)* négligent; **to be n. of one's duties** manquer à *ou* négliger ses devoirs **2** *(nonchalant ▸ attitude, manner)* nonchalant, négligent

negligently ['neglɪdʒəntlɪ] **ADV 1** *(carelessly)* négligemment, avec négligence; **he acted n.** il a fait preuve de légèreté; **they behaved n. towards their children** ils ont négligé leurs enfants **2** *(nonchalantly)* négligemment, nonchalamment

negligible ['neglɪdʒəbəl] **ADJ** négligeable, insignifiant

negotiability [nɪ,gəʊʃə'bɪlɪtɪ] **N** *Fin* négociabilité *f*

negotiable [nɪ'gəʊʃəbəl] **ADJ 1** *Fin (bonds, bill, document)* négociable; *(price, salary, fee)* négociable, à débattre; **not n.** non négociable; *Fin (on cheque)* non à ordre **2** *(road)* praticable; *(river ▸ navigable)* navigable; *(▸ crossable)* franchissable; **the path was not easily n.** le chemin n'était guère praticable
▸▸ *Fin* ***negotiable instrument*** instrument *m* négociable; *Fin* ***negotiable stock*** titres *mpl* négociables

negotiate [nɪ'gəʊʃɪeɪt] **VT 1** *(gen)* négocier; *Fin (business deal)* négocier, traiter; *(bill, document)* négocier, trafiquer; **price to be negotiated** prix *m* à débattre **2** *(manoeuvre round ▸ bend)* négocier; *(▸ rapids, obstacle)* franchir; *Fig (▸ difficulty)* franchir, surmonter
VI négocier; **the unions will have to n. with the management for higher pay** il faudra que les syndicats négocient une augmentation de salaire auprès de la direction; **to n. for peace** entreprer[illegible] dre des pourparlers de paix

negotiating table [nɪ'gəʊʃɪeɪtɪŋ-] **N** table *f* de négociations

negotiation [nɪ,gəʊʃɪ'eɪʃən] **N 1** *(discussion)* né[illegible]gociation *f*, pourparlers *mpl*; **to be in n. with s[illegible]** être en pourparler(s) avec qn; **to enter into n.[illegible] negotiations with sb** entamer des négociation[illegible] avec qn; **to break off/resume negotiations** rom[illegible]pre/reprendre les négociations; **pay/redu[illegible]dancy negotiations** négociations *fpl* sur le salaires/les licenciements; **peace negotiatior[illegible]** pourparlers *mpl* de paix; **the project is under [illegible]** le projet est en négociation **2** *(of bend, obstacle)* franchissement *m*

negotiator [nɪ'gəʊʃɪeɪtə(r)] **N** négociateu[illegible] (trice) *m,f*

Negress ['ni:grɪs] **N** *Old-fashioned* négresse *f*

Negro ['ni:grəʊ] *(pl* **Negroes)** *Old-fashioned* **N** nè[illegible]gre *m*
ADJ nègre
▸▸ ***Negro spiritual*** (negro) spiritual *m*

negroid ['ni:grɔɪd] **N** négroïde *mf*
ADJ négroïde

neigh [neɪ] **N** hennissement *m*
VI hennir

neighbour, *Am* **neighbor** ['neɪbə(r)] **N 1** *(wh[illegible] lives nearby)* voisin(e) *m,f*; **Britain's nearest n. [illegible] France** la France est le plus proche voisin de l[illegible] Grande-Bretagne **2** *Bible (fellow man)* prochai[illegible] (e) *m,f*; **love thy n. as thyself** aime ton prochai[illegible] comme toi-même
VT *Am* avoisiner
▸▸ ***neighbour states*** pays *mpl* voisins

▸ **neighbour on VT INSEP** *(adjoin)* avoisiner, êtr[illegible] contigu à; *(of country)* être limitrophe à

neighbourhood, *Am* **neighborhood** ['neɪbəhʊd] **N 1** *(district)* voisinage *m*, quartier *m*; **was in the n.** j'étais dans le coin *ou* dans le qua[illegible]tier *ou* dans le voisinage; **a very friendly n.** u[illegible] quartier très sympa; **the whole n.'s talking abou[illegible] it** tout le quartier en parle **2** *(vicinity)* **in the n. o[illegible]** *(place)* aux alentours de, dans les environs de; **there's some nice scenery in the n.** il y a de joli[illegible] paysages dans les environs **3** *Fig* **it'll cost you i[illegible] the n. of $1,000** cela vous coûtera dans les *ou* en[illegible]viron 1000 dollars; **a figure in the n. of £20,000** u[illegible] chiffre avoisinant les 20 000 livres
COMP *(police, shop, school)* du quartier
▸▸ ***Neighbourhood Watch*** = système par leque[illegible] les habitants d'un quartier s'entraident pour e[illegible] assurer la surveillance et la sécurité

neighbouring, *Am* **neighboring** ['neɪbərɪŋ] **ADJ** avoisinant, voisin

neighbourliness, *Am* **neighborliness** ['neɪbəlɪnɪs] **N** *(good)* **n.** (bons) rapports *mpl* de voi[illegible]sinage

neighbourly, *Am* **neighborly** ['neɪbəlɪ] **AD[illegible]** *(person)* amical; *(relations, visit)* de bon voisi[illegible]nage; **it was very n. of them** c'était très obligean[illegible] de leur part; **to be n.** être bon voisin, entreteni[illegible] de bonnes relations avec ses voisins; **peopl[illegible] used to be more n.** autrefois les gens entrete[illegible]naient de meilleurs rapports avec leurs voisins

neighing ['neɪɪŋ] **N** *(UNCOUNT)* hennisse[illegible]ment(s) *m(pl)*

neither ['ni:ðə(r), *Br* 'naɪðə(r)] **PRON** ni l'un ni l'au[illegible]tre; **n. of us is satisfied** nous ne sommes satisfait ni l'un ni l'autre; **n. (of them) eats fish** aucun de deux *ou* ni l'un ni l'autre ne mange de poisson; **which do you prefer? – n.!** lequel des deux préfères-tu? – ni l'un ni l'autre!
CONJ non plus; **Sandra can't swim and n. can I** Sandra ne sait pas nager, (et) moi non plus; **I haven't read it, n. do I intend to** je ne l'ai pas lu et d'ailleur[illegible] je n'en ai pas l'intention; **the funding wasn't avai[illegible]able and n. was the necessary expertise** ni le fonds ni les compétences nécessaires n'étaien[illegible] disponibles; **n. did/do/were we** (et) nous no[illegible] plus
ADV ni; **n.... nor... ni... ni...**; **it's n. good nor ba[illegible]** ce n'est ni bon ni mauvais; **that's n. here nor ther[illegible]** *(unimportant)* c'est sans importance; *(irrelevant)* là n'est pas la question; **I n. know nor care** c'es[illegible] vraiment le cadet de mes soucis; *Fam* **me n.** moi non plus!

ADJ aucun (des deux), ni l'un ni l'autre; **n. bottle is big enough** aucune des deux bouteilles n'est assez grande; **n. one of them has accepted** ni l'un ni l'autre n'a accepté

nelly ['nelɪ] N *Fam Br* **not on your n.!** jamais de la vie!, des clous!

nelson ['nelsən] N *(in wrestling)* double clé *f*; **full n.** nelson *m*; **half n.** simple prise *f* de tête à terre

nematode ['nemətəʊd] N nématode *m*

nemesis ['neməsɪs] N *Literary (person, organisation)* **she saw the British press as her n.** elle voyait dans la presse britannique l'instrument de sa perte; **to meet one's n.** *(be vanquished)* être vaincu; *(meet one's match)* trouver son maître

• **Nemesis** PR N *Myth* Némésis

neo- ['ni:əʊ] PREF néo-

neocapitalism [,ni:əʊ'kæpɪtəlɪzəm] N néocapitalisme *m*

neocapitalist [,ni:əʊ'kæpɪtəlɪst] N néocapitaliste *mf*

ADJ néocapitaliste

neoclassical [,ni:əʊ'klæsɪkəl] ADJ néoclassique

neoclassicism [,ni:əʊ'klæsɪsɪzəm] N néoclassicisme *m*

neocolonialism [,ni:əʊkə'ləʊnɪəlɪzəm] N néocolonialisme *m*

neofascism [,ni:əʊ'fæʃɪzəm] N néofascisme *m*

neofascist [,ni:əʊ'fæʃɪst] N néofasciste *mf*

ADJ néofasciste

neogothic [,ni:əʊ'gɒθɪk] *Archit* N néogothique *m*

ADJ néogothique

neoliberal [,ni:əʊ'lɪbərəl] *Pol* N néolibéral(e) *m,f*

ADJ néolibéral

neolithic, Neolithic [,ni:əʊ'lɪθɪk] ADJ néolithique; **the N. age** le néolithique

N néolithique *m*

neologism [ni:'ɒlədʒɪzəm] N néologisme *m*

neon ['ni:ɒn] N néon *m*

COMP *(lamp)* au néon

▸▸ ***neon lights*** néons *mpl*; ***neon sign*** enseigne *f* lumineuse (au néon)

neonatal [,ni:əʊ'neɪtəl] ADJ néonatal

neo-Nazi N néonazi(e) *m,f*

ADJ néonazi

neo-Nazism N néonazisme *m*

neophyte ['ni:əʊfaɪt] N néophyte *mf*

neoplasm ['ni:əʊ,plæzəm] N *Med* néoplasme *m*

neorealism [,ni:əʊ'rɪəlɪzəm] N néoréalisme *m*

neo-rural ADJ néorural

Nepal [nɪ'pɔ:l] N Népal *m*

Nepalese [,nepə'li:z] *(pl* **inv***)* N Népalais(e) *m,f*

ADJ népalais

Nepali [nɪ'pɔ:lɪ] N *(language)* népalais *m*

nephew ['nefju:] N neveu *m*

nephrite ['nefraɪt] N *Miner* néphrite *f*

nephritic [nɪ'frɪtɪk] ADJ *Med* néphrétique

nephritis [nɪ'fraɪtɪs] N *(UNCOUNT) Med* néphrite *f*; **to have n.** avoir une néphrite

nephron ['nefrɒn] N néphron *m*

nepotism ['nepətɪzəm] N népotisme *m*

Neptune ['neptju:n] PR N *Myth* Neptune

N *Astron* Neptune *f*

nerd [nɜ:d] N *Fam (stupid person)* crétin(e) *m,f*; *(unfashionable person)* ringard(e) *m,f*

nerdy ['nɜ:dɪ] ADJ *Fam (unfashionable)* ringard

Nereid ['nɪərɪɪd] *(pl* **Nereides** [nə'ri:ədi:z]*)* N *Astron & Myth* Néréide *f*

Nero ['nɪərəʊ] PR N *Antiq* Néron

nerve [nɜ:v] N **1** *(in body)* nerf *m*; **to take the n. out of a tooth** *(dentist)* dévitaliser une dent; *Fig* **to touch a raw n.** toucher une corde sensible

2 *(courage)* courage *m*; *(boldness)* audace *f*; *(self-control)* assurance *f*, sang-froid *m*; **it takes n. to say no to him** il faut du courage *ou* il faut avoir les nerfs solides pour lui dire non; **he didn't have the n. to say no** il n'a pas osé dire non, il n'a pas eu le courage de dire non; **his n. failed him, he lost his n.** *(backed down)* le courage lui a manqué; *(panicked)* il a perdu son sang-froid

3 *(cheek, audacity)* culot *m*; **he had the n. to refuse** il a eu le culot de refuser; *Fam* **you've got a n. coming here!** tu es gonflé de venir ici!; *Fam* **what a n.!** quel culot *ou* toupet!

4 *(vein ▸ in leaf, marble)* veine *f*, nervure *f*

VT *Formal* **to n. oneself to do sth** s'armer de courage pour faire qch; **to n. sb to do sth** encourager *ou* inciter qn à faire qch

• **nerves** NPL **1** *(agitated state)* nerfs *mpl*; *(anxiety)* nervosité *f*; *(before concert, exam, interview)* trac *m*; **to have a fit of nerves** avoir le trac; **to be in a state of nerves** être sur les nerfs; **to live on one's nerves** vivre sur les nerfs; **I'm a bundle of nerves** je suis un paquet de nerfs; **I need a drink to steady my nerves** il faut que je boive un verre pour me calmer **2** *(self-control)* nerfs *mpl*; **to have strong nerves/nerves of steel** avoir les nerfs solides/des nerfs d'acier; *Fam* **he gets on my nerves** il me tape sur les nerfs *ou* sur le système

▸▸ ***nerve cell*** cellule *f* nerveuse; ***nerve centre*** *Anat* centre *m* nerveux; *Fig (headquarters)* centre *m* névralgique; ***nerve ending*** terminaison *f* nerveuse; ***nerve fibre*** fibre *f* nerveuse; ***nerve gas*** gaz *m* neurotoxique *ou* innervant; ***nerve impulse*** influx *m* nerveux; *Med* ***nerve specialist*** neurologue *mf*

nerveless ['nɜ:vlɪs] ADJ **1** *(numb)* engourdi, inerte; **the revolver fell from his n. fingers** le revolver tomba de ses doigts inertes **2** *(weak)* sans force, mou (molle) **3** *(calm)* impassible, imperturbable; *(fearless)* intrépide

nerve-racking, nerve-wracking [-'rækɪŋ] ADJ *(experience)* éprouvant; *(suspense)* angoissant; **after a n. wait he was shown in** après une attente qui mit ses nerfs à rude épreuve, on le fit entrer

nerviness ['nɜ:vɪnɪs] N *Fam* **1** *Br (tension)* nervosité▫ *f* **2** *Am (impudence)* culot *m*

nervosity [nɜ:'vɒsɪtɪ] N *Med* nervosité *f*

nervous ['nɜ:vəs] ADJ **1** *(anxious, worried)* anxieux, appréhensif; *(shy)* timide, intimidé; *(uneasy)* mal à l'aise; *(agitated)* agité, tendu; *(tense)* tendu; **to be n.** *(before a performance, an exam etc)* avoir le trac; *(before going to the dentist etc)* avoir peur; **to be n. about sth** s'inquiéter à propos de qch; **I'm always n.** *or* **I always feel n. when he's around** je suis toujours tendu lorsqu'il est dans les parages; **don't be n.** détendez-vous, n'ayez pas peur; **I'm n. about speaking in public** j'ai peur *ou* j'appréhende de parler en public; **I was a bit n. about lending him the car** j'avais un peu d'appréhension à l'idée de lui prêter ma voiture; **he makes me n.** *(is intimidating)* il m'intimide; **don't hold your glass like that, you're making me n.** ne tiens pas ton verre comme ça, tu me rends nerveux *ou* tu me fais peur; **he is n. of Alsatians** les bergers allemands lui font peur; **he is n. of failure** il a peur de l'échec; **I'm always n. before exams** j'ai toujours le trac avant un examen; **airports make me n.** je me sens mal à l'aise dans les aéroports; *Fam* **he's a n. wreck** il est à bout de nerfs▫, il est à cran; **not for those of a n. disposition** à déconseiller aux âmes sensibles **2** *Anat (strain, illness)* nerveux

▸▸ ***nervous breakdown*** dépression *f* nerveuse; **to have a n. breakdown** avoir *ou* faire une dépression nerveuse; ***nervous disorder*** maladie *f* nerveuse; ***nervous energy*** énergie *f* nerveuse; ***nervous exhaustion*** fatigue *f* nerveuse; *Am Fam Pej* ***nervous Nellie*** poule *f* mouillée; ***the nervous system*** le système nerveux; ***nervous tension*** tension *f* nerveuse

nervously ['nɜ:vəslɪ] ADV *(anxiously)* anxieusement, avec inquiétude; *(tensely)* nerveusement; **he wondered n. if...** il se demanda, avec une certaine nervosité, si...

nervousness ['nɜ:vəsnɪs] N **1** *(worry)* anxiété *f*, inquiétude *f*; *(before exam, performance)* trac *m* **2** *(agitation)* nervosité *f*, agitation *f* (nerveuse), fébrilité *f*

nervy ['nɜ:vɪ] *(compar* **nervier**, *superl* **nerviest***)* ADJ *Fam* **1** *Br (tense)* énervé▫, excité▫ **2** *Am (cheeky)* culotté

nest [nest] N **1** *(of bird, wasps, snake etc)* nid *m*; *(nestful ▸ of fledgelings)* nichée *f*, couvée *f*; *(▸ of eggs)* couvée *f*; *Fig (den ▸ of brigands)* nid *m*, repaire *m*; *(▸ for machine guns)* nid *m*; *Fig* **the children have all left** *or* **flown the n.** les enfants ont tous quitté le nid familial **2** *(set)* **n. of tables** (série *f ou* ensemble *m* de) tables *fpl* gigognes

VI **1** *(bird)* (se) nicher, faire son nid **2** *(person)* **to go (bird) n.** *(find nests)* aller chercher des nids; *(steal eggs/birds)* aller dénicher des œufs/des oisillons **3** *(fit together)* s'emboîter

VT **1** *(tables, boxes)* emboîter **2** *Comput & Typ* imbriquer

▸▸ ***nest box*** *(in henhouse)* pondoir *m*; *(in birdhouse)* nichoir *m*; ***nest egg*** économies *fpl*, bas *m* de laine, pécule *m*

nested ['nestɪd] ADJ *Comput & Typ* imbriqué

nestful ['nestfʊl] N *(of fledgelings)* nichée *f*, couvée *f*; *(of eggs)* couvée *f*

nesting ['nestɪŋ] N *(building nests)* nidification *f*

COMP *(bird)* nicheur; *(time, instinct)* de (la) nidification

▸▸ ***nesting box*** *(in henhouse)* pondoir *m*; *(in birdhouse)* nichoir *m*

nestle ['nesəl] VT blottir; **to n. one's face against sb's shoulder** se blottir contre l'épaule de qn

VI **1** *(against person)* se blottir; *(in comfortable place)* se pelotonner; **to n. (up) close to sb** se pelotonner *ou* se blottir *ou* se serrer contre qn; **to n. (up) against sb's shoulder** se blottir contre l'épaule de qn; **to n. down in bed** se pelotonner dans son lit **2** *(land, house)* être niché *ou* blotti; **a village nestling in a valley** un village blotti *ou* tapi dans une vallée

nestling ['neslɪŋ] N oisillon *m*

.net ['dɒt'net] *Comput* = abréviation désignant les organismes officiels de l'Internet dans les adresses électroniques

net [net] *(pt & pp* **netted**, *cont* **netting***)* N **1** *(gen)* filet *m*; *Fig (trap)* filet *m*, piège *m*; *Fig* **to fall into the n.** tomber dans le piège; *Fig* **to slip through the n.** glisser *ou* passer à travers les mailles du filet

2 *Sport* filet *m*; **to come (up) to the n.** *(in tennis)* monter au filet; **to practise in the nets** *(in cricket)* = s'entraîner, un filet entourant les piquets; *Ftbl* **to put the ball in the (back of the) n.** marquer un but, envoyer la balle au fond des filets

3 *(for hair)* filet *m* à cheveux, résille *f*

4 *Tex* tulle *m*, filet *m*

5 *(network)* réseau *m*; **radio n.** ensemble *m* du réseau radiophonique

6 *(income, profit, weight)* net *m*; **n. payable** net *m* à payer

VT **1** *(catch ▸ fish, butterfly)* prendre *ou* attraper (au filet); *(▸ terrorist, criminal)* arrêter; **the police have netted the gang leaders** la police a mis la main sur les chefs de la bande

2 *(acquire ▸ prize)* ramasser, gagner; *(▸ fortune)* amasser

3 *Sport* **to n. the ball** *(in tennis)* envoyer la balle dans le filet; **he netted his service** *(in tennis)* son service échoua dans le filet; *Ftbl* **to n. a goal** marquer un but

4 *(cover with netting ▸ peas, strawberries etc)* recouvrir de filets *ou* d'un filet

5 *(of person, company)* gagner net; *(profit)* rapporter net; *(of sale)* produire net; **we netted over $10,000** nous avons réalisé un bénéfice net de plus de 10 000 dollars; **he nets £20,000 a year** il gagne 20 000 livres net par an

VI *Ftbl* marquer un but

ADJ **1** *(amount, weight, income, earnings, profit, loss)* net; **to earn £500 n.** gagner 500 livres net; **terms strictly n.** sans déduction **2** *(result)* final

ADV **n. of tax** net d'impôt; *Br* **n. of VAT** hors TVA

• **Net** N *Comput* **the N.** le Net, l'Internet *m*

▸▸ *Fin* ***net assets*** actif *m* net; *Br Formerly* ***the Net Book Agreement*** = accord entre maisons d'édition et libraires stipulant que ces derniers n'ont le droit de vendre aucun ouvrage à un prix inférieur à celui fixé par l'éditeur; *Fin* ***net book value*** valeur *f* comptable nette; *Fin* ***net capital expenditure*** mise *f* de fonds nette, dépenses *fpl* nettes d'investissement; ***net cord*** *(in tennis ▸ part of net)* corde *f* de filet; *(▸ shot)* let *m*, net *m*, filet *m*; ***net cord judge*** juge *m* de filet; *Fin* ***net cost*** prix *m* de revient; *Fin* ***net current assets*** actif *m* circulant net; ***net curtain*** rideau *m* (de tulle *ou* en filet), voilage *m*; *Fin* ***net dividend*** dividende *m* net; *Fin* ***net domestic product*** produit *m* intérieur net; *Fin* ***net national product*** produit *m* national net; *Sport* ***net play*** jeu *m* au filet; *Fin* ***net present value*** valeur *f* actuelle nette; *Fin* ***net realizable value*** valeur *f* réalisable nette

netball ['netbɔ:l] N net-ball *m (sport féminin proche du basket-ball)*

nethead ['nethed] N *Fam Comput* accro *mf* de l'Internet

nether ['neðə(r)] ADJ *Arch or Literary* bas, inférieur; *(lip)* inférieur; **the n. regions** les enfers *mpl*; *Hum (of body)* les parties *fpl* basses; *Hum (of building)* les profondeurs *fpl*

Netherlands ['neðələndz] NPL **the N.** les Pays-Bas *mpl*; **in the N.** aux Pays-Bas

netiquette ['netɪket] N *Fam Comput* netiquette *f*

netizen ['netɪzən] N *Comput* internaute *mf*

netspeak ['netspi:k] N langage *m* du Net, cyberjargon *m*

netting ['netɪŋ] N *(UNCOUNT)* **1** *(for strawberries, trees)* filet *m*, filets *mpl*; *(fencing)* treillis *m* (métallique), grillage *m* **2** *Tex (for curtains)* tulle *m*, filet *m* **3** *(of fish, butterfly)* prise *f* au filet

nettle ['netəl] N ortie *f*; *Br Fig* **to grasp the n.** prendre le taureau par les cornes
VT *Br* agacer, énerver
COMP *(soup)* aux orties
▸▸ ***nettle rash*** urticaire *f*

network ['netwɜ:k] N **1** *(gen), Elec & Rail* réseau *m*; *(of shops, hotels)* réseau *m*, chaîne *f*; *(of streets)* lacis *m*; *Mktg (for distribution, sales)* réseau *m*; **road n.** réseau *m* routier **2** *TV (national)* réseau *m*; *(channel)* chaîne *f* **3** *Comput* réseau *m*
VT **1** *TV (broadcast)* diffuser sur l'ensemble du réseau *ou* sur tout le territoire; **the programme wasn't networked** le programme n'a pas été diffusé (sur la chaîne nationale) **2** *Comput* mettre en réseau; **networked systems** systèmes *mpl* en réseau
VI **1** *Comput* faire partie du/d'un réseau, être raccordé au *ou* à un réseau **2** *(make contacts)* établir un réseau de contacts professionnels
▸▸ *Comput* ***network adaptor*** carte *f* réseau; *Comput* ***network administrator*** administrateur(trice) *m,f* de réseau; *Comput* ***network card*** carte *f* réseau; *Comput* ***network computer*** ordinateur *m* de réseau; *Comput* ***network interface card*** carte-adaptateur *f* réseau; *Comput* ***network traffic*** trafic *m* de réseau; ***network TV*** réseau *m* (de télévision) national

networking ['netwɜ:kɪŋ] N **1** *Comput (working method)* travail *m* en réseau; *(connecting as network)* mise *f* en réseau; **to have n. capabilities** *(terminal)* offrir la possibilité d'intégration à un réseau **2** *(gen) & Com* établissement *m* d'un réseau de liens *ou* de contacts

neural ['njʊərəl] ADJ neural
▸▸ *Comput* ***neural network*** réseau *m* neuronal

neuralgia [njʊ'rældʒə] N *(UNCOUNT) Med* névralgie *f*

neuralgic [njʊ'rældʒɪk] ADJ *Med* névralgique

neurasthenia [ˌnjʊərəs'θi:njə] N *(UNCOUNT) Old-fashioned Med* neurasthénie *f*

neurasthenic [ˌnjʊərəs'θenɪk] ADJ *Old-fashioned Med* neurasthénique

neuritis [ˌnjʊə'raɪtɪs] N *(UNCOUNT) Med* névrite *f*

neurobiology [ˌnjʊərəʊbaɪ'ɒlədʒɪ] N neurobiologie *f*

neurochemistry [ˌnjʊərəʊ'kemɪstrɪ] N neurochimie *f*

neurodegenerative [ˌnjʊərəʊdɪ'dʒenərətɪv] ADJ *Med* neurodégénératif

neurological [ˌnjʊərəʊ'lɒdʒɪkəl] ADJ neurologique

neurologist [ˌnjʊə'rɒlədʒɪst] N neurologue *mf*

neurology [ˌnjʊə'rɒlədʒɪ] N neurologie *f*

neuromuscular [ˌnjʊərəʊ'mʌskjʊlə(r)] ADJ neuromusculaire

neuron ['njʊərɒn], **neurone** ['njʊərəʊn] N *Biol* neurone *m*

neuropathology [ˌnjʊərəʊpə'θɒlədʒɪ] N neuropathologie *f*

neuropsychiatrist [ˌnjʊərəʊsaɪ'kaɪətrɪst] N neuropsychiatre *mf*

neuropsychologist [ˌnjʊərəʊsaɪ'kɒlədʒɪst] N neuropsychologue *mf*

neuroscience ['njʊərəʊsaɪəns] N neurosciences *fpl*

neurosis [ˌnjʊə'rəʊsɪs] *(pl* **neuroses** [-si:z]*)* N névrose *f*

neurosurgeon ['njʊərəʊˌsɜ:dʒən] N neurochirurgien(enne) *m,f*

neurosurgery [ˌnjʊərəʊ'sɜ:dʒərɪ] N neurochirurgie *f*

neurosurgical [ˌnjʊərəʊ'sɜ:dʒɪkəl] ADJ neurochirurgical

neurotic [ˌnjʊə'rɒtɪk] N névrosé(e) *m,f*
ADJ *(person)* névrosé; *(disease, behaviour)* névrotique; **a n. obsession** une névrose; *Fig* **he's positively n. about it** c'est une obsession chez lui; **don't be so n. about it!** tu ne vas pas en faire tout un plat *ou* une maladie!

neurotically [ˌnjʊə'rɒtɪkəlɪ] ADV de façon obsessionnelle; **to be n. obsessed with sth** avoir une obsession névrotique de qch

neuroticism [ˌnjʊə'rɒtɪsɪzəm] N neurasthénie *f*

neurotransmitter [ˌnjʊərəʊtrænz'mɪtə(r)] N neurotransmetteur *m*

neuter ['nju:tə(r)] N **1** *Gram* neutre *m*; **in the n.** au neutre **2** *(animal ▸ asexual)* animal *m* asexué; *(▸ castrated)* animal *m* châtré; *(insect, plant)* neutre *m*
ADJ **1** neutre **2** *Biol* neutre, asexué
VT châtrer

neutral ['nju:trəl] N **1** *Aut* point *m* mort; **in n.** au point mort **2** *Pol (person)* ressortissant(e) *m,f* d'un État neutre; *(state)* État *m ou* pays *m* neutre
ADJ neutre; *(policy)* de neutralité; **to remain n.** garder la neutralité, rester neutre

neutralism ['nju:trəlɪzəm] N neutralisme *m*

neutralist ['nju:trəlɪst] N neutraliste *mf*
ADJ neutraliste

neutrality [nju:'trælətɪ] N neutralité *f*

neutralization, -isation [ˌnju:trəlaɪ'zeɪʃən] N neutralisation *f*

neutralize, -ise ['nju:trəlaɪz] VT neutraliser; **to n. one another** *(chemical agents)* se neutraliser; *(forces)* se neutraliser, s'annuler

neutrino [nju:'tri:nəʊ] *(pl* **neutrinos***)* N *Phys* neutrino *m*

neutron ['nju:trɒn] N *Phys* neutron *m*
▸▸ ***neutron bomb*** bombe *f* à neutrons; ***neutron star*** étoile *f* à neutrons

Nev *(written abbr* **Nevada***)* le Nevada

never ['nevə(r)] ADV **1** *(not ever)* jamais; **I've n. been there** je n'y suis jamais allé; **I n. saw her again** je ne l'ai plus jamais *ou* jamais plus revue; **n. in (all) my life, n. in all my born days** jamais de la vie; **you n. know** on ne sait jamais; **n. before** *(until that moment)* jamais auparavant *ou* avant *ou* jusque-là; *(until now)* jamais jusqu'ici *ou* jusqu'à présent; **he's n. yet been wrong** jusqu'ici *ou* jusqu'à présent, il ne s'est jamais trompé; **n. ever do that again!** ne refais jamais cela!; **Darren, n. one to complain, said nothing** Darren, qui ne se plaint jamais, n'a rien dit; **n. again!** plus jamais ça!; *Fig* **n. say n.!** il ne faut jamais dire jamais!
2 *(used instead of "did not")* **she n. turned up** elle n'est pas venue; **I n. knew you cared** je ne savais pas que tu m'aimais
3 *(as intensifier)* **n. a one** pas même un seul; **I n. even asked if you wanted something to drink** je ne vous ai même pas offert (quelque chose) à boire; **he n. so much as blinked** il n'a même pas cillé; **n. fear** ne craignez rien, n'ayez crainte; **that will n. do!** *(it is unacceptable)* c'est inadmissible!; *(it is insufficient)* ça ne va pas!
4 *(in surprise, disbelief)* **you n. asked him to dinner!** vous ne l'avez quand même pas *ou* tout de même pas invité à dîner!; **you've n. lost your purse again!** ne me dis pas que tu as encore perdu ton porte-monnaie!; **she's n. 50!** ce n'est pas possible, elle ne peut pas avoir 50 ans!; *Br Fam* **well I n. (did)!** ça alors!, par exemple!
EXCLAM (ce n'est) pas possible!

never-ending ADJ *(complaints, noise)* incessant; *(task, sermon, evening)* interminable, qui n'en finit pas; **my problems seem to be n.** mes problèmes semblent ne pas en finir; **a n. supply of funny stories** un stock inépuisable d'histoires drôles; **housework is n.** le ménage n'est jamais fini

never-failing ADJ **1** *(infallible)* infaillible **2** *(en during)* inépuisable, intarissable

nevermore [ˌnevə'mɔ:(r)] ADV *Literary* jamai plus, plus jamais

never-never *Fam* N *Br & Austr (hire purchase)* **t buy sth on the n.** acheter qch à crédit[□] *ou* à tem pérament[□]
ADJ imaginaire, chimérique
▸▸ ***never-never land*** pays *m* de cocagne

nevertheless [ˌnevəðə'les] ADV **1** *(gen)* néan moins; **a small, but n. significant increase** une aug mentation faible mais néanmoins significative **we shall press on n. and hope things get bette** nous poursuivrons néanmoins nos efforts e espérant que les choses s'amélioreront; **she' not skied before but she insisted on coming wit us n.** elle n'avait jamais fait de ski mais elle quand même tenu à nous accompagner **2** *((start of clause or sentence)* cependant; **he says h never wants to see her again, n., I think he sti loves her** il dit qu'il ne veut plus jamais la revoi cependant je crois qu'il l'aime encore

NEW [nju:]

ADJ
- nouveau **1–5**
- neuf **1**
- autre **1**

N
- nouveau

(compar **newer**, *superl* **newest***)*
ADJ **1** *(gen)* nouveau(elle); *(different)* nouvea (elle), autre; *(unused)* neuf, nouveau(elle); **a r tablecloth** *(brand new)* une nouvelle nappe, un nappe neuve; *(fresh)* une nouvelle nappe, un nappe propre; **n. evidence** de nouvelles preuves **I don't want to get my n. gloves dirty** je ne veu pas salir mes nouveaux gants *ou* gants neufs **this dress isn't n.** ce n'est pas une robe neuve o une nouvelle robe, cette robe n'est pas neuve **would you like a n. glass?** *(for a different drink* désirez-vous un autre verre?; **we need some n ideas** il nous faut de nouvelles idées *ou* des idée neuves; **she likes her n. boss** elle aime bien so nouveau patron; **to look for n. business** faire d la prospection; **America was a n. country** *(just de veloping)* l'Amérique était un pays neuf; **under r management** *(sign)* changement de propriétaire **as** *or* **like n.** comme neuf; *(in advertisement)* éta neuf; **as good as n. (again)** *(clothing, carpet)* (nouveau) comme neuf; *(watch, electrical appl ance)* (à nouveau) en parfait état de marche; **t feel like a n. woman/man** se sentir revivre; **t make a n. woman/man of sb** transformer qn com plètement; *Prov* **there's nothing n. under the sun** n'y a rien de nouveau sous le soleil
2 *(latest, recent ▸ issue, recording, baby)* nouvea (elle); **is there anything n. on the catastrophe?** est ce qu'il y a du nouveau sur la catastrophe?; *Fan* **what's n.?** quoi de neuf?; *Fam* **(so) what's n.!, wha else is n.!** *(dismissive)* quelle surprise!; **that' nothing n.!** rien de nouveau à cela!
3 *(unfamiliar ▸ experience, environment)* nou veau(elle); **everything's still very n. to me her** tout est encore tout nouveau pour moi ici; *Far* **that's a n. one on me!** *(joke)* celle-là, on ne m l'avait jamais faite!; *(news)* première nouvelle *(experience)* on en apprend tous les jours!
4 *(recently arrived)* nouveau(elle); *(novice)* no vice; **you're n. here, aren't you?** vous êtes nou veau ici, n'est-ce pas?; **she's n. to the job** ell débute dans le métier; **we're n. to this area** nou venons d'arriver dans la région
5 *Culin (wine, potatoes, carrots)* nouveau(elle)
N nouveau *m*; **the cult of the n.** le culte du nou veau
ADV *(used to form compound adj)* nouvellement **n.-found** *(confidence, happiness)* tout neuf; *(frien etc)* nouveau(elle); **n.-laid egg** œuf fraîchemen pondu; **n. mown hay** foin fraîchement coupé
▸▸ *Fam* ***new blood*** sang *m* neuf; ***new boy Sc*** nouveau *m*, nouvel élève *m*; *(in office, team)* nou veau *m*; ***New Brunswick*** le Nouveau-Brunswick ***New Caledonia*** la Nouvelle-Calédonie *f*; ***the Nev Deal* 1** *Am Hist* le New Deal *(programme de ré formes sociales mises en place aux États-Unis pa le président Roosevelt au lendemain de la grand dépression des années 30)* **2** *Br Pol* = programm

du gouvernement Blair destiné à aider les jeunes à trouver un emploi; ***New Delhi*** New Delhi; ***New England*** la Nouvelle-Angleterre *f*; ***New Englander*** habitant(e) *m,f* de la Nouvelle-Angleterre; ***the New English Bible*** = texte de la Bible révisé dans les années 60; ***New Europe*** la nouvelle Europe; ***new girl*** *Sch* nouvelle (élève) *f*; *(in office, team)* nouvelle *f*; ***New Guinea*** la Nouvelle-Guinée; ***New Hampshire*** le New Hampshire; ***New Hebrides*** Nouvelles-Hébrides *fpl*; ***New Jersey*** le New Jersey; ***New Labour*** = nouveau nom donné au parti travailliste britannique vers le milieu des années quatre-vingt-dix dans le souci d'en moderniser l'image; *Br Pol* ***the New Left*** la nouvelle gauche; ***new look*** nouvelle image *f*; ***the New Look*** *(in post-war fashion)* le new-look; ***New Man*** homme *m* moderne *(qui participe équitablement à l'éducation des enfants et aux tâches ménagères)*; *Am* ***new math***, *Br* ***new maths*** les maths *fpl* modernes; ***the new media*** les nouveaux médias *mpl*; ***New Mexico*** le Nouveau-Mexique; ***new moon*** nouvelle lune *f*; ***New Orleans*** La Nouvelle-Orléans; *Com & Mktg* ***new product development*** développement *m* de nouveaux produits; ***the new rich*** les nouveaux riches *mpl*; *Pol* ***the New Right*** la nouvelle droite *f*; ***New Scotland Yard*** = siège de la police à Londres; ***New South Wales*** la Nouvelle-Galles du Sud; ***new technology*** nouvelle technologie *f*, technologie *f* de pointe; *Bible* ***New Testament*** Nouveau Testament *m*; *Br* ***new town*** ville *f* nouvelle; *Med* ***new variant CJD*** nouveau variant *m* de la maladie de Creutzfeld-Jacob; ***new wave*** *(in cinema)* nouvelle vague *f*; *(in pop music)* new wave *f*; ***the New World*** le Nouveau Monde; ***New Year*** Nouvel An *m*; **happy N. Year!** bonne année!; **to see in the N. Year** réveillonner *(le 31 décembre)*; *Am* ***New Year's*** *(day)* le premier de l'an; *(eve)* le soir du réveillon *ou* du 31 décembre; ***New Year's Day*** jour *m* de l'an; ***New Year's Eve*** Saint-Sylvestre *f*; *Br* ***the New Year's Honours List*** = titres et distinctions honorifiques décernés par la Reine à l'occasion de la nouvelle année et dont la liste est établie officieusement par le Premier ministre; ***New Year's resolutions*** résolutions *fpl* pour la nouvelle année; **have you made any N. Year's resolutions?** tu as des résolutions pour la nouvelle année?; ***New York (City)*** New York; ***New Yorker*** New-Yorkais(e) *m,f*; ***New York (State)*** l'État *m* de New York; ***New Zealand*** Nouvelle-Zélande *f*; ***New Zealander*** Néo-Zélandais(e) *m,f*

New Age ADJ New Age *(inv)*

▸▸ ***New Age traveller*** marginal(e) *m,f* itinérant *(vivant dans une communauté New Age)*

newbie ['nju:bɪ] N *Fam* **1** *Comput (Internet user)* internaute *mf* novice, cybernovice *mf* **2** *Am (new recruit)* bleu(e) *m,f*

newborn ['nju:bɔ:n] ADJ nouveau-né; **a n. baby** un(e) nouveau-né(e)

NPL **the n.** les nouveau-nés *mpl*

newcomer ['nju:ˌkʌmə(r)] N **1** *(new arrival)* nouveau(elle) venu(e) *m,f*; **she's a n. to the town** elle vient d'arriver dans la ville **2** *(beginner)* novice *mf*; **a good book for newcomers to computing** un bon livre pour les débutants en informatique; **I'm a n. to all this** tout cela est nouveau pour moi

newel ['nju:əl] N **1** *(on ordinary staircase)* pilastre *m* **2** *(in spiral staircase)* noyau *m* (d'escalier)

▸▸ ***newel post*** pilastre *m*

newfangled [ˌnju:'fæŋgəld] ADJ *Pej (idea, device)* nouveau(elle), dernier cri *(inv)*

Newfoundland ['nju:fəndlənd] N **1** *Geog* Terre-Neuve *f* **2** *(dog)* terre-neuve *m inv*

Newfoundlander ['nju:fəndləndə(r)] N Terre-Neuvien(enne) *m,f*

newish ['nju:ɪʃ] ADJ assez neuf *ou* nouveau(elle)

new-look ADJ new-look *(inv)*

newly ['nju:lɪ] ADV nouvellement, récemment; **n. arrived** récemment arrivé, arrivé de fraîche date; **the gate has been n. painted** la barrière vient d'être peinte; **n. dug** fraîchement creusé; **n. elected** nouvellement élu; **a n. discovered galaxy** une galaxie qu'on vient de découvrir *ou* récemment découverte; **their n. won independence** leur indépendance récemment conquise

▸▸ ***newly independent state*** nouvel État *m* indépendant; ***newly industrialized country*** pays *m* en voie d'industrialisation; ***newly industrialized economy*** économie *f* nouvellement industrialisée; *Br* ***newly qualified teacher*** = enseignant nouvellement formé

newlyweds ['nju:lɪwedz] NPL jeunes mariés *mpl*

newness ['nju:nɪs] N **1** *(of building)* nouveauté *f*; *(of shoes, carpet)* état *m* neuf **2** *(of ideas, experience, fashion)* nouveauté *f*, originalité *f*

news [nju:z] N *(UNCOUNT)* **1** *(information)* nouvelles *fpl*, informations *fpl*; **a piece of n.** une nouvelle, une information; **an interesting piece of n.** une nouvelle intéressante; **is there any more n. about** *or* **on the explosion?** est-ce qu'on a plus d'informations sur l'explosion?; **that's good/bad n.** c'est une bonne/mauvaise nouvelle; **to have n. of sb** avoir des nouvelles de qn; **have you had any n. of her?** avez-vous eu de ses nouvelles?; **what's your n.?** quoi de neuf (chez vous)?; **have I got n. for you!** j'ai du nouveau (à vous annoncer)!; **it's n. to me!** première nouvelle!, je l'ignorais!; **famine isn't n. any more** la famine ne fait plus la une (des journaux); **to be in the n., to make n.** faire parler de soi; **a city that is in the n. a lot these days** une ville dont on parle beaucoup ces jours-ci; **he's always in the n.** on parle toujours de lui dans la presse; **to break the n. (of sth) to sb** annoncer la nouvelle (de qch) à qn; **bad n. travels fast** les mauvaises nouvelles vont vite; *Fam* **he's bad n.** on a toujours des ennuis avec lui; *Prov* **no n. is good n.** pas de nouvelles, bonnes nouvelles

2 *Rad & TV* actualités *fpl*, informations *fpl*; *(bulletin)* journal *m*; **the 9 o'clock n.** *TV* le journal (télévisé) *ou* les informations de 21 heures; *Rad* le journal (parlé) *ou* les informations de 21 heures; **n. in brief** *(main headlines* ▸ *on news bulletin)* titres *mpl*; (▸ *in newspaper)* actualité *f* en résumé; *(miscellaneous news items)* faits *mpl* divers; **I heard it on the n.** je l'ai entendu aux informations; **the sports/financial n.** la page *ou* chronique sportive/financière

▸▸ ***news agency*** agence *f* de presse; *Am Rad & TV* ***news analyst*** commentateur(trice) *m,f*; ***news blackout*** black-out *m inv* sur l'actualité, censure *f* de l'actualité; **to impose a n. blackout on sth** empêcher la divulgation de qch; **the government has imposed a n. blackout** le gouvernement a fait le black-out; ***news broadcast*** informations *fpl*; ***news bulletin*** bulletin *m* d'informations; ***news channel*** chaîne *f* d'information continue; ***news conference*** conférence *f* de presse; ***news desk*** (salle *f* de) rédaction *f*; ***news editor*** rédacteur (trice) *m,f* en chef des actualités; ***news gathering*** collecte *f* de l'information; ***news headlines*** titres *mpl* de l'actualité; ***news item*** nouvelle *f*, information *f*; ***news magazine*** newsmagazine *m*; ***news programme*** magazine *m* d'actualités; *Comput* ***news reader*** logiciel *m* de lecture de nouvelles; ***news report*** bulletin *m* d'informations; ***news reporter*** reporter *m*; *Am* ***news service*** = agence de presse qui publie ses informations par le biais d'un syndicat de distribution; ***news stand*** kiosque *m* (à journaux); ***news story*** sujet *m*; ***news value*** intérêt *m* médiatique

newsagent ['nju:zˌeɪdʒənt] N *Br* marchand(e) *m,f* de journaux; *(shopkeeper also selling papers)* dépositaire *mf* de journaux; **n.'s (shop)** maison *f* de la presse; **at the n.'s** chez le marchand de journaux, à la maison de la presse

newscast ['nju:zkɑ:st] N *Rad* bulletin *m* d'informations; *TV* journal *m* télévisé, informations *fpl*

newscaster ['nju:zˌkɑ:stə(r)] N présentateur (trice) *m,f* du journal

newscasting ['nju:zˌkɑ:stɪŋ] N *Rad & TV* présentation *f* du journal

newsdealer ['nju:zˌdi:lə(r)] N *Am* marchand(e) *m,f* de journaux

newsflash ['nju:zflæʃ] N flash *m* d'informations

newsgroup ['nju:zgru:p] N *Comput* forum *m* de discussion, newsgroup *m*

newshawk ['nju:zhɔ:k], **newshound** ['nju:zhaʊnd] N *Fam* reporter[□] *m*, journaliste[□] *mf*

newsie ['nju:zɪ] N *Am Fam* **1** *(newspaper vendor)* vendeur(euse) *m,f* de journaux[□] **2** *(journalist)* journaleux(euse) *m,f*

newsletter ['nju:zˌletə(r)] N lettre *f*, bulletin *m* (d'informations); **monthly n.** bulletin *m* mensuel

newsman ['nju:zmən] *(pl* **newsmen** [-mən]) N journaliste *m*

newspaper ['nju:zˌpeɪpə(r)] N **1** *(publication)* journal *m*; **in the n.** dans le journal; **an evening n.** un journal du soir; **a daily n.** un quotidien **2** *(paper)* **wrapped in n.** enveloppé dans du papier journal

COMP *(article, report)* de journal

▸▸ ***newspaper advertisement*** publicité *f* presse; ***newspaper advertising*** *(UNCOUNT)* publicité *f* presse; ***newspaper clipping, newspaper cutting*** coupure *f* de presse; ***newspaper group*** groupe *m* de presse; ***newspaper kiosk*** kiosque *m* à journaux; ***newspaper rack*** porte-journaux *m*; ***newspaper reporter*** reporter *m* (de la presse écrite); ***newspaper stand*** kiosque *m* à journaux

newspaperman ['nju:zˌpeɪpəmæn] *(pl* **newspapermen** [-men]) N journaliste *m* (de la presse écrite)

newspaperwoman ['nju:zpeɪpəˌwʊmən] *(pl* **newspaperwomen** [-ˌwɪmɪn]) N journaliste *f* (de la presse écrite)

newsprint ['nju:zprɪnt] N papier *m* journal; **I got my hands covered in n.** *(ink)* je me suis mis de l'encre plein les mains

newsreader ['nju:zˌri:də(r)] N présentateur (trice) *m,f* du journal

newsreel ['nju:zri:l] N film *m* d'actualités

newsroom ['nju:zru:m] N **1** *Press* salle *f* de rédaction **2** *Rad & TV* studio *m*

newsstand ['nju:zstænd] N kiosque *m* (à journaux)

newswoman ['nju:zˌwʊmən] *(pl* **newswomen** [-ˌwɪmɪn]) N journaliste *f*

newsworthiness ['nju:zˌwɜ:ðɪnɪs] N intérêt *m* médiatique

newsworthy ['nju:zˌwɜ:ðɪ] ADJ **it's not n.** cela n'a aucun intérêt médiatique; **political scandal is always n.** les médias sont toujours friands *ou* la presse est toujours friande de scandales politiques

newsy ['nju:zɪ] *(compar* **newsier**, *superl* **newsiest)** ADJ *Fam (letter)* plein de nouvelles[□]

newt [nju:t] N *Zool* triton *m*; *Br very Fam* **pissed as a n.** soûl comme une bourrique, beurré comme un petit lu

new-wave ADJ *(cinema)* nouvelle vague *(inv)*; *(pop music)* new-wave *(inv)*

NEXT [nekst]

ADJ	
• prochain **1–3**	• suivant **1–3**
ADV	
• ensuite **1**	• la prochaine fois **2**
• la fois suivante **2**	
PRON	
• prochain, suivant	

ADJ **1** *(in time* ▸ *coming)* prochain; (▸ *already past)* suivant; **keep quiet about it for the n. few days** n'en parlez pas pendant les quelques jours qui viennent; **I had to stay in bed for the n. ten days** j'ai dû garder le lit pendant les dix jours qui ont suivi; **(the) n. day** le lendemain; **(the) n. morning/evening** le lendemain matin/soir; **n. Sunday, Sunday n.** dimanche prochain; **the n. Sunday** le dimanche suivant; **n. year** l'année prochaine; **this time n. year** d'ici un an; **the week/year after n.** dans deux semaines/ans; *Fam* **n. minute she was dashing off out again** une minute après, elle repartait[□]; **the situation's changing from one moment to the n.** la situation change sans arrêt; **(the) n. time I see him** la prochaine fois que je le vois *ou* verrai; **(the) n. time I saw him** quand je l'ai revu

2 *(in series* ▸ *in future)* prochain; (▸ *in past)* suivant; **the n. episode** *(in future)* le prochain épisode; *(in past)* l'épisode suivant; **the n. size up/down** la taille au-dessus/au-dessous; **their n. child was a girl** ensuite, ils eurent une fille; **your name is n. on the list** votre nom est le suivant *ou* prochain sur la liste; **the n. ten pages** les dix pages suivantes; **the n. before last** l'avant-dernier; **your train is the n. but one** ton train n'est pas le prochain, mais celui d'après; **ask the n. person you meet** demandez à la première personne que vous rencontrez; **(the) n. to arrive was Tanya** Tanya est arrivée à la suite; **the n. world** l'au-delà *m inv*; **(the) n. thing** ensuite; **and (the) n. thing I knew, I woke up in hospital** et l'instant d'après je me suis réveillé à l'hôpital

3 *(in space ▸ house, street)* prochain, suivant; **the n. room/house** *(next to this one)* la pièce/maison voisine *ou* d'à côté; **take the n. street on the left** prenez la prochaine à gauche; **after the kitchen, it's the n. room on your right** après la cuisine, c'est la première pièce à votre droite; **they live n. door to us** ils habitent à côté de chez nous, ce sont nos voisins; **I'm just going n. door** je vais juste chez les voisins; **the house n. door** la maison d'à côté *ou* des voisins; **we are n.-door neighbours** nous sommes voisins; **the girl/boy n. door** la fille/le garçon d'à côté; *Fig* **she was just the girl n. door** c'était une fille simple; *Fig* **that's n. door to madness/absurdity** ça frise la folie/l'absurde; **it's the man from n. door** c'est le voisin

4 *(in queue, line)* **I'm n.** c'est (à) mon tour, c'est à moi; **who's n.?** à qui le tour?; **I'm n. after you** je suis (juste) après vous; **Helen is n. in line for promotion** Helen est la suivante sur la liste des promotions; **I can take a joke as well as the n. person, but…** j'aime plaisanter comme tout le monde, mais…

ADV 1 *(afterwards)* ensuite, après; **what did you do n.?** et ensuite, qu'avez-vous fait?; **what shall we do n.?** qu'est-ce que nous allons faire maintenant?; **n. came Henry VII** puis vint *ou* il y eut Henri VII; *Hum* **what will they think of n.?** qu'est-ce qu'ils vont bien pouvoir inventer maintenant?; **what** *or* **whatever n.?** *(indignantly or in mock indignation)* et puis quoi encore?; *Fam* **you'll be asking me to give up my job (for you) n.!** tu n'as qu'à me demander de laisser tomber mon travail pendant que tu y es!

2 *(next time ▸ in future)* la prochaine fois; *(▸ in past)* la fois suivante *ou* d'après; **when I n. saw him, when n. I saw him** quand je l'ai revu; **when shall we meet n.?** quand nous reverrons-nous?

3 *(with superlative adj)* **the n. youngest/oldest child** l'enfant le plus jeune/le plus âgé ensuite; **who is the n. oldest/youngest after Mark?** qui est le suivant *ou* le prochain par ordre d'âge après Mark?; **the n. largest size** la taille juste au-dessus; **the n. fastest after the Ferrari was…** la voiture la plus rapide après la Ferrari était…; **the n. best thing would be to…** à défaut, le mieux serait de…; **watching the match on TV was the n. best thing to actually being there** l'idéal aurait été de pouvoir assister au match, mais ce n'était déjà pas mal de le voir à la télé

4 *Am Fam* **to get n. to sb** *(ingratiate oneself with)* faire de la lèche à qn; *(become emotionally involved with)* se lier avec qn; *(have sex with)* coucher avec qn

PRON *(next train, person, child)* prochain(e) *m,f*; **n., please!** au suivant, s'il vous plaît!

PREP *Am* = **next to**

• **next to PREP 1** *(near)* à côté de; **they live n. to a hospital** ils habitent à côté d'un hôpital; **come and sit n. to me** venez vous asseoir à côté de *ou* près de moi; **I love the feel of silk n. to my skin** j'adore le contact de la soie sur ma peau; **n. to him, everybody looks tiny** à côté de lui, tout le monde a l'air minuscule

2 *(in series)* **n. to last** avant-dernier; **the n. to bottom shelf** la deuxième étagère en partant du bas

3 *(in comparisons)* après; **n. to red, Lisa prefers white** après le rouge, Lisa préfère le blanc

4 *(almost)* presque; **n. to impossible** presque *ou* quasiment impossible; **I bought it for n. to nothing** je l'ai acheté pour trois fois rien *ou* presque rien; **they have n. to no proof** ils n'ont pratiquement aucune preuve; **in n. to no time** en un rien de temps

▸▸ *Law* **next friend** représentant *m* ad litem

next-day delivery N *Com* livraison *f* au lendemain

next-of-kin N *(relative)* parent *m* le plus proche; *(family)* famille *f*; **to inform the n.** prévenir la famille

NF [ˌen'ef] N *(abbr* **National Front***)* = parti britannique d'extrême droite

NGO [ˌendʒiː'əʊ] N *(abbr* **non-governmental organization***)* ONG *f*

NH *(written abbr* **New Hampshire***)* New Hampshire *m*

NHI [ˌeneɪtʃ'aɪ] N *Br (abbr* **National Health Insurance***)* = système britannique de sécurité sociale

NHS [ˌeneɪtʃ'es] N *Br (abbr* **National Health Service***)* ≃ Sécurité *f* sociale

NI¹ [ˌen'aɪ] N *Br (abbr* **national insurance***)* = système britannique de sécurité sociale

NI² *(written abbr* **Northern Ireland***)* Irlande *f* du Nord

Niagara Falls [naɪ'ægərə] NPL les chutes *fpl* du Niagara

nib [nɪb] N **1** *(of fountain pen)* (bec *m* de) plume *f*; *(of ballpoint, tool)* pointe *f*; **broad n.** grosse plume *f*, plume *f* à gros bec; **fine n.** plume *f* fine, plume *f* à bec fin **2** *Tech (of tool)* pointe *f*

nibble ['nɪbəl] VT **1** *(of person, caterpillar)* grignoter; *(of rodent)* grignoter, ronger; *(of goat, sheep)* brouter **2** *(playfully ▸ ear)* mordiller

VI **1** *(eat)* **to n. at** *or* **on sth** grignoter qch; **she nibbled at her food** elle mangeait du bout des dents; **the mice have nibbled through the wire** les souris ont entièrement rongé le fil **2** *(bite)* **to n. at sth** mordiller qch; *also Fig* **to n. at the bait** mordre à l'hameçon **3** *Fig (show interest)* **to n. at an offer** être tenté par une offre

N **1** *Fishing* touche *f*; **I didn't get** *or* **have a n. all day** le poisson n'a pas mordu *ou* je n'ai pas fait une seule touche de toute la journée **2** *(snack)* **I feel like a n. of something** j'ai envie de grignoter un petit morceau; **nibbles** amuse-gueule(s) *mpl*

nibbler ['nɪblə(r)] N *(person)* grignoteur(euse) *m,f*

nibs [nɪbz] N *Br Fam* **his/her n.** son altesse, cézigue

NIC [ˌenaɪ'siː] N **1** *(abbr* **national insurance contributions***)* cotisations *fpl* à la Sécurité sociale **2** *Comput (abbr* **network interface card***)* carte *f* (d')interface réseau **3** *(abbr* **newly-industrialized country***)* pays *m* en voie d'industrialisation, NPI *m*

Nicad battery [nɪ'kæd-] N batterie *f* au nickel-cadmium

NICAM ['naɪkæm] N *(abbr* **near-instantaneous companded audio multiplex***)* Nicam *m*

Nicaragua [ˌnɪkə'rægjuə] N Nicaragua *m*

Nicaraguan [ˌnɪkə'rægjuən] N Nicaraguayen(enne) *m,f*

ADJ nicaraguayen

COMP *(embassy, history)* du Nicaragua

NICE [naɪs] N *Br (abbr* **National Institute for Health and Clinical Excellence***)* = organisme dont le rôle est de veiller à la qualité des soins médicaux prodigués par le NHS

NICE [naɪs]

• bien **1, 2, 4, 5**	• beau **1**
• joli **1**	• bon **1**
• agréable **2**	• sympathique **2**
• gentil **3**	• subtil **7**

ADJ 1 *(expressing approval ▸ good)* bien; *(▸ attractive)* beau (belle); *(▸ pretty)* joli; *(▸ car, picture)* beau (belle); *(▸ food)* bon; *(▸ idea)* bon; *(▸ weather)* beau (belle); **they have a n. house** ils ont une belle maison; **very n.** *(visually)* très joli; *(food)* très bon; **to taste n.** avoir bon goût; **to smell n.** sentir bon; **she always looks n.** elle est toujours bien habillée *ou* mise; **we had a n. meal** on a bien mangé; **it's turned out n. again** *(weather)* il fait à nouveau beau

2 *(pleasant ▸ gen)* agréable, bien; *(▸ person)* bien, sympathique; **it's n. here** c'est bien, ici; **she's very n.** elle est très sympa; **have a n. time** amusez-vous bien; **have a n. day!** bonne journée!; **it's n. to be back again** cela fait plaisir d'être de retour; **(it was) n. meeting you** (j'ai été) ravi de faire votre connaissance; **it's not a n. thing to happen to anyone** ce n'est pas agréable quand ça arrive; **n. work!** beau travail!; *Br Fam* **n. one!** bravo!ᵅ

3 *(kind)* gentil, aimable; **to be n. to sb** être gentil avec qn; **that's n. of her** c'est gentil *ou* aimable de sa part; **she said some n. things** elle a dit des choses gentilles *ou* aimables; **it's n. of you to say so** vous êtes bien aimable de le dire

4 *(intensive)* **it's n. and cool** il fait bien frais; **a n. cold drink** une boisson bien fraîche; **it's n. and warm in here** il fait bon ici; **to have a n. long chat** faire une bonne petite causette; **n. long holiday** des vacances longues et agréables; **take it n. and easy** allez-y doucement

5 *(respectable)* bien (élevé), convenable; **n. people don't blow their noses at table** les gens bien élevés ne se mouchent pas à table

6 *Ironic* **we're in a n. mess** nous sommes dans de beaux draps *ou* un beau pétrin; **you're a n. one to talk!** toi, tu peux parler!; **that's a n. way to talk (to your father)!** en voilà une façon de parler (à ton père)!

7 *Formal (subtle ▸ distinction, point)* subtil, délicat

nice-looking ADJ *(place)* joli; *(person)* joli, beau (belle)

nicely ['naɪslɪ] ADV **1** *(well)* bien; **it fits her n.** cela lui va bien; **n. dressed** bien habillé; **n. done!** bien joué!, beau travail!; **n. put!** bien dit!; **to be coming along** *or* **doing n.** *(garden)* commencer à prendre tournure; *(investments)* bien se porter; *(invalid, pupil)* faire de bons progrès; **to do n. (for oneself)** bien s'en sortir; **he spoke very n. about you** il m'a parlé de vous en très bons termes; **this bag will do n.** ce sac fera très bien l'affaire

2 *(pleasantly)* gentiment, agréablement; **she smiled at me n.** elle me sourit gentiment

3 *(politely ▸ behave, eat)* bien, comme il faut; **ask n.** demandez gentiment

4 *(exactly)* exactement, avec précision; *(subtly)* avec précision; **they judged it n.** ils ne se sont pas trompés dans leur appréciation

niceness ['naɪsnɪs] N **1** *(of person ▸ kindness)* gentillesse *f*, amabilité *f*; *(▸ pleasantness)* caractère *m* agréable; *(of house, hotel etc)* caractère *m* agréable; **the n. of the weather** le temps agréable **2** *Formal (subtlety)* subtilité *f*

nicety ['naɪsətɪ] *(pl* **niceties***)* N **1** *(precision)* justesse *f*, précision *f*; **to a n.** exactement, à la perfection **2** *(usu pl) (subtlety)* subtilité *f*, finesse *f*; **diplomatic/legal niceties** des subtilités *fpl* diplomatiques/légales; **social niceties** *(etiquette)* règles *fpl* de la politesse; *(customs, refinements)* mondanités *fpl*

niche [niːʃ] N **1** *(recess ▸ in church, cliff)* niche *f*; *Fig* **to find one's n.** trouver sa voie **2** *Com & Mktg* créneau *m*

▸▸ *Com & Mktg* **niche market** niche *f*, créneau *m* spécialisé; *Com & Mktg* **niche marketing** marketing *m* de créneau, marketing *m* ciblé; *Com & Mktg* **niche product** produit *m* ciblé; *Rad & TV* **niche programming** = programmation d'émissions destinées à un public restreint; **niche publishing** = publication d'ouvrages destinés à un public restreint

nicher ['niːʃə(r)] N *Mktg* spécialiste *mf* dans une niche

niching ['niːʃɪŋ] N *Mktg* segmentation *f* en niches

nick [nɪk] N **1** *(notch ▸ in wood)* encoche *f*, entaille *f*; *(chip ▸ in crockery)* ébréchure *f*; *(cut ▸ on skin)* (petite) coupure *f*

2 *Br Fam (police station)* poste *m* (de police)ᵅ; *(prison)* taule *f*, bloc *m*; **in the n.** en taule, au bloc; **down the n.** au poste

3 *Br Fam (condition)* conditionᵅ *f*, étatᵅ *m*; **in good/bad n.** en bon/mauvais état; **he's in pretty good n. for his age** il est en bonne forme pour son âge

4 *(idiom)* **in the n. of time** juste à temps

VT 1 *(cut ▸ deliberately)* faire une entaille *ou* une encoche sur; *(accidentally ▸ crockery)* ébrécher; *(▸ metal, paint)* faire des entailles dans; *(▸ skin, face)* entailler, couper (légèrement); **he nicked his chin shaving** il s'est légèrement coupé le menton en se rasant

2 *Br Fam (arrest)* pincer, choper, épingler; **he got nicked outside the bank** il s'est fait épingler *ou* pincer devant la banque; **he got nicked for stealing a car** il s'est fait arrêter pour vol de voitureᵅ; **you're nicked!** tu es fait!

3 *Br Fam (steal)* piquer, faucher

4 *Am Fam (cheat)* arnaquer; **they nicked him for $1,000** il s'est fait arnaquer de 1000 dollars

nickel ['nɪkəl] (*Br pt & pp* **nickelled**, *cont* **nickelling**, *Am pt & pp* **nickeled**, *cont* **nickeling**) N **1** *(metal)* nickel *m* **2** *Am (coin)* pièce *f* de cinq cents; *Fam* **it's not worth a plugged n.** ça vaut pas un clou **3** *Am Fam (five dollars)* cinq dollars *mpl*
VT nickeler
▸▸ ***nickel plating*** nickelage *m*; ***nickel silver*** argentan *m*, maillechort *m*

nickel-and-dime *Am* ADJ de peu d'envergure
▸▸ ***nickel-and-dime store*** = magasin à prix unique

nickel-cadmium battery N batterie *f* au nickel-cadmium

nickel-plated ADJ nickelé

nickel-plating N nickelage *m*

nicker ['nɪkə(r)] (*pl* **inv**) *Br* N *Fam* livres *fpl* (sterling); **five n.** cinq livres
VI **1** *(neigh)* hennir doucement **2** *(snigger)* ricaner

nickname ['nɪkneɪm] N *(gen)* surnom *m*, sobriquet *m*; *(short form)* diminutif *m*; *Comput* surnom *m*
VT surnommer

nicotine ['nɪkəti:n] N nicotine *f*
▸▸ ***nicotine addiction*** tabagisme *m*; ***nicotine patch*** patch *m* ou timbre *m* anti-tabac; ***nicotine poisoning*** tabagisme *m*, intoxication *f* nicotinique

nicotine-stained ADJ jauni par la nicotine

nicotinism ['nɪkəti:nɪzəm] N *Med* nicotinisme *m*, tabagisme *m*

niece [ni:s] N nièce *f*

Nielsen Ratings ['ni:lsən-] NPL *Am TV* ≃ l'audimat *m*

niff [nɪf] *Br Fam* N mauvaise odeur *f*, puanteur *f*; **what a n.!** ça schlingue!
VI refouler, schlinguer, fouetter

niffy ['nɪfɪ] (*compar* **niffier**, *superl* **niffiest**) ADJ *Br Fam* qui fouette *ou* refoule; **it's a bit n. in here** ça pue là-dedans

nifty ['nɪftɪ] (*compar* **niftier**, *superl* **niftiest**) ADJ *Fam* **1** *(clever ▸ solution, idea)* astucieux; *(▸ person)* adroit, débrouillard; **a n. little gadget** un petit gadget très astucieux; **a n. piece of footwork** un beau jeu de jambes; **that was a n. piece of driving** ça c'est de la conduite!; **it's a very n. little car** c'est une petite voiture très commode *ou* pratique **2** *(quick)* rapide; *(agile)* agile **3** *(stylish)* chouette, classe *(inv)*

Niger N **1** [ni:'ʒeə(r)] *(country)* Niger *m* **2** ['naɪdʒə(r)] *(river)* **the (River) N.** le Niger

Nigeria [naɪ'dʒɪərɪə] N Nigeria *m*

Nigerian [naɪ'dʒɪərɪən] N Nigérian(e) *m,f*
ADJ nigérian
COMP *(embassy, history)* du Nigeria

niggard ['nɪgəd] N *Old-fashioned* pingre *mf*, avare *mf*

niggardliness ['nɪgədlɪnɪs] N *(of person)* pingrerie *f*, avarice *f*; *(of sum, budget, salary)* maigreur *f*; *(of quantity)* caractère *m* minuscule

niggardly ['nɪgədlɪ] ADJ *(person)* pingre, avare; *(sum, budget, salary)* maigre; *(quantity)* minime

nigger ['nɪgə(r)] N *Fam* nègre (négresse) *m,f*, = terme raciste désignant un Noir; *Br Old-fashioned* **there's a n. in the woodpile** *(problem)* il y a un hic; *(person)* il y a un empêcheur de tourner en rond; *Old-fashioned* **he's the n. in the woodpile** le problème, c'est lui

niggle ['nɪgəl] N **1** *(small criticism)* objection *f* mineure; **I've got one slight n.** il y a un point de détail sur lequel je ne suis pas d'accord **2** *(small worry, doubt)* tracasserie *f*, léger doute *m* **3** *(complaint)* protestation *f*; **to have a n. about sth** ronchonner à propos de qch
VT **1** *(worry ▸ of conscience)* harceler, travailler **2** *(nag)* harceler
VI **1** *(fuss over details)* ergoter, couper les cheveux en quatre; **to n. over** *or* **about sth** ergoter sur qch; **don't n. about details** ne chipote pas sur les détails **2** *(nag)* trouver à redire

niggler ['nɪgələ(r)] N *(who annoys people)* enquiquineur(euse) *m,f*; *(who worries about details)* coupeur(euse) *m,f* de cheveux en quatre, pinailleur(euse) *m,f*

niggling ['nɪgəlɪŋ] ADJ **1** *(petty ▸ person)* tatillon; *(▸ details)* insignifiant **2** *(fastidious ▸ job)* fastidieux **3** *(nagging ▸ pain, doubt)* tenace; **I've got a n. feeling that something is wrong** je n'arrive pas à m'ôter de la tête que quelque chose ne va pas
N chicanerie *f*, pinaillerie *f*

nigh [naɪ] *Literary* ADV **well n. impossible** presque impossible
ADJ proche; **the end is n.!** la fin est proche!; *Arch* **to be n. unto death** être à l'article de la mort
PREP près de, proche de
• **nigh on** ADV presque; **n. on six o'clock** presque six heures; **for n. on 80 years** pendant près de 80 ans

night [naɪt] N **1** *(evening)* soir *m*; *(late)* nuit *f*; **at n.** *(evening)* le soir; *(late)* la nuit; **ten o'clock at n.** dix heures du soir; **all n. (long)** toute la nuit; **by n.** de nuit; **during** *or* **in the n.** pendant la nuit; **(on) Tuesday n.** *(evening)* mardi soir; *(during night)* dans la nuit de mardi à mercredi; **last n.** *(evening)* hier soir; *(during night)* cette nuit; **the n. before** *(evening)* la veille au soir; *(late)* la nuit précédente; **far** *or* **late into the n.** jusqu'à une heure avancée de la nuit; **to work day and n.** *or* **n. and day** travailler nuit et jour; **to have a n. off** avoir une soirée libre; **I'm on nights next week** je suis de nuit la semaine prochaine; **to have a late/an early n.** se coucher tard/tôt; **too many late nights can be bad for you** se coucher tard trop souvent peut nuire à la santé; **to spend the n. together/with sb** passer la nuit ensemble/avec qn; **this has been going on n. after n.** cela s'est prolongé des nuits durant; **a good n.'s sleep** une bonne nuit de sommeil *ou* de repos; **I had a bad n.** j'ai passé une mauvaise nuit, j'ai mal dormi; **the n. is young** la nuit n'est pas très avancée, *Hum* on a toute la nuit devant nous
2 *(evening's entertainment)* soirée *f*; **to have a n. out** sortir; **that was a great n. last n.** on a passé une super soirée hier; **Tuesday's our poker n.** le mardi, c'est notre soirée poker, le mardi soir, nous faisons un poker; *Theat* **gala n.** soirée *f* de gala; **to make a n. of it** faire la fête toute la nuit
3 *(darkness)* obscurité *f*, *Fig* ténèbres *fpl*; **as n. was falling** alors que la nuit tombait; **n. falls early** il fait nuit tôt, la nuit tombe tôt; *Literary* **to go forth into the n.** s'en aller dans les ténèbres *ou* dans l'obscurité
COMP *(duty, flight, train, boat)* de nuit; *(sky)* nocturne
• **nights** ADV de nuit; **how can you sleep nights not knowing where he is?** comment arrives-tu à dormir sans même savoir où il est?; **to work nights** travailler de nuit; *Am* **to lie awake nights** ne pas dormir la nuit
▸▸ ***night bird*** *Orn* oiseau *m* nocturne *ou* de nuit; *Fig (person)* noctambule *mf*, oiseau *m* de nuit; ***night blindness*** *(UNCOUNT)* héméralopie *f*; ***night clerk*** *(in hotel)* réceptionniste *mf* de nuit; ***night driving*** conduite *f* de nuit; ***night editor*** rédacteur(trice) *m,f* de nuit *(dans un journal)*; *Mil & Aviat* ***night fighter*** chasseur *m* de nuit; ***night light*** lampe *f* veilleuse; ***night nurse*** infirmier(ère) *m,f* de nuit; *Fam* ***night owl*** couche-tard *mf inv*, oiseau *m* de nuit; ***night porter*** portier(ère) *m,f* de nuit; *Banking* ***night safe*** coffre(-fort) *m* de nuit; ***night school*** cours *mpl* du soir; **to go to n. school** suivre des cours du soir; ***night shift*** *(work force)* équipe *f* de nuit; *(period of duty)* poste *m* de nuit; **to be on the n. shift** être de nuit; ***night soil*** fumier *m (d'excréments humains)*; ***night storage heater*** radiateur *m* à accumulation; *Am* ***night table*** table *f* de chevet; ***night vision*** vision *f* nocturne; **to have good/bad n. vision** avoir une bonne/mauvaise vision nocturne; ***night watch*** *(period, guards)* garde *f* de nuit; *Naut* quart *m* de nuit; ***night watchman*** veilleur *m* de nuit; ***night work*** travail *m* de nuit

nightcap ['naɪtkæp] N **1** *(drink ▸ gen)* boisson *f (que l'on prend avant d'aller se coucher)*; *(▸ alcoholic)* dernier verre *m (avant d'aller se coucher)*; **would you like a n.?** prendrez-vous quelque chose avant de vous coucher? **2** *(headgear)* bonnet *m* de nuit

nightclothes ['naɪtkləʊðz] NPL *(pyjamas)* pyjama *m*; *(nightdress)* chemise *f* de nuit

nightclub ['naɪtklʌb] N night-club *m*, boîte *f* de nuit, *Can* club *m* de nuit

nightclubbing ['naɪt,klʌbɪŋ] N **to go n.** sortir en boîte

nightdress ['naɪtdres] N chemise *f* de nuit

nightfall ['naɪtfɔ:l] N tombée *f* de la nuit *ou* du jour; **at n.** à la tombée de la nuit *ou* du jour, à la nuit tombante; **we must get there by n.** il faut que nous y arrivions avant la tombée de la nuit *ou* du jour

nightgown ['naɪtgaʊn] N chemise *f* de nuit

nighthawk ['naɪthɔ:k] N **1** *Orn* engoulevent *m* (d'Amérique) **2** *Fam (person)* couche-tard *mf inv*, oiseau *m* de nuit

nightie ['naɪtɪ] N *Fam* chemise *f* de nuit

nightingale ['naɪtɪŋgeɪl] N *Orn* rossignol *m*

nightjar ['naɪtdʒɑ:(r)] N *Orn* engoulevent *m* (d'Europe)

nightlife ['naɪtlaɪf] N vie *f* nocturne; **what's the n. like round here?** qu'est-ce qu'on peut faire le soir, ici?

nightlight ['naɪtlaɪt] N veilleuse *f*

nightlong ['naɪtlɒŋ] ADJ qui dure toute la nuit; **a n. vigil** une nuit de veille

nightly ['naɪtlɪ] ADJ *(happening every night ▸ late)* de chaque nuit; *(▸ in the evening)* de tous les soirs; **it's a n. occurrence** c'est comme ça toutes les nuits/tous les soirs; **he would take his n. stroll** il faisait sa promenade nocturne
ADV *(late)* toutes les nuits, chaque nuit; *(in the evening)* tous les soirs, chaque soir; *Theat* **appearing n. at the Odeon** tous les soirs sur la scène de l'Odeon
▸▸ ***nightly performance*** *(sign)* représentation tous les soirs

nightmare ['naɪtmeə(r)] N *also Fig* cauchemar *m*; **I had a n.** j'ai fait un cauchemar; **to give sb nightmares** donner des cauchemars à qn; **everybody's worst n.** le cauchemar *ou* la hantise de tout un chacun; **the first day of the sales was a n.** la première journée de soldes fut un cauchemar
COMP *(vision, experience)* cauchemardesque, de cauchemar

nightmarish ['naɪt,meərɪʃ] ADJ cauchemardesque, de cauchemar

night-night EXCLAM *Fam* bonne nuit!

nightrobe ['naɪtrəʊb] N *Am* chemise *f* de nuit

nightshade ['naɪtʃeɪd] N *Bot* morelle *f*

nightshirt ['naɪtʃɜ:t] N chemise *f* de nuit

nightstand ['naɪtstænd] N *Am* table *f* de nuit

night-time N nuit *f*; **at n.** la nuit

nightwear ['naɪtweə(r)] N *(UNCOUNT)* *(pyjamas)* pyjama *m*; *(nightdress)* chemise *f* de nuit; *(department in store)* vêtements *mpl* de nuit

nihilism ['naɪɪlɪzəm] N nihilisme *m*

nihilist ['naɪɪlɪst] N nihiliste *mf*
ADJ nihiliste

nihilistic [,naɪɪ'lɪstɪk] ADJ nihiliste

> **SUFFIXE**
>
> **-NIK**
>
> Emprunté au yiddish et aux langues slaves, le suffixe **-nik** sert à former des noms décrivant des personnes associées à une CAUSE ou à une ACTIVITÉ. Il faut noter qu'il s'agit d'un procédé de formation de néologismes beaucoup plus courant en anglais américain qu'en anglais britannique.
> Les mots ainsi créés sont d'un registre légèrement familier et ont souvent une connotation péjorative, bien qu'humoristique.
> Parmi les termes formés sur ce modèle, citons **beatnik** beatnik; **peacenik** pacifiste; **refusenik** refuznik; **computernik** fada d'informatique; **no-goodnik** bon (bonne) à rien; **Vietnik** opposant(e) à la guerre du Vietnam.

Nikkei Index ['nɪkeɪ-] N *St Exch* indice *m* Nikkei

nil [nɪl] N *(gen) & Br Sport* zéro *m*; *(on written form)* néant *m*; *Br* **they won three n.** ils ont gagné par trois à zéro; *Med* **n. by mouth** *(on patient's chart)* ≃ ne rien administrer par voie orale; *Fin* **the balance is n.** le solde est nul
ADJ nul, zéro *(inv)*

Nile [naɪl] **N** *Br* **the (River) N.,** *Am* **the N. River** le Nil; **the Blue/White N.** le Nil Bleu/Blanc

nimble [ˈnɪmbəl] **ADJ 1** *(agile ▸ person, body)* agile, souple; *(▸ leap, movement)* leste, agile; *(▸ fingers)* adroit, habile; **she's very n. for (someone of) her age** elle est très alerte pour (quelqu'un de) son âge; **n.-fingered** aux doigts agiles *ou* souples *ou* de fée; **n.-footed** aux pieds agiles *ou* légers **2** *(quick ▸ thought, mind)* vif, prompt

nimbleness [ˈnɪmbəlnɪs] **N** *(of person, body)* agilité *f*, souplesse *f*; *(of leap, movement)* agilité *f*; *(of thought, mind)* vivacité *f*

nimbly [ˈnɪmblɪ] **ADV** agilement, lestement

nimbus [ˈnɪmbəs] *(pl* **nimbi** [-baɪ] *or* **nimbuses) N1** *Met* nimbus *m* **2** *(halo)* nimbe *m*, halo *m*, auréole *f*

Nimby [ˈnɪmbɪ] **N** *Fam (abbr* **not in my backyard)** = personne qui, tout en se montrant d'accord sur le principe, est peu encline à voir un projet (de construction le plus souvent) se réaliser à proximité de chez elle

nincompoop [ˈnɪŋkəmpuːp] **N** *Fam* cruche *f*, nigaud(e) *m,f*; **don't be such a n.** ne sois pas si nigaud

nine [naɪn] **N 1** *(number)* neuf *m inv*; **I couldn't stand a n.-to-five job** je ne supporterais pas de travailler de 9 à 5; **he was dressed up to the nines** il s'était mis sur son trente et un **2** *Am Sport* équipe *f* (de base-ball)

PRON neuf; **I need n. (of them)** il m'en faut neuf, j'en ai besoin de neuf

ADJ neuf; **a n.-hole golf course** un (parcours de) neuf trous; **n. times out of ten** neuf fois sur dix; **to have n. lives** *(cat)* avoir neuf vies; *(person)* avoir l'âme chevillée au corps; *Br* **a n. day wonder** un feu de paille; **to dial** *Br* **999** *or Am* **911** appeler les urgences; *see also* **five**

ninefold [ˈnaɪnfəʊld] **ADJ there was a n. increase in casualties** le nombre de victimes fut multiplié par neuf

ADV neuf fois; **to increase n.** (se) multiplier par neuf

ninepin [ˈnaɪnpɪn] **N** *(skittle)* quille *f*; *Br* **to go down like ninepins** tomber comme des mouches • **ninepins N** *(game)* quilles *fpl*

nineteen [ˌnaɪnˈtiːn] **N** dix-neuf *m inv*; *Br* **she talks n. to the dozen** elle n'arrête pas de parler; *Br* **they were talking n. to the dozen** ils étaient intarissables, il n'y avait pas moyen de les faire taire

PRON dix-neuf

ADJ dix-neuf; *see also* **five**

nineteenth [ˌnaɪnˈtiːnθ] **N 1** *(fraction)* dix-neuvième *m* **2** *(in series)* dix-neuvième *mf* **3** *(of month)* dix-neuf *m inv*

ADJ dix-neuvième; *Hum* **the n. hole** *(in golf)* le bar (du club)

ADV dix-neuvièmement; *(in contest)* en dix-neuvième position, à la dix-neuvième place; *see also* **fifth**

1922 Committee [ˌnaɪntiːntwentɪˈtuː-] **N** *Br Pol* = comité rassemblant les députés de base du parti conservateur

ninetieth [ˈnaɪntɪəθ] **N1** *(fraction)* quatre-vingt-dixième *m* **2** *(in series)* quatre-vingt-dixième *mf*

ADJ quatre-vingt-dixième

ADV quatre-vingt-dixièmement; *(in contest)* en quatre-vingt-dixième position, à la quatre-vingt-dixième place; *see also* **fifth**

ninety [ˈnaɪntɪ] *(pl* **nineties) N** quatre-vingt-dix *m inv*, *Belg & Suisse* nonante *m inv*; **the nineties** *(decade)* les années quatre-vingt-dix; **temperatures in the nineties** des températures autour de trente-cinq degrés; **she's in her nineties** elle est nonagénaire

PRON quatre-vingt-dix, *Belg & Suisse* nonante

ADJ quatre-vingt-dix, *Belg & Suisse* nonante

COMP n.-one quatre-vingt-onze; **n.-two** quatre-vingt-douze; **n.-nine** quatre-vingt-dix-neuf; *Law* **n.-nine-year lease** bail *m* emphytéotique de quatre-vingt-dix-neuf ans; **n.-first** quatre-vingt-onzième; **n.-second** quatre-vingt-douzième; *see also* **fifty**

NINJA loan [ˈnɪndʒə-] **N** *Fin (abbr* **no income, no job or assets)** = prêt à risque accordé à une personne sans revenu, sans travail et sans patrimoine

ninny [ˈnɪnɪ] *(pl* **ninnies) N** *Fam* niais(e) *m,f*, nigaud(e) *m,f*

ninth [naɪnθ] **ADJ** neuvième

N1 *(ordinal)* neuvième *mf* **2** *(fraction)* neuvième *m*

ADV *(in contest)* en neuvième position, à la neuvième place

▸▸ *Am Sch* **ninth grade** = classe de lycée pour les 13–14 ans; *see also* **fifth**

NIO [ˌenaɪˈəʊ] **N** *(abbr* **Northern Ireland Office)** = ministère des affaires d'Irlande du Nord

Nip [nɪp] **N** *very Fam* Jap *mf*, = terme injurieux désignant un Japonais

nip [nɪp] *(pt & pp* **nipped,** *cont* **nipping) N1** *(pinch)* pincement *m*; *(bite)* morsure *f*; **that dog gave me a n. on the leg** ce chien m'a mordu la jambe

2 *(cold)* froid *m* piquant; **there's a n. in the air** l'air est piquant

3 *(of alcohol)* goutte *f*

4 *(idioms) Fam Hum* **n. and tuck** *(plastic surgery)* chirurgie *f* esthétique[□]; **to be n. and tuck** être au coude à coude

VT1 *(pinch)* pincer; *(bite)* mordre (légèrement), mordiller; **she nipped her finger in the door** elle s'est pincé le doigt dans la porte **2** *Hort (plant, shoot)* pincer; *Fig* **to n. sth in the bud** tuer *ou* écraser *ou* étouffer qch dans l'œuf **3** *(numb, freeze)* geler, piquer; **the cold nipped our ears** le froid nous piquait les oreilles; **the vines were nipped by the frost** les vignes ont été grillées *ou* brûlées par le gel

VI 1 *(try to bite)* **the dog nipped at my ankles** le chien m'a mordillé les chevilles **2** *Br Fam (go)* faire un saut; **to n. (across** *or* **along** *or* **over) to the butcher's** faire un saut chez le boucher; **she nipped in to say hello** elle est passée en vitesse dire bonjour[□]; **could I just n. in in front of you?** *(in queue)* pourrais-je passer devant vous?[□]; **he always nips into the pub on the way home** il fait toujours un petit détour par le pub en rentrant chez lui[□]; **to n. in and out of the traffic** se faufiler entre les voitures[□]; **we just nipped out for a drink** on est sortis prendre un pot en vitesse; **she nipped off home** elle a filé chez elle

▸**nip in VT SEP** *(garment)* cintrer; **a dress nipped in at the waist** une robe cintrée

▸**nip off VT SEP** *(cut off)* couper; *Hort* pincer

nipper [ˈnɪpə(r)] **N1** *(of crab, lobster)* pince *f* **2** *Br Fam (child)* gosse *mf*, môme *mf*

• **nippers NPL** *(tool)* pince *f*, tenailles *fpl*; **a pair of nippers** une pince, des tenailles *fpl*

nipple [ˈnɪpəl] **N1** *(on breast)* mamelon *m*; *(on animal)* tétine *f*, mamelle *f*

2 *(teat ▸ on feeding bottle)* tétine *f*

3 *Am (baby's dummy)* tétine *f*

4 *Tech (of pump)* embout *m*; *(for greasing)* graisseur *m*; *(connector)* raccord *m*

5 *Geog* mamelon *m*

nippy [ˈnɪpɪ] *(compar* **nippier,** *superl* **nippiest) ADJ 1** *(weather)* frisquet; *(cold)* piquant; **it's a bit n. this morning** il fait frisquet ce matin **2** *Br Fam (quick)* vif[□], rapide[□]; **a n. little car** une petite voiture nerveuse **3** *Br (odour, flavour)* piquant, âpre

nirvana [ˌnɪəˈvɑːnə] **N** nirvana *m*

nisi [ˈnaɪsaɪ] **ADJ** *Law (rule, order)* provisoire; *(decision)* rendu sous condition; *see also* **decree**

nit [nɪt] **N1** *Entom & (in hair)* lente *f*; **to have nits** avoir des poux **2** *Br Fam (idiot)* andouille *f*, courge *f*

niter *Am* = **nitre**

nitery [ˈnaɪtərɪ] **N** *Am Fam* boîte *f* de nuit[□]

nitpick [ˈnɪtpɪk] **VI** *Fam* couper les cheveux en quatre, chercher la petite bête, pinailler

nitpicker [ˈnɪtˌpɪkə(r)] **N** *Fam* chipoteur(euse) *m,f*

nitpicking [ˈnɪtˌpɪkɪŋ] *Fam* **N** chipotage *m*

ADJ chipoteur

nitrate [ˈnaɪtreɪt] **N1** *Chem* nitrate *m*; **potassium n.** nitrate *m* de potassium, salpêtre *m* **2** *(fertilizer)* engrais *m* azoté

nitre, *Am* **niter** [ˈnaɪtə(r)] **N** *Chem* nitrate *m* de potassium

nitric [ˈnaɪtrɪk] **ADJ** *Chem* nitrique

▸▸ ***nitric acid*** acide *m* nitrique; ***nitric oxide*** oxyde *m* nitrique

nitro [ˈnaɪtrəʊ] **N** *Fam Chem* nitroglycérine[□]*f*

nitrogen [ˈnaɪtrədʒən] **N** *Chem* azote *m*

▸▸ ***nitrogen cycle*** cycle *m* de l'azote; ***nitrogen dioxide*** dioxyde *m* d'azote; ***nitrogen gas*** diazote *m*

nitroglycerin, nitroglycerine [ˌnaɪtrəʊˈglɪsəriːn] **N** *Chem* nitroglycérine *f*

nitrous [ˈnaɪtrəs] **ADJ** *Chem* nitreux, azoteux

▸▸ ***nitrous acid*** acide *m* nitreux; ***nitrous oxide*** oxyde *m* azoteux, protoxyde *m* d'azote

nitty-gritty [ˈnɪtɪ-] **N** *Fam* essentiel[□]*m*; **let's get down to the n.** passons aux choses sérieuses; **the n. of government** le gouvernement au quotidien[□]

nitwit [ˈnɪtwɪt] **N** *Br Fam* andouille *f*, courge *f*

nix [nɪks] *Am Fam* **EXCLAM** rien à faire!

N que dalle, rien[□]

VT *(refuse)* rejeter[□], refuser[□]; *(veto)* opposer un veto à[□]

NJ *(written abbr* **New Jersey)** New Jersey *m*

NLQ [ˌenelˈkjuː] **N** *Comput (abbr* **near letter quality)** = qualité quasi-courrier

NM *(written abbr* **New Mexico)** Nouveau-Mexique *m*

NMD [ˌenemˈdiː] **N** *(abbr* **National Missile Defense)** projet *m* NMD *(programme de défense antimissiles américain)*

NMR [ˌeneˈmɑː(r)] **N** *Med (abbr* **nuclear magnetic resonance)** RMN *f*

No., no. *(written abbr* **number)** n°

NO [nəʊ]

ADV
• non **1** • ne… pas **2**

ADJ
• ne… pas de **1, 2** • ne… aucun **1**
• ne… pas un **2**

N
• non

EXCLAM
• non

(pl **noes** *or* **nos)**

ADV1 *(expressing refusal, disagreement)* non; **do you like spinach? – no, I don't** aimez-vous les épinards? – non; **oh no you don't!** *(forbidding, stopping)* oh que non!; **to say no** dire non; **they won't take no for an answer** ils n'accepteront aucun refus

2 *(with comparative adj or adv)* **I can go no further** je ne peux pas aller plus loin; **how is she? – no better** comment va-t-elle? – pas mieux; **he's no longer here** il n'est plus ici; **this car is no more expensive than the other one** cette voiture ne coûte pas plus cher que l'autre

3 *Literary (not)* **whether you wish it or no** que vous le vouliez ou non

ADJ1 *(not any, not one)* **I have no family** je n'ai pas de famille; **she has no intention of leaving** elle n'a aucune intention de partir; **there are no letters for you today** il n'y a pas de courrier *ou* aucune lettre pour toi aujourd'hui; **no sensible person would dispute this** quelqu'un de raisonnable ne discuterait pas; **no other washing powder gets clothes so clean** aucune autre lessive ne laisse votre linge aussi propre; **it's of no importance/interest** ça n'a aucune importance/aucun intérêt; **no two experts ever come up with the same answer** il n'y a pas deux experts qui soient d'accord; **there's no denying it** c'est indéniable; **there's no pleasing him** il n'y a pas moyen de le satisfaire; **it's no distance** ce n'est pas loin

2 *(not a)* **I'm no expert, I'm afraid** malheureusement, je ne suis pas un expert; **she's no friend of mine** ce n'est pas une amie à moi; **it will be no easy task persuading them** ce ne sera pas une tâche facile que de les persuader; **that's no bad thing** ce n'est pas une mauvaise chose; *Fam* **no way!** pas question!

3 *(introducing a prohibition)* **no left turn** *(sign)* interdiction de tourner à gauche; **no smoking** *(sign)* défense de fumer; **no nonsense!** pas de bêtises!

N non *m inv*; **ayes and noes** *(in voting)* voix *fpl* pour et contre; **the noes have it** les non l'emportent

▸▸ ***no ball*** *(in cricket)* balle *f* nulle; ***'no' vote*** vote *m* défavorable

Noah ['nəʊə] **PR N** *Bible* Noé
▸▸ ***Noah's Ark*** l'arche *f* de Noé

nob [nɒb] **N** *Fam* **1** *Br (wealthy person)* rupin(e) *m,f*, richard(e) *m,f*; **the nobs** les rupins *mpl*, les richards *mpl* **2** *(head)* caboche *f*

nobble ['nɒbəl] **VT** *Br Fam* **1** *(jury, witness ▸ bribe)* graisser la patte à; *(▸ threaten)* manipuler (avec des menaces)▫ **2** *(racehorse)* mettre hors d'état de courir▫; *(with drugs)* droguer▫; *Fig* **to n. sb's chances of doing sth** bousiller *ou* saboter les chances que qn a de faire qch **3** *(grab) (thief)* pincer, choper, épingler; *(person)* accrocher (au passage), agrafer **4** *(steal)* faucher, barboter, chiper

Nobel [nəʊ'bel] **PR N**
▸▸ ***Nobel laureate*** lauréat(e) *m,f* du prix Nobel; ***Nobel Peace Prize*** prix *m* Nobel de la paix; ***Nobel prize*** prix *m* Nobel; **N. prize for Literature** prix *m* Nobel de littérature; ***Nobel prizewinner*** lauréat(e) *m,f* du prix Nobel

nobility [nə'bɪlətɪ] *(pl* **nobilities)** **N 1** *(aristocracy)* noblesse *f*, aristocratie *f* **2** *(loftiness)* noblesse *f*, majesté *f*, grandeur *f*

noble ['nəʊbəl] **ADJ 1** *(aristocratic)* noble; **of n. birth** de haute naissance, de naissance noble **2** *(fine, distinguished ▸ aspiration, purpose)* noble, élevé; *(▸ bearing, manner, proportions, building)* noble, majestueux; *(▸ mountain)* altier, imposant; *(▸ person, animal)* noble **3** *(generous ▸ gesture)* généreux, magnanime; *Hum* **that's very n. of you** c'est très généreux de votre part **4** *(brave ▸ deed, feat)* noble, héroïque; **the n. art** *or* **science** le noble art **5** *(impressive ▸ monument)* noble, majestueux **6** *Chem (gas, metal)* noble
N noble *mf*, aristocrate *mf*
▸▸ ***noble rot*** pourriture *f* noble; ***noble savage*** bon sauvage *m*; ***noble wine*** vin *m* noble, grand vin

nobleman ['nəʊbəlmən] *(pl* **noblemen** [-mən]) **N** noble *m*, aristocrate *m*

noble-minded **ADJ** magnanime, généreux

nobleness ['nəʊbəlnɪs] **N 1** *(of birth)* noblesse *f* **2** *(of mind, action)* noblesse *f*; *(of soul)* grandeur *f* **3** *(of statue, horse)* proportions *fpl* superbes *ou* magnifiques; *(of building)* aspect *m* majestueux

noblewoman ['nəʊbəl,wʊmən] *(pl* **noblewomen** [-,wɪmɪn]) **N** noble *f*, aristocrate *f*

nobly ['nəʊblɪ] **ADV 1** *(by birth)* noblement; **n. born** de haute naissance **2** *(majestically, superbly)* majestueusement, superbement; **n. proportioned** aux proportions majestueuses **3** *(generously)* généreusement, magnanimement; **she n. offered him the last piece of cake** elle lui a généreusement offert le dernier morceau de gâteau **4** *(bravely)* noblement, courageusement

nobody ['nəʊbədɪ] *(pl* **nobodies)** **PRON 1** *(no person, no one)* personne; **n. came** personne n'est venu; **n. knows** personne ne le sait; **n. else** personne d'autre; **there was n. there** il n'y avait personne; **n. who was there heard anything** aucun de ceux *ou* personne parmi tous ceux qui étaient là n'a entendu quoi que ce soit; **who was at the party? – n. you know** qui était à la fête? – personne que tu connais; **n. famous** personne de célèbre; **n. is perfect** nul *ou* personne n'est parfait; **she's n.'s fool** elle n'est pas née d'hier *ou* de la dernière pluie; *Fam* **to work like n.'s business** travailler comme un fou; *Fam* **to run like n.'s business** courir ventre à terre; *Fam* **the dogs were barking like n.'s business** les chiens aboyaient à vous rompre les tympans **2** *(obscure, insignificant)* **when he was n.** alors qu'il était encore inconnu; **as far as they're concerned, if you don't have money, you're n.** pour eux, si tu n'as pas d'argent tu es un zéro *ou* un moins que rien
N *(insignificant person)* zéro *m*; **he's just a n.** c'est un zéro; **they're (mere) nobodies** ce sont des gens de rien

no-brainer [-'breɪnə(r)] **N** *Am Fam* truc *m* pour débiles

no-claim(s) bonus **N** *Br Ins* bonus *m*

nocturnal [nɒk'tɜːnəl] **ADJ** nocturne
▸▸ *Physiol* ***nocturnal emission*** pollution *f* nocturne

nocturne ['nɒktɜːn] **N** nocturne *m*

nod [nɒd] *(pt & pp* **nodded**, *cont* **nodding)** **VT to n. one's head** *(as signal)* faire un signe de (la) tête; *(in assent)* faire oui de la tête, faire un signe de tête affirmatif; *(in greeting)* saluer d'un signe de tête; *(with fatigue)* dodeliner de la tête; **she nodded her approval** elle manifesta son approbation d'un signe de tête
VI 1 *(as signal)* faire un signe de (la) tête; *(in assent, approval)* faire un signe de tête affirmatif, faire oui de la tête; *(in greeting)* saluer d'un signe de tête; **to n. (in agreement/approval)** consentir/approuver d'un signe de tête; **she nodded at** *or* **to him through the window** elle lui fit un signe de tête de derrière la fenêtre **2** *(doze)* somnoler **3** *Fig (flowers)* danser, se balancer; *(crops, trees)* se balancer, onduler
N 1 *(sign)* signe *m* de (la) tête; **to give sb a n.** *(as signal)* faire un signe de tête à qn; *(in assent)* faire un signe de tête affirmatif à qn; *(in greeting)* saluer qn d'un signe de tête; **to answer with a n.** répondre d'un signe de tête; **a n. in sb's direction** un signe de tête à l'intention de qn; **a n. is as good as a wink (to a blind man)** inutile d'en dire plus; **to get** *Br* **the n.** *or Am* **a n.** *(gen)* obtenir le feu vert; *(in boxing)* gagner aux points; **to give sb** *Br* **the n.** *or Am* **a n.** donner le feu vert à qn; *Br* **to approve sth on the n.** *(without formality)* approuver qch d'un commun accord **2** *(sleep)* **the land of N.** le pays des rêves; *Hum* **to be in the land of N.** être dans les bras de Morphée
▸ **nod off** **VI** *Fam* s'assoupir▫, s'endormir▫

nodal ['nəʊdəl] **ADJ** nodal

nodding ['nɒdɪŋ] **ADJ** *Br* **to have a n. acquaintance with sb** connaître qn de vue *ou* vaguement; *Fig* **I have a n. acquaintance with marketing techniques** j'ai quelques notions des techniques de marketing; **we're on n. terms** nous nous saluons
▸▸ *Am Fam* ***nodding donkey*** pompe *f* à pétrole▫

noddle ['nɒdəl] **N** *Br Fam (head)* caboche *f*, ciboulot *m*; **use your n.!** fais marcher ton ciboulot *ou* tes méninges!

node [nəʊd] **N** *(gen)* nœud *m*; *Anat* nodosité *f*, nodule *m*

nodular ['nɒdjʊlə(r)] **ADJ** nodulaire

nodule ['nɒdjuːl] **N** nodule *m*

Noel, Noël [nəʊ'el] **N** *Literary (Christmas)* Noël *m*

no-fly zone **N** *Mil* zone *f* d'exclusion aérienne

no-frills **ADJ** *(airline, travel)* sans prestation de services; *(insurance policy)* de base; *(car, bicycle)* sans gadgets; *(service, wedding)* sans chichis, tout simple; **a n. hotel** un hôtel sans confort superflu

noggin ['nɒgɪn] **N 1** *(measure)* quart *m* de pinte **2** *Fam (drink)* pot *m*; **to have a n.** prendre un pot *ou* un verre **3** *Fam (head)* caboche *f*, ciboulot *m*

no-go area **N** zone *f* interdite; **this neighbourhood is a n. for the police** la police n'ose pas s'aventurer dans ce quartier

no-good *Fam* **N** bon (bonne) *m,f* à rien▫
ADJ bon à rien▫

no-holds-barred **ADJ** *(contest, fight)* où tous les coups sont permis; *(report, documentary)* sans fard

no-hoper [-'həʊpə(r)] **N** *Fam* raté(e) *m,f*, minable *mf*

nohow ['nəʊhaʊ] **ADV** *Fam* aucunement▫, en aucune façon▫

noise [nɔɪz] **N 1** *(sound)* bruit *m*; **a loud n.** un gros bruit; **the clock is making a funny n.** la pendule fait un drôle de bruit; **I thought I heard a n. downstairs** j'ai cru entendre du bruit en bas; **the humming n. of the engine** le ronronnement du moteur; *Theat* **noises off** bruitage *m* **2** *(din)* bruit *m*, tapage *m*, tintamarre *m*; *(very loud)* vacarme *m*; **to make a n.** faire du bruit; **do you call that n. music?** pour vous, ce vacarme c'est de la musique?; *Br Fam* **shut your n.!** fermela! **3** *Elec & Tel* parasites *mpl*; *(on line)* friture *f*, sifflement *m* **4** *Fam (idiom)* **to make a n. about sth** faire du tapage *ou* beaucoup de bruit autour de qch; **the critics made a lot of n. about the film** les critiques ont fait beaucoup de bruit autour de ce film
VT to n. sth about *or* **abroad** ébruiter qch
• **noises** **NPL** *Fam (indication of intentions)* **she's making noises about retiring** elle donne à entendre qu'elle va prendre sa retraite; **to make encouraging noises** dire des choses encourageantes▫; **they made all the right noises, but…** ils ont fait semblant de marcher à fond *ou* d'être tout à fait d'accord, mais…▫
▸▸ ***noise abatement*** lutte *f* contre le bruit; ***noise abatement campaign*** campagne *f ou* lutte *f* contre le bruit; ***noise level*** niveau *m* de bruit; ***noise pollution*** nuisances *fpl* sonores, pollution *f* sonore

noiseless ['nɔɪzlɪs] **ADJ** silencieux

noiselessly ['nɔɪzlɪslɪ] **ADV** silencieusement, sans faire de bruit

noiselessness ['nɔɪzlɪsnɪs] **N** silence *m*

noisily ['nɔɪzɪlɪ] **ADV** bruyamment

noisiness ['nɔɪzɪnɪs] **N** caractère *m* bruyant; **because of the n. of the street** à cause du bruit qu'il y a dans la rue; **I can't stand their n.** je ne peux pas supporter le bruit qu'ils font

noisome ['nɔɪsəm] **ADJ** *Literary (repellent)* répugnant, repoussant; *(smelly)* méphitique; *(noxious)* nocif, nuisible; **a n. smell** une odeur infecte *ou* pestilentielle

noisy ['nɔɪzɪ] *(compar* **noisier**, *superl* **noisiest)** **ADJ 1** *(machine, engine, person)* bruyant; **to be n.** *(of person)* faire du bruit; **my typewriter is very n.** ma machine à écrire est très bruyante *ou* fait beaucoup de bruit; **London was too n. for him** Londres était trop bruyant à son goût **2** *(colour)* criard

no-load fund **N** *St Exch* fonds *m* sans frais d'acquisition, fonds *m* qui ne prélève pas une commission

nomad ['nəʊmæd] **N** nomade *mf*

nomadic [nəʊ'mædɪk] **ADJ** nomade; *Fig* **a n. existence** une existence de nomade/nomades

no-man's-land **N** *also Fig* no man's land *m inv*

nom de plume [,nɒmdə'pluːm] **N** pseudonyme *m*, nom *m* de plume

nomenclature [*Br* ,nəʊ'menklətʃə(r), *Am* 'nəʊmən,kleɪtʃər] **N** nomenclature *f*

nominal ['nɒmɪnəl] **ADJ 1** *(in name only ▸ owner, leader)* de nom (seulement), nominal; *(▸ ownership, leadership)* nominal; **he was the n. president of the company** il n'était le président de la société que de nom **2** *(negligible)* insignifiant, nominal; *(rent)* insignifiant; **a n. amount** une somme insignifiante **3** *(token)* symbolique; **a n. contribution of one pound a year** une contribution symbolique d'une livre par an **4** *Gram* nominal
N *Gram* élément *m* nominal; *(noun phrase)* groupe *m* nominal; *(pronoun)* nominal *m*
▸▸ *Law* ***nominal damages*** dommages-intérêts *mpl* symboliques; ***nominal income*** revenu *m* nominal

nominally ['nɒmɪnəlɪ] **ADV 1** *(in name only)* nominalement **2** *(as token)* pour la forme **3** *(theoretically)* théoriquement

nominate ['nɒmɪneɪt] **VT 1** *(propose)* proposer (la candidature de); *Cin (for award)* sélectionner, nominer; **to n. sb for a post** proposer la candidature de qn à un poste; **the film was nominated for an Oscar** le film a été sélectionné *ou* nominé pour un oscar **2** *(appoint)* nommer, désigner; **to n. sb to a post** nommer *ou* désigner qn à un poste; **he was nominated chairman** *or* **to the chairmanship** il fut nommé président

nomination [,nɒmɪ'neɪʃən] **N 1** *(proposal ▸ of candidate etc)* proposition *f*; *Cin (▸ for an award)* nomination *f*; **who will get the Democratic n. (for president)?** qui obtiendra l'investiture démocrate (à l'élection présidentielle)?; **the film got three Oscar nominations** le film a obtenu trois nominations aux oscars **2** *(appointment ▸ of candidate)* nomination *f*; *(▸ of president, judge)* investiture *f*

nominative ['nɒmɪnətɪv] *Gram* **N** nominatif *m*; **in the n.** au nominatif

ADJ nominatif
▸▸ ***the nominative case*** le nominatif

nominator ['nɒmɪˌneɪtə(r)] **N** présentateur (trice) *m,f (d'un candidat)*; **his nominators** ceux qui ont proposé sa nomination

nominee [ˌnɒmɪ'ni:] **N 1** *(proposed)* candidat(e) *m,f* **2** *(appointed)* personne *f* désignée *ou* nommée; **the government nominees on the commission** les membres de la commission nommés par le gouvernement **3** *(at awards ceremony)* nominé(e) *m,f*, *Offic* nommé(e) *m,f*; **and the nominees are...** et les nominés sont..., *Offic* et les nommés sont...
▸▸ ***nominee company*** prête-nom *m*; *Fin* ***nominee name*** nom *m* de l'intermédiaire; *St Exch* ***nominee shareholder*** actionnaire *mf* intermédiaire

NON- PRÉFIXE

• Employé avec des adjectifs et des noms, le préfixe **non-** est extrêmement générateur en anglais. Il sert simplement à exprimer le CONTRAIRE du terme qu'il précède.
A l'inverse des préfixes **in-** et **un-**, qui ont fréquemment des connotations péjoratives, le préfixe **non-** est neutre.
A titre d'exemple, le terme **nonscientific** désigne une chose qui se situe en dehors du champ de la science, et n'a en lui-même aucune nuance péjorative, alors que l'adjectif **unscientific** signale un défaut de rigueur scientifique. La même dichotomie existe entre **nonhuman** (non humain) et **inhuman** (inhumain).
Le français utilise également le préfixe **non-**, mais de façon moins systématique que l'anglais:
nonalcoholic non alcoolisé, sans alcool; **nonexistent** non existant, inexistant; **nonessential** non essentiel; **non-dairy** qui ne contient aucun produit laitier; **nonfiction** ouvrages non romanesques; **a non-Muslim** un(e) non-musulman(e); **nonpayment** non-paiement, défaut de paiement; **noncooperation** refus de coopérer; **it rained nonstop** il a plu sans arrêt.
• On peut également employer le suffixe **non-** devant un verbe pour indiquer l'ABSENCE DE DÉFAUT d'un matériau ou d'une substance:
nonshrink irrétrécissable; **nonslip** antidérapant; **nonstick** antiadhésif; **nondrip paint** peinture qui ne coule pas. On notera l'exception: **a non-iron shirt** une chemise qui ne nécessite aucun repassage.
• Employé devant un nom, le préfixe **non-** sert à indiquer la NOTION INVERSE du terme qui suit, généralement avec des nuances péjoratives. Ce genre d'usage est générateur de très nombreux néologismes en anglais. Dans certains cas, le français utilise également le préfixe **non-** mais de façon moins systématique que l'anglais :
a non-event un non-événement; **his answers were non-answers** ses réponses n'en étaient pas; **it is a non-story with non-characters** c'est une histoire qui n'en est pas une avec des personnages qui n'en sont pas; **he treats his secretary like a nonperson** il se conduit envers sa secrétaire comme si elle n'existait pas.

non- [nɒn] **PREF 1** *(not)* non-; **the non-application of this rule** la non-application de cette règle; **all non-French nationals** tous les ressortissants de nationalité autre que française **2** *(against)* anti-; **non-rust** antirouille *(inv)*

nonabsorbent [ˌnɒnəb'zɔ:bənt] **ADJ** non absorbant

non-acceptance **N** non-acceptation *f*

non-accountability **N** *(of head of state)* irresponsabilité *f*

non-accountable **ADJ** *(unaccountable* ▸ *individual, institution)* qui n'a de comptes à rendre à personne; **to be n. to sb** ne pas avoir à répondre devant qn, ne pas avoir de comptes à rendre à qn

non-adopter **N** *Mktg* = consommateur qui n'essaie jamais de nouveaux produits

nonagenarian [ˌnəʊnədʒɪ'neərɪən] **N** nonagénaire *mf*
ADJ nonagénaire

nonaggression [ˌnɒnə'greʃən] **N** non-agression *f*
▸▸ ***nonaggression pact*** pacte *m* de non-agression

nonalcoholic [ˌnɒnælkə'hɒlɪk] **ADJ** non alcoolisé, sans alcool

nonaligned [ˌnɒnə'laɪnd] **ADJ** *Pol* non aligné

nonalignment [ˌnɒnə'laɪnmənt] **N** *Pol* non-alignement *m*

no-name product **N** *Mktg* produit *m* sans nom

nonappearance [ˌnɒnə'pɪərəns] **N 1** *(gen)* **how do you account for her n.?** comment expliquez-vous le fait qu'elle ne soit pas venue? **2** *Law* non-comparution *f*

nonarrival [ˌnɒnə'raɪvəl] **N** non-arrivée *f*

non-ASCII character **N** *Comput* caractère *m* non ASCII

nonattendance [ˌnɒnə'tendəns] **N** absence *f*; **n. at lectures** absence *f* aux cours

non-bank **ADJ** non-banque

non-business marketing **N** *Mktg* marketing *m* non commercial

nonce [nɒns] **N 1** *Literary or Hum* **for the n.** *(for the occasion)* pour la circonstance, pour l'occasion; *(for the moment)* pour l'instant **2** *Br Fam Crime slang (sex offender)* délinquant *m* sexuel[□] *(s'attaquant en particulier aux enfants)*
▸▸ *Ling* ***nonce word*** mot *m* créé pour l'occasion

nonchalance [*Br* 'nɒnʃələns, *Am* ˌnɒnʃə'lɑ:ns] **N** nonchalance *f*

nonchalant [*Br* 'nɒnʃələnt, *Am* ˌnɒnʃə'lɑ:nt] **ADJ** nonchalant

nonchalantly [*Br* 'nɒnʃələntlɪ, *Am* ˌnɒnʃə'lɑ:ntlɪ] **ADV** nonchalamment, avec nonchalance

noncombatant [*Br* ˌnɒn'kɒmbətənt, *Am* ˌnɒnkəm'bætənt] **N** non-combattant(e) *m,f*
ADJ non combattant

noncommissioned [ˌnɒnkə'mɪʃənd] **ADJ** *Mil* sans brevet
▸▸ ***noncommissioned officer*** sous-officier *m*

noncommittal [ˌnɒnkə'mɪtəl] **ADJ** *(statement)* évasif, qui n'engage à rien; *(attitude, person)* réservé; *(gesture)* peu révélateur; **to be n.** *(when answering)* ne pas s'engager; **he was very n. about his plans** il s'est montré très évasif sur ses projets

non-competition clause **N** clause *f* de non-concurrence

noncompletion [ˌnɒnkəm'pli:ʃən] **N** *(of job)* non-achèvement *m*; *(of contract)* non-exécution *f*

noncompliance [ˌnɒnkəm'plaɪəns] **N** non-respect *m*, non-observation *f* (**with** de); **n. with the orders of a superior** refus *m* d'obéir aux ordres d'un supérieur

nonconductor [ˌnɒnkən'dʌktə(r)] **N** *Phys* non-conducteur *m*, mauvais conducteur *m*; *Elec* isolant *m*

nonconformism [ˌnɒnkən'fɔ:mɪzəm] **N** non-conformisme *m*

nonconformist [ˌnɒnkən'fɔ:mɪst] **N** non-conformiste *mf*
ADJ non conformiste

nonconformity [ˌnɒnkən'fɔ:mətɪ] **N** non-conformité *f*

non-contributory **ADJ**
▸▸ *Br Fin* ***non-contributory pension (scheme)*** caisse *f* de retraite sans cotisations de la part des bénéficiaires

non-convertible **ADJ** inconvertible, non convertible

non-cumulative **ADJ** *Fin* non cumulatif

non-current liabilities **NPL** *Acct* passif *m* non exigible

noncustodial [ˌnɒnkʌs'təʊdɪəl] **ADJ** *(sentence)* n'entraînant pas l'emprisonnement

nondescript [*Br* 'nɒndɪskrɪpt, *Am* ˌnɒndɪ'skrɪp
ADJ *(person, object)* quelconque; *(colour)* neutr
Pej fade; **a n. little man** un petit homme que rie
ne distingue des autres *ou* tout à fait anodin; **th
street was lined with n. buildings** la rue était bo
dée de bâtiments quelconques *ou* dépourvu
de caractère

nondestructive [ˌnɒndɪ'strʌktɪv] **ADJ** *(test, tes
ing)* non destructif

nondetachable [ˌnɒndɪ'tætʃəbəl] **ADJ** inam
vible

non-DOS disk **N** *Comput* disque *m* à format i
compatible avec DOS

nondrip [ˌnɒn'drɪp] **ADJ** *(paint)* qui ne coule pa

non-dutiable **ADJ** exempt de droits d
douane

NONE [nʌn] **PRON 1** *(with countable nouns)* aucu
(e) *m,f*; **n. of the photos is** *or* **are for sale** aucur
des photos n'est à vendre; **he looked for clues b
found n.** il chercha des indices mais n'en trouv
aucun; **there are n. left** il n'en reste plus; **ho
many cigarettes have you got? – n. at all** combie
de cigarettes as-tu? – aucune *ou* pas une seul
2 *(with uncountable nouns)* **n. of her early wo
has been published** aucun de ses premiers text
n'a été publié; **n. of the milk was fresh** tout le la
avait tourné; **n. of the money was left** il ne resta
rien de l'argent; **how much of the wood did yo
use? – n. of it** quelle quantité du bois avez-vou
utilisée? – pas un seul morceau; **I've done a l
of work but you've done n.** j'ai beaucoup tr
vaillé, mais toi tu n'as rien fait; **she displayed
of her usual good humour** elle était loin d'affich
sa bonne humeur habituelle; **more soup anyon
– n. for me, thanks** encore un peu de soupe?
pas pour moi, merci; **(I'll have) n. of your chee
je ne tolérerai pas vos insolences!; **n. of tha
(stop it) pas de ça!; **she would have n. of it** elle n
voulait rien savoir; **n. of this concerns me** rien d
ceci ne me regarde
3 *(not one person)* aucun(e) *m,f*; **n. of them wor
or work hard enough** aucun d'eux ne travail
suffisamment; **n. of you can tell me** aucun d'ent
vous *ou* personne ne peut me le dire; *Literary*
can tell what the future holds nul ne sait ce qu
l'avenir nous réserve
ADV *Am Fam (in double negatives)* **you don't sca
me n.** tu ne me fais pas du tout peur[□]
• **none but** **ADV** *Formal or Literary* **we use n. bu
the finest ingredients** nous n'utilisons que l
meilleurs ingrédients; **I love n. but her** je n'aim
qu'elle
• **none other than** **PREP** personne d'aut
que; **he received a letter from n. other than th
Prime Minister himself** il reçut une lettre do
l'auteur n'était autre que le Premier ministre e
personne
• **none the** **ADV** *(with comparative adj)* **I lik
them n. the better/worse for it** je ne les en aim
pas plus/moins; **she's n. the worse for her adve
ture** son aventure ne lui a pas fait de mal
• **none too** **ADV** **I was n. too pleased with the**
j'étais loin d'être content d'eux; **he replied n. to
politely** sa réponse ne fut pas particulièreme
polie; **and n. too soon!** ce n'est pas trop tôt!

nonentity [nɒn'entətɪ] *(pl* **nonentities***)* **N 1** *(insi
nificant person)* personne *f* insignifiante, nulli
f; **she's a bit of a n.** elle est plutôt insignifiante
(insignificance) inexistence *f*

non-equity share **N** *St Exch* action *f* sans p
vilège de participation

non-erasable memory **N** *Comput* mémoi
f non effaçable

nonessential [ˌnɒnɪ'senʃəl] **ADJ** accessoire, no
essentiel
N **the nonessentials** l'accessoire *m*, le superfl
leave behind all nonessentials n'emportez qu
l'essentiel

nonetheless [ˌnʌnðə'les] = **nevertheless**

non-EU **ADJ** extracommunautaire; **n. countr**
pays *m* tiers

non-event **N** non-événement *m*; **the press co
ference was pretty much a n.** la conférence d
presse ne valait pas le déplacement

onexistence [ˌnɒnɪgˈzɪstəns] N non-existence

onexistent [ˌnɒnɪgˈzɪstənt] ADJ non existant, nexistant; *Fam* **his help has been almost n.** il ne 'est pas beaucoup foulé pour nous aider

on-ferrous ADJ non ferreux

onfiction [ˌnɒnˈfɪkʃən] N *(UNCOUNT)* ouvra-es *mpl* non romanesques

onflammable [ˌnɒnˈflæməbəl] ADJ ininflam-nable

on-floating exchange rate N *Econ* taux 1 de change fixe

on-fulfilment, *Am* **non-fulfillment** N *(of ontract)* non-exécution *f*

on-governmental organization, isation N organisation *f* non gouvernementale

on-Hodgkin's lymphoma N *Med* lym-phome *m* non-hodgkinien

on-impact printer N imprimante *f* sans mpact

oninflammable [ˌnɒnɪnˈflæməbəl] ADJ inin-ammable

on-interlaced display N *Comput* écran *m* on entrelacé

onintervention [ˌnɒnɪntəˈvenʃən] N non-ntervention *f*, non-ingérence *f*

oninterventionist [ˌnɒnɪntəˈvenʃənɪst] N on-interventionniste *mf*
ADJ *(policy)* non interventionniste, de non-ntervention

on-iron ADJ qui ne nécessite aucun repas-age

onjudgemental, nonjudgmental [ˌnɒn-ʒʌdʒˈmentəl] ADJ neutre, impartial; **to try to be .** s'efforcer de ne pas porter de jugements

on-linear ADJ non linéaire

onmalignant [ˌnɒnməˈlɪgnənt] ADJ bénin igne)

onmember [ˈnɒnˌmembə(r)] N non-membre *n*; *(of a club)* personne *f* étrangère (au club); **pen to nonmembers** ouvert au public

on-negotiable ADJ non négociable

on-nuclear ADJ *(country)* non nucléarisé; *war, defence, policy)* non nucléaire

o-no N *Fam* interdit*m*; **that subject is a n.** ce ujet est tabou; **dating someone from work is a .** sortir avec un collègue de travail, c'est l'erreur ne pas faire; **asking him for money is a definite .** il est hors de question de lui demander de l'ar-ent

onobservance [ˌnɒnəbˈzɜːvəns] N *(of rules)* on-observation *f*; *(of treaty)* non-respect *m*; *Rel* inobservance *f*

o-nonsense ADJ *(attitude, manner)* pratique; *person)* qui va droit au but; **she's got a very n. ap-roach** elle va droit au but; **she told him so in her sual n. way** elle le lui a dit très directement, comme à son habitude

onorganic [ˌnɒnɔːˈgænɪk] ADJ **1** *(food, farming, ertilizer)* non biologique **2** *Med* anorganique

onpareil [ˈnɒnpərəl] N *Literary (person)* per-onne *f* incomparable *ou* unique; *(thing)* chose incomparable *ou* unique

on-participating ADJ **1** *St Exch (share)* sans roit de participation **2** *(country, institution)* qui e participe pas **3** *Ins (policy)* sans participation ux bénéfices

onpartisan [ˈnɒnˌpɑːtɪˈzæn] ADJ impartial, ans parti pris

onpayment [ˌnɒnˈpeɪmənt] N non-paiement *n*, défaut *m* de paiement

on-performance N *(of contract)* non-exécution *f*, inexécution *f*

on-performing loan N *Banking* prêt *m* en ouffrance

onperson [ˌnɒnˈpɜːsən] N **1** *(stateless person)* = ersonne mise au ban de la société **2** *(insignifi-ant person)* personne *f* insignifiante, nullité *f*; **e treats his secretary like a n.** il se conduit envers a secrétaire comme si elle n'existait pas

onplus [ˌnɒnˈplʌs] *(Br pt & pp* **nonplussed,** *cont* **onplussing,** *Am pt & pp* **nonplused,** *cont* **nonplus-ng)** VT déconcerter, dérouter

non-poisonous ADJ non toxique; *(snake)* non venimeux; *(mushroom)* non vénéneux

nonpolitical [ˌnɒnpəˈlɪtɪkəl] ADJ apolitique

nonpolluting [ˌnɒnpəˈluːtɪŋ] ADJ non polluant, propre

non-printable character N caractère *m* non imprimable

non-probability ADJ
▸▸ ***non-probability method*** *(of sampling)* méthode *f* non probabiliste; ***non-probability sample*** échantillon *m* non probabiliste; ***non-probability sampling*** échantillonnage *m* non probabiliste

non-procedural language N *Comput* langage *m* non procédural

non-productive ADJ *Econ* improductif

non-profit-making ADJ *Br* à but non lucratif
▸▸ ***non-profit-making organization*** société *f* à but non lucratif

nonproliferation [ˈnɒnprəˌlɪfəˈreɪʃən] N non-prolifération *f*
▸▸ ***nonproliferation treaty*** traité *m* de non-prolifération

non-racial ADJ *(society, democracy, government)* qui ne pratique pas la discrimination raciale

non-random ADJ
▸▸ *Mktg* ***non-random sample*** échantillon *m* empirique; ***non-random sampling*** échantillonnage *m* empirique

non-recoverable N *Comput (file, data)* non récupérable

non-recurring ADJ exceptionnel, extraordinaire

non-reflecting ADJ antireflet *(inv)*

nonrefundable [ˌnɒnrɪˈfʌndəbəl] ADJ non remboursable; *(packaging)* perdu(e)

non-resident N **1** *(of country)* non-résident(e) *m,f* **2** *(of hotel)* **the dining room is open/closed to non-residents** le restaurant est ouvert au public/réservé aux clients de l'hôtel
ADJ non résident; *Banking & Fin* **n. account** compte *m* (de) non-résident

nonreturnable [ˌnɒnrɪˈtɜːnəbəl] ADJ sans réserve de retour; *(bottle, container)* non consigné; *(deposit)* non remboursable; *(packaging)* non consigné, perdu; **sales goods are n.** les articles en solde ne sont pas repris

non-return valve N *Tech* clapet *m* anti-retour

nonscheduled [*Br* nɒnˈʃedjuːld, *Am* nɒnˈskedjuːld] ADJ *(flight)* spécial
▸▸ ***nonscheduled stop*** étape *f* non prévue

nonsectarian [ˌnɒnsekˈteərɪən] ADJ tolérant, ouvert

nonsense [ˈnɒnsəns] N *(UNCOUNT)* **1** *(rubbish, absurdity)* absurdités *fpl*, sottises *fpl*; **a piece of n.** une sottise, une absurdité; **you're talking n.!** tu dis des sottises!, tu racontes n'importe quoi!; **his accusations are utter n.** ses accusations n'ont aucun sens; **it's n. to say that things will never improve** il est absurde de dire que les choses n'iront jamais mieux; **I've had enough of his n.** j'en ai assez de l'entendre raconter n'importe quoi; **what's all this n. about going to live in America?** qu'est-ce que c'est que cette histoire d'aller vivre en Amérique?; **to make a n. of sth** *(undo, go against etc)* ôter tout sens à qch **2** *(foolishness)* sottises *fpl*, bêtises *fpl*, enfantillages *mpl*; **stop this** *or* **no more of this n.!** arrêtez de vous conduire comme des imbéciles!; **she took no n. from her subordinates** elle ne tolérait aucun manquement de la part de ses subordonnés, elle menait ses subordonnés à la baguette; **the maths teacher doesn't stand for any n.** le prof de maths ne se laisse pas marcher sur les pieds
EXCLAM n'importe quoi!
▸▸ ***nonsense verse*** vers *mpl* amphigouriques; ***nonsense word*** mot *m* qui ne veut rien dire, nonsens *m*

nonsensical [ˌnɒnˈsensɪkəl] ADJ *(talk, idea, action)* absurde, qui n'a pas de sens, inepte

nonsensically [ˌnɒnˈsensɪkəlɪ] ADV absurdement

non sequitur [ˌnɒnˈsekwɪtə(r)] N *Ling* illogisme *m*; **that's a n.** ça manque de suite; **his argument was full of non sequiturs** son raisonnement était incohérent

nonsexist [ˌnɒnˈseksɪst] N non-sexiste *mf*
ADJ non sexiste

nonshrink [ˌnɒnˈʃrɪŋk] ADJ irrétrécissable

nonskid [ˌnɒnˈskɪd] ADJ antidérapant

nonslip [ˌnɒnˈslɪp] ADJ antidérapant

nonsmoker [ˌnɒnˈsməʊkə(r)] N **1** *(person)* non-fumeur(euse) *m,f* **2** *Rail* compartiment *m* non-fumeurs

nonsmoking [ˌnɒnˈsməʊkɪŋ] ADJ *(carriage, compartment, area)* non-fumeurs; *(seat)* non-fumeur; **we have a n. office** il est interdit de fumer dans notre bureau

non-speaking part N *Cin & TV* rôle *m* muet

nonspecialist [ˌnɒnˈspeʃəlɪst] N non-spécialiste *mf*
ADJ non spécialiste

nonstandard [ˌnɒnˈstændəd] ADJ **1** *Ling (use of word)* critiqué; **in n. English** *(colloquial)* en anglais familier *ou* populaire; *(dialectal)* en anglais dialectal **2** *(product, size, shape etc)* non standard

nonstarter [ˌnɒnˈstɑːtə(r)] N **1** *(horse)* non-partant *m*; *(athlete, cyclist)* = athlète ou cycliste qui ne prend pas le départ **2** *Fam Fig* **this project is a n.** ce projet est foutu d'avance

nonstick [ˌnɒnˈstɪk] ADJ *(coating)* antiadhésif; *(pan)* antiadhésif, qui n'attache pas

nonstop [ˌnɒnˈstɒp] ADJ *(journey)* sans arrêt; *(flight)* direct, sans escale, non-stop *(inv)*; *(train)* direct; *(show, radio programme)* non-stop *(inv)*, sans interruption; **they kept up a n. conversation** leur conversation se poursuivit sans interruption
ADV sans arrêt; **to fly n. from Rome to Montreal** faire Rome-Montréal sans escale

non-synchronous ADJ *Cin & TV* non-synchrone

non-taxable ADJ non imposable

nontransferability [ˌnɒntrænsfɜːrəˈbɪlɪtɪ] N *(of share)* caractère *m* nominatif; *(of property, right)* incessibilité *f*

nontransferable [ˌnɒntrænsˈfɜːrəbəl] ADJ *(share)* nominatif; *(property, right)* incessible

non-U ADJ *Br Old-fashioned* = façon de désigner "ce qui ne se fait pas" selon le code des bonnes manières

nonunion [ˌnɒnˈjuːnjən], **nonunionized, -ised** [ˌnɒnˈjuːnjənaɪzd] ADJ *(worker, labour)* non syndiqué; *(firm)* qui n'emploie pas de personnel syndiqué

non-user N *(person)* non-utilisateur *m*

nonverbal [ˌnɒnˈvɜːbəl] ADJ non verbal
▸▸ ***nonverbal communication*** communication *f* par les gestes

nonvintage [nɒnˈvɪntɪdʒ] ADJ *(wine)* non millésimé

nonviolence [ˌnɒnˈvaɪələns] N non-violence *f*

nonviolent [ˌnɒnˈvaɪələnt] ADJ non violent

non-voter N *(person* ▸ *not eligible to vote)* personne *f* qui n'a pas le droit de vote; *(*▸ *not exercising the right to vote)* abstentionniste *mf*

non-voting ADJ **1** *(person* ▸ *not eligible to vote)* qui n'a pas le droit de vote; *(*▸ *not exercising the right to vote)* abstentionniste **2** *Fin (shares)* sans droit de vote

non-wasting ADJ *(asset)* indéfectible

nonwhite [ˌnɒnˈwaɪt] N personne *f* de couleur
ADJ de couleur; **a n. neighbourhood** un quartier où vivent des gens de couleur (et très peu de Blancs)

non-working ADJ *Econ (population)* inactif

noodle [ˈnuːdəl] N **1** *Culin* nouille *f*; **chicken n. soup** soupe *f* de poulet aux vermicelles **2** *Fam (fool)* andouille *f*, nouille *f* **3** *Fam (head)* tronche *f*, caboche *f*
• **noodles** NPL *Culin* nouilles *fpl*

nook [nʊk] N **1** *(corner)* coin *m*, recoin *m*; **nooks and crannies** coins et recoins; **in every n. and cranny** dans le moindre recoin **2** *Literary (secluded spot)* retraite *f*

nookie, nooky ['nʊkɪ] **N** *Fam Hum* partie *f* de jambes en l'air; **to have a bit of n.** faire une partie de jambes en l'air

noon [nu:n] **N** *(midday)* midi *m*; **at twelve n.** à midi; **come at n.** venez à midi
COMP *(break, train, flight)* de midi

noonday ['nu:ndeɪ] **N** *Literary* midi *m*
COMP *(heat, sun)* de midi

no one, no-one = **nobody**

noose [nu:s] **N** *(gen)* nœud *m* coulant; *(snare)* collet *m*; *(lasso)* lasso *m*; **(hangman's) n.** corde *f* (de potence); *Fig* **to put one's head in the n., to put a n. around one's neck** creuser sa (propre) tombe
VT 1 *(rope)* faire un nœud coulant à **2** *(snare)* prendre au collet; *(lasso)* attraper *ou* prendre au lasso

nope [nəʊp] **EXCLAM** *Fam* non[a], nan

nor [nɔ:(r)] **CONJ** *(following "neither", "not")* ni; **neither he n. his wife has ever spoken to me** ni lui ni sa femme ne m'ont jamais adressé la parole; **she neither drinks n. smokes** elle ne boit ni ne fume; *Literary* **not a wave, n. even a ripple, disturbed the surface** pas une vague ni même une ride ne troublait la surface
ADV I don't believe him, n. do I trust him je ne le crois pas, et je n'ai pas confiance en lui non plus; **it's not the first time, n. will it be the last** ce n'est ni la première ni la dernière fois; **she couldn't see them, n. (could) they (see) her** elle ne les voyait pas, et eux non plus; **I don't like fish – n. do I** je n'aime pas le poisson – moi non plus; **I haven't read it, n. do I intend to** je ne l'ai pas lu et d'ailleurs je n'en ai pas l'intention; **n. was this all** et ce n'était pas tout

Nordic ['nɔ:dɪk] **N** Nordique *mf*
ADJ nordique
►► ***Nordic skiing*** ski *m* nordique; ***Nordic walking*** marche *f* nordique

nor'east [nɔ:'ri:st] *Naut* = **northeast**

nor'easterly [nɔ:'ri:stəlɪ] *Naut* = **northeasterly**

nor'eastern [nɔ:'ri:stən] *Naut* = **northeastern**

nork [nɔ:k] **N** *Br & Austr very Fam (breast)* nichon *m*

norm [nɔ:m] **N** norme *f*; **to deviate from the n.** s'écarter de la norme; **unemployment has become the n. in certain areas** dans certaines régions, le chômage est devenu la règle; **it's the n.** c'est la règle

normal ['nɔ:məl] **ADJ 1** *(common, typical, standard)* normal; **under n. conditions of use** dans des conditions normales d'utilisation; **this is not n. behaviour** ce n'est pas un comportement normal; *Fam* **he's just a n. kind of bloke** c'est un type tout ce qu'il y a de (plus) banal; **it's n. for it to rain in April** il est normal *ou* naturel qu'il pleuve en avril; **any n. person would have...** toute personne normalement constituée aurait...
2 *(habitual)* habituel, normal; **at the n. time** à l'heure habituelle
3 *Math (in statistics, geometry)* normal
4 *Chem* normal
N 1 *(gen)* normale *f*, état *m* normal; **temperatures above n.** des températures au-dessus de la normale; **to get back to n.** revenir à la normale, rentrer dans l'ordre; **he'll soon be back to n.** tout rentrera bientôt dans l'ordre; *(in health)* il sera bientôt remis sur pied; **things are back to n. again** tout est rentré dans l'ordre **2** *Geom* normale *f*
►► *Math* ***normal distribution*** distribution *f* normale

normal-angle lens **N** *Phot* objectif *m* à focale fixe

normality [nɔ:'mælətɪ], *Am* **normalcy** ['nɔ:məlsɪ] **N** normalité *f*; **a return to n.** un retour à la normale; **everything returned to n.** tout est redevenu normal, tout est rentré dans l'ordre

normalization, -isation [,nɔ:məlaɪ'zeɪʃən] **N** normalisation *f*

normalize, -ise ['nɔ:məlaɪz] **VT** normaliser
VI se normaliser, redevenir normal

normally ['nɔ:məlɪ] **ADV 1** *(in a normal manner)* normalement **2** *(ordinarily)* en temps normal, normalement; **I n. get up at 7.30** en temps normal *ou* normalement, je me lève à 7h30; **n. I would have offered you a lift, but...** je vous aurais bien proposé de vous emmener, mais...

Norman ['nɔ:mən] **N 1** *(person)* Normand(e) *m,f* **2** *Ling* normand *m*
ADJ 1 *Geog & Hist* normand **2** *Archit* roman (anglais)
►► *Hist* ***the Norman Conquest*** la conquête normande *(de l'Angleterre)*; *Ling* ***Norman French*** normand *m*

Normandy ['nɔ:məndɪ] **N** Normandie *f*
►► *Hist* ***the Normandy landings*** le débarquement

normative ['nɔ:mətɪv] **ADJ** normatif
►► ***normative economics*** économie *f* normative

nor'nor'east [nɔ:nɔ:'ri:st] *Naut* = **north-northeast**

nor'nor'west [nɔ:nɔ:'west] *Naut* = **north-northwest**

Norse [nɔ:s] **NPL** *Hist* **the N.** *(Norwegians)* les Norvégiens *mpl*; *(Vikings)* les Vikings *mpl*
N *Ling* norrois *m*, nordique *m*
ADJ *(Scandinavian)* scandinave, nordique; *(Norwegian)* norvégien
►► ***Norse legends*** légendes *fpl* scandinaves; ***Norse mythology*** mythologie *f* scandinave

Norseman ['nɔ:smən] *(pl* **Norsemen** [-mən]*)* **N** Viking *m*

north [nɔ:θ] **N** nord *m*; **in the n.** au nord, dans le nord; **20 miles to the n. of Sydney** ≃ 32 kilomètres au nord de Sydney; **in the n. of India** dans le nord de l'Inde; **the wind is in the n.** le vent est au nord; **the wind is coming from the n.** le vent vient *ou* souffle du nord; **the N.** *(in American Civil War)* = les États antiesclavagistes du nord des États-Unis; *(affluent countries)* l'hémisphère *m* nord; **the N.-South divide** *(in Britain)* = ligne fictive de démarcation, en termes de richesse, entre le nord de l'Angleterre (plus pauvre) et le sud (plus riche); *(in global economy)* le fossé Nord-Sud
ADJ 1 *Geog* nord *(inv)*, du nord; *(country, state)* du Nord; *(wall)* exposé au nord; **the n. coast** la côte nord; **on the n. side** du côté nord; **in n. London** dans le nord de Londres; **in N. India** en Inde du Nord; **the N. Atlantic/Pacific** l'Atlantique *m*/le Pacifique Nord; **n. transept** *(in church)* transept *m* septentrional **2** *(wind)* de nord, du nord
ADV au nord; *(travel)* vers le nord, en direction du nord; **this room faces n.** cette pièce est exposée au nord; **to go n.** aller vers le nord; **I drove n. for two hours** j'ai roulé pendant deux heures en direction du nord; **it's n. of here** c'est au nord d'ici; **to sail n.** naviguer cap sur le nord; **they live up n.** ils habitent dans le Nord; **n. by east/by west** nord-quart-nord-est/nord-quart-nord-ouest; **further n.** plus au nord
►► ***North Africa*** Afrique *f* du Nord; ***North African*** **N** Nord-Africain(e) *m,f* **ADJ** nord-africain, d'Afrique du Nord; ***North America*** Amérique *f* du Nord; ***North American*** **N** Nord-Américain(e) *m,f* **ADJ** nord-américain, d'Amérique du Nord; *Econ* ***North American Free Trade Agreement*** Accord *m* de libre-échange nord-américain; ***the North Atlantic Drift*** le Gulf Stream; ***North Atlantic Treaty Organization*** Organisation *f* du traité de l'Atlantique du Nord; ***North Carolina*** la Caroline du Nord; ***the North Country*** *(in England)* l'Angleterre *f* du Nord; *(in America)* = l'Alaska, le Yukon et les Territoires du Nord-Ouest; **he's got a N. Country accent** il a un accent du Nord; ***North Dakota*** le Dakota du Nord; ***North Island*** l'île *f* du Nord; ***North Korea*** Corée *f* du Nord; ***North Korean*** **N** Nord-Coréen(enne) *m,f* **ADJ** nord-coréen; ***the North Pole*** le pôle Nord; ***North Sea, the North Sea*** la mer du Nord; ***North Sea gas*** gaz *m* de la mer du Nord; ***the North Star*** l'étoile *f* Polaire; ***North Vietnam*** le Viêt-Nam du Nord; ***North Vietnamese*** **N** Nord-Vietnamien(enne) *m,f* **ADJ** nord-vietnamien

Northants *(written abbr* **Northamptonshire***)* Northamptonshire *m*

northbound ['nɔ:θbaʊnd] **ADJ** *(traffic)* en direction du nord; *(lane, carriageway)* du nord; *(road)* vers le nord; **n. traffic is subject to delays** la circulation est ralentie dans le sens nord; *Br* **the n. carriageway of the motorway is closed** l'axe nord de l'autoroute est fermé (à la circulation); **there's a jam on the n. carriageway** il y a un bouchon en direction du nord

northeast [nɔ:θ'i:st] **N** nord-est *m*; **in the n. of Scotland** dans le nord-est de l'Écosse
ADJ 1 *Geog* nord-est *(inv)*, du nord-est; **in n. Sc[otland]** dans le nord-est de l'Écosse **2** *(wind)* nord-est, du nord-est
ADV au nord-est; *(travel)* vers le nord-est, en [di]rection du nord-est; **it's 20 miles n. of Birmingh[am]** ≃ c'est à 32 kilomètres au nord-est de Birmi[ng]ham

northeaster [nɔ:θ'i:stə(r)] **N** vent *m* de *ou* nord-est

northeasterly [nɔ:θ'i:stəlɪ] **ADJ 1** *Geog* nord-[est] *(inv)*, du nord-est; **to travel in a n. direction** al[ler] vers le nord-est; *Naut* **to steer a n. course** fa[ire] route vers le nord-est; *(when setting out)* met[tre] le cap au nord-est **2** *(wind)* de nord-est, du no[rd-]est
ADV vers le nord-est, en direction du nord-es[t]
N vent *m* de *ou* du nord-est; *Naut* nordé *m*, n[or]det *m*

northeastern [nɔ:θ'i:stən] **ADJ** nord-est *(in[v])*, du nord-est; *(wind)* de nord-est, du nord-e[st]; **the n. suburbs** la banlieue nord-est

northerly ['nɔ:ðəlɪ] *(pl* **northerlies***)* **ADJ 1** *Ge[og]* nord *(inv)*, du nord; **to travel in a n. direction** al[ler] vers le nord; **the most n. point of the United Sta[tes]** le point situé le plus au nord des États-Unis[;] **room with a n. aspect** une pièce exposée [au] nord; *Naut* **to steer a n. course** faire route vers [le] nord; *(when setting out)* mettre le cap au nord[;] **these n. latitudes** sous ces latitudes boréale[s] **2** *(wind)* de nord, du nord
ADV vers le nord, en direction du nord
N vent *m* de *ou* du nord

northern ['nɔ:ðən] **ADJ 1** *Geog* nord *(inv)*, [du] nord; **she has a n. accent** elle a un accent du no[rd]; **the n. wing of the castle** l'aile nord du château[;] **n. Mexico** dans le nord du Mexique; **the n. mig[ra]tion of swallows in spring** la migration print[a]nière des hirondelles vers le nord **2** *(wind)* nord, du nord **3** *Hist (in American Civil War)* n[or]diste
►► ***northern hemisphere*** l'hémisphère *m* nord boréal; ***Northern Ireland*** Irlande *f* du Nord; ***Nor[th]ern Irish*** de l'Irlande du Nord; ***northern lights*** a[u]rore *f* boréale; *Geog* ***Northern Territory*** Territoire du Nord; **in N. Territory** dans le Ter[ri]toire du Nord

> **NORTHERN IRELAND**
>
> L'Irlande du Nord désigne la partie de l'Ir[]lande à majorité protestante restée ratta[]chée à la Grande-Bretagne lors de la partition du pays, en 1921. Les émeutes san[]glantes qui ont éclaté à Belfast et à London[]derry en 1969 à la suite de manifestations revendiquant l'égalité des droits pour la mi[]norité catholique ont marqué le début de trente ans de conflit entre catholiques e[t] protestants en Irlande du Nord. Ce confli[t] vit s'affronter les nationalistes de l'IRA, fa[]vorables à un rattachement avec la Répu[]blique d'Irlande, différents groupes para[]militaires protestants anti-catholiques, e[t] l'armée et la police, sous contrôle britan[]nique. Le processus de paix, amorcé en 1994 et qui aboutit au **Good Friday Agreement** (voir encadré à l'entrée "good") de 1998 marqua une nouvelle étape plus optimiste dans l'histoire de l'Irlande du Nord en dépi[t] des nombreuses tensions qui subsistent en[]tre catholiques et protestants.

Northerner, northerner ['nɔ:ðənə(r)] **N** *(ge[n])* habitant(e) *m,f* du Nord; **she is a n.** elle vient [du] Nord

north-facing **ADJ** *Br (house, wall)* (exposé) [au] nord

north-north-east **N** nord-nord-est *m*
ADJ 1 *Geog* nord-nord-est *(inv)*, du nord-no[rd-]est **2** *(wind)* de *ou* du nord-nord-est
ADV au nord-nord-est; *(travel)* vers le nord-no[rd-]est, en direction du nord-nord-est

north-north-west **N** nord-nord-ouest *m*
ADJ 1 *Geog* nord-nord-ouest *(inv)*, du nor[d-]nord-ouest **2** *(wind)* de *ou* du nord-nord-oues[t]

ADV au nord-nord-ouest; *(travel)* vers le nord-nord-ouest, en direction du nord-nord-ouest

Northumb *(written abbr* **Northumberland***)* Northumberland *m*

northward ['nɔːθwəd] **ADJ** vers le nord, en direction du nord

ADV = **northwards**

N nord *m*

northwards ['nɔːθwədz] **ADV** vers le nord, en direction du nord; **to sail n.** naviguer cap sur le nord

northwest [nɔːθ'west] **N** nord-ouest *m*; **in the n. of Canada** dans le nord-ouest du Canada

ADJ 1 *Geog* nord-ouest *(inv)*, du nord-ouest; **in n. Canada** dans le nord-ouest du Canada **2** *(wind)* de nord-ouest, du nord-ouest

ADV au nord-ouest; *(travel)* vers le nord-ouest, en direction du nord-ouest; **it's 20 miles n. of London** ≃ c'est à 32 kilomètres au nord-ouest de Londres

northwester [nɔː'westə(r)] **N** vent *m* de *ou* du nord-ouest; *Naut* noroît *m*

northwesterly [nɔːθ'westəlɪ] **ADJ 1** *Geog* nord-ouest *(inv)*, du nord-ouest; **to travel in a n. direction** aller vers le nord-ouest; *Naut* **to steer a n. course** faire route vers le nord-ouest; *(when setting out)* mettre le cap au nord-ouest **2** *(wind)* de nord-ouest, du nord-ouest

ADV vers le nord-ouest, en direction du nord-ouest

N vent *m* de *ou* du nord-ouest; *Naut* noroît *m*

northwestern [nɔːθ'westən] **ADJ** nord-ouest *(inv)*, du nord-ouest; **the n. frontier** la frontière nord-ouest

Norway ['nɔːweɪ] **N** Norvège *f*

►► *Ich* ***Norway lobster*** langoustine *f*; *Bot* ***Norway spruce*** épicéa *m* d'Europe

Norwegian [nɔː'wiːdʒən] **N 1** *(person)* Norvégien(enne) *m,f* **2** *(language)* norvégien *m*

ADJ norvégien

COMP *(embassy)* de Norvège; *(history)* de la Norvège; *(teacher)* de norvégien

nose [nəʊz] **N 1** *(part of body)* nez *m*; **to hold one's n.** se pincer le nez; **to blow one's n.** se moucher; **the dog has a wet n.** le chien a le nez *ou* la truffe humide; **your n. is bleeding** tu saignes du nez; **your n. is running** tu as le nez qui coule; **to speak through one's n.** parler du nez; **I punched him on** *or* **in the n.** je lui ai donné un coup de poing en pleine figure; **she's always got her n. in a book** elle a toujours le nez dans un livre; *Horseracing* **the favourite won by a n.** le favori a gagné d'une demi-tête

2 *(sense of smell)* odorat *m*, nez *m*; **these dogs have an excellent n.** ces chiens ont un excellent flair *ou* le nez fin; *Fig* **she's got a (good) n. for a bargain** elle a le nez creux *ou* du nez pour dénicher les bonnes affaires

3 *(aroma* ► *of wine)* arôme *m*, bouquet *m*, nez *m*

4 *(forward part* ► *of aircraft, ship)* nez *m*; *(*► *of car)* avant *m*; *(*► *of bullet, missile, tool)* pointe *f*; *(*► *of gun)* canon *m*; *Br* **the traffic was n. to tail all the way to London** les voitures étaient pare-chocs contre pare-chocs jusqu'à Londres

5 *Fam (snoop)* **to have a n. around** faire un tour d'inspection

6 *(idioms)* **it was (right) under my n. all the time** c'était en plein sous mon nez; *Fig* **they stole it from under the n. of the police** ils l'ont volé au nez et à la barbe de la police; **he can see no further than (the end of) his n.** il ne voit pas plus loin que le bout de son nez; *Br Fam* **to get up sb's n.** taper sur les nerfs à qn; *Fam* **he really gets** *or* **he gets right up my n.** il me tape sur les nerfs, il me pompe l'air; **you've got** *or* **hit it right on the n.** tu as mis en plein dans le mille; **to keep one's n. clean** se tenir à carreau; **keep your (big) n. out of my business!** mêle-toi de ce qui te regarde!; **to keep** *or* **to have one's n. to the grindstone** bosser (dur); **to lead sb by the n.** mener qn par le bout du nez; **to look down one's n. at sb/sth** traiter qn/qch avec condescendance; **to pay through the n. (for sth)** payer (qch) la peau des fesses; *Br Fam* **to put sb's n. out of joint** contrarier *ou* dépiter qn; *Fam* **to rub sb's n. in it** retourner le couteau dans la plaie; *Fam* **she's always sticking** *or* **poking her n. into our affairs** elle est toujours en train de fourrer son nez dans nos affaires; **to turn up one's n. at sth** faire la fine bouche devant qch; **that's cutting off your n. to spite your face** c'est toi le perdant; **he's always walking around with his n. in the air** il prend toujours un air hautain *ou* méprisant

VT 1 the ship nosed her way through the fog le navire avançait à l'aveuglette à travers le brouillard **2** *(push with nose)* pousser du nez; **the dog nosed the door open** le chien a ouvert la porte en la poussant du nez **3** *(smell)* flairer, renifler

VI 1 *(advance with care)* avancer précautionneusement; **the car nosed out into the traffic** la voiture se frayait un chemin au milieu des embouteillages **2** *Fam (snoop)* fouiner; **to n. through sb's papers** fouiner *ou* mettre son nez dans les papiers de qn

►► *Fam Drugs slang* ***nose candy*** *(cocaine)* coco *f*, neige *f*; ***nose cone*** *(of missile)* ogive *f*; *(of aircraft)* nez *m*; ***nose drops*** gouttes *fpl* nasales *ou* pour le nez; *Fam* ***nose job*** intervention *f* de chirurgie esthétique sur le nez; **she's had a n. job** elle s'est fait refaire le nez; ***nose ring*** anneau *m* de nez; ***nose stud*** piercing *m* de nez; *Aviat* ***nose wheel*** roue *f* avant

► **nose about, nose around VI** *Fam (snoop)* fureter, fouiner; **I don't want them nosing about in here!** je ne veux pas qu'ils viennent fourrer leur nez ici!

VT INSEP *(office, room, garden)* fureter dans, fouiner dans; **a policeman was nosing around the car** un agent de police fouinait *ou* furetait autour de la voiture

► **nose out VT SEP 1** *(of dog) (game)* flairer **2** *Fam (secret)* découvrir, éventer; *(person)* dépister, dénicher; *(good restaurant, bargain)* dénicher **3** *Fam (beat narrowly)* battre d'une courte tête

nosebag ['nəʊzbæg] **N** *(for horse)* musette *f*

noseband ['nəʊzbænd] **N** *(of bridle)* muserolle *f*

nosebleed ['nəʊzbliːd] **N** saignement *m* de nez, *Spec* épistaxis *f*; **I've got a n.** je saigne du nez

nosedive ['nəʊzdaɪv] **N 1** *(of plane, bird)* piqué *m*; **I did a n. onto the concrete** je suis tombé la tête la première sur le béton **2** *Fig (sharp drop)* chute *f*, dégringolade *f*; **prices took a n.** les prix ont considérablement chuté; **his popularity has taken a n.** sa cote de popularité s'est littéralement effondrée

VI 1 *(plane)* piquer, descendre en piqué **2** *Fig (drop sharply* ► *prices, popularity)* chuter, dégringoler

nosegay ['nəʊzgeɪ] **N** *Literary* (petit) bouquet *m*

nose-to-tail ADJ *(traffic)* pare-chocs contre pare-chocs

nosey = **nosy**

nosh [nɒʃ] *Fam Old-fashioned* **N** bouffe *f*

VI bouffer

no-show N *(for flight, voyage)* = passager qui ne se présente pas à l'embarquement; *(for show)* = spectateur qui a réservé sa place et qui n'assiste pas au spectacle; **there were so many no-shows that they cancelled the flight** il y a eu tellement de défections que le vol a été annulé

nosh-up N *Br Fam Old-fashioned* gueuleton *m*

nosily ['nəʊzɪlɪ] **ADV** *Fam* indiscrètement

nosiness ['nəʊzɪnɪs] **N** *Fam* curiosité *f*, indiscrétion *f*

no-smoking ADJ *(carriage, area)* non-fumeurs; *(seat)* non-fumeur

nostalgia [nɒ'stældʒə] **N** nostalgie *f*

nostalgic [nɒ'stældʒɪk] **ADJ** nostalgique; **a n. moment** un moment de nostalgie; **to be** *or* **feel n. for sth** avoir la nostalgie de qch

nostalgically [nɒs'tældʒɪkəlɪ] **ADV** avec nostalgie, nostalgiquement

nostril ['nɒstrɪl] **N** *(gen)* narine *f*; *(of horse, cow etc)* naseau *m*

nostrum ['nɒstrəm] **N** *also Fig* panacée *f*

nosy ['nəʊzɪ] *(compar* **nosier**, *superl* **nosiest***)* **ADJ** *Fam* curieux, indiscret(ète); **don't be so n.!** occupe-toi donc de tes affaires *ou* de tes oignons!; **I don't mean to be n. but...** je ne veux pas me mêler de ce qui ne me regarde pas mais...

►► *Br Fam Pej* ***nosy parker*** fouine *f*

NOT [nɒt]

- ne… pas **1, 2, 6, 8**
- pas **4, 5, 8**
- non **4, 6**
- moins de **7**

À l'oral, et à l'écrit dans un style familier, on utilise généralement **not** à la forme contractée lorsqu'il suit un modal ou un auxiliaire (**don't go!**; **she wasn't there**; **he couldn't see me**).

ADV 1 *(after verb or auxiliary)* ne... pas; **we are n.** *or* **aren't sure** nous ne sommes pas sûrs; **do n.** *or* **don't believe her** ne la croyez pas; **didn't he** *or* **did he n. hear you?** ne vous a-t-il pas entendu?; **is she coming? – no, she isn't** *or* **she's n.** est-ce qu'elle vient? – non(, elle ne vient pas); **you've been there already, haven't you** *or Formal* **have you n.?** vous y êtes déjà allé, non *ou* n'est-ce pas?; **n. wishing to be seen, I drew the curtain** comme je ne désirais pas être vu, j'ai tiré le rideau

2 *(with infinitive)* ne... pas; **I asked them n. to do it** je leur ai demandé de ne pas le faire; **they were annoyed, n. to say furious** ils étaient ennuyés, pour ne pas dire furieux; *Fam* **n. to worry!** ne vous en faites pas!

3 *(elliptically in answers etc)* **n. at all, n. a bit (of it)** pas du tout; **thank you so much! – n. at all!** merci beaucoup! – je vous en prie; **n. likely!** jamais de la vie!; **n. always** pas toujours; **n. any more** *or* **longer** plus maintenant; **n. even in France** (non) pas même en France; **n. so** pas du tout; **n. yet** pas encore

4 *(as phrase or clause substitute)* non, pas; **we hope n.** nous espérons que non; **are there any left? – I'm afraid n.** est-ce qu'il en reste? – j'ai bien peur que non; *Formal* **will it rain? – I think n.** est-ce qu'il va pleuvoir? – je crois que non *ou* je ne crois pas; **whether they like it or n.** que ça leur plaise ou non *ou* ou pas; **n. if I've got anything to do with it** pas si j'ai mon mot à dire

5 *(with adjective, adverb, noun)* pas; **it's Thomas, n. Jake** c'est Thomas, pas Jake; **the water is green, n. blue** l'eau est verte, pas bleue; **n. guilty** non coupable; **he is respected but n. loved** il est respecté mais (non) pas aimé; **n. a leaf stirred** pas une feuille ne bougeait; **n. a word was spoken** on n'a pas dit un mot; **n. all her books are good** ses livres ne sont pas tous bons, tous ses livres ne sont pas bons; **n. everyone would agree with you** tout le monde ne serait pas d'accord avec toi; **who wants some more? – n. me** qui en veut encore? – pas moi; *Formal* **n. I** pas moi; *Br Fam* **n. half!** et comment!, tu parles!

6 *(in double negatives)* **n. without some difficulty** non sans quelque difficulté; **it's n. unusual for him to be late** il n'est pas rare qu'il soit en retard; **I wasn't sorry to go** j'étais bien content de partir; **the two events are n. unconnected** les deux événements ne sont pas tout à fait indépendants l'un de l'autre

7 *(less than)* moins de; **n. ten metres away** à moins de dix mètres

8 n. that... ce n'est pas que... + *subjunctive*, non (pas) que... + *subjunctive*; **n. that I can remember** pas autant que je m'en souvienne

9 *Arch or Literary (following the verb)* **I know n.** je ne sais point; **fear n.!** n'ayez crainte!

10 *Fam Hum* **it was a great party, n.!** c'était pas vraiment génial comme soirée!; **he's really gorgeous, n.!** c'est pas exactement un Apollon!

notability [ˌnəʊtə'bɪlətɪ] *(pl* **notabilities***)* **N 1** *(importance)* importance *f* **2** *(important person)* notabilité *f*, notable *m*

notable ['nəʊtəbəl] **ADJ** *(thing)* notable, remarquable; *(person)* notable, éminent; **it is n. that...** il faut noter que...; **with a few n. exceptions** à part quelques exceptions notables; **the film was n. for its lack of violence** le film se distinguait par l'absence de scènes de violence

N notable *m*

notably ['nəʊtəblɪ] **ADV 1** *(particularly)* notamment, en particulier; **several officials were absent, n. the mayor** il manquait plusieurs personnalités, notamment le maire **2** *(markedly)* manifestement, de toute évidence

notarize, -ise ['nəʊtəraɪz] **VT** certifier, authentifier

▸▸ ***notarized copy*** ≃ copie *f* certifiée conforme *(par un notaire)*; ***notarized deed*** acte *m* notarié

notary [ˈnəʊtərɪ] *(pl* **notaries)** **N n. (public)** notaire *m*; **signed in the presence of a n.** signé par-devant notaire

notation [nəʊˈteɪʃən] **N 1** *(sign system)* notation *f*; **musical n.** notation *f* musicale; **mathematical n.** symboles *mpl* mathématiques; **in binary n.** en numération binaire, en base 2 **2** *Am (jotting)* notation *f*, note *f*

notch [nɒtʃ] **N 1** *(cut ▸ in stick)* entaille *f*, encoche *f*; *(hole ▸ in belt, rack)* cran *m*; *(of toothed wheel)* cran *m*, dent *f*; *(in blade)* brèche *f*; *Sewing* cran *m*; *(in diskette)* encoche *f*; **he let out/took in his belt a n.** il a desserré/resserré sa ceinture d'un cran; *Fig* **a n. on the bedpost** une conquête **2** *(degree)* cran *m*; **he's gone up a n. in my estimation** il est monté d'un cran dans mon estime; **turn the heating up a n.** monte un peu le chauffage; **her novel is a n. above the rest** son roman est meilleur que les autres **3** *Am (gorge)* défilé *m*

VT *(make cut in ▸ stick)* entailler, encocher; *(▸ gear wheel)* cranter, denteler; *(damage ▸ blade)* ébrécher

▸ **notch up VT SEP** *(point)* marquer; *(victory)* remporter; **they've notched up six wins in a row** ils ont six victoires consécutives à leur palmarès

NOTE [nəʊt]

N
- note **1, 3, 4, 6, 7, 8**
- mot **2**
- billet **5, 9**
- ton **6**
- touche **7**

VT
- remarquer **1, 3**
- noter **1, 2**
- observer **3**

N 1 *(record, reminder)* note *f*; **to take** *or* **to make notes** prendre des notes; **she spoke from/without notes** elle a parlé en s'aidant/sans s'aider de notes; **make a n. of everything you spend** notez toutes vos dépenses; **I must make a n. of it** il faut que je m'en souvienne; **he made a mental n. to look for it later** il se promit de le chercher plus tard; **they have no n. of any such meeting** ils n'ont aucune trace de cette réunion; *Fig* **to compare notes** échanger ses impressions; *Univ* **lecture notes** notes *fpl* (de cours)

2 *(short letter)* mot *m*; **she left a n. to say she'd call back later** elle a laissé un mot pour dire qu'elle repasserait plus tard

3 *(formal communication)* note *f*; **diplomatic n.** note *f* diplomatique; **a doctor's** *or* **sick n.** un certificat *ou* une attestation du médecin (traitant); *Sch* un certificat (médical)

4 *(annotation, commentary)* note *f*, annotation *f*; **editor's n.** note *f* de la rédaction; **to write** *or* **to make notes on a text** annoter un texte; **programme notes** notes *fpl* sur le programme

5 *Br (banknote)* billet *m* (de banque); **ten pound n.** billet *m* de dix livres

6 *(sound, tone)* ton *m*, note *f*; *Fig (feeling, quality)* note *f*; **there was a n. of contempt in her voice** il y avait du mépris dans sa voix; **the meeting began on a promising n.** la réunion débuta sur une note optimiste; **on a more serious/a happier n.** pour parler de choses plus sérieuses/plus gaies; **her speech struck a warning n.** son discours était un signal d'alarme; **to strike the right/a false n.** *(speech)* sonner juste/faux; *(behaviour)* être/ne pas être dans le ton

7 *Mus* note *f*; *Br (piano key)* touche *f*; **to hit a high n.** sortir un aigu

8 *(notice, attention)* **to take n. of sth** prendre (bonne) note de qch

9 *Com* **(promissory) n., n. of hand** billet *m* à ordre

VT 1 *(observe, notice)* remarquer, noter; **he noted that the window was open** il remarqua que la fenêtre était ouverte; **we have noted several omissions** nous avons relevé plusieurs oublis; **n. that she didn't actually refuse** notez (bien) qu'elle n'a pas vraiment refusé; **please n. that payment is now due** veuillez effectuer le règlement dans les plus brefs délais; **it should be noted that...** il est à noter que...

2 *(write down)* noter, écrire; **all sales are noted in this book** toutes les ventes sont enregistrées *ou* consignées dans ce carnet

3 *(mention)* (faire) remarquer *ou* observer; **as I noted earlier** comme je l'ai fait remarquer précédemment

• **of note ADJ a musician of n.** un musicien éminent *ou* renommé; **a musician of some n.** un musicien d'une certaine renommée; **nothing of n. has happened** il ne s'est rien passé d'important, aucun événement majeur ne s'est produit

▸▸ *Fin* ***note issue*** émission *f* fiduciaire

▸ **note down VT SEP** *(write down)* noter, écrire

notebook [ˈnəʊtbʊk] **N** carnet *m*, calepin *m*; *Sch* cahier *m*, carnet *m*; *Comput* agenda *m*

▸▸ ***notebook computer*** portable *m*, ordinateur *m* bloc-notes

notecase [ˈnəʊtkeɪs] **N** *Br Old-fashioned* portefeuille *m*

noted [ˈnəʊtɪd] **ADJ** *(person)* éminent, célèbre; *(place, object)* réputé, célèbre; *(fact, idea)* reconnu; **he's not n. for his subtlety** il ne passe pas pour quelqu'un de particulièrement subtil; **a region n. for its lakes** une région réputée *ou* connue pour ses lacs

notelet [ˈnəʊtlɪt] **N** *Br* carte-lettre *f*

notepad [ˈnəʊtpæd] **N** *(for notes)* bloc-notes *m*; *(for letters)* bloc *m* de papier à lettres

▸▸ ***notepad (computer)*** ardoise *f* électronique

notepaper [ˈnəʊtpeɪpə(r)] **N** papier *m* à lettres

note-taking N prise *f* de notes

noteworthy [ˈnəʊtˌwɜːðɪ] **ADJ** notable, remarquable; **it is n. that...** il convient de noter que...

not-for-profit *Am* = **non-profit-making**

NOTHING [ˈnʌθɪŋ] **PRON** ne... rien; **she forgets n.** elle n'oublie rien; **n. has been decided** rien n'a été décidé; **n. can beat French cooking** il n'y a rien de mieux que la cuisine française; **I have n. to drink** je n'ai rien à boire; **what are you doing? – n.** que faites-vous? – rien; **it's better than n.** c'est mieux que rien; **to have n. to do with sb/sth** n'avoir rien à voir avec qn/qch; **it's got n. to do with you** ça ne te concerne absolument pas; **I told them n. at all** je ne leur ai rien dit du tout; **you can't live on n.** on ne peut pas vivre de rien; **I have n. else to say** je n'ai rien d'autre à dire; **it looks like n. on earth** c'est ridicule; **n. serious** rien de grave; **that's n. new** ce n'est pas nouveau; **that's n. unusual** cela n'a rien d'anormal; **n. much** pas grand-chose; **there is n. more to be said** il n'y a plus rien à dire; **he's n. more than a petty crook** il n'est rien d'autre qu'un vulgaire escroc; **n. could be simpler** rien de plus simple, c'est tout ce qu'il y a de plus simple; **n. less than outright victory would satisfy him** seule une victoire écrasante le satisferait; **it was n. less than** *or* **short of a miracle** c'était tout simplement miraculeux/un miracle; **it's n. less than scandalous that...** c'est ni plus ni moins un scandale que...; **they're always fighting over n.** ils passent leur temps à se disputer pour des broutilles *ou* des riens; **she gets angry about n.** elle se fâche pour un rien; **reduced to n.** réduit à néant; **there's n. to cry/worry about** il n'y a pas de quoi pleurer/s'inquiéter; **n. else matters** tout le reste n'est rien, rien d'autre n'a d'importance; **there's n. (else) for it but to start again** il n'y a plus qu'à recommencer; **there's n. in it** *(no difference)* il n'y a aucune différence; *(in choosing between two candidates)* ils se valent, il n'y a aucune différence entre eux; *(in race)* ils sont à égalité; **there's n. in** *or* **to these rumours** ces rumeurs sont dénuées de tout fondement; **there's n. to it!** *(it's easy)* c'est simple (comme bonjour)!; **to come to n.** ne pas aboutir; *(of hopes etc)* s'anéantir; *(of scheme etc)* s'effondrer; **she says he's n.** *or* **he means n. to her** elle dit qu'il n'est rien pour elle; **the name means n. to me** le nom ne me dit rien; **a thousand pounds is n. to her** mille livres, ce n'est rien pour elle; **that's n. to what mum will say** ce n'est rien par rapport à ce que maman va dire; **in those days it was n. to see...** en ce temps-là, on voyait facilement...; **to think n. of doing sth** *(not hesitate to do)* ne pas hésiter à faire qch; **she thinks n. of walking 10 kilometres** pour elle 10 kilomètres à pied, ce n'est rien; **I can make n. of it** je n'y comprends rien du tout; **I'll take what's due to me, n. more, n. less** je prendrai mon dû, ni plus ni moins; **to have n. on** *(no engagement)* être libre; *(no clothes)* être tout nu; *Fam* **what a physique! Charles Atlas has got n. on you!** quel physique! tu n'as rien à envier à Charles Atlas *ou* Charles Atlas peut aller se rhabiller!; *Literary* **our sacrifices were as n. compared to his** nos sacrifices ne furent rien auprès des siens; *Fam* **n. doing!** pas question!

N 1 *(trifle)* rien *m*, vétille *f*; **a hundred euros? – a mere n.!** cent euros? – une bagatelle!; **to whisper sweet nothings to sb/in sb's ear** chuchoter des mots doux à qn/à l'oreille de qn

2 *Fam (person)* nullité *f*, zéro *m*

3 *Math* zéro *m*

ADJ *Fam (worthless)* nul; **it's a n. play!** c'est une pièce nulle!

• **for nothing ADV 1** *(gratis)* pour rien; **I got it for n. at the flea market** je l'ai eu pour (trois fois) rien aux puces

2 *(for no purpose)* pour rien; **all that work for n.** tout ce travail pour rien *ou* en pure perte!; **to count for n.** ne compter pour rien

3 *(for no good reason)* pour rien; **it's not for n. that...** ce n'est pas pour rien *ou* sans raison que...

• **nothing but ADV that car's been n. but trouble** cette voiture ne m'a attiré que des ennuis; **n. but a miracle can save us** seul un miracle pourrait nous sauver; **she wants n. but the best** elle ne veut que ce qu'il y a de meilleur

• **nothing if not ADV** rien de moins que; **she's n. if not honest** elle n'est rien de moins qu'honnête

• **nothing like PREP 1** *(completely unlike)* **she's n. like her mother** elle ne ressemble en rien à sa mère

2 *(nothing as good as)* **there's n. like a nice hot bath** rien de tel qu'un bon bain chaud **ADV** *Fam (nowhere near)* **this box is n. like big enough** cette boîte est beaucoup trop *ou* bien trop petite; **n. like as big** loin d'être aussi grand

nothingness [ˈnʌθɪŋnɪs] **N** néant *m*; **a feeling of sense of n.** un sentiment de vide

NOTICE [ˈnəʊtɪs]

N
- annonce **1**
- écriteau **1**
- affiche **1**
- attention **2**
- avis **3, 6**
- préavis **3**
- congé **4**
- démission **4**
- critique **5**

VT
- remarquer **1**
- faire attention à **2**

N 1 *(written announcement)* annonce *f*; *(sign)* écriteau *m*, pancarte *f*; *(poster)* affiche *f*; *(in newspaper ▸ article)* entrefilet *m*; *(▸ advertisement)* annonce *f*; **a n. was pinned to the door** il y avait une affiche sur la porte; **they put a birth n. in the local paper** ils ont passé un faire-part de naissance dans le quotidien régional

2 *(attention)* attention *f*; **to take n. of** faire *ou* prêter attention à; **to take not the slightest n. of sth** ne pas prêter la moindre attention à qch; **take no n. (of him)!** ne faites pas attention (à lui)!; **you never take any n. of what I say!** tu ne fais jamais attention à ce que je dis!; **to bring sth to sb's n.** faire remarquer qch à qn, attirer l'attention de qn sur qch; **certain facts have come to** *or* **been brought to our n.** on a attiré notre attention sur certains faits; **it has come to my n. that...** il est venu à ma connaissance que...; **her book attracted a great deal of/little n.** son livre a suscité beaucoup/peu d'intérêt; **to escape** *or* **to avoid n.** passer inaperçu; **my mistake did not escape his n.** mon erreur ne lui a pas échappé

3 *(notification, warning)* avis *m*, notification *f*; *(advance notification)* préavis *m*; **please give us n. of your intentions** veuillez nous faire part préalablement de vos intentions; *Formal* **n. is hereby given that...** le public est avisé que...; **he was given n.** *or* **n. was served on him to quit** on lui a fait savoir qu'il devait partir; **give me more n. next time you come up** préviens-moi plus tôt la prochaine fois que tu viens; **legally, they must give you a month's n.** d'après la loi, ils doivent vous donner un préavis d'un mois *ou* un mois de préavis; **without previous** *or* **prior n.** sans prévenir; **he turned up without any n.** il est arrivé à l'improviste; **at a moment's n.** sur-le-champ, im nédiatement; **at short n.** très rapidement; **it's impossible to do the work at such short n.** c'est un travail impossible à faire dans un délai aussi court; **that's rather short n.** c'est un peu court comme délai; **until further n.** jusqu'à nouvel ordre *ou* avis; **deposit at seven days' n.** dépôt *m* à sept jours de préavis

4 *(intent to terminate contract ▸ by employer, landlord, tenant)* congé *m*; *(▸ by employee)* démission *f*; **50 people have been given their n.** 50 personnes ont été licenciées; **to give in** *or* **to hand in one's n.** remettre sa démission; **has the landlord given you n.?** le propriétaire vous a-t-il donné congé?; **to give sb a week's n.** donner ses huit jours à qn; **we are under n. to quit** nous avons reçu notre congé; **what n. do you require?** quel est le terme du congé?; **employees must give three months' n.** les employés doivent donner trois mois de préavis

5 *(review)* critique *f*; **the play got excellent notices** la pièce a eu d'excellentes critiques

6 *(notifying document)* avis *m*, notification *f*; *(warning document)* avertissement *m*; *Law (served by bailiff)* dénonciation *f*; **n. to pay** avertissement *m*

VT 1 *(spot, observe)* remarquer, s'apercevoir de; **he noticed a scratch on the table** il remarqua que la table était rayée; **didn't anybody n. him leaving?** est-ce que personne n'a remarqué qu'il partait?; **hello, Sam, I didn't n. you in the corner** bonjour, Sam, je ne t'avais pas vu dans le coin; **so I've noticed!** c'est ce que j'ai remarqué!; **without his noticing it** sans qu'il s'en aperçoive; **she's beginning to get herself noticed** *(of writer, performer etc)* elle commence à être connue *ou* à percer

2 *(take notice of)* faire attention à; **he never notices what I wear!** il ne fait jamais attention à ce que je porte!

VI remarquer; **nobody will ever n.** personne ne s'en apercevra *ou* ne le remarquera jamais; **what happened? – I don't know, I didn't n.** qu'est-ce qui s'est passé? – je ne sais pas, je ne m'en suis pas rendu compte

▸▸ *Law* ***notice of appeal*** intimation *f* d'appel; *Com* ***notice period*** période *f* de préavis

> Note that the French word **notice** is a false friend and is never a translation for the English word **notice**. Its most common meaning is **directions (for use)**.

noticeable ['nəʊtɪsəbəl] **ADJ** *(mark, defect)* visible; *(effect, change, improvement)* sensible; **the stain is barely n.** la tache est à peine visible *ou* se voit à peine; **it was very n. that she didn't speak to her husband** on ne pouvait pas ne pas remarquer qu'elle ne parlait pas à son mari

noticeably ['nəʊtɪsəblɪ] **ADV** sensiblement; **to be n. absent** briller par son absence; **to be n. lacking in good manners** manquer totalement de savoir-vivre; **students did n. less well in these subjects** les étudiants ont obtenu des résultats nettement inférieurs dans ces matières

noticeboard ['nəʊtɪsbɔːd] **N** *Br* panneau *m* d'affichage

notifiable ['nəʊtɪfaɪəbəl] **ADJ** *Med (disease)* à déclaration obligatoire

notification [ˌnəʊtɪfɪ'keɪʃən] **N** notification *f*, avis *m*; **you will receive n. by post** vous serez averti par courrier

notify ['nəʊtɪfaɪ] *(pt & pp* **notified***)* **VT** notifier, avertir; **to n. sb of sth** avertir qn de qch, notifier qch à qn; **have you notified the authorities?** avez-vous averti *ou* prévenu les autorités?; **winners will be notified within ten days** les gagnants seront avisés dans les dix jours

notion ['nəʊʃən] **N 1** *(concept)* notion *f*, concept *m*; **the n. of evil** la notion du mal; **to have no n. of sth** ne pas avoir la moindre notion de qch; **I lost all n. of time** j'ai perdu la notion du temps

2 *(vague idea)* notion *f*, idée *f*; **have you any n. of what it will cost?** avez-vous une idée de ce que cela va coûter?; **where did she get the n.** *or* **whatever gave her the n. that we don't like her?** où est-elle allée chercher que nous ne l'aimions pas?

3 *(thought, whim)* idée *f*; **she has some pretty strange notions** elle a de drôles d'idées; **he hit upon the n. of buying a houseboat** il eut soudain l'idée d'acheter une péniche aménagée

4 *(urge)* envie *f*, désir *m*; **I've got a n. to paint it red** j'ai envie de le peindre en rouge

• **notions NPL** *Am (haberdashery)* mercerie *f*

notional ['nəʊʃənəl] **ADJ 1** *Br (hypothetical)* théorique, notionnel; **let's put a n. price of £2 a kilo on it** pour avoir un ordre d'idées, fixons-en le prix à 2 livres le kilo **2** *(imaginary)* imaginaire **3** *Ling (word)* sémantique, plein

▸▸ ***notional grammar*** grammaire *f* notionnelle; ***notional income*** revenu *m* fictif

notoriety [ˌnəʊtə'raɪətɪ] *(pl* **notorieties***)* **N** triste notoriété *f*; **to seek n.** chercher à se faire remarquer; **these measures brought** *or* **gained him n.** ces mesures l'ont rendu tristement célèbre

notorious [nəʊ'tɔːrɪəs] **ADJ** *Pej (ill-famed ▸ person)* tristement célèbre; *(▸ crime)* célèbre; *(▸ place)* mal famé; **a n. miser/spy/murderer** un avare/espion/meurtrier notoire; **she's n. for being late** elle est connue pour ne jamais être à l'heure; **a city n. for its slums** une ville connue *ou* célèbre pour ses bidonvilles; **the junction is a n. accident spot** ce croisement est réputé pour être très dangereux

notoriously [nəʊ'tɔːrɪəslɪ] **ADV** notoirement; **the trains here are n. unreliable** tout le monde sait qu'on ne peut pas se fier aux horaires des trains ici

Notting Hill [ˌnɒtɪŋ'hɪl] **N** = quartier de Londres

> **THE NOTTING HILL CARNIVAL**
>
> De nombreux immigrés en provenance des Caraïbes s'installèrent à Londres, dans le quartier de Notting Hill, au cours des années 50 et 60. Ils créèrent le carnaval de Notting Hill afin de célébrer leur culture d'origine. Aujourd'hui, Notting Hill est un quartier de Londres très à la mode et le carnaval attire des milliers de visiteurs chaque été. Des défilés de chars sont organisés, des stands vendent des spécialités culinaires des Caraïbes et les gens dansent dans les rues sur toutes sortes de musiques d'origine noire, du reggae au r'n'b, en passant par le calypso et le hip hop.

Notts *(written abbr* **Nottinghamshire***)* Nottinghamshire *m*

notwithstanding [ˌnɒtwɪθ'stændɪŋ] *Formal*
PREP en dépit de, nonobstant
ADV malgré tout, néanmoins

nougat ['nuːgɑː] **N** nougat *m*

nought [nɔːt] **N 1** *Br (zero)* zéro *m*; **n. point five** zéro virgule cinq **2** *Arch* = **naught**

▸▸ *Br* ***noughts and crosses*** *(UNCOUNT)* ≃ morpion *m (jeu)*

noughties ['nɔːtɪz] **NPL** *Fam* années *fpl* deux mille à deux mille dix□

noun [naʊn] **N** nom *m*, substantif *m*; **common/proper n.** nom *m* commun/propre

▸▸ ***noun clause*** proposition *f*; ***noun phrase*** groupe *m ou* syntagme *m* nominal

nourish ['nʌrɪʃ] **VT 1** *(feed)* nourrir; **nourished on grain** nourri au grain **2** *(entertain, foster)* nourrir, entretenir

nourishing ['nʌrɪʃɪŋ] **ADJ** nourrissant, nutritif

nourishment ['nʌrɪʃmənt] **N** *(UNCOUNT)* **1** *(food)* nourriture *f*, aliments *mpl*; **the patient has taken no n.** le malade ne s'est pas alimenté; **you're not getting enough n.** tu ne t'alimentes pas bien; **it's full of n.** c'est très nourrissant *ou* nutritif **2** *(act of nourishing)* alimentation *f*

nous [naʊs] **N** *Fam* bon sens□*m*, jugeote *f*; **she's got a lot of n.** elle a beaucoup de bon sens, elle est très sensée□; **anyone with any n.** n'importe qui doté d'un minimum de bon sens

Nov. *(written abbr* **November***)* nov

nova ['nəʊvə] *(pl* **novas** *or* **novae** [-viː]*)* **N** nova *f*

novel ['nɒvəl] **N** roman *m*
ADJ nouveau(elle), original; **what a n. idea!** quelle idée originale!; **it was a n. experience for me** ce fut une expérience nouvelle pour moi

> Note that the French noun **nouvelle** is a false friend. It means **short story**.

novelette [ˌnɒvə'let] **N 1** *(short novel)* nouvelle *f* **2** *Pej (easy reading)* roman *m* de hall de gare; *(love story)* roman *m* à l'eau de rose

novelist ['nɒvəlɪst] **N** romancier(ère) *m,f*

novelization, -isation [ˌnɒvəlaɪ'zeɪʃən] **N** *(of film)* novélisation *f*

novella [nə'velə] *(pl* **novellas** *or* **novelle** [-leɪ]*)* **N** ≃ nouvelle *f (texte plus court qu'un roman et plus long qu'une nouvelle)*

novelty ['nɒvəltɪ] *(pl* **novelties***)* **N 1** *(newness)* nouveauté *f*, originalité *f*; **the n. soon wore off** l'attrait de la nouveauté n'a pas duré; **there was no n. in it any more** cela n'avait plus rien de nouveau; **the n. of this scheme is that...** ce que ce programme a de nouveau *ou* d'innovateur c'est que... **2** *(thing, idea)* innovation *f*, nouveauté *f*; **it was a real n.** c'était une nouveauté, c'était tout nouveau; **as the only Chinese child, he was something of a n.** seul enfant chinois, il faisait figure de nouveauté **3** *(trinket)* nouveauté *f*, article *m* fantaisie; *(gadget)* gadget *m*

COMP *(object)* fantaisie *(inv)*

▸▸ ***novelty jewellery*** bijoux *mpl* fantaisie; ***novelty value*** attrait *m* de la nouveauté

November [nəʊ'vembə(r)] **N** novembre *m*; *see also* **February**

novena [nəʊ'viːnə] *(pl* **novenae** [-niː]*)* **N** neuvaine *f*

novice ['nɒvɪs] **N 1** *(beginner)* débutant(e) *m,f*, novice *mf*; **I'm still a n. at golf** en matière de golf, je ne suis encore qu'un novice; **a n. at skiing, a n. skier** un skieur débutant **2** *Rel* novice *mf*

novitiate, noviciate [nə'vɪʃɪət] **N** *Rel* **1** *(period)* noviciat *m*; *Fig* noviciat *m*, apprentissage *m* **2** *(place)* noviciat *m*

NOW [naʊ]

ADV	
• maintenant **1–3**	• aujourd'hui **2**
• alors **3**	• or **4**
CONJ	
• maintenant que	
ADJ	
• actuel **1**	• branché **2**

ADV 1 *(at this time)* maintenant; **what shall we do n.?** qu'est-ce qu'on fait maintenant?; **he hasn't seen her for a week n., it's a week n. since he's seen her** ça fait maintenant une semaine qu'il ne l'a pas vue; **she'll be here any moment** *or* **any time n.** elle va arriver d'un moment *ou* instant à l'autre; **he won't be long n.** il ne va plus tarder; **we are n. entering enemy territory** nous sommes désormais en territoire ennemi; **it's n. or never** c'est le moment ou jamais; **n. is the time to invest, the time to invest is n.** c'est maintenant le moment d'investir; *Hum* **n. she tells me!** c'est maintenant qu'elle me le dit!; **(and) n. for something completely different** (et) voici à présent quelque chose de tout à fait différent; **as of n.** désormais; **I'd never met them before n.** je ne les avais jamais rencontrés auparavant; **between n. and next August/next year** d'ici le mois d'août prochain/l'année prochaine; **they must have got the letter by n.** ils ont dû recevoir la lettre à l'heure qu'il est; **he ought to be here by n., he ought to have been here before n.** il devrait déjà être arrivé; **that's all for n.** c'est tout pour le moment; **from n. until Monday/next year** d'ici (à) lundi prochain/l'année prochaine; **in a few years from n.** d'ici quelques années; **from n. on** désormais, dorénavant, à partir de maintenant; **we've had no problems till n.** *or* **until n.** *or* **up to n.** nous n'avons eu aucun problème jusqu'ici

2 *(nowadays)* maintenant, aujourd'hui, actuellement; **he lives in London n.** il habite (à) Londres maintenant; **her n. famous first novel** son premier roman, aujourd'hui célèbre

3 *(marking a specific point in the past)* maintenant, alors, à ce moment-là; **by n. we were all exhausted** nous étions alors tous épuisés; **he was even n. on his way** il était déjà en route

4 *(before statement, argument)* **n. that's what I call a car!** voilà ce que j'appelle une voiture!; **n. it happened that...** *(in story)* or il advint que...; **n., what was I saying?** voyons, où en étais-je?; **there n.** *or* **n., n., you mustn't cry** allons, allons, il ne faut pas pleurer; **n. then, what's all the noise about?** eh bien alors, qu'est-ce que c'est que tout ce bruit?; **you be careful n.!** fais bien attention, hein!; **n. then...!** attention, hein...!; **n., n.!, stop quarrelling!** voyons, voyons!, assez de querelles!

CONJ maintenant que, à présent que; **she's happier n. (that) she's got a job** elle est plus heureuse depuis qu'elle travaille; **n. you come to mention it** maintenant que tu le dis

ADJ *Fam* **1** *(current)* actuel; **the n. president** le président actuel

2 *(fashionable)* branché; **golf is the n. thing to do** pour être branché, il faut se mettre au golf

• **now and again, now and then ADV** de temps en temps, de temps à autre

• **now... now CONJ** tantôt... tantôt; **n. happy, n. sad** tantôt gai, tantôt triste

nowadays ['naʊədeɪz] **ADV** aujourd'hui, de nos jours; **n. there is much more job insecurity** la précarité de l'emploi est un phénomène beaucoup plus courant de nos jours; **where's she working n.?** où travaille-t-elle actuellement?

nowhere ['nəʊweə(r)] **ADV 1** *(no place)* nulle part; **he goes n. without her** il ne va nulle part sans elle; **I've got n. to go** je n'ai nulle part où aller; **there's n. to hide** il n'y a pas d'endroit où se cacher; **n. else** nulle part ailleurs; **where are you going? – n. in particular** où vas-tu? – je ne sais pas exactement; **she's n. in the building** elle n'est pas dans l'immeuble; **she was n. to be found** on ne la trouvait nulle part, elle était introuvable; **she/the book was n. to be seen** elle/le livre avait disparu; **without your help we would be n.** sans votre aide nous serions perdus; **the horse I backed came n.** le cheval sur lequel j'ai parié est arrivé bon dernier *ou* loin derrière; **lying will get you n.** mentir ne vous servira à *ou* ne mènera à rien; *Fam* **we're getting n. fast** on pédale dans la choucroute *ou* la semoule; **he's going n. fast** il n'ira pas loin; **that kind of attitude will get you n.** ce genre d'attitude ne t'avancera *ou* ne te servira à rien **2** *(idioms)* **the hotel was n. near the beach** l'hôtel était bien loin de la plage; **dinner is n. near ready** le dîner est loin d'être prêt; **he's n. near as intelligent as his sister** il est loin d'être aussi intelligent que sa sœur

N a small place in the middle of n. un petit trou perdu; **he appeared from n.** *or* **out of n.** il est apparu comme par enchantement; **she rose to fame from n.** elle est devenue célèbre du jour au lendemain; **he came from n. to win the race** il a fait une remontée spectaculaire et a gagné la course

nowt [naʊt] **PRON** *NEng Fam (nothing)* rien; que dalle; **have you n. to say?** tu n'as rien à dire?

noxious ['nɒkʃəs] **ADJ** *(gas, substance)* nocif; *(influence)* néfaste

nozzle ['nɒzəl] **N** *(gen)* bec *m*, embout *m*; *(for hose, paint gun)* jet *m*, buse *f*; *(of bellows)* bec *m*, tuyau *m*, buse *f*; *(in carburettor)* gicleur *m*; *(in turbine)* tuyère *f*; *(of vacuum cleaner)* suceur *m*; *(for icing)* douille *f*

NPD [ˌenpiːˈdiː] **N** *Mktg* (*abbr* **new product development**) développement *m* de nouveaux produits

NPV [ˌenpiːˈviː] **N** *Acct* (*abbr* **net present value**) VAN *f*, valeur *f* actuelle nette

▸▸ ***NPV rate*** taux *m* d'actualisation

NQT [ˌenkjuːˈtiː] **N** *Br* (*abbr* **newly qualified teacher**) = enseignant nouvellement formé

NRS [ˌenɑːˈres] **N** (*abbr* **national readership survey**) étude *f* nationale sur le lectorat

NS (*written abbr* **Nova Scotia**) Nouvelle-Écosse *f*

NSPCC [ˌenesˌpiːsiːˈsiː] **N** *Br* (*abbr* **National Society for the Prevention of Cruelty to Children**) = association britannique de protection de l'enfance

nth [enθ] **ADJ 1** *Math* **to the n. power** à la puissance n **2** *Fam (umpteenth)* énième; **for the n. time** pour la énième fois; **to the n. degree** au énième degré

nuance ['njuːɒns] **N** nuance *f*; **a n. of meaning** une nuance

nuanced ['njuːɒnst] **ADJ** nuancé; **finely n.** subtilement nuancé

nub [nʌb] **N 1** *(crux)* essentiel *m*, cœur *m*; **the n. of the problem** le cœur *ou* le nœud du problème; **to get to the n. of the matter** entrer dans le vif du sujet **2** *(small piece)* petit morceau *m*, (petit) bout *m*; *(small bump)* petite bosse *f*

nubile [*Br* 'njuːbaɪl, *Am* 'nuːbəl] **ADJ 1** *(sexually attractive)* désirable **2** *Formal (marriageable)* nubile

nuclear ['njuːklɪə(r)] **ADJ 1** *Phys* nucléaire **2** *Mil* nucléaire; **France's n. deterrent** la force de dissuasion nucléaire française **3** *Biol* nucléaire

▸▸ ***nuclear bomb*** bombe *f* atomique; ***nuclear capability*** puissance *f ou* potentiel *m* nucléaire; ***nuclear disarmament*** désarmement *m* nucléaire; ***nuclear energy*** énergie *f* nucléaire; ***nuclear family*** famille *f* nucléaire; ***nuclear fission*** fission *f* nucléaire; ***nuclear fuel*** combustible *m* nucléaire; ***nuclear fusion*** fusion *f* nucléaire; ***nuclear industry*** industrie *f* nucléaire; *Med* ***nuclear magnetic resonance*** résonance *f* magnétique nucléaire; ***nuclear medicine*** médecine *f* nucléaire; ***Nuclear Non-Proliferation Treaty*** traité *m* de non-prolifération nucléaire; ***nuclear physicist*** physicien(enne) *m,f* nucléaire; ***nuclear physics*** *(UNCOUNT)* physique *f* nucléaire; ***nuclear power*** nucléaire *m*, énergie *f* nucléaire; *Am* ***nuclear power plant*** centrale *f* nucléaire *ou* atomique; ***nuclear powers*** puissances *fpl* nucléaires; ***nuclear power station*** centrale *f* nucléaire *ou* atomique; ***nuclear reaction*** réaction *f* nucléaire; ***nuclear reactor*** réacteur *m* nucléaire; ***nuclear reprocessing*** retraitement *m* (des déchets nucléaires); ***nuclear reprocessing plant*** usine *f* de retraitement (des déchets nucléaires); ***nuclear scientist*** physicien(enne) *m,f* nucléaire; ***nuclear shelter*** abri *m* antiatomique *ou* antinucléaire; ***nuclear submarine*** sous-marin *m* nucléaire; ***nuclear testing*** essais *mpl* nucléaires; ***nuclear umbrella*** parapluie *m* atomique *ou* nucléaire; ***nuclear war*** guerre *f* atomique; ***nuclear warhead*** ogive *f ou* tête *f* nucléaire; ***nuclear waste*** déchets *mpl* nucléaires; ***nuclear weapons*** armes *fpl* nucléaires; ***nuclear winter*** hiver *m* nucléaire

nuclear-free zone N = périmètre dans lequel une collectivité locale interdit l'utilisation, le stockage ou le transport de matières radioactives

nuclei ['njuːklɪaɪ] *pl of* **nucleus**

nucleic acid [njuːˈklɪɪk-] **N** *Biol* acide *m* nucléique

nucleus ['njuːklɪəs] (*pl* **nucleuses** *or* **nuclei** [-klɪaɪ]) **N 1** *Biol & Phys* noyau *m* **2** *Fig (of organization etc)* noyau *m*; *(of argument etc)* cœur *m*; **they form the n. of the team** ils forment le noyau de l'équipe; **the n. of a library** *(beginnings)* un commencement de bibliothèque; **the n. of a fine sales team** les premiers éléments d'une bonne équipe de vente; **a n. for regional development** un centre de développement régional

nuddy ['nʌdɪ] **N** *Br Fam Hum* **in the n.** à poil

nude [njuːd] **ADJ 1** *(naked)* nu; **there are several n. scenes in the film** il y a plusieurs scènes déshabillées dans le film; **to sunbathe n.** faire du bronzage intégral; **n. photos** nus *mpl*; *(soft pornography)* photos *fpl* érotiques **2** *(make-up)* nude

N 1 *Art* nu *m*; **a Matisse n.** un nu de Matisse **2 in the n.** (tout) nu; **to pose in the n.** poser nu

nudge [nʌdʒ] **VT 1** *(with elbow)* pousser du coude, donner un coup de coude à

2 *(push)* pousser; **he cautiously nudged the door open** il poussa tout doucement la porte (pour l'ouvrir); **the truck nudged its way through the crowd** le camion se fraya un passage à travers la foule

3 *(encourage)* encourager, pousser (**into doing sth** à faire qch); *Br* **to n. sb's memory** rafraîchir la mémoire de qn

4 *(approach)* approcher de; **he must be nudging fifty** il doit approcher de la cinquantaine; **temperatures nudging 40°C** des températures proches de 40°C

N 1 *(with elbow)* coup *m* de coude; *(with foot, stick etc)* petit coup *m* de pied/bâton/*etc*; **to give sb a n.** pousser qn du coude; *Br Hum* **he didn't come home last night, n. n., wink wink** il n'est pas rentré hier soir, si tu vois ce que je veux dire **2** *(encouragement)* **he needs a n. in the right direction** il a besoin qu'on le pousse dans la bonne direction

nudie ['njuːdɪ] **ADJ** *Fam* porno

▸▸ ***nudie book*** magazine *m* porno

nudism ['njuːdɪzəm] **N** nudisme *m*, naturisme *m*

nudist ['njuːdɪst] **N** nudiste *mf*, naturiste *mf*

ADJ nudiste, naturiste

▸▸ ***nudist beach*** plage *f* de nudistes; ***nudist camp***, ***nudist colony*** camp *m* de nudistes

nudity ['njuːdətɪ] **N** nudité *f*

nugatory ['njuːgətrɪ] **ADJ** *Formal* **1** *(trifling)* insignifiant, sans valeur **2** *(not valid)* non valable; *(ineffective)* inopérant, inefficace

nugget ['nʌgɪt] **N 1** *(piece)* pépite *f*; **gold n.** pépite *f* d'or **2** *Fig* **nuggets of wisdom** des trésors *mpl* de sagesse; **an interesting n. of information** un (petit) renseignement intéressant **3** *Culin* **chicken nuggets** morceaux *mpl* de poulet frit

nuisance ['njuːsəns] **N 1** *(annoying thing, situation)* **that noise is a n.** ce bruit est énervant; **it's (such) a n. having to attend all these meetings** c'est (vraiment) pénible de devoir assister à toutes ces réunions; **what a n.!** c'est énervant!; **it's a n. having to commute every day** c'est pénible de devoir faire le trajet tous les jours; **they are not politically important but they have a certain n. value** ils n'ont pas un grand poids politique, mais ils ont le mérite de déranger

2 *(annoying person)* casse-pieds *m inv*; **you're a n.!** tu m'embêtes!, tu me casses les pieds!; **he's nothing but a n.** c'est un véritable empoisonneur; **to make a n. of oneself** embêter *ou* empoisonner le monde; **stop being a n.** arrête de nous embêter

3 *(hazard)* nuisance *f*; **that rubbish dump is a public n.** cette décharge est une calamité

4 *Law* préjudice *m*

▸▸ *Tel* ***nuisance call*** appel *m* anonyme; *Tel* ***nuisance caller*** auteur *m* d'appels anonymes

NUJ [ˌenjuːˈdʒeɪ] **N** *Br* (*abbr* **National Union of Journalists**) = syndicat britannique des journalistes

nuke [njuːk] *Fam* **N 1** *(weapon)* arme *f* nucléaire **2** *Am (power plant)* centrale *f* nucléaire

VT 1 *(bomb)* atomiser **2** *(microwave)* faire cuire au four à micro-ondes **3** *(defeat)* ratatiner, battre à plates coutures

null [nʌl] **ADJ 1** *Law (invalid)* nul; *(lapsed)* caduc (caduque); **n. and void** nul et non avenu; **the contract was rendered n. (and void)** le contrat a été annulé *ou* invalidé **2** *(insignificant)* insignifiant, sans valeur; *(amounting to nothing)* nul **3** *Math* nul

▸▸ ***null set*** ensemble *m* vide; *Comput* ***null string*** chaîne *f* vide

nullification [ˌnʌlɪfɪˈkeɪʃən] **N** annulation *f*, invalidation *f*

nullify ['nʌlɪfaɪ] (*pt & pp* **nullified**) **VT 1** *Law (claim, contract, election)* annuler, invalider *(advantage)* neutraliser

nullity ['nʌlətɪ] (*pl* **nullities**) **N 1** *(worthlessness)* nullité *f* **2** *Law (of marriage)* nullité *f*, invalidité *f* *(of inheritance)* caducité *f* **3** *(person)* nullité *f*

▸▸ ***nullity suit*** demande *f* en nullité de mariage

NUM [ˌenjuːˈem] **N** (*abbr* **National Union of Mineworkers**) = syndicat britannique des mineurs

numb [nʌm] **ADJ** engourdi; **we were n. with cold** nous étions transis de froid; **my arm has gone n.** mon bras est tout engourdi; **is your jaw still n.** *(anaesthetized)* ta mâchoire est-elle encore anesthésiée?; *Fig* **n. with terror** paralysé par la peur; *Fig* **he was n. with shock** il était sous le choc; *Fig* **to become n. to sth** devenir insensible à qch

VT *(person, limbs, senses)* engourdir; *(pain)* atténuer, apaiser; **she was numbed by her father's death** elle était sous le choc après la mort de son père, la mort de son père l'a laissée sous le choc

NUMBER ['nʌmbə(r)]

N
- nombre **1, 3, 9**
- chiffre **1**
- numéro **2, 5, 7**

VT
- numéroter **1**
- compter **2–4**

VI
- compter

N 1 (gen) & Math nombre m; (figure, numeral) chiffre m; **a six-figure n.** un nombre de six chiffres; **in round numbers** en chiffres ronds; **to do sth by numbers** faire qch en suivant des instructions précises; **even/odd/rational/whole n.** nombre m pair/impair/rationnel/entier
2 (as identifier) numéro m; **have you got my work n.?** avez-vous mon numéro (de téléphone) au travail?; **we live at n. 80** nous habitons au (numéro) 80; **did you get the car's (registration) n.?** tu as relevé le numéro d'immatriculation de la voiture?; Fam **I've got your n.!** toi, je te vois venir!, j'ai repéré ton manège!; Fam **his n.'s up** son compte est bon
3 (quantity) nombre m; **any n. can participate** le nombre de participants est illimité; **they were eight in n.** ils étaient (au nombre de) huit; **in equal numbers** en nombre égal; **to be equal in n.** être à nombre égal; **we were many/few in n.** nous étions nombreux/en petit nombre; **a n. of people** un certain nombre de gens; **a large n. of people** un grand nombre de gens, de nombreuses personnes; **a small n. of people** un petit nombre de gens, peu de gens; **any n. of...** un grand nombre de..., bon nombre de...; **she is one of a n. of people who...** elle figure parmi les personnes qui...; **to be present in small numbers/in (great) numbers** être présents en petit nombre/en grand nombre; **times without n.** à maintes (et maintes) reprises; **they defeated us by force of** or **by sheer weight of numbers** ils l'ont emporté sur nous parce qu'ils étaient plus nombreux
4 (group) **one of their n.** (l')un d'entre eux
5 (issue ▸ of magazine, paper) numéro m
6 Fam (job) boulot m; **a cushy n.** une planque
7 (dance, act) numéro m; (song) chanson f; **a dance n.** un numéro de danse; **for my next n. I'd like to sing...** j'aimerais vous chanter maintenant...; **instrumental n.** morceau m instrumental
8 Fam (thing, person) **she was wearing a little black n.** elle portait une petite robe noire; **that car is a nice little n.** elle est pas mal, cette voiture; **who's that blonde n.?** qui est cette belle blonde?; **to do** or **to pull a n. on sb** rouler qn
9 Gram nombre m
VT 1 (assign number to) numéroter
2 (include) compter; **I n. him among the best jazz musicians** je le compte parmi les meilleurs musiciens de jazz; **I'm glad to n. her among my friends** je suis heureux de la compter parmi mes amis
3 (total) compter; **each team numbers six players** chaque équipe est composée de ou compte six joueurs; **the crowd numbered 5,000** il y avait une foule de 5000 personnes
4 (count) compter; **his days are numbered** ses jours sont comptés
VI she numbers among the great writers of the century elle compte parmi les grands écrivains de ce siècle; **the crowd numbered in thousands** il y avait des milliers de gens
▸▸ Am ***numbers game*** loterie f clandestine; Comput ***number key*** touche f numérique; Comput ***number lock*** verrouillage m du pavé numérique; Comput ***number lock key*** touche f de verrouillage du clavier numérique; ***number one*** **N** Fam (boss) boss m, patron(onne) m,f; Fam **to look out for** or **to take care of n. one** penser d'abord à soi; **her record got to n. one** son disque a été classé numéro un au hit-parade; Sport **the world n. one** le numéro un mondial; Fam (in children's language) **to do a n. one** (urinate) faire pipi **ADJ** premier; **it's our n. one priority** c'est la première de nos priorités; **the n. one oil exporter** le premier exportateur de pétrole; **my n. one choice** mon tout premier choix; Br Aut ***number plate*** plaque f minéralogique ou d'immatriculation; **the lorry had a foreign n. plate** le camion était immatriculé à l'étranger; Br Pol ***Number Ten (Downing Street)*** = résidence officielle du Premier ministre britannique; **N. Ten denied the rumour** le gouvernement a démenti la rumeur; Math ***number theory*** théorie f des nombres; ***number two*** (assistant) numéro m deux; Fam (in children's language) **to do a n. two** (defecate) faire la grosse commission
▸**number off** **VI** se numéroter; **n. off from the left** numérotez-vous en partant de la gauche

number-coded **ADJ** codé en chiffres

number-cruncher [-krʌntʃə(r)] **N** Fam ordinateur m puissant (pour le traitement de données numériques)

number-crunching [-krʌntʃɪŋ] **N** Fam traitement m en masse des chiffres

numbering ['nʌmbərɪŋ] **N** numérotation f, numérotage m
▸▸ ***numbering machine*** numéroteur m; ***numbering system*** système m de numérotation

numberless ['nʌmbəlɪs] **ADJ 1** Formal (countless) innombrable, sans nombre **2** (without a number) sans numéro, qui ne porte pas de numéro, non numéroté

numbly ['nʌmlɪ] **ADV** (react, say) mollement; (look, stare) d'un air engourdi

numbness ['nʌmnɪs] **N** (physical) engourdissement m; (mental) torpeur f, engourdissement m

numbskull ['nʌmskʌl] **N** Fam crétin(e) m,f, andouille f

numeracy ['nju:mərəsɪ] **N** (UNCOUNT) Br aptitudes fpl en calcul; **a high level of n.** un bon niveau en calcul

numeral ['nju:mərəl] **N** chiffre m, nombre m; **in Roman numerals** en chiffres romains
ADJ numéral

numerate ['nju:mərət] **ADJ** Br (skilled) bon en mathématiques; (having basics) sachant compter; **to be barely n.** savoir à peine compter; **applicants should be highly n.** les candidats doivent avoir des compétences élevées en calcul

numeration [ˌnju:mə'reɪʃən] **N** Math numération f; **binary n.** numération f binaire

numerator ['nju:məreɪtə(r)] **N** Math numérateur m

numeric [nju:'merɪk] Comput **ADJ** numérique
• **numerics** **NPL** chiffres mpl ou caractères mpl numériques
▸▸ ***numeric coding*** codage m numérique; ***numeric field*** champ m numérique; ***numeric keypad, numeric pad*** pavé m numérique

numerical [nju:'merɪkəl] **ADJ** numérique; **to have a n. advantage** avoir l'avantage du nombre; **in n. order** par ordre numérique
▸▸ ***numerical analysis*** analyse f numérique; Comput ***numerical keypad*** pavé m numérique

numerically [nju:'merɪkəlɪ] **ADV** numériquement

numerous ['nju:mərəs] **ADJ** nombreux; **for n. reasons** pour de nombreuses raisons

numismatic [ˌnju:mɪz'mætɪk] **ADJ** numismatique

numismatics [ˌnju:mɪz'mætɪks] **N** (UNCOUNT) numismatique f

numismatist [nju:'mɪzmətɪst] **N** numismate mf

num lock ['nʌm-] **N** Comput (abbr **number lock**) verr num; **the n. is on** le pavé numérique est verrouillé
▸▸ ***num lock key*** touche f de verrouillage du pavé numérique

numpty ['nʌmptɪ] **N** Scot Fam (idiot) crétin(e) m, f, cruche f, andouille f

numskull = **numbskull**

nun [nʌn] **N** religieuse f; **to become a n.** prendre le voile

nuncio ['nʌnsɪəʊ] (pl **nuncios**) **N** nonce m

nunnery ['nʌnərɪ] (pl **nunneries**) **N** couvent m ou monastère m (de femmes)

nuptial ['nʌpʃəl] Literary or Hum **ADJ** nuptial
• **nuptials** **NPL** noce f, noces fpl
▸▸ ***nuptial vows*** vœux mpl du mariage

NUR [ˌenju:'ɑ:(r)] **N** Formerly (abbr **National Union of Railwaymen**) = ancien syndicat britannique des employés des chemins de fer

nurse [nɜ:s] **N 1** Med (in hospital) infirmier(ère) m,f; (privately employed) infirmier(ère) m,f, garde-malade mf; **male n.** infirmier m; **thank you, n.** merci mademoiselle/madame **2** Br (nanny) nurse f, bonne f d'enfants **3** (wet nurse) nourrice f
VT 1 (care for) soigner; **he nursed her through the worst of it** il l'a soignée pendant qu'elle était au plus mal; **she nursed me back to health** elle a pris soin de moi jusqu'à ce que je guérisse; Fig **he was nursing a bad hangover** il essayait de faire passer sa gueule de bois; **to n. one's pride** panser ses blessures (d'amour-propre); **she nursed the boat back into harbour** elle ramena le bateau au port sans encombre; **he nursed the company through the crisis** il a permis à l'entreprise de traverser la crise
2 (harbour, foster ▸ grudge, hope, desire) entretenir; (▸ project) mijoter, couver
3 (breast-feed) allaiter
4 (hold) bercer (dans ses bras); **he sat nursing his fourth whisky** il sirotait son quatrième whisky
VI 1 (as profession) être infirmier(ère); **she spent a few years nursing** elle a travaillé pendant quelques années comme infirmière **2** (infant) téter

nursemaid ['nɜ:smeɪd] **N** nurse f, bonne f d'enfants; Fig **to play n. to sb** tenir qn par la main

nursery ['nɜ:sərɪ] (pl **nurseries**) **N 1** (room ▸ in house) nursery f, chambre f d'enfants
2 (day-care centre) crèche f, garderie f
3 (school) école f maternelle
4 (for plants, trees) & Fig pépinière f
▸▸ ***nursery education*** enseignement m de l'école maternelle; ***nursery garden*** pépinière f; ***nursery nurse*** puéricultrice f; ***nursery rhyme*** comptine f; ***nursery school*** (école f) maternelle f; ***nursery school teacher*** instituteur(trice) m,f de maternelle; Br ***nursery slopes*** pistes fpl pour débutants; ***nursery teacher*** instituteur(trice) m,f de maternelle

nurseryman ['nɜ:sərɪmən] (pl **nurserymen** [-mən]) **N** pépiniériste m

nursing ['nɜ:sɪŋ] **N 1** (profession) profession f d'infirmier; **when did she take up n.?** quand a-t-elle commencé ses études d'infirmière? **2** (care) soins mpl **3** (breast-feeding) allaitement m
ADJ 1 Med d'infirmier; **the n. staff** le personnel soignant **2** (suckling) allaitant
▸▸ ***nursing auxiliary*** aide-soignant(e) m,f; ***nursing bra*** soutien-gorge m d'allaitement; ***nursing home*** (for aged) maison f de retraite; (for convalescents) maison f de repos; (for mentally ill) maison f de santé; Br (private clinic) hôpital m privé, clinique f privée; ***nursing mother*** mère f qui allaite; Br ***nursing officer*** infirmier(ère) m,f en chef

nurture ['nɜ:tʃə(r)] **N 1** (upbringing) éducation f **2** (food) nourriture f
VT 1 (bring up) élever, éduquer; (nourish) nourrir (on de) **2** (foster ▸ hope, desire) entretenir; (▸ plan, scheme) mijoter, couver

nurturing ['nɜ:tʃərɪŋ] **ADJ** attentionné, maternel

NUS [ˌenju:'es] **N** Br (abbr **National Union of Students**) ≃ UNEF f

NUT [ˌenju:'ti:] **N** (abbr **National Union of Teachers**) = syndicat britannique d'enseignants

nut [nʌt] (pt & pp **nutted**, cont **nutting**) **N 1** Bot & Culin = terme générique pour les amandes, noisettes, noix etc; **nuts and raisins** mélange m de différents fruits secs (cacahouètes, noisettes, etc) et de raisins secs; Fam **a hard** or **tough n.** (person) une personne difficile ou peu commode; Fam **it's a hard** or **tough n. to crack** (problem) c'est difficile à résoudre
2 Tech écrou m; **nuts and bolts** des écrous mpl et des boulons mpl; Fig **the nuts and bolts of the problem** les détails pratiques du problème; **the nuts and bolts of a language** les éléments de base d'une langue
3 Fam (crazy person) cinglé(e) m,f, dingue mf; **what a n.!** il est complètement cinglé ou dingue!
4 Fam (enthusiast) fana mf; **she's a golf n.** c'est une fana de golf
5 Fam (head) caboche f, cafetière f; **to be off one's n.** (mad) être dingue ou cinglé; **to go off one's n.** (go insane) perdre la boule, devenir cinglé; (get angry) péter les plombs, piquer une crise; Br **to do one's n.** (get angry) péter les plombs, piquer une crise; **she really did her n.** elle a piqué une de ces crises
6 (small lump of coal) noix f, tête-de-moineau f
VT Fam donner un coup de boule à
▸▸ ***nut cutlet*** côtelette f végétarienne (à base de noix, noisettes etc); ***nut oil*** (from walnuts) huile f de noix; (from hazelnuts) huile f de noisettes; ***nut roast*** rôti m végétarien (à base de noix, noisettes, etc)

nutball ['nʌtbɔ:l] N *Am Fam* cinglé(e) *m,f*, dingue *mf*

nut-brown ADJ (couleur) noisette *(inv)*; *(hair)* châtain; *(skin)* brun

nutcase ['nʌtkeɪs] N *Fam* cinglé(e) *m,f*, dingue *mf*

nutcracker ['nʌtˌkrækə(r)] N **(pair of) nutcrackers** casse-noisette(s) *m inv*, casse-noix *m inv*

nuthatch ['nʌthætʃ] N *Orn* sittelle *f*

nuthouse ['nʌthaus, *pl* -hauzɪz] N *Fam* maison *f* de fous; **in the n.** chez les fous

nutmeg ['nʌtmeg] N **1** *Bot (nut)* (noix *f* de) muscade *f*; *(tree)* muscadier *m* **2** *(in football)* petit pont *m*

VT *(in football)* **to n. sb** faire un petit pont à qn

nutrient ['nju:trɪənt] N substance *f* nutritive

ADJ nutritif

nutriment ['nju:trɪmənt] N *(food)* nourriture *f*

nutrition [nju:'trɪʃən] N nutrition *f*

nutritional [nju:'trɪʃənəl] ADJ *(disorder, process, value)* nutritif; *(science, research)* nutritionnel; **cereals have a high n. content** les céréales sont très nourrissantes *ou* nutritives

▸▸ *Com* ***nutritional labelling*** étiquetage *m* de l'apport nutritionnel

nutritionist [nju:'trɪʃənɪst] N nutritionniste *mf*

nutritious [nju:'trɪʃəs] ADJ nutritif, nourrissant

nutritive ['nju:trətɪv] ADJ nutritif

nuts [nʌts] ADJ *Fam* dingue, cinglé, timbré; **that noise is driving me n.** ce bruit me rend dingue; **to go n.** *(go insane)* devenir cinglé, perdre la boule; *(get angry)* péter les plombs, piquer une crise; **to be n. about sb/sth** être dingue de qn/qch

NPL *very Fam (testicles)* couilles *fpl*, roupettes *fpl*

EXCLAM *Fam* mince!; **n. to that!** plutôt crever!

nutshell ['nʌtʃel] N coquille *f* de noix/noisette/*etc*; **in a n.** en un mot; **to put it in a n.** pour résumer l'histoire (en un mot)

nutso ['nʌtsəʊ] ADJ *Am Fam* dingue, cinglé, timbré; **to go n.** *(go insane)* devenir cinglé, perdre la boule; *(get angry)* péter les plombs, péter une durite; **to be n. about sb/sth** être dingue de qn/qch

nutter ['nʌtə(r)] N *Br Fam* cinglé(e) *m,f*, dingue *mf*; **he's a complete n.** il est complètement dingue *ou* cinglé *ou* timbré

nutty ['nʌtɪ] *(compar* **nuttier**, *superl* **nuttiest)** ADJ **1** *(tasting of or containing nuts)* aux noix/aux amandes/aux noisettes/*etc*; **a n. flavour** un goût de noix/noisette/*etc* **2** *Fam (mad)* dingue, cinglé, timbré; *Hum* **as n. as a fruitcake** complètement ravagé; **to be n. about sb/sth** raffoler de qn/qch

nuzzle ['nʌzəl] VT *(push with nose)* pousser du nez; *(sniff at)* renifler; *(of animal)* pousser du museau; **to n. sb's hand** fourrer son nez dans la paume de la main de qn; **he nuzzled her neck** il lui caressait le cou de ses lèvres

VI **1 to n. up against, to n. at** *(push with nose)* pousser du nez; *(sniff at)* renifler; *(of anima*l)* pousser du museau **2** *(nestle)* se blottir; **the**y **nuzzled (up) against their mother** ils se blottiren*t* contre leur mère

NY *(written abbr* **New York***)* *(city)* New York; *(state)* État *m* de New York

NYC *(written abbr* **New York City***)* New York

nylon ['naɪlɒn] N nylon *m*

COMP *(thread, shirt, stockings)* de *ou* en nylon

• **nylons** NPL *(stockings)* bas *mpl* nylon

NYMEX [ˌenwaɪ,emi:'eks] N *St Exch (abbr* **New Yor**k **Mercantile Exchange***)* = marché à terme des pro-duits pétroliers de New York

nymph [nɪmf] N *Myth & Zool* nymphe *f*; **sea n.** né-réide *f*; **tree** *or* **wood n.** hamadryade *f*; **water n.** naïade *f*

nymphet ['nɪmfət] N nymphette *f*

nympho ['nɪmfəʊ] N *Fam (abbr* **nymphomaniac***)* nympho *f*

nymphomania [ˌnɪmfə'meɪnɪə] N nymphoma-nie *f*

nymphomaniac [ˌnɪmfə'meɪnɪæk] N nympho-mane *f*

ADJ nymphomane

NYSE [ˌenwaɪ,es'i:] N *St Exch (abbr* **New York Stoc**k **Exchange***)* = la Bourse de New York

NZ *(written abbr* **New Zealand***)* Nouvelle-Zéland*e* *f*

¹, O [əʊ] **N 1** *(letter)* O, o *m inv*; **two o's** deux o; **O**
or orange ≃ comme Oscar **2** *(zero)* zéro *m*
² *(written abbr* **Ohio***)* Ohio *m*

2 [əʊ'tuː] **N the O2** = salle de spectacle géante, entre d'exposition et espace-loisirs au sud-est le Londres, anciennement nommé le "Millen-ium Dome"

af [əʊf] **N** *(clumsy man)* lourdaud *m*; *(uncouth nan)* rustre *m*, mufle *m*; **get out of the way, you reat o.!** pousse-toi, gros lourdaud!

afish ['əʊfɪʃ] **ADJ** *(clumsy)* lourdaud, balourd; *uncouth)* rustre, mufle

ak [əʊk] **N 1** *(tree, wood)* chêne *m* **2** *(colour)* hêne *m*
COMP *(furniture, door, panelling)* de *ou* en chêne
ADJ *(oak-coloured)* couleur chêne *(inv)*
▸▸ ***oak apple*** noix *f* de galle; ***oak forest*** forêt *f* de hênes, chênaie *f*; ***oak tree*** chêne *m*

aked [əʊkt] **ADJ** *(wine)* vieilli en fût de chêne

aken ['əʊkən] **ADJ** *Literary* de *ou* en chêne

akum ['əʊkəm] **N** étoupe *f*, filasse *f*; **to pick o.** émêler *ou* tirer l'étoupe

& M [ˌəʊənd'em] **N** *(abbr* **organization and meth-ds***)* O et M *f*

AP [ˌəʊeɪ'piː] **N** *Br (abbr* **old age pensioner***)* retrai-é(e) *m,f*; **students and OAPs half price** *(sign)* ≃ étudiants et carte Vermeil demi-tarif

ar [ɔː(r)] **N 1** *(for rowing)* rame *f*, aviron *m*; *Br am* **to stick** *or* **to put one's o. in** ramener sa fraise; **o rest on one's oars** lever les rames; *Fig* se repo-er sur ses lauriers **2** *(person)* rameur(euse) *m,f*

arlock ['ɔːlɒk] **N** *(U-shaped)* dame *f* de nage; *pin)* tolet *m*

arsman ['ɔːzmən] *(pl* **oarsmen** [-mən]*)* **N** rameur *n*

arswoman ['ɔːzˌwʊmən] *(pl* **oarswomen** [-ˌwɪmɪn]*)* **N** rameuse *f*

AS [ˌəʊeɪ'es] **N** *(abbr* **Organization of American States***)* OÉA *f*

asis [əʊ'eɪsɪs] *(pl* **oases** [-siːz]*)* **N** *also Fig* oasis *f*; **n o. of calm** une oasis *ou* un havre de paix

ast [əʊst] **N** *Br* **1** *(kiln)* séchoir *m* à houblon **2** *building)* sécherie *f* (de houblon)

asthouse ['əʊsthaʊs, *pl* -haʊzɪz] **N** sécherie *f* (de ioublon)

at [əʊt] **N** *(plant)* avoine *f*
▸ oats NPL avoine *f*; **a field of oats** un champ l'avoine; *Am Fam* **to be feeling one's oats** *(be self-mportant)* ne plus se sentir, faire l'important*ᵖ*; *be full of energy)* être en pleine forme*ᵖ*; *(be heerful)* avoir la pêche; *Br Fam* **to be off one's oats** *(be off form)* se sentir patraque, ne pas être lans son assiette; *(have no appetite)* avoir perdu 'appétit*ᵖ*; *Br Fam* **is he getting his oats?** est-ce qu'il a ce qu'il lui faut au lit?; *Fam Fig* **to sow one's wild) oats** jeter sa gourme*ᵖ*
▸▸ ***oat grass*** fromental *m*, avoine *f* élevée

atcake ['əʊtkeɪk] **N** gâteau *m* sec (d'avoine)

ath [əʊθ, *pl* əʊðz] **N 1** *(vow)* serment *m*; **he took or swore an o. never to return** il fit le serment *ou* il ura de ne jamais revenir; **to take the o. of alle-giance** faire (le) serment d'allégeance; **to swear on o.** jurer (sous serment); **it's true, on my o.!** c'est vrai, je vous le jure!; *Law* **to be on** *or* **under o.** être sous serment, être assermenté; *Law* **to put sb on** *or* **under o.** faire prêter serment à qn; **she swore/ testified under o. that...** elle a juré/témoigné sous serment que... **2** *(swearword)* juron *m*; **he let out a string of oaths** il a laissé échapper un torrent d'injures

oatmeal ['əʊtmiːl] **N** *(UNCOUNT)* **1** *(flakes)* flo-cons *mpl* d'avoine; *(flour)* farine *f* d'avoine **2** *(col-our)* beige *m* naturel
ADJ *(colour)* beige naturel
▸▸ ***oatmeal porridge*** bouillie *f* d'avoine, porridge *m*

OAU [ˌəʊeɪ'juː] **N** *(abbr* **Organization of African Unity***)* OUA *f*

OB [ˌəʊ'biː] **N** *TV (abbr* **outside broadcast***)* émission *f* réalisée en dehors des studios
▸▸ ***OB unit, OB van*** car *m* régie, unité *f* mobile de tournage

obduracy ['ɒbdjʊrəsɪ] **N** *Formal* **1** *(obstinacy)* obstination *f*, entêtement *m*; *(inflexibility)* inflexi-bilité *f*, intransigeance *f* **2** *(hardheartedness)* du-reté *f* (de cœur), insensibilité *f*

obdurate ['ɒbdjʊrət] **ADJ** *Formal* **1** *(obstinate)* obstiné, entêté; *(unyielding)* inflexible; **to remain o.** ne pas fléchir, rester inflexible **2** *(hardhearted)* insensible, dur

obdurately ['ɒbdjʊrətlɪ] **ADV** *Formal (obsti-nately)* avec entêtement; *(to resist)* inflexible-ment; **to remain o. silent** garder un silence obstiné *ou* têtu

OBE [ˌəʊbiː'iː] **N** *(abbr* **Officer of the Order of the British Empire***)* = distinction honorifique britan-nique

obedience [ə'biːdjəns] **N 1** *(gen)* obéissance *f*; **to show o. to sb** obéir à qn; **in o. to her wishes** conformément à ses vœux; **to command o.** sa-voir se faire obéir **2** *Rel* obédience *f*

> Note that the French word **obédience** is a false friend and is not normally used to translate the English word **obedience**.

obedient [ə'biːdjənt] **ADJ** obéissant, docile; **to be o. to sb** obéir à qn, être obéissant envers qn; *Formal Old-fashioned* **your o. servant** *(in letters)* votre humble serviteur

obediently [ə'biːdjəntlɪ] **ADV** docilement

obelisk ['ɒbəlɪsk] **N 1** *(column)* obélisque *m* **2** *Typ* croix *f*, obel *m*, obèle *m*

obese [əʊ'biːs] **ADJ** obèse

obesity [əʊ'biːsətɪ], **obeseness** [əʊ'biːsnɪs] **N** obésité *f*

obey [ə'beɪ] **VT** obéir à; **he always obeyed his mother/his intuition/the law** il a toujours obéi à sa mère/à son intuition/aux lois; **the plane is no longer obeying the controls** l'avion ne répond plus; **I want these instructions obeyed to the letter** je veux que ces instructions soient suivies à la lettre
VI obéir, obtempérer

obfuscate ['ɒbfʌskeɪt] **VT** *Formal (obscure ▸ is-sue)* obscurcir, embrouiller; *(▸ mind)* em-brouiller; *(perplex ▸ person)* embrouiller, dé-router

obfuscation [ˌɒbfʌs'keɪʃən] **N** *Formal (of issue)* obscurcissement *m*, embrouillement *m*; *(of mind)* embrouillement *m*; *(of person)* confusion *f*, embrouillement *m*

obituary [ə'bɪtʃʊərɪ] *(pl* **obituaries***)* **N** nécrologie *f*, notice *f* nécrologique; **the o. column, the obitu-aries** la rubrique nécrologique
ADJ nécrologique

object¹ ['ɒbdʒɪkt] **N 1** *(thing)* objet *m*, chose *f*; **an unidentified o.** un objet non identifié
2 *(aim)* objet *m*, but *m*, fin *f*; **with the sole o. of pleasing you** dans le seul but de *ou* à seule fin de vous plaire; **with this o. in mind** *or* **in view** dans ce but, à cette fin; **that's the (whole) o. of the ex-ercise** c'est (justement là) le but de l'opération; **money is no o.** peu importe le prix, le prix est sans importance; **time is no o.** peu importe le temps que cela prendra
3 *(focus)* objet *m*; **an o. of ridicule/interest** un ob-jet de ridicule/d'intérêt; **the o. of his love** l'objet *m* de son amour; **o. of study** objet *m ou* sujet *m* d'étude
4 *Gram (of verb)* complément *m* d'objet; *(of prep-osition)* objet *m*; **direct/indirect o.** complément *m* d'objet direct/indirect
5 *Comput (in document)* objet *m*
▸▸ ***object ball*** *(in snooker, pool, billiards)* bille *f* visée; ***object glass*** objectif *m*; ***object language*** *Ling (metalanguage)* métalangage *m*; *Comput* langage *m* objet; ***object lesson*** *(example)* démons-tration *f*, illustration *f (d'un principe)*; *Sch* leçon *f* de choses; **it was an o. lesson in how to lose votes** ce fut une illustration (parfaite) de la façon dont il faut s'y prendre pour perdre des voix; **it was an o. lesson in persistence** ce fut un parfait exemple de persévérance; *Comput* ***object program*** pro-gramme *m* objet

object² [əb'dʒekt] **VI** élever une objection; *(stronger)* protester; **to o. to sth** faire objection à qch; *(of demonstrators etc)* protester contre qch; **I o. to being treated like a child** je n'aime pas qu'on me prenne pour un gamin; **they o. to working overtime** ils ne sont pas d'accord pour faire des heures supplémentaires; **if you don't o.** si vous n'y voyez pas d'inconvénient; **I o.!** je proteste!; **I o. strongly to your attitude** je trouve votre atti-tude proprement inadmissible; **I wouldn't o. to a cup of tea** je ne dirais pas non à *ou* je prendrais volontiers une tasse de thé; **he objects to her smoking** il désapprouve qu'elle fume; **she objects to his coming** elle n'est pas d'accord pour qu'il vienne; **it's not her I o. to but her husband** ce n'est pas elle qui me déplaît, c'est son mari; **if no one objects** si personne n'y voit d'objection(s); *Law* **to o. to a witness** récuser un témoin
VT objecter; **I objected that it was too late** j'ai ob-jecté qu'il était trop tard

objectify [əb'dʒektɪfaɪ] *(pt & pp* **objectified***)* **VT** objectiver

objection [əb'dʒekʃən] **N 1** *(protest, argument against)* objection *f*; **are there any objections?** y a-t-il des objections?; **to make** *or* **to raise an o.** faire *ou* soulever une objection; **I have no o. to his coming** je ne vois pas d'objection à ce qu'il vienne; **I have no o. to his friends** je n'ai rien contre ses amis; **if you have no o.** si vous n'y voyez pas d'inconvénient; *Law* **o.!** objection!; *Law* **o. sustained/overruled!** objection retenue/ rejetée! **2** *(reason for objecting)* inconvénient *m*;

the chief o. to your plan is its cost le plus grand inconvénient de votre projet, c'est son coût

objectionable [əb'dʒekʃənəbəl] **ADJ** *(unpleasant)* désagréable; *(blameworthy)* répréhensible; **a highly o. smell/man** une odeur/un homme insupportable; **to use o. language** parler vulgairement; **I find his views o.** je n'aime pas sa façon de penser

objective [əb'dʒektɪv] **ADJ 1** *(unbiased)* objectif, impartial; **an o. observer** un observateur impartial **2** *(real, observable)* objectif **3** *Gram* objectif
N 1 *(aim)* objectif *m*, but *m*; **to achieve** *or* **to reach one's o.** atteindre son but; **our o. for this year is to increase sales by 10 percent** nous avons pour objectif d'augmenter nos ventes de 10 pour cent au cours de l'année prochaine **2** *Gram* accusatif *m*, cas *m* objectif **3** *Phot* objectif *m*
►► *Gram* ***the objective case*** le cas objectif; ***objective genitive*** génitif *m* objectif; ***objective reality*** la réalité objective; *Med* ***objective symptoms*** signes *mpl*; ***objective test*** test *m* objectif

objectively [əb'dʒektɪvlɪ] **ADV 1** *(unbiasedly)* objectivement, impartialement **2** *(really, externally)* objectivement

objectivism [əb'dʒektɪvɪzəm] **N** objectivisme *m*

objectivity [ˌɒbdʒek'tɪvətɪ] **N** objectivité *f*

objector [əb'dʒektə(r)] **N** opposant(e) *m,f*; **are there many objectors to the proposal?** y a-t-il beaucoup de gens contre la proposition?

object-orientated, *Am* **object-oriented ADJ** *Comput* orienté objet
►► ***object-orientated language*** langage *m* à objets; ***object-orientated programming*** programmation *f* par objets

oblate ['ɒbleɪt] **ADJ** *Geom* aplati (aux pôles)

obligate ['ɒblɪgeɪt] **VT 1** *Am Formal or Br (compel)* obliger, contraindre; **to be/to feel obligated to do sth** être/se sentir obligé de faire qch **2** *Am Fin (funds, credits)* affecter

obligation [ˌɒblɪ'geɪʃən] **N** obligation *f*; **to be under an o. to do sth** être dans l'obligation de faire qch; **you are under no o. to reply** vous n'êtes pas tenu de répondre, rien ne vous oblige à répondre; **to be under an o. to sb** avoir une dette de reconnaissance envers qn; **to put** *or* **to place sb under an o. to do sth** mettre qn dans l'obligation de faire qch; **family obligations** obligations *fpl* familiales; **to meet one's obligations** satisfaire à ses obligations, assumer ses engagements

obligatory [ə'blɪgətrɪ] **ADJ** obligatoire; **attendance is o.** la présence est obligatoire

oblige [ə'blaɪdʒ] **VT 1** *(constrain)* obliger; **to o. sb to do sth** obliger qn à faire qch; **you're not obliged to come** tu n'es pas obligé de venir **2** *(do a favour to)* rendre service à, *Formal* obliger; *Formal* **I would be obliged if you would refrain from smoking** vous m'obligeriez beaucoup en ne fumant pas; *Formal* **I would be obliged if you could send me the relevant details** je vous serais reconnaissant de bien vouloir m'envoyer les renseignements nécessaires; *Formal* **could you o. me with a match?** auriez-vous l'amabilité *ou* l'obligeance de me donner une allumette?; **much obliged!** merci beaucoup!; **to be obliged to sb for sth** être reconnaissant à qn pour qch, savoir gré à qn de qch
VI I would be only too glad to o. je serais ravi de vous rendre service

obliging [ə'blaɪdʒɪŋ] **ADJ** serviable, obligeant; **it was very o. of him** c'était très aimable à lui *ou* de sa part

obligingly [ə'blaɪdʒɪŋlɪ] **ADV** aimablement, obligeamment; **the letter you o. sent me** la lettre que vous avez eu l'obligeance de m'envoyer

oblique [ə'bliːk] **ADJ 1** *Geom (slanted)* oblique **2** *(indirect ► reference, hint etc)* indirect; **o. glance** regard *m* en biais **3** *Gram* oblique
N 1 *Geom* oblique *f*; *Anat* oblique *m* **2** *Typ & Comput* barre *f* oblique
►► ***oblique angle*** angle *m* oblique; **at an o. angle to the road** en biais par rapport à la route

obliquely [ə'bliːklɪ] **ADV 1** *Geom* obliquement, en biais **2** *(indirectly ► refer)* indirectement; *(► glance)* de *ou* en biais

obliqueness [ə'bliːknɪs], **obliquity** [ə'blɪkwətɪ] **N 1** *Astron & Geom* obliquité *f* **2** *(indirectness ► of reference, hint)* caractère *m* indirect

obliterate [ə'blɪtəreɪt] **VT 1** *(destroy, erase ► figures, footprints, traces etc)* effacer; *(► the past, a culture)* annihiler; *(► buildings, town, evidence)* détruire; **the town was all but obliterated during the war** la ville a été quasiment rayée de la carte pendant la guerre **2** *(cancel ► stamp)* oblitérer

obliteration [əˌblɪtə'reɪʃən] **N 1** *(destruction, erasure ► of figures, footprints, traces etc)* effacement *m*; *(of the past, a culture)* anéantissement *m*; *(of buildings, town, evidence)* destruction *f* **2** *(of stamp)* oblitération *f*

oblivion [ə'blɪvɪən] **N 1** *(being forgotten)* oubli *m*; **to fall** *or* **to sink into o.** tomber dans l'oubli; **to consign to o.** condamner à l'oubli; **to save sb/sth from o.** tirer *ou* sauver qn/qch de l'oubli **2** *(unconsciousness)* inconscience *f*, oubli *m*; **he had drunk himself into o.** il était abruti par l'alcool

oblivious [ə'blɪvɪəs] **ADJ** inconscient; **she was o. of** *or* **to what was happening** elle n'avait pas conscience de *ou* n'était pas consciente de ce qui se passait; **he remained o. to our comments** il est resté sourd à nos remarques; **he is o. to the fact that millions of people are starving** il n'est pas conscient du fait que des millions de gens meurent de faim

obliviously [ə'blɪvɪəslɪ] **ADV** en toute inconscience

oblong ['ɒblɒŋ] **N** *(rectangle)* rectangle *m*
ADJ *(rectangular)* rectangulaire; *(elongated)* allongé, oblong

obloquy ['ɒbləkwɪ] **N** *(UNCOUNT) Formal* **1** *(abuse)* insultes *fpl*, injures *fpl*; *(defamation)* diffamation *f* **2** *(disgrace)* opprobre *m*

obnoxious [əb'nɒkʃəs] **ADJ** *(person)* odieux, ignoble; *(behaviour)* odieux; *(smell)* ignoble, infect

oboe ['əʊbəʊ] **N** hautbois *m*
►► ***oboe d'amore*** hautbois *m* d'amour

oboist ['əʊbəʊɪst] **N** hautbois *m (musicien)*, hautboïste *mf*

obscene [əb'siːn] **ADJ** obscène; *Fig (profits, prices, demands etc)* scandaleux, indécent; *Fig* **it's o. to earn so much money** c'est indécent de gagner autant d'argent

obscenely [əb'siːnlɪ] **ADV** d'une manière obscène; **she gestured to o.** elle fit un geste obscène; *Fig* **he's o. rich** il est tellement riche que c'en est indécent

obscenity [əb'senətɪ] *(pl* **obscenities***)* **N 1** *(UNCOUNT) (obscene language)* obscénité *f*, obscénités *fpl* **2** *(obscene word)* obscénité *f*, grossièreté *f*; **to shout obscenities** crier des obscénités **3** *Fig* obscénité *f*; **the o. of war** l'obscénité *f* de la guerre; **war is an o.** la guerre est une chose obscène
►► ***obscenity laws*** lois *fpl* concernant les outrages à la pudeur

obscurantism [ˌɒbskjʊə'ræntɪzəm] **N** *Formal* obscurantisme *m*

obscurantist [ˌɒbskjʊə'ræntɪst] *Formal* **N** obscurantiste *mf*
ADJ obscurantiste

obscure [əb'skjʊə(r)] **ADJ 1** *(not clear)* obscur; **the meaning is rather o.** le sens n'est pas très clair; **for some o. reason he thought it would help** il pensait, pour d'obscures raisons, que ça serait utile **2** *(little-known ► writer, actor)* obscur; *(► place)* perdu; **of o. birth** de naissance obscure **3** *(dark)* obscur, sombre; **to grow** *or* **become o.** s'obscurcir, s'assombrir
VT 1 *(hide)* cacher; **to o. the truth** cacher *ou* dissimuler la vérité **2** *(confuse)* obscurcir, embrouiller; **to o. the facts/the issue** embrouiller les faits/la question **3** *(darken)* obscurcir, assombrir

obscurely [əb'skjʊəlɪ] **ADV 1** *(feel, see)* vaguement, obscurément **2** *(speak)* de façon obscure *ou* mystérieuse

obscurity [əb'skjʊərətɪ] *(pl* **obscurities***)* **N 1** *(insignificance)* obscurité *f*; **to rise from o. to fame** passer de l'anonymat à la célébrité; **to fall into o.** sombrer dans l'oubli **2** *(difficulty)* obscurité *f* **3** *(darkness)* obscurité *f*, ténèbres *fpl*

obsequies ['ɒbsɪkwɪz] **NPL** *Formal* obsèques *f*

obsequious [əb'siːkwɪəs] **ADJ** *Formal* obs quieux

obsequiously [əb'siːkwɪəslɪ] **ADV** *Formal* obs quieusement

obsequiousness [əb'siːkwɪəsnɪs] **N** *Formal* o séquiosité *f*

observable [əb'zɜːvəbəl] **ADJ** *(visible)* obse vable, visible; *(discernible)* perceptible, appr ciable; **behaviour o. in humans** u comportement observable *ou* que l'on peut o server chez les humains

observance [əb'zɜːvəns] **N 1** *(recognition ► custom, law etc)* observation *f*, observance *f*; *(of anniversary)* célébration *f* **2** *Rel (rite, ceremon* observance *f*

observant [əb'zɜːvənt] **ADJ** *(alert)* observateu **how o. of him!** comme il est observateur!, rie ne lui échappe!

observation [ˌɒbzə'veɪʃən] **N 1** *(study)* observ tion *f*, surveillance *f*; **the o. of nature** l'observ tion *f* de la nature; **to be under o.** *(patient)* êt en observation; *(by police)* être surveillé par police *ou* sous surveillance policière; **they a keeping the house under o.** ils ont placé la ma son sous surveillance
2 *(comment)* observation *f*, remarque *f*; **I have few observations to make** j'ai quelques rema ques à faire
3 *(perception)* observation *f*; **to have gre powers of o.** avoir de grandes facultés d'obse vation
4 *Naut* relèvement *m*
►► ***observation aircraft*** avion *m* de reconnai sance; ***observation balloon*** ballon *m* d'observ tion; *Rail* ***observation car*** voiture panoramique; ***observation deck*** terrasse *f* pan ramique; ***observation point*** point *m* d'observ tion; *Mil* ***observation post*** poste d'observation; ***observation satellite*** satellite d'observation; ***observation tower*** tour *f* de gue mirador *m*; *Med* ***observation ward*** salle *f* d'obse vation

observational [ˌɒbzə'veɪʃənəl] **ADJ** *(facultie powers)* d'observation; *(technique, researc data, study)* qui repose sur l'observation

observatory [əb'zɜːvətrɪ] *(pl* **observatories***)* observatoire *m*

observe [əb'zɜːv] **VT 1** *(see, notice)* observer, r marquer; **did you o. anything strange?** as-tu r marqué quelque chose d'anormal?
2 *(study, pay attention to)* observer; **the police a observing his movements** la police surveille s allées et venues
3 *(comment, remark)* (faire) remarquer, (fair observer; **"she seems worried," he observed** "el a l'air inquiet", fit-il remarquer
4 *(abide by, keep ► the law, the proprieties, a fas* observer; *(► the Sabbath)* respecter, observe *(► order)* se conformer à; **to o. a minute's silenc** observer une minute de silence

observer [əb'zɜːvə(r)] **N 1** *(watcher)* observate (trice) *m,f*; **to the casual o.** pour un non-initié **2** *(official ceremony, election)* observateur(trice) *m* **3** *(commentator)* spécialiste *mf*, expert *m*; **polit cal observers** experts *mpl ou* spécialistes *mfpl* e politique

obsess [əb'ses] **VT** obséder; **he's obsessed wit punctuality** c'est un maniaque de la ponctualit **she's obsessed with the idea of becoming an a tress** elle n'a qu'une idée, devenir actrice; **to b obsessed with death** être obsédé par la mort
VI to o. about sth être obsédé par qch

obsession [əb'seʃən] **N** *(fixed idea)* obsession idée *f* fixe; *(obsessive fear)* hantise *f*; **it's becomin an o. with him** ça devient une idée fixe *ou* un obsession chez lui; **she has an o. about punctua ity** c'est une maniaque de la ponctualité

obsessional [əb'seʃənəl] **ADJ** obsessionnel

obsessive [əb'sesɪv] **ADJ 1** *(person, behaviou jealousy)* obsessionnel; **he's o. about cleanline** c'est un maniaque de la propreté; **he was becon ing quite o. about it** ça devenait une obsessio chez lui **2** *(thought, image)* obsédant
N obsessionnel(elle) *m,f*; **you're turning into a o.** ça tourne à l'obsession chez toi

obsessively [əbˈsesɪvlɪ] ADV d'une manière obsessionnelle; **he's o. cautious** il est d'une prudence obsessionnelle; **he is o. tidy** c'est un maniaque de la propreté

obsolescence [ˌɒbsəˈlesəns] N *(of equipment, consumer goods)* obsolescence *f*; *Com* **planned** *or* **built-in o.** obsolescence *f* planifiée, désuétude *f* calculée; **to fall into o.** tomber en désuétude

►► *Ins* ***obsolescence clause*** clause *f* de vétusté

obsolescent [ˌɒbsəˈlesənt] ADJ qui tombe en désuétude; *(equipment, consumer goods)* obsolescent

obsolete [ˈɒbsəliːt] ADJ **1** *(practice, idea)* démodé, désuet(ète); *(law, idea)* dépassé; *(machinery)* dépassé, obsolète; *(institution)* archaïque, caduc (caduque) **2** *Ling* obsolète **3** *Biol* atrophié

obstacle [ˈɒbstəkəl] N obstacle *m*; **what are the obstacles to free trade?** qu'est-ce qui fait obstacle au libre-échange?; **to put obstacles in sb's way** mettre des bâtons dans les roues à qn

►► ***obstacle course*** parcours *m* d'obstacles; *Fig* parcours *m* du combattant; ***obstacle race*** course *f* d'obstacles

obstetric [ɒbˈstetrɪk] ADJ obstétrical; *(nurses)* en obstétrique

obstetrical [ɒbˈstetrɪkəl] ADJ obstétrical

obstetrician [ˌɒbstəˈtrɪʃən] N obstétricien(enne) *m,f*, médecin *m* accoucheur

obstetrics [ɒbˈstetrɪks] N *(UNCOUNT)* obstétrique *f*

obstinacy [ˈɒbstɪnəsɪ] N **1** *(stubbornness)* obstination *f*, entêtement *m*; *(tenacity)* opiniâtreté *f*, ténacité *f* **2** *(persistence)* persistance *f*; **the o. of an infection** le caractère persistant d'une infection

obstinate [ˈɒbstənət] ADJ **1** *(stubborn)* obstiné, entêté, têtu; *(tenacious)* obstiné, tenace, acharné; **an o. refusal** un refus obstiné; **to meet with o. resistance** se heurter à une résistance obstinée *ou* acharnée **2** *(persistent* ► *cold, illness)* persistant, tenace; *(*►*stain, grease)* rebelle; **an o. fever** une fièvre persistante

obstinately [ˈɒbstənətlɪ] ADV *(stubbornly)* obstinément, avec acharnement; **to behave o.** se montrer obstiné

obstreperous [əbˈstrepərəs] ADJ *Formal or Hum (noisy)* bruyant; *(disorderly)* turbulent, indiscipliné; *(recalcitrant)* récalcitrant; **to get o. about sth** faire du scandale à propos de qch; **don't (you) get o. with me!** tu ne vas pas me faire des histoires!

obstreperously [əbˈstrepərəslɪ] ADV *Formal or Hum (noisily)* bruyamment; *(in a disorderly manner)* avec turbulence; *(recalcitrantly)* à contrecœur

obstreperousness [əbˈstrepərəsnɪs] N *Formal or Hum (of crowd, children)* caractère *m* tapageur; *(of someone's tone)* agressivité *f*

obstruct [əbˈstrʌkt] VT **1** *(block* ► *passage, road, traffic)* bloquer, obstruer; *(*► *pipe)* boucher; *(*► *vein, artery)* obstruer, boucher; **don't o. the exits** ne bloquez pas les sorties; **the lane was obstructed by** *or* **with fallen trees** le chemin était bloqué par des arbres tombés; **her hat obstructed my view** son chapeau me cachait la vue **2** *(impede* ► *progress, measures)* faire obstruction *ou* obstacle à, entraver; **to o. progress/justice** entraver la marche du progrès/le cours de la justice; **he was arrested for obstructing a policeman in the course of his duty** on l'a arrêté pour avoir entravé un agent dans l'exercice de ses fonctions **3** *Sport (opponent)* faire obstruction à

obstruction [əbˈstrʌkʃən] N **1** *(impeding* ► *of progress, measures)* obstruction *f*
2 *(blockage, obstacle* ► *gen)* obstacle *m*; *(*► *in vein, artery)* obstruction *f*; *(*► *in pipe)* bouchon *m*; **the accident caused an o. in the road** l'accident a bloqué la route; *Med* **bowel o., o. of the bowel** occlusion *f* intestinale
3 *Sport* obstruction *f*
4 *Law* obstruction *f* de la voie publique

►► *Law* ***obstruction of justice*** rébellion *f*; ***obstruction lights*** feux *mpl* d'obstacle

obstructionism [əbˈstrʌkʃənɪzəm] N *Pol* obstructionnisme *m*

obstructionist [əbˈstrʌkʃənɪst] *Pol* N obstructionniste *mf*
ADJ obstructionniste

obstructive [əbˈstrʌktɪv] ADJ *(person)* qui fait de l'obstruction, qui met des bâtons dans les roues; *(tactic, attitude)* d'obstruction; *Med* obstructif, obstruant; **they are being very o.** ils nous mettent constamment des bâtons dans les roues; *Pol* **to use o. tactics** user de tactiques obstructionnistes

obtain [əbˈteɪn] VT obtenir; *(for oneself)* se procurer; **to o. sth for sb** obtenir qch pour qn, procurer qch à qn; **to o. sth from sb** obtenir qch de qn; **the book may be obtained from the publisher** on peut se procurer le livre chez l'éditeur
VI *Formal (practice)* avoir cours; *(rules)* être en vigueur; **this custom still obtains in Europe** cette coutume persiste en Europe; **the situation obtaining in Somalia** la situation (qui règne) en Somalie

obtainable [əbˈteɪnəbəl] ADJ **where is this drug o.?** où peut-on se procurer ce médicament?; **the catalogue is o. in our branches** le catalogue est disponible dans nos agences; **o. from your local supermarket** en vente dans votre supermarché; **this result is easily o.** ce résultat est facile à obtenir

obtrude [əbˈtruːd] *Formal* VT **1** *(impose)* imposer; **to o. itself** s'imposer **2** *(stick out)* sortir
VI **1** *(impose oneself)* s'imposer **2** *(stick out)* dépasser

obtrusion [əbˈtruːʒən] N *Formal* intrusion *f*

obtrusive [əbˈtruːsɪv] ADJ *(intrusive* ► *decor, advertising, hoarding, architecture)* trop voyant; *(*► *smell)* envahissant, pénétrant; *(*► *person, behaviour)* envahissant, importun

obtrusively [əbˈtruːsɪvlɪ] ADV importunément

obtrusiveness [əbˈtruːsɪvnɪs] N **1** *(of behaviour, presence)* importunité *f* **2** *(of smell)* caractère *m* pénétrant

obtuse [əbˈtjuːs] ADJ **1** *Formal (slow-witted)* obtus; **you're being deliberately o.** tu fais exprès de ne pas comprendre **2** *Geom (angle)* obtus; *(triangle)* obtusangle **3** *(indistinct)* vague, sourd; **an o. pain** une douleur sourde

obtuseness [əbˈtjuːsnɪs] N *Formal (slow-wittedness)* lenteur *f* d'esprit; *(stupidity)* stupidité *f*

obverse [ˈɒbvɜːs] N **1** *(of coin)* avers *m*, face *f* **2** *(of opinion, argument etc)* contraire *m*, opposé *m*
ADJ **the o. side** *(of coin)* le côté face *ou* l'avers *m*; *Fig (of opinion, argument etc)* le contraire

obviate [ˈɒbvɪeɪt] VT *Formal (difficulty, need)* obvier à; **this obviates the need for further action** cela rend toute autre démarche inutile

obvious [ˈɒbvɪəs] ADJ **1** *(evident)* évident, clair; **it's o. that he's wrong** il est évident *ou* clair qu'il a tort; **the o. choice** le choix évident *ou* qui s'impose; **an o. comparison would be with the French Revolution** la première comparaison qui vient à l'esprit est la révolution française; **her o. innocence** son innocence manifeste; **for o. reasons** pour des raisons évidentes; **the o. thing to do is to leave** la seule chose à faire, c'est de partir; **it was o. that he was going to resign** il était clair qu'il allait démissionner **2** *Pej (predictable)* prévisible; **his symbolism is too o.** son symbolisme manque de subtilité; **you were too o. about it** *(unsubtle)* tu n'as pas été très subtil; **the ending was a bit o.** la fin était prévisible
N **to state the o.** enfoncer une porte ouverte; **it would be stating the o. to say that** cela va sans dire

obviously [ˈɒbvɪəslɪ] ADV **1** *(of course)* évidemment, de toute évidence; **she's o. not lying** il est clair *ou* évident qu'elle ne ment pas; **o. not!** il semble que non!; **he o. got the wrong number** de toute évidence, il s'est trompé de numéro; **they were o. ill** on voyait tout de suite qu'ils étaient malades **2** *(plainly, visibly)* manifestement; **she's not o. lying** il n'est pas sûr qu'elle mente **3** *(beginning a sentence)* il va de soi; **o., we won't break even until next year** il va de soi que nous ne rentrerons pas dans nos frais avant un an

obviousness [ˈɒbvɪəsnɪs] N **1** *(evident nature)* évidence *f*, clarté *f*; *(of lie)* caractère *m* manifeste; **the o. of his displeasure** son mécontentement manifeste **2** *Pej (predictability)* caractère *m* trop prévisible

OC [ˌəʊˈsiː] N *Mil (abbr* **Officer Commanding***)* chef *m* de corps

ocarina [ˌɒkəˈriːnə] N ocarina *m*

occasion [əˈkeɪʒən] N **1** *(circumstance, time)* occasion *f*; **on this/that o.** cette fois-ci/là; **on the o. of her wedding** à l'occasion de son mariage; **on one o.** une fois; **on another o.** une autre fois; **I have been there on quite a few occasions** j'y suis allé à plusieurs occasions *ou* à plusieurs reprises; **on great occasions** dans les grandes occasions; **if the o. arises, should the o. arise** si l'occasion se présente, le cas échéant; **it wasn't a suitable o.** les circonstances n'étaient pas favorables; **to rise to the o.** se montrer à la hauteur (de la situation) **2** *(special event)* événement *m*; **his birthday is always a big o.** son anniversaire est toujours un événement important; **to have a sense of o.** savoir marquer le coup **3** *(reason, cause)* motif *m*, raison *f*, occasion *f*; **I had no o. to suspect her** je n'avais aucune raison de la soupçonner; **her return was the o. for great rejoicing** son retour donna lieu à de grandes réjouissances
VT occasionner, provoquer
• **on occasion, on occasions** ADV de temps en temps, de temps à autre

occasional [əˈkeɪʒənəl] ADJ **1** *(occurring from time to time)* occasionnel, épisodique; **he's an o. visitor/golfer** il vient/joue au golf de temps en temps; **I like an** *or* **the o. cigar** j'aime (fumer) un cigare à l'occasion *ou* de temps en temps; **she writes me the o. postcard** elle m'envoie une carte postale de temps à autre; **there will be o. showers** il y aura quelques averses *ou* pluies intermittentes **2** *(music, play)* de circonstance

►► ***occasional chair*** chaise *f* volante; *Br* ***occasional table*** table *f* d'appoint

occasionally [əˈkeɪʒənəlɪ] ADV de temps en temps, quelquefois, occasionnellement; **I smoke only very o.** je ne fume que très rarement

occident [ˈɒksɪdənt] N *Literary* occident *m*, couchant *m*
• **Occident** N **the O.** l'Occident *m*

occidental [ˌɒksɪˈdentəl] ADJ *Literary* occidental
• **Occidental** ADJ occidental N Occidental(e) *m,f*

occipital [ɒkˈsɪpɪtəl] *Anat* N os *m* occipital
ADJ occipital

►► ***occipital bone*** os *m* occipital; ***occipital lobe*** lobe *m* occipital

occiput [ˈɒksɪpʌt] *(pl* **occiputs** *or* **occipita** [ɒkˈsɪpɪtə]) N occiput *m*

occlude [ɒˈkluːd] VT occlure

occlusion [ɒˈkluːʒən] N occlusion *f*

occlusive [ɒˈkluːsɪv] N *Ling* (consonne *f*) occlusive *f*
ADJ occlusif

occult [ɒˈkʌlt] N **the o.** *(supernatural)* le surnaturel; *(mystical skills)* les sciences *fpl* occultes
ADJ occulte

occultism [ˈɒkʌltɪzəm] N occultisme *m*

occupancy [ˈɒkjʊpənsɪ] *(pl* **occupancies***)* N **1** *(of house, room etc)* occupation *f*; **hotel o. levels** *or* **rates** taux *m* d'occupation des hôtels **2** *Law* possession *f* à titre de premier occupant

occupant [ˈɒkjʊpənt] N **1** occupant(e) *m,f*; *(tenant)* locataire *mf*; *(of job)* titulaire *mf* **2** *Law* premier(ère) occupant(e) *m,f*

occupation [ˌɒkjʊˈpeɪʃən] N **1** *(employment)* emploi *m*, travail *m*; **what's his o.?** qu'est-ce qu'il fait comme travail *ou* dans la vie?; **please state your name and o.** veuillez indiquer votre nom et votre profession; **raising a family is a full-time o.** élever des enfants, c'est un travail à plein temps
2 *(activity, hobby)* occupation *f*; **a leisure o.** un loisir; **his favourite o. is listening to music** ce qu'il aime faire par-dessus tout, c'est écouter de la musique
3 *(of building, offices etc)* occupation *f*; **during Mr Gray's o. of the premises** lorsque M. Gray occu-

pait les locaux; **the offices are ready for o.** les bureaux sont prêts à être occupés

4 *Mil & Pol* occupation *f*; **the students have voted to continue their o.** les étudiants ont voté la poursuite de l'occupation des locaux; **under French o.** sous occupation française

• **Occupation** **N** *Hist* **the O.** l'Occupation *f*

occupational [ˌɒkjʊ'peɪʃənəl] **ADJ** professionnel

▸▸ ***occupational accident*** accident *m* du travail; ***occupational disease*** maladie *f* professionnelle; ***occupational hazard*** risque *m* professionnel *ou* du métier; ***occupational medicine*** médecine *f* du travail; *Br* ***occupational pension*** retraite *f* complémentaire; ***occupational pension scheme*** caisse *f* de retraite complémentaire; ***occupational psychology*** psychologie *f* du travail; ***occupational therapist*** ergothérapeute *mf*; ***occupational therapy*** ergothérapie *f*

occupied ['ɒkjʊpaɪd] **ADJ** *(country, town, territory)* occupé; **this seat is o.** cette place est prise; *Hist* **in o. France** dans la France occupée

occupier ['ɒkjʊpaɪə(r)] **N** occupant(e) *m,f*; *(tenant)* locataire *mf*; **to the o.** *(on letter)* à l'attention de l'occupant

occupy ['ɒkjʊpaɪ] *(pt & pp* **occupied***)* **VT 1** *(house, room etc)* occuper

2 *(keep busy* ▸ *person, mind)* occuper; **she occupies herself by doing crosswords** elle s'occupe en faisant des mots croisés; **to be occupied in** *or* **with sth/doing sth** être occupé à qch/faire qch; **try to keep them occupied for a few minutes** essaie de les occuper quelques minutes; **to keep one's mind occupied** s'occuper l'esprit; **find something to o. your mind** trouvez quelque chose qui vous occupe l'esprit; **reading keeps him occupied** ça l'occupe de lire

3 *(fill, take up* ▸ *time, space)* occuper; **the sofa occupies half the room** le canapé occupe *ou* prend la moitié de la pièce; **how do you o. your evenings?** comment *ou* à quoi occupez-vous vos soirées?

4 *Mil & Pol (enemy country)* occuper; *(strategic point)* s'emparer de; **occupying army** armée *f* d'occupation; **the workers have occupied the building** les ouvriers ont occupé le bâtiment

5 *(hold* ▸ *office, role, rank)* occuper

occur [ə'kɜː(r)] *(pt & pp* **occurred**, *cont* **occurring***)* **VI 1** *(happen* ▸ *event)* avoir lieu, arriver; *(*▸ *opportunity, vacancy)* se présenter; *(*▸ *accident)* avoir lieu, se produire; **this seldom occurs** cela arrive rarement; **misunderstandings often o. over the phone** il y a souvent des malentendus au téléphone; **many changes have occurred since then** beaucoup de choses ont changé depuis ce temps-là; **if a difficulty/the opportunity occurs** si une difficulté/l'occasion se présente; **I promise it won't o. again** je promets que ça ne se reproduira pas; **whatever occurs** quoi qu'il arrive **2** *(exist, be found)* se trouver, se rencontrer; **the mistake occurs at the end** l'erreur se trouve à la fin; **such phenomena often o. in nature** on rencontre souvent de tels phénomènes dans la nature **3** *(come to mind)* **to o. to sb** venir à l'esprit de qn; **it occurred to me later that he was lying** j'ai réalisé plus tard qu'il mentait; **didn't it o. to you to call me?** ça ne t'est pas venu à l'idée de m'appeler?; **it would never o. to me to use violence** il ne me viendrait jamais à l'idée d'avoir recours à la violence

occurrence [ə'kʌrəns] **N 1** *(incident)* événement *m*; **this was the first o. of its kind** c'était la première fois qu'un événement de cette espèce se produisait; **it's an everyday o.** ça arrive *ou* ça se produit tous les jours **2** *(fact or instance of occurring)* **the increasing o. of racial attacks** le nombre croissant d'agressions racistes; **the o. of leukaemia in this community is twice…** le nombre des cas de leucémie dans cette communauté est le double de…; **of rare o.** qui arrive *ou* se produit rarement **3** *Ling* occurrence *f*

OCD [ˌəʊsiː'diː] **N** *Psy (abbr* **obsessive compulsive disorder***)* TOC *m*

ocean ['əʊʃən] **N 1** *(body of water)* océan *m*; *Am* **the o.** la mer **2** *Fig* **oceans of** beaucoup de; **we've got oceans of time** nous avons beaucoup de temps

▸▸ ***ocean bed*** fond *m* de l'océan; ***ocean current*** courant *m* océanique; ***ocean floor*** fond *m* de l'océan; ***ocean liner*** paquebot *m*

oceangoing ['əʊʃənˌgəʊɪŋ] **ADJ** de haute mer

Oceania [ˌəʊʃɪ'ɑːnɪə] **N** Océanie *f*

oceanic [ˌəʊʃɪ'ænɪk] **ADJ** *(marine)* océanique

oceanographer [ˌəʊʃə'nɒgrəfə(r)] **N** océanographe *mf*

oceanography [ˌəʊʃə'nɒgrəfɪ] **N** océanographie *f*

ocelot ['əʊsɪlɒt] **N** *Zool* ocelot *m*

ochre, *Am* **ocher** ['əʊkə(r)] **N** *(ore)* ocre *f*; *(colour)* ocre *m*; **red o.** ocre *m* rouge; **yellow o.** jaune *m* d'ocre, ocre *m* jaune

ADJ ocre *(inv)*

ocker ['ɒkə(r)] *Austr Fam* **N** *(boor)* beauf *m*

ADJ *(boorish)* rustre

o'clock [ə'klɒk] **ADV 1** *(time)* **it's one/two o.** il est une heure/deux heures; **at precisely 9 o.** à 9 heures précises; **a flight at 4 o. in the afternoon** un vol à 16 heures; **the 8 o. bus** le bus de 8 heures; **at 12 o.** *(midday)* à midi; *(midnight)* à minuit **2** *(position)* **enemy fighter at 7 o.** chasseur ennemi à 7 heures

OCR [ˌəʊsiː'ɑː(r)] **N** *Comput* **1** *(abbr* **optical character reader***)* lecteur *m* (à reconnaissance) optique de caractères **2** *(abbr* **optical character recognition***)* OCR *f*

▸▸ ***OCR font*** fonte *f* reconnue optiquement; ***OCR reader*** lecteur *m* OCR; ***OCR software*** logiciel *m* d'OCR

Oct. *(written abbr* **October***)* oct.

octagon ['ɒktəgən] **N** octogone *m*

octagonal [ɒk'tægənəl] **ADJ** octogonal

octahedral [ˌɒktə'hiːdrəl] **ADJ** octaédrique

octahedron [ˌɒktə'hiːdrən] **N** octaèdre *m*

octane ['ɒkteɪn] **N** octane *m*

▸▸ ***octane number, octane rating*** indice *m* d'octane

octave ['ɒktɪv] **N** *Fencing, Mus & Rel* octave *f*; *Literature* huitain *m*; *Mus* **an o. apart** à une octave de différence

octavo [ɒk'teɪvəʊ] *(pl* **octavos***)* **N** in-octavo *m inv*

octet [ɒk'tet] **N 1** *(group)* octuor *m*

2 *Mus* octuor *m*

3 *Literature* huitain *m*

4 *Chem* octet *m*

October [ɒk'təʊbə(r)] **N** octobre *m*; *see also* **February**

▸▸ ***the October Revolution*** la révolution d'octobre

octogenarian [ˌɒktəʊdʒɪ'neərɪən] **N** octogénaire *mf*

ADJ octogénaire

octopod ['ɒktəpɒd] **N** octopode *m*

ADJ octopode

octopus ['ɒktəpəs] *(pl* **octopuses** *or* **octopi** [-paɪ]*)* **N 1** *Zool* pieuvre *f*, poulpe *m*; *Culin* poulpe *m* **2** *Fig* pieuvre *f*

octosyllabic [ˌɒktəʊsɪ'læbɪk] **ADJ** octosyllabique, octosyllabe; **in o. verse** en octosyllabes, en vers octosyllabiques

octuple ['ɒktjuːpəl] **N** octuple *m*

ADJ octuple

VT octupler

ocular ['ɒkjʊlə(r)] **N** oculaire *m*

ADJ oculaire

oculist ['ɒkjʊlɪst] **N** oculiste *mf*

OD [ˌəʊ'diː] *(pt & pp* **ODd**, *cont* **ODing***)* **N 1** *Fam (abbr* **overdose***)* overdose[□] *f* **2** *(abbr* **overdraft***)* découvert *m*

ADJ *(abbr* **overdrawn***)* à découvert

VI *Fam* faire une overdose (on de); **I've OD'd on pizzas/soap operas lately** j'ai tellement mangé de pizzas/regardé de feuilletons télé ces derniers temps que j'en suis dégoûté

ODA [ˌəʊdiː'eɪ] **N** *(abbr* **Official Development Assistance***)* APD *f*

odalisk, odalisque ['əʊdəlɪsk] **N** odalisque *f*

odd [ɒd] **ADJ 1** *(weird)* bizarre, curieux; **he's an o. character** c'est un drôle d'individu; **the o. thing is that the room was empty** ce qui est bizarre *ou* curieux, c'est que la pièce était vide; **it felt o. seeing her again** ça m'a fait (tout) drôle de la revoir; **an o. way of saying sorry** une drôle de manière de s'excuser; **(well,) that's o.!** (tiens,) c'est bizarre *ou* curieux!; *Fam* **he's a bit o. in the head** il lui manque une case

2 *(occasional, incidental)* **at o. moments** de temps en temps; **he has his o. moments of depression** il lui arrive d'avoir ses moments de déprime; **I smoke the o. cigarette** il m'arrive de fumer une cigarette de temps en temps; **we took the o. photo** nous avons pris deux ou trois photos; **she gives him a few o. jobs from time to time** de temps en temps, elle lui donne une ou deux choses à faire

3 *(not matching)* dépareillé; **he was wearing o. socks** ses chaussettes étaient dépareillées, il portait des chaussettes dépareillées

4 *(not divisible by two)* impair

5 *Fam (or so)* **twenty o.** vingt et quelques[□]; **thirty-o. pounds** trente livres et quelques, trente et quelques livres; **he must be forty-o.** il doit avoir la quarantaine *ou* dans les quarante ans

6 *(idioms)* **the o. one/man/woman out** l'exception *f*; **everyone else was in evening dress, I was the o. one out** ils étaient tous en tenue de soirée sauf moi; **which of these drawings is the o. one out?** parmi ces dessins, lequel est l'intrus?

▸▸ *Br Fam* ***odd bod*** allumé(e) *m,f*, farfelu(e) *m,f*; *Math* ***odd function*** fonction *f* impaire; ***odd jobs*** *(casual jobs)* petits boulots *mpl*; **to do o. jobs around the house** bricoler dans la maison; ***odd lot*** *Com* lot *m* dépareillé; *St Exch (of shares)* lot *m* de moins de cent actions; ***odd number*** nombre *m* impair

oddball ['ɒdbɔːl] *Fam* **N** allumé(e) *m,f*, farfelu(e) *m,f*; **he's a real o.** c'est un drôle de numéro

ADJ loufoque, farfelu

odd-even **ADJ**

▸▸ *Comput* ***odd-even check*** contrôle *m* de parité; *Mktg* ***odd-even price*** prix *m* magique; *Mktg* ***odd-even pricing*** fixation *f* des prix magiques

oddity ['ɒdɪtɪ] *(pl* **oddities***)* **N 1** *(strange person)* excentrique *mf*, original(e) *m,f*; *(strange thing)* curiosité *f*; **she's a bit of an o.** elle est un peu bizarre; **being the only woman there makes her something of an o.** on la remarque du simple fait qu'elle est la seule femme; **this movie is an o.** *(weird)* c'est un film bizarre; *(unusual)* ce film est une curiosité; **he has some little oddities** il a des côtés un peu bizarres **2** *(strangeness)* étrangeté *f*, bizarrerie *f*

odd-jobber [-'dʒɒbə(r)], **odd-job man** **N** homme *m* à tout faire

odd-looking **ADJ** à l'air bizarre

oddly ['ɒdlɪ] **ADV** bizarrement, curieusement; **o. shaped** d'une forme bizarre; **o. enough, he didn't recognize me** chose curieuse, il ne m'a pas reconnu

oddment ['ɒdmənt] **N** *Com (of matched set)* article *m* dépareillé; *(of lot, line)* fin *f* de série; *(of fabric)* coupon *m*

oddness ['ɒdnɪs] **N** bizarrerie *f*

odds [ɒdz] **NPL 1** *(in betting)* cote *f*; **the o. are ten to one against/on** la cote est de dix contre un/de un contre dix; **they're offering long/short o. against Jackson** Jackson a une bonne/faible cote; **I'll lay** *or* **give you o. of twenty to one that she'll leave him** je te parie à vingt contre un qu'elle le quittera; *Br* **I ended up paying over the o.** en fin de compte, je l'ai payé plus cher qu'il ne valait *ou* que sa valeur

2 *(chances)* chances *fpl*; **what are the o. on his getting the job?** quelles chances a-t-il d'avoir le poste?; **the o. are she's been lying to us all along** il y a de fortes chances qu'elle nous ait menti depuis le début; **the o. are on/against her accepting** il y a de fortes chances/il y a peu de chances (pour) qu'elle accepte; **the o. are that he'll succeed** il y a gros à parier qu'il réussira; **the o. are in favour of the socialists winning** il y a de fortes chances pour que les socialistes l'emportent

3 *(great difficulties)* **against all the o.** contre toute attente; **they won against overwhelming o.** ils ont gagné alors que tout était contre eux

4 *Br Fam (difference)* **it makes no o.** ça ne change rien[□]; **it makes no o. to me** ça m'est égal[□]; **it makes no o. what I say** ce que je dis ne sert à rien

5 *(idioms)* **o. and ends** *(miscellaneous objects)* objets *mpl* divers, bric-à-brac *m inv*; *(leftovers)* restes *mpl*; *Br Fam* **o. and sods** *(miscellaneous objects)* objets *mpl* divers□, bric-à-brac□*m inv*; *(people)* gens *mpl* divers□; **her desk is always covered with o. and ends** son bureau est toujours encombré de tout un bric-à-brac; **I've still a few o. and ends to do** j'ai encore quelques bricoles *ou* petites choses à faire

• **at odds** ADJ **to be at o. with sb (over sth)** *(be in disagreement)* ne pas être d'accord avec qn (à propos de qch); *(be on bad terms)* être brouillé avec qn (à propos de qch); **to be at o. with oneself** être mal dans sa peau; **to be at o. with the world** en vouloir au monde entier; **his latest statement is at o. with his earlier account** sa dernière déposition ne concorde pas avec son premier récit des faits; **his lavish lifestyle is totally at o. with his professed political beliefs** son train de vie luxueux est en contradiction avec les convictions politiques qu'il affiche

odds-on ADJ *Br* **it's o. that he'll win** il y a tout à parier qu'il gagnera

▸▸ ***odds-on favourite*** grand favori *m*

ode [əʊd] N ode *f*

odious ['əʊdɪəs] ADJ odieux

odiously ['əʊdɪəslɪ] ADV odieusement

odiousness ['əʊdɪəsnɪs] N caractère *m* odieux

odium ['əʊdjəm] N *Formal (condemnation)* réprobation *f*; *(hatred)* haine *f*; **to bring** *or* **cast o. upon sb** *(condemnation)* attirer à qn la réprobation générale; *(hatred)* rendre qn odieux (aux yeux des autres)

odometer [əʊ'dɒmɪtə(r)] N *Am Aut* compteur *m* kilométrique

odontology [,ɒdɒn'tɒlədʒɪ] N odontologie *f*

odor, odorless *Am* = **odour, odourless**

odorous ['əʊdərəs] ADJ *(fragrant)* odorant; *(malodorous)* malodorant

odour, *Am* **odor** ['əʊdə(r)] N **1** *(smell)* odeur *f* **2** *(pervasive quality)* odeur *f*, parfum *m*, arôme *m*; *Rel* **o. of sanctity** odeur *f* de sainteté **3** *Br (idiom) Formal* **to be in good/bad o. with sb** être bien/mal vu de qn; **you're not in good o. with the boss** tu n'es pas en odeur de sainteté auprès du patron

odourless, *Am* **odorless** ['əʊdəlɪs] ADJ inodore

odyssey ['ɒdɪsɪ] N odyssée *f*; *Fig* **a spiritual o.** une odyssée spirituelle

OECD [,əʊi:si:'di:] N *(abbr* **Organization for Economic Cooperation and Development**) OCDE *f*

oedema, *Am* **edema** [ɪ'di:mə] *(Br pl* **oedemata** [-mətə], *Am pl* **edemata** [-mətə]) N *Med* œdème *m*

Oedipal ['i:dɪpəl] ADJ œdipien

Oedipus ['i:dɪpəs] PR N *Myth* Œdipe

▸▸ ***Oedipus complex*** complexe *m* d'Œdipe

OEIC [,əʊi:aɪ'si:] N *Fin (abbr* **open-ended investment company**) ≃ SICAV *f*, sicav *f*

OEM [,əʊi:'em] N *(abbr* **original equipment manufacturer**) constructeur *m* de systèmes originaux, OEM *m*

o'er ['əʊə(r)] *Literary* = **over** ADV & PREP

oesophagus, *Am* **esophagus** [i:'sɒfəgəs] *(Br pl* **oesophaguses** *or* **oesophagi** [-gaɪ], *Am pl* **esophaguses** *or* **esophagi** [-gaɪ]) N œsophage *m*

oestrogen, *Am* **estrogen** ['i:strədʒən] N œstrogène *m*

oestrous, *Am* **estrous** ['i:strəs] ADJ œstral

▸▸ ***oestrous cycle*** cycle *m* œstral

oestrus, *Am* **estrus** ['i:strəs] N œstrus *m*

OF [əv, *stressed* ɒv] PREP **1** *(after nouns expressing quantity, number, amount)* de; **a pound of onions** une livre d'oignons; **a loaf of bread** un pain; **a piece of cake** un morceau de gâteau; **there are six of us** nous sommes six; **some/many/few of us were present** quelques-uns/beaucoup/peu d'entre nous étaient présents; **half of them failed** la moitié d'entre eux ont échoué; **how much of it do you want?** combien en voulez-vous?

2 *(indicating age)* de; **a boy/a girl of three** un garçon/une fille de trois ans; **at the age of 19** à 19 ans, à l'âge de 19 ans; **his wife of 20 years** la femme avec qui il est marié depuis 20 ans

3 *(indicating composition, content)* de; **a map of Spain** une carte d'Espagne; **a report of events in Parliament** un compte rendu de ce qui se passe au Parlement; **a rise of 25 percent** une augmentation de 25 pour cent; **a team of cricketers** une équipe de cricket; **a city of 120,000** une ville de 120000 habitants

4 *(created by)* de; **the poems of Byron** les poèmes de Byron

5 *(with words expressing attitude or emotion)* de; **I'm ashamed of it** j'en ai honte; **I'm proud of it** j'en suis fier; **I'm afraid of the dark** j'ai peur du noir; **she dreamt of one day becoming Prime Minister** elle rêvait de devenir un jour Premier ministre; **the fear of God** la crainte de Dieu

6 *(indicating possession, relationship)* de; **he's a friend of mine** c'est un ami à moi; **a friend of mine saw me** un de mes amis m'a vu; **I'd like a home of my own** j'aimerais avoir mon chez-moi; **cancer of the bowel** cancer des intestins; **the rights of man** les droits de l'homme; **she's head of department** elle est chef de service; **doctor of medicine** docteur en médecine

7 *(indicating subject of action)* **it was kind/mean of him** c'était gentil/méchant de sa part; **how clever of her** comme c'est intelligent de sa part

8 *(with names of places)* de; **the city of New York** la ville de New York; **the people of Chile** le peuple *ou* les habitants du Chili; **the University of Cambridge** l'université de Cambridge

9 *(after nouns derived from verbs)* de; **the arrival/departure of Flight 556** l'arrivée/le départ du vol 556; **we need the approval of the committee** nous devons obtenir l'autorisation du comité; **a lover of fine wine** un amateur de bons vins

10 *(describing a particular feeling or quality)* de; **a feeling of relief** un sentiment de soulagement; **she has the gift of mimicry** elle a un talent d'imitatrice; **a man of courage** un homme de courage; **people of foreign appearance** gens à l'air étranger; **a coat of many colours** un manteau multicolore; **a sort** *or* **kind** *or* **type of tree** un type d'arbre; **to be of a nervous disposition** avoir une prédisposition à la nervosité; **that fool of a sergeant** cet imbécile de sergent

11 *(made from)* **a ring of solid gold** une bague en or massif; **a heart of stone** un cœur de pierre; **made of wood** fait de *ou* en bois

12 *(after nouns of size, measurement etc)* de; **a width/length of 60 feet** une largeur/longueur de 60 pieds

13 *(indicating cause, origin, source)* de; **the consequence/the effects of the explosion** la conséquence/les effets de l'explosion; **to die of cancer** mourir du *ou* d'un cancer; **of royal descent** de lignée royale; **of which/whom** dont

14 *(indicating likeness, similarity)* de; **the colour of blood/of grass** la couleur du sang/de l'herbe; **the size of a tennis ball** de la taille d'une balle de tennis; **he reminds me of John Wayne** il me rappelle John Wayne; **it smells of coffee** ça sent le café; **a giant of a man** un homme très grand

15 *(indicating specific point in time or space)* de; **the 3rd of May** le 3 mai; **in the middle of August** à la mi-août; **the day of our wedding** le jour de notre mariage; *Am* **a quarter of nine** neuf heures moins le quart; **in the middle of the road** au milieu de la chaussée; **at the far end of the room** à l'autre bout de la pièce; **south of** au sud de; **within a mile of** à moins d'un mile de; *Naut* à moins d'un mille de

16 *(indicating deprivation or absence)* **a lack of food** un manque de nourriture; **to be cured of sth** être guéri de qch; **to rob sb of sth** voler qch à qn

17 *(indicating information received or passed on)* **I've never heard of him** je n'ai jamais entendu parler de lui; **to learn of sth** apprendre qch; **it was said of President Nixon that…** il a été dit du président Nixon que…

18 *(as intensifier)* **the best/the worst of all** le meilleur/le pire de tout; **today of all days!** il fallait que ça arrive aujourd'hui!; **he, of all men** *or* **people** lui entre tous; **you, of all people, should know…** toi, plus que quiconque, devrais savoir que…

19 *Old-fashioned or Hum* **I like to listen to the radio of a morning/an evening** j'aime écouter la radio le matin/le soir

ofay [əʊ'feɪ] N *Am Fam* sale Blanc (Blanche) *m,f*, = terme injurieux désignant un Blanc

Ofcom ['ɒf,kɒm] N *(abbr* **Office of Communications**) = organisme britannique chargé de réglementer le secteur des communications

OFEX ['əʊ,feks] N *St Exch (abbr* **off-exchange**) marché *m* secondaire

OFF [ɒf] ADV **1** *(indicating removal)* **to take sth o.** enlever *ou* ôter qch; **to come o.** *(sticker, handle)* se détacher; *(lipstick, paint)* partir; **you can leave your jacket o.** ce n'est pas la peine de remettre votre veste; **she kicked o. her shoes** elle ôta ses chaussures d'un coup de pied; **the knob had broken o.** la poignée était cassée; **she cut o. her hair** elle s'est coupé les cheveux; **could you take two centimetres o.?** *(off sleeves, hemline)* est-ce que vous pourriez enlever deux centimètres?; **o. with those wet clothes!** retire(-moi) *ou* enlève(-moi) ces vêtements humides!; **o. with his head!** coupez-lui la tête!

2 *(indicating departure)* **the truck drove o.** le camion démarra; **to run o.** partir en courant; **when are you o. to Dublin?** quand partez-vous pour Dublin?; **we'd better be o.** on doit partir; *Sport* **they're o.!** ils sont partis!; *Fam* **I'm o.!** j'y vais!□; **o. you go, you'll be late!** sauve-toi *ou* vas-y, tu vas être en retard!; **o. we go!** c'est parti!; **o. to bed with you!** au lit!; **isn't it time you were o. to bed?** n'est-il pas l'heure que tu ailles te coucher?; *Fam* **be o. with you!** va-t'en!□; **(get) o.!** enlevez-vous de là!; *Hum* **oh no, he's o. again!** ça y est, ça le reprend!

3 *(indicating movement away from a surface)* **the ball hit the wall and bounced o.** la balle a heurté le mur et a rebondi; **I knocked the glass o. with my elbow** j'ai fait tomber le verre d'un coup de coude

4 *(indicating location)* **it's o. to the right** c'est sur la droite; **she's o. playing tennis** elle est partie jouer au tennis

5 *(indicating disembarkment, dismounting etc)* **to get o.** descendre; **to jump o.** sauter

6 *(indicating absence, inactivity)* **to take a week o.** prendre une semaine de congé; **Monday's my day o.** le lundi est mon jour de congé; **have you any time o. during the week?** avez-vous des heures libres pendant la semaine?; **I get two hours o. for lunch** j'ai deux heures de libres pour le déjeuner

7 *(indicating distance in time or space)* **Paris/Christmas is still a long way o.** Paris/Noël est encore loin; **it's a few miles o.** c'est à quelques kilomètres d'ici

8 *Theat* off; **voice o.** voix *f* off; **noises/voices o.** bruits *mpl*/voix *fpl* en coulisses

9 *(indicating disconnection)* **to put** *or* **switch** *or* **turn the light o.** éteindre la lumière; **to turn the tap o.** fermer le robinet; **leave the lights o.** n'allume pas

10 *(indicating separation, partition)* **the playing area is divided o. by a low wall** l'aire de jeu est délimitée par un petit mur; **the police have cordoned o. the area** la police a bouclé le quartier

11 *(indicating price reduction)* **special offer: £5 o.** *(sign)* offre spéciale: 5 livres de réduction; **the salesman gave me $20/20 percent o.** le vendeur m'a fait une remise de 20 dollars/20 pour cent

12 *(indicating relief from discomfort)* **to sleep/to walk sth o.** faire passer qch en dormant/marchant

PREP **1** *(indicating movement away from)* de; **he fell o. his chair** il est tombé de sa chaise; **she knocked the vase o. the table** elle a fait tomber le vase de la table; **take your elbows o. the table** enlève tes coudes de la table; **o. the sofa!** *(don't stand on it)* descends du canapé!; *(don't sit on it)* lève-toi du canapé!; **drinks must not be taken o. the premises** *(sign)* les boissons doivent être consommées sur place; *Fig* **it'll take your mind o. it** ça te changera les idées

2 *(indicating removal)* de; **take the top o. the bottle** enlève le bouchon de la bouteille; **to cut a slice o. sth** couper une tranche de qch; **I've stripped the wallpaper o. the walls** j'ai décollé le papier peint des murs; **get that knife o. him!** prends-lui son couteau!; **o. the peg** en confection, en prêt-à-porter

3 *(from)* **to buy sth o. sb** acheter qch à qn; **I bought it o. a stall** je l'ai acheté sur le marché; **can I borrow £5 o. you?** je peux t'emprunter 5 livres?; **I caught a cold o. my brother** mon frère m'a passé son rhume

4 *(from the direction of)* de; **a cool breeze o. the sea** une brise fraîche venant du large
5 *(indicating location)* **a few miles o. the coast** à quelques kilomètres de la côte; **o. the coast of Spain** au large de la côte espagnole; **most students live o. campus** la plupart des étudiants vivent à l'extérieur du campus; **we ate in a small restaurant o. the main road** nous avons mangé dans un petit restaurant à l'écart de la grand-route; **the bathroom's o. the bedroom** la salle de bains donne dans la chambre; **just o. Oxford Street there's a pretty little square** à deux pas d'Oxford Street il y a une petite place ravissante
6 *(absent from)* **Mr Dale is o. work today** M. Dale est absent aujourd'hui; **you need a few days o. work** vous avez besoin de quelques jours de congé; **Wayne's o. school with the flu** Wayne est à la maison avec la grippe; **I'm o. duty at 6** je finis mon service à 6 heures; **I've been o. work for over a year now** voilà un an que je ne travaille plus
7 *(by means of)* **it runs o. gas/electricity/solar power** ça marche au gaz/à l'électricité/à l'énergie solaire; **the radio works o. the mains** la radio fonctionne sur secteur
8 *(indicating source of nourishment)* de; **to live o. vegetables** vivre de légumes; **we dined o. a leg of lamb** nous avons dîné d'une tranche de gigot
9 *(reduced from)* **I can get $20/20 percent o. the list price** je peux avoir une remise de 20 dollars/20 pour cent sur le prix de vente; *Fam* **they'll knock** *or* **take something o. it if you pay cash** ils vous feront une remise si vous payez en liquide□; **that's two seconds o. the record** c'est deux secondes de moins que le record
10 *Fam (no longer wanting or needing)* **to be o. one's food** ne pas avoir faim□; **I'm o. whisky** je n'aime plus le whisky□; **I'm o. him at the moment** j'en ai marre de lui en ce moment; **she's o. antibiotics now** elle ne prend plus d'antibiotiques maintenant□; **he's o. heroin now** il ne touche plus à l'héroïne maintenant□
ADJ 1 *(not working ▸ electricity, light, radio, TV)* éteint; *(▸ tap)* fermé; *(▸ engine, machine)* arrêté, à l'arrêt; *(▸ handbrake)* desserré; **the gas is o.** *(at mains)* le gaz est fermé; *(under saucepan)* le gaz est éteint; *(for safety reasons)* le gaz est coupé; **o.** *(on switch, appliance)* arrêt; **make sure the switches are in the o. position** vérifiez que les interrupteurs sont sur (la position) arrêt; **the o. button** le bouton d'arrêt
2 *(bad, tainted)* mauvais, avarié; **the milk is o.** le lait a tourné; **this beer's o.** cette bière est éventée; **it smells/tastes o.** on dirait que ce n'est plus bon
3 *(cancelled)* annulé; **tonight's match is o.** le match de ce soir est annulé; **if that's your attitude, the deal's o.!** si c'est comme ça que vous le prenez ma proposition ne tient plus!
4 *(on vacation, not working)* en congé, en vacances; **to be o. sick** être absent parce qu'on est malade, être malade; **he's o. today** il n'est pas là aujourd'hui; **are you o. tomorrow?** tu travailles demain?; *(no school)* tu (n')as (pas d')école demain?; *(no college)* tu (n')as (pas) cours demain?; **I'm o. from 3 to 5** je ne travaille pas entre 3 et 5 heures
5 *Br (not available)* **I'm afraid the salmon's o.** je regrette, mais il n'y a plus de saumon
6 *(unwell)* **I felt decidedly o. the next morning** le lendemain matin, je ne me sentais vraiment pas bien; **everyone has their o. days** on a tous nos mauvais jours
7 *(inaccurate)* **his timing was a bit o.** *(when he asked for a rise etc)* il n'a pas choisi un très bon moment
8 *Fam (unacceptable)* **that's a bit o.!** vous y allez un peu fort!; **I thought it was a bit o. the way she just ignored me** je n'ai pas apprécié qu'elle m'ignore comme ça□
9 *Br Aut (when driving on right)* (du côté) gauche; *(when driving on left)* (du côté) droit
10 *(having a certain amount of)* **how are we o. for milk?** combien de lait nous reste-t-il?
N *Fam (start)* départ□*m*; **they're ready for the o.** ils sont prêts à partir□; **right from the o.** dès le départ
VT *Am Fam (kill)* buter, refroidir, zigouiller
• **off chance N on the o. chance** au cas où, à tout hasard; **I phoned on the o. chance of catching him at home** j'ai appelé en espérant qu'il serait chez lui; **she kept it on the o. chance (that) it might prove useful** elle l'a gardé pour le cas où cela pourrait servir
• **off and on ADV** par intervalles; **we lived together o. and on for three years** on a plus ou moins vécu ensemble pendant trois ans
▸▸ *Cin & TV* ***off camera*** hors champ, off; *Br* ***off sales*** = vente à emporter de boissons alcoolisées

off-air ADJ hors-antenne
ADV hors antenne

offal [ˈɒfəl] **N** *(UNCOUNT) Br Culin* abats *mpl*

off-balance sheet ADJ *Acct* hors bilan
▸▸ ***off-balance sheet item*** poste *m ou* élément *m* hors bilan; ***off-balance sheet transaction*** opérations *f* de hors bilan

offbeat [ˈɒfbiːt] **ADJ** *(unconventional)* original, excentrique
N *Mus* temps *m* faible

off-Broadway ADJ *Am* **an o. show** = spectacle new-yorkais non conventionnel qui se démarque du style de ceux de Broadway, et qui n'est pas présenté dans un "Broadway Theater"

off-centre, *Am* **off-center ADJ 1** *(painting on wall)* décentré; *(rotation)* excentrique; *(gun sights)* désaligné; **the title is o.** le titre n'est pas centré **2** *Fig (imprecise ▸ analysis, description)* légèrement inexact, pas tout à fait exact; *(unconventional ▸ humour, style)* original
ADV de côté; **aim slightly o.** visez légèrement de côté

off-colour, *Am* **off-color ADJ 1** *Br (unwell)* **to be** *or* **feel o.** ne pas se sentir dans son assiette; **to look o.** ne pas avoir l'air dans son assiette **2** *Old-fashioned (joke)* d'un goût douteux

off-course ADJ *(bet)* effectué hors des champs de course

offcut [ˈɒfkʌt] **N** *(of cloth, wood, paper)* chute *f*; *(for animals)* rognures *fpl*; **offcuts** *(of meat)* restes *mpl* du découpage

off-day N he was having an o. il n'était pas en forme; **everyone has their off-days** il y a des jours "avec" et des jours "sans"

off-duty ADJ *(policeman, soldier, nurse)* qui n'est pas de service

offence, *Am* **offense** [əˈfens] **N 1** *Law (minor)* infraction *f*; *(more serious)* délit *m*; **it's his first o.** c'est la première fois qu'il commet un délit; **second** *or* **subsequent o.** récidive *f*; **arrested for drug offences** *(dealing)* arrêté pour trafic de drogue; *(use)* arrêté pour consommation de drogue; **indictable/nonindictable o.** infraction *f* majeure/mineure; **motoring** *or* **driving o.** infraction *f* au code de la route; **parking o.** contravention *f* au stationnement; **sex o.** ≃ attentat *m* à la pudeur
2 *(displeasure, hurt)* **to give** *or* **to cause o. to sb** *(person, personal remarks)* blesser *ou* offenser qn; *(film, book, programme)* heurter la sensibilité de qn; **to take o. at sth** s'offenser *ou* s'offusquer de qch; **he's very quick to take o.** il se vexe pour un rien; **no o. meant – none taken!** je n'avais pas l'intention de te vexer – il n'y a pas de mal!; **no o.!** il n'y a pas de mal!; **it's an o. against good taste** c'est un outrage au bon goût
3 *Mil (attack)* attaque *f*, offensive *f*
4 *Sport (attackers)* attaque *f*

offend [əˈfend] **VT** *(person)* offenser, blesser; *(senses, reason)* choquer; **to be offended at** *or* **by sth** se froisser *ou* s'offenser de qch; **she's easily offended** elle est susceptible, elle se vexe pour un rien; **I hope you won't be offended if I...** j'espère que vous ne vous froisserez *ou* offenserez pas si je…; **to o. the eye** choquer les regards *ou* la vue; **the film contains scenes which could o. some viewers** le film contient des scènes pouvant choquer certains spectateurs; **his behaviour offends my sense of fair play** son comportement choque mon sens du fair-play
VI 1 *Law* violer la loi, commettre un délit; **he is liable to o. again** il risque de récidiver **2** *(cause offence)* **I didn't mean to o.** *(give offence to the general public)* je ne voulais offenser personne; *(give offence to you)* je ne voulais pas t'offenser *ou* te froisser
▸ **offend against VT INSEP** *(law, regulation)* enfreindre, violer; *(custom)* aller à l'encontre de; *(good manners, good taste)* être un outrage à

offended [əˈfendɪd] **ADJ 1** *(insulted)* froissé, blessé; **don't be o. if I leave early** ne le prends pas mal si je pars de bonne heure; **she was very o. when he didn't come to her party** elle a été extrêmement vexée qu'il ne vienne pas à sa soirée **2** *Law* **the o. party** l'offensé(e) *m,f*

offender [əˈfendə(r)] **N 1** *Law* délinquant(e) *m,f*; **first o.** délinquant(e) *m,f* primaire; **13 percent of convicted offenders return to crime** 13 pour cent des condamnés récidivent; **drug o.** *(dealer)* trafiquant(e) *m,f* de drogue; *(user)* toxicomane *mf*; **traffic offenders** contrevenants *mpl* au code de la route **2** *(gen ▸ culprit)* coupable *mf*; **the chemical industry is the worst o.** l'industrie chimique est la première responsable

offending [əˈfendɪŋ] **ADJ** gênant; **the o. word was omitted** le mot gênant *ou* qui posait problème a été enlevé; **the o. object/article** l'objet *m*/l'article *m* incriminé; **the o. smell was traced to the drains** l'odeur suspecte venait des canalisations

offense *Am* = **offence**

offensive [əˈfensɪv] **ADJ 1** *(causing indignation, anger)* offensant, choquant; **to find sth o.** être choqué par qch; **to be o. to sb** *(person)* injurier *ou* insulter qn; **an o. remark** une remarque blessante; **this advertisement is o. to Muslims/women** cette publicité porte atteinte à la religion musulmane/à la dignité de la femme **2** *(disgusting ▸ smell)* nauséabond **3** *(aggressive)* offensif; **they took immediate o. action** ils sont immédiatement passés à l'offensive
N *Mil, Sport & Fig* offensive *f*; **to go on the o.** passer à l'offensive; **to take the o.** prendre l'offensive; **to be on the o.** attaquer
▸▸ ***offensive language*** propos *mpl* choquants; ***offensive weapon*** arme *f* offensive

offensively [əˈfensɪvlɪ] **ADV 1** *(behave, speak)* d'une manière offensante *ou* blessante **2** *Mil & Sport* offensivement

offensiveness [əˈfensɪvnɪs] **N** *(of sight, behaviour)* nature *f* offensante *ou* choquante; *(of smell)* nature *f* nauséabonde; *(of remark)* nature *f* injurieuse; **the o. of her tone** son ton injurieux

offer [ˈɒfə(r)] **VT 1** *(present)* offrir; *(excuses, advantages)* présenter; **to o. sth to sb, to o. sb sth** offrir qch à qn; **she offered me £800 for my car** elle m'a proposé 800 livres pour ma voiture; **he offered her a chair/his arm** il lui offrit une chaise/son bras; **can I o. you a drink?** puis-je vous offrir un verre?; **to o. sb one's sympathy** présenter ses condoléances à qn; **to have a lot to o.** *(town, person)* avoir beaucoup à offrir; **the town has little to o. in the way of entertainment** la ville n'a pas grand-chose à offrir pour ce qui est des divertissements; **candidates may o. one of the following foreign languages** les candidats peuvent présenter une des langues étrangères suivantes; **to o. goods for sale** mettre des marchandises en vente
2 *(propose)* proposer; **to o. to do sth** s'offrir pour faire qch, proposer de faire qch; **I offered to help them** je leur ai proposé mon aide; **it was kind of you to o.** c'est gentil de me l'avoir proposé; **to o. a suggestion** faire une suggestion; **to o. an opinion** émettre une opinion; **to o. sb advice** donner des conseils à qn; **nobody bothered to o. any explanation** personne ne s'est soucié de fournir une explication
N offre *f*; **o. of marriage** demande *f* en mariage; **I had several offers of help** plusieurs personnes m'ont proposé de m'aider; **we need somebody to help, any offers?** nous avons besoin de quelqu'un pour nous aider, est-ce qu'il y a des volontaires?; **£500 or near** *or* **nearest o.** 500 livres, à débattre; **she wants £500, but she's open to offers** elle veut 500 livres, mais elle est prête à négocier; **make me an o.!** faites-moi une offre!; **I made him an o. he couldn't refuse** je lui ai fait une offre qu'il ne pouvait pas refuser; **to be under o.** faire l'objet d'une proposition d'achat; **the house is under o.** on a reçu une offre pour la maison; *St Exch* **o. by prospectus** offre *f* publique de vente; **o. to purchase** offre *f* publique d'achat; **o. for sale** mise

f sur le marché; **offers in the region of £100** 100 livres à débattre

• **on offer** ADV *(on sale)* en vente; **there aren't many jobs on o.** les offres d'emploi sont peu nombreuses; **what is on o. in the negotiations?** qu'est-ce qui est proposé dans les négociations?

▸▸ ***offer price*** *St Exch* cours *m ou* prix *m* vendeur; *Mktg* prix *m* vendeur, prix *m* offert

▸ **offer up** VT SEP *(hymn, sacrifice)* offrir

offering [ˈɒfərɪŋ] N **1** *(action)* offre *f*; **the o. of gifts** le fait de s'offrir des cadeaux **2** *(thing offered)* offre *f*, don *m*; *Fig* **his latest o. is a novel set in Ireland** le dernier roman qu'il nous propose se déroule en Irlande; *Ironic* **let's hope this essay is better than your last o.** espérons que cette dissertation sera meilleure que votre dernier chef-d'œuvre **3** *Rel* offrande *f*

offertory [ˈɒfətrɪ] *(pl* **offertories)** N **1** *(prayers, ritual)* offertoire *m* **2** *(collection)* quête *f*

▸▸ ***offertory box*** tronc *m*

off-exchange ADJ *St Exch (transaction, contract, market)* hors Bourse, hors cote

offhand [ˌɒfˈhænd] ADJ *(nonchalant)* désinvolte, cavalier; *(abrupt)* brusque; **to be o. with sb** se montrer désinvolte *ou* cavalier à l'égard de qn

ADV spontanément, au pied levé; **I can't give you the figures o.** je ne peux pas vous citer les chiffres de mémoire *ou* de tête; **I don't know o.** comme ça de but en blanc, je ne le sais pas

offhanded [ˌɒfˈhændɪd] ADJ *(nonchalant)* désinvolte, cavalier; *(abrupt)* brusque; **to be o. with sb** se montrer désinvolte *ou* cavalier à l'égard de qn

offhandedly [ˌɒfˈhændɪdlɪ] ADV *(nonchalantly)* de façon désinvolte *ou* cavalière, avec désinvolture; *(with abruptness)* brusquement, sans ménagement

offhandedness [ˌɒfˈhændɪdnɪs] N *(casualness)* désinvolture *f*; *(brusqueness)* brusquerie *f*

off-highway ADJ *(driving)* hors route *(inv)*

ADV *(drive, cycle)* hors route

off-hook, offhook ADJ

▸▸ *Comput* ***off-hook signal*** signal *m* de réponse *ou* de décrochage

office [ˈɒfɪs] N **1** *(of firm)* bureau *m*; *(of solicitor)* étude *f*; *(of barrister)* cabinet *m*; *Am (of doctor, dentist)* cabinet *m* (de consultation); **the whole o. knows** tout le bureau est au courant; **he's out of the o. at the moment** il n'est pas dans le bureau en ce moment; **o. space is cheaper in the suburbs** les bureaux sont moins chers en banlieue; **for o. use only** *(on form)* (cadre) réservé à l'administration

2 *(government department)* bureau *m*, département *m*; **I have to send this to the tax o.** je dois envoyer ça au centre des impôts

3 *(position, power)* fonction *f*; **public o.** fonction *f* publique; **to rise to/hold high o.** être promu à/détenir un poste élevé; **to be in** *or* **to hold o.** *(political party)* être au pouvoir; *(mayor, minister, official)* être en fonction(s); **to be out of o.** avoir quitté ses fonctions; **to take o.** *(political party)* arriver au pouvoir; *(mayor, minister, official)* entrer en fonctions; **to resign/to leave o.** se démettre de/quitter ses fonctions; **to run for** *or* **to seek o.** se présenter aux élections; **elected to the o. of president** élu à la présidence

4 *Rel* office *m*; **o. for the dead** office *m* des morts; **last offices** *(for the dead)* derniers devoirs *mpl*; *(funeral)* obsèques *fpl*

COMP *(furniture, job, staff)* de bureau

• **offices** NPL **1** *(help, actions)* **I got the job through the (good) offices of Mrs Katz** j'ai obtenu ce travail grâce aux bons offices de Mme Katz **2** *Br (of large house, estate)* communs *mpl*

▸▸ *Fin* ***office account*** compte *m* commercial; ***office automation*** bureautique *f*; *Br* ***office bearer*** *(in club, association)* membre *m* du bureau; *Br* ***office block*** immeuble *m* de bureaux; *Old-fashioned* ***office boy*** garçon *m* de bureau; ***office building*** immeuble *m* de bureaux; ***office equipment*** matériel *m* de bureau; ***the Office of Fair Trading*** = organisme britannique de défense des consommateurs et de régulation des pratiques commerciales; *Am Pol* ***Office of Homeland Security*** = agence pour la sécurité intérieure des États-Unis; ***office hours*** heures *fpl* de bureau; **during o. hours** pendant les heures de bureau; *Comput* ***office IT*** bureautique *f*; ***office junior*** stagiaire *mf (en secrétariat)*; ***office manager*** chef *m* de bureau; ***office party*** = réception organisée dans un bureau à l'occasion des fêtes de fin d'année; ***office space*** locaux *mpl* pour bureaux; ***office supplies*** articles *mpl* de bureau; ***office work*** travail *m* de bureau; ***office worker*** employé *m* de bureau

officeholder [ˈɒfɪsˌhəʊldə(r)] N **1** *Pol* titulaire *mf* d'une fonction **2** *Am (in club, association)* membre *m* du bureau

officer [ˈɒfɪsə(r)] N **1** *Mil* officier *m* **2** *(policeman)* agent *m* de police; *(as form of address* ▸ *to policeman)* monsieur l'agent; *(*▸ *to policewoman)* madame l'agent **3** *(official* ▸ *in local government)* fonctionnaire *mf*; *(*▸ *of trade union)* représentant(e) *m,f* permanent(e); *(*▸ *of company)* membre *m* de la direction; *(*▸ *of association, institution)* membre *m* du bureau; **the officers of the association meet every month** le bureau de l'association se réunit tous les mois

VT *Mil* encadrer; **they were officered by young recruits** ils étaient encadrés par de jeunes recrues

▸▸ *Mil* ***officer of the day*** officier *m* de permanence; *Mil* ***officer of the guard*** officier *m* de la garde; *Mil* ***officers' mess*** mess *m*; *Br Mil* ***Officers' Training Corps*** = organisme fournissant une préparation militaire aux étudiants souhaitant devenir officiers; *Naut* ***officer of the watch*** officier *m* du quart

official [əˈfɪʃəl] ADJ **1** *(formal)* officiel; **she's here on o. business** elle est ici en visite officielle; **I can't understand this o. language** je ne comprends rien à ce jargon administratif; **the o. organist** le/la titulaire de l'orgue; **it's o., they're getting a divorce** c'est officiel, ils divorcent; **his appointment will be made o. tomorrow** sa nomination sera (rendue) officielle demain; **we decided to make it o. (and get married)** nous avons décidé de rendre notre liaison officielle (en nous mariant); **to act in one's o. capacity** agir dans l'exercice de ses fonctions; **she was speaking in her o. capacity as General Secretary** elle parlait en sa qualité de secrétaire général; **to go through the o. channels** suivre la filière (habituelle); **Spanish is the o. language of Mexico** l'espagnol est la langue officielle du Mexique **2** *(alleged)* officiel; **the o. reason for his visit is to discuss trade** officiellement, il est là pour des discussions ayant trait au commerce

N *(representative)* officiel *m*; *(civil servant)* fonctionnaire *mf*; *(subordinate employee)* employé(e) *m,f*; *Sport (referee)* arbitre *m*; *(linesman)* juge *m* de touche; *Sport* **the officials** l'arbitre *m* et les juges *mpl* de touche; **the o. at the entrance** le préposé à l'entrée; **a bank/club/union o.** un représentant de la banque/du club/du syndicat; **a government o.** un haut fonctionnaire; **minor officials** petits fonctionnaires *mpl*

▸▸ ***official biography*** biographie *f* officielle; ***the Official Birthday*** = jour de célébration officielle de l'anniversaire du souverain britannique (deuxième samedi de juin); ***official document*** document *m* officiel; *Fin* ***official exchange rate*** cours *m* officiel; ***official letter*** pli *m* officiel *ou* de service; *St Exch* ***Official List*** cote *f* officielle; *Fin* ***official market*** marché *m* officiel; ***official opening*** *(of new factory, museum etc)* inauguration *f*; *St Exch* ***official quotation*** cours *m* officiel; *Banking* ***official rate*** taux *m* officiel d'escompte; *Br* ***official receiver*** administrateur(trice) *m,f* judiciaire; **the o. receiver has been called in** on a fait appel à l'administration judiciaire; *Br* ***official receivership*** liquidation *f* judiciaire; *Br* ***official secret*** secret *m* d'État; ***the Official Secrets Act*** = loi britannique sur le secret-défense; ***official strike*** = grève soutenue par la direction du syndicat

officialdom [əˈfɪʃəldəm] N *(officials)* administration *f*; *Pej (bureaucracy)* bureaucratie *f*, fonctionnarisme *m*

officialese [əˌfɪʃəˈliːz] N *Pej* jargon *m* administratif

officially [əˈfɪʃəlɪ] ADV **1** *(formally)* officiellement; **he's now been o. appointed** sa nomination est désormais officielle; **we now have it o.** la nouvelle est maintenant officielle **2** *(allegedly)* théoriquement, en principe; **o., he's at the dentist's** en principe, il est chez le dentiste

officiate [əˈfɪʃɪeɪt] VI **1** *(gen)* **to o. as** remplir les fonctions de; **she officiated at the ceremony** elle a présidé la cérémonie; **the mayor will o. at the opening of the stadium** le maire inaugurera le stade **2** *Rel* officier; **officiating minister** (pasteur *m*) officiant *m*

officious [əˈfɪʃəs] ADJ **1** *(over-zealous)* zélé, empressé; *(interfering)* importun; *(overbearing)* impérieux, autoritaire; **to be o.** faire du zèle **2** *(in diplomacy* ▸ *unofficial)* officieux

officiously [əˈfɪʃəslɪ] ADV *(over-zealously)* avec zèle, avec empressement; *(interferingly)* d'une manière importune; *(overbearingly)* impérieusement, de manière autoritaire; **to behave o. towards sb** faire l'empressé auprès de qn

offie [ˈɒfɪ] N *Br Fam (abbr* **off-licence)** = magasin autorisé à vendre des boissons alcoolisées à emporter

offing [ˈɒfɪŋ] N **1** *Naut* large *m* **2** *(idioms)* **to be in the o.** être imminent, être dans l'air; **a confrontation had long been in the o.** une confrontation couvait depuis longtemps; **there could be some changes in the o.** il se pourrait qu'il y ait des changements en perspective

off-key ADJ **1** *Mus* faux (fausse); **he was o.** il n'était pas dans le ton, il jouait/chantait faux **2** *Fig (remark)* hors de propos, sans rapport

ADV faux; **to play/to sing o.** jouer/chanter faux

off-licence N *Br* **1** *(shop)* = magasin autorisé à vendre des boissons alcoolisées à emporter; **at the o.** ≃ chez le marchand de vins **2** *(licence)* licence *f (autorisant la vente de boissons alcoolisées à emporter)*

off-limits ADJ interdit; **o. to civilians** interdit aux civils

ADV en dehors des limites autorisées; **to go o.** sortir des limites autorisées

off-line, offline ADJ **1** *Comput* non connecté; *(processing)* en différé; *(printer)* déconnecté; **to be o.** ne pas être connecté; **to go o.** se déconnecter **2** *Ind (production)* hors ligne

ADV hors ligne, hors connexion; **to work o.** travailler sans se connecter à l'Internet

▸▸ *Cin & TV* ***off-line editing*** montage *m* offline; *Comput* ***off-line mode*** mode *m* autonome; *Comput* ***off-line reader*** lecteur *m* non connecté

offload [ɒfˈləʊd] VT **1** *(unload* ▸ *passengers)* débarquer; *(*▸ *cargo)* décharger **2** *(dump* ▸ *work, blame)* **she tends to o. responsibility onto other people** elle a tendance à se décharger de ses responsabilités sur les autres; **to o. the blame onto sb** rejeter la faute sur qn

off-message ADJ *Br Pol* = qui ne respecte pas scrupuleusement la ligne du parti

off-mike ADJ *Rad* hors-micro

off-off-Broadway ADJ *Am* à l'avant-garde de l'avant-garde; **o. show** spectacle *m* d'avant-garde

off-peak ADJ *(consumption, train)* aux heures creuses, en dehors des périodes de pointe

ADV pendant les heures creuses

▸▸ ***off-peak electricity*** électricité *f* consommée pendant les heures creuses; ***off-peak hours*** heures *fpl* creuses; *Elec* ***off-peak rate*** tarif *m* de nuit; ***off-peak times*** heures *fpl* creuses

off-piste *Ski* ADJ hors-piste(s)

ADV hors piste(s)

offprint [ˈɒfprɪnt] N tiré *m* à part

off-putting [-pʊtɪŋ] ADJ *Br (smell)* repoussant; *(manner)* rébarbatif; *(person, description)* peu engageant; *(experience)* démoralisant; **the idea of a five-hour stopover is very o.** l'idée d'une escale de cinq heures n'a rien d'enthousiasmant *ou* de réjouissant

off-ramp N sortie *f* d'autoroute

off-road ADJ *(driving)* hors route *(inv)*

ADV *(drive, cycle)* hors route

▸▸ ***off-road vehicle*** véhicule *m* tout-terrain

off-roader [-ˈrəʊdə(r)] N *Aut* tout-terrain *m inv*

off-screen *Cin & TV* ADJ **1** *(out of sight)* hors champ, off **2** *(romance, persona)* dans la vie; **their o. relationship mirrored their love affair in the film** la liaison qu'ils entretenaient dans la vie reflétait celle du film

ADV **1** *(out of sight)* hors champ, off **2** *(in real life)*

dans la réalité; **he's less handsome o.** il est moins séduisant dans la réalité

off-season N morte-saison *f*
ADJ hors saison *(inv)*
ADV pendant la morte-saison
►► ***off-season tariff*** tarif *m* hors saison

offset ['ɒfset] *(pt & pp* **offset**, *cont* **offsetting)** N **1** *(counterbalance)* contrepoids *m*
2 *Acct (compensation)* compensation *f*, dédommagement *m*
3 *Typ* offset *m*
4 *Bot (shoot)* rejeton *m*
5 *Constr* ressaut *m*
6 *Tech (of wheel)* désaxage *m*, décentrement *m*, déport *m*
VT **1** *(make up for)* contrebalancer, compenser; **the advantages tend to o. the difficulties** les avantages compensent presque les inconvénients; **to o. losses against tax** déduire le montant de ses pertes de ses impôts; **any wage increase will be o. by inflation** avec l'inflation, les augmentations de salaire n'en seront plus vraiment; **his faults are o. by his enthusiasm** son enthousiasme fait oublier ses défauts **2** *Typ* imprimer en offset **3** *Tech (wheel)* désaxer, décentrer; *(part)* déporter, décaler
►► *Acct* ***offset agreement*** accord *m* de compensation; *Typ* ***offset lithography*** lithographie *f* offset; *Typ* ***offset plate*** plaque *f* offset; *Typ* ***offset press*** offset *m*; *Typ* ***offset process*** offset *m*

offshoot ['ɒfʃuːt] N **1** *(of organization, political party, movement)* ramification *f*; *(of family)* branche *f*; *(spin-off)* application *f* secondaire; *(consequence* ► *of decision etc)* retombée *f*; **French and Spanish are offshoots of Latin** le français et l'espagnol sont issus *ou* dérivent du latin; **the company has offshoots in Asia** *(subsidiaries)* la société a des succursales en Asie **2** *Bot* rejeton *m*

offshore ['ɒfʃɔː(r)] ADJ **1** *(in or on sea)* marin; *(near shore* ► *shipping, fishing, waters)* côtier; *(*► *island)* près de la côte; *Petr (installation, platform)* offshore *(inv)*, marin **2** *(towards open sea* ► *current, direction)* vers le large; *(*► *wind)* de terre **3** *Fin (investment, company)* offshore *(inv)*, *Offic* extraterritorial
ADV *Petr (live, drill etc)* en mer, au large; *Fin* **to keep sth o.** garder qch offshore
►► ***offshore banking*** opérations *fpl* bancaires offshore; ***offshore company*** société *f* offshore; ***offshore fund*** fonds *m* offshore; ***offshore investment*** placement *m* offshore; *Petr* ***offshore oilfield*** champ *m* (pétrolifère) en mer *ou* offshore; ***offshore rig*** plate-forme *f* offshore

offshoring ['ɒfʃɔːrɪŋ] N délocalisation *f*

off-shot *TV & Cin* ADJ hors plan
ADV hors plan

offside N ['ɒfsaɪd] *Br Aut (when driving on right)* côté *m* gauche, côté *m* rue; *(when driving on left)* côté *m* droit, côté *m* rue
ADJ [ˌɒf'saɪd] *Sport* hors jeu *(inv)*; **to play the o. trap** jouer le hors-jeu
ADV [ˌɒf'saɪd] *Sport* hors jeu
►► ***the offside law*** *or* ***rule*** la règle du hors-jeu

offspring ['ɒfsprɪŋ] *(pl* **inv)** N *Arch or Hum (son or daughter)* rejeton *m*
NPL *(descendants)* progéniture *f*; **none of her o. were there** aucun de ses rejetons n'était là

offstage ADV ['ɒf,steɪdʒ] **1** *Theat* dans les coulisses; **she ran o.** elle quitta la scène en courant **2** *Fig (in private life)* en privé; **o., she was surprisingly reserved** en privé, elle était étonnamment réservée
ADJ ['ɒf,steɪdʒ] **1** *Theat* dans les coulisses; **an o. row** une querelle de coulisses **2** *Fig (life)* privé

off-street ADJ
►► ***off-street parking*** place *f* de parking *(située ailleurs que dans la rue)*

off-the-cuff ADJ impromptu, improvisé
ADV au pied levé, à l'improviste

off-the-peg, *Am* **off-the-rack** ADJ de prêt-à-porter
►► ***off-the-peg clothes*** prêt-à-porter *m*

off-the-record ADJ *(not to be made public)* confidentiel; *(not to be put in minutes)* à ne pas faire figurer dans le compte rendu; **on the understanding that it is strictly o.** à titre strictement officieux

off-the-shelf ADJ *(goods)* prêt à l'usage
►► ***off-the-shelf company*** société *f* tiroir

off-the-wall ADJ *Fam (crazy)* loufoque, bizarroïde; *(unexpected)* original□, excentrique□

off-white N blanc *m* cassé
ADJ blanc cassé *(inv)*

Ofgem ['ɒf,dʒem] N *(abbr* **Office of the Gas and Electricity Markets)** = nouvel organisme britannique qui a remplacé les anciens "Ofgas" et "Offer"

Ofsted ['ɒf,sted] N *(abbr* **Office for Standards in Education)** = organisme britannique chargé de contrôler le système d'éducation nationale

OFT [ˌəʊef'tiː] N *(abbr* **Office of FairTrading)** = organisme britannique de défense des consommateurs et de régulation des pratiques commerciales

oft [ɒft] ADV *Literary* maintes fois, souvent

oft- [ɒft] PREF **o.-repeated** *(warning)* réitéré; *(argument)* ressassé; **o.-quoted** souvent cité

Oftel ['ɒf,tel] N *Br (abbr* **Office of Telecommunications)** = organisme britannique chargé de contrôler les activités des sociétés de télécommunications

often ['ɒfən, 'ɒftən] ADV souvent; **I don't see her very o.** je ne la vois pas très souvent; **do you come here o.?** = expression toute faite dont l'équivalent français est "vous habitez chez vos parents?"; **how o.?** *(how many times)* combien de fois?; *(at what intervals)* tous les combien?; **how o. does he write to you?** est-ce qu'il t'écrit souvent?; **all too o. the money goes to the wrong people** trop souvent, l'argent va à ceux qui n'en ont pas besoin; **it cannot be repeated too o.** on ne saurait trop le répéter; **once too o.** une fois de trop
• **as often as not** ADV la plupart du temps
• **every so often** ADV de temps en temps, de temps à autre
• **more often than not** ADV la plupart du temps

Ofwat ['ɒf,wɒt] N *(abbr* **Office of Water Supply)** = organisme britannique chargé de contrôler les activités des compagnies régionales de distribution de l'eau

ogle ['əʊgəl] VT lorgner

O grade N *Scot Formerly Sch* = premier diplôme dans l'enseignement secondaire écossais

ogre ['əʊgə(r)] N ogre *m*

ogress ['əʊgrɪs] N ogresse *f*

oh [əʊ] EXCLAM oh!, ah!; **oh, what a surprise!** oh, quelle surprise!; **oh really?** vraiment?, ah bon?; **oh no!** oh non!; **oh yes you will!** ah si!

ohc [ˌəʊeɪtʃ'siː] N *(abbr* **overhead camshaft)**
►► ***ohc engine*** moteur *m* ACT

ohm [əʊm] N *Elec* ohm *m*

OHMS *(written abbr* **On His/Her Majesty's Service)** = tampon apposé sur le courrier administratif britannique

oho [ə'həʊ] EXCLAM *(expressing surprise)* oh!; *(expressing satisfaction)* ah!

> **-OHOLIC**
> *voir* **-AHOLIC**

OHP [ˌəʊeɪtʃ'piː] N *(abbr* **overhead projector)** rétroprojecteur *m*
►► ***OHP slide*** transparent *m*

OHS [ˌəʊeɪtʃ'es] N *Am Pol (abbr* **Office of Homeland Security)** = agence pour la sécurité intérieure des États-Unis

oi [ɔɪ] EXCLAM *Fam* hé!

OID [ˌəʊaɪ'diː] N *Fin (abbr* **original issue discount bond)** obligation *f* à prime d'émission

oik [ɔɪk] N *Br Fam Pej* pignouf *m*, plouc *mf*

oil [ɔɪl] N **1** *(petroleum)* pétrole *m* **2** *(in food, as lubricant)* huile *f*; *(as fuel)* mazout *m*, fuel *m ou* fioul *m* domestique; **sardines in o.** sardines *fpl* à l'huile; *Aut* **to change the o.** faire la vidange; **o. of lavender/turpentine** essence *f* de lavande/de térébenthine; *Fig* **to pour o. on troubled waters** ramener le calme **3** *Art (paint)* (peinture *f* à l')huile *f*; *(picture)* huile *f*; **a portrait in oils** un portrait (peint) à l'huile; **she works in oils** elle travaille avec de la peinture à l'huile
COMP **1** *(industry, production, corporation)* pétrolier; *(deposit, reserves)* de pétrole; *(magnate, sheikh)* du pétrole **2** *(level, pressure)* d'huile; *(filter)* à huile; *(heating, burner)* à mazout
VT *(machine, engine)* lubrifier, graisser; *(hinge, wood, skin)* huiler; *Fig* **it will help to o. the wheel[s]** cela facilitera les choses, cela mettra de l'huil[e] dans les rouages
►► ***oil bath*** bain *m* d'huile; ***oil cake*** tourteau *m* (pour bétail); ***oil change*** vidange *f*; ***oil cooling*** refroidissement *m* par huile; ***oil crisis*** choc *m* pétrolier; ***oil drum*** bidon *m* à pétrole; ***oil gland*** glande *f* uropygienne; ***oil gauge*** *(for measuring level)* jauge *f ou* indicateur *m* de niveau d'huile; *(for measuring pressure)* indicateur *m* de pression d'huile; ***oil lamp*** *(burning oil)* lampe *f* à huile; *(burning paraffin)* lampe *f* à pétrole; ***oil paint*** peinture *f* à l'huile *(substance)*; ***oil painting*** peinture *f* à l'huile; *Br Fam* **he's no o. painting** c'[est] n'est pas une beauté; ***oil palm*** éléis *m*; *Am Aut* ***oil pan*** carter *m*; ***oil pressure switch*** manocontact *m* d'huile; ***oil prices*** prix *mpl* du pétrole *ou* pétroliers; ***oil refinery*** raffinerie *f* de pétrole; ***oil rig*** *(onshore)* derrick *m*; *(offshore)* plate-forme pétrolière; *Fin* ***oil royalty*** redevance *f* pétrolière; ***oil shale*** schiste *m* bitumineux; ***oil slick*** *(on sea)* nappe *f* de pétrole; *(on beach)* marée *f* noire; ***oil spill*** *(event)* marée *f* noire; *(result)* nappe *f* de pétrole; *Br* ***oil stove*** *(using fuel oil)* poêle *m* à mazout; *(using paraffin, kerosene)* réchaud *m* à pétrole; ***oil sump*** carter *m* d'huile; ***oil tanker*** *(ship)* pétrolier *m*, tanker *m*; *(lorry)* camion-citerne *m* *(pour le pétrole)*; ***oil temperature gauge*** indicateur *m* de température d'huile; ***oil terminal*** terminal *m* (pétrolier); ***oil well*** puits *m* de pétrole

oil-bearing ADJ pétrolifère

oilcan ['ɔɪlkæn] N *(drum)* bidon *m* d'huile; *(oiler)* burette *f* (à huile)

oilcloth ['ɔɪlklɒθ] N toile *f* cirée

oil-cooled [-kuːld] ADJ refroidi par huile

oiled [ɔɪld] ADJ **1** *(machine)* lubrifié, graissé; *(hinge, silk)* huilé **2** *Fam (drunk)* bourré, beurré; **to be well o.** être complètement bourré **3** *esp Am (area, beach, animal)* mazouté

oiler ['ɔɪlə(r)] N **1** *(person)* graisseur(euse) *m,f*
2 *(tanker)* pétrolier *m*
3 *(can)* burette *f* (à huile)
4 *(well)* puits *m* de pétrole

oilfield ['ɔɪlfiːld] N gisement *m* de pétrole *ou* pétrolier

oil-fired ADJ à mazout

oiliness ['ɔɪlɪnɪs] N **1** *(greasiness)* nature *f* huileuse; **the o. of the dish makes it rather indigestible** ce plat contient tellement d'huile qu'il en devient indigeste **2** *Fig (obsequiousness)* obséquiosité *f*, patelinerie *f*

oilpaper ['ɔɪlpeɪpə(r)] N papier *m* huilé

oil-producing ADJ **1** *(shale etc)* pétrolifère; *(country)* producteur de pétrole **2** *(plant)* oléifère; *(substance etc)* oléifiant

oilrich ['ɔɪl,rɪtʃ] ADJ **1** *(made rich by oil trade)* enrichi par le pétrole **2** *(rich in oil resources)* riche en gisements pétrolifères

oilskin ['ɔɪlskɪn] N **1** *(cloth)* toile *f* cirée **2** *(garment)* ciré *m*
COMP en toile cirée

oilstone ['ɔɪlstəʊn] N *(for sharpening)* pierre *f* à huile

oily ['ɔɪlɪ] *(compar* **oilier**, *superl* **oiliest)** ADJ **1** *(substance)* huileux; *(rag, fingers)* graisseux; *(hair, skin, fish)* gras (grasse); *(salad dressing, sauce)* à base d'huile; **an o. stain** une tache de graisse **2** *Pej (smile, person)* mielleux, doucereux

oink [ɔɪŋk] N grognement *m*, grommellement *m*
ONOMAT krouik-krouik

ointment ['ɔɪntmənt] N pommade *f*, onguent *m*

OJ [ˌəʊ'dʒeɪ] N *Fam (abbr* **orange juice)** jus *m* d'orange□

OK[1] [ˌəʊ'keɪ] *(pt & pp* **OKed** [ˌəʊ'keɪd], *cont* **OKing** [ˌəʊ'keɪɪŋ]) *Fam* EXCLAM OK, d'accord□, d'ac; **well OK, I'm not a specialist, but...** bon, d'accord, je ne suis pas spécialiste, mais...; **in five minutes, OK?** dans cinq minutes, ça va *ou* c'est bon?
ADJ **1** *(in order, fine)* correct□, exact□; **everything's OK** tout est en règle□ *ou* OK; **to be OK** *(unhurt)* aller bien□; **are you OK?, did I hurt you/are**

ı upset? ça va?, je ne t'ai pas fait mal/tu es fâé?; **I'll be OK when I get home** ça ira une fois e je serai à la maison; **but is the car OK?** mais -ce que la voiture n'a rien?; **that's OK by** *or* **:h me** d'accord!; **is that OK by** *or* **with your ther?** est-ce que ta mère est d'accord?; **is it to bring my friend?** est-ce que ça vous déıge si je viens avec mon ami?; **no, it is NOT pas question; clothes like that are OK for a ·ty** des vêtements comme ça, c'est bon pour er à une soirée *(acceptable ▸ meal, film)* pas mal; *(▸ candidate, ger)* pas mauvais, pas mal; **how are things? –** comment ça va? – ça peut aller; **the meal/her ·formance was more than OK** le repas/sa presion était au-dessus de la moyenne; **was I ?** comment j'étais?; **an OK computer** un ordieur pas mal *(understanding)* **she was OK about it** elle n'a pas d'histoires; **are you sure he'll be OK about letg us use the car?** tu es sûr qu'il ne fera pas istoires pour nous laisser la voiture? *(likeable ▸ person)* **he's an OK sort of guy** c'est type plutôt bien; **she's OK but I wouldn't want live with her** elle est assez sympa mais je n'airais pas vivre avec elle **to be OK for work/money** *(have enough of)* oir assez de travail/d'argent; **is everybody for drink?** est-ce que tout le monde a à ire? ov bien; **is the engine working OK?** le moteur, va?; **everything is going OK** tout marche bien va bien; **you're doing OK!** tu t'en tires bien! *(approve)* approuver; *(initial)* parafer, pa·her; **his plan has been OKed** son projet a reçu eu vert *(agreement)* accord *m*; *(approval)* approban *f*; **I gave him the OK** je lui ai donné le feu ·t; **did you get her OK on the new plan?** elle d'accord pour le nouveau projet?

² *(written abbr* **Oklahoma***)* Oklahoma *m*

api [əʊ'kɑːpɪ] *(pl inv or* **okapis***)* N *Zool* okapi *m*

ay = **OK¹**

ay-dokay, okey-doke(y) [ˌəʊkɪ'dəʊk(ɪ)] EX-AM *Fam* OK, d'ac

ie ['əʊkɪ] N *Am Fam Pej* **1** *(inhabitant)* habitant *m,f* de l'Oklahoma **2** *Hist* **the Okies** = habiats de l'Oklahoma qui se sont déplacés vers Californie dans les années 30 pour échapper a pauvreté du "Dust Bowl"

la *(written abbr* **Oklahoma***)* Oklahoma *m*

ra ['əʊkrə] N gombo *m*

old [əʊld]

ADJ
vieux **1, 2, 5** • âgé de **3**
ancien **4**

NPL
vieux

mpar **older**, *superl* **oldest)**

ADJ **1** *(not new or recent)* vieux (vieille); **the o. traions of the countryside** les vieilles traditions mpagnardes; **there's an o. saying that…** il y a vieux dicton qui dit que…; **not that o. excuse ain!** tu ne vas pas/il ne va pas/*etc* ressortir ene une fois la même excuse!; **they're o. friends** sont de vieux amis *ou* des amis de longue te; **he's an o. friend of mine** c'est un de mes ux amis; **to go over o. ground** revenir sur un rain déjà parcouru; **an o. debt** une dette de ıgue date; **that's an o. dodge** c'est un coup ssique; **the o. country** la mère patrie *(not young)* vieux (vieille); **an o. man** un vieil mme; **an o. woman** une vieille femme; **I don't e that o. man/woman** je n'aime pas ce vieux/ tte vieille; **o. people** personnes *fpl* âgées; **the people next door** le couple âgé qui habite à té, *Fam* les vieux qui habitent à côté; **to get grow o.** vieillir; **who will look after me in my o. e?** qui s'occupera de moi quand je serai ux?; **I've got a little money put aside for my o. e** j'ai quelques économies de côté pour mes ux jours; **o. people's home** maison *f* de retraite *(referring to a particular age)* **how o. is she?** quel e a-t-elle?; **to be o. enough to do sth** être en âge faire qch; **she's o. enough to know better** elle devrait plus faire ce genre de chose à son âge; **he's o. enough to look after himself** il est (bien) assez grand pour se débrouiller tout seul; **he's o. enough to be my father!** il pourrait être mon père!; **you're as o. as you feel** on a l'âge de ses artères; **she is older than I am** elle est plus âgée *ou* vieille que moi; **she's two years older than him** elle a deux ans de plus que lui; **my boy wants to be a soldier when he's older** mon fils veut être soldat quand il sera grand; **the older generation** la vieille génération; **my older sister** ma sœur aînée; **the oldest of the tribe** l'aîné(e) *m,f* de la tribu; **she's six months/25 years o.** elle a six mois/25 ans, elle est âgée de six mois/25 ans; **at six years o.** à (l'âge de) six ans; **they have a 14-year-o. boy** ils ont un garçon de 14 ans

4 *(former)* ancien; **that's my o. address** c'est mon ancienne adresse; **an o. admirer of hers** un de ses anciens admirateurs; **in the o. days** autrefois, jadis; **the good o. days** le bon vieux temps; **a writer of the o. school** un écrivain de la vieille école

5 *Fam (expressing familiarity or affection)* vieux (vieille), brave; **o. Jimmy wants to speak to you** le vieux Jimmy veut te parler; **good o. Frank!** ce (bon) vieux Frank!; *Old-fashioned* **hello, o. thing** *or* **chap!** salut, mon vieux *ou* ma vieille branche!

6 *Fam (as intensifier)* **it's a funny o. life!** la vie est drôle, quand même!; *very Fam* **you o. bastard!** espèce de salaud!; **we had a fine o. time** nous avons passé un sacré bon moment; **any o. bit of wood will do** n'importe quel vieux bout de bois fera l'affaire; **any o. how** n'importe comment; **he's not just any o. scientist, he's a Nobel prizewinner** ce n'est pas n'importe quel scientifique, c'est un prix Nobel

NPL **the o.** les vieux *mpl*

• **of old** ADV **1** *Literary (of former times)* **in days of o.** autrefois, jadis; **the knights of o.** les chevaliers du temps jadis *ou* de jadis

2 *(for a long time)* **I know them of o.** je les connais depuis longtemps

▸▸ *Br* ***old age pension*** (pension *f* de) retraite *f*; *Br* ***old age pensioner*** retraité(e) *m,f*; ***the Old Bailey*** = la cour d'assises de Londres; *Br* ***old boy*** *(former pupil)* ancien élève *m*; *Fam (old man)* vieux *m*; *Fam Old-fashioned (form of address)* mon vieux; *Br Fam* ***old boy network*** = contacts privilégiés entre anciens élèves d'un même établissement privé; **he got the job through the o. boy network** il a obtenu ce poste en faisant jouer ses relations; *Br Fam* ***old dear*** *(elderly woman)* grand-mère *f*; *(mother)* vieille *f*; ***old economy*** vieille économie *f*; ***Old English*** vieil anglais *m*; ***Old English sheepdog*** bobtail *m*; ***Old Europe*** la vieille Europe; ***old flame*** ancien béguin *m*; ***Old French*** ancien français *m*; *Br* ***old girl*** *(former pupil)* ancienne élève *f*; *Fam (old woman)* vieille *f*; *Fam Old-fashioned (form of address)* ma chère, chère amie; *Am* ***Old Glory*** = surnom du drapeau américain; ***old gold*** *(colour)* vieil or *m inv*; ***old guard*** vieille garde *f*; ***old hand*** vieux routier *m*, vétéran *m*; **he's an o. hand at flying these planes** cela fait des années qu'il pilote ces avions; *Fam* ***old hat*** dépassé, vieux (vieille); ***Old High German*** ancien haut allemand *m*; ***Old Labour*** = appellation populaire du parti travailliste avant le passage au New Labour, insistant sur le fait qu'il se situait alors plus à gauche sur l'échiquier politique; *Fam* ***old lady*** *(wife)* bourgeoise *f*; *(mother)* vieille *f*; *Br Fam* ***old lag*** truand *m*; ***old maid*** vieille fille *f*; *Fam* ***old man*** *(husband)* homme *m*, jules *m*; *(father)* vieux *m*; *Br Old-fashioned (form of address)* mon cher, cher ami; *Bot* ***old man's beard*** *(Clematis vitalba)* clématite *f* des haies, clématite *f* vigne blanche; ***old master*** *(painter)* grand maître *m* (de la peinture); *(painting)* tableau *m* de maître; ***old money*** *(before decimalization)* ancien système *m* monétaire; **10 shillings in o. money** 10 shillings dans l'ancien système monétaire; **he married into o. money** *(wealth)* il a épousé une riche héritière; ***old moon*** vieille lune *f*; *Fam* ***Old Nick*** Satan *m*, Lucifer *m*; *Ling* ***Old Norse*** vieux norrois *m*; *Ling* ***Old Persian*** vieux perse *m*; *Br* ***old school tie*** *(garment)* cravate *f* aux couleurs de son ancienne école; *Fig Pej* = attitudes et système de valeurs typiques des anciens élèves des écoles privées britanniques; ***old stager*** vieux routier *m*, vétéran *m*; *Bible* ***Old Testament*** Ancien Testament *m*; ***old wives' tale*** conte *m* de bonne femme; *Fam* ***old woman*** *(wife)* patronne *f*, bourgeoise *f*; *(mother)* vieille *f*; *Fig Pej (timid, fussy man)* chochotte *f*; **he's such an o. woman** il est comme une petite vieille; ***the Old World*** l'Ancien Monde *m*

olden ['əʊldən] ADJ *Arch or Literary* d'autrefois, d'antan; **in o. times** *or* **days** autrefois, jadis

old-established ADJ ancien, établi depuis longtemps

olde-worlde [ˌəʊldɪ'wɜːldɪ] ADJ *Br Fam* pseudo-ancien

old-fashioned [-'fæʃənd] ADJ **1** *(out-of-date)* suranné, désuet(ète), démodé; *(idea)* périmé, démodé; **he's a bit o.** il est un peu vieux jeu; **you can call me o. but…** tu vas peut-être me trouver vieux jeu, mais… **2** *(of the past)* d'autrefois, ancien; *Fam Hum* **he needs a good o. kick in the pants** ce qu'il lui faudrait, c'est un bon coup de pied aux fesses **3** *(quizzical)* **to give sb an o. look** jeter un regard dubitatif à qn

N *Am* old-fashioned *m (cocktail composé de whisky, d'amers, de sucre et d'eau de Seltz)*

oldie ['əʊldɪ] N *Fam* **1** *(show, song)* vieux succès *m*; *(pop song)* vieux tube *m*; *(film)* classique *m* du cinéma populaire; **that's a real o.!** *(song, joke etc)* il ne date pas d'aujourd'hui celui-là! **2** *(old person)* petit(e) vieux (vieille) *m,f*

oldish ['əʊldɪʃ] ADJ vieillot

oldster ['əʊldstə(r)] N *Am Fam* ancien(enne) *m,f*, vieillard(e) *m,f*

old-style ADJ à l'ancienne (mode); *Hist* **the o. calendar** le calendrier ancien style

old-time ADJ d'autrefois, ancien

▸▸ ***old-time dancing*** danses *fpl* anciennes

old-timer N *Fam* **1** *(old person)* ancien(enne) *m,f*, vieillard(e) *m,f*; *(veteran)* vétéran *m*, vieux *m* de la vieille **2** *Fam (form of address)* vieux *m*

old-world ADJ *(of the past)* d'antan, d'autrefois; *(quaint)* pittoresque; **a village full of o. charm** un village au charme suranné

OLE [ˌəʊel'iː] N *Comput (abbr* **object linking and embedding***)* OLE *m*

ole [əʊl] *Fam* = **old** ADJ

oleaginous [ˌəʊlɪ'ædʒɪnəs] ADJ oléagineux

oleander [ˌəʊlɪ'ændə(r)] N *Bot* laurier-rose *m*

O level N *Formerly Sch (in England, Wales, Northern Ireland)* = examen qui sanctionnait autrefois la fin des études au niveau de la seconde, ≃ BEPC *m*

olfactory [ɒl'fæktərɪ] ADJ olfactif

▸▸ ***olfactory nerve*** nerf *m* olfactif

oligarchical [ˌɒlɪ'gɑːkɪkəl] ADJ oligarchique

oligarchy ['ɒlɪgɑːkɪ] *(pl* **oligarchies***)* N oligarchie *f*

oligopoly [ˌɒlɪ'gɒpəlɪ] *(pl* **oligopolies***)* N *Econ* oligopole *m*

oligopsony [ˌɒlɪ'gɒpsənɪ] *(pl* **oligopsonies***)* N *Econ* oligopsone *m*

olive ['ɒlɪv] N **1** *(fruit)* olive *f*; *(tree)* olivier *m*; *(wood)* (bois *m* d')olivier *m* **2** *(colour)* vert *m* olive *(inv)*

ADJ *(colour)* (vert) olive *(inv)*; **he has an o. complexion** il a le teint olive

▸▸ ***olive branch*** rameau *m* d'olivier; *Fig* **to hold out an o. branch to sb** proposer à qn de faire la paix; *Am* ***olive drab*** *(colour)* gris-vert *m* (olive); *(cloth)* toile *f* gris-vert (olive); *(uniform)* uniforme *m* gris-vert *(surtout celui de l'armée des États-Unis)*; ***olive green*** vert *m* olive *(inv)*; ***olive grove*** olivaie *f*, oliveraie *f*; ***olive oil*** huile *f* d'olive; *Bot* ***olive wood*** (bois *m* d')olivier *m*

Olympiad [ə'lɪmpɪæd] N olympiade *f*

Olympian [ə'lɪmpɪən] N **1** *Myth* Olympien(enne) *m,f* **2** *Am Sport* athlète *mf* olympique

ADJ olympien; *Fig* **it was an O. task** cela représentait un travail phénoménal

Olympic [ə'lɪmpɪk] ADJ olympique; **an O. champion** un champion olympique

• **Olympics** NPL **the Olympics** les jeux *mpl* Olympiques

▸▸ ***the Olympic flame*** la flamme olympique; ***the Olympic Games*** les jeux *mpl* Olympiques

Olympus [ə'lɪmpəs] N **(Mount) O.** l'Olympe *m*

Oman [əʊ'mɑːn] N Oman *m*

Omani [əʊ'mɑːnɪ] **N** Omanais(e) *m,f*
ADJ omanais

ombudsman ['ɒmbʊdzmən] *(pl* **ombudsmen** [-mən]) **N** ombudsman *m*, médiateur *m*; *(in Quebec)* protecteur *m* du citoyen

omega ['əʊmɪgə] **N** oméga *m*

omelette, *Am* **omelet** ['ɒmlɪt] **N** omelette *f*; **plain/mushroom o.** omelette *f* nature/aux champignons; *Prov* **you can't make an o. without breaking eggs** on ne fait pas d'omelette sans casser des œufs

omen ['əʊmen] **N** augure *m*, présage *m*; **a good/bad o.** un bon/mauvais présage; **the omens aren't good** cela ne laisse rien présager de bon

ominous ['ɒmɪnəs] **ADJ** *(threatening)* menaçant, inquiétant; *(boding ill)* de mauvais augure, de sinistre présage; **an o. silence** un silence lourd de menaces; **an o. sign** un signe inquiétant *ou* alarmant; **o. black clouds** des nuages menaçants; **an emergency meeting? – that sounds o.** une réunion d'urgence? – ça ne présage rien de bon

ominously ['ɒmɪnəslɪ] **ADV** de façon inquiétante *ou* menaçante; **the sea was o. calm** la mer était étrangement calme; **o., there was no answer when they rang** le téléphone ne répondait pas, ce qui ne présageait rien de bon; **the deadline was drawing o. close** la date limite se rapprochait dangereusement

omission [ə'mɪʃən] **N 1** *(exclusion ▸ accidental)* omission *f*, oubli *m*; *(▸ deliberate)* exclusion *f*; **there are several major omissions in his report** il y a plusieurs oublis importants dans son rapport **2** *Typ* bourdon *m*

omit [ə'mɪt] *(pt & pp* **omitted,** *cont* **omitting) VT 1** *(leave out)* omettre; **a name was omitted from the list** un nom a été omis sur la liste **2** *(fail)* **to o. to do sth** omettre de faire qch

omnibus ['ɒmnɪbəs] **N 1** *Old-fashioned (bus)* omnibus *m* **2** *TV & Rad* = rediffusion hebdomadaire des épisodes d'un feuilleton diffusés pendant la semaine **3** *(book)* recueil *m*; **an Edgar Allan Poe o.** un recueil d'œuvres d'Edgar Allan Poe

▸▸ ***omnibus edition*** *TV & Rad* = rediffusion hebdomadaire des épisodes d'un feuilleton diffusés pendant la semaine; *(of stories, poems)* gros recueil *m*; *Mktg* ***omnibus survey*** enquête *f* omnibus; ***omnibus volume*** *(of stories, poems etc)* gros recueil *m*

omnidirectional [ˌɒmnɪdɪ'rekʃənəl, ˌɒmnɪdaɪ'rekʃənəl] **ADJ** omnidirectionnel

omnipotence [ɒm'nɪpətəns] **N** omnipotence *f*

omnipotent [ɒm'nɪpətənt] **ADJ** omnipotent, tout-puissant
N the O. le Tout-Puissant

omnipresence [ˌɒmnɪ'prezəns] **N** omniprésence *f*

omnipresent [ˌɒmnɪ'prezənt] **ADJ** omniprésent

omniscience [ɒm'nɪsɪəns] **N** omniscience *f*

omniscient [ɒm'nɪsɪənt] **ADJ** omniscient

omnium ['ɒmnɪəm] **N** *Formerly St Exch* omnium *m*

omnivore ['ɒmnɪvɔː(r)] **N** *Zool* omnivore *m*

omnivorous [ɒm'nɪvərəs] **ADJ 1** *Zool* omnivore **2** *Fig* insatiable, avide; *(reader)* qui lit de tout

omnivorously [ɒm'nɪvərəslɪ] **ADV** *Zool* **to eat o.** se nourrir de tout; *Fig* **to read o.** lire de tout

ON [ɒn]

PREP
- sur **A1–4, 6, B1, C1, 4, D1–3, 10, 11**
- à **A3, D6, 8, 9, 10, F3, 6**
- en **A3, F7**
- par rapport à **C5**
- selon **D4**
- de **F4**

ADV
- allumé **5**
- ouvert **5**

ADJ
- allumé **1**
- ouvert **1**
- en marche **1**
- de garde **3**
- de service **3**

PREP A. 1 *(specifying position)* sur; **the vase is on the shelf** le vase est sur l'étagère; **on the floor** par terre; **on the ceiling** au plafond; **there are posters on the walls** il y a des affiches aux *ou* sur les murs; **there was blood on the walls** il y avait du sang sur les murs; **a coat was hanging on the hook** un manteau était accroché à la patère; **the post with the seagull on it** le poteau sur lequel il y a la mouette; **he has a ring on his finger** il a une bague au doigt; **to lie on one's back/side** être allongé sur le dos/côté; **on this side** de ce côté; **on the other side of the page** de l'autre côté de la page; **on page four** à la quatrième page, à la page quatre; **on the left/right** à gauche/droite

2 *(indicating writing or painting surface)* sur; **I had nothing to write on** je n'avais rien sur quoi écrire; **red on a green background** rouge sur un fond vert

3 *(indicating general location, area)* **he works on a building site** il travaille sur un chantier; **they live on a farm** ils habitent une ferme; **there's been an accident on the M1** il y a eu un accident sur la M1; **room on the second floor** chambre au second (étage); **on Arran/the Isle of Wight** sur Arran/l'île de Wight; **on Corsica/Crete** en Corse/Crète; **on Majorca/Minorca** à Majorque/Minorque

4 *(indicating part of body touched)* sur; **I kissed him on the cheek** je l'ai embrassé sur la joue

5 *(close to)* **the village is right on the lake/sea** le village est juste au bord du lac/de la mer

6 *(indicating movement, direction)* **put it on the shelf** mets-le sur l'étagère; **the mirror fell on the floor** la glace est tombée par terre; **to climb on (to) a wall** grimper sur un mur; **they marched on the capital** ils marchèrent sur la capitale; **don't tread on it** ne marchez pas dessus

B. 1 *(indicating thing carried)* sur; **I only had £10 on me** je n'avais que 10 livres sur moi; **she's got a gun on her** elle est armée

2 *(indicating facial expression)* **he had a scornful smile on his face** il affichait un sourire plein de mépris

C. 1 *(indicating purpose of money, time, effort spent)* sur; **I spent hours on that essay** j'ai passé des heures sur cette dissertation; **she spent £1,000 on her new stereo** elle a dépensé 1000 livres pour acheter sa nouvelle chaîne hi-fi; **to put money on a horse** parier *ou* miser sur un cheval; **what are you working on at the moment?** sur quoi travaillez-vous en ce moment?

2 *(indicating activity undertaken)* **I am here on business** je suis ici pour affaires; **he's off on a trip to Brazil** il part pour un voyage au Brésil; **she was sent on a course** on l'a envoyée suivre des cours; **I'm on nights next week** je suis de nuit la semaine prochaine; **he's on lunch/a break** il est en train de déjeuner/faire une pause; **she's been on the committee for years** ça fait des années qu'elle siège au comité

3 *(indicating special interest, pursuit)* **she's keen on music** elle a la passion de la musique; **he's good on modern history** il excelle en histoire moderne; **she's very big on equal opportunities** l'égalité des chances, c'est son cheval de bataille

4 *(indicating scale of activity)* **on a large/small scale** sur une grande/petite échelle

5 *(compared with)* par rapport à; **imports are up/down on last year** les importations sont en hausse/en baisse par rapport à l'année dernière

D. 1 *(about, on the subject of)* sur; **a book/film on the French Revolution** un livre/film sur la Révolution française; **we all agree on that point** nous sommes tous d'accord sur ce point; **could I speak to you on a matter of some delicacy?** pourrais-je vous parler d'une affaire assez délicate?; **the police have nothing on him** la police n'a rien sur lui

2 *(indicating person, thing affected)* sur; **it has no effect on them** cela n'a aucun effet sur eux; **a tax on alcohol** une taxe sur les boissons alcoolisées; **try it on your parents** essaie-le sur tes parents; **the government must act on inflation** le gouvernement doit prendre des mesures contre l'inflation; **he has survived two attempts on his life** il a échappé à deux tentatives d'assassinat; **it's unfair on women** c'est injuste envers les femmes; **the joke's on you!** c'est toi qui as l'air ridicule!

3 *(indicating cause of injury)* **I cut my finger on a piece of glass** je me suis coupé le doigt sur un morceau de verre

4 *(according to)* selon; **everyone will be judged on their merits** chacun sera jugé selon ses mérites; **candidates are selected on their examination results** les candidats sont choisis en fonction des résultats qu'ils ont obtenus à l'examen

5 *(indicating reason, motive for action)* **the po[lice] acted on information from abroad** la police es[t in]tervenue après avoir reçu des renseigneme[nts] de l'étranger

6 *(included in, forming part of)* **your name isn'[t on] the list** votre nom n'est pas sur la liste; **the bo[oks] on the syllabus** les livres au programme

7 *(indicating method, system)* **they work on a [rota] system** ils travaillent par roulement; **reorgan[ized] on a more rational basis** réorganisé sur une b[ase] plus rationnelle

8 *(indicating means of transport)* **on foot/ho[rse]back** à pied/cheval; **on the bus/train** dan[s le] bus/train; **she arrived on the midday bus/t[rain]** elle est arrivée par le bus/train de midi; **on a [bi]cycle** à bicyclette

9 *(indicating instrument played)* **to play a tun[e on] the flute** jouer un air à la flûte; **who's on guita[r/] drums?** qui est à la guitare/à la batterie?

10 *Rad, TV & Theat* **I heard it on the radio/on t[ele]vision** je l'ai entendu à la radio/à la télévision; **the first time she's been on television** c'est la [pre]mière fois qu'elle passe à la télévision; **what' [s on] the other channel** *or* **side?** qu'est-ce qu'il y a [sur] l'autre chaîne?

11 *(indicating where information is stored)* **it'[s all] on computer** tout est sur ordinateur; **on file** [sur] fichier

E. *INDICATING DATE, TIME ETC* **on the 6th of** [July] le 6 juillet; **on or about the 12th** vers le 12; [**on**] **Christmas Day** le jour de Noël; **I'll see her on M[on]day** je la vois lundi; **on Monday morning** lu[ndi] matin; **I don't work on Mondays** je ne trava[ille] pas le lundi; **on a Monday morning in Febru[ary]** un lundi matin (du mois) de février; **on a [fine] day in June** par une belle journée de juin; **ev[ery] hour on the hour** à chaque heure; **it's just on [five] o'clock** il est cinq heures pile; **just on a year** *(approximately)* il y a près d'un an

F. 1 *(indicating source of payment)* **have a drin[k on] me** prenez un verre, c'est moi qui offre; [**the**] **drinks are on me/the house!** c'est ma tournée[/la] tournée du patron!; **you can get it on the Natio[nal] Health** ≃ c'est remboursé par la Sécurité soc[iale]

2 *(indicating source or amount of income)* **to [live] on one's private income/a student grant** vivre [de] ses rentes/d'une bourse d'études; **you can't [live] on such a low wage** on ne peut pas vivre a[vec] des revenus aussi modestes; *Fam* **they're on [un]employment benefit** ils vivent du chômage[,] des allocations de chômage; **to retire on a p[en]sion of £5,000 a year** prendre sa retraite avec [une] pension de 5000 livres par an

3 *(indicating source of power)* à; **it works on e[lec]tricity** ça marche à l'électricité

4 *(indicating source of nourishment)* de; **they [live] on cereals** ils se nourrissent de céréales; [**we**] **dined on oysters and champagne** nous av[ons] dîné d'huîtres et de champagne

5 *(indicating drugs, medicine prescribed)* **is sh[e on] the pill?** est-ce qu'elle prend la pilule?; **I'm stil[l on] antibiotics** je suis toujours sous antibiotiqu[es]; **the doctor put her on tranquillizers** le méde[cin] lui a prescrit des tranquillisants; **he's on insu[lin/] heroin** il prend de l'insuline/de l'héroïne; **he's [on] drugs** il se drogue; *Fam Fig* **what's he on?** il se s[ent] bien?

6 *(at the same time as)* à; **he'll deal with it on [his] return** il s'en occupera à son retour; **on the de[ath] of his mother** à la mort de sa mère; **on my fi[rst/] last visit** lors de ma première/dernière vis[ite]; **on the count of three** à trois

7 *(with present participle)* en; **on hearing the ne[ws]** en apprenant la nouvelle; **on completing the [exam] candidates should...** quand ils auront fini l'e[xa]men les candidats devront...

ADV 1 *(in place)* **the lid wasn't on** le couve[rcle] n'était pas mis; **put the top back on afterwards** [re]mets le capuchon ensuite

2 *(referring to clothes)* **why have you got y[our] gloves on?** pourquoi as-tu mis tes gants?; [**the**] **woman with the blue dress on** la femme en r[obe] bleue; **what had she got on?** qu'est-ce qu'elle p[or]tait?, comment était-elle habillée?; **he's [got] nothing on** il est nu

3 *(indicating continued action)* **to read on** co[nti]nuer à lire; **the car drove on** la voiture ne s['est] pas arrêtée; **they walked on** ils poursuivir[ent]

leur chemin; **from now** *or* **this moment** *or* **this time on** désormais; **from that day on** à partir *ou* dater de ce jour; **well on in years** d'un âge avancé; **earlier/later/further on** plus tôt/tard/loin; **on with the show!** que le spectacle continue!

4 *(indicating activity)* **I've got a lot on this week** je suis très occupé cette semaine; **have you got anything on tonight?** tu fais quelque chose ce soir?

5 *(functioning, running)* **put** *or* **turn** *or* **switch the television on** allume la télévision; **turn the tap on** ouvre le robinet; **the lights had been left on** les lumières étaient restées allumées; **the tap had been left on** le robinet était resté ouvert; **the car had its headlights on** les phares de la voiture étaient allumés

6 *(in betting)* **I have a bet on** j'ai fait un pari

7 *Fam (idiom)* **to be** *or* **go on about sth** parler de qch sans arrêt▫; **he's on about his new car again** le voilà reparti sur sa nouvelle voiture; **what's she on about?** qu'est-ce qu'elle raconte?; **he's always on about the war/teenagers** il n'arrête pas de déblatérer sur la guerre/les adolescents; **my parents are always on at me about my hair** mes parents n'arrêtent pas de m'embêter avec mes cheveux; **I've been on at them for months to get it fixed** cela fait des mois que je suis sur leur dos pour qu'ils le fassent réparer

ADJ 1 *(working ▸ electricity, light, radio, TV)* allumé; *(▸ gas, tap)* ouvert; *(▸ engine, machine)* en marche; *(▸ handbrake)* serré; *(▸ alarm)* enclenché; **the radio was on very loud** la radio hurlait; **make sure the switches are in the "on" position** vérifiez que les interrupteurs sont sur (la position) "marche"; **the "on" button** *or* **switch** le bouton de mise en marche

2 *(happening, under way)* **to be on** *(actor)* être en scène; **we're on in ten minutes** c'est à nous dans dix minutes; **there's a conference on next week** il y a une conférence la semaine prochaine; **the meeting is on right now** la réunion est en train de se dérouler; **the match is still on** *(on TV)* le match n'est pas terminé; *(going ahead)* le match n'a pas été annulé; **it's on at the local cinema** ça passe au cinéma du quartier; **the play was on for weeks** la pièce a tenu l'affiche pendant des semaines; **your favourite TV programme is on tonight** il y a ton émission préférée à la télé ce soir; **there's nothing good on** *(on TV, radio)* il n'y a rien de bien; **is the party still on?** est-ce que la soirée se fait toujours?; **is our deal still on?** est-ce que notre affaire tient toujours?; **the kettle's on for tea** j'ai mis de l'eau à chauffer pour le thé; **hurry up, your dinner's on** dépêche-toi, ton dîner va être prêt

3 *(on duty ▸ in hospital, surgery)* de garde; *(▸ in shop, administration)* de service; **I'm on at three o'clock, then off at nine o'clock** je commence à trois heures et je finis à neuf heures

4 *(in betting)* **the odds are twenty to one on** la cote est de vingt contre un

5 *Fam (unacceptable)* **such behaviour just isn't on!** une telle conduite est tout à fait inadmissible!▫; *Br* **it's not on!** ça va pas du tout!

6 *Fam (feasible, possible)* **we'll never be ready by tomorrow, it just isn't on** nous ne serons jamais prêts pour demain, c'est tout bonnement impossible

7 *Fam (in agreement)* **are you still on for dinner tonight?** ça marche toujours pour le dîner de ce soir?; **shall we say £10? – you're on!** disons 10 livres? – d'accord *ou* tope là!; **if you wash the dishes, I'll dry them – you're on!** si tu fais la vaisselle, je l'essuie – ça marche!

8 *Br Fam* **to be on** *(menstruating)* avoir ses ragnagnas

• **on and off** ADV **we went out together on and off for a year** on a eu une relation irrégulière pendant un an

• **on and on** ADV sans arrêt; **he goes on and on about his minor ailments** il nous rebat les oreilles avec ses petits problèmes de santé; **the play dragged on and on** la pièce n'en finissait plus

on-air *TV & Rad* ADJ à l'antenne
ADV à l'antenne

onanism ['əʊnənɪzəm] N onanisme *m*

on-board ADJ *Comput (built-in)* intégré, embarqué
▸▸ *Aut & Transp* **on-board information** information *f* embarquée; *Fin* **on-board surcharge** surcharge *f* "on-board"

on-camera *TV & Cin* ADJ à l'image
ADV à l'image

once [wʌns] ADV **1** *(on a single occasion)* une fois; **I've been there o. before** j'y suis déjà allé une fois; **he's never o. said he was sorry** il ne s'est jamais excusé, il ne s'est pas excusé une seule fois; **more than o.** plus d'une fois; **o. or twice** une ou deux fois; **o. a week/month/year** une fois par semaine/mois/an; **I see her o. every three months** je la vois tous les trois mois; **o. in a while** occasionnellement, une fois de temps en temps; **o. more** *or* **again** encore une fois, une fois de plus; **for o. he isn't late** pour une fois, il n'est pas en retard; **o. a liar always a liar** qui a menti mentira; **I'll try anything o.** il faut bien tout essayer **2** *(formerly)* jadis, autrefois; **people o. believed that the world was flat** autrefois, on croyait que la terre était plate; **a o. famous poet** un poète autrefois célèbre; **o. upon a time there was a princess, there was o. a princess** il était une fois une princesse; **o. (upon a time) children used to respect their elders** il fut un temps où les enfants respectaient leurs aînés

CONJ une fois que, dès que; **it'll be easy o. we've started** une fois qu'on aura commencé, ce sera facile; **give me a call o. you get there** passe-moi un coup de fil quand tu arrives *ou* seras arrivé; **o. he reached home, he collapsed** une fois arrivé chez lui, il s'effondra

N **(just) this o.** (juste) pour cette fois-ci, (juste) pour une fois; **she did it just the o.** elle ne l'a fait qu'une seule fois

• **at once** ADV **1** *(at the same time)* à la fois, en même temps; **it was at o. fascinating and terrifying** c'était à la fois fascinant et terrifiant; **to do several things at o.** faire plusieurs choses à la fois *ou* en même temps; **it all happened at o.** tout est arrivé en même temps **2** *(immediately)* tout de suite

• **once and for all** ADV une fois pour toutes

once-over N *Fam* **1** *(glance)* coup *m* d'œil▫; **I gave the morning paper the o.** j'ai jeté un coup d'œil sur le journal du matin; **I could see her giving me the o.** je la voyais qui me regardait des pieds à la tête **2** *(clean)* **give the stairs/the bookcase a quick o.** passe un coup dans l'escalier/sur la bibliothèque **3** *(beating)* raclée *f*; **to give sb the** *or* **a o.** donner une bonne raclée à qn

oncology [ɒŋ'kɒlədʒɪ] N *Med* oncologie *f*

oncoming ['ɒn,kʌmɪŋ] ADJ **1 the o. traffic** *(for vehicle)* les véhicules venant en sens inverse; *(for pedestrian)* les véhicules qui approchent **2** *(year, season)* qui arrive, qui approche; **the o. generation of school-leavers** les jeunes qui vont quitter l'école à la fin de cette année scolaire
N approche *f*
▸▸ *Ind* **oncoming shift** poste *m* entrant

oncosts ['ɒnkɒsts] NPL *Com* frais *mpl* généraux

OND [,əʊen'di:] N *(abbr* **Ordinary National Diploma***)* = brevet de technicien en Grande-Bretagne

ONE [wʌn]

ADJ	
• un/une **1, 2, 5–8**	• seul **3**
• même **4**	
PRON	
• on **B1**	• vous **B1**

ADJ **1** *(in expressions of age, date, measurement etc)* un (une); **o. dollar** un dollar; **o. pound** une livre; **o. and a half kilos** un kilo et demi; **twenty-o. apples** vingt et une pommes; **o. million** un million; **o. thousand** mille; **at o. o'clock** à une heure; **he'll be o. (year old) in June** il aura un an en juin; **on page o.** *(of book)* (à la) page un; *(of newspaper)* à la une; **o. fifty** *(a hundred and fifty)* cent cinquante; *(one pound and fifty pence)* une livre cinquante (pence); *(one dollar fifty cents)* un dollar cinquante (cents); *(time)* deux heures moins dix, une heure cinquante; **o. or two** *(a few)* un/une ou deux; **a million** *or* **a thousand and o.** *(a lot)* un millier de

2 *(referring to a single object or person)* un (une); **o. American in two** un Américain sur deux; **only o. answer is correct** il n'y a qu'une seule bonne réponse; **at any o. time** au même moment; **o. car looks much like another to me** pour moi, toutes les voitures se ressemblent; *Pol* **o. member o. vote** = système de scrutin "un homme, une voix"

3 *(only, single)* seul, unique; **my o. mistake** ma seule erreur; **the o. woman who knows** la seule femme qui soit au courant; **no o. man should have that responsibility** c'est trop de responsabilité pour un seul homme; **not o. family was spared** pas une (seule) famille ne fut épargnée

4 *(same)* même; **they all arrived on the o. day** ils sont tous arrivés le même jour; **the two wanted men are in fact o. and the same person** les deux hommes recherchés sont en fait une seule et même personne; **it's all o. to me** ça m'est égal

5 *(instead of "a")* **if there's o. thing I hate it's rudeness** s'il y a une chose que je n'aime pas, c'est bien la grossièreté; **for o. thing it's too late** d'abord, c'est trop tard; **o. thing at a time** chaque chose en son temps; **we had o. customer once who wouldn't leave** une fois on a eu un client qui ne voulait pas partir

6 *(a certain)* **I was introduced to o. Ian Bell** on m'a présenté un certain Ian Bell

7 *(indicating indefinite time)* **o. day you'll understand** un jour, tu comprendras; **o. evening in July** un soir de juillet; **early o. morning** un matin de bonne heure

8 *Fam (as intensifier)* **that's o. fine car!** c'est une sacrée bagnole!; **the room was o. big mess!** il y avait une de ces pagailles dans la pièce!; **it's been o. hell of a day!** quelle journée!▫

PRON A. 1 *(person, thing)* **which o.** lequel (laquelle) *m,f*; **this o.** celui-ci (celle-ci) *m,f*; **that o.** celui-là (celle-là) *m,f*; **the other o.** l'autre *mf*; **the right o.** le (la) bon (bonne); **the wrong o.** le (la) mauvais(e); **which ones?** lesquels (lesquelles)?; **these ones** ceux-ci (celles-ci) *mpl,fpl*; **those ones** ceux-là (celles-là) *mpl,fpl*; **which dog? – the o. that's barking** quel chien? – celui qui aboie; **which cars? – the ones you like** quelles voitures? – celles que tu aimes; **the o. I spoke of** celui dont j'ai parlé; **he's the o. who did it** c'est lui qui l'a fait; **o. of my colleagues is sick** (l')un de mes collègues est malade; **o. of the bulbs has fused** (l')une des ampoules a grillé; **o. of them** l'un d'entre eux, l'un d'eux; **give me o. of them** donnez-m'en un; **she's o. of us** elle est des nôtres; **any o. of us** n'importe lequel d'entre nous; **that's o. of my favourite restaurants** c'est (l')un de mes restaurants préférés; **he's o. of my many admirers** c'est un de mes nombreux admirateurs; **I've only got o.** je n'en ai qu'un; **I was the only o. there** j'étais le seul à me trouver là; **have you seen o.?** en avez-vous vu un?; **two for the price of o.** deux pour le prix d'un; **o. or other** l'un d'eux; **o. after the other** l'un après l'autre; **you can't have o. without the other** l'un ne va pas sans l'autre; **take the new o.** prends le nouveau; **the scheme was a good o. on paper** le plan était excellent en théorie; **she's eaten all the ripe ones** elle a mangé tous ceux qui étaient mûrs/toutes celles qui étaient mûres; **our loved** *or* **dear ones** ceux qui nous sont chers; **the mother and her little ones** la mère et ses petits; **he's a strange o., that boy** il est bizarre, ce garçon; *Br Fam* **ooh, you are a o.!** toi, alors!; *Br Fam* **he's a right o. he is!** lui alors!; *Fam* **I'm not much of a o.** *or* **I'm not a great o. for cheese** je ne raffole pas du fromage; **she's a great o. for computers** c'est une mordue d'informatique; **she's o. in a million** *or* **thousand** c'est une perle rare; **I'm not o. to gossip but…** je ne suis pas du genre commère mais…; *Fam* **there's o. born every minute!** comment peut-on être aussi stupide!▫; **o. and all** tous (sans exception); **o. at a time** un à la fois; *Prov* **o. for all and all for o.** un pour tous et tous pour un; *Fam* **to get o. over on sb** avoir l'avantage sur qn▫

2 *(joke, story, question etc)* **have you heard the o. about the two postmen?** tu connais celle des deux facteurs?; **that's a good o.!** elle est bien bonne celle-là!; **that's a hard o.** *(a difficult question)* vous me posez une colle; **that's an easy o.** c'est facile; **the question is o. of great importance** cette question est d'une grande importance; **you'll have to solve this o. yourself** il faudra que tu règles ça tout seul

3 *Fam (drink)* **do you fancy a quick o.?** on prend un verre en vitesse?ᴰ; **to have had o. too many** avoir bu un coup de trop

4 *Fam (blow)* **to hit** *or* **thump** *or* **belt sb o.** en coller une à qn

5 *Br Fam* **to go into o., to go off on o.** *(lose one's temper)* péter les plombs, péter une durite

6 *very Fam* **to give sb o.** *(have sex with)* en glisser une paire à qn

7 *Knitting* **to make o.** faire une augmentation, augmenter d'une maille

8 *St Exch* unité *f*; **to issue shares in ones** émettre des actions en unités

B. 1 *Formal (as subject)* on; *(as object or after preposition)* vous; **o. can only do o.'s** *or Am* **his best** on fait ce qu'on peut; **it's enough to make o. weep** il y a de quoi vous faire pleurer; **it certainly makes o. think** ça fait réfléchir, c'est sûr

2 *(with infinitive forms)* **to wash o.'s hands** se laver les mains; **to put o.'s hands in o.'s pockets** mettre ses *ou* les mains dans les poches

• **at one** ADV *Formal* **to be at o. with sb/sth** être en harmonie avec qn/qch; **she felt at o. with the world** elle se sentait en harmonie avec le monde

• **for one** ADV **I for o. am disappointed** pour ma part, je suis déçu; **I know that Gillian for o. is against it** je sais que Gillian est contre en tout cas

• **in one** ADV **1** *(combined)* **all in o.** à la fois; **she's a writer, actress and director (all) in o.** elle est à la fois scénariste, actrice et metteur en scène; **two volumes in o.** deux volumes en un; **a useful three-in-o. kitchen knife** un couteau de cuisine très utile avec ses trois fonctions

2 *(at one attempt)* du premier coup; **he did it in o.** il l'a fait en un seul coup; *Fam* **got it in o.!** du premier coup!ᴰ

• **in ones and twos** ADV **they arrived in ones and twos** ils arrivèrent les uns après les autres; **people stood around in ones and twos** les gens se tenaient là par petits groupes

• **one another** PRON *(two people)* l'un l'autre (l'une l'autre) *m,f*; *(more than two people)* les uns les autres (les unes les autres) *mpl,fpl*; **they didn't dare talk to o. another** ils n'ont pas osé se parler; **we love o. another** nous nous aimons; **the group meet in o. another's homes** le groupe se réunit chez l'un ou chez l'autre; **they respect o. another** *(two people)* ils ont du respect l'un pour l'autre; *(more than two people)* ils se respectent les uns les autres; **you can copy o. another's notes** *(two people)* vous pouvez copier vos notes l'un sur l'autre; *(more than two people)* vous pouvez copier vos notes les uns sur les autres

• **one by one** ADV un par un (une par une)

one-act ADJ

▸▸ ***one-act play*** pièce *f* en un (seul) acte

one-armed ADJ manchot (d'un bras); **a o. man** un manchot

▸▸ ***one-armed bandit*** machine *f* à sous

one-day ADJ d'une journée

▸▸ *St Exch* ***one-day fall*** chute *f* enregistrée en un jour; ***one-day match*** *(of cricket)* = match de cricket joué sur une journée; *St Exch* ***one-day rise*** hausse *f* enregistrée en un jour

one-eyed ADJ borgne

one-hit wonder N = groupe ou chanteur qui n'a eu qu'un seul tube

one-horse ADJ **1** *(carriage)* à un cheval **2** *Fam (idiom)* **a o. town** un (vrai) trou, un bled paumé

one-legged ADJ unijambiste; **a o. man** un unijambiste

one-liner N *(quip)* bon mot *m*; **she has some very good one-liners** ses boutades sont très drôles; **there are some great one-liners in the film** il y a de très bonnes répliques dans ce film

one-man ADJ *(vehicle, canoe)* monoplace; *(task)* pour un seul homme; *(expedition)* en solitaire; **I'm a o. woman** je suis fidèle en amour

▸▸ ***one-man band*** homme-orchestre *m*; *Fig* **the company is very much a o. band** c'est une seule personne qui fait marcher cette entreprise; ***one-man show*** *(by artist)* exposition *f* individuelle; *(by performer)* spectacle *m* solo, one-man-show *m inv*

oneness ['wʌnnɪs] N **1** *(singleness)* unité *f*; *(uniqueness)* unicité *f*

2 *(agreement)* accord *m*

3 *(wholeness)* intégrité *f*

4 *(sameness)* identité *f*

one-night stand N **1** *Fam (sexual encounter)* aventure *f* (sans lendemain)ᴰ **2** *Mus & Theat* représentation *f* unique

one-off ADJ *(order, job)* unique; *(article)* spécial, hors-série *(inv)*; **he wants a o. payment** il veut être payé en une seule fois; **I'll do it if it's a o. job** je veux bien le faire mais seulement à titre exceptionnel; *Am* **this trip is definitely a o. deal** c'est la première et dernière fois que je fais ce voyage

N *(original)* **he's a complete o.** il n'y en a pas deux comme lui; **it's a o.** *(object)* c'est unique; *(situation)* c'est exceptionnel; **the mistake was a o.** cette erreur ne se reproduira pas; **her success was a o.** son succès sera sans lendemain

one-on-one ADV *Sport* **he was o. with the goalkeeper** il était seul face au gardien de but

ADJ *Am* = **one-to-one**

one-parent family N famille *f* monoparentale

one-party ADJ *Pol* à parti unique

▸▸ ***one-party rule*** = régime à parti unique; ***one-party state*** État *m* à parti unique; ***one-party system*** *(of government)* système *m* du parti unique

one-piece ADJ une pièce *(inv)*; *Tech (casting)* monobloc

N vêtement *m* une pièce

▸▸ ***one-piece swimsuit*** maillot *m* une pièce *(inv)*

oner ['wʌnə(r)] N *Br Fam* **to do sth in a o.** faire qch d'un seul coupᴰ; **to down a drink in a o.** faire cul sec; **he got it in a o.** *(understood)* il a tout de suite pigé; *(got answer)* il a tout de suite trouvé la solutionᴰ

onerous ['əʊnərəs] ADJ *Formal* lourd, pénible

> Note that the French word **onéreux** is a false friend and is never a translation for the English word **onerous**. It means **expensive**.

oneself [wʌn'self] PRON **1** *(reflexive)* se; *(after preposition)* soi, soi-même; *(emphatic)* soi-même; **to wash o.** se laver; **to enjoy o.** s'amuser; **to live for o.** vivre pour soi; **to be pleased with o.** être content de soi *ou* soi-même **2** *(one's normal self)* soi-même; **it's enough to be o.** il suffit d'être soi-même **3** *(idiom)* **to be (all) by o.** être tout seul

one-sided ADJ **1** *(unequal)* inégal; *Sport* **a o. match** un match inégal; **conversations with him tend to be pretty o.** avec lui, ce n'est pas une conversation, il n'y a que lui qui parle **2** *(biased)* partial **3** *(unilateral)* unilatéral

one-stop ADJ

▸▸ *Com & Mktg* ***one-stop buying*** achats *mpl* regroupés; *Comput* ***one-stop desktop connection*** connexion *f* directe à un ordinateur de bureau; *Com & Mktg* ***one-stop shop, one-stop store*** magasin *m* où l'on trouve de tout; *Com & Mktg* ***one-stop shopping*** achats *mpl* regroupés (dans un seul magasin)

one-time ADJ ancien; **a o. actor turned director** un ancien acteur devenu metteur en scène

one-to-one ADJ **1** *(discussion, meeting)* seul à seul, en tête à tête; *(relationship between people)* exclusif; **I'd prefer to talk to you on a o. basis** je préférerais vous parler seul à seul; **students receive o. instruction** le professeur travaille individuellement avec chaque étudiant **2** *(comparison, relationship)* terme à terme

ADV *(talk, meet)* seul à seul, en tête à tête; *(correspond)* de manière univoque, exclusivement

▸▸ ***one-to-one marketing*** marketing *m* one to one; ***one-to-one tuition*** cours *mpl* particuliers

one-track ADJ **1** *Rail* à voie unique **2** *Fam (idiom)* **he's got a o. mind** *(thinks only of one thing)* c'est une obsession chez luiᴰ; *(thinks only of sex)* il ne pense qu'à ça

one-trick pony N *Fig* = personne qui n'a qu'une seule corde à son arc; **he's quite funny in some of his films, but he's a bit of a o.** il est assez drôle dans certains films, mais il exploite toujours les mêmes procédés

one-upmanship [-'ʌpmənʃɪp] N = comportement d'une personne qui ne supporte pas de voir d'autres faire mieux qu'elle; **it's pure o. on her part** elle veut uniquement prouver qu'elle est la meilleure; **this is no time for o.** ce n'est pas le moment d'essayer de démontrer sa supériorité

one-way ADJ **1** *(street)* à sens unique; *(traffic)* en sens unique

2 *(ticket)* simple; **a o. ticket to Rome** un aller simple pour Rome

3 *(mirror)* sans tain

4 *(reaction, current)* irréversible; *(decision)* unilatéral

5 *(relationship, feeling)* à sens unique

6 *(packaging)* perdu

▸▸ ***one-way street*** (rue *f* à) sens *m* unique; **he went the wrong way up a o. street** il a pris un sens interdit

ongoing ['ɒn,gəʊɪŋ] ADJ **1** *(continuing)* continu; **it's an o. state of affairs** c'est une situation courante *ou* habituelle **2** *(current, in progress)* en cours; **the o. debate between supporters and adversaries of the system** le débat en cours entre partisans et adversaires du système

on-hook, onhook ADJ

▸▸ *Comput* ***on-hook signal*** signal *m* de fin de communication *ou* de raccrochage

onion ['ʌnjən] N oignon *m*; *Br Fam* **he knows his onions** il connaît son affaireᴰ

COMP *(soup)* à l'oignon

▸▸ *Archit* ***onion dome*** bulbe *m* (byzantin); ***onion rings*** rondelles *fpl* d'oignons frites

onionskin ['ʌnjənskɪn] N *(paper)* papier *m* pelure

▸▸ ***onionskin paper*** papier *m* pelure

oniony ['ʌnjənɪ] ADJ *(in smell)* qui sent l'oignon; *(in taste)* qui a un goût d'oignon

on-line, online ADJ *Comput* en ligne; **to be o.** *(person)* être connecté; **the disk contains all you need to get o.** cette disquette contient tout ce qu'il vous faut pour vous connecter; **to go o.** *(for the first time)* se raccorder à l'Internet; **to put the printer o.** connecter l'imprimante

ADV en ligne; **to buy/order o.** acheter/commander en ligne; **to pay o.** payer en ligne, télépayer; **to shop o.** faire un achat/des achats en ligne; **to work o.** travailler en étant connecté à l'Internet

▸▸ ***on-line bank*** banque *f* en ligne, cyberbanque *f*; ***on-line banking*** transactions *fpl* bancaires en ligne; *St Exch* ***on-line broker*** courtier(ère) *m,f* électronique; ***on-line cashdesk terminal*** terminal *m* de paiement connecté; *Mktg* ***on-line catalogue*** catalogue *m* en ligne; ***on-line dating*** rencontres *fpl* en ligne; ***on-line dating agency*** agence *f* de rencontres en ligne; *Cin & TV* ***on-line editing*** montage *m* on line; *Comput* ***on-line help*** aide *f* en ligne; *Fin* ***on-line investing*** investissement *m* en ligne; *Fin* ***on-line investor*** investisseur *m* en ligne; ***on-line marketing*** marketing *m* électronique; *Comput* ***on-line mode*** mode *m* connecté; *Comput* ***on-line newspaper*** journal *m* en ligne; ***on-line payment*** paiement *m* en ligne, télépaiement *m*; *Comput* ***on-line registration*** inscription *f* en ligne; ***on-line retailer*** société *f* de commerce en ligne; ***on-line retailing*** commerce *m* électronique; ***on-line selling*** vente *f* en ligne, vente *f* électronique; *Comput* ***on-line service*** service *m* en ligne; ***on-line shop*** magasin *m* électronique; ***on-line shopping*** achats *mpl* par Internet; ***on-line terminal*** terminal *m* de paiement connecté; *Comput* ***on-line time*** durée *f* de connexion; *St Exch* ***on-line trading*** transactions *fpl* boursières électroniques

onlooker ['ɒn,lʊkə(r)] N *(during event)* spectateur(trice) *m,f*; *(after accident)* badaud(e) *m,f*, curieux(euse) *m,f*

ONLY ['əʊnlɪ]

> ADJ
> • seul, unique
>
> ADV
> • seulement **1, 2** • ne... que **2, 3**
>
> CONJ
> • mais **1, 2** • seulement **2**

ADJ seul, unique; **he's/she's an o. child** il est fils/elle est fille unique; **she was the o. woman there** c'était la seule femme; **the o. coat I possess** le seul manteau que je possède; **he's the o. one who believes me** il est le seul à me croire; **I'm fed up! –**

you're not the o. one! j'en ai assez! – tu n'es pas le seul!; **her o. answer was to shrug her shoulders** pour toute réponse, elle a haussé les épaules; **it's our o. chance** c'est notre seule chance; **the o. thing is, I won't be there** le seul problème, c'est que je ne serai pas là; **the o. way I'll go is if it's free** je n'irai que si c'est gratuit; **her one and o. friend** son seul et unique ami; **the one and o. Billy Shears!** le seul, l'unique Billy Shears!; **Paris is the o. place to live** Paris est la ville idéale pour vivre

ADV 1 *(exclusively)* seulement; **o. if you agree** seulement si tu es d'accord; **she has o. one brother** elle n'a qu'un (seul) frère; **there are o. two people I trust** il n'y a que deux personnes en qui j'aie confiance; **o. an expert could advise us** seul un expert pourrait nous conseiller; **you'll o. get him to come if you offer him a lift** tu ne le feras venir que si tu lui proposes de l'amener; **staff o.** *(sign)* réservé au personnel

2 *(just, merely)* **he's o. a child!** ce n'est qu'un enfant!; **it's o. a scratch** c'est seulement une égratignure, ce n'est (rien) qu'une égratignure; **after all, it's o. money** après tout, ce n'est que de l'argent; **it's o. me!** c'est moi!; **I o. touched it** je n'ai fait que le toucher; **you've o. ruined my best silk shirt(, that's all)!** tu n'as fait qu'abîmer ma plus belle chemise en soie(, c'est tout)!; **go on, ask him, he can o. say no** vas-y, demande-lui, ce qui peut t'arriver de pire c'est qu'il refuse; **I was o. trying to help** je cherchais seulement à être utile; **it will o. make him sad** ça ne fera que l'attrister; **it's o. natural she should want to see him** c'est tout naturel qu'elle veuille le voir; **I shall be o. too pleased to come** je ne serai que trop heureux de venir; **I o. hope we're not too late** j'espère seulement que nous n'arrivons pas trop tard; **if o. they knew!, if they o. knew!** si (seulement) ils savaient!; **he has o. to ask for it** il n'a qu'à le demander; **you o. have to look at him to see he's guilty** il suffit de le regarder pour voir qu'il est coupable; **you're o. young once** il faut profiter de sa jeunesse

3 *(to emphasize smallness of amount, number etc)* ne… que; **it o. cost me £5** ça ne m'a coûté que 5 livres; **it o. took me half an hour** je n'ai mis qu'une demi-heure

4 *(to emphasize recentness of event)* **it seems like o. yesterday** c'est comme si c'était hier; **I saw her/used it o. yesterday** je l'ai vue/m'en suis servi pas plus tard qu'hier; **I o. found out this morning** je n'ai appris ça que ce matin; **o. last week he appeared to be quite happy** la semaine dernière encore, il semblait parfaitement heureux

5 *(with infinitive)* **I awoke o. to find he was gone** à mon réveil, il était parti

CONJ *Fam* **1** *(but, except)* mais[□]; **it's like Spain, o. cheaper** c'est comme l'Espagne, mais en moins cher; **go on then, o. hurry!** vas-y alors, mais dépêche-toi!

2 *(were it not for the fact that)* mais, seulement; **I'd do it, o. I don't have the time** je le ferais bien, seulement je n'ai pas le temps

• **not only** **CONJ** **she's not o. bright, she's funny too** elle est non seulement intelligente, mais en plus elle est drôle; **not o.… but also** non seulement… mais aussi

• **only if, only… if** **CONJ** seulement si; **I'll do it, but o. if you say sorry first** je le ferai, mais seulement si vous vous excusez d'abord; **he'll o. agree if the money's good enough** il n'acceptera que si on lui propose assez d'argent

• **only just** **ADV 1** *(not long before)* **I've o. just woken up** je viens (tout) juste de me réveiller

2 *(barely)* tout juste; **I o. just finished in time** je n'ai fini qu'au dernier moment; **did she win? – yes, but o. just** a-t-elle gagné? – oui, mais de justesse; **I've o. just got enough** j'en ai tout juste assez

• **only too** **ADV** **I'd be o. too delighted to come** je ne serai que trop heureux de venir; **I remember her o. too well** je ne risque pas de l'oublier

only-begotten **ADJ** *Rel* **the o. Son of the Father** le Fils unique du Père

on-message **ADJ** *Br Pol* = qui respecte scrupuleusement la ligne du parti

o.n.o. [ˌəʊen'əʊ] **ADV** *Br (abbr* **or near/nearest offer)** **£100 o.** 100 livres à débattre

on-off **ADJ** *(intermittent)* **they have a very o. relationship** ils ont une relation très peu suivie

►► *Elec* **on-off button, on-off switch** bouton *m* (de) marche-arrêt

onomatopoeia [ˈɒnəˌmætə'piːə] **N** onomatopée *f*

onomatopoeic [ˈɒnəˌmætə'piːɪk], **onomatopoetic** [ˈɒnəˌmætəpəʊ'etɪk] **ADJ** onomatopéique

on-pack **ADJ**

►► *Mktg* **on-pack offer** prime *f* différée; **on-pack promotion** promotion *f* on-pack

on-ramp **N** *Br (to motorway)* bretelle *f* d'accès

onrush ['ɒnˌrʌʃ] **N** *(of attackers, army)* attaque *f*, assaut *m*; *(of emotion, tears)* crise *f*; *(of anger)* accès *m*

ONS [ˌəʊen'es] **N** *Br (abbr* **Office for National Statistics)** ≃ INSEE *m*

on-screen **ADJ 1** *Comput* à l'écran **2** *Cin & TV* à l'écran; **her o. character bears a close resemblance to her real-life personality** le personnage qu'elle joue à l'écran ressemble beaucoup à ce qu'elle est en réalité

ADV 1 *Comput* sur (l')écran; **to work o.** travailler sur écran **2** *Cin & TV* à l'écran

►► *Comput* **on-screen help** aide *f* en ligne

onset ['ɒnˌset] **N 1** *(assault)* attaque *f*, assaut *m* **2** *(beginning)* début *m*, commencement *m*; **the o. of winter** le début de l'hiver

onshore ['ɒnˌʃɔː(r)] **ADJ** *(on land)* sur terre, terrestre

►► **onshore oil production** production *f* pétrolière à terre; **onshore wind** *(moving towards land)* vent *m* de mer

on-site **ADJ 1** *Comput* sur place **2** *(guarantee, warranty)* sur site

onslaught ['ɒnslɔːt] **N** attaque *f*, assaut *m*; **the opposition's o. on government policy** l'attaque violente de l'opposition contre la politique du gouvernement

Ont. *(written abbr* **Ontario)** Ontario *m*

on-target earnings **NPL** *Com & Mktg* salaire *m* de base plus commissions

on-the-job **ADJ** *(training)* en entreprise; *(experience)* sur le tas

on-the-spot **ADJ** *(fine)* immédiat; *(report)* sur place, sur le terrain

onto ['ɒntuː] **PREP 1** *(gen)* sur; **the bedroom looks out o. a garden** la chambre donne sur un jardin; **let's move o. the next point** passons au point suivant; **get o. the bus** montez dans le bus **2** *(indicating discovery)* **let's just hope the authorities don't get o. us** espérons qu'on ne sera pas découverts par les autorités; **we're o. something big** nous sommes sur le point de faire une importante découverte; **is he o. the fact that they're having an affair?** est-il au courant de leur liaison?; **he'd better watch out, I'm o. him!** qu'il fasse attention, je l'ai dans mon *ou* le collimateur! **3** *(in contact with)* **you should get o. head office about this** vous devriez contacter le siège à ce sujet; **she's been o. me about my poor marks** elle m'a enguirlandé à cause de mes mauvaises notes

ontological [ˌɒntə'lɒdʒɪkəl] **ADJ** ontologique

ontology [ɒn'tɒlədʒɪ] **N** ontologie *f*

on-trend **ADJ** à la mode

onus ['əʊnəs] **N** *(responsibility)* responsabilité *f*; *(burden)* charge *f*; **the o. is on you to make good the damage** c'est à vous qu'il incombe de réparer les dégâts; **the o. is now on United to attack** United se doit maintenant d'attaquer

onward ['ɒnwəd] **ADJ** **the o. journey** la suite du voyage; **there is an o. flight to Chicago** il y a une correspondance pour Chicago; **the o. march of time** la fuite du temps

ADV *Am* = **onwards**

EXCLAM en avant!

onwards ['ɒnwədz] **ADV** *(forwards)* en avant; *(further on)* plus loin; **to go o.** avancer; **o. and upwards!** en avant!

• **from… onwards** **ADV** à partir de; **from next July o.** à partir de juillet prochain; **from her childhood o.** dès *ou* depuis son enfance; **from now o.** désormais, dorénavant, à partir de maintenant; **from then o.** à partir de ce moment-là

onyx ['ɒnɪks] **N** onyx *m*

COMP en onyx, d'onyx

oodles ['uːdəlz] **NPL** *Fam* des masses *fpl*, des tas *mpl*; **there's o. of food left** il reste un tas de bouffe; **to have o. of money** avoir un paquet de fric, être plein aux as; **to have o. of time** avoir vachement de temps

ooh [uː] **EXCLAM** oh!

VI **they were all oohing and aahing over her baby** ils poussaient tous des cris d'admiration devant son bébé

oolite ['əʊəlaɪt] **N** *Geol* oolite *m ou f*, oolithe *m ou f*

oomph [ʊmf] **N** *Fam* **1** *(energy)* punch *m*, pêche *f*; **he's certainly got plenty of o.!** en tout cas, il a un sacré punch!; **their new album lacks the o. of the last one** leur nouvel album n'a pas la pêche du précédent **2** *(sex appeal)* sex-appeal[□] *m*; **she's got plenty of o.** elle est vachement sexy

oops [ʊps, uːps], **oops-a-daisy** ['ʊpsəˌdeɪzɪ] **EXCLAM** *Fam* **1** *(when stumbling, dropping something etc)* houp-là! **2** *(after someone has made a mistake)* oh là là!

ooze [uːz] **VI** suinter; **the mud oozed up between her toes** la boue lui passait entre les orteils; **blood oozed from the wound** du sang coulait de la blessure; *Fig* **the new father fairly oozed with pride** le nouveau père débordait de fierté

VT **the wound was oozing pus/blood** du pus/sang suintait de la plaie; **the walls o. moisture** l'humidité suinte des murs; *Fig* **to o. confidence** déborder d'assurance; **to o. charm** exsuder un charme mielleux; *Fig* **this place just oozes wealth** cet endroit sue l'opulence

N 1 *(mud)* boue *f*, vase *f* **2** *(flow* ► *of liquid)* suintement *m*

op [ɒp] **N** *Fam Med & Mil (abbr* **operation)** opération[□] *f*; **she has to have an op on her knee** il faut qu'elle se fasse opérer le *ou* du genou[□]

opacity [ə'pæsətɪ] **N** opacité *f*; *Fig (of text)* inintelligibilité *f*, obscurité *f*; *(of person)* stupidité *f*

opal ['əʊpəl] **N** opale *f*

COMP *(brooch, ring)* en opale

opalescence [ˌəʊpə'lesəns] **N** opalescence *f*

opalescent [ˌəʊpə'lesənt] **ADJ** opalescent, opalin

opaline ['əʊpəlaɪn] **N** *(glass)* opaline *f*

ADJ opalin

opaque [əʊ'peɪk] **ADJ** opaque; *Fig (text)* inintelligible, obscur; *(person)* stupide

►► *Am* **opaque projector** épiscope *m*, épidiascope *m*

opaqueness [əʊ'peɪknɪs] **N** opacité *f*; *Fig (of text)* inintelligibilité *f*, obscurité *f*; *(of person)* stupidité *f*

OPEC ['əʊpek] **N** *(abbr* **Organization of Petroleum Exporting Countries)** OPEP *f*; **the O. countries** les pays *mpl* membres de l'OPEP

op-ed **N** *(in newspaper)* page *f* face éditoriale; **an o. piece** article *m* d'opinion *(situé sur la page faisant face à l'éditorial)*

OPEIC [əʊpiːɪaɪ'siː] **N** *Fin (abbr* **open-ended investment company)** SICAV *f*, sicav *f*

OPEN ['əʊpən]

ADJ
- ouvert **1–4, 9, 10, 14, 15, 17–19**
- vacant **8**
- public **9, 15**
- franc **14**
- découvert **5**
- dégagé **7, 17**
- libre **8**
- non résolu **11**

VT
- ouvrir **1–7**
- écarter **3**
- engager **5**
- déboucher **1**
- commencer **5**
- dégager **7**

VI
- s'ouvrir **1–3**
- commencer **5**
- ouvrir **1, 4**

N
- grand air **1**
- open **3**
- grand jour **2**

ADJ 1 *(not shut* ► *window, cupboard, suitcase, jar, box, sore, valve)* ouvert; **her eyes were slightly o./wide o.** ses yeux étaient entrouverts/grands ouverts; **the panels slide o.** les panneaux s'ouvrent en coulissant; **to smash/lever sth o.** ouvrir qch en le fracassant/à l'aide d'un levier; **I can't get the bottle o.** je n'arrive pas à ouvrir la bouteille; **there's a bottle already o. in the fridge** il y a une bouteille entamée dans le frigo

2 *(not fastened* ▸ *coat, fly, packet)* ouvert; **his shirt was o. to the waist** sa chemise était ouverte *ou* déboutonnée jusqu'à la ceinture; **his shirt was o. at the neck** le col de sa chemise était ouvert; **the wrapping had been torn o.** l'emballage avait été arraché *ou* déchiré

3 *(spread apart, unfolded* ▸ *arms, book, magazine, umbrella)* ouvert; *(*▸ *newspaper)* ouvert, déplié; *(*▸ *legs, knees)* écarté; **the book lay o. at page 6** le livre était ouvert à la page 6; **I dropped the coin into his o. hand** *or* **palm** j'ai laissé tomber la pièce de monnaie dans le creux de sa main; **the seams had split o.** les coutures avaient craqué; **he ran into my o. arms** il s'est précipité dans mes bras

4 *(for business)* ouvert; **I couldn't find a bank o.** je n'ai pas pu trouver une banque qui soit ouverte; **are you o. on Saturdays?** ouvrez-vous le samedi?; **o. to the public** *(museum etc)* ouvert *ou* accessible au public; **o. late** ouvert en nocturne

5 *(not covered* ▸ *carriage, wagon, bus)* découvert; *(*▸ *car)* décapoté; *(*▸ *grave)* ouvert; *(*▸ *boat)* ouvert, non ponté; *(*▸ *courtyard, sewer)* à ciel ouvert; **the passengers sat on the o. deck** les passagers étaient assis sur le pont; **the wine should be left o. to breathe** il faut laisser la bouteille ouverte pour que le vin puisse respirer

6 *(not enclosed* ▸ *hillside, plain)* **the shelter was o. on three sides** l'abri était ouvert sur trois côtés; **the hill was o. to the elements** la colline était exposée à tous les éléments; **our neighbourhood lacks o. space** notre quartier manque d'espaces verts; **the wide o. spaces of Texas** les grands espaces du Texas; **shanty towns sprang up on every scrap of o. ground** des bidonvilles ont surgi sur la moindre parcelle de terrain vague; **o. countryside stretched away to the horizon** la campagne s'étendait à perte de vue; **o. grazing land** pâturages *mpl* non clôturés; **ahead lay a vast stretch of o. water** au loin s'étendait une vaste étendue d'eau; **in the o. air** en plein air; **nothing beats life in the o. air** il n'y a rien de mieux que la vie au grand air; **he took to the o. road** il a pris la route; **it'll do 150 on the o. road** elle monte à 150 sur l'autoroute; **the o. sea** la haute mer, le large

7 *(unobstructed* ▸ *road, passage)* dégagé; *(*▸ *mountain pass)* ouvert, praticable; *(*▸ *waterway)* ouvert à la navigation; *(*▸ *view)* dégagé; **only one lane on the bridge is o.** il n'y a qu'une voie ouverte à la circulation sur le pont

8 *(unoccupied, available* ▸ *job)* vacant; *(*▸ *period of time)* libre; **we have two positions o.** nous avons deux postes à pourvoir; **I'll keep this Friday o. for you** je vous réserverai ce vendredi; **she likes to keep her weekends o.** elle préfère ne pas faire de projets pour le week-end; **it's the only course of action o. to us** c'est la seule chose que nous puissions faire; **she used every opportunity o. to her** elle a profité de toutes les occasions qui se présentaient à elle; **he wants to keep his options o.** il ne veut pas s'engager

9 *(unrestricted* ▸ *competition)* ouvert (à tous); *(*▸ *meeting, trial)* public; *(*▸ *society)* ouvert, démocratique; **the contest is not o. to company employees** le concours n'est pas ouvert au personnel de la société; **club membership is o. to anyone** aucune condition particulière n'est requise pour devenir membre du club; **a career o. to very few** une carrière accessible à très peu de gens *ou* très fermée; **there are few positions of responsibility o. to immigrants** les immigrés ont rarement accès aux postes de responsabilité; **the field is wide o. for someone with your talents** pour quelqu'un d'aussi doué que vous, ce domaine offre des possibilités quasi illimitées; **to extend an o. invitation to sb** inviter qn à venir chez soi quand il le souhaite; **it's an o. invitation to tax-dodgers/thieves** c'est une invitation à la fraude fiscale/aux voleurs; *Am Fam* **Reno was a pretty o. town in those days** à cette époque, Reno était aux mains des hors-la-loi▫; **they have an o. marriage** ils forment un couple très libre

10 *(unprotected, unguarded* ▸ *flank, fire)* ouvert; *(*▸ *wiring)* non protégé; **the two countries share miles of o. border** les deux pays sont séparés par des kilomètres de frontière non matérialisée; *Sport* **he missed an o. goal** il n'y avait pas de défenseurs, et il a raté le but; **to lay oneself o. to criticism** prêter le flanc à la critique

11 *(undecided* ▸ *question)* non résolu, non tranché; **the election is still wide o.** l'élection n'est pas encore jouée; **it's still an o. question whether he'll resign or not** on ne sait toujours pas s'il va démissionner; **I prefer to leave the matter o.** je préfère laisser cette question en suspens; **he wanted to leave the date o.** il n'a pas voulu fixer de date

12 *(liable)* **his speech is o. to misunderstanding** son discours peut prêter à confusion; **the prices are not o. to negotiation** les prix ne sont pas négociables; **the plan is o. to modification** le projet n'a pas encore été finalisé; **it's o. to debate whether she knew about it or not** on peut se demander si elle était au courant; **o. to doubt** douteux

13 *(receptive)* **to be o. to suggestions** être ouvert aux suggestions; **I don't want to go but I'm o. to persuasion** je ne veux pas y aller mais je pourrais me laisser persuader; **I try to keep an o. mind about such things** j'essaie de ne pas avoir de préjugés sur ces questions; **o. to any reasonable offer** disposé à considérer toute offre raisonnable

14 *(candid* ▸ *person, smile, countenance)* ouvert, franc (franche); *(*▸ *discussion)* franc (franche); **let's be o. with each other** soyons francs l'un avec l'autre; **they weren't very o. about their intentions** ils se sont montrés assez discrets en ce qui concerne leurs intentions; **he is o. about his homosexuality** il ne cache pas son homosexualité

15 *(blatant* ▸ *contempt, criticism, conflict, disagreement)* ouvert; *(*▸ *attempt)* non dissimulé; *(*▸ *scandal)* public; *(*▸ *rivalry)* déclaré; **her o. dislike** son aversion déclarée; **the country is in a state of o. civil war** le pays est en état de véritable guerre civile; **they are in o. revolt** ils sont en révolte ouverte; **they showed an o. disregard for the law** ils ont fait preuve d'un manque de respect flagrant face à la loi

16 *(loose* ▸ *weave)* lâche

17 *Sport (play* ▸ *free-flowing)* ouvert, dégagé

18 *Ling (vowel, syllable)* ouvert

19 *Elec (circuit)* ouvert

20 *Br Fin (cheque)* non barré

21 *Mus (string)* à vide

VT 1 *(window, lock, shop, eyes, border)* ouvrir; *(wound)* rouvrir; *(bottle, can)* ouvrir, déboucher; *(wine)* déboucher; **o. quotations** *or* **inverted commas** ouvrez les guillemets; **she opened her eyes very wide** elle ouvrit grand les yeux, elle écarquilla les yeux; *Phot* **o. the aperture one more stop** ouvrez d'un diaphragme de plus; *Fig* **to o. one's heart to sb** se confier à qn; **we must o. our minds to new ideas** nous devons être ouverts aux idées nouvelles

2 *(unfasten* ▸ *coat, envelope, gift, collar)* ouvrir

3 *(unfold, spread apart* ▸ *book, umbrella, penknife, arms, hand)* ouvrir; *(*▸ *newspaper)* ouvrir, déplier; *(*▸ *legs, knees)* écarter

4 *(pierce* ▸ *hole)* percer; *(*▸ *breach)* ouvrir; *(*▸ *way, passage)* ouvrir, frayer; **to o. a road through the jungle** ouvrir une route à travers la jungle; **the agreement opens the way for peace** l'accord va mener à la paix

5 *(start* ▸ *campaign, discussion, account, trial)* ouvrir, commencer; *(*▸ *negotiations)* ouvrir, engager; *(*▸ *conversation)* engager, entamer; *Banking & Fin (*▸ *account, loan)* ouvrir; **her new film opened the festival** son dernier film a ouvert le festival; **to o. a file on sb** ouvrir un dossier sur qn; **to o. the bidding** *(in bridge)* ouvrir (les enchères); **to o. the betting** *(in poker)* lancer les enchères; **to o. Parliament** ouvrir la session du Parlement; *Law* **to o. the case** exposer les faits

6 *(set up* ▸ *shop, business)* ouvrir; *(inaugurate* ▸ *hospital, airport, library)* ouvrir, inaugurer

7 *(clear, unblock* ▸ *road, lane, passage)* dégager; *(*▸ *mountain pass)* ouvrir

VI 1 *(door, window)* (s')ouvrir; *(suitcase, valve, padlock, eyes)* s'ouvrir; **o. wide!** ouvrez grand!; **to o., press down and twist** pour ouvrir, appuyez et tournez; **both rooms o. onto the corridor** les deux chambres donnent *ou* ouvrent sur le couloir; *Fig* **the heavens opened and we got drenched** il s'est mis à tomber des trombes d'eau et on s'est fait tremper

2 *(unfold, spread apart* ▸ *book, umbrella, parachute)* s'ouvrir; *(*▸ *bud, leaf)* s'ouvrir, s'épanouir; **a new life opened before her** une nouvelle vie s'ouvrait devant elle

3 *(gape* ▸ *chasm)* s'ouvrir

4 *(for business)* ouvrir; **what time do you o. on Sundays?** à quelle heure ouvrez-vous le dimanche?; **the doors o. at 8 p.m.** les portes ouvrent à 20 heures; *Com* **to o. late** ouvrir en nocturne

5 *(start* ▸ *campaign, meeting, discussion, concert, play, story)* commencer; **the book opens with a murder** le livre commence par un meurtre; **the hunting season opens in September** la chasse ouvre en septembre; **she opened with a statement of the association's goals** elle commença par une présentation des buts de l'association; **the film opens next week** le film sort la semaine prochaine; *Theat* **when are you opening?** quand aura lieu la première?; **when it opened on Broadway, the play flopped** lorsqu'elle est sortie à Broadway, la pièce a fait un four; **the Dow Jones opened at 2461** le Dow Jones a ouvert à 2461; **to o. with two clubs** *(in bridge)* ouvrir de deux trèfles

N 1 *(outdoors, open air)* **(out) in the o.** *(gen)* en plein air, dehors; *(in countryside)* au grand air; **eating (out) in the o. gives me an appetite** manger au grand air me donne de l'appétit; **to sleep in the o.** dormir à la belle étoile

2 *(public eye)* **to bring sth (out) into the o.** exposer *ou* étaler qch au grand jour; **the riot brought the instability of the regime out into the o.** l'émeute a révélé l'instabilité du régime; **the conflict finally came out into the o.** le conflit a finalement éclaté au grand jour

3 *Sport* open *m*; **the British O.** *(golf)* l'open *m ou* le tournoi open de Grande-Bretagne; **the French O.** *(tennis)* Roland-Garros *m*

▸▸ ***open access*** libre accès *m*; *Banking* ***open account*** compte *m* ouvert; ***open bar*** buvette *f* gratuite, bar *m* gratuit; *Banking* ***open cheque*** chèque *m* ouvert *ou* non barré; *St Exch* ***open contract*** position *f* ouverte; *Law* ***open court*** audience *f* publique; *Fin* ***open credit*** crédit *m* à découvert; *Br* ***open day*** journée *f* portes ouvertes; ***open house*** *(party)* grande fête *f*; *Am (open day)* journée *f* portes ouvertes; *Br* **to keep o. house** tenir table ouverte; ***open inquiry*** enquête *f* publique; *Br* ***open learning*** enseignement *m* à la carte *(par correspondance ou à temps partiel)*; ***open letter*** lettre *f* ouverte; **an o. letter to the President** une lettre ouverte au Président; ***open market*** marché *m* libre; **to buy sth on the o. market** acheter qch sur le marché libre; *St Exch* **to buy shares on the o. market** acheter des actions en Bourse; ***open mesh*** mailles *fpl* lâches; *St Exch* ***open outcry system*** système *m* de criée; ***open pattern*** motif *m* aéré; *Ins* ***open policy*** police *f* flottante; *St Exch* ***open position*** position *f* ouverte; *Am Pol* ***open primary*** = élection primaire américaine ouverte aux non-inscrits d'un parti; ***open prison*** prison *f* ouverte; ***open sandwich*** *(gen)* tartine *f*; *(cocktail food)* canapé *m*; ***open season*** saison *f*; **the o. season for hunting** la saison de la chasse; *Fig* **the tabloid papers have declared o. season on the private lives of rock stars** les journaux à scandale se sont mis à traquer les stars du rock dans leur vie privée; *Aviat & Theat* ***open seating*** places *fpl* non réservées; *Br* ***open secret*** secret *m* de Polichinelle; **it's an o. secret that Alison will get the job** c'est Alison qui aura le poste, ce n'est un secret pour personne;

▸▸ ***open sesame*** EXCLAM sésame, ouvre-toi! **N** *Br (means to success)* sésame *m*; **good A level results aren't necessarily an o. sesame to university** de bons résultats aux "A levels" n'ouvrent pas forcément la porte de l'université; *Ind* ***open shop*** *Br (open to non-union members)* = entreprise ne pratiquant pas le monopole d'embauche; *Am (with no union)* établissement *m* sans syndicat; *Sport* ***open side*** *(in rugby)* grand côté *m*, côté *m* ouvert; *Comput* ***open source*** *(software)* logiciel *m* libre *ou* ouvert; ***open ticket*** billet *m* open; *Sport* ***open tournament*** (tournoi *m*) open *m*; *Br* ***Open University*** = enseignement universitaire par correspondance doublé d'émissions de télévision ou de radio; *Law* ***open verdict*** verdict *m* de décès sans cause déterminée

open out VI **1** *(unfold ▸ bud, petals)* s'ouvrir, s'épanouir; *(▸parachute)* s'ouvrir; *(▸sail)* se gonfler; **the sofa opens out into a bed** le canapé est convertible en lit; **the doors o. out onto a terrace** les portes donnent *ou* s'ouvrent sur une terrasse
2 *(lie ▸ vista, valley)* s'étendre, s'ouvrir; **miles of wheatfields opened out before us** des champs de blé s'étendaient devant nous à perte de vue
3 *(widen ▸ path, stream)* s'élargir; **the river opens out into a lake** la rivière se jette dans un lac; **the trail finally opens out onto a plateau** la piste débouche sur un plateau
4 *Br Fig (become less reserved)* s'ouvrir; **he opened out after a few drinks** quelques verres ont suffi à le faire sortir de sa réserve
VT SEP *(unfold ▸ newspaper, deck chair, fan)* ouvrir; **the peacock opened out its tail** le paon a fait la roue

open up VI **1** *(unlock the door)* ouvrir
2 *(become available ▸ possibility)* s'ouvrir; **we may have a position opening up in May** il se peut que nous ayons un poste disponible en mai; **new markets are opening up** de nouveaux marchés sont en train de s'ouvrir
3 *(for business ▸ shop, branch etc)* (s')ouvrir; **a new hotel opens up every week** un nouvel hôtel ouvre ses portes chaque semaine
4 *(start firing ▸ guns)* faire feu, tirer; *(▸ troops, person)* ouvrir le feu, se mettre à tirer
5 *(become less reserved ▸ person)* s'ouvrir; *(▸ discussion)* s'animer; **he needs to o. up about his feelings** il a besoin de dire ce qu'il a sur le cœur *ou* de s'épancher; **I got her to o. up about her doubts** j'ai réussi à la convaincre de me faire part de ses doutes
6 *(become interesting)* devenir intéressant; **things are beginning to o. up in my field of research** ça commence à bouger dans mon domaine de recherche; **the game opened up in the last half** le match est devenu plus ouvert après la mi-temps
VT SEP **1** *(crate, gift, bag, tomb)* ouvrir; **we're opening up the summer cottage this weekend** nous ouvrons la maison de campagne ce week-end
2 *(for business)* ouvrir; **each morning, Lucy opened up the shop** chaque matin, Lucy ouvrait la boutique; **he wants to o. up a travel agency** il veut ouvrir une agence de voyages
3 *(for development ▸ isolated region)* désenclaver; *(▸ quarry, oilfield)* ouvrir, commencer l'exploitation de; *(▸ new markets)* ouvrir; **irrigation will o. up new land for agriculture** l'irrigation permettra la mise en culture de nouvelles terres; **the airport opened up the island for tourism** l'aéroport a ouvert l'île au tourisme; **a discovery which opens up new fields of research** une découverte qui crée de nouveaux domaines de recherche; **the policy opened up possibilities for closer co-operation** la politique a créé les conditions d'une coopération plus étroite
4 *Fam (accelerate)* **he opened it** *or* **her up** il a accéléré à fond

---

open-access ADJ en libre accès

open-air ADJ *(market, concert)* en plein air; *(sports)* de plein air
▸▸ ***open-air cinema*** cinéma *m* en plein air; ***open-air restaurant*** restaurant *m* en terrasse; ***open-air swimming pool*** piscine *f* découverte

open-and-shut ADJ **it's an o. case** la solution est évidente *ou* ne fait pas l'ombre d'un doute

opencast ['əʊpənkɑːst] ADJ *Br Mining* à ciel ouvert
▸▸ ***opencast mining*** extraction *f* à ciel ouvert

open-date ticket N billet *m* open *inv ou* ouvert

open-door ADJ *(policy)* de la porte ouverte

open-ended [-'endɪd] ADJ *(flexible ▸ offer)* flexible; *(▸plan)* modifiable; *(▸question)* ouvert; *(▸ mortgage)* sans date limite; **could we keep the arrangement o.?** pourrions-nous garder une certaine flexibilité au niveau de notre arrangement?; **an o. discussion** une discussion libre
▸▸ *Fin* ***open-ended contract*** contrat *m* à durée indéterminée; *Fin* ***open-ended credit*** crédit *m* à durée indéterminée; *Fin* ***open-ended investment company, open-ended trust*** société *f* d'investissement à capital variable, SICAV *f*

opener ['əʊpənə(r)] N **1** *(tool)* outil *m ou* dispositif *m* servant à ouvrir; *(for cans)* ouvre-boîtes *m inv*
2 *(person ▸ in cards, games)* ouvreur(euse) *m,f*
3 *(first song, act etc)* lever *m* de rideau; **she chose her latest hit single as an o. for the show** elle a choisi son dernier tube pour ouvrir le spectacle
4 *Sport (in cricket)* premier batteur *m*
5 *(idiom) Br Fam* **for openers** pour commencer[□]; **I'm sacking the whole staff, and that's just for openers** je licencie toute l'équipe et ce n'est qu'un début[□]

open-eyed ADJ (qui a) les yeux ouverts; **they watched in o. amazement** ils ouvraient de grands yeux
ADV **to stare o.** regarder les yeux écarquillés

open-handed ADJ généreux

open-hearted [-'hɑːtɪd] ADJ **1** *(candid)* franc (franche), sincère **2** *(kind)* bon, qui a bon cœur

open-hearth ADJ
▸▸ *Metal* ***open-hearth furnace*** four *m* Martin; ***open-hearth process*** procédé *m* Martin

open-heart surgery N chirurgie *f* à cœur ouvert

opening ['əʊpənɪŋ] ADJ *(part, chapter)* premier; *(day, hours)* d'ouverture; *(ceremony)* d'ouverture, d'inauguration; *(remark)* préliminaire, préalable; *Theat* **the o. lines** les premières lignes
N **1** *(act of opening)* ouverture *f*; **at the play's New York o.** lors de la première de la pièce à New York; **the o. of negotiations has been postponed** l'ouverture *f* des négociations a été ajournée; **the o. of Parliament** l'ouverture *f* du Parlement
2 *(gap, hole, entrance)* ouverture *f*; **an o. in the clouds** une trouée *ou* une percée dans les nuages; **the o. to the mine** l'entrée *f* de la mine
3 *Am (in forest)* clairière *f*
4 *(start, first part)* ouverture *f*, début *m*; *Law (speech by lawyer)* exposition *f* des faits; **the o. of the film is in black and white** le début du film est en *ou* les premières scènes du film sont en noir et blanc
5 *(opportunity ▸ gen)* occasion *f*; *(▸ for employment)* débouché *m*; *Mktg (▸ in market)* débouché *m*, ouverture *f*; **we have exploited an o. in the market** nous avons exploité une ouverture sur le marché; **her remarks about the company gave me the o. I needed** ses observations au sujet de l'entreprise m'ont fourni le prétexte dont j'avais besoin; **there are lots of good openings in industry** l'industrie offre de nombreux débouchés intéressants; **there's an o. with Smith & Co** il y a un poste vacant chez Smith & Co
▸▸ *Acct* ***opening balance*** solde *m* d'ouverture; *Acct* ***opening balance sheet*** bilan *m* d'ouverture; ***opening batsman*** *(in cricket)* premier batteur *m*; *Cards* ***opening bid*** annonce *f* d'entrée *ou* d'indication; ***opening bracket*** parenthèse *f* ouvrante; *Cin & TV* ***opening credits*** générique *m* de début; *St Exch* ***opening day*** jour *m* d'ouverture; *Acct* ***opening entry*** écriture *f* d'ouverture; *Com* ***opening hours*** heures *fpl* d'ouverture; *Chess* ***opening gambit*** gambit *m*; *Fig* premier pas *m*; *St Exch* ***opening price*** *(at start of trading)* cours *m* d'ouverture, premier cours *m*; *(of new shares)* cours *m* d'introduction; ***opening quotation marks, opening quotes*** guillemets *mpl* ouvrants; *Fin* ***opening session*** séance *f* d'ouverture; *Fin* ***opening stock*** stock *m* initial *ou* d'ouverture; *Theat* ***opening night*** première *f*; *Comput* ***opening tag*** balise *f* de début; *Com* ***opening time*** heure *f* d'ouverture; *Cin* ***opening weekend*** premier week-end *m* d'exploitation

open-jaw ticket N billet *m* open *(inv)* ou ouvert

openly ['əʊpənlɪ] ADV visiblement; **drugs are on sale o.** la drogue est en vente libre; **to weep o.** pleurer sans retenue

open-minded ADJ *(receptive)* ouvert (d'esprit); *(unprejudiced)* sans préjugés; **my parents are pretty o. about mixed marriages** mes parents n'ont aucun a priori contre les mariages mixtes

open-mouthed [-'maʊðd] ADJ *(person)* stupéfait, interdit; **he was sitting there in o. astonishment** il était assis là, béant d'étonnement
ADV **to watch o.** regarder bouche bée

openness ['əʊpənnɪs] N **1** *(candidness)* franchise *f*
2 *(receptivity)* ouverture *f*; **I admire her for her o.** ce que j'admire chez elle, c'est qu'elle est très ouverte
3 *(spaciousness)* largeur *f*; **the picture window gives a feeling of o. to the room** la baie vitrée agrandit la pièce
4 *(of coastline)* situation *f* exposée; *(of terrain)* aspect *m* découvert

open-plan ADJ *Archit (design, house)* à plan ouvert, sans cloisons
▸▸ ***open-plan kitchen*** cuisine *f* américaine; ***open-plan office*** bureau *m* paysager

open-top ADJ décapotable

open-topped bus N autobus *m* à impériale

openwork ['əʊpənwɜːk] N *(UNCOUNT)* **1** *Sewing* jours *mpl*, ajours *mpl* **2** *Archit* claire-voie *f*, ajours *mpl*

opera ['ɒpərə] *pl of* **opus**
N **1** *(musical play)* opéra *m* **2** *(art)* opéra *m*; **she adores (the) o.** elle adore l'opéra **3** *(opera house)* opéra *m*
▸▸ ***opera cloak*** (grande) cape *f*; ***opera glasses*** jumelles *fpl* de théâtre; *Br* ***opera hat*** gibus *m*, (chapeau *m*) claque *m*; ***opera house*** (théâtre *m* de l')opéra *m*; ***opera singer*** chanteur(euse) *m,f* d'opéra

operable ['ɒprəbəl] ADJ **1** *Med (disease, tumour)* opérable **2** *(system)* utilisable

operand ['ɒpərænd] N *Math* opérande *m*

operate ['ɒpəreɪt] VT **1** *(machine, device)* faire fonctionner, faire marcher; **my husband doesn't even know how to o. the toaster!** mon mari ne sait même pas se servir du grille-pain!; **is it possible to o. the radio off the mains?** peut-on brancher cette radio sur le secteur?; **this clock is battery-operated** cette horloge fonctionne avec des piles; **a circuit-breaker operates the safety mechanism** un disjoncteur actionne *ou* déclenche le système de sécurité **2** *(business)* gérer, diriger; *(mine)* exploiter; *(drug ring)* contrôler; **they o. several casinos** ils tiennent plusieurs casinos; **she operates her business from her home** elle fait marcher son affaire depuis son domicile; **they o. a system of rent rebates for poorer families** ils ont un système de loyers modérés pour les familles les plus démunies
VI **1** *(machine, device)* marcher, fonctionner; *(system, process, network)* fonctionner; **it operates by itself** ça fonctionne tout seul; **the factory is operating at full capacity** l'usine tourne à plein rendement
2 *Med* opérer; **to o. on sb (for sth)** opérer qn (de qch); **he was operated on for cancer** on l'a opéré *ou* il a été opéré d'un cancer; **we'll have to o.** il va falloir opérer
3 *(be active)* opérer; **many crooks o. in this part of town** de nombreux malfaiteurs sévissent dans ce quartier; **the company operates out of Chicago** le siège de la société est à Chicago; **the company operates in ten countries** la société est implantée dans dix pays
4 *(produce an effect)* opérer, agir; **the drug operates on the nervous system** le médicament agit sur le système nerveux; **two elements o. in our favour** deux éléments jouent en notre faveur
5 *(be operative)* s'appliquer; **the rule doesn't o. in such cases** la règle ne s'applique pas à de tels cas; **the wage increase will o. from 1 January** l'augmentation des salaires prendra effet à partir du 1er janvier

operatic [,ɒpə'rætɪk] ADJ d'opéra
• **operatics** NPL *(amateur)* opéra *m* d'amateurs
▸▸ ***operatic repertoire*** répertoire *m* lyrique; ***operatic role*** rôle *m* lyrique; ***operatic society*** groupe *m* d'opéra d'amateurs

operating ['ɒpəreɪtɪŋ] ADJ *(costs, methods etc)* d'exploitation; **the factory has reached full o. capacity** l'usine a atteint sa pleine capacité de production
▸▸ *Am Fin* ***operating account*** compte *m* d'exploitation; *Acct* ***operating assets*** actif *m* d'exploitation; *Acct* ***operating budget*** budget *m* d'exploitation *ou* de fonctionnement; *Am* ***oper-***

ating capital capital *m* d'exploitation *ou* de roulement; *Acct* ***operating cash flow*** cash-flow *m* disponible; ***operating cost*** charge *f* opérationnelle; *Acct* ***operating costs*** frais *mpl ou* coûts *mpl* d'exploitation; *Fin* ***operating deficit*** déficit *m* d'exploitation; *Acct* ***operating expenses*** frais *mpl* d'exploitation; ***operating income*** produits *mpl* d'exploitation; ***operating instructions*** mode *m* d'emploi; *Fin* ***operating leverage*** levier *m* d'exploitation; *Acct & Fin* ***operating loss*** perte *f* d'exploitation; *Acct* ***operating margin*** marge *f* (nette) d'exploitation; *Acct & Fin* ***operating profit*** bénéfice *m* d'exploitation; *Acct* ***operating ratio*** coefficient *m ou* ratio *m* d'exploitation; *Am* ***operating room*** salle *f* d'opération; *Fin* ***operating statement*** compte *m ou* rapport *m* d'exploitation; *Comput* ***operating system*** système *m* d'exploitation; *Comput* ***operating system command*** commande *f* système d'exploitation; *Comput* ***operating system software*** logiciel *m* de système d'exploitation; ***operating table*** table *f* d'opération; *Br* ***operating theatre*** salle *f* d'opération

operation [ˌɒpəˈreɪʃən] **N 1** *(functioning ▸ of machine, device)* fonctionnement *m*, marche *f*; *(▸ of process, system)* fonctionnement *m*; *(▸ of drug, market force)* action *f*; **to be in o.** *(machine, train service)* être en service; *(firm, group, criminal)* être en activité; *(law)* être en vigueur; **the pit has been in o. for two years** le puits est exploité depuis deux ans; **the plant is in o. round the clock** l'usine fonctionne 24 heures sur 24; **to put into o.** *(machine, train service)* mettre en service; *(plan)* mettre en application *ou* en œuvre; *(law)* faire entrer en vigueur; **to come into o.** *(machine, train service)* entrer en service; *(law)* entrer en vigueur

2 *(running, management ▸ of firm)* gestion *f*; *(▸ of mine)* exploitation *f*; *(▸ of process, system)* application *f*; *(▸ of machine)* fonctionnement *m*

3 *(act, activity, deal etc)* opération *f*; *Mil* opération *f*; **a police/rescue o.** une opération de police/de sauvetage; **they are to close down their operations in Mexico** ils vont mettre un terme à leurs opérations *ou* activités au Mexique

4 *(company)* entreprise *f*, société *f*; **she works for a mining o.** elle travaille pour une exploitation minière

5 *Med* opération *f*, intervention *f*; **she had an o. for cancer** elle s'est fait opérer d'un cancer; **he had a heart o.** il a subi une opération *ou* il a été opéré du cœur; **to perform an o.** réaliser une intervention; **to perform an o. on sb (for sth)** opérer qn (de qch)

6 *Comput & Math* opération *f*

7 *Mktg (campaign)* opération *f*

▸▸ ***operations management*** gestion *f* des opérations; ***operations manager*** directeur(trice) *m,f* des exploitations; ***operations research*** recherche *f* opérationnelle; ***operations room*** base *f* d'opérations

operational [ˌɒpəˈreɪʃənəl] **ADJ 1** *Mil (gen)* opérationnel **2** *(equipment, engine, system)* opérationnel; **the new missiles are not yet o.** les nouveaux missiles ne sont pas encore opérationnels; **as soon as the engine is o.** dès que le moteur sera en état de marche; **o. difficulties** difficultés *fpl* d'ordre pratique **3** *(costs, requirements)* d'exploitation

▸▸ *Acct* ***operational audit*** audit *m* opérationnel; *Acct* ***operational cost accounting*** comptabilité *f* analytique d'exploitation; *Acct* ***operational cost centre*** centre *m* d'analyse opérationnel; ***operational marketing*** marketing *m* opérationnel; *Com* ***operational planning*** planification *f* des opérations; *Mktg* ***operational research*** recherche *f* opérationnelle

operative [ˈɒprətɪv] **ADJ 1** *(law)* en vigueur; **to become o.** entrer en vigueur, prendre effet; **parking restrictions became o. last year** les limitations de stationnement ont pris effet l'an dernier

2 *(operational ▸ system, scheme, skill)* opérationnel

3 *Med* opératoire

4 *(idiom)* **the o. word** le mot qui convient

N 1 *(worker)* ouvrier(ère) *m,f*; *(of machine)* opérateur(trice) *m,f*; **machine o.** conducteur(trice) *m,f* de machine; **textile o.** ouvrier(ère) *m,f* du textile **2** *Am (secret agent)* agent *m* secret; *(detective)* (détective *m*) privé *m*

operator [ˈɒpəreɪtə(r)] **N 1** *(technician)* opérateur(trice) *m,f*; **radio o.** radio *m*

2 *Tel* opérateur(trice) *m,f*; **(switchboard) o.** standardiste *mf*

3 *Com (director)* directeur(trice) *m,f*, dirigeant(e) *m,f*; *(organizer)* organisateur(trice) *m,f*; **there are too many small operators in real estate** l'immobilier compte trop de petites entreprises; **he's a big drug o.** c'est un grand caïd de la drogue; *Fam Pej* **he's a smooth o.** il sait s'y prendre *ou* se débrouiller, c'est un petit malin

4 *Math* opérateur *m*

5 *Am (in bus)* machiniste *mf*

operetta [ˌɒpəˈretə] **N** opérette *f*

ophthalmic [ɒfˈθælmɪk] **ADJ** *Anat (nerve)* ophtalmique; *Med (hospital, surgery)* ophtalmologique

▸▸ ***ophthalmic optician*** opticien(enne) *m,f* (optométriste)

ophthalmologist [ˌɒfθælˈmɒlədʒɪst] **N** oculiste *mf*, ophtalmologiste *mf*, ophtalmologue *mf*

ophthalmology [ˌɒfθælˈmɒlədʒɪ] **N** ophtalmologie *f*

opiate [ˈəʊpɪət] **N** *Pharm* opiacé *m*; *(soporific)* somnifère *m*

opine [əʊˈpaɪn] **VT** *Formal or Literary* (faire) remarquer

opinion [əˈpɪnjən] **N 1** *(estimation)* opinion *f*, avis *m*; *(viewpoint)* point *m* de vue; **in my o.** à mon avis; **in the o. of her teachers** de l'avis de ses professeurs, selon ses professeurs; **I am of the o. that we should wait** je suis d'avis que l'on attende; **what is your o. on *or* about the elections?** que pensez-vous des élections?; **my personal o. is that…** je suis d'avis que…, pour ma part, je pense que…; **well, if you want my honest o., I'll tell you** puisque tu veux savoir le fond de ma pensée, je vais te le dire; **can you give us your o. on the festival?** pouvez-vous nous dire ce que vous pensez du festival?; **to form an o. of sb/sth** se faire une opinion sur *ou* de qn/qch; **to have a good/bad o. of sth** avoir une bonne/mauvaise opinion de qch; **I have a rather low o. of him** je n'ai pas beaucoup d'estime pour lui; **he has too high an o. of himself** il a une trop haute opinion de lui-même

2 *(conviction, belief)* opinion *f*; **to have strong opinions** avoir des opinions tranchées *ou* bien arrêtées; **world/international o.** l'opinion *f* mondiale/internationale; **a matter of o.** une affaire d'opinion; **public o. is against them** ils ont l'opinion publique contre eux

3 *Law* avis *m*; **it is the o. of the court that…** la cour est d'avis que…

4 *(advice)* opinion *f*, avis *m*; **a medical/legal o.** un avis médical/juridique

▸▸ *Press* ***opinion column*** tribune *f* libre; *Mktg* ***opinion former, opinion leader*** leader *m* d'opinion, préconisateur *m*; *Mktg* ***opinion measurement*** sondage *m* d'opinion; *Mktg* ***opinion poll*** sondage *m* (d'opinion), enquête *f* (d'opinion); *Mktg* ***opinion pollster*** sondeur(euse) *m,f* (d'opinion); *Mktg* ***opinion survey*** sondage *m* d'opinion (publique), enquête *f* (d'opinion)

opinionated [əˈpɪnjəneɪtɪd] **ADJ** *Pej (tone)* dogmatique; *(person)* qui a des idées très arrêtées

opium [ˈəʊpjəm] **N** opium *m*

▸▸ ***opium addict*** opiomane *mf*; ***opium addiction*** opiomanie *f*; ***opium den*** fumerie *f* d'opium; ***opium poppy*** pavot *m* (somnifère)

Oporto [əˈpɔːtəʊ] **N** Porto

opossum [əˈpɒsəm] *(pl* **inv** *or* **opossums)** **N** *Zool* opossum *m*

opp *(written abbr* **opposite)** en face

opponent [əˈpəʊnənt] **N** *(gen)* adversaire *mf*; *(rival)* rival(e) *m,f*; *(competitor)* concurrent(e) *m,f*; *(in debate)* adversaire *mf*; **political o.** *(democratic)* adversaire *mf* politique; *(of regime)* opposant(e) *m,f* politique; **she has always been an o. of blood sports** elle a toujours été contre les sports sanguinaires; **opponents of the new marina held a rally** les opposants à la construction de la nouvelle marina ont organisé un meeting

opportune [ˈɒpətjuːn] **ADJ 1** *(coming at the right time)* opportun; **a very o. remark** une remarque tout à fait opportune **2** *(suitable for a particular purpose)* propice; **this seems an o. moment t break for coffee** le moment semble propice pou faire une pause-café

opportunely [ˈɒpətjuːnlɪ] **ADV** opportunémen au moment opportun

opportunism [ˌɒpəˈtjuːnɪzəm] **N** opportunism *m*

opportunist [ˌɒpəˈtjuːnɪst] **N** opportuniste *mf*
ADJ opportuniste

opportunistic [ˌɒpətjuːˈnɪstɪk] **ADJ** opportu niste

▸▸ *Med* ***opportunistic infection*** infection *f* oppo tuniste

opportunity [ˌɒpəˈtjuːnətɪ] *(pl* **opportunities)** **N** *(chance)* occasion *f*; **to have an o. to do *or* of doin sth** avoir l'occasion de faire qch; **we don't hav much o. of practising hang-gliding** nous avons ra rement l'occasion de faire du deltaplane; **if eve you get the o.** si jamais vous en avez l'occasior **to give sb an o. of doing sth *or* the o. to do sth** dor ner à qn l'occasion de faire qch; **should the arise** si l'occasion se présente; **I took every o. c travelling** je n'ai manqué aucune occasion de o j'ai saisi toutes les occasions de voyager; **I'd lik to take this o. to thank everyone** j'aimerais prof ter de cette occasion pour remercier tout l monde; **I'll leave at the first *or* earliest o.** je part rai à la première occasion *ou* dès que l'occasio se présentera; **at every o.** à la moindre occasio **2** *(prospect)* perspective *f*; **the opportunities fc advancement are excellent** les perspective d'avancement sont excellentes **3** *Mktg* opportu nité *f*; **o. to hear** occasion *f* d'entendre; **o. to se** occasion *f* de voir; **o. and threat analysis** analyse des opportunités et des menaces

▸▸ *Econ* ***opportunity cost*** coût *m* d'opportunit *ou* de renoncement

opposability [əˌpəʊzəbɪlətɪ] **N** opposabilité *f*

opposable [əˈpəʊzəbəl] **ADJ** opposable

oppose [əˈpəʊz] **VT 1** *(decision, plan, bill etc)* s'op poser à, être hostile à; *(verbally)* parler contre **the family opposed their marriage** la famille s'op posa à leur mariage; **the construction of th power station was opposed by local people** la cons truction de la centrale s'est heurtée à l'hostilit de la population locale **2** *(in contest, fight)* s'op poser à; *(combat)* combattre **3** *(contrast)* oppo ser; **the social sciences are often opposed to pur science** on oppose souvent les sciences humai nes aux sciences pures

opposed [əˈpəʊzd] **ADJ** opposé, hostile; **to be c to sth** être opposé *ou* hostile à qch; **she is ver much o. to the idea** c'est une idée à laquelle ell est totalement opposée; **his views are diametr cally o. to mine** il a des idées radicalement oppo sées aux miennes

• **as opposed to PREP** par opposition à, plutô que; **we will propose more science as o. to art courses** nous proposons de renforcer l'ense gnement des sciences plutôt que celui des ma tières littéraires

opposing [əˈpəʊzɪŋ] **ADJ 1** *(army, team)* adverse *(factions)* qui s'opposent; *(party, minority)* d'op position; **they're on o. sides** ils sont adversaires ils ne sont pas du même côté **2** *(contrasting views)* opposé, qui s'oppose

opposite [ˈɒpəzɪt] **ADJ 1** *(facing)* d'en face, op posé; **the o. side of the road** l'autre côté de l rue; **see illustration on o. page** *(in book, maga zine)* voir illustration ci-contre

2 *(opposing ▸ direction, position)* inverse, op posé; *(rival ▸ team)* adverse; **the letter-box is a the o. end of the street** la boîte à lettres se trouv à l'autre bout de la rue; **in the o. direction** en sen inverse, dans le sens opposé; **they went in o. d rections** ils ont pris des directions opposées

3 *(conflicting ▸ attitude, character, opinion* contraire, opposé; **I take the o. view** je suis d l'avis contraire; **his words had just the o. effec** ses paroles eurent exactement l'effet contraire

4 *Bot* opposé

5 *Math* opposé

ADV en face; **the houses o.** les maisons d'en face **the lady o.** la dame qui habite en face

PREP 1 *(across from)* en face de; **our houses are o each other** nos maisons se font face *ou* sont e face l'une de l'autre; **they sat o. each other** il taient assis l'un en face de l'autre; **we have a ark o. our house** nous avons un parc en face de hez nous; **put a tick o. the correct answer** mettre ne croix en face de la bonne réponse, cocher a bonne réponse **2** *Cin & Theat* **to play o. sb** doner la réplique à qn; **she played o. Richard Burton n many films** elle fut la partenaire de Richard urton dans de nombreux films

N opposé *m*, contraire *m*; **I understood quite the** . j'ai compris exactement le contraire; **she alvays does the o. of what she's told** elle fait touours le contraire de ce qu'on lui dit de faire; **Jill s the complete o. of her sister** Jill est tout à fait opposé de sa sœur; **what's the o. of "optimistic"?** uel est le contraire de "optimistic"?

▸ ***opposite number*** homologue *mf*; ***opposite sex*** exe *m* opposé; **a person** *or* **member of the o. sex** ne personne du sexe opposé

pposition [ˌɒpəˈzɪʃən] **N 1** *(physical)* opposiion *f*, résistance *f*; *(moral)* opposition *f*; **the army net with fierce o.** l'armée se heurta à une vive ésistance; **the besieged city put up little o.** la ille assiégée n'opposa guère de résistance; **in . to** en opposition avec; **the plans met with some .** les projets suscitèrent une certaine opposiion *ou* hostilité

2 *Pol* **the O.** l'opposition *f*; **Labour spent the 1980s n O.** les travaillistes furent dans l'opposition endant toutes les années 80; **the O. benches** es bancs *mpl* de l'opposition

3 *(rivals* ▸ *in sport)* adversaires *mpl*; *Com* oncurrents *mpl*, concurrence *f*

4 *(contrast)* (mise *f* en) opposition *f*

COMP *Pol (committee, spokesperson etc)* de l'oposition

ppositionist [ˌɒpəˈzɪʃənɪst] *Pol* **N** oppositionel(elle) *m,f*

ADJ oppositionnel

ppress [əˈpres] **VT 1** *(tyrannize)* opprimer **2** *Litrary (torment* ▸ *of anxiety, atmosphere)* accabler, ppresser

ppressed [əˈprest] **ADJ** *(people)* opprimé

NPL the o. les opprimés *mpl*

ppression [əˈpreʃən] **N 1** *(persecution)* oppresion *f* **2** *(sadness)* angoisse *f*, malaise *m*

ppressive [əˈpresɪv] **ADJ 1** *Pol (regime, governnent)* oppressif; *(tax)* accablant **2** *(hard to bear* ▸ *'ebt, situation)* accablant **3** *(weather, atmoshere)* lourd; **the heat was o.** il faisait une chaleur ccablante *ou* étouffante

ppressively [əˈpresɪvlɪ] **ADV** d'une manière ppressante *ou* accablante; **it was o. hot** il faiait une chaleur étouffante *ou* accablante

ppressiveness [əˈpresɪvnɪs] **N 1** *(of regime, overnment)* caractère *m* oppressif **2** *(of debt, sitation)* caractère *m* accablant **3** *(of weather, atnosphere)* lourdeur *f*; **the o. of the heat** la haleur accablante *ou* étouffante

ppressor [əˈpresə(r)] **N** oppresseur *m*

pprobrious [əˈprəʊbrɪəs] **ADJ** *Formal* **1** *(scornul)* méprisant **2** *(shameful)* honteux, scandaeux

pprobrium [əˈprəʊbrɪəm] **N** *Formal* opprobre *n*

pt [ɒpt] **VI to o. for sth** opter pour qch, choisir ch; **she opted to study maths** elle a choisi d'étulier les maths

opt in VI *(join)* choisir de participer

opt into VT INSEP *(join)* **to o. into an association/ he EU** entrer dans une association/l'Union uropéenne

opt out VI 1 *(gen)* se désengager, retirer sa paricipation; **to o. out of society** rejeter la société; **'m opting out!** ne comptez plus sur moi!, je me etire de la partie!; **many opted out of joining the nion** beaucoup ont choisi de ne pas adhérer au yndicat **2** *Pol (school, hospital)* = choisir l'autoomie vis-à-vis des pouvoirs publics

ptative [ˈɒptətɪv] **N** optatif *m*

ADJ optatif

ptic® [ˈɒptɪk] **N** *Br* mesure *f* transparente *(utiliée dans les bars)*

ptic [ˈɒptɪk] **ADJ** optique

▸▸ *Anat* ***optic nerve*** nerf *m* optique

optical [ˈɒptɪkəl] **ADJ** *(lens)* optique; *(instrument)* optique

▸▸ ***optical activity*** activité *f* optique; ***optical art*** art *m* optique; ***optical axis*** axe *m* optique; ***optical centre*** centre *m* optique; *Comput* ***optical character reader*** lecteur *m* optique de caractères; *Comput* ***optical character recognition*** reconnaissance *f* optique de caractères; *Comput* ***optical disk*** disque *m* optique; *Comput* ***optical drive*** lecteur *m* optique; ***optical fibre*** fibre *f* optique; ***optical fibre cable*** câble *m* à fibre optique; ***optical fibre technology*** fibre *f* optique; ***optical glass*** verre *m* optique; ***optical illusion*** illusion *f ou* effet *m* d'optique; *Comput* ***optical mouse*** souris *f* optique; *Comput* ***optical reader*** lecteur *m* optique; *Comput* ***optical resolution*** résolution *f* optique; *Comput* ***optical scanner*** scanneur *m* optique; ***optical scanning device*** lecteur *m* optique; ***optical sound*** son *m* optique

optician [ɒpˈtɪʃən] **N** opticien(enne) *m,f*; **at the o.'s** chez l'opticien

optics [ˈɒptɪks] **N** *(UNCOUNT)* optique *f*

optimal [ˈɒptɪməl] **ADJ** optimal, optimum

▸▸ *Mktg* ***optimal price*** prix *m* optimum

optimism [ˈɒptɪmɪzəm] **N** optimisme *m*

optimist [ˈɒptɪmɪst] **N** optimiste *mf*

optimistic [ˌɒptɪˈmɪstɪk] **ADJ** *(person, outlook)* optimiste; *(period)* d'optimisme; **things are looking quite o.** les choses se présentent plutôt bien

optimistically [ˌɒptɪˈmɪstɪklɪ] **ADV** avec optimisme, d'une manière optimiste; **they o. predicted record profits** ils se sont montrés optimistes et ont prédit des bénéfices record

optimize, -ise [ˈɒptɪmaɪz] **VT** optimiser, optimaliser

optimizer, -iser [ˈɒptɪmaɪzə(r)] **N** *Comput* optimiseur *m*

optimum [ˈɒptɪməm] *(pl* **optimums** *or* **optima** [-mə]) **N** optimum *m*

ADJ optimum, optimal

▸▸ ***optimum conditions*** conditions *fpl* optimales; *Econ* ***optimum population*** population *f* optimale

option [ˈɒpʃən] **N 1** *(alternative)* choix *m*; **he has no o.** il n'a pas le choix; **I have no o. but to refuse** je ne peux faire autrement que de refuser; **we have the o. of staying here** nous avons la possibilité de rester ici; **they were given the o. of adopting a child** on leur a proposé d'adopter un enfant; **you leave me no o.** vous ne me laissez pas le choix; **he didn't give me much o.** il ne m'a pas vraiment donné le choix

2 *(possible choice)* option *f*, possibilité *f*; *(accessory)* option *f*; *Sch & Univ* (matière *f* à) option *f*; **to keep** *or* **leave one's options open** ne pas prendre de décision, ne pas s'engager; **she has to choose between three foreign language options** elle doit choisir une option parmi trois langues étrangères; **power steering is an o.** la direction assistée est en option

3 *Com* option *f*; *St Exch* option *f*, (marché *m* à) prime *f*; *St Exch* **to take up an o.** lever une option; **to take an o. on sth** prendre une option sur qch; **the agency allowed her to take out an o. on the house until Monday** l'agence lui a laissé une option sur la maison jusqu'à lundi; **to declare an o.** répondre à une option; **o. on shares** option *f* sur actions; **Air France have an o. to buy 15 planes** Air France a une option d'achat sur 15 appareils

4 *Comput* option *f*

▸▸ *Comput* ***option box*** case *f* d'option; *Comput* ***option button*** case *f* d'option; ***option date*** jour *m* d'option; *St Exch* ***option day*** (jour *m* de la) réponse *f* des primes; ***option deal*** opération *f* à prime; ***options desk*** desk *m* d'options; *Comput* ***option key*** touche *f* Option; ***options market*** marché *m* à options *ou* à primes; *Comput* ***options menu*** menu *f* des options; *St Exch* ***option price*** prix *m* de l'option; *St Exch* ***options trading*** négociations *fpl* à prime, opérations *fpl* à option

optional [ˈɒpʃənəl] **ADJ** facultatif; *Sch & Univ (subject)* facultatif, optionnel; **evening dress is o.** la tenue de soirée n'est pas de rigueur; **the tinted lenses are o.** les verres teintés sont en option; **German is an o. subject** l'allemand est une matière optionnelle; **linguistics is o.** la linguistique est facultative

▸▸ ***optional extra*** option *f*; **the radio is an o. extra** la radio est en option *ou* en supplément

optionee [ˈɒpʃəniː] **N** *St Exch* bénéficiaire *mf* d'options

optomagnetic [ˌɒptəmægˈnetɪk] **ADJ** magnéto-optique

optometrist [ɒpˈtɒmətrɪst] **N** optométriste *mf*, réfractionniste *mf*

opt-out ADJ *(clause, provisions)* de désengagement

N 1 *(gen)* désengagement *m* **2** *Pol (of school, hospital)* = décision de choisir l'autonomie vis-à-vis des pouvoirs publics; **Britain's o. from the Social Chapter** la décision de la Grande-Bretagne de ne pas souscrire au chapitre social européen

opulence [ˈɒpjʊləns] **N** opulence *f*

opulent [ˈɒpjʊlənt] **ADJ** *(lifestyle, figure)* opulent; *(abundant)* abondant, luxuriant; *(house, clothes)* somptueux

opulently [ˈɒpjʊləntlɪ] **ADV** *(dress, decorate, dine)* avec opulence; *(live)* dans l'opulence

opus [ˈəʊpəs] *(pl* **opuses** *or Formal* **opera** [ˈɒpərə]) **N** opus *m*

-OR
voir **-ER**

or [ɔː(r)] **CONJ 1** *(in positive statements)* ou; *(in negative statements)* ni; **in New York or (in) London** à NewYork ou à Londres; **have you got any brothers or sisters?** avez-vous des frères et sœurs?; **he never laughs or smiles** il ne rit ni ne sourit jamais; **in a day or two** dans un ou deux jours; **Norma Jean Baker, or Marilyn Monroe as she became known** Norma Jean Baker ou Marilyn Monroe, puisque c'est le nom sous lequel elle est devenue célèbre; **or so I thought** du moins c'est ce que je pensais; **did she do it or not?** est-ce qu'elle l'a fait ou pas?; **...or not, as the case may be** ...ou non, peut-être **2** *(otherwise* ▸ *in negative statements)* ou; (▸ *in positive statements)* sinon; **don't hit it too hard or it'll break** ne tape pas trop fort dessus ou ça va casser; **she must have some talent or they wouldn't have chosen her** elle doit avoir un certain talent sinon ils ne l'auraient pas choisie

• **or else CONJ 1** *(otherwise)* sinon; **I'd better rush, or else I'll be late** je ferais mieux de me dépêcher, sinon je serai en retard **2** *(offering an alternative)* ou bien; **Monday, or else Tuesday** lundi, ou bien mardi **ADV** *Fam* **give us the money, or else!** donne-nous l'argent, sinon!

• **or no CONJ** ou pas; **I'm taking a holiday, work or no work** travail ou pas, je prends des vacances

• **or other ADV we stayed at San something or other** on s'est arrêté à San quelque chose; **somehow or other we made it home** on a fini par réussir à rentrer, Dieu sait comment; **somebody or other said that...** quelqu'un, je ne sais plus qui, a dit que...; **one or other of us will have to go** il faudra bien que l'un de nous s'en aille; **some actress or other** une actrice (quelconque)

• **or so ADV** environ; **ten minutes or so** environ dix minutes; **50 kilos or so** 50 kilos environ, dans les 50 kilos; **ten dollars or so** dix dollars environ, à peu près dix dollars

• **or something ADV** *Fam* ou quelque chose comme ça; **she's a lawyer or something** elle est avocate ou quelque chose comme ça; **are you deaf or something?** t'es sourd ou quoi?

• **or what ADV** *Fam* ou quoi; **are you stupid or what?** t'es bête ou quoi?

oracle [ˈɒrəkəl] **N** oracle *m*; **the Delphic o.** l'oracle de Delphes; **to consult the o.** consulter les oracles

oracular [ɒˈrækjʊlə(r)] **ADJ 1** *(relating to an oracle)* oraculaire **2** *Fig (wise)* prophétique; *(mysterious)* sibyllin

oracy [ˈɔːrəsɪ] **N** *Formal* facultés *fpl* orales

oral [ˈɔːrəl] **ADJ 1** *(spoken)* oral **2** *Anat (of mouth)* buccal, oral; *Pharm (medicine)* à prendre par voie orale; *Psy* **the o. stage** le stade oral **3** *Ling (in phonetics)* oral

N (examen *m*) oral *m*

▸▸ ***oral contraceptive*** contraceptif *m* oral; *Law* ***oral contract*** contrat *m* verbal; ***oral exam*** (examen *m*) oral *m*; ***oral literature*** littérature *f* orale; *Parl* ***oral question*** question *f* orale; *Med* ***oral rehydration therapy*** = réhydratation par ingestion d'une solution d'eau, de glucose et de sel; ***oral sex*** rapports *mpl* bucco-génitaux; *(fellatio)* fellation *f*; *(cunnilingus)* cunnilingus *m*; ***oral tradition*** tradition *f* orale

Attention: ne pas confondre avec **aural**.

orally ['ɔːrəlɪ] **ADJ 1** *(verbally)* oralement, verbalement, de vive voix **2** *Sch* oralement; *Med* par voie orale; **to be taken o.** *(on packaging)* par voie orale; **not to be taken o.** *(on packaging)* ne pas avaler

Orange ['ɒrɪndʒ] **N 1** *Geog* **the O. (River)** l'Orange *m* **2** *Hist* **the Prince of O.** le prince d'Orange; **William of O.** Guillaume d'Orange

ADJ *(in Ireland)* orangiste *(protestant)*

►► ***Orange Lodge*** association *f* d'orangistes; ***Orange march*** défilé *m* des orangistes; ***Orange Order*** Ordre *m* des orangistes

ORANGE MARCHES

Depuis des siècles, les orangistes (membres du Loyal Orange Order) défilent dans les villes d'Irlande du Nord et dans de nombreuses villes de l'ouest de l'Écosse pour commémorer les dates-clés de l'histoire du protestantisme en Irlande. L'événement le plus important fut la bataille de la Boyne en 1690 où le protestant Guillaume d'Orange l'emporta sur Jacques II, roi catholique déposé. Les orangistes sont farouchement attachés à la Couronne britannique et s'opposent à tout rapprochement avec la République d'Irlande. Organisés en loges, ils revendiquent chaque année ce qu'ils considèrent comme leur droit à défiler, même lorsque leurs parcours les conduisent dans des quartiers catholiques, ce qui donne souvent lieu à de violents affrontements.

orange ['ɒrɪndʒ] **N 1** *(fruit)* orange *f* **2** *(drink)* boisson *f* à l'orange; **vodka and o.** vodka-orange *f* **3** *(colour)* orange *m*

ADJ 1 *(colour)* orange *(inv)*, orangé **2** *(taste)* d'orange; *(liqueur, sauce, drink)* à l'orange

►► ***orange blossom*** fleur *f* ou fleurs *fpl* d'oranger; ***the Orange Free State*** l'État *m* libre d'Orange; ***orange grove*** orangeraie *f*; ***orange juice*** jus *m* d'orange; ***orange marmalade*** marmelade *f* d'orange, confiture *f* d'orange *ou* d'oranges; ***orange peel*** écorce *f ou* peau *f* d'orange; *Fig (cellulite)* peau *f* d'orange; ***orange pekoe*** pekoe *m* orange; ***Orange prize*** = prix accordé chaque année au meilleur roman d'expression anglaise écrit par une femme; ***orange squash*** boisson *f* à l'orange; ***orange stick*** bâtonnet *m* (de) manucure; ***orange tip*** *(butterfly)* aurore *f*; ***orange tree*** oranger *m*

orangeade [ˌɒrɪndʒ'eɪd] **N** *(still)* orangeade *f*; *(fizzy)* soda *m* à l'orange

Orangeman ['ɒrɪndʒmən] *(pl* **Orangemen** [-mən]) **N** *(in Ireland)* Orangiste *m (Protestant)*

orangery ['ɒrɪndʒərɪ] *(pl* **orangeries**) **N** orangerie *f*

orang-outang [ɒˌræŋuː'tæŋ], **orang-utan** [ɒˌræŋuː'tæn] **N** orang-outan(g) *m*

oration [ɒ'reɪʃən] **N** (long) discours *m*, allocution *f*; **funeral o.** oraison *f* funèbre

orator ['ɒrətə(r)] **N** orateur(trice) *m,f*

oratorial [ˌɒrə'tɔːrɪəl], **oratorical** [ˌɒrə'tɒrɪkəl] **ADJ** *Formal* oratoire

oratorio [ˌɒrə'tɔːrɪəʊ] *(pl* **oratorios**) **N** *Mus* oratorio *m*

oratory ['ɒrətrɪ] *(pl* **oratories**) **N 1** *(eloquence)* art *m* oratoire, éloquence *f*; **a superb piece of o.** un superbe morceau de rhétorique **2** *Rel* oratoire *m*

orb [ɔːb] **N 1** *(sphere)* globe *m* **2** *Astron & Literary* orbe *m*

orbit ['ɔːbɪt] **N 1** *Astron* orbite *f*; **to enter** *or* **to go into o.** se mettre *ou* se placer en orbite; *Fam Fig* **to go into o.** *(get angry)* piquer une crise; **to put** *or* **to send a satellite into o.** mettre un satellite sur *ou* en orbite; **in o.** en orbite **2** *(domain)* orbite *f*; **the countries within Washington's o.** les pays qui se situent dans la sphère d'influence de Washington; **that's not within the o. of my responsibility** cela n'est pas de mon ressort, cela ne relève pas de ma responsabilité **3** *Anat & Phys (of eye, electron)* orbite *f*

VT *(of planet, comet)* graviter *ou* tourner autour de; **the first man to o. the Earth** le premier homme à être placé *ou* mis en orbite autour de la Terre

VI décrire une orbite

orbital ['ɔːbɪtəl] **ADJ 1** *Astron* orbital **2** *Anat (cavity)* orbitaire

N *Br (road)* périphérique *m*

►► *Br* ***orbital motorway*** (autoroute *f*) périphérique *m*; *Br* ***orbital road*** périphérique *m*; ***orbital sander*** ponceuse *f* à disque, ponceuse *f* orbitale; ***orbital velocity*** vélocité *f* orbitale

Orcadian [ɔː'keɪdɪən] **N** *(inhabitant)* habitant(e) *m,f* des Orcades; *(native)* natif(ive) *m,f* des Orcades

ADJ des Orcades

orchard ['ɔːtʃəd] **N** verger *m*

orchestra ['ɔːkɪstrə] **N 1** *(band)* orchestre *m* **2** *(in theatre, cinema)* fauteuils *mpl* d'orchestre, parterre *m*

►► ***orchestra pit*** fosse *f* d'orchestre; *Am* ***orchestra stalls*** *(in theatre, cinema)* fauteuils *mpl* d'orchestre, parterre *m*

orchestral [ɔː'kestrəl] **ADJ** d'orchestre, orchestral

►► ***orchestral music*** musique *f* orchestrale

orchestrate ['ɔːkɪstreɪt] **VT** *Mus & Fig* orchestrer

orchestration [ˌɔːke'streɪʃən] **N** *Mus & Fig* orchestration *f*

orchid ['ɔːkɪd] **N** orchidée *f*

orchis ['ɔːkɪs] **N** orchis *m*

ordain [ɔː'deɪn] **VT 1** *Rel* ordonner; **to be ordained** être ordonné, recevoir les ordres **2** *(order)* ordonner, décréter; *(decide)* dicter, décider; **the judge ordained that the prisoner should be released** le juge ordonna que le prisonnier soit relâché; **fate ordained that they should meet** le destin a voulu qu'ils se rencontrent

ordeal [ɔː'diːl] **N 1** *(difficult experience)* épreuve *f*, calvaire *m*; **to go through an o.** subir une épreuve; **it was quite an o. for him** ce fut une épreuve assez pénible pour lui; **I always find family reunions an o.** j'ai toujours considéré les réunions de famille comme un (véritable) calvaire **2** *Hist* ordalie *f*, épreuve *f* judiciaire; **o. by fire** épreuve *f* du feu

ORDER ['ɔːdə(r)]

N
- ordre **1–3, 7, 8, 10–13**
- mandat **5**
- état **9**
- espèce **10**
- instruction **3**
- commande **4**
- ordonnance **6**
- classe **10**

VT
- ordonner **1**
- organiser **3**
- commander **2**
- classer **4**

VI
- commander

N 1 *(sequence, arrangement)* ordre *m*; **in alphabetical/chronological o.** par ordre alphabétique/chronologique; **in ascending o. of importance** par ordre croissant d'importance; **can you put the figures in the right o.?** pouvez-vous classer les chiffres dans le bon ordre?; **let's do things in o.** faisons les choses en ordre; **what was the o. of events?** dans quel ordre les événements se sont-ils déroulés?; **they have two boys and a girl, in that o.** ils ont deux garçons et une fille, dans cet ordre; *Theat* **in o. of appearance** par ordre d'entrée en scène; *Cin & TV* par ordre d'apparition à l'écran; **in o. of age** par rang d'âge; **battle o.** ordre *m* de bataille

2 *(organization, tidiness)* ordre *m*; **to put one's affairs/books in o.** mettre de l'ordre dans ses affaires/livres, ranger ses affaires/livres; **the magazines are all out of o.** les magazines sont tous dérangés; **to get one's ideas in o.** mettre de l'ordre dans ses idées; **she needs to get some o. into her life** elle a besoin de mettre un peu d'ordre dans sa vie; *Fig* **to set one's house in o.** remettre de l'ordre dans ses affaires

3 *(command)* ordre *m*; *(instruction)* instruction *f*; *Mil* ordre *m*, consigne *f*; **to give sb orders to do s[th]** ordonner à qn de faire qch; **to give the o. to op[en] fire** donner l'ordre d'ouvrir le feu; **the Queen ga[ve] the o. for the prisoner to be executed** la reine o[r]donna que le prisonnier soit exécuté; **Har[ry] loves giving orders** Harry adore donner des o[r]dres; **we have orders to wait here** on a reçu l'ord[re] d'attendre ici; **our orders are to...** nous avons l'o[r]dre de...; **I'm just following orders** je ne fa[is] qu'exécuter les ordres; **and that's an o.!** et c'e[st] un ordre!; **I don't have to take orders from you** [je] n'ai pas d'ordres à recevoir de vous; **orders a[re] orders** les ordres sont les ordres; **on my o., li[ne] up in twos** à mon commandement, mettez-vo[us] en rangs par deux; **on doctor's orders** sur ord[re] du médecin; **to be under sb's orders** être sous l[es] ordres de qn; **I am under orders to say nothing** j['ai] reçu l'ordre de ne rien dire; **by o. of the King** p[ar] ordre du roi, de par le roi; **until further orders** ju[s]qu'à nouvel ordre; *Fin* **o. to sell** ordre *m* de vent[e]; *Fin* **o. to pay** mandat *m ou* ordonnance *f* de paiement

4 *Com (request for goods)* commande *f*; *(goo[ds] ordered)* marchandises *fpl* commandées; *A[m] (portion)* part *f*; **to place an o. for sth** pass[er] (une) commande de qch; **to place an o. with s[b]**, **to give sb an o.** passer une commande à q[n], commander qch à qn; **another firm got the o.** [ils] ont passé la commande auprès d'une aut[re] compagnie; **the books are on o.** les livres o[nt] été commandés; **your o. has now arrived** vot[re] commande est arrivée; **to fill an o.** exécut[er] une commande; **as per o.** conformément à vot[re] commande; **can I take your o.?** *(in restauran[t])* avez-vous choisi?; **have you given your o.?** *(in re[staurant])* est-ce que vous avez commandé?; *A[m]* **an o. of French fries** une portion de frites

5 *Fin (money)* **o.** mandat *m*; **pay to the o. of Jones** payez à l'ordre de A. Jones; **pay A. Jones [or] o.** payer à A. Jones ou à son ordre; **cheque to o.** chèque *m* à ordre

6 *Law* ordonnance *f*, arrêté *m*; **he was serve[d] with an o. for the seizure of his property** il a reç[u] une ordonnance pour la saisie de ses biens

7 *(discipline, rule)* ordre *m*, discipline *f*; *(in mee[t]ing)* ordre *m*; **to keep o.** *(police)* maintenir l'ordr[e]; *Sch* maintenir la discipline; **children need to b[e] kept in o.** les enfants ont besoin de disciplin[e]; **to restore o.** rétablir l'ordre; **to call sb to o.** rapp[e]ler qn à l'ordre; **to be ruled out of o.** être en infraction avec le règlement; **o.! de l'ordre!**; **he's out [of] o.** ce qu'il a dit/fait était déplacé

8 *(system)* ordre *m* établi; **the old o.** l'ordre a[n]cien; **in the o. of things** dans l'ordre des chose[s]; *Pol* **o. of the day** ordre *m* du jour; **to be the o. [of] the day** *(common)* être à l'ordre du jour; *(fashio[n]able)* être au goût du jour

9 *(functioning state)* **in working o.** en état de ma[r]che *ou* de fonctionnement; **in good/perfect o.** e[n] bon/parfait état

10 *(class)* classe *f*, ordre *m*; *(rank)* ordre *m*; *(kin[d])* espèce *f*, genre *m*; **the lower orders** les ordres i[n]férieurs; **research work of the highest o.** un trava[il] de recherche de tout premier ordre; *Br* **a crook [of] the first o.** un escroc de grande envergure; **que[s]tions of a different o.** des questions d'un autre o[r]dre; **o. of magnitude** ordre *m* de grandeur; **disaster/a project/an investment of this o. (of ma[g]nitude)** un désastre/un projet/des investiss[e]ments de cette envergure

11 *(decoration)* ordre *m*

12 *Rel* ordre *m*; **the O. of St Benedict** l'ordre d[e] saint Benoît

13 *Archit, Bot & Zool* ordre *m*

VT 1 *(command)* ordonner; **to o. sb to do sth** o[r]donner à qn de faire qch; *Mil* donner l'ordre à q[n] de faire qch; **the Queen ordered that the prison[er] (should) be executed** la reine donna l'ordre d'exécuter le prisonnier; **the doctor ordered him to re[st] for three weeks** le médecin lui a prescrit trois se[maines] de repos; *Law* **he was ordered to pay cos[ts]** il a été condamné aux dépens; **the minister o[r]dered the drug to be banned** le ministre a o[r]donné de faire retirer le médicament de vente; **to o. sb back/in/out** donner à qn l'ord[re] de reculer/d'entrer/de sortir; **we were ordere[d]**

out of the room on nous a ordonné de quitter la pièce; **she ordered the children to bed** elle a ordonné aux enfants d'aller se coucher; **they were ordered (to return) home** on leur donna *ou* ils reçurent l'ordre de regagner leurs foyers

2 *Com (meal, goods)* commander; **he ordered himself a beer** il a commandé une bière

3 *(organize ▸ society)* organiser; *(▸ ideas, thoughts)* mettre de l'ordre dans; *(▸ affairs)* régler, mettre en ordre

4 *Bot & Zool* classer

VI commander, passer une commande; **would you like to o. now?** *(in restaurant)* voulez-vous commander maintenant?

• **by order of** PREP par ordre de; **by o. of the Court** sur décision du tribunal

• **in order** ADJ **1** *(valid)* en règle

2 *(acceptable)* approprié, admissible; **it is quite in o. for you to leave** rien ne s'oppose à ce que vous partiez; **I think lunch is in o.** je pense qu'il est temps de faire une pause pour le déjeuner; **an apology is in o.** des excuses s'imposent

• **in order that** CONJ afin que; **in o. that no one goes home empty-handed** afin que nul ne rentre chez soi les mains vides

• **in order to** CONJ afin de; **in o. to simplify things** afin de simplifier les choses; **in o. not to upset you** pour éviter de vous faire de la peine

• **in the order of, of the order of,** *Am* **on the order of** PREP de l'ordre de; **a sum** *Br* **in** *or* **of** *or Am* **on the o. of £500** une somme de l'ordre de 500 livres

• **out of order** ADJ *(machine, TV)* en panne; *(phone)* en dérangement; **out of o.** *(sign)* hors service, en panne

• **to order** ADV sur commande; **I can't do it to o.** ça ne se commande pas; *also Fig* **to be made to o.** être fait sur commande; **he had a suit made to o.** il s'est fait faire un costume sur mesures

▸▸ ***order book*** carnet *m* de commandes; **our o. books are empty/full** nos carnets de commandes sont vides/pleins; ***order of business*** ordre *m* du jour; ***order cycle time*** durée *f* du cycle de commande; ***order form*** bon *m* de commande; ***the Order of the Garter*** l'ordre *m* de la Jarretière; ***the Order of Merit*** l'ordre *m* du Mérite; ***order number*** numéro *m* de commande; *Pol* ***order paper*** (feuille *f* de l')ordre *m* du jour

▸ **order about, order around** VT SEP commander; **he likes ordering people about** il adore régenter son monde; **I refuse to be ordered about!** je n'ai pas d'ordres à recevoir!

▸ **order in** VT SEP **1** *(supplies)* commander **2** *(troops)* faire intervenir

▸ **order off** VT SEP *Sport* expulser

▸ **order up** VT SEP **1** *(troops, air support etc)* faire monter **2** *(stationery supplies, round of drinks etc)* commander

---

order-driven ADJ *St Exch (market)* dirigé par les ordres

ordered ['ɔ:dəd] ADJ ordonné; *(in good order)* en bon ordre; **an o. life** une vie régulière *ou* réglée

orderer ['ɔ:dərə(r)] N **France is the biggest o. of these parts** la France est le principal acheteur de ces pièces détachées

orderliness ['ɔ:dəlɪnɪs] N **1** *(of room, desk)* (bon) ordre *m* **2** *(of person, lifestyle, behaviour)* méticulosité *f* **3** *(of crowd, pupils)* discipline *f*, bonne conduite *f*

orderly ['ɔ:dəlɪ] *(pl* **orderlies***)* ADJ **1** *(tidy ▸ room)* ordonné, rangé; **a very o. kitchen** une cuisine très bien rangée **2** *(organized ▸ person, mind, lifestyle)* ordonné, méthodique; **try to work in an o. way** essayez de travailler méthodiquement; **an o. retreat/withdrawal** une retraite/un repli ordonné(e) **3** *(well-behaved)* ordonné, discipliné; **an o. crowd** une foule disciplinée; **in case of fire, leave the building in an o. fashion** en cas d'incendie, quitter les lieux sans précipitation

N 1 *Mil* officier *m* d'ordonnance **2** *Med* aide-infirmier *m*

▸▸ *Br Mil* ***orderly officer*** officier *m* de permanence

ordinal ['ɔ:dɪnəl] N ordinal *m*

ADJ ordinal

▸▸ ***ordinal number*** nombre *m* ordinal

ordinance ['ɔ:dɪnəns] N *Am Law* arrêté *m* municipal, arrêté *m* préfectoral

ordinand ['ɔ:dɪnænd] N *Rel* ordinand *m*

ordinarily ['ɔ:dənrəlɪ, *Am* ˌɔ:rdən'erəlɪ] ADV **1** *(in an ordinary way)* ordinairement, d'ordinaire; **a more than o. gifted child** un enfant d'une intelligence supérieure à la normale; **the questions were more than o. difficult** les questions étaient plus difficiles que d'ordinaire *ou* qu'à l'accoutumée **2** *(normally)* normalement, en temps normal; **isn't she due at 5 o'clock? – well, o., she would be** ne doit-elle pas être là *ou* arriver à 5 heures? – oui, normalement

ordinary ['ɔ:dənrɪ] ADJ **1** *(usual)* ordinaire, habituel; *(normal)* normal; **the o. run of things** le cours ordinaire *ou* normal des événements; **she remembered it as just an o. day** elle s'en souvenait comme d'un jour ordinaire; **2** *(average)* ordinaire, moyen; *Fam* **Ewan was just an o. guy before he got involved in films** Ewan était un type comme les autres avant de faire du cinéma; **Miss Brodie was no o. teacher** Miss Brodie était un professeur peu banal *ou* qui sortait de l'ordinaire **3** *(commonplace)* ordinaire; *Pej* quelconque; **they're very o. people** ce sont des gens très ordinaires; **it's a very o.-looking car** c'est une voiture qui n'a rien de spécial; **she's a very o.-looking girl** c'est une fille quelconque

N 1 *Rel* **the O. of the mass** l'ordinaire *m* de la messe **2** *Br Admin* **physician in o. to the king** médecin *m* (attitré) du roi **3** *Her* pièce *f* honorable

• **out of the ordinary** ADJ **as a pianist, she's really out of the o.** c'est vraiment une pianiste exceptionnelle *ou* hors du commun; **nothing out of the o. ever happens here** il ne se passe jamais rien de bien extraordinaire ici

▸▸ ***ordinary activities*** *Com* activités *fpl* ordinaires; *Acct (balance sheet item)* opérations *fpl* courantes; *Fin* ***ordinary creditor*** créancier(ère) *m,f* ordinaire; *Br* ***ordinary degree*** ≃ licence *f* sans mention *ou* avec mention passable; *Scot Formerly Sch* ***Ordinary grade*** = premier diplôme de l'enseignement secondaire écossais; *Formerly Sch* ***Ordinary level*** *(in England, Wales, Northern Ireland)* = examen qui sanctionnait autrefois la fin des études au niveau de la seconde, ≃ BEPC *m*; ***ordinary seaman*** matelot *m* breveté; *Br St Exch* ***ordinary share*** action *f* ordinaire; *Br St Exch* ***ordinary share capital*** capital *m* en actions ordinaires

ordinate ['ɔ:dənət] N ordonnée *f*

ordination [ˌɔ:dɪ'neɪʃən] N ordination *f*

ordnance ['ɔ:dnəns] N **1** *(supplies)* (service *m* de l')équipement *m* militaire; *Br* **Royal Army O. Corps,** *Am* **O. Service** Service *m* du Matériel **2** *(artillery)* artillerie *f*; **piece of o.** bouche *f* à feu, pièce *f* d'artillerie

▸▸ ***ordnance corps*** service *m* du matériel, ≃ train *m*; ***ordnance factory*** usine *f* d'artillerie; *Br* ***Ordnance Survey*** service *m* national de cartographie, ≃ IGN *m*; *Br* ***Ordnance Survey map*** carte *f* d'état-major

ordure ['ɔ:djʊə(r)] N *Literary* excrément *m*

Ore *(written abbr* **Oregon***)* Oregon *m*

ore [ɔ:(r)] N minerai *m*; **copper o.** minerai *m* de cuivre

▸▸ ***ore deposit*** gisement *m* de minerai

Oreg *(written abbr* **Oregon***)* Oregon *m*

oregano [*Br* ˌɒrɪ'gɑ:nəʊ, *Am* ə'regənəʊ] N *Bot & Culin* origan *m*

.org [ɔ:g] *Comput* = abréviation désignant les organisations à but non lucratif dans les adresses électroniques

organ ['ɔ:gən] N **1** *Mus* orgue *m*; *(large)* (grandes) orgues *fpl*

2 *Anat* organe *m*; **the organs of speech** les organes *mpl* phonatoires *ou* de la parole

3 *Euph or Hum (penis)* membre *m*

4 *Fig (means)* organe *m*, instrument *m*; *(mouthpiece)* organe *m*, porte-parole *m inv*; **the courts are the organs of justice** les tribunaux sont les organes *ou* les instruments de la justice; **the official o. of the Party** le porte-parole officiel du Parti

▸▸ ***organ builder*** facteur *m* d'orgues; ***organ donor*** donneur(euse) *m,f* d'organes; ***organ grinder*** joueur(euse) *m,f* d'orgue de Barbarie; *Br Fam* **I want to speak to the o. grinder, not the monkey!** je veux parler au responsable, pas au sous-fifre!; ***organ loft*** tribune *f* d'orgue; ***organ pipe*** tuyau *m* d'orgue; ***organ screen*** jubé *m*; ***organ stop*** jeu *m* d'orgue; ***organ transplant*** transplantation *f* d'organe

organdie, organdy ['ɔ:gəndɪ] *(pl* **organdies***)* N organdi *m*

COMP d'organdi, en organdi

organic [ɔ:'gænɪk] ADJ **1** *Biol & Chem* organique **2** *(natural ▸ food, produce)* biologique **3** *(structural)* organique; *(fundamental)* organique, fondamental; **an o. part** une partie intégrante; **an o. whole** un ensemble systématique, un tout intégré

▸▸ ***organic architecture*** architecture *f* organique; ***organic change*** changement *m* organique; ***organic chemist*** organicien(enne) *m,f*; ***organic chemistry*** chimie *f* organique; ***organic compound*** composé *m* organique; ***organic disease*** maladie *f* organique; ***organic farm*** ferme *f* biologique; ***organic farming*** culture *f* biologique; ***organic fertilizer*** engrais *m* organique; *Econ* ***organic growth*** croissance *f* interne; ***organic life*** vie *f* organique

> Note that the French word **organique** is never used in relation to food or farming.

organically [ɔ:'gænɪklɪ] ADV **1** *Biol & Chem* organiquement **2** *(naturally ▸ farm, garden)* avec des engrais organiques; **o. grown** cultivé sans engrais chimiques, biologique **3** *(structurally)* organiquement

organigram [ɔ:'gænɪgræm] N organigramme *m*

organism ['ɔ:gənɪzəm] N *Biol* organisme *m*

organist ['ɔ:gənɪst] N organiste *mf*

organization, -isation [ˌɔ:gənaɪ'zeɪʃən] N **1** *(organizing)* organisation *f*; **to have a flair for o.** avoir le sens de l'organisation; *Ind* **o. and method** organisation *f* scientifique du travail, OST *f*

2 *(association)* organisation *f*, association *f*; *(official body)* organisme *m*, organisation *f*; **a political o.** une organisation politique; **a charitable o.** une œuvre de bienfaisance

3 *Admin (personnel)* cadres *mpl*

4 *Ind (of labour)* syndicalisation *f*

▸▸ ***Organization of American States*** Organisation *f* des États américains; ***organization chart*** organigramme *m*; ***Organization for Economic Cooperation and Development*** Organisation *f* de Coopération et de Développement économique; ***organization man*** = employé ou cadre qui se dévoue entièrement à la société pour laquelle il travaille; ***Organization of Petroleum Exporting Countries*** Organisation *f* des pays exportateurs de pétrole; ***Organization for Security and Cooperation in Europe*** Organisation *f* sur la sécurité et la coopération en Europe; ***organization tree*** organigramme *m* en arborescence

organizational, -isational [ˌɔ:gənaɪ'zeɪʃənəl] ADJ *(skills, methods)* organisationnel, d'organisation; *(expenses)* d'organisation; *(change)* dans l'organisation, structurel; **the concert turned out to be an o. nightmare** l'organisation du concert fut un véritable cauchemar

▸▸ ***organizational buyer*** acheteur *m* (pour une organisation); ***organizational chart*** organigramme *m*

organizationally, -isationally [ˌɔ:gənaɪ'zeɪʃənəlɪ] ADV du point de vue de l'organisation; **he doesn't get involved o. in the project** il n'est pas impliqué au niveau de l'organisation du projet

organize, -ise ['ɔ:gənaɪz] VT **1** *(sort out, put into groups)* organiser; **to get organized** s'organiser; **he doesn't know how to o. himself** il ne sait pas s'organiser; **to o. one's thoughts** mettre de l'ordre dans ses idées; **she's good at organizing people** elle est douée pour la gestion du personnel **2** *(arrange, bring about ▸ concert, party etc)* organiser; *(▸ transport, food, accommodation)* s'occuper de; *(▸ money)* s'occuper de trouver; **I've organized a visit to a dairy for them** j'ai organisé la visite d'une laiterie à leur intention; **she organized it so that we got in free** elle s'est arrangée pour que nous puissions entrer sans payer; **don't worry, it's all organized** ne t'inquiète pas, tout est organisé **3** *Ind* syndiquer

VI *Ind* se syndiquer

organized, -ised ['ɔ:gənaɪzd] ADJ **1** *(trip)* organisé; **we went on an o. tour of Scottish castles**

nous avons visité les châteaux écossais en voyage organisé **2** *(unionized)* syndiqué **3** *(orderly)* organisé; *(methodical)* méthodique
▸▸ ***organized crime*** crime *m* organisé; ***organized labour*** main-d'œuvre *f* syndiquée; ***organized religion*** religion *f* organisée

organizer, -iser ['ɔːgənaɪzə(r)] **N 1** *(person)* organisateur(trice) *m,f*; **she's a born o.** elle a le sens de l'organisation, c'est une organisatrice née **2** *(diary)* organiseur *m*; *(electronic)* agenda *m* électronique **3** *Comput (software)* organiseur *m*

organizing, -ising ['ɔːgənaɪzɪŋ] **N** organisation *f*
▸▸ ***organizing committee*** comité *m* d'organisation

organophosphate [ˌɔːgənəʊ'fɒsfeɪt] *Chem* **N** organophosphoré *m*
ADJ organophosphoré

orgasm ['ɔːgæzəm] **N** orgasme *m*; **to have an o.** avoir un orgasme

orgasmic [ɔː'gæzmɪk] **ADJ** orgasmique, orgastique; *Fam Fig (food, experience etc)* jouissif

orgiastic [ˌɔːdʒɪ'æstɪk] **ADJ** orgiaque

orgy ['ɔːdʒɪ] *(pl* **orgies***)* **N** orgie *f*; **a drunken o.** une beuverie; **orgies** *(in ancient Greece, Rome)* orgies *fpl*, bacchanales *fpl*; *Fig* **an o. of killing** une orgie de meurtres

oriel ['ɔːrɪəl] **N** oriel *m*
▸▸ ***oriel window*** oriel *m*

orient ['ɔːrɪənt] **VT** orienter; **to o. oneself** s'orienter; **our firm is very much oriented towards the American market** notre société est très orientée vers le marché américain

oriental [ˌɔːrɪ'entəl] **ADJ** oriental
• **Oriental N** Asiatique *mf*
▸▸ ***oriental rug*** tapis *m* d'Orient

orientalist [ˌɔːrɪ'entəlɪst] **N** orientaliste *mf*

orientate ['ɔːrɪənteɪt] **VT** *Br* orienter; **to o. oneself** s'orienter; **the course is very much orientated towards the sciences** le cours est très orienté vers *ou* axé sur les sciences

orientation [ˌɔːrɪen'teɪʃən] **N** orientation *f*; **James is in charge of student o.** James est responsable de l'orientation des étudiants

oriented ['ɔːrɪentɪd] **ADJ** orienté

-oriented ['ɔːrɪentɪd] **SUFF** orienté vers…, axé sur…; **ours is a money-o. society** c'est l'argent qui mène notre société; **she's very work-o.** elle est très axée sur son travail; **pupil-o. teaching** enseignement adapté aux besoins des élèves; **profit-o.** axé sur le profit; **youth-o.** qui s'adresse à la jeunesse

orienteering [ˌɔːrɪen'tɪərɪŋ] **N** course *f* d'orientation

orifice ['ɒrɪfɪs] **N** orifice *m*

origami [ˌɒrɪ'gɑːmɪ] **N** origami *m*

origin ['ɒrɪdʒɪn] **N 1** *(source)* origine *f*; **the o. of the Nile** la source du Nil; **what's the o. of that word?** quelle est l'origine de ce mot?; **country of o.** pays *m* d'origine; **of unknown o.** d'origine inconnue; **this wine is of Australian o.** ce vin est d'origine australienne; **the present troubles have their o. in the proposed land reform** le projet de réforme agraire est à l'origine des troubles actuels; **the song is Celtic in o.** la chanson est d'origine celte **2** *(ancestry)* origine *f*; **he is of Canadian o.** il est d'origine canadienne; **to be of humble origins** avoir des origines modestes; **they can trace their origins back to the time of the Norman conquest** ils ont réussi à remonter dans leur arbre généalogique jusqu'à l'époque de la conquête normande **3** *Anat (of muscle)* attache *f*
▸▸ *Mktg* ***origin of goods label*** marque *f* d'origine

original [ɒ'rɪdʒɪnəl] **ADJ 1** *(initial)* premier, d'origine, initial; **the o. inhabitants of the country** les premiers habitants du pays; **the o. meaning of the word** le sens originel du mot; **my o. intention was to drive there** ma première intention *ou* mon intention initiale était d'y aller en voiture; **the fabric has lost its o. lustre** l'étoffe a perdu son éclat d'origine; **most of the o. 600 copies have been destroyed** la plupart des 600 exemplaires originaux ont été détruits; **to translate from the o. German** traduire d'après le texte allemand original; **the o. portrait by Rubens** le portrait original peint par Rubens **2** *(unusual, innovative)* original; *(strange)* singulier; **she has an o. approach to child-rearing** sa conception de l'éducation est originale
3 *(new ▸ play, writing)* original, inédit; *TV & Cin* **based on an o. idea by…** d'après une idée originale de…
N 1 *(painting, book, document)* original *m*; *Fin (of bill of exchange)* primata *m*; **the film was shown in the o.** le film a été projeté en version originale; **I prefer to read Proust in the o.** je préfère lire Proust dans le texte
2 *(model ▸ of hero, character)* **Catherine was the o. of the novel's heroine** Catherine inspira le personnage de l'héroïne du roman
3 *(unusual person)* original(e) *m,f*, excentrique *mf*; **she's a real o.** elle est vraiment spéciale *ou* originale
▸▸ *Fin* ***original capital*** capital *m* d'origine; *Fin* ***original cost*** coût *m* initial; *Acct* ***original document*** pièce *f* comptable; ***original edition*** édition *f* originale; *Mktg* ***original packaging*** emballage *m* d'origine; *Rel* ***original sin*** péché *m* originel; *Fin* ***original value*** valeur *f* initiale *ou* d'origine

> When translating **original**, note that the French words **originel** and **original** are not interchangeable.

originality [əˌrɪdʒɪ'nælətɪ] *(pl* **originalities***)* **N** originalité *f*

originally [ə'rɪdʒɪnəlɪ] **ADV 1** *(initially)* à l'origine, au début, initialement; **this room was o. the kitchen** à l'origine, cette pièce servait de cuisine; **o., I had planned to go to Greece** initialement *ou* au début, j'avais l'intention d'aller en Grèce; **where do you come from o.?** d'où êtes-vous originaire?; **that's what I o. thought** c'est ce que je pensais au début *ou* au départ; **I o. heard about it in Spain** c'est en Espagne que j'en ai entendu parler pour la première fois **2** *(unusually, inventively)* d'une façon *ou* d'une manière originale, originalement

originate [ə'rɪdʒɪneɪt] **VI 1** *(idea, rumour)* **to o. in** avoir *ou* trouver son origine dans; **to o. from** tirer son origine de; **where did the rumour o. from?** qu'est-ce qui a donné naissance à cette rumeur?; **the conflict originated in the towns** le conflit est né dans les villes; **this information originates from an official source** le renseignement émane d'une source officielle; **I wonder how that saying originated** je me demande d'où vient ce dicton **2** *(goods)* provenir; **the cocaine originates from South America** la cocaïne provient d'Amérique du Sud **3** *(person)* **he originates from Sydney** il est originaire de Sydney
VT *(give rise to)* être à l'origine de, donner naissance à; *(be author of)* être l'auteur de; **the experience originated the story of the invisible man** cette expérience donna naissance à l'histoire de l'homme invisible

originator [ə'rɪdʒɪneɪtə(r)] **N** *(of crime)* auteur *m*; *(of idea)* initiateur(trice) *m,f*, auteur *m*

oriole ['ɔːrɪəʊl] **N** *Orn* **1** *(European)* loriot *m* **2** *(North American)* troupiale *m*, *Can* oriole *m*

Orkney Islands ['ɔːknɪ-], **Orkneys** ['ɔːknɪz] **NPL** **the O.** les Orcades *fpl*

ormolu ['ɔːməluː] **N** chrysocale *m*, bronze *m* doré
COMP *(clock)* en chrysocale, en bronze doré

ornament N ['ɔːnəmənt] **1** *(decorative object)* objet *m* décoratif, bibelot *m*; *(jewellery)* colifichet *m* **2** *(embellishment)* ornement *m*; **rich in o.** richement orné **3** *Mus* ornement *m*
VT ['ɔːnəment] orner; **the ceiling was ornamented with frescoes** le plafond était orné de fresques; **his style is highly ornamented** il a un style très fleuri

ornamental [ˌɔːnə'mentəl] **ADJ** *(decorative)* ornemental, décoratif; *(plant)* ornemental; *(garden)* d'agrément; **o. lake** pièce *f* d'eau

ornamentation [ˌɔːnəmen'teɪʃən] **N** ornementation *f*

ornate [ɔː'neɪt] **ADJ** *(decoration)* (très) orné; *(style)* orné, fleuri; *(lettering)* orné

ornately [ɔː'neɪtlɪ] **ADV** d'une façon très ornée; **o. decorated room** pièce richement décorée; **o. carved furniture** meubles ornés *ou* rehaussés de nombreuses sculptures

ornery ['ɔːnərɪ] **ADJ** *Am Fam* **1** *(nasty)* méchant **an o. trick** un sale tour **2** *(stubborn)* obstiné, en têté **3** *(bad-tempered)* rouspéteur

ornithological [ˌɔːnɪθə'lɒdʒɪkəl] **ADJ** ornithologique

ornithologist [ˌɔːnɪ'θɒlədʒɪst] **N** ornithologiste *mf*, ornithologue *mf*

ornithology [ˌɔːnɪ'θɒlədʒɪ] **N** ornithologie *f*

orotund ['ɒrətʌnd] **ADJ** *Formal (voice)* sonore *(style)* ampoulé

orphan ['ɔːfən] **N 1** *(person)* orphelin(e) *m,f*; **to be left an o.** se retrouver *ou* devenir orphelin **2** *Typ & Comput* (ligne *f*) orpheline *f*
ADJ orphelin; **an o. child** un orphelin, une orpheline
VT to be orphaned se retrouver *ou* devenir orphelin; **they were orphaned by the war** ils ont perdu leurs parents pendant la guerre
▸▸ *Pharm* ***orphan drug*** médicament *m* orphelin

orphanage ['ɔːfənɪdʒ] **N** orphelinat *m*

Orpheus ['ɔːfɪəs] **PR N** *Myth* Orphée

orthodontics [ˌɔːθə'dɒntɪks] **N** *(UNCOUNT)* orthodontie *f*

orthodontist [ˌɔːθə'dɒntɪst] **N** orthodontiste *mf*

orthodox ['ɔːθədɒks] **ADJ** orthodoxe
▸▸ ***the Orthodox Church*** l'Église *f* orthodoxe

orthodoxy ['ɔːθədɒksɪ] *(pl* **orthodoxies***)* **N** orthodoxie *f*

orthogonal [ɔː'θɒgənəl] **ADJ** *Math* orthogonal
▸▸ ***orthogonal projection*** projection *f* orthogonale

orthographic [ˌɔːθə'græfɪk], **orthographical** [ˌɔːθə'græfɪkəl] **ADJ** orthographique

orthographically [ˌɔːθə'græfɪkəlɪ] **ADV** orthographiquement

orthography [ɔː'θɒgrəfɪ] *(pl* **orthographies***)* **N 1** *(spelling)* orthographe *f* **2** *Math* projection *f* orthogonale

orthopaedic, orthopaedics *Br* = **orthopedic, orthopedics**

orthopedic [ˌɔːθə'piːdɪk] **ADJ** orthopédique
▸▸ ***orthopedic surgeon*** chirurgien(enne) *m,f* orthopédiste; ***orthopedic surgery*** chirurgie *f* orthopédique

orthopedics [ˌɔːθə'piːdɪks] **N** *(UNCOUNT)* orthopédie *f*

orthoptist [ɔː'θɒptɪst] **N** orthoptiste *mf*

ortolan ['ɔːtələn] **N** *Orn* ortolan *m*

Orwellian [ɔː'welɪən] **ADJ** orwellien

oryx ['ɒrɪks] *(pl* **inv** *or* **oryxes***)* **N** *Zool* oryx *m*

OS[1] [ˌəʊ'es] **N 1** *(abbr* **ordinary seaman***)* matelot *m* breveté **2** *Comput (abbr* **operating system***)* système *m* d'exploitation **3** *(abbr* **Ordnance Survey***)* ≃ IGN *m*

OS[2] *(written abbr* **outsize***)* grande taille *f*

Oscar® ['ɒskə(r)] **N** *Cin* oscar *m*; **the Oscars** *(ceremony)* la cérémonie des oscars, les oscars *mpl*

Oscar-winning ADJ an O. picture un film primé aux oscars; **in her O. role** dans le rôle qui lui a valu l'oscar; *Fam Fig* **she really put on an O. performance!** elle a vraiment fait un numéro d'anthologie!

OSCE [ˌəʊesˌsiː'iː] **N** *(abbr* **Organization for Security and Cooperation in Europe***)* OSCE *f*

oscillate ['ɒsɪleɪt] **VI 1** *Elec & Phys* osciller **2** *(person)* osciller; **his mood oscillated between gloom and elation** son humeur oscillait entre la mélancolie et l'exultation
VT faire osciller

oscillating ['ɒsɪleɪtɪŋ] **ADJ** oscillateur

oscillation [ˌɒsɪ'leɪʃən] **N** oscillation *f*

oscillator ['ɒsɪleɪtə(r)] **N** oscillateur *m*

oscillatory [ɒ'sɪlətrɪ] **ADJ** oscillatoire

oscillogram [ɒ'sɪləgræm] **N** oscillogramme *m*

oscillograph [ɒ'sɪləgrɑːf] **N** oscillographe *m*

oscilloscope [ɒ'sɪləskəʊp] **N** oscilloscope *m*

osculate ['ɒskjʊleɪt] **VT** *Br Hum (kiss)* donner un baiser à, embrasser
VI 1 *Br Hum (kiss)* s'embrasser **2** *Math* **a curve that osculates with a line** une courbe osculatrice à une ligne

osculation [ˌɒskjʊ'leɪʃən] **N** *Math* osculation *f*

osier [ˈəʊzɪə(r)] N osier *m*
COMP *(basket)* d'osier
▸▸ *osier bed* oseraie *f*

osmosis [ɒzˈməʊsɪs] N *Chem & Fig* osmose *f*

osmotic [ɒzˈmɒtɪk] ADJ *Chem* osmotique
▸▸ *osmotic pressure* pression *f* osmotique

osprey [ˈɒsprɪ] N *Br* 1 *Orn* balbuzard *m*, *Can* aigle *m* pêcheur 2 *(feather)* aigrette *f*

ossicle [ˈɒsɪkəl] N *Anat & Zool* osselet *m*

ossification [ˌɒsɪfɪˈkeɪʃən] N ossification *f*

ossified [ˈɒsɪfaɪd] ADJ *(cartilage)* ossifié; *Fig (mind, ideas, social system)* sclérosé; *(person)* à l'esprit sclérosé; **the o. old fools who run this country** les vieux fossiles abrutis qui dirigent ce pays

ossify [ˈɒsɪfaɪ] *(pt & pp* **ossified***)* VT ossifier
VI *(cartilage)* s'ossifier; *Fig (government, mind)* se scléroser

ossuary [ˈɒsjʊərɪ] *(pl* **ossuaries***)* N *(vault)* ossuaire *m*; *(urn)* urne *f* (funéraire)

Ostend [ɒsˈtend] N Ostende

ostensible [ɒˈstensəbəl] ADJ *(apparent)* apparent; *(pretended)* prétendu; *(so-called)* soi-disant *(inv)*; **her o. reason for not coming was illness** elle a prétendu être malade pour éviter de venir

> Note that the French adjective **ostensible** is a false friend and is never a translation for the English adjective **ostensible**. It means **conspicuous**.

ostensibly [ɒˈstensəblɪ] ADV *(apparently)* apparemment; *(supposedly)* prétendument, soi-disant; **o. they are diplomats** ils se font passer pour des diplomates; **he left early, o. because he was sick** il est parti tôt, prétextant une indisposition *ou* soi-disant parce qu'il était souffrant

> Note that the French adverb **ostensiblement** is a false friend and is never a translation for the English adverb **ostensibly**. It means **conspicuously**.

ostentation [ˌɒstənˈteɪʃən] N ostentation *f*

ostentatious [ˌɒstənˈteɪʃəs] ADJ 1 *(showy ▸ display, appearance, decor)* ostentatoire, plein d'ostentation; *(▸ manner, behaviour)* prétentieux, ostentatoire 2 *(exaggerated)* exagéré, surfait; **with o. dislike** avec un mépris exagéré

ostentatiously [ˌɒstənˈteɪʃəslɪ] ADV avec ostentation; **to display sth o.** faire ostentation de qch; **to be o. rich** faire ostentation de sa richesse

ostentatiousness [ˌɒstənˈteɪʃəsnɪs] N ostentation *f*

osteoarthritis [ˌɒstɪəʊɑːˈθraɪtɪs] N *(UNCOUNT) Med* ostéoarthrite *f*

osteomyelitis [ˌɒstɪəʊmaɪˈlaɪtɪs] N *(UNCOUNT) Med* ostéomyélite *f*

osteopath [ˈɒstɪəpæθ] N ostéopathe *mf*

osteopathy [ˌɒstɪˈɒpəθɪ] N ostéopathie *f*

osteoplasty [ˈɒstɪəʊˌplæstɪ] N *Med* ostéoplastie *f*

osteoporosis [ˌɒstɪəʊpəˈrəʊsɪs] N *(UNCOUNT) Med* ostéoporose *f*

ostler [ˈɒslə(r)] N *Br Arch* valet *m* d'écurie

ostracism [ˈɒstrəsɪzəm] N ostracisme *m*

ostracize, -ise [ˈɒstrəsaɪz] VT frapper d'ostracisme, ostraciser; **he was ostracized by his workmates** ses collègues l'ont mis en quarantaine

ostrich [ˈɒstrɪtʃ] N *Orn* autruche *f*
▸▸ *ostrich farm* élevage *m* d'autruches; *ostrich feather* plume *f* d'autruche

OT [ˌəʊˈtiː] N 1 *(abbr* **Old Testament***)* AT *m* 2 *(abbr* **occupational therapy***)* ergothérapie *f*

OTC [ˌəʊtiːˈsiː] N *Br Sch (abbr* **Officer Training Corps***)* corps *m* de formation des officiers
ADJ *St Exch (abbr* **over the counter***)* hors cote

OTE [ˌəʊtiːˈiː] NPL *Mktg (abbr* **on-target earnings***)* salaire *m* de base plus commissions

OTH [ˌəʊtiːˈeɪtʃ] N *Mktg (abbr* **opportunity to hear***)* ODE *f*

OTHER [ˈʌðə(r)] ADJ 1 *(different)* autre, différent; **it's the same in o. countries** c'est la même chose dans les autres pays; **I had no o. choice** je n'avais pas le choix *ou* pas d'autre solution; **any o. book** tout autre livre; **by o. means** par d'autres moyens; **he doesn't respect o. people's property** il ne respecte pas le bien d'autrui; **it always happens to o. people** cela n'arrive qu'aux autres; **can't we discuss it some o. time?** on ne peut pas en parler plus tard?; **for this reason, if for no o.** pour cette raison, à défaut d'une autre; **in o. times** autrefois, à une autre époque; **the o. world** l'autre monde *m*, l'au-delà *m*
2 *(second of two)* autre; **give me the o. one** donnez-moi l'autre; **the o. woman/man** *(in relationship)* l'autre
3 *(additional)* autre; **can you get some o. cups?** pouvez-vous aller chercher d'autres tasses?; **some o. people came** d'autres personnes sont arrivées
4 *(remaining)* autre; **the o. three men** les trois autres hommes
5 *(in expressions of time)* autre; **the o. day/morning/month/week** l'autre jour/matin/mois/semaine
6 *(opposite)* **on the o. side of the room/of the river** de l'autre côté de la pièce/de la rivière; **a voice at the o. end (of the telephone)** une voix à l'autre bout (du fil)
PRON 1 *(additional person, thing)* autre; **he and two others got the sack** lui et deux autres ont été renvoyés; **some succeed, others fail** certains réussissent, d'autres échouent; **have you got any others?** *(any more)* en avez-vous encore?; *(any different ones)* en avez-vous d'autres?; **can you show me some others?** pouvez-vous m'en montrer d'autres?; **I have no o.** je n'en ai pas d'autre
2 *(opposite, far end)* autre; **I stood at this end of the room and she stood at the o.** j'étais à ce bout-ci de la pièce et elle était à l'autre (bout)
3 *(related person)* autre; **each thought the o. the better writer** chacun trouvait que l'autre était meilleur écrivain
N *(person, thing)* autre *mf*; *Phil* **the o.** l'autre; **the three others** les trois autres; **wait for the others** attendez les autres; **politicians, industrialists and others** les hommes politiques, les industriels et les autres; **she cares nothing for others** elle ne se soucie pas du tout des autres; **the property of others** le bien d'autrui; **to talk about this, that and the o.** parler de ci et ça; *Fam Hum* **to have a bit of the o.** *(sex)* prendre un peu son pied
• **other than** CONJ 1 *(apart from, except)* autrement que; **we had no alternative o. than to accept their offer** nous n'avions pas d'autre possibilité que celle d'accepter leur offre
2 *(differently from)* différemment de; **I think she should have behaved o. than she did** je pense qu'elle aurait dû se comporter différemment *ou* d'une autre façon; **she can't be o. than she is** elle est comme ça, c'est tout PREP sauf, à part; **o. than that** à part cela; **somebody o. than me/you/her/etc** quelqu'un d'autre; **all verbs o. than those in -er** tous les verbes autres que ceux en -er

otherwise [ˈʌðəwaɪz] ADV 1 *(differently)* autrement; **I think o.** *(in a different way)* je ne vois pas les choses de cette façon; *(don't agree)* je ne suis pas d'accord; **she is o. engaged** elle a d'autres engagements; **we'll have to invite everyone, we can hardly do o.** nous devrons inviter tout le monde, il nous serait difficile de faire autrement; **except where o. stated** *(on form)* sauf indication contraire
2 *(in other respects)* autrement, à part cela; *(in other circumstances)* sinon, autrement; **an o. excellent performance** une interprétation par ailleurs excellente; **it's a bit small, but o. it's a very nice house** c'est un peu petit, mais à part cela, c'est une maison très agréable; **the weather was bad, o. he might have stayed longer** il faisait mauvais, sans cela *ou* sinon il aurait pu rester plus longtemps
3 *(in other words)* autrement; **Louis XIV, o. known as the Sun King** Louis XIV, surnommé le Roi-Soleil
4 *(in contrast, opposition)* **through diplomatic channels or o.** par voie diplomatique ou autre
CONJ *(or else)* sinon, autrement; **you'd better phone your father, o. he'll worry** tu devrais appeler ton père, sinon il va s'inquiéter
ADJ autre; **the facts are o.** les faits sont autres
• **or otherwise** ADV **it is of no interest, financial or o.** ça ne présente aucun intérêt, que ce soit financier ou autre

otherworldly [ˌʌðəˈwɜːldlɪ] ADJ 1 *(remote from worldly matters)* détaché du monde 2 *(mystical)* mystique 3 *(ethereal, exotic)* irréel

otic [ˈəʊtɪk] ADJ *Anat* otique

otitis [əʊˈtaɪtɪs] N *(UNCOUNT) Med* otite *f*

otoplasty [ˈəʊtəʊˌplæstɪ] N *Med* otoplastie *f*

OTS [ˌəʊtiːˈes] N *Mktg (abbr* **opportunity to see***)* ODV *f*

OTT [ˌəʊtiːˈtiː] ADJ *Br Fam (abbr* **over-the-top***)* **that's a bit O.!** c'est un peu exagéré!; **the house is nice, but the decor's a bit O.** la maison est bien, mais la décoration est un peu lourdingue; **it's a bit O. to call him a fascist** c'est un peu exagéré de le traiter de fasciste

otter [ˈɒtə(r)] N *Zool* loutre *f*
▸▸ *otter hound* chien *m* pour la chasse aux loutres

ottoman [ˈɒtəmən] N *(seat)* ottomane *f*
• **Ottoman** N Ottoman(e) *m,f* ADJ ottoman

OU [ˌəʊˈjuː] N *Br Univ (abbr* **Open University***)* = organisme d'enseignement universitaire par correspondance doublé d'émissions de télévision et de radio

ouch [aʊtʃ] EXCLAM aïe!, ouille!, ouïe!

ought[1] [ɔːt]

> La forme négative **ought not** s'écrit **oughtn't** en forme contractée.

V AUX 1 *(indicating morally right action)* **you o. to tell her** vous devriez le lui dire; **you o. to talk to him** tu devrais lui parler, il faudrait que tu lui parles; **she thought she o. to tell you** elle a pensé qu'il valait mieux te le dire
2 *(indicating sensible or advisable action)* **perhaps we o. to discuss this further** peut-être devrions-nous en discuter plus longuement; **I really o. to be going** il faut vraiment que je m'en aille; *Formal* **do you think I o.?** pensez-vous que je doive le faire?; **he o. to know better** il devrait être plus sensé; **that's a nice car – it o. to be, it cost me a fortune!** c'est une belle voiture – j'espère bien, elle m'a coûté une fortune!
3 *(expressing expectation, likelihood)* **they o. to be home now** à l'heure qu'il est, ils devraient être rentrés; **it o. to be good** ça devrait être bien; **she o. to beat him easily** elle devrait le battre facilement; **that oughtn't to be too difficult** ça ne devrait pas être trop difficile
4 *(followed by "to have")* **you o. to have told me!** vous auriez dû me le dire!; **you o. to have seen her!** si vous l'aviez vue!, il fallait la voir!; **they o. not to have been allowed in** on n'aurait pas dû les laisser entrer

ought[2] = **aught**

oughtn't [ˈɔːtənt] = **ought not**

Ouija® [ˈwiːdʒə] N **O. (board)** oui-ja *m inv*

ounce [aʊns] N 1 *(unit of weight)* = 28,35 grammes, once *f* 2 *Fig* **there isn't an o. of truth in what she says** il n'y a pas une once de vérité dans ce qu'elle raconte; **you haven't got an o. of common sense** tu n'as pas (pour) deux sous de bon sens; **it took every o. of strength she had** cela lui a demandé toutes ses forces 3 *Zool* once *f*, léopard *m* des neiges

our [ˈaʊə(r)] ADJ *(singular)* notre; *(plural)* nos; **o. house** notre maison; **this is OUR house** cette maison est à nous; **we have a car of o. own** nous avons une voiture à nous; *Fam* **o. Debbie will be 16 next week** notre (petite) Debbie aura 16 ans la semaine prochaine; *Fam* **have you seen o. Ricky?** avez-vous vu Ricky?
▸▸ *Our Father (prayer)* Notre Père *m*

ours [ˈaʊəz] PRON 1 *(gen ▸ singular)* le (la) nôtre *mf*; *(▸ plural)* les nôtres *mfpl*; **that house is o.** *(we live there)* cette maison est la nôtre; *(we own it)* cette maison est à nous *ou* nous appartient; **those books are o.** ces livres sont à nous; **it's o. to spend as we like** nous pouvons le dépenser comme nous voulons; **it's all o.!** tout cela nous appartient!; **o. was a curious relationship** nous avions des rapports assez bizarres; **o. is a big family** nous sommes une grande famille; **it must be one of o.** ce doit être un des nôtres; **she's a friend of o.** c'est une de nos amies; **a friend of o.**

told us c'est un ami à nous qui nous l'a dit; *Fam* **those damned neighbours of o.** nos fichus voisins; **that wretched dog of o.** notre saleté de chien **2** *Fam (our house, flat)* chez nous

ourself [aʊə'self] PRON *Formal (regal or editorial plural)* nous-même

ourselves [aʊə'selvz] PRON **1** *(reflexive use)* nous; **we enjoyed o.** nous nous sommes bien amusés; **we built o. a log cabin** nous avons construit une cabane en rondins; **we said to o., why not wait here?** nous nous sommes dit *ou* on s'est dit: pourquoi ne pas attendre ici? **2** *(emphatic use)* nous-mêmes; **we welcomed him o.** nous l'avons accueilli nous-mêmes; **we were able to visit the caves o.** nous avons eu la chance de pouvoir visiter les grottes; **we o. have much to learn** nous-mêmes avons beaucoup à apprendre; **we want to see for o.** nous avons envie de nous en rendre compte (par) nous-mêmes; **(all) by o.** tout seuls; **we had the flat to o.** nous avions l'appartement pour nous tout seuls **3** *(replacing "us")* nous-mêmes; **apart from our parents and o., everyone was Russian** en dehors de nos parents et de nous-mêmes, tout le monde était russe

oust [aʊst] VT **1** *(opponent, rival)* évincer, chasser; **the president was ousted from power** le président a été évincé du pouvoir; **she has ousted her sister in Arthur's affections** elle a pris la place de *ou* a supplanté sa sœur dans le cœur d'Arthur **2** *(tenant, squatter)* déloger, expulser; *(landowner)* déposséder

> **OUT-** PRÉFIXE
>
> Employé avec des verbes transitifs, le préfixe **out-** a deux sens principaux :
>
> • Il peut signifier SURPASSER quelqu'un ou quelque chose dans un domaine donné. Bien qu'en français le préfixe **sur-** soit parfois employé pour rendre cette idée, il n'existe pas réellement de préfixe équivalent et l'on doit le plus souvent recourir à une périphrase :
>
> **to outclass someone** surclasser quelqu'un; **to outlive someone** survivre à quelqu'un; **to outjump someone** sauter plus haut/loin que quelqu'un; **to outsmart someone** se montrer plus malin que quelqu'un; **to outbid someone** enchérir sur quelqu'un; **to outscore someone** marquer plus de points que quelqu'un.
>
> On notera que ce procédé est très générateur et permet de créer des verbes à volonté, comme dans l'exemple suivant :
>
> **he can outdrink anybody** il peut boire plus que n'importe qui; **Blair is trying to out-Thatcher Thatcher** Blair essaie de se montrer plus thatchérien que Thatcher.
>
> • Il peut aussi véhiculer la notion de DÉPASSEMENT d'une limite :
>
> **he has outgrown his clothes** ses vêtements sont trop petits pour lui maintenant.

OUT [aʊt] ADV **A. 1** *(indicating movement from inside to outside)* dehors; **to go o.** sortir; **she ran/limped/strolled o.** elle est sortie en courant/en boitant/sans se presser; **I met her on my way o.** je l'ai rencontrée en sortant; **o. you go!** sortez!, hors d'ici!, allez, hop!; **the cork popped o.** le bouchon sauta; **she took o. a gun** elle a sorti un révolver; **I had my camera o. ready** j'avais sorti mon appareil; *Fam* **I'm o. of here** je me casse; *Fam* **let's get o. of here** allez, on se casse

2 *(away from home, office etc)* **Mr Powell's o., do you want to leave a message?** M. Powell est sorti, voulez-vous laisser un message?; **she's o. a lot in the daytime** elle est souvent absente pendant la journée; **she's o. picking mushrooms** elle est sortie (pour aller) cueillir des champignons; **a search party is o. looking for them** une équipe de secours est partie à leur recherche; **it's a long time since we had an evening o.** ça fait longtemps que nous ne sommes pas sortis; **the children are playing o. in the street** les enfants jouent dans la rue; *Fam* **to be o. to lunch** *(out of touch with reality)* être à côté de la plaque

3 *(no longer attending hospital, school etc)* sorti; **she's o. of hospital now** elle est sortie de l'hôpital maintenant; **what time do you get o. of school?** à quelle heure sors-tu de l'école?; **he's o. in September** *(of prisoner)* il sort en septembre

4 *(indicating view from inside)* **he was looking o. at the people in the street** il regardait les gens qui passaient dans la rue; **I stared o. of the window** je regardais par la fenêtre

5 *(in the open air)* dehors; **to sleep o.** dormir dehors; **it's cold o.** il fait froid dehors; **it's colder inside than o.** il fait plus froid à l'intérieur qu'à l'extérieur

6 *(indicating distance from land, centre, town etc)* **we were two days o. from Portsmouth** nous étions à deux jours de Portsmouth; **on the trip o.** à l'aller; **they live a long way o.** ils habitent loin du centre; **o. in the country** dans la campagne; **she's o. in Africa** elle est en Afrique; **o. there** là-bas

7 *(indicating extended position)* **she stuck her tongue o. at me** elle m'a tiré la langue; **he lay stretched o. on the bed** il était allongé (de tout son long) sur le lit; **hold your arms/your hand o.** tendez les bras/la main

B. 1 *(indicating distribution)* **the letter was sent o. yesterday** la lettre a été postée hier; **the book is o.** *(borrowed from library)* le livre est en prêt

2 *(indicating source of light, smell, sound etc)* **it gives o. a lot of heat** ça dégage beaucoup de chaleur; **music blared o. from the radio** la radio hurlait

3 *(loudly, audibly)* **read o. the first paragraph** lisez le premier paragraphe à haute voix; **I was thinking o. loud** je pensais tout haut

C. 1 *(indicating exclusion or rejection)* **traitors o.!** les traîtres, dehors!; **throw him o.!** jetez-le dehors!

2 *(indicating abandonment of activity)* **get o. before it's too late** abandonne avant qu'il ne soit trop tard; *Fam* **I want o.!** je laisse tomber!

3 *(extinguished)* **put** *or* **turn the lights o.** éteignez les lumières; **to stub o. a cigarette** écraser une cigarette

4 *(unconscious)* **to knock sb o.** assommer qn, mettre qn K-O; **several people passed o.** plusieurs personnes se sont évanouies

5 *(indicating disappearance)* **the stain will wash o.** la tache partira au lavage

D. 1 *(revealed, made public)* **the secret is o.** le secret a été éventé; **word is o. that he's going to resign** le bruit court qu'il va démissionner; **the truth will o.** la vérité se saura; *Fam* **o. with it!** alors, t'accouches?

2 *(published, on sale)* **is her new book/film/record o.?** est-ce que son nouveau livre/film/disque est sorti?; **the new model will be** *or* **come o. next month** le nouveau modèle sort le mois prochain

3 *(with superlative) Fam (in existence)* **it's the best computer o.** c'est le meilleur ordinateur qui existe❑; **she's the biggest liar o.** c'est la pire menteuse qui soit❑

E. *(of tide)* **the tide's on its way o.** la mer se retire, la marée descend

ADJ **1** *(flowering)* en fleurs; **the daffodils/cherry trees are o.** les jonquilles/cerisiers sont en fleurs

2 *(shining)* **the sun is o.** il y a du soleil; **the moon is o.** la lune s'est levée; **the stars are o.** on voit les étoiles

3 *(finished)* **before the year is o.** avant la fin de l'année

4 *(on strike)* en grève; **everybody o.!** tout le monde en grève!

5 *Sport* **if you score less than 3 points you're o.** si on marque moins de 3 points on est éliminé; **the ball was o.** la balle était dehors *ou* sortie, la balle était faute; **not o.** *(in cricket)* = encore au guichet *(à la fin de l'innings, de la journée)*

6 *(tide)* bas; **the tide's o.** la marée est basse

7 *(wrong)* **your calculations are (way) o., you're (way) o. in your calculations** vous vous êtes (complètement) trompé dans vos calculs; **I've checked the figures but I'm still £50 o.** j'ai vérifié les chiffres mais il manque toujours 50 livres; **it's a few inches o.** *(too long)* c'est trop long de quelques centimètres; *(too short)* c'est trop court de quelques centimètres; **it's only a few inches o.** c'est bon à quelques centimètres près; **the shot was only a centimetre o.** le coup n'a manqué le but que d'un centimètre

8 *Fam (impossible)* **that plan's o. because of the weather** ce projet est à l'eau à cause du temps

9 *Fam (unfashionable)* démodé❑; **long hair's (right) o.** les cheveux longs c'est (carrément) dépassé

10 *(indicating aim, intent)* **to be o. to do sth** avoir l'intention de faire qch; **we're o. to win** nous sommes partis pour gagner; **to be o. to get sb** en avoir après qn; **to be o. for sth** vouloir qch; **she was o. for a good time** elle cherchait à s'amuser; **she's o. for the presidency** elle vise le poste de président; **he's just o. for himself** il ne s'intéresse qu'à lui-même; **he's only o. for what he can get** il ne cherche qu'à servir ses propres intérêts

11 *Fam (unconscious)* **to be o.** être K-O

12 *(extinguished)* éteint; **the fire was o.** le feu était éteint

13 *Fam (openly gay)* qui ne cache pas son homosexualité❑, ouvertement homosexuel❑

N *(way of escape)* échappatoire *f*

EXCLAM **1** *(leave)* dehors!

2 *Tel* **(over and) o.!** terminé!

3 *Sport (in tennis)* faute!, out!

PREP *Fam* hors de; **she went o. that door** elle est sortie par cette porte; **look o. the window** regarde par la fenêtre

VT *(expose)* dénoncer; **to o. sb** *(reveal to be homosexual)* révéler que qn est homosexuel, outer qn; **to o. sb as a spy** dénoncer qn en tant qu'espion

• **out and about** ADV **where have you been? – oh, o. and about** où étais-tu? – oh, je suis allé faire un tour; **o. and about in Amsterdam** dans les rues d'Amsterdam

• **out of** PREP **1** *(indicating movement from inside to outside)* hors de; **she came o. of the office** elle est sortie du bureau; **he ran/limped/strolled o. of the office** il est sorti du bureau en courant/en boitant/sans se presser; **to look/to fall o. of a window** regarder/tomber par une fenêtre; **take your hands o. of your pockets!** sors *ou* ôte tes mains de tes poches!; **hardly were the words o. of my mouth** à peine avais-je prononcé ces mots

2 *(indicating location)* **we drank o. of china cups** nous avons bu dans des tasses de porcelaine; **to drink o. of the bottle** boire à (même) la bouteille; **she works o. of York** elle opère à partir de York; **he's o. of town** il n'est pas en ville; **she's o. of the country** elle est à l'étranger; **it's a long way o. of town** c'est loin de la ville

3 *(indicating source ▸ of feeling, profit, money etc)* **she did well o. of the deal** elle a trouvé son compte dans l'affaire; **what pleasure do they get o. of it?** quel plaisir en tirent-ils?; **you won't get anything o. of him** vous ne tirerez rien de lui; **she paid for it o. of company funds/o. of her own pocket** elle l'a payé avec l'argent de la société/payé de sa poche; **to copy sth o. of a book** copier qch dans un livre

4 *(indicating raw material)* **it's made o. of mahogany** c'est en acajou; **plastic is made o. of petroleum** on obtient le plastique à partir du pétrole; **hut made o. of a few old planks** cabane faite de quelques vieilles planches

5 *(indicating motive)* par; **he refused o. of sheer spite** il a refusé par pur dépit; **to act o. of fear** *(habitually)* agir sous l'emprise de la peur; *(on precise occasion)* agir sous le coup de la peur

6 *(indicating previous tendency, habit)* **I've got o. of the habit** j'en ai perdu l'habitude; **try and stay o. of trouble** essaie d'éviter les ennuis

7 *(lacking)* **I'm o. of cigarettes** je n'ai plus de cigarettes; *Com* **I am o. of this item** je n'ai plus cet article pour le moment; **o. of work** au chômage

8 *(in proportions, marks etc)* sur; **he got nine o. of ten in maths** il a eu neuf sur dix en maths; **ninety-nine times o. of a hundred** quatre-vingt-dix-neuf fois sur cent; **choose one o. of these ten** choisissez-en un parmi les dix; **three days o. of four** trois jours sur quatre; **one o. of every three** un sur trois; **o. of all the people there, only one spoke German** parmi toutes les personnes présentes, une seule parlait allemand

9 *(indicating similarity to book, film etc)* **it was like something o. of a Fellini film** on se serait cru dans un film de Fellini

10 *(indicating exclusion or rejection)* **he's o. of the race** il n'est plus dans la course; **you keep o. of this!** mêlez-vous de ce qui vous regarde!

11 *(indicating avoidance)* **come in o. of the rain** ne reste pas dehors sous la pluie; **stay o. of the sun** ne restez pas au soleil; **is there a way o. of it?** y a-t-il (un) moyen d'en sortir?

12 *(indicating recently completed activity)* **a young girl just o. of university** une jeune fille tout juste sortie de l'université

13 *(in breeding)* **Gladiator by Monarch o. of Gladia** Gladiateur par *ou* issu de Monarch et Gladia
14 *(idiom) Fam* **to be o. of it** *(unaware of situation)* être à côté de la plaque; *(drunk, on drugs)* être raide; **I felt a bit o. of it** *(excluded)* je me sentais un peu de trop
• **out there** ADJ *Fam* loufoque
►► *Comput* **out box** *(for e-mail)* corbeille *f* de départ; **out tray** corbeille *f* sortie

out- [aut] PREF **the government are attempting to out-Tory the Tories** le gouvernement essaie d'être plus conservatrice que les conservateurs eux-mêmes

outage ['autɪdʒ] N **1** *(breakdown)* panne *f*; *Elec* coupure *f ou* panne *f* de courant **2** *(of service)* interruption *f* **3** *Com (missing goods)* marchandises *fpl* perdues *(pendant le stockage ou le transport)*

out-and-out ADJ complet(ète), total; **it was an o. disaster** ce fut un désastre complet; **he's an o. crook** c'est un véritable escroc

outasight [,autə'saɪt] ADJ *Am Fam Old-fashioned* extra, super, génial

outback ['autbæk] N **the o.** l'arrière-pays *m inv*, l'intérieur *m* du pays

outbid [,aut'bɪd] *(pt* **outbid**, *pp* **outbid** *or* **outbidden** [-'bɪdən], *cont* **outbidding**) VT enchérir sur; **we were o. for the Renoir** nous voulions acheter le Renoir mais il est allé à plus offrant

outboard ['autbɔːd] N *(boat, motor)* hors-bord *m inv*
ADJ *(position, direction)* hors-bord
►► **outboard motor** moteur *m* hors-bord

outbound ['autbaund] ADJ en partance
►► *Com* **outbound freight** fret *m* de sortie; **outbound tourism** tourisme *m* émetteur

outbox [,aut'bɒks] VT boxer mieux que; **he was completely outboxed** il a été complètement dominé

outbreak ['autbreɪk] N **1** *(of fire, storm, war)* début *m*; *(of violence, disease, epidemic)* éruption *f*; **there have been outbreaks of violence throughout the country** il y a eu des explosions de violence dans tout le pays; **at the o. of war** au début de la guerre, lorsque la guerre a éclaté; **there's been an o. of flu** il y a eu de nombreux cas de grippe; **doctors fear an o. of meningitis** les médecins redoutent une épidémie de méningite **2** *Met (sudden shower)* **there will be outbreaks of rain/snow in many places** il y aura des chutes de pluie/de neige un peu partout

outbuilding ['aut,bɪldɪŋ] N *Br* (bâtiment *m*) annexe *f*; *(shed)* remise *f*; **the outbuildings** *(on farm, estate)* les dépendances *fpl*

outburst ['autbɜːst] N accès *m*, explosion *f*; **a sudden o. of violence** *(from a group)* une soudaine explosion de violence; *(from an individual)* un accès de brutalité; **a sudden o. of temper** un accès de mauvaise humeur; **you must control these outbursts** il faut que vous appreniez à garder votre sang-froid; **he apologized for his o.** il s'est excusé de s'être remporté

outcast ['autkɑːst] N paria *m*
ADJ proscrit, banni

outclass [,aut'klɑːs] VT surclasser, surpasser; **she outclassed all of the other athletes** elle a surclassé tous les autres athlètes

outcome ['autkʌm] N *(of election, competition)* résultat *m*; *(of sequence of events)* conséquence *f*; **the o. of it all was that they never visited us again** résultat, ils ne sont jamais revenus chez nous; **I don't know what the o. will be** je ne sais pas ce qui en résultera

outcrop *(pt & pp* **outcropped**, *cont* **outcropping**)
N ['autkrɒp] *Geol* affleurement *m*
VI [,aut'krɒp] affleurer

outcry ['autkraɪ] *(pl* **outcries**) N tollé *m*; **the government's decision was greeted by public o.** la décision du gouvernement fut accueillie par un tollé général

out-cue N *TV & Cin* signal *m* de sortie; *(on video)* point *m* de sortie

outdated [,aut'deɪtɪd] ADJ *(idea, attitude)* démodé, dépassé; *(clothes)* démodé; *(expression)* désuet(ète)

outdid [,aut'dɪd] *pt of* **outdo**

outdistance [,aut'dɪstəns] VT laisser derrière soi; **she was easily outdistanced by the Nigerian** elle fut facilement distancée par la Nigérienne

outdo [,aut'duː] *(pt* **outdid** [-'dɪd], *pp* **outdone** [-'dʌn]) VT surpasser, faire mieux que, l'emporter sur; **he's not easily outdone in an argument** il n'est pas facile d'avoir le dernier mot quand on discute avec lui; **Mark, not to be outdone, decided to be ill as well** Mark, pour ne pas être en reste, décida d'être malade lui aussi; **she wasn't to be outdone** *(in contest)* elle refusait de s'avouer vaincue; **she outdid all the other competitors** elle l'a emporté sur tous les autres concurrents

outdoor ['autdɔː(r)] ADJ **1** *(open-air* ► *games, sports)* de plein air; (► *work)* d'extérieur; (► *swimming pool)* en plein air, découvert **2** *(clothes)* d'extérieur **3** *(person, lifestyle)* **to lead an o. life** vivre au grand air; **Kate is a real o. type** Kate aime la vie au grand air
►► **outdoor advertising** publicité *f* extérieure; *Br* **outdoor aerial**, *Am* **outdoor antenna** antenne *f* extérieure; *Cin & TV* **outdoor scene** extérieur *m*, plan *m* d'extérieur; *Cin* **outdoor set** décor *m* en extérieur; **outdoor shoes** *(warm)* grosses chaussures *fpl*; *(waterproof)* chaussures *fpl* imperméables; *(for walking)* chaussures *fpl* de marche

> Attention: ne pas confondre avec l'adverbe **outdoors**.

outdoors [,aut'dɔːz] N **the great o.** les grands espaces naturels
ADV dehors, au dehors; **the scene takes place o.** la scène se déroule à l'extérieur; **to sleep o.** coucher à la belle étoile; **we were o. for most of the holiday** nous avons passé la plus grande partie de nos vacances au grand air
ADJ *(activity)* en *ou* de plein air; **she's an o. person** c'est quelqu'un qui aime le grand air *ou* qui aime être dehors

> Attention: ne pas confondre avec l'adjectif **outdoor**.

outdoorsy [,aut'dɔːzɪ] ADJ *Fam (activities)* de plein air; *(person)* qui aime le grand air□, qui aime être dehors□

outer ['autə(r)] ADJ **1** *(external)* extérieur, externe; **the o. man** l'homme dans son apparence extérieure; **o. packaging** suremballage *m* **2** *(peripheral)* périphérique; **o. London** la banlieue londonienne **3** *(furthest* ► *limits)* externe; (► *planets)* extérieur
N *(of target)* cercle *m* extérieur
►► *Br Law* **outer bar** = ensemble des avocats débutants qui ne plaident pas à la barre; *Archit* **outer door** avant-portail *m*; **outer ear** oreille *f* externe; **outer garments** vêtements *mpl* de dessus; **the Outer Hebrides** les Hébrides *fpl* extérieures; *Formerly* **Outer Mongolia** Mongolie-Extérieure *f*; **outer space** espace *m* intersidéral, cosmos *m*

outermost ['autəməust] ADJ **1** *(closest to outside)* le plus (à l')extérieur; **the o. layer was waterproofed** la première couche était imperméable; **make sure the coloured side is o.** assure-toi que le côté coloré se trouve à l'extérieur **2** *(most isolated)* le plus reculé *ou* isolé; **the o. limits of the galaxy** les limites les plus reculées de la galaxie

outfall ['autfɔːl] N *(of pipe)* embouchure *f*

outfit ['autfɪt] *(pt & pp* **outfitted**, *cont* **outfitting**) N **1** *(clothes)* ensemble *m*, tenue *f*; **she appears in a new o. every day** elle porte une tenue différente chaque jour; **riding/travelling o.** tenue *f* d'équitation/de voyage; **you should have seen the o. he had on!** tu aurais dû voir comment il était attifé *ou* fagoté!
2 *(child's disguise)* panoplie *f*; **cowboy/nurse's o.** panoplie *f* de cowboy/d'infirmière
3 *(equipment, kit* ► *for camping, fishing)* matériel *m*, équipement *m*; *(tools)* outils *mpl*, outillage *m*; *(case)* trousse *f*; **repair o.** trousse *f* de réparation
4 *Fam (group)* équipe *f*, bande *f*; *Am* **the O.** *(the Mafia)* la Mafia
5 *Mil* équipe *f*
VT *(with equipment)* équiper

outfitter ['aut,fɪtə(r)] N **1** *esp Br (for clothes)* spécialiste *mf* de la confection; **school o.** *or* **o.'s** = magasin qui vend des uniformes et autres vêtements scolaires; **sports o.** *or* **o.'s** magasin *m* de vêtements de sport; **(gentlemen's) o.** *or* **o.'s** magasin *m* de vêtements d'homme **2** *Am (for hunting equipment)* fournisseur *m*

outflank [,aut'flæŋk] VT **1** *Mil* déborder **2** *Fig (rival)* déjouer les manœuvres de

outflow ['autfləu] N **1** *(of fluid)* écoulement *m*; *(of lava)* coulée *f* **2** *(place)* décharge *f* **3** *(of capital)* sorties *fpl*, fuite *f*; *(of gold, currency)* sortie *f*; *(of population)* exode *m*, sorties *fpl*, fuite *f*; **o. per hour** débit *m* par heure

outfox [,aut'fɒks] VT se montrer plus rusé que

outgoing ['aut,gəuɪŋ] ADJ **1** *(departing* ► *government, minister, tenant)* sortant; (► *following resignation)* démissionnaire
2 *(train, ship, plane)* en partance; *(letters)* à expédier; *(telephone call)* sortant
3 *(tide)* descendant
4 *(extrovert)* extraverti, plein d'entrain; **she's a very o. person** elle a une personnalité très ouverte
►► *Ind* **outgoing shift** équipe *f* sortante *ou* relevée

outgoings ['aut,gəuɪŋz] NPL *Br* dépenses *fpl*, frais *mpl*; *Fin* dépenses *fpl*, décaissements *mpl*; **the o. exceed the incomings** les dépenses excèdent les recettes

outgrow [,aut'grəu] *(pt* **outgrew** [-'gruː], *pp* **outgrown** [-'grəun]) VT **1** *(game, habit, hobby)* ne plus s'intéresser à *(en grandissant)*; *(attitude, behaviour, phase)* abandonner (en grandissant *ou* en prenant de l'âge); **Abby has outgrown dolls** Abby est devenue trop grande pour s'intéresser aux poupées; **they soon outgrew their first computer** ils ont vite eu fait le tour (des possibilités) de leur premier ordinateur; **he has outgrown his protest phase** il a dépassé le stade de la contestation; **I think I simply outgrew our friendship** je crois qu'avec l'âge, notre amitié a tout simplement perdu son intérêt pour moi **2** *(clothes)* devenir trop grand pour; **she has outgrown three pairs of shoes this year** elle a pris quatre pointures cette année **3** *(grow faster than)* grandir plus (vite) que; **that boy is outgrowing his strength** ce garçon a une croissance beaucoup trop rapide pour sa constitution; **the world is outgrowing its resources** la population mondiale croît plus vite que les ressources dont elle dispose

outgrowth ['autgrəuθ] N excroissance *f*; *Fig (consequence)* conséquence *f*

outguess [aut'ges] VT *(person)* déjouer les intentions de

outgun [,aut'gʌn] *(pt & pp* **outgunned**, *cont* **outgunning**) VT *Mil* avoir une puissance de feu supérieure à; *Fig* vaincre, l'emporter sur

out-Herod VT *(idiom)* **to o. Herod** en rajouter *(dans la cruauté, la violence etc)*

outhouse ['authaus, *pl* -hauzɪz] N **1** *Br (outbuilding)* remise *f* **2** *Am (toilet)* toilettes *fpl* extérieures

outing ['autɪŋ] N **1** *(trip)* sortie *f*, *(organized)* excursion *f*; **to go on an o.** faire une excursion; **to go for an o. in the car** partir faire une balade en voiture; **school o.** sortie scolaire; **his first o. this season** *(of horse)* son premier concours de la saison **2** *(of homosexual)* = dénonciation d'un homosexuel dans le monde de la politique et du spectacle, outing *m*

outlandish [,aut'lændɪʃ] ADJ *(eccentric* ► *appearance, behaviour, idea)* bizarre, excentrique; *Pej (language, style)* barbare

outlast [,aut'lɑːst] VT *(of person)* survivre à; *(of machine)* durer plus longtemps que; **it has outlasted ten centuries of war, weather and vandalism** cela a résisté à dix siècles de guerres, d'intempéries et de vandalisme; **the theory has outlasted all its critics** cette théorie a résisté à l'assaut de tous les critiques

outlaw ['autlɔː] N hors-la-loi *m inv*
VT *(person)* mettre hors la loi; *(behaviour)* proscrire, interdire; *(organization)* interdire

outlay ['autleɪ] N *(expense)* dépenses *fpl*, frais *mpl*; *(investment)* investissement *m*, mise *f* de fonds; **to get back** *or* **recover one's o.** rentrer dans ses fonds

outlet ['aʊtlet] **N 1** *(for liquid, air, smoke)* bouche *f*; *(in reservoir, lock)* déversoir *m*, dégorgeoir *m*; *(tap)* vanne *f* d'écoulement; **air o.** bouche *f* d'aération; **the pipe/channel provides an o. for excess water** le tuyau/le canal permet l'écoulement du trop-plein d'eau
2 *(mouth of river)* embouchure *f*
3 *(for feelings, energy)* exutoire *m*; **children need an o. for their energies** les enfants ont besoin de se défouler; **writing is an o. for me** l'écriture est pour moi un exutoire
4 *(for talent)* débouché *m*; **the programme provides an o. for young talent** l'émission permet à de jeunes talents de se faire connaître
5 *Com (market)* débouché *m*; *(sales point)* point *m* de vente; **there are not many sales outlets in Japan** le Japon offre peu de débouchés commerciaux; **our North American outlets** notre réseau (de distribution) en Amérique du Nord
6 *Am Elec* prise *f* (de courant)
COMP *(for liquid)* d'écoulement; *(for gas, smoke)* d'échappement
▸▸ *Com* ***outlet village*** = centre commercial spécialisé dans les marques à prix réduit

outline ['aʊtlaɪn] **N 1** *(contour, shape)* silhouette *f*, contour *m*; *(of building, of mountains)* silhouette *f*; *(of face, figure)* profil *m*; *Art (sketch)* esquisse *f*, ébauche *f*; **to draw sth in o.** faire un croquis de qch
2 *(plan ▸ of project, essay)* plan *m* d'ensemble, esquisse *f*; *(▸ of book, play)* canevas *m*; **I've only written a rough o. of the chapter** je n'ai écrit que les grandes lignes du chapitre
3 *(general idea)* idée *f* générale, grandes lignes *fpl*; *(overall view)* vue *f* d'ensemble; **to give sb an o. of sth** expliquer les grandes lignes de qch à qn; **she gave us an o. of** *or* **she explained to us in o. what she intended to do** elle nous a expliqué dans les grandes lignes ce qu'elle avait l'intention de faire
VT 1 *(plan, theory)* expliquer dans les grandes lignes; *(facts)* résumer, passer en revue; **he outlined the situation briefly** il dressa un bref bilan de la situation; **could you o. your basic reasons for leaving?** pourriez-vous exposer brièvement les principales raisons de votre départ?
2 *(person, building, mountain)* **the trees were outlined against the blue sky** les arbres se détachaient sur le fond bleu du ciel
3 *Art* esquisser (les traits de), tracer; **to o. sth in pencil** faire le croquis de qch; **the figures are outlined in charcoal** les personnages sont esquissés au fusain; **to o. one's eyes in black** souligner le contour de ses yeux en noir
ADJ an o. history of Greece un précis d'histoire grecque
▸▸ ***outline agreement*** protocole *m* d'accord; ***outline drawing*** dessin *m* au trait; *Comput* ***outline font*** police *f* vectorielle; ***outline plan*** plan *m* schématique *ou* d'ensemble; ***outline script*** scénario *m* indicatif

outliner ['aʊtlaɪnə(r)] **N** *Comput* outliner *m*

outlive [ˌaʊt'lɪv] **VT** survivre à; **he'll o. us all at this rate** au train où il va, il nous enterrera tous; **the measures have outlived their usefulness** les mesures n'ont plus de raison d'être

outlook ['aʊtlʊk] **N 1** *(prospect)* perspective *f*; *Econ & Pol* horizon *m*, perspectives *fpl* (d'avenir); **the o. for the New Year is promising** cette nouvelle année s'annonce prometteuse; **it's a bleak o. for the unemployed** pour les sans-emploi, les perspectives d'avenir ne sont guère réjouissantes; **the o. for the future is grim** l'avenir est sombre
2 *Met* prévision *f*, prévisions *fpl*; **the o. for March is cold and windy** pour mars, on prévoit un temps froid avec beaucoup de vent
3 *(viewpoint)* point de vue *m*, conception *f*; **what's your o. on life?** quelle est votre conception de la vie?; **she has a pessimistic o.** elle voit les choses en noir *ou* de manière pessimiste
4 *(view ▸ from window)* perspective *f*, vue *f*; **we have a pleasant o. onto a small park** nous avons une vue agréable sur un petit parc

outlying ['aʊtˌlaɪɪŋ] **ADJ** *(remote ▸ area, village)* isolé, à l'écart; *(far from centre ▸ urban areas)* périphérique; **the o. suburbs** la grande banlieue

outmanoeuvre, *Am* **outmaneuver** [ˌaʊtmə'nuːvə(r)] **VT** *Mil* se montrer meilleur tacticien que; *Fig* déjouer les manœuvres de; **we were outmanoeuvred by the opposition** l'opposition nous a pris de vitesse

outmatch [ˌaʊt'mætʃ] **VT** surclasser, dominer

outmoded [ˌaʊt'məʊdəd] **ADJ** *(custom, beliefs)* désuet(ète), démodé; *(furniture, theory, word)* démodé

outnumber [ˌaʊt'nʌmbə(r)] **VT** être plus nombreux que; **they were outnumbered by the enemy** l'ennemi était supérieur en nombre; **women o. men by two to one** il y a deux fois plus de femmes que d'hommes

out-of-body experience **N** expérience *f* hors du corps, EHC *f*, autoscopie *f*

out-of-bounds **ADJ 1** *(barred)* interdit; **o. to civilians** interdit aux civils **2** *Am Sport* hors (du) terrain

out-of-court settlement **N** arrangement *m* à l'amiable

out-of-doors *Br* **ADJ = outdoor**
ADV = outdoors

out-of-focus **ADJ** flou

out-of-phase **ADJ** *TV & Cin* déphasé

out-of-pocket expenses **NPL** *Fin* menues dépenses *fpl*

out-of-shot **ADJ** *TV & Cin* en dehors du champ

out-of-sync **ADJ** désynchronisé, hors synchronisation

out-of-the-ordinary **ADJ** insolite

out-of-the-way **ADJ 1** *(isolated)* écarté, isolé; *(unknown to most people)* peu connu; *(not popular)* peu fréquenté **2** *(uncommon)* insolite

out-of-town **ADJ** *(shopping centre, retail park)* situé à la périphérie d'une ville

out-of-towner [-'taʊnə(r)] **N** *Am Fam* étranger (ère) *m,f* à la ville□; **he's an o.** il n'est pas d'ici□

outpace [ˌaʊt'peɪs] **VT** *(run faster than)* courir plus vite que; *(overtake)* dépasser, devancer; **demand has outpaced production** la demande a dépassé la production

outpatient ['aʊtˌpeɪʃənt] **N** malade *mf* en consultation externe; **he was being treated as an o.** il était traité en consultation externe
▸▸ ***outpatients' clinic, outpatients' department*** service *m* de consultation externe

outplacement ['aʊtpleɪsmənt] **N** *Com* outplacement *m*

outplay [ˌaʊt'pleɪ] **VT** jouer mieux que, dominer (au jeu); **she was outplayed** son adversaire a joué mieux qu'elle

outpoint **N** ['aʊtpɔɪnt] *(on tape, film)* point *m* de sortie
VT [ˌaʊt'pɔɪnt] *(in boxing)* battre aux points

outpost ['aʊtpəʊst] **N** avant-poste *m*; **the last outposts of civilization** les derniers bastions de la civilisation

outpouring ['aʊtˌpɔːrɪŋ] **N** *(of feelings)* épanchement *m*, effusion *f*; *(of ideas, creativity)* déluge *m*, flux *m*; **outpourings** effusions *fpl*

output ['aʊtpʊt] *(pt & pp* **output,** *cont* **outputting)**
N 1 *(production)* production *f*; *(productivity)* rendement *m*; **our o. is not keeping pace with demand** notre production est insuffisante pour répondre à la demande; **his writing o. is phenomenal** c'est un auteur très prolifique
2 *(power ▸ of machine)* rendement *m*, débit *m*; **this machine has an o. of 6,000 items an hour** cette machine débite 6000 pièces à l'heure
3 *Elec* puissance *f*; *(of amplifier)* puissance *f* (de sortie); **o. voltage** tension *f* de sortie
4 *Comput (device)* sortie *f*; *(printout)* sortie *f* papier, tirage *m*
VT 1 *(of factory etc)* produire **2** *Comput (data)* sortir (**to** sur)
VI *Comput* sortir des données
▸▸ *Comput* ***output buffer*** mémoire *f* tampon de sortie; *Comput* ***output card*** carte *f* sortie, carte *f* résultat; *Comput* ***output device*** périphérique *m* de sortie; *Comput* ***output file*** fichier *m* de sortie; *Comput* ***output formatting*** mise *f* en forme de sortie; *Econ* ***output gap*** écart *m* de production; *Comput* ***output port*** port *m* de sortie; *Tech* ***output shaft*** arbre *m* de sortie; *Elec* ***output signal*** signal *m* de sortie; *Acct* ***output tax*** TVA *f* encaissée, impôt *m* à la consommation

outrage ['aʊtreɪdʒ] **N 1** *(affront)* outrage *m*, affront *m*; **it's an o. against public decency** c'est un outrage aux bonnes mœurs; **it's an o. agains[t] humanity/society** c'est un affront à l'humanité/la société
2 *(scandal)* scandale *m*; **it's an o. that no on[e] came to their aid** c'est un scandale *ou* il est scandaleux que personne ne soit venu à leur secours
3 *(indignation)* indignation *f*
4 *(brutal act)* atrocité *f*, acte *m* de brutalité *ou d[e]* violence
VT 1 *(person)* scandaliser **2** *(moral sensibilit[y], feelings)* outrager, faire outrage à

outrageous [aʊt'reɪdʒəs] **ADJ 1** *(scandalous ▸ be[haviour], manners)* scandaleux; *(atrocious ▸ crime, attack etc)* monstrueux, atroce; **an o. viola[tion] of human rights** une violation scandaleus[e] des droits de l'homme; **it's o. that anyone shoul[d] believe him guilty!** il est scandaleux qu'on puiss[e] le croire coupable!
2 *(slightly offensive ▸ humour, style)* choquan[t]; *(▸ joke, remark)* outrageant
3 *(extravagant ▸ person, colour)* extravagant; **h[e] wears the most o. clothes** il porte les vêtement[s] les plus extravagants
4 *(price)* exorbitant

outrageously [aʊt'reɪdʒəslɪ] **ADV 1** *(scanda[lously])* de façon scandaleuse, scandaleuse[ment]; *(atrociously)* atrocement, monstrueuse[ment]; **we have been treated o.** on nous a traité d'une façon scandaleuse **2** *(extravagantly)* de fa[ç]on extravagante; **the shop is o. expensive** le[s] prix pratiqués dans ce magasin sont exorb[i]tants

outrageousness [aʊt'reɪdʒəsnɪs] **N** *(of behav[iour])* caractère *m* scandaleux *ou* outrageant; *(of crime, torture)* atrocité *f*; *(of dress, hairstyle)* extravagance *f*; *(of language)* outrance *f*; *(o[f] prices)* exagération *f*

outran [ˌaʊt'ræn] *pt of* **outrun**

outrank [ˌaʊt'ræŋk] **VT 1** *(be of higher rank than)* avoir un rang plus élevé que; *Mil* être supérieu[r] en grade à; **he was outranked by most of thos[e] present** la plupart des personnes présente[s] avaient un grade supérieur au sien **2** *(take prece[dence over])* avoir *ou* prendre le pas sur; **to be out[]ranked by** donner *ou* céder le pas à

outreach **VT** [ˌaʊt'riːtʃ] **1** *(exceed)* dépasser **2** *(i[n] arm length)* avoir le bras plus long que; *(in box[ing])* avoir l'allonge supérieure à
N ['aʊtriːtʃ] *Admin* = recherche des personne[s] qui ne demandent pas l'aide sociale dont elle[s] pourraient bénéficier
▸▸ ***outreach worker*** = employé ou bénévole dans un bureau d'aide sociale

outrider ['aʊtˌraɪdə(r)] **N** *Br (motorcyclist)* motar[d] *m* (d'escorte); *(horseman)* cavalier *m*

outrigger ['aʊtˌrɪgə(r)] **N** *Naut (gen)* balancier *m*; *(on racing boat)* portant *m*, outrigger *m*

outright **ADJ** ['aʊtraɪt] **1** *(absolute, utter ▸ dishon[esty], hypocrisy)* pur (et simple), absolu; *(▸ liar)* fieffé; *(▸ ownership)* total, absolu; *(frank ▸ de[nial], refusal)* net, catégorique; **he's an o. fascist** c'est un vrai fasciste!; **she's an o. opponent of cap[]ital punishment** c'est une adversaire incondi[]tionnelle de la peine de mort; **it was o. blackmai[l]** c'était purement et simplement du chantage, c'était du chantage, ni plus ni moins **2** *(clear ▸ win, winner)* incontesté; **it's an o. win for New Zealand** la victoire revient incontestablement à la Nouvelle-Zélande **3** *Com (purchase, sale ▸ fo[r] cash)* au comptant; *(▸ total)* en bloc
ADV [aʊt'raɪt] **1** *(frankly ▸ refuse)* net, carrément; *(▸ ask)* carrément, franchement
2 *(totally ▸ oppose)* absolument; *(▸ own)* totalement
3 *(clearly ▸ win)* nettement, haut la main
4 *Com (buy, sell ▸ for cash)* au comptant; *(▸ totally)* en bloc
5 *(instantly)* **they were killed o.** ils ont été tués sur le coup

outrival [ˌaʊt'raɪvəl] **VT** *(person)* surpasser, l'emporter sur

outrun [ˌaʊt'rʌn] *(pt* **outran** [-'ræn], *pp* **outrun,** *cont* **outrunning) VT 1** *(run faster than)* courir plus vite que; *(pursuer)* distancer **2** *(ability, energy, resources)* excéder, dépasser; **his zeal outruns his**

scretion son ardeur l'emporte sur son jugement

uts [aʊts] **NPL** *Am Fam* **to be on the o. with sb** être rouillé avec qn; **they're on the o.** ils sont rouillés

utsell [ˌaʊt'sel] (*pt & pp* **outsold** [-'səʊld]) **VT** *(of article)* se vendre mieux que; *(of company)* vendre davantage que, vendre plus que; **her book outsold all of this week's other publications** son livre a été la meilleure vente de la semaine

utset ['aʊtset] **N at the o.** au début, au départ; **om the o.** dès le début, d'emblée

utshine [ˌaʊt'ʃaɪn] (*pt & pp* **outshone** [-'ʃɒn]) **VT 1** *hine brighter than)* briller plus que **2** *Fig (surpass)* surpasser, éclipser

UTSIDE

ADV
- dehors **1–3**

PREP
- à l'extérieur de **1**
- devant **3**
- en dehors de **4**

ADJ
- extérieur **1, 2, 5**
- faible **3**
- maximum **4**

N
- extérieur **1, 4**
- dehors **1**

DV [aʊt'saɪd] **1** *(outdoors)* dehors, à l'extérieur; **'s cold o.** il fait froid dehors; **put the box o.** mettez la boîte dehors; **to go o.** sortir; **to run/to dash o.** sortir en courant/à toute vitesse; **seen from o.** u de l'extérieur; **the car is waiting o.** la voiture ttend dehors; **you'll have to park o.** il faudra ous garer dans la rue

2 *(on other side of door)* dehors; **there's a woman . in the hall** il y a une femme dehors dans le vestibule

3 *(out of prison)* dehors; **after ten years, it's hard o imagine life o.** après dix ans, c'est dur d'imaginer la vie dehors

PREP [aʊt'saɪd, 'aʊtsaɪd] **1** *(on or to the exterior)* à extérieur de, hors de; **nobody is allowed o. the ouse** personne n'a le droit de quitter la maison; **. my bedroom** *(at the door)* à la porte de ma hambre; *(below the windows)* sous les fenêtres e ma chambre; **put the eggs o. the window/the oor** mettez les œufs sur le rebord de la fenêtre/ evant la porte; **she was wearing her shirt o. her rousers** elle portait sa chemise par-dessus son antalon; **nobody o. the office must know** personne ne doit être mis au courant en dehors du ureau; *Fig* **the troublemakers were people from . the group** les fauteurs de troubles ne faisaient as partie du groupe

2 *(away from)* **we live some way o. the town** nous abitons assez loin de la ville; **I don't think anyody o. France has heard of him** je ne pense pas u'il soit connu ailleurs qu'en France

3 *(in front of)* devant; **they met o. the cathedral** *by chance)* ils se sont rencontrés devant la cahédrale; *(by arrangement)* ils se sont retrouvés levant la cathédrale

4 *(beyond)* en dehors de, au-delà de; **it's o. his ield** ce n'est pas son domaine; **it's o. my experince** ça ne m'est jamais arrivé; **the matter is o. ur responsibility** la question ne relève pas de otre responsabilité; **o. office hours** en dehors les heures de bureau

ADJ ['aʊtsaɪd] **1** *(exterior)* extérieur; **the o. world** le nonde extérieur; **she has few o. interests** elle 'intéresse à peu de choses à part son travail; **n o. toilet** des toilettes (situées) à l'extérieur; **he o. edge** le bord extérieur

2 *(from elsewhere ▸ help, influence)* extérieur; **to et an o. opinion** demander l'avis d'un tiers

3 *(poor ▸ possibility)* faible; **she has only an o. hance of winning** elle n'a que très peu de chanes de gagner

4 *(maximum ▸ price)* maximum; **the o. odds are 6 o 1** la cote maximum est de 6 contre 1

5 *(not belonging to a group)* extérieur, indépenlant; **an o. body** un organisme indépendant

N [aʊt'saɪd, 'aʊtsaɪd] **1** *(exterior ▸ of building, conainer)* extérieur *m*, dehors *m*; **the o. of the house needs repainting** l'extérieur de la maison a besoin d'être repeint; **on the o. of sth** à l'extérieur de qch; **the fruit is yellow on the o.** le fruit est aune à l'extérieur; **the door opens from (the) o.** la porte s'ouvre de l'extérieur *ou* du dehors; **the arms were flown in from o.** les armes ont été introduites dans le pays par avion; *Fig* **looking at the problem from (the) o.** quand on considère le problème de l'extérieur

2 *(out of prison)* **I've almost forgotten what life is like on the o.** j'ai presque oublié ce qu'est la vie dehors *ou* de l'autre côté des barreaux

3 *Aut* **to overtake on the o.** *(driving on left)* doubler à droite; *(driving on right)* doubler à gauche; *Sport* **to come up on the o.** *(in race)* arriver sur l'extérieur

4 *(outer edge)* extérieur *m*; **begin at the o. and work in** commencez par les bords et allez vers l'intérieur

• **at the outside ADV 1** *(in number)* tout au plus, au maximum; **20 people at the o.** 20 personnes tout au plus

2 *(in time)* au plus tard; **6:30 at the o.** 6 heures 30 au plus tard

• **outside of PREP** *esp Am* **1 = outside**

2 *(except for)* en dehors de; **nobody, o. of a few close friends, was invited** personne, en dehors de *ou* à part quelques amis intimes, n'était invité

3 *(more than)* au-delà de; **an offer o. of 10 million** une offre de plus de *ou* supérieure à 10 millions

▸▸ *TV* ***outside broadcast*** émission *f* réalisée en dehors des studios; *TV* ***outside broadcasting*** émissions *fpl* réalisées en dehors des studios; *TV* ***outside broadcasting unit, outside broadcasting van, outside broadcasting vehicle*** car *m* régie, unité *f* mobile de tournage; *St Exch* ***outside broker*** courtier(ère) *m,f* marron *ou* libre; ***outside half*** *(in rugby)* demi *m* d'ouverture; ***outside lane*** *(driving on left)* file *f ou* voie *f* de droite; *(driving on right)* file *f ou* voie *f* de gauche; *Sport* couloir *m* extérieur; *Ftbl* ***outside left*** ailier *m* gauche; *Tel* ***outside line*** ligne *f* extérieure; *Comput & Typ* ***outside margin*** marge *f* extérieure; *St Exch* ***outside market*** marché *m* hors cote *ou* en coulisse; *Ftbl* ***outside right*** ailier *m* droit

outsider [ˌaʊt'saɪdə(r)] **N 1** *(person)* étranger (ère) *m,f*; **he's always been a bit of an o.** il a toujours été plutôt marginal **2** *Sport* outsider *m* **3** *St Exch* courtier(ère) *m,f* marron

outsize ['aʊtsaɪz] *Br* **N** *(gen)* grande taille *f*, grandes tailles *fpl*; *(for men)* très grand patron *m*
ADJ 1 *(large)* énorme, colossal **2** *(in clothes sizes)* grande taille *(inv)*

outsized ['aʊtsaɪzd] **ADJ** énorme, colossal

outskirts ['aʊtskɜːts] **NPL** *(of town)* banlieue *f*, périphérie *f*; *(of forest)* orée *f*, lisière *f*; **we live on the o. of Copenhagen** nous habitons la banlieue de Copenhague

outsmart [ˌaʊt'smɑːt] **VT** *Fam* se montrer plus malin(igne) que

outsold [ˌaʊt'səʊld] *pt & pp of* **outsell**

outsource ['aʊtsɔːs] **VT** *Com* externaliser; **computer maintenance has been outsourced to another company** l'entretien du matériel informatique a été externalisé

outsourcing ['aʊtsɔːsɪŋ] **N** *Com* externalisation *f*

outspend [ˌaʊt'spend] (*pt & pp* **outspent** [-'spent]) **VT** dépenser plus que

outspoken [ˌaʊt'spəʊkən] **ADJ** franc (franche); **to be o.** parler franchement, avoir son francparler; **she was o. in her criticism of the project** elle a ouvertement critiqué le projet; **he has always been an o. critic of the reforms** il a toujours ouvertement critiqué les réformes

outspokenly [ˌaʊt'spəʊkənlɪ] **ADV** franchement, carrément

outspokenness [ˌaʊt'spəʊkənnɪs] **N** francparler *m*

outspread [ˌaʊt'spred] **ADJ** écarté; **with o. arms** les bras écartés; **with o. wings** les ailes déployées; **with o. fingers** les doigts écartés

outstanding [ˌaʊt'stændɪŋ] **ADJ 1** *(remarkable ▸ ability, performance)* exceptionnel, remarquable; *(notable ▸ event, feature)* marquant, mémorable; **an o. politician** un politicien hors pair *ou* exceptionnel; **she plays o. tennis** c'est une joueuse de tennis exceptionnelle *ou* remarquable

2 *(unresolved ▸ problem)* non résolu, en suspens; **there is still one o. matter** il reste encore un problème à régler

3 *(unfinished ▸ business, work)* inachevé, en cours; *Admin* en souffrance, en attente; **there are about 20 pages o.** il reste environ 20 pages à faire

4 *Fin (amount, account)* impayé, dû (due); *(bill)* impayé; *(payment)* en retard; *(invoice)* en souffrance; *(interest)* échu

5 *St Exch (shares)* en cours, en circulation

▸▸ *Fin* ***outstanding balance*** solde *m* à découvert; *Banking* ***outstanding cheque*** chèque *m* en circulation; *Fin* ***outstanding credits*** encours *m* de crédit; *Fin* ***outstanding debts*** créances *fpl* (à recouvrer); ***outstanding rent*** arriérés *mpl* de loyer

outstandingly [ˌaʊt'stændɪŋlɪ] **ADV** exceptionnellement, remarquablement

outstay [ˌaʊt'steɪ] **VT 1** *(of guests)* rester plus longtemps que; **to o. one's welcome** abuser de l'hospitalité de ses hôtes **2** *Br Sport (competitor)* tenir plus longtemps que

outstretched [ˌaʊt'stretʃt] **ADJ** *(limbs, body)* étendu, allongé; *(wings)* déployé; **to lie o.** s'allonger; **with arms o., with o. arms** *(gen)* les bras écartés; *(in welcome)* à bras (grand) ouverts; **the beggar stood outside the church with o. hands** le mendiant se tenait devant l'église, la main tendue

outstrip [ˌaʊt'strɪp] (*pt & pp* **outstripped**, *cont* **outstripping**) **VT** *Br* dépasser, surpasser; **they outstripped all their rivals** ils l'ont emporté sur tous leurs concurrents

out-supplier N *Com* fournisseur *m* potentiel

outta ['aʊtə] *Fam* = **out of**

outtake ['aʊtteɪk] **N** *Cin & TV* coupure *f*

outvote [ˌaʊt'vəʊt] **VT 1** *(bill, reform)* rejeter (à la majorité des voix); **the bill was outvoted** une majorité a voté contre le projet de loi **2** *(person)* mettre en minorité; **I wanted to go to the cinema, but I was outvoted** je voulais aller au cinéma, mais les autres ont voté contre

outward ['aʊtwəd] **ADJ 1** *(external)* extérieur, externe; *(apparent)* apparent; **to (all) o. appearances, she's very successful** selon toute apparence, elle réussit très bien; **she showed no o. signs of fear** elle ne montrait aucun signe de peur **2** *(in direction)* vers l'extérieur; **the o. journey** le voyage aller, l'aller *m*
ADV vers l'extérieur; **o. bound** *(ship, train)* en partance

▸▸ ***Outward Bound® course*** école *f* d'endurcissement (en plein air); ***outward cargo*** cargaison *f* d'aller; *Econ* ***outward investment*** investissement *m* à l'étranger; ***outward mail*** courrier *m* (en partance) pour l'étranger

outwardly ['aʊtwədlɪ] **ADV** en apparence; **she remained o. calm** elle est restée calme en apparence; **o. they seem to get on** ils donnent l'impression de bien s'entendre

outwards ['aʊtwədz] **ADV** vers l'extérieur; **his feet turn o.** il marche les pieds en dehors

outwear [aʊt'weə(r)] **VT 1** *(wear away)* user **2** *(last longer than)* durer plus longtemps que; **the system has outworn its usefulness** le système est désormais périmé

outweigh [ˌaʊt'weɪ] **VT 1** *(be more important than)* l'emporter sur; **the advantages easily o. the disadvantages** les avantages l'emportent largement sur les inconvénients **2** *(weigh more than)* peser plus que

outwit [ˌaʊt'wɪt] (*pt & pp* **outwitted**, *cont* **outwitting**) **VT** se montrer plus malin(igne) que; **we've been outwitted** on nous a eus

outwith [ˌaʊt'wɪð] **PREP** *Scot* **1** *(beyond)* en dehors de, au-delà de; **it's o. his field** ce n'est pas son domaine; **it's o. my experience** ça ne m'est jamais arrivé; **o. office hours** en dehors des heures de bureau **2** *(away from)* **we live some way o. the town** nous habitons assez loin de la ville; **I don't think anybody o. France has heard of him** je ne pense pas qu'il soit connu ailleurs qu'en France

outworn ['aʊtˌwɔːn] **ADJ** *(clothes)* usé; *(custom, idea)* dépassé, vieux-jeu *(inv)*

ouzel ['uːzəl] **N** *Orn* **ring o.** merle *m* à plastron *ou* à collier; **water o.** cincle *m* plongeur, merle *m* d'eau

ova ['əʊvə] *pl of* **ovum**

oval ['əʊvəl] ADJ (en) ovale
N ovale *m*
►► ***the Oval Office*** *(office)* le Bureau ovale; *(authority)* la présidence des États-Unis; **he has decided to make a bid for the O. Office** il a décidé de se présenter à la Maison-Blanche

ovarian [əʊ'veərɪən] ADJ ovarien
►► ***ovarian cancer*** cancer *m* de l'ovaire; ***ovarian cyst*** kyste *m* de l'ovaire

ovariectomy [ˌəʊvərɪ'ektəmɪ] (*pl* **ovariectomies**) N *Med* ovariectomie *f*

ovary ['əʊvərɪ] (*pl* **ovaries**) N ovaire *m*

ovate ['əʊveɪt] ADJ oviforme

ovation [əʊ'veɪʃən] N ovation *f*; **to give sb an o.** faire une ovation à qn

oven ['ʌvən] N four *m*; **to cook sth in the o.** faire cuire qch au four; **cook in a hot/medium o.** faire cuire à four chaud/à four moyen; **to put one's head in the o.** se suicider (au gaz); *Fig* **Athens is like an o. in summer** Athènes est une vraie fournaise en été
►► ***oven glove*** gant *m* isolant

ovenproof ['ʌvənpru:f] ADJ allant *ou* qui va au four

oven-ready ADJ prêt à cuire *ou* à mettre au four; *(chicken, meat)* prêt à rôtir

ovenware ['ʌvənweə(r)] N plats *mpl* allant au four

OVER- PRÉFIXE

Le préfixe **over-** peut s'employer avec des noms, des adjectifs, des verbes et des adverbes, et il véhicule la notion d'EXCÈS.

- Employé avec des noms, il est le plus souvent rendu en français par le préfixe **sur-** :
overpopulation surpopulation; **overconsumption** surconsommation; **overabundance** surabondance; **overfishing** surpêche; **overexposure** surexposition.
- Employé avec des adjectifs, des verbes et des adverbes, il est le plus souvent rendu en français par l'adverbe **trop** et parfois par le préfixe **sur-**:
overambitious trop ambitieux; **over-age** trop âgé; **overkeen** trop empressé; **to overcook** faire trop cuire; **to overheat** surchauffer; **to oversimplify** simplifier à l'excès; **to overemphasize** trop mettre l'accent sur; **overcautiously** avec une prudence excessive; **overcrowded** surpeuplé; **to overexpose** surexposer.

OVER ['əʊvə(r)]

PREP
- au-dessus de **A1**
- sur **A2, B1, 2**
- par-dessus **A2, 3**
- plus de **C1**
- pendant **C4**
- au sujet de **D1**
- à **D2**

ADV
- plus **B2**
- encore **B4**

ADJ
- fini

PREP **A. 1** *(above)* au-dessus de; **a bullet whistled o. my head** une balle siffla au-dessus de ma tête; **they live o. the shop** ils habitent au-dessus du magasin; **the plane came down o. France** l'avion s'est écrasé en France

2 *(on top of, covering)* sur, par-dessus; **put a lace cloth o. the table** mets une nappe en dentelle sur la table; **she wore a cardigan o. her dress** elle portait un gilet par-dessus sa robe; **she wore a black dress with a red cardigan o. it** elle avait une robe noire avec un gilet rouge par-dessus; **I put my hand o. my mouth** j'ai mis ma main devant ma bouche; **he had his jacket o. his arm** il avait sa veste sur le bras; **we painted o. the wallpaper** nous avons peint par-dessus la tapisserie; **she was hunched o. the wheel** elle était penchée sur la roue

3 *(across the top or edge of)* par-dessus; **he was watching me o. his newspaper** il m'observait par-dessus son journal; **I peered o. the edge** j'ai jeté un coup d'œil par-dessus le rebord; **he fell/jumped o. the cliff** il est tombé/a sauté du haut de la falaise

4 *(across the entire surface of)* **to cross o. the road** traverser la rue; **they live o. the road from me** ils habitent en face de chez moi; **there's a fine view o. the valley** on a une belle vue sur la vallée; **the bridge o. the river** le pont qui enjambe la rivière; **she ran her hand o. the smooth marble** elle passa la main sur le marbre lisse; **a strange look came o. her face** son visage prit une expression étrange

5 *(on the far side of)* **the village o. the hill** le village de l'autre côté de la colline; **they must be o. the border by now** ils doivent avoir passé la frontière maintenant

B. 1 *(indicating position of control)* **I have no control/influence o. them** je n'ai aucune autorité/influence sur eux; **she has some kind of hold o. him** elle a une certaine emprise sur lui; **she watched o. her children** elle surveillait ses enfants

2 *(indicating position of superiority, importance)* sur; **our project takes priority o. the others** notre projet a priorité sur les autres

C. 1 *(with specific figure or amount ► more than)* plus de; **it took me well/just o. an hour** j'ai mis bien plus/un peu plus d'une heure; **he must be o. 30** il doit avoir plus de30 ans; **children o. (the age of) seven** les enfants (âgés) de plus de sept ans; **think of a number o. 100** pensez à un chiffre supérieur à 100; **not o. 250 grams** *(in post office)* jusqu'à 250 grammes

2 *(louder than)* **his voice rang out o. the others** sa voix dominait toutes les autres; **I couldn't hear what she was saying o. the music** la musique m'empêchait d'entendre ce qu'elle disait

3 *Math (divided by)* **eight o. two** huit divisé par deux

4 *(during)* **I've got a job o. the long vacation** je vais travailler pendant les grandes vacances; **I'll do it o. the weekend** je le ferai pendant le week-end; **what are you doing o. Easter?** qu'est-ce que tu fais pour Pâques?; **it's improved o. the years** ça s'est amélioré au cours *ou* au fil des années; **o. the next few decades** au cours des prochaines décennies; **we discussed it o. a drink/o. lunch/o. a game of golf** nous en avons discuté autour d'un verre/pendant le déjeuner/en faisant une partie de golf

D. 1 *(concerning)* au sujet de; **a disagreement o. working conditions** un conflit portant sur les conditions de travail; **they're always quarrelling o. money** ils se disputent sans cesse pour des questions d'argent; **to laugh o. sth** rire (à propos) de qch

2 *(by means of, via)* **they were talking o. the telephone** ils parlaient au téléphone; **I heard it o. the radio** je l'ai entendu à la radio

3 *(recovered from)* **are you o. your bout of flu?** est-ce que tu es guéri *ou* est-ce que tu t'es remis de ta grippe?; **he's o. the shock now** il s'en est remis maintenant; **we'll soon be o. the worst** le plus dur sera bientôt passé; **don't worry, you'll be** *or* **get o. her soon** ne t'en fais pas, bientôt tu n'y penseras plus

ADV **A. 1** *(indicating movement or location, across distance or space)* **an eagle flew o.** un aigle passa au-dessus de nous; **she walked o. to him and said hello** elle s'approcha de lui pour dire bonjour; **he led me o. to the window** il m'a conduit à la fenêtre; **he must have seen us, he's coming o.** il a dû nous voir, il vient vers nous *ou* de notre côté; **pass my cup o., will you** tu peux me passer ma tasse?; **throw it o.!** *(over the wall etc)* lance-le par-dessus!; *(throw it to me)* lance-le moi!; **she glanced o. at me** elle jeta un coup d'œil dans ma direction; **o. in the States** aux États-Unis; **o. there** là-bas; **come o. here!** viens (par) ici!; **has Colin been o.?** est-ce que Colin est passé?; **she drove o. to meet us** elle est venue nous rejoindre en voiture; **let's have** *or* **invite them o. for dinner** si on les invitait à dîner?; **we have guests o. from Morocco** nous avons des invités qui viennent du Maroc

2 *(everywhere)* **she's travelled the whole world o.** elle a voyagé dans le monde entier; **people the world o. are watching the broadcast live** des téléspectateurs du monde entier assistent à cette retransmission en direct

3 *(indicating movement from a higher to a lower level)* **I fell o.** je suis tombé (par terre); **she knocked her glass o.** elle a renversé son verre; *Am Fam* **o. easy** *(egg)* cuit sur les deux côtés; **they rolled o. and o. in the grass** ils se roulaient dans l'herbe; **and o. I went** et me voilà par terre

4 *(so as to cover)* **we just whitewashed it o.** no[...] l'avons simplement passé à la chaux; **the bodi[...] were covered o. with blankets** les corps étaie[...] recouverts avec des couvertures

5 *(into the hands of another person, group etc)* **h[...] gone o. to the other side/to the opposition** il [...] passé de l'autre côté/dans l'opposition; **th[...] handed him o. to the authorities** ils l'ont rem[...] aux autorités *ou* entre les mains des autorité[...] *Rad & TV* **and now o. to Kirsty Jones in Paris** no[...] passons maintenant l'antenne à Kirsty Jones [...] Paris; **o. to you** *(it's your turn)* c'est votre to[...] c'est à vous; *Tel* **o. (to you)!** à vous!; **o. and ou[...]** terminé!

B. 1 *(left, remaining)* **there were/I had a fe[...] pounds (left) o.** il restait/il me restait quelqu[...] livres; **you will keep what is (left) o.** vous gard[...]rez l'excédent *ou* le surplus; **seven into fifty-tw[...] makes seven with three o.** cinquante-deux divi[...] par sept égale sept, il reste trois

2 *(with specific figure or amount ► more)* pl[...] **men of 30 and o.** les hommes âgés de 30 ans [...] plus; **articles costing £100 or o.** les articles de 1[...] livres et plus

3 *(through)* **read it o. carefully** lisez-le attentiv[...]ment; **do you want to talk the matter o.?** voule[...] vous en discuter?

4 *(again, more than once)* encore; *Am* **I had to [...] the whole thing o.** j'ai dû tout refaire; **she won t[...] tournament five times o.** elle a gagné le tourno[...] cinq reprises

ADJ fini; **the party's o.** la fête est finie; **the dang[...] is o.** le danger est passé; **the war was just o.** [...] guerre venait de finir *ou* de s'achever; **I'm gla[...] that's o. (with)!** je suis bien content que ça s[...] fini!; **that's o. and done with** voilà qui est fini [...] bien fini

N *(in cricket)* série *f* de six balles

• **overs** NPL *Typ (extra paper)* main *f* de pass[...] simple passe *f*; *(extra books)* exemplaires *m*[...] de passe

• **over and above** PREP en plus de; **o. and abo[...] what we've already paid** en plus de ce que no[...] avons déjà payé; **and o. and above that, he w[...] banned from driving for life** en plus, on lui a reti[...] son permis (de conduire) à vie

• **over and over** ADV **I've told you o. and [...] (again)** je te l'ai répété je ne sais combien de foi[...] **he did it o. and o. (again) until...** il a recommen[...] des dizaines de fois jusqu'à ce que...

overabundance [ˌəʊvərə'bʌndəns] N surabo[...]dance *f*

overabundant [ˌəʊvərə'bʌndənt] ADJ surabo[...]dant

overachieve [ˌəʊvərə'tʃi:v] VI réussir brillan[...]ment; **children who o.** les enfants surdoués

overachiever [ˌəʊvərə'tʃi:və(r)] N surdoué(e) *[...] f*

overact [ˌəʊvər'ækt] VI surjouer, en faire trop

overactive [ˌəʊvər'æktɪv] ADJ **to have an o. imag[...]nation** avoir une imagination débordante; *Me[...]* **to have an o. thyroid** faire de l'hyperthyroïdie

overaffectionate [ˌəʊvərə'fekʃənət] ADJ affe[...]tueux à l'excès

over-age ADJ *(too old)* trop âgé

overall ADV [ˌəʊvər'ɔ:l] **1** *(in general ► conside[...] examine)* en général, globalement **2** *(measur[...]* de bout en bout, d'un bout à l'autre; *(cos[...] amount)* en tout **3** *(in competition, sport)* au cla[...]sement général; **Britain finished third o.** [...] Grande-Bretagne a fini troisième au classe[...]ment général

ADJ ['əʊvərɔ:l] **1** *(general)* global, d'ensemble; **m[...] o. impression** mon impression d'ensemble; [...] **control of the region has fallen into the hands [...] the rebels** la plus grande partie de la région e[...] désormais aux mains des rebelles; **she has o. r[...]sponsibility for sales** elle est responsable de l'e[...]semble du service des ventes **2** *(total ► cos[...] amount)* total; *(► measurement)* total, hors tout

N ['əʊvərɔ:l] *(protective coat)* blouse *f*; *Am (boil[...] suit)* bleu *m* de travail

• **overalls** NPL ['əʊvərɔ:lz] *Br (boiler suit)* bleu [...] de travail; *Am (dungarees)* salopette *f*

►► ***overall budget*** budget *m* global; ***overall co[...]sumption*** consommation *f* totale; ***overall deman[...]***

demande *f* globale; *Pol* ***overall majority*** majorité *f* absolue

overanxious [ˌəʊvər'æŋkʃəs] **ADJ 1** *(worried)* trop inquiet(ète); **don't be o. about the exam** ne vous inquiétez pas trop au sujet de l'examen **2** *(keen)* **he did not seem o. to meet her** il n'avait pas l'air tellement pressé de faire sa connaissance; **she is o. to please** elle est trop désireuse *ou* soucieuse de plaire

overarm ['əʊvərɑːm] **ADV** *(serve, bowl)* par-dessus l'épaule; **to throw a ball o.** lancer une balle par-dessus sa tête; **to swim o.** nager à l'indienne

▸▸ *Sport* ***overarm bowling*** *(in cricket)* service *m* au-dessus de la tête; *Sport* ***overarm service*** *(in tennis, badminton)* service *m* au-dessus de la tête; *Swimming* ***overarm stroke*** brasse *f* indienne, nage *f* (à l')indienne

overassess [ˌəʊvərə'ses] **VT** *Fin (for tax)* surimposer

overassessment [ˌəʊvərə'sesmənt] **N** *Fin (for tax)* surimposition *f*

overate [ˌəʊvər'eɪt] *pt of* **overeat**

overawe [ˌəʊvər'ɔː] **VT** intimider; *(of prospect, difficulty, surroundings)* impressionner; **don't be overawed by what you are about to hear** ne vous laissez pas impressionner par ce que vous allez entendre

overbalance [ˌəʊvə'bæləns] **VT** *(person)* faire perdre l'équilibre à; *(pile, vehicle)* renverser, faire basculer

VI *(person)* perdre l'équilibre; *(load, pile)* basculer, se renverser; *(car)* capoter; *(boat)* chavirer

overbearing [ˌəʊvə'beərɪŋ] **ADJ** autoritaire, impérieux

overbite ['əʊvəbaɪt] **N** surocclusion *f*

overblown [ˌəʊvə'bləʊn] **ADJ 1** *(flower)* trop épanoui *ou* ouvert; *(beauty)* qui commence à se faner **2** *Pej (prose, style)* ampoulé, pompier

overboard ['əʊvəbɔːd] **ADV** *Naut* par-dessus bord; **to fall o.** passer par-dessus bord; **to jump o.** sauter à la mer; **man o.!** un homme à la mer!; **to throw sb/sth o.** jeter qn/qch par-dessus bord; *Fig* se débarrasser de qn/qch; *Fam* **to go o.** dépasser la mesure, exagérer; **the critics went o. about her first novel** les critiques se sont enthousiasmés *ou* emballés pour son premier roman

overbook [ˌəʊvə'bʊk] **VT** *(hotel, flight)* surbooker, surréserver

VI *(airline, hotel)* surbooker, surréserver

overbooking [ˌəʊvə'bʊkɪŋ] **N** surréservation *f*, surbooking *m*

overboot ['əʊvəbuːt] **N** couvre-chaussure *m*

overborrow [ˌəʊvə'bɒrəʊ] **VI** *Fin (of company)* emprunter de façon excessive

overborrowing [ˌəʊvə'bɒrəʊɪŋ] **N** *Fin (of company)* surendettement *m*

overbought [ˌəʊvə'bɔːt] **ADJ** *St Exch (market)* surévalué, suracheté

overburden [ˌəʊvə'bɜːdən] **VT** surcharger, accabler; **overburdened with work/worries** accablé de travail/de soucis; **overburdened with debts** criblé de dettes

overcame [ˌəʊvə'keɪm] *pt of* **overcome**

overcapacity [ˌəʊvəkə'pæsɪtɪ] **N** *Econ* surcapacité *f*

overcapitalization, -isation [ˌəʊvəˌkæpɪtəlaɪ'zeɪʃən] **N** *Fin* surcapitalisation *f*

overcapitalize, -ise [ˌəʊvə'kæpɪtəlaɪz] **VT** *Fin* surcapitaliser

overcast *(pt & pp* **overcast)** **VT** [ˌəʊvə'kɑːst] *Sewing* surfiler

ADJ ['əʊvəkɑːst] *(sky)* sombre, couvert; *(weather)* couvert; **it's getting o.** le temps se couvre; **the sky became o.** le ciel s'assombrit

overcautious [ˌəʊvə'kɔːʃəs] **ADJ** trop prudent, prudent à l'excès

overcautiously [ˌəʊvə'kɔːʃəslɪ] **ADV** avec trop de prudence, avec une prudence excessive

overcharge [ˌəʊvə'tʃɑːdʒ] **VT 1** *(customer)* faire payer trop cher à; *(goods)* survendre; **I've been overcharged!** on m'a fait payer trop cher!; **they overcharged me for the coffee** ils m'ont fait payer le café trop cher; **they overcharged me for the repair** ils m'ont pris trop cher pour la réparation **2** *Elec (circuit)* surcharger **3** *Br (description, picture)* surcharger; **the painting was overcharged with detail** le tableau était surchargé de détails

VI faire payer trop cher; **they overcharged for the tomatoes** ils ont fait payer les tomates trop cher

overcoat ['əʊvəkəʊt] **N** manteau *m*, pardessus *m*

overcome [ˌəʊvə'kʌm] *(pt* **overcame** [-'keɪm], *pp* **overcome)** **VT 1** *(vanquish ▸ enemy, opposition)* vaincre, triompher de; *(▸ difficulty, shyness)* surmonter; *(▸ fear, repulsion, prejudice)* vaincre, surmonter, maîtriser; *(master ▸ nerves)* maîtriser, contrôler **2** *(debilitate, weaken)* accabler; **the heat overcame me** la chaleur finit par me terrasser; **she was o. by the fumes** les émanations lui ont fait perdre connaissance **3** *(usu passive) (overwhelm)* **to be o. by the enemy** succomber à l'ennemi; **to be o. by fear** être paralysé par la peur; **to be o. with joy** être comblé de joie; **to be o. with grief** être accablé par la douleur; **I was o. by the news** la nouvelle m'a bouleversé; **in a voice o. with emotion** d'une voix tremblante d'émotion

VI vaincre

overcompensate [ˌəʊvə'kɒmpənseɪt] **VT 1** *Psy* surcompenser **2** *Law* verser des dommages-intérêts excessifs à

VI 1 *Psy* surcompenser; **to o. for sth** surcompenser qch **2** *(make amends)* **she feels guilty about being away so much and overcompensates by showering her children with gifts** elle se sent coupable d'être si souvent absente et essaie de se faire pardonner en couvrant ses enfants de cadeaux

overcomplicated [ˌəʊvə'kɒmplɪkeɪtɪd] **ADJ** trop *ou* excessivement compliqué

overconfidence [ˌəʊvə'kɒnfɪdəns] **N 1** *(arrogance)* suffisance *f*, présomption *f* **2** *(trust)* confiance *f* aveugle *ou* excessive

overconfident [ˌəʊvə'kɒnfɪdənt] **ADJ 1** *(arrogant)* suffisant, présomptueux; **you're being o. about the exam** tu présumes un peu trop de ta réussite à l'examen **2** *(trusting)* trop confiant; **I'm not o. of his chances of recovery** je ne crois pas trop en ses chances de guérison

overcook [ˌəʊvə'kʊk] **VT** faire trop cuire; **the vegetables are overcooked** les légumes sont trop cuits

VI trop cuire

over-correction **N** *(of air/fuel ratio etc)* surcorrection *f*

overcritical [ˌəʊvə'krɪtɪkəl] **ADJ** trop critique

overcrowd [ˌəʊvə'kraʊd] **VT** *(bus, train, room)* remplir au maximum, bourrer; *(city, streets, prison)* surpeupler; *(class)* surcharger

overcrowded [ˌəʊvə'kraʊdɪd] **ADJ** *(bus, train, room)* bondé, comble; *(city, country, prison)* surpeuplé; *(streets)* plein de monde; *(class)* surchargé; **Paris is o. with tourists in summer** en été, Paris est envahi par les touristes; **they live in very o. conditions** ils vivent très à l'étroit

overcrowding [ˌəʊvə'kraʊdɪŋ] **N** surpeuplement *m*, surpopulation *f*; *(in housing)* entassement *m*; *(in bus, train etc)* entassement *m* des voyageurs, affluence *f*; *(in schools)* effectifs *mpl* surchargés; *(in prisons)* surpeuplement *m*; **o. on trains means you sometimes have to stand** les trains sont tellement bondés qu'on est parfois contraint de voyager debout

overdemand [ˌəʊvədɪ'mɑːnd] **N** demande *f* excédentaire

overdeveloped [ˌəʊvədɪ'veləpt] **ADJ** *(gen) & Phot* surdéveloppé

overdo [ˌəʊvə'duː] *(pt* **overdid** [-'dɪd], *pp* **overdone** [-'dʌn]) **VT 1** *(exaggerate)* exagérer, pousser trop loin; **he rather overdoes the penniless student (bit)** il joue un peu trop l'étudiant pauvre; **the battle scenes are a bit overdone** les scènes de combat sont un peu exagérées; **all that jewellery is really overdoing it!** tous ces bijoux? c'est vraiment un peu trop!; **Maxine rather overdoes the make-up** Maxine se maquille un peu trop; **you've overdone the curry powder** tu as eu la main un peu lourde avec le curry; **she overdoes the jogging** elle force un peu trop sur le jogging

2 *(eat, drink too much of)* **don't o. the whisky** n'abuse pas du whisky

3 *(idiom)* **to o. it, to o. things** se surmener; **I've been overdoing it again** j'ai de nouveau un peu trop forcé; *Ironic* **don't o. it!** surtout ne te surmène pas!

4 *Culin* trop cuire

overdose **N** ['əʊvədəʊs] **1** *(of drugs)* dose *f* massive *ou* excessive; *(of hard drugs)* overdose *f*, surdose *f*; **to take an o.** *(of hard drugs)* faire une overdose; **she died from a drugs o.** elle est morte d'une overdose **2** *Fig* dose *f*; *Hum* **I think I've had an o. of culture today** je crois que j'ai eu ma dose de culture pour aujourd'hui

VI ['əʊvədəʊs] prendre une dose massive; *(on hard drugs)* prendre une overdose; **he overdosed on heroin/LSD** il a pris une overdose d'héroïne/de LSD; *Hum* **I've been overdosing on chocolate recently** j'ai trop forcé sur le chocolat ces derniers temps

VT [ˌəʊvə'dəʊs] *(patient)* administrer une dose excessive à

overdraft ['əʊvədrɑːft] **N** découvert *m* (bancaire); **to have an o.** avoir un découvert; **to allow** *or* **to give sb an o.** accorder à qn un découvert; **to pay off one's o.** rembourser son découvert

▸▸ ***overdraft facility*** autorisation *f* de découvert, facilités *fpl* de caisse; ***overdraft limit*** plafond *m* de découvert; ***overdraft loan*** prêt *m* à découvert

overdraw [ˌəʊvə'drɔː] *(pt* **overdrew** [-'druː], *pp* **overdrawn** [-'drɔːn]) **VT** *(account)* mettre à découvert

VI tirer à découvert; **to o. on one's account** mettre son compte à découvert

overdress **VI** [ˌəʊvə'dres] *Pej* s'habiller avec trop de recherche

N ['əʊvədres] robe-chasuble *f*

overdrew [ˌəʊvə'druː] *pt of* **overdraw**

overdrive ['əʊvədraɪv] **N** *Aut* (vitesse *f*) surmultipliée *f*, overdrive *m*; **in o.** en surmultipliée; *Fig* **to go into o.** mettre les bouchées doubles

overdub *(pt & pp* **overdubbed**, *cont* **overdubbing)** **VT** [ˌəʊvə'dʌb] *(in recording)* ajouter une piste/plusieurs pistes à, ajouter un overdub/des overdubs à

N ['əʊvədʌb] overdub *m*

overdubbing [ˌəʊvə'dʌbɪŋ] **N** overdubbing *m*, ajout *m* de pistes

overdue [ˌəʊvə'djuː] **ADJ 1** *(bus, flight, person)* en retard; *(amount, bill)* impayé, en souffrance; *(payment, rent)* en retard, impayé; *(library book)* non retourné; **she is long o.** elle devrait être là depuis longtemps; **the flight from Panama is half an hour o.** le vol de Panama a une demi-heure de retard; **our repayments are two months o.** nous avons un retard de deux mois dans nos remboursements **2** *(apology)* tardif; *(change, reform)* qui tarde, qui se fait attendre; **an explanation is o.** le moment semble venu de donner une explication, il est temps de donner une explication; **this reform is long o.** cette réforme aurait dû être appliquée il y a longtemps **3** *(in pregnancy)* **to be o.** avoir dépassé son terme; **the baby was two weeks o.** le bébé avait deux semaines de retard

overeat [ˌəʊvər'iːt] *(pt* **overate** [-'eɪt], *pp* **overeaten** [-'iːtən]) **VI** *(once)* trop manger, faire un repas trop copieux; *(habitually)* se suralimenter

overeating [ˌəʊvər'iːtɪŋ] **N** *(habitual)* suralimentation *f*

overelaborate [ˌəʊvərɪ'læbərɪt] **ADJ** *(dress, style)* trop recherché; *(ornamentation)* tarabiscoté; *(explanation, excuse)* tiré par les cheveux; *(description)* alambiqué, contourné

overemphasis [ˌəʊvə'remfəsɪs] **N** accentuation *f* excessive

overemphasize, -ise [ˌəʊvər'emfəsaɪz] **VT** trop mettre l'accent sur, trop insister sur; **I cannot o. the need for discretion** je n'insisterai jamais assez sur la nécessité de faire preuve de discrétion

overemployment [ˌəʊvərɪm'plɔɪmənt] **N** suremploi *m*

overenthusiastic ['əʊvərɪnˌθjuːzɪ'æstɪk] **ADJ** trop enthousiaste

overestimate [ˌəʊvər'estɪmeɪt] **VT** *(cost, person's talent, difficulty)* surestimer; *(one's strength)* trop présumer de; *Com (assets)* majorer; **to o. one's own importance** surestimer sa propre importance

overexcite [ˌəʊvərɪkˈsaɪt] VT surexciter

overexcited [ˌəʊvərɪkˈsaɪtɪd] ADJ surexcité; **to become** *or* **to get o.** (trop) s'énerver; **don't get o., they haven't arrived yet** ne vous excitez pas, ils ne sont pas encore arrivés

overexcitement [ˌəʊvərɪkˈsaɪtmənt] N surexcitation *f*

overexert [ˌəʊvərɪgˈzɜːt] VT surmener; **to o. oneself** se surmener, s'éreinter

overexertion [ˌəʊvərɪgˈzɜːʃən] N surmenage *m*

overexpose [ˌəʊvərɪkˈspəʊz] VT *Phot* surexposer

overexposed [ˌəʊvərɪkˈspəʊzd] ADJ *Phot* surexposé; *Fig (in the media)* surmédiatisé

overexposure [ˌəʊvərɪkˈspəʊʒə(r)] N **1** *Phot* surexposition *f*; *Fig (in the media)* surmédiatisation *f*; **to suffer from o.** faire trop parler de soi; **because of people's o. to advertising** parce que les gens sont bombardés de publicité **2** *Fin* risque *m* accru

overextend [ˌəʊvərɪkˈstend] VT *Fin* **to o. oneself** s'engager au-dessus de ses moyens

overfamiliar [ˌəʊvəfəˈmɪlɪə(r)] ADJ **1** *(too intimate, disrespectful)* trop familier; **to be o. with sb** se montrer trop familier *ou* prendre des libertés excessives avec qn **2** *(conversant)* **I'm not o. with the system** je ne connais pas très bien le système

overfeed [ˌəʊvəˈfiːd] *(pt & pp* **overfed** [-ˈfed]) VT suralimenter

VI se suralimenter, trop manger

overfishing [ˌəʊvə(r)ˈfɪʃɪŋ] N surpêche *f*

overflew [ˌəʊvəˈfluː] *pt of* **overfly**

overflow VI [ˌəʊvəˈfləʊ] **1** *(with liquid ▸ container, bath)* déborder; *(▸ river)* déborder, sortir de son lit; *(with people ▸ room, vehicle)* déborder, être plein à craquer; *(with objects ▸ box, wastebin)* déborder; **the river frequently overflows onto the surrounding plain** la rivière inonde souvent la plaine environnante; **the streets were overflowing with people** les rues regorgeaient de monde; **the demonstrators overflowed into the side streets** les manifestants ont débordé dans les rues transversales; **the glass is full to overflowing** le verre est plein à ras bord; **the shop was full to overflowing** le magasin était plein à craquer; **the contents of the bin overflowed onto the floor** le contenu de la poubelle s'est répandu par terre **2** *Fig (with emotion)* déborder; **his heart was overflowing with joy** son cœur débordait de joie

VT [ˌəʊvəˈfləʊ] déborder de; **the river overflowed its banks** la rivière est sortie de son lit *ou* a débordé

N [ˈəʊvəfləʊ] **1** *(drain ▸ from sink, cistern)* trop-plein *m*; *(▸ large-scale)* déversoir *m*

2 *(excess ▸ of population, production)* excédent *m*, surplus *m*; *(▸ of energy, emotion)* trop-plein *m*, débordement *m*

3 *(flooding)* inondation *f*; *(excess)* trop-plein *m*

4 *Comput* dépassement *m* de capacité, débordement *m*

▸▸ ***overflow pipe*** *(from sink, cistern)* trop-plein *m*; *(large-scale)* déversoir *m*

overflowing [ˌəʊvəˈfləʊɪŋ] ADJ *(water, river etc)* qui déborde; *(container)* plein à déborder; *(joy, gratitude)* débordant

overfly [ˌəʊvəˈflaɪ] *(pt* **overflew** [-ˈfluː], *pp* **overflown** [-ˈfləʊn]) VT survoler

overfond [ˌəʊvəˈfɒnd] ADJ **I'm not o. of oranges** je ne raffole pas des oranges; **she's not o. of children** on ne peut pas dire qu'elle ait une passion pour les enfants; **he's not o. of the cinema** il n'est pas très porté sur le cinéma

overfull [ˌəʊvəˈfʊl] ADJ trop plein, qui déborde

overgear [ˌəʊvəˈgɪə(r)] VT *Fin (company)* surendetter

overgearing [ˌəʊvəˈgɪərɪŋ] N *Fin* surendettement *m*

overgrown [ˌəʊvəˈgrəʊn] ADJ *(garden, path etc)* **the path was o. with weeds/brambles** le chemin était envahi par les mauvaises herbes/les ronces; **the garden has become very o.** le jardin est devenu une vraie jungle; **a wall o. with ivy** un mur recouvert de lierre; *Fig* **he's just an o. schoolboy** c'est un grand enfant

overhang *(pt & pp* **overhung** [-ˈhʌŋ]) VT [ˌəʊvəˈhæŋ] **1** *(of cliff, ledge, balcony)* surplomber, faire saillie au-dessus de; *(of cloud, mist, smoke)* planer sur, flotter au-dessus de **2** *Fig (of threat, danger)* planer sur, menacer

VI [ˌəʊvəˈhæŋ] être en surplomb, faire saillie

N [ˈəʊvəhæŋ] surplomb *m*; *(smaller)* dévers *m*; *Constr* **to have an o.** porter à faux

overhanging [ˌəʊvəˈhæŋɪŋ] ADJ **1** *(cliff, ledge, balcony)* en surplomb, en saillie; **we walked under the o. branches** nous marchions sous un dais *ou* une voûte de branches **2** *Fig (threat)* imminent

overhaul N [ˈəʊvəhɔːl] *(of car, machine)* révision *f*; *(of institution, system)* révision *f*, remaniement *m*; **the education system needs a complete o.** le système scolaire a besoin d'être complètement remanié

VT [ˌəʊvəˈhɔːl] **1** *(car, machine)* réviser; *(system)* revoir, remanier **2** *(catch up)* rattraper; *(overtake)* dépasser; *Naut* gagner

overhead ADV [ˌəʊvəˈhed] au-dessus; **we watched the hawk circling o.** nous regardions le faucon tournoyer dans le ciel *ou* au-dessus de nos têtes

ADJ [ˈəʊvəhed] *(cable, railway)* aérien; *(lighting)* au plafond; *Sport (racket stroke)* smashé; *Ftbl (kick)* retourné

N [ˈəʊvəhed] **1** *(cost)* charge *f* opérationnelle **2** *Am (costs)* frais *mpl* généraux **3** *(in tennis, badminton)* smash *m*

• **overheads** NPL *Br* frais *mpl* généraux; **to reduce overheads** réduire les frais généraux

▸▸ *Fin* ***overhead budget*** budget *m* des charges; *Tech* ***overhead camshaft*** arbre *m* à cames en tête; *Com* ***overhead costs*** frais *mpl* généraux; ***overhead door*** porte *f* basculante; *Com* ***overhead expenses*** frais *mpl* généraux; ***overhead projector*** rétroprojecteur *m*; *Cin & TV* ***overhead shot*** plan *m* en plongée

overhear [ˌəʊvəˈhɪə(r)] *(pt & pp* **overheard** [-ˈhɜːd]) VT *(gen)* entendre par hasard; *(conversation)* surprendre; **I couldn't help overhearing what you were saying** malgré moi, j'ai entendu votre conversation; **she overheard them talking about her** elle les a surpris à parler d'elle

overheat [ˌəʊvəˈhiːt] VT **1** *(oven etc)* surchauffer, trop chauffer **2** *(economy)* provoquer la surchauffe de

VI **1** *(engine etc)* chauffer **2** *(economy)* entrer en surchauffe

overheated [ˌəʊvəˈhiːtɪd] ADJ **1** *(too hot ▸ room)* surchauffé, trop chauffé; *(▸ engine)* qui chauffe **2** *Fig (angry)* passionné, violent, exalté; **to become** *or* **to get o.** *(person)* s'échauffer, s'énerver; *(situation)* devenir explosif; *(discussion, conversation)* s'animer **3** *(economy)* en surchauffe; **the economy is getting o.** l'économie est en surchauffe

overheating [ˌəʊvəˈhiːtɪŋ] N échauffement *m* excessif

overhung [ˌəʊvəˈhʌŋ] *pt & pp of* **overhang**

overhype [ˌəʊvəˈhaɪp] VT faire tout un tabac sur; *(counterproductively)* faire trop de battage sur

overindebted [ˌəʊvərɪnˈdetɪd] ADJ *Econ* surendetté

overindulge [ˌəʊvərɪnˈdʌldʒ] VT **1** *(appetite, desire)* céder à, succomber à, se laisser aller à; **she overindulges her passion for chocolate** elle cède *ou* succombe trop facilement à sa passion pour le chocolat **2** *(person)* (trop) gâter; **she overindulges her children** elle cède à tous les caprices de ses enfants; **he has a tendency to o. himself** il a tendance à faire des excès *ou* à se laisser aller

VI *(overeat)* faire des excès de table; *(drink)* trop boire; **you mustn't o.** il ne faut pas abuser des bonnes choses

overindulgence [ˌəʊvərɪnˈdʌldʒəns] N **1** *(in food and drink)* excès *m*, abus *m* **2** *(towards person)* indulgence *f* excessive, complaisance *f*

overinvest [ˌəʊvərɪnˈvest] *Fin* VT trop investir (**in** dans)

VI surinvestir (**in** dans)

overinvestment [ˌəʊvərɪnˈvestmənt] N *Fin* surinvestissement *m* (**in** dans)

overjoyed [ˌəʊvəˈdʒɔɪd] ADJ ravi, transporté, comblé; **she was o. at being home again** elle était ravie d'être rentrée; **I was o. at the news** cette nouvelle m'a ravi *ou* transporté; **I was o. to see him after so long** j'étais ravi de le voir après longtemps

overkeen [ˌəʊvəˈkiːn] ADJ empressé (**to do** faire); **he wasn't o. on her/the idea** elle/l'idée ne lui plaisait pas outre mesure

overkill [ˈəʊvəkɪl] N *Mil* surarmement *m*; *Fig* exagération *f*, excès *m*; **media o.** surmédiatisation *f*, médiatisation *f* excessive

overladen [ˌəʊvəˈleɪdən] *pp of* **overload**

ADJ surchargé

overlaid [ˌəʊvəˈleɪd] *pt & pp of* **overlay**

overlain [ˌəʊvəˈleɪn] *pp of* **overlie**

overland [ˈəʊvəlænd] ADJ par voie de terre; **the o. route to India** le voyage en Inde par la route

ADV par voie de terre

overlap *(pt & pp* **overlapped**, *cont* **overlapping**) VI [ˌəʊvəˈlæp] *(gen)* (se) chevaucher, se recouvrir partiellement; *(categories etc)* avoir un domaine commun, se recouper; *(in time)* coïncider; *(theories, evidence)* avoir des points communs, se recouper; **my responsibilities o. with hers** mes responsabilités et les siennes se recoupent; **the two systems o.** les deux systèmes font en partie double emploi

VT [ˌəʊvəˈlæp] *(in space)* faire se chevaucher; **the edges/tiles o. each other** les bords/les tuiles se chevauchent

N [ˈəʊvəlæp] **1** *(of tiles etc)* chevauchement *m*; *Fig* **there is some o. between philosophy and religion** il y a des points communs entre la philosophie et la religion; **the o. between two departments** les activités communes à deux services **2** *Geol* nappe *f* de charriage

overlapping [ˌəʊvəˈlæpɪŋ] ADJ *(tiles, planks etc)* qui se chevauchent; *(responsibilities)* qui se recoupent; *(holidays)* qui coïncident

overlay[1] [ˌəʊvəˈleɪ] *pt of* **overlie**

overlay[2] *(pt & pp* **overlaid** [-ˈleɪd]) VT [ˌəʊvəˈleɪ] recouvrir; **the shelf is overlaid with marble** l'étagère est recouverte de marbre

N [ˈəʊvəleɪ] **1** *(covering)* revêtement *m* **2** *Comput* recouvrement *m*

▸▸ *Comput* ***overlay program*** programme *m* à recouvrement; ***overlay segment*** segment *m* de recouvrement

overleaf [ˌəʊvəˈliːf] ADV au dos, au verso; **see o.** *(in book, magazine)* voir au verso; **continued o.** *(in book, magazine)* suite page suivante

overlie [ˌəʊvəˈlaɪ] VT *(pt* **overlay** [-ˈleɪ], *pp* **overlain** [-ˈleɪn]) recouvrir, couvrir

overload *(pp sense* **1 overloaded** *or* **overladen** [-ˈleɪdən], *pp sense* **2 overloaded**) VT [ˌəʊvəˈləʊd] **1** *(animal, vehicle)* surcharger; *(market)* surcharger **2** *(electric circuit)* surcharger; *(engine, machine)* surmener; *Fig (with work)* surcharger, écraser; **she's overloaded with work** elle est surchargée *ou* débordée de travail

N [ˈəʊvələʊd] *Elec* surcharge *f*; *Fig* surcharge *f*

overlong [ˌəʊvəˈlɒŋ] ADJ trop *ou* excessivement long (longue)

ADV trop longtemps

overlook VT [ˌəʊvəˈlʊk] **1** *(have view of)* avoir vue sur, donner sur; **villa overlooking the sea** *(in property advertisement)* villa avec vue sur la mer; **the bedroom window overlooks the garden** la fenêtre de la chambre donne sur le jardin; **the castle/hill overlooks the town** le château/la colline surplombe la ville; **our house is overlooked at the back** il y a une maison qui a vue sur l'arrière de la nôtre

2 *(fail to notice ▸ detail, small thing)* laisser échapper, oublier; *(neglect)* négliger, ne pas prendre en compte; **it's easy to o. the small print** on oublie souvent de lire ce qui est en petits caractères; **he seems to have overlooked the fact that I might have difficulties** l'idée que je puisse avoir des difficultés semble lui avoir échappé; **his work has been overlooked for centuries** cela fait des siècles que ses travaux sont ignorés

3 *(ignore)* laisser passer, passer sur; **I cannot o. this insolence** je ne peux pas laisser passer cette insolence; **she decided to o. the matter** elle décida de fermer les yeux sur l'affaire; **I'll o. it this time** je veux bien fermer les yeux cette fois-ci

4 *(supervise)* surveiller

N [ˈəʊvəlʊk] *Am* panorama *m*

overlord [ˈəʊvəlɔːd] **N 1** *Hist* suzerain *m* **2** *Fig* grand patron *m*

overly [ˈəʊvəlɪ] **ADJ** trop; **she was not o. friendly** elle ne s'est pas montrée particulièrement aimable

overlying [ˌəʊvəˈlaɪɪŋ] **ADJ** superposé; *(stratum)* surjacent

overmanned [ˌəʊvəˈmænd] **ADJ** *(factory, production line)* en sureffectif

overmanning [ˌəʊvəˈmænɪŋ] **N** *(UNCOUNT)* sureffectifs *mpl*

overmuch [ˌəʊvəˈmʌtʃ] *Formal* **ADJ** trop de

ADV outre mesure, trop

overnight ADV [ˌəʊvəˈnaɪt] **1** *(during the night)* pendant la nuit; *(until next day)* jusqu'au lendemain; **to drive/to fly o.** rouler/voler de nuit; **they stopped** *or* **stayed o. in Cork** ils ont passé la nuit à Cork; **the milk won't keep o.** le lait ne se conservera pas jusqu'à demain **2** *Fig (suddenly)* du jour au lendemain; **the situation grew worse o.** la situation a empiré du jour au lendemain *ou* a subitement empiré

ADJ [ˈəʊvənaɪt] **1** *(stay, guest)* d'une nuit; *(clothes, journey)* de nuit; **we had an o. stay in Paris** nous avons passé une nuit à Paris **2** *Fig (sudden)* soudain, subit; **to be an o. success** devenir célèbre du jour au lendemain; **there has been an o. improvement in the situation** la situation s'est subitement améliorée

▸▸ ***overnight bag*** sac *m ou* nécessaire *m* de voyage; *Fin* ***overnight loan*** prêt *m* du jour au lendemain; *Fin* ***overnight rate*** taux *m* de l'argent au jour le jour

overoptimism [ˌəʊvəˈrɒptɪmɪzəm] **N** optimisme *m* exagéré; **to suffer from** *or* **to be guilty of o.** être excessivement *ou* par trop optimiste

overoptimistic [ˌəʊvəˌrɒptɪˈmɪstɪk] **ADJ** excessivement *ou* par trop optimiste (**about** quant à); **I am not o. about their chances** je ne crois pas qu'ils aient de grandes chances

over-packaging N *Mktg* suremballage *m*

overpaid [ˌəʊvəˈpeɪd] *pt & pp of* **overpay**

overparticular [ˌəʊvəpəˈtɪkjʊlə(r)] **ADJ** (par) trop exigeant; **he's not o. about these things** il se moque un peu de ces choses-là

overpass [ˈəʊvəpɑːs] **N** *Aut* pont *m* routier

overpay [ˌəʊvəˈpeɪ] *(pt & pp* **overpaid** [-ˈpeɪd]) **VT** *(bill, employee)* surpayer, trop payer

overpayment [ˌəʊvəˈpeɪmənt] **N 1** *(of taxes, on bill)* trop-perçu *m* **2** *(of employee)* rémunération *f* excessive

overplay [ˌəʊvəˈpleɪ] **VT** *(importance)* exagérer; **to o. one's hand** présumer de ses forces *ou* de ses capacités

overpolite [ˌəʊvəpəˈlaɪt] **ADJ** trop poli

overpopulated [ˌəʊvəˈpɒpjʊleɪtɪd] **ADJ** surpeuplé

overpopulation [ˈəʊvəˌpɒpjʊˈleɪʃən] **N** surpeuplement *m*, surpopulation *f*

over-position VT *Mktg* surpositionner

over-positioning N *Mktg* surpositionnement *m*

overpower [ˌəʊvəˈpaʊə(r)] **VT 1** *(physically ▸ enemy, opponent)* maîtriser, vaincre **2** *(of smell)* suffoquer; *(of heat, emotion)* accabler; **they were overpowered by his charm** ils furent ensorcelés *ou* subjugués par son charme

overpowering [ˌəʊvəˈpaʊərɪŋ] **ADJ 1** *(heat, sensation)* accablant, écrasant; *(smell)* suffocant; *(perfume)* entêtant

2 *(desire, passion)* irrésistible; *(grief)* accablant; **an o. sense of guilt** un sentiment irrépressible de culpabilité

3 *(force)* irrésistible

4 *(personality, charisma)* dominateur; **I find him o.** je le trouve trop dominateur

overprice [ˌəʊvəˈpraɪs] **VT** vendre trop cher

overpriced [ˌəʊvəˈpraɪst] **ADJ** excessivement cher, trop cher

overpricing [ˌəʊvəˈpraɪsɪŋ] **N** fixation *f* d'un prix trop élevé

overprint VT [ˌəʊvəˈprɪnt] **1** *Typ (correction)* imprimer en surcharge; *Comput* surimprimer; *Phot* tirer en surimpression; **the old prices had been overprinted with new ones** les nouveaux prix avaient été imprimés sur les anciens **2** *(postage stamp)* surcharger

VI [ˌəʊvəˈprɪnt] *Comput* surimprimer

N [ˈəʊvəprɪnt] **1** *Typ* impression *f* en surcharge; *(on postage stamp etc)* surcharge *f*; *Phot* surimpression *f* **2** *(postage stamp)* timbre-poste surchargé

overprinting [ˌəʊvəˈprɪntɪŋ] **N** *Typ* impression *f* en surcharge; *Comput* surimpression *f*; *Phot* (tirage *m* en) surimpression *f*

overproduce [ˌəʊvəprəˈdjuːs] **VT** surproduire

overproduction [ˌəʊvəprəˈdʌkʃən] **N** surproduction *f*

overran [ˌəʊvəˈræn] *pt of* **overrun**

overrate [ˌəʊvəˈreɪt] **VT 1** *(person, person's abilities)* surestimer; *(book, film)* surfaire **2** *Admin* surtaxer

overrated [ˌəʊvəˈreɪtɪd] **ADJ** *(film, book)* surfait; **he is rather o. as a novelist** sa réputation de romancier est assez surfaite; **sex is o.** le sexe, ce n'est pas aussi formidable qu'on le dit

overreach [ˌəʊvəˈriːtʃ] **VT to o. oneself** présumer de ses forces, viser trop haut

overreact [ˌəʊvərɪˈækt] **VI** *(gen)* réagir de façon excessive, dramatiser; *(panic)* s'affoler; **I thought she overreacted to the news** j'ai pensé qu'elle réagissait de façon excessive à l'annonce de la nouvelle

overreaction [ˌəʊvərɪˈækʃən] **N** réaction *f* disproportionnée *ou* excessive; *(panic)* affolement *m*

overrepresentation [ˌəʊvəˌreprɪzenˈteɪʃən] **N** surreprésentation *f*

overrepresented [ˌəʊvəˌreprɪˈzentɪd] **ADJ** surreprésenté

override [ˌəʊvəˈraɪd] *(pt* **overrode** [-ˈrəʊd], *pp* **overridden** [-ˈrɪdən]) **VT 1** *(instruction, desire, authority)* passer outre à, outrepasser; *(decision)* annuler; *(rights)* fouler aux pieds, bafouer; **my objection was overridden** il n'a été tenu aucun compte de mon objection

2 *(fact, factor)* l'emporter sur; **this duty overrode all her other commitments** cette tâche a pris la priorité sur tous ses autres engagements

3 *(controls, mechanism)* annuler, neutraliser

4 *(horse)* surmener

overriding [ˌəʊvəˈraɪdɪŋ] **ADJ** *(importance)* primordial, capital; *(belief, consideration, factor)* prépondérant, dominant; **our o. desire is to avoid conflict** notre premier *ou* principal souci est d'éviter un conflit

overripe [ˌəʊvəˈraɪp] **ADJ** *(fruit)* trop mûr; *(cheese)* trop fait

overrode [ˌəʊvəˈrəʊd] *pt of* **override**

overrule [ˌəʊvəˈruːl] **VT** *(decision)* annuler; *(claim, objection)* rejeter; **I was overruled** mon avis a été rejeté

overruling [ˌəʊvəˈruːlɪŋ] **N** *(of decision)* annulation *f*; *(of claim, objection)* rejet *m*

overrun *(pt* **overran** [-ˈræn], *pp* **overrun**, *cont* **overrunning**) **VT** [ˌəʊvəˈrʌn] **1** *(invade)* envahir; **the garden is o. with weeds** le jardin est envahi par les mauvaises herbes; **the building was o. by rats** l'immeuble était infesté de rats; **the streets were o. by holidaymakers** les rues étaient envahies par les vacanciers

2 *(exceed ▸ time limit)* dépasser; **the programme overran the allotted time by ten minutes** l'émission a dépassé de dix minutes le temps qui lui était imparti

3 *(overshoot)* dépasser, aller au-delà de; **the plane overran the runway** l'avion a dépassé le bout de la piste d'atterrissage; *Rail* **to o. a signal** brûler un signal

4 *Typ (word, sentence ▸ over line)* reporter à la ligne suivante; *(▸ over page)* reporter à la page suivante

VI [ˌəʊvəˈrʌn] *(programme, speech)* dépasser le temps alloué *ou* imparti; *(meeting)* dépasser l'heure prévue; **the speech overran by ten minutes** le discours a duré dix minutes de plus que prévu

N [ˈəʊvərʌn] **1** *(in time, space)* dépassement *m*; *Com* **(cost) overruns** dépassement *m* du coût estimé **2** *Typ (at end of line)* chasse *f*; *(at end of page)* report *m*, ligne(s) *f(pl)* à reporter **3** *Ind (in production)* excédent *m*, surplus *m*

oversale [ˈəʊvəseɪl] **N** *Am* surlocation *f*

oversaw [ˌəʊvəˈsɔː] *pt of* **oversee**

overseas ADV [ˌəʊvəˈsiːz] à l'étranger; **to go o.** partir à l'étranger; **people who come back from o.** les gens qui reviennent de l'étranger

ADJ [ˈəʊvəsiːz] *(student, tourist, market)* étranger; *(travel, posting)* à l'étranger; *(mail ▸ from overseas)* (en provenance) de l'étranger; *(▸ to an overseas country)* pour l'étranger; *(trade)* extérieur; *(colony, possession)* d'outre-mer; **the French o. territories** les Territoires *mpl* français d'outre-mer

▸▸ ***overseas aid*** aide *f* au tiers-monde; ***overseas business*** = affaires réalisées avec l'étranger; ***overseas development*** développement *m* outre-mer; ***overseas investment*** investissement *m* extérieur; *Mktg* ***overseas market*** marché *m* étranger *ou* extérieur *ou* d'outremer

oversee [ˌəʊvəˈsiː] *(pt* **oversaw** [-ˈsɔː], *pp* **overseen** [-ˈsiːn]) **VT** *(watch)* surveiller, contrôler; *(supervise)* superviser

overseer [ˈəʊvəˌsiːə(r)] **N** *(foreman)* contremaître *m*, chef *m* d'équipe; *(in mine)* porion *m*; *(in printing works)* prote *m*; *Hist (of slaves)* surveillant(e) *m,f*

oversell [ˌəʊvəˈsel] *(pt & pp* **oversold** [-ˈsəʊld]) **VT 1** *(exaggerate ▸ person, quality)* mettre trop en valeur, faire trop valoir; **to o. oneself** se mettre trop en avant; **personally, I think the Costa Brava is oversold** personnellement, je pense que la Costa Brava est surfaite **2** *Com* **the concert was oversold** on a vendu plus de billets pour le concert qu'il n'y avait de places

oversensitive [ˌəʊvəˈsensɪtɪv] **ADJ** trop sensible *ou* susceptible, hypersensible; **you're being o.!** tu es trop susceptible!

oversew [ˈəʊvəsəʊ] *(pp* **oversewn** [-səʊn]) **VT** surjeter; **oversewn seam** surpiqûre *f*

oversexed [ˌəʊvəˈsekst] **ADJ he's o.** il ne pense qu'au sexe; *Pej* c'est un obsédé sexuel

overshadow [ˌəʊvəˈʃædəʊ] **VT 1** *(eclipse ▸ person, event)* éclipser; **the peace talks were overshadowed by the presidential election** l'élection présidentielle a éclipsé les pourparlers de paix **2** *(darken)* ombrager; **the negotiations were overshadowed by gloom** une atmosphère morose planait sur les négociations; *Fig* **their lives had been overshadowed by the death of their father** leur vie avait été endeuillée par la mort de leur père

overshoe [ˈəʊvəʃuː] **N** galoche *f*; **rubber overshoes** caoutchoucs *mpl*

overshoot *(pt & pp* **overshot** [-ˈʃɒt]) **VT** [ˌəʊvəˈʃuːt] dépasser, aller au-delà de; **the plane overshot the runway** l'avion a dépassé la piste; **to o. the mark** dépasser le but; *Fig* mettre à côté de la plaque

VI [ˌəʊvəˈʃuːt] *(aircraft)* dépasser la piste

N [ˈəʊvəʃuːt] dépassement *m*

overshooting [ˌəʊvəˈʃuːtɪŋ] **N** *Econ* surréaction *f*

overshot [ˈəʊvəʃɒt] *pt & pp of* **overshoot**

ADJ *Tech (wheel)* mû (mue) par en dessus

oversight [ˈəʊvəsaɪt] **N 1** *(error)* omission *f*, oubli *m*; **by** *or* **through an o.** par mégarde, par négligence; **due to an o. your tickets have been sent to your old address** vos billets ont été envoyés par erreur à votre ancienne adresse **2** *(supervision)* surveillance *f*, supervision *f*

oversimplification [ˌəʊvəˌsɪmplɪfɪˈkeɪʃən] **N** simplification *f* excessive

oversimplify [ˌəʊvəˈsɪmplɪfaɪ] *(pt & pp* **oversimplified**) **VT** simplifier à l'excès

oversize, oversized [ˌəʊvəˈsaɪz(d)] **ADJ 1** *(very big)* énorme, démesuré **2** *(too big)* trop grand

oversleep [ˌəʊvəˈsliːp] *(pt & pp* **overslept** [-ˈslept]) **VI** se réveiller en retard, ne pas se réveiller à temps

oversleeve [ˈəʊvəsliːv] **N** manchette *f*

overslept [ˌəʊvəˈslept] *pt & pp of* **oversleep**

oversold [ˌəʊvəˈsəʊld] *pt & pp of* **oversell**

ADJ *St Exch (market)* sousévalué(e)

overspend *(pt & pp* **overspent** [-ˈspent]) **N** [ˈəʊvəspend] *Fin* dépenses *fpl* excessives

VI [ˌəʊvə'spend] *(gen)* trop dépenser; *Fin* dépasser le budget; **I've overspent by £5** j'ai dépensé 5 livres de trop
VT [ˌəʊvə'spend] *(allowance)* dépasser; *(money)* dépenser trop de; *Fin* **to have overspent one's budget** être en dépassement budgétaire

overspending [ˌəʊvə'spendɪŋ] **N** dépense *f* excessive; *Fin* dépassement *m* budgétaire

overspent [ˌəʊvə'spent] *pt & pp of* **overspend**

overspill **VI** [ˌəʊvə'spɪl] déborder, se répandre
N ['əʊvəspɪl] excédent *m* de population (urbaine); **the London o.** l'excédent *m* de la population londonienne
▸▸ ***overspill population*** excédent *m* de population; ***overspill town*** = ville servant à décongestionner une agglomération surpeuplée

overstaffed [ˌəʊvə'stɑːft] **ADJ** en sureffectif; **the firm is o.** le personnel de la firme est trop nombreux, la firme connaît un problème de sureffectifs

overstaffing [ˌəʊvə'stɑːfɪŋ] **N** excédents *mpl* de personnel, sureffectifs *mpl*

overstate [ˌəʊvə'steɪt] **VT** exagérer; **the importance of this factor cannot be overstated** on ne saurait insister suffisamment sur l'importance de ce facteur

overstay [ˌəʊvə'steɪ] **VT to o. one's welcome** abuser de l'hospitalité de ses hôtes; *Mil* **to o. one's leave** dépasser la durée de sa permission

oversteer *Aut* **N** ['əʊvəstɪə(r)] survirage *m*
VI [ˌəʊvə'stɪə(r)] survirer

overstep [ˌəʊvə'step] *(pt & pp* **overstepped,** *cont* **overstepping)** **VT** dépasser, outrepasser; **to o. one's authority** outrepasser ses pouvoirs; *Fig* **to o. the mark** *or* **the limit** dépasser les bornes, aller trop loin

overstock [ˌəʊvə'stɒk] **VT 1** *Com (warehouse)* trop approvisionner; *(market)* encombrer (**with** de); *(outlet)* munir de stocks excessifs **2** *(farm)* mettre trop de bétail dans; *(pond, river)* mettre trop de poissons dans

overstocking [ˌəʊvə'stɒkɪŋ] **N** *Com* stockage *m* excessif

overstrike *(pt & pp* **overstruck** [-'strʌk], *cont* **overstriking)** *Comput* **N** ['əʊvəstraɪk] *(character)* caractère *m* superposé; *(action)* frappe *f* superposée
VT [ˌəʊvə'straɪk] superposer un caractère à

oversubscribe [ˌəʊvəsəb'skraɪb] **VT to be oversubscribed** *(concert, play)* être en surlocation; *St Exch* **the share issue was oversubscribed** l'offre d'actions a été sursouscrite; **the school trip is oversubscribed** il y a trop d'élèves inscrits à l'excursion organisée par l'école

oversubscription [ˌəʊvəsəb'skrɪpʃən] **N** *St Exch (of loan, share issue)* sursouscription *f*

oversupply ['əʊvəsəplaɪ] **N** *Econ* suroffre *f*

overt ['əʊvɜːt, əʊ'vɜːt] **ADJ** manifeste
▸▸ *Law* ***overt act*** acte *m* manifeste

overtake [ˌəʊvə'teɪk] *(pt* **overtook** [-'tʊk], *pp* **overtaken** [-'teɪkən]) **VT 1** *(pass beyond)* dépasser, devancer; *esp Br Aut* dépasser, doubler; **he overtook all the other runners** il a dépassé tous les autres coureurs; **France has overtaken Spain as the main exporter of these products** la France a supplanté l'Espagne au rang de premier exportateur de ces produits **2** *(surprise)* surprendre; *(strike)* frapper; **overtaken by events** dépassé par les événements; **catastrophe overtook the community** la catastrophe a frappé *ou* s'est abattue sur la communauté; **their plans/we were overtaken by fate** le sort s'est joué de leurs projets/nous

overtaking [ˌəʊvə'teɪkɪŋ] **N** *esp Br Aut* dépassement *m*; **no o.** *(sign)* interdiction de dépasser
▸▸ ***overtaking lane*** *(when driving on right)* voie *f* de gauche; *(when driving on left)* voie *f* de droite

overtax [ˌəʊvə'tæks] **VT 1** *Fin (person)* surimposer; *(goods)* surtaxer **2** *(strain* ▸ *patience, hospitality)* abuser de; (▸ *person, heart)* surmener; **don't o. your strength** *or* **yourself** ne te fatigue pas inutilement, ne te surmène pas; **don't o. his brain!** ne lui usez pas la cervelle!

over-the-counter **ADJ 1** *(medicines)* vendu sans ordonnance, en vente libre **2** *Am St Exch* hors cote
▸▸ *Am St Exch* ***over-the-counter market*** marché *m* hors cote, marché *m* des transactions hors séance

over-the-top **ADJ** *Br Fam* **that's a bit o.!** c'est un peu exagéré!; **the house is nice, but the decor's a bit o.** la maison est bien, mais la décoration est un peu lourdingue; **it's a bit o. to call him a fascist** c'est un peu exagéré de le traiter de fasciste; **his latest film is a bit o.** il dépasse un peu la mesure dans son dernier film

overthrow *(pt* **overthrew** [-'θruː], *pp* **overthrown** [-'θrəʊn]) **VT** [ˌəʊvə'θrəʊ] *(regime, government)* renverser; *(rival, enemy army)* vaincre; *(values, standards)* bouleverser; *(plans)* réduire à néant
N ['əʊvəθrəʊ] *(of enemy)* défaite *f*; *(of regime, government)* renversement *m*, chute *f*; *(of values, standards)* bouleversement *m*

overtime ['əʊvətaɪm] **N** *(UNCOUNT)* **1** *(work)* heures *fpl* supplémentaires; **to do** *or* **to work o.** faire des heures supplémentaires; *Fig* **he'll have to work o. to get those two to agree!** s'il veut mettre ces deux-là d'accord, il a intérêt à se lever de bonne heure!; **your imagination seems to have been working o.** on dirait que tu as laissé ton imagination s'emballer **2** *(overtime pay)* rémunération *f* des heures supplémentaires; **after 6 p.m. we're on o. (pay)** après 18 heures, on nous paie en heures supplémentaires; **to be paid o.** être payé en heures supplémentaires **3** *Am Sport* prolongations *fpl*; **the match went into o.** ils ont joué les prolongations
▸▸ *Ind* ***overtime ban*** refus *m* de faire des heures supplémentaires; ***overtime pay*** rémunération *f* des heures supplémentaires; ***overtime rate*** tarif *m* des heures supplémentaires

overtire [ˌəʊvə'taɪə(r)] **VT** *(person)* surmener; **to o. oneself** se surmener, trop se fatiguer

overtiredness [ˌəʊvə'taɪədnɪs] **N** surmenage *m*

overtly [əʊ'vɜːtlɪ] **ADV** franchement, ouvertement

overtness [əʊ'vɜːtnɪs] **N** franchise *f*

overtone ['əʊvətəʊn] **N 1** *(nuance)* nuance *f*, accent *m*; **there was an o. of aggression in what she said** il y avait une pointe d'agressivité dans ses propos; **his speech was full of racist overtones** son discours était truffé de sous-entendus racistes **2** *Mus* harmonique *m*

overtook [ˌəʊvə'tʊk] *pt of* **overtake**

overtrade [ˌəʊvə'treɪd] **VI** avoir une marge d'exploitation trop étroite

overture ['əʊvəˌtjʊə(r)] **N 1** *Mus* ouverture *f* **2** *Fig (proposal)* ouverture *f*, avance *f*; **to make overtures to sb** *(sexually)* faire des avances à qn; *(in business, politics etc)* faire des démarches auprès de qn; *(friendly)* essayer de lier connaissance avec qn; **romantic overtures** avances *fpl* amoureuses; **peace overtures** propositions *fpl* de paix **3** *Fig (prelude)* prélude *m*, début *m*

overturn [ˌəʊvə'tɜːn] **VT 1** *(lamp, car, furniture)* renverser; *(ship)* faire chavirer **2** *(overthrow* ▸ *regime, government, plans)* renverser; *Law* (▸ *judgment, sentence)* casser; **the bill was overturned by the Senate** le projet de loi a été rejeté par le Sénat
VI *(lamp, furniture)* se renverser; *(car)* se retourner, capoter; *(ship)* chavirer

overuse **VT** [ˌəʊvə'juːz] abuser de
N [ˌəʊvə'juːs] abus *m*, usage *m* excessif; **the phrase has become meaningless by o.** l'expression a perdu tout son sens à force d'être trop employée

overvaluation [ˌəʊvəˌvæljuː'eɪʃən] **N** *(of currency)* surévaluation *f*; *(of house, painting)* surestimation *f*

overvalue [ˌəʊvə'væljuː] **VT 1** *(currency)* surévaluer; *(house, painting)* surestimer **2** *(overrate)* surestimer, faire trop de cas de; **his influence has been overvalued** son influence a été surestimée *ou* exagérée

overview ['əʊvəvjuː] **N** vue *f* d'ensemble, panorama *m*

overwater [ˌəʊvə'wɔːtə(r)] **VT** *(plant)* trop arroser

overwatering [ˌəʊvə'wɔːtərɪŋ] **N** *(of plant)* arrosage *m* excessif

overweening [ˌəʊvə'wiːnɪŋ] **ADJ** *Br* **1** *(pride, ambition etc)* sans bornes, démesuré **2** *(person)* outrecuidant, présomptueux

overweight **ADJ** [ˌəʊvə'weɪt] **1** *(person)* (trop) gros (grosse); **I'm a few pounds o.** j'ai quelques kilos de trop **2** *(luggage, parcel)* trop lourd
N ['əʊvəweɪt] excès *m* de poids

overwhelm [ˌəʊvə'welm] **VT 1** *(devastate)* accabler, terrasser; *(astound)* bouleverser; *(with kindness)* combler; **overwhelmed with grief** accablé de chagrin; **grief overwhelmed us** le chagrin nous a terrassés; **your generosity overwhelms me** votre générosité me bouleverse *ou* me va droit au cœur **2** *also Fig (submerge)* submerger; **our switchboard has been overwhelmed by the number of calls** notre standard a été submergé par les appels; **I'm completely overwhelmed with work** je suis débordé de travail **3** *(defeat)* écraser; **we fought back but our attackers overwhelmed us** nous nous sommes débattus mais nos agresseurs ont eu le dessus

overwhelming [ˌəʊvə'welmɪŋ] **ADJ 1** *(crushing* ▸ *victory, defeat)* écrasant; **to win by an o. majority** gagner avec une majorité écrasante; **the o. majority (of people) oppose these measures** la grande majorité des gens est opposée à ces mesures **2** *(extreme, overpowering* ▸ *grief, heat)* accablant; (▸ *joy)* extrême; (▸ *love)* passionnel (▸ *desire, urge, passion)* irrésistible; **an o. sense of frustration** un sentiment d'extrême frustration; **their friendliness is somewhat o.** leur amabilité a quelque chose d'excessif

overwhelmingly [ˌəʊvə'welmɪŋlɪ] **ADV 1** *(crushingly)* de manière écrasante; **the House of Lords voted o. against the bill** la Chambre des lords a voté contre le projet à une écrasante majorité **2** *(as intensifier)* extrêmement; *(predominantly)* surtout

overwind [ˌəʊvə'waɪnd] *(pt & pp* **overwound** [-'waʊnd]) **VT** *(clock, watch)* trop remonter

overwork **VT** ['əʊvəˌwɜːk] **1** *(person)* surmener; **don't o. yourself** n'en fais pas trop; **to be overworked and underpaid** être surchargé de travail et sous-payé **2** *(word)* abuser de, utiliser trop souvent; **it's one of the most overworked phrases in the English language** c'est une des expressions les plus utilisées de la langue anglaise
VI ['əʊvəˌwɜːk] se surmener
N ['əʊvəˌwɜːk] surmenage *m*

overworking [ˌəʊvə'wɜːkɪŋ] **N** surmenage *m*

overwound [ˌəʊvə'waʊnd] *pt & pp of* **overwind**

overwrite [ˌəʊvə'raɪt] *(pt* **overwrote** [-'rəʊt], *pp* **overwritten** [-'rɪtən]) **VT 1** *(write on top of)* écrire sur, repasser sur **2** *Comput (file)* écraser
VI écrire dans un style ampoulé
▸▸ *Comput* ***overwrite mode*** mode *m* de superposition

overwrought [ˌəʊvə'rɔːt] **ADJ** sur les nerfs, à bout; **to get o. about sth** se mettre dans tous ses états à propos de qch

overzealous [ˌəʊvə'zeləs] **ADJ** trop zélé

Ovid ['ɒvɪd] **PR N** *Antiq* Ovide

oviduct ['əʊvɪdʌkt] **N** oviducte *m*

ovine ['əʊvaɪn] **ADJ** ovin

oviparous [əʊ'vɪpərəs] **ADJ** ovipare

ovoid ['əʊvɔɪd] **N** figure *f* ovoïde
ADJ ovoïde, ovoïdal

ovulate ['ɒvjʊleɪt] **VI** ovuler

ovulation [ˌɒvjʊ'leɪʃən] **N** ovulation *f*

ovule ['ɒvjuːl] **N** ovule *m*

ovum ['əʊvəm] *(pl* **ova** [-və]) **N** *Biol* ovule *m*

ow [aʊ] **EXCLAM** aïe!

owe [əʊ] **VT** devoir; **to o. sth to sb, to o. sb sth** devoir qch à qn; **you o. me £10** tu me dois 10 livres; **how much** *or* **what do I o. you?** combien est-ce que *ou* qu'est-ce que je vous dois?; **how much do we still o. him for** *or* **on the car?** combien nous reste-t-il à lui payer pour la voiture?; **I still o. you for the petrol** je vous dois encore l'essence; **he thinks society owes him a living** il s'imagine avoir le droit de vivre aux crochets de la société; **I think you o. him an explanation** je pense qu'il a droit à une explication de ta part *ou* que tu lui dois une explication; **we o. them an apology** nous leur devons des excuses; **you o. it to yourself to do your best** vous vous devez à vous-même de faire de votre mieux; **to what do we o. the honour of your visit?** qu'est-ce qui nous vaut l'honneur de votre visite?; **I o. it all to my parents** je suis redevable de tout cela à mes parents; **to o. sb a favour** être redevable d'un service à qn; **I o. my life to you** je vous dois la vie; **I o. you one!** à charge de revanche!

VI être endetté; **he still owes for** *or* **on the house** il n'a pas encore fini de payer la maison

owing ['əʊɪŋ] ADJ *(after n)* dû; **the sum o. on the car** la somme qui reste due sur le prix de la voiture; **all the money o. to me** tout l'argent qui m'est dû; **to have a lot of money o.** *(to owe)* devoir beaucoup d'argent; *(to be owed)* avoir beaucoup d'argent à récupérer

• **owing to** PREP à cause de, en raison de

owl [aʊl] N *Orn* hibou *m*, chouette *f*; **he's a wise old o.** c'est la sagesse faite homme, c'est l'image même de la sagesse

owlet ['aʊlɪt] N *Orn* jeune hibou *m*, jeune chouette *f*

owlish ['aʊlɪʃ] ADJ de hibou; **those glasses give you an o. look** tu as l'air d'un hibou avec ces lunettes

OWN [əʊn]

> ADJ
> • propre
> PRON
> • le mien/le sien/*etc*
> VT
> • posséder **1** • admettre **2**

ADJ propre; **I have my o. bedroom** j'ai ma propre chambre; **a flat with its o. entrance** un appartement avec une porte d'entrée indépendante; **these are my o. skis** ces skis sont à moi *ou* m'appartiennent; **I'll do it (in) my o. way** je le ferai à ma façon; **it's all my o. work** c'est moi qui ai tout fait; **she makes all her o. clothes** elle fait elle-même tous ses vêtements; **it's your o. fault!** tu n'as à t'en prendre qu'à toi-même!; **you'll have to make up your o. mind** c'est à toi et à toi seul de décider, personne ne pourra prendre cette décision à ta place; **I saw it with my o. eyes** je l'ai vu de mes propres yeux; **to be one's o. man/woman** vivre à sa façon *ou* à son idée

PRON **is that car your o.?** est-ce que cette voiture est à vous?; **I don't need a pen, I've brought my o.** je n'ai pas besoin de stylo, j'ai apporté le mien; **if you want a car, you'll have to buy your o.** si tu veux une voiture, tu n'as qu'à t'en acheter une; **a house/a room/a garden of one's (very) o.** une maison/une pièce/un jardin (bien) à soi; **their son has a car of his o.** leur fils a sa propre voiture; **a child of his o.** un enfant à lui; **his ideas are his o.** ses idées lui sont propres; **the town has a character of its o.** *or* **all (of) its o.** la ville possède un charme qui lui est propre *ou* un charme bien à elle; **my time is not my o.** je ne suis pas maître de mon temps; **I haven't a single thing I can call my o.** je n'ai rien à moi; **you're on your o. now!** à toi de jouer maintenant!; **to come into one's o.** *(show one's capabilities)* montrer de quoi on est capable; *(inherit)* toucher son héritage; **on bad roads the four-wheel-drive model really comes into its o.** sur les mauvaises routes, le modèle à quatre roues motrices montre vraiment ses capacités; **to get one's o. back (on sb)** se venger (de qn); **I'll get my o. back on him for that** je lui revaudrai ça; **to look after one's o.** s'occuper des siens; **to make sth one's o.** s'approprier qch; **she has made the role her o.** elle en a fait son rôle

VT **1** *(possess)* posséder; **they o. 51 per cent of the shares** ils détiennent 51 pourcent des actions; **does she o. the house?** est-elle propriétaire de la maison?; **who owns this car?** à qui appartient cette voiture?; **the land owned by the Crown** les terres qui appartiennent à la Couronne; *Fam* **they walked in as if they owned the place** ils sont entrés comme (s'ils étaient) chez eux; **you don't o. me!** je ne t'appartiens pas!

2 *Literary (admit)* admettre, reconnaître; **she owned that I was right** elle a reconnu que j'avais raison

• **on one's own** ADJ (tout) seul; **are you here on your o.?** êtes-vous seul ici?; **he left me on my o. all evening** il m'a laissé seul toute la soirée; **I'm trying to get him on his o.** j'essaie de le voir seul à seul; **I did it (all) on my o.** je l'ai fait tout seul; **she's setting up in business on her o.** elle monte une affaire toute seule; **you're on your o.!** c'est à toi de te débrouiller!

▸▸ *Mktg* ***own brand*** marque *f* de distributeur; *Ftbl* ***own goal*** but *m* marqué contre son camp, *Suisse* autogoal *m*; **to score an o. goal** marquer contre son camp, *Suisse* marquer un autogoal; *Fig* agir contre ses propres intérêts

▸ **own up** VI avouer, faire des aveux; **if the culprit doesn't o. up...** si le coupable n'avoue pas *ou* ne passe pas aux aveux...; **to o. up to sth** avouer qch; **he owned up to his mistake** il a reconnu son erreur; **to o. up to having done sth** avouer avoir fait qch

own-brand ADJ *Br* **the supermarket's o. jam is cheaper** la confiture que le supermarché vend sous sa propre marque coûte moins cher

▸▸ *Mktg* ***own-brand label*** marque *f* de distributeur; ***own-brand product*** produit *m* à marque de distributeur

own-branding N *Mktg* apposition *f* de sa propre marque

owner ['əʊnə(r)] N propriétaire *mf*; **at the o.'s risk** aux risques du propriétaire; **who is the o. of this jacket?** à qui appartient cette veste?; **they are all car owners** ils possèdent *ou* ils ont tous une voiture; **dog owners should be aware that...** les propriétaires de chiens sont priés de noter que...

▸▸ *Acct* ***owner's capital account*** compte *m* de l'exploitant

ownerless ['əʊnəlɪs] ADJ sans propriétaire

owner-occupancy N = fait d'être propriétaire du logement qu'on occupe; **o. has increased** de plus en plus de gens sont propriétaires de leurs logements

owner-occupier N occupant(e) *m,f* propriétaire

ownership ['əʊnəʃɪp] N possession *f*; **we require proof of o.** nous demandons un titre de propriété; **the o. of the house is contested** les droits de propriété sont contestés; **to be in private/public o.** appartenir au secteur privé/public; **change of o.** changement de propriétaire; **under new o.** *(sign)* changement de propriétaire

own-label ADJ *Mktg* à marque de distributeur

owt [aʊt] PRON *NEng Fam* quelque chose▫; **he never said o.** il n'a rien dit▫; **is there o. the matter?** il y a quelque chose qui va pas?

ox [ɒks] *(pl* **oxen** ['ɒksən]) N bœuf *m*; **(as) strong as an ox** fort comme un bœuf

▸▸ ***ox tongue*** langue *f* de bœuf

oxalic acid [ɒk'sælɪk-] N *Chem* acide *m* oxalique

oxblood ['ɒksblʌd] N *(colour)* rouge *m* sang

ADJ rouge sang *(inv)*

oxbow (lake) ['ɒksbəʊ-] N bras *m* mort *(d'un cours d'eau)*

Oxbridge ['ɒksbrɪdʒ] N = désignation collective des universités d'Oxford et de Cambridge

ADJ *(graduate etc)* de l'université d'Oxford ou de Cambridge; **the privileges of an O. education** les privilèges que confère un diplôme d'Oxford ou de Cambridge

> **OXBRIDGE**
>
> Oxbridge désigne conjointement les universités d'Oxford et de Cambridge, les plus anciennes et les plus prestigieuses d'Angleterre. Le terme est généralement employé pour les différencier des universités de création plus récente. Oxford et Cambridge se distinguent encore des autres établissements d'enseignement supérieur, notamment de par leur structure collégiale et leurs conditions d'admission très rigoureuses. De nos jours, Oxbridge est toujours synonyme d'élitisme en dépit des efforts entrepris pour élargir le recrutement des deux universités. Jusqu'à une époque très récente, un diplôme d'Oxbridge était considéré comme indispensable pour accéder à des postes importants dans le monde de la politique ou de la diplomatie.

oxen ['ɒksən] *pl of* **ox**

Oxfam ['ɒksfæm] N *(abbr* **Oxford Committee for Famine Relief**) = association caritative britannique

▸▸ ***Oxfam shop*** = magasin où l'œuvre de bienfaisance Oxfam vend des articles d'occasion et d'artisanat au profit du tiers-monde

Oxford ['ɒksfəd] N Oxford

▸▸ ***Oxford bags*** *(trousers)* pantalon *m* très large; ***Oxford blue*** *(colour)* bleu *m* foncé; *(sportsperson)* = sportif qui porte ou a porté les couleurs de l'université d'Oxford; ***Oxford English*** = l'anglais de l'université d'Oxford, servant parfois de référence pour la "bonne" prononciation; ***the Oxford Movement*** le puseyisme, le mouvement d'Oxford; ***Oxford Street*** = une des grandes artères commerçantes de Londres

oxhide ['ɒkshaɪd] N cuir *m* de bœuf

oxidation [ˌɒksɪ'deɪʃən] N *Chem* oxydation *f*

oxide ['ɒksaɪd] N *Chem* oxyde *m*

oxidization, -isation [ˌɒksɪdaɪ'zeɪʃən] N *Chem* oxydation *f*

oxidize, -ise ['ɒksɪdaɪz] *Chem* VT oxyder

VI s'oxyder

Oxonian [ɒk'səʊnjən] N *(student)* étudiant(e) *m,f* de l'université d'Oxford; *(townsperson)* Oxfordien(enne) *m,f*

ADJ oxfordien, d'Oxford

oxtail ['ɒksteɪl] N queue *f* de bœuf

▸▸ ***oxtail soup*** soupe *f* de queue de bœuf

oxyacetylene [ˌɒksɪə'setɪliːn] ADJ oxyacétylénique

▸▸ ***oxyacetylene burner, oxyacetylene lamp, oxyacetylene torch*** chalumeau *m* oxyacétylénique

oxygen ['ɒksɪdʒən] N oxygène *m*

▸▸ *Physiol* ***oxygen debt*** dette *f* d'oxygène; ***oxygen mask*** masque *m* à oxygène; ***oxygen tent*** tente *f* à oxygène

oxygenate ['ɒksɪdʒəneɪt] VT *Physiol & Chem* oxygéner

oxygenation [ˌɒksɪdʒə'neɪʃən] N *Physiol & Chem* oxygénation *f*

oxygenize, -ise ['ɒksɪdʒənaɪz] VT *Physiol & Chem* oxygéner

oxymoron [ˌɒksɪ'mɔːrɒn] *(pl* **oxymora** [-rə]) N *Ling* oxymoron *m*

oyez [əʊ'jes] EXCLAM *Arch* oyez!

oyster ['ɔɪstə(r)] N **1** *(seafood)* huître *f*; **the world is her o.** le monde lui appartient **2** *(colour)* gris *m* perle *inv* **3** *(part of fowl)* sot-l'y-laisse *m inv*

ADJ *(colour)* gris perle *(inv)*

▸▸ ***oyster basket*** bourriche *f*; ***oyster bed*** parc *m* à huîtres; ***oyster farm*** parc *m* à huîtres; ***oyster farmer*** ostréiculteur(trice) *m,f*; ***oyster farming*** ostréiculture *f*; ***oyster knife*** couteau *m* à huîtres; ***oyster mushroom*** pleurote *f*; *Culin* ***oyster sauce*** sauce *f* d'huître

Oyster® card ['ɔɪstə-] N *Transp* = carte de transport à puce utilisée dans les transports en commun à Londres

oystercatcher ['ɔɪstəˌkætʃə(r)] N *Orn* huîtrier *m*, pie *f* de mer

Oz [ɒz] N *Fam (Australia)* Australie▫*f*

oz. *(written abbr* **ounce**) once *f*

ozone ['əʊzəʊn] N **1** *(gas)* ozone *m* **2** *Fam (sea air)* bon air *m* marin▫

▸▸ ***ozone depletion*** diminution *f* de l'ozone; ***ozone layer, ozone shield*** couche *f* d'ozone; **the hole in the o. layer** le trou d'ozone

ozone-friendly ADJ qui préserve la couche d'ozone

Ozzie ['ɒzɪ] N *Fam (Australian)* Australien (enne)▫*m,f*

P, p [piː] **N** *(letter)* P, p *m inv*; **two p's** deux p; *Br* **to mind one's p's and q's** se surveiller, bien se tenir

p. *(written abbr* **page***)* p.

P2P [ˌpiːtuːˈpiː] **ADJ** *Comput (abbr* **peer to peer***)* P2P

P45 [ˌpiːfɔːtiˈfaɪv] **N** *Br* = document administratif donné à tout employé lorsqu'il quitte un emploi et devant être présenté à tout nouvel employeur, où figurent le total des rémunérations versées par l'employeur ainsi que les sommes payées par l'employé en impôts et cotisations sociales; *Fig* **to be handed one's P.** se faire licencier

PA[1] [ˌpiːˈeɪ] **N 1** *Br (abbr* **personal assistant***)* *(of executive)* assistant(e) *m,f*; *(with secretarial duties)* secrétaire *mf* de direction

2 *(abbr* **public address system***)* système *m* de sonorisation, sono *f*; **departure times will be announced over the PA** les horaires de départ seront annoncés par haut-parleur

3 *(abbr* **public appearance***)* **to do a PA** venir en personne

4 *(abbr* **Press Association***)* = la principale agence de presse britannique

5 *(abbr* **production assistant***)* assistant(e) *m,f* de production

PA[2] *(written abbr* **Pennsylvania***)* Pennsylvanie *f*

pa [pɑː] **N** *Fam* papa *m*

p.a. *(written abbr* **per annum***)* par an

pace[1] [peɪs] **N 1** *(speed)* allure *f*, vitesse *f*, train *m*; **she quickened/slackened her p.** elle pressa/ralentit le pas; **at a good** *or* **brisk** *or* **smart p.** à vive allure; **at a slow p.** à petite allure; **at walking p.** au pas; **the slower p. of country life** le rythme plus paisible de la vie à la campagne; **don't walk so fast, I can't keep p. with you** ne marche pas si vite, je n'arrive pas à te suivre; **to keep p. with new developments** se tenir au courant des derniers développements; **output is keeping p. with demand** la production se maintient au niveau de *ou* répond à la demande; **our incomes haven't kept p. with inflation** nos revenus n'ont pas augmenté au même rythme que l'inflation; **he couldn't stand** *or* **take the p.** il n'arrivait pas à suivre le rythme; **do it at your own p.** faites-le à votre propre rythme; **to force the p.** forcer l'allure; **to make** *or* **to set the p.** *Sport* donner l'allure, mener le train; *Fig* donner le ton

2 *(step)* pas *m*; **take two paces to the left** faites deux pas à gauche; **he was a few paces from me** il était à quelques pas de moi; *Br* **to put sb through his/her paces** mettre qn à l'épreuve; **to put a horse through its paces** faire passer un cheval à la montre; **to put a car/machine through its paces** mettre une voiture/une machine à l'épreuve; **to go through** *or* **to show one's paces** montrer ce dont *ou* de quoi on est capable

VI marcher (à pas mesurés); **he paced up and down the corridor** il arpentait le couloir

VT 1 *(corridor, cage, room)* arpenter **2** *(regulate)* régler l'allure de; *(runner)* tirer; **the action is well paced** le suspense ne faiblit pas; **to p. oneself** *(when running, drinking)* trouver son rythme; *(when eating)* garder de la place pour la suite

►► ***pace bowler*** *(in cricket)* lanceur *m* rapide *or* puissant; ***pace car*** *(in motor racing)* pace-car *m or f*

pace[2] [ˈpɑːtʃeɪ] **PREP** *Formal* n'en déplaise à

▸**pace off, pace out VT SEP** mesurer en pas; **she paced out ten steps** elle compta dix pas

pacemaker [ˈpeɪsˌmeɪkə(r)] **N 1** *Med* pacemaker *m*, stimulateur *m* cardiaque **2** *Sport* meneur (euse) *m,f* de train; *Fig (leader)* leader *m*

pacesetter [ˈpeɪsˌsetə(r)] **N** *Sport* meneur(euse) *m,f* de train; *Fig (leader)* leader *m*

pacey [ˈpeɪsɪ] *(compar* **pacier**, *superl* **paciest***)* **ADJ** *(vehicle, runner, horse)* rapide; *(story, film)* mouvementé, vivant

pachyderm [ˈpækɪdɜːm] **N** pachyderme *m*

Pacific [pəˈsɪfɪk] **N** *(ocean)* **the P.** le Pacifique, l'océan *m* Pacifique

ADJ du Pacifique

►► ***Pacific Daylight Time*** heure *f* d'été du Pacifique; ***the Pacific Ocean*** le Pacifique, l'océan *m* Pacifique; ***the Pacific Rim*** = groupe de pays situés au bord du Pacifique, pariculièrement les pays industrialisés d'Asie; ***Pacific (Standard) Time*** heure *f* d'hiver du Pacifique

pacific [pəˈsɪfɪk] **ADJ** *Formal* pacifique

pacifically [pəˈsɪfɪklɪ] **ADV** *Formal* pacifiquement

pacification [ˌpæsɪfɪˈkeɪʃən] **N 1** *(of anger, person)* apaisement *m* **2** *(of crowd, country, region)* pacification *f*

pacifier [ˈpæsɪfaɪə(r)] **N 1** *(person)* pacificateur (trice) *m,f* **2** *Am (for baby)* tétine *f*, sucette *f*

pacifism [ˈpæsɪfɪzəm] **N** pacifisme *m*

pacifist [ˈpæsɪfɪst] **N** pacifiste *mf*

ADJ pacifiste

pacify [ˈpæsɪfaɪ] *(pt & pp* **pacified***)* **VT 1** *(anger, person)* apaiser, calmer; **she refused to be pacified** elle n'a jamais voulu se calmer **2** *(crowd, country, region)* pacifier

PACK [pæk]

VT
- remplir **1**
- emballer **2**
- charger **5**
- bourrer **1, 3**
- tasser **4**
- condenser **8**

VI
- faire sa valise **1**
- s'entasser **3**
- rentrer **2**
- former une mêlée **4**

N
- sac à dos **1**
- jeu **3**
- meute **4**
- pack **5, 7**
- paquet **2**
- bande **4**
- peloton **4**
- compresse **6**

VT 1 *(fill)* remplir, bourrer (**with** de); *Constr & Mining (trench)* remblayer; **to p. one's case/one's bags** faire sa valise/ses bagages; *Fig* **to p. one's bags** *(leave)* plier bagages; **we're not packed** nous n'avons pas fait nos bagages; *Theat* **she packs the house every night** elle fait salle comble chaque soir

2 *(put into box, carton etc)* emballer, empaqueter; *(put into suitcase, bag, trunk etc)* mettre dans sa valise/son sac/sa malle/*etc*; **I've already packed the towels** j'ai déjà mis les serviettes dans la valise; **shall I p. the camera?** est-ce que j'emporte *ou* je prends l'appareil photo?; **I've packed a lunch for you** je t'ai préparé de quoi déjeuner; **the equipment is packed in polystyrene** le matériel est emballé dans du polystyrène; **shall I p. these for you?** *(in supermarket)* je vous emballe vos achats?

3 *(cram tightly ► cupboard, container)* bourrer; *(► belongings, people)* entasser; **he packed his pockets with sweets, he packed sweets into his pockets** il a bourré ses poches de bonbons; **commuters p. the morning trains** les banlieusards s'entassent dans les trains du matin; *Fig* **we managed to p. a lot into a week's holiday** on a réussi à faire énormément de choses en une semaine de vacances

4 *(compress ► soil, snow)* tasser

5 *(load ► horse, donkey)* charger

6 *(rig)* **to p. a jury** se composer un jury favorable; **to p. a meeting** s'assurer un nombre prépondérant de partisans à une réunion; *Cards* **to p. the cards** apprêter les cartes

7 *Tech (packing box)* garnir, étouper

8 *Comput (database)* condenser, compacter

9 *Am (carry in a backpack)* transporter dans un sac à dos

10 *(idioms)* **he packs a lot of influence in cabinet/ministerial circles** il a beaucoup d'influence au conseil des ministres/dans les milieux ministériels; *Fam* **to p. a punch** *(person)* cogner dur; *(drink)* donner un coup de fouet; *Am Fam* **to p. a gun** être armé[□], être chargé

VI 1 *(for journey)* faire sa valise *ou* ses bagages; **have you finished packing?** as-tu fini tes bagages?

2 *(fit ► into container)* rentrer; **the keyboard will p. easily into a briefcase** on peut facilement faire tenir le clavier dans un attaché-case

3 *(crowd together ► spectators, passengers)* s'entasser; **we all packed into her car** nous nous sommes tous entassés dans sa voiture

4 *(in rugby)* former une mêlée

N 1 *(rucksack)* sac *m* à dos; *(bundle)* ballot *m*; *(bale)* balle *f*; *(on animal)* charge *f*

2 *(packet)* paquet *m*; *Br* **a p. of washing powder** un paquet de lessive; *Am* **a p. of cigarettes** un paquet de cigarettes; **a four-/six-p. of beer** un pack de quatre/six

3 *Br (deck of cards)* jeu *m*

4 *(group ► of people)* bande *f*; *(► of cub scouts)* meute *f*; *(► of hunting hounds)* meute *f*; *(► of wolves)* meute *f*, bande *f*; *(► of runners, cyclists)* peloton *m*; **wolves hunt in packs** les loups chassent en meute; **a p. of fools** une bande *ou* un tas d'imbéciles; *Br* **that's a p. of lies!** c'est un tissu de mensonges!

5 *(in rugby)* pack *m*

6 *Med* compresse *f*; **wet/cold p.** enveloppement *m* humide/froid

7 *(pack ice)* pack *m*, banquise *f*

8 *(in snooker)* = triangle formé par les boules rouges

►► ***pack animal*** bête *f* de somme; *Mil* ***pack drill*** exercice *m* avec paquetage *(à titre de punition)*; ***pack ice*** pack *m*, banquise *f*; ***pack leader*** *(in rugby)* responsable *m* des avants; *Am Zool* ***pack rat*** rat *m* des bois, néotome *m*; *Fam Fig* **to be a p. rat** *(person)* avoir la manie de tout garder[□]; *TV & Cin* ***pack shot*** pack shot *m*; ***pack train*** convoi *m* de bêtes de somme

▸**pack away VT SEP 1** *(tidy up)* ranger; *(bed, folding table, chair)* replier **2** *Fam (eat)* bouffer; **he really packs it away!** qu'est-ce qu'il bouffe!; **she**

an really p. away the food when she gets going ce qu'elle peut engouffrer quand elle s'y met **3** *Fam (send away)* expédier; **I packed the kids away to bed/school** j'ai envoyé les gosses au lit/à l'école
VI *(bed, folding table, chair)* se replier

pack down VT SEP *(soil, snow)* tasser
VI *(in rugby)* former une mêlée

pack in VT SEP *Br* **1** *(cram in)* entasser; **I couldn't p. anything more in** je ne pouvais pas en faire entrer plus; **the play is packing them in** la pièce fait salle comble **2** *Fam (task)* laisser tomber; *(job, boyfriend, girlfriend)* plaquer; **you should p. in smoking** tu devrais arrêter de fumer; **p. it in!** arrête!, ça suffit!
VI 1 *(crowd in)* s'entasser (à l'intérieur) **2** *Br Fam (break down ▸ machine, engine)* tomber en panne; **the photocopier's just packed in on me** la photocopieuse vient de me lâcher

pack off VT SEP *Fam* expédier; **I packed the kids off to bed/school** j'ai envoyé les gosses au lit/à l'école

pack out VT SEP *Fam (fill completely ▸ room)* remplir à craquer; **the hall was packed out** la salle était pleine à craquer *ou* comble *ou* bondée; **the theatre had been packed out for weeks** le théâtre faisait salle comble depuis des semaines; **the show was completely packed out** il n'y avait plus un seul billet pour ce spectacle

pack up VI 1 *(pack one's suitcase)* faire sa valise *ou* ses bagages
2 *(tidy up)* ranger
3 *Br Fam (break down)* tomber en panne; **my car's packed up** ma voiture m'a lâché; **her heart has packed up** son cœur a lâché *ou* cédé
4 *Br Fam (stop work)* dételer; **I'm packing up for today** j'arrête pour aujourd'hui
VT SEP 1 *(suitcase, bags)* faire **2** *(tidy up ▸ clothes, belongings, tools)* ranger; **help me p. up the tent** aide-moi à plier la tente

package ['pækɪdʒ] **N 1** *(small parcel)* paquet *m*, colis *m*; *Am (packet)* paquet *m*
2 *(set of proposals, items)* ensemble *m*; **financial p.** ensemble *m* de mesures financières; **aid p.** ensemble *m* de mesures d'aide; **the p. includes a company car** l'offre comprend une voiture de société; **we offered them a generous p.** nous leur avons proposé un contrat global très avantageux
3 *(holiday)* voyage *m* organisé *ou* à prix forfaitaire
4 *Comput* **(software) p.** logiciel *m*
5 *(on TV or radio)* sujet *m*
6 *Fam (male genitals)* service *m* trois-pièces
VT 1 *(wrap)* emballer, conditionner **2** *(pop star, candidate etc)* créer l'image de marque de; **she has packaged herself as a sex symbol** elle s'est créé *ou* fabriqué une image de sex-symbol
▸▸ ***package deal*** transaction *f* globale, accord *m* global; **the p. deal put forward by the management** l'ensemble des mesures proposées par la direction; **we bought up the lot in a p. deal** nous avons tout acheté en un seul lot; ***package holiday, package tour*** voyage *m* organisé *or* à prix forfaitaire

packager ['pækɪdʒə(r)] **N** *(in advertising, publishing)* packager *m*, packageur *m*

packaging ['pækɪdʒɪŋ] **N 1** *(wrapping materials)* emballage *m*, conditionnement *m* **2** *(in advertising, publishing)* packaging *m*; **the p. of the project is all wrong** la façon dont on a présenté le projet ne marche pas du tout
▸▸ *Com* ***packaging charges, packaging costs*** frais *mpl* d'emballage

packed [pækt] **ADJ 1** *(crowded ▸ train, room)* bondé; *(▸ theatre)* comble; *Br* **the cinema was p.** la salle était comble *ou* pleine à craquer; *Theat etc* **to play to a p. house** faire salle comble; **the meeting was p.** la réunion a fait salle comble; **the book was p. with information** le livre était truffé *ou* bourré de renseignements **2** *(packaged)* emballé, conditionné **3** *(jury)* favorable
▸▸ ***packed lunch*** panier-repas *m*, casse-croûte *m inv*

packer ['pækə(r)] **N** *(worker)* emballeur(euse) *m,f*, conditionneur(euse) *m,f*; *(machine)* emballeuse *f*, conditionneuse *f*

packet ['pækɪt] **N 1** *(box)* paquet *m*; *(bag, envelope)* sachet *m*; *Br* **a p. of cigarettes** un paquet de cigarettes; **a p. of soup/seeds** un sachet de soupe/graines
2 *(parcel)* paquet *m*, colis *m*
3 *Br Fam (lot of money)* paquet *m*; **that must have cost you a p.** ça a dû te coûter les yeux de la tête *ou* un paquet d'argent; **to earn** *or* **make a p.** gagner des mille et des cents
4 *Naut (boat, steamer)* paquebot *m*
5 *Comput (of data)* paquet *m*
6 *Fam (male genitals)* service *m* trois-pièces; **what a p.!** quel entrejambe!
▸▸ *Naut* ***packet boat*** paquebot *m*; ***packet soup*** soupe *f* en sachet; *Comput* ***packet switching*** commutation *f* de paquets

packhorse ['pækhɔːs, *pl* -hɔːsɪz] **N** cheval *m* de bât

packing ['pækɪŋ] **N** *(UNCOUNT)* **1** *(of personal belongings)* **have you done your p.?** as-tu fait tes bagages?; **there isn't much p. (to do)** il n'y a pas beaucoup de bagages à faire; **the removal men will do the p.** les déménageurs se chargeront de l'emballage
2 *(of parcel)* emballage *m*; *(of commercial goods)* emballage *m*, conditionnement *m*; **the fish/meat p. industry** les conserveries *fpl* de poisson/viande
3 *(wrapping material)* emballage *m*
4 *Tech (of piston, joint)* garniture *f*
5 *Med (to help blood clotting)* méchage *m*
▸▸ ***packing case*** caisse *f* d'emballage; *Com* ***packing charges, packing costs*** frais *mpl* d'emballage; *Am* ***packing house*** usine *f* de conditionnement; ***packing materials*** matériaux *mpl* d'emballage; *Tech* ***packing ring*** *(of cylinder)* rondelle *f ou* bague de garniture; *(of piston)* segment *m*, bague *f*, garniture *f*; *Com* ***packing slip*** bon *m* de livraison

packsaddle ['pækˌsædəl] **N** bât *m*

pact [pækt] **N** pacte *m*; **we made a p. to stop smoking** nous avons convenu de nous arrêter de fumer; **to make a p. with the Devil** faire un pacte *ou* pactiser avec le Diable

pacy = **pacey**

pad [pæd] *(pt & pp* **padded**, *cont* **padding)** **N 1** *(to cushion shock)* coussinet *m*; *(for brake)* plaquette *f*; **the skaters wear pads on their knees and elbows** les patineurs portent des genouillères et des protège-coudes
2 *(for absorbing liquid, polishing etc)* tampon *m*; **a p. of cotton wool** un tampon de coton hydrophile
3 *(on body ▸ of finger, toe)* pulpe *f*; *(▸ of dog, fox, hare etc)* coussinet *m*
4 *(of paper)* bloc *m*; *(on desktop)* sous-main *m inv*; **(inking) p.** tampon *m* encreur
5 *Aviat & Astron* aire *f*; **helicopter p.** aire *f* d'atterrissage pour hélicoptères
6 *Fam (home)* casbah *f*; **let's go to my p.** allons chez moi; **you can crash at my p.** tu peux pieuter chez moi
7 *Bot (leaf)* feuille *f*; **(water) lily p.** feuille *f* de nénuphar
8 *(noise ▸ of animal)* pas *mpl* sourds; *(▸ of person)* pas *mpl* feutrés; **the p. of footsteps behind me** des pas feutrés derrière moi
9 *Fam (sanitary towel)* serviette *f* hygiénique
VT *(clothing)* matelasser; *(shoulder)* rembourrer; *(armchair, door, wall)* capitonner
VI *(walk)* avancer à pas feutrés; **he padded downstairs in his slippers** il descendit l'escalier en pantoufles; **the dog padded along beside the cyclist** le chien trottinait à côté du cycliste

▸ **pad out VT SEP** *(essay, article, speech)* étoffer; **he padded out the talk with anecdotes** il a étoffé son discours en le truffant d'anecdotes; **they padded out the meal with some rice** ils ont complété le repas avec du riz

padded ['pædɪd] **ADJ 1** *(door, bench, wall, steering wheel)* capitonné; *(garment, envelope, oven glove)* matelassé; *(sofa)* bien rembourré **2** *(fat)* **he's well p.** il est bien en chair
▸▸ ***padded bra*** soutien-gorge *m* à bonnets renforcés; ***padded cell*** cellule *f* capitonnée; ***padded shoulders*** *(of dress, jacket)* épaulettes *fpl*

padding ['pædɪŋ] **N 1** *(material) (for cushion etc)* bourre *f*, rembourrage *m*; *(for seat, jacket etc)* rembourrage *m*; *(on walls, door)* capitonnage *m*
2 *(in speech, essay etc)* délayage *m*

paddle ['pædəl] **N 1** *(for boat, canoe)* pagaie *f*
2 *(of waterwheel, paddleboat)* palette *f*, aube *f*
3 *Am (table tennis bat)* raquette *f* (de ping-pong)
4 *(of turtle, penguin, seal)* nageoire *f*; *(of duck)* patte *f*
5 *(walk in water)* **to go for** *or* **to have a p.** aller patauger
VI 1 *(in canoe)* pagayer; *(in rowing boat)* tirer en douce; *(duck)* nager; **he paddled across the lake** il a traversé le lac en pagayant **2** *(walk in water)* patauger
VT 1 *(boat)* **to p. a canoe** pagayer; *Fig* **to p. one's own canoe** se débrouiller tout seul, mener sa barque **2** *Am Fam (spank)* donner une fessée à; *very Fam* **I'll p. your ass!** tu vas prendre une fessée!
▸▸ ***paddle steamer*** bateau *m* à aubes *ou* à roues; *Naut* ***paddle wheel*** roue *f* à aubes

paddleboat ['pædəlbəʊt] **N 1** *(boat)* bateau *m* à aubes *ou* à roues **2** *(pedalo)* Pédalo® *m*

paddling pool ['pædəlɪŋ-] **N** *Br* pataugeoire *f*, *Can* barboteuse *f*

paddock ['pædək] **N 1** *(gen)* enclos *m*; *(at racetrack)* paddock *m* **2** *Austr (field)* champ *m*

Paddy ['pædɪ] *(pl* **Paddies)** **N** *Br Fam (Irishman)* Irlandais *m*, = terme injurieux désignant un Irlandais; **hey, P.!** hé, l'Irlandais!

paddy ['pædɪ] *(pl* **paddies)** **N 1** *(field)* rizière *f* **2** *(rice)* paddy *m*, riz *m* non décortiqué **3** *Br Fam (fit of temper)* **to be/get in a p. (about)** être/se mettre en rogne (pour)
▸▸ *Am Fam* ***paddy wagon*** panier *m* à salade

PADI ['pædɪ] **N** *(abbr* **Professional Association of Diving Instructors)** PADI *m*; **P. course/certificate** cours *m*/certificat *m* PADI

padlock ['pædlɒk] **N** *(for door, gate)* cadenas *m*; *(for bicycle)* antivol *m*
VT *(door, gate)* cadenasser; *(bicycle)* mettre un antivol à; **she padlocked her bicycle to a lamppost** elle a attaché sa bicyclette à un réverbère avec son antivol

padre ['pɑːdrɪ] **N 1** *(gen ▸ Catholic)* prêtre *m*, curé *m*; *(▸ Protestant)* pasteur *m*; *(term of address)* (mon) Père *m* **2** *Mil* aumônier *m*

paean ['piːən] **N 1** *Hist* péan *m* **2** *Literary (expressing praise)* dithyrambe *m*

paediatric, *Am* **pediatric** [ˌpiːdɪ'ætrɪk] **ADJ** pédiatrique

paediatrician, *Am* **pediatrician** [ˌpiːdɪə'trɪʃən] **N** pédiatre *mf*

paediatrics, *Am* **pediatrics** [ˌpiːdɪ'ætrɪks] **N** pédiatrie *f*

paedology *Br* = **pedology**[2]

paedophile, *Am* **pedophile** ['piːdəʊˌfaɪl] **N** pédophile *m*

paedophilia, *Am* **pedophilia** [ˌpiːdəʊ'fɪlɪə] **N** pédophilie *f*

pagan ['peɪgən] **N** païen(enne) *m,f*
ADJ païen

paganism ['peɪgənɪzəm] **N** paganisme *m*

page [peɪdʒ] **N 1** *(of book, newspaper, Web site etc)* page *f*; **on p. two** *(of book)* (à la) page deux; *(of newspaper)* (en) page deux; **p. one** *(of newspaper)* la une; **the sports/business pages** *(in newspaper)* la section sport/économie; *Fig* **a glorious p. in our history** une page glorieuse de notre histoire **2** *(at court)* page *m*; *(in hotel)* chasseur *m*, groom *m*; *(at wedding)* page *m*; *(in legislative body)* (jeune) huissier *m*
VT 1 *Typ (paginate)* paginer **2** *(call ▸ of pageboy)* appeler; *(▸ with loudspeaker)* appeler par haut-parleur; *(▸ by sending messenger)* envoyer chercher par un chasseur; *(▸ with pager)* biper; **I'm having her paged** je la fais appeler; **paging Mrs Clark!** on demande Mme Clark!
▸▸ *Comput* ***page break*** saut *m* de page; *Typ* ***page depth*** hauteur *f* de page; *Comput* ***page description language*** langage *m* de description de page; *Typ & Comput* ***page design*** mise *f* en page; *Comput* ***page down*** page suivante; *Comput* ***page down key*** touche *f* page suivante; *Typ & Comput* ***page format*** format *m* de page; *Comput* ***page layout*** mise *f* en page; *Typ* ***page length*** longueur *f* de

page; *Typ* **page make-up** mise *f* en pages; **page number** numéro *m* de page; *Typ* **page numbering** numérotage *m* des pages, pagination *f*; *Typ* **page plan** plan *m* de mise en page, chemin *m* de fer; *Comput* **page preview** aperçu *m* avant l'impression; *Comput* **page printer** imprimante *f* page par page, imprimante *f* par pages; *Typ* **page proofs** épreuves *fpl* en pages; *Comput* **page scanner** lecteur *m* de pages; *Comput* **page setup** format *m* de page; *Typ* **page size** format *m* de la page; *Press* **page three** = page sur laquelle une femme pose seins nus dans certains quotidiens de la presse populaire britannique; *Press* **page three girl** = jeune femme posant seins nus dans certains quotidiens de la presse populaire britannique; *Comput* **page up** page précédente; *Comput* **page up key** touche *f* page précédente

> **PAGE THREE**
>
> "The Sun" est le tabloïd (voir encadré à cette entrée) le plus connu et le plus vendu de Grande-Bretagne. Il se distingue notamment par le fait qu'il publie en page trois une photo d'une jeune femme posant les seins nus. Ces modèles sont connus sous le nom de "Page Three Girls".

▸ **page down** VI *Comput* feuilleter en avant

▸ **page off** VT SEP *Typ* paginer

▸ **page up** VI *Comput* feuilleter en arrière

pageant ['pædʒənt] N *(display)* spectacle *m* grandiose *ou* majestueux; *(of historical events)* cortège *m* historique; *Fig* **the rich p. of our country's history** la riche galerie de tableaux de l'histoire de notre pays

pageantry ['pædʒəntrɪ] N apparat *m*, pompe *f*

pageboy ['peɪdʒ,bɔɪ] N **1** *(servant)* page *m*; *(in hotel)* chasseur *m*, groom *m*; *(at wedding)* garçon *m* d'honneur **2** *(hairstyle)* coupe *f* à la Jeanne d'Arc
▸▸ **pageboy cut** coupe *f* à la Jeanne d'Arc

pager ['peɪdʒə(r)] N pager *m*, bip *m*

page-turner N *Fam (book)* livre *m* passionnant❑ *ou* captivant❑

paginate ['pædʒɪneɪt] VT *Typ & Comput (make into pages)* mettre en pages; *(number pages in)* paginer

pagination [,pædʒɪ'neɪʃən] N *Typ & Comput (page make-up)* mise *f* en pages; *(numbering)* pagination *f*

pagoda [pə'gəʊdə] N pagode *f*

pah [pɑː] EXCLAM pouah!

paid [peɪd] *pt & pp of* **pay**
ADJ **1** *(person, work)* payé, rétribué, rémunéré; **to get p. maternity leave** avoir droit aux congés de maternité; **to get p. sick leave** avoir droit aux congés de maladie **2** *Com (goods, bill)* payé; **p.** *(on bill)* pour acquit **3 to put p. to sb's chances/hopes** réduire les chances/espoirs de qn en poussière; **well, that's put p. to that!** et voilà, tout tombe à l'eau!
▸▸ **paid holidays** congés *mpl* payés; *Am* **paid political broadcast** = émission d'un parti politique

paid-out ADJ *Com & Fin*
▸▸ **paid-out form** bon *m* de décaissement; **paid-out voucher** bon *m* de débours

paid-up ADJ **1** *(member)* à jour de ses cotisations; *Fig* **he's a (fully) p. member of the Communist Party** *(committed)* il a sa carte au Parti Communiste **2** *Fin (capital)* versé; *(shares)* libéré; **fully p. policy** police *f* d'assurance dont les primes sont à jour
▸▸ **paid-up share capital** capital *m* appelé et libéré

pail [peɪl] N **1** *(bucket)* seau *m* **2** *(bucketful)* plein seau *m*

pailful ['peɪlfʊl] N plein seau *m*; **a p. of water** un plein seau d'eau

pain [peɪn] VT **1** *(mentally)* faire de la peine à, peiner, attrister; **it pained her to see them quarrel** ça lui faisait de la peine *ou* ça la peinait de les voir se disputer; **it pains me to have to tell you that...** je regrette infiniment d'avoir à vous dire que... **2** *Old-fashioned (physically)* faire souffrir, faire mal à
N **1** *(physical)* douleur *f*; **he has a p. in his ear** il a mal à l'oreille; **I have a p. in my side** j'ai une douleur au côté; **are you in p.?** avez-vous mal?, est-ce que vous souffrez?; **to be in great p.** souffrir beaucoup; **to cry out in p.** crier *ou* hurler de douleur; **to cause sb p.** faire mal à qn; *Hum* **no p., no gain!** on n'a rien sans rien!
2 *(emotional)* peine *f*, douleur *f*, souffrance *f*; **to cause sb p.** faire de la peine à qn; **he went through a lot of p. when his son left home** il a eu beaucoup de peine quand son fils a quitté la maison; **I can't bear the p. of losing her** je ne supporterai pas de la perdre
3 *Fam (annoying person or thing)* **what a p. he is!** qu'est-ce qu'il est enquiquinant!; **it's a (real) p.** *or* **such a p. trying to cross London during the rush hour** traverser Londres aux heures de pointe, c'est la galère; **to be a p. (in the neck)** être casse-pieds; *Am* **to give sb a p. (in the neck)** taper sur le système à qn; *very Fam* **to be a p. in the** *Br* **arse** *or Am* **ass** être casse-couilles *ou* chiant; *very Fam* **it's a real p. in the** *Br* **arse** *or Am* **ass having to get up so early** ça fait vraiment chier de devoir se lever si tôt
4 *Law* **on p. of death** sous peine de mort
• **pains** NPL *(efforts)* peine *f*, mal *m*; **he went to great pains to help us** il s'est donné beaucoup de mal pour nous aider; **she took great pains over her work/the dinner** elle s'est donné beaucoup de mal pour son travail/pour ce dîner; **is that all we get for our pains?** c'est comme cela que nous sommes récompensés de nos efforts?; **he was at** *or* **he took pains to avoid her** il a tout fait pour l'éviter
▸▸ **pain barrier** seuil *m* de douleur; **pain relief** soulagement *m*; **aspirin for fast p. relief** aspirine pour soulager rapidement la douleur

pained [peɪnd] ADJ peiné, affligé

painful ['peɪnfʊl] ADJ **1** *(sore)* douloureux; **my burns are still p.** mes brûlures me font toujours mal; **these shoes are really p.** ces chaussures me font vraiment mal; **is your back still p.?** avez-vous toujours mal au dos?; **that looked p.!** ça a dû faire mal!
2 *(unpleasant ▸ spectacle, effort, subject)* pénible; **a p. memory** un souvenir désagréable; **it was p. to see (it)** c'était pénible à voir; **it's p. to have to admit it** c'est dur à admettre; **the expensive shops were a p. reminder of their poverty** les boutiques chères leur rappelaient péniblement leur pauvreté
3 *(laborious ▸ task)* pénible, difficile, laborieux
4 *Fam (bad ▸ performance, singing)* atroce❑

painfully ['peɪnfʊlɪ] ADV **1** *(hit, strike, rub)* durement; *(move, walk)* péniblement; **her head throbbed p.** elle sentait une douleur lancinante à la tête **2** *(laboriously)* laborieusement, avec difficulté **3** *(as intensifier)* horriblement, atrocement; **a p. slow journey** un voyage horriblement *ou* atrocement long; **a p. boring speech** un discours mortellement ennuyeux; **it was p. obvious that he didn't understand** il n'était que trop évident qu'il ne comprenait pas; **she's p. shy/thin** elle est d'une timidité/maigreur maladive

painkiller ['peɪn,kɪlə(r)] N analgésique *m*, calmant *m*

painkilling ['peɪn,kɪlɪŋ] ADJ analgésique, calmant; **to give sb a p. injection** injecter un analgésique à qn

painless ['peɪnləs] ADJ **1** *(injection, operation)* sans douleur, indolore; *(death)* sans souffrance **2** *(unproblematic)* facile; **it was a p. decision** la décision n'a pas été dure à prendre; **the p. way to pay your bills** la manière commode de payer vos factures

painlessly ['peɪnləslɪ] ADV **1** *(without hurting)* sans douleur **2** *(unproblematically)* sans peine, sans mal

painstaking ['peɪnz,teɪkɪŋ] ADJ *(research, investigation, care)* rigoureux, méticuleux; *(worker)* assidu, soigneux; *(accuracy, attention to detail)* extrême

painstakingly ['peɪnz,teɪkɪŋlɪ] ADV soigneusement, méticuleusement; **to be p. accurate in one's work** faire preuve d'une extrême minutie dans son travail

paint [peɪnt] N **1** *(gen)* peinture *f*; *Art* couleur *f*; **a set** *or* **box of paints** une boîte de couleurs **2** *Fam (make-up)* peinture *f* **3** *Med* badigeon *m*
VT **1** *(gen)* peindre; **the door was painted yellow** la porte était peinte en jaune; **the kitchen needs painting** la cuisine a besoin d'être repeinte; *Theat* **to p. the scenery for a play** brosser les décors d'une pièce; **to p. a picture** peindre un tableau; **to p. (a picture of) sb** faire le portrait de qn; **to p. one's nails** se vernir les ongles; **to p. one's face** se peindre le visage; *(with make-up)* se maquiller; *Fam* **to p. the town red** faire la noce *ou* la foire; *Fig* **to p. oneself into a corner** se mettre dans une impasse
2 *(apply ▸ varnish)* appliquer (au pinceau)
3 *Med (throat)* badigeonner
4 *Fig (describe)* dépeindre, décrire; **the author paints a bleak picture of suburban life** l'auteur dresse un sombre portrait *ou* brosse un sombre tableau de la vie des banlieusards; **to p. everything in rosy colours** peindre tout en rose
VI peindre, faire de la peinture; **to p. in oils** faire de la peinture à l'huile; **to p. in watercolours** faire de l'aquarelle; **I've always wanted to p.** j'ai toujours voulu faire de la peinture
▸▸ **paint gun** pistolet *m* à peinture; *Br* **paint pot** pot *m* de peinture; *Comput* **paint program** programme *m* de dessin bitmap; *Ind* **paint shop** atelier *m* de peinture; **paint stripper** décapant *m*

paintball ['peɪntbɔːl] N paintball *m*

paintballing ['peɪnt,bɔːlɪŋ] N **to go p.** faire du paintball

paintbox ['peɪntbɒks] N boîte *f* de couleurs

paintbrush ['peɪntbrʌʃ] N pinceau *m*

painter ['peɪntə(r)] N **1** *(artist, decorator)* peintre *m*; **p. and decorator** peintre-décorateur(trice) *m,f* **2** *Naut (rope)* bosse *f*; **to cut the p.** couper l'amarre

painting ['peɪntɪŋ] N **1** *(activity)* peinture *f*; **to study p.** étudier la peinture **2** *(picture)* peinture *f*, tableau *m* **3** *Med (of skin ▸ with antiseptic etc)* badigeonnage *m*

paintwork ['peɪntwɜːk] N *(UNCOUNT)* peinture *f*; **the house with the white p.** la maison peinte en blanc

pair [peə(r)] N **1** *(two related objects or people)* paire *f*; **a p. of shoes/gloves** une paire de chaussures/de gants; **these two pictures are a p.** *(match)* ces deux tableaux se font pendant; **where's the p. to this sock?** où est la chaussette qui va avec celle-ci?; **to work in pairs** travailler par deux; **line up in pairs!** mettez-vous en rang (deux) par deux!; **the p. of you** vous deux; **they can go to bed without their supper, the p. of them** qu'ils aillent au lit sans manger tous les deux; **you're a p. of idiots!** vous faites une belle paire d'imbéciles!; **I've only got one p. of hands!** je n'ai que deux mains!
2 *(single object in two parts)* **a p. of trousers/shorts/tights** un pantalon/short/collant; **a p. of pliers** une pince; **a p. of scissors** une paire de ciseaux
3 *(husband and wife)* couple *m*
4 *(in rowing)* deux *m*
5 *(of animals)* paire *f*; *(of horses)* attelage *m*; *(of birds)* couple *m*
6 *Math* paire *f*
7 *Br Pol* = deux membres de partis adverses qui se sont entendus pour ne pas participer à un vote ou pour s'abstenir de voter durant une période déterminée
8 *(in cards, dice)* paire *f*; **a p. of kings/sevens** une paire de rois/de sept; *Fam* **two p.** deux paires❑
VT *(socks)* assortir; *(animals, birds)* apparier, accoupler
VI *(animals, birds)* s'apparier, s'accoupler
▸▸ **pair bond** *(between animals)* monogamie *f*; **pair bonding** *(between animals)* monogamie *f*; *Cards* **pair royal** brelan *m*

▸ **pair off** VT SEP *(arrange in couples ▸ dancers)* répartir en couples; *(▸ team members, children in class)* mettre deux par deux; **I got paired off with Roger** on m'a mis avec Roger; **he's trying to pair them off** *(in a relationship)* il essaie de les mettre ensemble
VI *(dancers)* former des couples; *(team members, children in class)* se mettre deux par deux

▸ **pair up** VT SEP *(socks)* assortir
VI *(people)* se mettre par deux; **to p. up with sb** s'associer avec qn, se mettre avec qn; **he paired**

up with Bob for the car rally il a choisi Bob comme équipier pour le rallye

paisley ['peɪzlɪ] **N** *(pattern)* (impression *f*) cachemire *m*; *(material)* tissu *m* cachemire; **a p. tie** une cravate impression cachemire

pajama *Am* = **pyjama**

Paki ['pækɪ] **N** *Br very Fam (abbr* **Pakistani***)* = terme raciste désignant une personne d'origine pakistanaise

►► ***Paki shop*** = épicerie de quartier tenue par une personne d'origine pakistanaise

Paki-basher **N** *Br very Fam* = individu qui attaque des personnes d'origine pakistanaise

Paki-bashing **N** *Br very Fam* = violences à l'encontre de personnes d'origine pakistanaise

Pakistan [ˌpɑːkɪ'stɑːn] **N** Pakistan *m*

Pakistani [ˌpɑːkɪ'stɑːnɪ] **N** Pakistanais(e) *m,f*

ADJ pakistanais

COMP *(embassy, history)* du Pakistan

pakora [pə'kɔːrə] **N** = spécialité indienne de beignets de légumes, de poulet etc

pal [pæl] *(pt & pp* **palled**, *cont* **palling***)* **N** *Fam* **1** *(friend)* copain (copine) *m,f*; **we're great pals** on est très copains; **be a p. and fetch my coat** sois sympa, va me chercher mon manteau **2** *(term of address)* **watch it, p.!** fais gaffe, mec!; **watch where you're going, p.!** hé, regarde où tu vas!; **thanks, p.** *(to friend)* merci, vieux; *(to stranger)* merci, chef

► **pal about, pal around** **VI** *Fam* **to p. about** *or* **around with sb** copiner avec qn, être pote avec qn; **they p. about together** ils sont toujours fourrés ensemble

► **pal up** **VI** *Br Fam (two people)* devenir copains (copines); **to p. up with sb** devenir copain (copine) avec qn

palace ['pælɪs] **N** palais *m*; *Br* **the P.** *(Buckingham Palace)* le palais de Buckingham *(et par extension ses habitants)*; *Br* **the P. raised no objections to the visit** Buckingham n'a élevé aucune objection concernant la visite

►► ***palace guard*** *(person)* garde *m* du palais; *(all guards)* garde *f* du palais; ***palace revolution*** révolution *f* de palais; *Br* ***Palace spokesperson*** porte-parole *mf* (du palais) de Buckingham; ***the Palace of Westminster*** le palais de Westminster *(siège du Parlement britannique)*

> Note that the French word **palace** is a false friend and is never a translation for the English word **palace**. It means **luxury hotel**.

paladin ['pælədɪn] **N** paladin *m*

palatable ['pælətəbəl] **ADJ** **1** *(food)* savoureux; *(wine)* qui se laisse boire **2** *Fig (idea, doctrine)* acceptable

palatal ['pælətəl] **ADJ** **1** *Anat* palatin **2** *Ling* palatal

N *Ling* palatale *f*

palatalize, -ise ['pælətəlaɪz] **VT** palataliser

palate ['pælət] **N** **1** *Anat* palais *m* **2** *(sense of taste)* palais *m*; **to have a good p.** avoir le palais fin

palatial [pə'leɪʃəl] **ADJ** grandiose, magnifique; **she lives alone in a p. house** elle vit toute seule dans un véritable palais *ou* palace

palatinate [pə'lætɪnət] **N** palatinat *m*

• **Palatinate** **N** **the P.** le Palatinat

palaver [pə'lɑːvə(r)] *Br* **N** *(UNCOUNT)* **1** *Fam (fuss)* histoires *fpl*; **what a p.!** quelle histoire!; **it was a real p. getting a work permit** ça a été la croix et la bannière pour obtenir un permis de travail; **we had the usual p. about who was going to pay** ça a été le cirque habituel pour décider qui allait payer **2** *Old-fashioned (discussion)* palabre *m ou f*; *(tedious)* palabres *mpl ou fpl*

pale [peɪl] **ADJ** **1** *(face, complexion)* pâle; *(from fright, shock, sickness)* blême, blafard; **to grow** *or* **become p.** pâlir; **to turn p. with fright** pâlir de terreur; **(as) p. as death** blanc comme un linge **2** *(colour)* pâle, clair; *(light)* pâle, blafard; **a p. blue dress** une robe bleu pâle **3** *(feeble)* pâle; **it was a p. imitation of the real thing** c'était une pâle copie de l'original

VI *(person, face)* pâlir, blêmir; *(sky, colour)* pâlir; **my adventures p. beside yours** mes aventures semblent bien pâles auprès des vôtres; **our problems p. into insignificance beside hers** nos problèmes sont insignifiants comparés aux siens *ou* à côté des siens

N **1** *(post)* pieu *m* **2** *(fence)* palissade *f*; *Br Fig* **he's beyond the p.** il n'est pas fréquentable; **I find such behaviour beyond the p.** je trouve un tel comportement inadmissible

►► ***pale ale*** pale-ale *f*, bière *f* blonde légère

paleface ['peɪlfeɪs] **N** *Pej or Hum* Visage *m* pâle

palefaced ['peɪlfeɪst] **ADJ** (au teint) pâle

paleness ['peɪlnɪs] **N** pâleur *f*

paleographer [ˌpælɪ'ɒgrəfə(r)] **N** paléographe *mf*

paleographic [ˌpælɪəʊ'græfɪk] **ADJ** paléographe

paleography [ˌpælɪ'ɒgrəfɪ] **N** paléographie *f*

Paleolithic [ˌpælɪəʊ'lɪθɪk] **ADJ** paléolithique

N **the P.** le paléolithique

paleontologist [ˌpælɪɒn'tɒlədʒɪst] **N** paléontologiste *mf*, paléontologue *mf*

paleontology [ˌpælɪɒn'tɒlədʒɪ] **N** paléontologie *f*

Palestine ['pæləˌstaɪn] **N** Palestine *f*

►► ***Palestine Liberation Organization*** Organisation *f* de libération de la Palestine

Palestinian [ˌpælə'stɪnɪən] **N** Palestinien(enne) *m,f*

ADJ palestinien

palette ['pælət] **N** *Art & Comput* palette *f*

►► ***palette knife*** *Art* couteau *m* (à palette); *Culin* spatule *f*

palimony ['pælɪmənɪ] **N** pension *f* alimentaire *(accordée à un ex-concubin ou une ex-concubine)*

palimpsest ['pælɪmpsest] **N** palimpseste *m*

palindrome ['pælɪndrəʊm] **N** *Literature* palindrome *m*

paling ['peɪlɪŋ] **N** *(stake)* pieu *m*; *(fence)* palissade *f*

• **palings** **NPL** *(fence)* palissade *f*

palisade [ˌpælɪ'seɪd] **N** *(fence)* palissade *f*

• **palisades** **NPL** *Am (cliffs)* ligne *f* de falaises

pall [pɔːl] **N** **1** *(over coffin)* drap *m* mortuaire, poêle *m* **2** *(of smoke)* voile *m*; *(of snow, darkness, gloom)* manteau *m*; **a p. of silence hung over the room** il régnait dans la pièce un silence profond **3** *Am (coffin)* cercueil *m*

VI *Br* perdre son charme; **it began to p. on me** j'ai commencé à m'en lasser

pallbearer ['pɔːlˌbeərə(r)] **N** porteur *m (du cercueil)*; **the pallbearers** *(accompanying coffin)* le cortège funèbre

pallet ['pælɪt] **N** **1** *(bed)* grabat *m*; *(mattress)* paillasse *f*

2 *(for loading, transportation)* palette *f*

3 *(potter's instrument)* palette *f*

4 *Art & Comput* palette *f*

►► ***pallet truck*** chariot *m* élévateur, transpalette *m*

palletizable, -isable [ˌpælɪ'taɪzəbəl] **ADJ** *Com* palettisable

palletization, -isation [ˌpælɪtaɪ'zeɪʃən] **N** *Com* palettisation *f*

palletize, -ise ['pælɪtaɪz] **VT** *Com* palettiser

palletizer, -iser ['pælɪtaɪzə(r)] **N** *Com* palettiseur *m*

palliasse ['pælɪæs] **N** paillasse *f*

palliate ['pælɪeɪt] **VT** **1** *Med* pallier, lénifier **2** *Formal (fears)* apaiser; *(fault, offence)* pallier, atténuer; **her words had a palliating effect** ses paroles ont eu un effet lénifiant

palliative ['pælɪətɪv] **ADJ** palliatif; **to have a p. effect** *(medicine)* avoir un effet palliatif *ou* lénifiant; *(words)* avoir un effet lénifiant

N palliatif *m*

pallid ['pælɪd] **ADJ** **1** *(person, face, complexion)* pâle, blême, blafard; *(skin, hands)* pâle; *(light, moon)* blafard **2** *(performance)* insipide

pallidness ['pælɪdnɪs], **pallor** ['pælə(r)] **N** pâleur *f*

pally ['pælɪ] *(compar* **pallier**, *superl* **palliest***)* **ADJ** *Br Fam* **to be p. with sb** être pote avec qn; **they're very p. all of a sudden** ils sont très potes tout d'un coup

palm [pɑːm] **N** **1** *(of hand)* paume *f*; *(of glove)* empaumure *f*; **to have sweaty palms** avoir les mains moites; **to read sb's p.** lire les lignes de la main à qn; **he had them in the p. of his hand** il les tenait à sa merci *ou* sous sa coupe; **to grease sb's p.** graisser la patte à qn **2** *(tree)* palmier *m* **3** *(branch)* palme *f*; *Rel* rameau *m*; *Br Fig* **to carry off the p.** remporter la palme

VT *(coin)* cacher dans le creux de la main; **to p. a card** *(in conjuring)* filer une carte

►► ***palm grove*** palmeraie *f*; ***palm house*** serre *f* à palmiers, palmarium *m*; ***palm leaf*** feuille *f* de palmier; ***palm oil*** huile *f* de palme; ***palm plantation*** palmeraie *f*; ***palm sugar*** sucre *m* de palme; *Rel* ***Palm Sunday*** le dimanche des Rameaux, les Rameaux *mpl*; ***palm tree*** palmier *m*; ***palm wine*** vin *m* de palme

► **palm off** **VT SEP** *Fam (unwanted objects)* refiler; *(inferior goods)* fourguer; **to p. sb off with sth, to p. sth off on sb** refiler qch à qn; **they're palming the children off on us for the weekend** ils vont nous refiler les enfants pour le week-end; **she tried to p. me off with some ridiculous excuse** elle a essayé de me faire avaler une excuse ridicule

palmist ['pɑːmɪst] **N** chiromancien(enne) *m,f*

palmistry ['pɑːmɪstrɪ] **N** chiromancie *f*

palmtop ['pɑːmtɒp] **N** *(computer)* ordinateur *m* de poche

►► ***palmtop computer*** ordinateur *m* de poche

palmy ['pɑːmɪ] *(compar* **palmier**, *superl* **palmiest***)* **ADJ** **1** *(pleasant)* agréable, doux (douce); **in the p. days of our youth** aux jours heureux de notre jeunesse **2** *(beach, coast)* bordé de palmiers

palpable ['pælpəbəl] **ADJ** **1** *(tangible)* palpable, tangible **2** *(obvious)* évident, manifeste, flagrant; **a p. lie** un mensonge grossier

palpably ['pælpəblɪ] **ADV** **1** *(tangibly)* tangiblement **2** *(obviously)* manifestement

palpate ['pælpeɪt] **VT** *Med* palper

palpation [pæl'peɪʃən] **N** *Med* palpation *f*, palper *m*

palpitate ['pælpɪteɪt] **VI** palpiter

palpitating ['pælpɪteɪtɪŋ] **ADJ** *Med* palpitant

palpitation [ˌpælpɪ'teɪʃən] **N** palpitation *f*; *Med* **to have** *or* **to get palpitations** avoir des palpitations; *Hum* **I get palpitations whenever I see her** mon cœur bat la chamade *ou* s'emballe chaque fois que je la vois

palsied ['pɔːlzɪd] **ADJ** **1** *(paralysed)* paralysé **2** *Literary (trembling)* tremblant, tremblotant

palsy ['pɔːlzɪ] **N** paralysie *f*; **shaking p.** maladie *f* de Parkinson

palsy-walsy ['pælzɪ'wælzɪ] **ADJ** *Fam* **to be p. with sb** être comme cul et chemise avec qn, être à tu et à toi avec qn

paltry ['pɔːltrɪ] **ADJ** **1** *(meagre* ► *wage, sum)* misérable, dérisoire; **it'll cost you a p. $100** ça vous coûtera cent malheureux dollars **2** *(worthless* ► *person, attitude)* insignifiant, minable; **a p. excuse** une piètre excuse

pampas ['pæmpəz] **NPL** pampa *f*

►► ***pampas grass*** herbe *f* de la pampa

pamper ['pæmpə(r)] **VT** choyer, dorloter; **to p. oneself** se dorloter

pamphlet ['pæmflɪt] **N** *(gen)* brochure *f*, *(literary, scientific)* opuscule *m*; *Pol* pamphlet *m*

> Note that the French word **pamphlet** always refers to a satirical tract.

pamphleteer [ˌpæmflə'tɪə(r)] **N** auteur *m* de brochures; *Pol* pamphlétaire *mf*

Pan [pæn] **PR N** *Myth* Pan

pan [pæn] *(pt & pp* **panned**, *cont* **panning***)* **N** **1** *Culin* casserole *f*; *Am* **cake p.** moule *m* à gâteau

2 *Mining (for gold)* batée *f*

3 *(of scales)* plateau *m*

4 *Br (toilet bowl)* **(lavatory) p.** cuvette *f* de W-C; *Fam Fig* **to go down the p.** être foutu en l'air; *Fam* **that's six months' work down the p.!** voilà six mois de travail qui s'en vont en fumée!; **that's our holidays down the p.!** on peut faire une croix sur nos vacances!

5 *TV & Cin* panoramique *m*

6 *Geol* cuvette *f*, bassin *m* de déposition *ou* de

sédimentation; **salt p.** marais *m* salant, saline *f*, salin *m*

VI 1 *Mining* laver le gravier à la batée; **to p. for gold** chercher de l'or **2** *TV & Cin* faire un panoramique; **to p. across the room** prendre la salle en panoramique, faire un panoramique de la salle

VT 1 *TV & Cin* **to p. the camera** faire un panoramique, *Spec* panoramiquer **2** *Mining (gravel etc)* laver à la batée **3** *Fam (criticize)* descendre (en flammes), éreinter; **the movie was panned by the critics** le film a été descendu par les critiques

►► ***pan scourer, pan scrubber*** tampon *m* à récurer

► **pan down** **VI** *TV & Cin* faire un panoramique vers le bas

► **pan out** **VI** *Br Fam (work out)* se dérouler[□], marcher[□]; *(succeed)* réussir[□]; **if things p. out as planned** si tout marche comme prévu; **it depends how things p. out** ça dépend de comment les choses vont s'arranger[□]

► **pan up** **VI** *TV & Cin* faire un panoramique vertical

panacea [ˌpænəˈsɪə] **N** panacée *f*

panache [pəˈnæʃ] **N** panache *m*

Pan-African **ADJ** panafricain

Pan-Africanism **N** panafricanisme *m*

Panama [ˈpænəmɑː] **N 1** *Geog* Panama *m*; **the Isthmus of P.** l'isthme *m* de Panama **2** *(hat)* panama *m*

►► ***the Panama Canal*** le canal de Panama; ***Panama City*** Panama; ***Panama hat*** panama *m*

Panamanian [ˌpænəˈmeɪnɪən] **N** Panaméen (enne) *m,f*

ADJ panaméen

COMP *(embassy, history)* du Panama

Pan-American **ADJ** panaméricain

►► ***the Pan-American Games*** les jeux *mpl* Panaméricains; ***the Pan-American Highway*** la route panaméricaine

Pan-Americanism **N** panaméricanisme *m*

Pan-Arab **ADJ** panarabe

Pan-Arabism [-ˈærəbɪzəm] **N** panarabisme *m*

Pan-Asian, Pan-Asiatic **ADJ** panasiatique

panatella [ˌpænəˈtelə] **N** panatela *m*, panatella *m*

pancake [ˈpæŋkeɪk] **N 1** *Culin (thin)* crêpe *f*; *(thick)* = sorte de petite galette épaisse; **(as) flat as a p.** plat comme une galette **2** *(make-up)* fond *m* de teint solide **3** *Aviat* atterrissage *m* à plat *or* brutal

VI *Aviat* atterrir sur le ventre

►► *Br* ***Pancake Day*** mardi gras *m*; ***pancake ice*** glace *f* en crêpes; *Aviat* ***pancake landing*** atterrissage *m* à plat *or* brutal; ***pancake race*** = course traditionnelle du mardi gras britannique consistant à courir avec une poêle dans laquelle se trouve une crêpe qu'il faut retourner; ***pancake roll*** rouleau *m* de printemps; *Br* ***Pancake Tuesday*** mardi gras *m*

panchromatic [ˌpænkrəʊˈmætɪk] **ADJ** *Phot* panchromatique

pancreas [ˈpæŋkrɪəs] **N** *Anat* pancréas *m*

pancreatic [ˌpæŋkrɪˈætɪk] **ADJ** *Anat* pancréatique

►► ***pancreatic cancer*** cancer *m* du pancréas; ***pancreatic juice*** suc *m* pancréatique

pancreatitis [ˌpæŋkrɪəˈtaɪtəs] **N** *Med* pancréatite *f*

panda [ˈpændə] **N 1** *Zool* panda *m* **2** *Br (car)* voiture *f* de police

►► *Br* ***panda car*** voiture *f* de police

pandemic [ˌpænˈdemɪk] *Med* **ADJ** pandémique

N pandémie *f*

pandemonium [ˌpændɪˈməʊnɪəm] **N** *(UNCOUNT) (chaos)* chaos *m*, *Literary* pandémonium *m*; *(uproar)* tumulte *m*, tohu-bohu *m*; **p. broke out** cela a déclenché un véritable tumulte; **the whole office is in p.** le bureau est sens dessus dessous

pander [ˈpændə(r)] **VI these films p. to our worst instincts** ces films font appel à nos pires instincts; **to p. to sb** encourager bassement qn; **to p. to sb's whims** se prêter aux exigences de qn

N *(pimp)* entremetteur(euse) *m,f*, proxénète *mf*

P & L [ˌpiːənˈel] **N 1** *(abbr* **profit and loss)** pertes *fpl* et profits *mpl* **2** *(abbr* **profit and loss account, profit and loss statement)** compte *m* de résultat

►► ***P & L account, P & L statement*** compte *m* de résultat

Pandora [pænˈdɔːrə] **PR N** *Myth* Pandore

►► ***Pandora's box*** la boîte de Pandore

p & p [ˌpiːənˈpiː] **N** *Br (abbr* **postage and packing)** frais *mpl* de port et d'emballage

pane [peɪn] **N** vitre *f*, carreau *m*; **a p. of glass** un carreau

►► *Am* ***pane glass window*** fenêtre *f* panoramique

panegyric [ˌpænɪˈdʒɪrɪk] **N** *Formal* panégyrique *m*; **he launched into a p. of** *or* **about French cuisine** il s'est lancé dans un éloge dithyrambique de la cuisine française

panel [ˈpænəl] *(Br pt & pp* **panelled,** *cont* **panelling,** *Am pt & pp* **paneled,** *cont* **paneling) N 1** *(flat section ► of wood, glass etc)* panneau *m*; *(in ceiling)* caisson *m*; *(of cartoon strip)* case *f*; *(in book, magazine)* encadré *m*; **sliding p.** panneau *m* coulissant

2 *(group, committee ► gen)* comité *m*; *(► to judge exam, contest)* jury *m*; *(► in radio or TV quiz)* invités *mpl*; *(► in public debate)* panel *m*; *(► in public inquiry)* commission *f* (d'enquête); **a p. of experts** un comité d'experts; **our p. for tonight's show** nos invités à l'émission de ce soir

3 *Mktg (for market research)* panel *m*

4 *(set of controls)* **(control) p.** tableau *m* de bord; *Aviat & Aut* **(instrument) p.** tableau *m* de bord

5 *Sewing* panneau *m*, lé *m*

6 *Law (selection list)* liste *f* de jurés

7 *Art (backing)* panneau *m*; *(picture)* (peinture *f* sur) panneau *m*

VT *(wall, hall)* lambrisser, revêtir de panneaux; *(surface)* plaquer; **a panelled door** une porte à panneaux; **the room is in panelled oak** la pièce est lambrissée de chêne

►► *BrAut* ***panel beater*** carrossier *m*, tôlier *m*; ***panel discussion*** débat *m*, table *f* ronde; *Br* ***panel game*** *Rad* jeu *m* radiophonique; *TV* jeu *m* télévisé; ***panel heating*** chauffage *m* à panneaux; ***panel member*** *(jury member)* juré *m*; *(in radio or TV quiz)* invité(e) *m,f*; *(in public debate)* panéliste *mf*; *(of committee)* membre *m* du comité; *Br* ***panel pin*** pointe *f* à tête d'homme, clou *m* à panneau; ***panel research*** recherches *fpl* par panel; *Am* ***panel truck,*** *Austr* ***panel van*** camionnette *f*

panelling, *Am* **paneling** [ˈpænəlɪŋ] **N** *(UNCOUNT)* **1** *(wall covering)* lambris *m*, boiseries *fpl*, placage *m*; **oak p.** lambris *mpl* de chêne **2** *(material)* panneaux *mpl*

panellist, *Am* **panelist** [ˈpænəlɪst] **N** *(jury member)* juré *m*; *(in radio or TV quiz)* invité(e) *m,f*; *(in public debate)* panéliste *mf*; *(of committee)* membre *m* du comité

Pan-European **ADJ** paneuropéen

pan-fries **NPL** *Am* pommes *fpl* (de terre) sautées

pan-fry *(pt & pp* **pan-fried) VT** (faire) sauter; **pan-fried chicken** poulet *m* sauté

pang [pæŋ] **N 1** *(of emotion)* coup *m* au cœur, pincement *m* de cœur; **I felt a p. of sadness** j'ai eu un serrement de cœur; **to feel pangs of conscience** *or* **guilt** éprouver des remords **2** *(of pain)* élancement *m*; **hunger pangs** tiraillements *mpl* d'estomac

Pan-German, Pan-Germanic **ADJ** pangermanique

Pan-Germanism [-ˈdʒɜːmənɪzəm] **N** pangermanisme *m*

panhandle [ˈpænˌhændəl] *Am* **N** *Geog* langue *f* de terre; **the Alaska p.** la région sud de l'Alaska; **the Texas p.** = la langue de terre correspondant à la partie nord-ouest du Texas

VI *Fam* faire la manche

VT *Fam* **to p. money from sb, to p. sb** taper qn

panhandler [ˈpænˌhændlə(r)] **N** *Am Fam* mendiant(e)[□] *m,f*

Panhellenic [ˌpænheˈlenɪk] **ADJ** panhellénique, panhellénien

Panhellenism [ˌpænˈhelənɪzəm] **N** panhellénisme *m*

panic [ˈpænɪk] *(pt & pp* **panicked,** *cont* **panicking) N 1** *(alarm)* panique *f*, affolement *m*; **to get into a p. over** *or* **about sth** s'affoler à cause de qch; **to throw sb into a p.** affoler qn; *Fam* **it was p. stations!** ça a été la panique générale! **2** *Fam (rush)* hâte[□] *f*; **I was in a mad p. to get to the airport** c'était la panique pour aller à l'aéroport[□]; **what's the p.?** ne vous affolez pas![□]; **there's no p.!** il n'y a pas le feu! **3** *Am Fam (funny thing)* **it was a p.!** c'était à hurler de rire!

VI s'affoler; **don't p.!** ne vous affolez pas!; **he's starting to p. about the wedding** il commence à s'affoler à la perspective de ce mariage

VT affoler; **the news panicked the government into action** la panique provoquée par cette nouvelle a poussé le gouvernement à l'action; **she was panicked into accepting** sous le coup de la panique, elle a accepté

►► ***panic attack*** crise *f* de panique; ***panic bolt*** barre *f* antipanique; ***panic button*** signal *m* d'alarme; *Fam* **to hit the p. button** paniquer[□], flipper; ***panic buying*** *(gén)* = achats massifs provoqués par la crainte de la pénurie; *St Exch* achats *mpl* de précaution; *Bot* ***panic grass*** panic *m*; ***panic measures*** mesures *fpl* dictées par la panique; ***panic reaction*** réaction *f* de panique; ***panic room*** = pièce où les occupants d'une maison peuvent se réfugier en cas de danger; *St Exch* ***panic selling*** ventes *fpl* de précaution

panicky [ˈpænɪkɪ] **ADJ** *(person, crowd)* paniqué; *(voice, answer, message)* affolé; *(feeling, reaction)* de panique; *(market)* enclin à la panique; **I get p. every time I have to speak to him** je panique chaque fois que je dois lui parler

panic-stricken **ADJ** affolé, pris de panique; *(reaction, answer, look)* affolé

Pan-Islamic **ADJ** panislamique

Pan-Islamism **N** panislamisme *m*

panjandrum [ˌpænˈdʒændrəm] **N** *Fam* grand manitou *m*, ponte *m*

pannier [ˈpænɪə(r)] **N 1** *(bag ► on bicycle, motorbike)* sacoche *f*; *(► on donkey)* panier *m* de bât **2** *(basket)* panier *m*, corbeille *f*

panning [ˈpænɪŋ] **N 1** *TV & Cin* panoramique *m* **2** *Mining* lavage *m* **3** *Fam (criticism)* descente *f* en flammes; **the movie got a real p.** le film s'est fait descendre (en flammes)

►► *TV & Cin* ***panning shot*** prise *f* panoramique

panoply [ˈpænəplɪ] **N** panoplie *f*

panorama [ˌpænəˈrɑːmə] **N** *also Fig* panorama *m*

panoramic [ˌpænəˈræmɪk] **ADJ** panoramique

►► ***panoramic photograph*** photo *f* panoramique; *Cin* ***panoramic screen*** écran *m* panoramique; ***panoramic sight*** viseur *m* panoramique; ***panoramic view*** vue *f* panoramique

panpipes [ˈpænpaɪps] **NPL** flûte *f* de Pan

pansy [ˈpænzɪ] *(pl* **pansies) N 1** *Bot* pensée *f* **2** *Br Fam Pej (sissy)* poule *f* mouillée, femmelette *f*; *(effeminate man)* chochotte *f*; *(homosexual)* tante *f*

pant [pænt] **VI 1** *(puff)* haleter, souffler; *(of animal)* battre du flanc; **he panted up the stairs** il monta l'escalier en soufflant; **to p. for breath** chercher son souffle **2** *Fam (be eager)* **he's panting to do it** il meurt d'envie de le faire

VT *(say)* dire en haletant *ou* d'une voix haletante

N *(breath)* halètement *m*

► **pant out** **VT SEP** *(say)* dire en haletant

pantechnicon [pænˈteknɪkən] **N** *Br Old-fashioned (van)* camion *m* de déménagement

pantheism [ˈpænθiːɪzəm] **N** panthéisme *m*

pantheist [ˈpænθiːɪst] **N** panthéiste *mf*

pantheistic [ˌpænθiːˈɪstɪk] **ADJ** panthéiste

pantheon [ˈpænθɪən] **N** panthéon *m*; **he belongs in the p. of great movie stars** il mérite de figurer au panthéon des stars du cinéma

panther [ˈpænθə(r)] *(pl* **inv** *or* **panthers) N 1** *(leopard)* panthère *f* **2** *Am (puma)* puma *m*; **the (Black) Panthers** = mouvement politique fondé par des militants noirs américains dans les années soixante

panties [ˈpæntɪz] **NPL** (petite) culotte *f*; **a pair of p.** un slip, une culotte; *Am Fam Hum* **don't get your p. in a wad!** *(don't panic)* ne t'affole pas![□]; *(don't get angry)* du calme![□], calme-toi![□]

pantihose = **pantyhose**

panting [ˈpæntɪŋ] **ADJ** *(person, dog)* haletant

N halètement *m*

panto ['pæntəʊ] (*pl* **pantos**) **N** *Br Fam (Christmas show)* = spectacle de Noël pour enfants

pantograph ['pæntəgrɑːf] **N** pantographe *m*

pantomime ['pæntəmaɪm] **N 1** *Br (Christmas show)* = spectacle de Noël pour enfants **2** *(mime)* pantomime *f* **3** *Br Fam Fig* comédie *f*, cirque *m*; **there was a bit of a p. over who should pay** ça a été tout un cirque pour savoir qui devait payer

▸▸ ***pantomime dame*** = rôle travesti outré et ridicule dans la "pantomime"; ***pantomime horse*** = personnage de cheval joué par deux comédiens dans la "pantomime"

> Note that the French word **pantomime** never refers to a Christmas show.

> **PANTOMIME**
>
> Le genre typiquement britannique de la "pantomime" est très conventionnel; certains personnages-types ("pantomime dame", "principal boy") et certaines rengaines ("Behind you!", "Oh yes he is! – Oh no he isn't!") apparaissent dans toutes les pièces. Ces pièces, qui se jouent au moment des fêtes de fin d'année, sont généralement inspirées d'un conte de fées.

Pantone® [pæn'təʊn] **N** *Typ* Pantone® *m*

▸▸ ***Pantone® number*** numéro *m* de Pantone®

pantry ['pæntrɪ] (*pl* **pantries**) **N** *(cupboard)* garde-manger *m inv*; *(walk-in cupboard)* cellier *m*, office *m*

pants [pænts] **NPL 1** *Br* **(pair of) p.** slip *m*, culotte *f*; *(boxer shorts)* caleçon *m* **2** *esp Am (trousers)* **(pair of) p.** pantalon *m*; **a kick in the p.** un coup de pied aux fesses; **he's still in short p.** il est encore à l'âge des culottes courtes **3** *Fam (idioms)* **to beat the p. off sb** battre qn à plates coutures; **to scare the p. off sb** foutre une trouille pas possible à qn; **to bore the p. off sb** ennuyer qn à mourir; **to be caught with one's p. down** être pris sur le fait en train de faire une bêtise[▫]; **it's clear who wears the p. around here** il n'y a pas de doute sur qui porte le pantalon ici; **he charmed the p. off my parents** il a conquis mes parents[▫]

ADJ *Br Fam Hum (of poor quality)* nul

EXCLAM *Br Fam Hum* zut!, mince!

▸▸ *esp Am* ***pants leg*** jambe *f* de pantalon

panty ['pæntɪ-] **COMP**

▸▸ ***panty girdle*** gaine-culotte *f*; ***panty liner*** protège-slip *m*

pantyhose ['pæntɪˌhəʊz] **N** *Am* collant *m*, collants *mpl*

panzer ['pænzə(r)] **N** panzer *m*, blindé *m*

▸▸ ***panzer division*** division *f* blindée

Pap [pæp] **ADJ** *esp Am*

▸▸ *Med* ***Pap smear, Pap test*** frottis *m* vaginal

pap[1] [pæp] **N 1** *(mush)* bouillie *f* **2** *(UNCOUNT) Fig (nonsense)* bêtises *fpl*, imbécillités *fpl*; **his films are p.** ses films sont stupides; **what a load of p.!** n'importe quoi!

pap[2] (*pt & pp* **papped**, *cont* **papping**) **VT** *Fam* **he was papped coming out of a club** des paparazzi l'ont pris en photo alors qu'il sortait d'une boîte

papa [pə'pɑː] **N** *Old-fashioned or Hum* papa *m*

papacy ['peɪpəsɪ] (*pl* **papacies**) **N** *(system, institution)* papauté *f*; *(term of office)* pontificat *m*

papadum = **poppadom**

papal ['peɪpəl] **ADJ** papal

▸▸ ***papal bull*** bulle *f* papale; ***papal cross*** croix *f* papale; ***papal interdict*** interdit *m* papal; ***papal nuncio*** nonce *m* du Pape; ***papal throne*** trône *m* pontifical

paparazzi [ˌpæpə'rætsɪ] **NPL** paparazzi *mpl*

papaw [pə'pɔː] **N 1** *(asimina triloba* ▸ *fruit)* asimine *f*, pomme-cannelle *f*; (▸ *tree)* asiminier *m* **2** *(carica papaya* ▸ *fruit)* papaye *f*; (▸ *tree)* papayer *m*

papaya [pə'paɪə] **N** *(fruit)* papaye *f*; *(tree)* papayer *m*

paper ['peɪpə(r)] **N 1** *(UNCOUNT) (material)* papier *m*; **a piece/sheet of p.** un bout/une feuille de papier; **the p. industry** l'industrie *f* papetière, la papeterie; **he wants it on p.** il veut que ce soit écrit; **to put sth down on p.** mettre qch par écrit; **on p., they're by far the better side** sur le papier *ou* a priori, c'est de loin la meilleure équipe; **it's a good plan on p.** ce projet est excellent en théorie **2** *(newspaper)* journal *m*; **it's in all the morning papers** c'est dans tous les journaux du matin **3** *(usu pl) (document)* papier *m*, document *m*; **could you fill out this p.?** pourriez-vous remplir ce formulaire?; **once you've got the necessary papers together** une fois que vous aurez réuni les pièces nécessaires; **Virginia Woolf's private papers** les écrits *mpl* personnels de Virginia Woolf; **(identity) papers** papiers *mpl* (d'identité); **ship's papers** papiers *mpl* de bord **4** *Sch & Univ (exam paper)* épreuve *f*; *(questions)* questions *fpl* d'examen; *(answer)* copie *f*; **hand in your papers** rendez vos copies **5** *(academic treatise* ▸ *published)* article *m*; (▸ *oral)* communication *f*; **to give** *or* **to read a p. on sth** faire un exposé sur qch **6** *(wallpaper)* papier *m* peint **7** *Fin* papier *m* valeur; *(banknotes)* billets *mpl* de banque; **long/short p.** papier *m* à long/court terme

ADJ 1 *(theoretical)* sur le papier, théorique **2** *Pej (worthless)* sans valeur

COMP *(napkin, towel)* en *ou* de papier

VT *(room, walls)* tapisser

▸▸ *Comput* ***paper advance*** *(on printer)* entraînement *m* du papier; ***paper aeroplane*** avion *m* en papier; ***paper bag*** sac *m* en papier; ***paper chains*** guirlandes *fpl* de papier; ***paper chase*** rallye-papier *m*, ≃ jeu *m* de piste; *Fig* **education has become an academic p. chase** l'éducation est devenue une véritable course aux diplômes; ***paper clip*** trombone *m*; ***paper copy*** copie *f* sur papier, sortie *f* papier; ***paper cup*** gobelet *m* en carton; ***paper currency*** papier-monnaie *m*; ***paper dart*** avion *m* en papier; *Comput & Typ* ***paper feed*** alimentation *f* du papier; *Comput & Typ* ***paper format*** format *m* de papier; ***paper handkerchief***, *Fam* ***paper hankie*** mouchoir *m* en papier[▫]; *Comput* ***paper jam*** bourrage *m* de papier; ***paper knife*** coupe-papier *m inv*; *Fin* ***paper loss*** moins-value *f*; ***paper mill*** papeterie *f*, usine *f* à papier; *Fin* ***paper money*** papier-monnaie *m*, monnaie *f* fiduciaire; ***paper plate*** assiette *f* en carton; ***paper profits*** profits *mpl* fictifs; ***paper qualifications*** diplômes *mpl*; ***paper round*** livraison *f* de journaux; **to have** *or* **do a p. round** distribuer les journaux; *Fin* ***paper securities*** titres *mpl* fiduciaires, papiers *mpl* valeurs; *Br* ***paper shop*** marchand *m* de journaux; **to go to the p. shop** aller chez le marchand de journaux; **he works in a p. shop** il travaille dans un magasin de journaux; ***paper shredder*** broyeur *m*; *Comput* ***paper tape*** bande *f* perforée; ***paper tiger*** tigre *m* de papier; ***paper tissue*** mouchoir *m* en papier; ***paper transaction*** jeu *m* d'écritures; *Comput* ***paper tray*** bac *m* à feuilles; ***paper victory*** victoire *f* inutile

▸ **paper over VT SEP 1** *(with wallpaper)* recouvrir de papier peint **2** *Fig (dispute, facts)* dissimuler; **to p. over the cracks** *(disguise faults)* masquer les défauts; *(disguise disagreements)* masquer les mésententes

paperback ['peɪpəbæk] **N** livre *m* de poche; **it's in p.** c'est en (édition de) poche

ADJ *(book)* de poche; **p. edition** édition *f* de poche

paperboard ['peɪpəbɔːd] **N** *(UNCOUNT)* carton *m*, carton-pâte *m*

paperboy ['peɪpəbɔɪ] **N** *(delivering papers)* livreur *m* de journaux; *(selling papers)* vendeur *m* de journaux

papergirl ['peɪpəgɜːl] **N** *(delivering papers)* livreuse *f* de journaux; *(selling papers)* vendeuse *f* de journaux

paperhanger ['peɪpəˌhæŋə(r)] **N 1** *(decorator)* peintre-décorateur(trice) *m,f* **2** *Am Fam (counterfeiter)* faux-monnayeur[▫] *m*

paperless ['peɪpəlɪs] **ADJ** *(electronic* ▸ *communication, record-keeping)* informatique

▸▸ ***paperless office*** bureau *m* entièrement informatisé; *St Exch* ***paperless trading*** marché *m* ou cotation *f* électronique

paperweight ['peɪpəweɪt] **N** presse-papiers *m inv*

paperwork ['peɪpəwɜːk] **N** travail *m* de bureau, *Pej* paperasserie *f*; **to do the p.** s'occuper du travail de bureau; **I'm drowning in p.** je suis dans la paperasserie jusqu'au cou

papery ['peɪpərɪ] **ADJ** qui ressemble à du papier; *(thin)* mince comme du papier; **p. skin** peau *f* parcheminée

papier-mâché [ˌpæpjer'mæʃeɪ] **N** papier *m* mâché

papilloma [ˌpæpɪ'ləʊmə] **N** *Med* papillome *m*

papillomavirus [ˌpæpɪ'ləʊməˌvaɪrəs] **N** *Med* papillomavirus *m*

papist ['peɪpɪst] *Pej* **N** papiste *mf*

ADJ papiste

papistry ['peɪpɪstrɪ] **N** *Pej* papisme *m*

paprika ['pæprɪkə] **N** paprika *m*

Papua ['pæpjʊə] **N** Papouasie *f*

▸▸ ***Papua New Guinea*** Papouasie-Nouvelle-Guinée *f*

Papuan ['pæpjʊən] **N 1** *(person)* Papou(e) *m,f* **2** *Ling* langue *f* papoue

ADJ papou

papyrus [pə'paɪrəs] (*pl* **papyruses** *or* **papyri** [-raɪ]) **N** papyrus *m*

par [pɑː(r)] (*pt & pp* **parred**, *cont* **parring**) **N 1** *(equality)* égalité *f*; **to be on a p. (with sb/sth)** être au même niveau (que qn/qch); **you can't put him on a p. with Mozart!** tu ne peux pas le comparer à Mozart! **2** *(normal, average)* normale *f*, moyenne *f*; **I'm feeling a bit below** *or* **under p. these days** je ne me sens pas en forme ces jours-ci; **the film isn't really up to p.** le film n'est pas aussi bon qu'on aurait pu s'y attendre **3** *Golf* par *m*; **a p.-three (hole)** un par trois; **she got a p. four** elle a fait un par quatre; **she was two under/over p.** elle était à deux coups en-dessous/au-dessus du par; *Fam Fig* **that's about p. for the course** c'est ce à quoi il faut s'attendre[▫]; **his behaviour was about p. for the course** son comportement n'a rien eu de vraiment surprenant[▫] **4** *Fin & St Exch (of bills, shares)* pair *m*; **above/below p.** au-dessus/au-dessous du pair; **at p.** au pair

VT *Golf (hole)* faire le par à

▸▸ *Fin & St Exch* ***par of exchange*** pair *m* du change; *Fin & St Exch* ***par value*** valeur *f* au pair *ou* nominale

para ['pærə] **N 1** *(abbr* **paragraph***)* par. **2** *Fam Mil (abbr* **paratrooper***)* para *m*

paraben ['pærəben] **N** *Chem* paraben *m*

parable ['pærəbəl] **N** *Rel & Fig* parabole *f*

parabola [pə'ræbələ] **N** *Math* parabole *f*

parabolic [ˌpærə'bɒlɪk] **ADJ** *Math & Literature* parabolique

▸▸ *TV* ***parabolic dish*** antenne *f* parabolique, parabole *f*

paracetamol [ˌpærə'siːtəmɒl] **N** paracétamol *m*; **take two p.** *or* **paracetamols** prenez deux cachets de paracétamol

parachute ['pærəʃuːt] **N** parachute *m*; **to drop sb/sth by p.** larguer qn/qch par parachute, parachuter qn/qch

COMP *(harness)* de parachute; *(troops, regiment)* de parachutistes

VT parachuter

VI sauter en parachute; **they parachuted into occupied France** ils se sont fait parachuter en France occupée

▸▸ *Can Pol* ***parachuted candidate*** candidat *m* parachuté; ***parachute drop*** parachutage *m*; ***parachute jump*** saut *m* en parachute; **to make a p. jump** sauter en parachute; ***parachute pack*** *(parachute)* parachute *m* (plié et prêt à servir); *(container)* enveloppe *f* ou sac *m* de parachute

▸ **parachute in VT SEP** *(troops, supplies etc)* parachuter, envoyer par parachute; *Fig (new manager, candidate)* parachuter

VI descendre en parachute

parachuting ['pærəʃuːtɪŋ] **N** *(of person, supplies)* parachutage *m*; *Sport* parachutisme *m*; **to go p.** faire du parachutisme

parachutist ['pærəʃuːtɪst] **N** parachutiste *mf*

parade [pə'reɪd] **N 1** *(procession)* défilé *m*; **fashion p.** défilé *m* de mode

2 *Mil (on parade ground)* exercice *m*; *(procession)* défilé *m*, parade *f*; **to be on p.** *(on parade ground)* être à l'exercice; **to go on p.** *(in procession)* défiler

3 *(along beach)* boulevard *m*; **a p. of shops** une rangée de magasins

4 *(show, ostentation)* étalage *m*; **to make a p. of one's grief** faire étalage de son chagrin; **all the world leaders were on p.** il y avait tout une panoplie de chefs d'états

5 *(in fencing)* parade *f*

VI 1 *(march ▸ gen) & Mil* défiler; **supporters paraded through the streets** les supporters défilaient dans les rues **2** *(show off)* se pavaner, parader; **he was parading up and down as if he owned the place** il se pavanait comme s'il était chez lui

VT 1 *(troops, prisoners etc)* faire défiler; **the prisoners were paraded through the streets** on fit défiler les prisonniers dans les rues **2** *(show off)* faire étalage de

▸▸ *Horseracing* ***parade ring*** terrain *m* de manœuvres

paradigm ['pærədaɪm] **N** paradigme *m*

▸▸ ***paradigm shift*** changement *m* radical

paradigmatic [ˌpærədɪg'mætɪk] **ADJ** paradigmatique

paradise ['pærədaɪs] **N 1** *(heaven)* paradis *m*; *(Eden)* le paradis terrestre; **to go to P.** aller *ou* monter au paradis **2** *Fig* paradis *m*; **it's p. (here) on earth** c'est le paradis sur terre; **a whole week away from the kids was p.!** une semaine entière loin des enfants, quel paradis!; **this river is a fisherman's p.** cette rivière est le paradis des pêcheurs

▸▸ *Ich* ***paradise fish*** poisson-paradis *m*, macropode *m*

paradisiac [ˌpærə'dɪsɪæk], **paradisiacal** [ˌpærədɪ'saɪəkəl] **ADJ** paradisiaque, édénique

paradox ['pærədɒks] **N** paradoxe *m*

paradoxical [ˌpærə'dɒksɪkəl] **ADJ** paradoxal

▸▸ ***paradoxical sleep*** sommeil *m* paradoxal

paradoxically [ˌpærə'dɒksɪkəlɪ] **ADV** paradoxalement

paraffin ['pærəfɪn] **N 1** *Br (fuel ▸ for lamp)* pétrole *m*; *(▸ for stove)* mazout *m*; *(▸ for aircraft)* kérosène *m* **2** *Chem (alkane)* paraffine *f*, alcane *m* **3** *(paraffin wax)* paraffine *f*

COMP *(heater)* à mazout

▸▸ ***paraffin lamp*** lampe *f* à pétrole; ***paraffin stove*** poêle *m* à mazout; ***paraffin wax*** paraffine *f*

paragliding ['pærəˌglaɪdɪŋ] **N** parapente *m*; **to go p.** faire du parapente

paragon ['pærəgən] **N** modèle *m*; **a p. of virtue** un modèle *ou* un parangon de vertu

paragraph ['pærəgrɑːf] **N 1** *(in writing)* paragraphe *m*, alinéa *m*; **new p.** *(when dictating)* (allez) à la ligne; **to start a new p.** aller à la ligne; **section A, p. 3 (of the contract)** article A, alinéa 3 (du contrat) **2** *(short article)* entrefilet *m* **3** *Typ (mark)* pied *m* de mouche, alinéa *m*

VT diviser en paragraphes *ou* en alinéas

▸▸ *Comput* ***paragraph break*** fin *f* de paragraphe; ***paragraph format*** format *m* de paragraphe; *Typ* ***paragraph mark*** pied *m* de mouche, alinéa *m*

Paraguay ['pærəgwaɪ] **N** Paraguay *m*

Paraguayan [ˌpærə'gwaɪən] **N** Paraguayen (enne) *m,f*

ADJ paraguayen

COMP *(embassy, history)* du Paraguay

parakeet ['pærəkiːt] **N** *Orn* perruche *f*

parallel ['pærəlel] **ADJ 1** *(gen) & Math* parallèle (**to***ou***with** à); **there is a ditch p. with** *or* **to the fence** il y a un fossé qui longe la clôture; **to run p. to sth** longer qch **2** *(analogous)* pareil, semblable; *(case, situation)* analogue (**to** *or* **with** à); **a p. investigation was mounted in England and Scotland** une enquête a été menée simultanément en Angleterre et en Écosse **3** *Comput* parallèle

N 1 *(equivalent)* équivalent *m*; *(similarity)* ressemblance *f*, similitude *f*; **there are obvious parallels between the two cases** les deux cas présentent des similitudes frappantes; **a tradition which has no p. in our own culture** une tradition qui n'a pas d'équivalent dans notre culture; **the two industries have developed in p.** ces deux industries se sont développées en parallèle; **the disaster is without p.** une telle catastrophe est sans précédent; **in p. to** *or* **with sth** parallèlement à qch

2 *(comparison)* parallèle *m*; **to draw a p. between** faire *ou* établir un parallèle entre

3 *Math* (ligne *f*) parallèle *f*

4 *Geog & Astron* parallèle *m*; **the 48th p.** le 48ème parallèle

5 *Elec* parallèle *m*; **in p.** en parallèle; **out of p.** déphasé, hors de phase

VT 1 *(be similar to)* être analogue à; **his career has paralleled his father's** sa carrière a suivi une trajectoire semblable à celle de son père **2** *(equal)* égaler; **the victory has not been paralleled** cette victoire est restée sans égal

ADV to ski p., to p. ski skier parallèle; **to p. park** faire un créneau

▸▸ ***parallel bars*** barres *fpl* parallèles; *Elec* ***parallel circuit*** circuit *m* en parallèle; ***parallel computer*** ordinateur *m* à traitement parallèle; *Elec* ***parallel connection*** couplage *m ou* montage *m* en parallèle *ou* en dérivation; ***parallel importing*** importations *fpl* parallèles; *Comput* ***parallel interface*** interface *f* parallèle; ***parallel lines*** lignes *fpl* parallèles; ***parallel parking*** stationnement *m* en créneau; *Comput* ***parallel port*** port *m* parallèle; ***parallel printer*** imprimante *f* en parallèle; *Comput* ***parallel processing*** traitement *m* en parallèle *or* en simultanéité; *Fin* ***parallel rate of exchange*** cours *m* parallèle; ***parallel ruler*** règle *f* parallèle, règles *fpl* parallèles; *Mktg* ***parallel selling*** vente *f* parallèle; *Ski* ***parallel slalom*** slalom *m* parallèle; *Ski* ***parallel turn*** virage *m* en parallèle

parallelism ['pærəlelɪzəm] **N** parallélisme *m*

parallelogram [ˌpærə'leləgræm] **N** *Geom* parallélogramme *m*

Paralympics [ˌpærə'lɪmpɪks] **NPL the P.** les jeux *mpl* Paralympiques

paralyse, *Am* **paralyze** ['pærəlaɪz] **VT 1** *Med* paralyser **2** *Fig (city, industry etc)* paralyser, immobiliser; *(person)* paralyser, pétrifier

paralysing, *Am* **paralyzing** ['pærəˌlaɪzɪŋ] **ADJ** *Med & Fig* paralysant

paralysis [pə'rælɪsɪs] **N 1** *Med* paralysie *f* **2** *Fig (of industry, business)* immobilisation *f*; *(of government)* paralysie *f*

paralytic [ˌpærə'lɪtɪk] **ADJ 1** *Med* paralytique **2** *Br Fam (very drunk)* pété à mort, bourré comme un coing

N *Med* paralytique *mf*

▸▸ ***paralytic stroke*** attaque *f* de paralysie

paralytically [ˌpærə'lɪtɪkəlɪ] **ADV** *Br Fam* **p. drunk** pété à mort, bourré comme un coing

paralyze, paralyzing *etc Am* = **paralyse, paralysing** *etc*

paramedic [ˌpærə'medɪk] **N** auxiliaire *mf* médical(e); *Am* **the paramedics** les services *mpl* de secours, ≃ le SAMU

ADJ paramédical

parameter [pə'ræmɪtə(r)] **N** *(gen) & Ling, Math & Comput* paramètre *m*; **to set the parameters of sth** paramétrer qch; **within the parameters of the enquiry** dans les limites fixées par les paramètres de l'enquête

paramilitary [ˌpærə'mɪlɪtrɪ] *(pl* **paramilitaries***)* **ADJ** paramilitaire

N *(group)* formation *f* paramilitaire; *(person)* paramilitaire *mf*

NPL the p. la milice

paramount ['pærəmaʊnt] **ADJ 1** *(asset, necessity, concern)* primordial; **it is of p. importance** c'est d'une importance primordiale; **it is p. that we do this** il est primordial que nous fassions ceci; **the children's interests are p.** l'intérêt des enfants passe avant tout **2** *(ruler)* suprême

paramour ['pærəˌmʊə(r)] **N** *Literary or Hum (man)* amant *m*; *(woman)* maîtresse *f*

paranoia [ˌpærə'nɔɪə] **N** *(UNCOUNT)* paranoïa *f*

paranoiac [ˌpærə'nɔɪæk], **paranoic** [ˌpærə'nəʊɪk] **ADJ** paranoïaque

N paranoïaque *mf*

paranoid ['pærənɔɪd] **ADJ** *(disorder, delusion)* paranoïde; *(person)* paranoïaque; *Fig* **he's p. about being cheated** il est obsédé par l'idée qu'on cherche à l'avoir; **you're being p.** tu es parano

N paranoïaque *mf*

paranormal [ˌpærə'nɔːməl] **ADJ** paranormal

N the p. le paranormal

parapet ['pærəpet] **N 1** *Mil (in fortress)* parapet *m* *(of trench)* berge *f* **2** *(wall)* parapet *m*; *(railing)* garde-fou *m*; *(of bridge)* garde-corps *m inv*

paraphernalia [ˌpærəfə'neɪlɪə] **N** *(UNCOUNT)* **1** *(equipment)* attirail *m*; *(belongings)* fourbi *m* **2** *Fam (trappings)* tralala *m*; **it was a society wedding with all the p.** ce fut un mariage mondain avec tout le tralala

paraphrase ['pærəfreɪz] **N** paraphrase *f*

VT paraphraser

paraplegia [ˌpærə'pliːdʒə] **N** *Med* paraplégie *f*

paraplegic [ˌpærə'pliːdʒɪk] *Med* **ADJ** paraplégique

N paraplégique *mf*

parapsychology [ˌpærəsaɪ'kɒlədʒɪ] **N** parapsychologie *f*

parasite ['pærəsaɪt] **N 1** *Biol* parasite *m* **2** *Fig (person)* parasite *m*; **to be a p. on society** *(person)* parasiter la société

parasitic [ˌpærə'sɪtɪk], **parasitical** [ˌpærə'sɪtɪkəl] **ADJ 1** *Biol* parasite; **to be p. on an organism** parasiter un organisme **2** *Fig (person)* parasite; *(existence)* de parasite **3** *(illness ▸ caused by parasites)* parasitaire

parasitism ['pærəsaɪˌtɪzəm] **N** *Biol* parasitisme *m*

parasitize, -ise ['pærəsɪtaɪz] **VT** *Biol* parasiter

parasitology [ˌpærəsaɪ'tɒlədʒɪ] **N** *Biol* parasitologie *f*

parasol ['pærəsɒl] **N** *(for woman)* ombrelle *f*; *(for beach, table)* parasol *m*

▸▸ *Bot* ***parasol mushroom*** coulemelle *f*, lépiote *f*; ***parasol pine*** pin *m* parasol

paratroop ['pærətruːp] *Mil* **COMP** de parachutistes; *(regiment)* parachutiste, de parachutistes; *(commander)* parachutiste

• **paratroops NPL** parachutistes *mpl*

paratrooper ['pærətruːpə(r)] **N** *Mil* parachutiste *m*

paratyphoid [ˌpærə'taɪfɔɪd] **N** *Med* paratyphoïde *f*

▸▸ ***paratyphoid fever*** paratyphoïde *f*

parboil ['pɑːbɔɪl] **VT** *Culin* faire bouillir pendant quelques minutes

parcel ['pɑːsəl] *(Br pt & pp* **parcelled,** *cont* **parcelling,** *Am pt & pp* **parceled,** *cont* **parceling)** **N 1** *(package)* colis *m*, paquet *m*; **to send sth by p. post** envoyer qch par colis postal *or* en paquet-poste

2 *(portion of land)* parcelle *f*

3 *(group ▸ gen)* groupe *m*, lot *m*; *(▸ of shares)* paquet *m*

4 *(integral part)* partie *f* (intégrante)

5 *Culin* chausson *m*

VT 1 *(wrap up)* emballer, faire un colis de **2** *(divide up)* diviser en parcelles

▸▸ ***parcel bomb*** colis *m* piégé; ***parcel delivery*** livraison *f* de colis à domicile; ***parcel(s) office*** bureau *m* des messageries, messageries *fpl*; ***parcel rates*** tarif *m* colis postal; *Aut* ***parcel shelf*** tablette *f*

▸ **parcel out VT SEP 1** *(share out)* distribuer, partager **2** *(divide up ▸ land)* diviser en parcelles, lotir

▸ **parcel up VT SEP** emballer, mettre en colis

parch [pɑːtʃ] **VT 1** *(scorch)* dessécher, brûler; **the sun had parched the hills** le soleil avait brûlé les collines **2** *(usu passive) (make thirsty)* assoiffer **3** *Culin* griller légèrement

parched [pɑːtʃt] **ADJ 1** *(grass, earth)* desséché; *(throat, lips)* sec (sèche) **2** *Fam (person)* **I'm p.** je crève de soif

parchment ['pɑːtʃmənt] **N** *(material, document)* parchemin *m*; **skin like p.** peau *f* parcheminée

pardon ['pɑːdən] **VT 1** *(forgive ▸ fault)* pardonner; *(▸ person)* pardonner à; **to p. sb for sth** pardonner qch à qn; **please p. my rudeness** veuillez excuser mon impolitesse; **p. me for asking, but...** excusez-moi de vous poser cette question, mais...; *Ironic* **p. me for speaking!** hou là là, excuse-moi d'avoir osé m'exprimer!; **p. me for breathing!** excuse-moi d'avoir osé ouvrir la bouche!; **you could be pardoned for thinking so** il est facile de croire cela **2** *Law* gracier **3** *Rel (person)* absoudre; *(sin)* pardonner; **to p. sb sth** absoudre qn de qch

N 1 *(forgiveness)* pardon *m* **2** *Law* grâce *f*; *(document)* lettre *f* de grâce; **he was granted a p.** il fut gracié **3** *Rel* indulgence *f*

EXCLAM p. (me)? *(what?)* pardon?, comment?; **p. (me)!** *(sorry)* pardon!, excusez-moi!

pardonable ['pɑ:dənəbəl] **ADJ 1** *(forgivable)* pardonnable, excusable **2** *Law* graciable

pardonably ['pɑ:dənəblɪ] **ADV** de façon bien pardonnable *ou* excusable

pare [peə(r)] **VT 1** *(fruit, vegetable)* peler, éplucher; *(nails)* ronger, couper; *(horseshoe)* parer; **p. the rind off the cheese** enlever la croûte du fromage **2** *(reduce* ▸ *budget)* réduire; **staff levels have already been pared to the bone** on a déjà réduit les effectifs au minimum

pare down VT SEP *(expenses, activity)* réduire; *(text, speech)* raccourcir; **we've got to p. the report down to 50 pages** il va falloir ramener le rapport à 50 pages; **the budget has been pared down to the bone** le budget a été réduit *ou* ramené au strict minimum

parent ['peərənt] **N 1** *(mother)* mère *f*; *(father)* père *m*; **parents** parents *mpl*; **when you first become a p.** quand on devient père/mère; **Janet and Angus have become parents** Janet et Angus ont eu un enfant; **the p.-child relationship** la relation parents-enfant; **if neither p. can attend the meeting** si ni le père ni la mère ne peuvent assister à la réunion **2** *Phys* parent *m*

COMP 1 *(cooperation, participation)* des parents, parental **2** *(organization)* mère **3** *(animal)* parent; **one of the p. birds/seals** un des parents de l'oiseau/du phoque

▸▸ *Com* ***parent company*** société *f ou* maison *f* mère; ***parent plant*** plante *f* mère; **cuttings from the p. plant** des boutures *fpl* de la plante mère; ***parent tree*** arbre *m* d'origine

parentage ['peərəntɪdʒ] **N** origine *f*; **a child of unknown p.** un(e) enfant de père et mère inconnus; **children of racially mixed p.** des enfants *mpl* issus de mariages mixtes

parental [pə'rentəl] **ADJ** parental, des parents

▸▸ ***parental guidance*** contrôle *m* parental

parenthesis [pə'renθɪsɪs] *(pl* **parentheses** [-si:z]*)* **N** parenthèse *f*; **in parentheses** entre parenthèses

parenthesize, -ise [pə'renθɪsaɪz] **VT** *(word, explanation)* mettre entre parenthèses

parenthetic [,pærən'θetɪk], **parenthetical** [,pærən'θetɪkəl] **ADJ** entre parenthèses

▸▸ *Gram* ***parenthetic clause*** incidente *f*

parenthetically [,pærən'θetɪklɪ] **ADV** entre parenthèses

parenthood ['peərənthʊd] **N** *(fatherhood)* paternité *f*; *(motherhood)* maternité *f*; **the responsibilities of p.** les responsabilités *fpl* parentales

parenting ['peərəntɪŋ] **N** *(art)* art *m* d'être parent; *(activity)* métier *m* de parent; **the problems of p.** les problèmes qu'on a quand on est parent *ou* quand on a des enfants; **I put it down to bad p.** d'après moi, c'est parce que les parents remplissent mal leur rôle

▸▸ ***parenting skills*** capacités *fpl* à élever des enfants

pariah [pə'raɪə] **N** paria *m*

▸▸ ***pariah dog*** (chien *m*) paria *m*

paring ['peərɪŋ] **N** *(activity* ▸ *of fruit, vegetables)* épluchage *m*; *(*▸ *of nails)* fait *m* de ronger

• **parings NPL** *(of fruit, vegetables)* épluchures *fpl*, pelures *fpl*; *(of nails)* rognures *fpl*; *(of metal)* cisaille *f*

▸▸ ***paring knife*** couteau *m* à légumes

pari passu [,pærɪ'pæsu] **ADV 1** *Literary* **to go p. with sth** marcher de pair avec qch **2** *Fin & St Exch* pari passu (**with** avec)

Paris ['pærɪs] **N** *(city)* Paris

PR N *Myth* Pâris

▸▸ ***the Paris Basin*** le Bassin parisien

parish ['pærɪʃ] **N 1** *Rel* paroisse *f* **2** *Pol* ≃ commune *f (en Angleterre)*

COMP *(funds) & Rel* paroissial

▸▸ ***parish church*** église *f* paroissiale; ***parish clerk*** bedeau *m*; ***parish council*** ≃ conseil *m* municipal *(d'une petite commune, en Angleterre)*; ***parish hall*** salle *f* paroissiale; ***parish priest*** *(Catholic)* curé *m*; *(Protestant)* pasteur *m*; ***parish register*** registre *m* paroissial; ***parish school*** école *f* communale

parishioner [pə'rɪʃənə(r)] **N** paroissien(enne) *m,f*

Parisian *[Br* pə'rɪzɪən, *Am* pə'ri:ʒən] **N** Parisien (enne) *m,f*

ADJ parisien

parity ['pærətɪ] *(pl* **parities) N 1** *(equality)* égalité *f*, parité *f*; **we have achieved p. of productivity with Japan** nous avons atteint le niveau de productivité du Japon; **ambulance staff want p. with firemen** les ambulanciers veulent obtenir l'égalité de statut avec les pompiers

2 *Econ & Fin* parité *f*; **the two currencies were at p.** les deux monnaies étaient à parité; **euro-dollar p.** parité *f* euro-dollar

3 *(analogy)* **p. of reasoning** raisonnement *m* analogue

4 *Comput, Math & Phys* parité *f*

▸▸ *Comput* ***parity bit*** bit *m* de parité; ***parity error*** erreur *f* de parité; *Econ & Fin* ***parity of exchange*** parité *f* de change; ***parity ratio*** rapport *m* de parité; ***parity table*** table *f* des parités; ***parity value*** valeur *f* au pair

park [pɑ:k] **N 1** *(public* ▸ *large)* parc *m*; *(*▸ *smaller)* jardin *m* public; *(private estate)* parc *m*, domaine *m* **2** *Aut (on automatic gearbox)* position *f* (de) stationnement; **leave the car in p.** laisse la voiture en position (de) stationnement **3** *Br Fam Sport* **the p.** le terrain[□]

VT 1 *(car)* garer

2 *Fam (dump* ▸ *person, box)* laisser[□]; **she parked her bags in the hall** elle a laissé ses sacs dans l'entrée; **to p. oneself beside sb/on sth** se poser *ou* poser ses fesses à côté de qn/sur qch

3 *(sheep)* parquer

4 *Mil (artillery etc)* mettre en parc

5 *Comput (hard disk)* parquer, effectuer le parcage de

6 *St Exch* mettre en attente

VI *Aut* se garer, stationner; **I couldn't find anywhere to p.** je n'ai pas trouvé à me garer

▸▸ *Br* ***park keeper*** *(of large park)* gardien(enne) *m,f* de parc; *(of smaller park)* gardien(enne) *m,f* de jardin public; ***Park Lane*** = avenue résidentielle très chic à Londres; ***park officer*** gardien (enne) *m,f* de parc

parka ['pɑ:kə] **N** parka *m*

park-and-ride N = système de contrôle de la circulation qui consiste à garer les voitures à l'extérieur des grandes villes, puis à utiliser les transports en commun

parked [pɑ:kt] **ADJ** *(vehicle)* en stationnement, garé; **he was p. by a fire hydrant** il s'était garé devant une bouche d'incendie

parker ['pɑ:kə(r)] **N she's a good p.** elle sait très bien faire les créneaux

parking ['pɑ:kɪŋ] **N 1** *(of vehicle)* stationnement *m*; **no p.** *(sign)* stationnement interdit, défense de stationner; **p. is a problem in town** il est difficile de se garer *ou* de stationner en ville; **there's plenty of underground p.** il y a de nombreuses places dans les parkings souterrains; **I'm not very good at p.** je ne suis pas très doué pour me garer **2** *St Exch* mise *f* en attente

COMP de stationnement

▸▸ ***parking area*** aire *f* de stationnement, parking *m*; ***parking attendant*** *(in car park)* gardien (enne) *m,f*; *(at hotel)* voiturier *m*; ***parking bay*** aire *f* de stationnement; *Am* ***parking brake*** frein *m* à main; ***parking fine*** amende *f* de stationnement; *Am* ***parking garage*** parking *m* couvert; ***parking light*** feu *m* de position; *Am* ***parking lot*** parking *m*, parc *m* de stationnement; ***parking meter*** parcmètre *m*, parcomètre *m*, *Can* compteur *m* de stationnement; ***parking offence*** contravention *f* au stationnement; *Astron* ***parking orbit*** orbite *f* d'attente; ***parking place, parking space*** place *f* de stationnement, *Suisse* place *f* de parc; **to look for/to find a p. place** chercher/trouver à se garer; ***parking ticket*** contravention *f (pour stationnement irrégulier)*, P-V *m*

Parkinson's disease, Parkinson's ['pɑ:kɪnsənz-] **N** maladie *f* de Parkinson; **to have P.** avoir la maladie de Parkinson *ou* un parkinson

parkland ['pɑ:klænd] **N** *(UNCOUNT)* espace *m* vert, espaces *mpl* verts

parkour ['pɑ:kɔ:(r)] **N** parkour *m*

parkway ['pɑ:kweɪ] **N** *Am* grand boulevard *m* bordé d'arbres

parky ['pɑ:kɪ] *(compar* **parkier**, *superl* **parkiest)** **ADJ** *Br Fam (cold)* frisquet; **it's p. today** il fait frisquet aujourd'hui

parlance ['pɑ:ləns] **N** *Formal* langage *m*, parler *m*; **in common p.** dans la langue de tous les jours, en langage courant; **in legal p.** en langage juridique

parley ['pɑ:lɪ] **VI** parlementer

N conférence *f*; *(with enemy)* pourparlers *mpl*

parliament ['pɑ:ləmənt] **N** parlement *m*; **P. has decided that…** le Parlement a décidé que…; **in P.** au Parlement; **she was elected to P. in 2001** elle a été élue député en 2001; **the French P.** l'Assemblée nationale (française)

parliamentarian [,pɑ:ləmen'teərɪən] **N** parlementaire *mf*

parliamentary [,pɑ:lə'mentərɪ] **ADJ** *(system, debate, democracy)* parlementaire

▸▸ ***parliamentary candidate*** candidat *m* aux (élections) législatives; *Br* ***Parliamentary committee*** commission *f* parlementaire; ***parliamentary correspondent*** journaliste *mf* parlementaire; ***parliamentary elections*** élections *fpl* législatives; ***parliamentary group*** groupe *m* parlementaire; *Br* ***Parliamentary Labour Party*** députés *mpl* du Parti travailliste; ***parliamentary majority*** majorité *f* parlementaire; ***parliamentary minority*** minorité *f* parlementaire; ***parliamentary party*** parti *m* parlementaire; *Br* ***parliamentary private secretary*** = député qui assure la liaison entre un ministre et la Chambre des communes; ***parliamentary privilege*** immunité *f* parlementaire; *Br* ***parliamentary question*** = question posée au cours d'un débat parlementaire; ***Parliamentary recess*** vacances *fpl* parlementaires; *Br* ***parliamentary secretary (of state)*** ≃ sous-secrétaire *m* d'État; *Br* ***parliamentary undersecretary of state*** ≃ sous-secrétaire *mf* d'État

parlour, *Am* **parlor** ['pɑ:lə(r)] **N 1** *Old-fashioned (in house)* salon *m*

2 *Old-fashioned (in hotel, club)* salon *m*; *(in pub)* arrière-salle *f*

3 *(in convent)* parloir *m*

4 *Am Com* **beer p.** bar *m*; **billiard p.** salle *f* de billard; **ice-cream p.** salon *m* de dégustation de glaces

▸▸ *Am Rail* ***parlor car*** pullman *m (dans un train)*; *Br* ***parlour game*** jeu *m* de société

parlourmaid ['pɑ:ləmeɪd] **N** bonne *f (affectée au service de table)*

parlous ['pɑ:ləs] **ADJ** *Arch or Literary (state)* précaire; *(situation)* périlleux

Parma ['pɑ:mə] **N** Parme

▸▸ ***Parma ham*** jambon *m* de Parme; ***Parma violet*** violette *f* de Parme

Parmesan (cheese) [,pɑ:mɪ'zæn-] **N** parmesan *m*

Parnassus [pɑ:'næsəs] **N** Parnasse *m*; **(Mount) P.** le (mont) Parnasse

parochial [pə'rəʊkɪəl] **ADJ 1** *Rel* paroissial **2** *Pej* borné; **p. attitudes** attitudes *fpl* de clocher *ou* bornées

▸▸ *Am* ***parochial school*** école *f* religieuse

parochialism [pə'rəʊkɪəlɪzəm] **N** *Pej* esprit *m* de clocher, étroitesse *f* d'esprit

parodist ['pærədɪst] **N** parodiste *mf*

parody ['pærədɪ] *(pl* **parodies**, *pt & pp* **parodied)** **N** parodie *f*, pastiche *m*; *(of truth)* travestissement *m*

VT parodier, pasticher

parole [pə'rəʊl] **N 1** *Law* liberté *f* conditionnelle *ou* sur parole; **to be released** *or* **put on p.** être mis en liberté conditionnelle, être libéré conditionnellement; **to break one's p.** manquer à sa parole; **he's up for p. next year** il devrait être mis en liberté conditionnelle l'année prochaine **2** *Am Mil (password)* mot *m* de passe **3** *Ling* parole *f*

VT mettre en liberté conditionnelle, libérer sur parole

▸▸ ***parole board*** ≃ comité *m* de probation et d'assistance aux libérés

parolee [pərəʊ'li:] N*Am* prisonnier(ère) *m,f* en liberté conditionnelle

paroxysm ['pærəksɪzəm] N**1** *(of rage, despair)* accès *m*; *(of jealousy, grief, tears)* crise *f*; **to be in paroxysms of laughter** avoir le fou rire; **to send sb into paroxysms of laughter** donner le fou rire à qn **2** *Med* paroxysme *m*

parquet ['pɑ:keɪ] N**1** *Constr (floor)* parquet *m* **2** *Am Theat* parterre *m*
VTparqueter
▸▸ ***parquet floor, parquet flooring*** parquet *m*

parricide ['pærɪsaɪd] N**1** *(crime)* parricide *m* **2** *(person)* parricide *mf*

parrot ['pærət] N*Orn* perroquet *m*; *Fam* **I was as sick as a p.** *(disappointed)* ça m'a rendu malade; **to repeat sth p. fashion** répéter qch comme un perroquet; **to learn sth p. fashion** *(by repetition)* apprendre qch en le répétant
VT*(words)* répéter comme un perroquet; *(person, actions)* imiter
▸▸ ***parrot disease, parrot fever*** psittacose *f*; *Ich* ***parrot fish*** perroquet *m* de mer, poisson-perroquet *m*

parry ['pærɪ] *(pt & pp* **parried**, *pl* **parries***)* VT**1** *(in fencing, boxing)* parer **2** *(problem)* tourner, éviter; *(question)* éluder; *(manoeuvre)* parer à, contrer
VI*(in fencing, boxing)* parer; **he parried with his right** il a paré l'attaque *ou* le coup d'une droite; **to p. and thrust** parer et tirer
N*(in fencing, boxing)* parade *f*

parse [pɑ:z] VT**1** *Gram (word)* faire l'analyse (grammaticale) de; *(sentence)* faire l'analyse logique de **2** *Comput* analyser

Parsee, Parsi [,pɑ:'si:] NParsi(e) *m,f*
ADJparsi

parser ['pɑ:zə(r)] N*Comput* analyseur *m* syntaxique

parsimonious [,pɑ:sɪ'məʊnɪəs] ADJ*Formal* parcimonieux; **to be p. with one's money** dépenser son argent avec parcimonie

parsimoniously [,pɑ:sɪ'məʊnɪəslɪ] ADV*Formal* avec parcimonie, parcimonieusement

parsimony ['pɑ:sɪmənɪ] N*Formal* parcimonie *f*

parsing ['pɑ:zɪŋ] N**1** *Gram (of word)* analyse *f* grammaticale; *(of sentence)* analyse *f* logique **2** *Comput* analyse *f* syntaxique

parsley ['pɑ:slɪ] Npersil *m*
COMP*(sauce, butter)* au persil

parsnip ['pɑ:snɪp] Npanais *m*

parson ['pɑ:sən] N*(gen)* ecclésiastique *m*; *(Protestant)* pasteur *m*
▸▸ *Culin* ***parson's nose*** croupion *m*

parsonage ['pɑ:sənɪdʒ] Npresbytère *m*

PART [pɑ:t]

N
- partie **1, 9, 10**
- rôle **2**
- pièce **3**
- région **4**
- quartier **4**
- épisode **5**
- mesure **6**
- parti **7**
- raie **8**

ADV
- en partie

VI
- s'entrouvrir **1**
- s'ouvrir **1**
- se quitter **2**
- se casser **3**
- se déchirer **3**

VT
- entrouvrir **1**
- écarter **1**
- séparer **2**

NPL
- talents

N**1** *(gen* ▸ *portion, subdivision)* partie *f*; **the exam is in two parts** l'examen est en deux parties; **see p. one, section two** voir première partie, section deux; **the parts of the body** les parties *fpl* du corps; **(a) p. of the garden is flooded** une partie du jardin est inondée; **(a) p. of me strongly agrees with them** sur un certain plan, je suis tout à fait d'accord avec eux; **that's only p. of the problem** ce n'est qu'un des aspects du problème; **it's very much p. of the game/of the process** ça fait partie du jeu/du processus; **it's all p. of growing up** c'est ce qui se passe quand on grandit; **we've finished the hardest p.** nous avons fait le plus dur; **the best/worst p. was when he started laughing** le mieux/le pire ça a été quand il s'est mis à rire; **in the early p. of the week** au début *ou* dans les premiers jours de la semaine; **for the best** *or* **greater p. of five years** *(to wait, last etc)* presque cinq ans; **the greater p. of the population** la plus grande partie de la population; **to be (a) p. of sth** *(be involved with)* faire partie de qch; **to form p. of sth** faire partie de qch; **to be p. and parcel of sth** faire partie (intégrante) de qch
2 *(role)* rôle *m*; **who played the p. of Hamlet?** qui a joué le rôle de Hamlet?; *Fig* **he's just playing a p.** il joue la comédie; **to know one's p.** connaître son texte; **work plays a large p. in our lives** le travail joue un rôle important dans notre vie; **she played a large p. in persuading the company to relocate** c'est surtout elle qui a persuadé l'entreprise de se relocaliser; **to take p. (in sth)** prendre part *ou* participer (à qch); **she takes an active p. in decision-making** elle participe activement au processus de prise de décision; **I had no p. in that affair** je n'ai joué aucun rôle dans cette affaire; **he has no p. in the running of the company** il ne participe pas à *ou* il n'intervient pas dans la gestion de la société; **Joe had no p. in it** Joe n'y était pour rien; **I want no p. in** *or* **of their schemes** je ne veux pas être mêlé à leurs projets; **to do one's p.** y mettre du sien; **to dress the p.** se mettre en tenue de circonstance; **to look the p.** avoir la tenue de circonstance; **for my/his p.** pour ma/sa part
3 *(component* ▸ *of machine)* pièce *f*; **parts and labour warranty** garantie *f* pièces et main-d'œuvre
4 *(area* ▸ *of country, town etc)* **which p. of England are you from?** vous êtes d'où en Angleterre?, de quelle région de l'Angleterre venez-vous?; **in some parts of Sydney/Australia** dans certains quartiers de Sydney/certaines régions de l'Australie; **it's a dangerous p. of town** c'est un quartier dangereux; **are you new to these parts?** vous êtes nouveau ici?; **they are not from our p. of the world** ils ne sont pas de chez nous; **she's travelling in foreign parts** elle est en voyage à l'étranger
5 *(instalment* ▸ *of encyclopedia)* fascicule *m*; *(*▸ *of serial)* épisode *m*; **don't miss p. two!** *(of serial)* ne manquez pas le deuxième épisode!; *(of programme in two parts)* ne manquez pas la deuxième partie!
6 *(measure)* mesure *f*; **one p. of pastis and four parts of water** une mesure de pastis et quatre mesures d'eau; *Chem* **a concentration of six parts per million** une concentration de six pour un million; **the bottle was three parts empty** la bouteille était aux trois quarts vide
7 *(side)* parti *m*, part *f*; **he always takes his mother's p.** il prend toujours le parti de sa mère; **to take sth in good p.** bien prendre qch
8 *Am (in hair)* raie *f*
9 *Gram* partie *f*
10 *Mus* partie *f*; **the vocal/violin p.** la partie vocale/(pour) violon; **to sing in three parts** chanter à trois voix
ADVen partie, partiellement; **the jacket is p. cotton, p. polyester** la veste est un mélange de coton et de polyester *ou* un mélange coton-polyester; **he's p. English, p. Chinese** il est moitié anglais, moitié chinois; **a mythical creature, p. woman, p. fish** une créature mythique mi-femme, mi-poisson
VI**1** *(move apart* ▸ *lips, curtains)* s'entrouvrir; *(*▸ *legs)* s'écarter, s'ouvrir; *(*▸ *crowd)* s'ouvrir; *(disengage* ▸ *fighters)* se séparer; **the clouds parted** il y eut une éclaircie
2 *(leave one another)* se quitter; **they parted good friends** ils se sont quittés bons amis
3 *(break* ▸ *rope)* se casser; *(tear* ▸ *fabric)* se déchirer
VT**1** *(move apart, open* ▸ *curtains)* entrouvrir; *(*▸ *branches, legs)* écarter; **her lips were slightly parted** ses lèvres étaient entrouvertes
2 *(separate)* séparer **(from** de**)**; **the children were parted from their parents** les enfants ont été séparés de leurs parents; *Hum* **he's not easily parted from his cash** il ne se sépare pas facilement de son argent
3 *(hair)* faire une raie à; **her hair's parted in the middle** elle a la raie au milieu
• **parts** NPL*(talents)* talents *mpl*; **a man/woman of many parts** un homme/une femme de talent
• **for the most part** ADVdans l'ensemble
• **in part** ADVen partie; **it's in large p. true** c'est en grande partie vrai
• **in parts** ADVpar endroits; **the book is good in parts** le livre est bon par endroits, certains passages du livre sont bons
• **on the part of** PREPde la part de
▸▸ *Com* ***part consignment*** expédition *f* partielle; *Com* ***part exchange*** reprise *f*; **they'll take your old TV set in p. exchange** ils vous font une reprise sur *or* ils reprennent votre ancien téléviseur; **will you take it in p. exchange?** voulez-vous le reprendre?; *Com* ***part load*** chargement *m* partiel; ***part music*** musique *f* d'ensemble; ***part owner*** copropriétaire *mf*; ***part ownership*** copropriété *f*; ***part payment*** acompte *m*, paiement *m* partiel; **I received £500 in p. payment for the car** j'ai reçu un acompte de 500 livres pour la voiture; *Com* ***part shipment*** expédition *f* partielle; ***part singing*** chant *m* polyphonique *or* à plusieurs voix; ***part song*** chant *m* polyphonique *or* à plusieurs voix; ***part of speech*** partie *f* du discours; *Br* ***part work*** ouvrage *m* à fascicules; **they published it as a p. work** ils l'ont publié sous forme de fascicules

partake [pɑ:'teɪk] *(pt* **partook** [-'tʊk], *pp* **partaken** [-'teɪkən]*)* VI*Arch or Formal* **1** *(eat, drink)* **to p. of sth** prendre qch; **I no longer p.** *(don't drink)* je ne bois plus; *Rel* **to p. of the Sacrament** s'approcher des sacrements, fréquenter les sacrements **2** *(participate)* **to p. in** *(event)* participer à; *(joy, grief)* partager **3** *(share quality)* **to p. of** relever de, tenir à; **it partakes of a certain grandeur** c'est empreint d'une certaine grandeur

parterre [pɑ:'teə(r)] N*Am (in theatre)* parterre *m*

parthenogenesis [,pɑ:θənəʊ'dʒenɪsɪs] N*Bio* parthénogenèse *f*

Parthian ['pɑ:θɪən] NParthe *mf*
▸▸ ***Parthian shot*** flèche *f* du Parthe

partial ['pɑ:ʃəl] ADJ**1** *(incomplete)* partiel; **the exhibition was only a p. success** l'exposition n'a connu qu'un succès mitigé **2** *(biased)* partial **(towards** envers**)** **3** *(fond)* **to be p. to sth** avoir un penchant *ou* un faible pour qch; **I am rather p. to a spot of whisky after dinner** je bois volontiers un petit verre de whisky après dîner
▸▸ *Math* ***partial derivative*** dérivée *f* partielle; ***partial eclipse*** éclipse *f* partielle; ***partial fraction*** petite partie *f* d'une fraction; *Ins* ***partial loss*** perte partielle, sinistre *m* partiel; *Fin* ***partial payment*** paiement *m* partiel

> When translating the English word **partial**, note that the French words **partial** and **partiel** are not interchangeable. **Partial** means **biased** and **partiel** is the opposite of **complete**.

partiality [,pɑ:ʃɪ'ælətɪ] *(pl* **partialities***)* N**1** *(bias)* partialité *f* **(towards** envers**)**; *(favouritism)* favoritisme *m* **2** *(fondness)* faible *m*, penchant *m* **(for** pour**)**

partially ['pɑ:ʃəlɪ] ADV**1** *(partly)* en partie, partiellement **2** *(in biased way)* partialement, avec partialité

partially-sighted ADJmalvoyant
NPL**the partially sighted** les malvoyants *mpl*

participant [pɑ:'tɪsɪpənt] Nparticipant(e) *m,f*; **the participants in the debate** les participants au débat

participate [pɑ:'tɪsɪpeɪt] VIparticiper, prendre part; **to p. in** *(race, discussion)* prendre part à, participer à; *Literary* **to p. in sb's joy** s'associer à la joie de qn

participating interest [pɑ:'tɪsɪpeɪtɪŋ-] N*Fin* intérêt *m* de participation; **to hold a p. in a company** avoir un intérêt de participation dans une société

participation [pɑ:,tɪsɪ'peɪʃən] Nparticipation **(in** à**)**; **they should encourage greater student participation** ils devraient encourager les étudiants à participer plus activement

participial [,pɑ:tɪ'sɪpɪəl] ADJ*Gram* participial

participle ['pɑ:tɪsɪpəl] N*Gram* participe *m*

particle ['pɑ:tɪkəl] N**1** *(tiny piece* ▸ *gen)* particule *f*, parcelle *f*; *(*▸ *of blood)* goutte *f*; *(*▸ *of metal)* paillette *f*; *(*▸ *of dust, sand)* grain *m*; *Fig (jot)* brin

m, grain *m*; **food particles** particules *fpl* de nourriture; **there's not a p. of truth in the story** il n'y a pas une ombre de vérité dans ce récit
2 *Gram* particule *f*
3 *Phys* particule *f*
4 *Rel* hostie *f*
▸▸ *Phys* ***particle accelerator*** accélérateur *m* de particules; *Phys* ***particle beam*** faisceau *m* de particules; *Constr* ***particle board*** (panneau *m* d')aggloméré *m*, panneau *m* de particules; ***particle physics*** physique *f* des particules

parti-coloured ['pɑːtɪ-] **ADJ** bariolé, bigarré

particular [pə'tɪkjʊlə(r)] **ADJ 1** *(specific)* particulier; **that p. book** ce livre-là, ce livre en particulier; **for no p. reason** sans raison particulière *ou* précise; **why did you insist on this p. one?** pourquoi as-tu insisté sur celui-là en particulier?; **my own p. feelings** mes sentiments personnels; **I've got no p. place to go** je ne vais nulle part en particulier, je n'ai pas de destination précise
2 *(special)* particulier, spécial; **it's an issue of p. importance to us** c'est une question qui revêt une importance toute particulière à nos yeux; **this one is a p. favourite of mine** j'affectionne tout particulièrement celui-ci; **to take p. care to do sth** mettre un soin (tout) particulier à faire qch
3 *(person* ▸ *exacting)* méticuleux, minutieux, soigneux; *(*▸ *about rules etc)* pointilleux; *(*▸ *about choice of friends, methods used etc)* difficile, exigeant; **I have to be quite p. about what I eat** je dois faire très attention à ce que je mange; **it had to be pure silk, he was most p. about it** il fallait que ce soit de la soie pure, il a insisté; **to be p. about one's food** *(demanding)* être exigeant pour la nourriture; *(difficult)* être difficile pour la nourriture; **to be p. about one's dress** soigner sa mise *ou* sa tenue; *Fam* **I'm not p. (about it)** *(I don't care)* je n'y tiens pas plus que ça; *Fam* **he's not p. about where the goods come from** l'origine des marchandises lui importe peu❑
N 1 *(specific)* **from the general to the p.** du général au particulier
2 *(detail)* détail *m*; **alike in every p.** semblables en tout point; **they differ in several particulars** ils diffèrent en plusieurs points; **to go into particulars** entrer dans les détails; **to give particulars of sth** donner les détails de qch; **to take down sb's particulars** prendre les coordonnées de qn; **for further particulars apply to...** pour plus amples détails *ou* renseignements s'adresser à...
• **in particular ADV** en particulier; **what are you thinking about? – nothing in p.** à quoi penses-tu? – à rien en particulier; **what happened? – nothing in p.** que s'est-il passé? – rien de particulier *ou* rien de spécial; **no one in p.** personne en particulier; **where are you going? – nowhere in p.** où vas-tu? – je vais juste faire un tour

particularity [pə,tɪkjʊ'lærətɪ] *(pl* **particularities)** **N 1** *(special quality)* particularité *f* **2** *(exacting nature)* méticulosité *f* **3** *(detailed nature* ▸ *of description)* minutie *f*

particularize, -ise [pə'tɪkjʊləraɪz] **VT** spécifier
VI entrer dans les détails, préciser

particularly [pə'tɪkjʊləlɪ] **ADV** particulièrement; **I don't know him p. well** je ne le connais pas spécialement bien; **I was surprised he wasn't there, p. as he'd received an official invitation** son absence m'a surpris, d'autant plus qu'il avait reçu une invitation officielle; **not p.** pas particulièrement *ou* spécialement; **she's not p. rich** elle n'est pas tellement riche

particulate [pə'tɪkjʊlɪt] **ADJ** particulaire
N particule *f*
▸▸ ***particulate emissions*** émissions *fpl* de particules

parting ['pɑːtɪŋ] **N 1** *(leave-taking)* séparation *f*; **they had a tearful p. at the station** ils se quittèrent en larmes à la gare; **p. from his family was hard** il a eu du mal à quitter sa famille
2 *(division)* séparation *f*; *Fig* **to be at** *or* **to have come to the p. of the ways** être à la croisée des chemins
3 *(opening* ▸ *in clouds)* trouée *f*; *Bible* **the p. of the Red Sea** le partage des eaux de la mer Rouge
4 *Br (in hair)* raie *f*; **centre/side p.** raie *f* au milieu/sur le côté
ADJ *Literary (words, kiss)* d'adieu; **he gave me a p. handshake** il m'a serré la main en partant
▸▸ *Fig* ***parting shot*** flèche *f* du Parthe; **that was his p. shot** et sur ces mots, il s'en alla

partisan [,pɑːtɪ'zæn] **ADJ** partisan
N 1 *(supporter)* partisan *m*; **to act in a p. spirit** *(politician etc)* faire preuve d'esprit de parti; *(be prejudiced)* faire preuve de parti pris **2** *Mil* partisan *m*
▸▸ ***partisan politics*** politique *f* partisane

partisanship [,pɑːtɪ'zænʃɪp] **N** partialité *f*; *(of politician etc)* esprit *m* de parti

partition [pɑː'tɪʃən] **N 1** *(screen)* paravent *m*; *(wall)* cloison *f*; *(of ship's hold etc)* compartiment *m* **2** *(dividing* ▸ *of country)* partition *f*; *(*▸ *of room)* séparation *f*; *(*▸ *of property)* division *f*; *(*▸ *of power)* répartition *f*, morcellement *m* **3** *Comput (of hard disk)* partition *f*
VT 1 *(country, property)* diviser, partager
2 *(room)* séparer en deux
3 *(power)* partager
4 *Comput (hard disk)* diviser en partitions
▸▸ ***partition wall*** cloison *f*

> Note that the French word **partition** never means **wall.**

▸ **partition off VT SEP** *(room)* cloisonner; *(part of a room)* séparer par une cloison; **a small office had been partitioned off** on avait aménagé un petit bureau derrière une cloison

partitive ['pɑːtɪtɪv] *Gram* **N** partitif *m*
ADJ partitif

partly ['pɑːtlɪ] **ADV** en partie, partiellement; **wholly or p.** en tout ou en partie; **p. by force, p. by persuasion** moitié par la force, moitié par la persuasion; **a p. eaten sandwich** un sandwich à moitié mangé; **she was only p. convinced** elle n'était qu'à moitié convaincue
▸▸ *Fin* ***partly paid-up capital*** capital *m* non entièrement versé; *St Exch* ***partly paid-up shares*** actions *fpl* non entièrement libérées

partner ['pɑːtnə(r)] **N 1** *(spouse)* époux (épouse) *m,f*, conjoint(e) *m,f*; *(boyfriend, girlfriend)* ami(e) *m,f*; **sexual p.** partenaire *mf* (sexuel(elle))
2 *(in game, dance)* partenaire *mf*; **his p. in the waltz** sa partenaire *ou* sa cavalière pour la valse; *Cards* **to cut** *or* **draw for partners** = faire les rois
3 *Com* associé(e) *m,f*
4 *(in common undertaking)* partenaire *mf*; *(of cowboy, bank robber etc)* acolyte *m*; **our European partners** nos partenaires européens; **to be partners in crime** être complices dans le crime
VT 1 *(be the partner of)* être partenaire de **2** *(dance with)* danser avec; *(in games)* faire équipe avec, être le partenaire de; **she partnered him in a foxtrot** elle a dansé un fox-trot avec lui; **Wilson partnered Bailey to victory in the men's doubles** Wilson et Bailey ont remporté le double messieurs

partnership ['pɑːtnəʃɪp] **N 1** *(gen)* association *f*; **to work in p. with sb/sth** travailler en association avec qn/qch; **a winning doubles p.** une équipe de double gagnante; **their relationship has lasted so long because they're a p.** s'ils sont ensemble depuis si longtemps, c'est qu'ils ont une vraie relation de partenariat **2** *Com (association)* association *f*; *(company)* ≃ société *f* en nom collectif; **to go into p. with sb** s'associer avec qn; **they've gone into p. together** ils se sont associés; **they offered him a p.** ils lui ont proposé de devenir leur associé
▸▸ ***partnership agreement*** accord *m* de partenariat; *St Exch* ***partnership share*** part *f* d'association

partook [pɑː'tʊk] *pt of* **partake**

partridge ['pɑːtrɪdʒ] *(pl* **inv** *or* **partridges)** **N** perdrix *f*; *(immature)* perdreau *m*

part-time ADJ à temps partiel; **a p. teacher** un professeur à temps partiel; **on a p. basis** à temps partiel; **she's got a p. job** elle travaille à temps partiel
ADV à temps partiel

parturition [,pɑːtjʊ'rɪʃən] **N** parturition *f*

partway ['pɑːtweɪ] **ADV** en partie, partiellement; **p. through the year, she resigned** elle a démissionné en cours d'année; **I'm only p. through the book** je n'ai pas fini le livre; **they had gone p. towards an agreement** ils s'acheminaient vers un accord; **this will go p. towards covering the costs** cela couvrira une bonne partie des coûts

party ['pɑːtɪ] *(pl* **parties**, *pt & pp* **partied)** **N 1** *(social event)* fête *f*; *(more formal)* soirée *f*, réception *f*; **to give a p.** *(formal)* donner une réception *ou* une soirée; *(informal)* faire une fête; **to have** *or* **to throw a p. for sb** organiser une fête en l'honneur de qn; **he's caught the p. spirit** il s'est abandonné aux joies de la fête; **he's a real p. person** il adore faire la fête; **New Year's Eve p.** réveillon *m* de fin d'année
2 *Pol* parti *m*; **he joined the Socialist P. in 1936** il est entré au parti socialiste en 1936
3 *(group* ▸ *of tourists, climbers)* groupe *m*; *(*▸ *of miners, workers etc)* brigade *f*, équipe *f*, groupe; *Mil* détachement *m*; **will you join our p.?** voulez-vous être des nôtres?; **we're a small p.** nous sommes peu nombreux; **I was one of the p.** j'étais de la partie; **a tour p.** un groupe de touristes; **the funeral p.** le cortège funèbre; **the rescue p.** l'équipe *f* de secours; **the wedding p.** les invités *mpl (à un mariage)*; **to make dinner reservations for a p. of six** réserver une table pour six personnes
4 *Formal or Law (participant)* partie *f*; **to be a p. to** *(conversation)* prendre part à; *(crime)* être complice de; *(conspiracy, enterprise)* être mêlé à, tremper dans; *also Fig* **the guilty p.** le (la) coupable; **I would never be (a) p. to such a thing** je ne me ferais jamais complice d'une chose pareille, je ne m'associerais jamais à une chose pareille
5 *(person)* individu *m*
COMP 1 *(atmosphere, clothes)* de fête **2** *Pol (leader, leadership, funds)* du parti; *(system)* des partis
VI *Fam* faire la fête❑; **let's p.!** faisons la fête!; **she's a great one for partying** elle adore faire la fête
▸▸ *Fam* ***party animal*** fêtard(e) *m,f*; **she's a real p. animal** elle adore faire la fête, c'est une sacrée fêtarde; *Pol* ***party chairman*** premier secrétaire *m* du parti; *Pol* ***Party Conference*** Congrès *m* du parti; *Pol* ***party convention*** Congrès *m* du parti; ***party dress*** robe *f* habillée; *Pol* ***party faithful*** fidèles *mfpl* du parti; ***party games*** = jeux auxquels on joue dans les soirées ou les fêtes; ***party invitation*** invitation *f*; ***party line*** *Tel* ligne *f* commune *(à plusieurs abonnés)*; *Pol* ligne *f* du parti; **to toe** *or* **follow the p. line** suivre la ligne du parti; *Pol* ***party machine*** machine *f* du parti; *Pol* ***party man*** homme *m* de parti; *Pol* ***party member*** membre *m* du parti; *Br Fam* ***party piece*** numéro❑*m (à l'occasion d'une fête)*; *Ironic* **that's his p. piece** c'est son numéro habituel; *Pol* ***party platform*** = annonce du programme d'un parti politique; *Pol* ***party politics*** politique *f* de parti; *Pej* politique *f* politicienne; *Fam* ***party pooper*** rabat-joie *m inv*; ***party snacks*** amuse-gueule(s) *mpl*; ***party wall*** mur *m* mitoyen

partygoer ['pɑːtɪgəʊə(r)] **N** fêtard(e) *m,f*; *(more formal)* habitué(e) *m,f* des soirées; **the streets were full of partygoers** les rues étaient pleines de gens se rendant à des soirées

party-list system N *Pol (of voting)* scrutin *m* de liste

PASCAL [pæ'skæl] **N** *Comput* PASCAL *m*

paschal, Paschal ['pæskəl] **ADJ** pascal
▸▸ ***Paschal candle*** cierge *m* pascal; ***Paschal Lamb*** agneau *m* pascal

pashmina [pæʃ'miːnə] **N** *(wool, garment)* pashmina *m*

PASS [pɑːs]

N
• col **1** • laissez–passer **2**
• moyenne **3** • passe **5–7**
VT
• passer devant **1** • dépasser **1**
• passer **2–5, 10, 12** • être reçu à **6**
• voter **7** • admettre **7**
• prononcer **8**
VI
• passer **1, 2, 4, 5, 7, 8, 10, 11, 14** • dépasser **3**
• se passer **4, 6**
• être voté **9** • être reçu **9**
• se faire passer **12** • faire une passe **13**

N 1 *(in mountains)* col *m*, défilé *m*; **the Brenner P.** le col du Brenner

2 *(authorization* ▸ *for worker, visitor)* laissez-passer *m inv*; *Theat* invitation *f*, billet *m* de faveur; *Mil* (▸ *for leave of absence)* permission *f*; (▸ *for safe conduct)* sauf-conduit *m*; **rail/bus p.** carte *f* d'abonnement (de train)/de bus

3 *Sch & Univ (in exam)* moyenne *f*, mention *f* passable; **to get a p.** être reçu; **I got three passes** j'ai été reçu dans trois matières

4 *(state of affairs)* **things have come to a pretty p.** on est dans une bien mauvaise passe, la situation s'est bien dégradée; **things came to such a p. that…** les choses en vinrent à ce point *ou* à tel point que…

5 *Sport (with ball, puck)* passe *f*; *(in fencing)* botte *f*; *(in bullfighting)* passe *f*; **to make a p. at** *(in fencing)* porter une botte à

6 *(by magician)* passe *f*

7 *Comput* passe *f*

8 *Aviat (overflight)* survol *m*; *(attack)* attaque *f*

9 *Fam* **to make a p. at sb** *(sexual advances)* faire du plat à qn

VT 1 *(move past, go by* ▸ *building, window, table)* passer devant; (▸ *person)* croiser; *(overtake)* dépasser, doubler; **if you p. a chemist's, get some aspirin** si tu passes devant une pharmacie, achète de l'aspirine; **the ships passed each other in the fog** les navires se sont croisés dans le brouillard

2 *(go beyond* ▸ *finishing line, frontier)* passer; **we've passed the right exit** nous avons dépassé la sortie que nous aurions dû prendre; **contributions have passed the $100,000 mark** les dons ont franchi la barre des 100 000 dollars; **not a word about it had passed her lips** elle n'en avait pas dit un mot; **to p. understanding** dépasser l'entendement

3 *(move, run)* passer; **to p. one's hand between the bars** passer *ou* glisser sa main à travers les barreaux; **to p. a rope round sth** passer une corde autour de qch; **she passed her hand over her hair** elle s'est passé la main dans les cheveux

4 *(hand)* passer; *(transmit* ▸ *message)* transmettre; **to p. sth from hand to hand** passer qch de main en main; **p. me the sugar, please** passez-moi le sucre, s'il vous plaît; **p. the list around the office** faites passer *ou* circuler la liste dans le bureau; **can you p. her the message?** pourriez-vous lui transmettre *ou* faire passer le message?

5 *(spend* ▸ *life, time, visit)* passer; **it passes the time** cela fait passer le temps

6 *(succeed in* ▸ *exam, driving test)* être reçu à, réussir; **he didn't p. his history exam** il a échoué *ou* il a été recalé à son examen d'histoire; **to p. a test** *(vehicle, product)* passer une épreuve avec succès

7 *(approve* ▸ *bill, law)* voter; (▸ *motion, resolution)* adopter; *Sch & Univ* (▸*student)* recevoir, admettre; **the drug has not been passed by the Health Ministry** le médicament n'a pas reçu l'autorisation de mise sur le marché du ministère de la Santé; **the censor has passed the film** le film a obtenu son visa de censure; *Typ* **to p. for press** donner le bon à tirer pour; *Mil etc* **to be passed fit** être reconnu apte

8 *(pronounce* ▸ *verdict, sentence)* prononcer, rendre; (▸*remark, compliment)* faire; **he declined to p. comment** il s'est refusé à tout commentaire; *Law* **to p. sentence** prononcer le jugement; **to p. judgment on sb** porter un jugement sur qn, juger qn

9 *(counterfeit money, stolen goods)* écouler

10 *Sport (ball, puck)* passer

11 *Physiol* **to p. blood** avoir du sang dans les urines; **to p. water** uriner

12 *Mil* **to p. troops in review** passer des troupes en revue

VI 1 *(move in specified direction)* passer; **a cloud passed across the moon** un nuage est passé devant la lune; **alcohol passes rapidly into the bloodstream** l'alcool passe rapidement dans le sang; **his life passed before his eyes** il a vu sa vie défiler devant ses yeux; **to p. into history/legend** entrer dans l'histoire/la légende; **the expression has passed into the language** l'expression est passée dans la langue

2 *(move past, go by)* passer; **let me p.** laissez-moi passer; **the road was too narrow for two cars to p.** la route était trop étroite pour que deux voitures se croisent; **everyone smiles as he passes** tout le monde sourit à son passage; **I happened to be passing, so I thought I'd call in** il s'est trouvé que je passais, alors j'ai eu l'idée de venir vous voir

3 *(overtake)* dépasser, doubler; **no passing** défense de doubler

4 *(elapse* ▸ *months, years)* (se) passer, s'écouler; (▸ *holiday)* se passer; **the weekend passed uneventfully** le week-end s'est passé sans surprises; **time passed rapidly** le temps a passé très rapidement; **when five minutes had passed** au bout de cinq minutes

5 *(be transformed)* passer, se transformer; **it then passes into a larval stage** il se transforme par la suite en larve; **the oxygen then passes to a liquid state** ensuite l'oxygène passe à l'état liquide

6 *(take place)* se passer, avoir lieu; **harsh words passed between them** ils ont eu des mots; **I don't know what passed between them** je ne sais pas ce qui s'est passé entre eux; **the party, if it ever comes to p., should be quite something** la fête, si elle a jamais lieu, sera vraiment un grand moment; *Bible* **and it came to p. that…** et il advint que…

7 *(end, disappear* ▸ *pain, crisis, fever)* passer; (▸ *anger, desire)* disparaître, tomber; (▸ *dream, hope)* disparaître; **the moment of tension passed** le moment de tension est passé; **I was about to say something witty, but the moment passed** j'allais dire quelque chose de spirituel, mais j'ai laissé passer l'occasion; **to let the opportunity p.** laisser passer l'occasion

8 *(be transferred* ▸ *power, responsibility)* passer; (▸ *inheritance)* passer, être transmis; **authority passes to the Vice-President when the President is abroad** c'est au vice-président que revient la charge du pouvoir lorsque le président se trouve à l'étranger; **the turn passes to the player on the left** c'est ensuite au tour du joueur placé à gauche

9 *(get through, be approved* ▸ *proposal)* être approuvé; (▸ *bill, law)* être voté; (▸ *motion)* être adopté; *Sch & Univ* (▸*student)* être reçu *ou* admis

10 *(go unchallenged)* passer; **the insult passed unnoticed** personne ne releva l'insulte; **he let the remark/mistake p.** il a laissé passer la remarque/l'erreur sans la relever; **I don't like it, but I'll let it p.** je n'aime pas ça, mais je préfère ne rien dire *ou* me taire; **let it p.!** passe pour cela!

11 *(be adequate, acceptable* ▸ *behaviour)* convenir, être acceptable; (▸*repair job)* passer; **in your grey suit you might just p.** avec ton costume gris, ça peut aller

12 *(substitute)* **don't try to p. as an expert** n'essaie pas de te faire passer pour un expert; **you could easily p. for your sister** on pourrait très bien te prendre pour ta sœur; **he could p. for 30** on lui donnerait 30 ans; **she could p. for a Scandinavian** on pourrait la prendre pour une Scandinave

13 *Sport* faire une passe

14 *Cards* passer; *(at dominoes)* bouder; **(I) p.!** *(in cards, quiz)* je passe!; *Fig* aucune idée!; *Fig* **I'll p. on that** *(declining offer)* non merci; *(declining to answer question)* je préfère ne pas répondre à cette question

▸▸ *Banking* **pass book** livret *m* de banque; **pass laws** = lois qui anciennement restreignaient la liberté de mouvement de la population noire en Afrique du Sud; *Br Sch* **pass mark** moyenne *f*

> Note that the French expression **passer un examen** does not mean **to pass an exam**. It means **to sit an exam**.

▸ **pass around** VT SEP *(cake, cigarettes)* faire passer

▸ **pass away** VT SEP *(while away)* passer; **we read to p. the time away** nous avons lu pour tuer *ou* passer le temps

VI 1 *Euph (die)* s'éteindre **2** *(elapse* ▸ *time)* passer, s'écouler

▸ **pass by** VT SEP *(disregard)* ignorer, négliger; **life is passing me by** je n'ai pas l'impression de vivre; **life has passed her by** elle n'a pas vraiment vécu; **whenever a chance comes, don't let it p. you by** quand une occasion se présente, ne la laissez pas échapper

VT INSEP *(go past* ▸ *house etc)* passer devant

VI 1 *(go past)* passer; *(carry on without stopping)* continuer son chemin; **luckily a taxi was passing by** heureusement un taxi passait par là; **he passed by without a word!** il est passé à côté de moi sans dire un mot! **2** *(visit)* passer; **she passed by to say hello** elle est passée dire bonjour **3** *(of time)* passer

▸ **pass down** VT SEP **1** *(reach down)* passer; **he passed me down my suitcase** il m'a tendu *ou* passé ma valise **2** *(transmit* ▸ *inheritance, disease, tradition)* transmettre, passer; **the songs were passed down from generation to generation** les chansons ont été transmises de génération en génération

▸ **pass off** VT SEP *(represent falsely)* faire passer; **she passed him off as a duke** elle l'a fait passer pour un duc; **to p. oneself off as an artist** se faire passer pour (un) artiste; **to p. sth off as a joke** *(accept as a joke)* prendre qch en riant *ou* comme une plaisanterie; *(claim to be a joke)* dire qu'on a fait/dit qch pour rire

VI 1 *(take place* ▸ *conference, attack)* se passer, se dérouler; **the meeting passed off without incident** la réunion s'est déroulée sans incident; **everything passed off well** tout s'est bien passé **2** *(end* ▸ *fever, fit)* passer; **the effects of the drug had passed off** les effets du médicament s'étaient dissipés

▸ **pass on** VT SEP **1** *(hand on* ▸ *box, letter)* (faire) passer; **read this and p. it on** lisez ceci et faites circuler **2** *(transmit* ▸ *disease, message, tradition)* transmettre; **they p. the costs on to their customers** ils répercutent les coûts sur leurs clients; **these cost reductions have been passed on to the consumer** le consommateur a bénéficié de ces réductions des coûts; **we meet at eight o'clock, p. it on** nous avons rendez-vous à huit heures, fais passer (la consigne)

VI 1 *Euph (die)* trépasser, s'éteindre **2** *(proceed* ▸ *on journey)* continuer son chemin *ou* sa route; **to p. on to another subject** passer à un autre sujet

▸ **pass out** VT SEP **1** *(hand out)* distribuer **2** *Ir Aus (overtake)* dépasser

VI 1 *(faint)* s'évanouir, perdre connaissance; *(from drunkenness)* tomber ivre mort; *(go to sleep)* s'endormir **2** *Mil (cadet)* ≃ finir ses classes

▸ **pass over** VT SEP *(overlook* ▸ *person)* ne pas prendre en considération; **he was passed over for promotion** on ne lui a pas accordé la promotion qu'il attendait

VT INSEP 1 *(ignore)* passer sous silence; *(difficulty etc)* passer sur, glisser sur; **they passed over the subject in silence** ils ont passé la question sous silence **2** *(cross* ▸ *river etc)* traverser, franchir; (▸*obstacle)* franchir, passer sur

VI 1 *(end* ▸ *storm)* se dissiper, finir **2** *(defect)* **to p. over to the enemy** passer à l'ennemi

▸ **pass round** = **pass around**

▸ **pass through** VT INSEP *(country, area, difficult period)* traverser; *(barrier)* franchir; **the bullet passed through his shoulder** la balle lui a traversé l'épaule; **he passed through the checkpoint without any trouble** il a passé le poste de contrôle sans encombre

VI passer; **I'm not staying in Boston, I'm just passing through** je ne reste pas à Boston, je suis juste de passage

▸ **pass up** VT SEP **1** *(hand up)* passer; **p. me up the light bulb** passe-moi l'ampoule **2** *(not take* ▸ *opportunity)* laisser passer; (▸*job)* refuser; **I'll have to p. up their invitation** je vais devoir décliner leur invitation

passable [ˈpɑːsəbəl] **ADJ 1** *(acceptable)* passable, acceptable; **it's p.** ce n'est pas trop mal; **he does a p. impression of the boss** il imite plutôt bien le chef **2** *(road)* praticable; *(river, canyon)* franchissable; **the road is p. with difficulty** la route est difficilement praticable

passably [ˈpɑːsəblɪ] **ADV** passablement, pas trop mal; **to perform p.** offrir une performance passable

passage [ˈpæsɪdʒ] **N 1** *(way through)* passage *m*; **they cleared a p. through the crowd** ils ouvrirent un passage à travers la foule

2 *(corridor)* passage *m*, couloir *m*; *(alley)* ruelle *f*; **an underground p.** un passage souterrain

3 *(from book, music)* passage *m*; **selected passages from Churchill's speeches** morceaux *mpl* choisis des discours de Churchill; **the most touching p. in the book** l'endroit le plus touchant du livre

4 *Anat & Tech* conduit *m*; **nasal passages** conduits *mpl* nasaux; *Anat* **air p.** conduit *m* aérifère

5 *(passing ▸ gen)* passage *m*; *Pol (▸ of bill)* adoption *f*; **with the p. of time** avec le temps; **their friendship has survived the p. of time** leur amitié a survécu au temps; **the bill had an uninterrupted p. through parliament** la loi a été adoptée sans encombre par le Parlement

6 *(voyage)* voyage *m*; *(crossing)* traversée *f*; *Naut* **to work one's p.** gagner son passage (en travaillant à bord)

7 *Formal (access)* libre passage *m*; **to grant sb safe p. through a country** accorder à qn le libre passage à travers un pays; *Arch or Fig* **p. of** *or* **at arms** passe *f* d'armes

passageway ['pæsɪdʒweɪ] **N 1** *(space)* passage *m*; **to leave a p.** laisser le passage libre **2** *(corridor)* passage *m*, couloir *m*; *(alleyway)* ruelle *f*; **don't block the p.!** n'obstruez pas le passage!, laissez le passage libre!

passé [*Br* 'pæseɪ, *Am* pæ'seɪ] **ADJ** *Pej* dépassé, vieillot, désuet(ète)

passenger ['pæsɪndʒə(r)] **N 1** *(in car, bus, aircraft, ship)* passager(ère) *m,f*; *(in train)* voyageur (euse) *m,f* **2** *Br Pej (worker, team member)* poids *m* mort; **we can't carry passengers** on ne peut pas traîner de poids morts

▸▸ *Am Rail* ***passenger car*** wagon *m ou* voiture *f* de voyageurs; ***passenger and cargo plane*** avion *m* mixte; ***passenger and cargo ship*** bateau *m* mixte; *Br Rail* ***passenger coach*** wagon *m ou* voiture *f* de voyageurs; ***passenger compartment*** *(of car)* habitacle *m*; ***passenger list*** liste *f* des passagers; ***passenger mile*** *Aviat* ≃ kilomètre-passager *m*; *Rail* ≃ kilomètre-voyageur *m*; *Aut* ***passenger seat*** *(in front)* siège *m* du passager; *(in back)* siège *m* arrière; ***passenger train*** train *m* de voyageurs; *Aut* ***passenger wagon*** voiture *f* familiale

passe-partout [,pæspɑː'tuː] **N 1** *(card, gummed paper)* passe-partout *m inv* **2** *(key)* passe-partout *m inv*

passer-by [,pɑːsə'baɪ] *(pl* **passers-by***)* **N** passant(e) *m,f*

passim ['pæsɪm] **ADV** passim

passing ['pɑːsɪŋ] **ADJ 1** *(going by)* qui passe; **she watched the p. crowd** elle regardait la foule qui passait; **she flagged down a p. car** elle a fait signe à une voiture qui passait de s'arrêter; **with each p. day he grew more worried** son inquiétude croissait de jour en jour **2** *(fancy, infatuation)* éphémère, passager; **a p. whim** un caprice passager; **he didn't give her absence a p. thought** c'est tout juste s'il a remarqué son absence, il a à peine remarqué son absence; **he made only a p. reference to her absence** il a fait mention de son absence en passant **3** *(slight)* **to have a p. acquaintance with sb** connaître qn de vue; **to bear a p. resemblance to sb** ressembler vaguement à qn

N 1 *(of train, birds etc)* passage *m*; *(overtaking ▸ of another car)* dépassement *m*, doublement *m*

2 *(of time)* écoulement *m*; *(of beauty)* disparition *f*; **with the p. of time** avec le temps

3 *(approval ▸ of bill, resolution)* adoption *f*; *(▸ of law)* vote *m*; *Fin & Com (▸ of accounts)* approbation *f*

4 *(giving ▸ of message etc)* transmission *f*; *(▸ of judgment)* prononcé *m*

5 *Sport* passes *fpl*

6 *Euph (death)* trépas *m*, mort *f*

ADV *Arch* fort, extrêmement; **p. fair** de toute beauté

• **in passing ADV** en passant; **I'd like to say in p.... ...**soit dit en passant

▸▸ *Literary* ***passing bell*** glas *m*; ***passing customer*** client(e) *m,f* de passage; *Am* ***passing lane*** voie *f* de dépassement; ***passing place*** *Aut (on narrow road)* aire *f* de croisement; *(in general)* endroit *m* pour doubler; *Rail* voie *f* d'évitement *ou* de dédoublement; ***passing shot*** *(in tennis)* passing-shot *m*; *Com* ***passing trade*** clients *mpl ou* clientèle *f* de passage

passion ['pæʃən] **N 1** *(love)* passion *f*; **to have a p. for sb** aimer qn passionnément; *Fig* **to have a p. for music/painting/cars** avoir la passion de la musique/de la peinture/des voitures; **to have a p. for Chinese cooking** adorer la cuisine chinoise **2** *(emotion)* passion *f*; **to play with great p.** jouer avec beaucoup d'enthousiasme *ou* d'ardeur; **passions are running high on this issue** ce sujet déchaîne les passions; **to hate sb/sth with a p.** avoir horreur de qn/qch **3** *Literary (fit of anger)* (accès *m* de) colère *f*; **he tore it up in a (fit of) p.** il l'a déchiré dans un accès de colère; **to be in a p. about sth** être fou de colère à cause de qch; **to fly into a p.** s'emporter

• **Passion N** *Mus & Rel* **the P.** la Passion

▸▸ ***passion fruit*** fruit *m* de la Passion; ***Passion play*** mystère *m* de la Passion; ***Passion Sunday*** le dimanche de la Passion; ***Passion Week*** la semaine de la Passion

passionate ['pæʃənɪt] **ADJ 1** *(love, lover)* passionné, ardent; *(embrace, kiss)* passionné; *(relationship)* passionnel; **to make p. love** faire l'amour avec passion; **a p. weekend** un week-end de passion **2** *(speech)* véhément; *(advocate, believer)* fervent, ardent; **he is p. in his commitment to peace** c'est un fervent *ou* ardent défenseur de la paix; **a p. plea for justice** un véhément appel à la justice; **she's p. about human rights** elle est dévouée à la cause des droits de l'homme

passionately ['pæʃənɪtlɪ] **ADV 1** *(love, kiss)* passionnément; **to be p. in love with sb** aimer qn passionnément **2** *(believe, committed)* ardemment, avec ferveur; *(speak, argue)* avec passion, avec véhémence; *(sing)* avec passion; **to be p. fond of sth/doing sth** adorer qch/faire qch; **he is p. devoted to the cause** il est dévoué à la cause corps et âme

passionflower ['pæʃən,flaʊə(r)] **N** passiflore *f*, fleur *f* de la Passion

passionless ['pæʃənlɪs] **ADJ** sans passion

passive ['pæsɪv] **ADJ 1** *(gen) & Chem & Electron* passif **2** *Gram* passif; **the p. voice** la voix passive

N *Gram* passif *m*; **in the p.** au passif

▸▸ *Psy* ***passive aggression, passive aggressivity*** comportement *m* passif-agressif; *Med* ***passive immunity*** immunité *f* passive; *Comput* ***passive matrix screen*** écran *m* à matrice passive; ***passive resistance*** résistance *f* passive; *Comput* ***passive security*** sécurité *f* passive; ***passive smoker*** = non-fumeur dans un environnement fumeur; ***passive smoking*** tabagisme *m* passif

passive-aggressive ADJ *Psy* passif-agressif

passively ['pæsɪvlɪ] **ADV 1** *(gen)* passivement **2** *Gram* au passif

passiveness ['pæsɪvnɪs], **passivity** [pæ'sɪvətɪ] **N** passivité *f*

passkey ['pɑːskiː] **N** passe-partout *m inv*

Passover ['pɑːs,əʊvə(r)] **N** la Pâque (juive), Pesah *m*

passport ['pɑːspɔːt] **N 1** *(document)* passeport *m*; **British p. holders** les détenteurs *mpl* de passeports britanniques **2** *Fig* clé *f*; **the p. to happiness** la clé du bonheur; **this job was her p. to fame** ce travail a été son passeport pour la célébrité

▸▸ ***passport control*** contrôle *m* des passeports; ***passport number*** numéro *m* de passeport; ***passport photo*** photo *f* d'identité

passport-sized photograph N photo *f* d'identité

password ['pɑːswɜːd] **N** mot *m* de passe

▸▸ *Comput* ***password protection*** protection *f* par mot de passe

password-protected ADJ *Comput* protégé par mot de passe

past [pɑːst] **N 1** *(former time)* passé *m*; **to live in the p.** vivre dans le passé; **the great empires of the p.** les grands empires de l'histoire; **it is a thing of the p.** *(institution, custom)* ça n'existe plus; *(relationship)* c'est du passé; *(is old-fashioned)* c'est périmé; **politeness seems to have become a thing of the p.** la politesse semble être une chose démodée **2** *(background ▸ of person)* passé *m*; **woman with a p.** femme *f* qui a vécu *ou* qui a un passé chargé; **town with a p.** ville *f* historique; **our country's glorious p.** le glorieux passé de notre pays **3** *Gram* passé *m*; **in the p.** au passé

ADJ 1 *(former, gone by ▸ life)* antérieur; *(▸ quarrels, differences)* vieux (vieille), d'autrefois; *(▸ generation, centuries, mistakes, event)* passé; **in centuries p.** autrefois; **the time for negotiating is p.** l'heure n'est plus à la négociation; **those days are p.** ces temps sont révolus; **from p. experience** par expérience; **in p. time** *or* **times p.** autrefois, (au temps) jadis; **to be p.** *(ended)* être passé *ou* terminé; **the crisis is now p.** la crise est maintenant passée; **the p. mayors of the town** les anciens maires de la ville **2** *(last)* dernier; **the p. week** la semaine dernière *ou* passée; **the p. two months** les deux derniers mois; **this p. month has been very busy** le mois qui vient de s'achever a été très chargé; **I've not been feeling well for the p. few days** ça fait quelques jours que je ne me sens pas très bien **3** *Gram* passé

PREP 1 *(in time)* après; **it's ten/quarter/half p. six** il est six heures dix/et quart/et demie; **it is p. four (o'clock)** il est quatre heures passées; **it's quarter p. the hour** il est le *ou* et quart; **it's already p. midnight** il est déjà plus de minuit *ou* minuit passé; **it's long** *or* **way p. my bedtime** je devrais être au lit depuis longtemps; **he's p. fifty** il a plus de cinquante ans, il a dépassé la cinquantaine; **these beans are p. their best** ces haricots ne sont plus très frais

2 *(further than)* plus loin que, au-delà de; **just p. the bridge** un peu plus loin que le pont, un peu au-delà du pont; **turn right just p. the school** prenez à droite juste après l'école; **he can't count p. ten** il ne sait compter que jusqu'à dix; **I didn't manage to get p. the first page** je n'ai pas réussi à lire plus d'une page; **he knocked the ball p. the defender** il a envoyé la balle derrière le défenseur

3 *(in front of)* devant; **he walked right p. my table** il est passé juste devant ma table

4 *(beyond scope of)* au-delà de; **it's p. all understanding** ça dépasse l'entendement; **p. endurance** insupportable; **that's p. all belief** c'est incroyable

5 *(incapable of)* **I'm p. caring** ça ne me fait plus ni chaud ni froid; **I'm p. work** *(too old)* je ne suis plus d'âge à travailler; *(too ill)* je ne peux plus travailler; *Fam* **to be p. it** *(person)* avoir passé l'âge□; *(car, machine)* avoir fait son temps□; **I wouldn't put it p. him** il en est bien capable; **I wouldn't put anything p. this government** ce gouvernement est capable de tout *ou* du pire

ADV 1 *(by)* **to go p.** passer; **they ran p.** ils passèrent en courant; **the years flew p.** les années passaient à une vitesse prodigieuse **2** *(ago)* **one night about three years p.** une nuit il y a environ trois ans; **it had long p. struck midnight** minuit avait sonné depuis longtemps

• **in the past ADV** autrefois, dans le temps

▸▸ ***past master*** expert *m*; *Hum* **he's a p. master at doing as little as possible** il est passé maître dans l'art d'en faire le moins possible; *Gram* ***past participle*** participe *m* passé; *Gram* ***past perfect*** plus-que-parfait *m*; *Gram* ***past tense*** passé *m*; **in the p. tense** au passé

pasta ['pæstə] **N** *(UNCOUNT)* pâtes *fpl* (alimentaires)

▸▸ ***pasta machine*** machine *f* à fabriquer les pâtes; ***pasta salad*** salade *f* de pâtes; ***pasta sauce*** sauce *f* pour pâtes

paste [peɪst] **N 1** *(smooth substance)* pâte *f*; *Cer* **hard/soft p.** pâte *f* dure/tendre

2 *Culin (dough)* pâte *f*; **fish/meat p.** = pâte à tartiner à base de poisson/viande; **tomato p.** concentré *m* de tomate

3 *(glue)* colle *f*

4 *(for jewellery)* strass *m*, stras *m*; **p. necklace/diamonds** collier *m*/diamants *mpl* en strass *ou* strass

VT 1 *(stick ▸ stamp, poster)* coller; *(▸ wallpaper)* encoller; **p. the labels on the parcel** collez les étiquettes sur le colis

2 *(cover ▸ wall)* recouvrir; **the crate was pasted with stickers** la caisse était couverte d'autocollants

3 *Comput (text)* coller (**into/onto** dans)

4 *Fam (beat up)* tabasser, casser la figure à; *(defeat)* battre à plate(s) couture(s), mettre la pâtée à; **to get pasted** *(beaten up)* se faire tabasser; *(defeated)* être battu à plate(s) couture(s)

▸ **paste up VT SEP** *(poster)* coller; *(notice, list)* afficher; *(wallpaper)* poser

pasteboard ['peɪstbɔːd] **N 1** *(cardboard)* carton *m* **2** *Am (for pastry)* planche *f* à pâtisserie

COMP de *ou* en carton-pâte

pastel [ˈpæstəl] N *(crayon)* pastel *m*; *(drawing)* (dessin *m* au) pastel *m*; **a portrait in pastels** un portrait au pastel; **pastels suit her** les couleurs *ou* teintes pastel lui vont bien

ADJ pastel *(inv)*; **p. pink skirts** des jupes *fpl* rose pastel

▸▸ ***pastel drawing*** (dessin *m* au) pastel *m*; ***pastel shade*** ton *m ou* teinte *f* pastel

pastern [ˈpæstɜːn] N paturon *m*

paste-up N *Typ* maquette *f*

pasteurization, -isation [ˌpɑːstʃəraɪˈzeɪʃən] N pasteurisation *f*

pasteurize, -ise [ˈpɑːstʃəraɪz] VT pasteuriser

pastiche [pæˈstiːʃ] N pastiche *m*

pastille, pastil [ˈpæstɪl] N pastille *f*; **cough pastilles** pastilles *fpl* pour *ou* contre la toux

pastime [ˈpɑːstaɪm] N passe-temps *m*

pastiness [ˈpeɪstɪnɪs] N **1** *(of face)* teint *m* terreux **2** *(of bread etc)* consistance *f* pâteuse

pasting [ˈpeɪstɪŋ] N **1** *(gluing ▸ of poster etc)* collage *m*; *(▸ of wallpaper)* encollage *m* **2** *Fam (beating)* rossée *f*, raclée *f*; **to give sb a p.** *(beat up)* tabasser qn, mettre une raclée à qn; *(defeat)* battre qn à plate(s) couture(s); **to** *Br* **get** *or Am* **take a p.** *(be beaten up)* se faire tabasser; *(be defeated)* être battu à plate(s) couture(s)

pastor [ˈpɑːstə(r)] N *Rel* pasteur *m*

pastoral [ˈpɑːstərəl] ADJ **1** *(gen) & Art, Literature & Mus* pastoral; **they are a p. people** c'est un peuple de bergers **2** *Rel* pastoral; *Fig* **teachers also have a p. role** les enseignants ont également un rôle de conseillers

N **1** *Art, Literature & Mus* pastorale *f* **2** *Rel* (lettre *f*) pastorale *f*

▸▸ *Sch* ***pastoral care*** ≃ tutorat *m*; ***pastoral land*** pâturages *mpl*; *Rel* ***pastoral letter*** (lettre *f*) pastorale *f*; *Rel* ***pastoral staff*** crosse *f* (d'évêque); *Rel* ***pastoral visit*** visite *f* pastorale

pastrami [pəˈstrɑːmɪ] N pastrami *m*

pastry [ˈpeɪstrɪ] *(pl* **pastries***)* N **1** *(dough)* pâte *f* **2** *(cake)* pâtisserie *f*, gâteau *m*

▸▸ ***pastry board*** planche *f* à pâtisserie; ***pastry brush*** pinceau *m* (à pâtisserie); ***pastry case*** croûte *f*; ***pastry chef, pastry cook*** pâtissier(ère) *m,f*; ***pastry cream, pastry custard*** crème *f* pâtissière; ***pastry cutter*** emporte-pièce *m inv*

pasturage [ˈpɑːstjʊrɪdʒ] N pâturage *m*

pasture [ˈpɑːstʃə(r)] N pâture *f*, pâturage *m*; **to put out to p.** *(animal)* mettre au pâturage; *Hum (person)* mettre au vert; *Hum (car)* mettre à la casse; **he left for greener pastures** *or* **pastures new** il est parti vers des horizons plus favorables

VT *(animal)* faire paître

VI paître, pâturer, pacager

pasty[1] [ˈpeɪstɪ] *(compar* **pastier**, *superl* **pastiest***)* ADJ **1** *(face, complexion)* terreux; *(person)* qui a le teint terreux **2** *(texture)* pâteux

pasty[2] [ˈpæstɪ] *(pl* **pasties***)* N *Br Culin* ≃ petit pâté *m (en croûte)*

pasty-faced [ˈpeɪstɪ-] ADJ au teint terreux

pat [pæt] *(pt & pp* **patted**, *cont* **patting***)* VT tapoter; *(animal)* caresser, flatter (de la main); **"sit here," she said, patting the seat beside her** "assieds-toi ici", dit-elle, désignant la place à côté d'elle; **p. the fish/vegetables dry** séchez le poisson/les légumes avec de l'essuie-tout; **she patted her hair** elle se tapota les cheveux; **to p. sb on the back** donner une tape dans le dos à qn; *Fig (congratulate)* féliciter qn; *Fig* **to p. oneself on the back** se féliciter

N **1** *(tap)* (légère) tape *f*; **he gave me a friendly p. on the shoulder** il m'a donné une tape amicale sur l'épaule; **to give sb a p. on the back** donner une tape dans le dos à qn; *Fig (congratulate)* féliciter qn; *Fig* **to give oneself a p. on the back** se féliciter **2** *(lump)* a **p. of butter** une noix de beurre

ADJ **1** *(glib ▸ remark)* tout fait; *(▸ answer)* tout prêt; **his story is a little too p.** son histoire colle un peu trop bien **2** *(in poker)* **a p. hand** une main servie

ADV **1** *(exactly)* parfaitement, avec facilité; **to know** *or* **have sth off p.** savoir qch par cœur; **he had his explanation off p.** il avait une explication toute prête **2** *Am* **to stand p.** *(on decision)* rester intraitable; **dealer stands p.** *(in poker)* pas de cartes pour le donneur, donneur servi

▸ **pat down** VT SEP *(soil, sand etc)* tasser (doucement)

Patagonia [ˌpætəˈgəʊnɪə] N Patagonie *f*

patch [pætʃ] N **1** *(of fabric)* pièce *f*; *(on garment)* pièce *f* (rapportée); *(on sail)* placard *m*; *(on inner tube)* Rustine® *f*; **a jacket with suede patches on the elbows** une veste avec des pièces en daim aux coudes; *Fam Fig* **he's not a p. on you** il ne t'arrive pas à la cheville; **his last novel isn't a p. on the others** son dernier roman est loin de valoir les autres[□]

2 *(over eye)* bandeau *m*; **he wore a black eye p.** il avait un bandeau noir sur l'œil

3 *(sticking plaster)* pansement *m* (adhésif)

4 *(beauty spot)* mouche *f*

5 *Mil (on uniform)* insigne *m*

6 *(plot of land)* parcelle *f*, lopin *m*; **cabbage/strawberry/vegetable p.** carré *m* de choux/de fraises/de légumes

7 *(of light, colour, grease, dampness)* tache *f*; *(of fog, mist)* nappe *f*; *(of oil)* flaque *f*; *(of ice)* plaque *f*; **there were damp patches on the ceiling** il y avait des taches d'humidité au plafond; **p. of blue sky** pan *m ou* coin *m ou* échappée *f* de ciel bleu; **snow still lay in patches on the slopes** les pistes étaient encore enneigées par endroits

8 *Br (period)* période *f*, moment *m*; **to go through a bad** *or* **sticky** *or* **rough p.** traverser une période difficile *ou* une mauvaise passe; **the company had a bad p. in 2004** la firme a connu des moments difficiles en 2004

9 *Br (of prostitute, salesperson, police officer)* secteur *m*; *Fam* **keep off my p.!** ne mets pas les pieds sur mon territoire!

10 *Comput* modification *f* (de programme); *(correction)* correction *f*

11 *Med (for administering substance through skin)* patch *m*, timbre *m*

VT **1** *(mend ▸ clothes)* rapiécer; *(▸ tyre, canoe)* réparer; *Naut (▸ sail)* placarder; **his jeans were patched at the knees** son jean avait des pièces *ou* était rapiécé aux genoux; **they patched the hole in the roof** ils ont colmaté *ou* bouché le trou dans la toiture **2** *Comput (program)* modifier **3** *Tel* raccorder; **I'll p. you through** je vous passe votre communication

▸▸ *Tel* ***patch board*** tableau *m* de raccordement; *Sewing* ***patch pocket*** poche *f* plaquée; *Med* ***patch test*** test *m* cutané

▸ **patch together** VT SEP *Fam (temporary shelter, broken object)* assembler[□]; *(business plan, team, government)* mettre sur pied[□]; **they patched together a documentary** ils ont monté un documentaire tant bien que mal; *Pej* **the whole thing is a bit patched together** tout est un peu mal fichu

▸ **patch up** VT SEP *Fam* **1** *(repair ▸ clothes)* rapiécer[□]; *(▸ car, boat)* réparer[□]; *(▸ in makeshift way)* rafistoler; **they patched him up in hospital** ils l'ont rafistolé à l'hôpital **2** *(relationship)* **he's trying to p. things up with his wife** il essaie de se rabibocher avec sa femme; **they patched up their differences** ils ont réglé leurs différends[□]

patching [ˈpætʃɪŋ] N *(of piece of clothing)* rapiéçage *m*, rapiècement *m*; **we can use that old jacket for p.** nous pouvons utiliser cette vieille veste pour faire du rapiècement *ou* rapiéçage

patchwork [ˈpætʃwɜːk] N **1** *Sewing* patchwork *m*; *Fig (of colours, fields)* mosaïque *f* **2** *(collection)* collection *f*; **the book is a p. of previously published writings** le livre rassemble des écrits déjà publiés; **a p. team** une équipe disparate *ou* hétéroclite

▸▸ ***patchwork quilt*** couverture *f* en patchwork

patchy [ˈpætʃɪ] *(compar* **patchier**, *superl* **patchiest***)* ADJ **1** *(performance, novel, TV coverage)* inégal **2** *(paintwork)* inégal, irrégulier; **p. fog** des nappes *fpl* de brouillard; **p. rain** des averses *fpl* éparses; **p. cloud** nuages *mpl* épars **3** *(evidence)* incomplet (ète); *(knowledge)* imparfait

pate [peɪt] N *Arch or Hum* tête *f*; **bald p.** crâne *m* chauve

pâté [ˈpæteɪ] N pâté *m*; **liver p.** pâté *m* de foie

patella [pəˈtelə] *(pl* **patellas** *or* **patellae** [-liː]) N *Anat* rotule *f*

paten [ˈpætən] N *Rel* patène *f*

patent [*Br* ˈpeɪtənt, *Am* ˈpætənt] N **1** *(on invention)* brevet *m* (d'invention); *(thing patented)* invention *f*/fabrication *f* brevetée; **to take out a p. on sth** prendre un brevet sur qch, faire breveter qch; **p. pending** *(on packaging)* demande de brevet déposée **2** *(leather)* cuir *m* verni, vernis *m* **3** *Am (on land)* concession *f*

ADJ **1** *(product, procedure)* breveté **2** *Law* **letters p.** lettres *fpl* patentes **3** *(evident ▸ lack of concern, disrespect)* manifeste; *(▸ fact)* évident; **that's a p. lie!** c'est un mensonge éhonté!

VT *(of authorities)* protéger par un brevet, breveter; *(of inventor)* faire breveter, prendre un brevet pour

▸▸ ***patent agent*** agent *m* en brevets; ***patent application*** demande *f ou* dépôt *m* de brevet; *Am* ***patent attorney*** conseil *m* en matière de brevets; ***patent goods*** articles *mpl* brevetés; ***patent leather*** cuir *m* verni, vernis *m*; **p. leather boots** bottes *fpl* vernies *or* en cuir verni; ***patent medicine*** médicament *m* vendu sans ordonnance; *Pej (cure-all)* élixir *m* universel, remède *m* de charlatan; ***Patent Office*** ≃ Institut *m* national de la propriété industrielle; ***patent register*** registre des brevets; ***patent rights*** propriété *f* industrielle; *Am* ***Patent and Trademark Office*** ≃ Institut *m* national de la propriété industrielle

patentability [*Br* ˌpeɪtəntəˈbɪlətɪ, *Am* ˌpætəntəˈbɪlətɪ] N brevetabilité *f*

patentable [*Br* ˈpeɪtəntəbəl, *Am* ˈpætəntəbəl] ADJ brevetable

patented [*Br* ˈpeɪtəntɪd, *Am* ˈpætəntɪd] ADJ *(product, procedure)* breveté

patentee [*Br* ˌpeɪtənˈtiː, *Am* ˌpætənˈtiː] N détenteur (trice) *m,f ou* titulaire *mf* d'un/du brevet (d'invention)

patently [*Br* ˈpeɪtəntlɪ, *Am* ˈpætəntlɪ] ADV manifestement, de toute évidence; **he was p. lying** il était manifeste qu'il mentait; **it was p. obvious that...** il était absolument évident que... + *indicative*

patentor [*Br* ˈpeɪtəntə(r), *Am* ˈpætəntə(r)] N organisme *m* délivrant un brevet

pater [ˈpeɪtə(r)] N *Br Fam Old-fashioned* pater *m*, paternel *m*

paterfamilias [ˌpeɪtəfəˈmɪlæs] N *Formal* paterfamilias *m*

paternal [pəˈtɜːnəl] ADJ **1** *(fatherly ▸ love, instinct)* paternel; *(▸ role, responsibilities)* de père **2** *(related through father)* paternel; **p. grandparents** grands-parents *mpl* paternels

paternalism [pəˈtɜːnəlɪzəm] N paternalisme *m*

paternalist [pəˈtɜːnəlɪst] N = personne qui fait preuve de paternalisme

ADJ paternaliste

paternalistic [pəˌtɜːnəˈlɪstɪk] ADJ paternaliste

paternalistically [pəˌtɜːnəˈlɪstɪklɪ] ADV *(govern)* avec paternalisme; *(say)* d'un ton paternaliste; *(smile)* d'un air paternaliste

paternally [pəˈtɜːnəlɪ] ADV paternellement

paternity [pəˈtɜːnətɪ] N paternité *f*; **there are doubts about his p.** on n'est pas sûr de l'identité de son père

▸▸ ***paternity leave*** congé *m* de paternité; *Law* ***paternity order*** (ordonnance *f* de) reconnaissance *f* de paternité; *Law* ***paternity suit*** action *f* en recherche de paternité; ***paternity test*** test *m* de recherche de paternité

path [pɑːθ, *pl* pɑːðz] N **1** *(in garden, park)* allée *f*; *(in country)* chemin *m*, sentier *m*; *(pavement)* trottoir *m*

2 *(way ahead or through)* chemin *m*, passage *m*; *(of inquiry, investigation)* ligne *f*; **his career p.** son choix de carrière; **to cut a p. through sth** se tailler *ou* se frayer un chemin à travers qch; **a tree blocked his p.** un arbre lui bloquait le passage *ou* chemin; **he stepped into the p. of an oncoming vehicle** il est allé sur la chaussée au moment où arrivait un véhicule; **the hurricane destroyed everything in its p.** l'ouragan a tout détruit sur son passage; *Fig* **the p. to fame** *or* **glory** la route *ou* le chemin qui mène à la gloire

3 *(trajectory ▸ of moving body)* trajet *m*, course *f*; *(▸ of projectile, planet)* trajectoire *f*; *(▸ of ray of*

light) passage *m*, trajet *m*; (▸ *of sun)* route *f*; **our paths first crossed in 1985** nos chemins se sont croisés *ou* nous nous sommes rencontrés pour la première fois en 1985
4 *Comput* chemin *m* (d'accès)

pathetic [pəˈθetɪk] **ADJ 1** *(pitiable* ▸ *lament, waif, smile, story)* pitoyable; **it was p. to see how they lived** cela serrait le cœur *ou* c'était un crève-cœur de voir dans quelles conditions ils vivaient **2** *Fam (poor, useless* ▸ *excuse, game, person etc)* lamentable, pitoyable; **you're p.!** tu es lamentable!; **how p.!, it's p.!** c'est (vraiment) lamentable!
▸▸ *Literature* ***pathetic fallacy*** = attribution à la nature de sentiments humains

> Note that the French word **pathétique** never means **appalling**.

pathetically [pəˈθetɪklɪ] **ADV 1** *(touchingly)* pitoyablement; **she looked at him p.** elle lui jeta un regard pitoyable **2** *Fam (atrociously)* lamentablement; **p. bad** *(performance, speech etc)* lamentable; **p. easy** si facile que c'en est ridicule; **that's a p. weak excuse** c'est une excuse lamentable; **they performed p.** ils ont offert une performance lamentable *ou* pitoyable

pathfinder [ˈpɑːθˌfaɪndə(r)] **N 1** *(scout)* éclaireur *m* **2** *Fig (pioneer)* pionnier *m* **3** *(aircraft)* avion *m* éclaireur

pathname [ˈpɑːθneɪm] **N** *Comput* chemin *m* d'accès

pathological [ˌpæθəˈlɒdʒɪkəl] **ADJ** pathologique; **he's a p. liar** il ne peut pas s'empêcher de mentir

pathologically [ˌpæθəˈlɒdʒɪklɪ] **ADV** pathologiquement; **to be p. afraid of sth** avoir une peur pathologique de qch

pathologist [pəˈθɒlədʒɪst] **N** pathologiste *mf*; **(forensic) p.** médecin *m* légiste

pathology [pəˈθɒlədʒɪ] *(pl* **pathologies)** **N** pathologie *f*

pathos [ˈpeɪθɒs] **N** pathétique *m*

pathway [ˈpɑːθweɪ] **N** *(in garden)* allée *f*; *(in country)* chemin *m*, sentier *m*; *(pavement)* trottoir *m*

patience [ˈpeɪʃəns] **N 1** *(tolerance)* patience *f*; **to lose p. (with sb)** perdre patience (avec qn); **(have) p.!** (prenez) patience!; **I haven't the p. to redo it** je n'ai pas la patience de le refaire; **he has no p. with children** les enfants l'exaspèrent; **don't try my p. any further!** ne mets pas davantage ma patience à l'épreuve!, n'abuse pas davantage de ma patience!; **my p. is wearing thin** ma patience a des limites, je suis à bout de patience **2** *Br (card game)* réussite *f*; **she was playing p.** elle faisait des réussites

patient [ˈpeɪʃənt] **ADJ** patient; **to be p.** *(naturally)* être patient, avoir de la patience; *(on specific occasion)* être patient, patienter, prendre patience; **be p.!** (un peu de) patience!, soyez patient!; **if you'll be p. a few moments longer** veuillez patienter encore quelques instants
N *Med* malade *mf*, patient(e) *m,f*; *(after operation)* opéré(e) *m,f*
▸▸ ***patient care*** soins *mpl* administrés aux patients

patiently [ˈpeɪʃəntlɪ] **ADV** patiemment; **a long illness, p. borne** une longue maladie, endurée avec patience

patina [ˈpætɪnə] *(pl* **patinas** *or* **patinae** [-niː]) **N** patine *f*

patio [ˈpætɪəʊ] *(pl* **patios)** **N** patio *m*
▸▸ ***patio doors*** porte-fenêtre *f*; ***patio furniture*** meubles *mpl* de jardin

patriarch [ˈpeɪtrɪɑːk] **N** patriarche *m*

patriarchal [ˌpeɪtrɪˈɑːkəl] **ADJ** patriarcal
▸▸ ***patriarchal cross*** croix *f* patriarcale

patriarchy [ˈpeɪtrɪɑːkɪ] *(pl* **patriarchies)** **N** patriarcat *m*

patrician [pəˈtrɪʃən] **ADJ** patricien
N patricien(enne) *m,f*

patricide [ˈpætrɪsaɪd] **N 1** *(crime)* parricide *m* **2** *(person)* parricide *mf*

patrimony [*Br* ˈpætrɪmənɪ, *Am* ˈpætrɪməʊnɪ] *(pl* **patrimonies)** **N 1** *(inheritance)* patrimoine *m* **2** *(of church)* biens-fonds *mpl*, revenu *m*

patriot [*Br* ˈpætrɪət, *Am* ˈpeɪtrɪət] **N** patriote *mf*
▸▸ ***Patriot Act*** = loi qui donne aux agences gouvernementales américaines des pouvoirs exceptionnels dans la lutte contre le terrorisme

patriotic [*Br* ˌpætrɪˈɒtɪk, *Am* ˌpeɪtrɪˈɒtɪk] **ADJ** *(person)* patriote; *(song, action, speech)* patriotique

patriotically [*Br* ˌpætrɪˈɒtɪkəlɪ, *Am* ˌpeɪtrɪˈɒtɪkəlɪ] **ADV** patriotiquement, en patriote

patriotism [*Br* ˈpætrɪətɪzəm, *Am* ˈpeɪtrɪətɪzəm] **N** patriotisme *m*

patrol [pəˈtrəʊl] *(pt & pp* **patrolled**, *cont* **patrolling)** **N 1** *(group)* patrouille *f*; *Am* **highway p.** police *f* des autoroutes **2** *(task* ▸ *gen)* patrouille *f*; (▸ *of nightwatchman, police officer on foot)* ronde *f*; **to be on p.** être de patrouille, patrouiller
VI patrouiller, être en patrouille
VT *(area, streets)* patrouiller dans; **the border is patrolled by armed guards** des gardes armés patrouillent le long de la frontière
▸▸ ***patrol boat*** patrouilleur *m*; ***patrol car*** voiture *f* de police; ***patrol leader*** chef *m* de patrouille; *Am, Austr & NZ* **patrol wagon** fourgon *m* cellulaire

patrolman [pəˈtrəʊlmən] *(pl* **patrolmen** [-mən]) **N 1** *Am (policeman)* agent *m* de police *(qui fait sa ronde)* **2** *Br (from motoring organization)* = dépanneur employé par une association d'automobilistes

patrolwoman [pəˈtrəʊlˌwʊmən] *(pl* **patrolwomen** [-ˌwɪmɪn]) **N** *Am* femme *f* agent de police *(qui fait sa ronde)*

patron [ˈpeɪtrən] **N 1** *(sponsor* ▸ *of the arts)* mécène *m*; (▸ *of festival)* parrain *m*, sponsor *m*; (▸ *of charity)* patron(onne) *m,f*; **he's a p. of the arts** c'est un mécène *ou* un protecteur des arts; **many multinational companies are becoming patrons of the arts** de nombreuses multinationales se lancent dans le mécénat; **the mayor is one of the patrons of our association** *(supporter)* le maire est une des personnes qui ont accordé leur patronage à notre association **2** *(customer* ▸ *of restaurant, hotel, shop)* client(e) *m,f*; (▸ *of library)* usager *m*; (▸ *of museum)* visiteur(euse) *m,f*; (▸ *of theatre, cinema)* spectateur(trice) *m,f*; **patrons only** *(sign)* réservé aux clients
▸▸ ***patron saint*** (saint(e) *m,f*) patron(onne) *m,f*

> Note that the French word **patron** is a false friend and is never a translation for the English word **patron**. It means **boss**.

patronage [ˈpeɪtrənɪdʒ] **N 1** *(support* ▸ *gen)* patronage *m*, parrainage *m*; (▸ *of art)* mécénat *m*; (▸ *of charity)* patronage *m*
2 *Com (custom)* clientèle *f*; **I shall take my p. elsewhere** j'irai me fournir ailleurs
3 *Pol* pouvoir *m* de nomination; *Pej* népotisme *m*; **he got the promotion through the Minister's p.** il a obtenu de l'avancement grâce à l'influence du ministre
4 *(sponsorship)* mécénat *m*
5 *(condescension)* condescendance *f*
6 *(in Church of England)* droit *m* de présentation (à un bénéfice)

patroness [ˈpeɪtrənɪs] **N** *Old-fashioned (of the arts)* protectrice *f*, mécène *m*; *(of charity)* (dame *f*) patronnesse *f*

patronize, -ise [ˈpætrənaɪz] **VT 1** *(business)* donner *ou* accorder sa clientèle à; *(cinema)* être un(e) habitué(e) de, fréquenter; **a restaurant patronized by the famous** un restaurant fréquenté par des gens célèbres; **we no longer p. the local shops** nous ne faisons plus nos courses dans le quartier, nous ne nous fournissons plus dans les magasins du quartier **2** *(condescend to)* traiter avec condescendance; **don't p. me!** ne prenez pas ce ton condescendant avec moi! **3** *(sponsor* ▸ *gen)* parrainer; (▸ *artist)* soutenir

patronizing, -ising [ˈpætrənaɪzɪŋ] **ADJ** condescendant; **to be p. towards sb** se montrer condescendant envers qn, traiter qn avec condescendance

patronizingly, -isingly [ˈpætrənaɪzɪŋlɪ] **ADV** *(smile)* avec condescendance; *(say)* d'un ton condescendant

patronymic [ˌpætrəˈnɪmɪk] **N** patronyme *m*
ADJ patronymique

patsy [ˈpætsɪ] *(pl* **patsies)** **N** *Am Fam (gullible person)* pigeon *m*, gogo *m*; *(scapegoat)* bouc *m* émissaire[□]

patten [ˈpætən] **N** socque *m (pour protéger les chaussures contre la boue)*

patter [ˈpætə(r)] **N 1** *(sound* ▸ *of footsteps)* petit bruit *m*; (▸ *of mice)* trottinement *m*; (▸ *of rain)* crépitement *m*; *(gentler)* tambourinement *m*; *Hum* **we'll soon be hearing the (pitter) p. of tiny feet** nous attendons un heureux événement **2** *Fam (of entertainer)* bavardage *m*, baratin *m*; *Pej (of salesman)* baratin *m*, boniment *m* **3** *Fam (jargon)* jargon[□] *m*
VI 1 *(raindrops)* crépiter; *(more gently)* tambouriner **2** *(person, mouse)* trottiner; **she pattered down the corridor in her slippers** elle trottinait dans le couloir en pantoufles **3** *Fam (talk)* bavarder, baratiner

pattern [ˈpætən] **N 1** *(design* ▸ *decorative)* motif *m*; (▸ *natural)* dessin *m*; (▸ *on animal)* marques *fpl*; **a geometric/herringbone p.** un motif géométrique/à chevrons
2 *(physical arrangement)* disposition *f*, configuration *f*; **to form a p.** former un motif *ou* un dessin; **the p. of light and shade on the ground** le dessin que forment les effets d'ombre et de lumière sur le sol; **the p. of footprints on the sand** la disposition des empreintes de pas sur le sable
3 *(standard way of occurring or being arranged)* système *m*, configuration *f*; **p. of events** cheminement *m* des événements; **sometimes there seems to be no p. to our lives** notre existence semble parfois être régie par le hasard; **research has established that there is a p. in** *or* **to the data** la recherche a établi que les données ne sont pas aléatoires; **some clear patterns emerge from the statistics** des tendances nettes ressortent des statistiques; **weather patterns** grandes tendances *fpl* climatiques; **there is a definite p. to the burglaries** on observe une constante bien précise dans les cambriolages; **to follow a set p.** se dérouler toujours de la même façon; **the evening followed the usual p.** la soirée s'est déroulée selon le schéma habituel; **p. of trade** structure *f* des échanges; **voice p.** empreintes *fpl* vocales
4 *(diagram, shape which guides) & Tech* modèle *m*, gabarit *m*; *Sewing* patron *m*; **dress p.** patron *m* de robe; **to cut out a shirt from a p.** tailler une chemise sur un patron
5 *Fig (example)* exemple *m*, modèle *m*; **to set a p. for** *(of company, method, work)* servir de modèle à; *(of person)* instaurer un modèle pour; **this opening debate set the p. for what followed** ce débat d'ouverture a donné le ton de ce qui allait suivre
6 *Mktg (sample)* échantillon *m*
VT 1 *(mark* ▸ *fabric)* décorer d'un motif **2** *(copy)* modeler; **to p. oneself on** *or* **after sb** prendre modèle *ou* exemple sur qn
▸▸ *Mil* ***pattern bombing*** bombardement *m* systématique; ***pattern book*** livre *m* d'échantillons; *(for dressmaking)* catalogue *m* de patrons; *Ind* ***pattern designer*** dessinateur(trice) *m,f* de patrons

patterned [ˈpætənd] **ADJ** à motifs; **p. wallpaper** papier *m* peint à motifs

pattie, patty [ˈpætɪ] *(pl* **patties)** **N 1** *Am* **(hamburger) p.** = portion de steak haché **2** *(pasty)* ≃ (petit) pâté *m*

pattypan [ˈpætɪpæn] **N** *Culin* petit moule *m* à pâté
▸▸ ***pattypan squash*** pâtisson *m*

paucity [ˈpɔːsətɪ] **N** *Formal* pénurie *f*; *(of information, proof, evidence)* manque *m*

paunch [pɔːntʃ] **N 1** *Pej or Hum (stomach)* (gros) ventre *m*, bedaine *f*; **he's getting a p.** il prend du ventre **2** *Zool* panse *f*

paunchy [ˈpɔːntʃɪ] *(compar* **paunchier**, *superl* **paunchiest)** **ADJ** *Pej or Hum* ventru, pansu, bedonnant; **he's getting p.** il prend du ventre

pauper [ˈpɔːpə(r)] **N** *(man)* pauvre *m*, indigent *m*; *(woman)* pauvre *f*, pauvresse *f*, indigente *f*; **to die a p.** mourir dans l'indigence
▸▸ ***pauper's grave*** fosse *f* commune

pause [pɔːz] **N 1** *(break)* pause *f*, temps *m* d'arrêt; **p.** *(on tape recorder, video etc)* pause *f*; **there will be a ten-minute p. after the second lecture** il y aura *ou* nous ferons une pause de dix minutes après le deuxième cours; **without a p.** sans s'arrêter, sans interruption; **there was a long p. before she answered** elle garda longtemps le silence avant de répondre; *Formal* **to give sb p., to give p. to sb** donner à réfléchir à qn
2 *Mus* point *m* d'orgue
3 *Literature* césure *f*
4 *Comput* pause *f*
VI faire *ou* marquer une pause; **he paused in the middle of his explanation** il s'arrêta *ou* s'interrompit au milieu de son explication; **without pausing for breath** sans même reprendre son souffle; **she paused on the doorstep** elle hésita sur le pas de la porte
VT *(DVD, video, CD)* mettre sur pause
►► ***pause button*** *(on cassette player, video etc)* bouton *m* pause; *Comput* ***pause key*** touche *f* pause

pave [peɪv] **VT** *(street, floor ► with flagstones, tiles)* paver; *(► with concrete, asphalt)* revêtir; *Fig* **to p. the way for sth** ouvrir la voie à *ou* préparer le terrain pour qch

pavement ['peɪvmənt] **N 1** *Br (footpath)* trottoir *m* **2** *Am (roadway)* chaussée *f* **3** *(surfaced area ► of cobbles)* pavé *m*; *(► of stones, marble, granite)* dallage *m*; *(► of concrete)* (dalle *f* de) béton *m*; *(► of mosaic)* pavement *m*
►► *Br* ***pavement artist*** artiste *mf* de rue *(qui dessine sur les trottoirs)*; ***pavement café*** café *m*, terrasse *f* d'un café; **we sat at a p. café** on s'est assis à une terrasse de café; ***pavement light*** = blocs de verre encastrés dans un trottoir pour éclairer une cave se trouvant au-dessous

pavilion [pə'vɪljən] **N 1** *(building)* pavillon *m*; *(at sports ground)* vestiaires *mpl*; **the Japanese p. at the exhibition** le pavillon du Japon à l'exposition; **(cricket) p.** = bâtiment abritant les vestiaires et parfois le bar sur un terrain de cricket **2** *(tent)* pavillon *m*, tente *f*

paving ['peɪvɪŋ] **N** *(cobbles)* pavage *m*; *(flagstones)* dallage *m*; *(tiles)* carrelage *m*; *(concrete)* dallage *m*, béton *m*
ADJ *(measure, legislation)* préparatoire
►► ***paving stone*** pavé *m*; ***paving tile*** carreau *m* (de pavage); *(bigger)* dalle *f* (de pavage)

pavlova [pæv'ləʊvə] **N** *Culin* vacherin *m*; **raspberry p.** vacherin *m* à la framboise

Pavlovian [pæv'ləʊvɪən] **ADJ** pavlovien

paw [pɔː] **N 1** *(of animal)* patte *f* **2** *Fam (hand)* pogne *m*, patte *f*; *Br* **paws off!**, *Am* **keep your (big) paws off!** bas les pattes!; **you're not getting your dirty** *or* **sweaty paws on my new bike!** il n'est pas question que tu touches à mon nouveau vélo!
VT 1 *(of animal)* donner un coup de patte à; **the horse pawed the ground** le cheval piaffait **2** *Fam (touch, maul)* tripoter; *(sexually)* peloter
VI the dog pawed at the door le chien grattait à la porte

pawky ['pɔːkɪ] *(compar* **pawkier**, *superl* **pawkiest)** **ADJ** *Scot* pince-sans-rire *(inv)*

pawl [pɔːl] **N** cliquet *m*

pawn [pɔːn] **N 1** *(in chess)* pion *m*; *Fig* **to be sb's p.** être le jouet de qn; **they are mere pawns in the hands of the politicians** ils ne sont que des pions sur l'échiquier politique **2** *(at pawnbroker's)* **my watch is in p.** ma montre est en gage; **to put sth in p.** mettre qch en gage; **I got my watch out of p.** j'ai dégagé ma montre (du mont-de-piété)
VT engager au mont-de-piété; *Fig (one's life, honour)* engager
►► ***pawn ticket*** reconnaissance *f* du mont-de-piété

pawnbroker ['pɔːn,brəʊkə(r)] **N** prêteur *m* sur gages; **at the p.'s** au mont-de-piété

pawnbroking ['pɔːn,brəʊkɪŋ] **N** prêt *m* sur gages

pawnshop ['pɔːnʃɒp] **N** boutique *f* de prêteur sur gages, mont-de-piété *m*

pawpaw ['pɔːpɔː] = **papaw**

pax [pæks] **EXCLAM** *Br Fam School slang* pouce!

PAY [peɪ]

VT
• payer **1** • régler **1**
• rapporter à **2** • rendre **3**
VI
• payer
N
• salaire • paie
• traitement
COMP
• salarial **1** • de salaire **1**
• payant **2**

(pt & pp **paid** [peɪd]*)*
VT 1 *(person)* payer; *(bill, debt)* payer, régler; *(fine, rent, taxes, fare, sum of money)* payer; *St Exch (dividend)* distribuer; *(premium)* verser, acquitter; **she's paid £2,000 a month** elle est payée *ou* elle touche 2000 livres par mois; **to be paid by the hour/the week** être payé à l'heure/la semaine; **badly paid job** travail *m* mal payé; **I wouldn't do it if you paid me** je ne le ferais pas même si on me payait; **I paid her £20** je lui ai payé 20 livres; **he paid £20 for the watch** il a payé la montre 20 livres; **to p. cash (down)** payer en liquide *ou* en espèces; **they've paid their debt to society** ils ont payé leur dette envers la société; **to p. one's way** payer sa part; **is the business paying its way?** cette affaire est-elle rentable?; **it's a small price to p. for peace of mind** c'est faire un bien petit sacrifice pour avoir sa tranquillité d'esprit; *Fam Hum* **you pays your money and you takes your choice** *or* **chances** c'est à chacun de décider selon ce qu'il veut faire
2 *Fig (benefit)* rapporter à; **it pays them to use immigrant labour** cela leur rapporte d'utiliser la main-d'œuvre immigrée; **it'll p. you to keep quiet!** tu as intérêt à tenir ta langue!
3 *(give)* **p. attention!** faites attention!; **nobody pays any attention to me** personne ne m'écoute; **to p. a call on sb, to p. sb a visit** rendre visite à qn; **to p. one's respects to sb** présenter ses respects à qn; **to p. one's (last) respects to sb** rendre les derniers devoirs à qn; **to p. tribute** *or* **homage to sb** rendre hommage à qn
VI payer, régler; **to p. by cheque** payer *ou* régler par chèque; **to p. in cash** payer en liquide *ou* en espèces; **how would you like to p.?** comment souhaitez-vous régler? **to p. on delivery** payer à la livraison; **to p. in advance** payer d'avance; **to p. in full** payer intégralement *ou* en totalité; **to p. on demand** *or* **on presentation** payer à vue *ou* à présentation; *Fin* **p. to bearer** payez au porteur; **the job pays very well** le travail est très bien payé; **to p. on the nail** payer rubis sur ongle; **after two years the business was beginning to p.** après deux ans, l'affaire était devenue rentable; *Fig* **it pays to be honest** l'honnêteté est toujours récompensée; **crime doesn't p.** le crime ne paie pas
N *(gen)* salaire *m*, paie *f*; *(of domestic staff)* gages *mpl*; *(of civil servant)* traitement *m*; *Mil* solde *f*; **my first month's p.** ma première paie, mon premier salaire; **the p. is good** c'est bien payé; **he's in the p. of the enemy** il est à la solde de l'ennemi
COMP 1 *(demand, negotiations)* salarial; *(increase, cut)* de salaire
2 *(not free)* payant
3 *Mining (deposit)* exploitable
►► ***pay advice slip*** fiche *f* de paie; ***pay award*** augmentation *f* de salaire; *Br* ***pay bed*** lit *m* payant; *TV* ***pay channel*** chaîne *f* payante, chaîne *f* à péage; *Br* ***pay cheque***, *Am* ***pay check*** chèque *m* de salaire; ***pay day*** jour *m* de paie; ***pay dirt*** *(earth)* gisement *m*; *Fam (discovery)* trouvaille *f*; **to hit p. dirt** trouver un bon filon; *Am* ***pay envelope*** *(envelope)* enveloppe *f* contenant le salaire; *(money)* paie *f*, salaire *m*; ***pay formula*** formule *f* de paie; ***pay freeze*** gel *m ou* blocage *m* des salaires; ***pay increase*** augmentation *f* de salaire; ***pay ledger*** livre *m* de paie; *Br* ***pay packet*** *(envelope)* enveloppe *f* contenant le salaire; *(money)* paie *f*, salaire *m*; ***pay rise*** augmentation *f* de salaire; ***pay slip*** bulletin *m* de paie; *Am* ***pay station*** téléphone *m* public; ***pay television, pay TV*** chaîne *f* à péage

►**pay back VT SEP 1** *(loan, lender)* rembourser; **she paid her father back the sum she had borrowed** elle remboursa à son père la somme qu'elle avait empruntée **2** *(retaliate against)* rendre la monnaie de sa pièce à; **I'll p. you back for that** tu me le paieras!

►**pay for VT INSEP 1** *(item, task)* payer; **who paid for the drinks?** qui est-ce qui a payé les consommations?; **I paid good money for that!** ça m'a coûté cher!; **you get what you p. for** la qualité est en rapport avec le prix (que vous payez); **it's all paid for** *(someone has paid for everything)* tout a été réglé; *(I've paid for everything)* c'est à mes frais; **a free holiday with everything paid for** des vacances gratuites tout compris; **the ticket pays for itself after two trips** le billet est amorti dès le deuxième voyage **2** *(crime, mistake)* payer; **he'll p. for this!, I'll make him p. for this!** il me le paiera!; **you'll p. for this tomorrow** *(for drinking too much etc)* tu vas en subir les conséquences demain; **he paid for his mistake with his life** il a payé son erreur de sa vie

►**pay in VT SEP** *Br (cheque)* déposer sur un compte; *(money)* verser sur un compte; **I'd like to p. this cheque in** j'aimerais déposer ce chèque sur mon compte

►**pay off VT SEP 1** *(debt)* payer, régler, s'acquitter de; *(loan, mortgage)* rembourser **2** *(dismiss, lay off)* licencier, congédier; **he threatened to p. us all off** il a menacé de nous mettre tous à la porte **3** *Fam (bribe)* acheter
VI être payant, porter ses fruits; **moving the company out of London really paid off** le transfert de la société hors de Londres a été bénéfique; **all these years of work have paid off at last** nous sommes enfin récompensés après toutes ces années de travail

►**pay out VT SEP 1** *(money)* payer, débourser **2** *(rope)* laisser filer

►**pay up VI** payer; **p. up or else!** payez, sinon...!
VT SEP *(sum)* payer

payable ['peɪəbəl] **ADJ** payable; **p. in 24 monthly instalments/in advance** payable en 24 mensualités/d'avance; **refunds are p. in certain cases** vous pouvez être remboursé sous certaines conditions; **to make a cheque p. to sb** faire *ou* libeller un chèque à l'ordre de qn; **cheque p. to bearer** chèque *m* payable au porteur; **cheques should be made p. to Mr Brown** les chèques devraient être libellés *ou* établis à l'ordre de M. Brown; **p. at sight** payable à vue; **p. to order** payable à ordre; **p. in cash** payable comptant; **p. on delivery with order** payable à la livraison/à la commande; **the interest p. on the loan** les intérêts *mpl* à payer sur le prêt
• **payables NPL** *Am* factures *fpl* à payer

pay-as-you-earn N *Br Fin* prélèvement *m* de l'impôt à la source

pay-as-you-go N 1 *Br Tel* paiement *m* par carte prépayée **2** *Am Fin* prélèvement *m* de l'impôt à la source

pay-as-you-talk N *Am Tel* paiement *m* par carte prépayée

payback ['peɪbæk] **N 1** *Fin* récupération *f* du capital investi **2** *esp Am (revenge)* revanche *f*; **it's p. time** c'est le moment de la revanche
►► ***payback period*** délai *m* de récupération, période *f* de remboursement

payday ['peɪdeɪ] **N** jour *m* de paie; **tomorrow is p.** nous sommes payés demain

PAYE [,piːeɪ,waɪ'iː] **N** *Br Fin (abbr* **pay-as-you-earn)** prélèvement *m* de l'impôt à la source

payee [peɪ'iː] **N** *(of postal order, cheque)* bénéficiaire *mf*; *Fin (of bill)* porteur *m*, preneur *m*

payer ['peɪə(r)] **N 1** *(gen)* payeur(euse) *m,f*; **a good/bad p.** un bon/mauvais payeur **2** *(of cheque)* tireur(euse) *m,f*

paying ['peɪɪŋ] **N** paiement *m*
ADJ 1 *(who pays)* payant **2** *(profitable)* payant, rentable; **it's not a p. proposition** cette proposition n'est pas avantageuse *ou* profitable
►► *Fin* ***paying bank*** domiciliataire *m*, établissement *m* payeur, domiciliation *f* bancaire; ***paying guest*** hôte *m* payant, pensionnaire *mf*

payload ['peɪləʊd] **N 1** *(gen)* chargement *m*; **he was transporting a p. of cement** il transportait un chargement de ciment **2** *Tech (of vehicle, aircraft)* charge *f* payante; *(of rocket)* charge *f* utile; *(of missile, warhead)* charge *f* marchande

paymaster ['peɪˌmɑːstə(r)] N *(gen)* payeur(euse) *m,f*, intendant(e) *m,f*; *(in school, institution)* économe *mf*; *(in army)* trésorier *m*; *Naut* commissaire *m*; *(in administration)* trésorier-payeur *m*; *Pej (of criminals, terrorists)* commanditaire *mf*; **the World Bank acts as p. of the project** la Banque mondiale fait office de bailleur de fonds pour ce projet
▸▸ ***the Paymaster General*** le Trésorier-payeur-général britannique

payment ['peɪmənt] N **1** *(sum paid, act of paying)* paiement *m*; *(when paying in instalments)* versement *m*; **48 monthly payments** 48 versements mensuels, 48 mensualités; **on p. of £100** contre paiement de 100 livres; **on p. of a deposit** moyennant des arrhes; **in p. of your invoice** en règlement de votre facture; **to make a p.** effectuer un versement; **to present a bill for p.** présenter un effet au paiement *ou* à l'encaissement; **she would not accept p.** elle n'a pas voulu qu'on la paie; **they offered their services without p.** ils ont offert leurs services à titre gracieux; **to stop p. on a cheque** faire opposition à un chèque; **p. by instalments** paiement *m* échelonné *ou* par versements, paiement *m* à tempérament; **in easy payments** avec facilités de paiement; **p. on account** paiement *m* partiel; **p. in advance** paiement *m* d'avance, paiement *m* par anticipation; **p. in arrears** paiement *m* arriéré; **p. in cash** paiement *m* en espèces; **p. by cheque** paiement *m* par chèque; **p. on delivery** livraison *f* contre remboursement; **p. in full** paiement *m* intégral; **p. in kind** paiement *m ou* avantages *mpl* en nature **2** *(reward, compensation)* récompense *f*
▸▸ ***payment advice*** avis *m* de paiement; ***payment card*** carte *f* de paiement; ***payment day*** jour *m* de paiement, jour *m* de règlement; ***payment facilities*** facilités *fpl* de paiement; ***payment order*** ordre *m* de paiement; ***payment schedule*** échéancier *m* de paiement

payoff ['peɪɒf] N **1** *(act of paying off)* paiement *m*; **the p. is set for tomorrow night** *(gen)* le paiement sera effectué demain soir; *(ransom)* la remise de la rançon est fixée à demain soir
2 *(profit)* bénéfice *m*, profit *m*
3 *(consequence)* conséquence *f*, résultat *m*; *(reward)* récompense *f*
4 *Fam (climax)* dénouement▫*m*
5 *Fam (bribe)* pot-de-vin▫*m*

payola [peɪ'əʊlə] N *(UNCOUNT) Am Fam* pots-de-vin *mpl*, dessous-de-table *mpl*

pay-per-use ADJ facturé à l'utilisation

pay-per-view *TV* N système *m* de télévision à la carte
ADJ à la carte
▸▸ ***pay-per-view channel*** chaîne *f* à la carte; ***pay-per-view television*** télévision *f* à la carte

payroll ['peɪrəʊl] N **1** *(list of employees)* liste *f* du personnel, registre *m* des salaires; *(employees collectively)* personnel *m*; **he's been on our p. for years** il fait partie du personnel depuis des années; **they've added 500 workers to their p.** ils ont embauché 500 travailleurs supplémentaires; **to be taken off the p.** *(voluntarily)* quitter l'entreprise; *(be laid off)* être licencié; **to do the p.** faire la paie, établir les bulletins de paie **2** *(money paid)* masse *f* salariale
▸▸ *Fin* ***payroll ledger*** journal *m ou* livre *m* de paie; *Fin* ***payroll tax*** impôt *m* sur la masse salariale

PBX [ˌpiːbiː'eks] N *Br Tel (abbr* **private branch exchange***)* = autocommutateur privé

PC¹, pc¹ [ˌpiː'siː] N **1** *Comput (abbr* **personal computer***)* PC *m*, micro *m*; **available for the PC** disponible en version PC **2** *(abbr* **postcard***)* carte *f* postale
▸▸ *Comput* ***PC disk*** disquette *f* pour PC

PC² N *(abbr* **police constable***)* agent *m* de police
ADJ *(abbr* **politically correct***)* politiquement correct

pc² *(written abbr* **per cent***)* pc

PCA [ˌpiːsiː'eɪ] N *EU (abbr* **Partnership and Cooperation Agreements***)* Accords *mpl* de partenariat et de coopération

PCB [ˌpiːsiː'biː] N *Electron (abbr* **printed circuit board***)* carte *f* de *ou* à circuits imprimés

PC-compatible ADJ compatible PC

PCI [ˌpiːsiː'aɪ] N *Comput (abbr* **peripheral component interface***)* PCI *m*

PCMCIA [ˌpiːsiːˌemˌsiːaɪ'eɪ] N *Comput (abbr* **PC memory card international association***)* PCMCIA *m*

PCOS [ˌpiːsiːəʊ'es] N *Med (abbr* **polycystic ovary syndrome***)* SOPK *m*

PD [ˌpiː'diː] N *Am (abbr* **police department***)* service *m* de police

PDA [ˌpiːdiː'eɪ] N *Comput (abbr* **personal digital assistant***)* PDA *m*, agenda *m* électronique de poche, assistant *m* numérique personnel

PDF [ˌpiːdiː'ef] N *Comput (abbr* **portable document format***)* (format *m*) PDF *m*

PDL [ˌpiːdiː'el] N *Comptr (abbr* **page description language***)* PDL *m*

pdq [ˌpiːdiː'kjuː] ADV *Fam (abbr* **pretty damn quick***)* illico presto

PDSA [ˌpiːdiːˌes'eɪ] N *Br (abbr* **People's Dispensary for Sick Animals***)* = association de soins aux animaux malades

PE [ˌpiː'iː] N *(abbr* **physical education***)* EPS *f*

pea [piː] N *Bot* pois *m*; *Culin* (petit) pois *m*; **frozen peas** petits pois *mpl* surgelés; **they are as alike as two peas in a pod** ils se ressemblent comme deux gouttes d'eau
▸▸ ***pea green*** vert *m* pomme *(inv)*; ***pea jacket*** caban *m*; ***pea soup*** soupe *f* aux pois; *Fam* ***pea souper*** *(fog)* purée *f* de pois

peace [piːs] N **1** *(not war)* paix *f*; *(treaty)* (traité *m* de) paix *f*; **in time of p.** en temps de paix; **the country is at p. now** la paix est maintenant rétablie dans le pays; **I come in p.** je viens en ami; **to make p.** faire la paix; *Fig* **he made (his) p. with his father** il a fait la paix *ou* il s'est réconcilié avec son père; **to win the p.** gagner la paix; **they wanted to sign a separate p. with the invaders** ils voulaient conclure *ou* signer une paix séparée avec les envahisseurs
2 *(tranquillity)* paix *f*, tranquillité *f*; **to be at p. with oneself/the world** être en paix avec soi-même/le reste du monde; **to be at p.** *(dead person)* reposer en paix; **we haven't had a moment's p. all morning** nous n'avons pas eu un moment de tranquillité de toute la matinée; **all I want is a bit of p. and quiet** tout ce que je veux, c'est un peu de tranquillité; **p. of mind** tranquillité *f* d'esprit; **to have p. of mind** avoir l'esprit tranquille; **he'll give you no p. until you pay him** tant que tu ne l'auras pas payé, il ne te laissera pas tranquille; **leave us in p.!** laisse-nous tranquilles!, laisse-nous en paix!; *Rel* **p. be with you!** que la paix soit avec vous!; **go in p.!** allez en paix!
3 *(silence)* **to hold** *or* **to keep one's p.** garder le silence, se taire; **hold your p.!** silence!
4 *(law and order)* paix *f*, ordre *m* public; **to disturb the p.** troubler l'ordre public; **to keep the p.** *(army, police)* maintenir l'ordre
▸▸ ***peace activist*** activiste *mf* en faveur de la paix; ***peace agreement*** accord *m* de paix; ***peace camp*** = camp installé près d'une base militaire en signe de protestation contre les activités qui s'y déroulent; *Br* ***peace campaigner*** militant(e) *m,f* pour la paix; ***Peace Corps*** = organisation américaine de coopération avec les pays en voie de développement; ***peace dividend*** dividende *m* de paix; ***peace formula*** formule *f* de paix; ***peace initiative*** initiative *f* de paix; ***peace movement*** mouvement *m* pour la paix; ***peace negotiations*** négociations *fpl* pour la paix; ***peace offering*** offrande *f* de paix; ***peace pipe*** calumet *m* (de la paix); ***peace process*** processus *m* de paix; ***peace proposal*** proposition *f* de paix; ***peace rally*** rassemblement *m* pour la paix; ***peace sign*** signe *m* de la paix; ***peace studies*** = discipline universitaire consistant à étudier les rapports stratégiques entre pays, le rôle de l'armée et la promotion de la paix dans le monde; ***peace talks*** pourparlers *mpl* de paix; ***peace treaty*** traité *m* de paix

peaceable ['piːsəbəl] ADJ **1** *(peace-loving* ▸ *nation, person)* pacifique; **a p. man** un homme de paix **2** *(calm* ▸ *atmosphere)* paisible, tranquille; *(*▸ *demonstration, methods)* pacifique; *(*▸ *discussion)* calme

peaceably ['piːsəblɪ] ADV *(live)* paisiblement, tranquillement; *(discuss, listen)* calmement, paisiblement; *(assemble, disperse)* pacifiquement, sans incident

peaceful ['piːsfʊl] ADJ **1** *(calm, serene)* paisible, tranquille; **he had a p. death** il est mort sans souffrir **2** *(non-violent* ▸ *solution, protest, means)* pacifique; **we are a p. nation** nous sommes une nation pacifique; **the p. uses of nuclear energy** les utilisations pacifiques de l'énergie nucléaire

peacefully ['piːsfʊlɪ] ADV *(live, rest)* paisiblement, tranquillement; *(protest)* pacifiquement; **the rally went off p.** le meeting s'est déroulé dans le calme *ou* sans incident; **he died p.** il est mort sans souffrir; **p., at home** *(in death notice)* survenu à son domicile

peacefulness ['piːsfʊlnɪs] N paix *f*, calme *m*, tranquillité *f*

peacekeeping ['piːsˌkiːpɪŋ] N maintien *m* de la paix
ADJ de maintien de la paix; **a United Nations p. force** des forces des Nations unies pour le maintien de la paix

peace-loving ADJ pacifique

peacemaking ['piːsˌmeɪkɪŋ] ADJ pacificateur

peacenik ['piːsnɪk] N *Fam Pej* pacifiste▫*mf*

peacetime ['piːstaɪm] N temps *m* de paix; **in p.** en temps de paix

peach [piːtʃ] N **1** *(fruit)* pêche *f*; **she has a peaches and cream complexion** elle a un teint de pêche
2 *(tree)* pêcher *m*
3 *(colour)* couleur *f* pêche
4 *Fam (expressing approval)* **he played a p. of a shot** il a joué un coup superbe▫; **a p. of a goal/dress** un but/une robe magnifique▫; **she's a p.** elle est jolie comme un cœur
COMP *(yoghurt)* aux pêches; *(jam)* de pêches
ADJ *(colour)* pêche *(inv)*
VI *Fam (inform)* cafarder; **to p. on sb** cafarder qn
▸▸ ***peach blossom*** fleurs *mpl* de pêcher; ***peach melba*** pêche *f* melba; ***peach tree*** pêcher *m*

peachy ['piːtʃɪ] *(compar* **peachier**, *superl* **peachiest***)* ADJ **1** *(taste, flavour, complexion)* de pêche **2** *esp Am Fam* **p. (keen)** *(excellent)* chouette, super; **everything's just p.!** tout baigne (dans l'huile)!
ADV *Am Fam (well)* super

peacock ['piːkɒk] *(pl inv or* **peacocks***)* N **1** *Orn* paon *m* (bleu) **2** *(colour)* bleu *m* canard
ADJ bleu canard *(inv)*
▸▸ ***peacock blue*** bleu *m* canard; ***peacock butterfly*** paon *m* de jour

peahen ['piːhen] N paonne *f*

peak [piːk] N **1** *(mountain top)* pic *m*, sommet *m*; *(mountain)* pic *m*; **the highest peaks** les plus hauts sommets; **snowy peaks** pics *mpl ou* sommets *mpl* enneigés
2 *(pointed part* ▸ *of roof)* faîte *m*; **beat the egg whites until they form peaks** battez les blancs d'œuf en neige très ferme
3 *(high point* ▸ *of fame, career)* sommet *m*, apogée *m*; *(*▸ *on graph)* sommet *m*; **emigration was at its p. in the 1890s** l'émigration a atteint son point culminant *ou* son sommet dans les années 1890; **the gardens are at their p. in July** c'est en juillet que les jardins sont au faîte *ou* à l'apogée de leur splendeur; **the team will be at its p. in a few weeks** l'équipe sera à son top niveau dans quelques semaines; **the party was at its p.** la fête battait son plein; **sales have reached a new p.** les ventes ont atteint un nouveau record
4 *(of cap)* visière *f*
VI *(production, demand)* atteindre un maximum; **his popularity peaked just before the elections** sa cote a atteint un *ou* son maximum juste avant les élections; **she peaked too soon** *(athlete)* elle s'est lancée trop tôt; *(musician, actress)* elle a donné le maximum trop tôt
ADJ maximum; **the team is in p. condition** l'équipe est à son top niveau
▸▸ ***peak demand*** demande *f* maximum; ***the Peak District*** = région de moyenne montagne dans le nord de l'Angleterre; *Med* ***peak flow*** débit *m* expiratoire de pointe; ***peak hours, peak period*** *(of*

electricity use) période *f* de pointe; *(of traffic)* heures *fpl* de pointe *or* d'affluence; *(in restaurant)* coup *m* de feu; *St Exch* ***peak price*** prix *m* maximum; ***peak rate*** tarif *m* heures pleines; ***peak season*** haute saison *f*; *Br TV* ***peak time*** heures *fpl* de grande écoute, prime time *m*; *Br TV* ***peak time advertisement*** publicité *f* aux heures de grande écoute *ou* en prime time; *Br TV* ***peak time advertising*** publicité *f* aux heures de grande écoute *ou* en prime time; *Br TV* ***peak viewing hours, peak viewing time*** heures *fpl* de grande écoute; ***peak year*** année-record *f*

▸**peak out** VI *(reach top limit)* atteindre son maximum

peaked [pi:kt] ADJ *(roof)* pointu; *(cap)* à visière

peaky ['pi:kɪ] *(compar* **peakier**, *superl* **peakiest***)* ADJ *Br Fam (unwell)* patraque; *(tired)* fatigué□; **I feel a little p. this morning** je ne me sens pas en forme *ou* je ne me sens pas dans mon assiette ce matin

peal [pi:l] N **1** *(sound ▸ of bells)* carillonnement *m*; *(▸ of doorbell)* sonnerie *f*; *(▸ of organ)* grondement *m*; **the p. of bells** la sonnerie de cloches; **a p. of thunder** un coup de tonnerre; **peals of laughter came from the living room** des éclats de rire s'échappaient du salon; **they burst into peals of laughter** ils ont éclaté de rire **2** *(set of bells)* carillon *m*

VI *(bells ▸ chime)* carillonner; *(▸ ring out loudly)* sonner à toute volée; *(thunder, organ)* retentir, gronder; *(laughter)* résonner

VT *(bells)* sonner à toute volée

▸**peal out** VI *(bells ▸ chime)* carillonner; *(▸ ring out loudly)* sonner à toute volée; *(thunder, organ)* retentir, gronder; *(laughter)* résonner

peanut ['pi:nʌt] N *(nut)* cacahouète *f*, cacahuète *f*; *(plant)* arachide *f*; *Fam* **peanuts** *(small sum)* clopinettes *fpl*, cacahuètes *fpl*; **to work for peanuts** travailler pour des clopinettes; **it's worth peanuts** ça ne vaut pas un clou; **£100 is peanuts for a return ticket** 100 livres, ce n'est rien pour un billet aller-retour□

▸▸ ***peanut butter*** beurre *m* de cacahuètes; *Am Fam* ***peanut gallery*** *(in theatre)* poulailler *m*; ***peanut oil*** huile *f* d'arachide

pear [peə(r)] N **1** *(fruit)* poire *f* **2** *(tree, wood)* poirier *m*

COMP *(yoghurt, tart)* aux poires

peardrop ['peədrɒp] N *Br* = bonbon parfumé à la poire

pearl [pɜ:l] N **1** *(gem)* perle *f*; **to cast pearls before swine** donner de la confiture aux cochons, donner des perles aux cochons; *Fig* **pearls of dew** perles *fpl* de rosée **2** *(mother-of-pearl)* nacre *f* **3** *Fig* perle *f*; **Hong Kong, p. of the East** Hongkong, perle de l'Orient; *Literary* **a p. amongst women** une perle; **pearls of wisdom** trésors *mpl* de sagesse; *Ironic* inepties *fpl*

ADJ **1** *(made of pearls)* de perles; **p. earrings** perles *fpl* montées en boucles d'oreilles; **a p. necklace** un collier de perles **2** *(made of mother-of-pearl)* de *ou* en nacre; **p. buttons** boutons *mpl* en nacre

VI **1** *(form drops)* perler **2** *(search for pearls)* pêcher des perles

▸▸ ***pearl barley*** orge *m* perlé; ***pearl diver*** pêcheur (euse) *m,f* de perles; ***pearl diving*** pêche *f* aux perles; ***pearl grey*** gris *m* perle *(inv)*; ***pearl light-bulb*** ampoule *f* opale; ***pearl mussel*** mulette *f*, moule *f* d'eau douce *ou* de rivière; ***pearl oyster*** huître *f* perlière, méléagrine *f*

pearly ['pɜ:lɪ] *(compar* **pearlier**, *superl* **pearliest***)* ADJ **1** *(pearl-like)* nacré; **p. white teeth** dents *fpl* de perle *ou* éclatantes **2** *(decorated with pearls)* perlé; *(made of mother-of-pearl)* en *ou* de nacre

▸▸ *Fam* ***the Pearly Gates*** les portes *fpl* du paradis□; ***pearly king/queen*** = marchand/marchande des quatre-saisons "cockney" dont les vêtements sont ornés d'une profusion de boutons de nacre

pear-shaped ADJ en forme de poire, *Spec* piriforme; *(female figure)* plus fort au niveau des hanches

ADV *Br Fam Fig* **to go p.** *(go wrong)* partir en eau de boudin; **it all went p. after they wouldn't lend us the money** ça s'est gâté quand ils ont refusé de nous prêter l'argent□

peasant ['pezənt] N **1** *(from the country)* paysan (anne) *m,f* **2** *Fam Pej (uncouth person)* péquenaud(e) *m,f*, plouc *m*

ADJ paysan; **p. life** la vie des paysans; **p. dress** des vêtements *mpl* de paysans

▸▸ ***peasant farmer*** paysan *m*; ***peasant farming*** petite agriculture *f*; *Br Hist* ***the Peasants' Revolt*** la guerre des Gueux

> **THE PEASANTS' REVOLT**
>
> Il s'agit de la première grande révolte populaire de l'histoire d'Angleterre (en 1381), provoquée par la mise en vigueur de la capitation. Son meneur, Wat Tyler, fut assassiné lors de pourparlers avec le roi Richard II et la révolte s'éteignit sans avoir apporté de changements.

peasantry ['pezəntrɪ] N paysannerie *f*, paysans *mpl*

pease pudding [pi:z-] N *Culin* = purée de pois au jambon

peashooter ['pi:ʃu:tə(r)] N sarbacane *f*

peat [pi:t] N tourbe *f*; **turf** *or* **sod** *or* **block of p.** motte *f* de tourbe; **to cut** *or* **dig p.** tourber

▸▸ ***peat bog*** tourbière *f*; *Bot* ***peat moss*** sphaigne *f*

peaty ['pi:tɪ] *(compar* **peatier**, *superl* **peatiest***)* ADJ *(soil, water, stream)* tourbeux; *(taste)* de fumée de tourbe

pebble ['pebəl] N **1** *(stone)* caillou *m*; *(water-worn)* galet *m*; **a p. beach** une plage de galets; **he's not the only p. on the beach** un de perdu, dix de retrouvés **2** *Opt (lens)* lentille *f* en cristal de roche

VT **1** *(road, path)* caillouter; **a pebbled drive** une allée de gravillons **2** *(leather)* greneler

▸▸ *Fam* ***pebble glasses*** lunettes *fpl* à verres très épais□

pebbledash ['pebəldæʃ] *Br* N crépi *m (incrusté de cailloux)*

VT crépir

pebbly ['peblɪ] *(compar* **pebblier**, *superl* **pebbliest***)* ADJ **1** *(stony ▸ soil, path)* caillouteux; **a p. beach** une plage de galets **2** *(grainy)* grené, grenu

pecan [*Br* 'pi:kən, *Am* pɪ'kæn] N **1** *(nut)* (noix *f* de) pecan *m*, (noix *f* de) pacane *f* **2** *(tree)* pacanier *m*

ADJ *(pie, ice cream)* à la noix de pecan

peccadillo [,pekə'dɪləʊ] *(pl* **peccadillos** *or* **peccadilloes***)* N peccadille *f*

peccary ['pekərɪ] *(pl* **inv** *or* **peccaries***)* N *Zool* pécari *m*

peck [pek] VT **1** *(pick up)* picorer, picoter; *(strike with beak)* donner un coup de bec à; **chickens were pecking the ground** des poulets picoraient le sol; **be careful, it'll p. you!** fais attention, tu vas recevoir un coup de bec! **2** *(kiss)* faire une bise à

N **1** *(with beak)* coup *m* de bec **2** *(kiss)* bise *f*, (petit) baiser *m*; **she gave me a p. on the cheek** elle m'a fait une bise **3** *(measure)* picotin *m*

▸▸ *also Fig Am* ***peck order***, *Br* ***pecking order*** hiérarchie *f*

pecker ['pekə(r)] N **1** *Br Fam (spirits)* **to keep one's p. up** ne pas se laisser abattre□; **keep your p. up!** (du) courage!□ **2** *Am very Fam (penis)* queue *f*, quéquette *f*

peckerwood ['pekəwʊ:d] N *Fam Black Am slang* **to be a p.** être génial *ou* super

peckish ['pekɪʃ] ADJ *esp Br Fam* **to be** *or* **to feel p.** avoir un petit creux

pecs [peks] NPL *Fam (abbr* **pectoral muscles***)* pectoraux□ *mpl*; **he's got a great set of p.** il a des super pectoraux

pectin ['pektɪn] N *Biol & Chem* pectine *f*

pectoral ['pektərəl] ADJ *Mil & Rel* pectoral

N *Anat, Mil & Rel* pectoral *m*

▸▸ ***pectoral cross*** *(of bishop)* croix *f* pectorale; *Ich* ***pectoral fin*** nageoire *f* pectorale; *Anat* ***pectoral muscle*** muscle *m* pectoral

peculate ['pekjʊleɪt] *Formal* VI détourner les fonds *ou* deniers publics

VT *(funds)* détourner

peculation [,pekjʊ'leɪʃən] N *Formal* détournement *m* de fonds publics

peculiar [pɪ'kju:lɪə(r)] ADJ **1** *(strange)* étrange, bizarre; **he/she is a little p.** il/elle est un peu bizarre; **well, that's p.** tiens, c'est bizarre *ou* curieux!, voilà qui est singulier!; **I feel a bit p.** je me sens un peu bizarre **2** *(specific, exclusive)* particulier; **to be p. to** être spécifique *ou* particulier à; **this species is p. to Scandinavia** cette espèce n'existe qu'en Scandinavie; **it has a p. taste** ça a un goût spécial

peculiarity [pɪ,kju:lɪ'ærətɪ] *(pl* **peculiarities***)* N **1** *(oddness)* étrangeté *f*, bizarrerie *f*; **I should explain the p. of my situation** il faut que je vous explique ce qu'il y a d'étrange dans ma situation; **we all have our little peculiarities** nous avons tous nos petites manies **2** *(specific characteristic)* particularité *f*; **each region has its own peculiarities** chaque région a son particularisme *ou* ses particularités

peculiarly [pɪ'kju:lɪəlɪ] ADV **1** *(oddly)* étrangement, bizarrement **2** *(especially)* particulièrement, singulièrement; **a p. French institution/obsession** une institution/obsession bien française

pecuniary [pɪ'kju:nɪərɪ] ADJ *Formal* pécuniaire

pedagogic [,pedə'gɒdʒɪk], **pedagogical** [,pedə'gɒdʒɪkəl] ADJ pédagogique

pedagogically [,pedə'gɒdʒɪkəlɪ] ADV pédagogiquement

pedagogue ['pedəgɒg] N pédagogue *mf*

pedagogy ['pedəgɒdʒɪ] N pédagogie *f*

pedal ['pedəl] *(Br pt & pp* **pedalled**, *cont* **pedalling**, *Am pt & pp* **pedaled**, *cont* **pedaling***)* N pédale *f*

VI pédaler; **we pedalled along the back roads** nous roulions (à bicyclette) sur les routes de l'arrière-pays; **he pedalled off** il est parti (à vélo)

VT faire avancer en pédalant; **he pedalled his bike up the hill** il a pédalé jusqu'en haut de la côte sur son vélo

▸▸ *Br* ***pedal bin*** poubelle *f* à pédale; ***pedal boat*** pédalo *m*; ***pedal car*** voiture *f* à pédales; ***pedal cycle*** bicyclette *f*; ***pedal keyboard*** *(of organ)* pédalier *m*; *Mus* ***pedal point*** pédale *f*; ***pedal pushers*** (pantalon *m*) corsaire *m*; ***pedal steel (guitar)*** guitare *f* hawaïenne, pedal-steel *f*

pedalo ['pedələʊ] *(pl* **pedalos** *or* **pedaloes***)* N pédalo *m*

pedal-operated ADJ commandé par pédale(s)

pedant ['pedənt] N pédant(e) *m,f*

pedantic [pɪ'dæntɪk] ADJ pédant

pedantically [pɪ'dæntɪkəlɪ] ADV de manière pédante; *(say)* d'un ton pédant

pedantry ['pedəntrɪ] *(pl* **pedantries***)* N **1** *(behaviour)* pédantisme *m*, pédanterie *f* **2** *(remark)* pédanterie *f*

peddle ['pedəl] VT **1** *Old-fashioned (wares)* colporter; **he didn't want to p. encyclopedias all his life** il ne voulait pas passer sa vie à faire du porte à porte pour vendre des encyclopédies **2** *(drugs)* revendre, faire le trafic de **3** *Pej (promote ▸ idea, opinion)* propager; *(▸ gossip, scandal)* colporter

VI faire du colportage

peddler ['pedlə(r)] N **1** *(seller)* colporteur(euse) *m,f* **2** *(drug pusher)* trafiquant(e) *m,f* (de drogue), revendeur(euse) *m,f* **3** *Pej (promoter ▸ of ideas, opinions)* propagateur(trice) *m,f*; *(▸ of gossip, scandal)* colporteur(euse) *m,f*; **peddlers of dreams** marchands *mpl* de rêves

pederast ['pedəræst] N pédéraste *m*

pederasty ['pedəræstɪ] N pédérastie *f*

pedestal ['pedɪstəl] N piédestal *m*, socle *m*; *Fig* piédestal *m*; **to place** *or* **to put sb on a p.** mettre qn sur un piédestal; **that knocked him off his p.** cela l'a fait tomber de son piédestal

▸▸ ***pedestal basin*** lavabo *m* sur colonne; ***pedestal desk*** bureau *m* ministre; ***pedestal table*** guéridon *m*

pedestrian [pɪ'destrɪən] N piéton *m*; **pedestrians only** *(sign)* réservé aux piétons

COMP *(street, area)* piéton, piétonnier

ADJ *(prosaic)* prosaïque; *(commonplace)* banal; **a p. style** un style prosaïque

▸▸ *Br* ***pedestrian crossing*** passage *m* clouté *ou* piétons; ***pedestrian overpass*** passerelle *f*; *Br* ***pe***

destrian precinct, *Am* **pedestrian zone** zone *f* piétonnière *ou* piétonne

pedestrian-controlled crossing N passage *m* pour piétons à bouton d'appel

pedestrianization, -isation [pəˌdestrɪənaɪˈzeɪʃən] N transformation *f* en zone piétonne *ou* piétonnière

pedestrianize, -ise [pəˈdestrɪənaɪz] VT transformer en zone piétonne *ou* piétonnière
▸▸ ***pedestrianized streets*** rues *fpl* piétonnes *or* piétonnières

pediatric, pediatrician *etc Am* = **paediatric, paediatrician** *etc*

pedicure [ˈpedɪˌkjʊə(r)] N *(treatment)* soins *mpl* des pieds; **to have a p.** se faire soigner les pieds, aller chez le/la pédicure

pedigree [ˈpedɪgriː] N **1** *(descent ▸ of animal)* pedigree *m*; *(▸ of person)* ascendance *f*, lignée *f*; *Fig (background ▸ of person)* origine *f*; **she had an impeccable political p.** ses antécédents politiques étaient irréprochables **2** *(document for animal)* pedigree *m* **3** *(genealogical table)* arbre *m* généalogique
ADJ *(horse, cat, dog)* de (pure) race

pediment [ˈpedɪmənt] N **1** *Archit* fronton *m* **2** *Geol* pédiment *m*

pedlar = **peddler**

pedology[1] [pɪˈdɒlədʒɪ] N *Geol* pédologie *f*

pedology[2] N *(study of child growth, development etc)* pédologie *f*

pedometer [pɪˈdɒmɪtə(r)] N pédomètre *m*, podomètre *m*

pedophile, pedophilia *Am* = **paedophile, paedophilia**

pee [piː] *Fam* N pipi *m*; **to have** *or* **to take a p.** faire pipi; **to go for a p.** aller faire pipi
VI faire pipi; **it's peeing down** *(raining)* il pleut comme vache qui pisse
VT **to p. oneself** *or Br* **one's pants** faire pipi dans sa culotte; **to p. oneself (laughing)** rire à en faire dans sa culotte

▸**pee off** VT SEP *very Fam (annoy)* **to p. sb off** faire chier qn; **to be peed off** être fumasse *ou* furibard; **to be peed off at sb/about sth** être en pétard contre qn/à cause de qch; **to be peed off with sb/sth** *(have had enough of)* en avoir ras le bol de qn/qch

peek [piːk] VI *(glance)* jeter un coup d'œil; *(look furtively)* regarder furtivement; **to p. at sth** jeter un coup d'œil à *ou* sur qch; **someone was peeking through the keyhole** quelqu'un regardait par le trou de la serrure; **turn around and no peeking!** retourne-toi et n'essaie pas de voir ce que je fais!
N coup *m* d'œil; **to have** *or* **to take a p. at sth** jeter un coup d'œil à *ou* sur qch

peekaboo [ˈpiːkəbuː] *Fam* EXCLAM coucou!
N **to play p.** jouer à faire coucou
ADJ *(see-through)* transparent□; *(with holes)* avec *ou* en broderie(s) ajourée(s)□

peel [piːl] N **1** *(of banana)* peau *f*; *(of orange, lemon)* écorce *f*; *(of apple, onion, potato)* pelure *f*; **add a twist of lemon p.** ajouter un zeste de citron **2** *(UNCOUNT) (peelings)* épluchures *fpl*
VT *(fruit, vegetable)* peler, éplucher; *(boiled egg)* écaler, éplucher; *(shrimp)* décortiquer; *(twig)* écorcer; *(skin, bark)* enlever; **to keep one's eyes peeled** ouvrir l'œil; **we were all keeping our eyes peeled for a pub** nous guettions tous un pub, nous étions tous à l'affût d'un pub
VI **1** *(fruit, vegetable)* se peler **2** *(plaster on wall, ceiling etc)* s'écailler, se craqueler; *(paint, varnish)* s'écailler; *(wallpaper)* se décoller **3** *(skin on back, face etc)* peler; **I'm peeling all over** je pèle de partout

▸**peel off** VI **1** *(plaster on wall, ceiling etc)* s'écailler, se craqueler; *(paint, varnish)* s'écailler; *(wallpaper)* se décoller **2** *Fam (undress)* se déshabiller□ **3** *(turn away)* se détacher; **two aircraft peeled off from the main group** deux avions se détachèrent du gros de l'escadre
VT SEP **1** *(label, wallpaper)* détacher, décoller; *(bandage)* enlever, ôter **2** *(item of clothing)* enlever; **to p. off one's clothes** se déshabiller

peeler [ˈpiːlə(r)] N **1** *(device)* éplucheur *m*; *(electric)* éplucheuse *f*; **potato p.** économe *m* **2** *Am Fam (stripper)* effeuilleuse *f* **3** *Br Fam Old-fashioned (policeman)* flic *m*

peeling [ˈpiːlɪŋ] N **1** *Med (of skin)* desquamation *f* **2 peelings** *(of potato etc)* épluchures *fpl*, pelures *fpl*
ADJ *(nose, back etc)* qui pèle/pelait

peep [piːp] N **1** *(glance)* coup *m* d'œil; **to have a p. at sth** jeter un coup d'œil à qch; **I got a p. at the file before he came in** j'ai réussi à jeter un coup d'œil sur le dossier avant qu'il arrive **2** *(of bird)* pépiement *m*; *Fam Fig* **any news from him? – not a p.!** tu as eu de ses nouvelles? – pas un mot *ou* que dalle!; *Fam* **one more p. out of you and you've had it!** encore un mot et ton compte est bon!
VI **1** *(glance)* jeter un coup d'œil; **to p. at/over/under sth** jeter un coup d'œil (furtif) à/par-dessus/sous qch; **the children were peeping through the keyhole** les enfants épiaient à travers le trou de la serrure; **someone was peeping at her from behind the curtains** quelqu'un l'observait, caché derrière les rideaux; **no peeping!** on ne regarde pas! **2** *(emerge)* se montrer; **snowdrops were beginning to p. through** des perce-neiges commençaient à pointer **3** *(bird)* pépier; *(mouse)* couiner

▸**peep out** VI *(be visible)* se laisser entrevoir, se montrer; *(flower)* percer, pointer; **the moon peeped out through the clouds** la lune a percé *ou* est apparue à travers les nuages; **his feet were peeping out from beneath the curtains** ses pieds dépassaient de derrière les rideaux; **his big toe was peeping out through a hole in his sock** son gros doigt de pied pointait par un trou de sa chaussette; **her nose peeped out over her scarf** le bout de son nez pointait *ou* apparaissait par-dessus son écharpe

peepbo [ˈpiːpˌbəʊ] *Fam* EXCLAM coucou!
N **to play p.** jouer à faire coucou

pee-pee N *Am Fam (in children's language)* **to go p.** faire pipi

peepers [ˈpiːpəz] NPL *Fam (eyes)* mirettes *fpl*

peephole [ˈpiːphəʊl] N trou *m*; *(in house door, cell)* judas *m*
▸▸ ***peephole bra*** soutien-gorge *m* seins nus

peeps [piːps] NPL *Fam (people)* populo *m*; **hi, p.** salut tout le monde; **my p.** ma bande

peepshow [ˈpiːpʃəʊ] N *(device)* stéréoscope *m (pour images érotiques)*; *(pictures)* vues *fpl* stéréoscopiques; *(form of entertainment)* peep-show *m*

peer [pɪə(r)] N **1** *(noble)* pair *m*, noble *mf*; **he was made a p.** il a été élevé à la pairie; *Pol* **the Conservative Peers** les pairs *mpl* conservateurs *(en Grande-Bretagne)*; **p. of the realm** pair *m* du royaume **2** *(equal)* pair *m*; **a jury of one's peers** un jury formé *ou* composé de ses pairs; **as a negotiator she has no p.** c'est une négociatrice hors pair, comme négociatrice elle n'a pas son pareil
VI *(look ▸ intently)* regarder attentivement; *(▸ with difficulty)* s'efforcer de voir; **to p. at sb/sth** scruter qn/qch du regard; **she peered out into the darkness** elle scruta l'obscurité; **he peered at the suspects' faces** il dévisagea les suspects; **she peered at the small print** elle s'efforça de lire ce qui était écrit en petits caractères
▸▸ ***peer group*** pairs *mpl*; ***peer pressure*** influence *f* des pairs *ou* du groupe; ***peer review*** révision *f* par un collègue

peerage [ˈpɪərɪdʒ] N **1** *(title)* pairie *f*; **he was given a p.** *or* **raised to the p.** il a été élevé à la pairie **2** *(body of peers)* pairs *mpl*, noblesse *f* **3** *(book)* nobiliaire *m*

peeress [ˈpɪərɪs] N pairesse *f*

peerless [ˈpɪəlɪs] ADJ sans pareil, incomparable

peer-to-peer ADJ *Comput* peer-to-peer

peeve [piːv] VT *Fam* mettre en rogne; **it really peeves me that he got the job** ça me met en rogne qu'il ait eu le poste

peevish [ˈpiːvɪʃ] ADJ *(person)* irritable, grincheux; *(child)* grognon; *(report, expression)* irrité; **in a p. mood** de mauvaise humeur

peevishly [ˈpiːvɪʃlɪ] ADV *(say, refuse)* d'un ton irrité; *(behave)* de façon désagréable; **to complain p.** ronchonner

peevishness [ˈpiːvɪʃnɪs] N mauvaise humeur *f*, irritabilité *f*

peewit [ˈpiːwɪt] N *Orn* vanneau *m*

peg [peg] *(pt & pp* **pegged**, *cont* **pegging)** N **1** *(for hat, coat)* patère *f*; *Fig* **a p. to hang an argument on** un prétexte de dispute, une excuse pour se disputer
2 *Br (clothespeg)* pince *f* à linge
3 *(dowel ▸ wooden)* cheville *f*; *(▸ metal)* fiche *f*
4 *(for tent)* piquet *m*
5 *(in mountaineering)* piton *m*
6 *(in croquet)* piquet *m*
7 *(of barrel)* fausset *m*, fosset *m*
8 *Mus (on string instrument)* cheville *f*
9 *Fig (degree, notch)* degré *m*, cran *m*; **she's gone down a p. (or two) in my estimation** elle a baissé d'un cran dans mon estime; **to bring** *or* **to take sb down a p. or two** rabattre le caquet à qn, remettre qn à sa place
10 *Br Fam (of spirits)* petit verre□ *m*
VT **1** *(fasten ▸ gen)* attacher; *(▸ with dowels)* cheviller; *(insert ▸ stake)* enfoncer, planter; *(in mountaineering)* pitonner; **he was pegging the washing on the line** il accrochait le linge à la corde avec des pinces; **to p. a tent** fixer une tente avec des piquets **2** *(set ▸ price, increase)* fixer; *(tie ▸ currency)* indexer; **oil was pegged at $20 a barrel** le prix du pétrole était fixé à 20 dollars le baril; **to p. sth to the rate of inflation** indexer qch sur le taux de l'inflation; **export earnings are pegged to the exchange rate** le revenu des exportations varie en fonction du taux de change **3** *Am Fam (classify)* classer□
▸▸ *Fam* ***peg leg*** *(wooden leg)* jambe *f* de bois□, pilon□ *m*; *(artificial leg)* jambe *f* artificielle□; *(person)* = personne qui a une jambe de bois ou une jambe artificielle

▸**peg away** VI *Br Fam* travailler sans relâche□; *(student)* bûcher; **she pegged away at her Latin** elle bûchait son latin; **we're pegging away at the backlog** petit à petit, nous rattrapons notre retard□

▸**peg down** VT SEP *(fasten down)* fixer *ou* attacher (avec des piquets); **he pegged the tarpaulin down** il fixa la bâche au sol avec des piquets

▸**peg out** VT SEP **1** *(hang out ▸ washing)* étendre **2** *(mark out with pegs)* piqueter
VI **1** *Fam (die)* crever, claquer **2** *Fam (give up)* laisser tomber□, abandonner□ **3** *(in croquet)* toucher le piquet final *(et se retirer de la partie)*

pegboard [ˈpegbɔːd] N plaquette *f* perforée *(utilisée dans certains jeux)*

pegging [ˈpegɪŋ] N **1** *(fixing ▸ of prices, increase)* fixation *f*; *(tying ▸ of currency)* indexation *f* **2** *Br Sport & Fig* **it's level p.** ils sont à égalité

PEI *(written abbr* **Prince Edward Island)** l'île *f* du Prince-Édouard

pejorative [pɪˈdʒɒrətɪv] ADJ péjoratif
N péjoratif *m*

pejoratively [pɪˈdʒɒrətɪvlɪ] ADV péjorativement

peke [piːk] N *Fam* pékinois□ *m (chien)*

Pekinese [ˌpiːkəˈniːz], **Pekingese** [ˌpiːkɪŋˈiːz] N **1** *(person)* Pékinois(e) *m,f* **2** *Ling* pékinois *m* **3** *(dog)* pékinois *m*
ADJ pékinois

Peking [ˌpiːˈkɪŋ] N Pékin
▸▸ ***Peking duck*** canard *m* laqué

pelagic [peˈlædʒɪk] ADJ **1** *(fauna, sediment)* pélagien, pélagique; **p. life forms** pelagos *m* **2** *(not coastal)* hauturier, de haute mer

pelargonium [ˌpeləˈgəʊnɪəm] N pélargonium *m*

pelican [ˈpelɪkən] N *Orn* pélican *m*
▸▸ *Br* ***pelican crossing*** = passage piétons à commande manuelle

pellagra [pəˈlægrə] N *Med* pellagre *f*

pellet [ˈpelɪt] N **1** *(small ball)* boulette *f*; **wax/paper pellets** boulettes *fpl* de cire/de papier; **pellets of rabbit dung** crottes *fpl* de lapin
2 *(for gun)* (grain *m* de) plomb *m*
3 *(pill)* pilule *f*
4 *Zool (regurgitated food of owl etc)* pelote *f* de régurgitation
▸▸ ***pellet gun*** fusil *m* à plombs

pell-mell [ˌpelˈmel] ADV *Br (pile, throw)* pêle-mêle; **the crowd ran p. into the square** la foule s'est ruée sur la place dans une cohue indescriptible

pellucid [pe'lu:sɪd] ADJ *(membrane, zone)* pellucide; *(water)* limpide; *Fig (prose, style)* clair, limpide

pelmet ['pelmɪt] N *(for curtains)* cantonnière *f*; *(wood, board)* lambrequin *m*

Peloponnese [,peləpə'ni:z] N the P. le Péloponnèse

Peloponnesian [,peləpə'ni:zɪən] ADJ péloponnésien, du Péloponnèse
▸▸ ***the Peloponnesian War*** la guerre du Péloponnèse

pelota [pə'lɒtə] N pelote *f* basque
▸▸ ***pelota court*** fronton *m*

pelt [pelt] VT *(person, target)* bombarder; **they were pelting each other with snowballs** ils se bombardaient de boules de neige
VI *Fam* **1** *(rain)* **it was pelting with rain** il pleuvait à verse□, il tombait des cordes; **I changed the tyre in the pelting rain** j'ai changé le pneu sous la pluie battante□ **2** *(run)* courir à fond de train *ou* à toute allure; **she came pelting up the stairs** elle grimpa l'escalier quatre à quatre; **she came pelting down the stairs** elle dévala l'escalier
N **1** *(skin)* peau *f*; *(fur)* fourrure *f* **2** *Br (idiom)* **at full p.** à fond de train

▸**pelt down** VI *Fam (rain)* tomber à verse□; **the rain** *or* **it was pelting down** la pluie tombait à verse, il pleuvait à verse□

pelvic ['pelvɪk] ADJ pelvien
▸▸ ***pelvic bone*** ilion *m*; *Ich* ***pelvic fins*** pelviennes *fpl*; ***pelvic floor*** plancher *m* pelvien; ***pelvic floor exercises*** exercices *mpl* de musculation du plancher pelvien; ***pelvic girdle*** ceinture *f* pelvienne; ***pelvic inflammatory disease*** syndrome *m* inflammatoire pelvien

pelvis ['pelvɪs] *(pl* **pelvises** *or* **pelves** [-vi:z]) N bassin *m*, pelvis *m*

pen [pen] *(pt & pp* **penned**, *sense* **2** *also* **pent** [pent], *cont* **penning**) N **1** *(for writing)* stylo *m*; **fountain p.** stylo *m* à plume, stylo-plume *m*; **ball(point) p.** stylo *m* à bille, stylo-bille *m*; **felt(-tip) p.** (crayon *m ou* stylo *m*) feutre *m*; **to put p. to paper** écrire, prendre sa plume; **another novel from the p. of Muriel Spark** un nouveau roman de la plume de Muriel Spark; **she lives by her p.** elle vit de sa plume; *Prov* **the p. is mightier than the sword** un coup de langue est pire qu'un coup de lance
2 *(female swan)* cygne *m* femelle
3 *(for animals)* enclos *m*, parc *m*; **sheep p.** parc *m* à moutons
4 *(for submarines)* **(submarine) p.** bassin *m* protégé
5 *Am Fam (penitentiary)* taule *f*, tôle *f*; **in the p.** en taule, en cabane; **he spent ten years in the p.** il a passé dix ans en taule, il a fait dix ans de taule
VT **1** *(write)* écrire; **a letter penned in a childish hand** une lettre d'une écriture enfantine **2** *(enclose)* **to p. in** *or* **up** *(livestock)* parquer, enfermer dans un enclos; *(dog)* enfermer; *(person)* enfermer, cloîtrer, claquemurer
▸▸ *Comput* ***pen drive*** clé *f* USB; *Br* ***pen friend*** correspondant(e) *m,f (épistolaire)*; ***pen name*** nom *m* de plume, pseudonyme *m*; ***pen nib*** plume *f (de stylo)*; *Fam* ***pen pal*** correspondant(e)□*m,f (épistolaire)*

penal ['pi:nəl] ADJ **1** *(law)* pénal; *(establishment)* pénitentiaire **2** *(severe ▸ taxation, fine)* écrasant
▸▸ ***penal code*** code *m* pénal; ***penal colony*** colonie *f* pénitentiaire, bagne *m*; ***penal offence*** infraction *f* pénale; *Fin* ***penal rate*** taux *m* d'usure; ***penal servitude*** travaux *mpl* forcés, bagne *m*; ***penal settlement*** colonie *f* pénitentiaire, bagne *m*

penalization, -isation [,pi:nəlaɪ'zeɪʃən] N pénalisation *f*, sanction *f*

penalize, -ise ['pi:nəlaɪz] VT **1** *(punish)* pénaliser, sanctionner **2** *(disadvantage)* pénaliser, défavoriser, désavantager; **the new tax penalizes large families** le nouvel impôt pénalise les familles nombreuses

penalty ['penəltɪ] *(pl* **penalties**) N **1** *Law (punishment)* peine *f*; *(fine)* amende *f*; **on p. of** sous peine de; **under p. of death** sous peine de mort; **p. for improper use: £25** *(sign)* tout abus est passible d'une amende de 25 livres
2 *Admin & Com (for breaking contract)* pénalité *f*, sanction *f*
3 *Fig (unpleasant consequence)* **to pay the p. (for sth)** subir les conséquences (de qch); **that's the p. for being famous** c'est la rançon de la gloire
4 *Sport (gen)* pénalisation *f*; *(kick ▸ in football)* penalty *m*; (▸ *in rugby)* pénalité *f*; **to award a p.** *(in football)* accorder un penalty; *(in rugby)* accorder une pénalité; **to score (from) a p.** *(in football)* marquer un penalty; **a two-minute (time) p.** *(in ice hockey)* une pénalité de deux minutes
▸▸ *Ftbl* ***penalty area*** surface *f* de réparation; ***penalty bench*** *(in ice hockey)* banc *m* de pénalité; ***penalty box*** *Ftbl* surface *f* de réparation; *(in ice hockey)* banc *m* de pénalité; *Law* ***penalty clause*** clause *f* pénale; ***penalty corner*** *(in hockey)* coup *m* de coin de pénalité; ***penalty double*** *(in bridge)* contre *m* de pénalité; *Sport* ***penalty goal*** but *m* sur pénalité; *Fin* ***penalty interest*** pénalité *f* de retard, intérêts *mpl* moratoires; ***penalty kick*** *(in football)* penalty *m*; *(in rugby)* (coup *m* de pied de) pénalité *f*; ***penalty points*** *(in quiz, game)* gage *m*; *(for drivers)* points *mpl* de pénalité *(dans le système du permis à points)*; ***penalty rate*** *(of taxation)* taux *m* de pénalité; *Am, Austr & Can (for overtime)* tarif *m* des heures supplémentaires; *Ftbl* ***penalty shootout*** épreuve *f* des penalties; ***penalty shot*** *(in ice hockey)* pénalité *f*; *Ftbl* ***penalty spot*** point *m* de réparation; *Golf* ***penalty stroke*** coup *m* d'amende; *Sport* ***penalty throw*** penalty *m*; ***penalty try*** *(in rugby)* essai *m* de pénalité

penance ['penəns] N pénitence *f*; **to do p. for one's sins** faire pénitence; **to do sth as a p.** faire qch par pénitence

pence [pens] NPL *(pl of* **penny**) pence *mpl*

pencil ['pensəl] *(Br pt & pp* **pencilled**, *cont* **pencilling**, *Am pt & pp* **penciled**, *cont* **penciling**) N **1** *(for writing, makeup)* crayon *m*; **the corrections are in p.** les corrections sont (faites) au crayon **2** *Fig (narrow beam)* **a p. of light** un pinceau de lumière
COMP *(drawing)* au crayon
VT écrire au crayon; *(hastily)* crayonner; **question marks were pencilled in the margin** on avait mis des points d'interrogation au crayon dans la marge; **to p. one's eyebrows** se dessiner les sourcils (au crayon)
▸▸ ***pencil box*** plumier *m*; ***pencil case*** trousse *f*; ***pencil holder*** porte-crayon *m*; *Am Fam Pej* ***pencil pusher*** gratte-papier *m inv*; ***pencil sharpener*** taille-crayon *m*; ***pencil sketch*** croquis *m* au crayon

▸**pencil in** VT SEP *(date, name, address)* noter *ou* inscrire au crayon; *Fig* fixer provisoirement; **I'll p. the meeting/you in for 6 June** retenons provisoirement la date du 6 juin pour la réunion/notre rendez-vous

pendant ['pendənt] N **1** *(necklace)* pendentif *m* **2** *(piece of jewellery ▸ on necklace)* pendentif *m*; (▸ *on earring)* pendeloque *f* **3** *(chandelier)* lustre *m*
ADJ **1** *(hanging)* pendant, qui pend **2** *(overhanging)* en surplomb, en saillie
▸▸ ***pendant earrings*** pendants *mpl* d'oreille

pending ['pendɪŋ] ADJ **1** *(waiting to be settled ▸ gen)* en attente; *Law* en instance, pendant; (▸ *documents)* en souffrance; **a p. court case** une affaire en instance *ou* en cours **2** *(imminent)* imminent
PREP en attendant
▸▸ *Br* ***pending tray*** corbeille *f* des dossiers en attente; **mail is piling up in the p. tray** le courrier en attente s'accumule

Pendolino® [,pendəʊ'li:nəʊ] N Pendolino® *m*

pendulous ['pendjʊləs] ADJ **1** *(sagging ▸ breasts)* tombant; (▸ *lips)* pendant **2** *(swinging)* oscillant

pendulum ['pendjʊləm] N pendule *m*; *(in clock)* balancier *m*; *Fig* **the p. of fashion has swung back to a sixties look** la mode des années soixante est revenue au goût du jour
▸▸ ***pendulum bob*** lentille *f* de pendule *ou* de balancier; ***pendulum clock*** horloge *f* à pendule *ou* à balancier

penes ['pi:ni:z] *pl of* **penis**

penetrable ['penɪtrəbəl] ADJ **1** *(material, defences)* pénétrable; **easily p.** facile à pénétrer **2** *(prose, style)* **barely p.** difficilement compréhensible

penetrate ['penɪtreɪt] VT **1** *(find way into or through ▸ jungle, region)* pénétrer dans; (▸ *blockade, enemy defences)* pénétrer; **they penetrated unknown territory** ils ont pénétré en territoire inconnu
2 *(infiltrate ▸ party, movement)* s'infiltrer dans, noyauter; **penetrated by an informer** infiltré par un indicateur
3 *(pierce ▸ of missile)* percer, transpercer; **the bullet penetrated his right lung** la balle lui a perforé le poumon droit
4 *(pass through ▸ of sound, light etc)* traverser, transpercer; **the child's cries penetrated the silence** les cris de l'enfant déchiraient le silence; **the cold wind penetrated her clothing** le vent glacial passait à travers ses vêtements; **the ship's lights failed to p. the fog** les lumières du bateau ne parvenaient pas à percer le brouillard
5 *(see through ▸ darkness, disguise, mystery)* percer; **to p. sb's thoughts** lire dans les pensées de qn
6 *Mktg (market)* pénétrer
7 *(sexually)* pénétrer
VI **1** *(break through)* pénétrer; **the troops penetrated deep into enemy territory** les troupes ont pénétré très avant en territoire ennemi **2** *(ideas, beliefs)* s'implanter; **the custom has not penetrated to this part of the country** cette coutume n'est pas parvenue jusqu'à cette partie du pays **3** *(sink in)* **I heard what you said but it didn't p. at the time** j'ai entendu ce que tu as dit, mais je n'ai pas saisi sur le moment; **I had to explain it to him several times before it finally penetrated** j'ai dû le lui expliquer plusieurs fois avant que ça (ne) rentre

penetrating ['penɪtreɪtɪŋ] ADJ **1** *(sound ▸ pleasant)* pénétrant; (▸ *unpleasant)* perçant **2** *(cold)* pénétrant, perçant; *(rain, wind)* pénétrant **3** *(look)* pénétrant, perçant; *(mind, question)* pénétrant; **she had p. eyes** elle avait un regard pénétrant
▸▸ ***penetrating oil*** dégrippant *m*

penetration [,penɪ'treɪʃən] N **1** *(gen)* & *Mktg* pénétration *f* **2** *Mil* percée *f* **3** *Phot* profondeur *f* de champ
▸▸ *Mktg* ***penetration price*** prix *m* de pénétration

penetrative ['penɪtrətɪv] ADJ *(force)* de pénétration
▸▸ ***penetrative sex*** relations *fpl* sexuelles avec pénétration

penetrator ['penɪtreɪtə(r)] N *Astron (spacecraft)* pénétrateur *m*

penguin ['peŋgwɪn] N manchot *m*
▸▸ *Br Fam* ***penguin suit*** costard *m* chic

penholder ['pen,həʊldə(r)] N porte-plume *m inv*

penicillin [,penɪ'sɪlɪn] N pénicilline *f*

peninsula [pə'nɪnsjʊlə] N *(large)* péninsule *f*; *(small)* presqu'île *f*

peninsular [pə'nɪnsjʊlə(r)] ADJ péninsulaire
▸▸ ***the Peninsular War*** la guerre d'Espagne *(1808–14)*

penis ['pi:nɪs] *(pl* **penises** *or* **penes** [-i:z]) N pénis *m*
▸▸ *Psy* ***penis envy*** envie *f* du pénis

penitence ['penɪtəns] N pénitence *f*, repentir *m*

penitent ['penɪtənt] ADJ **1** *(gen)* contrit **2** *Rel* pénitent
N *Rel* pénitent(e) *m,f*

penitential [,penɪ'tenʃəl] ADJ pénitentiel
N *(book)* pénitentiel *m*

penitentiary [,penɪ'tenʃərɪ] *(pl* **penitentiaries**) N **1** *Am (prison)* prison *f* **2** *Rel (priest)* pénitencier *m*
ADJ **1** *Am (life, conditions)* pénitentiaire; *(offence)* passible d'une peine de prison **2** *(penitential)* pénitentiel
▸▸ *Am* ***penitentiary guard*** gardien(enne) *m,f* de prison

penitently ['penɪtəntlɪ] ADV *(say)* d'un ton contrit; *(submit, kneel)* avec contrition

penknife ['pennaɪf] *(pl* **penknives** [-naɪvz]) N canif *m*

penmanship ['penmənʃɪp] N calligraphie *f*

Penn, Penna *(written abbr* **Pennsylvania**) Pennsylvanie *f*

pennant ['penənt] N **1** *(flag ▸ gen)* fanion *m* **2** *Naut (for identification)* flamme *f*; *(for signalling)* pavillon *m* **3** *Am Sport* = drapeau servant de trophée dans certains championnats; **to win the p.** remporter le championnat

penne ['peneɪ] **NPL** *(pasta)* penne *mpl*

penniless ['penɪlɪs] **ADJ** sans le sou; **they're absolutely p.** ils n'ont pas un sou; **the stock market crash left him p.** le krach boursier l'a mis sur la paille

Pennines ['penaɪnz] **NPL the P.** les Pennines *fpl*

pennon ['penən] **N 1** *(flag ▸ gen)* fanion *m*; *(▸ on lance)* pennon *m* **2** *Naut (for identification)* flamme *f*; *(for signalling)* pavillon *m*

Pennsylvania [,pensɪl'veɪnɪə] **N** la Pennsylvanie; **1600 P. Avenue** = adresse de la Maison Blanche, utilisée par les médias américains pour faire référence au gouvernement

penny ['penɪ] *(pl sense* **1** **pence** [pens], *pl sense* **2** **pennies) N 1** *(unit of currency ▸ in Britain, Ireland)* penny *m*; **it cost me 44 pence** ça m'a coûté 44 pence **2** *(coin ▸ in Britain, Ireland)* penny *m*, pièce *f* d'un penny; *(▸ in US)* cent *m*, pièce *f* d'un cent; **it was expensive, but it was worth every p.** c'était cher, mais j'en ai vraiment eu pour mon argent; **it won't cost you a p.** ça ne vous coûtera pas un centime *ou* un sou; **every p. counts** un sou est un sou; **they haven't got a p. to their name** *or* **two pennies to rub together** ils n'ont pas un sou vaillant; **to earn** *or Am* **to turn an honest p.** gagner honnêtement sa vie; *Br Fam* **people like him are two** *or* **ten a p.** des gens comme lui, ce n'est pas ça qui manque; **a p. for your thoughts** à quoi penses-tu?; *Br Fam* **suddenly the p. dropped** d'un seul coup ça a fait tilt; *Br Fam* **he keeps turning up like a bad p.** c'est un vrai pot de colle; *Br Prov* **in for a p. in for a pound** quand le vin est tiré, il faut le boire; *Br Prov* **take care of the pennies and the pounds will take care of themselves** les petits ruisseaux font les grandes rivières; **to be p. wise and pound foolish** chipoter sur les petites dépenses sans regarder aux grandes

▸▸ *Am* ***penny arcade*** galerie *f* de jeux; ***Penny Black*** = premier timbre-poste britannique; *Br Fam Old-fashioned* ***penny dreadful*** *(novel)* = roman d'amour ou d'aventures à quatre sous; *(magazine)* magazine *m* à sensation[❑]; *Br St Exch* ***penny shares*** actions *fpl* d'une valeur de moins d'une livre sterling; *Am St Exch* ***penny stocks*** actions *fpl* d'une valeur de moins d'un dollar; ***penny whistle*** pipeau *m*

penny-pincher [-'pɪntʃə(r)] **N** *Fam* pingre *mf*, radin(e) *m,f*

penny-pinching [-'pɪntʃɪŋ] *Fam* **N** *(UNCOUNT)* économies *fpl* de bouts de chandelle; **government p. will ruin the education system** à force de serrer les cordons de la bourse, le gouvernement finira par étrangler le système éducatif

ADJ *(person)* radin, pingre, qui fait des économies de bouts de chandelle; *(action, step)* mesquin; *(lifestyle, measures)* de lésine, d'économie de bouts de chandelle

pennyworth ['penɪwɜːθ, 'penəθ] *(pl* **inv** *or* **pennyworths) N** *Br* **1** *Old-fashioned* **she asked for a p. of toffees** elle demanda pour un penny de caramels **2** *Fig (small quantity)* **if he had a p. of sense** s'il avait une once de bon sens

penology [piː'nɒlədʒɪ] **N** pénologie *f*

pen-pusher N *Fam Pej* gratte-papier *m inv*, scribouillard(e) *m,f*

pen-pushing ADJ *Fam Pej (job)* de gratte-papier

pension ['penʃən, *sense* **2** *also* 'pɑ̃sjɔ̃] **N 1** *(for retired people)* retraite *f*; *(for disabled people)* pension *f*; **to draw a p.** *(retired person)* toucher une retraite; *(disabled person)* toucher une pension, être pensionné; **to pay sb a p.** verser une pension à qn; **widow's p.** *(before retiring age)* allocation *f* de veuvage; *(at retiring age)* pension *f* de réversion **2** *(small hotel)* pension *f* de famille

VT *(for retirement)* verser une pension de retraite à; *(for disability)* pensionner, verser une pension à

▸▸ *Br* ***pension book*** ≃ titre *m* de pension *(carnet permettant de retirer sa pension de retraite)*; ***pension fund*** caisse *f* de retraite, fonds *m* de pension; ***pension plan*** plan *m ou* régime *m* de retraite; ***pension scheme*** plan *m ou* régime *m* de retraite

▸ **pension off VT SEP** *Br* **1** *(person)* mettre à la retraite **2** *Hum (old car, machine)* mettre au rancart

pensionable ['penʃənəbəl] **ADJ 1** *(person ▸ gen)* qui a droit à une pension; *(▸ for retirement)* qui a atteint l'âge de la retraite **2** *(job)* qui donne droit à une retraite

▸▸ ***pensionable age*** âge *m* de la mise à la retraite; **teachers of p. age** les enseignants qui ont atteint l'âge de la retraite

pensioner ['penʃənə(r)] **N** *Br* **(old age) p.** retraité(e) *m,f*; **war p.** ancien combattant *m (titulaire d'une pension militaire d'invalidité)*

> Note that the French term **pensionnaire** is never a translation for the English word **pensioner**.

pensive ['pensɪv] **ADJ** pensif, méditatif, songeur

pensively ['pensɪvlɪ] **ADV** pensivement

pent [pent] *pt & pp of* **pen**

pentagon ['pentəgən] **N** *Geom* pentagone *m*

• **Pentagon N** *Pol* **the P.** le Pentagone

pentagonal [pen'tægənəl] **ADJ** pentagonal

pentameter [pen'tæmɪtə(r)] **N** *Literature* pentamètre *m*

Pentateuch ['pentətjuːk] **N the P.** le Pentateuque

pentathlete [pen'tæθliːt] **N** pentathlonien (enne) *m,f*

pentathlon [pen'tæθlən] **N** pentathlon *m*

Pentecost ['pentɪkɒst] **N** Pentecôte *f*

pentecostal [pentɪ'kɒstəl] **ADJ** *Rel* de la Pentecôte

▸▸ ***the Pentecostal Church*** l'église *f* pentecôtiste

penthouse ['penthaus, *pl* -hauzɪz] **N 1** *(flat)* = appartement de luxe avec terrasse, généralement au dernier étage d'un immeuble **2** *(on roof)* **elevator p.** machinerie *f* d'ascenseur *(installée sur un toit)* **3** *(doorway shelter)* auvent *m*; *(shed)* appentis *m*

▸▸ ***penthouse suite*** *(in hotel)* suite *f* avec terrasse

Pentium® ['pentɪəm] **N** *Comput* Pentium® *m*

pent-up ADJ *(emotion)* refoulé, réprimé; *(force)* contenu, réprimé; **his anger is a product of p. frustration** sa colère vient de ce qu'il est frustré; **to get rid of p. energy** se défouler

penultimate [pe'nʌltɪmət] **ADJ 1** *(gen)* avant-dernier **2** *Ling* pénultième

N 1 *(gen)* avant-dernier(ère) *m,f* **2** *Ling* pénultième *f*

penumbra [pɪ'nʌmbrə] *(pl* **penumbras** *or* **penumbrae** [-briː]) **N** *Astron & Phys* pénombre *f*

penurious [pɪ'njuərɪəs] **ADJ** *Formal* **1** *(impoverished)* indigent, sans ressources **2** *(miserly)* parcimonieux, avare

penury ['penjurɪ] **N** *Formal* **1** *(poverty)* indigence *f*, dénuement *m* **2** *(scarcity)* pénurie *f*

peony ['piːənɪ] *(pl* **peonies) N** pivoine *f*

PEOPLE ['piːpəl]

> **NPL**
> • personnes **1** • gens **1, 3**
> • on **2** • peuple **4**
> • famille **5**
> **N**
> • peuple **1** • nation **1**
> • population **2**
> **VT**
> • peupler

NPL 1 *(gen)* personnes *fpl*, gens *mpl*; **500 p.** 500 personnes; **there were p. everywhere** il y avait des gens *ou* du monde partout; **how many p. were there?** combien de personnes y avait-il?; **there were a lot of p. there** il y avait beaucoup de monde; **some p. think it's true** certaines personnes *ou* certains pensent que c'est vrai; **a lot of p. think that…** beaucoup de gens pensent que…; **I've talked to several p. about it** j'en ai parlé à plusieurs personnes; **to have p. skills** avoir le sens du contact; **she's a real p. person** elle a vraiment le sens du contact; **many/most p. disagree** beaucoup de gens/la plupart des gens ne sont pas d'accord; **are you p. coming or not?** et vous (autres), vous venez ou pas?; **it's Meg, of all p.!** ça alors, c'est Meg!; **you of all p. should know that!** si quelqu'un doit savoir ça, c'est bien toi!

2 *(in indefinite uses)* on; **p. say it's impossible** on dit que c'est impossible; **I don't want p. to know about this** je ne veux pas qu'on le sache *ou* que cela se sache; **p. won't like it** les gens ne vont pas aimer ça

3 *(with qualifier)* gens *mpl*; **clever/sensitive p.** les gens *mpl* intelligents/sensibles; **rich/poor/blind p.** les riches/pauvres/aveugles *mpl*; **young p.** les jeunes *mpl*; **old p.** les personnes *fpl* âgées; **city/country p.** les citadins/campagnards *mpl*; **p. who know her** ceux qui la connaissent; **p. like you** les gens comme toi; **p. of taste** les gens *mpl* de goût; **p. with large cars** ceux qui ont de grandes voitures; **they are nice p.** ce sont des gens sympathiques; **nice p. don't do that!** les gens bien *ou* comme il faut ne font pas ce genre de chose!; **they are theatre/circus p.** ce sont des gens de théâtre/du cirque; **Danish p.** les Danois *mpl*; **the p. of Brazil** les Brésiliens *mpl*; **the p. of Glasgow** les habitants *mpl* de Glasgow; **the p. of Yorkshire** les gens *mpl* du Yorkshire; **I'll call the electricity/gas p. tomorrow** je téléphonerai à la compagnie d'électricité/de gaz demain; **the President's financial p.** les conseillers *mpl* financiers du Président

4 *Pol* **the p.** le peuple; **power to the p.!** le pouvoir au peuple!; **a p.'s government/democracy** un gouvernement/une démocratie populaire; *Am Law* **the P. vs Smith** le ministère public contre Smith

5 *Old-fashioned (family)* famille *f*, parents *mpl*; **her p. emigrated in 1801** sa famille a émigré en 1801

N 1 *(nation)* peuple *m*, nation *f*; **a seafaring p.** un peuple de marins

2 *(ethnic group)* population *f*; **the native peoples of Polynesia** les populations *fpl* indigènes *ou* autochtones de Polynésie; **the French-speaking peoples** les populations *fpl* francophones

VT *(usu passive) (inhabit)* peupler; **peopled by** peuplée de, habité par; *Fig* **the monsters that p. his dreams** les monstres qui hantent ses rêves

▸▸ ***people carrier*** *(car)* monospace *m*; ***people mover*** *(car)* monospace *m*; *(transport)* système *m* de transport automatique; *(moving pavement)* trottoir *m* roulant; ***people power*** pouvoir *m* populaire; ***the People's Republic of China*** la République populaire de Chine; ***people skills*** aptitudes *fpl* relationnelles; ***people smuggling, people trafficking*** traite *f* d'êtres humains

people-focused ADJ centré sur l'humain

PEP [pep] **N** *Br Formerly Fin (abbr* **personal equity plan)** ≃ PEA *m*

pep [pep] *(pt & pp* **pepped**, *cont* **pepping) N** *Fam* punch *m*; **to have a lot of** *or* **to be full of p.** avoir du punch

▸▸ ***pep pill*** stimulant[❑] *m*, excitant[❑] *m*; ***pep talk*** discours *m* d'encouragement[❑]; **their boss gave them a p. talk** leur patron leur a dit quelques mots pour leur remonter le moral[❑]

▸ **pep up VT SEP** *Fam* **1** *(depressed person)* remonter le moral à[❑]; *(ill, tired person)* requinquer, retaper; **a cup of tea will soon p. you up** une tasse de thé aura vite fait de te ravigoter *ou* retaper **2** *(business)* faire repartir[❑], dynamiser[❑]; *(party)* dynamiser[❑], remettre de l'entrain dans[❑]; *(conversation)* égayer[❑], ranimer[❑], relancer[❑]

pepper ['pepə(r)] **N 1** *(condiment)* poivre *m* **2** *(vegetable ▸ sweet)* poivron *m*; *(▸ hot)* piment *m*; **green/red/yellow p.** poivron *m* vert/rouge/jaune

VT 1 *Culin* poivrer **2** *(scatter, sprinkle)* émailler, parsemer; **her text was peppered with quotations** son texte était émaillé de citations **3** *(pelt)* **the walls were peppered with lead shot** les murs étaient criblés d'impacts de balles; **they peppered the houses with machine-gun fire** ils ont mitraillé les maisons

▸▸ ***pepper mill*** moulin *m* à poivre; ***pepper pot*** poivrier *m*, poivrière *f*; ***pepper sauce*** sauce *f* au poivre; *Br Culin* ***pepper steak*** steak *m* au poivre

pepper-and-salt ADJ 1 *(hair, beard)* poivre et sel *(inv)* **2** *(jacket)* marengo *(inv)*

▸▸ ***pepper-and-salt cloth*** marengo *m*

peppercorn ['pepəkɔːn] **N** grain *m* de poivre

▸▸ *Br* ***peppercorn rent*** loyer *m* modique

peppermint ['pepəmɪnt] **N 1** *Bot* menthe *f* poivrée **2** *(sweet)* bonbon *m* à la menthe

ADJ à la menthe; **p.** *or* **p.-flavoured toothpaste** dentifrice *m* au menthol

►► *peppermint cream* bonbon *m* à la crème de menthe; *peppermint tea* thé *m* à la menthe

peppery ['pepərɪ] ADJ **1** *Culin* poivré **2** *(quick-tempered)* coléreux, irascible **3** *(incisive)* mordant, piquant

peppy ['pepɪ] *(compar* **peppier**, *superl* **peppiest**) ADJ *Fam (person)* qui a du punch

pepsin ['pepsɪn] N *Biol & Chem* pepsine *f*

peptic ['peptɪk] ADJ *Biol & Chem* peptique

►► *Med* **peptic ulcer** ulcère *m* gastro-duodénal *ou* de l'estomac

peptide ['peptaɪd] N *Biol & Chem* peptide *m*

peptone ['peptəʊn] N *Biol & Chem* peptone *f*

per [pɜː(r)] PREP *(for each)* par; **p. person** par personne; **p. head** par tête; **p. day/week/month/year** par jour/semaine/mois/an; **they are paid £6 p. hour** ils sont payés 6 livres de l'heure; **100 miles p. hour** ≃ 160 kilomètres à l'heure; **it costs £8 p. kilo** ça coûte 8 livres le kilo; **output p. worker has increased** la production individuelle des ouvriers a augmenté; **p. annum** par an, annuellement; **$5,000 p. annum** 5000 dollars par an; *Formal* **p. capita** par personne, par tête; **p. capita consumption** consommation *f* par tête; **p. capita growth** croissance *f* par tête; **p. capita income is higher in the south** le revenu par habitant est plus élevé dans le sud

• **as per** PREP suivant, selon; **as p. specifications** *(on bill)* conformément aux spécifications requises; **as p. your instructions/letter** conformément à vos instructions/votre lettre; **the work is going ahead as p. schedule** le travail avance selon le calendrier prévu; *Fam* **as p. normal** *or* **usual** comme d'habitude[□]

peradventure [pərəd'ventʃə(r)] ADV *Arch* par hasard, d'aventure

perambulate [pə'ræmbjʊleɪt] *Literary or Hum* VI se promener, (se) baguenauder

VT **1** *(estate, boundary)* inspecter **2** *(sea, region)* parcourir

perambulator [pə'ræmbjʊleɪtə(r)] N *Old-fashioned* landau *m*

p/e ratio [,piː'iː-] N *St Exch (abbr* **price-earnings ratio**) ratio *m ou* rapport *m* cours-bénéfices, PER *m*

perceive [pə'siːv] VT **1** *(see)* distinguer; *(hear, smell etc)* percevoir

2 *(notice)* s'apercevoir de, remarquer; **few people perceived the differences** peu de gens ont remarqué les différences

3 *(conceive, understand)* percevoir, comprendre; **their presence is perceived as a threat** leur présence est perçue comme une menace

4 *Mktg (product, brand)* percevoir

perceived [pə'siːvd] ADJ perçu; **public reaction to p. injustice in the trial** la réaction du public à ce qu'il a perçu comme une injustice au cours du procès; **the government's p. failure to resolve the conflict** ce qui est perçu comme l'incapacité du gouvernement à résoudre le conflit

►► *perceived noise decibel* perceived noise decibel *m*; *Mktg* **perceived performance** résultats *mpl* perçus; *Mktg* **perceived quality** qualité *f* perçue; **perceived risk** risque *m* perçu; *Mktg* **perceived value** valeur *f* perçue

percent [pə'sent] *(pl* **inv**) ADV pour cent; **prices went up (by) 10 p.** les prix ont augmenté de 10 pour cent; **it's 50 p. cotton** il y a 50 pour cent de coton, c'est du coton à 50 pour cent; **a 9 p. interest rate** un taux d'intérêt à 9 pour cent; **I'm 99 p. certain** j'en suis à 99 pour cent sûr

N *(percentage)* pourcentage *m*; **what p. of people own a mobile phone?** quel est le pourcentage des propriétaires de téléphones portables?

percentage [pə'sentɪdʒ] N **1** *(proportion)* proportion *f*; *(expressed in %)* pourcentage *m*; **to express sth as a p.** exprimer qch en pourcentage; **in a high/tiny p. of cases** dans une vaste/petite proportion des cas; **a high p. of the staff** une grande partie du personnel **2** *(share of profits, investment)* pourcentage *m*; **his manager takes a p. of his winnings** son directeur prend un pourcentage sur ses gains; **to get a p. on sth** toucher un pourcentage sur qch **3** *Br Fam (advantage)* avantage[□] *m*, intérêt[□] *m*; **there's no p. in kicking up a fuss** ça ne sert à rien de faire des histoires

ADJ *Am (profitable)* payant

►► *percentage increase* augmentation *f* en pourcentage; **percentage point** point *m*; **percentage reduction** réduction *f* en pourcentage

percenter [pə'sentə(r)] N *Am Fam (agent)* agent *m* artistique[□]

percentery [pə'sentərɪ] N *Am Fam (talent agency)* agence *f* artistique

percentile [pə'sentaɪl] N centile *m*

perceptibility [pə,septə'bɪlɪtɪ] N perceptibilité *f*

perceptible [pə'septəbəl] ADJ perceptible; *(difference, change)* sensible

perceptibly [pə'septəblɪ] ADV *(diminish, change)* sensiblement; *(move)* de manière perceptible; **she was p. thinner** elle avait sensiblement maigri

perception [pə'sepʃən] N **1** *(faculty)* perception *f*; **visual/aural p.** perception *f* visuelle/auditive; **organs of p.** organes *mpl* percepteurs; **powers of p.** facultés *fpl* perceptives **2** *(notion, conception)* perception *f*, conception *f*; *Mktg (of product, brand)* perception *f*; **her p. of the problem is different from mine** sa façon de voir le problème diffère de la mienne; **the general public's p. of the police** l'image que le grand public a de la police, la façon dont le grand public perçoit la police **3** *(insight)* perspicacité *f*, intuition *f*; **a man of great p.** un homme très perspicace

perceptive [pə'septɪv] ADJ **1** *(observant* ► *person)* perspicace; *(*► *remark)* judicieux; *(analysis, article)* tout en finesse **2** *(sensitive)* sensible **3** *(organ)* sensoriel

perceptively [pə'septɪvlɪ] ADV avec perspicacité

perceptiveness [pə'septɪvnɪs] N perspicacité *f*, pénétration *f*

perceptual [pə'septjʊəl] ADJ **1** *(organ)* percepteur **2** *Mktg* perceptuel

perch [pɜːtʃ] *(pl sense* **4 inv** *or* **perches**) N **1** *(for bird* ► *in cage)* perchoir *m*; *(*► *on tree)* branche *f*; **the bird flew from its p. on the roof** l'oiseau s'envola du toit où il était perché

2 *Fam (for person* ► *seat)* perchoir *m*; **to knock sb off his/her p.** *(depose)* détrôner qn[□]; *(force to abandon pretensions)* rabattre son caquet à qn; *Hum* **to fall** *or* **drop off one's p.** *(die)* passer l'arme à gauche

3 *(linear or square measure)* ≃ perche *f*

4 *Ich* perche *f*

VI *(bird, person)* se percher; **he perched on the edge of the table** il se percha *ou* se jucha sur le bord de la table

VT *(person, object)* percher, jucher; **she was perched on a stool/on the arm of the chair** elle était juchée sur un tabouret/sur le bras du fauteuil; **castle perched on a hill** château perché sur (le sommet d')une colline; **with his glasses perched on the end of his nose** avec ses lunettes perchées sur le bout du nez

perchance [pə'tʃɑːns] ADV *Arch or Literary* **1** *(perhaps)* peut-être **2** *(by accident)* par hasard, fortuitement

percipient [pə'sɪpɪənt] ADJ **1** *Formal (person)* perspicace **2** *Anat (organ)* sensoriel

percolate ['pɜːkəleɪt] VI **1** *(liquid)* filtrer, s'infiltrer; *(coffee)* passer; **toxic chemicals had percolated through the soil** des produits chimiques toxiques s'étaient infiltrés dans le sol **2** *(ideas, news)* filtrer; **his ideas percolated through to the rank and file** ses idées ont gagné la base **3** *Am Fam (be excited)* être (tout) excité[□]; **he is percolating with joy** il déborde de joie[□]; **she percolates with ideas** elle bouillonne d'idées

VT *(coffee)* préparer, faire *(dans une cafetière à pression)*

►► *percolated coffee* café *m* fait avec une cafetière à pression

percolator ['pɜːkəleɪtə(r)] N cafetière *f* à pression; *(for large quantities)* percolateur *m*

percussion [pə'kʌʃən] N **1** *Mus* percussion *f*; **Jane Stowell on p.** aux percussions, Jane Stowell **2** *(collision, shock)* percussion *f*, choc *m* **3** *Med & Mil* percussion *f*

►► *Mil* **percussion cap** amorce *f* fulminante; **percussion drill** perceuse *f* à percussion; *Mus* **percussion instrument** instrument *m* à percussion; *Mil* **percussion lock** percuteur *m*; *Mus* **percussion player** percussionniste *mf*; *Mus* **the percussion section** les percussions *fpl*; **percussion tool** outil *m* à percussion

percussionist [pə'kʌʃənɪst] N *Mus* percussionniste *mf*

percussive [pə'kʌsɪv] ADJ *(instrument)* à percussion; *(force)* de percussion

perdition [pə'dɪʃən] N **1** *Literary (spiritual ruin)* perdition *f*; *(hell)* enfer *m*, damnation *f* **2** *Arch (ruin)* perte *f*, ruine *f*

peregrination [,perɪgrɪ'neɪʃən] N *Formal or Hum* pérégrination *f*

peregrine ['perɪgrɪn] N *Orn* **p. (falcon)** (faucon *m*) pèlerin *m*

peremptorily [pə'remptərəlɪ] ADV de façon péremptoire, impérieusement

peremptory [pə'remptərɪ] ADJ *(tone, manner, person)* péremptoire, impérieux; **there was a p. knock at the door** on a frappé à la porte de façon péremptoire

►► *Br Law* **peremptory writ** assignation *f* à comparaître en personne

perennial [pə'renɪəl] ADJ **1** *Bot* vivace **2** *Fig (everlasting)* éternel; *(recurrent, continual)* perpétuel, sempiternel; **a p. subject of debate** un éternel *ou* perpétuel sujet de discussion

N *Bot* plante *f* vivace

perennially [pə'renɪəlɪ] ADV *(everlastingly)* éternellement; *(recurrently, continually)* perpétuellement, continuellement

perestroika [,perə'strɔɪkə] N perestroïka *f*

perfect ADJ ['pɜːfɪkt] **1** *(flawless* ► *person, performance, English etc)* parfait; **a p. circle** un cercle parfait; **to be in p. condition** *(engine, appliance)* être en parfait état de marche; *(painting, antique, teeth)* être en parfait état; **in p. health** en excellente *ou* parfaite santé; **her hearing is still p.** elle entend encore parfaitement; **try it yourself, since you think you're (so) p.!** essaie toi-même, puisque tu te crois *ou* tu es si fort!; **nobody's p.** personne n'est parfait

2 *(complete* ► *agreement, mastery etc)* parfait, complet(ète); *(as intensifier)* véritable, parfait; **there was p. silence** il y avait un silence total; **you have a p. right to be here** vous avez parfaitement *ou* tout à fait le droit d'être ici; **it makes p. sense (to me)** ça me semble tout à fait logique; **he's a p. idiot** c'est un parfait imbécile

3 *(fine, lovely* ► *conditions)* parfait, idéal; *(*► *weather)* idéal, superbe; **it was a p. day** *(weather)* il faisait un temps magnifique; *(activities)* nous avons passé une excellente journée

4 *(fitting, right* ► *example)* parfait, approprié; **the p. gift** le cadeau idéal; **the p. opportunity** l'occasion idéale *ou* rêvée; **tonight at 7? – that will be p.** ce soir à 7 heures? – c'est parfait; **Monday is p. for me** lundi me convient parfaitement; **the colour is p. on you** cette couleur te va à merveille *ou* à la perfection

5 *(exemplary* ► *gentleman, host)* parfait, exemplaire

6 *Mus* **to have p. pitch** avoir l'oreille absolue

7 *Bot* parfait

N ['pɜːfɪkt] *Gram* parfait *m*; **in the p.** au parfait

VT [pə'fekt] **1** *(improve* ► *knowledge, skill)* perfectionner, parfaire **2** *(bring to final form* ► *plans, method)* mettre au point

►► *Mus* **perfect cadence** cadence *f* parfaite; *Econ* **perfect competition** concurrence *f* parfaite; *Mus* **perfect fifth** quinte *f* juste; *Mus* **perfect fourth** quarte *f* juste; *Math* **perfect number** nombre *m* parfait; *Gram* **perfect participle** participe *m* passé; *Gram* **the perfect tense** le parfait

perfectibility [pə,fektə'bɪlɪtɪ] N perfectibilité *f*

perfectible [pə'fektəbəl] ADJ perfectible

perfection [pə'fekʃən] N **1** *(quality)* perfection *f*; **to attain p.** atteindre la perfection; **this cake is p.!** ce gâteau est un vrai délice!; **to do sth to p.** faire qch à la perfection **2** *(perfecting* ► *of skill, knowledge)* perfectionnement *m*; *(*► *of plans, method)* mise *f* au point

perfectionism [pə'fekʃənɪzəm] N perfectionnisme *m*

perfectionist [pə'fekʃənɪst] N perfectionniste *mf*

ADJ perfectionniste

erfective [pə'fektɪv] ADJ *Gram* perfectif

erfectly ['pɜːfɪktlɪ] ADV **1** *(speak, understand)* ·arfaitement; **p. formed** d'une forme parfaite **2** *as intensifier)* tout à fait, parfaitement; **you are . right** vous avez parfaitement *ou* tout à fait rai-on; **to be p. honest/frank with you** pour être tout fait honnête/franc avec vous; **you know p. well** *what I mean)* tu le sais parfaitement bien *ou* très ·ien; **it's a p. good raincoat** cet imperméable est ɔut à fait mettable

erfecto [pɜː'fektəʊ] *(pl* **perfectos)** N *Am (cigar)* = ·igare effilé aux deux bouts

erfidious [pə'fɪdɪəs] ADJ *Literary* perfide
·► *perfidious Albion* la perfide Albion

erfidiously [pə'fɪdɪəslɪ] ADV *Literary* perfide-nent

erfidiousness [pə'fɪdɪəsnɪs], **perfidy** ['pɜːfɪdɪ] *pl* **perfidies)** N *Literary* perfidie *f*

erforate ['pɜːfəreɪt] VT **1** *(pierce)* perforer, per-:er **2** *Tech (punch holes in)* perforer

erforated ['pɜːfəreɪtɪd] ADJ perforé, percé; *Aed* **to have a p. eardrum** avoir un tympan per-ɔré *ou* crevé; **tear along the p. line** *(on form)* déta-·her suivant les pointillés
·► *Comput* ***perforated paper*** papier *m* à bandes ·erforées; *Comput* ***perforated tape*** bande *f* per-ɔrée; *Med* ***perforated ulcer*** perforation *f* ulcé-euse

erforation [,pɜːfə'reɪʃən] N perforation *f*

erforce [pə'fɔːs] ADV *Literary* forcément, né-·essairement

erform [pə'fɔːm] VT **1** *(carry out ► manoeuvre, ask)* exécuter, accomplir; *(► calculation)* effec-uer, faire; *(► miracle)* accomplir; *(► wedding, rit-al)* célébrer; **the robot can p. complex move-nents** le robot peut exécuter des mouvements omplexes; *Med* **to p. an operation** opérer **2** *(fulfil · function, duty)* remplir; **the agency performs a ·ital service** l'agence remplit une fonction vitale **3** *(stage ► play)* jouer, donner; *(► ballet, opera)* in-erpréter, jouer; *(► concert)* donner; *(► piece of music)* exécuter; **to p. a part** *Theat* jouer *ou* inter-·réter un rôle; *(in ballet)* danser un rôle

VI **1** *(actor, comedian, musician)* jouer; *(dancer)* lanser; *(singer)* chanter; **the Berlin Philharmonic s performing tonight** l'Orchestre philharmo-ique de Berlin donne un concert *ou* joue ce oir; **she performed superbly in the role of Lady racknell** elle a magnifiquement interprété le ôle de Lady Bracknell

2 *(person ► in job, situation)* se débrouiller; **to p. vell/badly** bien/ne pas bien s'en tirer; **how does he p. under pressure?** comment réagit-elle lors-u'elle est sous pression?; **I couldn't p.** *(sexually)* e n'ai pas pu

3 *(company, business)* fonctionner; *(shares, in-estment, currency)* se comporter; **to p. well/ ·adly** *(company)* avoir de bons/mauvais résul-ats; **the Miami branch is not performing well** les ésultats de la succursale de Miami ne sont pas rès satisfaisants; **how did the company p. in the irst quarter?** comment la société a-t-elle fonc-ionné au premier trimestre?

4 *(function ► vehicle, machine)* marcher, fonc-ionner; **the car performs well/badly in wet condi-ions** cette voiture a une bonne/mauvaise tenue le route par temps de pluie

erformance [pə'fɔːməns] N **1** *(show)* spectacle *n*, représentation *f*; *Cin* séance *f*; **there is no p. on Mondays** il n'y a pas de représentation le lundi, e lundi est jour de relâche

2 *(rendition ► by actor, musician, dancer)* inter-·rétation *f*; **he gave an excellent p. in the role of Othello** son interprétation du rôle d'Othello fut emarquable

3 *(showing ► by sportsman, politician etc)* perfor-nance *f*, prestation *f*; *(► by pupil, economy, ex-·orts, company)* résultats *mpl*, performances *pl*; *(► by employee)* rendement *m*, performance ; *(► by shares, investment, currency)* perfor-nance *f*; **to put up a good p.** *(team, athlete etc)* ac-omplir une bonne performance; *(in exam, nterview, court case)* bien s'en tirer; **another poor . by the French team** encore une contre-·erformance de l'équipe française; **the country's ·oor economic p.** les mauvais résultats économi-ues du pays; **sterling's p. on the Stock Exchange** le comportement en Bourse de la livre sterling; **sexual p.** prouesses *fpl* sexuelles

4 *(of machine, computer, car)* performance *f*

5 *(carrying out ► of task, manoeuvre)* exécution *f*; *(► of miracle, duties)* accomplissement *m*; *(► of ritual)* célébration *f*

6 *Fam (rigmarole)* histoire *f*, cirque *m*; **it's such a p. getting a visa!** quelle histoire *ou* quel cirque pour avoir un visa!; **what a p.!** quel cirque!

7 *Ling* performance *f*

►► ***performance appraisal*** *(system)* système *m* d'évaluation; *(individual)* évaluation *f*; ***performance art*** performance *f*, action *f*; ***performance artist*** = artiste spécialisé dans la performance; *Fin* ***performance bond*** garantie *f* de bonne fin *ou* de bonne exécution; *Aut* ***performance car*** voiture *f* puissante, voiture *f* haute performance; ***performance indicator*** indice *m* de performance; ***performance pay*** prime *f* de mérite *or* de résultat; *Fin* ***performance ratio*** coefficient *m ou* ratio *m* d'exploitation; *Psy & Mktg* ***performance test*** test *m* de performance

> Note that the French word **performance** never means **show**.

performance-enhancing ADJ *(drug)* qui améliore les performances

performance-related ADJ en fonction du mérite *ou* résultat
►► ***performance-related pay*** salaire *m* au mérite

performative [pə'fɔːmətɪv] ADJ *Ling & Phil* performatif
N *Ling (verb)* performatif *m*; *(utterance)* énoncé *m* performatif

performer [pə'fɔːmə(r)] N *(singer, dancer, actor)* interprète *mf*; **nightclub p.** artiste *mf* de cabaret; **he's a good stage p. but awful on camera** il est très bon sur la scène mais il ne passe pas du tout à l'écran; **he has been a consistent p.** *(in sport)* il a toujours été régulier

performing [pə'fɔːmɪŋ] ADJ *(bear, dog etc)* savant
►► ***performing arts*** arts *mpl* du spectacle; ***performing rights*** *Theat* droits *mpl* de représentation; *Mus* droits *mpl* d'exécution

perfume N ['pɜːfjuːm] **1** *(bottled)* parfum *m*; **I don't usually wear p.** d'habitude je ne me parfume pas; **what p. does she wear** *or* **use?** quel parfum met-elle?, quel est son parfum? **2** *(smell)* parfum *m*
VT [pə'fjuːm] parfumer
►► ***perfume counter*** *(in shop)* rayon *m* parfumerie; ***perfume spray*** atomiseur *m* de parfum

perfumed [*Br* 'pɜːfjuːmd, *Am* pɜː'fjuːmd] ADJ parfumé

perfumery [pə'fjuːmərɪ] *(pl* **perfumeries)** N parfumerie *f*

perfunctorily [pə'fʌŋktərəlɪ] ADV *(wave, greet)* machinalement; *(explain, apologize, search)* sommairement; *(read out, announce)* sans conviction

perfunctory [pə'fʌŋktərɪ] ADJ *(greeting, gesture)* machinal; *(explanation, apology, letter)* sommaire; *(effort)* de pure forme; *(interrogation, search)* fait pour la forme; *(manner)* brusque; **he greeted me with a p. nod** il me salua machinalement d'un signe de la tête

pergola ['pɜːgələ] N pergola *f*

perhaps [pə'hæps] ADV peut-être; **p. he's forgotten** peut-être qu'il a oublié, il a peut-être oublié; **p. not** peut-être que non; **p. you'd be kind enough to close the door** peut-être aurais-tu la gentillesse de fermer la porte

perigee ['perɪdʒiː] N *Astron* périgée *m*

perihelion [,perɪ'hiːlɪən] N *Astron* périhélie *m*

peril ['perɪl] N péril *m*, danger *m*; **the perils of hard drugs** le danger des drogues dures; **to be in p.** être en péril *ou* danger; **in p. of one's life** en danger de mort; *Br* **you do it at your p.** c'est à vos risques et périls

perilous ['perɪləs] ADJ périlleux, dangereux

perilously ['perɪləslɪ] ADV périlleusement, dangereusement; **he came p. close to defeat/drowning** il s'en est fallu d'un cheveu qu'il ne perde/qu'il ne se noie; **to come p. close to disaster** frôler la catastrophe

perimeter [pə'rɪmɪtə(r)] N périmètre *m*
►► ***perimeter fence*** grillage *m*

perinatal [,perɪ'neɪtəl] ADJ périnatal

perineum [,perɪ'niːəm] *(pl* **perinea** [-'niːə]) N *Anat* périnée *m*

period ['pɪərɪəd] N **1** *(length of time)* période *f*; *(historical epoch)* période *f*, époque *f*; **within a p. of a few months** en l'espace de quelques mois; **we have a two-month p. in which to do it** nous avons un délai de deux mois pour le faire; **he's going through a difficult p.** il traverse une période difficile; **he found a job after a long p. of unemployment** il a trouvé un emploi après avoir été au chômage pendant longtemps; **a p. of colonial expansion** une période d'expansion coloniale; **the Elizabethan p.** l'époque élisabéthaine; **at that p. in her life** à cette époque de sa vie; **his cubist/jazz p.** sa période cubiste/jazz

2 *Geol* période *f*; **the Jurassic p.** la période jurassique

3 *Sch (lesson)* cours *m*; **during the Latin p.** pendant le cours de latin; **a free p.** *(for pupil)* une heure de permanence; *(for teacher)* une heure de battement

4 *(in ice hockey)* période *f*

5 *Astron* **p. of rotation** période *f* de rotation

6 *(menstruation)* règles *fpl*; **I've got my p.** j'ai mes règles; **my periods have stopped** je n'ai plus mes règles

7 *Am (full stop)* point *m*

8 *(sentence)* période *f*

9 *Chem (in periodic table)* période *f*

10 *Mus* période *f*

COMP *(furniture, costume)* d'époque; *(novel)* historique; **the play has a definite p. flavour** la pièce nous transporte vraiment dans une autre époque

ADV *Fam* **you're not going out alone, p.!** tu ne sortiras pas tout seul, un point c'est tout!; **I said no, p.** j'ai dit non, point final

►► *Fin* ***period bill*** effet *m* à terme; ***period detail*** détail *m* historique; *Fin* ***period of grace*** délai *m* de grâce; ***period pains*** règles *fpl* douloureuses; ***period piece*** *(object, antique)* objet *m* d'époque; *(film)* film *m* historique; *(play)* pièce *f* historique

periodic [,pɪərɪ'ɒdɪk] ADJ **1** *(gen)* périodique **2** *Chem & Math* périodique
►► ***periodic function*** fonction *f* périodique; ***periodic law*** loi *f* périodique; *Chem* ***periodic table*** classification *f* périodique (des éléments), tableau *m* de Mendeleïev; *Econ* ***periodic unemployment*** chômage *m* récurrent

periodical [,pɪərɪ'ɒdɪkəl] N *(publication)* périodique *m*
ADJ périodique
►► ***periodical press*** presse *f* périodique

periodically [,pɪərɪ'ɒdɪkəlɪ] ADV périodiquement, de temps en temps

periodontal [,perɪə'dɒntəl] ADJ *Med* parodontal

peripatetic [,perɪpə'tetɪk] ADJ *(itinerant)* itinérant
►► *Br Sch* ***peripatetic teacher*** = professeur qui enseigne dans plusieurs établissements scolaires

peripheral [pə'rɪfərəl] ADJ **1** *(gen)* périphérique **2** *Fig (unimportant)* secondaire; **of purely p. importance** d'une importance tout à fait secondaire; **this issue is p. to the central debate** ce problème est accessoire au débat principal
N *Comput* périphérique *m*
►► *Comput* ***peripheral device, peripheral unit*** unité *f* périphérique; ***peripheral vision*** vue *f* périphérique

periphery [pə'rɪfərɪ] *(pl* **peripheries)** N **1** *(of circle, vision, city etc)* périphérie *f*; **on the p.** à la périphérie **2** *(of group, movement)* frange *f*; **on the p. of society** en marge de la société

periphrasis [pə'rɪfrəsɪs] *(pl* **periphrases** [-siːz]) N périphrase *f*, circonlocution *f*

periphrastic [,perɪ'fræstɪk] ADJ périphrastique

periscope ['perɪskəʊp] N périscope *m*; **up p.!** sortez le périscope!

perish ['perɪʃ] VI **1** *Br (rot ► rubber, leather etc)* s'abîmer, se détériorer; *(► food)* se gâter, pourrir **2** *Literary (die)* périr; **p. the thought!** loin de moi cette pensée!; **you're not pregnant, are you? – p.**

the thought! tu n'es pas enceinte au moins? – tu veux rire *ou* j'espère bien que non!; **if, p. the thought, he were to die** si, Dieu nous en préserve, il venait à mourir

VT *(rubber, leather)* abîmer, détériorer; *(food)* gâter

perishability [ˌperɪʃə'bɪlɪtɪ] **N** *Com* périssabilité *f*

perishable ['perɪʃəbəl] **ADJ** périssable

• **perishables NPL** denrées *fpl* périssables

perished ['perɪʃt] **ADJ** *Br Fam (very cold)* frigorifié; **I'm p.** je meurs de froid, je suis frigorifié

perisher ['perɪʃə(r)] **N** *Br Fam* galopin *m*

perishing ['perɪʃɪŋ] **ADJ** *Br Fam* **1** *(very cold ▸ person, hands)* frigorifié; **it's p. (cold)** il fait un froid de canard *ou* de loup **2** *Old-fashioned (as intensifier)* sacré, fichu, foutu; **that p. telephone** ce fichu téléphone; **what a p. nuisance!** c'est vraiment casse-pied!

peristalsis [ˌperɪ'stælsɪs] *(pl* **peristalses** [-siːz]) **N** *Physiol* péristaltisme *m*

peristyle ['perɪstaɪl] **N** *Archit* péristyle *m*

peritoneum [ˌperɪtə'niːəm] *(pl* **peritoneums** *or* **peritonea** [-'niːə]) **N** *Anat* péritoine *m*

peritonitis [ˌperɪtə'naɪtɪs] **N** *(UNCOUNT) Med* péritonite *f*; **to have p.** avoir une péritonite

periwig ['perɪwɪg] **N** *Hist* perruque *f*

periwinkle ['perɪˌwɪŋkəl] **N 1** *Bot* pervenche *f* **2** *Zool* bigorneau *m*

▸▸ ***periwinkle blue*** bleu *m* pervenche

perjure ['pɜːdʒə(r)] **VT to p. oneself** faire un faux témoignage

perjurer ['pɜːdʒərə(r)] **N** faux témoin *m*

perjury ['pɜːdʒərɪ] *(pl* **perjuries) N** faux témoignage *m*; **to commit p.** faire un faux témoignage

perk [pɜːk] *Fam* **N** *(from job)* avantage *m* en nature ▫; *(advantage)* avantage ▫ *m*; **cheap air travel is one of the perks of his job** un des avantages de son boulot, c'est qu'il peut prendre l'avion pour trois fois rien

VT *(coffee)* passer ▫

VI *(coffee)* passer ▫

▸ **perk up VT SEP** *(cheer up)* remonter, ragaillardir, revigouer; *(liven up)* revigorer; **the news really perked me up** la nouvelle m'a vraiment remonté le moral; **some wine will p. you up** un peu de vin te remontera

VI 1 *(cheer up)* se ragaillardir, retrouver le moral; **he perked up in the afternoon** il a retrouvé son entrain l'après-midi **2** *(become interested)* dresser l'oreille *ou* la tête **3** *(ears, head)* se dresser

perkily ['pɜːkɪlɪ] **ADV** *(in a lively manner)* d'un air animé; *(answer, say)* d'un ton dégagé *ou* désinvolte

perky ['pɜːkɪ] *(compar* **perkier,** *superl* **perkiest) ADJ** *(lively)* plein d'entrain, animé; *(cheerful)* guilleret; *(tone)* dégagé, désinvolte

perm [pɜːm] **VT** *(hair)* permanenter; **her hair is permed** elle a les cheveux permanentés; **I've had my hair permed** je me suis fait faire une permanente

N 1 *(in hair)* permanente *f*; **to have a p.** se faire faire une permanente **2** *Br (permutation)* = combinaison jouée dans les paris sur les matches de football en Grande-Bretagne

permafrost ['pɜːməfrɒst] **N** permagel *m*, permafrost *m*, pergélisol *m*

permanence ['pɜːmənəns] **N** permanence *f*, caractère *m* permanent

permanency ['pɜːmənənsɪ] *(pl* **permanencies) N 1** *(person, thing)* **they predicted that computers would be a p. in every office** ils avaient prévu que les ordinateurs deviendraient indispensables dans tous les bureaux **2** *(state, quality)* permanence *f*, caractère *m* permanent

permanent ['pɜːmənənt] **ADJ** permanent; **no p. damage was caused** aucun dégât irréparable n'a été occasionné; **are you here on a p. basis?** êtes-vous ici à titre définitif?; **she has taken up p. residence abroad** elle s'est installée définitivement à l'étranger

N *Am (in hair)* permanente *f*

▸▸ ***permanent address*** domicile *m*; *Fin* ***permanent assets*** actif *m* immobilisé; *Fin* ***permanent credit*** accréditif *m* permanent; *Ins* ***permanent health insurance*** assurance *f* longue maladie; ***permanent ink*** encre *f* indélébile; ***permanent magnet*** aimant *m* permanent; ***permanent post*** *(gen)* emploi *m* permanent; *(in public service)* poste *f* de titulaire; *Pol* ***permanent representation*** représentation *f* permanente; *Pol* ***permanent representative*** représentant *m* permanent; *Br* ***Permanent Secretary*** chef *m* de cabinet; ***permanent staff*** *(gen)* personnel *m* permanent; *(in public service)* personnel *m* titulaire; ***permanent tooth*** dent *f* permanente; *Br* ***Permanent Undersecretary*** ≃ secrétaire *mf* général(e) *(dans la fonction publique)*; ***permanent wave*** permanente *f*; *Br* ***permanent way*** voie *f* ferrée

permanganate [pɜː'mæŋgəneɪt] **N** *Chem* permanganate *m*

permatan ['pɜːmətæn] **N** *Fam Hum* bronzage *m* permanent ▫

permeability [ˌpɜːmɪə'bɪlətɪ] **N** perméabilité *f*

permeable ['pɜːmɪəbəl] **ADJ** perméable

permeate ['pɜːmɪeɪt] **VT 1** *(of gas, smell)* se répandre dans; **a lovely smell permeated the kitchen** une merveilleuse odeur emplissait la cuisine **2** *(of liquid)* s'infiltrer dans; **damp had permeated the floorboards** le plancher était imprégné *ou* gorgé d'humidité; **the sand is permeated with oil** le sable est imbibé de pétrole **3** *Fig (of ideas)* imprégner; *(of feelings)* envahir, emplir; **an atmosphere of gloom permeates his novels** ses romans sont empreints d'une mélancolie profonde; **the optimism that permeated the sixties** l'optimisme qui prévalait *ou* dominait dans les années soixante

VI 1 *(gas)* se répandre, se diffuser; *(smell)* se répandre **2** *(liquid)* filtrer; **rain water had permeated through the walls** les eaux de pluie avaient filtré à travers les murs **3** *Fig (ideas, feelings)* se répandre, se propager

Permian ['pɜːmɪən] *Geol* **N** permien *m*

ADJ permien

permissible [pə'mɪsəbəl] **ADJ** *Formal* **1** *(allowed)* permis, autorisé; **is it p. for him to take two days off?** est-ce qu'il est autorisé à prendre deux jours de congé? **2** *(tolerable ▸ behaviour)* admissible, acceptable; **degree of p. error** marge *f* d'erreur admissible *ou* admise

permission [pə'mɪʃən] **N** permission *f*, autorisation *f*; **to ask for p. to do sth** demander la permission *ou* l'autorisation de faire qch; **to have p. to do sth** avoir la permission *ou* l'autorisation de faire qch; **to give sb p. to do sth** donner à qn la permission de faire qch; **who gave them p.?** qui le leur a permis?; **who gave him p. to go out?** qui lui a permis de *ou* l'a autorisé à sortir?; **with your p.** avec votre permission, si vous le permettez; **without my/your/her p.** sans ma/votre/sa permission; **photos published by kind p. of Picturebank** photos publiées avec l'aimable autorisation de Picturebank; **you need written p. to work at home** il faut une autorisation écrite pour travailler chez soi; *St Exch* **p. to deal** visa *m (de la COB)*

permissive [pə'mɪsɪv] **ADJ** *(tolerant ▸ behaviour, parent etc)* permissif; **the p. society** la société permissive

▸▸ ***permissive path*** = sentier privé dont le propriétaire autorise l'accès au public

permissively [pə'mɪsɪvlɪ] **ADV** de manière permissive

permissiveness [pə'mɪsɪvnɪs] **N** *(morally)* permissivité *f*

permit *(pt & pp* **permitted,** *cont* **permitting) VT** [pə'mɪt] **1** *(allow)* permettre, autoriser; **to p. sb to do sth** permettre à qn de faire qch, autoriser qn à faire qch; **she was permitted to take two weeks off** on l'a autorisée à prendre deux semaines de congé; **p. me to inform you that…** laissez-moi vous apprendre que…; **he won't p. it** il ne le permettra pas; **you are not permitted to enter the building** vous n'avez pas le droit de pénétrer dans l'immeuble; **smoking is not permitted upstairs** il est interdit de fumer à l'étage; **the hotel won't p. animals in the bedrooms** l'hôtel n'autorise pas la présence d'animaux dans les chambres **2** *(enable)* permettre; **the computer permits her to take more time off** l'ordinateur lui laisse plus de temps libre

VI [pə'mɪt] permettre; **weather permitting** si le temps le permet; **if time permits** si j'ai/nous avons/*etc* le temps

N ['pɜːmɪt] *(authorization)* autorisation *f*, perm[is] *m*; *(pass)* laissez-passer *m inv*; **export/drinks** [p.] licence *f* d'exportation/pour la vente de boi[s]sons alcoolisées; **p. holders only** *(on sign)* r[é]servé aux personnes autorisées

▸▸ *BrAdmin* ***permitted hours*** *(for selling alcoho[l])* = heures légales de vente des boissons alcool[i]sées

▸ **permit of VT INSEP** *Formal (admit possibility o[f])* admettre; **this permits of only one explanation** c[e]ci n'admet qu'une explication

permutation [ˌpɜːmjuː'teɪʃən] **N** *Math* permuta[]tion *f*

permute [pə'mjuːt] **VT** permuter

pernicious [pə'nɪʃəs] **ADJ 1** *(harmful)* pern[i]cieux **2** *(malicious ▸ gossip, lie)* malveillant

▸▸ *Med* ***pernicious anaemia*** anémie *f* pernicieus[e]

perniciously [pə'nɪʃəslɪ] **ADV** pernicieuseme[nt]

pernickety [pə'nɪkətɪ], *Am* **persnickety** [p[ə]'snɪkɪtɪ] **ADJ** *Fam* **1** *Pej (person ▸ fussy)* tatillon, ch[i]poteur; *(▸ hard to please)* difficile ▫; **to be about one's food** être difficile sur la nourriture *(fiddly ▸ job)* délicat ▫, minutieux ▫

perorate ['perəreɪt] **VI** *Formal* **1** *(conclude speec[h])* faire la péroraison **2** *(speak at length)* discour[ir] longuement, pérorer

peroration [ˌperə'reɪʃən] **N** *Formal* **1** *(conclusio[n])* péroraison *f* **2** *(long speech)* long discours *m*, di[s]cours *m* de longue haleine

peroxide [pə'rɒksaɪd] **N 1** *Chem* peroxyde *m* *(for hair)* eau *f* oxygénée

VT *(bleach ▸ hair)* décolorer, *Spec* oxygéner

▸▸ *Pej* ***peroxide blonde*** *(woman)* blonde *f* décol[o]rée

perp [pɜːp] **N** *Am Fam Crime slang (abbr* **perpetr[a]tor)** auteur ▫ *m*

perpendicular [ˌpɜːpən'dɪkjʊlə(r)] **ADJ 1** *Geo[m]* perpendiculaire **(to** à) **2** *(vertical ▸ cliff)* e[s]carpé, abrupt, à pic; *(▸ slope)* raide, à pic

N perpendiculaire *f*; **the tower is out of (the) p.** [la] tour n'est pas verticale *ou Spec* est hors d'aplom[b]

• **Perpendicular ADJ** *Archit* perpendiculaire

perpendicularly [ˌpɜːpən'dɪkjʊləlɪ] **ADV** pe[r]pendiculairement; *(rise, fall, drop)* verticale[]ment, à la verticale; *(be built)* d'aplomb; **the cl[iff] rose p.** la falaise s'élevait tout droit

perpetrate ['pɜːpɪtreɪt] **VT** *Formal (commit crime)* commettre, *Literary* perpétrer; *(▸ erro[r])* commettre; **she perpetrated several frauds** elle [a] escroqué plusieurs personnes; **to p. a hoax** ét[re] l'auteur d'une farce

perpetration [ˌpɜːpɪ'treɪʃən] **N** *Formal* perpétr[a]tion *f*

perpetrator ['pɜːpɪtreɪtə(r)] **N** *Formal* auteur *[m]*; **the p. of the crime** l'auteur du délit

perpetual [pə'petʃʊəl] **ADJ 1** *(state, worry)* pe[r]pétuel; *(noise, questions)* continuel, incessan[t]; **her p. coughing kept me awake all night** sa tou[x] incessante m'a gardé éveillé toute la nuit; **it's p. worry to us** c'est pour nous un sujet d'inqui[é]tude *ou* un souci permanent; **p. snows** neiges *f* éternelles **2** *Hort* perpétuel

▸▸ ***perpetual calendar*** calendrier *m* perpétue[l]; *Chess* ***perpetual check*** échec *m* perpétuel; *F[in]* ***perpetual loan*** emprunt *m* perpétuel; ***perpetu[al] motion*** mouvement *m* perpétuel

perpetually [pə'petʃʊəlɪ] **ADV** perpétuell[e]ment, sans cesse; **they're p. complaining** ils so[nt] toujours à se plaindre, ils se plaignent sans a[r]rêt

perpetuate [pə'petʃʊeɪt] **VT** perpétuer

perpetuation [pəˌpetʃʊ'eɪʃən] **N** perpétuation

perpetuity [ˌpɜːpɪ'tjuːətɪ] *(pl* **perpetuities) N** *(eternity)* perpétuité *f*; **in** *or* **for p.** à perpétuité *(annuity)* rente *f* perpétuelle

perplex [pə'pleks] **VT 1** *(puzzle)* rendre *ou* laiss[er] perplexe; **his questions perplexed us** ses que[s]tions nous ont laissés perplexes *ou* nous o[nt] plongés dans la perplexité **2** *(complicate)* co[m]pliquer

perplexed [pə'plekst] **ADJ** perplexe; **I'm p. abo[ut] what to do** je ne sais pas trop quoi faire

perplexing [pə'pleksɪŋ] ADJ inexplicable, incompréhensible; **I find their silence rather p.** je me demande bien ce que peut signifier leur silence; **he asked us some p. questions** il a posé des questions qui nous ont laissés perplexes

perplexity [pə'pleksətɪ] N **1** *(confusion)* perplexité *f* **2** *(complexity ▸ of problem)* complexité *f*

perquisite ['pɜːkwɪzɪt] N *Formal (from job)* avantage *m* en nature; *(advantage)* avantage *m*

perry ['perɪ] *(pl* **perries***)* N poiré *m*

persecute ['pɜːsɪkjuːt] VT **1** *(oppress)* persécuter; **they were persecuted for their religious beliefs** ils ont été persécutés à cause de leurs convictions religieuses **2** *(pester)* persécuter, harceler; **they persecuted her with questions** ils l'ont harcelée de questions

persecution [ˌpɜːsɪ'kjuːʃən] N persécution *f*

▸▸ *Psy* ***persecution complex*** délire *m* de persécution; *Psy* ***persecution mania*** manie *f* de la persécution

persecutor ['pɜːsɪkjuːtə(r)] N persécuteur(trice) *m,f*

perseverance [ˌpɜːsɪ'vɪərəns] N persévérance *f*

persevere [ˌpɜːsɪ'vɪə(r)] VI persévérer; **p. in your efforts** persévérez dans vos efforts; **you must p. with your studies** il faut persévérer dans vos études

persevering [ˌpɜːsɪ'vɪərɪŋ] ADJ persévérant, obstiné

Persia ['pɜːʃə] N Perse *f*

Persian ['pɜːʃən] N **1** *(person)* Persan(e) *m,f*; *Antiq* Perse *mf* **2** *Ling (modern)* persan *m*; *(ancient)* perse *m*

ADJ persan; *Antiq* perse

▸▸ ***Persian blinds*** persiennes *fpl*; ***Persian carpet*** tapis *m* persan; ***Persian cat*** chat *m* persan; ***the Persian Gulf*** le golfe Persique; ***persian lamb*** *(animal, fur)* karakul *m*, caracul *m*

persimmon [pə'sɪmən] N **1** *(fruit)* plaquemine *f*, kaki *m* **2** *(tree)* plaqueminier *m*

persist [pə'sɪst] VI **1** *(person)* persister; **to p. in doing sth** persister *ou* s'obstiner à faire qch; **he persists in the belief that...** il persiste à croire que... **2** *(weather, problem, fever etc)* persister

persistence [pə'sɪstəns], **persistency** [pə'sɪstənsɪ] N **1** *(perseverance)* persistance *f*, persévérance *f*; *(insistence)* persistance *f*, insistance *f*; *(obstinacy)* obstination *f*; **his p. in asking awkward questions** son obstination à poser des questions embarrassantes **2** *(continuation ▸ of rain, problem, belief etc)* persistance *f*

▸▸ *Cin* ***persistence of vision*** persistance *f* rétinienne, rémanence *f*

persistent [pə'sɪstənt] ADJ **1** *(continual ▸ demands, rain etc)* continuel, incessant

2 *(lingering ▸ smell, fever, pain etc)* persistant, tenace

3 *(persevering)* persévérant

4 *Bot* persistant

▸▸ *Law* ***persistent cruelty*** sévices *mpl* répétés; ***persistent offender*** récidiviste *mf*; *Med* ***persistent vegetative state*** état *m* végétatif chronique

persistently [pə'sɪstəntlɪ] ADV **1** *(continually)* continuellement, sans cesse; **I've warned you p.** je me suis acharné à vous prévenir; **they p. insult him** ils ne cessent de l'insulter **2** *(perseveringly)* avec persévérance *ou* persistance, obstinément

persnickety [pə'snɪkɪtɪ] *Am* = **pernickety**

person ['pɜːsən] *(pl* **people** ['piːpəl] *or Formal* **persons***)* N **1** *(individual)* personne *f*; **he's just the p. we need** c'est exactement la personne qu'il nous faut; **a young p.** *(female)* une jeune personne; *(male)* un jeune homme; *Law* **by a p. or persons unknown** par des personnes inconnues *ou* non identifiées; **she is a nice/strange p.** c'est une personne gentille/étrange, c'est quelqu'un de gentil/d'étrange; **I like him as a p.** je l'aime bien en tant que personne; **he's not that sort of p.** ce n'est pas du tout son genre; *Fam* **I'm not a great eating-out p.** je n'aime pas beaucoup manger au restaurant ▫; *Fam* **are you a cat p. or a dog p.?** est-ce que tu préfères les chats ou chiens? ▫; **in the p. of** en la personne de

2 *Formal (body)* personne *f*; **to have sth on** *or* **about one's p.** avoir qch sur soi; **she had the wallet concealed about her p.** le portefeuille était caché sur elle

3 *Gram* personne *f*; **in the first p. plural** à la première personne du pluriel

4 *Rel* personne *f*

• **in person** ADV en personne; **she came in p.** elle est venue en personne; **this letter must be delivered to him in p.** cette lettre doit lui être remise en mains propres

persona [pə'səʊnə] *(pl* **personas** *or* **personae** [-niː]*)* N *Literature & Psy* personnage *m*; **to take on a new p.** se créer un personnage

personable ['pɜːsənəbəl] ADJ plaisant, charmant; **he's a very p. young man** c'est un jeune homme qui présente très bien

personage ['pɜːsənɪdʒ] N *Formal* personnage *m* *(individu)*

personal ['pɜːsənəl] ADJ **1** *(individual ▸ experience, belief etc)* personnel; **my p. opinion is that he drowned** personnellement, je crois qu'il s'est noyé; **you get more p. attention in small shops** on s'occupe mieux de vous dans les petits magasins; **will you do me a p. favour?** pourriez-vous m'accorder une faveur?

2 *(in person)* personnel; **under the p. supervision of the author** supervisé personnellement par l'auteur; **the boss made a p. visit to the scene** le patron est venu lui-même *ou* en personne sur les lieux; **p. callers welcome** *(sign)* vente en gros et au détail

3 *(private ▸ message, letter)* personnel; **p. and private** *(on letter)* strictement confidentiel

4 *(for one's own use)* personnel; **to be careless about one's p. appearance** négliger sa tenue; **this is for my p. use** ceci est destiné à mon usage personnel

5 *(intimate ▸ feelings, reasons, life)* personnel; **for p. reasons** pour des raisons personnelles; **I'd like to see her on a p. matter** je voudrais la voir pour des raisons personnelles; **just a few p. friends** rien que quelques amis intimes

6 *(offensive)* désobligeant; **there's no need to be so p.!** ce n'est pas la peine de t'en prendre à moi!; **nothing p.!** ne le prenez pas pour vous!, n'y voyez rien de personnel!; **it's nothing p. but...** ça n'a rien de personnel mais...; **the discussion was getting rather p.** la discussion prenait un tour un peu trop personnel

7 *Gram* personnel; **p. pronoun** pronom *m* personnel

N *Am (advert)* petite annonce *f (pour rencontres)*

▸▸ ***personal accident insurance*** assurance *f* contre les accidents corporels; ***personal account*** *Banking* compte *m* personnel; *St Exch* compte *m* de tiers; *Acct* compte *m* propre; *Fam* ***personal ad*** petite annonce ▫ *f (pour rencontres)*; *Fin* ***personal allowance*** abattement *m (sur l'impôt sur le revenu)*; *Banking* ***personal assets*** patrimoine *m*; ***personal assistant*** *(of executive)* assistant(e) *m,f*; *(with secretarial duties)* secrétaire *mf* de direction; ***personal belongings*** objets *mpl* personnels, affaires *fpl*; *Sport* ***personal best*** record *m* personnel; **he ran a p. best in the 200 m** il a battu son propre record *or* record personnel sur 200 m; *Tel* ***personal call*** appel *m* personnel *ou* privé; **is this a p. call?** c'est personnel?; ***personal column*** petites annonces *fpl (pour rencontres)*; **to put an ad in the p. column** passer une petite annonce; *Comput* ***personal computer*** ordinateur *m* individuel *ou* personnel, PC *m*; ***personal computing*** informatique *f* individuelle; ***personal credit*** crédit *m* personnel; *Comput* ***personal digital assistant*** agenda *m* électronique de poche, assistant *m* numérique de poche; ***personal effects*** effets *mpl* personnels; *Br Formerly Fin* ***personal equity plan*** ≃ plan *m* d'épargne en actions; ***personal estate*** biens *mpl* mobiliers personnels; ***personal foul*** *(in basketball)* faute *f* personnelle; *Comput* ***personal home page*** page *f* personnelle, page *f* perso; ***personal hygiene*** hygiène *f* corporelle; **he has a p. hygiene problem** il ne doit pas se laver bien souvent; *Banking* ***personal identification number*** code *m* confidentiel *(d'une carte bancaire)*; ***personal loan*** prêt *m* personnel, prêt *m* personnalisé; ***personal maid*** femme *f* de chambre; ***personal organizer*** organiseur *m*; *(electronic)* agenda *m* électronique, organiseur *m*; *Fin* ***personal pension plan*** retraite *f* personnelle; ***personal possessions*** objets *mpl* personnels, affaires *fpl*; ***personal property*** biens *mpl* mobiliers personnels; ***personal shopper*** acheteur(euse) *m,f* personnel(elle); ***personal stereo*** Walkman® *m*, *Offic* baladeur *m*; ***personal trainer*** entraîneur(euse) *m,f* personnel(elle); *Am* ***personal watercraft*** scooter *m* des mers, jet-ski *m*

personality [ˌpɜːsə'nælətɪ] *(pl* **personalities***)* N **1** *(character ▸ of person)* personnalité *f*, caractère *m*; *(▸ of thing, animal etc)* caractère *m*; **a woman with a lot of p.** une femme dotée d'une forte personnalité; **he's got no p.** il n'a aucune personnalité **2** *(famous person)* personnalité *f*; *Cin & TV* vedette *f*; **sports p.** vedette *f* du monde du sport; **media p.** vedette *f* des médias **3** *Psy* personnalité *f*

▸▸ ***personality cult*** culte *m* de la personnalité; ***personality disorder*** trouble *m* de la personnalité; **he has a serious p. disorder** il a de graves problèmes psychologiques; ***personality profile*** profil *m* de personnalité; ***personality test*** test *m* de personnalité, *Spec* test *m* projectif; ***personality type*** configuration *f* psychologique

personalize, -ise ['pɜːsənəlaɪz] VT **1** *(make personal ▸ gen)* personnaliser; *(▸ luggage, clothes)* marquer (à son nom) **2** *(argument, campaign)* donner un tour personnel à **3** *(personify)* personnifier

personally ['pɜːsnəlɪ] ADV **1** *(speaking for oneself)* personnellement, pour ma/sa/*etc* part; **p. (speaking), I think it's a silly idea** pour ma part *ou* en ce qui me concerne, je trouve que c'est une idée stupide

2 *(in person, directly)* en personne, personnellement; **I was not p. involved in the project** je n'ai pas participé directement au projet; **I want to speak to him p.** j'aimerais lui parler personnellement; **deliver the letter to the director p.** remettez la lettre en mains propres au directeur

3 *(not officially)* sur le plan personnel

4 *(individually)* personnellement; **I was talking about the whole team, not you p.** je parlais de toute l'équipe, pas de toi personnellement *ou* en particulier; **to take things p.** prendre les choses trop à cœur; **don't take it p.** *(what was said/done)* n'en faites pas une affaire personnelle; **don't take it p., but...** ne vous sentez pas visé, mais...; **I didn't mean it p.** ma remarque n'avait rien de personnel

personalty ['pɜːsənəltɪ] *(pl* **personalties***)* N *Law* biens *mpl* mobiliers; **to convert realty into p.** ameublir un bien

personification [pəˌsɒnɪfɪ'keɪʃən] N personnification *f*; **he is the p. of evil** c'est le mal personnifié *ou* en personne

personify [pə'sɒnɪfaɪ] *(pt & pp* **personified***)* VT personnifier; **he is evil personified** c'est le mal personnifié *ou* incarné

personnel [ˌpɜːsə'nel] N **1** *(staff)* personnel *m* **2** *(department)* service *m* du personnel; **she works in p.** elle travaille au service du personnel **3** *Mil (troops)* troupes *fpl*

▸▸ *Mil* ***personnel carrier*** (véhicule *m* de) transport *m* de troupes; ***personnel consultant*** conseiller(ère) *m,f* du travail; ***personnel department*** service *m* du personnel; ***personnel management*** direction *f ou* administration *f* du personnel; ***personnel officer*** responsable *mf* du personnel

perspective [pə'spektɪv] N **1** *Archit & Art* perspective *f*; **to draw sth in p.** dessiner qch en perspective; **the houses are out of p.** la perspective des maisons est fausse

2 *(opinion, viewpoint)* perspective *f*, optique *f*; **it gives you a different p. on the problem** cela vous permet de voir le problème sous un angle *ou* un jour différent; **from a psychological p.** d'un point de vue psychologique; **the latest developments put a new p. on the case** les derniers événements éclairent l'affaire d'un jour nouveau

3 *(proportion)* **we must try to keep our (sense of) p.** *or* **to keep things in p.** nous devons nous efforcer de garder notre sens des proportions; **to get things out of p.** perdre le sens des proportions; **it should help us to get** *or* **to put the role she played into p.** cela devrait nous aider à mesurer le rôle qu'elle a joué; **the figures must be looked at in (their proper) p.** il faut étudier les chiffres dans leur contexte

4 *Formal (view, vista)* perspective *f*, panorama *m*, vue *f*; **a fine p. opened out before his eyes** une belle perspective s'ouvrit devant ses yeux
ADJ *(drawing)* perspectif

Perspex® [ˈpɜːspeks] *Br* **N** Plexiglas® *m*
COMP *(window, windscreen etc)* en Plexiglas®

perspicacious [ˌpɜːspɪˈkeɪʃəs] **ADJ** *Formal (person)* perspicace; *(remark, judgment)* pénétrant, lucide

perspicaciously [ˌpɜːspɪˈkeɪʃəslɪ] **ADV** *Formal* avec perspicacité

perspicacity [ˌpɜːspɪˈkæsətɪ] **N** *Formal* perspicacité *f*

perspicuity [ˌpɜːspɪˈkjuːətɪ] **N** *Formal* clarté *f*, lucidité *f*

perspicuous [pəˈspɪkjuəs] **ADJ** *Formal* clair, lucide

perspicuously [pəˈspɪkjuəslɪ] **ADV** *Formal* clairement, nettement

perspiration [ˌpɜːspəˈreɪʃən] **N 1** *(sweat)* transpiration *f*, sueur *f*; **bathed in** *or* **dripping with p.** trempé de sueur, en nage **2** *(act)* transpiration *f*, perspiration *f*

perspire [pəˈspaɪə(r)] **VI** transpirer; **his hands were perspiring** il avait les mains moites; **she was perspiring freely** *or* **heavily** elle transpirait à grosses gouttes

persuadable [pəˈsweɪdəbəl] **ADJ** facile à persuader

persuade [pəˈsweɪd] **VT** persuader, convaincre; **to p. sb to do sth** persuader *ou* convaincre qn de faire qch; **to p. sb not to do sth** persuader qn de ne pas faire qch, dissuader qn de faire qch; **I managed to p. him (that) I was right** j'ai réussi à le persuader *ou* convaincre que j'avais raison; **I let myself be persuaded into coming** je me suis laissé convaincre qu'il fallait venir; **she persuaded herself that everything would work out** elle s'est persuadée *ou* convaincue elle-même que tout marcherait bien; *Fig* **she finally persuaded the car to start** elle a réussi à faire démarrer la voiture; *Formal* **I was persuaded of her innocence** j'étais convaincu *ou* persuadé qu'elle était innocente

persuasion [pəˈsweɪʒən] **N 1** *(act of convincing)* persuasion *f*; **the art of gentle p.** l'art de convaincre en douceur; **I used all my powers of p. on him** j'ai fait tout mon possible *ou* tout ce qui était en mon pouvoir pour le convaincre; **I wouldn't need much p. to give it up** il ne faudrait pas insister beaucoup pour que j'abandonne; **to be open to p.** être disposé à se laisser convaincre **2** *(belief) & Rel* confession *f*, religion *f*; *Pol* tendance *f*; **men and women of many persuasions** des hommes et des femmes de nombreuses confessions; **people, regardless of their political p.** les gens, quelles que soient leurs convictions politiques **3** *Formal (conviction)* conviction *f*

persuasive [pəˈsweɪsɪv] **ADJ** *(manner, speaker)* persuasif, convaincant; *(argument)* convaincant

persuasively [pəˈsweɪsɪvlɪ] **ADV** de façon convaincante *ou* persuasive; **she argues p.** elle emploie des arguments convaincants

persuasiveness [pəˈsweɪsɪvnəs] **N** *(of person)* force *f* persuasive *ou* de persuasion; *(of argument)* caractère *m* convaincant

pert [pɜːt] **ADJ 1** *(cheeky ▸ person, reply)* effronté **2** *(stylishly neat ▸ garment, hat)* coquet **3** *(nose)* mutin; *(bottom)* (petit et) ferme

pertain [pəˈteɪn] **VI 1** *(apply)* s'appliquer **2 to p. to** *(concern)* avoir rapport à, se rapporter à; *Law (of land, property)* se rattacher à, dépendre de; **the evidence pertaining to the case** les témoignages se rattachant *ou* se rapportant à l'affaire

pertinacious [ˌpɜːtɪˈneɪʃəs] **ADJ** *Formal* opiniâtre

pertinaciously [ˌpɜːtɪˈneɪʃəslɪ] **ADV** *Formal* opiniâtrement

pertinence [ˈpɜːtɪnəns] **N** pertinence *f*, à-propos *m*; **I don't see the p. of that remark** cette remarque ne me semble pas pertinente

pertinent [ˈpɜːtɪnənt] **ADJ** pertinent, à propos; **a very p. question** une question très pertinente

pertinently [ˈpɜːtɪnəntlɪ] **ADV** pertinemment, avec justesse *ou* à-propos

pertly [ˈpɜːtlɪ] **ADV** *(reply)* avec effronterie; *(dress)* coquettement

pertness [ˈpɜːtnɪs] **N** *(of reply, manner)* effronterie *f*; *(of garment, hat)* coquetterie *f*

perturb [pəˈtɜːb] **VT 1** *(worry)* inquiéter, troubler; **they were very perturbed by his disappearance** sa disparition les a beaucoup inquiétés **2** *Astron & Electron* perturber

perturbation [ˌpɜːtəˈbeɪʃən] **N 1** *Formal (anxiety)* trouble *m*, inquiétude *f* **2** *Astron & Electron* perturbation *f*

perturbed [pəˈtɜːbd] **ADJ** troublé, inquiet(ète); **I was p. to hear that he is ill** ça m'a troublé *ou* inquiété d'apprendre qu'il est malade

Peru [pəˈruː] **N** Pérou *m*

perusal [pəˈruːzəl] **N** *(thorough reading)* lecture *f* approfondie, examen *m*; *(quick reading)* lecture *f* sommaire, survol *m*; **he left the document for her p.** il lui a laissé le document pour information

peruse [pəˈruːz] **VT** *(read thoroughly)* lire attentivement, examiner; *(read quickly)* parcourir, survoler

Peruvian [pəˈruːvɪən] **N** Péruvien(enne) *m,f*
ADJ péruvien
COMP *(embassy, history)* du Pérou

perv [pɜːv] **N** *Br & Austr Fam* pervers(e)▫ *m,f*, détraqué(e) *m,f*
▸ **perv over VT INSEP** *Br & Austr Fam* baver devant *ou* sur; **there were all these horrible old men perving over us in the club** il y avait plein de vieux dégueulasses qui bavaient devant nous dans le club

pervade [pəˈveɪd] **VT 1** *(of gas, smell)* se répandre dans; **the scent of pine trees pervaded the air** l'air était embaumé de l'odeur des pins **2** *(of ideas)* se répandre dans, se propager à travers; *(of feelings)* envahir; **the fundamental error that pervades their philosophy** l'erreur fondamentale qui imprègne leur philosophie; **such attitudes p. British business** ces attitudes sont omniprésentes dans *ou* se retrouvent à tous les niveaux de l'entreprenariat britannique

pervading [pəˈveɪdɪŋ] **ADJ** *(smell)* pénétrant; *(influence, feeling, idea)* dominant; **the p. nostalgia of his work** la nostalgie qui est omniprésente dans son œuvre

pervasive [pəˈveɪsɪv] **ADJ** *(feeling)* envahissant; *(influence)* omniprésent; *(effect)* général; *(smell)* envahissant, omniprésent; **a p. atmosphere of pessimism** une atmosphère de pessimisme général

perverse [pəˈvɜːs] **ADJ 1** *(stubborn ▸ person)* têtu, entêté; *(▸ desire)* tenace; *(contrary, wayward)* contrariant; **he felt a p. urge to refuse** il fut pris d'une envie de refuser simplement pour le plaisir; **she takes a p. delight in doing this** elle y prend un malin plaisir; **you're just being p.!** tu fais ça juste pour embêter le monde! **2** *(sexually deviant)* pervers

> Note that the French word **pervers** never means **stubborn** or **contrary**.

perversely [pəˈvɜːslɪ] **ADV** *(stubbornly)* obstinément; *(unreasonably, contrarily)* par esprit de contradiction; **to p. believe that...** s'entêter à croire que...

perverseness [pəˈvɜːsnɪs] **N** *(stubbornness)* entêtement *m*, obstination *f*; *(unreasonableness, contrariness)* esprit *m* de contradiction

perversion [pəˈvɜːʃən] **N 1** *(sexual abnormality)* perversion *f* **2** *(distortion ▸ of truth)* déformation *f*

perversity [pəˈvɜːsətɪ] *(pl* **perversities**) **N 1** *(stubbornness)* entêtement *m*, obstination *f*; *(unreasonableness, contrariness)* esprit *m* de contradiction **2** *(sexual abnormality)* perversité *f*

pervert **VT** [pəˈvɜːt] **1** *(corrupt morally ▸ person)* pervertir, corrompre; *Psy* pervertir **2** *(distort ▸ truth, ideals)* déformer; *(▸ words)* dénaturer; *Law* **to p. the course of justice** entraver le cours de la justice
N [ˈpɜːvɜːt] pervers(e) *m,f*, *Hum* **you p.!** espèce d'obsédé!

perverted [pəˈvɜːtɪd] **ADJ** *Psy* pervers

pervious [ˈpɜːvɪəs] **ADJ 1** *Geol (permeable)* perméable **2** *Literary (receptive)* ouvert, perméable

pervy [ˈpɜːvɪ] **ADJ** *Br Fam* pervers▫

pescatarian [ˌpeskəˈteərɪən] **N** pesco-végétarien(enne) *m,f*

peseta [pəˈseɪtə] **N** *Formerly* peseta *f*

pesky [ˈpeskɪ] *(compar* **peskier**, *superl* **peskiest**) **ADJ** *esp Am Fam* fichu; **p. weather!** fichu temps!; **p. flies!** maudites *ou* satanées mouches!

peso [ˈpeɪsəʊ] *(pl* **pesos**) **N** peso *m*

pessary [ˈpesərɪ] *(pl* **pessaries**) **N** *Med* pessaire *m*

pessimism [ˈpesɪmɪzəm] **N** pessimisme *m*; **there is growing p. about the prospects for peace** on est de plus en plus pessimiste quant aux chances de paix

pessimist [ˈpesɪmɪst] **N** pessimiste *mf*

pessimistic [ˌpesɪˈmɪstɪk] **ADJ** pessimiste; **I feel very p. about her chances of getting the job** je doute fort qu'elle obtienne ce poste

pessimistically [ˌpesɪˈmɪstɪklɪ] **ADV** avec pessimisme

PEST [pest] **N** *Mktg* (*abbr* **political, economic, sociological, technological**) = facteurs politiques, économiques, sociaux et technologiques

pest [pest] **N 1** *(insect)* insecte *m* nuisible; *(animal)* animal *m* nuisible **2** *Fam (nuisance)* plaie *f*, peste *f*; **what a p. he is!** quelle plaie!, qu'est-ce qu'il est casse-pieds!; **that dog is a real p.** ce chien est une véritable plaie; **having to take the dog for a walk every day is a real p.** c'est vraiment empoisonnant *ou* embêtant d'avoir à promener le chien tous les jours
▸▸ ***pest control*** *(action ▸ of rats)* dératisation *f*; *(▸ of insects)* désinsectisation *f*; *(department ▸ for rats)* service *m* de dératisation; *(▸ for insects)* service *m* de désinsectisation

> Note that the French word **peste** also means **plague**.

pester [ˈpestə(r)] **VT** importuner, harceler; **to p. sb with questions** importuner *ou* assommer *ou* harceler qn de (ses) questions; **stop pestering your mother!** arrête d'embêter ta mère!; **they're always pestering me for money** ils sont toujours à me réclamer de l'argent; **the children pestered me to tell them a story** les enfants n'ont eu de cesse que je leur raconte une histoire; **he pestered me into buying him a computer** il m'a harcelé jusqu'à ce que je lui achète un ordinateur

pesticide [ˈpestɪsaɪd] **N** pesticide *m*

pestiferous [pesˈtɪfərəs] **ADJ 1** *Literary (unhealthy)* pestilentiel **2** *(pernicious ▸ doctrine)* pernicieux

pestilence [ˈpestɪləns] **N** *Literary* pestilence *f*

pestilential [ˌpestɪˈlenʃəl] **ADJ 1** *Med* pestilentiel **2** *Literary (annoying)* agaçant

pestle [ˈpesəl] **N** *Culin* pilon *m*

pet [pet] *(pt & pp* **petted**, *cont* **petting**) **N 1** *(animal)* animal *m* domestique *ou* familier *ou* de compagnie; **we don't keep pets** nous n'avons pas d'animaux à la maison; **he keeps** *or* **has a snake as a p.** il a un serpent apprivoisé; **sorry, no pets** *(sign, in advertisement)* les animaux ne sont pas admis
2 *(favourite)* favori(ite) *m,f*, *Pej* chouchou(oute) *m,f*; **the teacher's p.** le (la) chouchou(oute) du prof
3 *Fam (term of endearment)* chéri(e)▫ *m,f*; **how are you, p.?** comment ça va, mon chou?; **be a p. and close the door** tu seras un chou de fermer la porte; **she's a real p.** elle est adorable▫
4 *Fam (temper)* crise *f* de colère▫; **to be in a p.** être de mauvais poil *ou* en rogne
ADJ 1 *(hawk, snake etc)* apprivoisé; **they have a p. budgerigar/hamster** ils ont une perruche/un hamster chez eux **2** *Fam (favourite ▸ project, theory)* favori▫; **it's my p. ambition to write a novel** ma grande ambition, c'est d'écrire un roman▫; **Lauren is the teacher's p. pupil** Lauren est la chouchoute du prof; **his p. subject** *or* **p. topic** son dada
VT 1 *(pamper)* chouchouter **2** *(stroke ▸ animal)* câliner, caresser **3** *Fam (caress sexually)* caresser▫
VI *Fam (sexually)* se caresser▫
▸▸ ***pet food*** aliments *mpl* pour animaux (domestiques); ***pet hate*** bête *f* noire; ***pet name*** sur

nom *m* affectueux; **her p. name for him was "honeybun"** elle l'appelait "honeybun"; ***pet passport*** = sorte de passeport pour animal domestique, visant à éviter la période de quarantaine après un séjour à l'étranger; *Am* ***pet peeve*** bête *f* noire; ***pet shop*** magasin *m* d'animaux domestiques, animalerie *f*; ***pet sitter*** garde *mf* d'animaux familiers

petal ['petəl] **N 1** *(of flower)* pétale *m* **2** *Br Fam (term of affection)* mon chou; **thanks, p.** merci, mon chou

petard [pə'tɑːd] **N** pétard *m*; *Fig* **to be hoist with one's own p.** être pris à son propre piège

Pete [piːt] **PR N** *Fam* **for P.'s sake!** mais nom d'un chien!, mais bon sang!

Peter ['piːtə(r)] **PR N** Pierre
►► ***Peter the Great*** Pierre le Grand

peter ['piːtə(r)] **N 1** *Fam (safe)* coffiot *m* **2** *Am very Fam (penis)* quéquette *f*, zizi *m*

►**peter out VI 1** *(run out* ► *supplies, money)* s'épuiser; *(come to end* ► *path)* se perdre; *(*► *stream)* tarir; *(*► *line)* s'estomper, s'évanouir; *(*► *conversation)* tarir **2** *(die away* ► *voice)* s'éteindre; *(*► *fire)* s'éteindre, mourir **3** *(come to nothing* ► *plan)* tomber à l'eau

peterman ['piːtəmæn] *(pl* **petermen** [-mən]) **N** *Fam Crime slang (safe-breaker)* perceur *m* de coffres-forts

petersham ['piːtəʃəm] **N** *Tex* gros-grain *m*

Pete Tong [-tɒŋ] **ADJ** *Br Fam (rhyming slang* **wrong)** **to go P.** partir en eau de boudin, se gâter; **it all went a bit P. when her ex turned up at the party** les choses se sont gâtées quand son ex s'est pointé à la fête

petite [pə'tiːt] **ADJ** *(woman)* menue
N *(clothing size)* petites tailles *fpl (pour adultes)*

petition [pɪ'tɪʃən] **N 1** *(with signatures)* pétition *f*; **to hand in/sign a p.** remettre/signer une pétition; **they got up a p. against the council's plans** ils ont préparé une pétition pour protester contre les projets de la municipalité
2 *(request)* requête *f*
3 *Law* requête *f*, pétition *f*; **p. for divorce** demande *f* de divorce; **p. in bankruptcy** demande *f* de mise en liquidation judiciaire; **to file a p. in bankruptcy** déposer son bilan; **p. for mercy** recours *m* en grâce
4 *Rel* prière *f*
VT 1 *(court, sovereign etc)* adresser une pétition à; **they petitioned the government for the release of** *or* **to release the political prisoners** ils ont adressé une pétition au gouvernement pour demander la libération des prisonniers politiques; **we are going to p. to have the wall demolished** nous allons demander que le mur soit démoli **2** *Formal (beg)* **they petitioned the king to save them** ils ont imploré le roi de les sauver **3** *Law* **to p. the court** déposer une requête auprès du tribunal
VI 1 *(with signatures)* faire signer une pétition; **they petitioned for his release** ils ont fait circuler une pétition demandant sa libération **2** *(take measures)* **why don't you p. against the plan?** pourquoi n'engagez-vous pas un recours contre le projet? **3** *Law* **to p. for divorce** faire une demande de divorce

petitioner [pɪ'tɪʃənə(r)] **N 1** *Law* pétitionnaire *mf*; *(in divorce)* demandeur(eresse) *m,f* de divorce **2** *(on petition)* signataire *mf* d'une/de la pétition

petrel ['petrəl] **N** *Orn* pétrel *m*

Petri dish ['piːtrɪ-] **N** boîte *f* de Petri

petrifaction [ˌpetrɪ'fækʃən] **N 1** *(fossilization)* pétrification *f* **2** *(shock)* ébahissement *m*, *Literary* pétrification *f*

petrified ['petrɪfaɪd] **ADJ 1** *(fossilized)* pétrifié **2** *(terrified)* paralysé *ou* pétrifié de peur; *(weaker use)* terrifié
►► ***petrified forest*** forêt *f* pétrifiée

petrify ['petrɪfaɪ] *(pt & pp* **petrified) VT 1** *(fossilize)* pétrifier **2** *(terrify)* paralyser *ou* pétrifier de peur; *(weaker use)* terrifier; **the noise petrified me** le bruit me glaça le sang

petrifying ['petrɪfaɪɪŋ] **ADJ** *Fam (frightening)* paralysant

petrochemical [ˌpetrəʊ'kemɪkəl] **ADJ** *(industry etc)* pétrochimique
• **petrochemicals NPL** produits *mpl* pétrochimiques

petrocurrency [ˌpetrəʊ'kʌrənsɪ] *(pl* **petrocurrencies) N** devise *f* pétrolière, pétromonnaie *f*

petrodollar ['petrəʊˌdɒlə(r)] **N** pétrodollar *m*

petrol ['petrəl] *Br* **N** essence *f*; **to fill up with p.** faire le plein d'essence; **to run out of p.** tomber en panne d'essence
COMP *(fumes, rationing, shortage)* d'essence
►► ***petrol blue*** bleu *m* pétrole *(inv)*; ***petrol bomb*** cocktail *m* Molotov; ***petrol bomber*** lanceur (euse) *m,f* de cocktail Molotov; ***petrol can*** bidon *m* d'essence; ***petrol cap*** bouchon *m* d'essence; ***petrol coupon*** bon *m* d'essence; ***petrol engine*** moteur *m* à essence; ***petrol filler cap*** bouchon *m* d'essence; ***petrol gauge*** jauge *f* à essence; ***petrol pump*** *(at service station)* pompe *f* à essence; **prices at the p. pump have risen** le prix de l'essence à la pompe a augmenté; ***petrol station*** station-service *f*; *Aut* ***petrol tank*** réservoir *m* (d'essence); ***petrol tanker*** *(lorry)* camion-citerne *m*; *(ship)* pétrolier *m*, tanker *m*

> Note that the French word **pétrole** is a false friend and is never a translation for the English word **petrol**. It means **oil**.

petrol-bomb VT *Br* attaquer au cocktail Molotov, lancer un cocktail Molotov contre *ou* sur; **the police station was petrol-bombed during the night** le commissariat a été attaqué à coups de cocktails Molotov pendant la nuit

petroleum [pɪ'trəʊlɪəm] **N** pétrole *m*
COMP *(industry)* du pétrole, pétrolier; *(imports)* de pétrole
►► *Br* ***petroleum jelly*** vaseline *f*

petrolhead ['petrəlhed] **N** *Br Fam* dingue *mf* de bagnoles

petrology [pe'trɒlədʒɪ] **N** pétrologie *f*

petticoat ['petɪkəʊt] **N** *(waist slip)* jupon *m*; *(full-length slip)* combinaison *f*
COMP *Pej (government, politics)* de femmes

pettifogging ['petɪfɒgɪŋ] **ADJ 1** *(petty* ► *person)* chicanier; *(*► *details)* insignifiant **2** *(dishonest)* louche; **a p. lawyer** un avocat marron

pettiness ['petɪnɪs] **N 1** *(triviality* ► *of details)* insignifiance *f*; *(*► *of rules)* caractère *m* pointilleux **2** *(small-mindedness)* mesquinerie *f*, étroitesse *f* d'esprit

petting ['petɪŋ] **N** *(UNCOUNT) Fam (sexual)* caresses *fpl*
►► *Am* ***petting zoo*** = partie d'un zoo où les enfants peuvent s'approcher des animaux

pettish ['petɪʃ] **ADJ** *Br (person)* grincheux, acariâtre; *(mood)* maussade; *(remark)* hargneux, désagréable

pettishly ['petɪʃlɪ] **ADV** avec humeur

petty ['petɪ] *(compar* **pettier**, *superl* **pettiest) ADJ 1** *Pej (trivial* ► *detail)* insignifiant, mineur; *(*► *difficulty)* mineur; *(*► *question)* tatillon; *(*► *regulation)* tracassier; *(*► *ambitions)* médiocre **2** *Pej (mean* ► *behaviour, mind, spite)* mesquin **3** *(minor, small-scale)* petit; **p. acts of vandalism** de petits actes *mpl* de vandalisme; **p. annoyances** tracasseries *fpl*, petits ennuis *mpl*
►► ***petty bourgeois*** **N** petit-bourgeois (petite-bourgeoise) *m,f* **ADJ** petit-bourgeois; ***petty bourgeoisie*** petite-bourgeoisie *f*; ***petty cash*** petite caisse *f*; **I took the money out of p. cash** j'ai pris l'argent dans la petite caisse; **they'll pay you back out of p. cash** ils vous rembourseront avec la petite caisse; ***petty cash book*** livre *m* de petite caisse; ***petty cash box*** petite caisse *f*; ***petty cash voucher*** bon *m* de petite caisse; ***petty crime*** actes *mpl* délictueux; ***petty expenses*** menues dépenses *fpl*; *Law* ***petty larceny*** larcin *m*; ***petty offence*** infraction *f* mineure; *Br Naut* ***petty officer*** ≃ second maître *m*; ***petty thief*** petit(e) délinquant(e) *m,f*

petty-mindedness [-'maɪndɪdnɪs] **N** mesquinerie *f*

petulance ['petjʊləns] **N** irritabilité *f*, mauvaise humeur *f*

petulant ['petjʊlənt] **ADJ** *(bad-tempered* ► *person)* irritable, acariâtre; *(*► *remark)* acerbe, désagréable; *(*► *behaviour)* désagréable, agressif; *(sulky)* maussade; **in a p. mood** de mauvaise humeur

> Note that the French word **pétulant** is a false friend and is never a translation for the English word **petulant**. It means **exuberant**.

petulantly ['petjʊləntlɪ] **ADV** *(act, speak* ► *irritably)* avec irritation; *(*► *sulkily)* avec mauvaise humeur; **"no!" she said p.** "non!" dit-elle avec mauvaise humeur

petunia [pə'tjuːnɪə] **N** *Bot* pétunia *m*

pew [pjuː] **N** banc *m* d'église; *Br Fam Hum* **take** *or* **have a p.!** pose-toi quelque-part!

pewter ['pjuːtə(r)] **N 1** *(metal)* étain *m* **2** *(UNCOUNT) (ware)* étains *mpl*, vaisselle *f* d'étain **3** *(colour)* gris étain *m*
COMP *(tableware, tankard)* en étain

PFI [ˌpiːef'aɪ] **N** *(abbr* **private finance initiative)** partenariat *m* public-privé

PG [ˌpiː'dʒiː] **ADJ** *Cin (abbr* **parental guidance)** = désigne un film dont certaines scènes peuvent choquer, ≃ tous publics *(l'accord des parents étant souhaitable)*

PG-13 [-ˌθɜː'tiːn] **ADJ** *Am Cin* = désigne un film dont certaines scènes peuvent choquer *(accord des parents exigé pour les moins de 13 ans)*

PGCE [ˌpiːdʒiːˌsiː'iː] **N** *Br Sch (abbr* **postgraduate certificate in education)** = diplôme d'enseignement

PGD [ˌpiːdʒiː'diː] **N** *Med (abbr* **pre-implantation genetic diagnosis)** DPI *m*

PGP [ˌpiːdʒiː'piː] **N** *Comput (abbr* **Pretty Good Privacy)** (logiciel *m* de chiffrement) PGP *m*

pH [piː'eɪtʃ] **N** *Chem* pH *m*; **a pH of 9** un pH de 9; **pH balanced** *(soap, shampoo etc)* (à) pH neutre

phalanx ['fælæŋks] *(pl* **phalanxes** *or* **phalanges** [-lændʒiːz]) **N 1** *Antiq & Mil* phalange *f* **2** *Anat* phalange *f* **3** *Pol* phalange *f*

phallic ['fælɪk] **ADJ** phallique
►► ***phallic symbol*** symbole *m* phallique

phallocentric [ˌfæləʊ'sentrɪk] **ADJ** phallocentrique

phallus ['fæləs] *(pl* **phalluses** *or* **phalli** [-laɪ]) **N** phallus *m*

phantasm ['fæntæzəm] **N** fantasme *m*

phantasmagoria [ˌfæntæzmə'gɔːrɪə] **N** fantasmagorie *f*

phantasy = **fantasy**

phantom ['fæntəm] **N 1** *(ghost)* fantôme *m*, spectre *m* **2** *(threat, source of dread)* spectre *m* **3** *Literary (illusion)* illusion *f*
ADJ imaginaire, fantôme
►► *Med* ***phantom limb*** membre *m* fantôme; *Br* ***phantom pregnancy*** grossesse *f* nerveuse; ***phantom ship*** vaisseau *m* fantôme

Pharaoh ['feərəʊ] **N** pharaon *m*

Pharisee ['færɪsiː] **N** Pharisien(enne) *m,f*

pharmaceutical [ˌfɑːmə'sjuːtɪkəl] **ADJ** pharmaceutique
• **pharmaceuticals NPL** *(medicines)* produits *mpl* pharmaceutiques, médicaments *mpl*; *(industry)* industrie *f* pharmaceutique
►► ***pharmaceutical company*** société *f* pharmaceutique

pharmacist ['fɑːməsɪst] **N** pharmacien(enne) *m,f*

pharmacological [ˌfɑːməkəʊ'lɒdʒɪkəl] **ADJ** pharmacologique

pharmacologist [ˌfɑːmə'kɒlədʒɪst] **N** pharmacologiste *mf*, pharmacologue *mf*

pharmacology [ˌfɑːmə'kɒlədʒɪ] **N** pharmacologie *f*
COMP *(laboratory, studies)* de pharmacologie, pharmacologique

pharmacopoeia, *Am* **pharmacopeia** [ˌfɑːməkəʊ'piːə] **N** pharmacopée *f*

pharmacy ['fɑːməsɪ] *(pl* **pharmacies) N 1** *(science)* pharmacie *f* **2** *(dispensary, shop)* pharmacie *f*

pharyngitis [ˌfærɪn'dʒaɪtɪs] **N** *(UNCOUNT) Med* pharyngite *f*; **to have p.** avoir une pharyngite

pharynx ['færɪnks] *(pl* **pharynxes** *or* **pharynges** [fæ'rɪndʒiːz]) **N** *Anat* pharynx *m*

phase [feɪz] **N 1** *(period ▸ gen)* phase *f*, période *f*; *(▸ of illness)* phase *f*, stade *m*; *(▸ of career, project, campaign)* étape *f*; *(▸ of civilization)* période *f*; **the project is going through a critical p.** le projet traverse une phase critique; **it's still in the development p.** c'est encore en cours de développement; **p. two of the restoration project/rebuilding programme** la deuxième tranche des travaux de restauration/de reconstruction; **the investigation/trial has entered a new p.** l'enquête/le procès est désormais dans une nouvelle phase; **their daughter's going through a difficult p.** leur fille traverse une période difficile; **don't worry, it's just a p. she's going through** ne vous inquiétez pas, ça lui passera **2** *Astron (of moon)* phase *f* **3** *Chem, Elec & Phys* phase *f*; **in the solid p.** en phase *ou* à l'état solide; *also Fig* **to be in p.** être en phase; *also Fig* **to be out of p.** être déphasé; **the government is out of p. with the mood of the country** le gouvernement est en décalage complet avec les sentiments de la population

VT 1 *(changes, new methods)* introduire progressivement; *(project)* développer en phases successives; *(schedule, introduction of technology etc)* échelonner; **the closure of the plant will be phased over three years** la fermeture de l'usine se fera progressivement, sur trois ans

2 *(synchronize)* synchroniser, faire coïncider; **the two operations have to be perfectly phased** les deux opérations doivent être parfaitement synchronisées

3 *Am (prearrange ▸ delivery, development)* planifier, programmer

4 *Elec & Tech* mettre en phase

▸**phase in VT SEP** *(new methods)* introduire progressivement *ou* par étapes; *(new systems, new equipment)* mettre progressivement en place; **the increases will be phased in over five years** les augmentations seront échelonnées sur cinq ans

▸**phase out VT SEP** *(stop using ▸ machinery, weapon)* cesser progressivement d'utiliser; *(stop producing ▸ car, model)* abandonner progressivement la production de; *(do away with ▸ jobs, tax)* supprimer progressivement *ou* par étapes; *(▸ grant)* retirer progressivement; **when the use of these pesticides has been phased out** quand ces pesticides auront cessé d'être utilisés; **the system is being phased out** ce système est en cours d'abandon

phased [feɪzd] **ADJ** *(withdrawal, development)* progressif, par étapes; *(evacuation)* progressif

phasing ['feɪzɪŋ] **N**

▸▸ ***phasing in*** *(of new methods)* adoption *f ou* introduction *f* progressive; *(of new systems, new equipment)* mise *f* en place progressive; ***phasing out*** *(of old methods, systems, equipment etc)* abandon *m* progressif; *(of jobs)* suppression *f* progressive

phat [fæt] **ADJ** *Am Fam* super, génial

PhD [ˌpiːeɪtʃ'diː] **N** *(abbr* **Doctor of Philosophy***)* *(person)* = titulaire d'un doctorat de 3ème cycle; *(qualification)* = doctorat de 3ème cycle; **to have a P. in Maths** avoir un doctorat en maths

▸▸ ***PhD student*** étudiant(e) *m,f* inscrit(e) en doctorat; ***PhD thesis*** thèse *f* de doctorat

pheasant ['fezənt] *(pl* **inv** *or* **pheasants***)* **N** faisan *m*; *(hen)* (poule *f*) faisane *f*

▸▸ ***pheasant poult*** faisandeau *m*; ***pheasant shoot*** faisanderie *f*; ***pheasant shooting*** chasse *f* au faisan

phenix *Am* = **phoenix**

phenobarbitone [ˌfiːnəʊ'bɑːbɪtəʊn], *Am* **phenobarbital** [ˌfiːnəʊ'bɑːbɪtəl] **N** *Pharm* phénobarbital *m*, Gardénal® *m*

phenol ['fiːnɒl] **N** *Chem* phénol *m*

phenomena [fɪ'nɒmɪnə] *pl of* **phenomenon**

phenomenal [fɪ'nɒmɪnəl] **ADJ** phénoménal; **a p. success** un immense succès

phenomenally [fɪ'nɒmɪnəlɪ] **ADV** phénoménalement; **it's p. expensive** ça coûte horriblement cher

phenomenological [fɪˌnɒmɪnə'lɒdʒɪkəl] **ADJ** phénoménologique

phenomenologist [fɪˌnɒmə'nɒlədʒɪst] **N** phénoménologue *mf*

phenomenology [fɪˌnɒmɪ'nɒlədʒɪ] **N** phénoménologie *f*

phenomenon [fɪ'nɒmɪnən] *(pl* **phenomena** [-nə]*)* **N** phénomène *m*; **the credit card p.** le phénomène des cartes de crédit

pheromone ['ferəməʊn] **N** phéromone *f*, phérormone *f*

phew [fjuː] **EXCLAM** *(in relief)* ouf!; *(from heat)* pff!; *(in disgust)* berk!, beurk!

phial ['faɪəl] **N** fiole *f*

Phil *(written abbr* **Philadelphia***)* Philadelphie *f*

Philadelphia [ˌfɪlə'delfɪə] **N** Philadelphie *f*

philander [fɪ'lændə(r)] **VI** *Pej* courir le jupon

philanderer [fɪ'lændərə(r)] **N** *Pej* coureur *m* (de jupons)

philandering [fɪ'lændərɪŋ] *Pej* **N she had had enough of his p.** elle en avait assez qu'il coure le jupon

ADJ *(ways, habits)* de coureur de jupon; **her p. husband** son coureur de jupon de mari

philanthropic [ˌfɪlən'θrɒpɪk] **ADJ** philanthropique

philanthropist [fɪ'lænθrəpɪst] **N** philanthrope *mf*

philanthropy [fɪ'lænθrəpɪ] **N** philanthropie *f*

philatelic [ˌfɪlə'telɪk] **ADJ** philatélique

philatelist [fɪ'lætəlɪst] **N** philatéliste *mf*

philately [fɪ'lætəlɪ] **N** philatélie *f*

-phile [faɪl] **SUFF** -phile; **Anglophile** anglophile *mf*; **Francophile** francophile *mf*

philharmonic [ˌfɪlɑː'mɒnɪk] **ADJ** philharmonique

N orchestre *m* philharmonique

▸▸ ***philharmonic orchestra*** orchestre *m* philharmonique

-philia ['fɪlɪə] **SUFF** -philie; **necrophilia** nécrophilie *f*; **anglophilia** anglophilie *f*

Philippines ['fɪlɪpiːnz] **NPL the P.** les Philippines *fpl*

Philistine [*Br* 'fɪlɪstaɪn, *Am* 'fɪlɪstiːn] **N 1** *Hist* Philistin *m* **2** *Fig* béotien(enne) *m,f*

ADJ philistin

Philistinism ['fɪlɪstɪnɪzəm] **N** philistinisme *m*

Phillips® ['fɪlɪps] **N**

▸▸ ***Phillips® screw*** vis *f* cruciforme; ***Phillips® screwdriver*** tournevis *m* cruciforme

philodendron [ˌfɪlə'dendrən] *(pl* **philodendrons** *or* **philodendra** [-drə]*)* **N** *Bot* philodendron *m*

philological [ˌfɪlə'lɒdʒɪkəl] **ADJ** philologique

philologist [fɪ'lɒlədʒɪst] **N** philologue *mf*

philology [fɪ'lɒlədʒɪ] **N** philologie *f*

philosopher [fɪ'lɒsəfə(r)] **N** philosophe *mf*; **the p.'s stone** la pierre philosophale

philosophic [ˌfɪlə'sɒfɪk] **ADJ** *Phil* philosophique

philosophical [ˌfɪlə'sɒfɪkəl] **ADJ 1** *Phil* philosophique **2** *(calm, resigned)* philosophe; **I feel quite p. about the situation** j'envisage la situation avec philosophie

philosophically [ˌfɪlə'sɒfɪklɪ] **ADV 1** *Phil* philosophiquement **2** *(calmly)* philosophiquement, avec philosophie

philosophize, -ise [fɪ'lɒsəfaɪz] **VI** philosopher; **to p. about sth** philosopher sur qch

philosophy [fɪ'lɒsəfɪ] *(pl* **philosophies***)* **N** philosophie *f*; **she's a p. student** elle est étudiante en philosophie; *Fig* **we share the same p. of life** nous avons la même conception de la vie

philtre, *Am* **philter** ['fɪltə(r)] **N** *Literary* philtre *m*

phisher ['fɪʃə(r)] **N** *Fam Comput* = escroc qui pratique le phishing

phishing ['fɪʃɪŋ] **N** *Fam Comput* phishing *m*, filoutage *m*, = extorsion de données confidentielles par e-mail

phiz [fɪz], **phizog** ['fɪzɒg] **N** *Br Fam Old-fashioned (face)* tronche *f*, poire *f*

phlebitis [flɪ'baɪtɪs] **N** *(UNCOUNT) Med* phlébite *f*

phlegm [flem] **N 1** *Med (in respiratory passages)* glaire *f*; **to cough up p.** tousser gras **2** *Fig (composure)* flegme *m*

phlegmatic [fleg'mætɪk] **ADJ** flegmatique

phlegmatically [fleg'mætɪkəlɪ] **ADV** avec flegme, flegmatiquement

phlox [flɒks] **N** *Bot* phlox *m inv*

-phobe [fəʊb] **SUFF** -phobe; **xenophobe** xénophobe *mf*; **Anglophobe** anglophobe *mf*

-phobia ['fəʊbɪə] **SUFF** -phobie; **claustrophobia** claustrophobie *f*; **xenophobia** xénophobie *f*

phobia ['fəʊbɪə] **N** phobie *f*; **he has a p. of spiders** il a la phobie des araignées; *Fam Fig* **she's got a p. about work** elle est allergique au travail

phobic ['fəʊbɪk] **ADJ** phobique

N phobique *mf*

Phoenician [fɪ'nɪʃɪən] **N 1** *(person)* Phénicien(enne) *m,f* **2** *Ling* phénicien *m*

ADJ phénicien

phoenix, *Am* **phenix** ['fiːnɪks] **N** phénix *m*

-phone [fəʊn] **SUFF** -phone; **Anglophone** anglophone *mf*; **Francophone** francophone *mf*

phone [fəʊn] **N 1** *(telephone)* téléphone *m*; **I answered the p.** j'ai répondu au téléphone; **just a minute, I'm on the p.** un instant, je suis au téléphone; **he was on the p. for an hour** il a passé une heure au téléphone; **you're wanted on the p.** on vous demande au téléphone; **to get on the p. to sb** téléphoner à qn; **I don't wish to discuss it over the p.** je préfère ne pas en parler au téléphone; *Fam* **to give sb a p.** donner un coup de téléphone *ou* de fil à qn☐; **get off the p.!** raccroche! **2** *Ling* phone *m*

COMP *(bill)* de téléphone; *(line, message)* téléphonique

VI *Br* téléphoner; **to p. for a plumber/a taxi** appeler un plombier/un taxi *(par téléphone)*; **to p. home** téléphoner à la maison

VT *Br* téléphoner à; **to p. Paris** téléphoner à Paris; **can you p. me the answer?** pouvez-vous me donner la réponse par téléphone?

▸▸ ***phone book*** annuaire *m* (téléphonique); ***phone booth*** cabine *f* téléphonique; *Br* ***phone box*** cabine *f* téléphonique; **I'm calling from a p. box** j'appelle d'une cabine; ***phone call*** coup *m* de téléphone, appel *m* (téléphonique); ***phone number*** numéro *m* de téléphone; *Fam Comput* ***phone phreak*** pirate *m* du téléphone☐; ***phone zap*** zapping *m (par un groupe de pression)*

▸**phone in VI** téléphoner; **to p. in sick** téléphoner pour dire qu'on est malade

▸**phone up VT SEP** téléphoner à

VI téléphoner

phonecard ['fəʊnkɑːd] **N** Télécarte® *f*, carte *f* de téléphone

phone-in **N** *Rad & TV* **p. (programme)** = émission au cours de laquelle les auditeurs ou les téléspectateurs peuvent intervenir par téléphone

phoneme ['fəʊniːm] **N** *Ling* phonème *m*

phonemic [fə'niːmɪk] **ADJ** *Ling* phonémique, phonématique

phonetic [fə'netɪk] **ADJ** phonétique

▸▸ ***phonetic alphabet*** alphabet *m* phonétique

phonetically [fə'netɪkəlɪ] **ADV** phonétiquement

phonetician [ˌfəʊnɪ'tɪʃən] **N** phonéticien(enne) *m,f*

phonetics [fə'netɪks] **N** *(UNCOUNT)* phonétique *f*

phoney ['fəʊnɪ] *(compar* **phonier,** *superl* **phoniest,** *pl* **phonies***)* *Fam* **ADJ 1** *(false ▸ banknote, jewel, name)* faux (fausse)☐; *(▸ title, company, accent)* bidon; *(▸ tears)* de crocodile; *(▸ laughter)* qui sonne faux☐; **his story sounds p.** son histoire a tout l'air d'être (du) bidon; **the p. war** la drôle de guerre **2** *(spurious ▸ person)* bidon

N 1 *(impostor)* imposteur☐*m*; *(charlatan)* charlatan☐*m* **2** *(pretentious person)* frimeur(euse) *m,f*, m'as-tu-vu *mf inv* **3** *(fake object)* faux☐*m*

phonic ['fəʊnɪk] **ADJ** phonique

phonograph ['fəʊnəgrɑːf] **N 1** *(early gramophone)* phonographe *m* **2** *Am Old-fashioned (record player)* tourne-disque *m*, électrophone *m*

phonology [fə'nɒlədʒɪ] *(pl* **phonologies***)* **N** phonologie *f*

phony = **phoney**

phooey ['fuːɪ] **EXCLAM** *Fam (expressing irritation)* zut!, flûte!; *(expressing disbelief)* mon œil!

phosgene [ˈfɒsdʒiːn] **N** *Chem* phosgène *m*

phosphate [ˈfɒsfeɪt] **N** *Agr & Chem* phosphate *m*

phosphide [ˈfɒsfaɪd] **N** *Chem* phosphure *m*

phosphite [ˈfɒsfaɪt] **N** *Chem* phosphite *m*

phosphoresce [ˌfɒsfəˈres] **VI** être phosphorescent

phosphorescence [ˌfɒsfəˈresəns] **N** phosphorescence *f*

phosphorescent [ˌfɒsfəˈresənt] **ADJ** phosphorescent

phosphoric [fɒsˈfɒrɪk] **ADJ** *Chem* phosphorique
▸▸ ***phosphoric acid*** acide *m* orthophosphorique

phosphorous [ˈfɒsfərəs] **ADJ** *Chem* phosphorique

phosphorus [ˈfɒsfərəs] **N** *Chem* phosphore *m*

photo [ˈfəʊtəʊ] *(pl* **photos***)* **N** photo *f*; **to take good photos** prendre de bonnes photos; **to take a good p.** *(be photogenic)* être photogénique; **it was a good p. opportunity** c'était une bonne occasion de se faire prendre en photo
▸▸ ***photo album*** album *m* de photos; *Comput* ***photo CD*** CD-Photo *m*, Photo-CD *m*; *Comput* ***photo editing*** retouche *f* d'images; ***photo finish*** *Sport* arrivée *f* groupée; *Fig* partie *f* serrée; **the race was a p. finish** il a fallu départager les vainqueurs de la course avec la photo-finish; **the election is going to be a p. finish** pour les élections, la partie sera serrée; ***photo library*** photothèque *f*; *Tel* ***photo messaging*** = prise et envoi de photos par téléphone portable; ***photo printer*** imprimante *f* photo; ***photo report*** reportage *m* photo; ***photo shoot*** séance *f* photos

photo- [ˈfəʊtəʊ] **PREF** photo-

photobooth [ˈfəʊtəʊbuːð] **N** Photomaton® *m*

photocard [ˈfəʊtəʊkɑːd] **N** = carte portant une photo d'identité du titulaire

photocell [ˈfəʊtəʊsel] **N** cellule *f* photoélectrique

photocompose [ˌfəʊtəʊkəmˈpəʊz] **VT** *Typ* photocomposer

photocomposer [ˈfəʊtəʊˌkəmˈpəʊzə(r)] **N** *Typ (person)* photocompositeur(trice) *m,f*

photocomposition [ˈfəʊtəʊˌkɒmpəˈzɪʃən] **N** *Typ* photocomposition *f*

photocompositor [ˈfəʊtəʊˌkəmˈpɒzɪtə(r)] **N** *Typ (machine)* photocomposeuse *f*

photocopier [ˈfəʊtəʊˌkɒpɪə(r)] **N** photocopieur *m*, photocopieuse *f*

photocopy [ˈfəʊtəʊˌkɒpɪ] *(pl* **photocopies**, *pt &* *pp* **photocopied***)* **N** photocopie *f*; **to take** *or* **make a p. of sth** faire une photocopie de qch, photocopier qch
VT photocopier

photoelectric [ˌfəʊtəʊɪˈlektrɪk] **ADJ** photoélectrique
▸▸ ***photoelectric cell*** cellule *f* photoélectrique; ***photoelectric effect*** effet *m* photoélectrique

photoelectron [ˌfəʊtəʊɪˈlektrɒn] **N** *Phys* photoélectron *m*

photoengraving [ˌfəʊtəʊɪnˈgreɪvɪŋ] **N** photogravure *f*

Photofit® [ˈfəʊtəʊfɪt] **N** *(picture)* photo-robot *f*, portrait-robot *m*
▸▸ ***Photofit® picture*** photo-robot *f*, portrait-robot *m*

photogenic [ˌfəʊtəʊˈdʒenɪk] **ADJ 1** *(person)* photogénique **2** *Biol* photogène

photograph [ˈfəʊtəgrɑːf] **N** photographie *f (image)*, photo *f (image)*; **to take a p.** prendre *ou* faire une photo; **to take a p. of sb** prendre qn en photo, photographier qn; **they took our p.** ils nous ont pris en photo; **to have one's p. taken** se faire photographier; **I'm in this p.** je suis sur cette photo; **she takes a good p.** *(is photogenic)* elle est photogénique
VT photographier, prendre en photo; **she doesn't like being photographed** elle n'aime pas qu'on la prenne en photo
VI he photographs well *(is photogenic)* il est photogénique; **the trees won't p. well in this light** il n'y a pas assez de lumière pour faire une bonne photo des arbres
▸▸ ***photograph album*** album *m* de photos; ***photograph library*** photothèque *f*

> Note that the French word **photographe** is a false friend and is never a translation for the English word **photograph**. It means **photographer**.

photographer [fəˈtɒgrəfə(r)] **N** photographe *mf*; **I'm not much of a p.** je ne suis pas très doué pour la photographie

photographic [ˌfəʊtəʊˈgræfɪk] **ADJ** photographique; **to have a p. memory** avoir une bonne mémoire visuelle
▸▸ ***photographic agency*** agence *f* photographique; ***photographic library*** photothèque *f*; ***photographic shop*** magasin *m* de photo; ***photographic society*** club *m* d'amateurs de photo

photographically [ˌfəʊtəʊˈgræfɪkəlɪ] **ADV** photographiquement

photography [fəˈtɒgrəfɪ] **N** photographie *f (art)*, photo *f (art)*; **an exhibition of French p.** une exposition de photographie française

photogravure [ˌfəʊtəʊgrəˈvjʊə(r)] **N** photogravure *f*

photojournalism [ˌfəʊtəʊˈdʒɜːnəlɪzəm] **N** photojournalisme *m*

photojournalist [ˌfəʊtəʊˈdʒɜːnəlɪst] **N** reporter *m* photographe, photojournaliste *mf*

photolithograph [ˌfəʊtəʊˈlɪθəgrɑːf] **N** photolithographie *f (image)*

photolithography [ˌfəʊtəʊlɪˈθɒgrəfɪ] **N** photolithographie *f (art)*

photoluminescence [ˈfəʊtəʊˌluːmɪˈnesəns] **N** photoluminescence *f*

photometer [fəʊˈtɒmɪtə(r)] **N** photomètre *m*

photometry [fəʊˈtɒmɪtrɪ] **N** photométrie *f*

photomontage [ˌfəʊtəʊmɒnˈtɑːʒ] **N** photomontage *m*

photon [ˈfəʊtɒn] **N** *Phys* photon *m*

photonovel [ˈfəʊtəʊˌnɒvəl] **N** roman-photo *m*, photo-roman *m*

photosensitive [ˌfəʊtəʊˈsensɪtɪv] **ADJ** photosensible

photoset [ˈfəʊtəʊset] *(pt & pp* **photoset**, *cont* **photosetting***)* **VT** photocomposer

photosetter [ˈfəʊtəʊˌsetə(r)] **N** *Br* photocomposeuse *f*, photocompositeur *m*

photosetting [ˈfəʊtəʊˌsetɪŋ] **N** *Br* photocomposition *f*
▸▸ ***photosetting machine*** photocomposeuse *f*

Photoshop® [ˈfəʊtəʊʃɒp] *(pt & pp* **Photoshopped**, *cont* **Photoshopping***)* **N** Photoshop® *m*
VT to P. a picture retoucher une photo *(avec le logiciel Photoshop®)*; **they've Photoshopped me out of the picture!** ils m'ont effacé de la photo!

photostat [ˈfəʊtəʊstæt] *(pt & pp* **photostatted**, *cont* **photostatting***)* **VT** photocopier
• **Photostat**® **N** photocopie *f*

photo-story **N** roman-photo *m*

photosynthesis [ˌfəʊtəʊˈsɪnθəsɪs] **N** *Biol & Bot* photosynthèse *f*

photosynthesize, -ise [ˌfəʊtəʊˈsɪnθəsaɪz] **VT** *Biol & Bot* fabriquer par photosynthèse

phototropism [ˌfəʊtəʊˈtrəʊpɪzəm] **N** *Biol* phototropisme *m*

phototypesetter [ˌfəʊtəʊˈtaɪpsetə(r)] **N** photocompositeur *m*

phototypesetting [ˌfəʊtəʊˈtaɪpsetɪŋ] **N** photocomposition *f*

photovoltaic [ˌfəʊtəʊvɒlˈteɪɪk] **ADJ** photovoltaïque
▸▸ ***photovoltaic cell*** cellule *f* photovoltaïque, photopile *f*; ***photovoltaic effect*** effet *m* photovoltaïque

phrasal verb [ˈfreɪzəl-] *Gram* verbe *m* à particule

phrase [freɪz] **N 1** *(expression)* expression *f*, locution *f*; **I can't find the right p.** je ne trouve pas l'expression que je cherche **2** *Ling* syntagme *m*, groupe *m* **3** *Mus* phrase *f*
VT 1 *(letter)* rédiger, tourner; *(idea)* exprimer, tourner; **couldn't you p. it differently?** ne pourriez-vous pas trouver une autre formule?; **how shall I p. it?** comment dire ça?; **he phrased it very elegantly** il a trouvé une tournure très élégante (pour le dire) **2** *Mus* phraser
▸▸ *Ling* ***phrase marker*** indicateur *m* syntagmatique; *Ling* ***phrase structure grammar*** grammaire *f* syntagmatique

> Note that the French noun **phrase** is a false friend. It means **sentence**.

phraseology [ˌfreɪzɪˈɒlədʒɪ] *(pl* **phraseologies***)* **N** phraséologie *f*

phrasing [ˈfreɪzɪŋ] **N 1** *(expressing)* choix *m* des mots; **with careful p.** en choisissant ses mots avec le plus grand soin *ou* soigneusement ses mots; **the p. of her refusal was very elegant** son refus était formulé de manière très élégante **2** *Mus* phrasé *m*

phreaker [ˈfriːkə(r)] **N** *Fam Comput* pirate *m* du téléphone ◻

phreaking [ˈfriːkɪŋ] **N** *Fam* piratage *m* téléphonique ◻

phrenic [ˈfrenɪk] **ADJ** *Anat* phrénique
▸▸ ***phrenic nerve*** nerf *m* phrénique

phrenology [frɪˈnɒlədʒɪ] **N** phrénologie *f*

phthisis [ˈθaɪsɪs] **N** *(UNCOUNT) Old-fashioned* phtisie *f*

phut [fʌt] **ADV** *Fam* **to go p.** *(break down)* rendre l'âme, lâcher

phwoar [fwɔː(r)] **EXCLAM** *Fam* wouaouh!

phyla [ˈfaɪlə] *pl of* **phylum**

phylactery [fɪˈlæktərɪ] *(pl* **phylacteries***)* **N** *Rel* phylactère *m*

phylloxera [fɪˈlɒksərə] **N** *Entom* phylloxéra *m*, phylloxera *m*

phylum [ˈfaɪləm] *(pl* **phyla** [-lə]*)* **N** *Biol & Bot* phylum *m*

physalis [ˌfaɪˈseɪlɪs, ˈfɪsəlɪs] **N** physalis *m*

Phys Ed [ˈfɪzˌed] **N** *Am (abbr* **physical education***)* éducation *f* physique

physic [ˈfɪzɪk] **N** *Arch* médicament *m*, remède *m*

physical [ˈfɪzɪkəl] **ADJ 1** *(bodily)* physique; **a p. examination** un examen médical, une visite médicale; **I don't get enough p. exercise** je ne fais pas assez d'exercice (physique); **rugby is a very p. sport** le rugby est un sport dans lequel il y a beaucoup de contacts physiques; **it left him a p. wreck** ça lui a détruit la santé
2 *(natural, material* ▸ *forces, property, presence)* physique; *(*▸ *manifestation, universe)* physique, matériel; **it's a p. impossibility** c'est physiquement *ou* matériellement impossible
3 *Chem & Phys* physique
4 *Geog* physique; **the p. features of the desert** la topographie du désert
N visite *f* médicale; **to go for a p.** passer une visite médicale
▸▸ ***physical abuse*** sévices *mpl*; ***physical access control*** contrôle *m* d'accès physique; ***physical anthropology*** anthropologie *f* physique; *Fin* ***physical assets*** immobilisations *fpl* non financières; ***physical chemistry*** chimie *f* physique; *Comput* ***physical disk cache*** cache *m* disque physique; ***physical education*** éducation *f* physique; ***physical fitness*** (bonne) forme *f* physique; ***physical geography*** géographie *f* physique; ***physical handicap*** infirmité *f*; *Br Fam Old-fashioned* ***physical jerks*** mouvements *mpl* de gym ◻; **to do p. jerks** faire des mouvements de gym; ***physical presence*** présence *f* physique; ***physical property*** propriété *f* physique; ***physical sciences*** sciences *fpl* physiques; ***physical strength*** force *f* physique; ***physical therapist*** kinésithérapeute *mf*; ***physical therapy*** kinésithérapie *f*; *(after accident or illness)* rééducation *f*; ***physical training*** éducation *f* physique

physically [ˈfɪzɪklɪ] **ADV** physiquement; **to be p. fit** être en bonne forme physique; **she is p. handicapped** elle a un handicap physique

physician [fɪˈzɪʃən] **N** médecin *m*

> Note that the French word **physicien** is a false friend and is never a translation for the English word **physician**. It means **physicist**.

physicist [ˈfɪzɪsɪst] **N** physicien(enne) *m,f*

physics [ˈfɪzɪks] **N** *(UNCOUNT)* physique *f*

physio ['fɪzɪəʊ] (*pl sense* **2 physios**) **N** *Fam* **1** (*abbr* **physiotherapy**) kiné *f* **2** (*abbr* **physiotherapist**) kiné *mf*

physiognomy [ˌfɪzɪ'ɒnəmɪ] (*pl* **physiognomies**) **N 1** *(facial features)* physionomie *f* **2** *Geog* topographie *f*, configuration *f*; **the p. of London is changing** la physionomie de Londres est en train de changer

physiological [ˌfɪzɪəʊ'lɒdʒɪkəl] **ADJ** physiologique

physiologically [ˌfɪzɪə'lɒdʒɪklɪ] **ADV** physiologiquement

physiologist [ˌfɪzɪ'ɒlədʒɪst] **N** physiologiste *mf*

physiology [ˌfɪzɪ'ɒlədʒɪ] **N** physiologie *f*

physiopathology [ˌfɪzɪəʊpə'θɒlədʒɪ] **N** physiopathologie *f*

physiotherapist [ˌfɪzɪəʊ'θerəpɪst] **N** kinésithérapeute *mf*

physiotherapy [ˌfɪzɪəʊ'θerəpɪ] **N** kinésithérapie *f*; *(after accident or illness)* rééducation *f*; **to go for** *or* **to have p.** faire des séances de kinésithérapie

physique [fɪ'ziːk] **N** constitution *f* physique, physique *m*; **to have a fine p.** avoir un beau corps; **to have a poor p.** être chétif; **he hasn't the p. for it** il n'a pas le physique de l'emploi

pi [paɪ] **N** *Math* pi *m*

PIA [ˌpiːaɪ'eɪ] **N** *Br Formerly Fin* (*abbr* **personal investment authority**) = organisme chargé de surveiller les activités des conseillers financiers indépendants et de protéger les petits investisseurs

pianissimo [ˌpɪə'nɪsɪməʊ] *Mus* **N** pianissimo *m*
ADV pianissimo

pianist ['pɪənɪst] **N** pianiste *mf*

piano¹ [pɪ'ænəʊ] (*pl* **pianos**) **N** piano *m*
COMP *(duet, lesson, stool, teacher, tuner)* de piano; *(music)* pour piano; *(lid, leg)* du piano
►► ***piano accordion*** accordéon *m* (à touches); ***piano concerto*** concerto *m* pour piano; ***piano key*** touche *f*; **the p. keys** le clavier (du piano); ***piano organ*** piano *m* mécanique; ***piano player*** pianiste *mf*; ***piano roll*** bande *f* perforée *(pour piano mécanique)*

piano² ['pjɑːnəʊ] *Mus* **ADJ** piano *(inv)*
ADV piano

piastre [pɪ'æstə(r)] **N** piastre *f*

piazza [pɪ'ætsə] **N 1** *(square)* place *f*, piazza *f* **2** *Br (gallery)* galerie *f*

PIBOR ['paɪbɔː(r)] **N** (*abbr* **Paris Interbank Offered Rate**) TIOP *m*, PIBOR *m*

pic [pɪk] (*pl* **pics** *or* **pix** [pɪks]) **N** *Fam (photograph)* photo ◻ *f*; *(picture)* illustration ◻ *f*; *(film)* film ◻ *m*

pica ['paɪkə] **N 1** *Typ (unit)* pica *m* **2** *(on typewriter)* pica *m*

picador ['pɪkədɔː(r)] **N** picador *m*

Picardy ['pɪkədɪ] **N** Picardie *f*

picaresque [ˌpɪkə'resk] **ADJ** picaresque

piccalilli [ˌpɪkə'lɪlɪ] **N** piccalilli *m (pickles à la moutarde)*

piccaninny [ˌpɪkə'nɪnɪ] (*pl* **piccaninnies**) **N** *Fam* négrillon(onne) *m,f*, = terme raciste désignant un enfant noir

piccolo ['pɪkələʊ] (*pl* **piccolos**) **N** piccolo *m*, piccolo *m*

piccy ['pɪkɪ] (*pl* **piccies**) **N** *Br Fam (photograph)* photo ◻ *f*

PICK [pɪk]

VT
- choisir **1**
- cueillir **2**
- enlever **3**
- gratter **4**
- crocheter **6**
- pincer **7**

VI
- choisir

N
- choix **1**
- meilleur **2**
- pic **3**
- médiator **4**

VT 1 *(select)* choisir; **to p. one's words (carefully)** (bien) choisir ses mots; **she's been picked for the England team** elle a été sélectionnée pour l'équipe d'Angleterre; **to p. a team** former une équipe; **to p. a winner** *(in horseracing)* choisir un cheval gagnant; *Fig* **we've certainly picked a winner in Paul Rodger** nous avons vraiment tiré le bon numéro avec Paul Rodger; *Ironic* **you really (know how to) p. them!** tu les choisis bien!; *Ironic* **you picked a fine time to tell me** tu as bien choisi ton moment pour me le dire

2 *(gather* ► *fruit, flowers)* cueillir; *(*► *mushrooms)* ramasser; **to p. cherries/grapes** *(for pleasure)* cueillir des cerises/du raisin; *(as job)* faire la cueillette des cerises/les vendanges; **p. your own** *(sign)* cueillette à la ferme

3 *(remove)* enlever; **I had to p. the cat hairs off my dress** il a fallu que j'enlève les poils de chat de ma robe

4 *(poke at* ► *spot, scab)* gratter; **to p. one's nose** se mettre les doigts dans le nez; **to p. one's teeth** se curer les dents; **they picked the bones clean** ils n'ont rien laissé sur les os; **she picked a hole in her jumper** elle a fait un trou à son pull en tirant sur la laine

5 *(walk carefully)* **they picked their way along the narrow ridge** ils avancèrent prudemment le long de la crête étroite; **he picked his way through the crowd** il se fraya un chemin à travers la foule

6 *(lock)* crocheter

7 *(pluck* ► *guitar string)* pincer; *(*► *guitar)* pincer les cordes de

8 *(idioms)* **to have a bone to p. with sb** avoir un compte à régler avec qn; **to p. sb's brains** tirer parti de l'intelligence *ou* des connaissances de qn; **can I p. your brains a minute?** est-ce que je peux faire appel à tes connaissances une minute?; **to p. a fight** chercher la bagarre; **to p. holes in sth** *(in argument, theory, book etc)* trouver des failles dans qch; **to p. sb's pocket** faire les poches à qn; **to p. a quarrel with sb** chercher noise *ou* querelle à qn

VI *(choose)* choisir; **to p. and choose** *(be fussy)* faire le/la difficile, faire la fine bouche; **with your qualifications you can p. and choose** avec vos diplômes, toutes les portes vous sont ouvertes

N 1 *(choice)* choix *m*; **take your p.** faites votre choix, choisissez; **you can have your p. of them** vous pouvez choisir celui qui vous plaît; **he could have his p. of any job he wanted** il pourrait obtenir n'importe quel emploi; **we had first p.** nous avons été les premiers à choisir

2 *(best)* meilleur(e) *m,f*; **the p. of France's footballers/writers** *(one)* le meilleur footballer/écrivain français; *(several)* les meilleurs footballers/écrivains français; *Fam* **the p. of the bunch** *(people)* le dessus du panier, le gratin; *(things)* ce qui se fait de mieux ◻

3 *(tool)* pic *m*, pioche *f*; *(of miner)* pic *m* à main; *(of mason)* smille *f*; *(of climber)* piolet *m*

4 *(plectrum)* plectre *m*, médiator *m*

►**pick at VT INSEP 1** *(pull at* ► *loose end)* tirer sur; *(*► *flake of paint, scab)* gratter **2** *(food)* manger du bout des dents; **he only picked at the fish** il a à peine touché au poisson **3** *(criticize pettily)* être sur le dos de

►**pick off VT SEP 1** *(shoot)* abattre **2** *(remove* ► *scab, paint)* gratter; *(*► *flowers, leaves)* enlever, ôter; **p. those papers off the ground** ramassez ces papiers qui sont par terre; **to p. the meat off a bone** décortiquer un os; **she picked herself off the floor** elle s'est relevée

►**pick on VT INSEP 1** *(victimize)* harceler, s'en prendre à; **p. on someone your own size!** ne t'en prends pas à un plus petit que toi! **2** *(single out)* choisir

►**pick out VT SEP 1** *(choose)* choisir

2 *(spot, identify* ► *person in crowd)* repérer; *(*► *person in photo)* reconnaître; *(*► *person in identification parade)* identifier; *(*► *landmark, object)* distinguer; **she was easy to p. out in her orange coat** elle était facilement reconnaissable *ou* facile à repérer avec son manteau orange

3 *(highlight, accentuate)* rehausser; **the stitching is picked out in bright green** un vert vif fait ressortir les coutures

4 *(play)* **to p. out a tune on the piano** retrouver un air au piano

►**pick over VT INSEP** *(examine* ► *fruit, vegetables etc)* trier; *(*► *performance, evidence, details)* décortiquer, analyser

►**pick up VT SEP 1** *(lift)* prendre; *(something from the ground)* ramasser; *(something that has fallen over)* relever; *Knitting (stitch)* relever; **p. up those books!** ramassez ces livres!; **to p. up the telephone** décrocher le téléphone; **to p. up a child** *(in one's arms)* prendre un enfant dans ses bras; *(after falling)* relever un enfant; **to p. oneself up** *(after falling)* se relever; *Fig (recover from crisis)* se remettre; **they left me to p. up the** *Br* **bill** *or Am* **tab** ils m'ont laissé l'addition; *Fig* **to p. up the pieces** recoller les morceaux

2 *(collect* ► *gen)* passer prendre; *(*► *children from school, people from airport etc)* aller chercher; **my father picked me up at the station** mon père est venu me chercher à la gare; **helicopters were sent to p. up the wounded** on a envoyé des hélicoptères pour ramener les blessés; **I never p. up hitchhikers** je ne prends jamais d'auto-stoppeurs

3 *(acquire, come by* ► *skill, information, language)* apprendre; *(*► *reputation)* gagner, acquérir; *(*► *prize)* gagner, remporter; **to p. up bad habits** prendre de mauvaises habitudes; **I don't know where he's picking up these funny ideas from** je ne sais pas où il va chercher ces idées bizarres; **to p. up a parking ticket** attraper un PV; **our country picked up most of the medals** notre pays a remporté la plupart des médailles

4 *Fam (buy cheaply)* **to p. up a bargain** dénicher une bonne affaire; **to p. sth up cheap** acheter qch bon marché ◻; **I picked it up at the flea market** je l'ai trouvé au marché aux puces ◻

5 *(catch* ► *illness, infection)* attraper

6 *Fam (earn)* se faire; **you can p. up good money working on the rigs** on peut se faire pas mal de fric en travaillant sur les plates-formes pétrolières

7 *Fam (arrest)* pincer, agrafer

8 *Fam* **to p. sb up** *(sexual partner)* lever qn; **he tried to p. her up** il l'a draguée; **to p. up a customer** *(of prostitute)* racoler *ou* raccrocher un client

9 *(detect)* détecter; **he picked up the sound of a distant bell** il perçut le son d'une cloche dans le lointain; **the dogs picked up the scent again** les chiens ont retrouvé la piste

10 *Rad & TV (receive)* capter

11 *(notice)* relever; **the proofreaders p. up most of the mistakes** les correcteurs repèrent *ou* relèvent la plupart des erreurs

12 *(criticize)* reprendre; **nobody picked him up on his sexist comments** personne n'a relevé ses remarques sexistes

13 *(resume)* reprendre

14 *(return to)* revenir sur, reprendre; **I'd like to p. up a point you made earlier** j'aimerais revenir sur une remarque que vous avez faite tout à l'heure

15 *(gather* ► *speed, momentum)* prendre; **to p. up strength** *(person)* reprendre des forces

16 *Fam (revive)* remonter ◻, requinquer; **that will p. you up** voilà qui vous remontera

VI 1 *(get better* ► *sick person)* se rétablir, se sentir mieux

2 *(improve* ► *conditions, weather)* s'améliorer; *(*► *business, trade)* reprendre; **the market is picking up after a slow start** après avoir démarré doucement le marché commence à prendre; **the game certainly picked up in the second half** la partie s'est animée pendant la deuxième mi-temps

3 *(resume)* reprendre; **they picked up where they had left off** *(in conversation)* ils ont repris la conversation là où ils l'avaient laissée; *(in game)* ils ont repris le jeu là où ils l'avaient laissé

4 *(notice)* **she didn't p. up on the criticism** elle n'a pas relevé la critique

---

pickaback ['pɪkəbæk] **N to give sb a p.** porter qn sur le dos; **can I have a p.?** est-ce que je peux monter sur ton dos?
ADJ *(ride)* sur le dos

pickaninny (*pl* **pickaninnies**) = **piccaninny**

pickaxe, *Am* **pickax** ['pɪkæks] **N** pic *m*, pioche *f*

picker ['pɪkə(r)] **N** *(of fruit, cotton etc)* cueilleur(euse) *m,f*, ramasseur(euse) *m,f*; **grape-p.** vendangeur(euse) *m,f*; **strawberry-p.** cueilleur(euse) *m,f* de fraises; **mushroom-p.** ramasseur(euse) *m,f* de champignons

pickerel ['pɪkərəl] (*pl* **inv** *or* **pickerels**) **N** *Ich* brochet *m*

picket [ˈpɪkɪt] **N 1** *Ind (group)* piquet *m* de grève; *(individual)* gréviste *mf* (en faction); **there was a p. outside the factory** il y avait un piquet de grève devant l'usine; **20 pickets stood in front of the factory** 20 grévistes se tenaient devant l'usine
2 *(outside embassy, ministry ▸ group)* groupe *m* de manifestants; *(▸ individual)* manifestant(e) *m,f*
3 *Mil* piquet *m*
4 *(stake)* piquet *m*
VT 1 *Ind (workplace, embassy)* **the strikers picketed the factory** les grévistes ont mis en place un piquet de grève devant l'usine; **demonstrators picketed the consulate at the weekend** des manifestants ont bloqué le consulat ce week-end **2** *(fence)* palissader
VI *Ind* mettre en place un piquet de grève
▸▸ ***picket duty*** piquet *m*; **to be on p. duty** faire partie d'un piquet de grève; ***picket fence*** clôture *f* de piquets, palissade *f*; ***picket line*** piquet *m* de grève; **to be** *or* **to stand on a p. line** faire partie d'un piquet de grève; **to cross a p. line** franchir un piquet de grève

picketing [ˈpɪkətɪŋ] **N** *(UNCOUNT)* **1** *(of workplace)* piquets *mpl* de grève; **there is heavy p. at the factory gates** les piquets de grève sont très nombreux aux portes de l'usine **2** *(of ministry, embassy)* **there was p. outside the embassy today** aujourd'hui, il y a eu des manifestations devant l'ambassade

picking [ˈpɪkɪŋ] **N 1** *(selection ▸ of object)* choix *m*; *(▸ of team)* sélection *f* **2** *(of fruit, vegetables)* cueillette *f*, ramassage *m*; **cherry-/strawberry-p.** cueillette *f* des cerises/des fraises; **mushroom-/potato-p.** ramassage *m* des champignons/des pommes de terre **3** *(of lock)* crochetage *m*

pickings **NPL 1** *(remains)* restes *mpl*; **you can have the pickings** vous pouvez prendre ce qui reste **2** *Fam (spoils)* gratte *f*; **there are rich** *or* **easy pickings to be had** on pourrait se faire pas mal d'argent, ça pourrait rapporter gros

pickle [ˈpɪkəl] **N 1** *Am (gherkin)* cornichon *m*
2 *(vinegar)* vinaigre *m*; *(brine)* saumure *f*
3 *Fam (mess, dilemma)* pétrin *m*; **to be in a p.** être dans le pétrin *ou* dans de beaux draps
4 *(UNCOUNT) Br Culin (food)* pickles *mpl (petits oignons, cornichons, morceaux de choux-fleurs etc, macérés dans du vinaigre)*
VT 1 *Culin (in vinegar)* conserver dans le vinaigre; *(in brine)* conserver dans la saumure **2** *Tech (metal)* nettoyer à l'acide ou dans un bain d'acide

pickled [ˈpɪkəld] **ADJ 1** *Culin (in vinegar)* au vinaigre; *(in brine)* conservé dans la saumure **2** *Am (wood, furniture)* cérusé **3** *Fam (drunk)* bourré, pété
▸▸ ***pickled cabbage*** chou *m* rouge au vinaigre; ***pickled herring*** rollmops *m inv*; ***pickled onion*** oignon *m* au vinaigre

pickling [ˈpɪklɪŋ] **N** saumurage *m*, conservation *f* au vinaigre
▸▸ ***pickling onions*** petits oignons *mpl*

picklock [ˈpɪklɒk] **N 1** *(instrument)* crochet *m*, passe-partout *m inv* **2** *(burglar)* crocheteur *m* (de serrures)

pick-me-up **N** *Fam* remontant□ *m*

pick-'n'-mix **N** *(sweets, cheese etc)* assortiment *m (composé par l'acheteur lui-même)*

pickpocket [ˈpɪkˌpɒkɪt] **N** pickpocket *m*, voleur (euse) *m,f* à la tire

pick-up **N 1** *Aut (vehicle)* pick-up *m inv*, camionnette *f* (découverte)
2 *Fam (casual acquaintance)* partenaire *mf* de rencontre□
3 *(act of collecting)* **the truck made several pick-ups on the way** le camion s'est arrêté plusieurs fois en route pour charger des marchandises; **where will the p. be made?** où est-ce qu'on doit passer prendre les marchandises?
4 *(on record player)* pick-up *m inv*, lecteur *m*
5 *(on guitar)* micro *m*
6 *(UNCOUNT) Am Aut (acceleration)* reprises *fpl*; **this car has got good p.** cette voiture a de bonnes reprises
7 *(improvement ▸ of business, economy)* reprise *f*; **we're hoping for a p. in sales** nous espérons une reprise des ventes
8 *Fam (arrest)* arrestation□ *f*
9 *Tech (detector)* détecteur *m*, capteur *m*
10 *Rad & TV (reception)* réception *f*
ADJ *Am (impromptu)* **sometimes I try and get a p. game of squash with the pro** de temps en temps j'improvise une petite partie de squash avec le pro; **a p. musician** un(e) musicien(enne) amateur
▸▸ ***pick-up arm*** *(on record player)* pick-up *m inv*; *Am* ***pick-up line*** = formule d'entrée en matière pour commencer à draguer quelqu'un; ***pick-up point*** *(for cargo)* aire *f* de chargement; *(for passengers)* point *m* de ramassage, lieu *m* de rendez-vous; ***pick-up truck*** pick-up *m inv*, camionnette *f* (découverte)

picky [ˈpɪkɪ] *(compar* **pickier**, *superl* **pickiest)** **ADJ** *Fam* difficile□; **she's really p. about her food** elle est très difficile pour la nourriture; **don't be so p.!** arrête de faire le/la difficile!

picnic [ˈpɪknɪk] *(pt & pp* **picnicked**, *cont* **picnicking)** **N 1** *(in open air)* pique-nique *m*; **to go on** *or* **for a p.** faire un pique-nique; **we took a p. lunch** nous avons emporté de quoi faire un pique-nique; **let's have a p.** faisons un pique-nique **2** *Fam Fig (easy task)* **it was no p.!** c'était pas de la tarte!; **it's no p. showing tourists around London** ce n'est pas une partie de plaisir que de faire visiter Londres aux touristes; **it was no p. cleaning all the pans** ça n'a pas été du gâteau de nettoyer toutes les casseroles
VI pique-niquer
▸▸ ***picnic area*** aire *f* de pique-nique; ***picnic basket, picnic hamper*** panier *m* à pique-nique; *(filled)* panier *m* garni; ***picnic site*** aire *f* de pique-nique

picnicker [ˈpɪknɪkə(r)] **N** pique-niqueur(euse) *m,f*

Pict [pɪkt] **N** Picte *mf*

Pictish [ˈpɪktɪʃ] **N** langue *f* picte
ADJ picte

pictogram [ˈpɪktəgræm], **pictograph** [ˈpɪktəgrɑːf] **N 1** *Ling (symbol)* pictogramme *m*, idéogramme *m* **2** *(chart)* graphique *m*

pictorial [pɪkˈtɔːrɪəl] **ADJ 1** *(in pictures)* en images; *(magazine, newspaper)* illustré **2** *(vivid ▸ style)* vivant **3** *Art* pictural
N illustré *m*

pictorially [pɪkˈtɔːrɪəlɪ] **ADV** en images

PICTURE [ˈpɪktʃə(r)]

N
- image **1, 4**
- peinture **1**
- photo **1**
- portrait **3**
- dessin **1**
- tableau **1, 3**
- film **2**
- situation **5**

VT
- s'imaginer **1**
- représenter **2, 3**
- dépeindre **2**

N 1 *(gen)* image *f*; *(drawing)* dessin *m*; *(painting)* peinture *f*, tableau *m*; *(in book)* illustration *f*; *(photograph)* photo *f*; **he used pictures to illustrate his talk** il a illustré sa conférence à l'aide d'images; **to draw/to paint a p.** faire un dessin/une peinture; **to draw a p. of sb/sth** dessiner qn/qch; **to paint a p. of sb** peindre le portrait de qn; **to take a p.** prendre une photo; **to take a p. of sb, to take sb's p.** prendre une photo de qn, prendre qn en photo; **to have one's p. taken** se faire prendre en photo; **the p.'s blurred** *(on television)* l'image est floue
2 *(film)* film *m*; *Br Fam* **the pictures** *(the cinema)* le cinoche, le ciné
3 *(description)* tableau *m*, portrait *m*; **his novels give a vivid p. of the period** l'époque est peinte de façon très vivante dans ses romans, ses romans brossent un portrait très vivant de l'époque; **the TV series gives a good p. of life in a mining town** cette série télévisée donne un bon aperçu de la vie dans une ville minière; **the p. he painted was a depressing one** il a brossé *ou* fait un tableau déprimant de la situation; **to paint a bleak p. of the future** présenter une triste image de l'avenir
4 *(idea, image)* image *f*; **I have a strong mental p. of what war was like** je m'imagine très bien ce qu'était la guerre; **he's the p. of health** il respire la santé, il est resplendissant de santé; **she was the p. of despair** elle était l'image vivante du désespoir; **he's the p. of his elder brother** c'est (tout) le portrait de son frère aîné
5 *(situation)* situation *f*; **the economic p. is bleak** la situation économique est inquiétante
6 *Fam (idioms)* **to be in the p.** être au courant□; **she hates being left out of the p.** elle déteste qu'on la laisse dans l'ignorance□; **to put sb in the p.** mettre qn au courant□; **I get the p.!** je pige!, j'y suis!; **doesn't she look a p.!** n'est-elle pas adorable *ou* ravissante!□; **her face was a real p. when she heard the news!** il fallait voir sa tête quand elle a appris la nouvelle!; **the big p.** *(overview)* une vue d'ensemble□
VT 1 *(imagine)* s'imaginer, se représenter; **I can't quite p. him as a teacher** j'ai du mal à me l'imaginer comme enseignant; **p. yourself at 80** imagine-toi à 80 ans; **just p. the scene** imaginez un peu la scène
2 *(describe)* dépeindre, représenter
3 *(paint, draw etc)* représenter; **he was pictured with her on the front page of all the papers** une photo où il était en sa compagnie s'étalait à la une de tous les journaux
▸▸ ***picture book*** livre *m* d'images; *Cards* ***picture card*** figure *f*; ***picture cheque*** image-chèque *f*; *Journ* ***picture desk*** bureau *m* des illustrations; ***picture dictionary*** dictionnaire *m* en images; *TV* ***picture distortion*** distorsion *f* de l'image; ***picture editor*** illustrateur(trice) *m,f*; ***picture frame*** cadre *m* (pour tableaux); ***picture framer*** encadreur (euse) *m,f*; ***picture gallery*** musée *m* de peinture; ***picture hat*** capeline *f*; *Br Old-fashioned* ***picture house*** cinéma *m*; ***picture library*** banque *f* d'images; *Comput* ***picture memory*** mémoire *f* d'images; *Tel* ***picture messaging*** = prise et envoi de photos par téléphone portable; ***picture monitor*** écran *m* de contrôle de l'image; *Br Old-fashioned* ***picture palace*** cinéma *m*; *Old-fashioned* ***picture postcard*** carte *f* postale (illustrée); ***picture puzzle*** rébus *m*; *Phot & TV* ***picture quality*** qualité *f* d'image; ***picture rail*** cimaise *f*; ***picture research*** documentation *f* iconographique; ***picture researcher*** documentaliste *mf* iconographique; ***picture restorer*** restaurateur(trice) *m,f* de tableaux; *TV* ***picture signal*** signal *m* d'image; *TV* ***picture tube*** tube *m* image; ***picture window*** fenêtre *f* *ou* baie *f* panoramique; ***picture writing*** écriture *f* idéographique

picturesque [ˌpɪktʃəˈresk] **ADJ** pittoresque

picturesquely [ˌpɪktʃəˈresklɪ] **ADV** de façon pittoresque; **the village is p. situated** le village se trouve dans un site pittoresque

picturesqueness [ˌpɪktʃəˈresknɪs] **N** pittoresque *m*

piddle [ˈpɪdəl] *Fam* **VI** faire pipi
N pipi *m*; **to have a p.** faire pipi; **to go for a p.** aller faire pipi

piddling [ˈpɪdlɪŋ], **piddly** [ˈpɪdlɪ] **ADJ** *Fam (details)* insignifiant□; *(job, pay)* minable

pidgin [ˈpɪdʒɪn] **N** *Ling* pidgin *m*
▸▸ *Ling* ***pidgin English*** pidgin *m*, pidgin-english *m*; *Pej* **to speak p. English** parler de façon incorrecte

pie [paɪ] **N** *Culin (with fruit)* tarte *f*; *(with meat, fish etc)* tourte *f*; **chicken p.** tourte *f* au poulet; *Fig* **I want my piece of the p.** je veux ma part du gâteau; *Fam* **it's just p. in the sky** ce sont des paroles *ou* promesses en l'air
▸▸ ***pie chart*** graphique *m* circulaire, camembert *m*; ***pie dish*** plat *m* à tarte; *(for meat)* terrine *f*; *(oven-proof)* plat *m* allant au four; ***pie funnel*** = sorte de cheminée en céramique que l'on place au centre d'une tourte avant de la faire cuire; *Am* ***pie plate*** plat *m* allant au four

piebald [ˈpaɪbɔːld] **ADJ** pie *(inv)*
N cheval *m* pie

PIECE [piːs]

- morceau **1, 3, 5**
- parcelle **1**
- pion **4**
- bout **1**
- pièce **2–5, 7, 8, 11**
- article **6**

N 1 *(bit ▸ of bread, chocolate, paper, wood)* morceau *m*, bout *m*; *(▸ of cake, pie)* morceau *m*, tranche *f*; *(▸ of land)* parcelle *f*, lopin *m*; *(of string, ribbon)* bout *m*; *(▸ of cloth)* morceau *m*, coupon *m*; *(▸ of glass)* morceau *m*, fragment *m*, éclat *m*; **a**

p. of advice un conseil; **a p. of information** un renseignement; **a p. of news** une nouvelle; **that was a real p. of luck** cela a vraiment été un coup de chance; **it's a superb p. of craftsmanship** *or* **workmanship** c'est du très beau travail; **to be in pieces** *(in parts)* être en pièces détachées; *(broken)* être en pièces *ou* en morceaux; **to be in one p.** *(undamaged)* être intact; *(uninjured)* être indemne; *(safe)* être sain et sauf; **to be all of a p.** *(in one piece)* être tout d'une pièce *ou* d'un seul tenant; *(consistent)* être cohérent; *(alike)* se ressembler; *Br* **his actions are of a p. with his opinions** ses actes sont conformes à ses opinions; **to be still in one p.** *(person, car etc after accident)* être encore entier; **to break sth into pieces** mettre qch en morceaux *ou* en pièces; **to pull sth to pieces** *(doll, garment, book)* mettre qch en morceaux; *(flower)* effeuiller qch; *Fig (argument, suggestion, idea)* démolir qch; **to pull sb to pieces** descendre qn en flammes; **to come to pieces** *(into separate parts)* se démonter; *(break)* se briser; **to fall to pieces** partir en morceaux; **to take sth to pieces** démonter qch; *Fam* **to go (all) to pieces** *(person)* s'effondrer❑, craquer; *(team)* se désintégrer❑; *(market)* s'effondrer❑; *Fam* **it's a p. of cake** c'est du gâteau; *Br very Fam* **a p. of piss** un jeu d'enfant❑; *Br Fam* **he's a nasty p. of work** c'est un sale type; **I gave him a p. of my mind** *(spoke frankly)* je lui ai dit ma façon de penser; *(spoke harshly)* je lui ai passé un savon; **to say one's p.** dire ce qu'on a sur le cœur

2 *(item)* pièce *f*; **a p. of clothing** un vêtement; **a p. of furniture** un meuble; **a p. of luggage** *(suitcase)* une valise; *(bag)* un sac; **how many pieces of luggage do you have?** combien de bagages avez-vous?; **one p. of hand luggage** un bagage à main; **to sell sth by the p.** vendre qch à la pièce *ou* au détail; **to be paid by the p.** être payé à la pièce *ou* à la tâche

3 *(part ▸ of machine, set)* pièce *f*; *(▸ of jigsaw)* pièce *f*, morceau *m*; **to put sth together p. by p.** assembler qch pièce par pièce *ou* morceau par morceau; **an 18-p. dinner service** un service de table de 18 pièces; **an 18-p. band** un orchestre de 18 musiciens

4 *(for games ▸ in chess)* pièce *f*; *(▸ in draughts)* pion *m*; *(▸ in backgammon)* dame *f*; *(▸ in dominoes)* domino *m*

5 *(performance)* morceau *m*; *(musical composition)* morceau *m*, pièce *f*; *(sculpture)* pièce *f* (de sculpture); **a piano p.** un morceau pour piano

6 *(newspaper article)* article *m*

7 *(coin)* pièce *f*; **a 50p p.** une pièce de 50 pence

8 *Mil (firearm, cannon)* pièce *f*; *Fam Crime slang (gun)* flingue *m*

9 *very Fam (girl)* **she's a nice** *or* **tasty p.** c'est un beau brin de fille❑

10 *Am (time)* moment *m*; *(distance)* bout *m* de chemin; **he walked with me a p.** il a fait un bout de chemin avec moi

11 *Metal* **punched/shaped p.** pièce *f* estampée/profilée; **to cast cylinders in one p.** couler des cylindres d'un seul jet *ou* en bloc

►► ***piece rate*** paiement *m* à la pièce; **to be on p. rate** être payé aux pièces

▸**piece together** VT SEP **1** *(from parts ▸ broken object)* recoller; *(▸ jigsaw)* assembler; **the collage was pieced together from scraps of material** le collage était fait *ou* constitué de petits bouts de tissu **2** *(story, facts)* reconstituer; **detectives are piecing together a picture of the events** les enquêteurs sont en train de se faire une idée des événements

piecemeal ['pi:smi:l] ADV *(little by little)* peu à peu, petit à petit; **he told the story p.** il a raconté l'histoire par bribes; **the town was rebuilt p. after the war** la ville a été reconstruite par étapes après la guerre; **the collection was sold p.** les pièces de la collection ont été vendues séparément

ADJ *(fragmentary)* fragmentaire, parcellaire; *(work)* fait petit à petit; *(funding, transformation)* morcelé, fragmenté

piecework ['pi:swɜ:k] N *(UNCOUNT)* travail *m* à la pièce; **to be on p.** travailler à la pièce

pieceworker ['pi:swɜ:kə(r)] N travailleur(euse) *m,f* à la pièce

piecrust ['paɪkrʌst] N couche *f* de pâte *(pour recouvrir une tourte)*

pied [paɪd] ADJ *(gen)* bariolé, bigarré; *(animal)* pie *(inv)*

►► *Orn* ***pied wagtail*** bergeronnette *f* de Yarrell

pied-à-terre [,pjeɪdæ'teə(r)] *(pl* **pieds-à-terre** [,pjeɪdæ'teə(r)]*)* N pied-à-terre *m inv*

Piedmont ['pi:dmənt] N Piémont *m*

pie-eyed ADJ *Fam (drunk)* bourré, rond

pier [pɪə(r)] N **1** *Br (at seaside)* jetée *f* **2** *(jetty)* jetée *f*; *(landing stage)* embarcadère *m*; *(breakwater)* digue *f* **3** *(pillar)* pilier *m*, colonne *f*; *(of bridge)* pile *f*

pierce [pɪəs] VT **1** *(make hole in)* percer, transpercer; **to p. a hole in sth** faire *ou* percer un trou dans qch; **the knife pierced her lung** le couteau lui a perforé *ou* transpercé le poumon; **she had her ears pierced** elle s'est fait percer les oreilles; **his words pierced my heart** ses paroles me fendirent le cœur **2** *(of sound, scream, light)* percer; **a cry pierced the silence** un cri perça *ou* déchira le silence; **the beam pierced the darkness** le faisceau perça l'obscurité; **the biting wind pierced his clothing** le vent glacial transperçait ses vêtements **3** *(penetrate ▸ defence, barrier)* percer

piercing ['pɪəsɪŋ] ADJ *(scream, eyes, look)* perçant; *(question)* lancinant; *(wind)* glacial

N *(on face, body)* piercing *m*

pierhead ['pɪəhed] N musoir *m*

Pierrot ['pɪərəʊ] PR N Pierrot

piety ['paɪətɪ] *(pl* **pieties***)* N piété *f*

piffle ['pɪfəl] *Br Fam* N *(UNCOUNT)* balivernes *fpl*, niaiseries *fpl*; **don't talk p.!** ne dis pas de bêtises!❑

EXCLAM des sottises tout ça!

piffling ['pɪflɪŋ] ADJ *Br Fam (excuse, amount, mistake)* insignifiant❑; **a p. little man** un moins que rien

pig [pɪg] *(pt & pp* **pigged**, *cont* **pigging***)* N **1** *(animal)* cochon *m*, porc *m*; *Am (young pig)* cochonnet *m*, porcelet *m*; **pigs might fly!** quand les poules auront des dents!; *Br Fam* **to make a p.'s ear of sth** saloper qch, foirer qch; **he made a p.'s ear of laying the carpet** il a posé la moquette comme un vrai sagouin; **to buy a p. in a poke** acheter chat en poche

2 *Fam (greedy person)* goinfre *mf*; *(dirty eater)* cochon(onne) *m,f*; **to eat like a p.** manger comme un cochon *ou* un porc; **to make a p. of oneself** se goinfrer, s'empiffrer

3 *Fam (dirty person)* cochon(onne) *m,f*; **to live like pigs** vivre dans une écurie *ou* porcherie

4 *Fam (unpleasant person)* ordure *f*, chameau *m*; **fascist p.!** sale fasciste!; **what a selfish p.!** quel sale égoïste!

5 *Br Fam (unpleasant thing, task)* truc *m* chiant; **it's a real p. of a job** ce travail est un véritable cauchemar; **the filing cabinet was a p. to move** ça a été vachement difficile de déplacer le classeur

6 *Fam Pej (policeman)* flic *m*, poulet *m*; **the pigs** les flics *mpl*, les poulets *mpl*

7 *Metal (of casting)* gueuse *f*; *(of lead, tin etc)* saumon *m*

8 *Fam (ugly person)* mocheté *f*

VT *Fam* **1** *(stuff)* **to p. oneself (on sth)** s'empiffrer (de qch), se goinfrer (de qch) **2 to p. it** *(dirty person)* vivre comme des cochons

VI *(sow)* mettre bas, cochonner

►► ***pig farm*** porcherie *f*, élevage *m* de porcs; ***pig iron*** fonte *f* brute; *Culin* ***pig's trotter*** pied *m* de porc

▸**pig out** VI *Fam* s'empiffrer, se goinfrer (**on sth** de qch)

pigeon ['pɪdʒɪn] N **1** *Orn* pigeon *m* **2** *Br Fam (business)* **it's not my p.** ce n'est pas mon problème❑; **that's their p.** c'est leurs affaires *ou* leurs oignons

►► ***pigeon droppings*** fiente *f* de pigeon; ***pigeon fancier*** colombophile *mf*; ***pigeon loft*** pigeonnier *m*; ***pigeon post*** transport *m* de dépêches par pigeons voyageurs; ***pigeon shooting*** tir *m ou* chasse *f* aux pigeons

pigeon-breasted [-'brestɪd], **pigeon-chested** [-'tʃestɪd] ADJ **to be p.** avoir la poitrine bombée

pigeonhole ['pɪdʒɪnhəʊl] N casier *m* (à courrier); *Fig* **he tends to put people in pigeonholes** il a tendance à étiqueter les gens *ou* à mettre de étiquettes aux gens

VT **1** *(file)* classer **2** *(postpone)* différer, remettr (à plus tard); **the scheme had been pigeonhole until further notice** le projet avait été remis jus qu'à nouvel ordre **3** *(classify)* étiqueter, cata loguer; **they pigeonholed me as a feminist** il m'avaient étiquetée comme féministe

pigeon-toed ADJ **to be p.** avoir les pieds tou nés en dedans

piggery ['pɪgərɪ] *(pl* **piggeries***)* N **1** *(for pigs)* po cherie *f* **2** *(greediness)* gloutonnerie *f*

piggish ['pɪgɪʃ] ADJ *Fam Pej* **1** *(dirty)* cochon *(greedy)* glouton❑ **2** *Br (stubborn)* têtu❑

piggy ['pɪgɪ] *(pl* **piggies***)* *Fam* N *(in children's lan guage ▸ pig)* (petit) cochon❑ *m*; *(▸ toe)* doigt *n* de pied❑; *(▸ finger)* doigt❑ *m*; **p. in the middle** = jeu d'enfants au cours duquel deux enfants s lancent un ballon alors qu'un troisième plac au milieu essaie de l'attraper; *Fig* **I'm tired o being p. in the middle** j'en ai assez d'être pris en tre deux feux

ADJ **1** *(greedy)* glouton❑, goinfre **2** *(features)* **p eyes** de petits yeux *mpl* porcins❑

piggyback ['pɪgɪbæk] ADV **1** *(on one's back)* sur l dos; **to ride** *or* **to be carried p.** se faire porter sur l dos de qn **2** *Comput* **to mount sth p. on sth** supe poser qch sur qch

N **to give sb a p.** porter qn sur le dos; **can I have p.?** est-ce que je peux monter sur ton dos?

ADJ *(ride)* sur le dos

VT **1** *(carry)* porter sur son dos; *Fig* **the new musi festival was piggybacked onto the main theatr festival** ils ont profité de l'existence du festiva de théâtre pour lancer le nouveau festival d musique; **this provision was piggybacked ont the new legislation** cette disposition a été incor porée à la nouvelle loi **2** *esp Am Transp* ferroute

►► *Comput* ***piggyback board*** carte *f* fille

piggybacking ['pɪgɪ,bækɪŋ] N **1** *Banking* por tage *m* **2** *(in export)* exportation *f* kangourou **3** *esp Am Transp* ferroutage *m*

pigheaded [pɪg'hedɪd] ADJ têtu, obstiné

pigheadedly [pɪg'hedɪdlɪ] ADV obstinément avec entêtement

pigheadedness [pɪg'hedɪdnɪs] N obstination *f* entêtement *m*

piglet ['pɪglɪt] N cochonnet *m*, porcelet *m*

pigment N ['pɪgmənt] **1** *Art* couleur *f*, colorant *m* pigment *m* **2** *Physiol* pigment *m*

VT [pɪg'ment] pigmenter

►► ***pigment cell*** cellule *f* pigmentaire

pigmentation [,pɪgmən'teɪʃən] N pigmentatio *f*

pigmy = **pygmy**

pigpen ['pɪgpen] N *Am also Fig* porcherie *f*

pigskin ['pɪgskɪn] N **1** *(leather)* peau *f* de porc; **it' made of p.** c'est en (peau de) porc **2** *Am (football* ballon *m (de football américain)*

COMP *(bag, watchstrap)* en (peau de) porc

pigsty ['pɪgstaɪ] *(pl* **pigsties***)* N *also Fig* porcherie

pigswill ['pɪgswɪl] N *Br* pâtée *f* (pour les co chons); *Fig* **our school meals are p.** ce qu'o (nous) sert à la cantine de l'école est bon pou les cochons

pigtail ['pɪgteɪl] N natte *f*

pig-thick ADJ *Br Fam* con comme un balai

pig-ugly ADJ *Br Fam* moche comme un pou

pike [paɪk] *(pl* **inv** *or* **pikes***)* N **1** *Ich* brochet *m*

2 *(spear)* pique *f*

3 *NEng (hill)* pic *m*

4 *(barrier)* barrière *f* de péage

5 *(in diving)* plongeon *m* groupé

pikestaff ['paɪkstɑ:f] N **1** *(weapon)* bois *m o* hampe *f* de pique **2** *(for walking)* bâton *m* à pointe de fer

pikey ['paɪkɪ] N *Br Fam* voyou *m*

pilaf, pilaff ['pɪlæf] = **pilau**

pilaster [pɪ'læstə(r)] N pilastre *m*

Pilates [pɪ'lɑ:teɪz] N Pilates *m*, méthode *f* Pilates; **to do P.** pratiquer la méthode Pilates; **a P. class** u cours de Pilates

pilau [pɪ'laʊ] N pilaf *m*

►► ***pilau rice*** riz *m* pilaf

pilchard ['pɪltʃəd] **N** *Ich* pilchard *m*

PILE [paɪl]

N
- pile **1, 5–7**
- tas **1, 2**
- fortune **3**
- édifice **4**
- pieu **7**
- poil **8**

VT
- empiler
- entasser

N 1 *(neat stack)* pile *f*; *(heap)* tas *m*; **to put books/magazines in a p.** empiler des livres/magazines; **she left her clothes/records in a p. on the floor** elle a laissé ses vêtements/disques en tas par terre; *Fam Fig* **to be at the top/bottom of the p.** être en haut/en bas de l'échelle□

2 *(usu pl) Fam (large quantity)* tas *m ou mpl*, masses *fpl*; **to have piles of money** avoir plein d'argent, être plein aux as; **I've got piles of work to do** j'ai un tas de boulot *ou* un boulot dingue

3 *Fam (fortune)* fortune□*f*; **he made his p. in the fur trade** il a fait fortune dans le commerce de la fourrure; **she must have made a p. out of that deal** elle a dû gagner une fortune dans ce contrat

4 *(large building)* édifice *m*; **she owns a huge Jacobean p. in the country** elle a un immense manoir du XVIIème siècle à la campagne

5 *(battery)* pile *f*

6 *Nucl* **(atomic) p.** pile *f*, réacteur *m* (atomique)

7 *Constr* pieu *m*; *(for bridge)* pile *f*; **built on piles** sur pilotis

8 *(UNCOUNT) Tex* fibres *fpl*, poil *m*; **a deep-p. carpet** une moquette épaisse

VT *(stack)* empiler; *(put in a heap)* entasser; **don't p. those records on top of one another** n'empilez pas ces disques les uns sur les autres; **she piled her clothes into the suitcase** elle a mis tous ses habits pêle-mêle dans la valise; **the table was piled high with papers** il y avait une grosse pile de papiers sur la table; **he piled more coal on the fire** il a remis du charbon dans le feu; **he piled spaghetti onto his plate** il a rempli son assiette de spaghettis

VI *Fam* **they piled into the car** ils se sont entassés dans la voiture; **they all piled off the bus** ils sont tous descendus du bus en se bousculant□; **we piled up the stairs** nous avons monté l'escalier en nous bousculant□

►► *Constr* **pile driver** sonnette *f*; *Fam Fig (blow)* coup *m* violent□; ***pile dwelling*** habitation *f* lacustre *ou* sur pilotis

►**pile in VI** *Fam (enter)* entrer en se bousculant□; **they opened the doors and we all piled in** ils ont ouvert les portes et nous nous sommes tous bousculés pour entrer; **p. in!** *(into car)* montez!□, en voiture!□; **once the first punch was thrown we all piled in** *(joined the fight)* après le premier coup de poing, on s'est tous lancés dans la bagarre□

►**pile off VI** *Fam (from bus, train)* descendre en se bousculant□

►**pile on** *Fam* **VT SEP** *(increase ► suspense)* faire durer□; *(► pressure)* faire monter□; **to p. on the agony** forcer la dose, dramatiser (à l'excès)□; **to p. on the pounds** grossir□, prendre du poids□; **to p. it on** *(exaggerate)* exagérer□, en rajouter

VI *(onto bus, train)* s'entasser, monter en s'entassant

►**pile out VI** *Fam (off bus, train)* descendre en se bousculant□; *(from cinema, lecture hall)* sortir en se bousculant□

►**pile up VI 1** *(crash ► cars)* se rentrer dedans, se caramboler **2** *(accumulate ► work, debts)* s'accumuler, s'entasser; *(► washing, clouds)* s'amonceler; **work was piling up on her desk** le travail s'amoncelait sur son bureau

VT SEP 1 *(stack)* empiler; *(put in a heap)* entasser **2** *(accumulate ► evidence, examples)* accumuler

piles [paɪlz] **NPL** *(haemorrhoids)* hémorroïdes *fpl*; **to have p.** avoir des hémorroïdes

pile-up N carambolage *m*; **there was a 50-car p. in the fog** 50 voitures se sont télescopées *ou* carambolées dans le brouillard

pilfer ['pɪlfə(r)] **VT** chaparder (**from sb** à qn)

VI chaparder

pilferage ['pɪlfərɪdʒ] **N** petits vols *mpl*, larcins *mpl*; **the percentage lost through p.** le pourcentage perdu imputable aux petits vols

pilferer ['pɪlfərə(r)] **N** chapardeur(euse) *m,f*

pilfering ['pɪlfərɪŋ] = **pilferage**

pilgrim ['pɪlgrɪm] **N** pèlerin *m*; **the Pilgrims** les Pèlerins *mpl*

►► ***the Pilgrim Fathers*** les Pères Pèlerins *mpl*

pilgrimage ['pɪlgrɪmɪdʒ] **N** pèlerinage *m*; **to make** *or* **to go on a p.** faire un pèlerinage; **they made** *or* **went on a p. to Lourdes** ils sont allés en pèlerinage à Lourdes; *Fig* **I made a p. to my childhood home** je suis retourné visiter la maison de mon enfance

pill [pɪl] **N 1** *Med* pilule *f*, comprimé *m*; *Fig* **to sugar** *or* **to sweeten the p. (for sb)** dorer la pilule (à qn) **2** *(contraceptive pill)* **the p.** la pilule; **to go on the p.** commencer à prendre la pilule; **to be on the p.** prendre la pilule

►► *Fam* ***pill popper*** accro *mf* aux tranquillisants

pillage ['pɪlɪdʒ] **VT** mettre à sac, piller

VI se livrer au pillage

N pillage *m*

pillager ['pɪlɪdʒə(r)] **N** pilleur(euse) *m,f*, pillard (e) *m,f*

pillar ['pɪlə(r)] **N 1** *(structural support)* pilier *m*; *(ornamental)* colonne *f*; **to go from p. to post** tourner en rond; **he was sent from p. to post** on l'a envoyé à droite et à gauche **2** *(of smoke)* colonne *f*; *(of water)* trombe *f*; **p. of rock** colonne *f* rocheuse; *Bible* **a p. of salt** une statue de sel **3** *Fig (mainstay)* pilier *m*; **a p. of society** un pilier de la société; **you've been a real p. of strength** vous avez été un soutien précieux

►► *Br* ***pillar box*** boîte *f* à lettres

pillared ['pɪləd] **ADJ** à piliers, à colonnes

pillbox ['pɪlbɒks] **N 1** *Med* boîte *f* à pilules **2** *Mil* blockhaus *m inv*, casemate *f* **3** *(hat)* toque *f*

pillhead ['pɪlhed] **N** *Fam* = accro aux tranquillisants ou aux speeds

pillion ['pɪljən] **N 1** *(on motorbike)* siège *m* arrière **2** *(on horse)* selle *f* de derrière

ADV to ride p. *(on motorbike)* voyager sur le siège arrière; *(on horse)* monter en croupe

►► ***pillion passenger, pillion rider*** passager(ère) *m,f* *(sur une moto)*; ***pillion seat*** siège *m* arrière

pillock ['pɪlək] **N** *Br Fam (idiot)* andouille *f*, courge *f*

pillory ['pɪlərɪ] *(pl* **pillories,** *pt & pp* **pilloried)** **N** pilori *m*

VT *Hist & Fig* mettre *ou* clouer au pilori

pillow ['pɪləʊ] **N 1** *(on bed)* oreiller *m* **2** *Tex (for lace)* carreau *m* (de dentellière)

VT *(rest)* reposer; **he pillowed his head on his arms** il posa sa tête sur ses bras; **her head was pillowed on a mound of leaves** sa tête reposait sur un oreiller de feuilles

►► ***pillow fight*** bataille *f* de polochons; *Am* ***pillow sham*** taie *f* d'oreiller; ***pillow talk*** *(UNCOUNT)* confidences *fpl* sur l'oreiller

pillowcase ['pɪləʊkeɪs], *Br* **pillowslip** ['pɪləʊslɪp] **N** taie *f* d'oreiller

pilot ['paɪlət] **N 1** *Aviat & Naut* pilote *m*; *Fig (guide)* guide *m*

2 *Tech (on tool)* guidage *m*

3 *(pilot light)* veilleuse *f*

4 *TV* émission *f* pilote

COMP *(error)* de pilotage

VT 1 *Aviat & Naut* piloter **2** *(guide)* piloter, guider; **he's piloted the company through several crises** il a sorti l'entreprise de la crise *ou* de ses difficultés à plusieurs reprises; **she piloted the bill through parliament** elle s'est assurée que le projet de loi serait voté **3** *(test)* tester, expérimenter; **the project was piloted at Harvard University** le projet a été testé à l'Université de Harvard

ADJ *(trial ► programme)* d'essai, pilote, expérimental

►► *Met* ***pilot balloon*** ballon-sonde *m*; ***pilot boat*** bateau-pilote *m*; ***pilot burner*** veilleuse *f*; *Ich* ***pilot fish*** pilote *m*, poisson-pilote *m*; ***pilot flame*** veilleuse *f*; *Naut* ***pilot house*** poste *m* de pilotage; ***pilot lamp*** veilleuse *f* (électrique); ***pilot light*** veilleuse *f*; *Br Aviat* ***pilot officer*** ≃ sous-lieutenant *m*; ***pilot project*** projet-pilote *m*; *Aviat, Ind & Com* ***pilot run*** présérie *f*; *Br* ***pilot scheme*** projet-pilote *m*; ***pilot study*** étude *f* pilote, avant-projet *m*, pré-étude *f*; ***pilot waters*** zone *f* de pilotage; *Zool* ***pilot whale*** globicéphale *m*

pimento [pɪ'mentəʊ] *(pl* **pimentos)** **N** piment *m*

pimp [pɪmp] **N** maquereau *m*, souteneur *m*

VI faire le maquereau

pimpernel ['pɪmpənel] **N** *Bot (scarlet)* mouron *m*; *(yellow)* lysimaque *f*

pimple ['pɪmpəl] **N** bouton *m*; **to come out in pimples** boutonner, bourgeonner

pimply ['pɪmplɪ] *(compar* **pimplier,** *superl* **pimpliest)** **ADJ** boutonneux

PIMS [pɪmz] **N** *Mktg (abbr* **profit impact of marketing strategy)** IRSM *m*

PIN [pɪn] **N** *(abbr* **personal identification number)** code *m* confidentiel *(d'une carte bancaire)*

►► ***PIN number*** code *m* confidentiel *(d'une carte bancaire)*

PIN [pɪn]

N
- épingle **1**
- punaise **1**
- broche **2, 5, 6**
- cheville **4**
- goujon **4**
- goupille **4**
- quille **7**

VT
- épingler **1**
- punaiser **1**
- immobiliser **2**
- cheviller **3**
- étayer **4**

(pt & pp **pinned,** *cont* **pinning)**

N 1 *(for sewing, fastening)* épingle *f*; *(drawing pin)* punaise *f*; *(hairpin)* épingle *f* à cheveux; **she took a p. from her hair** elle enleva une épingle de ses cheveux; **you could have heard a p. drop** on aurait entendu voler une mouche; **as bright** *or* **clean as a new p.** propre comme un sou neuf; **for two pins I'd let the whole thing drop** il ne faudrait pas beaucoup me pousser pour que je laisse tout tomber; **he doesn't care two pins about it** il s'en moque complètement

2 *Am (brooch)* broche *f*; *(badge)* insigne *m*

3 *Fam* **pins** *(legs)* cannes *fpl*, guibolles *fpl*, gambettes *fpl*; **he's a bit unsteady on his pins** il ne tient pas bien sur ses guibolles

4 *(peg ► in piano, violin)* cheville *f*; *(► in hinge, pulley)* goujon *m*; *(► in hand grenade)* goupille *f*; **(firing) p.** percuteur *m*

5 *Elec (on plug)* broche *f*; **two-p. plug** prise *f* à deux broches

6 *Med (for broken bone)* broche *f*

7 *(in skittles, bowling)* quille *f*

8 *(in wrestling ► gen)* prise *f*; *(► with shoulders on floor)* tombé *m*

9 *Chess* clouage *m*

10 *Golf* drapeau *m*

VT 1 *(attach ► with pin or pins)* épingler; *(► with drawing pin or pins)* punaiser; **she had a brooch pinned to her jacket** elle portait une broche épinglée à sa veste; **there was a sign pinned to the door** un écriteau était punaisé sur la porte; *Fig* **to p. one's hopes on sb/sth** mettre tous ses espoirs dans qn/qch; **to p. one's faith on sb** placer sa foi en qn; **the crime was pinned on James** c'est James qu'on a accusé du délit, on a mis le délit sur le dos de James; **they pinned the blame on the shop assistant** ils ont rejeté la responsabilité sur la vendeuse, ils ont mis ça sur le dos de la vendeuse; **you can't p. this on me** tu ne peux pas me mettre ça sur le dos

2 *(immobilize)* immobiliser, coincer; **they pinned his arms behind his back** ils lui ont coincé les bras derrière le dos; **to p. sb to the ground/against a wall** clouer qn au sol/contre un mur; **she was pinned under a boulder** elle était coincée *ou* bloquée sous un rocher

3 *Tech* cheviller, goupiller, mettre une goupille à

4 *Constr (wall)* étayer, étançonner

5 *Chess* clouer

►► ***pin money*** argent *m* de poche; **she works at weekends to earn a bit of p. money** elle travaille le week-end pour se faire un peu d'argent pour ses menus plaisirs; *Fam* ***pins and needles*** fourmillements□*mpl*; **I've got pins and needles in my arm** j'ai des fourmis dans le bras□, je ne sens plus mon bras; *Am* **to be on pins and needles** trépigner d'impatience□, ronger son frein□; *Sew-*

ing **pin tuck** nervure *f*; **pin wheel** *(on printer)* roue *f* à picots

▸ **pin back** VT SEP **to have one's ears pinned back** se faire recoller les oreilles; *Fam* **p. back your ears!** ouvrez vos oreilles!, écoutez bien!□

▸ **pin down** VT SEP **1** *(with pin or pins)* fixer avec une épingle/des épingles; *(with drawing pin or pins)* fixer avec une punaise/des punaises

2 *(trap)* coincer; **his legs were pinned down by the fallen tree** ses jambes étaient coincées sous l'arbre; **he had me pinned down** il m'avait coincé; **pinned down by enemy fire** coincé par le feu de l'ennemi

3 *(define clearly ▸ difference, meaning)* mettre le doigt sur, cerner avec précision; **a feeling that's difficult to p. down** un sentiment qu'il est difficile d'isoler *ou* d'identifier; **it's difficult to p. it down** c'est difficile de mettre le doigt dessus

4 *(commit)* amener à se décider; **try to p. her down to a definite schedule** essayez d'obtenir d'elle un planning définitif; **he doesn't want to be pinned down** il veut avoir les coudées franches, il tient à garder sa liberté de manœuvre

▸ **pin up** VT SEP **1** *(poster)* punaiser; *(results, names)* afficher **2** *(hem)* épingler; *(hair)* relever (avec des épingles); **she wears her hair pinned up** elle porte ses cheveux relevés en chignon

pinafore ['pɪnəfɔː(r)] *Br* N **1** *(apron)* tablier *m* **2** *(dress)* robe-chasuble *f*

▸▸ ***pinafore dress*** robe-chasuble *f*

pinball ['pɪnbɔːl] N *(game)* flipper *m*; **to play p.** jouer au flipper

▸▸ ***pinball machine, pinball table*** flipper *m*

pincer ['pɪnsə(r)] N *(of crab)* pince *f*

• **pincers** NPL *(tool)* tenaille *f*, tenailles *fpl*; **a pair of pincers** une tenaille, des tenailles *fpl*

▸▸ *Mil* ***pincer movement*** manœuvre *f ou* mouvement *m* d'encerclement

pinch [pɪntʃ] VT **1** *(squeeze)* pincer; **he pinched her cheek** il lui a pincé la joue; **I had to p. myself to make sure I wasn't dreaming** je me suis pincé pour voir si je ne rêvais pas; **these new shoes p. my feet** ces chaussures neuves me font mal aux pieds

2 *Br Fam (steal)* piquer, faucher; **to p. sth from sb** piquer qch à qn; **I had my stereo pinched** on m'a piqué ma chaîne stéréo

3 *Am Fam (arrest)* pincer, agrafer; **they got pinched for shoplifting** ils se sont fait pincer pour vol à l'étalage

4 *Hort* pincer

VI **1** *(shoes)* serrer, faire mal (aux pieds); *Fig* **that's where the shoe pinches** c'est là que le bât blesse **2** *(economize)* **to p. and scrape** économiser sur tout, regarder (de près) à la dépense

N **1** *(squeeze)* pincement *m*; **if it comes to the p.** s'il le faut vraiment, en cas de nécessité absolue; **we're beginning to feel the p.** nous commençons à devoir nous priver **2** *(of salt, snuff)* pincée *f*

• **at a pinch,** *Am* **in a pinch** ADV à la rigueur

▸ **pinch back, pinch off, pinch out** VT SEP *Hort* pincer

pinchbeck ['pɪntʃbek] N **1** *Metal* chrysocale *m* **2** *Fig (sham)* toc *m*

ADJ **1** *Metal* en chrysocale **2** *Fig (sham)* en toc

pinched [pɪntʃt] ADJ **1** *(features)* tiré; **his face looked pale and p.** il était pâle et avait les traits tirés; **p. with cold** transi de froid **2** *(lacking)* **I'm a bit p. for money** je suis à court d'argent; **I'm a bit p. for time** je n'ai pas beaucoup de temps; **they're p. for space in their flat** ils sont à l'étroit *ou* ils n'ont pas beaucoup de place dans leur appartement

pinch-hit VI *Am* **1** *Sport* remplacer un joueur **2** *Fig (act as replacement)* effectuer un remplacement; **he's pinch-hitting for Joe** il remplace Joe

pinch-hitter N *Am Sport* remplaçant(e) *m,f*

pinch-runner N *Am Sport* coureur(euse) *m,f* d'urgence *ou* suppléant

pincushion ['pɪnˌkʊʃən] N pelote *f* à épingles

pine [paɪn] N *Bot (tree, wood)* pin *m*

COMP *(furniture)* en pin

VI **1** *(long)* **to p. for sth** désirer qch ardemment, soupirer après qch; **he was pining for home** il avait le mal du pays **2** *(grieve)* languir; **she was pining for her lover** elle se languissait de son amant

▸▸ ***pine cone*** pomme *f* de pin, *Can* cocotte *f*; ***pine forest*** forêt *f* de pins, pinède *f*; ***pine grove*** pinède *f*; ***pine kernel*** pignon *m*, pigne *f*; ***pine marten*** martre *f*; ***pine needle*** aiguille *f* de pin; ***pine nut*** pignon *m*, pigne *f*

▸ **pine away** VI dépérir

pineapple ['paɪnˌæpəl] N *(fruit)* ananas *m*

COMP *(juice)* d'ananas; *(ice cream, yoghurt)* à l'ananas

▸▸ ***pineapple chunks*** ananas *m* en morceaux

ping [pɪŋ] ONOMAT ding

N tintement *m*

VI **1** *(make pinging sound)* faire ding; *(timer)* sonner **2** *Am (car engine)* cliqueter

pinger ['pɪŋə(r)] N minuteur *m* (de cuisine)

ping-pong, ping pong ['pɪŋpɒŋ] N ping-pong *m*

▸▸ ***ping-pong ball*** balle *f* de ping-pong; ***ping-pong player*** pongiste *mf*; ***ping-pong table*** table *f* de ping-pong

pinhead ['pɪnhed] N **1** *(of pin)* tête *f* d'épingle **2** *Fam (fool)* andouille *f*, crétin(e) *m,f*

pinhole ['pɪnhəʊl] N trou *m* d'épingle

▸▸ ***pinhole camera*** appareil *m* à sténopé

pining ['paɪnɪŋ] N langueur *f*, languissement *m*; *(strong desire)* désir *m* ardent (**for** de); *(for home)* nostalgie *f*

pinion ['pɪnjən] N **1** *Orn (wing tip)* aileron *m*; *(flight feather)* penne *f*, rémige *f* **2** *Tech* pignon *m*

VT *(hold fast)* retenir de force; **two policemen pinioned his arms** deux policiers le retenaient par le bras; **we were pinioned against the wall by the crowd** la foule nous coinçait contre le mur

▸▸ *Tech* ***pinion wheel*** roue *f* à pignon

pink [pɪŋk] N **1** *(colour)* rose *m* **2** *Fig* **to be in the p. (of health)** se porter à merveille **3** *Bot* œillet *m*; **garden p.** mignardise *f*

ADJ **1** *(in colour)* rose; **to paint a room p.** peindre une pièce en rose; **the sky turned p.** le ciel vira au rose *ou* rosit; **to go** *or* **to turn p. with anger/embarrassment** rougir de colère/confusion; *Hum* **to see p. elephants** voir des éléphants roses **2** *Fam (left-wing)* de gauche□, gauchisant□ **3** *Fam (gay)* gay, homo

VT **1** *(wound)* **he pinked my shoulder with his sword** il m'a éraflé *ou* égratigné l'épaule d'un coup d'épée **2** *Sewing* cranter

VI *Br (car engine)* cliqueter

▸▸ ***pink champagne*** champagne *m* rosé; ***pink economy*** = activités économiques générées par le pouvoir d'achat des homosexuels; ***pink gin*** = cocktail à base de gin et d'angustura; ***pink lady*** = cocktail à base de gin et de grenadine; ***pink noise*** bruit *m* rose; *Br* ***pink pound*** = le pouvoir d'achat des homosexuels; *Am Fam* ***pink slip*** lettre *f ou* avis *m* de licenciement□; **to get a p. slip** se faire virer

pinkeye ['pɪŋkaɪ] N *Med* conjonctivite *f* aiguë contagieuse; *Vet* ophtalmie *f* périodique

pinkie = **pinky**

pinking[1] ['pɪŋkɪŋ] N *Br Aut* cliquetis *m*, cliquetement *m*

pinking[2] ADJ *Sewing*

▸▸ ***pinking scissors, pinking shears*** ciseaux *mpl* à cranter

pinkish ['pɪŋkɪʃ] ADJ **1** *(in colour)* rosâtre, rosé **2** *Fam (left-wing)* gauchisant□

pinko ['pɪŋkəʊ] *(pl* **pinkos** *or* **pinkoes**) *Fam Pej* N gaucho *mf*

ADJ gaucho

pinky ['pɪŋkɪ] *(pl* **pinkies**) N *Am, Can & Scot* petit doigt *m*

pinnace ['pɪnɪs] N chaloupe *f*

pinnacle ['pɪnəkəl] N **1** *(mountain peak)* pic *m*, cime *f*; *(rock formation)* piton *m*, gendarme *m* **2** *Fig (of fame, career)* apogée *m*, sommet *m*; *(of technology)* fin *m* du fin **3** *Archit* pinacle *m*

pinny ['pɪnɪ] *(pl* **pinnies**) N *Fam* tablier□ *m*

pinout ['pɪnaʊt] N *Comput* broche *f* de sortie

pinpad ['pɪnpæd] N terminal *m* de paiement électronique, TPE *m*

pinpoint ['pɪnpɔɪnt] VT **1** *(locate ▸ smell, leak)* localiser; *(▸ on map)* localiser, repérer **2** *(identify ▸ difficulty, source of rumour, cause of problem)* identifier

N pointe *f* d'épingle; **a p. of light** un minuscule point lumineux

ADJ **1** *(precise)* très précis; **with p. accuracy** avec une précision parfaite **2** *(tiny)* minuscule

▸▸ *Mil* ***pinpoint bombing*** bombardement *m* de précision

pinprick ['pɪnprɪk] N **1** *(puncture)* piqûre *f* d'épingle **2** *(irritation)* agacement *m*, tracasserie *f*

pinstripe ['pɪnstraɪp] *Tex* N rayure *f* (très fine)

ADJ rayé

pint [paɪnt] N **1** *(measure)* pinte *f*, ≃ demi-litre *m*; *Br Fam (beer)* bière□ *f*; **I had a few pints last night** j'ai bu quelques bières hier soir; **I'm going for a p.** je vais prendre une bière

▸▸ ***pint mug, pint pot*** chope *f* d'une pinte

pinta ['paɪntə] N *Br Fam (pint of milk)* pinte *f* de lait□

pintail ['pɪnteɪl] N *Orn* pilet *m*

pinto ['pɪntəʊ] *(pl* **pintos** *or* **pintoes**) N *Am* cheval *m* pie

ADJ *Am (gen)* tacheté; *(horse)* pie *(inv)*

▸▸ ***pinto bean*** = variété de haricot moucheté de rose

pint-sized ADJ *Fam Pej* tout petit□, minuscule□

pin-up N pin-up *f inv*

ADJ *(photo)* de pin-up

▸▸ ***pin-up girl*** pin-up *f inv*

Pinyin [ˌpɪn'jɪn] N *Ling* pinyin *m*

pioneer [ˌpaɪə'nɪə(r)] N **1** *(explorer, settler)* pionnier(ère) *m,f* **2** *(of technique, activity)* pionnier(ère) *m,f*; **she was a p. in the field of psychoanalysis** elle a été une pionnière de la psychanalyse; **they were pioneers in the development of heart surgery** ils ont ouvert la voie en matière de chirurgie cardiaque

COMP *(work, research)* novateur, original; **a p. researcher in the field of genetics** un chercheur à l'avant-garde dans le domaine de la génétique

VT **to p. research in nuclear physics** être à l'avant-garde de la recherche en physique nucléaire; **the town is pioneering a job-creation scheme** la municipalité expérimente un nouveau programme de création d'emplois; **the factory pioneered the use of robots** l'usine a été la première à utiliser des robots

pioneering [ˌpaɪə'nɪərɪŋ] ADJ *(work, spirit)* novateur, original

▸▸ ***pioneering company*** entreprise *f* innovatrice

pious ['paɪəs] ADJ **1** *(person, act, text)* pieux **2** *(falsely devout)* hypocrite **3** *(unrealistic)* irréel; **to have p. hopes** avoir de vains espoirs, nourrir des espoirs chimériques

piously ['paɪəslɪ] ADV pieusement

piousness ['paɪəsnɪs] N piété *f*

PIP [pɪp] N *Comput* (*abbr* **peripheral interchange program**) logiciel *m* de commutation de périphérique

pip [pɪp] *(pt & pp* **pipped**, *cont* **pipping**) N **1** *(in fruit)* pépin *m*; **orange p.** pépin *m* d'orange

2 *Br (sound)* bip *m*; *Tel* **the pips** *(time signal)* le signal sonore, le signal horaire

3 *(on playing card, domino)* point *m*

4 *(on radar screen)* spot *m*

5 *Br Fam Mil slang (on uniform)* ficelle *f*; **to get one's third p.** recevoir sa troisième ficelle

6 *Br Fam Old-fashioned (idiom)* **to give sb the p** courir sur le haricot à qn

7 *Vet* pépie *f*

VT *Br* **1** *(defeat)* battre, vaincre; **to p. sb at the post** coiffer qn au poteau **2** *Fam (hit with bullet)* atteindre□; **he got pipped in the leg** il a pris une balle dans la jambe□

pipe [paɪp] N **1** *(for smoking)* pipe *f*; **he smokes a p** il fume la pipe; **he smokes four pipes a day** il fume quatre pipes par jour; *Fam* **put that in your p. and smoke it!** mets ça dans ta poche et ton mouchoir par-dessus!

2 *(for gas, liquid etc)* tuyau *m*, conduite *f*; *(for stove)* tuyau *m*; **to lay gas pipes** poser des conduites de gaz; **the pipes have frozen** les canalisations ont gelé

3 *Mus (gen)* pipeau *m*; *(boatswain's whistle)* sifflet *m*; *(on organ)* tuyau *m*; **the pipes** *(bagpipes)* la cornemuse
4 *Anat & Zool* tube *m*; **respiratory p.** tube *m* respiratoire
5 *(birdsong)* pépiement *m*, gazouillis *m*
6 *Comput (symbol)* barre *f* verticale
COMP *(bowl, stem)* de pipe; *(tobacco)* à pipe
VT 1 *(convey ▸ liquid)* acheminer par tuyau; **natural gas is piped to the cities** le gaz naturel est acheminé jusqu'aux villes par gazoducs; **untreated sewage is piped into the lake** les égouts se déversent directement dans le lac
2 *Mus (tune)* jouer
3 *Naut (order)* siffler; **to p. sb aboard** rendre à qn les honneurs du sifflet *(quand il monte à bord)*
4 *(say)* dire d'une voix flûtée
5 *Sewing* passepoiler
6 *Culin (cake)* décorer avec une (poche à) douille; **p. the cream onto the sponge** avec une poche à douille, versez la crème sur le gâteau
7 *Comput (commands)* chaîner
VI *Mus (on bagpipes)* jouer de la cornemuse; *(on simple pipe)* jouer du pipeau
▸▸ *Mus* ***pipe band*** orchestre *m* de cornemuses; ***pipe bomb*** = bombe artisanale fabriquée à partir d'un morceau de tuyau contenant des explosifs; ***pipe cleaner*** cure-pipe *m*; ***pipe dream*** chimère *f*; ***pipe fitter*** tuyauteur(euse) *m,f*; ***pipe major*** cornemuse *f* principale; ***pipe organ*** grandes orgues *fpl*; ***pipe of peace*** calumet *m* de la paix; ***pipe rack*** râtelier *m* à pipes
▸pipe down **VI** *Fam* **1** *(make less noise)* faire moins de bruit□; **p. down!** moins de bruit! **2** *(not talk so much)* rabattre son caquet; **p. down!** boucle-la!
▸pipe in **VT SEP** *(with bagpipes)* **to p. in the guests** = jouer de la cornemuse en tête de la procession (lors de l'entrée solennelle des invités)
▸pipe up **VI** *(person)* se faire entendre; **"me too!" he piped up** "moi aussi!" dit-il, sortant de son silence

pipeclay ['paɪpkleɪ] **N** terre *f* de pipe

pipeline ['paɪplaɪn] **N 1** *(gen)* pipeline *m*; *(for oil)* oléoduc *m*; *(for gas)* gazoduc *m* **2** *Am Fam Fig* **to have a p. to sb** avoir l'oreille de qn□ **3** *(idiom)* **they have a new model in the p.** ils sont en train de mettre un nouveau modèle au point; **he's got another movie/project in the p.** il travaille actuellement sur un autre film/projet; **changes are in the p. for next year** des changements sont prévus pour l'année prochaine

piper ['paɪpə(r)] **N** *(gen)* joueur(euse) *m,f* de pipeau; *(of bagpipes)* joueur(euse) *m,f* de cornemuse, cornemuseur *m*; *Prov* **he who pays the p. calls the tune** celui qui paie les pipeaux commande la musique

pipette, *Am* **pipet** [pɪ'pet] **N** pipette *f*

piping ['paɪpɪŋ] **N 1** *(system of pipes)* tuyauterie *f*, canalisations *fpl*; **a piece of copper p.** un tuyau de cuivre
2 *Sewing* passepoil *m*
3 *Mus (gen)* son *m* du pipeau *ou* de la flûte; *(of bagpipes)* son *m* de la cornemuse
4 *Culin* décoration *f* (appliquée à la douille)
5 *Comput (of commands)* chaînage *m*
ADV *(as intensifier)* **p. hot** très chaud, brûlant; **a cup of p. hot tea** une tasse de thé bien chaud
ADJ *(sound, voice)* flûté
▸▸ *Culin* ***piping bag*** poche *f* à douille; *Culin* ***piping nozzle*** douille *f*

pipistrelle ['pɪpɪstrel] **N** *Zool* pipistrelle *f*

pipit ['pɪpɪt] **N** *Orn* pipit *m*

pippin ['pɪpɪn] **N** *(apple)* (pomme *f*) reinette *f*

pipsqueak ['pɪpskwi:k] **N** *Fam Pej* demi-portion *f*

piquancy ['pi:kənsɪ] **N 1** *(interest)* piquant *m*, piment *m*; **it adds p. to the situation** cela corse un peu la situation **2** *(taste)* goût *m* piquant

piquant ['pi:kənt] **ADJ** piquant

piquantly ['pi:kəntlɪ] **ADV** d'une manière piquante, avec du piquant

pique [pi:k] **N** dépit *m*, ressentiment *m*; **he resigned in a fit of p.** il a démissionné par pur dépit, il était tellement dépité qu'il a démissionné
VT 1 *(vex)* dépiter, irriter, froisser **2** *(arouse)* piquer, exciter; **my curiosity was piqued** cela a piqué ma curiosité **3** *(pride)* **to p. oneself on sth/on doing sth** se piquer de qch/de faire qch

piquet [pɪ'ket] **N** piquet *m* *(jeu de cartes)*

piracy ['paɪrəsɪ] *(pl* **piracies)** **N 1** *(of vessel)* piraterie *f*; **air p.** piraterie *f* aérienne **2** *(of copyright)* atteinte *f* au droit d'auteur; *(of software, book, cassette etc)* piratage *m*; *(of idea)* copie *f*, vol *m*

piranha [pɪ'rɑ:nə] *(pl* **inv** *or* **piranhas)** **N** *Ich* piranha *m*, piraya *m*

pirate ['paɪrət] **N 1** *(person ▸ on ship, plane)* pirate *m*; *(ship)* navire *m* de pirates **2** *(of software, book, cassette etc)* pirate *m*; *(of idea)* voleur(euse) *m,f*
COMP 1 *(raid, flag)* de pirates **2** *(software, book, cassette etc)* pirate
VT *(software, book, cassette etc)* pirater; *(idea)* s'approprier, voler
▸▸ ***pirate edition*** édition *f* pirate; ***pirate radio*** radio *f* pirate; ***pirate station*** poste *m* *ou* émetteur *m* pirate

pirated ['paɪrɪtɪd] **ADJ** pirate
▸▸ ***pirated edition*** édition *f* pirate

piratical [paɪ'rætɪkəl] **ADJ** de pirate

pirating ['paɪrɪtɪŋ] **N** *(of software etc)* piratage *m*

pirouette [,pɪrʊ'et] **N** pirouette *f*
VI pirouetter

Pisa ['pi:zə] **N** Pise

piscatorial [,pɪskə'tɔ:rɪəl], **piscatory** ['pɪskətrɪ] **ADJ** *Formal* halieutique; *(tribe)* de pêcheurs

Piscean ['paɪsɪən] *Astrol* **N to be a P.** être (du signe des) Poissons
ADJ des Poissons; **the P. male** l'homme *m* Poissons

Pisces ['paɪsi:z] **N 1** *Astron* Poissons *mpl* **2** *Astrol* Poissons *mpl*; **he's a P.** il est (du signe des) Poissons
ADJ *Astrol* des Poissons; **he's P.** il est (du signe des) Poissons

pish [pɪʃ] **EXCLAM** *Old-fashioned* peuh!

piss [pɪs] *very Fam* **VI 1** *(urinate)* pisser; **to p. in the wind** se fatiguer pour rien□; *Am* **p. on it!** *(forget it)* laisse béton!; *(I'm fed up)* j'en ai plein le cul! **2** *(rain)* **it's pissing with rain** il pleut comme vache qui pisse **3 to p. all over sb** *(defeat)* battre qn à plates coutures
VT pisser; **to p. one's pants** pisser dans sa culotte; **to p. oneself** se pisser dessus; **to p. oneself (laughing)** rire à en pisser dans sa culotte
N 1 *(urine, act of urinating)* pisse *f*; *Br* **to have** *or* *Am* **to take a p.** pisser (un coup); **to go for a p.** aller pisser
2 *Br* **to go on the p.** *(go out drinking)* aller se bourrer la gueule, aller prendre une cuite; *Br* **to be on the p.** se bourrer la gueule, prendre une cuite
3 to take the p. out of sb *Br (mock)* se foutre de la gueule de qn; *Am (calm down)* calmer qn□
4 *Br (worthless thing)* **the film/book was p.** le film/le bouquin ne valait pas un clou; **their beer is p.** leur bière, c'est du pipi de chat
ADV *Br* **p. easy** fastoche
▸▸ *Br* ***piss artist*** *(drunkard)* poivrot(e) *m,f*; **he's a real p. artist** *(fool)* il n'arrête pas de déconner
▸piss about, piss around *very Fam* **VI** *(fool around)* déconner, faire le con; *(waste time)* glander, glandouiller; **we don't have time to p. about** on n'a pas de temps à perdre en conneries; **don't p. around with my stuff** arrête de tripoter mes affaires *ou* de foutre le bordel dans mes affaires
VT SEP emmerder; **to p. sb about** *(cause problems for)* se foutre de la gueule de qn; *(waste time of)* faire perdre son temps à qn
▸piss down *very Fam* **VT SEP it's pissing it down** il pleut comme vache qui pisse
VI it's pissing down il pleut comme vache qui pisse
▸piss off *very Fam* **VI** *(go away)* se casser, se tirer, foutre le camp; **p. off!** *(go away)* casse-toi!, tire-toi!, fous(-moi) le camp!; *(expressing contempt, disagreement)* va te faire foutre!
VT SEP faire chier; **to be pissed off** *(bored)* s'emmerder; *(angry)* être en rogne, être fumasse; **to be pissed off with sb/sth** *(have had enough of)* en avoir ras le bol de qn/qch; **to be pissed off at sb/about sth** être en pétard contre qn/à cause de qch

pissbucket ['pɪsbʌkɪt] **N** *very Fam* **1** *(toilet)* chiottes *fpl* **2** *(person)* ordure *f*, raclure *f*

pissed [pɪst] **ADJ** *very Fam* **1** *Br (drunk)* bourré, pété; **to get p.** se soûler *ou* se péter la gueule; **as p. as a fart** *or* **a newt, p. out of one's head** *or* **mind** bourré comme un coing, plein comme une barrique **2** *Am (angry)* en rogne; **to be p.** être fumasse; **I was pretty p. about it** ça m'a vraiment foutu en rogne; **to be p. at sb/about sth** être en pétard contre qn/à cause de qch; **to be p. with sb/sth** *(have had enough of)* en avoir ras le bol de qn/qch

pisser ['pɪsə(r)] **N** *very Fam (annoying situation)* **what a p.!** quelle merde!; **it was a real p. that the weather wasn't better** c'était vraiment chiant qu'il fasse pas plus beau

pisshead ['pɪshed] **N** *Br very Fam (drunkard)* poivrot(e) *m,f*, soûlard(e) *m,f*

pisshole ['pɪshəʊl] **N** *very Fam* **his eyes are like pissholes in the snow** il a des petits yeux□

piss-poor **ADJ** *very Fam* minable, nul

piss-take **N** *Br very Fam (mockery)* mise *f* en boîte; *(of book, film)* parodie□*f*; **this is a p., isn't it?** non mais tu te fous de ma gueule ou quoi?

piss-taker **N** *Br very Fam (mocker)* personne *f* qui se fout du monde; **he's a real p.** il se fout vraiment de la gueule du monde

piss-up **N** *Br very Fam* beuverie *f*; **to go on** *or* **to have a p.** se soûler *ou* se bourrer la gueule, prendre une cuite; *Hum* **he couldn't organize a p. in a brewery** il n'est pas foutu d'organiser quoi que ce soit, c'est un incompétent de première

pistachio [pɪ'stɑ:ʃɪəʊ] *(pl* **pistachios)** **N 1** *(nut)* pistache *f*; *(tree)* pistachier *m*; **p.-flavoured** à la pistache **2** *(colour)* (vert *m*) pistache *m*
COMP *(ice cream)* à la pistache
ADJ *(in colour)* (vert) pistache *(inv)*

piste [pi:st] **N** piste *f* (de ski)

pistil ['pɪstɪl] **N** *Bot* pistil *m*

pistol ['pɪstəl] **N** *(gun)* pistolet *m*; **I heard p. shots** j'ai entendu des coups de feu; *Fig* **he's holding a p. to her head** il lui met le couteau sur la gorge
▸▸ ***pistol grip*** *(of tool, camera)* crosse *f*

pistol-whip **VT** frapper (au visage) avec un pistolet

piston ['pɪstən] **N** piston *m*
▸▸ ***piston engine*** moteur *m* à pistons; ***piston head*** tête *f* *ou* fond *m* du piston; ***piston ring*** segment *m* (de piston); ***piston rod*** tige *f* de piston, bielle *f*

pit [pɪt] *(pt & pp* **pitted,** *cont* **pitting)** **N 1** *(hole in ground)* fosse *f*, trou *m*; *(pothole in road)* nid *m* de poule; **to dig a p.** creuser un trou
2 *(shallow mark ▸ in metal)* marque *f*, piqûre *f*; *(▸ on skin)* cicatrice *f*, marque *f*
3 *(mine)* mine *f*, puits *m*; *(mineshaft)* puits *m* de mine; **to go down the p.** descendre dans la mine; *(work as miner)* travailler à la mine; **to work down the p.** travailler à la mine
4 *Br Theat (for orchestra)* fosse *f* (d'orchestre); *(seating section)* parterre *m*
5 *St Exch* parquet *m*, corbeille *f*
6 *(usu pl) (at motor-racing track)* stand *m* (de ravitaillement)
7 *(in cockfighting)* arène *f*
8 *Sport (for long jump)* fosse *f*
9 *Anat* creux *m*; **the p. of the stomach** le creux de l'estomac; *Fig* **her rejection hit him in the p. of his stomach** son rejet lui a fait l'effet d'un coup de poing dans l'estomac
10 *Br Fam (bed)* plumard *m*, pieu *m*; **in one's p.** au pieu
11 *Fam (untidy place)* foutoir *m*
12 *Am (in fruit)* noyau *m*
COMP *(closure)* de mine; *(worker)* de fond; *(accident)* minier
VT 1 *(mark)* cribler; **his face was pitted with acne** son visage était criblé d'acné; **meteors have pitted the surface of the moon** la lune est criblée de cratères laissés par les météores; **a road pitted with potholes** une route criblée de nids-de-poule; **pitted with rust** piqué par la rouille **2** *(oppose)* opposer, dresser; **she was pitted against the champion** on l'a opposée à la championne; **to p. oneself against sb** se mesurer à qn; **to p. one's**

wits against sb se mesurer à *ou* avec qn **3** *Am (fruit)* dénoyauter

• **pits** NPL *Fam* **to be the pits** être complètement nul; **it's the pits!** c'est l'horreur!; **this town is the pits** cette ville est un vrai trou

►► ***pit bull (terrier)*** pit bull *m*; ***pit pony*** cheval *m* de mine; ***pit prop*** poteau *m ou* étau *m* de mine, étançon *m*; ***pit stop*** *(in motor racing)* arrêt *m* au stand; **to make a p. stop** s'arrêter au stand

pita = **pitta**

pit-a-pat ['pɪtə'pæt] = **pitter-patter**

pitch [pɪtʃ] VT **1** *(throw)* lancer, jeter; *(in cricket)* lancer; *Fig* **she found herself pitched into the political arena** elle se trouva propulsée dans l'arène politique; **he pitched a great game last night** *(in baseball)* il a très bien joué hier soir

2 *Mus (note)* donner; *(tune)* donner le ton de; *(one's voice)* poser; **I can't p. my voice any higher** je n'arrive pas à chanter dans un ton *ou* un registre plus aigu; **the music was pitched too high/low for her** le ton était trop haut/bas pour elle

3 *(set level of)* **we must p. the price at the right level** il faut fixer le prix au bon niveau; **he pitched his speech at the level of the man in the street** son discours était à la portée de l'homme de la rue, il avait rendu son discours accessible à l'homme de la rue; **stories pitched at older children** histoires écrites pour des enfants plus âgés

4 *(set up ► camp)* établir; **let's p. camp here** établissons notre camp *ou* dressons nos tentes ici

5 *(in golf)* pitcher

6 *Fam (tell)* raconter[□]

7 *(product)* promouvoir; *(idea)* présenter, soumettre

VI **1** *(fall over)* tomber; **to p. headlong** tomber la tête la première; **the passengers pitched forwards/backwards** les passagers ont été projetés en avant/en arrière

2 *(bounce ► ball)* pitcher

3 *Aviat & Naut* tanguer

4 *(in baseball ► player)* lancer, être lanceur; *Am Fam Fig* **to be in there pitching** y mettre du sien[□]

5 *(slope ► roof)* être incliné

6 *(for contract)* faire une soumission (**for** pour)

7 *(in golf ► player)* pitcher

N **1** *(tone)* ton *m*; **to give the orchestra the p.** donner le ton à l'orchestre; **to rise in p.** monter de ton

2 *(particular level or degree)* niveau *m*, degré *m*; *(highest point)* comble *m*; **a high p. of excitement was reached** l'excitation était presque à son comble; **how did their relationship reach such a p.?** comment leurs relations ont-elles pu se détériorer à ce point?; **the suspense was at its highest p.** le suspense était à son comble

3 *Br (sports field)* terrain *m*; **rugby p.** terrain *m* de rugby

4 *(act of throwing)* lancer *m*, lancement *m*; **the ball went full p. through the window** la balle passa à travers la vitre sans rebondir

5 *Br Fam (street vendor's place)* place[□]*f*, emplacement[□]*m*

6 *Mktg (of product)* promotion *f*; *(of idea)* présentation *f*, soumission *f*; **the salesman's p.** le boniment du vendeur

7 *(slope ► of roof)* pente *f*, inclinaison *f*; *(► of staircase)* pente *f*, rampant *m*; *Tech (► of plane)* inclinaison *f*, basile *f*

8 *(movement ► of boat, aircraft)* tangage *m*; **angle of p.** angle *m* de tangage

9 *Tech (of rivets, holes)* espacement *m*, écartement *m*; *(of screw, cogwheel, rotor)* pas *m*; *Typ (of characters)* pas *m*

10 *Archit (of ceiling)* hauteur *f*

11 *(in golf)* pitch *m*

12 *(natural tar)* poix *f*; *(distillation residue)* brai *m*

13 *Am Fam (idiom)* **to make a p. for sth** jeter son dévolu sur qch[□]; **he made a p. at her** il lui a fait du plat, il a essayé de la draguer

►► ***pitch circle*** cercle *m* primitif; *(of wheel)* ligne *f* d'engrènement; ***pitch pine*** pitchpin *m*; *Mus* ***pitch pipe*** diapason *m (sifflet)*

►**pitch in** VI *(start work)* s'attaquer au travail; *(lend a hand)* donner un coup de main; **everybody is expected to p. in** on attend de chacun qu'il mette la main à la pâte

►**pitch into** VT INSEP *(attack)* s'en prendre à; **to p. into a task** se mettre à une tâche

►**pitch on** VT INSEP choisir, opter pour

►**pitch out** VT SEP *(rubbish)* jeter; *(person)* expulser, mettre à la porte

pitch-black ADJ *(water)* noir comme de l'encre; **the cave was p.** la caverne était plongée dans l'obscurité totale; **it's p. in here** il fait noir comme dans un four ici

pitch-dark ADJ *(night)* noir; **it was p. inside** à l'intérieur, il faisait noir comme dans un four

pitched [pɪtʃt] ADJ *(roof)* en pente

►► *Mil & Fig* ***pitched battle*** bataille *f* rangée; ***pitched roof*** toit *m* en pente

pitcher ['pɪtʃə(r)] N **1** *(jug ► earthenware)* cruche *f*; *(► metal, plastic)* broc *m*; *Am (smaller ► for milk)* pot *m* **2** *(in baseball)* lanceur *m*

►► *Sport* ***pitcher's mound*** monticule *m*

pitchfork ['pɪtʃfɔːk] N fourche *f* (à foin)

VT **1** *(hay)* fourcher **2** *Fig (person)* propulser; **she was pitchforked into the job** elle a été parachutée à ce poste

piteous ['pɪtɪəs] ADJ pitoyable; *(situation)* triste

piteously ['pɪtɪəslɪ] ADV pitoyablement

pitfall ['pɪtfɔːl] N **1** *(hazard)* embûche *f*, piège *m*; **the pitfalls of English** les pièges *mpl* de l'anglais **2** *Hunt* piège *m*, trappe *f*

pith [pɪθ] N **1** *(in citrus fruit)* peau *f* blanche *(sous l'écorce des agrumes)*

2 *(crux)* substance *f*, moelle *f*; **this is the p. of the matter** c'est le cœur *ou* le fond du problème

3 *(force)* vigueur *f*, force *f*; **his argument lacks p.** son argument manque de force

4 *Bot (in stem)* moelle *f*

►► ***pith helmet*** casque *m* colonial

pithead ['pɪthed] N carreau *m* de mine

►► ***pithead ballot*** vote *m* des mineurs

pithiness ['pɪθɪnɪs] N concision *f*

pithy ['pɪθɪ] *(compar* **pithier**, *superl* **pithiest)** ADJ **1** *(fruit)* couvert de peau blanche **2** *(style, phrase, writing etc)* concis, lapidaire **3** *Bot (stem)* moelleux

pitiable ['pɪtɪəbəl] ADJ **1** *(arousing pity)* pitoyable **2** *(arousing contempt)* piteux, lamentable

pitiful ['pɪtɪfʊl] ADJ **1** *(arousing pity)* pitoyable; **it's p. to see people living on the street** cela fait pitié de voir des gens à la rue **2** *(arousing contempt)* piteux, lamentable; **they're paid a p. wage** ils touchent un salaire de misère

pitifully ['pɪtɪfʊlɪ] ADV **1** *(touchingly)* pitoyablement; **she was p. thin** sa maigreur faisait peine à voir, elle était maigre à faire pitié **2** *(contemptibly)* lamentablement; **he was p. bad at drawing** il était lamentable en dessin; **she earns a p. small salary** elle gagne un salaire de misère

pitiless ['pɪtɪlɪs] ADJ *(person)* impitoyable, sans pitié; *(weather)* rude, rigoureux

pitilessly ['pɪtɪlɪslɪ] ADV impitoyablement, sans pitié

piton ['piːtɒn] N piton *m* (d'alpiniste)

pitta ['pɪtə] N **p. (bread)** pita *m*

pittance ['pɪtəns] N somme *f* misérable *ou* dérisoire; **to work for a p.** travailler pour un salaire de misère; **to live on a p.** vivre de presque rien

> Note that the French word **pitance** is a false friend and is never a translation for the English word **pittance**. It means **sustenance**.

pitted ['pɪtɪd] ADJ **1** *(metal etc)* piqué, alvéolé; *(surface of moon)* alvéolé; *(skin ► by smallpox)* grêlé; *(► by acne)* couvert de marques **2** *(fruit, olives)* dénoyauté

pitter-patter ['pɪtə-] N *(of rain, hail)* crépitement *m*; *(of feet)* trottinement *m*; *(of heart)* battement *m*

ADV **to go p.** *(feet)* trottiner; *(heart)* palpiter

pitting ['pɪtɪŋ] N *(on metal surface)* piquage *m*

pituitary [pɪ'tjuːɪtərɪ] N *(gland)* glande *f* pituitaire, hypophyse *f*

ADJ pituitaire

►► ***pituitary gland*** glande *f* pituitaire, hypophyse *f*

pity ['pɪtɪ] *(pl* **pities**, *pt & pp* **pitied)** N **1** *(compassion)* pitié *f*, compassion *f*; **I feel great p. for them** j'ai beaucoup de pitié pour eux, je les plains énormément; **the sight moved her to p.** le spectacle l'a apitoyée *ou* attendrie; **out of p.** par pitié; **to take** *or* **to have p. on sb** avoir pitié de qn **2** *(mercy)* pitié *f*, miséricorde *f*; **have p. on the children!** ayez pitié des enfants!; **he showed no p. to the traitors** il s'est montré impitoyable envers les traîtres; **for p.'s sake!** *(as entreaty)* pitié!; *(in annoyance)* par pitié! **3** *(misfortune, shame)* dommage *m*; **what a p.!** c'est dommage!; **it's a p. (that) she isn't here** quel dommage qu'elle ne soit pas là; **it seems a p. not to finish the bottle** ce serait dommage de ne pas finir la bouteille; **we're leaving tomorrow, more's the p.** nous partons demain, malheureusement

VT avoir pitié de, s'apitoyer sur; **he pities himself** il s'apitoie sur son sort; **they are greatly to be pitied** ils sont bien à plaindre

pitying ['pɪtɪɪŋ] ADJ *(look, smile)* de pitié, compatissant

pityingly ['pɪtɪɪŋlɪ] ADV avec compassion, avec pitié

Pius ['paɪəs] PR N Pie

pivot ['pɪvət] N **1** *Tech* pivot *m*, axe *m*; *(of crane)* pivot *m*; *(of axle)* tourillon *m* **2** *Fig (person in company etc)* pivot *m*, cheville *f* ouvrière; *Mil* pivot *m*, guide *m*, homme *m* de base

VI **1** *(turn)* pivoter; **p. on your left foot** pivotez sur votre pied gauche **2** *Fig* **his life pivots around his family** toute son existence tourne autour de sa famille

VT faire pivoter

►► ***pivot bridge*** pont *m* tournant; *Mil* ***pivot man*** pivot *m*, guide *m*, homme *m* de base

pivotal ['pɪvətəl] ADJ *(crucial)* crucial, central; **she is p. in their plans** elle joue un rôle central dans leurs projets

pix [pɪks] *pl of* **pic**

pixel ['pɪksəl] N pixel *m*

►► ***pixel density*** densité *f* en pixels

pixelize, -ise ['pɪksəlaɪz] VT *TV (to hide identity)* mosaïquer

pixellated ['pɪksəleɪtɪd] ADJ *Comput (image)* pixélisé, bitmap, en mode point

pixellization, -isation [ˌpɪksəlaɪ'zeɪʃən] N *TV (to hide identity)* mosaïquage *m*

pixellize, -ise ['pɪksəlaɪz] VT *TV (to hide identity)* mosaïquer

pixie ['pɪksɪ] N fée *f*, lutin *m*

►► ***pixie boots*** bottines *fpl* à bout pointu; ***pixie hat*** bonnet *m* pointu

pixilated ['pɪksɪleɪtɪd] ADJ *Am Fam (drunk)* bourré, pété

pixillation [ˌpɪksɪ'leɪʃən] N *Cin & TV* pixillation *f*, prise *f* de vue image par image

pixy *(pl* **pixies)** = **pixie**

pizza ['piːtsə] N pizza *f*

►► ***pizza base*** pâte *f* à pizza; ***pizza parlour*** pizzeria *f*

pizzazz [pɪ'zæz] N *Fam (dynamism)* tonus[□]*m*, punch *m*; *(panache)* panache[□]*m*

pizzeria [ˌpiːtsə'rɪə] N pizzeria *f*

PJs ['piːdʒeɪz] NPL *Fam (abbr* **pyjamas)** pyjama[□]*m*

pkg *(written abbr* **package)** paquet *m*, colis *m*

pkt *(written abbr* **packet)** paquet *m*

Pl. *(written abbr* **place)** rue *f*

pl *(written abbr* **plural)** pl

placard ['plækɑːd] N *(on wall)* affiche *f*, placard *m*; *(hand-held)* pancarte *f*

VT *(wall, town)* placarder

> Note that the French word **placard** is a false friend and is rarely a translation for the English word **placard**. Its most common meaning is **cupboard**.

placate [plə'keɪt] VT apaiser, calmer

PLACE [pleɪs]

N
- endroit **1**
- lieu **1, 11**
- maison **3**
- appartement **3**
- place **4–6, 8, 9**
- couvert **7**
- poste **8**

VT
- placer **1–4, 7**
- (se) remettre **5**
- passer **6**

N 1 *(gen ▸ spot, location)* endroit *m*, lieu *m*; **this is the p.** c'est ici; **p. of death/amusement** lieu *m* de décès/de divertissement; **the p. where the accident happened** l'endroit où a eu lieu l'accident; **this is neither the time nor the p. to discuss it** ce n'est ni le moment ni le lieu pour en discuter; **this looks like a good p. to pitch the tent** l'endroit semble parfait pour monter la tente; **I had no particular p. to go** je n'avais nulle part où aller; **you can't be in two places at once** on ne peut pas être en deux endroits à la fois; **her leg is fractured in two places** elle a deux fractures à la jambe; **there are still one or two places where the text needs changing** le texte doit encore être modifié en un ou deux endroits; **to go places** *(travel)* aller quelque part; *Fig* **that girl will go places!** cette fille ira loin!
2 *(locality)* **do you know the p. well?** est-ce que tu connais bien le coin?; **she comes from a p. called Barton** elle vient d'un endroit qui s'appelle Barton; **the whole p. went up in flames** *(building)* tout l'immeuble s'est embrasé; *(house)* toute la maison s'est embrasée; **how long have you been working in this p.?** depuis combien de temps travaillez-vous ici?; **we had lunch at a little p. in the country** nous avons déjeuné dans un petit restaurant de campagne; **can you recommend a p. to eat?** pouvez-vous me recommander un restaurant?; **I'm looking for a p. to stay** je cherche un logement; *Fam* **to shout** *or* **to scream the p. down** hurler comme un forcené; **the other p.** *Br Univ (at Oxford)* Cambridge; *(at Cambridge)* Oxford; *Br Parl (in House of Commons)* la Chambre des Lords; *(in House of Lords)* la Chambre des Communes
3 *(house)* maison *f*; *(flat)* appartement *m*; **they have a p. in the country** ils ont une maison de campagne; *Fam* **nice p. you've got here** c'est joli chez toi❑; *Fam* **your p. or mine?** on va chez toi ou chez moi?❑; *Fam* **they met up at Ali's p.** ils se sont retrouvés chez Ali❑
4 *(position)* place *f*; **take your places!** prenez vos places!; **everything is in its p.** tout est à sa place; **put it back in its proper p.** remets-le à sa place; **it occupies a central p. in his philosophy** cela occupe une place centrale dans sa philosophie; **I lost my p. in the queue** j'ai perdu ma place dans la file d'attente; **I've lost my p.** *(in a book)* je ne sais plus où j'en étais; **push the lever till it clicks into p.** poussez le levier jusqu'au déclic; *Fig* **suddenly everything fell** *or* **clicked into p.** *(I understood)* tout à coup, ça a fait tilt; *(everything went well)* tout d'un coup, tout s'est arrangé; **what would you do (if you were) in my p.?** que feriez-vous (si vous étiez) à ma place?; **try and put yourself in his p.** essaie de te mettre à sa place; **I wouldn't change places with her for anything** pour rien au monde je n'aimerais être à sa place; **his anger gave p. to pity** sa colère a fait place à un sentiment de pitié
5 *(role, function)* place *f*; **robots took the p. of human workers** des robots ont remplacé les hommes dans l'accomplissement de leur tâche; **if she leaves there's nobody to take** *or* **to fill her p.** si elle part, il n'y a personne pour la remplacer; **it's not really my p. to say** ce n'est pas à moi de le dire
6 *(seat ▸ on train, in theatre etc)* place *f*; (▸ *on committee)* siège *m*; **she gave up her p. to an old man** elle a offert sa place à un vieux monsieur; **save me a p.** garde-moi une place; **she has a p. on the new commission** elle siège à la nouvelle commission; **to change places with sb** changer de place avec qn; **we changed places so that he could sit by the window** nous avons échangé nos places pour qu'il puisse s'asseoir près de la fenêtre
7 *(table setting)* couvert *m*; **how many places should I set?** combien de couverts dois-je mettre?
8 *(post, vacancy)* place *f*, poste *m*; **to get a p. at university** être admis à l'université; **there is keen competition for university places** il y a une forte compétition pour les places en faculté
9 *(ranking ▸ in competition, hierarchy etc)* place *f*; **the prize for second p.** le prix pour la deuxième place; **Brenda took third p. in the race/exam** Brenda a terminé troisième de la course/a été reçue troisième à l'examen; **the team is in fifth p.** l'équipe est en cinquième position; *Horseracing* **to back a horse for a p.** jouer un cheval placé; **for me, work takes second p. to my family** pour moi, la famille passe avant le travail; **he needs to find his p. in society** il a besoin de trouver sa place dans la société; **I'll soon put him in his p.** j'aurai vite fait de le remettre à sa place; **to know one's p.** savoir se tenir à sa place
10 *Math* **to three decimal places, to three places of decimals** jusqu'à la troisième décimale
11 to take p. *(to happen)* avoir lieu; **many changes have taken p.** il y a eu beaucoup de changements; **while this was taking p.** tandis que cela se passait
12 *Am (in adverbial phrases)* **no p.** nulle part; **I'm not going any p.** je ne vais nulle part; **some p.** quelque part; **I've looked every p.** j'ai cherché partout

VT 1 *(put, set)* placer, mettre; **she placed the vase on the shelf** elle a mis le vase sur l'étagère; **to p. a book back on a shelf** remettre un livre (en place) sur un rayon; **he placed an ad in the local paper** il a fait passer *ou* mis une annonce dans le journal local; **the proposals have been placed before the committee** les propositions ont été soumises au comité; **to p. a matter in sb's hands** mettre une affaire dans les mains de qn
2 *(find work or a home for)* placer; **to p. sb in care** placer qn
3 *(usu passive) (situate)* placer, situer; **the house is well placed** la maison est bien située; **strategically placed airfields** des terrains d'aviation stratégiquement situés; **you are better placed to judge than I am** vous êtes mieux placé que moi pour en juger; **British industry is well placed to...** l'industrie britannique est à même de...; **how are we placed for time?** combien de temps avons-nous?; **how are you placed for money at the moment?** quelle est ta situation financière en ce moment?
4 *(usu passive) (rank ▸ in competition, race etc)* placer, classer; **she was placed third** elle était en troisième position; **the runners placed in the first five go through to the final** les coureurs classés dans les cinq premiers participent à la finale; **the horse we bet on wasn't even placed** le cheval sur lequel nous avions parié n'est même pas arrivé placé; **I would p. her amongst the best writers of our time** je la classerais parmi les meilleurs écrivains de notre époque
5 *(identify)* (se) remettre; **I can't p. him** je n'arrive pas à (me) le remettre
6 *(order, contract)* passer (**with** à); **to p. an order for sth** passer commande de qch; **to p. a bet** faire un pari; **to p. a bet on sb/sth** parier sur qn/qch; **p. your bets!** *(in casino)* faites vos jeux!
7 *(invest ▸ funds)* placer; *(sell ▸ goods, shares)* placer, vendre

VI *Am (in racing)* être placé

• **all over the place** **ADV** *Fam (everywhere)* partout❑; *(untidy)* en désordre❑; **you always leave your things all over the p.!** tu laisses toujours traîner tes affaires partout!; **my hair's all over the p.** je suis complètement décoiffé❑; *Fig* **the team were all over the p.** l'équipe a joué n'importe comment❑; **at the interview he was all over the p.** *(panicking, unclear)* il a raconté n'importe quoi à l'entretien❑

• **in place** **ADV** *(steady)* en place; **hold it in p. while I nail it in** tiens-le en place pendant que je le cloue

• **in place of** **PREP** à la place de

• **in places** **ADV** par endroits

• **in the first place** **ADV** **what drew your attention to it in the first p.?** qu'est-ce qui a attiré votre attention à l'origine *ou* en premier lieu?; **I didn't want to come in the first p.** d'abord, je ne voulais même pas venir; **in the first p., it's too big, and in the second p....** premièrement, c'est trop grand, et deuxièmement..., primo, c'est trop grand, et secundo...

• **out of place** **ADJ** **the wardrobe looks out of p. in such a small room** l'armoire n'a pas l'air à sa place dans une pièce aussi petite; **he felt out of p. amongst so many young people** il ne se sentait pas à sa place parmi tous les jeunes; **he didn't look out of p.** il ne déparait pas; **such remarks are out of p. at a funeral** de telles paroles sont déplacées lors d'un enterrement

▸▸ ***place of birth*** lieu *m* de naissance; ***place of business*** lieu *m* de travail; ***place card*** = carte marquant la place de chaque convive à table; *Mktg* ***place of delivery*** lieu *m* de livraison; *Fin* ***place of issue*** lieu *m* d'émission; *Sport* ***place kick*** coup *m* de pied placé; ***place mat*** set *m* (de table); ***place of residence*** résidence *f*, domicile *m* (réel); *Br Law* ***place of safety order*** = ordonnance autorisant une personne ou un organisme à garder des enfants maltraités en lieu sûr; ***place setting*** couvert *m*; ***place of work*** lieu *m* de travail; ***place of worship*** lieu *m* de culte

placebo [plə'si:bəʊ] *(pl* **placebos** *or* **placeboes)** **N** *also Fig* placebo *m*
▸▸ *Med* ***placebo effect*** effet *m* placebo

placement ['pleɪsmənt] **N 1** *(gen ▸ act of putting, sending)* placement *m*; *(situation, position)* situation *f*, localisation *f*; *Mktg (of product)* placement *m*; *St Exch (of shares)* placement *m* **2** *(job-seeking)* placement *m* **3** *(work experience)* stage *m* (en entreprise)
▸▸ *Am Univ* ***placement office*** centre *m* d'orientation (professionnelle); ***placement service*** agence *f* pour l'emploi

placenta [plə'sentə] *(pl* **placentas** *or* **placentae** [-ti:]) **N** *Anat, Zool & Bot* placenta *m*

placid ['plæsɪd] **ADJ** *(person, attitude)* placide; *(lake, town)* tranquille, calme

placidity [plə'sɪdətɪ] **N** *(of person, attitude)* placidité *f*; *(of place)* calme *m*, tranquillité *f*

placidly ['plæsɪdlɪ] **ADV** placidement

placing ['pleɪsɪŋ] **N** *(act of putting)* placement *m*; *(situation, position)* situation *f*, localisation *f*; *(arrangement)* disposition *f*

placket ['plækɪt] **N** *Sewing* patte *f* (de boutonnage)

plagiarism ['pleɪdʒərɪzəm] **N** plagiat *m*; **it's a crude piece of p.** c'est un plagiat grossier

plagiarist ['pleɪdʒərɪst] **N** plagiaire *mf*

plagiarize, -ise ['pleɪdʒəraɪz] **VT** plagier
VI plagier

plague [pleɪg] **N 1** *(bubonic)* **the p.** la peste; **to avoid sb/sth like the p.** fuir qn/qch comme la peste; *Hum* **he avoids work like the p.** il est allergique au travail; *Arch* **a p. on them!** qu'ils crèvent! **2** *(epidemic)* épidémie *f*; *Fig* **there's been a veritable p. of burglaries** il y a eu toute une série de cambriolages **3** *(scourge)* fléau *m*; *Bible* plaie *f*; **a p. of rats** une invasion de rats
VT 1 *(afflict)* tourmenter; **the region is plagued by floods** la région est en proie aux inondations; **we are plagued with tourists in the summer** l'été, nous sommes envahis par les touristes; **we are plagued with mosquitoes in the summer** l'été, nous sommes infestés de moustiques; **it's an old injury that still plagues him** c'est une vieille blessure dont il souffre encore; **the industry has been plagued with strikes this year** l'industrie a beaucoup souffert des grèves cette année **2** *(pester)* harceler; **to p. sb with telephone calls** harceler qn de coups de téléphone

plaice [pleɪs] *(pl* **inv** *or* **plaices)** **N** *Ich* carrelet *m*, plie *f*

plaid [plæd, *Scot & Ir* pleɪd] **N 1** *(fabric, design)* tartan *m*, tissu *m* écossais **2** *(worn over shoulder)* plaid *m*
ADJ (en tissu) écossais

Plaid Cymru [,plaɪd'kʌmrɪ] **N** = parti nationaliste gallois

PLAIN [pleɪn]

N	
• plaine **1**	
ADJ	
• simple **1**	• nature **1**
• clair **2**	• uni **3**
• franc **4**	• quelconque **5**
• pur **6**	
ADV	
• franchement **1**	• complètement **2**

N 1 *Geog* plaine *f*
2 *(in knitting)* maille *f* à l'endroit
ADJ 1 *(simple ▸ style, furniture, dress)* simple; *(with nothing added ▸ omelette, rice, yoghurt)* nature *(inv)*; **he's just a p. soldier** il n'est que simple soldat; **she was just p. Sarah then** elle s'appelait

tout simplement Sarah à l'époque; **I like good p. cooking** j'aime la cuisine simple; **it's p. sailing from now on** maintenant ça va marcher tout seul *or* comme sur des roulettes; **to be in** *or* **to wear p. clothes** être en civil

2 *(clear, obvious)* clair, évident, manifeste; **it's p. (to see) that he's lying** il est clair *ou* évident qu'il ment; **it soon became p. that I was lost** j'ai vite réalisé *ou* je me suis vite rendu compte que j'étais égaré; **his embarrassment was p. to see** on pouvait voir qu'il était gêné, sa gêne était évidente; **the facts are p.** c'est clair, les choses sont claires; **I want to make our position absolutely p. to you** je veux que vous compreniez bien notre position; **she made her intentions p.** elle n'a pas caché ses intentions; **he made it p. to us that he wasn't interested** il nous a bien fait comprendre que cela ne l'intéressait pas; **I thought I'd made myself p.** je croyais avoir été assez clair; *Fam* **it's as p. as a pikestaff** *or* **as the nose on your face** c'est clair comme de l'eau de roche, ça saute aux yeux

3 *(of one colour, not patterned)* uni; **p. blue wallpaper** papier peint bleu uni; **under p. cover, in a p. envelope** sous pli discret

4 *(blunt, unambiguous)* franc (franche); **the p. truth of the matter is I'm bored** la vérité, c'est que je m'ennuie; **let me be p. with you** je vais être franc avec vous; **I want a p. yes or no answer** je veux une réponse claire et nette; **the time has come for p. words** *or* **speaking** le moment est venu de parler franchement; **in p. language** de manière claire; **I told him in p. English what I thought** je lui ai dit ce que je pensais sans mâcher mes mots

5 *(unattractive)* pas très beau (belle), quelconque; **she's a bit of a p. Jane** ce n'est pas une beauté *ou* une Vénus

6 *(pure, sheer)* pur (et simple); **that's just p. foolishness/ignorance** c'est de la pure bêtise/ignorance

7 *Knitting* **one p., two purl** une maille à l'endroit, deux à l'envers; **p. knitting** tricot *m* à l'endroit

ADV 1 *(clearly)* franchement, carrément; **you couldn't have put it any plainer** tu n'aurais pas pu être plus clair

2 *Fam (utterly)* complètement□, carrément; **he's just p. crazy** il est complètement cinglé; **he's just p. ignorant** il est tout simplement ignorant□; **I just p. forgot!** j'ai tout bonnement oublié!□

►► ***plain chocolate*** chocolat *m* noir; ***plain flour*** farine *f* (sans levure); ***plain paper*** *(unheaded)* papier *m* sans en-tête; *(unruled)* papier *m* non réglé; *Knitting* ***plain row*** rang *m* à l'endroit; *Knitting* ***plain stitch*** maille *f* à l'endroit

plainchant ['pleɪntʃɑːnt] **N** plain-chant *m*

plainly ['pleɪnlɪ] **ADV 1** *(manifestly)* clairement, manifestement; **you p. weren't listening** manifestement, vous n'écoutiez pas, il est évident que vous n'écoutiez pas; **he was p. tired** il était visiblement fatigué; **she's p. his favourite** il est clair qu'elle est sa préférée

2 *(distinctly ► remember, hear)* clairement, distinctement

3 *(simply ► dress, lunch)* simplement

4 *(bluntly, unambiguously)* franchement, carrément, sans ambages

plainness ['pleɪnnɪs] **N 1** *(of clothes, cooking)* simplicité *f* **2** *(clarity, obviousness)* clarté *f* **3** *(unattractiveness)* physique *m* quelconque *ou* ingrat

plainsong ['pleɪnsɒŋ] **N** plain-chant *m*

plain-spoken ADJ qui a son franc-parler

plaint [pleɪnt] **N** *Literary* plainte *f*, lamentation *f*

plaintiff ['pleɪntɪf] **N** *Law* demandeur(eresse) *m,f*, plaignant(e) *m,f*

plaintive ['pleɪntɪv] **ADJ** *(voice, sound)* plaintif

plaintively ['pleɪntɪvlɪ] **ADV** plaintivement

plaintiveness ['pleɪntɪvnɪs] **N** ton *m* plaintif

plait [plæt] **N** *(of hair)* natte *f*, tresse *f*; *(of straw)* tresse *f*

VT *(hair, rope, grass)* natter, tresser; *(garland)* tresser

plan [plæn] (*pt & pp* **planned**, *cont* **planning**) **N 1** *(strategy)* plan *m*, projet *m*; **to draw up** *or* **to make a p.** dresser *ou* établir un plan; **what's your p. of action?** qu'est-ce que vous comptez faire?; **to go according to p.** se dérouler comme prévu *ou* selon les prévisions; **we'll have to try p. B** il faudra qu'on essaie l'autre solution; **I've thought of a p.** j'ai un plan

2 *(intention, idea)* projet *m*; **I had to change my holiday plans** j'ai dû changer mes projets de vacances; **we had made plans to stay at a hotel** nous avions prévu de descendre à l'hôtel; **what are your plans for Monday?** qu'est-ce que tu as prévu pour lundi?; **to have other plans** avoir d'autres projets; **the p. is to meet up at Rachel's** l'idée, c'est de se retrouver chez Rachel

3 *(diagram, map)* plan *m*

4 *(outline ► of book, essay, lesson)* plan *m*; **rough p.** canevas *m*, esquisse *f*

5 *Archit* plan *m*; **drawn in p. and in elevation** dessiné en plan et en élévation

VT 1 *(organize in advance ► project)* élaborer; *(► concert, conference)* organiser, monter; *(► crime, holiday, trip, surprise, lesson)* préparer; *(► campaign)* organiser, preparer; *Econ* planifier; **everything had been planned down to the last detail** tout avait été planifié dans les moindres détails; **p. your time carefully** organisez votre emploi du temps avec soin; **they're planning a surprise for you** ils te préparent une surprise; **they're planning a new venture** ils ont en projet une nouvelle entreprise; **the Pope's visit is planned for March** la visite du pape doit avoir lieu en mars; **an industrial estate is planned for this site** il est prévu d'aménager un parc industriel sur ce site; **everything went as planned** tout s'est déroulé comme prévu

2 *(intend)* projeter; **we're planning to go to the States** nous projetons d'aller aux États-Unis; **p. to finish it in about four hours** comptez environ quatre heures pour le terminer

3 *(design ► house, garden, town)* concevoir, dresser les plans de

4 *(make outline of ► book, essay)* faire le plan de, esquisser; *(► lesson)* préparer

VI faire des projets

►**plan on VT INSEP 1** *(intend)* projeter; **what are you planning on doing?** qu'est-ce que vous projetez de faire *ou* vous avez l'intention de faire?; **we're planning on going to Brazil** *or* **on a trip to Brazil** nous projetons de *ou* nous avons l'intention de partir au Brésil, nous projetons un voyage au Brésil **2** *(expect)* compter sur; **we hadn't planned on it raining** nous n'avions pas prévu qu'il pleuvrait; **we hadn't planned on staying long** nous n'avions pas prévu de *ou* nous ne comptions pas rester longtemps

►**plan out VT SEP** *(make detailed plans for)* prévoir (en détail); **he had planned it all out** il avait tout prévu, il en avait établi tous les détails

plane [pleɪn] **N 1** *(aeroplane)* avion *m*; **by p.** en avion; **it's just a short p. ride** c'est un court voyage en avion

2 *Archit, Art & Math* plan *m*; **vertical p.** plan *m* vertical

3 *(level, degree)* plan *m*; **she's on a higher intellectual p.** elle est d'un niveau intellectuel plus élevé

4 *(tool)* rabot *m*

5 *(tree)* platane *m*

ADJ *(flat)* plan, plat; *Geom* plan

VI *(glide)* planer

VT *(in carpentry)* **to p. sth (down)** raboter qch

►► ***plane crash*** accident *m* d'avion; ***plane geometry*** géométrie *f* plane; ***plane ticket*** billet *m* d'avion; ***plane tree*** platane *m*

planet ['plænɪt] **N** planète *f*; **the biggest country on the p.** le plus grand pays de la planète

planetarium [ˌplænɪ'teərɪəm] (*pl* **planetariums** *or* **planetaria** [-rɪə]) **N** planétarium *m*

planetary ['plænɪtrɪ] **ADJ** planétaire

plangent ['plændʒənt] **ADJ** *Literary* **1** *(loud)* sonore, retentissant **2** *(plaintive)* plaintif, mélancolique

planing ['pleɪnɪŋ] **N** *(of wood)* rabotage *m*, planage *m*, aplanissage *m*; *(of metal)* planage *m*, aplanissage *m*

►► ***planing machine*** raboteuse *f*

planisphere ['plænɪˌsfɪə(r)] **N** planisphère *m*

plank [plæŋk] **N 1** *(board)* planche *f*; **to walk the p.** subir le supplice de la planche **2** *Pol* article *m*; **the main p. of their policy** la pièce maîtresse de leur politique

VT *(floor, room)* planchéier

►**plank down VT SEP** *(put down heavily)* poser brusquement

planking ['plæŋkɪŋ] **N** *(UNCOUNT)* planches *fpl*, planchéiage *m*

plankton ['plæŋktən] **N** plancton *m*

planned [plænd] **ADJ** *(trip)* projeté; *(murder)* prémédité; *(baby)* désiré, voulu; **news of the p. sale was leaked** le projet de vente s'est ébruité; **a demonstration against the p. nuclear power station** une manifestation contre le projet de centrale nucléaire

►► *Econ* ***planned economy*** économie *f* planifiée; *Ind* ***planned obsolescence*** obsolescence *f* planifiée, désuétude *f* calculée

planner ['plænə(r)] **N 1** *(gen) & Econ* planificateur(trice) *m,f*; *Rad & TV* **programme p.** programmateur(trice) *m,f*; **(town) p.** urbaniste *mf* **2** *(in diary, on wall)* planning *m*

planning ['plænɪŋ] **N 1** *(of project)* élaboration *f*; *(of concert, conference)* organisation *f*; *(of crime, holiday, trip, surprise, lesson)* préparation *f*; *(of campaign)* organisation *f*, préparation *f*; **the expedition will require careful p.** il faudra une organisation minutieuse pour mener à bien cette expédition; **the new product is still at the p. stage** le nouveau produit n'en est encore qu'au stade de projet **2** *(of economy, production)* planification *f*; **demographic p.** planification *f* des naissances **3** *(of town, city)* urbanisme *m*

►► *Br* ***planning blight*** = effets négatifs possibles de l'urbanisation; ***planning permission*** *(UNCOUNT)* permis *m* de construire

plant [plɑːnt] **N 1** *Bot* plante *f*

2 *(factory)* usine *f*

3 *(UNCOUNT) (industrial equipment)* équipement *m*, matériel *m*; *(buildings and equipment)* bâtiments *mpl* et matériel

4 *Fam (thing)* = objet caché dans le but d'incriminer quelqu'un; **he claims the heroin was a p. by the police** il prétend que l'héroïne a été mise là par la police (pour le compromettre)□

5 *Fam (infiltrator)* agent *m* infiltré□, taupe *f*; *(from police)* mouchard *m*; *(of magician, memory man)* compère□*m*

VT 1 *(flowers, crops, seed)* planter; **fields planted with wheat** des champs (plantés) de blé

2 *Fam (place firmly)* planter□; **she planted herself in the doorway** elle se planta *ou* se campa dans l'entrée□

3 *Br Fam (offload)* **don't try and p. the blame on me!** n'essaie pas de me faire porter le chapeau!

4 *Fam (give ► kick, blow)* envoyer□, donner□; *(► kiss)* planter□; **he planted a punch on his nose** il lui a mis un coup de poing sur le nez□

5 *(in someone's mind)* mettre, introduire; **her talk planted doubts in their minds** son discours a semé le doute dans leur esprit; **who planted that idea in your head?** qui t'a mis cette idée dans la tête?

6 *(hide ► bomb)* poser; *(► microphone)* cacher; *(infiltrate ► spy)* infiltrer; **he says the weapons were planted in his flat** il prétend que les armes ont été placées dans son appartement pour le compromettre; **to p. evidence on sb** cacher un objet compromettant sur qn pour l'incriminer

►► ***plant biology*** phytobiologie *f*; ***plant breeder*** phytogénéticien(enne) *m,f*; ***plant food*** engrais *m (pour plantes d'appartement)*; ***plant hire*** location *f* de matériel industriel; ***the plant kingdom*** le règne végétal; ***plant life*** flore *f*; ***plant louse*** puceron *m*; ***plant physiology*** physiologie *f* végétale; ***plant pot*** pot *m* (de fleurs); ***plant stand*** jardinière *f*

►**plant out VT SEP** *(young plants)* repiquer

plantain¹ ['plæntɪn] **N** *(plant)* plantain *m*

plantain² **N 1** *(fruit)* banane *f* plantain **2** *(tree)* plantain *m*

►► ***plantain tree*** plantain *m*

plantar ['plæntə(r)] **ADJ** *Anat* plantaire

plantation [plæn'teɪʃən] **N** plantation *f*; **sugar p.** plantation *f* de canne à sucre

planter ['plɑːntə(r)] **N 1** *(person)* planteur(euse) *m,f*; **tea p.** planteur(euse) *m,f* de thé **2** *(machine)* planteuse *f* **3** *(flowerpot holder)* cache-pot *m inv*; *(for several plants)* bac *m* à fleurs

plaque [plɑːk] **N 1** *(on wall, monument)* plaque *f* **2** *(on teeth)* **(dental) p.** plaque *f* dentaire

plash [plæʃ] *Literary* **N** *(of waves, oars)* clapotement *m*, clapotis *m*; *(of stream, fountain)* murmure *m*
VI *(waves)* clapoter; *(oars)* frapper l'eau avec un bruit sourd; *(stream, fountain)* murmurer

plasm ['plæzəm] **N** *Biol* protoplasme *m*

plasma ['plæzmə] **N** *Biol & Phys* plasma *m*
▸▸ *Comput* ***plasma display*** affichage *m* à plasma; ***plasma screen*** écran *m* (à) plasma; ***plasma TV*** télévision *f* à plasma

plasmapheresis [,plæzməˈferəsɪs] **N** *Med* plasmaphérèse *f*, échange *m* plasmatique

plaster ['plɑːstə(r)] **N 1** *(for walls, modelling)* plâtre *m* **2** *(for broken limbs)* plâtre *m*; *Br* **her arm was in p.** elle avait le bras dans le plâtre **3** *Br (for cut) (sticking)* **p.** pansement *m* (adhésif)
COMP *(model, statue)* de *ou* en plâtre
VT 1 *Constr & Med* plâtrer
2 *(smear* ▸ *ointment, cream)* enduire; **she had plastered make-up on her face, her face was plastered with make-up** elle avait une belle couche de maquillage sur la figure; **they were plastered with mud** ils étaient couverts de boue
3 *(make stick)* coller; **the rain had plastered his shirt to his back** la pluie lui avait plaqué la chemise sur le dos; **he tried to p. his hair down with oil** il mit de l'huile sur ses cheveux pour essayer de les plaquer sur sa tête
4 *(cover)* **to p. sth with sth** couvrir qch de qch; **to p. a wall with notices, to p. notices over a wall** couvrir un mur d'affiches; **her name was plastered over the front pages** son nom s'étalait en première page
▸▸ ***plaster cast*** *Med* plâtre *m*; *Art* moule *m* (en plâtre); ***plaster of Paris*** plâtre *m* de Paris *or* à mouler

plasterboard ['plɑːstəbɔːd] **N** Placoplâtre® *m*

plastered ['plɑːstəd] **ADJ** *Fam (drunk)* bourré, pété; **to get p.** se soûler

plasterer ['plɑːstərə(r)] **N** plâtrier *m*

plasterwork ['plɑːstəwɜːk] **N** *(UNCOUNT) Constr* plâtre *m*, plâtres *mpl*

plastic ['plæstɪk] **N 1** *(material)* plastique *m*, matière *f* plastique; **the plastics industry** l'industrie *f* du plastique **2** *(UNCOUNT) Fam (credit cards)* cartes *fpl* de crédit ᵔ; **she pays for everything with p.** elle règle tous ses achats avec des cartes de crédit; **do they take p.?** est-ce qu'ils acceptent *ou* prennent les cartes de crédit?
ADJ 1 *(made of plastic)* en *ou* de plastique
2 *(malleable)* plastique, malléable; *(adaptable)* influençable
3 *Art* plastique
4 *Fam Pej (artificial)* synthétique ᵔ; **the p. rubbish they call bread** cette espèce de caoutchouc qu'ils appellent du pain
▸▸ *Art* ***the plastic arts*** les arts *mpl* plastiques; ***plastic bomb*** charge *f* de plastique, bombe *f* au plastique; ***plastic bullet*** balle *f* en plastique; ***plastic cup*** gobelet *m* en plastique; ***plastic explosive*** plastic *m*; **the laboratory was blown up with p. explosives** le laboratoire a été plastiqué; *Fam* ***plastic money*** *(UNCOUNT)* cartes *fpl* de crédit ᵔ; ***plastic surgeon*** *(cosmetic)* chirurgien(enne) *m,f* esthétique; *(therapeutic)* plasticien(enne) *m,f*; ***plastic surgery*** *(cosmetic)* chirurgie *f* esthétique; *(therapeutic)* chirurgie *f* plastique *ou* réparatrice; **she had p. surgery on her nose** elle s'est fait refaire le nez; ***plastic wrap*** film *m* alimentaire

Plasticine® ['plæstɪsiːn] **N** pâte *f* à modeler

plasticity [plæsˈtɪsətɪ] **N** plasticité *f*

plastinate ['plæstɪneɪt] **VT** plastiner

plastination [,plæstɪˈneɪʃən] **N** plastination *f*

plate [pleɪt] **N 1** *(for eating)* assiette *f*; *(for serving)* plat *m*; **he ate a huge p. of spaghetti** il a mangé une énorme assiette de spaghettis; *Fig* **to hand sth to sb on a p.** donner *ou* apporter qch à qn sur un plateau (d'argent); **she was handed the job on a p.** on lui a offert cet emploi sans qu'elle ait à lever le petit doigt; *Fig* **to have a lot on one's p.** avoir du pain sur la planche
2 *(piece of metal, glass etc)* plaque *f*; *(rolled metal)* tôle *f*; *(for microscope)* lamelle *f*; **he has a metal p. in his thigh** il a une plaque en métal dans la cuisse
3 *(with inscription)* plaque *f*; **a car with foreign plates** une voiture avec une plaque d'immatriculation étrangère *ou* immatriculée à l'étranger
4 *(on cooker)* plaque *f* (de cuisson)
5 *(dishes, cutlery* ▸ *silver)* vaisselle *f* en argent; *(▸ gold)* vaisselle *f* en or; **the burglars took all the (silver) p.** les cambrioleurs ont pris toute l'argenterie
6 *(coated metal)* plaqué *m*; *(metal coating)* placage *m*; **the knives are silver p.** les couteaux sont en plaqué argent
7 *Typ (for printing)* cliché *m*; *(for engraving)* planche *f*; *(illustration)* planche *f*, hors-texte *m inv*; **offset p.** plaque *f* offset
8 *Phot* plaque *f* (sensible)
9 *(for church collection)* plateau *m* (de quête)
10 *Anat & Zool* plaque *f*
11 *(denture)* dentier *m*, appareil *m ou* prothèse *f* dentaire; *(for straightening teeth)* appareil *m* (orthodontique)
12 *(in earth's crust)* plaque *f*
13 *(trophy, race)* trophée *m*
14 *Elec & Electron* plaque *f*
15 *(in baseball* ▸ *home plate)* bâton *m*, = plaque qui marque le début et la fin du parcours que doit effectuer le batteur pour marquer un point; *Fig* **to step up to the p.** prendre ses responsabilités
VT 1 *(coat with metal* ▸ *gen)* plaquer; *(▸ in gold)* dorer; *(▸ in silver)* argenter; *(▸ in nickel)* nickeler; *(▸ in copper)* cuivrer **2** *(cover with metal plates)* garnir de plaques; *(armour-plate)* blinder
▸▸ ***plate armour*** armure *f (en plaques de fer)*; ***plate glass*** verre *m* (à vitres); ***plate rack*** égouttoir *m*; ***plate tectonics*** *(UNCOUNT)* tectonique *f* des plaques

plateau ['plætəʊ] (*pl* **plateaus** *or* **plateaux** [-təʊz]) **N** *Geog & Fig* plateau *m*; **to reach a p.** *(activity, process)* atteindre un palier

plated ['pleɪtɪd] **ADJ 1** *(covered with metal plates)* recouvert *ou* garni de plaques; *(armour-plated)* blindé **2** *(coated with metal)* plaqué

plateful ['pleɪtfʊl] **N** assiettée *f*, assiette *f*

platelayer ['pleɪt,leɪə(r)] **N** *Br Rail* poseur *m* de rails

plateless printing ['pleɪtlɪs-] **N** *Typ* impression *f* sans presse

platelet ['pleɪtlɪt] **N** *Biol* plaquette *f* (sanguine)

plate-maker **N** *Typ* copiste *mf*

plate-making **N** *Typ* préparation *f* des plaques offset

platen ['plætən] **N 1** *(on typewriter)* rouleau *m*, cylindre *m* **2** *(in printing press)* platine *f*

platform ['plætfɔːm] **N 1** *(stage)* estrade *f*; *(for speakers)* tribune *f*; *Fig* tribune *f*; **she shared the p. with her rival** elle était à la même tribune que son rival; *Fig* **it serves as a p. for their racist views** cela sert de tribune pour propager leurs opinions racistes
2 *(raised structure)* plate-forme *f*; *(of weighing machine)* tablier *m*; *(of crane)* passerelle *f*; **gun p.** plate-forme *f* de tir; **loading p.** quai *m* de chargement
3 *(at station)* quai *m*; **what p. is it for York?** quel quai est-ce pour York?; **the train waiting at p. one** le train au départ voie numéro un
4 *Pol (programme)* plate-forme *f*
5 *Br (on bus)* plate-forme *f*
6 *Comput (hardware standard)* plate-forme *f*; **on the Macintosh p.** sur la plate-forme Macintosh
• **platforms** **NPL** chaussures *fpl* à semelle compensée
▸▸ *Am Rail* ***platform car*** *(wagon m)* plate-forme *f*; ***platform shoes*** chaussures *fpl* à semelle compensée; ***platform soles*** semelles *fpl* compensées; ***platform ticket*** ticket *m* de quai

plating ['pleɪtɪŋ] **N 1** *(coating with metal* ▸ *gen)* placage *m*; *(▸ in gold)* dorage *m*, dorure *f*; *(▸ in silver)* argentage *m*, argenture *f*; *(▸ in nickel)* nickelage *m*; *(▸ in copper)* cuivrage *m* **2** *(covering with metal plates)* placage *m*; *(armour-plating)* blindage *m*

platinum ['plætɪnəm] **N** platine *m*
COMP *(jewellery, pen)* en platine
ADJ *(colour)* platine *(inv)*
ADV to go p. *(record)* devenir disque de platine
▸▸ ***platinum blonde*** blonde *f* platine; *Mus* ***platinum disc, platinum record*** disque *m* de platine

platitude ['plætɪtjuːd] **N** *(trite remark)* platitude *f*, lieu *m* commun

platitudinous [,plætɪˈtjuːdɪnəs] **ADJ** *Formal* banal, d'une grande platitude

Plato ['pleɪtəʊ] **PR N** Platon

platonic [pləˈtɒnɪk] **ADJ** *(love, relationship)* platonique
• **Platonic** **ADJ** *Phil* platonicien

platoon [pləˈtuːn] **N** *Mil* section *f*; *(of bodyguards, firemen etc)* armée *f*

platter ['plætə(r)] **N 1** *(for serving)* plat *m*; **seafood p.** plateau *m* de fruits de mer **2** *Am Fam (record)* disque ᵔ *m*

platypus ['plætɪpəs] **N** *Zool* ornithorynque *m*

plaudits ['plɔːdɪts] **NPL** *Formal* **1** *(applause)* applaudissements *mpl* **2** *(praise)* éloges *mpl*; **her poetry won her p. from the critics** ses poésies lui ont valu les éloges de la critique

plausibility [,plɔːzəˈbɪlətɪ] **N** plausibilité *f*; **the plot is lacking in p.** l'intrigue n'est guère plausible

plausible ['plɔːzəbəl] **ADJ** *(excuse, alibi, theory)* plausible; *(person)* crédible; **he's a very p. liar** il ment de façon très convaincante

plausibly ['plɔːzəblɪ] **ADV** de façon convaincante

PLAY [pleɪ]

N
- jeu **1, 5, 6, 8, 9**
- tour **3**
- stratagème **4**
- pièce (de théâtre) **7**
- intérêt **10**

VT
- jouer à **1, 8**
- jouer **2, 3, 5–7, 9–11, 13**
- faire jouer **4**
- jouer de **13**
- mettre **14**

VI
- jouer **1–5, 8**
- s'amuser **1**
- se jouer **6**

N 1 *(fun, recreation)* jeu *m*; **I like to watch the children at p.** j'aime regarder les enfants jouer; **the aristocracy at p.** l'aristocratie en train de se détendre; **to say sth in p.** dire qch en plaisantant *ou* pour rire; **p. on words** jeu *m* de mots, calembour *m*
2 *Sport* **p. starts at one o'clock** le match commence à une heure; **there was some nice p. from Brooks** Brooks a réussi de belles actions *ou* a bien joué; **to keep the ball in p.** garder la balle en jeu; **out of p.** sorti, hors jeu; **rain stopped p.** la partie a été interrompue par la pluie; *Am* **she scored off a passing p.** elle a marqué un but après une combinaison de passes
3 *(turn)* tour *m*; **whose p. is it?** c'est à qui de jouer?
4 *(manoeuvre)* stratagème *m*; **he is making a p. for the presidency** il se lance dans la course à la présidence; **she made a p. for my boyfriend** elle a fait des avances à mon copain
5 *(gambling)* jeu *m*; **I lost heavily at last night's p.** j'ai perdu gros au jeu hier soir
6 *(activity, interaction)* jeu *m*; **the result of a complex p. of forces** le résultat d'un jeu de forces complexe; **to come into p.** entrer en jeu; **to bring sth into p.** mettre qch en jeu
7 *Theat* pièce *f* (de théâtre); **Shakespeare's plays** les pièces *fpl ou* le théâtre de Shakespeare; **to be in a p.** jouer dans une pièce; **it's been ages since I've seen** *or* **gone to see a p.** ça fait des années que je ne suis pas allé au théâtre; **television p.** dramatique *f*
8 *Tech (slack, give)* jeu *m*; **there's too much p. in the socket** il y a trop de jeu dans la douille; **give the rope more p.** donnez plus de mou à la corde; *Fig* **to give** *or* **to allow full p. to sth** donner libre cours à qch
9 *(of sun, colours)* jeu *m*; **I like the p. of light and shadow in his photographs** j'aime les jeux d'ombre et de lumière dans ses photos
10 *Fam (attention, interest)* intérêt ᵔ *m*; **the summit meeting is getting a lot of media p.** les médias font beaucoup de tapage *ou* battage autour de ce sommet; **they made a lot of p.** *or* **a big p. about his war record** ils ont fait tout un plat de son passé militaire
VT 1 *(games, cards)* jouer à; **to p. football/tennis** jouer au football/tennis; **to p. poker/chess** jouer

au poker/aux échecs; **the children were playing dolls/soldiers** les enfants jouaient à la poupée/aux soldats; **how about playing some golf after work?** si on faisait une partie de golf après le travail?; **do you p. any sports?** pratiquez-vous un sport?; **squash is played indoors** le squash se pratique en salle; **to p. the game** *Sport* jouer selon les règles; *Fig* jouer le jeu; **I won't p. his game** je ne vais pas entrer dans son jeu; **she's playing games with you** elle te fait marcher; *Fam* **to p. it cool** ne pas s'énerver□, garder son calme□; *Am* **to p. favorites** faire du favoritisme; *Fam* **the meeting's next week, how shall we p. it?** la réunion aura lieu la semaine prochaine, quelle va être notre stratégie?□; **to p. it safe** ne pas prendre de risque, jouer la sécurité

2 *(opposing player or team)* jouer contre, rencontrer; **I played him at chess** j'ai joué aux échecs avec lui; **he will p. Karpov** il jouera contre Karpov; **I'll p. you for the drinks** je vous joue les consommations

3 *(match)* jouer, disputer; **to p. a match against sb** disputer un match avec *ou* contre qn; **how many tournaments has he played this year?** à combien de tournois a-t-il participé cette année?; **the next game will be played on Sunday** la prochaine partie aura lieu dimanche

4 *(include on the team ▸ player)* faire jouer; **the coach didn't p. her until the second half** l'entraîneur ne l'a fait entrer (sur le terrain) qu'à la deuxième mi-temps

5 *(card, chess piece, hand)* jouer; **to p. spades/trumps** jouer pique/atout; **she played her ace** elle a joué son as; *Fig* elle a abattu sa carte maîtresse; *Fig* **he plays his cards close to his chest** il cache son jeu

6 *(position)* jouer; **he plays winger/defence** il joue ailier/en défense

7 *(shot, stroke)* jouer; **she played a chip shot to the green** elle a fait un coup coché jusque sur le green; **try playing your backhand more** essayez de faire plus de revers; **to p. a six iron** *(in golf)* jouer un fer numéro six; **he played the ball to me** il m'a envoyé la balle

8 *(gamble on ▸ stock market, slot machine)* jouer à; **to p. the horses** jouer aux courses; **to p. the property market** spéculer sur le marché immobilier; **he played the red/the black** il a misé sur le rouge/le noir

9 *(joke, trick)* **to p. a trick/joke on sb** jouer un tour/faire une farce à qn; **your memory's playing tricks on you** votre mémoire vous joue des tours

10 *Cin & Theat (act ▸ role, part)* jouer, interpréter; **Cressida was played by Joan Dobbs** le rôle de Cressida était interprété par Joan Dobbs; **who played the godfather in Coppola's movie?** qui jouait le rôle du parrain dans le film de Coppola?; *Fig* **to p. a part** *or* **role in sth** prendre part *ou* contribuer à qch; **an affair in which prejudice plays its part** une affaire dans laquelle les préjugés entrent pour beaucoup *ou* jouent un rôle important

11 *Cin & Theat (perform at ▸ theatre, club)* **they played Broadway last year** ils ont joué à Broadway l'année dernière; **'Othello' is playing the Strand for another week** 'Othello' est à l'affiche du Strand pendant encore une semaine; **he's now playing the club circuit** il se produit maintenant dans les clubs

12 *(act as)* **to p. the fool** faire l'idiot *ou* l'imbécile; **some doctors p. God** il y a des médecins qui se prennent pour Dieu sur terre; **to p. host to sb** recevoir qn; **to p. the hero** jouer les héros; **don't p. the wise old professor with me!** ce n'est pas la peine de jouer les grands savants avec moi!

13 *(instrument)* jouer de; *(note, melody, waltz)* jouer; **to p. the violin** jouer du violon; **to p. the blues** jouer du blues; **they're playing our song/Strauss** ils jouent notre chanson/du Strauss; **to p. scales on the piano** faire des gammes au piano

14 *(put on ▸ record, tape)* passer, mettre; *(▸ radio)* mettre, allumer; *(▸ tapedeck, jukebox)* faire marcher; **don't p. the stereo so loud** ne mets pas la chaîne si fort; **he's in his room playing records** il écoute des disques dans sa chambre; **can you p. some Pink Floyd?** tu peux mettre quelque chose des Pink Floyd?

15 *(direct ▸ beam, nozzle)* diriger (**on** sur); **he played his torch over the cave walls** il promena le faisceau de sa lampe sur les murs de la grotte

16 *(fish)* fatiguer

VI 1 *(amuse oneself)* jouer, s'amuser; *(frolic ▸ children, animals)* folâtrer, s'ébattre; **I like to work hard and p. hard** quand je travaille, je travaille, quand je m'amuse, je m'amuse; **he didn't mean to hurt you, he was only playing** il ne voulait pas te faire de mal, c'était juste pour jouer; **don't p. on the street!** ne jouez pas dans la rue!; **to p. with dolls/with guns** jouer à la poupée/à la guerre

2 *Sport* jouer; **to p. against sb/a team** jouer contre qn/une équipe; **to p. in goal** être goal; **it's her (turn) to p.** c'est à elle de jouer, c'est (à) son tour; **to p. in a tournament** participer à un tournoi; **he plays in the Italian team** il joue dans l'équipe d'Italie; **try playing to his backhand** essayez de jouer son revers; **to p. high/low** *(in cards)* jouer une forte/basse carte; **do you p.?** est-ce que tu sais jouer?; **to p. to win** jouer pour gagner; **to p. dirty** ne pas jouer franc jeu; *Fig* ne pas jouer le jeu; **to p. fair** jouer franc jeu; *Fig* jouer le jeu; **to p. into sb's hands** faire le jeu de qn; **you're playing right into his hands!** tu entres dans son jeu!; **to p. for time** essayer de gagner du temps; **to p. safe** ne pas prendre de risques, jouer la sécurité

3 *(gamble)* jouer; **to p. high** *or* **for high stakes** jouer gros (jeu); **to p. for drinks/for money** jouer les consommations/de l'argent

4 *Mus (person, band, instrument)* jouer; *(record)* passer; **I heard a guitar playing** j'entendais le son d'une guitare; **music played in the background** *(recorded)* des haut-parleurs diffusaient de la musique d'ambiance; *(band)* un orchestre jouait en fond sonore; **is that Strauss playing?** est-ce que c'est du Strauss que l'on entend?; **a radio was playing upstairs** on entendait une radio en haut; **the stereo was playing full blast** on avait mis la chaîne à fond

5 *Cin & Theat (act)* jouer; **the last movie she played in** le dernier film dans lequel elle a joué

6 *Cin & Theat (show, play, movie)* se jouer; **'Hamlet' is playing tonight** on joue 'Hamlet' ce soir; **the movie is playing to full** *or* **packed houses** le film fait salle comble; **the same show has been playing there for five years** cela fait cinq ans que le même spectacle est à l'affiche; **what's playing at the Rex?** qu'est-ce qui passe au Rex?

7 *(feign)* faire semblant; **to p. dead** faire le mort; **to p. innocent** *or Fam* **dumb** faire l'innocent, jouer les innocents; *Fam* **to p. hard to get** se faire désirer□

8 *(breeze, sprinkler, light)* **to p. (on)** jouer (sur); **a smile played on** *or* **about** *or* **over his lips** un sourire jouait sur ses lèvres

▸▸ ***play area*** aire *f* de jeux

▸ **play about** **VI** *Br (have fun ▸ children)* jouer, s'amuser; *(frolic)* s'ébattre, folâtrer; **it's time he stopped playing about and settled down** il est temps qu'il arrête de s'amuser et qu'il se fixe

▸ **play along** **VT SEP** *(tease, deceive)* faire marcher

VI *(cooperate)* coopérer; **to p. along with sb** *or* **with sb's plans** entrer dans le jeu de qn; **you'd better p. along** tu as tout intérêt à te montrer coopératif

▸ **play around** = **play about**

▸ **play at** **VT INSEP 1** *(of child)* jouer à; **to p. at cops and robbers** jouer aux gendarmes et aux voleurs; *Fam* **just what do you think you're playing at?** à quoi tu joues exactement? **2** *(dabble in ▸ politics, journalism)* faire en dilettante; **you're just playing at being an artist** tu joues les artistes

▸ **play back** **VT SEP** *(cassette, film)* repasser

▸ **play down** **VT SEP** *(role, victory)* minimiser; *(problem)* dédramatiser; **we've been asked to p. down the political aspects of the affair** on nous a demandé de ne pas insister sur le côté politique de l'affaire; **her book rightly plays down the conspiracy theory** son livre minimise à juste titre la thèse du complot

▸ **play in** **VT SEP 1** *(in basketball)* **to p. the ball in** remettre la balle en jeu **2** *Br Fig* **to p. oneself in** s'habituer, se faire la main **3** *(with music)* accueillir en musique

▸ **play off** **VI** *(teams, contestants)* disputer un match de barrage

▸ **play on** **VT INSEP** *(weakness, naivety, trust, fee ings)* jouer sur; **the waiting began to p. on m nerves** l'attente commençait à me porter sur le nerfs; **the title plays on a line from Shakespeare** l titre est un jeu de mots sur une phrase de Sha kespeare

VI continuer à jouer

▸ **play out** **VT SEP 1** *(enact ▸ scene)* jouer; *(▸ far tasy)* satisfaire; **the events being played out on th world's stage** les événements qui se dérouler dans le monde; **the drama was played out be tween rioters and police** les incidents ont eu lie entre les émeutiers et les forces de police **2** *(us passive) Fam (exhaust)* **to be played out** *(perso horse etc)* être vanné *ou* éreinté□; *(idea)* êtr vieux jeu□ *ou* démodé□; *(story)* avoir perdu tou intérêt□ **3** *(with music)* **they were played out t the strains of...** leur départ a été accompagn par l'air de...

▸ **play up** **VT SEP 1** *(exaggerate ▸ role, importance* exagérer; *(stress)* souligner, insister sur; **in th interview, p. up your sales experience** pendar l'entretien, mettez en avant *ou* insistez sur votr expérience de la vente; **his speech played up h working-class background** son discours metta l'accent sur ses origines populaires; **the pres played up her divorce** la presse a monté son d vorce en épingle **2** *Br Fam (bother)* tracasser□ **my back is playing me up** mon dos me joue er core des tours; **don't let the kids p. you up** ne lais sez pas les enfants vous marcher sur les pieds

VI *Br Fam (car, child, TV, machine etc)* faire de siennes; **my back is playing up** mon dos me jou encore des tours

▸ **play upon** **VT INSEP** = **play on**

▸ **play with** **VT INSEP 1** *(toy with ▸ pencil, hai* jouer avec; **he was playing with the radio dials** i jouait avec les boutons de la radio; **he onl played with his food** il a à peine touché à son as siette; *Fig* **to p. with fire** jouer avec le feu

2 *(manipulate ▸ words)* jouer sur; *(▸ rhyme, lar guage)* manier; **she plays with language in bol and startling ways** elle manipule la langue ave une audace saisissante

3 *(consider ▸ idea)* caresser; **we're playing wit the idea of buying a house** nous pensons à ache ter une maison; **here are a few suggestions to p with** voici quelques suggestions que je soumet à votre réflexion

4 *(treat casually)* **to p. with sb's affections** joue avec les sentiments de qn; **don't you see he's jus playing with you?** tu ne vois pas qu'il se moqu de toi *ou* qu'il te fait marcher?

5 *(have available ▸ money, time)* disposer de **how much time have we got to p. with?** de com bien de temps disposons-nous?; **they've got $ million to p. with** ils disposent de deux million de dollars

6 *Fam* **to p. with oneself** *(masturbate)* se touche

playability [,pleɪə'bɪlɪtɪ] **N** jouabilité *f*

playable ['pleɪəbəl] **ADJ** jouable; *(sports pitch* praticable

play-act **VI 1** *Fig (pretend)* jouer la comédie **stop play-acting!** arrête ton cinéma *ou* de joue la comédie! **2** *(act in plays)* faire du théâtre

play-acting **N 1** *(pretence)* (pure) comédie *f* cinéma *m* **2** *(acting in play)* théâtre *m*

playback ['pleɪbæk] **N 1** *(replay)* enregistremen *m* **2** *(function)* lecture *f*; **put it on p.** mettez-le e position lecture

▸▸ ***playback deck*** magnétoscope *m* de lecture ***playback head*** tête *f* de lecture

playbill ['pleɪbɪl] **N 1** *(poster)* affiche *f* (de théâ tre) **2** *(programme)* programme *m*

playboy ['pleɪbɔɪ] **N** playboy *m*

playdate ['pleɪdeɪt] **N** *(for young children)* = séance de jeu entre jeunes enfants organisée par les parents

Play-Doh® ['pleɪ,dəʊ] **N** = sorte de pâte à mode ler

player ['pleɪə(r)] **N 1** *(of game, sport)* joueu (euse) *m,f*; **are you a poker p.?** est-ce que vou jouez au poker?

2 *(of musical instrument)* joueur(euse) *m,f*; **she' a piano/guitar p.** elle joue du piano/de la guitare **3** *(participant)* participant(e) *m,f*; *Mktg* acteu *m*; **France has been a major p. in this debate** la France a eu un rôle clé dans ce débat; **who are the key players in this market?** qui sont les acteurs principaux sur ce marché?

4 *Arch (actor)* acteur(trice) *m,f*

►► ***player piano*** piano *m* mécanique

playfellow [ˈpleɪˌfeləʊ] **N** *Br Old-fashioned* camarade *mf* (de jeux)

playful [ˈpleɪfʊl] **ADJ** *(lively ► person)* gai, espiègle; *(► animal)* espiègle; *(good-natured ► answer)* en forme de plaisanterie; *(► nudge)* complice; **to be in a p. mood** être d'humeur enjouée

playfully [ˈpleɪfʊlɪ] **ADV** *(answer, remark)* d'un ton taquin; *(smile)* d'un air enjoué; *(act)* avec espièglerie

playfulness [ˈpleɪfʊlnɪs] **N** enjouement *m*, espièglerie *f*

playgoer [ˈpleɪˌgəʊə(r)] **N** amateur *m* de théâtre; **disappointed playgoers were demanding their money back** des spectateurs déçus demandaient à être remboursés

playground [ˈpleɪgraʊnd] **N** *(at school)* cour *f* de récréation; *(in park)* aire *f* de jeu; *Fig* **the islands are a p. for the rich** les îles sont des lieux de villégiature pour les riches

playgroup [ˈpleɪgruːp] **N** = réunion régulière d'enfants d'âge préscolaire généralement surveillés par une mère

playhouse [ˈpleɪhaʊs, *pl* -haʊzɪz] **N 1** *(theatre)* théâtre *m* **2** *(children's)* maison *f* de poupée

playing [ˈpleɪɪŋ] **N** *Mus* **the pianist's p. was excellent** le pianiste jouait merveilleusement bien; **guitar p. is becoming more popular** de plus en plus de gens jouent de la guitare

►► ***playing card*** carte *f* à jouer; *Br* ***playing field*** terrain *m* de sport; *Fig* **to have a level p. field** être sur un pied d'égalité; **to create a level p. field** créer une situation qui n'avantage personne en particulier

playlist [ˈpleɪlɪst] **N** *Rad* playlist *f (programme des disques à passer)*; *Comput* playlist *f*, liste *f* de lecture

playmaker [ˈpleɪmeɪkə(r)] **N** *Sport* meneur (euse) *m,f* de jeu

playmate [ˈpleɪmeɪt] **N** camarade *mf* (de jeux)

play-off N *Sport* match *m* de barrage

playpen [ˈpleɪpen] **N** parc *m (pour bébés)*

playroom [ˈpleɪrʊm] **N** *(in house)* salle *f* de jeux

playschool [ˈpleɪskuːl] **N** *Br* = réunion régulière d'enfants d'âge préscolaire généralement surveillés par une mère

playsuit [ˈpleɪsuːt] **N** combi-short *m*

plaything [ˈpleɪθɪŋ] **N** *also Fig* jouet *m*; **she's just his p.** il se sert d'elle comme d'un jouet

playtime [ˈpleɪtaɪm] **N** récréation *f*; **at p.** pendant la récréation

playwright [ˈpleɪraɪt] **N** dramaturge *m*, auteur *m* dramatique

plaza [ˈplɑːzə] **N 1** *(open square)* place *f* **2** *Am (shopping centre)* centre *m* commercial; **toll p.** péage *m* (d'autoroute)

plc, PLC [ˌpiːelˈsiː] **N** *Br Com (abbr* **public limited company**) ≃ SA *f*; **Scandia p.** ≃ Scandia SA

plea [pliː] **N 1** *(appeal)* appel *m*, supplication *f*; **they ignored his p. for help** ils n'ont pas répondu à son appel au secours; **she made a p. to the nation not to forget the needy** elle conjura la nation de ne pas oublier les nécessiteux **2** *Law (argument)* argument *m*; *(defence)* défense *f*; **what is your p.?** plaidez-vous coupable ou non coupable?; **to enter a p. of guilty/not guilty/insanity** plaider coupable/non coupable/la démence **3** *(excuse, pretext)* excuse *f*, prétexte *m*; **his p. of ill health didn't fool anyone** sa prétendue maladie n'a trompé personne; **they did not accept his p. that he had simply forgotten** ils n'ont pas accepté son excuse, à savoir qu'il avait simplement oublié

►► *Law* ***plea bargaining*** = possibilité pour un inculpé de se voir notifier un chef d'inculpation moins grave s'il accepte de plaider coupable

plead [pliːd] *(Br pt & pp* **pleaded**, *Scot & Am pt & pp* **pleaded** *or* **pled** [pled]) **VI 1** *(beg)* supplier; **to p. for forgiveness** implorer le pardon; **she pleaded to be given more time** elle supplia qu'on lui accorde plus de temps; **to p. with sb** supplier *ou* implorer qn; **I pleaded with her to give me a second chance** je la suppliai de me donner une deuxième chance **2** *Law* plaider; **to p. in court** plaider devant le tribunal; **to p. guilty/not guilty** plaider coupable/non coupable; **to p. for the defence** plaider pour la défense; **how does the accused p.?** l'accusé plaide-t-il coupable ou non coupable?

VT 1 *(beg)* implorer, supplier; **"please let me go," he pleaded** "laissez-moi partir, je vous en prie", implora-t-il; **she pleaded that her son be forgiven** elle supplia que l'on pardonne à son fils **2** *(gen) & Law* plaider; **to p. sb's case** *Law* défendre qn; *Fig* plaider la cause de qn; **to p. self-defence** plaider la légitime défense **3** *(put forward as excuse)* invoquer, alléguer; *(pretend)* prétexter; **we could always p. ignorance** nous pourrions toujours prétendre que nous ne savions pas; **she pleaded a prior engagement** elle a prétendu qu'elle était déjà prise

pleading [ˈpliːdɪŋ] **ADJ** implorant, suppliant

N 1 *(entreaty)* supplication *f*, prière *f*; **I couldn't resist her p.** *or* **pleadings** je n'ai pas pu résister à ses prières **2** *Law (presentation of case)* plaidoyer *m*, plaidoirie *f*

pleadingly [ˈpliːdɪŋlɪ] **ADV** *(look)* d'un air suppliant *ou* implorant; *(ask)* d'un ton suppliant *ou* implorant

pleasant [ˈplezənt] **ADJ 1** *(enjoyable, attractive)* agréable, plaisant; **thank you for a most p. evening** merci pour cette merveilleuse soirée; **it was p. to be out in the countryside again** c'était agréable de se retrouver de nouveau à la campagne; **p. dreams!** fais de beaux rêves! **2** *(friendly ► person, attitude, smile)* aimable, agréable; **she was very p. to us as a rule** elle était en général très aimable à notre égard

pleasantly [ˈplezəntlɪ] **ADV 1** *(attractively)* agréablement; **the room was p. arranged** la pièce était aménagée de façon agréable **2** *(enjoyably)* agréablement; **p. surprised** agréablement surpris, surpris en bien **3** *(kindly ► speak, smile)* aimablement

pleasantness [ˈplezəntnɪs] **N 1** *(attractiveness)* attrait *m*, charme *m* **2** *(enjoyableness)* agrément *m* **3** *(friendliness)* amabilité *f*, affabilité *f*

pleasantry [ˈplezəntrɪ] *(pl* **pleasantries**) **N** *(agreeable remark)* propos *m* aimable; **to exchange pleasantries** échanger des civilités

please [pliːz] **ADV 1** *(requesting or accepting)* s'il vous/te plaît; **another cup of tea? – (yes) p.!** une autre tasse de thé? – oui, s'il vous plaît! *ou* volontiers!; **may I sit beside you? – p. do** puis-je m'asseoir près de vous? – mais bien sûr; **p., make yourselves at home** faites comme chez vous, je vous en prie; **p., Miss!** s'il vous plaît, Mademoiselle!; **p. ring** *(sign)* sonnez SVP, veuillez sonner; **quiet p.** *(sign)* silence

2 *(pleading)* **p. don't hurt him** je vous en prie, ne lui faites pas de mal

3 *(in indignation, disgust etc)* **(oh) p.!** c'est pas vrai!

4 *(remonstrating)* **Henry, p., we've got guests!** Henry, voyons *ou* je t'en prie, nous avons des invités!

5 *(hoping)* **p. let them arrive safely!** faites qu'ils arrivent sains et saufs!

VT 1 *(give enjoyment to)* plaire à, faire plaisir à; *(satisfy)* contenter; **he only did it to p. his mother** il ne l'a fait que pour faire plaisir à sa mère; **you can't p. everybody** on ne peut pas faire plaisir à tout le monde; **to be easy/hard to p.** être facile/difficile à satisfaire **2** *(idioms)* **to p. oneself** faire comme on veut; **p. yourself!** comme tu veux!; **I can p. myself what I do** je fais ce qui me plaît; **everything will be all right, p. God!** tout ira bien, plaise à Dieu!

VI 1 *(give pleasure)* plaire, faire plaisir; **to be eager to p.** chercher à faire plaisir **2** *(choose)* **she does as** *or* **what she pleases** elle fait ce qu'elle veut *ou* ce qui lui plaît; **I'll talk to whoever I p.!** je parlerai avec qui je veux!; *Formal* **as you p.!** comme vous voudrez!, comme bon vous semblera!; *Formal* **if you p.** *(requesting)* s'il vous/te plaît; **she told me I was fat, if you p.!** figure-toi qu'elle m'a dit que j'étais gros!

N without so much as a p. or thank you sans même dire merci

pleased [pliːzd] **ADJ** *(satisfied)* satisfait, content; *(happy)* heureux; **a p. smile** un sourire satisfait; **to be p. with sb/sth** être content de qn/qch; **to be p. for sb** être content pour qn; **you're looking very p. with yourself!** tu as l'air très content de toi!; **I am not at all p. with the results** je ne suis pas du tout satisfait des résultats; **I'm very p. to be here this evening** je suis très heureux d'être ici ce soir; *Formal* **Mr & Mrs Adams are p. to announce...** M. et Mme Adams sont heureux de *ou* ont le plaisir de vous faire part de...; **she would be only too p. to help us** elle ne demanderait pas mieux que de nous aider; **I'm very p. (that) you could come** je suis ravi que tu aies pu venir; **I'm afraid they were none too p.!** je crains qu'ils n'aient pas été très contents!; **p. to meet you!** enchanté (de faire votre connaissance)!; **as p. as Punch** heureux comme un roi

pleasing [ˈpliːzɪŋ] **ADJ** *(meal, film, conversation etc)* agréable; *(person, manner)* agréable, plaisant; *(news, result)* qui fait plaisir

pleasingly [ˈpliːzɪŋlɪ] **ADV** agréablement, plaisamment

pleasurable [ˈpleʒərəbəl] **ADJ** agréable, plaisant

pleasurably [ˈpleʒərəblɪ] **ADV** agréablement, plaisamment

pleasure [ˈpleʒə(r)] **N 1** *(enjoyment, delight)* plaisir *m*; **to write/to paint for p.** écrire/peindre pour le plaisir; **are you here on business or for p.?** êtes-vous là pour affaires ou pour le plaisir?; **to take** *or* **to find p. in doing sth** prendre plaisir *ou* éprouver du plaisir à faire qch; **I'd accept your invitation with p., but...** j'accepterais votre invitation avec plaisir, seulement...; **another beer? – with p.!** une autre bière? – avec plaisir *ou* volontiers!; **it's one of my few pleasures in life** c'est un de mes rares plaisirs dans la vie; **thank you very much – my p.!** *or* **it's a p.!** merci beaucoup – je vous en prie!; **it's a great p. (to meet you)** ravi de faire votre connaissance; **I haven't the p. of knowing her** je n'ai pas le plaisir de la connaître; *Formal* **would you do me the p. of having lunch with me?** me feriez-vous le plaisir de déjeuner avec moi?; *Formal* **may I have the p. (of this dance)?** m'accorderez-vous *ou* voulez-vous m'accorder cette danse?; *Formal* **Mr and Mrs Evans request the p. of your company at their daughter's wedding** M. et Mme Evans vous prient de leur faire l'honneur d'assister au mariage de leur fille **2** *Formal (desire)* **at your p.** à votre guise; **they are appointed at the chairman's p.** ils sont nommés selon le bon vouloir du président; *Br Euph* **detained at His/Her Majesty's p.** emprisonné pour longtemps **3** *Euph (sexual gratification)* plaisir *m*

COMP *(boat, yacht)* de plaisance; *(park)* de loisirs; *(cruise, tour)* d'agrément

VT *Arch or Literary* plaire à, faire plaisir à

►► ***pleasure beach*** parc *m* d'attractions en bord de mer; ***the pleasure principle*** le principe de plaisir; ***pleasure trip*** excursion *f*

pleat [pliːt] **N** pli *m*

VT plisser

pleated [ˈpliːtɪd] **ADJ** plissé; **a p. skirt** une jupe plissée

pleating [ˈpliːtɪŋ] **N** *(UNCOUNT) (pleats)* plis *mpl*, plissé *m*

pleb [pleb], *Am* **plebe** [pliːb] **N 1** *Pej (plebeian)* plébéien(enne) *m,f* **2** *Br Fam Pej (vulgar, uncultured person)* plouc *m*; **you p.!** espèce de plouc! **3** *Antiq* **the plebs** la plèbe

plebby [ˈplebɪ] **ADJ** *Br Fam* prolo

plebeian [plɪˈbiːən] **N** plébéien(enne) *m,f*

ADJ 1 *Pej (vulgar)* plébéien; **his tastes are rather p.** il a des goûts plutôt vulgaires **2** *Antiq* plébéien

plebiscite [ˈplebɪsaɪt] **N** plébiscite *m*; **to hold a p.** organiser un plébiscite; **to vote for sth by p.** plébisciter qn/qch

plectrum [ˈplektrəm] *(pl* **plectrums** *or* **plectra** [-trə]) **N** médiator *m*, plectre *m*

pled [pled] *Scot & Am pt & pp of* **plead**

pledge [pledʒ] **VT 1** *(promise)* promettre; **they have pledged £500 to the relief fund** ils ont promis

500 livres à la caisse de secours; **she pledged never to see him again** *(to herself)* elle s'est promis de ne plus jamais le revoir; *(to someone else)* elle a promis de ne plus jamais le revoir; *Formal* **her heart is pledged to another** son cœur est déjà pris

2 *Formal (commit)* engager; **he pledged himself to fight for the cause** il s'engagea à lutter pour la cause; **I am pledged to secrecy** j'ai juré de garder le secret; **to p. one's word** donner *ou* engager sa parole; **to p. one's loyalty/support** accorder sa loyauté/son soutien

3 *Fin (offer as security)* donner en gage *ou* garantie; *(pawn)* mettre en gage, engager; **to p. one's property** engager son bien

4 *Formal (toast)* porter un toast à, boire à la santé de

N1 *(promise)* promesse *f*; **manifesto p.** promesse *f* électorale; **a £10 p.** un gage de 10 livres; **thousands of people phoned in with pledges of money** des milliers de personnes ont téléphoné en promettant de donner de l'argent; **I am under a p. of secrecy** j'ai juré de garder le secret; **to sign** *or* **to take the p.** *(stop drinking)* cesser de boire

2 *Fin (security, collateral)* gage *m*, garantie *f*; **in p.** en gage

3 *(token, symbol)* gage *m*; **as a p. of our sincerity** comme gage de notre sincérité

4 *Formal (toast)* toast *m*; **let us drink a p. to their success** portons un toast *ou* buvons à leur réussite

►► *Fin* ***pledge holder*** détenteur(trice) *m,f* de gage(s)

pledgee [ple'dʒiː] **N** *Fin* gagiste *mf*

pledger, pledgor ['pledʒə(r)] **N** *Fin* gageur (euse) *m,f*

Pleiades ['plaɪədiːz] **NPL** *Myth & Astron* **the P.** les Pléiades *fpl*

plenary ['pliːnərɪ] **ADJ** *(meeting)* plénier

►► ***plenary assembly*** assemblée *f* plénière; *Rel* ***plenary indulgence*** indulgence *f* plénière; *Pol* ***plenary powers*** pleins pouvoirs *mpl*; ***plenary session*** *(at conference)* séance *f* plénière; **in p. session** en séance plénière

plenipotentiary [ˌplenɪpə'tenʃərɪ] *(pl* **plenipotentiaries)** **ADJ** plénipotentiaire; **ambassador p.** ministre *m* plénipotentiaire

N plénipotentiaire *mf*

plenitude ['plenɪtjuːd] **N** *Literary* plénitude *f*

plentiful ['plentɪful] **ADJ** *(gen)* abondant; *(meal)* copieux; **we have a p. supply of food** nous avons de la nourriture en abondance

plentifully ['plentɪfʊlɪ] **ADV** abondamment, copieusement; **weeds grow p. there** les mauvaises herbes y poussent en abondance

plenty ['plentɪ] **PRON1** *(enough)* (largement) assez, plus qu'assez; **no thanks, I've got p.** non merci, j'en ai (largement) assez; **£20 should be p.** 20 livres devraient suffire (amplement); **they have p. to live on** ils ont largement de quoi vivre; **to arrive in p. of time** arriver de bonne heure; **we've got p. of time** nous avons largement le temps **2** *(a great deal)* beaucoup; **there'll be p. of other opportunities** il y aura beaucoup d'autres occasions; **you've got p. of explaining to do** tu vas devoir t'expliquer

N *Literary (abundance)* abondance *f*; **the years of p.** les années *fpl* d'abondance

ADV *Fam* **1** *(a lot)* beaucoup▫; **there's p. more food in the fridge** il y a encore plein de choses à manger dans le frigo; **there's p. more where that came from!** *(food etc)* quand il y en a plus, il y en a encore; *Am* **he sure talks p.** c'est un vrai moulin à paroles **2** *(easily)* **the room is p. big enough for two** la pièce est largement assez grande pour deux▫

• **in plenty** **ADV** en abondance

pleonasm ['pliːənæzəm] **N** pléonasme *m*

pleonastic [ˌplɪə'næstɪk] **ADJ** pléonastique

plethora ['pleθərə] **N** pléthore *f*

pleural ['plʊərəl] **ADJ** *Anat* pleural

►► ***pleural membrane*** plèvre *f*

pleurisy ['plʊərəsɪ] **N** *(UNCOUNT) Med* pleurésie *f*; **to have p.** avoir *ou* faire une pleurésie

plex [pleks] **N** *Am Fam Cin* complexe *m* multisalles, cinéma *m* multisalle, multiplexe *m*

Plexiglas® ['pleksɪglɑːs] **N** Plexiglas® *m*

plexus ['pleksəs] **N1** *Anat* plexus *m* **2** *Formal (intricate network)* enchevêtrement *m*, dédale *m*

pliability [ˌplaɪə'bɪlətɪ] **N1** *(of material)* flexibilité *f* **2** *(of person)* malléabilité *f*, docilité *f*

pliable ['plaɪəbəl] **ADJ 1** *(material)* flexible, pliable **2** *(person)* malléable, accommodant, docile

pliers ['plaɪəz] **NPL** pince *f*; **a pair of p.** une pince

plight [plaɪt] **N** *(bad situation)* situation *f* désespérée; **the p. of the young homeless** la situation désespérée dans laquelle se trouvent les jeunes sans-abri; **to be in a sad** *or* **sorry p.** être dans une situation désespérée

VT *Arch (pledge)* **to p. one's troth (to sb)** se fiancer (à qn)

plimsoll ['plɪmsəl] **N** *Br (shoe)* tennis *m*

plinth [plɪnθ] **N** *(of statue)* socle *m*; *(of column, pedestal)* plinthe *f*; *Mktg (for displaying goods)* plinthe *f*

Pliny ['plɪnɪ] **PR NP. the Elder** Pline l'Ancien; **P. the Younger** Pline le Jeune

plip key [plɪp-] **N** *Aut* plip *m*

PLO [ˌpiːel'əʊ] **N** *(abbr* **Palestine Liberation Organization)** OLP *f*

plod [plɒd] *(pt & pp* **plodded**, *cont* **plodding)** **VI1** *(walk)* marcher lourdement **2** *Fam (carry on)* **he'd been plodding along in the same job for years** ça faisait des années qu'il faisait le même boulot; **she kept plodding on until it was finished** elle s'est accrochée jusqu'à ce que ce soit fini; **I plodded through the first five chapters** je me suis coltiné les cinq premiers chapitres

N1 *(heavy walk)* **we could hear the p. of feet** on entendait des pas lourds; **we maintained a steady p.** nous avons gardé un pas régulier **2** *Br Fam (policeman)* flic *m*, poulet *m*; **the p.** *(the police)* les flics *mpl*, les poulets *mpl*

plodder ['plɒdə(r)] **N** *Fam Pej* **he's a bit of a p.** il est plutôt lent à la tâche▫

plodding ['plɒdɪŋ] **ADJ** *Pej (walk, rhythm, style)* lourd, pesant; *(worker)* lent

plonk [plɒŋk] **N1** *(heavy sound)* bruit *m* sourd **2** *Br Fam (cheap wine)* pinard *m*, piquette *f*

VT *Fam (put, place)* flanquer, coller; *(put down)* poser bruyamment▫; **just p. your stuff on the table** t'as qu'à foutre tes affaires sur la table; **he plonked his glass down** il posa son verre bruyamment; **she plonked herself down on the sofa** elle s'est affalée sur le canapé▫

VI **to p. away on the piano** jouer du piano (mal et assez fort)

plonker ['plɒŋkə(r)] **N** *Br Fam* **1** *(penis)* quéquette *f*, zizi *m* **2** *(fool)* andouille *f*, courge *f*

plook [pluk] **N** *Scot & NEng Fam (pimple)* bouton▫*m*

plop [plɒp] *(pt & pp* **plopped**, *cont* **plopping)** **N** plouf *m*, floc *m*

ADV **to go p.** faire plouf

VI *(splash)* faire plouf *ou* floc

VT *(put)* poser, mettre

plosive ['pləʊsɪv] *Ling* **ADJ** occlusif

N occlusive *f*

plot [plɒt] *(pt & pp* **plotted**, *cont* **plotting)** **N1** *(conspiracy)* complot *m*, conspiration *f*; **to hatch a p.** tramer *ou* ourdir un complot; **a p. to overthrow the government** un complot pour renverser le gouvernement

2 *(story line* ► *of novel, play)* intrigue *f*; **the p. thickens** l'affaire se corse

3 *(piece of land)* terrain *m*; **vacant/building p.** terrain *m* vague/à bâtir; **the land has been split up into 12 plots** le terrain a été divisé en 12 lotissements; **we have a small vegetable p.** nous avons un petit potager *ou* carré de légumes

4 *Am (graph)* graphique *m*

5 *Am Archit* plan *m*

VT1 *(conspire)* comploter; **they were accused of plotting to overthrow the government** ils ont été accusés de complot *ou* de conspiration contre le gouvernement; **I think they're plotting something** je crois qu'ils préparent quelque chose

2 *(course, position)* déterminer; *Fig* **they're trying to p. the company's development over the next five years** ils essaient de prévoir le développement de la société dans les cinq années à venir

3 *(curve, diagram, graph)* tracer, faire le tracé de; **to p. figures on** *or* **onto a graph** reporter des coordonnées sur un graphique

4 *(map, plan)* lever

VI *(conspire)* comploter, conspirer; **to p. against sb** conspirer contre qn

plotter ['plɒtə(r)] **N1** *(conspirator)* conspirateur (trice) *m,f* **2** *(device)* traceur *m*

plotting ['plɒtɪŋ] **N** *(UNCOUNT)* **1** *(conspiring)* complots *mpl*, conspirations *fpl* **2** *Comput & Math* traçage *m*

►► *Comput & Math* ***plotting board, plotting table*** table *f* traçante, traceur *m* de courbes

plough, *Am* **plow** [plaʊ] **N1** *(farm implement)* charrue *f*; **large areas of moorland have gone under the p.** de larges portions de lande ont été labourées; *Fig* **to put one's hand to the p.** s'atteler à la tâche **2** *Astron* **the P.** la Grande Ourse

VT1 *(land)* labourer; *(furrow)* creuser; *(of ship* ► *waves)* fendre, sillonner **2** *Fig (invest)* investir; **to p. money into sth** investir de l'argent dans qch

VI *Agr* labourer

▸**plough back,** *Am* **plow back** **VT SEP** *(profits)* réinvestir (**into** dans)

▸**plough in,** *Am* **plow in** **VT SEP1** *(earth, crops stubble)* enfouir (en labourant) **2** *(money)* investir

▸**plough into,** *Am* **plow into** **VT INSEP1** *(of vehicle)* rentrer dans, foncer dans **2** *(attack* ► *physically)* se jeter sur; *(*► *verbally)* s'en prendre à

▸**plough on,** *Am* **plow on** **VI** *(continue laboriously)* **to p. on with one's work/one's book** pour suivre laborieusement son travail/sa lecture; **let's p. on another 15 minutes** encore un petit effort d'un quart d'heure

▸**plough through,** *Am* **plow through** **VT INSEP 1** *(move laboriously through)* **to p. through the snow** avancer péniblement dans la neige; **the ship ploughed through the waves** le navire fendait les flots **2** *(progress laboriously through)* **to p. through a book** lire laborieusement un livre; **they were ploughing through their work** ils avançaient laborieusement dans leur travail; **I've got all this to p. through** j'ai tout ça à me taper

VT SEP **to p. one's way through the snow** avance péniblement dans la neige; **to p. one's way through a book** lire un livre à grand peine; **he was ploughing his way through a huge plate of spaghetti** il s'efforçait de finir une énorme assiette de spaghettis

▸**plough up,** *Am* **plow up** **VT SEP1** *Agr (field footpath)* labourer **2** *(rip up)* labourer; **the grass had been ploughed up by the motorbikes** le gazon avait été labouré par les motos

ploughback, *Am* **plowback** ['plaʊbæk] **N** *Fin* bénéfices *mpl* réinvestis

ploughing, *Am* **plowing** ['plaʊɪŋ] **N** labourage *m*

ploughland, *Am* **plowland** ['plaʊlænd] **N** *(UNCOUNT)* terre *f* de labour, labours *mpl*

ploughman, *Am* **plowman** ['plaʊmən] *(pl* **ploughmen,** *Am* **plowmen** [-mən]) **N** laboureur *m*

►► *Br* ***ploughman's (lunch)*** = assiette de fromage de pain et de pickles (généralement servie dans un pub)

ploughshare, *Am* **plowshare** ['plaʊʃeə(r)] **N** soc *m*

plover ['plʌvə(r)] **N** *Orn* pluvier *m*

plow, plowback *etc Am* = **plough, ploughback** *etc*

ploy [plɔɪ] **N** *(stratagem, trick)* ruse *f*, stratagème *m*; **it's just a p. to get us to leave** ce n'est qu'une ruse pour nous faire partir

pluck [plʌk] **VT1** *(pick* ► *flower, fruit)* cueillir

2 *(pull)* tirer, retirer; **to p. sb from obscurity** arracher qn à l'obscurité; **he plucked the cigarette from my mouth** il m'a arraché la cigarette de la bouche; **the ten survivors were plucked from the sea by helicopter** les dix survivants ont été récupérés en mer par un hélicoptère; **these figures have been plucked from the air** ces chiffres ne reposent sur rien de concret

3 *(chicken)* plumer; *(feathers)* arracher

4 *(instrument)* pincer les cordes de; *(string)* pincer

5 *(eyebrow)* épiler; **to p. one's eyebrows** s'épiler les sourcils

VI he plucked at my sleeve il m'a tiré par la manche; **she was plucking at (the strings of) her guitar** elle pinçait les cordes de sa guitare

N 1 *(courage)* courage *m*; **it takes p. to do that** il faut du courage pour faire ça **2** *(tug)* petite secousse *f*; *(at string)* pincement *m* **3** *Culin* fressure *f*

▸**pluck up VT SEP 1** *(uproot)* arracher, extirper **2** *Fig* **to p. up (one's) courage** prendre son courage à deux mains; **to p. up the courage to do sth** trouver le courage de faire qch

pluckily ['plʌkɪlɪ] **ADV** courageusement

pluckiness ['plʌkɪnɪs] **N** courage *m*

plucky ['plʌkɪ] *(compar* **pluckier,** *superl* **pluckiest)** **ADJ** courageux

plug [plʌg] *(pt & pp* **plugged,** *cont* **plugging)** **N 1** *Elec (on appliance, cable)* fiche *f*, prise *f* (mâle); *(wall socket)* prise *f* (de courant); **to pull the p. out** *(disconnect electrical appliance)* débrancher; *Comput* **p. compatible** compatible au niveau du matériel

2 *(stopper ▸ gen)* bouchon *m*; *(▸ in barrel)* bonde *f*; *(▸ for nose, wound)* tampon *m*

3 *(for sink, bath)* bonde *f*; **to pull the p. out** retirer la bonde; *Fig* **this will pull the p. on our competitors** cela va couper l'herbe sous le pied de nos concurrents; **he pulled the p. on our plan** *(stopped it)* il a mis le holà à notre projet

4 *(of toilet)* chasse *f* d'eau; **to pull the p.** tirer la chasse

5 *Aut* **(spark) p.** bougie *f*

6 *(for fixing screws)* cheville *f*

7 *Fam (advertising)* coup *m* de pub; **their products got another p. on TV** on a encore fait du battage *ou* de la pub pour leurs produits à la télé

8 *(of tobacco)* carotte *f*

9 *Geol* **(volcanic) p.** culot *m*

10 *Am* **(fire) p.** bouche *f* d'incendie

VT 1 *(block ▸ hole, gap)* boucher; *(▸ leak)* colmater; *(▸ wound)* tamponner; **they plugged (up) the hole in the dam** ils ont colmaté la brèche dans le barrage

2 *(insert)* enficher; **p. the cable into the socket** branchez le câble sur la prise

3 *Fam (advertise)* faire du battage *ou* de la pub pour; **the radio stations are continually plugging her record** les stations de radio passent son disque sans arrêt▫

4 *Am Fam (shoot)* flinguer

▸▸ *Aut* ***plug spanner*** clé *f* à bougies

▸**plug away VI** travailler dur; **he keeps plugging away at his work** il s'acharne sur son travail

▸**plug in VT SEP** brancher

▸**plug into VT SEP** *(connect)* **to p. sth into sth** brancher qch sur qch

VT INSEP 1 *(connect)* **the TV plugs into that socket** la télé se branche sur cette prise; *Fig* **to p. into a computer network** avoir accès à un réseau informatique **2** *(be in touch with)* **to p. into public opinion** se mettre à l'écoute de l'opinion publique; **we try to p. into people's needs** nous essayons d'être à l'écoute des besoins de la population

plug-and-play *Comput* **N** plug and play *m inv*

ADJ plug and play *(inv)*

plughole ['plʌghəʊl] **N** trou *m* d'écoulement; *Br Fam* **that's all our work gone down the p.!** tout notre travail est fichu!; **that's £300 down the p.!** voilà 300 livres par la fenêtre!; **his company's going down the p.** sa société se casse la figure

plug-in ADJ *(radio)* qui se branche sur le secteur; *(accessory for computer, stereo etc)* qui se branche sur l'appareil

N *Comput* module *m* d'extension, *Can* plugiciel *m*

plug-in-and-go ADJ *Comput* prêt à brancher

plug-ugly *Fam* **ADJ** moche comme un pou

N *Am (ruffian)* voyou▫ *m*, loubard *m*

plum [plʌm] **N 1** *(fruit)* prune *f* **2** *(tree)* prunier *m* **3** *(colour)* couleur *f* prune

COMP *(tart)* aux prunes; *(jam)* de prunes

ADJ 1 *(colour)* prune *(inv)* **2** *Fam (desirable)* **it's a p. job** c'est un boulot en or

▸▸ ***plum brandy*** (eau *f* de vie de) prune *f*; ***plum cake*** cake *m*; *Br* ***plum duff, plum pudding*** plum-pudding *m*; ***plum sauce*** sauce *f* aux prunes; ***plum tomato*** olivette *f*; ***plum tree*** prunier *m*

plumage ['plu:mɪdʒ] **N** plumage *m*

plumb [plʌm] **N 1** *(weight)* plomb *m* **2** *(verticality)* aplomb *m*; **the wall is out of p.** le mur n'est pas d'aplomb *ou* à l'aplomb

ADJ 1 *(vertical)* vertical, à l'aplomb **2** *Am Fam (utter, complete)* complet(ète)▫, absolu▫; **it's a p. nuisance!** c'est la barbe!

ADV 1 *(in a vertical position)* à l'aplomb, d'aplomb; **p. with** d'aplomb avec **2** *Fam (exactly, right)* exactement▫, en plein▫; **p. in the middle of the first act** en plein *ou* au beau milieu du premier acte▫ **3** *Am Fam (utterly, completely)* complètement▫, tout à fait▫; **I'm p. exhausted!** je suis complètement crevé!; **she's p. crazy!** elle est complètement dingue!

VT 1 *(measure depth of)* sonder; **to p. the depths** toucher le fond; **his films p. the depths of bad taste** ses films sont d'un mauvais goût inimaginable **2** *(test for verticality)* vérifier l'aplomb de; *(wall)* vérifier l'aplomb de, plomber

▸▸ ***plumb bob*** plomb *m*; ***plumb line*** *Constr* fil *m* à plomb; *Naut* sonde *f*

▸**plumb in VT SEP** effectuer le raccordement de; *(washing machine)* raccorder

plumbago [plʌm'beɪgəʊ] *(pl* **plumbagos)** **N 1** *(plant)* plumbago *m* **2** *(graphite)* plombagine *f*

plumber ['plʌmə(r)] **N** plombier *m*

plumbing ['plʌmɪŋ] **N 1** *(job)* plomberie *f* **2** *(pipes)* plomberie *f*, tuyauterie *f*; *(toilets, washbasins)* installations *fpl* sanitaires **3** *Fam Euph (urinary system)* voies *fpl* urinaires▫; **I'm having a bit of trouble with my p.** j'ai des problèmes de vessie▫

plume [plu:m] **N 1** *(feather)* plume *f*; **ostrich p.** plume *f* d'autruche **2** *(on helmet)* plumet *m*, panache *m*; *(on hat)* plumet *m*; *(on woman's hat)* plume *f* **3** *(of smoke)* volute *f*; *(of water)* jet *m*

VT 1 *(preen)* lisser; **the swan plumed itself** *or* **its feathers** le cygne se lissait les plumes **2** *Fig Literary (pride)* **to p. oneself on sth** se glorifier de qch

plummet ['plʌmɪt] **VI 1** *(plunge, dive)* tomber, plonger, piquer; **he plummeted from the roof** il est tombé du toit; **the plane plummeted towards the earth** l'avion piqua vers le sol **2** *(drop, go down ▸ price, rate, amount)* chuter, dégringoler; *(▸ blood pressure)* tomber soudainement; **his popularity has plummeted** sa cote de popularité a beaucoup baissé; **educational standards have plummeted** le niveau d'instruction a considérablement baissé

N *(weight)* plomb *m*; *(plumb line)* fil *m* à plomb

plummy ['plʌmɪ] *(compar* **plummier,** *superl* **plummiest)** **ADJ 1** *Br Pej (voice, accent)* snob **2** *Old-fashioned (job)* agréable, bien payé

plump [plʌmp] **ADJ** *(person)* rondelet, dodu; *(arms, legs)* dodu, potelé; *(fowl)* dodu, bien gras; *(fruit)* charnu

ADV *(heavily)* lourdement; *(directly)* exactement, en plein; **he ran p. into me** il m'a heurté de plein fouet; **it landed p. in the middle** ça a atterri en plein milieu

VT *(pillow, cushion)* retaper

▸**plump down VT SEP she plumped herself/her bag down next to me** elle s'est affalée/a laissé tomber son sac à côté de moi

VI se laisser tomber (lourdement), s'affaler

▸**plump for VT INSEP** *Fam* arrêter son choix sur▫, opter pour▫

▸**plump out VI** s'arrondir, engraisser

▸**plump up VT SEP** *(pillow, cushion)* retaper

VI *(become fat)* devenir dodu

plumpness ['plʌmpnɪs] **N** rondeur *f*, embonpoint *m*; **to be inclined to p.** avoir tendance à prendre de l'embonpoint

plunder ['plʌndə(r)] **VT** piller; *Fig (bookshelves, fridge)* faire une descente dans

VI piller

N 1 *(booty)* butin *m* **2** *(act of pillaging)* pillage *m*

plundering ['plʌndərɪŋ] **N** pillage *m*

ADJ pillard

plunge [plʌndʒ] **VI 1** *(dive)* plonger

2 *(throw oneself)* se jeter, se précipiter; *(fall, drop)* tomber, chuter; **the bus plunged into the river** le bus est tombé dans la rivière; **the lorry plunged over the cliff** le camion plongea par-dessus la falaise; **the helicopter plunged to the ground** l'hélicoptère piqua vers le sol; **to p. to one's death** faire une chute mortelle; **I slipped and plunged forward** j'ai glissé et je suis tombé la tête la première *ou* la tête en avant

3 *Fig* **he plunged into a long and complicated story** il s'est lancé dans une histoire longue et compliquée; **the neckline plunges deeply at the front** le devant est très décolleté

4 *(price, rate, currency)* chuter, dégringoler; **sales have plunged by 30 percent** les ventes ont chuté de 30 pour cent

VT 1 *(immerse)* plonger **2** *Fig* plonger; **he plunged his hands into his pockets** il enfonça les mains dans ses poches; **he was plunged into despair by the news** la nouvelle l'a plongé dans le désespoir; **the office was plunged into darkness** le bureau fut plongé dans l'obscurité

N 1 *(dive)* plongeon *m*; *Fig* **to take the p.** *(dare)* se jeter à l'eau; *(get married)* faire le grand saut, se mettre la corde au cou **2** *(fall, drop)* chute *f*; **a ten-metre p.** une chute de dix mètres; **prices have taken a p.** les prix ont chuté *ou* se sont effondrés

plunger ['plʌndʒə(r)] **N 1** *(for sinks, drains)* ventouse *f*, déboucheur *m* **2** *(piston ▸ in coffee-maker, syringe)* piston *m*; *(▸ of detonator)* manette *f*

plunging ['plʌndʒɪŋ] **ADJ** plongeant; **a p. neckline** un décolleté plongeant

plunk [plʌŋk] *Fam* **N 1** *(sound)* bruit *m* sourd▫; **I could hear the p. of a guitar** j'entendais quelqu'un gratter sa guitare **2** *Am (blow)* beigne *f*, gnon *m*

VT 1 *(put down)* poser lourdement▫ **2** *(guitar, banjo)* gratter **3** *Am (hit)* flanquer une beigne à; *(shoot)* flinguer

▸**plunk down VT SEP** *Fam* poser lourdement▫

pluperfect [,plu:'pɜ:fɪkt] **N** *Gram* plus-que-parfait *m*; **in the p.** au plus-que-parfait

▸▸ ***pluperfect subjunctive*** plus-que-parfait *m* du subjonctif; ***pluperfect tense*** plus-que-parfait *m*

plural ['plʊərəl] **ADJ 1** *Gram (form, ending)* pluriel, du pluriel; *(noun)* au pluriel **2** *(multiple)* multiple; *(heterogeneous)* hétérogène, pluriel; **a p. society** une société plurielle; **a p. system of education** un système d'éducation diversifié

N *Gram* pluriel *m*; **in the p.** au pluriel

▸▸ *Pol* ***plural vote*** vote *m* plural; *Pol* ***plural voting*** vote *m* plural

pluralism ['plʊərəlɪzəm] **N 1** *(gen) & Phil* pluralisme *m* **2** *(holding of several offices)* cumul *m* des fonctions

plurality [plʊə'rælətɪ] *(pl* **pluralities)** **N 1** *(multiplicity)* pluralité *f* **2** *Am Pol* majorité *f* relative **3** *(holding of several offices)* cumul *m* des fonctions

plus [plʌs] *(pl* **pluses** *or* **plusses)** **PREP 1** *Math* plus; **two p. two is** *or* **equals** *or* **makes four** deux plus deux *ou* deux et deux font quatre **2** *(as well as)* plus; **there were six of us, p. the children** nous étions six, sans compter les enfants; **£97 p. VAT** 97 livres plus la TVA

ADJ 1 *Elec & Math* positif **2** *(good, positive)* positif; **on the p. side, it's near the shops** un des avantages, c'est que c'est près des magasins; **it certainly is a big p. point** c'est incontestablement un gros avantage **3** *(after n) (over, more than)* plus; **children of 12 p.** les enfants de 12 ans et plus

N 1 *Math* plus *m* **2** *(bonus, advantage)* plus *m*, avantage *m*; **there are a number of pluses to the new plan** le nouveau projet comporte un certain nombre d'avantages

CONJ *Fam* (et) en plus▫; **he's stupid, p. he's ugly** il est bête, et en plus il est laid

▸▸ ***plus factor*** facteur *m* positif, plus *m*; ***plus fours*** pantalon *m* de golf; *Comput* ***plus key*** touche *f* plus; ***plus sign*** signe *m* plus, plus *m*

plush [plʌʃ] **ADJ 1** *Fam (luxurious ▸ apartment)* luxueux▫; *(▸ restaurant, hotel)* de luxe▫ **2** *(made of plush)* en peluche

N peluche *f*

plushy ['plʌʃɪ] *(compar* **plushier,** *superl* **plushiest)** **ADJ** *Fam (luxurious ▸ apartment)* luxueux▫; *(▸ restaurant, hotel)* de luxe▫

Plutarch ['plu:tɑ:k] **PR N** Plutarque

Pluto ['plu:təʊ] **PR N** *Myth* Pluton

N *Astron* Pluton *f*

plutocracy [pluːˈtɒkrəsɪ] *(pl* **plutocracies***)* **N** ploutocratie *f*

plutocrat [ˈpluːtəkræt] **N** ploutocrate *mf*

plutocratic [ˌpluːtəˈkrætɪk] **ADJ** ploutocratique

plutonium [pluːˈtəʊnɪəm] **N** *Chem* plutonium *m*

pluviometer [ˌpluːvɪˈɒmɪtə(r)] **N** pluviomètre *m*

ply [plaɪ] *(pl* **plies,** *pt & pp* **plied***)* **N 1** *(thickness)* épaisseur *f*; *(layer ▸ of plywood, tyre)* pli *m*; *(strand ▸ of rope, wool)* brin *m* **2** *Fam (plywood)* contreplaqué *m*

VT 1 *(supply insistently)* **she plied us with food all evening** elle nous a gavés toute la soirée; **he plied us with drinks** il nous versait sans arrêt à boire; **we plied her with questions** nous l'avons assaillie de questions

2 *Literary (perform, practise)* exercer; **to p. one's trade** exercer son métier

3 *Literary (use ▸ tool)* manier; *(▸ needle)* faire courir

4 *Literary (travel ▸ river, ocean)* naviguer sur; **the barges that p. the Thames** les péniches qui descendent et remontent le cours de la Tamise

VI 1 *(seek work)* **to p. for hire** *(taxi)* prendre des clients **2** *(travel ▸ ship, boat)* **to p. between** faire la navette entre

plywood [ˈplaɪwʊd] **N** contreplaqué *m*

PM [ˌpiːˈem] **N 1** *(abbr* **Prime Minister***)* Premier ministre *m* **2** *(abbr* **post mortem***)* autopsie *f*

p.m. [ˌpiːˈem] **ADV** *(abbr* **post meridiem***)* de l'après-midi; **3 p.m.** 3 heures de l'après-midi, 15 heures; **at 11 p.m.** à 11 heures du soir, à 23 heures

PMS [ˌpiːemˈes] **N** *Am (abbr* **premenstrual syndrome***)* syndrome *m* prémenstruel

PMT [ˌpiːemˈtiː] **N** *Br (abbr* **premenstrual tension***)* syndrome *m* prémenstruel

P/N *Com (written abbr* **promissory note***)* billet *m* à ordre, effet *m* à ordre

pneumatic [njuːˈmætɪk] **ADJ** pneumatique

▸▸ ***pneumatic brakes*** freins *mpl* à air comprimé; ***pneumatic drill*** marteau-piqueur *m*; ***pneumatic tyre*** pneu *m*

pneumatically [njuːˈmætɪkəlɪ] **ADV** pneumatiquement

pneumatics [njuːˈmætɪks] **N** *(UNCOUNT)* pneumatique *f*

pneumonia [njuːˈməʊnɪə] **N** *(UNCOUNT) Med* pneumonie *f*; **you'll catch** *or* **get p.!** tu vas attraper une pneumonie!

PO¹ [ˌpiːˈəʊ] **N** *(abbr* **Post Office***)* poste *f*

▸▸ ***PO Box*** BP *f*, boîte *f* postale

PO² 1 *(written abbr* **postal order***)* mandat *m* postal **2** *Naut (written abbr* **petty officer***)* second maître *m*

po [pəʊ] *(pl* **pos***)* **N** *Br Fam* pot *m* (de chambre)

POA [ˌpiːəʊˈeɪ] **N** *Br (abbr* **Prison Officers' Association***)* = syndicat des agents pénitentiaires en Grande-Bretagne

poach [pəʊtʃ] **VT 1** *(hunt illegally)* prendre en braconnant **2** *Fig (steal ▸ idea)* voler; *(▸ employee)* débaucher; **to p. sb's shots** *(in tennis)* piquer les balles de qn **3** *Culin* pocher; **a poached egg** un œuf poché; **poached salmon** saumon *m* poché

VI braconner; **to p. for hare** chasser le lièvre sur une propriété privée; **to p. for salmon** prendre du saumon en braconnant; *Fig* **to p. on sb's territory** *or* **preserves** braconner sur les terres de qn, empiéter sur le territoire de qn

poacher [ˈpəʊtʃə(r)] **N 1** *(person)* braconnier *m* **2** *Culin* **(egg) p.** pocheuse *f*

poaching [ˈpəʊtʃɪŋ] **N** *(hunting)* braconnage *m*

pock [pɒk] = **pockmark**

pocket [ˈpɒkɪt] **N 1** *(on clothing)* poche *f*; *(on car door)* compartiment *m*; **it's in your coat p.** c'est dans la poche de ton manteau; **I went through his pockets** j'ai fouillé *ou* regardé dans ses poches; **he tried to pick her p.** il a essayé de lui faire les poches; **the maps are in the p. of the car door** les cartes sont dans (le compartiment de) la portière de la voiture; **to have sb in one's p.** avoir qn dans sa poche; **we had the deal in our p.** le marché était dans la poche; **they live in each other's pockets** ils sont tout le temps ensemble; **to line one's pockets** se remplir les poches, s'en mettre plein les poches; *Fig* **to put one's hand in one's p.** mettre la main au portefeuille; **he doesn't like putting his hand in his p.** il est du genre radin; **to be out of p.** en être de sa poche; **how much are you out of p.?** combien ça vous a coûté?

2 *Fig (financial resources)* portefeuille *m*, porte-monnaie *m*; **we have prices to suit all pockets** nous avons des prix pour toutes les bourses

3 *Mining (of ore, water, gas)* poche *f*; *(of fire-damp)* nid *m*; **p. of air** trou *m* d'air

4 *(small area ▸ of resistance, rebellion, unemployment)* poche *f*

5 *(of snooker or pool table)* blouse *f*

COMP *(diary, camera, revolver etc)* de poche

VT 1 *(put in one's pocket)* mettre dans sa poche, empocher; **I paid up and pocketed the change** j'ai payé et j'ai mis la monnaie dans ma poche; *Fig* **to p. one's pride** mettre son amour-propre dans sa poche; **to p. an insult** encaisser une insulte sans rien dire

2 *(steal)* voler

3 *(in snooker, pool)* mettre dans la blouse

4 *Am Pol* **to p. a bill** = garder un projet de loi sous le coude pour l'empêcher d'être adopté

▸▸ ***pocket battleship*** cuirassé *m* de poche; *Br* ***pocket billiards*** *(pool)* billard *m* américain; *Hist* ***pocket borough*** = circonscription électorale contrôlée par une personne ou une famille; ***pocket calculator*** calculatrice *f* de poche; ***pocket computer*** ordinateur *m* de poche; ***pocket dictionary*** dictionnaire *m* de poche; ***pocket edition*** édition *f* de poche; ***pocket handkerchief*** mouchoir *m* de poche; *Br* ***pocket money*** argent *m* de poche; ***pocket notebook*** carnet *m*; *Am* ***pocket pool*** billard *m* américain; ***pocket size*** *(in bookbinding)* format *m* de poche; *Am* ***pocket veto*** = refus par le Président de signer une proposition de loi, pour l'empêcher d'être adoptée

pocketbook [ˈpɒkɪtbʊk] **N 1** *(notebook)* calepin *m*, carnet *m* **2** *Am (handbag)* sac *m* à main; *(wallet)* portefeuille *m*; *(purse)* porte-monnaie *m*

pocketful [ˈpɒkɪtfʊl] **N** poche *f* pleine; **I've got pocketfuls of small change** j'ai les poches pleines de petite monnaie

pocketknife [ˈpɒkɪtnaɪf] *(pl* **pocketknives** [-naɪvz]*)* **N** canif *m*

pockmark [ˈpɒkmɑːk] **N** *(on surface)* marque *f*, petit trou *m*; *(from smallpox)* cicatrice *f* de variole; **his face is covered with pockmarks** il a le visage grêlé *ou* variolé

pockmarked [ˈpɒkmɑːkt] **ADJ** *(face)* grêlé; *(surface)* criblé de petits trous; **p. with rust** piqué par la rouille

pod [pɒd] *(pt & pp* **podded,** *cont* **podding***)* **N 1** *Bot* cosse *f*; **bean p.** cosse *f* de haricot **2** *Zool* oothèque *f* **3** *Aviat* nacelle *f*; *Astron* capsule *f*

VT *Br (peas)* écosser

podcast [ˈpɒdkɑːst] *(pt & pp* **podcast***) Comput* **N** podcast *m*

VT podcaster

podcasting [ˈpɒdkɑːstɪŋ] **N** podcasting *m*

podgy [ˈpɒdʒɪ] *(compar* **podgier,** *superl* **podgiest***)* **ADJ** *Br* grassouillet

podiatrist [pəˈdaɪətrɪst] **N** pédicure *mf*

podium [ˈpəʊdɪəm] *(pl* **podiums** *or* **podia** [-dɪə]*)* **N 1** *(stand)* podium *m* **2** *Am (desk, counter)* guichet *m*; **next p. please** *(sign)* passez au guichet suivant

▸▸ ***podium dancer*** danseur(euse) *m,f* professionnel(elle) de boîte de nuit

poem [ˈpəʊɪm] **N** poème *m*

poet [ˈpəʊɪt] **N** poète *m*

▸▸ ***Poets' Corner*** = partie de l'abbaye de Westminster où reposent plusieurs poètes anglais; ***poet laureate*** poète *m* lauréat

poetaster [ˌpəʊɪˈtæstə(r)] **N** *Pej* rimailleur(euse) *m,f*

poetess [ˈpəʊɪtɪs] **N** *Old-fashioned* poétesse *f*

poetic [pəʊˈetɪk] **ADJ** poétique

▸▸ ***poetic justice*** justice *f* immanente; **it's p. justice that they ended up losing** ce n'est que justice qu'ils aient fini par perdre; ***poetic licence*** licence *f* poétique

poetical [pəʊˈetɪkəl] **ADJ** poétique

poetically [pəʊˈetɪkəlɪ] **ADV** poétiquement

poetics [pəʊˈetɪks] **N** *(UNCOUNT)* poétique *f*

poetry [ˈpəʊɪtrɪ] **N** poésie *f*; **to write p.** écrire des poèmes; **the art of p.** l'art *m* poétique; **it was p. in motion** c'était un vrai plaisir pour les yeux; *Ironic* c'était beau à voir!

▸▸ ***poetry reading*** lecture *f* de poèmes; ***poetry slam*** slam *m*

po-faced **ADJ** *Br Fam* à l'air pincé

pogo [ˈpəʊgəʊ] **N** *(dance)* pogo *m (danse punk)*

VI *(dance)* danser le pogo

▸▸ ***pogo stick*** bâton *m* sauteur

pogrom [ˈpɒgrəm] **N** pogrom *m*

poignancy [ˈpɔɪnjənsɪ] **N** caractère *m* poignant; **a moment of great p.** un moment d'intense émotion

poignant [ˈpɔɪnjənt] **ADJ** poignant

poignantly [ˈpɔɪnjəntlɪ] **ADV** de façon poignante

poinsettia [pɔɪnˈsetɪə] **N** *Bot* poinsettia *m*

POINT [pɔɪnt]

N	
• pointe **1, 16, 20**	• point **2, 3, 5, 6, 9–12, 14, 15, 21**
• endroit **3**	• essentiel **7**
• moment **4**	• virgule **13**
• but **8**	
• prise **18**	
VT	
• diriger **1**	• pointer **1**
• indiquer **2**	
VI	
• montrer du doigt **1**	• être braqué **3**

N 1 *(tip ▸ of sword, nail, pencil etc)* pointe *f*; **trim one end of the stick into a p.** taillez un des bouts de la branche en pointe; **his beard ended in a neat p.** sa barbe était soigneusement taillée en pointe; **draw a star with five points** dessinez une étoile à cinq branches; **a dog with white points** un chien aux pattes et aux oreilles blanches; **to dance on points** faire des pointes; **on (full) p.** *(ballet dancer)* sur la pointe; **not to put too fine a p. on it...** pour dire les choses clairement...

2 *(small dot)* point *m*; **a tiny p. of light** un minuscule point de lumière

3 *(specific place)* point *m*, endroit *m*, lieu *m*; **meeting p.** *(sign)* point rencontre; **the runners have passed the halfway p.** les coureurs ont dépassé la mi-parcours; **we're back to our p. of departure** *or* **our starting p.** nous sommes revenus au *ou* à notre point de départ; **the p. where the accident occurred** l'endroit où l'accident a eu lieu; **at that p. you'll see a church on the left** à ce moment-là, vous verrez une église sur votre gauche; **the bus service to Dayton and points west** le service de bus à destination de Dayton et des villes situées plus à l'ouest

4 *(particular moment)* moment *m*; *(particular period)* période *f*; **the country is at a critical p. in its development** le pays traverse une période *ou* phase critique de son développement; **we are at a critical p.** nous voici à un point critique; **there comes a p. when a decision has to be made** il arrive un moment où il faut prendre une décision; **when it comes to the p. of actually doing it** quand vient le moment de passer à l'acte; **when it came to the p.** quand le moment critique est arrivé; **at one p. in the discussion** à un moment de la discussion; **at one p. in my travels** au cours de mes voyages; **at one p., I thought the roof was going to cave in** à un moment (donné), j'ai cru que le toit allait s'effondrer; **at one p. in the book** à un moment donné dans le livre; **at this p. the phone rang** c'est alors que le téléphone a sonné, à ce moment-là le téléphone a sonné; **at that p., I was still undecided** à ce moment-là, je n'avais pas encore pris de décision; **at that p. in China's history** à ce moment précis de l'histoire de la Chine; **it's too late by this p.** il est déjà trop tard à l'heure qu'il est; **by that p., I was too tired to move** j'étais alors tellement fatigué que je ne pouvais plus bouger

5 *(stage in development or process)* point *m*; **she had reached the p. of wanting a divorce** elle en était (arrivée) au point de vouloir divorcer; **to reach the p. of no return** atteindre le point de non-retour; **to be at the p. of death** être sur le point de mourir; **the conflict has gone beyond the p. where negotiations are possible** le conflit a atteint le stade où toute négociation est impossible; **the regime is on the p. of collapse** le régime est au bord de l'effondrement; **I was on the p. of admitting everything** j'étais sur le point de tout avouer; **she had worked to the p. of exhaustion** elle avait travaillé jusqu'à l'épuisement; **he stuffed himself to the p. of being sick** il s'est gavé à en être malade

6 *(for discussion or debate)* point *m*; **a seven-p. memorandum** un mémorandum en sept points; **let's go on to the next p.** passons à la question suivante *ou* au point suivant; **on this p. we disagree** sur ce point nous ne sommes pas d'accord; **I want to emphasize this p.** je voudrais insister sur ce point; **are there any points I haven't covered?** y a-t-il des questions que je n'ai pas abordées?; **to make** *or* **to raise a p.** faire une remarque; **to make the p. that...** faire remarquer que... + *indicative*; **my p.** *or* **the p. I'm making is that...** là où je veux en venir c'est que...; **all right, you've made your p.!** d'accord, on a compris!; **let me illustrate my p.** laissez-moi illustrer mon propos; **to prove his p. he showed us a photo** pour prouver ses affirmations, il nous a montré une photo; **I see** *or* **take your p.** je vois ce que vous voulez dire *ou* où vous voulez en venir; **p. taken!** c'est juste!; **he may not be home – you've got a p. there!** il n'est peut-être pas chez lui – ça c'est vrai!; **the fact that he went to the police is a p. in his favour/a p. against him** le fait qu'il soit allé à la police est un bon/mauvais point pour lui; **I corrected her on a p. of grammar** je l'ai corrigée sur un point de grammaire; **she was disqualified on a technical p.** elle a été disqualifiée pour *ou* sur une faute technique; **to make a p. of doing sth** tenir à faire qch; **kindly make a p. of remembering next time** faites-moi le plaisir de ne pas oublier la prochaine fois

7 *(essential part, heart ▸ of argument, explanation)* essentiel *m*; *(conclusion ▸ of joke)* chute *f*; **I get the p.** je comprends, je vois; **the p. is (that) we're overloaded with work** le fait est que nous sommes débordés de travail; **we're getting off** *or* **away from the p.** nous nous éloignons *ou* écartons du sujet; **that's the (whole) p.!** *(that's the problem)* c'est là (tout) le problème!; *(that's the aim)* c'est ça, le but!; **that's not the p.!** là n'est pas la question!; **the money is/your feelings are beside the p.** l'argent n'a/vos sentiments n'ont rien à voir là-dedans; **get** *or* **come to the p.!** dites ce que vous avez à dire!, ne tournez pas autour du pot!; **I'll come straight to the p.** je serai bref; **to keep to the p.** ne pas s'écarter du sujet

8 *(purpose)* but *m*; *(meaning, use)* sens *m*, intérêt *m*; **the p. of the game is to get rid of all your cards** le but du jeu est de se débarrasser de toutes ses cartes; **there's no p. in asking him now** ça ne sert à rien *ou* ce n'est pas la peine de le lui demander maintenant; **what's the p. of all this?** à quoi ça sert tout ça?; **I don't see the p. (of re-doing it)** je ne vois pas l'intérêt (de le refaire); **oh, what's the p. anyway!** oh, et puis à quoi bon, après tout!

9 *(feature, characteristic)* point *m*; **the boss has his good points** le patron a ses bons côtés; **it's my weak/strong p.** c'est mon point faible/fort; **tact has never been one of your strong points** la délicatesse n'a jamais été ton fort

10 *(unit ▸ in scoring, measuring)* point *m*; *Mktg (▸ on customer loyalty card)* point *m*; **the Dow Jones index is up/down two points** l'indice Dow Jones a augmenté/baissé de deux points; **who scored the winning p.?** qui a marqué le point gagnant?; **to win/to lead on points** *(in boxing)* gagner/mener aux points; *Am Fam* **to make points with sb** *(find favour with)* faire bonne impression à qn ☐; *Sch* **merit points** bons points *mpl*; **points competition** *(in cycling)* classement *m* par points

11 *(on compass)* point *m*; **the four points of the compass** les quatre points *mpl* cardinaux; **the 32 points of the compass** les 32 points *mpl* de la rose des vents; **to alter course 16 points** venir de 16 quarts; **our people were scattered to all points of the compass** notre peuple s'est retrouvé éparpillé aux quatre coins du monde

12 *Geom* point *m*

13 *(in decimals)* virgule *f*; **five p. one** cinq virgule un

14 *(punctuation mark)* point *m*; **three** *or* **ellipsis points** points *mpl* de suspension

15 *Typ & Comput (measurement)* point *m*; **6-p. type** caractères *mpl* de 6 points

16 *Geog (promontory)* pointe *f*, promontoire *m*

17 *Aut* vis *f* platinée

18 *Br Elec (socket)* **(power) p.** prise *f* (de courant); **eight-p. distributor** *(in engine)* distributeur *m* (d'allumage) à huit plots

19 *Br Rail* **points** aiguillage *m*

20 *(on backgammon board)* flèche *f*, pointe *f*

21 *Her* point *m*

VT 1 *(direct, aim ▸ vehicle)* diriger; *(▸ flashlight, hose)* pointer, braquer; *(▸ finger)* pointer, tendre; *(▸ telescope)* diriger, braquer; **to p. one's finger at sb/sth** montrer qn/qch du doigt; **he pointed his finger accusingly at Gus** il pointa un doigt accusateur vers Gus, il montra *ou* désigna Gus d'un doigt accusateur; **he pointed the rifle/the camera at me** il braqua le fusil/l'appareil photo sur moi; **she pointed the truck towards the garage** elle tourna le camion vers le garage; **if anybody shows up, just p. them in my direction** si quelqu'un arrive, tu n'as qu'à me l'envoyer; **just p. me in the right direction** dites-moi simplement quelle direction je dois prendre

2 *(indicate)* **to p. the way** indiquer la direction *ou* le chemin; *Fig* montrer le chemin, indiquer la direction à suivre; **her research points the way to a better understanding of the phenomenon** ses recherches vont permettre une meilleure compréhension du phénomène

3 *(in dance)* **to p. one's toes** tendre le pied

4 *Constr (wall, building)* jointoyer

5 *(sharpen ▸ stick, pencil)* tailler

VI 1 *(person)* **to p. at** *or* **to** *or* **towards sth** montrer qch du doigt; **she pointed left** elle fit un signe vers la gauche; **he pointed back down the corridor** il fit un signe vers le fond du couloir; **he pointed at** *or* **to me with his pencil** il pointa son crayon vers moi; **he was pointing at me** son doigt était pointé vers moi; **it's rude to p.** ce n'est pas poli de montrer du doigt

2 *(road sign, needle on dial)* **the signpost points up the hill** le panneau est tourné vers le haut de la colline; **the weather vane is pointing north** la girouette est orientée au nord; **when the big hand points to 12** quand la grande aiguille est sur le 12

3 *(be directed, face ▸ gun, camera)* être braqué; *(▸ vehicle)* être dirigé, être tourné; **hold the gun with the barrel pointing downwards** tenez le canon de l'arme pointé vers le bas; **the rifle/the camera was pointing straight at me** la carabine/la caméra était braquée sur moi; **p. your flashlight over there** éclaire là-bas; **insert the disk with the arrow pointing right** insérez la disquette, la flèche pointée *ou* pointant vers la droite; **the aerial should be pointing in the direction of the transmitter** l'antenne devrait être tournée dans la direction de *ou* tournée vers l'émetteur; **he walks with his feet pointing outwards** il marche les pieds en dehors

4 *(dog)* tomber en arrêt

• **at this point in time** ADV pour l'instant

• **in point of fact** ADV en fait, à vrai dire

• **to the point** ADJ pertinent

• **up to a point** ADV jusqu'à un certain point; **did the strategy succeed? – up to a p.** est-ce que la stratégie a réussi? – dans une certaine mesure; **she can be persuaded, but only up to a p.** il est possible de la convaincre, mais seulement jusqu'à un certain point

►► *Mktg* ***point of delivery*** lieu *m* de livraison; *Br* ***point duty*** *(of police officer, traffic warden)* service *m* de la circulation; **to be on p. duty** diriger la circulation; ***point guard*** *(in basketball)* meneur(euse) *m,f*; ***point of intersection*** point *m* d'intersection; *Br Rail* ***point lever*** levier *m* d'aiguille; ***point of order*** point *m* de procédure; **he rose on a p. of order** il a demandé la parole pour soulever un point de procédure; *Am* ***point man*** *(in the forefront)* précurseur *m*; *Comput* ***point of presence*** point *m* de présence *ou* d'accès; *Mktg* ***point of purchase*** lieu *m* d'achat, lieu *m* de vente; ***point of reference*** point *m* de référence; *Mktg* ***point of sale*** lieu *m* de vente, point *m* de vente; **at the p. of sale** sur le lieu de vente; ***point shoes*** *(for ballet)* (chaussons *mpl* à) pointes *fpl*; *Typ & Comput* ***point size*** corps *m*; ***point source*** source *f* ponctuelle; ***point of view*** *TV & Cin* angle *m* du regard; *(opinion)* point *m* de vue, opinion *f*; **from my p. of view, it doesn't make much difference** en ce qui me concerne, ça ne change pas grand-chose; **to consider sth from all points of view** considérer qch sous tous ses aspects; ***point work*** *(of ballet dancer)* pointes *fpl*

▸ **point off** VT SEP *Math (decimals)* séparer par une virgule

▸ **point out** VT SEP **1** *(indicate)* indiquer, montrer; **I'll p. the church out to you as we go by** je vous montrerai *ou* vous indiquerai l'église quand nous passerons devant **2** *(mention, call attention to ▸ error)* signaler; *(▸ fact)* faire remarquer; **she pointed out several mistakes to us** elle nous a signalé plusieurs erreurs, elle a attiré notre attention sur plusieurs erreurs; **I'd like to p. out that it was my idea in the first place** je vous ferai remarquer que l'idée est de moi; **he pointed out that two people were missing** il fit remarquer qu'il manquait deux personnes

▸ **point up** VT SEP *(of person, report)* souligner, mettre l'accent sur; *(of event)* faire ressortir; **his account points up the irony of the defeat** son exposé met l'accent sur l'ironie de la défaite; **the accident points up the need for closer cooperation** l'accident fait ressortir le besoin d'une coopération plus étroite

point-and-click *Comput* VT pointer et cliquer sur

VI pointer et cliquer

ADJ **p. interface** interface *f* souris

point-blank ADJ **1** *(shot)* à bout portant; **he was shot at p. range** on lui a tiré dessus à bout portant **2** *(refusal, denial)* catégorique; *(question)* (posé) de but en blanc, (posé) à brûle-pourpoint

ADV **1** *(shoot)* à bout portant **2** *(refuse, deny)* catégoriquement; *(ask)* de but en blanc, à brûle-pourpoint

point-by-point ADJ méthodique

pointed ['pɔɪntɪd] ADJ **1** *(sharp)* pointu; *(beard)* (taillé) en pointe **2** *Fig (comment, remark, look)* qui en dit long, lourd de sous-entendus; *(reference)* peu équivoque

►► *Archit* ***pointed arch*** arche *f* en ogive

pointedly ['pɔɪntɪdlɪ] ADV *(comment)* de façon explicite; **she looked at me p.** elle m'a lancé un regard qui en disait long; **she p. ignored me all evening** elle m'a ostensiblement ignoré pendant toute la soirée

pointedness ['pɔɪntɪdnɪs] N *(of comment, reference)* caractère *m* explicite

pointer ['pɔɪntə(r)] N **1** *(for pointing ▸ stick)* baguette *f*; *(▸ arrow)* flèche *f*

2 *(on dial)* aiguille *f*

3 *(indication, sign)* indice *m*, signe *m*; *(tip)* tuyau *m*; **there are several pointers as to what really happened** plusieurs indices nous permettent de deviner ce qui s'est réellement passé; **all the pointers indicate an impending economic recovery** tout indique que la reprise économique est imminente; **he gave me a few pointers on how to use the computer** il m'a donné quelques tuyaux sur la façon d'utiliser l'ordinateur

4 *Comput* pointeur *m*

5 *(dog)* pointer *m*

6 *Constr (bricklayer's tool)* pointe *f*

pointillism ['pɔɪntɪlɪzəm] N *Art* pointillisme *m*

pointing ['pɔɪntɪŋ] N *(UNCOUNT) Constr (act, job)* jointoiement *m*; *(cement work)* joints *mpl*

►► *Comput* ***pointing device*** pointeur *m*

pointless ['pɔɪntlɪs] ADJ inutile, vain; *(crime, violence, vandalism)* gratuit; *(story, joke)* qui ne rime à rien; **it's p. trying to convince him** ça ne sert à rien *ou* il est inutile d'essayer de le convaincre

pointlessly ['pɔɪntlɪslɪ] ADV *(gen)* inutilement, vainement; *(hurt, murder, vandalize)* gratuitement

pointlessness ['pɔɪntlɪsnɪs] N *(gen)* inutilité *f*; *(of remark)* manque *m* d'à-propos; *(of crime, violence, vandalism)* gratuité *f*

point-of-purchase ADJ sur le point *ou* sur le lieu de vente

►► ***point-of-purchase advertising*** publicité *f* sur le lieu de vente, PLV *f*; ***point-of-purchase display*** exposition *f* sur le lieu de vente; ***point-of-purchase information*** informations *fpl* sur le lieu de vente;

point-of-purchase material matériel *m* de publicité sur le lieu de vente *ou* de PLV

point-of-sale ADJ sur le point *ou* sur le lieu de vente

▸▸ ***point-of-sale advertising*** publicité *f* sur le lieu de vente, PLV *f*; ***point-of-sale display*** exposition *f* sur le lieu de vente; ***point-of-sale information*** informations *fpl* sur le lieu de vente; ***point-of-sale material*** matériel *m* de publicité sur le lieu de vente *ou* de PLV; ***point-of-sale terminal*** terminal *m* point de vente, TPV *m*

point-of-view shot N *Cin & TV* plan *m* subjectif

pointsman ['pɔɪntsmən] (*pl* **pointsmen** [-mən]) N *Br Rail* aiguilleur *m*

point-to-point N *Br* rallye *m* hippique

pointy-headed [,pɔɪntɪ'-] ADJ *Am Fam Pej* intello

poise [pɔɪz] N **1** *(composure, coolness)* calme *m*, aisance *f*, assurance *f*; **to recover one's p.** retrouver son aplomb **2** *(physical bearing)* port *m*, maintien *m*; *(gracefulness)* grâce *f*

VT *(balance)* mettre en équilibre; *(hold suspended)* tenir suspendu; **she poised herself on the arm of my chair** elle s'est assise gracieusement sur le bras de mon fauteuil

poised [pɔɪzd] ADJ **1** *(balanced)* en équilibre; *(suspended)* suspendu; **her hand was p. over the telephone** sa main était suspendue au-dessus du téléphone; **she held her glass p. near her lips** elle tenait son verre près de ses lèvres; **the cat was p. ready to spring** le chat se tenait prêt à bondir **2** *(ready, prepared)* prêt; **p. for action** prêt à agir **3** *(composed, self-assured)* calme, assuré

poison ['pɔɪzən] N **1** *(substance)* poison *m*; *(of reptile)* venin *m* **2** *Fig* poison *m*, venin *m*; **the p. spreading through our society** le mal qui se propage dans notre société; **they hate each other like p.** ils se détestent cordialement; *Fam* **he's absolute p.!** c'est un vrai poison!; *Fam Hum* **name your p.**, *Br* **what's your p.?** qu'est-ce que tu bois?ᵅ, qu'est-ce que je t'offre?ᵅ

COMP *(mushroom, plant)* vénéneux; *(gas)* toxique

VT **1** *(give poison to)* empoisonner; **to p. sb with sth** empoisonner qn à qch; **a poisoned arrow/drink** une flèche/boisson empoisonnée; **all these pesticides are poisoning the air** tous ces pesticides empoisonnent l'atmosphère **2** *Fig* envenimer, gâcher; **his arrival poisoned the atmosphere** son arrivée rendit l'atmosphère insupportable; **he poisoned our minds against her** il nous a montés contre elle

▸▸ *Fig* ***poisoned chalice*** cadeau *m* empoisonné; *Zool* ***poison gland*** glande *f* à venin; *Bot* ***poison ivy*** sumac *m* vénéneux, *Can* herbe *f* à puces *ou* à la puce; *Fam Fin* ***poison pill*** *(strategy)* pilule *f* empoisonnée

poisoner ['pɔɪzənə(r)] N empoisonneur(euse) *m,f*

poisoning ['pɔɪzənɪŋ] N empoisonnement *m*

poisonous ['pɔɪzənəs] ADJ **1** *(mushroom, plant)* vénéneux; *(snake, lizard)* venimeux; *(gas, chemical)* toxique; **mercury is highly p.** le mercure est très toxique **2** *Fig (person)* malveillant, venimeux; *(remark, allegation)* venimeux; *(doctrine)* pernicieux; **he's got a p. tongue** il a une langue de vipère

> When translating the English word **poisonous**, note that the French words **vénéneux** and **venimeux** are not interchangeable. **Vénéneux** applies to plants whereas **venimeux** applies to animals.

poke [pəʊk] VT **1** *(push, prod* ▸ *gen)* donner un coup à; *(*▸ *with elbow)* donner un coup de coude à; **somebody poked me in the back** quelqu'un m'a donné un coup dans le dos

2 *(stick, insert)* enfoncer; **she poked her finger/knife into the tart** elle enfonça son doigt/son couteau dans la tarte; **to p. a hole in sth** faire un trou dans qch; **he poked his finger at the map** il a pointé le doigt vers la carte; **he poked his stick at me** il fit un mouvement avec son bâton dans ma direction; **she opened the door and poked her head in/out** elle ouvrit la porte et passa sa tête à l'intérieur/à l'extérieur; **he's always poking his nose in other people's business** il se mêle toujours de ce qui ne le regarde pas

3 *(fire)* tisonner

4 *Am Fam (punch)* flanquer un coup de poing à; **I poked him in the nose** je lui ai flanqué un coup de poing sur le nez

5 *Vulg (have sex with)* tirer un coup avec, tringler

6 *(idiom)* **to p. fun at sb/sth** se moquer de qn/qch

VI *(prod)* **to p. at sth** *(with finger)* toucher qch du doigt; *(with stick)* donner un petit coup dans qch

N **1** *(push, prod)* poussée *f*, (petit) coup *m*; **he gave me a p. in the back** il m'a donné un (petit) coup dans le dos; **give the fire a p.** donne un coup de tisonnier dans le feu; *Fam Hum* **it's better than a p. in the eye with a sharp stick** c'est mieux que rienᵅ

2 *Am Fam (punch)* gnon *m*, marron *m*; **he's asking for a p. in the nose!** il va prendre un marron s'il continue!

3 *Scot (bag)* sac *m*

4 *Vulg (sexual intercourse)* **to have a p.** tirer un coup

▸**poke about** VI **1** *(search)* fouiller, fureter; **a dog was poking about in the bushes** un chien fouinait *ou* furetait dans les buissons; **she was poking about in the wardrobe for something to wear** elle fouillait dans l'armoire pour trouver quelque chose à mettre **2** *(make unwanted enquiries)* fourrer son nez partout, fouiner; **that social worker is always poking about** cette assistante sociale est toujours en train de fourrer son nez partout

VT INSEP *(search in)* fouiller dans; **she loves poking about antique shops** elle adore fouiner *ou* farfouiller dans les magasins d'antiquités

▸**poke out** VI *(stick out)* dépasser; **the new shoots were just poking out of the ground** les nouvelles pousses commençaient tout juste à sortir de terre; **her umbrella was poking out of her bag** son parapluie sortait *ou* dépassait de son sac

VT SEP *(remove)* déloger; **to p. sb's eye out** crever un œil à qn

poker ['pəʊkə(r)] N **1** *(card game)* poker *m* **2** *(for fire)* tisonnier *m*

▸▸ ***poker dice*** N *(game)* poker *m* d'as; NPL *(set of dice)* dés *mpl* pour le poker d'as; ***poker face*** visage *m* impassible *or* impénétrable; **she kept a p. face** son visage n'a pas trahi la moindre émotion *ou* est resté totalement impassible

poker-faced ADJ *(person)* au visage impassible; *(reply, response)* qui ne trahit aucune émotion

pokey, poky ['pəʊkɪ] *(compar* **pokier**, *superl* **pokiest**) *Fam*

N *Am (prison)* taule *f*, cabane *f*; **in p.** en taule, en cabane

ADJ *Br (cramped)* exigu(ë)

pol [pɒl] N *Am Fam* politicienᵅ *m*

Polack ['pəʊlæk] N *very Fam* Polaque *mf*, = terme injurieux désignant un Polonais

Poland ['pəʊlənd] N Pologne *f*

polar ['pəʊlə(r)] ADJ **1** *Chem, Elec, Geog & Math* polaire **2** *Fig (completely different* ▸ *opinions, attitudes)* diamétralement opposé; **they are p. opposites** ils sont diamétralement opposés

▸▸ *Zool* ***polar bear*** ours *m* polaire *ou* blanc; ***the Polar Circle*** le cercle polaire; ***polar coordinates*** coordonnées *fpl* polaires; ***the polar lights*** l'aurore *f* polaire; ***polar regions*** les régions *fpl* polaires

polarity [pəʊ'lærətɪ] (*pl* **polarities**) N *Phys* polarité *f*; *Fig* **there is a growing p. between the two parties** les deux partis sont en opposition de plus en plus nette

polarization, -isation [,pəʊləraɪ'zeɪʃən] N polarisation *f*

polarize, -ise ['pəʊləraɪz] VT polariser; *Fig (people, opinion)* diviser

VI se polariser; *Fig (opinion)* se diviser

Polaroid® ['pəʊlərɔɪd] ADJ *(camera)* Polaroid®; *(film)* pour Polaroid®; *(glasses)* à verre polarisé

N *(camera)* Polaroid®; *(photo)* photo *f ou* cliché *m* Polaroid®

• **Polaroids**® NPL *(sunglasses)* lunettes *fpl* de soleil à verre polarisé

polder ['pəʊldə(r)] N *Geog* polder *m*

Pole [pəʊl] N Polonais(e) *m,f*

pole [pəʊl] N **1** *Elec & Geog* pôle *m*; **to travel from p. to p.** parcourir la terre entière; *Fig* **they are poles apart** ils n'ont absolument rien en commun; **their positions on disarmament are poles apart** leurs positions sur le désarmement sont diamétralement opposées

2 *(rod)* bâton *m*, perche *f*; *(for tent)* montant *m*; *(in fence, construction)* poteau *m*, pieu *m*; *(for gardening)* tuteur *m*; *(for climbing plants)* rame *f*; *(for pole-vaulting, punting)* perche *f*; *(for skier)* bâton *m*; *(of stretcher)* bras *m*

3 *(mast* ▸ *for phonelines)* poteau *m*; *(*▸ *for flags, circus tent)* mât *m*

4 *(for climbing)* mât *m*; *(in fire-station)* perche *f*

5 *Br Fam* **to be up the p.** *(crazy)* être cinglé *ou* dingue; **to be up the p. with worry** être fou *ou* malade d'inquiétude; **he's driving me up the p.!** il me rend dingue!

6 *Am (on racecourse)* corde *f*

7 *(unit of measure)* ≃ perche *f*

VT **1** *(punt)* faire avancer (avec une perche) **2** *(plants)* ramer

▸▸ *Am* ***pole bean*** haricot *m* à rames; ***pole dancer*** = danseuse qui pratique le "pole dancing"; ***pole dancing*** = style de danse de strip-tease qui s'exécute autour d'une barre verticale; ***pole jump*** saut *m* à la perche; ***pole position*** *(in motor racing)* pole position *f*; **to be in p. position** être en pole position; ***Pole Star*** (étoile *f*) Polaire *f*; ***pole vault*** saut *m* à la perche

poleaxe, *Am* **poleax** ['pəʊlæks] N **1** *(weapon)* hache *f* d'armes **2** *(for slaughter)* merlin *m*

VT *(hit* ▸ *person)* assommer; *(*▸ *animal)* abattre avec un merlin; *Fig* **she was poleaxed by the news** la nouvelle l'a abasourdie *ou* assommée

polecat ['pəʊlkæt] (*pl* **inv** *or* **polecats**) N *Zool* **1** *(European, African)* putois *m* **2** *Am (skunk)* mouffette *f*, mouffette *f*

polemic [pə'lemɪk] ADJ polémique

N *(argument)* polémique *f*

• **polemics** N *(UNCOUNT) (skill, practice)* art *m* de la polémique

polemical [pə'lemɪkəl] ADJ polémique

polemicist [pə'lemɪsɪst] N polémiste *mf*

polenta [pə'lentə] N polenta *f*

pole-vault VI *(as activity)* faire du saut à la perche; *(on specific jump)* faire un saut à la perche

pole-vaulter [-'vɔːltə(r)] N perchiste *mf*

police [pə'liːs] NPL **1** *(police force)* police *f*; **the p. are on their way** la police arrive, les gendarmes arrivent; **he's in the p.** il est dans la police, c'est un policier; **a man is helping p. with their enquiries** un homme est entendu par les policiers dans le cadre de leur enquête **2** *(police officers)* policiers *mpl*; **18 p. were injured** 18 policiers ont été blessés

COMP *(vehicle, patrol, spy)* de police; *(protection, work)* de la police, policier; *(harassment)* policier; **he was taken into p. custody** il a été emmené en garde à vue; **all p. leave was cancelled** les permissions des policiers ont été annulées; **p. powers were extended** les pouvoirs de la police ont été étendus; **there was a heavy p. presence** d'importantes forces de police se trouvaient sur place

VT **1** *(of policemen)* surveiller, maintenir l'ordre dans; **the streets are being policed 24 hours a day** les rues sont surveillées par la police 24 heures sur 24; **the match was heavily policed** d'importantes forces de police étaient présentes lors du match

2 *(of guards, vigilantes)* surveiller, maintenir l'ordre dans; **the factory is policed by security guards** l'usine est surveillée par des vigiles; **vigilante groups p. the neighbourhood** des groupes d'autodéfense maintiennent l'ordre dans le quartier

3 *(of army, international organization)* surveiller, contrôler; **the area is policed by army patrols** des patrouilles militaires veillent au maintien de l'ordre dans la région

4 *(regulate* ▸ *prices)* contrôler; *(*▸ *agreement)* veiller à l'application *ou* au respect de

5 *Am (clean* ▸ *military camp)* nettoyer

▸▸ *Am* ***police academy*** école *f* de police; *Am po-*

lice captain ≃ commissaire *m* de police; ***police car*** voiture *f* de police; ***police cell*** cellule *f* d'un poste de police; ***police chief*** ≃ préfet *m* de police; *Am* ***police commissioner*** commissaire *m* de police; *Br* ***police constable*** ≃ gardien *m* de la paix, ≃ agent *m* (de police); ***police court*** tribunal *m* de police; *Am* ***police department*** service *m* de police; ***police dog*** chien *m* policier; ***a police escort*** une escorte policière; ***police force*** police *f*; **the local p. force** la police locale; **to join the p. force** entrer dans la police; ***police informer*** indicateur(trice) *m,f*; ***police inspector*** inspecteur (trice) *m,f* de police; *Br (in the CID)* commissaire *m* de police; *Am* ***police line*** cordon *m* de police *(sur le lieu du crime)*; ***police officer*** policier *m*, agent *m* de police; ***police record*** casier *m* judiciaire; **she has no p. record** elle n'a pas de casier judiciaire, son casier judiciaire est vierge; ***police sergeant*** ≃ brigadier *m* (de police); ***police state*** État *m ou* régime *m* policier; ***police station*** *(urban)* poste *m* de police, commissariat *m* (de police); *(rural)* gendarmerie *f*; ***police van*** *(for transporting prisoners)* voiture *f* cellulaire; *Am* ***police wagon*** fourgon *m* cellulaire

oliceman [pəˈliːsmən] *(pl* **policemen** [-mən]) **N** agent *m* (de police), policier *m*

olicewoman [pəˈliːsˌwʊmən] *(pl* **policewomen** [-ˌwɪmɪn]) **N** femme *f* policier

olicing [pəˈliːsɪŋ] **N 1** *(by police)* maintien *m* de l'ordre; **the p. of the match/demonstration was inadequate** le service d'ordre du match/de la manifestation était inadéquat **2** *Fig* **the p. of these regulations** la responsabilité de veiller au respect de cette réglementation

▸▸ ***policing policy*** politique *f* de maintien de l'ordre

olicy [ˈpɒləsɪ] *(pl* **policies) N 1** *Pol* politique *f*; **the government's economic policies** la politique économique du gouvernement

2 *Com (of company, organization)* politique *f*, orientation *f*; **they don't know what p. to adopt** ils ne savent pas quelle politique adopter; **this is in line with company p.** ça va dans le sens de la politique de l'entreprise; **our p. is to hire professionals only** nous avons pour politique de n'engager que des professionnels

3 *(personal principle, rule of action)* principe *m*, règle *f*; **her p. has been always to tell the truth** elle a toujours eu pour principe de dire la vérité; **it's bad p. to reveal your objectives early on** c'est une mauvaise tactique de dévoiler vos objectifs à l'avance

4 *(for insurance)* police *f*; **to take out a p.** souscrire à une police d'assurance

COMP *(decision)* de principe; *(debate)* de politique générale

▸▸ ***policy adviser*** conseiller(ère) *m,f* politique; ***policy document*** document *m* de politique générale; ***policy machine*** machine *f* politique; ***policy meeting*** séance *f* de concertation; ***policy paper*** = document énonçant une position de principe; ***policy position*** position *f* de principe; ***policy statement*** déclaration *f* de principe; ***policy unit*** comité *m* politique; *Am Pej* ***policy wonk*** conseiller(ère) *m,f* politique

olicyholder [ˈpɒləsɪˌhəʊldə(r)] **N** assuré(e) *m,f*

olio [ˈpəʊlɪəʊ] **N** *(UNCOUNT) Med* polio *f*; **to have p.** avoir la polio

oliomyelitis [ˌpəʊlɪəʊmaɪəˈlaɪtɪs] **N** *(UNCOUNT) Med* poliomyélite *f*

olish [ˈpəʊlɪʃ] **NPL the P.** les Polonais *mpl*

N *(language)* polonais *m*

ADJ polonais

COMP *(embassy)* de Pologne; *(history)* de la Pologne; *(teacher)* de polonais

olish [ˈpɒlɪʃ] **VT 1** *(furniture, floor, tiles)* cirer, encaustiquer; *(brass, car, mirror)* astiquer; *(shoes)* cirer, brosser; *(gemstone, wood, metal)* polir; *(gold, silver)* brunir

2 *Culin (rice)* décortiquer

3 *Fig (perfect)* polir, perfectionner; **to p. one's prose/style** polir sa prose/son style

4 *Fig (person)* parfaire l'éducation de; **his manners could do with polishing** ses manières laissent à désirer

N 1 *(product ▸ for wood, furniture)* encaustique *f*, cire *f*; *(▸ for shoes)* cirage *m*; *(▸ for brass, car, silverware)* produit *m* d'entretien; *(▸ for fingernails)* vernis *m*

2 *(act of polishing)* **to give sth a p.** *(furniture, floor, tiles)* cirer qch, encaustiquer qch; *(brass, car, mirror)* astiquer qch; *(shoes)* cirer qch, brosser qch; **give your shoes a quick p.** donne un petit coup de brosse à tes chaussures; **the brass could do with a p.** les cuivres auraient besoin d'être astiqués

3 *(shine, lustre)* brillant *m*, éclat *m*; **the silver has a lovely p.** l'argent a un bel éclat; **his shoes have lost their p.** ses chaussures ont perdu leur lustre; **to put a p. on sth** faire briller qch

4 *Fig (of prose, style, performance)* brio *m*

5 *Fig (of person)* raffinement *m*, élégance *f*; **she has a lot of p.** elle est très raffinée

▸ **polish off VT SEP** *Fam* **1** *(finish ▸ meal)* finir[□], avaler[□]; **they polished off half a loaf between them** ils ont avalé la moitié d'un pain à eux seuls; **they soon polished off the rest of the beer** ils ont eu vite fait de finir ce qui restait de bière **2** *(complete ▸ job)* expédier[□]; *(▸ book, essay)* en finir avec[□] **3** *(defeat)* se débarrasser de, écraser; *(kill)* liquider, descendre

▸ **polish up VI brass polishes up well** le cuivre est facile à faire briller

VT SEP 1 *(furniture, shoes)* faire briller; *(diamond)* polir **2** *Fig (perfect ▸ maths, language)* perfectionner, travailler; *(▸ technique)* parfaire, améliorer

polished [ˈpɒlɪʃt] **ADJ 1** *(surface)* brillant, poli

2 *Culin (rice)* poli

3 *(person)* qui a du savoir-vivre, raffiné; *(manners)* raffiné

4 *(prose, style)* raffiné, élégant; *(performance)* parfait, impeccable; *(performer)* accompli

polisher [ˈpɒlɪʃə(r)] **N** *(person)* cireur(euse) *m,f*; *(machine)* polissoir *m*; *(for floors)* cireuse *f*

Politburo [ˈpɒlɪtˌbjʊərəʊ] *(pl* **Politburos) N** Politburo *m*

polite [pəˈlaɪt] **ADJ 1** *(person)* poli, courtois; *(refusal)* poli; *(remark, conversation)* poli, aimable; **to be p. to sb** être poli envers *ou* avec qn; **it is p. to ask first** quand on est poli, on demande d'abord; **to make p. conversation** faire la conversation; **she was very p. about my poems** elle s'est montrée très diplomate dans ses commentaires sur mes poèmes **2** *(refined ▸ manners)* raffiné, élégant

▸▸ ***polite society*** la bonne société, le beau monde

politely [pəˈlaɪtlɪ] **ADV** poliment, de manière courtoise

politeness [pəˈlaɪtnɪs] **N** politesse *f*, courtoisie *f*; **out of p.** par politesse

politic [ˈpɒlətɪk] **ADJ** *Formal (shrewd)* habile, avisé; *(wise)* judicieux, sage; **it would not be p. to refuse** ce ne serait pas prudent de refuser

political [pəˈlɪtɪkəl] **ADJ 1** *(relating to politics)* politique; **p. beliefs** opinions *fpl* politiques; **things are getting far too p. in the office** il y a vraiment trop de manigances au bureau en ce moment **2** *(tactical ▸ decision, appointment)* stratégique, tactique **3** *(interested in politics)* **he's always been very p.** il s'est toujours intéressé à la politique

▸▸ ***political activity*** activité *f* politique; ***political affiliations*** attaches *fpl* politiques; ***political agenda*** agenda *m* politique; ***political allegiance*** allégeance *f* politique; ***political analyst*** analyste *mf* politique; ***political asylum*** asile *m* politique; **to request/be granted p. asylum** demander/se voir accorder l'asile politique; ***political awareness*** politisation *f*; ***political commentator*** journaliste *mf* politique; ***political correctness*** le politiquement correct; ***political correspondent*** journaliste *mf* politique; ***political crisis*** crise *f* politique; ***political economy*** économie *f* politique; ***political editor*** rédacteur(trice) *m,f* en chef politique; ***political élite*** élite *f* politique; ***political establishment*** classe *f* politique dirigeante; ***political geography*** géographie *f* politique; ***political group*** formation *f* politique; ***political institution*** institution *f* politique; ***political journalist*** journaliste *mf* politique; ***political leader*** responsable *mf* politique; ***political map*** carte *f* politique; ***political observer*** expert *m ou* spécialiste *mf* en politique; ***political offence*** délit *m* politique; ***political opponent*** *(democratic)* adversaire *mf* politique; *(of regime)* opposant(e) *m,f* politique; ***political organization*** organisation *f* politique; ***political party*** parti *m* politique; ***political prisoner*** prisonnier(ère) *m,f* politique; ***political reform*** réforme *f* politique; ***political rival*** rival(e) *m,f* politique; ***political science*** *(UNCOUNT)* sciences *fpl* politiques; ***political scientist*** spécialiste *mf* en sciences politiques; ***political structure*** structure *f* politique; ***political suicide*** suicide *f* politique; ***political tendency*** tendance *f* politique; ***political theory*** théorie *f* politique

politically [pəˈlɪtɪkəlɪ] **ADV** politiquement; **p. informed** au courant des choses de la politique; **to be p. aware** avoir une conscience politique, être politisé; **p. correct** politiquement correct

politician [ˌpɒlɪˈtɪʃən] **N 1** *(gen ▸ man)* homme *m* politique, politique *m*; *(▸ woman)* femme *f* politique, politique *f* **2** *Am Pej* politicien(enne) *m,f*

politicize, -ise [pəˈlɪtɪsaɪz] **VT** politiser; **the whole issue has become highly politicized** on a beaucoup politisé toute cette question

VI faire de la politique

politicking [ˈpɒlətɪkɪŋ] **N** *Pej* politique *f* politicienne

politico [pəˈlɪtɪkəʊ] *(pl* **politicos** *or* **politicoes) N** *Fam Pej* politicard(e) *m,f*

politico- [pəˈlɪtɪkəʊ] **PREF** politico-

politico-economic(al) **ADJ** politico-économique

politics [ˈpɒlətɪks] **N** *(UNCOUNT)* **1** *(as a profession)* politique *f*; **to go into p.** faire de la politique; **local p.** la politique locale **2** *(art or science)* politique *f*; **she studied p. at university** elle a étudié les sciences politiques à l'université **3** *(activity)* politique *f*; **I tried not to be drawn into office p.** j'ai essayé de ne pas me laisser entraîner dans les intrigues de bureau

NPL 1 *(opinions)* idées *fpl ou* opinions *fpl* politiques; **what exactly are her p.?** quelles sont ses opinions politiques au juste?; **his p. are right of centre** politiquement parlant il se situe à droite **2** *(political aspects)* dimension *f* politique; **the politics of fighting terrorism** la dimension politique de la lutte contre le terrorisme

polity [ˈpɒlətɪ] *(pl* **polities) N** *Formal (state)* État *m*; *(administration)* organisation *f* politique *ou* administrative; *(political unit)* entité *f* politique

polka [ˈpɒlkə] **N** polka *f*

VI danser la polka

▸▸ ***polka dot*** pois *m*

polka-dot ADJ à pois

poll [pəʊl] **N 1** *Pol (elections)* élection *f*, élections *fpl*, scrutin *m*; **the p. took place in June** les élections ont eu lieu en juin; **to go to the polls** voter, se rendre aux urnes; **the party is likely to be defeated at the polls** le parti sera probablement battu aux élections **2** *(vote)* vote *m*; *(votes cast)* suffrages *mpl* (exprimés), nombre *m* de voix; **there was an unexpectedly heavy p.** contrairement aux prévisions, il y a eu un fort taux de participation au scrutin; **the ecology candidate got three percent of the p.** le candidat écologiste a obtenu *ou* recueilli trois pour cent des suffrages *ou* des voix **3** *(survey ▸ of opinion, intentions)* sondage *m* (d'opinion); **to conduct a p. (on** *or* **about sth)** faire un sondage (sur qch); **the latest p. puts the Socialists in the lead** le dernier sondage donne les socialistes en tête

VT 1 *Pol (votes)* recueillir, obtenir; **the Greens polled 14 percent of the vote** les verts ont obtenu 14 pour cent des voix

2 *(person)* sonder, recueillir l'opinion de; **most of those polled were in favour of the plan** la plupart des personnes interrogées *ou* sondées étaient favorables au projet

3 *Comput (terminal)* appeler; *(data)* recueillir

4 *(tree)* étêter; *(cattle)* décorner

VI 1 *(cast one's vote)* voter **2** *(receive votes)* **the party polled well** le parti a remporté une bonne proportion des suffrages *ou* des voix

▸▸ ***poll tax*** *(in UK)* = impôt aboli en 1993, regroupant taxe d'habitation et impôts locaux, payable par chaque occupant adulte d'une même habitation; *(in US)* = impôt, aboli en 1964, donnant droit à être inscrit sur les listes électorales; *Hist* capitation *f*

pollack ['pɒlək] **N** *Ich* merlu *m*, colin *m*, *Can* goberge *f*

pollard ['pɒləd] **N 1** *Bot* têtard *m (arbre)* **2** *Zool* animal *m* sans cornes
VT 1 *Bot* étêter **2** *Zool* décorner

pollen ['pɒlən] **N** pollen *m*
▸▸ ***pollen analysis*** analyse *f* pollinique; ***pollen count*** taux *m* de pollen; ***pollen sac*** sac *m* pollinique; ***pollen tube*** tube *m* pollinique

pollinate ['pɒlɪneɪt] **VT** polliniser

pollination [ˌpɒlɪ'neɪʃən] **N** pollinisation *f*

polling ['pəʊlɪŋ] **N** *(UNCOUNT)* **1** *Pol (voting)* vote *m*, suffrage *m*; *(elections)* élections *fpl*, scrutin *m*; **the result of the p.** le résultat du scrutin *ou* des élections; **p. takes place every five years** le scrutin a lieu tous les cinq ans; **p. is up on last year** la participation au vote est plus élevée que l'année dernière **2** *(for opinion poll)* sondage *m* **3** *Comput (querying)* interrogation *f*
▸▸ ***polling booth*** isoloir *m*; *Br* ***polling card*** carte *f* d'électeur; ***polling company*** institut *m* de sondage; ***polling day*** jour *m* des élections *or* du scrutin; *Am* ***polling place***, *Br* ***polling station*** bureau *m* de vote

polliwog ['pɒlɪwɒg] **N** *Am Zool* têtard *m*

pollock = **pollack**

pollster ['pəʊlstə(r)] **N** *Fam* enquêteur(euse) *m,f*, sondeur(euse) *m,f*; **the pollsters are predicting a high turnout** les sondages prévoient un fort taux de participation

pollutant [pə'luːtənt] **N** polluant *m*

pollute [pə'luːt] **VT 1** *(environment, river, atmosphere)* polluer; **the rivers are polluted with toxic waste** les cours d'eau sont pollués par les déchets toxiques **2** *(language, mind)* contaminer

polluted [pə'luːtɪd] **ADJ** *Am Fam (drunk)* pété, bourré, rond

polluter [pə'luːtə(r)] **N** pollueur(euse) *m,f*
▸▸ ***polluter pays principle*** principe *m* pollueur-payeur

pollution [pə'luːʃən] **N 1** *(of environment, river, atmosphere)* pollution *f* **2** *(UNCOUNT) (pollutants)* polluants *mpl*; **volunteers are helping to clear the beach of p.** des volontaires participent aux opérations d'assainissement de la plage **3** *(of language, mind)* contamination *f*

pollution-free **ADJ** non pollué

Polly ['pɒlɪ] **PR N** = nom typique pour un perroquet, ≃ Jacquot

Pollyanna [ˌpɒlɪ'ænə] **N** = individu naïvement optimiste

pollywog = **polliwog**

polo ['pəʊləʊ] *(pl* **polos***)* **N 1** *Sport* polo *m* **2** *Am (shirt)* polo *m (chemise)*
COMP *(match, pony)* de polo
▸▸ *Br* ***polo neck*** *(collar)* col *m* roulé; *(sweater)* (pull *m* à) col *m* roulé; ***polo shirt*** polo *m (chemise)*; *Sport* ***polo stick*** maillet *m*

polonaise [ˌpɒlə'neɪz] **N** *Mus & Sewing* polonaise *f*

poltergeist ['pɒltəgaɪst] **N** esprit *m* frappeur, poltergeist *m*

poly ['pɒlɪ] *(pl* **polys***)* **N** *Br Fam Formerly (polytechnic)* = en Grande-Bretagne, avant 1993, établissement d'enseignement supérieur qui appartenait à un système différent de celui des universités

poly- ['pɒlɪ] **PREF** poly-

polyacrylic [ˌpɒlɪə'krɪlɪk] *Chem* **N** polyacrylique *m*
ADJ polyacrylique

polyamory [ˌpɒlɪ'æmərɪ] **N** polyamour *m*

polyandrous [ˌpɒlɪ'ændrəs] **ADJ** polyandre

polyandry ['pɒlɪændrɪ] **N** polyandrie *f*

polyanthus [ˌpɒlɪ'ænθəs] *(pl* **polyanthuses** *or* **polyanthi** [-θaɪ]*)* **N** *(primrose)* primevère *f*

poly bag **N** *Br Fam* sac *m* (en) plastique[□]

polychromatic [ˌpɒlɪkrəʊ'mætɪk] **ADJ** *(multicoloured)* multicolore, polychrome

polychrome ['pɒlɪkrəʊm] **ADJ** polychrome
N 1 *(object)* objet *m* polychrome **2** *(colouring)* polychromie *f*

polychromy ['pɒlɪkrəʊmɪ] **N** polychromie *f*

polyclinic [ˌpɒlɪ'klɪnɪk] **N** polyclinique *f*

polycystic [ˌpɒlɪ'sɪstɪk] **ADJ** *Med* polykystique
▸▸ ***polycystic ovaries*** ovaires *mpl* polykystiques; ***polycystic ovary syndrome*** syndrome *m* des ovaires polykystiques

polyester [ˌpɒlɪ'estə(r)] *Chem* **N** polyester *m*
ADJ (de *ou* en) polyester

polyethylene [ˌpɒmɪ'eθɪliːn] **N** *Chem* polyéthylène *m*, Polythène® *m*

polygamist [pə'lɪgəmɪst] **N** polygame *m*

polygamous [pə'lɪgəməs] **ADJ** polygame

polygamy [pə'lɪgəmɪ] **N** polygamie *f*

polyglot ['pɒlɪglɒt] **ADJ** *(person)* polyglotte; *(edition)* multilingue
N *(person)* polyglotte *mf*; *(book)* édition *f* multilingue

polygon ['pɒlɪgɒn] **N** *Geom* polygone *m*

polygonal [pɒ'lɪgənəl] **ADJ** *Geom* polygonal

polygraph ['pɒlɪgrɑːf] **N** *(lie detector)* détecteur *m* de mensonges; **to take a p. test** subir un test au détecteur de mensonges

polyhedron [ˌpɒlɪ'hiːdrən] *(pl* **polyhedrons** *or* **polyhedra** [-drə]*)* **N** *Geom* polyèdre *m*

polymath ['pɒlɪmæθ] **N** *Formal* esprit *m* universel

polymer ['pɒlɪmə(r)] **N** *Chem* polymère *m*

polymerism ['pɒlɪmərɪzəm] **N** *Chem* polymérie *f*

polymerization, -isation [ˌpɒlɪməraɪ'zeɪʃən] **N** *Chem* polymérisation *f*

polymorphic [ˌpɒlɪ'mɔːfɪk] **ADJ** polymorphe

polymorphism [ˌpɒlɪ'mɔːfɪzəm] **N** *(gen)* polymorphisme *m*; *Chem* polymorphie *f*

polymorphous [ˌpɒlɪ'mɔːfəs] **ADJ** polymorphe

Polynesia [ˌpɒlɪ'niːzjə] **N** Polynésie *f*; **French P.** la Polynésie française

Polynesian [ˌpɒlɪ'niːzjən] **N 1** *(person)* Polynésien(enne) *m,f* **2** *Ling* polynésien *m*
ADJ polynésien

polyneuritis [ˌpɒlɪnjʊ'raɪtɪs] **N** *Med* polynévrite *f*

polynomial [ˌpɒlɪ'nəʊmɪəl] *Math* **ADJ** polynomial
N polynôme *m*

polyp ['pɒlɪp] **N** *Med & Zool* polype *m*

polyphase ['pɒlɪfeɪz] **ADJ** *Elec* polyphasé

polyphonic [ˌpɒlɪ'fɒnɪk], **polyphonous** [pə'lɪfənəs] **ADJ** polyphonique
▸▸ *Tel* ***polyphonic ringtone*** sonnerie *f* polyphonique

polyphony [pə'lɪfənɪ] **N** polyphonie *f*

polypropylene [ˌpɒlɪ'prəʊpəliːn] **N** polypropylène *m*

polysaccharide [ˌpɒlɪ'sækəraɪd] **N** *Chem* polysaccharide *m*, polyoside *m*, polyholoside *m*

polystyrene [ˌpɒlɪ'staɪriːn] **N** polystyrène *m*
▸▸ ***polystyrene cement*** colle *f* polystyrène; ***polystyrene tiles*** carreaux *mpl* de polystyrène

polysyllabic [ˌpɒlɪsɪ'læbɪk] **ADJ** polysyllabe, polysyllabique

polysyllable ['pɒlɪˌsɪləbəl] **N** polysyllabe *m*

polytechnic [ˌpɒlɪ'teknɪk] **N** *Br Formerly* = en Grande-Bretagne, avant 1993, établissement d'enseignement supérieur qui appartenait à un système différent de celui des universités

> Note that the French noun **Polytechnique** is a false friend and is never a translation for the word **polytechnic**. It is the name of one of France's most prestigious **grandes écoles**.

polytheism ['pɒlɪθiːɪzəm] **N** polythéisme *m*

polytheistic [ˌpɒlɪθiː'ɪstɪk] **ADJ** polythéiste

polythene ['pɒlɪθiːn] **N** polyéthylène *m*, Polythène® *m*
COMP en polyéthylène, en Polythène®
▸▸ ***polythene bag*** sac *m* (en) plastique

polyunsaturated [ˌpɒlɪʌn'sætʃəreɪtɪd] **ADJ** polyinsaturé

polyurethane [ˌpɒlɪ'jʊərəθeɪn], **polyurethan** [ˌpɒlɪ'jʊərəθæn] **N** *Chem* polyuréthane *m*, polyuréthanne *m*
▸▸ ***polyurethane foam*** mousse *f* de polyuréthane

polyvalent [ˌpɒlɪ'veɪlənt] **ADJ** *Chem* polyvalent

polyvinyl [ˌpɒlɪ'vaɪnɪl] **N** chlorofibre *f*
ADJ polyvinylique
▸▸ ***polyvinyl chloride*** chlorure *m* de polyvinyle

pom [pɒm] = **pommie**

pomegranate ['pɒmɪˌgrænɪt] **N** *(fruit)* grenad[e] *f*; *(tree)* grenadier *m*
▸▸ ***pomegranate tree*** grenadier *m*

Pomerania [ˌpɒmə'reɪnjə] **N** Poméranie *f*

Pomeranian [ˌpɒmə'reɪnjən] **N 1** *(person)* Poméranien(enne) *m,f* **2** *(dog)* loulou *m* (de Poméranie)
ADJ poméranien

pommel ['pɒməl] *(Br pt & pp* **pommelled**, *cont* **pommelling**, *Am pt & pp* **pommeled**, *cont* **pommeling***)* **N** pommeau *m*
VT = **pummel**
▸▸ ***pommel horse*** cheval-d'arçons *m inv*

pommie, pommy ['pɒmɪ] *(pl* **pommies***)* *Austr & NZ Fam* **N** angliche *mf*
ADJ angliche

pomp [pɒmp] **N** pompe *f*, faste *m*; **with great p. (and circumstance)** en grande pompe

Pompeii [ˌpɒm'peɪiː] **N** Pompéi

pompom ['pɒmˌpɒm] **N** *(flower, bobble)* pompon *m*

pom-pom **N** *Mil* canon-mitrailleuse *m*

pomposity [ˌpɒm'pɒsətɪ] *(pl* **pomposities***)* **N** *(UNCOUNT) (of person)* comportement *m* pompeux, manières *fpl* pompeuses **2** *(of ceremony)* apparat *m*, pompe *f*; *(of style, comment)* caractère *m* pompeux

pompous ['pɒmpəs] **ADJ** *(pretentious)* pompeux, prétentieux

pompously ['pɒmpəslɪ] **ADV** pompeusement

pompousness ['pɒmpəsnɪs] **N 1** *(of person)* comportement *m* pompeux, manières *fpl* pompeuses **2** *(of ceremony)* apparat *m*, pompe *f*; *(of style, comment)* caractère *m* pompeux

ponce [pɒns] *Br Fam* **N 1** *(pimp)* maquereau *m* **2** *Pej (effeminate man)* chochotte *f*
VI 1 *(pimp)* faire le maquereau **2** *Pej (behave effeminately)* minauder, faire chochotte
▸ **ponce about, ponce around** *Br Fam* **VI** *(waste time)* traîner, glander; **stop poncing around and get on with it** arrête un peu de traîner et dépêche-toi **2** *Pej (behave effeminately)* minauder, faire chochotte
▸ **ponce up** **VT SEP** *Br Fam (dress up)* **to get all ponced up** se mettre sur son trente-et-un

poncey ['pɒnsɪ] **ADJ** *Br Fam Pej* **1** *(effeminate)* qui fait chochotte **2** *(pretentious)* chichiteux; **I hate restaurants that serve p. food** j'ai horreur de restos qui servent de la cuisine chichiteuse

poncho ['pɒntʃəʊ] *(pl* **ponchos***)* **N** poncho *m*

poncy = **poncey**

pond [pɒnd] **N** *(small)* mare *f*; *(large)* étang *m*; *(in garden, park)* bassin *m*; *Fam* **the P.** *(the Atlantic)* l'Atlantique[□] *m*; *Fam* **across the p.** outre-Atlantique[□]
▸▸ ***pond life*** la faune des étangs; *Fam Hum Pej (disreputable people)* minables *mpl*; *Bot* ***pond lily*** nénuphar *m*

ponder ['pɒndə(r)] **VI** *(think)* réfléchir; *(meditate)* méditer; **he spent hours pondering over the meaning of it all** il passa des heures à méditer sur le sens de tout cela; **she had plenty of time to p. on** *or* **upon the folly of her ways** elle a eu tout le temps de réfléchir à la stupidité de ses actes
VT réfléchir à; **I sat down and pondered what to do** je m'assis et considérai ce que j'allais faire; **she retreated to her own room to p. her next move** elle se retira dans sa chambre pour réfléchir à la décision qu'elle allait prendre

ponderable ['pɒndərəbəl] *Formal* **ADJ** pondérable
• **ponderables** **NPL** données *fpl* mesurables

ponderous ['pɒndərəs] **ADJ** *(heavy)* pesant, lourd; *(slow)* lent, laborieux; *(dull)* lourd; **with p. steps** d'un pas lourd; **a p. style** un style lourd *ou* laborieux

ponderously ['pɒndərəslɪ] **ADV** *(heavily)* lourdement; *(laboriously)* laborieusement; **he walked p. across the yard** il traversa la cour d'un pas pesant

pondweed ['pɒndwi:d] **N** *Bot* potamot *m*

pone [pəʊn] **N** *Am (bread)* pain *m* au maïs

▸▸ ***pone bread*** pain *m* au maïs

pong [pɒŋ] *Br Fam* **N** puanteur◻*f*; **what a p.!** ça pue!◻, ça schlingue!; **there's a terrible p. of fish!** ça pue le poisson à plein nez!

VI puer◻, schlinguer; **the room still pongs of cigarettes** la pièce pue encore la cigarette

pongy ['pɒŋɪ] **ADJ** *Br Fam (smelly)* **it's a bit p. in here** ça pue◻ *ou* schlingue là-dedans

pontiff ['pɒntɪf] **N** souverain pontife *m*, pape *m*

pontifical [pɒn'tɪfɪkəl] **ADJ 1** *Rel* pontifical **2** *(pompous)* pompeux

N *Rel (book)* pontifical *m*

pontificate VI [pɒn'tɪfɪkeɪt] *(gen) & Rel* pontifier; *Pej* **he's always pontificating about** *or* **on something or other** il faut toujours qu'il pontifie

N [pɒn'tɪfɪkɪt] pontificat *m*

Pontius Pilate [pɒnʃəs-] **PR N** Ponce Pilate

pontoon [pɒn'tu:n] **N 1** *(float)* ponton *m*; *(on seaplane)* flotteur *m* **2** *(card game)* vingt-et-un *m inv*

▸▸ ***pontoon bridge*** pont *m* flottant

pony ['pəʊnɪ] *(pl* **ponies) N 1** *Zool* poney *m*; *Am (small horse)* petit cheval *m*; **we went for a p. ride** nous avons fait une promenade à dos de poney

2 *Fam (glass)* verre *m* à liqueur◻

3 *Br Fam (£25)* vingt-cinq livres◻*fpl*; *(bet)* pari *m* de vingt-cinq livres◻

4 *Am Fam (crib)* antisèche *f*

▸▸ ***pony express*** = service postal américain à cheval mis en place en 1860 et détrôné par l'apparition du télégraphe

ponytail ['pəʊnɪteɪl] **N** queue *f* de cheval; **she wears her hair in a p.** elle a *ou* se fait une queue de cheval

poo [pu:] *Fam* **N 1** *(excrement)* caca *m*; **to do** *or Br* **have** *or Am* **take a p.**, *Am* **to make p.** faire caca **2** *Br (worthless things)* **it's a load of p.** c'est de la merde; **he's talking a load of p.** il raconte n'importe quoi◻

VI faire caca

pooch [pu:tʃ] **N** *Fam (dog)* toutou *m*

poodle ['pu:dəl] **N** *Zool* caniche *m*; *Fig* **I'm not your p.!** je ne suis pas ton chien!

poof¹ [pʊf] **N** *Br very Fam* pédé *m*, tapette *f*, = terme injurieux désignant un homosexuel

poof² EXCLAM *Fam* **and then it was gone, p., just like that!** et puis hop! il a disparu d'un coup

poofter ['pʊftə(r)] **N** *Br very Fam* pédé *m*, tapette *f*, = terme injurieux désignant un homosexuel

poofy ['pʊfɪ] *(compar* **poofier**, *superl* **poofiest) ADJ** *Br very Fam Pej* qui fait pédé *ou* tapette; **he's a bit p.** il fait un peu pédé *ou* tapette

pooh [pu:] *Br Fam* **EXCLAM** *(with disgust)* pouah!; *(with disdain)* peuh!

N *(excrement)* caca *m*

VI faire caca

pooh-pooh VT *Br* rire de, ricaner de

pool [pu:l] **N 1** *(pond ▸ small)* mare *f*; *(▸ large)* étang *m*; *(▸ ornamental)* bassin *m*

2 *(puddle)* flaque *f*; **a p. of blood** une flaque *ou* une mare de sang; **a p. of light** un rond de lumière

3 *(swimming pool)* piscine *f*

4 *(in harbour)* bassin *m*; *(in canal, river)* plan *m* d'eau

5 *(of money)* cagnotte *f*; *(in card games)* cagnotte *f*, poule *f*

6 *(of workmen, babysitters)* groupe *m*, groupement *m*; *(of experts, advisers)* équipe *f*; *(of typists)* pool *m*; *(of company cars, computers)* parc *m*; *(of ideas)* réserve *f*; *(of talent)* pépinière *f*, réserve *f*

7 *(consortium)* cartel *m*, pool *m*; *(group of producers)* groupement *m* de producteurs

8 *Am Fin (group)* groupement *m*; *(agreement)* entente *f*, accord *m*

9 *(game)* billard *m* américain; *Br* **to have a game of p.**, *Am* **to shoot (some) p.** jouer au billard (américain)

VT *(resources, cars, capital, profits)* mettre en commun; *(efforts, ideas)* unir

▸▸ ***pool cue*** queue *f* de billard; ***pool hall*** salle *f* de billard; ***pool party*** = fête organisée autour d'une piscine; ***pool table*** (table *f* de) billard *m*

pooling ['pu:lɪŋ] **N** *Am Fin* **p. of interests** (absorption-)fusion *f*, unification *f*

poolroom ['pu:l,ru:m] **N** salle *f* de billard

pools [pu:lz] **NPL** *Br* **the (football) p.** les concours *mpl* de pronostics (au football); **to win the (football) p.** gagner aux pronostics (au football)

poon, poonani [pu:n], [pu:'nænɪ] **N** *esp Am Vulg* chatte *f*

poop [pu:p] **N 1** *Am Fam (excrement)* caca *m*; **to take a p.** faire caca **2** *Naut (deck)* (pont *m* de) dunette *f*, gaillard *m* d'arrière **3** *Naut (raised part)* poupe *f*

VI *Am Fam (defecate)* faire caca; **p. and scoop** *(sign)* nettoyer derrière votre chien!

▸▸ *Naut* ***poop deck*** (pont *m* de) dunette *f*, gaillard *m* d'arrière

pooped [pu:pt] **ADJ** *esp Am Fam (exhausted)* claqué, crevé

pooper-scooper ['pu:pə,sku:pə(r)] **N** ramasse-crotte *m*

POOR [pʊə(r)]

ADJ
- pauvre **1, 6**
- médiocre **2**
- peu doué **4**
- faible **2, 5**
- mauvais **3**

NPL
- pauvres

ADJ 1 *(not rich ▸ person, area, country)* pauvre; **a p. man/woman** un pauvre/une pauvre; **p. people** les pauvres *mpl*; **they're too p. to own a car** ils n'ont pas les moyens d'avoir une voiture; **I'm 100 euros poorer, I'm poorer by 100 euros** j'en suis pour 100 euros; **the oil crisis made these countries considerably poorer** la crise du pétrole a considérablement appauvri ces pays; **p. as a church mouse** pauvre comme Job

2 *(mediocre ▸ output, sales figures)* faible, médiocre; *(▸ land, soil)* maigre, pauvre; *(▸ effort, excuse)* piètre; *(▸ piece of work)* médiocre; *(▸ results)* médiocre, piètre; *(▸ weather, summer)* médiocre; *(▸ quality, condition)* mauvais; **the match took place in p. light** le match a eu lieu alors qu'on n'y voyait pratiquement rien; **the joke was in extremely p. taste** la plaisanterie était du plus mauvais goût; **she has very p. taste in clothes** elle s'habille avec un goût douteux; **a p. excuse** une piètre excuse; **p. reception** *(unwelcoming)* mauvais accueil *m*; *Rad & TV* mauvaise transmission *f*; **p. performance** *(of company)* contre-performance *f*; **the team put in a p. performance** l'équipe n'a pas très bien joué; **our side put up a very p. show** notre équipe a donné un piètre spectacle; **to come a p. second** *(in race)* se classer deuxième, loin derrière le vainqueur; **in terms of exports, Britain comes a p. second to Japan** en matière d'exportations, la Grande-Bretagne est en deuxième position, loin derrière le Japon; **it's a p. substitute for the real thing** c'est loin de valoir l'original; **he gave a p. account of himself** il ne s'en est pas très bien tiré; **there was a p. turnout** peu de gens sont venus; **his pay is very p.** il est très mal payé; **don't be such a p. loser!** *(in game)* ne sois pas si mauvais perdant!; **I have only a p. understanding of economics** je ne comprends pas grand-chose à l'économie; *Sch* **p. work** travail *m* insuffisant; **our chances of success are very p.** nos chances de réussite sont bien maigres

3 *(weak ▸ memory, sight)* mauvais; **to be in p. health** être en mauvaise santé; **I have rather p. sight** j'ai une mauvaise vue; **I have rather p. hearing** j'entends mal

4 *(in ability)* peu doué; **I'm a p. cook** je ne suis pas doué pour la cuisine; **my spelling/French is p.** je ne suis pas fort en orthographe/en français; **she's a p. sailor** elle n'a pas le pied marin; **she's a p. traveller** elle supporte mal les voyages; **he is very p. at maths/at making speeches** il n'est pas doué en maths/pour les discours

5 *(inadequate)* faible; **their food is p. in vitamins** leur alimentation est pauvre en vitamines

6 *(pitiful)* pauvre; **p. you!, you p. thing!** *(to man)* mon pauvre (vieux)!; *(to woman)* ma pauvre (vieille)!; **the p. girl!** la pauvre (fille)!; **p. me!** pauvre de moi!; **p. (old) Bill** le pauvre Bill; **to cut a p. figure** faire piètre figure

NPL the p. les pauvres *mpl*; **the new p.** les nouveaux pauvres *mpl*

▸▸ ***poor box*** tronc *m* des pauvres; *Hist* ***poor law*** = loi sociale dictant les conditions dans lesquelles les pauvres étaient pris en charge par les communes; ***poor relation*** parent *m* pauvre; **we're definitely considered the p. relations of the publishing world** on nous considère vraiment comme les parents pauvres de l'édition; *Am Pej* ***poor White*** petit(e) Blanc (Blanche) *m,f*

poorhouse ['pʊəhaʊs, *pl* -haʊzɪz] **N** *Hist* asile *m* des pauvres

poorly ['pʊəlɪ] *(compar* **poorlier**, *superl* **poorliest) ADJ** *Br* malade, souffrant; *Med* **his condition is described as p.** son état est considéré comme sérieux

ADV *(badly)* mal; **p. lit** mal éclairé; **p. dressed** pauvrement *ou* mal vêtu; **to be p. off** *(financially)* avoir des problèmes d'argent; **I did p. in the maths test** je n'ai pas bien réussi à l'interrogation de maths; **to think p. of sb** avoir une mauvaise opinion de qn

poorness ['pʊənɪs] **N 1** *(financially)* pauvreté *f* **2** *(mediocrity)* médiocrité *f*, pauvreté *f*

POP [,pi:əʊ'pi:] **N 1** *Comput (abbr* **post office protocol)** protocole *m* POP **2** *Comput (abbr* **point of presence)** point *m* de présence, point *m* d'accès **3** *Mktg (abbr* **point of purchase)** lieu *m* d'achat, lieu *m* de vente

POP [pɒp]

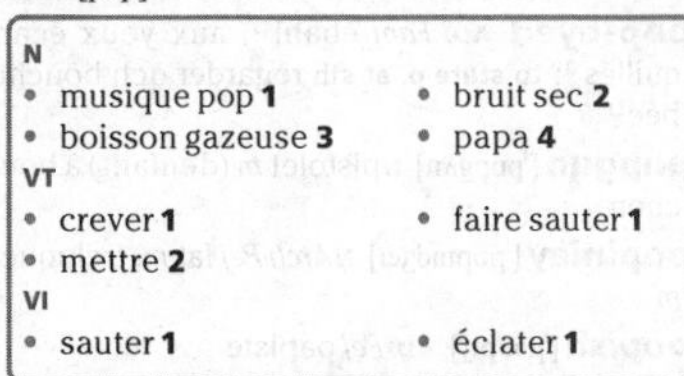
N
- musique pop **1**
- boisson gazeuse **3**
- bruit sec **2**
- papa **4**

VT
- crever **1**
- mettre **2**
- faire sauter **1**

VI
- sauter **1**
- éclater **1**

(pt & pp **popped**, *cont* **popping)**

ONOMAT pan!

N 1 *Mus* musique *f* pop, pop *f*

2 *(sound)* bruit *m* sec; **to go p.** *(cork)* sauter; *(balloon)* éclater

3 *(drink)* boisson *f* gazeuse, soda *m*; **ginger p.** boisson *f* gazeuse au gingembre

4 *Am Fam (father)* papa *m*

5 *Fam* **to take a p. at sb/sth** débiner qn/qch

COMP *(singer, song)* pop *(inv)*

VT 1 *(balloon, bag)* crever; *(button, cork)* faire sauter; **to p. some corn** faire du pop-corn

2 *Fam (put)* mettre◻, fourrer; **she popped her purse into her bag** elle a fourré son porte-monnaie dans son sac; **just p. the paper through the letterbox** vous n'avez qu'à glisser le journal dans la boîte aux lettres; **she kept popping tablets into her mouth** elle n'arrêtait pas de se fourrer des comprimés dans la bouche; **to p. one's head out of the window** passer la tête par la fenêtre◻; *Am* **let's p. open a bottle of beer** ouvrons une bouteille de bière◻; **to p. the question** proposer le mariage◻; *Br Fam* **to p. one's clogs** casser sa pipe

3 *Fam (hit)* **he popped me one on the chin** il m'a fichu un coup de poing au menton

4 *Fam Drugs slang* **to p. pills** prendre des pilules◻ *(pour se droguer)*

5 *Br Fam Old-fashioned (pawn)* mettre au clou

VI 1 *(cork, buttons)* sauter; *(bulb, balloon)* éclater; *(ears)* se déboucher d'un seul coup; **to make a popping noise** faire un bruit de bouchon qui saute; **to p. open** *(box, bag)* s'ouvrir tout d'un coup; *(buttons)* sauter

2 *(eyes)* s'ouvrir tout grand; **his eyes were popping out of his head** les yeux lui sortaient de la tête

3 *Br Fam (go)* **to p. into town** faire un saut en ville; **she popped into the butcher's on her way home** elle a fait un saut chez *ou* elle est passée en vitesse chez le boucher sur le chemin du retour; **they popped by** *or* **round to see us** ils sont passés nous voir◻

▸▸ ***pop art*** pop art *m*; ***pop concert*** concert *m* pop; ***pop group*** groupe *m* pop; ***pop music*** musique *f* pop, pop music *f*; ***pop poetry*** = poésie destinée à être dite en public; ***pop psychology*** psychologie *f* vulgarisée; ***pop science*** science *f* vulgarisée; *Fam Old-fashioned* ***pop shop*** mont-de-piété◻*m*; ***pop star*** vedette *f* de la musique pop; ***pop video*** clip *m* (vidéo)

▸**pop in** VI *Fam* passer◻, faire une petite visite◻; **p. in on your way home** passez chez moi en rentrant (à la maison); **to p. in to see sb/say hello** passer voir qn/dire bonjour; **I've just popped in** je ne fais que passer

▸**pop off** VI **1** *Fam (leave)* s'en aller◻, filer; **he popped off home to get his tennis things** il est allé chez lui chercher ses affaires de tennis **2** *Br Fam (die)* casser sa pipe, calancher **3** *Am Fam (shout)* gueuler

▸**pop out** VI *Fam* sortir un instant◻; **I only popped out for five minutes** je ne suis sorti que cinq minutes; **to p. out to the tobacconist's** faire un saut au bureau de tabac

▸**pop up** VI *Fam (appear suddenly)* surgir◻; **a head popped up through the trap door** une tête a surgi de la trappe; **this question has popped up again** cette question est revenue sur le tapis; **he popped up again some years later in Miami** il est réapparu quelques années après à Miami◻

popcorn ['pɒpkɔːn] N pop-corn *m inv*

pope [pəʊp] N **1** *(in Catholic Church)* pape *m*; *Fam Hum* **is the P. Catholic?** à ton avis? **2** *(in Eastern Orthodox Church)* pope *m*

▸▸ *Am Culin* ***pope's nose*** croupion *m*

popemobile ['pəʊpməbiːl] N *Fam* papamobile *f*

popery ['pəʊpərɪ] N *Pej* papisme *m*

pop-eyed ADJ *Fam* ébahi◻, aux yeux écarquillés◻; **to stare p. at sth** regarder qch bouche bée◻

popgun ['pɒpgʌn] N pistolet *m* (d'enfant) à bouchon

popinjay ['pɒpɪndʒeɪ] N *Arch Pej* fat *m*, freluquet *m*

popish ['pəʊpɪʃ] ADJ *Pej* papiste

poplar ['pɒplə(r)] N peuplier *m*

poplin ['pɒplɪn] N popeline *f*

COMP *(coat, jacket)* en popeline

popover ['pɒp,əʊvə(r)] N **1** *(garment)* débardeur *m* **2** *Am Culin* chausson *m*; **apple p.** chausson *m* aux pommes

poppadom, poppadum ['pɒpədəm] N *Culin* papadum *m*, papadam *m (galette indienne)*

popper ['pɒpə(r)] N **1** *Br (press-stud)* bouton-pression *m*, pression *f* **2** *Am (for popcorn)* appareil *m* à pop-corn **3** *Fam Drugs slang* popper *m*

poppet ['pɒpɪt] N **1** *Br Fam* chéri(e)◻ *m,f*, mignon (onne) *m,f*; **be a p. and fetch my bag for me** sois mignon et va me chercher mon sac; **her new puppy's an absolute p.** son nouveau petit chien est mignon à croquer; **thanks, p.** *(to male)* merci, mon mignon; *(to female)* merci, ma mignonne **2** *Tech (valve)* soupape *f* à champignon

▸▸ ***poppet valve*** soupape *f* à champignon

popping ['pɒpɪŋ] N *(in audio)* saturation *f* acoustique

poppy ['pɒpɪ] *(pl* **poppies***)* N **1** *(flower)* coquelicot *m*; *(opium poppy)* pavot *m* **2** *(paper flower)* coquelicot *m* en papier *(vendu à l'occasion du "Poppy Day")* **3** *(colour)* rouge *m* coquelicot *(inv)*

▸▸ *Br* ***Poppy Day*** = journée de commémoration (le dimanche suivant ou précédant le 11 novembre) pendant laquelle on porte un coquelicot en papier en souvenir des soldats britanniques morts lors des guerres mondiales; ***poppy seed*** graine *f* de pavot

> **POPPIES**
>
> Les Britanniques marquent généralement l'armistice de la Première Guerre mondiale en observant deux minutes de silence le 11 novembre à 11 heures du matin. Les cérémonies religieuses liées à l'Armistice, elles, ont lieu le deuxième dimanche de novembre (baptisé "Remembrance Sunday"). A cette occasion l'on dépose des couronnes de coquelicots ("poppies") artificiels au pied des monuments aux morts; par ailleurs nombreux sont ceux et celles qui portent un coquelicot à la boutonnière dans les jours qui précèdent les commémorations. L'argent collecté grâce à la vente des ces coquelicots va à la British Legion, association britannique d'anciens combattants. L'on associe les coquelicots à la Première Guerre mondiale parce qu'ils étaient nombreux dans les champs de Belgique et du nord de la France, où tant de combats ont se sont déroulés.

poppycock ['pɒpɪkɒk] N *(UNCOUNT) Br Fam Old-fashioned* sottises *fpl*, balivernes *fpl*

Popsicle® ['pɒpsɪkəl] N *Am* glace *f* à l'eau

popstrel ['pɒpstrəl] N *Br Fam* jeune chanteuse *f* pop◻

popsy ['pɒpsɪ] *(pl* **popsies***)* N *Br Fam Old-fashioned* pépée *f*

populace ['pɒpjʊləs] N **1** *(population)* population *f*; *Fig* **the whole p. is up in arms** la population entière s'est rebellée **2** *(masses)* peuple *m*, *Pej* masses *fpl*, populace *f*

popular ['pɒpjʊlə(r)] ADJ **1** *(well-liked* ▸ *person)* populaire; **she's very p. with her pupils** elle est très populaire auprès de ses élèves, ses élèves l'aiment beaucoup; **Britain's most p. TV personality** la personnalité la plus populaire de la télévision britannique; **to make oneself p. (with)** se rendre populaire (auprès de); **his views have not made him p. with the authorities** à cause de ses opinions, il est mal vu des autorités; **he isn't very p. with his men** il n'est pas très bien vu de ses hommes, ses hommes ne l'aiment pas beaucoup; **I'm not going to be very p. when they find out it's my fault!** je ne vais pas être bien vu quand ils découvriront que c'est de ma faute!

2 *(appreciated by many* ▸ *product, colour)* populaire; *(*▸ *restaurant, resort)* très couru, très fréquenté; **the movie was very p. in Europe** le film a été un très grand succès en Europe; **the most p. book of the year** le livre le plus vendu *ou* le best-seller de l'année; **DVDs are a p. present** les DVD sont des cadeaux très appréciés; **it's very p. with the customers** les clients l'apprécient beaucoup; **a p. line** un article qui se vend bien; **it's always been a p. café with young people** ce café a toujours été très populaire auprès des jeunes

3 *(common)* courant, répandu; *(general)* populaire; **contrary to p. belief** contrairement à ce que les gens croient; **a p. misconception** une erreur répandue *ou* fréquente; **on** *or* **by p. demand** à la demande générale; **it's an idea that enjoys great p. support** c'est une idée qui a l'approbation générale *ou* de tous; **p. unrest** mécontentement *m* populaire

4 *(of or for the people)* populaire; **quality goods at p. prices** marchandises *fpl* de qualité à des prix abordables

▸▸ *Pol* ***popular front*** front *m* populaire; ***Popular Front for the Liberation of Palestine*** Front *m* populaire de libération de la Palestine; ***popular music*** musique *f* populaire; ***the popular press*** la presse à grand tirage et à sensation; ***popular vote*** vote *m* populaire

popularity [,pɒpjʊ'lærətɪ] N popularité *f*; **to grow/decline in p.** devenir plus/moins populaire; **they enjoy a certain p. with young people** ils jouissent d'une certaine popularité auprès des jeunes; **the sport has gained in p.** le sport est de plus en plus populaire

popularization, -isation [,pɒpjʊləraɪ'zeɪʃən] N **1** *(of trend, activity)* popularisation *f*; *(of science, philosophy)* vulgarisation *f* **2** *(book)* œuvre *f* de vulgarisation

popularize, -ise ['pɒpjʊləraɪz] VT **1** *(make popular)* populariser; *(fashion)* mettre en vogue; **a sport popularized by television** un sport que la télévision a rendu populaire **2** *(science, philosophy, knowledge)* vulgariser

popularizer, -iser ['pɒpjʊləraɪzə(r)] N *(of fashion, ideas)* promoteur(trice) *m,f*

popularly ['pɒpjʊləlɪ] ADV généralement; *(commonly)* couramment, communément; **antirrhinums are p. known as snapdragons** les antirrhinums sont plus connus sous le nom de gueules-de-loup; **once the earth was p. thought to be flat** autrefois tout le monde croyait que la Terre était plate

populate ['pɒpjʊleɪt] VT *(inhabit)* peupler, habiter; *(colonize)* peupler, coloniser; **a town populated by miners and their families** une ville habitée par des mineurs et leurs familles; **a densely populated country** un pays fortemen peuplé *ou* à forte densité de population

population [,pɒpjʊ'leɪʃən] N population *f*; **th whole p. is in mourning** tous les habitants po tent *ou* toute la population porte le deuil; **Edir burgh has a p. of about half a million** Édimbour compte environ un demi-million d'habitant **the prison p.** la population carcérale; **the beave p. is declining** la population de castors est e baisse

COMP *(control, fall, increase)* démographique, d la population

▸▸ ***population census*** recensement *m* démogra phique *ou* de la population; ***population explosio*** explosion *f* démographique; ***population growt*** croissance *f* démographique; ***population statis tics*** statistiques *fpl* démographiques

populism ['pɒpjʊlɪzəm] N populisme *m*

populist ['pɒpjʊlɪst] N populiste *mf*

▸▸ ***populist support*** support *m* populaire

populous ['pɒpjʊləs] ADJ populeux

pop-up ADJ *(book, card)* en relief; *(toaste* automatique

N *Comput* pop-up *m ou f*

▸▸ *Comput* ***pop-up ad*** pop-up *m ou f*; *Comput* ***po up menu*** menu *m* local; *Aut* ***pop-up sunroof*** toit ouvrant dépliant

porcelain ['pɔːsəlɪn] N porcelaine *f*

COMP *(dish, vase, lamp)* en porcelaine

▸▸ ***porcelain clay*** kaolin *m*; ***porcelain manufa turer*** porcelainier(ère) *m,f*

porch [pɔːtʃ] N **1** *(entrance)* porche *m* **2** *Am (ve randa)* véranda *f*

▸▸ ***porch roof*** auvent *m*

porchscreen ['pɔːtʃskriːn] N *Am* moustiquaire *(autour d'une véranda)*

porchswing ['pɔːtʃswɪŋ] N *Am* balançoire *f (su une véranda, typique de certaines maisons au États-Unis)*

porcine ['pɔːsaɪn] ADJ porcin

porcupine ['pɔːkjʊpaɪn] N *Zool* porc-épic *m*

▸▸ *Ich* ***porcupine fish*** poisson *m* porc-épic

pore [pɔː(r)] N *(in skin, plant, fungus, rock)* pore

VI **to p. over sth** *(book)* être plongé dans *ou* ab sorbé par qch; *(picture, details)* étudier qch d près

pork [pɔːk] N *Culin* porc *m*

COMP *(chop, sausage)* de porc

▸▸ *Am Pol* ***pork barrel*** = projet local entrepri par un parlementaire ou un parti à des fins élec torales; ***pork butcher*** ≃ charcutier(ère) *m,f*; ***por pie*** ≃ pâté *m* en croûte *(à la viande de porc)*; *Ar* ***pork rinds***, *Br* ***pork scratchings*** = petits morceau croustillants de couenne de porc consommé comme amuse-gueule

pork-barrel ADJ *Am Pol (politics, spending* électoraliste

▸▸ ***pork-barrel legislation*** = action menée par u parlementaire pour favoriser des intérêts lo caux dans sa circonscription

porker ['pɔːkə(r)] N **1** *(animal)* porcelet *m (en graissé par la boucherie)* **2** *Fam (man)* gros lar *m*; *(woman)* grosse vache *f*

porkpie hat ['pɔːkpaɪ-] N = chapeau de feutr rond et aplati

porky ['pɔːkɪ] *(pl* **porkies**, *compar* **porkier**, *supe* **porkiest***)* N *Br Fam* **p. (pie)** *(rhyming slang* **lie***)* bo bard *m*, craque *f*

ADJ **1** *(resembling pork)* semblable au porc **2** *Fa Pej (fat)* gros (grosse)◻, mastard

porn [pɔːn] *Fam* N porno *m*

ADJ porno

▸▸ ***porn shop*** sex-shop *m*

porno ['pɔːnəʊ] ADJ *Fam* porno

pornographer [pɔː'nɒgrəfə(r)] N pornograph *mf*

pornographic [,pɔːnə'græfɪk] ADJ pornogra phique

pornography [pɔː'nɒgrəfɪ] N pornographie *f*; **the customs officers impounded a large consig ment of p.** les douaniers ont saisi une grand quantité de revues pornographiques

porosity [pɔː'rɒsɪtɪ] *(pl* **porosities***)* N porosité *f*

porous ['pɔːrəs] ADJ poreux

porousness ['pɔːrəsnɪs] N porosité *f*

porphyry ['pɔːfɪrɪ] (*pl* **porphyries**) N *Miner* porphyre *m*

porpoise ['pɔːpəs] (*pl inv or* **porpoises**) N *Zool* marsouin *m*

porridge ['pɒrɪdʒ] N **1** *Br Culin* porridge *m* **2** *Br Fam Crime slang (prison sentence)* peine *f* de prison❑; **to do p.** faire de la tôle

►► *porridge oats* flocons *mpl* d'avoine

porringer ['pɒrɪndʒə(r)] N = récipient à porridge

port [pɔːt] N **1** *(harbour, town)* port *m*; **to come into p.** entrer dans le port; **we put into p. at Naples** nous avons relâché dans le port de Naples; **we left p. before dawn** nous avons appareillé avant l'aube; *Prov* **any p. in a storm** nécessité fait loi

2 *(wine)* porto *m*

3 *(window ► on ship, plane)* hublot *m*

4 *(for loading)* sabord *m* (de charge)

5 *Mil (in wall)* meurtrière *f*; *(in tank)* fente *f* de visée

6 *Comput* port *m*; **input/output p.** port *m* entrée/sortie

7 *Tech (in engine)* orifice *m*; **inlet/outlet p.** orifice *m* d'admission/d'échappement

8 *Naut (left side)* bâbord *m*; **the ship listed to p.** le navire donnait de la gîte à bâbord; **on the p. side** à bâbord; **ship to p.!** navire à bâbord!

9 *Aviat* côté *m* gauche, bâbord *m*

COMP *(activity, facilities)* portuaire; *(bow, quarter)* de bâbord

VT **1** *Comput* transférer **2** *Mil* **p. arms!** présentez armes!

►► *port of arrival* port *m* d'arrivée; *port authority* autorité *f* portuaire; *Naut* ***port of call*** escale *f*; *Fig* **her last p. of call was the bank** elle est passée à la banque en dernier; ***port charges*** droits *mpl* de port, frais *mpl* portuaires; ***port of departure*** port *m* de départ; ***port of discharge*** port *m* d'arrivée; ***port dues*** droits *mpl* de port, frais *mpl* portuaires; ***port of embarkation*** port *m* d'embarquement; ***port of entry*** port *m* de débarquement; ***port of loading*** port *m* d'embarquement; ***port of refuge*** port *m* de refuge; ***port of registry*** port *m* d'attache; *Old-fashioned* ***port wine stain*** *(birthmark)* tache *f* de vin

portability [,pɔːtə'bɪlətɪ] N *(gen) & Comput* portabilité *f*

portable ['pɔːtəbəl] ADJ **1** *(easily carried, moved)* portatif, portable; *Fin (pension, mortgage)* transférable **2** *Comput (software, program)* compatible

N *(typewriter)* machine *f* portative; *(TV)* télévision *f* portative; *(computer)* portable *m*

►► ***portable jukebox*** lecteur *m* audio portable; ***portable TV (set)*** télévision *f* portative

portage ['pɔːtɪdʒ] N **1** *(transport)* transport *m*; *(cost)* (frais *mpl* de) port *m* **2** *Naut* portage *m*

Portakabin® ['pɔːtə,kæbɪn] N *Br* baraquement *m* préfabriqué

portal ['pɔːtəl] N **1** *Archit (of cathedral)* portail *m* **2** *Comput* portail *m*

►► *Anat* ***portal vein*** veine *f* porte

Portaloo® ['pɔːtəluː] N toilettes *fpl* provisoires

portcullis [,pɔːt'kʌlɪs] N herse *f (de château fort)*

portend [pɔː'tend] VT *Literary* (laisser) présager, annoncer; **who knows what mysteries these events may p.?** qui sait quels mystères ces événements présagent?

portent ['pɔːtənt] N *Literary* **1** *(omen)* présage *m*, augure *m*; *(bad omen)* mauvais présage *m*; **a p. of evil** un très mauvais présage **2** *(significance)* portée *f*, signification *f*

portentous [pɔː'tentəs] ADJ *Literary* **1** *(ominous ► sign)* de mauvais présage *ou* augure

2 *(momentous ► event)* capital, extraordinaire; **I've nothing very p. to announce** je n'ai rien d'extraordinaire *ou* de très important à annoncer

3 *(serious)* grave, solennel; **her face took on a p. air** elle prit un air solennel

4 *(pompous)* pompeux

portentously [pɔː'tentəslɪ] ADV *Literary* **1** *(ominously)* sinistrement

2 *(momentously)* mémorablement

3 *(seriously)* solennellement

4 *(pompously)* pompeusement

porter ['pɔːtə(r)] N **1** *(of luggage)* porteur(euse) *m,f*

2 *Br (door attendant ► in hotel)* portier(ère) *m,f*; *(► in block of flats)* concierge *mf*, gardien(enne) *m,f*; *(► on private estate)* gardien(enne) *m,f*; *(► in university, college)* appariteur *m*

3 *(in hospital)* brancardier(ère) *m,f*

4 *Am Rail (on train)* employé(e) *m,f* des wagons-lits

5 *Old-fashioned (beer)* porter *m*, bière *f* brune

porterage ['pɔːtərɪdʒ] N **1** *(transport)* portage *m*, transport *m* (par porteurs) **2** *(cost)* coût *m* du transport

►► ***porterage facilities*** service *m* de porteurs

porterhouse ['pɔːtəhaʊs, *pl* -haʊzɪz] N *(steak)* chateaubriand *m*, châteaubriant *m*

►► *Culin* ***porterhouse steak*** chateaubriand *m*, châteaubriant *m*

portfolio [,pɔːt'fəʊljəʊ] (*pl* **portfolios**) N **1** *(briefcase)* porte-documents *m inv*

2 *(of artist ► dossier)* carton *m* à dessins; *(► collection of work)* book *m*; *(of model, actor, photographer)* book *m*

3 *Pol* portefeuille *m*; **minister without p.** ministre *m* sans portefeuille

4 *St Exch* portefeuille *m* (financier *ou* d'investissements); **securities in p.** valeurs *fpl* en portefeuille

5 *Mktg* portefeuille *m*

►► ***portfolio analysis*** analyse *f* de portefeuille; ***portfolio diversification*** diversification *f* de portefeuille; ***portfolio insurance*** assurance *f* de portefeuille; ***portfolio investment*** investissement *m* de portefeuille; ***portfolio management*** gestion *f* de portefeuille; ***portfolio manager*** gestionnaire *mf* de portefeuille; ***portfolio mix*** portefeuille *m* d'activités; ***portfolio securities*** valeurs *fpl* de portefeuille; ***portfolio worker*** = personne ayant plusieurs emplois ou travailleur indépendant ayant plusieurs employeurs

porthole ['pɔːthəʊl] N hublot *m*

portico ['pɔːtɪkəʊ] (*pl* **porticos** *or* **porticoes**) N *Archit* portique *m*

portion ['pɔːʃən] N **1** *(part, section)* partie *f*; **this p. to be given up** *(on ticket)* côté *m* à détacher

2 *(share)* part *f*; *(measure)* mesure *f*, dose *f*; *Law* **p. (of inheritance)** part *f* d'héritage; **he cut the cake into five portions** il a coupé le gâteau en cinq (parts); **three portions of flour to one p. of sugar** trois mesures *ou* doses de farine pour une mesure *ou* dose de sucre

3 *(helping ► of food)* portion *f*

4 *Literary (fate)* sort *m*, destin *m*; **suffering is our p. here below** la souffrance est notre part ici-bas

5 *Arch (dowry)* **(marriage) p.** dot *f*

►**portion out** VT SEP distribuer, répartir

portliness ['pɔːtlɪnɪs] N corpulence *f*, embonpoint *m*

portly ['pɔːtlɪ] (*compar* **portlier**, *superl* **portliest**) ADJ corpulent, fort; **a p. gentleman** un monsieur corpulent

portmanteau [,pɔːt'mæntəʊ] (*pl* **portmanteaus** *or* **portmanteaux** [-təʊz]) N grande valise *f*

ADJ qui combine plusieurs éléments *ou* styles

►► ***portmanteau word*** mot-valise *m*

portrait ['pɔːtreɪt] N **1** *(gen) & Art* portrait *m*; **he had his p. painted** il a fait faire son portrait; **a p. of 18th century society** un portrait de la société du XVIIIème siècle **2** *Comput & Typ (paper format)* (format *m*) portrait *m*; **to print sth in p.** *Comput* imprimer qch en portrait; *Typ* imprimer qch à la française

ADJ *Comput* au format portrait; *Typ* à la française

►► ***portrait bust*** (portrait *m* en) buste *m*; ***portrait gallery*** galerie *f* de portraits; *Comput* ***portrait mode*** mode *m* portrait; ***portrait painter*** portraitiste *mf*; ***portrait painting*** le portrait; ***portrait photograph*** portrait *m* photographique, photo-portrait *f*; ***portrait photographer*** photographe *mf* portraitiste

portraitist ['pɔːtreɪtɪst] N portraitiste *mf*

portraiture ['pɔːtrɪtʃə(r)] N art *m* du portrait

portray [pɔː'treɪ] VT **1** *(represent)* représenter; **he portrayed John as a scoundrel** il a représenté John sous les traits d'un voyou

2 *(act role of)* jouer le rôle de;

3 *(depict)* dépeindre; **she vividly portrays medieval life** elle fait une vivante description de la vie au Moyen Âge; **in the movie the soldiers are portrayed as monsters** dans le film, les soldats sont dépeints comme des monstres

4 *(of artist)* peindre, faire le portrait de

portrayal [pɔː'treɪəl] N **1** *(description)* portrait *m*, description *f*; **he disputes the p. of the protesters as extremists** il conteste la façon dont les médias présentent les protestataires comme des extrémistes **2** *Art* portrait *m* **3** *Theat & Cin* interprétation *f*

Portugal ['pɔːtʃʊgəl] N Portugal *m*

Portuguese [,pɔːtʃʊ'giːz] NPL **the P.** les Portugais *mpl*

N **1** (*pl inv*) *(person)* Portugais(e) *m,f* **2** *(language)* portugais *m*

ADJ portugais

COMP *(embassy, history)* du Portugal; *(teacher)* de portugais

►► *Zool* ***Portuguese man-of-war*** physalie *f*

POS [,piːəʊ'es] N *Mktg (abbr* **point of sale***)* PDV *m*

pose [pəʊz] N **1** *(position ► gen)* pose *f*; **to take up** *or* **to strike a p.** prendre une pose **2** *(pretence)* façade *f*; **their puritanism is only a p.** leur puritanisme n'est qu'une façade

VI **1** *Art & Phot* poser; **to p. for a photograph/for an artist** poser pour une photographie/pour un artiste; **to p. in the nude** poser nu; **she posed as a nymph** elle a posé en nymphe **2** *(masquerade)* **he posed as a hero** il s'est posé en héros, il s'est fait passer pour un héros; **a man posing as a policeman** un homme se faisant passer pour un policier **3** *(behave affectedly)* frimer; **look at him posing in his designer suit!** regarde-le frimer avec son costume de marque!

VT *(constitute ► problem)* poser, créer; *(► threat)* constituer; *(set ► question)* poser; *(put forward ► claim, idea)* formuler

poser ['pəʊzə(r)] N *Br Fam* **1** *(question ► thorny)* question *f* épineuse❑; *(► difficult)* colle *f*; **that's a bit of a p.!** alors ça, c'est une colle! **2** *Pej (show-off)* poseur(euse) *m,f*

poseur [pəʊ'zɜː(r)] N *Pej* poseur(euse) *m,f*

posh [pɒʃ] *Br Fam* ADJ *(clothes, car, restaurant)* chic❑ *(inv)*; *Pej (person, accent)* snob❑; *(neighbourhood)* rupin; **he's joined a p. tennis club** il s'est inscrit à un club de tennis huppé *ou* chic; **he moves in some very p. circles** il fréquente des milieux très huppés *ou* des gens de la haute; **p. people don't usually come here** généralement les gens de la haute ne viennent pas ici

ADV **to talk p.** parler avec un accent snob

posit ['pɒzɪt] VT *Formal (put forward ► idea)* avancer; *(► theory)* avancer, postuler

POSITION [pə'zɪʃən]

N
- position **1, 2, 4, 5, 8–10**
- point de vue **5**
- guichet **7**
- situation **1, 3, 4, 6**
- place **4**
- poste **6**

VT
- mettre en place **1**
- situer **2**
- positionner **4, 5**
- placer **1, 2**
- orienter **3**

N **1** *(place ► gen)* position *f*; *(► of town, house etc)* situation *f*, emplacement *m*; **in p.** en place; **to put sth in(to) p.** mettre qch en place; *Aviat & Naut* **to fix** *or* **work out one's p.** faire le point; **you've changed the p. of the lamp** vous avez changé la lampe de place; **white is now in a strong p.** *(in chess)* les blancs sont maintenant très bien placés; **they put the machine guns in** *or* **into p.** ils mirent les mitrailleuses en batterie; **take up your positions!, get into p.!** *(actors, dancers)* à vos places!; *(soldiers, guards)* à vos postes!

2 *(posture, angle)* position *f*; **to change** *or* **to shift p.** changer de position; **in a sitting p.** en position assise; **hold the spray can in an upright p.** tenez le vaporisateur en position verticale; **the lever should be in the on/off p.** le levier devrait être en position marche/arrêt

3 *(circumstances)* situation *f*; **the p. as I see it is this** voici comment je vois la situation *ou* les choses; **to be in a bad/good p.** être en mauvaise/bonne posture; **you're in no p. to judge** vous êtes mal placé pour (en) juger; **to be in a p. to do sth** être en mesure de faire qch; **to be in a strong p.** être bien placé; **put yourself in my p.** mettez-vous à ma place; **it's an awkward p. to be in** c'est une drôle de situation; **our financial p. is improving** notre situation financière s'améliore; **the present economic p.** la conjoncture économique actuelle

4 *(rank ▸ in table, scale)* place *f*, position *f*; *(▸ in hierarchy)* position *f*, situation *f*; *(social standing)* position *f*, place *f*; **they're in tenth p. in the championship** ils sont à la dixième place *ou* ils occupent la dixième place du championnat; **his p. in the firm is unclear** sa situation au sein de l'entreprise n'est pas claire; **what exactly is his p. in the government?** quelles sont exactement ses fonctions au sein du gouvernement?; **a person in my p. can't afford a scandal** une personne de mon rang ne peut se permettre un scandale

5 *(standpoint)* position *f*, point *m* de vue; **try to see things from my p.** essayez de voir les choses de mon point de vue; **to take up a p. on sth** adopter une position *ou* prendre position sur qch; **I have no p. on the matter** je n'ai pas d'idée bien arrêtée sur le sujet; **could you make your p. clear on this point?** pouvez-vous préciser votre position à ce sujet?; **his p. on the death penalty is indefensible** son point de vue sur la peine de mort est indéfendable; **her p. is that...** ce qu'elle pense c'est que..., son point de vue est que...

6 *(job)* poste *m*, situation *f*; **there were four candidates for the p. of manager** il y avait quatre candidats au poste de directeur; **it is a p. of great responsibility** c'est un poste à haute responsabilité; **p. of trust** poste *m* de confiance; **what was your previous p.?** quel était votre poste précédent?

7 *Admin (in bank, post office)* guichet *m*; **p. closed** *(sign)* guichet fermé

8 *Sport (in team, on field)* position *f*; **he can play in any p.** il peut jouer à n'importe quelle position *ou* place; **the full back was out of p.** l'arrière était mal placé

9 *Mil* position *f*; **to move into p.** se mettre en place *ou* en position; **the men took up p. on the hill** les hommes prirent position sur la colline; **to jockey** *or* **to jostle** *or* **to manoeuvre for p.** chercher à occuper le terrain; *Fig* chercher à obtenir la meilleure place

10 *St Exch* position *f*; **to take a long/short p.** prendre une position longue/courte

VT 1 *(put in place ▸ cameras, equipment)* mettre en place, placer, disposer; *(▸ guests, officials, players)* placer; *(▸ guards, police, troops)* poster, mettre en position; **the TV cameras were positioned round the square** les caméras de télé ont été disposées autour de la place; **he positioned himself on the roof** il a pris position sur le toit; **they have positioned their ships in the gulf** ils ont envoyé leurs navires dans le golfe

2 *(usu passive) (situate ▸ house, building)* situer, placer; **the school is positioned near a dangerous crossroads** l'école est située *ou* placée près d'un carrefour dangereux; **the flat is well positioned** l'appartement est bien situé; **we are well positioned to take advantage of this opportunity** nous sommes bien placés pour tirer parti de cette opportunité

3 *(adjust angle of ▸ lamp, aerial)* orienter

4 *(locate)* déterminer la position de, positionner

5 *Mktg (product)* positionner

▸▸ *St Exch* ***position limit*** limite *f* de position; *Pol* ***position paper*** déclaration *f* de principe; *St Exch* ***position trader*** spéculateur(trice) *m,f* sur plusieurs positions

---

positioning [pəˈzɪʃənɪŋ] **N 1** *(putting in place)* mise *f* en place *ou* en position

2 *(adjusting position)* positionnement *m*; *(of aerial)* orientation *f*

3 *Mktg* positionnement *m*

4 *Gram (of word)* **end p.** rejet *m*

▸▸ *Constr* ***positioning angle*** cornière *f* de mise en place *ou* de centrage; *Comput* ***positioning arm*** bras *m* de positionnement *ou* de lecture-écriture; *Comput* ***positioning macro*** macro-commande *f* de position; *Mil* ***positioning map*** carte *f* de positionnement; *Mktg* ***positioning study*** étude *f* de positionnement

positive [ˈpɒzɪtɪv] **ADJ 1** *(sure)* sûr, certain; **are you p. about that?** en êtes-vous sûr?; **are you absolutely sure? – yes, p.** en êtes-vous absolument sûr? – sûr et certain; **I'm p. (that) he wasn't there** je suis absolument sûr qu'il n'y était pas

2 *(constructive)* positif, constructif; **haven't you got any p. suggestions?** n'avez-vous rien à proposer qui fasse avancer les choses?; **she has a very p. approach to the problem** son approche du problème est très positive *ou* constructive

3 *(affirmative ▸ reply, response)* positif, affirmatif; *(▸ test, result)* positif; **there was a tremendously p. response to this idea** cette idée a été extrêmement bien accueillie *ou* reçue

4 *(definite ▸ fact, progress)* réel, certain; *(clear ▸ change, advantage)* réel, effectif; *(precise ▸ instructions)* formel, clair; **we have p. evidence of his involvement** nous avons des preuves irréfutables de son implication; **his intervention was a p. factor in the release of the hostages** son intervention a efficacement contribué à la libération des otages; **p. proof,** *Br* **proof p.** preuve *f* formelle

5 *(as intensifier ▸ absolute)* absolu, véritable, pur; **the whole thing was a p. nightmare** tout cela était un véritable cauchemar; **a p. delight** un pur délice; **a p. pleasure** un véritable plaisir

6 *(assured)* assuré, ferme; **she answered in a very p. tone** elle a répondu d'un ton très assuré *ou* très ferme

7 *Elec, Math & Phot* positif

8 *Am Pol (progressive)* progressiste

9 *Gram* **p. degree** *(of adjective, adverb)* degré *m* positif

N 1 *Gram* positif *m*; **in the p.** à la forme positive

2 *(answer)* réponse *f* positive *ou* affirmative, oui *m*; **to reply in the p.** répondre par l'affirmative *ou* affirmativement

3 *Phot* épreuve *f* positive

4 *Elec* borne *f* positive

▸▸ ***positive discrimination*** *(UNCOUNT)* discrimination *f* positive *(mesures favorisant les membres de groupes minoritaires)*; **p. discrimination in favour of people with disabilities** mesures *fpl* en faveur des handicapés; ***positive feedback*** *(in electronic circuit)* réaction *f* positive; *(in mechanical or cybernetic system)* feed-back *m inv* positif, rétroaction *f* positive; *Fig* **I didn't get much p. feedback on my suggestion** ma proposition n'a pas enthousiasmé grand monde; *Phot* ***positive film*** film *m* positif; *Am* ***positive ID*** papiers *mpl* d'identité *(avec photo)*; ***positive pole*** *(magnet)* pôle *m* nord; *(anode)* anode *f (pôle positif)*; *Phot* ***positive print*** positif *m*, épreuve *f* positive; ***positive proof*** preuve *f* formelle; *Psy* ***positive reinforcement*** renforcement *m* positif; ***positive thinking*** idées *fpl* constructives; ***positive vetting*** contrôle *m ou* enquête *f* de sécurité *(sur un candidat à un poste touchant à la sécurité nationale)*

positively [ˈpɒzɪtɪvlɪ] **ADV 1** *(absolutely)* absolument, positivement; *(definitely)* incontestablement, positivement; **it's p. ridiculous** c'est absolument ridicule; **her behaviour was p. disgraceful** elle s'est comportée de manière absolument scandaleuse; **smiling? she was p. beaming!** souriante? elle était carrément *ou* littéralement radieuse!

2 *(constructively)* positivement, de façon constructive; **it's important to act p.** il est important d'agir de façon positive; **to think p.** positiver; **people have responded quite p. to our suggestions** nos suggestions ont été fort bien accueillies

3 *(affirmatively)* affirmativement; *(with certainty)* avec certitude, positivement; **the body has been p. identified** le cadavre a été formellement identifié; **he had been p. vetted on three occasions** il avait fait l'objet de trois enquêtes de sécurité qui s'étaient avérées satisfaisantes

4 *Elec* positivement; **p. charged** chargé positivement

positivism [ˈpɒzɪtɪvɪzəm] **N** positivisme *m*

positivist [ˈpɒzɪtɪvɪst] **N** positiviste *mf*

ADJ positiviste

posology [pəˈsɒlədʒɪ] **N** *Med* posologie *f*

poss [pɒs] **ADJ** *Fam* possible; **as soon as p.** dès que possible

posse [ˈpɒsɪ] **N 1** *Am Hist* = autrefois, peti groupe d'hommes rassemblés par le shérif er cas d'urgence; **to round up a p.** réunir un groupe d'hommes; *Fig* **a p. of fans were in hot pursuit** de fans en détachement spécial s'étaient lancé dans une poursuite échevelée **2** *Fam (group o friends)* bande *f*; **he's out with the p.** il est sort avec ses potes *ou* avec sa bande **3** *Fam Black Am slang (entourage)* clique *f*; *(criminal gang* gang *m*

possess [pəˈzes] **VT 1** *(have possession of ▸ per manently)* posséder, avoir; *(▸ temporarily)* être en possession de, détenir, avoir; **what proof do you p.?** quelles preuves avez-vous?; **she possesses a clear understanding of the subject** elle connaît bien son sujet, elle a une bonne connaissance du sujet **2** *(obsess)* obséder; **he was completely possessed by the idea of going to India** il était complètement obsédé par l'idée d'aller en Inde; **what on earth possessed him to do such a thing?** qu'est-ce qui lui a pris de faire une chose pareille? **3** *Formal or Literary* **to p. oneself of sth** se munir de qch

possession [pəˈzeʃən] **N 1** *(gen)* possession *f*; **to be in p. of sth** être en possession de qch; **to have sth in one's p.** avoir qch en sa possession; **he was found in p. of a flick-knife, a flick-knife was found in his p.** il a été trouvé en possession d'un couteau à cran d'arrêt; **he's been arrested for p.** *(of drugs)* il a été arrêté pour détention de drogue; **she was charged with p. of illegal substances** elle a été inculpée pour détention de stupéfiants; **the file is no longer in my p.** le dossier n'est plus en ma possession, je ne suis plus en possession du dossier; **how did the car come into your p.?** comment la voiture est-elle entrée en votre possession?; **certain documents have come into my p.** certains documents sont tombés en ma possession; **to be in full p. of one's senses** être en pleine possession de ses moyens; *Sport* **to be in** *or* **to have p.** **(of the ball)** avoir le ballon; **she got p. of the house two weeks ago** elle a pris possession de la maison il y a deux semaines; **do they have p. of the necessary documents?** ont-ils *ou* possèdent-ils les documents nécessaires?; **to take p. of sth** *(acquire)* prendre possession de qch; *(by force)* s'emparer de *ou* s'approprier qch; *(confiscate)* confisquer qch; *Br* **p. is nine points** *or* **parts of tenths of the law** possession vaut titre **2** *Law (of property)* possession *f*, jouissance *f*; **to take p.** prendre possession; **immediate p.** jouissance immédiate **3** *(by evil)* possession *f*

• **possessions NPL 1** *(belongings)* affaires *fpl* biens *mpl*; **the jade vases are our most precious possessions** les vases en jade sont ce que nous possédons de plus précieux **2** *(colonies)* possessions *fpl*; *(land)* terres *fpl*

▸▸ *Law* ***possession of stolen goods*** recel *m*

possessive [pəˈzesɪv] **ADJ 1** *(gen)* possessif; **he's p. about his belongings** il a horreur de prêter ses affaires; **she's p. about her children** c'est une mère possessive **2** *Gram* possessif

N *Gram (case)* (cas *m*) possessif *m*; *(word)* possessif *m*

▸▸ *Gram* ***possessive adjective*** adjectif *m* possessif; *Gram* ***possessive pronoun*** pronom *m* possessif

possessiveness [pəˈzesɪvnɪs] **N** caractère *m* possessif, possessivité *f*

possessor [pəˈzesə(r)] **N** possesseur *m*, propriétaire *mf*; **I found myself the p. of an old manor house** je me suis trouvé propriétaire d'un vieux manoir

possibility [ˌpɒsəˈbɪlətɪ] *(pl* **possibilities)** **N 1** *(chance)* possibilité *f*, éventualité *f*; **it's a p.** c'est une possibilité, c'est bien possible; **within the bounds of p.** dans la limite du possible; **the p. of a settlement is fading fast** la perspective d'un règlement est de moins en moins probable; **is there any p. of you coming up for the weekend?** pourriez-vous venir ce week-end?, y a-t-il des chances que vous veniez ce week-end?; **if there's any p. of leaving early, I'll let you know** s'il y a moyen de partir de bonne heure, je vous le ferai savoir; **there's no p. of that happening** il n'y a aucune chance *ou* aucun risque que cela se produise; **there's little p. of any changes being made to the budget** il est peu probable que le budget soit modifié; **there's a strong p. we'll know the results tomorrow** il est fort possible que nous connaissions les résultats demain; **they hadn't even considered the p. that he might leave** ils n'avaient même pas envisagé qu'il puisse partir **2** *(person ▸ for job)* candidat(e) *m,f* possible; *(▸ as choice)* choix *m* possible; **she's still a p.** elle conserve toutes ses chances **3** *(possible event, outcome)* éventualité *f*; **that is a distinct p.** c'est bien possible; **to allow for all possibilities** parer à toute éventualité; **the possibilities are endless!** les possibilités sont innombrables!

• **possibilities** NPL *(potential)* possibilités *fpl*; **the job has a lot of possibilities** le poste offre de nombreuses perspectives; **job possibilities** possibilités *fpl* d'emploi

possible ['pɒsəbəl] ADJ possible; **if p.** si possible; **I'll be there, if at all p.** j'y serai, dans la mesure du possible; **that's p.** c'est possible, ça se peut; **anything's p.** tout est possible; **it's quite p. to complete the job in two months** il est tout à fait possible de terminer le travail en deux mois; **it wasn't p. to achieve our objectives** il ne nous a pas été possible d'atteindre nos objectifs; **it isn't p. for her to come** il ne lui est pas possible *ou* il lui est impossible de venir; **it's p. (that) he won't come** il se peut qu'il ne vienne pas; **it's just p. she's forgotten** il n'est pas impossible qu'elle ait oublié; **it doesn't seem p. that anyone could be so stupid** il est difficile d'imaginer que l'on puisse être aussi bête; **he comes to see me whenever p.** il vient me voir quand il le peut; **the grant made it p. for me to continue my research** la bourse m'a permis de poursuivre mes recherches; **the doctors did everything p. to save her** les médecins ont fait tout leur possible *ou* tout ce qu'ils ont pu pour la sauver; **as far as p.** *(within one's competence)* dans la mesure du possible; *(at maximum distance)* aussi loin que possible; **as long/cheap as p.** aussi longtemps/bon marché que possible; **as much** *or* **as many as p.** autant que possible; **to give as many details as p.** donner le plus de détails possible *ou* tous les détails possibles; **as soon as p.** dès que *ou* le plus tôt possible; **the best/the smallest p.** le meilleur/le plus petit possible; **the shortest p. route** l'itinéraire le plus court possible; **I mean that in the nicest p. way** je dis cela sans méchanceté (aucune); **the best of all p. worlds** le meilleur des mondes possibles; **he tried all p. means** il a essayé tous les moyens possibles (et imaginables); **there's no p. way out** il n'y a absolument aucune issue; **what p. benefit can we get from it?** quel bénéfice *ou* quel profit peut-on bien en tirer?; **to insure against p. accidents** s'assurer contre les accidents éventuels

N **1** *(activity)* possible *m*; **it's in the realms of the p.** c'est dans le domaine du possible **2** *(choice)* choix *m* possible; *(candidate)* candidature *f* susceptible d'être retenue; *Sport (player)* joueur (euse) *m,f* susceptible d'être choisi; **we looked at ten houses, of which two are possibles** nous avons visité dix maisons dont deux nous intéressent *ou* sont à retenir; **she is still a p. for the prize/job** elle garde toutes ses chances d'avoir le prix/d'obtenir le poste; **the England possibles** les joueurs *mpl* susceptibles de faire partie de l'équipe d'Angleterre

possibly ['pɒsəblɪ] ADV **1** *(perhaps)* peut-être; **he is p. the greatest musician of his time** c'est peut-être le plus grand musicien de son temps; **p. (so)/p. not, but he had no other choice** peut-être (bien)/peut-être pas, mais il n'avait pas le choix; **will you be there tomorrow? – p.** vous serez là demain? – c'est possible; **could you p. lend me £5?** vous serait-il possible de me prêter 5 livres? **2** *(conceivably)* **what advantage can we p. get from it?** quel avantage pouvons-nous espérer en tirer?; **she can't p. get here on time** elle ne pourra jamais arriver à l'heure; **where can they p. have got to?** où peuvent-ils bien être passés?; **run as fast as you p. can** cours aussi vite que tu peux; **the doctors did all they p. could to save her** les médecins ont fait tout ce qu'ils ont pu *ou* tout leur possible pour la sauver; **I'll come whenever I p. can** je viendrai chaque fois que cela me sera possible; **I couldn't p. accept your offer** je ne puis accepter votre proposition; **she might p. still be here** il se pourrait qu'elle soit encore ici

possum ['pɒsəm] N *(American)* opossum *m*; *(Australian)* phalanger *m*; *Fam* **to play p.** faire le mort

POST [pəʊst]

N	
• courrier **1**	• poste **1, 6, 7**
• poteau **3–5**	• pieu **3**
• montant **3, 5**	
VT	
• poster **1, 2**	• muter **3**
• affecter **3**	• afficher **4**

N **1** *Br (letters)* courrier *m*; *(postal service)* poste *f*, courrier *m*; *(delivery)* (distribution *f* du) courrier *m*; *(collection)* levée *f* (du courrier); **has the p. come?** est-ce que le facteur est passé?; **there's no p. today** il n'y a pas de courrier aujourd'hui; **did it come through the p.** *or* **by p.?** est-ce que c'est arrivé par la poste?; **I sent it by p.** je l'ai envoyé par la poste; **it's in the p.** c'est parti au courrier; **can you put the cheque in the p.?** pouvez-vous envoyer le chèque par la poste?; **do you want the letters to go first or second class p.?** voulez-vous envoyer ces lettres au tarif normal ou au tarif lent?; **a parcel came in this morning's p.** un paquet est arrivé au courrier de ce matin; **I don't want to miss the p.** je ne veux pas manquer la levée; **will we still catch the p.?** pourrons-nous poster le courrier à temps *ou* avant la levée?; **I missed the p.** quand je suis arrivé, la levée était déjà faite *ou* le courrier était déjà parti; **can you take the letters to the p.?** *(post office)* pouvez-vous porter les lettres à la poste?; *(post them)* pouvez-vous poster les lettres *ou* mettre les lettres à la boîte?

2 *Hist (station)* relais *m* de poste; *(rider)* courrier *m*

3 *(of sign, street lamp)* poteau *m*; *(of fence)* pieu *m*; *(of four-poster bed)* colonne *f*; *(upright ▸ of door, window)* montant *m*

4 *(in racing)* poteau *m*; **starting/finishing** *or* **winning p.** poteau *m* de départ/d'arrivée; *also Fig* **to be left at the p.** rater le départ; *also Fam Fig* **to be beaten** *or* **pipped at the p.** se faire coiffer *ou* battre sur le poteau

5 *Ftbl* poteau *m*, montant *m*; **the near/back p.** le premier/deuxième poteau

6 *(job)* poste *m*, emploi *m*; **he got a p. as an economist** il a obtenu un poste d'économiste; **a university/diplomatic p.** un poste universitaire/de diplomate; **a government p.** un poste au gouvernement

7 *Mil etc (duty station)* poste *m*; *Am (permanent station)* camp *m*, fort *m*; *(garrison)* garnison *f*; **remain at your p.** restez à votre poste; **a sentry p.** un poste de sentinelle; **advanced** *or* **outlying p.** *(place, group of men)* poste *m* avancé

8 *Comput (on blog, message board)* commentaire *m*, contribution *f*

9 *Am (trading post)* comptoir *m*

10 *Mil (bugle call)* **first p.** première partie *f* de la sonnerie de la retraite; **last p.** *(at night)* extinction *f* des feux; *(at funeral)* sonnerie *f* aux morts; **to sound the last p. (over the grave)** jouer la sonnerie aux morts

VT **1** *esp Br (letter ▸ put in box)* poster, mettre à la poste; *(▸ send by post)* envoyer par la poste; **to p. sth to sb** envoyer qch à qn par la poste, poster qch à qn

2 *Mil etc (station ▸ guard, sentry)* poster; *Fig* **she posted herself at the window** elle s'est postée à la fenêtre

3 *(assign ▸ gen)* muter, affecter; *Mil* affecter; **to be posted to a different branch** être muté dans une autre succursale; *Mil* **to be posted to a unit/a ship** être affecté à une unité/un navire; **to be posted overseas** être en poste à l'étranger

4 *(display ▸ on bulletin board, wall)* afficher; *(▸ banns, names)* publier; **he has been posted missing** il a été porté disparu; *Am* **p. no bills** *(sign)* défense d'afficher; *Fig* **to keep sb posted** tenir qn au courant

5 *(publicize ▸ results)* annoncer; **they have posted a ten percent increase in profits** ils ont annoncé une augmentation des bénéfices de dix pour cent

6 *Acct (amount)* passer; *(ledger)* tenir à jour; **to p. an entry** passer une écriture; **to p. the books** passer les écritures

7 *Am (issue)* **to p. bail** déposer une caution

8 *St Exch* **to p. security** déposer des garanties

9 *Comput (on Internet)* poster

▸▸ ***post chaise*** chaise *f* de poste; *Am Mil* ***post exchange*** = économat pour les militaires et leurs familles; ***post horn*** trompe *f* (de la malle-poste); ***post house*** relais *m* de poste; ***post office*** *(place)* (bureau *m* de) poste *f*; *(service)* (service *m* des) postes *fpl*, poste *f*; ***the Post Office*** *(government department)* ≃ la Poste; ***post office account*** compte *m* chèque postal; ***post office box*** boîte *f* postale; ***post office and general store*** = petite épicerie de village faisant office de bureau de poste; *Comput* ***post office protocol*** protocole *m* POP; *Br* ***post office savings*** ≃ Caisse *f* (nationale) d'épargne; **we have a little money in p. office savings** nous avons un peu d'argent à la Caisse d'épargne

▸ **post on** VT SEP *(letters)* faire suivre; **can you p. my letters on to me?** pouvez-vous faire suivre mon courrier?

postage ['pəʊstɪdʒ] N *(UNCOUNT) (postal charges)* tarifs *mpl* postaux *ou* d'affranchissement; *(cost of posting)* frais *mpl* d'expédition *ou* d'envoi *ou* de port; **what's the p. on this parcel?** c'est combien pour envoyer ce paquet?; *Br* **p. and packing,** *Am* **p. and handling** frais *mpl* de port et d'emballage; **p. included** port compris; **p. paid** franco, port payé

COMP *(rates)* postal

▸▸ ***postage due stamp*** timbre *m* taxe; *Am* ***postage meter*** machine *f* à affranchir; ***postage stamp*** timbre *m*, timbre-poste *m*

postal ['pəʊstəl] ADJ **1** *(charge, district)* postal; *(administration, service, strike)* des postes; *(delivery)* par la poste **2** *Am Fam* **to go p.** *(get angry)* piquer une crise

▸▸ *Br Pol* ***postal ballot*** vote *m* par correspondance; ***postal charges*** frais *mpl* d'envoi *ou* de port; ***postal code*** code *m* postal; *Am* ***postal meter*** machine *f* à affranchir; *Br* ***postal order*** mandat *m* postal, mandat *m* poste; ***postal rates*** tarifs *mpl* postaux; *Am* ***the Postal Service*** ≃ la Poste; *Mktg* ***postal survey*** enquête *f* postale; *Br* ***postal vote*** vote *m* par correspondance; ***postal worker*** employé(e) *m,f* des postes

postbag ['pəʊstbæg] N *Br* **1** *(sack)* sac *m* postal **2** *(correspondence)* courrier *m*; **we've got a full p. this morning** nous avons reçu énormément de lettres *ou* une avalanche de courrier ce matin

postbox ['pəʊstbɒks] N *Br* boîte *f* à *ou* aux lettres

postcard ['pəʊstkɑːd] N carte *f* postale

postcode ['pəʊstkəʊd] N *Br* code *m* postal

▸▸ ***postcode discrimination*** = forme d'ostracisme social qui frappe les habitants des quartiers défavorisés; ***postcode lottery*** = fait de pouvoir accéder ou non à des services publics de qualité (notamment en matière de santé et d'éducation) en fonction de l'endroit où l'on habite

Post-Cold War ADJ après la guerre froide; **the P. period** l'après-guerre froide *m ou f*

post-colonial ADJ post-colonial

post-colonialism N post-colonialisme *m*

post-colonialist N post-colonialiste *mf*

ADJ post-colonialiste

postdate [ˌpəʊst'deɪt] VT **1** *(letter, cheque)* postdater **2** *(event)* assigner une date postérieure à; **historians now p. the event by several centuries** les historiens pensent aujourd'hui que l'événement a eu lieu des siècles plus tard

post-doctoral ADJ *Univ* postdoctoral

post-doctorate *Univ* N post-doctorat *m*

ADJ post-doctoral

postedit [ˌpəʊst'edɪt] VT *(in machine translation)* post-éditer

posted price ['pəʊstəd-] N *Mktg* prix *m* public

poster ['pəʊstə(r)] N **1** *(informative)* affiche *f*; *(decorative)* poster *m* **2** *(idiom)* **to be a p. boy/girl for sth** incarner qch **3** *Comput (on blog, message board)* contributeur(trice) *m,f*

▸▸ *Mktg* ***poster advertising*** publicité *f* par affichage *ou* par voie d'affiches; ***poster art*** l'art *m* de l'affiche; *Mktg* ***poster campaign*** campagne *f* d'affichage; ***poster colour*** gouache *f*; ***poster paint*** gouache *f*

poste restante [ˌpəʊstresˈtɒnt] N poste *f* restante; **you can write to me p. Florence** vous pouvez m'écrire poste restante à Florence

posterior [pɒˈstɪərɪə(r)] ADJ **1** *Formal (in time)* postérieur **2** *Tech (rear)* arrière

N *Fam Hum (of person)* postérieur *m*, arrière-train *m*

posterity [pɒˈsterɪtɪ] N postérité *f*; **for p.** pour la postérité; **to go down in** *or* **to p.** entrer dans la postérité *ou* l'histoire

postern [ˈpɒstən] N poterne *f*

post-free ADJ **1** *Br (prepaid)* port payé **2** *(free of postal charge)* dispensé d'affranchissement

ADV **1** *Br (prepaid)* en port payé **2** *(free of postal charge)* en franchise postale

postgrad [ˌpəʊstˈgræd] *Fam* = **postgraduate**

postgraduate [ˌpəʊstˈgrædʒʊət] N étudiant(e) *m,f* de troisième cycle

ADJ *(diploma, studies)* de troisième cycle

posthaste [ˌpəʊstˈheɪst] ADV *Literary* à toute vitesse, en toute hâte

posthumous [ˈpɒstjʊməs] ADJ posthume

posthumously [ˈpɒstjʊməslɪ] ADJ après la mort; **the poems were published p.** les poèmes ont été publiés après la mort de l'auteur; **the prize was awarded p.** le prix a été décerné à titre posthume

post-ignition N auto-allumage *m*

postilion, postillion [pəˈstɪljən] N postillon *m*

Postimpressionism [ˌpəʊstɪmˈpreʃənɪzəm] N postimpressionnisme *m*

Postimpressionist [ˌpəʊstɪmˈpreʃənɪst] N postimpressionniste *mf*

ADJ postimpressionniste

postindustrial [ˌpəʊstɪnˈdʌstrɪəl] ADJ postindustriel

►► ***postindustrial society*** société *f* postindustrielle

posting [ˈpəʊstɪŋ] N **1** *Br (of diplomat)* nomination *f*, affectation *f*; *(of soldier)* affectation *f*; *(of guards)* mise *f* en faction; **to get an overseas p.** être nommé en poste à l'étranger; **he had been given a p. as sales manager in Eastern Europe** on l'avait envoyé en Europe de l'Est comme directeur des ventes **2** *Com (in ledger)* inscription *f*, enregistrement *m* **3** *Br (of letter) (putting in the post)* mise *f* à la boîte *ou* à la poste; *(sending by mail)* envoi *m* par la poste

►► ***posting date*** date *f* de la poste

Post-it® N Post-it® *m*

postman [ˈpəʊstmən] (*pl* **postmen** [-mən]) N facteur *m*, *Admin* préposé *m*

►► *Br* ***postman's knock*** = jeu d'enfant dans lequel un des joueurs fait semblant de distribuer des lettres, en échange desquelles il reçoit un baiser

postmark [ˈpəʊstmɑːk] N *(on letter)* cachet *m* de la poste; **date as p.** le cachet de la poste faisant foi

VT oblitérer; **the letter is postmarked Phoenix** la lettre vient de *ou* a été postée à Phoenix

postmaster [ˈpəʊstˌmɑːstə(r)] N **1** *Admin* receveur *m* des Postes **2** *Comput (for e-mail)* maître *m* de poste

►► ***Postmaster General*** ≃ ministre *m* des Postes et Télécommunications, *Can* ministre *m* des Postes

post meridiem [-məˈrɪdɪəm] ADV *Formal (in afternoon)* de l'après-midi; *(in evening)* du soir

postmillennial [pəʊstmɪˈlenjəl] ADJ **1** *Rel* qui suit le millénium **2** *(after the millennium)* qui suit le passage à un nouveau millénaire

postmistress [ˈpəʊstˌmɪstrɪs] N receveuse *f* des Postes

postmodern [ˌpəʊstˈmɒdən] ADJ postmoderne

postmodernism [ˌpəʊstˈmɒdənɪzəm] N postmodernisme *m*

postmodernist [ˌpəʊstˈmɒdənɪst] N postmoderniste *mf*

ADJ postmoderniste

post-mortem [-ˈmɔːtəm] N **1** *Med* autopsie *f*; **to carry out a p.** pratiquer une autopsie **2** *Fig* autopsie *f*; **they held a p. on the game** ils ont disséqué *ou* analysé le match après coup

ADJ après le décès, post mortem

►► ***post-mortem examination*** autopsie *f*

postnatal [ˌpəʊstˈneɪtəl] ADJ postnatal

►► ***postnatal depression*** dépression *f* postnatale

post-op ADJ postopératoire

N salle *f* de réveil

postoperative [ˌpəʊstˈɒpərətɪv] ADJ postopératoire

postpaid [ˌpəʊstˈpeɪd] ADJ & ADV franc de port, en port payé

postpartum [ˌpəʊstˈpɑːtəm] N *Med* postpartum *m*

postpone [ˌpəʊstˈpəʊn] VT *(meeting, holiday)* remettre (à plus tard), reporter; *(match, game)* reporter; *(decision)* différer; **the meeting was postponed for three weeks/until a later date** la réunion a été reportée de trois semaines/remise à une date ultérieure

postponement [ˌpəʊstˈpəʊnmənt] N *(of meeting, match)* renvoi *m* (à une date ultérieure), report *m*; *(of holiday)* report *m*

postposition [ˌpəʊstpəˈzɪʃən] N *Gram* postposition *f*

postprandial [ˌpəʊstˈprændɪəl] ADJ *Formal or Hum* postprandial; **I like to take a p. nap/walk** j'aime faire une petite sieste/promenade après le déjeuner

postproduction [ˌpəʊstprəˈdʌkʃən] N *Cin & TV* postproduction *f*

►► ***postproduction editing*** montage *m* de postproduction; ***postproduction mixer*** mélangeur *m* de postproduction; ***postproduction studio*** studio *m* de postproduction

post-purchase ADJ *Mktg* post-achat

►► ***post-purchase behaviour*** comportement *m* post-achat; ***post-purchase evaluation*** évaluation *f* post-achat

PostScript® [ˈpəʊstskrɪpt] N *Comput* PostScript® *m*

►► ***PostScript® font*** police *f* de caractères PostScript®; ***PostScript® printer*** imprimante *f* PostScript®

postscript [ˈpəʊstskrɪpt] N **1** *(in letter)* postscriptum *m inv*; **by way of p.** en post-scriptum **2** *(in book)* postface *f*; *Fig (additional events)* suite *f*

post-synch N *Fam Cin & TV* postsynchronisation □*f*

post-synchronization, -isation N *Cin & TV* postsynchronisation *f*

post-test *Mktg* N post-test *m*

VT post-tester

post-traumatic stress disorder N *(UNCOUNT) Psy* syndrome *m* de stress post-traumatique, névrose *f* post-traumatique

postulant [ˈpɒstjʊlənt] N *Rel* postulant(e) *m,f*

postulate *Formal* VT [ˈpɒstjʊleɪt] **1** *(hypothesize)* poser comme hypothèse; **to p. the existence of an underground lake** soutenir l'hypothèse d'un lac souterrain; **we p. that a cure will soon be found** nous sommes sûrs qu'on trouvera bientôt un remède

2 *(take as granted)* postuler, poser comme principe; **the charter postulates that all men are equal** la charte part du principe que tous les hommes sont égaux

3 *Rel (nominate)* postuler

4 *(claim)* demander

N [ˈpɒstjʊlət] postulat *m*

posture [ˈpɒstʃə(r)] N **1** *(body position)* posture *f*, position *f*; **to keep an upright p.** se tenir droit **2** *Fig (attitude)* attitude *f*

VI se donner des airs, poser

posturing [ˈpɒstʃərɪŋ] N pose *f*, affectation *f*

postwar [ˌpəʊstˈwɔː(r)] ADJ d'après-guerre, après la guerre; **the p. period** l'après-guerre *m ou f*; **in the immediate p. period** au cours des années qui ont immédiatement suivi la guerre, tout de suite après la guerre

posy [ˈpəʊsɪ] (*pl* **posies**) N petit bouquet *m* (de fleurs)

pot [pɒt] (*pt & pp* **potted**, *cont* **potting**) VT **1** *(jam)* mettre en pot *ou* pots; *(fruit)* mettre en conserve **2** *(plant)* mettre en pot

3 *Br (in snooker, pool, billiards)* **to p. a ball** empocher une bille

4 *Br (shoot)* tuer; **she potted a partridge** elle a abattu une perdrix; **he's out potting rabbits** il est à la chasse au lapin

VI *Br (shoot)* **to p. at sth** tirer sur qch

N **1** *(container* ► *for paint, plant, jam etc)* pot *m*; *(teapot)* théière *f*; *(coffee pot)* cafetière *f*; **a p. of paint/mustard** un pot de peinture/de moutarde; **I drank a whole p. of tea/coffee** j'ai bu une théière/une cafetière entière; **I'll make another p. of tea/coffee** je vais refaire du thé/café; **a p. of tea for two** du thé pour deux personnes

2 *(saucepan)* casserole *f*; **pots and pans** batterie de cuisine; **(cooking) p.** marmite *f*, fait-tout *m inv*

Br Prov **it's a case of the p. calling the kettle black** c'est l'hôpital qui se moque de la charité

3 *(pottery object)* poterie *f*, pot *m*; **to throw a p.** tourner une poterie

4 *Fam (trophy)* trophée□*m*, coupe□*f*

5 *(in card games)* cagnotte *f*

6 *Fam (belly)* bedaine *f*, brioche *f*

7 *Br Fam* **to take a p. (shot) at sth** *(shoot at)* tirer à l'aveuglette sur qch□; *(attempt)* faire qch à l'aveuglette□

8 *Fam (marijuana)* herbe *f*, beu *f*

9 *Br (in snooker, pool, billiards)* blousage *m*, empochage *m*

10 *Elec* potentiomètre *m*

11 *Fam (idiom)* **to go to p.** *(deteriorate* ► *country)* aller à la dérive□; *(*► *morals)* dégénérer□; *(*► *plans)* tomber à l'eau; *(*► *person)* se laisser aller□; **everything has gone to p.** tout est fichu; **his health has gone to p.** sa santé s'est délabrée□; **her marriage has gone to p.** ça ne va plus du tout avec son mari□

• **pots** NPL *Br Fam (large amount)* tas *mpl*, tonnes *fpl*; **to have pots of money** avoir plein de fric, être plein aux as

►► *Am* ***pot cheese*** fromage *m* blanc (égoutté), cottage cheese *m*; *Am* ***pot pie*** tourte *f* à la viande et aux légumes; *Br* ***pot plant*** plante *f* d'intérieur; *esp Am* ***pot roast*** rôti *m* à la cocotte

►**pot on** VT SEP *(plant)* rempoter

►**pot up** VT SEP *(plant)* empoter

potable [ˈpəʊtəbəl] ADJ *Literary or Hum* potable, buvable

potash [ˈpɒtæʃ] N *Chem (UNCOUNT)* potasse *f*

potassium [pəˈtæsɪəm] N *Chem (UNCOUNT)* potassium *m*

►► ***potassium bromide*** bromure *m* de potassium; ***potassium chloride*** chlorure *m* de potassium; ***potassium hydroxide*** hydroxyde *m* de potassium, ***potassium nitrate*** nitrate *m* de potassium

potato [pəˈteɪtəʊ] (*pl* **potatoes**) N pomme *f* de terre

COMP *(farming, salad, soup)* de pommes de terre

►► *Entom* ***potato beetle*** doryphore *m*, *Can* bête à patates; ***potato blight*** mildiou *m* de la pomme de terre; ***potato cake*** = sorte de galette de pomme de terre; ***potato chip*** *Br (French fry)* (pomme *f*) frite *f*; *Am (crisp)* (pomme *f*) chips *f*; *Br* ***potato crisp*** (pomme *f*) chips *f*; ***potato masher*** presse-purée *m inv*; ***potato peeler*** *(tool)* éplucheur *m*, épluche-légumes *m inv*, (couteau *m*) économe *m*; *(machine)* éplucheuse *f*; ***potato scone*** = sorte de galette de pomme de terre

potbellied [ˈpɒtˌbelɪd] ADJ *(person)* bedonnant; **to be p.** avoir du ventre

►► ***potbellied stove*** poêle *m*

potbelly [ˈpɒtˌbelɪ] (*pl* **potbellies**) N **1** *(stomach)* ventre *m*, bedon *m*; **to have a p.** avoir du ventre **2** *Am (stove)* poêle *m*

potboiler [ˈpɒtˌbɔɪlə(r)] N *Fam* gagne-pain *m*; **he only writes potboilers** il n'écrit que pour faire bouillir la marmite

poteen [pɒˈtʃiːn] N *Ir* = whisky fabriqué clandestinement

potency [ˈpəʊtənsɪ] (*pl* **potencies**) N **1** *(strength* ► *of spell, influence, argument)* force *f*, puissance *f*; *(*► *of medicine)* efficacité *f*; *(*► *of drink)* (forte) teneur *f* en alcool **2** *(virility)* puissance *f*, virilité *f*

potent [ˈpəʊtənt] ADJ **1** *(spell, influence)* fort, puissant; *(argument)* convaincant; *(medicine, poison, antidote)* actif; *(drink)* fort (en alcool); **p. stuff, this rum!** il est fort, ce rhum! **2** *(virile)* viril

potentate [ˈpəʊtənteɪt] N *Pol* potentat *m*; *Fig* magnat *m*

potential [pəˈtenʃəl] ADJ **1** *(possible)* possible, potentiel, éventuel; **that boy is a p. genius** ce garçon est un génie en puissance; **we mustn't discourage p. investors** il ne faut pas décourager les investisseurs éventuels *ou* potentiels **2** *Ling* potentiel **3** *Elec & Phys* potentiel

N *(UNCOUNT)* **1** *(of person)* promesse *f*, possibilités *fpl* (d'avenir); **your son has p.** votre fils a de l'avenir *ou* un avenir prometteur; **she has the p. to succeed** elle a la capacité de réussir; **she has great p. as an actress** *or* **great acting p.** elle a toutes les qualités d'une grande actrice; **she has p. as an athlete** elle peut devenir une grande athlète; **to fulfil one's p.** donner toute sa mesure; **he never achieved his full p.** il n'a jamais exploité pleinement ses capacités

2 *(of concept, discovery, situation)* possibilités *fpl*; **the idea has p.** l'idée a de l'avenir; **your latest invention has great p. for developing countries** votre dernière invention ouvre de grandes perspectives dans les pays en voie de développement; **the scheme has no p.** le projet n'a aucun avenir; **there is little p. for development in the firm** l'entreprise offre peu de possibilités de développement; **the country's military p.** le potentiel militaire du pays

3 *(of place)* possibilités *fpl*; **the area/garden has real p.** le quartier/le jardin offre de nombreuses possibilités; **the building has a lot of p.** le bâtiment offre de grandes possibilités d'aménagement

4 *Elec, Math, Phys & Physiol* potentiel *m*

►► *Com & Mktg* ***potential buyer*** acheteur(euse) *m,f* éventuel(elle); *Elec & Phys* ***potential difference*** différence *f* de potentiel; *Elec & Phys* ***potential energy*** énergie *f* potentielle; *Econ* ***potential GDP*** PIB *m* potentiel

potentiality [pəˌtenʃɪˈælətɪ] *(pl* **potentialities***)* N **1** *(likelihood)* potentialité *f* **2** *(potential)* possibilités *fpl*, perspective *f* (d'avenir); **to have potentialities** offrir de nombreuses possibilités

potentially [pəˈtenʃəlɪ] ADV potentiellement; **she's p. a great writer** elle pourrait être un grand écrivain; **p. lethal poisons** des poisons *mpl* qui peuvent être mortels

potentiometer [pəˌtenʃɪˈɒmɪtə(r)] N potentiomètre *m*

pothead [ˈpɒthed] N *Fam Drugs slang* gros (grosse) fumeur(euse) *m,f* de haschisch

pother [ˈpɒðə(r)] N agitation *f*; **to get into a p. over sth** se mettre dans tous ses états au sujet de qch

pothole [ˈpɒthəʊl] N **1** *(in road)* fondrière *f*, nid-de-poule *m* **2** *(underground)* caverne *f*, grotte *f* **3** *(in river)* marmite *f* de géants

potholer [ˈpɒtˌhəʊlə(r)] N *Br* spéléologue *mf*

potholing [ˈpɒtˌhəʊlɪŋ] N *(UNCOUNT) Br* spéléologie *f*; **to go p.** faire de la spéléologie

pothook [ˈpɒthʊk] N **1** *(in fireplace)* crémaillère *f* *(crochet en forme de s)* **2** *(in writing)* boucle *f*

pothunter [ˈpɒtˌhʌntə(r)] N *Pej* **1** *Hunt* chasseur(euse) *m,f* sans scrupules **2** *(archaeologist)* archéologue *mf* amateur **3** *Sport* chasseur(euse) *m,f* de médailles

potion [ˈpəʊʃən] N **1** *Med* potion *f* **2** *Fig* potion *f*, breuvage *m*; **magic p.** potion *f* magique

potluck [ˌpɒtˈlʌk] N *Fam* **to take p.** *(for meal)* manger à la fortune du pot; *(take what one finds)* s'en remettre au hasard[□]; **it was just p.** c'était un pur hasard[□]; *Am* **p. lunch/supper** déjeuner *m*/dîner *m* où chacun apporte un plat

potpourri [ˌpəʊˈpʊərɪ] N pot-pourri *m*

pottage [ˈpɒtɪdʒ] N *Culin* potage *m* épais

potted [ˈpɒtɪd] ADJ **1** *Hort* en pot

2 *Culin (cooked)* (cuit) en terrine; *(conserved)* (conservé) en terrine *ou* en pot

3 *Fam (condensed* ► *version)* condensé[□], abrégé[□]; **a p. history of the Second World War** un abrégé d'histoire de la Seconde Guerre mondiale; **she gave me a p. version of the truth** elle m'a donné une version sommaire des faits

4 *Am Fam (drunk)* pété, bourré

►► ***potted meat*** ≃ terrine *f*; ***potted palm*** palmier *m* en pot; ***potted plant*** plante *f* verte; ***potted shrimps*** crevettes *fpl* en conserve

potter [ˈpɒtə(r)] N potier(ère) *m,f*

VI *Br Fam* **1** *(do odd jobs)* bricoler; **I spent the evening just pottering** j'ai passé la soirée à bricoler **2** *(move about slowly)* traîner, traînasser; **after lunch, I'll p. down to the post office** après le déjeuner, je ferai un saut à la poste

►► ***potter's clay*** argile *f* de potier, terre *f* glaise; *Am* ***potter's field*** cimetière *m* des pauvres; ***potter's wheel*** tour *m* de potier

► **potter about** *Br Fam* VI **1** *(do odd jobs)* s'occuper[□], bricoler; **to p. about in the garden** faire de petits travaux *ou* bricoler dans le jardin **2** *(move about slowly)* traîner, traînasser; **pottering about in country lanes in her car** en se baladant dans les chemins de campagne au volant de sa voiture

VT INSEP **to p. about the house/garden** faire des petits travaux *ou* bricoler dans la maison/le jardin

► **potter along** VI *Br Fam* aller son petit bonhomme de chemin; **I'd better be pottering along now** bon, il faudrait que je commence à y aller; **I might p. along to the library later** j'irai peut-être faire un tour à la bibliothèque tout à l'heure

pottery [ˈpɒtərɪ] *(pl* **potteries***)* N **1** *(UNCOUNT) (craft)* poterie *f* **2** *(UNCOUNT) (earthenware)* poterie *f*, poteries *fpl*; *(ceramics)* céramiques *fpl*; **a beautiful piece of p.** une très belle poterie **3** *(workshop)* atelier *m* de poterie

potting [ˈpɒtɪŋ] N *(UNCOUNT)* **1** *Hort* rempotage *m* **2** *(pottery)* poterie *f*

►► *Br* ***potting shed*** remise *f ou* resserre *f* (de jardin)

potty [ˈpɒtɪ] *(pl* **potties**, *compar* **pottier**, *superl* **pottiest***)* N *(for children)* pot *m* (de chambre)

ADJ *Br Fam (crazy)* timbré, dingue; **to go p.** devenir timbré *ou* dingue; **to be p. about sb/sth** être timbré *ou* dingue de qn/qch; **you're driving me p.** tu me rends dingue, tu me fais tourner en bourrique

►► *Fam* ***potty mouth*** = personne qui jure comme un charretier; **to be a p. mouth** jurer comme un charretier

potty-mouthed ADJ *Fam* **to be p.** jurer comme un charretier

POTUS [ˈpəʊtʌs] N *(abbr* **President of the United States***)* = président des États-Unis d'Amérique

pouch [paʊtʃ] N **1** *(bag)* (petit) sac *m*; *(for tobacco)* blague *f*; *(for money)* sac *m*, bourse *f*; *(for ammunition)* cartouchière *f*, giberne *f*; *(for gunpowder)* sacoche *f*, sac *m*; *(for mail)* sac *m* (postal) **2** *Zool (of rodent* ► *in cheeks)* poche *f*, abajoue *f*; *(of marsupial* ► *pocket of skin)* poche *f* **3** *Am (for diplomats)* valise *f* diplomatique

pouf, pouffe [puːf] N *Br* **1** *(cushion)* pouf *m* **2** *very Fam* pédé *m*, tapette *f*, = terme injurieux désignant un homosexuel

poult [pəʊlt] N *(young chicken)* (jeune) poulet *m*; *(young turkey)* dindonneau *m*; *(young pheasant, partridge)* pouillard *m*

poulterer [ˈpəʊltərə(r)] N *Br* volailler(ère) *m,f*

poultice [ˈpəʊltɪs] N *Med* cataplasme *m*

poultry [ˈpəʊltrɪ] N *(UNCOUNT) (meat)* volaille *f*

NPL *(birds)* volaille *f*, volailles *fpl*

►► ***poultry farm*** élevage *m* de volaille *or* de volailles; ***poultry farmer*** éleveur(euse) *m,f* de volaille *or* de volailles, aviculteur(trice) *m,f*; ***poultry farming*** élevage *m* de volaille *or* de volailles, aviculture *f*

pounce [paʊns] VI sauter, bondir; **a man pounced (out) from behind the bush** un homme a surgi de derrière le buisson

N bond *m*; **with a sudden p.** d'un bond

POUND [paʊnd]

N	
• livre **1, 2**	• fourrière **3**
VT	
• broyer **1**	• cogner sur **2**
• bombarder **3**	• faire les cent pas dans **4**
VI	
• cogner **1**	• taper **1**
• battre **2**	

N **1** *(unit of weight)* = 453,6 grammes, livre *f*; **to sell goods by the p.** vendre des marchandises à la livre; **three p.** *or* **pounds of apples** trois livres *fpl* de pommes; **two dollars a p.** deux dollars la livre; *Fig* **to get one's p. of flesh** obtenir ce que l'on exigeait; **he wants his p. of flesh** il veut son dû à n'importe quel prix

2 *(money)* livre *f*; **have you got change for a p.?** avez-vous la monnaie d'une livre?; **two for a p.** deux pour une livre; **p. coin** pièce *f* d'une livre; **the Lebanese/Maltese p.** la livre libanaise/maltaise; **the p. sterling** la livre sterling

3 *(for dogs, cars)* fourrière *f*

VT **1** *(crush, pulverize* ► *grain)* broyer, concasser; *(*► *spices, drugs etc)* piler, broyer; *(*► *rocks)* concasser, broyer, piler; **to p. sth to a powder/a paste** réduire qch en poudre/en bouillie

2 *(hammer, hit)* cogner sur, marteler; *(flatten* ► *earth)* pilonner, tasser; **she pounded the table with her fist** elle martelait la table du poing; **the waves pounded the rocks/boat** les vagues battaient les rochers/venaient s'écraser violemment contre le bateau; **he began pounding the typewriter keys** il commença à taper sur *ou* à marteler le clavier de la machine à écrire

3 *(bombard, shell)* bombarder, pilonner; **they pounded the enemy positions with mortar fire** ils ont bombardé les positions ennemies au mortier

4 *(walk* ► *corridor)* faire les cent pas dans, aller et venir dans; **to p. the streets** battre le pavé; **to p. the beat** *(policeman)* faire sa ronde

VI **1** *(hammer* ► *on table, ceiling)* cogner, taper; *(*► *on piano, typewriter)* taper; **the neighbours started pounding on the ceiling** les voisins ont commencé à cogner au plafond; **we had to p. on the door before anyone answered** il a fallu frapper à la porte à coups redoublés avant d'obtenir une réponse; **the waves pounded against the rocks** les vagues battaient les rochers; **the rain was pounding on the roof** la pluie tambourinait sur le toit

2 *(rhythmically* ► *drums)* battre; *(*► *heart)* battre fort; *(*► *with fear, excitement)* battre la chamade; **my head was pounding from the noise** le bruit me martelait la tête

3 *(run noisily)* **he pounded up/down the stairs** il monta/descendit l'escalier bruyamment; **the horses came pounding along the track** les chevaux arrivaient au grand galop dans un bruit de tonnerre

►► *Culin* ***pound cake*** ≃ quatre-quarts *m inv*; ***pound sign*** *(£)* symbole *m* de la livre (sterling); *Am (on telephone)* dièse *m*

► **pound away** VI **1** *(on typewriter, piano, drums)* **he was pounding away at the piano** il martelait les touches du piano; **she's been pounding away at her typewriter since eight o'clock** elle s'acharne sur sa machine à écrire depuis huit heures; **every weekend, he pounds away on his drums** il passe ses week-ends à taper sur sa batterie **2** *(with artillery)* **to p. away at the enemy lines** pilonner sans arrêt les lignes ennemies; **we heard the guns pounding away** nous entendions le bruit incessant des canons

poundage [ˈpaʊndɪdʒ] N *(UNCOUNT)* **1** *(on weight)* droits *mpl* perçus par livre de poids **2** *(on value)* droits *mpl* perçus par livre de valeur **3** *(weight)* poids *m (en livres)*

-pounder [ˈpaʊndə(r)] SUFF **a fifteen-p.** *(fish)* un poisson de quinze livres; **a two-hundred-p.** *(shell)* un obus de deux cents livres; **a six-p.** *(gun)* un canon *ou* une pièce de six

pounding [ˈpaʊndɪŋ] N **1** *(noise)* martèlement *m*

2 *(UNCOUNT) (beating* ► *of heart)* battements *mpl*; **I could hear the p. of her heart** j'entendais son cœur qui battait à tout rompre

3 *Fam (battering)* rossée *f*; **he took a real p. in the first five rounds** il a pris une bonne volée *ou* il s'est drôlement fait rosser pendant les cinq premières reprises; **the jetty/harbour took a p. in the storm** la jetée/le port en a pris un coup pendant la tempête; **the dollar took a severe p. last week** le dollar a été sérieusement malmené la semaine dernière

4 *Fam (severe defeat)* déculottée *f*, piquette *f*; **the team took a real p. last week** l'équipe a subi une lourde défaite *ou* s'est fait battre à plate couture la semaine dernière

pour [pɔː(r)] VT **1** *(liquid)* verser; *(serve)* servir, verser; *Metal* couler; **to p. a drink for sb** servir à boire à qn; **p. yourself a drink** servez-vous *ou* versez-vous à boire; **may I p. you some wine?** je vous sers du vin?; **would you p. the tea?** voulez-vous servir le thé?; **she poured milk into their mugs** elle a versé du lait dans leurs tasses; **we poured the water/wine down the sink** nous avons vidé l'eau/jeté le vin dans l'évier; **her jeans were so tight she looked as if she'd been poured into them** son jean était tellement serré qu'elle semblait avoir été coulée dedans; **to p. cold water on** *or* **over sb's plans** décourager *ou* refroidir qn dans ses projets; **to p. scorn on sb** traiter qn avec mépris

2 *(supply in large amounts)* **he poured all his energies into the project** il a mis toute son énergie dans le projet; **the government poured money into the industry** le gouvernement a investi des sommes énormes dans cette industrie; **they poured reinforcements into the area** ils ont envoyé des renforts en masse dans la région

VI 1 *(liquid)* se déverser, couler à flots; **water poured from the gutters** l'eau débordait des gouttières; **water was pouring into the cellar** l'eau entrait à flots dans la cave; **tears poured down her face** elle pleurait à chaudes larmes; **blood poured from the wound** la blessure saignait abondamment; **the sweat was pouring off him/his back** il/son dos ruisselait de sueur; **light poured into the church** l'église était inondée de lumière; **smoke poured out of the blazing building** des nuages de fumée s'échappaient de l'immeuble en flammes

2 *(rain)* pleuvoir à verse; **it's pouring (with rain)** il pleut à verse *ou* à torrents

3 *(crowd)* affluer; **reporters p. into Cannes for the festival** les journalistes affluent à Cannes pour le festival; **spectators poured into/out of the cinema** une foule de spectateurs entrait dans le cinéma/sortait du cinéma; **thousands of cars poured out of Paris** des milliers de voitures se pressaient aux portes de Paris

4 *(pan, jug)* **to p. well/badly** verser bien/mal

5 *(serve a drink)* **shall I p.?** je fais le service?

▸**pour down VI** *(rain)* tomber à verse; **it's been pouring down for days** il pleut à verse depuis des jours et des jours

▸**pour in VI 1** *(rain, light, water)* entrer à flots **2** *(cars, refugees, spectators)* arriver en masse; *(information, reports)* affluer, arriver en masse; **the crowd came pouring in** la foule est entrée en masse; **offers of help poured in from all sides** des offres d'aide ont afflué de toutes parts; **money poured in for the disaster victims** des milliers de dons ont été envoyés pour les victimes de la catastrophe

▸**pour off VT SEP** *(liquid, excess)* vider

▸**pour out VT SEP 1** *(liquid)* verser **2** *(information, propaganda)* répandre, diffuser; *(of chimney* ▸ *clouds of smoke)* cracher, vomir; **the industry pours out tons of dangerous chemicals** l'industrie déverse des tonnes de produits chimiques dangereux **3** *(emotions)* donner libre cours à; **she poured out all her troubles to me** elle m'a raconté tout ce qu'elle avait sur le cœur; **to p. out one's heart to sb** parler à qn à cœur ouvert; **to p. out a torrent of abuse at sb** déverser un torrent d'injures sur qn

VI 1 *(water)* jaillir, couler à flots; *(tears)* couler abondamment; *(light)* jaillir; **smoke was pouring out of the window** des nuages de fumée s'échappaient de la fenêtre; **the words just poured out** les mots sont sortis en flots; **all his feelings came pouring out** il a laissé libre cours à ses émotions **2** *(people)* sortir en masse

pouring ['pɔːrɪŋ] **ADJ 1** *(rain)* battant, diluvien; **we were stranded in the p. rain** nous étions coincés sous une pluie battante **2** *(cream)* liquide

pout [paʊt] **VI** faire la moue

VT dire en faisant la moue

N *(facial expression)* moue *f*; **with a p.** en faisant la moue

pouter ['paʊtə(r)] **N** *Orn* boulant *m*

POV [,piːəʊ'viː] **N** *TV & Cin (abbr* **point of view***)* angle *m* du regard

poverty ['pɒvətɪ] **N 1** *(financial)* pauvreté *f*, misère *f*; **to live in p.** vivre dans le besoin **2** *(shortage* ▸ *of resources)* manque *m*; *(*▸ *of ideas, imagination)* pauvreté *f*, manque *m*; *(weakness* ▸ *of style, arguments)* pauvreté *f*, faiblesse *f* **3** *(of soil)* pauvreté *f*, aridité *f*

▸▸ ***poverty line*** seuil *m* de pauvreté; **to live on/below the p. line** vivre à la limite/en dessous du seuil de pauvreté; ***poverty trap*** = situation inextricable de ceux qui dépendent de prestations sociales qu'ils perdent pour peu qu'ils trouvent une activité, même peu rémunérée

poverty-stricken ADJ *(person)* dans la misère, dans le plus grand dénuement; *(areas)* misérable, où sévit la misère

POW [,piːəʊ'dʌbəljuː] **N** *(abbr* **prisoner of war***)* PG *m*

powder ['paʊdə(r)] **N 1** *(gen) & Mil* poudre *f*; **in p. form** en poudre, sous forme de poudre; **to grind sth to a p.** réduire qch en poudre, pulvériser qch; *Br Fig* **to keep one's p. dry** se tenir prêt, être aux aguets

2 *(snow)* poudreuse *f*

3 *(for face)* poudre *f*

4 *Old-fashioned* **to take a headache p.** prendre un médicament (en sachet) contre le mal de tête

5 *Am Fam (idiom)* **to take a p.** *(disappear)* ficher le camp, décamper

VT 1 *(crush, pulverize)* pulvériser, réduire en poudre **2** *(make up)* poudrer; **to p. one's face** se poudrer le visage; *Euph* **to p. one's nose** *(go to the toilet)* aller se repoudrer le nez **3** *(sprinkle)* saupoudrer; **the Christmas tree was powdered with artificial snow** le sapin de Noël était saupoudré de neige artificielle

▸▸ ***powder blue*** bleu *m* pastel; ***powder compact*** poudrier *m*; ***powder eyeshadow*** ombre *f* à paupières en poudre; ***powder horn*** corne *f*, cartouche *f* à poudre; ***powder keg*** *(of gunpowder)* baril *m* de poudre; *Fig* poudrière *f*; ***powder puff*** houppette *f*; *Euph* ***powder room*** toilettes *fpl* (pour dames)

powdered ['paʊdəd] **ADJ 1** *(milk)* en poudre; *(coffee)* instantané **2** *(hair, face)* poudré

▸▸ *Am* ***powdered sugar*** sucre *m* glace

powdery ['paʊdərɪ] **ADJ 1** *(covered in powder)* couvert de poudre **2** *(like powder)* poudreux; **p. snow** (neige *f*) poudreuse *f* **3** *(crumbling)* friable

POWER ['paʊə(r)]

> **N**
> - puissance **1, 3, 4, 10**
> - pouvoir **2, 5, 6, 9**
> - faculté **6**
> - énergie **8**
> - force **1**
> - capacité **5**
> - courant **7**
>
> **VT**
> - faire fonctionner
>
> **VI**
> - foncer

N 1 *(strength, force* ▸ *gen)* puissance *f*, force *f*; *Phys (*▸ *of engine, lens, microscope)* puissance *f*; *(*▸ *of magnet)* force *f*; **I underestimated the p. of the explosion** j'ai sous-estimé la puissance *ou* la force de l'explosion; **we want greater economic and industrial p.** nous voulons renforcer la puissance économique et industrielle; **at full p.** à plein régime; **the vehicle moves under its own p.** le véhicule se déplace par ses propres moyens *ou* de façon autonome; **sea/air p.** puissance *f* maritime/aérienne; *Fam* **the holiday did me a p. of good** les vacances m'ont fait un bien fou; *Br Fam* **more p. to your elbow!** bonne chance!☐, bon courage!☐

2 *(influence, control) & Pol* pouvoir *m*; *(authority)* autorité *f*, pouvoir *m*; **to have sb in one's p.** avoir qn en son pouvoir; **to be in sb's p.** être à la merci de qn; **to fall into sb's p.** tomber au pouvoir de qn; **to be in p.** être au pouvoir; **to come (in)to/to take p.** arriver au/prendre le pouvoir; **to lose p.** perdre le pouvoir; **to have the p. to decide/judge** avoir le pouvoir de décider/juger, avoir autorité pour décider/juger; **absolute/executive/legislative p.** pouvoir *m* absolu/exécutif/législatif; **the committee doesn't really have much p.** le comité n'a pas grand pouvoir; **to act with full powers** agir de pleine autorité; **the police have been given greater powers** la police a reçu des pouvoirs plus importants; **it's beyond** *or* **outside my p.** *or* **powers** cela dépasse ma compétence *ou* ne relève pas de mon autorité; **it's beyond my p. to do anything** je n'ai pas compétence en la matière, je ne suis pas habilité à intervenir

3 *(influential group or person)* puissance *f*; **th[e] President is the real p. in the land** c'est le présiden[t] qui détient le véritable pouvoir dans le pays; **t[o] be a p. in the land** avoir une grande influence o[u] être très puissant dans un pays; **the powers o[f] darkness** les forces *fpl ou* puissances *fpl* des té[-]nèbres; **the (real) p. behind the throne** *(individ[u]ual)* l'éminence *f* grise, celui (celle) *m,f* qui tir[e] les ficelles; *(group)* ceux *mpl* qui tirent les fice[l]les, les véritables acteurs *mpl*; *also Hum* **th[e] powers that be** les autorités *fpl* constituées; **n[o] p. on earth will persuade me to go** rien au mond[e] ne me persuadera d'y aller

4 *Pol (state)* puissance *f*; **the great Wester[n] powers** les grandes puissances occidentales; **i[n]dustrial/nuclear/world p.** *(country)* puissance in[-]dustrielle/nucléaire/mondiale

5 *(ability, capacity)* capacité *f*, pouvoir *m*; **he ha[s] great powers as an orator** *or* **great oratorica[l] powers** il a de grands talents oratoires; **to be a[t] the height** *or* **peak of one's powers** être à l'apogé[e] de sa puissance; **it's within her p. to do it** c'est e[n] son pouvoir, elle est capable de le faire; **I'll d[o] everything in my p. to help you** je ferai tout mo[n] possible *ou* tout ce qui est en mon pouvoir pou[r] vous aider; **magical/aphrodisiac powers** pouvoir[s] *mpl* magiques/aphrodisiaques; **to have grea[t] powers of persuasion/suggestion** avoir un gran[d] pouvoir *ou* une grande force de persuasion[/] suggestion; **the body's powers of resistance** la ca[-]pacité de résistance du corps; **she has great i[n]tellectual powers** elle a de grandes capacité[s] intellectuelles; *Phys & Chem* **p. of absorption** ca[-]pacité *f* d'absorption

6 *(faculty)* faculté *f*, pouvoir *m*; **her powers ar[e] failing** ses facultés déclinent; **the p. of sight** l[a] vue; **the p. of hearing** l'ouïe *f*; **the p. of reason** l[a] raison; **he lost the p. of speech** il a perdu l'usag[e] de la parole

7 *Elec (current)* courant *m*; **to turn on/cut off th[e] p.** mettre/couper le courant

8 *Elec & Phys (energy)* énergie *f*; **the p. industr[y]** l'industrie *f* de l'énergie

9 *Law (proxy)* pouvoir *m*

10 *Math* puissance *f*; **5 to the p. (of) 6** 5 puis[-]sance 6; **raised to the 5th p.** élevé à la puissanc[e] 5

COMP *(source, consumption)* d'énergie; *(cable)* électrique; *(brakes)* assisté

VT *(give power to)* faire fonctionner *ou* marche[r]; *(propel)* propulser; **powered by solar energ[y]** fonctionnant à l'énergie solaire; **the boat is pow[-]ered by gas turbines** le bateau est propulsé pa[r] des turbines à gaz

VI avancer à toute vitesse, foncer; **he powere[d] into his opponent** il fonça sur son adversaire; **the leading cars powered down the home straigh[t]** les voitures de tête foncèrent dans la dernièr[e] ligne

▸▸ ***power amplifier,*** *Fam* ***power amp*** amplifica[-]teur *m* de puissance; *Law* ***power of attorney*** pro[-]curation *f*; **to give sb p. of attorney** donne[r] procuration à qn; ***power base*** assise *f* politique[;] ***power breakfast*** = petit déjeuner d'affaires entr[e] personnes importantes; ***power broker*** décideu[r] (euse) *m,f* politique; ***power cut*** coupure *f* de cou[-]rant; *Aviat* ***power dive*** (descente *f* en) piqué *m*; *B[r]* ***power dressing*** = façon de s'habiller qu'adopten[t] certaines femmes cadres dans le but de proje[-]ter une image d'autorité; ***power drill*** perceuse électrique; ***power failure*** panne *f* de courant[;] ***power game*** lutte *f* d'influence, course *f* au pou[-]voir; ***power line*** ligne *f* à haute tension; ***powe[r] lunch*** = déjeuner d'affaires entre personnes im[-]portantes; *Am* ***power outage*** rupture *f* de l'ali[-]mentation; *Elec* ***power pack*** bloc *m* d'alimentation électrique; ***power plant*** *(factory)* centrale *f* électrique; *(generator)* groupe *m* élec[-]trogène; *(engine)* groupe *m* moteur; ***power pla[y]*** *(in ice hockey)* coup *m* de force; ***power point*** pris[e] *f* de courant; ***power politics*** *(UNCOUNT)* poli[-]tique *f* du coup de force; *Math* ***power set*** en[-]semble *m* des sous-ensembles; *Pol* ***powe[r] sharing*** partage *m* du pouvoir; ***power showe[r]*** douche *f* à jet puissant; ***power station*** centrale (électrique); *Aut* ***power steering*** direction *f* assis[-]tée; ***power strike*** grève *f* des employés de l'élec[-]tricité; ***power structure*** *(system)* hiérarchie *f*[,] répartition *f* des pouvoirs; *(people with power)* =

ensemble des personnes qui détiennent le pouvoir; ***power struggle*** lutte *f* pour le pouvoir; ***power suit*** = costume pour homme ou femme d'affaires; *Elec* ***power supply*** alimentation *f* (électrique); ***power tool*** outil *m* électrique; *Comput* ***power unit*** dispositif *m* d'alimentation; ***power user*** gros (grosse) utilisateur(trice) *m,f*; *Comput* = personne qui sait utiliser au mieux les ressources de son ordinateur; ***power walking*** marche *f* sportive; ***power worker*** employé(e) *m,f* de l'électricité; ***power yoga*** power yoga *m* *(forme de yoga où l'on travaille en puissance)*

▸ **power down, power off** VT SEP éteindre, mettre hors tension

VI *(computer, machine)* s'éteindre, se mettre hors tension

▸ **power up** VT SEP mettre sous tension, allumer

VI *(computer, machine)* se mettre sous tension, s'allumer

power-assisted ADJ assisté

powerboat ['paʊəbəʊt] N *(outboard)* hors-bord *m inv*; *(inboard)* vedette *f* (rapide)

powerbroker ['paʊə,brəʊkə(r)] N décideur *m* politique

power-down N *Comput* mise *f* hors tension

powered ['paʊəd] SUFF **high/low-p.** de haute/faible puissance; **a high-p. executive** un cadre très haut placé; **steam/wind-p.** mû (mue) par la vapeur/le vent; **jet-p.** propulsé par un moteur à réaction

powerful ['paʊəfʊl] ADJ **1** *(strong ▸ gen)* puissant; *(▸ smell)* fort; *(▸ kick)* violent; *(▸ imagination)* débordant; *(▸ language, prose style)* vigoureux, qui a de l'impact; **a p. swimmer** un excellent nageur; **she has a very p. voice** elle a une voix très puissante; **the engine isn't p. enough** le moteur n'est pas assez puissant; **p. binoculars** jumelles *fpl* puissantes *ou* à fort grossissement; **p. drugs** médication *f* puissante *ou* active; **he has been a p. influence in her life** il a exercé une influence décisive dans sa vie **2** *(influential ▸ person)* fort, influent; *(▸ country, firm)* puissant

powerfully ['paʊəfʊlɪ] ADV puissamment; **he's p. built** il est d'une stature imposante

powerhouse ['paʊəhaʊs, *pl* -haʊzɪz] N **1** *Elec* centrale *f* électrique **2** *Fig (person)* personne *f* énergique, locomotive *f*; *(place)* pépinière *f*; **she's a p. of energy** elle déborde d'énergie; **the university became a p. of new ideas** l'université est devenue une vraie pépinière d'idées nouvelles

powerless ['paʊəlɪs] ADJ impuissant, désarmé; **they were p. to prevent the scandal** ils n'ont rien pu faire pour éviter le scandale; **our arguments were p. in the face of such conviction** nos arguments sont restés lettre morte devant une telle conviction

power-on key N *Br Comput* touche *f* d'alimentation

power-sharing ADJ *(deal, coalition, talks)* de partage du pouvoir

▸▸ ***power-sharing arrangement*** accord *m* de partage du pouvoir

powertrain ['paʊətreɪn] N *Aut* groupe *m* motopropulseur

power-up N *Comput* mise *f* sous tension

powwow ['paʊwaʊ] N *(of American Indians)* assemblée *f*; *Fam Fig (meeting)* réunion ▫ *f*; *(discussion)* discussion ▫ *f*, pourparlers ▫ *mpl*; **to have** *or* **to hold a p.** *(American Indians)* tenir une assemblée; *Fam Fig* discuter ▫

VI *(American Indians)* tenir une assemblée; *Fam Fig (talk)* discuter ▫

pox [pɒks] N *Fam* vérole ▫ *f*; *Arch* **a p. on him!** qu'il aille au diable!

poxy ['pɒksɪ] *(compar* **poxier**, *superl* **poxiest)** ADJ *Fam* **1** *Med* vérolé ▫ **2** *Br (worthless)* minable; **he only gave me a p. five pounds for it** il me l'a acheté (pour) cinq malheureuses livres

pp [,piː'piː] *(abbr* **per procurationem**) ADV **pp Jane Smith** pp Jane Smith

VT **shall I pp it?** est-ce que je signe à votre/sa place?

PPB [,piːpiː'biː] N *Acct (abbr* **planning-programming-budgeting system**) système *m* de planification-programmation-budgétisation, rationalisation *f* des choix budgétaires

PPD, ppd [,piːpiː'diː] ADJ *Com (abbr* **prepaid**) port payé par le destinataire

PPE [,piːpiː'iː] N *Br (abbr* **philosophy, politics and economics**) = philosophie, science politique et science économique (cours à l'université d'Oxford)

ppi [,piːpiː'aɪ] N *Comput (abbr* **pixels per inch**) pixels *mpl* par pouce

ppm **1** *Chem (written abbr* **parts per million**) ppm **2** *Comput (written abbr* **pages per minute**) ppm

PPP [,piːpiː'piː] N **1** *Comput (abbr* **point-to-point protocol**) protocole *m* PPP, protocole *m* point à point **2** *Com (abbr* **public-private partnership**) partenariat *m* public-privé

PPS [,piːpiː'es] N *(abbr* **post postscriptum**) PPS

PQ [,piː'kjuː] N *Can* **1** *(abbr* **Province of Quebec**) province *f* de Québec **2** *(abbr* **Parti québécois**) PQ *m*

PR[1] [,piː'ɑː(r)] N **1** *(abbr* **public relations**) relations *fpl* publiques, RP *fpl*; **we need better PR** il nous faut améliorer nos relations publiques; **a skilful PR man** un homme qui excelle dans les relations publiques **2** *Pol (abbr* **proportional representation**) RP *f*

▸▸ ***PR agency*** agence *f* conseil en communication; ***PR company*** société *f* conseil en communication; ***PR consultancy*** agence *f* conseil en communication; ***PR consultant*** conseil *m* en communication

PR[2] **1** *(written abbr* **Puerto Rico**) Porto Rico *m* **2** *Am Pej (written abbr* **Puerto Rican**) Portoricain(e) *m,f*

practicability [,præktɪkə'bɪlətɪ] N **1** *(of plan, action)* faisabilité *f*, viabilité *f* **2** *(of road)* praticabilité *f*

practicable ['præktɪkəbəl] ADJ **1** *(feasible)* réalisable, praticable; *(possible)* possible; **as far as p.** autant que possible, autant que faire se peut **2** *(road)* praticable

practical ['præktɪkəl] ADJ **1** *(convenient, easy to use)* pratique, commode

2 *(sensible, commonsense ▸ person)* (qui a le sens) pratique, doué de sens pratique; *(▸ mind, suggestion)* pratique; **now, be p., we can't afford a new car** allons, un peu de bon sens, nous n'avons pas les moyens de nous offrir une nouvelle voiture; **is white the most p. colour?** le blanc, c'est ce qu'il y a de plus pratique comme couleur?

3 *(training, experience, question)* pratique, concret(ète); **does it have any p. application?** est-ce qu'il y a une application pratique?; **for all p. purposes** à toutes fins utiles; **he has a p. knowledge of German** il connaît l'allemand usuel

4 *(virtual)* **it's a p. impossibility** c'est pratiquement impossible

N *Br Sch & Univ (class)* travaux *mpl* pratiques, TP *mpl*; *(exam)* épreuve *f* pratique

▸▸ ***practical joke*** farce *f*; **to play a p. joke on sb** faire une farce *ou* jouer un tour à qn; ***practical joker*** farceur(euse) *m,f*; *Am* ***practical nurse*** aide-soignant(e) *m,f*

practicality [,præktɪ'kælətɪ] *(pl* **practicalities**) N *(of person)* sens *m* pratique; *(of ideas)* nature *f* pratique; **I'm not too sure about the p. of his suggestions** je doute que ses propositions puissent trouver une application pratique

• **practicalities** NPL *(details)* détails *mpl* pratiques

practically ['præktɪkəlɪ] ADV **1** *(sensibly)* de manière pratique; **she very p. suggested telephoning home** elle a eu la bonne idée de suggérer qu'on téléphone chez elle; **to be p. dressed** être habillé de façon pratique

2 *(based on practice)* pratiquement; **the whole course is very much p. based** le cours est fondé en grande partie sur la pratique

3 *(almost)* presque, pratiquement; **p. the whole of the audience** la quasi-totalité de l'auditoire; **we're p. there** nous y sommes presque, nous sommes pratiquement arrivés

4 *(in practice)* dans la pratique; **p. speaking** en fait

practice ['præktɪs] N **1** *(habit)* pratique *f*, habitude *f*; *(custom)* pratique *f*, coutume *f*, usage *m*; **tribal/religious practices** pratiques *fpl* tribales/religieuses; **they make a regular p. of going jogging on Sundays** ils font régulièrement du jogging le dimanche; **he makes a p. of voting against** *or* **he makes it a p. to vote against the government** il se fait une règle de voter contre le gouvernement; **it's not company p. to refund deposits** il n'est pas dans les habitudes de la société de rembourser les arrhes; **it's normal p. among most shopkeepers** c'est une pratique courante chez les commerçants; **it's our usual p.** c'est ce que nous faisons habituellement, c'est notre politique habituelle; **it's standard p. to make a written request** la procédure habituelle veut que l'on fasse une demande par écrit

2 *(exercise ▸ of profession, witchcraft, archery)* pratique *f*

3 *(training)* entraînement *m*; *(rehearsal)* répétition *f*; *(study ▸ of instrument)* étude *f*, travail *m*; **I've had a lot of p. at** *or* **in dealing with difficult negotiations** j'ai une grande habitude des négociations difficiles; **it's good p. for your interview** c'est un bon entraînement pour votre entrevue; **to be in p.** être bien entraîné; **to be out of p.** manquer d'entraînement; **I'm getting out of p.** *(on piano)* je commence à avoir les doigts rouillés; *(at sport)* je commence à manquer d'entraînement; *(at skill)* je commence à perdre la main; **it's time for your piano p.** c'est l'heure de travailler ton piano; *Sport* **Schumacher was fastest in p.** Schumacher a été le plus rapide aux essais; *Prov* **p. makes perfect** c'est en forgeant qu'on devient forgeron

4 *(training session)* (séance *f* d')entraînement *m*; *(rehearsal ▸ of choir)* répétition *f*

5 *(practical application)* pratique *f*; **to put sth in** *or* **into p.** mettre qch en pratique; **in p.** dans la pratique

6 *(professional activity)* exercice *m*; **to be in p. as a doctor** exercer en tant que médecin; **to go into** *or* **to set up in p. as a doctor** s'installer comme médecin, ouvrir un cabinet de médecin; **medical/legal p.** l'exercice *m* de la médecine/de la profession d'avocat

7 *Br (office, surgery)* cabinet *m*; *(clientele)* clientèle *f*; **he has a country p.** il a un cabinet à la campagne

COMP *(game, run, session)* d'entraînement

VT & VI *Am* = **practise**

▸▸ *Golf* ***practice ground*** practice *m*; *Sport* ***practice match*** match *m* d'entraînement

practiced, practicing *Am* = **practised, practising**

practise, *Am* **practice** ['præktɪs] VT **1** *(for improvement ▸ musical instrument)* s'exercer à, travailler; *(▸ song)* travailler, répéter; *(▸ foreign language)* travailler, pratiquer; *(▸ stroke, shot)* travailler; **she was practising a Chopin nocturne** elle travaillait un nocturne de Chopin; **can I p. my French on you?** est-ce que je peux parler français *ou* pratiquer mon français avec vous?; **to p. speaking French** s'entraîner à parler français

2 *(put into practice ▸ principle, virtue)* pratiquer, mettre en pratique; **in this school, we p. self-discipline** dans cette école, on pratique l'autodiscipline; **you should p. what you preach** vous devriez donner l'exemple; **he doesn't p. what he preaches** il ne met pas en pratique ce qu'il prêche

3 *(profession)* exercer, pratiquer; **he practises medicine** il pratique *ou* exerce la médecine; **to p. law** exercer le métier de notaire/d'avocat

4 *(inflict)* infliger; **the cruelty they practised on their victims** les cruautés qu'ils infligeaient à *ou* les sévices qu'ils faisaient subir à leurs victimes

5 *(customs, beliefs)* observer, pratiquer; **pagan rituals are still practised in the area** on pratique encore certains rites païens dans la région

6 *Rel* pratiquer

7 *(magic)* pratiquer

VI **1** *(gen) & Mus* s'entraîner, s'exercer; *Sport* s'entraîner; **I'm just practising** je ne fais que m'entraîner; **to p. on the guitar** faire des exercices à la guitare **2** *(professionally)* exercer **3** *Rel* être pratiquant

practised, *Am* **practiced** ['præktɪst] ADJ **1** *(experienced)* expérimenté, chevronné; *(skilled)* habile; **p. in the arts of seduction/deception** rompu aux arts de la séduction/tromperie **2** *(expert ▸ aim, movement)* expert; *(▸ ear, eye)* exercé;

with a p. hand d'une main exercée *ou* habile; with p. ease avec une grande aisance 3 *(artificial ▸ smile, charm)* factice, étudié

practising, *Am* **practicing** [ˈpræktɪsɪŋ] ADJ 1 *Rel* pratiquant; he's a p. Jew c'est un juif pratiquant 2 *(professionally ▸ doctor)* exerçant; *(▸ lawyer, solicitor)* en exercice 3 *(homosexual)* actif

practitioner [prækˈtɪʃənə(r)] N 1 *Med* (medical) p. médecin *m* 2 *(gen)* praticien(enne) *m,f*

pragmatic [prægˈmætɪk] ADJ pragmatique; from a p. point of view d'un point de vue pratique

pragmatism [ˈprægmətɪzəm] N pragmatisme *m*

pragmatist [ˈprægmətɪst] N pragmatiste *mf*

prairie [ˈpreərɪ] N plaine *f* (herbeuse)

• **Prairie** N the P. *or* Prairies *(in US)* la Grande Prairie; *(in Canada)* les Prairies *fpl*

▸▸ *Zool* **prairie dog, prairie marmot** chien *m* de prairie; **prairie oyster** *(drink)* = boisson à base d'œuf cru (remède contre les excès d'alcool); **Prairie Provinces** les provinces *fpl* des Prairies *(au Canada)*; in the P. Provinces dans les (provinces des) Prairies; *Zool* **prairie wolf** coyote *m*

praise [preɪz] N 1 *(compliments)* éloge *m*, louanges *fpl*; she was full of p. for their kindness elle ne tarissait pas d'éloges sur leur gentillesse; I have nothing but p. for him je n'ai rien pour lui que des éloges *ou* louanges; she deserves special p. elle mérite tous les éloges *ou* toutes les louanges; her film has received high p. from the critics son film a été couvert d'éloges par la critique 2 *Rel* louange *f*, louanges *fpl*, gloire *f*; to give p. to the Lord rendre gloire à Dieu; p. (be to) the Lord! Dieu soit loué!; *Old-fashioned* p. be! Dieu merci!; hymn *or* song of p. cantique *m*

VT 1 *(gen)* louer, faire l'éloge de; he praised her for her patience il la loua de *ou* pour sa patience; he praised her for having been so patient il la loua d'avoir été si patiente; to p. sb to high heaven *or* to the skies couvrir qn d'éloges, porter qn aux nues 2 *Rel* louer, glorifier, rendre gloire à

• **in praise of** PREP à la louange de; the director spoke in p. of his staff le directeur fit l'éloge de son personnel

praiseworthiness [ˈpreɪzˌwɜːðɪnɪs] N mérite *m*

praiseworthy [ˈpreɪzˌwɜːðɪ] ADJ *(person)* digne d'éloges; *(action, intention, sentiment)* louable, méritoire

praline [ˈprɑːliːn] N pralin *m*

pram [præm] N *Br (for baby)* voiture *f* d'enfant, landau *m*

prance [prɑːns] VI 1 *(cavort ▸ horse)* caracoler, cabrioler; *(▸ person)* caracoler, gambader; the horses came prancing into the circus ring les chevaux sont entrés en caracolant sur la piste du cirque 2 *(strut)* se pavaner, se dandiner; he came prancing into the room il entra dans la pièce en se pavanant

N sautillement *m*

▸ **prance about** VI *(horse)* caracoler; *(person)* se pavaner

prang [præŋ] *Br Fam* VT *(car)* esquinter; *(plane)* bousiller

N accrochage◻ *m*; to have a p. avoir un accrochage◻

prank [præŋk] N farce *f*, tour *m*; to play a p. on sb jouer un tour *ou* faire une farce à qn; they used to get up to all kinds of pranks when they were at school ils faisaient toutes sortes de farces quand ils étaient à l'école

prankster [ˈpræŋkstə(r)] N farceur(euse) *m,f*; he's a little p. c'est un petit farceur *ou* polisson

prat [præt] *(pt & pp* pratted, *cont* pratting*)* N *Br Fam* andouille *f*, crétin(e) *m,f*; I feel like a right p. j'ai vraiment l'air d'une andouille

▸ **prat about, prat around** VI *Br Fam (act foolishly)* faire l'idiot; *(waste time)* glander, glandouiller

prate [preɪt] VI *Old-fashioned Pej* jacasser, bavarder

pratfall [ˈprætfɔːl] N *Fam (fall)* gadin *m*, pelle *f*; *(blunder)* gaffe *f*

prattish [ˈprætɪʃ] ADJ *Br Fam* crétin, idiot

prattle [ˈprætəl] *Br Fam Pej* VI *(child)* babiller; *(adult)* jacasser; *(converse)* papoter; she prattles away *or* on about her children for hours elle radote pendant des heures au sujet de ses enfants

N *(babble)* babillage *m*; *(conversation)* papotage *m*, bavardage *m*

prawn [prɔːn] N 1 *(seafood)* crevette *f* (rose); *(bigger)* bouquet *m*; p. curry curry *m* de crevettes 2 *Fam (person)* I felt a right p. je me suis senti vraiment bête◻

▸▸ **prawn cocktail** cocktail *m* de crevettes; *Br* **prawn cracker** beignet *m* de crevette

pray [preɪ] VI prier; to p. to God prier Dieu; to p. for sb/for sb's soul prier pour qn/pour l'âme de qn; she prayed to God to save her child elle pria Dieu qu'il sauve son enfant; I've been praying for you to say that j'espérais de tout mon cœur que tu dises cela; she's past praying for *(will die)* elle est perdue; the country is past praying for at this stage il n'y a plus d'espoir pour le pays à ce stade; to p. for rain prier pour qu'il pleuve; let's just p. for fine weather espérons qu'il fasse beau

VT 1 *Rel* she prayed God he might live elle pria Dieu pour qu'il vive; I prayed that they wouldn't hear me j'ai prié pour qu'ils ne m'entendent pas; I p. we are on time je prie pour que nous arrivions à l'heure 2 *Arch or Formal (request)* prier; to p. sb to do sth prier qn de faire qch; I p. you je vous (en) prie

EXCLAM *Arch or Formal* p. be seated asseyez-vous, je vous en prie; p., do tell me dites-le-moi, je vous (en) prie; *Literary or Ironic* and what, p., would you suggest I do? et que suggérerais-tu donc que je fasse?

prayer [preə(r)] N 1 *Rel* prière *f*; Morning/Evening P. office *m* du matin/du soir; to be at p. être en prière, prier; to kneel in p. prier à genoux, s'agenouiller pour prier; they believe he can be made well through p. ils croient qu'on peut le guérir par la prière; to say a p. for sb dire une prière pour qn; to say one's prayers faire sa prière; remember me in your prayers pensez à moi *ou* ne m'oubliez pas dans vos prières; her p. was granted *or* answered sa prière fut exaucée; *Fam* he doesn't have a p. il n'a pas la moindre chance *ou* l'ombre d'une chance◻ 2 *(wish)* souhait *m*; it is my earnest p. that you will succeed j'espère de tout cœur que vous réussissiez, je souhaite sincèrement que vous réussissiez

• **prayers** NPL *(at church)* office *m* (divin), prière *f*; *Br Sch* prière *f* du matin; *Parl* prière *f*

▸▸ **prayer beads** chapelet *m*; **prayer book** livre *m* de prières; **prayer mat** tapis *m* de prière; **prayer meeting** réunion *f* de prière; **prayer rug** tapis *m* de prière; **prayer shawl** talith *m*, tallith *m*; **prayer stool** prie-Dieu *m inv*; **prayer wheel** moulin *m* à prières

praying [ˈpreɪɪŋ] ADJ en prières

N prière *f*, prières *fpl*

▸▸ *Entom* **praying mantis** mante *f* religieuse

pre- [priː] PREF pré-

pre-accession N *EU* préadhésion *f*

▸▸ **pre-accession agreement** accord *m* de préadhésion; **pre-accession funding** financement *m* de préadhésion

preach [priːtʃ] VI 1 *Rel* prêcher; to p. to sb prêcher qn; *Fig* to p. to the converted prêcher un converti 2 *(lecture)* prêcher, sermonner; stop preaching at me! arrête tes sermons *ou* de me faire la leçon!

VT 1 *Rel* prêcher; to p. a sermon prêcher, faire un sermon 2 *Fig (recommend)* prêcher, prôner; to p. a new doctrine prêcher une doctrine nouvelle; she preaches austerity and lives in luxury elle prêche l'austérité mais elle vit dans le luxe

preacher [ˈpriːtʃə(r)] N *(gen)* prédicateur(trice) *m,f*, *esp Am (minister)* pasteur *m*

preachify [ˈpriːtʃɪfaɪ] *(pt & pp* preachified*)* VI *Fam Pej* faire la morale◻

preaching [ˈpriːtʃɪŋ] N *(UNCOUNT)* *(sermon)* prédication *f*, *Fam Pej (moralizing)* sermons *mpl*

preachy [ˈpriːtʃɪ] *(compar* preachier, *superl* preachiest*)* ADJ *Fam Pej* prêcheur, sermonneur

preamble [ˌpriːˈæmbəl] N 1 *Formal (to legal text)* préambule *m*; *(of book)* introduction *f*, préface *f*; *(of treaty)* préliminaires *mpl*; *(to speech)* préambule *m*, entrée *f* en matière; P. to the Constitution Préambule *m* de la Constitution des États-Unis 2 *Law (of bill)* exposé *m*

preamplifier [ˌpriːˈæmplɪfaɪə(r)] N préamplificateur *m*

prearrange [ˌpriːəˈreɪndʒ] VT fixer *ou* régler à l'avance; at a prearranged time à une heure fixée à l'avance *ou* au préalable

prebend [ˈprebənd] N *Rel* prébende *f*

prebendary [ˈprebəndərɪ] *(pl* prebendaries*)* N *Rel* prébendier *m*

prebill [ˌpriːˈbɪl] VT *Acct* préfacturer

prebilling [ˌpriːˈbɪlɪŋ] N *Acct* préfacturation *f*

pre-board VT pré-embarquer

pre-budget N *Br Parl* avant-projet *m* de budget

▸▸ **pre-budget report** rapport *m* pré-budgétaire, **pre-budget statement** = déclaration prébudgétaire ayant lieu en novembre

precancerous [ˌpriːˈkænsərəs] ADJ précancéreux

precarious [prɪˈkeərɪəs] ADJ précaire; to make a p. living gagner sa vie précairement

precariously [prɪˈkeərɪəslɪ] ADV précairement; p. balanced en équilibre précaire

precariousness [prɪˈkeərɪəsnɪs] N précarité *f*

precast [ˌpriːˈkɑːst] ADJ *(concrete)* prémoulé

precaution [prɪˈkɔːʃən] N précaution *f*, *(attitude)* prévoyance *f*; as a p. par précaution; to take precautions prendre des précautions; *(use contraceptive)* se protéger; she took the p. of informing her solicitor elle prit la précaution d'avertir son avocat; fire precautions mesures *fpl* de prévention contre l'incendie

precautionary [prɪˈkɔːʃənərɪ] ADJ de précaution; as a p. measure par mesure de précaution; to take p. measures *or* steps against sth prendre des mesures préventives contre qch

precede [prɪˈsiːd] VT 1 *(in order, time)* précéder; the conference was preceded by a reception une réception a eu lieu avant la conférence 2 *(in importance, rank)* avoir la préséance sur, prendre le pas sur 3 *(preface)* (faire) précéder

precedence [ˈpresɪdəns], **precedency** [ˈpresɪdənsɪ] N *(UNCOUNT)* 1 *(priority)* priorité *f*; this job takes p. over everything else ce travail est à faire en priorité; her health must take p. over all other considerations sa santé doit passer avant toute autre considération 2 *(in rank, status)* préséance *f*; in order of p. par ordre de préséance; to have *or* to take p. over sb avoir la préséance *ou* prendre le pas sur qn

precedent [ˈpresɪdənt] N 1 *Law* précédent *m*, jurisprudence *f*; to set a p. faire jurisprudence; there is no p. il n'y a pas de jurisprudence; to follow a p. s'appuyer sur un précédent, suivre la jurisprudence 2 *(example case)* précédent *m*; to create *or* to set *or* to establish a p. créer un précédent; without p. sans précédent 3 *(tradition)* tradition *f*; to break with p. rompre avec la tradition

preceding [prɪˈsiːdɪŋ] ADJ précédent; the p. day le jour précédent, la veille; the p. evening le soir précédent, la veille au soir; on the p. page à la page précédente; the p. week/year la semaine, l'année *f* précédente

precentor [prɪˈsentə(r)] N *Rel* préchantre *m*

precept [ˈpriːsept] N précepte *m*

pre-check-in N pré-inscription *f*

precinct [ˈpriːsɪŋkt] N 1 *(area ▸ round castle, cathedral)* enceinte *f*; (shopping) p. centre *m* commercial; (pedestrian) p. zone *f* piétonnière *ou* piétonne; within the castle precincts dans l'enceinte du château

2 *(boundary)* pourtour *m*; the question falls within the precincts of philosophy la question est du domaine *ou* relève de la philosophie

3 *Am (police district)* arrondissement *m*, circonscription *f* administrative; 7th p. 7ème arrondissement *m*

4 *Am Pol* circonscription *f* électorale

• **precincts** NPL environs *mpl*, alentours *mpl*; somewhere in the precincts quelque part dans les environs *ou* alentours

▸▸ *Am* **precinct police** police *f* de quartier *ou* d'arrondissement; *Am* **precinct station** commissariat *m* de quartier *ou* d'arrondissement

preciosity [ˌpreʃɪˈɒsətɪ] N *Formal* préciosité *f*

precious [ˈpreʃəs] ADJ 1 *(jewel, material, object)* précieux, de grande valeur; the world's most precious resources les ressources les plus précieuses de la planète

2 *(friend, friendship, moment)* précieux; **my time** s **p.** mon temps est précieux; **a few p. drops of** water quelques précieuses gouttes d'eau; **that** hoto is very p. to me je tiens beaucoup à cette hoto
3 *(affected ▸ style, person)* précieux
4 *Fam (expressing irritation)* **I don't want your p.** dvice je ne veux pas de vos fichus conseils; ere's your p. book! le voilà ton sacré livre!
ADV *Fam* très[□]; **there's p. little chance of that hap-** ening il y a bien peu *ou* très peu de chances pour) que cela se produise; **p. few of them** urned up il y en a très peu qui sont venus
N *(term of affection)* **(my) p.** mon trésor
▸ ***precious metal*** métal *m* précieux; ***precious*** ***tone*** pierre *f* précieuse

recipice ['presɪpɪs] N précipice *m*; *Fig* catas- rophe *f*; **the car fell over the p.** la voiture est tom- ée dans le précipice
▸ *Fin* ***precipice bond*** obligation *f* à très haut isque

recipitance [prɪ'sɪpɪtəns], **precipitancy** [prɪ- sɪpɪtənsɪ] N *Formal (hastiness)* précipitation *f*; **the** **. of his decision** sa précipitation à prendre une écision

recipitant [prɪ'sɪpɪtənt] ADJ *Formal (action)* récipité; *(decision, judgment)* hâtif; *(remark)* ir- éfléchi
N *Chem* précipitant *m*

recipitate VT [prɪ'sɪpɪteɪt] **1** *(downfall, ruin, cri- is)* précipiter, hâter **2** *(person, vehicle, object)* récipiter **3** *Chem* précipiter
VI [prɪ'sɪpɪteɪt] **1** *Chem* se précipiter **2** *Met* se con- lenser
N [prɪ'sɪpɪteɪt, prɪ'sɪpɪtət] *Chem* précipité *m*
ADJ [prɪ'sɪpɪtət] *Formal (hasty ▸ action)* précipité; ▸ *decision, judgement)* hâtif; (▸ *remark)* irréflé- hi; **let's not be p.** ne précipitons pas les choses

Attention: ne pas confondre avec **precipitous**.

recipitately [prɪ'sɪpɪtətlɪ] ADV *Formal* précipi- amment, avec précipitation

recipitation [prɪˌsɪpɪ'teɪʃən] N *(UNCOUNT)* **1** *ormal (haste)* précipitation *f*; **to act with p.** agir vec précipitation *ou* précipitamment **2** *Chem* récipitation *f* **3** *Met* précipitations *fpl*

recipitous [prɪ'sɪpɪtəs] ADJ **1** *(steep ▸ cliff)* à pic, scarpé; (▸ *road, stairs)* raide; (▸ *fall)* à pic **2** *hasty)* précipité

Attention: ne pas confondre avec **precipitate**.

recipitously [prɪ'sɪpɪtəslɪ] ADV **1** *(steeply)* à pic, bruptement **2** *Formal (hastily)* précipitamment

récis [*Br* 'preɪsiː, *Am* 'preɪsiː] (*pl* inv [*Br* 'preɪsiːz, *Am* resiːz]) N précis *m*, résumé *m*
VT faire un résumé de
▸ ***précis writing*** compte rendu *m* de lecture

recise [prɪ'saɪs] ADJ **1** *(exact ▸ amount, detail)* récis; (▸ *location)* exact; (▸ *pronunciation)* xact, juste; **eleven, to be p.** onze, pour être pré- is; **be more p.!** soyez plus précis!; **he was very p.** n **his description** il a donné une description très récise *ou* détaillée; **at that p. moment** à ce mo- nent précis **2** *(meticulous ▸ person, manner, nind, movement)* précis, méticuleux **3** *Pej (fussy)* ointilleux, maniaque

recisely [prɪ'saɪslɪ] ADV *(exactly ▸ explain, cost)* récisément, exactement; (▸ *describe, draw, neasure)* avec précision; **that's p. the reason why) I'm not going** c'est précisément pourquoi e n'y vais pas; **she speaks very p.** elle s'exprime vec beaucoup de précision; **at four o'clock p.** à uatre heures précises
EXCLAM précisément!, exactement!; **do you** hink it's too risky? – p.! pensez-vous que ce soit rop risqué? – tout à fait! *ou* exactement!

reciseness [prɪ'saɪsnɪs] N **1** *(exactness)* préci- ion *f* **2** *(meticulousness)* méticulosité *f* **3** *(fussi- ess)* formalisme *m*

recision [prɪ'sɪʒən] N précision *f*; **with mathe- natical p.** avec une précision (toute) mathéma- ique
COMP *(instrument, engineering, tool, bombing)* de récision

recision-engineered ADJ de haute préci- ion

precision-made ADJ de (haute) précision

preclude [prɪ'kluːd] VT *Formal* exclure, prévenir; **this rule precludes any possibility of a misunder- standing** cette règle exclut toute possibilité de malentendu; **the crisis precludes her (from) going to Moscow** la crise rend impossible son départ pour Moscou, la crise l'empêche de partir pour Moscou

precocious [prɪ'kəʊʃəs] ADJ précoce

precociously [prɪ'kəʊʃəslɪ] ADV précocement, avec précocité

precociousness [prɪ'kəʊʃəsnɪs], **precocity** [prɪ'kɒsətɪ] N précocité *f*

precognition [ˌpriːkɒg'nɪʃən] N *(gift)* pres- cience *f*, don *m* de seconde vue; *(knowledge)* connaissance *f* préalable

precombustion [ˌpriːkəm'bʌstʃən] N précom- bustion *f*

preconceive [ˌpriːkən'siːv] VT préconcevoir

preconception [ˌpriːkən'sepʃən] N préconcep- tion *f*, idée *f* préconçue; *(prejudice)* préjugé *m*; **to free oneself from all preconceptions** se libérer de toute opinion préconçue

precondition [ˌpriːkən'dɪʃən] N condition *f* préalable, condition *f* sine qua non; **a university degree is a p. for a diplomatic career** il est impos- sible de faire carrière dans la diplomatie si l'on n'a pas un diplôme universitaire
VT conditionner

pre-configured [ˌpriːkən'fɪgəd] ADJ préconfi- guré

precooked [ˌpriː'kʊkt] ADJ précuit

precursor [ˌpriː'kɜːsə(r)] N *(person)* précurseur *m*; *(invention, machine)* ancêtre *m*; *(event)* signe *m* avant-coureur *ou* précurseur; **the stock ex- change crash was a p. to worldwide recession** le krach boursier fut le signe précurseur de la ré- cession à l'échelle mondiale

precursory [ˌpriː'kɜːsərɪ] ADJ **1** *(anticipatory)* précurseur, annonciateur **2** *(introductory)* préli- minaire, préalable

precut [ˌpriː'kʌt] ADJ *(gen)* prédécoupé; *(ham, fish, bread)* prédécoupé, prétranché

predate [ˌpriː'deɪt] VT **1** *(give earlier date to ▸ cheque)* antidater; (▸ *historical event)* attribuer une date antérieure à **2** *(precede)* être antérieur à

predator ['predətə(r)] N **1** *(animal, bird)* préda- teur *m* **2** *Fig (person)* rapace *m*

predatory ['predətərɪ] ADJ **1** *(animal, bird)* pré- dateur **2** *Fig (person, instinct)* rapace; *(attacker)* pillard; **the p. world of advertising** le milieu ra- pace de la publicité
▸▸ *Mktg* ***predatory pricing*** fixation *f* de prix pré- dateurs

predecease [ˌpriːdɪ'siːs] VT prédécéder

predecessor ['priːdɪsesə(r)] N *(person, model)* prédécesseur *m*; *(event)* précédent *m*; **my (im- mediate) p. (in the job)** mon prédécesseur (à ce poste); **my new desk is much better than its p.** mon nouveau bureau est bien mieux que le pré- cédent

predestination ['priːˌdestɪ'neɪʃən] N prédesti- nation *f*

predestine [ˌpriː'destɪn] VT prédestiner; **it was as if they were predestined to lose** on aurait dit qu'ils étaient prédestinés à perdre

predetermination ['priːdɪˌtɜːmɪ'neɪʃən] N pré- détermination *f*

predetermine [ˌpriːdɪ'tɜːmɪn] VT prédétermi- ner

predetermined [ˌpriːdɪ'tɜːmɪnd] ADJ déter- miné; **at a p. date** à une date déterminée *ou* arrê- tée d'avance

predicament [prɪ'dɪkəmənt] N situation *f* diffi- cile; **to be in a p.** être dans une situation difficile; **we'll have to find some way out of this p.** il va nous falloir trouver un moyen de nous sortir de ce mauvais pas

predicate VT ['predɪkeɪt] *Formal* **1** *(state)* affir- mer **2** *(base)* **to p. one's arguments/policy on sth** fonder ses arguments/sa politique sur qch **3** *Phil* **to p. a quality of sth** attribuer une qualité à qch
N ['predɪkət] *Phil* prédicat *m*; *Gram* attribut *m*
ADJ ['predɪkət] prédicatif
▸▸ *Math* ***predicate calculus*** calcul *m* fonctionnel

predicative [prɪ'dɪkətɪv] ADJ prédicatif

predict [prɪ'dɪkt] VT prédire; **you could have pre- dicted she would be late** il était à prévoir qu'elle serait en retard; **she predicted that he would have a long life** elle a prédit qu'il vivrait longtemps; **the weathermen are predicting rain** les météoro- logues annoncent de la pluie

predictable [prɪ'dɪktəbəl] ADJ prévisible; **the outcome was p.** le résultat était prévisible; **the film was too p.** ce film était sans surprise; *Pej* **you're so p.!** avec toi au moins, on n'est jamais surpris!; **there was the p. standing ovation** comme on pouvait le prévoir, le public s'est levé pour l'ovationner/les ovationner

predictably [prɪ'dɪktəblɪ] ADV *(behave, happen)* de manière prévisible; **p., she forgot to tell him** comme on pouvait le prévoir *ou* comme on pou- vait s'y attendre, elle a oublié de le lui dire; **the evening proceeded entirely p.** la soirée s'est dé- roulée sans surprise aucune

prediction [prɪ'dɪkʃən] N *(gen)* prévision *f*; *(supernatural)* prédiction *f*

predictive [prɪ'dɪktɪv] ADJ **1** *(anticipating)* de prédiction **2** *(prophetic)* prophétique; **to be p. of sth** être annonciateur de qch
▸▸ *Tel* ***predictive texting, predictive text (input)*** écriture *f* prédictive, T9 *m*

predigested [ˌpriːdaɪ'dʒestɪd] ADJ prédigéré; *Fig (idea)* tout fait

predilection [ˌpriːdɪ'lekʃən] N prédilection *f* **(for** pour)

predispose [ˌpriːdɪs'pəʊz] VT prédisposer; **to be predisposed to do sth** être prédisposé à faire qch; **I was not predisposed in his favour** je n'étais pas prédisposé en sa faveur

predisposition ['priːˌdɪspə'zɪʃən] N prédisposi- tion *f* **(to** à)

predominance [prɪ'dɒmɪnəns], **predomi- nancy** [prɪ'dɒmɪnənsɪ] N prédominance *f*; **there is a p. of women in the profession** il y a une prédo- minance de femmes dans ce métier

predominant [prɪ'dɒmɪnənt] ADJ prédominant

predominantly [prɪ'dɒmɪnəntlɪ] ADV principa- lement; **the population is p. English-speaking** la population est majoritairement anglophone; **cars sold here are p. Italian** la plupart des voitures vendues ici sont italiennes; **a p. Jewish area** un quartier à majorité juive; **to be p. concerned with a particular problem** être essentiellement préoc- cupé par un problème particulier

predominate [prɪ'dɒmɪneɪt] VI **1** *(be greater in number)* prédominer; **males still p. over females in industry** les hommes continuent à être plus nombreux que les femmes dans l'industrie **2** *(prevail)* prédominer, prévaloir, l'emporter; **a sense of apathy predominated at the meeting** lors de la réunion, un sentiment d'apathie a prédo- miné

predominating [prɪ'dɒmɪneɪtɪŋ] ADJ prédomi- nant

pre-election ADJ préélectoral
▸▸ ***pre-election campaign*** campagne *f* préélecto- rale

preemie ['priːmɪ] N *Am Fam Obst (premature baby)* prématuré(e)[□] *m,f*

pre-eminence N prééminence *f*; **this country's sporting p.** la prééminence de ce pays sur le plan sportif; **to achieve p. in the field of ecology** obtenir une place prééminente dans le do- maine de l'écologie

pre-eminent ADJ prééminent

pre-eminently ADV essentiellement, avant tout; **the reasons are p. economic** les raisons sont avant tout économiques

pre-empt [-'empt] VT **1** *(plan, decision)* antici- per, devancer; *(person)* devancer **2** *Law (land, property)* acquérir par (droit de) préemption
VI *Cards (in bridge)* faire une annonce de bar- rage

pre-emption [-'empʃən] N *Law* préemption *f*

pre-emptive [-'emptɪv] ADJ **1** *Law (right)* de préemption **2** *Mil (attack, war)* préventif

►► *Cards* ***pre-emptive bid*** *(in bridge)* annonce *f* de barrage; *Mil* ***pre-emptive strike*** attaque *f* préemptive

preen [pri:n] **VT 1** *(plumage)* lisser; **the bird was preening its feathers** *or* **was preening itself** l'oiseau se lissait les plumes; *Fig* **to p. oneself** *(person)* se faire beau, se pomponner **2** *(pride)* **to p. oneself on sth** s'enorgueillir de qch

pre-establish VT préétablir

pre-established ADJ préétabli

pre-exist VT préexister

pre-existence N préexistence *f*

pre-existent, pre-existing ADJ préexistant

prefab ['pri:fæb] **N** *Fam* (bâtiment *m*) préfabriqué□*m*; **they live in a p.** ils habitent une maison préfabriquée

prefabricate [ˌpri:'fæbrɪkeɪt] **VT** préfabriquer

preface ['prefɪs] **N 1** *(to text)* préface *f*, avant-propos *m inv*; *(to speech)* introduction *f*, préambule *m* **2** *Rel* préface *f*

VT *(book)* préfacer; *(speech)* faire précéder; **she has prefaced the book with a reply to her critics** la préface de son livre est une réponse à ses critiques; **he usually prefaces his speeches with a joke** d'habitude, il commence ses discours par une histoire drôle

prefade ['pri:feɪd] **N** *TV & Cin* pré-fondu *m*

prefaded [ˌpri:'feɪdɪd] **ADJ** *(fabric)* délavé

prefatory ['prefətərɪ] **ADJ** *(remarks)* préliminaire, préalable; *(note)* liminaire; *(page)* de préface

prefect ['pri:fekt] **N 1** *Sch* = élève chargé de la discipline **2** *Admin (in France, Italy etc)* préfet *m*

prefectship ['pri:fektʃɪp] **N** *Sch* = responsabilité de maintenir la discipline, attribuée à un ou une élève des grandes classes

prefecture ['pri:fekˌtjʊə(r)] **N** *Admin* préfecture *f*

prefer [prɪ'fɜ:(r)] **VT 1** *(like better)* préférer, aimer mieux; **to p. sth to sth** préférer qch à qch, aimer mieux qch que qch; **which would you p., wine or beer?** tu préfères du vin ou de la bière?; **she prefers living** *or* **to live alone** elle préfère vivre seule; **he prefers to walk rather than take the bus** il préfère marcher plutôt que prendre le bus; **I much p. his first movie** je préfère de loin *ou* de beaucoup son premier film; **many people p. watching TV to going out** *or* **rather than going out** beaucoup de gens préfèrent regarder la télévision plutôt que de sortir; **do you mind if I smoke? – I'd p. (it) if you didn't** cela vous dérange si je fume? – j'aimerais mieux que vous ne le fassiez pas; **I'd p. you not to go, I would p. it if you didn't go** je préférerais que vous n'y alliez pas

2 *Law* **to p. charges against sb** *(civil action)* porter plainte contre qn; *(police action)* ≃ déférer qn au parquet

3 *Fin (creditor)* privilégier

4 *Formal (appoint)* nommer, élever

preferable ['prefərəbəl] **ADJ** préférable; **it is p. to book seats** il est préférable de *ou* il vaut mieux retenir des places

preferably ['prefərəblɪ] **ADV** de préférence, préférablement; **come tomorrow, p. in the evening** venez demain, de préférence dans la soirée; **would you like to make the presentations? – p. not** voudriez-vous faire les présentations? – je n'y tiens pas

preference ['prefərəns] **N 1** *(liking)* préférence *f*; **what is your p.?** que préférez-vous?; **this is my p.** voilà celui que je préfère; **to have** *or* **to show a p. for sth** avoir une préférence pour qch; **his p. is for Mozart** il préfère Mozart; **women will be given p.** les femmes auront la préférence; **in order of p.** par ordre de préférence; **he chose the first candidate in p. to the second** il a choisi le premier candidat plutôt que le second; **to express a p.** se prononcer

2 *(priority)* préférence *f*, priorité *f*; **to have** *or* **to be given p. over** avoir la priorité sur

3 *Econ* tarif *m ou* régime *m* de faveur; *(preferential treatment)* traitement *m* préférentiel *ou* de faveur; **imports entitled to p.** importations *fpl* bénéficiant d'un régime de faveur

4 *St Exch* droit *m* de priorité

►► *Br St Exch* ***preference dividend*** dividende *m* privilégié *ou* prioritaire; *Br St Exch* ***preference share*** action *f* privilégiée *ou* de priorité

preferential [ˌprefə'renʃəl] **ADJ** *(treatment, rate)* préférentiel, de faveur; **to get p. treatment** *(of person)* bénéficier d'un traitement préférentiel *ou* de faveur

►► *Law* ***preferential claim*** privilège *m*; *Fin* ***preferential creditor*** créancier(ère) *m,f* privilégié(e); *Fin* ***preferential dividend*** dividende *m* privilégié *ou* de priorité; *Customs* ***preferential duty*** préférences *fpl* douanières; *Com* ***preferential price*** prix *m* de faveur *ou* préférentiel; *Fin* ***preferential rate*** tarif *m* préférentiel; *Law* ***preferential right*** privilège *m*; *Pol* ***preferential voting*** vote *m* préférentiel

preferment [prɪ'fɜ:mənt] **N** *(gen) & Rel* avancement *m*, promotion *f*

preferred [prɪ'fɜ:d] **ADJ** préféré

►► *Fin* ***preferred creditor*** créancier(ère) *m,f* privilégié; *Fin* ***preferred debt*** dette *f ou* créance *f* privilégiée; *Am St Exch* ***preferred stock*** *(UNCOUNT)* actions *fpl* privilégiées *ou* de priorité

prefiguration [ˌpri:ˌfɪgə'reɪʃən] **N** préfiguration *f*

prefigure [ˌpri:'fɪgə(r)] **VT** *(foreshadow)* préfigurer

pre-financing N *Acct* préfinancement *m*

prefix ['pri:fɪks] **N** préfixe *m*; *(before name)* particule *f*; *(title)* titre *m*

VT préfixer; **to p. sth to sth** faire précéder qch de qch; **compounds prefixed with the word mega-** les composés commençant par le mot méga-; **telephone numbers prefixed with the code 0800** les numéros de téléphone commençant par le code 0800

preflight ['pri:flaɪt] **ADJ** préalable au décollage

►► ***preflight checks*** vérifications *fpl* avant décollage

preformatted [ˌpri:'fɔ:mætɪd] **ADJ** *Comput (disk)* préformaté

prefrontal [ˌpri:'frʌntəl] **ADJ** *Anat* préfrontal

preggers ['pregəz] **ADJ** *Fam (pregnant)* en cloque

pregnancy ['pregnənsɪ] *(pl* **pregnancies)** **N** *(of woman)* grossesse *f*; *(of animal)* gestation *f*

►► ***pregnancy test*** test *m* de grossesse

pregnant ['pregnənt] **ADJ 1** *(woman)* enceinte; *(animal)* pleine, grosse; **to get** *or* **to become p.** tomber enceinte; **to get a woman p.** faire un enfant à une femme; **to be six months p.** être enceinte de six mois; **she was p. with Kyle then** à cette époque, elle attendait Kyle **2** *Literary (pause, silence)* lourd *ou* chargé de sens; **p. with meaning/tension** chargé de sens/tension; **p. with possibilities** riche de possibilités

preheat [ˌpri:'hi:t] **VT** préchauffer

preheated [ˌpri:'hi:tɪd] **ADJ** préchauffé

prehensile [ˌprɪ'hensaɪl] **ADJ** *Zool* préhensile

prehistoric [ˌpri:hɪ'stɒrɪk] **ADJ** *also Fig* préhistorique

prehistory [ˌpri:'hɪstərɪ] **N** préhistoire *f*

pre-ignition N *Aut* préallumage *m*

pre-implantation ADJ *Biol & Med* préimplantatoire

►► *Med* ***pre-implantation genetic diagnosis*** diagnostic *m* génétique préimplantatoire

pre-installed ADJ *Comput (software)* préinstallé

pre-inventory balance N *Acct* balance *f* avant inventaire

prejudge [ˌpri:'dʒʌdʒ] **VT** *(issue, topic)* préjuger de; *(person)* porter un jugement prématuré sur

prejudice ['predʒʊdɪs] **N 1** *(bias)* préjugé *m*; **to have a p. in favour of/against** avoir un préjugé en faveur de/contre; **he's full of/without p.** il est plein de/sans préjugés; **racial p.** préjugés *mpl* raciaux, racisme *m* **2** *Formal (harm)* préjudice *m*, tort *m*; **to the p. of sb's rights** au préjudice *ou* au détriment des droits de qn; *Law* **without p. to your guarantee** sans préjudice de votre garantie

VT 1 *(bias* ► *person, outcome, decision)* influencer; **to p. sb against/in favour of sth** prévenir qn contre/en faveur de qch **2** *(harm* ► *reputation etc)* nuire à, faire du tort à, porter préjudice à; *(*► *interests)* nuire à; **without prejudicing my righ** sans préjudice de mes droits

> Note that the French word **préjudice** neve means **bias.**

prejudiced ['predʒʊdɪst] **ADJ** *(person)* qui a de préjugés *ou* des idées préconçues; *(idea, opi ion)* partial, préconçu; **to be p. against sth** avo des préjugés contre qch; **let's not be p. about th** essayons de ne pas avoir d'idées préconçues l dessus; **her politics are p.** ses idées politique sont fondées sur des préjugés

prejudicial [ˌpredʒʊ'dɪʃəl] **ADJ** préjudiciabl nuisible (**to** à); **this decision is p. to world pea** cette décision risque de compromettre la pa mondiale

prelacy ['preləsɪ] *(pl* **prelacies)** **N 1** *(office)* prél ture *f* **2** *(prelates generally)* **the p.** les prélats *mp*

prelate ['prelɪt] **N** *Rel* prélat *m*

prelim ['pri:lɪm] **N** (*abbr* **preliminary exam**) *Un* examen *m* préliminaire; *Scot Sch* examen blanc

• **prelims NPL** *Typ* (*abbr* **preliminary pages**) page *fpl* liminaires *(précédant le corps de l'ouvrage)*

preliminary [prɪ'lɪmɪnərɪ] *(pl* **preliminaries)** **A** préliminaire, préalable; **after a few p. remar** après quelques remarques préliminaires; **th p. stages of the inquiry** les étapes préliminair *ou* les débuts de l'enquête

N 1 *(gen)* préliminaire *m*; **to go through all th preliminaries** passer par tous les préliminaire **as a p.** en guise de préliminaire, au préalabl **the measure is seen by many as a p. to...** cette m sure est considérée par beaucoup comme ur action préliminaire à… **2** *(eliminating contes* épreuve *f* éliminatoire

►► ***preliminary contract*** avant-contrat *m*; ***pre minary exam*** *Univ* examen *m* préliminaire; *Sc Sch* examen *m* blanc; *Law* ***preliminary hearir*** première audience *f*; *Law* ***preliminary investig tion*** instruction *f* (d'une affaire); *Typ* ***prelimina pages*** pages *fpl* liminaires *(précédant le corps c l'ouvrage)*

preloaded [ˌpri:'ləʊdɪd] **ADJ** *Comput* précharg

prelude ['prelju:d] **N** *(gen) & Mus* prélude *m* (**to**

VT préluder à

premarital [ˌpri:'mærɪtəl] **ADJ** prénuptial, ava le mariage

►► ***premarital sex*** rapports *mpl* sexuels avant mariage

pre-marketing N *Mktg* précommercialis tion *f*, prémarketing *m*

premature ['preməˌtjʊə(r)] **ADJ 1** *(birth, chil* prématuré, avant terme; **three months p.** né tro mois avant terme, prématuré de trois mois *(death, decision, judgment)* prématuré; *(bal ness, senility, ejaculation)* précoce; **you're bei a bit p.!** tu vas trop vite!; **it was a bit p. of hi** c'était un peu prématuré de sa part

prematurely ['preməˌtjʊəlɪ] **ADV** prématur ment; **he was born p.** il est né avant terme; **to b p. senile/bald** souffrir de sénilité/calvitie pr coce

premed ['pri:ˌmed] *Fam Med* **ADJ** ≃ de premiè année de médecine

N 1 *(medication)* prémédication□*f* **2** *(student)* étudiant(e) *m,f* en première année de médecir **3** *(studies)* ≃ études *fpl* de première année c médecine

premedicate [pri:'medɪkeɪt] **VT** *Med* préméd quer

premedication [ˌpri:ˌmedɪ'keɪʃən] **N** *Med* pr médication *f*

premeditate [ˌpri:'medɪteɪt] **VT** préméditer

premeditated [ˌpri:'medɪteɪtɪd] **ADJ** prémédit

►► ***premeditated murder*** meurtre *m* avec prém ditation

premeditation ['pri:ˌmedɪ'teɪʃən] **N** prémédit tion *f*; **without p.** sans préméditation

premenstrual [ˌpri:'menstruəl] **ADJ** prémen truel; **I think she's feeling p.** je crois que ses r gles ne vont pas tarder à arriver

►► *Am* ***premenstrual syndrome***, *Br* ***premenstru tension*** syndrome *m* prémenstruel

premier ['premjə(r)] **ADJ 1** *(earliest)* premier **2** *(most important)* **this is our p. product** c'est notre produit haut de gamme
N Premier ministre *m*
▸▸ *Ftbl* ***Premier Division*** = première division du football professionnel écossais; ***Premier League*** *(in Scotland)* = première division du football professionnel écossais; *(in England)* = ancienne appellation de la première division du football professionnel anglais

premiere ['premɪeə(r)] **N** *Cin & Theat* première *f*; **the film's London/television p.** la première londonienne/télévisée du film
VT donner la première de; **the play was premiered in Paris** la première de la pièce a eu lieu à Paris
VI the play premiered in New York la première de la pièce a eu lieu à New York

premiership ['premjəʃɪp] **N** poste *m* de Premier ministre; **to be elected to the p.** être élu Premier ministre; **during her p.** alors qu'elle était Premier ministre; **he had a successful p.** il a rempli son mandat de Premier ministre avec succès
• **Premiership N the P.** = première division du football professionnel anglais

premillennial [ˌpri:mɪ'lenɪəl] **ADJ 1** *Rel* d'avant le millénium **2** *(preceding the millennium)* qui précède le passage à un nouveau millénaire

premise ['premɪs] **N** *(hypothesis)* prémisse *f*; **on the p. that...** en partant du principe que...
VT *Formal* **to p. that...** poser en principe que...; *(in logic)* poser en prémisse que...; **to be premised on sth** être basé *ou* fondé sur qch

premises ['premɪsɪz] **NPL 1** *(place)* locaux *mpl*, lieux *mpl*; **business p.** locaux *mpl* commerciaux; **on the p.** sur les lieux, sur place; **she's still on the p.** elle est encore dans le bâtiment **2** *Law* préalable *m*

> Note that the French word **prémices** is a false friend and never refers to a location.

premiss = **premise**

premium ['pri:mɪəm] **N 1** *(insurance payment)* prime *f* (d'assurance); **to pay an additional p.** payer une surprime **2** *(additional sum* ▸ *on price)* supplément *m*; *(*▸ *on salary)* prime *f*; *St Exch* **to pay a p.** verser *ou* acquitter un premium; **to issue shares at a p.** émettre des actions au-dessus du pair *ou* de leur valeur nominale; **to sell sth at a p.** vendre qch à prime *ou* à bénéfice; **antiques are at a p.** *(are sought after)* les antiquités sont très recherchées; *(sell at high prices)* les antiquités se vendent à prix d'or; **time is at a p.** le temps presse; **her time is at a p.** son temps est précieux; **good translators are at a p.** les bons traducteurs ne courent pas les rues *ou* sont rares; *Fig* **to put** *or* **place a p. on sth** *(of people, government etc)* accorder beaucoup d'importance à qch; *(of circumstances, nature of work etc)* mettre l'accent sur qch **3** *Am (fuel)* supercarburant *m*
▸▸ *Br* ***premium bonds*** obligations *fpl* à lots; *Com* ***premium price*** prix *m* de prestige; *Mktg* ***premium product*** produit *m* de prestige; ***premium quality*** qualité *f* extra; *Tel* ***premium rate*** tarif *m* surtaxé; *Com* ***premium rebate*** ristourne *f* de prime; *Mktg* ***premium selling*** vente *f* avec prime; *Mktg* ***premium service*** service *m* premier

premium-rate ADJ *Tel (call)* vers un numéro surtaxé; *(number)* surtaxé

premolar [ˌpri:'məʊlə(r)] **N** *Anat* prémolaire *f*
▸▸ ***premolar tooth*** prémolaire *f*

premonition [ˌpremə'nɪʃən] **N** prémonition *f*, pressentiment *m*; **to have a p. of sth** pressentir qch, avoir le pressentiment de qch; **I had a p. he wouldn't come** j'avais le pressentiment qu'il ne viendrait pas

premonitory [prɪ'mɒnɪtərɪ] **ADJ** prémonitoire

prenatal [ˌpri:'neɪtəl] **ADJ** prénatal

prenup ['pri:nʌp] **N** *Fam* contrat *m* de mariage▫

prenuptial [ˌpri:'nʌpʃəl] **ADJ** prénuptial
▸▸ ***prenuptial agreement*** contrat *m* de mariage

preoccupation [pri:ˌɒkjʊ'peɪʃən] **N** préoccupation *f*; **to have a p. with sth** être préoccupé par qch; **I don't understand his p. with physical fitness** je ne comprends pas qu'il soit si préoccupé par sa forme physique

preoccupied [ˌpri:'ɒkjʊpaɪd] **ADJ** préoccupé; **to be p. by** *or* **with sth** être préoccupé par qch; **he seems p. with the idea** il semble que cette idée le préoccupe

preoccupy [ˌpri:'ɒkjʊpaɪ] *(pt & pp* **preoccupied***)* **VT** préoccuper

preordain [ˌpri:ɔ:'deɪn] **VT** *(destine)* prédéterminer; **she felt preordained to be a missionary** elle se sentait prédestinée à devenir missionnaire; **our defeat was preordained** il était dit que nous perdrions

prep [prep] *Fam* **N** *(UNCOUNT) Br* **1** *(homework)* devoirs▫*mpl* **2** *(study period)* étude▫*f (après les cours)*
VT *Am* préparer▫; *Med* **to p. sb for an operation** préparer qn pour une opération
VI *Am* = faire ses études dans un établissement privé
▸▸ ***prep period*** (heure *f* de) permanence▫*f*; ***prep room*** (salle *f* d')étude▫*f*; ***prep school*** *(in UK)* école *f* primaire privée▫*(pour enfants de sept à treize ans, préparant généralement à entrer dans une "public school")*; *(in US)* = école privée qui prépare à l'enseignement supérieur

pre-pack, pre-package VT préemballer, préconditionner; **the fruit is all pre-packed** les fruits sont entièrement conditionnés

prepaid [ˌpri:'peɪd] *pt & pp of* **prepay**
ADJ ['pri:peɪd] prépayé; *Acct* payé (d'avance), constaté d'avance
▸▸ ***prepaid card*** carte *f* prépayée; ***prepaid envelope*** enveloppe *f* affranchie; ***prepaid income*** produit *m* constaté d'avance; ***prepaid reply*** réponse *f* payée

preparation [ˌprepə'reɪʃən] **N 1** *(UNCOUNT) (gen)* préparation *f*; *(of plane, car etc)* mise *f* en état; **to be in p.** être en préparation; **in p. for publication** en vue d'une publication; **in p. for Christmas** pour préparer Noël; **as a p. for public life** pour préparer à la vie publique **2** *Chem & Pharm* préparation *f*; **to make up a p.** faire une préparation **3** *(UNCOUNT) Br Sch (homework)* devoirs *mpl*; *(study period)* étude *f (après les cours)*
• **preparations NPL** *(arrangements)* préparatifs *mpl*, dispositions *fpl*; **preparations for war** préparatifs *mpl* de guerre; **she attended to the wedding preparations** elle s'est occupée des préparatifs du mariage; **to make preparations for sth** faire des préparatifs en vue de qch

> When translating the English word **preparation**, note that the French words **préparatifs** and **préparation** are not interchangeable.

preparatory [prɪ'pærətərɪ] **ADJ** *(work)* préparatoire; *(measure)* préalable, préliminaire; **the report is still at the p. stage** le rapport en est encore au stade préliminaire *ou* préparatoire; *Formal* **p. to the launch** avant le lancement; *Formal* **p. to travelling abroad** avant de partir en voyage à l'étranger
▸▸ ***preparatory school*** *(in UK)* école *f* primaire privée *(pour enfants de sept à treize ans, préparant généralement à entrer dans une "public school")*; *(in US)* = école privée qui prépare à l'enseignement supérieur

prepare [prɪ'peə(r)] **VT** *(plan, food, lesson, person)* préparer; *(attack)* monter, préparer; *(plane, car)* mettre en état; **to p. a meal for sb** préparer un repas à *ou* pour qn; **to p. a surprise for sb** préparer une surprise à qn; **we are preparing to leave tomorrow** nous nous préparons à partir demain; **she's preparing them for the exam** elle les prépare à l'examen; **to p. oneself for sth** se préparer à qch; **p. yourself for a surprise** attendez-vous à une surprise; **p. yourself for the worst** préparez-vous *ou* attendez-vous au pire; **you'd better p. yourself for some bad news** préparez-vous à recevoir de mauvaises nouvelles; **their training had prepared them for most eventualities** leur entraînement les avait préparés à presque toutes les éventualités; **prepared from the finest ingredients** préparé avec les meilleurs ingrédients
VI to p. for sth faire des préparatifs en vue de *ou* se préparer à qch; **to p. to do sth** se préparer *ou* s'apprêter à faire qch; **to p. for departure** faire des préparatifs en vue d'un départ, se préparer à partir; **the country is preparing for war** le pays se prépare à la guerre; **to p. for a meeting/an exam** préparer une réunion/un examen; **p. for the worst!** préparez-vous au pire!

prepared [prɪ'peəd] **ADJ 1** *(ready* ▸ *gen)* préparé, prêt; *(*▸ *answer, excuse)* tout prêt; **to be p. for anything** être prêt à tout; **be p.** *(Scouts' motto)* toujours prêt; **I was p. to leave** j'étais préparé *ou* prêt à partir; **he wasn't p. for what he saw** *(hadn't expected)* il ne s'attendait pas à ce spectacle; *(was shocked)* il n'était pas préparé à voir cela; **a p. statement** une déclaration préparée à l'avance; **p. timber** bois *m* refait **2** *(willing)* prêt, disposé; **I am p. to cooperate** je suis prêt *ou* disposé à coopérer; **he was not p. to lie** il n'était pas disposé à mentir

preparedness [prɪ'peədnɪs] **N** état *m* de préparation; **p. for war** préparation *f* à la guerre; **I am unsure of their p. to deal with such an eventuality** je doute qu'ils soient prêts à faire face à une telle éventualité

prepay [ˌpri:'peɪ] *(pt & pp* **prepaid** [-'peɪd]*)* **VT** payer d'avance

prepayment [ˌpri:'peɪmənt] **N** paiement *m* d'avance, paiement *m* préalable; *Acct* charge *f* constatée d'avance
▸▸ *Fin* ***prepayment penalty*** indemnité *f* de remboursement par anticipation

preponderance [prɪ'pɒndərəns] **N** *(in importance)* prépondérance *f*; *(in number)* supériorité *f* numérique; **there was a p. of boys in the science subjects** les garçons étaient majoritaires dans les disciplines scientifiques

preponderant [prɪ'pɒndərənt] **ADJ** prépondérant; **boys tend to be p.** il tend à y avoir une majorité de garçons

preponderantly [prɪ'pɒndərəntlɪ] **ADV** *(in importance)* de façon prépondérante; *(especially)* surtout; **the guests were p. French** les invités étaient pour la majeure partie français

preponderate [prɪ'pɒndəreɪt] **VI** être prépondérant, prédominer; **to p. over sth** l'emporter sur qch

preposition [ˌprepə'zɪʃən] **N** *Gram* préposition *f*

prepositional [ˌprepə'zɪʃənəl] **ADJ** *Gram* prépositionnel
▸▸ ***prepositional phrase*** locution *f* prépositive

prepositionally [ˌprepə'zɪʃənəlɪ] **ADV** *Gram* prépositivement

prepossess [ˌpri:pə'zes] **VT** *Formal* **1** *(engross)* préoccuper **2** *(influence)* influencer

prepossessing [ˌpri:pə'zesɪŋ] **ADJ** *(person)* avenant; *(smile, behaviour)* avenant, engageant; **a most p. young man** un jeune homme très présentable

preposterous [prɪ'pɒstərəs] **ADJ** absurde, grotesque; **that's a p. lie!** c'est complètement absurde *ou* grotesque!

preposterously [prɪ'pɒstərəslɪ] **ADV** absurdement, ridiculement; **it was p. easy** ça a été un jeu d'enfant

preposterousness [prɪ'pɒstərəsnɪs] **N** absurdité *f*

preppie, preppy ['prepɪ] *(pl* **preppies**, *compar* **preppier**, *superl* **preppiest***)* *Am Fam* **N** BCBG *mf inv*
ADJ BCBG *(inv)*

pre-press N *Typ* prépresse *m*

pre-printed form N pré-imprimé *m*

preproduction [ˌpri:prə'dʌkʃən] **N** *TV & Cin* préproduction *f*; **the movie is in p.** le film est en préproduction

preprogram [ˌpri:'prəʊgræm] *(pt & pp* **preprogrammed**, *cont* **preprogamming***)* **VT** *Comput* préprogrammer; *Fig* **humans are preprogrammed to behave in certain ways** les êtres humains sont conditionnés à se comporter d'une certaine façon

preprogrammed [ˌpri:'prəʊgræmd] **ADJ** *Comput* préprogrammé

prepubescent [ˌpri:pju:'besənt] **ADJ** prépubère; *Fig Pej (immature)* puéril

prepublication [ˌpri:pʌblɪ'keɪʃən] **N** prépublication *f*

prepuce ['pri:ˌpju:s] **N** *Anat* prépuce *m*

prequel ['pri:kwəl] **N** = film qui reprend les thèmes et les personnages d'un film réalisé précédemment, mais dont l'action est antérieure

Pre-Raphaelite [,pri:'ræfəlaɪt] *Art* **ADJ** préraphaélite
N préraphaélite *mf*

prerecord [,pri:rɪ'kɔ:d] **VT** préenregistrer

prerecording [,pri:rɪ'kɔ:dɪŋ] **N** préenregistrement *m*; *TV & Rad* (émission *f* en) différé *m*

preregistration [,pri:redʒɪ'streɪʃən] **N** *Univ* préinscription *f*

prerelease [,pri:rɪ'li:s] **N** *(of film)* avant-première *f*; *(of record)* sortie *f* précommerciale

prerequisite [,pri:'rekwɪzɪt] **N** (condition *f*) préalable *m*, condition *f* sine qua non; **to be a p. for** *or* **of sth** être une condition préalable à qch; **a knowledge of foreign languages is not a p.** la connaissance de langues étrangères n'est pas indispensable
ADJ préalablement nécessaire, indispensable; **p. condition** condition *f* préalable

prerogative [prɪ'rɒgətɪv] **N** prérogative *f*, apanage *m*; **the royal p.** la prérogative royale; **to exercise one's p.** exercer ses prérogatives; **it's a woman's p. to be late** les femmes ont le droit d'être en retard

Pres. *(written abbr* **president***)* président *m*

presage ['presɪdʒ] *Literary* **N** *(sign)* présage *m*; *(foreboding)* pressentiment *m*; **to have a p. of doom** pressentir un malheur
VT présager, annoncer

Presbyterian [,prezbɪ'tɪərɪən] *Rel* **N** presbytérien(enne) *m,f*
ADJ presbytérien

Presbyterianism [,prezbɪ'tɪərɪənɪzəm] **N** *Rel* presbytérianisme *m*

presbytery ['prezbɪtrɪ] **N 1** *(residence)* presbytère *m* **2** *(court)* consistoire *m* **3** *(part of church)* presbyterium *m*

preschool [,pri:'sku:l] **ADJ** *(playgroup, age)* préscolaire; *(child)* d'âge préscolaire
N *Am* école *f* maternelle

prescience ['presɪəns] **N** *Formal* prescience *f*

prescient ['presɪənt] **ADJ** *Formal* prescient

prescribe [prɪ'skraɪb] **VT 1** *Med* prescrire; **to p. sth for sb** prescrire qch à qn; **the doctor prescribed her a month's rest** le médecin lui a prescrit un mois de repos; **what can you p. for migraine?** que prescrivez-vous contre la migraine?; **do not exceed the prescribed dose** *(on packaging)* ne pas dépasser la dose prescrite
2 *(advocate)* préconiser, recommander; **what cure would you p. for the current economic problems?** quelles mesures préconiseriez-vous pour remédier aux problèmes économiques actuels?
3 *(set ▸ punishment)* infliger; *Br Sch & Univ (▸ books)* inscrire au programme; **in the prescribed time** dans le délai prescrit
4 *Law* prescrire

prescription [prɪ'skrɪpʃən] **N 1** *Med* ordonnance *f*; **the doctor wrote out a p. for her** le médecin lui a rédigé *ou* fait une ordonnance; **to make up a p. for sb** exécuter *ou* préparer une ordonnance pour qn; **I'll give you a p. for some antibiotics** je vais vous prescrire des antibiotiques; **to get sth on p.** obtenir qch sur ordonnance; **available** *or* **obtainable only on p.** délivré seulement sur ordonnance **2** *(recommendation)* prescription *f*; **what's your p. for a happy life?** quelle est votre recette du bonheur?
▸▸ *Br* ***prescription charge*** = partie du coût des médicaments délivrés sur ordonnance qui est à la charge du patient; ***prescription drug*** = médicament délivré seulement sur ordonnance

prescriptive [prɪ'skrɪptɪv] **ADJ 1** *Ling (grammar, rule)* normatif **2** *(dogmatic)* dogmatique, strict **3** *(customary)* consacré par l'usage
▸▸ *Law* ***prescriptive right*** droit *m* consacré par l'usage

prescriptivism [prɪ'skrɪptɪvɪzəm] **N** normativisme *m*

preselect [,pri:sə'lekt] **VT** *(tracks, channels)* présélectionner

pre-selector **N** *Aut* présélecteur *m*
▸▸ ***pre-selector gearbox*** boîte *f* à présélection

presence ['prezəns] **N 1** *(gen)* présence *f*; **in the p. of sb** en présence de qn; **it happened in my p.** cela s'est passé en ma présence; **don't say anything about it in his p.** n'en parlez pas devant lui; **your p. is requested at Saturday's meeting** vous êtes prié d'assister à la réunion de samedi; *Formal* **to be admitted to the p. of sb** être admis en présence de qn; **to show/to have great p. of mind** faire preuve d'une/avoir une grande présence d'esprit; **to have the p. of mind to do sth** avoir la présence d'esprit de faire qch
2 *(number of people present)* présence *f*; **there was a large student/police p. at the demonstration** il y avait un nombre important d'étudiants/un important service d'ordre à la manifestation; **the police maintained a discreet p.** la police a assuré une surveillance discrète; **America has maintained a strong military p. in the area** l'Amérique a maintenu une forte présence militaire dans la région
3 *(personality, magnetism)* présence *f*; **she has great stage p.** elle a beaucoup de présence sur scène; **to make one's p. felt** se faire remarquer, faire sentir sa présence
4 *(entity)* présence *f*; **I could sense a p. in the room** je sentais comme une présence dans la pièce

presenile dementia [,pri:'si:naɪl-] **N** *Med* démence *f* présénile

PRESENT

N	
• cadeau **1**	• présent **2, 3**
ADJ	
• présent **1**	• actuel **2**
VT	
• donner **1, 3**	• remettre **1**
• présenter **2, 3–8, 10**	
VI	
• se présenter **1**	• consulter le médecin **2**
• se manifester **3**	

N ['prezənt] **1** *(gift)* cadeau *m*; **to give sb a p.** faire un cadeau à qn; **we gave her a pony as a p.** nous lui avons offert un *ou* fait cadeau d'un poney; **to make sb a p. of sth** faire cadeau de qch à qn; **it's for a p.** *(in shop)* c'est pour offrir
2 *(in time)* présent *m*; **at p.** actuellement, à présent; **that's all I can tell you at p.** c'est tout ce que je peux vous dire pour l'instant *ou* pour le moment; **as things are at p.** *(at this stage)* au point où en sont les choses; *(nowadays)* par les temps qui courent; **up to the p.** jusqu'à présent, jusqu'à maintenant; **that's enough for the p.** ça suffit pour le moment *ou* pour l'instant; **to live only in** *or* **for the p.** vivre pour l'instant présent *ou* au présent; **(there's) no time like the p.!** il ne faut pas remettre au lendemain ce qu'on peut faire le jour même!
3 *Gram* présent *m*; **in the p.** au présent
4 *Law* **by these presents** par les présentes
ADJ ['prezənt] **1** *(in attendance)* présent; **to be p. at a meeting** être présent à *ou* assister à une réunion; **how many were p.?** combien de personnes étaient là *ou* étaient présentes?; **those p. were very moved** les personnes présentes étaient très émues, l'assistance était très émue; **he cannot be interviewed without a lawyer being p.** on ne peut pas l'interroger sans la présence d'un avocat; **p. company excepted** à l'exception des personnes présentes
2 *(current ▸ job, government, price)* actuel; **in the p. case** dans le cas présent; **at the p. time** actuellement, à l'époque actuelle; **up to the p. day** jusqu'à présent, jusqu'à aujourd'hui; **the p. year** l'année *f* en cours; *Fin* l'année *f* courante; **given the p. circumstances** étant donné les circonstances actuelles, dans l'état actuel des choses; **in the p. writer's opinion** de l'avis de l'auteur de ces lignes
3 *Gram* au présent
VT [prɪ'zent] **1** *(gift)* donner, offrir; *(prize)* remettre, décerner; *(medal, diploma)* remettre; **to p. sth to sb** *or* **sb with sth** donner *ou* offrir qch à qn; **they presented him with a clock** ils lui ont offert une *ou* fait cadeau d'une pendule; **he presented his collection to the museum** il a fait cadeau de sa collection au musée; **the singer was presented with a bunch of flowers** la chanteuse s'est vu offrir *ou* remettre un bouquet de fleurs; **who is going to p. the prizes?** qui va procéder à la remise des prix?; **she was presented with first prize** on lui a décerné le premier prix; **the project presents us with a formidable challenge** le projet constitue pour nous un formidable défi; **he presented us with a fait accompli** il nous a mis devant le fait accompli; **they were presented with an empty goalmouth** ils se trouvèrent devant un but vide; **this presented her with no option but to agree** ceci ne lui a pas laissé d'autre alternative que d'accepter; *Fig* **to p. sb with an easy target** offrir une bonne cible à qn; **she presented him with a daughter** elle lui a donné une fille
2 *Formal (introduce)* présenter; **to p. sb to sb** présenter qn à qn; **allow me to p. Mr Jones** permettez-moi de vous présenter M. Jones; **to be presented at Court** être présenté à la Cour
3 *(put on ▸ play, film)* donner; *(▸ exhibition)* présenter, monter
4 *Rad & TV* présenter; **the programme was presented by Ian King** l'émission était présentée par Ian King
5 *(offer ▸ entertainment)* présenter; **we proudly p. Donna Stewart** nous avons le plaisir *ou* nous sommes heureux de vous présenter Donna Stewart; **presenting Vanessa Brown in the title role** avec Vanessa Brown dans le rôle principal
6 *(put forward ▸ apology, view, report)* présenter; *(▸ plan)* soumettre; *(orally)* exposer; **the essay is well presented** la dissertation est bien présentée; **I wish to p. my complaint in person** je tiens à déposer plainte moi-même; **to p. a bill in Parliament** présenter *ou* introduire un projet de loi au Parlement; *Law* **to p. a plea** introduire une instance
7 *(pose, offer ▸ problem, difficulty)* présenter, poser; *(▸ chance, view)* offrir; **if the opportunity presents itself** si l'occasion se présente; **a strange idea presented itself to her** une idée étrange lui est venue; **to p. sb/sth in a good/bad light** présenter qn/qch sous un jour favorable/défavorable
8 *(show ▸ passport, ticket)* présenter; **you must p. proof of ownership** vous devez présenter un certificat de propriété *ou* prouver que cela vous appartient; *Mil* **p. arms!** présentez armes!
9 *(arrive, go)* **to p. oneself** se présenter; **to p. oneself at** *or* **for an examination** se présenter à *ou* pour un examen
10 *Com (invoice)* présenter; **to p. a cheque for payment** présenter un chèque à l'encaissement; **to p. a bill for acceptance** présenter une traite à l'acceptation
VI [prɪ'zent] **1** *Obst (foetus)* se présenter
2 *Med (patient)* consulter le médecin; **the patient presented with bruises and multiple fractures** cette patiente présentait des contusions et des fractures multiples
3 *Med (illness, condition)* se manifester (**as** par)
▸▸ *Gram* ***present indicative*** présent *m* de l'indicatif; *Gram* ***present participle*** participe *m* présent; *Gram* ***present perfect*** passé *m* composé; **in the p. perfect** au passé composé; *Gram* ***present subjunctive*** présent *m* du subjonctif; *Gram* ***present tense*** présent *m*; **in the p. tense** au présent; *Acct* ***present value*** valeur *f* actuelle *ou* actualisée

presentable [prɪ'zentəbəl] **ADJ** *(person, room)* présentable; *(clothes)* présentable, mettable; **do I look p.?** est-ce que j'ai l'air présentable?; **make yourself p.** arrange-toi un peu

presentation [,prezən'teɪʃən] **N 1** *(showing)* présentation *f*; *(putting forward ▸ of ideas, facts)* présentation *f*, exposition *f*; *(▸ of petition)* présentation *f*, soumission *f*; *(talk)* exposé *m*; **to give a p.** faire un exposé; **cheque payable on p.** chèque *m* payable à vue; **he made a very clear p. of the case** il a très clairement présenté l'affaire; **payable on p. of the coupon** payable contre remise du coupon
2 *Com (of product, policy, invoice)* présentation *f*; **on p. of the invoice** au vu de *ou* sur présentation de la facture; **p. for acceptance** présentation *f* à l'acceptation; **p. for payment** présentation *f* au paiement
3 *(introduction)* présentation *f*; **can you make the presentations?** pouvez-vous faire les présentations?

4 *(performance ▸ of play, film)* représentation *f*; **in a new p. of 'Hamlet'** dans une nouvelle mise en scène de 'Hamlet'
5 *(of piece of work)* présentation *f*; **she lost marks for poor p.** elle a perdu des points parce que sa présentation n'était pas assez soignée
6 *(award ▸ of prize, medal, diploma, gift)* remise *f*; **to make sb a p. of sth** remettre qch à qn
7 *(award ceremony)* cérémonie *f* de remise *(d'un prix)*
8 *Med (of foetus)* présentation *f*
▸▸ ***presentation ceremony*** cérémonie *f* de remise *(d'un prix)*; ***presentation copy*** *(specimen)* spécimen *m* (gratuit); *(from writer)* exemplaire *m* gratuit; *Fin* ***presentation date*** date *f* de présentation; *Comput* ***presentation graphics*** graphiques *mpl* de présentation; *Mktg* ***presentation pack*** paquet *m* de présentation

present-day **ADJ** actuel, contemporain; **p. London/Brazil** le Londres/Brésil d'aujourd'hui

presenteeism [prezən'tiːɪzəm] **N** zèle *m (fait de faire beaucoup d'heures, par opposition à "absenteeism")*

presenter [prɪ'zentə(r)] **N** présentateur(trice) *m,f*

presentiment [prɪ'zentɪmənt] **N** pressentiment *m*; **to have a p. of danger** avoir le pressentiment qu'il y a du danger

presently ['prezəntlɪ] **ADV 1** *(soon)* bientôt, tout à l'heure; **he will be here p.** il sera bientôt là; **p., she got up and left** au bout de quelques minutes elle se leva et s'en alla **2** *(now)* à présent, actuellement

> Note that the French word **présentement** always means **at present**.

presentment [prɪ'zentmənt] **N 1** *Law* déclaration *f* **2** *Fin (of bill)* présentation *f*

preservation [,prezə'veɪʃən] **N 1** *(maintenance ▸ of tradition)* conservation *f*; *(▸ of leather, building, wood)* entretien *m*; *(▸ of peace, order, life)* maintien *m*; *(▸ of specimen, plant)* naturalisation *f*; **the mummy was in a good state of p.** la momie était en bon état de conservation *ou* était bien conservée; **to put a p. order on a building** classer un édifice *(monument historique)* **2** *(of food)* conservation *f* **3** *(protection)* préservation *f*
▸▸ ***preservation society*** = association pour la protection des sites et monuments

preservative [prɪ'zɜːvətɪv] **N** conservateur *m*; *(in foods)* agent *m* de conservation, conservateur *m*, préservateur *m*; **contains no artificial preservatives** *(on packaging)* sans conservateurs
ADJ conservateur

> Note that the French word **préservatif** is a false friend and is never a translation for the English word **preservative**. It means **condom**.

preserve [prɪ'zɜːv] **VT 1** *(maintain ▸ tradition, building)* conserver; *(▸ leather)* conserver, entretenir; *(▸ silence)* garder, observer; *(▸ peace, order, life)* maintenir; *(▸ dignity)* garder, conserver; *(▸ specimen, plant)* naturaliser; **to be well preserved** *(building, specimen)* être en bon état de conservation; *(person)* être bien conservé; **they tried to p. some semblance of normality** ils essayaient de faire comme si de rien n'était **2** *(protect)* préserver, protéger; **Saints p. us!** le Ciel *ou* Dieu nous préserve! **3** *Culin* mettre en conserve
N 1 *Hunt* réserve *f* (de chasse) **2** *(privilege)* privilège *m*, apanage *m*; **it's still very much a male p.** c'est encore un domaine essentiellement réservé aux hommes; **cruises are the p. of the rich** les croisières sont réservées aux *ou* sont le privilège des riches **3** *Culin (jam)* confiture *f*; *(of vegetables)* conserve *f*
• **preserves** **NPL** *Culin (jam)* confitures *fpl*; *(vegetables, fruit)* conserves *fpl*; *(pickles)* pickles *mpl*
▸▸ *Culin* ***preserved fruit*** fruits *mpl* en conserve

preserver [prɪ'zɜːvə(r)] **N** sauveur *m*; *(of tradition)* gardien(enne) *m,f*

preset [,priː'set] *(pt & pp* **preset***)* **VT** prérégler, régler à l'avance
ADJ préréglé, réglé d'avance; *Comput* présélectionné

preshrink [,priː'ʃrɪŋk] **VT** *(pt* **preshrank** [-'ʃræŋk], *pp* **preshrunk** [-'ʃrʌŋk]) *(fabric)* rendre irrétrécissable

preshrunk [,priː'ʃrʌŋk] **ADJ** irrétrécissable

preside [prɪ'zaɪd] **VI** présider; **to p. at a meeting/at table** présider une réunion/la table

presidency ['prezɪdənsɪ] *(pl* **presidencies***)* **N** présidence *f*; **during his p.** durant sa présidence; **the Clinton p.** la présidence de Clinton; **to assume the p.** assumer la présidence

president ['prezɪdənt] **N 1** *(of state)* président(e) *m,f*; **P. Simpson** le président Simpson; **Mr P.** Monsieur le Président **2** *(of organization, club)* président(e) *m,f* **3** *Am (of company, bank)* président-directeur général *m*, P-DG *m*
▸▸ *Br Pol* ***President of the Board of Trade*** ministre *mf* du Commerce et de l'Industrie; *EU* ***President of the Commission*** président(e) *m,f* de la Commission; *Am* ***Presidents' Day*** = jour férié en l'honneur des anniversaires des présidents Washington et Lincoln; ***President of the European Parliament*** président(e) *m,f* du Parlement européen; *Am* ***President of the Senate*** président *m* du Sénat

president-elect **N** *Am* = titre du président des États-Unis entre son élection et son investiture

presidential [,prezɪ'denʃəl] **ADJ** *(candidate)* présidentiel; *(aeroplane, suite)* présidentiel, du président; **to nurse p. ambitions** *or* **aspirations** aspirer à *ou* ambitionner la présidence; **it's a p. year** c'est l'année des élections présidentielles
▸▸ ***presidential appointment*** = poste à pourvoir sur nomination présidentielle; ***presidential contest*** élection *f* présidentielle; ***presidential elections*** (élections *fpl*) présidentielles *fpl*; ***presidential hopeful*** présidentiable *mf*; ***presidential pardon*** grâce *f* présidentielle; ***presidential term of office*** mandat *m* présidentiel; ***presidential veto*** veto présidentiel

presidium [prɪ'sɪdɪəm] *(pl* **presidiums** *or* **presidia** [-dɪə]) **N** praesidium *m*, présidium *m*

PRESS [pres]

N	
• presse **1–5, 7, 15**	• pressoir **7**
• serrement **9**	• foule **10**
• bousculade **10**	• coup de fer **11**
COMP	
• de presse	
VT	
• appuyer sur **1**	• presser **2, 3, 7, 8**
• forcer **4**	• insister sur **5**
• repasser **6**	
VI	
• appuyer **1**	• faire pression **2**
• insister **3**	• se repasser **4**

N 1 *(newspapers)* presse *f*; **freedom of the p.** la liberté de la presse; **they advertised in the p.** ils ont fait passer une annonce dans les journaux; **they managed to keep her name out of the p.** ils ont réussi à ce que son nom ne paraisse pas dans la presse
2 *(journalists)* presse *f*; **the p. were there** la presse était là; **she's a member of the p.** elle a une carte de presse; *Ironic* **the gentlemen of the p.** ces messieurs de la presse
3 *(report, opinion)* presse *f*; **to get (a) good/bad p.** avoir bonne/mauvaise presse; **to give sb (a) good/bad p.** faire l'éloge/la critique de qn
4 *(printing)* presse *f*; **to go to p.** *(book)* être mis sous presse; *(newspaper)* partir à l'impression; **we go to p. at 5 p.m.** on est mis sous presse à 5 heures; *(copy deadline)* on boucle à 5 heures; **in** *or* **at (the) p.** sous presse; **hot** *or* **straight from the p.** tout frais; **ready for p.** prêt à mettre sous presse; **prices correct at time of going to p.** prix corrects au moment de la mise sous presse
5 *(machine)* **(printing) p.** presse *f*
6 *(publisher)* presses *fpl*
7 *(for tennis racket, handicrafts, woodwork, trousers)* presse *f*; *(for cider, oil, wine)* pressoir *m*
8 *(push)* **the machine dispenses hot coffee at the p. of a button** il suffit d'appuyer sur un bouton pour que la machine distribue du café chaud; **give it a slight p.** appuyez légèrement là-dessus
9 *(squeeze)* serrement *m*; **he gave my hand a quick p.** il m'a serré la main rapidement
10 *(crowd)* foule *f*; *(rush)* bousculade *f*; *Literary (of battle)* mêlée *f*; **in the p. for the door we became separated** dans la ruée de la foule vers la porte, nous avons été séparés; **to force one's way through the p.** fendre la foule, se frayer un chemin à travers la foule
11 *(ironing)* coup *m* de fer; **to give sth a p.** donner un coup de fer à qch
12 *Ir & Scot (cupboard)* placard *m*, armoire *f*
13 *(in weightlifting)* développé *m*
14 *(in basketball)* pressing *m*; **full court p.** zone-presse *f* (tout terrain); *Am Fig* **it was the full court p.** on faisait le maximum
15 *Ind (forming machine)* presse *f*
COMP *(reporter, photographer)* de presse; *(advertising)* dans la presse
VT 1 *(push ▸ button, bell, trigger, accelerator)* appuyer sur; **try pressing it** essayez d'appuyer dessus; **he pressed the lid shut** il a fermé le couvercle (en appuyant dessus); **to p. sth flat** aplatir qch; **to p. sth home** enfoncer qch; **to p. sth (back) into shape** rendre sa forme à qch; **to p. one's way through a crowd/to the front** se frayer un chemin à travers une foule/jusqu'au premier rang; **he was pressed (up) against the railings** il s'est trouvé coincé contre le grillage; **I pressed myself against the wall** je me suis collé contre le mur; **she pressed a note into my hand** elle m'a glissé un billet dans la main; **he pressed his nose (up) against the window** il a collé son nez à la vitre; **he pressed his hat down on his head** il rabattit *ou* enfonça son chapeau sur sa tête; **she pressed the papers down into the bin** elle a enfoncé les papiers dans la poubelle
2 *(squeeze ▸ hand, arm)* presser, serrer; *(▸ grapes, lemon, olives)* presser; **she pressed her son to her** elle serra son fils contre elle
3 *(urge)* presser, pousser; *(harass)* harceler, talonner; **to p. sb for payment/an answer** presser qn de payer/répondre; **she pressed me to tell her the truth** elle me pressa de lui dire la vérité; **if you p. her she'll tell you** si tu insistes, elle te le dira; **if pressed, he would admit…** quand on insistait *ou* le poussait, il admettait…
4 *(force)* forcer, obliger; **I was pressed into signing the contract** j'ai été obligé de signer le contrat; **don't let yourself be pressed into going** ne laissez personne vous forcer à y aller
5 *(impose, push forward ▸ claim)* appuyer, pousser; *(▸ opinions)* insister sur; **can I p. a cup of tea on you?** puis-je vous offrir une tasse de thé?; **to p. a gift on sb** forcer qn à accepter un cadeau; **to p. (home) one's advantage** profiter d'un avantage; **to p. one's attentions on sb** poursuivre qn de ses assiduités; **I don't want to p. the point** je ne veux pas insister; *Law* **to p. charges against sb** engager des poursuites contre qn
6 *(iron ▸ shirt, tablecloth)* repasser
7 *(manufacture in mould ▸ component)* mouler; *(▸ record)* presser
8 *(preserve by pressing ▸ flower)* presser, faire sécher *(dans un livre ou un pressoir)*
9 *(in weightlifting)* soulever
10 *Mil (enlist by force)* recruter *ou* enrôler de force; *Fig* **to p. into service** réquisitionner
VI 1 *(push)* appuyer; **p. here** appuyez *ou* pressez ici; **he pressed (down) on the accelerator** il appuya sur l'accélérateur; **the crowd pressed against the barriers/round the President** la foule se pressait contre les barrières/autour du président; **they pressed forward to get a better view** ils poussaient pour essayer de mieux voir; **to p. through a crowd** se frayer un chemin à travers une foule; **to p. close against sb** se serrer contre qn
2 *(weight, burden)* faire pression (**on** sur); *(troubles)* peser (**on** à); **the rucksack pressed on his shoulders** le sac à dos pesait sur ses épaules; **her problems pressed on her mind** ses problèmes lui pesaient; **time presses!** le temps presse!
3 *(insist)* **he pressed hard to get the grant** il a fait des pieds et des mains pour obtenir la bourse; **to p. for an answer** insister pour avoir une réponse immédiate; **to p. for an adjournment/the law to be tightened up** exiger un ajournement/que la loi soit renforcée
4 *(iron)* se repasser; **some shirts p. easily** il y a des chemises qui se repassent facilement
▸▸ ***press agency*** agence *f* de presse; ***press agent*** attaché(e) *m,f* de presse; ***press attaché*** attaché(e) *m,f* de presse; ***press badge*** macaron *m* de

presse; ***press baron*** magnat *m* de la presse; ***press book*** press-book *m*; ***press box*** tribune *f* de (la) presse; ***press button*** bouton-poussoir *m*; ***press campaign*** campagne *f* de presse; ***press card*** carte *f* de presse *ou* de journaliste; ***press clipping*** coupure *f* de presse *or* de journal; ***press conference*** conférence *f* de presse; ***press copy*** *(of book)* exemplaire *m* de service de presse; ***press corps*** journalistes *mpl*; **the White House p. corps** = les journalistes accrédités à la Maison-Blanche; ***press correspondent*** correspondant(e) *m,f* de presse; ***press coverage*** couverture-presse *f*; **the resignation got a lot of p. coverage** la démission a été largement couverte dans la presse; *Br* ***press cutting*** coupure *f* de presse *ou* de journal; **a collection of p. cuttings** une collection de coupures de journaux, un dossier de presse; *Br* ***press cuttings agency*** agence *f* de coupures de presse; ***press gallery*** tribune *f* de (la) presse; ***press handout*** communiqué *m* de presse; ***press insert*** encart *m* presse; ***press kit*** dossier *m* de presse *(distribué aux journalistes)*; ***press lord*** magnat *m* de la presse; ***press office*** service *m* de presse; ***press officer*** responsable *mf* des relations avec la presse; ***press pack*** dossier *m* de presse *(distribué aux journalistes)*; ***press pass*** carte *f* de presse; *Typ* ***press proof*** tierce *f*; ***press relations*** relations *fpl* presse; ***press release*** communiqué *m* de presse; ***press report*** reportage *m*; **p. reports of the incident were inaccurate** les articles de presse relatant l'incident étaient inexacts; ***press run*** tirage *m*; *Pol* ***press secretary*** ≃ porte-parole *m inv* du gouvernement; ***press stand*** tribune *f* de (la) presse; *Br* ***press stud*** bouton-pression *m*, pression *f*

▸**press down** VT SEP appuyer sur; *(with force)* enfoncer

VI **to p. down on sb** peser sur qn

▸**press on** VI *(continue* ▸ *on journey)* poursuivre *ou* continuer son chemin; *(*▸ *with activity)* continuer; *(persevere* ▸ *in enterprise, job)* poursuivre, persévérer; **we must p. on to York** *or* **as far as York** il faut poursuivre jusqu'à York; **we pressed on regardless** nous avons continué malgré tout

▸**press out** VT SEP **1** *(juice etc)* exprimer **2** *Tech (holes)* percer; *(shapes, parts)* découper

press-button ADJ à touches, à boutons-poussoirs

pressed [prest] ADJ **1** *(flower)* pressé, séché **2** *(hurried)* pressé; *(overworked)* débordé; **to be p. for time/money** être à court de temps/d'argent; **we're p. for space** nous manquons de place

▸▸ ***pressed steel*** acier *m* embouti

press-gang N *Mil & Hist* racoleurs *mpl*, recruteurs *mpl*

VT **1** *Br (force)* **to p. sb into doing sth** obliger qn à faire qch (contre son gré); **I was press-ganged into taking part** on m'a obligé à participer **2** *Mil & Hist* racoler, recruter de force

pressie ['prezɪ] N *Br Fam* cadeau ᵒ*m*

pressing ['presɪŋ] ADJ **1** *(urgent* ▸ *appointment, business, debt)* urgent; **there is a p. need for action** il faut agir vite **2** *(insistent* ▸ *demand, danger, need)* pressant **3** *(imminent* ▸ *danger)* imminent

N **1** *(gen)* pression *f*; *(of grapes)* pressurage *m*; *(with feet)* foulage *m*; *(of record)* pressage *m* **2** *(ironing)* repassage *m*

pressman ['presmæn] *(pl* **pressmen** [-men]*)* N **1** *(journalist)* journaliste *m* **2** *(printer)* typographe *m*

pressmark ['presmɑːk] N cote *f (d'un livre)*

press-up N *Br Sport* pompe *f*; **to do press-ups** faire des pompes

pressure ['preʃə(r)] N **1** *(strain, stress)* pression *f*; **the pressures of city life** le stress de la vie en ville; **I can't take all this p.** je ne supporte pas d'être sous une telle pression; **he's been under a lot of p. lately** il est très stressé *ou* vraiment sous pression ces derniers temps; **he pleaded p. of work** il s'est excusé en disant qu'il était débordé de travail; **to work under p.** travailler sous pression; **we're under p. to finish on time** on nous presse de respecter les délais; **the p. of work is too much for me** la charge de travail est trop lourde pour moi; **there's a lot of p. on her to succeed** on fait beaucoup pression sur elle pour qu'elle réussisse; **the p.'s on!** il va falloir mettre les bouchées doubles!

2 *Met & Phys* pression *f*; *(of blood)* tension *f*; **high/low p. area** *(on weather chart)* zone *f* de hautes/basses pressions; *Fig* **to work at full p.** *(person)* travailler à plein régime; *(machine, factory)* tourner à plein régime

3 *(squeezing)* pression *f*; **she could feel the p. of his grip on her arm** elle sentait la pression de sa poigne sur son bras

4 *(force, influence)* pression *f*; *Formal* **to bring p. to bear** *or* **to put p. on sb** faire pression *ou* exercer une pression sur qn; **they put p. on me to come** ils ont fait pression sur moi pour que je vienne; **she did it under p.** elle l'a fait contrainte et forcée; **there's no p., don't come if you don't want to** rien ne t'oblige, si tu ne veux pas venir, ne viens pas; **they're putting too much p. on him** ils le soumettent à trop de pression; *Sport* **they came under sustained p. in the second half** ils ont été constamment sous pression pendant la deuxième mi-temps

VT faire pression sur; **stop pressuring me!** arrête de me presser comme ça!; **they pressured him into resigning** ils l'ont contraint à démissionner

▸▸ *Med* ***pressure bandage*** bandage *m* compressif; *Aviat* ***pressure cabin*** cabine *f* pressurisée *ou* sous pression; *Tech* ***pressure chamber*** réservoir *m* d'air comprimé; ***pressure cooker*** Cocotte-minute® *f*, autocuiseur *m*; *Fig* **a p. cooker atmosphere** une ambiance lourde de tension; ***pressure gauge*** jauge *f* de pression, manomètre *m*; ***pressure group*** groupe *m* de pression; ***pressure point*** *(on artery)* point *m* de compression; *Med* ***pressure sore*** escarre *f*; ***pressure suit*** scaphandre *m* pressurisé; ***pressure washer*** karcher® *m*

pressure-cook VT faire cuire à la Cocotte-minute® *ou* à l'autocuiseur

pressurization, -isation [ˌpreʃəraɪ'zeɪʃən] N pressurisation *f*

pressurize, -ise ['preʃəraɪz] VT **1** *(person, government)* faire pression sur; **to p. sb to do sth** *or* **into doing sth** faire pression sur qn pour qu'il/elle fasse qch; **don't p. me** ne me force pas; **a pressurized environment** un environnement stressant **2** *Aviat & Astron* pressuriser

Prestel® ['prestel] N = service de vidéotexte et fournisseur d'accès à l'internet de BT

prestidigitation ['prestɪˌdɪdʒɪ'teɪʃən] N *Formal or Hum* prestidigitation *f*

prestidigitator [ˌprestɪ'dɪdʒɪteɪtə(r)] N *Formal or Hum* prestidigitateur(trice) *m,f*

prestige [pre'stiːʒ] N prestige *m*; **it would mean a loss of p.** ce serait déchoir *ou* déroger

ADJ de prestige; **p. apartments** appartements *mpl* de grand standing; **a p. job** un poste prestigieux; **it has p. value** c'est prestigieux

▸▸ ***prestige goods*** produits *mpl* prestigieux; ***prestige model*** modèle *m* de prestige; *Mktg* ***prestige product*** produit *m* de prestige

prestigious [pre'stɪdʒəs] ADJ prestigieux

presto ['prestəʊ] *(pl* **prestos***)* ADV **1** *Mus* presto **2 hey p.!** et voilà, le tour est joué! **3** *Fam* **p. (pronto)** *(immediately)* illico presto

N *Mus* presto *m*

prestress [ˌpriː'stres] VT *Constr* précontraindre; **prestressed concrete** béton *m* précontraint

presumably [prɪ'zjuːməblɪ] ADV vraisemblablement; **p., he isn't coming** apparemment, il ne viendra pas; **p. you told him that…** je suppose que vous lui avez dit que…; **have they left? – p.** ils sont partis? – je pense *ou* vraisemblablement

presume [prɪ'zjuːm] VT **1** *(suppose)* présumer, supposer; **I p. he isn't coming** je présume *ou* suppose qu'il ne viendra pas; **I presumed them to be aware** *or* **that they were aware of the difficulties** je supposais qu'ils étaient au courant des difficultés; *Mil* **missing, presumed dead** manque à l'appel *ou* porté disparu, présumé mort; **he was presumed dead** *(by family etc)* on le croyait mort; *(by authorities)* on a présumé qu'il était mort, on l'a considéré comme décédé; *Law* **every man is presumed innocent until proven guilty** tout homme est présumé innocent tant qu'il n'a pas été déclaré coupable; **I p. so** je suppose, je présume que oui **2** *(take liberty)* oser, se permettre; **I wouldn't p. to contradict you** je ne me permettrais pas de vous contredire; **you're presuming rather a lot** tu es bien présomptueux **3** *(presuppose)* présupposer; **presuming they agree** à supposer qu'ils soient d'accord

VI **I don't want to p.** je ne voudrais pas m'imposer; **to p. on** *or* **upon sb** abuser de la gentillesse de qn

presumption [prɪ'zʌmpʃən] N **1** *(supposition)* présomption *f*, supposition *f*; **the p. is that he was drowned** on pense *ou* suppose qu'il s'est noyé; **there is a strong p. that he is guilty** on le soupçonne d'être coupable; **it's only a p.** ce n'est qu'une hypothèse; **to act on a false p.** agir sur une *ou* à partir d'une fausse supposition; **we worked on the p. that she would agree** nous avons agi en supposant qu'elle serait d'accord; *Law* **p. of innocence** présomption *f* d'innocence; *Law* **p. of fact** présomption *f* de fait; *Law* **p. of law** présomption *f* légale **2** *(UNCOUNT) (arrogance)* audace *f*, présomption *f*, prétention *f*; **she had the p. to say I was lying** elle a eu l'audace de dire que je mentais

presumptive [prɪ'zʌmptɪv] ADJ *(heir)* présomptif

▸▸ ***presumptive proof*** preuve *f* par déduction *ou* par présomption

presumptuous [prɪ'zʌmptʃʊəs] ADJ présomptueux, arrogant

presumptuously [prɪ'zʌmptʃʊəslɪ] ADV présomptueusement, avec arrogance; **she p. assumed that…** elle a eu la présomption de croire que…

presumptuousness [prɪ'zʌmptʃʊəsnɪs] N présomption *f*, arrogance *f*

presuppose [ˌpriːsə'pəʊz] VT présupposer

presupposition [ˌpriːsʌpə'zɪʃən] N présupposition *f*

pre-tax ADJ brut, avant (le prélèvement des) impôts

▸▸ ***pre-tax profits*** bénéfices *mpl* bruts *ou* avant impôts

pretence, *Am* **pretense** [prɪ'tens] N **1** *(false display)* simulacre *m*, faux-semblant *m*; **to make a p. of doing sth** faire semblant *ou* mine de faire qch; **he's not really ill, it's only** *or* **all (a) p.!** il n'est pas vraiment malade, il fait seulement semblant *ou* c'est (simplement) de la comédie!; **at least SHE made some p. of sympathy!** elle au moins elle a fait comme si ça la touchait!; **she made no p. of being interested** elle n'a aucunement feint d'être intéressée

2 *(pretext)* prétexte *m*; **under** *or* **on the p. of doing sth** sous prétexte de faire qch; **he criticizes her on the slightest p.** il la critique pour un rien *ou* à la moindre occasion

3 *(claim)* prétention *f*; **he has** *or* **makes no p. to musical taste** il ne prétend pas *ou* il n'a pas la prétention de s'y connaître en musique

4 *(UNCOUNT) (arrogance)* prétention *f*

pretend [prɪ'tend] VT **1** *(make believe)* **to p. to do sth** faire semblant de faire qch, feindre de faire qch; **they p. to be rich** ils font semblant d'être riches; **they pretended not to see** *or* **to have seen us** ils ont fait semblant *ou* mine de ne pas nous voir; **he pretended not to be interested** il a fait semblant de ne pas être intéressé, il a joué les indifférents; **they pretended to be ill/shocked** ils ont fait semblant d'être malades/choqués; **he pretended to be** *or* **that he was their uncle** il s'est fait passer pour leur oncle; **she pretends that everything is all right** elle fait comme si tout allait bien; **it's no use pretending things will improve** cela ne sert à rien de faire comme si les choses allaient s'améliorer; **I'll p. I didn't hear that last remark** je vais faire comme si je n'avais pas entendu cette dernière remarque; **let's p. we're astronauts** *(children playing)* on dirait qu'on était astronautes **2** *(claim)* prétendre; **I don't p. to be an expert** je ne prétends pas être un expert, je n'ai pas la prétention d'être un expert; **I don't p. to understand** je ne prétends pas comprendre **3** *(feign* ▸ *indifference, ignorance)* feindre, simuler

VI **1** *(feign)* faire semblant; **there's no point in pretending (to me)** inutile de faire semblant (avec moi); **I'm only pretending!** c'est juste pour rire!; **let's p.** faisons semblant *ou* comme si **2** *(lay claim)* prétendre; **to p. to sth** prétendre à qch; **I don't p. to great knowledge on the matter/any special expertise** je ne prétends pas savoir grand-chose sur la question/avoir des connaissances particulières

ADJ *Fam (fight)* pour faire semblant□, pour jouer□; **it was only p.!** c'était pour rire *ou* pour faire semblant!; **it's only p. money/a p. gun** ce n'est pas du vrai argent/un vrai pistolet□

> Note that the French verb **prétendre** is a false friend and is not usually a translation for the English verb **to pretend**. It usually means **to claim.**

pretended [prɪ'tendɪd] **ADJ** *(emotion, interest)* feint, simulé; *(doctor, wealth, ignorance etc)* prétendu, soi-disant

pretender [prɪ'tendə(r)] **N 1** *(to throne, title, right)* prétendant(e) *m,f* **2** *(impostor)* imposteur *m*

pretense *Am* = **pretence**

pretension [prɪ'tenʃən] **N 1** *(claim)* prétention *f*; **to have pretensions to sth** avoir des prétentions *ou* prétendre à qch; **a film with intellectual pretensions** un film qui a des prétentions intellectuelles; **to have social pretensions** vouloir arriver; **I make no pretensions to expert knowledge** je n'ai pas la prétention *ou* je ne me flatte pas d'être expert en la matière; **he has literary pretensions** il se prend pour un écrivain **2** *(UNCOUNT) (pretentiousness)* prétention *f*

pretentious [prɪ'tenʃəs] **ADJ** prétentieux

pretentiously [prɪ'tenʃəslɪ] **ADV** prétentieusement

pretentiousness [prɪ'tenʃəsnɪs] **N** *(UNCOUNT)* prétention *f*

preterite, *Am* **preterit** ['pretərət] *Gram* **ADJ** *(form)* du prétérit

N prétérit *m*; **in the p.** au prétérit

▸▸ ***preterite tense*** prétérit *m*

preternatural [,pri:tə'nætʃərəl] **ADJ** *Literary* surnaturel

pre-test N pré-test *m*

VT pré-tester

pretext ['pri:tekst] **N** prétexte *m*; **on** *or* **under the p. of doing sth** sous prétexte de faire qch; **it's just a p. for avoiding work** ce n'est qu'un prétexte pour ne pas travailler

Pretoria [prɪ'tɔ:rɪə] **N** Pretoria

pre-trial ADJ *Law* avant procès

▸▸ ***pre-trial conference*** conférence *f* avant procès; ***pre-trial detention*** détention *f* préventive

prettify ['prɪtɪfaɪ] *(pt & pp* **prettified)** **VT** *Pej (room, garden)* enjoliver; **to p. oneself** se pomponner

prettily ['prɪtɪlɪ] **ADV** joliment; **p. dressed** joliment habillé; **to smile p.** faire un/des sourire(s) charmeur(s); **she sang very p.** elle a chanté avec beaucoup de charme

prettiness ['prɪtɪnɪs] **N 1** *(of appearance)* beauté *f*; **the p. of her smile** son joli sourire **2** *Pej (of style)* mièvrerie *f*

pretty ['prɪtɪ] *(compar* **prettier,** *superl* **prettiest,** *pt & pp* **prettied)** **ADJ 1** *(attractive* ▸ *clothes, girl, place, picture, song)* joli; **she's a p. little thing** elle est mignonne comme tout; *Fam* **I'm not just a p. face!** qu'est-ce que tu crois?, il y en a, là-dedans!; **to be as p. as a picture** *(person)* être mignon comme tout; *(place)* être ravissant

2 *Ironic* **it was not a p. sight** ce n'était pas beau à voir; **this is a p. state of affairs!** c'est du joli *ou* du propre!; **things have come to a p. pass!** nous voilà bien!; **it cost a p. penny** ça a coûté une jolie petite somme; **that'll cost me a p. penny!** ça va me coûter cher!; **to make a p. penny out of sth** tirer une petite fortune de qch

3 *Pej (style, expression)* précieux; **it's not enough to make p. speeches** il ne suffit pas de faire de beaux discours; *Pej* **his p.-boy good looks** son physique de jeune minet

ADV *Fam* **1** *(quite)* assez□; **it's p. good** c'est pas mal du tout□; **it's p. difficult** c'est plutôt difficile□; **you did p. well for a beginner** tu t'en es plutôt bien tiré pour un débutant; **we've got a p. good idea of what she was like** nous nous imaginons assez bien comment elle était□

2 *(almost)* presque□, à peu près□, pratiquement□; **I'm p. certain I'm right** je suis presque sûr d'avoir raison; **it's p. much the same team as last week** c'est à peu près la même équipe que la semaine dernière; **he told her p. well everything** il lui a raconté pratiquement *ou* à peu près tout

3 *(idiom)* **to be sitting p.** ne pas avoir de souci à se faire□

N *Fam Old-fashioned (girl, animal)* mignon (onne) *m,f*; **come here, my p.** viens ici, mon (ma) mignon(onne)

▸ **pretty up VT SEP** enjoliver; **to pretty oneself up** se faire beau (belle)

pretty-pretty ADJ *Fam Pej (person)* gentillet□, mignonnet□; *(dress)* cucul la praline *(inv)*; *(painting)* gentillet□; *(garden)* mignon, gentil□

pretzel ['pretsəl] **N** *Culin* bretzel *m*

prevail [prɪ'veɪl] **VI 1** *(triumph)* l'emporter, prévaloir; **to p. against/over sb** l'emporter *ou* prévaloir contre/sur qn; **luckily, common sense prevailed** heureusement, le bon sens a prévalu *ou* l'a emporté **2** *(exist* ▸ *situation, opinion, belief)* régner, avoir cours; **the conditions prevailing in the Third World** les conditions que l'on rencontre le plus souvent dans le tiers monde

prevailing [prɪ'veɪlɪŋ] **ADJ 1** *(wind)* dominant **2** *(belief, opinion)* courant, répandu; *(fashion)* en vogue; **according to p. opinion** selon l'opinion la plus répandue **3** *(current)* actuel; **the p. exchange rate** le taux de change actuel; **in the p. conditions** *(now)* dans les conditions actuelles; *(then)* à l'époque

prevalence ['prevələns] **N** *(widespread existence)* prédominance *f*; *(of disease)* prévalence *f*; *(frequency)* fréquence *f*; **the p. of rented property surprised him** il fut surpris de constater à quel point les locations étaient répandues; **the p. of these theories can only do harm** la popularité de ces théories ne peut qu'être nuisible

prevalent ['prevələnt] **ADJ 1** *(widespread)* répandu, courant; *(frequent)* fréquent; **violence is p. in big cities** la violence est monnaie courante dans les grandes villes; **this opinion is p. among teenagers** cette opinion est très répandue parmi les adolescents; **to become p.** se généraliser **2** *(current)* actuel, d'aujourd'hui; *(in past)* de *ou* à l'époque

prevaricate [prɪ'værɪkeɪt] **VI** tergiverser, user de faux-fuyants; **stop prevaricating!** assez de faux-fuyants!

prevaricating [prɪ'værɪkeɪtɪŋ], **prevarication** [prɪ,værɪ'keɪʃən] **N** tergiversation *f*, faux-fuyants *mpl*; **I'm fed up with your p.** j'en ai assez de tes faux-fuyants *ou* tergiversations

prevaricator [prɪ'værɪkeɪtə(r)] **N** personne *f* qui tergiverse *ou* qui use de faux-fuyants

prevent [prɪ'vent] **VT** *(accident, catastrophe, scandal)* empêcher, éviter; *(illness)* prévenir; **to p. sb (from) doing sth** empêcher qn de faire qch; **there is nothing to p. our going** *or* **to p. us from going** rien ne nous empêche d'y aller; **to p. a disease from spreading** empêcher une maladie de s'étendre, éviter qu'une maladie ne s'étende; **I couldn't p. her** je n'ai pas pu l'en empêcher; **we were unable to p. the bomb from exploding** nous n'avons rien pu faire pour empêcher la bombe d'exploser; **they couldn't p. his departure** ils n'ont pu l'empêcher de partir

preventable [prɪ'ventəbəl] **ADJ** évitable; **it would have been easily p.** ç'aurait été facile à éviter; **a p. disease** une maladie que l'on peut prévenir

preventative [prɪ'ventətɪv] **ADJ** préventif; **to take p. measures** prendre des mesures préventives

prevention [prɪ'venʃən] **N** prévention *f*; **the p. of cruelty to animals** la protection des animaux; *Prov* **p. is better than cure** mieux vaut prévenir que guérir

preventive [prɪ'ventɪv] **ADJ** *(medicine)* préventif, prophylactique; *(measure)* préventif; **as a p. measure** à titre préventif

N 1 *(measure)* mesure *f* préventive; **as a p.** à titre préventif **2** *Med* médicament *m* préventif *ou* prophylactique

▸▸ *Law* ***preventive custody*** détention *f* préventive; *Br Law* ***preventive detention*** détention *f* préventive; *Comput* ***preventive security*** sécurité *f* préventive; ***preventive war*** guerre *f* préventive

preventively [prɪ'ventɪvlɪ] **ADV** préventivement; **to act p. against sth** prendre des mesures préventives contre qch

preview ['pri:vju:] **N 1** *(of movie, show, exhibition)* avant-première *f*; *(of art exhibition)* vernissage *m*; **and here is a p. of tomorrow's programmes** et voici un aperçu des programmes de demain **2** *Am Cin (trailer)* bande-annonce *f* **3** *Comput* prévisualisation *f*, aperçu *m* avant impression

VT 1 to p. a movie *(put on)* donner un film en avant-première; *(see)* voir un film en avant-première; **to p. the evening's television viewing** passer en revue les programmes télévisés de la soirée **2** *Comput* prévisualiser, faire un aperçu avant impression de

▸▸ *Comput* ***preview mode*** mode *m* de prévisualisation; *TV* ***preview monitor*** écran *m* de prévisualisation

previous ['pri:vjəs] **ADJ 1** *(prior)* précédent; **on a p. occasion** auparavant; **on the p. occasion we had met** la dernière fois que nous nous étions rencontrés; **I have a p. engagement** j'ai déjà un rendez-vous, je suis déjà pris; **she has had several p. accidents** elle a déjà eu plusieurs accidents; **do you have any p. experience of this kind of work?** avez-vous déjà une expérience de ce genre de travail?; **the two months p. to your arrival** les deux mois précédant votre arrivée; *Law* **he has no p. convictions** il n'a pas de casier judiciaire, il a un casier judiciaire vierge; **he has had several p. convictions** il a déjà fait l'objet de plusieurs condamnations

2 *(former)* antérieur; **in a p. life** dans une vie antérieure; **his p. marriages ended in divorce** ses autres mariages se sont soldés par des divorces

3 *(with days and dates)* précédent; **the p. Monday** le lundi précédent; **the p. June** au mois de juin précédent; **the p. day** le jour précédent, la veille; **the p. evening** le soir précédent, la veille au soir

4 *Br Fam (hasty* ▸ *decision, judgment)* prématuré□, hâtif□; *(*▸ *person)* expéditif□; **aren't you being a little p.?** n'êtes-vous pas un peu pressé?□, n'allez-vous pas un peu vite?□

ADV antérieurement; *Formal* **p. to his death** avant sa mort, avant qu'il ne meure

N *Fam Crime slang (previous convictions)* casier□ *m*

previously ['pri:vjəslɪ] **ADV 1** *(in the past)* auparavant, précédemment; **six weeks p.** six semaines auparavant *ou* plus tôt; **p., the country was under British rule** auparavant, le pays était sous autorité britannique **2** *(already)* déjà; **we've met p.** nous nous sommes déjà rencontrés

prewar [,pri:'wɔ:(r)] **ADJ** d'avant-guerre; **the p. years** l'avant-guerre *m ou f*

prey [preɪ] **N** *(UNCOUNT) also Fig* proie *f*; **hens are often (a) p. to foxes** les poules sont souvent la proie des renards; **the sheep fell (a) p. to some marauding beast** les moutons ont été attaqués par un animal maraudeur; **to be (a) p. to doubts/nightmares** être en proie au doute/à des cauchemars; **she was an easy p. for** *or* **to fast-talking salesmen** elle était une proie facile pour le boniment des vendeurs; **to fall p. to temptation** tomber en proie à la tentation

▸ **prey on, prey upon VT INSEP 1** *(of predator)* faire sa proie de; *Fig* **he preyed on her fears** il exploita ses angoisses; *Fig* **the thieves preyed upon old women** les voleurs s'en prenaient aux vieilles dames **2** *(of fear, doubts)* ronger; **the thought continued to p. on his mind** l'idée continuait à lui ronger l'esprit

prez [prez] **N** *Fam* **the p.** le président□

prezzie = **pressie**

PRICE [praɪs]

> **N**
> - prix **1, 2, 4** • valeur **2**
> - cours **3** • cote **3, 5**
> - devis **6**
>
> **COMP**
> - de(s) prix
>
> **VT**
> - fixer le prix de **1** • évaluer **1**
> - marquer le prix de **2** • étiqueter **2**
> - demander le prix de **3**

N **1** *(cost)* prix *m*; **what p. is the clock?** quel est le prix de cette pendule?; **what is the p. of petrol?** à quel prix est l'essence?; **to rise** *or* **increase** *or* **go up in p.** augmenter; **petrol has gone down in p.** le prix de l'essence a baissé; **prices are rising/falling** les prix sont en hausse/baisse; **I paid a high p. for it** je l'ai payé cher; **he charges reasonable prices** ses prix sont raisonnables; **they pay top prices for antique china** ils achètent la porcelaine ancienne au prix fort; **if the p. is right** si le prix est correct; **she got a good p. for her car** elle a obtenu un bon prix de sa voiture; **to sell sth at a reduced p.** vendre qch à prix réduit; **I'll let you have the carpet at a reduced p.** je vous ferai un prix d'ami pour le tapis; **I got the chair at a reduced/at half p.** j'ai eu la chaise à prix réduit/à moitié prix; **her jewels fetched huge prices at auction** ses bijoux ont atteint des sommes folles aux enchères; **that's my p., take it or leave it** c'est mon dernier prix, à prendre ou à laisser; **name** *or* **state your p.!** votre prix sera le mien!; **every man has his p.** tout homme s'achète; **he gave us a p. for repairing the car** il nous a donné le prix des réparations à faire sur la voiture

2 *(value)* prix *m*, valeur *f*; **to put a p. on sth** *(definite)* fixer le prix *ou* la valeur de qch; *(estimate)* évaluer le prix *ou* estimer la valeur de qch; **I wouldn't like to put a p. on that fur coat** je n'ose pas imaginer le prix de ce manteau de fourrure; **to put a p. on sb's head** mettre la tête de qn à prix; **there's a p. on his head** sa tête a été mise à prix; **you can't put a p. on love/health** l'amour/la santé n'a pas de prix; **what p. all her hopes now?** que valent tous ses espoirs maintenant?; **he puts a high p. on loyalty** il attache beaucoup d'importance *ou* il accorde beaucoup de valeur à la loyauté; **to be beyond** *or* **without p.** être (d'un prix) inestimable *ou* hors de prix, ne pas avoir de prix

3 *St Exch* cours *m*, cote *f*; **today's prices** les cours *mpl* du jour; **what is the p. of gold?** quel est le cours de l'or?

4 *Fig (penalty)* prix *m*; **it's a small p. to pay for peace of mind** c'est bien peu de chose pour avoir l'esprit tranquille; **this must be done at any p.** il faut que cela se fasse à tout prix *ou* coûte que coûte; **it's a high p. to pay for independence** c'est bien cher payer l'indépendance; **that's the p. of** *or* **the p. paid for fame** c'est la rançon de la gloire

5 *(chance, odds)* cote *f*; *Horseracing* **what p. are they giving on Stardust?** quelle est la cote de Stardust?; *Horseracing* **long/short p.** forte/faible cote *f*; **what p. he'll keep his word?** combien pariez-vous qu'il tiendra parole?; **what p. peace now?** quelles sont les chances de paix maintenant?; **what p. my chances of being appointed?** quelles sont mes chances d'être nommé?

6 *(quotation)* devis *m*

COMP *(bracket)* de prix; *(rise)* des prix

VT **1** *(set cost of)* fixer *ou* établir *ou* déterminer le prix de; *(estimate value of)* évaluer, estimer la valeur de; **the book is priced at £17** le livre coûte 17 livres; **his paintings are rather highly priced** le prix de ses tableaux est un peu élevé; **a reasonably priced hotel** un hôtel aux prix raisonnables; **how would you p. that house?** à combien estimeriez-vous cette maison?

2 *(indicate cost of)* marquer le prix de, mettre le prix sur; *(with label)* étiqueter; **all goods must be clearly priced** le prix des marchandises doit être clairement indiqué; **the book is priced at £10** le livre est vendu (au prix de) 10 livres; **this book isn't priced** le prix de ce livre n'est pas indiqué

3 *(ascertain price of)* demander le prix de, s'informer du prix de; **she priced the stereo in several shops before buying it** elle a comparé le prix de la chaîne dans plusieurs magasins avant de l'acheter

4 *Econ (quantity)* valoriser

• **at any price** ADV **she wants a husband at any p.** elle veut un mari à tout prix *ou* coûte que coûte; **he wouldn't do it at any p.!** il ne voulait le faire à aucun prix *ou* pour rien au monde!

• **at a price** ADV en y mettant le prix; **she'll help you, at a p.** elle vous aidera, à condition que vous y mettiez le prix; **you can get real silk, but only at a p.** vous pouvez avoir de la soie véritable, à condition d'y mettre le prix; **you got what you wanted, but at a p.!** vous avez eu ce que vous souhaitiez, mais à quel prix! *ou* mais vous l'avez payé cher!

►► ***price agreement*** accord *m* sur les prix; ***price ceiling*** plafond *m* de prix; ***price comparison*** comparaison *f* des prix; ***price control*** contrôle *m* des prix; ***price cut*** rabais *m*, réduction *f* (des prix), baisse *f* des prix; **huge p. cuts!** *(in advertisement)* prix sacrifiés!; *Mktg* ***price differential*** écart *m* de prix; ***price discount*** remise *f* sur les prix; ***price discrimination*** tarif *m* discriminatoire; ***price escalation*** flambée *f* des prix; ***price ex-works*** prix *m* départ usine; ***price floor*** prix *m* plancher; ***price freeze*** blocage *m* des prix, gel *m* des prix; ***price hike*** hausse *f* de prix; *Fin* ***prices and incomes policy*** politique *f* des prix et des salaires; ***price increase*** hausse *f* des prix, augmentation *f* des prix; ***price(s) index*** indice *m* des prix, *Belg* index *m* des prix; ***price indicator*** indicateur *m* de prix; *Fin* ***price inflation*** inflation *f* des prix; ***price instability*** instabilité *f* des prix; *Mktg* ***price label*** étiquette *f* de prix; *Mktg* ***price leadership*** commandement *m* des prix; ***price level*** niveau *m* de prix; ***price list*** tarif *m*, liste *f* des prix; *Mktg* ***price mark-up*** majoration *f* de prix; ***price mechanism*** mécanisme *m* des prix; *Fin* ***price of money*** prix *m ou* loyer *m* de l'argent; ***price pegging*** soutien *m* des prix; *Mktg* ***price policy*** politique *f* de prix; ***price range*** gamme *f ou* échelle *f* des prix; **what is your p. range?** combien voulez-vous mettre?; **it's not in my p. range** ce n'est pas dans mes prix; ***price reduction*** réduction *f* (des prix); ***price regulation*** réglementation *f* des prix; *Fin* ***price ring*** monopole *m* des prix; *Mktg* ***price scale*** barème *m* des prix, échelle *f* des prix; *Mktg* ***price setting*** détermination *f* des prix, fixation *f* des prix; *Mktg* ***price stability*** stabilité *f* des prix; *Fin* ***price structure*** structure *f* des prix; ***price support*** soutien *m* des prix; ***price tag*** *(label)* étiquette *f* de prix; *(value)* prix *m*, valeur *f*; **what's the p. tag on a Rolls these days?** combien vaut une Rolls de nos jours?; ***price theory*** théorie *f* des prix; ***price ticket*** étiquette *f* de prix; ***price war*** guerre *f* des prix

► **price down** VT SEP *Br* baisser le prix de, démarquer; **everything has been priced down by 10 percent for the sales** tous les articles ont été démarqués de 10 pour cent pour les soldes

► **price up** VT SEP *Br (raise cost of)* augmenter *ou* majorer le prix de, majorer; *(on label)* indiquer un prix plus élevé sur

price-conscious ADJ attentif aux prix

price-cutting N *(UNCOUNT)* réductions *fpl* de prix

-priced [praɪst] SUFF **high-p.** à prix élevé, (plutôt) cher; **low-p.** à bas prix, peu cher

price-elastic ADJ *Mktg* au prix élastique

price-fixing N *(control)* contrôle *m* des prix; *(rigging)* entente *f* sur les prix

price-inelastic ADJ *Mktg* au prix stable

priceless ['praɪslɪs] ADJ **1** *(precious* ► *jewels, friendship)* d'une valeur inestimable **2** *Fam (funny* ► *joke)* tordant, bidonnant; *(*► *person)* impayable, crevant

> Attention: ne pas confondre avec **worthless**, qui signifie **sans aucune valeur**.

price-sensitive ADJ *Mktg* sensible au prix

pricey ['praɪsɪ] *(compar* **pricier**, *superl* **priciest)** ADJ *Fam* chérot

pricing ['praɪsɪŋ] N détermination *f* du prix, fixation *f* du prix

►► ***pricing policy*** politique *f* de(s) prix

prick [prɪk] VT **1** *(jab, pierce)* piquer, percer; **she pricked her finger/herself with the needle** elle s'est piqué le doigt/elle s'est piquée avec l'aiguille; **to p. holes in sth** faire des trous dans qch; **the kids were pricking balloons with pins** les gosses crevaient des ballons avec des épingles; **the thorns pricked their legs** les épines leur piquaient les jambes **2** *(irritate)* piquer, picoter; **the smoke was pricking my eyes** la fumée me piquait les yeux; *Fig* **his conscience was pricking him** il n'avait pas la conscience tranquille, il avait mauvaise conscience

VI **1** *(pin, cactus, thorn)* piquer **2** *(be irritated)* picoter; **my eyes are pricking from the smoke** j'ai les yeux qui me piquent *ou* brûlent à cause de la fumée

N **1** *(from insect, pin, thorn)* piqûre *f*; **he felt a sudden p. in his finger** soudain il a senti quelque chose lui piquer le doigt; *Fig* **pricks of conscience** remords *mpl*; **to have a p. of conscience** être titillé par sa conscience **2** *Vulg (penis)* bite *f*, queue *f* **3** *very Fam (man)* con *m*, connard *m*; **stop making such a p. of yourself!** arrête de faire le con!; *Vulg* **to feel like a spare p. (at a wedding)** tenir la chandelle

► **prick out** VT SEP *Hort (seedlings)* repiquer

► **prick up** VI *(ears)* se dresser

VT SEP dresser; **the dog pricked up its ears** le chien a dressé les oreilles; **she pricked up her ears at the sound of her name** elle a dressé *ou* tendu l'oreille en entendant son nom

pricking ['prɪkɪŋ] N *(piercing)* piquage *m*; *(sensation)* picotement *m*; **she felt a p. in her fingers** elle avait des picotements dans les doigts; **the prickings of conscience** les remords *mpl*

ADJ piquant; **a p. sensation** un picotement, un fourmillement

►► *Hort* ***pricking out*** *(of seedlings)* repiquage *m*

prickle ['prɪkəl] N **1** *(of rose, cactus)* épine *f*, piquant *m*; *(of hedgehog, porcupine)* piquant *m*; *(sensation)* picotement *m*; *(of anticipation, excitement)* fourmillement *m*

VT piquer

VI *(skin)* picoter, fourmiller; **her skin prickled with excitement** elle eu un frisson d'excitation; *Fig* **to p. with indignation** se hérisser

prickling ['prɪklɪŋ] ADJ *(sensation)* de picotement; *(of anticipation, excitement)* de fourmillement *m*

N picotement *m*

prickly ['prɪkəlɪ] *(compar* **pricklier**, *superl* **prickliest)** ADJ **1** *(cactus, plant)* épineux; *(hedgehog)* couvert de piquants; *(beard)* piquant; *(clothes)* qui pique; **his fingers felt p.** il avait des fourmillements dans les doigts; **his skin felt p.** sa peau le démangeait; **the surface felt p.** la surface était piquante; **a p. sensation** une sensation de picotement **2** *Fam (irritable* ► *person)* ombrageux[□], irritable[□]; *(*► *character)* ombrageux[□]; **he's very p.** il se froisse facilement[□], il est très susceptible[□]; **she's a bit p. today** elle est plutôt irritable aujourd'hui[□] **3** *(delicate* ► *subject, topic, problem, situation)* épineux, délicat

►► *Med* ***prickly heat*** *(UNCOUNT)* fièvre *f* miliaire, miliaire *f*, suette *f* miliaire; ***prickly pear*** *(fruit)* figue *f* de Barbarie; *(tree)* figuier *m* de Barbarie

pride [praɪd] N **1** *(satisfaction)* fierté *f*; **she takes great p. in her son** elle est très fière de son fils; **they take p. in their town** ils sont fiers de leur ville; **to take (a) p. in one's appearance** prendre soin de sa personne; **he takes no p. in his work** il ne prend pas du tout son travail à cœur; **to take (a) p. in doing sth** mettre de la fierté à faire qch, s'enorgueillir de faire qch; **she pointed with p. to her new car** elle montra fièrement du doigt sa nouvelle voiture

2 *(self-respect)* fierté *f*, amour-propre *m*; **a sense of p.** un sentiment d'amour-propre; **he has no p.** il n'a pas d'amour-propre; **I have my p.!** j'ai ma fierté!; **her p. was hurt** elle était blessée dans son amour-propre

3 *Pej (arrogance)* orgueil *m*; *Prov* **p. comes** *or* **goes before a fall** = plus on est fier, plus dure est la chute

4 *(most valuable thing)* orgueil *m*, fierté *f*; **she is her parents' p. and joy** elle fait la fierté de ses parents; **that antique table is her p. and joy** elle est très fière de cette table ancienne; **this painting is the p. of the collection** ce tableau est le joyau de la collection; **to have** *or* **to take p. of place** occuper la place d'honneur

5 *(of lions)* troupe *f*

VT **to p. oneself on** *or* **upon sth** être fier *ou* s'enorgueillir de qch; **she prided herself on being the youngest member of the team** elle s'enorgueillissait *ou* était fière d'être la plus jeune de l'équipe

priest [priːst] N prêtre *m*; **parish p.** *(Catholic)* curé *m*; **a Buddhist p.** un prêtre bouddhiste

►► *Hist* ***priest hole*** = cachette pour les prêtres à l'époque des persécutions contre les catholiques

riestess ['pri:stɪs] N prêtresse *f*

riesthood ['pri:sthʊd] N *(as vocation)* prêtrise **the p.** *(priests)* le clergé; **to enter the p.** se faire rêtre

riestly ['pri:stlɪ] *(compar* **priestlier,** *superl* **priest-est)** ADJ sacerdotal, de prêtre

rig [prɪg] N *Br* **he's such a p.!** il fait toujours son etit saint!; **don't be such a p.!** ne sois pas aussi égueule!

riggish ['prɪgɪʃ] ADJ *(prudish)* pudibond, bé-ueule; *(smug)* suffisant

riggishness ['prɪgɪʃnɪs] N *(prudishness)* pudi-onderie *f*; *(smugness)* suffisance *f*

rim [prɪm] *(compar* **primmer,** *superl* **primmest)** DJ *Pej* **1** *(person)* collet monté *(inv)*; *(attitude, be-aviour)* guindé, compassé; *(voice)* affecté; **she's ery p. and proper** elle est très collet monté **2** *ıeat ▸ clothes)* (très) comme il faut, (très) clas-ique; *(▸ house, hedge, lawn)* impeccable

rima ['pri:mə] ADJ

▸ ***prima ballerina*** danseuse *f* étoile; ***prima donna*** *pera singer)* prima donna *f*; *Pej (temperamental erson)* diva *f*; **don't be such a p. donna** arrête de uer les divas; **he's a real p. donna** c'est une vraie iva

rimacy ['praɪməsɪ] *(pl* **primacies)** N **1** *(pre-emi-ence)* primauté *f*, prééminence *f*; *Ling* **the p. of** peech la primauté de la parole **2** *Rel* primatie *f*

rimaeval = **primeval**

rima facie [ˌpraɪmə'feɪʃi:] ADV à première vue, e prime abord

DJ *Law* **a p. case** une affaire simple a priori; **it's p. case of mistaken identity** a priori, il s'agit une erreur sur la personne; **p. evidence** com-encement *m* de preuve, *Can* preuve *f* prima fa-ie; **there is no p. evidence** a priori, il n'y a aucune reuve

rimal ['praɪməl] ADJ **1** *(original)* primitif, pre-ier **2** *(main)* primordial, principal

▸ *Psy* ***primal scream*** cri *m* primal; *Psy* ***primal cream therapy, primal therapy*** thérapie *f* primale

rimarily [*Br* 'praɪmərɪlɪ, *Am* praɪ'merəlɪ] ADV **1** *nainly)* principalement, avant tout **2** *(origi-ally)* primitivement, à l'origine

rimary ['praɪmərɪ] *(pl* **primaries)** ADJ **1** *(main)* rincipal, premier; *(basic)* principal, fonda-ental; **our p. objective** notre premier objectif, otre objectif principal; **our p. duty** notre pre-ier devoir; **the p. meaning of this word** le sens remier de ce mot; **this question is of p. impor-ance** cette question revêt une importance capi-ale; **the p. cause of the accident** la cause rincipale de l'accident

2 *Biol, Chem & Phys* primaire

3 *Sch* primaire

4 *Econ* primaire

N **1** *Am Pol (election)* (élection *f*) primaire *f*

2 *(school)* école *f* primaire

3 *(colour)* couleur *f* primaire

4 *Zool* rémige *f*

5 *Elec* bobine *f* primaire

▸ *Mus* ***primary accent*** accent *m* principal; *Br* ***pri-ary care trust*** = administration qui gère les ser-ices de santé au niveau local; *Elec* ***primary cell*** ile *f* primaire; *Elec* ***primary circuit*** circuit *m* pri-aire; *Elec* ***primary coil*** bobine *f* primaire; ***pri-ary colour*** couleur *f* primaire; *Mktg* ***primary ata*** informations *fpl* primaires, données *fpl* pri-aires; *Sch* ***primary education*** enseignement *m* rimaire; *Am Pol* ***primary election*** (élection *f*) pri-aire *f*; *Econ* ***primary employment*** activité *f* pri-aire; *Orn* ***primary feather*** rémige *f*; ***primary ealth care*** soins *mpl* primaires; *Econ* ***primary in-ustry*** industrie *f* primaire; *Med* ***primary infection*** rimo-infection *f*; *Com* ***primary product*** matière *f* remière, produit *m* brut; *Geol* ***primary rocks*** ro-hes *fpl* primaires; ***primary school*** école *f* pri-aire; ***primary school teacher*** instituteur(trice) *,f*; *Econ* ***primary sector*** secteur *m* primaire; *con* **the p. sector industries** les industries *fpl* du ecteur primaire; *Ling* ***primary stress*** accent *m* rincipal

> **PRIMARY ELECTIONS**
>
> Les élections primaires américaines (directes ou indirectes selon les États) aboutissent à la sélection des candidats qui seront en lice pour représenter les deux grands partis nationaux à l'élection présidentielle. Ces élections ont lieu entre les mois de février et de mai chaque année d'élections présidentielles. Certains États tiennent des meetings électoraux appelés "caucuses" au lieu des élections primaires.

primate ['praɪmeɪt] N **1** *Zool* primate *m* **2** *Rel* primat *m*; **the P. of All England** = titre officiel de l'archevêque de Cantorbéry

prime [praɪm] ADJ **1** *(foremost)* premier, primordial; *(principal)* premier, principal; *(fundamental)* fondamental; **one of the p. causes of heart disease** une des principales causes des maladies cardiaques; **our p. concern is to avoid loss of life** notre préoccupation principale est d'éviter de faire des victimes; **of p. importance** de la plus haute importance, d'une importance primordiale **2** *(perfect)* parfait; *(excellent)* excellent; **in p. condition** *(person)* en parfaite santé; *(athlete)* en parfaite condition; *(car, antique, stamp)* en parfait état; **it's a p. example of what I mean** c'est un excellent exemple de ce que je veux dire; **3** *Math (number)* premier; **10 is p. to 11** 10 et 11 sont premiers entre eux

N **1** *(best moment)* **to be in one's p. or in the p. of life** être dans la fleur de l'âge; **I'm past my p.** je ne suis plus dans la fleur de l'âge; **these roses look a bit past their p.** ces roses sont plutôt défraîchies; **these curtains look a bit past their p.** ces rideaux ont vu des jours meilleurs; **when Romantic poetry was in its p.** lorsque la poésie romantique était à son apogée

2 *Math (prime number)* nombre *m* premier; *(mark)* prime *f*

3 *Rel* prime *f*; **to say/sing the p.** dire/chanter prime

4 *Fencing* prime *f*

5 *Mus* son *m* fondamental

VT **1** *(gun, machine, pump)* amorcer; **to p. sb with drink** faire boire qn; *Fam* **he was well primed** il était bien parti; *Fig* **to p. the pump** faire repartir la machine, remettre les choses en route **2** *(brief ▸ person)* mettre au courant; **to p. sb for a meeting** préparer qn à une réunion; **he is well primed in local politics** il est bien renseigné sur la politique locale; **the witnesses had all been primed by the police** les dépositions des témoins leur avaient été suggérées par la police **3** *(with paint, varnish)* apprêter

▸▸ ***prime beef*** bœuf *m* de première catégorie; *Fin* ***prime bond*** obligation *f* de premier ordre; ***prime cost*** prix *m* de revient; ***prime cut*** *(of meat)* morceau *m* de premier choix; *Fin* ***prime lending rate*** taux *m* de base bancaire; ***prime location*** site *m* idéal; ***prime meridian*** premier méridien *m*, méridien *m* origine; ***prime minister*** Premier ministre *m*; ***Prime Minister's Question Time*** = session hebdomadaire du Parlement britannique réservée aux questions des députés au Premier ministre; ***prime ministership, prime ministry*** fonctions *fpl* de Premier ministre; **during her p. ministership** pendant qu'elle était Premier ministre; ***prime mover*** *Phys* force *f* motrice; *Phil* cause *f* première; *Fig (person)* instigateur(trice) *m,f*; *Math* ***prime number*** nombre *m* premier; ***prime quality*** première qualité *f*; *Fin* ***prime rate*** taux *m* d'escompte bancaire préférentiel, prime rate *m*; *Am* ***prime rib*** *(UNCOUNT)* ≃ côte *f* de bœuf; *TV* ***prime time*** heures *fpl* de grande écoute, prime time *m*

primer ['praɪmə(r)] N **1** *(paint)* apprêt *m* **2** *(for explosives)* amorce *f* **3** *(book ▸ elementary)* manuel *m* (élémentaire); *(▸ for reading)* abécédaire *m*; **a Latin p.** un manuel de latin pour débutants

prime-time ADJ *TV* diffusé à une heure de grande écoute *ou* de prime time

▸▸ ***prime-time advertisement*** publicité *f* aux heures de grande écoute *ou* en prime time; ***prime-time advertising*** publicité *f* aux heures de grande écoute *ou* en prime time

primeval [praɪ'mi:vəl] ADJ **1** *(prehistoric)* primitif, des premiers âges *ou* temps **2** *(primordial ▸ fears, emotions)* atavique, instinctif

▸▸ ***primeval forest*** forêt *f* vierge

priming ['praɪmɪŋ] N *(UNCOUNT)* **1** *(of pump)* amorçage *m*; *(of gun)* amorce *f* **2** *(of wood etc)* apprêtage *m*, apprêt *m*; *(paint)* apprêt *m*

primitive ['prɪmɪtɪv] ADJ *(gen)* primitif; *(manners)* grossier, rude; *(understanding)* rudimentaire

N **1** *(primitive person)* primitif(ive) *m,f* **2** *(artist, picture)* primitif *m* **3** *Comput & Math* primitive *f*

▸▸ ***primitive art*** art *m* primitif

primitively ['prɪmɪtɪvlɪ] ADV *(gen)* primitivement; *(constructed, equipped)* de manière rudimentaire

primitiveness ['prɪmɪtɪvnɪs] N *(gen)* caractère *m* primitif; *(of plumbing, understanding)* caractère *m* rudimentaire; *(of manners)* grossièreté *f*, rudesse *f*

primitivism ['prɪmɪtɪvɪzəm] N *Art* primitivisme *m*

primly ['prɪmlɪ] ADV *Pej* d'une manière guindée *ou* collet monté; **to be p. dressed** être habillé très comme il faut; **she sat p. in the corner** elle se tenait assise très sagement dans le coin; **"no thank you," he said p.** "non merci", dit-il d'une voix affectée

primness ['prɪmnɪs] N *Pej (of person)* air *m* collet monté *ou* compassé; *(of behaviour)* caractère *m* maniéré *ou* compassé; *(of dress)* aspect *m* collet monté *ou* très comme il faut; *(of voice)* caractère *m* affecté

primogeniture [ˌpraɪməʊ'dʒenɪtʃə(r)] N primogéniture *f*; **(right of) p.** droit *m* d'aînesse

primordial [praɪ'mɔ:dɪəl] ADJ primordial

▸▸ *Biol* ***primordial ooze, primordial soup*** soupe *f* primitive

primordially [praɪ'mɔ:dɪəlɪ] ADV primordialement, originellement

primp [prɪmp] *Old-fashioned* VI se faire beau (belle)

VT **to p. oneself (up)** se faire beau (belle)

primrose ['prɪmrəʊz] N **1** *Bot* primevère *f* **2** *(colour)* jaune *m* pâle

ADJ jaune pâle *(inv)*

▸▸ *Literary* ***the primrose path*** la voie de la facilité; ***primrose yellow*** jaune *m* pâle

primula ['prɪmjʊlə] *(pl* **primulas** *or* **primulae** [-li:]) N *Bot* primevère *f*

Primus® ['praɪməs] N *Br (stove)* réchaud *m* (de camping)

▸▸ ***Primus® stove*** réchaud *m* (de camping)

prince [prɪns] N *also Fig* prince *m*; **P. Rupert** le prince Rupert; **he is a p. among men** c'est un prince parmi les hommes; **to live like a p.** vivre comme un prince; *Am Fam* **thanks, you're a p.** merci, vous êtes très généreux

▸▸ ***Prince Charming*** le Prince Charmant; ***prince consort*** prince *m* consort; ***the Prince of Darkness*** le prince des ténèbres; ***Prince Edward Island*** l'île *f* du Prince-Édouard; ***the Prince of Peace*** le prince de la paix; ***prince regent*** prince *m* régent; ***the Prince of Wales*** le prince de Galles

princeling ['prɪnslɪŋ] N petit prince *m*

princely ['prɪnslɪ] ADJ princier

▸▸ ***princely sum*** somme *f* princière

princess [prɪn'ses] N princesse *f*; **P. Anne** la princesse Anne; **the P. of Wales** la princesse de Galles

▸▸ ***princess dress*** robe *f* princesse; ***the princess royal*** la princesse royale *(fille aînée du monarque)*

principal ['prɪnsɪpəl] ADJ **1** *(gen)* principal; **the p. cause of the problem** la cause principale du problème **2** *Mus (violin, oboe)* premier

N **1** *(head ▸ of school)* directeur(trice) *m,f*; *(▸ of university)* doyen(enne) *m,f*

2 *Law (employer of agent)* mandant(e) *m,f*, commettant *m*; *St Exch* donneur(euse) *m,f* d'ordre

3 *(main character ▸ in play)* acteur(trice) *m,f* principal(e); *(▸ in orchestra)* chef *m* de pupitre; *(▸ in crime)* auteur *m*

4 *Fin (capital ▸ gen)* capital *m*; *(▸ of debt)* principal *m*; **p. and interest** capital *m* et intérêts *mpl*

▸▸ ***principal boy*** = jeune héros d'une pantomime dont le rôle est traditionnellement joué par une femme; *Gram* ***principal clause*** (proposition *f*) principale *f*; *Gram* ***principal parts*** temps *mpl* primitifs; *Br Pol* ***principal private secretary*** ≃ directeur(trice) *m,f* de cabinet

principality [ˌprɪnsɪ'pælətɪ] N principauté *f*; **the P.** *(Wales)* le pays de Galles

principally ['prɪnsɪpəlɪ] ADV principalement, surtout; **p., it's a question of money** c'est principalement *ou* essentiellement une question d'argent

principle ['prɪnsɪpəl] N **1** *(for behaviour)* principe *m*; **she has high principles** elle a des principes; **she was a woman of p.** c'était une femme de principes *ou* qui avait des principes; **he has no principles** il n'a pas de principes; **it's not the money, it's the p.** ce n'est pas pour l'argent, c'est pour le principe; **on p., as a matter of p.** par principe; **it's a matter of p., it's the p. of the thing** c'est une question de principe; **it's against my principles to eat meat** j'ai pour principe de ne pas manger de viande; **she makes it a p. never to criticize others** elle a pour principe de ne jamais critiquer les autres; **to stick to one's principles** rester fidèle à ses principes **2** *(fundamental law)* principe *m*; **to go back to first principles** remonter jusqu'au principe; *Phil* **p. of causality** loi *f* de causalité **3** *(theory)* principe *m*; **basic p.** principe *m* de base; **to be based on false principles** reposer sur de faux principes *ou* de fausses prémisses; **machines that work on the same p.** machines qui fonctionnent sur *ou* d'après le même principe; **we acted on the p. that everybody knew** nous sommes partis du principe que tout le monde était au courant

• **in principle** ADV en principe; **to reach an agreement in p.** parvenir à un accord de principe

principled ['prɪnsɪpəld] ADJ *(behaviour)* dicté par des principes; *(person)* qui a des principes; **to take a p. stand** adopter une position de principe; **it was very p. of her to refuse** elle a démontré de hauts principes en refusant

print [prɪnt] N **1** *(UNCOUNT) (of publications)* **to appear in p.** *(book)* être publié *ou* imprimé; **he appeared in p. for the first time in 2001** son premier ouvrage/roman a été publié en 2001; **to see oneself/one's name in p.** voir ses écrits imprimés/son nom imprimé; **her work will soon be in p.** son œuvre sera bientôt publiée; **to be in/out of p.** *(book)* être disponible/épuisé; **his unguarded comments got into p.** ses propos irréfléchis ont été publiés *ou* imprimés; **he refused to believe the story until he saw it in p.** il a refusé de croire à l'histoire tant qu'il ne l'a pas vue publiée; **the newspapers had already gone to p. before the news broke** les journaux étaient déjà sous presse lorsque la nouvelle est tombée

2 *(UNCOUNT) (characters)* caractères *mpl*; *(text)* texte *m* (imprimé); **in large p.** en gros caractères; **in bold p.** en caractères gras; **I had to read through twenty pages of p.** j'ai dû lire vingt pages imprimées; **the p. was so small I could barely read it** il était imprimé en caractères si petits que j'avais du mal à le lire; **always read the small p.** *(of contract, guarantee etc)* il faut toujours lire ce qu'il y a d'écrit en petits caractères

3 *Phot* épreuve *f*, tirage *m*; **to make a p. from a negative** tirer une épreuve d'un négatif

4 *Art (engraving)* gravure *f*, estampe *f*; *(reproduction)* poster *m*

5 *Tex (fabric)* imprimé *m*; *(dress)* robe *f* imprimée; **a floral p.** un imprimé à fleurs

6 *(mark ▸ from tyre, foot)* empreinte *f*; *(fingerprint)* empreinte *f* digitale; **the thief left his prints all over the door handle** le voleur a laissé ses empreintes partout sur la poignée de la porte

ADJ *(dress)* en tissu imprimé

VT **1** *(book, newspaper, money)* imprimer; *(copies)* tirer; *(publish ▸ story, article)* publier; **the novel is being printed** le roman est sous presse *ou* en cours d'impression; **1,000 copies of the book have already been printed** on a déjà tiré le livre à 1000 exemplaires; **printed in France** imprimé en France

2 *Comput* imprimer; **to p. sth to disk** imprimer qch sur disque

3 *(write)* écrire en caractères d'imprimerie; **p. your name clearly** écrivez votre nom lisiblement

4 *Phot* tirer

5 *Tex* imprimer

6 *(mark)* imprimer; *Fig (in memory)* graver, imprimer; **the mark of a man's foot was printed in the wet sand** la trace d'un pied d'homme était imprimée dans le sable humide; **the incident remained printed in their memory** l'incident est resté gravé dans leur mémoire

VI **1** *(book, text)* imprimer; *Comput (document)* s'imprimer; *(printer)* imprimer; **the book is now printing** le livre est à l'impression *ou* est actuellement sous presse; **the drawing should p. well** le dessin devrait bien ressortir à l'impression **2** *(in handwriting)* écrire en caractères d'imprimerie **3** *Phot (negative)* **to p. well** sortir bien au tirage

▸▸ *Mktg* ***print ad, print advertisement*** publicité *f* presse; *Mktg* ***print advertising*** publicité *f* presse; *Comput* ***print buffer*** mémoire *f* tampon d'imprimante; *Comput* ***print cartridge*** cartouche *f*; *Comput* ***print drum*** tambour *m* d'impression; *Comput* ***print file*** fichier *m* d'impression; *Comput* ***print format*** format *m* d'impression; *Comput* ***print head*** tête *f* d'impression; *Comput* ***print job (file)*** fichier *m* à imprimer; ***print journalist*** journaliste *mf* de la presse écrite; *Comput* ***print list*** liste *f* de fichiers à imprimer; ***the print media*** la presse écrite et l'édition; *Comput* ***print menu*** menu *m* d'impression; *Comput* ***print option*** option *f* d'impression; *Comput* ***print preview*** prévisualisation *f*, aperçu *m* avant impression; *Comput* ***print quality*** qualité *f* d'impression; *Comput* ***print queue*** liste *f* de fichiers à imprimer; *Comput* ***print queuing*** mise *f* en attente à l'impression; *Typ* ***print room*** cabinet *m* d'estampes; ***print run*** tirage *m*; **a p. run of 5,000** un tirage à 5000 exemplaires; *Comput* ***print screen*** copie *f* d'écran; *Comput* ***print screen key*** touche *f* d'impression d'écran; **to do a p. screen** imprimer un écran; ***print shop*** imprimerie *f*; *Comput* ***print speed*** vitesse *f* d'impression; ***print union*** syndicat *m* des typographes; ***print worker*** imprimeur *m*

▸ **print off** VT SEP **1** *Typ* imprimer; *(copies)* tirer **2** *Comput* imprimer **3** *Phot* tirer

▸ **print out** VT SEP *Comput* imprimer

printable ['prɪntəbəl] ADJ imprimable, publiable; **some of their remarks were hardly p.** certaines de leurs remarques étaient difficilement publiables; **my opinion on the matter is not p.** mon avis sur la question n'est pas très agréable à entendre

printed ['prɪntɪd] ADJ **1** *(gen)* imprimé; **the p. word** l'écrit *m* **2** *(notepaper)* à en-tête

▸▸ *Elec* ***printed circuit*** circuit *m* imprimé; *Elec* ***printed circuit board*** carte *f* de *ou* à circuits imprimés; *Tex* ***printed cotton*** coton *m* imprimé; ***printed form*** imprimé *m*, formulaire *m*; ***printed matter*** imprimés *mpl*

printer ['prɪntə(r)] N **1** *(person ▸ gen)* imprimeur *m*; *(▸ typographer)* typographe *mf*; *(▸ compositor)* compositeur(trice) *m,f*; **it's at the p.'s** c'est chez l'imprimeur *ou* à l'impression **2** *Comput* imprimante *f* **3** *Phot (person)* tireur(euse) *m,f* d'épreuves; *(machine)* tireuse *f*

▸▸ ***printer cable*** câble *m* d'imprimante; ***printer's devil*** apprenti *m* imprimeur; *Comput* ***printer driver*** programme *m* de commande d'impression; ***printer drum*** tambour *m* d'impression; ***printer's error*** coquille *f*; ***printer font*** fonte *f* imprimante; ***printer's ink*** encre *f* d'imprimerie; ***printer's mark*** marque *f* d'imprimeur; ***printer paper*** papier *m* d'impression; *Comput* ***printer port*** port *m* d'imprimante; ***printer's proofs*** épreuves *fpl* d'imprimerie; ***printer's reader*** correcteur(trice) *m,f* d'épreuves; ***printer ribbon*** ruban *m* d'impression; *Comput* ***printer server*** serveur *m* d'imprimante; ***printer speed*** vitesse *f* d'impression; ***printer spooler*** spouleur *m* d'imprimante, pilote *m* de mise en attente des fichiers à imprimer; ***printer spooling*** mise *f* en attente des fichiers à imprimer

printing ['prɪntɪŋ] N **1** *(industry, craft)* imprimerie *f*; **he works in p.** il travaille dans l'imprimerie

2 *(process)* impression *f*

3 *(copies printed)* impression *f*, tirage *m*; **fourth p.** quatrième impression *f*

4 *Phot* tirage *m*

5 *(UNCOUNT) (handwriting)* (écriture *f* en) caractères *mpl* d'imprimerie

▸▸ ***printing error*** erreur *f* typographique; ***printing house*** imprimerie *f*; ***printing ink*** encre *f* d'imprimerie; ***printing office*** imprimerie *f*; ***printing plate*** plaque *f*; ***printing press*** presse *f* (d'imprimerie)

printout ['prɪntaʊt] N *(act of printing out)* tirage *m*, sortie *f* sur imprimante; *(printed version)* sortie *f* (sur) papier, tirage *m*; *(results of calculation)* listing *m*; **to do a p.** sortir un document sur imp[rimante], imprimer (un document); **here's the p. [of] the results** voici le listing des résultats

print-through paper N *Comput* papier *m* effet d'empreinte, liasse *f* carbonnée

prior ['praɪə(r)] ADJ **1** *(earlier)* antérieur, préc[é]dent; **she had a p. engagement** elle était dé[jà] prise; **to have p. knowledge of sth** être déjà [au] courant de qch; **without p. notice** sans préav[is]; **without his p. agreement** sans son accord pré[a]lable **2** *(more important)* **to have a p. claim to on sth** avoir un droit de priorité *ou* d'antériori[té] sur qch; **her son had a p. claim on her attention** s[on] fils passait avant tout

N *Rel* (père *m*) prieur *m*

• **prior to** PREP avant, antérieurement à, pré[a]lablement à; **p. to (his) departure...** avant son d[é]part *ou* avant de partir...; **p. to today** ava[nt] aujourd'hui; **p. to any discussion** préalableme[nt] à *ou* avant toute discussion; **p. to his winning/a[p]pointment** avant qu'il ne gagne/ne soit nomm[é], avant sa victoire/sa nomination

prioress ['praɪərɪs] N *Rel* (mère *f*) prieure *f*

prioritization, -isation [ˌpraɪɒrɪtaɪ'zeɪʃən] **the p. of all these jobs** la définition d'un ordre [de] priorité pour toutes ces tâches; **they opted fo[r] p. of expansion** ils ont décidé de donner la pr[io]rité à l'expansion

prioritize, -ise [praɪ'ɒrɪtaɪz] VT **1** *(give priority)* donner *ou* accorder la priorité à; **they've prio[ri]tized those who've been waiting longest** ils [ont] donné la priorité à ceux qui avaient attendu [le] plus longtemps **2** *(arrange according to priori[ty])* donner un ordre de priorité à; **it depends h[ow] you p. them** tout dépend de l'ordre de prior[ité] que tu établis; **it was wrongly prioritized** on [a] mal jugé de son importance

VI *(evaluate priorities)* établir un ordre de prio[ri]tés

priority [praɪ'ɒrətɪ] (*pl* **priorities**) N priorité *f*; **give p. to** donner *ou* accorder la priorité à; **have p.** *(of job etc)* être prioritaire; *(of driver)* av[oir] la priorité; **to have** *or* **to take p. over** avoir la pri[o]rité sur; **to do sth as a (matter of) p.** faire qch [en] priorité; **the matter has top p.** l'affaire a la prior[ité] absolue *ou* est absolument prioritaire; **the [li]brary came high/low on the list of priorities** la [bi]bliothèque venait en tête/venait loin sur la lis[te] des priorités; **you should get your priorities righ[t]** [il] faudrait que tu apprennes à distinguer ce q[ui] est important de ce qui ne l'est pas; **the gove[rn]ment has got its priorities all wrong** le gouvern[e]ment n'accorde pas la priorité aux choses [les] plus importantes; **according to p.** selon l'ord[re] de priorité

COMP **to get p. treatment** *(task)* être exécuté [en] fait en priorité

▸▸ ***priority booking*** réservation *f* prioritai[re]; ***priority holder*** prioritaire *mf*; *Am* ***priority m[ail]*** courrier *m* prioritaire; *Law* ***priority rights*** dro[its] *mpl* de priorité *ou* de préférence; *St Exch* ***prior[ity] share*** action *f* privilégiée, action *f* de priorité

priory ['praɪərɪ] (*pl* **priories**) N *Rel* prieuré *m*

prise [praɪz] VT *Br* **to p. sth open** ouvrir qch [à] l'aide d'un levier; **he tried to p. open the door** i[l a] essayé de forcer la porte; **she managed to p. h[er] leg free** elle a réussi à dégager sa jambe; **th[ey] had to p. his hand open to get the key** ils ont [dû] ouvrir sa main de force pour avoir la clé; **[we] prised the top off with a spoon** on a enlevé le co[u]vercle à l'aide d'une cuillère; *Fig* **we managed [to] p. the information out of her** on a réussi à lui ar[ra]cher le renseignement; **I managed to p. £10 o[ut] of him** j'ai réussi à lui soutirer 10 livres

prism ['prɪzəm] N prisme *m*

prismatic [prɪz'mætɪk] ADJ prismatique

prison ['prɪzən] N *also Fig* prison *f*; **to be in p.** êt[re] en prison; **he's been in p.** il a fait de la prison; **go to p.** aller en prison, être emprisonné; **to se[nd] sb to p., to put sb in p.** envoyer *ou* mettre qn [en] prison; **to be sent to** *or* **put in p.** être incarcé[ré]; **to sentence sb to three years in p.** condamner [qn] à trois ans de prison

COMP *(director, warder, cell)* de prison; *(foo[d], conditions)* en prison, dans les prisons; *(syste[m], regulations, administration)* pénitentiaire, carc[é]ral

►► *prison camp* camp *m* de prisonniers; *prison colony* bagne *m*, colonie *f* pénitentiaire; *prison officer* gardien(enne) *m,f* de prison; *prison sentence* peine *f* de prison; **his assignment to Vladivostok had become a p. sentence** son séjour à Vladivostok, où il est en poste, est devenu un long exil; *prison van* fourgon *m* cellulaire; *prison visitor* visiteur(euse) *m,f* de prison; *prison yard* cour *f* de prison

prisoner ['prɪzənə(r)] **N 1** *(captive)* prisonnier (ère) *m,f*; **to take sb p.** faire qn prisonnier; **to hold sb p.** retenir qn prisonnier, détenir qn; **to be taken p.** être fait prisonnier; **to be held p.** être détenu; *Fig* **she became a p. of her own fears** elle devint prisonnière de ses propres peurs; *Fig* **to take no prisoners** ne faire aucune concession **2** *Law* détenu(e) *m,f*; *(after sentence)* détenu(e) *m,f*, prisonnier(ère) *m,f*; **p. at the bar** prévenu(e) *m,f*; *(for serious crimes)* accusé(e) *m,f*

►► *prisoner of conscience* prisonnier(ère) *m,f* d'opinion; *prisoner of war* prisonnier(ère) *m,f* de guerre; *prisoner of war camp* camp *m* de prisonniers de guerre

prissy ['prɪsɪ] *(compar* **prissier**, *superl* **prissiest)** **ADJ** *(fussy)* pointilleux, maniaque; *(prudish)* bégueule

pristine ['prɪsti:n] **ADJ 1** *(immaculate)* parfait, immaculé; **in p. condition** en parfait état **2** *(original)* primitif, premier

prithee ['prɪðɪ] **EXCLAM** *Arch* je vous prie, s'il vous plaît

privacy ['prɪvəsɪ, 'praɪvəsɪ] **N 1** *(seclusion)* solitude *f*; **lack of p.** manque *m* d'intimité; **there is no p. here** on n'est jamais seul ici; **can I have some p. for a few hours?** pouvez-vous me laisser seul quelques heures?; **she hates having her p. disturbed** elle déteste qu'on la dérange chez elle **2** *(private life)* vie *f* privée; **I value my p.** je tiens à ma vie privée; **you can't have any p. if you're a star** les stars n'ont pas de vie privée; **an intrusion on sb's p.** une ingérence dans la vie privée de qn **3** *(secrecy)* intimité *f*, secret *m*; **to get married in the strictest p.** se marier dans la plus stricte intimité; **in the p. of one's home** dans l'intimité de son foyer

►► *Can Privacy Commissioner* Commissaire *m* à la protection de la vie privée; *privacy laws* lois *fpl* sur la protection de la vie privée

PRIVATE ['praɪvɪt]

ADJ
- privé **1–4, 6**
- particulier **5**
- personnel **3–5**
- intime **6**

N
- soldat

ADJ 1 *(not for the public)* privé; **p.** *(sign)* privé, interdit au public; **the funeral will be p.** les obsèques auront lieu dans la plus stricte intimité; **they want a p. wedding** ils veulent se marier dans l'intimité

2 *(not state-run)* privé; **they operate a p. pension scheme** ils ont leur propre caisse de retraite; **the p. sector** le secteur privé

3 *(personal)* privé, personnel; **for p. reasons** pour des raisons personnelles; **don't interfere in my p. affairs** *or* **business** ne vous mêlez pas de mes affaires personnelles; **a p. agreement** un accord à l'amiable; **it's my p. opinion** c'est mon opinion personnelle; **it's a p. joke** c'est une blague entre nous/eux/*etc*; **she keeps her p. thoughts to herself** elle garde pour elle ses opinions personnelles

4 *(confidential)* privé, confidentiel, personnel; **a p. conversation** une conversation privée *ou* à caractère privé; **we had a p. meeting** nous nous sommes vus en privé; **keep it p.** gardez-le pour vous; **can I tell him? – no, it's p.** je peux le lui dire? – non, c'est personnel; **p. and confidential** secret et confidentiel; **p.** *(on envelope)* personnel

5 *(individual ► bank account)* personnel; *(► bathroom, lessons, tuition)* particulier; **she has p. lessons in French** elle prend des cours particuliers de français; **this is a p. house** c'est une maison particulière *ou* qui appartient à des particuliers; **in my p. capacity** à titre personnel; **for your p. use** pour votre usage personnel; **this is his own p. room** c'est sa pièce à lui

6 *(quiet, intimate)* intime, privé; **a p. place** un endroit tranquille; **he's a very p. person** c'est quelqu'un de très discret; **do you have a p. room where we can talk?** avez-vous une pièce où l'on puisse parler tranquillement?

7 *(ordinary)* **a p. citizen** *or* **individual** un (simple) citoyen, un particulier

N *Mil* (simple) soldat *m*, soldat *m* de deuxième classe; **it belongs to P. Hopkins** ça appartient au soldat Hopkins; **the privates and the NCOs** la troupe et les gradés; **P. Murdoch!** soldat Murdoch!

• **privates NPL** *Fam Euph* parties *fpl* génitales

• **in private ADV** *(confidentially)* en privé, en confidence; *(in private life)* en privé, dans la vie privée; *(with close family)* dans l'intimité; *(with friends, not in public)* dans le privé; **to sit in p.** *(assembly)* se réunir en séance privée *ou* à huis clos; *Law* **to hear a case in p.** juger une affaire à huis clos; **to speak to sb in p.** parler à qn en privé; **in p. she admitted she was worried** en privé, elle a admis qu'elle était inquiète; *(to herself)* dans son for intérieur elle a admis qu'elle était inquiète

►► *private address* adresse *f* personnelle, domicile *m*; *Law* *private agreement* acte *m* sous seing privé; *Tel* *private automatic exchange* central *m* automatique privé; *private bank* banque *f* privée; *private bar* = salon dans un pub; *private car* voiture *f* particulière; *private citizen* simple particulier *m*; *private company* entreprise *f ou* société *f* privée; *private dance* bal *m* sur invitation; *private detective* détective *m* privé; *private education* enseignement *m* privé; *private enterprise* entreprise *f* privée; *(principle)* libre entreprise *f*; *Fam* *private eye (private detective)* privé *m*; *private finance initiative* partenariat *m* public-privé; *private fishing* pêche *f* gardée; *private health insurance* assurance *f* maladie privée; *private hotel* ≃ pension *f* de famille; *private income* rentes *fpl*; **to live on** *or* **off a p. income** vivre de ses rentes; *private industry* privé *m*; *private investigator* détective *m* privé; *Fin* *private investment* investissement *m ou* placement *m* privé; *Fin* *private investor* investisseur(euse) *m,f* privé(e); *private land* terrain *m* privé; *private law* droit *m* privé; *private life* vie *f* privée; **in (his) p. life** dans sa vie privée, en privé; **she has no p. life** elle n'a pas de vie privée; *Fin* *private limited company* société *f* à responsabilité limitée; *Tel* *private line* ligne *f* privée; *private means* rentes *fpl*, fortune *f* personnelle; **a man of p. means** un rentier; *private medical insurance* assurance-maladie *f* privée; *Parl* *private member* = simple député *m*; *Parl* *private member's bill* = proposition de loi faite par un simple député; *private ownership* propriété *f* privée; *Fam Euph* *private parts* parties *fpl* génitales; *private party (gathering)* réunion *f* privée *ou* intime; *(group)* groupe *m* de particuliers; *private patient* = patient d'un médecin dont les consultations ne sont pas prises en charge par les services de santé; *Fin* *private pension* retraite *f* complémentaire; *Theat* *private performance* représentation *f* privée; *Med* *private practice* médecine *f* privée *or* non conventionnée; **she's in p. practice** elle a un cabinet (médical) privé; *private property* propriété *f* privée; **p. property, keep out!** *(sign)* propriété privée, défense d'entrer; *private pupil* élève *mf (à qui l'on donne des cours particuliers)*; **he has a lot of p. pupils** il donne beaucoup de cours particuliers; *private road* voie *f* privée; *private room (in hospital)* chambre *f* particulière; *private sale* vente *f* à l'amiable; *private school* école *f* privée; *Cin* *private screening* projection *f* privée; *private secretary* secrétaire *mf* particulier(ère); *Br Pol* = haut fonctionnaire dont le rôle est d'assister un ministre; *Cin* *private showing* projection *f* privée; *private soldier* simple soldat *m*, (soldat *m* de) deuxième classe *m*; *private teacher* précepteur(trice) *m,f*; *Art* *private view* vernissage *m*; *Law* *private wrong* atteinte *f* aux droits d'un individu

privateer [ˌpraɪvə'tɪə(r)] **N** corsaire *m*

private-label brand N *Mktg* marque *f* de distributeur

privately ['praɪvɪtlɪ] **ADV 1** *(not publicly)* **a p. owned company** une entreprise privée; **I had it done p.** *(treatment at doctor's, dentist's)* je l'ai fait faire à mes frais; **she sold her house p.** elle a vendu sa maison de particulier à particulier; **they were married p.** leur mariage a eu lieu dans l'intimité; **to be p. educated** *(at school)* faire ses études dans une école privée; *(with tutor)* avoir un précepteur; **the jury's deliberations took place p.** les délibérations du jury se sont déroulées à huis clos

2 *(personally)* dans *ou* en mon/son/*etc* for intérieur, en moi-même/lui-même/*etc*; **p., he didn't agree** dans son for intérieur *ou* intérieurement, il n'était pas d'accord

3 *(secretly)* secrètement

4 *(confidentially)* en privé; **she informed me p. that...** elle m'a informé en toute confidence que...; **we met p.** nous avons eu une entrevue privée; **can I see you p.?** puis-je vous voir en privé *ou* en tête-à-tête?; **I spoke to her p.** je lui ai parlé en tête-à-tête

5 *(as a private individual)* à titre personnel

privation [ˌpraɪ'veɪʃən] **N** privation *f*; **to live in p.** vivre dans la privation, vivre de privations

privatization, -isation [ˌpraɪvɪtaɪ'zeɪʃən] **N** privatisation *f*

privatize, -ise ['praɪvɪtaɪz] **VT** privatiser

privet ['prɪvɪt] **N** *Bot* troène *m*

►► *privet hedge* haie *f* de troènes

privilege ['prɪvɪlɪdʒ] **N 1** *(right, advantage)* privilège *m*; **to grant sb the p. of doing sth** accorder à qn le privilège de faire qch

2 *(UNCOUNT)* *(unfair advantage)* **a struggle against p.** une lutte contre les privilèges

3 *(honour)* honneur *m*; **it was a p. doing business with you** ce fut un honneur de travailler avec vous; **I had the p. of attending his wedding** j'ai eu le bonheur *ou* la chance d'assister à son mariage; **it is my p. to introduce...** j'ai le grand honneur *ou* le privilège de vous présenter...

4 *Law (of lawyer)* droit *m* de tenir une information secrète; *Pol* **parliamentary p.** immunité *f* parlementaire

5 *Comput (for access to network, database)* droits *mpl* d'accès

VT privilégier; **I am privileged to be able to present to you...** j'ai l'honneur *ou* le privilège de vous présenter...

privileged ['prɪvɪlɪdʒd] **ADJ 1** *(person, position)* privilégié; **he comes from a p. background** il est issu d'un milieu privilégié; **only a p. few were invited** seuls quelques privilégiés ont été invités; **a p. minority** une minorité privilégiée, quelques privilégiés *mpl* **2** *Law (document, information)* laissé à la discrétion du témoin; **such information is p.** le témoin n'est pas obligé de divulguer une telle information

NPL the p. les privilégiés *mpl*

►► *Fin* *privileged debt* dette *f* privilégiée

privily ['prɪvɪlɪ] **ADV** *Arch* en secret

privy ['prɪvɪ] *(pl* **privies) ADJ** *Formal (informed)* **to be p. to sth** avoir connaissance de qch, être au courant de qch; **an officer who had been p. to the plot was arrested** un officier qui était au courant du complot fut arrêté

N *Old-fashioned (toilet)* lieux *mpl* d'aisances *(souvent en dehors de la maison)*

►► *Privy Council* = le Conseil privé du souverain en Grande-Bretagne; *Privy Councillor* = membre du Conseil privé; *Privy Purse* cassette *f* royale; *the Privy Seal* le Petit Sceau

prize[1] [praɪz] **N 1** *(for merit)* prix *m*; **to award a p. to sb** décerner un prix à qn; **to win (the) first p. in a contest** remporter le premier prix d'un concours; **she won the p. for the best pupil** elle s'est vu décerner *ou* elle a reçu le prix d'excellence; *Fig* **no prizes for guessing who won** vous n'aurez aucun mal à deviner le nom du gagnant **2** *(in game)* prix *m*; *(in lottery)* lot *m*; **to win first p.** gagner le gros lot; **the first p. is a week in London** le premier prix est une semaine à Londres **3** *Naut* prise *f*

VT *(cherish ► gen)* chérir, attacher une grande valeur à; *(► for quality, rarity)* priser; **I p. his friendship very highly** son amitié m'est très précieuse; **her most prized possession** l'objet qu'elle chérit plus que tout; **original editions are highly prized** les éditions originales sont très prisées *ou* recherchées

ADJ 1 *(prizewinning)* primé, médaillé; **p. lamb**

agneau *m* primé *ou* médaillé **2** *(excellent)* parfait, typique; a **p. specimen of manhood** un superbe mâle; **that's a p. example of what not to do!** c'est un parfait exemple de ce qu'il ne faut pas faire!; *Fam* **a p. fool** un parfait imbécile **3** *(valuable)* de valeur; *(cherished)* prisé; **it's my p. possession** c'est l'objet que je prise au-dessus de tout

▸▸ *Br Sch* ***prize day*** (jour *m* de la) distribution *f* des prix; ***prize draw*** tombola *f*, loterie *f*; ***prize list*** liste *f* des gagnants; ***prize money*** prix *m (en argent)*; *Boxing* ***prize ring*** ring *m (pour la boxe professionnelle)*

prize[2] = **prise**

prizefight ['praɪzfaɪt] **N** *Boxing* combat *m* professionnel

prizefighter ['praɪzfaɪtə(r)] **N** *Boxing* boxeur (euse) *m,f* professionnel(elle)

prizefighting ['praɪzfaɪtɪŋ] **N** *Boxing* boxe *f* professionnelle

prize-giving **N** distribution *f ou* remise *f* des prix

▸▸ ***prize-giving ceremony*** cérémonie *f* de distribution *ou* de remise des prix

prizewinner ['praɪzwɪnə(r)] **N** *(of exam, essay contest)* lauréat(e) *m,f*; *(of game, lottery)* gagnant(e) *m,f*

prizewinning ['praɪzwɪnɪŋ] **ADJ** *(novel, entry)* primé; *(ticket, number, contestant)* gagnant

PRO [,piːɑːr'əʊ] **N 1** *(abbr* **public relations officer)** responsable *mf* des relations publiques **2** *Br (abbr* **Public Record Office)** ≃ Archives *fpl* nationales

pro [prəʊ] *(pl* **pros) N** *Fam* **1** *(abbr* **professional)** pro *mf*; **to turn p.** passer pro; **she was a real p.** *(actress, singer etc)* c'était une vraie pro **2** *(abbr* **professional)** *(at sports club)* pro *mf* **3** *(abbr* **prostitute)** professionnelle *f*

ADJ *Fam (abbr* **professional)** pro

PREP *(in favour of)* pour; **he's very p. capital punishment** c'est un partisan convaincu de la peine capitale

• **pros NPL the pros and cons** le pour et le contre; **the pros and the antis** ceux qui sont pour et ceux qui sont contre

▸▸ *Am* ***pro ball*** *(baseball)* base-ball *m* professionnel; *Golf* ***pro shop*** pro shop *m*, *Can* boutique *f* du pro

pro- [prəʊ] **PREF** *(in favour of)* pro-; **p.-American** proaméricain; **p.-Europe** pro-européen; **they were p.-Stalin** ils étaient pour Staline, c'étaient des partisans de Staline

proactive [,prəʊ'æktɪv] **ADJ 1** *(not reactive)* dynamique, qui prend des initiatives; **you should be more p.** tu devrais prendre plus souvent des initiatives **2** *Psy* proactif

pro-am [,prəʊ'æm] *Sport* **ADJ** professionnel et amateur

N = tournoi opposant des équipes composées chacune d'un professionnel et d'un amateur

▸▸ ***pro-am tournament*** = tournoi opposant des équipes composées chacune d'un professionnel et d'un amateur

prob [prɒb] **N** *Fam (problem)* problème□*m*, blème *m*; *Br* **no probs!** pas de problèmes!

probability [,prɒbə'bɪlətɪ] *(pl* **probabilities) N 1** *(likelihood)* probabilité *f*; **the p. is that he won't come** il est probable qu'il ne viendra pas, il y a de fortes chances (pour) qu'il ne vienne pas; **there is little** *or* **not much p. of her changing her mind** il est peu probable qu'elle *ou* il y a peu de chance (pour) qu'elle change d'avis; **there is a strong p. of that happening** il y a de fortes chances que cela se produise; **in all p.** selon toute probabilité **2** *Math* probabilité *f*; **what is the p.** *or* **what are the probabilities of such a result?** quelle est la probabilité d'un tel résultat?; **what is the p. of 10 percent proving defective?** quelle probabilité y a-t-il que 10 pour cent s'avèrent défectueux?

▸▸ ***probability method*** *(of sampling)* méthode *f* probabiliste; ***probability sample*** échantillon *m* probabiliste; ***probability sampling*** échantillonnage *m* probabiliste; *Math* ***probability theory*** théorie *f* des probabilités

probable ['prɒbəbəl] **ADJ 1** *(likely)* probable; **the most p. hypothesis** l'hypothèse la plus vraisemblable; **it's highly p. that we won't arrive before 2 o'clock** il est fort probable *ou* plus que probable que nous n'arriverons pas avant 14 heures; **that's quite p.** c'est tout à fait probable; **p. cause of death** cause *f* probable de la mort **2** *(plausible)* vraisemblable; **it doesn't sound very p. to me** ça ne me paraît pas très vraisemblable

N he's a p. for the team next Saturday il y a de fortes chances pour qu'il joue dans l'équipe samedi prochain; **she's one of the probables for the job** elle fait partie des candidats qui ont de bonnes chances

▸▸ *Law* ***probable cause*** motif *m* raisonnable

probably ['prɒbəblɪ] **ADV** probablement; **p. not** probablement pas; **will you be able to come? – p.** pourrez-vous venir? – probablement; **will he write to you? – very p.** il t'écrira? – c'est très probable; **she's p. left already** elle est probablement déjà partie, il est probable qu'elle soit déjà partie

probate ['prəʊbeɪt] *Law* **N** *(authentification)* homologation *f*, authentification *f*, validation *f*; **to grant/to take out p. of a will** homologuer/faire homologuer un testament

VT *Am (will)* homologuer, faire authentifier

▸▸ ***probate court*** tribunal *m* des successions et des tutelles

probation [prə'beɪʃən] **N 1** *Law* sursis *m* avec mise à l'épreuve, *Spec* probation *f*; **to be on p.** ≃ être en sursis avec mise à l'épreuve; **to put sb on p.** ≃ condamner qn avec sursis et mise à l'épreuve **2** *(trial employment)* essai *m*; **period of p.** période *f* d'essai; **to be on p.** être en période d'essai **3** *Rel* probation *f*

▸▸ ***probation officer*** ≃ agent *m* de probation

probationary [prə'beɪʃənərɪ] **ADJ 1** *(trial)* d'essai **2** *Law* de probation **3** *Rel* de probation, de noviciat

▸▸ ***probationary period*** période *f* d'essai; ***probationary teacher*** professeur *m* stagiaire; *Br Sch* ***probationary year*** année *f* probatoire

probationer [prə'beɪʃənə(r)] **N 1** *(employee)* employé(e) *m,f* à l'essai *ou* en période d'essai; *Br (teacher)* (professeur *m*) stagiaire *mf*; *(trainee nurse)* élève *mf* infirmier(ère) **2** *Law* probationnaire *mf* **3** *Rel* novice *mf*

probe [prəʊb] **N 1** *(investigation)* enquête *f*, investigation *f*; **there has been a newspaper p. into corruption** la presse a fait une enquête sur la corruption **2** *(question)* question *f*, interrogation *f*; **he didn't respond to our probes into** *or* **about his past** il est resté muet lorsque nous avons essayé de l'interroger sur son passé **3** *Astron, Electron & Med* sonde *f*; *Zool* trompe *f*

VT 1 *(investigate)* enquêter sur; **police are probing the company's accounts** la police épluche les comptes *ou* examine la comptabilité de la société **2** *(examine, sound out* ▸ *person, motive, reasons)* sonder; **to p. sb about sth** sonder qn sur qch **3** *(explore)* explorer, fouiller, sonder; *Med* sonder; **she probed the snow with her umbrella** elle fouilla la neige avec la pointe de son parapluie; **to p. the mysteries of the mind** sonder les mystères de l'esprit

VI 1 *(investigate)* enquêter, faire une enquête; **the police are probing for clues** les policiers recherchent des indices; **to p. into sth** enquêter sur qch; **if you p. into his past, you'll have some surprises** si vous fouillez dans son passé, vous aurez des surprises; **to p. into people's private lives** fouiller dans la vie des gens **2** *Med* faire un sondage

probing ['prəʊbɪŋ] **ADJ** *(look)* inquisiteur, perçant; *(mind)* pénétrant, clairvoyant; *(analysis)* pénétrant; **after hours of p. questioning** après des heures d'un interrogatoire très poussé *ou* approfondi

N *(UNCOUNT)* **1** *(investigation)* enquête *f*, investigations *fpl*; *(questioning)* questions *fpl*, interrogatoire *m*; **she didn't react to my p.** je l'ai sondée, mais elle n'a pas réagi; **I'll do some p. and try to find out why she's so reluctant** je ferai ma petite enquête pour savoir pourquoi elle est si réticente; **no amount of p. will persuade him to reveal the truth** on aura beau insister, rien ne le persuadera à révéler la vérité **2** *Med* sondage *m*

probity ['prəʊbətɪ] **N** *Formal* probité *f*

problem ['prɒbləm] **N** problème *m*; **a maths p.** un problème de mathématique; **a technical/financial p.** un problème technique/financier; **to cause problems for sb** causer des ennuis *ou* poser des problèmes à qn; **he's got problems with the police** il a des problèmes *ou* ennuis avec la police; **that's your p.** ça, c'est ton problème; **their p. is that they don't have enough time** leur problème c'est qu'ils n'ont pas assez de temps; **money isn't a p.** l'argent n'est pas un problème; **I can't pay until next week – that's not a p.** je ne pourrai payer avant la semaine prochaine – pas de problème *ou* ce n'est pas un problème; *Fam* **haven't got a car – no p., I'll take you** je n'ai pas de voiture – pas de problème, je t'emmènerai; **the housing p.** la crise du logement; **it's a p. to know what to do** il est bien difficile de savoir quoi faire; **he's a p.** c'est un cas *ou* c'est un problème, celui-là; **I don't want to be a p.** je ne veux pas causer *ou* créer de problème(s); **what seems to be the p.?** qu'est-ce qu'il y a?, où est le problème?; **has anyone got a p. with that?** est-ce que quelqu'un a une objection?, est-ce que ça dérange quelqu'un?; *Fam* **what's your p.?** tu as un problème ou quoi?; **to have a drink/drug p.** (trop) boire/se droguer; **she has a bit of a weight p.** elle a des problèmes de poids; **it's a real p. case** c'est un cas qui pose de réels problèmes

COMP *(family, hair)* à problèmes; *(play)* à thèse

▸▸ ***problem area*** *(in town)* quartier *m* à problèmes; *(in project)* source *f* de problèmes; ***problem child*** *(child)* enfant *mf* à problèmes, enfant *m* difficile; *Mktg (company, product)* dilemme *m*; *Br* ***problem page*** courrier *m* du cœur

problematic [,prɒblə'mætɪk], **problematical** [,prɒblə'mætɪkəl] **ADJ** problématique, incertain; **staying the night there could be a bit p.** ça paraît compliqué d'y passer la nuit

problematically [,prɒblə'mætɪkəlɪ] **ADV** problématiquement

problem-oriented, problem-orientated **ADJ** *Comput* orienté problème

▸▸ ***problem-oriented language*** langage *m* orienté problème

problem-solving [-'sɒlvɪŋ] **N** résolution *f* de problèmes

ADJ this job requires good p. skills ce travail demande de bonnes aptitudes à résoudre les problèmes

pro bono [-'bəʊnəʊ] **ADJ** *Am Law (legal work)* à titre gratuit; *(lawyer)* exerçant à titre gratuit

proboscis [prəʊ'bɒsɪs] *(pl* **proboscises** [-sɪsiːz] *or* **proboscides** [-sɪdiːz]) **N** *Zool* trompe *f*; *Hum (nose)* appendice *m*

▸▸ *Zool* ***proboscis monkey*** nasique *m*

procedural [prə'siːdʒərəl] **ADJ** de procédure, procédural; **the delays were merely p.** les retards étaient dus à de simples questions de procédure

▸▸ ***procedural agreement*** accord *m* de procédure *ou* sur la procédure; ***procedural motion*** motion *f* d'ordre

procedure [prə'siːdʒə(r)] **N 1** *(course of action)* procédure *f*; **you must follow (the) normal p.** vous devez suivre la procédure normale; **what's the correct p.?** comment doit-on procéder?, quelle est la marche à suivre?; **what's the p. for renewing a passport?** quelle est la marche à suivre pour faire renouveler un passeport?; **rules** *or* **order of p.** règles *fpl* de procédure; *(of assembly)* règlement *m* intérieur; *Law* **criminal/civil (law) p.** procédure *f* pénale/civile **2** *Comput* procédure *f*, sous-programme *m*

procedure-oriented, procedure-orientated **ADJ** *Comput* orienté procédure

▸▸ ***procedure-oriented language*** langage *m* procédural

proceed [prə'siːd] **VI 1** *(continue)* continuer, poursuivre; **you may p.** vous pouvez poursuivre *ou* continuer; **the play proceeded without further interruption** la pièce se poursuivit sans autre interruption; **the project is proceeding well** le projet se déroule bien; **negotiations are now proceeding** des négociations sont en cours; **before proceeding any further with our investigations...** avant de poursuivre nos investigations..., avant de pousser plus avant nos investigations…; **before I p.** avant d'aller plus loin

2 *(happen)* se passer, se dérouler; **is the meeting proceeding according to plan?** est-ce que la réunion se déroule comme prévu?

3 *(move on)* passer; **let's p. to item 32** passons à la question 32; **to p. to do sth** *(start)* se mettre à faire qch; *(do next)* passer à qch; **he proceeded to tear up my report** puis, il a déchiré mon rapport

4 *(act)* procéder, agir; **how should we p.?** comment devons-nous procéder?, quelle est la marche à suivre?; **I'm not sure how to p.** je ne vois pas très bien comment faire; **p. with caution** agissez avec prudence

5 *(go, travel)* avancer, aller; *(car)* avancer, rouler; **they proceeded at a slow pace** ils ont avancé lentement; **she proceeded on her way** elle a poursuivi son chemin; **they are proceeding towards Calais** ils se dirigent vers Calais; **to p. with caution** avancer prudemment; **I then proceeded to the post office** je me suis ensuite rendu au bureau de poste

6 *Law* **to p. with charges against sb** poursuivre qn en justice, intenter un procès contre qn

7 *(originate)* **to p. from** provenir de, découler de; **smells proceeding from the kitchen** des odeurs provenant de la cuisine

8 *Comput (in dialog box)* continuer

proceeding [prəˈsiːdɪŋ] **N 1** *Formal (way of acting)* manière *f* de procéder, façon *f* d'agir **2** *(event)* événement *m*

• **proceedings NPL 1** *(events)* **proceedings were interrupted by…** le déroulement des événements a été interrompu par…; **we watched the proceedings on television** nous avons regardé la retransmission télévisée de la cérémonie

2 *(meeting)* réunion *f*, séance *f*; **I missed some of the proceedings** j'ai manqué une partie de la réunion *ou* des débats

3 *(records ▸ of meeting)* compte rendu *m*, procès-verbal *m*; *(▸ of conference, learned society)* actes *mpl*

4 *Law (legal action)* procès *m*, poursuites *fpl*; *(legal process)* procédure *f*; **to take** *or* **to institute (legal) proceedings against sb** intenter une action (en justice) contre qn, engager des poursuites contre qn

proceeds [ˈprəʊsiːdz] **NPL** recette *f*, bénéfices *mpl*; **all p. will go to charity** tous les bénéfices seront versés aux associations caritatives

process N [ˈprəʊses] **1** *(series of events, operation)* processus *m*; **the democratic p.** le processus démocratique; **by a p. of elimination** en procédant par élimination; **to be in the p. of doing sth** être en train de faire qch; **they're in the p. of getting a divorce** ils sont en instance de divorce; **the building is in the p. of being repaired** le bâtiment est en cours de réparation; **in the p. of time** avec le temps, à la longue; **he lost most of his friends in the p.** il a perdu presque tous ses amis en faisant cela; **but you ruined the carpet in the p.** mais tu as abîmé la moquette par la même occasion; **during the p. of dismantling** au cours du démontage; **the work is in p.** le travail est en cours

2 *Tech (industrial)* procédé *m*; *(chemical)* réaction *f*; *Typ & Phot* procédés *mpl* photomécaniques; *Comput* procédé *m*, opération *f*, traitement *m*

3 *Law* procès *m*, action *f* en justice; *(summons)* sommation *f* de comparaître; **by due p. of law** par voies légales

4 *Biol (outgrowth)* processus *m*

VT [ˈprəʊses] **1** *(transform ▸ raw materials)* traiter, transformer; *(▸ cheese, meat, milk)* traiter; *(▸ nuclear waste)* retraiter; *Comput (data)* traiter

2 *Admin & Com (deal with ▸ order, information, cheque)* traiter; **my insurance claim is still being processed** ma déclaration de sinistre est toujours en cours de règlement; **we p. thousands of applications every week** nous traitons des milliers de demandes chaque semaine; **your request is being processed** votre demande est en cours de traitement

3 *Law (person)* intenter un procès à, poursuivre (en justice)

4 *Phot* développer

5 *Fig (come to terms with)* faire face à

VI [prəˈses] *(march)* défiler; *Rel* défiler en procession; **the bishops processed slowly down the aisle** la procession des évêques avançait lentement dans l'allée centrale

▸▸ *Phot* **process camera** tireuse *f* optique; *Comput & Typ* **process colours** impression *f* en quadrichromie; **process engineer** ingénieur *m* en procédés; **process engineering** ingénierie *f* de procédés; **process printing** impression *f* en couleurs; *Cin & TV* **process shot** prise *f* de vue par transparence

> Note that the French noun **procès** is a false friend. It only means **trial**.

processing [ˈprəʊsesɪŋ] **N 1** *(of raw material, product)* traitement *m*, transformation *f*; *Comput (of data)* traitement *m* **2** *Admin (of application)* traitement *m* **3** *Phot (of film)* développement *m*, traitement *m*

▸▸ **processing industry** industrie *f* de transformation; *Comput* **processing language** langage *m* de traitement; **processing plant** *(for sewage, nuclear waste etc)* usine *f* de traitement; *Comput* **processing power** puissance *f* de traitement; *Comput* **processing speed** vitesse *f* de traitement; *Comput* **processing time** temps *m* de traitement; *Comput* **processing unit** unité *f* de traitement

procession [prəˈseʃən] **N 1** *(ceremony)* procession *f*, cortège *m*; *Rel* procession *f* **2** *(demonstration)* défilé *m*, cortège *m*; **to go** *or* **walk in p.** aller en cortège *ou* en procession, défiler **3** *(continuous line)* procession *f*, défilé *m*; **the soldiers marched in p. through the town** les soldats ont défilé à travers la ville; **I've had a p. of people through my office all day** toute la journée, ça a été un défilé permanent dans mon bureau

processional [prəˈseʃənəl] **ADJ** processionnel

N *Rel (hymn)* hymne *m* processionnel; *(book)* processional *m*

processor [ˈprəʊsesə(r)] **N 1** *Comput* processeur *m* **2** *Culin* robot *m* ménager

▸▸ *Comput* **processor chip** microprocesseur *m*; *Comput* **processor speed** vitesse *f* du processeur

process-server N *Law* huissier *m (qui dresse des exploits)*

pro-choice ADJ en faveur du droit à l'avortement, *Can* pro-choix *(inv)*

proclaim [prəˈkleɪm] **VT 1** *(declare)* proclamer, déclarer; **to p. independence** proclamer l'indépendance; **to p. a state of emergency** proclamer l'état d'urgence; **a holiday was proclaimed for the investiture** une journée de congé fut octroyée pour l'investiture; **many proclaimed that he was mad** *or* **proclaimed him to be mad** beaucoup de gens ont déclaré qu'il était fou; **he proclaimed himself emperor** il s'est proclamé empereur; **she proclaimed her innocence** elle a clamé son innocence **2** *(reveal)* révéler, manifester, trahir; **his behaviour proclaimed his nervousness** son comportement trahissait sa nervosité

proclamation [ˌprɒkləˈmeɪʃən] **N** proclamation *f*, déclaration *f*; **by public p.** par proclamation publique; **to issue** *or* **to make a p.** faire une proclamation

proclivity [prəˈklɪvətɪ] *(pl* **proclivities**) **N** *Formal* propension *f*, inclination *f*, tendance *f*; **to have a p. to** *or* **towards sth** avoir une propension à qch; **sexual proclivities** penchant *m* pour certaines pratiques sexuelles

proconsul [ˌprəʊˈkɒnsəl] **N** *Hist* proconsul *m*

procrastinate [prəˈkræstɪneɪt] **VI** remettre les choses au lendemain; **if you hadn't procrastinated** *(wasted time)* si vous n'aviez pas fait traîner les choses; *(hesitated)* si vous n'aviez pas hésité

procrastination [prəˌkræstɪˈneɪʃən] **N** tendance *f* à tout remettre au lendemain; **there's too much p.** on a trop tendance à remettre les choses au lendemain; *Prov* **p. is the thief of time** ≃ il ne faut pas remettre au lendemain ce que l'on peut faire le jour même

procrastinator [prəʊˈkræstɪneɪtə(r)] **N** indécis (e) *m,f*, velléitaire *mf*; **he's a terrible p.!** il a une fâcheuse tendance à toujours tout remettre au lendemain!

procreate [ˈprəʊkrɪeɪt] **VI** *Formal* procréer

procreation [ˌprəʊkrɪˈeɪʃən] **N** *Formal* procréation *f*

proctor [ˈprɒktə(r)] **N 1** *Law (agent)* ≃ fondé(e) *m,f* de pouvoir **2** *Univ (in UK)* représentant(e) *m,f* du conseil de discipline; *(in US ▸ invigilator)* surveillant(e) *m,f* (à un examen) **3** *Rel* procureur *m*

VT *Am Univ* surveiller

VI *Am Univ* surveiller

procurable [prəˈkjʊərəbəl] **ADJ** que l'on peut se procurer *ou* obtenir; **these goods are p. only from an overseas supplier** on ne peut se procurer ces denrées qu'auprès d'un fournisseur à l'étranger

procuration [ˌprɒkjʊˈreɪʃən] **N 1** *(acquisition)* obtention *f*, acquisition *f* **2** *Law* procuration *f* **3** *(of prostitutes)* proxénétisme *m*

procurator [ˈprɒkjʊreɪtə(r)] **N 1** *Law* fondé(e) *m,f* de pouvoir; *Scot* = en Écosse, magistrat qui fait office de procureur et qui remplit les fonctions du "coroner" en Angleterre **2** *Antiq* procurateur *m*

▸▸ **procurator fiscal** = en Écosse, magistrat qui fait office de procureur et qui remplit les fonctions du "coroner" en Angleterre

procure [prəˈkjʊə(r)] **VT 1** *Formal (obtain)* procurer, obtenir; *(buy ▸ for oneself)* se procurer, acheter; *(▸ for someone else)* procurer, acheter; **to p. sth (for oneself)** se procurer qch; **to p. sth for sb** procurer qch à qn; **the defence lawyers procured his acquittal** les avocats de la défense ont obtenu son acquittement **2** *Law (prostitutes)* procurer, prostituer

VI *Law* faire du proxénétisme

procurement [prəˈkjʊəmənt] **N 1** *Formal (acquisition)* obtention *f*, acquisition *f* **2** *Com (buying)* achat *m*, acquisition *f*; *Mil* acquisition *f* de matériel; *(department)* service *m* des achats

▸▸ *Mil* **procurement department** service *m* des achats; *Mil* **procurement officer** agent *m* des achats

procurer [prəˈkjʊərə(r)] **N** *Law* proxénète *m*

procuress [prəˈkjʊərɪs] **N** *Law* proxénète *f*

procuring [prəˈkjʊərɪŋ] **N 1** *Formal (acquisition)* acquisition *f*, obtention *f* **2** *Law* proxénétisme *m*

Prod [prɒd] **N** *Ir & Scot Fam* = terme péjoratif désignant un Protestant

prod [prɒd] *(pt & pp* **prodded**, *cont* **prodding**) **N 1** *(with finger)* petit coup *m* (avec le doigt); *(with stick)* petit coup *m* de bâton; **I gave him a p. with my walking stick** je lui ai donné un petit coup avec ma canne **2** *Fig (urging)* **to give sb a p.** pousser qn; **he needs an occasional p.** il a besoin qu'on le pousse de temps en temps **3** *(stick)* bâton *m*, pique *f*; *(for cattle)* aiguillon *m*

VT 1 *(with finger)* donner un coup avec le doigt à, pousser (du doigt); *(with stick)* pousser avec la pointe d'un bâton; **he prodded me in the back with his pen** il m'a donné un (petit) coup dans le dos avec son stylo; **he prodded the sausages with a fork** il a piqué les saucisses avec une fourchette **2** *Fig (urge)* pousser, inciter; **to p. sb into doing sth** pousser *ou* inciter qn à faire qch; **to p. sb into action** pousser qn à agir

prodigal [ˈprɒdɪgəl] **ADJ** prodigue; *Formal* **to be p. with** *or* **of sth** être prodigue de qch

N prodigue *mf*

▸▸ *Bible* **the prodigal son** le fils prodigue

prodigality [ˌprɒdɪˈgælətɪ] **N** prodigalité *f*

prodigally [ˈprɒdɪgəlɪ] **ADV** avec prodigalité

prodigious [prəˈdɪdʒəs] **ADJ** prodigieux; **a p. reader** un lecteur avide

prodigiously [prəˈdɪdʒəslɪ] **ADV** prodigieusement

prodigy [ˈprɒdɪdʒɪ] *(pl* **prodigies**) **N 1** *(person)* prodige *m*; **child** *or* **infant p.** enfant *mf* prodige **2** *(marvel)* prodige *m*

PRODUCE

N
- produits

VT
- produire **1–3, 6, 7, 9**
- publier **3**
- causer **5**
- provoquer **5**
- réaliser **7**
- rapporter **2**
- donner naissance à **4**
- présenter **6**

VI
- produire **1**
- assurer la production **2**
- assurer la réalisation **2**

N ['prɒdju:s] *(UNCOUNT)* produits *mpl* (alimentaires); **agricultural/dairy p.** produits *mpl* agricoles/laitiers; **home p.** produits *mpl* du pays; **they eat their own p.** ils mangent ce qu'ils produisent; **p. of Spain** *(on packaging)* produit en Espagne

VT [prə'dju:s] **1** *(manufacture, make)* produire, fabriquer; **we aren't producing enough spare parts** nous ne produisons pas assez de pièces détachées; **our factory produces spare parts for washing machines** notre usine fabrique des pièces détachées pour machines à laver; **Denmark produces dairy products** le Danemark est un pays producteur de produits laitiers; **we have produced three new models this year** nous avons sorti trois nouveaux modèles cette année

2 *(yield ▸ minerals, crops)* produire; *(▸ interest, profit)* rapporter; **this mine is producing less and less coal** la production de charbon de cette mine est en déclin; **this region produces good wine** cette région produit du bon vin; **halogen lamps p. a lot of light** les lampes halogènes donnent beaucoup de lumière; **my investments p. a fairly good return** mes investissements sont d'un assez bon rapport

3 *(bring out ▸ book, record)* produire, sortir; *(publish)* publier, éditer; **he hasn't produced a new painting for over a year now** cela fait maintenant plus d'un an qu'il n'a rien peint; **the publishers produced a special edition** les éditeurs ont publié *ou* sorti une édition spéciale

4 *Biol (give birth to ▸ of woman)* donner naissance à; *(▸ of animal)* produire, donner naissance à; *(secrete ▸ saliva, sweat etc)* secréter; **she produced many children** elle a eu de nombreux enfants

5 *(bring about ▸ situation, problem)* causer, provoquer, créer; *(▸ illness, death)* causer, provoquer; *(▸ anger, pleasure, reaction)* susciter, provoquer; *(▸ effect)* provoquer, produire; **the team has produced some good results/some surprises this season** l'équipe a obtenu quelques bons résultats/provoqué quelques surprises cette saison; **she can p. a meal from nothing** il lui suffit d'un rien pour cuisiner un bon repas; **to p. a sensation** *(of book etc)* faire sensation; **the drug produces a sensation of well-being** cette drogue procure une sensation de bien-être

6 *(present, show ▸ evidence, documents)* présenter, produire; **he produced a £5 note from his pocket** il a sorti un billet de 5 livres de sa poche; **you have to be able to p. identification** vous devez pouvoir présenter une pièce d'identité; **the defendant was unable to p. any proof** l'accusé n'a pu fournir *ou* apporter aucune preuve; **to p. a witness** faire comparaître un témoin; **they produced some excellent arguments** ils ont avancé d'excellents arguments; **he finally managed to p. the money** il a enfin réussi à trouver l'argent *ou* réunir la somme nécessaire

7 *(finance ▸ film, play, programme)* produire; *(make ▸ documentary, current affairs programme)* réaliser; **a well-produced play** une pièce bien montée

8 *Geom (line)* prolonger, continuer

9 *Chem, Elec & Phys (reaction, spark)* produire; *(discharge)* produire, provoquer; *(vacuum)* faire, créer

VI [prə'dju:s] **1** *(yield ▸ factory, mine)* produire, rendre

2 *(organize production of a film, play, radio or TV programme)* assurer la production; *(make film or programme)* assurer la réalisation

producer [prə'dju:sə(r)] N **1** *Agr & Ind* producteur (trice) *m,f*; **the country is a major p. of coffee** *or* **coffee p.** ce pays est un important producteur de café; **this region is Europe's biggest wine p.** cette région est la plus grande productrice de vin d'Europe **2** *(of film)* producteur(trice) *m,f*; *(of play, TV or radio programme ▸ organizer, financer)* producteur(trice) *m,f*; *(▸ director)* réalisateur(trice) *m,f*

▸▸ ***producers' association*** syndicat *m* de producteurs; ***producers' cooperative*** coopérative *f* de production; ***producer gas*** gaz *m* de gazogène; ***producer goods*** biens *mpl* de production; ***producer price index*** indice *m* des prix à la production

-producing [prə'dju:sɪŋ] SUFF producteur de; **oil-p.** producteur de pétrole; *Anat* **tear/sweat-p. glands** glandes *fpl* lacrymales/sudoripares

product ['prɒdʌkt] N **1** *Agr, Chem, Com & Ind* produit *m*; **finished p.** *Ind* produit *m* fini; *(piece of work)* résultat *m* final; **p. of India** *(on packaging)* produit d'Inde **2** *(result)* produit *m*, résultat *m*; **this book is the p. of many years' hard work** ce livre est le fruit de longues années d'un travail acharné; **she's the p. of an unhappy childhood** elle est le produit d'une enfance malheureuse; **that's the p. of a lively imagination** c'est le produit d'une imagination débordante; **she was a p. of her age** c'était un pur produit de son époque **3** *Math* produit *m*; **the p. of x and y** le produit de x par y

▸▸ ***product advertising*** publicité *f* de produit; ***product awareness*** notoriété *f ou* mémorisation *f* du produit; ***product bundling*** groupage *m* de produits; ***product depth*** profondeur *f* de produit; ***product design*** conception *f* du produit; ***product development*** élaboration *f* du produit; ***product development cost*** coût *m* de l'élaboration du produit; ***product development programme*** programme *m* de mise au point du produit; ***product differentiation*** différenciation *f* du produit; ***product display*** présentation *f* du produit; ***product diversification*** diversification *f* des produits; ***product features*** caractéristiques *fpl* du produit; ***product group manager*** directeur(trice) *m,f* de groupe de produits; ***product hierarchy*** hiérarchie *f* des produits; ***product image*** image *f* de produit; ***product information sheet*** fiche *f* technique; ***product innovation*** innovation *f* de produit; *EU* ***product liability*** responsabilité *f* du produit; ***product liability insurance*** assurance *f* de responsabilité du produit; ***product life cycle*** cycle *m* de vie du produit; ***product line*** ligne *f* de produits; ***product management*** gestion *f* de produits; ***product manager*** chef *m ou* directeur(trice) *m,f* de produit, responsable *mf* produit; ***product mapping*** carte *f* perceptuelle de produits; ***product market*** marché *m* de produit; ***product marketing*** marketing *m* du produit; ***product mix*** assortiment *m ou* mix *m* de produits; ***product orientation*** optique *f* produit; ***product placement*** placement *m* de produit; ***product planning*** plan *m* de développement des produits; ***product policy*** politique *f* de lancement de produit; ***product portfolio*** portefeuille *m* de produits; ***product positioning*** positionnement *m* du produit; ***product promotion*** communication *f* produit; ***product range*** gamme *f* de produits; ***product specialist*** spécialiste *mf* produit; ***product test*** test *m* de produit, essai *m* de produits; ***product testing*** essais *mpl ou* tests *mpl* de produit

production [prə'dʌkʃən] N **1** *(process of producing ▸ of goods)* production *f*, fabrication *f*; *(▸ of crops, electricity, heat)* production *f*; **the workers have halted p.** les travailleurs ont arrêté la production; **to go into/out of p.** être/ne plus être fabriqué; **the model is now in p.** le modèle est en cours de production; **this model went into/out of p. in 1999** on a commencé la fabrication de ce modèle/ce modèle a été retiré de la production en 1999; **to move** *or* **shift p.** relocaliser son unité de production

2 *(amount produced)* production *f*; **an increase/fall in p.** une hausse/baisse de la production *ou* du rendement

3 *(of film)* production *f*; *(of play, of radio or TV programme ▸ organization, financing)* production *f*; *(▸ artistic direction)* réalisation *f*, mise *f* en scène

4 *(show, work of art) & Cin, Rad, Theat & TV* production *f*; *Art & Literature* œuvre *f*; **the RSC's p. of 'Macbeth'** le 'Macbeth' de la RSC; *Fam Fig* **there's no need to make such a (big) p. out of it!** il n'y a pas de quoi en faire un plat *ou* toute une histoire!; *Cin* **a film with high/low p. values** un film à gros/petit budget

5 *(presentation ▸ of document, passport, ticket)* présentation *f*; **on p. of this voucher** sur présentation de ce bon

▸▸ *Cin, Rad, TV & Theat* ***production assistant*** assistant(e) *m,f* de production; *Cin, Rad, TV & Theat* ***production associate*** producteur(trice) *m,f* associé(e); *Ind* ***production budget*** budget *m* de production; *Cin, Rad, TV & Theat* ***production buyer*** responsable *mf* des achats; ***production capacity*** capacité *f* de production; ***production car*** voiture *f* de série; *Cin, Rad, TV & Theat* ***production company*** société *f* de production; *Cin, Rad, TV & Theat* ***production control*** direction *f* de la production; ***production cost*** coût *m* de production; ***production department*** service *m* (de) production; ***production director*** directeur(trice) *m,f* de production; *Journ* directeur(trice) *m,f* de la fabrication; *TV* administrateur(trice) *m,f* de la production; ***production editor*** rédacteur(trice) *m,f* en chef technique; ***production flowchart*** organigramme *m* de production; ***production lead time*** délai *m* de production; ***production line*** chaîne *f* de fabrication; **to work on the p. line** travailler à la chaîne; ***production manager*** directeu(trice) *m,f* de la production; ***production meeting*** conférence *f* de production; ***production mixer*** mélangeur *m* (de production); ***production overheads*** frais *mpl* généraux de production; ***production platform*** plate-forme *f* de production; ***production secretary*** secrétaire *mf* de production; ***production switcher*** mélangeur *m* (de production); ***production team*** équipe *f* de production

productive [prə'dʌktɪv] ADJ **1** *(gen)* productif; *Formal* **to be p. of sth** engendrer qch, créer qch; **such methods are p. of stress** de telles méthodes favorisent le stress

2 *(land)* fertile; *(imagination)* fertile, fécond; *(writer, artist)* prolifique

3 *(useful)* fructueux, utile; **our visit/meeting has been very p.** notre visite/réunion a été très fructueuse

4 *Econ* productif; **the p. forces** les forces *fpl* productives *ou* de production

5 *Ling* productif

▸▸ *Econ* ***productive labour*** travail *m* productif; ***productive life*** *(of machine)* vie *f* physique

productively [prə'dʌktɪvlɪ] ADV **1** *Econ* d'une manière productive **2** *(usefully)* utilement; *(fruitfully)* fructueusement, profitablement; **to use one's time p.** employer son temps de façon efficace

productivity [ˌprɒdʌk'tɪvətɪ] N productivité *f*, rendement *m*; **p. is up/down** la productivité est en augmentation/en baisse

COMP *(fall, rise, level)* de productivité

▸▸ ***productivity agreement*** contrat *m* de productivité; ***productivity bargaining*** négociation *f* syndicale d'un contrat de productivité; ***productivity bonus*** prime *f* de rendement; ***productivity deal*** contrat *m* de productivité; ***productivity drive*** campagne *f* de productivité

product/market pair N *Mktg* couple *m* produit/marché

product/price policy N *Mktg* politique *f* de produit/prix

Prof. *(written abbr* **professor***)* Pr

prof [prɒf] N *Fam (abbr* **professor***)* prof *mf*

profanation [ˌprɒfə'neɪʃən] N *Rel* profanation *f*

profane [prə'feɪn] ADJ **1** *(irreligious)* sacrilège **2** *(secular)* profane, laïque; **things sacred and p.** le sacré et le profane **3** *(language ▸ vulgar)* vulgaire, grossier; *(▸ blasphemous)* blasphématoire; *(person)* qui blasphème à tout propos

VT profaner; **to p. the name of God** blasphémer le saint nom de Dieu

profanity [prə'fænətɪ] *(pl* **profanities***)* N **1** *(UNCOUNT) (profane nature ▸ of text)* nature *f ou* caractère *m* profane; *(▸ of action)* impiété *f*; **an act of p.** une profanation **2** *(oath)* grossièreté *f*, juron *m*; **to utter profanities** *(swear)* proférer des grossièretés; *(blaspheme)* blasphémer

profess [prə'fes] VT **1** *(declare)* déclarer, proclamer, *Literary* professer; **to p. hatred for** *or* **of sb** professer sa haine pour qn; **to p. oneself satisfied** se déclarer satisfait; **to p. ignorance** avouer son ignorance; **to p. an opinion** professer *ou* proclamer une opinion **2** *(claim)* prétendre, déclarer; **he professes to be a socialist** il se prétend *ou* se déclare socialiste; **I don't p. to be an expert (in the subject)** je ne prétends pas être expert en la matière

professed [prə'fest] ADJ **1** *(avowed)* déclaré; **a p. Marxist** un marxiste déclaré; **that is my p. aim** c'est mon but avoué **2** *(alleged)* supposé, prétendu; **a p. friend** un soi-disant ami; **she's a p. expert in the field** elle se dit experte en la matière **3** *Rel* profès; **a p. nun** une religieuse professe

professedly [prəˈfesɪdlɪ] **ADV 1** *(avowedly)* **they are p. anarchists;** de leur propre aveu, ce sont des anarchistes; **she has p. killed three people** d'après elle *ou* d'après ses dires, elle aurait tué trois personnes **2** *(allegedly)* soi-disant, prétendument; **he came here p. to help me** à l'en croire, il est venu pour m'aider; **she's p. rich** c'est une femme prétendument riche

profession [prəˈfeʃən] **N 1** *(occupation)* profession *f*, métier *m*; **what's your p.?** quelle est votre profession *ou* métier?; **she's a lawyer by p.** elle exerce la profession d'avocat, elle est avocate (de profession); **the (liberal) professions** les professions *fpl* libérales; **learned p.** profession *f* intellectuelle; *Hum* **the oldest p. (in the world)** le plus vieux métier du monde
2 *(body)* (membres *mpl* d'une) profession *f*, corps *m*; **those in the p. think that…** les membres de la profession pensent que…
3 *(declaration)* profession *f*, déclaration *f*; **professions of love** des déclarations *fpl* d'amour
4 *Rel* **p. of faith** profession *f* de foi

professional [prəˈfeʃənəl] **ADJ 1** *(relating to a profession)* professionnel; **the surgeon demonstrated his great p. skill** le chirurgien a montré ses grandes compétences professionnelles; **a lawyer is a p. man** un avocat exerce une profession libérale; **a club for p. people** un club réservé aux membres des professions libérales; **p. person wanted for flat share** *(in advertisement)* recherchons personne avec emploi pour partager un appartement; **to take a p. interest in sth** s'intéresser professionnellement à qch; **it would be against p. etiquette to tell you** vous le dire serait contraire aux usages *ou* à la déontologie de la profession; **to take** *or* **to get p. advice** *(gen)* consulter un professionnel; *(from doctor, lawyer)* consulter un médecin/un avocat; **his work is not up to p. standards** son travail n'est pas ce qu'on peut attendre d'un professionnel
2 *(as career, full-time)* professionnel, de profession; *(soldier, diplomat)* de carrière; **she's a p. writer/photographer** elle est écrivain professionnel/photographe professionnelle; **he's a p. painter** il vit de sa peinture; *Fig* **he's a p. drunk** il passe son temps à boire
3 *Sport* professionnel; **to go** *or* **to turn p.** passer professionnel; **p. golf** le golf professionnel
4 *(in quality, attitude)* professionnel; **a p. piece of work** un travail de professionnel; **they made a very p. job of the repair** la réparation qu'ils ont faite est digne de professionnels; **she is very p. in her approach to the problem** elle aborde le problème de façon très professionnelle; **he works in a very p. manner** il travaille en professionnel
N professionnel(elle) *m,f*; **it's best to leave such work to the professionals** il vaut mieux laisser ce genre de travail à des professionnels *ou* à des gens du métier; **a golf/rugby p.** un golfeur/rugbyman professionnel
▸▸ ***professional army*** armée *f* de métier; ***professional association*** association *f* professionnelle; ***professional body*** organisme *m* professionnel; ***professional code of ethics*** déontologie *f*; *Ftbl* ***professional foul*** faute *f* délibérée; ***professional hospitality*** industrie *f* de l'hôtellerie; ***professional indemnity insurance*** assurance *f* d'indemnisation professionnelle; ***professional misconduct*** faute *f* professionnelle

professionalism [prəˈfeʃənəlɪzəm] **N** professionnalisme *m*; **this burglary shows great p.** ce cambriolage est l'œuvre d'un professionnel

professionally [prəˈfeʃənəlɪ] **ADV 1** *(as profession)* professionnellement; **he writes p.** il vit de sa plume; **she's a p. qualified doctor** elle est médecin diplômé; *Sport* **he plays p.** c'est un joueur professionnel; **I've only ever met her p.** mes seuls rapports avec elle ont été d'ordre professionnel *ou* ont été des rapports de travail; **we had the house painted p.** on a fait peindre la maison par un professionnel *ou* un homme de métier **2** *(skilfully, conscientiously)* de manière professionnelle, comme un professionnel; **this work has been done very p.** c'est le travail d'un professionnel; **she works very p.** elle travaille en vraie professionnelle, elle fait un vrai travail de professionnel

professor [prəˈfesə(r)] **N** *Univ (in UK* ▸ *head of department)* titulaire *mf* d'une chaire, professeur *m*; *(in US* ▸ *lecturer)* enseignant(e) *m,f* (de faculté *ou* d'université); **p. of sociology** *(in UK)* titulaire *mf* de la chaire de sociologie, professeur *m* responsable du département de sociologie; *(in US)* professeur *m* de sociologie; **P. Colin Appleton** le professeur Colin Appleton; **Dear P. Appleton** Monsieur le Professeur; *(less formally)* (Cher) Monsieur

professorial [ˌprɒfɪˈsɔːrɪəl] **ADJ** professoral

professorship [prəˈfesəʃɪp] **N** chaire *f*; **she has a p. in French at Durham** elle occupe la chaire *ou* est titulaire de la chaire de français à l'Université de Durham

proffer [ˈprɒfə(r)] **VT** *Formal* **1** *(offer, present* ▸ *drink, present)* offrir, tendre; *(*▸ *resignation)* remettre; *(*▸ *advice)* donner; *(*▸ *excuses)* présenter, offrir; **to p. one's hand to sb** tendre la main à qn **2** *(put forward* ▸ *idea, opinion)* émettre; *(*▸ *remark, suggestion)* émettre, faire

proficiency [prəˈfɪʃənsɪ] **N** compétence *f*, maîtrise *f*; **she attained a high degree of p. in French** elle a acquis une grande maîtrise du français; **p. in driving is essential** une maîtrise de la conduite (automobile) est indispensable

proficient [prəˈfɪʃənt] **ADJ** *(worker)* compétent, expérimenté; *(driver)* expérimenté, chevronné; **she's a very p. pianist** c'est une excellente pianiste; **to be p. at German** avoir une bonne maîtrise de l'allemand; **to be a p. liar** avoir le mensonge facile

proficiently [prəˈfɪʃəntlɪ] **ADV** de façon (très) compétente, avec (beaucoup de) maîtrise; **she speaks French p.** elle parle couramment le français; **to swim p.** être un excellent nageur

profile [ˈprəʊfaɪl] **N 1** *Art & Archit* profil *m*; **to look at/to draw sb in p.** regarder/dessiner qn de profil
2 *(description* ▸ *of person)* profil *m*, portrait *m*; **psychiatrists came up with a p. of the killer** les psychiatres ont établi un profil du tueur
3 *(of candidate, employee, company, product etc)* profil *m*; **to have the right p. for the job** avoir le bon profil pour le poste; **to keep a high p.** occuper le devant de la scène, faire parler de soi; **to raise one's p.** se mettre plus en vue; **to keep a low p.** adopter un profil bas, se faire tout petit; **when the boss is in a bad mood I keep a low p.** lorsque le patron est de mauvaise humeur, je me fais tout petit *ou* je ne me fais pas remarquer
4 *(graph)* profil *m*
5 *Geog & Geol* profil *m*; **a soil p.** le profil d'un sol
6 *Tech* profil *m*
VT 1 *(show in profile)* profiler; **his shadow was profiled against the wall** son ombre se profilait *ou* se découpait sur le mur **2** *(write profile of)* brosser le portrait de; **she was profiled in a recent TV programme** une émission télévisée récente a présenté son portrait

profit [ˈprɒfɪt] **N 1** *(financial gain)* profit *m*, bénéfice *m*; **to make a p. out of sth** faire un bénéfice sur qch; **we made a £200 p. on the sale** nous avons réalisé un bénéfice de 200 livres sur cette vente; **to be in p.** être bénéficiaire; **to move into p.** *(business)* devenir rentable; **to make** *or* **to turn out a p.** réaliser *ou* faire un bénéfice *ou* des bénéfices; **£100 clear p.** 100 livres de bénéfice net; **to show a p.** rapporter (un bénéfice *ou* des bénéfices); **profits were down/up this year** les bénéfices ont diminué/augmenté cette année; **to sell sth at a p.** vendre qch à profit, faire un bénéfice sur la vente de qch; **he only writes for p.** il n'écrit que pour l'argent; **I don't do it for p.** je ne le fais pas dans un but lucratif; *Com* **p. and loss** pertes *fpl* et profits *mpl*; *Fin* **p. and loss account, p. and loss form, p. and loss statement** compte *m* de résultat; **p. before tax** bénéfices *mpl* avant impôts **2** *Formal (advantage)* profit *m*, avantage *m*; **to turn sth to one's p., to gain p. from sth** tirer profit *ou* avantage de qch; **what p. is there in it for her?** quel avantage cela présente-t-il pour elle?, qu'est-ce que cela peut lui rapporter?
VT *Formal or Arch* profiter à, bénéficier à; **it won't p. you to tell lies** cela ne vous servira à rien de mentir
VI profiter, tirer un profit *ou* avantage; **to p. from** *or* **by sth** tirer profit *ou* avantage de qch, profiter de qch; **to p. from others' misfortunes** tirer profit du malheur des autres; **you could well p. by being more careful** vous avez tout intérêt à faire plus attention
▸▸ *Acct* ***profit balance*** solde *m* bénéficiaire; *Acct* ***profit centre*** centre *m* de profit; *Fin* ***profit equation*** équation *f* de bénéfice; *Fin* ***profit indicator*** indice *m* de profit; *Fin* ***profit margin*** marge *f* bénéficiaire; *Fin* ***profit motive*** motivation *f* par le profit; *Fin* ***profit optimization*** optimisation *f* du profit *ou* des profits; *Fin* ***profit outlook*** perspectives *fpl* de profit; *Fin* ***profit rate*** taux *m* de profit *ou* de bénéfice; *Fin* ***profit squeeze*** compression *f* des bénéfices, étranglement *m* des marges; *Fin* ***profit tax*** impôt *m* sur les bénéfices; *Fin* ***profit warning*** = annonce d'une baisse prochaine des bénéfices d'une entreprise

profitability [ˌprɒfɪtəˈbɪlətɪ] **N** *Fin* rentabilité *f*; *(of ideas, action)* caractère *m* profitable *ou* fructueux
▸▸ ***profitability index*** indice *m* de rentabilité; ***profitability value*** *(of a company)* valeur *f* de rendement

profitable [ˈprɒfɪtəbəl] **ADJ 1** *(lucrative)* rentable, lucratif; **this shop is no longer p.** ce magasin n'est plus rentable; **it wouldn't be very p. for me to sell** cela ne me rapporterait pas grand-chose de vendre **2** *(beneficial)* profitable, fructueux; **we had a very p. discussion** nous avons eu une discussion très fructueuse; **this is the most p. way to do it** c'est la manière la plus avantageuse de le faire; **it would be a more p. use of your time** ça serait pour vous une meilleure manière d'utiliser votre temps

profitably [ˈprɒfɪtəblɪ] **ADV 1** *Fin* avec profit, d'une manière rentable; **we sold it very p.** on l'a vendu en faisant un bénéfice confortable **2** *(usefully)* utilement, avec profit, profitablement; **use your time p.** ne gaspillez pas votre temps

profit-driven **ADJ** *Com* poussé par les profits

profiteer [ˌprɒfɪˈtɪə(r)] **N** profiteur(euse) *m,f*
VI faire des bénéfices exorbitants

profiteering [ˌprɒfɪˈtɪərɪŋ] **N** **they were accused of p.** on les a accusés de profiter de la situation pour faire des bénéfices excessifs

profitless [ˈprɒfɪtlɪs] **ADJ** sans profit; **we spent a p. afternoon** nous avons perdu *ou* gaspillé notre après-midi

profit-making **ADJ 1** *(aiming to make profit)* à but lucratif; **p. organization** association *f* à but lucratif; **non p. organization** association *f* à but non lucratif **2** *(profitable)* rentable

profit-sharing **N** participation *f ou* intéressement *m* aux bénéfices; **we have a p. agreement/scheme** nous avons un accord/un système de participation (aux bénéfices)

profit-taking **N** prise *f* de bénéfices

profit-volume ratio **N** *Fin* rapport *m* profit sur ventes

profligacy [ˈprɒflɪgəsɪ] **N** *Formal* **1** *(dissoluteness)* débauche *f*, licence *f* **2** *(extravagance)* (extrême) prodigalité *f*

profligate [ˈprɒflɪgət] *Formal* **ADJ 1** *(dissolute)* débauché, dévergondé; **to behave in a p. manner** se comporter en débauché; **a p. way of life** une vie dissolue *ou* de débauche **2** *(extravagant)* (très) prodigue, dépensier; *(wasteful)* (très) gaspilleur; **the p. use of natural resources** le gaspillage des ressources naturelles; **she's p. with her riches** elle gaspille ses richesses
N 1 *(dissolute person)* débauché(e) *m,f*, libertin(e) *m,f* **2** *(spendthrift)* dépensier(ère) *m,f*

pro forma [-ˈfɔːmə] **ADJ** pro forma *(inv)*
ADV pour la forme
N *(invoice)* facture *f* pro forma
▸▸ *Fin* ***pro forma bill*** traite *f* pro forma; ***pro forma invoice*** facture *f* pro forma

profound [prəˈfaʊnd] **ADJ** profond

profoundly [prəˈfaʊndlɪ] **ADV** profondément; **the p. deaf** les sourds *mpl* profonds

profundity [prəˈfʌndətɪ] *(pl* **profundities)** **N** *Formal* profondeur *f*

profuse [prəˈfjuːs] **ADJ 1** *(copious)* abondant, *Literary* profus; **p. vegetation** végétation *f* abondante; **p. sweating** transpiration *f* profuse **2** *(generous* ▸ *praise, apologies)* prodigue, profus;

to be p. in one's praise se répandre en compliments; **to be p. in one's apologies** se confondre en excuses

profusely [prəˈfjuːslɪ] **ADV 1** *(copiously)* abondamment, profusément; **to sweat p.** transpirer abondamment **2** *(generously)* **they thanked her p.** ils la remercièrent avec effusion; **to praise sb p.** se répandre en éloges sur qn; **she was p. apologetic** elle s'est confondue en excuses

profuseness [prəˈfjuːsnɪs] **N** profusion *f*

profusion [prəˈfjuːʒən] **N** profusion *f*, abondance *f*; **in p.** à profusion, en abondance

prog[1] [prɒg] **N** *Fam TV & Rad* émission *f*

prog[2] **ADJ** *(abbr* **progressive***)* **p. rock** rock *m* progressif

progenitor [prəʊˈdʒenɪtə(r)] **N** *Formal* **1** *(ancestor)* ancêtre *m* **2** *(originator)* auteur *m*; *(precursor)* précurseur *m*; *Hum (parent)* géniteur(trice) *m,f*

progeny [ˈprɒdʒənɪ] **N** *Formal (offspring)* progéniture *f*; *(descendants)* descendants *mpl*, lignée *f*

progesterone [prəˈdʒestərəʊn] **N** *Biol & Chem* progestérone *f*

prognosis [prɒgˈnəʊsɪs] *(pl* **prognoses** [-siːz]*)* **N 1** *Med* pronostic *m*; *(art)* prognose *f* **2** *(forecast)* prévision(s) *f(pl)*, pronostic *m*; **to make a p.** faire un pronostic *ou* des prévisions

prognostic [prɒgˈnɒstɪk] **N 1** *Med (symptom)* signe *m* pronostique **2** *Formal (sign)* présage *m*; *(forecast)* pronostic *m*

ADJ *Med* pronostique

prognostication [prɒgˌnɒstɪˈkeɪʃən] **N** *Formal* pronostic *m*

program[1] [ˈprəʊgræm] *(pt & pp* **programmed** *or* **programed**, *cont* **programming** *or* **programing***)* *Comput* **N** programme *m*

VT programmer; **to p. a computer to do sth** programmer un ordinateur pour qu'il fasse qch; **to be programmed to do sth** être programmé pour faire qch

VI programmer

▸▸ ***program card*** carte *f* programme; ***program disk*** disquette *f* programme; ***program error*** erreur *f* de programmation; ***program file*** fichier *m* programme; ***program language*** langage *m* de programmation; ***program library*** bibliothèque *f* de programmes; ***program manager*** gestionnaire *m* de programmes

program[2] *Am* = **programme**

programmable, *Am* **programable** [ˌprəʊˈgræməbəl] **ADJ** *Comput* programmable

▸▸ ***programmable function key*** touche *f* de fonction programmable; ***programmable ROM*** mémoire *f* morte programmable

programme, *Am* **program** [ˈprəʊgræm] **N 1** *Mus, Pol & Theat* programme *m*; **the p. of the day's events** le programme des manifestations de la journée; **there's a change in the p.** il y a un changement de programme; **the p. includes three pieces by Debussy** il y a trois morceaux de Debussy au programme; *esp Am* **an election p.** un programme électoral; **the party has adopted a new p.** le parti a adopté un nouveau programme; **what's (on) the p. for next week?** quel est l'emploi du temps prévu pour la semaine prochaine?; *esp Am Fam* **get with the p.!** un peu d'attention!

2 *(booklet)* programme *m*; *(syllabus)* programme *m*; *(timetable)* emploi *m* du temps; **to draw up a p.** arrêter un programme; **p. of study** programme *m*

3 *Rad & TV (broadcast)* émission *f*; **there's a good p. about** *or* **on opera on TV tonight** il y a une bonne émission sur l'opéra à la télévision ce soir

4 *(TV station)* chaîne *f*; *(radio station)* station *f*; **to change p.** *TV* changer de chaîne; *Rad* changer de station

VT programmer; **the heating is programmed to switch itself off at night** le chauffage est programmé pour s'arrêter la nuit; **his arrival wasn't programmed** son arrivée n'était pas prévue; **all children are programmed to learn language** chez les enfants, la capacité d'apprentissage du langage est innée

▸▸ *TV & Rad* ***programme controller*** directeur (trice) *m,f* des programmes *ou* d'antenne; ***programme grid*** grille *f* de programmes; ***programmed learning*** enseignement *m* programmé; *Mus* ***programme music*** musique *f* à programme; *Theat* ***programme notes*** notes *fpl* sur le programme; **the p. notes are very useful** les commentaires donnés dans le programme sont très utiles; *TV & Rad* ***programme planner*** programmateur(trice) *m,f*; *TV & Rad* ***programme planning*** programmation *f*; *TV & Rad* ***programme researcher*** recherchiste *mf*; ***programme schedule*** grille *f* de programmes; *TV & Rad* ***programme scheduler*** programmateur(trice) *m,f*; *Theat* ***programme seller*** vendeur(euse) *m,f* de programmes; ***programme supervisor*** chef *m* d'antenne; ***programme trail*** annonce *f* de programme

programme-maker, *Am* **program-maker** **N** *TV & Rad* réalisateur(trice) *m,f*

programmer, *Am* **programer** [ˈprəʊgræmə(r)] **N** *Comput* **1** *(person)* programmeur(euse) *m,f* **2** *(device)* programmateur *m*

programming, *Am* **programing** [ˈprəʊgræmɪŋ] **N 1** *Comput* programmation *f* **2** *TV & Rad* programmation *f*

▸▸ *Comput* ***programming error*** erreur *f* de programmation; *Comput* ***programming language*** langage *m* de programmation

progress N [ˈprəʊgres] **1** *(UNCOUNT) (headway)* progrès *mpl*; **they have made fast p.** ils ont avancé *ou* ils ont progressé rapidement; **it was slow p.** ça n'avançait pas vite; **to make good p.** *(in journey, process)* bien avancer; **negotiations are making good p.** les négociations sont en bonne voie; **the patient is making good p.** le patient donne de bons signes de récupération; **he is making p. in English** il fait des progrès en anglais; **we'll never make any p. this way** nous ne ferons jamais de progrès *ou* jamais aucun progrès de cette façon

2 *(UNCOUNT) (evolution)* progrès *m*; **to hinder p.** entraver *ou* freiner le progrès; **you can't stop p.** on ne peut arrêter le progrès; *Ironic* **that's p. for you!** c'est ça le progrès!

3 *(UNCOUNT) (forward movement)* progression *f*; *(of time, disease etc)* marche *f*; *(of events)* cours *m*; *(of plan, project)* déroulement *m*; **we watched the p. of the boat along the canal** nous avons regardé le bateau avancer le long du canal

4 *Arch (journey)* voyage *m*

VI [prəˈgres] **1** *(make headway* ▸ *negotiations, research)* progresser, avancer; *(*▸ *situation)* progresser, s'améliorer; *(*▸ *patient)* aller mieux; *(*▸ *student)* progresser, faire des progrès; **the talks are progressing well** les pourparlers sont en bonne voie; **the patient is progressing satisfactorily** le malade fait des progrès satisfaisants **2** *(move forward)* avancer; **to p. towards a place/an objective** se rapprocher d'un lieu/d'un objectif; **as the day progressed** à mesure que la journée avançait; **to p. onto more difficult tasks** passer à des tâches plus difficiles; **I never progressed beyond the first lesson** je ne suis jamais allé au-delà de la première leçon

VT [prəˈgres] *Com (advance)* faire progresser; **we need to p. this issue as quickly as possible** il nous faut accélérer les choses le plus possible

• **in progress ADJ to be in p.** être en cours; **work in p.** travaux *mpl* en cours; **while the exam is in p.** pendant l'examen; **service in p.** *(in cathedral)* office en cours

▸▸ *Ind* ***progress chart*** diagramme *m* de l'avancement des travaux; ***progress chaser*** responsable *mf* du (suivi d'un) planning; *Ind* ***progress payment*** paiement *m* proportionnel (à l'avancement des travaux); ***progress report*** compte-rendu *m*; *(on work)* rapport *m* sur l'avancement des travaux; *(on patient)* bulletin *m* de santé; *(on pupil)* bulletin *m* scolaire

progression [prəˈgreʃən] **N 1** *(advance* ▸ *of disease, army)* progression *f*

2 *Math & Mus* progression *f*; *Mus* **melodic p.** progression *f* mélodique

3 *(series)* série *f*, suite *f*; **I watched the endless p. of suburban houses from the taxi** du taxi, j'ai regardé la succession sans fin des pavillons de banlieue

4 *(of star)* marche *f*

progressive [prəˈgresɪv] **ADJ 1** *(forward-looking* ▸ *idea, teacher, politician, jazz)* progressiste; *(*▸ *education, method)* nouveau(elle), moderne; **he has a very p. outlook** sa vision des choses est très moderne; **to be p.** *(person)* avoir des idées progressistes

2 *(gradual* ▸ *change)* progressif; **to do sth in p. steps** *or* **stages** faire qch par étapes successives

3 *Med (disease)* progressif, évolutif; **p. hardening of the arteries** artériosclérose *f* progressive

4 *Gram (aspect)* progressif

N 1 *Pol* progressiste *mf* **2** *Gram* forme *f* progressive, progressif *m*; **in the p.** à la forme progressive

▸▸ *Fin* ***progressive tax*** impôt *m* progressif; *Econ* ***progressive taxation*** imposition *f* progressive

progressively [prəˈgresɪvlɪ] **ADV 1** *Pol & Sch* d'une manière progressiste; **to think p.** avoir des idées progressistes **2** *(gradually)* progressivement, graduellement, petit à petit; **taxes were p. increased** les impôts ont augmenté progressivement

progressiveness [prəˈgresɪvnɪs] **N 1** *(of ideas, teaching)* caractère *m* progressiste **2** *(gradualness)* progressivité *f*

prohibit [prəˈhɪbɪt] **VT 1** *(forbid)* interdire, défendre, prohiber; **to p. sb from doing sth** défendre *ou* interdire à qn de faire qch; **drinking alcohol at work is prohibited** il est interdit de boire de l'alcool sur le lieu de travail; **smoking is strictly prohibited** il est formellement interdit de fumer; **smoking prohibited** *(sign)* défense de fumer; **parking prohibited** *(sign)* stationnement interdit **2** *(prevent)* interdire, empêcher; **to p. sb from doing sth** empêcher qn de faire qch; **my promise to her prohibits me from saying more** la promesse que je lui ai faite m'interdit *ou* m'empêche d'en dire plus

prohibition [ˌprəʊɪˈbɪʃən] **N** interdiction *f*, prohibition *f*; **the p. of alcohol** la prohibition de l'alcool; **there should be a p. on the sale of such goods** il devrait y avoir une loi qui interdise la vente de ce genre de marchandises

• **Prohibition N** *Am Hist* la Prohibition

prohibitionist [ˌprəʊɪˈbɪʃənɪst] **ADJ** prohibitionniste

N prohibitionniste *mf*

prohibitive [prəˈhɪbətɪv] **ADJ** prohibitif; **the price of flowers is p.** les fleurs sont hors de prix

▸▸ ***prohibitive price*** prix *m* prohibitif *ou* inabordable

prohibitively [prəˈhɪbətɪvlɪ] **ADV p. expensive** d'un coût prohibitif

PROJECT

N
- projet **1**
- travaux pratiques **2**
- étude **3**

VT
- prévoir **1, 2**
- projeter **3–5, 7**
- présenter **4**

VI
- dépasser **1**

N [ˈprɒdʒekt] **1** *(plan)* projet *m*; *(enterprise, undertaking)* opération *f*, entreprise *f*; **they're working on a new building p.** ils travaillent sur un nouveau projet de construction; **a fund-raising p. to save** *or* **for saving the shipyard** une collecte de fonds pour sauver le chantier naval

2 *Sch (class work)* travaux *mpl* pratiques; *(individual work)* dossier *m*; **the class has just finished a nature p.** la classe vient de terminer des travaux pratiques de sciences naturelles

3 *(study, research)* étude *f*

4 *Am* **(housing) p.** cité *f* HLM

VT [prəˈdʒekt] **1** *(plan)* prévoir; **two new airports are projected for the next decade** il est prévu de construire deux nouveaux aéroports durant la prochaine décennie

2 *(forecast* ▸ *figures, output)* prévoir

3 *(send forth* ▸ *gen)* projeter, envoyer; *(*▸ *film, slide etc)* projeter; **to p. one's voice** projeter sa voix; **the missile was projected into space** le missile a été envoyé dans l'espace; **the explosion projected debris high into the air** l'explosion a projeté des débris très haut dans les airs; *Art* **projected shadow** ombre *f* portée; *Fig* **try to p. yourself forward into the 25th century** essayez d'imaginer que vous êtes au 25ème siècle

4 *(present)* présenter, projeter; **football hooligans p. a poor image of our country abroad** les

ooligans donnent une mauvaise image de no-
e pays à l'étranger; **she projects an image of self-onfidence** elle donne d'elle-même l'image d'une ersonne pleine d'assurance; **to p. one's personality** mettre sa personnalité en avant; **he tries to . himself as a great humanist** il essaie de se faire asser pour un grand humaniste
5 *Psy (transfer)* projeter; **to p. one's feelings onto b** projeter ses sentiments sur qn
6 *(cause to jut out)* faire dépasser
7 *Geom* projeter; **to p. a cylinder on** *or* **onto a lane** projeter un cylindre sur un plan
VI [prə'dʒekt] **1** *(protrude, jut out)* faire saillie, dé-asser; **the barrel of his gun projected from his vercoat** le canon de son revolver dépassait de on pardessus; **the balcony projects over the pave-ient** le balcon surplombe le trottoir
2 *Psy* se projeter
3 *(show personality)* **she doesn't p. well** elle pré-ente mal
4 *(with voice)* projeter sa voix
▸ ***project analysis*** étude *f* de projet; ***project man-gement*** gestion *f* de projets; ***project manager*** *gen)* chef *m* de projet; *Constr* maître *m* d'œuvre; ***roject milestone*** étape *f* principale du projet

rojected [prə'dʒektɪd] **ADJ 1** *(planned ▸ under-aking, visit)* prévu; **they are opposed to the p. uilding scheme** ils sont contre le projet de con-truction **2** *(forecast ▸ figures, production)* prévu; **he p. growth of the economy** la croissance éco-omique prévue, les prévisions de croissance conomique; *Fin* **p. turnover** chiffre *m* d'affaires révisionnel
▸ *Geom* ***projected angle*** angle *m* projeté

rojectile [prə'dʒektaɪl] **ADJ** *(force)* impulsif, rojectif
N projectile *m*
▸ *Mil* ***projectile weapons*** armes *fpl* de jet

rojecting [prə'dʒektɪŋ] **ADJ** *(roof, balcony etc)* aillant, en saillie, qui fait saillie; *(teeth)* en vant

rojection [prə'dʒekʃən] **N 1** *Cin, Geom & Psy* rojection *f*
2 *(estimate)* projection *f*, prévision *f*; **here are my rojections for the next ten years** voici mes prévi-ions pour les dix années à venir; **demographic rojections** projections *fpl* démographiques
3 *(of missile)* lancement *m*, envoi *m*; *(of one's oice)* projection *f*
4 *(protrusion)* saillie *f*, avancée *f*; *(overhang)* sur-lomb *m*
▸ *Cin* ***projection room*** cabine *f* de projection

rojectionist [prə'dʒekʃənɪst] **N** *Cin* projection-iste *mf*

rojective [prə'dʒektɪv] **ADJ** *Math (plane)* de rojection
▸ *Math* ***projective geometry*** géometrie *f* projec-ive; ***projective test*** test *m* projectif

rojector [prə'dʒektə(r)] **N** projecteur *m*

rolapse ['prəʊlæps] *Med* **N** prolapsus *m*, ptôse **p. (of the uterus)** prolapsus *m* ou descente *f* de utérus
VI descendre, tomber

rolapsed ['prəʊlæpst] **ADJ** *Med* prolabé

role [prəʊl] *Fam Pej* **ADJ** prolo
N prolo *mf*

roletarian [ˌprəʊlɪ'teərɪən] **N** prolétaire *mf*
ADJ prolétarien; *Pej* de prolétaire

roletarianize, -ise [ˌprəʊlɪ'teərɪənaɪz] **VT** pro-étariser

roletariat [ˌprəʊlɪ'teərɪət] **N** prolétariat *m*

ro-life **ADJ** contre l'interruption volontaire de rossesse
▸ ***pro-life movement*** mouvement *m* pour le res-ect de la vie

ro-lifer **N** *Fam* = adversaire de l'interruption olontaire de grossesse

roliferate [prə'lɪfəreɪt] **VI** proliférer

roliferation [prəˌlɪfə'reɪʃən] **N 1** *(rapid increase)* rolifération *f* **2** *(large amount or number)* grande uantité *f* **3** *Biol & Nucl* prolifération *f*

rolific [prə'lɪfɪk] **ADJ** prolifique, fécond; **the ountry has been a p. producer of inventors** le pays été fécond en inventeurs; **a p. goalscorer** un ros buteur

prolifically [prə'lɪfɪkəlɪ] **ADV** *(write, compose)* abondamment; *(grow)* en abondance; **he has been a p. successful goalscorer** il a marqué énormément de buts

prolix ['prəʊlɪks] **ADJ** *Formal* prolixe

prolixity [prəʊ'lɪksətɪ] **N** *Formal* prolixité *f*

prologue, *Am* **prolog** ['prəʊlɒg] **N** *also Fig* prologue *m*, prélude *m* (**to** de); **her arrival was the p. to yet another row** son arrivée allait être le prélude d'une *ou* préluder à une nouvelle querelle

prolong [prə'lɒŋ] **VT** prolonger; *Fig Hum* **to p. the agony** faire durer le suspense

prolongation [ˌprəʊlɒŋ'geɪʃən] **N** *(in time)* prolongation *f*, *(in space)* prolongement *m*, extension *f*

prolonged [prə'lɒŋd] **ADJ** long (longue); **after a p. absence** après une longue absence

PROM [prɒm] **N** *Comput (abbr* **programmable read-only memory***)* PROM *f inv*

prom [prɒm] **N 1** *Br Fam (at seaside)* front *m* de mer[□], promenade[□] *f* **2** *Br Fam Mus (concert)* concert-promenade[□] *m* **3** *Am (dance)* bal[□] *m (de lycéens ou d'étudiants)*
• **Proms** **NPL** **the Proms** = série de concerts-promenades, qui a lieu au mois de juillet au Albert Hall de Londres
▸▸ *Am Sch & Univ* ***prom king*** roi *m* du bal; *Am Sch & Univ* ***prom queen*** reine *f* du bal

> **PROM**
>
> Aux États-Unis, on célèbre la fin des études secondaires par un grand bal formel appelé le "senior prom". Ce bal a lieu à la fin des examens de dernière année et c'est un événement important auquel assistent élèves et professeurs. Les étudiantes et leurs cavaliers sont en tenue de soirée et, au cours de la fête, on élit un roi et une reine du bal ("prom king" et "prom queen").

pro-marketeer **N** *Br Pol* partisan(e) *m,f* du Marché commun

promenade [ˌprɒmə'nɑːd] **N 1** *Br (at seaside)* front *m* de mer, promenade *f* **2** *(walk)* promenade *f* **3** *Am (dance)* bal *m (de lycéens ou d'étudiants)*
COMP *(performance)* = où les auditeurs doivent se déplacer pour suivre l'action de la pièce
VI 1 *Formal or Hum (walk)* se promener **2** *(in dancing)* marcher
VT *(show off)* faire parade de, exhiber
▸▸ ***promenade concert*** concert-promenade *m*; *Naut* ***promenade deck*** pont *m* promenade

promenader [ˌprɒmə'nɑːdə(r)] **N** *Mus* auditeur (trice) *m,f* d'un concert-promenade

Promethean [prə'miːθjən] **ADJ** prométhéen

Prometheus [prə'miːθɪəs] **PR N** *Myth* Prométhée

prominence ['prɒmɪnəns] **N 1** *(importance)* importance *f*, *(fame)* célébrité *f*; **to rise to p.** se hisser au premier rang; **to come into** *or* **to p.** *(become important)* prendre de l'importance; *(become famous)* devenir célèbre; **to give p. to sth** faire ressortir qch, donner une place importante à qch; **to bring sb/sth into p.** attirer l'attention sur qn/qch; **to occupy a position of p.** *(politician etc)* occuper une position éminente; *(house)* être situé sur une éminence **2** *(of land, feature etc)* proéminence *f*, *(part sticking up)* saillie *f*, protubérance *f*; **a rocky p.** une saillie rocheuse **3** *Astron* protubérance *f* solaire

prominent ['prɒmɪnənt] **ADJ 1** *(well-known)* célèbre; *(eminent)* éminent; *(obvious)* saillant, frappant; **a scandal involving a p. politician** un scandale impliquant un éminent homme politique; **he has a p. position in the government** il est très haut placé au gouvernement; **he was very p. in the campaign** il a joué un rôle très important dans la campagne; **rice is p. in Eastern cuisine** le riz est l'un des principaux ingrédients de la cuisine asiatique; **to play a p. part** *or* **role in sth** jouer un rôle important *ou* de tout premier plan dans qch **2** *(striking ▸ detail, difference)* frappant, remarquable; *(▸ fact, feature)* saillant, marquant; **put that poster in a p. position** mettez cette affiche (dans un endroit) bien en vue; **the title needs to be more p.** il faut que le titre ressorte plus **3** *(projecting)* saillant, en saillie, proéminent; *(land, structure, nose)* proéminent; *(teeth)* qui avance, proéminent

prominently ['prɒmɪnəntlɪ] **ADV** bien en vue; **he figures p. in French politics** il occupe une position importante *ou* de premier plan dans la vie politique française; **the medal was p. displayed** la médaille était mise en évidence

promiscuity [ˌprɒmɪ'skjuːətɪ] **N** promiscuité *f* sexuelle

> Note that the French word **promiscuité** is a false friend and is never a translation for the English word **promiscuity**. It means **lack of privacy**.

promiscuous [prə'mɪskjʊəs] **ADJ 1** *(sexually)* **to be p.** *(person)* avoir des mœurs dissolues; *(society, group)* être permissif; **he's very p.** il couche avec n'importe qui; **p. behaviour** promiscuité *f* sexuelle **2** *Formal (mixed)* confus, mêlé; *(crowd)* hétérogène

promiscuously [prə'mɪskjʊəslɪ] **ADV 1** *(sexually)* **to behave p.** avoir des mœurs dissolues **2** *Formal (in a random or confused way)* confusément

promise ['prɒmɪs] **N 1** *(pledge)* promesse *f*; **to make** *or* **to give sb a p.** faire une promesse à qn, donner sa parole à qn; **to keep a p.** respecter *ou* tenir une promesse; **she always keeps her promises** elle tient toujours ses promesses, elle tient toujours (sa) parole; **I'm not making any promises but I'll try my best** je ne promets rien, mais je ferai de mon mieux; **I kept** *or* **held him to his p.** j'ai fait en sorte qu'il tienne parole; **to break one's p.** manquer à sa parole, ne pas tenir ses promesses; **a p. of help** une promesse d'assistance; **to hold out the p. of sth to sb** laisser espérer qch à qn, faire miroiter qch à qn; **he did it under (the) p. of a Parliamentary seat** il l'a fait parce qu'on lui a promis un siège de député; **a p. is a p.** chose promise, chose due; **promises, promises!** toujours des promesses!
2 *(potential)* promesse *f*; **she is full of p., she shows p.** elle est pleine de promesse *ou* promesses; **an artist of p.** un artiste qui promet
VT 1 *(pledge)* promettre; **to p. sth to sb, to p. sb sth** promettre qch à qn; **to p. (sb) to do sth** promettre (à qn) de faire qch; **I can't p. (you) anything** je ne peux rien vous promettre; **he promised himself a good meal** il se promit mentalement de faire un bon repas; **she promised him (that) she would come** elle lui a promis de venir *ou* qu'elle viendrait; **you'll get into trouble, I p. you!** tu auras des ennuis, je te le promets *ou* tu verras ce que je te dis!
2 *(indicate)* promettre, annoncer; **it promises to be hot today** le temps promet d'être *ou* s'annonce chaud aujourd'hui; **next week already promises to be difficult** la semaine prochaine promet déjà d'être difficile *ou* s'annonce déjà difficile
3 *(in marriage)* **she was promised to the King's son at birth** dès sa naissance, elle fut promise au fils du roi
VI 1 *(gen)* promettre; **he wanted to come but he couldn't p.** il espérait pouvoir venir mais ne pouvait rien promettre; **I'll wait for you – (do you) p.?** je t'attendrai – tu le promets? *ou* promis?; **OK, I p.!** d'accord, c'est promis!; **but you promised!** mais tu avais promis!
2 to p. well *(enterprise)* promettre, s'annoncer bien; *(person)* être prometteur *ou* plein de promesses; *(results, harvest, negotiations)* s'annoncer bien; **his first article promises well** son premier article promet *ou* est prometteur
▸▸ *Bible & Fig* ***Promised Land*** Terre *f* promise

promising ['prɒmɪsɪŋ] **ADJ 1** *(full of potential ▸ person)* prometteur, qui promet, plein de promesses; **she's a p. actress** c'est une actrice pleine de promesses *ou* qui promet **2** *(encouraging)* prometteur, qui promet; **these are p. signs** ce sont des signes prometteurs; **she got off to a p. start** elle a fait des débuts prometteurs; **her work is very p.** son travail est très prometteur; **the forecast isn't very p. for tomorrow** les prévisions météo n'annoncent rien de bon pour demain

promisingly ['prɒmɪsɪŋlɪ] **ADV** d'une façon prometteuse; **France started the match p.** la France a bien débuté la partie

promissory note ['prɒmɪsərɪ-] N *Com* billet *m* à ordre, effet *m* à ordre

promo ['prəʊməʊ] (*pl* **promos**) N *Fam* **1** (*video*) vidéo *f* promotionnelle; (*for record*) clip *m* **2** (*sales promotion*) promo *f*

promontory ['prɒməntərɪ] (*pl* **promontories**) N promontoire *m*

promote [prə'məʊt] VT **1** (*in profession, army*) promouvoir; **to be** *or* **to get promoted** être promu, monter en grade, obtenir de l'avancement; **Blyth has been promoted to (the rank of) captain** Blyth a été promu (au grade de) capitaine; **she's been promoted to regional manager** elle a été promue (au poste de) directrice régionale

2 *Sport* **to be promoted to the first division** passer *ou* monter en première division; **to get** *or* **be promoted** passer *ou* monter dans la division supérieure

3 (*encourage* ▸ *peace, growth, justice, cause*) promouvoir; (▸ *the arts, a project*) encourager; (▸ *success*) favoriser; (▸ *person's interests*) servir; **to p. international cooperation** promouvoir *ou* favoriser *ou* encourager la coopération internationale; **cleanliness promotes health** la propreté est un facteur de santé; *Parl* **to p. a bill** prendre l'initiative d'un projet de loi

4 *Com* (*advertise, publicize*) promouvoir, faire la promotion de; **she's in England to p. her new record** elle est en Angleterre pour faire la promotion de son nouveau disque

5 (*in chess*) promouvoir

promoter [prə'məʊtə(r)] N **1** *Com* promoteur(trice) *m,f* (des ventes) **2** (*organizer* ▸ *of match, concert*) organisateur(trice) *m,f*; (*sponsor*) parrain *m* **3** (*of peace, scheme*) promoteur(trice) *m, f*; **to be a p. of sth** (*theory, idea, cause*) promouvoir qch

promotion [prə'məʊʃən] N **1** (*advancement*) promotion *f*, avancement *m*; **to get p.** être promu, obtenir de l'avancement; **there are good prospects of p. in this company** il y a de réelles possibilités de promotion *ou* d'avancement dans cette société

2 *Sport* promotion *f*; **the team won p. to the first division** l'équipe a gagné sa place en première division; **to get** *or* **win p.** passer *ou* monter dans la division supérieure

3 (*encouragement*) promotion *f*, développement *m*; **the p. of good international relations** le développement de bonnes relations internationales

4 *Com & Mktg* promotion *f*; **this week's p.** la promotion de la semaine; **I helped in the p. of her new book** j'ai contribué à la promotion *ou* au lancement de son nouveau livre

5 (*in chess*) promotion *f*

▸▸ ***promotions agency*** agence *f* de promotion; ***promotion budget*** budget *m* promotionnel; ***promotion campaign*** campagne *f* de promotion; ***promotion team*** équipe *f* promotionnelle; ***promotion techniques*** techniques *fpl* de promotion des ventes

promotional [prə'məʊʃənəl] ADJ *Com & Mktg* promotionnel, publicitaire

▸▸ ***promotional campaign*** campagne *f* de promotion; ***promotional costs*** coûts *mpl* de promotion; ***promotional discount*** remise *f* promotionnelle; ***promotional literature*** prospectus *mpl* promotionnels; ***promotional material*** matériel *m* de promotion; ***promotional offer*** offre *f* promotionnelle; ***promotional price*** prix *m* promotionnel; ***promotional sample*** échantillon *m* promotionnel; ***promotional video*** (cassette *f*) vidéo *f* promotionnelle

prompt [prɒmpt] ADJ **1** (*quick*) rapide, prompt; **a p. answer/decision** une réponse/décision rapide; **Carrie was p. to answer our letter** Carrie a répondu rapidement *ou* sans attendre à notre lettre; **to take p. action** prendre des mesures immédiates; **her p. action saved his life** la rapidité de sa réaction lui a sauvé la vie; **to be p. in paying one's debts** être prompt à payer ses dettes **2** (*punctual*) exact, à l'heure

ADV (*exactly*) **at nine o'clock p.** à neuf heures précises

VT **1** (*provoke* ▸ *person*) pousser, inciter; (▸ *reaction, reply*) provoquer; **to p. sb to do sth** pousser *ou* porter qn à faire qch; **I felt prompted to intervene** je me suis senti obligé d'intervenir; **the wave of strikes has prompted the Government to step up its reform programme** la vague de grèves a incité le gouvernement à accélérer son programme de réformes; **his letter prompts me to think that he's mad** sa lettre m'incite à penser qu'il est fou; **what prompted you to suggest such a thing?** qu'est-ce qui vous a incité à proposer une chose pareille?; **the scandal prompted his resignation** le scandale a provoqué sa démission **2 to p. sb** (*actor*) souffler sa réplique à qn; (*speaker, pupil*) souffler à qn; **she needed no prompting when asked her opinion on the subject** elle n'avait pas besoin d'encouragement pour donner son opinion sur le sujet

N **1** *Theat* **to give an actor a p.** souffler une réplique à un acteur **2** *Comput* invite *f*; (*with wording*) message *m* d'invite *ou* d'attente; **DOS p.** invite *f* du DOS; **return to the C:\ p.** revenir au message d'attente du DOS **3** *Fin* (*for payment*) délai *m* (de paiement)

▸▸ *Theat* ***prompt box*** trou *m* (du souffleur); *Fin* ***prompt note*** rappel *m* d'échéance; *Com* ***prompt payment*** paiement *m* dans les délais; *Theat* ***prompt side*** (*in UK*) côté *m* cour; (*in US*) côté *m* jardin; **opposite p. side** (*in UK*) côté *m* jardin; (*in US*) côté *m* cour

prompter ['prɒmptə(r)] N *Theat* souffleur(euse) *m,f*; *TV* téléprompteur *m*

prompting ['prɒmptɪŋ] N **1** (*persuasion*) incitation *f*; **they will not do it without the p. of the international community** ils ne le feront pas si la communauté internationale ne les y pousse pas; **to do sth at sb's p.** faire qch sur les instances *ou* à l'instigation de qn; **the promptings of conscience** l'aiguillon *m* de la conscience; **he needed no p.** il n'a pas été nécessaire de le pousser **2** (*of actor, pupil, speaker*) **he needed a lot of p.** (*actor*) on devait lui souffler tout le temps; **to answer a question without p.** répondre à une question sans que personne ne souffle; *Sch* **no p.!** ne soufflez pas!

promptitude ['prɒmptɪtju:d] N *Formal* **1** (*quickness*) promptitude *f*, rapidité *f* **2** (*punctuality*) ponctualité *f*

promptly ['prɒmptlɪ] ADV **1** (*quickly*) promptement, rapidement; **he p. sent off the telegram** il a rapidement envoyé le télégramme; **he paid up p.** il a payé immédiatement **2** (*punctually*) ponctuellement; **he always gets up p. at seven o'clock** il se lève toujours à sept heures précises **3** (*immediately*) aussitôt, tout de suite; **I p. forgot what I was meant to do** j'ai aussitôt oublié ce que j'étais supposé faire

promptness ['prɒmptnɪs] N **1** (*quickness*) promptitude *f*, rapidité *f* **2** (*punctuality*) ponctualité *f*

promulgate ['prɒməlgeɪt] VT *Formal* **1** (*decree, law*) promulguer **2** (*belief, idea, opinion*) répandre, diffuser

promulgation [ˌprɒməl'geɪʃən] N *Formal* **1** (*of decree, law*) promulgation *f* **2** (*of belief, idea, opinion*) diffusion *f*, dissémination *f*

prone [prəʊn] ADJ **1** (*inclined*) sujet, enclin; **to be p. to do sth** être sujet *ou* enclin à faire qch; **p. to a disease** prédisposé à une maladie **2** (*prostrate*) à plat ventre; **in a p. position** couché sur le ventre

-prone [prəʊn] SUFF **to be accident/disaster-p.** être enclin aux accidents/désastres; **a strike-p. industry** une industrie sujette aux grèves

proneness ['prəʊnnɪs] N tendance *f*, prédisposition *f*; **he has a certain p. to accidents/to letting himself be influenced** il est assez enclin aux accidents/à se laisser influencer

prong [prɒŋ] N (*of fork*) dent *f*; (*of tuning fork*) branche *f*; (*of antler*) pointe *f*; (*of attack, argument*) pointe *f*

pronged [prɒŋd] ADJ à dents, à pointes

pronominal [prə'nɒmɪnəl] ADJ pronominal

pronominally [prə'nɒmɪnəlɪ] ADV pronominalement

pronoun ['prəʊnaʊn] N pronom *m*

pronounce [prə'naʊns] VT **1** (*say*) prononcer; **his name is hard to p.** son nom est difficile à prononcer; **how's it pronounced?** comment est-ce que ça se prononce?; **you don't p. the "p" in "psalm"** on ne prononce pas le "p" de "psalm", le "p" d[e] "psalm" est muet **2** *Formal* (*declare*) déclare[r] prononcer; **the doctor pronounced him dead** [le] médecin l'a déclaré mort; **judgment has not y[et] been pronounced** le jugement n'est pas enco[re] prononcé *ou* rendu; **I now p. you man and wi[fe]** (*in marriage service*) je vous déclare mari [et] femme

VI (*declare*) se prononcer; **to p. for/against sth** [se] prononcer pour/contre qch; *Law* pronon[cer] pour/contre qch; **to p. on** *or* **upon sth** se prono[n]cer sur qch; *Law* statuer *ou* prononcer sur qch

pronounceable [prə'naʊnsəbəl] ADJ prono[n]çable

pronounced [prə'naʊnst] ADJ (*squint, accen[t], liking*) prononcé, marqué; (*features*) accus[é]; (*views, opinions*) arrêté; **the change is becomi[ng] more p.** le changement s'accentue; **he walks wi[th] a p. limp** il boite de façon prononcée

pronouncement [prə'naʊnsmənt] N décl[a]ration *f*

pronouncing [prə'naʊnsɪŋ] N *Law* (*of sentenc[e]*) prononcé *m*

▸▸ ***pronouncing dictionary*** dictionnaire *m* [de] prononciation

pronto ['prɒntəʊ] ADV *Fam* illico (presto), pron[to]

pronuclear [ˌprəʊ'nju:klɪə(r)] ADJ (*policy, stat[e]ment*) en faveur du nucléaire; **he is p.** il est po[ur] le nucléaire

pronunciation [prəˌnʌnsɪ'eɪʃən] N prononci[a]tion *f*; **his French p. was good** il avait une bon[ne] prononciation en français

proof [pru:f] N **1** (UNCOUNT) (*evidence*) preuve [*f*]; **to show** *or* **to give p. of sth** faire *ou* donner [la] preuve de qch; **do you have any p.?** vous en av[ez] la preuve *ou* des preuves?; **you need p. of identi[ty]** vous devez fournir une pièce d'identité; **can yo[u] produce any p. for your accusations?** avez-vo[us] des preuves pour justifier vos accusations[?]; **we have written p. of it** nous en avons la preuv[e] écrite *ou* par écrit; **that's no p.!** ce n'est pas u[ne] preuve!; **by way of p.** comme *ou* pour preuve; **[he] cited several other cases in p. of his argument** il [a] cité plusieurs autres cas pour défendre s[a] thèse; **he gave her a locket as p. of his love** il lu[i a] offert un médaillon comme preuve de so[n] amour pour elle *ou* en gage d'amour; *Prov* **t[he] p. of the pudding is in the eating** il faut juger s[ur] pièces **2** *Phot & Typ* épreuve *f*; **to correct** *or* **[to] read the proofs** corriger les épreuves; **to pa[ss] the proofs** donner le bon à tirer; **at the p. stage** la correction des épreuves **3** (*of alcohol*) teneu[r] (en alcool); **45 percent p. brandy** ≃ cognac *m* 45 degrés

ADJ *Br* **to be p. against** (*fire, acid, rust*) être à l'épreuve de; (*danger, temptation*) être à l'abri [de] *ou* insensible à

VT **1** (*fabric*) imperméabiliser **2** *Typ* (*proofrea[d]*) corriger les épreuves de; (*produce proof of*) pr[é]parer les épreuves de

▸▸ *Typ* ***proof correction mark*** signe *m* de corre[c]tion; ***proof of delivery*** bordereau *m* de livraiso[n]; ***proof of payment*** justificatif *m* de paiemen[t]; ***proof of postage*** certificat *m* d'expédition; ***pro[of] of purchase*** reçu *m*; ***proof spirit*** (*in UK*) alcool *m* 57°; (*in US*) alcool *m* à 50°

-proof [pru:f] SUFF à l'épreuve de; **acid-p.** [à] l'épreuve des acides; **an idiot-p. mechanism** u[n] mécanisme (totalement) indéréglable

proofing ['pru:fɪŋ] N **1** (*action* ▸ *of fabric*) impe[r]méabilisation *f* **2** (*coating*) enduit *m* impe[r]méable **3** *Typ* (*reading*) correction *f* d[es] épreuves; (*production*) tirage *m* des épreuves

proofread ['pru:fri:d] (*pt & pp* **proofread** [-red]) VT corriger (les épreuves de)

proofreader ['pru:fˌri:də(r)] N correcteur(tric[e]) *m,f* (d'épreuves *ou* d'imprimerie)

proofreading ['pru:fˌri:dɪŋ] N correction (d'épreuves)

▸▸ ***proofreading mark, proofreading symb[ol]*** signe *m* de correction

prop [prɒp] (*pt & pp* **propped**, *cont* **propping**) N [**1**] (*gen*) support *m*; *Constr* (*for tunnel, wall*) étai [*m*], étançon *m*; (*in pit*) étai *m*

2 (*pole, stick* ▸ *for plant, flowers*) tuteur *m*; (▸ *f* beans, peas) rame *f*; (▸ *for vines*) échalas *m*; (▸ *for washing line*) perche *f*

3 *Sport (in rugby)* pilier *m*

4 *Fig* soutien *m*; **he uses alcohol as a p.** il boit pour se donner du courage; **he was the p. of his father's old age** il était le bâton de vieillesse de son père

5 *Theat (property)* accessoire *m*

6 *Fam (propeller)* hélice*f*

VT 1 *(lean)* appuyer; **she propped her bike (up) against the wall** elle a appuyé son vélo contre le mur; **p. yourself** *or* **your back against these cushions** calez-vous contre *ou* adossez-vous à ces coussins; **he was propping his head (up) in his hands** il tenait sa tête calée entre ses mains **2** *(support)* **to p. (up)** *(wall, tunnel)* étayer, étançonner, consolider; *(plants)* mettre un tuteur à; *(peas, beans)* ramer; **I propped the door open with a chair** j'ai maintenu la porte ouverte avec une chaise

▸▸ *Sport* ***prop forward*** *(in rugby)* pilier *m*; *Cin & TV* ***props person*** accessoiriste *mf*, ensemblier *m*; *Aut* ***prop shaft*** arbre *m* de transmission

prop up VT SEP *(regime, family, business, currency)* soutenir; *Fam Hum* **he's always propping up the bar** c'est un vrai pilier de bar *ou* de bistro

propaganda [ˌprɒpəˈgændə] **N** propagande *f*

COMP *(film, machine, material, exercise)* de propagande

propagandist [ˌprɒpəˈgændɪst] **ADJ** propagandiste

N propagandiste *mf*

propagandize, -ise [ˌprɒpəˈgændaɪz] **VI** faire de la propagande

VT *(ideas, views)* faire de la propagande pour *ou* en faveur de; *(person, masses)* faire de la propagande auprès de

propagate [ˈprɒpəgeɪt] **VT** *Bot & Phys* propager; *Fig (ideas etc)* propager, disséminer

VI se propager

propagation [ˌprɒpəˈgeɪʃən] **N** *Bot, Phys & Fig* propagation *f*

propagator [ˈprɒpəgeɪtə(r)] **N 1** *(gen)* propagateur(trice) *m,f* **2** *Bot* germoir *m*

propane [ˈprəʊpeɪn] **N** *Chem* propane *m*

propel [prəˈpel] *(pt & pp* **propelled**, *cont* **propelling)** **VT 1** *(machine, vehicle etc)* propulser, faire avancer **2** *(person)* propulser, pousser; **she was propelled along the road by the crowd** elle fut poussée par la foule sur toute la longueur de la rue; **the sudden stop propelled us all forward** l'arrêt subit nous a tous propulsés vers l'avant; **he was propelled into the position of manager** on l'a bombardé directeur

propellant, propellent [prəˈpelənt] **N** *(for rocket)* propergol *m*; *(for gun)* poudre *f* propulsive; *(in aerosol)* (agent *m*) propulseur *m*

ADJ propulsif, propulseur

propeller [prəˈpelə(r)] **N** hélice *f*

▸▸ ***propeller engine*** moteur *m* à hélice; ***propeller shaft*** *Aviat* arbre *m* porte-hélice; *Naut* arbre *m* d'hélice; *Aut* arbre *m* de transmission

propelling pencil [prəˈpelɪŋ-] **N** *Br* portemine *m*

propensity [prəˈpensətɪ] *(pl* **propensities)** **N** *Formal* propension *f*, tendance *f*, penchant *m*; **he has a p. for** *or* **towards drink** il a tendance à boire (plus que de raison); **my p. not to trust** *or* **for not trusting other people** ma propension *ou* ma tendance à ne pas faire confiance aux autres

PROPER [ˈprɒpə(r)]

• bon **1**	• correct **1, 3**
• convenable **1, 3**	• vrai **2, 4**
• proprement dit **5**	

ADJ 1 *(correct)* bon, juste, correct; *(appropriate)* convenable, approprié; **the p. answer** la bonne réponse, la réponse correcte; **you're not doing it in the p. way** vous ne vous y prenez pas comme il faut; **to apply to the p. person** s'adresser à qui de droit; **to put sth in the p. place** mettre qch à sa place; **John wasn't waiting at the p. place** John n'attendait pas au bon endroit *ou* là où il fallait; **she didn't come at the p. time** elle s'est trompée d'heure; **to think it p. to do sth** juger bon de faire qch; **do as you think p.** faites comme bon vous semble; **that wasn't the p. thing to say/to do** ce n'était pas ce qu'il fallait dire/faire; **she thanked him, as is only p.** elle l'a remercié, comme il se devait; **that noisy pub isn't a p. place for a meeting** ce pub bruyant n'est pas un endroit approprié pour tenir une réunion; **paid at the p. rate** payé au taux *ou* au prix convenable; **he wasn't wearing the p. clothes** il n'était pas vêtu pour la circonstance; **you must go through the p. channels** il faut suivre la filière officielle; **I don't have the p. tools for this engine** je n'ai pas les outils appropriés pour *ou* qui conviennent pour ce moteur; **I can't find the p. word to describe him** je n'arrive pas à trouver le mot juste *ou* qui convient pour le décrire; *Old-fashioned or Hum* **he did the p. thing by her** *(he married her)* il a réparé

2 *(real)* vrai, véritable; **I haven't had a p. meal in ages** il y a une éternité que je n'ai pas fait un vrai repas; **we must give the President a p. welcome** nous devons réserver au président un accueil digne de ce nom; **it's a toy, not a p. rifle** c'est un jouet, pas un vrai fusil; **they call him Tommy but his p. name's Thomas** on l'appelle Tommy mais son vrai nom c'est Thomas; **he's not a p. doctor** ce n'est pas un vrai docteur; **in the p. sense of the word** au sens propre du mot; **putting letters in envelopes isn't a p. job** mettre des lettres dans des enveloppes n'a rien d'un vrai travail

3 *(respectable)* correct, convenable, comme il faut; **that's not p. behaviour** ce n'est pas convenable, cela ne se fait pas; **she's a very p. young woman** c'est une jeune femme très bien; **she's a bit too p.** elle est un peu trop comme il faut; **may I take my shoes off? – no, that's not the p. thing to do here** puis-je ôter mes chaussures? – non, ça ne se fait pas *ou* ce serait déplacé ici

4 *Br Fam (as intensifier)* vrai, véritable, complet(ète); **it's a p. catastrophe** c'est une vraie *ou* véritable catastrophe; **you're a p. idiot** tu es un parfait imbécile *ou* un imbécile fini; **he made a p. fool of himself** il s'est couvert de ridicule; **a p. little madam** une vraie petite madame; **we're in a p. mess** nous voilà dans de beaux draps!; **I gave him a p. telling-off** je lui ai passé un bon savon

5 *(predicative use* ▸ *specifically)* proprement dit; **he lives outside the city p.** il habite en dehors de la ville même *ou* proprement dite

6 *(characteristic)* **p. to** propre à, typique de; **illnesses p. to tropical climates** maladies propres aux climats tropicaux

ADV *Br Fam* **they got it good and p.** ils ont reçu ce qu'ils méritaient; **to talk p.** parler correctement; *NEng* **he was p. angry with me** il était très *ou* vraiment en colère contre moi

▸▸ *Math* ***proper fraction*** fraction *f* inférieure à l'unité; *Astron* ***proper motion*** mouvement *m* propre; ***proper name*** nom *m* propre; ***proper noun*** nom *m* propre

> Note that the French word **propre** never means **right** or **adequate**. Its most common meaning is **clean**.

properly [ˈprɒpəlɪ] **ADV 1** *(well, correctly)* bien, juste, correctement; **the lid isn't on p.** le couvercle n'est pas bien mis; **the engine isn't working p.** le moteur ne marche pas bien; **for once they pronounced my name p.** pour une fois, ils ont prononcé mon nom correctement *ou* ils ont bien prononcé mon nom; **I haven't slept p. in weeks** ça fait des semaines que je n'ai pas bien dormi; **she quite p. intervened** c'est avec raison *ou* à juste titre qu'elle est intervenue

2 *(decently, suitably)* correctement, convenablement; *(correctly in behaviour)* comme il faut; **patrons must be p. dressed** une tenue vestimentaire correcte est exigée de nos clients; **eat p.!** mange proprement *ou* comme il faut!; **he didn't behave p. towards her** il ne s'est pas comporté correctement envers elle; **I haven't thanked you p.** je ne vous ai pas remercié comme il faut *ou* comme il convient

3 *(strictly)* proprement; **he isn't p. speaking an expert** il n'est pas à proprement parler un expert

4 *Br Fam (as intensifier)* vraiment, complètement, tout à fait; **I'm p. exhausted** je suis complètement crevé; **they were p. told off** ils en ont pris pour leur grade

propertied [ˈprɒpətɪd] **ADJ** *Formal* possédant; **a p. gentleman** un homme fortuné; **the p. classes** les classes *fpl* possédantes

property [ˈprɒpətɪ] *(pl* **properties)** **N 1** *(UNCOUNT) (belongings)* propriété *f*, biens *mpl*; *(objects)* objets *mpl*; *Law* biens *mpl*; **hands off! that's my p.!** n'y touchez pas, c'est à moi *ou* ça m'appartient!; **this book is the p. of Theresa Lloyd** ce livre appartient à Theresa Lloyd; **government p.** propriété *f* de l'État; **she left him all her p.** elle lui a laissé tous ses biens; **this is stolen p.** ce sont des objets volés

2 *(UNCOUNT) (buildings)* propriété *f*, *(real estate)* biens *mpl* immobiliers, immobilier *m*; *(land)* terres *fpl*, propriété *f* (foncière); **Smythe is investing his money in p.** Smythe investit son argent dans l'immobilier; **they own a lot of p. in the country** *(houses)* ils ont de nombreuses propriétés à la campagne; *(land)* ils ont de nombreuses terres à la campagne; **a man of p.** un homme qui possède des biens immobiliers *ou* une fortune personnelle; **to get (a foot) on the p. ladder** accéder à la propriété, devenir propriétaire

3 *(plot of land)* terrain *m*; *(house, building)* propriété *f*; **to be on sb's p.** être dans la propriété de qn; **get off my p.!** sortez de chez moi!

4 *(quality)* propriété *f*; **what are the chemical properties of cobalt?** quelles sont les propriétés chimiques du cobalt?; **healing properties** vertus *fpl* thérapeutiques *ou* curatives

5 *Law (right)* (droit *m* de) propriété *f*; **literary/intellectual p.** propriété *f* littéraire/intellectuelle

6 *Theat* accessoire *m*

▸▸ *Br* ***property assets*** patrimoine *m* immobilier; ***property centre*** centre *m* de vente immobilière; ***property developer*** promoteur(trice) *m,f* (immobilier(ère)); ***property development*** promotion *f* immobilière; *Br* ***property loan*** prêt *m* immobilier; *Theat* ***property man*** accessoiriste *m*; ***property market*** marché *m* immobilier; *Theat* ***property mistress*** accessoiriste *f*; ***property owner*** propriétaire *mf*; ***property shares*** valeurs *fpl* immobilières; ***property speculation*** spéculation *f* immobilière; ***property speculator*** spéculateur (trice) *m,f* immobilier(ère); ***property surveyor*** (architecte *mf*) expert(e) *m,f*; ***property tax*** impôt *m* foncier

> Attention: ne pas confondre avec **propriety**, qui signifie **bienséance**.

prophecy [ˈprɒfɪsɪ] *(pl* **prophecies)** **N** prophétie *f*

prophesy [ˈprɒfɪsaɪ] *(pt & pp* **prophesied)** **VT** prophétiser, prédire; **scaremongers prophesied the end of the world** des alarmistes ont annoncé la fin du monde; **to p. that sth will happen** prédire que qch va arriver

VI faire des prophéties

prophet [ˈprɒfɪt] **N** prophète *m*; **the P.** *(in Islam)* le Prophète (Mahomet); **a p. of doom** un prophète de malheur

• **Prophets N** *Bible* **(the Book of) Prophets** le livre des Prophètes

prophetess [ˈprɒfɪtɪs] **N** prophétesse *f*

prophetic [prəˈfetɪk] **ADJ** prophétique

prophetically [prəˈfetɪkəlɪ] **ADV** prophétiquement

prophylactic [ˌprɒfɪˈlæktɪk] **ADJ** prophylactique

N 1 *(drug)* médicament *m* prophylactique **2** *(condom)* préservatif *m*

prophylaxis [ˌprɒfɪˈlæksɪs] *(pl* **prophylaxes** [-siːz]) **N** prophylaxie *f*

propinquity [prəˈpɪŋkwətɪ] **N** *Formal* **1** *(in space, time)* proximité *f* **2** *(in kinship)* consanguinité *f*

propitiate [prəˈpɪʃɪeɪt] **VT** *Formal* apaiser

propitiation [prəˌpɪʃɪˈeɪʃən] **N** *Formal* propitiation *f*

propitiatory [prəˈpɪʃɪətrɪ] **ADJ** *Formal* propitiatoire

propitious [prəˈpɪʃəs] **ADJ** *Formal* propice, favorable (**for** à); **it wasn't really a p. moment to ask for a rise** le moment était plutôt mal choisi pour demander une augmentation

propitiously [prəˈpɪʃəslɪ] **ADV** *Formal* d'une manière propice

propman ['prɒpmæn] (*pl* **propmen** [-mən]) **N** *Cin, Theat & TV* accessoiriste *mf*

proponent [prə'pəʊnənt] **N** avocat(e) *m,f*, partisan(e) *m,f*

proportion [prə'pɔːʃən] **N 1** *(gen) & Math (ratio)* proportion *f*, rapport *m*; **in the p. of 6 parts water to 1 part shampoo** dans la proportion de 6 mesures d'eau pour 1 mesure de shampooing; **the sentence is out of all p. to the crime** la peine est disproportionnée par rapport au *ou* est sans commune mesure avec le délit; **the p. of income to** *or* **over expenditure** le rapport entre les revenus et les dépenses

2 *(perspective)* proportion *f*; **to have a sense of p.** avoir le sens des proportions; **he has no sense of p.** il n'a pas le sens de la mesure; **you seem to have got** *or* **blown the problem out of (all) p.** vous semblez avoir exagéré *ou* grossi le problème; **you must try to see things in p.** vous devez essayer de ramener les choses à leur juste valeur; **the artist has got the tree out of p.** l'artiste n'a pas respecté les proportions de l'arbre

3 *(dimension)* proportion *f*, dimension *f*; **a ship of vast proportions** un navire de grande dimension; **the affair has assumed worrying proportions** l'affaire a pris des proportions alarmantes; **the disease has reached epidemic proportions** la maladie est devenue une véritable épidémie; **the problem has reached epidemic proportions** le problème s'est étendu tel une épidémie

4 *(part)* partie *f*; **a large p. of the staff/population** une grande partie du personnel/de la population; **she only got a small p. of the profits** elle n'a touché qu'une petite part *ou* partie des bénéfices; **what p. of your income do you spend on clothes?** quel pourcentage de vos revenus dépensez-vous en vêtements?

VT proportionner; **to p. one's expenditure to one's resources** proportionner ses dépenses à ses ressources, calculer ses dépenses en fonction de ses ressources

• **in proportion to, in proportion with PREP** par rapport à; **the office block is huge in p. to the houses around it** l'immeuble de bureaux est énorme par rapport aux maisons qui l'entourent; **the job is badly paid in p. to the effort required** cet emploi est mal payé vu le travail exigé; **his salary is in p. to his experience** son salaire correspond à son expérience; **the monthly payments are calculated in p. to your income** les mensualités sont calculées en fonction de *ou* sont proportionnelles à vos revenus; **inflation may increase in p. with wage rises** l'inflation risque d'augmenter proportionnellement aux augmentations de salaire

proportional [prə'pɔːʃənəl] **ADJ** proportionnel, en proportion; **p. to** proportionnel à

►► *Pol* ***proportional representation*** représentation *f* proportionnelle; *Typ* ***proportional spacing*** espacement *m* proportionnel; ***proportional tax*** impôt *m* proportionnel

proportionally [prə'pɔːʃənəlɪ] **ADV** proportionnellement; **they spend p. more of their budget on research than does Chemco** ils accordent à la recherche une proportion de leur budget supérieure à celle que dépense Chemco

proportionate [prə'pɔːʃənət] **ADJ** proportionné

proportionately [prə'pɔːʃənətlɪ] **ADV** proportionnellement, en proportion

proportioned [prə'pɔːʃənd] **ADJ well/badly p.** bien/mal proportionné

proposal [prə'pəʊzəl] **N 1** *(offer)* proposition *f*, offre *f*; **to make a p.** faire *ou* formuler une proposition

2 *(of marriage)* demande *f* en mariage; **she refused his p.** elle a rejeté sa demande en mariage, elle a refusé de l'épouser

3 *(suggestion)* proposition *f*, suggestion *f*; **he accepted her p. to go on holiday** il a accepté de partir en vacances, comme elle l'avait suggéré

4 *(plan, scheme)* proposition *f*, projet *m*, plan *m*; **the p. for a car park/to build a car park** le projet de parking/de construction d'un parking

propose [prə'pəʊz] **VT 1** *(suggest)* proposer, suggérer; **to p. sth to sb** proposer qch à qn; **to p. doing sth** proposer de faire qch; **it was proposed that we might like to stay a few days longer** on nous a proposé de rester quelques jours de plus; **I p. (that) we all go for a drink** je propose *ou* suggère que nous allions tous prendre un verre **2** *(present* ► *policy, resolution, scheme)* proposer, présenter, soumettre; **to p. sb's health, to p. a toast to sb** porter un toast à (la santé de) qn; **I p. Jones as** *or* **for treasurer** je propose Jones comme trésorier; **to p. marriage to sb** demander qn en mariage, faire une demande en mariage à qn **3** *(intend)* se proposer, avoir l'intention, compter; **I p. taking** *or* **to take a few days off work** je me propose de prendre quelques jours de congé; **they p. leaving early** ils ont l'intention de partir de bonne heure

VI 1 *(offer marriage)* faire une demande en mariage; **to p. to sb** demander qn en mariage **2** *(idiom)* **man proposes, God disposes** l'homme propose, Dieu dispose

proposed [prə'pəʊzd] **ADJ** projeté; **the p. visit** la visite prévue; **the building of the p. car park has been delayed** le projet de construction d'un parking a été suspendu

proposer [prə'pəʊzə(r)] **N 1** *(of motion)* auteur *m* (d'une proposition) **2** *(of candidate* ► *man)* parrain *m*; *(*► *woman)* marraine *f*

proposition [ˌprɒpə'zɪʃən] **N 1** *(proposal, statement)* proposition *f*

2 *(task)* affaire *f*; **that's quite a p.** c'est une tout autre affaire; **climbing that mountain will be no easy p.** ce ne sera pas une petite *ou* mince affaire que de gravir cette montagne; *Fig* **the boss is a tough p.** le patron n'est pas quelqu'un de commode *ou* facile, le patron est du genre coriace

3 *(available choice)* solution *f*; **solar power is not an economic p.** l'énergie solaire n'est pas une solution rentable; **the deal wasn't a paying p.** l'affaire n'était pas rentable

4 *(offer of sex)* proposition *f*; **to make sb a p.** faire des propositions (malhonnêtes) *ou* des avances à qn

5 *Math* proposition *f*

VT faire des propositions (malhonnêtes) *ou* des avances à

propound [prə'paʊnd] **VT** *Formal (argument, theory)* avancer, mettre en avant; *(opinion)* avancer, émettre; *(problem)* poser

proprietary [prə'praɪətərɪ] **ADJ 1** *Com* de marque déposée **2** *(attitude, behaviour, function)* de propriétaire; **his manner towards her was rather p.** il était plutôt possessif avec elle

►► *Com* ***proprietary article*** article *m* de marque (déposée); *Com* ***proprietary brand*** marque *f* déposée; *Am* ***proprietary hospital*** hôpital *m* privé, clinique *f* privée; ***proprietary information*** informations *fpl* confidentielles, informations *fpl* exclusives à la société; *Pharm* ***proprietary medicine*** spécialité *f* pharmaceutique; *Com* ***proprietary name*** marque *f* déposée

proprietor [prə'praɪətə(r)] **N** propriétaire *mf*

proprietorial [prəˌpraɪə'tɔːrɪəl] **ADJ** de propriétaire; **he's very p. about it** il est très possessif avec ça

proprietorship [prə'praɪətəʃɪp] **N** propriété *f*, possession *f*; *Law* (droit *m* de) propriété *f*; **under new p.** *(sign)* changement de propriétaire

proprietress [prə'praɪətrɪs] **N** propriétaire *f*

propriety [prə'praɪətɪ] (*pl* **proprieties**) **N** *Formal* **1** *(decorum)* bienséance *f*, convenance *f*; **his behaviour is lacking in p.** son comportement est tout à fait inconvenant *ou* déplacé; **to have a sense of p.** avoir le sens des convenances; **contrary to the proprieties** contraire aux bienséances *ou* convenances **2** *(suitability* ► *of action, measure)* opportunité *f*; *(*► *of word, remark)* justesse *f* **3** *(rectitude)* rectitude *f*; **to behave with p.** respecter les convenances

> Note that the French word **propriété** is a false friend and is never a translation for the English word **propriety**. It means **property**.
>
> Attention: ne pas confondre avec **property**, qui signifie **propriété**.

propshaft ['prɒpʃɑːft] **N** *Tech* arbre *m* de transmission

propulsion [prə'pʌlʃən] **N** propulsion *f*

propulsive [prə'pʌlsɪv] **ADJ** propulseur, propu sif

pro rata [-'rɑːtə] **ADJ** au prorata **ADV** au prorata

prorogation [ˌprəʊrə'geɪʃən] **N** prorogation *f*

prorogue [prə'rəʊg] **VT** proroger

prosaic [ˌprəʊ'zeɪɪk] **ADJ** prosaïque

prosaically [ˌprəʊ'zeɪkəlɪ] **ADV** prosaïquemen

proscenium [prə'siːnjəm] (*pl* **prosceniums** *c* **proscenia** [-njə]) **N** *Theat* avant-scène *f*; *Ant* proscenium *m*

►► *Theat* ***proscenium arch*** ≃ manteau *m* d'Arle quin

proscribe [prəʊ'skraɪb] **VT** proscrire

proscription [prəʊ'skrɪpʃən] **N** proscription *f*

prose [prəʊz] **N 1** *Literature* prose *f*; **to write in** écrire en prose, faire de la prose; **the writer's el gant/rhythmic p. style** la prose élégante/ryth mée de l'auteur **2** *Br Sch & Univ (translatio* thème *m*

►► ***prose poem*** poème *m* en prose

pro se [-seɪ] **N** *Am Law* = personne qui se repré sente elle-même

prosecute ['prɒsɪkjuːt] **VT 1** *Law* poursuivre (e justice), engager des poursuites contre; **to p. for sth** poursuivre qn (en justice) pour qch; **h was prosecuted for disturbing the peace** il a ét poursuivi pour tapage nocturne **2** *Formal (pu sue* ► *war, investigation)* poursuivre

VI *Law (lawyer* ► *in civil case)* représenter la pa tie civile; *(*► *in criminal case)* représenter le m nistère public *ou* le parquet; **to decide to** décider d'engager des poursuites judiciaires

prosecution [ˌprɒsɪ'kjuːʃən] **N 1** *Law (procee ings)* poursuites *fpl* (judiciaires); *(indictmen* accusation *f*; **to be liable to p.** s'exposer à de poursuites (judiciaires); **to bring a p. against s** poursuivre qn en justice, engager des poursu tes judiciaires contre qn; **this is her second** c'est la deuxième fois qu'elle est poursuivie *Law (lawyer* ► *in civil case)* avocat *m*/avoca *mpl* représentant les plaignants *ou* la parti plaignante; *(*► *in criminal case)* ministère *m* pu blic, accusation *f* **3** *Formal (pursuit)* poursuite **the p. of the war** la poursuite de la guerre; **in th p. of his duties** dans l'exercice *ou* l'accomplisse ment de ses fonctions

►► ***prosecution witness*** témoin *m* à charge

prosecutor ['prɒsɪkjuːtə(r)] **N** *Law* **1** *(perso bringing case)* plaignant(e) *m,f* **2** *(lawyer)* **(publi p.** procureur *m*

proselyte ['prɒsəlaɪt] **N** prosélyte *mf*

proselytism ['prɒsəlɪtɪzəm] **N** prosélytisme *m*

proselytize, -ise ['prɒsəlɪtaɪz] **VI** faire du prosé lytisme

VT faire un prosélyte de

proselytizing, -ising ['prɒsəlɪtaɪzɪŋ] **N** prosély tisme *m*

prosodic [prə'sɒdɪk] **ADJ** prosodique

prosody ['prɒsədɪ] **N** prosodie *f*

prospect N ['prɒspekt] **1** *(possibility)* chance perspective *f*; **what are his prospects of success** quelles chances a-t-il de réussir?; **there's little of their winning the match** ils ont peu de chance de remporter *ou* il y a peu d'espoir (pour) qu'il remportent le match; **we had given up all p. o hearing from you** nous avions renoncé à tout es poir d'avoir *ou* nous pensions ne jamais plus re cevoir de vos nouvelles

2 *(impending event, situation)* perspective *f*; **don't relish the p. of working for him** la perspec tive de travailler pour lui ne m'enchante guère **to have sth in p.** avoir qch en vue *ou* en perspec tive; **he has a bright future in p.** il a un bel aven en perspective *ou* devant lui; **what are th weather prospects for tomorrow?** quelles sor les prévisions météorologiques pour demain?

3 *(usu pl) (chance of success)* perspectives *f* d'avenir; **the prospects are not very good** les cho ses se présentent plutôt mal; **the prospect(s) fo the automobile industry** les perspectives d'aven de l'industrie automobile; **she's a woman wit good prospects** c'est une femme qui a de l'aven *ou* une femme d'avenir; **this company has goo prospects/no prospects** cette entreprise a un b avenir devant elle/n'a pas d'avenir; **a job with prospects** un poste qui offre des perspectives d'avenir; **it's a job without any prospects of promotion** c'est un poste qui n'offre aucune perspective d'avancement; **this job has good promotion prospects** ce poste offre de réelles possibilités d'avancement

4 *(person ▸ customer)* client(e) *m,f* potentiel (elle) *ou* éventuel(elle), prospect *m*; *(▸ candidate)* espoir *m*; *Old-fashioned (▸ marriage partner)* parti *m*; **he's a good p. for the manager's job** c'est un candidat potentiel au poste de directeur; **there are two young prospects in the team** l'équipe compte deux joueurs prometteurs *ou* qui ont un bel avenir devant eux

5 *(view)* perspective *f*, vue *f*

VI [prə'spekt] prospecter; **to p. for oil** chercher du pétrole; *Mktg* **to p. for new customers** prospecter la clientèle

VT [prə'spekt] *(area, land)* prospecter

▸▸ *Mktg* ***prospect pool*** groupe *m* de prospects

prospecting [prə'spektɪŋ] **N** prospection *f*; *Mining & Petr* **oil/gold p.** prospection *f* pétrolière/d'or

prospective [prə'spektɪv] **ADJ 1** *(future)* futur; **my p. mother-in-law** ma future belle-mère **2** *(possible ▸ customer)* potentiel, éventuel; *(▸ candidate)* éventuel; **he's a p. customer** c'est un client potentiel **3** *(intended, expected)* en perspective; **my p. trip to Ireland** le voyage que je projette de faire en Irlande

prospector [prə'spektə(r)] **N** prospecteur(trice) *m,f*, chercheur(euse) *m,f*; **gold prospectors** chercheurs *mpl* d'or

prospectus [prə'spektəs] **N** *Mktg (about company, product)* prospectus *m*; *(about university)* brochure *f* de présentation; *St Exch (about share issue)* appel *m* à la souscription publique

prosper ['prɒspə(r)] **VI** prospérer

prosperity [prɒ'sperətɪ] **N** prospérité *f*

prosperous ['prɒspərəs] **ADJ** *(business, area, family)* prospère; *(period)* prospère, de prospérité; *Literary* **p. winds** vents *mpl* favorables

prosperously ['prɒspərəslɪ] **ADV** de manière prospère; **they live p.** ils vivent dans la prospérité

prosperousness ['prɒspərəsnɪs] **N** prospérité *f*

prostaglandin [ˌprɒstə'glændɪn] **N** *Physiol* prostaglandine *f*

prostate ['prɒsteɪt] **N** *Anat (gland)* prostate *f*

▸▸ ***prostate cancer*** cancer *m* de la prostate; ***prostate gland*** prostate *f*

prosthesis [prɒs'θiːsɪs] *(pl* **prostheses** [-siːz]) **N 1** *Med* prothèse *f* **2** *Ling* prosthèse *f*

prosthetics [prɒs'θetɪks] **N** *(UNCOUNT) Med* prothétique *f*

prostitute ['prɒstɪtjuːt] **N** prostituée *f*; **male p.** prostitué *m*

VT *also Fig* prostituer; **to p. oneself** se prostituer

prostitution [ˌprɒstɪ'tjuːʃən] **N** prostitution *f*

prostrate ADJ ['prɒstreɪt] **1** *(lying flat)* (couché) à plat ventre; *(in submission)* prosterné; **to lie p. before sb** être prosterné devant qn **2** *(exhausted)* épuisé, abattu; *(overwhelmed)* prostré, accablé, atterré; **p. with grief** accablé de chagrin

VT [prɒ'streɪt] **1** *(in obedience, respect)* **to p. oneself before sb** se prosterner devant qn **2** *(overwhelm)* accabler, abattre; **to be prostrated by illness** être accablé *ou* abattu par la maladie; **to be prostrated with grief** être accablé de chagrin

prostration [prɒ'streɪʃən] **N 1** *(lying down)* prosternement *m*; *Rel* prostration *f* **2** *(exhaustion)* prostration *f*, épuisement *m*; **the country was in a state of economic p.** l'économie du pays était en ruine

prosy ['prəʊzɪ] *(compar* **prosier**, *superl* **prosiest)** **ADJ** *(dull)* ennuyeux, prosaïque; *(long-winded)* verbeux

protagonist [prə'tægənɪst] **N** protagoniste *mf*; *(of book, film)* personnage *m* principal

protean [prəʊ'tiːən] **ADJ** *Literary* changeant

protease ['prəʊtɪeɪz] **N** *Physiol* protéase *f*

▸▸ *Pharm* ***protease inhibitor*** antiprotéase *f*, inhibiteur *m* de protéase

protect [prə'tekt] **VT** protéger; **to p. sb/sth from** *or* **against sth** protéger qn/qch de *ou* contre qch; **she protected her eyes from the sun** elle se protégea les yeux du soleil; **to p. oneself from sth** se protéger de *ou* contre qch; **it is important to p. your civil rights** il est important de veiller à ce que vos droits civiques ne soient pas bafoués

protected [prə'tektɪd] **ADJ** protégé

▸▸ ***protected industries*** industries *fpl* protégées; ***protected species*** espèce *f* protégée

protection [prə'tekʃən] **N 1** *(safeguard)* protection *f*; **this drug offers p. against** *or* **from the virus** ce médicament vous protège *ou* vous immunise contre le virus; **cyclists often wear face masks for p. against car fumes** les cyclistes portent souvent des masques pour se protéger des gaz d'échappement des voitures; **to be under sb's p.** être sous la protection de qn; **she travelled under police p.** elle a voyagé sous la protection de la police; **environmental p.** protection *f* de l'environnement; **society for the p. of birds** société *f* protectrice des oiseaux

2 *(insurance)* protection *f*; **p. against fire and theft** protection *f* contre l'incendie et le vol

3 *(run by gangsters)* argent *m* versé aux racketteurs; **all the shopkeepers have to pay p. (money)** tous les commerçants sont rackettés

4 *(contraception)* protection *f*; **did you use any p.?** tu as pris tes précautions?

▸▸ ***protection factor*** *(of suntan lotion)* indice *m* de protection; ***protection money*** argent *m* versé aux racketteurs; ***protection racket*** racket *m*; **to run a p. racket** être à la tête d'un racket

protectionism [prə'tekʃənɪzəm] **N** *Econ* protectionnisme *m*

protectionist [prə'tekʃənɪst] *Econ* **ADJ** protectionniste

N protectionniste *mf*

protective [prə'tektɪv] **ADJ 1** *(person)* protecteur; *(behaviour, attitude)* protecteur, de protection; **to be p. towards sb** avoir une attitude protectrice envers qn; **she's too p. towards her children** elle a trop tendance à couver ses enfants; **to be p. of one's interests** sauvegarder ses intérêts **2** *(material, clothes)* de protection; *(cover)* protecteur, de protection **3** *Econ (duty, measure)* protecteur

▸▸ *Aut* ***protective cage*** cage *f* de sécurité; *Zool* ***protective coloration*** homochromie *f*; *Law* ***protective custody*** détention *f* dans l'intérêt de la personne

protectively [prə'tektɪvlɪ] **ADV** *(behave, act)* de façon protectrice; **he put an arm p. around her shoulder** il entoura son épaule d'un bras protecteur

protector [prə'tektə(r)] **N 1** *(person)* protecteur(trice) *m,f* **2** *(on machine)* dispositif *m* de protection, protecteur *m*

protectorate [prə'tektərət] **N** protectorat *m*

> **THE PROTECTORATE**
>
> Il s'agit de la période allant de 1653 à 1658, succédant à la guerre civile, pendant laquelle Oliver Cromwell, se proclamant "Lord Protector", exerça son autorité sur l'Angleterre. En dépit de l'existence du Parlement, le gouvernement de Cromwell était quasiment dictatorial et s'appuyait avant tout sur l'armée. Le Protectorat, qui vit l'essor du puritanisme dans la société anglaise, prit fin en 1659 lorsqu'un nouveau Parlement rétablit la monarchie.

protectress [prə'tektrɪs] **N** protectrice *f*

protégé, protégée ['prɒteʒeɪ] **N** protégé(e) *m,f*

protein ['prəʊtiːn] **N** protéine *f*

▸▸ ***protein deficiency*** carence *f* en protéines

proteinaceous [ˌprəʊtiː'neɪʃəs] **ADJ** *Med* protéique

protest N ['prəʊtest] **1** *(gen)* protestation *f*; **to make a p. against** *or* **about sth** élever une protestation contre qch, protester contre qch; **to register** *or* **to lodge a p. with sb** protester auprès de qn; **in p. against** *or* **at sth** en signe de protestation contre qch; **they did it without the slightest p.** ils l'ont fait sans élever la moindre protestation *ou* sans protester le moins du monde; **to stage a p.** *(complaint)* organiser une protestation; *(demonstration)* organiser une manifestation; **she resigned in p. (at this decision)** elle a démissionné en signe de protestation (contre cette décision); **to do sth under p.** faire qch en protestant **2** *Com & Law* protêt *m*

COMP ['prəʊtest] *(letter, meeting)* de protestation

VT [prə'test] **1** *(innocence, love etc)* protester de; **"no one told me," she protested** "personne ne me l'a dit", protesta-t-elle; **she protested that it was unfair** elle déclara que ce n'était pas juste **2** *Am (measures, law etc)* protester contre

VI [prə'test] protester; **to p. at** *or* **against/about sth** protester contre qch; **I must p. in the strongest terms at** *or* **about...** je m'élève avec la dernière énergie *ou* énergiquement contre...; **really, I p., that's too much!** non, vraiment, je proteste, c'est trop!

▸▸ ***protest demonstration*** manifestation *f*; ***protest march*** manifestation *f*; ***protest marcher*** manifestant(e) *m,f*; ***protest movement*** mouvement *m* de contestation *ou* de protestation; ***protest rally*** mouvement *m* de protestation; ***protest singer*** chanteur(euse) *m,f* engagé(e); ***protest song*** chanson *f* engagée; ***protest vote*** vote *m* de protestation

Protestant ['prɒtɪstənt] **ADJ** protestant

N Protestant(e) *m,f*

▸▸ ***the Protestant Church*** l'Église *f* protestante; ***the Protestant (work) ethic*** l'éthique *f* protestante (du travail)

Protestantism ['prɒtɪstənˌtɪzəm] **N** protestantisme *m*

protestation [ˌprɒte'steɪʃən] **N** protestation *f*; **in spite of his protestations of innocence** en dépit de ses protestations d'innocence

protester [prə'testə(r)] **N** *(demonstrator)* manifestant(e) *m,f*; *(complainer)* protestataire *mf*; **anti-nuclear/peace p.** manifestant(e) *m,f* contre le nucléaire/pour la paix

prothorax [ˌprəʊ'θɔːræks] **N** *Entom* prothorax *m*

protocol ['prəʊtəkɒl] **N** *(gen) & Comput* protocole *m*

proton ['prəʊtɒn] **N** *Phys* proton *m*

▸▸ ***proton microscope*** microscope *m* protonique; ***proton number*** numéro *m* atomique

protoplasm ['prəʊtəʊplæzəm] **N** *Biol* protoplasme *m*, protoplasma *m*

prototype ['prəʊtətaɪp] **N** prototype *m*

protozoan [ˌprəʊtə'zəʊən] *(pl* **protozoans** *or* **protozoa** [-'zəʊə]) **N** *Zool* protozoaire *m*

protract [prə'trækt] **VT** *(prolong)* prolonger, faire durer

protracted [prə'træktɪd] **ADJ** *(stay)* prolongé; *(argument, negotiations)* qui dure, (très) long (longue); *(illness)* long (longue); **a p. death** une longue agonie

protraction [prə'trækʃən] **N 1** *(of trial etc)* prolongation *f*; *(of procedure etc)* longueur *f* **2** *Anat (of muscle)* protraction *f*

protractor [prə'træktə(r)] **N 1** *Geom* rapporteur *m* **2** *Anat (muscle)* (muscle *m*) protracteur *m*

▸▸ *Anat* ***protractor muscle*** (muscle *m*) protracteur *m*

protrude [prə'truːd] **VI** *(rock, ledge)* faire saillie, dépasser; *(eyes, chin)* saillir; *(teeth)* avancer; **the promontory protrudes into the sea** le promontoire s'avance dans la mer; **his belly protruded over his trousers** son ventre débordait de son pantalon; **his feet protruded from under the bedclothes** ses pieds dépassaient de sous les couvertures

VT avancer, pousser en avant

protruding [prə'truːdɪŋ] **ADJ** *(ledge)* en saillie; *(chin, ribs)* saillant; *(eyes)* globuleux; *(teeth)* proéminent, protubérant; *(belly)* protubérant; **the p. end of the nail** le bout du clou qui dépasse

protrusion [prə'truːʒən] **N** *(ledge)* saillie *f*; *(bump)* bosse *f*, protrusion *f*

protuberance [prə'tjuːbərəns] **N** *Formal* protubérance *f*

protuberant [prə'tjuːbərənt] **ADJ** *Formal* protubérant

proud [praʊd] **ADJ 1** *(pleased)* fier; **to be p. of sb/sth** être fier de qn/qch; **to be p. of oneself** être fier de soi; *Ironic* I hope you're p. of yourself! tu peux être fier de toi!; he was p. to have won *or* of having won il était fier d'avoir gagné; I'm p. (that) you didn't give up je suis fier que tu n'aies pas abandonné; it's nothing to be p. of! il n'y a vraiment pas de quoi être fier!; she was too p. to accept elle était trop fière pour accepter; I'll do anything, I'm not p. je ferai n'importe quoi, je ne suis pas fier; they are now the p. parents of a daughter ils sont désormais les heureux parents d'une petite fille; we are p. to present this concert nous sommes heureux de vous présenter ce concert; it was a p. moment for me pour moi, ce fut un moment de grande fierté; it was her proudest possession c'était son bien le plus précieux

2 *(arrogant)* fier, orgueilleux; he's a p. man c'est un orgueilleux; as p. as a peacock fier comme un coq *ou* comme Artaban

3 *Literary (stately ▸ tree, mountain)* majestueux, altier; *(▸ bearing, stallion, eagle)* fier, majestueux

4 *Br (protruding)* qui dépasse; it's a few millimetres p. ça dépasse de quelques millimètres; to stand p. faire saillie

ADV *Fam* to do sb p. *(entertain lavishly)* recevoir qn comme un roi/une reine□; *(honour)* faire honneur à qn□; the caterers did us p. les traiteurs nous ont fait un festin de rois□; to do oneself p. se dépasser□

▸▸ *Med* **proud flesh** bourgeon *m* conjonctif *ou* charnu

proudly ['praudlı] ADV 1 *(with pride)* fièrement, avec fierté; we p. present… nous avons le plaisir de vous présenter… 2 *(arrogantly)* orgueilleusement 3 *(majestically)* majestueusement

prove [pru:v] *(Br pt & pp* proved, *Am pt* proved, *pp* proved *or* proven ['pru:vən]) VT 1 *(verify, show)* prouver; *(by demonstration, argument)* démontrer; *(one's identity)* justifier de; the facts p. her (to be) guilty les faits prouvent qu'elle est coupable; the autopsy proved that it was suicide l'autopsie prouva que c'était un suicide; the accused is innocent until proved *or* proven guilty l'accusé est innocent jusqu'à preuve du contraire *ou* tant que sa culpabilité n'est pas prouvée; to p. sb right/wrong donner raison/tort à qn; they can't p. anything against us ils n'ont aucune preuve contre nous; to do sth to p. a point faire qch pour prouver qu'on a raison; I think I've proved my point je crois avoir apporté la preuve de ce que j'avançais; it remains to be proved whether the decision was correct rien ne prouve que cette décision était la bonne; she quickly proved herself indispensable elle s'est vite montrée indispensable; he has already proved his loyalty il a déjà prouvé sa fidélité, sa fidélité n'est plus à prouver

2 *(proposition, theorem ▸ in maths, logic)* démontrer

3 *(put to the test)* mettre à l'épreuve; the method has not yet been proved la méthode n'a pas encore fait ses preuves; to p. oneself faire ses preuves

4 *Law (will)* homologuer

VI 1 *(turn out)* s'avérer, se révéler; your suspicions proved (to be) well-founded vos soupçons se sont avérés fondés; the arrangement proved (to be) unworkable cet arrangement s'est révélé impraticable; he may p. (to be) of help to you il pourrait bien vous être utile; it has proved impossible to find him il a été impossible de le retrouver; if that proves to be the case s'il s'avère que tel est le cas 2 *Culin (dough)* lever

proven ['pru:vən] *pp of* prove

ADJ 1 ['pru:vən] *(tested)* éprouvé; a woman of p. courage une femme qui a fait preuve de courage; a candidate with p. experience un candidat qui a déjà fait ses preuves; a p. method une méthode qui a fait ses preuves 2 ['prəuvən] *Scot Law* a verdict of not p. ≃ un non-lieu

provenance ['prɒvənəns] N provenance *f*

Provençal [ˌprɒvɒn'sɑ:l] N 1 *(person)* Provençal(e) *m,f* 2 *Ling* provençal *m*

ADJ provençal

provender ['prɒvındə(r)] N 1 *(fodder)* fourrage *m*, provende *f* 2 *(food)* nourriture *f*

proverb ['prɒvɜ:b] N proverbe *m*

• **Proverbs** N *Bible* (the Book of) Proverbs le Livre des Proverbes

proverbial [prə'vɜ:bjəl] ADJ proverbial, légendaire

N *Fam Euph* we're really up the p. now! on est vraiment dans le pétrin maintenant!

proverbially [prə'vɜ:bjəlı] ADV proverbialement

provide [prə'vaıd] VT 1 *(supply)* fournir; to p. sth for sb, to p. sb with sth fournir qch à qn; who provided them with that information? qui leur a fourni *ou* transmis ces renseignements?; to p. jobs fournir des emplois; this factory will p. 500 new jobs cette usine créera 500 emplois; they p. a car for her use ils mettent une voiture à sa disposition; the plane is provided with eight emergency exits l'avion dispose de huit sorties de secours; write the answers in the spaces provided écrivez les réponses dans les blancs prévus à cet effet

2 *(offer)* offrir; a small summerhouse provides some privacy un petit pavillon dans le jardin offre une certaine intimité; I want to p. my children with a good education je veux pouvoir offrir *ou* donner une bonne éducation à mes enfants; the book provides a good introduction to maths ce livre est une bonne introduction aux maths; milk provides a good source of protein le lait constitue un bon apport en protéines

3 *(stipulate ▸ of contract, law)* stipuler; the rules p. that… le règlement stipule que…

VI to p. against sth se prémunir contre qch; the Lord will p. Dieu y pourvoira

▸ **provide for** VT INSEP 1 *(support)* to p. for sb pourvoir *ou* subvenir aux besoins de qn; I have a family to p. for j'ai une famille à nourrir; an insurance policy that will p. for your children's future une assurance qui subviendra aux besoins de vos enfants; his widow was left well provided for sa veuve était à l'abri du besoin

2 *(prepare)* to p. for sth se préparer à qch; they hadn't provided for the drop in demand la baisse de la demande les a pris au dépourvu; expenses provided for in the budget dépenses *fpl* prévues au budget; we try to p. for all eventualities nous nous efforçons de parer à toute éventualité

3 *(contract, law)* to p. for sth stipuler *ou* prévoir qch; the bill provides for subsidies to be reduced le projet de loi prévoit une baisse des subventions

provided [prə'vaıdıd] CONJ p. (that) pourvu que + *subjunctive*, à condition que + *subjunctive*; I'll wait for you p. (that) it doesn't take too long je t'attendrai à condition que ce ne soit pas trop long; you can leave early p. (that) you finish your work vous pouvez partir plus tôt à condition d'avoir fini votre travail

providence ['prɒvıdəns] N 1 *(fate)* la providence 2 *Old-fashioned (foresight)* prévoyance *f*; *(thrift)* économie *f*

• **Providence** N *(fate)* la Providence; P. smiled on us la Providence nous a souri

provident ['prɒvıdənt] ADJ *(foresighted)* prévoyant; *(thrifty)* économe

▸▸ *Br* **provident club** = système d'achat à tempérament proposé par certains grands magasins; *Fin* **provident fund** caisse *f* de prévoyance; *Br* **provident society** société *f* de prévoyance

providential [ˌprɒvı'denʃəl] ADJ providentiel

providentially [ˌprɒvı'denʃəlı] ADV providentiellement

providently ['prɒvıdəntlı] ADV avec prévoyance, prudemment

provider [prə'vaıdə(r)] N 1 *(person)* pourvoyeur (euse) *m,f*, *Com* fournisseur(euse) *m,f*; she's the family's sole p. elle subvient seule aux besoins de la famille 2 *Comput* fournisseur *m* d'accès à l'Internet

providing [prə'vaıdıŋ] = provided

province ['prɒvıns] N 1 *(region, district)* province *f*; the P. of Ontario/Ulster la province d'Ontario/d'Ulster 2 *(field, sphere ▸ of activity)* domaine *m*; *(▸ of responsability)* compétence *f*; politics was once the sole p. of men autrefois, la politique était un domaine exclusivement masculin; staff supervision is not within my p. la gestion du personnel n'est pas de mon ressort 3 *Rel* province *f* ecclésiastique

• **provinces** NPL *Br (not the metropolis)* the provinces la province; in the provinces en province

provincial [prə'vınʃəl] ADJ provincial

N 1 *(from provinces)* provincial(e) *m,f* 2 *Rel* provincial *m*

provincialism [prə'vınʃəlızəm] N provincialisme *m*

proving ['pru:vıŋ] N *(of truth of something)* preuve *f*, démonstration *f*; *(of fact)* constatation *f*; *Law (of a will)* homologation *f*; the p. of a theory/a hypothesis la démonstration d'une théorie/d'une hypothèse

▸▸ **proving ground** terrain *m* d'essai

provirus ['prəuvaırəs] N *Biol* provirus *m*

provision [prə'vıʒən] VT approvisionner, ravitailler

N 1 *(act of supplying)* approvisionnement *m*, fourniture *f*, ravitaillement *m*; p. of supplies in wartime is a major problem le ravitaillement en temps de guerre pose de graves problèmes; one of their functions is the p. of meals for the homeless un de leurs rôles est de distribuer des repas aux sans-abri; the p. of new jobs la création d'emplois

2 *(stock, supply)* provision *f*, réserve *f*; to lay in provisions for the winter faire des provisions pour l'hiver; the US sent medical provisions les États-Unis envoyèrent des stocks de médicaments; I have a week's p. of firewood left il me reste du bois *ou* assez de bois pour une semaine

3 *(arrangement)* disposition *f*; they are making provisions for a crisis ils prennent des dispositions en vue d'une crise; no p. had been made for the influx of refugees aucune disposition n'avait été prise pour faire face à l'afflux de réfugiés; social service p. has been cut again les services sociaux ont à nouveau connu des compressions budgétaires; to make provisions for one's family pourvoir aux besoins de sa famille; you should think about making provisions for the future vous devriez penser à assurer votre avenir

4 *Fin (allowance)* provision *f*; to make p. for sth prévoir qch

5 *(condition, clause)* disposition *f*, clause *f*; under the provisions of the UN charter/his will selon les dispositions de la charte de l'ONU/de son testament; *Law* notwithstanding any p. to the contrary nonobstant toute clause contraire

• **provisions** NPL *(food)* vivres *mpl*, provisions *fpl*

▸▸ *Acct* **provision for bad debts** provision *f* pour créances douteuses; *Acct* **provision for depreciation** provision *f* pour dépréciation *ou* amortissement; *Acct* **provision for liabilities** provision *f* pour sommes exigibles

provisional [prə'vıʒənəl] ADJ provisoire

• **Provisional** *Pol* N membre *m* de l'IRA provisoire

ADJ provisoire

▸▸ *Fin* **provisional budget** budget *m* prévisionnel; *Br* **provisional (driving) licence** permis *m* de conduire provisoire *(autorisation que l'on doit obtenir avant de prendre des leçons)*; *Pol* **provisional government** gouvernement *m* provisoire; *Pol* **the Provisional IRA** l'IRA *f* provisoire *(branche de l'IRA favorable à la lutte armée)*

provisionally [prə'vıʒənəlı] ADV provisoirement

proviso [prə'vaızəu] *(pl* provisos *or* provisoes) N stipulation *f*, condition *f*; with the p. that the goods be delivered à la condition expresse *ou* sous réserve que les marchandises soient livrées; they accept, with one p. ils acceptent, à une condition

provisory [prə'vaızərı] ADJ 1 *(conditional)* conditionnel 2 *(provisional)* provisoire

Provo ['prəuvəu] *(pl* Provos) N *Fam* = membre de l'IRA provisoire, la branche de l'IRA favorable à la lutte armée

provocation [ˌprɒvə'keıʃən] N provocation *f*; he loses his temper at *or* given the slightest p. il se met en colère à la moindre provocation; the crime was committed under p. ce crime a été commis en réponse à une provocation

provocative [prə'vɒkətıv] ADJ 1 *(challenging)* provocateur, provocant; his early films were very p. ses premiers films étaient très provocants; she doesn't really think that, she was just being p.

elle ne le pense pas vraiment, c'est simplement de la provocation **2** *(sexually ▸ behaviour, dress, person)* provocant; *(▸ smile, look)* aguichant **3** *(obscene)* **a p. gesture** un geste obscène

provocatively [prəˈvɒkətɪvlɪ] ADV *(write, dress)* d'une manière provocante; *(say)* sur un ton provocateur *ou* provocant

provoke [prəˈvəʊk] VT **1** *(goad)* provoquer; *(infuriate)* enrager; *(vex)* exaspérer; **to p. sb into doing sth** pousser qn à faire qch; **they'll shoot if in any way provoked** ils tireront à la moindre provocation; **I was provoked** on m'a provoqué; **the dog is dangerous when provoked** le chien devient méchant si on le provoque *ou* l'excite **2** *(cause ▸ accident, quarrel, anger)* provoquer; **to p. a reaction** provoquer une réaction; **the revelations provoked a public outcry** les révélations ont soulevé un tollé général

provoking [prəˈvəʊkɪŋ] ADJ *(situation)* contrariant; *(person, behaviour)* exaspérant

provost N **1** [ˈprɒvəst] *Univ Br* ≃ recteur *m*; *Am* ≃ doyen *m*
2 [ˈprɒvəst] *Rel* doyen *m*
3 [ˈprɒvəst] *Scot* maire *m*
4 [prəˈvəʊ] *Mil* ≃ gendarme *m*
5 [ˈprɒvəst] *Hist* prévôt *m*
▸▸ *Mil* ***provost court*** tribunal *m* prévôtal; *Am Mil* ***provost guard*** ≃ prévôté *f*; *Mil* ***provost marshal*** prévôt *m*

prow [praʊ] N *Naut* proue *f*

prowess [ˈpraʊɪs] N *(UNCOUNT)* **1** *(skill)* (grande) habileté *f*; **p. in negotiating** habileté *f ou* savoir-faire *m inv* en matière de négociations; **he showed great p. on the sports field** il s'est révélé d'une adresse remarquable sur le terrain de sport; **sexual p.** prouesses *fpl* sexuelles **2** *Literary (bravery)* vaillance *f*

prowl [praʊl] VI rôder
VT *(street, jungle)* rôder dans; **cats prowled the rooftops** des chats rôdaient sur les toits
N **to be on the p.** rôder; **to be on the p. for sth** être en quête *ou* à la recherche de qch; *also Fig* **to go on the p.** partir en chasse
▸▸ *Am* ***prowl car*** voiture *f* de police en patrouille

prowler [ˈpraʊlə(r)] N rôdeur(euse) *m,f*

prox *Old-fashioned (written abbr* **proximo***)* du mois prochain

proximity [prɒkˈsɪmətɪ] N proximité *f*; **its p. to London** sa situation à proximité de Londres; **in p. to, in the p. of** à proximité de; **in close p. to** juste à proximité *ou* tout près de
▸▸ *Mil* ***proximity fuse*** fusée *f* à influence, fusée *f* de proximité; *Pol* ***proximity talks*** négociations *fpl* rapprochées

proximo [ˈprɒksɪməʊ] ADV *Old-fashioned Admin* du mois prochain; **the 4th p.** le 4 du mois prochain

proxy [ˈprɒksɪ] *(pl* **proxies***)* N *(person)* mandataire *mf*, fondé(e) *m,f* de pouvoir; *(authorization)* procuration *f*, mandat *m*; *Comput* mandataire *m*; **to vote by p.** voter par procuration
▸▸ ***proxy bomb*** = bombe amenée sur les lieux par une personne agissant sous la contrainte; *Comput* ***proxy server*** serveur *m* proxy, serveur *m* mandataire *ou* de procuration; ***proxy vote*** vote *m* par procuration

Prozac® [ˈprəʊzæk] N *Pharm* Prozac® *m*

PRP [ˌpiːɑːˈpiː] N *(abbr* **performance-related pay***)* salaire *m* au mérite

prude [pruːd] N prude *mf*, bégueule *mf*; **don't be such a p.!** ne sois pas si prude *ou* bégueule!

prudence [ˈpruːdəns] N prudence *f*, circonspection *f*

prudent [ˈpruːdənt] ADJ prudent, circonspect

prudential [pruːˈdenʃəl] ADJ
▸▸ *Am* ***prudential committee*** *(of municipality, company)* = comité de surveillance

prudently [ˈpruːdəntlɪ] ADV prudemment

prudery [ˈpruːdərɪ] N pruderie *f*, pudibonderie *f*

prudish [ˈpruːdɪʃ] ADJ prude, pudibond

prudishness [ˈpruːdɪʃnɪs] N pruderie *f*, pudibonderie *f*

prune [pruːn] N **1** *(fruit)* pruneau *m*; **stewed prunes** pruneaux *mpl* cuits; *Fam Fig* **to look like an old p.** être ridé comme une vieille pomme **2** *Br Fam (fool)* patate *f*, ballot *m*
VT **1** *(hedge, tree)* tailler; *(branch)* élaguer **2** *Fig (text, budget, staff)* élaguer, faire des coupes sombres dans; **to p. (back** *or* **down) expenditure** réduire les dépenses

> Note that the French word **prune** is a false friend and is never a translation for the English word **prune**. It means **plum**.

pruning [ˈpruːnɪŋ] N *(of hedge, tree)* taille *f*; *(of branches)* élagage *m*; *Fig (of text, budget, staff)* élagage *m*; **there will have to be some p. in this department** il va falloir faire du nettoyage dans ce service
▸▸ ***pruning hook*** ébranchoir *m*; ***pruning knife*** serpette *f*

prurience [ˈprʊərɪəns] N lubricité *f*, lascivité *f*

prurient [ˈprʊərɪənt] ADJ lubrique, lascif

Prussia [ˈprʌʃə] N Prusse *f*

Prussian [ˈprʌʃən] N Prussien(enne) *m,f*
ADJ prussien
▸▸ ***Prussian blue*** bleu *m* de Prusse

prussic acid [ˈprʌsɪk-] N acide *m* prussique

pry[1] [praɪ] *(pt & pp* **pried***)* VI fouiller, fureter; **I didn't mean to p.** je ne voulais pas être indiscret; **I told him not to p. into my affairs** je lui ai dit de ne pas venir mettre le nez dans mes affaires; **he doesn't like people prying into his past** il n'aime pas qu'on aille fouiller dans son passé

pry[2] *Am* = **prise**

prying [ˈpraɪɪŋ] ADJ indiscret(ète); **away from p. eyes** à l'abri des regards indiscrets

PS [ˌpiːˈes] N *(abbr* **postscript***)* PS *m*

psalm [sɑːm] N psaume *m*; **(the Book of) Psalms** (le Livre des) Psaumes

psalmist [ˈsɑːmɪst] N psalmiste *m*

psalmody [ˈsælmədɪ] *(pl* **psalmodies***)* N psalmodie *f*

psalter [ˈsɔːltə(r)] N psautier *m*

PSB [ˌpiːesˈbiː] N *Rad & TV (abbr* **public-service broadcasting***)* émissions *fpl* de service public

PSBR [ˌpiːesˌbiːˈɑː(r)] N *Br Econ (abbr* **public sector borrowing requirement***)* = besoins d'emprunt du secteur public non couverts par les rentrées fiscales

psephological [ˌsefəˈlɒdʒɪkəl] ADJ = relatif à l'étude statistique et sociologique des élections

psephologist [seˈfɒlədʒɪst] N spécialiste *mf* des élections

psephology [seˈfɒlədʒɪ] N = étude statistique et sociologique des élections

pseud [sjuːd] N *Fam* poseur(euse)□ *m,f*, prétentieux(euse)□ *m,f*

pseudo [ˈsjuːdəʊ] ADJ *Fam (kindness, interest)* prétendu; *(person)* faux (fausse)

pseudonym [ˈsjuːdənɪm] N pseudonyme *m*; **to write under a p.** écrire sous un pseudonyme *ou* sous un nom d'emprunt

pseudonymous [sjuːˈdɒnɪməs] ADJ *(writer)* qui écrit sous un pseudonyme; *(column, article)* écrit sous un pseudonyme

pseudy [ˈsjuːdɪ] ADJ *Fam Pej* prétentieux□

pshaw [(p)ʃɔː] EXCLAM *Old-fashioned* peuh!

PSHE [ˌpiːesˌeɪtʃˈiː] N *Br (abbr* **personal, social and health education***)* éducation *f* civique et sexuelle

psi [ˌpiːesˈaɪ] N *Phys (abbr* **pounds per square inch***)* = livres au pouce carré (mesure de pression)

psittacosis [ˌsɪtəˈkəʊsɪs] N *(UNCOUNT)* psittacose *f*

psoriasis [sɒˈraɪəsɪs] N *(UNCOUNT)* psoriasis *m*

psst [pst] EXCLAM *(to attract attention)* psitt!, pst!; *(to warn)* chut!

PST [ˌpiːesˈtiː] N *Am (abbr* **Pacific Standard Time***)* heure *f* du Pacifique

PSV [ˌpiːesˈviː] N *Br Formerly (abbr* **public service vehicle***)* véhicule *m* de transport en commun

▸ **psych out** VT SEP *Fam* **1** *(sense ▸ someone's motives)* deviner□; *(▸ situation)* comprendre□, piger **2** *(intimidate)* **he soon psyched out his opponent and the game was his** très vite il a décontenancé son adversaire et il a gagné□

▸ **psych up** VT SEP *Fam (motivate)* **to p. oneself up for sth/to do sth** se préparer psychologiquement à qch/à faire qch□; **he had to p. himself up to tell her** il a dû prendre son courage à deux mains pour arriver à le lui dire□; **she psyched herself up before the race** elle s'est concentrée avant la course□

psyche[1] [ˈsaɪkɪ] N *Psy (mind)* psyché *f*, psychisme *m*

psyche[2] [saɪk] = **psych**

psychedelic [ˌsaɪkəˈdelɪk] ADJ psychédélique

psychiatric [ˌsaɪkɪˈætrɪk] ADJ psychiatrique; **he needs p. help** il devrait consulter un psychiatre
▸▸ ***psychiatric nurse*** infirmier(ère) *m,f* psychiatrique; ***psychiatric patient*** patient(e) *m,f* en psychiatrie; *Br* ***psychiatric social worker*** assistant(e) *m,f* social(e) en psychiatrie

psychiatrist [saɪˈkaɪətrɪst] N psychiatre *mf*

psychiatry [saɪˈkaɪətrɪ] N psychiatrie *f*

psychic [ˈsaɪkɪk] ADJ **1** *(supernatural)* parapsychique; **to be p., to have p. powers** avoir le don de double vue *ou* un sixième sens; *Hum* **I'm not p.!** je ne suis pas devin! **2** *(mental)* psychique
N médium *m*

psychical [ˈsaɪkɪkəl] = **psychic** ADJ

psycho [ˈsaɪkəʊ] *(pl* **psychos***)* *Fam* N psychopathe□ *mf*, cinglé(e) *m,f*
ADJ psychopathe□

psychoanalyse, *Am* **psychoanalyze** [ˌsaɪkəʊˈænəlaɪz] VT psychanalyser

psychoanalysis [ˌsaɪkəʊəˈnæləsɪs] N psychanalyse *f*; **to undergo p.** suivre une psychanalyse, se faire psychanalyser; **he spent five years in p.** il a été en psychanalyse pendant cinq ans

psychoanalyst [ˌsaɪkəʊˈænəlɪst] N psychanalyste *mf*

psychoanalytic [ˈsaɪkəʊˌænəˈlɪtɪk], **psychoanalytical** [ˈsaɪkəʊˌænəˈlɪtɪkəl] ADJ psychanalytique

psychoanalyze *Am* = **psychoanalyse**

psychobabble [ˈsaɪkəʊˌbæbəl] N *Fam Pej* jargon *m* des psychologues□

psychodrama [ˈsaɪkəʊˌdrɑːmə] N psychodrame *m*

psychographic [ˌsaɪkəʊˈɡræfɪk] N psychographique

psychographics [ˌsaɪkəʊˈɡræfɪks] N *(UNCOUNT)* psychographie *f*

psychological [ˌsaɪkəʊˈlɒdʒɪkəl] ADJ psychologique
▸▸ ***psychological block*** blocage *m* psychologique; **I have a p. block about driving** je fais un blocage quand il s'agit de conduire; ***the psychological moment*** le bon moment, le moment favorable *ou* psychologique; *Mktg* ***psychological price*** prix *m* psychologique *ou* d'acceptabilité; ***psychological profile*** profil *m* psychologique; ***psychological warfare*** guerre *f* psychologique

psychologically [ˌsaɪkəʊˈlɒdʒɪkəlɪ] ADV psychologiquement; **inflation has fallen below the p. important 5 percent level** l'inflation est passée sous le seuil psychologique de 5 pour cent

psychologist [saɪˈkɒlədʒɪst] N psychologue *mf*

psychology [saɪˈkɒlədʒɪ] N psychologie *f*; **it would be good/bad p. to tell them** ce serait faire preuve de psychologie/d'un manque de psychologie que de le leur dire

psychometric [ˌsaɪkəʊˈmetrɪk] ADJ psychométrique
▸▸ ***psychometric test*** test *m* psychométrique

psychomotor [ˌsaɪkəʊˈməʊtə(r)] ADJ psychomoteur

psychoneurosis [ˌsaɪkəʊnjʊəˈrəʊsɪs] *(pl* **psychoneuroses** [-siːz]*)* N psychonévrose *f*

psychopath [ˈsaɪkəʊpæθ] N psychopathe *mf*

psychopathic [ˌsaɪkəʊˈpæθɪk] ADJ *(person)* psychopathe; *(disorder, personality)* psychopathique

psychopathology [ˌsaɪkəʊpəˈθɒlədʒɪ] N psychopathologie *f*

psychophysiology [ˌsaɪkəʊfɪsɪˈɒlədʒɪ] N psychophysiologie *f*

psychosis [saɪˈkəʊsɪs] (*pl* **psychoses** [-siːz]) N psychose *f*

psychosomatic [ˌsaɪkəʊsəˈmætɪk] ADJ psychosomatique

psychotherapist [ˌsaɪkəʊˈθerəpɪst] N psychothérapeute *mf*

psychotherapy [ˌsaɪkəʊˈθerəpɪ] N psychothérapie *f*

psychotic [saˈkɒtɪk] ADJ psychotique
N psychotique *mf*

psychotropic [ˌsaɪkəʊˈtrɒpɪk] ADJ psychotrope

PT [ˌpiːˈtiː] N **1** (*abbr* **physical training**) EPS *f* **2** *Am* (*abbr* **physical therapy**) kinésithérapie *f*
▸▸ ***PT instructor*** professeur *mf* d'éducation physique

PTA [ˌpiːtiːˈeɪ] N *Sch* (*abbr* **parent-teacher association**) = association de parents d'élèves et de professeurs

ptarmigan [ˈtɑːmɪgən] (*pl* **inv** *or* **ptarmigans**) N *Orn* lagopède *m* des Alpes, ptarmigan *m*, perdrix *f* des neiges

Pte. *Br Mil* (*written abbr* **private**) soldat *m* de deuxième classe

pterodactyl [ˌterəˈdæktɪl] N ptérodactyle *m*

PTO[1] [ˌpiːtiːˈəʊ] N *Am Sch* (*abbr* **parent-teacher organization**) = association de parents d'élèves et de professeurs

PTO[2] *Br* (*written abbr* **please turn over**) TSVP

ptomaine [ˈtəʊmeɪn] N *Biol* ptomaïne *f*
▸▸ *Med **ptomaine poisoning*** intoxication *f* alimentaire

Pty (*written abbr* **proprietary company**) SARL *f*

pub [pʌb] N pub *m*; **we had a p. lunch** nous avons déjeuné dans un pub
▸▸ *Br Fam **pub crawl*** tournée *f* des bars□; **to go on a p. crawl** faire la tournée des bars; *Br Fam **pub grub*** = nourriture (relativement simple) servie dans un pub; ***pub quiz*** jeu *m* de culture générale organisé dans un pub

> **PUBS**
>
> Les Britanniques aiment aller prendre quelques verres entre amis, que ce soit dans un pub traditionnel ou dans un "wine bar" (bar à vin moderne), ce qui a un côté plus branché. Lorsque l'on sort entre amis, la coutume est pour chacun de payer une tournée ("to buy a round"). On commande et on règle les consommations directement au bar – cependant de nombreux pubs servent désormais des repas le midi, qui eux sont le plus souvent apportés jusqu'à la table du client. De nombreux établissements proposent des "pub quizzes" – généralement une fois par semaine – au cours desquels des équipes d'habitués se retrouvent pour répondre à des questions portant sur la culture générale, le sport etc, posées par un animateur, le "quiz master". Ces mini-concours durent entre deux et trois heures et l'équipe gagnante reçoit un prix d'une valeur modique; parfois le prix consiste en des consommations gratuites. Il faut noter que tous les pubs sont désormais non-fumeurs.

pubalgia [ˌpjuːˈbældʒə] N *Med* pubalgie *f*

pub-crawl VI *Br Fam* faire la tournée des bars□, aller de bar en bar□

puberty [ˈpjuːbətɪ] N puberté *f*; **to reach p.** atteindre l'âge de la puberté

pubescence [pjuːˈbesəns] N **1** (*puberty*) (âge *m* de la) puberté *f* **2** (*of plant, animal*) pubescence *f*

pubescent [pjuːˈbesənt] ADJ **1** (*at puberty*) pubère **2** (*plant, animal*) pubescent

pubic [ˈpjuːbɪk] ADJ pubien
▸▸ ***pubic bone*** symphyse *f* pubienne; ***pubic hair*** poils *mpl* pubiens *ou* du pubis; (*single*) poil *m* pubien *ou* du pubis; ***pubic louse*** pou *m* du pubis

pubis [ˈpjuːbɪs] (*pl* **pubes** [-biːz]) N pubis *m*

public [ˈpʌblɪk] ADJ **1** (*of, by the state* ▸ *education, debt*) public; **built at p. expense** construit aux frais du contribuable; **to hold p. office** avoir des fonctions officielles
2 (*open or accessible to all* ▸ *place, meeting*) public; **was it a p. trial?** le public pouvait-il assister au procès?; **let's talk somewhere less p.** allons discuter dans un endroit plus tranquille; **these gardens are p. property!** ces jardins appartiennent à tout le monde!
3 (*of, by the public*) public; **the p. interest** *or* **good** le bien *ou* l'intérêt *m* public; **in the p. interest** dans l'intérêt du public; **to make a p. protest** protester publiquement; **the increase in crime is generating great p. concern** la montée de la criminalité inquiète sérieusement la population; **to restore p. confidence** regagner la confiance de la population; **to be in the** *Br* **p.** *or Am* **p.'s eye** être très en vue; **to disappear from the** *Br* **p.** *or Am* **p.'s eye** tomber dans les oubliettes; **a p. outcry** un tollé général; **it created a p. scandal** ça a provoqué un scandale retentissant; **p. awareness of the problem has increased** le public est plus sensible au problème maintenant; **the bill has p. support** l'opinion publique est favorable au projet de loi
4 (*publicly known, open*) public; **to make sth p.** rendre qch public; **to make a p. appearance** paraître en public; **to go into p. life** se lancer dans les affaires publiques; **she's active in p. life** elle prend une part active aux affaires publiques; **the contrast between his p. and his private life** le contraste entre sa vie publique et sa vie privée; **his first p. statement** sa première déclaration publique; **it's p. knowledge that...** il est de notoriété publique que...
ADV **to go p.** (*company*) s'introduire en Bourse; (*reveal information*) tout dire *ou* raconter; **to go p. with the story** raconter toute l'histoire
N public *m*; **the (general) p.** le (grand) public; **the p. is** *or* **are tired of political scandals** la population est lasse des scandales politiques; *Fin* **to issue shares to the p.** placer des actions dans le public; **her books reach a wide p.** ses livres touchent un public très large; **the movie-going p.** les amateurs de *ou* les gens qui vont au cinéma; **the viewing p.** les téléspectateurs
• **in public** ADV en public
▸▸ *Am TV **public access channel*** = chaîne du réseau câblé sur laquelle des particuliers peuvent diffuser leurs propres émissions; *Am TV **public access television*** = chaînes télévisées câblées non commerciales; ***public affairs*** affaires *fpl* publiques; *Am **public assistance*** aide *f* sociale; ***public authorities*** pouvoirs *mpl* publics; *Br **public bar*** salle *f* de bar (*dans un "pub" qui contient deux bars séparés, l'expression désigne le plus populaire des deux*); ***public baths*** bains *mpl* publics; *Br Pol **public bill*** ≃ projet *m* de loi d'intérêt général; ***public body*** corporation *f* de droit public; *Br **public call box*** cabine *f* (téléphonique) publique; ***public company*** ≃ société *f* anonyme; *Br **public convenience*** toilettes *fpl* publiques; *Br & Can **public corporation*** entreprise *f* publique; *Fin **public debt*** dette *f* publique *ou* de l'État; *Am Law **public defender*** avocat *m* commis d'office; ***public domain*** domaine *m* public; **to be in the p. domain** (*publication*) être dans le domaine public; *Comput **public domain software*** logiciel *m* (du domaine) public, *Can* publiciel *m*; ***public enemy*** ennemi *m* public; **p. enemy number one** ennemi *m* public numéro un; *Fin **public enterprise*** (*company*) entreprise *f* publique; ***public examination*** examen *m* national de l'enseignement public; ***public expenditure*** dépenses *fpl* publiques; ***public figure*** personnalité *f* très en vue; ***public finance*** finances *fpl* publiques; *Br **public footpath*** sentier *m* public; ***public funds*** fonds *mpl* publics; ***public gallery*** tribune *f* réservée au public; ***public health*** santé *f* publique; ***public health authorities*** = administration régionale des services publics de santé; ***public health clinic*** centre *m* d'hygiène publique; ***public health hazard*** risque *m* pour la santé publique; *Old-fashioned **public health inspector*** inspecteur(trice) *m,f* sanitaire; ***public health official*** représentant(e) *m,f* de la santé publique; ***public holiday*** jour *m* férié, fête *f* légale; ***public house*** *Br* (*pub*) pub *m*, bar *m*; *Am* (*inn*) auberge *f*; *Am **public housing*** logements *mpl* sociaux, ≃ HLM *f inv*; *Am **public housing project*** ≃ cité *f* HLM; *Law **public indecency*** outrage *m* public à la pudeur; **to be arrested for p. indecency** se faire arrêter pour outrage public à la pudeur; ***public inquiry*** enquête *f* officielle; **to hold a p. inquiry** faire une enquête officielle; *Br **public lavatory*** toilettes *fpl* publiques; ***public law*** droit *m* public; ***public lending right*** = droits que touche un auteur ou un éditeur pour le prêt de ses livres en bibliothèque; ***public liability*** responsabilité *f* civile; ***public liability insurance*** assurance responsabilité civile; ***public library*** bibliothèque *f* municipale; ***public limited company*** ≃ société anonyme; ***public loan*** emprunt *m* public; ***public money*** deniers *mpl ou* fonds *mpl* publics; ***public nuisance*** (*person*) fléau *m* public, empoisonneur(euse) *m,f*; **the pub's late opening hours were creating a p. nuisance** (*act*) les heures d'ouverture tardives du pub portaient atteinte à la tranquillité générale; *St Exch **public offering*** offre *f* publique; ***public official*** fonctionnaire *mf*; ***public opinion*** opinion *f* publique; ***public opinion poll*** sondage *m* (d'opinion); ***public order*** ordre *m* public; ***public ownership*** nationalisation *f*, étatisation *f*; **most airports are under p. ownership** la plupart des aéroports appartiennent à l'État; ***public park*** jardin *m* public; *Law **public prosecutor*** ≃ procureur *m* général, ≃ ministère *m* public; *Br **the public purse*** le Trésor (public); *Br **Public Record Office*** ≃ Archives *fpl* nationales; ***public relations*** relations *fpl* publiques; **giving them a free meal was great p. relations** en leur offrant le repas, nous avons fait un excellent travail de relations publiques; ***public relations agency, public relations consultancy*** agence *f* conseil en communication; ***public relations consultant*** conseil *m* en relations publiques, conseil *m* en communication; ***public relations exercise*** opération *f* de relations publiques; **it was a good p. relations exercise** ce fut une réussite pour ce qui est des relations publiques; ***public relations manager*** directeur(trice) *m,f* des relations publiques; ***public relations officer*** responsable *mf* des relations publiques; ***public room*** (*in hotel, institution*) salle *f* de réception; *Scot* (*in house*) salon *m*; ***public school*** (*in UK*) public school *f*, école *f* privée (*prestigieuse*); (*in US*) école *f* publique; *Br **public schoolboy*** = élève d'une "public school"; *Br **public schoolgirl*** = élève d'une "public school"; ***public sector*** secteur *m* public; *Br Fin **public sector borrowing requirement*** = besoins d'emprunt du secteur public non couverts par les rentrées fiscales; *Fin **public sector deficit*** déficit *m* du secteur public; *Fin **public sector earnings*** revenus *mpl* du secteur public; ***public servant*** fonctionnaire *mf*; ***public service*** (*amenity*) service *m* public *ou* d'intérêt général; *Br* (*civil service*) fonction *f* publique; **she's in p. service** elle est fonctionnaire; *Admin* **our organization performs a p. service** notre association assure un service d'intérêt général; *St Exch **public share offer*** offre publique de vente; ***public speaker*** orateur(trice) *m,f*; **he's a very good p. speaker** c'est un excellent orateur; ***public speaking*** art *m* oratoire; *Fin **public spending*** (UNCOUNT) dépenses *fpl* publiques *ou* de l'État; ***public spirit*** sens *m* civique, civisme *m*; *Am **public television*** (télévision *f* du) service *m* public; ***public transport*** (UNCOUNT) transports *mpl* en commun; **he went by p. transport** (*bus*) il est allé en bus; (*train*) il est allé en train; ***public utility*** *Am* (*company*) = société privée assurant un service public et réglementée par une commission d'État; *Br* (*amenity*) service *m* public; *Br **public utility company*** société *f* d'utilité publique; ***public works*** travaux *mpl* publics

> Note that the French expression **école publique** is never a translation for the British sense of the expression **public school**. It means **state school**.

> **PUBLIC SCHOOL**
>
> En Angleterre et au pays de Galles, le terme "public school" désigne une école privée de type traditionnel. Certaines de ces écoles (Eton et Harrow, par exemple) sont très prestigieuses et élitistes. Les "public schools" sont censées former l'élite de la nation. Aux États-Unis et parfois en Écosse, le terme désigne une école publique.

publican [ˈpʌblɪkən] N **1** *Br* (*pub owner*) patron(onne) *m,f* de pub; (*manager*) tenancier(ère) *m,f* de pub **2** *Bible* (*tax collector*) publicain *m*

ublication [ˌpʌblɪˈkeɪʃən] **N 1** *(of book, statis-ics, banns)* publication *f*; *(of edict)* promulgation *f*; **her article has been accepted for p.** son article va être publié; **this isn't for p.** ceci n'est pas destiné à la publication **2** *(work)* publication *f*, ouvrage *m* publié
▸▸ ***publication date*** *(of book)* date *f* de parution ou de publication

ublicist [ˈpʌblɪsɪst] **N 1** *(press agent)* (agent *m*) publicitaire *mf* **2** *(journalist)* journaliste *mf*

ublicity [pʌbˈlɪsɪtɪ] **N 1** *(media interest, expo-ure)* publicité *f*; **it'll give us free p. for the product** ça fera de la publicité gratuite pour notre pro-duit; **she/her movie is getting** *or* **attracting a lot of p.** c'est un procès/un film dont on a beaucoup parlé; **the incident will mean bad p. for us** cet inci-dent va être mauvais pour *ou* va faire du tort à notre image de marque; **an actress who shuns p.** une actrice qui fuit les médias; **they don't want any p.** ils ne veulent pas faire parler d'eux **2** *(ad-vertising material, information)* matériel *m* publi-citaire; **advance p.** promotion *f*
▸▸ ***publicity brochure*** brochure *f* publicitaire; ***publicity budget*** budget *m* publicitaire; ***publicity campaign*** *(for new product)* campagne *f* publici-taire, campagne *f* de publicité; *(by government)* campagne *f* d'information; ***publicity department*** service *m* de publicité; ***publicity director*** atta-ché(e) *m,f* de presse de plateau; *Press* ***publicity editor*** annoncier(ère) *m,f*; ***publicity expenses*** dé-penses *fpl* de la publicité; ***publicity gimmick*** as-tuce *f* publicitaire; ***publicity manager*** chef *m* de (la) publicité; ***publicity photograph*** photogra-phie *f* publicitaire; *Cin* ***publicity still*** photo *f* pu-blicitaire; ***publicity stunt*** coup *m* de pub

ublicize, -ise [ˈpʌblɪsaɪz] **VT 1** *(make known)* faire connaître (au public); **her father is a minis-ter, but she doesn't p. the fact** son père est minis-tre, mais elle ne tient pas spécialement à ce que cela se sache *ou* elle ne le crie pas sur les toits; **his much publicized blunders don't help his image** ses célèbres gaffes ne font rien pour arranger son image de marque; **the government's environ-mental reforms have been well publicized in the press** la presse a beaucoup parlé des réformes du gouvernement en matière d'environnement **2** *Mktg (advertise ▸ product, event)* faire de la pu-blicité pour; **the festival was well publicized** le festival a été annoncé à grand renfort de publi-cité; **the launch of the their new product has been widely publicized** leur nouveau produit a été lancé à grand renfort de publicité

ublicly [ˈpʌblɪklɪ] **ADV** publiquement, en pu-blic; **his p. declared intentions** les intentions qu'il avait affichées; *Econ* **p. owned** nationalisé; **the company is 51 percent p. controlled** la compagnie est contrôlée à 51 pour cent par des capitaux publics

ublic-Private Partnership N partenariat *m* public-privé

ublic-spirited ADJ *(gesture)* d'esprit civique; *(person)* **to be p.** faire preuve de civisme

ublish [ˈpʌblɪʃ] **VT 1** *(book, journal)* publier, éditer; *(author)* éditer; *Comput (Web page)* pu-blier; **her latest novel has just been published** son dernier roman vient de paraître; **he's a published author** ses livres sont publiés; **it's published by Orion** c'est édité chez Orion; **the magazine is pub-lished quarterly** la revue paraît tous les trois mois; **the newspaper published my letter** le jour-nal a publié ma lettre **2** *(of author)* **he's published poems in several magazines** ses poèmes ont été publiés dans plusieurs revues **3** *(make known ▸ statistics, statement, banns)* publier
VI *(newspaper)* paraître; *(author)* être publié; **she publishes regularly in women's magazines** ses arti-cles sont régulièrement publiés dans la presse féminine
▸▸ ***published price*** prix *m* de vente

ublishable [ˈpʌblɪʃəbəl] **ADJ** publiable; **her re-marks aren't p.!** ses commentaires sont impu-bliables!, on ne peut pas publier ses commentaires!

ublisher [ˈpʌblɪʃə(r)] **N 1** *(person)* éditeur(trice) *m,f*; *(company)* maison *f* d'édition **2** *(newspaper owner)* patron *m* de presse
▸▸ ***publisher's reader*** lecteur(trice) *m,f* de manus-crits *(dans une maison d'édition)*

publishing [ˈpʌblɪʃɪŋ] **N 1** *(industry)* édition *f*; **she's** *or* **she works in p.** elle travaille dans l'édi-tion; **a p. giant** un géant de l'édition; **a p. empire** un empire de l'édition **2** *(of book, journal)* publi-cation *f*
▸▸ ***publishing company*** maison *f* d'édition; ***pub-lishing house*** maison *f* d'édition; ***publishing man-ager*** directeur(trice) *m,f* éditorial(e)

puce [pju:s] **N** couleur *f* puce
ADJ puce *(inv)*

puck [pʌk] **N 1** *(in ice hockey)* palet *m* **2** *(sprite)* lutin *m*, farfadet *m*

pucker [ˈpʌkə(r)] **VI** *(face, forehead)* se plisser; *(fabric, collar)* goder, godailler
VT *(face, forehead)* plisser; *(fabric, collar)* faire goder, faire godailler; **to p. one's lips** faire une bouche en cul de poule; **she puckered her lips at the sour taste** elle fit la grimace en sentant le goût acide; **the seam/hem is puckered** la cou-ture/l'ourlet fait des plis
N *(crease)* pli *m*

▸**pucker up VI 1** *(face, forehead)* se plisser; *(fab-ric, collar)* goder, godailler **2** *Fam (for kiss)* avan-cer les lèvres□
VT SEP *(face, forehead)* plisser; *(fabric, collar)* faire goder, faire godailler

puckish [ˈpʌkɪʃ] **ADJ** espiègle

pud [pʊd] **N** *Br Fam (abbr* **pudding***)* dessert□*m*

pudding [ˈpʊdɪŋ] **N 1** *(cooked sweet dish)* **jam p.** pudding *m ou* pouding *m* à la confiture; **rice/ta-pioca p.** riz *m*/tapioca *m* au lait
2 *Br (part of meal)* dessert *m*; **what are we having for p.?** qu'est-ce qu'il y a comme dessert?
3 *Br (savoury dish)* = tourte cuite à la vapeur
4 *Br (sausage)* boudin *m*; **white p.** boudin *m* blanc
5 *Br Fam (podgy person)* patapouf *m*
6 *Br Fam (idiom)* **to be in the p. club** avoir un poli-chinelle dans le tiroir
▸▸ *Br* ***pudding basin, pudding bowl*** = jatte dans laquelle on fait cuire le pudding; ***pudding basin haircut, pudding bowl haircut*** coupe *f* au bol; ***pud-ding rice*** riz *m* rond; *Geol* ***pudding stone*** poudin-gue *m*

puddle [ˈpʌdəl] **N** *(of water, oil)* flaque *f*; *(small pool)* petite mare *f*; *Fam* **the dog's made a p. on the carpet** le chien a fait pipi sur le tapis
VT *(clay)* malaxer

pudendum [pju:ˈdendəm] *(pl* **pudenda** [-də]*)* **N** *(usu pl)* parties *fpl* génitales

pudgy [ˈpʌdʒɪ] *(compar* **pudgier**, *superl* **pudgiest***)* **ADJ** *Br Fam* grassouillet

puerile [ˈpjʊəraɪl] **ADJ** puéril

puerility [pjʊəˈrɪlətɪ] **N** puérilité *f*

puerperal [pju:ˈɜ:pərəl] **ADJ** *Med* puerpéral
▸▸ ***puerperal fever*** fièvre *f* puerpérale

Puerto Rican [ˌpwɜ:təʊˈri:kən] **N** Portoricain(e) *m,f*
ADJ portoricain
COMP *(embassy, history)* du Puerto Rico

Puerto Rico [ˌpwɜ:təʊˈri:kəʊ] **N** Porto Rico, Puer-to Rico

puff[1] [pʌf] **VT 1** *(smoke ▸ cigar, pipe)* tirer des bouffées de
2 *(emit, expel)* **to p. (out) smoke/steam** envoyer des nuages de fumée/des jets de vapeur; **he sat opposite me puffing smoke in my face!** il était as-sis en face de moi et m'envoyait sa fumée en pleine figure!
3 *(pant)* **"I can't go on," he puffed** "je n'en peux plus", haleta-t-il
4 *Fam Old-fashioned (laud)* vanter□, faire mous-ser
VI 1 *(blow ▸ person)* souffler; *(▸ wind)* souffler en bourrasques; **to p. (away) at one's pipe** tirer sur sa pipe, tirer des bouffées de sa pipe
2 *(pant)* haleter; *(breathe heavily)* souffler; **he was puffing and panting** il soufflait comme un phoque; **I puffed along beside her** je courais, tout essoufflé, à ses côtés
3 *(smoke)* **to p. on one's cigar** tirer sur son cigare
4 *(issue ▸ smoke, steam)* sortir
5 *(train)* **the train puffed into the station** le train entra en gare dans un nuage de fumée; **the steam engine puffed into view** la fumée indiqua l'arrivée du train
N 1 *(gust, whiff)* bouffée *f*; *(gasp)* souffle *m*; **her breath came in short puffs** elle haletait; **a p. of dust/smoke on the horizon** un nuage de pous-sière/fumée à l'horizon; *Fig* **all our plans went up in a p. of smoke** tous nos projets sont partis en fumée *ou* se sont évanouis
2 *(on cigarette, pipe)* bouffée *f*; **to have** *or* **to take a p.** tirer une bouffée; **give me a p.** *(of your ciga-rette)* passe-moi une bouffée
3 *(sound ▸ of train)* teuf-teuf *m*
4 *Br Fam (breath)* souffle□*m*; **to be out of p.** être à bout de souffle *ou* essoufflé□
5 *(fluffy mass)* **puffs of cloud in the sky** des mou-tons *mpl ou* des petits nuages *mpl* dans le ciel
6 *(for make-up)* **(powder) p.** houppe *f* (à pou-drer), houpette *f*
7 *(pastry)* chou *m*; **cream p.** chou *m* à la crème
8 *Am (eiderdown)* édredon *m*
9 *Fam (free endorsement)* **to give sth a p.** faire de la pub gratuite pour qch
10 *Br Fam Drugs slang (marijuana)* herbe *f*, beu *f*; *(cannabis)* shit *m*, hasch *m*
▸▸ *Zool* ***puff adder*** vipère *f* heurtante; *Culin Am* ***puff paste***, *Br* ***puff pastry*** pâte *f* feuilletée; ***puff sleeves*** manches *fpl* ballon

puff[2] [pʊf] = **poof**[1]

▸**puff out VT SEP 1** *(extinguish)* souffler, éteindre (en soufflant) **2** *(inflate, make rounded ▸ cheeks, sail)* gonfler; *(▸ chest)* bomber; *(▸ cushion, hair)* faire bouffer; **the pigeon puffed out its feathers** le pigeon fit gonfler ses plumes; **the wind puffed out the sails** les voiles se gonflèrent **3** *(emit)* **to p. out smoke/steam** envoyer des nuages de fumée/de vapeur
VI 1 *(parachute, sail)* se gonfler **2** *(be emitted ▸ smoke)* s'échapper

▸**puff up VT SEP 1** *(inflate, make rounded ▸ cheeks, sail)* gonfler; *(▸ cushion, hair)* faire bouf-fer **2** *(usu passive) (swell ▸ lip, ankle etc)* enfler; **her eyes were puffed up** elle avait les yeux bouf-fis; *Fig* **to be puffed up with pride** être bouffi d'or-gueil
VI *(lip, ankle etc)* enfler, bouffir

Puffa jacket® [ˈpʌfə-] **N** blouson *m* de rappeur

puffball [ˈpʌfbɔ:l] **N** *Bot* vesse-de-loup *f*
▸▸ ***puffball skirt*** = jupe plus évasée en bas qu'en haut

puffed [pʌft] **ADJ 1** *(oats, wheat)* soufflé; *(rice)* gonflé **2** *Br Fam (out of breath)* **p. (out)** essoufflé□, à bout de souffle□; **we were p. (out) after the climb** la montée nous a essoufflés
▸▸ ***puffed sleeves*** manches *fpl* ballon

puffer [ˈpʌfə(r)] **N 1** *Ich* **p. (fish)** poisson-globe *m* **2** *Br Fam (train)* train□*m*

puffin [ˈpʌfɪn] **N** *Orn* macareux *m*

puffiness [ˈpʌfɪnɪs] **N** boursouflure *f*

puffy [ˈpʌfɪ] *(compar* **puffier**, *superl* **puffiest***)* **ADJ** *(face)* bouffi, boursouflé; *(lip, cheek)* enflé; *(eye)* bouffi; **p. clouds** moutons *mpl*

pug [pʌg] **N** *(dog)* carlin *m*
▸▸ ***pug nose*** nez *m* camus

pugilism [ˈpju:dʒɪlɪzəm] **N** *Literary* pugilat *m*, boxe *f*

pugilist [ˈpju:dʒɪlɪst] **N** *Literary* pugiliste *mf*, boxeur(euse) *m,f*

pugnacious [pʌgˈneɪʃəs] **ADJ** *Formal* pugnace, agressif

pugnaciously [pʌgˈneɪʃəslɪ] **ADV** *Formal* avec pugnacité *ou* agressivité

pugnacity [pʌgˈnæsətɪ] **N** *Formal* pugnacité *f*

pug-nosed ADJ *(face, person)* au nez camus; **to be p.** avoir le nez camus

puh-lease [pəˈli:z] **EXCLAM** *Fam* je t'en/vous en prie!□; **oh, p.!, did you really think I'd believe that?** oh, je t'en prie! tu pensais vraiment que j'allais avaler ça?

puke [pju:k] *Fam* **VT** dégueuler, gerber
VI dégueuler, gerber; *Fig* **you make me p.!** tu me dégoûtes!
N dégueulis *m*

pukey [ˈpju:kɪ] **ADJ** *Fam* dégueulasse

pukka [ˈpʌkə] ADJ *Br Old-fashioned or Hum* **1** *(genuine)* réglo *(inv)*, régulier; **a p. sahib** un vrai gentleman; **p. information** des renseignements *mpl* exacts **2** *(done well)* bien fait, très correct; *(excellent)* de premier ordre, super *(inv)* **3** *(socially acceptable)* (très) comme il faut

pulchritude [ˈpʌlkrɪtjuːd] N *Literary* beauté *f*, splendeur *f*

PULL [pʊl]

N
- traction **2**
- résistance **3**
- attrait **4**
- influence **5**
- coup de rame **7**
- bouffée **8**
- gorgée **8**
- accroc **10**

VT
- tirer **1–3, 4, 10, 15**
- traîner **1**
- arracher **4**
- se déchirer **5**
- réussir **6**
- retenir **7**
- retirer **12**
- attirer **13**

VI
- tirer **1**
- se mettre **3**
- ramer **7**

N **1** *(tug, act of pulling)* **to give sth a p., to give a p. on sth** tirer (sur) qch; **give it a hard** *or* **good p.!** tirez fort!; **give it one more p.** tire encore un coup; **we'll need a p. to get out of the mud** nous aurons besoin que quelqu'un nous remorque *ou* nous prenne en remorque pour nous désembourber; **with a p. the dog broke free** le chien tira sur sa laisse et s'échappa; **she felt a p. at** *or* **on her handbag** elle a senti qu'on tirait sur son sac à main; **I felt a p. on the fishing line** ça mordait

2 *(physical force ▸ of machine)* traction *f*; *(▸ of sun, moon, magnet)* (force *f*) d'attraction *f*; **the winch applies a steady p.** le treuil exerce une traction continue; **we fought against the p. of the current** nous luttions contre le courant qui nous entraînait

3 *(resistance ▸ of bowstring)* résistance *f*; **adjust the trigger if the p. is too stiff for you** réglez la détente si elle est trop dure pour vous

4 *(psychological, emotional attraction)* attrait *m*; **the p. of city life** l'attrait *m* de la vie en ville; **he resisted the p. of family tradition and went his own way** il a résisté à l'influence de la tradition familiale pour suivre son propre chemin

5 *Fam (influence, power)* influence[❑]*f*, piston *m*; **to have a lot of p.** avoir le bras long; **he has a lot of p. with the Prime Minister** il a beaucoup d'influence sur le Premier ministre; **his money gives him a certain political p.** son argent lui confère une certaine influence *ou* un certain pouvoir politique; **his father's p. got him in** son père l'a pistonné

6 *(prolonged effort)* **it'll be a long p. to the summit** la montée sera longue (et difficile) pour atteindre le sommet; **it will be a hard p. upstream** il faudra ramer dur pour remonter le courant; **it's going to be a long uphill p. to make the firm profitable** ça sera difficile de remettre l'entreprise à flot

7 *(in rowing ▸ stroke)* coup *m* de rame *ou* d'aviron; **with another p. he was clear of the rock** d'un autre coup de rame, il évita le rocher

8 *(at cigar)* bouffée *f*; *(at drink, bottle)* gorgée *f*; **to take a p. at** *or* **on one's beer** boire *ou* prendre une gorgée de bière; **to take a p. at** *or* **on one's cigarette/pipe** tirer sur sa cigarette/pipe

9 *(usu in compounds) (knob, handle)* poignée *f*; *(cord)* cordon *m*; *(strap)* sangle *f*

10 *(snag ▸ in sweater)* accroc *m*; **my cardigan has a p. in it** j'ai fait un accroc à mon cardigan

11 *Typ* épreuve *f*

12 *Fam* **to be on the p.** *(man)* chercher à lever une nana; *(woman)* chercher à lever un mec

VT **1** *(object ▸ yank, tug)* tirer; *(▸ drag)* traîner; *(person)* tirer, entraîner; **she pulled my hair** elle m'a tiré les cheveux; **to p. the blinds** baisser les stores; **to p. the** *Br* **curtains** *or Am* **drapes** tirer *ou* fermer les rideaux; **p. the lamp towards you** tirez la lampe vers vous; **he pulled his chair closer to the fire** il approcha sa chaise de la cheminée; **she pulled the hood over her face** elle abaissa le capuchon sur son visage; **he pulled his hat over his eyes** il enfonça *ou* rabattit son chapeau sur ses yeux; **he pulled the steering wheel to the right** il a donné un coup de volant à droite; **to p. a drawer open** ouvrir un tiroir; **she came in and pulled the door shut behind her** elle entra et ferma la porte derrière elle; **p. the rope taut** tendez la corde; **p. the knot tight** serrez le nœud; **p. the tablecloth straight** tendez la nappe; **he pulled the wrapping from the package** il arracha l'emballage du paquet; **he pulled the sheets off the bed** il enleva les draps du lit; **she pulled her hand from mine** elle retira (brusquement) sa main de la mienne; **she pulled the box from his hands** elle lui a arraché la boîte des mains; **he was pulling her towards the exit** il l'entraînait vers la sortie; **he pulled her closer (to him)** il l'a attirée plus près de lui; **he pulled himself onto the riverbank** il se hissa sur la berge; *Fig* **he was pulled off the first team** on l'a écarté *ou* exclu de la première équipe; *Br Fam* **p. the other one (it's got bells on)!** mon œil!, à d'autres!; **to p. to bits** *or* **pieces** *(toy, appliance)* démolir, mettre en morceaux; *(book, flower)* déchirer; *Fig (book, play, person)* démolir

2 *(operate ▸ lever, handle)* tirer; **p. the trigger** appuyez *ou* pressez sur la détente

3 *(tow, draw ▸ load, trailer, carriage, boat)* tirer, remorquer; **carts pulled by mules** des charrettes tirées par des mules; **a suitcase with wheels that you p. behind you** une valise à roulettes qu'on tire *ou* traîne derrière soi; **the barges were pulled along the canals** les péniches étaient halées le long des canaux

4 *(take out ▸ tooth)* arracher, extraire; *(▸ weeds)* arracher; *(▸ weapon)* tirer, sortir; **he pulled a dollar bill from his wad/wallet** il a tiré un billet d'un dollar de sa liasse/sorti un billet d'un dollar de son portefeuille; **he pulled a gun on me** il a braqué un revolver sur moi; **to p. a cork** déboucher une bouteille; **to have a tooth pulled** se faire arracher une dent; **it was like pulling teeth** c'était pénible comme tout; *Fam* **can you p. that file for me?** pourriez-vous me sortir ce dossier?[❑]

5 *(strain ▸ muscle, tendon)* se déchirer; **she pulled a muscle** elle s'est déchiré un muscle, elle s'est fait un claquage; **a pulled muscle** un claquage

6 *Fam (bring off)* réussir[❑]; **he pulled a big bank job in Italy** il a réussi un hold-up de première dans une banque italienne; **to p. a trick on sb** jouer un tour à qn[❑]; **what are you trying to p.?** qu'est-ce que tu es en train de combiner *ou* manigancer?[❑]; **don't try and p. anything!** n'essayez pas de jouer au plus malin!; **don't ever p. a stunt like that again** ne me/nous/*etc* refais jamais un tour comme ça[❑]; **to p. a fast one on sb** avoir qn, rouler qn; *Am* **I pulled an all-nighter** j'ai bossé toute la nuit

7 *(hold back) Horseracing* **to p. a horse** retenir un cheval; *also Fig* **to p. one's punches** retenir ses coups, ménager son adversaire; *Fig* **she didn't p. any punches** elle n'y est pas allée de main morte

8 *(in golf, tennis ▸ ball)* puller; **to p. a shot** puller

9 *(in rowing ▸ boat)* faire avancer à la rame; **he pulls a good oar** c'est un bon rameur; **the boat pulls eight oars** c'est un bateau à huit avirons

10 *Typ (proof)* tirer

11 *Comput* extraire

12 *Fam (withdraw)* retirer[❑]; **people complained and they had to p. the commercial** ils ont dû retirer la pub suite à des plaintes

13 *Fam (attract ▸ customers, spectators)* attirer[❑]; **the festival pulled a big crowd** le festival a attiré beaucoup de monde

14 *Br (serve ▸ draught beer)* tirer; **he pulls pints at the Crown** il est barman au Crown

15 *Fam (sexual partner)* lever, emballer

VI **1** *(exert force, tug)* tirer; **p. harder!** tirez plus fort!; **to p. on** *or* **at a rope** tirer sur un cordage; **the steering pulls to the right** la direction tire à droite; *Aut* **the 2-litre model pulls very well** le modèle 2 litres a de bonnes reprises; *Fig* **they're pulling in different directions** ils tirent à hue et à dia

2 *(rope, cord)* **the rope pulled easily** la corde filait librement

3 *(go, move)* **p. into the space next to the Mercedes** mettez-vous *ou* garez-vous à côté de la Mercedes; **he pulled into the right-hand lane** il a pris la file de droite; **p. into the garage** entrez dans le garage; **when the train pulls out of the station** quand le train quitte la gare; **she pulled clear of the pack** elle s'est détachée du peloton; **he pulled clear of the traffic and sped on** il est sor[ti] du flot de la circulation et a accéléré; **he pulle[d] sharply to the left** il a viré brutalement sur l[a] gauche; **the lorry pulled slowly up the hill** le ca[mion] gravissait lentement la côte

4 *(strain, labour ▸ vehicle)* peiner; *(▸ horse)* tire[r] sur le mors; **the engine's pulling** le moteur fatigu[e] *ou* peine

5 *Fam (exert influence, give support)* **the head o[f] personnel is pulling for you** *or* **on your behalf** vou[s] avez le chef du personnel derrière vous[❑]

6 *(snag ▸ sweater)* filer; **my sweater's pulled in [a] couple of places** mon pull a plusieurs mailles f[i]lées

7 *(row)* ramer; **to p. for shore** ramer vers la côt[e]

8 *Br Fam (find sexual partner)* **did you p. las[t] night?** t'as levé une nana/un mec hier soir?

▸▸ *Am* **pull date** date *f* limite de vente; *Mktg* **pu[ll] strategy** stratégie *f* pull; **pull tab** *(on can)* annea[u] *m*, bague *f*

▸ **pull about** VT SEP *(handle roughly ▸ person)* malmener; *(▸ object)* tirer dans tous les sens, t[i]railler; **stop pulling me about!** mais lâche-mo[i] donc!

▸ **pull ahead** VI prendre de l'avance; **to p. ahea[d] of sb** prendre de l'avance sur qn

▸ **pull along** VT SEP *(load, vehicle)* tirer; *(perso[n])* entraîner; **he was pulling the suitcase along by th[e] strap** il tirait la valise derrière lui par la sangl[e]; **she pulled me along by my arm** elle m'entraîna[it] en me tirant par le bras

▸ **pull apart** VT SEP **1** *(take to pieces ▸ machine, furniture)* démonter

2 *(destroy, break ▸ object)* mettre en morceau[x] *ou* en pièces; *(▸ clothing)* déchirer; *(body, flesh)* déchiqueter; **the wreck was pulled apart by th[e] waves** les vagues ont disloqué l'épave; **tell hi[m] where it's hidden or he'll p. the place apart** dites[-]lui où c'est (caché) sinon il va tout saccager

3 *(criticize ▸ essay, performance, theory)* démoli[r]; *(▸ person)* éreinter

4 *(separate ▸ fighters, dogs)* séparer; *(▸ papers)* détacher, séparer

5 *(make suffer)* déchirer

VI *(furniture)* se démonter, être démontable; **th[e] shelves simply p. apart** les étagères se démonten[t] sans outils

▸ **pull away** VT SEP *(withdraw ▸ covering, hand)* retirer; *(grab)* arracher; **he pulled me away fro[m] the window** il m'éloigna de la fenêtre; **she pulle[d] the book away from him** elle lui arracha le livre

VI **1** *(withdraw ▸ person)* s'écarter; **I put out m[y] hand but she pulled away** j'ai tendu la main ver[s] elle mais elle s'est détournée; **he had me by th[e] arm but I managed to p. away** il me tenait par l[e] bras mais j'ai réussi à me dégager **2** *(move off ▸ vehicle, ship)* démarrer; *(▸ train, convoy)* s'ébran[ler]; **the boat pulled away from the bank** le batea[u] quitta la rive; **the train pulled away from the sta[tion]** le train a quitté la gare **3** *(get ahead ▸ runne[r], competitor)* prendre de l'avance; **she's pullin[g] away from the pack** elle prend de l'avance sur l[e] peloton, elle se détache du peloton

▸ **pull back** VT SEP **1** *(draw backwards or toward[s] one)* retirer; **he pulled his hand back** il retira *ou* ôt[a] sa main; **she pulled back the curtains** elle ouvr[it] les rideaux; **p. the lever back** tirez le levier (ve[rs] l'arrière); **he pulled me back from the railing** il m['a] éloigné de la barrière; **to p. sb/a company bac[k] from the brink** faire refaire surface à qn/une en[treprise], tirer qn/une entreprise d'affaire **2** *(withdraw ▸ troops)* retirer

VI **1** *(withdraw ▸ troops, participant)* se retire[r]; **it's too late to p. back now** il est trop tard pour s[e] retirer *ou* pour faire marche arrière maintenan[t]; **they pulled back from committing themselves full[y]** ils ont renoncé à s'engager complètement **2** *(step backwards)* reculer; **to p. back involuntari[ly]** avoir un mouvement de recul involontaire **3** *(jib ▸ horse, person)* regimber

▸ **pull down** VT SEP **1** *(lower ▸ lever, handle)* tire[r] (vers le bas); *(▸ trousers, veil)* baisser; *(▸ sui[t]case, book)* descendre; *(▸ blind, window)* bais[ser]; **with his hat pulled down over his eyes** so[n] chapeau rabattu sur les yeux; **she pulled her ski[rt] down over her knees** elle ramena sa jupe sur se[s] genoux; **I pulled him down onto the chair** je l'ai fa[it] asseoir sur la chaise; **he's pulling the whole tear[m]** down il fait baisser le niveau de toute l'équipe; ny marks in the oral exam will pull me down mes notes à l'oral vont baisser *ou* descendre ma moyenne

2 *(demolish ▸ house, wall)* démolir, abattre; they're pulling down the whole neighbourhood ils démolissent tout le quartier; *Fig* it'll p. down the government ça va renverser le gouvernement

3 *Fam (weaken ▸ of illness)* affaiblir❑, abattre❑; *(depress)* déprimer❑, abattre❑

4 *Am Fam (earn)* gagner❑, se faire

5 *Comput (menu)* dérouler

VI *(blind)* descendre

pull in VT SEP **1** *(line, fishing net)* ramener; **they pulled the rope in** ils tirèrent la corde à eux; **to p. sb in** *(into building, car)* tirer qn à l'intérieur, faire entrer qn; *(into water)* faire tomber qn à l'eau

2 *(stomach)* rentrer; **to p. oneself in** rentrer son ventre

3 *(attract ▸ customers, investors, investment)* attirer; **the show's really pulling them in** le spectacle attire les foules

4 *Fam (earn ▸ of person)* gagner❑, se faire; *(▸ of business)* rapporter❑

5 *Fam (arrest)* arrêter❑, embarquer; **they pulled him in for questioning** ils l'ont arrêté pour l'interroger

6 *(stop ▸ horse)* retenir, tirer les rênes de; **to p. one's car in to the kerb** se ranger près du trottoir; **to be pulled in for speeding** être arrêté pour excès de vitesse

VI *(vehicle, driver ▸ stop)* s'arrêter; *(▸ park)* se garer; *(▸ move to side of road)* se rabattre; *(arrive ▸ train)* entrer en gare; **I pulled in for petrol** je me suis arrêté pour prendre de l'essence; **the car in front pulled in to let me past** la voiture devant moi s'est rabattue pour me laisser passer; **p. in here** arrête-toi là; **to p. in to the kerb** se ranger près du trottoir; **the express pulled in two hours late** l'express est arrivé avec deux heures de retard

pull off VT SEP **1** *(clothes, boots, ring)* enlever, retirer; *(cover, bandage, knob, wrapping)* enlever; *(page from calendar, sticky backing)* détacher; **to p. the sheets off the bed** retirer *ou* enlever les draps du lit; **I pulled her hat off** je lui ai enlevé son chapeau; *(more violently)* je lui ai arraché son chapeau **2** *Fam (accomplish ▸ deal, stratagem, mission, shot)* réussir❑; *(▸ press conference, negotiations)* mener à bien❑; *(▸ plan)* réaliser❑; *(▸ prize)* décrocher, gagner❑; **the deal will be difficult to p. off** cette affaire ne sera pas facile à négocier; **will she (manage to) p. it off?** est-ce qu'elle va y arriver?; **he pulled it off** il a réussi **3** *Vulg (masturbate)* **to p. sb off** branler qn; **to p. oneself off** se branler

VI **1** *(move off)* démarrer; *(after halt)* redémarrer **2** *(stop)* s'arrêter; *(leave main road)* quitter la route; **he pulled off onto a side road** il bifurqua sur une petite route; **there's no place to p. off** il n'y a pas de place pour s'arrêter **3** *(come off)* **the lid simply pulls off** il suffit de tirer pour enlever le couvercle; **the top pulls off to reveal...** le dessus se retire et on peut voir...

pull on VT SEP *(clothes, boots, pillow slip)* mettre, enfiler

VT INSEP **1** *(tug at ▸ rope, handle etc)* tirer sur **2** *(draw on ▸ cigarette, pipe)* tirer sur

pull out VT SEP **1** *(remove ▸ tooth, hair, weeds)* arracher; *(▸ splinter, nail)* enlever; *(▸ plug, cork)* ôter, enlever; *(produce ▸ wallet, weapon)* sortir, tirer; **she pulled a map out of her bag** elle a sorti une carte de son sac; **he pulled a page out of his notebook** il a déchiré une feuille de son carnet; **p. the paper gently out of the printer** retirez doucement le papier de l'imprimante; **to p. a nail out of a plank** arracher un clou d'une planche; **the tractor pulled us out of the mud/ditch** le tracteur nous a sortis de la boue/du fossé; **to p. the country out of recession** (faire) sortir le pays de la récession; **to p. sb out of a tight spot** tirer qn d'un mauvais pas; *Fam* **to p. out all the stops (to do sth)** faire le maximum (pour faire qch); *Br Fam* **p. your finger out!** remue-toi!

2 *(draw towards one ▸ drawer, leaf of table, shelf)* tirer; *(unfold)* déplier; **p. the bed out from the wall** écartez le lit du mur; **he pulled a chair out from under the table** il a écarté une chaise de la table

3 *(withdraw ▸ troops, contestant)* retirer; **he threatened to p. the party out of the coalition** il menaça de retirer le parti de la coalition

4 *Comput (select, produce ▸ data)* sortir

VI **1** *(withdraw ▸ troops, ally, participant)* se retirer; *(▸ company from project, buyer)* se désister; *(▸ company from place)* quitter une/la région/ville/*etc*; **she's pulling out of the election** elle retire sa candidature; **they've pulled out of the deal** ils se sont retirés de l'affaire

2 *(move off ▸ car, ship)* démarrer; *(▸ train, convoy)* s'ébranler; *(move out to overtake)* déboîter; **she was pulling out of the garage** elle sortait du garage; **a truck suddenly pulled out in front of me** soudain, un camion m'a coupé la route; **to p. out into traffic** s'engager dans la circulation; *Aviat* **to p. out of a dive** sortir d'un piqué, se rétablir

3 *(economy)* **to p. out of a recession/a crisis** sortir de la récession/d'une crise

4 *(be extendible or detachable ▸ drawer)* s'ouvrir; *(▸ handle)* s'allonger; *(▸ map)* se déplier; **the sofa pulls out into a bed** le canapé se transforme en lit; **the shelves p. out** on peut retirer les étagères; **the table top pulls out** c'est une table à rallonges

▸ **pull over** VT SEP **1** *(draw into specified position)* tirer, traîner; **p. the chair over to the window** amenez la chaise près de la fenêtre; **she pulled the dish over and helped herself** elle a tiré le plat vers *ou* à elle et s'est servie **2** *(make fall ▸ pile, person, table)* faire tomber, renverser; **watch out you don't p. that lamp over** fais attention de ne pas faire tomber cette lampe **3** *(usu passive) (stop ▸ vehicle, driver)* arrêter; **I got pulled over for speeding** je me suis fait arrêter pour excès de vitesse

VI *(vehicle, driver ▸ stop)* s'arrêter; *(▸ move to side of road)* se ranger, se rabattre; **p. over and let the fire engine past** rangez-vous *ou* rabattez-vous sur le côté et laissez passer les pompiers

▸ **pull round** *Br* VT SEP *(revive)* ranimer; **a drop of brandy will p. her round** un peu de cognac la remettra *ou* remontera

VI *(regain consciousness)* revenir à soi, reprendre connaissance; *(recover)* se remettre

▸ **pull through** VT SEP **1** *(draw through ▸ rope, thread)* faire passer; **p. the needle through to the other side** faites sortir l'aiguille de l'autre côté **2** *(help survive or surmount)* tirer d'affaire; **he says his faith pulled him through** il dit que c'est sa foi qui lui a permis de s'en sortir

VI *(recover)* s'en sortir, s'en tirer

▸ **pull to** VT SEP *(shut ▸ door, gate)* fermer

▸ **pull together** VT SEP **1** *(place together, join)* joindre **2** *(organize ▸ demonstration, rescue team)* organiser; *(prepare)* préparer; **I've pulled together a few suggestions** j'ai préparé *ou* noté quelques propositions **3 to p. oneself together** se reprendre, se ressaisir; **p. yourself together!** ressaisissez-vous!, ne vous laissez pas aller!

VI **1** *(on rope)* tirer ensemble; *(on oars)* ramer à l'unisson; **p. together!** *(in rowing)* avant partout! **2** *(combine efforts, cooperate)* concentrer ses efforts, agir de concert; **we've all got to p. together on this one** il faut que nous nous y mettions tous ensemble, il faut que nous nous attelions tous ensemble à la tâche

▸ **pull up** VT SEP **1** *(draw upwards ▸ trousers, sleeve, blanket, lever)* remonter; *(▸ blind)* hausser, lever; *(▸ skirt)* retrousser, relever; *(hoist oneself)* hisser; **they pulled the boat up onto the beach** ils ont tiré le bateau sur la plage; **she pulled herself up onto the ledge** elle s'est hissée sur le rebord; **to p. one's socks up** tirer *ou* remonter ses chaussettes; *Fam Fig* se remuer, s'activer

2 *(move closer ▸ chair)* approcher; **I pulled a chair up to the desk** j'ai approché une chaise du bureau; **why don't you p. up a chair and join us?** prenez donc une chaise et joignez-vous à nous!; **he pulled the crate up to the scales** il a traîné la caisse jusqu'à la balance

3 *(uproot ▸ weeds)* arracher; *(▸ bush, stump, tree)* arracher, déraciner; *(rip up ▸ floorboards)* arracher

4 *(stop ▸ person, vehicle, horse)* arrêter; *(check ▸ person)* retenir; **to be pulled up (by the police)** se faire arrêter (par un agent); **his warning pulled me up short** je me suis arrêté net lorsqu'il m'a crié de faire attention; **he was about to tell them everything but I pulled him up (short)** il était sur le point de tout leur dire mais je lui ai coupé la parole

5 *Fam (improve ▸ score, mark)* améliorer❑; *(▸ average)* remonter❑; **his good marks in maths pulled him up again** ses bonnes notes en maths ont remonté sa moyenne

6 *Br Fam (rebuke)* réprimander❑, enguirlander; **he was pulled up for being late** il s'est fait enguirlander pour être arrivé en retard; **if your work is sloppy, they'll p. you up on it** si ton travail est bâclé, tu vas te faire taper sur les doigts

VI **1** *(stop)* s'arrêter; **as I was pulling up at the red light** alors que j'allais m'arrêter au feu rouge; **to p. up short** s'arrêter net *ou* brusquement

2 *Fam (ease up)* se détendre❑, se relâcher❑

3 *(draw even)* rattraper; **to p. up with sb** rattraper qn; **Sun Boy is pulling up on the outside!** Sun Boy remonte à l'extérieur!

4 *(improve ▸ student, athlete, performance)* s'améliorer

---

pull-back N *Mil* repli *m*, retraite *f*

pull-down ADJ *(bench, counter)* à abattant

▸▸ *Comput* ***pull-down menu*** menu *m* déroulant; ***pull-down seat*** strapontin *m*; *Comput* ***pull-down window*** fenêtre *f* déroulante

pullet ['pʊlɪt] N *Orn* poulette *f*

pulley ['pʊlɪ] N *(wheel, device)* poulie *f*; *Tech (set of parallel wheels)* molette *f*

▸▸ ***pulley block*** palan *m*, moufle *f*; ***pulley wheel*** réa *m*, rouet *m*

pull-in N *Br Aut (café)* café *m* au bord de la route, ≃ restaurant *m* routier

Pullman ['pʊlmən] *(pl* **Pullmans***)* N **1** *(sleeping car)* (voiture *f*) pullman *m* **2** *(train)* rapide *m* de nuit

▸▸ ***Pullman car, Pullman carriage*** voiture *f* pullman

pull-off N *Am Aut (rest area)* aire *f* de repos

pull-out N **1** *(magazine supplement)* supplément *m* détachable

2 *(fold-out)* hors-texte *m inv (qui se déplie)*

3 *(withdrawal ▸ gen) & Mil* retrait *m*; *(▸ of candidate)* désistement *m*; *(evacuation)* évacuation *f*; *Fin* **investment p.** désinvestissement *m*

4 *Aviat* rétablissement *m*

ADJ *(magazine section)* détachable; *(map, advertising page)* hors texte *(inv)*; *(legs, shelf)* rétractable

▸▸ ***pull-out bed*** canapé-lit *m*; ***pull-out leaf*** *(on desk, table)* rallonge *f*

pullover ['pʊl,əʊvə(r)] N pullover *m*, pull *m*

pullulate ['pʌljʊleɪt] VI **1** *Literary (teem, breed)* pulluler **2** *Bot (germinate)* germer

pull-up N **1** *Sport* traction *f (sur une barre ou sur des anneaux)*; **to do pull-ups** faire des tractions **2** *Br Aut (café)* café *m* au bord de la route, ≃ restaurant *m* routier

pulmonary ['pʌlmənərɪ] ADJ *Med* pulmonaire

▸▸ *Med* ***pulmonary embolism*** embolie *f* pulmonaire; *Med* ***pulmonary emphysema*** emphysème *m* pulmonaire; *Med* ***pulmonary tuberculosis*** tuberculose *f* pulmonaire, bacillose *f*

pulp [pʌlp] N **1** *(in fruit)* pulpe *f*

2 *(for paper)* pâte *f* à papier, pulpe *f*; **p. and paper mill** fabrique *f* de papier

3 *(in tooth)* pulpe *f*

4 *(mush)* bouillie *f*; **to beat** *or* **to smash to a p.** réduire en bouillie *ou* en marmelade

VT **1** *(crush ▸ wood)* réduire en pâte; *(▸ fruit, vegetables)* réduire en pulpe; *(▸ book)* mettre au pilon, pilonner **2** *(remove pulp from)* ôter la pulpe de

▸▸ ***pulp fiction*** romans *mpl* de gare; ***pulp magazine*** magazine *m* à sensation; ***pulp writer*** auteur *m* de romans de gare

pulping ['pʌlpɪŋ] N *(of books)* pilonnage *m*

pulpit ['pʊlpɪt] N *Rel* chaire *f*; *Fig* **the p.** *(clergy)* le clergé, les ecclésiastiques *mpl*

pulpwood ['pʌlpwʊd] N bois *m* à pâte, bois *m* de papeterie

pulpy ['pʌlpɪ] *(compar* **pulpier**, *superl* **pulpiest***)* ADJ **1** *(fruit, tissue)* pulpeux **2** *Fam Pej (novel, magazine)* à sensation❑

pulsar ['pʌlsɑː(r)] N *Astron* pulsar *m*

pulsate [pʌl'seɪt] VI **1** *(throb ▸ heart)* battre fort, palpiter; *(▸ music, room)* vibrer; **the pulsating rhythm of jazz** le rythme syncopé du jazz; **the pulsating beat of the drums** le rythme lancinant des tambours **2** *Phys* subir des pulsations; *Astron (variable star)* pulser

pulsation [pʌl'seɪʃən] **N** *(of heart, arteries)* battement *m*, pulsation *f*; *Astron & Phys* pulsation *f*

pulse [pʌls] **N 1** *Med* pouls *m*; *(single throb)* pulsation *f*; **he took my p.** il m'a pris le pouls, il a pris mon pouls; **her p. (rate) is a hundred** son pouls est à cent (pulsations par minute); **my p. quickens when I see her** quand je la vois, j'ai le cœur qui bat plus fort; *Fig* **to have one's finger on the p.** être à la page; *Fig* **to keep one's finger on the p.** se tenir au courant

2 *Electron & Phys (series)* série *f* d'impulsions; *(single)* impulsion *f*

3 *(vibration)* rythme *m* régulier; **I felt the p. of the ship's motors** je sentais le rythme régulier des moteurs du navire

4 *(bustle, life)* animation *f*

5 *Bot (plant)* légumineuse *f*; *Culin* **(dried) pulses** légumes *mpl* secs

VI *(blood)* battre; *(music, room)* vibrer; **a vein pulsed in his temple** une veine palpitait sur sa tempe; **the whole place pulsed with life** il y avait partout une animation extraordinaire

►► ***pulse rate*** fréquence *f* du pouls; **an exercise that increases the p. rate** un exercice qui fait accélérer le rythme cardiaque

pulverization, -isation [ˌpʌlvəraɪ'zeɪʃən] **N** pulvérisation *f*

pulverize, -ise ['pʌlvəraɪz] **VT** *also Fig* pulvériser

puma ['pju:mə] *(pl* **inv** *or* **pumas) N** *Zool* puma *m*, couguar *m*, cougouar *m*

pumice ['pʌmɪs] **N** ponce *f*

VT poncer, passer à la pierre ponce

►► ***pumice stone*** pierre *f* ponce

pummel ['pʌməl] *(Br pt & pp* **pummelled**, *cont* **pummelling**, *Am pt & pp* **pummeled**, *cont* **pummeling**) **VT 1** *(punch)* donner des coups de poing à, marteler à coups de poing; *Fig (thrash)* battre à plate(s) couture(s); **she pummelled his chest** elle lui martelait la poitrine à coups de poings *ou* de ses poings; **to be pummelled by artillery** être pilonné par les tirs d'artillerie **2** *(in massage)* masser, palper **3** *(knead ▸ dough)* pétrir

pummelling, *Am* **pummeling** ['pʌməlɪŋ] **N** volée *f* de coups, raclée *f*; **to give sb a good p.** donner une bonne raclée à qn; **to get a p.** *(boxer)* se faire taper dessus; *Fig (team)* se faire battre à plate(s) couture(s)

pump [pʌmp] **N 1** *Tech* pompe *f*; **hand/water p.** pompe *f* à main/à eau **2** *(shoe ▸ for dancing)* chausson *m*; *(▸ for gym)* (chaussure *f* de) tennis *m* **3** *Am Fam (heart)* cœur◻ *m*, palpitant *m*

VT 1 *(liquid, gas)* pomper; **to p. sth out of sth** pomper *ou* aspirer qch de qch; **the water is pumped into a tank** l'eau est acheminée dans un réservoir au moyen d'une pompe; **the factory pumps its waste directly into the river** l'usine déverse ses déchets directement dans la rivière; **they pumped air into the football** ils ont gonflé le ballon de foot; **the heart's function is to p. blood around the body** le cœur a pour fonction de pomper le sang dans tout le corps; **coolant is pumped through the system** une pompe fait circuler le liquide de refroidissement dans le système; *Am* **to p. gas** travailler comme pompiste

2 *Med* **to p. sb's stomach** faire un lavage d'estomac à qn; **he had to have** *or* **to get his stomach pumped** on a dû lui faire un lavage d'estomac

3 *(inflate ▸ tyre, ball etc)* gonfler

4 *(move back and forth ▸ pedal, handle)* appuyer sur *ou* actionner (plusieurs fois); **p. the brakes or they'll lock** freinez progressivement ou les freins se bloqueront; *Fig* **to p. sb's hand** secouer vigoureusement la main de qn; *Fam* **to p. iron** faire de la gonflette

5 *Fam (shoot)* **to p. sb full of lead** cribler qn de plomb

6 *Fam (money)* investir◻; **public money is being pumped into the area** la région reçoit d'importantes subventions du gouvernement◻; **the government has pumped money into the project** le gouvernement a injecté des capitaux dans ce projet◻

7 *Fam (interrogate)* interroger◻, tirer les vers du nez à; **they pumped her for information** ils l'ont cuisinée

VI 1 *(machine, person)* pomper; *(heart)* battre fort **2** *(liquid)* couler à flots, jaillir; **blood pumped from the wound** du sang coulait de la blessure

►► ***pump attendant*** pompiste *mf*; ***pump gun*** fusil *m* à pompe; *Econ* ***pump priming*** = relance de l'économie par injection de fonds publics; ***pump room*** *(building)* pavillon *m*; *(room)* buvette *f* *(dans une station thermale)*

▸**pump in VT SEP 1** *(liquid, gas)* refouler; **the village pumps in water from the river** l'eau du village est amenée de la rivière à l'aide d'un système de pompage **2** *Fam (funds, capital)* investir◻, injecter◻

▸**pump out VT SEP 1** *(liquid, gas)* pomper; *(stomach)* vider **2** *Fam Pej (mass-produce ▸ music, graduates, products)* produire◻; *(▸ books, essays)* produire à la chaîne◻, pondre en série◻

VI *(liquid, blood)* couler à flots

▸**pump up VT SEP 1** *(liquid, mixture)* pomper **2** *(inflate)* gonfler **3** *Am Fam (excite)* **to be all pumped up** être tout excité◻

pump-action shotgun N fusil *m* à pompe

pumped [pʌmpt] **ADJ 1** *(gen)* pompé **2** *Fam (exhausted)* **p. (out)** épuisé◻, éreinté, pompé **3** *Am Fam (excited)* surexcité◻; *(enthusiastic)* emballé

pumping ['pʌmpɪŋ] **N**

►► ***pumping station*** station *f* de pompage; *(machinery)* installation *f* de pompage

pumpkin ['pʌmpkɪn] **N** potiron *m*; *(smaller)* citrouille *f*

COMP *(soup)* au potiron

►► *Am Culin* ***pumpkin pie*** tarte *f* au potiron

pun [pʌn] *(pt & pp* **punned**, *cont* **punning**) **N** calembour *m*, jeu *m* de mots

VI faire des calembours, faire des jeux de mots;

Punch [pʌntʃ] **PR N** ≃ Polichinelle; **P.-and-Judy show** ≃ (spectacle *m* de) guignol *m*; **as pleased as P.** heureux comme un roi

> **PUNCH AND JUDY**
>
> En Grande-Bretagne, le "Punch and Judy show" est un spectacle pour enfants semblable aux Guignols en France. Il est souvent présenté dans un jardin public ou sur une plage. On y retrouve Punch le bossu, sa femme Judy avec laquelle il se querelle constamment, et leur chien Toby.

punch [pʌntʃ] **N 1** *(blow)* coup *m* de poing; **he gave him a p. on the chin/in the stomach** il lui a donné un coup de poing dans le menton/dans l'estomac; *Fam* **to pack a powerful** *or* **mean p.** *(hit hard)* cogner dur◻; *Boxing* avoir du punch◻; *(drink, cocktail)* être costaud; *(film)* être percutant◻

2 *Fig (effectiveness ▸ of person)* punch *m inv*; *(of speech, cartoon, play)* mordant *m*; **find a slogan with a bit more p.** trouvez un slogan un peu plus accrocheur

3 *(for holes ▸ in paper)* perforateur *m inv*; *(▸ in metal)* poinçonneuse *f*; *(for tickets ▸ by hand)* poinçonneuse *f*; *(▸ machine)* composteur *m*; *(steel rod, die)* poinçon *m*

4 *(for stamping design)* machine *f* à estamper

5 *(for nails, bolts)* chasse-clou *m*

6 *(drink)* punch *m*

VT 1 *(hit ▸ once)* donner un coup de poing à; *(▸ repeatedly)* marteler à coups de poing; **he punched him on the chin/nose** il lui a donné un coup de poing au menton/sur le nez; **to p. the air** lever le bras en signe de victoire

2 *(key, button)* appuyer sur

3 *(pierce ▸ ticket)* poinçonner; *(▸ in machine)* composter; *(▸ paper, computer card)* perforer; *(▸ sheet metal)* poinçonner; **to p. a hole in sth** faire un trou dans qch; **to p. the time clock** *or* **one's time card** pointer

4 *(stamp)* estamper

5 *Am* **to p. cattle** être cowboy

VI *(strike)* frapper; **no punching!** pas de coups de poing!; **they were punching away at each other** ils se donnaient des coups de poing

►► ***punch bowl*** *(container)* coupe *f* à punch; *Br Geog (between two hills)* cuvette *f*; *Am Comput* ***punch card*** carte *f* perforée; ***punch line*** chute *f* *(d'une histoire drôle)*; **I've forgotten the p. line** j'ai oublié la chute *ou* comment ça finit

▸**punch in VT SEP 1** *(enter ▸ code, number)* tape composer; *(▸ figures, data)* introduire; **p. yo number in** composez votre numéro **2** *(knock ▸ door)* défoncer (à coups de poing); *(▸ nail* enfoncer; *Fam* **I'll p. your face** *or* **head** *or* **teeth i** je vais te casser la figure!

VI *Am (on time clock)* pointer (en arrivant)

▸**punch out VT SEP 1** *(enter ▸ code, number)* ta per, composer

2 *(cut out ▸ form, pattern)* découper; **the hole are punched out by a machine** les trous sont fai par une machine

3 *(remove ▸ nail, bolt)* enlever au chasse-clou

4 *(stamp)* estamper, emboutir

5 *Fam Br* **to p. sb's lights out**, *Am* **to p. sb out** *(be up)* tabasser qn, amocher qn; *Am* **to get punche out** se faire tabasser *ou* amocher; *Am* **to p. it o with sb** échanger des coups de poing avec qn

VI *Am (on time clock)* pointer (en partant)

punchbag ['pʌntʃbæg] **N** *Br Sport* sac *m* de sabl punching-bag *m*; *Fig (victim)* souffr douleur *m inv*

punchball ['pʌntʃbɔ:l] **N** *Sport* **1** *Br (used for trai ing)* punching-ball *m* **2** *Am (game)* = versio simplifiée du base-ball, qui se joue sans batt et avec une balle moins dure

punch-drunk ADJ *(boxer)* groggy *(inv)*; *F* abruti, sonné; **I was p. after seeing four films in row** après avoir vu quatre films d'affilée, j'éta complètement abruti

puncher ['pʌntʃə(r)] **N 1** *Tech (person ▸ of she metal)* poinçonneur(euse) *m,f*, perceur(euse *m,f*; *(▸ in metalworking)* estampeur(euse) *m,f*

2 *Tech (device ▸ for sheet metal)* poinçonneuse *(▸ for cardboard, leather)* emporte-pièce *m in Comput (for cards, tapes)* perforatrice *f*

3 *Boxing* puncheur *m*

4 *Am* **cow p.** cow-boy *m*

punchiness ['pʌntʃɪnɪs] **N** *Fam* punch *m*, pêche

punching ['pʌntʃɪŋ] **N**

►► *Am* ***punching bag*** *Sport* sac *m* de sabl punching-bag *m*; *Fig (victim)* souffre-douleur *inv*; *Am Sport* ***punching ball*** punching-ball *m*

punchtape reader ['pʌntʃteɪp-] **N** lecteur *m* d ruban perforé

punch-up N *Fam* bagarre◻ *f*; **they had a p.** ils s sont bagarrés

punchy ['pʌntʃɪ] *(compar* **punchier**, *superl* **punc iest) ADJ** *Fam* **1** *(slogan, speech, novel)* percutant **2** *(boxer)* groggy◻ *(inv)*; *Fig* abruti, sonné

punctilious [pʌŋk'tɪlɪəs] **ADJ** pointilleux, mét culeux

punctiliously [pʌŋk'tɪlɪəslɪ] **ADV** pointilleuse ment, de façon pointilleuse

punctiliousness [pʌŋk'tɪlɪəsnɪs] **N** grande a tention *f* portée aux détails, méticulosité *f*

punctual ['pʌŋktʃuəl] **ADJ** *(bus)* à l'heure; *(pe son)* ponctuel; **be p. for the interview** soyez l'heure pour l'entretien

punctuality [ˌpʌŋktʃu'ælətɪ] **N** ponctualité exactitude *f*

punctually ['pʌŋktʃuəlɪ] **ADV** *(begin, arrive)* l'heure; *(pay)* ponctuellement; **the flight left at nine/at noon** le vol est parti à neuf heure pile/à midi juste

punctuate ['pʌŋktʃueɪt] **VT 1** *(sentence etc)* ponc tuer **2** *Fig* **a speech punctuated with anecdotes/ap plause** un discours ponctué *ou* agrément d'anecdotes/entrecoupé d'applaudissement **a landscape punctuated with clumps of trees** u paysage avec ça et là un bouquet d'arbres

punctuation [ˌpʌŋktʃu'eɪʃən] **N** ponctuation *f*

►► ***punctuation mark*** signe *m* de ponctuation

puncture ['pʌŋktʃə(r)] **N 1** *(in tyre, ball, balloor* crevaison *f*; **one of the front tyres had a p.** un de pneus avant était crevé; **I had a p. on the way t work** j'ai crevé en allant travailler; **the garage ha repaired the p.** le garage a réparé le pneu crevé *(gen ▸ hole)* perforation *f* **3** *Med* ponction *f*, ponc ture *f*

VT 1 *(gen)* perforer; **the bullet punctured his lun** la balle lui a perforé le poumon **2** *(tyre, ball, ba loon)* crever **3** *Fig (pride, self-esteem)* blesse porter atteinte à

VI crever

►► ***puncture patch*** *(for repairing inner tube)* rus

tine® *f*; ***puncture repair kit*** trousse *f* de réparation pour crevaisons; *Med* ***puncture wound*** blessure *f* pénétrante

pundit [ˈpʌndɪt] **N 1** *(expert)* expert *m (qui pontifie)* **2** *(Brahmin)* pandit *m*

pungency [ˈpʌndʒənsɪ] **N 1** *(of smell, taste, food ▸ sourness)* âcreté *f*; *(▸ spiciness)* piquant *m* **2** *(of wit, remark)* causticité *f*, mordant *m*

pungent [ˈpʌndʒənt] **ADJ 1** *(smell, taste ▸ sour)* âcre; *(▸ spicy)* piquant **2** *(wit, remark)* caustique, mordant

pungently [ˈpʌndʒəntlɪ] **ADV** d'une manière piquante

Punic [ˈpjuːnɪk] **ADJ** punique
▸▸ *Hist* ***the Punic Wars*** les guerres *fpl* puniques

puniness [ˈpjuːnɪnɪs] **N** faiblesse *f*

punish [ˈpʌnɪʃ] **VT 1** *(person, crime)* punir; **to p. sb for having done sth** *or* **for doing sth** punir qn pour avoir fait qch; **they will be punished for their mistakes** ils seront punis pour leurs erreurs; **such offences are punished by imprisonment** ce genre de délit est passible d'une peine de prison **2** *Fam Fig (opponent, enemy)* malmener; *(engine)* fatiguer, forcer; **he really punishes himself in training** il se donne à fond à l'entraînement; *Hum* **to p. a bottle of wine/whisky** faire un sort à une bouteille de vin/de whisky

punishable [ˈpʌnɪʃəbəl] **ADJ** punissable; **p. by prison/a £50 fine** passible d'emprisonnement/d'une amende de 50 livres
▸▸ ***punishable offence*** délit *m*

punishing [ˈpʌnɪʃɪŋ] **N 1** *(punishment)* punition *f* **2** *Fam Fig* **to take a p.** *(opponent, team)* se faire malmener; **the car's suspension/this bottle of wine has taken a p.** la suspension de la voiture/cette bouteille de vin en a pris un coup
ADJ *(heat, climb, effort)* exténuant; *(defeat)* écrasant; **a p. race** une course exténuante; **a p. schedule** un emploi du temps très éprouvant

punishment [ˈpʌnɪʃmənt] **N 1** *(act of punishing)* punition *f*, châtiment *m* **2** *(means of punishment)* punition *f*, châtiment *m*, sanction *f*; *Law* peine *f*; **I had to dig the garden as a p.** comme punition, j'ai dû bêcher le jardin; **to take one's p. like a man** recevoir sa punition sans broncher; **no p. is harsh enough for them** aucune peine n'est assez sévère pour eux; **to make the p. fit the crime** adapter le châtiment au délit **3** *Fam Fig* **to take a lot of p.** *(boxer)* encaisser; *(army, warship, tank, car, boat etc)* être malmené; *(shoes, clothes)* être soumis à rude épreuve

punitive [ˈpjuːnɪtɪv] **ADJ 1** *(expedition, method)* punitif **2** *(measures, tax)* écrasant; **to take p. action** avoir recours à des sanctions
▸▸ *Law* ***punitive damages*** dommages et intérêts *mpl* dissuasifs

Punjab [ˌpʌnˈdʒɑːb] **N the P.** le Pendjab

Punjabi [ˌpʌnˈdʒɑːbɪ] **N 1** *(person)* Pendjabi *mf* **2** *Ling* pendjabi *m*
ADJ pendjabi, du Pendjab

punk [pʌŋk] **N 1** *(music, fashion)* punk *m* **2** *(punk rocker)* punk *mf* **3** *Am very Fam (worthless person)* vaurien(enne) *m,f*; *(hoodlum)* voyou *m*
ADJ 1 *(music, fashion)* punk *(inv)* **2** *Am Fam (worthless)* nul **3** *Am very Fam (ill)* **he's feeling kind of p.** il se sent un peu nase
▸▸ ***punk rock*** punk *m*; ***punk rocker*** punk *mf*

punnet [ˈpʌnɪt] **N** *Br* barquette *f*

punster [ˈpʌnstə(r)] **N** faiseur(euse) *m,f* de calembours *ou* de jeux de mots

punt¹ [pʌnt] **N 1** *(boat)* = longue barque à fond plat manœuvrée à la perche **2** *Sport (kick)* coup *m* de pied de volée **3** *Br Fam (bet)* **to have a p. (on sth)** parier (sur qch)
VT 1 *(boat)* faire avancer à la perche **2** *Sport (kick)* envoyer d'un coup de pied de volée
VI 1 *(in boat)* **to go punting** faire un tour en barque **2** *Br Fam (gamble)* jouer
▸▸ ***punt pole*** perche *f (pour la conduite d'un bateau à fond plat)*

punt² [pʊnt] **N** *Formerly (currency)* livre *f* irlandaise

punter [ˈpʌntə(r)] **N** *Br Fam* **1** *(gambler)* parieur(euse) *m,f*
2 *(consumer, customer)* client(e) *m,f*; **the average p.** *(typical customer)* le client type *ou* moyen; *(typical person)* l'homme *m* de la rue; **the punters** le public
3 *St Exch (speculator)* boursicoteur(euse) *m,f*, boursicotier(ère) *m,f*
4 *(prostitute's client)* micheton *m*

puny [ˈpjuːnɪ] *(compar* **punier**, *superl* **puniest)** **ADJ 1** *(frail ▸ person, animal, plant)* malingre, chétif; *(▸ arms, legs)* maigre, grêle **2** *(feeble ▸ effort)* pitoyable; *(▸ argument, excuse)* piètre

pup [pʌp] *(pt & pp* **pupped**, *cont* **pupping)** **N 1** *(young dog)* chiot *m*; *(young animal)* jeune animal *m*; **spaniel p.** jeune *ou* petit épagneul *m*; **seal p.** jeune *ou* bébé phoque *m*; **to be in p.** *(bitch)* être pleine; *Br Fam Fig* **to be sold a p.** se faire avoir **2** *Fam (youth ▸ self-important)* freluquet *m*; *(▸ inexperienced)* blanc-bec *m*; **you cheeky young p.!** espèce de petit impertinent!
VI mettre bas
▸▸ ***pup tent*** canadienne *f*

pupa [ˈpjuːpə] *(pl* **pupas** *or* **pupae** [-piː]) **N** *Entom* nymphe *f*, chrysalide *f*, pupe *f*

pupate [pjuːˈpeɪt] **VI** *Entom* se métamorphoser (en nymphe *ou* en chrysalide)

pupil [ˈpjuːpəl] **N 1** *Sch* élève *mf* **2** *Law (minor ward)* pupille *mf* **3** *Anat* pupille *f*
COMP *Sch (participation, power)* des élèves

pupilage, pupillage [ˈpjuːpɪlɪdʒ] **N** *Law* **1** *(of minor ward)* pupillarité *f*; **a child in p.** un enfant en pupille *ou* en tutelle **2** *(of junior lawyer)* stage *m (d'avocat)*

pupilometer [ˌpjuːpɪˈlɒmɪtə(r)] **N** pupillomètre *m*

puppet [ˈpʌpɪt] **N 1** *(gen)* marionnette *f*; *(string puppet)* fantoche *m*, pantin *m* **2** *Fig* pantin *m*, fantoche *m*
COMP *Pol (government, president)* fantoche
▸▸ *Pol* ***puppet monarch*** souverain(e) *m,f* fantoche; ***puppet show*** (spectacle *m* de) marionnettes *fpl*; ***puppet theatre*** théâtre *m* de marionnettes

puppeteer [ˌpʌpɪˈtɪə(r)] **N** marionnettiste *mf*

puppetry [ˈpʌpɪtrɪ] **N** *(art ▸ of making)* fabrication *f* de marionnettes; *(▸ of manipulating)* art *m* du marionnettiste

puppy [ˈpʌpɪ] *(pl* **puppies)** **N** chiot *m*
▸▸ ***puppy farm*** chenil *m*, élevage *m* de chiens; *Br* ***puppy fat*** *(UNCOUNT)* rondeurs *fpl* de l'adolescence; ***puppy love*** amourette *f*, amour *m* d'adolescent; **it's only p. love** ce n'est qu'une amourette *ou* qu'un amour de jeunesse

purblind [ˈpɜːblaɪnd] **ADJ 1** *(poorly sighted)* malvoyant **2** *Literary (obtuse)* obtus, borné

purchase [ˈpɜːtʃəs] **VT** acheter; **to p. sth from sb** acheter qch à qn; **to p. sth for sb, to p. sb sth** acheter qch à *ou* pour qn; **to p. sth on credit** acheter qch à crédit; *Acct* **to p. a debt** racheter une créance
N 1 *(act of buying, thing bought)* achat *m*; **to make a p.** faire un achat; **date of p.** date *f* d'achat **2** *(of company)* rachat *m* **3** *(grip)* prise *f*; **she managed to gain (a) p. on a small ledge** elle parvint à trouver une prise sur une petite corniche
VI acheter; **now is the time to p.** c'est maintenant qu'il faut acheter
▸▸ *Acct* ***purchase account*** compte *m* d'achats; *Am Acct* ***purchase accounting*** = méthode de comptabilité utilisée lors de l'acquistion d'une entreprise, dans laquelle les résultats de la filiale n'apparaissent pas dans le bilan de la société mère; ***purchase agreement*** engagement *m* d'achat; *Acct* ***purchase budget*** budget *m* des approvisionnements; ***purchase cost*** coût *m* d'achat; *Acct* ***purchase of debts*** rachat *m* des créances; *Mktg* ***purchase decision*** décision *f* d'achat; *Mktg* ***purchase diary*** relevé *m* d'achat journalier; *Acct* ***purchase entry*** écriture *f* d'achats; *Mktg* ***purchase environment*** environnement *m* d'achat; *Acct* ***purchase invoice*** facture *f* d'achat; *Acct* ***purchase invoice ledger*** journal *m* factures-fournisseurs; *Acct* ***purchase ledger*** (grand-)livre *m* d'achats, journal *m* des achats; *Acct* ***purchase method*** méthode *f* d'achat; *Fin* ***purchase note*** bordereau *m* d'achat; ***purchase order*** *Fin (for goods, service)* bon *m* de commande; *St Exch (for shares)* ordre *m* d'achat; ***purchase price*** prix *m* d'achat; *Fin* ***purchase tax*** taxe *f* à l'achat; *Fin* ***purchase value*** valeur *f* d'achat

> Note that the French verb **pourchasser** is a false friend and is never a translation for the English word **to purchase**. It means **to chase**.

purchaser [ˈpɜːtʃəsə(r)] **N** acheteur(euse) *m,f*

purchasing [ˈpɜːtʃəsɪŋ] **N** achat *m*; *(of company)* rachat *m*
▸▸ *Am* ***purchasing agent*** acheteur(euse) *m,f*; *Mktg* ***purchasing behaviour*** comportement *m* d'achat; ***purchasing costs*** frais *mpl* de passation de commande; *Mktg* ***purchasing decision*** décision *f* d'achat; ***purchasing department*** service *m* des achats; ***purchasing manager*** chef *m* des achats; *Econ* ***purchasing power*** pouvoir *m* d'achat, capacité *f* d'achat; *Mktg* ***purchasing process*** processus *m* d'achat; ***purchasing rights*** droits *mpl* d'achat

purdah [ˈpɜːdə] **N** = chez certains peuples hindous et musulmans, système qui astreint les femmes à une vie retirée; **to be in p.** être reclus; *Fig* vivre en reclus

pure [pjʊə(r)] **ADJ 1** *(unadulterated, untainted)* pur; **a p. silk tie** une cravate (en) pure soie; **p. new wool** laine *f* vierge; **p. air** air *m* pur; **p. water** eau *f* pure; **p. white** blanc *m* immaculé; **the p. tones of the flute** le son clair *ou* pur de la flûte
2 *(chaste ▸ person, mind, life)* pur; **p. thoughts** pensées *fpl* pures; *Bible* **the p. in heart** ceux qui ont le cœur pur; **as p. as the driven snow** *(not guilty)* blanc (blanche) comme neige; *(chaste)* innocent comme l'enfant *ou* l'agneau qui vient de naître
3 *(science, maths, research)* pur
4 *(as intensifier)* pur; **by p. chance** par (un) pur hasard; **it's the truth, p. and simple** c'est la vérité pure et simple

pure-blood **ADJ** *(horse)* pur-sang *inv*
N *(horse)* pur-sang *m inv*

pure-blooded **ADJ** pur-sang *(inv)*

purebred [ˈpjʊəbred] **ADJ** de race (pure); *(horse)* pur-sang *(inv)*

puree, purée [ˈpjʊəreɪ] *(pt & pp* **pureed** *or* **puréed**, *cont* **pureeing** *or* **puréeing)** **N** purée *f*; **tomato p.** *(gen)* purée *f* de tomates; *(in tube)* concentré *m* de tomates
VT réduire en purée; **pureed carrots** purée *f* de carottes

purely [ˈpjʊəlɪ] **ADJ** purement; **p. and simply** purement et simplement; **ours is a p. professional relationship** nos rapports sont purement *ou* strictement professionnels; **it was p. by chance that we met** notre rencontre n'était qu'un pur hasard

pureness [ˈpjʊənɪs] **N** pureté *f*

purgation [pɜːˈgeɪʃən] **N 1** *Med (of intestine)* purge *f* **2** *Rel (in purgatory)* purgation *f* de l'âme

purgative [ˈpɜːgətɪv] *Med* **N** purgatif *m*
ADJ purgatif

purgatory [ˈpɜːgətərɪ] **N** *Rel* purgatoire *m*; *Fig* enfer *m*; **the souls in p.** les âmes du purgatoire, les âmes en peine; **rush hour is absolute p.!** les heures de pointe sont un véritable enfer!

purge [pɜːdʒ] **VT 1** *Pol (party, organization)* purger, épurer; *(undesirable elements)* éliminer; **the extreme right was purged from the party** le parti s'est débarrassé de son extrême droite
2 *(free, rid)* débarrasser, délivrer; **p. your mind of such morbid ideas** chassez ces idées morbides de votre esprit; *Rel* **to p. oneself of** *or* **from sin** se laver de ses péchés
3 *Law (clear)* disculper, innocenter; *Am Law* **to p. one's contempt** faire amende honorable *(pour outrage aux magistrats)*
4 *Med (bowels)* purger
N 1 *(gen) & Pol* purge *f*, épuration *f*; **he carried out a p. of the army** il procéda à une purge au sein de l'armée **2** *Med* purge *f*

purging [ˈpɜːdʒɪŋ] **N** *Med (of body)* purge *f*, purification *f*; *Pol (of party, organization)* épuration *f*

purification [ˌpjʊərɪfɪˈkeɪʃən] **N 1** *(of water, oil)* épuration *f* **2** *Rel* purification *f*; **the P. (of the Virgin Mary)** la Purification (de la Vierge Marie)

purifier [ˈpjʊərɪfaɪə(r)] **N** *(device ▸ for water, oil)* épurateur *m*; *(▸ for air, atmosphere)* purificateur *m*, assainisseur *m*

purify ['pjʊərɪfaɪ] (*pt & pp* **purified**) **VT** *(water, oil)* épurer; *(air, soul, mind)* purifier; *(blood)* dépurer

purist ['pjʊərɪst] **ADJ** puriste

N puriste *mf*; **a linguistic p.** un(e) puriste en matière de linguistique

puritan ['pjʊərɪtən] **N** puritain(e) *m,f*

ADJ puritain

• **Puritan** *Rel* **N** puritain(e) *m,f* **ADJ** puritain

puritanical [,pjʊərɪ'tænɪkəl] **ADJ** puritain, de puritain

puritanism ['pjʊərɪtənɪzəm] **N** puritanisme *m*

purity ['pjʊərɪtɪ] **N** pureté *f*; **degree of p.** *(of water etc)* (degré *m* de) pureté *f*; *(of gold)* titre *m*

purl [pɜːl] *Knitting* **N** maille *f* à l'envers

VT tricoter à l'envers; **knit one, p. one** une maille à l'endroit, une maille à l'envers

►► ***purl stitch*** maille *f* à l'envers

purlieus ['pɜːljuːz] **NPL** *Literary* alentours *mpl*, environs *mpl*; **in the p. of** aux alentours de, dans les environs de

purloin [pɜː'lɔɪn] **VT** *Formal or Hum* dérober, voler

purple ['pɜːpəl] **N 1** *(colour* ► *gen)* violet *m*; *(*► *reddish)* pourpre *m* **2** *(dye, cloth)* pourpre *f* **3** *(high rank)* **the p.** la pourpre

ADJ 1 *(in colour* ► *gen)* violet; *(*► *reddish)* pourpre; **he turned** *or* **went p. (with rage)** il est devenu cramoisi (de rage) **2** *(prose)* emphatique, ampoulé

►► *Entom* ***purple emperor*** grand mars *m* (changeant); *Mil* ***Purple Heart*** = médaille décernée aux blessés de guerre de l'armée américaine; *Fam Drugs slang* ***purple heart*** pilule *f* d'amphétamine; *Br* ***purple passage, purple patch*** *(of writing)* morceau *m* de bravoure; *(period of success)* **he's been going through a p. patch recently: he's won five out of the last six tournaments he's entered** il est dans une bonne période: il a gagné cinq des six tournois auxquels il a participé; ***purple sprouting broccoli*** brocoli *m* violet

purplish ['pɜːplɪʃ], **purply** ['pɜːplɪ] **ADJ** *(gen)* violacé, violâtre; *(reddish)* pourpré, purpurin; *(of the face)* cramoisi; **p. red** rouge violacé; **p. blue** hyacinthe *(inv)*

purport *Formal* **VT** [pə'pɔːt] *(claim)* prétendre; *(of film, book)* se vouloir; **he purports to be an expert** il prétend être un expert, il se fait passer pour un expert; **her book purports to be the definitive work on the French Revolution** son livre se veut la somme de ce qui a été écrit sur la Révolution française

N ['pɜːpɔːt] signification *f*, teneur *f*

purpose ['pɜːpəs] **N 1** *(objective, reason)* but *m*, objet *m*; **what's the p. of your visit?** quel est le but *ou* l'objet de votre visite?; **for** *or* **with the p. of doing sth** dans l'intention *ou* le but de faire qch; **he buys real estate for tax purposes** il investit dans l'immobilier pour des raisons fiscales; **it suits my purposes to stay here** j'ai de bonnes raisons de rester ici; **to do sth with a p. in mind** *or* **for a p.** faire qch dans un but précis; **for this p.** dans ce but, à cet effet; **but that's the whole p. of the exercise!** mais tout l'intérêt de l'exercice est là!; **to have a sense of p.** être motivé; **to give sb a sense of p.** motiver qn; **his life lacked any real sense of p.** sa vie était dépourvue de but précis; **to have a p. in life** avoir un but dans la vie; **her remarks were to the p./not to the p.** ses remarques étaient pertinentes/hors de propos

2 *(use, function)* usage *m*; *(end, result)* fin *f*; **what is the p. of this room/object?** à quoi sert cette pièce/cet objet?; **the hangar wasn't built for that p.** le hangar n'était pas destiné à cet usage; **for all purposes** à toutes fins, à tous usages; **for our purposes** pour ce que nous voulons faire; **for the purposes of this demonstration** pour les besoins de cette démonstration; **£5,000 will be enough for present purposes** 5000 livres suffiront à couvrir nos besoins actuels; **the funds are to be used for humanitarian purposes** les fonds seront utilisés à des fins humanitaires; **intended p.** *(of building, amount of money)* destination *f*, affectation *f*; **they were never used for their intended p.** ils n'ont jamais servi à l'usage auquel on les destinait; **does it serve any useful p.?** est-ce que ça sert à quelque chose?; **to serve no p.** ne servir à rien; **this will suit** *or* **serve your p.** cela fera votre affaire; **once she had served her p. they abandoned her** une fois qu'elle eut tenu son rôle, ils l'abandonnèrent; **the money will be put** *or* **used to good p.** l'argent sera bien employé; **he will use his knowledge to good p. there** il pourra y mettre à profit ses connaissances; **we are arguing to no p.** nous discutons inutilement; **my efforts had been to no p.** mes efforts étaient restés vains; **the negotiations have been to little p.** les négociations n'ont pas abouti à grand-chose

3 *(determination)* résolution *f*, détermination *f*; **she has great strength of p.** elle a une volonté de fer, c'est quelqu'un de très déterminé

VT *Literary* **to p. to do sth** *or* **doing sth** se proposer de faire qch

• **on purpose** **ADV** exprès; **I did it on p.** je l'ai fait exprès; **I avoided the subject on p.** j'ai fait exprès d'éviter *ou* j'ai délibérément évité la question

purpose-built **ADJ** *Br* construit *ou* conçu pour un usage spécifique; **a p. conference centre** un centre de conférence entièrement conçu pour cet usage; **p. flats for the disabled** appartements *mpl* spécialement adaptés aux besoins des handicapés

purposeful ['pɜːpəsfʊl] **ADJ** *(person)* résolu, déterminé; *(look, walk)* résolu, décidé; *(act)* réfléchi

purposefully ['pɜːpəsfʊlɪ] **ADV** *(for a reason)* dans un but précis, délibérément; *(determinedly)* d'un air résolu; **she walked forward p.** elle avança d'un pas résolu

> Attention: ne pas confondre avec **purposely**, qui signifie **délibérément**.

purposeless ['pɜːpəslɪs] **ADJ** *(life)* sans but, vide de sens; *(act, violence)* gratuit

purposely ['pɜːpəslɪ] **ADV** exprès, délibérément; **they p. didn't invite her** ils ont fait exprès de ne pas l'inviter

> Attention: ne pas confondre avec **purposefully**, qui signifie **avec détermination**.

purr [pɜː(r)] **VI** *(cat, engine)* ronronner

VT susurrer; **"do have another drink," she purred** "vous prendrez bien encore un verre", susurra-t-elle

N *(of cat)* ronronnement *m*, ronron *m*; *(of engine)* ronronnement *m*

purring ['pɜːrɪŋ] **N** *(UNCOUNT) (of cat)* ronronnement *m*, ronron *m*; *(of engine)* ronronnement *m*

ADJ qui ronronne

purse [pɜːs] **N 1** *Br (for coins)* porte-monnaie *m inv*

2 *Am (handbag)* sac *m* à main

3 *Fig (wealth, resources)* bourse *f*; **to hold** *or* **to control the p. strings** tenir les cordons de la bourse; **the public p.** le Trésor public; *Old-fashioned* **it is beyond my p.** c'est au-dessus de mes moyens

4 *Sport (prize money)* prix *m*

VT to p. (up) one's lips *or* **mouth** pincer les lèvres

►► ***purse net*** bourse *f*; *Fishing* ***purse seine*** bourse *f*; *Am* ***purse snatching*** vol *m* à l'arraché

purser ['pɜːsə(r)] **N** *Naut* commissaire *m* du bord

pursuance [pə'sjuːəns] **N** *Formal* exécution *f*, accomplissement *m*; **in (the) p. of his duties** dans l'exercice de ses fonctions; *Law* **in p. of this contract/clause** conformément au présent contrat/à la présente clause

pursuant [pə'sjuːənt] **pursuant to** **PREP** *Formal (following)* à la suite de, suivant; *(in accordance with)* conformément à

pursue [pə'sjuː] **VT 1** *(chase, follow)* poursuivre; *Fig* suivre, poursuivre; **he was being pursued by dogs** il était poursuivi par des chiens; *Literary* **she was pursued by ill fortune/ill health** elle était poursuivie par la malchance/la maladie

2 *(strive for* ► *pleasure, happiness)* rechercher; *(*► *aim)* poursuivre

3 *(studies)* poursuivre; *(course of action)* suivre; *(policy)* mener; **I have no time to p. any hobbies** je n'ai pas de temps à consacrer à des hobbies; **to p. a career in law/journalism** faire carrière dans le droit/le journalisme

4 *(take further* ► *enquiry, matter)* poursuivre; **he became so upset that she decided not to p. the matter** il s'est mis dans un état tel qu'elle a préféré ne pas insister; **if I may p. that line of argument** si je peux me permettre de pousser plus loin *ou* de développer ce raisonnement; **to p. a point** insister sur *ou* revenir sur un point

pursuer [pə'sjuːə(r)] **N** poursuivant(e) *m,f*

pursuit [pə'sjuːt] **N 1** *(chasing)* poursuite *f*; **they went out in p. of the vandals** ils se sont lancés à la poursuite des vandales; **with a pack of dogs in hot p.** avec une meute de chiens à leurs trousses

2 *(of pleasure, knowledge etc)* quête *f*, recherche *f*; **the p. of knowledge/happiness** la quête du savoir/du bonheur; **in p. of fame/glory** en quête de renommée/de gloire

3 *(pastime)* occupation *f*; **leisure pursuits** loisirs *mpl*, passe-temps *mpl*

4 *Sport (in cycling)* poursuite *f*

►► *Mil & Aviat* ***pursuit plane*** avion *m* de chasse; *Cycling* ***pursuit race*** poursuite *f*

purulence ['pjʊərʊləns] **N** purulence *f*

purulent ['pjʊərʊlənt] **ADJ** purulent

purvey [pə'veɪ] **VT 1** *(sell)* vendre, fournir; **to p. sth to sb** fournir qch à qn, approvisionner qn en qch **2** *(communicate* ► *information, news)* communiquer; *(*► *lies, rumours)* colporter

purveyance [pə'veɪəns] **N** fourniture *f*, approvisionnement *m*

purveyor [pə'veɪə(r)] **N** *Formal* **1** *(supplier)* fournisseur(euse) *m,f*; **purveyors of marmalade to HM the Queen** fournisseurs en confiture de Sa Majesté la Reine **2** *(spreader* ► *of gossip, lies)* colporteur(euse) *m,f*

purview ['pɜːvjuː] **N 1** *Formal (scope)* champ *m*, domaine *m*; **the matter falls within/outside the p. of the committee** la question relève/ne relève pas de la compétence du comité **2** *Law (body of statute)* texte *m*

pus [pʌs] **N** pus *m*

PUSH [pʊʃ]

N
- poussée **1**
- effort **5**
- poussée **6**
- mot d'encouragement **2**
- campagne **5**
- dynamisme **7**

VT
- pousser **1, 4**
- appuyer sur **2**
- prôner **5**
- insister sur **6**
- enfoncer **1**
- forcer **4**
- promouvoir **5**
- friser **8**

VI
- pousser **1**
- avancer **3**
- appuyer **2**
- s'étendre **4**

N 1 *(shove)* poussée *f*; **to give sb/sth a p.** pousser qn/qch; **the door opens at the p. of a button** il suffit d'appuyer sur un bouton pour que la porte s'ouvre

2 *(encouragement)* mot *m* d'encouragement; **he'll do it, but he needs a little p.** il le fera, mais il a besoin qu'on le pousse un peu; **he just needs a p. in the right direction** il a juste besoin qu'on le mette sur la bonne voie

3 *Br Fam* **to give sb the p.** *(from job)* virer qn; *(in relationship)* plaquer qn; **he got the p.** *(from job)* il s'est fait virer; *(from relationship)* il s'est fait plaquer

4 *Fam (critical moment)* **when it comes to the p., when p. comes to shove** au moment critique *ou* crucial; **I can lend you the money if it comes to the p.** au pire, je pourrai vous prêter l'argent; **if it comes to the p., he'll choose Sarah, not Gillian** s'il fallait qu'il choisisse, il prendrait Sarah et pas Gillian; **at a p.** à la limite; **I can do it at a p.** je peux le faire si c'est vraiment nécessaire

5 *(effort)* effort *m*, coup *m* de collier; *(campaign)* campagne *f*; **the final p. for the summit** le dernier effort pour atteindre le sommet; **to make a p. for change** lutter pour le changement; **the club's p. for promotion** les efforts soutenus du club pour être promu; **a sales p.** une campagne de promotion des ventes; **the p. towards protectionism is gathering strength** la tendance au protectionnisme se renforce

6 *Mil (advance)* poussée *f*; **the platoon made a p. to capture the airfield** la section a fait une poussée pour s'emparer de l'aérodrome

7 *(drive, dynamism)* dynamisme *m*; **he has a lot of p.** il est très dynamique

8 *(billiards)* coup *m* queuté

9 *Austr Fam (gang)* bande *f*, clique *f*

VT 1 *(shove, propel)* pousser; *(thrust)* enfoncer; **she pushed the door open/shut** elle ouvrit/ferma la porte (en la poussant); **he pushed her onto the chair/into the room** il la poussa sur la chaise/(pour la faire entrer) dans la pièce; **to p. sb into a corner** acculer qn; **to p. sb out of the way** écarter qn; **don't p. (me)!** ne (me) poussez pas!, ne (me) bousculez pas!; **a man was pushed out of the window** quelqu'un a poussé un homme par la fenêtre; *Fig* **did he leave or was he pushed?** *(from job)* il est parti de lui-même ou on l'y a poussé?; **p. all that mess under the bed** pousse tout ce bazar sous le lit; **he pushed the branches apart** il a écarté les branches; **she pushed her way to the bar** elle se fraya un chemin jusqu'au bar; **p. one tube into the other** enfoncez un tube dans l'autre; **he pushed a gun into my ribs** il m'enfonça un revolver dans les côtes; **he pushed his hands into his pockets** il enfonça ses mains dans ses poches; **to p. an attack home** pousser à fond une attaque; **to p. home one's advantage** tirer le meilleur parti possible de son avantage

2 *(press ▸ doorbell, pedal, button)* appuyer sur

3 *(cause to move in specified direction)* **it will p. inflation upwards** cela va relancer l'inflation; **the crisis is pushing the country towards chaos** la crise entraîne le pays vers le chaos; **buying the car will p. us even further into debt** en achetant cette voiture, nous allons nous endetter encore plus; **economic conditions have pushed the peasants off the land** les paysans ont été chassés des campagnes par les conditions économiques

4 *(pressurize)* pousser; *(force)* forcer, obliger, contraindre; **to p. sb to do sth** pousser qn à faire qch; **to p. sb into doing sth** forcer *ou* obliger qn à faire qch; **he needs pushing** il faut toujours le pousser; **their coach doesn't p. them hard enough** leur entraîneur ne les pousse pas assez; **I like to p. myself hard** j'aime me donner à fond; **he pushed the car to its limits** il a poussé la voiture à la limite de ses possibilités; **you're still weak, so don't p. yourself** tu es encore faible, vas-y doucement; **he won't do it if he's pushed too hard** il ne le fera pas si l'on insiste trop; **don't p. him too far** ne le poussez pas à bout; **I won't be pushed, I need time to think it over!** je ne me laisserai pas bousculer, j'ai besoin de temps pour y réfléchir!; **when I pushed her, she admitted it** quand j'ai insisté, elle a avoué; **he keeps pushing me for the rent** il me relance sans cesse au sujet du loyer; *Fam* **don't p. your luck!** n'exagère pas!

5 *(advocate, argue for ▸ idea, method)* prôner, préconiser; *(promote ▸ product)* promouvoir; **he's trying to p. his own point of view** il essaie d'imposer son point de vue personnel; **the mayor is pushing his town as the best site for the conference** le maire présente sa ville comme le meilleur endroit pour tenir la conférence; **the government is pushing the idea of people setting up small businesses** le gouvernement favorise la création de petites entreprises; **he's pushing himself as a compromise candidate** il se présente comme le candidat du compromis

6 *(stretch, exaggerate ▸ argument, case)* présenter avec insistance, insister sur; **if we p. the comparison a little further** si on pousse la comparaison un peu plus loin; *Fam* **that's pushing it a bit!** *(going too far)* c'est un peu exagéré!; **I'll try to arrive by 7 p.m. but it's pushing it a bit** je tâcherai d'arriver à 19 heures, mais ça va être juste□

7 *Fam (sell ▸ drugs)* revendre□, dealer

8 *Fam (approach)* friser; **to be pushing thirty** friser la trentaine; **the car was pushing 100 mph** ≃ la voiture frisait les 160

9 *St Exch* **to p. shares** placer des valeurs douteuses

VI 1 *(shove)* pousser; **to p. against sth** pousser qch; **p.** *(on door)* poussez; **people were pushing to get in** les gens se bousculaient pour entrer; **he pushed through the crowd to the bar** il s'est frayé un chemin jusqu'au bar à travers la foule; **somebody pushed past me** quelqu'un est passé en me bousculant; **we'll have to get out and p.** il va falloir descendre pousser

2 *(press ▸ on button, bell, knob)* appuyer

3 *(advance)* avancer; **the army pushed towards the border** l'armée a avancé jusqu'à la frontière

4 *(extend ▸ path, fence)* s'étendre; **the road pushed deep into the hills** la route s'enfonçait dans les collines

▸▸ ***push button*** bouton-poussoir *m*; *Com* ***push money*** prime *f* au vendeur; ***push stroke*** *(in billiards, snooker)* coup *m* queuté; *Comput* ***push technology*** technologie *f* du push de données

▸ **push about** **VT SEP 1** *(physically)* malmener **2** *Fam (bully)* marcher sur les pieds à; **I won't be pushed about!** je ne vais pas me laisser marcher sur les pieds!

▸ **push ahead** **VI 1** *(continue)* continuer, persévérer; **to p. ahead with the work** poursuivre les travaux; **they decided to p. ahead with the plans to extend the school** ils ont décidé d'activer les projets d'extension de l'école **2** *(advance)* avancer, progresser (**with** dans); **research is pushing ahead** les recherches avancent

▸ **push along** **VT SEP** *(trolley, pram)* pousser (devant soi)

VI *Fam (leave)* filer; **I'll be pushing along now** bon, il est temps que je file

▸ **push around** = **push about**

▸ **push aside** **VT SEP 1** *(objects)* pousser, écarter **2** *(reject ▸ proposal)* écarter, rejeter; **you can't just p. aside the problem like that** vous ne pouvez pas faire comme si le problème n'existait pas; **I pushed my doubts aside** je n'ai pas tenu compte de mes doutes

▸ **push away** **VT SEP** repousser; **he pushed his chair away from the fire** il éloigna sa chaise du feu

▸ **push back** **VT SEP 1** *(person)* repousser (en arrière); *(crowd)* faire reculer, refouler; *(curtains)* écarter; *(bedclothes)* rejeter, repousser; **he pushed me back from the door** il m'a éloigné de la porte **2** *(repulse ▸ troops)* repousser; **the enemy was pushed back ten miles/to the river** l'ennemi a été repoussé d'une quinzaine de kilomètres/jusqu'à la rivière **3** *(postpone)* repousser; **the meeting has been pushed back to Friday** la réunion a été repoussée à vendredi

▸ **push down** **VT SEP 1** *(lever, handle, switch)* abaisser; *(pedal)* appuyer sur; **she pushed the clothes down in the bag** elle a tassé les vêtements dans le sac; **he pushed down the lid but it wouldn't shut** il a appuyé sur le couvercle mais il ne voulait pas fermer **2** *(knock over)* renverser, faire tomber **3** *(prices)* faire baisser

VI *(pedal, lever)* s'abaisser; *(person ▸ on pedal, lever)* appuyer (**on** sur)

▸ **push for** **VT INSEP** *(argue for)* demander; *(campaign for)* faire campagne pour; **to p. for a 35-hour week** demander la semaine de 35 heures; **I'm going to p. for a bigger budget** je vais faire tout ce qui est en mon pouvoir pour obtenir un budget plus important; **the unions are pushing for 10 percent** les syndicats font pression pour obtenir 10 pour cent; **to p. for a decision** exiger qu'une décision soit prise

▸ **push forward** **VT SEP** pousser (en avant); **he was pushed forward by the crowd** la foule l'a poussé en avant; *Fig* **to p. oneself forward** se mettre en avant, se faire valoir

VI 1 *(advance ▸ person, car)* avancer; *(▸ crowd, herd)* se presser en avant **2** = **push ahead**

▸ **push in** **VT SEP 1** *(drawer)* pousser; *(electric plug, key)* enfoncer, introduire; *(disk)* insérer; *(knife, stake, spade)* enfoncer; *(button, switch)* appuyer sur; **p. the button right in** appuyer à fond sur le bouton **2** *(person)* **they pushed me in the water** ils m'ont poussé dans l'eau; **he opened the door and pushed me in** il ouvrit la porte et me poussa à l'intérieur **3** *(break down ▸ panel, cardboard, door)* enfoncer

VI *(in queue)* **to p. in ahead of sb** doubler qn; **no pushing in!** faites la queue!; **she's always pushing in where she's not wanted** il faut toujours qu'elle s'immisce *ou* s'impose là où on ne veut pas d'elle

▸ **push off** **VT SEP 1** *(knock off)* faire tomber; **they pushed me off the ladder** ils m'ont fait tomber de l'échelle **2** *(boat)* déborder **3** *(remove)* pousser; **p. the lid off** soulève le couvercle; **they tried to p. her (car) off the road** ils ont essayé de faire sortir sa voiture de la route; **to p. sb off a committee** exclure *ou* écarter qn d'un comité

VI 1 *Fam (go away)* filer, mettre les bouts; **time for me to p. off** il faut que je file; **p. off!** de l'air!, dégage! **2** *(in boat)* pousser au large

▸ **push on** **VT SEP** *(urge on)* **to p. sb on to do sth** pousser *ou* inciter qn à faire qch

VI *(on journey ▸ set off again)* reprendre la route, se remettre en route; *(▸ continue)* poursuivre *ou* continuer son chemin; *(keep working)* continuer, persévérer; **let's p. on to Dundee** poussons jusqu'à Dundee; **they're pushing on with the reforms** ils poursuivent leurs efforts pour faire passer les réformes

▸ **push out** **VT SEP 1** *(person, object)* pousser dehors; **they pushed the car out of the mud** ils ont désembourbé la voiture en la poussant; **to p. one's way out** se frayer un chemin vers la sortie; **to p. the boat out** déborder l'embarcation; *Fig* faire la fête

2 *(stick out ▸ hand, leg)* tendre

3 *(grow ▸ roots, shoots)* faire, produire

4 *(oust)* évincer; *(dismiss from job)* mettre à la porte; **we've been pushed out of the Japanese market** nous avons été évincés du marché japonais

VI *(appear ▸ roots, leaves)* pousser; *(▸ snowdrops, tulips)* pointer

▸ **push over** **VT SEP 1** *(pass ▸ across table, floor)* pousser; **he pushed the book over to me** il poussa le livre vers moi **2** *(knock over)* faire tomber, renverser; *(from ledge, bridge)* pousser, faire tomber; **many cars had been pushed over onto their sides** beaucoup de voitures avaient été renversées sur le côté

▸ **push through** **VT SEP 1** *(project, decision)* faire accepter; *(deal)* conclure; *(bill, budget)* réussir à faire voter *ou* passer **2** *(thrust ▸ needle)* passer; **she eventually managed to p. her way through (the crowd)** elle réussit finalement à se frayer un chemin (à travers la foule)

VI *(car, person)* se frayer un chemin; *(troops, army)* avancer

▸ **push to** **VT SEP** *(door, drawer)* fermer

▸ **push up** **VT SEP 1** *(push upwards ▸ handle, lever)* remonter, relever; *(▸ sleeves)* remonter, retrousser; **she pushed herself up onto her feet** elle se releva; *Fam* **he's pushing up (the) daisies** il mange les pissenlits par la racine **2** *(increase ▸ taxes, sales, demand)* augmenter; *(▸ prices, costs, statistics)* faire monter; **the effect will be to p. interest rates up** cela aura pour effet de faire grimper les taux d'intérêt

pushbike [ˈpʊʃbaɪk] **N** *Br Fam* vélo□ *m*, bécane *f*

push-button **ADJ** *(telephone)* à touches, à boutons-poussoirs; *(car window)* à commande automatique

▸▸ ***push-button controls*** commandes *fpl* automatiques; ***push-button warfare*** guerre *f* presse-bouton

pushcart [ˈpʊʃkɑːt] **N** *Am* charrette *f* à bras

pushchair [ˈpʊʃtʃeə(r)] **N** *Br* poussette *f*

pusher [ˈpʊʃə(r)] **N** *Fam (drug dealer)* trafiquant (e) *m,f* (de drogue)□, dealer *m*

pushiness [ˈpʊʃɪnɪs] **N** *Fam (ambitiousness)* arrivisme□ *m*; *(forwardness)* insistance□ *f*; **I can't stand his p.** je ne supporte pas sa façon de s'imposer□

pushing [ˈpʊʃɪŋ] **N** bousculade *f*; **no p.!** ne poussez pas!; **there was a lot of p. and shoving** ça poussait et ça se bousculait dans tous les sens

pushover [ˈpʊʃˌəʊvə(r)] **N 1** *Fam (easy thing)* jeu *m* d'enfant; **the exam was a p.** l'examen était un jeu d'enfant; **the match will be a p.** le match, c'est du tout cuit *ou* ça va être du gâteau; **that team are no p.** cette équipe n'est pas du genre à se laisser battre **2** *Fam (gullible person)* poire *f*, pigeon *m*; **he's no p.** il ne se laisse pas avoir facilement; **when it comes to flattery, I'm a complete p.** la flatterie marche à tous les coups avec moi

▸▸ ***pushover try*** *(in rugby)* essai *m* collectif (par les avants)

pushpin [ˈpʊʃpɪn] **N** *Am* punaise *f*

push-pull ADJ
►► *Elec* ***push-pull amplifier*** amplificateur *m* push-pull; ***push-pull circuit*** montage *m* symétrique, push-pull *m inv*; ***push-pull train*** train *m* réversible

pushrod ['pʊʃrɒd] N *Aut* tige *f* de poussoir, tige *f* de culbuteur

push-start N *Aut* **to give sb a p.** pousser la voiture de qn pour la faire démarrer
VT faire démarrer en poussant

push-up N *esp Am* pompe *f (exercice physique)*; **to do push-ups** faire des pompes

pushy ['pʊʃɪ] (*compar* **pushier**, *superl* **pushiest**) ADJ *Fam* **1** *Pej (ambitious)* arriviste▫; *(self-serving)* qui cherche à se faire mousser, qui se met en avant▫; **don't be so p.** arrête de te faire valoir comme ça!▫ **2** *(self-assertive)* **you have to be pretty p. in this work** il faut savoir s'imposer dans ce travail▫

pusillanimity [,pju:sɪlə'nɪmətɪ] N *Formal* pusillanimité *f*

pusillanimous [,pju:sɪ'lænɪməs] ADJ *Formal* pusillanime

puss [pʊs] N **1** *Fam (cat)* minou *m*, minet(ette) *m,f* **2** *Fam (mouth, face)* gueule *f*, binette *f*

pussy ['pʊsɪ] (*pl* **pussies**) N **1** *Fam (cat)* minou *m*, minet(ette) *m,f* **2** *Vulg (female sex organs)* chatte *f*, chagatte *f* **3** *Vulg (women)* nanas *fpl*, cuisse *f*; **they're looking out for p.** ils cherchent des meufs
►► *Bot* ***pussy willow*** saule *m* blanc

pussyfoot ['pʊsɪfʊt] VI *Fam* ne pas se mouiller; **stop pussyfooting (about** *or* **around)!** assez tergiversé!

pussy-whipped ADJ *very Fam* dominé par sa femme▫; **he's totally p.** c'est sa femme qui porte la culotte

pustule ['pʌstju:l] N *Med* pustule *f*

PUT [pʊt]

VT
- mettre **1, 3–6, 9, 10**
- soumettre **8**
- placer **9, 12**
- consacrer **11**
- lancer **14**
- dire **7**
- présenter **8**
- investir **11, 12**
- miser **13**

N
- lancer (du poids) **1**

(*pt & pp* **put**, *cont* **putting**)
VT **1** *(into specified place or position)* mettre; **p. the saucepan on the shelf** mets la casserole sur l'étagère; **she p. her hand on my shoulder** elle a mis sa main sur mon épaule; **p. the chairs nearer the table** approche les chaises de la table; **he p. his arm around my shoulders** il passa son bras autour de mes épaules; **she p. her arms around him** elle l'a pris dans ses bras; **to p. one's head round the door/through the window** passer la tête par la porte/par la fenêtre; **did you p. any salt in?** as-tu mis du sel (dedans)?; **p. some more water on to boil** remettez de l'eau à chauffer; **to p. a coin/a letter/a gun into sb's hand** glisser *ou* mettre une pièce/une lettre/un revolver dans la main de qn; **she p. a match to the wood** elle a allumé le bois; **to p. an advert in the paper** mettre une annonce dans le journal; **they want to p. me in an old folks' home** ils veulent me mettre dans une maison pour les vieux; **to p. a child to bed** mettre un enfant au lit, coucher un enfant; **to p. a man on the moon** envoyer un homme sur la lune; **he p. the telescope to his eye** il a porté la longue-vue à son œil; **to p. honour before riches** préférer l'honneur à l'argent; **to p. a play on the stage** monter une pièce; **to p. a guard on the door** faire surveiller la porte; *Fig* **I didn't know where to p. myself!** je ne savais plus où me mettre!; **p. yourself in my position** *or* **place** mettez-vous à ma place; **to p. oneself into sb's hands** s'en remettre à qn; **p. it out of your mind** *or* **head** sors-le-toi de la tête; **I had long p. this thought out of my mind** ça faisait longtemps que je m'étais sorti cette idée de la tête; **we p. a lot of emphasis on creativity** nous mettons beaucoup l'accent sur la créativité; **don't p. too much trust in what he says** ne te fie pas trop à ce qu'il dit; *Fam* **p. it there!** *(shake hands)* tope-là!, serrons-nous la pince!

2 *(push or send forcefully)* **he p. his fist through the window** il a passé son poing à travers le carreau; **he p. a bullet through his head** il s'est mis une balle dans la tête; **she p. her pen through the whole paragraph** elle a rayé tout le paragraphe d'un coup de stylo

3 *(impose ► limit, responsibility, tax)* mettre; **to p. a ban on sth** interdire qch; **it puts an extra burden on our department** c'est un fardeau de plus pour notre service; **the new tax will p. five pence on a packet of cigarettes** la nouvelle taxe augmentera de cinq pence le prix d'un paquet de cigarettes

4 *(into specified state)* mettre; **you're putting me in an awkward position** vous me mettez dans une situation délicate; **I hope I've not p. you to too much trouble** j'espère que je ne vous ai pas trop dérangé; **music always puts him in a good mood** la musique le met toujours de bonne humeur; **to p. sb out of a job** mettre qn au chômage; **to p. a prisoner on bread and water** mettre un prisonnier au pain sec et à l'eau; **the money will be p. to good use** l'argent sera bien employé

5 *(write down)* mettre, écrire; **I forgot to p. my address** j'ai oublié de mettre mon adresse; **what date shall I p.?** quelle date est-ce que je mets?

6 *(bring about)* **to p. an end** *or* **a stop to sth** mettre fin *ou* un terme à qch

7 *(say, express)* dire, exprimer; **I wouldn't p. it quite like that** je ne dirais pas cela; **I don't know how to p. it** je ne sais comment dire; **to p. one's thoughts into words** exprimer sa pensée, s'exprimer; **let me p. it this way** laissez-moi l'exprimer ainsi; **it was, how shall I p. it, rather long** c'était, comment dirais-je, un peu long; **to p. it another way,...** en d'autres termes,...; **he p. it better than that** il l'a dit *ou* formulé mieux que ça; **she p. it politely but firmly** elle l'a dit poliment mais clairement; **as Churchill once p. it** comme l'a dit Churchill un jour; **to p. it briefly** *or* **simply, they refused** bref *ou* en un mot, ils ont refusé; **to p. it bluntly** pour parler franc

8 *(present, submit ► suggestion, question)* soumettre; *(► motion)* proposer, présenter; **to p. a proposal to the board** présenter une proposition au conseil d'administration; **he p. his case very well** il a très bien présenté son cas; *Law* **I p. it to you that...** n'est-il pas vrai que...?; **I p. it to the delegates that now is the time to act** je tiens à dire aux délégués que c'est maintenant qu'il faut agir

9 *(class, rank)* placer, mettre; **I wouldn't p. them in the same class as the Beatles** je ne les mettrais *ou* placerais pas dans la même catégorie que les Beatles; **I p. my family above my job** je fais passer ma famille avant mon travail

10 *(set to work)* **to p. sb to work** mettre qn au travail; **they p. her on the Jones case** ils l'ont mise sur l'affaire Jones

11 *(devote ► effort)* investir, consacrer; **to p. a lot of time/energy into sth** consacrer beaucoup de temps/d'énergie à qch, investir beaucoup de temps/d'énergie dans qch; **she puts more into their relationship than he does** elle s'investit plus que lui dans leur relation; **to p. a lot of work into sth/doing sth** beaucoup travailler à qch/pour faire qch; *Sport* **he p. everything he had into his first service** il a tout mis dans son premier service

12 *(invest ► money)* placer, investir; **she had p. all her savings into property** elle avait investi *ou* placé toutes ses économies dans l'immobilier

13 *(bet)* miser, parier; **to p. money on a horse** miser *ou* parier sur un cheval; **he p. all his winnings on the red** il misa tous ses gains sur le rouge

14 *Sport* **to p. the shot** lancer le poids

15 *Naut* **to p. a ship into port** rentrer un bateau au port

VI *Naut* **to p. to sea** lever l'ancre, appareiller; **they had to p. back into harbour** ils ont dû rentrer au port; **we p. into port at Bombay** nous avons relâché *ou* fait relâche à Bombay

N **1** *Sport* lancer *m* (du poids); **his third p.** son troisième lancer

2 *St Exch* option *f* de vente, put *m*; **p. and call** stellage *m*, double option *f*
►► *St Exch* ***put option*** option *f* de vente

►**put about** VT SEP **1** *(spread ► gossip, story)* faire courir; *(► rumour)* faire circuler; **to p. it about that...** faire circuler le bruit que...; **it is being p about that he intends resigning** le bruit court qu' a l'intention de démissionner **2** *Naut* **to p. a boa about** virer de bord **3** *Fam* **to p. it** *or* **oneself abou** *(be promiscuous)* coucher à droite à gauche
VI *Naut* virer de bord

►**put across** VT SEP **1** *(communicate ► gen)* fair comprendre; *(► feeling)* communiquer; **to p. st across to sb** faire comprendre qch à qn; **sh knows how to p. her ideas across** elle sait bie faire passer ses idées; **she's good at putting he self across** elle sait se mettre en valeur **2** *Br Fa* **to p. one across on sb** avoir qn, rouler qn; **don't tr putting anything across on me!** ne me prends pa pour un imbécile!

►**put around** VT SEP = **put about** *vt sep* 1

►**put aside** VT SEP **1** *(book, piece of work)* mettr de côté, poser **2** *(disregard, ignore)* écarter, lais ser de côté; **let's p. aside our differences of opinio for the moment** laissons nos différends de côt pour le moment; **p. aside all gloomy thought** oublie toutes ces pensées maussades **3** *(save keep)* mettre de côté; **we have a little money p aside** nous avons un peu d'argent de côté

►**put away** VT SEP **1** *(tidy)* ranger; *(return to it place)* remettre à sa place; *(car)* garer; **p. you toys away!** range tes jouets!; **p. your money/wa let away** *(I'm paying)* range ton argent/ton por tefeuille

2 *(save)* mettre de côté; **I have a few pounds p away** j'ai un peu d'argent de côté, j'ai quelque économies; **to p. something away for one's ol age** mettre quelque chose de côté pour sa re traite

3 *Fam (lock up ► in prison)* coffrer; *(► in menta home)* enfermer▫

4 *Fam (eat)* enfourner, s'envoyer; *(drink)* des cendre, écluser; **he can really p. it away!** *(food* il a un sacré appétit!; *(drink)* qu'est-ce qu'il des cend!

►**put back** VT SEP **1** *(replace, return)* remettre; **p that record back where you found it!** remets c disque où tu l'as trouvé!

2 *(postpone)* remettre; **the meeting has been p back to Thursday** la réunion a été repoussée *o* remise à jeudi

3 *(slow down, delay)* retarder; **the strike has p our schedule back at least a month** la grève nou a fait perdre au moins un mois sur notre plan ning

4 *(turn back ► clock)* retarder; **we p. the clock back next weekend** le week-end prochain, o passe à l'heure d'hiver; *Fig* **this decision has p the clock back** cette décision nous a ramené en arrière
VI *Naut* **to p. back (to port)** rentrer au port

►**put by** VT SEP *(save ► money)* mettre de côté; *(► supplies)* mettre en réserve; **have you got any thing p. by?** avez-vous un peu d'argent de côté?

►**put down** VT SEP **1** *(on table, floor etc)* poser; **p that knife down at once!** pose ce couteau tout d suite!; **p. me down!** lâche-moi!; **p. that down** laisse (ça)!; **to p. the phone down** raccrocher **he p. the phone down on me** il m'a raccroché a nez; **I couldn't p. it down** *(book)* j'ai trouvé ça pas sionnant

2 *(drop off ► passenger)* déposer, laisser

3 *(write down)* écrire, inscrire; *(enrol, enter o list)* inscrire; **p. down your name and address** écri vez votre nom et votre adresse; **she p. us down a Mr and Mrs Smith** elle nous a inscrits sous le nom de M. et Mme Smith; **it's never been p. down i writing** ça n'a jamais été mis par écrit; **I can p. i down as expenses** je peux le faire passer dan mes notes de frais

4 *(on agenda)* inscrire à l'ordre du jour; **to p down a motion of no confidence** déposer une mo tion de censure

5 *(quell)* réprimer, étouffer; **the revolt was p down by armed police** la révolte a été réprimée par les forces de police

6 *(belittle)* rabaisser, critiquer; **he's always put ting students down** il passe son temps à critique les étudiants; **you shouldn't p. yourself down** t ne devrais pas te sous-estimer

7 *Br Euph (kill)* **to have a cat/dog p. down** faire piquer un chat/chien

(pay as deposit) verser; **I've already p. £50 down**
n the sofa j'ai déjà versé 50 livres pour le ca-
apé
(store ▸ wine) mettre en cave
0 (put to bed ▸ baby) coucher
1 (land ▸ plane) poser
2 (close ▸ umbrella) fermer
vi (land ▸ plane, pilot) atterrir, se poser

ut forward **VT SEP 1** (suggest ▸ proposal, idea,
ypothesis) avancer; (▸ candidate) proposer; **she**
her name forward for the post of treasurer elle a
osé sa candidature au poste de trésorière; **to p.**
ne's best foot forward (walk faster) presser le
as; Fig se mettre en devoir de faire de son
nieux **2** (turn forward ▸ clock, hands of clock)
vancer; **we p. the clocks forward next weekend**
week-end prochain, on passe à l'heure d'été
(bring forward) avancer; **the meeting has been**
forward to early next week la réunion a été
vancée au début de la semaine prochaine

ut in **VT SEP 1** (place inside bag, container, cup-
oard etc) mettre dans; **he p. the eggs in the fridge**
a mis les œufs dans le réfrigérateur; **to p. one's**
ontact lenses in mettre ses lentilles de contact;
p. one's head in at the window passer la tête
ar la fenêtre; Sport (in rugby) **to p. the ball in** re-
ettre la balle en jeu
(insert, include) insérer, inclure; **have you p. in**
e episode about the rabbit? as-tu inclus l'épi-
ode du lapin?
(interject) placer; **"her name was Alicia," the**
om-
n p. in "elle s'appelait Alicia", ajouta la femme
(install) installer; **we're having central heating**
in nous faisons installer le chauffage central;
e voters p. the Tories in les électeurs ont mis les
onservateurs au pouvoir; **they've p. in a new**
anager at the factory ils ont nommé un noueau directeur à l'usine
(devote ▸ time) passer; **I've p. in a lot of work on**
at car j'ai beaucoup travaillé sur cette voiture;
. in a few hours' revision before supper j'ai passé
uelques heures à réviser avant le dîner; **to p. in**
n hour's work faire une heure de travail; **to p. in**
full day at the office passer toute la journée au
ureau; **you only get out what you p. in** on ne ré-
olte que ce qu'on sème
(submit ▸ request, demand) déposer, soumet-
e; **they p. in a claim for a 10 per cent pay rise** ils
nt déposé une demande d'augmentation de
alaire de 10 pour cent; **to p. in an application for**
job déposer sa candidature pour ou se présen-
r pour un emploi
vi Naut relâcher, faire relâche; **we p. in at Wel-**
ngton nous avons relâché ou fait relâche à Wel-
ngton

ut off **VT SEP 1** (drop off ▸ passenger) déposer,
isser; **just p. me off at the corner** vous n'avez
u'à me laisser ou me déposer au coin
(postpone ▸ meeting, appointment) remettre à
lus tard, repousser; (▸ decision, payment) re-
ettre à plus tard, différer; (▸ work) remettre à
lus tard; (▸ guests) décommander; **the meeting**
as been p. off until tomorrow la réunion a été
envoyée ou remise à demain; **I kept putting off**
lling him the truth je continuais à repousser le
oment de lui dire la vérité; **I can't p. him off**
gain je ne peux pas encore annuler un
ndez-vous avec lui
(dissuade) **once he's made up his mind nothing**
the world can p. him off une fois qu'il a pris
ne décision, rien au monde ne peut le faire
hanger d'avis
(distract) déranger, empêcher de se concen-
er; **he deliberately tries to p. his opponent off** il
it tout pour empêcher son adversaire de se
oncentrer; **the noise p. her off her service** le bruit
a gênée ou dérangée pendant son service
(repel) dégoûter, rebuter; **it's the smell that**
uts me off c'est l'odeur qui me rebute; **don't be**
off by his odd sense of humour ne te laisse pas
ebuter par son humour un peu particulier; **it p.**
e off skiing for good ça m'a définitivement dé-
oûté du ski; **it p. me off my dinner** ça m'a coupé
appétit
(switch off ▸ television, radio etc) éteindre
vi Naut déborder du quai, pousser au large; **to**
. off from the shore quitter la côte, prendre le
rge

▸**put on** **VT SEP 1** (clothes, make-up, ointment) mettre; **to p. on one's make-up** se maquiller

2 (present, stage ▸ play, opera) monter; (▸ poetry reading, slide show etc) organiser; **why can't they p. something decent on for a change?** (on TV, radio) ils ne pourraient pas passer quelque chose d'intéressant pour une fois?

3 (lay on, provide ▸ train) mettre en service; **they p. on excellent meals on Sundays** ils servent d'excellents repas le dimanche; **they have p. on 20 extra trains** ils ont ajouté 20 trains

4 (gain ▸ speed, weight) prendre; **I've p. on a few pounds** j'ai pris quelques kilos

5 (turn on, cause to function ▸ light, radio, gas) allumer; (▸ record, tape) mettre; (▸ handbrake) mettre, serrer; **p. the heater on** mets ou allume le chauffage; **he p. on some Vivaldi/the news** il a mis du Vivaldi/les informations; **I've p. the kettle on for tea** j'ai mis de l'eau à chauffer pour le thé; **to p. on the brakes** freiner

6 (start cooking) mettre (à cuire); **I forgot to p. the peas on** j'ai oublié de mettre les petits pois à cuire

7 (bet) parier; **I p. £10 on the favourite** j'ai parié 10 livres sur le favori

8 (assume) prendre; **to p. on airs** prendre des airs; **he p. on a silly voice** il a pris une voix ridicule; **to p. on an act** jouer la comédie; Fam **don't worry, he's just putting it on** ne t'inquiète pas, il fait du cinéma ou du chiqué

9 Am Fam (tease) faire marcher; **you're putting me on!** là, tu me fais marcher!

10 (apply ▸ pressure) exercer

11 (add) ajouter; **the tax increase will p. another ten pence on a gallon of petrol** l'augmentation de la taxe va faire monter le prix du gallon d'essence de dix pence

12 (impose) imposer; **new restrictions have been p. on bringing animals into the country** de nouvelles restrictions ont été imposées à l'importation d'animaux dans le pays

13 (attribute) **it's hard to p. a price on it** c'est difficile d'en évaluer ou estimer le prix

14 (advance ▸ clock) avancer

15 (on telephone) **could you p. him on, please?** pouvez-vous me le passer, s'il vous plaît?

▸**put out** **VT SEP 1** (place outside) mettre dehors, sortir; **have you p. the dustbin out?** as-tu sorti la poubelle?; **I'll p. the washing out (to dry)** je vais mettre le linge (dehors) à sécher; **to p. a cow out to grass** mettre une vache en pâture

2 (remove) **to p. sb's eye out** éborgner qn; **you almost p. my eye out!** tu as failli m'éborgner!

3 (issue ▸ apology, announcement) publier; (▸ story, rumour) faire circuler; (▸ new record, edition, model etc) sortir; (▸ appeal, request) faire; (broadcast) émettre; **police have p. out a description of the wanted man** la police a publié une description de l'homme qu'elle recherche; **to p. out an SOS** lancer un SOS

4 (extinguish ▸ fire, light, candle) éteindre; (▸ cigarette) éteindre, écraser; (▸ gas) fermer; **don't forget to p. the light out when you leave** n'oubliez pas d'éteindre (la lumière) en partant

5 (lay out, arrange) sortir; **the valet had p. out a suit for me** le valet de chambre m'avait sorti un costume

6 (stick out, stretch out ▸ arm, leg) étendre, allonger; (▸ hand) tendre; (▸ tongue) tirer; **she walked up to me and p. out her hand** elle s'approcha de moi et me tendit la main; **she p. out a foot to trip him up** elle a mis un pied en avant pour le faire trébucher

7 (dislocate) **to p. one's back/shoulder out** se démettre le dos/l'épaule; **I've p. my back out** je me suis déplacé une vertèbre

8 (annoy, upset) **to be p. out about sth** être fâché à cause de qch; **he seems quite p. out about it** on dirait que ça l'a vraiment contrarié

9 (inconvenience) déranger; **she's always ready to p. herself out for other people** elle est toujours prête à rendre service

10 (sprout ▸ shoots, leaves) produire

11 (make unconscious ▸ with drug, injection) endormir

12 (subcontract) sous-traiter; **we p. most of our work out** nous confions la plus grande partie de notre travail à des sous-traitants

13 Hort (plant out) repiquer

VI 1 Naut prendre le large; **to p. out to sea** faire appareiller **2** Am Fam (woman) accepter de coucher (**for** avec); **did she p. out?** est-ce qu'elle a bien voulu coucher?; **she'd p. out for anybody** elle coucherait avec le premier venu

▸**put over** = **put across**

▸**put through** **VT SEP 1** Tel (connect) passer la communication à; **hold on, I'll try to p. you through** ne quittez pas, je vais essayer de vous le/la passer; **p. the call through to my office** passez-moi la communication dans mon bureau; **I'll p. you through to Mrs Powell** je vous passe Mme Powell

2 (carry through, conclude) conclure; **we finally p. through the necessary reforms** nous avons fini par faire passer les réformes nécessaires

3 (subject to) soumettre à; **he was p. through a whole battery of tests** on l'a soumis à toute une série d'examens; **I'm sorry to p. you through this** je suis désolé de vous imposer ça; **have you any idea what you're putting him through?** as-tu la moindre idée de ce que tu lui fais subir?; Fam **to p. sb through it** en faire voir de toutes les couleurs à qn; (at interview) faire passer un mauvais quart d'heure à qn; **he really p. me through it** il m'en a vraiment fait voir (de toutes les couleurs)

4 (pay for) **he p. himself through college** il a payé ses études

▸**put together** **VT SEP 1** (place side by side ▸ two objects) mettre côte à côte; (▸ facts) rapprocher, comparer; **he's more trouble than the rest of them p. together** il nous crée plus de problèmes à lui seul que tous les autres réunis **2** (kit, furniture, engine) monter, assembler; (meal) préparer, confectionner; (menu) élaborer; (dossier) réunir; (proposal, report) préparer; (story, facts) reconstituer; (show, campaign) organiser, monter; **to p. sth (back) together again** remonter qch; **we're trying to p. together enough evidence to convict him** nous essayons de réunir assez de preuves pour le faire condamner; **to p. together a convincing picture of what happened** reconstituer une idée convaincante de ce qui s'est passé; **the programme is nicely p. together** ce programme est bien fait; **I'll just p. a few things together (in my bag)** je vais faire rapidement ma valise

▸**put up** **VT SEP 1** (raise ▸ hand) lever; (▸ flag) hisser; (▸ hood) relever; (▸ umbrella) ouvrir; (▸ one's hair, coat collar) relever; **could all those going p. up their hands?** que tous ceux qui y vont lèvent la main; **p. your hands up!** haut les mains!; Fam **p. 'em up!** (in surrender) haut les mains!; (to fight) défends-toi!; **I'm going to p. my feet up for a few minutes** je vais me reposer un peu

2 (erect ▸ tent) dresser, monter; (▸ house, factory) construire; (▸ monument, statue) ériger; (▸ scaffolding) installer, monter; (▸ ladder) dresser; **they p. up a statue to her** ils érigèrent une statue en son honneur

3 (install, put in place) mettre; (curtains) poser, accrocher; (wallpaper) poser; **they've already p. up the Christmas decorations** ils ont déjà installé les décorations de Noël; **the shopkeeper p. up the shutters** le commerçant a baissé le rideau de fer

4 (send up ▸ rocket, satellite) lancer

5 (display ▸ sign) mettre; (▸ poster) afficher; **the results will be p. up tomorrow** les résultats seront affichés demain

6 (show ▸ resistance) offrir, opposer; **to p. up a good show** bien se défendre; **to p. up a struggle** se défendre, se débattre

7 (present ▸ argument, proposal) présenter; **he puts up a good case for abstention** il a des arguments convaincants en faveur de l'abstention

8 (offer for sale) **to p. sth up for sale/auction** mettre qch en vente/aux enchères

9 (put forward ▸ candidate) présenter; (▸ person, name) proposer (comme candidat)

10 Fam (provide ▸ capital) fournir; **who's putting the money up for the new business?** qui finance la nouvelle entreprise?; **we p. up our own money** nous sommes auto-financés

11 (increase) faire monter, augmenter; **this will p. up the price of meat** ça va faire augmenter ou monter le prix de la viande

12 (give hospitality to) loger, héberger; **to p. sb up for the night** coucher qn

13 *(urge, incite)* **to p. sb up to (doing) sth** pousser qn à (faire) qch
14 *Arch (put away ▸ sword, pistol)* rengainer
VI 1 *Br* **to p. up at a hotel** descendre dans un hôtel; **where are you putting up?** où est-ce que tu loges?; *(in hotel)* où es-tu descendu?; **I'm putting up at Gary's for the moment** je loge chez Gary pour le moment **2** *(stand ▸ in election)* se présenter, se porter candidat; **she p. up as a Labour candidate** elle s'est présentée comme candidate du parti travailliste **3** *Fam* **p. up or shut up!** assez parlé, agissez!

▸ **put up with** VT INSEP supporter, tolérer; **I refuse to p. up with this noise any longer!** je ne supporterai pas ce bruit une minute de plus!; **we'll have to p. up with it** il faut l'accepter *ou* nous y résigner

▸ **put upon** VT INSEP *(usu passive)* **to p. upon sb** *(abuse)* abuser de qn; *(exploit)* exploiter qn; **you shouldn't let yourself be p. upon like that!** tu ne devrais pas te laisser marcher sur les pieds comme ça!

---

putative ['pju:tətɪv] ADJ *Formal* présumé, putatif

put-down N *Fam (snub)* rebuffade *f*

put-in N *Sport (in rugby)* introduction *f*

put-on ADJ affecté, simulé
N *Fam* **1** *(pretence)* simulacre *m*; **it's just a p.** c'est du chiqué, c'est de la comédie; **the whole thing was a p. to gain sympathy** toute l'histoire n'était qu'un subterfuge pour s'attirer de la sympathie **2** *(hoax)* canular *m*

put-put ['pʌtˌpʌt] *(pt & pp* **put-putted**, *cont* **put-putting**) *Br Fam* N teuf-teuf *m*
VI **to p. along** avancer en faisant teuf-teuf

putrefaction [ˌpju:trɪ'fækʃən] N putréfaction *f*

putrefy ['pju:trɪfaɪ] *(pt & pp* **putrefied**) VI se putréfier
VT putréfier

putrescence [pju:'tresəns] N *Formal* putrescence *f*

putrescent [pju:'tresənt] ADJ *Formal* putrescent

putrid ['pju:trɪd] ADJ **1** *(decaying)* putride; **a p. smell** une odeur nauséabonde **2** *Fam (awful)* dégueulasse

putsch [pʊtʃ] N putsch *m*, coup *m* d'État

putt [pʌt] *Golf* N putt *m*; **to hole a long p.** rentrer un long putt
VT putter
VI putter

putter[1] ['pʌtə(r)] N *Golf* **1** *(club)* putter *m* **2** *(person)* **he's a good p.** il putte bien

putter[2] *Am* = **potter VI**

putting ['pʌtɪŋ] N *Golf* putting *m*
▸▸ ***putting green*** green *m*

putto ['pʊtəʊ] *(pl* **putti** [-ti:]) N *Art* putto *m*

putty ['pʌtɪ] *(pt & pp* **puttied**) N **1** *(for cracks, holes)* mastic *m*; *(for walls)* enduit *m*; **my legs feel like p.** j'ai les jambes en coton; **Max is p. in her hands** elle fait de Max (tout) ce qu'elle veut, Max ne sait pas lui résister **2** *(colour)* (couleur *f*) mastic *m*
VT mastiquer
▸▸ ***putty knife*** couteau *m* à mastiquer, spatule *f* de vitrier

put-upon ADJ *Br* exploité; **he's very p.** tout le monde l'exploite; **his poor p. wife** sa pauvre femme qui lui sert de bonne à tout faire; **she was feeling p.** elle avait l'impression qu'on abusait de sa gentillesse; **a p. expression** une tête de martyr

put-you-up N *Br* canapé-lit *m*

putz [pʌts] N *Am Fam* andouille *f*, truffe *f*

▸ **putz around** VI *Am Fam* **1** *(act foolishly)* faire l'idiot, faire l'imbécile **2** *(waste time)* glander, glandouiller

puzzle ['pʌzəl] N **1** *(game ▸ gen)* jeu *m* de patience; *(▸ jigsaw)* puzzle *m*; *(▸ brainteaser)* casse-tête *m inv*; *(▸ riddle)* devinette *f* **2** *(problem)* question *f* (difficile); *(enigma, mystery)* énigme *f*, mystère *m*; **how he escaped remains a p.** la façon dont il s'y est pris pour s'évader reste un mystère *ou* une énigme **3** *(perplexity)* perplexité *f*; **he was in a p. about what to do** il ne savait pas trop quoi faire
VT laisser *ou* rendre perplexe; **he puzzles me** il m'intrigue, c'est une énigme pour moi; **I'm still puzzled to know how he got out** j'essaie toujours de comprendre comment il s'y est pris pour sortir; **don't p. your head over** *or* **about it** ne vous tracassez pas pour ça
VI *(wonder)* se poser des questions; *(ponder)* réfléchir; **to p. about sth** chercher à comprendre qch
▸▸ ***puzzle book*** *(gen)* livre *m* de jeux; *(of crosswords)* livre *m* de mots croisés

▸ **puzzle out** VT SEP *Br (meaning, solution, route, way)* trouver, découvrir; *(code, enigma, handwriting)* déchiffrer; *(problem)* résoudre; *(behaviour, intentions)* comprendre; **I'm still trying to p. out how he did it** je cherche toujours à comprendre comment il l'a fait; **I was never able to p. her out** je ne suis jamais arrivé *ou* parvenu à la comprendre

▸ **puzzle over** VT INSEP *(answer, explanation)* essayer de trouver; *(absence, letter, theory)* essayer de comprendre; *(enigma, crossword)* essayer de résoudre; *(code, handwriting)* essayer de déchiffrer; **we're still puzzling over why he did it** nous nous demandons toujours ce qui a bien pu le pousser à faire cela; *Br* **he puzzled over the list of figures** la liste des chiffres le laissait perplexe; *Br* **that'll give you something to p. over!** cela vous donnera de quoi réfléchir!

puzzlement ['pʌzəlmənt] N perplexité *f*; **to look at sb in p.** regarder qn d'un air perplexe

puzzler ['pʌzlə(r)] N énigme *f*, casse-tête *m inv*; **his statement is a real p.** sa déclaration est des plus ambiguës

puzzling ['pʌzlɪŋ] ADJ *(behaviour, remark)* curieux, qui laisse perplexe; *(symbol, machine)* incompréhensible; **it's p. that he hasn't sent word** c'est curieux qu'il n'ait pas donné signe de vie; **it remains a p. phenomenon** c'est un phénomène encore inexpliqué; **it's a p. affair** c'est une affaire difficile à éclaircir

PVC [ˌpi:vi:'si:] N *(abbr* **polyvinyl chloride**) PVC *m*

PVS [ˌpi:vi:'es] N *Med (abbr* **persistent vegetative state**) état *m* végétatif chronique

PW [ˌpi:'dʌbəlju:] N *Br (abbr* **policewoman**) femme *f* policier

PWR [ˌpi:dʌbəlju:'ɑ:(r)] N *Nucl & Phys (abbr* **press ized-water reactor**) REP *m*

PX [ˌpi:'eks] N *Am Mil (abbr* **post exchange**) = éc nomat pour les militaires et leurs familles

pygmy ['pɪgmɪ] *(pl* **pygmies**) N **1** *Zool (small a mal)* nain(e) *m,f* **2** *Fig Pej (person)* nain(e) *m* **he's a political p.** c'est un homme politique sa importance
ADJ *Zool* pygmée, nain
• **Pygmy** N Pygmée *mf* ADJ pygmée
▸▸ *Zool* ***pygmy chimpanzee*** chimpanzé *m* py mée; *Zool* ***pygmy hippo*** hippopotame *m* na *Orn* ***pygmy owl*** chevêchette *f*

pyjama, *Am* **pajama** [pə'dʒɑ:mə] COMP *(jack trousers)* de pyjama
• **pyjamas,** *Am*
• **pajamas** NPL pyjama *m*; **a pair of pyjamas** pyjama; **he was in his pyjamas** il était en pyjam
▸▸ ***pyjama party*** = fête où l'on doit venir en py ma; ***pyjama top*** *(jacket)* veste *f* de pyjama; *(p on type)* haut *m* de pyjama

pylon ['paɪlən] N *(gen) & Archeol* pylône *m*

pyorrhoea, *Am* **pyorrhea** [ˌpaɪə'rɪə] N *M* pyorrhée *f*

pyramid ['pɪrəmɪd] N pyramide *f*; **age** *or* **popu tion p.** pyramide *f* des âges
▸▸ *Com* ***pyramid selling*** vente *f* pyramidale

pyramidal [pɪ'ræmɪdəl], **pyramidical** [ˌpɪ 'mɪdɪkəl] ADJ pyramidal

pyre ['paɪə(r)] N **(funeral) p.** bûcher *m* funéraire

Pyrenean [ˌpɪrə'ni:ən] ADJ pyrénéen, des Py nées
▸▸ ***Pyrenean mountain dog*** chien *m ou* berger des Pyrénées

Pyrenees [ˌpɪrə'ni:z] NPL **the P.** les Pyrénées *fp*

pyrethrum [paɪ'ri:θrəm] N *Bot* pyrèthre *m*

pyretic [paɪ'retɪk] ADJ *Med* pyrétique

Pyrex® ['paɪreks] N Pyrex® *m*
COMP *(dish, bowl)* en Pyrex

pyrite ['paɪˌraɪt], **pyrites** [ˌpaɪ'raɪti:z] N *Miner* p rite *f*

pyritic [paɪ'rɪtɪk] ADJ *Miner* pyriteux

pyromaniac [ˌpaɪrə'meɪnɪæk] N pyromane *mf*

pyrotechnic [ˌpaɪərəʊ'teknɪk] ADJ pyrotec nique

pyrotechnics [ˌpaɪrəʊ'teknɪks] N *(UNCOUN (process)* pyrotechnie *f*
NPL **1** *(display)* feu *m* d'artifice **2** *Fig (display skill)* performance *f* éblouissante

Pyrrhic victory ['pɪrɪk-] N victoire *f* à la P rhus

Pythagoras [paɪ'θægərəs] PR N Pythagore
▸▸ ***Pythagoras' theorem*** théorème *m* de Pyth gore

Pythagorean [paɪˌθægə'ri:ən] ADJ *(relating Pythagoras)* pythagoricien; *(relating to Pytha oras' theorem)* pythagorique
N pythagoricien(enne) *m,f*
▸▸ ***Pythagorean numbers*** nombres *mpl* pythag riques

python ['paɪθən] N *Zool* python *m*

pyx [pɪks] N *Rel* ciboire *m*

pzazz [pə'zæz] N *Fam (flair)* punch *m inv*

Q, q[1] [kjuː] **N** *(letter)* Q, q *m inv*; **two q's** deux q

q[2] *(written abbr* **quart**) ≃ litre *m*

Qatar [kæˈtɑː(r)] **N** Qatar *m*

Qatari [kæˈtɑːrɪ] **N** Quatari *mf*
ADJ quatari

QB [ˌkjuːˈbiː] **N** *Law (abbr* **Queen's Bench**) = en Angleterre et au pays de Galles, l'une des trois divisions de la "High Court", ≃ tribunal *m* de grande instance

QBD [ˌkjuːbiːˈdiː] **N** *Law (abbr* **Queen's Bench Division**) = en Angleterre et au pays de Galles, l'une des trois divisions de la "High Court", ≃ tribunal *m* de grande instance

QC [ˌkjuːˈsiː] **N** *Br Law (abbr* **Queen's Counsel**) ≃ bâtonnier *m* de l'ordre

QE2 [ˌkjuːiːˈtuː] **N** *Br Naut (abbr* **Queen Elizabeth II**) = grand paquebot de luxe

QED [ˌkjuːiːˈdiː] **ADV** *(abbr* **quod erat demonstrandum**) CQFD

QIP [ˌkjuːaɪˈpiː] **N** *(abbr* **quality improvement programme**) programme *m* d'amélioration de la qualité

QM [ˌkjuːˈem] **N** *Mil (abbr* **Quartermaster**) **1** *(in army)* commissaire *m* **2** *(in navy)* officier *m* de manœuvre

QMG [ˌkjuːemˈdʒiː] **N** *Mil (abbr* **Quartermaster General**) ≃ Directeur *m* de l'Intendance (militaire)

QMV [ˌkjuːemˈviː] **N** *EU (abbr* **qualified majority voting**) vote *m* à la majorité qualifiée

qt[1] *(written abbr* **quart**) *Br* = 1,136 l; *Am* = 0,946 l

qt[2], **QT** [ˌkjuːˈtiː] **ADV** *Br Fam* en douce; **this is strictly on the qt** c'est confidentiel

Q-T interval **N** *Med* intervalle *m* QT

Q-tip® **N** *Am* coton-tige® *m*

qty *(written abbr* **quantity**) qté

qua [kweɪ] **PREP** *Formal* en tant que; **alcohol q. alcohol** l'alcool en tant que tel

quack [kwæk] **VI** *(duck)* cancaner, faire coincoin
N 1 *(of duck)* cancanement *m*, coin-coin *m inv* **2** *(charlatan)* charlatan *m* **3** *Br & Austr Fam Hum (doctor)* toubib *m*
ADJ *(medicine, method, remedy)* de charlatan
ONOMAT q. (q.)! coin-coin!
▸▸ ***quack doctor*** charlatan *m*

quackery [ˈkwækərɪ] **N** charlatanisme *m*

quad [kwɒd] **N 1** *(abbr* **quadruplet**) quadruplé(e) *m,f* **2** *(abbr* **quadrangle**) cour *f*
▸▸ ***quad bike*** quad *m*; ***quad biking*** quad *m*; **to go q. biking** faire du quad

quadragenarian [ˌkwɒdrədʒəˈneərɪən] **N** quadragénaire *mf*
ADJ quadragénaire

Quadragesima [ˌkwɒdrəˈdʒesɪmə] **N Q. (Sunday)** quadragésime *f*

quadrangle [ˈkwɒdræŋgəl] **N 1** *Geom* quadrilatère *m*; **complete q.** quadrangle *m* **2** *(courtyard)* cour *f* carrée

quadrangular [kwɒˈdræŋgjʊlə(r)] **ADJ** quadrangulaire

quadrant [ˈkwɒdrənt] **N 1** *Geom* quadrant *m* **2** *Astron & Naut* quart-de-cercle *m*, quadrant *m*

quadraphonic [ˌkwɒdrəˈfɒnɪk] **ADJ** quadriphonique, tétraphonique; **in q. sound** en quadriphonie

quadraphonics [ˌkwɒdrəˈfɒnɪks], **quadraphony** [kwɒˈdrɒfənɪ] **N** *(UNCOUNT)* quadriphonie *f*, quadri *f*, tétraphonie *f*

quadrasonic [ˌkwɒdrəˈsɒnɪk] **ADJ** quadriphonique, tétraphonique

quadratic [kwɒˈdrætɪk] *Math* **ADJ** quadratique
N équation *f* quadratique *ou* du second degré
▸▸ ***quadratic equation*** équation *f* quadratique *ou* du second degré

quadrature [ˈkwɒdrətʃə(r)] **N** *Geom & Astron* quadrature *f*

quadrennial [kwɒˈdrenɪəl] **ADJ** quadriennal

quadri- [ˈkwɒdrɪ] **PREF** quadri-

quadrilateral [ˌkwɒdrɪˈlætərəl] *Geom* **ADJ** quadrilatère, quadrilatéral
N quadrilatère *m*

quadrille [kwəˈdrɪl] **N** quadrille *m*

quadrillion [kwɒˈdrɪlɪən] **N** mille billions *mpl* (10^{15}); *Br Old-fashioned* quatrillion *m* (10^{24})

quadriplegia [ˌkwɒdrɪˈpliːdʒə] **N** *Med* tétraplégie *f*, quadriplégie *f*

quadriplegic [ˌkwɒdrɪˈpliːdʒɪk] *Med* **ADJ** tétraplégique
N tétraplégique *mf*

quadroon [kwɒˈdruːn] **N** quarteron(onne) *m,f*

quadruped [ˈkwɒdruped] **ADJ** quadrupède
N quadrupède *m*

quadruple [kwɒˈdruːpəl] **ADJ** quadruple
N quadruple *m*
VT quadrupler
VI quadrupler

quadruplet [ˈkwɒdrʊplɪt] **N** quadruplé(e) *m,f*

quadruplicate **ADJ** [kwɒˈdruːplɪkət] quadruple
N [kwɒˈdruːplɪkət] **in q.** en quatre exemplaires
VT [kwɒˈdruːplɪkeɪt] **1** *(multiply by four)* quadrupler, multiplier par quatre **2** *(make four copies of ▸ letter etc)* faire *ou* tirer quatre exemplaires de

quaff [kwɒf] **VT** *(wine)* boire à longs traits; *(glass)* vider d'un trait

quaffable [ˈkwɒfəbəl] **ADJ** *Fam* qui se laisse boire

quagmire [ˈkwægmaɪə(r)] **N** marécage *m*; *Fig* bourbier *m*

quail [kweɪl] *(pl* **inv or quails**) **N** *Orn* caille *f*
VI *(feel afraid)* trembler; *(give way, lose heart)* fléchir, faiblir; **to q. before sb/sth** trembler devant qn/qch; **he quailed at the thought of having to talk to her** il tremblait à l'idée d'avoir à lui parler

quaint [kweɪnt] **ADJ 1** *(picturesque)* pittoresque; *(old-fashioned)* au charme désuet; **a q. little cottage** un mignon petit cottage; **a q. old lady** une vieille dame aux manières désuètes **2** *(odd)* bizarre, étrange

quaintly [ˈkweɪntlɪ] **ADV 1** *(picturesquely)* de façon pittoresque; **the q. old-fashioned villages** les vieux villages pittoresques; **rather q. worded** formulé de façon assez désuète **2** *(oddly)* bizarrement, étrangement

quaintness [ˈkweɪntnɪs] **N 1** *(picturesqueness)* pittoresque *m*; *(old-fashioned charm)* charme *m* vieillot *ou* désuet **2** *(oddness)* bizarrerie *f*, étrangeté *f*

quake [kweɪk] **VI 1** *(person)* trembler, frémir; **to q. with fear** trembler de peur; **he was quaking in his boots** il était mort de peur; **I was quaking at the thought of having to confront her** je tremblais à l'idée d'avoir à lui faire face **2** *(earth)* trembler
N *Fam* tremblement *m* de terre

Quaker [ˈkweɪkə(r)] *Rel* **N** quaker(eresse) *m,f*
ADJ des quakers

Quakerish [ˈkweɪkərɪʃ] **ADJ** de quaker, des quakers; **Q. dress** costume *m* sobre digne d'un quaker

Quakerism [ˈkweɪkərɪzəm] **N** *Rel* quakerisme *m*

qualification [ˌkwɒlɪfɪˈkeɪʃən] **N 1** *(diploma, degree)* diplôme *m*; **candidates with formal qualifications in translating** des candidats possédant un diplôme de traducteur; **he has no academic or professional qualifications** il n'a ni diplôme universitaire ni qualification professionnelle
2 *(ability, quality)* aptitude *f*, compétence *f*; *(for job)* qualification *f*; **one of the qualifications for this job is a sense of humour** une des qualités requises pour ce poste est le sens de l'humour
3 *(restriction)* réserve *f*; **they accepted the idea with some/without q.** ils acceptèrent l'idée avec quelques réserves/sans réserve
4 *(graduation)* **most of our students find jobs after q.** la plupart de nos étudiants trouvent du travail dès qu'ils ont obtenu leur diplôme
5 *(act of qualifying)* qualification *f*; **her q. for the semi-final** sa qualification pour la demi-finale

qualified [ˈkwɒlɪfaɪd] **ADJ 1** *(trained)* qualifié, diplômé; **q. teachers** professeurs *mpl* qualifiés *ou* diplômés; **our staff are highly q.** notre personnel est hautement qualifié; **suitably q. persons for...** des personnes qualifiées pour... **2** *(able, competent)* compétent, qualifié; **I don't feel q. to discuss such matters** je ne suis pas à même de discuter de cela **3** *(limited, conditional)* mitigé; **their efforts met with q. praise** leurs efforts ont recueilli des louanges mitigées *ou* réservées
▸▸ *Banking* ***qualified acceptance*** acceptation *f* conditionnelle *ou* sous condition; *EU* ***qualified majority voting*** vote *m* à la majorité qualifiée; *Acct* ***qualified report*** rapport *m* réservé; ***qualified success*** demi-succès *m*

qualifier [ˈkwɒlɪfaɪə(r)] **N 1** *Sport (person)* qualifié(e) *m,f*; *(contest)* (épreuve *f*) éliminatoire *f* **2** *Gram* qualificatif *m*

qualify [ˈkwɒlɪfaɪ] *(pt & pp* **qualified**) **VI 1** *(pass exams, complete training)* obtenir son diplôme; **only 10 percent of the students go on to q.** seuls 10 pour cent des étudiants finissent par obtenir leur diplôme; **to q. as an accountant/a vet** obtenir son diplôme de comptable/vétérinaire; **to q. as a pilot** obtenir son brevet de pilote **2** *(be eligible)* **to q. for a pension** avoir droit à la retraite; **none of the candidates really qualifies for the post** aucun candidat ne répond véritablement aux conditions requises pour ce poste; *Fig* **it hardly qualifies as a mountain** on ne peut pas vraiment appeler cela une montagne, ça ne mérite pas le nom de montagne **3** *(in competition)* se qualifier; **he qualified for the finals** il s'est qualifié pour la finale
VT 1 *(make able or competent)* qualifier, habiliter;

to q. sb for sth/for doing *or* **to do sth** *(of training, course etc)* donner à qn les compétences voulues pour qch/pour faire qch, qualifier qn pour qch/pour faire qch; *Law* donner qualité à qn pour qch/pour faire qch; **her experience qualifies her for the post** son expérience lui permet de prétendre à ce poste; **this diploma qualifies you to practise acupuncture** par ce diplôme, vous êtes habilité à pratiquer l'acupuncture; **what qualifies him to talk about French politics?** en quoi est-il qualifié pour parler de la politique française?
2 *(modify ▸ statement, criticism)* mitiger, atténuer; *(put conditions on)* poser des conditions à; **they qualified their acceptance of the plan** ils ont accepté le projet sous conditions
3 *(describe)* qualifier; **I wouldn't q. the play as a masterpiece** je n'irai pas jusqu'à qualifier cette pièce de chef-d'œuvre
4 *Gram* qualifier

qualifying ['kwɒlɪfaɪŋ] **ADJ 1** *Gram* qualificatif **2** *(modifying)* modificateur
▸▸ ***qualifying examination*** *(at end of course)* examen *m* de fin d'études; *(to get onto course)* examen *m* d'entrée; *Br Sch* ***qualifying mark*** moyenne *f*; *Sport* ***qualifying round*** (épreuve *f*) éliminatoire *f*; ***qualifying statement*** déclaration *f* corrective

qualitative ['kwɒlɪtətɪv] **ADJ** qualitatif
▸▸ ***qualitative analysis*** analyse *f* qualitative; *Mktg* ***qualitative forecasting*** prévisions *fpl* qualitatives; *Mktg* ***qualitative research*** études *fpl* qualitatives; *Mktg* ***qualitative study*** étude *f* qualitative

qualitatively ['kwɒlɪtətɪvlɪ] **ADV** qualitativement

quality ['kwɒlɪtɪ] *(pl* **qualities***)* **N 1** *(standard, nature)* qualité *f*; **the high/poor q. of the workmanship** la bonne/mauvaise qualité du travail; **q. of life** qualité *f* de la vie
2 *(high standard, excellence)* qualité *f*; **q. matters more than quantity** la qualité importe plus que la quantité; **we have a reputation for q.** nous sommes réputés pour la qualité de nos produits
3 *(feature, attribute)* qualité *f*; **these are the qualities we are looking for in our candidates** voici les qualités que nous recherchons chez nos candidats; **he has a lot of good qualities** il a de nombreuses qualités; **I don't doubt her intellectual qualities** je ne doute pas de ses capacités intellectuelles
4 *Br (newspaper)* = quotidien ou journal du dimanche de qualité (par opposition à la presse populaire)
5 *Arch (high social status)* qualité *f*; **a gentleman of q.** un homme de qualité; **the q.** les gens *mpl* de qualité, *Pej* le beau linge
6 *(tone)* timbre *m*
COMP *(goods, work, shop)* de qualité; **to spend q. time together** passer de bons moments ensemble; **I only spend an hour in the evening with my kids, but it's q. time** je ne passe qu'une heure avec mes gosses le soir, mais je profite bien d'eux
▸▸ ***quality assurance*** garantie *f* de qualité; ***quality audit*** audit *m* de qualité; *Br* ***quality circle*** cercle *m* de qualité; ***quality control*** contrôle *m* de (la) qualité; ***quality controller*** responsable *mf* du contrôle de (la) qualité, qualiticien(enne) *m,f*; ***quality improvement*** l'amélioration *f* de la qualité; ***quality label*** label *m* de qualité; ***quality management*** gestion *f* qualité; *Br* ***quality newspaper*** = quotidien ou journal du dimanche de qualité (par opposition à la presse populaire); *Mktg* ***quality positioning*** positionnement *m* par la qualité; *Br* ***quality press*** presse *f* d'opinion

quality-assurance manager N directeur (trice) *m,f* de l'assurance-qualité

qualm [kwɑːm] **N** *(scruple)* scrupule *m*; *(misgiving)* appréhension *f*, inquiétude *f*; **I occasionally have qualms about the job I do** il m'arrive d'avoir des scrupules à faire le travail que je fais; **he had no qualms about laying off his staff** il n'avait aucun scrupule à licencier ses employés; **she has no qualms about going out alone** elle ne craint pas de sortir seule

quandary ['kwɒndərɪ] *(pl* **quandaries***)* **N** dilemme *m*; **I'm in a dreadful q.** je suis confronté à un terrible dilemme; **she was in a q. over** *or* **about whether or not to tell him** elle ne parvenait pas à décider si elle devait le lui dire

quango ['kwæŋgəʊ] *(pl* **quangos***)* **N** *Br (abbr* **quasi-autonomous non-governmental organization***)* = organisme semi-public

quantifiable [ˌkwɒntɪ'faɪəbəl] **ADJ** quantifiable

quantifier ['kwɒntɪfaɪə(r)] **N 1** *Gram* quantificateur *m*, quantifieur *m* **2** *(in logic) & Math* quantificateur *m*

quantify ['kwɒntɪfaɪ] *(pt & pp* **quantified***)* **VT 1** *(estimate)* quantifier, évaluer quantitativement; **it is hard to q. the damage** il est difficile d'évaluer l'ampleur des dégâts **2** *(in logic)* quantifier

quantitative ['kwɒntɪtətɪv] **ADJ** quantitatif
▸▸ ***quantitative analysis*** analyse *f* quantitative; ***quantitative forecasting*** prévisions *fpl* quantitatives; ***quantitative research*** études *fpl* quantitatives; ***quantitative study*** étude *f* quantitative

quantitatively ['kwɒntɪtətɪvlɪ] **ADV** quantitativement

quantity ['kwɒntɪtɪ] *(pl* **quantities***)* **N** *(gen) & Ling & Math* quantité *f*; **what q. of sugar do you need for the cake?** de quelle quantité de sucre avez-vous besoin pour le gâteau?; **large quantities of** de grandes quantités de; **to buy sth in large quantities** acheter qch en grande quantité
▸▸ ***quantity discount*** remise *f ou* escompte *m* sur la quantité *ou* sur les achats en gros; ***quantity mark*** signe *m* de quantité; ***quantity rebate*** remise *f* sur la quantité; ***quantity surveying*** métrage *m*; ***quantity surveyor*** métreur(euse) *m,f*; *Econ* ***quantity theory (of money)*** théorie *f* quantitative (de la monnaie)

quantum ['kwɒntəm] *(pl* **quanta** [-tə]*)* **N** *Math & Phys* quantum *m*
▸▸ ***quantum jump, quantum leap*** progrès *m* énorme, bond *m* en avant; *Fig* **the new model represents a q. jump** le nouveau modèle représente un grand bond en avant; ***quantum mechanics*** *(UNCOUNT)* (mécanique *f*) quantique *f*; ***quantum number*** nombre *m* quantique; ***quantum physics*** physique *f* quantique; ***quantum theory*** théorie *f* des quanta *ou* quantique

quarantinable ['kwɒrənˌtiːnəbəl] **ADJ** *Med & Vet* quarantenaire

quarantine ['kwɒrəntiːn] **N** *Med & Vet* quarantaine *f*; **our dog is in q.** notre chien est en quarantaine
VT mettre en quarantaine

quark [kwɑːk] **N 1** *Phys* quark *m* **2** *(cheese)* fromage *m* blanc

quarrel ['kwɒrəl] *(Br pt & pp* **quarrelled***, cont* **quarrelling***, Am pt & pp* **quarreled***, cont* **quarreling***)*
N 1 *(dispute)* querelle *f*, dispute *f*; **they had a q. over money** ils se sont disputés pour des histoires d'argent; **are you trying to start a q.?** tu cherches la dispute?; **to pick a q. with sb** chercher querelle à qn **2** *(cause for complaint)* **I have no q. with him** je n'ai rien à lui reprocher; **I have no q. with her proposal** je n'ai rien contre sa proposition
VI 1 *(argue)* se disputer, se quereller; **I don't want to q. with you over** *or* **about this** je ne veux pas me disputer avec toi à ce sujet *ou* à propos de cela; **they're always quarrelling over money** ils se disputent sans cesse pour des histoires d'argent **2** *(take issue)* **I can't q. with your figures** je ne peux pas contester vos chiffres; **critics might q. with parts of the introduction** les critiques pourraient trouver à redire à certains passages de l'introduction

quarrelling, *Am* **quarreling** ['kwɒrəlɪŋ] **N** *(UNCOUNT)* disputes *fpl*, querelles *fpl*
ADJ *(children, parents, lovers)* qui se disputent

quarrelsome ['kwɒrəlsəm] **ADJ** querelleur

quarrier ['kwɒrɪə(r)] **N** carrier *m*

quarry ['kwɒrɪ] *(pl* **quarries***, pt & pp* **quarried***)* **N 1** *(for stone, slate, sand, marble etc)* carrière *f* **2** *(prey)* proie *f*
VT 1 *(stone, slate, sand, marble etc)* extraire **2** *(land, mountain)* exploiter; **the hills have been extensively quarried** de nombreuses carrières ont été ouvertes dans les collines
VI exploiter; **they are quarrying for marble** ils exploitent une carrière de marbre
▸▸ ***quarry tile*** carreau *m*

quarrying ['kwɒrɪɪŋ] **N** *(UNCOUNT)* **1** *(of stone, slate, sand, marble etc)* extraction *f* **2** *(of land, mountain)* exploitation *f*; **the countryside has been spoilt by q.** les carrières ont défiguré *ou* massacré le paysage

quarryman ['kwɒrɪmən] *(pl* **quarrymen** [-mən]*)* **N** carrier *m*

quart [kwɔːt] **N** *(liquid measurement) Br* = 1,136 l; *Am* = 0,946 l

quarte [kɑːt] **N** *Fencing* quarte *f*

quarter ['kwɔːtə(r)] **ADJ a q. hour/century/pound** un quart d'heure/de siècle/de livre
VT 1 *(divide into four)* diviser en quatre; *(beef etc)* diviser par quartiers, équarrir; **to q. a cake** couper un gâteau en quatre parts égales
2 *(divide by four ▸ figure, price)* diviser par quatre
3 *(lodge)* loger; *Mil* cantonner; **the troops are quartered in the town** les soldats sont logés en ville
4 *Hist (dismember)* écarteler
N 1 *(one fourth)* quart *m*; *(portion ▸ of apple, circle, century etc)* quart *m*; (▸ *of orange, moon)* quartier *m*; **during the first q. of the century** au cours du premier quart de ce siècle; **a q. of an hour** un quart d'heure; **a q. (of a) century** un quart de siècle; **a ton and a q., one and a q. tons** une tonne un quart; **he ate a q./three quarters of the cake** il a mangé le quart/les trois quarts du gâteau; **it's a q./three quarters empty** c'est au quart/aux trois quarts vide; **we've only done (a) q. of the work** nous n'avons fait que le quart du travail
2 *(in telling time)* quart *m*; *Br* **(a) q. to six,** *Am* **(a) q. of six** six heures moins le quart; *Br* **(a) q. past six,** *Am* **(a) q. after six** six heures et quart; **it's a q. past** il est le quart
3 *(three-month period)* trimestre *m*; **published every q.** publié tous les trimestres *ou* tous les trois mois; **profits were up during the last q.** les bénéfices ont augmenté au cours du dernier trimestre
4 *(US and Canadian money)* (pièce *f* de) 25 cents *mpl*
5 *(unit of weight ▸ quarter of hundredweight)* = 12 kg; (▸ *quarter pound)* = 113 g
6 *Naut (direction)* **the wind is in the port/starboard q.** le vent souffle par la hanche de bâbord/tribord
7 *(milieu)* **the decision has been criticized in certain quarters** la décision a été critiquée dans certains milieux; **offers of help poured in from all quarters** des offres d'aide affluèrent de tous côtés
8 *(part of town)* quartier *m*
9 *(phase of moon)* quartier *m*; **the moon is in the first/last q.** la lune est dans le premier/dernier quartier
10 *Sport (period of play)* quart-temps *m inv*
11 *(part of butchered animal)* quartier *m*
12 *(usu neg) Literary (mercy)* quartier *m*; **they gave no q.** ils ne firent pas de quartier
• **quarters NPL** *(accommodation)* domicile *m*, résidence *f*; *Mil* quartiers *mpl*, cantonnement *m*, logement *m*; **the servants' quarters** les appartements *mpl* des domestiques; **she took up quarters in central London** elle a élu domicile *ou* s'est installée dans le centre de Londres; **many families live in very cramped quarters** de nombreuses familles vivent dans des conditions de surpeuplement
▸▸ ***quarter binding*** *(in bookbinding)* demi-reliure *f*; *Br Fin* ***quarter day*** (jour *m* du) terme *m*; *Am Mus* ***quarter note*** noire *f*; *Law* ***quarter sessions*** *Formerly (in England and Wales)* ≃ cour *f* d'assises *(remplacée en 1972 par la "Crown Court")*; *(in US)* = dans certains États, tribunal local à compétence criminelle, pouvant avoir des fonctions administratives; *Mus* ***quarter tone*** quart *m* de ton

quarterback ['kwɔːtəˌbæk] **N** *Sport* quarterback *m*, *Can* quart-arrière *m*
VT *Am* **1** *Sport (team)* jouer quarterback dans **2** *Fig* être le stratège de, diriger la stratégie de

quarterdeck ['kwɔːtəˌdek] **N 1** *Naut (part of ship)* plage *f* arrière **2** *(personnel)* **the q.** les officiers *mpl*

quarterfinal [ˌkwɔːtəˈfaɪnəl] **N** quart *m* de finale; **knocked out in the quarterfinals** éliminé en quart de finale

quarterfinalist [ˌkwɔːtəˈfaɪnəlɪst] **N** quart-de-finaliste *mf*

quartering [ˈkwɔːtərɪŋ] *(UNCOUNT)* **N 1** *(dividing up)* division *f* en quatre **2** *Mil (billeting)* cantonnement *m*

quarterlight [ˈkwɔːtəˌlaɪt] **N** *Br Aut* déflecteur *m*

quarterly [ˈkwɔːtəlɪ] **ADJ** trimestriel
N publication *f* trimestrielle
ADV trimestriellement, tous les trimestres

quartermaster [ˈkwɔːtəˌmɑːstə(r)] **N 1** *(in army)* commissaire *m* **2** *(in navy)* officier *m* de manœuvre
▸▸ *Mil* ***Quartermaster General*** Directeur *m* de l'Intendance *(militaire)*

quarter-pounder **N** gros hamburger *m*

quarterwindow [ˈkwɔːtəwɪndəʊ] **N** *Aut* glace *f* de custode, custode *f*

quartet, quartette [kwɔːˈtet] **N 1** *Mus (players* ▸ *classical)* quatuor *m*; *(*▸ *jazz)* quartette *m* **2** *Mus (piece of music)* quatuor *m* **3** *(group of four people)* quatuor *m*

quartile [ˈkwɔːtaɪl] **N** *Math* quartile *m*

quarto [ˈkwɔːtəʊ] *(pl* **quartos***)* **N** in-quarto *m inv*
ADJ in-quarto *(inv)*

quartz [kwɔːts] *Miner* **N** quartz *m*
COMP *(clock, watch)* à quartz
▸▸ ***quartz crystal*** cristal *m* de quartz

quartz-halogen **N** halogène *m* à quartz

quartzite [ˈkwɔːtsaɪt] **N** *Miner* quartzite *m*

quasar [ˈkweɪzɑː(r)] **N** *Astron* quasar *m*

quash [kwɒʃ] **VT** *Br* **1** *(annul* ▸ *verdict, decision)* casser, annuler **2** *(suppress* ▸ *revolt)* étouffer, écraser; *(*▸ *emotion)* réprimer, refouler; *(*▸ *suggestion)* rejeter, repousser; **their creativity is quashed at an early age** leur créativité est étouffée dès leur jeune âge

quasi- [ˈkweɪzaɪ] **PREF** quasi-; **a q.-official organization** une organisation quasi officielle

quatercentenary [ˌkwætəsenˈtiːnərɪ] *(pl* **quatercentenaries***)* **N** quatrième centenaire *m*

quaternary [kwəˈtɜːnərɪ] **ADJ** *Chem & Math* quaternaire
• **Quaternary** *Geol* **ADJ** quaternaire **N the Q.** le quaternaire

quatrain [ˈkwɒtreɪn] **N** *Literature* quatrain *m*

quaver [ˈkweɪvə(r)] **VI** *(voice)* trembloter, chevroter; *(person)* parler d'une voix tremblotante *ou* chevrotante
N 1 *(of sound, in voice)* chevrotement *m*, tremblement *m* **2** *Br Mus* croche *f*

quay [kiː] **N** quai *m*

quayside [ˈkiːsaɪd] **N** quai *m*; **we walked along the q.** nous nous sommes promenés le long du quai; **at** *or* **on the q.** sur le quai

queasiness [ˈkwiːzɪnɪs] **N** *(UNCOUNT)* **1** *(nausea)* nausée *f* **2** *(uneasiness)* scrupules *mpl*

queasy [ˈkwiːzɪ] *(compar* **queasier**, *superl* **queasiest***)* **ADJ 1** *(nauseous)* nauséeux; **I** *or* **my stomach felt a little q.** j'avais un peu mal au cœur; **the drugs make him q.** les médicaments lui donnent des nausées; **the very sight of meat makes her feel q.** la simple vue de la viande lui donne la nausée; **she was looking a bit q.** elle avait l'air d'avoir mal au cœur **2** *(uneasy)* mal à l'aise, gêné

Quebec [kwɪˈbek] **N 1** *(city)* Québec **2** *(province)* le Québec

Quebecker, Quebecer [kwɪˈbekə(r)] **N** Québécois(e) *m,f*

Quebecois, Québecois [ˌkebeˈkwɑː] *(pl* **inv***)* **N** Québécois(e) *m,f*

queen [kwiːn] **N 1** *(sovereign, king's wife)* reine *f*; **the Q. of Spain/Belgium** la reine d'Espagne/de Belgique; **Q. Elizabeth II** la reine Élisabeth II; **she was q. to Charles II** elle fut la reine *ou* l'épouse de Charles II; *Br* **the Q.'s Christmas message** = discours télévisé et radiodiffusé de la reine le jour de Noël; *Br Law* **to turn Q.'s evidence** témoigner contre ses complices *(sous promesse de pardon)*
2 *(woman, place, thing considered best)* reine *f*; **the q. of the blues** la reine du blues; **the rose is the q. of flowers** la rose est la reine des fleurs
3 *Cards & Chess* dame *f*, reine *f*; **q. of clubs** dame *f* de trèfle
4 *(of bees, ants)* reine *f*
5 *Fam Pej (any homosexual)* pédé *m*, tantouze *f*; *(effeminate homosexual)* folle *f*
VT 1 *Chess* **to q. a pawn** aller à dame **2** *Br Fam (idiom)* **to q. it** prendre des airs de (grande) marquise; **she thinks she can q. it over us!** elle s'imagine qu'elle est supérieure à nous!□
VI *Chess (pawn)* aller à dame
▸▸ ***Queen Anne*** = style d'architecture et de mobilier du XVIIIème siècle caractérisé par des lignes sobres; *Entom* ***queen bee*** reine *f* des abeilles; *Fam Fig* **she's the q. bee round here** c'est elle la patronne ici; *Law* ***Queen's Bench (Division)*** = en Angleterre et au pays de Galles, l'une des trois divisions de la "High Court", ≃ tribunal *m* de grande instance; *Am Culin* ***queen cake*** = petit gâteau aux raisins secs; ***queen consort*** reine *f* *(épouse du roi)*; ***Queen's Counsel*** avocat(e) *m,f* de la Couronne *(en Grande-Bretagne)*; ***Queen's English*** = l'anglais britannique correct; **she speaks the Q.'s English** elle s'exprime dans un anglais très soigné; ***Queen Mother*** reine *f* mère; *Br Fam* ***the Queen Mum*** la reine mère□; ***queen regent*** reine *f* régente; ***Queen's Speech*** *(in UK)* = allocution prononcée par la reine (mais préparée par le gouvernement) lors de la rentrée parlementaire et dans laquelle elle définit les grands axes de la politique gouvernementale

> **QUEEN'S CHRISTMAS MESSAGE/QUEEN'S SPEECH**
>
> Le message de Noël de la Reine ("the Queen's Christmas Message", dont l'appellation officielle est "the Royal Christmas Message") est diffusé à la télévision et à la radio le 25 décembre au Royaume-Uni et dans les pays du Commonwealth. Dans son discours, la Reine revient sur le grands événements de l'année et transmet ses vœux à la nation pour l'année à venir. Bien que l'on fasse souvent référence au message de Noël de la Reine en employant le terme "the Queen's speech", cette appellation désigne en fait quelque chose de bien différent. En effet, le Queen's Speech est le discours (écrit par le gouvernment) que lit la Reine lors de la rentrée parlementaire et dans laquelle elle définit les grands axes de la politique gouvernementale.

queenly [ˈkwiːnlɪ] **ADJ** royal, majestueux

queen-size bed **N** grand lit *m* double *(de 2 mètres sur 1,50 mètre)*

queer [kwɪə(r)] **ADJ 1** *(strange)* étrange, bizarre; **he's a q. fish!** c'est un drôle d'individu!; **he's got some q. ideas** il a de drôles d'idées, il a des idées bizarres; **she's a q.-looking person** elle a une drôle de tête
2 *(suspicious)* suspect, louche; **there've been some q. goings-on around here** il s'est passé des choses bizarres ici
3 *Fam (queasy)* mal fichu, patraque
4 *Fam (crazy)* timbré, cinglé; **he's a bit q. in the head** il lui manque une case
5 *very Fam (homosexual)* homo, pédé
N *very Fam (homosexual)* pédé *m*, pédale *f*
VT *Fam* gâter□, gâcher□; *Br* **to q. sb's pitch** couper l'herbe sous les pieds de qn
▸▸ *Am Fam* ***queer money*** *(counterfeit)* fausse monnaie□*f*

queer-basher **N** *Br very Fam* = individu qui se livre à des violences à l'encontre d'homosexuels

queer-bashing **N** *Br very Fam* = violences à l'encontre d'homosexuels

queerly [ˈkwɪəlɪ] **ADV** étrangement, bizarrement; **she looked at me q.** elle me regarda d'un drôle d'air

queerness [ˈkwɪənɪs] **N 1** *(strangeness)* étrangeté *f*, bizarrerie *f* **2** *(queasiness)* nausée *f*

quell [kwel] **VT 1** *(quash* ▸ *revolt, opposition)* réprimer, étouffer **2** *(overcome* ▸ *emotion)* dompter, maîtriser **3** *(allay* ▸ *pain)* apaiser, soulager; *(*▸ *doubts, fears)* dissiper

quench [kwentʃ] **VT 1 to q. one's thirst** étancher sa soif, se désaltérer
2 *(fire)* éteindre
3 *Metal* tremper
4 *Fig (enthusiasm)* atténuer; *(desire)* réprimer, étouffer

querulous [ˈkwerʊləs] **ADJ** *(person)* pleurnicheur; *(voice, tone)* plaintif, gémissant

querulously [ˈkwerʊləslɪ] **ADV** d'un ton plaintif

query [ˈkwɪərɪ] *(pl* **queries**, *pt & pp* **queried***)* **N 1** *(question)* question *f*; *(doubt)* doute *m*; **I have a q.** j'ai une question; **these facts raise a q. about his honesty** ces faits qui ont été mis au jour jettent un doute sur son honnêteté; **there was a note of q. in her voice** il y avait une note d'interrogation dans sa voix **2** *Br (question mark)* point *m* d'interrogation **3** *Comput* interrogation *f*
VT 1 *(express doubt about)* mettre en doute; **it is not for me to q. their motives** ce n'est pas à moi de mettre en doute leurs mobiles; **the accountant queried the figures** le comptable posa des questions sur les chiffres; **I would q. it if I were you** à votre place je le vérifierais
2 *(ask)* demander; **"how much is it?" she queried** "combien est-ce?" demanda-t-elle
3 *(mark with question mark)* marquer d'un point d'interrogation
4 *Am (interrogate)* interroger; **he queried me about my trip** il m'a posé des questions sur mon voyage
5 *Comput (database)* interroger
▸▸ *Comput* ***query language*** langage *m* d'interrogation; *Am* ***query mark*** point *m* d'interrogation

quest [kwest] **N** quête *f*; **to go in q. of sb/sth** se mettre *ou* aller *ou* partir à la recherche de qn/qch *ou* en quête de qn/qch; **her q. for justice** sa bataille pour que justice soit faite; **in q. of the truth** en quête de *ou* à la recherche de la vérité
VI *Literary* **to q. for** *or* **after sth** se mettre en quête de qch

QUESTION [ˈkwestʃən]

> **N**
> • question **1, 2, 4, 5** • problème **2**
> • doute **3**
> **VT**
> • interroger **1** • mettre en doute **2**

N 1 *(query)* question *f*; **to ask sb a q.** poser une question à qn; **I wish to put a q. to the chairman** j'aimerais poser une question au président; *Parl* **to put down a q. for sb** adresser une interpellation à qn; **you haven't answered my q.** vous n'avez pas répondu à ma question; **they obeyed without q.** ils ont obéi sans poser de questions; **a q. and answer session** une séance questions-réponses; *Gram* **direct/indirect q.** interrogation *f* directe/indirecte; *Br Parl* **(Prime Minister's) Q. Time, Prime Minister's Questions** = session hebdomadaire du Parlement britannique réservée aux questions des députés au Premier ministre
2 *(matter, issue)* question *f*; *(problem)* problème *m*; **her article raises some important questions** son article soulève d'importantes questions *ou* d'importants problèmes; **it raises the q. of how much teachers should be paid** cela soulève *ou* pose le problème du salaire des enseignants; **the place/time/person in q.** le lieu/l'heure/la personne en question; **the person in q. is away at the moment** la personne en question est absente en ce moment; **the Jewish q.** la question juive; **the q. is, will he do it?** toute la question est de savoir s'il le fera; **that is the q.** voilà la question; **that's another** *or* **a different q.** c'est une autre histoire; **but that's not the q.** mais là n'est pas la question, il ne s'agit pas de cela; **it's not a q. of who's right** la question n'est pas de savoir qui a raison; **it's a q. of how much you want to spend** tout dépend de la somme que vous voulez mettre; **it's only a q. of money/time** ce n'est qu'une question d'argent/de temps
3 *(UNCOUNT) (doubt)* doute *m*; **there's no q. about it, he was murdered** il a été assassiné, cela ne fait aucun doute; **his honesty was never in q.** son honnêteté n'a jamais été mise en doute *ou* remise en question; **to bring** *or* **to call sth into q.** remettre qch en question; **she is without** *or* **beyond q. the best** elle est incontestablement la meilleure; **whether they are happier now is open to q.** sont-ils plus heureux maintenant? on peut se le demander; **the wisdom of this decision is**

open to q. le bien-fondé de la décision est discutable

4 *(possibility)* **there was some q. of...** il a été question de...; **there's no q. of our making the same mistake again** nous ne sommes pas près de refaire la même erreur; **there's no q. of his coming with us, it's out of the q. that he should come with us** il est hors de question qu'il vienne avec nous; **there was never any q. of his coming with us** il n'a jamais été question qu'il nous accompagne; **I'm sorry, you can't go, it's out of the q.!** je regrette, vous ne pouvez pas y aller, c'est hors de question!

VT 1 *(interrogate)* interroger, poser des questions à; *(of police)* interroger; *Sch* interroger; *Mktg (consumer)* interroger; **to be questioned** être interrogé; *(suspect)* subir un interrogatoire; **the people questioned in the survey** les personnes interrogées dans le cadre du sondage; **she was questioned on her views** on l'a interrogée sur ses opinions

2 *(doubt ▸ motives, honesty, wisdom)* mettre en doute, mettre en question; *(▸ statement, claim)* mettre en doute, contester; **nobody is questioning your motives** personne ne met en doute *ou* en question vos motivations; **I questioned whether it was wise to continue** je me suis demandé s'il était bien sage de continuer

▸▸ *Gram* ***question form*** forme *f* interrogative; ***question mark*** *(punctuation mark)* point *m* d'interrogation; *Mktg (product)* point *m* d'interrogation, dilemme *m*; *Fig* **a q. mark hangs over the future of this country** il est impossible de prédire quel sort attend ce pays *ou* sera réservé à ce pays; **there is a q. mark over her reasons for leaving** on ignore les raisons qui l'ont poussée à partir; ***question master*** meneur(euse) *m,f* de jeu; *Rad & TV* animateur(trice) *m,f (d'un jeu)*; *Ling* ***question tag*** question tag *m*, = tournure interrogative en fin de phrase, équivalent du "n'est-ce pas" français

---

questionable ['kwestʃənəbəl] **ADJ 1** *(doubtful)* contestable, douteux; **his involvement in the affair is q.** sa participation dans cette affaire reste à démontrer *ou* à prouver; **it is q. whether she knew** rien ne prouve qu'elle était au courant; **this is the most democratic country – that's q.** c'est le pays le plus démocratique – c'est discutable **2** *(suspicious ▸ motives)* douteux, louche; *(▸ behaviour)* louche **3** *(strange ▸ taste, style)* douteux

questioner ['kwestʃənə(r)] **N** *(gen, in quiz show)* animateur(trice) *m,f*; *Law* interrogateur(trice) *m,f*; *Rad & TV* **our next q. is from Belfast** la question suivante nous vient de Belfast

questioning ['kwestʃənɪŋ] **ADJ** interrogateur; **to have a q. mind** avoir un esprit curieux

N interrogation *f*; *Law* **he was taken in for q.** il a été interpellé pour être interrogé

questioningly ['kwestʃənɪŋlɪ] **ADV** de manière interrogative

questionnaire [ˌkwestʃə'neə(r)] **N** questionnaire *m*

▸▸ ***questionnaire analysis*** dépouillement *m* de questionnaire; ***questionnaire construction*** construction *f* de questionnaire; ***questionnaire survey*** enquête *f* par questionnaire

quetzal ['ketsəl] **N 1** *Orn* quetzal *m* **2** *(currency)* quetzal *m*

queue [kjuː] **N 1** *Br* queue *f*, file *f* d'attente; **they were standing in a q.** ils faisaient la queue; **to form a q.** former une queue; **a long q. of cars** une longue file de voitures; **I was first in the q.** j'étais le premier de la file; **we joined the q. for foreign exchange** nous avons fait la queue devant le bureau de change **2** *Comput* file *f* d'attente

VT *Comput (print jobs)* mettre en file d'attente

VI *Br* faire la queue; **I spent ages queuing for a bus** j'ai passé des heures à attendre le bus; **q. here for tickets** *(sign)* file d'attente pour les billets

▸**queue up VI** *Br* faire la queue; **people queued up to shake his hand** les gens faisaient la queue pour lui serrer la main; **people are queuing up for a job like yours** les gens se battent pour décrocher un emploi comme le vôtre

queue-jump VI *Br* essayer de passer avant son tour, resquiller

queue-jumper N *Br* resquilleur(euse) *m,f (qui n'attend pas son tour)*

quibble ['kwɪbəl] **VI** chicaner; **to q. over details** chicaner sur des détails; **he didn't q. about the price** il n'a pas chipoté sur le prix

N chicane *f*; **I have one small q.** il y a juste une petite chose qui me gêne

quibbler ['kwɪblə(r)] **N** chicaneur(euse) *m,f*, chicanier(ère) *m,f*

quibbling ['kwɪblɪŋ] **ADJ** chicaneur, chicanier

N chicanerie *f*

quiche [kiːʃ] **N** quiche *f*

quick [kwɪk] **ADJ 1** *(rapid)* rapide; *(easy ▸ profits)* rapide, facile; **he's a q. worker** il travaille vite; *Fig* il ne perd pas de temps; **be q. (about it)!** faites vite!, dépêchez-vous!; **to have a q. look** jeter un rapide coup d'œil; **can I have a q. word?** est-ce que je peux vous parler un instant?; **we had a q. lunch** nous avons déjeuné sur le pouce; *Fam* **let's have a q. one** *or* **a q. drink** prenons un verre en vitesse[□]; **she did the job in double q. time** elle a fait le travail en deux temps, trois mouvements *ou* en un rien de temps; **the questions came in q. succession** les questions se sont succédé à un rythme très rapide; **q. march** marche *f* rapide *ou* au pas accéléré; **(as) q. as lightning** *or* **as a flash** rapide *ou* vif comme l'éclair

2 *(sharp)* alerte, éveillé, vif; **he is q. to learn** il apprend vite; **she has a q. ear** elle a l'oreille fine; **she has a q. eye for detail** aucun détail ne lui échappe; **thanks to his q. eye for bargains** grâce au chic qu'il a pour dénicher *ou* pour faire de bonnes affaires; **I was q. to notice the difference** j'ai tout de suite remarqué la différence; **she's too q. for me** elle est trop rapide pour moi; *Br* **they were very q. off the mark** ils n'ont pas perdu de temps; **he wasn't exactly q. off the mark when it came to ordering drinks** il était plutôt lent à la détente quand il s'agissait de commander les boissons

3 *(hasty ▸ judgment)* hâtif, rapide; **he has a q. temper** il s'emporte facilement; **he is q. to take offence** il est prompt à s'offenser, il se vexe pour un rien

ADV *Fam* rapidement[□]; **as q. as possible** aussi vite que possible; **come q.!** venez vite!; **to get rich q.** s'enrichir rapidement

N *(of fingernail)* vif *m*; **his nails were bitten to the q.** il s'était rongé les ongles jusqu'au sang; **her remark cut him to the q.** sa remarque l'a piqué au vif

NPL *Arch (living)* **the q. and the dead** les vivants *mpl* et les morts *mpl*

▸▸ ***quick fix*** solution *f* miracle; *Comput* ***quick launch bar*** barre *f* de lancement rapide

quick-change artist N = artiste qui change plusieurs fois de costume au cours d'un spectacle

quicken ['kwɪkən] **VT 1** *(hasten)* accélérer, hâter; *(▸ pulse)* accélérer; *Mus (▸ tempo)* presser; **to q. one's pace** *or* **step** hâter *ou* presser le pas **2** *(stir ▸ imagination, appetite, interest)* stimuler; *(▸ hatred, desire)* exciter; *(▸ resolve)* hâter; **the incident quickened his sense of injustice** l'incident a aiguisé son sentiment d'injustice

VI 1 *(step, pulse)* s'accélérer; **my heart** *or* **pulse quickened** mon cœur se mit à battre plus vite **2** *Literary (hopes, fire)* se ranimer

quickening ['kwɪkənɪŋ] **ADJ 1** *(pace, pulse)* qui s'accélère **2** *Literary (hopes, fire)* qui se ranime

N *(of pace, pulse)* accélération *f*

quickfire ['kwɪkfaɪə(r)] **ADJ he directed q. questions at me** il m'a mitraillé de questions; **a series of q. questions** un feu roulant de questions

quick-freeze *(pt* **quick-froze**, *pp* **quick-frozen) VT** surgeler

quickie ['kwɪkɪ] **N** *Fam* **1** *(gen)* truc *m* vite fait; *(question)* question *f* rapide[□] **2** *(sex)* coup *m* en vitesse *ou* entre deux portes; **to have a q.** tirer un coup vite fait **3** *(drink)* pot *m* rapide; **to have a q.** prendre un pot en vitesse; **we stopped at a pub for a q.** on s'est arrêtés dans un bar pour prendre un pot en vitesse

▸▸ ***quickie divorce*** divorce *m* express[□]

quicklime ['kwɪklaɪm] **N** chaux *f* vive

quickly ['kwɪklɪ] **ADV** rapidement, vite; **come as q. as possible** venez aussi vite que possible; **he q. telephoned the doctor** il se dépêcha d'appele[r] le médecin

quickness ['kwɪknɪs] **N 1** *(rapidity ▸ of movement, pulse)* rapidité *f*; *(▸ of thought, reaction)* rapidité *f*, vivacité *f* **2** *(acuteness ▸ of wit)* vivacité *f*; *(▸ of sight)* acuité *f*; *(▸ of hearing)* finesse *f*; *(hastiness)* **his q. of temper** sa promptitude à s'emporter

quicksand ['kwɪksænd] **N** sables *mpl* mouvants; **to get caught** *or* **stuck in q.** être pris dans des sables mouvants

• **quicksands NPL** sables *mpl* mouvants

quickset hedge ['kwɪkset-] **N** *Br* haie *f* vive

quicksilver ['kwɪkˌsɪlvə(r)] **N** vif-argent *m*, mercure *m*

quickstep ['kwɪkstep] **N** quickstep *m*

quick-tempered ADJ emporté, coléreux; **to be q.** s'emporter facilement

quick-witted ADJ à l'esprit vif; **she is very q.** *(in answers)* elle a de la repartie; *(in intelligence)* elle a l'esprit vif

quid [kwɪd] *(pl sense* **1 inv) N 1** *Br Fam (pound sterling)* livre *f* sterling[□]; **could you lend me ten q.** t'as pas dix livres à me prêter? **2** *(tobacco)* chique *f* **3** *Br Fam (idiom)* **to be quids in** être à l'aise, avoir du fric

quid pro quo [ˌkwɪdprəʊ'kwəʊ] *(pl* **quid pro quos) N** contrepartie *f*, récompense *f*; **what did she get as a q. for her silence?** qu'est-ce qu'elle a reçu en contrepartie de son silence?

quiescence [kwaɪ'esəns] **N** *Literary* tranquillité *f*, quiétude *f*

quiescent [kwaɪ'esənt] **ADJ** *Literary (passive)* passif; *(peaceful)* tranquille

QUIET ['kwaɪət]

N	
• tranquillité	• silence
ADJ	
• tranquille **1, 2**	• silencieux **1, 3**
• doux **1**	• calme **2, 3**
• docile **3**	• dans l'intimité **4**
• discret **5**	• sobre **6**
VT	
• calmer	• faire taire

N *(calm)* tranquillité *f*, calme *m*; *(silence)* silence *m*; **to ask for q.** demander le silence; **perfect peace and q.** une parfaite tranquillité; *Br Fam* **on the q.** *(in secrecy)* en douce, en cachette[□]; *(discreetly)* discrètement[□], en douceur[□]; *(in confidence)* en confiance[□]

ADJ 1 *(silent)* tranquille, silencieux; *(not loud ▸ music)* doux (douce); *(▸ voice)* bas, doux (douce); **be** *or* **keep q.!** taisez-vous!; **could you try to keep them q.?** pourriez-vous essayer de les faire taire?; **q. please!** silence, s'il vous plaît!; **you're very q.** vous ne dites pas grand-chose; **keep q. about what you've seen** ne dites rien de ce que vous avez vu; **it was as q. as the grave** il régnait un silence de mort; **she was as q. as a mouse** elle ne faisait pas le moindre bruit; **the wind grew q.** le vent s'est apaisé; **we were having a q. conversation** nous bavardions tranquillement; **in a q. voice** d'une voix douce

2 *(calm, tranquil)* calme, tranquille, paisible; *Fin (market, business)* calme; **to lead a q. life** mener une vie paisible *ou* tranquille; **anything for a q. life** tout pour avoir la paix; **the TV keeps the children q.** pendant qu'ils regardent la télé, les enfants se tiennent tranquilles; **sit q. for ten minutes** restez assis tranquillement pendant dix minutes; **he's a very q. kind of chap** c'est un type très tranquille; **q. disposition** caractère *m* doux *ou* calme; **to have a q. drink** boire un verre tranquillement; **we had a q. Christmas** nous avons passé un Noël tranquille; **it's very pretty countryside, in a q. sort of way** c'est un très joli paysage dans le genre paisible; **she had a q. night** elle a passé une nuit tranquille *ou* paisible; **all is q.** tout va bien, rien à signaler

3 *(docile ▸ animal)* docile; *(easy ▸ baby)* calme; *(uncommunicative)* silencieux, peu communicatif; **you're very q., is anything wrong?** tu es drôlement silencieux, il y a quelque chose qui ne va pas?

4 *(private ▸ wedding)* dans l'intimité; *(▸ party)*

avec quelques intimes, avec peu d'invités; *(secret)* secret(ète), dissimulé; **can I have a q. word with you?** est-ce que je peux vous dire un mot en particulier?; **keep the news q.** gardez la nouvelle pour vous; **she was very q. about her background** elle n'a pas dit grand-chose de ses antécédents

5 *(subtle, discreet ▸ irony)* voilé, discret(ète); *(▸ optimism)* discret(ète); *(▸ anger)* sourd; *(▸ despair, resentment)* secret(ète); **he had a q. smile on his lips** il avait un petit sourire aux lèvres

6 *(muted ▸ colour, style)* sobre; **he's a q. dresser** il s'habille sobrement *ou* sans ostentation

VT *(calm)* calmer; *(silence)* faire taire

▸ **quiet down** *Am* = **quieten down**

quieten ['kwaɪətən] **VT** *Br (child, audience)* calmer, apaiser; *(conscience)* tranquilliser, apaiser; *(doubts)* dissiper; **does that q. your fears?** est-ce que cela dissipe vos craintes?

VI *(child)* se calmer; *(music)* devenir plus doux (douce)

▸ **quieten down VI 1** *(become quiet ▸ person)* se calmer; *(▸ storm, wind)* se calmer, s'apaiser; **the meeting gradually quietened down** peu à peu, l'assemblée s'est calmée **2** *(become reasonable)* s'assagir; **he's quietened down a lot since he got married** il s'est beaucoup assagi depuis son mariage

VT SEP *(calm)* calmer, apaiser; *(shut up)* faire taire

quietly ['kwaɪətlɪ] **ADV 1** *(silently)* silencieusement, sans bruit

2 *(calmly)* doucement, calmement; **a q. flowing river** une rivière au cours paisible; **to be q. determined to do sth** être froidement décidé à faire qch

3 *(peacefully)* tranquillement, paisiblement; **sit q.** restez assis tranquillement

4 *(discreetly)* simplement, discrètement; **they got married q.** ils se sont mariés dans l'intimité

quietness ['kwaɪətnɪs] **N 1** *(silence)* silence *m* **2** *(calmness, tranquillity)* tranquillité *f*, calme *m* **3** *(of colour, style)* caractère *m* sobre

quietude ['kwaɪətju:d] **N** *Literary* quiétude *f*

quietus [kwaɪ'i:təs] *(pl* **quietuses** [-si:z]) **N** *Literary (death)* trépas *m*

quiff [kwɪf] **N** *(hairstyle)* banane *f*

quill [kwɪl] **N 1** *(feather)* penne *f*; *(shaft of feather)* tuyau *m*; *(of hedgehog, porcupine)* piquant *m* **2** *(pen)* plume *f* (d'oie)

▸▸ ***quill pen*** plume *f* d'oie

quilt [kwɪlt] **N** *(eiderdown)* édredon *m*; *(bedspread)* dessus-de-lit *m inv*; *(duvet)* couette *f*, *Suisse* duvet *m*

▸▸ ***quilt cover*** housse *f* de couette

quilting ['kwɪltɪŋ] **N 1** *(fabric)* tissu *m* matelassé; *(on furniture)* capitonnage *m* **2** *(of clothing)* ouatinage *m*; *(of furniture covering)* capitonnage *m* **3** *(hobby)* = réalisation d'ouvrages (vêtements, dessus-de-lit) en tissu matelassé

quin [kwɪn] **N** *Br (abbr* **quintuplet**) quintuplé(e) *m,f*

quince [kwɪns] **N** *(fruit)* coing *m*; *(tree)* cognassier *m*

COMP *(jam, jelly)* de coings

quincentenary [,kwɪnsen'ti:nərɪ] *(pl* **quincentenaries**) **N** cinq-centième anniversaire *m*

quinine [kwɪ'ni:n] **N** *Pharm* quinine *f*

quinquagenarian [,kwɪŋkwədʒə'neərɪən] **N** quinquagénaire *mf*

ADJ quinquagénaire

Quinquagesima [,kwɪŋkwə'dʒesɪmə] **N** *Rel* Quinquagésime *f*

quintal ['kwɪntəl] **N** quintal *m*

quinte [kænt] **N** *Fencing* quinte *f*

quintessence [kwɪn'tesəns] **N** *Literary* quintessence *f*

quintessential [,kwɪntɪ'senʃəl] **ADJ** typique, type; **she's the q. Parisian** c'est la Parisienne type

quintessentially [,kwɪntɪ'senʃəlɪ] **ADV** fondamentalement

quintet, quintette [kwɪn'tet] **N 1** *(players ▸ classical)* quintette *m*; *(▸ jazz)* quintet *m* **2** *(piece of music)* quintette *m*

quintillion [,kwɪn'tɪlɪən] **N** trillion *m* (10^{18}); *Br Old-fashioned* quintillion *m* (10^{30})

quintuple [,kwɪn'tju:pəl] **ADJ** quintuple

N quintuple *m*

VT quintupler

VI quintupler

quintuplet [,kwɪn'tju:plɪt] **N** quintuplé(e) *m,f*

quip [kwɪp] *(pt & pp* **quipped**, *cont* **quipping**) **N** *(remark ▸ witty)* bon mot *m*, mot *m* d'esprit; *(▸ sarcastic)* sarcasme *m*; *(gibe)* quolibet *m*; **to make a q.** faire un bon mot *ou* de l'esprit; **he made a nasty q. about her humble origins** il a fait une remarque désobligeante sur ses origines modestes

VT *(say sarcastically)* dire de façon sarcastique; *(say wittily)* dire avec esprit

quire ['kwaɪə(r)] **N** *(in bookbinding)* cahier *m*; *(of paper)* main *f* (de papier)

quirk [kw3:k] **N 1** *(idiosyncrasy)* manie *f*, excentricité *f*; **he's got a lot of little quirks** il y a plein de choses bizarres chez lui **2** *(accident)* bizarrerie *f*, caprice *m*; **by a strange q. of fate we met in Sydney** par un caprice du destin, nous nous sommes rencontrés à Sydney

quirky ['kw3:kɪ] *(compar* **quirkier**, *superl* **quirkiest**) **ADJ** bizarre, original

quisling ['kwɪzlɪŋ] **N** *Pej* collaborateur(trice) *m,f*

quit [kwɪt] *(pt & pp* **quit** *or* **quitted**, *cont* **quitting**) **VT 1** *(leave)* quitter; **we have to q. the premises by the end of the month** nous devons quitter les lieux avant la fin du mois **2** *Am (give up, stop)* quitter, cesser; **he q. school at 15** il a quitté l'école à 15 ans; **he q. his job** il a quitté son travail; **I've q. smoking** j'ai arrêté *ou* cessé de fumer; **q. it!** arrête!, ça suffit! **3** *Comput (database, program)* sortir de, quitter

VI 1 *(give up)* renoncer, abandonner; *(resign)* démissionner; *Fam* **I q.!** j'abandonne!; **I want to q.** j'ai envie de tout laisser tomber; **you shouldn't q. so easily** vous ne devriez pas abandonner la partie si facilement **2** *(leave)* partir; **to receive notice to q.** *(tenant)* recevoir son congé **3** *Comput* sortir

ADJ *Formal* **to be q. of sb/sth** être débarrassé de qn/qch

QUITE [kwaɪt]

> **ADV**
> • assez **1**
> • exactement **3**
> • tout à fait **2, 3**
>
> **EXCLAM**
> • tout à fait!

ADV 1 *(moderately)* assez; **the movie is q. good** le film est assez bon; **it's q. cold today** il fait assez froid aujourd'hui; **q. frequently/recently** assez fréquemment/récemment; **I'd q. like to go** ça me plairait assez d'y aller; **q. a difficult job** un travail assez difficile; **q. a good job** un assez bon emploi; **q. a lot of people seem to believe it** un bon nombre de gens semblent le croire; **there were q. a few good paintings** il y avait un assez grand nombre de bons tableaux; **there was q. a crowd** il y avait pas mal de monde; **I've been here for q. some time** je suis ici depuis un bon moment *ou* depuis assez longtemps; **he was in France for q. some time** il a passé pas mal de temps en France

2 *(completely, absolutely)* tout à fait; **she's q. right** elle a tout à fait *ou* parfaitement raison; **the story isn't q. true** l'histoire n'est pas tout à fait *ou* entièrement vraie; **I q. understand** je comprends tout à fait *ou* parfaitement; **we've always been q. happy together** nous avons toujours été parfaitement heureux ensemble; **he's q. happy to let others do the work** ça ne le dérange absolument pas de laisser les autres faire le travail; **he was q. obviously drunk** il était manifestement ivre; **if you've q. finished** si vous avez terminé; **that's q. another matter!** ça, c'est autre chose!; **q. the opposite** bien au contraire; **in q. another tone** sur un tout autre ton; **not q. a month ago** il y a un peu moins d'un mois; **not q. 300** pas tout à fait 300; **it's not q. 2 o'clock** il n'est pas tout à fait 2 heures; **that's q. enough (of that)!** ça suffit comme ça!; **I'm afraid I'll be a bit late – that's q. all right** je crains d'être un peu en retard – ce n'est pas grave; **q. apart from the fact that...** en dehors du fait que...; **q. the best story of its kind** sans aucun doute la meilleure histoire de ce genre; **he's q. the young gentleman** c'est le parfait jeune homme

3 *(exactly)* exactement, tout à fait; **that wasn't q. what I had in mind** ce n'est pas exactement ce que j'avais en tête; **I'm not q. sure what you mean** je ne vois pas très bien ce que vous voulez dire; **I can't q. remember when it happened** je ne me souviens pas bien *ou* tout à fait quand ça s'est passé

4 *(expressing approval, appreciation)* **that was q. a party!** ça a été une sacrée soirée!; **it's been q. a day** quelle journée!; **that movie was q. something** ce film, c'était vraiment quelque chose; **his speech was q. something** son discours était tout à fait remarquable

EXCLAM q. (so)! tout à fait!, parfaitement!

quits [kwɪts] **ADJ** quitte; **now we're q.** maintenant nous sommes quittes; **double or q.** quitte ou double; **let's call it q.** *(financially)* disons que nous sommes quittes; *(in fight, argument)* restons-en là

quittance ['kwɪtəns] **N** *Fin & Law* quittance *f*

quitter ['kwɪtə(r)] **N** *Fam* dégonflé(e) *m,f*

quiver ['kwɪvə(r)] **VI 1** *(tremble ▸ person)* frémir, trembler; *(▸ lips, hands, voice)* trembler; *(▸ flesh)* palpiter, frémir; **to q. with fear/rage** trembler de peur/de rage; **to q. with emotion** frissonner d'émotion; **the quivering tones of the violin** les trémolos *mpl* du violon **2** *(flutter ▸ heart)* trembler, frémir; *(▸ leaves)* frémir, frissonner; *(▸ flame)* trembler, vaciller

N 1 *(tremble)* tremblement *m*; *(of violin)* trémolo *m*, frémissement *m*; **a q. of fear went down my spine** un frisson de peur me parcourut le dos; **he had a q. in his voice** sa voix tremblait d'émotion **2** *(for arrows)* carquois *m*

quivering ['kwɪvərɪŋ] **ADJ** *(person)* frémissant, tremblant; *(lips, voice)* tremblant; *(flesh)* palpitant, frémissant; *(leaves)* frémissant, frissonnant; *(flame)* tremblant, vacillant; **the experience had reduced him to a q. mass** *or* **jelly** l'épreuve l'avait réduit à l'état de loque

N *(UNCOUNT) (gen)* tremblement *m*; *(of flesh)* palpitation *f*, frémissement *m*

qui vive [,ki:'vi:v] **N** *Br* **on the q.** sur le qui-vive

Quixote ['kwɪksət] **PR N Don Q.** Don Quichotte

quixotic [kwɪk'sɒtɪk] **ADJ** *(idealistic)* idéaliste, chimérique; *(chivalrous)* généreux, chevaleresque

quixotically [kwɪk'sɒtɪklɪ] **ADV** à la (manière de) Don Quichotte

quiz [kwɪz] *(pl* **quizzes**, *pt & pp* **quizzed**, *cont* **quizzing**) **N 1** *(game ▸ on TV)* jeu *m* télévisé; *(▸ on radio)* jeu *m* radiophonique; *(▸ in newspaper)* quiz *m*, questionnaire *m*; **q. shows** *or* **programmes** les jeux *mpl* télévisés/radiophoniques **2** *Am Sch (test)* interrogation *f* écrite

VT 1 *(question)* interroger, questionner; **to q. sb about sth** interroger qn au sujet de qch **2** *Am Sch (test)* interroger

quizmaster ['kwɪz,mɑ:stə(r)] **N** *Rad & TV* animateur(trice) *m,f (d'un jeu)*

quizzical ['kwɪzɪkəl] **ADJ** *(questioning)* interrogateur; *(ironic)* ironique, narquois; **to give sb a q. look** lancer un regard narquois à qn

quizzically ['kwɪzɪklɪ] **ADV** *(questioningly)* d'un air interrogateur; *(ironically)* d'un air ironique *ou* narquois

quod [kwɒd] **N** *Br Fam (jail)* tôle *f*; **in q.** en tôle

quoin [kɔɪn] **N** *(cornerstone)* pierre *f* d'angle; *(keystone)* clef *f* de voûte

quoit [kɔɪt] **N** *(in game)* anneau *m*; **to play quoits** jouer aux anneaux

quorate ['kwɔ:reɪt] **ADJ** *Br Formal* **to be q.** être en nombre

Quorn® [kwɔ:n] **N** = aliment aux protéines végétales servant de substitut à la viande

quorum ['kwɔ:rəm] **N** quorum *m*; **to have a q.** être en nombre; **to form a q.** constituer un quorum

quota ['kwəʊtə] **N 1** *(limited quantity)* quota *m*, contingent *m*; **they are admitted on a q. system** il y a un numerus clausus *ou* un quota pour les

admissions; **to apportion** *or* **to fix quotas for import** déterminer les quotas d'importation **2** *(share)* part *f*, quota *m*; **I've had my q. of bad luck** j'ai eu ma dose *ou* ma part de malchance; **we've had more than our q. of rain recently** nous avons eu plus que notre quota *ou* notre dose de pluie dernièrement
▸▸ *Mktg* ***quota method*** *(of sampling)* méthode *f* des quotas; *Mktg* ***quota sample*** échantillon *m* par quotas; *Mktg* ***quota sampling*** échantillonnage *m* par quotas

quotable ['kwəʊtəbəl] ADJ **1** *(worth quoting)* digne d'être cité; **a very q. phrase** une phrase tout à fait digne d'être citée; **the press find him very q.** les journalistes adorent ses petites phrases **2** *(on the record)* que l'on peut citer; **are these figures q.?** peut-on citer ces chiffres?; **what he said is not q.** ce qu'il a dit ne peut être répété **3** *St Exch* cotable

quotation [kwəʊ'teɪʃən] N **1** *(remark, sentence)* citation *f* **2** *St Exch* cours *m*, cotation *f*; **the latest quotations** les derniers cours; **to seek a share q.** faire une demande d'admission *ou* d'inscription à la cote **3** *Com (estimate)* devis *m*; *(for insurance)* cotation *f*; **to get a q.** faire faire un devis; **they gave me a q. of £500** ils m'ont fait un devis de 500 livres
▸▸ ***quotation marks*** guillemets *mpl*; **in q. marks** entre guillemets

quote [kwəʊt] VT **1** *(cite ▸ words, example, statistics)* citer; **can I q. you on that?** vous me permettez de citer ce que vous venez de dire?; **don't q. me on that** *(don't repeat it)* ne le répétez pas; *(don't say who told you)* ne dites pas que c'est moi qui vous l'ai dit; **she quoted several passages from the book** elle cita plusieurs passages du livre; **he said, q., get lost, unquote** il a dit, je cite, allez vous faire voir; **their leader was quoted as denying the allegation** leur leader aurait rejeté l'accusation **2** *Admin & Com* **in reply please q. this number** prière de rappeler ce numéro dans toute correspondance ultérieure **3** *(specify ▸ price)* indiquer; *St Exch* (▸ *shares)* coter; **gold prices were quoted at £500** l'or a été coté à 500 livres; **quoted on the Stock Exchange** coté en Bourse; **can you q. me a price?** pouvez-vous me donner *ou* m'indiquer un prix?
VI **1** *(cite)* faire des citations; **to q. from Yeats** citer Yeats **2** *Com* **to q. for a job** faire un devis pour un travail
N **1** *(quotation)* citation *f*; *(statement)* déclaration *f*; **a q. from Shakespeare** une citation de Shakespeare **2** *(estimate)* devis *m* **3** *(quotation mark)* guillemet *m*; **in quotes** entre guillemets
▸▸ *Br St Exch* ***quoted company*** société *f* cotée en Bourse; *Fin* ***quoted investment*** valeur *f* cotée en Bourse; *Fin* ***quoted price*** cours *m* inscrit à la cote officielle; *Fin* ***quoted securities*** valeurs *fpl* de Bourse; *St Exch* ***quoted share*** action *f* cotée, action *f* inscrite à la cote officielle

quoth [kwəʊθ] VT *Arch* **"nay," q. the King** "non", fit *ou* dit le roi

quotidian [kwɒ'tɪdɪən] ADJ *Formal* quotidien

quotient ['kwəʊʃənt] N quotient *m*

Qur'an, Qur'anic = **Koran, Koranic**

qv *(written abbr* **quod vide)** = expression renvoyant le lecteur à une autre entrée dans une encyclopédie

qwerty, Qwerty ['kwɜːtɪ] N
▸▸ ***qwerty keyboard*** clavier *m* QWERTY

qwertz, Qwertz [kwɜːts] N
▸▸ ***qwertz keyboard*** clavier *m* QWERTZ

R[1], **r** [ɑː(r)] N (letter) R, r *m inv*; **two r's** deux r; **R for Robert** ≃ R comme Raoul; *Br Sch* **the three Rs** = la lecture, l'écriture et l'arithmétique *(qui constituent les fondements de l'enseignement primaire)*

R[2] [ɑː(r)] ADJ *Am* (*abbr* **restricted**) = indique qu'un film est interdit aux moins de 17 ans

R[3] **1** (*written abbr* **right**) dr
2 (*written abbr* **river**) rivière *f*
3 (*written abbr* **Réaumur**) R
4 *Am* (*written abbr* **Republican**) républicain
5 *Br* (*written abbr* **Rex**) = suit le nom d'un roi
6 *Br* (*written abbr* **Regina**) = suit le nom d'une reine
7 *Geom* (*written abbr* **radius**) R
8 (*written abbr* **road**) rue *f*
9 (*written abbr* **rand**) R

RA [ɑːˈreɪ] N **1** (*abbr* **rear admiral**) contre-amiral *m* **2** (*abbr* **Royal Academician**) = membre de la "Royal Academy" **3** (*abbr* **Royal Academy**) Académie *f* royale britannique *(académie des beaux-arts)*

rabbet [ˈræbɪt] *Carp* N *(groove)* feuillure *f*
VT feuiller
▸▸ ***rabbet plane*** feuilleret *m*

rabbi [ˈræbaɪ] N rabbin *m*; **chief r.** grand rabbin *m*

rabbinic [rəˈbɪnɪk] ADJ rabbinique
• **Rabbinic** N hébreu *m* rabbinique

rabbinical [rəˈbɪnɪkəl] ADJ rabbinique

rabbit [ˈræbɪt] N *(animal)* lapin(e) *m,f*; **doe r.** lapine *f*; **young r.** lapereau *m*; **wild r.** lapin *m* de garenne; *Fig* **they breed like rabbits** ils se reproduisent comme des lapins; **to produce a r. out of a hat** *(conjuror)* faire sortir un lapin d'un chapeau; *Fig* trouver une solution miracle
COMP *(coat)* en (peau de) lapin; *(stew)* de lapin
VI **to go rabbiting** chasser le lapin
▸▸ ***rabbit burrow*** terrier *m* (de lapin); *Am* ***rabbit ears*** antenne *f* téléscopique; ***rabbit food*** aliments *mpl* pour lapins; *Fam Hum Pej (salad, green vegetables)* verdure *f*; ***rabbit hole*** terrier *m* de lapin; ***rabbit hutch*** clapier *m*, cage *f ou* cabane à lapins; *Br Fam Fig (accommodation)* cage *f* à lapins; ***rabbit punch*** coup *m* du lapin; ***rabbit warren*** garenne *f*; *Fig* labyrinthe *m*, dédale *m*

rabbit on VI *Br Fam (talk)* jacasser, bavasser (**about** à propos de); **what's she rabbiting on about?** qu'est-ce qu'elle raconte *ou* bave?; **do stop rabbiting on** tais-toi un peu; **he's been rabbiting on about his money problems** il me rebat les oreilles de ses problèmes d'argent

rabble [ˈræbəl] N **1** *(disorderly mob)* foule *f* **2** *Old-fashioned Pej (lower classes)* **the r.** la populace, la canaille **3** *Tech (in foundry)* râble *m*

rabble-rouser [-raʊzə(r)] N agitateur(trice) *m,f*

rabble-rousing N incitation *f* à la révolte
ADJ *(speech)* incendiaire; *(leader)* qui incite à la révolte

Rabelaisian [ˌræbəˈleɪzɪən] ADJ rabelaisien

rabid [ˈræbɪd, ˈreɪbɪd] ADJ **1** *Med (animal)* enragé; *(person)* atteint de la rage **2** *Fig (extremist, revolutionary)* enragé; *(hatred)* farouche; *(anger)* féroce

rabies [ˈreɪbiːz] N *(UNCOUNT)* rage *f*; **the dog is a r. carrier** le chien est porteur de la rage
▸▸ ***rabies vaccine*** vaccin *m* contre la rage

RAC [ɑːreɪˈsiː] N *Br* (*abbr* **Royal Automobile Club**) = automobile club britannique et compagnie d'assurances qui garantit le dépannage de ses adhérents et propose des services touristiques et juridiques, ≃ ACF *m*, ≃ TCF *m*

raccoon [rəˈkuːn] N *Zool* raton *m* laveur
COMP *(coat, stole)* en (fourrure de) raton laveur
▸▸ *Zool* ***raccoon dog*** chien *m* viverrin

race [reɪs] N **1** *(competition)* course *f*; **an 800-metre r.** une course de *ou* sur 800 mètres; **the 100 metres r.** le 100 mètres, la course de 100 mètres; **to run a r.** courir, participer à une course; **it's anybody's r.** il n'y a pas de favori; *Horseracing* **a day at the races** une journée aux courses; **a r. against time** une course contre la montre; **it'll be a r. to finish on time** il faudra se dépêcher pour finir à temps; **the r. for the Presidency** la course à la présidence
2 *(ethnic group)* race *f*; *(in anthropology)* ethnie *f*; **the human r.** la race humaine
3 *Literary (passing ▸ of sun, moon)* course *f*; *(▸ of life)* cours *m*
4 *(swift current)* fort courant *m*; *(in sea)* raz *m*
5 *Aviat (slipstream)* sillage *m*; *(turbulence)* turbulence *f*
COMP *(discrimination, hatred, prejudice)* racial
VT **1** *(compete against)* faire la course avec; **I'll r. you home!** le premier arrivé à la maison a gagné!; **he raced me round the block** il a fait la course avec moi autour du pâté de maisons
2 *(rush)* **he raced me to the airport** il m'a emmené à l'aéroport à toute vitesse; **the casualties were raced to hospital** les blessés ont été transportés d'urgence à l'hôpital; **to r. a bill through Parliament** faire adopter un projet de loi en toute hâte
3 *(put into a race)* **to r. a horse** faire courir un cheval; **this colt hasn't been raced yet** ce poulain n'a pas encore couru; **to r. pigeons** faire des courses de pigeons
4 *Aut* **to r. the engine** accélérer; *(excessively)* faire s'emballer le moteur
VI **1** *(compete)* courir; **the cars/drivers were racing against each other** les voitures/les conducteurs faisaient la course; **his horse will be racing at Ascot** son cheval courra à Ascot **2** *(go fast, rush)* aller à toute allure *ou* vitesse; **to r. in/out/past** entrer/sortir/passer à toute allure; **they raced out of the café** ils se précipitèrent hors du café; **to r. for a bus** courir pour attraper un bus; **she raced downstairs** elle a dévalé l'escalier; **she raced up the stairs** elle a monté les escaliers quatre à quatre; **he raced through his meal** il a avalé son repas à toute vitesse; **my pulse was racing** mon cœur battait à tout rompre; **the ambulance raced to the scene of the accident** l'ambulance fonça sur les lieux de l'accident; **the car was racing along** la voiture allait à toute vitesse; **the work is racing ahead** le travail avance très vite; **the clouds are racing across the sky** les nuages filent dans le ciel **3** *(engine)* s'emballer
▸▸ ***race baiting*** = dans un débat, une campagne électorale etc, fait d'exploiter des stéréotypes raciaux pour déstabiliser son adversaire; *Am* ***race car*** voiture *f* de course; ***race card*** programme *m* (des courses); *Am* ***race driver*** pilote *m* de course; ***race meeting*** courses *fpl*; **there is a r. meeting at Newmarket tomorrow** on court *ou* il y a des courses demain à Newmarket; ***race norming*** égalité *f* des chances; ***race relations*** relations *fpl* interraciales; *Br* ***race relations board*** = organisme luttant contre la discrimination raciale; ***race riot*** émeute *f* raciale

racecourse [ˈreɪskɔːs] N **1** *(for horses)* champ *m* de courses, hippodrome *m* **2** *Am (for cars, motorbikes)* circuit *m*; *(for runners, cycles)* piste *f*

racegoer [ˈreɪsˌgəʊə(r)] N turfiste *mf*

racehorse [ˈreɪshɔːs, *pl* -hɔːsɪz] N cheval *m* de course

raceme [ˈræsiːm] N *Bot* grappe *f (inflorescence)*

racer [ˈreɪsə(r)] N *(runner)* coureur(euse) *m,f*; *(horse)* cheval *m* de course; *(car)* voiture *f* de course; *(cycle)* vélo *m* de course

racetrack [ˈreɪstræk] N *(gen)* piste *f*; *(for horses)* champ *m* de courses, hippodrome *m*

racewalking [ˈreɪsˌwɔːkɪŋ] N marche *f* (athlétique)

raceway [ˈreɪsweɪ] N **1** *(channel for water)* canal *m* **2** *Am (for car racing)* circuit *m* **3** *esp Am Horseracing* champ *m* de courses, hippodrome *m*

racial [ˈreɪʃəl] ADJ **1** *(concerning a race)* racial, ethnique **2** *(between races)* racial
▸▸ ***racial discrimination*** discrimination *f* raciale; ***racial engineering*** = pratiques visant à favoriser l'égalité des races dans l'emploi, l'éducation etc; ***racial harmony*** harmonie *f ou* entente *f* raciale; *Am* ***racial profiling*** = pratique policière qui consiste à contrôler l'identité des membres de la communauté noire américaine en priorité; ***racial violence*** violence *f* raciale

racialism [ˈreɪʃəlɪzəm] N racisme *m*

racialist [ˈreɪʃəlɪst] ADJ raciste
N raciste *mf*

racially [ˈreɪʃəlɪ] ADV du point de vue racial; **a r. motivated attack** une agression raciste; **r. prejudiced** raciste

raciness [ˈreɪsɪnɪs] N **1** *(liveliness)* verve *f* **2** *(suggestiveness)* grivoiserie *f*

racing [ˈreɪsɪŋ] N *(of horses)* courses *fpl* de chevaux
COMP *(bicycle, yacht)* de course
▸▸ ***racing car*** voiture *f* de course; *Horseracing* ***racing colours*** couleurs *fpl* de l'écurie; ***racing cyclist*** coureur(euse) *m,f* cycliste; ***racing driver*** coureur(euse) *m,f* automobile, pilote *mf* (de course); ***racing pigeon*** pigeon *m* voyageur *(de compétition)*; ***racing stable*** écurie *f* de courses; ***racing tip*** pronostic *m*

racism [ˈreɪsɪzəm] N racisme *m*

racist [ˈreɪsɪst] ADJ raciste
N raciste *mf*

rack [ræk] N **1** *(shelf)* étagère *f*; *(in shop)* présentoir *m*; *(on cycle)* porte-bagages *m inv*; *(for cooling, drying)* grille *f*, claie *f*; *(for fodder, bicycles, test tubes, pipes)* râtelier *m*; *(for bottles)* casier *m*; **(luggage) r.** *(in train, bus)* filet *m* (à bagages); **(tool) r.** porte-outils *m inv*; **(clothes) r.** triangle *m* (à vêtements); **to buy a suit off the r.** acheter un costume en prêt-à-porter
2 *Hist* chevalet *m*; **to put sb on the r.** faire subir à qn le supplice du chevalet; *Fig* mettre qn au supplice; **that question put him on the r.** cette question l'a mis dans une position très difficile
3 *Tech* crémaillère *f*

4 *Culin* **r. of lamb** carré *m* d'agneau
5 *Br Fam (woman's breasts)* nénés *mpl*
6 *Am Fam* **to hit the r.** *(go to bed)* se pieuter, se bâcher
7 *(idiom)* **to go to r. and ruin** *(house)* tomber en ruine; *(garden)* être à l'abandon; *(person)* dépérir; *(company)* péricliter; *(country, institution)* aller à vau-l'eau

VT 1 *(torture)* faire subir le supplice du chevalet à; *Fig* tenailler, ronger; **to be racked with pain** être perclus de douleur; **racked by guilt** tenaillé par un sentiment de culpabilité; **her body was racked with sobs** son corps était secoué de sanglots; **to r. one's brains** se creuser la tête **2** *(wine)* soutirer

▸▸ *Cin & TV* ***rack focus*** changement *m* de focale *(en cours de prise)*; ***rack and pinion*** crémaillère *f*; ***rack and pinion railway*** chemin *m* de fer à crémaillère; ***rack railway*** chemin *m* de fer à crémaillère; *Br* ***rack rent*** loyer *m* exorbitant

▸ **rack back VT SEP** *Am Fam* **to r. sb back** passer un savon à qn, remonter les bretelles à qn

▸ **rack off VI** *Austr Fam* dégager, se casser; **r. off!** dégage!, casse-toi!

▸ **rack up VT SEP** *(points)* marquer

racket ['rækɪt] **N 1** *Sport (bat)* raquette *f*
2 *(snowshoe)* raquette *f*
3 *Fam (din)* boucan *m*, barouf *m*; **to make a r.** faire du boucan *ou* du barouf; **will you turn that r. off!** arrêtez ce boucan!
4 *Fam (extortion)* racket☐*m*; *(fraud)* escroquerie☐*f*; *(traffic)* trafic☐*m*; **protection r.** racket *m*; **drugs r.** trafic *m* de drogue; **this lottery is such a r.** cette loterie, c'est de l'arnaque; **he's involved in some money-laundering r.** il trempe dans des affaires de blanchiment d'argent
5 *Fam (job)* boulot *m*; **what's your r.?** vous travaillez dans quoi?; **is she still in the teaching r.?** est-ce qu'elle est encore dans l'enseignement?☐

VI *Fam (be noisy)* faire du boucan

• **rackets N** *(UNCOUNT) (game)* racquet-ball *m*

▸▸ *Sport* ***racket cover*** housse *f* de raquette; *Sport* ***racket press*** presse-raquette *m*

racketeer [ˌrækə'tɪə(r)] **N** racketteur(euse) *m,f*
VI racketter

racketeering [ˌrækə'tɪərɪŋ] **N** racket *m*

racking ['rækɪŋ] **ADJ** *(pain)* atroce, déchirant

racoon = **raccoon**

racquet ['rækət] **N** *Sport (bat)* raquette *f*

racy ['reɪsɪ] *(compar* **racier**, *superl* **raciest***)* **ADJ 1** *(lively)* plein de verve *ou* de brio **2** *(suggestive)* osé **3** *(wine)* racé

rad [ræd] **N** *Phys* rad *m*
ADJ *Am Fam* génial, géant

RADA ['rɑːdə] **N** *Br (abbr* **Royal Academy of Dramatic Art***)* = conservatoire britannique d'art dramatique

radar ['reɪdɑː(r)] **N** radar *m*; **to navigate by r.** naviguer au radar
COMP *(image)* radar
▸▸ ***radar astronomy*** radarastronomie *f*; ***radar beacon*** radiophare *m*; ***radar blip*** top *m* d'écho (radar); ***radar detection*** détection *f* radar; ***radar gun*** radar gun *m*; ***radar imaging*** imagerie *f* radar; *Am* ***radar man***, *Br* ***radar operator*** radariste *mf*; ***radar scanner*** antenne *f* radar; ***radar screen*** écran *m* (de) radar; ***radar speed trap*** contrôle *m* radar; ***radar station*** station *f* radar; ***radar trap*** contrôle *m* radar

raddled ['rædəld] **ADJ** ravagé

radial ['reɪdɪəl] **ADJ 1** *Tech & Math* radial **2** *Anat (artery etc)* radial
N 1 *(tyre)* pneu *m* radial *ou* à carcasse radiale **2** *(line)* rayon *m*
▸▸ ***radial engine*** moteur *m* en étoile; ***radial roads*** routes *fpl* en étoile; ***radial symmetry*** symétrie *f* radiée *ou* radiaire; ***radial tyre*** pneu *m* radial *ou* à carcasse radiale; *Astron* ***radial velocity*** vitesse *f* radiale

radially ['reɪdɪəlɪ] **ADV** radialement

radiance ['reɪdɪəns], **radiancy** ['reɪdɪənsɪ] **N** *(of light, sun)* éclat *m*, rayonnement *m*; *Fig (beauty, happiness)* éclat *m*

radiant ['reɪdɪənt] **ADJ 1** *Literary (bright)* radieux; *Fig* **her r. beauty** sa beauté éclatante **2** *(happy)* radieux, rayonnant; **he was r. with joy** il rayonnait de joie **3** *Phys* radiant, rayonnant
N 1 *Phys* point *m* radiant **2** *Astron* radiant *m*
▸▸ *Phys* ***radiant energy*** énergie *f* de rayonnement; *Phys* ***radiant flux*** flux *m* de rayonnement; *Phys* ***radiant heat*** chaleur *f* rayonnante; ***radiant heating*** chauffage *m* par rayonnement

radiantly ['reɪdɪəntlɪ] **ADV** *(shine, glow)* avec éclat; *(smile)* d'un air radieux; **r. beautiful** d'une beauté éclatante

radiate ['reɪdɪeɪt] **VI 1** *(emit energy)* émettre de l'énergie; *(be emitted)* rayonner, irradier; **heat radiates from the centre** le centre dégage de la chaleur **2** *(spread)* rayonner; **the roads which r. from Chicago** les routes qui partent de Chicago
VT 1 *(heat)* émettre, dégager; *(light)* émettre **2** *Fig* **the children r. good health/happiness** les enfants respirent la santé/rayonnent de bonheur; **his manner radiated confidence** il semblait très sûr de lui

radiation [ˌreɪdɪ'eɪʃən] **N 1** *Phys (act of radiating)* rayonnement *m*; *(energy radiated)* rayonnement (s) *m(pl)*, rayons *mpl*; **low-level r.** radiations *fpl* de faible intensité; **ultraviolet r.** rayons *mpl* ultraviolets **2** *Nucl* radiation *f*; **to be exposed to r.** être exposé à des radiations **3** *Med* rayons *mpl*
▸▸ ***radiation sickness*** mal *m* des rayons; ***radiation therapy*** radiothérapie *f*

radiator ['reɪdɪeɪtə(r)] **N** *(gen) & Aut* radiateur *m*
▸▸ ***radiator cap*** bouchon *m* du radiateur; ***radiator core*** faisceau *m* de radiateur; ***radiator grille*** calandre *f*; ***radiator key*** = petite clé servant à purger les radiateurs; ***radiator matrix*** faisceau *m* de radiateur

radical ['rædɪkəl] **ADJ 1** *(gen)* radical **2** *Am Fam (excellent)* génial, géant
N 1 *Pol* radical(e) *m,f* **2** *Ling, Math & Chem* radical *m*
▸▸ ***radical chic*** ≃ socialisme *m* de salon

radicalism ['rædɪkəlɪzəm] **N** radicalisme *m*

radicalization, -isation [ˌrædɪkəlaɪ'zeɪʃən] **N** radicalisation *f*

radicalize, -ise ['rædɪkəlaɪz] **VT** radicaliser

radically ['rædɪkəlɪ] **ADV** radicalement

radical-socialism N *Pol* radical-socialisme *m*

radical-socialist *Pol* **N** radical-socialiste *mf*
ADJ radical-socialiste

radicle ['rædɪkəl] **N 1** *Bot (part of plant embryo)* radicule *f*; *(rootlet)* radicelle *f* **2** *Chem* radical *m*

radio ['reɪdɪəʊ] *(pl* **radios***)* **N 1** *(apparatus)* radio *f*; **to turn the r. on/off** allumer/éteindre la radio **2** *(system, industry, activity)* radio *f*; **by r.** par radio; **I heard it on the r.** je l'ai entendu à la radio; **to be on the r.** passer à la radio
COMP *(play)* radiophonique; *(contact, link, silence)* radio *(inv)*; *(announcer, technician)* à la radio
VT 1 *(person)* appeler *ou* contacter par radio **2** *(message)* envoyer par radio; *(position, movement)* signaler par radio
VI envoyer un message radio; **she radioed for help** elle demanda de l'aide par radio
▸▸ *Mktg* ***radio advertising*** publicité *f* à la radio; ***radio alarm (clock)*** radio-réveil *m*; ***radio astronomer*** radioastronome *mf*; ***radio astronomy*** radioastronomie *f*; ***radio beacon*** radiobalise *f*; ***radio beam*** faisceau *m* hertzien; ***radio broadcast*** émission *f* de radio, émission *f* radiophonique; ***radio broadcasting*** radiodiffusion *f*; ***radio button*** bouton *m* radio, bouton *m* d'option; ***radio car*** voiture *f* radio; ***radio cassette*** radiocassette *f*; ***radio chip*** puce *f* radio; ***radio communication*** contact *m* radio, liaison *f* radio, radiocommunications *fpl*; ***radio compass*** radiocompas *m*; ***radio control*** télécommande *f* (par) radio, radiocommande *f*; ***radio data system*** *(for motorists)* système *m* radio de transmission de données; ***radio engineer*** ingénieur *m* radio; ***radio frequency*** fréquence *f* radioélectrique, radiofréquence *f*; *Astron* ***radio galaxy*** radiogalaxie *f*; ***radio ham*** radioamateur *m*; ***radio journalism*** journalisme *m* de radio; ***radio journalist*** journaliste *mf* de radio; ***radio listener*** auditeur(trice) *m,f*; ***radio microphone, radio mike*** microphone-émetteur *m*, microphone *m* sans fil; ***radio navigation*** radionavigation *f*; ***radio news*** informations *fpl* radiodiffusées; ***radio officer*** radionavigant *m*; ***radio operator*** *(on plane)* radio *m* *(on ship)* radionavigant *m*; ***radio producer*** producteur(trice) *m,f* d'émissions de radio; ***radio programme*** émission *f* de radio, émission *f* radiophonique; ***radio receiver*** radiorécepteur *m*; ***radio relay system*** réseau *m* hertzien; ***radio report*** radioreportage *m*; ***radio reporter*** radioreporter *m*; *Naut* ***radio room*** poste *m* radio de bord; ***radio satellite*** satellite *m* radio; ***radio signal*** signal *m* radiophonique; ***radio source*** radiosource *f*; ***radio spectrum*** spectre *m* radio *ou* radioélectrique *ou* des fréquences radioélectriques; ***radio star*** radiosource *f*; ***radio station*** station *f* de radio; ***radio taxi*** radio-taxi *m*; ***radio telescope*** radiotélescope *m*; ***radio transmitter*** (poste *m*) émetteur *m*; ***radio vehicle*** véhicule *m* radio; ***radio waves*** ondes *fpl* hertziennes

> **RADIO**
>
> Les principales stations de radio de la BBC sont: Radio 1 (musique pop et rock); Radio 2 (variétés); Radio 3 (musique classique); Radio 4 (actualités, reportages, théâtre, programmes éducatifs); Radio 5 Live (sports, programmes éducatifs, musique pop et rock). La BBC comprend également de très nombreuses stations locales, ainsi que plusieurs stations de radio numériques spécialisées. Il existe d'autre part plus de cent stations indépendantes.

radioactive [ˌreɪdɪəʊ'æktɪv] **ADJ** radioactif
▸▸ ***radioactive bomb*** bombe *f* radioactive *ou* sale; ***radioactive decay*** désintégration *f* radioactive; ***radioactive dust*** poussières *fpl* radioactives; ***radioactive fallout*** retombées *fpl* radioactives; ***radioactive waste*** déchets *mpl* radioactifs *ou* nucléaires

radioactivity [ˌreɪdɪəʊæk'tɪvɪtɪ] **N** radioactivité

radiocarbon [ˌreɪdɪəʊ'kɑːbən] **N** radiocarbone *m*, carbone *m* 14
▸▸ ***radiocarbon dating*** datation *f* au carbone 14

radio-controlled ADJ radioguidé

radiogram ['reɪdɪəʊgræm] **N 1** *Old-fashioned (radio and record player)* radio *f* avec pick-up *(message)* radiogramme *m* **3** *(radiograph)* radiographie *f*

radiograph ['reɪdɪəʊgrɑːf] **N** radiographie *f*

radiographer [ˌreɪdɪ'ɒgrəfə(r)] **N** radiologue *m* radiologiste *mf*

radiographic [ˌreɪdɪəʊ'græfɪk] **ADJ** radiographique

radiography [ˌreɪdɪ'ɒgrəfɪ] **N** radiographie *f*

radioisotope [ˌreɪdɪəʊ'aɪsətəʊp] **N** radio-isotope *m*, isotope *m* radioactif

radiological [ˌreɪdɪəʊ'lɒdʒɪkəl] **ADJ** radiologique

radiologist [ˌreɪdɪ'ɒlədʒɪst] **N** radiologue *mf*, radiologiste *mf*

radiology [ˌreɪdɪ'ɒlədʒɪ] **N** radiologie *f*

radiopager ['reɪdɪəʊˌpeɪdʒə(r)] **N** récepteur *m* d'appel *ou* de poche

radiopaging ['reɪdɪəʊˌpeɪdʒɪŋ] **N** radiomessagerie *f*

radioscopic [ˌreɪdɪəʊ'skɒpɪk] **ADJ**
▸▸ ***radioscopic image*** radiophotographie *f*

radioscopy [ˌreɪdɪ'ɒskəpɪ] **N** radioscopie *f*

radiotelegram [ˌreɪdɪəʊ'telɪgræm] **N** radiotélégramme *m*, radiogramme *m*

radiotelephone [ˌreɪdɪəʊ'telɪfəʊn] **N** radiotéléphone *m*

radiotelephony [ˌreɪdɪəʊtɪ'lefənɪ] **N** radiotéléphonie *f*

radiotherapist [ˌreɪdɪəʊ'θerəpɪst] **N** radiothérapeute *mf*

radiotherapy [ˌreɪdɪəʊ'θerəpɪ] **N** radiothérapie

radish ['rædɪʃ] **N** radis *m*

radium ['reɪdɪəm] **N** *Chem* radium *m*
▸▸ ***radium therapy*** curiethérapie *f*

radius ['reɪdɪəs] *(pl* **radiuses** *or* **radii** [-dɪaɪ]*)* **N** *(gen) & Math* rayon *m*; **within** *or* **in a r. of 20 km** dans un rayon de 20 km **2** *Anat* radius *m* **3** *(of crane)* portée *f*

▸▸ *Mil* **radius of action** rayon *m* d'action; *Math* **radius vector** rayon *m* vecteur

adix ['reɪdɪks] (*pl* **radices** [-dɪsiːz]) **N 1** *Math* base *f* **2** *Ling* radical *m*

adon ['reɪdɒn] **N** *Chem* radon *m*

AF [ˌɑːreɪ'ef] **N** *Br* (*abbr* **Royal Air Force**) = armée de l'air britannique

affia ['ræfiə] **N** raphia *m*

affish ['ræfɪʃ] **ADJ** dissolu

affle ['ræfəl] **N** tombola *f*

VT to r. (off) mettre en tombola

▸▸ ***raffle ticket*** billet *m* de tombola

aft [rɑːft] **N 1** (*craft* ▸ *gen*) radeau *m*; (▸ *inflatable*) matelas *m* pneumatique; *Sport* raft *m*

2 (*logs*) train *m* de flottage

3 *Fam* (*large amount*) tas *m*, flopée *f*; **we've got rafts of** *or* **a r. of mail** nous avons reçu des tas de lettres

4 *Constr* radier *m*

VT they r. wood down the river ils envoient le bois en aval dans des trains de flottage

VI voyager en radeau

after ['rɑːftə(r)] **N** *Constr* chevron *m*; **main r.** arbalétrier *m*; **the rafters** le chevronnage; *Fam* **to raise the rafters** (*make noise*) faire un boucan de tous les diables

afting ['rɑːftɪŋ] **N 1** *Sport* rafting *m*; **to go r.** faire du rafting **2** (*of wood*) flottage *m* (de bois) en trains

ag [ræg] (*pt & pp* **ragged**, *cont* **ragging**) **N 1** (*cloth*) chiffon *m*; **he wiped his hands on a r.** il s'essuya les mains avec un chiffon; **a piece of r.** un bout de chiffon; *Fam* **to chew the r.** discuter le bout de gras; *Fam* **to feel like** *Br* **a wet r.** *or Am* **a dish r.** (*physically*) être crevé; (*emotionally*) être vidé; *Br Fam* **to lose one's** *or* **the r.** piquer une crise, péter les plombs; **when he said that to her it was like a red r. to a bull** elle a vu rouge après ce qu'il lui a dit

2 (*worn-out garment*) loque *f*

3 (*shred, scrap*) lambeau *m*; **torn to rags** mis en lambeaux

4 *Fam Pej* (*newspaper*) feuille *f* de chou, torchon *m*

5 *Br very Fam* (*sanitary towel*) serviette *f* hygiénique; **to be on the r.** avoir ses ragnagnas

6 *Br Univ* = semaine pendant laquelle les étudiants préparent des divertissements, surtout au profit d'œuvres charitables

7 *Br* (*joke*) farce *f*, canular *m*

8 *Mus* ragtime *m*

VT (*tease*) taquiner

• **rags NPL** (*worn-out clothes*) guenilles *fpl*, haillons *mpl*, loques *fpl*; *Am Fam* (*clothes*) fringues *fpl*; **a tramp dressed in rags** un clochard vêtu de haillons; **in rags and tatters** en loques; **to go from rags to riches** passer de la misère à la richesse; **a rags-to-riches story** un véritable conte de fées

▸▸ ***rag book*** livre *m* en tissu; ***rag content*** (*of paper*) pourcentage *m* de peille; ***rag doll*** poupée *f* de chiffon; ***rag paper*** papier *m* à base de peille; ***rag picker*** chiffonnier(ère) *m,f*; ***rag rug*** catalogne *f*; *Fam* ***rag trade*** confection ◻ *f*; **he's in the r. trade** il est *or* travaille dans les fringues; ***rag week*** = semaine pendant laquelle les étudiants préparent des divertissements, surtout au profit d'œuvres charitables

aga ['rɑːgə] **N** *Mus* raga *m inv*

agamuffin ['rægəˌmʌfɪn] **N** (*vagrant*) va-nu-pieds *m inv*, gueux (gueuse) *m,f*; (*urchin*) galopin *m*, polisson(onne) *m,f*

ag-and-bone man N *Br* chiffonnier *m*

agbag ['rægbæg] **N** *Br Fig* ramassis *m*, bric-à-brac *m inv*, fouillis *m*; **a r. of ideas** un fouillis d'idées (confuses); **they were a r. team** ils formaient une équipe hétéroclite

age [reɪdʒ] **N 1** (*anger*) rage *f*, fureur *f*; **the boss was in a r.** le patron était furieux; **to fly into a r.** piquer une colère; **a fit of r.** un accès *ou* une crise de rage **2** *Fam* (*fashion*) **to be all the r.** faire fureur **3** (*of sea, elements*) furie *f*

VI 1 (*person*) être furieux, s'emporter; **he was raging against the Government** il pestait contre le gouvernement **2** (*sea, river*) se déchaîner; (*fire, storm, war*) faire rage; **the plague was raging throughout Europe** la peste ravageait l'Europe; **the argument still rages** la question est toujours très controversée

ragga ['rægə] **N** *Mus* ragga *m*

ragged ['rægɪd] **ADJ 1** (*tattered* ▸ *clothes*) en lambeaux, en loques, en haillons; (▸ *person*) loqueteux, vêtu de loques *ou* de haillons; **she was beginning to look rather r.** elle commençait à avoir l'air dépenaillé

2 (*uneven*) irrégulier; **the r. coastline** la côte échancrée

3 (*erratic* ▸ *performance*) inégal, décousu

4 *Typ* **r. right/left** non-justifié à droite/à gauche; **to print sth r.** imprimer qch sans justification

5 *Fam* (*idiom*) **to run sb r.** éreinter *ou* crever qn; **to run oneself r.** s'éreinter; **I've been running myself r. for you!** je me suis vraiment décarcassé pour toi!

▸▸ *Bot* ***ragged robin*** fleur *f* de coucou (*lychnis*); *Br Formerly* ***ragged school*** = école primaire pour les pauvres

ragging ['rægɪŋ] **N** (*teasing*) taquineries *fpl*; **to give sb a r.** mettre qn en boîte, taquiner qn; **he took a lot of r.** on l'a beaucoup taquiné

raggle-taggle [-'tægəl] **ADJ** *Br Fam* (*band, army*) disparate ◻; (*person*) débraillé ◻, dépenaillé ◻

raghead ['ræghed] **N** *Am Fam* **1** (*Arab*) raton *m*, bicot *m*, = terme injurieux désignant un Arabe du Proche-Orient **2** (*gypsy*) romanichel(elle) *m,f*, = terme injurieux désignant un Tsigane

raging ['reɪdʒɪŋ] **ADJ 1** (*intense* ▸ *pain*) insupportable, atroce; (▸ *fever*) violent; **I had a r. headache** j'avais affreusement mal à la tête; **I've got a r. thirst** je meurs de soif; **r. anticlericalism** un anticléricalisme virulent; **r. toothache** rage *f* de dents **2** (*storm*) déchaîné, violent; (*sea*) démonté; (*torrent*) furieux **3** (*person*) furieux; **to be in a r. temper** être furieux

raglan ['ræglən] **N** raglan *m*

ADJ raglan (*inv*)

ragman ['rægmən] (*pl* **ragmen** [-mən]) **N** chiffonnier *m*

ragout ['ræguː] **N** ragoût *m*

rag-roll VT peindre au chiffon

ragtag ['rægtæg] *Br Fam* **ADJ** (*band, army*) disparate ◻; (*person*) débraillé ◻, dépenaillé ◻

N the r. and bobtail la racaille, la populace

ragtime ['rægtaɪm] **N** *Mus* ragtime *m*

ragtop ['rægtɒp] **N** *Am Fam Aut* décapotable ◻ *f*

ragweed ['rægwiːd] **N** *Bot* ambroisie *f*, ambrosia *f*

ragwort ['rægwɜːt] **N** *Bot* jacobée *f*, herbe *f* de Saint-Jacques

rah-rah [rɑː-] **ADJ** *Am* enthousiaste; **he's very r. about the President** c'est un fervent admirateur du Président

▸▸ ***rah-rah skirt*** jupe *f* à volants

raid [reɪd] **N 1** *Mil* raid *m*, incursion *f*; **they made a r. over the border** ils ont fait une incursion de l'autre côté de la frontière; **bombing r.** raid *m* aérien

2 (*by police*) descente *f*, rafle *f*; **a drugs r.** une descente de police (pour saisir de la drogue)

3 (*robbery*) hold-up *m inv*, braquage *m*; **a r. on a bank** un hold-up dans une banque; *Hum* **a r. on the fridge** une razzia dans le frigo

4 *St Exch* raid *m*

VT 1 *Mil* (*of army*) faire un raid *ou* une incursion dans; (*of airforce*) bombarder

2 (*of police*) faire une descente *ou* une rafle dans

3 (*of thieves*) **to r. a bank** dévaliser une banque; **somebody's raided my locker** quelqu'un a fouillé dans mon casier; *Hum* **to r. the fridge** dévaliser le frigo

4 *Fin* (*pension funds*) puiser dans

raider ['reɪdə(r)] **N 1** *Mil* (*soldier*) membre *m* d'un commando; (*boat*) raider *m*; (*plane*) bombardier *m*; **the raiders were repelled** le commando a été repoussé **2** (*thief*) voleur(euse) *m,f*; **the bank raiders have all been arrested** les auteurs du hold-up (de la banque) ont tous été arrêtés **3** *St Exch* **(corporate) r.** raider *m*

rail [reɪl] **N 1** (*bar* ▸ *gen*) barre *f*; (▸ *in window, on bridge*) garde-fou *m*; (▸ *on ship*) bastingage *m*; (▸ *on balcony*) balustrade *f*; (▸ *on stairway*) rampe *f*; (▸ *for carpet*) tringle *f*; **towel r.** porte-serviettes *m inv* **2** (*for train, tram*) rail *m*; **to travel by r.** voyager en train; **to send goods by r.** envoyer des marchandises par chemin de fer; **to go off the rails** (*train*) dérailler; *Br Fig* (*person*) perdre la tête *ou* le nord; **to get the economy back on the rails** remettre l'économie sur les rails; **I did my best to get him back on the rails after his breakdown** j'ai fait de mon mieux pour le remettre sur pieds après sa dépression nerveuse

COMP (*traffic, link, tunnel*) ferroviaire; (*ticket, fare*) de train; (*journey, travel*) en train; (*employee, union*) des chemins de fer

VT (*enclose*) clôturer

VI (*complain bitterly*) **to r. against** *or* **at** pester contre

• **rails NPL** (*fencing*) grille *f*; (*in horseracing*) corde *f*; **he was pushed to the rails by the other jockeys** il a été forcé de tenir la corde par les autres jockeys; *Fig* **to be on the rails** (*in difficult situation*) être sur la corde raide

▸▸ ***rail network*** réseau *m* ferroviaire *ou* de chemin de fer; ***rail strike*** grève *f* des chemins de fer; ***rail transport*** transport *m* par chemin de fer *ou* par train; ***rail worker*** (*gen*) employé(e) *m,f* des chemins de fer; (*for track, rolling stock*) cheminot *m*

▸ **rail in VT SEP** clôturer

▸ **rail off VT SEP** fermer (au moyen d'une barrière); **the end of the hall was railed off** une barrière interdisait l'accès au fond de la salle

railcar ['reɪlkɑː(r)] **N** autorail *m*

railcard ['reɪlkɑːd] **N** *Br* = carte permettant de bénéficier de tarifs avantageux sur les chemins de fer britanniques; **student r.** carte *f* de réduction pour étudiant

railhead ['reɪlhed] **N** tête *f* de ligne

railing ['reɪlɪŋ] **N 1** (*barrier* ▸ *gen*) barrière *f*; (▸ *on bridge*) garde-fou *m*; (▸ *on balcony*) balustrade *f* **2** (*upright bar*) barreau *m* **3** (*fence*) grille *f*

• **railings NPL** (*fence*) grille *f*; **she squeezed through the railings** elle se glissa entre les barreaux de la grille

raillery ['reɪlərɪ] (*pl* **railleries**) **N** raillerie *f*

railman ['reɪlmən] (*pl* **railmen** [-men]) **N** *Br & Can* (*gen*) employé(e) *m,f* des chemins de fer; (*technical employee*) cheminot *m*

railroad ['reɪlrəʊd] **N** *Am* (*system*) chemin *m* de fer; (*track*) voie *f* ferrée; **to travel by r.** voyager en chemin de fer

VT 1 *Fam* (*force acceptance of*) **to r. a bill through Parliament** imposer un projet de loi au Parlement ◻

2 *Fam* (*force into action*) **to r. sb into doing sth** faire pression sur qn pour qu'il fasse qch ◻; **to be railroaded into doing sth** être forcé à faire qch ◻; **I don't want to r. you, but...** je ne voudrais pas te forcer mais...; **she was railroaded into this job** on a fait pression sur elle pour qu'elle prenne ce poste

3 *esp Am Fam Law* (*convict by false charges*) condamner à l'aide de fausses inculpations ◻; (*hastily*) juger sommairement ◻

4 *Am* (*transport*) transporter par chemin de fer

▸▸ *Am* ***railroad apartment*** = appartement dont les pièces sont en enfilade; ***railroad car*** wagon *m*

railway ['reɪlweɪ] **N 1** (*system, organization*) chemin *m* de fer; **I'd never travelled by Russian r.** *or* **on the Russian railways** je n'avais jamais pris le train en Russie; **he works on the railways** il est cheminot **2** (*track*) voie *f* ferrée

COMP (*bridge, traffic, link, tunnel*) ferroviaire; (*company*) ferroviaire, de chemin de fer; (*journey, travel*) en train; (*employee, union*) des chemins de fer

▸▸ ***railway carriage*** wagon *m*, voiture *f*; ***railway crossing*** passage *m* à niveau; ***railway cutting*** tranchée *f* en déblai; ***railway embankment*** remblai *m*; ***railway engine*** locomotive *f*; ***railway engineer*** ingénieur *m* des chemins de fer; ***railway guide*** indicateur *m* des chemins de fer; ***railway line*** (*route*) ligne *f* de chemin de fer; (*track*) voie *f* ferrée; (*rail*) rail *m*; ***railway network*** réseau *m* ferroviaire *ou* de chemin de fer; ***railway signal*** signal *m* ferroviaire; ***railway station*** (*gen*) gare *f* (de chemin de fer); (*in France*) gare *f* SNCF; ***railway strike*** grève *f* des chemins de fer; ***railway system*** réseau *m* ferroviaire *ou* de chemin de fer; ***railway ticket*** billet *m* de train; ***railway timetable*** horaires *mpl* des chemins de fer; ***railway track*** voie *f* ferrée; ***railway worker*** *(gen)* employé(e) *m,f* des chemins de fer; *(for track, rolling stock)* cheminot *m*; ***railway yard*** dépôt *m*

railwayman ['reɪlweɪmən] *(pl* **railwaymen** [-mən]) **N** *Br & Can (gen)* employé(e) *m,f* des chemins de fer; *(technical employee)* cheminot *m*

raiment ['reɪmənt] **N** *(UNCOUNT) Literary* atours *mpl*

rain [reɪn] **N 1** *(precipitation)* pluie *f*; **it was pouring with r.** il pleuvait à verse; **the r. was heavy** il pleuvait beaucoup; **a light r. was falling** il tombait une pluie fine; **come in out of the r.** rentre, ne reste pas sous la pluie; **it looks like r.** on dirait qu'il va pleuvoir; **Venice in the r.** Venise sous la pluie; **the rains** la saison des pluies; **come r. or shine** *(whatever the weather)* qu'il pleuve ou qu'il vente; *(whatever the circumstances)* quoiqu'il arrive; *Fam* **don't worry, you'll be as right as r. in a minute** ne t'inquiète pas, ça va passer□ **2** *Fig (of projectiles, blows)* pluie *f*

VI pleuvoir; **it's raining** il pleut; *Fam* **it's raining cats and dogs** il pleut des cordes, il tombe des hallebardes; *Prov Br* **it never rains but it pours,** *Am* **when it rains, it pours** = tout arrive en même temps

VT faire pleuvoir; **they rained blows on his head** ils firent pleuvoir des coups sur sa tête

►► *Am* ***rain check*** = bon pour un autre match (ou spectacle) donné par suite d'une annulation à cause de la pluie; *Fam Fig* **I'll take a r. check on that** ça sera pour une autre fois□; ***rain cloud*** nuage *m* de pluie; ***rain dance*** danse *f* de la pluie; ***rain gauge*** pluviomètre *m*; ***rain shadow*** région *f* sous le vent *(dans les montagnes)*

►**rain down VI** *(projectiles, blows etc)* pleuvoir

VT SEP *(projectiles, blows etc)* faire pleuvoir

►**rain off VT SEP** *Br* **the game was rained off** *(cancelled)* la partie a été annulée à cause de la pluie; *(abandoned)* la partie a été abandonnée à cause de la pluie

►**rain out VT SEP 1** *(campers)* **to be rained out** être chassé par la pluie **2** *Am* **the game was rained out** *(cancelled)* la partie a été annulée à cause de la pluie; *(abandoned)* la partie a été abandonnée à cause de la pluie

rainbow ['reɪmbəʊ] **N** arc-en-ciel *m*; *Fig* **it's at the end of the r.** c'est un mirage; *Fig* **to chase rainbows** se bercer d'illusions

►► ***rainbow coalition*** = coalition représentant un large éventail de tendances; *Ich* ***rainbow trout*** truite *f* arc-en-ciel

rainbow-coloured, *Am* **rainbow-colored ADJ** arc-en-ciel *(inv)*, multicolore

raincoat ['reɪnkəʊt] **N** imperméable *m*

raindrop ['reɪndrɒp] **N** goutte *f* de pluie

rainfall ['reɪnfɔːl] **N** *(amount of rain)* pluviosité *f*; **after three days of heavy r.** après trois jours de fortes pluies

rainforest ['reɪnˌfɒrɪst] **N** forêt *f* pluviale, forêt *f* tropicale humide

rainless ['reɪnlɪs] **ADJ** sans pluie

rainmaker ['reɪnˌmeɪkə(r)] **N 1** *(in tribe)* faiseur *m* de pluie **2** *Fam (in company)* cadre *m* hyperperformant

rainmaking ['reɪnˌmeɪkɪŋ] **ADJ** *(ritual, dance)* pour faire pleuvoir

rainout ['reɪnaʊt] **N 1** *(UNCOUNT) (pollution)* = retombées entraînées par la pluie **2** *Am Sport* = match annulé à cause du mauvais temps

rainproof ['reɪnpruːf] **ADJ** imperméable

VT imperméabiliser

rainslicker ['reɪnslɪkə(r)] **N** *Am* ciré *m*

rainstorm ['reɪnstɔːm] **N** pluie *f* torrentielle

rainwater ['reɪnˌwɔːtə(r)] **N** eau *f* de pluie *ou* pluviale

rainwear ['reɪnweə(r)] **N** *(UNCOUNT)* vêtements *mpl* de pluie

rainy ['reɪnɪ] *(compar* **rainier**, *superl* **rainiest) ADJ** pluvieux; **a r. day** un jour de pluie; *Fig* **to save sth for a r. day** garder qch pour les mauvais jours

►► ***rainy season*** saison *f* des pluies

RAISE [reɪz]

N
- augmentation (de salaire) **1**
- enchère **2**

VT
- lever **1, 5, 6, 14**
- soulever **1, 11**
- relever **1, 2**
- remonter **1, 3**
- augmenter **2**
- élever **3, 4, 9, 10, 12, 18**
- ressusciter **13**
- contacter **15**
- monter sur **16**
- faire lever **17**

VI
- enchérir

N 1 *Am (pay increase)* augmentation *f* (de salaire); **to get a r.** être augmenté, avoir une augmentation

2 *Cards (in bridge)* enchère *f*; *(in poker)* relance *f*

VT 1 *(lift, move upwards* ► *gen)* lever; *(*► *burden, lid)* soulever; *(*► *veil)* relever; *(*► *weight)* lever, soulever; *(*► *blind)* remonter; *(*► *flag)* hisser; *(*► *sunken ship)* renflouer; **to r. one's head** *(from lowered position)* lever la tête; *(hold erect)* dresser la tête; **she didn't r. her eyes from her book** elle n'a pas levé les yeux de son livre; **he tried to r. himself from the sofa** il essaya de se lever du canapé; **she raised herself to her full height** elle se dressa de toute sa hauteur; **to r. a patient to a sitting position** soulever un malade pour l'asseoir; **to r. one's glass (to sb)** lever son verre (à la santé de qn); **to r. one's glass to one's lips** porter son verre à ses lèvres; **to r. one's fist to sb** menacer qn du poing; **to r. sb's hackles** hérisser qn; **to r. one's hand to sb** lever la main sur qn; **to r. one's hat to sb** soulever son chapeau pour saluer qn; *Fig* tirer son chapeau à qn; **to r. a cloud of dust** soulever un nuage de poussière; *Mil & Fig* **to r. one's sights** viser plus haut

2 *(increase* ► *offer, price, tax, salaries)* augmenter; *(*► *interest rates)* relever; *(*► *temperature, tension)* faire monter; *(*► *volume)* augmenter; **the speed limit has been raised to 150 km/h** la limitation de vitesse est passée à 150 km/h; **to r. the school-leaving age** prolonger la scolarité; **to r. a credit limit** déplafonner un crédit; **to r. the ceiling on wage increases** augmenter le plafond des salaires; **to r. production to a maximum** porter la production au maximum; **to r. the stakes** faire monter les enjeux; **to r. the pass mark** élever le niveau requis; **to r. (the level of) a wall** rehausser *ou* surélever un mur; **to r. the level of the ground** rehausser le niveau du sol; **to r. one's voice** *(speak more loudly)* élever la voix; *(speak in anger)* hausser le ton; **no one raised their voice (to answer** *or* **to speak)** personne ne souffla mot

3 *(boost, improve)* remonter, élever; **to r. standards** *(of education, morality)* élever le niveau; *(of cleanliness, safety)* améliorer les conditions; **to r. the standard of living** améliorer le niveau de vie; **to r. sb's spirits/hopes** remonter le moral/donner des espoirs à qn; **to r. the tone** *or* **the level of the conversation** élever le niveau de la conversation

4 *(promote)* élever, promouvoir; *Mil & Fig* **to r. sb from the ranks** promouvoir qn; **raised to the rank of colonel** élevé au rang de colonel

5 *(collect together* ► *support)* réunir; *(*► *army)* lever; **we have raised over a million signatures** nous avons recueilli plus d'un million de signatures

6 *(obtain* ► *money)* trouver, obtenir; *(*► *capital)* mobiliser, procurer; *(*► *taxes)* lever; **to r. funds (for)** *(for charity)* collecter des fonds (pour *ou* au profit de); *(for business, government programme)* se procurer des fonds (pour *ou* au profit de); **to r. a loan (on)** *(of government)* émettre *ou* lancer un emprunt (sur); *(of individual)* faire un emprunt (sur)

7 *(make, produce)* **they raised a cheer when she came in** ils ont poussé des bravos quand elle est entrée; **he managed to r. a smile when he saw us** il a réussi à sourire en nous voyant

8 *(cause as reaction* ► *laugh, welt, blister, rebellion)* provoquer; **his jokes didn't even r. a smile** ses plaisanteries n'ont même pas fait sourire; **to r. a storm of protest** déclencher *ou* soulever une tempête de protestations

9 *(rear* ► *children, family)* élever

10 *(breed* ► *livestock)* élever; *(grow* ► *crops)* cultiver

11 *(introduce, bring up* ► *point, subject, question objection)* soulever; *(*► *doubts)* soulever, susciter; **his attitude raises certain questions** son attitude pose *ou* soulève certaines questions; **his attitude raises questions about his loyalty** son attitude remet en question sa loyauté

12 *(erect)* élever, ériger; **to r. a statue to sb** élever une statue à qn

13 *(resuscitate)* ressusciter; *(evoke* ► *spirit)* évoquer; **they were making enough noise to r. the dead** ils faisaient un bruit à réveiller les morts

14 *(end* ► *ban, embargo, siege)* lever

15 *(contact)* contacter; **the radio officer was trying to r. Boston** le radio essayait de contacter Boston

16 *(in bridge)* monter sur; *(in poker)* relancer; **I'll r. you £5** je relance de 5 livres

17 *Culin (dough, bread)* faire lever

18 *Math* élever; **to r. a number to the power of n** élever un nombre à la puissance n

19 *Naut* **to r. land** arriver en vue de terre

20 *(cheque)* faire

VI *(in bridge)* monter, enchérir; *(in poker)* relancer

►**raise up VT SEP to r. oneself up** se soulever; **she raised herself up onto the chair** elle se hissa sur la chaise

Attention: ne pas confondre avec le verbe **to rise**, qui n'est jamais suivi d'un complément d'objet.

raised [reɪzd] **ADJ 1** *(elevated* ► *ground, platform, jetty etc)* surélevé

2 *(embossed* ► *pattern, letter, motif)* en relief

3 *Am Culin* levé, à la levure

4 *Ling (vowel)* haut

►► *Typ* ***raised bands*** nerfs *mpl*

raiser ['reɪzə(r)] **N** *(of livestock)* éleveur(euse) *m,f*; *(of crops)* cultivateur(trice) *m,f*

raisin ['reɪzən] **N** raisin *m* sec

►► ***raisin bread*** pain *m* aux raisins *(miche)*

Note that the French word **raisin** is a false friend and is never a translation for the English word **raisin**. It means **grapes**.

raising ['reɪzɪŋ] **N 1** *(lifting* ► *of curtain)* lever *m*; *(*► *of sunken ship)* renflouage *m*; *(*► *of standards)* élévation *f*

2 *(of offer, price, tax, salaries)* augmentation *f*; **r. of the school-leaving age** prolongation *f* de la scolarité

3 *(of army)* levée *f*; *(collecting* ► *of funds for charity)* collecte *f*; *(*► *of taxes)* levée *f*

4 *(of barn, building)* construction *f*; *(of monument, statue)* érection *f*

5 *(of animals)* élevage *m*; *(of children)* éducation *f*; *(of crops)* culture *f*

6 *(of blockade, embargo, siege)* levée *f*

7 r. of the dead résurrection *f* des morts

►► *Culin* ***raising agent*** levure *f*

raison d'état [ˌreɪzɔ̃deɪ'tɑː] **N** *Pol* raison *f* d'État

raison d'être [ˌreɪzɔ̃'detrə] **N** raison *f* d'être

Raj [rɑːdʒ] **N the R.** l'empire *m* britannique (en Inde)

raja, rajah ['rɑːdʒə] **N** raja *m*, rajah *m*, radjah *m*

rake [reɪk] **N 1** *(in garden, casino)* râteau *m*; **as thin as a r.** maigre comme un clou

2 *(libertine)* roué *m*, libertin *m*

3 *(slope* ► *of seating, terrace)* pente *f*

4 *Naut (of mast, funnel)* quête *f*

VT 1 *(soil, lawn, path)* ratisser, râteler; **she raked the leaves into a pile** elle ratissa les feuilles en tas

2 *(search)* fouiller (dans); **to r. one's memory** fouiller dans ses souvenirs

3 *(scan)* balayer; **his eyes raked the audience** son regard parcourut l'assistance

4 *(strafe)* balayer; **machine-gun fire raked the trench** le feu d'une mitrailleuse balaya la tranchée

VI 1 *(search)* **to r. among** *or* **through** fouiller dans

2 *(slope)* être en pente, être incliné

►**rake about, rake around VI** *(search)* fouiller (**among** *or* **in** dans)

►**rake in VT SEP** *Fam (money)* amasser□; **that shop is raking in a fortune** ce magasin ramasse une fortune; **they must be raking it in** ils doivent s'en mettre plein les poches

▸**rake off** VT SEP *Fam (share of profits)* empocher□, ramasser□

▸**rake out** VT SEP **1** *(fire)* enlever les cendres de; *(ashes)* enlever **2** *(search out)* dénicher

▸**rake over** VT SEP **1** *(soil, lawn, path)* ratisser **2** *Fig* remuer; **why r. over the past?** pourquoi remuer le passé?

▸**rake up** VT SEP **1** *(collect together* ▸ *leaves, weeds)* ratisser; *(*▸ *people)* réunir, rassembler **2** *(dredge up)* déterrer; **to r. up sb's past** fouiller dans le passé de qn; **to r. up an old quarrel** raviver une ancienne querelle

rake-off N *Fam* ristourne□*f*, petit profit□*m*; **to get a r. on each sale** toucher un pourcentage *ou* une commission sur chaque vente

raki ['rɑːkiː, 'rækɪ] N *(drink)* raki *m*

rakish ['reɪkɪʃ] ADJ **1** *(dissolute)* débauché; *(jaunty)* désinvolte, insouciant; **he wore his hat at a r. angle** il portait son chapeau avec désinvolture **2** *(boat)* à la forme élancée, allongé

rakishly ['reɪkɪʃlɪ] ADV *(dissolutely)* d'un air débauché; *(jauntily)* d'un air désinvolte

rally ['rælɪ] *(pl* **rallies**, *pt & pp* **rallied***)* N **1** *(gathering* ▸ *gen)* rassemblement *m*; *Mil (during battle)* ralliement *m*; *Pol* rassemblement *m*, (grand) meeting *m*

2 *(recovery* ▸ *gen)* amélioration *f*; *(*▸ *of prices, shares, business)* reprise *f*; **the England team staged a r. in the second half** l'équipe anglaise s'est reprise au cours de la deuxième mi-temps

3 *Aut* rallye *m*; **the Monte Carlo r.** le rallye de Monte-Carlo

4 *Sport (in tennis, squash etc)* long échange *m*

VI **1** *(assemble, gather* ▸ *gen)* se rassembler; *(*▸ *troops, supporters)* se rallier; **they rallied to the party/to the defence of their leader** ils se sont ralliés au parti/pour défendre leur chef **2** *(recover* ▸ *gen)* s'améliorer; *(*▸ *sick person)* aller mieux, reprendre des forces; *(*▸ *currency, prices, shares, business)* se redresser, reprendre; *(*▸ *stock market)* se reprendre; **the pound rallied in the afternoon** la livre est remontée dans l'après-midi; **the market rallied** les cours ont repris **3** *Aut* faire des rallyes

VT **1** *(gather)* rallier, rassembler; **she's trying to r. support for her project** elle essaie de rallier des gens pour soutenir son projet **2** *(summon up)* reprendre; *(boost)* ranimer; **to r. one's spirits** reprendre ses esprits; **the news rallied their morale** la nouvelle leur a remonté le moral **3** *Arch (tease)* taquiner

▸▸ ***rally driver*** pilote *m* de rallye

rallycross ['rælɪkrɒs] N *Br* rallye-cross *m*

rallyer ['rælɪə(r)] N *Sport* concurrent(e) *m,f* d'un rallye

rallying ['rælɪɪŋ] N *Sport* rallyes *mpl*; **to go r.** faire un rallye

ADJ de ralliement

▸▸ ***rallying cry*** cri *m* de ralliement; ***rallying point*** point *m* de ralliement

ralph [rælf] VI *Fam (vomit)* gerber, dégueuler

RAM[1] [ræm] N *Comput (abbr* **random-access memory***)* RAM *f*, mémoire *f* vive

▸▸ ***RAM chip*** puce *f* de mémoire vive; ***RAM disk*** mémoire *f* à disque

RAM[2] [ˌɑːreɪ'em] N *(abbr* **Royal Academy of Music***)* = conservatoire national de musique de Londres

ram [ræm] *(pt & pp* **rammed**, *cont* **ramming***)* N **1** *Zool* bélier *m* **2** *Hist (for breaking doors, walls)* bélier *m* **3** *Tech (piston)* piston *m*; *(flattening tool)* hie *f*, dame *f*; *(pile driver)* mouton *m*; *(lifting pump)* bélier *m* hydraulique

VT **1** *(bang into)* percuter; *Naut* aborder; *(in battle)* éperonner; **he rammed the trolley into my ankles** il m'a heurté les chevilles avec son caddie® **2** *(push)* pousser (violemment); **a table had been rammed up against the door** une table avait été poussée contre la porte; **she rammed the bolt home** elle repoussa le verrou (violemment); **she rammed the papers into her bag** elle fourra les papiers dans son sac; **he rammed his pipe with tobacco** il bourra sa pipe; *Fig* **in order to r. home the point** pour enfoncer le clou; **she's always ramming religion down my throat** elle me rebat toujours les oreilles avec sa religion

VI **to r. into sth** entrer dans *ou* percuter qch; **a Jag rammed into the back of me** une Jaguar a embouti l'arrière de ma voiture

▸▸ *Aut* ***ram air*** air *m* forcé; *Aut* ***ram air induction*** introduction *f* d'air par forçage; ***ram cylinder*** vérin *m*

Ramadan [ˌræmə'dæn] N *Rel* ramadan *m*; **during R.** pendant (le) ramadan

ramble ['ræmbəl] N *(hike)* randonnée *f* (pédestre); *(casual walk)* promenade *f*; **to go for a r.** aller faire un tour

VI **1** *(hike)* faire une randonnée

2 *(wander)* se balader

3 *(talk)* divaguer, radoter; **he rambled on and on about nothing** il n'arrêtait pas de parler pour ne rien dire; **what are you rambling on about now?** qu'est-ce que tu racontes maintenant?

4 *(be delirious)* divaguer

5 *(plant)* pousser à tort et à travers

6 *(path, stream)* serpenter

rambler ['ræmblə(r)] N **1** *(hiker)* randonneur (euse) *m,f* **2** *(in speech)* **he's a bit of a r.** il est du genre radoteur **3** *Bot* plante *f* sarmenteuse

rambling ['ræmblɪŋ] ADJ **1** *(building)* plein de coins et de recoins; *(path, stream)* sinueux **2** *(conversation, style)* décousu; *(ideas, book, thoughts)* incohérent, sans suite; *(person)* qui divague, qui radote **3** *(plant)* sarmenteux

N **1** *(hiking)* randonnée *f*; **to go r.** partir en randonnée **2 ramblings** *(delirium)* divagations *fpl*; **the ramblings of old age** les radotages *mpl* de la vieillesse

▸▸ ***rambling rose*** rosier *m* sarmenteux

rambunctious [ræm'bʌŋkʃəs] ADJ *Fam* **1** *(boisterous)* turbulent□, chahuteur, tapageur **2** *(noisy)* bruyant□

RAMC [ˌɑːreɪˌem'siː] N *Br (abbr* **Royal Army Medical Corps***)* = service de santé des armées britanniques

ramekin ['ræmɪkɪn] N ramequin *m*

ramie ['ræmɪ] N *Tex* ramie *f*

ramification [ˌræmɪfɪ'keɪʃən] N **1** *(implication)* implication *f*, conséquence *f* **2** *(branching)* ramification *f*

ramify ['ræmɪfaɪ] *(pt & pp* **ramified***)* VT ramifier

VI se ramifier

ramjet ['ræmdʒet] N *(engine)* statoréacteur *m*, tuyère *f* thermopropulsive; *(aircraft)* avion *m* à statoréacteur

rammed [ræmd] ADJ *Br Fam (very crowded)* plein à craquer, bondé

rammer ['ræmə(r)] N *(for road-making)* dame *f*; *(for metal-working)* fouloir *m*, batte *f*; *(for civil engineering)* engin *m* de compactage du sol

ramp [ræmp] N **1** *(slope)* rampe *f*

2 *Aut (in garage)* pont *m* élévateur

3 *Am (connecting road)* bretelle *f* (d'accès)

4 *(bump on road)* dos *m* d'âne; *(difference in level)* dénivellation *f*, dénivellement *m*; *(to slow traffic down)* ralentisseur *m*

rampage [ræm'peɪdʒ] N fureur *f*; **to be on the r.** être déchaîné; **to go on the r.** se livrer à des actes de violence; **football fans went on the r. through the town** des supporters de football ont saccagé la ville

VI se déchaîner; **a herd of elephants rampaged through the bush** un troupeau d'éléphants avançait dans la brousse en balayant tout sur son passage; **they rampaged through the town** ils ont saccagé la ville

rampaging [ræm'peɪdʒɪŋ] ADJ déchaîné

rampancy ['ræmpənsɪ] N *(of corruption, vice)* prolifération *f*; *(of plant)* exubérance *f*

rampant ['ræmpənt] ADJ **1** *(unrestrained)* déchaîné, effréné; *(plant)* exubérant, luxuriant; **they're r. Marxists** ce sont des marxistes purs et durs; **corruption is r.** la corruption sévit; **the disease is r.** la maladie fait des ravages; *Fam* **he's a bit r. tonight** *(sexually)* il est émoustillé ce soir **2** *(exuberant* ▸ *vegetation)* exubérant, foisonnant **3** *(after n) Her* rampant; **the Lion R.** le Lion rampant

rampart ['ræmpɑːt] N *also Fig* rempart *m*

VT fortifier

ramraid ['ræmreɪd] VT *Br* cambrioler *(en enfonçant la vitrine avec un véhicule)*

RAM-resident [ræm-] ADJ *Comput* résident en mémoire vive

ramrod ['ræmrɒd] N *(for cleaning rifle)* écouvillon *m*; *(for loading cannon)* refouloir *m*; **to sit/to stand as stiff as a r.** être assis/se tenir raide comme un piquet

ADV **the sentry stood r. straight** la sentinelle se tenait debout, raide comme un piquet

ramshackle ['ræmˌʃækəl] ADJ délabré

ran [ræn] *pt of* **run**

ranch [rɑːntʃ] N ranch *m*; **chicken r.** élevage *m* de poulets

VI exploiter un ranch

VT **to r. cattle** élever du bétail (sur un ranch)

▸▸ *Culin* ***ranch dressing*** = mayonnaise crémeuse à l'ail; ***ranch hand*** ouvrier(ère) *m,f* agricole; ***ranch house*** *(bungalow)* maison *f* sans étage; *(on ranch)* maison *f*; *Am* ***ranch mink*** vison *m* d'élevage

rancher ['rɑːntʃə(r)] N *(owner)* propriétaire *mf* de ranch; *(manager)* exploitant(e) *m,f* de ranch; *(worker)* garçon *m* de ranch, cow-boy *m*

ranching ['rɑːntʃɪŋ] N exploitation *f* d'un ranch; **cattle/chicken r.** élevage *m* de bétail/de poulets

rancid ['rænsɪd] ADJ rance; **to go** *or* **to turn r.** rancir

rancidity [ræn'sɪdɪtɪ], **rancidness** ['rænsɪdnɪs] N rancidité *f*, rancissure *f*

rancorous ['ræŋkərəs] ADJ rancunier

rancour, *Am* **rancor** ['ræŋkə(r)] N rancœur *f*, rancune *f*

rand [rænd] *(pl* **inv***)* N *(money)* rand *m*

R & B [ˌɑːrən'biː] N *(abbr* **rhythm and blues***)* R&B *m*, R'n'B *m*

R & D [ˌɑːrən'diː] N *(abbr* **research and development***)* recherche *f* et développement *m*, R-D *f*

COMP *(manager, director)* de recherche et développement; *(expenditure)* pour la recherche et le développement

▸▸ ***R & D department*** bureau *m* d'études

random ['rændəm] ADJ **1** *(choice)* fait au hasard; *(pattern)* irrégulier; *Math (error, number)* aléatoire; **I just made a r. guess** j'ai deviné tout à fait par hasard; **a r. selection of people were asked if…** on a demandé à des gens choisis au hasard si…; **a r. selection of goods** des marchandises prises au hasard, une sélection arbitraire de marchandises; **a r. shot** une balle perdue **2** *Fam (unknown)* **she was talking to some r. guy** elle parlait à un type quelconque **3** *Fam (strange)* **it turns out we went to the same school, how r.!** il se trouve qu'on était à la même école, c'est dingue!

• **at random** ADV au hasard; **chosen at r.** choisi au hasard; **to lash out at r.** distribuer des coups à l'aveuglette

▸▸ *Comput* ***random access*** accès *m* aléatoire; *Mktg* ***random check*** contrôle *m* par sondage(s); *Comput* ***random error*** erreur *f* aléatoire; ***random killings*** tuerie *f* aveugle *ou* au hasard; *Mktg* ***random sample*** échantillon *m* aléatoire; *Mktg* ***random sampling*** échantillonnage *m* aléatoire; *Mktg* ***random selection*** sélection *f* au hasard; *Math* ***random variable*** variable *f* aléatoire; ***random violence*** violence *f* aveugle; *Math & St Exch* ***random walk*** marche *f* aléatoire

randomize, -ise ['rændəmaɪz] VT randomiser

R and R, R & R [ˌɑːrən'dɑː(r)] N *Am Mil (abbr* **rest and recreation***)* permission *f*; *Fam Fig* **she went on holiday for some R.** elle est allée en vacances pour se reposer un peu□

randy ['rændɪ] *(compar* **randier**, *superl* **randiest***)* ADJ *Fam* excité□; **to get** *or* **to become r.** commencer à s'exciter; **he's a r. devil** c'est un chaud lapin; **a r. old man** un vieux satyre

ranee = **rani**

RANGE [reɪndʒ]

N

• portée **1**	• échelle **2**
• gamme **3**	• choix **3**
• étendue **4**	• domaine **4**

- chaîne **5** • habitat **6**
- champ de tir **7** • fourneau **8**
- rang **9**

VT
- parcourir **1** • ranger **2, 3, 6**
- mettre en rangs **2** • braquer **4**
- aligner **5**

VI
- aller (de... à) **1** • varier (entre... et) **1**
- parcourir **2**

N 1 *(of missile, sound, transmitter, telescope)* portée *f*; *(of vehicle, aircraft)* autonomie *f*; **medium-r.** *or* **intermediate-r. missiles** missiles *mpl* à portée intermédiaire; **short-/medium-/long-r. aircraft** court-/moyen-/long-courrier *m*; *Met* **short-/long-r. forecast** prévisions *fpl* météorologiques à court/long terme; **at long/short r.** à longue/courte portée; **out of r.** hors de portée; **within (firing) r.** à portée de tir; **to be within hearing r.** être à portée de voix; **it can kill a man at a r. of 800 metres** ça peut tuer un homme à une distance de 800 mètres; **at point blank r.** à bout portant; **r. of vision** champ *m* visuel; **it gives you some idea of the r. of their powers** ça vous donne une petite idée de l'étendue de leurs pouvoirs

2 *(scale ▸ of prices, salaries)* échelle *f*, éventail *m*; *(of instrument, voice)* tessiture *f*; **there is a wide r. of temperatures in these parts** il existe de très grands écarts de température dans ces régions; **children in the same age r.** les enfants dans la même tranche d'âge; **beyond/within one's r.** *(note)* hors de/dans son registre; **it's within my price r.** c'est dans mes prix; **what is your price r.?** quel prix voulez-vous mettre?; *St Exch* **opening/closing r.** fourchette *f* de cours d'ouverture/de clôture

3 *(series, selection ▸ of colours, feelings, products)* gamme *f*; (▸ *of patterns, sizes)* choix *m*; **the new autumn r.** *(of clothes)* la nouvelle collection d'automne; **this car is (at) the top/bottom of the r.** cette voiture est le modèle haut/bas de gamme; **the coat comes in a wide r. of colours/sizes** le manteau existe dans une gamme variée de couleurs/un grand choix de tailles; **we talked on a wide r. of topics** nous avons discuté de sujets très divers; **she has a wide r. of interests** elle s'intéresse à beaucoup de choses; **to experience the full r. of emotions** passer par toute la gamme des émotions; **the r. of possibilities is almost infinite** l'éventail des possibilités est presque infini

4 *(scope ▸ of activity)* champ *m*; (▸ *of knowledge, research)* étendue *f*; (▸ *of inquiry, investigation)* domaine *m*; *Mktg* (▸ *of advertising campaign)* rayon *m* d'action; **that is beyond the r. of the present inquiry** cela ne relève pas de cette enquête; **that lies outside the r. of my responsibility** ça dépasse les limites de ma responsabilité

5 *(of mountains)* chaîne *f*

6 *(territory ▸ of animal, plant)* habitat *m*; *Am (prairie)* prairie *f*

7 *(for target practice)* champ *m* de tir; **missile r.** champ *m* de tir de missiles

8 *(cooker)* fourneau *m* (de cuisine)

9 *(row, line)* rang *m*, rangée *f*

10 *(in surveying)* alignement *m*, direction *f*

VT 1 *(roam over)* parcourir

2 *(put in a row or in rows)* ranger, mettre *ou* disposer en rang *ou* en rangs; **the troops ranged themselves in front of the embassy** les troupes se rangèrent devant l'ambassade; **the desks are ranged in threes** les pupitres sont en rangées de trois

3 *(join, ally)* ranger, rallier; **to r. oneself with sb** se ranger du côté de qn; *(ideologically)* s'aligner sur la position de qn; **to r. oneself against sb** s'opposer à qn; **the forces ranged against them** les forces ralliées contre eux

4 *(aim ▸ cannon, telescope)* braquer (**on** sur)

5 *Typ* aligner, justifier; **ranged left/right** justifié à gauche/à droite

6 *(classify)* classer, ranger

7 *Am* **to r. cattle** élever du bétail dans la prairie

VI 1 *(extend, vary)* aller (**from... to** de... à), varier (**from...** to entre... et); **prices r. from £15 to £150** les prix vont de 15 à 150 livres; **their ages r. from 5 to 12** *or* **between 5 and 12** ils ont de 5 à 12 *ou* entre 5 et 12 ans; **the quality ranges from mediocre to excellent** la qualité varie de médiocre à excellent; **the survey ranged over the whole country** l'enquête couvrait la totalité du pays; **our conversation ranged over a large number of topics** nous avons discuté d'un grand nombre de sujets

2 *(roam)* **to r. over sth** parcourir qch; **they r. over the countryside** ils parcourent la campagne; **his eyes ranged over the audience** il parcourut l'auditoire des yeux

3 *(gun, missile)* **to r. over** avoir une portée de

▸▸ *Mktg* ***range addition*** ajout *m* à la gamme; *Am* ***range cattle*** bétail *m* élevé dans la prairie; *Mktg* ***range extension*** déclinaison *f* de la gamme; *Phot* ***range finding*** télémétrie *f*; ***range pole, range rod*** *(surveying instrument)* jalon *m*; *Mktg* ***range stretching*** extension *f* de la gamme

rangefinder ['reɪndʒˌfaɪndə(r)] **N** télémètre *m*

rangeland ['reɪndʒlænd] **N** *Am* prairie *f*

ranger ['reɪndʒə(r)] **N 1** *(in park, forest)* garde *m* forestier **2** *Am (lawman)* ≃ gendarme *m* **3** *Am Mil* ranger *m*

• **Ranger (Guide) N** guide *m*

ranging ['reɪndʒɪŋ] **ADJ**

▸▸ *Mil* ***ranging fire*** tir *m* de réglage; ***ranging pole, ranging rod*** *(surveying instrument)* jalon *m*

rangy ['reɪndʒɪ] *(compar* **rangier**, *superl* **rangiest)** **ADJ 1** *(tall and thin)* grand et élancé **2** *(roomy)* spacieux

rani ['rɑːnɪ] **N** rani *f*

rank [ræŋk] **N 1** *(grade)* rang *m*, grade *m*; **promoted to the r. of colonel** promu (au rang de *ou* au grade de) colonel; **the r. of manager** le titre de directeur; **to pull r.** faire valoir sa supériorité hiérarchique; **I don't want to have to pull r. on you** je ne veux pas avoir à user de mon autorité sur vous

2 *(quality)* rang *m*; **we have very few players in the first** *or* **top r.** nous avons très peu de joueurs de premier ordre

3 *(social class)* rang *m*, condition *f* (sociale); **the lower ranks of society** les couches inférieures de la société

4 *(row, line)* rang *m*, rangée *f*; *(on chessboard)* rangée *f*; **to break ranks** *Mil* rompre les rangs; *Fig* se désolidariser; *Mil & Fig* **to close ranks** serrer les rangs; *Mil* **close ranks!** serrez!

5 *Br* **(taxi) r.** station *f* (de taxis)

6 *Math (in matrix)* rang *m*

7 *Fin (of debt, mortgage)* rang *m*

VT 1 *(rate)* classer; **she is ranked among the best contemporary writers** elle est classée parmi les meilleurs écrivains contemporains; **I r. this as one of our finest performances** je considère que c'est une de nos meilleures représentations; **he is ranked number 3** il est classé numéro 3 **2** *(arrange)* ranger **3** *Am (outrank ▸ in army)* avoir un grade supérieur à; (▸ *in office, organization etc)* être le supérieur de; **a general ranks a captain** un général est au-dessus d'un capitaine

VI 1 *(rate)* figurer; **to r. above/below sb** être le supérieur de/occuper un rang inférieur à qn; **to r. equally (with sb)** être au même niveau (que qn); **it ranks high/low on our list of priorities** c'est/ce n'est pas une de nos priorités; **he hardly ranks as an expert** on ne peut guère le qualifier d'expert; *Chess* **a castle ranks above a bishop** la tour est plus forte que le fou

2 *Fin (creditor, claimant)* **to r. before/after sb** prendre rang *ou* passer avant/après qn; **to r. equally (with sb)** prendre *ou* avoir le même rang (que qn)

3 *Fin (share)* **to r. after/before sth** être primé par/avoir la priorité sur qch

4 *Am Mil* être officier supérieur; *Fig* **he doesn't r.** ce n'est pas quelqu'un d'important

ADJ 1 *(as intensifier)* complet(ète), véritable; **it's a r. injustice** c'est une injustice flagrante

2 *(foul-smelling)* infect, fétide; *(rancid)* rance; **to smell r.** sentir fort; **his shirt was r. with sweat** sa chemise empestait la sueur

3 *Br Fam (worthless)* merdique

4 *(coarse ▸ person, language)* grossier

5 *Literary (profuse ▸ vegetation)* luxuriant; (▸ *weeds)* prolifique

• **ranks NPL 1** *(members)* rangs *mpl*; **to join the ranks of the opposition** rejoindre les rangs de l'opposition **2** *Mil (rank and file)* **the ranks, other ranks** les hommes *mpl* du rang; **to have served in the ranks** avoir servi comme simple soldat; **to come up through** *or* **to rise from the ranks** sortir du rang; **to reduce an officer to the ranks** dégrader un officier

▸ **rank on VT INSEP** *Am Fam* **to r. on sb** traiter qn de tous les noms

rank-and-file ADJ *(party member)* de la base; **r. soldiers** simples soldats *mpl*

rank-and-filer N *(in army)* simple soldat *m*; *(in political party, union)* membre *m* de la base

ranker ['ræŋkə(r)] **N** *Br Mil (private)* homme *m* du rang; *(officer)* officier *m* sorti du rang

ranking ['ræŋkɪŋ] **N** classement *m*; **his r. is number four** il est classé quatrième

ADJ *Am (prominent)* de premier ordre

▸▸ *Am Mil* ***ranking officer*** officier *m* responsable

rankle ['ræŋkəl] **VI** rester sur le cœur; **it rankled with me** je ne l'ai pas digéré

rankness ['ræŋknɪs] **N 1** *(smell)* puanteur *f*; *(taste)* rance *m* **2** *Literary (luxuriance ▸ of vegetation)* luxuriance *f*, profusion *f*

ransack ['rænsæk] **VT 1** *(plunder)* saccager, mettre à sac **2** *(search)* mettre sens dessus dessous; **he ransacked the wardrobe for his tie** il mit l'armoire sens dessus dessous pour trouver sa cravate

ransom ['rænsəm] **N** rançon *f*; **they held her to r.** ils l'ont kidnappée pour avoir une rançon; *Fig* **they're holding the country to r.** ils tiennent le pays en otage; *Fig* **a king's r.** une fortune

VT *(hold to ransom)* rançonner; *(pay ransom for release of)* racheter

rant [rænt] **VI** fulminer; **they ranted on and on** ils n'arrêtaient pas de fulminer; **to r. at sb** fulminer contre qn; **to r. and rave** tempêter, tonitruer

ranting ['ræntɪŋ] **N** *(UNCOUNT)* vociférations *fpl*

ADJ déclamatoire

ranunculus [rə'nʌŋkjʊləs] **N** *Bot* renoncule *f*

rap [ræp] *(pt & pp* **rapped**, *cont* **rapping**) **VT 1** *(strike)* frapper sur, cogner sur; *Fig* **to r. sb's knuckles, to r. sb over the knuckles** sermonner qn **2** *(in newspaper headlines)* réprimander **3** *Am Fam (criticize)* éreinter, descendre

VI 1 *(knock)* frapper, cogner; **somebody rapped on the door** quelqu'un a frappé (à la porte) **2** *Am Fam (chat)* bavarder□, discuter le bout de gras; **what's he rapping about now?** qu'est-ce qu'il raconte maintenant? **3** *Mus* faire du rap

N 1 *(blow, sound)* coup *m* (sec); **I heard a r. at the door** j'ai entendu frapper à la porte; *Fig* **to be given a r. over** *or* **on the knuckles** se faire taper sur les doigts

2 *Fam (blame)* **to take the r. (for sth)** écoper (pour qch)

3 *Am Fam (legal charge)* accusation□ *f*; **he's up on a murder r.** il est accusé de meurtre□; **to beat the r.** échapper à la justice□, échapper à la condamnation□, être acquitté□

4 *Am Fam (speech)* **don't give me that r.!** raconte pas n'importe quoi!; **he was laying down some r. about the new model** il était en train de faire un baratin sur le nouveau modèle

5 *Mus* rap *m*

6 *Br Fam (idiom)* **I don't care a r.!** je m'en fiche (pas mal)!

▸▸ *Mus* ***rap artist*** chanteur(euse) *m,f* de rap; *Mus* ***rap music*** rap *m*; ***rap session*** bavardage *m*; **we had a good r. session** on a discuté pendant un bon bout de temps; *Am Fam* ***rap sheet*** casier *m* judiciaire□

▸ **rap out VT SEP 1** *(say sharply)* lancer, lâcher; **she rapped out an order** elle lança un ordre **2** *(tap out ▸ message)* taper

rapacious [rə'peɪʃəs] **ADJ** rapace

rapaciously [rə'peɪʃəslɪ] **ADV** avec rapacité *ou* avidité

rapaciousness [rə'peɪʃəsnɪs], **rapacity** [rə'pæsɪtɪ] **N** rapacité *f*

rape[1] [reɪp] **N 1** *(sex crime)* viol *m*; **to commit r.** perpétrer un viol; *Fig* **the r. of the countryside** la dévastation de la campagne **2** *Arch (abduction)* rapt *m*, enlèvement *m*

VT violer

▸▸ ***rape crisis centre*** centre *m* d'accueil pour femmes violées; ***rape suite*** pièce *f* réservée aux victimes de viols *(dans un commissariat)*; **rape victim** personne *f* violée, victime *f* d'un viol

rape² **N 1** *Bot (crop)* colza *m* **2** *(remains of grapes)* marc *m* (de raisin)
▸▸ ***rape oil*** huile *f* de colza

rapeseed ['reɪpsi:d] **N** graine *f* de colza
▸▸ ***rapeseed oil*** huile *f* de colza

raphia ['ræfiə] **N** *Bot* raphia *m*
ADJ en raphia

rapid ['ræpɪd] **ADJ** rapide; **a r. pulse** un pouls rapide; *Fig* **we are making r. strides towards a cure for cancer** la recherche contre le cancer fait des progrès rapides
• **rapids NPL** rapide *m*, rapides *mpl*; **to shoot the rapids** franchir le rapide *ou* les rapides
▸▸ *Mil* ***rapid deployment force*** force *f* d'intervention rapide; ***rapid eye movement*** mouvements *mpl* oculaires rapides; ***rapid reaction force*** forces *fpl* d'action rapide; *Am* ***rapid transit*** transport *m* urbain rapide

rapid-fire ADJ *Mil* à tir rapide; *Fig (questions, jokes)* qui se succèdent à toute allure

rapidity [rə'pɪdɪtɪ] **N** rapidité *f*

rapidly ['ræpɪdlɪ] **ADV** rapidement

rapier ['reɪpjə(r)] **N** rapière *f*
▸▸ ***rapier thrust*** coup *m* de rapière; ***rapier wit*** esprit *m* acerbe

rapist ['reɪpɪst] **N** violeur *m*

▸**rappel down VI** descendre en rappel

rapper ['ræpə(r)] **N 1** *(on door)* heurtoir *m* **2** *Mus* chanteur(euse) *m,f* de rap, rappeur(euse) *m,f*

rapport [ræ'pɔ:(r)] **N** rapport *m*; **I have a good r. with him** j'ai de bons rapports avec lui; **there was an instant r. between them** ils ressentirent une sympathie immédiate

rapprochement [ræ'prɒʃmɑ̃] **N** rapprochement *m*

rapscallion [ræp'skæljən] **N** *Arch* fripon(onne) *m,f*, gredin(e) *m,f*

rapt [ræpt] **ADJ 1** *(engrossed)* absorbé, captivé; **the clown held the children r.** le clown fascinait les enfants; **with r. attention** complètement absorbé; **to be r. in contemplation** être plongé dans ses pensées **2** *(delighted)* ravi; **r. with joy** transporté de joie

raptor ['ræptə(r)] **N** rapace *m*

rapture ['ræptʃə(r)] **N** ravissement *m*, extase *f*; **to be filled with r.** être enchanté; **to go into raptures over** *or* **about sth** s'extasier sur qch; **they were in raptures about their presents** leurs cadeaux les ont ravis

rapturous ['ræptʃərəs] **ADJ** *(feeling)* intense, profond; *(gaze)* ravi, extasié; *(praise, applause)* enthousiaste; **the champions were given a r. welcome** on a réservé un accueil délirant aux champions; **they were r. about their daughter's success** le succès de leur fille les rendait fous de joie

rare [reə(r)] **ADJ 1** *(uncommon)* rare; **it's r. to see such marital bliss nowadays** un tel bonheur conjugal est rare de nos jours; **on r. occasions** en de rares occasions; **on the r. occasions when I've seen him angry** les rares fois où je l'ai vu en colère; **a r. opportunity** une occasion exceptionnelle; **that r. bird, the man who does the housework** cet oiseau rare qu'est l'homme qui fait le ménage
2 *(exceptional)* rare, exceptionnel; **she has a r. gift** elle a un don exceptionnel
3 *Fam (extreme)* énorme□; **you gave me a r. fright!** tu m'as fait une de ces peurs!
4 *(excellent)* fameux, génial; **we had a r. old time** on s'est amusés comme des fous
5 *(meat)* saignant; **very r.** bleu
6 *(rarefied* ▸ *air, atmosphere)* raréfié
▸▸ *Chem* ***rare earth*** terre *f* rare

rarebit ['reəbɪt] **N** ≃ toast *m* au fromage

rarefied ['reərɪfaɪd] **ADJ 1** *(air, atmosphere)* raréfié; **to become r.** se raréfier **2** *(refined)* raffiné; **the r. circles in which she moves** les milieux raffinés dans lesquels elle évolue

rarefy ['reərɪfaɪ] *(pt & pp* **rarefied)** **VT** raréfier
VI se raréfier

rarely ['reəlɪ] **ADV** rarement; **r. have I** *or* **I have r. encountered anyone like him** j'ai rarement rencontré quelqu'un comme lui

rareness ['reənɪs] **N** rareté *f*

raring ['reərɪŋ] **ADJ** *Fam* impatient□; **to be r. to go** ronger son frein

rarity ['reərɪtɪ] *(pl* **rarities) N 1** *(uncommon person, thing)* rareté *f*; **a foreigner's a r. in these parts** les étrangers sont rares par ici **2** *(scarcity)* rareté *f*

rascal ['rɑ:skəl] **N 1** *(naughty child)* coquin(e) *m,f*, polisson(onne) *m,f* **2** *(rogue)* vaurien *m*, gredin *m*

rascally ['rɑ:skəlɪ] **ADJ** *(person)* coquin; *(deed)* de coquin

rash [ræʃ] **N 1** *Med* rougeur *fpl*, éruption *f*; **to come out in a r.** avoir une éruption; **oysters bring me out in a r.** les huîtres me donnent des éruptions; **I've got a r. on my face** j'ai des rougeurs sur le visage **2** *(wave, outbreak)* vague *f*; **a r. of strikes** une vague de grèves
ADJ imprudent; **that was a bit r. of you** c'était un peu risqué de ta part; **don't do anything r.** ne faites pas de bêtises; **don't make any r. promises!** ne faites pas de promesses en l'air!; **I bought it in a r. moment** je l'ai acheté sur un coup de tête; **r. words** des paroles *fpl* irréfléchies

rasher ['ræʃə(r)] **N** tranche *f (de bacon)*

rashly ['ræʃlɪ] **ADV** imprudemment; **I rather r. offered to drive her home** dans un moment de folie, j'ai offert de la reconduire chez elle

rashness ['ræʃnɪs] **N** imprudence *f*; **I paid for my r.** j'ai payé cher mes imprudences

rasp [rɑ:sp] **N 1** *(file)* râpe *f* **2** *(sound)* bruit *m* de râpe; **the r. in his voice** sa voix rauque **3** *Scot Fam (raspberry)* framboise□*f*
VT 1 *(scrape, file)* râper; *Fig* **the cat rasped its tongue over my face** le chat m'a léché la figure de sa langue râpeuse; **he rasped his hand over his unshaven chin** il frotta sa main sur son menton râpeux **2** *(say)* dire d'une voix rauque; **to r. out an answer** répondre d'une voix rauque
VI *(make rasping noise)* grincer, crisser; **her breath rasped in her lungs** elle avait une respiration sifflante

raspberry ['rɑ:zbərɪ] *(pl* **raspberries) N 1** *(fruit)* framboise *f* **2** *Fam (noise)* **to blow a r.** faire pfft *(en signe de dérision)*; **the announcement was greeted with a chorus of raspberries** la nouvelle fut accueillie par des sifflements□
COMP *(jam)* de framboises; *(tart, ice-cream)* aux framboises
ADJ *(colour)* framboise *(inv)*
▸▸ ***raspberry bush, raspberry cane*** framboisier *m*; ***raspberry vinegar*** vinaigre *m* de framboise

rasping ['rɑ:spɪŋ] **ADJ** *(noise)* grinçant, crissant; *(voice)* rauque, grinçant
N *(noise)* grincement *m*, crissement *m*

raspings ['rɑ:spɪŋz] **NPL** *Culin (breadcrumbs)* chapelure *f*

Rasta ['ræstə] *(abbr* **Rastafarian) N** rasta *mf*
ADJ rasta *(inv)*

Rastafarian [,ræstə'feərɪən] **N** rastafari *mf*
ADJ rastafari *(inv)*

Rastafarianism [,ræstə'feərɪənɪzəm] **N** rastafarisme *m*

raster ['ræstə(r)] **N** *Comput, Typ & TV* trame *m*
▸▸ *Comput & Typ* ***raster image*** image *f* tramée; *Comput & Typ* ***raster image processor*** processeur *m* d'image tramée; *Comput & Typ* ***raster scan*** balayage *m* de trame

rasterize, -ise ['ræstəraɪz] **VT** *Comput, Typ & TV* rastériser

rat [ræt] *(pt & pp* **ratted**, *cont* **ratting) N 1** *Zool* rat *m*; **female r., she-r.** rate *f*; **baby r.** raton *m*; **black r.** rat *m* noir; **grey** *or* **sewer r.** rat *m* d'égout, surmulot *m*; **to look like a drowned r.** avoir l'air d'un chien mouillé; **to be caught like a r. in a trap** être fait comme un rat; **with her hair all in rats' tails** avec ses mèches collées; *Am very Fam* **I don't give a r.'s ass** je m'en fous pas mal, je m'en balance
2 *Fam (despicable person)* ordure *f*; **you dirty r.!** espèce d'ordure!
3 *Am Fam Pej (informer)* mouchard(e) *m,f*, indic *m*
4 *Fam Pej (strikebreaker)* jaune *mf*, briseur(euse) *m,f* de grève□
5 *Br Fam Old-fashioned* **rats!** zut!
VI *Fam Fig* retourner sa veste
▸▸ *Zool* ***rat kangaroo*** rat-kangourou *m*, potoroo *m*, potorou *m*; ***rat pack*** *(paparazzi)* paparazzi(s) *mpl*; ***rat poison*** mort-aux-rats *f inv*; ***rat race*** foire *f* d'empoigne; **she dropped out of the r. race to live in the country** elle quitta le monde impitoyable du travail et partit vivre à la campagne; ***rat run*** = rue résidentielle empruntée par les automobilistes qui veulent éviter les bouchons aux heures de pointe; *Zool* ***rat snake*** serpent *m* ratier; ***rat trap*** *(for rats)* piège *m* à rats, ratière *f*; *Am (building)* taudis *m*

▸**rat on VT INSEP** *Fam* **1** *(betray)* vendre; *(inform on)* moucharder **2** *(go back on)* revenir sur□; **they ratted on our deal** ils nous ont laissé tomber dans cette affaire

▸**rat out VT SEP** *Am Fam* **to r. sb out** balancer qn, moucharder qn

ratable = **rateable**

ratafia [,rætə'fɪə] **N 1** *(liqueur)* ratafia *m* **2** *(biscuit)* macaron *m*
▸▸ ***ratafia biscuit*** macaron *m*

rat-arsed [-ɑ:st] **ADJ** *Br very Fam* bourré comme un coing, pété à mort; **to get r.** se bourrer la gueule

rat-a-tat(-tat) ['rætə,tæt('tæt)] **N** *(on door)* toc-toc *m*; *(of machine gun)* pétarade *f*; *(of typewriter)* tac-tac-tac *m*

ratatouille [,rætə'tu:ɪ] **N** *Culin* ratatouille *f*

ratbag ['rætbæg] **N** *Br Fam* peau *f* de vache, ordure *f*; **the old r.!** la vieille chouette!

ratcatcher ['ræt,kætʃə(r)] **N** *(gen)* chasseur(euse) *m,f* de rats; *(official)* agent *m* de la dératisation

ratchet ['rætʃɪt] **N** rochet *m*; *Fig* **this had a r. effect on prices** cela a entraîné une augmentation irréversible des prix
▸▸ ***ratchet mechanism*** (dispositif *m* d')encliquetage *m*; ***ratchet screwdriver*** tournevis *m* à cliquet; ***ratchet wheel*** roue *f* à rochet; ***ratchet wrench*** clé *f* à rochet

-rate [reɪt] **SUFF first-r.** de premier ordre; **second-r.** de deuxième ordre

rate [reɪt] **N 1** *(ratio, level)* taux *m*; **the birth/death/suicide r.** le taux de natalité/de mortalité/de suicide; **the success r. is falling** le taux de réussite est en baisse; **the hourly r. is going to be increased** le taux horaire va être augmenté
2 *(cost, charge)* tarif *m*; **his rates have gone up** ses prix ont augmenté; **to strike for higher rates of pay** faire la grève pour obtenir une augmentation de salaire; **the r. is 60p in the pound** le taux est de 60 pence par livre; **postal** *or* **postage r.** tarifs *mpl* postaux; **standard/reduced r.** tarif *m* normal/réduit; **the going r.** le tarif courant
3 *(speed)* vitesse *f*, train *m*; **at this r. we'll never get there** au rythme où nous allons, nous n'y arriverons jamais; **she shot past at a terrific r.** elle est passée comme une flèche; *Fam* **at a r. of knots** à toute allure
4 *(idiom) Fam* **(at) any r.** enfin bref
VT 1 *(reckon, consider)* considérer; **she's rated as one of the best players in the world** elle est classée parmi les meilleures joueuses du monde; **I r. him among my closest friends** je le considère comme un de mes amis les plus proches; **to r. sb/sth highly** avoir une haute opinion de qn/qch, faire grand cas de qn/qch
2 *(deserve)* mériter; **her film rates better reviews** son film mérite de meilleures critiques; **that performance should r. him third place** cette prestation devrait lui assurer la troisième place
3 *Fam (have high opinion of)* **I don't r. him as an actor** à mon avis, ce n'est pas un bon acteur□; **I don't r. their chances much** je ne pense pas qu'ils aient beaucoup de chance□
4 *Br (fix rateable value of)* fixer la valeur locative imposable de; **their house has been rated higher this year** leur maison a été classée dans la tranche supérieure cette année
5 *Literary (scold)* tancer
VI *(rank high)* se classer; **he rates highly in my estimation** je le tiens en très haute estime; **in terms of efficiency, she rates higher than anyone else** pour ce qui est de l'efficacité, elle bat tout le monde

• **rates** NPL *Br Formerly* impôts *mpl* locaux
• **at any rate** ADV de toute façon, de toute manière, en tout cas
►► *Mkfg* ***rate of adoption*** *(of product)* taux *m* d'adoption; *Mktg* ***rate of awareness*** taux *m* de notoriété; *Fin* ***rate band*** plage *f ou* fourchette *f* de taux; *Br Formerly* ***rate collector*** receveur(euse) *m,f* municipal(e); *Fin* ***rate of depreciation*** taux *m* d'amortissement; *Fin* ***rate of exchange*** cours *m ou* taux *m* de change; *Fin* ***rate of growth*** taux *m* d'accroissement *ou* de croissance; *Fin* ***rate of increase*** taux *m* d'accroissement; *Fin & Econ* ***rate of inflation*** taux *m* d'inflation; *Fin* ***rate of interest*** taux *m* d'intérêt; *Mktg* ***rate of penetration*** taux *m* de pénétration; *Chem* ***rate of reaction*** vitesse *f* de réaction; *Br Formerly* ***rate rebate*** dégrèvement *m* d'impôts locaux; *Mktg* ***rate of renewal*** taux *m* de renouvellement; *Fin* ***rate of return*** *(on investment)* taux *m* de rendement; *Fin* ***rate of return analysis*** analyse *f* du rendement; *Fin* ***rate of return pricing*** fixation *f* de prix au taux de rendement établi; *Br* ***rate support grant*** = subvention à une collectivité locale; ***rate of taxation*** taux *m* d'imposition; ***rate of uptake*** taux *m* de succès

rateable ['reɪtəbəl] ADJ
►► *Br* ***rateable value*** ≃ valeur *f* locative imposable

rate-cap VT *Br Admin (local authority)* fixer un taux plafond pour les impôts locaux de

rate-capping [-'kæpɪŋ] N *Br Admin* plafonnement *m* des impôts locaux

rated ['reɪtɪd] ADJ *Tech (load, speed, voltage)* nominal

ratepayer ['reɪt,peɪə(r)] N *Br Formerly* contribuable *mf*

ratfink ['rætfɪŋk] N *Am very Fam* salaud *m*, salopard *m*

rather ['rɑːðə(r)] ADV **1** *(slightly, a bit)* assez, un peu; **I was r. tired** j'étais assez fatigué; **it's r. too small for me** c'est un peu trop petit pour moi; **she cut me a r. large slice** elle m'a coupé une tranche plutôt grande; **it tastes r. like honey** ça a un peu le goût du miel; **I am r. inclined to agree with you** je suis plutôt de votre avis; **I r. rashly volunteered** j'ai offert mes services un peu rapidement
2 *Br (as intensifier)* **I r. like this town** je trouve cette ville plutôt agréable; **she's r. nice** elle est plutôt sympa
3 *(expressing preference)* plutôt; **I'd r. go by car** je préférerais *ou* j'aimerais mieux y aller en voiture; **I'd r. not do it today** je préférerais *ou* j'aimerais mieux ne pas le faire aujourd'hui; **would you r. go to Scotland?** préféreriez-vous aller en Écosse?; **I would r. that you came** je préférerais que vous veniez; **I'd r. you didn't do it** je préférerais que tu ne le fasses pas; **shall we go out tonight? – I'd r. not** si on sortait ce soir? – je n'ai pas très envie; **you should congratulate his wife r. than him** c'est sa femme que tu devrais féliciter, pas lui; **r. than walk I took the bus** plutôt que d'y aller à pied, j'ai pris le bus; **r. you than me!** plutôt toi que moi!
4 *(more exactly)* plutôt, plus exactement; **my parents, or r. my mother and stepfather** mes parents, ou plutôt ma mère et mon beau-père
PREDET plutôt; **it was r. a long film** le film était plutôt long
EXCLAM *Br Old-fashioned* et comment!; **fancy a drink? – r.!** tu veux boire quelque chose? – je ne dis pas non! *ou* ce n'est pas de refus!

ratification [,rætɪfɪ'keɪʃən] N ratification *f*

ratify ['rætɪfaɪ] *(pt & pp* **ratified***)* VT ratifier

ratine [ræ'tiːn] N *Tex* ratine *f*

rating ['reɪtɪŋ] N **1** *(ranking)* classement *m*; *Fin (of bank, company)* notation *f*; **popularity r.** cote *f* de popularité
2 *(appraisal)* évaluation *f*, estimation *f*
3 *Br Naut* matelot *m*; **the ratings** les matelots *mpl* et gradés *mpl*
4 *(scolding) Literary* réprimande *f*, admonestation *f*
• **ratings** NPL *Rad & TV* indice *m* d'écoute; **to boost the ratings** améliorer l'indice d'écoute; **to be high in the ratings** avoir un fort indice d'écoute
►► ***rating agency*** agence *f* de notation *ou* de rating; *Rad & TV* ***ratings battle*** course *f* à l'Audimat®; *Mktg* ***rating scale*** *(in market research)* échelle *f* de classement; *Cin* ***rating system*** = système de classement des films en fonction de l'âge du public autorisé; *Rad & TV* ***ratings war*** course *f* à l'Audimat®

ratio ['reɪʃɪəʊ] *(pl* **ratios***)* N **1** *(proportion)* proportion *f*, rapport *m*; **in the r. of 6 to 1** dans la proportion de 6 contre 1; **the teacher-student r. is 1 to 10** le rapport enseignants-étudiants est de 1 pour 10 **2** *Math* raison *f*, proportion *f* **3** *Econ* ratio *m*

ratiocination [,rætɪɒsɪ'neɪʃən] N *Formal* raisonnement *m*

ration ['ræʃən] N *also Fig* ration *f*; **you've had your r. of television for today** tu as eu ta dose de télévision pour aujourd'hui
VT **1** *(food)* rationner; **they are rationed to one pound of meat a week** ils sont rationnés à une livre de viande par semaine; **she rations herself to one film a week** elle se limite *ou* se rationne à un film par semaine **2** *(funds)* limiter
• **rations** NPL *(food)* vivres *mpl*; **to be on double/short rations** toucher une ration double/réduite; **full rations** rations *fpl* complètes; **half rations** demi-rations *fpl*
►► ***ration book*** carnet *m* de tickets de rationnement; ***ration card*** carte *f* de rationnement

rational ['ræʃənəl] ADJ **1** *(capable of reason)* doué de raison, raisonnable; **a r. being** un être doué de raison
2 *(reasonable, logical* ► *person)* raisonnable; *(*► *behaviour, explanation)* rationnel; **it seemed like the r. thing to do** il me semblait que c'était ce qu'il y avait de plus logique à faire; **he is incapable of r. thought** il est incapable de raisonner logiquement
3 *(of sound mind, sane)* lucide
4 *Math (number)* rationnel

rationale [,ræʃə'nɑːl] N **1** *(underlying reason)* logique *f*; **what is the r. for** *or* **behind their decision?** quelle logique sous-tend leur décision? **2** *(exposition)* exposé *m*

rationalism ['ræʃənəlɪzəm] N rationalisme *m*

rationalist ['ræʃənəlɪst] ADJ rationaliste
N rationaliste *mf*

rationalistic [,ræʃənə'lɪstɪk] ADJ rationaliste

rationality [,ræʃə'nælɪtɪ] N *(of belief, system etc)* rationalité *f*

rationalization, -isation [,ræʃənəlaɪ'zeɪʃən] N rationalisation *f*

rationalize, -ise ['ræʃənəlaɪz] VT **1** *(action, behaviour, dislike, fear etc)* rationaliser, trouver une explication logique *ou* rationnelle à **2** *Br Ind (company etc)* rationaliser **3** *Math* rendre rationnel
VI **stop rationalizing!** arrête de chercher des excuses!

rationally ['ræʃənəlɪ] ADV rationnellement

rationing ['ræʃənɪŋ] N **1** *(of food)* rationnement *m*; **(food) r.** rationnement *m* alimentaire **2** *(of funds)* rationnement *m*

ratlin, ratline ['rætlɪn] N enfléchure *f*

ratrack ['rætræk] N *Ski* ratrack *m*

rattan [rə'tæn] N *Bot* rotang *m*; *(substance)* rotin *m*
COMP *(furniture)* en rotin

rat-tat ['ræt,tæt] = **rat-a-tat(-tat)**

ratted ['rætɪd] ADJ *Br Fam* bourré comme un coing, pété à mort; **to get r.** se péter, se torcher

ratteen = **ratine**

ratter ['rætə(r)] N *(dog, cat)* chasseur *m* de rats

rattiness ['rætɪnɪs] N *Br Fam (irritability)* irritabilité *f*

ratting ['rætɪŋ] N **to go r.** faire la chasse aux rats

rattle ['rætəl] VI *(gen)* faire du bruit; *(car, engine)* faire un bruit de ferraille; *(chain, machine, dice)* cliqueter; *(gunfire, hailstones)* crépiter; *(door, window)* vibrer; **the trains make the windows r.** les trains font vibrer les fenêtres; **somebody was rattling at the door** quelqu'un secouait la porte
VT **1** *(box)* agiter *(en faisant du bruit)*; *(key)* faire cliqueter; *(chain, dice)* agiter, secouer; *(door, window)* faire vibrer; *Fam* **who rattled your cage?** quelle mouche te pique? **2** *(disconcert)* ébranler, secouer; **to get rattled** perdre son sang froid; **don't get rattled!** pas de panique!
N **1** *(noise* ► *of chains)* bruit *m*; *(*► *of car, engine)* bruit *m* de ferraille; *(*► *of coins, keys)* cliquetis *m*; *(*► *of gunfire, hailstones)* crépitement *m*; *(*► *of window, door)* vibration *f*, vibrations *fpl* **2** *(for baby)* hochet *m*; *(for sports fan)* crécelle *f* **3** *Zool (of rattlesnake)* cascabelle *f*

► **rattle along** VI **1** *(move noisily* ► *of car, train)* rouler dans un bruit de ferraille **2** *(move quickly* ► *in car, train)* rouler à toute allure

► **rattle around** VI **you'll be rattling around in that big old house!** tu seras perdu tout seul dans cette grande maison!

► **rattle off** VT SEP *(speech, list)* débiter, réciter à toute allure; *(piece of work)* expédier; *(letter, essay)* écrire en vitesse

► **rattle on** VI jacasser

► **rattle through** VT INSEP *(speech, meeting etc)* expédier

rattlebrain ['rætəlbreɪn] N *Fam Old-fashioned* écervelé(e) *m,f*

rattlesnake ['rætəlsneɪk] N serpent *m* à sonnette, crotale *m*

rattletrap ['rætəltræp] N *Br Fam Old-fashioned (car)* tacot *m*

rattling ['rætəlɪŋ] N = **rattle** *n* 1
ADJ **1** *(sound)* **there was a r. noise** on entendait un cliquetis **2** *(fast)* rapide; **at a r. pace** à vive allure
ADV *Fam Old-fashioned* **we had a r. good time** on s'est drôlement amusés; **this book is a r. good read** ce livre est vraiment formidable

ratty ['rætɪ] *(compar* **rattier**, *superl* **rattiest***)* AD[J] *Fam* **1** *(irritable)* de mauvais poil, râleur; **don't get r.!** ne commence pas à râler! **2** *Am (shabby)* miteux

raucous ['rɔːkəs] ADJ **1** *(noisy)* bruyant; **r. laughter** rires *mpl* gras; **a r. party** une soirée tapageuse *ou* bruyante; **things got a bit r. as the evening wore on** la soirée est devenue de plus en plus bruyante **2** *(hoarse)* rauque

raucously ['rɔːkəslɪ] ADV **1** *(noisily)* bruyammen[t] **2** *(hoarsely)* d'une voix rauque

raucousness ['rɔːkəsnɪs] N **1** *(noisiness)* tapage *m* **2** *(hoarseness)* ton *m* rauque

raunchiness ['rɔːntʃɪnɪs] N sensualité *f*

raunchy ['rɔːntʃɪ] *(compar* **raunchier**, *super[l]* **raunchiest***)* ADJ *Fam* **1** *(lewd)* cochon; *(in more light-hearted way)* grivois **2** *(sexy)* sexy **3** *Am (slovenly)* négligé

ravage ['rævɪdʒ] VT ravager, dévaster; **the city had been ravaged by war** la ville avait été ravagée par la guerre; **ravaged face** visage *m* ravagé
• **ravages** NPL **the ravages of time** les ravages *mpl* du temps

rave [reɪv] VI **1** *(be delirious)* délirer
2 *(talk irrationally)* divaguer
3 *(shout)* se déchaîner; **she started raving at me** elle a commencé à vitupérer
4 *Fam (praise)* s'extasier; **to r. about sb/sth** s'extasier sur qn/qch
N *Fam* **1** *(praise)* critique *f* élogieuse **2** *(fashion craze)* mode *f*; **the latest r.** la dernière mode, le dernier cri **3** *Br (party)* rave *f*
ADJ *Fam* **1** *(enthusiastic)* élogieux; **the play got r. reviews** les critiques de la pièce furent très élogieuses **2** *(trendy)* branché

raven ['reɪvən] N *Orn* (grand) corbeau *m*
ADJ noir comme un corbeau *ou* comme du jais; **a r.-haired beauty** une beauté aux cheveux noirs corbeau *ou* de jais

ravening ['rævənɪŋ] ADJ *Literary* vorace

ravenous ['rævənəs] ADJ **1** *(hungry)* affamé; **I was r.!** j'avais une faim de loup!; *Fig* **to be r. for sth** *(fame, power)* être assoiffé *ou* avide de qch **2** *(rapacious)* vorace

ravenously ['rævənəslɪ] ADV voracement; **to be r. hungry** avoir une faim de loup

raver ['reɪvə(r)] N *Br* **1** *Fam (socially active person)* fêtard(e) *m,f*, noceur(euse) *m,f*; **he's a bit of a r.** il est noceur **2** *(who goes to raves)* raver *mf*, raveu[r](euse) *m,f*

rave-up N *Br Fam Old-fashioned* fête f; **to have a r.** faire une fête

ravine [rəˈviːn] N ravin m

raving [ˈreɪvɪŋ] ADJ **1** *(mad)* délirant **2** *(as intensifier)* **she is a r. beauty** elle est d'une grande beauté; *Fam* **he's a r. lunatic** c'est un fou furieux, il est fou à lier; **to be a r. success** avoir un succès fou

ADV *Fam* **r. mad** fou à lier

• **ravings** NPL divagations fpl; **the ravings of a madman** les divagations fpl d'un fou

ravioli [ˌrævɪˈəʊlɪ] N *(UNCOUNT)* ravioli mpl, raviolis mpl

ravish [ˈrævɪʃ] VT **1** *Literary (delight)* ravir, transporter de joie **2** *Arch or Literary (abduct)* ravir, enlever; *(rape)* violer

ravishing [ˈrævɪʃɪŋ] ADJ ravissant, éblouissant

ravishingly [ˈrævɪʃɪŋlɪ] ADV de façon ravissante; **r. beautiful** d'une beauté éblouissante

raw [rɔː] ADJ **1** *(uncooked)* cru; **r. vegetables** légumes mpl crus; *(as hors d'oeuvre)* crudités fpl

2 *(untreated ▸ sugar, latex, leather)* brut; *(▸ spirits)* pur; *(▸ cotton, linen)* écru; *(▸ silk)* grège, écru; *(▸ sewage)* non traité

3 *(unprocessed ▸ data, statistics)* brut

4 *(sore ▸ gen)* sensible, irrité; *(▸ wound, blister)* à vif; *(▸ nerves)* à fleur de peau; **her hands were r. with the cold** ses mains étaient rougies par le froid; *Fig* **the memory was still r.** le souvenir était encore cuisant *ou* douloureux; *Fig* **the remark touched a r. nerve (in him)** la remarque l'a touché *ou* piqué au vif; **my nerves are r.** j'ai les nerfs à vif *ou* à fleur de peau

5 *(emotion, power, energy)* brut

6 *(inexperienced)* inexpérimenté; **a r. recruit** un bleu

7 *(weather)* rigoureux, rude; **a r. wind** un vent âpre *ou* pénétrant; **a r. February night** une froide nuit de février

8 *(forthright)* franc (franche), direct

9 *Am (rude, coarse)* grossier, cru; **the movie paints a r. picture of penitentiary life** le film peint la vie carcérale de façon crue *ou* brutale *ou* réaliste

10 *(idioms)* **to give sb a r. deal** traiter qn de manière injuste; **the unemployed get a r. deal** les chômeurs n'ont pas la part belle; **he's had a r. deal out of life** il n'a pas été gâté par la vie

N *(idioms) Fam* **in the r.** à poil; **life in the r.** la vie telle qu'elle est; *Br* **to touch sb on the r.** toucher *ou* piquer qn au vif

▸▸ ***raw edge*** *(of material)* bord m coupé; ***raw material*** matière f première; **her marriage provided her with r. material for her novel** son mariage lui a servi de matière première pour son roman

rawboned [ˈrɔːbəʊnd] ADJ décharné

rawhide [ˈrɔːhaɪd] N **1** *(skin)* cuir m vert *ou* brut **2** *(whip)* fouet m (de cuir)

Rawlplug® [ˈrɔːlplʌg] N cheville f, fiche f

rawness [ˈrɔːnɪs] N **1** *(natural state)* nature f brute **2** *(soreness)* irritation f

3 *(inexperience)* inexpérience f, manque m d'expérience

4 *(of weather)* rigueur f, rudesse f; *(of wind)* âpreté

5 *(frankness)* franchise f, brutalité f

ray [reɪ] N **1** *(of light)* rayon m **2** *Fig (of hope, intelligence)* lueur f; **a r. of comfort** une petite consolation; **a r. of hope** une lueur d'espoir; *Ironic* **he's a little r. of sunshine** il est de charmante humeur **3** *Ich* raie f

▸▸ ***ray gun*** pistolet m à rayons

rayon [ˈreɪɒn] *Tex* N rayonne f

COMP en rayonne

raze [reɪz] VT raser; **the village was razed to the ground** le village fut entièrement rasé

razor [ˈreɪzə(r)] N rasoir m; **electric/safety r.** rasoir m électrique/de sûreté; **to be on a** *or* **the r.'s edge** être sur le fil du rasoir; **these people are living on the r.'s edge** ces gens vivent dans la peur et l'incertitude

VT raser

▸▸ ***razor blade*** lame f de rasoir; *Am Zool* ***razor clam*** couteau m; ***razor cut*** *(hairstyle)* coupe f au rasoir; ***razor wire*** *(UNCOUNT)* barbelés mpl tranchants

razorback [ˈreɪzəbæk] N **1** *(whale)* balénoptère m, rorqual m **2** *Am (pig)* sanglier m

razorbill [ˈreɪzəbɪl] N *Orn* petit pingouin m, (pingouin m) torda m

razor-cut VT *(hair)* couper au rasoir

razor-sharp ADJ **1** *(blade)* tranchant comme un rasoir *ou* comme une lame de rasoir; *(nails)* acéré **2** *(person, mind)* vif

razz [ræz] N *Br Fam* **to be** *or* **to go on the r.** faire la bringue *ou* la nouba

VT *Am Fam (jeer at)* chambrer

razzle [ˈræzəl] N *Br Fam* **to be** *or* **to go on the r.** faire la bringue *ou* la nouba

razzle-dazzle N *Fam (flashy display)* tape-à-l'œil m *inv*, clinquant m; *Br* **to be** *or* **to go on the r.** faire la bringue *ou* la fête *ou* la nouba

razzmatazz [ˈræzməˌtæz] N *Fam (flashy display)* tape-à-l'œil m *inv*, clinquant m

RC [ˌɑːˈsiː] N *(abbr* **Roman Catholic***)* catholique mf

RCMP [ˌɑːsiːˌemˈpiː] N *Can (abbr* **Royal Canadian Mounted Police***)* Gendarmerie f royale du Canada

Rd *(written abbr* **road***)* rue f

RDA [ˌɑːdiːˈeɪ] N *(abbr* **recommended daily allowance***)* recommandation f quotidienne officielle *(en vitamines, sels minéraux etc)*

RDBMS [ˌɑːdiːˌbiːemˈes] N *Comput (abbr* **relational database management system***)* SGBDR m

RDS [ˌɑːdiːˈes] N *(abbr* **radio data system***)* RDS m

> **RE-** — PRÉFIXE
>
> **Re-** est un préfixe très productif qui s'emploie avec des verbes et des noms et qui se traduit généralement par **re-**, **ré-** ou **r-**.
> En anglais il est courant d'employer un trait d'union après **re** lorsque celui-ci précède un mot qui commence par **e** comme dans **to re-employ**, **to re-evaluate** et **re-election**.
> Le trait d'union est également utilisé pour éviter la confusion avec d'autres verbes, comme dans les exemples suivants :
> **to re-sign a document** signer un document une nouvelle fois (ne pas confondre avec **to resign** = démissionner) ; **to re-cover an armchair** recouvrir un fauteuil (ne pas confondre avec to **to recover** = récupérer).
> • **Re-** s'emploie pour exprimer l'idée de RÉPÉTITION :
> **to reread** relire; **to re-elect** réélire; **re-election** réélection ; **to rearrest** arrêter de nouveau; **he remarried** il s'est remarié.
> Parfois à l'idée de répétition vient s'ajouter la notion d'AMÉLIORATION :
> **to rewrite a letter** réécrire une lettre; **he repainted the walls a lighter colour** il a repeint les murs avec une couleur plus claire; **a rethink of the whole policy is necessary** il faut repenser le projet dans son ensemble.
> • **Re-** peut également exprimer l'idée de RETOUR A UN ÉTAT ANTÉRIEUR :
> **to rearm** réarmer; **to rebuild** reconstruire; **to re-establish order** rétablir l'ordre; **reinstatement** réintégration ; **reforestation** reboisement.

re[1] [reɪ] N *Mus* ré m *inv*

re[2] [riː] PREP **1** *Admin & Com* **re your letter of 6 June** en réponse à *ou* suite à votre lettre du 6 juin; **Re: job application** *(in letter heading)* Objet: demande d'emploi **2** *Law* **(in) re** en l'affaire de

REACH [riːtʃ]

> **N**
> • portée **1, 5** • extension **2**
> **VT**
> • arriver à **1, 3, 4** • atteindre **1–3**
> • parvenir à **1, 4** • passer **5**
> • joindre **6**
> **VI**
> • tendre la main **1** • s'étendre **2**
> • porter **2**
> **NPL**
> • étendue

N **1** *(range)* portée f, atteinte f; **within (arm's) r.** à portée de la main; **within r. of** à la portée de; *(of place)* à proximité de, proche de; **the house is within easy r. of the shops** la maison est à proximité des magasins; **within everyone's r.** *(affordable by all)* à la portée de toutes les bourses; **out of** *or* **beyond r.** hors de portée; **out of r. of** hors de (la) portée de; **keep out of the r. of children** *(on packaging)* ne pas laisser à la portée des enfants; **nuclear physics is beyond my r.** la physique nucléaire, ça me dépasse complètement; **beyond the r. of the authorities** à l'abri des *ou* hors de la portée des autorités

2 *(arm's length)* extension f; *(in boxing)* allonge f; **a good** *or* **long r.** une bonne allonge

3 *(action)* **she made a r. for the gun** elle étendit la main pour prendre le revolver

4 *Naut* bordée f, bord m

5 *TV & Rad (audience size)* portée f

VT **1** *(arrive at ▸ destination)* arriver à, atteindre; *(letter, news, parcel)* parvenir à; **they reached port** ils arrivèrent au *ou* gagnèrent le port; **easy/difficult to r.** facile/difficile d'accès; **the town could only be reached by sea** on ne pouvait accéder à *ou* atteindre la ville que par la mer; **I've reached the end of chapter one** je suis arrivé à la fin du premier chapitre; **the letter hasn't reached him yet** la lettre ne lui est pas encore parvenue; **it has reached my ears that...** j'ai entendu dire *ou* appris que... + *indicative*

2 *(get as far as ▸ age, goal, point, level)* atteindre; **to r. the age of 80** atteindre l'âge de 80 ans; **to r. the semi-finals** atteindre les demi-finales; **production has reached an all-time low** la production est descendue à son niveau le plus bas; **to r. a younger/wider audience** toucher un public plus jeune/large

3 *(extend to)* arriver (jusqu')à; *(be able to touch)* atteindre; **the water reached my knees** l'eau m'arrivait aux genoux; **can you r. the top shelf?** est-ce que tu peux atteindre la dernière étagère?; **his feet don't r. the floor** ses pieds ne touchent pas par terre

4 *(come to ▸ agreement, decision, conclusion)* arriver à, parvenir à; *(▸ compromise)* arriver à, aboutir à; *(▸ verdict)* parvenir à

5 *(pass, hand)* passer; **could you r. me that book?** pourriez-vous me passer ce livre?

6 *(contact)* joindre; **to r. sb by telephone** joindre qn par *ou* au téléphone; **you can always r. me at this number** vous pouvez toujours me joindre à ce numéro

7 *Am (bribe ▸ witness)* soudoyer

VI **1** *(with hand)* **to r. for sth** *or* **to get sth** tendre la main pour prendre qch; **he reached across the table for the mustard** il allongea le bras par-dessus la table pour prendre la moutarde; **the policeman reached for his gun** l'agent de police mit la main sur son revolver; **to r. into sth (for sth)** *(drawer, pocket)* mettre la main dans qch (pour prendre qch); **can you r.?** est-ce que tu peux y arriver?; **r. for the sky!** haut les mains!; **to r. for the stars** viser haut

2 *(forest, property etc)* s'étendre (**to** jusqu'à); *(noise, voice)* porter (**to** jusqu'à)

3 *(be long enough)* **it won't r.** ce n'est pas assez long

4 *Naut* faire une bordée

• **reaches** NPL étendue f; **vast reaches of water/moorland** de vastes étendues fpl d'eau/de lande; **the upper/the lower reaches of a river** l'amont m/l'aval m d'une rivière; **in the further reaches of the empire** au fin fond de l'empire

▸ **reach back** VI *(in time)* remonter; **a family reaching back to the 16th century** une famille qui remonte au XVIème siècle

▸ **reach down** VT SEP descendre; **can you r. me down that saucepan?** est-ce que tu peux me passer la casserole là-haut?

VI **1** *(coat, hair)* descendre; **her skirt reached down to her ankles** sa jupe lui descendait jusqu'aux chevilles **2** *(person)* tendre *ou* étendre le bras (**for** pour prendre)

▸ **reach out** VT SEP *(arm, hand)* tendre, étendre; **he reached out his hand and took the money** il étendit la main et prit l'argent

VI tendre *ou* étendre le bras; **to r. out to people in need** venir en aide aux nécessiteux

▸ **reach up** VI **1** *(raise arm)* lever le bras (**for** pour prendre) **2** *(rise ▸ of water, snow etc)* **to r. up to** arriver à; **the water reached up to my waist** l'eau m'arrivait à la taille

reachable [ˈriːtʃəbəl] ADJ **1** *(town, destination)* accessible; **is it r. by boat?** peut-on y aller *ou* accéder par bateau? **2** *(person)* joignable; **he's r. at the following number** on peut le joindre au numéro suivant

reach-me-down N *Br Fam* vieux vêtement *m (que les aînés passent aux cadets)*

react [rɪˈækt] VI réagir (**against** contre; **on** sur; **to** à); **to be slow to r.** *(chemical)* avoir une réaction lente; *(person)* être lent à réagir; **the acid reacts with the metal** l'acide réagit avec le métal

VT *Chem* faire réagir (**sth with sth** qch avec qch)

reactance [rɪˈæktəns] N réactance *f*

reactant [rɪˈæktənt] N réactif *m*

reaction [rɪˈækʃən] N **1** *(gen)* réaction *f*; *Mktg (of consumer to product)* réaction *f*; **their r. to the news was unexpected** ils ont réagi à la nouvelle de façon inattendue; **what was her r.?** quelle a été sa réaction?, comment a-t-elle réagi?; **her work is a r. against abstract art** son œuvre est une réaction par rapport à l'art abstrait **2** *(reflex)* réflexe *m*; **it slows down your reactions** cela ralentit vos réflexes **3** *Pol* réaction *f*; **the forces of r.** les forces *fpl* réactionnaires

▸▸ *Tech* ***reaction engine, reaction motor*** moteur *m* à réaction, réacteur *m*; ***reaction time*** temps *m* de réaction; *Tech* ***reaction turbine*** turbine *f* à réaction

reactionary [rɪˈækʃənrɪ] (*pl* **reactionaries**) ADJ réactionnaire

N réactionnaire *mf*

reactivate [rɪˈæktɪveɪt] VT **1** *(start again ▸ group, club)* reconstituer, reformer; *(▸ economy)* relancer; *(revive ▸ feelings, memories)* raviver, réveiller **2** *Chem, Electron & Med* réactiver **3** *Comput* relancer **4** *esp Am Mil (return to active status ▸ ship)* remettre en service

reactive [rɪˈæktɪv] ADJ *(gen) & Chem & Phys* réactif; *Psy* réactionnel

reactiveness [rɪˈæktɪvnɪs], **reactivity** [ˌriːækˈtɪvɪtɪ] N réactivité *f*

reactor [rɪˈæktə(r)] N réacteur *m*

READ¹ [riːd]

VT	
• lire **1, 2, 6, 10**	• interpréter **3**
• comprendre **3**	• recevoir **4**
• étudier **5**	• indiquer **7**
• annoncer **8**	• corriger **9**
VI	
• lire **1, 2**	• se lire **3**

(*pt & pp* **read** [red])

N **1** *(act of reading)* **to have a r.** lire; **I enjoy a good r.** j'aime lire; **he was having a quiet r.** il lisait tranquillement; **can I have a r. of your paper?** est-ce que je peux jeter un coup d'œil sur ton journal? **2** *(reading matter)* **it's an easy r.** c'est facile à lire; **her books are a good r.** ses livres se lisent bien

VT **1** *(book, magazine etc)* lire; *(bad handwriting, music)* lire, déchiffrer; **I r. it in the paper** je l'ai lu dans le journal; **have you got anything to r.?** avez-vous de quoi lire *ou* quelque chose à lire?; **have you got enough to r.?** avez-vous assez de lecture?; **to r. sth over and over (again)** lire et relire qch; **everything I've r. about the subject** tout ce que j'ai lu à ce sujet; **she r. herself to sleep** elle a lu jusqu'à ce qu'elle s'endorme; **for "Barry" r. "Harry"** lire "Harry" à la place de "Barry"; **can you r. music/braille/Italian?** savez-vous lire la musique/le braille/l'italien?; **to r. sb's lips** lire sur les lèvres de qn; *Fig* **r. my lips!** écoutez-moi bien!; *Admin* **r. and approved** *(stamp on document)* lu et approuvé; **to take sth as r.** *(evident)* considérer qch comme allant de soi; *(agreed upon)* considérer qch comme entendu

2 *(aloud)* lire (à haute voix); **to r. sb sth, to r. sth to sb** lire qch à qn; **r. me a story** lis-moi une histoire; **to r. a paper at a conference** présenter un exposé à une conférence; *Rel* **to r. the lesson** lire un passage de l'Évangile; **to r. the news** *Rad* lire les informations; *TV* présenter le journal; *Law* **to r. a will** exécuter la lecture d'un testament

3 *(interpret ▸ situation, behaviour)* interpréter; *(understand ▸ person, mood)* comprendre; **I r. it this way** c'est comme ça que je l'interprète; **to r. sb's mind** *or* **thoughts** lire dans les pensées de qn; **to r. sb's palm** *or* **hand** lire les lignes de la main à qn; **I can r. him like a book!** je sais comment il fonctionne!; *Sport* **he reads the game very well** c'est un très bon stratège; **he r. that well** il a bien anticipé

4 *(via radio)* recevoir; **do you r. me?** est-ce que vous me recevez?; *Fig* est-ce que tu me comprends?; **I r. you loud and clear** je vous reçois cinq sur cinq; *Fig* oui, oui j'ai compris

5 *Br (at university)* étudier; **he r. history** il a étudié l'histoire, il a fait des études d'histoire; **to r. law/medicine** faire son droit/sa médecine, faire des études de droit/de médecine

6 *(temperature, thermometer, barometer)* lire; **to r. the meter** relever le compteur

7 *(register ▸ of gauge, dial, barometer)* indiquer; **the thermometer is reading 40°** le thermomètre indique 40°

8 *(announce ▸ of notice)* annoncer; **a sign on the door r. "staff only"** un écriteau sur la porte indiquait "réservé au personnel"; **the inscription on the monument reads…** on peut lire sur le monument…

9 *(proofs)* corriger

10 *Comput (data, disk)* lire

VI **1** *(person)* lire; **she's learning to r.** elle apprend à lire; **to r. to sb** faire la lecture à qn; **to r. aloud** lire à haute voix; **to r. to oneself** lire; **r. quietly to yourselves** lisez en silence; **I enjoy reading** j'aime beaucoup lire *ou* la lecture; **I'd r. about it in the papers** je l'avais lu dans les journaux; **we r. of his death in the newspaper** nous avons appris sa mort dans le journal; **we've all r. about** *or* **of such phenomena** nous avons tous lu des textes qui traitent de tels phénomènes

2 *(interpret)* **to r. between the lines** lire entre les lignes; **she r. in the cards that I would be famous** elle a lu dans les cartes que je serais célèbre

3 *(text)* **her article reads well/badly** son article est bien/mal écrit; **the table reads from left to right** le tableau se lit de gauche à droite; **the book reads like a translation** à la lecture, on sent que ce roman est une traduction; **article 22 reads as follows** voici ce que dit l'article 22; **her life story reads like a fairytale** sa vie ressemble à un conte de fées

4 *(gauge, meter etc)* **the dials r. differently** les cadrans n'indiquent pas le même chiffre

5 *Br (at university)* **to r. for a degree** préparer un diplôme; **to r. for the Bar** faire des études de droit

▸▸ *Comput* ***read head*** tête *f* de lecture

▸ **read in** VT SEP *Comput (data)* lire (en mémoire)

▸ **read into** VT SEP **you shouldn't r. too much into their silence** vous ne devriez pas accorder trop d'importance à leur silence; **you're reading far too much into it** tu interprètes beaucoup trop

▸ **read off** VT SEP **1** *(names etc)* énumérer (**from** sur) **2** *(figure on dial, scale etc)* relever

▸ **read on** VI lire la suite

▸ **read out** VT SEP **1** *(aloud)* lire (à haute voix) **2** *Comput (data)* sortir, extraire de la mémoire

▸ **read over** VT SEP *(quickly)* parcourir; *(with special care)* examiner; *esp Am (read again)* relire

▸ **read through** VT SEP *(skim)* parcourir; *(examine closely)* lire en détail, examiner; *Theat* **to r. through a play** faire la lecture d'une pièce

▸ **read up** VT SEP étudier

▸ **read up on** VT INSEP étudier

read² [red] *pt & pp of* **read**

ADJ **he's widely r.** c'est un homme cultivé; **her books are widely r.** ses livres sont très lus

readability [ˌriːdəˈbɪlɪtɪ] N lisibilité *f*

readable [ˈriːdəbəl] ADJ **1** *(handwriting, disk)* lisible **2** *(book)* qui se laisse lire

readdress [ˌriːəˈdres] VT *(mail, e-mail)* faire suivre

reader [ˈriːdə(r)] N **1** *(of book)* lecteur(trice) *m,f*; *Am (company librarian)* documentaliste *mf*; **she's an avid r.** c'est une passionnée de lecture; **he's not a great r.** il ne lit pas beaucoup; **publisher's r.** lecteur(trice) *m,f* de manuscrits *(dans une maison d'édition)*

2 *Comput* lecteur *m*; **optical character r.** lecteur *m* optique

3 *(reading book)* livre *m* de lecture; *(anthology)* recueil *m* de textes; **German r.** recueil *m* de textes allemands

4 *Br Univ* ≃ maître-assistant(e) *m,f*

5 *Am Univ* ≃ assistant(e) *m,f*; *Can Univ* chargé(e) *m,f* de cours

6 *Rel (Protestant)* lecteur(trice) *m,f*; *(Jewish)* chantre *m*

readership [ˈriːdəʃɪp] N **1** *(of newspaper, magazine)* nombre *m* de lecteurs, lectorat *m*; **what is their r. (figure)?** combien ont-ils de lecteurs?; **this book should attract a wide r.** ce livre devrait intéresser un grand nombre de lecteurs **2** *Br Univ* ≃ poste *m* de maître-assistant **3** *Am Univ* ≃ fonction *f* d'assistant(e); *Can Univ* fonction *f* de chargé(e) de cours

▸▸ ***readership survey*** étude *f* du lectorat

readies [ˈredɪz] NPL *Br Fam (cash)* fric *m*, liquide *m*; **£500 in r.** 500 livres en liquide; **I want the r. first** je veux le fric d'abord

readily [ˈredɪlɪ] ADV **1** *(willingly)* volontiers **2** *(with ease)* facilement, aisément; **r. understandable ideas** des idées qu'on comprend facilement; **our products are r. available** nos produits sont en vente partout

readiness [ˈredɪnɪs] N **1** *(preparedness)* **to be in r. for sth** être préparé à qch; **to be in a state of r.** être fin prêt **2** *(willingness)* empressement *m*; **their r. to assist us** leur empressement à nous aider

reading [ˈriːdɪŋ] N **1** *(activity)* lecture *f*; **r., writing and arithmetic** la lecture, l'écriture et le calcul; **I have a lot of r. to catch up on** j'ai beaucoup de retard à rattraper dans mes lectures; **I have a r. knowledge of Italian** je peux lire l'italien; **take some r. matter** emmenez de quoi lire; **the r. public** le public des lecteurs

2 *(reading material)* lecture *f*; **light r.** lecture *f* facile *ou* distrayante; **his autobiography makes fascinating/dull r.** son autobiographie est passionnante/ennuyeuse à lire

3 *(recital)* lecture *f*

4 *(from instrument, gauge)* relevé *m*; **the r. on the dial was wrong** les indications qui apparaissaient sur le cadran étaient fausses; **to take a r.** faire un relevé

5 *Pol* lecture *f*; **to give a bill its first/second r.** examiner un projet de loi en première/deuxième lecture

6 *(interpretation)* interprétation *f*; **my r. of the situation** la manière dont j'interprète la situation

7 *(variant)* variante *f*

▸▸ *Br* ***reading age*** niveau *m* de lecture; **she has a r. age of eleven** elle a le niveau de lecture d'un enfant de onze ans; ***reading book*** livre *m* de lecture; ***reading desk*** pupitre *m*; *Rel* lutrin *m*; ***reading glass*** *(magnifying glass)* loupe *f (pour lire)*; ***reading glasses*** *(spectacles)* lunettes *fpl* pour lire; ***reading lamp*** lampe *f* de bureau; *(by bed)* lampe *f* de chevet; ***reading light*** liseuse *f*; ***reading list*** *(syllabus)* liste *f* des ouvrages au programme; *(for further reading)* liste *f* des ouvrages recommandés; ***reading room*** salle *f* de lecture

readjust [ˌriːəˈdʒʌst] VT **1** *(readapt)* **to r. oneself** se réadapter **2** *(alter ▸ controls, prices, clothing)* rajuster, réajuster

VI se réadapter; **to r. to sth** se réadapter à qch

readjustment [ˌriːəˈdʒʌstmənt] N **1** *(readaptation)* réadaptation *f* **2** *(alteration)* rajustement *m*, réajustement *m*

read-me document, read-me file N *Comput* (fichier *m*) lisez-moi *m*, ouvrez-moi *m*

readmission [ˌriːədˈmɪʃən] N *(to political party)* réintégration *f*; *(to hospital)* réadmission *f*; **no r.** *(on ticket)* ce ticket ne sera accepté qu'une seule fois à l'entrée

readmit [ˌriːədˈmɪt] VT *(to political party)* réintégrer; *(to hospital)* réadmettre; **she has been readmitted to hospital** elle a été réadmise à l'hôpital

read-only ADJ *Comput* (à) lecture seule; **that file is r.** ce fichier est protégé en écriture; **to make a file r.** mettre un fichier en lecture seule

▸▸ ***read-only disk*** *(hard)* disque *m* en lecture seule; *(floppy)* disquette *f* en lecture seule; ***read-only file*** fichier *m* en lecture seule; ***read-only***

memory mémoire *f* morte; ***read-only mode*** mode *m* lecture seule

readout ['riːdaʊt] N *Comput (gen)* lecture *f*; *(on screen)* affichage *m*; *(on paper)* sortie *f* papier *ou* sur imprimante, listing *m*

read-through N *(of script)* lecture *f* du scénario; **to give sth a quick r.** parcourir qch rapidement

readvertise [ˌriː'ædvətaɪz] VT repasser une annonce de; **no suitable candidates applied, so they had to r. the post** comme aucune candidature ne convenait, ils ont dû repasser une annonce pour le poste

VI repasser l'annonce

readvertisement [ˌriːəd'vɜːtɪsmənt] N deuxième annonce *f*; **this is a r.** *(in job advertisement)* deuxième annonce d'offre d'emploi

read-write ADJ *Comput*

►► ***read-write head*** tête *f* de lecture-écriture; ***read-write memory*** mémoire *f* lecture-écriture; ***read-write protection notch*** encoche *f* de protection lecture-écriture

ready ['redɪ] *(compar* **readier**, *superl* **readiest**, *pt & pp* **readied)** ADJ **1** *(prepared)* prêt; **are you r.?** êtes-vous prêt?; **he's just getting r.** il est en train de se préparer; **to be r. to do sth** être prêt à faire qch; **to be r. for anything** être prêt à tout; **to get sth r.** préparer qch; **I'll get the room/the dinner r.** je vais préparer la chambre/le dîner; **to get r. to do sth** se préparer *ou* s'apprêter à faire qch; **to get r. for bed** s'apprêter à aller au lit; **r. when you are!** quand tu veux!; *Arch or Literary* **to make r. (for sth/to do sth)** se préparer (pour qch/pour faire qch); **dinner's r.!** c'est prêt!; **are you r. to order?** vous avez choisi?; **the tomatoes are r. for eating** les tomates sont bonnes à manger; **r., steady, go!** à vos marques, prêts, partez!; *Com* **r. for delivery** livrable; *Com* **r. for shipping** sous palan; **r. for use** prêt à l'usage

2 *(willing)* prêt, disposé; **to be r. to do sth** être prêt à faire qch; **they are always r. to find fault** ils sont toujours prêts à critiquer; **don't be so r. to believe him** ne le crois pas systématiquement; **I'm r. for bed!** j'ai envie d'aller me coucher

3 *(quick)* prompt; **to be always r. with an answer** avoir la réplique prompte; **you're always a bit too r. with advice** tu donnes toujours trop de conseils; **he's very r. with his fists** il est prompt à se battre; **don't be too r. to condemn him** ne le condamnez pas trop rapidement, ne soyez pas trop prompt à lui jeter la pierre; **she has a r. wit** elle a l'esprit d'à-propos; **he had a r. smile** il souriait facilement

4 *(likely)* **to be r. to do sth** être sur le point de faire qch; **she looks r. to explode** on dirait qu'elle va exploser

5 *(easily accessible)* **a r. market for our products** un marché tout trouvé pour nos produits; **r. to hand** *(within reach)* à portée de main; *(available)* à disposition; **r. cash** *or* **money** argent *m* comptant *ou* liquide; **a r. source of income** une source de revenu facile

ADV *Br* **r. cut ham** jambon *m* prétranché; **r. salted crisps** chips *fpl* nature

VT préparer; **to r. oneself for sth** se préparer pour qch

• **at the ready** ADJ (tout) prêt; **the reporter had her notebook at the r.** la journaliste avait son carnet tout prêt; **with their guns at the r.** prêts à tirer

►► ***ready meal*** plat *m* cuisiné; *Br* ***ready reckoner*** barème *m*

ready-made ADJ **1** *(clothes)* de prêt-à-porter; *(food)* précuit; *(curtains)* tout fait **2** *(excuse, solution, argument)* tout prêt

N *(garment)* vêtement *m* de prêt-à-porter

ready-mix ADJ *(cake)* fait à partir d'une préparation; *(concrete)* prémalaxé

ready-to-serve ADJ prêt à l'emploi

ready-to-wear ADJ

►► ***ready-to-wear clothing*** prêt-à-porter *m*

reaffirm [ˌriːə'fɜːm] VT réaffirmer

reafforest [ˌriːə'fɒrɪst] VT reboiser

reafforestation ['riːəˌfɒrɪ'steɪʃən] N reboisement *m*, reforestation *f*

Reaganite ['reɪgənaɪt] N partisan *m* de Reagan

ADJ reaganien; **R. budget/programme** budget *m*/programme *m* reaganien

Reaganomics [ˌreɪgə'nɒmɪks] N = politique reaganienne selon laquelle l'argent des riches finit par profiter aux pauvres

reagent [riː'eɪdʒənt] N *Chem* réactif *m*

real [rɪəl] ADJ **1** *(authentic)* vrai, véritable; *(not imitation* ► *diamond, pearl)* vrai; *(*► *gold, leather)* véritable; *(*► *silk, flowers)* naturel; **a r. friend/idiot** un véritable ami/idiot; **a r. disaster/shock** un véritable *ou* vrai désastre/choc; **a r. man** un vrai homme; **I don't know his r. name** je ne connais pas son vrai nom; **my first r. job** mon premier vrai travail; **she has no r. feeling for poetry** elle n'a pas le sens de la poésie; **he's made a r. effort** il a fait un véritable effort, il a fait un effort réel; **that's what I call a r. cup of tea!** ça, c'est ce que j'appelle une tasse de thé!; *Fam* **she's a r. pain** elle est vraiment rasante; **it's the r. thing** *(authentic object)* c'est du vrai de vrai; *(true love)* c'est le grand amour; **this orange drink is not bad but it's poor stuff compared to the r. thing** cette boisson à l'orange n'est pas mauvaise, mais ça ne vaut pas le vrai jus d'orange; **this is not a drill, it's the r. thing** ce n'est pas un exercice, c'est pour de vrai; *Fam* **get r.!** arrête de délirer *ou* de rêver!, redescends sur terre!

2 *(actual* ► *cost, salary, income)* réel; **the r. world** le monde réel; **salaries have fallen in r. terms** les salaires ont baissé en termes réels; **in r. life** dans la réalité, dans la vie

3 *Comput, Math, Phil & Phys* réel

ADV *Am Fam (very)* vachement; **we had a r. good time** on s'est vachement bien amusés; **that's r. nice of you** c'est vraiment *ou* très gentil de votre part[□]; **I'll see you r. soon** à très bientôt[□]

N *Phil* **the r.** le réel

• **for real** ADJ & ADV *Fam* pour de vrai[□], pour de bon; **this time it's for r.** cette fois-ci c'est la bonne; **is he for r.?** d'où il sort, celui-là?; **is that for r.?** c'est vrai?

►► *Br* ***real ale*** bière *f* artisanale; ***real estate*** *(UNCOUNT) Br Law* biens *mpl* fonciers; *Am (property)* biens *mpl* immobiliers; **he works in r. estate** il travaille dans l'immobilier; ***real estate agent*** agent *m* immobilier; ***real estate developer*** promoteur *m* immobilier; *Am* ***real property*** *(UNCOUNT)* biens *mpl* immobiliers *ou* immeubles; ***real tennis*** jeu *m* de paume; **to play r. tennis** jouer à la paume; *Comput* ***real time*** temps *m* réel; ***real value*** valeur *f* effective

realign [ˌriːə'laɪn] VT aligner (de nouveau); *Fin (currencies)* réaligner; *Pol* regrouper

VI s'aligner (de nouveau); *Pol* se regrouper

realignment [ˌriːə'laɪnmənt] N (nouvel) alignement *m*; *Fin* réalignement *m*; *Pol* regroupement *m*

►► ***realignment of currencies*** réalignement *m* monétaire

realism ['rɪəlɪzəm] N réalisme *m*

realist ['rɪəlɪst] ADJ réaliste

N réaliste *mf*

realistic [ˌrɪə'lɪstɪk] ADJ **1** *(reasonable)* réaliste **2** *(lifelike)* ressemblant

realistically [ˌrɪə'lɪstɪklɪ] ADV de façon réaliste; **the film portrays wartime London very r.** le film dépeint de façon très réaliste Londres en temps de guerre; **they can't r. expect us to do all this** ils ne peuvent pas s'attendre sérieusement à ce que nous fassions tout cela

reality [rɪ'ælətɪ] *(pl* **realities)** N réalité *f*; **the r.** *or* **realities of living in today's Britain** les réalités de la vie dans la Grande-Bretagne d'aujourd'hui; **will our dream ever become (a) r.?** notre rêve deviendra-t-il un jour réalité?; **to bring sb back to r.** ramener qn à la réalité; **you have to face r.** il faut que tu regardes la réalité en face; **it was a r. check for him** ça l'a ramené à la réalité

• **in reality** ADV en réalité

►► *TV* ***reality show*** reality show *m*; ***reality TV*** téléréalité *f*

realizable, -isable ['rɪəlaɪzəbəl] ADJ *also Fin* réalisable

►► ***realizable assets*** actif *m* réalisable; ***realizable securities*** valeurs *fpl* réalisables

realization, -isation [ˌrɪəlaɪ'zeɪʃən] N **1** *(awareness)* **this sudden r. left us speechless** cette découverte nous a laissés sans voix; **there has been a growing r. on the part of the government that...** le gouvernement s'est peu à peu rendu compte que... + *indicative*; **his r. that he was gay** la prise de conscience de son homosexualité **2** *(of aim, dream, project)* réalisation *f* **3** *Fin (of assets)* réalisation *f*

realize, -ise ['rɪəlaɪz] VT **1** *(be or become aware of)* se rendre compte de; **do you r. what time it is?** tu te rends compte de *ou* tu as vu l'heure qu'il est?; **I didn't r. how late it was** je ne m'étais pas rendu compte qu'il était si tard; **it made me r. what a fool I had been** cela m'a fait comprendre quel imbécile j'avais été; **I r. you're busy, but...** je sais que tu es occupé mais... **2** *(achieve)* réaliser; **my worst fears were realized** ce que je craignais le plus s'est produit *ou* est arrivé; **a job where you could r. your full potential** un travail qui te permettrait de te réaliser complètement **3** *Fin (yield financially)* rapporter; *(convert into cash)* réaliser; **to r. a high price** *(goods)* atteindre un prix élevé; *(seller)* obtenir un prix élevé; **how much did they r. on the sale?** combien est-ce qu'ils ont gagné sur la vente?

VI **I'm sorry, I didn't r.** je suis désolé, je ne m'en étais pas rendu compte

really ['rɪəlɪ] ADV **1** *(actually)* vraiment, réellement; **did you r. say that?** as-tu vraiment dit ça?; **things that r. exist** des choses qui existent réellement; **that's r. a matter for the manager** c'est là proprement l'affaire du gérant

2 *(as intensifier)* vraiment; **these cakes are r. delicious** ces gâteaux sont vraiment délicieux; **he r. likes you** il t'aime beaucoup; **you r. ought to see it** il faut vraiment que vous le voyiez

3 *(softening negative statements)* **I don't r. know** je ne sais pas vraiment

4 *(tentative use)* **he's quite nice, r.** il est plutôt sympa, en fait

EXCLAM **1** *(in irritation)* **(well) r.!** enfin! **2** *(in surprise, interest)* **(oh) r.?** oh, vraiment?, c'est pas vrai?

realm [relm] N **1** *(field, domain)* domaine *m*; **it is within the realms of possibility** c'est du domaine du possible; **health is no longer exclusively the r. of doctors** la santé n'est plus l'apanage du médecin **2** *Literary (kingdom)* royaume *m*

real-time ADJ *(system, control, processing)* en temps réel

►► ***real-time clock*** horloge *f* (en) temps réel; ***real-time graphics*** graphiques *mpl* en temps réel; ***real-time management*** gestion *f* en temps réel

realtone ['rɪəltəʊn] N sonnerie *f* hi-fi

Realtor® ['rɪəltə(r)] N *Am* agent *m* immobilier

realty ['rɪəltɪ] N *(UNCOUNT) Am* biens *mpl* immobiliers

ream [riːm] N *(of paper)* rame *f*; *Fam Fig* **to write reams** écrire des tartines; *Fam* **reams of statistics/information** des quantités *fpl* de statistiques/d'informations

VT **1** *Tech* fraiser **2** *Am (lemon)* presser **3** *Am Fam (person)* rouler

▸ **ream out** VT SEP *Am Fam* **to r. sb out** *(scold)* passer un savon à qn, remonter les bretelles à qn

reamer ['riːmə(r)] N **1** *Tech* fraise *f* **2** *(juice extractor)* presse-citron *m inv*

reanimate [ˌriː'ænɪmeɪt] VT réanimer

reap [riːp] VT **1** *(crop)* moissonner, faucher **2** *Fig* récolter, tirer; **to r. the benefit** *or* **the benefits of sth** récolter les bénéfices de qch; **to r. the rewards of one's labours** recueillir le fruit de ses travaux; **you r. what you sow** comme tu auras semé tu moissonneras

VI moissonner, faire la moisson

reaper ['riːpə(r)] N **1** *(machine)* moissonneuse *f*; **r. and binder** moissonneuse-lieuse *f* **2** *(person)* moissonneur(euse) *m,f*; *Literary* **the (Grim) R.** la Faucheuse

reaping ['riːpɪŋ] N moisson *f*

►► ***reaping hook*** faucille *f*; ***reaping machine*** moissonneuse *f*

reappear [ˌriːə'pɪə(r)] VI *(person, figure, sun)* réapparaître; *(lost object)* refaire surface

reappearance [ˌriːə'pɪərəns] N réapparition *f*

reapply [ˌriːə'plaɪ] *(pt & pp* **reapplied)** VT *(cream, lotion etc)* réappliquer

VI **to r. for a grant/loan** faire une nouvelle demande de bourse/de prêt; **previous applicants need not r.** les personnes ayant déjà posé leur candidature n'ont pas besoin de le faire à nouveau

reappoint [ˌriːəˈpɔɪnt] **VT** réengager, rengager

reappointment [ˌriːəˈpɔɪntmənt] **N since her r. as minister for the arts** depuis qu'elle a été nommée à nouveau ministre de la Culture

reappraisal [ˌriːəˈpreɪzəl] **N 1** *Fin (of property)* réévaluation *f* **2** *(of policy)* réexamen *m*

reappraise [ˌriːəˈpreɪz] **VT 1** *Fin (property)* réévaluer **2** *(policy)* réexaminer

rear [rɪə(r)] **N 1** *(of place)* arrière *m*; **at the r. of the bus** à l'arrière du bus; **the garden** *Br* **at the r.** *or Am* **in the r. of the house** le jardin qui est derrière la maison; **from the r.** par derrière; *(to recognize)* de derrière; **they attacked them from the r.** ils les ont attaqués par derrière **2** *Mil* arrière *m*, arrières *mpl*; *Mil & Fig* **to bring up the r.** fermer la marche; **to protect one's r.** *Mil* protéger ses arrières; *Fig* assurer ses arrières **3** *Fam* **r. (end)** *(buttocks)* arrière-train *m*

ADJ *(door, wheel)* arrière *(inv)*, de derrière; *(engine)* arrière *(inv)*; *(carriages)* de queue; **is there a r. entrance?** est-ce qu'il y a une entrée par derrière?

VT 1 *(children, animals)* élever; *(plants)* cultiver **2** *(head, legs)* lever, relever; *Fig* **racism has reared its ugly head again** le spectre du racisme a refait son apparition

VI 1 *(horse)* **to r. (up) (on its hind legs)** se cabrer **2** *(mountain, skyscraper)* **to r. (up)** se dresser

▸▸ ***rear admiral*** contre-amiral *m*; ***rear drive axle*** pont *m* arrière; ***rear gunner*** mitrailleur *m* arrière; *BrAut* ***rear lamp, rear light*** feu *m* arrière; *Cin & TV* ***rear projection*** projection *f* en transparence; ***rear spoiler*** aileron *m ou* spoiler *m* arrière; ***rear window*** lunette *f* arrière

rear-drive **ADJ** à traction arrière

rear-end **VT** *(drive into back of)* emboutir à l'arrière

rear-engined **ADJ** avec moteur à l'arrière

rearguard [ˈrɪəgɑːd] **N** arrière-garde *f*

▸▸ ***rearguard action*** combat *m* d'arrière-garde; *also Fig* **to fight** *or* **mount a r. action** mener un combat d'arrière-garde

rearing [ˈrɪərɪŋ] **N 1** *(of children)* éducation *f*; *(of animals)* élevage *m*; *(of plants)* culture *f* **2 r. (up)** *(of horse)* cabrage *m*

rearm [ˌriːˈɑːm] **VT** *(nation, ship)* réarmer

VI réarmer

rearmament [ˌriːˈɑːməmənt] **N** réarmement *m*

rearmost [ˈrɪəməʊst] **ADJ** dernier

rear-mounted **ADJ** monté à l'arrière

rearrange [ˌriːəˈreɪndʒ] **VT 1** *(arrange differently* ▸ *furniture, objects)* réarranger, changer la disposition de; *(*▸ *flat, room)* réaménager **2** *(put back in place)* réarranger; **she rearranged her hair** elle se recoiffa **3** *(reschedule)* changer la date/l'heure de; **the meeting has been rearranged for Monday** la réunion a été remise à lundi; **we'll have to r. our schedule** il faudra réaménager notre programme

rearrangement [ˌriːəˈreɪndʒmənt] **N 1** *(different arrangement)* réarrangement *m*, réaménagement *m* **2** *(rescheduling)* changement *m* de date/d'heure

rear-view mirror [ˈrɪəvjuː-] **N** rétroviseur *m*

rearward [ˈrɪəwəd] **ADJ** *(part, end)* arrière *(inv)*; *(motion)* en arrière, vers l'arrière

ADV en arrière, vers l'arrière

rearwards [ˈrɪəwədz] **ADV** en arrière, vers l'arrière

rear-wheel **ADJ** *Aut*

▸▸ ***rear-wheel drive*** traction *f* arrière; ***rear-wheel steering*** roues *fpl* arrière directrices

REASON [ˈriːzən]

> **N**
> • raison **1, 2**
> **VT**
> • maintenir **1** • calculer **1**
> • conclure **1** • persuader **2**
> **VI**
> • raisonner

N 1 *(cause, motive)* raison *f* (**for** de); **did he give a r. for being so late?** a-t-il donné la raison d'un tel retard?; **she's my r. for living** elle est ma raison de vivre; **there is a r. for his doing that** il y a une raison pour qu'il fasse ça; **what r. did you give for your absence?** comment as-tu expliqué ton absence?; **I (can) see no r. to disagree** je ne vois pas pourquoi je ne serais pas d'accord; **all the more r. to try again** raison de plus pour réessayer; **to have r. enough (to do sth)** avoir de bonnes raisons (de faire qch); **you have every r.** *or* **good r. to be angry** vous avez de bonnes raisons d'être en colère; **that's no r. to get annoyed** ce n'est pas une raison pour s'énerver; **we have/there is r. to believe he is lying** nous avons de bonnes raisons de croire/il y a lieu de croire qu'il ment; **the r. (why) they refused** la raison de leur refus, la raison pour laquelle ils ont refusé; **she wouldn't tell me the r. why** elle ne voulait pas me dire pourquoi; **for reasons of space/national security** pour des raisons de place/de sécurité nationale; **for reasons best known to herself** pour des raisons qu'elle est seule à connaître; **for some r. (or other), for one r. or another** pour une raison ou pour une autre; **for no other r. than that I forgot** pour la simple raison que j'ai oublié; **for no particular r.** sans raison particulière; **why do you ask? – oh, no particular r.** pourquoi est-ce que tu me demandes ça? – oh, comme ça; **for no r. at all** sans aucune raison; **but that's the only r. I came!** mais c'est pour ça que je suis venue!; **they were upset, and with (good) r.** ils étaient bouleversés, et pour cause; **give me one good r. why I should!** donne-moi une raison valable pour que je le fasse!

2 *(common sense, rationality)* raison *f*; **he lost his r.** il a perdu la raison; **he won't listen to r.** il refuse d'entendre raison; **I can't make her see r.** je n'arrive pas à lui faire entendre raison *ou* à la raisonner; **it stands to r. (that...)** il va de soi *ou* sans dire (que...+ *indicative*); **that stands to r.** c'est logique, ça va de soi

VT 1 *(maintain)* maintenir, soutenir; *(work out)* calculer, déduire; *(conclude)* conclure; **they reasoned that the fault must be in the cooling system** ils en ont déduit que la défaillance devait provenir du système de refroidissement

2 *(persuade)* **she reasoned me into/out of going** elle m'a persuadé/dissuadé d'y aller

VI raisonner; **to r. with sb** raisonner qn; **I tried to r. with them** j'ai essayé de les raisonner *ou* de leur faire entendre raison; *Hum* **ours is not to r. why** il ne faut pas chercher à comprendre

• **by reason of** **PREP** en raison de; **to be found not guilty by r. of insanity** être déclaré non-coupable pour cause de démence

• **within reason** **ADV** dans la limite du raisonnable; **you can do what you like, within r.** vous pouvez faire ce que vous voulez, dans la limite du raisonnable

▸ **reason out** **VT SEP** *(maths problem)* résoudre; *(one's differences)* résoudre en discutant

---

reasonable [ˈriːzənəbəl] **ADJ 1** *(sensible* ▸ *person, behaviour, attitude)* raisonnable; *(*▸ *explanation, decision)* raisonnable, sensé; **be r.!** soyez raisonnable!; **you must be r. in your demands** vos revendications doivent être raisonnables **2** *(moderate* ▸ *price)* raisonnable, correct; *(*▸ *restaurant)* qui pratique des prix raisonnables; **with a r. amount of luck** avec un peu de chance **3** *(fair, acceptable* ▸ *offer, suggestion)* raisonnable, acceptable; **the weather/meal was r.** le temps/le repas était passable; **we've had quite a r. day** nous avons passé une journée plutôt agréable

▸▸ *Law* ***reasonable care*** diligence *f* raisonnable; *Law* ***reasonable doubt*** doute *m* raisonnable; **beyond a** *or* **all r. doubt** indubitablement

reasonableness [ˈriːzənəbəlnɪs] **N 1** *(of person, behaviour)* caractère *m* raisonnable **2** *(of price)* modération *f*

reasonably [ˈriːzənəblɪ] **ADV 1** *(behave, argue)* raisonnablement; **one can r. expect...** on est en droit d'attendre...; **r. priced** à un prix raisonnable **2** *(quite, rather)* assez; **r. good** assez bien, pas mal; **r. fit** en assez bonne forme

reasoned [ˈriːzənd] **ADJ** *(argument, decision)* raisonné

reasoning [ˈriːzənɪŋ] **N** raisonnement *m*; **the r. behind the decision** les raisons de cette décision

reassemble [ˌriːəˈsembəl] **VT 1** *(people, arguments)* rassembler **2** *(machinery)* remonter; *(frame)* réassembler

VI se rassembler; **Parliament reassembles in September** la rentrée parlementaire a lieu en septembre

reassembly [ˌriːəˈsemblɪ] **N 1** *(of group)* rassemblement *m*; *Pol* rentrée *f* **2** *(of machine)* remontage *m*; *(of frame)* réassemblage *m*

reassert [ˌriːəˈsɜːt] **VT** *(authority)* réaffirmer; **you'll have to r. yourself** vous devrez imposer à nouveau *ou* réaffirmer votre autorité; **her self-confidence reasserted itself** sa confiance est revenue

reassess [ˌriːəˈses] **VT 1** *(position, opinion)* réexaminer **2** *Fin (damages)* réévaluer; *(taxation)* réviser; **you have been reassessed** votre situation fiscale a été réexaminée

reassessment [ˌriːəˈsesmənt] **N 1** *(of position, opinion)* réexamen *m* **2** *Fin (of damages)* réévaluation *f*; *(of taxes)* révision *f*

reassign [ˌriːəˈsaɪn] **VT** *(employee)* muter (**to** à); *(work, project)* confier (**to** à); *(funds)* réaffecter (**to** à); **the work has been reassigned** le travail a été confié à quelqu'un d'autre

reassignment [ˌriːəˈsaɪnmənt] **N** *(transfer)* mutation *f*; *(of duties)* nouveau poste *m*, nouvelles fonctions *fpl*; *(of funds)* réaffectation *f*

reassume [ˌriːəˈsjuːm] **VT** *(one's duties)* reprendre

reassurance [ˌriːəˈʃɔːrəns] **N 1** *(comforting)* réconfort *m*; **she turned to me for r.** elle s'est tournée vers moi *ou* est venue à moi pour que je la rassure **2** *(guarantee)* assurance *f*, confirmation *f*; **despite his r.** *or* **reassurances that the contract is still valid** bien qu'il affirme que le contrat est toujours valable; **the government has given reassurances that...** le gouvernement a assuré que...+ *indicative* **3** *Br Fin* réassurance *f*

reassure [ˌriːəˈʃɔː(r)] **VT 1** *(gen)* rassurer; **to r. sb of one's esteem** assurer qn de son estime; **I feel reassured now** je me sens rassuré maintenant **2** *Br Fin* réassurer

reassuring [ˌriːəˈʃɔːrɪŋ] **ADJ** rassurant

reassuringly [ˌriːəˈʃɔːrɪŋlɪ] **ADV** d'une manière rassurante; **he smiled at me r.** il me fit un sourire pour me rassurer; **r. simple** d'une grande simplicité

reawaken [ˌriːəˈweɪkən] **VT** *(person, interest)* réveiller; *(feelings)* faire renaître, raviver

VI *(person)* se réveiller de nouveau; *(feelings, interest)* se raviver

reawakening [ˌriːəˈweɪkənɪŋ] **N** *(of person, interest)* regain *m*; **the r. of national pride** le réveil de l'orgueil national

rebate [ˈriːbeɪt] **N 1** *(reduction* ▸ *on goods)* remise *f*, ristourne *f*; *(*▸ *on tax)* dégrèvement *m* **2** *(refund)* remboursement *m* **3** *(groove)* feuillure *f*

rebel *(pt & pp* **rebelled**, *cont* **rebelling**) **N** [ˈrebəl] *(in revolution)* rebelle *mf*, insurgé(e) *m,f*; *Fig* rebelle *mf*; *Am Hist* **the Rebels** les confédérés *mpl*

ADJ [ˈrebəl] *(soldier)* rebelle; *(camp, territory)* des rebelles; *(attack)* de rebelles

VI [rɪˈbel] se rebeller; **to r. against sb/sth** se révolter contre qn/qch; *Hum* **my stomach rebelled** mon estomac a protesté

▸▸ ***rebel forces*** forces *fpl* rebelles; ***rebel leader*** chef *m* des rebelles; ***rebel MP*** parlementaire *m* rebelle

rebellion [rɪˈbeljən] **N** rébellion *f*, révolte *f*; **in open r.** en rébellion ouverte; **to rise (up) in r. against sb/sth** se révolter contre qn/qch

rebellious [rɪˈbeljəs] **ADJ** *(behaviour, child, politician, hair, inhabitants)* rebelle; *(troops)* insoumis; **a r. act** un acte de rébellion

rebelliously [rɪˈbeljəslɪ] **ADV** *(reply)* d'un ton de défi; *(act)* en rebelle

rebelliousness [rɪˈbeljəsnɪs] **N** *(of child, politician)* esprit *m* de rébellion; *(of troops)* insoumission *f*; *(of inhabitants)* disposition *f* à la rébellion

rebirth [ˌriːˈbɜːθ] **N** renaissance *f*

reboot [ˌriːˈbuːt] *Comput* **VT** réamorcer

VI se réamorcer

rebore VT [ˌriːˈbɔː(r)] réaléser
N [ˈriːbɔː(r)] réalésage *m*; **my car needs a r.** le cylindre de ma voiture a besoin d'être réalésé *ou* d'un réalésage

reborn [ˌriːˈbɔːn] ADJ réincarné; **to be r.** renaître; **I feel r.** je me sens renaître

rebound VI [rɪˈbaʊnd] **1** *(ball)* rebondir (**against** contre) **2** *Fig* **to r. on sb** se retourner contre qn; **the situation rebounded on us** la situation s'est retournée contre nous **3** *(recover ▸ business)* reprendre, repartir; *(▸ prices)* remonter
N [ˈriːbaʊnd] **1** *(of ball)* rebond *m*; **to catch a ball on the r.** attraper une balle au rebond; **he headed in the r.** il a marqué un but de la tête en prenant la balle au rebond **2** *(idioms)* **to be on the r.** *(after relationship)* être sous le coup d'une déception sentimentale; **he married her on the r.** il l'a épousée à la suite d'une déception sentimentale

rebrand [ˌriːˈbrænd] VT *Mktg (product)* changer la marque de

rebranding [ˌriːˈbrændɪŋ] N *Mktg (of product)* changement *m* de marque

rebuff [rɪˈbʌf] VT *(snub)* rabrouer; *(reject)* repousser
N rebuffade *f*; **to meet with** *or* **to suffer a r.** *(person)* essuyer une rebuffade; *(request)* être repoussé

rebuild [ˌriːˈbɪld] *(pt & pp* **rebuilt** [-ˈbɪlt]*)* VT *(town, economy)* rebâtir, reconstruire; *(company, relationship, life)* reconstruire; *(confidence)* faire renaître

rebuilding [ˌriːˈbɪldɪŋ] N *(of town, economy, relationship)* reconstruction *f*
COMP *(project, work)* de réfection, de reconstruction

rebuke [rɪˈbjuːk] VT *(reprimand)* réprimander; **to r. sb for sth** reprocher qch à qn; **to r. sb for doing** *or* **having done sth** reprocher à qn d'avoir fait qch
N reproche *m*, réprimande *f*

rebus [ˈriːbəs] N rébus *m*

rebut [rɪˈbʌt] *(pt & pp* **rebutted**, *cont* **rebutting***)* VT réfuter

rebuttal [rɪˈbʌtəl] N réfutation *f*

rebuy [ˈriːbaɪ] N *Mktg* réachat *m*

rec [rek] N *Fam* **1** *Br (ground)* terrain *m* de jeux◻ **2** *Am Sch (break)* récré *f*
▸▸ *Br* **rec ground** terrain *m* de jeux◻; *Am* **rec room** *(in home)* salle *f* de jeux◻

recalcitrance [rɪˈkælsɪtrəns] N *Formal* caractère *m ou* esprit *m* récalcitrant

recalcitrant [rɪˈkælsɪtrənt] ADJ *Formal* récalcitrant

recall VT [rɪˈkɔːl] **1** *(remember)* se rappeler, se souvenir de; **I don't r. seeing** *or* **having seen her** je ne me rappelle pas l'avoir vue; **as far as I can r.** aussi loin que je m'en souvienne; **as I r.** si mes souvenirs sont bons; **as you may r.** comme vous vous en souvenez peut-être
2 *(evoke ▸ past)* rappeler, évoquer; **paintings that r. the past** des tableaux qui évoquent le passé
3 *(summon back ▸ ambassador, faulty goods)* rappeler; *(▸ Parliament)* rappeler (en session extraordinaire); *(▸ library book, hire car)* demander le retour de; **the sound of the telephone recalled her to the present** la sonnerie du téléphone la ramena à la réalité
4 *Mil (troops)* rappeler; *Sport (player)* rappeler, sélectionner à nouveau
N [ˈriːkɔːl] **1** *(memory)* rappel *m*, mémoire *f*; **to have instant r.** avoir une excellente mémoire; **total r.** aptitude à se souvenir des moindres détails; **to be beyond** *or* **past r.** être oublié à tout jamais
2 *Mktg (of brand name)* mémorisation *f*
3 *(summoning back ▸ of ambassador, faulty goods)* rappel *m*; *(▸ of library book)* fait *m* de demander le retour de; *(▸ of Parliament)* reconvocation *f*
4 *Mil (of troops)* rappel *m*; *Sport (of player)* **he was expecting a r. to the team** il s'attendait à ce qu'on le rappelle dans l'équipe
▸▸ ***recall button*** *(on phone)* rappel *m* automatique; ***recall slip*** *(for library book)* fiche *f* de rappel; *Mktg* **recall test** test *m* de rappel *ou* de mémorisation

recant [rɪˈkænt] VT *(religion)* abjurer; *(opinion)* rétracter
VI *(from religion)* abjurer; *(from opinion)* se rétracter

recantation [ˌriːkænˈteɪʃən] N *(of religion)* abjuration *f*; *(of statement)* rétractation *f*

recap [ˈriːkæp] *(pt & pp* **recapped**, *cont* **recapping***)* N **1** *(summary)* récapitulation *f* **2** *Am (tyre)* pneu *m* rechapé
VT **1** *(summarize)* récapituler; **so, to r.** donc, pour récapituler *ou* résumer **2** *Am (tyre)* rechaper

recapitalization, -isation [riːˌkæpɪtəlaɪˈzeɪʃən] N *Fin (of company)* recapitalisation *f*, changement *m* de la structure financière

recapitalize, -ise [ˌriːˈkæpɪtəlaɪz] VT *Fin (company)* recapitaliser, changer la structure financière de

recapitulate [ˌriːkəˈpɪtjʊleɪt] VT **1** *(summarize ▸ discussion etc)* récapituler **2** *Mus (theme)* reprendre
VI récapituler

recapitulation [ˌriːkəˌpɪtjʊˈleɪʃən] N **1** *(of discussion etc)* récapitulation *f* **2** *Mus* reprise *f*

recapture [ˌriːˈkæptʃə(r)] VT **1** *(prisoner, town)* reprendre; *(animal)* capturer **2** *(regain ▸ confidence)* reprendre; *(▸ feeling, spirit)* retrouver; *(evoke ▸ of film, book, play)* recréer, faire revivre
N *(of escapee, animal)* capture *f*; *(of town)* reprise *f*

recarpet [ˌriːˈkɑːpət] VT changer la moquette de, remoquetter

recast [ˌriːˈkɑːst] *(pt & pp* **recast***)* VT **1** *(redraft)* remanier **2** *(play)* changer la distribution de; *(actor)* donner un nouveau rôle à; **he was r. in the role of Prospero** on lui a donné un nouveau rôle, celui de Prospero; **the part has been r.** le rôle a été donné à quelqu'un d'autre **3** *Metal* refondre
N *Metal* refonte *f*

recce [ˈrekɪ] *(pt & pp* **recced** *or* **recceed***)* *Fam* VT reconnaître◻
VI faire une reconnaissance◻
N reconnaissance◻ *f*; **to go on a r.** *(gen)* faire la reconnaissance des lieux; *Mil* aller en reconnaissance

recede [rɪˈsiːd] VI **1** *(move away ▸ coastline, person, object)* s'éloigner; *(▸ waters)* refluer; *(▸ tide)* descendre; **to r. into the distance** disparaître dans le lointain
2 *(fade ▸ hopes)* s'évanouir; *(▸ fears)* s'estomper; *(▸ danger)* s'éloigner; **as memories of the past r.** à mesure que les souvenirs du passé s'effacent
3 *(hairline)* **his hair has started to r.** son front commence à se dégarnir; **to have a receding chin/forehead** avoir le menton/front fuyant *ou* qui fuit
4 *Fin* baisser

receipt [rɪˈsiːt] N **1** *(for purchase, meal, taxi fare)* reçu *m* (**for** de); *(in supermarket, bar)* ticket *m* de caisse, reçu *m*; *(for bill)* acquit *m*; *(for rent, insurance)* quittance *f*; *(from customs)* récépissé *m*; *(for letter, parcel)* récépissé *m*, accusé *m* de réception **2** *(reception ▸ of letter, parcel etc)* réception *f*; **to pay on r.** payer à la réception; **to be in r. of sth** avoir reçu qch; *Com* **I am in r. of the goods** j'ai bien reçu les marchandises; *Com* **to acknowledge r. of sth** accuser réception de qch; **on r. of your results** dès que vous aurez reçu vos résultats; **within one week of r.** dans un délai d'une semaine après réception
VT *Br* acquitter, quittancer; **to r. a bill** acquitter une facture
• **receipts** NPL *(takings)* recettes *fpl*, rentrées *fpl*; **receipts and expenditure** recettes *fpl* et dépenses *fpl*
▸▸ *Fin* ***receipt book*** carnet *m* de quittances

receivable [rɪˈsiːvəbəl] ADJ recevable; *Com (outstanding)* à recevoir; **accounts r.** comptes *mpl* clients, créances *fpl*
• **receivables** NPL *(debts)* comptes *mpl* clients, créances *fpl*; *(bills)* effets *mpl* à recevoir

receive [rɪˈsiːv] VT **1** *(gift, letter)* recevoir; *(salary, money)* toucher, recevoir; **to r. sth from sb** recevoir qch de qn; **we received your letter on Monday** nous avons reçu votre lettre *ou* votre lettre nous est parvenue lundi; **to r. a high salary** recevoir *ou* toucher un salaire élevé; *Com* **received with thanks** *(on receipt)* acquitté, pour acquit; *Law* **she received ten years** elle a été condamnée à dix ans de réclusion; *St Exch* **to r. a premium** encaisser un premium
2 *(blow)* recevoir; *(insult, refusal)* essuyer; *(criticism)* être l'objet de; **to r. treatment (for sth)** se faire soigner (pour qch); **he received excellent treatment** il a été traité avec beaucoup d'égards; **she received injuries from which she has since died** elle est morte des suites de ses blessures
3 *(greet, welcome)* accueillir, recevoir; *(into club, organization)* admettre; **to be cordially received** *(visitor etc)* trouver un accueil chaleureux, être bien reçu; **the new movie was enthusiastically received** le nouveau film a été accueilli avec enthousiasme; **their offer was not well received** leur proposition n'a pas reçu un accueil favorable; **to be received into the Church** être reçu *ou* admis dans le sein de l'Église
4 *(signal, broadcast)* recevoir, capter; **are you receiving me?** *(on radio)* est-ce que vous me recevez?; **I'm receiving you loud and clear** je vous reçois cinq sur cinq
5 *Sport* **to r. service** recevoir le service
6 *Law (stolen goods)* receler
7 *Formal (accommodate)* recevoir, prendre; **holes were drilled to r. the pegs** des trous étaient percés pour recevoir les chevilles
VI **1** *Prov* **it is better to give than to r.** il y a plus de joie à donner qu'à recevoir
2 *Formal (have guests)* recevoir
3 *Sport* relancer, être le relanceur
4 *Rel* recevoir la communion
5 *Law (thief)* receler; **to be accused of receiving** être accusé de recel

received [rɪˈsiːvd] ADJ *(idea, opinion)* reçu, tout fait; **the r. wisdom is that…** de l'avis général, …
▸▸ *Br* ***Received Pronunciation*** prononciation *f* standard (de l'anglais); *Am* ***Received Standard*** prononciation *f* standard (de l'américain)

receiver [rɪˈsiːvə(r)] N **1** *(gen) & Sport* receveur (euse) *m,f*; *(of consignment)* destinataire *mf*, consignataire *mf*; *(of stolen goods)* receleur (euse) *m,f*
2 *(on telephone)* combiné *m*, récepteur *m*; **to lift / to replace the r.** décrocher/raccrocher (le téléphone)
3 *TV* récepteur *m*, poste *m* de télévision; *Rad* récepteur *m*, poste *m* de radio
4 *Fin* **(official) r.** administrateur(trice) *m,f* judiciaire, syndic *m* de faillite; **to be in the hands of the r.** *or* **receivers** être sous administration judiciaire; **they have been placed in the hands of the r., the r. has been called in** ils ont été placés sous administration judiciaire
5 *Chem* récipient *m*
▸▸ ***receiver rest*** *(for telephone)* berceau *m* (du combiné)

receivership [rɪˈsiːvəʃɪp] N *Fin* **to go into r.** être placé sous administration judiciaire

receiving [rɪˈsiːvɪŋ] ADJ **1** *(office)* de réception; *(country)* d'accueil **2** *Fam* **to be on the r. end** écoper; **it's different when you're on the r. end** c'est tout autre chose quand c'est à toi que ça arrive; **she was on the r. end of his bad temper** c'est sur elle qu'il a passé sa mauvaise humeur, c'est elle qui a fait les frais de sa mauvaise humeur
N *(of stolen property)* recel *m*
▸▸ *Rad* ***receiving set*** poste *m* récepteur; *Rad* ***receiving station*** station *f* réceptrice

recent [ˈriːsənt] ADJ *(new)* récent, nouveau(elle); *(modern)* récent, moderne; **in r. months** ces derniers mois; **in r. times** récemment; **one of the most charismatic leaders of r. times** l'un des dirigeants les plus charismatiques de ces dernières années; **r. developments** les derniers événements *mpl*; **her most r. novel** son dernier roman; **have you any r. news of them?** avez-vous eu de leurs nouvelles récemment?

recently [ˈriːsəntlɪ] ADV récemment, dernièrement, ces derniers temps; **I saw her quite r.** je l'ai vue tout dernièrement **as r. as yesterday** pas plus tard qu'hier; **until r.** jusqu'à ces derniers temps

receptacle [rɪˈseptəkəl] N *Formal (container)* récipient *m*

reception [rɪˈsepʃən] N **1** *(welcome)* réception *f*, accueil *m*; **to get a warm r.** recevoir un accueil chaleureux; **to get a frosty r.** être reçu froidement; **the movie got an enthusiastic r. from the critics** le film a été accueilli avec enthousiasme par la critique

2 *(formal party)* réception *f*; *(in the evening)* réception *f*, soirée *f*; **to hold a r.** donner une réception

3 *(in hotel)* réception *f*; *(in office, hospital)* accueil *m*; **at r., in r.** à la réception

4 *Rad & TV* réception *f*

5 *Am Sport (of ball)* réception *f*

6 *Br Sch* ≃ cours *m* préparatoire

►► *Br* ***reception centre*** centre *m* d'accueil; *Br Sch* ***reception class*** première année *f* de maternelle; *Am* ***reception clerk*** réceptionniste *mf*; *also Hum* ***reception committee*** comité *m* d'accueil; ***reception desk*** *(in hotel)* réception *f*; *(in office, hospital)* accueil *m*; ***reception room*** *(in hotel)* salle *f* de réception; *Br (in house)* salon *m*

receptionist [rɪ'sepʃənɪst] **N** *(in hotel)* réceptionniste *mf*; *(in office)* hôtesse *f* d'accueil

receptive [rɪ'septɪv] **ADJ** *(open)* réceptif; **to be r. to new ideas** être ouvert aux idées nouvelles

receptiveness [rɪ'septɪvnɪs], **receptivity** [ˌrɪsep'tɪvɪtɪ] **N** réceptivité *f*

receptor [rɪ'septə(r)] **N** *Phys & Physiol* récepteur *m*

►► ***receptor site*** (site *m*) récepteur *m*

recess [*Br* rɪ'ses, *Am* 'riːses] **N 1** *(alcove ► gen)* renfoncement *m*; *(► in bedroom)* alcôve *f*; *(► for statue)* niche *f*; *(in doorway)* embrasure *f*; **dining r.** coin *m* repas, coin *m* salle à manger

2 *(of mind, memory)* recoin *m*, tréfonds *m*; **in the innermost recesses of the soul** dans les replis *ou* les recoins les plus secrets de l'âme

3 *Am Law* suspension *f* d'audience; **the court went into r.** l'audience a été suspendue

4 *Am Sch* récréation *f*

5 *(closure ► of Parliament)* vacances *fpl* parlementaires, intersession *f* parlementaire; *(► of courts)* vacances *fpl* judiciaires, vacations *fpl*; **Parliament is in r. for the summer** le Parlement est en vacances pour l'été

VI *Am Law* suspendre l'audience; *Pol* suspendre la séance; **Parliament will r. next week** *(begin holiday)* les vacances parlementaires commenceront la semaine prochaine

VT *(lighting, switch etc)* encastrer

recession [rɪ'seʃən] **N 1** *Econ* récession *f*; **the economy is in r.** l'économie est en récession **2** *Formal (retreat)* recul *m*, retraite *f*

recessionary [rɪ'seʃənərɪ] **ADJ** *Econ* de crise, de récession; **to have a r. effect** *(of policy etc)* entraîner une récession

►► ***recessionary gap*** écart *m* déflationniste

recession-proof **ADJ** *(business, market, industry)* à l'abri de la crise

VT *(business)* protéger contre les effets de la crise

recessive [rɪ'sesɪv] **ADJ 1** *(gene)* récessif **2** *(backward ► measure)* rétrograde

recharge **VT** [ˌriː'tʃɑːdʒ] *(battery, rifle)* recharger; **to r. one's batteries** recharger ses batteries

VI [ˌriː'tʃɑːdʒ] *(battery)* se recharger

N ['riːtʃɑːdʒ] recharge *f*

rechargeable [ˌriː'tʃɑːdʒəbəl] **ADJ** rechargeable

recharger [riː'tʃɑːdʒə(r)] **N** *(for battery)* chargeur *m*

recherché [rə'ʃeəʃeɪ] **ADJ** *(film, topic)* recherché

recidivism [rɪ'sɪdɪvɪzəm] **N** *Law* récidive *f*

recidivist [rɪ'sɪdɪvɪst] *Law* **ADJ** récidiviste

N récidiviste *mf*

recipe ['resɪpɪ] **N** *Culin* recette *f*; *Fig* recette *f*, secret *m*; **a r. for success/long life** le secret de la réussite/de la longévité; **it's a r. for disaster** c'est le meilleur moyen d'aller droit à la catastrophe

►► ***recipe book*** livre *m* de recettes; ***recipe card*** fiche-recette *f*, fiche-cuisine *f*

recipient [rɪ'sɪpɪənt] **N 1** *(of letter, e-mail)* destinataire *mf*; *(of cheque, bill)* bénéficiaire *mf*; *(of award, honour)* récipiendaire *m*; **he was the proud r. of a gold watch** il a eu la chance de se voir remettre une montre en or **2** *Med (of transplant)* receveur(euse) *m,f*

> Note that the French word **récipient** is a false friend and is never a translation for the English word **recipient**. It means **container**.

reciprocal [rɪ'sɪprəkəl] **ADJ** *(mutual)* réciproque, mutuel; *(bilateral)* réciproque, bilatéral; *Gram* réciproque; *Math* réciproque, inverse; **he dislikes me and it's r.** il ne m'aime pas et c'est réciproque *ou* je le lui rends bien

N *Math* réciproque *f*, inverse *f*

►► ***reciprocal agreement*** accord *m* réciproque; *Econ* ***reciprocal demand*** demande *f* réciproque; ***reciprocal trading*** commerce *m* réciproque

reciprocally [rɪ'sɪprəkəlɪ] **ADV** réciproquement

reciprocate [rɪ'sɪprəkeɪt] **VT 1** *(favour, invitation, smile)* rendre; *(love, sentiment)* répondre à, rendre; **to r. sb's kindness** payer la gentillesse de qn de retour; **he had great admiration for her but his feelings were not reciprocated** il avait beaucoup d'admiration pour elle mais ce n'était pas réciproque **2** *Tech* actionner d'un mouvement alternatif

VI 1 *(in praise, compliments)* retourner le compliment; *(in fight)* rendre coup pour coup; *(in dispute)* rendre la pareille; *(in argument)* répondre du tac au tac **2** *Tech* avoir un mouvement de va-et-vient

reciprocating [rɪ'sɪprəˌkeɪtɪŋ] **ADJ** *Tech* alternatif

►► ***reciprocating engine*** moteur *m* alternatif

reciprocation [rɪˌsɪprə'keɪʃən] **N 1** *(of feeling)* réciprocité *f*; **in r. for** en retour de; **his r. of her feelings was clear** il était clair que leurs sentiments étaient réciproques **2** *Tech* mouvement *m* alternatif, va-et-vient *m inv*

reciprocity [ˌresɪ'prɒsɪtɪ] **N** réciprocité *f*

recirculated air [ˌriː'sɜːkjʊleɪtɪd-] **N** air *m* recyclé

recital [rɪ'saɪtəl] **N 1** *Mus & Literature* récital *m*; **to give a r.** donner un récital; **piano/poetry r.** récital *m* de piano/poésie **2** *(narrative)* narration *f*, relation *f*; *(of details)* énumération *f*

• **recitals** **NPL** *Law* préambule *m* *(à un acte notarié)*

recitation [ˌresɪ'teɪʃən] **N** récitation *f*

recitative [ˌresɪtə'tiːv] **N** *Mus* récitatif *m*

recite [rɪ'saɪt] **VT** *(play, poem)* réciter, déclamer; *(details, facts)* réciter, énumérer

VI réciter

reckless ['reklɪs] **ADJ** *(foolhardy)* téméraire; *(rash)* imprudent; *(thoughtless)* irréfléchi; **to make r. promises** s'engager à la légère; **to be a r. spender** dépenser sans compter; **it would be r. to ignore the consequences/the danger** il serait imprudent de ne pas tenir compte des conséquences/du danger

►► *Law* ***reckless driver*** conducteur(trice) *m,f* imprudent(e); *Law* ***reckless driving*** conduite *f* imprudente

recklessly ['reklɪslɪ] **ADV** *(fearlessly)* avec témérité; *(rashly)* imprudemment; *(thoughtlessly)* sans réfléchir; **to spend r.** dépenser sans compter; **they rather r. promised to contribute £500** ils ont promis assez imprudemment *ou* un peu hâtivement de donner 500 livres

recklessness ['reklɪsnɪs] **N** *(foolhardiness)* témérité *f*; *(rashness)* imprudence *f*; *(thoughtlessness)* insouciance *f*, étourderie *f*

reckon ['rekən] **VT 1** *(estimate)* estimer; **there were reckoned to be about 50,000 demonstrators** on a estimé à 50000 le nombre des manifestants

2 *(consider)* considérer; **he is reckoned to be one of the richest men in England** ce serait l'un des hommes les plus riches d'Angleterre

3 *Fam (suppose, think)* croire[□], supposer[□]; **I r. you're right** je crois bien que tu as raison[□]; **I r. the omelette is ready** je crois que l'omelette est prête[□]; **how old do you r. he is?** quel âge lui donnez-vous?[□]; **it's all over, I r.** je suppose que tout est fini[□]; **what do you r.?** qu'en pensez-vous?[□]

4 *Fam (regard favourably)* **I don't r. her chances** je ne crois pas qu'elle ait beaucoup de chances[□]

5 *Formal (calculate)* calculer

VI 1 *(calculate)* calculer, compter; **reckoning from today** à partir *ou* à compter d'aujourd'hui **2** *(expect)* compter, penser; **they had reckoned t make more profit from the venture** ils comptaien *ou* pensaient que l'entreprise leur rapporterai de plus gros bénéfices; **you should r. to be there by six o'clock at the latest** il faut que tu prévoi d'arriver à six heures au plus tard

► **reckon in** **VT SEP** *Br* compter, inclure

► **reckon on** **VT INSEP 1** *(rely on)* compter sur; **yo can r. on him making a mess of it** tu peux compte sur lui pour tout gâcher **2** *(expect)* s'attendre à espérer; **she had reckoned on going next week** elle avait prévu d'y aller la semaine prochaine **I didn't r. on that extra cost** je n'avais pas prévu ces frais supplémentaires

► **reckon up** **VT SEP** *(column of figures)* additionner; *(change, coins)* compter; *(total, cost)* calculer; **to r. up a bill** faire une facture

VI faire ses comptes; **to r. up with sb** régler se comptes avec qn

► **reckon with** **VT INSEP** compter avec; *(as oppo nent)* avoir affaire à; **you'll have to r. with anothe guest** il faudra compter avec un invité supplé mentaire; **you'll have his brother to r. with** vous aurez affaire à son frère; **he hadn't reckoned wit this response** il ne s'attendait pas à cette réac tion; **she's a force to be reckoned with** c'est une femme avec laquelle il faut compter

► **reckon without** **VT INSEP** *Br* **1** *(do without)* se passer de, se débrouiller sans **2** *Fam (ignore overlook)* ne pas tenir compte de[□]; **he had reck oned without his rivals** il n'avait pas tenu compte de ses rivaux; **she had reckoned without the fac that they had no car** elle n'avait pas pris e compte le fait qu'ils n'avaient pas de voiture

reckoning ['rekənɪŋ] **N 1** *(UNCOUNT) (calcula tion)* calcul *m*, compte *m*; **you are way out in you r.** vous vous êtes complètement trompé dans vos comptes *ou* dans vos calculs; **by my r., yo owe us £50** d'après mes calculs, vous nous de vez 50 livres; **in the final r.** en fin de compte **2** *(es timation)* estimation *f*; *(opinion)* avis *m*; **to th best of my r.** pour autant que je puisse en juger **by** *or* **on any r. she's a fine pianist** personne ne nie ra que c'est une excellente pianiste; *Rel* **day of r** jour *m* du Jugement dernier **3** *Naut* estime *f*

reclaim [rɪ'kleɪm] **VT 1** *(land ► gen)* mettre en va leur; *(► from undergrowth)* défricher; *(► fro marsh)* assécher; **they have reclaimed 1,000 hec tares of land from the sea/the desert** ils ont gagné 1000 hectares de terres sur la mer/le désert

2 *(salvage)* récupérer; *(recycle)* recycler

3 *(deposit, baggage)* récupérer; *(tax, expenses* se faire rembourser; **to r. sth from sb** récupére qch auprès de qn

4 *Literary (sinner, drunkard)* ramener dans l droit chemin

5 *(rehabilitate ► term, word)* se réapproprier; **i their election campaign they want to r. the issue o law and order** dans leur campagne ils veulent se réapproprier le thème de la sécurité et du maintien de l'ordre

6 *Ind (rubber etc)* régénérer; *(by-product)* récupérer

> Note that the French verb **réclamer** is a false friend and is never a translation for the English verb **to reclaim**. It means **to claim, to demand**.

reclamation [ˌreklə'meɪʃən] **N 1** *(of land ► gen* remise *f* en valeur; *(► from forest)* défrichemen *m*; *(► from sea, marsh)* assèchement *m*, drainage *m*; *(► from desert)* reconquête *f*

2 *(salvage)* récupération *f*; *(recycling)* recyclage *m*

3 *(of tax, expenses)* remboursement *m*

4 *Ind (of rubber etc)* régénération *f*; *(of by product)* récupération *f*

reclassify [ˌriː'klæsɪfaɪ] *(pt & pp* **reclassified***)* **V** *(plant etc)* reclasser; *(document etc)* reclassifier

recline [rɪ'klaɪn] **VT 1** *(head)* appuyer **2** *(seat* baisser, incliner

VI 1 *(be stretched out)* être allongé, être étendu *(lie back)* s'allonger; **he was reclining on the sofa i** était allongé *ou* étendu sur le canapé **2** *(seat* être inclinable, avoir un dossier inclinable

ecliner [rɪ'klaɪnə(r)] **N** *(for sunbathing)* chaise *f* longue; *(armchair)* fauteuil *m* à dossier inclinable, fauteuil *m* relax

eclining [rɪ'klaɪnɪŋ] **ADJ** *(seat)* inclinable, à dossier inclinable; **to be in a r. position** *(person)* être en position allongée *ou* couchée; *(seat)* être incliné

▸▸ ***reclining chair*** chaise *f* longue

ecluse [rɪ'klu:s] **N** reclus(e) *m,f*; **to live like a r.** vivre en reclus *ou* en ermite; **she's a bit of a r.** elle aime la solitude

ecognition [ˌrekəg'nɪʃən] **N 1** *(identification)* reconnaissance *f*; **he gave no sign of r.** il n'a pas eu l'air de me/le/*etc* reconnaître; **the town has changed beyond** *or* **out of all r.** la ville est méconnaissable

2 *(acknowledgment)* reconnaissance *f*; **in r. of** en reconnaissance de; **there is a growing r. that this is a serious social problem** de plus en plus de gens reconnaissent qu'il s'agit là d'un grave problème social

3 *(appreciation)* **to win** *or* **to achieve r.** être (enfin) reconnu; **to seek r. (for oneself)** chercher à être reconnu; **a composer who received no r. during his lifetime** un compositeur méconnu de son vivant; **public r.** la reconnaissance du public

4 *(of state, organization, trade union)* reconnaissance *f*; **to withhold r. from** *(government)* refuser de reconnaître

ecognizable, -isable [ˌrekəgˌnaɪzəbəl] **ADJ** reconnaissable; **she was barely r. as the woman he had known 20 years before** il reconnaissait à peine la femme qu'il avait rencontrée 20 ans auparavant; **his style was instantly r.** son style était immédiatement reconnaissable

ecognizably, -isably ['rekəgˌnaɪzəblɪ] **ADV** d'une manière *ou* d'une façon reconnaissable; **the car was not r. Japanese** on n'aurait pas dit une voiture japonaise, cette voiture ne ressemblait pas à une voiture japonaise

ecognizance, -isance [rɪ'kɒgnɪzəns] **N** *Law (bond)* engagement *m*; *(monies)* caution *f*; **to enter into recognizances for sb** *(with money)* verser une caution pour qn; *(personally)* se porter garant de qn; **to be released on one's own recognizances** être remis en liberté sur engagement personnel

ecognize, -ise ['rekəgnaɪz] **VT 1** *(identify ▸ person, place, voice etc)* reconnaître; **you'll r. him by his hat** vous le reconnaîtrez à son chapeau; **they recognized him for what he was** ils le reconnurent pour ce qu'il était; **he can certainly r. a good business opportunity** il sait repérer les bonnes affaires

2 *(acknowledge ▸ person)* reconnaître les talents de; *(▸ achievement)* reconnaître; *Sport (record)* homologuer; **to r. sb as king** reconnaître qn comme *ou* en tant que roi

3 *(be aware of, admit)* reconnaître; **I r. (that) I made a mistake** je reconnais *ou* j'admets que je me suis trompé; **the scale of the disaster has finally been recognized** on a fini par se rendre compte de l'étendue du désastre

4 *Admin & Pol (state, diploma)* reconnaître

5 *Am (in debate)* donner la parole à

6 *Comput* reconnaître

ecognized, -ised ['rekəgnaɪzd] **ADJ 1** *(acknowledged)* reconnu, admis; **it is a r. fact that...** c'est un fait avéré *ou* reconnu que... + *indicative*; **she's a r. authority on medieval history** c'est une autorité en histoire médiévale **2** *(official)* officiel, attitré; **that's not the r. legal term** ce n'est pas le terme juridique officiel

▸▸ *Com* ***recognized agent*** agent *m* accrédité; ***recognized professional body*** = organisme professionnel agréé

ecoil **VI** [rɪ'kɔɪl] **1** *(person)* reculer, avoir un mouvement de recul; **she recoiled in horror** horrifiée, elle recula; **to r. from doing sth** reculer devant l'idée de faire qch **2** *(firearm)* reculer; *(spring)* se détendre

N ['ri:kɔɪl] **1** *(of gun)* recul *m*; *(of spring)* détente *f* **2** *(of person)* mouvement *m* de recul; *Fig* répugnance *f*

ecoilless, *Am* **recoiless** [ri:kɔɪlɪs] **ADJ** *Mil & Tech* sans recul

recollect [ˌrekə'lekt] **VT 1** *(remember)* se souvenir de, se rappeler; **I don't r. having asked her** je ne me rappelle pas le lui avoir demandé; **she was unable to r. what had happened** elle était incapable de se souvenir de ce qui s'était passé **2** *Literary (gather ▸ courage)* rassembler; **to r. oneself** se ressaisir

VI se souvenir; **as far as I (can) r.** autant que je m'en souvienne, autant qu'il m'en souvienne

recollection [ˌrekə'lekʃən] **N** *(memory)* souvenir *m*; **I have no r. of it** je n'en ai aucun souvenir; **I have some r. of it** j'en ai un vague souvenir; **to the best of my r.** (pour) autant que je m'en souvienne

recombinant [rɪ'kɒmbɪnənt] **ADJ**

▸▸ *Biol* ***recombinant DNA*** ADN *m* recombinant

recommend [ˌrekə'mend] **VT 1** *(speak in favour of)* recommander (**to/for** à/pour); **she recommended him for the job** elle l'a recommandé pour cet emploi; **I'll r. you to the Minister** j'appuyerai votre candidature auprès du ministre; **the book has been highly recommended to me** le livre m'a été fortement recommandé; **it's a restaurant I can thoroughly r.** c'est un restaurant que je recommande vivement; **the town has little to r. it** la ville est sans grand intérêt; **the proposal has a lot to r. it** la proposition a beaucoup d'avantages *ou* d'attrait **2** *(advise)* recommander, conseiller; **I r. you (to) see the film** je vous recommande *ou* conseille d'aller voir ce film; **not (to be) recommended** à déconseiller; **recommended** *(in film or book review etc)* à voir/lire/*etc* **3** *Arch or Formal (entrust)* recommander; **to r. one's soul to God** recommander son âme à Dieu; **the orphans were recommended to the care of their grandmother** les orphelins ont été confiés à leur grand-mère

▸▸ *Com & Mktg* ***recommended retail price*** prix *m* recommandé *ou* conseillé

recommendable [ˌrekə'mendəbəl] **ADJ** recommandable

recommendation [ˌrekəmen'deɪʃən] **N 1** *(personal)* recommandation *f*; **on your/his r.** sur votre/sa recommandation; **my r. is that...** ce que je recommande *ou* conseille c'est que... + *subjunctive* **2** *(of committee, advisory body)* recommandation *f*; **to make a r.** faire une recommandation **3** *(commendation)* recommandation *f*; **the hotel's sole r. is its location** l'emplacement de l'hôtel est son seul intérêt

recompense ['rekəmpens] **N 1** *(reward)* récompense *f*; **in r. for your trouble** en récompense de *ou* pour vous récompenser de votre peine **2** *Law (compensation)* dédommagement *m*, compensation *f*

VT récompenser; **to r. sb for sth** *(gen)* récompenser qn de qch; *Law* dédommager qn de *ou* pour qch

reconcilable ['rekənsaɪləbəl] **ADJ** *(opinions)* conciliable, compatible; *(people)* compatible

reconcile ['rekənsaɪl] **VT 1** *(people)* réconcilier; *(ideas, opposing principles)* concilier; **Peter and Jane are reconciled at last** Peter et Jane se sont enfin réconciliés; **to be reconciled with sb** se réconcilier avec qn; témoignage qui ne cadre pas avec les faits connus; **you cannot r. morality with politics** on ne saurait concilier moralité et politique

2 *(resign)* **to r. oneself** *or* **to become reconciled to sth** se résigner à qch; **she reconciled herself to the idea of leaving** elle s'est faite à l'idée de partir

3 *(win over)* **to r. sb to sth** faire accepter qch à qn

4 *(settle ▸ dispute)* régler

5 *Fin (figures, bank statements)* rapprocher; *Acct (accounts, entries)* faire cadrer, faire accorder

> When translating the English verb **to reconcile**, note that the French verbs **concilier** and **réconcilier** are not interchangeable.

reconciliation [ˌrekənsɪlɪ'eɪʃən] **N 1** *(between people)* réconciliation *f*; *(of ideas, opinions, principles)* conciliation *f* **2** *Fin (of figures, bank statements)* rapprochement *m*; *Acct (of accounts, entries)* ajustement *m*

recondite ['rekəndaɪt] **ADJ** *Formal (obscure ▸ text, style)* abscons, obscur; *(▸ taste)* ésotérique

recondition [ˌri:kən'dɪʃən] **VT** remettre en état *ou* à neuf

reconditioned [ˌri:kən'dɪʃənd] **ADJ** remis à neuf; *Br (tyre)* rechapé

▸▸ *Aut* ***reconditioned engine*** (moteur *m*) échange *m* standard

reconditioning [ˌri:kən'dɪʃənɪŋ] **N** remise *f* en état *ou* à neuf

reconfiguration [ˌri:kənfɪgə'reɪʃən] **N** *Comput* reconfiguration *f*

reconfigure [ˌri:kən'fɪgə(r)] **VT** *Comput* reconfigurer

reconnaissance [rɪ'kɒnɪsəns] **N** *Mil* reconnaissance *f*; **to be on r.** être en reconnaissance; **aerial r.** reconnaissance *f* aérienne

▸▸ ***reconnaissance flight*** vol *m* de reconnaissance; ***reconnaissance satellite*** satellite *m* de reconnaissance

reconnect [ˌri:kə'nekt] **VT** rebrancher; **to r. the water supply** rétablir l'alimentation en eau; *Tel* **the operator reconnected us** l'opérateur a rétabli la communication; **the telephone company reconnected us** la compagnie de téléphone nous a reconnectés

VI *Comput* se reconnecter

reconnection [ˌri:kə'nekʃən] **N** *(of cable, telephone etc)* rebranchement *m*; *(of pipe)* raccordement *m*; *(of water supply, telephone call)* rétablissement *m*

▸▸ *Tel* ***reconnection charge*** frais *mpl* de rebranchement

reconnoitre, *Am* **reconnoiter** [ˌrekə'nɔɪtə(r)] *Mil*

VT reconnaître

VI effectuer une reconnaissance

reconquer [ˌri:'kɒŋkə(r)] **VT** reconquérir

reconquest [ˌri:'kɒŋkwest] **N** reconquête *f*

reconsider [ˌri:kən'sɪdə(r)] **VT** *(decision, problem)* réexaminer; *(topic)* se repencher sur; *(judgment)* réviser, revoir

VI reconsidérer la question; **I advise you to r.** je vous conseille de revoir votre position

reconsideration ['ri:kənˌsɪdə'reɪʃən] **N** *(reexamination)* nouvel examen *m*, nouveau regard *m*; *(of judgment)* révision *f*

reconstitute [ˌri:'kɒnstɪtju:t] **VT** reconstituer

reconstitution ['ri:ˌkɒnstɪ'tju:ʃən] **N** reconstitution *f*

reconstruct [ˌri:kən'strʌkt] **VT 1** *(make again ▸ house, bridge)* reconstruire, rebâtir **2** *(form picture of ▸ crime, event)* reconstituer; *(▸ government, system)* reconstituer; *(▸ one's life, a country)* reconstruire

reconstruction [ˌri:kən'strʌkʃən] **N 1** *(of demolished building)* reconstruction *f*; *(of old building)* reconstitution *f*; *(of façade, shop)* réfection *f* **2** *(of crime, event, government)* reconstitution *f*; *(of economy)* restauration *f*

reconstructive surgery [ˌri:kən'strʌktɪv-] **N** chirurgie *f* réparatrice

reconvene [ˌri:kən'vi:n] **VT** reconvoquer

VI se réunir à nouveau; **the meeting reconvenes at three** la réunion reprend à trois heures

RECORD

N
- rapport **1**
- procès-verbal **1**
- casier (judiciaire) **2**
- record **4**
- dossier **1, 2**
- antécédents **2**
- disque **3**
- article **5**

ADJ
- record

VT
- noter **1**
- rapporter **1**
- enregistrer **1–3**
- marquer **2, 4**

VI
- enregistrer

N ['rekɔ:d] **1** *(account, report)* rapport *m*; *(file)* dossier *m*; *(note)* note *f*; *(of attendance)* registre *m*; *(of proceedings, debate)* procès-verbal *m*, compte rendu *m*; **records** *(of government, police, hospital)* archives *fpl*; *(of learned society)* actes *mpl*; **to make a r. of sth** noter qch; *Law* **to strike sth from the r.** rayer qch du procès-verbal; **they keep a r. of all deposits/all comings and goings** ils enregistrent tous les versements/toutes les allées et venues; **there is no r. of their visit** il n'existe aucune trace de leur visite; **do you have any r. of the transaction?** avez-vous gardé une trace de la transaction?; **there's no r. of it anywhere** ce n'est mentionné nulle part; **the book provides a r. of 19th-century Parisian society** le livre évoque la société parisienne du XIXème siècle; **the wettest June since records began** le mois de juin le plus humide depuis que l'on tient des statistiques; **public records office** archives *fpl* nationales; **to put** *or* **to set the r. straight** mettre les choses au clair

2 *(past history)* passé *m*, antécédents *mpl*; *(reputation)* réputation *f*; *(criminal or police file)* casier *m* (judiciaire); **his past r.** *(behaviour)* ses antécédents; *(achievements)* ses résultats antérieurs; **his past r. with the firm** son passé dans l'entreprise; **given your r. as a late payer** vu vos antécédents de mauvais payeur; **she has an excellent attendance r.** elle a été très assidue, elle n'a presque jamais été absente; **the plane has a good safety r.** l'avion est réputé pour sa sécurité; **to have a (criminal) r.** avoir un casier judiciaire; **to have a clean r.** avoir un casier judiciaire vierge; **he has a r. of previous convictions** il a déjà été condamné; **case r.** *Med* dossier *m* médical; *Law* dossier *m* judiciaire; *Mil* **service** *or* **army r.** états *mpl* de service; **school r.** dossier *m* scolaire

3 *(disc)* disque *m*; *(recording)* enregistrement *m*; **to play** *or* **to put on a r.** mettre *ou* passer un disque; **to make** *or* **to cut a r.** faire *ou* graver un disque

4 *(gen) & Sport* record *m*; **to set a r.** établir un record; **to break** *or* **beat the record** battre le record; **to hold the r. (for)** détenir le record (de); **the 200 m r.** le record du 200 m

5 *Comput (in database)* article *m*, enregistrement *m*

ADJ ['rekɔːd] *(summer, temperature)* record *(inv)*; **in r. time** en un temps record; **to reach r. levels** atteindre un niveau record; **unemployment is at a r. high/low** le chômage a atteint son chiffre le plus haut/bas

VT [rɪ'kɔːd] **1** *(take note of ▸ fact, complaint, detail)* noter, enregistrer, consigner; *(▸ in archives, on computer)* enregistrer; *(give account of ▸ events)* attester, rapporter; *(▸ thoughts, ideas)* noter (par écrit), consigner, mettre sur papier; *Law (judgment)* minuter; **your objection has been recorded** nous avons pris acte de votre objection; **no biography records the visit** aucune biographie ne fait mention de *ou* n'atteste la visite; **their answer was not recorded** leur réponse n'a pas été enregistrée; **a photograph was taken to r. the event** une photographie a été prise pour rappeler cet événement; **the book records life in medieval England** le livre dépeint *ou* évoque la vie en Angleterre au Moyen Âge; **history records that 30,000 soldiers took part** selon les livres d'histoire, 30000 soldats y ont participé; **throughout recorded history** aussi loin que les archives remontent; **to r. one's opposition** indiquer par écrit son opposition; *(in speech)* faire part de son opposition; *Parl* **to r. a vote** *(MP)* voter

2 *(register ▸ of equipment)* enregistrer; *(▸ of dial, gauge)* indiquer, marquer; **temperatures of 50° were recorded** on a relevé des températures de 50°

3 *(music, tape, TV programme)* enregistrer; **recorded** *(not live)* différé; **this is a recorded message** *(on telephone)* ceci est un message enregistré; **recorded highlights** extraits *mpl* préenregistrés

4 *Sport (score)* marquer; **he recorded a time of 10.7 seconds for the 100 metres** il a couru le 100 m en 10,7 secondes

VI [rɪ'kɔːd] *(on tape, video)* enregistrer; **leave the video, it's recording** laisse le magnétoscope, il est en train d'enregistrer; **his voice doesn't r. well** sa voix ne se prête pas bien à l'enregistrement

• **for the record ADV** pour mémoire, pour la petite histoire; **just for the r., you started it!** je te signale au passage que c'est toi qui as commencé!

• **off the record ADJ** confidentiel; **this is strictly off the r.** ceci est strictement confidentiel, ceci doit rester strictement entre nous **ADV to say sth off the r.** dire qch en confidence; **he admitted off the r. that he had known** il a admis en privé qu'il était au courant

• **on record ADV** enregistré; **it's on r. that you were informed** il est établi que vous étiez au courant; **we have it on r. that...** il est attesté *ou* établi que...+ *indicative*; **to put** *or* **to place sth on r.** *(say)* dire *ou* déclarer qch officiellement; *(write)* consigner qch par écrit; **I wish to go on r. as saying that...** je voudrais dire officiellement *ou* publiquement que...+ *indicative*; **it's the only example on r.** c'est le seul exemple connu

▸▸ *record book* *(for official information)* registre *m*; *Fam* **that's one for the r. books!** c'est un nouveau record!; ***record card*** fiche *f*; ***record company*** maison *f* de disques; ***record deck*** platine *f* (tourne-disque); ***record holder*** *(man)* recordman *m*, détenteur *m* d'un/du record; *(woman)* recordwoman *f*, détentrice *f* d'un/du record; ***record label*** label *m*; ***record library*** discothèque *f (de prêt)*; ***record player*** tourne-disque *m*, platine *f* (disques); ***record producer*** producteur *m* de disques; ***record shop*** magasin *m* de disques; ***record token*** chèque-disque *m*

---

record-breaker N *Sport (man)* nouveau recordman *m*; *(woman)* nouvelle recordwoman *f*; *Br Fig* **the new product is a r.** le nouveau produit bat tous les records

record-breaking ADJ 1 *Sport* **a r. jump** un saut qui a établi un nouveau record **2** *(year, temperatures)* record *(inv)*

recorded [rɪ'kɔːdɪd] **ADJ 1** *(music, message, tape)* enregistré; *(programme)* préenregistré; *(broadcast)* transmis en différé **2** *(fact)* attesté, noté; *(history)* écrit; *(votes)* exprimé; **throughout r. history** pendant toute la période couverte pour laquelle on dispose de documents écrits

▸▸ *Br* ***recorded delivery*** recommandé *m*; **to send sth (by) r. delivery** envoyer qch en recommandé avec accusé de réception

recorder [rɪ'kɔːdə(r)] **N 1** *(apparatus)* enregistreur *m*

2 *(musical instrument)* flûte *f* à bec

3 *(keeper of records)* archiviste *mf*; *Law* **court r.** greffier *m*

4 *Br Law* = avocat nommé à la fonction de magistrat (à temps partiel)

recording [rɪ'kɔːdɪŋ] **N** *(of music, data)* enregistrement *m*

COMP *Mus & TV (equipment, session)* d'enregistrement; *(company)* de disques; *(star)* du disque

▸▸ *Bible & Fig* ***Recording Angel*** = l'ange qui tient le livre des actes (bons et mauvais) de chacun; ***recording artist*** musicien(enne) *m,f* qui enregistre des disques; ***recording deck*** magnétoscope *m* d'enregistrement; ***recording engineer*** ingénieur *m* du son; ***recording head*** tête *f* d'enregistrement; ***recording studio*** studio *m* d'enregistrement; ***recording tape*** ruban *m ou* bande *f* d'enregistrement

recount [rɪ'kaʊnt] **VT** *(story, experience)* raconter

re-count VT [,riː'kaʊnt] *(count again)* recompter, compter de nouveau

N ['riːkaʊnt] *Pol* nouveau décompte *m*; **to do a r.** *(of money, people, votes etc)* recompter; **to demand a r.** *(of votes)* exiger un nouveau décompte; **there were four re-counts** on a compté le nombre de bulletins de vote à quatre reprises

recoup [rɪ'kuːp] **VT 1** *(get back ▸ losses, cost)* récupérer; **to r. one's investments** rentrer dans ses fonds; **to r. one's costs** rentrer dans *ou* couvrir ses frais **2** *(pay back)* rembourser, dédommager **3** *Law (deduct)* défalquer, déduire

recourse [rɪ'kɔːs] **N 1** *(gen)* recours *m*; **to have r. to sth** recourir à qch, avoir recours à qch; **right of r.** droit *m* de recours **2** *Fin* recours *m*; **endorsement without r.** endossement *m* à forfait

recover [rɪ'kʌvə(r)] **VT 1** *(get back ▸ property)* récupérer, retrouver; *(▸ debt, loan, deposit)* récupérer, recouvrer; *(take back)* reprendre; *(regain ▸ territory, ball)* regagner; *(▸ control, hearing, appetite)* retrouver; *(▸ advantage)* reprendre; **50 bodies have been recovered** 50 corps ont été retrouvés; **to r. one's breath/footing** reprendre haleine/pied; **to r. one's balance** retrouver son équilibre; **to r. one's composure** se ressaisir; **to r. one's health** guérir, se rétablir, recouvrer la santé; **to r. one's strength** reprendre des forces; *also Fig* **to r. lost ground** regagner du terrain; **to r. one's expenses** rentrer dans ses fonds

2 *(salvage ▸ wreck, waste)* récupérer; *(▸ from water)* récupérer, repêcher

3 *Law* **to r. damages** obtenir des dommages intérêts

4 *(extract ▸ from ore)* extraire

5 *Comput (file, data)* récupérer

VI 1 *(after accident, shock, setback)* se remettr *(after illness)* se rétablir, guérir; **to r. from sth** s remettre de qch; **to be fully recovered** être com plètement guéri *ou* rétabli **2** *(currency, economy* se redresser; *(market)* reprendre, se redresse *(prices, shares)* se redresser, remonter **3** *Law* ga gner son procès, obtenir gain de cause

re-cover [,riː-] **VT** *(chair etc)* recouvrir

recoverable [rɪ'kʌvrəbəl] **ADJ** *(debt)* recou vrable; *(losses, mistake)* réparable; *(by-produc computer file)* récupérable

recovery [rɪ'kʌvərɪ] *(pl* **recoveries**) **N 1** *(of lo property, wreck)* récupération *f*; *(of debt)* recou vrement *m*, récupération *f*; *(of money, depos* récupération *f*; **the r. of his sight changed his lif** le fait de recouvrer la vue a transformé sa vie

2 *(from illness)* rétablissement *m*, guérison *f*; **make a speedy r.** se remettre vite; **to be on the wa** *or* **the road to r.** être en voie de guérison; **she making a good r.** elle est en bonne voie de guér son; **he is past** *or* **beyond r.** *(patient)* on ne peu plus rien faire pour lui, il est dans un état dése péré

3 *(of economy)* relance *f*, redressement *m*; *(prices, shares)* redressement *m*, remontée *f*; *(currency)* redressement *m*; *(of market, busines* reprise *f*; *Sport* **to stage** *or* **to make a r.** reprendr le dessus; **the country made a slow r. after the wa** le pays s'est rétabli lentement après la guerr **to be past** *or* **beyond r.** *(situation)* être irrémé diable *ou* sans espoir; *(loss)* être irrécupérab *ou* irréparable

4 *(of wreck, waste)* récupération *f*; *(from wate* récupération *f*, repêchage *m*

5 *Comput (of file, data)* récupération *f*

6 *Law (of damages)* obtention *f*

▸▸ *Med* ***recovery position*** position *f* latérale d sécurité; *Med* ***recovery room*** salle *f* de réanima tion; *Br Aut* ***recovery service*** service *m* de dépan nage; ***recovery ship*** navire *m* de récupération; ***recovery vehicle*** dépanneuse *f*; ***recovery vess*** navire *m* de récupération

re-create [,riː-] **VT** *(past event)* reconstitue *(place, scene)* recréer

recreation [,rekrɪ'eɪʃən] **N 1** *(relaxation)* récréa tion *f*, détente *f*; **she only reads for r.** elle ne lit qu pour se délasser *ou* se détendre **2** *Sch* récréatio *f*

COMP *(activities, facilities)* de loisirs

▸▸ *recreation centre* centre *m* de loisirs; *Br **re creation ground*** terrain *m* de jeux; ***recreatio room*** *(in school, hospital)* salle *f* de récréation *(in hotel) & Am (at home)* salle *f* de jeux

re-creation ['riː-] **N** *(of event, scene)* recréatio *f*, reconstitution *f*

recreational [,rekrɪ'eɪʃənəl] **ADJ** *(activities, fac ities)* de loisirs

▸▸ *recreational drug* drogue *f* à usage récréati ***recreational therapy*** thérapie *f* par le jeu; *Am **re creational vehicle*** camping-car *m*

recriminate [rɪ'krɪmɪneɪt] **VT** *Formal* récrimine **to r. against sb** récriminer contre qn

recrimination [rɪ,krɪmɪ'neɪʃən] **N** *(usu pl)* **re criminations** récriminations *fpl*

recriminatory [rɪ'krɪmɪnətrɪ] **ADJ** *Formal* récr minateur

recrudescence [,riːkruː'desəns] **N** *Formal* recru descence *f*

recrudescent [,riːkruː'desənt] **ADJ** *Formal* recru descent

recruit [rɪ'kruːt] **N** *(gen) & Mil* recrue *f*

VT *(member, army)* recruter; *(worker)* recrute embaucher (**as** pour le poste de); **to r. sb to d sth** embaucher *ou* recruter qn pour faire qch

recruiting [rɪ'kruːtɪŋ] **N** recrutement *m*

▸▸ *recruiting office* bureau *m* de recrutemen ***recruiting officer*** *Mil* recruteur(euse) *m,f*; *Hist* ra coleur *m*; *Mil* ***recruiting sergeant*** sergent *m* re cruteur

recruitment [rɪ'kruːtmənt] **N** recrutement *m*

▸▸ *Br* ***recruitment agency*** cabinet *m* de recrute ment; ***recruitment campaign*** campagne *f* de re crutement; ***recruitment consultant*** conseil *m* e recrutement; ***recruitment drive*** campagne *f* de recrutement; ***recruitment officer*** recruteur (euse) *m,f*

rectal ['rektəl] **ADJ** rectal
▸▸ ***rectal cancer*** cancer *m* du rectum; ***rectal examination*** examen *m* rectal *ou* du rectum

rectangle ['rekˌtæŋgəl] **N** rectangle *m*

rectangular [ˌrek'tæŋgjʊlə(r)] **ADJ** rectangulaire

rectification [ˌrektɪfɪ'keɪʃən] **N 1** *(correction)* rectification *f*, correction *f* **2** *Chem & Math* rectification *f*; *Elec* redressement *m* **3** *Acct (of entry)* modification *f*, rectification *f*

rectifier ['rektɪfaɪə(r)] **N** *Elec* redresseur *m*; *Chem* rectificateur *m*

rectify ['rektɪfaɪ] *(pt & pp* **rectified)** **VT 1** *(mistake)* rectifier, corriger; *(oversight)* réparer; *(situation)* redresser **2** *Chem & Math* rectifier; *Elec* redresser **3** *Acct (entry)* modifier, rectifier

rectilineal [ˌrektɪ'lɪnɪəl], **rectilinear** [ˌrektɪ'lɪnɪə(r)] **ADJ** rectiligne

rectitude ['rektɪtjuːd] **N** rectitude *f*; **moral r.** droiture *f*

recto ['rektəʊ] *(pl* **rectos)** **N** *Typ* recto *m*

rector ['rektə(r)] **N 1** *Rel (Anglican, Presbyterian)* pasteur *m*; *(Catholic)* recteur *m* **2** *Scot Sch* proviseur *m*, directeur(trice) *m,f* **3** *Scot Univ* = personnalité élue par les étudiants pour les représenter

rectorial [rek'tɔːrɪəl] **ADJ** *(decision, duties)* rectoral

rectory ['rektərɪ] *(pl* **rectories)** **N** presbytère *m*

rectoscope ['rektəskəʊp] **N** *Med* rectoscope *m*

rectum ['rektəm] *(pl* **rectums** *or* **recta** [-tə]) **N** rectum *m*

recumbent [rɪ'kʌmbənt] **ADJ** couché, étendu, allongé

recuperate [rɪ'kuːpəreɪt] **VI 1** *(person)* se remettre, récupérer (**from** de); **he had gone to the South of France to r.** il était allé en convalescence dans le Midi; **she is still recuperating** elle est encore en convalescence **2** *Fin (market)* reprendre
VT *(materials, money)* récupérer; *(loss)* compenser; *(strength)* reprendre

recuperation [rɪˌkuːpə'reɪʃən] **N 1** *(of person)* rétablissement *m* **2** *(of materials, money)* récupération *f* **3** *Fin (of market)* reprise *f*

recuperative [rɪ'kuːpərətɪv] **ADJ** *(medicine)* régénérateur, reconstituant; *(rest)* réparateur; *(powers)* de récupération

recur [rɪ'kɜː(r)] *(pt & pp* **recurred**, *cont* **recurring)** **VI 1** *(occur again ▸ event)* se reproduire; *(reappear ▸ theme, image)* réapparaître, revenir; **come back if the problem recurs** revenez si le problème réapparaît *ou* se représente **2** *(to memory)* revenir à la mémoire **3** *Math* se reproduire, se répéter

recurrence [rɪ'kʌrəns] **N** *(of mistake, notion, event)* répétition *f*; *(of disease, symptoms)* réapparition *f*; *(of theme)* répétition *f*, réapparition *f*; *(of subject, problem)* retour *m*; **there must be no r. of such behaviour** ce genre de comportement ne devra jamais se reproduire; **has there been any r. of the symptoms?** les symptômes se sont-ils manifestés à nouveau?

recurrent [rɪ'kʌrənt] **ADJ 1** *(event)* périodique, qui revient *ou* se répète périodiquement; *(theme)* récurrent; *(dream, nightmare)* qui revient souvent; **I get r. headaches/bouts of flu** j'ai souvent des maux de tête/la grippe **2** *Anat & Med* récurrent
▸▸ ***recurrent expenses*** *(gen)* dépenses *fpl* courantes; *Com* frais *mpl* généraux

recurring [rɪ'kɜːrɪŋ] **ADJ 1** *(persistent ▸ problem)* qui revient *ou* qui se reproduit souvent; *(▸ dream, nightmare)* qui revient souvent **2** *Math* périodique; **33. 33 r.** 33, 33 à l'infini; **2 point 7 r.** 2 virgule 7 périodique
▸▸ ***recurring decimal*** fraction *f* périodique

recusant ['rekjʊzənt] *Rel* **ADJ** réfractaire
N rebelle *mf* à l'Église

recyclability [ˌriːsaɪklə'bɪlɪtɪ] **N** recyclabilité *f*

recyclable [ˌriː'saɪkləbəl] **ADJ** recyclable

recycle [ˌriː'saɪkəl] **VT** *(materials)* recycler; *(money)* réinvestir; *(funds)* remettre en circulation
▸▸ *Comput* ***recycle bin*** corbeille *f*

recycling [ˌriː'saɪklɪŋ] **N** recyclage *m*; *(of funds)* remise *f* en circulation
▸▸ ***recycling facility*** installation *f* de recyclage; ***recycling plant*** usine *f* de recyclage

red [red] *(compar* **redder**, *superl* **reddest)** **ADJ 1** *(gen)* rouge; *(hair, beard)* roux (rousse); **to turn** *or* **to go r.** *(person, litmus paper)* rougir, devenir rouge; *(leaves)* roussir; *(sky)* rougeoyer; **wait till the lights turn r.** attend que le feu passe au rouge; **r. with anger/shame** rouge de colère/honte; **to take a r. pen to sth** corriger qch à l'encre rouge; **to be r. in the face** *(after effort)* avoir la figure toute rouge; *(with embarrassment)* être rouge de confusion; *(permanent state)* être rougeaud; **there will be some r. faces on the Opposition benches** cela va causer de l'embarras dans les rangs de l'opposition; **to bring** *or* **to raise a metal to r. heat** chauffer *ou* porter un métal au rouge; **to be as r. as a beetroot** *(with embarrassment)* être rouge comme une tomate *ou* une pivoine; **to be as r. as a lobster** *(with sunburn)* être rouge comme une écrevisse; *Prov* **r. sky at night, shepherd's delight** = ciel rouge le soir est signe de beau temps; *Prov* **r. sky in the morning, shepherd's warning** = ciel rouge le matin est signe de mauvais temps; *Am Fam* **it's not worth a r. cent** ça ne vaut pas un clou *ou* un centime; **the mere mention of his name was like a r. rag to a bull (to him)** le simple fait d'entendre son nom le mettait dans une colère noire **2** *Fam (communist)* rouge **3** *Am* **to go into r. ink** *(person)* être à découvert; *(company)* être en déficit; *(account)* avoir un solde déficitaire
N 1 *(colour)* rouge *m*; **dressed in r.** habillé en rouge; *Fam* **to see r.** *(be angry)* voir rouge
2 *(in roulette)* rouge *m*; *(in snooker)* (bille *f*) rouge *f*
3 *(wine)* rouge *m*
4 *Fam Pej (communist)* rouge *mf*, coco *mf*; **reds under the bed** = expression évoquant la psychose du communisme; **the reds-under-the-bed syndrome** la phobie anti-communiste
5 *(deficit)* **to be in the r.** *(person)* avoir un découvert, être dans le rouge; *(company)* être en déficit; *(account)* avoir un solde déficitaire; **to be £5,000 in the r.** *(person)* avoir un découvert de 5000 livres; *(company)* avoir un déficit de 5000 livres; *(account)* avoir un solde déficitaire de 5000 livres; **to get out of the r.** *(person)* combler son découvert; *(company)* sortir du rouge
▸▸ *Entom* ***red admiral*** vulcain *m*; ***red alert*** alerte *f* rouge; **to be on r. alert** être en état d'alerte maximale; ***the Red Army*** l'Armée *f* rouge; ***red cabbage*** chou *m* rouge; ***red card*** *(in football, rugby)* carton *m* rouge, *Belg* carte *f* rouge; **to get** *or* **to be shown the r. card** recevoir le carton *ou Belg* la carte rouge; ***red carpet*** tapis *m* rouge; **to roll out the r. carpet for sb** *(for VIP)* dérouler le tapis rouge en l'honneur de qn; *(for guest)* mettre les petits plats dans les grands en l'honneur de qn; ***red channel*** *(at airport etc)* file *f* pour les passagers qui ont des objets à déclarer à la douane; *Fam* ***Red China*** la Chine communiste *ou* populaire▫; ***red corpuscle*** globule *m* rouge, hématie *f*; ***the Red Crescent*** le Croissant-Rouge; ***the Red Cross (Society)*** la Croix-Rouge; *Zool* ***red deer*** cerf *m* commun *ou* d'Europe; *Astron* ***red dwarf*** naine *f* rouge; ***Red Ensign*** = pavillon de la marine marchande britannique; *Phot* ***red eye*** *(UNCOUNT)* = phénomène provoquant l'apparition de taches rouges dans les yeux des personnes photographiées au flash; ***red flag*** drapeau *m* rouge; ***the Red Flag*** = hymne du parti travailliste britannique; *Astron* ***red giant*** géante *f* rouge; ***the Red Guard*** la garde rouge; ***red herring*** *(fish)* hareng *m* saur; *Fig* diversion *f*; **it's just a r. herring** ce n'est qu'un truc pour nous dépister *ou* pour brouiller les pistes; *Old-fashioned* ***Red Indian*** Peau-Rouge *mf*; ***red lead*** minium *m*; *Aut* ***red light*** feu *m* rouge; **to go through a r. light** passer au rouge, brûler le feu rouge; ***red light district*** quartier *m* des prostituées, quartier *m* chaud; ***red meat*** viande *f* rouge; *Ich* ***red mullet*** rouget barbet *m*; *Zool* ***red panda*** petit panda *m*; ***red pepper*** *(spice)* (poivre *m* de) cayenne *m*; *(vegetable)* poivron *m* rouge; ***the Red Planet*** *(Mars)* la planète rouge; ***(Little) Red Riding Hood*** le Petit Chaperon Rouge; ***the Red Sea*** la mer Rouge; ***red setter*** setter *m* irlandais; ***Red Square*** la place Rouge; *Zool* ***red squirrel*** écureuil *m* roux; ***red tape*** *(bureaucracy)* paperasserie *f*; **there's too much r. tape** il y a trop de paperasserie *ou* de bureaucratie

red-blooded [-'blʌdɪd] **ADJ** vigoureux, viril; **the average r. male** n'importe quel homme digne de ce nom

redbreast ['redbrest] **N** *Orn* rouge-gorge *m*

redbrick ['redbrɪk] **ADJ** *Br (building)* en brique rouge
▸▸ *Br Univ* ***redbrick university*** = université de province (par opposition à Oxford et Cambridge) fondée à la fin du XIXème siècle

redcap ['redkæp] **N 1** *Br Fam* policier *m* militaire▫ **2** *Am Rail* porteur *m*

red-carpet **ADJ** **to give sb the r. treatment** réserver un accueil fastueux *ou* princier à qn; **r. event** événement *m* prestigieux *(pour lequel on déroule le tapis rouge)*

redcoat ['redkəʊt] **N** *Br* **1** *Hist* soldat *m* anglais **2** *(in holiday camp)* animateur(trice) *m,f*

redcurrant ['redkʌrənt] **N** groseille *f* (rouge)
COMP *(tart, sauce)* aux groseilles
▸▸ ***redcurrant bush*** groseillier *m* rouge; ***redcurrant jelly*** gelée *f* de groseille

redden ['redən] **VT** rougir, rendre rouge; *(hair)* teindre en roux
VI *(person, face)* rougir, devenir (tout) rouge; *(sky)* rougeoyer; *(leaves)* devenir roux (rousse), roussir

reddish ['redɪʃ] **ADJ** *(light, colour)* rougeâtre; *(fur)* roussâtre; *(hair)* roussâtre, qui tire sur le roux

redecorate [ˌriː'dekəreɪt] **VT** *(gen ▸ room, house)* refaire; *(repaint)* refaire les peintures de; *(re-wallpaper)* retapisser; **we're redecorating the flat** nous sommes en train de repeindre et de retapisser l'appartement
VI *(repaint)* refaire les peintures; *(re-wallpaper)* refaire les papiers peints

redecoration [riːˌdekə'reɪʃən] **N** *(painting)* remise *f* à neuf des peintures; *(wallpapering)* remise *f* à neuf des papiers peints

redeem [rɪ'diːm] **VT 1** *(from pawn)* dégager, retirer
2 *(cash ▸ voucher)* encaisser; *(▸ share)* réaliser, racheter; *(exchange ▸ coupon, savings stamps)* échanger; *(▸ banknote)* compenser
3 *(annuity, mortgage)* rembourser; *(debt)* amortir, se libérer de; *(bill)* honorer; *(loan)* rembourser, amortir
4 *(make up for ▸ mistake, failure)* racheter, réparer; *(▸ crime, sin)* expier; **to r. oneself** se racheter; **it's his sole redeeming feature** c'est sa seule qualité
5 *(save ▸ situation, position)* sauver; *(▸ loss)* récupérer, réparer; *(▸ honour)* sauver; *Rel (▸ sinner)* racheter
6 *(fulfil ▸ promise)* s'acquitter de, tenir; *(▸ obligation)* satisfaire à, s'acquitter de
7 *(free ▸ slave)* racheter

redeemable [rɪ'diːməbəl] **ADJ 1** *(loan, mortgage)* remboursable; *(voucher)* encaissable; *(share)* réalisable, rachetable; *(debt)* remboursable, amortissable; **the stamps are not r. for cash** les timbres ne peuvent être échangés contre des espèces **2** *(mistake)* réparable; *(sin, crime)* expiable; *(sinner)* rachetable

redeemer [rɪ'diːmə(r)] **N** rédempteur *m*; *Rel* **the R.** le Rédempteur

redefine [ˌriːdɪ'faɪn] **VT** *(restate ▸ objectives, terms)* redéfinir; *(modify)* modifier

redefinition [ˌriːdefɪ'nɪʃən] **N** *(restatement ▸ of objectives, terms)* redéfinition *f*; *(modification)* modification *f*

redemption [rɪ'dempʃən] **N 1** *(from pawn)* dégagement *m*
2 *Fin (of annuity, debt, loan, mortgage)* remboursement *m*; *(of shares)* rachat *m*
3 *(gen) & Rel* rédemption *f*, rachat *m*; **past** *or* **beyond r.** *(person)* perdu à tout jamais, qui ne peut être racheté; *(situation, position)* irrémédiable, irrécupérable; *(book, furniture)* irréparable, irrécupérable; *Fig* **this setback proved his r.** ce revers de fortune fut son salut
4 *(of slave)* rachat *m*
▸▸ *Fin* ***redemption date*** date *f* d'échéance; *Fin* ***redemption fee, redemption premium*** prime *f* de

remboursement; *Fin* ***redemption value*** valeur *f* de remboursement *ou* de rachat

redemptive [rɪˈdemptɪv] **ADJ** rédempteur

redeploy [ˌriːdɪˈplɔɪ] **VT** *(troops, forces, resources)* redéployer; *(workers ▸ to new job)* reconvertir; *(▸ to new location)* réaffecter

redeployment [ˌriːdɪˈplɔɪmənt] **N** *(of troops, resources)* redéploiement *m*; *(of workers ▸ to new job)* reconversion *f*; *(▸ to new location)* réaffectation *f*

redesign [ˌriːdɪˈzaɪn] **VT** *(plan of room, garden etc)* redessiner; *(layout of furniture, rooms etc)* réagencer; *(system)* repenser; *(book cover, poster etc)* refaire le design de

redevelop [ˌriːdɪˈveləp] **VT 1** *(urban area, site)* réaménager; *(region)* revaloriser; *(tourism, industry)* relancer **2** *(argument)* réexposer **3** *Phot* redévelopper

redevelopment [ˌriːdɪˈveləpmənt] **N 1** *(of urban area, site)* réaménagement *m*; *(of region)* revalorisation *f*; *(of tourism, industry)* relance *f*; **urban r.** rénovation *f* urbaine, réaménagement *m* urbain **2** *Phot* redéveloppement *m*

▸▸ ***redevelopment area*** zone *f* de réaménagement

red-eye [ˈredaɪ] *Am Fam* **N 1** *(whisky)* mauvais whisky[a] *m*, ≃ gnôle *f* **2** *(night flight)* vol *m* de nuit

▸▸ ***red-eye flight*** vol *m* de nuit

red-eyed **ADJ** aux yeux rouges; **she was r. from crying/staying up all night** elle avait les yeux rouges d'avoir pleuré/d'avoir passé une nuit blanche

red-faced **ADJ** *(naturally)* rougeaud; *Fig (with anger, embarrassment)* rouge de confusion *ou* de honte

red-haired **ADJ** roux (rousse), aux cheveux roux; **a r. girl** une rousse

red-handed **ADV to be caught r.** être pris en flagrant délit *ou* la main dans le sac

redhead [ˈredhed] **N** *(person)* roux (rousse) *m,f*, rouquin(e) *m,f*

red-headed **ADJ** roux (rousse), aux cheveux roux; **a r. girl** une rousse

red-hot **ADJ 1** *(metal)* chauffé au rouge

2 *(very hot)* brûlant

3 *Fam Fig (keen)* passionné[a], enthousiaste[a]

4 *Fam (recent ▸ news, information)* de dernière minute[a]

5 *Fam (sure ▸ tip, favourite)* certain[a], sûr[a]; **Rangers are the r. favourites to win the cup** Rangers sont les grandissimes favoris de la coupe

6 *Fam (expert)* calé; **he's r. on the best investments** c'est un expert en matière d'investissements

7 *(strong ▸ passion)* fort, puissant

8 *Fam (sensational ▸ scandal, story)* croustillant, sensationnel[a]

N *Am Fam (hot dog)* hot-dog *m* épicé[a]

▸▸ *Bot* ***red-hot poker*** tritoma *m*

redial *Tel* **VT** [ˌriːˈdaɪəl] **to r. a number** refaire un numéro

VI [ˌriːˈdaɪəl] refaire le numéro

N [ˈriːdaɪəl] rappel *m* du dernier numéro; **the latest model has automatic r.** le dernier modèle est muni du système de rappel du dernier numéro

▸▸ ***redial feature*** rappel *m* du dernier numéro

redirect [ˌriːdɪˈrekt] **VT 1** *(mail)* faire suivre, réexpédier; *(telephone call etc)* réacheminer; *Comput (e-mail)* faire suivre (**to** à); *(aeroplane, traffic)* dérouter (**to** sur) **2** *Fig (efforts, attentions)* réorienter

redirection [ˌriːdɪˈrekʃən] **N 1** *(of letter etc)* réacheminement *m*, réexpédition *f* **2** *(of plane)* déroutement *m*

rediscount *Com* **N** [ˈriːdɪskaʊnt] réescompte *m*

VT [ˌriːˈdɪskaʊnt] réescompter

rediscover [ˌriːdɪˈskʌvə(r)] **VT** redécouvrir

redistribute [ˌriːdɪˈstrɪbjuːt] **VT** *(money, wealth, objects)* redistribuer; *(tasks)* réassigner; *Pol* **to r. seats** redécouper les circonscriptions électorales

redistribution [ˈriːˌdɪstrɪˈbjuːʃən] **N** redistribution *f*; **the r. of wealth** la redistribution *ou* la répartition des richesses

redistrict [ˌriːˈdɪstrɪkt] **VT** *Am Admin (into new administrative districts)* modifier le découpage administratif de; *(into new electoral districts)* modifier le découpage électoral de

redistricting [ˌriːˈdɪstrɪktɪŋ] **N** *Am Admin (of administrative districts)* redécoupage *m* administratif; *(of electoral districts)* redécoupage *m* électoral

red-letter day **N** jour *m* à marquer d'une pierre blanche; **this has been a r. for everyone** ceci a été un jour mémorable pour tout le monde

redneck [ˈrednek] *Am Fam Pej* **N** plouc *mf*, bouseux(euse) *m,f (du Sud des États-Unis)*; **a r. politician/cop** un homme politique/flic tout ce qu'il y a de plus réactionnaire

COMP *(attitude)* de plouc, borné[a]

redness [ˈrednɪs] **N** *(UNCOUNT) (of face, sky etc)* rougeur *f*; *(of hair)* rousseur *f*; *(inflammation)* rougeurs *fpl*

redo [ˌriːˈduː] (*pt* **redid** [-ˈdɪd], *pp* **redone** [-ˈdʌn]) **VT** refaire; *(hair)* recoiffer; *(repaint)* refaire, repeindre; *Comput* rétablir, refaire

redolent [ˈredələnt] **ADJ 1** *(perfumed)* **r. of** *or* **with lemon** qui sent le citron, qui a une odeur de citron **2** *(evocative, reminiscent)* **a house r. of the past** une maison qui évoque le passé

redouble [ˌriːˈdʌbəl] **VT 1** *(in intensity)* redoubler; **to r. one's efforts** redoubler ses efforts *ou* d'efforts **2** *Cards* surcontrer

VI *Cards* surcontrer

N *Cards* surcontre *m*

redoubt [rɪˈdaʊt] **N** *Mil* redoute *f*; *Fig* forteresse *f*

redoubtable [rɪˈdaʊtəbəl] **ADJ** *(formidable)* redoutable, terrifiant; *(awe-inspiring)* impressionnant

redound [rɪˈdaʊnd] **VI** *Formal* **to r. on** *or* **upon sb** *(negatively)* retomber sur qn; *(positively)* rejaillir sur qn; **to r. to sb's advantage** être *ou* rejaillir à l'avantage de qn; **her behaviour can only r. to her credit** sa conduite ne peut qu'être portée à son crédit

red-pencil **VT** *(correct)* biffer au crayon rouge; *(censor)* censurer

redraft **VT** [ˌriːˈdrɑːft] *(bill, contract)* rédiger de nouveau; *(demand)* reformuler; *(text)* remanier

N [ˈriːdrɑːft] *(rewriting)* nouvelle rédaction *f*; *(reformulation)* reformulation *f*

redress [rɪˈdres] **VT** *(grievance, errors)* réparer; *(wrong)* réparer, redresser; *(situation)* rattraper; **to r. the balance** rétablir l'équilibre

N *(gen) & Law* réparation *f*; **to seek r. for sth** demander réparation de qch; **there is no r.** il n'y a pas de recours

re-dress [ˈriː-] **VT to r. a wound** refaire le pansement d'une blessure

redshank [ˈredʃæŋk] **N** *Orn* chevalier *m* gambette

redskin [ˈredskɪn] **N** *Fam Old-fashioned* Peau-Rouge *mf*, = terme raciste désignant un Amérindien

redstart [ˈredstɑːt] **N** *Orn* rouge-queue *m*, rossignol *m* des murailles

redtop [ˈredtɒp] **N** *Br Fam* tabloïde[a] *m*, journal *m* à sensation[a]

reduce [rɪˈdjuːs] **VT 1** *(risk, scale, time, workload)* réduire, diminuer; *(temperature)* abaisser; *(speed)* réduire, ralentir; *(in length)* réduire, raccourcir; *(in size)* réduire, rapetisser, diminuer; *(in weight)* réduire, alléger; *(in height)* réduire, abaisser; *(in thickness)* réduire, amenuiser; *(in strength)* réduire, affaiblir; **the record has been reduced by two seconds** le record a été amélioré de deux secondes; **I'm trying to r. my sugar consumption by half** j'essaie de réduire ma consommation de sucre de moitié; **his prison sentence was reduced to two years** sa peine de prison a été ramenée à deux ans; **to r. the risk (of sth)** réduire le risque (de qch); **to r. output** ralentir la production; **to r. speed** *(driver)* diminuer *ou* réduire la vitesse, ralentir

2 *Com & Fin (price)* baisser, réduire; *(rate, expenses, cost, investment)* réduire; *(tax)* alléger, réduire; *(goods)* solder, réduire le prix de; *(output)* ralentir; **the shirt was reduced to £15** la chemise était soldée à 15 livres

3 *(render)* **to r. sth to ashes/to a pulp** réduire qch en cendres/en bouillie; **to r. sb to silence/to poverty/to submission** réduire qn au silence/à la pauvreté/à l'obéissance; **his words reduced her to tears** ses paroles l'ont fait fondre en larmes; **we were reduced to helpless laughter** nous riions sans pouvoir nous arrêter; **she was reduced to buying her own pencils** elle en était réduite à acheter ses crayons elle-même; **is this what I've been reduced to?** j'en suis donc réduit à cela?

4 *Culin (sauce)* faire réduire

5 *Chem & Math* réduire; **to r. fractions to a common denominator** réduire des fractions à un dénominateur commun

6 *Med (fracture)* réduire; *(swelling)* résorber, résoudre

7 *(dilute)* diluer

8 *Arch or Literary (subjugate)* soumettre

9 *Mil* **to r. sb to the ranks** rétrograder *ou* casser qn

VI 1 *Culin* réduire **2** *(slim)* maigrir

reduced [rɪˈdjuːst] **ADJ** *(price, rate, scale)* réduit; *(goods)* soldé, en solde; **at r. prices** à prix réduits; **to buy sth at a r. price** acheter qch à prix réduit; **on a r. scale** à une échelle réduite; **r. to clear** *(sign)* articles en solde; **to buy/sell sth at a r. rate** acheter/vendre qch à tarif réduit; *Euph* **to be/to live in r. circumstances** être/vivre dans la gêne

reducer [rɪˈdjuːsə(r)] **N** *Tech* réducteur *m*; *Phot* affaiblisseur *m*; *(for slimmer)* appareil *m* d'amaigrissement

reducible [rɪˈdjuːsəbəl] **ADJ** réductible

reduction [rɪˈdʌkʃən] **N 1** *(lessening ▸ gen)* réduction *f*, diminution *f*; *(▸ in temperature)* baisse *f*, diminution *f*; *(▸ in length)* réduction *f*, raccourcissement *m*; *(▸ in weight)* réduction *f*, diminution *f*; *(▸ in strength)* réduction *f*, affaiblissement *m*; *(▸ in speed)* réduction *f*, ralentissement *m*; **staff reductions** compression *f* de personnel; **the r. of the argument to basic principles** la réduction du débat à des principes fondamentaux

2 *Com & Fin (of price)* baisse *f*, diminution *f*; *(of rate, expenses, cost, investment)* réduction *f*; *(of taxes)* allègement *m*; *(on goods)* rabais *m*, remise *f*; **to make a 5 percent r. on an article** faire une remise de 5 pour cent sur un article; **cash r.** *(discount)* remise *f ou* escompte *m* au comptant; *(refund)* remise *f* en espèces; **I'll give you a r.** *(on purchase)* je vous fais un prix; **big reductions** *(sign)* rabais, soldes

3 *Chem, Math & Phot* réduction *f*

4 *Tech (of gear)* démultiplication *f*

5 *Med (of fracture)* réduction *f*; *(of swelling)* résorption *f*

reductionism [rɪˈdʌkʃənɪzəm] **N** *Phil* réductionnisme *m*

reductionist [rɪˈdʌkʃənɪst] *Phil* **N** réductionniste *mf*

ADJ réductionniste

redundancy [rɪˈdʌndənsɪ] (*pl* **redundancies**) **N** *Br (layoff)* licenciement *m*; *(unemployment)* chômage *m*; **there is a high level of r. here** il y a un fort taux de chômage ici; **5,000 redundancies have been announced** on a annoncé 5000 licenciements **2** *(superfluousness)* caractère *m* superflu; *(tautology)* pléonasme *m* **3** *Comput, Ling & Tel* redondance *f*

▸▸ *Br* ***redundancy notice*** préavis *m* de licenciement; *Br* ***redundancy payment*** indemnité *f* de licenciement

redundant [rɪˈdʌndənt] **ADJ 1** *Br (worker)* licencié, au chômage; **to make sb r.** *(of employer)* licencier qn, mettre qn au chômage; *(of technology etc)* entraîner le licenciement de qn; **to be made r.** être licencié, être mis au chômage; **2** *(superfluous)* redondant, superflu; *(tautologous)* pléonastique; **much of what you write is r.** il y a beaucoup de redites *ou* de répétitions dans ce que vous écrivez **3** *Comput, Ling & Tel* redondant

redwood [ˈredwʊd] **N** *Bot* séquoia *m*

re-echo [ˌriː-] **VT** répercuter, renvoyer

VI retentir; **the wood re-echoed with his shouts** le bois retentit *ou* résonna de ses cris

reed [riːd] **N 1** *Bot* roseau *m* **2** *Mus* anche *f*; **the reeds** les instruments *mpl* à anche **3** *(idiom)* **he's a broken r.** on ne peut pas compter sur lui

COMP *(chair, mat)* en roseau *ou* roseaux, fait de roseaux
▸▸ *Orn* ***reed bunting*** bruant *m* des roseaux; ***reed instrument*** instrument *m* à anche; *Orn* ***reed warbler*** fauvette *f* des roseaux, rousserolle *f* effarvatte

re-edit **VT** [ˌriː-] rééditer

re-educate **VT** [ˌriː-] rééduquer

re-education **N** [riː-] rééducation *f*

reedy [ˈriːdɪ] *(compar* **reedier**, *superl* **reediest)** **ADJ** **1** *(place)* envahi par les roseaux **2** *(voice, sound)* flûté, aigu(uë)

reef [riːf] **N 1** *(in sea)* récif *m*, écueil *m*; *Fig* écueil *m*; **to hit a r.** *(ship)* faire naufrage sur un récif; *Fig (plans etc)* se heurter à un écueil **2** *Mining* filon *m* **3** *Naut* ris *m*
VT *(spar)* rentrer; **to r. a sail** prendre un ris dans une voile
▸▸ ***reef knot*** nœud *m* plat

reefer [ˈriːfə(r)] **N 1** *(garment)* caban *m* **2** *Fam (cannabis cigarette)* joint *m*, stick *m* **3** *Am Fam (for transporting goods* ▸ *truck)* camion *m* frigorifique; *(*▸ *ship)* navire *m* frigorifique; *(*▸ *train compartment)* wagon *m* frigorifique; *(refrigerator)* chambre *f* frigorifique
▸▸ ***reefer jacket*** caban *m*

reek [riːk] **VI** *(smell)* puer, empester; **it reeks of tobacco in here** ça empeste *ou* ça pue le tabac ici; *Fig* **the whole affair reeks of corruption** toute cette affaire sent la corruption à plein nez; *Fam Fig* **this place reeks of money** cet endroit pue le fric
N puanteur *f*

reel [riːl] **N 1** *(for thread, film, tape)* bobine *f*; *(for hose)* dévidoir *m*, enrouleur *m*; *(for cable)* enrouleur *m*; *(for rope-making)* caret *m*; **(fishing) r.** moulinet *m* (de pêche) **2** *(film, tape)* bande *f*, bobine *f*; **r. to r. (tape recorder)** magnétophone *m* à bobines **3** *(dance)* quadrille *m (écossais ou irlandais)*; *Mus* branle *m (écossais ou irlandais)*
VI 1 *(stagger)* tituber; *(sway)* chanceler; **the blow sent me reeling across the room** le coup m'a envoyé valser à travers la pièce; **to r. back/down/out** reculer/descendre/sortir en chancelant; **a drunk came reeling downstairs** un ivrogne descendait l'escalier en titubant **2** *Fig (whirl* ▸ *head, mind)* tournoyer; **my head is reeling** j'ai la tête qui tourne; **he is still reeling from the shock** il ne s'est pas encore remis du choc; **the room started reeling before her** la pièce a commencé à tournoyer autour d'elle; **to make sb's senses r.** donner le vertige à qn
VT bobiner
▸ **reel in** **VT SEP** *(cable, hose)* enrouler; *(fish)* remonter, ramener; *(line)* enrouler, remonter; *Fig* **he charmed her for months, then he just reeled her in** il lui a fait du charme pendant des mois, puis il l'a tout simplement cueillie
▸ **reel off** **VT SEP** *(list, speech, story)* débiter

re-elect [ˈriː-] **VT** réélire; **she is sure to be re-elected** sa réélection est assurée

re-election [ˈriː-] **N** réélection *f*; **to stand** *or* **to run for r.** se représenter aux élections

reeling [ˈriːlɪŋ] **ADJ** *(gait)* titubant

re-embark [ˈriː-] **VT** *(passengers)* rembarquer
VI rembarquer; *Fig* **to r. on sth** recommencer qch

re-embarkation [ˈriː-] **N** rembarquement *m*

re-emerge [ˈriː-] **VI** *(new facts)* ressortir; *(idea, clue)* réapparaître; *(problem, question)* se reposer; *(person, sun)* réapparaître; *(from hiding, tunnel)* ressortir, ressurgir

re-employ [ˈriː-] **VT** *(worker)* réembaucher, rembaucher

re-employment [ˈriː-] **N** *(of worker)* réembauche *f*

re-enact [ˈriː-] **VT 1** *(accident, crime, battle)* reconstituer; *(scene, mistakes)* reproduire **2** *Admin & Pol (regulation, legislation)* remettre en vigueur

re-enactment [ˈriː-] **N 1** *(of accident, crime, battle)* reconstitution *f*; *(of scene, mistakes)* reproduction *f* **2** *Admin, Law & Pol (of regulation, legislation)* remise *f* en vigueur

re-engage [ˈriː-] **VT 1** *(troops)* rengager; *(employee)* réengager, rengager, réembaucher **2** *(mechanism)* rengrener; **to r. the clutch** rembrayer

re-engagement [ˈriː-] **N 1** *(of troops, of worker)* réengagement *m*, rengagement *m*, réembauche *f* **2** *Tech* rengrènement *m*

re-engineer [ˈriː-] **VT** *(process, system, company)* réorganiser

re-engineering [ˈriː-] **N** *(of process, system, company)* réorganisation *f*

re-enlist [ˈriː-] *Mil* **VT** réengager, rengager
VI se réengager, se rengager

re-enter [ˈriː-] **VI 1** *(gen)* rentrer, entrer à nouveau; *Astron* rentrer dans l'atmosphère; *(musical instrument)* faire une *ou* sa rentrée; *Theat* **r. Macbeth** Macbeth rentre **2** *(candidate)* **to r. for an exam** se réinscrire à un examen
VT 1 *(room, country)* rentrer dans, entrer à nouveau dans; *(atmosphere)* rentrer dans; **the spacecraft re-entered the atmosphere** le vaisseau spatial est rentré dans l'atmosphère; **to r. the job market** se remettre à chercher du travail **2** *(date, name)* réinscrire, inscrire de nouveau; *Comput (data)* saisir à nouveau, réintroduire

re-entrant [ˈriː-] *Math* **N** angle *m* rentrant
ADJ rentrant

re-entry [ˈriː-] *(pl* **re-entries)** **N 1** *(gen) & Astron* rentrée *f* **2** *Mus (of theme)* reprise *f*
▸▸ *Astron* ***re-entry point*** point *m* de rentrée

re-establish [ˈriː-] **VT 1** *(relations, order)* rétablir; *(custom, practice)* restaurer; *(law)* remettre en vigueur **2** *(person)* réhabiliter, réintégrer; **the team have re-established themselves as the best in the country** l'équipe s'est imposée de nouveau comme la meilleure du pays; **to r. oneself** *or* **one's position** rétablir sa position

re-establishment [ˈriː-] **N 1** *(of relations, order)* rétablissement *m*; *(of custom, practice)* restauration *f*; *(of law)* remise *f* en vigueur **2** *(of person)* réintégration *f*

reeve [riːv] *(pt & pp* **reeved** *or* **rove** [rəʊv]) **N 1** *Br Hist (in town)* premier magistrat *m*; *(in manor)* intendant *m* **2** *Can* président *m* (du conseil municipal)
VT *Naut (rope* ▸ *pass)* passer; *(*▸ *fasten)* capeler

re-examination [ˈriː-] **N** *(of question, case)* réexamen *m*; *Law (of witness)* nouvel interrogatoire *m*

re-examine [ˈriː-] **VT** *(question, case)* réexaminer, examiner de nouveau; *(candidate)* faire repasser un examen à; *Law (witness)* réinterroger, interroger de nouveau

re-export **VT** [ˈriː-] réexporter
N [ˌriːˈekspɔːt] **1** *(of goods)* réexportation *f* **2** *(product)* marchandise *f* de réexportation

re-exportation [ˈriː-] **N** réexportation *f*

ref[1], **ref.** *(written abbr* **reference)** réf.; **your r.** v/réf.; **our r.** n/réf.

ref[2] [ref] **N** *Br Fam Sport (abbr* **referee)** arbitre [□] *m*

reface [ˌriːˈfeɪs] **VT** *(wall, building)* ravaler

refashion [ˌriːˈfæʃən] **VT** *(object)* refaçonner; *(image)* reconstruire

refectory [rɪˈfektərɪ] *(pl* **refectories)** **N 1** *(in monastery, school)* réfectoire *m* **2** *(university canteen)* restaurant *m* universitaire
▸▸ ***refectory table*** = table longue et étroite *(souvent en chêne massif)*

refer [rɪˈfɜː(r)] *(pt & pp* **referred**, *cont* **referring)** **VT 1** *(submit* ▸ *matter, proposal etc)* soumettre (**to** à); **the dispute has been referred to arbitration** le litige a été soumis à arbitrage *ou* à l'arbitrage d'un médiateur; **I r. the matter to you for a decision** je m'en remets à vous pour prendre une décision sur la question; **the question has been referred to Jane** la question a été soumise à Jane; **to r. a case to a higher court** renvoyer *ou* déférer une affaire à une instance supérieure; **the contract has been referred to us** le contrat nous a été soumis; *Banking* **to r. a cheque to drawer** refuser d'honorer un chèque; **r. to drawer** *(on cheque)* voir le tireur
2 *(send, direct* ▸ *person)* renvoyer; **my doctor referred me to the hospital/to a specialist** mon docteur m'a envoyé à l'hôpital/chez un spécialiste; **the doctor's going to r. me** le docteur va m'envoyer chez un spécialiste; **I r. you to Ludlow's book** je vous renvoie au livre de Ludlow
3 *Law* **to r. the accused** déférer l'accusé
4 *Univ (student)* refuser, recaler; *(thesis)* renvoyer pour révision
5 *Med* **the pain may be referred to another part of the body** il peut y avoir irradiation de la douleur dans d'autres parties du corps
▸ **refer to** **VT INSEP 1** *(allude to)* faire allusion *ou* référence à, parler de; **I don't know what you are referring to** je ne sais pas à quoi vous faites allusion *ou* de quoi vous parlez; **we won't r. to it again** nous n'en reparlons plus; **he keeps referring to me as Dr Rayburn** il ne cesse de m'appeler Dr Rayburn; **he never refers to it** il n'en parle jamais; **that comment refers to you** cette remarque s'adresse à vous; **they r. to themselves as martyrs** ils se qualifient eux-mêmes de martyrs; *Com* **referring to your letter** suite à votre lettre **2** *(relate to)* correspondre à, faire référence à; *(apply, be connected to)* s'appliquer à, s'adresser à; **the numbers r. to footnotes** les chiffres renvoient à des notes en bas de page; **these measures only r. to taxpayers** ses mesures ne s'appliquent qu'aux contribuables **3** *(consult* ▸ *notes)* consulter; *(*▸ *book, page, instructions)* se reporter à; **I shall have to r. to my boss** je dois en référer à *ou* consulter mon patron

referee [ˌrefəˈriː] **N 1** *Sport* arbitre *m*; *(in tennis)* juge-arbitre *m*
2 *Br (for job)* = personne pouvant fournir des références; **I was r.** *or* **I acted as his r. for his last job** je lui ai fourni des références pour son dernier emploi; **please give the names of three referees** veuillez nous donner le nom de trois personnes susceptibles de fournir des références
3 *Law* conciliateur *m*, médiateur *m*
4 *Fin* **r. in case of need** *(on bill of exchange)* adresse *f* au besoin
VT *Sport* arbitrer; **he refereed the game well** il a bien arbitré
VI *Sport* être arbitre, servir d'arbitre

reference [ˈrefrəns] **N 1** *(allusion)* allusion *f* (**to** à); *(mention)* mention *f* (**to** de); **to make r. to sth** faire allusion à qch; **if any r. is made to me** si on parle de moi; **a talk on the environment with particular r. to...** un exposé sur l'environnement abordant tout particulièrement...; **with r. to your request for more funding** en ce qui concerne votre demande de fonds supplémentaires; *Com* **with r. to your letter of 25 June...** suite à votre courrier du 25 juin...; **with r. to what was said at the meeting** à propos de *ou* en ce qui concerne ce qui a été dit au cours de la réunion
2 *(consultation)* consultation *f*; **without r. to me** sans me consulter; **for r. only** *(on library book)* consultation sur place; *(on document etc in circulation)* pour information seulement; **to keep sth for future r.** garder qch à titre d'information; **for future r., please note...** pour votre information à l'avenir, veuillez noter...
3 *(in code, catalogue)* référence *f*; *(on map)* coordonnées *fpl*; *(in book* ▸ *allusion)* référence *f*, allusion *f*; *(*▸ *footnote, cross-reference)* renvoi *m*; **it's a biblical r.** c'est une allusion *ou* une référence biblique
4 *Com* référence *f*; **quote this r.** rappelez cette référence; **your/our r.** votre/notre référence
5 *Banking (testimonial)* référence *f*
6 *(recommendation* ▸ *for job)* références *fpl*; **to give sb a r.** fournir des références à qn; **to give sb as a r.** se recommander de qn; **I'm often asked for references** on me demande souvent de fournir des références; **to take up references** prendre contact avec *ou* contacter les personnes dont un candidat se recommande; **you can use my name as a r.** vous pouvez me citer comme référence; **banker's r.** références *fpl* bancaires
7 *(remit* ▸ *of commission)* compétence *f*, pouvoirs *mpl*; **the question is outside the committee's (terms of) r.** la question n'est pas de la compétence du comité
8 *Ling* référence *f*
9 *Law (of case)* renvoi *m*
COMP *(material, section)* de référence; *(value, quantity)* de référence, étalon
VT 1 *(refer to)* faire référence à **2** *(thesis)* établir la liste des citations dans; *(quotation)* donner la référence de **3** *Comput* référencer

▸▸ ***reference book*** ouvrage *m* de référence; ***reference library*** bibliothèque *f* d'ouvrages de référence; *Typ* ***reference mark*** appel *m* de note; ***reference number*** numéro *m* de référence; ***reference point*** point *m* de repère; ***reference room*** *(in public library)* salle *f* de lecture; *(in university)* salle *f* de consultation; ***reference work*** ouvrage *m* de référence

referendum [ˌrefəˈrendəm] *(pl* **referendums** *or* **referenda** [-də]) **N** référendum *m*; **to hold a r.** organiser un référendum

referral [rɪˈfɜːrəl] **N 1** *(forwarding)* renvoi *m*
2 *(consultation)* consultation *f*
3 *Univ (of thesis)* renvoi *m* pour révision
4 *(person)* patient(e) *m,f (envoyé par son médecin chez un spécialiste)*

refill VT [ˌriːˈfɪl] *(glass)* remplir (à nouveau); *(lighter, canister)* recharger
N [ˈriːfɪl] *(for pen, lighter, notebook)* recharge *f*; *(for propelling pencil)* mine *f* de rechange; **do you need a r.?** *(drink)* je vous en ressers un?
COMP [ˈriːfɪl] de rechange

refillable [ˌriːˈfɪləbəl] **ADJ** rechargeable

refinance [ˌriːˈfaɪnæns] **VT** *(loan)* refinancer
VI *(company)* se refinancer

refinancing [ˌriːˈfaɪnænsɪŋ] **N** refinancement *m*; **to get r. from a bank** se refinancer auprès d'une banque

refine [rɪˈfaɪn] **VT 1** *(oil, sugar)* raffiner; *(ore, metal)* affiner; *(by distillation)* épurer **2** *(model, manners)* améliorer; *(judgment, taste)* affiner; *(lecture, speech)* parfaire, peaufiner; *(technique, machine)* perfectionner

▸**refine on, refine upon VT INSEP** parfaire, peaufiner

refined [rɪˈfaɪnd] **ADJ 1** *(oil, sugar)* raffiné; *(ore)* affiné; *(by distillation)* épuré **2** *(style, person, taste)* raffiné

refinement [rɪˈfaɪnmənt] **N 1** *(of oil, sugar)* raffinage *m*; *(of metals, ore)* affinage *m*; *(by distillation)* épuration *f*
2 *(of person)* délicatesse *f*, raffinement *m*; *(of taste, culture)* raffinement *m*; *(of morals)* pureté *f*; **a man of r.** un homme raffiné; **his lack of r.** ses manières peu raffinées
3 *(of style, discourse, language)* subtilité *f*, raffinement *m*
4 *(improvement)* perfectionnement *m*, amélioration *f*; **to make refinements to** *(machine)* perfectionner; *(plan, tactics etc)* parfaire; **all the latest technical refinements** tous les derniers perfectionnements techniques

refiner [rɪˈfaɪnə(r)] **N** *(of oil, sugar)* raffineur (euse) *m,f*; *(of metal)* affineur(euse) *m,f*

refinery [rɪˈfaɪnərɪ] *(pl* **refineries**) **N** *(for oil, sugar)* raffinerie *f*; *(for metals)* affinerie *f*

refining [rɪˈfaɪnɪŋ] **N** *(of oil, sugar)* raffinage *m*; *(of metal)* affinage *m*

refit *(pt & pp* **refitted**, *cont* **refitting**) **VT** [ˌriːˈfɪt] **1** *(repair)* remettre en état **2** *(refurbish)* rééquiper, renouveler l'équipement de
VI [ˌriːˈfɪt] *(ship)* être remis en état
N [ˈriːfɪt] *(of plant, factory)* rééquipement *m*, nouvel équipement *m*; *(of ship)* remise *f* en état, réparation *f*; **the yacht is under r.** le yacht est en cours de réparation

reflate [ˌriːˈfleɪt] **VT 1** *(ball, tyre)* regonfler **2** *Econ* relancer

reflation [ˌriːˈfleɪʃən] **N** *Econ* relance *f*

reflationary [ˌriːˈfleɪʃənərɪ] **ADJ** *Econ (policy)* de relance
▸▸ *Econ* ***reflationary pressure*** pression *f* pour une relance (économique)

reflect [rɪˈflekt] **VT 1** *(image)* refléter; *(sound, heat)* renvoyer; *(light)* réfléchir; **her face was reflected in the mirror/the water** son visage se reflétait dans la glace/dans l'eau; **she saw herself reflected in the window** elle a vu son image dans la vitre
2 *Fig (credit)* faire jaillir, faire retomber; **the behaviour of a few reflects discredit on us all** le comportement de quelques-uns porte atteinte à l'honneur de tous; *Fig* **he bathed in the reflected glory of his wife's achievements** il tira gloire de la réussite de sa femme
3 *Fig (personality, reality)* traduire, refléter; **the graph reflects population movements** le graphique traduit les mouvements de population; **her personal problems are reflected in her poor performance at school** elle a des problèmes personnels et ses résultats scolaires s'en ressentent
4 *(think)* penser, se dire; *(say)* dire, réfléchir; **I often r. that...** je me dis souvent *ou* je me fais souvent la réflexion que...; **Peter might know, she reflected** Peter saura peut-être, songeait-elle
VI 1 *(light)* se réfléchir **2** *(think)* réfléchir; (**on** à *ou* sur)

▸**reflect on, reflect upon VT INSEP** *(negatively)* porter atteinte à, nuire à; *(positively)* rejaillir sur; *(cast doubt on)* mettre en doute, jeter le doute sur; **their behaviour reflects well on them** leur comportement leur fait honneur; **this will reflect badly upon the company** ceci va porter atteinte à l'image de l'entreprise; **how is that going to r. on the company?** quelles en seront les conséquences *ou* les répercussions pour l'image de l'entreprise?

reflecting [rɪˈflektɪŋ] **ADJ**
▸▸ *Astron* ***reflecting telescope*** téléscope *m* réflecteur

reflection [rɪˈflekʃən] **N 1** *(image)* reflet *m*; **can you see your r. in the mirror?** voyez-vous votre reflet *ou* votre image dans le miroir?; **there is some r. on the screen** il y a des reflets sur l'écran; *Fig* **the result was not a fair r. of the game** le résultat ne reflétait pas la manière dont le match s'était joué; *Fig* **this report is not an accurate r. of the situation** ce rapport ne donne pas un aperçu exact de la situation
2 *(action ▸ of light, sound, heat)* réflexion *f*
3 *(comment)* réflexion *f*, remarque *f*, observation *f*; **reflections on James Joyce/on Communism** réflexions sur James Joyce/sur le communisme
4 *(criticism)* critique *f*; **his book was seen as a r. on the government** son livre a été perçu comme une critique du gouvernement; **it's a good r. on the school** c'est bon pour la réputation de l'école; **their conduct is a (bad) r. on all of us** leur conduite nous fait du tort à tous; **it's no r. on their integrity** leur intégrité n'est pas en cause
5 *(deliberation)* réflexion *f*; *(thought)* pensée *f*; **on r.** après *ou* à la réflexion, en y réfléchissant; **to do sth without due r.** faire qch sans avoir suffisamment réfléchi

reflective [rɪˈflektɪv] **ADJ 1** *Opt (surface)* réfléchissant, réflecteur; *(power, angle)* réflecteur; *(light)* réfléchi **2** *(mind, person)* pensif, réfléchi; *(faculty)* de réflexion

reflectively [rɪˈflektɪvlɪ] **ADV** *(say)* d'un ton pensif; *(look at)* d'un air songeur

reflector [rɪˈflektə(r)] **N** réflecteur *m*; *Aut* catadioptre *m*
▸▸ ***reflector board*** panneau *m* réflecteur

reflex [ˈriːfleks] **N 1** *(gen) & Physiol* réflexe *m*; **to have good reflexes** avoir de bons réflexes; **to test sb's reflexes** tester les réflexes de qn **2** *Phot* (appareil *m*) reflex *m*
ADJ 1 *Physiol* réflexe
2 *Opt & Phys* réfléchi
3 *Phot* reflex *(inv)*
4 *Math* rentrant
▸▸ *Physiol* ***reflex action*** réflexe *m*; *Phot* ***reflex camera*** (appareil *m*) reflex *m*

reflexion *Br* = **reflection**

reflexive [rɪˈfleksɪv] **ADJ 1** *Gram* réfléchi **2** *Physiol* réflexe **3** *(in logic) & Math* réflexif
N *Gram (verb)* verbe *m* réfléchi; *(pronoun)* pronom *m* (personnel) réfléchi
▸▸ *Gram* ***reflexive pronoun*** pronom *m* réfléchi; *Gram* ***reflexive verb*** verbe *m* réfléchi

reflexively [rɪˈfleksɪvlɪ] **ADV** *Gram (in meaning)* au sens réfléchi; *(in form)* à la forme réfléchie

reflexology [ˌriːflekˈsɒlədʒɪ] **N** réflexologie *f*

refloat [ˌriːˈfləʊt] **VT 1** *(ship)* renflouer, mettre *ou* remettre à flot **2** *Fin (loan)* émettre de nouveau; *(company)* renflouer, remettre à flot; *(economy)* renflouer
VI être renfloué

reflux [ˈriːflʌks] **N** reflux *m*

refocus [ˌriːˈfəʊkəs] *(pt & pp* **refocused** *or* **refocussed**, *cont* **refocusing** *or* **refocussing**) **VT** *(projector, camera)* refaire la mise au point de; *Fig* **it has refocused attention on the problem** cela a attiré une nouvelle fois l'attention sur ce problème
VI refaire la mise au point

reforest [ˌriːˈfɒrɪst] = **reafforest**

reforestation [riːˌfɒrɪˈsteɪʃən] = **reafforestation**

reform [rɪˈfɔːm] **VT 1** *(modify ▸ law, system, institution)* réformer **2** *(person)* faire perdre ses mauvaises habitudes à; *(drunkard)* faire renoncer à la boisson; *(habits, behaviour)* corriger; **to r. oneself** s'amender, se corriger; **he's a reformed character** il s'est assagi, il a changé en bien
VI se corriger, s'amender
N réforme *f*
▸▸ *Am* ***reform school*** ≃ centre *m* d'éducation surveillée

re-form [riː-] **VT 1** *Mil (ranks)* remettre en rang, reformer; *(men)* rallier **2** *(return to original form)* rendre sa forme primitive *ou* originale à; *(in new form)* donner une nouvelle forme à; *(form again ▸ battalion, group etc)* reformer
VI 1 *Mil (men)* se remettre en rangs; *(ranks)* se reformer **2** *(group, band, battalion)* se reformer

reformat [ˌriːˈfɔːmæt] *(pt & pp* **reformatted**, *cont* **reformatting**) *Comput* **VT** reformater
VI reformater

reformation [ˌrefəˈmeɪʃən] **N 1** *(of law, institution)* réforme *f* **2** *(of behaviour)* réforme *f*; *(of criminal, addict etc)* réinsertion *f*
• **Reformation N the R.** la Réforme

reformatory [rɪˈfɔːmətrɪ] **ADJ** réformateur
N *Br* ≃ maison *f* de redressement, *Am* ≃ centre *m* d'éducation surveillée

reformatting [ˌriːˈfɔːmætɪŋ] **N** *Comput* reformatage *m*

reformer [rɪˈfɔːmə(r)] **N** réformateur(trice) *m,f*

reformism [rɪˈfɔːmɪzəm] **N** réformisme *m*

reformist [rɪˈfɔːmɪst] **ADJ** réformiste
N réformiste *mf*

refract [rɪˈfrækt] **VT** réfracter; **to be refracted** être réfracté
VI se réfracter

refracting [rɪˈfræktɪŋ] **ADJ** *(material, prism)* réfringent; *(angle)* de réfraction
▸▸ ***refracting telescope*** réfracteur *m*, lunette *f* astronomique

refraction [rɪˈfrækʃən] **N** *(phenomenon)* réfraction *f*; *(property)* réfringence *f*

refractive [rɪˈfræktɪv] **ADJ** *Phys* réfringent
▸▸ ***refractive index*** indice *m* de réfraction

refractivity [ˌriːfrækˈtɪvɪtɪ] **N** *Phys* réfringence *f*

refractor [rɪˈfræktə(r)] **N 1** *Opt & Phys (apparatus)* appareil *m* de réfraction; *(material, medium)* milieu *m* réfringent **2** *Astron (telescope)* réfracteur *m*, lunette *f* astronomique

refractory [rɪˈfræktərɪ] **ADJ 1** *Formal (person)* réfractaire, récalcitrant, rebelle **2** *Physiol & Tech* réfractaire

refrain [rɪˈfreɪn] **VI** *(hold back)* **to r. from sth/doing sth** s'abstenir de qch/de faire qch; **to r. from comment** s'abstenir de tout commentaire; **he couldn't r. from smiling** il n'a pu s'empêcher de sourire; **please r. from smoking** *(sign)* prière de ne pas fumer
N *Mus, Literature & Fig* refrain *m*

refrangible [rɪˈfrændʒɪbəl] **ADJ** *Phys & Opt* réfrangible

refreeze [ˌriːˈfriːz] *(pt* **refroze** [-ˈfrəʊz], *pp* **refrozen** [-ˈfrəʊzən]) **VT** *(ice, ice-cream)* remettre au congélateur; *(food)* recongeler

refresh [rɪˈfreʃ] **VT 1** *(revive ▸ of drink, shower, ice)* rafraîchir; *(▸ of exercise, swim)* revigorer; *(▸ of sleep)* reposer, détendre; **I feel refreshed** *(after shower, drink)* je me sens rafraîchi; *(after exercise)* je me sens revigoré; *(after rest)* je me sens reposé; **they woke refreshed** ils se sont réveillés frais et dispos **2** *(memory, experience)* rafraîchir; **to r. one's memory** se rafraîchir la mémoire; **let me r. your memory** laissez-moi vous rafraîchir la mémoire; **she wanted to r. her German** elle voulait se remettre à niveau en allemand; **can I r.**

your drink for you? voulez-vous que je vous resserve? **3** *Comput (screen)* actualiser, rafraîchir
N *Comput* actualisation *f*, rafraîchissement *m*
▸▸ *Comput* ***refresh rate*** taux *m* d'actualisation *ou* de rafraîchissement

efresher [rɪˈfreʃə(r)] **N** *(drink)* boisson *f* rafraîchissante
▸▸ ***refresher course*** stage *m ou* cours *m* de recyclage

efreshing [rɪˈfreʃɪŋ] **ADJ 1** *(physically ▸ breeze)* rafraîchissant; *(▸ exercise)* tonique, revigorant; *(▸ bath, shower, cup of tea)* revigorant, ravigotant; *(▸ sleep)* réparateur, reposant; *(▸ holiday)* reposant **2** *(mentally ▸ idea)* original, stimulant; *(▸ sight)* réconfortant; *(▸ performance)* plein de vie; **a r. change** un changement agréable *ou* appréciable; **his honesty is r.** son honnêteté est comme une bouffée d'air frais *ou* est réconfortante

efreshingly [rɪˈfreʃɪŋlɪ] **ADV r. honest** d'une honnêteté rassurante; **she is r. different from most politicians/actresses** cela fait plaisir de voir qu'elle est différente de la plupart des politiques/des actrices

efreshment [rɪˈfreʃmənt] **N** *(of body, mind)* repos *m*, délassement *m*; **would you like some r.?** *(food)* voulez-vous manger un morceau?; *(drink)* voulez-vous boire quelque chose?
• **refreshments NPL** *(drinks)* rafraîchissements *mpl*; *(snacks)* collation *f*; **refreshments available** *(sign)* buvette
▸▸ ***refreshment bar, refreshment stall*** buvette *f*

efrigerant [rɪˈfrɪdʒərənt] **ADJ** réfrigérant
N 1 *(substance)* mélange *m* réfrigérant **2** *Med* réfrigérant *m*

efrigerate [rɪˈfrɪdʒəreɪt] **VT** *(in cold store)* frigorifier, réfrigérer; *(freeze)* congeler; *(put in fridge)* mettre au réfrigérateur; **keep refrigerated** *(on packaging)* conserver au réfrigérateur
▸▸ ***refrigerated lorry*** camion *m* frigorifique; ***refrigerated meat*** viande *f* frigorifiée *ou* réfrigérée; ***refrigerated ship*** navire *m* frigorifique

efrigeration [rɪˌfrɪdʒəˈreɪʃən] **N** réfrigération *f*; **to keep sth under r.** garder qch au réfrigérateur
▸▸ ***refrigeration plant*** installation *f* frigorifique

efrigerator [rɪˈfrɪdʒəreɪtə(r)] **N** *(in kitchen)* réfrigérateur *m*, Frigidaire® *m*; *(storeroom)* chambre *f* froide *ou* frigorifique
COMP *(ship, lorry, unit)* frigorifique

efuel [ˌriːˈfjʊəl] *(Br pt & pp* **refuelled**, *cont* **refuelling**, *Am pt & pp* **refueled**, *cont* **refueling**) **VT** ravitailler (en carburant); *Fig* **to r. speculation** alimenter les conjectures
VI se ravitailler en carburant; *Fig (eat, drink)* se restaurer; **the aeroplane refuelled in mid-flight** l'avion s'est ravitaillé en vol

efuelling, *Am* **refueling** [ˌriːˈfjʊəlɪŋ] **N** ravitaillement *m* (en carburant); **to make a r. stop** *Aut* s'arrêter pour prendre de l'essence; *Aviat* faire une escale technique
COMP *(boom, tanker)* de ravitaillement
▸▸ ***refuelling aircraft*** avion *m* de ravitaillement (en vol)

efuge [ˈrefjuːdʒ] **N 1** *(shelter ▸ gen)* refuge *m*, abri *m*; *(▸ in mountains)* refuge *m*; *Br (▸ for crossing road)* refuge *m*; **(battered) women's r.** foyer *m* pour femmes battues **2** *(protection ▸ from weather)* **to take r. from the rain** s'abriter de la pluie; **she took r. in the tent** elle s'est réfugiée sous la tente; **to seek r.** *(from attack, reality)* chercher refuge; **he sought r. from his persecutors** il chercha un asile pour échapper à ses persécuteurs; **to seek r. in drugs** chercher refuge dans la drogue; **to take r. in fantasy** se réfugier dans l'imagination; **place of r.** *(from rain)* abri *m*; *(from pursuit)* (lieu *m* d')asile *m*; *Literary* **God is my r.** Dieu est mon refuge

efugee [ˌrefjʊˈdʒiː] **N** réfugié(e) *m,f*; **economic r.** migrant(e) *m,f* économique
▸▸ ***refugee camp*** camp *m* de réfugiés; ***refugee status*** statut *m* de réfugié

efund VT [rɪˈfʌnd] **1** *(expenses, excess, person)* rembourser; **to r. sth to sb, to r. sb sth** rembourser qch à qn; **they refunded me the postage** ils m'ont remboursé les frais de port **2** *Fin & Law (monies)* restituer
N [ˈriːfʌnd] **1** *Com* remboursement *m*; **to get a r.** se faire rembourser **2** *Fin & Law (of monies)* restitution *f* **3** *Am (of tax)* bonification *f* de trop-perçu

refundable [ˌriːˈfʌndəbəl] **ADJ** remboursable

refunding [ˌriːˈfʌndɪŋ] **N** remboursement *m*

refurbish [ˌriːˈfɜːbɪʃ] **VT** remettre à neuf

refurbishment [ˌriːˈfɜːbɪʃmənt] **N** remise *f* à neuf

refusable [rɪˈfjuːzəbəl] **ADJ** *(offer, request)* refusable, rejetable

refusal [rɪˈfjuːzəl] **N 1** *(of request, suggestion)* refus *m*, rejet *m*; **to meet with a r.** *(person)* se heurter à *ou* essuyer un refus; **my offer/invitation met with a r.** je me suis vu refuser mon offre/mon invitation; **to receive a r.** recevoir une réponse négative; **we don't understand your r. to compromise** nous ne comprenons pas les raisons pour lesquelles vous vous opposez à un compromis
2 *Horseriding* refus *m*
3 *(denial ▸ of justice, truth)* refus *m*, déni *m*
4 *Com* **to have first r. (on sth)** avoir la priorité (sur qch); **to give sb first r.** donner la priorité à qn; **you promised me first r. on the car** tu m'as promis que je serais le premier à qui tu proposerais (d'acheter) la voiture
▸▸ *Mktg* ***refusal rate*** taux *m* de refus

refuse[1] [rɪˈfjuːz] **VT 1** *(turn down ▸ invitation, gift)* refuser; *(▸ offer)* refuser, décliner; *(▸ request, proposition)* refuser, rejeter; **to r. to do sth** refuser de *ou Formal* se refuser à faire qch; **I r. to accept that all is lost** je refuse de croire que tout soit perdu; **to r. to comment** se refuser à tout commentaire; **I refused to take delivery of the parcel** j'ai refusé le paquet; **to r. to fight** refuser le combat; **the car refuses to start** la voiture ne veut pas démarrer; **to be refused** essuyer un refus; **she refused him** *(would not marry him)* elle l'a rejeté **2** *(deny ▸ permission)* refuser (d'accorder); *(▸ help, visa)* refuser; **he was refused entry** on lui a refusé l'entrée; **they were refused a loan** on leur a refusé un prêt; **we were refused permission to see him** on nous a refusé la permission de le voir; **I don't see how we can r. them** je ne vois pas comment on peut le leur refuser **3** *Horseriding* refuser; **to r. a jump** refuser de sauter
VI *(person)* refuser; *(horse)* refuser l'obstacle

refuse[2] [ˈrefjuːs] **N** *Br (household)* ordures *fpl* (ménagères); *(garden)* détritus *mpl*; *(industrial)* déchets *mpl*; **household/garden r.** ordures *fpl* ménagères; **no r.** *(sign)* défense de déposer les ordures
▸▸ ***refuse bag*** sac *m* à ordures; *Br* ***refuse bin*** poubelle *f*; *Br* ***refuse chute*** vide-ordures *m inv*; *Br* ***refuse collection*** ramassage *m* d'ordures; *Br* ***refuse collector*** éboueur *m*; *Br* ***refuse disposal*** traitement *m* des ordures; ***refuse disposal unit*** broyeur *m* d'ordures; *Br* ***refuse dump*** *(public)* décharge *f* (publique), dépotoir *m*

> Note that the French word **refus** is a false friend and is never a translation for the English word **refuse**. It means **refusal**.

refusenik, refusnik [rɪˈfjuːznɪk] **N** refuznik *mf*

refutation [ˌrefjuːˈteɪʃən] **N** réfutation *f*

refute [rɪˈfjuːt] **VT** *(disprove)* réfuter; *(deny)* nier

regain [rɪˈgeɪn] **VT 1** *(territory)* reconquérir; *(health)* recouvrer; *(strength)* retrouver; *(sight, composure)* retrouver, recouvrer; *(glory)* retrouver; **to r. possession of sth** rentrer en possession de qch; **to r. consciousness** reprendre connaissance; **to r. one's balance** retrouver l'équilibre; **to r. one's footing** reprendre pied **2** *Formal (get back to ▸ road, place, shelter)* regagner

regal [ˈriːgəl] **ADJ** royal; *Fig (person, bearing)* majestueux; *(banquet, decor)* somptueux

regale [rɪˈgeɪl] **VT to r. sb with sth** régaler qn de qch

regalia [rɪˈgeɪljə] **NPL 1** *(insignia)* insignes *mpl* **2** *(finery, robes)* accoutrement *m*, atours *mpl*; **to be in full r.** *(judge, general)* être en grande tenue; *Fig Hum (woman)* être paré de tous ses atours

regally [ˈriːgəlɪ] **ADV** royalement, majestueusement

regard [rɪˈgɑːd] **VT 1** *(consider)* considérer, regarder; *(treat)* traiter; **I r. him as a brother** je le considère comme un frère; **I r. their conclusions as correct** *or* **to be correct** je tiens leurs conclusions pour correctes; **I prefer to r. the whole thing as a joke** je préfère considérer toute l'affaire comme une plaisanterie; **he regards himself as an expert** il se considère comme *ou* il se prend pour un expert
2 *(esteem)* estimer, tenir en estime; **to r. sb highly** tenir qn en grande estime; **highly regarded** très estimé
3 *Formal (observe)* regarder, observer
N 1 *(notice, attention)* considération *f*, attention *f*; **to pay r. to sth** tenir compte de qch, faire attention à qch; **they paid scant r. to my explanations** ils n'ont guère fait attention à mes explications; **having r. to his age** en tenant compte de *ou* eu égard à son âge
2 *(care, respect)* souci *m*, considération *f*, respect *m*; **they have no r. for your feelings** ils ne se soucient pas de vos sentiments; **to have scant r. for human rights** se soucier peu des droits de l'homme; **they showed no r. for our wishes** ils n'ont tenu aucun compte de nos souhaits; **without r. to race or colour** sans distinction de race ni de couleur; **with no r. for his health** sans se soucier de sa santé; **out of r. for** par égard pour; **without due r. to** sans tenir compte de
3 *(connection)* **in this r.** à cet égard
4 *(esteem)* estime *f*, considération *f*; **to have great r. for sb** avoir beaucoup d'estime pour qn; **I hold them in high r.** je les tiens en grande estime
5 *Formal (eyes, look)* regard *m*
• **regards NPL 1** *(in letter)* **regards, Peter** bien cordialement, Peter; **kind regards, best regards** bien à vous, amitiés, bien amicalement **2** *(in greetings)* **give them my regards** transmettez-leur mon bon souvenir; **he sends his regards** vous avez le bonjour de sa part
• **as regards PREP** en ce qui concerne, pour ce qui est de; **as regards the cost** en ce qui concerne le coût, quant au coût
• **in regard to, with regard to PREP** en ce qui concerne

> Note that the French word **regard** is a false friend and is never a translation for the English word **regard**. It means **look, gaze**.
>
> Note that the French verb **regarder** is a false friend and is never a translation for the English verb **to regard**. It means **to look at, to watch**.

regardful [rɪˈgɑːdfʊl] **ADJ** *Formal* **to be r. of** *(needs, wishes, difficulties)* être attentif à, faire attention à; *(children, interests, image)* s'occuper de, soigner, se soucier de

regarding [rɪˈgɑːdɪŋ] **PREP** quant à, en ce qui concerne, pour ce qui est de; **questions r. management** des questions relatives à la gestion

regardless [rɪˈgɑːdlɪs] **ADV** *(in any case)* quand même, en tout cas; *(without worrying)* sans s'occuper *ou* se soucier du reste; **they carried on r.** ils continuèrent quand même
• **regardless of PREP** *(consequences, danger, noise etc)* sans se soucier de; **r. of what you think** *(without bothering)* sans se soucier de ce que vous pensez; *(whatever your opinion)* indépendamment de ce que vous pouvez penser; **r. of the danger** sans se soucier du danger; **r. of the expense** sans regarder à la dépense

regatta [rɪˈgætə] **N** régate *f*

regency [ˈriːdʒənsɪ] *(pl* **regencies**) **N** régence *f*
• **Regency COMP** *(style, furniture, period)* Regency *(inv)*, de la Régence anglaise *(1811–20)*

regenerate VT [rɪˈdʒenəreɪt] régénérer; **to r. interest in sth** provoquer un regain d'intérêt pour qch, raviver l'intérêt pour qch
VI [rɪˈdʒenəreɪt] *(industry, party etc)* se régénérer; *(tail, organ etc)* repousser

regeneration [rɪˌdʒenəˈreɪʃən] **N** *(gen)* régénération *f*; *(of interest)* regain *m*; *(of urban area)* reconstruction *f*, rénovation *f*

regenerative [rɪˈdʒenərətɪv] **ADJ** régénérateur

regent [ˈriːdʒənt] **N 1** *Hist* régent(e) *m,f*; **prince r.** prince *m* régent **2** *Am* = membre du conseil d'administration d'une université

reggae [ˈregeɪ] **N** reggae *m*
COMP *(song, group, singer)* reggae *(inv)*

regicide ['redʒɪsaɪd] **N** *(person)* régicide *mf*; *(crime)* régicide *m*

regime, régime [reɪ'ʒiːm] **N 1** *Pol & (in sociology)* régime *m*; **under the present r.** sous le régime actuel **2** *Med* régime *m (sous surveillance médicale)*
►► ***regime change*** changement *m* de régime

regimen ['redʒɪmen] **N** régime *m (sous surveillance médicale)*

regiment N ['redʒɪmənt] *Mil & Fig* régiment *m*; **there's enough to feed a r.** il y a de quoi nourrir un régiment
VT ['redʒɪment] *(organize)* enrégimenter; *(discipline)* soumettre à une discipline trop stricte

regimental [ˌredʒɪ'mentəl] *Mil* **ADJ** *(mess, dress, flag)* régimentaire, du régiment; *(band, mascot)* du régiment; *Fig (organization)* trop discipliné, enrégimenté
• **regimentals NPL** uniforme *m ou* tenue *f* (militaire); **in full regimentals** en grande tenue
►► ***regimental sergeant major*** ≃ adjudant-chef *m*

regimentation [ˌredʒɪmen'teɪʃən] **N** *Pej (of business, system)* organisation *f* quasi militaire; *(in school)* discipline *f* étouffante *ou* trop sévère

regimented ['redʒɪmentɪd] **ADJ** *Pej (lifestyle etc)* strict; **it's a very r. organization** c'est une organisation très rigide *ou* stricte

region ['riːdʒən] **N 1** *Geog & Admin* région *f*; **in the Liverpool r.** dans la région de Liverpool; **the regions** les provinces **2** *(in body)* région *f*; **in the lower back r.** dans la région lombaire **3** *(of knowledge, sentiments)* domaine *m*
• **in the region of PREP** environ; **in the r. of 10 kg** dans les 10 kg (environ); **in the r. of £500** aux environs de *ou* dans les 500 livres

regional ['riːdʒənəl] **ADJ** régional
►► *Br* ***regional development*** *(building, land development)* aménagement *m* du territoire; *(for jobs)* action *f* régionale; *Br* ***regional development corporation*** = organisme pour l'aménagement du territoire

regionalism ['riːdʒənəlɪzəm] **N** régionalisme *m*

regionalization, -isation [ˌriːdʒənəlaɪ'zeɪʃən] **N** régionalisation *f*

REGISTER ['redʒɪstə(r)]

N
• registre **1, 3–6** • liste **1**
• cahier d'appel **1** • livre de bord **1**
• enregistreur **2** • caisse **2**

VT
• enregistrer **1, 6** • inscrire **1**
• indiquer **2** • exprimer **2**
• piger **4** • envoyer en recommandé **5**

VI
• s'inscrire **1** • donner une indication **2**

N 1 *(book)* registre *m*; *(list)* liste *f*; *Sch* registre *m* de présences, cahier *m* d'appel; *(on ship)* livre *m* de bord; **to keep a r.** tenir un registre; **to enter sth in a r.** inscrire qch dans un registre; *Sch* **to call** *or* **to take the r.** faire l'appel; **electoral r.** liste *f* électorale; **r. of shipping** registre *m* maritime; **r. of births, marriages and deaths** registre *m* de l'état civil
2 *(gauge)* enregistreur *m*; *(counter)* compteur *m*; *(cash till)* caisse *f* (enregistreuse)
3 *(pitch ► of voice)* registre *m*, tessiture *f*; *(► of instrument)* registre *m*
4 *Ling* registre *m*, niveau *m* de langue
5 *Typ* registre *m*; **to be in/out of r.** être/ne pas être en registre
6 *Comput (of memory)* registre *m*
VT 1 *(record ► name)* (faire) enregistrer, (faire) inscrire; *(► on list)* inscrire; *(► birth, death)* déclarer; *(► vehicle)* (faire) immatriculer; *(► trademark)* déposer; *(► readings)* relever, enregistrer; *Fin (► shares)* immatriculer; *Comput (► software)* inscrire; **to r. a complaint** déposer une plainte; **to r. a protest** protester; **to r. one's vote** exprimer son vote, voter; **is the car registered in your name?** est-ce que la voiture est à votre nom?; **she is not registered at this hotel** elle n'est pas descendue à cet hôtel
2 *(indicate ► of thermometer, dial etc)* indiquer; *(► of person, face)* exprimer; **the needle is registering 700 kg** l'aiguille indique 700 kg; **the earthquake registered seven on the Richter scale** le séisme a atteint sept sur l'échelle de Richter; **winds registering 100 mph** ≃ des vents atteignant 160 km/h; **her face registered disbelief** l'incrédulité se lisait sur son visage
3 *(obtain ► success)* remporter; *(► defeat)* essuyer
4 *Fam (understand)* saisir, piger; **she hadn't registered the danger she was in** elle ne s'était pas rendue compte du danger qu'elle courait
5 *(parcel, letter)* envoyer en recommandé
6 *(at railway station, airport etc ► suitcase)* (faire) enregistrer
7 *Typ* mettre en registre
8 *Tech* (faire) aligner, faire coïncider
VI 1 *(for course)* s'inscrire, se faire inscrire (**for** à); *(at hotel)* s'inscrire sur *ou* signer le registre (de l'hôtel); *(voter)* se faire inscrire sur la liste électorale; **foreign nationals must r. with the police** les ressortissants étrangers doivent se faire enregistrer au commissariat de police; **to r. with a GP** se faire inscrire auprès d'un médecin traitant
2 *(instrument)* donner une indication; **the current was too weak to r.** le courant était trop faible pour donner une indication; **the quake was so small it barely even registered** la secousse a été à peine perceptible
3 *Fam (be understood)* **I did give them the address but I don't think it registered** je leur ai bien donné l'adresse mais je ne crois pas qu'ils l'aient retenue□; **he explained it to me yesterday but it didn't r.** il me l'a expliqué hier, mais je n'ai pas fait attention; **her success didn't really r. with her** elle ne s'était pas vraiment rendu compte de son succès□
4 *Tech* coïncider, être aligné; *Typ* être en registre
►► *Admin* ***register office*** bureau *m* de l'état civil; *Naut* ***register ton*** tonneau *m* (de jauge)

registered ['redʒɪstəd] **ADJ 1** *(student, elector)* inscrit; *Br (charity)* ≃ reconnu d'utilité publique; *Fin (bond, securities, stocks)* nominatif; **r. unemployed** inscrit au chômage; *Br* **to be r. disabled** avoir une carte d'invalidité **2** *(letter, parcel, mail)* recommandé; *Br* **send it r.** envoyez-le en recommandé
►► ***registered address*** domicile *m*; *Fin* ***registered capital*** capital *m* déclaré; ***registered childminder*** nourrice *f* agréée; ***registered company*** société *f* inscrite au registre du commerce; ***registered name*** nom *m* déposé; ***Registered Nurse*** infirmier (ère) *m,f* diplômé(e) d'État; *Br* ***registered office*** siège *m* social; *Br* ***registered post*** envoi *m* recommandé; *St Exch* ***registered stock*** titres *mpl* nominatifs, valeurs *fpl* nominatives; ***registered trademark*** marque *f* déposée; *Comput* ***registered user*** utilisateur(trice) *m,f* disposant d'une licence

registrar [ˌredʒɪ'strɑː(r)] **N 1** *Br Admin* officier *m* de l'état civil; **r.'s office** bureau *m* de l'état civil
2 *Br & NZ Med* chef *m* de clinique
3 *Law* greffier *m*
4 *Am Univ* chef *m* du service *ou* du bureau des inscriptions; *Br Univ* secrétaire *m* général
5 *Com & Fin* **companies' r.** responsable *mf* du registre des sociétés
►► ***the Registrar General*** le Conservateur des actes de l'état civil

registration [ˌredʒɪ'streɪʃən] **N 1** *(of name)* enregistrement *m*; *(of student)* inscription *f*; *(of voter)* inscription *f* sur la liste électorale; *(of trademark)* dépôt *m*; *(of vehicle, shares, company)* immatriculation *f*; *(of luggage)* enregistrement *m*; *(of birth, death, marriage)* déclaration *f*; **when does r. start?** *(for university, evening classes)* quand les inscriptions commencent-elles? **2** *Br Sch* appel *m* **3** *(of mail)* recommandation *f*
►► ***registration card*** *(for enrolling on course etc)* fiche *f* d'inscription; *(for foreign guests)* fiche *f* voyageur; *(for non-EU guests)* fiche *f* de police; *Comput* licence *f*; *Br Aut* ***registration document*** ≃ carte *f* grise; *Fin* ***registration fees*** droits *mpl* d'inscription; *Br* ***registration number*** *(of vehicle)* numéro *m* d'immatriculation; **the car has the r. number E123 SYK** la voiture est immatriculée E123 SYK

registry ['redʒɪstrɪ] *(pl* **registries) N 1** *(registra-tion)* enregistrement *m*; *Univ* inscription *f*
2 *(office)* bureau *m* d'enregistrement
3 *Naut* immatriculation *f*; **a ship of Japanese r.** un navire immatriculé au Japon; **port of r.** port *m* d'attache
4 *Comput (Windows® file)* registre *m*
►► *Br Admin* ***registry office*** bureau *m* de l'éta[t] civil; **to be married at a r. office** se marier civile[-]ment, ≃ se marier à la mairie

regrade [ˌriː'greɪd] **VT** *Am Sch (essay)* renoter, no[-]ter de nouveau; *(employee, nurse, officer, objects)* reclasser

regrading [ˌriː'greɪdɪŋ] **N** *(of employee, nurse, o[f-]ficer)* reclassement *m*

regress VI [rɪ'gres] **1** *Biol & Psy* régresser; **to r. t[o] childhood** régresser à un stade infantile **2** *Sch (g[o] back)* reculer, revenir en arrière
N ['riːgres] **1** *Biol & Psy* régression *f* **2** *(retreat)* re[-]cul *m*, régression *f*

regression [rɪ'greʃən] **N 1** *Biol & Psy* régression **2** *(retreat)* recul *m*, régression *f*

regressive [rɪ'gresɪv] **ADJ** *Biol, Fin & Psy* régres[-]sif; *(movement)* de recul
►► *Econ* ***regressive tax*** impôt *m* régressif; *Eco[n]* ***regressive taxation*** imposition *f* régressive

regret [rɪ'gret] *(pt & pp* **regretted**, *cont* **regretting) VT** *(be sorry about ► action, behaviour)* regretter; **r. to say** *(apologize)* j'ai le regret de *ou* je regrett[e] de dire; *(unfortunately)* hélas, malheureuse[-]ment; **we r. to inform you that…** nous avons l[e] regret de vous informer que…; **to r. doing** *or* **hav[-]ing done sth** regretter d'avoir fait qch; **I r. eve[r] mentioning it** je regrette d'en avoir jamais parlé; **I r. not being able to come** je regrette *ou* je sui[s] désolé de ne pouvoir venir; **she regrets that sh[e] never met Donovan** elle regrette de n'avoir jamai[s] rencontré Donovan; **it is to be regretted that…** i[l] est regrettable *ou* à regretter que… + *subjonc[-]tive*; **you'll live to r. this!** vous le regretterez!; **th[e] airline regrets any inconvenience caused to passen[-]gers** la compagnie s'excuse pour la gêne occa[-]sionnée
N *(sorrow, sadness)* regret *m*; **with r.** avec regre[t] **we announce with r. the death of our chairma[n]** nous avons le regret de vous faire part de l[a] mort de notre directeur; **much to our r.** à notr[e] grand regret; **to express one's regrets at** *or* **abou[t] sth** exprimer ses regrets devant qch; **I have n[o] regrets** je n'ai pas de regrets, je ne regrette rie[n] **do you have any regrets about** *or* **for what you did** regrettez-vous ce que vous avez fait?; **my only r[.] is that I didn't resign earlier** je n'ai qu'un regre[t] c'est de ne pas avoir donné ma démission plu[s] tôt; **to send sb one's regrets** *(condolences)* expri[-]mer ses regrets à qn; *(apologies)* s'excuser au[-]près de qn

regretful [rɪ'gretfʊl] **ADJ** *(person)* plein de re[-]grets; *(expression, attitude)* de regret; **to be** *or* **t[o] feel r. about sth** regretter qch

regretfully [rɪ'gretfʊlɪ] **ADV** *(sadly)* avec regre[t] *(unfortunately)* malheureusement

regrettable [rɪ'gretəbəl] **ADJ** *(unfortunate)* re[-]grettable, malencontreux; *(inconvenient)* fâ[-]cheux, ennuyeux; **it is most r. that you were no[t] informed** il est fort regrettable que vous n'aye[z] pas été informé

regrettably [rɪ'gretəblɪ] **ADV** *(unfortunately)* malheureusement, malencontreusement; *(in[-]conveniently)* fâcheusement; **r. few people wer[e] present** il est regrettable que si peu de person[-]nes soient venues; **a joke in r. poor taste** une pla[i-]santerie dont le mauvais goût est à déplorer

regroup [ˌriː'gruːp] **VT** regrouper
VI se regrouper

regrouping [riː'gruːpɪŋ] **N** regroupement *m*

REGULAR ['regjʊlə(r)]

N
• habitué **1** • militaire de carrière **3**
• régulier **4** • ordinaire **5**

ADJ
• régulier **1–3, 5, 8** • habituel **2**
• fidèle **2** • permanent **3**
• uni **4** • vrai **6**
• sympa **7**

N **1** *(customer ▸ in bar, restaurant)* habitué(e) *m,f*; *(▸ in shop)* client(e) *m,f* fidèle
2 *(contributor, player)* **she's a r. on our column** elle contribue régulièrement à notre rubrique; **he's a r. in the team** il joue régulièrement dans l'équipe
3 *Mil (soldier)* militaire *m* de carrière
4 *Rel* religieux *m* régulier, régulier *m*
5 *Am (fuel)* ordinaire *m*
6 *Am Pol (loyal party member)* membre *m* fidèle (du parti)
ADJ **1** *(steady, even ▸ features, footsteps, movement, sound)* régulier; *(▸ breathing, pulse)* régulier, égal; *(▸ meetings, service, salary)* régulier; **at r. intervals** à intervalles réguliers; **on a r. basis** régulièrement; **it's a r. occurrence** cela arrive régulièrement; **she has r. treatment** elle suit régulièrement un traitement; **he was a man of r. habits** il avait ses habitudes; **to keep r. hours** se lever et se coucher à heures régulières; **to have r. bowel movements** aller régulièrement à la selle; **bran will keep you r.** le son vous fera aller régulièrement à la selle; **to be as r. as clockwork** être réglé comme une horloge
2 *(usual ▸ brand, dentist, procedure, supplier)* habituel; *(▸ customer)* régulier, fidèle; *(▸ listener, reader)* fidèle; *(▸ price, model)* courant; *(▸ size)* courant, standard; **my r. bedtime** l'heure à laquelle je me couche habituellement; **who is your r. doctor?** qui est votre médecin traitant?; **a r. visitor to the house** un/une des habitué(e)s de la maison; **a r. Coke** un Coca® normal; **to go through the r. channels** suivre la filière normale *ou* habituelle
3 *(permanent ▸ agent)* attitré, permanent; *(▸ police force)* permanent, régulier; *(▸ army)* de métier; *(▸ soldier)* de carrière
4 *(smooth, level)* uni, égal
5 *Gram & Math* régulier
6 *Fam (as intensifier)* vrai□, véritable□; **a r. mess** une vraie pagaille
7 *Am Fam (pleasant)* sympa, chouette; **a r. guy** un type sympa
8 *Rel (clergy)* régulier
9 *Am Pol (loyal to party)* fidèle au parti
ADV *Fam* régulièrement□
▸▸ *Am Aut* **regular (grade) gas** (essence *f*) ordinaire *m*; *Gram* **regular verb** verbe *m* régulier

---

egularity [ˌregjʊ'lærɪtɪ] *(pl* **regularities***)* N régularité *f*; **to do sth with unfailing r.** faire qch avec une régularité infaillible

egularize, -ise ['regjʊləraɪz] VT régulariser

egularly ['regjʊləlɪ] ADV régulièrement

egulate ['regjʊleɪt] VT **1** *(control, adjust ▸ machine, expenditure)* régler; *(▸ flow)* réguler **2** *(organize ▸ habit, life)* régler; *(▸ with rules)* réglementer; **he followed a well regulated diet** il suivit un régime équilibré; **rules regulating the use of additives** les réglementations qui régissent l'emploi des additifs

egulating ['regjʊleɪtɪŋ] ADJ *(knob, switch, valve)* de réglage; *(hormone, mechanism)* régulateur; **self-r.** à réglage automatique
▸▸ ***regulating body*** autorité *f* de régulation

egulation [ˌregjʊ'leɪʃən] N **1** *(ruling)* règlement *m*; **it's contrary to** *or* **against (the) regulations** c'est contraire au règlement; **it complies with EU regulations** c'est conforme aux dispositions communautaires; **safety regulations** règles *fpl* de sécurité; **fire regulations** consignes *fpl* en cas d'incendie; **building regulations** normes *fpl* de construction; **(food) hygiene regulations** normes *fpl* d'hygiène alimentaire **2** *(adjustment, control ▸ of machine)* réglage *m*; *(▸ of flow, voltage)* régulation *f* **3** *(by law ▸ of food additives etc)* réglementation *f*; *(▸ of information)* contrôle *m*
COMP *(size, haircut, issue, dress)* réglementaire; *(pistol, helmet)* d'ordonnance

egulator ['regjʊleɪtə(r)] N **1** *(person)* régulateur (trice) *m,f* **2** *(body)* instance *f* de contrôle **3** *(apparatus)* régulateur *m*
▸▸ ***regulator valve*** régulateur *m*

egulatory ['regjʊlətərɪ] ADJ *(framework)* réglementaire; *(authority)* de contrôle
▸▸ ***regulatory body*** instance *f* de contrôle

egulo ['regjʊləʊ] N *Br* **r. 4** thermostat 4

regurgitate [rɪ'gɜːdʒɪteɪt] VT *(food)* régurgiter; *Fig (facts)* régurgiter, reproduire
VI *(bird)* dégorger

regurgitation [rɪˌgɜːdʒɪ'teɪʃən] N régurgitation *f*

rehab ['riːhæb] N **to be in r.** faire une cure de désintoxication
▸▸ ***rehab centre*** centre *m* de désintoxication

rehabilitate [ˌriːə'bɪlɪteɪt] VT **1** *(convict, drug addict, alcoholic)* réhabiliter; *(restore to health)* rééduquer; *(find employment for)* réinsérer **2** *(reinstate ▸ idea, style)* réhabiliter **3** *(renovate ▸ area, building)* réhabiliter

rehabilitation [ˈriːəˌbɪlɪ'teɪʃən] N **1** *(of disgraced person, memory, reputation)* réhabilitation *f*; *(of convict, alcoholic, drug addict)* réhabilitation *f*; *(of disabled person)* rééducation *f*; *(of unemployed)* réinsertion *f* **2** *(of idea, style)* réhabilitation *f* **3** *(of area, building)* réhabilitation *f*
▸▸ ***rehabilitation centre*** *(for work training)* centre *m* de réadaptation; *(for drug addicts)* centre *m* de désintoxication

rehash *Fam Pej* VT [ˌriː'hæʃ] **1** *Br (rearrange)* remanier□ **2** *(repeat ▸ argument)* ressasser□; *(▸ programme)* reprendre□; *(▸ artistic material)* remanier□
N ['riːhæʃ] réchauffé *m*; **it's just a r.** ce n'est que du réchauffé; **it was a r. of her first novel** c'était une resucée de son premier roman

rehearsal [rɪ'hɜːsəl] N **1** *also Fig (practice)* répétition *f*; **to have** *or* **to hold a r.** faire une répétition; **the play is currently in r.** ils sont en train de répéter; *Fig* **the naval exercises were just a r. for the real thing** les exercices navals n'étaient qu'une répétition **2** *Literary (recital ▸ of list, facts, complaints)* récit *m*, énumération *f*; *(▸ of old arguments)* répétition *f*
▸▸ ***rehearsal room*** salle *f* de répétition; ***rehearsal script*** scénario *m* de répétition

rehearse [rɪ'hɜːs] VT **1** *also Fig (play, music, speech, coup d'état)* répéter; *(actors, singers, orchestra)* faire répéter; **well rehearsed** *(play, performance)* bien répété, répété avec soin; *(actor)* qui a bien répété son rôle, qui sait son rôle sur le bout des doigts; *(request, coup d'état, applause)* bien *ou* soigneusement préparé; **I rehearsed what I was going to say** j'ai préparé ce que j'allais dire **2** *Literary (recite ▸ list, facts, complaints)* réciter, énumérer; *(▸ old arguments)* répéter, ressasser
VI *Mus & Theat* répéter

reheat [ˌriː'hiːt] VT réchauffer

rehouse [ˌriː'haʊz] VT reloger

rehousing [ˌriː'haʊzɪŋ] N relogement *m*

rehydration [ˌriːhaɪ'dreɪʃən] N *Med* réhydratation *f*

reign [reɪn] N règne *m*; **in** *or* **under the r. of** sous le règne de; **r. of terror** règne *m* de terreur
VI **1** *(rule)* régner **2** *Fig (predominate)* régner; **silence reigned** le silence régnait; **to r. supreme** *(monarch, champion)* régner en maître; **it's the usual situation in the office: chaos reigns** c'est comme d'habitude au bureau: il y règne le plus grand chaos
▸ **reign over** VT INSEP *(of monarch, silence etc)* régner sur

reigning ['reɪnɪŋ] ADJ **1** *(monarch, emperor)* régnant **2** *(present ▸ champion)* en titre **3** *(predominant ▸ attitude, idea)* régnant, dominant

reimburse [ˌriːɪm'bɜːs] VT rembourser; **to r. sb (for) sth** rembourser qch à qn *ou* qn de qch; **I was reimbursed** je me suis fait rembourser

reimbursement [ˌriːɪm'bɜːsmənt] N remboursement *m*

reimplant [ˌriː'implɑːnt] VT *Med* réimplanter

reimplantation [riːˌimplɑːn'teɪʃən] N *Med* réimplantation *f*

reimport VT [ˌriːɪm'pɔːt] réimporter
N [ˌriː'impɔːt] réimportation *f*

reimportation [ˌriːɪmpɔː'teɪʃən] N réimportation *f*

reimpose [ˌriːɪm'pəʊz] VT réimposer

rein [reɪn] N **1** *(for horse)* rêne *f* **2** *Fig (control)* bride *f*; **to give (a) free r. to sb** laisser à qn la bride sur le cou; **to give free r. to one's emotions/imagination** donner libre cours à ses émotions/son imagination; **to keep a r. on sth** tenir qch en bride, maîtriser qch; **to keep a tight r. on sb** tenir la bride haute à qn; **to keep a tight r. on one's spending** surveiller étroitement ses dépenses
• **reins** NPL *(for horse, child)* rênes *f*; *Fig* **the reins of government** les rênes du gouvernement; **to hand over the reins** passer les rênes
▸ **rein back** VI tirer sur les rênes, serrer la bride
VT SEP faire ralentir, freiner
▸ **rein in** VI ralentir
VT SEP **1** *(horse)* serrer la bride à, ramener au pas **2** *Fig (person)* ramener au pas; *(emotions)* maîtriser, refréner

reincarnate VT [riː'ɪnkɑːneɪt] réincarner; **to be reincarnated** se réincarner (**as** sous les traits de *ou* sous la forme de)
ADJ [ˌriːɪn'kɑːnɪt] réincarné

reincarnation [ˌriːɪnkɑː'neɪʃən] N réincarnation *f*

reindeer ['reɪndɪə(r)] *(pl* **inv***)* N *Zool* renne *m*

reinforce [ˌriːɪn'fɔːs] VT **1** *Mil* renforcer **2** *(gen) & Constr (wall, heel)* renforcer **3** *Fig (demand)* appuyer; *(argument)* renforcer
▸▸ ***reinforced concrete*** béton *m* armé

reinforcement [ˌriːɪn'fɔːsmənt] N **1** *(strengthening ▸ of army, wall, fabric)* renforcement *m*; *(▸ of foundations)* consolidation *f*; *(▸ of concrete, glass)* armature *f* **2** *(gen) & Mil* renfort *m*; **reinforcements** renforts *mpl*
COMP *(troops, ships, supplies)* de renfort

reinitialize, -ise [ˌriːɪ'nɪʃəlaɪz] VT *Comput* réinitialiser

reinsert [ˌriːɪn'sɜːt] VT réinsérer

reinstall, *Am* **reinstal** [ˌriːɪn'stɔːl] VT *Comput* réinstaller

reinstallation [ˌriːɪnstə'leɪʃən] N *Comput* réinstallation

reinstate [ˌriːɪn'steɪt] VT *(employee)* réintégrer, rétablir (dans ses fonctions); *(idea, system)* rétablir, restaurer; *(clause etc)* réintroduire

reinstatement [ˌriːɪn'steɪtmənt] N réintégration *f*

reinstitute [ˌriː'ɪnstɪtjuːt] VT réintroduire

reinstitution [ˌriːɪnstɪ'tjuːʃən] N réintroduction *f*

reinsurance [ˌriːɪn'ʃɔːrəns] N réassurance *f*

reinsure [ˌriːɪn'ʃɔː(r)] VT réassurer

reintegrate [ˌriː'ɪntɪgreɪt] VT réintégrer; *(criminal, addict)* réinsérer

reintegration ['riːˌɪntɪ'greɪʃən] N réintégration *f*; *(of criminal, addict)* réinsertion *f*

reinterpret [ˌriːɪn'tɜːprɪt] VT réinterpréter

reinterpretation [ˌriːɪntɜːprɪ'teɪʃən] N réinterprétation *f*

reintroduce ['riːˌɪntrə'djuːs] VT réintroduire

reintroduction ['riːˌɪntrə'dʌkʃən] N réintroduction *f*

reinvent [ˌriːɪn'vent] VT *Fig* **to r. the wheel** refaire ce qui a déjà été fait; **to r. oneself** changer d'image

reinvest [ˌriːɪn'vest] VT réinvestir

reinvestigate [ˌriːɪn'vestɪgeɪt] VT *(question, problem)* examiner de nouveau; *(crime)* faire une nouvelle enquête sur

reinvestigation [ˌriːɪnˌvestɪ'geɪʃən] N *(of crime)* nouvelle enquête *f*

reinvestment [ˌriːɪn'vestmənt] N réinvestissement *m*

reinvigorate [ˌriːɪn'vɪgəreɪt] VT revigorer

reissue [ˌriː'ɪʃuː] VT **1** *(book)* rééditer; *(film)* rediffuser, ressortir **2** *Admin & Fin (banknotes, shares, stamps)* réémettre, émettre de nouveau
N **1** *(of book)* réédition *f*, *(of film)* rediffusion *f* **2** *Admin & Fin (of banknotes, shares, stamps)* nouvelle émission *f*

reiterate [ˌriː'ɪtəreɪt] VT réitérer, répéter

reiteration [ˌriːɪtə'reɪʃən] N réitération *f*, répétition *f*

reiterative [ˌriː'ɪtərətɪv] ADJ réitératif

reject VT [rɪ'dʒekt] **1** *(offer, suggestion, unwanted article)* rejeter; *(advances, demands)* rejeter, repousser; *(application, manuscript)* rejeter, refuser; *(suitor)* éconduire, repousser; *(belief,* *system, values)* rejeter; **to feel rejected** se sentir rejeté; **the machine keeps rejecting my coin** pas moyen que la machine accepte ma pièce

2 *Med (foreign body, transplant)* rejeter

3 *Comput* rejeter

4 *Mktg (goods)* refuser

N [ˈriːdʒekt] **1** *Com (in factory)* article *m ou* pièce *f* de rebut; *(in shop)* (article *m* de) second choix *m*; *Fig (person)* personne *f* marginalisée; *Fig* **I'm not going out with one of your rejects!** *(former boyfriend or girlfriend)* ne crois pas que je vais sortir avec un/une de tes ex! **2** *Comput* rejet *m*

COMP [ˈriːdʒekt] *(merchandise)* de rebut; *(for sale)* (de) second choix; *(shop)* d'articles de second choix

►► ***reject shop*** magasin *m* d'articles de second choix

rejection [rɪˈdʒekʃən] **N 1** *(of offer, manuscript)* refus *m*; *(of advances, demands)* rejet *m*; **to meet with r.** *(applicant etc)* essuyer un refus; *(offer, suggestion)* être rejeté; **to be afraid of r.** *(emotional)* avoir peur d'être rejeté **2** *Med* rejet *m*

►► ***rejection letter, rejection slip*** lettre *f* de refus

rejig [ˌriːˈdʒɪg] *(pt & pp* **rejigged,** *cont* **rejigging***)* **VT** *Br* **1** *(re-equip)* rééquiper, réaménager **2** *(reorganize)* réarranger, revoir

rejoice [rɪˈdʒɔɪs] **VI** se réjouir; **to r. at** *or* **over sth** se réjouir de qch; *Formal* **we r. to hear that you are safe** nous sommes ravis d'apprendre que vous êtes sain et sauf; *Hum* **he rejoices in the name of French-Edwardes** il a le privilège de porter le nom de French-Edwardes

rejoicing [rɪˈdʒɔɪsɪŋ] **N 1** *(joy)* réjouissance *f*; **it was the occasion of much r.** ce fut l'occasion de grandes réjouissances **2 rejoicings** *(festivities)* réjouissances *fpl*, festivités *fpl*; **there were great rejoicings on the day of the Coronation** il y a eu de grandes réjouissances le jour du couronnement

rejoin[1] [ˌriːˈdʒɔɪn] **VT 1** *(go back to)* rejoindre; *Mil* **to r. one's regiment** rallier *ou* rejoindre son régiment; *Naut* **to r. ship** rallier le bord; **we rejoined the main road a few miles later** nous avons rejoint la nationale quelques kilomètres plus loin **2** *(join again)* rejoindre; *(club, political party)* se réinscrire à

VI *(roads, lines etc)* se rejoindre

rejoin[2] [rɪˈdʒɔɪn] **VT** *(reply)* répliquer

VI *(reply)* répliquer

rejoinder [rɪˈdʒɔɪndə(r)] **N** réplique *f*

rejuvenate [rɪˈdʒuːvəneɪt] **VT** rajeunir

rejuvenating [rɪˈdʒuːvəneɪtɪŋ] **ADJ** rajeunissant

►► ***rejuvenating cream*** crème *f* de beauté rajeunissante

rejuvenation [rɪˌdʒuːvəˈneɪʃən] **N** rajeunissement *m*

rekey [ˌriːˈkiː] **VT** *Comput* refrapper

rekeying [ˌriːˈkiːɪŋ] **N** *Comput* refrappe *f*

rekindle [ˌriːˈkɪndəl] **VT** *(fire)* rallumer, attiser; *Fig (enthusiasm, desire, hatred)* raviver, ranimer

VI *(fire)* se rallumer; *Fig (feelings)* se ranimer

relapse [rɪˈlæps] **N** *Med & Fig* rechute *f*; **to have a r.** faire une rechute, rechuter

VI 1 *Med* rechuter, faire une rechute **2** *(go back)* retomber; **to r. into alcoholism** retomber dans l'alcoolisme; **to r. into unconsciousness** reperdre connaissance; **to r. into silence** redevenir silencieux

relate [rɪˈleɪt] **VT 1** *(tell ► events, story)* relater, raconter; *(► details, facts)* rapporter; **strange to r....** chose curieuse... **2** *(connect ► ideas, events)* rapprocher, établir un rapport *ou* un lien entre; **we can r. this episode to a previous scene in the novel** nous pouvons établir un lien entre cet épisode et une scène antérieure du roman

VI 1 *(connect ► idea, event)* se rapporter, se rattacher; **I don't understand how the two ideas r.** je ne comprends pas la relation entre les deux idées; **this relates to what I was just saying** ceci est lié à *ou* est en rapport avec ce que je viens de dire **2** *(have relationship, interact)* **he finds it difficult to r. to others** il lui est difficile de communiquer avec les autres **3** *Fam (respond, appreciate)* **I can't r. to his music** je n'accroche pas à sa musique; **I can r. to that** je comprends tout à fait□

related [rɪˈleɪtɪd] **ADJ 1** *(in family)* parent (**to** de); *(animal, species)* apparenté; *(language)* de même famille, proche; **are you two r.?** êtes-vous apparentés *ou* parents *ou* de la même famille?; **to be r. by marriage to sb** être parent de qn par alliance; **they aren't r.** ils n'ont aucun lien de parenté; **they are closely r.** ils sont proches parents; **an animal r. to the cat** un animal apparenté au *ou* de la famille du chat **2** *(connected)* connexe, lié; *(neighbouring)* voisin; **psychoanalysis and r. areas** la psychanalyse et les domaines qui s'y rattachent; **problems r. to health** problèmes qui se rattachent *ou* qui touchent à la santé; **the cost of the project is directly r. to...** le coût du projet est directement lié à; **the two events are not r.** les deux événements n'ont aucun rapport **3** *Mus* relatif

-related [rɪˈleɪtɪd] **SUFF** lié à; **stress-/industry-r.** lié au stress/à l'industrie; **performance-r. bonus** prime *f* d'encouragement

relating [rɪˈleɪtɪŋ] **relating to PREP** ayant rapport à, relatif à, concernant; *Admin & Law* afférent à

relation [rɪˈleɪʃən] **N 1** *(member of family)* parent (e) *m,f*; **they have relations in Paris** ils ont de la famille à Paris; **he's a r.** il est de ma famille; **she is no r. to me** *or* **of mine** il n'y a aucun lien de parenté entre nous; **is she a r. of yours?** est-elle de votre famille?

2 *(kinship)* parenté *f*; **what r. is he to you?** quelle est votre lien de parenté?

3 *(connection)* rapport *m*, relation *f*; **to have** *or* **to bear a r. to sth** avoir (un) rapport à qch, être en rapport avec qch; **to bear little/no relation to sth** avoir peu de/n'avoir aucun rapport avec qch; **your answer bore no r. to the question** votre réponse n'avait rien à voir avec la question

4 *(relationship, contact)* rapport *m*, relation *f*; *(between people, countries)* rapport *m*, rapports *mpl*; **to enter into relations with sb** entrer *ou* se mettre en rapport avec qn; **their relations are somewhat strained** ils ont des rapports assez tendus; *Formal* **to have (sexual) relations with sb** avoir des rapports (sexuels) avec qn; **to break off all relations with sb** rompre toute relation *ou* cesser tout rapport avec qn

5 *Formal (narration ► of events, story)* récit *m*, relation *f*; *(► of details)* rapport *m*

● **in relation to, with relation to PREP** par rapport à, relativement à

relational [rɪˈleɪʃənəl] **ADJ** relationnel

►► *Comput* ***relational database*** base *f* de données relationnelle

relationship [rɪˈleɪʃənʃɪp] **N 1** *(between people, countries)* rapports *mpl*, relations *fpl*; **to have a good/bad r. with sb** *(gen)* avoir de bonnes/mauvaises relations avec qn; **our r. is purely a business one** nos relations sont simplement des relations d'affaires; **they have a good r.** ils s'entendent bien; **she has a good r. with her class** elle a de bons rapports avec sa classe

2 *(sexual)* relation *f* amoureuse; **a r. is something you have to work at** être en couple, ça demande des efforts; **to have a r. (with sb)** *(affair)* avoir une liaison (avec qn); **I'm already in a r.** j'ai déjà quelqu'un, je suis déjà avec quelqu'un

3 *(kinship)* **family r.** lien *m ou* liens *mpl* de parenté; **blood r.** parenté *f*, (degré *m* de) consanguinité *f*

4 *(connection ► between ideas, events, things)* rapport *m*, relation *f*, lien *m*

relative [ˈrelətɪv] **ADJ 1** *(comparative)* relatif; **to live in r. comfort** vivre dans un confort relatif; **the r. advantages of electricity as opposed to gas** les avantages relatifs de l'électricité par rapport au gaz; **taxation is r. to income** l'imposition est proportionnelle au revenu; **the r. qualities of the two candidates** les qualités respectives des deux candidats

2 *(not absolute)* relatif

3 *Mus* relatif

4 *Gram* relatif

N 1 *(person)* parent(e) *m,f*; **r. by marriage** parent (e) *m,f* par alliance; **she is my closest living r.** c'est la plus proche parente qui me reste; **she has relatives in Canada** elle a de la famille au Canada; **he's a r. of mine** il fait partie de ma famille **2** *Gram* relatif *m*

● **relative to PREP** relativement à

►► *Gram* ***relative clause*** (proposition *f*) relative; ***relative density*** densité *f* relative; ***relative humidity*** humidité *f* relative; *Pol* ***relative majority*** majorité *f* relative *ou* simple; *Mktg* ***relative market share*** part *f* de marché relative; *Econ* ***relative poverty*** pauvreté *f* relative; *Gram* ***relative pronoun*** pronom *m* relatif

> Note that the French word **relatif** is never used to refer to members of one's family.

relatively [ˈrelətɪvlɪ] **ADV** relativement; **r. difficult** relativement *ou* assez difficile; **r. speaking** relativement parlant

relativism [ˈrelətɪvɪzəm] **N** relativisme *m*

relativistic [ˌreləttɪˈvɪstɪk] **ADJ** relativiste

relativity [ˌreləˈtɪvɪtɪ] **N** relativité *f*; **theory of r.** théorie *f* de la relativité

relaunch *Com & Mktg* **N** [ˈriːlɔːntʃ] *(of product, company)* relancement *m*, relance *f*

VT [ˌriːˈlɔːntʃ] *(product, company)* relancer

relax [rɪˈlæks] **VI 1** *(person)* se détendre, se délasser; *(in comfort, on holiday)* se relaxer, se détendre; *(calm down)* se calmer, se détendre; **you need to r.** vous avez besoin de détente *ou* de vous détendre; **r.!** *(calm down)* du calme!; *(don't worry)* ne t'inquiète pas! **2** *(grip)* se relâcher, se desserrer; *(muscle)* se relâcher, se décontracter; *Tech (spring)* se détendre; **his face relaxed into a smile** son visage s'est détendu et il a souri

VT 1 *(person, mind)* détendre, délasser; *(muscles)* relâcher, décontracter

2 *(grip)* relâcher, desserrer; **to r. one's hold** *or* **one's grip** relâcher son étreinte; *Fig* **to r. one's grip on** relâcher son emprise sur

3 *Med (bowels)* relâcher

4 *Fig (discipline, restriction)* assouplir, relâcher; *(concentration, effort)* relâcher; **the government has relaxed the laws on immigration** le gouvernement a assoupli les lois sur l'immigration

relaxant [rɪˈlæksənt] **N** (médicament *m*) relaxant *m*; *Med* **muscle r.** myorelaxant *m*, décontracturant *m*

ADJ relaxant

relaxation [ˌriːlækˈseɪʃən] **N 1** *(rest)* détente *f*, relaxation *f*; **he plays golf for r.** il joue au golf pour se détendre; **she finds r. in gardening** pour elle, le jardinage est une détente; **reading is one of my favourite forms of r.** lire est une de mes façons préférées de me détendre **2** *(loosening ► of grip)* relâchement *m*, desserrement *m*; *Fig (► of authority, law, discipline)* relâchement *m*, assouplissement *m*

►► ***relaxation therapy*** relaxation *f*

relaxed [rɪˈlækst] **ADJ 1** *(person, atmosphere)* détendu, décontracté; *(smile)* détendu; *(attitude)* décontracté; **to feel/to look r.** se sentir/avoir l'air détendu; **he's very r. about the whole business** cette affaire n'a pas l'air de beaucoup le perturber **2** *(muscle)* relâché; *(discipline)* assoupli

relaxing [rɪˈlæksɪŋ] **ADJ** *(restful ► atmosphere, afternoon, holiday)* reposant; *(► bath, music)* relaxant; **she finds gardening r.** elle trouve le jardinage reposant; **a r. place for a holiday** un endroit tranquille pour passer des vacances

relay *(pt & pp senses* **1, 2 relayed,** *pt & pp sense* **3 relaid** [-leɪd]*)* **N** [ˈriːleɪ] **1** *(team ► of athletes, workers, horses)* relais *m*; *Br* **to work in relays** travailler par relais, se relayer

2 *Rad & TV (transmitter)* réémetteur *m*, relais *m*; *(broadcast)* émission *f* relayée

3 *Elec & Tech* relais *m*

4 *Sport (race)* (course *f* de) relais *m*; **the 4 x 100 m r.** le relais 4 x 100 m

VT 1 [ˈriːleɪ] *(pass on ► message, news)* transmettre **2** [ˈriːleɪ] *Rad & TV (broadcast)* relayer, retransmettre **3** [ˌriːˈleɪ] *(cable, carpet)* reposer

►► *Sport* ***relay race*** course *f* de relais *m*; *Rad & TV* ***relay station*** relais *m*; *Rad & TV* ***relay transmitter*** réémetteur *m*

release [rɪˈliːs] **N 1** *(from captivity)* libération *f*; *(from prison)* libération *f*, mise *f* en liberté; *Admin* élargissement *m*; *(from custody)* mise *f* en liberté, relaxe *f*; *(from debt)* libération *f*; *(from obligation, promise)* libération *f*, dispense *f*; *(from pain, suffering)* délivrance *f*; **on his r. from prison** lors de sa mise en liberté, dès sa sorti

de prison; **r. on bail** mise *f* en liberté provisoire (sous caution); **r. on parole** libération *f* conditionnelle; **order of r.** ordre *m* de levée d'écrou; **death was a r. for her** pour elle, la mort a été une délivrance
2 *Fin (of credits, funds)* déblocage *m*, dégagement *m*
3 *(distribution ▸ of film, record)* sortie *f*; *(▸ of book)* sortie *f*, parution *f*; *(▸ of document)* diffusion *f*; **the film is on general r.** le film est sorti
4 *(new film, book, record)* nouveauté *f*; *(software)* version *f*; **her latest r. is called...** son dernier disque s'appelle...; **it's a new r.** ça vient de sortir
5 *(of handle, switch)* déclenchement *m*; *(of brake)* desserrage *m*; *(of clutch)* débrayage *m*; *(of spring)* détente *f*; *(of bomb)* largage *m*; *(of balloons, pigeons)* lâcher *m*; *(of gas etc)* dégagement *m*; *(of steam)* échappement *m*; *(of pressure)* relâchement *m*; *(of energy)* libération *f*
6 *Tech (lever)* levier *m*; *(safety catch)* cran *m* de sûreté
COMP *(button, switch)* de déclenchement
VT 1 *(prisoner)* libérer, relâcher; *(from custody)* remettre en liberté, relâcher, relaxer; *(captive person, animal)* libérer; *(employee, schoolchild)* libérer, laisser partir; *(hospital patient)* laisser sortir; *(from obligation)* libérer, dégager; *(from promise)* dégager, relever; *(from vows)* relever, dispenser; **to r. sb from captivity** libérer qn; *Law* **to be released on bail** être libéré sous caution; **to be released on parole** être mis en liberté conditionnelle; **to r. sb from a debt** remettre une dette à qn
2 *(let go ▸ from control, grasp)* lâcher; *(▸ feelings)* donner *ou* laisser libre cours à; *(▸ bomb)* larguer, lâcher; *(▸ gas, heat)* libérer, dégager; **he released his grip on my hand** il m'a lâché la *ou* il a lâché ma main; **to r. one's hold** desserrer son étreinte, lâcher prise; **the explosion released chemicals into the river** l'explosion a libéré des agents chimiques dans la rivière; **playing squash is a good way of releasing tension** le squash est un bon moyen de se détendre
3 *(issue ▸ film)* sortir; *(▸ book)* sortir, faire paraître, mettre en vente; *(▸ record)* sortir, mettre en vente; *(▸ goods, new model)* mettre en vente *ou* sur le marché; *(▸ stamps, coins)* émettre
4 *(make public ▸ statement)* publier; *(▸ information, story)* dévoiler, annoncer; **the company refuses to r. details of the contract** la société refuse de divulguer *ou* de faire connaître les détails du contrat
5 *(lever, mechanism)* déclencher; *(brake)* desserrer; *(jammed part etc)* dégager; *(spring)* détendre; *Aut* **to r. the clutch** débrayer; **to r. the safety catch** *(on gun)* libérer le cran de sûreté
6 *Fin (credits, funds)* dégager, débloquer
▸▸ ***release date*** *(of film, record)* date *f* de sortie; *(of book)* date *f* de parution; *Cin* ***release print*** copie *f* d'exploitation

relegate ['relɪgeɪt] **VT 1** *(person, thought)* reléguer; **to r. sb/sth to sth** reléguer qn/qch à qch; *Fig* **we relegated the old bed to the spare room** on a relégué le vieux lit dans la chambre d'amis **2** *Sport (team)* reléguer, déclasser; *Ftbl* **to be relegated** descendre en *ou* être relégué à la division inférieure **3** *(refer ▸ issue, question)* renvoyer

relegation [,relɪ'geɪʃən] **N 1** *(demotion ▸ of person, team, thing)* relégation *f* **2** *(referral ▸ of issue, matter)* renvoi *m*

relent [rɪ'lent] **VI 1** *(person)* se laisser fléchir, céder; **the prime minister shows no sign of relenting** le premier ministre ne semble pas vouloir céder; **he finally relented and let us go** il a finalement accepté de nous laisser partir **2** *(storm)* s'apaiser, se calmer

relentless [rɪ'lentlɪs] **ADJ 1** *(merciless)* implacable, impitoyable **2** *(sustained ▸ activity, effort)* acharné, opiniâtre; *(▸ noise)* ininterrompu; *(▸ rain)* incessant; *(▸ pain)* tenace; *(▸ advance)* inexorable

relentlessly [rɪ'lentlɪslɪ] **ADV 1** *(mercilessly)* impitoyablement, implacablement **2** *(persistently)* avec acharnement *ou* opiniâtreté; **he worked r.** il travailla avec acharnement; **the rain beat down r.** il n'a pas cessé de pleuvoir à verse

relet [,riː'let] **VT** relouer

relevance ['reləvəns], **relevancy** ['reləvənsɪ] **N 1** *(of facts, remarks etc)* pertinence *f*, intérêt *m*; **I don't see the r. of your remark** la pertinence de votre remarque m'échappe; **what is the r. of this to the matter under discussion?** quel est le rapport avec ce dont on parle?; **to have no r. to sth** n'avoir aucun rapport avec qch; **this question has little r. for us** cette question ne nous concerne pas vraiment **2** *(usefulness, significance)* intérêt *m*; **many students fail to see the practical r. of such courses** de nombreux étudiants considèrent que ces formations n'ont pas d'intérêt *ou* d'utilité pratique; **Shakespeare's plays are still full of r.** les pièces de Shakespeare sont toujours d'actualité

relevant ['reləvənt] **ADJ 1** *(pertinent ▸ comment, beliefs, ideas)* pertinent; **to be r. (to sth)** avoir un rapport (avec qch); **that's not r.** ça n'a rien à voir **2** *(appropriate)* approprié; **she did not have the r. experience for the job** elle n'avait pas l'expérience requise pour le poste; **you should report the matter to the r. department** vous devriez en référer au service compétent; **to refer sb to the r. chapter of a book** renvoyer qn au chapitre correspondant; **the r. documents** les documents qui se rapportent à l'affaire; *Law* les pièces justificatives **3** *(useful, significant)* **to be highly r. (for)** *(experience, qualifications)* être très utile (pour); **to be/remain r.** *(book, play, idea, ideology etc)* être/rester d'actualité

reliability [rɪ,laɪə'bɪlɪtɪ] **N 1** *(of person, company)* sérieux *m*; *(of information)* sérieux *m*, fiabilité *f*; *(of memory, judgment)* sûreté *f*, fiabilité *f*; **I'm not altogether sure about the r. of our witnesses** je ne suis pas vraiment sûr qu'on puisse faire confiance à nos témoins **2** *(of clock, machine, car)* fiabilité *f*

reliable [rɪ'laɪəbəl] **ADJ 1** *(trustworthy ▸ friend)* sur qui on peut compter, sûr; *(▸ worker)* à qui on peut faire confiance, sérieux; *(▸ witness)* digne de confiance *ou* de foi; *(▸ information)* sérieux, sûr; *(▸ memory, judgment)* fiable, auquel on peut se fier; *(▸ company)* sérieux; **he's very r.** on peut toujours compter sur lui *ou* lui faire confiance; **the news came from a r. source** la nouvelle provenait d'une source sûre; **my memory isn't r.** je n'ai pas bonne mémoire **2** *(clock, machine, car)* fiable

reliably [rɪ'laɪəblɪ] **ADV** *(operate, perform etc)* de façon fiable; **we are r. informed that...** nous avons appris de bonne source *ou* de source sûre que...

reliance [rɪ'laɪəns] **N 1** *(trust)* confiance *f*; **to place r. in** *or* **on sb/sth** faire confiance à qn/qch **2** *(dependence)* dépendance *f*; **because of the country's r. on the arms industry** parce que l'économie du pays dépend de l'industrie de l'armement

reliant [rɪ'laɪənt] **ADJ** dépendant; **to be r. on sb (for sth)** dépendre de qn (pour qch); **he is too r. on tranquillizers** il a trop recours aux tranquillisants

relic ['relɪk] **N 1** *(reminder of past, remnant)* vestige *m*; **the last surviving r. of** les derniers vestiges de; *Hum* **their old r. of a car** leur vieille bagnole toute pourrie; *Literary* **relics** *(corpse)* dépouille *f* mortelle **2** *Rel* relique *f*

relief [rɪ'liːf] **N 1** *(from anxiety, pain)* soulagement *m*; **to bring r. to sb** soulager qn, apporter un soulagement à qn; **to our great r., much to our r.** à notre grand soulagement; **it was a great r. to her when the exams ended** la fin des examens fut un grand soulagement pour elle; **that's** *or* **what a r.!** quel soulagement!
2 *(aid)* secours *m*, aide *f*; **to send r. to Third-World countries** apporter de l'aide aux pays du tiers-monde; **famine r.** aide *f* aux victimes de la famine
3 *Am (state benefit)* aide *f* sociale; **to be on r.** recevoir des aides sociales *ou* des allocations
4 *(diversion)* divertissement *m*, distraction *f*; **to provide light** *or* **comic r.** détendre l'atmosphère, introduire une note comique; **by way of light r.** pour se détendre un peu, pour détendre l'atmosphère
5 *(of besieged city)* libération *f*, délivrance *f*
6 *(of guard, team)* relève *f*; **my r. didn't show up** mon remplaçant/ma remplaçante ne s'est pas présenté(e)
7 *Art* relief *m*; **the inscription stood out in r.** l'inscription était en relief; **the mountains stood out in bold r. against the sky** les montagnes se détachaient *ou* se découpaient nettement sur le ciel; *Fig* **to bring** *or* **to throw sth into r.** mettre qch en relief *ou* en valeur, faire ressortir qch; *Art* **high r.** haut-/bas-relief *m*
8 *Geog* relief *m*; **an area of low r.** une zone au relief peu élevé
9 *Law (redress)* réparation *f*; *(exemption)* dérogation *f*, exemption *f*
COMP *(extra ▸ transport, service)* supplémentaire; *(replacement ▸ employee, troops, team)* de relève; *(▸ bus, machine)* de remplacement
▸▸ ***relief agency*** organisme *m* d'aide humanitaire; ***relief driver*** chauffeur *m* qui assure la relève; ***relief fund*** caisse *f* de secours; ***relief map*** carte *f* en relief; ***relief organization*** organisation *f* humanitaire; ***relief road*** itinéraire *m* bis, route *f* de délestage; ***relief valve*** soupape *f* de sûreté, clapet *m* de décharge; ***relief work*** coopération *f*; ***relief worker*** *(in humanitarian organization)* = membre d'une organisation humanitaire qui travaille sur le terrain

> Note that the French word **relief** never means **assistance.**

relieve [rɪ'liːv] **VT 1** *(anxiety, distress, pain)* soulager, alléger; *(poverty)* soulager; *Med & Transp* **to r. congestion** décongestionner
2 *(gloom)* dissiper; *(boredom)* tromper; *(monotony)* briser; **the darkness of the room was relieved only by the firelight** la pièce n'était éclairée que par la lueur du feu; **black dress relieved by** *or* **with white lace** robe noire agrémentée de dentelle blanche
3 *(unburden)* **to r. sb of sth** soulager *ou* débarrasser qn de qch; **he relieved her of her suitcase/coat** il l'a débarrassée de sa valise/de son manteau; **to r. sb of a burden** soulager qn d'un fardeau; *Hum* **to r. sb of their wallet** délester qn de son portefeuille; **to r. sb of his/her duties** *or* **position** relever qn de ses fonctions
4 *(aid ▸ population, refugees, country)* secourir, venir en aide à
5 *(replace ▸ worker, team)* relayer, prendre la relève de; *(▸ guard, sentry)* relever
6 *(liberate ▸ fort, city)* délivrer, libérer; *(from siege)* lever le siège de
7 *Euph* **to r. oneself** *(urinate)* se soulager

relieved [rɪ'liːvd] **ADJ** soulagé; **to feel r.** se sentir soulagé; **I'm very r. to hear it** je suis très soulagé de l'apprendre, c'est un grand soulagement pour moi de l'apprendre

religion [rɪ'lɪdʒən] **N 1** *Rel* religion *f*; *(Catholic, Protestant)* religion *f*, culte *m*; *(heading on form)* confession *f*; **the Jewish r.** la religion *ou* la confession juive; *Am* **to get r.** découvrir Dieu; *Fig* devenir un modèle de vertu; *Hum* **it's against his r. to do the washing-up!** c'est contraire à sa religion de faire la vaisselle! **2** *Fig (obsession)* religion *f*, culte *m*; **to make a r. of sth** se faire une religion de qch; **sport is a r. with him** le sport est son dieu

religiosity [rɪ,lɪdʒɪ'ɒsɪtɪ] **N** religiosité *f*

religious [rɪ'lɪdʒəs] **ADJ 1** *(belief, order, ceremony, art)* religieux; *(war)* de religion **2** *(devout)* pieux, croyant **3** *Fig (scrupulous)* religieux; **to do sth with r. care, to be r. about doing sth** faire qch avec un soin religieux
N *(monk, nun)* religieux(euse) *m,f*
▸▸ ***religious education, religious instruction*** instruction *f* religieuse; ***religious persuasion*** confession *f*

religiously [rɪ'lɪdʒəslɪ] **ADV** *also Fig* religieusement

religiousness [rɪ'lɪdʒəsnɪs] **N** *(of person)* piété *f*, dévotion *f*; *(of music, art)* caractère *m* religieux; *Fig (of attendance, obedience)* caractère *m* scrupuleux; *(in carrying out task)* extrême méticulosité *f*

reline [,riː'laɪn] **VT** *(garment)* mettre une nouvelle doublure à, redoubler; *Aut* **to r. the brakes** changer les garnitures de freins

relinquish [rɪ'lɪŋkwɪʃ] **VT 1** *(give up ▸ claim, hope, power)* abandonner, renoncer à; *(▸ property, possessions)* se dessaisir de; *(▸ right)* renoncer à; **he relinquished his voting rights to the**

chairman il a cédé son droit de vote au président; **they are reluctant to r. control of monetary policy** ils sont peu enclins à laisser à d'autres le contrôle de la politique monétaire **2** *(release ▸ grip, hold)* **to r. one's hold of** *or* **on sth** lâcher qch; *Fig* relâcher l'étreinte que l'on a sur qch

relinquishment [rɪ'lɪŋkwɪʃmənt] **N** abandon *m*, renonciation *f*; **the r. of one's rights** l'abandon de *ou* la renonciation à ses droits

reliquary ['relɪkwərɪ] *(pl* **reliquaries)** **N** reliquaire *m*

relish ['relɪʃ] **N 1** *(pleasure, enthusiasm)* goût *m*, plaisir *m*, délectation *f*; **to do sth with r.** faire qch avec délectation *ou* avec grand plaisir, adorer faire qch; **... she said with great r.** ... ditelle avec délectation; **he ate with r.** il mangea avec délice *ou* avec délectation **2** *(condiment, sauce)* condiment *m*, sauce *f* **3** *(flavour)* goût *m*, saveur *f*; *Fig* **life had lost its r. for her** la vie avait perdu toute saveur pour elle

VT 1 *(enjoy)* savourer; **I bet he's relishing this moment** je parie qu'il savoure cet instant; **to r. doing sth** trouver du plaisir à *ou* aimer faire qch; **I don't r. the idea** *or* **the prospect** *or* **the thought of seeing them again** l'idée *ou* la perspective de les revoir ne m'enchante *ou* ne me réjouit guère **2** *(savour ▸ food, drink)* savourer, se délecter de

relive [ˌri:'lɪv] **VT** revivre

rellies ['relɪz] **NPL** *Br & Austr Fam (relatives)* famille *f*; **are you seeing your r. at Christmas?** tu vas voir ta famille à Noël?

reload [ˌri:'ləʊd] **VT** *(ship, camera, rifle, software etc)* recharger

VI *(ship, photographer etc)* recharger; *(gun, software)* se recharger

relocate [ˌri:ləʊ'keɪt] **VT** réimplanter, délocaliser

VI se réimplanter, déménager; **the company has relocated to Idaho** l'entreprise a déménagé dans l'Idaho

relocation [ˌri:ləʊ'keɪʃən] **N** *(of premises, industry)* délocalisation *f*, déménagement *m*; *(of population)* relogement *m*

▸▸ ***relocation allowance*** *(for employee)* indemnité *f* de déménagement; ***relocation expenses*** *(for employee)* frais *mpl* de déménagement

reluctance [rɪ'lʌktəns] **N 1** *(unwillingness)* réticence *f*, répugnance *f*; **to do sth with r.** faire qch à contrecœur *ou* de mauvais gré; **to show (some) r. to do sth** se montrer peu disposé *ou* peu empressé à faire qch; **to do sth with a show of r.** faire qch avec une réticence feinte **2** *Phys* réluctance *f*

reluctant [rɪ'lʌktənt] **ADJ 1** *(unwilling)* réticent; **to be r. to do sth** être peu enclin à faire qch, n'avoir pas envie de faire qch; **to feel r. (to do sth)** hésiter (à faire qch) **2** *(against one's will ▸ commitment, promise, approval)* accordé à contrecœur; **she gave a r. smile** elle eut un sourire contraint; **he was a r. sex symbol** c'est bien malgré lui qu'il était devenu un sex-symbol

reluctantly [rɪ'lʌktəntlɪ] **ADV** à contrecœur; **to do sth r.** faire qch à contrecœur

rely on, rely upon [rɪ'laɪ] *(pp & pt* **relied)** **VT INSEP 1** *(count on ▸ person's help, discretion)* compter sur; *(have confidence in ▸ person)* compter sur, avoir confiance en; *(▸ judgment, opinion etc)* avoir confiance en; *(be dependent on ▸ person)* dépendre de (**for sth** pour qch); **she can always be relied upon to give good advice** on peut toujours compter sur elle pour donner de bons conseils; **you can't r. on the weather** on ne peut jamais savoir quel temps il va faire; **he can never be relied upon to keep a secret** on ne peut lui confier aucun secret; **I'm relying on it** j'y compte (bien); **he relies on his family for everything** il dépend de sa famille pour tout; *Ironic* **you can always r. on him to be late** tu peux compter sur lui pour arriver en retard à chaque fois **2** *Law (call on)* invoquer

REM [ˌɑ:ri:'em] **N** *(abbr* **rapid eye movement)** mouvements *mpl* oculaires rapides

▸▸ ***REM sleep*** sommeil *m* paradoxal

remailer [ˌri:'meɪlə(r)] **N** *Comput* service *m* de courrier électronique anonyme

remain [rɪ'meɪn] **VI 1** *(be left)* rester; *(doubts)* rester, subsister; **very little remains** *or* **there remains very little of the original building** il ne reste pas grand-chose du bâtiment d'origine; **much remains to be discussed** il y a encore beaucoup de choses à discuter; **that remains to be seen** cela reste à voir; **it remains to be seen whether he will agree** (il) reste à savoir s'il sera d'accord; **the fact remains that we can't afford this house** il n'en reste pas moins que *ou* toujours est-il que nous ne pouvons pas nous offrir cette maison; **it only remains for me to thank you** il ne me reste plus qu'à vous remercier **2** *(stay)* rester, demeurer; **please r. seated** *or* **in your seats** veuillez rester assis; **to r. faithful to sb** rester fidèle à qn; **to r. silent** garder le silence, rester silencieux; **the weather remained settled** le temps est resté stable; **he remained behind after the meeting** il est resté après la réunion; **it remains a mystery whether...** on ignore toujours si...; **the crime remains unsolved** le crime n'a toujours pas été élucidé; **to r. a problem** demeurer un problème; **one thing remains certain** une chose demeure certaine; *Formal Old-fashioned* **I r., Sir, your most faithful servant** veuillez agréer *ou* je vous prie d'agréer, Monsieur, l'expression de mes sentiments les plus respectueux

remainder [rɪ'meɪndə(r)] **N 1** *(leftover ▸ supplies, time)* reste *m*; *(▸ money)* solde *m*; *(▸ debt)* reliquat *m*; **the r.** *(remaining people)* les autres *mfpl*; **for the r. of his life** pour le restant de ses jours; **she spent the r. on sweets** elle a dépensé ce qui restait en bonbons **2** *Math* reste *m* **3** *(unsold book)* invendu *m*; *(unsold product)* fin *f* de série

VT *Com* solder

remaining [rɪ'meɪnɪŋ] **ADJ** *(food, money, wine etc)* qui reste, restant; **her only r. relative** la seule personne de sa famille (qui soit) encore en vie; **the r. guests/travellers** le reste des invités/des voyageurs; **it's our only r. hope** c'est le seul espoir qui nous reste, c'est notre dernier espoir

remains [rɪ'meɪnz] **NPL 1** *(of meal, fortune)* restes *mpl*; *(of building)* restes *mpl*, vestiges *mpl* **2** *Euph Formal (corpse)* restes *mpl*, dépouille *f* mortelle; **(human) r.** restes *mpl* humains **3** *Old-fashioned* **(literary) r.** œuvres *fpl* posthumes

remake *(pt & pp* **remade** [-'meɪd]) **VT** [ˌri:'meɪk] refaire

N ['ri:meɪk] *(film)* remake *m*

remand [rɪ'mɑ:nd] *Br* **VT** *Law (case)* renvoyer; *(defendant)* déférer; **to r. sb in custody** placer qn en détention préventive; **to r. sb on bail** mettre qn en liberté *ou* libérer qn sous caution

N renvoi *m*; **to be on r.** *(in custody)* être en détention préventive; *(on bail)* avoir été libéré sous caution

▸▸ *Br* ***remand centre*** = centre de détention préventive; *Br Old-fashioned* ***remand home*** maison *f* de correction

remark [rɪ'mɑ:k] **N 1** *(comment)* remarque *f*, réflexion *f*; **to make** *or* **to pass a r.** faire une remarque; **to make** *or* **to pass remarks about sb/sth** faire des réflexions sur qn/qch; **to let sth pass without r.** laisser passer qch sans faire de commentaire; **no remarks, please!** pas de commentaires, s'il vous plaît! **2** *Formal (attention)* attention *f*, intérêt *m*; **worthy of r.** digne d'attention; **his behaviour did not escape r.** son comportement n'est pas passé inaperçu

VT 1 *(comment)* (faire) remarquer, (faire) observer; **"the days are getting longer," she remarked** "les jours rallongent", fit-elle remarquer **2** *Formal (notice)* remarquer; **it may be remarked that...** constatons que... + *indicative*

> Note that the French verb **remarquer** is a false friend and is never a translation for the English verb **to remark**. Its most common meaning is **to notice**.

remarkable [rɪ'mɑ:kəbəl] **ADJ** *(quality, aspect)* remarquable; *(event, figure)* remarquable, marquant; **they are r. for their modesty** ils sont d'une rare modestie *ou* remarquablement modestes; **these birds are r. for their bright plumage** ces oiseaux se distinguent par leur plumage éclatant

remarkably [rɪ'mɑ:kəblɪ] **ADV** remarquablement; **she was looking r. well** elle avait l'air très en forme; **r., most of the population survived the earthquake** la majorité de la population a survécu au tremblement de terre, ce qui est remarquable

remarket [ˌri:'mɑ:kɪt] **VT** *Mktg* recommercialiser

remarketing [ˌri:'mɑ:kɪtɪŋ] **N** *Mktg* marketing *m* de relance

remarriage [ˌri:'mærɪdʒ] **N** remariage *m*

remarry [ˌri:'mærɪ] *(pt & pp* **remarried)** **VT 1** *(first spouse)* se remarier avec, épouser de nouveau **2** *(registrar, priest ▸ divorced couple)* remarier

VI se remarier

remaster [ˌri:'mɑ:stə(r)] **VT** *(album)* remastériser

rematch *Sport* **VT** [ˌri:'mætʃ] *(players, contestants)* opposer de nouveau

N ['ri:mætʃ] *(return)* match *m* retour; *(second)* deuxième match *m*

remediable [rɪ'mi:djəbəl] **ADJ** remédiable

remedial [rɪ'mi:djəl] **ADJ 1** *(measures, action)* de redressement; **to take r. action** prendre des mesures de redressement **2** *Br Sch (classes)* de rattrapage, de soutien; *(education)* spécialisé; *(pupil, student)* qui n'a pas le niveau; **she teaches r. maths** elle donne des cours de rattrapage *ou* de soutien en maths **3** *Med (treatment)* correctif, curatif

▸▸ *Med* ***remedial exercises*** gymnastique *f* corrective; *Br Sch* ***remedial teacher*** enseignant(e) *m,f* chargé(e) d'une classe de rattrapage; *Br Sch* ***remedial teaching*** rattrapage *m* scolaire

remedy ['remədɪ] *(pl* **remedies**, *pt & pp* **remedied)** **N 1** *also Fig* remède *m*; **it's a good r. for insomnia** c'est un bon remède contre l'insomnie; **to find a r. for sth** trouver un remède à qch; **it's past** *or* **beyond r.** c'est irrémédiable *ou* sans remède **2** *Br Law* recours *m*

VT *Med* remédier à; *Fig* rattraper, remédier à; **the situation cannot be remedied** la situation est sans issue

remember [rɪ'membə(r)] **VT 1** *(recollect ▸ face, past event)* se souvenir de, se rappeler; *(▸ person)* se souvenir de; **don't you r. me?** *(in memory)* vous ne vous souvenez pas de moi?; *(recognize)* vous ne me reconnaissez pas?; **I r. him as a child** je me souviens de lui enfant; **I r. her as a very elegant woman** je me souviens d'elle comme de quelqu'un de très élégant; **I r. locking the door** je me rappelle avoir *ou* je me souviens d'avoir fermé la porte à clé; **do you r. me knocking on your door?** vous souvenez-vous que j'ai frappé à votre porte?; **I r. when there was no such thing as a paid holiday** je me souviens de l'époque où les congés payés n'existaient pas; **I can't r. her name** son nom m'échappe, je ne me souviens pas de son nom; **I can never r. names** je n'ai aucune mémoire des noms; **I'll r. his name in a minute** son nom me reviendra dans une minute; **we have nothing to r. him by** nous n'avons aucun souvenir de lui; **nobody could r. such a thing happening before** personne n'avait jamais vu une chose pareille se produire

2 *(not forget)* penser à, songer à; **r. my advice** n'oubliez pas mes conseils; **r. to close the door** n'oubliez pas de *ou* pensez à fermer la porte; **a night/holiday to r.** une nuit mémorable/des vacances mémorables; **you must r. (that) he's only ten years old** n'oubliez pas qu'il n'a que dix ans; **we can't be expected to r. everything** nous ne pouvons quand même pas penser à tout; **that's worth remembering** c'est à noter; **r. where you are!** un peu de tenue, voyons!; **r. who you're talking to!** à qui croyez-vous parler?; **he remembered himself just in time** il s'est repris juste à temps; **let us r. them in our prayers** prions pour eux

3 *(give regards to)* **r. me to your parents** rappelez-moi au bon souvenir de vos parents; **she asked to be remembered to you** elle vous envoie son meilleur souvenir

4 *(give tip or present to)* **she always remembers me on my birthday** elle n'oublie jamais le jour de mon anniversaire; **he remembered me in his will** il a pensé à moi dans son testament

5 *(commemorate ▸ war)* commémorer; *(▸ victims)* se souvenir de

VI se souvenir; **I r. now** maintenant, je m'en souviens; **as far as I can r.** autant qu'il m'en souvienne; **not that I r.** pas que je m'en souvienne; **if I r. rightly** si je me *ou* si je m'en souviens bien, si j'ai bonne mémoire; **for as long as I can r.** aussi loin que remontent mes souvenirs

remembrance [rɪ'membrəns] **N 1** *(recollection)* souvenir *m*, mémoire *f*; **I have no r. of it** je n'en ai gardé aucun souvenir

2 *(memory)* souvenir *m*

3 *(keepsake)* souvenir *m*; **as a r. of sb/sth** en souvenir de qn/qch

4 *(commemoration)* souvenir *m*, commémoration *f*; **in r. of sb/sth** en souvenir *ou* en mémoire de qn/qch; **r. service, service of r.** cérémonie *f* du souvenir, commémoration *f*

5 *Old-fashioned (greeting)* **give my kind remembrances to him** rappelez-moi à son bon souvenir

►► ***Remembrance Day,*** *Br* ***Remembrance Sunday*** (commémoration *f* de) l'Armistice *m (le dimanche avant ou après le 11 novembre)*

remind [rɪ'maɪnd] **VT** rappeler à; **to r. sb to do sth** rappeler à qn de faire qch, faire penser à qn qu'il faut faire qch; **to r. sb about sth** rappeler qch à qn; **he reminds me of my brother** il me fait penser à *ou* me rappelle mon frère; **the music reminded them of Greece** la musique leur rappelait la Grèce; **can you r. me about the bills/to pay the bills?** pouvez-vous me faire penser aux factures/me rappeler qu'il faut payer les factures?; **she reminded herself that he was still very young** elle se dit qu'il était encore très jeune; **do I need to** *or* **need I r. you of the necessity for discretion?** inutile de vous rappeler que la discrétion s'impose; **that reminds me!** à propos!, pendant que j'y pense!; **passengers are reminded that...** nous rappelons aux voyageurs que...

reminder [rɪ'maɪndə(r)] **N** *(of event)* rappel *m*; *(to jog memory)* pense-bête *m*; *Admin & Com (of unpaid bill)* rappel *m*; **final r.** dernier rappel *m*; **to give sb a r. to do sth** rappeler à qn qu'il doit faire qch; **she tied a knot in her handkerchief as a r.** elle a fait un nœud à son mouchoir pour ne pas oublier; **we gave him a gentle r. that it's her birthday tomorrow** nous lui avons discrètement rappelé que demain, c'est son anniversaire; **the exhibition is a stark** *or* **a grim r. of the horrors of war** l'exposition rappelle la guerre dans toute son horreur

reminisce [ˌremɪ'nɪs] **VI** évoquer *ou* raconter ses souvenirs; **to r. about the past** évoquer le passé, parler du passé

reminiscence [ˌremɪ'nɪsəns] **N** *(memory)* réminiscence *f*, souvenir *m*

• **reminiscences NPL** *(memoirs)* mémoires *mpl*

reminiscent [ˌremɪ'nɪsənt] **ADJ 1** *(suggestive)* **r. of** qui rappelle, qui fait penser à; **parts of the book are r. of Proust** on trouve des réminiscences de Proust dans certaines parties du livre, certaines parties du livre rappellent Proust **2** *(nostalgic* ► *person, smile)* nostalgique; **to be in a r. mood** être enclin à *ou* d'humeur à évoquer des souvenirs

reminiscently [ˌremɪ'nɪsəntlɪ] **ADV** *(smile, say)* avec nostalgie; **to talk r. of sth** évoquer des souvenirs de qch

remiss [rɪ'mɪs] **ADJ** *Formal* négligent; **he is r. in his duties** il néglige ses devoirs; **that was very r. of her** c'était de la négligence de sa part; **it was rather r. of you to forget her birthday** c'était un peu négligent *ou* léger de votre part d'oublier son anniversaire

remission [rɪ'mɪʃən] **N 1** *Br Law (release* ► *from prison sentence)* remise *f* (de peine); *(*► *from debt, claim)* remise *f*; *Admin (dispensation)* dispense *f*; **he was granted five years' r. for good behaviour** on lui a accordé une remise de peine de cinq ans pour bonne conduite **2** *Med & Rel* rémission *f*; **to be in/go into r.** *(disease, patient)* être/entrer en phase de rémission

remit *(pt & pp* **remitted,** *cont* **remitting) VT** [rɪ'mɪt] **1** *(release* ► *from penalty)* remettre; *Rel (*► *from sins)* remettre, pardonner; **to r. sb's sentence** accorder une remise de peine à qn

2 *(dispense, exonerate* ► *fees, tax)* remettre; *Fin (*► *debt)* remettre, faire remise de; **to r. sb's fees** dispenser qn de ses frais; **to r. sb's income tax** dispenser *ou* exempter qn d'impôt

3 *(send* ► *money)* envoyer; **to r. a sum of money to sb** envoyer une somme (d'argent) à qn

4 *Law (case)* renvoyer (à une instance inférieure)

5 *Formal (defer)* différer, remettre

VI [rɪ'mɪt] **1** *(lessen* ► *zeal)* diminuer; *(*► *attention, efforts)* se relâcher; *(*► *storm)* s'apaiser, se calmer **2** *Med (fever)* tomber, diminuer; *(disease)* régresser

N ['ri:mɪt] attributions *fpl*, pouvoirs *mpl*; **that's outside their r.** cela n'entre pas dans (le cadre de) leurs attributions; **our r. is to...** il nous incombe de...

remittance [rɪ'mɪtəns] **N 1** *(payment)* versement *m*; *(settlement)* paiement *m*, règlement *m*; **return the form with your r.** renvoyez le formulaire avec votre paiement *ou* votre règlement **2** *(delivery* ► *of papers, documents)* remise *f*

►► *Fin* ***remittance advice*** avis *m* de remise; *Fin* ***remittance of funds*** remise *f* de fonds

remix VT [ˌri:'mɪks] *(record, recording)* remixer, refaire le mixage de

N ['ri:mɪks] remix *m*

remnant ['remnənt] **N** *(remains* ► *of meal, material)* reste *m*; *(vestige* ► *of beauty, culture)* vestige *m*; **the remnants of the army/his fortune** ce qui reste de l'armée/de sa fortune

• **remnants NPL** *Com (unsold goods)* invendus *mpl*; *(fabric)* coupons *mpl* (de tissus); *(oddments)* fins *fpl* de série

remodel [ˌri:'mɒdəl] *(Br pt & pp* **remodelled,** *cont* **remodelling,** *Am pt & pp* **remodeled,** *cont* **remodeling) VT** *(bill, draft)* remanier; *(structure, legislation)* modifier

remonstrate ['remənstreɪt] **VI** *Formal* protester; **to r. with sb** faire des remontrances à qn (**about** au sujet de); **to r. against sth** protester contre qch

VT to r. that... protester en disant que... + *indicative*

remorse [rɪ'mɔ:s] **N** remords *m*; **to feel r. (for having done sth)** éprouver *ou* avoir du *ou* des remords (d'avoir fait qch); **he was filled with r. at what he had done** il était pris de remords en songeant à ce qu'il avait fait; **without r.** *(with no regret)* sans remords; *(pitilessly)* sans pitié; **in a fit of r.** dans un accès de remords; **to show r.** manifester des remords

remorseful [rɪ'mɔ:sfʊl] **ADJ** plein de remords

remorsefully [rɪ'mɔ:sfʊlɪ] **ADV** avec remords

remorseless [rɪ'mɔ:slɪs] **ADJ 1** *(relentless* ► *person, wind)* impitoyable; *(*► *cruelty, persecution)* incessant; *Fig (*► *ambition, logic, self-interest etc)* implacable; **he was r. in the demands that he made on his employees** il ne laissait aucun répit à ses employés **2** *(with no regret)* sans remords

remorselessly [rɪ'mɔ:slɪslɪ] **ADV 1** *(relentlessly)* impitoyablement, implacablement **2** *(with no regret)* sans remords

remorselessness [rɪ'mɔ:slɪsnɪs] **N 1** *(relentlessness)* acharnement *m* **2** *(lack of regret)* absence *f* de remords

remortgage [ˌri:'mɔ:gɪdʒ] **VT** *(house, property)* hypothéquer de nouveau, prendre une nouvelle hypothèque sur

remote [rɪ'məʊt] **ADJ 1** *(far away)* éloigné, lointain; *(isolated)* reculé, isolé; *(ancestor)* lointain; **in the remotest parts of the continent** au fin fond du continent; **r. from** loin *ou* éloigné de; **r. from civilization** loin de la civilisation; **in the r. future/past** dans un avenir/un passé lointain

2 *(aloof* ► *person, manner)* distant, froid; *(faraway* ► *look)* lointain, vague; *(*► *voice)* lointain; **she seems very r.** elle semble être très distante *ou* d'un abord difficile

3 *(unconnected* ► *idea, comment)* éloigné; **his plays are r. from everyday life** ses pièces sont éloignées de la vie quotidienne

4 *(slight* ► *chance)* petit, faible; *(*► *ressemblance)* vague, lointain; **our chances of success are rather r.** nos chances de réussite sont assez minces, nous n'avons que peu de chances de réussir; **there is a r. possibility that...** il y a une vague possibilité que... + *subjunctive*; **I haven't the remotest idea** je n'en ai pas la moindre idée

5 *Comput (terminal)* distant; *(user)* à distance

6 *Fin (payment)* à distance

N *Fam (remote control)* télécommande *f*, commande *f* à distance

►► ***remote access*** accès *m* à distance; *Tel* **this telephone has an answering machine with a r. access facility** ce répondeur est interrogeable à distance; ***remote control*** télécommande *f*, commande *f* à distance; *Nucl* ***remote handling equipment*** équipement *m* de télémanipulation; *Comput* ***remote sensing*** télédétection *f*; *Comput* ***remote server*** serveur *m* distant; *Comput* ***remote terminal*** terminal *m* distant

remote-controlled ADJ télécommandé

remotely [rɪ'məʊtlɪ] **ADV 1** *(slightly)* faiblement, vaguement; **the two subjects are only very r. linked** il n'y a qu'un rapport très lointain entre les deux sujets; **it is r. possible that I'm mistaken** il n'est pas absolument impossible que je fasse erreur; **she's not r. interested** ça ne l'intéresse pas le moins du monde *ou* absolument pas; **I'm not even r. tired** je ne suis pas fatigué du tout *ou* absolument pas fatigué **2** *(distantly)* **the house is r. situated** la maison se trouve dans un coin isolé; **they are r. related** ils sont parents éloignés **3** *(aloofly)* de façon distante *ou* hautaine; *(dreamily)* vaguement, de façon songeuse

remoteness [rɪ'məʊtnɪs] **N 1** *(distance* ► *in space)* éloignement *m*, isolement *m*; *(*► *in time)* éloignement *m* **2** *(aloofness* ► *of person)* distance *f*, froideur *f*; **her air of r.** *(aloofness)* son air distant; *(absent-mindedness)* son air absent **3** *(of resemblance)* faible degré *m*

remould, *Am* **remold VT** [ˌri:'məʊld] **1** *Art & Tech* refaçonner **2** *Aut (tyre)* rechaper **3** *Fig (person, character)* changer, remodeler

N ['ri:məʊld] *(tyre)* pneu *m* rechapé

remount [ˌri:'maʊnt] **VT 1** *(bicycle)* remonter sur; **to r. one's horse** se remettre en selle **2** *(picture)* rentoiler; *(photograph)* remplacer le support de; *(jewel)* remonter

VI *(on horse, bicycle)* remonter à cheval/à bicyclette

removability [rɪˌmu:və'bɪlətɪ] **N** *(of official)* amovibilité *f*

removable [rɪ'mu:vəbəl] **ADJ 1** *(detachable* ► *lining, cover)* amovible, détachable **2** *(mark, spot, stain etc)* qui peut partir; **the stain is not r.** la tache est indélébile **2** *(transportable* ► *furniture, fittings)* mobile, transportable

►► *Comput* ***removable disk*** disque *m* amovible *ou* extractible

removal [rɪ'mu:vəl] **N 1** *(of garment, stain, object)* enlèvement *m*; *(of abuse, evil, threat)* suppression *f*; *(of doubt, fear)* dissipation *f*; *Med (of organ, tumour)* ablation *f*; **for stain r., for the r. of stains** pour enlever les taches, pour détacher; **after r. of the bandages** une fois les bandages enlevés; **make-up r.** démaquillage *m* **2** *(change of residence)* déménagement *m*; *(transfer)* transfert *m*; **their r. from/to Dublin** leur départ de/pour Dublin **3** *(dismissal)* renvoi *m*; *(of civil servant, judge etc)* destitution *f*; **r. from office** révocation *f*, renvoi *m*

COMP *(expenses, firm)* de déménagement

►► *Br* ***removal man*** déménageur *m*; *Br* ***removal van*** camion *m* de déménagement

remove [rɪ'mu:v] **VT 1** *(take off, out* ► *clothes, object)* enlever, retirer, ôter; *(*► *stain)* enlever, faire partir; *Med (*► *organ, tumour)* enlever, retirer; *(take or send away* ► *rubbish, plates etc)* enlever; *(*► *person)* emmener (**to** à); **to r. one's make-up** se démaquiller; **to r. hair from one's legs** s'épiler les jambes; **to have a mole/wart removed** se faire enlever un grain de beauté/une verrue; **the chairs were removed to the attic** les chaises ont été mises au grenier; **she was removed to hospital** elle a été transportée à l'hôpital *ou* hospitalisée; **to r. a child from school** retirer un enfant de l'école; **the soldiers were removed to the front** on envoya les soldats au front; **police removed the demonstrators** la police a fait partir les manifestants; **the judge ordered her to be removed from the court room** le juge a ordonné qu'on la fasse sortir de la salle d'audience

2 *(suppress* ► *clause, paragraph)* supprimer; *(*► *suspicion, doubt, fear)* dissiper; *(*► *worry, obstacle, threat, word)* supprimer, éliminer; **to r. sb's name from a list** rayer qn d'une liste

3 *(dismiss* ► *employee)* renvoyer; *(*► *official)* révoquer, destituer; **his opponents had him removed from office** ses opposants l'ont fait révoquer

4 *Euph (kill)* faire disparaître, tuer

VI *Formal (firm, premises, family)* déménager;

our office removed to Glasgow notre service s'est installé à Glasgow

N 1 *(distance)* distance *f*; **to experience sth at one r.** faire indirectement l'expérience de qch; **this is but one r. from blackmail** ça frôle le chantage; **her account is several removes from the truth** son récit est assez loin de la vérité; **it's several removes** *or* **a far r. from what we need** ce n'est vraiment pas ce qu'il nous faut **2** *(degree of kinship)* degré *m* de parenté

removed [rɪ'muːvd] **ADJ to be far r. from** être très éloigné *ou* loin de; **what you say is not far r. from the truth** ce que vous dites n'est pas bien éloigné de la vérité; **first cousin once/twice r.** cousin(e) *m,f* au deuxième/troisième degré

remover [rɪ'muːvə(r)] **N 1** *(of furniture)* déménageur *m*; **a company of furniture removers** une entreprise de déménagement **2** *(solvent)* **paint r.** décapant *m (pour peinture)*; **stain r.** détachant *m*

remunerate [rɪ'mjuːnəreɪt] **VT** rémunérer

remuneration [rɪˌmjuːnə'reɪʃən] **N** rémunération *f* (**for** de); **to receive r. for sth** être rémunéré *ou* payé pour qch

▸▸ ***remuneration package*** = salaire et avantages complémentaires

remunerative [rɪ'mjuːnərətɪv] **ADJ** rémunérateur

renaissance [rə'neɪsəns] **N** renaissance *f*

• **Renaissance** *Art & Hist* **N the R.** la Renaissance

COMP *(art, painter, literature)* de la Renaissance; *(palace, architecture, style)* Renaissance *(inv)*

▸▸ ***Renaissance man*** esprit *m* universel

renal ['riːnəl] **ADJ** rénal

▸▸ ***renal failure*** insuffisance *f* rénale

rename [ˌriː'neɪm] **VT** *(person, street)* rebaptiser; *Comput (file)* changer le nom de, renommer

renascence [rɪ'næsəns] **N** renaissance *f*

renascent [rɪ'næsənt] **ADJ** renaissant

renationalization, -isation [riːˌnæʃənəlaɪ'zeɪʃən] **N** renationalisation *f*

renationalize, -ise [ˌriː'næʃənəlaɪz] **VT** renationaliser

rend [rend] *(pt & pp* **rent** [rent]) **VT** *Literary* **1** *(tear ▸ fabric)* déchirer; *(▸ wood, armour)* fendre; *Fig (▸ silence, air)* déchirer; **the air was rent with her screams** l'air était déchiré par ses hurlements; **the country was rent in two by political strife** le pays était profondément divisé par les conflits politiques; **a flash of lightning rent the sky** un éclair déchira le ciel; **to r. sb's heart** fendre le cœur à qn **2** *(wrench)* arracher; **the child was rent from its mother's arms** on a arraché l'enfant des bras de sa mère

render ['rendə(r)] **VT 1** *(deliver ▸ homage, judgment, verdict)* rendre; *(▸ assistance)* prêter; *(▸ help)* fournir; *(submit ▸ bill, account)* présenter, remettre; **to r. sb a service** rendre (un) service à qn; **for services rendered** *(on invoice)* pour services rendus; **to r. assistance to sb** prêter secours à qn; **to r. an account of sth** *(explain)* rendre compte de qch; *Com* remettre *ou* présenter le compte de qch; **to r. an explanation of sth** fournir une explication à qch; **to r. thanks to sb** remercier qn, faire des remerciements à qn; **to r. thanks to God** rendre grâce à Dieu; *Bible* **r. unto Caesar the things that are Caesar's** rendez à César ce qui appartient à César

2 *(cause to become)* rendre; **a misprint rendered the text incomprehensible** une coquille rendait le texte incompréhensible; **the news rendered her speechless** la nouvelle l'a laissée sans voix

3 *(perform ▸ song, piece of music)* interpréter; *(convey ▸ atmosphere, spirit)* rendre, évoquer

4 *(translate)* rendre, traduire (**in** *or* **into** en)

5 *Culin* faire fondre

6 *Constr* crépir, enduire de crépi

rendering ['rendərɪŋ] **N 1** *(performance ▸ of song, play, piece of music)* interprétation *f*

2 *(evocation ▸ of atmosphere, spirit)* évocation *f*

3 *(translation)* traduction *f*

4 *Constr* enduit *m*

5 *Comput* rendu *m*

6 *(of meat)* équarrissage *m*

▸▸ ***rendering plant*** usine *f* d'équarrissage

rendezvous ['rɒndɪvuː] *(pl* **inv** [-vuːz], *pp & pt* **rendezvoused** [-vuːd], *cont* **rendezvousing** [-vuːɪŋ]) **N 1** *(meeting)* rendez-vous *m*; **to make** *or* **arrange a r. with sb** prendre rendez-vous avec qn **2** *(meeting place)* lieu *m* de rendez-vous

VI *(friends)* se retrouver; *(group, party)* se réunir; **to r. with sb** rejoindre qn; **the boats rendezvoused successfully after the operation** les bateaux se sont retrouvés comme prévu après l'opération

rendition [ren'dɪʃən] **N 1** *(of poem, piece of music)* interprétation *f*; **to give a r. of** *(role etc)* interpréter; **they finished with a r. of the Marseillaise** ils ont terminé en chantant/jouant la Marseillaise **2** *(translation)* traduction *f*

renegade ['renɪgeɪd] **N 1** *(traitor)* renégat(e) *m,f* **2** *(outlaw)* hors-la-loi *m inv*

ADJ renégat

▸▸ ***renegade priest*** prêtre *m* parjure

renege [rɪ'niːg] **VI 1** manquer à *ou* revenir sur sa promesse; **to r. on sth** *(on promise)* manquer à qch; *(on deal)* revenir sur qch **2** *Cards* faire une renonce

renegotiate [ˌriːnɪ'gəʊʃɪeɪt] **VI** renégocier

VT renégocier

renegotiation ['riːnɪˌgəʊʃɪ'eɪʃən] **N** renégociation *f*

renew [rɪ'njuː] **VT 1** *(extend validity of ▸ passport)* renouveler; *(▸ library book)* faire prolonger; *(▸ contract, lease)* renouveler, reconduire; **to r. one's subscription to sth** renouveler son abonnement *ou* se réabonner à qch; **to r. one's wardrobe** renouveler sa garde-robe

2 *(repeat ▸ attack, promise, threat)* renouveler; *(restart ▸ correspondence, negotiations)* reprendre; *(restate ▸ request, promise)* renouveler; **to r. one's acquaintance with sb** renouer avec qn

3 *(increase ▸ strength)* reconstituer, reprendre; **to r. one's efforts to do sth** redoubler d'efforts pour faire qch; **to r. pressure on sb (to do sth)** recommencer à faire pression sur qn (pour qu'il fasse qch)

4 *(replace ▸ supplies)* renouveler, remplacer; *(▸ batteries, mechanism)* remplacer, changer

renewable [rɪ'njuːəbəl] **ADJ** *(passport etc)* renouvelable; *(lease, contract)* reconductible, renouvelable

▸▸ ***renewable energy*** énergie *f* renouvelable; ***renewable resources*** ressources *fpl* renouvelables

renewal [rɪ'njuːəl] **N 1** *(extension ▸ of validity)* renouvellement *m*; *(restart ▸ of negotiations, hostilities)* reprise *f*; *(▸ of acquaintance)* fait *m* de renouer; *(increase ▸ of energy, hope)* regain *m*; *(repetition ▸ of promise, threat)* renouvellement *m*; **r. of subscription** réabonnement *m*, renouvellement *m* d'abonnement; **r. of activity** reprise *f ou* regain *m* d'activité **2** *(renovation)* rénovation *f* **3** *Rel* renouveau *m*

▸▸ *Ins* ***renewal notice*** avis *m* de renouvellement; *Ins* ***renewal premium*** prime *f* de renouvellement

renewed [rɪ'njuːd] **ADJ** *(confidence, hope)* renouvelé; *(vigour, force)* accru; **with r. enthusiasm** avec un regain d'enthousiasme; **r. outbreaks of violence** une reprise des violences; **there is r. interest in...** il y a un regain d'intérêt pour...

rennet ['renɪt] **N** *(for cheese, junket)* présure *f*

renounce [rɪ'naʊns] **VT** *(claim, title)* abandonner, renoncer à; *(faith, principle, habit)* renoncer à, renier; *(treaty)* dénoncer; *Law (nationality, inheritance)* répudier; **to r. the world** renoncer au monde; *Rel* **to r. Satan and all his works** renoncer à Satan, à ses pompes et à ses œuvres

VI *Cards* renoncer

renovate ['renəveɪt] **VT** remettre à neuf, rénover

renovation [ˌrenə'veɪʃən] **N** *(of house etc)* remise *f* à neuf, rénovation *f*; **to be under r.** être en cours de rénovation; **closed for r.** *or* **renovations** *(sign)* fermé pour cause de travaux de rénovation; **to carry out renovations** faire des travaux de rénovation

renovator ['renəveɪtə(r)] **N** rénovateur(trice) *m,f*

renown [rɪ'naʊn] **N** renommée *f*, renom *m*; **a man of great r.** un homme de grand renom; **to win r. (as/for)** acquérir une renommée, se faire une renommée (en tant que/pour)

renowned [rɪ'naʊnd] **ADJ** renommé, célèbre, réputé; **to be r. for sth** être connu *ou* célèbre pour qch; **an internationally-r.** *or* **a world-r. expert** un expert célèbre dans le monde entier

rent [rent] *pt & pp of* **rend**

VT 1 *(of tenant, hirer)* louer, prendre en location; **to r. sth from sb** louer qch à qn; **their house must be expensive to r.** le loyer de leur maison doit être élevé **she lives in a rented house** elle habite dans une maison qu'elle loue; **rented accommodation** logement *m* en location **2** *(of owner)* louer, donner en location; **to r. sth (out) to sb** louer qch à qn

VI 1 *(tenant)* louer **2** *(property)* se louer

N 1 *(for flat, house)* loyer *m*; *(for farm)* loyer *m*, fermage *m*; *(for car, TV)* (prix *m* de) location *f*; **for r.** à louer; **how much do you pay in r.?, how much r. do you pay?** combien est-ce que tu paies de loyer?; **to be behind with the r.** être en retard pour (payer) le loyer

2 *Econ* loyer *m*

3 *(tear ▸ in clothing)* déchirure *f*; *(▸ in clouds)* déchirure *f*, trouée *f*

4 *(split ▸ in movement, party)* rupture *f*, scission *f*

▸▸ ***rent book*** carnet *m* de quittances de loyer; *Fam* ***rent boy*** jeune prostitué *m* homosexuel[□]; ***rent collector*** receveur(euse) *m,f* des loyers; ***rent rebate*** réduction *f* de loyer; ***rent strike*** grève *f* des loyers; ***rent tribunal*** commission *f* de contrôle des loyers

rentability [ˌrentə'bɪlɪtɪ] **N** *Com* rentabilité *f* locative

rent-a-crowd, rent-a-mob N *Br Fam (protesters)* agitateurs *mpl* professionnels[□]; *(audience, supporters)* claque *f*

rental ['rentəl] **N 1** *(hire agreement ▸ for car, house, TV, telephone)* location *f*

2 *(payment ▸ for property, land)* loyer *m*; *(▸ for TV, car, holiday accommodation)* (prix *m* de) location *f*; *(▸ for telephone)* abonnement *m*, redevance *f*

3 *(income)* (revenu *m* des) loyers *mpl*

4 *Am (apartment)* appartement *m* en location; *(house)* maison *f* en location; *(land)* terrain *m* en location

ADJ *(agency)* de location; *(property)* à louer

▸▸ ***rental agreement*** contrat *m* de location; ***rental car*** voiture *f* de location; ***rental charge*** *(for telephone)* abonnement *m*; *(for TV, car)* prix *m* de location; ***rental income*** revenus *mpl* locatifs

rent-free ADJ exempt de loyer

ADV sans payer de loyer, sans avoir de loyer à payer; **to live in an apartment r.** habiter un appartement sans payer de loyer

rents [rents] **NPL** *Am Fam (parents)* vieux *mpl*

renunciation [rɪˌnʌnsɪ'eɪʃən] **N 1** *(of authority, claim, title)* renonciation *f*, abandon *m*; *(of faith, religion)* renonciation *f*, abjuration *f*; *(of principle)* abandon *m*, répudiation *f*; *(of treaty)* dénonciation *f* **2** *Law (of nationality, inheritance)* répudiation *f*

reoccupy [ˌriː'ɒkjʊpaɪ] *(pt & pp* **reoccupied**) **VT** réoccuper

reopen [ˌriː'əʊpən] **VT 1** *(door, border, book, bank account)* rouvrir; *Fig* **to r. an old wound** rouvrir une plaie **2** *(restart ▸ hostilities)* reprendre; *(▸ debate, negotiations)* reprendre, rouvrir

VI 1 *(door, wound)* se rouvrir; *(shop, theatre)* rouvrir; *(school ▸ after holiday)* reprendre; **the border has reopened** la frontière a été rouverte **2** *(negotiations)* reprendre

reopening [ˌriː'əʊpənɪŋ] **N** *(of shop, theatre, border, investigations)* réouverture *f*; *(of negotiations)* reprise *f*

reorder **VT** [ˌriː'ɔːdə(r)] **1** *Com (goods, supplies)* commander de nouveau, faire une nouvelle commande de **2** *(rearrange ▸ numbers, statistics, objects)* reclasser, réorganiser

N ['riːɔːdə(r)] *Com* nouvelle commande *f*

reorganization, -isation [ˈriːˌɔːgənaɪ'zeɪʃən] **N** réorganisation *f*

reorganize, -ise [ˌriː'ɔːgənaɪz] **VT** réorganiser

VI se réorganiser

Rep *Am* **1** *(written abbr* **Representative**) ≃ député *m* **2** *(written abbr* **Republican**) républicain(e) *m,f*

rep [rep] **N 1** *Fam (abbr* **representative**) représentant(e)[□] *m,f*, VRP[□] *m*

2 *Br Fam (abbr* **repertory**) *(theatre)* théâtre *m* de répertoire[□]; **to be** *or* **to work in r.** faire partie d'une troupe de répertoire, faire du théâtre de répertoire

3 *Tex* reps *m*

4 *Fam (abbr* **reputation***)* réputation *f*

5 *Fam (abbr* **repetition***) (in physical training)* mouvement *m*

repackage [ˌriːˈpækɪdʒ] **VT** *(goods)* remballer; *Mktg (product)* reconditionner, repenser l'emballage de; *Fig (company, image)* redorer

repaginate [ˌriːˈpædʒɪneɪt] **VT** remettre en pages; *(renumber)* repaginer

repaint [ˌriːˈpeɪnt] **VT** repeindre

repair [rɪˈpeə(r)] **VT 1** *(mend ▸ car, tyre, watch, machine)* réparer; *(▸ road, roof)* réparer, refaire; *(▸ clothes)* raccommoder; *(▸ hull)* radouber, caréner; *(▸ tights)* repriser; **to have one's shoes repaired** faire réparer ses chaussures **2** *(make amends for ▸ error, injustice)* réparer, remédier à

VI *Formal or Hum* aller, se rendre; **let us r. to bed** allons nous coucher

N 1 *(mending ▸ of car, machine, building, roof)* réparation *f*, remise *f* en état; *(▸ of clothes)* raccommodage *m*; *(▸ of shoes)* réparation *f*; *(▸ of road)* réfection *f*, remise *f* en état; *Naut* radoub *m*; **to carry out repairs to** *or* **on sth** effectuer des réparations sur qch; **to be under r.** être en réparation; **road under r.** *(sign)* travaux; **closed for repairs** *(sign)* fermé pour (cause de) travaux; **(shoe) repairs while you wait** *(sign)* cordonnerie minute; **the bridge was damaged beyond r.** le pont avait subi des dégâts irréparables **2** *(condition)* état *m*; **to be in good/bad r.** être en bon/mauvais état; **to keep sth in good r.** bien entretenir qch

▸▸ ***repair kit*** trousse *f* à outils; ***repair shop*** atelier *m* de réparations

repairer [rɪˈpeərə(r)] **N** *(of shoes)* cordonnier (ère) *m,f*; *(of watch, machine etc)* réparateur (trice) *m,f*

repairman [rɪˈpeəmən] *(pl* **repairmen** [-mən]*)* **N** réparateur *m*

repaper [ˌriːˈpeɪpə(r)] **VT** retapisser

reparation [ˌrepəˈreɪʃən] **N 1** *Formal (amends)* réparation *f*; *Fig* **to make r.** *or* **reparations for sth** réparer qch **2** *(usu pl) (damages ▸ after war, invasion etc)* réparations *fpl*

▸▸ ***reparation payments*** réparations *fpl*

repartee [ˌrepɑːˈtiː] **N 1** *(witty conversation)* esprit *m*, repartie *f*; **to engage in r.** faire de l'esprit; **to be good** *or* **quick at r.** avoir la repartie (facile) **2** *(witty comment)* repartie *f*, réplique *f*

repast [rɪˈpɑːst] **N** *Literary* repas *m*

repatriate VT [ˌriːˈpætrɪeɪt] rapatrier (**to** vers)

N [riːˈpætrɪət] rapatrié(e) *m,f*

repatriated [ˌriːˈpætrɪeɪtɪd] **ADJ** rapatrié

repatriation [ˌriːpætrɪˈeɪʃən] **N** rapatriement *m*

repay [ˌriːˈpeɪ] *(pt & pp* **repaid** [-ˈpeɪd]*)* **VT 1** *(refund ▸ creditor, loan)* rembourser; *(▸ money)* rendre, rembourser; **to r. a debt** rembourser une dette; *Fig* s'acquitter d'une dette **2** *(return ▸ visit)* rendre; *(▸ hospitality, kindness)* rendre, payer de retour; **how can I ever r. you (for your kindness)?** comment pourrai-je jamais vous remercier (pour votre gentillesse)?; **to r. good for evil** rendre le bien pour le mal **3** *(reward ▸ efforts, help)* récompenser; **to be repaid for one's efforts/one's persistence** être récompensé de ses efforts/de sa persévérance; **her generosity was repaid with indifference** tout ce qu'elle a obtenu en échange de sa générosité, c'est de l'indifférence

repayable [ˌriːˈpeɪəbəl] **ADJ** remboursable; **r. in** *or* **over five years** remboursable sur cinq ans *ou* en cinq annuités

repayment [ˌriːˈpeɪmənt] **N 1** *(of money, loan)* remboursement *m*; **repayments can be spread over twelve months** les remboursements peuvent être échelonnés sur douze mois **2** *(reward ▸ for kindness, effort)* récompense *f*

▸▸ *Br* ***repayment mortgage*** prêt-logement *m (qui n'est pas lié à une assurance-vie)*; ***repayment options*** formules *fpl* de remboursement; ***repayment plan*** calendrier *m* des paiements

repeal [rɪˈpiːl] **VT** *(law)* abroger, annuler; *(prison sentence)* annuler; *(decree)* rapporter, révoquer

N *(of law)* abrogation *f*; *(of prison sentence)* annulation *f*; *(of decree)* révocation *f*

repeat [rɪˈpiːt] **VT 1** *(say again ▸ word, secret, instructions, question)* répéter; *(▸ demand, promise, threat)* répéter, réitérer; **you're repeating yourself** vous vous répétez; **don't r. this, but...** ne le répète pas, mais... **it can't be repeated too often** on ne saurait trop le répéter; **it doesn't bear repeating** *(rude)* c'est trop grossier pour être répété; *(trivial)* ça ne vaut pas la peine d'être répété

2 *(redo, re-execute ▸ action, attack, mistake)* répéter, renouveler; *Mus* reprendre; **I wouldn't like to r. the experience** je n'aimerais pas renouveler l'expérience; **it's history repeating itself** c'est l'histoire qui se répète; **the pattern repeats itself** le motif se répète

3 *Rad & TV (broadcast)* rediffuser

4 *Com (order, offer)* renouveler

5 *Sch & Univ (class, year)* redoubler; **to r. a year** redoubler (une année)

VI 1 *(say again)* répéter; **I r., I have never heard of him** je le répète, je n'ai jamais entendu parler de lui; **I shall never, r. never, go there again** je n'y retournerai jamais, mais alors ce qui s'appelle jamais

2 *(recur)* se répéter, se reproduire; *Math* se reproduire périodiquement

3 *(food)* donner des renvois; **onions always r. on me** les oignons me donnent toujours des renvois

4 *Am Pol* voter plus d'une fois *(à une même élection)*

5 *(watch, clock)* être à répétition

N 1 *(gen)* répétition *f*; **it will be a r. of last year's final** ça sera comme la finale de l'année dernière **2** *Mus (passage)* reprise *f*; *(sign)* signe *m* de reprise **3** *Rad & TV (broadcast)* rediffusion *f*, reprise *f*

COMP *(order, visit)* renouvelé; **we get a lot of r. business** beaucoup de nos clients reviennent

▸▸ *Comput* ***repeat function*** fonction *f* de répétition; *Law* ***repeat offender*** récidiviste *mf*; *Theat* ***repeat performance*** deuxième représentation *f*; *Fig* **we don't want a r. performance of last year's chaos** nous ne voulons pas que le désordre de l'année dernière se reproduise; ***repeat prescription*** ordonnance *f (de renouvellement d'un médicament)*; **she gave me a r. prescription** elle a renouvelé mon ordonnance

repeat-action key N *Comput* touche *f* de répétition

repeated [rɪˈpiːtɪd] **ADJ** *(action)* répété; *(question, statement)* réitéré; *(effort)* renouvelé

repeatedly [rɪˈpiːtɪdlɪ] **ADV** à plusieurs *ou* à maintes reprises; **you have been told r. not to play by the canal** on vous a dit cent fois de ne pas jouer près du canal

repeater [rɪˈpiːtə(r)] **N 1** *(clock)* pendule *f* à répétition; *(alarm)* réveil *m* à répétition

2 *(gun)* fusil *m* à répétition

3 *Elec* répéteur *m*

4 *Am Sch* redoublant(e) *m,f*

5 *Am Pol* électeur(trice) *m,f* qui vote plus d'une fois *(à une même élection)*

repeating [rɪˈpiːtɪŋ] **ADJ 1** *Math* périodique **2** *(gun)* à répétition

▸▸ *Math* ***repeating decimal*** fraction *f* décimale périodique

repel [rɪˈpel] *(pt & pp* **repelled**, *cont* **repelling***)* **VT 1** *(drive back ▸ attacker, advance, suggestion)* repousser; **a spray that repels greenfly** un aérosol qui éloigne les pucerons; **to r. moisture** empêcher l'infiltration de l'humidité **2** *(disgust ▸ of unpleasant sight, smell etc)* rebuter, dégoûter; **the sight of blood repelled him** la vue du sang lui soulevait le cœur *ou* le dégoûtait **3** *Elec & Phys* repousser

VI *Elec & Phys* se repousser

repellent, repellant [rɪˈpelənt] **ADJ** repoussant, répugnant; **he finds her/the idea quite r.** elle/l'idée lui répugne

N 1 *(for insects)* insecticide *m*; *(for mosquitoes)* anti-moustiques *m inv* **2** *(for waterproofing)* imperméabilisant *m*

repent [rɪˈpent] **VI** se repentir; **to r. of sth** se repentir de qch

VT se repentir de

repentance [rɪˈpentəns] **N** repentir *m*; **to show no sign of r.** ne manifester aucun signe de repentir

repentant [rɪˈpentənt] **ADJ** repentant

repentantly [rɪˈpentəntlɪ] **ADV** *(say)* d'un ton repentant; *(look at)* d'un air repentant

repercussion [ˌriːpəˈkʌʃən] **N 1** *(consequence)* répercussion *f*, retentissement *m*, contrecoup *m*; **to have repercussions (for** *or* **on)** avoir des répercussions (sur); **the repercussions of the affair** les répercussions *ou* le contrecoup de l'affaire **2** *(echo)* répercussion *f*

repertoire [ˈrepətwɑː(r)] **N** *also Fig* répertoire *m*; **to have a wide/a limited r.** avoir un vaste répertoire/un répertoire restreint

repertory [ˈrepətərɪ] *(pl* **repertories***)* **N 1** *Theat* **to be** *or* **to work** *or* **to act in r.** faire partie d'une troupe de répertoire, faire du théâtre de répertoire; *(theatre)* théâtre *m* de répertoire **2** *(repertoire)* répertoire *m*

▸▸ ***repertory company*** compagnie *f ou* troupe *f* de répertoire; ***repertory theatre*** théâtre *m* de répertoire

répétiteur [ˌrepetɪˈtɜː(r)] **N** *Theat* maître *m* de musique

repetition [ˌrepɪˈtɪʃən] **N 1** *(of words, orders)* répétition *f* **2** *(of action)* répétition *f*, renouvellement *m*; **I don't want any r. of this behaviour!** que cela ne se reproduise pas! **3** *Mus* reprise *f*

repetitious [ˌrepɪˈtɪʃəs] **ADJ** plein de répétitions *ou* de redites

repetitive [rɪˈpetɪtɪv] **ADJ** *(activity, work, rhythm)* répétitif, monotone; *(song, speech)* plein de répétitions

▸▸ ***repetitive strain injury, repetitive stress injury*** lésions *fpl* attribuables au travail répétitif

rephrase [ˌriːˈfreɪz] **VT** reformuler; **perhaps I should r. that** peut-être devrais-je m'exprimer autrement

repine [rɪˈpaɪn] **VI** *Literary (be sad)* languir, dépérir; *(complain)* maugréer

replace [rɪˈpleɪs] **VT 1** *(put back)* replacer, remettre (à sa place *ou* en place); **to r. the receiver** *(on telephone)* reposer le combiné, raccrocher (le téléphone) **2** *(person)* remplacer; *(mechanism, tyres)* remplacer; **she replaced him as head of department/leader** elle lui a succédé à la tête du service/en tant que leader; **to r. a worn part by** *or* **with a new one** remplacer une pièce usée par une pièce neuve; **it can be replaced** *(of broken cup etc)* on peut retrouver le/la même **3** *Comput* remplacer; **r. all** *(command)* tout remplacer

> When translating the English verb **to replace**, note that the French verbs **replacer** and **remplacer** are not interchangeable. **Replacer** means **to put back** and **remplacer** means **to take the place of**.

replaceable [rɪˈpleɪsəbəl] **ADJ** remplaçable; **he is easily r.** on peut le remplacer facilement

replacement [rɪˈpleɪsmənt] **N 1** *(putting back)* remise *f* en place

2 *(substitution)* remplacement *m*

3 *(person)* remplaçant(e) *m,f*; **we are looking for a r. for our secretary** nous cherchons quelqu'un pour remplacer notre secrétaire

4 *(engine or machine part)* pièce *f* de rechange; *(product)* produit *m* de remplacement

COMP *(part)* de rechange; *(staff)* de remplacement

▸▸ *Ins* ***replacement cost*** coût *m* de remplacement; *Med* ***replacement hip joint*** prothèse *f* de (la) hanche; *Med* ***replacement knee joint*** prothèse *f* de (la) rotule; *Sch* ***replacement teacher*** professeur *m* suppléant, suppléant(e) *m,f*, remplaçant(e) *m,f*; *Ins* ***replacement value*** valeur *f* de remplacement

replant [ˌriːˈplɑːnt] **VT** replanter

replay N [ˈriːpleɪ] **1 (action** *or Am* **instant) r.** répétition *f* immédiate d'une séquence; *(in slow motion)* ralenti *m*; *TV* **(slow-motion) r.** répétition *f* au ralenti; **the r. clearly shows the foul** on voit bien la faute au ralenti **2** *Sport* match *m* rejoué

VT [ˌriːˈpleɪ] **1** *(record, piece of film, video)* repasser **2** *(match, point)* rejouer

replenish [rɪ'plenɪʃ] VT *Formal* **1** *(restock ▸ cellar, stock)* réapprovisionner; **to r. one's supplies of sth** se réapprovisionner en qch **2** *(refill ▸ glass)* remplir de nouveau; **she kept his glass replenished** elle veillait à ce que son verre fût toujours plein

replenishment [rɪ'plenɪʃmənt] N *Formal (of glass)* remplissage *m*; **r. of supplies/stocks** réapprovisionnement *m*

replete [rɪ'pli:t] ADJ *Formal (full)* rempli, plein; *(person ▸ full up)* rassasié; **to be r. with** *(food)* être repu *ou* rassasié de; *(fuel, supplies)* être (bien) ravitaillé en

repletion [rɪ'pli:ʃən] N *Formal* satiété *f*; *Physiol* réplétion *f*; **to eat to r.** se rassasier, manger à satiété

replica ['replɪkə] N *(of painting, model, sculpture)* réplique *f*, copie *f*; *(of document)* copie *f* (exacte), fac-similé *m*; **she is the exact r. of her mother** c'est la réplique vivante *ou* exacte de sa mère

COMP **a r. Messerschmitt** la réplique d'un Messerschmitt

replicate ['replɪkeɪt] VT *(document)* copier; *(experiment, cell, gene)* reproduire; *Comput (in spreadsheet)* recopier à l'identique; **the gene can r. itself** le gène peut se reproduire

VI *Biol* se reproduire par mitose

reply [rɪ'plaɪ] *(pl* **replies**, *pt & pp* **replied***)* N **1** *(answer)* réponse *f*; *(retort)* réplique *f*; **he made no r.** il n'a pas répondu; **his r. to that was to march out of the room** il a réagi à cela en sortant d'un air furieux de la pièce; **there was no r.** *(to telephone call)* on n'a pas répondu, ça ne répondait pas; *(to knock on door)* on n'a pas ouvert; **in r. to your letter** en réponse à votre lettre; **what did he say in r.?** qu'est-ce qu'il a répondu? **2** *Law* réplique *f*

VT *(answer)* répondre; *(retort)* répliquer, rétorquer; **"I don't know," she replied** "je ne sais pas", répondit-elle

VI répondre (**to** à)

▸▸ *Mktg* ***reply coupon*** coupon-réponse *m*; ***reply slip*** talon *m* à retourner

reply-paid ADJ *Br* avec réponse payée

▸▸ ***reply-paid envelope*** enveloppe *f* T, enveloppe-retour *f*; ***reply-paid letter*** lettre *f* avec réponse payée

repo ['ri:pəʊ] N **1** *Am Fam St Exch (abbr* **repossession***)* réméré[□] *m* **2** *(abbr* **repurchase***)* rachat *m*; *St Exch & Banking* réméré *m*

VT *Fam (abbr* **reposses***)* saisir[□]

▸▸ *Am Fam* ***repo man*** ≃ huissier *m (chargé par une société de saisir des meubles etc non payés)*

REPORT [rɪ'pɔ:t]

> **N**
> • rapport **1** • compte rendu **1**
> • procès-verbal **1, 4** • reportage **2**
> • bulletin **2, 3** • rumeur **2**
> • nouvelle **2**
> **VT**
> • annoncer **1, 2** • rendre compte de **1**
> • faire un reportage sur **2** • signaler **3**
> **VI**
> • faire un/son rapport **1** • faire un reportage **1**
> • se présenter **3**

N **1** *(account)* rapport *m*; *(summary ▸ of speech, meeting)* compte rendu *m*; *(official record)* procès-verbal *m*; *Com & Fin (review)* rapport *m*; *(balance sheet)* bilan *m*; **to draw up** *or* **to make a r. on sth** faire *ou* rédiger un rapport sur qch; **he gave an accurate r. of the situation** il a fait un rapport précis sur la situation; **official/police r.** rapport *m* officiel/de police; **his r. on the meeting** son compte rendu de la réunion; **sales r.** rapport *m ou* bilan *m* commercial

2 *(in media)* reportage *m*; *(investigation)* enquête *f*, *(bulletin)* bulletin *m*; *(rumour)* rumeur *f*, *(news)* nouvelle *f*; **to do a r. on sth** faire un reportage *ou* une enquête sur qch; **according to newspaper/intelligence reports** selon les journaux/les services de renseignements; **there are reports of civil disturbances in the North** il y aurait des troubles dans le Nord; **I only know it by r.** je ne le sais que par ouï-dire, j'en ai seulement entendu parler

3 *Br Sch* **(school) r.** bulletin *m* (scolaire); **end of term r.** bulletin *m* trimestriel

4 *Law (of court proceedings)* procès-verbal *m*; **law reports** recueil *m* de jurisprudence

5 *(sound ▸ of explosion, shot)* détonation *f*

6 *Comput (of database)* état *m*

7 *Formal (repute)* renom *m*, réputation *f*; **of good r.** de bonne réputation

VT **1** *(announce)* annoncer, déclarer, signaler; *(give account of)* faire état de, rendre compte de; **to r. one's findings** *(in research)* rendre compte des résultats de ses recherches; *(in inquiry, commission)* présenter ses conclusions; **to r. the position of a ship** signaler la position d'un navire; **to r. a profit** *(of company)* annoncer un bénéfice; **the doctors r. his condition as comfortable** les médecins déclarent son état satisfaisant; **little progress has been reported so far** jusqu'à présent on n'a obtenu que peu de résultats

2 *(of press, media ▸ event, match)* faire un reportage sur; *(▸ winner)* annoncer; *(▸ debate, speech)* faire le compte rendu de; **the newspapers r. heavy casualties** les journaux font état de nombreuses victimes; **our correspondent reports that troops have left the city** notre correspondant nous signale que des troupes ont quitté la ville; **her resignation is reported in several papers** sa démission est annoncée dans plusieurs journaux; **a woman is reported to have drowned, it is reported that a woman has drowned** une femme se serait noyée; **the version reported in the press** la version parue dans la presse

3 *(accident, burglary, disappearance, murder)* signaler; *(wrongdoer)* dénoncer, porter plainte contre; **to r. sb missing (to the police)** signaler la disparition de qn (à la police); **ten people were reported dead** on a annoncé la mort de dix personnes; **she was reported missing five years ago** elle a été portée disparue il y a cinq ans; **nothing to r.** rien à signaler; **they were reported to the police for vandalism** on les a dénoncés à la police pour vandalisme; **to r. a pupil to the headmaster** *(of teacher)* signaler la mauvaise conduite d'un élève au directeur

VI **1** *(make a report ▸ committee)* faire son rapport, présenter ses conclusions; *(▸ police)* faire un rapport; *(▸ journalist)* faire un reportage; **to r. on sth** *Admin* faire un rapport sur qch; *Press* faire un reportage sur qch; **he reports for the BBC** il est reporter *ou* journaliste à la BBC; **this is Keith Owen, reporting from Moscow for CBS** de Moscou, pour la CBS, Keith Owen

2 *(in hierarchy)* **to r. to sb** être sous les ordres de qn; **who do you r. to?** qui est votre supérieur?; **I r. directly to the sales manager** je dépends directement du chef des ventes

3 *(present oneself)* se présenter; **please r. to reception** veuillez vous présenter à la réception; **you've to r. to the headmaster** tu dois aller chez le directeur; **to r. for duty** prendre son service, se présenter au travail; **to r. sick** se faire porter malade; *Mil* **to r. to base** *(go)* se présenter à la base; *(contact)* contacter la base; *Mil* **to r. to barracks** *or* **to one's unit** rallier son unité

▸▸ *Sch* ***report card*** bulletin *m ou* carnet *m* scolaire; *Comput* ***report form*** rapport *m* (d'édition), fiche *f* d'état; *Comput* ***report form generator*** générateur *m* d'états; *Br Pol* ***report stage*** = examen d'un projet de loi avant la troisième lecture; **the bill has reached r. stage** ≃ le projet de loi vient de passer en commission

> Note that the French word **report** is a false friend and is never a translation for the English word **report**. Its most common meaning is **postponement**.
>
> Note that the French verb **reporter** is a false friend and is never a translation for the English verb **to report**. Its most common meaning is **to postpone**.

▸ **report back** VI **1** *(return ▸ soldier)* regagner ses quartiers, rallier son régiment; *(▸ journalist, salesman)* rentrer; **I have to r. back to the office** il faut que je repasse au bureau **2** *(present report ▸ committee)* présenter son rapport; **please r. back to me before you decide anything** veuillez vous en référer à moi avant de prendre une décision

VT SEP *(results, decision)* rapporter, rendre compte de

reportage [,repɔ:'tɑ:ʒ] N reportage *m*

reported [rɪ'pɔ:tɪd] ADJ **there have been r. sightings of dolphins off the coast** on aurait vu des dauphins près des côtes; **what was their last r. position?** où ont-ils été signalés pour la dernière fois?

▸▸ *Gram* ***reported speech*** style *m ou* discours *m* indirect

reportedly [rɪ'pɔ:tɪdlɪ] ADV **he is r. about to resign** il serait sur le point de démissionner; **300 people have r. been killed** 300 personnes auraient été tuées

reporter [rɪ'pɔ:tə(r)] N **1** *(for newspaper)* journaliste *mf*, reporter *m*; *Rad & TV* reporter *m* **2** *(scribe ▸ in court)* greffier(ère) *m,f*; *(▸ in parliament)* sténographe *mf*

reporting [rɪ'pɔ:tɪŋ] N *(of news)* reportage *m*; **she is noted for her objective r.** elle est connue pour l'objectivité de ses reportages

▸▸ ***reporting restrictions*** restrictions *fpl* journalistiques; **r. restrictions have been imposed** on a imposé des restrictions quant aux reportages; ***reporting structure*** *(within company)* structure hiérarchique

repose [rɪ'pəʊz] VT *Formal* **1** *(rest)* **to r. oneself** se reposer **2** *(place ▸ confidence, trust)* mettre, placer; **to r. (one's) trust in sb** placer *ou* mettre sa confiance en qn

VI **1** *(rest ▸ person)* se reposer; *(▸ the dead)* reposer **2** *(be founded ▸ belief, theory)* reposer

N *Formal or Literary (rest)* repos *m*; *(sleep)* sommeil *m*; **in r.** au *ou* en repos; **to pray for the r. of sb's soul** prier pour le repos de l'âme de qn

reposition [,ri:pə'zɪʃən] VT **1** *(move)* **to r. sth** changer qch de place; **she repositioned herself nearer the door** elle a changé de place pour aller se placer près de la porte **2** *Com (change image of ▸ product, brand, political party)* repositionner

repositioning [,ri:pə'zɪʃənɪŋ] N *Com (of product, brand, political party)* repositionnement *m*

repository [rɪ'pɒzɪtərɪ] *(pl* **repositories***)* N **1** *(storehouse ▸ large)* entrepôt *m*; *(▸ smaller)* dépôt *m* **2** *Literary (of knowledge)* mine *f*; *(person ▸ of secret)* dépositaire *mf*

repossess [,ri:pə'zes] VT reprendre possession de; *Law* saisir; **they have been repossessed, their house has been repossessed** leur maison a été mise en saisie immobilière

repossession [,ri:pə'zeʃən] N reprise *f* de possession; *Law* saisie *f*

▸▸ ***repossession order*** ordre *m* de saisie

repot [,ri:'pɒt] *(pt & pp* **repotted**, *cont* **repotting***)* VT *(plant)* rempoter

reprehend [,reprɪ'hend] VT *(person)* réprimander; *(conduct, action)* condamner, désavouer

reprehensible [,reprɪ'hensəbəl] ADJ répréhensible

reprehensibly [,reprɪ'hensəblɪ] ADV de façon répréhensible

represent [,reprɪ'zent] VT **1** *(symbolize ▸ of diagram, picture, symbol)* représenter; **the statue represents peace** la statue représente *ou* symbolise la paix

2 *(constitute ▸ achievement, change)* représenter, constituer; **this represents a great improvement** cela constitue un grand progrès; **the book represents five years' work** le livre représente cinq années de travail

3 *Pol (voters, members)* représenter; **she represents Tooting** elle est député de *ou* elle représente la circonscription de Tooting

4 *(be delegate for ▸ of person)* représenter; **the President was represented by the ambassador** le Président était représenté par l'ambassadeur; **the best lawyers are representing the victims** les victimes sont représentées par les meilleurs avocats

5 *(opinion)* représenter; **the voice of women is not represented on the committee** les femmes ne sont pas représentées au comité; **the government's policy does not r. my opinions** la politique du gouvernement n'est pas représentative de mes opinions

6 *(in numbers)* représenter; **foreign students are well represented in the university** il y a une forte proportion d'étudiants étrangers à l'université

7 *(depict)* représenter, dépeindre; *(describe)* décrire

8 *Formal (express, explain ▸ advantages, prospect, theory)* présenter; **they represented their grievances to the director** ils ont fait part de *ou* présenté leurs griefs au directeur
9 *Theat (of actor)* jouer, interpréter

e-present [riː-] **VT** *Fin* présenter de nouveau

epresentation [ˌreprɪzen'teɪʃən] **N 1** *Pol* représentation *f*; **they have increased their r. to six** le nombre de leurs délégués est passé à six; **they still lacked r. in Parliament** ils n'étaient toujours pas représentés au parlement **2** *(description, presentation)* représentation *f* **3** *(of facts)* exposé *m* des faits; **this is a fair r. of their point of view** cela représente bien leur point de vue
• **representations NPL** *(complaints)* plaintes *fpl*, protestations *fpl*; *(intervention)* démarche *f*, intervention *f*; **to make representations to sb** *(complain)* se plaindre auprès de qn; *(intervene)* faire des démarches auprès de qn

epresentational [ˌreprɪzen'teɪʃənəl] **ADJ** *(gen)* représentatif; *Art* figuratif

epresentative [ˌreprɪ'zentətɪv] **ADJ** *(typical)* typique, représentatif; **to be r. of sth** être représentatif de qch; **a r. cross-section of the population** un échantillon représentatif de la population
N 1 *(gen)* représentant(e) *m,f*; **he is our country's r. abroad** il représente notre pays à l'étranger **2** *Com* **(sales) r.** représentant(e) *m,f* (de commerce)
• **Representative** *Am Pol* **N** = membre de la Chambre des représentants, ≃ député *m*
▸▸ *Pol* ***representative assembly*** assemblée *m* représentative

epress [rɪ'pres] **VT 1** *(impulse, desire)* réprimer **2** *Psy* refouler

epressed [rɪ'prest] **ADJ 1** *(gen)* réprimé **2** *Psy* refoulé; **she had a very r. adolescence** elle a été refoulée à l'adolescence

epression [rɪ'preʃən] **N 1** *(gen)* répression *f* **2** *Psy* refoulement *m*

epressive [rɪ'presɪv] **ADJ** *(authority, system, law)* répressif; *(measures)* de répression, répressif

eprieve [rɪ'priːv] **VT 1** *Law (prisoner ▸ remit)* gracier; *(▸ postpone)* accorder un sursis à **2** *Fig (give respite to ▸ company)* accorder un sursis à; **the shipyard has been reprieved** *(temporarily)* le chantier naval bénéficie d'un sursis; *(definitively)* le chantier naval a été sauvé
N 1 *Law (permanent)* remise *f* de peine, grâce *f*; *(temporary)* sursis *m*; **to be given a r.** *(permanent)* être gracié, obtenir une remise de peine; *(temporary)* obtenir un sursis **2** *Fig (respite ▸ from danger, illness)* sursis *m*, répit *m*; *(extra time)* sursis *m*, délai *m*; **this is a r. for the government** cela constitue un sursis pour le gouvernement

eprimand ['reprɪmɑːnd] **VT** *(rebuke)* réprimander (**for** pour); *(employee, accused person)* blâmer (**for** pour); **he was reprimanded for being late** *(schoolchild)* on lui a donné un avertissement pour son retard; *(employee)* il a reçu un blâme pour son retard
N *(rebuke)* réprimande *f*; *(professional)* blâme *m*

eprint VT [ˌriː'prɪnt] *(book)* réimprimer; *(article)* faire paraître *ou* publier à nouveau; **the book is being reprinted** le livre est en réimpression; **an article reprinted from The Times** un article reproduit du Times
VI [ˌriː'prɪnt] *(book)* être en réimpression
N ['riːprɪnt] *(of book)* réimpression *f*; *(of article)* nouvelle parution *f*, nouvelle publication *f*; **her novel is in its tenth r.** son roman en est à sa dixième réimpression

eprisal [rɪ'praɪzəl] **N** représailles *fpl*; **to take reprisals (against sb)** user de représailles *ou* exercer des représailles (contre qn); **by way of** *or* **in r., as a r.** par représailles; **there have been threats of r.** il y a eu des menaces de représailles
COMP *(attack, raid)* de représailles

eprise [rɪ'priːz] **N** *Mus* reprise *f*

epro ['riːprəʊ] *(pl* **repros) N** *Fam Typ (abbr* **reproduction)** (épreuve *f*) repro *f*
▸▸ ***repro head*** tête *f* de lecture□

eproach [rɪ'prəʊtʃ] **N 1** *(criticism)* reproche *m*; **in a tone of r.** sur un ton réprobateur *ou* de reproche; **a look of r.** un regard plein de reproche; **to heap reproaches on sb** accabler qn de reproches; **above** *or* **beyond r.** au-dessus de tout reproche, irréprochable **2** *(source of shame)* honte *f*; **to be a r. to** être la honte de; **it is a r. to the government that...** c'est une honte pour le gouvernement que...; **things that have brought r. upon his** des choses qui ont jeté le discrédit sur lui
VT faire des reproches à; **to r. sb with sth** reprocher qch à qn; **I r. myself for failing to warn them** je m'en veux de ne pas les avoir prévenus; **I have nothing to r. myself for** *or* **with** je n'ai rien à me reprocher; **he was reproached for his insensitivity** on lui a reproché son manque de sensibilité

reproachful [rɪ'prəʊtʃfʊl] **ADJ** *(voice, look, attitude)* réprobateur; *(tone, words)* de reproche, réprobateur

reproachfully [rɪ'prəʊtʃfʊlɪ] **ADV** avec reproche; *(say, look at)* d'un ton/d'un air de reproche *ou* plein de reproche

reprobate ['reprəbeɪt] **ADJ** dépravé
N *Formal* réprouvé(e) *m,f*; *Hum* vaurien(enne) *m,f*

reprocess [ˌriː'prəʊses] **VT** retraiter

reprocessing [ˌriː'prəʊsesɪŋ] **N** retraitement *m*; **nuclear r.** retraitement *m* des déchets nucléaires
▸▸ ***reprocessing plant*** usine *f* de retraitement

reproduce [ˌriːprə'djuːs] **VT** *(painting, document)* reproduire
VI 1 *Biol* se reproduire **2** *(photocopier)* reproduire; **this print will r. well** cette estampe se prêtera bien à la reproduction

reproduction [ˌriːprə'dʌkʃən] **N 1** *Biol* reproduction *f* **2** *(of painting, document)* reproduction *f*, copie *f*; **thousands of reproductions have been made of this picture** ce tableau a été reproduit à des milliers d'exemplaires; **a r. Regency armchair** une reproduction *ou* une copie d'un fauteuil Régence
▸▸ ***reproduction furniture*** reproduction *f ou* copie *f* de meubles d'époque; ***reproduction rights*** droits *mpl* de reproduction

reproductive [ˌriːprə'dʌktɪv] **ADJ** *Biol* reproducteur, de reproduction
▸▸ ***reproductive organs*** organes *mpl* reproducteurs; ***reproductive system*** appareil *m* reproducteur

reprogram [ˌriː'prəʊgræm] **VT** *Comput* reprogrammer; **to r. a computer to do sth** reprogrammer un ordinateur pour qu'il fasse qch

reprogrammable [ˌriːˌprəʊ'græməbəl] **ADJ** *Comput (key)* reprogrammable

reprographic [ˌriːprəʊ'græfɪk] **ADJ** *Typ* reprographique

reprographics [ˌriːprəg'ræfɪks], **reprography** [rɪ'prɒgrəfɪ] **N** reprographie *f*

reproof[1] [rɪ'pruːf] **N** *(reproach)* réprimande *f*, reproche *m*

reproof[2] [ˌriː'pruːf] **VT** *(raincoat)* réimperméabiliser

reprove [rɪ'pruːv] **VT** *(person)* réprimander; *(action, behaviour)* réprouver; **he was reproved for his conduct** on lui a reproché sa conduite

reproving [rɪ'pruːvɪŋ] **ADJ** réprobateur

reprovingly [rɪ'pruːvɪŋlɪ] **ADV** *(look)* d'un air réprobateur *ou* de reproche; *(say)* d'un ton réprobateur *ou* de reproche

reptile ['reptaɪl] **ADJ** reptile
N reptile *m*
▸▸ ***reptile house*** vivarium *m*

reptilian [rep'tɪlɪən] **ADJ 1** *Zool* reptilien **2** *Fig Pej* reptile
N reptile *m*

Repub. *Am (written abbr* **Republican)** républicain

republic [rɪ'pʌblɪk] **N** *Pol & Fig* république *f*

republican [rɪ'pʌblɪkən] **ADJ** républicain
N républicain(e) *m,f*
• **Republican** *Pol* **N** républicain(e) *m,f* **ADJ** républicain
▸▸ ***the Republican party*** le Parti républicain

> **REPUBLICAN**
>
> Aux États-Unis, un républicain est un partisan du parti républicain. Ce parti est le plus conservateur des deux principaux partis politiques des États-Unis: son origine remonte à 1854 et à l'alliance des opposants à l'extension de l'esclavage dans l'Ouest américain. En Irlande, le terme républicain désigne une personne qui souhaite le rattachement de l'Irlande du Nord à la république d'Irlande. Au Royaume-Uni et en Australie, le terme désigne les personnes favorables à l'abolition de la monarchie et à l'établissement d'une république.

republicanism [rɪ'pʌblɪkənɪzəm] **N** républicanisme *m*

republication ['riːˌpʌblɪ'keɪʃən] **N** *(of book)* réédition *f*, nouvelle édition *f*; *(of banns)* nouvelle publication *f*

republish [ˌriː'pʌblɪʃ] **VT** *(book)* rééditer; *(banns)* republier, publier de nouveau

repudiate [rɪ'pjuːdɪeɪt] **VT 1** *(reject ▸ opinion, belief, friend)* renier, désavouer; *(▸ authority, accusation, charge, evidence)* rejeter; *(▸ spouse)* répudier; *(▸ gift, offer)* refuser, rejeter **2** *(go back on ▸ obligation, debt, treaty)* refuser d'honorer

repudiation [rɪˌpjuːdɪ'eɪʃən] **N 1** *(of opinion, belief, friend)* reniement *m*, désaveu *m*; *(of spouse)* répudiation *f*; *(of authority, accusation, charge, evidence)* rejet *m*; *(of gift, offer)* refus *m*, rejet *m* **2** *(of obligation, debt, treaty)* refus *m* d'honorer

repugnance [rɪ'pʌgnəns] **N** répugnance *f* (**for** pour)

repugnant [rɪ'pʌgnənt] **ADJ** répugnant; **to be r. to sb** répugner à qn; **I find the idea r.** cette idée me répugne

repulse [rɪ'pʌls] **VT** *(attack, offer)* repousser; **to be repulsed by sth** *(disgusted)* être révolté par qch
N *Mil (defeat)* défaite *f*, échec *m*; *Fig (refusal)* refus *m*, rebuffade *f*

repulsion [rɪ'pʌlʃən] **N 1** *(disgust)* répulsion *f* (**for** à l'égard de); **to feel r. for sb/sth** éprouver de la répulsion à l'égard de qn/qch **2** *Phys* répulsion *f*

repulsive [rɪ'pʌlsɪv] **ADJ 1** *(disgusting)* répugnant, repoussant **2** *Phys* répulsif

repulsively [rɪ'pʌlsɪvlɪ] **ADV** de façon repoussante *ou* répugnante; **r. ugly** d'une laideur repoussante

repulsiveness [rɪ'pʌlsɪvnɪs] **N 1** *(disgusting quality)* caractère *m* repoussant *ou* répugnant **2** *Phys* force *f* répulsive

repurchase [ˌriː'pɜːtʃɪs] **N** rachat *m*; *Mktg* réachat *m*; *St Exch & Banking* réméré *m*; **sale with option of r.** vente *f* avec faculté de rachat
VT racheter; *Mktg* réacheter
▸▸ *St Exch & Banking* ***repurchase agreement*** pension *f* livrée, opération *f* de réméré *ou* de prise en pension; ***repurchase right*** droit *m* de rachat

reputable ['repjʊtəbəl] **ADJ** *(person, family)* qui a bonne réputation, honorable, estimable; *(firm, tradesman)* qui a bonne réputation; *(profession)* honorable; *(source)* sûr; **they're a very r. firm** c'est une entreprise d'excellente réputation

reputation [ˌrepjʊ'teɪʃən] **N** réputation *f*; **to have a good/bad r.** avoir (une) bonne/mauvaise réputation; **to know sb by r.** connaître qn de réputation; **his r. had gone before him** sa réputation l'avait précédé; **she has a r. as a cook** sa réputation de cuisinière n'est plus à faire; **they have a r. for good service** ils sont réputés pour la qualité de leur service; **she has a r. for being difficult** elle a la réputation d'être difficile; *Pej* **he has a bit of a r.** il n'a pas très bonne réputation; **to live up to one's r.** *(person)* se montrer à la hauteur de sa réputation; *(book, restaurant etc)* être à la hauteur de sa réputation; *Old-fashioned* **to ruin a girl's r.** entacher l'honneur d'une jeune fille

repute [rɪ'pjuːt] **N** réputation *f*, renom *m*; **to be of good/ill r.** avoir (une) bonne/mauvaise réputation; **a firm of some r.** une entreprise d'un certain renom; *Hum Euph* **a house of ill r.** une maison close; **I only know her by r.** je ne la connais que de réputation; **she is held in high r. by all her colleagues** elle jouit d'une excellente réputation auprès de ses collègues
VT *(rumoured)* **she is reputed to be wealthy** elle passe pour riche; **he is reputed to be a good doc-**

tor il a la réputation d'être (un) bon médecin, il est réputé pour être bon médecin

reputed [rɪ'pju:tɪd] ADJ réputé

►► *Law* ***reputed father*** père *m* putatif

reputedly [rɪ'pju:tɪdlɪ] ADV d'après ce qu'on dit; **he is r. a millionaire** on le dit milliardaire; **she is r. the best heart specialist** elle a la réputation d'être la meilleure cardiologue

request [rɪ'kwest] N1 *(demand)* demande *f*, requête *f*; **to make a r.** faire une demande; **to grant** *or* **to meet sb's r.** accéder à la demande *ou* à la requête de qn; **at sb's r.** à la demande *ou* à la requête de qn; **to do sth on r.** faire qch sur simple demande; **tickets are available on r.** des billets peuvent être obtenus sur simple demande; **any last requests?** quelles sont vos dernières volontés?; **by popular r.** à la demande générale **2** *(record ▸ on radio)* = disque demandé par un auditeur; *(▸ at dance)* = disque ou chanson demandé(e) par un membre du public; **to play a r. for sb** passer un disque à l'intention de qn

VT demander; **to r. sb to do sth** demander à qn *ou* prier qn de faire qch; **visitors are requested not to touch the objects on display** les visiteurs sont priés de ne pas toucher aux objets exposés; **Mr and Mrs Booth r. the pleasure of your company** M. et Mme Booth vous prient de leur faire l'honneur de votre présence; **I enclose a postal order for £5, as requested** selon votre demande, je joins un mandat postal de 5 livres; *Formal* **to r. sth of sb** demander qch à qn

►► *Rad* ***request programme, request show*** programme *m* des auditeurs, émission *f* de disques à la demande; *Br* ***request stop*** arrêt *m* facultatif

requiem ['rekwɪəm] N *Mus* requiem *m*; *Rel (mass)* messe *f* de requiem *ou* des morts

►► *Rel* ***requiem mass*** messe *f* de requiem, messe *f* des morts

require [rɪ'kwaɪə(r)] VT1 *(need ▸ attention, care etc)* exiger, nécessiter, demander; *(▸ of person)* avoir besoin de; **extreme caution is required** une extrême vigilance s'impose; **is that all you r.?** c'est tout ce qu'il vous faut?, c'est tout ce dont vous avez besoin?; **if required** si besoin est, s'il le faut; **your presence is urgently required** on vous réclame d'urgence; **my services are no longer required** on n'a plus besoin de mes services; *Euph (I've been dismissed)* j'ai été remercié **2** *(demand ▸ qualifications, standard, commitment)* exiger, requérir, réclamer; **to r. sth of sb** exiger qch de qn; **to r. sb to do sth** exiger que qn fasse qch; **candidates are required to provide three photographs** les candidats doivent fournir trois photographies; **the law requires you to wear seatbelts** la loi exige que vous portiez une ceinture de sécurité; **this job requires skill and experience** ce travail demande *ou* requiert *ou* réclame compétence et expérience; **what do you r. of me?** que voulez-vous *ou* qu'attendez-vous de moi?; **formal dress required** *(on invitation)* tenue correcte exigée

required [rɪ'kwaɪəd] ADJ *(conditions, qualifications, standard)* requis, exigé; **in** *or* **by the r. time** dans les délais (prescrits); **to reach the r. standard** atteindre le niveau requis

►► *Sch & Univ* ***required reading*** lectures *fpl* à faire

requirement [rɪ'kwaɪəmənt] N1 *(demand)* exigence *f*, besoin *m*; **to meet sb's requirements** satisfaire aux exigences *ou* aux besoins de qn; **this doesn't meet our requirements** ceci ne répond pas à nos exigences **2** *(necessity)* besoin *m*, nécessité *f*; **energy requirements** besoins *mpl* énergétiques **3** *(condition, prerequisite)* condition *f* requise; **she doesn't fulfil the requirements for the job** elle ne remplit pas les conditions requises pour le poste; **what are the course requirements?** *(for enrolment)* quelles conditions faut-il remplir pour s'inscrire à ce cours?; *(as student)* quel niveau doit-on avoir pour suivre ce cours?; **a qualification in Greek is no longer a r.** un diplôme de grec n'est plus nécessaire

requisite ['rekwɪzɪt] *Formal* N1 *(for travel etc)* article *m*; **toilet requisites** articles *mpl ou* nécessaire *m* de toilette **2** *(condition)* condition *f* (requise)

ADJ requis, nécessaire; **he didn't have the r. amount of money** il n'avait pas assez d'argent *ou* l'argent qu'il fallait

requisition [ˌrekwɪ'zɪʃən] N1 *Mil* réquisition *f*; **to make a r. for supplies** réquisitionner des provisions **2** *Com* demande *f*; **the boss put in a r. for staplers** le patron a fait une demande d'agrafeuses

VT1 *Mil & Fig* réquisitionner (**to do sth** pour faire qch) **2** *Com* commander, faire la demande de

►► ***requisition number*** numéro *m* de référence

requisitioning [ˌrekwɪ'zɪʃənɪŋ] N

►► *Mil* ***requisitioning officer*** officier *m* chargé des réquisitions

requital [rɪ'kwaɪtəl] N *Formal (repayment)* récompense *f*; *(retaliation)* revanche *f*; **in r. of** *or* **for sth** *(as reward)* en récompense de *ou* pour qch; *(in retaliation)* pour se venger de qch

requite [rɪ'kwaɪt] VT *Formal* **1** *(return ▸ payment, kindness)* récompenser, payer de retour; **her love had never been requited** son amour n'avait jamais été payé de retour **2** *(avenge ▸ injury)* venger

reread [ˌri:'ri:d] *(pt & pp* **reread** [-'red]) VT relire

reredos ['rɪədɒs] N retable *m*

rerelease VT [ˌri:rɪ'li:s] *(film, record)* ressortir

N ['ri:rɪli:s] *(film, record)* reprise *f*

reroute [ˌri:'ru:t] VT dérouter, changer l'itinéraire de; **the flight was rerouted to Shannon** le vol a été dérouté sur Shannon

rerouting [ˌri:'ru:tɪŋ] N *(of flight etc)* déroutement *m*; *(of goods)* déroutage *m*

rerun *(pt* **reran** [-'ræn], *pp* **rerun**, *cont* **rerunning**) N ['ri:rʌn] *(of film)* reprise *f*; *(of TV serial)* rediffusion *f*; *Fig* **it's just a r. of last year's final** la finale prend la même tournure que celle de l'année dernière

VT [ˌri:'rʌn] **1** *(film)* passer de nouveau; *(TV series)* rediffuser **2** *(race)* courir de nouveau **3** *Comput (program)* relancer

res [reɪs] N *Law* res *m*, chose *f*

►► ***res judicata*** chose *f* jugée

resale ['ri:seɪl] N revente *f*; **not for r.** *(on packaging)* ne peut être vendu

►► *Mktg* ***resale price maintenance*** prix *m* de vente imposé; ***resale value*** valeur *f* à la revente

resaleable [ˌri:'seɪləbəl] ADJ *Mktg* revendable

reschedule [*Br* ˌri:'ʃedju:l, *Am* ˌri:'skedʒʊl] VT1 *(appointment, meeting)* modifier l'heure/la date de; *(bus, train, flight)* modifier l'horaire de; *(planned event)* modifier le programme de; **the meeting has been rescheduled for next week** la réunion a été déplacée à la semaine prochaine **2** *Fin (debt)* rééchelonner

rescheduling [*Br* ri:'ʃedju:lɪŋ, *Am* ˌri:'skedʒʊlɪŋ] N **1** *(of appointment, meeting)* modification *f* de l'heure/de la date; *(of bus, train, flight)* modification *f* de l'horaire; *(of planned event)* modification *f* du programme **2** *Fin (of debt)* rééchelonnement *m*

rescind [rɪ'sɪnd] VT *Formal (judgment)* casser, annuler; *(agreement)* annuler; *(law)* abroger; *(contract)* résilier

rescindable [rɪ'sɪndəbəl] ADJ *Formal (judgment)* cassable, annulable; *(law)* abrogeable; *(contract)* résiliable

rescue ['reskju:] VT *(from danger)* sauver; *(from captivity)* délivrer; *(from need, difficulty)* secourir, venir au secours de; **to r. sb from drowning** sauver qn de la noyade; **they were rescued from a potentially dangerous situation** on les a tirés d'une situation qui aurait pu être dangereuse; *Fig* **thanks for rescuing me from that boring conversation** merci de m'avoir délivré, cette conversation m'assommait; **to r. sb from poverty** tirer qn de la misère

N *(from danger, drowning)* sauvetage *m*; *(from captivity)* délivrance *f*; *(from need, difficulty)* secours *m*; **to go/to come to sb's r.** aller/venir au secours *ou* à la rescousse de qn; **r. was impossible** toute opération de sauvetage était impossible

COMP *(attempt, mission, operation, party, team)* de sauvetage, de secours

►► ***rescue package*** plan *m* de sauvetage (financier); ***rescue services*** services *mpl* de secours; ***rescue worker*** sauveteur *m*

rescuer ['reskjʊə(r)] N sauveteur *m*

resealable [ˌri:'si:ləbəl] ADJ refermable

research [rɪ'sɜ:tʃ] N *(UNCOUNT) (concept, acti[v]ity)* recherche *f*; *(work involved)* recherches *fp[l]*; **to do r. into sth** faire des recherches sur qch; **t[o] do** *or* **be engaged in r.** faire des recherches (**o[n]** **into** sur); **when I finish my degree I'd like to do** quand j'aurai mon diplôme, j'aimerais faire d[e] la recherche *ou* devenir chercheur; **an excellen[t] piece of r.** un excellent travail de recherche; **scientific r.** la recherche scientifique

COMP *(establishment, work, programme, tech[]nique, tool)* de recherche

VT *(article, book, problem, subject)* faire des re[]cherches sur; **your essay is not very well re[]searched** votre travail n'est pas très bie[n] documenté

VI faire des recherches *ou* de la recherche

►► ***research assistant*** assistant(e) *m,f* de reche[r]che; ***research budget*** budget *m* consacré à la re[]cherche; ***research department*** service *m* d[e] recherche; ***research and development*** recherch[e] *f* et développement *m*, recherche-développe[]ment *f*; ***research fellow*** chercheur(euse) *m,f (q[ui] a reçu une bourse)*; ***research laboratory*** labora[]toire *m* de recherches; ***research scientist*** cher[]cheur(euse) *m,f*; ***research student*** étudiant(e) *m[,] f* qui fait de la recherche *(après la licence)*; ***re[]search worker*** *(scientific)* chercheur(euse) *m,[f]*; *Am (literary)* documentaliste *mf*

researcher [rɪ'sɜ:tʃə(r)] N chercheur(euse) *m,f*

reseat [ˌri:'si:t] VT1 *(person ▸ sit again)* faire ras[]seoir; *(▸ change place)* assigner une nouvell[e] place à; **to r. the guests** *(put in different position[s])* refaire les tables **2** *(chair)* refaire le fond de; *(trousers)* remettre un fond à **3** *Tech (valve)* rode[r]

resection [ri:'sekʃən] N *Med* résection *f*

reselection [ˌri:sɪ'lekʃən] N *Pol (of candidate)* fait d'être à nouveau choisi par son parti en tan[t] que candidat pour des élections

resell [ˌri:'sel] *(pt & pp* **resold** [-'səʊld]) VT revendr[e]

resemblance [rɪ'zembləns] N ressemblance[;] **to bear a r. to sb/sth** ressembler à qn/qch; **th[e] brothers show a strong family r.** les frères se res[]semblent beaucoup; **the newspaper accoun[t] bears little r. to the actual interview** il n'y a qu'un[e] vague ressemblance entre l'article du journal e[t] l'interview proprement dite

resemble [rɪ'zembəl] VT ressembler à; **they [r.] each other** *or* **one another** ils se ressemblent

resend [ˌri:'send] VT *(e-mail, text message)* ren[]voyer

resent [rɪ'zent] VT *(person)* en vouloir à, éprou[]ver du ressentiment à l'égard de; *(remark, criti[]cism)* ne pas apprécier; **to r. sth strongly** avoi[r] beaucoup de mal à supporter *ou* à accepte[r] qch; **I r. him being there** le fait qu'il soit là me dé[]plaît; **I r. that remark!** je n'apprécie pas du tou[t] cette remarque!; **I r. that!** je n'apprécie pas d[u] tout!; **they r. her enjoying herself** ils lui en veulen[t] de s'amuser, ils supportent mal qu'elle s'amuse[;] **he resents having to take orders from a woman** [il] accepte mal d'avoir une femme comme supé[]rieur

> Note that the French verb **ressentir** is a false friend. It means **to feel, to experience**.

resentful [rɪ'zentfʊl] ADJ plein de ressentimen[t] *ou* d'amertume; **to feel r. about** *or* **at sth** mal sup[]porter *ou* accepter qch; **to be r. about** *or* **of sb'[s] achievements** en vouloir à qn parce qu'il a réuss[i]

resentfully [rɪ'zentfʊlɪ] ADV avec ressentiment

resentment [rɪ'zentmənt] N ressentiment *m*

reservation [ˌrezə'veɪʃən] N1 *(doubt)* réserve [*f*,] restriction *f*; **to have reservations about sth** fair[e] *ou* émettre des réserves sur qch; **I have reserva[]tions about letting them go abroad** j'hésite à le[s] laisser partir à l'étranger; **without r.** *or* **reserva[]tions** sans réserve; **with (some) reservations** ave[c] certaines réserves; **he expressed some reserva[]tions about the plan** il a émis quelques doutes à propos *ou* au sujet du projet

2 *(booking)* réservation *f*; **to make a r.** *(on train)* réserver une *ou* sa place; *(in hotel)* réserver *o[u]* retenir une chambre; *(in restaurant)* réserve[r] une table; **the secretary made all the reservation[s]** la secrétaire s'est occupée de toutes les réser[]vations; **I have a r.** *(at hotel)* j'ai une réservation[,] j'ai réservé une chambre

3 *(enclosed area)* réserve *f*; **Indian r.** réserve *f* indienne
4 *Br (on road)* **(central) r.** terre-plein *m* central
5 *Rel* **the R. (of the sacrament)** la Sainte Réserve
▸▸ ***reservation desk*** bureau *m* des réservations

reserve [rɪ'zɜːv] **VT 1** *(keep back)* réserver, mettre de côté; **to r. one's strength** garder *ou* ménager ses forces; **to r. the right to do sth** se réserver le droit de faire qch; **to r. (one's) judgment about sth** ne pas se prononcer sur qch **2** *(book)* réserver, retenir; **these seats are reserved for VIPs** ces places sont réservées aux personnalités
N 1 *(store ▸ of energy, money, provisions)* réserve *f*; **to draw on one's reserves** puiser dans ses réserves; **the nation's coal reserves** les réserves de charbon du pays; **he has great reserves of energy** il a beaucoup d'énergie en réserve *ou* de grandes réserves d'énergie; **cash reserves** réserves *fpl* de caisse
2 *(storage)* réserve *f*; **to have** *or* **to keep in r.** avoir *ou* garder en réserve
3 *Br (doubt, qualification)* réserve *f*; **without r.** sans réserve, sans restriction
4 *(reticence)* réserve *f*, retenue *f*; **to break through sb's r.** amener qn à sortir de sa réserve; **with typical English r.** avec une réserve toute britannique
5 *Mil* réserve *f*; **to call up the r.** *or* **reserves** faire appel à la réserve *ou* aux réservistes
6 *(area of land)* réserve *f*; **nature r.** réserve *f* naturelle
7 *Sport* remplaçant(e) *m,f*; **to play for the reserves** jouer dans l'équipe de réserve
8 *(at auction)* prix *m* minimum; **to put a r. on sth** fixer un prix minimum à qch; **the item did not reach its r.** l'article n'a pas atteint le prix minimum fixé
COMP 1 *Fin (funds, resources)* de réserve **2** *Sport* remplaçant; **the r. goalkeeper** le gardien de but remplaçant
▸▸ *Fin* ***reserve account*** compte *m* de réserve; ***reserve bank*** banque *f* de réserve; *Mil* ***reserve list*** cadre *m* de réserve; ***reserve price*** prix *m* minimum; *Aut* ***reserve tank*** réservoir *m* de secours; *Sport* ***reserve team*** équipe *f* de réserve

reserved [rɪ'zɜːvd] **ADJ 1** *(shy ▸ person)* timide, réservé; **she is very r.** elle est très réservée **2** *(doubtful)* **to be r. in one's opinion about sth** ne pas se prononcer sur qch; **he has always been rather r. about the scheme** il a toujours exprimé des doutes sur ce projet **3** *(room, seat)* réservé; **all rights r.** tous droits réservés

reservedly [rɪ'zɜːvɪdlɪ] **ADV** avec réserve, avec retenue

reservist [rɪ'zɜːvɪst] **N** réserviste *m*

reservoir ['rezəvwɑː(r)] **N** *also Fig* réservoir *m*

reset *(pt & pp* **reset**, *cont* **resetting)** **VT** [ˌriː'set] **1** *(jewel)* remonter
2 *(watch, clock)* remettre à l'heure; *(alarm)* réenclencher; *(stopwatch, counter)* remettre à zéro
3 *Comput* réinitialiser
4 *(limb)* remettre en place; *(fracture)* réduire
5 *Typ* recomposer
N ['riːset] *Comput* réinitialisation *f*
▸▸ *Comput* ***reset button, reset switch*** bouton *m* de remise à zéro, bouton *m* de réinitialisation

resettle [ˌriː'setəl] **VT** *(refugees, population)* établir *ou* implanter (dans une nouvelle région); *(territory)* repeupler
VI se réinstaller (**in** dans)

resettlement [ˌriː'setəlmənt] **N** *(of refugees, population)* établissement *m ou* implantation *f* (dans une nouvelle région); *(of territory)* repeuplement *m*

reshape [ˌriː'ʃeɪp] **VT 1** *(clay, material)* refaçonner **2** *(novel, policy, industry, company, department)* réorganiser, remanier **3** *(sweater)* redonner sa forme à

reshaping [ˌriː'ʃeɪpɪŋ] **N 1** *(of clay, material)* refaçonnage *m* **2** *(of novel, policy, industry, company, department)* réorganisation *f*, remaniement *m* **3** **the r. of a sweater** le fait de redonner sa forme à un pull

reshuffle [ˌriː'ʃʌfəl] **VT 1** *Pol (cabinet)* remanier **2** *(cards)* rebattre, battre de nouveau
N *Pol* remaniement *m*; **a Cabinet r.** un remaniement ministériel

reside [rɪ'zaɪd] **VI** *Formal* **1** *(live)* résider; (**at, in** à) **2** *Fig (be located)* **authority resides in** *or* **with the Prime Minister** c'est le Premier ministre qui est investi de l'autorité; **the problem resides in the fact that...** le problème est dû au fait que... + *indicative*

residence ['rezɪdəns] **N 1** *(home)* résidence *f*, demeure *f*; **country/official r.** résidence *f* à la campagne/officielle; **desirable r. for sale** *(in advertisement)* belle demeure *ou* demeure de caractère à vendre; **to be in r.** *(monarch)* être en résidence; **writer/artist in r.** écrivain *m*/artiste *mf* en résidence; **place of r.** lieu *m* de résidence; *(on form)* domicile *m* **2** *Univ* **(university) r., (hall of) r.,** *Am* **r. hall** résidence *f* (universitaire) **3** *(period of stay)* résidence *f*, séjour *m*; **after three years' r. abroad** après avoir résidé pendant trois ans à l'étranger; **they took up r. in Oxford** ils se sont installés *ou* ils ont élu domicile à Oxford
▸▸ ***residence permit*** ≃ permis *m* de séjour

residency ['rezɪdənsɪ] *(pl* **residencies) N 1** *Formal (home)* résidence *f* officielle **2** *Am Med* = période d'études spécialisées après l'internat **3** *Mus & Theat (engagement)* contrat *m* (à long terme)

resident ['rezɪdənt] **N 1** *(of town)* habitant(e) *m,f*; *(of street)* riverain(e) *m,f*; *(in hotel, hostel)* pensionnaire *mf*; *(foreigner)* résident(e) *m,f*; **(local) residents' association** *(in building)* association *f* des copropriétaires; *(in neighbourhood)* association *f* de riverains; **are you a r. of an EU country?** êtes-vous ressortissant d'un pays membre de l'Union européenne?; **residents only** *(sign ▸ in street)* interdit sauf aux riverains; (▸ *in hotel)* réservé à la clientèle de l'hôtel **2** *Am Med* interne *mf (qui poursuit une spécialité)* **3** *Zool* résident *m*
ADJ 1 *(as inhabitant)* résidant; **to be r. in a country** résider dans un pays; **r. population** population *f* résidante *ou* fixe **2** *(staff)* qui habite sur place, à demeure; **our r. pianist** notre pianiste attitré; **he's our r. expert on football** c'est notre expert attitré pour le football **3** *Comput* résident

residential [ˌrezɪ'denʃəl] **ADJ 1** *(area, accommodation)* résidentiel; *(status)* de résident; **the building is reverting to r. use** l'édifice va être à nouveau utilisé comme habitation **2** *(course)* avec résidence sur place; **a r. post** un travail qui oblige à rester sur les lieux
▸▸ ***residential care*** = mode d'hébergement supervisé pour handicapés, délinquants etc

residual [rɪ'zɪdjʊəl] **ADJ 1** *(gen)* restant **2** *Chem & Geol* résiduel; *Phys (magnetism)* rémanent
N *Math* reste *m*; *Chem & Geol* résidu *m*
• **residuals NPL** *Cin & TV (repeat fees)* droits *mpl* de seconde diffusion
▸▸ *Fin* ***residual income*** revenu *m* résiduel

residuary [rɪ'zɪdjʊərɪ] **ADJ** *(gen)* restant; *Chem* résiduaire; *Geol* résiduel
▸▸ *Law* ***residuary estate*** = montant de la succession après déduction des charges; *Law* ***residuary legatee*** légataire *mf* universel(elle)

residue ['rezɪdjuː] **N 1** *(leftovers)* reste *m*, restes *mpl*; *Law (of estate)* reliquat *m* **2** *Chem & Phys* résidu *m*; *Math* reste *m*, reliquat *m*

residuum [rɪ'zɪdjʊəm] *(pl* **residua** [-djʊə]) **N** *Chem* résidu *m*

resign [rɪ'zaɪn] **VI 1** *(from post)* démissionner, donner sa démission; (**from** de); **he has resigned as Prime Minister** il a démissionné de son poste de Premier ministre **2** *Chess* abandonner
VT 1 *(give up ▸ advantage)* renoncer à; (▸ *job)* démissionner de; (▸ *function)* se démettre de, démissionner de **2** *(give away)* céder; **I resigned my voting rights to the chairman** j'ai cédé mon droit de vote au président **3** *(reconcile)* **to r. oneself to sth/to doing sth** se résigner à qch/à faire qch

resignation [ˌrezɪg'neɪʃən] **N 1** *(from job)* démission *f*; *Formal* **to hand in** *or* **to tender one's r.** donner sa démission **2** *(acceptance ▸ of fact, situation)* résignation *f*

> Note that the French word **résignation** never means **giving up one's job**.

resigned [rɪ'zaɪnd] **ADJ** résigné; **to be r. to sth/to doing sth** s'être résigné à qch/à faire qch; **to become r. to sth/to doing sth** se résigner à qch/à faire qch

resignedly [rɪ'zaɪnɪdlɪ] **ADV** avec résignation

resilience [rɪ'zɪlɪəns] **N 1** *(of rubber, metal ▸ springiness)* élasticité *f*; (▸ *toughness)* résistance *f* **2** *(of character, person)* énergie *f*, ressort *m*; *(of institution)* résistance *f*; *(of economy etc)* faculté *f* de reprise

resilient [rɪ'zɪlɪənt] **ADJ 1** *(rubber, metal ▸ springy)* élastique; (▸ *tough)* résistant **2** *(person ▸ in character)* qui a du ressort, qui ne se laisse pas abattre *ou* décourager; (▸ *in health, condition)* très résistant; **children are more r. than adults** les enfants se remettent plus vite que les adultes

resin ['rezɪn] **N** résine *f*

resinated ['rezɪneɪtɪd] **ADJ** *(wine)* résiné

resinous ['rezɪnəs] **ADJ** résineux

resist [rɪ'zɪst] **VT** *(temptation, attack, pressure)* résister à; *(reform, change, influence, attempt)* s'opposer à; **I can't r. chocolates** je ne peux pas résister aux chocolats; **he couldn't r. having just one more drink** il n'a pas pu résister à l'envie de prendre un dernier verre; **I can't r. it!** c'est plus fort que moi!; *Formal* **he was charged with resisting arrest** il a été inculpé de résistance aux forces de l'ordre
VI résister, offrir de la résistance

resistance [rɪ'zɪstəns] **N** résistance *f*; **their r. to all reform** leur opposition (systématique) à toute réforme; **they offered no r. to the new measures** ils ne se sont pas opposés aux nouvelles mesures; **they put up fierce r. to their attackers** ils opposèrent une vive résistance à leurs agresseurs; **to meet with no r.** ne rencontrer aucune résistance; **her r. to infection is low** elle offre peu de résistance à l'infection; *Fig* **to take the line of least r.** aller au plus facile, choisir la facilité; **air/wind r.** résistance *f* de l'air/du vent; *Hist* **the (French) R.** la Résistance (française)
COMP *(movement)* de résistance; *(group)* de résistants
▸▸ ***resistance fighter*** résistant(e) *m,f*

resistant [rɪ'zɪstənt] **ADJ** résistant; **she is very r. to change** elle est très hostile au changement; **r. to antibiotics** résistant aux antibiotiques

-resistant [rɪ'zɪstənt] **SUFF heat-r.** qui résiste à la chaleur; **water-r.** résistant à l'eau; **flame-r.** ignifugé

resistor [rɪ'zɪstə(r)] **N** *Elec* résistance *f (objet)*

resit *(pt & pp* **resat** [-'sæt], *cont* **resitting)** *Br* **VT** [ˌriː'sɪt] *(exam, driving test)* repasser
N ['riːsɪt] examen *m* de rattrapage; **the resits are scheduled for August** la session de rattrapage est prévue pour le mois d'août; **how many resits do you have?** combien d'examens est-ce que tu as à repasser?

resizable [riː'saɪzəb(ə)l] **ADJ** *Comput (window)* redimensionnable

resize [ˌriː'saɪz] **VT** *Comput (window)* redimensionner
▸▸ ***resize box*** case *f* de redimensionnement

resole [ˌriː'səʊl] **VT** ressemeler

resolute ['rezəluːt] **ADJ** *(determined ▸ person, expression, jaw)* résolu; *(steadfast ▸ faith, courage)* inébranlable; (▸ *refusal)* ferme; **he is r. in his decision** il est inébranlable dans sa décision; **to be r. in one's efforts** être déterminé dans ses efforts

resolutely ['rezəluːtlɪ] **ADV** *(oppose, struggle, believe)* résolument; *(refuse)* fermement

resoluteness ['rezəluːtnɪs] **N** résolution *f*, détermination *f*

resolution [ˌrezə'luːʃən] **N 1** *(decision)* résolution *f*, décision *f*; **to be full of good resolutions** être plein de bonnes résolutions; **she made a r. to stop smoking** elle a pris la résolution d'arrêter de fumer
2 *(formal motion)* résolution *f*; **they passed/adopted/rejected a r. to limit the budget** ils ont voté/adopté/rejeté une résolution pour limiter le budget; **to put a r. to the meeting** soumettre *ou* proposer une résolution à l'assemblée; **the statutes can only be changed by r.** les statuts ne peuvent être modifiés que par l'adoption d'une résolution
3 *(determination)* résolution *f*; **a note of r. entered her voice** sa voix a pris un ton résolu; **he always showed r.** il a toujours fait preuve de résolution

4 *(settling, solving)* résolution *f*
5 *Comput, Opt & TV (of image)* résolution *f*; **high r. screen** écran *m* à haute résolution *ou* définition
6 *Med (of tumour)* résolution *f*
7 *Mus* résolution *f*

resolve [rɪ'zɒlv] **VT 1** *(work out ▸ quarrel, difficulty, dilemma)* résoudre; *(▸ doubt)* dissiper; *Math (▸ equation)* résoudre
2 *(decide)* (se) résoudre; **to r. to do sth** décider de *ou* se résoudre à faire qch; **I resolved to resign** j'ai pris la décision de démissionner; **it was resolved that a final decision would be taken later** il a été résolu *ou* on a décidé qu'une décision finale serait prise ultérieurement
3 *(break down, separate)* résoudre, réduire; **the problem can be resolved into three simple questions** le problème peut se résoudre en *ou* être ramené à trois questions simples
4 *Med* résoudre, faire disparaître
5 *Mus* résoudre
VI 1 *(separate, break down)* se résoudre **2** *Mus (chord)* être résolu
N 1 *(determination)* résolution *f*; **it only strengthened our r.** ça n'a fait que renforcer notre détermination **2** *(decision)* résolution *f*, décision *f*; **to make a (firm) r. to do sth** prendre la résolution de faire qch

resolved [rɪ'zɒlvd] **ADJ** résolu, décidé, déterminé; **to be r. to do sth** être résolu *ou* décidé à faire qch

resolving [rɪ'zɒlvɪŋ] **N**
▸▸ *Opt* ***resolving power*** *(of lens)* pouvoir *m* de résolution

resonance ['rezənəns] **N** résonance *f*; *(of voice)* sonorité *f*
▸▸ *Aut* ***resonance chamber*** *(in silencer)* pot *m* de résonance; *Electron* ***resonance curve*** courbe *f* de résonance

resonant ['rezənənt] **ADJ 1** *(loud, echoing)* retentissant, sonore; *Fig* **to be r. with** résonner de **2** *Mus & Phys* résonant, résonnant
▸▸ *Mus & Phys* ***resonant frequency*** fréquence *f* de résonance

resonate ['rezəneɪt] **VI** *(noise, voice, laughter, place)* résonner, retentir (**with** de)

resonator ['rezəneɪtə(r)] **N** résonateur *m*

resort [rɪ'zɔːt] **N 1** *(recourse)* recours *m*; **without r. to threats** sans avoir recours aux menaces; **the doctor is our last r.** le médecin est notre dernier recours; **as a last r., in the last r.** en dernier ressort **2** *(for holidays)* lieu *m* de villégiature; **(holiday) r.** lieu *m* de vacances; **health r.** station *f* climatique *ou* thermale; **ski r.** station *f* de sports d'hiver **3** *(haunt, hang-out)* repaire *m*
VI to r. to sth avoir recours à qch, recourir à qch; **to r. to doing sth** en venir à faire qch; **to r. to sb (for help)** avoir recours *ou* faire appel *ou* recourir à qn
▸▸ ***resort development*** aménagement *m* touristique; ***resort hotel*** hôtel *m* de tourisme; ***resort tax*** taxe *f* sur l'hôtellerie

resound [rɪ'zaʊnd] **VI 1** *(noise, words, explosion)* retentir, résonner; *Fig* **the declaration resounded throughout the country** la déclaration a eu un retentissement national **2** *(hall, cave, hills, room)* retentir (**with** de); **the woods resounded with birdsong** les bois étaient pleins de chants d'oiseaux

resounding [rɪ'zaʊndɪŋ] **ADJ 1** *(loud ▸ noise, applause, blow, wail)* retentissant; *(▸ voice, laugh)* sonore, claironnant; *(▸ explosion)* violent; **with a r. splash** avec un grand plouf **2** *(unequivocal)* retentissant, éclatant; **her first novel was a r. success/failure** son premier roman a connu un succès/échec retentissant

resoundingly [rɪ'zaʊndɪŋlɪ] **ADV 1** *(loudly)* bruyamment **2** *(unequivocally ▸ win)* d'une manière retentissante *ou* décisive; *(▸ criticize, condemn)* sévèrement; **to be r. successful** connaître un succès retentissant

resource [rɪ'sɔːs] **N 1** *(asset)* ressource *f*; **your health is a precious r.** ta santé est un précieux capital; **natural/energy/human resources** ressources *fpl* naturelles/énergétiques/humaines **2** *(human capacity)* ressource *f*; **after lunch I'll leave you to your own resources** après le déjeuner, je vous laisserai vous débrouiller tout seul; **left to their own resources, they're likely to mess everything up** livrés à eux-mêmes, ils risquent de tout gâcher **3** *(ingenuity)* ressource *f*; **a man of r.** un homme plein de ressource *ou* de ressources
VT *(project)* accorder les ressources nécessaires à
▸▸ ***resource allocation*** allocation *f* des ressources; *Sch & Univ* ***resource centre*** centre *m* de documentation; ***resource management*** gestion *f* des ressources

resourceful [rɪ'sɔːsfʊl] **ADJ** *(person)* ingénieux, plein de ressource *ou* de ressources; *(solution etc)* habile, ingénieux; **that was very r. of you** tu as fait preuve de beaucoup de débrouillardise

resourcefully [rɪ'sɔːsfʊlɪ] **ADV** ingénieusement; **he acted r. in a difficult situation** dans cette situation difficile, il s'est montré très ingénieux

resourcefulness [rɪ'sɔːsfʊlnɪs] **N** ressource *f*, ingéniosité *f*

resourcing [rɪ'sɔːsɪŋ] **N** financement *m*

respect [rɪ'spekt] **VT 1** *(esteem ▸ person, judgment, right, authority)* respecter (**for** pour); **he was greatly respected** il était très respecté; **if you don't r. yourself, no one else will** si vous ne vous respectez pas vous-même, personne ne vous respectera **2** *(comply with ▸ rules, customs, wishes, the law)* respecter; **to r. sb's wishes** respecter les volontés de qn
N 1 *(esteem)* respect *m*, estime *f*; **I have enormous** *or* **the greatest r. for her competence** je respecte infiniment sa compétence; **she is held in great r. by her colleagues** elle est très respectée *ou* elle est tenue en haute estime par ses collègues; **you have to get** *or* **to gain the children's r.** il faut savoir se faire respecter par les enfants; **he knows how to command r.** il sait se faire respecter; **he has no r. for authority/money** il méprise l'autorité/l'argent
2 *(care, politeness)* respect *m*, égard *m*; **show a little r.!** un peu de respect!; **he shows little r. for his parents** il ne se montre guère respectueux avec *ou* envers ses parents; **they have no r. for public property** ils n'ont aucun respect pour le bien public; **he took his hat off as a mark of r.** il a ôté son chapeau en signe de respect; **to do sth out of r. for sb/sth** faire qch par respect *ou* égard pour qn/qch; **guns should be treated with r.** les armes à feu doivent être maniées avec précaution; **with all due r., Mr Clark...** sauf votre respect, M. Clark…, sans vouloir vous vexer *ou* offenser, M. Clark…
3 *(regard, aspect)* égard *m*; **in every r.** à tous les égards; **in some/other respects** à certains/d'autres égards; **in many respects** à bien des égards
4 *(compliance, observance)* respect *m*, observation *f*
• **respects NPL** *(salutations)* respects *mpl*, hommages *mpl*; **give my respects to your father** présentez mes respects à votre père; **to pay one's respects to sb** présenter ses respects *ou* ses hommages à qn; **I went to the funeral to pay my last respects** je suis allé à l'enterrement pour lui rendre un dernier hommage
• **with respect to PREP** quant à, en ce qui concerne

respectability [rɪ,spektə'bɪlɪtɪ] **N** respectabilité *f*

respectable [rɪ'spektəbəl] **ADJ 1** *(socially proper, worthy)* respectable, convenable, comme il faut; **I'm a r. married woman!** je suis une femme mariée et respectable!; **that's not done in r. society** ça ne se fait pas dans la bonne société; **to be outwardly r.** avoir l'apparence de la respectabilité; **to make oneself (look) r.** se préparer; **I'm not r., YOU answer the door** va ouvrir, je ne suis pas présentable **2** *(fair ▸ speech, athlete)* assez bon; *(▸ amount, wage etc)* respectable, correct; **a r. first novel** un premier roman qui n'est pas dénué d'intérêt; **I play a r. game of golf** je joue passablement bien au golf; **he left a r. tip** il a laissé un pourboire correct

respectably [rɪ'spektəblɪ] **ADV 1** *(properly)* de manière respectable; *(to behave, dress)* convenablement, comme il faut; *(brought up)* comme il faut; **to live r.** mener une existence respectable **2** *(rather well)* plutôt bien

respecter [rɪ'spektə(r)] **N she is no r. of tradition** elle ne fait pas partie de ceux qui respectent la tradition; **disease is no r. of class** nous sommes tous égaux devant la maladie; **to be no r. of persons** *(death, taxes etc)* ne faire acception de personne; *(person)* ne s'en laisser imposer par personne

respectful [rɪ'spektfʊl] **ADJ** respectueux (**to** *or* **towards** envers; **of** de)

respectfully [rɪ'spektfʊlɪ] **ADV** respectueusement; *Old-fashioned* **(I remain,) yours r.** *(at end of letter)* veuillez agréer l'expression de mes sentiments respectueux

respectfulness [rɪ'spektfʊlnɪs] **N** respect *m*

respecting [rɪ'spektɪŋ] **PREP** *Formal* concernant en ce qui concerne, relatif à

respective [rɪ'spektɪv] **ADJ** respectif

respectively [rɪ'spektɪvlɪ] **ADV** respectivement

respiration [,respə'reɪʃən] **N** respiration *f*

respirator ['respəreɪtə(r)] **N** *(mask, machine)* respirateur *m*; **to be on a r.** être sous respirateur

respiratory [*Br* rɪ'spɪrətərɪ, *Am* 'respərətɔːrɪ] **ADJ** respiratoire
▸▸ ***respiratory failure*** insuffisance *f* respiratoire; ***respiratory system*** système *m* respiratoire

respire [rɪ'spaɪə(r)] **VI** respirer
VT respirer

respite ['respaɪt] **N 1** *(pause, rest)* répit *m*; **without r.** sans répit *ou* relâche; **there wasn't a moment's r. from the noise** il y avait un bruit ininterrompu; **the weekend was a welcome r.** le weekend a constitué un répit bienvenu **2** *(delay)* répit *m*, délai *m*; *(stay of execution)* sursis *m*; **to get/grant a r.** obtenir/accorder un délai
▸▸ ***respite care*** *(UNCOUNT)* = accueil temporaire, dans un établissement médicalisé, de personnes malades, handicapées etc, destiné à prendre le relais des familles

resplendence [rɪ'splendəns] **N** *Literary (splendour)* splendeur *f*; *(brightness)* resplendissement *m*

resplendent [rɪ'splendənt] **ADJ** *(splendid)* magnifique, splendide; *(bright)* resplendissant; **Joe, r. in his new suit** Joe, resplendissant *ou* magnifique dans son nouveau costume

resplendently [rɪ'splendəntlɪ] **ADV** *(dress, decorate)* somptueusement; *(shine)* avec éclat

respond [rɪ'spɒnd] **VI 1** *(answer ▸ person, guns)* répondre (**to** à); **she responded with a smile** elle a répondu par un sourire **2** *(react)* répondre, réagir; **the steering is slow to r.** la direction ne répond pas bien; **the patient is responding to treatment** le malade réagit positivement au traitement; **her condition isn't responding to treatment** le traitement ne semble pas agir sur sa maladie; **they'll r. to the crisis by raising taxes** ils répondront à la crise en augmentant les impôts; **children r. well to responsibility** les enfants aiment bien qu'on leur donne des responsabilités; **he doesn't r. well to criticism** il réagit mal à la critique; **to r. to flattery** être sensible à la flatterie
VT répondre; **"who cares?" he responded angrily** "qu'est-ce que ça peut bien faire?" répondit-il avec colère

respondent [rɪ'spɒndənt] **N 1** *Law* défendeur (eresse) *m,f* **2** *(in survey)* sondé(e) *m,f*, personne *f* interrogée, répondant(e) *m,f*

response [rɪ'spɒns] **N 1** *(answer)* réponse *f*; **have you had any r. to your request yet?** avez-vous obtenu une réponse à votre demande?; **she gave** *or* **made no r.** elle n'a pas répondu; **he smiled in r.** il a répondu par un sourire; **in r. to your question** en réponse à votre question, pour répondre à votre question; **in r. to your letter** suite à votre lettre
2 *(reaction)* réponse *f*, réaction *f*; **the decision was taken in r. to public demand** la décision a été prise en réaction à la demande du public; **their proposals met with a favourable/lukewarm r.** leurs propositions ont été accueillies favorablement/ont reçu un accueil mitigé; **r. from the public was disappointing** la réponse du public a été décevante
3 *(in bridge)* réponse *f*
4 *Rel* répons *m*; **to make the responses at Mass** répondre la messe

5 *Med* réaction *f*

►► *Mktg* ***response rate*** *(to questionnaire)* taux *m* de réponse; ***response time*** *Comput* temps *m* de réponse; *Med & Psy* temps *m* de réaction

responsibility [rɪˌspɒnsəˈbɪlɪtɪ] (*pl* **responsibilities**) **N 1** *(control, authority)* responsabilité *f*; **r. for the campaign has been transferred to her** c'est à elle qu'incombe désormais la responsabilité de la campagne; **to have r. for sth** avoir la charge *ou* la responsabilité de qch; **a position of great r.** un poste à haute responsabilité; **can he handle all that r.?** est-il capable d'assumer toutes ces responsabilités?; **he authorized it on his own r.** il l'a autorisé de son propre chef, il a pris sur lui de l'autoriser

2 *(accountability)* responsabilité *f*; **he has no sense of r.** il n'a aucun sens des responsabilités; **to take r. for sth** prendre *ou* assumer la responsabilité de qch; **I take full r. for the defeat** je prends (sur moi) l'entière responsabilité de la défaite; **they refused to accept any r. for the accident** ils ont décliné toute responsabilité pour *ou* quant à l'accident; **we accept no r. for lost or stolen items** *(sign)* nous déclinons toute responsabilité pour les objets perdus ou volés; **no one has yet claimed r. for the attack** personne n'a encore revendiqué l'attaque

3 *(task, duty)* responsabilité *f*; **responsibilities include product development** vous assurerez entre autres le développement des nouveaux produits; **answering the phone is your r., not mine** c'est à toi de répondre au téléphone, pas à moi; **they have a r. to the shareholders/the electors** ils ont une responsabilité envers les actionnaires/les électeurs; **children are a big r.** c'est une lourde responsabilité que d'avoir des enfants

responsible [rɪˈspɒnsəbəl] **ADJ 1** *(in charge, in authority)* responsable; **who's r. for research?** qui est chargé de la recherche?; **a r. position** un poste à responsabilité **2** *(accountable)* responsable (**for** de); **he's not r. for his actions** il n'est pas responsable de ses actes; **who's r. for this mess?** qui est responsable de ce désordre?; **he can be held legally r. for the accident** il peut être tenu légalement responsable de l'accident; **I hold you personally r.** je vous tiens personnellement responsable; **he is r. only to the managing director** il n'est responsable que devant le directeur général **3** *(serious, trustworthy)* sérieux, responsable; **it wasn't very r. of him** ce n'était pas très sérieux de sa part; **they aren't r. parents** ce ne sont pas des parents dignes de ce nom

responsibly [rɪˈspɒnsɪblɪ] **ADV** de manière responsable; **to behave r.** avoir un comportement responsable

responsive [rɪˈspɒnsɪv] **ADJ 1** *(person* ► *sensitive)* sensible; *(*► *receptive)* réceptif, ouvert; **I asked him for advice, but he wasn't very r.** je lui ai demandé des conseils mais il semblait peu disposé à me répondre; **to be r. to praise** être sensible aux compliments; **he is very r. to my needs** il est très attentif à mes besoins; **people become more r. if...** les gens sont plus réceptifs si...; **they're not very r. tonight** *(of audience)* ils ne réagissent pas beaucoup *ou* ils sont plutôt amorphes ce soir; **the industry is not r. to market signals** l'industrie ne réagit *ou* ne répond pas aux sollicitations du marché **2** *(brakes, controls, keyboard)* sensible

responsiveness [rɪˈspɒnsɪvnɪs] **N 1** *(of person* ► *sensitivity)* sensibilité *f*; *(*► *receptiveness)* ouverture *f* **2** *(of brakes, controls, keyboard)* sensibilité *f*

respray **VT** [ˌriːˈspreɪ] *(car)* repeindre

N [ˈriːspreɪ] **I took the car in for a r.** j'ai donné la voiture à repeindre

REST [rest]

> **N**
> • reste **1** • repos **2**
> • paix **3** • support **4**
> • silence **5**
> **VT**
> • laisser se reposer **1** • reposer **2**
> • appuyer **2** • fonder **2, 3**
> **VI**
> • se reposer **1** • reposer **2, 3, 7**
> • s'appuyer **2** • être **4**
> • résider **5** • se poser **6**

N 1 the r. *(remainder)* le reste; *(others)* les autres *mfpl*; **take the r. of the cake** prenez le reste *ou* ce qui reste du gâteau; **take the r. of the cakes** prenez les autres gâteaux *ou* les gâteaux qui restent; **I'm keeping the r. of it for tomorrow** je garde le reste *ou* le restant pour demain; **the r. of the time they watch television** le reste du temps, ils regardent la télévision; **the r. of us** nous autres, le reste (d'entre nous); **it's just another day like all the r.** c'est un jour comme un autre; **(as) for the r.** pour le reste, quant au reste; **and all the r. (of it), and the r.** et tout le reste *ou* tout le tralala

2 *(relaxation)* repos *m*; *(pause)* repos *m*, pause *f*; **you need a week's r./a good night's r.** vous avez besoin d'une semaine de repos/d'une bonne nuit de sommeil; **try to get some r.** essayez de vous reposer (un peu); **I had** *or* **I took a ten-minute r.** je me suis reposé pendant dix minutes, j'ai fait une pause de dix minutes; **my arms need a r.** j'ai besoin de me reposer les bras; **after her afternoon r.** après sa sieste; **a day of r.** une journée de repos; **he needs a r. from the pressure/the children** il a besoin de se détendre/d'un peu de temps sans les enfants; **he gave her no r. until she consented** il ne lui a pas laissé une minute de répit jusqu'à ce qu'elle accepte; **you'd better give the skiing a r.** vous feriez mieux de ne pas faire de ski pendant un certain temps; *Fam* **give it a r.!** arrête, tu veux?; **r. and recuperation** *Am Mil* permission *f*; *Hum* vacances *fpl*; **to put** *or* **to set sb's mind at r.** tranquilliser *ou* rassurer qn; **to come to r.** *(vehicle, pendulum, ball)* s'immobiliser, s'arrêter; *(bird, falling object)* se poser

3 *Euph (death)* paix *f*; **he's finally at r.** il a finalement trouvé la paix; **to lay sb to r.** porter qn en terre; **to lay** *or* **to put sth to r.** *(doubts, rumour, suspicions)* dissiper qch; *(allegation, notion)* abandonner qch

4 *(support)* support *m*, appui *m*; *(in snooker)* chevalet *m*

5 *Mus* silence *m*; *Br* **crotchet** *or Am* **quarter r.** soupir *m*

6 *(in poetry)* césure *f*

VT 1 *(allow to relax)* laisser se reposer; **to r. oneself** se reposer; **to r. one's men/horses** laisser ses hommes/chevaux se reposer; **the coach wanted to r. his players** l'entraîneur voulait que son équipe se repose; **to r. one's eyes/legs** se reposer les yeux/les jambes; **(God) r. his soul!** que Dieu ait son âme!, qu'il repose en paix!; **I r. my case** *Law* j'ai conclu mon plaidoyer; *Fig* je n'ai rien d'autre à ajouter

2 *(support, lean* ► *gen)* appuyer; *(*► *one's head)* reposer (**on** sur); *(*► *one's hopes, confidence etc)* fonder (**on** sur); **she rested her bicycle against a lamppost** elle appuya sa bicyclette contre un réverbère; **he rested his arm on the back of the sofa** son bras reposait sur le dossier du canapé

3 *(base* ► *argument, theory)* fonder (**on** sur)

VI 1 *(relax)* se reposer; **they set off again after resting for an hour** ils se sont remis en route après s'être reposés pendant une heure; **to be resting** *(actor)* = se trouver sans engagement; **we shall not r. until the fight is won** nous n'aurons de cesse que la lutte ne soit gagnée

2 *(be held up or supported)* reposer; *(lean* ► *person)* s'appuyer; *(*► *bicycle, ladder)* être appuyé; **his head was resting on her shoulder** il avait la tête appuyée contre son épaule; **she was resting on her broom** elle était appuyée sur son balai

3 *(be based)* **to r. on** *(argument, hope)* reposer sur; **the theory rests on a false assumption** la théorie repose sur une hypothèse fausse

4 *(be, remain)* être; **r. assured we're doing our best** soyez certain que nous faisons de notre mieux; **their fate rests in your hands** leur sort est entre vos mains; **can't you let the matter r.?** ne pouvez-vous pas abandonner cette idée?; **he just won't let it r.** il y revient sans cesse

5 *(reside, belong)* résider; **power rests with the committee** c'est le comité qui détient le pouvoir; **the choice rests with you** c'est à vous de choisir; **the decision doesn't r. with me** la décision ne dépend pas de moi

6 *(alight* ► *eyes, gaze)* se poser (**on** sur)

7 *Euph (lie dead)* reposer; **may they r. in peace!** qu'ils reposent en paix!

8 *Law* **the defence/the prosecution rests** = formule de fin de plaidoyer ou de réquisitoire

9 *Agr (lie fallow)* être en repos *ou* en jachère; **to let a field r.** laisser un champ en repos *ou* en jachère

►► *Aut* ***rest area*** aire *f* de repos; ***rest cure*** cure *f* de repos; *Fig* **this job is no r. cure** ce travail n'est pas une sinécure; ***rest day*** jour *m* de repos; ***rest home*** *(for convalescents)* maison *f* de repos; *(for elderly)* maison *f* de retraite; *Am* ***rest room*** toilettes *fpl*; *Am Aut* ***rest stop*** aire *f* de stationnement *ou* de repos; **to make a r. stop** faire une pause pour se détendre

restart **VT** [ˌriːˈstɑːt] **1** *(activity)* reprendre, recommencer; *(engine, mechanism)* remettre en marche **2** *Comput (system)* relancer, redémarrer; *(program)* reprendre

VI [ˌriːˈstɑːt] **1** *(job, project)* reprendre, recommencer; *(engine, mechanism)* redémarrer **2** *Comput (system)* redémarrer; *(program)* reprendre

N [ˈriːstɑːt] **1** *(of engine, mechanism)* remise *f* en marche **2** *Comput (of system)* redémarrage *m*; *(of program)* reprise *f*

restate [ˌriːˈsteɪt] **VT 1** *(reiterate* ► *argument, case, objection)* répéter, réitérer; *(*► *one's intentions, innocence, faith)* réaffirmer; **the unions restated their position** les syndicats ont réaffirmé leur position **2** *(formulate differently)* reformuler

restatement [ˌriːˈsteɪtmənt] **N 1** *(repetition* ► *of argument, case, objection)* répétition *f*, réitération *f*; *(*► *of intentions, innocence, faith)* réaffirmation *f* **2** *(different formulation)* reformulation *f*; **a r. of our objectives is perhaps necessary** nous devrions peut-être reformuler nos objectifs

restaurant [ˈrestrɒnt] **N** restaurant *m*

►► *Br* ***restaurant car*** wagon-restaurant *m*, voiture-restaurant *f*

restaurateur [ˌrestərəˈtɜː(r)] **N** restaurateur (trice) *m,f* *(tenant un restaurant)*

rested [ˈrestɪd] **ADJ** reposé; **to feel r.** se sentir (bien) reposé

restful [ˈrestfʊl] **ADJ** *(holiday, weekend etc)* reposant, délassant; *(place)* paisible, tranquille; **r. to the eyes** *(colour, lighting)* qui repose les yeux, reposant pour la vue

restfully [ˈrestfʊlɪ] **ADV** paisiblement, tranquillement

resting [ˈrestɪŋ] **N**

►► ***resting place*** lieu *m* de repos; *Fig Literary* **(last) r. place** *(grave)* dernière demeure *f*

restitution [ˌrestɪˈtjuːʃən] **N** *Formal (of stolen property)* restitution *f*; *(compensation)* réparation *f*; **the company was ordered to make full r. of the monies** la société a été sommée de restituer l'intégralité de la somme

restive [ˈrestɪv] **ADJ 1** *(nervous, fidgety)* nerveux, agité **2** *(unmanageable)* rétif, difficile

restively [ˈrestɪvlɪ] **ADV** nerveusement

restiveness [ˈrestɪvnɪs] **N 1** *(of person)* nervosité *f*, agitation *f* **2** *(of horse)* caractère *m* rétif

restless [ˈrestlɪs] **ADJ 1** *(fidgety)* nerveux, agité; *(impatient)* impatient; **I get r. after a few days in the country** après quelques jours à la campagne, je ne tiens plus en place; **the audience was beginning to grow r.** le public commençait à s'impatienter; **to be a r. sleeper** avoir un *ou* le sommeil agité **2** *(constantly moving)* agité; **her r. mind** son esprit en ébullition **3** *(giving no rest)* **a r. night** une nuit agitée

restlessly [ˈrestlɪslɪ] **ADV 1** *(nervously)* nerveusement, avec agitation; *(impatiently)* impatiemment, avec impatience; **to pace r. up and down** faire les cent pas **2** *(sleeplessly)* **she tossed r. all night** elle a eu une nuit très agitée

restlessness [ˈrestlɪsnɪs] **N** *(fidgeting, nervousness)* nervosité *f*, agitation *f*; *(impatience)* impatience *f*

restock [ˌriːˈstɒk] **VT 1** *(with food, supplies)* réapprovisionner; **to r. a freezer** regarnir un congélateur **2** *Com (shop)* réassortir **3** *(with fish)* empoissonner; *(with game)* réapprovisionner en gibier

VI *(shop)* se réapprovisionner

restocking [ˌriːˈstɒkɪŋ] **N** *Com (of shop)* réassortiment *m*

restoration [ˌrestəˈreɪʃən] **N 1** *(giving back)* restitution *f* **2** *(re-establishment)* restauration *f*, rétablissement *m*; *(of law and order, monarchy)* restauration *f* **3** *(repairing, cleaning ▸ of work of art, building)* restauration *f*

• **Restoration** *Hist* **N the R.** la Restauration anglaise **COMP** *(literature, drama)* de (l'époque de) la Restauration (anglaise); *(fund, project, work)* de restauration

▸▸ ***Restoration comedy*** *(genre)* théâtre *m* de la Restauration anglaise *(caractérisé par la satire des mœurs du temps)*; *(play)* comédie *f* de l'époque de la Restauration anglaise *(caractérisée par la satire des mœurs du temps)*

restorative [rɪˈstɒrətɪv] **ADJ** fortifiant, remontant

N fortifiant *m*, remontant *m*

restore [rɪˈstɔː(r)] **VT 1** *(re-establish ▸ peace, confidence etc)* restaurer, rétablir; *(▸ monarchy)* restaurer; *(▸ monarch)* remettre sur le trône; **to r. sb's sight/hearing** rendre la vue/l'ouïe à qn; **restored to his former post** rétabli *ou* réintégré dans ses anciennes fonctions; **if the left-wing government is restored to power** si le gouvernement de gauche revient au pouvoir; **it restored my faith in human nature** cela m'a redonné confiance en la nature humaine; **to r. sb's sight/hearing** rendre la vue/l'ouïe à qn; **the treatment should soon r. his health** *or* **him to health** le traitement devrait très vite le remettre sur pied; **she managed to r. the company to profitability** grâce à elle, l'entreprise fait de nouveau des profits

2 *(repair, clean ▸ work of art, building)* restaurer; **to r. sth to its former glory** redonner son éclat d'antan à qch

3 *Comput (file, text, data)* restaurer

4 *(give back)* rendre, restituer

N *Comput* restauration *f*

restorer [rɪˈstɔːrə(r)] **N** *(of work of art, building)* restaurateur(trice) *m,f*

restrain [rɪˈstreɪn] **VT 1** *(hold back, prevent)* retenir, empêcher; **to r. sb from doing sth** empêcher qn de faire qch; **I couldn't r. myself from making a remark** je n'ai pas pu m'empêcher de faire une remarque; **I had to r. an impulse to laugh out loud** il a fallu que je me retienne pour ne pas rire tout haut

2 *(overpower, bring under control ▸ person)* maîtriser; **he had to be forcibly restrained** il a fallu le retenir de force

3 *(repress ▸ emotion, anger, laughter)* contenir, réprimer

4 *(imprison)* interner, emprisonner

restrained [rɪˈstreɪnd] **ADJ 1** *(person)* retenu, réservé; *(emotion)* contenu, maîtrisé; *(tone, terms, response)* mesuré; **her manner was very r.** son attitude était très réservée **2** *(colour, style)* sobre, discret(ète)

restraining order [rɪˈstreɪnɪŋ-] **N** *Law* injonction *f*

restraint [rɪˈstreɪnt] **N 1** *(moderation) (of person)* modération *f*, mesure *f*; *(of style)* retenue *f*, sobriété *f*; **to show** *or* **exercise great r.** faire preuve de beaucoup de modération **2** *(restriction)* restriction *f*, contrainte *f*; **to put a r. on sb** contraindre qn; **certain restraints should be put on the committee's powers** il faudrait restreindre les pouvoirs du comité; **the right to travel without r.** le droit de se déplacer en toute liberté *ou* librement; *Law* **to place** *or* **to keep sb under r.** interner qn **3** *(control)* contrôle *m*; **a policy of price r.** une politique de contrôle des prix

restrict [rɪˈstrɪkt] **VT** restreindre, limiter; **I r. myself to ten cigarettes a day** je me limite à dix cigarettes par jour; **fog is restricting visibility** le brouillard limite la visibilité; **airlines r. the amount of luggage you can take** les lignes aériennes limitent la quantité de bagages qu'on peut emporter

restricted [rɪˈstrɪktɪd] **ADJ 1** *(limited)* limité, restreint; **the choice is too r.** le choix est trop restreint; **to be on a r. diet** suivre un régime sévère *ou* strict; **she feels less r. wearing trousers** elle se sent plus libre de ses mouvements lorsqu'elle porte un pantalon; **r. access** *(sign)* accès réservé **2** *Admin (secret ▸ document, information)* secret (ète), confidentiel **3** *(narrow ▸ ideas, outlook)* étroit, borné

▸▸ ***restricted area*** *(out of bounds)* zone *f* interdite; *Br Aut (with parking restrictions)* zone *f* à stationnement réglementé; *(with speed limit)* zone *f* à vitesse limitée

restriction [rɪˈstrɪkʃən] **N** *(limitation)* restriction *f*, limitation *f*; **to put** *or* **to place** *or* **to impose restrictions on sth** imposer des restrictions sur qch; **speed r.** limitation *f* de vitesse

restrictive [rɪˈstrɪktɪv] **ADJ 1** *(clause, list)* restrictif, limitatif; *(interpretation)* strict **2** *Ling (clause)* déterminatif

▸▸ ***restrictive practice*** *(by union)* pratique *f* syndicale restrictive; *(by traders)* atteinte *f* à la libre concurrence

restring [ˌriːˈstrɪŋ] *(pt & pp* **restrung** [-ˈstrʌŋ]) **VT** *(bow)* remplacer la corde de; *(musical instrument)* remplacer les cordes de; *(tennis racket)* recorder; *(beads)* renfiler

restructure [ˌriːˈstrʌktʃə(r)] **VT** restructurer

restructuring [ˌriːˈstrʌktʃərɪŋ] **N** restructuration *f*

restyle [ˌriːˈstaɪl] **VT** *(car)* changer le design de; *(hair, clothes)* changer le style de; *(magazine)* changer la présentation de

result [rɪˈzʌlt] **N 1** *(consequence)* résultat *m*, conséquence *f*; **this paint gives excellent results** cette peinture donne d'excellents résultats; **the net r.** le résultat final; **I tried making jam, with disastrous results** j'ai essayé de faire de la confiture mais ça a été un désastre; **these problems are the r. of a misunderstanding** ces problèmes sont dus à un malentendu; **I overslept, with the r. that I was late for work** je ne me suis pas réveillé à temps, et du coup, je suis arrivé à mon travail en retard

2 *(success)* résultat *m*; **our policy is beginning to get** *or* **to show results** notre politique commence à porter ses fruits; **they're looking for sales staff who can get results** ils cherchent des vendeurs capables d'obtenir de bons résultats; *Fam* **we need a r.** *(a successful outcome)* il faut qu'on fasse un résultat

3 *(of match, exam, election)* résultat *m*; **the football results** les résultats des matches de football; *Br* **she got good A level results** ≃ elle a obtenu de bons résultats au baccalauréat; *Fam* **our team needs a r. next week** *(win)* notre équipe a besoin de gagner la semaine prochaine; *Fin* **the company's results** les résultats financiers de l'entreprise

4 *Math (of sum, equation)* résultat *m*

VI résulter (**from** de); **the fire resulted from a short circuit** c'est un court-circuit qui a provoqué l'incendie; **a price rise would inevitably r.** il en résulterait *ou* il s'ensuivrait inévitablement une augmentation des prix; **to r. in** entraîner, avoir pour résultat; **the attack resulted in heavy losses on both sides** l'attaque s'est soldée par d'importantes pertes des deux côtés; **the resulting protests** les protestations qui s'ensuivirent

• **as a result ADV as a r., I missed my flight** à cause de cela, j'ai manqué mon avion

• **as a result of PREP** à cause de; **I was late as a r. of the strike** j'ai été en retard en raison de la grève

resultant [rɪˈzʌltənt] **ADJ** *(gen)* qui en résulte, résultant; *Math & Mus* résultant

N *Math & Phys* résultante *f*

resume [rɪˈzjuːm] **VT 1** *(activity, duties, negotiations, speech, discussions)* reprendre; *(trip, journey, walk)* continuer, poursuivre; *(relations)* renouer; *Comput* reprendre; *Formal* **kindly r. your seats** veuillez regagner vos places *ou* vous rasseoir; **to r. work** se remettre au travail; **she resumed her maiden name** elle a repris son nom de jeune fille **2** *Arch (sum up)* résumer

VI reprendre, continuer; **the meeting will r. after lunch** la réunion reprendra après le déjeuner; **play resumed at four** le match a repris à quatre heures

> Note that the French verb **résumer** is a false friend and is never a translation for the English verb **to resume**. It means **to summarize**.

résumé [ˈrezjuːmeɪ] **N 1** *(summary)* résumé *m*; **to give a r. of sth** faire un résumé de qch **2** *Am (curriculum vitae)* curriculum vitae *m inv*

resummon [riːˈsʌmən] **VT** réassigner

resummons [riːˈsʌmənz] *(pl* **resummonses**) **N** réassignation *f*

VT réassigner

resumption [rɪˈzʌmpʃən] **N** reprise *f*

resurface [ˌriːˈsɜːfɪs] **VI** *also Fig* refaire surface; **the stolen jewels resurfaced in Australia** les bijoux volés ont refait surface en Australie

VT *(road)* refaire

resurgence [rɪˈsɜːdʒəns] **N** *(of ideology, trend, party)* résurgence *f*, réapparition *f*; *(of disease)* réapparition *f*; *(of interest)* renouveau *m*; *(of company)* reprise *f*

resurgent [rɪˈsɜːdʒənt] **ADJ** *(ideology, trend, party)* qui connaît un nouvel essor; *(interest, nationalism)* renaissant

resurrect [ˌrezəˈrekt] **VT** *also Fig* ressusciter; *(quarrel, argument)* réveiller; *(career)* redémarrer; **resurrected from the dead** ressuscité des *ou* d'entre les morts

resurrection [ˌrezəˈrekʃən] **N** *also Fig* résurrection *f*; **the R. (of Christ)** la résurrection du Christ, la Résurrection

resuscitate [rɪˈsʌsɪteɪt] **VT** *Med* réanimer; *(company)* faire repartir

> Note that the French verb **ressusciter** is a false friend and is never a translation for the English verb **to resuscitate**. It means **to resurrect** or **to revive**.

resuscitation [rɪˌsʌsɪˈteɪʃən] **N** *Med* réanimation *f*; **all attempts at r. failed** toutes les tentatives de réanimation ont échoué

resuscitator [rɪˈsʌsɪteɪtə(r)] **N** *(apparatus)* respirateur *m*

retail [ˈriːteɪl] **N** (vente *f* au) détail *m*; **he has a background in r.** il a une expérience de la vente

ADJ de détail; **a wholesale and r. business** un commerce de gros et de détail; *Hum* **I indulged in a little r. therapy this weekend** j'ai fait un peu de shopping pour me remonter le moral ce week-end

ADV au détail

VT 1 *(goods)* vendre au détail **2** *Formal (gossip, scandal)* répandre, *Pej* colporter

VI *(goods)* se vendre (au détail); **they r. at £10 each** ils se vendent à 10 livres la pièce

▸▸ ***retail banking*** banque *f* de détail; ***retail chain*** chaîne *f* de vente au détail, chaîne *f* de détail; ***retail dealer*** détaillant(e) *m,f*; ***retail goods*** marchandises *fpl* vendues au détail, marchandises *fpl* au détail; ***retail industry*** secteur *m* de la vente; ***retail outlet*** magasin *m* de (vente au) détail, point *m* de (vente au) détail; *Br* ***retail park*** zone *f* commerciale; ***retail price*** prix *m* de *ou* au détail; *Br Fin* **Retail Price Index** indice *m* des prix de détail; ***retail price maintenance*** prix *m* imposé; ***retail sales*** ventes *fpl* au détail; ***retail trade*** commerce *m* (de détail)

retailer [ˈriːteɪlə(r)] **N** détaillant(e) *m,f*

retailing [ˈriːteɪlɪŋ] **N** vente *f* au détail

retain [rɪˈteɪn] **VT 1** *(keep)* garder; **the village has retained its charm** le village a conservé son charme

2 *(hold, keep in place)* retenir; **to r. heat** retenir la chaleur; *Constr* **retaining wall** mur *m* de soutènement *ou* de retenue

3 *(remember)* retenir, garder en mémoire

4 *(reserve ▸ place, hotel room)* retenir, réserver

5 *(engage ▸ solicitor)* engager; **to r. sb's services** s'assurer les services de qn; *Law* **retaining fee** avance *f*, provision *f*

retained [rɪˈteɪnd] **ADJ** *Acct*

▸▸ ***retained earnings*** revenu *m* non distribué; ***retained profit*** bénéfices *mpl* non distribués

retainer [rɪˈteɪnə(r)] **N 1** *(retaining fee)* provision *f*, avance *f*; **to pay sb a r.** verser une provision *ou* avance à qn **2** *(servant)* domestique *mf*, *Arch* serviteur *m* **3** *(nominal rent)* loyer *m* nominal

retake *(pt* **retook** [-ˈtʊk], *pp* **retaken** [-ˈteɪkən]) **VT** [ˌriːˈteɪk] **1** *(town, fortress)* reprendre **2** *(exam)* repasser **3** *Cin (shot)* reprendre, refaire; *(scene)* refaire une prise (de vues) de

N ['ri:teɪk] **1** *(exam)* examen *m* à repasser; **how many retakes did you have?** combien d'examens est-ce que tu as dû repasser? **2** *Cin* nouvelle prise *f* (de vues); **it took several retakes** il a fallu plusieurs prises

etaliate [rɪ'tælɪeɪt] VI se venger, riposter (**by doing** en faisant); **the goalkeeper was sent off for retaliating** le gardien de but a été expulsé pour avoir riposté à l'agression; **she retaliated against her critics** elle a riposté à l'attaque de ses critiques

etaliation [rɪˌtælɪ'eɪʃən] N *(UNCOUNT)* représailles *fpl*, vengeance *f*; **in r.** par mesure de représailles; **in r. for** en représailles de

etaliatory [rɪ'tælɪətərɪ] ADJ de représailles, de rétorsion; **to take r. measures** exercer des représailles, riposter

▸▸ ***retaliatory attack*** riposte *f*; ***retaliatory bombing*** des représailles *fpl* sous forme de bombardements

etard [rɪ'tɑ:d] VT retarder; **to be severely (mentally) retarded** être très attardé *ou* arriéré

N *Fam* débile *mf* mental(e)ᵒ, demeuré(e)ᵒ *m,f*

etardant [rɪ'tɑ:dənt] N retardateur *m*

ADJ retardateur

etardation [ˌri:tɑ:'deɪʃən] N **1** *(mental)* arriération *f* **2** *(delaying)* retardement *m*

etch [retʃ] VI avoir un *ou* des haut-le-cœur; **the smell made me r.** l'odeur m'a donné des haut-le-cœur *ou* m'a soulevé l'estomac

N haut-le-cœur *m inv*

etching ['retʃɪŋ] N haut-le-cœur *m inv*

etd *(written abbr* **retired***)* à la retraite

etell [ˌri:'tel] *(pt & pp* **retold** [-'təʊld]*)* VT raconter de nouveau

etelling [ˌri:'telɪŋ] N nouvelle version *f*; **the story gained in the r.** l'histoire gagnait à être racontée de nouveau

etention [rɪ'tenʃən] N **1** *(keeping)* conservation *f*; *(of authority, provisions, restrictions)* maintien *m*; *(of fact, impression etc)* mémoire *f*; **to have limited/great powers of r.** *(memory)* avoir peu de mémoire/une excellente mémoire; *Com* **r. of title** réserve *f* de propriété **2** *Med (holding)* rétention *f*; **fluid** *or* **water/urine r.** rétention *f* d'eau/d'urine **3** *(memory)* rétention *f*

etentive [rɪ'tentɪv] ADJ *(memory)* fidèle, qui retient bien; *(person)* qui a une bonne mémoire

etentiveness [rɪ'tentɪvnɪs] N mémoire *f*

ethink *(pt & pp* **rethought** [-'θɔ:t]*)* VT [ˌri:'θɪŋk] repenser

N ['ri:θɪŋk] **to have a r. (about sth)** réfléchir de nouveau (à qch); **we need a complete r. of our strategy** il nous faut repenser *ou* revoir entièrement notre stratégie

eticence ['retɪsəns] N *(on one occasion)* réticence *f*; *(character trait)* réserve *f*

eticent ['retɪsənt] ADJ réservé; **he's r. about explaining his reasons** il hésite *ou* est peu disposé à expliquer ses raisons

> Note that the French word **réticent** is a false friend and is never a translation for the English word **reticent**. It means **hesitant**.

eticently ['retɪsəntlɪ] ADV avec réticence *ou* réserve

reticular [rɪ'tɪkjʊlə(r)] ADJ réticulé

reticulation [rɪˌtɪkjʊ'leɪʃən] N réticulation *f*

reticule ['retɪkju:l] N **1** *Hist (bag)* réticule *m* **2** *Opt* réticule *m*

retina ['retɪnə] *(pl* **retinas** *or* **retinae** [-ni:]*)* N rétine *f*

retinal ['retɪnəl] ADJ rétinien

▸▸ *Med* ***retinal detachment*** décollement *m* de la rétine

etinitis [ˌretɪ'naɪtəs] N *Med* rétinite *f*

retinue ['retɪnju:] N suite *f*, cortège *m*

retire [rɪ'taɪə(r)] VI **1** *(from job)* prendre sa retraite; *(from business, politics)* se retirer; **to r. at 65** prendre sa retraite à 65 ans; **to have retired** être à la retraite; **to r. from the political scene** se retirer de la scène politique; **to r. from boxing/from motor racing** abandonner la boxe/la course automobile; **to r. early** prendre une retraite anticipée

2 *Formal or Hum (go to bed)* aller se coucher

3 *(leave)* se retirer; **the jury retired to consider its verdict** les jurés se sont retirés pour délibérer; *Formal or Hum* **shall we r. to the lounge?** si nous passions au salon?; **to r. to a monastery** se retirer dans un monastère; *Sport* **to r. from the race** abandonner la course

4 *Mil (pull back)* se replier

VT **1** *(employee)* mettre à la retraite **2** *Mil (troops)* retirer **3** *Fin (coins, bill, bonds, shares)* retirer

retired [rɪ'taɪəd] ADJ **1** *(from job)* retraité, à la retraite; **to be r.** être à la retraite; *Mil* **to put** *or* **to place sb on the r. list** mettre qn à la retraite **2** *Fin (coins, bill, bonds, shares)* retiré **3** *(secluded ▸ life)* retiré; *(▸ place)* retiré, isolé

retiree [ˌrɪtaɪə'ri:] N *Am* retraité(e) *m,f*

retirement [rɪ'taɪəmənt] N **1** *(from job)* retraite *f*; **how do you plan to spend your r.?** comment comptez-vous passer votre retraite?; **to take early r.** prendre une retraite anticipée; **to come out of r.** reprendre sa carrière

2 *(seclusion)* isolement *m*, solitude *f*

3 *Mil (withdrawal)* repli *m*

4 *Sport (from match, competition)* abandon *m*

5 *Fin (of coins, bill, bonds, shares)* retrait *m*

▸▸ ***retirement age*** âge *m* de la retraite; *Br* ***retirement flat*** appartement *m* pour retraités; ***retirement home*** maison *f* de retraite; ***retirement pay*** retraite *f*; ***retirement pension*** (pension *f* de) retraite *f*; *Am* ***retirement plan*** régime *m* de retraite

retiring [rɪ'taɪərɪŋ] ADJ **1** *(reserved)* réservé **2** *(leaving ▸ official, MP)* sortant **3** *(employee)* qui part à la retraite; **to reach r. age** atteindre l'âge de la retraite

retool [ˌri:'tu:l] VT **1** *Ind* rééquiper **2** *Am Fam (company)* réorganiserᵒ

VI **1** *Ind* se rééquiper **2** *Am (company)* se réorganiser

retort [rɪ'tɔ:t] VI rétorquer, riposter

VT rétorquer, riposter

N **1** *(reply)* riposte *f*, réplique *f* **2** *Chem & Ind* cornue *f*

retouch [ˌri:'tʌtʃ] VT *(photograph)* retoucher

retouching [ˌri:'tʌtʃɪŋ] N *(of photograph)* retouche *f*

retrace [rɪ'treɪs] VT **1** *(go back over ▸ route)* refaire; **to r. one's steps** rebrousser chemin, revenir sur ses pas **2** *(reconstitute ▸ past events, someone's movements)* reconstituer

retract [rɪ'trækt] VT **1** *(withdraw ▸ statement, confession)* retirer, rétracter; *(go back on ▸ promise, agreement)* revenir sur **2** *(draw in ▸ claws, horns)* rétracter, rentrer; *Aviat (▸ wheels, undercarriage)* escamoter, rentrer

VI **1** *(recant)* se rétracter, se désavouer **2** *(be drawn in ▸ claws, horns)* se rétracter; *Aviat (▸ wheels, undercarriage)* rentrer, s'escamoter

retractable [rɪ'træktəbəl] ADJ *(aerial, undercarriage, handle)* escamotable; *(ballpoint pen)* à pointe rétractable

retraction [rɪ'trækʃən] N *(of statement)* rétractation *f*; *(of opinion)* désaveu *m*, reniement *m*; **to publish a r.** *(newspaper)* publier un désaveu

retrain [ˌri:'treɪn] VT recycler

VI se recycler

retraining [ˌri:'treɪnɪŋ] N recyclage *m*

retread *(pt* **retrod** [-'trɒd], *pp* **retrodden** [-'trɒdən] *or* **retrod** [-'trɒd]*)* *Aut* VT [ˌri:'tred] rechaper

N ['ri:tred] pneu *m* rechapé

retreat [rɪ'tri:t] VI **1** *Mil* battre en retraite, se replier; *Fig* **the management was forced to r. on this point** la direction a été obligée de céder sur ce point **2** *(gen)* se retirer; **to r. to the country** se retirer à la campagne; **to r. into a world of one's own** s'isoler dans son petit monde (à soi); **to r. from the public eye** se retirer du monde **3** *(flood waters)* reculer

N **1** *Mil & (withdrawal)* retraite *f*, repli *m*; **to beat/to sound the r.** battre/sonner la retraite; **to beat a hasty r.** prendre ses jambes à son cou

2 *(refuge)* refuge *m*, asile *m*; **a mountain r.** un refuge de montagne; **a holiday/a weekend r.** un lieu paisible pour les vacances/le week-end

3 *Rel* retraite *f*; **to go on** *or* **into r.** faire une retraite

4 *(of flood waters)* retrait *m*, recul *m*

retrench [ˌri:'trentʃ] VT **1** *(costs, expenses)* réduire, restreindre **2** *(literary work)* faire des coupures dans; *(passage)* supprimer

VI *(economize)* faire des économies, restreindre ses dépenses

retrenchment [ˌri:'trentʃmənt] N **1** *(of costs, expenses)* réduction *f*, compression *f*; **a policy of r.** une politique d'économies **2** *(of literary passage)* suppression *f*

retrial [ˌri:'traɪəl] N nouveau procès *m*

retribution [ˌretrɪ'bju:ʃən] N punition *f*, châtiment *m*; **in r. for sth** comme châtiment pour qch; **it is divine r.** c'est le châtiment de Dieu

> Note that the French word **rétribution** is a false friend and is never a translation for the English word **retribution**. It means **remuneration** or **reward**.

retributive [rɪ'trɪbjʊtɪv], **retributory** [rɪ'trɪbjʊtərɪ] ADJ *(involving punishment)* punitif, de châtiment; *(avenging)* vengeur

retrievable [rɪ'tri:vəbəl] ADJ *(object)* récupérable; *(fortune, health)* recouvrable; *(error, loss)* réparable; *(situation)* rattrapable; *Comput (data, file)* accessible; *(lost file)* récupérable

retrieval [rɪ'tri:vəl] N **1** *(getting back ▸ of object)* récupération *f*; *(▸ of fortune, health)* recouvrement *m* **2** *Comput (of data, file)* recherche *f*; *(of lost data)* récupération *f* **3** *(making good ▸ of error, loss)* réparation *f*; **the situation is beyond r.** il n'y a plus rien à faire (pour sauver la situation)

▸▸ *Comput* ***retrieval system*** système *m* de recherche

retrieve [rɪ'tri:v] VT **1** *(get back ▸ lost object)* récupérer; *(▸ fortune, health)* recouvrer, retrouver; *Fin (assets)* recouvrer; **I retrieved my bag from the lost property office** j'ai récupéré mon sac au bureau des objets trouvés

2 *(save)* sauver

3 *(of dog ▸ ball, stick, game bird)* rapporter

4 *Comput (data, file)* rechercher; *(lost data)* récupérer

5 *(make good ▸ error, loss)* réparer; *(▸ situation)* rattraper, sauver

VI *Hunt (dog)* rapporter le gibier

retriever [rɪ'tri:və(r)] N *(dog)* retriever *m*

retro ['retrəʊ] ADJ rétro *(inv)*

▸▸ ***retro chic*** la mode rétro

retro- ['retrəʊ] PREF rétro-

retroactive [ˌretrəʊ'æktɪv] ADJ rétroactif; **the increase is r. to last January** l'augmentation a un effet rétroactif à compter de janvier dernier

retroactively [ˌretrəʊ'æktɪvlɪ] ADV rétroactivement

retrofit ['retrəʊfɪt] *(pt & pp* **retrofitted***)* VT moderniser

retroflex ['retrəʊfleks], **retroflexed** ['retrəʊflekst] ADJ **1** *Ling* rétroflexe **2** *Anat* rétrofléchi

retroflexion [ˌretrəʊ'flekʃən] N *Ling* rétroflexion *f*

retrograde ['retrəʊgreɪd] ADJ rétrograde

retrogress ['retrəʊgres] VI *Formal* **1** *(degenerate)* régresser **2** *(move backwards)* rétrograder

retrogression [ˌretrəʊ'greʃən] N rétrogression *f*, rétrogradation *f*

retrogressive [ˌretrəʊ'gresɪv] ADJ rétrogressif, régressif

retrorocket ['retrəʊˌrɒkɪt] N rétrofusée *f*

retrospect ['retrəʊspekt] **in retrospect** ADV rétrospectivement, avec le recul

retrospective [ˌretrəʊ'spektɪv] ADJ *(fear, analysis)* rétrospectif; *(law, effect)* rétroactif

N *Art & Cin* rétrospective *f*

retrospectively [ˌretrəʊ'spektɪvlɪ] ADV *(wonder, acknowledge)* rétrospectivement; *(apply, increase)* rétroactivement; **the law will not be applied r.** la loi n'aura pas d'effet rétroactif

retroussé [rə'tru:seɪ] ADJ *(nose)* retroussé

retrovirus ['retrəʊˌvaɪrəs] N *Med* rétrovirus *m*

retry [ˌri:'traɪ] *(pt & pp* **retried***)* VT *Law* refaire le procès de, juger à nouveau

VI *Comput* réessayer

retsina [ret'si:nə] N retsina *m*

retune [ˌriːˈtjuːn] **VT 1** *Mus* réaccorder **2** *Rad* régler **3** *(engine)* régler
VI *Rad* **to r. to medium wave** régler son poste sur ondes moyennes
N *(of engine)* réglage *m*; **the engine needs a r.** il faut faire régler le moteur

RETURN [rɪˈtɜːn]

N
- retour **1, 2, 5, 6, 8–10**
- renvoi **2**
- rendu **3**
- aller et retour **4**
- réapparition **5**
- rendement **6**
- déclaration d'impôts **7**

VT
- rendre **1, 3, 4, 8**
- rapporter **1, 9**
- renvoyer **1, 5**
- remettre **2**
- élire **6**
- répondre **7**

VI
- retourner
- revenir
- réapparaître

NPL
- résultats **1**
- bénéfices **2**
- invendus **4**

N 1 *(going or coming back)* retour *m*; **on her r.** à son retour; **on his r. to France** à son retour en France; **the r. to school** la rentrée (des classes); **the point of no r.** le point de non-retour; *Br* **by r. (of post)** par retour du courrier; **a r. to traditional methods** un retour aux méthodes traditionnelles; **the strikers' r. to work** la reprise du travail par les grévistes; **r. to office** *(of politician)* reprise *f* de fonctions; **on his r. to office** quand il a été réélu
2 *(giving or taking back)* retour *m*; *(sending back)* renvoi *m*, retour *m*; *(of stolen property)* restitution *f*; *(of overpayment)* remboursement *m*; **on sale or r.** *(goods)* vendu avec possibilité de retour; **no deposit, no r.** *(on bottle)* ni retour, ni consigne; **it's a small r. for all your kindness** c'est une modeste récompense pour votre bonté
3 *(returned article)* rendu *m*; *(library book)* livre *m* (de bibliothèque) que l'on rapporte; *Theat* **returns may be available on the day of the performance** des places peuvent se libérer le jour de la représentation
4 *Br (round trip, ticket)* aller et retour *m*; **two returns to York, please** deux allers et retours pour York, s'il vous plaît
5 *(reappearance ▸ of fever, pain, good weather)* réapparition *f*, retour *m*
6 *Fin (yield)* rendement *m*, rapport *m*; **a 10 per cent r. on investment** un rendement de 10 pour cent sur la somme investie; **to bring a good r.** être d'un bon rapport; **r. on capital** retour *m* sur capital
7 *(for income tax)* (formulaire *m* de) déclaration *f* d'impôts
8 *Sport (in tennis)* retour *m*; **r. of serve** *or* **service** retour *m* de service; **to make a good r. (of serve** *or* **service)** bien renvoyer le service
9 *Archit* retour *m*
10 *(on keyboard)* touche *f* retour
VT 1 *(give back)* rendre; *(take back)* rapporter; *(send back)* renvoyer, retourner; *Mktg (goods)* renvoyer; **r. to sender** *(on envelope)* retour à l'expéditeur; *Tel* **to r. sb's call** rappeler qn; **returned cheque** chèque *m* retourné; **she returned my look** elle me regarda à son tour
2 *(replace, put back)* remettre; **she returned the book to its place** elle remit le livre à sa place; **to r. an animal to the wild** remettre un animal en liberté
3 *(repay ▸ kindness, compliment)* rendre (en retour); **how can I r. your kindness?** comment vous remercier?; *Fig* **to r. the favour** rendre la pareille; **to r. sb's greeting** rendre un salut à qn; **to r. good for evil** rendre le bien pour le mal; **they returned our visit the following year** ils sont venus nous voir à leur tour l'année suivante
4 *(reciprocate ▸ affection)* rendre; **she did not r. his love** l'amour qu'il éprouvait pour elle n'était pas partagé
5 *Sport (in tennis ▸ serve)* renvoyer; **to r. service** renvoyer le service
6 *Br (elect)* élire
7 *(reply)* répondre
8 *Law (pronounce ▸ verdict)* rendre, prononcer; **the jury returned a verdict of guilty/not guilty** le jury a déclaré l'accusé coupable/non coupable
9 *Fin (yield ▸ profit, interest)* rapporter
10 *Cards (in bridge)* rejouer
VI *(go back)* retourner; *(come back)* revenir; *(reappear ▸ fever, pain, good weather, fears)* revenir, réapparaître; **as soon as she returns** dès son retour; **to r. home** rentrer (à la maison *ou* chez soi); **let's r. to your question** revenons à votre question; **to r. to work** reprendre le travail; **she returned to her reading** elle reprit sa lecture; **he soon returned to his old ways** il est vite retombé dans *ou* il a vite repris ses anciennes habitudes; **the situation should r. to normal next week** la situation devrait redevenir normale la semaine prochaine; **her colour returned** elle a repris des couleurs; *Naut* **to r. to port** rentrer au port; **to r. from the dead** ressusciter d'entre les morts
• returns NPL 1 *(results)* résultats *mpl*; *(statistics)* statistiques *fpl*, chiffres *mpl*; **first returns indicate a swing to the left** les premiers résultats du scrutin indiquent un glissement à gauche
2 *Fin (profit)* bénéfices *mpl*
3 *(birthday greetings)* **many happy returns (of the day)!** bon *ou* joyeux anniversaire!
4 *(unsold books, newspapers etc)* invendus *mpl*
• in return ADV en retour, en échange
• in return for PREP en échange de, en récompense de
▸▸ *return address* adresse *f* de l'expéditeur; *Br* ***return fare*** tarif *m* aller (et) retour; ***return flight*** vol *m* de retour; ***return journey*** (voyage *m* du) retour *m*; *Comput* ***return key*** touche *f* retour; *Sport* ***return match*** match *m* retour, revanche *f*; ***return ticket* 1** *(used for return journey)* billet *m* de retour **2** *Br (round-trip ticket)* (billet *m* d')aller (et) retour *m*

returnable [rɪˈtɜːnəbəl] **ADJ 1** *(container, bottle)* consigné; *(purchase, ticket)* qui peut être rendu; **sale items are not r.** *(sign)* les articles en solde ne sont ni échangés ni repris **2** *(document)* à retourner; **r. by 1 July** à renvoyer avant le 1er juillet
▸▸ *Com* ***returnable packaging*** emballage *m* consigné

returning officer [rɪˈtɜːnɪŋ-] **N** président(e) *m,f* du bureau de vote

reunification [ˈriːjuːnɪfɪˈkeɪʃən] **N** réunification *f*

reunify [ˌriːˈjuːnɪfaɪ] *(pt & pp* **reunified***)* **VT** réunifier

reunion [ˌriːˈjuːnjən] **N** réunion *f*; **a family r.** une réunion familiale; *Am* **class r.** = réunion d'anciens élèves de la même classe ou promotion; **r. celebration/dinner** célébration *f*/dîner *m* de retrouvailles

reunite [ˌriːjuːˈnaɪt] **VT** réunir; **when the hostages were reunited with their families** quand les otages ont retrouvé leur famille; **he reunited the band for one last gig** il a reformé le groupe pour un ultime concert
VI se réunir; *(band)* se reformer

reupholster [ˌriːʌpˈhəʊlstə(r)] **VT** *(furniture)* refaire

reusable [riːˈjuːzəbəl] **ADJ** réutilisable, recyclable

re-use VT [ˌriːˈjuːz] réutiliser, remployer, recycler
N [ˌriːˈjuːs] réutilisation *f*, remploi *m*, recyclage *m*

Rev. *(written abbr* **Reverend***)* révérend *m*

rev [rev] *(pt & pp* **revved**, *cont* **revving***)* *Fam* **N** *Aut* *(abbr* **revolution***)* tour□ *m*; **to do three thousand revs** faire trois mille tours (à la) minute
VT *(engine)* faire monter le régime de□
VI *(driver)* appuyer sur l'accélérateur□; *(engine)* monter en régime□
▸▸ *rev counter* compte-tours□ *m inv*; ***rev limiter*** limiteur *m* de régime
▸ rev up VT SEP *(engine)* faire monter le régime de
VI *(driver)* appuyer sur l'accélérateur; *(engine)* monter en régime

revalidate [riːˈvælɪdeɪt] **VT** revalider

revaluation [ˌriːvæljʊˈeɪʃən] **N** *(of currency, property)* réévaluation *f*

revalue [ˌriːˈvæljuː] **VT** *(currency)* réévaluer; *(property)* réévaluer, estimer à nouveau la valeur de

revamp *Fam* **N** [ˈriːvæmp] *(of method, play)* remaniement□ *m*; *(of policy)* modification□ *f*, remaniement□ *m*; *(of company)* réorganisation□ *f*, restructuration□ *f*; *(of house, furniture, room)* retapage *m*
VT [ˌriːˈvæmp] *(method, play)* remanier□; *(policy)* modifier□, remanier□; *(company)* réorganiser□, restructurer□; *(house, furniture)* retaper; *(room)* donner un coup de frais à

revanchism [rɪˈvæntʃɪzəm] **N** revanchisme *m*

revanchist [rɪˈvæntʃɪst] **ADJ** revanchiste
N revanchiste *mf*

Revd *(written abbr* **Reverend***)* révérend *m*

reveal [rɪˈviːl] **VT 1** *(disclose, divulge)* révéler; **to r. a secret** révéler *ou* divulguer un secret; **the police do not want to r. the identity of the victim** la police ne veut pas révéler l'identité de la victime **2** *(show)* révéler, découvrir, laisser voir; **she removed the veil to r. her face** elle enleva son voile pour découvrir son visage; **he tried hard not to r. his true feelings** il s'efforça de ne pas révéler ses vrais sentiments; **the undertaking revealed itself to be impossible** l'entreprise s'est révélée impossible; **a medical examination revealed two cracked ribs** un examen médical a permis de découvrir deux côtes fêlées
N *(moment result is revealed)* moment *m* de vérité

revealing [rɪˈviːlɪŋ] **ADJ 1** *(experience, action, comment)* révélateur **2** *(dress)* décolleté, qui ne cache rien; *(neckline)* décolleté

revealingly [rɪˈviːlɪŋlɪ] **ADV 1** *(significantly)* **r. not one of them speaks a foreign language** il est révélateur qu'aucun d'entre eux ne parle une langue étrangère **2** *(exposing the body)* **a r. short dress** une robe courte qui laisse tout voir

reveille [*Br* rɪˈvælɪ, *Am* ˈrevəlɪ] **N** *Mil* réveil *m*; **to sound (the) r.** sonner *ou* battre le réveil

revel [ˈrevəl] *(Br pt & pp* **revelled**, *cont* **revelling**, *Am pt & pp* **reveled**, *cont* **reveling***)* **VI 1** *(bask, wallow)* se délecter; **to r. in sth/in doing sth** se délecter de *ou* à qch/à faire qch; **to r. in one's freedom** savourer pleinement sa liberté **2** *(make merry)* s'amuser
• revels NPL festivités *fpl*

revelation [ˌrevəˈleɪʃən] **N** révélation *f*; **her talent was a r. to me** son talent a été une révélation pour moi; *Bible* **the R. (of Saint John the Divine), (the Book of) Revelations** l'Apocalypse *f* (de saint Jean l'Évangéliste)

reveller, *Am* **reveler** [ˈrevələ(r)] **N** fêtard(e) *m,f*, noceur(euse) *m,f*

revenge [rɪˈvendʒ] **N 1** *(vengeance)* vengeance *f*, revanche *f*; **r. is sweet** c'est bon de se venger; **I'll get** *or* **I'll take my r. on him for this!** il va me le payer!; **she did it out of** *or* **in r.** elle l'a fait pour se venger *ou* par vengeance **2** *Sport* revanche *f*; **Liverpool got their r. for last week's defeat** Liverpool a pris la revanche de sa défaite de la semaine dernière
VT venger; **to r. oneself, to be revenged** se venger (**on** sur; **for** de)

revengeful [rɪˈvendʒfʊl] **ADJ** vengeur, vindicatif

revengefully [rɪˈvendʒfʊlɪ] **ADV** vindicativement, par vengeance; *(say)* d'un ton vengeur

revenger [rɪˈvendʒə(r)] **N** vengeur(eresse) *m,f*

revenue [ˈrevənjuː] **N** revenu *m*; *(from land, property)* revenu *m*, rentes *fpl*; *(from sales)* recettes *fpl*; **advertising r.** recettes *fpl* de publicité; **oil r.** revenu *m* pétrolier; **state r.** *or* **revenues** les recettes *fpl* publiques *ou* de l'État
COMP *(department, official)* du fisc
• Revenue N *Br Fam Fin* **the R.** ≃ le fisc□
▸▸ *Fin* ***revenue account*** *(from land, property)* compte *m* de recettes; *(profit and loss account)* compte *m* d'exploitation; ***revenue man*** agent *m* du fisc; ***revenue stamp*** timbre *m* fiscal

reverberate [rɪˈvɜːbəreɪt] **VI 1** *(sound)* résonner, retentir; **the building reverberated with their cries** l'immeuble retentissait de leurs cris **2** *(light)* se réverbérer **3** *Fig (spread)* retentir; *Fig* **the scandal reverberated through the country** ce scandale a secoué tout le pays *(had an effect)* ce scandale a eu des répercussions partout dans le pays
VT 1 *(sound)* renvoyer, répercuter **2** *(light)* réverbérer

reverberation [rɪˌvɜːbəˈreɪʃən] **N 1** *(of sound, light)* réverbération *f* **2** *Fig (repercussion)* retenissement *m*, répercussion *f*; **the crisis had reverberations in neighbouring countries** la crise a eu des répercussions dans les pays voisins

evere [rɪˈvɪə(r)] **VT** révérer, vénérer; **she was a much revered figure** c'était une personnalité très respectée

everence [ˈrevərəns] **N 1** *(respect)* révérence *f*, vénération *f*; **they hold her in r.** ils la révèrent *ou* vénèrent **2** *(term of address)* **Your R.** mon révérend (père); **His R. the Archbishop** Son Excellence l'archevêque
VT révérer, vénérer

everend [ˈrevərənd] **ADJ 1** *Rel* **a r. gentleman** un révérend père; **the R. Paul James** le révérend Paul James; *Br* **the Right R. James Brown** *(bishop ▸ Protestant)* le très révérend James Brown; *(▸ Catholic)* monseigneur Brown; **Very R.** *(dean)* très révérend; **Most R.** *(archbishop)* révérendissime
2 *(gen ▸ respected)* vénérable, révéré
N *(Protestant)* pasteur *m*; *(Catholic)* curé *m*; **yes, R.** *(Protestant)* oui, Monsieur le pasteur; *(Catholic)* oui, Monsieur le curé
▸▸ ***Reverend Mother*** révérende mère *f*

everent [ˈrevərənt] **ADJ** respectueux, *Literary* révérencieux

everential [ˌrevəˈrenʃəl] **ADJ** respectueux, *Literary* révérencieux

everently [ˈrevərəntlɪ] **ADV** avec révérence

everie [ˈrevərɪ] **N** *(gen)* & *Mus* rêverie *f*; **to be lost in r.** être perdu dans ses rêveries

evers [rɪˈvɪə(r)] *(pl inv* [-ˈvɪəz]) **N** revers *m*

eversal [rɪˈvɜːsəl] **N 1** *(change ▸ of situation)* retournement *m*; *(▸ of opinion)* revirement *m*; *(▸ of order, roles)* interversion *f*, inversion *f*; *(▸ of policy)* changement *m*
2 *(setback)* revers *m*; **r. of fortune** revers *m* de fortune; **the patient has suffered a r.** le malade a fait une rechute
3 *Law (annulment)* annulation *f*
4 *Phot* inversion *f*
▸▸ ***reversal film*** film *m* inversible

EVERSE [rɪˈvɜːs]

N
- marche arrière **1**
- envers **3**
- échec **4**
- contraire **2**
- revers **3, 4**

ADJ
- inverse

VT
- renverser **1**
- inverser **1**
- retourner **1, 2**
- mettre en marche arrière **4**

VI
- faire marche arrière

N 1 *Aut* marche *f* arrière; **in r.** en marche arrière; **he put the bus into r.** le conducteur de l'autobus passa en marche arrière; *Fig* **the company's fortunes are going into r.** l'entreprise connaît actuellement un revers de fortune
2 *(contrary)* contraire *m*, inverse *m*, opposé *m*; **unfortunately, the r. is true** malheureusement, c'est le contraire qui est vrai; **did you enjoy it? – quite the r.** cela vous a-t-il plu? – pas du tout; **she is the r. of shy** elle est tout sauf timide; **try to do the same thing in r.** essayez de faire la même chose dans l'ordre inverse
3 *(other side ▸ of cloth, leaf)* envers *m*; *(▸ of sheet of paper)* verso *m*; *(▸ of coin, medal)* revers *m*
4 *(setback)* revers *m*, échec *m*; *(defeat)* échec *m*, défaite *f*; **to suffer a r.** essuyer un revers de fortune; *(be defeated)* essuyer un échec
5 *Typ* noir *m* au blanc; **in r.** inversé (en noir au blanc)
ADJ *(opposite, contrary)* inverse, contraire, opposé; *(turned around)* inversé; **in r. order** dans l'ordre inverse; **in the r. direction** en sens inverse; **the r. side** *(of cloth, leaf)* l'envers; *(of sheet of paper)* le verso; *(of coin, medal)* le revers
VT 1 *(change ▸ process, trend)* renverser; *(▸ situation)* retourner; *(▸ order, roles, decline)* inverser; **this could r. the effects of all our policies** ceci pourrait annuler les effets de toute notre politique; **the unions have reversed their policy** les syndicats ont fait volte-face; *Mil* **to r. arms** renverser les fusils; *Tech* **to r. steam** renverser la vapeur
2 *(turn around ▸ garment)* retourner; *(▸ photo)* inverser
3 *(annul ▸ decision)* annuler; *Law* casser, annuler
4 *(cause to go backwards ▸ car)* mettre en marche arrière; *(▸ machine)* renverser la marche de; **she reversed the car up the street/out of the garage** elle remonta la rue/elle sortit du garage en marche arrière; **he reversed the truck into a lamppost** en faisant marche arrière avec le camion, il est rentré dans un réverbère
5 *BrTel* **to r. the charges** appeler en PCV, faire un appel en PCV
6 *Acct (entry)* contre-passer
7 *Typ* **reversed out** inversé (en noir au blanc)
VI *Aut (car, driver)* faire marche arrière; **she reversed up the street/out of the garage** elle remonta la rue/elle sortit du garage en marche arrière; **the driver in front reversed into me** la voiture qui était devant moi m'est rentrée dedans en marche arrière
▸▸ ***reverse discrimination*** = discrimination à l'encontre d'un groupe normalement privilégié; *Aut* ***reverse gear*** marche *f* arrière; *Comput* ***reverse mode*** inversion *f* vidéo; ***reverse planning*** rétroplanning *m*; *Comput* ***reverse slash*** barre *f* oblique inversée; *Comput* ***reverse sort*** tri *m* en ordre décroissant; *Fin* ***reverse takeover*** contre-OPA *f*; *Aviat* ***reverse thrust*** poussée *f* inversée; *Aut* ***reverse turn*** virage *m* en marche arrière; **to do** *or* **to make a r. turn** faire un virage en marche arrière; *Comput* ***reverse video*** vidéo *f* inverse
▸ **reverse out VT SEP** *Typ* inverser (en noir au blanc)

reverse-charge call **N** *Br* communication *f* en PCV, *Can* appel *m* à frais virés

reversible [rɪˈvɜːsəbəl] **ADJ** *(garment, process)* réversible; *(decision, decree, judgment, sentence)* révocable; *Phot (film)* inversible
▸▸ *Chem* ***reversible reaction*** réaction *f* réversible

reversing light [rɪˈvɜːsɪŋ-] **N** *Br* feu *m* de recul

reversion [rɪˈvɜːʃən] **N 1** *(to former condition, practice)* retour *m* **2** *Law* réversion *f*; **right of r.** réversion *f*; **estate in r.** bien *m* grevé d'une réversion **3** *Biol* réversion *f*; **r. to type** retour *m* au type primitif; *Fig* **this was a not unexpected r. to type** comme on s'y attendait, le naturel a repris le dessus

reversionary [rɪˈvɜːʃənərɪ] **ADJ 1** *Law (right)* de réversion, réversible **2** *Biol (characteristic, organ)* atavique
▸▸ *Fin* ***reversionary bonus*** prime *f* d'intéressement

revert [rɪˈvɜːt] **VI 1** *(gen)* retourner, revenir; **they reverted to barbarism** ils ont à nouveau sombré dans la barbarie; **to r. to childhood** retomber en enfance; **the field has reverted to a wild meadow** le champ est retourné à l'état de prairie **2** *Law (of property)* revenir, retourner **(to à) 3** *Biol* **to r. to type** revenir *ou* retourner au type primitif; *Fig* **he soon reverted to type** le naturel a vite repris le dessus

revertible [rɪˈvɜːtəbəl] **ADJ** *Law* réversible

revetment [rɪˈvetmənt] **N** revêtement *m*

review [rɪˈvjuː] **N 1** *(critical article)* critique *f*; **he gave it a good r.** il en a fait une bonne critique
2 *(magazine)* revue *f*; *(radio or TV programme)* magazine *m*
3 *(assessment ▸ of situation, conditions)* étude *f*, examen *m*, bilan *m*; **the annual r. of expenditure** le bilan annuel des dépenses; **she gave us a brief r. of the situation** elle nous a présenté un court bilan de la situation; **pollution controls are under r.** on est en train de réexaminer la réglementation en matière de pollution; **a r. of the year** une rétrospective des événements de l'année
4 *(reassessment ▸ of salary, prices, case)* révision *f*; **all our prices are subject to r.** tous nos prix sont susceptibles d'être révisés; **my salary comes** *or* **is up for r. next month** mon salaire doit être révisé le mois prochain; *Law* **he asked for a r. of his case** il a demandé la révision de son procès
5 *Mil (inspection)* revue *f*; **to pass troops in r.** passer des troupes en revue
6 *Am Sch & Univ (revision)* révision *f*
7 *Theat* revue *f*
VT 1 *(write critical article on)* faire la critique de; **she reviews books for an Australian paper** elle est critique littéraire pour un journal australien
2 *(assess)* examiner, étudier, faire le bilan de; *(reassess)* réviser, revoir; *Law (case)* réviser; **they should r. their security arrangements** ils devraient revoir leurs dispositifs de sécurité; **to r. a decision** reconsidérer une décision
3 *(go back over, look back on)* passer en revue
4 *Mil (troops)* passer en revue
5 *(revise)* réviser; **she quickly reviewed her notes before the speech** elle jeta un dernier coup d'œil sur ses notes avant le discours
VI 1 *(write reviews)* **he reviews for the Sunday Times** il rédige des critiques pour le Sunday Times **2** *Am (revise for exam, test)* réviser, faire des révisions
▸▸ ***review board, review body*** commission *f* d'étude; ***review copy*** exemplaire *m* de service de presse; *TV* ***review screen*** écran *m* de vision

> Attention: ne pas confondre avec le mot anglais **revue**, qui signifie uniquement **spectacle de cabaret**.

reviewable [rɪˈvjuːəbəl] **ADJ** *Law (case)* révisable

reviewer [rɪˈvjuːə(r)] **N** *(of film, play etc)* critique *m*; **book/film r.** critique *m* littéraire/de cinéma

revile [rɪˈvaɪl] **VT** vilipender, injurier; **our much reviled education system** notre système scolaire tellement décrié *ou* dont on dit tant de mal

revise [rɪˈvaɪz] **VT 1** *(alter ▸ policy, belief, offer, price)* réviser; **to r. figures upwards/downwards** corriger des chiffres *ou* des calculs à la hausse/à la baisse; **to r. one's opinion of sb** changer d'opinion à l'égard de qn
2 *(read through ▸ text, manuscript)* revoir, corriger
3 *(update)* mettre à jour, corriger
4 *Br Sch & Univ* réviser
VI *Br Sch & Univ* réviser; **she's revising for her end-of-year exams** elle révise pour ses examens de fin d'année
N *Typ* deuxième épreuve *f*

revised [rɪˈvaɪzd] **ADJ 1** *(figures, estimate)* révisé **2** *(edition)* revu et corrigé
▸▸ ***Revised Standard Version*** = traduction américaine de la Bible établie en 1952; ***Revised Version*** = traduction anglaise de la Bible faite en 1885

reviser [rɪˈvaɪzə(r)] **N** *(gen)* réviseur(euse) *m,f*; *Typ* correcteur(trice) *m,f*

revision [rɪˈvɪʒən] **N 1** *(alteration etc)* révision *f*; **the book has undergone several revisions** ce livre a été révisé *ou* remanié plusieurs fois **2** *Br Sch & Univ* révision *f*; **to do some r.** faire des révisions

revisionism [rɪˈvɪʒənɪzəm] **N** révisionnisme *m*

revisionist [rɪˈvɪʒənɪst] **ADJ** révisionniste
N révisionniste *mf*

revisit [ˌriːˈvɪzɪt] **VT** *(place)* revisiter; *(person)* retourner voir; *Fig* **Dickens revisited** Dickens revisité, une nouvelle perspective sur Dickens

revitalization, -isation [ˌriːvaɪtəlaɪˈzeɪʃən] **N** *(of economy)* relance *f*; *(of region)* revitalisation *f*; *(of industry, arts, trade unionism)* nouvel essor *m*

revitalize, -ise [ˌriːˈvaɪtəlaɪz] **VT** *(person)* revigorer; *(economy)* relancer; *(region)* revitaliser; *(industry, arts, trade unionism)* donner un nouvel essor à

revival [rɪˈvaɪvəl] **N 1** *(resurgence)* renouveau *m*, renaissance *f*; **a r. of interest in Latin poets** un regain d'intérêt pour les poètes latins; **a religious r.** un renouveau de la religion
2 *(bringing back ▸ of custom, language)* rétablissement *m*; *(▸ of fashion)* réapparition *f*, renouveau *m*; **they would like to see a r. of Victorian values** ils souhaitent le retour aux valeurs de l'époque victorienne
3 *(of play, TV series)* reprise *f*
4 *(recovery ▸ from a faint)* reprise *f* de connaissance; *(▸ from illness)* récupération *f*; *(resuscitation)* réanimation *f*

revivalism [rɪˈvaɪvəlɪzəm] **N** *Rel* revivalisme *m*

revivalist [rɪˈvaɪvəlɪst] *Rel*
N revivaliste *mf*
ADJ revivaliste; **a r. meeting** une réunion revivaliste

revive [rɪ'vaɪv] VI **1** *(regain consciousness)* reprendre connaissance, revenir à soi; *(regain strength or form)* récupérer **2** *(flourish again ▸ business, economy)* reprendre; *(▸ movement, group)* renaître, ressusciter; *(▸ custom, expression)* réapparaître; **their interest revived when the clowns came on** ils ont recommencé à trouver le spectacle intéressant quand les clowns sont entrés en scène; **hopes have revived of finding the miners alive** l'espoir renaît de trouver les mineurs vivants

VT **1** *(restore to consciousness)* ranimer; *Med* réanimer; *(restore strength to)* remonter; **this will r. you!** *(drink)* voilà qui te remontera!; **to r. sb's spirits** remonter le moral à qn

2 *(make flourish again ▸ discussion, faith etc)* ranimer, raviver; *(▸ business, economy)* relancer, faire redémarrer; *(▸ interest, hope etc)* raviver, faire renaître; **a plan to r. the city centre** un projet destiné à dynamiser le centre-ville; **this role could r. his flagging career** ce rôle pourrait faire redémarrer sa carrière sur le déclin

3 *(bring back ▸ law)* remettre en vigueur; *(▸ fashion)* relancer; *(▸ style, look)* remettre en vogue; *(▸ custom, language, movement)* raviver, ressusciter; **prewar fashions have been revived** on est revenu à la mode de l'avant-guerre

4 *(play, TV series)* reprendre

revivify [ˌriː'vɪvɪfaɪ] *(pt & pp* **revivified***)* VT revivifier

revocable [rɪ'vəʊkəbəl] ADJ *Law (contract, law, will)* révocable; *(decision)* sur laquelle on peut revenir; *(order)* que l'on peut annuler

revocation [ˌrevə'keɪʃən] N *Law (of decision)* annulation *f*; *(of measure, law)* abrogation *f*, annulation *f*, révocation *f*; *(of will)* révocation *f*, annulation *f*; *(of title, diploma, permit)* retrait *m*

re-voice ['riː-] VT *TV & Cin* doubler

revoke [rɪ'vəʊk] VT *Law (decision)* annuler; *(measure, law)* abroger, annuler, révoquer; *(will)* révoquer, annuler; *(title, diploma, permit)* retirer

revolt [rɪ'vəʊlt] VI *(rise up)* se révolter, se rebeller, se soulever (**against** contre)

VT dégoûter; **she is revolted by the idea** l'idée la dégoûte *ou* la révolte; **the sight of food revolts me at the moment** la vue de la nourriture m'écœure *ou* me dégoûte en ce moment

N **1** *(uprising)* révolte *f*, rébellion *f*; **the peasants rose up in r.** les paysans se sont révoltés *ou* soulevés; **they are in r. against the system** ils se rebellent contre le système **2** *(disgust)* dégoût *m*; *(indignation)* indignation *f*

revolting [rɪ'vəʊltɪŋ] ADJ **1** *(disgusting ▸ story, scene)* dégoûtant; *(▸ person, act)* ignoble; *(▸ food, mess)* écœurant, immonde; *(▸ taste, smell)* infect, écœurant; **that sounds r.!** ça semble répugnant **2** *Fam (nasty, ugly)* affreux[□]

revoltingly [rɪ'vəʊltɪŋlɪ] ADV **1** *(disgustingly)* de façon dégoûtante; **he's r. ugly/dirty** il est d'une laideur/d'une saleté repoussante **2** *Fam (as intensifier)* **she's so r. clever!** ça m'écœure qu'on puisse être aussi intelligent!

revolution [ˌrevə'luːʃən] N **1** *Pol & Fig* révolution *f*; **the French/Russian R.** la Révolution française/russe; **a r. in computer technology** une révolution dans le domaine de l'informatique **2** *(turn ▸ of wheel)* révolution *f*, tour *m*; *(▸ of record, turntable, propeller)* tour *m*; *(▸ of planet)* révolution *f*; *Tech* **100 revolutions per minute** 100 tours *ou* révolutions à la minute **3** *(turning)* révolution *f*

revolutionary [ˌrevə'luːʃənərɪ] *(pl* **revolutionaries***)* ADJ révolutionnaire

N révolutionnaire *mf*

revolutionize, -ise [ˌrevə'luːʃənaɪz] VT *(change radically)* révolutionner, transformer complètement

revolve [rɪ'vɒlv] VI **1** *(rotate)* tourner; **the moon revolves around** *or* **round the earth** la Lune tourne autour de la Terre **2** *(centre, focus)* tourner; **their conversation revolved around** *or* **round two main points** leur conversation tournait autour de deux points principaux; **his whole life revolves around his work** sa vie tout entière est centrée *ou* axée sur son travail **3** *(recur)* revenir; **ideas revolved in her mind** elle tournait et retournait les idées dans sa tête

VT **1** *(rotate)* faire tourner **2** *Formal (ponder)* considérer, ruminer; **to r. a problem in one's mind** retourner un problème dans son esprit

revolver [rɪ'vɒlvə(r)] N revolver *m*

revolving [rɪ'vɒlvɪŋ] ADJ *(gen)* tournant; *(chair)* pivotant; *Tech* rotatif; *Astron* en rotation

▸▸ ***revolving credit*** crédit *m* renouvelable, crédit *m* revolving; ***revolving door*** tambour *m (porte)*; *Am Fig* = le va-et-vient de fonctionnaires hautplacés entre les services publics et le secteur privé; ***revolving light*** *(on ambulance, police car)* gyrophare *m*; ***revolving stand*** *(to display goods)* tourniquet *m*

revue [rɪ'vjuː] N *Theat* revue *f*

> Attention: ne pas confondre avec **review.**

revulsion [rɪ'vʌlʃən] N répulsion *f*, dégoût *m*; **she turned away in r.** elle s'est détournée, dégoûtée; **to be filled with r.** être rempli de dégoût;

reward [rɪ'wɔːd] N récompense *f*; **they're offering a $500 r.** ils offrent 500 dollars de récompense *ou* une récompense de 500 dollars; **as a r. for his efforts** en récompense de ses efforts; **I do everything for him, and what do I get in r.** *or* **what r. do I get?** je fais tout pour lui, et tu vois comment il me remercie?

VT récompenser; **that's how he rewards me for my loyalty** voilà comment il me récompense de mon dévouement; **his alibi might r. investigation** ça vaut peut-être la peine d'enquêter sur son alibi

rewarding [rɪ'wɔːdɪŋ] ADJ *(job, career)* gratifiant; *(experience, conference)* enrichissant; **financially r.** rémunérateur, lucratif; **a r. book** un livre qui vaut la peine d'être lu

rewind *(pt & pp* **rewound** [-'waʊnd]*)* VT [ˌriː'waɪnd] rembobiner

VI [ˌriː'waɪnd] se rembobiner

N ['riːwaɪnd] rembobinage *m*; **it has automatic r.** ça se rembobine automatiquement

▸▸ ***rewind button*** bouton *m* de rembobinage

rewire [ˌriː'waɪə(r)] VT *(house)* refaire l'électricité dans; *(machine)* refaire les circuits électriques de; **we had to get the place rewired** nous avons dû faire refaire l'électricité

reword [ˌriː'wɜːd] VT reformuler; **let me r. that** je vais essayer de m'exprimer autrement

rework [ˌriː'wɜːk] VT **1** *(speech, text)* retravailler; **his last novel reworks the same theme** son dernier roman reprend le même thème **2** *Ind* retraiter

rewritable [ˌriː'raɪtəbəl] ADJ *Comput* réinscriptible

rewrite *(pt* **rewrote** [-'rəʊt], *pp* **rewritten** [-'rɪtən]*)* VT [ˌriː'raɪt] récrire, réécrire; *(for publication)* récrire, rewriter; *Fig* **to r. history** réécrire l'histoire

N ['riːraɪt] **1** *(act)* réécriture *f*, rewriting *m*; **can you do a r. of this?** pouvez-vous me récrire *ou* rewriter ça? **2** *(text)* nouvelle version *f*

▸▸ ***rewrite rule*** règle *f* de réécriture

rewriter [ˌriː'raɪtə(r)] N *Journ* réviseur *m*, rewriter *m*

rewriting [ˌriː'raɪtɪŋ] N *Journ* récriture *f*, rewriting *m*

Reykjavik ['rekjəvɪk] N Reykjavik

RFL [ˌɑːref'el] N *Br Sport (abbr* **Rugby Football League***)* = fédération britannique de rugby à treize

RFU [ˌɑːref'juː] N *Br Sport (abbr* **Rugby Football Union***)* = fédération anglaise de rugby

RGB [ˌɑːdʒiː'biː] N *Comput (abbr* **red, green and blue***)* RVB *m*

Rgt *(written abbr* **regiment***)* rég

rhapsodic [ræp'sɒdɪk] ADJ **1** *(ecstatic)* extatique; *(full of praise)* dithyrambique **2** *Mus* rhapsodique, rapsodique

rhapsodize, -ise ['ræpsədaɪz] VI s'extasier; **to r. about** *or* **over sth** s'extasier sur qch

rhapsody ['ræpsədɪ] *(pl* **rhapsodies***)* N **1** *(ecstasy)* extase *f*; **to go into rhapsodies about sth** s'extasier sur qch; **to send sb into rhapsodies** rendre qn extatique **2** *Mus & Literature* rhapsodie *f*, rapsodie *f*

rhea [rɪə] N *Orn* nandou *m*

Rhenish ['riːnɪʃ] ADJ rhénan, du Rhin

N vin *m* du Rhin

▸▸ ***Rhenish wine*** vin *m* du Rhin

rhesus ['riːsəs] N *Zool (monkey)* rhésus *m*; **R positive/negative** Rhésus positif/négatif

▸▸ ***Rhesus baby*** = enfant rhésus positif sou frant d'incompatibilité avec le rhésus négat de la mère; *Physiol* ***Rhesus factor*** (facteur *m*) rhé sus *m*; *Zool* ***rhesus macaque, rhesus monkey*** (ma caque *m*) rhésus *m*

rhetoric ['retərɪk] N **1** *Pej (bombast)* emphase rhétorique *f*; **it's just empty r.** ce ne sont que de mots **2** *(art of speaking)* rhétorique *f*

rhetorical [rɪ'tɒrɪkəl] ADJ *(question)* rhétorique *(term)* de rhétorique; **his question was purely r.** s question était purement rhétorique

▸▸ ***rhetorical question*** question *f* posée pour l forme

rhetorically [rɪ'tɒrɪklɪ] ADV en rhétoricien; *(ask* pour la forme; **"who knows?" she asked r.** "qu sait?" demanda-t-elle sans vraiment attendr de réponse

rhetorician [ˌretə'rɪʃən] N **1** *(speaker)* rhétor cien(enne) *m,f*; *Pej (who uses over-elaborate lar guage)* rhéteur *m* **2** *(teacher of rhetoric)* rhéteur *r*

rheumatic [ruː'mætɪk] ADJ *(pain, symptom)* rhu matismal; *(person)* rhumatisant; *(finger, join limb)* atteint de rhumatismes; **his r. fingers** se doigts déformés par les rhumatismes

N rhumatisant(e) *m,f*

▸▸ ***rheumatic fever*** rhumatisme *m* articulaire a gu

rheumaticky [ruː'mætɪkɪ] ADJ *Br Fam (person* rhumatisant[□]; *(finger, joint, limb)* atteint de rhu matismes[□]

rheumatics [ruː'mætɪks] NPL *Fam* rhumatis mes[□] *mpl*; **to have** *or* **to suffer from r.** avoir de *ou* souffrir de rhumatismes[□]

rheumatoid ['ruːmətɔɪd] ADJ rhumatoïde

▸▸ ***rheumatoid arthritis*** polyarthrite *f* rhuma toïde

rheumatologist [ˌruːmə'tɒlədʒɪst] N rhumato logue *mf*

rheumatology [ˌruːmə'tɒlədʒɪ] N rhumatologi *f*

rheumy ['ruːmɪ] *(compar* **rheumier**, *superl* **rheu miest***)* ADJ chassieux

Rhine [raɪn] N **the (River) R.** le Rhin

▸▸ ***Rhine wine*** vin *m* du Rhin

Rhineland ['raɪnlænd] N Rhénanie *f*

rhinestone ['raɪnstəʊn] N faux diamant *n (smaller)* strass *m*

COMP en strass

rhino ['raɪnəʊ] *(pl* inv *or* **rhinos***)* N *Zool* rhinocéro *m*

▸▸ ***rhino bars*** pare-buffles *m inv*

rhinoceros [raɪ'nɒsərəs] *(pl* **inv** *or* **rhinocerose** *or* **rhinoceri** [-raɪ]*)* N *Zool* rhinocéros *m*; *Fig* **t have skin** *or* **a hide like a r.** manquer totalemen de *ou* être complètement dépourvu de sensibi lité

rhizome ['raɪzəʊm] N *Bot* rhizome *m*

Rhode Island [rəʊd-] N le Rhode Island

▸▸ ***Rhode Island Red*** poule *f* Rhode-Island

Rhodes [rəʊdz] N Rhodes

▸▸ ***Rhodes scholar*** = titulaire d'une "Rhode Scholarship"; ***Rhodes Scholarship*** = bourse pe mettant à certains étudiants étrangers d'étu dier à l'université d'Oxford

Rhodesia [rəʊ'diːʃə] N *Formerly* Rhodésie **Northern/Southern R.** Rhodésie *f* du Nord/du Su

Rhodesian [rəʊ'diːʃən] N Rhodésien(enne) *m,f*

ADJ rhodésien

rhododendron [ˌrəʊdə'dendrən] N *Bot* rhodo dendron *m*

▸▸ ***rhododendron bush*** rhododendron *m*

rhomb [rɒm] N **1** *Geom (rhombus)* losange *m (in crystallography)* rhomboèdre *m*

rhombic ['rɒmbɪk] ADJ **1** *Geom* rhombique **2** *(i crystallography)* orthorhombique

rhomboid ['rɒmbɔɪd] *Geom* N parallélogramm *m (dont les côtés adjacents sont inégaux)*

ADJ rhomboïdal, rhombiforme

rhombus ['rɒmbəs] *(pl* **rhombuses** *or* **rhomb** [-baɪ]*)* N *Geom* losange *m*

Rhône [rəʊn] N **the (River) R.** le Rhône

rhubarb ['ru:bɑ:b] **N 1** *Bot* rhubarbe *f* **2** *Theat* **r., r.** = mots répétés par les acteurs lorsqu'ils doivent avoir l'air de parler entre eux sur scène
COMP *(jam)* de rhubarbe; *(tart)* à la rhubarbe

rhyme [raɪm] **N 1** *(sound)* rime *f*; **give me a r. for "mash"** trouve-moi un mot qui rime avec "mash"; *Fig* **without r. or reason** sans rime ni raison; **there's neither r. nor reason to their demands** leurs revendications ne riment à rien **2** *(UNCOUNT) (poetry)* vers *mpl*; **in r.** en vers **3** *(poem)* poème *m*; **to speak in r.** faire des vers
VI 1 *(word, lines)* rimer; **what rhymes with "orange"?** qu'est-ce qui rime avec "orange"? **2** *(write verse)* écrire *ou* composer des poèmes
VT faire rimer (**with** avec)
►► ***rhyme scheme*** combinaison *f* de rimes

rhymed [raɪmd] **ADJ** rimé
►► ***rhymed verse*** vers *mpl* rimés

rhymer ['raɪmə(r)], **rhymester** ['raɪmstə(r)] **N** *Pej* rimeur(euse) *m,f*, rimailleur(euse) *m,f*

rhyming ['raɪmɪŋ] **ADJ**
►► ***rhyming couplet*** distique *m*; ***rhyming slang*** = sorte d'argot qui consiste à remplacer un mot par un groupe de mots choisis pour la rime

> **RHYMING SLANG**
>
> Il s'agit d'un procédé complexe consistant à remplacer un mot par une expression dont le dernier terme rime avec le mot en question; bien souvent n'est prononcé que le premier terme de l'expression, à savoir celui qui ne rime pas avec le mot remplacé. Exemple: kids = dustbin lids = dustbins; head = loaf of bread = loaf. À l'origine ce type d'argot était pratiqué par les Cockneys (habitants de l'est de Londres) mais certains termes sont maintenant passés dans la langue courante et sont connus de la plupart des Britanniques.

rhythm ['rɪðəm] **N** rythme *m*; **she's got (a sense of) r.** elle a le sens du rythme
►► ***rhythm and blues*** rhythm and blues *m inv*; ***rhythm guitar*** guitare *f* rythmique; ***rhythm method*** *(of contraception)* méthode *f* des températures; ***rhythm section*** section *f* rythmique

rhythmic ['rɪðmɪk], **rhythmical** ['rɪðmɪkəl] **ADJ** *(pattern, exercice)* rythmique; *(music, noise)* rythmé; **rhythmical structure/movement** structure *f*/mouvement *m* rythmique; **Greek music is less r.** la musique grecque est moins rythmée
►► ***rhythmic gymnastics*** gymnastique *f* rythmique, GRS *f*

rhythmically ['rɪðmɪklɪ] **ADV** rythmiquement, de façon rythmée

RI[1] [ɑ:'raɪ] **N** *(abbr* **religious instruction**) instruction *f* religieuse

RI[2] *(written abbr* **Rhode Island**) Rhode Island *m*

rib [rɪb] *(pt & pp* **ribbed**, *cont* **ribbing**) **N 1** *Anat* côte *f*; **he dug** *or* **he poked her in the ribs** il lui a donné un petit coup de coude; **his ribs stick out** on lui voit les côtes; **floating r.** côte *f* flottante; **true/false r.** vraie/fausse côte *f*
2 *Culin* côte *f*; **r. of beef** côte *f* de bœuf
3 *(of vault, leaf, aircraft or insect wing)* nervure *f*; *(of ship's hull)* couple *m*, membre *m*; *(of umbrella)* baleine *f*
4 *Knitting* côte *f*; **knit fifteen rows in r.** tricotez quinze rangs en côtes
5 *(on mountain ► spur)* éperon *m*; *(► crest)* arête *f*
6 *(vein of ore)* veine *f*, filon *m*
VT *Fam (tease)* taquiner, mettre en boîte
VI *Knitting* **r. for fifteen rows** tricotez quinze rangs en côtes
►► ***rib roast*** côte *f* de bœuf

ribald ['rɪbəld, 'raɪbəld] **ADJ** *Literary (joke, language)* grivois, paillard; *(laughter)* égrillard

ribaldry ['rɪbəldrɪ, 'raɪbəldrɪ] **N** *Literary* paillardises *fpl*, grivoiserie *f*

ribbed [rɪbd] **ADJ 1** *(vault, leaf)* à nervures **2** *(garment, fabric)* à côtes

ribbing ['rɪbɪŋ] **N 1** *(UNCOUNT) (of fabric, knitting)* côtes *fpl* **2** *Fam (teasing)* taquinerie *f*, mise *f* en boîte; **to get** *or* **take a r. from sb** être mis en boîte par qn

ribbon ['rɪbən] **N 1** *(for hair, typewriter, parcel etc)* ruban *m*; *Horseriding* **ribbons** *(reins)* guides *fpl*
2 *(on medal)* ruban *m*; *(of order)* cordon *m*
3 *Fig (of road)* ruban *m*; *(of land)* bande *f*; *(of cloud)* traînée *f*; *(of smoke)* filet *m*; **her dress hung in ribbons** sa robe était en lambeaux *ou* en loques; **to tear sth to ribbons** mettre qch en lambeaux; **I've cut my hand to ribbons** je me suis charcuté la main
4 *Comput (under menu bar)* ruban *m*, barre *f* d'outils
►► ***ribbon cartridge*** ruban *m* encreur; ***ribbon cassette*** cassette *f* de ruban; *Br* ***ribbon development*** croissance *f* urbaine linéaire *(le long des grands axes routiers)*; ***ribbon guide*** *(on printer)* guide-ruban *m*

ribcage ['rɪbkeɪdʒ] **N** cage *f* thoracique

ribeye ['rɪbaɪ] **N** *Culin* faux-filet *m*

riboflavin [ˌraɪbəʊ'fleɪvɪn], **riboflavine** [ˌraɪbəʊ'fleɪvi:n] **N** riboflavine *f*

ribonucleic acid [ˌraɪbəʊnju:'kli:ɪk-] **N** *Chem* acide *m* ribonucléique

rice [raɪs] **N** riz *m*; **long/short grain r.** riz *m* à grains longs/courts; **brown r.** riz *m* complet
VT *Am (potatoes)* faire une purée de
►► ***rice bowl*** *(dish)* bol *m* à riz; *Fig (region)* région *f* productrice de riz; **this province was the r. bowl of Burma** cette province était le grenier à riz de la Birmanie; ***rice grower*** riziculteur(trice) *m,f*; ***rice growing*** riziculture *f*; ***rice paddy*** rizière *f*; ***rice paper*** papier *m* de riz; ***rice pudding*** riz *m* au lait; ***rice water*** eau *f* de riz; ***rice wine*** alcool *m* de riz, saké *m*

rice-growing **ADJ** *(country, region)* rizicole

ricer ['raɪsə(r)] **N** presse-purée *m inv*

rich [rɪtʃ] **ADJ 1** *(wealthy, affluent)* riche; **r. people** les riches *mpl*; **to get** *or* **grow r.** s'enrichir; **they want to get r. quick** ils veulent s'enrichir très vite; **the r. part of town** les quartiers riches, les beaux quartiers; **I'm a hundred pounds richer** j'ai une centaine de livres de plus
2 *(elegant, luxurious ► costume, dress)* riche, somptueux; *(► furnishings)* luxueux; *(► tapestries)* somptueux
3 *(abundant, prolific)* riche, abondant; *(► vegetation)* luxuriant; **r. in vitamins/in protein(s)** riche en vitamines/en protéines
4 *(fertile ► soil, imagination)* riche, fertile
5 *(strong, intense ► colour)* riche, chaud, vif; *(► voice, sound)* chaud, riche; *(► smell)* fort
6 *Culin (food)* riche; *(meal)* lourd; **your diet is too r.** vous mangez trop d'aliments riches
7 *(funny)* drôle; *Fam Ironic* **that's r. coming from you!** venant de toi, c'est un peu fort!
NPL the r. les riches *mpl*
• riches NPL richesses *fpl*
►► *Aut & Tech* ***rich mixture*** *(in engine)* mélange *m* riche

> **-RICH** — SUFFIXE
>
> Le suffixe **-rich**, très courant et générateur en anglais, sert à indiquer une GRANDE TENEUR en une substance donnée, comme dans les exemples suivants :
>
> **protein-rich foods** aliments riches en protéines; **nutrient-rich soil** sol riche en substances nutritives; **oil-rich countries** pays riches en gisements pétrolifères.
>
> Ce suffixe s'emploie également de façon plus large pour indiquer une abondance d'une chose déterminée :
>
> **I'm time-rich but cash-poor** j'ai beaucoup de temps libre mais peu d'argent; **technology-rich countries** les pays disposant d'importants moyens technologiques.

-rich [rɪtʃ] **SUFF** riche en…; **vitamin-r. foods** aliments *mpl* riches en vitamines

Richard ['rɪtʃəd] **PR N R. the Lionheart** Richard Cœur de Lion

richly ['rɪtʃlɪ] **ADV 1** *(handsomely, generously)* largement, richement; **they will be r. rewarded** ils seront largement *ou* généreusement récompensés
2 *(thoroughly)* largement, pleinement; **the punishment she so r. deserved** le châtiment qu'elle méritait amplement
3 *(abundantly)* abondamment, richement; **r. illustrated** richement illustré
4 *(elegantly, luxuriously)* somptueusement, luxueusement
5 *(vividly)* **r. coloured** aux couleurs riches *ou* vives

richness ['rɪtʃnɪs] **N 1** *(wealth, affluence)* richesse *f*
2 *(elegance, luxury)* luxe *m*, richesse *f*
3 *(abundance)* abondance *f*, richesse *f*; **an amazing r. of detail** une étonnante abondance de détails
4 *(fertility)* richesse *f*, fertilité *f*
5 *(fullness, eventfulness)* richesse *f*; **the r. of his experience** la richesse de son expérience
6 *(strength, intensity ► of colour, sound)* richesse *f*; *(► of smell)* intensité *f*

Richter scale ['rɪktə-] **N** échelle *f* de Richter; **it measured six on the R.** il mesurait six sur l'échelle de Richter

ricin ['raɪsɪn] **N** *Chem* ricine *f*

rick [rɪk] **N** *Agr* meule *f (de foin etc)*
VT 1 *Agr* mettre en meules **2** *Br (sprain)* se faire une entorse à; **to r. one's neck** attraper un torticolis; **to r. one's back** se donner un tour de reins

rickets ['rɪkɪts] **N** *(UNCOUNT) Med* rachitisme *m*; **to have r.** souffrir de rachitisme, être rachitique

rickety ['rɪkətɪ] **ADJ 1** *(shaky ► structure)* branlant; *(► chair)* bancal; *(► vehicle)* (tout) bringuebalant **2** *Fig (alliance, alibi)* bancal, boiteux **3** *Med* rachitique

rickshaw ['rɪkʃɔ:] **N** *(pulled)* pousse *m inv*, pousse-pousse *m inv*; *(pedalled)* cyclo-pousse *m inv*

ricochet ['rɪkəʃeɪ] *(pt & pp* **ricocheted** [-ʃeɪd] *or* **ricochetted** [-ʃetɪd], *cont* **ricocheting** [-eɪɪŋ] *or* **ricochetting** [-ʃetɪŋ]) **N** ricochet *m*
VI ricocher; **to r. off sth** ricocher sur qch

rictus ['rɪktəs] **N** rictus *m*

rid [rɪd] *(pt & pp* **rid** *or* **ridded**, *cont* **ridding**) **VT** débarrasser; **to r. a house of rats** débarrasser une maison de ses rats, dératiser une maison; **to r. the world of poverty** délivrer le monde de la pauvreté; **we must r. the country of corruption** il faut débarrasser le pays de la corruption; **you should r. yourself of such illusions!** arrêtez de vous bercer d'illusions!
ADJ to get r. of se débarrasser de; **I'll get r. of it for you** je vais t'en débarrasser; **I can't seem to get r. of this cold** je n'arrive pas à me débarrasser de ce rhume; **I thought we were never going to get r. of them!** *(guests)* j'ai cru que nous n'allions jamais arriver à nous en débarrasser *ou* à nous débarrasser d'eux!; **we can't get r. of the house** nous n'arrivons pas à vendre la maison; **to be r. of** être débarrassé de; **I was glad to be r. of them** j'étais content d'être débarrassé d'eux; **to be well r. of sb/sth** être bien débarrassé de qn/qch; **you're well r. of him!** tu en es bien débarrassé!

riddance ['rɪdəns] **N** débarras *m*; *Fam* **good r. (to bad rubbish)!** bon débarras!

ridden ['rɪdən] *pp of* **ride**
ADJ affligé, atteint; **to be r. with** *or* **by guilt** être bourrelé de remords *ou* accablé par le remords

> **-RIDDEN** — SUFFIXE
>
> Le suffixe **-ridden** vient s'ajouter à des noms pour former des adjectifs qui véhiculent deux notions apparentées :
>
> (a) d'une part la notion d'INFESTATION, comme dans les exemples suivants :
>
> **flea-ridden** infesté de puces; **disease-ridden** infesté de maladies; **a drug-ridden area** un quartier infesté par la drogue; **crime-ridden areas** des zones de forte criminalité
>
> (b) d'autre part la notion d'ABONDANCE et d'EXCÈS, comme dans les exemples suivants :
>
> **guilt-ridden** accablé par le remord; **a cliché-ridden article** un article truffé de clichés; **debt-ridden families** des familles criblées de dettes.

-ridden ['rɪdən] **SUFF flea-r.** infesté de puces; **disease-r.** infesté de maladies; **debt-r.** criblé de dettes

riddle [ˈrɪdəl] **N 1** *(poser)* devinette *f*; **to ask sb a r.** poser une devinette à qn **2** *(mystery)* énigme *f*; **to talk** *or* **to speak in riddles** parler par énigmes **3** *(sieve)* crible *m*, tamis *m*

VT 1 *(pierce)* cribler; **they riddled the car with bullets** ils criblèrent la voiture de balles; **riddled with** *(holes)* criblé de; *(spelling mistakes)* cousu de; *(corruption)* en proie à; *(cancer)* rongé par **2** *(sift)* passer au crible, cribler

RIDE [raɪd]

N
- tour **1, 5**
- promenade **1**
- parcours **2**
- trajet **2**
- manège **5**

VT
- monter à **1**
- monter sur **2**
- parcourir **3**
- faire **3, 4**
- faire un tour de **5**
- prendre **5**
- amener **11**

VI
- faire du cheval **1**
- aller **2**
- voguer **3**
- dépendre **4**
- miser **5**

(*pt* **rode** [rəʊd], *pp* **ridden** [ˈrɪdən])

N 1 *(trip ▸ on bicycle, motorbike, in car)* tour *m*, promenade *f*; *(▸ in taxi)* course *f*; *(▸ on horse)* promenade *f*; *(▸ in train)* voyage *m*; *(▸ in boat, helicopter, plane)* tour *m*; **to go for a car r.** *or* **a r. in a car** (aller) faire un tour *ou* une promenade en voiture; **we went on long bicycle rides** nous avons fait de longues promenades à bicyclette; **a donkey r.** une promenade à dos d'âne; **to go for a r.** *(on horse)* faire une promenade à cheval; *(on bicycle, motorbike)* aller se promener *ou* aller faire un tour à bicyclette/à moto; **give Tom a r.** *or* **let Tom have a r. on your tricycle** laisse Tom monter sur ton tricycle; **give me a r. on your back** portemoi sur ton dos; **his sister came along for the r.** sa sœur est venue faire un tour avec nous; **this type of suspension gives a smoother r.** ce type de suspension est plus confortable; **we're in for a bumpy r.** *(in plane, car etc)* ça va secouer; *Fig* ça promet!; **the journalists gave her a rough r.** *or* **didn't give her an easy r.** les journalistes ne l'ont pas ménagée; *Fam* **to take sb for a r.** *(deceive)* faire marcher qn; *(cheat)* arnaquer *ou* rouler qn; *Am (kill)* descendre *ou* liquider qn

2 *(distance)* parcours *m*, trajet *m*; **she has a long car/bus r. to work** elle doit faire un long trajet en voiture/en bus pour aller travailler; **it's a long bus r. to Mexico** c'est long d'aller en car au Mexique; **it's only a short r. away by car** il n'y en a pas pour longtemps en voiture; **it's a 30-minute r. by bus/train/car** il faut 30 minutes en bus/train/voiture

3 *Am (lift ▸ in car)* **can you give me a r. to the station?** peux-tu me conduire à la gare?; **don't accept rides from strangers** ne montez pas dans la voiture de quelqu'un que vous ne connaissez pas

4 *Am Fam (car)* bagnole *f*, caisse *f*

5 *(in fairground ▸ attraction)* manège *m*; *(▸ turn)* tour *m*; **he wanted to go on all the rides** il a voulu faire un tour sur chaque manège; **it's 50p a r.** c'est 50 pence le tour

6 *(bridle path)* piste *f* cavalière; *(wider)* allée *f* cavalière

7 *(passenger in taxi)* client(e) *m,f*

8 *Vulg (sexual partner)* **to be a good r.** être un bon coup

VT 1 *(horse)* monter à; *(camel, donkey, elephant)* monter à dos de; **I don't know how to r. a horse** je ne sais pas monter à cheval; **they were riding horses/donkeys/camels** ils étaient à cheval/à dos d'âne/à dos de chameau; **she rode her horse at the fence** elle a dirigé son cheval sur la barrière; **to r. a horse into the ground** monter un cheval jusqu'à l'épuisement; **witches r. broomsticks** les sorcières chevauchent des balais *ou* des manches à balai

2 *(bicycle, motorcycle)* monter sur; **he won't let me r. his bike** il ne veut pas que je monte sur *ou* que je me serve de son vélo; **I don't know how to r. a bike/a motorbike** je ne sais pas faire du vélo/conduire une moto; **she was riding a motorbike** elle était à *ou* en moto; **she rides her bicycle everywhere** elle se déplace toujours à bicyclette; **he rides his bike to work** il va travailler à vélo, il va au travail à vélo

3 *(go about ▸ fields, valleys)* parcourir; *(cover ▸ distance)* faire

4 *(participate in ▸ race)* faire; **he rode a good race** *(jockey, horse)* il a fait une bonne course

5 *Am (have a go on ▸ roundabout, fairground attraction)* faire un tour de; *(use ▸ bus, lift, subway, train)* prendre; **she rides a bus to work** elle prend le bus pour aller travailler, elle va travailler en bus; **he spent three hours riding the subway** il a passé trois heures dans le métro

6 *(move with)* **to r. the waves** *(ship)* voguer sur les flots; *(surfer)* glisser sur les vagues; **to r. the rapids** descendre les rapides

7 *(take, recoil with ▸ punch, blow)* encaisser

8 *Am Fam (nag)* harceler□; **stop riding her!** laisse-la tranquille!; **you r. the kids too hard** tu es trop dur avec les gosses

9 *(copulate with ▸ of animal)* monter

10 *Vulg (have sex with)* **to r. sb** se faire qn

11 *Am (give a lift to)* amener; **hop in and I'll r. you home** monte, je te ramène chez toi

VI 1 *(ride a horse)* monter (à cheval), faire du cheval; **can you r.?** est-ce que vous savez monter à cheval *ou* faire du cheval; **he rides well** il monte bien (à cheval), il est bon cavalier; **he's riding in the 3:30** *(in horserace)* il dispute la course de 3 h 30; **to r. to hounds** faire de la chasse à courre

2 *(go ▸ on horseback)* aller (à cheval); *(▸ by bicycle)* aller (à bicyclette); *(▸ by car)* aller (en voiture); **we rode along the canal and over the bridge** nous avons longé le canal et traversé le pont; **he rode by on a bicycle/on a white horse/on a donkey** il passa à bicyclette/sur un cheval blanc/monté sur un âne; **they r. to work on the bus/the train** ils vont travailler en autobus/en train; **I want to r. in the front seat/in the first carriage** je veux monter à l'avant/dans la voiture de tête; **I'll r. up/down in the lift** je monterai/descendrai en ascenseur; **they rode to the top in the cable car** ils ont pris la télécabine pour aller au sommet; **to r. on an elephant** aller à dos d'éléphant; **to r. off** *(leave)* partir; *(move away)* s'éloigner

3 *(float, sail)* voguer; **to r. with the current** voguer au fil de l'eau; **to r. at anchor** être ancré; **the moon was riding high in the sky** la lune était haut dans le ciel

4 *(depend)* dépendre; **everything rides on whether the meeting is successful** tout dépend de la réussite de la réunion; **my reputation is riding on the outcome** ma réputation est en jeu

5 *(money in bet)* miser; **I've $5 riding on the favourite** j'ai misé 5 dollars sur le favori; **they have a fortune riding on this project** ils ont investi une fortune dans ce projet

6 *(idioms)* **to be riding high** avoir le vent en poupe; **to be riding for a fall** courir à l'échec; **he decided to let the matter r.** il a décidé de laisser courir; **she was riding on a wave of popularity** elle était portée par une vague de popularité

▸ **ride out VT INSEP** *(difficulty, crisis)* surmonter; *(recession)* survivre à; **if we can r. out the next few months** si nous pouvons tenir *ou* nous maintenir à flot encore quelques mois; **to r. out the storm** *Naut* étaler la tempête; *Fig* surmonter la crise, tenir

VI sortir *(à cheval, à bicyclette etc)*; **we rode out to meet them** nous sommes partis à leur rencontre en vélo/à cheval

▸ **ride up VI** *(garment)* remonter

rider [ˈraɪdə(r)] **N 1** *(of horse, donkey)* cavalier (ère) *m,f*; *(of racehorse)* jockey *m*; *(of bicycle)* cycliste *mf*; *(of motorcycle)* motocycliste *mf*; **to be a good r.** *(on horse)* bien monter à cheval, être bon cavalier

2 *(proviso)* condition *f*, stipulation *f*; **I'd like to add one small r. to what my colleague said** j'aimerais apporter une petite précision à ce qu'a dit mon collègue

3 *(for band, artist)* liste *f* de requêtes

4 *(annexe ▸ to contract)* annexe *f*; *Br Law (jury recommendation)* recommandation *f*; **to add a r. (recommending) that...** ajouter une clause recommandant que...

5 *(on scales)* curseur *m*

riderless [ˈraɪdəlɪs] **ADJ** *(horse)* sans cavalie *(racehorse)* sans jockey

ridership [ˈraɪdəʃɪp] **N** *Am* nombre *m* de voya geurs

ridesharing [ˈraɪdˌʃeərɪŋ] **N** *Am* = partage d'u véhicule pour se rendre sur son lieu de travail

ridge [rɪdʒ] **N 1** *(of mountains)* crête *f*, ligne *f* d faîte; *(leading to summit)* crête *f*, arête *f* **2** *(raise strip or part)* arête *f*, crête *f*; *(on sand)* ride *f*; *Ag (in ploughed field)* crête *f*; *Met* **a r. of high pressur** une crête de haute pression, *Spec* une dorsal barométrique **3** *(of roof)* faîte *m*

VT 1 *(roof)* enfaîter **2** *(surface)* strier, sillonne *(sand)* rider

▸▸ ***ridge tent*** tente *f* à faîtière; ***ridge tile*** (tuile *f* faîtière *f*

ridged [rɪdʒd] **ADJ** ridé, strié

ridgepole [ˈrɪdʒpəʊl] **N** *(of roof)* panne *f* faîtière *(of tent)* mât *m* de faîte

ridgetree [ˈrɪdʒtriː] **N** *(of roof)* panne *f* faîtière

ridgeway [ˈrɪdʒweɪ] **N** = chemin de randonné qui suit une ligne de faîte

ridicule [ˈrɪdɪkjuːl] **N** ridicule *m*; **to hold sb/sth u to r.** tourner qn/qch en ridicule; **to lay onesel open to r.** s'exposer au ridicule

VT ridiculiser, tourner en ridicule (**for** à caus de)

ridiculous [rɪˈdɪkjʊləs] **ADJ** ridicule; **you look r. i that hat** tu as l'air ridicule avec ce chapeau; **it's that I should have to pay a fine** il est absurde qu j'aie à payer une amende; **£500? don't be r.!** 50 livres? vous plaisantez!; **to make sb/sth look** rendre qn/qch ridicule, ridiculiser qn/qch; **t make oneself look r.** se ridiculiser, se couvrir d ridicule

N the r. le ridicule; **to verge on the r.** friser le rid cule

ridiculously [rɪˈdɪkjʊləslɪ] **ADV** ridiculement; **it' r. expensive** *(price)* c'est un prix exorbitant; *(ar icle, shop)* c'est beaucoup trop cher; **it's r. chea** *(price)* c'est un prix dérisoire; *(article, shop)* c'es très bon marché

ridiculousness [rɪˈdɪkjʊləsnɪs] **N** ridicule *m*; **th r. of the situation** le (côté) ridicule de la situatio

riding [ˈraɪdɪŋ] **N 1** *Horseriding* **(horse) r.** équita tion *f*; **to go r.** faire de l'équitation *ou* du cheva **do you like r.?** aimez-vous l'équitation *ou* monte à cheval? **2** *(in Yorkshire)* division *f* administra tive **3** *(in Canada, New Zealand)* circonscriptio *f* électorale

COMP *(boots, jacket)* de cheval; *(lesson, tech niques)* d'équitation

▸▸ ***riding breeches*** culotte *f* de cheval; ***riding cro*** cravache *f*; ***riding habit*** tenue *f* d'amazone; ***ridin instructor*** professeur *m* d'équitation; ***riding kit*** te nue *f* de cheval; ***riding school*** école *f* d'équitation ***riding whip*** cravache *f*

RIE [ˌɑːraɪˈiː] **N** *Fin* (*abbr* **recognized investment ex change**) marché *m* d'investissement agréé

RIF [ˌɑːraɪˈef] (*abbr* **reduction in force**) **N** licencie ment *m* économique

VT *(usu passive)* **to get RIFed** être licencié pou raisons économiques

rife [raɪf] **ADJ 1** *(widespread)* **to be r.** *(corruption crime, disease etc)* régner, sévir; *(rumours)* alle bon train **2** *(full)* **the garden is r. with caterpillar** le jardin est envahi par les chenilles; **the office i r. with rumour** les langues vont bon train au bu reau; **the city was r. with disease** la ville était e proie à la maladie, la maladie régnait dans l ville

riff [rɪf] **N** riff *m*

riffle [ˈrɪfəl] **VT 1** *(magazine, pages)* feuilleter **2** *(cards)* battre **3** *Am (water, lake)* rider

N *Am* **1** *(rapids)* rapide *m*, rapides *mpl* **2** *(on sur face of water)* ride *f*, ondulation *f*

▸ **riffle through VT INSEP** feuilleter

riffraff [ˈrɪfræf] **N** racaille *f*

rifle [ˈraɪfəl] **VT 1** *(search ▸ flat, office etc)* mettr sens dessus dessous; *(▸ person's pockets, filin cabinet, drawer)* fouiller (dans); *(tomb)* violer **2** *(rob)* dévaliser; **they rifled the safe** ils ont déva lisé le coffre-fort

VI to r. through sth fouiller dans qch

N *(gun)* fusil *m*

COMP *(bullet, butt, shot)* de fusil
• **rifles** **NPL** *Mil (unit)* fusiliers *mpl*
▸▸ ***rifle club*** société *f* de tir; *Mil* ***Rifle Corps*** corps *m* des fusiliers *ou* des chasseurs à pied; ***rifle practice*** (exercice *m* de) tir *m* au fusil; ***rifle range*** *Mil (for practice)* champ *m* de tir; *(at funfair)* stand *m* de tir; **within r. range** *(distance)* à portée de tir *ou* de fusil

rifleman ['raɪfəlmən] *(pl* **riflemen** [-mən]) **N** fusilier *m*

rifling ['raɪflɪŋ] **N** *(UNCOUNT) (in gun barrel)* rayures *fpl*

rift [rɪft] **N 1** *(gap, cleavage)* fissure *f*, crevasse *f*; *Geol (fault)* faille *f*; **a r. in the clouds** une trouée dans les nuages **2** *Fig (split)* cassure *f*, faille *f*; *(in relationship)* rupture *f*; *Pol* scission *f*; *(quarrel)* désaccord *m*, querelle *f*; **there is a deep r. between them** un abîme les sépare; **to heal the r. between two people/in the party** réconcilier deux personnes/les adversaires au sein du parti
▸▸ ***rift valley*** fossé *m* d'effondrement; ***the Rift Valley*** la Rift Valley

rig [rɪg] *(pt & pp* **rigged**, *cont* **rigging)** **VT 1** *(fiddle* ▸ *election, match)* truquer; *(*▸ *prices)* fixer illégalement; **the dice were rigged** les dés étaient truqués *ou* pipés; **the whole affair was rigged!** c'était un coup monté du début jusqu'à la fin!; **to r. a jury** manipuler un jury; *St Exch* **to r. the market** manipuler la Bourse **2** *Naut* gréer **3** *(install)* monter, bricoler
N 1 *(gen* ▸ *equipment)* matériel *m*
2 *Naut* gréement *m*
3 *Petr (on land)* derrick *m*; *(offshore)* plate-forme *f*
4 *Fam (clothes)* tenue□ *f*, fringues *fpl*
5 *Fam (large truck)* semi-remorque□ *m*, gros-cul *m*
6 *St Exch (rise)* hausse *f* factice; *(fall)* baisse *f* factice
▸ **rig out** **VT SEP 1** *Fam (clothe)* habiller□; **he was rigged out in a cowboy costume** il était habillé *ou* déguisé en cowboy **2** *(equip)* équiper
▸ **rig up** **VT SEP** *(install)* monter, installer

rigamarole ['rɪgəmərəʊl] *Am* = **rigmarole**

rigger ['rɪgə(r)] **N 1** *Naut* gréeur *m* **2** *Aviat* monteur-régleur *m* **3** *Petr* = personne qui travaille sur un chantier de forage

rigging ['rɪgɪŋ] **N 1** *Naut (on ship)* gréement *m*; *(of ship)* gréage *m* **2** *Theat* machinerie *f* **3** *(fiddling* ▸ *of election, match)* trucage *m*; *(*▸ *of market)* hausse *f ou* baisse *f* factice; *(*▸ *of prices)* fixation *f* illégale

RIGHT [raɪt]

> **N**
> • droite **1–3** • droit **4**
> • bien **5**
> **NPL**
> • droits **1, 2**
> **ADJ**
> • droit **1, 8** • bon **2, 3**
> • juste **2, 4** • bien **4–7**
> • vrai **9**
> **VT**
> • redresser **1, 2** • réparer **2**
> • corriger **2**
> **ADV**
> • à droite **1** • bien **2, 3, 7**
> • juste **2, 4** • tout de suite **6**

N 1 *(in directions)* droite *f*; **on the r.** à droite; **look to the** *or* **your r.** regardez à droite *ou* sur votre droite; **keep to the** *or* **your r.** restez à droite; **take a r.** tournez à droite; **he was seated on your r.** il était assis à ta droite; **from r. to left** de droite à gauche
2 *Pol* **the r.** la droite; **the r. is** *or* **are divided** la droite est divisée; **to be to** *or* **on the r.** être à droite; **he's to the r. of the party leadership** il est plus à droite que les dirigeants du parti; **the party has moved** *or* **shifted to the r.** le parti s'est droitisé
3 *(in boxing)* droite *f*; **with a r. to the jaw** d'une droite à la mâchoire
4 *(entitlement)* droit *m*; **to have a r. to sth** avoir droit à qch; **to have a** *or* **the r. to do sth** avoir le droit de faire qch; **you've no r. to talk to me like that!** tu n'as pas le droit de me parler ainsi!; **you have every r. to be angry** tu as toutes les raisons d'être en colère; **by what r.?** de quel droit?; **what r. have you to do that?** de quel droit faites-vous cela?; **r. of abode/asylum** droit *m* de séjour/d'asile; **the r. to vote/to know** le droit de vote/de savoir; **the r. to life** le droit à la vie; *Law* **r. of appeal** droit *m* d'appel; *Law* **with no r. of appeal** sans appel; **r. of reply** droit *m* de réponse *ou* de rectification; **as of r.** de (plein) droit; **you'd be within your rights to demand a refund** vous seriez dans votre (bon) droit si vous réclamiez un remboursement; **she's rich in her own r.** elle a une grande fortune personnelle; **he became a leader in his own r.** il est devenu leader par son seul talent
5 *(what is good, moral)* bien *m*; **to know r. from wrong** faire la différence entre le bien et le mal; **to be in the r.** être dans le vrai, avoir raison; **he put himself in the r. by apologizing** il s'est racheté en s'excusant
NPL 1 *Com & Law* **rights** droits *mpl*; **film/distribution rights** droits *mpl* d'adaptation cinématographique/de distribution; **to hold the translation rights to a book** détenir les droits de traduction d'un livre; **all rights reserved** tous droits réservés
2 *(proper order)* **to put** *or* **to set to rights** *(room)* mettre en ordre; *(firm, country)* redresser; *(situation)* arranger; **I'll soon have this kitchen set to rights** j'aurai vite fait de remettre de l'ordre dans la cuisine; **to put** *or* **to set the world to rights** refaire le monde
ADJ 1 *(indicating location, direction)* droit; **on my r. hand** sur *ou* à ma droite; **he's my r. hand** c'est mon bras droit; **the r. side of the stage** le côté droit de *ou* la droite de la scène; **take the next r. turn** prenez la prochaine à droite
2 *(accurate, correct* ▸ *answer, address)* bon; *(*▸ *prediction)* juste, exact; **the weather forecasts are never r.** les prévisions météo ne sont jamais exactes; **have you got the r. change?** avez-vous le compte exact?; **is this the r. house?** est-ce la bonne maison?, est-ce bien la maison?; **the station clock is r.** l'horloge de la gare est juste *ou* à l'heure; **have you got the r. time?** est-ce que vous avez l'heure (exacte)?; **that can't be r.** ça ne peut pas être ça, ça ne peut pas être juste; **the sentence doesn't sound/look quite r.** la phrase sonne/a l'air un peu bizarre; **to be r.** *(person)* avoir raison; **you're quite r.!** vous avez bien raison!; **you were r. about the bus schedules/about him/about what she would say** vous aviez raison au sujet des horaires de bus/à son sujet/sur ce qu'elle dirait; **am I r. in thinking you're German?** vous êtes bien allemand, ou est-ce que je me trompe?; **I owe you $5, r.?** je te dois 5 dollars, c'est (bien) ça?; **he's sick today, r.?** il est malade aujourd'hui, non?; **that's r.** c'est juste, oui; *Fam* **r.?** d'accord?; **she got the answer r.** elle a donné la bonne réponse; **he's on the r. side of 40** il n'a pas encore 40 ans; **to get on the r. side of sb** s'insinuer dans les bonnes grâces de qn; **to keep on the r. side of the law** respecter la loi; **you're not doing it the r. way!** ce n'est pas comme ça qu'il faut faire *ou* s'y prendre!; **get your facts r.!** vérifiez vos renseignements!; **he got it r. this time** il ne s'est pas trompé cette fois-ci; **let's get this r.** mettons les choses au clair; **time proved her r.** le temps lui a donné raison; **how r. you are!** vous avez cent fois raison!; **to put sb r. (about sb/sth)** détromper qn (au sujet de qn/qch); **to put** *or* **to set r.** *(fallen or tilting object)* redresser, remettre d'aplomb; *(clock)* remettre à l'heure; *(machine, mechanism)* réparer; *(text, mistake, record)* corriger; *(oversight, injustice)* réparer; **to put things** *or* **matters r.** *(politically, financially etc)* redresser *ou* rétablir la situation; *(in relationships)* arranger les choses; **he made a mess of it and I had to put things r.** il a raté son coup et j'ai dû réparer les dégâts
3 *(most appropriate* ▸ *diploma, tool, sequence, moment)* bon; *(*▸ *choice, decision)* meilleur; **when the time is r.** au bon moment, au moment voulu; **to be in the r. place at the r. time** être là où il faut quand il faut; **I can't find the r. word** je ne trouve pas le mot juste; **we're on the r. road** nous sommes sur le bon chemin *ou* la bonne route; **if the price is r.** si le prix est intéressant; **the colour is just r.** la couleur est parfaite; **she's the r. woman for the job** c'est la femme qu'il faut pour ce travail; **the frame is r. for the picture** le cadre convient tout à fait au tableau; **teaching isn't r. for you** l'enseignement n'est pas ce qu'il vous faut; **it wasn't the r. thing to say** ce n'était pas la chose à dire; **you did the r. thing to tell us about it** vous avez bien fait de nous en parler
4 *(fair, just)* juste, équitable; *(morally good)* bien *(inv)*; *(socially correct)* correct; **it's not r. to steal** ce n'est pas bien de voler; **I thought it r. to ask you first** j'ai cru bon de vous demander d'abord; **I don't feel r. leaving you alone** ça me gêne de te laisser tout seul; **it's only r. that you should know** il est juste que vous le sachiez; **I only want to do what is r.** je ne cherche qu'à bien faire; **to do the r. thing (by sb)** agir correctement (envers qn)
5 *(healthy)* bien *(inv)*; **I don't feel r.** je ne me sens pas très bien, je ne suis pas dans mon assiette; **my knee doesn't feel r.** j'ai quelque chose au genou; **nobody in their r. mind would refuse such an offer!** aucune personne sensée ne refuserait une telle offre!; *Fam* **he's not quite r. in the head** ça ne va pas très bien dans sa tête
6 *(satisfactory)* bien *(inv)*; **things aren't r. between them** ça ne va pas très bien entre eux; **I can't get this hem r.** je n'arrive pas à faire un bel ourlet; **there's something not quite r. with the motor** le moteur ne marche pas très bien
7 *(indicating social status)* bien *(inv)*, comme il faut; **she took care to be seen in all the r. places** elle a fait en sorte d'être vue partout où il fallait; **to know the r. people** connaître des gens bien placés
8 *Geom (angle, line, prism, cone)* droit
9 *Br Fam (as intensifier)* vrai□, complet(ète)□; **I felt like a r. idiot** je me sentais vraiment bête□; **the government made a r. mess of it** le gouvernement a fait un beau gâchis; **there was a r. one in here this morning!** on a eu un vrai cinglé ce matin!
VT 1 *(set upright again* ▸ *chair, ship)* redresser; **the raft will r. itself** le radeau se redressera (tout seul)
2 *(redress* ▸ *situation)* redresser, rétablir; *(*▸ *damage, injustice)* réparer; *(*▸ *mistake)* corriger, rectifier; **to r. a wrong** redresser un tort; **the problem won't just r. itself** ce problème ne va pas se résoudre de lui-même *ou* s'arranger tout seul
EXCLAM come tomorrow – r. (you are)! venez demain – d'accord!; **r., let's get to work!** bon *ou* bien, au travail!; **r. (you are) then, see you later** bon alors, à plus tard; *Fam* **too r.!** tu l'as dit!; *Fam* **r. on!** bravo!
ADV 1 *(in directions)* à droite; **turn r. at the traffic lights** tournez à droite au feu (rouge); **look r.** regardez à droite; **the party is moving further r.** le parti est en train de virer plus à droite; *Fam* **r., left and centre** *(everywhere)* de tous les côtés; *Fam* **he owes money r. and left** *or* **r., left and centre** il doit de l'argent à droite et à gauche
2 *(accurately, correctly* ▸ *hear)* bien; *(*▸ *guess)* juste; *(*▸ *answer, spell)* bien, correctement; **if I remember r.** si je me rappelle bien; **he predicted the results r.** il a vu juste en ce qui concernait les résultats; **he's to blame r. enough** c'est bien de sa faute (à lui)
3 *(properly)* bien, comme il faut; **the top isn't on r.** le couvercle n'est pas bien mis; **you're not holding the saw r.** tu ne tiens pas la scie comme il faut; **nothing is going r. today** tout va de travers aujourd'hui; **he can't do anything r.** il ne peut rien faire correctement *ou* comme il faut; *Fam* **to come r.** s'arranger□
4 *(exactly)* **the lamp's shining r. in my eyes** j'ai la lumière de la lampe en plein dans les yeux *ou* en pleine figure; **I left it r. here** je l'ai laissé juste ici; **the hotel was r. on the beach** l'hôtel donnait directement sur la plage; **r. in the middle of the film** au beau milieu du film **it's r. opposite the post office** c'est juste en face de la poste; **it's r. in front of/behind you** c'est droit devant vous/juste derrière vous; **stay r. there** ne bougez pas
5 *(completely, all the way)* **it's r. at the back of the drawer** c'est tout au fond du tiroir; **r. down to the bottom** jusqu'au fond; **r. at the top** tout en haut; **a wall r. round the house** un mur tout autour de la maison; **he turned r. round** il a fait un tour complet; **r. from the start** dès le début; **to go r. through sth** *(to pierce)* traverser qch de part en

part; **his shoes were worn r. through** ses chaussures étaient usées jusqu'à la corde; **the water came r. up to the window** l'eau est montée jusqu'à la fenêtre; **she walked r. up to me** elle se dirigea tout droit vers moi; **we worked r. up until the last minute** nous avons travaillé jusqu'à la toute dernière minute; *Fig* **I'm r. behind you there** je suis entièrement d'accord avec vous là-dessus; *Fig* **you have to go r. to the top if you want to get anything done** il faut aller tout en haut de la hiérarchie pour arriver à quelque chose

6 *(immediately)* tout de suite; **I'll be r. back** je reviens tout de suite; **I'll be r. with you** je suis à vous tout de suite

7 *(justly, fairly)* bien; *(decently, fittingly)* correctement; **you did r.** tu as bien fait; **to see sb r.** *(financially)* veiller à ce que qn ne soit pas à court d'argent; **to do r. by sb** agir correctement envers qn

8 *Br (in titles)* **the R. Reverend William Walker** le très révérend William Walker; **my R. Honourable Friend** *(form of address in Parliament)* mon distingué collègue; **the R. Honourable Member for Edinburgh West** le député de la circonscription "Edinburgh West"

9 *Br Fam (for emphasis)* très[□], vachement; **I was r. glad to hear it** j'étais très heureux de l'apprendre; **I was r. angry** j'étais vachement en colère;

• **by right, by rights** ADV en principe; **she ought, by rights, to get compensation** en principe, elle devrait toucher une compensation

• **right away** ADV *(at once)* tout de suite, aussitôt; *(from the start)* dès le début; *(first go)* du premier coup; **r. away, sir!** tout de suite, monsieur!

• **right now** ADV **1** *(at once)* tout de suite **2** *(at the moment)* pour le moment

• **right off** *Am* = **right away**

►► ***right angle*** angle *m* droit; **a line at r. angles to the base** une ligne perpendiculaire à la base; *Comput* ***right arrow*** flèche *f* vers la droite; *Comput* ***right arrow key*** touche *f* de déplacement vers la droite; *Comput & Typ* ***right indent*** indentation *f* à droite; *Fin* ***rights issue*** émission *f* de nouvelles actions à taux préférentiel; *Comput & Typ* ***right justification*** justification *f* à droite; ***rights manager*** *(in publishing)* responsable *mf* des droits; *Comput & Typ* ***right margin*** marge *f* droite; ***right of way*** *Aut* priorité *f*; *(right to cross land)* droit *m* de passage; *(path, road)* chemin *m*; *Am (for power line, railroad etc)* voie *f*; **it's your r. of way** vous avez (la) priorité; **to have (the) r. of way** avoir (la) priorité; *Zool* ***right whale*** baleine *f* franche; ***right wing*** *Pol* droite *f*; *Sport (position)* aile *f* droite; *(player)* ailier *m* droit; **the r. wing of the party** l'aile droite du parti

right-angled ADJ *(hook, turn)* à angle droit
►► *Br* ***right-angled triangle*** triangle *m* rectangle

right-click *Comput* VT cliquer avec le bouton droit de la souris sur
VI cliquer avec le bouton droit de la souris (**on** sur)

righteous ['raɪtʃəs] ADJ **1** *(just)* juste; *(virtuous)* vertueux; **r. indignation** colère *f* justifiée **2** *Pej (self-righteous)* suffisant **3** *Fam Black Am slang (genuine)* authentique[□]; *(excellent)* génial, super *inv*
NPL **the r.** les bons *mpl*, les justes *mpl*

righteously ['raɪtʃəslɪ] ADV **1** *(virtuously)* vertueusement **2** *Pej (self-righteously)* avec suffisance

righteousness ['raɪtʃəsnɪs] N vertu *f*, rectitude *f*

rightful ['raɪtfʊl] ADJ *(owner, king, claim)* légitime; *(inheritance)* auquel on a droit; **to have one's r. share** avoir sa juste part
►► ***rightful heir*** héritier(ère) *m,f* légitime *ou* naturel(elle)

rightfully ['raɪtfʊlɪ] ADV légitimement; **it is r. mine** cela m'appartient légitimement

right-hand ADJ droit; *(drawer, margin)* de droite; **on the r. side** à droite; **the r. side of the road** le côté droit de la route; **a r. bend** un virage à droite
►► *Aut* ***right-hand drive*** conduite *f* à droite; **a r. drive vehicle** un véhicule avec la conduite à droite; ***right-hand man*** bras *m* droit

right-handed ADJ **1** *(person)* droitier **2** *(punch)* du droit **3** *(scissors, golf club)* pour droitiers; *(screw)* fileté à droite
ADV *(to play, hit etc)* de la main droite

right-hander N **1** *(person)* droitier(ère) *m,f* **2** *(blow)* coup *m* du droit

rightism ['raɪtɪzəm] N idées *fpl* de droite

rightist ['raɪtɪst] N homme *m*/femme *f* de droite; **they're rightists** ils sont de droite
ADJ de droite

rightly ['raɪtlɪ] ADV **1** *(correctly)* correctement, bien; **r. or wrongly** à tort ou à raison; **r. dressed for the occasion** habillé pour la circonstance; *Fam* **I don't r. know** je ne sais pas bien[□] **2** *(with justification)* à juste titre, avec raison; **he was r. angry, he was angry and r. so** il était en colère à juste titre

right-minded ADJ raisonnable, sensé; **every r. citizen/Christian** tout citoyen/chrétien honnête

rightness ['raɪtnɪs] N **1** *(accuracy ► of answer)* exactitude *f*, justesse *f*; *(► of guess)* justesse *f* **2** *(justness ► of decision, judgment)* équité *f*; *(► of claim)* légitimité *f*

righto ['raɪtəʊ] EXCLAM *Br Fam* OK!, d'ac!

right-of-centre ADJ de centre-droite

right-on ADJ *Fam (socially aware)* politiquement correct[□]

rightsize ['raɪtsaɪz] VT dégraisser

rightsizing ['raɪt,saɪzɪŋ] N dégraissage *m*

right-thinking ADJ raisonnable, sensé

right-to-lifer N adversaire *mf* de l'avortement

right-wing ADJ *Pol* de droite; **she's more r. than the others** elle est plus à droite que les autres

right-winger N **1** *Pol* homme *m*/femme *f* de droite; **measures unpopular with right-wingers** mesures peu appréciées par la droite **2** *Sport* ailier *m* droit

righty-ho [,raɪtɪ'həʊ] EXCLAM *Br Fam* OK!, d'accord!

rigid ['rɪdʒɪd] ADJ **1** *(structure, material)* rigide; *(body, muscle)* raide; **he was r. with fear** il était paralysé par la peur; *Fam* **it shook me r.!** ça m'a fait un de ces coups! **2** *(person, ideas, policy)* rigide, inflexible; *(discipline)* strict, sévère; **she's very r. in her ideas** elle a des idées très rigides *ou* inflexibles; *Br Fam* **to be bored r.** s'ennuyer ferme

rigidity [rɪ'dʒɪdɪtɪ] N **1** *(of structure, material)* rigidité *f*; *(of body, muscle)* raideur *f* **2** *(of person, ideas, policy)* rigidité *f*, inflexibilité *f*; *(of discipline)* sévérité *f*

rigidly ['rɪdʒɪdlɪ] ADV rigidement, avec raideur; *(censored, controlled)* sévèrement, strictement; **the rules are r. applied** le règlement est rigoureusement appliqué

rigmarole ['rɪgmərəʊl], *Am* **rigamarole** ['rɪgəmərəʊl] N **1** *(procedure)* cirque *m*; **I don't want to go through all the r. of applying for a licence** je ne veux pas m'embêter à déposer une demande de permis **2** *(talk)* charabia *m*, galimatias *m*

rigor[1] ['rɪgə(r)] N *(UNCOUNT) Med (before fever)* frissons *mpl*; *(in muscle)* crampe *f*
►► ***rigor mortis*** rigidité *f* cadavérique

rigor[2] *Am* = **rigour**

rigorous ['rɪgərəs] ADJ rigoureux

rigorously ['rɪgərəslɪ] ADV rigoureusement, avec rigueur

rigorousness ['rɪgərəsnɪs] N rigueur *f*

rigour, *Am* **rigor** ['rɪgə(r)] N rigueur *f*; **the r. of the law** la sévérité de la loi; **the rigours of prison life/the Scottish climate** les rigueurs de la vie en prison/du climat écossais

rigout ['rɪgaʊt] N *Fam* accoutrement[□] *m*; **you can't go in that r.!** tu ne peux pas y aller accoutré comme ça!

rile [raɪl] VT *(person)* agacer, énerver; **don't get riled!** ne t'énerve pas!

Riley ['raɪlɪ] N *Fam* **to live the life of R.** se la couler douce, avoir la belle vie

rill [rɪl] N *Literary (brook)* ruisselet *m*

rim [rɪm] *(pt & pp* **rimmed**, *cont* **rimming)** N **1** *(of bowl, cup)* bord *m*; *(of eye, lake)* bord *m*, pourtour *m*; *(of well)* margelle *f*
2 *(of spectacles)* monture *f*
3 *(of wheel)* jante *f*
4 *(of dirt)* marque *f*; **a r. of coffee left in the cup** des traces de café à l'intérieur de la tasse; **there was a black r. around the bath** il y avait une trace de crasse tout autour de la baignoire
VT border; **trees r. the lake** le lac est bordé *ou* entouré d'arbres
►► ***rim brake*** frein *m* sur jante

rime[1] [raɪm] *Literary* N *(frost)* givre *m*, gelée *f* blanche
VT givrer

rime[2] *Arch* = **rhyme**

rimless ['rɪmlɪs] ADJ *(spectacles)* sans monture

-rimmed [rɪmd] SUFF **gold-/steel-r. spectacles** lunettes *fpl* à monture en or/d'acier; **to have red-r. eyes** avoir les yeux rouges

rimming ['rɪmɪŋ] N *TV & Cin* éclairage *m* frisant

rind [raɪnd] N *(on bacon)* couenne *f*; *(on cheese)* croûte *f*; *(on fruit)* écorce *f*; *(of bark)* couche *f* extérieure

RING [rɪŋ]

N	
• sonnerie **1**	• tintement **1**
• coup de fil **2**	• anneau **4–6**
• bague **4, 5**	• rond **5, 6**
• cercle **6, 9**	• ring **7**
VT	
• sonner **1**	• téléphoner à **2**
• entourer **3, 4**	
VI	
• sonner **1, 3**	• tinter **1**
• résonner **2**	• téléphoner **4**

(senses **VT 1,2, VI** *pt* **rang** [ræŋ], *pp* **rung** [rʌŋ]*, senses* **VT 3–5** *pt & pp* **ringed)**

N **1** *(sound ► of bell, telephone)* sonnerie *f*; *(► of small bell, coins)* tintement *m*; **there was a r. at the door** on a sonné (à la porte); **she answered the phone after just one r.** le téléphone n'avait sonné qu'une fois quand elle a décroché; *Fig* **it has a hollow r.** cela sonne creux; **his words had a r. of truth** il y avait un accent de vérité dans ses paroles; **the name has a familiar r. to it** ce nom me dit quelque chose

2 *Br Fam (telephone call)* coup *m* de fil[□]; **give me a r. tomorrow** passe-moi un coup de fil *ou* appelle-moi demain

3 *(set of bells)* **a r. of bells** un jeu de cloches

4 *(on finger)* anneau *m*; *(with stone)* bague *f*; *(in nose, ear)* anneau *m*; **a diamond r.** une bague de diamant(s)

5 *(round object)* anneau *m*; *(for serviette)* rond *m*; *(for swimmer)* bouée *f*; *(for identifying bird)* bague *f*; *(of piston)* segment *m*; *Tech* **retaining r.** plaquette *f* de fixation; **the rings** *(in gym)* les anneaux *mpl*

6 *(circle ► of people, chairs)* cercle *m*; *(► in water, of smoke)* rond *m*; *(► in or around tree trunk, around planet)* anneau *m*; *(► around sun, moon)* halo *m*; **all stand in a r.** mettez-vous tous en cercle *ou* en rond; **to draw** *or* **put a r. round sth** entourer qch d'un cercle; **she looked round the r. of faces** elle regarda les visages tout autour d'elle; **the glasses left rings on the piano** les verres ont laissé des ronds *ou* des marques sur le piano; **the rings of Saturn** les anneaux de Saturne; **he has rings round his eyes** il a les yeux cernés; *Fam* **to run rings round sb** éclipser *ou* écraser qn

7 *(for boxing, wrestling)* ring *m*; *(in circus)* piste *f*; *(for bullfight)* arène *f*; *(for showjumping)* enceinte *f*; **the r.** *(boxing as sport)* la boxe; *St Exch* **the R.** le Parquet

8 *Br (for cooking ► electric)* plaque *f*; *(► gas)* feu *m*, brûleur *m*

9 *(group ► of people)* cercle *m*; *(► gang)* bande *f*; *(► of spies, drug traffickers)* réseau *m*; *Com* cartel *m*

VT **1** *(bell, alarm)* sonner; **I rang the doorbell** j'ai sonné à la porte; **the name/title rings a bell** ce nom/titre me dit quelque chose; **to r. the changes** *(on church bells)* carillonner; *Fig* changer; **to r. the changes on sth** apporter des changements à qch

2 *Br (phone)* téléphoner à, appeler

3 *(surround)* entourer, encercler; **a lake ringed with trees** un lac entouré *ou* bordé d'arbres

4 *(draw circle round)* entourer d'un cercle; **r. the right answer** entourez la bonne réponse

5 *(bird)* baguer; *(bull, pig)* anneler

VI 1 *(chime, peal ▸ bell, telephone, alarm)* sonner; *(▸ with high pitch)* tinter; *(▸ long and loud)* carillonner; **to r. at the door** sonner à la porte; **the doorbell rang** on a sonné (à la porte); **the bell is ringing for dinner** on sonne pour le dîner; **the line is ringing for you** ne quittez pas, je vous le/la passe

2 *(resound ▸ gen)* résonner, retentir; *(▸ ears)* bourdonner; **their laughter rang through the house** leurs rires résonnaient dans toute la maison; **my ears are ringing** j'ai les oreilles qui bourdonnent; **her words still r. in my ears** ses paroles résonnent encore à mes oreilles; **to r. true/false/hollow** sonner vrai/faux/creux

3 *(summon)* sonner; **to r. for the maid** sonner la bonne; **I rang for a glass of water** j'ai sonné pour qu'on m'apporte un verre d'eau; **you rang, Sir?** Monsieur a sonné?

4 *Br (phone)* téléphoner; **to r. round** passer une série de coups de fil

▸▸ ***ring binder*** classeur *m* (à anneaux); *Mus* ***the Ring Cycle*** la Tétralogie; ***ring finger*** annulaire *m*; ***ring main*** conducteur *m* de bouclage; *Br* ***ring road*** périphérique *m*; *Br* ***ring spanner*** clé *f* polygonale

ring back *Br* **VT SEP** *(phone back)* rappeler
VI *(phone back)* rappeler

ring down **VT SEP** *Theat* **to r. down the curtain** baisser le rideau; *Fig* **to r. down the curtain on sth** marquer la fin de qch

ring in **VT SEP 1 to r. the new year in** sonner les cloches pour annoncer la nouvelle année **2** *Austr & NZ (rope in)* enrôler
VI *Br* téléphoner; **listeners are encouraged to r. in** on encourage les auditeurs à téléphoner (au studio); **to r. in sick** téléphoner pour dire qu'on est malade

ring off **VI** *Br* raccrocher

ring out **VT SEP to r. out the old year** sonner les cloches pour annoncer la fin de l'année; *Fig* **to r. out the old and ring in the new** se débarrasser du vieux pour faire place au neuf
VI *(bell, telephone)* sonner; *(voice, shot)* retentir

ring up *Br* **VT SEP 1** *(phone)* téléphoner à, appeler **2** *(on cash register ▸ sale, sum)* enregistrer; **to r. up a profit** réaliser un bénéfice **3** *Theat* **to r. up the curtain** lever le rideau; *Fig* **to r. up the curtain on sth** marquer le début de qch
VI téléphoner

ring-bound **ADJ** *(notebook, file)* à anneaux

ringed [rɪŋd] **ADJ** *(bird ▸ wearing ring)* bagué; *(▸ with marking)* à collier
▸▸ *Orn* ***ringed plover*** grand gravelot *m*, grand pluvier *m* à collier

ringer ['rɪŋə(r)] **N 1** *(of bells)* sonneur *m*, carillonneur(euse) *m,f* **2** *Fam (double)* **he's a dead r. for you** vous vous ressemblez comme deux gouttes d'eau **3** *Am Fam Sport (horse)* = cheval qui participe frauduleusement à une course; *(player)* = joueur participant frauduleusement à un match

ringing ['rɪŋɪŋ] **ADJ** sonore, retentissant; **I still have a r. sound in my ears** j'ai encore les oreilles qui sifflent; **in r. tones** d'une voix vibrante
N 1 *(of doorbell, phone, alarm)* sonnerie *f*; *(of cowbell)* tintement *m*; *(of church bells)* carillonnement *m* **2** *(of cries, laughter)* retentissement *m*; *(in ears)* bourdonnement *m*
▸▸ *Br Tel* ***ringing tone*** sonnerie *f*, signal *m* d'appel

ringleader ['rɪŋ,li:də(r)] **N** *(of gang)* chef *m* de bande; *(of rebellion, in mischief etc)* meneur (euse) *m,f*

ringlet ['rɪŋlɪt] **N** *(curl)* anglaise *f*, boucle *f* (de cheveux); **to wear one's hair in ringlets** porter les cheveux en boucles, porter des anglaises

ringmaster ['rɪŋ,mɑ:stə(r)] **N** ≃ Monsieur Loyal *m*

ringnecked ['rɪŋnekt] **ADJ** *(bird, snake)* à collier
▸▸ *Orn* ***ringnecked dove*** pigeon *m* ramier, palombe *f*

ring-pull **N** *Br* anneau *m*, bague *f* *(sur une boîte de conserve, de boisson etc)*
▸▸ ***ring-pull can*** cannette *f*, boîte *f* *(qu'on ouvre en tirant sur une bague)*

ringside ['rɪŋsaɪd] **N** *(UNCOUNT) Sport* premiers rangs *mpl*; **at the r.** au premier rang; **to have a r. seat** *(at circus, boxing match)* avoir une place au premier rang; *Fig* être aux premières loges; **to have a r. view of sth** être bien placé pour voir qch

ring-tailed lemur **N** *Zool* lémur *m* catta, maki *m*

ringtone ['rɪŋtəʊn] **N** *Tel* (tonalité *f* de) sonnerie *f*; **to download a r.** *(for a mobile phone)* télécharger une sonnerie

ringworm ['rɪŋwɜ:m] **N** teigne *f*

rink [rɪŋk] **N** *(for ice-skating)* patinoire *f*; *(for roller-skating)* piste *f*

rinky-dink ['rɪŋkɪdɪŋk] **ADJ** *Am Fam (goods)* merdique; *(business, businessman)* minable

rinse [rɪns] **VT** rincer; **she rinsed her hands/her mouth** elle se rinça les mains/la bouche; **r. the soap out of the clothes** rincez les vêtements
N 1 *(gen)* rinçage *m*; **I gave the shirt a good r.** j'ai bien rincé la chemise; **put the washing machine on r.** mettez le lave-linge sur rinçage **2** *(for hair)* rinçage *m*; **to have a r.** se faire faire un rinçage (colorant)
▸▸ ***rinse cycle*** *(in washing machine)* cycle *m* de rinçage, rinçage *m*

▸**rinse down** **VT SEP** *(meal, pill)* **a little glass of something to r. it down?** un petit verre de quelque chose pour le faire passer?

▸**rinse out** **VT SEP** *(cup, bucket)* rincer; **to r. out the dirt/the soap** rincer pour enlever la saleté/le savon; *Fig* **go and r. your mouth out!** va te laver la bouche!
VI *(stain, dye)* partir à l'eau

riot ['raɪət] **N 1** *(civil disturbance)* émeute *f* **2** *Fam (entertaining person, event, situation)* **the party was a r.** on s'est éclatés à la fête, la soirée était vraiment démente; **Alex is a r.** Alex est tordant *ou* impayable **3** *(profusion)* profusion *f*; **the garden is a r. of colour** le jardin offre une véritable débauche de couleurs
VI *(gen)* se livrer à de violentes manifestations; *(at football match)* se battre; *(in prison)* se mutiner; **they are afraid the people will r.** ils craignent des émeutes populaires
ADV to run r. *(people)* se déchaîner; *(imagination)* se débrider; *(plant)* proliférer, envahir le terrain; **a group of youths ran r. through the streets** un groupe de jeunes a semé la panique dans les rues; **my imagination was running r.** j'ai commencé à imaginer toutes sortes de choses
▸▸ *Br Hist* ***the Riot Act*** loi *f* antiémeutes, loi *f* contre les rasssemblements séditieux; *Fam Fig* **to read sb the r. act** souffler dans les bronches à qn, passer un savon à qn; ***riot gear*** matériel *m* antiémeutes; ***riot gun*** flash-ball *m*; ***riot police*** police *f* *ou* forces *fpl* antiémeutes; ***riot shield*** bouclier *m* antiémeutes; ***riot squad*** brigade *f* antiémeutes

rioter ['raɪətə(r)] **N** émeutier(ère) *m,f*

rioting ['raɪətɪŋ] **N** *(UNCOUNT)* émeutes *fpl*; *(fighting)* bagarres *fpl*
ADJ r. football hooligans des hooligans qui cassent tout sur leur passage; **a r. mob** une bande d'émeutiers; *(of football fans)* une bande de vandales *ou* de casseurs

riotous ['raɪətəs] **ADJ 1** *(mob)* déchaîné; *(behaviour)* séditieux **2** *(debauched)* débauché; *(exuberant, noisy)* tapageur, bruyant; **to lead a r. life** mener une vie déréglée *ou* dissolue; **a r. party was going on upstairs** à l'étage au-dessus, des fêtards s'en donnaient à cœur joie; **bursts of r. laughter** des éclats de rire bruyants; **we had a r. time** on a bien rigolé **3** *(funny)* désopilant, tordant
▸▸ *Law* ***riotous assembly*** attroupement *m* séditieux

riotously ['raɪətəslɪ] **ADV 1** *(seditiously)* de façon séditieuse **2** *(noisily)* bruyamment **3** *Fam (as intensifier)* **it's r. funny** c'est à mourir *ou* à hurler de rire

RIP [,ɑ:raɪ'pi:] **N** *(abbr* **rest in peace***)* RIP

rip [rɪp] *(pt & pp* **ripped***, cont* **ripping***)* **VT 1** *(tear)* déchirer (violemment); **he ripped the envelope open** il déchira l'enveloppe; **to r. sth to shreds** *or* **to pieces** *(garment, letter)* mettre qch en morceaux *ou* en lambeaux; *Fig (criticize)* éreinter **2** *(snatch)* arracher; **she ripped the book from my hands** elle m'arracha le livre des mains
VI 1 *(tear)* se déchirer **2** *Fam (go fast)* aller à fond de train *ou* à fond la caisse; **the explosion ripped through the building** le choc de l'explosion s'est propagé dans tout le bâtiment; **let her** *or* **it r.!** *(car, motorboat etc)* mets les gaz!, fonce! **3** *Br Fam* **to let r.** *(be angry)* laisser éclater sa colère; *(behave unrestrainedly)* se déchaîner; *(pass wind)* larguer une caisse; **to let r. at sb** se mettre en pétard contre qn; **to let r. (with) a stream of abuse** lancer une bordée d'injures
N 1 *(tear)* déchirure *f* (**in** à) **2** *(ocean current)* zone *f* de forts courants

▸**rip apart** **VT SEP** déchirer; *Fig* éreinter, mettre en pièces
VI se déchirer

▸**rip off** **VT SEP 1** *(tear off)* arracher; *(one's jacket)* enlever en toute hâte; **they ripped off their clothes** ils se sont déshabillés en toute hâte **2** *Fam (cheat, overcharge)* arnaquer; **you were ripped off** tu t'es fait arnaquer **3** *Fam (rob)* dévaliser[◻]; *(steal)* faucher, piquer; **he ripped off our idea** il nous a piqué notre idée

▸**rip out** **VT SEP** arracher

▸**rip up** **VT SEP** *(paper, cloth)* déchirer *(violemment)*, mettre en pièces; *(floorboards)* arracher; *(road surface, street)* éventrer

riparian [rɪ'peərɪən] *Formal* **ADJ** *(person, property)* riverain; *(rights)* des riverains
N riverain(e) *m,f*

ripcord ['rɪpkɔ:d] **N** poignée *f* d'ouverture *(de parachute)*

ripe [raɪp] **ADJ 1** *(fruit, vegetable)* mûr; *(cheese)* fait, à point
2 *(age)* **to live to a r. old age** vivre jusqu'à un âge avancé; **he married at the r. old age of 80** il s'est marié au bel âge de 80 ans
3 *(ready)* prêt, mûr; **the country is r. for a change of regime** le pays est mûr pour un changement de régime; **this land is r. for development** ce terrain ne demande qu'à être aménagé; **the company is r. for takeover** la société est prête pour être rachetée; **the time is r. to sell** c'est le moment de vendre; **the time is not yet r.** le temps n'est pas encore venu
4 *(full ▸ lips)* sensuel, charnu; *(▸ breasts)* plantureux
5 *(pungent ▸ smell)* âcre
6 *Fam (vulgar)* égrillard

ripen ['raɪpən] **VI** *(fruit, grain)* mûrir; *(cheese)* se faire
VT *(of sun)* mûrir; *(of farmer)* (faire) mûrir; **sun-ripened oranges** oranges *fpl* mûries au soleil

ripeness ['raɪpnɪs] **N** maturité *f*

ripening ['raɪpənɪŋ] **N** *(of fruit, grain)* maturation *f*, mûrissage *m*, mûrissement *m*; *(of cheese)* affinage *m*
ADJ 1 *Literary (sun)* qui fait mûrir **2** *(fruit, grain)* mûrissant, qui mûrit; *(cheese)* qui se fait

rip-off **N** *Fam* **1** *(swindle)* escroquerie[◻] *f*, arnaque[◻] *f*; **that restaurant's a r.** ce restaurant est une arnaque; **what a r.!** quelle arnaque!; **r. prices** des prix astronomiques **2** *(theft)* vol[◻] *m*, fauche *f*; **it's a r. from an Osborne play** ils ont pompé l'idée dans une pièce d'Osborne
▸▸ ***rip-off merchant*** arnaqueur(euse) *m,f*

riposte [*Br* rɪ'pɒst, *Am* rɪ'pəʊst] **N 1** *(retort)* riposte *f*, réplique *f* **2** *Fencing* riposte *f*
VI riposter

ripped [rɪpt] **ADJ** *Fam (drunk)* bourré, pété; *(on drugs)* raide, défoncé; *Br very Fam* **r. to the tits** *(drunk)* bourré comme un coing, plein comme une barrique; *(on drugs)* complètement raide *ou* défoncé

ripper ['rɪpə(r)] **N** *(criminal)* éventreur *m*; **Jack the R.** Jack l'Éventreur

ripping ['rɪpɪŋ] **ADJ** *Br Fam Old-fashioned* épatant, sensass *(inv)*; **a r. yarn** une histoire épatante

ripple ['rɪpəl] **N 1** *(on water)* ride *f*, ondulation *f*; *(on wheatfield, hair, sand)* ondulation *f*
2 *(sound ▸ of waves)* clapotis *m*; *(▸ of brook)* gazouillis *m*; *(▸ of conversation)* murmure *m*; *Fig* **a r. of excitement ran through the crowd** un murmure d'excitation parcourut la foule; **a r. of laughter ran through the audience** des rires discrets parcourent l'assistance

3 *(repercussion)* répercussion *f*, vague *f*; **her resignation hardly caused a r.** sa démission a fait très peu de bruit
4 *Culin* **strawberry/chocolate r. (ice cream)** glace *f* marbrée à la fraise/au chocolat
5 *Electron* oscillation *f*
VI 1 *(undulate ▸ water)* se rider; *(▸ wheatfield, hair)* onduler; **moonlight rippled on the surface of the lake** le clair de lune scintillait sur la surface du lac; **rippling muscles** muscles *mpl* saillants *ou* puissants **2** *(murmur ▸ water, waves)* clapoter **3** *(resound, have repercussions)* se répercuter
VT *(water, lake)* rider
▸▸ *TV & Cin* ***ripple dissolve*** fondu *m* par ondulation; ***ripple effect*** répercussions *fpl*

rip-roaring **ADJ** *Fam (noisy)* bruyant□, tapageur; *(great, fantastic)* génial, super *(inv)*; **we had a r. time** on s'est amusés comme des fous; **a r. success** un succès monstre

ripsaw ['rɪpsɔː] **N** scie *f* à refendre

riptide ['rɪptaɪd] **N** contre-courant *m*, turbulence *f*

RISC [rɪsk] **N** *Comput (abbr* **reduced instruction set chip** *or* **computer)** RISC *m*

RISE [raɪz]

N	
• hauteur **1**	• lever **2**
• montée **2**	• hausse **3**
• augmentation (de salaire) **3**	• source **4**
VI	
• se lever **1, 2**	• se relever **1**
• s'élever **2, 6**	• augmenter **3**
• monter **3, 4, 7**	• se hérisser **5**
• se dresser **6**	• se soulever **8**
• lever la séance **9**	

(pt **rose** [rəʊz], *pp* **risen** ['rɪzən])
N 1 *(high ground)* hauteur *f*, éminence *f*; *(slope)* pente *f*; *(hill)* côte *f*
2 *(of moon, sun, curtain)* lever *m*; *(to power, influence)* montée *f*, ascension *f*; *(in rank)* avancement *m*, promotion *f*; *(of industry, technology)* essor *m*; **the r. and fall of the tide** le flux et le reflux de la marée; **the r. and fall of the Roman Empire** la croissance et la chute *ou* la grandeur et la décadence de l'Empire romain; *Br Fam* **to get** *or* **to take a r. out of sb** faire marcher qn, faire enrager qn
3 *(increase ▸ in price, cost of living, crime, accidents)* hausse *f*, augmentation *f*; *(▸ in bank rate, interest)* relèvement *m*, hausse *f*; *(▸ in temperature, pressure)* hausse *f*; *(▸ in level of river)* crue *f*; *(▸ in affluence, wealth)* augmentation *f*; *Br (▸ in salary)* augmentation *f* (de salaire); **to be on the r.** être en hausse; **there has been a steep r. in house prices** les prix de l'immobilier ont beaucoup augmenté; **the r. in the price of petrol** la hausse du prix de l'essence; **r. in value** appréciation *f*; *Br* **to be given a r.** être augmenté
4 *(origin ▸ of river)* source *f*; *Fig* **to give r. to sth** donner lieu à qch, entraîner qch; **it gave r. to a lot of hostility/difficulties** cela a provoqué une forte hostilité/beaucoup de difficultés
VI 1 *(get up ▸ from chair, bed)* se lever; *(▸ from knees, after fall)* se relever; **to r. to one's feet** se lever, se mettre debout; **he rises late every morning** il se lève tard tous les matins; **all r.!** *(in courtroom)* levez-vous, s'il vous plaît!; **the horse rose on its hind legs** le cheval s'est cabré; **r. and shine!** debout!; *Rel* **to r. from the dead** ressusciter d'entre les morts
2 *(sun, moon, star, fog)* se lever; *(smoke, balloon)* s'élever, monter; *(land)* s'élever; *(fish)* mordre; *Theat (curtain)* se lever; **to r. into the air** *(bird, balloon)* s'élever (dans les airs); *(plane)* monter *ou* s'élever (dans les airs); **to r. to the surface** *(swimmer, whale)* remonter à la surface; *(anger)* faire surface; *(doubts, conflict)* se faire jour; *also Fig* **to r. to the bait** mordre à l'hameçon; **the colour rose in** *or* **to her cheeks** le rouge lui est monté aux joues; **his eyebrows rose in surprise** il leva les sourcils de surprise; **a murmur rose from the crowd** une rumeur s'est élevée de la foule; **disturbing images rose in my mind** des images troublantes me vinrent à l'esprit; **to r. to the occasion/challenge/task** se montrer à la hauteur de la situation/du défi/de la tâche; **try to r. above it** tâche de rester au-dessus de la mêlée; *Fig* **to r. from the ashes** renaître de ses cendres
3 *(increase ▸ value)* augmenter; *(▸ number, amount)* augmenter, monter; *(▸ prices, costs)* monter, augmenter, être en hausse; *(▸ temperature, pressure)* monter; *(▸ barometer)* monter, remonter; *(▸ wind)* se lever; *(▸ tide, river level)* monter; *(▸ tension, tone)* monter; *(▸ voice)* s'élever; **to r. in price** augmenter (de prix); **the pound has risen against the dollar** la livre s'est appréciée vis-à-vis du dollar; **the river has risen by two metres** la rivière est montée de deux mètres; **the wind rose to gale force** le vent se mit à souffler en tempête; **his voice rose above the noise of the crowd** sa voix s'élevait au-dessus du bruit de la foule; **his spirits rose when he heard the news** il a été soulagé *ou* heureux d'apprendre la nouvelle
4 *Culin (dough)* lever; *(soufflé)* monter
5 *(become erect ▸ hair)* se hérisser; **the dog's hackles rose** le chien s'est hérissé de colère; **the hair on the back of her neck rose** ses poils se sont hérissés
6 *(mountains, buildings)* se dresser, s'élever; **the trees rose above our heads** les arbres se dressaient au-dessus de nos têtes; **the mountain rises to 2,500 m** la montagne a une altitude de *ou* culmine à *ou* s'élève à 2500 m; **the steeple rises 200 feet into the air** ≃ le clocher a *ou* fait 60 mètres de haut
7 *(socially, professionally)* monter, réussir; **to r. in society** réussir socialement; **to r. to fame** devenir célèbre; **to r. to power** accéder au pouvoir; **to r. in sb's esteem** monter dans l'estime de qn; **to r. to the rank of colonel** monter jusqu'au grade de colonel; **to r. through the ranks** monter les échelons un à un; **she rose to the position of personnel manager** elle a réussi à devenir chef du personnel
8 *(revolt)* se soulever, se révolter (**against** contre); **to r. in protest against sth** se soulever contre qch
9 *(adjourn ▸ assembly, meeting)* lever la séance; *(▸ Parliament, court)* clore la session; **Parliament rose for the summer recess** la session parlementaire est close pour les vacances d'été
10 *(originate ▸ river)* prendre sa source
▸ rise up VI 1 *(get up)* se lever; **to r. up from one's chair** se lever de sa chaise
2 *(go up ▸ smoke, balloon etc)* monter, s'élever
3 *(revolt)* se soulever, se révolter; (**against** contre); **to r. up in arms** prendre les armes
4 *Rel* ressusciter
5 *(appear)* apparaître; **a shadowy figure rose up out of the mist** une ombre surgit de la brume

Attention: ne pas confondre avec le verbe **to raise**, qui est toujours accompagné d'un complément d'objet.

riser ['raɪzə(r)] **N 1** *(person)* **to be an early/late r.** être un(e) lève-tôt *(inv)*/lève-tard *(inv)* **2** *(of step)* contremarche *f* **3** *(in plumbing)* conduite *f* montante

risibility [ˌrɪzə'bɪlətɪ] *(pl* **risibilities) N** *Formal (of situation)* caractère *m* risible *ou* ridicule; *(of offer)* caractère dérisoire

risible ['rɪzəbəl] **ADJ** *Formal (idea, plan etc)* risible, ridicule; *(offer)* dérisoire

rising ['raɪzɪŋ] **N 1** *(revolt)* insurrection *f*, soulèvement *m*
2 *(of sun, moon, theatre curtain)* lever *m*
3 *(of prices)* augmentation *f*, hausse *f*
4 *(of river)* crue *f*, *(of ground)* élévation *f*, *(of sap)* montée *f*
5 *(from dead)* résurrection *f*
6 *(of Parliament, an assembly)* ajournement *m*, clôture *f* de séance
ADJ 1 *(sun)* levant; **they were up early to see the r. sun** ils se levèrent de bonne heure pour voir le soleil se lever *ou* le soleil levant; **the land of the r. sun** *(Japan)* l'empire *m* du Soleil-Levant
2 *(tide)* montant; *(water level)* ascendant
3 *(ground, road)* qui monte
4 *(increasing ▸ temperature, prices)* en hausse; *Fin (▸ market)* orienté à la hausse; **the r. number of homeless people/tourists** le nombre croissant de sans-logis/de touristes
5 *(up-and-coming)* qui monte; **the r. generation** la nouvelle génération, la génération montante
6 *(emotion)* croissant
ADV *Br Fam* **she's r. 40** elle va sur ses 40 ans
▸▸ ***rising damp*** humidité *f* ascensionnelle *ou* par capillarité; *Br* ***rising fives*** = enfants allant sur leurs cinq ans (âge où ils doivent commencer l'école); ***rising star*** *Astron* étoile *f* montante; *Mkt (product)* produit *m* d'avenir; *Horseriding* ***rising trot*** trot *m* enlevé *ou* à l'anglaise

risk [rɪsk] **N 1** *(gen)* risque *m*; **to take a r.** prendre un risque; **to run the r.** courir le risque; **to run the r. of losing everything** courir le risque *ou* risquer de tout perdre; **is there any r. of him making another blunder?** est-ce qu'il risque de commettre un nouvel impair?; **there's no r. of that happening** pas de danger que ça se passe, ça ne risque pas d'arriver; **it's not worth the r.** c'est trop risqué; **that's a r. we'll have to take** c'est un risque à courir; **I'm not taking any risks** je ne veux prendre aucun risque, je ne veux rien risquer; **I'll take that r.** j'en prends le risque; **it's too much of a r.** c'est un trop grand risque; **cars may be parked here at the owner's r.** *(sign)* les automobilistes peuvent stationner ici à leurs risques (et périls); **at the r. of one's life** au péril de sa vie; **at considerable r. to herself** en courant (elle-même) un risque considérable; **at the r. of sounding ignorant, how does one open this box?** au risque de passer pour un idiot, j'aimerais savoir comment on ouvre cette boîte?
2 *(in insurance)* risque *m*; **to underwrite a r.** souscrire un risque; **to be a fire/health/security r.** constituer un risque d'incendie/pour la santé/pour la sécurité; **he's a bad r.** c'est un client à risques; **risks and perils at sea** fortune *f* de mer
VT 1 *(endanger ▸ life, reputation, job)* risquer, hasarder; **don't r. your career/reputation on a shady deal** ne risquez pas votre carrière/réputation sur une affaire louche; **to r. one's neck** *or* **skin, to r. life and limb** risquer sa peau
2 *(take the chance of ▸ defeat, failure)* courir le risque de; **to r. sb's anger** s'exposer à la colère de qn; **she won't r. leaving** elle ne se risquera pas à partir; **to r. breaking one's leg** risquer de *ou* courir le risque de se casser une jambe
• at risk ADJ to place *or* **put sth at r.** risquer qch; **to place** *or* **put sb at r.** faire courir un danger à qn; **our children are at r. from all kinds of violence** nos enfants ont toutes sortes de violences à craindre; **all our jobs are at r.** tous nos emplois sont menacés; *Med & Admin* **to be at r.** être vulnérable, être une personne à risque
▸▸ ***risk analysis*** analyse *f* des risques; ***risk assessment*** évaluation *f* des risques; ***risk aversion*** aversion *f* pour le risque; *Br Fin* ***risk capital*** *(UNCOUNT)* capital *m* à risque; ***risk factor*** facteur *m* de risque; ***risk management*** gestion *f* des risques

riskiness ['rɪskɪnɪs] **N** *(UNCOUNT)* risques *mpl*

risk-taker N = personne qui aime prendre des risques

risky ['rɪskɪ] *(compar* **riskier**, *superl* **riskiest) ADJ** *(hazardous)* risqué, hasardeux; **r. business** entreprise *f* hasardeuse

risotto [rɪ'zɒtəʊ] *(pl* **risottos) N** *Culin* risotto *m*

risqué ['riːskeɪ] **ADJ** *(story, joke)* risqué, osé, scabreux

rissole ['rɪsəʊl] **N** *Culin* rissole *f*

Ritalin® ['rɪtəlɪn] **N** *Pharm* Ritaline® *f*

rite [raɪt] **N** rite *m*; **initiation/fertility rites** rites *mpl* d'initiation/de fertilité; **r. of passage** cérémonie *f* d'initiation

ritual ['rɪtʃʊəl] **N** rituel *m*; **to make a r. of sth** (se) faire un rituel de qch; **it's become a bit of a r.** c'est devenu comme un rituel; **he went through his nightly r. of locking the doors** il a verrouillé les portes selon son rituel de tous les soirs
ADJ rituel; *Fig* **there was r. condemnation of him in the press** la presse l'a condamné pour la forme

ritualism ['rɪtʃʊəlɪzəm] **N** ritualisme *m*

ritualist ['rɪtʃʊəlɪst] **N** ritualiste *mf*

ritualistic [ˌrɪtʃʊə'lɪstɪk] **ADJ** ritualiste

ritually ['rɪtʃʊəlɪ] **ADV** rituellement

ritz [rɪts] **N** *Am Fam* tape-à-l'œil *m inv*; **to put on the r.** se mettre sur son trente et un, *Pej* faire du tape-à-l'œil

tzy ['rɪtsɪ] *(compar* **ritzier**, *superl* **ritziest)** ADJ *am* tape-a-l'œil *inv*, clinquant

val ['raɪvəl] *(Br pt & pp* **rivalled**, *cont* **rivalling**, *Am* *t & pp* **rivaled**, *cont* **rivaling)** N *(gen)* rival(e) *m,f*; *om* rival(e) *m,f*, concurrent(e) *m,f*; **rivals in busi-ess/love** rivaux *mpl* en affaires/amour; **to be riv-ls for sth** être en compétition pour qch;
ADJ *(gen)* rival; *Com* concurrent, rival
VT *(gen)* rivaliser avec; *Com* être en concur-ence avec; **no one can r. her when it comes to usiness acumen** son sens des affaires n'a pas 'égal; **it rivals anything to be seen in Paris** ça vaut argement tout ce que l'on peut voir à Paris; **New ork cannot r. London for historic interest** New ork ne vaut pas Londres du point de vue de intérêt historique; **your stubbornness is rivalled nly by your narrow-mindedness** votre entête-ent n'a d'égal que votre étroitesse d'esprit

valry ['raɪvəlrɪ] *(pl* **rivalries)** N rivalité *f* (**be-ween** entre); **the party is torn by personal rivalries** e parti est divisé par des rivalités d'ordre per-onnel; **in r. with sb** en concurrence *ou* rivalité vec qn

ven ['rɪvən] ADJ déchiré, divisé; **the party was r. y deep ideological divisions** le parti était déchiré ar de profondes divergences idéologiques

ver ['rɪvə(r)] N **1** *(as tributary)* rivière *f*; *(flowing o sea)* fleuve *m*; **we sailed up/down the r.** nous vons remonté/descendu la rivière; *Am Fam* **to e up the r.** *(in prison)* être en taule *ou* en cabane; *am* **to sell sb down the r.** trahir qn[□], vendre qn[□] **2** *Fig (of mud, lava)* coulée *f*; **rivers of blood** des euves de sang
COMP *(port, system, traffic)* fluvial; *(fish)* d'eau ouce
▸▸ ***river bank*** rive *f*; ***river basin*** bassin *m* fluvial; *Med* ***river blindness*** cécité *f* des rivières; *Zool* ***river dolphin*** dauphin *m* d'eau douce; ***river mouth*** *(of ributary)* embouchure *f* de la rivière *ou* du leuve; ***river police*** police *f* fluviale

verbed ['rɪvəbed] N lit *m* de rivière *ou* de fleuve

verside ['rɪvəsaɪd] N bord *m* de la rivière *ou* du leuve, bord *m* de l'eau, rive *f*; **we walked along he r.** nous nous sommes promenés le long de a rivière
ADJ au bord d'une rivière *ou* d'un fleuve; **a r. park** ın parc situé au bord de l'eau *ou* d'une rivière
▸▸ ***riverside properties*** propriétés *fpl* riveraines

vet ['rɪvɪt] N rivet *m*
VT **1** *Tech* riveter, river; **riveted joint** rivure *f* **2** *Fig* **o be riveted to the spot** rester cloué *ou* rivé sur lace; **the children were riveted to the television et** les enfants étaient rivés au poste de télévi-ion **3** *(fascinate)* fasciner; **to be absolutely iveted (by)** être absolument fasciné (par)
▸▸ ***rivet gun*** pistolet *m* à river; ***rivet head*** tête *f* de ivet; ***rivet hole*** trou *m* de rivet

iveter ['rɪvɪtə(r)] N *(person)* riveur(euse) *m,f*; *machine)* riveteuse *f*

iveting ['rɪvɪtɪŋ] N rivetage *m*
ADJ *Fig (fascinating)* fascinant, passionnant, aptivant
▸▸ ***riveting machine*** riveteuse *f*

iviera [,rɪvɪ'eərə] N **the French R.** la Côte d'Azur; **he Italian R.** la Riviera italienne; **the British R.** = a côte sud-ouest de l'Angleterre

ivulet ['rɪvjʊlɪt] N (petit) ruisseau *m*, *Literary* ru *n*

iyadh [rɪ'æd] N Riyad, Riad

iyal [rɪ'jæl] N rial *m*

N [,ɑː'ren] N *Br* **1** *(abbr* **Royal Navy)** marine *f* natio-ale britannique **2** *(abbr* **registered nurse)** *(nurse)* nfirmier(ère) *m,f* diplômé(e) (d'État) **3** *(qualifi-ation)* diplôme *m* (d'État) d'infirmier

NA [,ɑːren'eɪ] N *Biol (abbr* **ribonucleic acid)** ARN *n*

NLI [,ɑːren,el'aɪ] N *(abbr* **Royal National Lifeboat nstitution)** = société britannique de sauvetage en mer

oach [rəʊtʃ] *(pl sense* **1 inv** *or* **roaches)** N **1** *Ich* gar-don *m* **2** *Am (cockroach)* cafard *m*, cancrelat *m* **3** *am Drugs slang (of cannabis cigarette)* mégot[□] *m d'une cigarette de marijuana)*
▸▸ *Fam Drugs slang* ***roach clip*** fume-joint *m*; *Am am* **roach motel** piège *m* à cafards; ***roach powder*** oudre *f* pour tuer les cafards

road [rəʊd] N **1** *(gen)* route *f*; *(small)* chemin *m*; **minor r.** route *f* secondaire; **by r.** par la route; **the Liverpool r.** la route de Liverpool; **is this the (right) r. for** *or* **to Liverpool?** est-ce la (bonne) route pour Liverpool?; **are we on the right r.?** sommes-nous sur la bonne route?; **on the r. to Liverpool, the car broke down** en allant à Liverpool, la voiture est tombée en panne; **we took the r. from Manchester to Liverpool** on a pris la route qui va de Manchester à Liverpool *ou* qui relie Manchester à Liverpool; **to take to the r.** *(driver)* prendre la route *ou* le volant; *(tramp)* partir sur les routes; **to be on the r.** *(travelling)* être en route *ou* chemin *ou* voyage; *(salesman)* être sur la route; *(pop star, troupe)* être en tournée; **we've been on the r. since six o'clock this morning** nous roulons depuis six heures ce matin; **his car shouldn't be on the r.** sa voiture devrait être retirée de la circulation; *Br* **the price on the r.** *(of new car)* le prix clés en mains; **my car is off the r. at the moment** ma voiture est en panne *ou* chez le garagiste
2 *(street)* rue *f*; **a r. of shops/of houses** une rue de magasins/de maisons, une artère commerçante/résidentielle; **he lives just down the r.** il habite un peu plus loin dans la même rue; **Mr James from across the r.** M. James qui habite en face
3 *(roadway)* route *f*, chaussée *f*; **to stand in the middle of the r.** se tenir au milieu de la route *ou* de la chaussée; *Fam* **one for the r.** un petit coup avant de partir; *Prov* **the r. to hell is paved with good intentions** l'enfer est pavé de bonnes intentions
4 *Fig (path)* chemin *m*, voie *f*; **we don't want to go down the r. of military intervention** nous ne voulons pas nous engager dans la voie d'une intervention armée; **to be on the right r.** être sur la bonne voie; **to be on the r. to success/recovery** être sur le chemin de la réussite/en voie de guérison; **he is on the r. to an early death** il est (bien) parti pour mourir jeune; **down the r.** *(in the future)* à l'avenir; **a few years down the r.** dans quelques années; **yes, when I'm 70, but that's a long way down the r. (yet)** oui, quand j'aurai 70 ans, mais ce n'est pas pour tout de suite; *Br Fam* **you're in my r.!** *(I can't pass)* vous me bouchez le passage![□]; *(I can't see)* vous me bouchez la vue![□]; *Br Fam* **get out (of) my r.!** poussez-vous![□], dégagez!; *Prov* **all roads lead to Rome** tous les chemins mènent à Rome
5 *Am (railway)* chemin *m* de fer, voie *f* ferrée
6 *(usu pl) Naut* rade *f*
7 *NEng Fam (idiom)* **any r.** de toute façon
COMP *(traffic, bridge)* routier; *(accident)* de la route; *(conditions, construction, repairs)* des routes
▸▸ ***road atlas*** atlas *m* routier; ***road haulage*** camionnage *m*, transports *mpl* routiers; ***road haulage company*** entreprise *f* de transports routiers; ***road haulier*** transporteur *m* routier, affréteur *m* routier; *Fam* ***road kill*** = animaux écrasés par des voitures; ***road manager*** responsable *mf* de tournée *(d'un chanteur ou d'un groupe pop)*; ***road metal*** *(for road)* empierrement *m*; *Rail* terre-plein *m*, ballast *m*; ***road movie*** road-movie *m*; ***road pricing*** = instauration d'un système de routes à péage; ***road race*** *(in cycling)* course *f* cycliste sur route; ***road racer*** *(bicycle)* bicyclette *f* de compétition; *(cyclist)* routier(ère) *m,f*; ***road racing*** *(cycling)* cyclisme *m* sur route; *(motor racing)* compétition *f* automobile *(sur route)*; ***road rage*** rage *f* au volant; ***road roller*** rouleau *m* compresseur; ***road safety*** sécurité *f* routière; ***road sense*** *(for driver)* sens *m* de la conduite; **children have to be taught r. sense** on doit apprendre aux enfants à faire attention à la circulation; ***road sign*** panneau *m* de signalisation; *Br* ***road tax*** taxe *f* sur les automobiles; **have you paid your r. tax?** ≃ est-ce que tu as acheté ta vignette?; ***road tax disc*** ≃ vignette *f* (automobile); ***road test*** essai *m* sur route; ***road train*** train *m ou* convoi *m* routier; ***road transport*** transports *mpl* routiers; ***road user*** usager *m* de la route; *Am Fam* ***road warrior*** *(businessman)* = homme d'affaires constamment en déplacement; *Comput & Tel* nomade *m*; *Am* ***road work***, *Br* ***road works*** travaux *mpl* (d'entretien des routes)

roadbed ['rəʊdbed] N *Constr* empierrement *m*; *Rail* ballast *m*

roadblock ['rəʊdblɒk] N barrage *m* routier

roadbuilding ['rəʊd,bɪldɪŋ] N construction *f* de routes
▸▸ ***roadbuilding programme*** programme *m* pour construire des routes

road-fund ADJ *Br*
▸▸ ***road-fund licence*** ≃ vignette *f*; ***road-fund tax*** taxe *f* routière

roadholding ['rəʊd,həʊldɪŋ] N *Aut* tenue *f* de route

roadhouse ['rəʊdhaʊs, *pl* -haʊzɪz] N relais *m* routier

roadie ['rəʊdɪ] N *Fam* = technicien qui accompagne les groupes de rock en tournée

roadmap ['rəʊdmæp] N carte *f* routière; *Fig* **a r. for peace** un plan de paix

roadshow ['rəʊdʃəʊ] N *(gen)* tournée *f*; *(radio show)* = animation en direct proposée par une station de radio en tournée; *Mktg* tournée *f* de présentation

roadside ['rəʊdsaɪd] N bord *m* de la route, bas-côté *m*; **we stopped the car by the r.** nous avons arrêté la voiture au bord *ou* sur le bord de la route
ADJ au bord de la route
▸▸ ***roadside advertising*** affichage *m* routier; *Aut* ***roadside assistance*** assistance *f* technique aux véhicules, assistance *f* dépannage; ***roadside camera*** caméra *f* en bord de route; ***roadside inn*** auberge *f* située au bord de la route; ***roadside repairs*** *(by driver)* réparations *fpl* de fortune; *(by mechanic)* dépannage *m*

roadstead ['rəʊdsted] N *Naut* rade *f*

roadster ['rəʊdstə(r)] N **1** *(car)* roadster *m* **2** *(bicycle)* bicyclette *f* (de tourisme)

roadsweeper ['rəʊd,swiːpə(r)] N *(person)* balayeur(euse) *m,f*; *(vehicle)* balayeuse *f*

road-test VT essayer sur route; *Fig* tester

roadtrip ['rəʊdtrɪp] N *Am (short)* promenade *f* en voiture; *(longer)* voyage *m* en voiture

roadway ['rəʊdweɪ] N chaussée *f*

roadwork ['rəʊdwɜːk] N *(by boxer, athlete etc)* = entraînement consistant à courir le long de la route; **to do r.** courir le long de la route

roadworthiness ['rəʊd,wɜːðɪnɪs] N état *m* général *(d'un véhicule)*

roadworthy ['rəʊd,wɜːðɪ] ADJ *(vehicle)* en état de rouler

roam [rəʊm] VT **1** *(travel* ▸ *world)* courir; *(*▸ *streets)* errer dans; **to r. the seven seas** aller aux quatre coins du monde **2** *(hang about* ▸ *streets)* traîner dans
VI **1** *(wander)* errer, voyager sans but; **to r. about the world** courir le monde; *Fig* **he allowed his imagination/his thoughts to r.** il a laissé vagabonder son imagination/ses pensées **2** *Tel (mobile phone user)* itinérer

roamer ['rəʊmə(r)] N vagabond(e) *m,f*

roaming ['rəʊmɪŋ] ADJ vagabond, errant
N **1** *(wandering)* vagabondage *m* **2** *Tel (of mobile phone)* roaming *m*, itinérance *f*; *Comput (on Internet)* roaming *m*

roan [rəʊn] ADJ rouan
N *(horse)* (cheval *m*) rouan *m*; *(cow)* vache *f* rouanne

roar [rɔː(r)] VI *(lion)* rugir; *(bull)* beugler, mugir; *(elephant)* barrir; *(person, crowd)* hurler; *(radio, music)* beugler, hurler; *(sea, wind)* mugir; *(storm, thunder)* gronder; *(fire, furnace)* ronfler; *(cannon)* tonner, gronder; *(car, motorcycle, engine)* vrombir; **to r. with laughter** rire aux éclats, rire à gorge déployée; **to r. with pain** hurler de douleur; **it made everyone r. (with laughter)** ça a déclenché un tonnerre d'hilarité *ou* l'hilarité générale; **the car roared past** *(noisily)* la voiture est passée en vrombissant; *(fast)* la voiture est passée à toute allure
VT *(feelings, order)* hurler; **the sergeant roared (out) an order to the men** le sergent a hurlé un ordre aux hommes; **the crowd roared their delight** la foule hurlait de joie; **they roared their team on** *(encouraged)* ils ont crié de toutes leurs forces pour encourager leur équipe

N *(of lion)* rugissement *m*; *(of bull)* mugissement *m*, beuglement *m*; *(of elephant)* barrissement *m*; *(of sea, wind)* mugissement *m*; *(of thunder, storm, cannons)* grondement *m*; *(of fire, furnace)* ronflement *m*; *(of crowd)* clameur *f*; *(hostile)* grondement *m*; *(of engine)* vrombissement *m*; **to give a r.** *(person)* hurler; *(lion)* rugir; **roars of laughter** gros *ou* grands éclats *mpl* de rire; **the r. of the traffic** le vacarme de la circulation

roaring ['rɔːrɪŋ] **ADJ 1** *(lion)* rugissant; *(bull)* mugissant, beuglant; *(elephant)* qui barrit; *(person, crowd)* hurlant; *(sea, wind)* mugissant; *(thunder, storm)* qui gronde; *(engine)* vrombissant; **a r. fire** une bonne flambée **2** *Fig (excellent)* **a r. success** un succès fou; *Br* **to do a r. trade** faire des affaires en or; **they did a r. trade in pancakes** ils ont vendu énormément de crêpes

ADV *Fam* **r. drunk** ivre mort, complètement bourré

►► *Naut* ***Roaring Forties*** quarantièmes *mpl* rugissants; ***Roaring Twenties*** les Années *fpl* folles

roast [rəʊst] **VT 1** *(meat)* rôtir, faire rôtir; *(peanuts, almonds, chestnuts)* griller, faire griller; *(coffee)* griller, torréfier; **I decided to r. a chicken for dinner** j'ai décidé de faire un poulet rôti pour le dîner

2 *(minerals)* calciner

3 *Fig (by sun, fire)* griller, rôtir; **I sat roasting my toes by the fire** j'étais assis devant le feu pour me réchauffer les pieds

4 *Fam (criticize ► book, film)* éreinter

5 *Am Fam (tease ► person)* railler[□], mettre en boîte

VI 1 *(meat)* rôtir **2** *Fig (person)* avoir très chaud; **we spent a week roasting in the sun** nous avons passé une semaine à nous rôtir au soleil

ADJ rôti; **medium/high r. coffee** café *m* torréfié/torréfié à cœur

N 1 *(joint of meat)* rôti *m*; **a pork r., a r. of pork** un rôti de porc **2** *Am (barbecue)* barbecue *m* **3** *Am Fam (of celebrity)* = soirée ou émission en l'honneur d'une vedette, et au cours de laquelle cette dernière fait l'objet de taquineries et de flatteries

►► ***roast beef*** rôti *m* de bœuf, rosbif *m*; ***roast chestnuts*** marrons *mpl* chauds; ***roast chicken*** poulet *m* rôti; ***roast pork*** rôti *m* de porc; ***roast potatoes*** pommes *fpl* de terre rôties au four

roaster ['rəʊstə(r)] **N 1** *Br Culin (chicken)* volaille *f* à rôtir; *(pan)* cocotte *f* **2** *(for coffee)* brûloir *m*, torréfacteur *m*

roasting ['rəʊstɪŋ] **N 1** *(of meat)* rôtissage *m*; *(of coffee)* torréfaction *f* **2** *Br Fam Fig* **to give sb a r.** *(tell off)* souffler dans les bronches à qn, passer un savon à qn; *(criticize)* éreinter qn; **to get a r.** *(get told off)* se faire souffler dans les bronches, prendre *ou* se faire passer un savon; *(get criticized)* se faire éreinter

ADJ *Fam (weather)* torride[□]; **it was r. in her office** il faisait une chaleur à crever dans son bureau; **I'm r.!** je crève de chaud!

►► ***roasting pan*** plat *m* à rôtir; ***roasting spit*** tournebroche *m*; ***roasting tin*** plat *m* à rôtir

rob [rɒb] *(pt & pp* **robbed**, *cont* **robbing)** **VT 1** *(person)* voler; *(bank)* dévaliser; *(house)* cambrioler; **to r. sb of sth** voler *ou* dérober qch à qn; *(deprive)* priver qn de qch; **someone has robbed the till!** on a volé l'argent de la caisse! **2** *Fig (deprive)* priver; **to r. sb of sth** priver qn de qch; **the illness had robbed him of his good looks** la maladie lui avait fait perdre sa beauté; **the team was robbed of its victory** l'équipe s'est vue ravir la victoire; **we were robbed!** *(after match)* on nous a volé la victoire!; **to r. Peter to pay Paul** déshabiller Pierre pour habiller Paul

robber ['rɒbə(r)] **N** *(of property)* voleur(euse) *m,f*

►► ***robber baron*** *Hist* baron *m* pillard; *Fig (tough businessman)* requin *m* de l'industrie

robbery ['rɒbərɪ] *(pl* **robberies)** **N 1** *(of property)* vol *m*; *(of bank)* hold-up *m inv*; *(of house)* cambriolage *m*; **r. with violence** vol *m* avec coups et blessures, *Spec* vol *m* qualifié **2** *Fam (overcharging)* vol *m*; **it's highway** *or* **daylight r.!** c'est du vol (organisé)!, c'est de l'arnaque!; **it's nothing short of r.!** c'est du vol!

robe [rəʊb] **N 1** *(dressing gown ► heavy)* robe *f* de chambre; *(► light, for women)* peignoir *m*; *(► bathrobe)* sortie *f* de bain, peignoir *m* (de bain) **2** *(long garment ► gen)* robe *f*; *(► for judge, academic)* robe *f*, toge *f*

VT 1 *Literary (dress)* habiller, vêtir; **robed in red** vêtu de rouge **2** *(judge, priest)* vêtir d'une robe

VI *(judge)* revêtir sa robe

> Note that the most common meaning of the French word **robe** is **dress**.

robin ['rɒbɪn] **N** *Orn* **1** *(European)* rouge-gorge *m* **2** *(American)* merle *m* américain; **r.'s-egg blue** *(colour)* bleu-vert *m inv* pâle

►► *Orn* ***robin redbreast*** rouge-gorge *m*

robing room ['rəʊbɪŋ-] **N** *(of judge)* vestiaire *m*

Robin Hood PR N Robin des bois

robot ['rəʊbɒt] **N** *also Fig (automaton)* robot *m*, automate *m*

COMP *(pilot, vehicle, system)* automatique

►► ***robot arm*** bras-robot *m*; ***robot bomb*** bombe *f* volante

robotics [rəʊ'bɒtɪks] **N** *(UNCOUNT) (science)* robotique *f*

robotize, -ise ['rəʊbətaɪz] **VT** robotiser

robust [rəʊ'bʌst] **ADJ** *(person)* robuste, vigoureux, solide; *(furniture, structure, health)* solide; *(appetite)* robuste, solide; *(wine)* robuste, corsé; *(economy, style, car)* robuste; *(response, defence)* vigoureux, énergique

robustness [rəʊ'bʌstnɪs] **N** *(of person)* robustesse *f*, vigueur *f*; *(of furniture, structure, health)* solidité *f*; *(of appetite)* robustesse *f*, solidité *f*; *(of economy, style, car)* robustesse *f*; *(of response, defence)* vigueur *f*

roc [rɒk] **N** *Myth (bird)* rock *m*

ROCE [ˌɑːrəʊˌsiː'iː] **N** *Fin (abbr* **return on capital employed)** retour *m* sur capital immobilisé

rock [rɒk] **N 1** *(substance ► gen)* roche *f*; *(► hard)* roc *m*; **cut into/hewn out of the r.** creusé dans le roc; **a layer of r.** une couche rocheuse

2 *(boulder, rock face)* rocher *m*; *Am (stone)* pierre *f*; **to run onto the rocks** *(ship)* s'échouer sur des rochers; **fall of rocks** chute *f* de pierres, éboulis *m* rocheux; *Fig* **she was an absolute r. during the crisis** elle nous a été d'un grand secours pendant cette épreuve; *Fig* **to be as solid as a r.** être solide comme le roc; **the R. (of Gibraltar)** le rocher de Gibraltar; *Fam* **to be on the rocks** *(company)* être au bord de la faillite[□]; *(relationship, marriage)* mal tourner[□], tourner à la catastrophe[□]; **on the rocks** *(drink)* avec des glaçons, *Can* sur glace; **to be between a r. and a hard place** être pris entre deux feux, être entre le marteau et l'enclume

3 *(music)* rock *m*; **r. and roll** rock *m* (and roll)

4 *Br (sweet)* ≃ sucre *m* d'orge; **a stick of r.** ≃ un bâton de sucre d'orge

5 *Fam (diamond)* diam *m*

6 *very Fam* **rocks** *(testicles)* couilles *fpl*, boules *fpl*; **to get one's rocks off** *(have sex)* baiser, s'envoyer en l'air; *(have orgasm)* prendre son pied, jouir; *(enjoy oneself)* s'éclater, prendre son pied

7 *Fam Drugs slang (crack cocaine)* crack *m*; *Br (cocaine)* coco *f*, neige *f*

COMP *(film)* rock *(inv)*; *(band, record, concert, guitarist)* (de) rock *(inv)*

VT 1 *(swing to and fro ► baby)* bercer; *(► chair, cradle)* balancer; *(► lever)* basculer; **to r. a baby to sleep** bercer un bébé pour l'endormir; **he rocked himself in the rocking chair** il se balançait dans le fauteuil à bascule; **the boat was rocked by the waves** *(gently)* le bateau était bercé par les flots; *(violently)* le bateau était ballotté par les vagues; *Fig* **to r. the boat** jouer les troublefête, semer le trouble; **don't r. the boat** ne fais pas de vagues **2** *(shake)* secouer, ébranler; **the village was rocked by an explosion/an earthquake** le village fut secoué par une explosion/un tremblement de terre; **the Government has been rocked by the latest sex scandal** le gouvernement a été secoué par la dernière histoire de mœurs

VI 1 *(sway)* se balancer; **to r. on a chair** se balancer sur une chaise; **to r. with laughter** se tordre de rire

2 *(building, ground)* trembler

3 *(jive)* danser le rock

4 *Fam (be excellent)* **the party was really rocking** *(animated)* il y avait une ambiance d'enfer à la soirée

ADV *(idiom)* **to hit r. bottom** *(person, morale)* avoir le moral à zéro, toucher le fond; *(fir… funds)* atteindre le niveau le plus bas

►► *Culin* ***rock bun, rock cake*** rocher *m* (gâtea… *Am* ***rock candy*** sucre *m* d'orge; *Fam* ***rock ch…*** mordue *f* de hard rock; ***rock climber*** varappe… (euse) *m,f*; ***rock climbing*** escalade *f* (de rocher… varappe *f*; **to go r. climbing** faire de l'escalade… de la varappe; ***rock crystal*** cristal *m* de roche; *O…* ***rock dove*** (pigeon *m*) biset *m*; ***rock face*** paroi *f* r… cheuse; ***rock garden*** (jardin *m* de) rocaille *f*; ***ro… music*** rock *m*; *Bot* ***rock plant*** plante *f* de rocail… ***rock pool*** flaque *f* dans les rochers; *Bot* ***rock ro…*** hélianthème *m*; *Ich* ***rock salmon*** roussette *f*; ***ro… salt*** sel *m* gemme; ***rock slide*** *(action)* éboulemen… *m* de rochers; *(result)* éboulis *m*; ***rock star*** ro… star *f*

> When translating the English word **rock**, not… that the French words **rocher** and **roche** ar… not interchangeable. **Rocher** describes an in… dividual piece of rock whereas with **roche** th… emphasis is on the matter or the type of rock

rock-bottom ADJ *(price)* défiant toute concu… rence, le plus bas, sacrifié

rock-bound ADJ encerclé de rochers

rock-climb VI faire de la varappe

rocker ['rɒkə(r)] **N 1** *(of cradle, chair)* bascule… *Fam* **to be off one's r.** être cinglé, débloque… *Fam* **to go off one's r.** *(go mad)* devenir ding… *ou* cinglé, perdre la boule; *(lose one's temper)* p… ter une durit, piquer une crise

2 *(rocking chair)* fauteuil *m* à bascule, *Can* be… çante *f*

3 *Mus (person)* rocker *m*, rockeur(euse) *m,f*

4 *Aut & Tech* culbuteur *m*

5 *Br (youth)* rocker *m*, rockeur(euse) *m,f*; **th… Rockers** = jeunes motards aux cheveux lon… qui rivalisaient avec les "Mods" dans les anné… 60

►► *Aut & Tech* ***rocker arm*** culbuteur *m*

rockery ['rɒkərɪ] *(pl* **rockeries)** **N** (jardin *m* de) r… caille *f*

rocket ['rɒkɪt] **N 1** *Aviat & Astron* fusée *f*; **to fire… launch a r.** lancer une fusée; **to go off like a r.** pa… tir comme une fusée

2 *Mil (missile)* roquette *f*

3 *(signal, firework)* fusée *f*

4 *Br Fam (telling off)* engueulade *f*; **to get a… (from sb)** se faire engueuler (par qn), prend… *ou* se faire passer un savon (par qn); **to give s… a r.** engueuler qn, passer un savon a qn

5 *Br Bot & Culin* roquette *f*

COMP *(propulsion)* par fusée; *(engine)* de fusée

VT 1 *(missile, astronaut)* lancer (dans l'espace)… *(record, singer)* faire monter en flèche; **the reco… rocketed the group into the top 10** grâce à c… disque, le groupe est monté en flèche jusqu'a… top 10

VI *(price, sales)* monter en flèche; **to r. to fam…** devenir célèbre du jour au lendemain; **the c… rocketed down the road/round the track** la voitu… a descendu la rue/fait le tour de la piste à un… vitesse incroyable

►► *Mil* ***rocket attack*** attaque *f* à la roquette; *Avi… & Astron* ***rocket fuel*** propergol *m*; ***rocket gun*** fus… *m* lance-roquettes; ***rocket launcher*** *Aviat & Astro…* lance-fusées *m inv*; *Mil* lance-roquettes *m in…* *Mil* ***rocket range*** base *f* de lancement de missile… ***rocket science*** fuséologie *m*; *Fam Fig* **it's not e… actly r. science** ce n'est pas sorcier; ***rocket scienti…*** spécialiste *mf* de fuséologie

rocketry ['rɒkɪtrɪ] **N 1** *(science)* fuséologie *f* *(rockets collectively)* arsenal *m* de fusées

rockfall ['rɒkfɔːl] **N** chute *f* de pierres *ou* de r… chers, éboulement *m*

rock-hard ADJ dur comme le roc

rockhouse ['rɒkhaʊs, *pl* -haʊzɪz] **N** *Am Fam Drug… slang* = lieu où l'on achète, vend et consomm… du crack

Rockies ['rɒkɪz] **NPL the R.** les Rocheuses *fpl*

rocking ['rɒkɪŋ] **ADJ** *(movement)* oscillan… *(building)* branlant; **a r. movement** des oscill… tions *fpl*

N 1 *(of chair, boat, cradle)* balancement *m*; *(… baby)* bercement *m*; *(of head ► to rhythm)* balan… cement *m* **2** *Tech* oscillation *f*

►► ***rocking chair*** fauteuil *m* à bascule, rockin…

chair *m*, *Can* berçante *f*; ***rocking horse*** cheval *m* à bascule

rock-solid ADJ inébranlable

rockumentary [ˌrɒkjuˈmentərɪ] N *Cin* rockumentaire *m (documentaire sur un groupe de rock)*

rocky [ˈrɒkɪ] (*compar* **rockier**, *superl* **rockiest**) ADJ **1** *(seabed, mountain, shoreline)* rocheux; *(path, track)* rocailleux; *(soil)* rocailleux, pierreux; **r. outcrop** affleurement *m* rocheux **2** *(unstable ▸ situation)* précaire, instable; *(▸ government)* peu stable; *(relationship, marriage)* difficile; **it's been a r. year for the oil industry** ça a été une année difficile pour l'industrie pétrolière; **to have a r. road ahead** avoir des problèmes en perspective; **to go through a r. patch** traverser une période difficile

N *Br Fam Drugs slang (cannabis)* marocain *m*

▸▸ ***the Rocky Mountains*** les montagnes *fpl* Rocheuses

rococo [rəˈkəʊkəʊ] ADJ rococo *(inv)*

N rococo *m*

rod [rɒd] N **1** *(of metal)* tige *f*; *(of wood)* baguette *f*; *(for curtains, carpet)* tringle *f*; *(for fishing)* canne *f*; *(for punishment ▸ stiff)* baguette *f*; *(▸ flexible)* verge *f*; *Sch (pointer)* baguette *f*; **to fish with r. and line** pêcher à la ligne; **r. fishing** pêche *f* à la ligne; **rods** *(mechanism)* tringlerie *f*, timonerie *f*; *Fig* **to rule with a r. of iron** gouverner d'une main *ou* poigne de fer; *Fig* **to make a r. for one's own back** s'attirer des ennuis; *Fig* **a r. to beat oneself with** des verges pour se faire battre

2 *(of uranium)* barre *f*

3 *(symbol of office)* verge *f*

4 *(for surveying)* mire *f*

5 *Anat (in eye)* bâtonnet *m*

6 *(linear or square measure)* ≃ perche *f*

7 *Am Fam (gun)* flingue *m*

8 *Fam (car)* voiture *f* gonflée

9 *Vulg (penis)* bite *f*, tige *f*

rode [rəʊd] *pt of* **ride**

rodent [ˈrəʊdənt] ADJ rongeur

N rongeur *m*

▸▸ ***rodent control*** dératisation *f*; *Br Admin* ***rodent operative*** spécialiste *mf* de la dératisation; *Med* ***rodent ulcer*** carcinome *m* basocellulaire ulcéreux

rodent-like ADJ qui fait penser à un rongeur

rodeo [ˈrəʊdɪəʊ] (*pl* **rodeos**) N rodéo *m*

▸▸ ***rodeo rider*** cavalier(ère) *m,f* pratiquant le rodéo

rodomontade [ˌrɒdəmɒnˈteɪd] N *Literary* rodomontade *f*

roe [rəʊ] (*pl sense* **2** inv *or* **roes**) N **1** *(UNCOUNT)* *(eggs)* œufs *mpl* de poisson; *(sperm)* laitance *f*; **cod r.** œufs *mpl* de cabillaud **2** *(deer)* chevreuil *m*

▸▸ *Zool* ***roe deer*** chevreuil *m*

roebuck [ˈrəʊbʌk] (*pl* inv *or* **roebucks**) N *Zool* chevreuil *m* mâle

roentgen [ˈrɜːntgən] N *Phys* röntgen *m*, rœntgen *m*

▸▸ ***roentgen rays*** rayons *mpl* X

rogation [rəʊˈgeɪʃən] N *(usu pl)* rogations *fpl*

▸▸ ***Rogation Days*** rogations *fpl*; ***Rogation Sunday*** dimanche *m* des rogations

roger [ˈrɒdʒə(r)] EXCLAM *Tel* reçu et compris, d'accord; **r. and out** message reçu, terminé

VT *Br very Fam (have sex with)* baiser, sauter

rogue [rəʊg] N **1** *(scoundrel)* escroc *m*, filou *m*; *(mischievous child)* polisson(onne) *m,f*, coquin(e) *m,f*; *(maverick)* franc-tireur *m* **2** *(animal)* solitaire *m*

ADJ **1** *(animal)* solitaire; **a r. elephant** un éléphant solitaire **2** *Am (delinquent)* dévoyé

▸▸ *Tel & Comput* ***rogue dialling*** détournement *m* de modem; ***rogues' gallery*** *(in police files)* photographies *fpl* de repris de justice; *Fig Hum* **they're a real rogues' gallery!** ils ont des mines patibulaires!; *Biol* ***rogue gene*** gène *m* aberrant; ***rogue policeman*** policier *m* corrompu; ***rogue state*** État *m* voyou, État *m* paria; *St Exch* ***rogue trader*** trader *m* fou, trader *m* fraudeur

roguery [ˈrəʊgərɪ] N *(UNCOUNT)* *(dishonesty)* malhonnêteté *f*; *(mischievousness)* côté *m* farceur; *(of child)* espièglerie *f*

roguish [ˈrəʊgɪʃ] ADJ *(mischievous)* espiègle, malicieux, coquin

roguishly [ˈrəʊgɪʃlɪ] ADV *(smile, wink)* avec espièglerie, d'un air coquin

roguishness [ˈrəʊgɪʃnɪs] N *(dishonesty)* malhonnêteté *f*; *(mischievousness)* côté *m* farceur; *(of child)* espièglerie *f*

ROI [ˌɑːrəʊˈaɪ] N **1** *Fin (abbr* **return on investment***)* retour *m* sur investissement(s) **2** *(abbr* **Republic of Ireland***)* République *f* de l'Irlande

roisterer [ˈrɔɪstərə(r)] N noceur(euse) *m,f*

role, rôle [rəʊl] N rôle *m*; **to have** *or* **to play the leading r.** jouer le rôle principal; **she had** *or* **she played an important r. in this project** elle a joué un rôle important dans ce projet; **to have a r. in life** avoir un rôle dans la vie

▸▸ ***role model*** modèle *m*; **children need a r. model** les enfants ont besoin de quelqu'un à qui s'identifier; ***role play*** *(gén)* jeu *m* de rôles; *Psy* psychodrame *m*; ***role playing*** *(UNCOUNT)* *(gén)* jeux *mpl* de rôles; *Psy* psychodrames *mpl*; ***role reversal*** inversion *f* des rôles

rolf [rɒlf] VI *Am very Fam (vomit)* dégueuler

ROLL [rəʊl]

N
- rouleau **1**
- roulement **3, 5**
- petit pain **2**
- liste **4**

VT
- rouler **1, 2**
- faire tourner **3**

VI
- rouler **1, 4**
- tourner **3**
- avoir du roulis **2**

N **1** *(of carpet, paper)* rouleau *m*; *(of banknotes)* liasse *f*; *(of tobacco)* carotte *f*; *(of butter)* coquille *f*; *(of fat, flesh)* bourrelet *m*; *(of tools)* trousse *f*; **a r. of film** une pellicule photo

2 *(bread)* petit pain *m*; **ham/cheese r.** ≃ sandwich *m* au jambon/fromage

3 *(movement ▸ of ball)* roulement *m*; *(▸ of dice)* lancement *m*; *(▸ of car, ship)* roulis *m*; *(▸ of plane)* *(in turbulence)* roulis *m*; *(in aerobatics)* tonneau *m*; *(▸ of hips, shoulders)* balancement *m*; *(▸ of sea)* houle *f*; **to have a r. on the ground** *(horse)* se rouler par terre; **to do a r.** *(in high jump)* sauter en rouleau; **to walk with a r.** se balancer *ou* se dandiner en marchant; *Fam* **to have a r. in the hay** *(have sex)* se rouler dans le foin, se faire une partie de jambes en l'air; *Fam* **to be on a r.** être bien parti

4 *(list ▸ of members)* liste *f*, tableau *m*; *Admin & Naut* rôle *m*; *Sch* liste *f* des élèves; **to call the r.** faire l'appel; *Law* **to strike sb off** *or* **from the rolls** rayer qn du tableau; *Sch* **falling rolls** baisse *f* d'effectifs; **r. of honour** *Mil* liste *f* des combattants morts pour la patrie; *Sch* tableau *m* d'honneur

5 *(noise ▸ of drum)* roulement *m*; *(▸ of thunder)* grondement *m*; **I can hear the rolls of thunder** j'entends gronder le tonnerre

VT **1** *(ball)* (faire) rouler; *(dice)* jeter, lancer; *(cigarette, paper, carpet, umbrella)* rouler; *(coil)* enrouler; **to r. sth along the ground** faire rouler qch sur le sol; **to r. yarn into a ball** faire des pelotes de laine; **the hedgehog rolled itself into a ball** le hérisson s'est mis en boule; **to r. sth in** *or* **between one's fingers** rouler qch entre ses doigts; **he rolled his sleeves above his elbows** il a roulé *ou* retroussé ses manches au-dessus du coude; **to r. the presses** faire tourner les presses; **to r. dice** *(to play)* jouer aux dés; **to r. one's r's** rouler les r; **to r. one's hips/shoulders** rouler les hanches/épaules; *Br* **to r. one's own** *(cigarettes)* se rouler ses cigarettes; **this room is a bedroom and study rolled into one** cette pièce sert à la fois de chambre et de bureau

2 *(flatten ▸ grass)* rouler; *(▸ pastry, dough)* étendre; *(▸ gold, metal)* laminer; *(▸ road)* cylindrer

3 *Cin (camera)* faire tourner; **r. 'em!** moteur!

4 *Am Fam (rob)* dévaliser[□], faire les poches à *(une personne ivre ou endormie)*

VI **1** *(ball, coin etc)* rouler; **to r. on the ground/in the grass** *(person, animal)* se rouler par terre/dans l'herbe; **to r. in the mud** *(gén)* se rouler dans la boue; *(wallow)* se vautrer dans la boue; **the ball rolled under the car/down the stairs/along the floor** la balle roula sous la voiture/en bas de l'escalier/sur le sol; **the car rolled down the hill** la voiture dévalait la colline; **the parade rolled slowly past the window** le défilé passait lentement devant la fenêtre; **the bus rolled into the yard** le bus est entré dans la cour; **the car rolled to a halt** la voiture s'est arrêtée lentement; **tears rolled down her face** des larmes roulaient sur ses joues; **sweat rolled off his back** la sueur lui dégoulinait dans le dos; **to r. with the punches** *(boxer)* encaisser les coups de l'adversaire; *Fig* encaisser; *Fam* **to be rolling in money** *or* **rolling in it** rouler sur l'or, être plein aux as; **he had them rolling in the aisles** il les faisait mourir de rire

2 *(ship)* avoir du roulis; *(plane ▸ with turbulence)* avoir du roulis; *(▸ in aerobatics)* faire un tonneau/des tonneaux; *Astron* tourner sur soi-même

3 *(camera, machine)* tourner; **to keep the cameras/the presses rolling** laisser tourner les caméras/les presses; *TV & Cin* **r.!** moteur!; **the credits started to r.** *(of film)* le générique commença à défiler; *Fig* **OK, we're ready to r.!** bon, on est prêt, allons-y!; *Fig* **to get** *or* **to start things rolling** mettre les choses en marche; **let the good times r.** que la fête continue

4 *(drums)* rouler; *(thunder)* gronder; *(voice)* retentir; *(music)* retentir, résonner; *(organ)* résonner, sonner

▸▸ *Aut* ***roll bar*** arceau *m* de sécurité; ***roll call*** appel *m*; **to take (the) r. call** faire l'appel; ***roll collar*** col *m* roulé; ***roll film*** pellicule *f* en bobine; ***roll neck*** col *m* roulé

▸ **roll about** VT SEP **to r. sth about** faire rouler qch

VI *(marble, ball etc)* rouler çà et là; *(ship)* rouler; **to r. about on the floor** *or* **ground/grass** *(person)* se rouler par terre/dans l'herbe; **to r. about laughing/in pain** se tordre de rire/de douleur

▸ **roll along** VT SEP *(hoop, ball)* faire rouler; *(car, wheelbarrow)* pousser

VI **1** *(river)* couler; *(car)* rouler **2** *(project)* avancer **3** *Fam (visit)* passer[□], se pointer

▸ **roll around = roll about**

▸ **roll away** VT SEP *(take away)* emmener; *(put away)* ranger

VI *(clouds)* s'éloigner; *(marble, ball etc)* rouler au loin; *(mist)* se retirer; **the hills rolled away into the distance** les collines disparaissaient au loin

▸ **roll back** VT SEP **1** *(push back ▸ carpet)* rouler, enrouler; *(▸ blankets)* replier; *(▸ enemy, difficulties)* faire reculer; *(▸ trolley, wheelchair)* reculer; **to r. back the frontiers of science** faire reculer les frontières de la science

2 *(time)* faire reculer; **it would be nice to r. back the years** ce serait bien de revenir des années en arrière

3 *Am (prices)* casser

4 *(bring back)* ramener

VI *(waves)* se retirer; *(car)* reculer, rouler en arrière; *(memories, time)* revenir; **her eyes rolled back in her head** ses yeux se révulsèrent

▸ **roll by** VI **1** *(time)* s'écouler, passer **2** *(car)* passer

▸ **roll down** VT SEP *(blind, car window)* baisser; *(sleeves)* redescendre

VI *(tears, sweat)* couler; **to r. down a hill** *(car, children)* débouler une pente; **the tears rolled down his cheeks** les larmes coulaient le long de ses joues

▸ **roll in** VT SEP *(bring in)* faire entrer; *(barrel)* faire entrer en roulant; **to r. the ball in** *(in hockey)* remettre la balle en jeu

VI **1** *(waves)* déferler; *(mist, clouds, train)* arriver

2 *(pour in ▸ money, crowds)* affluer

3 *Fam (person ▸ arrive)* se pointer; *(▸ come back)* rentrer[□]; **they finally rolled in at three o'clock in the morning** ils sont finalement rentrés à trois heures du matin; **she rolled in to work three hours late** elle s'est amenée au travail avec trois heures de retard

4 *(in hockey)* remettre la balle en jeu

▸ **roll off** VT SEP *Typ (print)* imprimer

VI *(fall on floor)* rouler par terre; **the top rolled off into the bath** le bouchon a roulé dans la baignoire; **to r. off the shelf/the table** rouler de l'étagère/de la table; **cars are rolling off the production line** les voitures sortent de la chaîne de production

▸ **roll on** VT SEP **1** *(paint)* appliquer au rouleau; *(deodorant)* appliquer **2** *(stockings)* enfiler

VI **1** *(time)* s'écouler **2** *Br Fam* **r. on Christmas!** vivement (qu'on soit à) Noël!□; **r. on the day when I'm my own boss!** vivement que je sois mon propre patron!□

▸**roll out** VT SEP **1** *(ball)* rouler (dehors); *(map)* dérouler; *(pastry)* étendre (au rouleau) **2** *(produce ▸ goods, speech)* débiter **3** *(launch ▸ product)* lancer; *(extend ▸ new scheme)* étendre; *(▸ production)* accroître; **the new scheme will be rolled out nationwide** le nouveau système s'étendra à tout le pays

VI sortir; **to r. out of bed** *(person)* sortir du lit; **the ball rolled out from under the sofa** la balle est sortie de sous le canapé; **the train rolled out of the station** le train quitta la gare; *Fam* **we rolled out of the pub at midnight** nous sommes sortis du pub à minuit□

▸**roll over** VT SEP **1** *(person, animal, object)* retourner **2** *Fin (credit, interest rates)* renouveler

VT INSEP rouler sur; *(of car)* écraser

VI *(person, animal)* se retourner; *(car)* faire un tonneau; **to r. over and over** *(in bed)* se retourner plusieurs fois; *(car)* faire une série de tonneaux

▸**roll round** VI *(season etc)* arriver

▸**roll up** VT SEP *(map, carpet)* rouler; *(sleeves)* retrousser; *(trousers)* remonter, retrousser; *(blind, car window)* remonter; **to r. sth up in a blanket** enrouler *ou* envelopper qch dans une couverture

VI **1** *(carpet)* se rouler; *(blind)* remonter; **to r. up into a ball** se rouler en boule **2** *Fam (arrive ▸ guests)* rappliquer, se pointer, s'amener; *(▸ customers, spectators)* rappliquer en foule; **r. up! r. up!** approchez!□

---

rollaway ['rəʊləweɪ] ADJ à roulettes

▸▸ ***rollaway bed*** lit *m* pliant sur roulettes

rollback ['rəʊlbæk] N *Am* réduction *f*, baisse *f*

rolled [rəʊld] ADJ **1** *(paper)* en rouleau; *(carpet)* roulé; *(umbrella)* plié **2** *(iron, steel)* laminé **3** *(tobacco)* en carotte

▸▸ ***rolled gold*** plaqué *m* or; **a r. gold bracelet** un bracelet en plaqué or; ***rolled oats*** flocons *mpl* d'avoine; *Constr* ***rolled steel joist*** solive *f* en I

rolled-up ADJ roulé, enroulé

Roller ['rəʊlə(r)] N *Br Fam (Rolls-Royce®)* Rolls Royce®□*f*

roller ['rəʊlə(r)] N **1** *(cylinder ▸ for paint, pastry, garden, hair)* rouleau *m*; *(▸ for blind)* enrouleur *m*; *(▸ of typewriter)* rouleau *m*, cylindre *m*; *Tex* calandre *f*; *Metal* laminoir *m*; **to put rollers in (one's hair), to put one's hair in rollers** se mettre des rouleaux *ou* des bigoudis; **my hair's in rollers** j'ai des rouleaux *ou* des bigoudis sur la tête

2 *(wheel ▸ for marking, furniture)* roulette *f*; *(▸ in machine)* galet *m*

3 *(wave)* rouleau *m*

4 *Orn (pigeon)* pigeon *m* culbutant, (pigeon *m*) rouleur *m*; *(European)* rollier *m* d'Europe

▸▸ ***roller bandage*** bandage *m* enroulé; ***roller blind*** store *m* à enrouleur; ***roller derby*** course *f* en patins à roulettes; ***roller disco*** = discothèque où l'on tourne en patins à roulettes sur une piste; ***roller hockey*** hockey *m* sur patins à roulettes; ***roller map*** carte *f* sur rouleau; ***roller skate*** patin *m* à roulettes; ***roller towel*** essuie-mains *m inv (monté sur un rouleau)*

rollerblader ['rəʊlə,bleɪdə(r)] N patineur(euse) *m,f* en rollers

rollerblades ['rəʊlə,bleɪdz] NPL patins *mpl* en ligne, rollerblades *mpl*, rollers *mpl*

rollerblading ['rəʊlə,bleɪdɪŋ] N roller *m*; **to go r.** faire du roller

rollercoaster ['rəʊlə,kəʊstə(r)] N montagnes *fpl* russes, grand huit *m*; **the r. fortunes of a company/a party** les hauts et les bas que connaît une société/un parti; **to be on an emotional r.** être ballotté par ses émotions

VI *esp Am (road)* faire des montagnes russes; *(economy)* connaître des hauts et des bas prononcés

roller-skate VI faire du patin à roulettes

roller-skating N patinage *m* à roulettes; **to go r.** aller faire du patin à roulettes

rollick ['rɒlɪk] *Fam* VI *(romp)* s'ébattre□; *(celebrate)* faire la noce

VT *Br (scold)* engueuler, remonter les bretelles à

▸**rollick about** VI *Br Fam* s'ébattre□, faire le fou (la folle)

rollicking ['rɒlɪkɪŋ] *Fam* ADV **to get r. drunk** se soûler; **it's a r. good read!** *(book)* c'est un livre excellent!□; **to have a r. good time** s'amuser comme des fous

N *Br (scolding)* **to get a r.** se faire engueuler, se faire remonter les bretelles; **to give sb a r.** engueuler qn, remonter les bretelles à qn

rollie ['rəʊlɪ] N *Br Fam* cigarette *f* roulée à la main□

rolling ['rəʊlɪŋ] ADJ **1** *(object)* roulant, qui roule; *Culin* **bring to a r. boil** maintenir à ébullition

2 *(hills)* ondulant; *(countryside)* valonné; **to have a r. gait** rouler les hanches

3 *(sea)* houleux; *(boat)* qui a du roulis

4 *(fog)* enveloppant; *(thunder)* grondant

5 *(mobile ▸ target)* mobile, mouvant; **a r. plan for development** un plan de développement constamment remis à jour

N **1** *(of dice)* lancement *m*

2 *(of boat)* roulis *m*

3 *(of thunder)* grondement *m*

4 *(of shoulders)* roulement *m*

5 *(of road, lawn)* cylindrage *m*

6 *Metal* laminage *m*

ADV *Br Fam* **to be r. drunk** être complètement soûl□

▸▸ *Acct* ***rolling budget*** budget *m* glissant; *Cin & TV* ***rolling credits*** générique *m* déroulant; ***rolling mill*** *(factory)* usine *f* de laminage; *(equipment)* laminoir *m*; ***rolling pin*** rouleau *m* à pâtisserie; *Rail* ***rolling stock*** matériel *m* roulant; ***rolling stone*** *(person)* vadrouilleur(euse) *m,f*; **to be a r. stone** rouler sa bosse, avoir une âme de vagabond; *Prov* **a r. stone gathers no moss** pierre qui roule n'amasse pas mousse; ***rolling strikes*** grèves *fpl* tournantes

rollmop ['rəʊlmɒp] N rollmops *m*

roll-neck(ed) ADJ à col roulé

roll-on N **1** *(deodorant)* déodorant *m* à bille **2** *(corset)* gaine *f*, corset *m*

▸▸ ***roll-on deodorant*** déodorant *m* à bille

roll-on/roll-off N *(ship)* (navire *m*) transbordeur *m*, ferry-boat *m*; *(system)* roll on-roll off *m inv*, manutention *f* par roulage

ADJ *(ferry)* transbordeur, ro-ro *(inv)*; *(port)* à roulage direct

rollover ['rəʊl,əʊvə(r)] N **1** *Br (in National Lottery)* = à la loterie nationale, situation où, personne n'ayant gagné le gros lot, celui-ci est ajouté à l'enjeu du tirage suivant **2** *Fin (in taxation)* (disposition *f* de) roulement *m*; *(of loan)* reconduction *f*

ADJ *Am (renewable)* renouvelable; *(renegotiable)* renégociable; *(credit, loan)* à taux révisable

▸▸ *Fin* ***rollover credit*** crédit *m* renouvelable; *Br* ***rollover jackpot*** *(in National Lottery)* jackpot *m* roulant; *Fin* ***rollover loan*** prêt *m* renouvelable; *Br* ***rollover week*** *(in National Lottery)* tirage *m* du jackpot roulant

Rolls [rəʊlz] N *Br Fam (Rolls-Royce®)* Rolls Royce®□*f*

roll-up ADJ *(map)* qui s'enroule

N *Br Fam* cigarette *f* roulée à la main□; **she smokes roll-ups** elle roule elle-même ses cigarettes

roly-poly [,rəʊlɪ'pəʊlɪ] *(pl* **roly-polies***)* ADJ *Fam* grassouillet, rondelet

N **1** *Fam (plump person)* **she's a real r.** elle est vraiment grassouillette **2** *Culin* gâteau *m* roulé à la confiture

▸▸ *Culin* ***roly-poly pudding*** gâteau *m* roulé à la confiture

ROM [rɒm] N *Comput (abbr* **read-only memory***)* mémoire *f* morte, (mémoire *f*) ROM *f*

romaine [rəʊ'meɪn] N *Am (lettuce)* romaine *f*

▸▸ ***romaine lettuce*** laitue *f* romaine

Roman ['rəʊmən] N **1** *(person from Rome)* Romain(e) *m,f*; *Bible* **the Epistle of Paul to the Romans** l'Épître de saint Paul aux Romains **2** *Typ* romain *m*

ADJ **1** *(gen) & Typ & Rel* romain **2** *(nose)* aquilin

▸▸ ***Roman alphabet*** alphabet *m* romain; ***Roman calendar*** calendrier *m* romain; ***Roman candle*** chandelle *f* romaine; *Rel* ***Roman Catholic*** ADJ catholique

N catholique *mf*; *Rel* ***Roman Catholicism*** catholicisme *m*; *Hist* ***the Roman Empire*** l'Empire *m* romain; ***Roman law*** droit *m* romain; ***Roman numeral*** chiffre *m* romain; ***Roman road*** voie *f* romaine

> Note that the French adjective **roman** is a false friend and is never a translation for the English word **Roman**. It means **Romanesque**.

roman ['rəʊmən] *Typ* N romain *m*; **in r.** en romain

ADJ romain; **r. type** caractères *mpl* romains

romance [rəʊ'mæns] N **1** *(love affair)* liaison (amoureuse); **to have a r. with sb** *(affair)* avoir une liaison avec qn; *(idyll)* vivre un roman d'amour avec qn; **a holiday r.** un amour de vacances

2 *(love)* amour *m* (romantique); **r. is in the air** il y a de l'amour dans l'air

3 *(romantic novel)* roman *m* d'amour; *(film)* film *m* romantique; **historical r.** = roman d'amour situé à une époque ancienne

4 *(charm)* charme *m*, poésie *f*; *(excitement)* attrait *m*; **after a while the r. wore off** après quelque temps, le charme s'estompa

5 *Literature* roman *m* de chevalerie *ou* d'aventures

6 *Mus* romance *f*

VI laisser vagabonder son imagination, fabuler; **to r. on** *or* **about sth** fabuler *ou* broder sur qch

VT *(person)* courtiser

• **Romance** N *Ling* roman *m* ADJ **the R. languages** les langues *fpl* romanes; **student of R. languages** romaniste *mf*

romancing [rəʊ'mænsɪŋ] N *(UNCOUNT) (invention)* fabulations *fpl*, affabulations *fpl*; *(exaggeration)* exagérations *fpl*

Romanesco [,rəʊmə'neskəʊ] N *Bot & Culin* chou *m* romanesco

Romanesque [,rəʊmə'nesk] *Archit* ADJ roman

N roman *m*

Romania [ru:'meɪnɪə] N Roumanie *f*

Romanian [ru:'meɪnɪən] N **1** *(person)* Roumain(e) *m,f* **2** *(language)* roumain *m*

ADJ roumain

COMP *(embassy)* de Roumanie; *(history)* de la Roumanie; *(teacher)* de roumain

romanize, -ise ['rəʊmənaɪz] VT *Typ* transcrire en caractères romains

Romansch, Romansh [rəʊ'mænʃ] N romanche *m*

ADJ romanche

romantic [rəʊ'mæntɪk] ADJ **1** *(relating to romance, love)* romantique; **a r. dinner for two** un dîner romantique *ou* en tête à tête **2** *(unrealistic)* romanesque; **she still has some r. ideas about life** elle a encore des idées romanesques sur l'existence

N romantique *mf*; **he's an incurable r.** c'est un éternel romantique

• **Romantic** ADJ *Art, Literature & Mus* romantique; **the French R. poets** les poètes *mpl* romantiques français

▸▸ ***romantic adventure*** aventure *f* romanesque; ***romantic comedy*** comédie *f* romantique; ***romantic love*** l'amour *m* romantique; ***romantic novelist*** auteur *m* de romans d'amour; ***romantic play*** pièce *f* romantique

> When translating the English adjective **romantic**, note that the French words **romantique** and **romanesque** are not interchangeable. **Romantique** relates to sentiment and romance, whereas **romanesque** is used to describe people or situations that one could expect to find in a novel.

romantically [rəʊ'mæntɪkəlɪ] ADV de manière romantique; **to be r. involved with sb** avoir des relations amoureuses avec qn; **the two celebrities have been r. linked** les deux célébrités ont eu une liaison amoureuse; **a hotel set r. by the side of a lake** un hôtel situé dans un cadre romantique tout près d'un lac

romanticism [rəʊ'mæntɪsɪzəm] N *(of person)* idées *fpl* romanesques

• **Romanticism** N *Art, Literature & Mus* romantisme *m*

romanticist [rəʊ'mæntɪsɪst] **N** romantique *mf*

romanticize, -ise [rəʊ'mæntɪsaɪz] **VT** *(idea, event)* idéaliser; **to r. war** glorifier la guerre; **they have a romanticized view of life in Britain** ils ont une vision très romantique de la vie en Grande-Bretagne
VI donner dans le romanesque

Romany ['rəʊmənɪ] *(pl* **Romanies***)* **N 1** *(person)* Bohémien(enne) *m,f*, Rom *mf inv* **2** *Ling* rom *m*
ADJ bohémien, rom *(inv)*

rom-com ['rɒmkɒm] **N** *Fam Cin (abbr* **romantic comedy***)* comédie *f* romantique

Rome [rəʊm] **N 1** *(city)* Rome; *Prov* **when in R.(, do as the Romans do)** = il faut adopter les usages de l'endroit où l'on se trouve; *Prov* **R. wasn't built in a day** Rome ne s'est pas faite *ou* Paris ne s'est pas fait en un jour **2** *Rel* **(the Church of) R.** l'Église *f* de Rome; **to go over to R.** passer au catholicisme

Romeo ['rəʊmɪəʊ] **PR N** Roméo
N *Hum* **he's a bit of a R.** c'est un Roméo

romp [rɒmp] **VI** s'ébattre (bruyamment), gambarder; **to r. home** *(candidate, horse, runner)* arriver dans un fauteuil; **the favourite romped home ten lengths ahead** le favori est arrivé avec dix bonnes longueurs d'avance; **to r. through an examination** passer un examen sans effort
N 1 *(frolic)* ébats *mpl*, gambades *fpl*; **sex romps** ébats *mpl* amoureux; *Fig* **the film/play is an enjoyable r.** ce film/cette pièce constitue un divertissement agréable **2** *(film, play)* farce *f*, comédie *f*

rompers ['rɒmpəz] **NPL** barboteuse *f*

romper suit ['rɒmpə-] **N** barboteuse *f*

rondo ['rɒndəʊ] *(pl* **rondos***)* **N** *Mus* rondo *m*

Roneo® ['rəʊnɪəʊ] *(pl* **Roneos**, *pt & pp* **Roneoed***)* **N** Ronéo® *f*
VT ronéotyper, ronéoter

roo [ruː] *(pl* **roos***)* **N** *Austr Fam* kangourou *m*
▸▸ *Aut* ***roo bars*** pare-buffles *m inv*

rood [ruːd] **N 1** *(cross)* crucifix *m* **2** *Br (unit of measurement)* = 1000 m^2
▸▸ ***rood screen*** jubé *m*

roof [ruːf] *(pl* **roofs** *or* **rooves** [ruːvz]*)* **N 1** *(of building)* toit *m*; *(of cave, tunnel, mine)* plafond *m*; *(of branches, trees)* voûte *f*; *(of car)* toit *m*, pavillon *m*; *(of furnace)* dôme *m*; **to live under the same r.** vivre sous le même toit; **shops and sports facilities under one** *or* **the same r.** des boutiques et des aménagements sportifs dans un même endroit; **I won't have this sort of behaviour under my r.** je ne tolérerai pas ce genre de comportement sous mon toit *ou* chez moi; **to be without a r. over one's head** être à la rue; **at least you have a r. over your head** au moins, tu as un endroit pour vivre; *Fig* **the r. of the world** le toit du monde; *Fam* **to go through** *or* **to hit the r.** *(person)* piquer une crise, sortir de ses gonds; *(prices)* flamber; *Fam* **to raise the r.** *(make noise)* faire le diable à quatre; *(cause fuss)* protester à grands cris **2** *(roof covering)* toiture *f* **3** *Anat* **r. of the mouth** voûte *f* du palais
VT couvrir d'un toit; **to r. sth in** *or* **over** recouvrir qch d'un toit; **a house roofed with slate/thatch** une maison à toit d'ardoises/de chaume
▸▸ ***roof garden*** jardin *m* sur le toit; ***roof light*** *(of vehicle)* plafonnier *m*; *(window)* lucarne *f*; ***roof rack*** *(on car)* galerie *f*; ***roof support*** solive *f*; ***roof timbers*** combles *mpl*

-roofed [ruːft] **SUFF flat-r. warehouses** des entrepôts *mpl* à toits plats *ou* en terrasse

roofer ['ruːfə(r)] **N** *Constr* couvreur *m*

roofie ['ruːfɪ] **N** *Fam Drugs Slang (abrév* **Rohypnol®***)* Rohypnol® *m*

roofing ['ruːfɪŋ] **N** *(operation)* pose *f* de la toiture; *(material)* toiture *f*
▸▸ ***roofing felt*** carton *m* bitumé *ou* goudronné, *Belg* roofing *m*; ***roofing materials*** matériaux *mpl* pour toitures; ***roofing tiles*** tuiles *fpl* de couverture

roofless ['ruːflɪs] **ADJ** sans toit, à ciel ouvert

rooftop ['ruːftɒp] **N** toit *m*; *Fig* **to shout** *or* **to proclaim sth from the rooftops** crier qch sur les toits; **police marksmen have taken up r. positions** des tireurs d'élite ont pris position sur le toit

rooftree ['ruːftriː] **N** *Constr* poutre *f* de faîte, faîtage *m*

rook [rʊk] **N 1** *Orn* freux *m*, corbeau *m* **2** *(in chess)* tour *f*
VT *Fam* rouler, escroquer

rookery ['rʊkərɪ] *(pl* **rookeries***)* **N** *(of rooks)* colonie *f* de freux; **a r. of seals/penguins** une colonie de phoques/manchots

rookie ['rʊkɪ] **N** *Am Fam (recruit)* bleu *m*; *(inexperienced person)* novice *mf*; *(addition to a team)* nouveau membre *m*; **r. cop** flic *m* débutant, bleu *m*

room [ruːm, rʊm] **N 1** *(in building, public place)* salle *f*; *(in house)* pièce *f*; *(bedroom, in hotel)* chambre *f*; **r. to let** *or* **to rent** *(sign)* chambre à louer; **his rooms are in Bayswater** il habite à Bayswater; **to live in rooms** vivre dans un meublé; **r. and board** chambre *f* avec pension; **the whole r. burst out laughing** toute la salle a éclaté de rire; *Fam Euph* **the smallest r. in the house** *(toilet)* le petit coin; *Fam Hum* **get a r.!** ne faites pas ça en public!
2 *(space)* place *f*; **is there enough r. for everybody?** y a-t-il assez de place pour tout le monde?; **there's plenty of r.** il y a beaucoup de place; **it takes up too much r.** ça prend trop de place; *Fam* **there isn't (enough) r. to swing a cat in here** c'est grand comme un placard ici; **to make r. for sb** faire une place *ou* de la place pour qn; *Fig* laisser la place à qn; *Fig* **it's time to make r. for young people with fresh ideas** il est temps de laisser la place à des gens jeunes avec des idées neuves; **is there r. for one more?** *(person)* est-ce qu'il y a encore de la place pour une personne?; **r. to** *or* **for manoeuvre** place *f* pour manœuvrer; *Fig* marge *f* de manœuvre; **there's r. for improvement** il y a des progrès à faire; **there's still r. for discussion/hope** on peut encore discuter/espérer; **there's no r. for doubt** il n'y a plus aucun doute possible; **there's no r. for slackers in this company** les fainéants n'ont pas leur place dans cette société
VI *Am* loger; **to r. with sb** *(share apartment)* partager un appartement avec qn; *(in hotel)* partager une chambre avec qn; **to r. together** vivre ensemble dans le même appartement
▸▸ *Am* ***room clerk*** réceptionniste *mf*; ***room divider*** cloison *f*, écran *m*; ***room key*** clé *f* de la chambre; **your r. key** la clé de votre chambre; ***room number*** *(in hotel)* numéro *m* de chambre; ***room service*** service *m* de chambre; **to call r. service** appeler le service de chambre; ***room temperature*** température *f* ambiante; **to keep sth at r. temperature** garder qch à la température ambiante *ou* de la pièce; **serve at r. temperature** *(on packaging)* servir chambré

-roomed [ruːmd] **SUFF a five-r. flat** un appartement de cinq pièces, un cinq-pièces

roomer ['ruːmə(r)] **N** *Am* pensionnaire *mf*

roomette [ruː'met] **N** *Am* = petit wagon-lit à une place

roomful ['ruːmfʊl] **N** pleine salle *f ou* pièce *f*; **a r. of furniture** une pièce pleine de meubles; **a r. of people** une salle pleine de monde

roomie ['ruːmɪ] **N** *Am Fam (room-mate)* colocataire *mf*, coloc *mf*

roominess ['ruːmɪnɪs] **N** *(of house etc)* dimensions *fpl* spacieuses *ou* généreuses; *(of clothes)* coupe *f* confortable *ou* ample; *(of car)* dimensions *fpl* spacieuses

rooming house ['ruːmɪŋ-] **N** *Am* immeuble *m (avec chambres à louer)*

room-mate **N** *(in boarding school, college)* camarade *mf* de chambre; *Am (in apartment)* colocataire *mf*

roomy ['ruːmɪ] *(compar* **roomier**, *superl* **roomiest***)* **ADJ** *(house, office, car)* spacieux; *(suitcase, bag)* grand; *(clothes)* ample

roost [ruːst] **N** perchoir *m*; *(for domestic fowl)* juchoir *m*; *Fig (for person)* logement *m*, gîte *m*
VI *(bird)* se percher; *(domestic fowl)* (se) jucher; *Fig* **to come home to r.** *(crime, mistake)* se retourner contre son auteur; *Fig* **your chickens have come home to r.** ça s'est retourné contre toi, ça a fait boomerang

rooster ['ruːstə(r)] **N** *Am* coq *m*

root [ruːt] **N 1** *(of plant)* & *Fig* racine *f*; **to pull up a plant by its roots** déraciner une plante; **to take r.** *(plant)* & *Fig* prendre racine; **to put down roots** *(plant)* & *Fig* prendre racine, s'enraciner
2 *Anat (of tooth, hair etc)* racine *f*; **to touch up one's roots** *(person with dyed hair)* refaire ses racines; **to get one's roots done** se faire refaire les racines
3 *(source)* source *f*; *(cause)* cause *f*; *(bottom)* fond *m*; **to have its roots in sth** *(of crisis etc)* avoir ses origines dans qch; **the r. of all evil** la source de tous les maux; **to get at** *or* **to the r. of the problem** aller au fond du problème
4 *Ling (in etymology)* racine *f*; *(base form)* radical *m*, base *f*
5 *Comput (directory)* racine *f*, répertoire *m* principal
6 *Math* racine *f*
7 *Mus* fondamentale *f*
8 *(idiom)* **corruption must be eliminated r. and branch** il faut éradiquer la corruption; **a r. and branch reform** une réforme complète
VT 1 *(fix)* enraciner; *Fig* **he stood rooted to the spot** il est resté cloué sur place; **her political convictions are rooted in her upbringing** c'est dans son éducation qu'il faut chercher les racines de ses convictions politiques **2** *Austr very Fam (have sex with)* s'envoyer en l'air avec
VI 1 *(plant)* s'enraciner, prendre racine **2** *(animal)* fouiller *(avec le museau)*; **to r. for truffles** chercher des truffes
• **roots** **NPL** *(of person* ▸ *origin)* racines *fpl*, origines *fpl*; **he has no real roots** il n'a pas de véritables racines; **she is in search of her roots** elle est à la recherche de ses origines; **to get back to one's roots** retrouver ses racines
▸▸ *Am* ***root beer*** = boisson gazeuse à base d'extraits végétaux; *Anat* ***root canal*** canal *m* dentaire; *Med* ***root canal treatment, root canal work*** traitement *m* canalaire; ***root cause*** cause *f* première; ***root crop*** racine *f* comestible; *Comput* ***root directory*** racine *f*, répertoire *m* principal; ***roots music*** musique *f* "roots" *(influencée par la musique traditionnelle)*; ***root vegetable*** légume *m* à racine comestible

▸ **root about, root around** **VI** *(animal)* fouiller *(avec le museau)*; *(person)* fouiller; **to r. about for sth** fouiller pour trouver qch

▸ **root for** **VT INSEP** *(team)* encourager, soutenir; **to r. for a candidate** appuyer un candidat; **we're all rooting for you** nous sommes de votre côté

▸ **root out** **VT SEP 1** *(from earth)* déterrer; *(from hiding place)* dénicher **2** *(suppress)* supprimer, extirper

▸ **root through** **VT INSEP** *(search through)* fouiller dans

▸ **root up** **VT SEP** *(plant)* déraciner; *(of pig)* déterrer

rooted ['ruːtɪd] **ADJ** *(plant, prejudice, belief, habits)* enraciné; **deeply r. superstitions** des superstitions *fpl* bien enracinées *ou* profondément ancrées

rooting ['ruːtɪŋ] **N** enracinement *m*
▸▸ *Hort* ***rooting compost*** compost *m* spécial pour boutures; ***rooting out*** *(of abuse, malpractice)* extirpation *f*, éradication *f*

rootless ['ruːtlɪs] **ADJ** sans racine *ou* racines

rootstock ['ruːtstɒk] **N** *Bot* **1** *(rhizome)* rhizome *m* **2** *(stem receiving graft)* porte-greffe *m*, sujet *m*; *(plant from which graft is taken)* plante *f* mère *(sur laquelle on prélève un greffon)*

rooves [ruːvz] *pl of* **roof**

rope [rəʊp] **N 1** *(gen)* corde *f*; *(collectively)* cordage *m*; *(of steel, wire)* filin *m*; *(cable)* câble *m*; *(for bell, curtains)* cordon *m*; **a piece** *or* **length of r.** un bout de corde, une corde; **the r.** *(death by hanging)* la pendaison; **to bring back the r.** remettre la pendaison en vigueur; *Fig* **to come to the end of one's r.** être au bout du rouleau; *Fig* **to give sb more r.** laisser à qn une plus grande liberté d'action, lâcher la bride à qn; *Fig* **give him enough r. and he'll hang himself** si on le laisse faire, il creusera sa propre tombe **2** *(in mountaineering)* cordée *f* **3** *(of pearls)* collier *m*; *(long)* sautoir *m*; *(of onions)* chapelet *m*
VT 1 *(package)* attacher avec une corde, corder; **the climbers were roped together** les alpinistes étaient encordés; **he was roped to a post** il a été attaché à un poteau **2** *Am (cattle, horses)* prendre au lasso

• **ropes** NPL **1** *Boxing* cordes *fpl*; **to be on the ropes** *(boxer)* se retrouver dans les cordes; *Fig (company, economy etc)* battre de l'aile; *Fig* **to be up against the ropes** être le dos au mur; **to have sb on the ropes** *Boxing* mettre qn dans les cordes; *Fig* acculer qn, mettre qn dans une position difficile **2** *(know-how)* **to know the ropes** connaître les ficelles *ou* son affaire; **to show** *or* **to teach sb the ropes** montrer les ficelles du métier à qn; **to learn the ropes** se mettre au courant, apprendre à se débrouiller

►► ***rope bridge*** pont *m* de corde; ***rope ladder*** échelle *f* de corde; ***rope maker*** cordier(ère) *m,f*; ***rope trick*** = tour de prestidigitation réalisé avec une cordelette

► **rope in** VT SEP **1** *(land)* entourer de cordes, délimiter par des cordes **2** *(cattle)* mettre dans un enclos **3** *Fig* **to r. sb in to do sth** enrôler qn pour faire qch; **he got himself roped in as chairman** il a été forcé d'accepter la présidence

► **rope off** VT SEP *(part of hall, of church)* délimiter par une corde; *(street, building)* interdire l'accès de

► **rope up** VI *(climbers)* s'encorder

VT SEP **1** *(parcel)* attacher avec une corde, corder **2** *(climbers)* encorder

rope-soled [-səʊld] ADJ *(sandals)* à semelles de corde

ropey, ropy ['rəʊpɪ] *(compar* **ropier**, *superl* **ropiest)** ADJ *Br* **1** *(substance)* visqueux **2** *Fam (mediocre)* médiocre ▫, pas fameux; *(ill)* mal fichu, patraque; **to feel a bit r.** se sentir patraque, ne pas être dans son assiette

ro-ro ['rəʊrəʊ] *(pl* **ro-ros)** N *(ship)* (navire *m*) transbordeur *m*, ferry-boat *m*; *(system)* roll on-roll off *m inv*, manutention *f* par roulage

ADJ *(ferry)* transbordeur, ro-ro *(inv)*; *(port)* à roulage direct

ROS [,ɑːrəʊ'es] N *Fin (abbr* **return on sales)** retour *m* sur ventes

rosary ['rəʊzərɪ] *(pl* **rosaries)** N **1** *Rel (beads)* chapelet *m*, rosaire *m*; *(prayers)* rosaire *m*; **to tell** *or* **to say the r.** dire son rosaire **2** *(rose garden)* roseraie *f*

rose [rəʊz] *pt of* **rise**

N **1** *(flower)* rose *f*; *(bush)* rosier *m*; **life's not a bed of roses** *or* **all roses** tout n'est pas rose dans la vie; **there's no r. without a thorn** il n'y a pas de roses sans épines, chaque médaille a son revers; *Fig* **to always come up smelling of roses** s'en sortir toujours très bien; **to come up roses** *(enterprise)* marcher comme sur des roulettes; *(person)* réussir, avoir le vent en poupe; *Literary* **under the r.** en cachette, en confidence; **that'll put the roses back into your cheeks** ça va te redonner des couleurs

2 *(rose shape* ► *on hat, dress)* rosette *f*; *(*► *on ceiling)* rosace *f*

3 *(colour)* rose *m*

4 *(on hosepipe, watering can)* pomme *f*

ADJ rose, de couleur rose

►► ***rose bush*** rosier *m*; ***rose garden*** roseraie *f*; ***rose grower*** rosiériste *mf*; ***rose pink*** rose *m*; *Miner* ***rose quartz*** quartz *m* rose; ***rose red*** vermillon *m*; ***rose tree*** rosier *m*; *Archit* ***rose window*** rosace *f*

rosé ['rəʊzeɪ] N (vin *m*) rosé *m*

roseate ['rəʊzɪət] ADJ *Literary* rose; **to take a r. view of things** voir la vie en rose

rosebay ['rəʊzbeɪ] N *Bot* laurier-rose *m*

►► ***rosebay willowherb*** épilobe *m* en épis, laurier *m* de Saint-Antoine

rosebud ['rəʊzbʌd] N bouton *m* de rose

►► ***rosebud mouth*** bouche *f* en cerise

rose-coloured, *Am* **rose-colored** ADJ rose, rosé; **to see life through r. spectacles** voir la vie en rose

rose-cut ADJ *(diamond etc)* (taillé) en rose

rosehip ['rəʊzhɪp] N *Bot* gratte-cul *m inv*, *Spec* cynorhodon *m*

►► ***rosehip syrup*** sirop *m* d'églantine

rosemary ['rəʊzmərɪ] N *Bot* romarin *m*

►► ***rosemary bush*** buisson *m* de romarin

rose-pink ADJ (couleur de) rose

rose-red ADJ vermeil

rose-tinted ADJ teinté en rose; **to see life through r. glasses** *or* **spectacles** voir la vie en rose

rosette [rəʊ'zet] N **1** *(made of ribbons)* rosette *f*; *Sport* cocarde *f* **2** *Archit (carving)* rosette *f*; *(window)* rosace *f*

rosewater ['rəʊzwɔːtə(r)] N eau *f* de rose

rosewood ['rəʊzwʊd] *Bot* N bois *m* de rose

COMP en bois de rose

rosie ['rəʊzɪ] N *SEng Fam (rhyming slang* **rosie lee** = **tea)** thé ▫ *m*

rosin ['rɒzɪn] N colophane *f*, arcanson *m*

VT traiter à la colophane, enduire de colophane

rosiness ['rəʊzɪnɪs] N couleur *f* rose, rose *m*; *Literary* roseur *f*; **the r. of her cheeks** le rose de ses joues

roster ['rɒstə(r)] N *(list)* liste *f*; *(for duty)* tableau *m* de service; **by r.** à tour de rôle

VT inscrire au tableau de service *ou* au planning; **I'm rostered on Sunday** je suis de service dimanche

rostrum ['rɒstrəm] *(pl* **rostrums** *or* **rostra** [-trə]) N **1** *(platform* ► *for speaker)* estrade *f*, tribune *f*; *(*► *for conductor)* estrade *f*; *Sport* podium *m*; **to take the r.** monter sur l'estrade *ou* à la tribune **2** *Antiq (of ship)* rostre *m*; *(platform in forum)* rostres *mpl*

►► *Cin & TV* ***rostrum camera*** banc-titre *m*; *Cin & TV* ***rostrum cameraman*** opérateur *m* banc-titre

rosy ['rəʊzɪ] *(compar* **rosier**, *superl* **rosiest)** ADJ *(in colour)* rose, rosé; *Fig (future, situation)* prometteur, qui se présente bien; **to have r. cheeks** avoir les joues roses; **her r. complexion** son teint de rose; *Fig* **to paint a r. picture of sth** dépeindre qch sous un jour optimiste; **to have a r. view of life** voir la vie en rose

rot [rɒt] *(pt & pp* **rotted**, *cont* **rotting)** VI **1** *(gen)* pourrir; *(meat, body)* se putréfier; *(compost matter)* se décomposer; *(teeth)* se carier **2** *Fig (person)* pourrir; **to r. in prison** pourrir *ou* croupir en prison; *Fam* **let them r.!** qu'ils crèvent!

VT *(vegetable, fibres)* (faire) pourrir; *(tooth)* carier, gâter; **sugar rots your teeth** le sucre gâte les dents *ou* donne des caries

N **1** *(of fruit, vegetable, wood)* pourriture *f*; *(of tooth)* carie *f* **2** *Fig (in society)* pourriture *f*; **the r. has set in** ça commence à se gâter; **to stop the r.** empêcher les choses de se dégrader, remonter la pente; **we've stopped the r.** on remonte la pente **3** *(UNCOUNT) Fam* foutaises *fpl*; **don't talk r.!** arrête de raconter n'importe quoi!; **that's utter r.!, what r.!** c'est vraiment n'importe quoi!

► **rot away** VI & VT SEP = **rot** VI & VT

► **rot down** VI *(compost material)* se décomposer

rota ['rəʊtə] N *Br (system)* roulement *m*; *(for duty* ► *list)* tableau *m* de service, planning *m*; **we have a r. for the housework** nous faisons le ménage (chacun) à tour de rôle; **on a r. basis** à tour de rôle, par roulement

• **Rota** N *Rel* rote *f*

Rotarian [rəʊ'teərɪən] ADJ rotarien

N rotarien(enne) *m,f*

rotary ['rəʊtərɪ] *(pl* **rotaries)** ADJ rotatif

N *Am* rond-point *m*

►► ***the Rotary Club*** le Rotary Club; ***Rotary Club member*** rotarien(enne) *m,f*; ***rotary cultivator*** motoculteur *m*; ***rotary engine*** moteur *m* rotatif; *Typ* ***rotary press*** rotative *f*; *Typ* ***rotary printer*** *(person)* rotativiste *mf*

rotate [rəʊ'teɪt] VT **1** *(turn)* faire tourner; *(on pivot)* faire pivoter **2** *Agr (crops)* alterner **3** *(staff)* faire un roulement de; *(jobs)* faire à tour de rôle *ou* par roulement

VI **1** *(turn)* tourner; *(on pivot)* pivoter **2** *(staff)* changer de poste par roulement; **the presidency rotates every two years among the members** les membres assument la présidence à tour de rôle tous les deux ans

rotating [rəʊ'teɪtɪŋ] ADJ **1** *(turning)* tournant, rotatif; **r. body** corps *m* en rotation **2 on a r. basis** *(in turns)* à tour de rôle

N **1** *(turning)* rotation *f* **2** *Agr (of crops)* alternance *f*

rotation [rəʊ'teɪʃən] N **1** *(of machinery, planets)* rotation *f*; **rotations per minute** tours *mpl* par minute **2** *(of staff, jobs)* roulement *m*; **in** *or* **by r.** par roulement, à tour de rôle **3** *Agr (of crops)* alternance *f*

rotator [rəʊ'teɪtə(r)] N **1** *(spindle)* axe *m* rotatif; *(machine)* appareil *m* rotateur; *(propeller)* hélice *f* **2** *Anat* (muscle *m*) rotateur *m*

rotatory ['rəʊtətərɪ] ADJ rotatoire

rote [rəʊt] N routine *f*; **to learn sth by r.** apprendre qch par cœur

►► ***rote learning*** apprentissage *m* par cœur

rotgut ['rɒtgʌt] N *Fam (spirits)* tord-boyaux *m inv*, gnôle *f*; *(wine)* piquette *f*

rotisserie [rəʊ'tiːsərɪ] N *(spit)* rôtissoire *f*

rotogravure [,rəʊtəgrə'vjʊə(r)] N rotogravure *f*

rotor ['rəʊtə(r)] N rotor *m*

►► ***rotor arm*** *(of helicopter)* rotor *m*; *(of engine)* rotor *m*, balai *m*; ***rotor blade*** pale *f* de rotor

Rotovator® ['rəʊtəveɪtə(r)] N *Br* motoculteur *m*

rotten ['rɒtən] ADJ **1** *(fruit, egg, wood)* pourri; *(tooth)* carié, gâté; **to smell r.** sentir le pourri; **to go r.** pourrir

2 *(corrupt)* pourri, corrompu; **r. through and through** *or* **to the core** complètement pourri, corrompu jusqu'à la moelle

3 *Fam (person* ► *unkind)* vache, dégueulasse; **to be r. to sb** être vache *ou* dégueulasse avec qn; **don't be r.!** ne sois pas vache!; **that was a r. thing to do** c'était un sale tour, c'est vraiment vache *ou* dégueulasse d'avoir fait ça; **what a r. thing to say!** c'est moche de dire des choses pareilles!; **what a r. trick!** quel sale tour!; *Fam* **you r. so-and-so!** espèce de salaud!

4 *Fam (guilty)* **to feel r.** se sentir coupable ▫; **I felt r. about it** j'en étais malade

5 *Fam (ill)* **to feel r.** se sentir patraque; **you look r.** vous n'avez pas l'air en forme ▫

6 *Fam (worthless)* nul, pourri; *(weather)* pourri; **the weather was r.** il a fait un temps de chien, le temps était vraiment pourri; **he's a r. goalkeeper** il est nul *ou* il ne vaut rien comme gardien de but; **what r. luck!** quelle poisse!; **I've had a r. time recently** j'ai traversé une sale période récemment

7 *Fam (in indignation)* fichu; **keep your r. (old) sweets!** tes bonbons pourris, tu peux te les garder!

►► *Hist* ***rotten borough*** = circonscription électorale britannique dont les électeurs, bien que peu nombreux, pouvaient élire un député (avant 1832)

rottenly ['rɒtənlɪ] ADV abominablement; **to behave r. to sb** se conduire d'une manière inqualifiable avec qn

rottenness ['rɒtənnɪs] N **1** *(of wood, fruit, vegetable)* pourriture *f* **2** *Fam (poor quality)* caractère *m* lamentable ▫, nullité ▫ *f*

rotter ['rɒtə(r)] N *Br Fam Old-fashioned* crapule *f*, sale type *m*

rotting ['rɒtɪŋ] ADJ qui pourrit, pourri

rottweiler ['rɒtvaɪlə(r)] N *(dog)* rottweiler *m*

rotund [rəʊ'tʌnd] ADJ **1** *(shape)* rond, arrondi; *(person)* rondelet; **his r. figure** ses formes arrondies **2** *(style, speech)* grandiloquent

rotunda [rəʊ'tʌndə] N *Archit* rotonde *f*

rotundity [rəʊ'tʌndətɪ] N **1** *(of person)* embonpoint *m*, rotondité *f* **2** *(of style, speech)* grandiloquence *f*

rouble ['ruːbəl] N rouble *m*

roué ['ruːeɪ] N *Arch or Hum* roué *m*, débauché *m*

rouge [ruːʒ] N rouge *m* (à joues)

VT **she had rouged cheeks** elle s'était mis du rouge aux joues

ROUGH [rʌf]

ADJ
- rêche **1, 6**
- accidenté **1**
- mal fréquenté **2**
- rude **3–5**
- rauque **6**
- patraque **8**
- rugueux **1**
- brutal **2**
- dur **2, 4**
- agité **5**
- approximatif **7**

N
- terrain rocailleux **1**
- voyou **3**
- brouillon **2**

ADJ **1** *(uneven ▸ skin, cloth, paper)* rêche; *(▸ surface)* rugueux; *(▸ ground, road)* raboteux, rocailleux; *(▸ terrain)* accidenté; *(▸ edge)* rugueux **2** *(violent ▸ behaviour, person, treatment)* brutal; *(▸ neighbourhood)* dur, mal fréquenté; **they came in for some r. treatment** ils ont été malmenés; **she's terribly r. with the children** elle est très brutale avec les enfants; **he's a r. customer** c'est un dur; **to give sb the r. edge** *or* **side of one's tongue** réprimander qn, ne pas ménager ses reproches à qn

3 *(unrefined ▸ person, manners)* rude, fruste; *(▸ speech, accent)* rude, grossier; **to knock the r. edges off sb/sth** dégrossir qn/qch

4 *(unpleasant, hard)* rude, dur; **she's had a r. time of it** elle en a vu des dures *ou* de toutes les couleurs; **they gave him a r. time** *or* **ride** ils lui ont mené la vie dure; **he's had a r. deal** ça a été très dur pour lui; **he received some r. handling from the press** la presse l'a présenté de façon défavorable; **it's r. on her** *(unlucky)* c'est dur pour elle; *(unjust)* c'est injuste pour elle; **it's r. on the skin** c'est mauvais pour la peau; **you were too r. on them** tu as été trop sévère avec eux; **it's r. having to work on Saturdays** c'est dur de devoir travailler le samedi; *Br* **r. luck!** pas de veine!

5 *(sea)* agité, houleux; *(climate)* rude; **a r. crossing** *or* **passage** une traversée agitée; *Fig* **the bill had a r. passage through the House** le projet de loi a eu des difficultés à passer à la Chambre; **r. weather** gros temps *m*

6 *(harsh ▸ sound, voice)* rauque; *(▸ tone)* brusque; *(▸ taste)* âpre; *(▸ wine)* rêche

7 *(approximate ▸ calculation, estimate, translation)* approximatif; **at a r. guess** grosso modo, approximativement; **I only need a r. estimate** je n'ai pas besoin d'une réponse précise; **could you give me a r. idea of how long it will take?** pourriez-vous me donner une idée approximative du temps que ça va prendre?, pourriez-vous me dire en gros combien de temps cela va prendre?; **I have a r. idea of what it's about** j'ai une petite idée de ce dont il s'agit

8 *Br Fam (ill)* patraque; **I'm feeling a bit r.** je ne suis pas dans mon assiette; **to look r.** ne pas avoir l'air dans son assiette

N **1** *(ground)* terrain *m* rocailleux; *Golf* rough *m*; *Golf* **to be in the r.** être dans l'herbe longue; *Fig* **to take the r. with the smooth** prendre les choses comme elles viennent

2 *(draft)* brouillon *m*; *(of design)* crayonné *m*, esquisse *f*; *(of drawing)* ébauche *f*; **in r.** à l'état de brouillon/d'ébauche; **he drafted the proposal in r.** il rédigea un brouillon de la proposition

3 *Fam (hoodlum)* dur *m*, voyou *m*

4 *Fam* **she likes a bit of r.** *(person)* elle aime s'envoyer un prolo de temps en temps; *(sexual activity)* elle aime qu'on la malmène un peu pendant l'amour

ADV **to play r.** *(children etc)* jouer brutalement; *(in business, relationship)* ne pas faire de cadeaux; **to live r.** vivre à la dure; **to sleep r.** coucher à la dure *ou* dans la rue

VT *Br Fam* **to r. it** vivre à la dure; **we'll just have to r. it** il faudra qu'on fasse avec les moyens du bord□

▸▸ ***rough copy*** brouillon *m*; ***rough diamond*** diamant *m* brut; *Br Fig* **he's a r. diamond** il est bourru mais il a un cœur d'or; ***rough draft*** brouillon *m*; ***rough justice*** justice *f* sommaire; ***rough paper*** papier *m* brouillon; ***rough sketch*** croquis *m*, ébauche *f*; *Fam* ***rough stuff*** brutalités□*fpl*; *Fam* ***rough trade*** *(male prostitute)* = jeune prostitué homosexuel à tendances violentes; *(working-class male homosexual)* homosexuel *m* prolo; ***rough work*** brouillon *m*

▸ **rough out** VT SEP *Br (drawing, plan)* ébaucher, esquisser

▸ **rough up** VT SEP **1** *(hair)* ébouriffer; *(clothes)* mettre en désordre **2** *Fam (person)* tabasser, passer à tabac

roughage ['rʌfɪdʒ] N *(UNCOUNT)* fibres *fpl* (alimentaires)

rough-and-ready ADJ **1** *(makeshift ▸ equipment, apparatus)* rudimentaire, de fortune; *(careless ▸ work)* grossier, fait à la hâte; *(▸ methods)* grossier, expéditif **2** *(unrefined ▸ person)* fruste, rustre; *(▸ living conditions)* dur

rough-and-tumble ADJ *(life ▸ hectic)* mouvementé; *(▸ disorderly)* désordonné

N *(fight)* bagarre *f*; *(hurly-burly)* tohu-bohu *m inv*; **the children were having a bit of a r.** les enfants chahutaient; **the r. of politics** le bouillonnement de la politique; **the r. world of publishing** la jungle de l'édition

roughcast ['rʌfkɑːst] *(pt & pp* **inv**) ADJ crépi

N crépi *m*

VT crépir

roughen ['rʌfən] VT *(surface)* rendre rugueux; *(hands)* rendre rugueux *ou* rêche

VI **1** *(surface)* devenir rugueux **2** *(sea)* grossir, devenir houleux

rough-hewn ADJ taillé grossièrement, dégrossi; *Fig* **his r. features** son visage taillé à coups de serpe

rough-house *Am Fam* N [-haus, *pl* -hauzɪz] bagarre□*f*

VT [-hauz] bousculer□

VI [-hauz] *(children)* faire du chahut

roughly ['rʌflɪ] ADV **1** *(brutally)* avec brutalité, brutalement; **they treated us very r.** ils nous ont traités avec brutalité; **he answered her very r.** il lui a répondu sur un ton très sec **2** *(sketchily ▸ draw)* grossièrement; *(crudely ▸ make)* grossièrement, sans soin; **to sketch sth r.** faire un croquis sommaire de qch **3** *(approximately)* approximativement, à peu près; **r. 500** à peu près *ou* environ 500; **r. speaking** en gros, approximativement; **she told me r. how to get there** elle m'a expliqué en gros comment y aller; **they live in r. the same area** ils habitent plus ou moins le même quartier

roughneck ['rʌfnek] N **1** *Fam (thug)* voyou□*m*, dur *m* **2** *(oil-rig worker)* = ouvrier travaillant sur une plate-forme pétrolière

roughness ['rʌfnɪs] N **1** *(of surface)* caractère *m* rugueux; *(of skin, cloth, paper)* caractère *m* rêche; *(of road, ground)* inégalités *fpl* **2** *(of manner)* rudesse *f*; *(of reply, speech)* brusquerie *f*; *(of person)* rudesse *f*, brutalité *f*; *(of living conditions)* rudesse *f*, dureté *f* **3** *(turbulence)* **because of the r. of the sea** parce que la mer est/était agitée

roughrider ['rʌf,raɪdə(r)] N dresseur(euse) *m,f* de chevaux

roughshod ['rʌfʃɒd] ADJ *Br (horse)* ferré à glace

ADV *(idiom)* **to ride r. over** *(person)* traiter cavalièrement, fouler aux pieds; *(objections)* fouler aux pieds

rough-spoken ADJ *(vulgar)* au langage grossier

roulette [ruː'let] N roulette *f*; **to play r.** jouer à la roulette

▸▸ ***roulette table*** table *f* de roulette; ***roulette wheel*** roulette *f*

Roumania, Roumanian = **Romania, Romanian**

ROUND [raʊnd]

ADJ
- rond **1–3**
- rondelette **4**
- net **5**
- sonore **6**

PREP
- autour de **1**
- aux environs de **4**

ADV
- autour **1**

N
- rond **1, 11**
- tranche **2**
- série **3**
- tournée **4, 8**
- ronde **4**
- tour **6**
- partie **7**
- round **7**
- cartouche **9**

VT
- arrondir **1**

ADJ **1** *(circular)* rond, circulaire; *(spherical)* rond, sphérique; **to have a r. face** avoir la figure ronde; **she looked up, her eyes r. with surprise** elle leva des yeux écarquillés de surprise; **r. hand** *or* **handwriting** écriture *f* ronde

2 *(curved ▸ belly, cheeks)* rond; **to have r. shoulders** avoir le dos rond *ou* voûté

3 *(figures)* rond; **in r. figures** en chiffres ronds; **that's 500, in r. figures** ça fait 500 tout rond; **a r. dozen** une douzaine tout rond

4 *(considerable)* **a r. sum** une somme rondelette

5 *Literary (candid)* net, franc (franche); **they gave a r. denial** ils ont nié tout net

6 *(rich, sonorous ▸ tone, voice)* sonore

PREP **1** *(surrounding, circular motion)* autour de; **sitting r. the fire/table** assis autour du feu/de la table; **the pillar is three feet r. the base** la base du pilier fait trois pieds de circonférence; **he's 95 cm r. the chest** il fait 95 cm de tour de poitrine; **the countryside r. Bath is lovely** la campagne autour de Bath est très belle; **he put his arm r. her waist** il a passé son bras autour de sa taille; **he put a blanket r. her legs** il lui enveloppa les jambes d'une couverture; **Drake sailed r. the world** Drake a fait le tour du monde en bateau; **we drove r. and r. the field** on a fait plusieurs tours dans le champ; **the earth goes** *or* **moves r. the sun** la terre tourne autour du soleil; **to go r. an obstacle** contourner un obstacle; **there must be a way r. the problem** il doit y avoir un moyen de contourner ce problème

2 *(indicating position)* **it's just r. the corner** c'est juste au coin de la rue; **they live somewhere r. here** ils habitent quelque part par ici; **the orchard is r. the back** le verger est derrière; *Br* **he's r. the pub** il est au pub; *Br* **he's r. his brother's** il est chez son frère

3 *(all over, everywhere in)* **she looked r. the room** elle a promené son regard autour de la pièce; **to walk r. the town** faire le tour de la ville (à pied); **we went for a stroll r. the garden** nous avons fait une balade dans le jardin; **there's a rumour going r. the school** une rumeur circule dans l'école

4 *(approximately)* environ, aux environs de; **r. about** environ; **r. (about) six o'clock** aux environs de *ou* vers les six heures

ADV **1** *(on all sides)* autour; **there were trees all r.** il y avait des arbres tout autour; **the villages r. about** les villages alentour *ou* des alentours; **taking things all r., taken all r.** à tout prendre, tout compte fait; **all r., it was a good result** dans l'ensemble, c'était un bon résultat

2 *(indicating circular motion)* **turn the wheel right r.** *or* **all the way r.** faites faire un tour complet à la roue; **to go r. and r.** tourner; **we drove r. and r. for hours** on a tourné en rond pendant des heures; **you'll have to go r., the door's locked** il faudra faire le tour, la porte est fermée à clé; **she looked r. at us** elle se retourna pour nous regarder; **we had to take the long way r.** on a dû faire le grand tour *ou* un grand détour; **all year r.** tout au long de *ou* toute l'année; **summer will soon be** *or* **come r. again** l'été reviendra vite

3 *(indicating position)* **to have one's hat/jumper on the wrong way r.** avoir son chapeau/son pull à l'envers; **it's the other way r.** *(quite the opposite)* c'est (tout) le contraire; **try the key the other way r.** essaie la clef dans l'autre sens; **she's always moving the furniture r.** elle passe son temps à changer les meubles de place

4 *(to various parts)* **we spent the summer just travelling r.** on a passé l'été à voyager; **can I have a look r.?** je peux jeter un coup d'œil?

5 *(from one person to another)* **hand the sweets r.** faites passer les bonbons; **there wasn't enough to go r.** il n'y en avait pas assez pour tout le monde

6 *(to somebody's house)* **she came r. to see me** elle est passée me voir; **let's invite some friends r.** et si on invitait des amis?; **come r. for dinner some time** viens dîner un soir

7 *(in circumference)* **the tree is five metres r.** l'arbre fait cinq mètres de circonférence

N **1** *(circle)* rond *m*, cercle *m*

2 *Br (slice ▸ of ham, cheese, bread, toast)* tranche *f*; **a r. of sandwiches** = un sandwich au pain de mie coupé en deux ou en quatre

3 *(one in a series ▸ of discussions, negotiations)* série *f*, *(▸ of elections, voting)* tour *m*; *(▸ of increases)* série *f*, train *m*; **the next r. of talks will be held in Moscow** les prochains pourparlers auront lieu à Moscou

4 *(regular route ▸ for delivery)* tournée *f*; *(▸ of sentry, patrol)* ronde *f*; **to do a paper/milk r.** distribuer les journaux/le lait à domicile; **to go on** *or* **do one's rounds** *(doctor)* faire ses visites; *(guard, policeman)* faire sa ronde; **to go** *or* **do** *or* **make the rounds** *(story, rumour, cold)* circuler; **to do** *or* **go the rounds of the travel agencies** faire le tour des agences de voyages

5 *(routine)* **the daily r.** le train-train quotidien, la routine quotidienne; **the daily r. of cooking and cleaning** les travaux quotidiens de cuisine et de ménage; **his life is one long r. of parties** il passe sa vie à faire la fête

6 *(stage of competition)* tour *m*, manche *f*; **to be/get through to the next r.** se qualifier/s'être qualifié pour la manche suivante

7 *(of golf, cards)* partie *f*; *(in boxing, wrestling)* round *m*, reprise *f*; *Horseriding* **there were six clear rounds** six chevaux avaient fait un sans-faute; *Boxing* **he only went three rounds** il n'a fait que trois rounds; **to play a r. of golf** faire une partie de golf

8 *(of drinks)* tournée *f*; **to buy** *or* **stand a r. of drinks** payer une tournée (générale); **whose r. is it?** qui paye cette tournée?; **it's my r.** c'est ma tournée

9 *(of ammunition)* cartouche *f*

10 *(song)* canon *m*

11 *Theat* **theatre in the r.** théâtre *m* en rond

12 *Art* **sculpture in the r.** ronde-bosse *f*

VT 1 *(lips, vowel)* arrondir

2 *Naut (cape)* doubler, franchir; **to r. a corner** *(of car)* prendre un virage; *(of person)* tourner un coin

▸▸ ***a round of applause*** des applaudissements *mpl*; **give her a r. of applause!** on peut l'applaudir! *Archit* ***round arch*** arc *m* en plein cintre; *Culin* ***round of beef*** gîte *m* à la noix; *Typ* ***round brackets*** parenthèses *fpl*; ***round dance*** ronde *f*; ***round robin*** *(petition)* pétition *f (où les signatures sont disposées en rond)*; *(social letter)* = lettre standard qu'une personne envoie à ses nombreux amis pour donner de ses nouvelles; *esp Am (contest)* poule *f*; ***the Round Table*** la Table ronde; ***round table*** *(discussion, conference)* table *f* ronde; ***round trip*** (voyage *m*) aller et retour *m*

▸round down VT SEP arrondir au chiffre inférieur; **their prices were rounded down to the nearest £10** ils ont arrondi leurs prix aux 10 livres inférieures

▸round off VT SEP **1** *(finish, complete)* terminer, clore; *(speech)* achever; **he rounded off his meal with a glass of brandy** il a terminé son repas par un verre de cognac **2** *(figures)* arrondir

VI *(conclude)* conclure, finir; **and to r. off…** et pour conclure…, et pour finir…

▸round on VT INSEP attaquer, s'en prendre à; **she rounded on him for no reason** elle lui est tombée dessus sans aucune raison

▸round up VT SEP **1** *(cattle, people)* rassembler; *(criminals)* ramasser **2** *(figures)* arrondir au chiffre supérieur

---

roundabout ['raʊndəbaʊt] N *Br* **1** *(at fairground, playground)* manège *m* **2** *Aut* rond-point *m*, *Suisse* giratoire *m*

ADJ détourné, indirect; **to take a r. route** prendre un chemin détourné; **to hear of sth in a r. way** apprendre qch indirectement; **to lead up to a question in a r. way** aborder une question de biais

rounded ['raʊndɪd] ADJ **1** *(shape)* arrondi; *(shoulders)* voûté; *(breasts)* plein; *(vowel)* arrondi **2** *(education)* complet(ète) **3** *(style)* harmonieux

roundel ['raʊndəl] N **1** *Literature* rondeau *m* **2** *Aviat* cocarde *f* **3** *(window)* œil-de-bœuf *m*; *(panel, medal)* médaillon *m*

rounders ['raʊndəz] N *(UNCOUNT) Br* = sport proche du base-ball

round-eyed ADJ aux yeux ronds; **to listen in r. amazement** écouter les yeux ronds

Roundhead ['raʊndhed] N *Hist* **the Roundheads** les Têtes rondes *(partisans du Parlement pendant la guerre civile anglaise, de 1642 à 1646)*

roundhouse ['raʊndhaʊs, *pl* -haʊzɪz] N rotonde *f*

roundly ['raʊndlɪ] ADV **1** *(severely)* vivement, sévèrement; **the film was r. attacked for its racist content** le film fut vivement critiqué pour son caractère raciste; **r. beaten** battu à plate(s) couture(s) **2** *Br (plainly)* carrément

roundness ['raʊndnɪs] N **1** *(shape)* rondeur *f* **2** *(of sound, voice)* richesse *f*, ampleur *f*

round-shouldered [-'ʃəʊldəd] ADJ **to be r.** avoir le dos rond, être voûté

roundsman ['raʊndzmən] *(pl* **roundsmen** [-mən]) N *Br* livreur *m*; *Am* **night r.** gardien *m* de nuit

round-the-clock ADJ 24 heures sur 24; **a r. vigil** une permanence nuit et jour

ADV *(work, study)* 24 heures sur 24; **open r.** ouvert 24 heures sur 24

round-trip ticket N *Am* (billet *m*) aller-retour *m*

round-up N **1** *(of cattle, people)* rassemblement *m*; *(of criminals)* rafle *f* **2** *(of news)* résumé *m* de l'actualité

roundworm ['raʊndwɜːm] N *Zool* ascaride *m*

rouse [raʊz] VT **1** *(wake ▸ person)* réveiller; **he was roused from his thoughts by the doorbell** la sonnette l'a arraché à ses pensées; **to r. oneself** se secouer; **to r. oneself to do sth** s'efforcer de faire qch; **to r. sb from his/her apathy** faire sortir qn de son apathie; **to r. the camp** donner l'alerte au camp **2** *(provoke ▸ interest, passion)* éveiller, exciter; *(▸ hope)* éveiller; *(▸ suspicion)* éveiller, susciter; *(▸ admiration, anger, indignation)* susciter, provoquer; **to r. sb to action** pousser *ou* inciter qn à agir; **to r. sb to anger, to r. sb's anger** susciter la colère de qn, mettre qn en colère **3** *Hunt (game)* lever

roused [raʊzd] ADJ *(angry)* en colère; **now she's r., sparks will fly** maintenant qu'elle s'est mise en colère, ça va barder

rousing ['raʊzɪŋ] ADJ *(speech)* vibrant, passionné; *(march, music)* entraînant; *(applause, welcome)* enthousiaste

roust [raʊst] VT **1 to r. sb (out) from bed** faire sortir qn du lit **2** *Am Fam (harass)* harceler▫ **3** *Am Fam (arrest)* agrafer, gauler, alpaguer

roustabout ['raʊstəbaʊt] N ouvrier *m*, manœuvre *m*; *(on farm)* ouvrier *m* agricole; *Austr & NZ* = ouvrier agricole dans un élevage ovin

rout [raʊt] N **1** *Mil* déroute *f*, débâcle *f*; **to put an enemy/army to r.** mettre un ennemi/une armée en déroute; *Fig* **the election was a r. for the government** l'élection a été une débâcle pour le gouvernement **2** *Law* attroupement *m* illégal

VT *Mil* mettre en déroute *ou* en fuite; *Fig (team, opponent)* battre à plate couture, écraser

▸rout out VT SEP **1** *(find)* dénicher **2** *(remove, force out)* déloger, expulser; **they routed us out of our hiding-place** ils nous ont délogés de notre cachette

route [*Br* ruːt, *Am* raʊt] N **1** *(way ▸ gen)* route *f*, itinéraire *m*; *(▸ of plane, ship)* route *f*, voie *f*; *(▸ of procession, demonstration)* parcours *m*; **what is the best r. to Manchester?** quel est le meilleur itinéraire pour aller à Manchester?; **all routes** *(road sign)* toutes directions; *Fig* **giving up one's studies is hardly the best r. to success** le meilleur moyen de réussir ce n'est pas d'abandonner ses études; **sea/air r.** voie *f ou* route *f* maritime/aérienne

2 *(for buses)* trajet *m*, parcours *m*; **a map of the bus routes** un plan des lignes d'autobus; **are they on a bus r.?** sont-ils desservis par les autobus?

3 *Am (for deliveries)* tournée *f*; **he's got a paper r.** il livre des journaux à domicile

4 *Am (highway)* ≃ route *f* (nationale), ≃ nationale *f*; **R. 66** ≃ la nationale 66

VT 1 *(procession, motorist)* fixer l'itinéraire de, diriger; *(train, bus)* fixer l'itinéraire de; **the police routed the marchers via Post Street** la police a fait passer les manifestants par Post Street **2** *(luggage, parcel)* expédier, acheminer; **our bags have been routed to Hong Kong** nos bagages ont été expédiés sur *ou* à Hongkong; **the flight was routed via Turkey** notre itinéraire passait par la Turquie

• en route ADV en route; *Fig* **he's en r. for success** il est sur la voie du succès

▸▸ ***route map*** *(for roads)* carte *f* routière; *(for buses)* plan *m* du réseau; *(for trains)* carte *f* du réseau; *Mil* ***route march*** marche *f* d'entraînement

> Note that the French word **route** also means **road**.

router¹ ['raʊtə(r)] N *Carp (tool)* détoureuse *f*

router² ['ruːtə(r)] N *Comput* routeur *m*

routine [ruː'tiːn] N **1** *(habit)* routine *f*, habitude *f*; **to do sth as a matter of r.** faire qch de façon systématique; **it has become a regular r.** c'est deven une habitude

2 *Pej (dull habit)* routine *f*; **the daily r.** la routin quotidienne, le train-train quotidien

3 *(formality)* formalité *f*; **it's just r.** c'est une sim ple formalité

4 *(performance)* numéro *m*, séquence *f*; *(c dancer)* enchaînement *m*

5 *(insincere act)* **don't give me that old r.!** toujour la même chose *ou* le même refrain, change d disque!

6 *Comput* sous-programme *m*, routine *f*

ADJ 1 *(ordinary)* de routine; *(investigation, exam ination)* de routine, d'usage; **can I ask you some questions?** puis-je vous poser quelques ques tions de routine?; **r. enquiries** *(of police)* consta tations *fpl* d'usage; **she comes in once a year for r. check-up** elle vient une fois par an pour un exa men de routine; **it was a r. flight** c'était un vo sans histoire **2** *(everyday)* de routine **3** *(monoto nous)* routinier, monotone

routinely [ruː'tiːnlɪ] ADV systématiquement

routing ['ruːtɪŋ] N *(action)* routage *m*; *(route)* it néraire *m*; *(of parcel, goods)* acheminement *m*

rove [rəʊv] *pt & pp of* **reeve** VI **1** *(person)* erre vagabonder **2** *(eyes)* errer; **her eyes roved ove the page/the crowd** son regard errait sur l page/parmi la foule

VT *(country)* parcourir, errer dans; *(streets)* erre dans; *(the seas)* écumer

rover ['rəʊvə(r)] N vagabond(e) *m,f*

roving ['rəʊvɪŋ] ADJ vagabond, nomade; **he has r. commission** il a toute liberté de manœuvre; *Fi* **he has a r. eye** il aime bien lorgner les filles; **r. lif** vie *f* de nomade; **to lead a r. life** mener une vie d nomade

N vagabondage *m*

▸▸ ***roving reporter*** reporter *m (qui va sur le te rain)*

row¹ [rəʊ] N **1** *(of chairs, trees, houses)* rangée *(of vegetables, seeds)* rang *m*; *(of people ▸ next t one another)* rangée *f*; *(▸ behind one another)* fil *f*, queue *f*; *(of cars)* file *f*; *(in knitting)* rang *m*; **fo the third time in a r.** pour la troisième fois d suite; **she put the boxes in a r.** elle aligna les boî tes; **they sat/stood in a r.** ils étaient assis/debou en rang; **in rows** par rangs; **in two rows** sur deu rangs

2 *(in cinema, hall)* rang *m*; **in the third r.** au troi sième rang

3 *Sport (in rugby)* ligne *f*

4 *Br (in street names)* rue *f*

5 *Comput (in spreadsheet)* ligne *f*

6 *(in boat)* promenade *f* (en bateau à rames); **t go for a r.** faire une promenade en canot à ra mes; **to have a r. round the island** faire le tour d l'île à la rame

VI *(in boat)* ramer; *Sport* faire de l'aviron; **to across a lake** traverser un lac à la rame; **to r. har** ramer de toutes ses forces, faire force de rame

VT *(boat)* faire avancer à la rame *ou* à l'aviron *(passengers)* transporter en canot; **he rowed th tourists across the lake** il fit traverser le lac au touristes dans un bateau à rames; **Redgrav rowed a great/poor race** Redgrave a fait un belle/mauvaise course

▸▸ *Am* ***row house*** = maison attenante aux mai sons voisines

row² [raʊ] N *Br* **1** *(quarrel)* dispute *f*, querelle *f*; **t have a r. with sb** se disputer avec qn; **I got into a with the bus driver** je me suis disputé avec l chauffeur du bus; **the r. in Parliament over de fence policy** la controverse au Parlement au su jet de la politique de défense **2** *(noise)* tapage *m* vacarme *m*; **to make a r.** *(be noisy)* faire du tapag *ou* du vacarme; *(protest)* faire toute une histoire **stop that r.!** arrêtez ce boucan!; **what's all the about?** qu'est-ce que c'est que tout ce raffut?

VI se disputer; **to r. with sb** se disputer avec qn

rowan ['raʊən, 'rəʊən] N *Bot (tree)* sorbier *m* de oiseleurs *ou* des oiseaux; *(fruit)* sorbe *f*

rowboat ['rəʊbəʊt] N *Am* bateau *m* à rames

rowdiness ['raʊdɪnɪs] N tapage *m*, chahut *m*

rowdy ['raʊdɪ] *(compar* **rowdier**, *superl* **rowdies** *pl* **rowdies)** ADJ *(person)* chahuteur, bagarreur *(behaviour)* chahuteur; **to be r.** chahuter; **what**

r. bunch! quelle bande de chahuteurs!
N bagarreur(euse) *m,f*, voyou *m*

owdyism ['raʊdɪɪzəm] **N** *Br* tapage *m*, chahut *m*

owel ['raʊəl] **N** *(on spur)* molette *f*

ower ['rəʊə(r)] **N** rameur(euse) *m,f*

owing ['rəʊɪŋ] **N** canotage *m*; *Sport* aviron *m*; **to go r.** faire du canotage/de l'aviron
▸▸ *Br* ***rowing boat*** bateau *m* à rames; ***rowing club*** club *m* d'aviron; ***rowing machine*** rameur *m*

owlock ['rɒlək] **N** *(U-shaped)* dame *f* de nage; *(pin)* tolet *m*

oyal ['rɔɪəl] **ADJ 1** *(seal, residence, visit)* royal; *(horse, household, vehicle)* royal, du roi/de la reine; **Your/Her R. Highness** Votre/Son Altesse Royale; **by r. charter** par acte du souverain; **the r. "we"** le "nous" de majesté
2 *Fig Formal (splendid)* royal, princier; **they gave us a (right) r. welcome** ils nous ont accueillis comme des rois; **to be in r. spirits** être d'excellente humeur
3 *Fam (for emphasis)* sombre, de première; **that guy is a right r. pain in the neck** ce type est un véritable emmerdeur; **he's a r. idiot** c'est un sombre crétin *ou* un crétin de première
4 *(paper)* (format *m*) grand raisin *m*; **r. octavo/quarto** in-huit *m*/in-quarto *m* raisin
N *Fam* = membre de la famille royale; **the Royals** la famille royaleᵓ
▸▸ *Br* ***the Royal Academy (of Arts)*** l'Académie *f* royale des beaux-arts; ***the Royal Air Force*** = armée de l'air britannique; ***royal assent*** = signature royale qui officialise une loi; ***royal blue*** bleu *m* roi; ***the Royal Canadian Mounted Police*** la Gendarmerie royale du Canada; ***the Royal Commission*** = commission nommée par le monarque sur recommandation du Premier ministre; ***the Royal Family*** la famille royale; *Cards* ***royal flush*** quinte *f* royale; *(in poker)* flush *m* royal; *Br Culin* ***royal icing*** = glaçage à base de sucre glace et de blancs d'œufs (utilisé pour les cakes); ***royal jelly*** gelée *f* royale; ***the Royal Mail*** = la Poste britannique; ***the Royal Marines*** les Marines *mpl* (britanniques); ***the Royal Mint*** = la Monnaie britannique, ≃ (l'hôtel *m* de) la Monnaie; ***the Royal Navy*** la marine *f* nationale britannique; *Bot* ***royal palm*** palmier *m* royal; ***royal prerogative*** prérogative *f* du souverain; **to exercise the r. prerogative** faire acte de souverain; ***the Royal Society*** l'Académie *f* des sciences britannique; ***the Royal Ulster Constabulary*** = corps de police d'Irlande du Nord; ***royal warrant*** brevet *m* de fournisseur du souverain

oyalism ['rɔɪəlɪzəm] **N** royalisme *m*

oyalist ['rɔɪəlɪst] **ADJ** royaliste
N royaliste *mf*

oyally ['rɔɪəlɪ] **ADV 1** *also Fig (regally)* royalement; *(like a king)* en roi; *(like a queen)* en reine **2** *Fam (for emphasis)* dans les grandes largeurs; **they messed up r.** ils se sont plantés dans les grandes largeurs, ils se sont plantés, et pas qu'un peu

oyalty ['rɔɪəltɪ] **N 1** *(UNCOUNT) (royal family)* famille *f* royale; **a hotel patronized by r.** un hôtel fréquenté par les membres de la famille royale; **is he r.?** est-ce qu'il fait partie de la famille royale?; **we were treated like r.** nous avons été traités comme des princes **2** *(rank)* royauté *f*
• **royalties** **NPL** *(for writer, musician)* droits *mpl* d'auteur; *(for patent)* royalties *fpl*, redevance *f*
▸▸ ***royalty payments*** *(for writer, musician)* (paiement *m* des) droits *mpl* d'auteur; *(for patent)* (paiement *m* des) royalties *fpl*

ozzer ['rɒzə(r)] **N** *Br Fam Old-fashioned* flic *m*, poulet *m*

RP [ˌɑːˈpiː] **N** *Ling* (*abbr* **received pronunciation**) = prononciation de l'anglais britannique considérée comme la norme

RPI [ˌɑːpiːˈaɪ] **N** *Br Fin* (*abbr* **Retail Price Index**) indice *m* des prix de détail

rpm [ˌɑːpiːˈem] **N** *Tech* (*abbr* **revolutions per minute**) tr/min

RRP [ˌɑːrɑːˈpiː] **N** *Br* (*abbr* **recommended retail price**) prix *m* recommandé, prix *m* conseillé

RS [ɑːˈres] **N** *Br* (*abbr* **Royal Society**) Académie *f* des sciences britannique

RSA [ˌɑːresˈeɪ] **N 1** *Br* (*abbr* **Royal Society of Arts**) Société *f* royale des arts **2** (*abbr* **Republic of South Africa**) Afrique *f* du Sud

RSI [ˌɑːresˈaɪ] **N** *(UNCOUNT) Med* (*abbr* **repetitive strain** *or* **stress injury**) lésions *fpl* attribuables au travail répétitif

RSM [ˌɑːresˈem] **N** *Mil* (*abbr* **regimental sergeant major**) ≃ adjudant-chef *m*

RSPB [ˌɑːresˌpiːˈbiː] **N** (*abbr* **Royal Society for the Protection of Birds**) = ligue britannique pour la protection des oiseaux, ≃ LPO *f*

RSPCA [ˌɑːresˌpiːsiːˈeɪ] **N** (*abbr* **Royal Society for the Prevention of Cruelty to Animals**) = société britannique protectrice des animaux, ≃ SPA *f*

RSPCC [ˌɑːresˌpiːsiːˈsiː] **N** *Br* (*abbr* **Royal Society for the Prevention of Cruelty to Children**) ≃ Fondation *f* pour l'enfance

RSS [ˌɑːresˈes] **N** *Comput* (*abbr* **Really Simple Syndication**) RSS *m*

RSVP [ˌɑːresˌviːˈpiː] (*abbr* **répondez s'il vous plaît**) RSVP

RT [ˌɑːˈtiː] **N** *Biol* (*abbr* **reverse transcriptase**) transcriptase *f* inverse

Rt Hon *Br* (*written abbr* **Right Honourable**) = titre utilisé pour s'adresser à certains hauts fonctionnaires ou à quelqu'un ayant un titre de noblesse

RTM [ˌɑːtiːˈem] **N** (*abbr* **registered trademark**) marque *f* déposée

Rt Rev (*written abbr* **Right Reverend**) **the R. James Brown** le très révérend James Brown

rub [rʌb] (*pt & pp* **rubbed**, *cont* **rubbing**) **N 1** *(rubbing)* frottement *m*; *(massage)* friction *f*, massage *m*; *(with rag, duster)* coup *m* de chiffon; *(with brush)* coup *m* de brosse; *(with tea towel)* coup *m* de torchon; **to give sth a r.** frotter qch; *(massage)* frictionner qch; *(to dry it)* donner un coup de torchon à qch; *(to polish it)* astiquer qch; **can you give my back a r.?** pouvez-vous me frotter le dos? **2** *Sport (unevenness)* inégalité *f* (du terrain) **3** *(difficulty)* **there's the r.!** voilà le nœud du problème!, c'est là que le bât blesse!
VT 1 *(gen)* frotter; *(massage)* frictionner; **the cat rubbed itself against my leg** le chat s'est frotté contre ma jambe; **to r. one's eyes/chin** se frotter les yeux/le menton; **to r. one's hands (in glee)** se frotter les mains (en jubilant); **we rubbed ourselves dry with a towel** nous nous sommes séchés *ou* essuyés avec une serviette; **to r. sth through a sieve** passer qch au tamis; **r. it better!** *(to child)* frotte!; **r. the ointment into the skin** faire pénétrer la pommade; **r. your chest with the ointment** frottez-vous la poitrine avec la pommade; **these shoes r. my heels** ces chaussures me blessent aux talons; *Fig* **to r. shoulders with millionaires/movie stars** côtoyer des millionnaires/des stars du cinéma; *Fam* **he hasn't got two brain cells to r. together** il n'a pas deux sous de jugeote **2** *(polish)* astiquer, frotter
VI frotter; **her leg rubbed against mine** sa jambe a effleuré la mienne; **my shoe is rubbing** ma chaussure me fait mal

▸ **rub along** **VI** *Br Fam* **1** *(manage)* se débrouillerᵓ **2** *(get on ▸ people)* s'entendreᵓ; **they r. along (together)** ils s'entendent tant bien que mal

▸ **rub away** **VT SEP 1** *(stain, writing)* faire disparaître en frottant; **the inscription has been rubbed away** l'inscription a été effacée **2** *(wipe ▸ tears, sweat)* essuyer
VI disparaître en frottant

▸ **rub down** **VT SEP 1** *(horse)* bouchonner; *(dog)* frotter *(pour sécher)*; *(person)* frictionner; **to r. oneself down** se sécher **2** *(clean ▸ wall)* frotter, nettoyer en frottant; *(with sandpaper)* frotter, poncer

▸ **rub in** **VT SEP** *(lotion, oil)* faire pénétrer (en frottant); *Culin (butter)* incorporer; **r. the ointment in** faites bien pénétrer la pommade; **to r. a hole in sth** faire un trou dans qch à force de frotter; *Culin* **r. the butter into the mixture** travailler la pâte (du bout des doigts) pour incorporer le beurre; *Fig* **there's no need to r. it in** inutile de remuer le couteau dans la plaie

▸ **rub off** **VT SEP** *(erase ▸ writing)* effacer; *(▸ mark, dirt)* enlever en frottant
VI 1 *(mark)* s'en aller, partir; **these stains won't r. off** on a beau frotter, ces taches ne partent pas; **the red dye has rubbed off on my shirt/hands** la teinture rouge a déteint sur ma chemise/m'a déteint sur les mains **2** *Fig* **with a bit of luck, her common sense will r. off on him** avec un peu de chance, son bon sens déteindra sur lui; **some of it is bound to r. off** il y aura forcément des influences

▸ **rub out** **VT SEP 1** *(erase ▸ stain, writing)* effacer **2** *Am Fam (kill)* liquider, descendre
VI *(mark, stain)* partir, s'en aller (en frottant)

▸ **rub up** **VT SEP 1** *(polish)* frotter, astiquer; *Fig* **to r. sb up the wrong way** prendre qn à rebrousse-poil **2** *Fam (revise)* potasser; **it's time you rubbed up your Greek** il est temps que tu potasses ton grec
VI *(animal)* se frotter (**against** contre); *Fig* **to r. up against sb** côtoyer qn, coudoyer qn

rubber ['rʌbə(r)] **ADJ** *(ball, gloves, hose)* en *ou* de caoutchouc; *(bullet)* en caoutchouc
N 1 *(material)* caoutchouc *m*; *Fig* **my legs feel like r.** j'ai les jambes en coton; *Am Fam Aut* **to burn** *or* **lay r.** démarrer en trombe *ou* sur les chapeaux de roue
2 *Br (eraser ▸ for pencil)* gomme *f*; **(board) r.** *(with wooden back)* tampon *m (pour essuyer le tableau)*; *(rag)* chiffon *m*
3 *Am Fam (condom)* préservatifᵓ *m*, capote *f* (anglaise)
4 *(in bridge, whist)* robre *m*, rob *m*
• **rubbers** **NPL** *Am (boots)* caoutchoucs *mpl*, bottes *fpl* en caoutchouc
▸▸ ***rubber band*** élastique *m*; *Am* ***rubber boots*** bottes *fpl* en caoutchouc; *Fam Br* ***rubber cheque***, *Am* ***rubber check*** chèque *m* sans provisionᵓ, chèque *m* en bois; ***rubber dinghy*** canot *m* pneumatique; ***rubber gloves*** gants *mpl* de *ou* en caoutchouc; *Bot* ***rubber plant*** caoutchouc *m*, ficus *m*; ***rubber plantation*** plantation *f* d'hévéas; ***rubber planter*** planteur(euse) *m,f* d'hévéas; ***rubber ring*** bouée *f* (de natation); ***rubber stamp*** tampon *m* *ou* timbre *m* en caoutchouc; *Bot* ***rubber tree*** hévéa *m*

rubberize, -ise ['rʌbəraɪz] **VT** caoutchouter

rubberneck ['rʌbənek] *Fam* **N 1** *(onlooker)* badaud(e)ᵓ *m,f*; *(at scene of accident)* curieux (euse)ᵓ *m,f (qui s'attarde sur le lieu d'un accident)* **2** *(tourist)* touristeᵓ *mf (qui assiste à des visites guidées)*
VI 1 *(look on)* faire le badaudᵓ; *(at accident)* = faire le curieux sur le lieu d'un accident **2** *(tourist)* faire le touristeᵓ *(en assistant à des visites guidées)*

rubber-stamp **VT** tamponner; *Fig (decision)* approuver sans discussion

rubbery ['rʌbərɪ] **ADJ** caoutchouteux

rubbing ['rʌbɪŋ] **N 1** *(gen)* frottement *m* **2** *Art* frottis *m*; **to take a r. of an inscription** décalquer une inscription *(en frottant)*
▸▸ *Am* ***rubbing alcohol*** alcool *m* à 90 (degrés)

rubbish ['rʌbɪʃ] **N** *(UNCOUNT)* **1** *(from household)* ordures *fpl* (ménagères); *(from garden)* détritus *mpl*; *(from factory)* déchets *mpl*; *(from building site)* gravats *mpl* **2** *Fam (worthless goods)* camelote *f*, pacotille *f*; **shall I keep this? – no, it's just r.** je garde ça? – non, c'est bon à jeter; **it's amazing how much r. one accumulates** c'est incroyable toutes les cochonneries qu'on peut accumuler **3** *Fam (nonsense)* foutaises *fpl*, sottises *fpl*; **don't talk r.!** ne dis pas de bêtises!, arrête de raconter n'importe quoi!; **(what) r.!, what a load of (old) r.!** quelles foutaises!; **her latest book is a load of r.** son dernier livre est vraiment nul
ADJ *Fam* nul, pourri; **that was a r. film/meal** ce film/repas était nul
VT *Fam* éreinter; **he always rubbishes my ideas** il faut toujours qu'il débine mes idées
EXCLAM *Fam* n'importe quoi!
▸▸ *Br* ***rubbish bin*** poubelle *f*; *Br* ***rubbish chute*** *(in building)* vide-ordures *m inv*; *(at building site)* gaine *f* d'évacuation des gravats; ***rubbish collection*** ramassage *m* des ordures; *Br* ***rubbish dump*** décharge *f* (publique), dépotoir *m*; *Br* ***rubbish heap*** *(in garden)* tas *m* de détritus; *(for public use)* décharge *f* (publique), dépotoir *m*; *Fig* **to throw sb/sth on the r. heap** se débarrasser de

qn/qch; *Br* **rubbish tip** décharge *f* (publique), dépotoir *m*

rubbishy [ˈrʌbɪʃɪ] ADJ *Br Fam (worthless)* sans valeur□; *(poor quality)* de mauvaise qualité□; *(book, play)* nul

rubble [ˈrʌbəl] N *(UNCOUNT)* **1** *(ruins)* décombres *mpl*; *(debris)* débris *mpl*; *(stones)* gravats *mpl*; **the building was reduced to (a heap of) r.** l'immeuble n'était plus qu'un amas de décombres **2** *(for roadmaking, building)* blocage *m*, blocaille *f*

rubdown [ˈrʌbdaʊn] N friction *f*; **to give sb a r.** frictionner qn; **to give a horse a r.** bouchonner un cheval

rube [ru:b] N *Am Fam* plouc *m*, péquenot *m*

Rube Goldberg [ˌru:bˈgəʊldbɜ:g] ADJ *Am (device)* de bric et de broc; *(plan, idea)* tarabiscoté

rubella [ru:ˈbelə] N *(UNCOUNT) Med* rubéole *f*
COMP *(injection, vaccine)* contre la rubéole

Rubicon [ˈru:bɪkən] N Rubicon *m*; *Fig* **to cross** *or* **to pass the R.** franchir le Rubicon

rubicund [ˈru:bɪkənd] ADJ *Literary* rubicond

ruble = **rouble**

rub-out N *Am Fam* assassinat□ *m*

rubric [ˈru:brɪk] N rubrique *f*

ruby [ˈru:bɪ] *(pl* **rubies***)* N **1** *(jewel)* rubis *m* **2** *(colour)* couleur *f* (de) rubis, couleur *f* vermeille
ADJ **1** *(in colour)* vermeil, rubis *(inv)*; **r. (red) lips** des lèvres *fpl* vermeilles **2** *(made of rubies)* de *ou* en rubis; **r. earrings/necklace** boucles *fpl* d'oreille/collier *m* en rubis
▸▸ ***ruby port*** porto *m* rouge; ***ruby wedding (anniversary)*** noces *fpl* de vermeil

RUC [ˌɑ:ju:ˈsi:] N *Formerly (abbr* **Royal Ulster Constabulary***)* = corps de police d'Irlande du Nord

ruche [ru:ʃ] N ruché *m*
VT garnir d'un ruché

ruck [rʌk] N **1** *(in rugby)* mêlée *f* ouverte
2 *Br Fam (fight)* bagarre□*f*, baston *m ou f*; **there was a bit of a r. last night** il y a eu de la bagarre hier soir
3 *(crease)* faux pli *m*, godet *m*
4 *(masses)* **the (common) r.** les masses *fpl*, la foule
VI **1** *(in rugby)* former une mêlée ouverte **2** *(crease)* se froisser, se chiffonner
VT *(crease)* froisser, chiffonner

rucksack [ˈrʌksæk] N *esp Br* sac *m* à dos

ruckus [ˈrʌkəs] N *esp Am Fam (argument, controversy)* bagarre□*f*; *(noise)* chahut *m*, vacarme□*m*; **to make a r.** faire du chahut *ou* du vacarme; *(complain noisily)* faire un scandale; **to cause a r.** *(of news etc)* faire du foin

ructions [ˈrʌkʃənz] NPL *Fam* grabuge *m*; **there'll be r. if they find out** il va y avoir du grabuge *ou* ça va barder s'ils l'apprennent

rudder [ˈrʌdə(r)] N *(of boat)* gouvernail *m*; *(plane)* gouverne *f*

rudderless [ˈrʌdəlɪs] ADJ *(boat)* sans gouvernail; *Fig* à la dérive

ruddiness [ˈrʌdɪnɪs] N teint *m* rouge

ruddy [ˈrʌdɪ] *(compar* **ruddier**, *superl* **ruddiest***)*
ADJ **1** *(red ▸ gen)* rougeâtre, rougeoyant; *(▸ face)* rougeaud, rubicond; **to have a r. complexion** avoir le teint rouge, être rougeaud; **a r. glow** *(of fire)* une lueur rouge **2** *Br Fam (as intensifier)* fichu, sacré; **he's eaten the r. lot!** il a tout mangé, ce sale goinfre!; **r. hell!** nom de Dieu!; **you r. idiot!** espèce d'andouille!
ADV *Br Fam (as intensifier)* sacrément, vachement; **he was r. marvellous!** il a été super chouette!; **it's r. cold** il fait rudement froid

rude [ru:d] ADJ **1** *(ill-mannered)* impoli, mal élevé; *(stronger)* grossier; *(insolent)* insolent; **r. words** gros mots *mpl*; **to be r. to sb** être impoli envers qn; **it's r. to talk with your mouth full** c'est mal élevé de parler la bouche pleine; **he was very r. about my new hairstyle** il a fait des commentaires très désagréables sur ma nouvelle coiffure
2 *Br (indecent)* indécent, obscène, grossier; **to make a r. gesture** faire un geste obscène; **a r. joke** une histoire grivoise *ou* scabreuse
3 *(sudden)* rude, violent, brutal; **a r. shock** un choc brutal; **to receive a r. awakening** recevoir un choc; **it was a bit of a r. awakening** le réveil a été brutal
4 *Literary (rudimentary ▸ tool, hut)* rudimentaire, grossier; *(▸ drawing)* primitif
5 *Literary (primitive ▸ tribesman, lifestyle)* primitif, rude
6 *Literary (vigorous)* vigoureux; **to be in r. health** être en pleine santé

> Note that the French word **rude** is a false friend and is never a translation for the English word **rude**. It means **harsh, rough.**

rudely [ˈru:dlɪ] ADV **1** *(impolitely)* impoliment, de façon mal élevée; *(stronger)* grossièrement; *(insolently)* insolemment; **as I was saying, before I was so r. interrupted,...** comme je le disais, avant qu'on ne m'interrompe aussi impoliment,...
2 *(indecently)* indécemment, d'une manière obscène
3 *(suddenly)* violemment, brutalement; **to be r. awakened** être réveillé brusquement; *Fig* sortir brusquement de sa torpeur; **they were r. awakened to the difficulties which such an operation entails** ils se rendirent soudain compte des difficultés qu'une telle opération implique
4 *(in a rudimentary way ▸ made, drawn)* grossièrement

rudeness [ˈru:dnɪs] N **1** *(impoliteness)* impolitesse *f*; *(stronger)* grossièreté *f*; *(insolence)* insolence *f*
2 *Br (indecency)* indécence *f*, obscénité *f*
3 *(suddenness)* violence *f*, brutalité *f*
4 *(rudimentary nature)* caractère *m* rudimentaire; *(primitive nature)* caractère *m* primitif

rudiment [ˈru:dɪmənt] N *Anat* rudiment *m*
• **rudiments** NPL *(of a language, a skill)* rudiments *mpl*, notions *fpl* élémentaires

rudimentary [ˌru:dɪˈmentərɪ] ADJ *(gen) & Anat* rudimentaire; **to have a r. grasp of sth** comprendre les rudiments de qch; **I speak r. Chinese** j'ai des rudiments de chinois

rue [ru:] VT *Literary or Hum* regretter; **I lived to r. my words** toute ma vie, j'ai regretté mes propos; **I r. the day I met him** je maudis le jour où je l'ai rencontré; **you'll r. the day** *(that you did this)* tu vas le regretter
N *Bot & Culin* rue *f*

rueful [ˈru:fʊl] ADJ *(sad)* triste; *(regretful)* plein de regret

ruefully [ˈru:fʊlɪ] ADV *(sadly)* tristement; *(regretfully)* avec regret

ruefulness [ˈru:fʊlnɪs] N *(sadness)* tristesse *f*

ruff [rʌf] N **1** *(collar)* collerette *f*; *Hist* fraise *f*
2 *Zool (on bird, animal)* collier *m*
3 *Orn* (chevalier *m*) combattant *m*
4 *(in cards)* action *f* de couper
VT *(in cards)* couper

ruffian [ˈrʌfɪən] N voyou *m*; *Hum (naughty child)* petit(e) vaurien(enne) *m,f*

ruffle [ˈrʌfəl] VT **1** *(hair, fur, feathers)* ébouriffer; *(clothes)* friper, froisser, chiffonner; **the parrot ruffled its feathers** le perroquet hérissa ses plumes; *Fig* **to r. sb's feathers** froisser qn; **to r. sb's composure** faire perdre contenance à qn **2** *(surface of water)* troubler, rider; *(grass)* agiter **3** *(upset ▸ person)* troubler, décontenancer
N **1** *(frill ▸ at wrist)* manchette *f* (en dentelle); *(▸ at throat)* jabot *m* plissé **2** *(of bird)* collier *m*, cravate *f* **3** *(ripple ▸ on lake, sea)* ride *f*

ruffled [ˈrʌfəld] ADJ **1** *(flustered)* décontenancé; *(annoyed)* irrité; **to get r.** *(flustered)* perdre contenance; *(annoyed)* s'irriter **2** *(rumpled ▸ sheets)* froissé; *(▸ hair)* ébouriffé; *Fig* **to smooth sb's r. feathers** apaiser qn **3** *(decorated with frill)* ruché, plissé

rug [rʌg] N **1** *(for floor)* carpette *f*, (petit) tapis *m*; *Fig* **to pull the r. (out) from under sb's feet** faire capoter les projets de qn; *Am Fig* **to sweep sth under the r.** enterrer qch **2** *Br (blanket)* couverture *f*; **tartan r.** plaid *m*; **travelling r.** couverture *f* de voyage, plaid *m* **3** *Fam (hairpiece)* moumoute *f*

rugby [ˈrʌgbɪ] N rugby *m*
COMP *(ball, match, team)* de rugby
▸▸ ***rugby football*** rugby *m*; ***rugby league*** rugby *m* *ou* jeu *m* à treize; ***rugby player*** joueur(euse) *m,f* de rugby, rugbyman *m*; ***rugby shirt*** maillot *m* de rugby; ***rugby tackle*** plaquage *m*; ***rugby union*** rugby *m* à quinze

rugged [ˈrʌgɪd] ADJ **1** *(countryside, region)* accidenté; *(road, path ▸ bumpy)* cahoteux, défoncé; *(coastline)* échancré, découpé
2 *(face, features)* rude; **he had r. good looks** il était d'une beauté virile
3 *(unrefined ▸ person, character, manners)* rude, mal dégrossi; *(▸ lifestyle)* rude, fruste; *(determined ▸ resistance)* acharné; **r. individualist** individualiste *mf* farouche *ou* forcené(e)
4 *(clothing, equipment, vehicle)* solide, robuste

ruggedness [ˈrʌgɪdnɪs] N *(UNCOUNT)* **1** *(of countryside, region)* caractère *m* accidenté; *(of road, path)* inégalités *fpl*; *(of coastline)* échancrures *fpl*; **the r. of the terrain** les inégalités *fpl* du terrain
2 *(of face, features)* irrégularité *f*
3 *(of person, manners, lifestyle)* rudesse *f*
4 *(of clothing, equipment, vehicle)* solidité *f*, robustesse *f*

rugger [ˈrʌgə(r)] N *Br Fam* rugby□*m*

rugrat [ˈrʌgræt] N *Fam* môme *mf*, chiard *m*

ruin [ˈru:ɪn] N **1** *(usu pl) (remains)* ruine *f*; **the monastery is now a r.** le monastère n'est plus qu'une ruine; **the ruins of an old castle** les ruines *fpl* d'un vieux château; **to be** *or* **lie in ruins** *(building, economy)* être en ruine(s); *(career)* être fini; *(hopes)* être anéanti **2** *(destruction)* ruine *f*; **this spelt the r. of our hopes** c'était la fin de nos espoirs; **to fall into r.** tomber en ruine(s); **to go to r.** *(economy, country)* tomber en ruine(s); *(person)* sombrer; **to be the r. of sb** être la perte de qn; **it will be the r. of him** ça le perdra **3** *(bankruptcy)* ruine *f*; **the business was on the brink of (financial) r.** l'affaire était au bord de la ruine
VT **1** *(destroy ▸ health, economy, country)* ruiner; *(▸ person, career)* détruire; *(damage ▸ clothes)* abîmer; *(spoil ▸ event, meal, holiday)* gâcher; **that's ruined our chances** ça nous a fait perdre toutes nos chances; **you're ruining your eyesight** tu es en train de t'abîmer la vue *ou* les yeux; **to r. one's health** se ruiner la santé; **the meal's ruined** le repas est gâché; **to r. sb's plans** faire échouer les projets de qn; **the small villages along the coast have been ruined by mass tourism** les petits villages de la côte ont perdu tout leur charme à cause du tourisme de masse **2** *(bankrupt)* ruiner

ruination [ˌru:ɪˈneɪʃən] N ruine *f*, perte *f*; **you'll be the r. of me!** tu me perdras!

ruinous [ˈru:ɪnəs] ADJ **1** *(expensive)* ruineux **2** *(disastrous)* désastreux; **in a r. condition** *or* **state** *(of building, economy)* en ruine; **tobacco and alcohol are r. to the health** le tabac et l'alcool ruinent la santé

ruinously [ˈru:ɪnəslɪ] ADV de façon ruineuse; **r. expensive** ruineux

RULE [ru:l]

N
• règle **1, 2, 4, 5** • règlement **1**
• gouvernement **3** • règne **3**
• mètre **4**
VT
• gouverner **1** • dominer **2**
• juger **3** • tirer à la règle **4**
VI
• régner **1, 2** • statuer **3**

N **1** *(principle)* règle *f*; *(regulation)* règlement *m*; **the rules of chess/grammar** les règles *fpl* du jeu d'échecs/de la grammaire; **to break the rules** ne pas respecter les règles; **to play according to the rules** *or* **by the rules (of the game)** jouer suivant les règles (du jeu); **the rules and regulations** le règlement; **the club rules are very strict on this point** le règlement du club est très strict sur ce point; *Br* **against the rules**, *Am* **against the r.** contraire au règlement; **to work to r.** faire la grève du zèle; **to stretch** *or* **to bend the rules (for sb)** faire une entorse au règlement (pour qn); *Math* **r. of three** règle *f* de trois; **r. of thumb** point *m* de repère; **as a r. of thumb, allow one pound of meat for four people** en règle générale, compter une livre de viande pour quatre personnes
2 *(usual practice, custom)* règle *f*; **as a (general) r.** en règle générale; **rules of conduct** règles *fpl* de conduite; **he makes it a r. not to trust anyone** il a comme *ou* pour règle de ne faire confiance à personne; **tipping is the r. here** les pourboires

ont de règle ici; **long hair was the r. in those days** out le monde avait les cheveux longs à cette poque; **there's no hard and fast r.** il n'y a pas de ègle absolue; **politeness seems to be the exception rather than the r.** on dirait que la politesse st l'exception plutôt que la règle; **the exception roves the r.** l'exception confirme la règle
3 *(government)* gouvernement *m*, autorité *f*; *eign)* règne *m*; **the territories under French r.** les erritoires *mpl* sous autorité française; **majority ., the r. of the majority** la règle majoritaire; **the . of law** (l'autorité *f* de) la loi
4 *(for measuring)* règle *f*; **folding r.** mètre *m* liant; **pocket r.** règle *f ou* mètre *m* de poche
5 *(of religious order)* règle *f*
VT 1 *(govern ▸ country, people)* gouverner; **if I uled the world** si j'étais maître du monde
2 *(dominate ▸ person)* dominer; *(▸ emotion)* maîriser; **their lives are ruled by fear** leur vie est dominée par la peur; **don't let him r. your life** ne le aisse pas mener ta vie; **don't be ruled by what he ays** ce n'est pas à lui de vous dire ce que vous vez à faire; **don't let your heart r. your head** ne aisse pas tes émotions l'emporter sur la raison; **o r. the roost** faire la loi
3 *(judge, decide)* juger, décider; **the referee ruled he ball out** *or* **that the ball was out** l'arbitre a dé-laré *ou* jugé que la balle était hors jeu; **the strike vas ruled illegal** la grève a été jugée illégale; **the ourt ruled that he should have custody of the children** c'est à lui que la cour a accordé la garde des nfants
4 *(draw ▸ line, margin)* tirer à la règle; *(draw lines n ▸ paper)* régler; **ruled paper** papier *m* rayé *ou* églé
VI 1 *(govern ▸ monarch, dictator)* régner (**over ur**); *(▸ elected government)* gouverner; *Fam* **Chelea r. OK!** vive Chelsea!◻
2 *(prevail)* régner; **chaos ruled** le désordre ré-nait; **the philosophy currently ruling in the party** a philosophie actuellement en vigueur au parti
3 *Law (decide)* statuer (**on sth** sur qch); **to r. on a ispute** statuer sur un litige; **to r. against/in faour of sb** décider *ou* prononcer contre/en faeur de qn

rule off VT SEP tirer une ligne sous; *Fin (acount)* clore, arrêter

rule out VT SEP *(possibility, suggestion, suspect)* xclure, écarter; **we cannot r. out that possibility** n ne saurait exclure *ou* écarter cette éventuaité; **the police have ruled out murder** la police exlut la possibilité d'un meurtre; **the presence of ostages ruled out an attack** la présence d'otages endait toute attaque impossible; **the injury ules him out of Saturday's game** sa blessure ne ui permettra pas de jouer samedi

le-governed [-gʌvənd] ADJ qui suit des règles

ler [ˈruːlə(r)] N **1** *(sovereign)* souverain(e) *m,f*; *resident, prime minister etc)* chef *m* d'État, dirieant(e) *m,f* **2** *(for measuring)* règle *f*; *Comput (in ord processor, in DTP)* règle *f*
▸ *Comput* **ruler line** règle *f*

ling [ˈruːlɪŋ] ADJ **1** *(monarch)* régnant; *(party)* u pouvoir; *(class)* dirigeant **2** *(passion, factor)* ominant
N *(of judge, umpire)* décision *f*; **to give** *or* **hand own a r. in favour of sb** décider en faveur de qn
▸ **ruling body** instances *fpl* (dirigeantes)

um [rʌm] (*compar* **rummer**, *superl* **rummest**) N *drink)* rhum *m*
COMP *(ice cream, toddy)* au rhum
ADJ *Br Fam Old-fashioned (odd)* bizarre◻; **a r. haracter** un drôle de type; **it was a bit of a r. do** était un peu louche
▸ *Br Culin* **rum baba** baba *m* au rhum; **rum runer** trafiquant(e) *m,f* d'alcool

umania, Rumanian = **Romania, Romaian**

umba [ˈrʌmbə] N rumba *f*
VI danser la rumba

umble [ˈrʌmbəl] N **1** *(of thunder, traffic, cannons)* rondement *m*; *(of conversation)* bourdonnenent *m*, bruit *m* confus; *(of cart)* roulement *m*; *in stomach)* borborygme *m*, gargouillis *m*, garouillement *m*; **this caused rumbles of discontent n the press/party** cela a soulevé des vagues dans la presse/au sein du parti **2** *Fam (fight)* baston *m ou f*
VI 1 *(thunder, traffic, cannons)* gronder; *(stomach)* gargouiller; **trucks were rumbling past all night** toute la nuit, on entendait le grondement des camions **2** *Fam (fight)* se bagarrer◻, se friter
VT 1 *Br Fam (see through ▸ scheme, plot)* flairer◻; *(▸ person)* voir venir◻; **we've been rumbled** on a deviné notre jeu; **I soon rumbled their little game** j'ai tout de suite pigé leur petit jeu **2** *(comment, remark)* grommeler, bougonner
▸▸ *Am* **rumble seat** strapontin *m*; *Aut* **rumble strip** bande *f* rugueuse

▸ **rumble on** VI *(person)* palabrer; *(conversation, debate)* ne pas en finir; **the dispute's been rumbling on for weeks now** le conflit dure depuis des semaines

rumbling [ˈrʌmbəlɪŋ] N *(of thunder, traffic, cannons)* grondement *m*; *(of stomach)* borborygmes *mpl*, gargouillis *mpl*, gargouillements *mpl*
ADJ **a r. noise** un grondement
• **rumblings** NPL *(of discontent)* grondement *m*, grondements *mpl*; *(omens)* présages *mpl*

rumbustious [rʌmˈbʌstʃəs] ADJ *Br Fam (boisterous)* exubérant◻; *(unruly)* turbulent◻, indiscipliné◻; *Theat (farce)* joyeux◻

rum-dum [-dʌm] N *Am Fam* **1** *(idiot)* abruti(e) *m, f*, crétin(e) *m,f* **2** *(drunken tramp)* **he's a r.** c'est un clodo et un poivrot

ruminant [ˈruːmɪnənt] ADJ **1** *Zool* ruminant **2** *Literary (person)* pensif, méditatif; *(look, mood)* pensif
N *Zool* ruminant *m*

ruminate [ˈruːmɪneɪt] VI **1** *Zool* ruminer **2** *Formal (person)* ruminer; **to r. over** *or* **about** *or* **on sth** ruminer qch, réfléchir longuement à qch
VT **1** *Zool* ruminer **2** *Formal (of person)* ruminer

rumination [ˌruːmɪˈneɪʃən] N **1** *Zool* rumination *f* **2** *Formal (of person)* rumination *f*

ruminative [ˈruːmɪnətɪv] ADJ *(person)* pensif, méditatif; *(look, mood)* pensif

ruminatively [ˈruːmɪnətɪvlɪ] ADV pensivement

rummage [ˈrʌmɪdʒ] N **1** *(search)* **to have a r. through sth** *or* **around in sth** fouiller (dans) qch; **I had a quick r. in his suitcase** j'ai rapidement fouillé sa valise **2** *Am (jumble)* bric-à-brac *m inv*
VI fouiller; **he rummaged in** *or* **through his pockets** il fouilla dans ses poches
▸▸ *Am* **rummage sale** vente *f* de charité

▸ **rummage about, rummage around** VI fouiller; **what are you rummaging around in here for?** qu'est-ce que tu farfouilles?

rummy [ˈrʌmɪ] (*pl* **rummies**) N **1** *(card game)* rami *m*; **to play r.** jouer au rami **2** *Am Fam (drunk)* alcolo *mf*, poivrot(e) *m,f*

rumour, Am rumor [ˈruːmə(r)] N **1** *(information)* rumeur *f*, bruit *m* (qui court); **there's a r. going round that..., r. has it that...** le bruit court que... + *indicative*; **so r. has it** c'est ce qu'on dit; **to hear a r. that...** entendre dire que... + *indicative*; **there are rumours of a takeover** on parle de *ou* d'un rachat **2** *Arch or Literary (sound)* **the r. of the sea/wind** la rumeur des flots/du vent
VT **it is rumoured that...** le bruit court que... + *indicative*; **she is rumoured to be extremely rich** on la dit extrêmement riche; **he is rumoured to have killed a man** on dit *ou* le bruit court qu'il a tué un homme; **so it was rumoured** c'est ce qu'on a dit
▸▸ **rumour monger** colporteur(euse) *m,f* de rumeurs

rumoured, Am rumored [ˈruːməd] ADJ **the r. takeover of the company/cancellation of the project** la rumeur selon laquelle l'entreprise serait rachetée/le projet serait annulé; **the table was sold for a r. £2m** selon la rumeur, la table aurait été vendue 2 millions de livres

rump [rʌmp] N **1** *(of mammal)* croupe *f*; *Culin* culotte *f*; *(of bird)* croupion *m*; *Hum (of person)* croupe *f* **2** *(of army, political party)* restant *m*; **the r. Yugoslavia** ce qui reste de la Yougoslavie; **the organization was reduced to a r.** il ne restait pas grand-chose de l'organisation
▸▸ *Br Hist* **the Rump Parliament** le Parlement croupion *(nom du Parlement anglais pendant la période du Protectorat de Cromwell, de 1649 à 1660)*; *Pol* **rump party** parti *m* croupion; **rump state** État *m* croupion; **rump steak** romsteck *m*, rumsteck *m*

rumple [ˈrʌmpəl] VT *(clothes)* friper, froisser, chiffonner; *(sheets, banknote, letter)* froisser; *(hair, fur)* ébouriffer; **the wind had rumpled my hair** le vent m'avait décoiffé

rumpled [ˈrʌmpəld] ADJ *(clothes)* fripé, froissé, chiffonné; *(sheets, banknote, letter)* froissé; *(hair, fur)* ébouriffé; **to look r.** *(person)* avoir l'air ébouriffé

rumpus [ˈrʌmpəs] N *Fam (noise)* chahut *m*, vacarme◻ *m*; *(argument, protest)* bagarre◻ *f*; **to kick up** *or* **make** *or* **raise** *or* **cause a r.** *(be noisy)* faire un chahut à tout casser; *(protest)* faire du raffut; **there's been a bit of a r. about her appointment** il y a eu toute une histoire à propos de sa nomination
▸▸ *esp Am* **rumpus room** salle *f* de jeu *(souvent située au sous-sol et également utilisée pour des fêtes)*

rumpy-pumpy [ˌrʌmpɪˈpʌmpɪ] N *Br Fam Hum (sex)* zig-zig *m*, crac-crac *m*; **to have a bit of r.** faire une partie de jambes en l'air, faire zig-zig *ou* crac-crac

RUN [rʌn]

N	
• course **1, 2**	• excursion **3**
• parcours **4**	• trajet **4**
• vol **5**	• piste **7**
• suite **8, 9**	• série **8, 10**
• tirage **10**	• tendance **11**
• ruée **12**	• candidature **14**
• enclos **16**	
VT	
• diriger **1**	• organiser **2**
• faire marcher **3**	• effectuer **4**
• courir **5**	• chasser **7**
• transporter **8**	• conduire **8, 10**
• faire le trafic de **9**	• passer **11**
• faire passer **12**	• faire couler **14**
• publier **15**	• présenter **16**
VI	
• courir **1, 2**	• se sauver **3**
• passer **4**	• rouler **5**
• se répandre **7**	• couler **8**
• déteindre **9**	• marcher **10**
• circuler **11**	• durer **12**
• être à l'affiche **13**	• se présenter **16**
• faire un tour **17**	

(*pt* **ran** [ræn], *pp* **run**, *cont* **running**)
N 1 *(action)* course *f*; **at a r.** en courant; **to go for a r.** aller faire du jogging; **to go for a five-mile r.** ≃ courir huit kilomètres; **I took the dog for a r. in the park** j'ai emmené le chien courir dans le parc; **to break into a r.** se mettre à courir; **to make a r. for it** prendre la fuite, se sauver; **the murderer is on the r.** le meurtrier est en cavale; **she was on the r. from her creditors/the police** elle essayait d'échapper à ses créanciers/à la police; **we've got them on the r.!** nous les avons mis en déroute!; *Fig* **we have the r. of the house while the owners are away** nous disposons de toute la maison pendant l'absence des propriétaires; **you've had a good r. (for your money), it's time to step down** tu en as bien profité, maintenant il faut laisser la place à un autre; **they gave the Russian team a good r. for their money** ils ont donné du fil à retordre à l'équipe soviétique; *Fam* **to have the runs** *(diarrhoea)* avoir la courante
2 *(race)* course *f*; **a charity r.** une course de charité
3 *(drive)* excursion *f*, promenade *f*; **we went for a r. down to the coast** nous sommes allés nous promener au bord de la mer; **she took me for a r. in her new car** elle m'a emmené faire un tour dans sa nouvelle voiture; **I do the school r. in the morning** c'est moi qui emmène les enfants à l'école tous les matins
4 *(route, itinerary)* trajet *m*, parcours *m*; **the buses on the London to Glasgow r.** les cars qui font le trajet *ou* qui assurent le service Londres–Glasgow; **he used to do the London (to) Glasgow r.** *(pilot, bus or train driver)* il faisait la ligne Londres–Glasgow; **it's only a short r. into town** le trajet jusqu'au centre-ville n'est pas long

5 *Aviat (flight)* vol *m*, mission *f*; **a bombing r.** une mission de bombardement
6 *Sport (in cricket, baseball)* point *m*; **to make ten runs** marquer dix points
7 *(track ▸ for skiing, bobsleighing)* piste *f*
8 *(series, sequence)* série *f*, succession *f*, suite *f*; **they've had a r. of ten defeats** ils ont connu dix défaites consécutives; **the recent r. of events** la récente série d'événements; **a r. of bad luck** une série *ou* suite de malheurs; **you seem to be having a r. of good/bad luck** on dirait que la chance est/n'est pas de ton côté en ce moment; **the play had a triumphant r. on Broadway** la pièce a connu un succès triomphal à Broadway; **to have a long r.** *(of fashion, person in power)* tenir longtemps; *(of play)* tenir longtemps l'affiche; **in the long/short r.** à long/court terme
9 *(in card games)* suite *f*
10 *(of product)* lot *m*, série *f*; *(of book)* tirage *m*
11 *(general tendency, trend)* tendance *f*; **to score against the r. of play** marquer contre le jeu; **I was lucky and got the r. of the cards** j'avais de la chance, les cartes m'étaient favorables; **the usual r. of colds and upset stomachs** les rhumes et les maux de ventre habituels; **she's well above the average** *or* **ordinary r. of students** elle est bien au-dessus de la moyenne des étudiants; **in the ordinary r. of things** normalement, en temps normal
12 *(great demand ▸ on product, currency, Stock Exchange)* ruée *f* (**on** sur); **the heatwave caused a r. on suntan cream** la vague de chaleur provoqua une ruée sur les crèmes solaires; **a r. on the banks** un retrait massif des dépôts bancaires; *St Exch* **there was a r. on the dollar** il y a eu une ruée sur le dollar
13 *(operation ▸ of machine)* opération *f*; **computer r.** passage *m* machine
14 *(bid ▸ in election)* candidature *f*; **his r. for the presidency** sa candidature à la présidence
15 *(ladder ▸ in stocking, tights)* échelle *f*, maille *f* filée; **I've got a r. in my tights** mon collant est filé
16 *(enclosure ▸ for animals)* enclos *m*; **chicken r.** poulailler *m*
17 *(of salmon)* remontée *f*
18 *Mus* roulade *f*
VT 1 *(manage ▸ company, office)* diriger, gérer; *(▸ shop, restaurant, club)* tenir; *(▸ theatre)* diriger; *(▸ farm)* exploiter; *(▸ newspaper, magazine)* rédiger; *(▸ house)* tenir; *(▸ country)* gouverner, diriger; **the library is r. by volunteer workers** la bibliothèque est tenue par des bénévoles; **the farm was too big for him to r. alone** la ferme était trop grande pour qu'il puisse s'en occuper seul; **who's running this outfit?** qui est le patron ici?; **I wish she'd stop trying to r. my life!** j'aimerais bien qu'elle arrête de me dire comment vivre ma vie!
2 *(organize, lay on ▸ service, course, contest)* organiser; *(▸ train, bus)* mettre en service; **they r. evening classes in computing** ils organisent des cours du soir en informatique; **they r. extra trains in the summer** l'été ils mettent (en service) des trains supplémentaires; **several private companies r. buses to the airport** plusieurs sociétés privées assurent un service d'autobus pour l'aéroport
3 *(operate ▸ piece of equipment)* faire marcher, faire fonctionner; *Comput (program)* exécuter, faire tourner; **you can r. it off solar energy/the mains** vous pouvez le faire fonctionner à l'énergie solaire/sur secteur; **this computer runs most software** on peut utiliser la plupart des logiciels sur cet ordinateur; **I can't afford to r. a car any more** je n'ai plus les moyens d'avoir une voiture; **she runs a Porsche** elle roule en Porsche
4 *(conduct ▸ experiment, test)* effectuer
5 *(do or cover at a run ▸ race, distance)* courir; **I can still r. two kilometres in under seven minutes** j'arrive encore à courir *ou* à couvrir deux kilomètres en moins de sept minutes; **the race will be r. in Paris next year** la course aura lieu à Paris l'année prochaine; **to r. messages** *or* **errands** faire des commissions *ou* des courses; **he'd r. a mile if he saw it** il prendrait ses jambes à son cou s'il voyait ça; **to be r. off one's feet** être débordé
6 *(enter for race ▸ horse, greyhound)* faire courir
7 *(hunt, chase)* chasser; **to r. a fox to earth** chasser un renard jusqu'à son terrier; **the outlaws were r. out of town** les hors-la-loi furent chassés de la ville
8 *(transport ▸ goods)* transporter; *(give lift to ▸ person)* conduire, emmener; **I'll r. you to the bus stop** je vais te conduire à l'arrêt de bus; **to r. sb home** reconduire qn chez lui
9 *(smuggle)* faire le trafic de; **he's suspected of running drugs/guns** il est soupçonné de trafic de drogue/d'armes
10 *(drive ▸ vehicle)* conduire; **I ran the car into the driveway** j'ai mis la voiture dans l'allée; **I ran my car into a lamppost** je suis rentré dans un réverbère (avec ma voiture); **he tried to r. me off the road!** il a essayé de me faire sortir de la route!
11 *(pass, quickly or lightly)* passer; **he ran his hand through his hair** il se passa la main dans les cheveux; **he ran a comb through his hair** il se donna un coup de peigne; **she ran her finger down the list/her eye over the text** elle parcourut la liste du doigt/le texte des yeux
12 *(send via specified route)* faire passer; **it would be better to r. the wires under the floorboards** ce serait mieux de faire passer les fils sous le plancher; **we could r. a cable from the house** nous pourrions amener un câble de la maison
13 *(go through or past ▸ blockade)* forcer; *(▸ rapids)* franchir; *Am (▸ red light)* brûler
14 *(cause to flow ▸ water)* faire couler; **to r. a bath** faire couler un bain
15 *(publish ▸ article)* publier; **to r. an ad (in the newspaper)** passer *ou* faire passer une annonce (dans le journal)
16 *(enter for election ▸ candidate)* présenter
17 *Med* **to r. a temperature** *or* **fever** avoir de la fièvre
VI 1 *(gen)* courir; **to come running towards sb** accourir vers qn; **to r. upstairs/downstairs** monter/descendre l'escalier en courant; **I had to r. for the train** j'ai dû courir pour attraper le train; **I'll just r. across** *or* **over to the shop** je fais un saut à l'épicerie; **to r. to meet sb** courir *ou* se précipiter à la rencontre de qn; **don't come running to me with your problems** ne viens pas m'embêter avec tes problèmes
2 *(compete in race)* courir; **to r. in a race** *(horse, person)* participer à une course
3 *(flee)* se sauver, fuir; **r. for your lives!** sauve qui peut!; *Fam* **if he sees you, r. for it!** s'il te voit, tire-toi *ou* file!
4 *(pass ▸ road, railway, boundary)* passer; **the railway line runs through a valley** le chemin de fer passe dans une vallée; **the pipes r. under the road** les tuyaux passent sous la route; **the road runs alongside the river/parallel to the coast** la route longe la rivière/la côte; **the road runs due north** la route va droit vers le nord; **a high fence runs around the building** une grande barrière fait le tour du bâtiment
5 *(move, go ▸ ball, vehicle)* rouler; *(slip, slide ▸ rope, cable)* filer; **the crane runs on rails** la grue se déplace sur des rails; **the truck ran off the road** le camion a quitté la route; **a shiver ran down my spine** un frisson me parcourut le dos
6 *(words, text)* **how does that last verse r.?** c'est quoi la dernière strophe?; **their argument runs something like this** voici plus ou moins leur raisonnement
7 *(spread ▸ rumour, news)* se répandre
8 *(flow ▸ river, water, tap, nose)* couler; *(paint)* goutter; **let the water r. until it's hot** laisse couler l'eau jusqu'à ce qu'elle soit chaude; **the water's r. cold** l'eau est froide au robinet; **your nose is running** tu as le nez qui coule; **the cold made our eyes r.** le froid nous piquait les yeux; **her mascara had r.** son mascara avait coulé **the hot water runs along/down this pipe** l'eau chaude passe/descend dans ce tuyau; **their faces were running with sweat** leurs visages ruisselaient de transpiration; **tears ran down her face** des larmes coulaient sur son visage; **the river runs into a lake** la rivière débouche *ou* se jette dans un lac
9 *(in wash ▸ colour, fabric)* déteindre
10 *(operate ▸ engine, machine, business)* marcher, fonctionner; **to r. on** *or* **off electricity/gas/diesel** fonctionner à l'électricité/au gaz/au diesel; **this machine runs off the mains** cet appareil se branche sur (le) secteur; **the tape recorder was still running** le magnétophone était encore en marche; **leave the engine running** laissez tourner le moteur; *Comput* **do not interrupt the program while it is running** ne pas interrompre le programme en cours d'exécution; *Comput* **this software runs on DOS** ce logiciel tourne so DOS; *Fig* **everything is running smoothly** to marche très bien
11 *(public transport)* circuler; **this train doesn't on Sundays** ce train ne circule pas le dimanch **some bus lines r. all night** certaines lignes d'aut bus sont en service toute la nuit; **the buses st running at midnight** après minuit il n'y a plus c bus
12 *(last)* durer; *(be valid ▸ contract)* être *ou* re ter valide; *(▸ agreement)* être *ou* rester en v gueur; **the meeting ran for an hour longer tha expected** la réunion a duré une heure de pl que prévu; **I'd like the ad to r. for a week** je vo drais que l'annonce passe pendant une s maine; **the lease has another year to r.** le ba n'expire pas avant un an; **your subscription w r. for two years** votre abonnement sera valab deux ans
13 *Cin & Theat (be performed ▸ play, film)* être l'affiche; **the play has been running for a year** pièce est à l'affiche depuis un an; *TV* **this soa opera has been running for 20 years** ça fait ans que ce feuilleton est diffusé; **America's lon est-running TV series** la plus longue série télév sée américaine
14 *(occur ▸ inherited trait, illness)* **twins r. in o family** les jumeaux sont courants dans la f mille; **heart disease runs in the family** les mal dies cardiaques sont fréquentes dans not famille
15 *(indicating current state or condition)* **feelin** *or* **tempers were running high** les esprits étaie échauffés; **our stores are running low** nos prov sions s'épuisent *ou* tirent à leur fin; **the river ha r. dry** la rivière s'était asséchée; **he's runnir scared** il a la frousse; **programmes are runnir ten minutes late** les émissions ont toutes dix m nutes de retard; **sorry, I can't stop, I'm running a b late** désolé, je ne peux pas rester, je suis un pe en retard; **inflation was running at 18 percent** taux d'inflation était de 18 pour cent
16 *(be candidate, stand)* se présenter; **to r. f president** *or* **the presidency** se présenter au élections présidentielles, être candidat au élections présidentielles *ou* à la présidence; **r. for office** se porter candidat
17 *(drive)* faire un tour *ou* une promenade; **wh don't we r. down to the coast?** si on faisait un to jusqu'à la mer?
18 *(ladder ▸ stocking, tights)* filer
19 *(salmon)* remonter les rivières
20 *(tide)* monter

▸**run about** **VI** *Br* courir (çà et là); **the childre were running about all over the place** les enfan couraient partout

▸**run across** **VT INSEP** *(meet ▸ acquaintance)* re contrer par hasard, tomber sur; *(find ▸ boo reference)* trouver par hasard, tomber sur

▸**run after** **VT INSEP** *also Fig* courir après; **it's n like her to r. after a man** ce n'est pas son genre c courir après un homme; **she spends half her li running after her kids** elle passe son temps à êt derrière les enfants; **he's got all these assistan running after him the whole time** il a tout un t d'assistants qui passent sans arrêt derrière c qu'il fait

▸**run around** **VI** *Fam* courir (çà et là)[□]; **I've bee running around all day looking for you!** j'ai pass ma journée à te chercher partout![□]

▸**run around with** **VT INSEP** *Fam (be friend with)* fréquenter[□]; *(have affair with)* sortir avec **he's always running around with other women** est toujours en train de courir après d'autre femmes

▸**run away** **VI 1** *(flee)* se sauver, s'enfuir; **their so has r. away from home** leur fils a fait une fugue; **away and play now, children** allez jouer ailleur les enfants; *Fig* **to r. away from one's responsib ities** fuir ses responsabilités; *Fig* **to r. away fro the facts** se refuser à l'évidence; **to r. away wi sth** emporter qch, partir avec qch; **the favouri ran away with the race** le favori a gagné la cours haut la main; **don't r. away with the idea that I' rich** ne va pas t'imaginer que je suis riche; **h imagination runs away with him** il a une imagin tion galopante; **she lets her enthusiasm r. awa** with her elle se laisse emporter par son enthousiasme **2** *(elope)* partir (**with sb** avec qn)

run back VT SEP **1** *(drive back)* raccompagner (en voiture); **he ran me back on his motorbike** il m'a raccompagné en moto **2** *(rewind* ▸ *tape, film)* rembobiner

VI *(return)* retourner *ou* revenir en courant; *Fam* **to come running back** *(errant husband etc)* revenir❑

run by VT SEP **to r. sth by sb** *(submit)* soumettre qch à qn; **r. that by me again** répétez-moi ça

run down VT SEP **1** *(reduce, diminish* ▸ *gen)* réduire; *(*▸ *number of employees)* diminuer; *(*▸ *stocks)* laisser s'épuiser; *(*▸ *industry, factory)* fermer progressivement; **you've r. the battery down** vous avez déchargé la pile; *(of car)* vous avez vidé *ou* déchargé la batterie, vous avez mis la batterie à plat

2 *Fam (criticize, denigrate)* rabaisser❑; **they're always running her friends down** ils passent leur temps à dire du mal de *ou* à dénigrer ses amis❑; **stop running yourself down all the time** cesse de te rabaisser constamment

3 *(in car* ▸ *pedestrian, animal)* renverser, écraser; **he was r. down by a bus** il s'est fait renverser par un bus

4 *(track down* ▸ *animal, criminal)* (traquer et) capturer; *(*▸ *person, object)* dénicher

VI **1** *(person)* descendre en courant **2** *(clock, machine)* s'arrêter; *(battery* ▸ *through use)* s'user; *(*▸ *through a fault)* se décharger; **the batteries are beginning to r. down** les piles commencent à être usées

run in VT SEP **1** *Br (car, engine)* roder **2** *Fam (arrest)* pincer

VI **1** *(person)* entrer en courant **2** *Br (car, engine)* **running in** en rodage

run into VT INSEP **1** *(encounter* ▸ *problem, difficulty)* rencontrer

2 *(meet* ▸ *acquaintance)* rencontrer (par hasard), tomber sur; **to r. into debt** faire des dettes, s'endetter

3 *(collide with* ▸ *of car, driver)* percuter, rentrer dans; **you should be more careful, you nearly ran into me!** tu devrais faire attention, tu as failli me rentrer dedans!

4 *(amount to)* s'élever à; **debts running into millions of dollars** des dettes qui s'élèvent à des millions de dollars; **takings r. into five figures** la recette atteint les cinq chiffres

5 *(merge into)* se fondre dans, se confondre avec; **the words began to r. into each other before my eyes** les mots commençaient à se confondre devant mes yeux

run off VT SEP **1** *(print)* tirer, imprimer; *(photocopy)* photocopier; **r. me off five copies of this report** faites-moi cinq copies de ce rapport

2 *(write quickly* ▸ *article)* pondre

3 *Sport (race)* disputer

4 *(lose by running* ▸ *excess weight, fat)* perdre en courant

5 *(liquid)* laisser s'écouler

VI **1** *(flee)* se sauver, s'enfuir; **to r. off with the cash** partir en emportant l'argent; **to r. off with sb** *(elope with)* s'enfuir avec qn **2** *(liquid)* s'écouler

run on VT SEP *(lines of writing)* ne pas découper en paragraphes; *(letters, words)* ne pas séparer, lier

VI **1** *(continue)* continuer, durer; *(drag on)* s'éterniser; **the meeting ran on for an extra hour** la réunion a duré une heure de plus que prévu **2** *Fam (talk non-stop)* parler sans cesse❑; **he can r. on for hours if you let him** si tu le laisses faire il peut tenir le crachoir pendant des heures **3** *(line of text)* suivre sans alinéa; *Typ (of words)* se rejoindre, être liés; *(verse)* enjamber

run out VT SEP **1** *(cable, rope)* laisser filer **2** *(in cricket)* **to r. a batsman out** mettre un batteur hors jeu

VI **1** *(person, animal)* sortir en courant; *(liquid)* s'écouler; *Fig* **to r. out on sb** abandonner qn **2** *(be used up* ▸ *supplies, money etc)* s'épuiser, (venir à) manquer; *(*▸ *time)* filer; **hurry up, time is running out!** dépêchez-vous, il ne reste plus beaucoup de temps!; **their luck finally ran out** la chance a fini par tourner, leur chance n'a pas duré **3** *(expire* ▸ *contract, passport, agreement)* expirer, venir à expiration

▸ **run out of** VT INSEP manquer de; **we're running out of ammunition** nous commençons à manquer de munitions; **we're running out of sugar** nous allons nous trouver à court de sucre; **we're running out of time** il nous reste peu de temps; **he's r. out of money** il n'a plus d'argent; **to r. out of petrol** tomber en panne d'essence

▸ **run over** VT SEP *(pedestrian, animal)* écraser; **I nearly got r. over** j'ai failli me faire écraser

VT INSEP **1 the car ran over his legs** la voiture lui est passé sur les jambes **2** *(review)* revoir; *(rehearse)* répéter; *(recap)* récapituler; **let's r. over the arguments one more time** reprenons les arguments une dernière fois; **could you r. over the main points for us?** pourriez-vous nous récapituler les principaux points? **3** *(exceed)* **to r. over the allotted time** excéder le temps imparti

VI **1** *(overflow)* déborder; *Literary* **my cup runneth over** je nage dans le bonheur **2** *(run late)* dépasser l'heure; *Rad & TV* dépasser le temps d'antenne, déborder sur le temps d'antenne; **the programme ran over by 20 minutes** l'émission a dépassé son temps d'antenne de 20 minutes

▸ **run past** VT SEP = **run by**

VI passer en courant

▸ **run through** VT INSEP **1** *(cross* ▸ *of person)* traverser en courant

2 *(pervade* ▸ *of thought, feeling)* **an angry murmur ran through the crowd** des murmures de colère parcoururent la foule; **his words kept running through my head** ses paroles ne cessaient de retentir dans ma tête; **an air of melancholy runs through the whole film** une atmosphère de mélancolie imprègne tout le film

3 *(review)* revoir; *(rehearse)* répéter; *(recap)* récapituler; **she ran through the arguments in her mind** elle repassa les arguments dans sa tête; **let's just r. through the procedure one more time** reprenons une dernière fois la marche à suivre; **I'll r. through your speech with you** je vous ferai répéter votre discours

4 *(read quickly)* parcourir (des yeux), jeter un coup d'œil sur

5 *(use up* ▸ *money)* dépenser; *(*▸ *case of wine, coffee)* consommer; *(squander* ▸ *fortune)* gaspiller; **he runs through a dozen shirts a week** il lui faut une douzaine de chemises par semaine

VT SEP **to r. sb through (with a sword)** transpercer qn (d'un coup d'épée)

▸ **run to** VT INSEP **1** *(amount to)* se chiffrer à; **her essay ran to 20 pages** sa dissertation faisait 20 pages **2** *Br (afford, be enough for)* **your salary should r. to a new computer** ton salaire devrait te permettre d'acheter un nouvel ordinateur; **the budget won't r. to champagne** le budget ne nous permet pas d'acheter du champagne

▸ **run up** VT SEP **1** *(debt, bill)* laisser s'accumuler; **I've r. up a huge overdraft** j'ai un découvert énorme **2** *(flag)* hisser **3** *(sew quickly)* coudre rapidement *ou* à la hâte

VI *(climb rapidly)* monter en courant; *(approach)* approcher en courant; **a young man ran up to me** un jeune homme s'approcha de moi en courant

▸ **run up against** VT INSEP *(encounter* ▸ *problems, difficulties)* se heurter à

---

runabout ['rʌnəbaʊt] N *Fam (car)* petite voiture❑ *f*, voiture *f* de ville❑; *(boat)* runabout❑*m*

runaround ['rʌnəraʊnd] N *Fam* **to give sb the r.** raconter des salades à qn; *(lover, husband, wife)* tromper qn❑

runaway ['rʌnəweɪ] N *(gen)* fugitif(ive) *m,f*; *(child, teenager)* fugueur(euse) *m,f*; *(horse)* cheval *m* emballé *ou* échappé

ADJ **1** *(convict)* fugitif; *(child, teenager)* fugueur; *(horse)* emballé, échappé; *(train, car)* fou (folle); **a r. marriage** un mariage clandestin **2** *(inflation)* galopant; *(success)* fou (folle); **her book was this year's r. bestseller** son livre a été le best-seller de l'année; **a r. victory** une victoire remportée haut la main

run-down ADJ **1** *(tired)* vanné, crevé; **I think you're just a bit r.** je pense que c'est juste un peu de surmenage; **I'm feeling very r.** je me sens complètement à plat **2** *(building)* délabré **3** *(battery)* à plat

rundown ['rʌndaʊn] N **1** *(reduction)* réduction *f*, déclin *m* **2** *Fam (report)* compte rendu❑*m*; **to give sb a r. of** *or* **on sth** mettre qn au courant de qch❑

rune [ruːn] N rune *f*; **to read the runes** déchiffrer les runes

run-flat ADJ *(tyre)* anti-crevaison *(inv)*

rung [rʌŋ] *pp of* **ring**

N *(of ladder)* barreau *m*, échelon *m*; *(of chair)* barreau *m*; *Fig (in hierarchy)* échelon *m*; **on the bottom** *or* **lowest r. of the ladder** *(in organization etc)* tout en bas de l'échelle; **it's the first r. on the ladder to becoming a qualified vet** c'est la première étape pour devenir vétérinaire

runic ['ruːnɪk] ADJ runique

run-in N **1** *Fam (quarrel)* engueulade *f*, prise *f* de bec; **I had a bit of a r. with the police last week** j'ai eu un petit accrochage avec la police la semaine dernière **2** *(period before)* période *f* préparatoire; **the r. to the elections** la période qui précède les élections *ou* pré-électorale

runnel ['rʌnəl] N *Literary* ruisselet *m*, ru *m*

runner ['rʌnə(r)] N **1** *(in race* ▸ *person)* coureur (euse) *m,f*; *(*▸ *horse)* partant *m*; **he's a good/fast r.** il court bien/vite; **the runners and riders for the 3.00 race** les partants pour la course de 15 heures; *Fig* **the runners and riders** *(in election)* les candidats *mpl*; *(in competition)* les concurrents *mpl*

2 *(messenger)* coursier(ère) *m,f*; *(for film crew)* stagiaire *mf*, grouillot *m*

3 *(usu in compounds) (smuggler)* contrebandier (ère) *m,f*, trafiquant(e) *m,f*; **drug r.** trafiquant(e) *m,f* de drogue

4 *(for door, car seat)* glissière *f*; *(for drawer)* coulisseau *m*; *(of sledge)* patin *m*; *(of skate)* lame *f*

5 *Bot* coulant *m*, stolon *m*; *(on strawberry)* marcotte *f*

6 *(for table)* chemin *m* de table; *(carpet* ▸ *for stairs)* chemin *m* d'escalier; *(*▸ *for passage)* chemin *m* de couloir

7 *(for desk)* rallonge *f*

8 *Br Fam (idiom)* **to do a r.** *(run away)* décaniller, se débiner; *(leave without paying)* partir sans payer❑

▸▸ *Br* **runner bean** haricot *m* d'Espagne

runner-up *(pl* **runners-up***)* N second(e) *m,f*; **her novel was r. for the Prix Goncourt** son roman était le second favori pour le prix Goncourt; **there will be 50 consolation prizes for the runners-up** il y aura 50 lots de consolation pour les autres gagnants

running ['rʌnɪŋ] N **1** *(on foot)* course *f* (à pied); **I like r.** j'aime courir; **I go r. every weekend** je vais courir tous les week-ends; **to make the r.** *Sport* mener le train; *Fig* prendre l'initiative; **to make all the r.** *(in contest)* être en tête; *(in relationship)* toujours prendre les devants; **to be in the r. for sth** être sur les rangs pour qch, être dans la course pour qch; **he's in the r. to get the job** il a des chances d'obtenir le poste; **to be out of the r.** ne plus être dans la course

2 *(management)* gestion *f*, direction *f*; *(organization)* organisation *f*

3 *(working, functioning)* marche *f*, fonctionnement *m*; **we apologize for the late r. of this train** nous vous prions d'excuser le retard de ce train

4 *(operating)* conduite *f*, maniement *m*

5 *(usu in compounds) (smuggling)* contrebande *f*; **drug r.** trafic *m* de drogue

6 *(of water)* écoulement *m*, ruissellement *m*

7 *Comput (of program)* exécution *f*

COMP *(shorts, vest)* de course (à pied)

ADJ **1** *(at a run* ▸ *person, animal)* courant, qui court

2 *(continuous)* continu, ininterrompu

3 *(flowing)* **the sound of r. water** *(stream)* le bruit de l'eau qui coule; **all the rooms have r. water** toutes les chambres ont l'eau courante; **a r. tap** un robinet qui coule; **a r. sore** *Med* une plaie suppurante; *Fig* une source de problèmes

4 *(working, operating)* **in r. order** en état de marche; **to be up and r.** être opérationnel

5 *(handwriting)* cursif

ADV *(after n) (consecutive)* de suite; **three times/weeks/years r.** trois fois/semaines/années de suite

▸▸ *Fin* **running account** compte *m* courant; *Am*

running back *(in American football)* demi *m* à l'attaque; ***running battle*** lutte *f* continuelle; **they have a r. battle about housework** ils se bagarrent continuellement à propos des travaux ménagers; ***running board*** marchepied *m*; *Rad & TV* ***running commentary*** commentaire *m* en direct; *Fig* **she gave us a r. commentary on what the neighbours were doing** elle nous a expliqué en détail ce que les voisins étaient en train de faire; ***running costs*** frais *mpl* d'exploitation; *(of car)* frais *mpl* d'entretien; ***running down*** *(criticism ▸ of person, play)* dénigrement *m*; *(reduction ▸ of staff)* réduction *f*, diminution *f*; *(▸ of industry, factory)* réduction *f ou* diminution *f* de la production; *Typ* ***running footer*** titre *m* courant en bas de page; *Typ* ***running head*** titre *m* courant; ***running jump*** saut *m* avec élan; *Fam* **(go) take a r. jump** *or Am* **a r. jump at the moon!** va te faire voir (ailleurs)!, va voir ailleurs si j'y suis!; ***running knot*** nœud *m* coulant; *Naut* ***running lights*** feux *mpl* de position; *Am Pol* ***running mate*** candidat(e) *m,f* à la vice-présidence; *TV* ***running order*** ordre *m* de passage; ***running repairs*** réparations *fpl* courantes; ***running shoe*** chaussure *f* de course; *Sewing* ***running stitch*** point *m* droit; *Rad & TV* ***running time*** durée *f*; *Typ* ***running title*** titre *m* courant; ***running total*** total *m* cumulé; **to keep a r. total of sth** calculer qch au fur et à mesure; **the r. total of the number of casualties is 32** on dénombre jusqu'à présent 32 victimes; ***running track*** piste *f*

runny ['rʌnɪ] *(compar* **runnier**, *superl* **runniest)**
ADJ 1 *(sauce, honey)* liquide; *(liquid)* (très) fluide; *(omelette)* baveux; **a r. egg** un œuf dont le jaune coule **2** *(nose)* qui coule; *(eye)* qui pleure; **I've got a r. nose** j'ai le nez qui coule

run-off **N 1** *Sport (final)* finale *f*; *(after tie)* belle *f*; *Pol* élection *f* pour départager deux candidats **2** *(water)* trop-plein *m*
▸▸ *Pol* ***run-off election*** élection *f* pour départager deux candidats; ***run-off race*** finale *f*

run-of-the-mill **ADJ** ordinaire, banal

run-on **N 1** *Typ (text)* texte *m* composé à la suite *(sans alinéa)* **2** *Typ (extra quantity of books)* exemplaires *mpl* supplémentaires **3** *(in dictionary)* sous-entrée *f*

run-out **N 1** *Ski* zone *f* d'arrivée **2** *(of film, tape)* amorce *f* de fin de bobine

run-proof **ADJ** *(tights)* indémaillable; **r. mascara** mascara *m* waterproof *ou* résistant à l'eau

run-resist **ADJ** *(tights)* indémaillable

runt [rʌnt] **N 1** *(animal)* avorton *m* **2** *Fam Pej (person)* avorton *m*

run-through **N** *(review)* révision *f*; *(rehearsal)* répétition *f*; *(recap)* récapitulation *f*; **to have a r.** *(rehearse)* répéter

runtime ['rʌntaɪm] **N** *Comput*
▸▸ ***runtime system*** système *m* en phase d'exécution; ***runtime version*** version *f* exécutable

run-up **N 1** *Sport* élan *m*; **she only takes a short r.** elle ne prend pas beaucoup d'élan **2** *(period before)* période *f* préparatoire; **the r. to the elections** la période qui précède les élections *ou* préélectorale **3** *Am (increase)* augmentation *f*, hausse *f*

runway ['rʌnweɪ] **N 1** *Aviat* piste *f* (d'atterrissage *ou* d'envol) **2** *Sport* piste *f* d'élan **3** *Am (catwalk)* passerelle *f* (de défilé de mode)
▸▸ *Aviat* ***runway lights*** feux *mpl* de piste

rupee [ru:'pi:] **N** roupie *f*

rupture ['rʌptʃə(r)] **N 1** *(split ▸ gen)* rupture *f*; *Med (▸ of artery)* éclatement *m*, rupture *f* **2** *Med (hernia)* hernie *f*
VT 1 *(split)* rompre; *Med (blood vessel, appendix)* se rompre; *(spleen)* se faire éclater **2** *Med* **to r. oneself** se faire une hernie
VI *(split)* éclater, se rompre; *Med (blood vessel, appendix)* se rompre; *(spleen)* éclater

ruptured ['rʌptʃəd] **ADJ** *Med (organ)* hernié; *(blood vessel, appendix)* rompu; *(spleen)* éclaté

rural ['rʊərəl] **ADJ** *(life, economy, community, area)* rural; *(landscape, scene, atmosphere)* champêtre
▸▸ *Br Rel* ***rural dean*** doyen *m* rural; *Br* ***rural district*** ≃ canton *m*; *Br* ***rural district council*** conseil *m* municipal rural; ***rural planning*** aménagement *m* rural

ruse [ru:z] **N** ruse *f*

RUSH [rʌʃ]

N
- précipitation **1**
- heure de pointe **4**
- jaillissement **6**
- ruée **2, 3**
- attaque **5**
- montée **6**

VT
- expédier **1**
- bousculer **2**
- attaquer **3**
- envoyer d'urgence **4**
- faire à la hâte **1**
- presser **2**
- transporter d'urgence **4**

VI
- se précipiter **1**
- s'engouffrer **2**
- monter **2**
- se ruer **1**
- jaillir **2**

N 1 *(hurry)* précipitation *f*, hâte *f*; **to do sth in a r.** faire qch à la hâte; **to be in a r.** être (très) pressé; **what's the r.?** pourquoi tant de précipitation?; **there's no (great) r.** rien ne presse; **it'll be a bit of a r., but we should make it** il faudra se dépêcher mais on devrait y arriver; **in the r. to finish the article, he forgot to check the spelling** dans sa hâte de terminer l'article, il a oublié de vérifier l'orthographe; **we left in such a r. that…** nous sommes partis avec une telle précipitation que… + *indicative*
2 *(dash, stampede)* ruée *f*, bousculade *f*; **there was a r. for the door** tout le monde s'est rué *ou* précipité vers la porte; **he made a r. for the exit** il s'est rué *ou* précipité vers la sortie; **I lost a shoe in the r.** j'ai perdu une chaussure dans la bousculade; **let's leave before the r. starts** partons avant la bousculade
3 *(great demand)* ruée *f* (**on** sur); **there's been a r. on** *or* **for tickets** les gens se sont rués sur les billets; **there's a r. on that particular model** ce modèle est très demandé
4 *(busy period)* heure *f* de pointe *ou* d'affluence; **I try to avoid the lunchtime r.** j'essaie d'éviter la foule de l'heure du déjeuner; **we had a r. (of customers) in the afternoon** les clients sont arrivés en masse l'après-midi; **the holiday r.** les grands départs *mpl* en vacances
5 *(attack)* attaque *f*, assaut *m*; **to make a r. at** *or* **for sb** se jeter sur qn
6 *(surge ▸ of water)* jaillissement *m*; *(▸ of air)* bouffée *f*; *(▸ of emotion, nausea)* accès *m*, montée *f*; **I could hear nothing above the r. of water** le bruit de l'eau (qui bouillonnait) m'empêchait d'entendre quoi que ce soit; **she had a r. of blood to the head** le sang lui est monté à la tête
7 *Bot* jonc *m*; *(for chair)* jonc *m*, paille *f*
8 *Fam Drugs slang (from drugs)* flash *m*; *Fam* **I got a real r. from that coffee** ce café m'a donné un coup de fouet
VT 1 *(do quickly)* expédier; *(do overhastily)* faire à la hâte *ou* à la va-vite; **they had obviously rushed the work** à l'évidence, ils avaient travaillé trop vite; **don't r. your food** ne mange pas trop vite; **a horse that rushes its fences** un cheval qui se précipite sur les obstacles avec trop d'impétuosité
2 *(cause to hurry)* bousculer, presser; *(pressurize)* faire pression sur, forcer la main à; **don't r. me!** ne me bouscule pas!; **let's not r. things** ne nous précipitons pas; **I've been rushed off my feet all day** j'ai passé ma journée à courir à droite et à gauche
3 *(attack ▸ person)* attaquer, agresser; *(▸ place)* attaquer, prendre d'assaut; **a group of prisoners rushed the guards** un groupe de prisonniers s'attaqua aux gardiens; **the audience rushed the platform** le public a envahi l'estrade
4 *(transport quickly)* transporter d'urgence; *(send quickly)* envoyer *ou* expédier d'urgence; **the injured were rushed to hospital** les blessés ont été transportés d'urgence à l'hôpital; **please r. me your new catalogue** veuillez me faire parvenir au plus vite votre nouveau catalogue
5 *Br Fam (charge a lot)* **how much did they r. you for that?** combien est-ce qu'ils t'ont fait cracher pour ça?
VI 1 *(hurry, dash ▸ individual)* se précipiter; *(▸ crowd)* se ruer, se précipiter; *(▸ vehicle)* foncer; **I rushed home after work** je me suis précipité chez moi après le travail; **there's no need to r.** pas besoin de se presser; **passers-by rushed to help the injured man** des passants se sont précipités au secours du blessé; **he came rushing down the stairs** il a dégringolé l'escalier; **I must r.** il faut que je me dépêche; **to r. forward** se précipiter (en avant); **he rushed past** il est passé à toute allure; **to r. to conclusions** conclure trop hâtivement; *Prov* **fools r. in (where angels fear to tread)** = agir sans réfléchir peut avoir des conséquences fâcheuses
2 *(surge ▸ air)* s'engouffrer; *(▸ liquid)* jaillir; **could hear the wind rushing through the trees** j'entendais le vent s'engouffrer dans les branches; **a stream that rushes down the mountain side** un ruisseau qui dévale le flanc de la montagne; **the blood rushed to her head** le sang lui est monté à la tête
3 *(in American football)* **he rushed for 137 yards** il a fait une course de 137 yards avec le ballon
• **rushes** **NPL** *Cin* rushes *mpl*, épreuves *fpl* de tournage
▸▸ ***rush hour*** heures *fpl* de pointe *ou* d'affluence; ***rush job*** *(urgent)* travail *m* urgent; *(hurried)* travail *m* bâclé; **I'm afraid it's a bit of a r. job** je suis désolé, le travail a été fait un peu vite *ou* a été un peu bâclé; ***rush light*** chandelle *f* à mèche de jonc; ***rush mat*** natte *f* (de jonc); ***rush matting*** *(UNCOUNT)* nattes *fpl* (de jonc); ***rush order*** commande *f* urgente

▸**rush about, rush around** **VI** courir çà et là

▸**rush away** **VI & VT SEP** = **rush off**

▸**rush into** **VT INSEP** **to r. into a room** entrer précipitamment *ou* faire irruption dans une pièce; *Fig* **to r. into things** agir sans réfléchir; **now don't r. into anything** ne va pas foncer tête baissée; **to r. into marriage/divorce** se marier/divorcer trop vite
VT SEP **to r. sb into doing sth** forcer qn à faire qch à la hâte; **to be rushed into a decision/an answer** être contraint à *ou* obligé de prendre une décision/donner une réponse à la hâte; **don't let yourself be rushed into anything** ne te sens pas obligé de faire quoi que ce soit à la hâte; **don't be rushed into signing** ne signez pas sous la pression

▸**rush off** **VI** partir précipitamment; **do you have to r. off?** est-ce qu'il faut vraiment que vous partiez aussi vite?
VT SEP *(person)* emmener d'urgence

▸**rush out** **VT SEP** *(book, new product, advertisement)* sortir rapidement; *(troops)* envoyer d'urgence
VI sortir précipitamment *ou* à toute allure

▸**rush through** **VT SEP** *(job)* expédier; *(goods ordered)* envoyer d'urgence; *(order, application)* traiter d'urgence; *(bill, legislation)* faire voter à la hâte

▸**rush up** **VT SEP** *(troops, reinforcements)* envoyer d'urgence
VI accourir; **to r. up to sb** *(to say hello etc)* se précipiter sur qn

rushing ['rʌʃɪŋ] **ADJ** *(wind, river)* déchaîné, *Literary* impétueux

rusk [rʌsk] **N** = biscuit pour bébés

russet ['rʌsɪt] **N 1** *(colour)* brun *m* roux *inv* **2** *(apple)* reinette *f*
ADJ *(colour)* brun roux *(inv)*

Russia ['rʌʃə] **N** Russie *f*

Russian ['rʌʃən] **N 1** *(person)* Russe *mf* **2** *(language)* russe *m*
ADJ russe
COMP *(embassy)* de Russie; *(history)* de la Russie; *(teacher)* de russe
▸▸ ***Russian dolls*** poupées *fpl* russes, poupées *fpl* gigognes; *Culin* ***Russian dressing*** sauce *f* (de salade) relevée au piment; ***the Russian Federation*** la Fédération de Russie; *Rel* ***the Russian Orthodox Church*** l'Église *f* orthodoxe russe; *Hist* ***the Russian Revolution*** la révolution russe; ***Russian roulette*** roulette *f* russe; *Culin* ***Russian salad*** salade *f* russe

Russianization, -isation [ˌrʌʃənaɪ'zeɪʃən] **N** russification *f*

Russianize, -ise ['rʌʃənaɪz] **VT** russifier

Russify ['rʌsɪfaɪ] *(pt & pp* **Russified)** **VT** russifier

Russky ['rʌskɪ] *(pl* **Russkies)** **N** *Fam* Ruskof *m*, Ruski *mf*

Russophil, Russophile ['rʌsəʊfaɪl] **N** russophile *mf*
ADJ russophile

Russophobe ['rʌsəʊfəʊb] **N** russophobe *mf*
ADJ russophobe

rust [rʌst] **N 1** *(on metal) & Bot* rouille *f* **2** *(colour)* couleur *f* rouille
ADJ r. (coloured) rouille *(inv)*
VI rouiller, se rouiller; **the car was left to r. away** la voiture fut abandonnée à la rouille
VT rouiller; **badly rusted** très rouillé; **it's completely rusted through** il est complètement mangé par la rouille
▸▸ ***Rust Belt*** = États du Nord des États-Unis (principalement le Michigan et l'Illinois) dont l'industrie (sidérurgie et automobile) a périclité; *Br Fam* ***rust bucket, rust heap*** *(car)* poubelle *f*, tas *m* de ferraille; ***rust inhibitor, rust preventer*** antirouille *m*

rustic ['rʌstɪk] **ADJ** rustique
N paysan(anne) *m,f*, campagnard(e) *m,f*

rusticate ['rʌstɪkeɪt] *Formal* **VT** *Br Univ (student)* renvoyer *ou* expulser temporairement
VI *(retire to country)* se retirer à la campagne; *(live in country)* vivre à la campagne

rustication [ˌrʌstɪ'keɪʃən] **N** *Br Formal Univ (of student)* renvoi *m* temporaire

rusticity [rʌ'stɪsɪtɪ] **N** rusticité *f*

rustiness ['rʌstɪnɪs] **N** rouille *f*; *Fig* **because of the r. of my French** parce que mon français est un peu rouillé

rustle ['rʌsəl] **VI 1** *(leaves)* bruire, frémir; *(silk, dress)* faire frou-frou, froufrouter; *(paper)* froisser; **to hear papers rustling** entendre des froissements de papier; **something was rustling against the window** quelque chose frottait contre la fenêtre **2** *(steal cattle)* voler du bétail
VT 1 *(leaves)* faire bruire; *(silk, dress)* faire froufrouter; *(paper)* froisser **2** *(cattle)* voler
N *(of leaves)* bruissement *m*, frémissement *m*; *(of silk, dress)* frou-frou *m*; *(of paper)* froissement *m*
▸ **rustle up VT SEP** *Fam (meal)* faire en vitesse◻; **to r. up some coffee** faire du café◻; **to r. up support** rassembler des partisans◻

rustler ['rʌsələ(r)] **N 1** *(of cattle)* voleur(euse) *m,f* (de bétail); **horse r.** voleur(euse) *m,f* de chevaux **2** *Am Fam (dynamic person)* homme *m*/femme *f* dynamique◻

rustling ['rʌsəlɪŋ] **N 1** *(of leaves)* bruissement *m*, frémissement *m*; *(of silk, dress)* frou-frou *m*; *(of paper)* froissement *m* **2** *(of cattle)* vol *m* (de bétail); **horse r.** vol *m* de chevaux

rustproof ['rʌstpru:f] **ADJ** *(metal, blade)* inoxydable; *(paint)* antirouille *(inv)*
VT traiter contre la rouille

rustproofing ['rʌstpru:fɪŋ] **N** *(product)* (produit *m*) antirouille *m*; *(process)* traitement *m* antirouille

rust-resistant ADJ *(metal, blade)* inoxydable; *(paint)* antirouille *(inv)*

rusty ['rʌstɪ] (*compar* **rustier**, *superl* **rustiest**) **ADJ 1** *(metal)* rouillé; **to go** *or* **get r.** se rouiller; *Fig* **my French is a bit r.** mon français est un peu rouillé; **my playing is very/a bit r.** je suis très/un peu rouillé; **the pianist sounded/the batsman looked a bit r.** le pianiste était/le batteur semblait un peu rouillé **2** *(colour)* rouille *(inv)*; **a r. red** un marron rouille
▸▸ ***rusty nail*** *(cocktail)* rusty nail *m (cocktail à base de whisky et de Drambuie®)*

rut [rʌt] (*pt & pp* **rutted**, *cont* **rutting**) **N 1** *(in ground)* ornière *f* **2** *Fig* routine *f*; **to get into a r.** s'encroûter; **to be (stuck) in a r.** être prisonnier d'une routine; **to get out of the r.** sortir de l'ornière **3** *(of stag)* rut *m*; **in r.** en rut
VT *(ground)* sillonner; **the track had been deeply rutted by tractors** des tracteurs avaient creusé de profondes ornières dans le chemin
VI *(stag)* être en rut

rutabaga [ˌru:tə'beɪgə] **N** *Am* rutabaga *m*, chounavet *m*

ruthless ['ru:θlɪs] **ADJ** *(person)* impitoyable, sans pitié; *(act)* brutal; *(determination, schedule, pace)* impitoyable; **to be r. in enforcing the law** être impitoyable dans l'application de la loi; **he was r. in shortening the text** il n'a pas fait de sentiments quand il s'est agi d'abréger le texte; **I'm going to have to be r.** il faut que j'y aille carrément

ruthlessly ['ru:θlɪslɪ] **ADV** *(pitilessly)* impitoyablement, sans pitié

ruthlessness ['ru:θlɪsnɪs] **N** *(of person, behaviour)* caractère *m* impitoyable, dureté *f*

rutted ['rʌtɪd] **ADJ** sillonné; **a badly r. road** une route complètement défoncée

rutting ['rʌtɪŋ] **N** *(of stag)* rut *m*
▸▸ ***rutting season*** saison *f* du rut

RV [ˌɑ:'vi:] **N 1** *Bible (abbr* **Revised Version**) = traduction anglaise de la Bible faite en 1885 **2** *Am (abbr* **recreational vehicle**) camping-car *m*

Rwanda [ru'ændə] **N 1** *(country)* Rwanda *m* **2** *(language)* rwanda *m*

Rwandan [ru'ændən] **N** Rwandais(e) *m,f*
ADJ rwandais
COMP *(embassy, history)* du Rwanda; *(teacher)* de rwanda

rye [raɪ] **N 1** *(cereal)* seigle *m* **2** *(bread)* pain *m* de seigle **3** *(drink)* whisky *m* (de seigle)
▸▸ ***rye bread*** pain *m* de seigle; ***rye whiskey*** whisky *m* (de seigle)

S

S¹, s [es] **N** S, s *m inv*; **two s's** deux s; **S for Susan** ≃ S comme Suzanne

S² **1** *(written abbr* **south***)* S **2** *(written abbr* **small***)* *(on clothes label)* S

SA¹ [ˌesˈeɪ] **N** *(abbr* **Salvation Army***)* Armée *f* du salut

SA² **1** *(written abbr* **South Africa***)* Afrique *f* du Sud **2** *(written abbr* **South America***)* Amérique *f* du Sud

Saar [sɑː(r)] **N the S.** la Sarre

Sabbath [ˈsæbəθ] **N** *Rel* **1** *(Christian)* dimanche *m*, jour *m* du Seigneur; *(Jewish)* sabbat *m*; **to observe/to break the S.** *(Christian)* observer/violer le repos du dimanche; *(Jew)* observer/violer le sabbat **2 witches' S.** sabbat *m* (de sorcières)

sabbatical [səˈbætɪkəl] **ADJ** *(gen)* & *Rel* sabbatique; **to take a s. year** prendre une année sabbatique

N congé *m* sabbatique; **to be on s.** être en congé sabbatique

saber *Am* = **sabre**

sable [ˈseɪbəl] **N 1** *(animal, fur)* zibeline *f* **2** *(colour)* noir *m*

COMP *(coat)* de *ou* en zibeline; *(paintbrush)* en poil de martre

ADJ *(colour)* noir; *Her* sable *(inv)*

►► *Zool* ***sable fur*** zibeline *f*

sabot [ˈsæbəʊ] **N 1** *(shoe)* sabot *m* **2** *Mil* sabot *m*

sabotage [ˈsæbətɑːʒ] **N** sabotage *m*

VT saboter

saboteur [ˌsæbəˈtɜː(r)] **N** saboteur(euse) *m,f*

sabre, *Am* **saber** [ˈseɪbə(r)] **N** sabre *m*

sac [sæk] **N** *Anat* & *Bot* sac *m*

saccharin [ˈsækərɪn] **N** *Chem* saccharine *f*

saccharine [ˈsækəriːn] **ADJ 1** *Chem* saccharin **2** *Fig Pej (exaggeratedly sweet* ► *smile)* mielleux; *(*►*politeness)* onctueux; *(*►*sentimentality)* écœurant; *(*►*story, film etc)* à l'eau de rose

N *Chem* saccharine *f*

sacerdotal [ˌsæsəˈdəʊtəl] **ADJ** sacerdotal

sachet [ˈsæʃeɪ] **N** sachet *m*

sack [sæk] **N 1** *(bag)* (grand) sac *m*; **two sacks of potatoes** deux sacs *mpl* de pommes de terre; *Am* **grocery s.** sac *m* à provisions

2 *Br Fam (dismissal)* licenciement▫*m*; **to give sb the s.** virer qn; **to get the s.** se faire virer

3 *(pillage)* sac *m*, pillage *m*

4 *Fam (bed)* pieu *m*, plumard *m*; **to hit the s.** se pieuter; *very Fam* **to be good/no good in the s.** être/ne pas être une affaire au pieu

5 *Arch (wine)* vin *m* blanc sec *(d'Espagne ou du Portugal)*

VT 1 *Fam (dismiss)* virer, mettre à la porte▫ **2** *(pillage)* mettre à sac, piller

►► ***sack race*** course *f* en sac

sackcloth [ˈsækklɒθ] **N** toile *f* à sac *ou* d'emballage; *Rel* **to wear s. and ashes** faire pénitence avec le sac et la cendre; *Fig* **to be in s. and ashes** être contrit

sackful [ˈsækfʊl] **N** sac *m*; **(whole) sackfuls of flour** des sacs *mpl* entiers de farine; **we've been getting letters by the s.** nous avons reçu des sacs entiers de lettres

sacking [ˈsækɪŋ] **N 1** *Tex* toile *f* à sac *ou* d'emballage **2** *Fam (dismissal)* licenciement▫*m* **3** *(pillaging)* sac *m*, pillage *m*

sackload [ˈsækləʊd] = **sackful**

sacra [ˈseɪkrə] *pl of* **sacrum**

sacrament [ˈsækrəmənt] **N** sacrement *m*; **to take** *or* **receive the sacraments** communier

• **Sacrament N the Blessed** *or* **Holy S.** le saint sacrement

sacramental [ˌsækrəˈmentəl] **ADJ** sacramentel

N sacramental *m*

sacred [ˈseɪkrɪd] **ADJ 1** *(holy)* sacré, saint; **a s. place** un lieu saint; **s. to the memory of…** *(on tombstone)* à la mémoire de… **2** *(solemn, important* ► *task, duty)* sacré, solennel; *(*► *promise, right)* inviolable, sacré; *(revered, respected)* sacré; **nothing was s. in his eyes** il n'y avait rien de sacré pour lui; **is nothing s. any more?** on ne respecte donc plus rien aujourd'hui?

N the s. and the profane le sacré et le profane

►► *Fig* ***sacred cow*** vache *f* sacrée; *Rel* ***Sacred Heart*** Sacré-Cœur *m*

sacredness [ˈseɪkrɪdnɪs] **N 1** *(holiness)* caractère *m* sacré **2** *(solemness, importance)* inviolabilité *f*

sacrifice [ˈsækrɪfaɪs] **N** *Rel* & *Fig* sacrifice *m*; **to offer sth (up) as a s. to the gods** offrir qch en sacrifice aux dieux; **I've made a lot of sacrifices for you** j'ai fait beaucoup de sacrifices pour vous; **human s.** sacrifice *m* humain

VT *Rel* & *Fig* sacrifier; **she sacrificed herself for her children** elle s'est sacrifiée pour ses enfants; **to s. one's career/independence** sacrifier sa carrière/son indépendance

sacrificial [ˌsækrɪˈfɪʃəl] **ADJ** *(rite, dagger)* sacrificiel; *(victim)* offert en sacrifice

►► ***sacrificial lamb*** agneau *m* pascal; *Fig* victime *f* expiatoire

sacrilege [ˈsækrɪlɪdʒ] **N** *also Fig* sacrilège *m*; **to commit s.** commettre un sacrilège

sacrilegious [ˌsækrɪˈlɪdʒəs] **ADJ** *also Fig* sacrilège

sacristan [ˈsækrɪstən] **N** sacristain *m*

sacristy [ˈsækrɪstɪ] *(pl* **sacristies***)* **N** sacristie *f*

sacrosanct [ˈsækrəʊˌsæŋkt] **ADJ** *also Fig* sacrosaint

sacrum [ˈseɪkrəm] *(pl* **sacra** [-krə]*)* **N** *Anat* sacrum *m*

SAD [sæd] **N** *(abbr* **seasonal affective disorder***)* dépression *f* saisonnière

sad [sæd] *(compar* **sadder,** *superl* **saddest***)* **ADJ 1** *(unhappy, melancholy)* triste; *(stronger)* affligé; **it makes me s. to see what's become of them** ça me rend triste *ou* m'attriste de voir ce qu'ils sont devenus; **to be s. at heart** avoir le cœur gros; **he came through the experience a sadder and a wiser man** l'expérience a été dure mais profitable

2 *(depressing* ► *news, day, story)* triste; *(*► *sight, occasion)* triste, attristant; *(*► *painting, music etc)* lugubre, triste; *(*► *loss)* cruel, douloureux; **but s. to say it didn't last long** mais, malheureusement, cela n'a pas duré; **that's very s. news** c'est bien triste; **she came to a s. end** elle a eu une triste fin; **the s. fact is that he's incompetent** c'est malheureux à dire, mais c'est un incapable

3 *(regrettable)* triste, regrettable; **it's a s. state of affairs when this sort of thing can go unpunished** il est vraiment regrettable que de tels actes restent impunis; **it's a s. reflection on modern society** malheureusement, cela en dit long sur la société moderne; **it's a s. day for trade unionism** c'est un jour bien sombre pour le mouvement syndical; **it's a s. day when you can't walk the streets at night in safety** c'est quand même triste de ne pas pouvoir se sentir en sécurité dans les rues le soir

4 *Fam (pathetic)* minable; **to be a s. case** être minable; **he's still living with his parents, how s. can you get?** il habite toujours chez ses parents, il est grave *ou* il craint!; *very Fam* **what a s. bastard!** quel gros nullard!; **they've got really s. taste in music** ils écoutent de la musique vraiment craignos

►► *Am Fam* ***sad sack*** *(person)* raté(e) *m,f*

sadden [ˈsædən] **VT** rendre triste, attrister *(stronger)* affliger

saddle [ˈsædəl] **N 1** *(on horse, bicycle)* selle *f*; *also Fig* **to be in the s.** être en selle; **you'll soon be back in the s. again** vous serez bientôt à nouveau d'attaque **2** *Culin (of lamb, mutton)* selle *f*; *(of hare)* râble *m* **3** *Geog* col *m*

VT 1 *(horse)* seller **2** *Fam (lumber)* **to s. sb with sth** refiler qch à qn; **I always get saddled with doing the nasty jobs** c'est toujours moi qui fais le sale boulot; **she was saddled with the children** elle s'est retrouvée avec les enfants sur les bras; **I don't want to s. myself with any more work** je ne veux pas m'encombrer de travail supplémentaire▫; **saddled with debts** grevé de dettes▫

►► *Am* ***saddle blanket*** tapis *m* de selle; ***saddle horse*** cheval *m* de selle; *Am* ***saddle shoes*** chaussures *fpl* basses bicolores; ***saddle sore*** *(on rider)* = meurtrissures provoquées par de longues heures en selle; *(on horse)* écorchure *f ou* excoriation *f* sous la selle; ***saddle stitch*** *(in needlework)* point *m* sellier; *(in bookbinding)* piqûre *f* à cheval

► **saddle up VI** *(rider)* seller sa monture

VT SEP *(horse)* seller

saddlebag [ˈsædəlbæg] **N** *(for bicycle, motorcycle)* sacoche *f*; *(for horse)* sacoche *f* de selle

saddlecloth [ˈsædəlklɒθ] **N** tapis *m* de selle

saddler [ˈsædlə(r)] **N** sellier *m*

saddlery [ˈsædlərɪ] *(pl* **saddleries***)* **N** *(trade, shop, goods)* sellerie *f*

saddle-sore ADJ he was s. il avait les fesses meurtries par de longues heures à cheval/à vélo

saddling [ˈsædəlɪŋ] **N** *(of horse)* sellage *m*

saddo [ˈsædəʊ] *(pl* **saddos** *or* **saddoes***)* **N** *Br Fam* ringard(e) *m,f*, nul (nulle) *m,f*

Sadducee [ˈsædjʊsiː] **N** *Rel* Saducéen(enne) *m,f* Sadducéen(enne) *m,f*

sadism [ˈseɪdɪzəm] **N** sadisme *m*

sadist [ˈseɪdɪst] **N** sadique *mf*

sadistic [səˈdɪstɪk] **ADJ** sadique

sadistically [səˈdɪstɪkəlɪ] **ADV** sadiquement avec sadisme

sadly [ˈsædlɪ] **ADV 1** *(unhappily)* tristement; **she looked at me s.** elle m'a regardé tristement *ou* d'un air triste; **he is s. missed** il nous/leur manque beaucoup **2** *(unfortunately)* malheureusement; **s., I won't be able to come** malheureusement, je ne pourrai pas venir; **my aunt, who s. died two years ago** ma tante qui, hélas *ou* malheureusement, est morte il y a deux ans **3** *(regrettably)* déplorablement; **you are s. mistaken** vous vous trompez lourdement; **the house had been s. neglected** la maison était dans un état déplorable; **compassion is s. lacking in our society** la compassion fait tristement défaut dans notre société

adness [ˈsædnɪs] **N** tristesse *f*

adomasochism [ˌseɪdəʊˈmæsəkɪzəm] **N** sadomasochisme *m*

adomasochist [ˌseɪdəʊˈmæsəkɪst] **N** sadomasochiste *mf*

adomasochistic [ˌseɪdəʊˌmæsəˈkɪstɪk] **ADJ** sadomasochiste

.a.e., sae, SAE [ˌeseɪˈiː] **N** *(abbr* **stamped addressed envelope)** enveloppe *f* timbrée *(portant l'adresse à laquelle elle doit être renvoyée)*; **please return the form with an s.** veuillez renvoyer le formulaire ainsi qu'une enveloppe timbrée à votre adresse

afari [səˈfɑːrɪ] **N** safari *m*; **they've gone on** *or* **they're on s.** ils font un safari

►► ***safari jacket*** saharienne *f*; ***safari park*** réserve *f* d'animaux sauvages; ***safari suit*** ensemble *m* avec saharienne

AFE [seɪf]

ADJ	
• sûr **1, 4–6**	• solide **1**
• pas dangereux **1**	• sans danger **1, 5**
• en sécurité **2**	• hors de danger **2**
• sain et sauf **3**	• sans risques **5**
N	
• coffre-fort **1**	• garde-manger **2**

ADJ 1 *(not dangerous ► car, machine, area)* sûr; *(► structure, building, fastening)* solide; *(► beach)* pas dangereux; *(►chemical, water)* sans danger; **this part of town is/isn't s. at night** ce quartier est/ n'est pas sûr la nuit; **the staircase doesn't look very s.** l'escalier n'a pas l'air très sûr; **this medicine is/isn't s. for young children** ce médicament convient/ne convient pas aux enfants en bas âge; **she assured me the water was perfectly s. to drink** elle m'a assuré qu'on pouvait boire l'eau sans danger *ou* sans risque; **is it s. to come out now?** est-ce qu'on peut sortir (sans danger *ou* sans crainte) maintenant?; **is it s. to swim here?** est-ce qu'on peut nager ici?, ce n'est pas dangereux de nager ici?; **it isn't s. to play in the street** il est dangereux de jouer dans la rue; **the bomb has been made s.** la bombe a été désamorcée; **the police kept the crowd at a s. distance** les policiers ont empêché la foule d'approcher; **the s. period** = période du cycle pendant laquelle la femme est censée ne pas être féconde

2 *(protected, not in danger)* en sécurité; *(no longer in danger)* hors de danger; **I don't feel s. alone at night** je ne me sens pas en sécurité toute seule la nuit; **the money's s. in the bank** l'argent est en sécurité à la banque; *Am* **keep s.!** prends bien soin de toi!; **the secret will be s. with her** elle ne risque pas d'ébruiter le secret; **s. from attack/ from suspicion** à l'abri d'une attaque/des soupçons; **I don't feel s. on that chair** je ne me sens pas en sécurité sur cette chaise; **(have a) s. journey!** bon voyage!; *Hum* **no woman is s. with him** c'est un coureur invétéré

3 *(unharmed, undamaged ► person)* sain et sauf; **s. and sound** sain et sauf; **I'm glad to hear you're s.** je suis content d'apprendre qu'il ne t'est rien arrivé; **we shall pay upon s. delivery of the goods** nous payerons après réception des marchandises

4 *(secure ► place)* sûr; **keep it in a s. place** gardez-le en lieu sûr; **in s. custody** *(child)* sous bonne garde; *(securities, assets etc)* en dépôt; **in s. hands** en de bonnes mains; **in s. keeping** en lieu sûr, en sûreté; **to give sth to sb for s. keeping** confier qch à qn

5 *(not risky, certain ► course of action)* sans risque *ou* risques, sans danger; *(► investment)* sûr; *(►estimate)* raisonnable; **I played it s. and arrived an hour early** pour ne pas prendre de risques, je suis arrivé une heure en avance; **a s. winner** un (une) gagnant(e) certain(e); **the steak's a s. bet here** le steak est toujours bon ici; **it's a s. bet that he'll be late** on peut être sûr qu'il arrivera en retard; **I think it's s. to say that everybody enjoyed themselves** je pense que l'on peut dire avec certitude que ça a plu à tout le monde; **take an umbrella (just) to be on the s. side** prends un parapluie, c'est plus sûr *ou* au cas où; **it's as s. as houses** cela ne présente pas le moindre risque; *Prov* **better s. than sorry** deux précautions valent mieux qu'une

6 *(reliable ► driver)* sûr, prudent; **is he s. with the money/the children?** est-ce qu'on peut lui confier l'argent/les enfants (sans crainte)?; **she's a very s. driver** c'est une conductrice très sûre *ou* très prudente; **he's a s. pair of hands** *(goalkeeper)* il a les mains très sûres; *(manager, minister etc)* il est très fiable

7 *Br Fam (good)* chouette, cool *(inv)*; **are we still on for tonight? – yeah, s.** ça marche toujours pour ce soir? – ouais, pas de problème

N 1 *(for money, valuables etc)* coffre-fort *m*; **night** *or* **deposit s.** coffre *m* de nuit

2 *(for food)* garde-manger *m inv*

►► ***safe area*** zone *f* de sécurité; ***safe deposit box*** coffre-fort *m (à la banque)*; ***safe haven*** *(gen)* refuge *m*; *Mil* zone *f* de sécurité; ***safe house*** *(for spies, wanted man)* refuge *m*; *Br Pol* ***safe seat*** = siège de député qui traditionnellement va toujours au même parti; ***safe sex*** rapports *mpl* sexuels protégés

safeblower [ˈseɪfˌbləʊə(r)] **N** perceur(euse) *m,f* de coffres-forts *(qui emploie des explosifs)*

safebreaker [ˈseɪfˌbreɪkə(r)] **N** perceur(euse) *m, f* de coffres-forts

safe-conduct [-ˈkɒndʌkt] **N** sauf-conduit *m*

safecracker [ˈseɪfˌkrækə(r)] *Am* = **safebreaker**

safeguard [ˈseɪfgɑːd] **VT** *(interests, rights)* sauvegarder; **to s. sb/sth against sth** protéger qn/qch contre qch

VI to s. against sth se protéger contre qch

N sauvegarde *f*; **as a s. against theft** comme précaution contre le vol

►► *Law* ***safeguard clause*** clause *f* de sauvegarde

safekeeping [ˌseɪfˈkiːpɪŋ] **N** (bonne) garde *f*; **she was given the documents for s.** on lui a confié les documents; **to place securities in the bank for s.** mettre des valeurs en dépôt à la banque; **the money is in your s.** je vous confie l'argent

safely [ˈseɪflɪ] **ADV 1** *(without danger)* en toute sécurité; **drive s.!** sois prudent sur la route!; **an area where women can s. go out at night** un quartier où les femmes peuvent sortir la nuit en toute sécurité; **you can s. invest with them** vous pouvez investir chez eux en toute tranquillité

2 *(without incident)* **to arrive s.** *(person ► gen)* bien arriver; *(► after dangerous journey)* arriver sain et sauf; *(parcel)* arriver sans dommage; *(ship)* arriver à bon port; **I'm just phoning to say I've arrived s.** je téléphone juste pour dire que je suis bien arrivé; **the bill was seen s. through Parliament** le projet de loi fut voté sans problème par le Parlement

3 *(securely)* en sécurité, à l'abri; **I've put the money away s.** j'ai mis l'argent en sécurité; **all the doors and windows are s. locked** toutes les portes et les fenêtres sont bien fermées; **the kids are s. tucked up in bed** les enfants sont bien couchés

4 *(confidently, certainly)* avec confiance *ou* certitude; **we can s. predict that...** nous pouvons prédire avec certitude que... + *indicative*

safeness [ˈseɪfnɪs] **N 1** *(absence of danger)* sécurité *f* **2** *(of structure, building)* solidité *f*; *(of nuclear power, electrical appliances)* sûreté *f* **3** *(certainty ► of deal, investment, choice)* sûreté *f*

safety [ˈseɪftɪ] **N** *(absence of danger)* sécurité *f*; **there are fears for the s. of the hostages** on craint pour la sécurité des otages; **we are concerned about the s. of imported toys** nous craignons que les jouets importés présentent certains dangers; **to seek s. in flight** chercher son salut dans la fuite; **he ran for s.** il a couru se mettre à l'abri; **he reached s.** il arriva en lieu sûr; **in a place of s.** en lieu sûr; **there's s. in numbers** plus on est nombreux, plus on est en sécurité; **s. in the home/workplace** la sécurité à la maison/au travail; **road s.** sécurité *f* routière; **to guarantee sb's s.** *(of police etc)* assurer la protection de qn; **s. first!** la sécurité d'abord!

COMP *(device, mechanism, measures etc)* de sécurité

►► ***safety belt*** ceinture *f* de sécurité; ***safety catch*** *(on gun)* cran *m* de sécurité; *(on window, door)* cran *m* de sûreté; *(on bonnet)* crochet *m* de sécurité; ***safety chain*** *(on door)* chaîne *f* de sûreté; *(on bracelet)* chaînette *f* de sûreté; *Theat* ***safety curtain*** rideau *m* de fer; ***safety drill*** exercice *m* d'évacuation; *Tech* ***safety factor*** facteur *m* de sécurité; ***safety feature*** *(device)* dispositif *m* de sécurité; ***safety glass*** verre *m* de sécurité; ***safety helmet*** casque *m* (de protection); *Am* ***safety island*** refuge *m (sur une route)*; ***safety lamp*** lampe *f* de mineur; ***safety margin*** marge *f* de sécurité; ***safety match*** allumette *f* de sûreté; ***safety net*** filet *m*; *Fig* filet *m* de sécurité; **without a s. net** sans filet; ***safety pin*** *(fastener)* épingle *f* de nourrice *ou* de sûreté; *(of grenade, bomb)* goupille *f* de sûreté; ***safety procedures*** procédures *fpl* de sécurité; ***safety razor*** rasoir *m* de sûreté; ***safety regulations*** consignes *fpl* de sécurité; ***safety standards*** normes *fpl* de sécurité; *also Fig* ***safety valve*** soupape *f* de sûreté

saffron [ˈsæfrən] **N 1** *Bot & Culin* safran *m* **2** *(colour)* jaune *m* safran

ADJ (jaune) safran *(inv)*

►► ***saffron rice*** riz *m* au safran

sag [sæg] *(pt & pp* **sagged**, *cont* **sagging) VI 1** *(roof, beam, shelf, bridge)* s'affaisser; *(branch)* ployer; *(cable, rope ► state)* être détendu, pendre; *(► action)* se détendre; *(jowls, cheeks, hemline)* pendre; *(breasts)* tomber; **the bed sags in the middle** le lit s'affaisse au milieu **2** *(prices, stocks, demand)* fléchir, baisser; *(conversation)* traîner; **the novel sags a bit in the middle** le roman perd un peu de son intérêt au milieu; **their spirits sagged** ils perdirent courage

N 1 *(of structure)* affaissement *m* **2** *(in prices, stocks, demand)* fléchissement *m*, baisse *f*

saga [ˈsɑːgə] **N 1** *(legend, film)* saga *f*; *(novel)* saga *f*, roman-fleuve *m* **2** *(complicated story)* **I heard the whole s. of her trip to France** elle m'a raconté son voyage en France en long et en large; **it's a s. of bad management and wrong decisions** c'est une longue histoire de mauvaise gestion et de mauvaises décisions; **the continuing s. of the minister's resignation still dominates the headlines** le feuilleton de la démission du ministre domine toujours l'actualité

sagacious [səˈgeɪʃəs] **ADJ** *Literary (person)* sagace, perspicace, avisé; *(remark)* judicieux

sagaciously [səˈgeɪʃəslɪ] **ADV** *Literary* avec sagacité, judicieusement

sagaciousness [səˈgeɪʃəsnɪs], **sagacity** [səˈgæsətɪ] **N** *Literary* sagacité *f*

sage [seɪdʒ] **N 1** *Literary (wise person)* sage *m* **2** *Bot & Culin* sauge *f*; **s. and onion stuffing** farce *f* à la sauge et à l'oignon

ADJ *Literary (wise)* sage, judicieux

►► ***sage green*** vert *m* cendré

sagely [ˈseɪdʒlɪ] **ADV** avec sagesse, avec sagacité

sagging [ˈsægɪŋ], **saggy** [ˈsægɪ] *(compar* **saggier**, *superl* **saggiest) ADJ 1** *(bed, roof, bridge)* affaissé; *(shelf, beam)* qui ploie; *(rope)* détendu; *(hemline)* qui pend; *(jowls, cheeks)* pendant; *(breasts)* tombant **2** *(prices, demand)* en baisse; *(spirits)* abattu, découragé; *(enthusiasm)* fléchissant, faiblissant

Sagittarian [ˌsædʒɪˈteərɪən] *Astrol* **N to be a S.** être (du signe du) Sagittaire

ADJ du Sagittaire; **the S. male** les hommes *mpl* du Sagittaire

Sagittarius [ˌsædʒɪˈteərɪəs] **N 1** *Astron* Sagittaire *m* **2** *Astrol* Sagittaire *m*; **he's a S.** il est (du signe du) Sagittaire

ADJ *Astrol* du Sagittaire; **he's S.** il est (du signe du) Sagittaire

sago [ˈseɪgəʊ] **N** sagou *m*

►► *Bot* ***sago palm*** sagoutier *m*; ***sago pudding*** sagou *m* au lait

Sahara [səˈhɑːrə] **N** le (désert du) Sahara

►► ***the Sahara Desert*** le désert du Sahara

SAHD [ˌeseɪˌeɪtʃˈdiː] **N** *(abbr* **stay-at-home dad)** père *m* au foyer

sahib [ˈsɑːɪb] **N** sahib *m*

SAHM [ˌeseɪˌeɪtʃˈem] **N** *(abbr* **stay-at-home mum/mom)** mère *f* au foyer

said [sed] *pt & pp of* **say**
ADJ the s. Howard Riley le dit *ou* dénommé Howard Riley; **the s. Anne Smith** la dite *ou* dénommée Anne Smith; **the s. articles** les dits articles *mpl*

sail [seɪl] **N 1** *(on boat)* voile *f*; **to set s.** prendre la mer, appareiller; **to set s. for…** partir pour…, appareiller pour…; **in full s., with all sails set** toutes voiles dehors; **they rounded the cape under s.** ils doublèrent le cap à la voile
2 *(journey)* voyage *m* en bateau; *(pleasure trip)* promenade *f* en bateau; **to go for a s.** faire un tour en bateau; **it's a few hours' s. from here** c'est à quelques heures d'ici en bateau
3 *(of windmill)* aile *f*
VI 1 *(move over water* ▸ *boat, ship)* naviguer; **the trawler was sailing north** le chalutier se dirigeait *ou* cinglait vers le nord; **the boat sailed up/down the river** le bateau remonta/descendit le fleuve; **the ferry sailed into Dover** le ferry-boat entra dans le port de Douvres; **they sailed around the Mediterranean** ils ont fait le tour de la Méditerranée en bateau; **to s. close to the wind** naviguer au (plus) près; *Fig* jouer un jeu dangereux
2 *(set off* ▸ *boat, passenger)* partir, prendre la mer, appareiller
3 *(travel by boat)* voyager (en bateau); **are you flying or sailing?** est-ce que vous y allez en avion ou en bateau?; **they sailed from Liverpool to Boston** ils ont fait le voyage de Liverpool à Boston en bateau
4 *(as sport or hobby)* **to s., to go sailing** faire de la voile
5 *Fig* **swans sailed by on the lake** des cygnes glissaient sur le lac; **there were clouds sailing by** des nuages voguaient dans le ciel; **a sports car sailed past me** une voiture de sport m'a doublé à toute vitesse; **the ball sailed over the wall** la balle est passée par-dessus le mur; **to s. into a room** entrer majestueusement dans une pièce; **she sailed across the room to greet me** elle traversa la pièce d'un pas majestueux pour venir à ma rencontre
VT 1 *(boat* ▸ *of captain)* commander; *(*▸ *of helmsman, yachtsman)* barrer; **have you ever sailed a catamaran before?** est-ce que vous avez déjà fait du catamaran?; **she sailed the boat into port** elle a manœuvré *ou* piloté le bateau jusque dans le port **2** *(cross* ▸ *sea, lake)* traverser; **to s. the Atlantic single-handed** traverser l'Atlantique en solitaire; **to s. the seas** parcourir les mers

sailboard [ˈseɪlbɔːd] *Sport* **N** planche *f* à voile
VI faire de la planche à voile

sailboarder [ˈseɪlbɔːdə(r)] **N** véliplanchiste *mf*

sailboarding [ˈseɪlbɔːdɪŋ] **N** planche *f* à voile *(activité)*

sailboat [ˈseɪlbəʊt] **N** *Am* voilier *m*, bateau *m* à voiles

sailcloth [ˈseɪlklɒθ] **N** toile *f* à voile *ou* à voiles

sailing [ˈseɪlɪŋ] **N 1** *(activity)* navigation *f*; *(hobby)* voile *f*, navigation *f* de plaisance; *(sport)* voile *f*; **to go s.** faire de la voile **2** *(departure)* départ *m*; **there are three sailings a day for Cherbourg** il y a trois départs par jour pour Cherbourg; **the 12 o'clock s.** le bateau de midi
▸▸ *Br* ***sailing boat*** voilier *m*, bateau *m* à voiles; ***sailing dinghy*** canot *m* à voile, dériveur *m*; ***sailing ship*** (grand) voilier *m*, navire *m* à voile *ou* à voiles

sailmaker [ˈseɪlmeɪkə(r)] **N** voilier *m (personne)*

sailor [ˈseɪlə(r)] **N 1** *(gen)* marin *m*, navigateur (trice) *m,f*; **I'm a good/bad s.** j'ai/je n'ai pas le pied marin **2** *(as rank)* matelot *m*
▸▸ ***sailor hat*** *(for boys)* béret *m* de marin; *(for women)* canotier *m*; ***sailor suit*** costume *m* marin

sainfoin [ˈsænfɔɪn] **N** *Bot* sainfoin *m*

saint [seɪnt] **N** saint(e) *m,f*; *Fig* **he's no s.** ce n'est pas un petit saint; *Fam* **it would try the patience of a s.** cela ferait s'impatienter le plus patient des hommes
▸▸ ***Saint Augustine*** saint Augustin; ***the Saint Bartholomew's Day Massacre, the Massacre of Saint Bartholomew*** le massacre de la Saint-Barthélemy; ***Saint Bernard (dog)*** saint-bernard *m inv*; ***saint's day*** fête *f (d'un saint)*; ***Saint Elmo's fire*** feu *m* Saint-Elme; ***Saint Francis (of Assisi)*** saint François (d'Assise); ***Saint Helena (island)*** Sainte-Hélène; **on S. Helena** à Sainte-Hélène; ***Saint John*** saint Jean; ***Saint John the Baptist*** saint Jean-Baptiste; *Bot* ***Saint John's wort*** millepertuis *m*; ***the Saint Lawrence (River)*** le Saint-Laurent; ***Saint Lucia*** Sainte-Lucie; ***Saint Mark's Square*** la place Saint-Marc; ***Saint Patrick*** saint Patrick *(saint patron de l'Irlande)*; ***Saint Patrick's Day*** la Saint-Patrick *(fête nationale de l'Irlande, le 17 mars)*; ***Saint Peter's Basilica*** la basilique Saint-Pierre; ***Saint Petersburg*** Saint-Pétersbourg; *Ich* ***Saint Peter's fish*** saint-pierre *m inv*; ***Saint Pierre and Miquelon*** Saint-Pierre-et-Miquelon; ***Saint Stephen*** saint Étienne; *Ir* ***Saint Stephen's Day*** = le 26 décembre; ***Saint Thomas Aquinas*** saint Thomas d'Aquin; ***Saint Valentine's Day*** la Saint-Valentin; *Geog* ***Saint Vincent*** Saint-Vincent-et-les Grenadines; *Med* ***Saint Vitus' dance*** danse *f* de Saint-Guy, chorée *f*

> **SAINT PATRICK'S DAY**
>
> Patrick, le saint patron de l'Irlande, est célébré le 17 mars, qui est le jour de sa mort, en l'an 461. Saint Patrick convertit les Irlandais au christianisme et établit monastères, églises et écoles dans tout le pays. Selon la légende, il aurait également réussi à chasser tous les serpents d'Irlande. Chômée en Irlande, la St Patrick est également fêtée dans certaines villes américaines comptant une forte proportion de personnes d'origine irlandaise.

sainted [ˈseɪntɪd] **ADJ** *(person)* sanctifié; *(place)* sacré, consacré; *Fam Old-fashioned* **my s. aunt!** vingt dieux!

sainthood [ˈseɪnthʊd] **N** sainteté *f*

saintliness [ˈseɪntlɪnɪs] **N** sainteté *f*

saintly [ˈseɪntlɪ] *(compar* **saintlier**, *superl* **saintliest) ADJ** *(life, behaviour, humility, virtue)* de saint; **she was a s. woman** c'était une vraie sainte; **to put on a s. air** prendre un air de petit saint

sake¹ [seɪk] **N for sb's s.** *(for their good)* pour (le bien de) qn; *(out of respect for)* par égard pour qn; *(out of love for)* pour l'amour de qn; **do it for my s./for your own s.** fais-le pour moi/pour toi; **please come, for both our sakes** viens s'il te plaît, fais-le pour nous deux; **for all our sakes, tell no one** ne le dis à personne dans notre intérêt à tous; **they decided not to divorce, for the s. of the children** ils ont décidé de ne pas divorcer à cause des enfants; **I walk to work for its own s., not to save money** je vais travailler à pied pour le plaisir, pas par esprit d'économie; **they're just talking for the s. of talking** *or* **of it** ils parlent pour ne rien dire; **art for art's s.** l'art pour l'art; **all that for the s. of a few dollars** tout ça pour quelques malheureux dollars; **for old times' s.** en souvenir du passé; **for the s. of argument, let's assume it costs £100** à titre d'exemple, admettons que ça coûte 100 livres; **for goodness** *or* **God's** *or* **Christ's** *or* **pity's** *or* **heaven's s.!** pour l'amour du ciel *ou* de Dieu!

sake² [ˈsɑːkɪ] **N** *(drink)* saké *m*

sal [sæl] **N** *Chem* sel *m*
▸▸ ***sal ammoniac*** sel *m* ammoniac; ***sal volatile*** sel *m* volatile, sels *mpl* (anglais)

salaam [səˈlɑːm] **N** salutation *f* à l'orientale
VT saluer à l'orientale
VI saluer à l'orientale
EXCLAM salam!

salacious [səˈleɪʃəs] **ADJ** *Formal (joke, book, look)* salace, grivois, obscène

salaciousness [səˈleɪʃəsnɪs], **salacity** [səˈlæsɪtɪ] **N** *Formal* salacité *f*, grivoiserie *f*, obscénité *f*

salad [ˈsæləd] **N** salade *f*; **green s.** salade *f* (verte); **cheese/ham s.** salade *f* au fromage/jambon; **tomato/fruit/mixed s.** salade *f* de tomates/de fruits/mixte
▸▸ ***salad bar*** *(restaurant)* = restaurant où l'on mange des salades; *(area)* salad bar *m*; ***salad bowl*** saladier *m*; *Br* ***salad cream*** = sorte de mayonnaise (vendue en bouteille); ***salad days*** années *fpl* de jeunesse; *Fam Hum* ***salad dodger*** *(man)* gros patapouf *m*; *(woman)* grosse vache *f*; ***salad dressing*** *(gen)* sauce *f (pour salade)*; *(French dressing)* vinaigrette *f*; ***salad oil*** huile pour assaisonnement; ***salad servers*** couvert *mpl* à salade; ***salad spinner*** essoreuse *f* à salade

salamander [ˈsæləˌmændə(r)] **N** *Zool* salamandre *f*

salami [səˈlɑːmɪ] **N** salami *m*, saucisson *m* sec

salaried [ˈsælərɪd] **ADJ** salarié
▸▸ ***salaried employee*** salarié(e) *m,f*

salary [ˈsælərɪ] *(pl* **salaries) N** salaire *m*; **I have to bring up a family on a teacher's s.** je dois faire vivre ma famille avec un salaire d'enseignant
COMP *(bracket, level)* des salaires
▸▸ ***salary earner*** salarié(e) *m,f*; ***salary scale*** échelle *f* de salaires; ***salary structure*** structure des salaires

sale [seɪl] **N 1** *(gen)* vente *f*; **to make a s.** conclure une vente; **the s. of alcohol is forbidden** la vente d'alcool est interdite; **for s.** *(sign)* à vendre; **I'm afraid that article is not for s.** je regrette, cet article n'est pas à vendre; **to put sth up for s.** mettre qch en vente; **our house is up for s.** nous avons mis notre maison en vente; **on s.** en vente; **on s. at a supermarket near you** en vente dans tous les supermarchés; **s. by auction** vente *f* aux enchères **2** *(event)* soldes *mpl*; **the sales are on in London** les soldes ont commencé à Londres; **I got it in s.** je l'ai acheté en solde; **closing-down s.** liquidation *f* **3** *(auction)* vente *f* (aux enchères)
COMP *(goods)* soldé
• **sales COMP** *(campaign, force, team)* de vente *(promotion, forecasts)* des ventes
▸▸ ***sales acumen*** sens *m* du commerce; ***sales agent*** agent *m* commercial; ***sales assistant*** vendeur(euse) *m,f*; *Am* ***sales clerk*** vendeur(euse) *m,f*; ***sales conference*** réunion *f* du personnel de ventes; ***sales department*** service *m* commercial, service *m* des ventes; ***sales director*** directeur(trice) *m,f* des ventes; ***sales drive*** campagne *f* de vente; ***sales executive*** cadre *m* commercial; ***sales figures*** chiffre *m* de vente; ***sales manager*** directeur(trice) *m,f* commercial(e); ***sales and marketing*** vente-marketing *f*; ***sales network*** réseau *m* de vente; ***sales pitch*** arguments *mpl* de vente *(verbal)* boniment *m*, argumentation *f*; ***sales rep, sales representative*** représentant(e) *m,f* (de commerce); ***sales resistance*** réticence *f* de la part du consommateur; **our product met with some initial sales resistance** le public n'a pas accepté notre produit tout de suite; *Am* ***sales slip*** ticket *m* de caisse; ***sales staff*** personnel *m* de vente; ***sales talk*** boniment *m*; ***sales target*** objectif *m* de vente; *Am* ***sales tax*** TVA *f*

saleability [ˌseɪləˈbɪlɪtɪ] **N** *Com* qualité *f* marchande

saleable [ˈseɪləbəl] **ADJ** *Br* vendable

saleroom [ˈseɪlrʊm] **N** *Br* salle *f* des ventes

salesclerk [ˈseɪlzklɜːrk] **N** *Am* vendeur(euse) *m,f*

salesgirl [ˈseɪlzgɜːl] **N** vendeuse *f*

salesman [ˈseɪlzmən] *(pl* **salesmen** [-mən]) **N** *(in shop)* vendeur *m*; *(rep)* représentant *m* (de commerce); **an insurance s.** un représentant en assurances

salesmanship [ˈseɪlzmənʃɪp] **N** art *m* de la vente, technique *f* de vente

salesmen [ˈseɪlzmən] *pl of* **salesman**

salesperson [ˈseɪlzpɜːsən] *(pl* **salespeople** [-piːpəl]) **N** *(in shop)* vendeur(euse) *m,f*; *(rep)* représentant(e) *m,f* (de commerce)

salesroom [ˈseɪlzrʊm] **N** *Am* salle *f* des ventes

saleswoman [ˈseɪlzwʊmən] *(pl* **saleswomen** [-wɪmɪn]) **N** *(in shop)* vendeuse *f*; *(rep)* représentante *f* (de commerce)

Salic law [ˈsælɪk-] **N** *Hist* loi *f* salique

salient [ˈseɪlɪənt] **ADJ** *Formal* saillant, principal
N *Archit & Mil* saillant *m*

saline [ˈseɪlaɪn] **ADJ** salin
N *Med (salt solution)* sérum *m* physiologique
▸▸ *Med* ***saline drip*** perfusion *f* saline; ***saline solution*** solution *f* saline

salinity [səˈlɪnɪtɪ] **N** salinité *f*

saliva [səˈlaɪvə] **N** salive *f*

salivary gland [ˈsælɪvərɪ-] **N** glande *f* salivaire

salivate [ˈsælɪveɪt] **VI** *also Fig* saliver

salivation [ˌsælɪˈveɪʃən] **N** salivation *f*

allow ['sæləʊ] **ADJ** *(gen)* jaunâtre; *(face, complexion)* jaunâtre, cireux
N *Bot* saule *m*

allowness ['sæləʊnɪs] **N** *(of person, complexion)* eint *m* cireux

ally ['sælɪ] **PR N**
▸ *Br Fam* ***the Sally Army*** l'Armée *f* du salut[□]

ally ['sælɪ] *(pl* **sallies,** *pt & pp* **sallied) N 1** *Mil* sortie *(excursion)* excursion *f*, sortie *f*; **his first s. into** **ravel writing** sa première tentative de récit de oyage **2** *Formal (quip)* boutade *f*, saillie *f*

sally forth, sally out VI *Literary* sortir; **we all allied forth** *or* **out into the snow** nous sommes ous partis gaillardement sous la neige

almon ['sæmən] *(pl* **inv** *or* **salmons) N** *Ich* saunon *m*; **young s.** tacon *m*
▸ ***salmon farm*** élevage *m* de saumons; ***salmon*** ***ink*** (rose *m*) saumon *m*; ***salmon steak*** darne *f* le saumon; *Ich* ***salmon trout*** truite *f* saumonée

almonella [,sælmə'nelə] *(pl* **salmonellae** [-liː]) **N** *iol* salmonella *f inv*, salmonelle *f*
▸ *Med* ***salmonella poisoning*** salmonellose *f*

alon ['sælɒn] **N** salon *m*

aloon [sə'luːn] **N 1** *Br Aut* berline *f*
2 *(public room)* salle *f*, salon *m*; *(on ship)* salon *m*
3 *Am (bar)* bar *m*; *(in Wild West)* saloon *m*; **to be drinking) in the last chance s.** n'avoir plus qu'une eule chance
4 *Br (in pub)* salle *f* de pub *(plus confortable que le ar principal)*
▸ *Br* ***saloon bar*** salle *f* de pub *(plus confortable ue le bar principal)*; *Br* ***saloon car*** *Aut* berline *f*; *ail* voiture-salon *f*

alsa ['sælsə] **N 1** *(music, dance)* salsa *f* **2** *(sauce)* alsa *f* mexicaine
VI danser la salsa

alsify ['sælsɪfɪ] *(pl* **salsifies) N** *Bot* salsifis *m*

ALT [sɔːlt, sɒlt] **N** *(abbr* **Strategic Arms Limitation alks** *or* **Treaty)** SALT *m*
▸ ***SALT talks*** négociations *fpl* SALT

alt [sɔːlt, sɒlt] **N 1** *Chem & Culin* sel *m*; **kitchen s.** ros sel *m*; **there's too much s. in the soup** la soupe st trop salée; *Bible* **the s. of the earth** le sel de la erre; **she's the s. of the earth, that woman!** cette emme est la bonté même!; *Fig* **to rub s. into the wound** remuer le couteau dans la plaie; *Fig* **you nust take what he says with a pinch of s.** il ne faut as prendre ce qu'il dit pour argent comptant; **ny athlete worth his/her s.** n'importe quel(le) thlète digne de ce nom *ou* qui se respecte **2** *am (sailor)* **old s.** (vieux) loup *m* de mer
VT 1 *(food)* saler **2** *(roads)* saler, répandre du sel ur
ADJ salé; *Literary* **to weep s. tears** pleurer amèrenent
• **salts NPL** *Pharm* sels *mpl*; *Fam* **like a dose of alts** rapidement[□]; **to get through sth like a dose of salts** faire qch en deux temps trois mouvenents *ou* en deux coups de cuillère à pot; **that urry went through me like a dose of salts** sitôt valé, le curry m'a donné la courante
▸ *Chem* ***salt ammoniac*** sel *m* ammoniaque; ***salt box*** *(object)* salière *f*, *Am Archit* = maison à toit nansardé ayant deux étages à l'avant et un tage à l'arrière; ***salt cellar*** salière *f*; ***salt flat*** saant *m*; ***salt lake*** lac *m* salé; ***salt marsh*** marais *m* alant; ***salt mine*** mine *f* de sel; ***salt pork*** porc *m* salé, petit salé *m*; *Am* ***salt shaker*** salière *f*; ***salt water*** eau *f* salée

salt away VT SEP *Fam Fig (money)* mettre de ôté[□]

salt down VT SEP saler, conserver dans du sel

alted ['sɔːltɪd] **ADJ** salé

alt-free ADJ sans sel

altine® ['sɔːltiːn] **N** ≃ cracker *m*

altiness ['sɔːltɪnɪs] **N** *(of water)* salinité *f*; *(taste)* oût *m* salé

alting ['sɔːltɪŋ] **N 1** *(of food ▸ for preserving)* saaison *f*; *(▸ for flavouring)* salage *m* **2** *Geog* **saltngs** marais *m* salant

altmill ['sɔːltmɪl] **N** moulin *m* à sel

altpetre, *Am* **saltpeter** [,sɔːlt'piːtə(r)] **N** salpêre *m*

altwater ['sɔːltwɔːtə(r)] **ADJ** *(fish, plant)* de mer
▸ *Zool* ***saltwater crocodile*** crocodile *m* marin

saltworks ['sɔːltwɜːks] *(pl* **inv) N** saline *f*

salty ['sɔːltɪ] *(compar* **saltier,** *superl* **saltiest) ADJ 1** *(food, taste)* salé; *(deposit)* saumâtre **2** *Fam (anecdote, book)* piquant[□]; *Old-fashioned (licentious)* salé, corsé[□]

salubrious [sə'luːbrɪəs] **ADJ 1** *(respectable)* respectable, bien; **it's not the most s. of bars** c'est un bar plutôt mal famé **2** *(healthy)* salubre, sain

salubriousness [sə'luːbrɪəsnɪs] **N** salubrité *f*

saluki [sə'luːkɪ] **N** *(dog)* sloughi *m*

salutary ['sæljʊtərɪ] **ADJ** salutaire; **a s. lesson** une leçon salutaire

salutation [,sæljʊ'teɪʃən] **N 1** *(greeting)* salut *m*, salutation *f* **2** *(on letter)* formule *f* de début de lettre

salute [sə'luːt] **N 1** *Mil (with hand)* salut *m*; *(with guns)* salve *f*; **to give (sb) a s.** faire un salut (à qn); **to stand at s.** garder le salut; **to take the s.** passer les troupes en revue; **to fire a s.** tirer une salve; **a 21-gun s.** une salve de 21 coups de canon **2** *(greeting)* salut *m*, salutation *f* **3** *(tribute)* hommage *m*; **a s. to British artists** un hommage aux artistes britanniques
VT 1 *Mil (with hand)* saluer; *(with guns)* tirer une salve en l'honneur de; **to s. the flag** saluer le drapeau **2** *(greet)* saluer; **she saluted me with a wave** elle m'a salué d'un geste de la main **3** *(acknowledge, praise)* saluer, acclamer; **the press today salutes a new world champion** la presse salue aujourd'hui un nouveau champion du monde
VI *Mil* faire un salut

salvage ['sælvɪdʒ] **VT 1** *(vessel, cargo, belongings)* sauver; *(old newspapers, scrap metal)* récupérer; **they managed to s. some furniture from the fire** ils ont réussi à sauver quelques meubles de l'incendie; **a counter salvaged from an old butcher's shop** un comptoir récupéré dans une ancienne boucherie **2** *Fig (mistake, meal)* rattraper; *(situation)* rattraper, sauver; **to s. one's reputation** sauver sa réputation
N 1 *(recovery ▸ of vessel, cargo, belongings, furniture)* sauvetage *m*; *(▸ of old newspapers, scrap metal)* récupération *f* **2** *(UNCOUNT) (things recovered ▸ from shipwreck, disaster)* objets *mpl* sauvés; *(▸ for re-use, recycling)* objets *mpl* récupérés **3** *(payment)* indemnité *f ou* prime *f* de sauvetage; *(paid to salvage tug)* indemnité *f* de remorquage
COMP *(company, operation)* de sauvetage
▸▸ ***salvaged goods*** matériel *m* récupéré; ***salvage tug*** remorqueur *m (pour les sauvetages)*; ***salvage vessel*** navire *m* de relevage

salvation [sæl'veɪʃən] **N 1** *Rel* salut *m* **2** *Fig* salut *m*; **writing has always been my s.** c'est l'écriture qui me sauve; **the country's s. does not lie in rearmament** ce n'est pas le réarmement qui va sauver le pays
▸▸ ***the Salvation Army*** l'Armée *f* du salut

salvationist [sæl'veɪʃənɪst] **N 1** *(member of evangelical sect)* salutiste *mf* **2** *(member of Salvation Army)* salutiste *mf*

salve [sælv] **N 1** *(ointment)* baume *m*, pommade *f* **2** *Fig (relief)* baume *m*
VT 1 *(relieve)* calmer, soulager; **I did it to s. my conscience** je l'ai fait pour soulager ma conscience **2** *(salvage)* sauver

salver ['sælvə(r)] **N** plateau *m* (de service); **a silver s.** un plateau en argent

salvia ['sælvɪə] **N** *Bot* salvia *f*, sauge *f*

salvo ['sælvəʊ] *(pl* **salvos** *or* **salvoes) N 1** *Mil* salve *f* **2** *Fig (of applause)* salve *f*, *(of laughter)* éclat *m*; *(of insults)* torrent *m*

salwar kameez ['sælwɑkæ'miːz] **N** = tenue traditionnelle des femmes indiennes composée d'une longue tunique et d'un pantalon ample

SAM [sæm] **N** *(abbr* **surface-to-air missile)** missile *m* sol–air

Samaritan [sə'mærɪtən] **N** *Rel* Samaritain(e) *m,f*
ADJ samaritain
• **Samaritans NPL the Samaritans** = association proposant un soutien moral par téléphone aux personnes déprimées, ≃ SOS Amitié

samba ['sæmbə] **N** samba *f*
VI danser la samba

sambo ['sæmbəʊ] *(pl* **sambos) N** *Br very Fam Old-fashioned* nègre (négresse)[□] *m,f*, bamboula *m*, = terme raciste désignant un Noir

SAME [seɪm]

> **ADJ**
> - même
>
> **PRON**
> - le/la même **1**
> - identique **2**
> - la même chose **3**
>
> **ADV**
> - de la même façon

ADJ même; **she's wearing the s. glasses as you** elle porte les mêmes lunettes que toi; **you saw the s. movie I did** tu as vu le même film que moi; **their son is the s. age as ours** leur fils a le même âge que le nôtre; **we are going the s. way** nous allons dans la même direction; **they are one and the s. thing** c'est une seule et même chose; **it is always the s. thing** c'est toujours la même chose; **see you s. time, s. place** je te retrouve à la même heure, au même endroit; **she's still the s. (old) Sarah** c'est toujours notre bonne vieille Sarah; *Fam* **s. difference!** c'est du pareil au même!
PRON 1 the s. *(unchanged ▸ singular)* le même (la même) *m,f*; *(▸ plural)* les mêmes *mfpl*; **it's the s. as before** c'est comme avant; **life's just not the s. now they're gone** les choses ont changé depuis qu'ils sont partis; **the city centre is still exactly the s.** le centre-ville n'a pas changé du tout; **he had an accident and he's never been the s. since** il a eu un accident et il n'est plus le même depuis
2 *(identical)* identique; **the two vases are exactly the s.** les deux vases sont identiques
3 *(used in comparisons)* **the s.** la même chose; **it's the s. in Italy** c'est la même chose *ou* c'est pareil en Italie; **it's always the s.** c'est toujours la même chose *ou* toujours pareil; **it's not a bit the s.** ce n'est pas du tout la même chose *ou* pas du tout pareil; **aren't you Freddie Fortescue? – the very s.** vous n'êtes pas Freddie Fortescue? – lui-même; **(the) s. again, please** la même chose(, s'il vous plaît); **if it's all the s. to you, I'll go now** si cela ne vous fait rien, je vais partir maintenant; **it's all** *or* **just the s. to me what you do** tu peux faire ce que tu veux, ça m'est bien égal; *Fam* **I was really cross – s. here!** j'étais vraiment fâché – et moi donc!; **Happy Christmas – (and the) s. to you!** Joyeux Noël – à vous aussi *ou* de même!; *Fam* **stupid idiot! – and the s. to you!** espèce d'imbécile! – imbécile toi-même!
4 *Law* **the s.** *(aforementioned)* le (la) susdit(e)
5 *Com* **and for delivery of s.** et pour livraison de ces (mêmes) articles
ADV the s. de la même façon; **it's not spelt the s.** ça ne s'écrit pas de la même façon; **they all taste the s.** ils ont tous le même goût; **all these houses look the s. to me** je trouve que ces maisons se ressemblent toutes; **all her songs sound the s.** toutes ses chansons se ressemblent
• **all the same, just the same ADV** quand même; **all** *or* **just the s., I would like to know what happened** quand même, j'aimerais bien savoir ce qui s'est passé; **all the s., I still like her** je l'aime bien quand même; **thanks all the s.** merci quand même

same-day ADJ *Com (processing, delivery)* dans la journée
▸▸ *Com* ***same-day delivery*** livraison *f* le jour même; *Banking* ***same-day value*** valeur *f* jour

sameness ['seɪmnɪs] **N 1** *(similarity)* similitude *f*, ressemblance *f* **2** *(tedium)* monotonie *f*, uniformité *f*

samey ['seɪmɪ] **ADJ** *Br Fam Pej* monotone[□], ennuyeux[□]

Samoa [sə'məʊə] **N** Samoa *m*

Samoan [sə'məʊən] **N 1** *(person)* Samoan(e) *m,f* **2** *Ling* samoan *m*
ADJ samoan

samosa [sə'məʊsə] *(pl* **inv** *or* **samosas) N** samosa *m (petit pâté indien à la viande ou aux légumes)*

samovar ['sæmə,vɑː(r)] **N** samovar *m*

sampan ['sæmpæn] **N** sampan *m*, sampang *m*

sample ['sɑːmpəl] **N 1** *(gen) & Com* échantillon *m*; **a free s.** un échantillon gratuit; **a representative s. of the population** un échantillon représentatif de la population; **please bring a s. of your work** veuillez apporter un échantillon de votre travail **2** *Geol, Med & (science)* échantillon *m*, prélèvement *m*; *(of blood)* prélèvement *m*; *(of urine)* échantillon *m*; **water/rock samples** prélèvements *mpl* d'eau/de roche; **to take a s.** prélever un échantillon, faire un prélèvement; **to take a blood s.** faire une prise de sang **3** *Mus* sample *m*; **he uses a lot of samples** il utilise beaucoup de samples

COMP a s. bottle/pack un échantillon; **a s. question from last year's exam paper** un exemple de question tiré de l'examen de l'année dernière

VT 1 *(food, drink)* goûter (à), déguster; *(experience)* goûter à **2** *Mus* échantillonner **3** *(public opinion)* sonder

VI *Mus* échantillonner

►► *Com* ***sample book*** catalogue *m* d'échantillons, livre *m* d'échantillons; *Mktg* ***sample survey*** enquête *f* par sondage

sampler ['sɑːmplə(r)] **N 1** *Sewing* modèle *m* de broderie **2** *Mus* échantillonneur *m* **3** *(person)* échantillonneur(euse) *m,f*

sampling ['sɑːmplɪŋ] **N 1** *(gen) & Com* échantillonnage *m* **2** *Mus* sampling *m*

►► ***sampling error*** erreur *f* d'échantillonnage

samurai ['sæmʊraɪ] *(pl* **inv***)* **N** samouraï *m*, samourai *m inv*

►► *Fin* ***samurai bond*** obligation *f* samouraï

San Andreas Fault [ˌsænæn'dreɪəs-] **N the S.** la faille de San Andreas

sanatorium [ˌsænə'tɔːrɪəm] *(pl* **sanatoriums** *or* **sanatoria** [-rɪə]), *Am* **sanitarium** [ˌsænɪ'teərɪəm] *(pl* **sanitariums** *or* **sanitaria** [-rɪə]) **N** *(for TB patients)* sanatorium *m*; *(for convalescents)* maison *f* de santé; *(sick bay)* infirmerie *f*

sancta ['sæŋktə] *pl of* **sanctum**

sanctification [ˌsæŋktɪfɪ'keɪʃən] **N** sanctification *f*

sanctified ['sæŋktɪfaɪd] **ADJ** sanctifié

sanctify ['sæŋktɪfaɪ] *(pt & pp* **sanctified***)* **VT** sanctifier

sanctimonious [ˌsæŋktɪ'məʊnɪəs] **ADJ** moralisateur; **I hate his s. manner** je ne supporte pas ses airs de petit saint

sanctimoniously [ˌsæŋktɪ'məʊnɪəslɪ] **ADV** *(look)* d'un air de petit saint; *(speak)* d'un ton bigot *ou* moralisateur

sanction ['sæŋkʃən] **N 1** *(approval)* sanction *f*, accord *m*, consentement *m*; **with the s. of the government** avec l'accord du gouvernement; **it hasn't yet been given official s.** ceci n'a pas encore été officiellement approuvé *ou* sanctionné, ceci n'a pas encore eu l'approbation *ou* la sanction officielle **2** *(punitive measure)* sanction *f*; **to impose (economic) sanctions on a country** prendre des sanctions (économiques) à l'encontre d'un pays

VT *(authorize)* sanctionner, entériner; *(approve* ► *behaviour)* approuver; **to s. a plan** donner son accord *ou* son aval à un plan

►► ***sanctions busting*** violation *f* des sanctions

sanctity ['sæŋktɪtɪ] **N** *(of person, life)* sainteté *f*; *(of marriage, property, place* ► *holiness)* caractère *m* sacré; *(*► *inviolability)* inviolabilité *f*

sanctuary ['sæŋktʃʊərɪ] *(pl* **sanctuaries***)* **N 1** *(holy place)* sanctuaire *m* **2** *(refuge)* refuge *m*, asile *m*; **to seek s.** chercher asile *ou* refuge; **to take s.** trouver asile **3** *(for animals)* réserve *f*

sanctum ['sæŋktəm] *(pl* **sanctums** *or* **sancta** [-tə]) **N 1** *(holy place)* sanctuaire *m* **2** *Hum (private place)* refuge *m*, retraite *f*, tanière *f*; **he's in his inner s.** il s'est retiré dans sa tanière

sand [sænd] **N 1** *(gen)* sable *m*; **miles of golden sands** des kilomètres *mpl* de sable doré; **shifting s.** sables *mpl* mouvants; **the sands of time** le temps qui passe; **the sands of time are running out for us** nous n'aurons bientôt plus le temps; *Fig* **to build on s.** bâtir sur le sable; *Fig* **to draw a line in the s.** fixer une limite à ne pas dépasser **2** *Am Fam (courage)* cran *m*

VT 1 *(with sandpaper)* poncer au papier de verre **2** *(spread sand on)* sabler

►► *Zool* ***sand dollar*** clypéastéroïde *m*; ***sand dune*** dune *f*; *Zool* ***sand eel*** lançon *m*, équille *f*; *Zool* ***sand flea*** *(sandhopper)* puce *f* de mer, talitre *m*; *(chigoe)* chique *f*; *Entom* ***sand fly*** phlébotome *m*, mouche *f* des sables; *Zool* ***sand lizard*** lézard *m* agile; *Am* ***sand lot*** terrain *m* vague; *Br Orn* ***sand martin*** hirondelle *f* de rivage; *Ich* ***sand tiger shark*** requin-taureau *m*; *Am Golf* ***sand trap*** bunker *m* (de sable); ***sand yacht*** char *m* à voile

► **sand down VT SEP** *(wood, metal)* poncer au papier de verre, décaper

sandal ['sændəl] **N 1** *(footwear)* sandale *f* **2** = **sandalwood**

sandalwood ['sændəlwʊd] **N** bois *m* de santal

►► ***sandalwood oil*** essence *f* de bois de santal

sandbag ['sændbæg] *(pt & pp* **sandbagged,** *cont* **sandbagging***)* **N** sac *m* de sable *ou* de terre

VT 1 *(shore up)* renforcer avec des sacs de sable; *(protect)* protéger avec des sacs de sable **2** *Fam (hit)* assommer[□] *(d'un coup de gourdin sur la nuque)* **3** *Am Fam (coerce)* **to s. sb into doing sth** forcer qn à faire qch[□]

sandbank ['sændbæŋk] **N** banc *m* de sable

sandblast ['sændblɑːst] **VT** décaper à la sableuse, sabler

N jet *m* de sable

sandblasting ['sændblɑːstɪŋ] **N** décapage *m* à la sableuse, sablage *m*

sandboy ['sændbɔɪ] **N** *see* **happy**

sander ['sændə(r)] **N** *(tool)* ponceuse *f*

sandglass ['sændglɑːs] **N** sablier *m*

Sandhurst ['sændhɜːst] **N** = centre de formation militaire britannique établi à Sandhurst, dans le Berkshire

sanding ['sændɪŋ] **N 1** *(of wood, plaster)* ponçage *m* **2** *(of roads)* sablage *m*

S&L [ˌesə'nel] **N** *Am (abbr* **savings and loan association***)* ≃ société *f* de crédit immobilier

sandman ['sændmæn] *(pl* **sandmen** [-men]) **N** *Fig* marchand *m* de sable; **the s. is coming** le marchand de sable va passer

sandpail ['sændpeɪl] **N** *Am* seau *m (pour faire des châteaux de sable)*

sandpaper ['sændpeɪpə(r)] **N** papier *m* de verre

VT poncer (au papier de verre)

sandpiper ['sændpaɪpə(r)] **N** *Orn* bécasseau *m*, chevalier *m*

sandpit ['sændpɪt] **N** *Br* **1** *(for children)* bac *m* à sable **2** *(quarry)* sablière *f*, sablonnière *f*

sandshoe ['sændʃuː] **N** *Br* tennis *m ou f* en toile

sandstone ['sændstəʊn] **N** grès *m*; **red/grey s.** grès *m* rouge/gris

sandstorm ['sændstɔːm] **N** tempête *f* de sable

sandwich ['sænwɪdʒ] **N 1** *(bread)* sandwich *m*; **a ham s.** un sandwich au jambon; *Br Fam Hum* **to be one s. short of a picnic** ne pas être net **2** *Br (cake)* gâteau *m* fourré

VT 1 *Fam (place)* intercaler[□]; **I'll try to s. you (in) between appointments** j'essaierai de vous caser entre deux rendez-vous **2** *Fam (trap)* prendre en sandwich, coincer; **I was sandwiched (in) between two people** j'étais coincé *ou* pris en sandwich entre deux personnes **3** *(join* ► *gen)* joindre; *(*► *with glue)* coller; **we sandwiched the boards together with glue** nous avons collé les planches

►► *Br* ***sandwich bar*** ≃ snack *m (où on vend des sandwichs)*; ***sandwich board*** panneau *m* publicitaire *(porté par un homme-sandwich)*; *Br* ***sandwich cake*** gâteau *m* fourré; *Br* ***sandwich course*** = stage de formation professionnelle en alternance; ***sandwich generation*** génération *f* sandwich; ***sandwich loaf*** ≃ pain *m* de mie; ***sandwich man*** homme-sandwich *m*; ***sandwich toaster*** appareil *m* à croque-monsieur

sandy ['sændɪ] *(compar* **sandier,** *superl* **sandiest***)* **ADJ 1** *(beach, desert)* de sable; *(soil, road)* sablonneux; *(water, alluvium)* sableux; *(floor, clothes)* couvert de sable **2** *(in colour)* (couleur) sable *(inv)*; **s. bottom** *(of sea, river)* fond de sable; **he has s.** *or* **s.-coloured hair** il a les cheveux blond roux

sane [seɪn] **ADJ 1** *(person)* sain d'esprit; **how do you manage to stay s. in this environment?** comment fais-tu pour ne pas devenir fou dans une ambiance pareille? **2** *(action)* sensé; *(attitude, approach, policy)* raisonnable, sensé

sanely ['seɪnlɪ] **ADV** raisonnablement

sang [sæŋ] *pt of* **sing**

sangfroid [ˌsɒŋ'frwɑː] **N** sang-froid *m inv*

sanguinary ['sæŋgwɪnərɪ] **ADJ** *Literary (mu derer, tyrant)* sanguinaire; *(battle)* sanglant

sanguine ['sæŋgwɪn] **ADJ 1** *(optimistic* ► *perso temperament)* optimiste, confiant; *(*► *attitud prospect)* **he was s. about the company's prospec** il voyait l'avenir de l'entreprise avec optimism **2** *Literary (ruddy* ► *complexion)* sanguin, rub cond

> Note that the French adjective **sanguin** is false friend and is almost never a translatio for the English adjective **sanguine**.

sanguinely ['sæŋgwɪnlɪ] **ADV** avec optimism *ou* confiance

sanitarium [ˌsænɪ'teərɪəm] *(pl* **sanitariums sanitaria** [-rɪə]) *Am* = **sanatorium**

sanitary ['sænɪtərɪ] **ADJ 1** *(hygienic)* hygiéniqu **the kitchen didn't look very s.** la cuisine n'ava pas l'air très propre **2** *(conditions, measure equipment)* sanitaire; **s. arrangements/faciliti** dispositions *fpl*/installations *fpl* sanitaires

►► ***sanitary engineer*** technicien(enne) *m,f* c service sanitaire; ***sanitary inspector*** inspecte (trice) *m,f* de la santé publique; *Am* ***sanitary na kin***, *Br* ***sanitary towel*** serviette *f* hygiénique

sanitation [ˌsænɪ'teɪʃən] **N** *(public health)* h giène *f* publique; *(sewers)* système *m* sanitair *(toilets, showers)* sanitaires *mpl*

►► *Am* ***sanitation department*** service *m* de cc lecte des ordures ménagères; *Am* ***sanitatic worker*** éboueur *m*

sanitize, -ise ['sænɪtaɪz] **VT 1** *(disinfect)* dési fecter; *Fig* **this is the sanitized image he would li to project** c'est l'image aseptisée qu'il voudra présenter **2** *Fig (expurgate* ► *document, nove* expurger; **the original tapes had been sanitize** les bandes originales avaient été expurgées

sanity ['sænɪtɪ] **N 1** *(mental health)* santé *f* me tale; **to lose one's s.** perdre la raison **2** *(reaso ableness)* bon sens *m*, rationalité *f*

sank [sæŋk] *pt of* **sink**

Sanskrit ['sænskrɪt] **ADJ** sanskrit

N sanskrit *m*

Santa ['sæntə] **PR N** *Fam* le père Noël[□]

►► ***Santa Claus*** le père Noël

sap [sæp] *(pt & pp* **sapped,** *cont* **sapping***)* **N 1** *B* sève *f*

2 *Am Fam (fool)* bêta(asse) *m,f*, andouille *f*; *(gu lible person)* nigaud(e) *m,f*, poire *f*

3 *Am Fam (cosh)* matraque[□] *f*, gourdin[□] *m*

4 *Mil (trench)* sape *f*

VT 1 *Fig (strength, courage)* saper, miner; **the f ver has sapped (him of) his strength** la fièvre miné **2** *Am Fam (cosh)* assommer (d'un coup c gourdin)[□]

saphead ['sæphed] **N** *Am Fam* bêta(asse) *m,f*, a douille *f*

sapless ['sæplɪs] **ADJ** *(plant, wood)* sans sèv desséché

sapling ['sæplɪŋ] **N 1** *Bot* jeune arbre *m* **2** *Litera (youth)* jouvenceau *m*

sapper ['sæpə(r)] **N** *Br Mil (engineer)* soldat *m* d génie; *(who makes saps)* sapeur *m*

Sapphic ['sæfɪk] **ADJ 1** *(relating to Sappho)* s phique **2** *Old-fashioned (lesbian)* saphique

sapphire ['sæfaɪə(r)] **N** *(gem, colour)* saphir *m*

COMP *(ring, pendant)* de saphir

ADJ *(in colour)* (bleu) saphir *(inv)*

►► ***sapphire blue*** (bleu *m*) saphir

sappiness ['sæpɪnɪs] **N** *(of tree etc)* abondance de sève, teneur *f* en sève

sappy ['sæpɪ] *(compar* **sappier,** *superl* **sappies ADJ 1** *(tree, leaves)* plein de sève; *(wood)* vert *Am Fam (corny)* nunuche

saraband(e) ['særəbænd] **N** *Mus* sarabande *f*

Saracen ['særəsən] **N** Sarrasin(e) *m,f*

ADJ sarrasin

Saran wrap® [sə'ræn-] **N** *Am* film *m* alimentai transparent

sarcasm ['sɑːkæzəm] **N** sarcasme *m*

sarcastic [sɑː'kæstɪk] **ADJ** sarcastique

arcastically [sɑːˈkæstɪkəlɪ] ADV d'un ton sar-castique

arcoma [sɑːˈkəʊmə] (*pl* **sarcomas** *or* **sarcomata** [-mətə]) N *Med* sarcome *m*

arcophagus [sɑːˈkɒfəgəs] (*pl* **sarcophaguses** *or* **sarcophagi** [-gaɪ]) N sarcophage *m*

ardine [sɑːˈdiːn] N sardine *f*; **we were packed in like sardines** nous étions serrés comme des sar-dines

▸ **sardines** N *Br (game)* = jeu de cache-cache dans lequel une seule personne se cache, cha-cun des autres participants devant la chercher et se cacher avec elle quand ils la trouvent

ardinia [sɑːˈdɪnɪə] N Sardaigne *f*

ardinian [sɑːˈdɪnɪən] N **1** *(person)* Sarde *mf* **2** *Ling* sarde *m*

ADJ sarde

ardonic [sɑːˈdɒnɪk] ADJ sardonique

ardonically [sɑːˈdɒnɪkəlɪ] ADV sardonique-ment

arge [sɑːdʒ] N *Fam (abbr* **sergeant***)* sergent□ *m*

ari [ˈsɑːrɪ] N sari *m*

ark [sɑːk] N Sercq

arky [ˈsɑːkɪ] (*compar* **sarkier**, *superl* **sarkiest**) ADJ *Br Fam* sarcastique□

arnie [ˈsɑːnɪ] N *Br Fam (abbr* **sandwich***)* sand-wich□ *m*, casse-dalle *m inv*

arong [səˈrɒŋ] N sarong *m*

ARS [sɑːz] N *Med (abbr* **severe acute respiratory syndrome***)* SRAS *m*

arsaparilla [ˌsɑːspəˈrɪlə] N *(plant)* salsepa-reille *f*; *(drink)* boisson *f* à la salsepareille

artorial [sɑːˈtɔːrɪəl] ADJ vestimentaire; **his s. ele-gance** son élégance vestimentaire, l'élégance *f* de sa mise

AS [ˌeseɪˈes] N *Br Mil (abbr* **Special Air Service***)* = commando d'intervention spéciale de l'armée britannique

ASE [ˌeseɪˌesˈiː] N *Am (abbr* **self-addressed stamped envelope***)* enveloppe *f* timbrée *(portant l'adresse à laquelle elle doit être renvoyée)*

ash [sæʃ] N **1** *(belt)* ceinture *f* (en étoffe); *(sign of office)* écharpe *f* **2** *(frame of window)* châssis *m* à guillotine

▸▸ ***sash window*** fenêtre *f* à guillotine

ashay [ˈsæʃeɪ] VI **1** *(walk indolently)* marcher d'un pas nonchalant; *(walk with swaying motion)* marcher en se déhanchant **2** *Am Fam* **I'll just s. down to Joe's place** *(go)* je vais juste faire un tour chez Joe

ashimi [ˈsæʃɪmɪ] N *Culin* sashimi *m*

ask *(written abbr* **Saskatchewan***)* Saskatchewan *m*

asquatch [ˈsæskwætʃ] N = animal légendaire (sorte de yéti) du Canada et du nord des États-Unis

ass [sæs] *Am Fam* N culot *m*, toupet *m*

VT répondre (avec impertinence) à□; **don't you s. me!** ne me réponds pas sur ce ton!□

assenach [ˈsæsənæk] N *Scot Fam Pej* = terme péjoratif par lequel les Écossais désignent les Anglais

assy [ˈsæsɪ] (*compar* **sassier**, *superl* **sassiest**) ADJ *Fam* **1** *(lively)* plein de pêche; **she looks s. in that dress** elle en jette dans cette robe **2** *Am (cheeky)* culotté, gonflé

at. *(written abbr* **Saturday***)* sam

at [sæt] *pt & pp of* **sit**

N *(abbr* **satellite***)* satellite *m*

▸▸ *Fam* ***sat nav*** *(concept)* navigation *f* GPS□; *(de-vice)* GPS *m*

atan [ˈseɪtən] PR N Satan; *Hum* **get thee behind me, S.!** n'essaie pas de me tenter!

atanic [səˈtænɪk] ADJ satanique

atanically [səˈtænɪkəlɪ] ADV sataniquement, d'une manière satanique

atanism [ˈseɪtənɪzəm] N satanisme *m*

atanist [ˈseɪtənɪst] ADJ sataniste

N sataniste *mf*

atay [ˈsæteɪ] N *Culin* satay *m*

▸▸ ***satay sauce*** sauce *f* satay

atchel [ˈsætʃəl] N cartable *m*

sate [seɪt] VT *(satisfy ▸ person)* rassasier; *(▸ hun-ger)* assouvir; *(▸ thirst)* étancher

sateen [sæˈtiːn] N satinette *f*

satellite [ˈsætəlaɪt] N **1** *Astron & Tel* satellite *m*; **(tele)communications s.** satellite *m* de télécom-munications; **meteorological** *or* **weather s.** satel-lite *m* météorologique; **broadcast live by s.** transmis en direct par satellite **2** *(country)* pays *m* satellite; **the country is a s. of the United States** c'est un pays satellite des États-Unis **3** *(in air-port)* satellite *m*

COMP **1** *(broadcast, broadcasting, network, relay)* par satellite; **ten s. channels** dix chaînes *fpl* (de télévision) par satellite **2** *(country, nation)* satel-lite

▸▸ ***satellite dish*** antenne *f* parabolique; ***satellite link*** liaison *f* par satellite; ***satellite navigation*** na-vigation *f* GPS; ***satellite picture*** photo *f* satellite; ***satellite television*** télévision *f* par satellite

satiate [ˈseɪʃɪeɪt] VT *Literary* **1** *(satisfy ▸ hunger, desire)* assouvir; *(▸ thirst)* étancher **2** *(gorge)* ras-sasier

satiated [ˈseɪʃɪeɪtɪd] ADJ *Formal (with food)* ras-sasié; *(with pleasure)* comblé

satiation [ˌseɪʃɪˈeɪʃən] N satiété *f*; **to the point of s.** à satiété, jusqu'à satiété

satiety [səˈtaɪətɪ] N satiété *f*

satin [ˈsætɪn] N satin *m*

COMP *(dress, shirt, sheets)* en *ou* de satin

▸▸ ***satin finish*** *(of paper etc)* apprêt *m* satiné; **to have a s. finish** être satiné

satinet, satinette [ˌsætɪˈnet] N satinette *f*

satire [ˈsætaɪə(r)] N satire *f*; **it's a s. on the English** c'est une satire contre les Anglais; **her novels are full of s.** ses romans sont pleins d'observations satiriques

satirical [səˈtɪrɪkəl] ADJ satirique

satirically [səˈtɪrɪkəlɪ] ADV satiriquement

satirist [ˈsætərɪst] N *(writer)* satiriste *mf*; *(comed-ian)* chansonnier(ère) *m,f*, comédien(enne) *m,f* satirique

satirize, -ise [ˈsætəraɪz] VT faire la satire de; **in her book, she satirizes English manners** son livre est une satire *ou* fait la satire des mœurs anglai-ses

satisfaction [ˌsætɪsˈfækʃən] N **1** *(fulfilment ▸ of curiosity, hunger, demand, conditions)* satisfac-tion *f*; *(▸ of contract)* exécution *f*, réalisation *f*; *(▸ of debt)* acquittement *m*, remboursement *m*; **the s. of the union's demands** la satisfaction des revendications syndicales

2 *(pleasure)* satisfaction *f*, contentement *m*; **to have the s. of doing sth** avoir la satisfaction de faire qch; **is everything to your s.?** est-ce que tout est à votre convenance?; **the plan was agreed to everyone's s.** le projet fut accepté à la satisfac-tion générale; **I don't get much job s.** je ne tire pas beaucoup de satisfaction de mon travail; *Com* **s. guaranteed** satisfaction *f* garantie

3 *(pleasing thing)* satisfaction *f*

4 *(redress ▸ of a wrong)* réparation *f*; *(▸ of dam-age)* dédommagement *m*; *(▸ of an insult)* répara-tion *f*; **to demand s.** *(gen)* exiger réparation; *(in a duel)* demander satisfaction

satisfactorily [ˌsætɪsˈfæktərəlɪ] ADV de façon sa-tisfaisante; **the trip went off most s.** le voyage s'est déroulé de manière tout à fait satisfaisante

satisfactory [ˌsætɪsˈfæktərɪ] ADJ satisfaisant; **their progress is only s.** leurs progrès sont satis-faisants, sans plus; **I hope she has a s. excuse** j'es-père qu'elle a une excuse valable; **the patient's condition is s.** l'état du malade est satisfaisant

> Attention: ne pas confondre avec **satisfying.**

satisfied [ˈsætɪsfaɪd] ADJ **1** *(happy)* satisfait, con-tent; **a s. sigh** un soupir de satisfaction; **the tea-cher isn't s. with their work** le professeur n'est pas satisfait de leur travail; **are you s. now you've made her cry?** tu es content de l'avoir fait pleu-rer?; **they'll have to be s. with what they've got** ils devront se contenter de ce qu'ils ont; *Ironic* **not s. with that she then broke the other chair** comme ça ne lui suffisait pas, elle a cassé l'autre chaise **2** *(convinced)* convaincu, persuadé; **I'm not en-tirely s. with the truth of his story** je ne suis pas tout à fait convaincu que son histoire soit vraie

satisfy [ˈsætɪsfaɪ] (*pt & pp* **satisfied**) VT **1** *(please)* satisfaire, contenter; **nothing satisfies him** il n'est jamais content; *Sch* **to s. the examiners** *(of exam-inee)* être reçu à l'examen **2** *(fulfil ▸ curiosity, de-sire, hunger)* satisfaire; *(▸ thirst)* étancher; *(▸ demand, need, requirements)* satisfaire à, répon-dre à; *(▸ conditions, terms of contract)* remplir; *(▸ debt)* s'acquitter de **3** *(prove to ▸ gen)* persuader, convaincre; **I am satisfied that he was telling the truth** je suis convaincu *ou* persuadé *ou* sûr qu'il disait la vérité; **you have to s. the authorities that you have been resident here for three years** vous devez prouver aux autorités que vous résidez ici depuis trois ans; **I satisfied myself that all the windows were closed** je me suis assuré que tou-tes les fenêtres étaient fermées

VI donner satisfaction

satisfying [ˈsætɪsfaɪɪŋ] ADJ *(job, outcome, eve-ning)* satisfaisant; *(meal)* substantiel

> Attention: ne pas confondre avec **satisfac-tory.**

satsuma [ˌsætˈsuːmə] N *Br* mandarine *f*

saturate [ˈsætʃəreɪt] VT **1** *Fig (swamp)* saturer; **to s. sb with sth** saturer qn de qch; **the market is sa-turated** le marché est saturé **2** *(drench)* tremper **3** *Chem* saturer

saturated [ˈsætʃəreɪtɪd] ADJ **1** *Chem* saturé **2** *(very wet ▸ person, cloth)* trempé; *(▸ ground)* dé-trempé **3** *(colour)* saturé

▸▸ ***saturated fats*** graisses *fpl* saturées

saturation [ˌsætʃəˈreɪʃən] N saturation *f*

▸▸ ***saturation bombing*** bombardement *m* inten-sif; *Mktg* ***saturation campaign*** campagne *f* inten-sive, campagne *f* de saturation; *TV* ***saturation coverage*** couverture *f* maximum; *also Fig* ***satura-tion point*** point *m* de saturation; **we've reached s. point** nous sommes arrivés à saturation; **the market is at** *or* **has reached s. point** le marché est saturé

Saturday [ˈsætədɪ] N samedi *m*; *see also* **Friday**

▸▸ *Am Fam* ***Saturday night special*** *(gun)* flingue *m* *(bon marché et de qualité médiocre, que l'on peut se procurer facilement)*

Saturn [ˈsætən] PR N *Myth* Saturne

N *Astron* Saturne *f*

saturnalia [ˌsætəˈneɪlɪə] N saturnales *fpl*

saturnine [ˈsætənaɪn] ADJ *Literary* saturnien

saturnism [ˈsætənɪzəm] N *Med* saturnisme *m*, in-toxication *f* par le plomb

satyr [ˈsætə(r)] N satyre *m*

sauce [sɔːs] N **1** *Culin (with savoury dishes)* sauce *f*; *(with desserts)* coulis *m*; **tomato s.** sauce *f* to-mate; **raspberry s.** coulis *m* de framboises; **choco-late s.** sauce *f* au chocolat; *Prov* **what's s. for the goose is s. for the gander** = ce qui vaut pour l'un vaut aussi pour les autres **2** *Br Fam Old-fashioned (insolence)* culot *m*, toupet *m*; **that's enough of your s.!** arrête de faire l'insolent!□ **3** *Fam (alco-hol)* alcool□ *m*, bibine *f*; **to hit the s.** se mettre à picoler; **to be off the s.** être au régime sec

▸▸ ***sauce boat*** saucière *f*

sauced [sɔːst] ADJ *Fam (drunk)* beurré, bourré, pété

saucepan [ˈsɔːspən] N casserole *f*

saucer [ˈsɔːsə(r)] N soucoupe *f*, sous-tasse *f*

saucily [ˈsɔːsɪlɪ] ADV *Fam* **1** *(cheekily)* avec effron-terie□ **2** *(suggestively)* d'un air coquin□

sauciness [ˈsɔːsɪnɪs] N *Fam* **1** *(cheekiness)* effron-terie□ *f* **2** *(suggestiveness ▸ of joke, clothes)* côté *m* coquin□

saucy [ˈsɔːsɪ] (*compar* **saucier**, *superl* **sauciest**) ADJ *Fam* **1** *(cheeky, pert)* effronté□; **a s. little hat** un pe-tit chapeau aguichant□ **2** *(suggestive ▸ postcard, joke, clothes)* coquin□

Saudi [ˈsaʊdɪ] ADJ saoudien

N *Fam* **1** *(person)* Saoudien(enne)□ *m,f* **2** *(coun-try)* Arabie *f* Saoudite□

▸▸ ***Saudi Arabia*** Arabie *f* Saoudite; ***Saudi Arabian*** N Saoudien(enne) *m,f* ADJ saoudien

sauerkraut [ˈsaʊəkraʊt] N choucroute *f*

sauna [ˈsɔːnə] N sauna *m*

saunter [ˈsɔːntə(r)] VI se promener d'un pas nonchalant, flâner; **to s. in/out/across** entrer/ sortir/traverser d'un pas nonchalant; **I think I'll**

s. down to the library je pense que je vais aller faire un petit tour jusqu'à la bibliothèque; **she sauntered in, half an hour late** elle est arrivée tranquillement, avec une demi-heure de retard

N petit tour *m*; **to go for a s.** (aller) faire un petit tour

saurian ['sɔːrɪən] **ADJ** saurien

N saurien *m*

sausage ['sɒsɪdʒ] **N 1** *(food)* saucisse *f*; *(of pre-cooked meats)* saucisson *m*; **pork sausages** saucisses *fpl* de porc; *Br Fam* **not a s.!** que dalle!, des clous!; *Br Fam* **you silly s.!** espèce de nouille! **2** *Br Fam Hum (penis)* chipolata *f*

►► *Br Fam* ***sausage dog*** saucisse *f* à pattes, teckel[□] *m*; ***sausage machine*** machine *f* à saucisses; ***sausage meat*** chair *f* à saucisse; ***sausage roll*** = sorte de friand à la saucisse

sauté [*Br* 'səʊteɪ, *Am* səʊ'teɪ] *(pt & pp* **sautéed,** *cont* **sautéing) VT** faire sauter; **s. the potatoes in a little butter** faire sauter les pommes de terre dans un peu de beurre

N sauté *m*

►► ***sauté potatoes*** pommes *fpl* de terre sautées

sautéed ['səʊteɪd] **ADJ** sauté

savage ['sævɪdʒ] **ADJ 1** *(ferocious ► person)* féroce, brutal; *(► dog)* méchant; *(► fighting, tiger)* féroce; *(► reply, attack)* violent, féroce; **he came in for some s. criticism from the press** il a été violemment critiqué dans la presse **2** *(primitive ► tribe)* primitif; *(► customs)* barbare, primitif

N sauvage *mf*; **they behaved like savages** ils se sont comportés comme des sauvages

VT 1 *(of animal)* attaquer; **she was savaged by a tiger** elle a été attaquée par un tigre **2** *(of critics, press)* éreinter, attaquer violemment; **the opposition leader savaged the government's latest proposals** le chef de l'opposition a violemment attaqué les dernières propositions du gouvernement

savagely ['sævɪdʒlɪ] **ADV** sauvagement, brutalement

savanna, savannah [sə'vænə] **N** savane *f*

SAVE [seɪv]

N	
• arrêt **1**	• sauvegarde **2**
VT	
• sauver **1, 7**	• économiser **2, 3**
• épargner **2, 4**	• mettre de côté **2**
• faire des économies de **3**	• éviter **4**
	• arrêter **6**
• sauvegarder **8**	
VI	
• économiser **1**	• faire des économies **1, 2**
• épargner **2**	
• sauvegarder **3**	
PREP	
• sauf	

N 1 *Ftbl* arrêt *m*; **great s.!** superbe arrêt!

2 *Comput* sauvegarde *f*; **s. command** commande *f* de sauvegarde

VT 1 *(rescue)* sauver; **she saved my life** elle m'a sauvé la vie; **to s. sb from a fire/from drowning** sauver qn d'un incendie/de la noyade; **he saved me from making a terrible mistake** il m'a empêché de faire une erreur monstrueuse; **to s. a species from extinction** sauver une espèce en voie de disparition; **saved by the bell!** sauvé par le gong!; *Fam* **to s. one's neck** *or* **skin** *or* **hide** *or* **bacon** sauver sa peau; *Fam* **I couldn't climb up there to s. my life** je serais incapable de grimper là-haut[□]; *Fam* **he can't sing/play tennis to s. his life** il chante/joue au tennis comme un pied; **to s. face** sauver la face; **to s. the day** sauver la mise

2 *(put by, keep ► money)* économiser, épargner, mettre de côté; *(► food, papers, old jars etc)* garder, mettre de côté; *(collect ► stamps, cards)* collectionner; **how much money have you got saved?** combien d'argent avez-vous mis de côté?; **I'm saving money to buy a car** je fais des économies pour acheter une voiture; **I'll s. you a place** je te garderai une place; **I always s. the best part till last** je garde toujours le meilleur pour la fin; **to s. oneself for sth** se réserver pour qch; **s. a dance for me** réserve-moi une danse; **do you still s. stamps?** est-ce que tu collectionnes toujours les timbres?

3 *(economize on ► fuel, electricity)* économiser, faire des économies de; *(► money)* économiser; *(► time, space)* gagner; *(► strength)* ménager, économiser; **buy now and s. £15!** achetez dès maintenant et économisez 15 livres!; **their advice saved me a fortune** leurs conseils m'ont fait économiser une fortune; **a computer would s. you a lot of time** un ordinateur vous ferait gagner beaucoup de temps; **I might as well have saved my breath** j'aurais mieux fait d'économiser ma salive

4 *(spare ► trouble, effort)* éviter, épargner; *(► expense)* éviter; **it'll s. you getting up early/going into town** ça t'évitera de te lever tôt/d'aller en ville; **this has saved him a great deal of expense/trouble** cela lui a évité *ou* épargné beaucoup de dépense/peine

5 *(protect ► eyes, shoes)* ménager; **God s. the King/the Queen!** vive le Roi/la Reine!

6 *Ftbl (shot, penalty)* arrêter; **to s. a goal** arrêter *ou* bloquer un tir

7 *Rel (sinner, mankind)* sauver, délivrer; *(soul)* sauver

8 *Comput (document)* sauvegarder, enregistrer; **to s. sth to the hard disk** sauvegarder qch sur le disque dur; **s. as...** enregistrer sous...

VI 1 *(spend less)* faire des économies, économiser; **you s. if you buy in bulk** on fait des économies en achetant en gros; **to s. on fuel** faire des économies de carburant

2 *(put money aside)* faire des économies, épargner; **I'm saving for a new car** je fais des économies pour acheter une nouvelle voiture

3 *Comput* sauvegarder, enregistrer

PREP *Formal* sauf, hormis; **we'd thought of every possibility s. one** nous avions pensé à tout sauf à une chose

• **save for PREP** à part; **s. for the fact that we lost, it was a great match** à part le fait qu'on a perdu, c'était un très bon match; **she was utterly alone, s. for one good friend** à part une seule amie, elle n'avait personne

► **save up VT SEP** *(put by, keep ► money)* économiser, épargner, mettre de côté; *(► food, papers, old jars etc)* garder, mettre de côté; *(collect ► stamps, cards)* collectionner; **I'm saving up money to buy a car** je fais des économies pour acheter une voiture

VI faire des économies, épargner; **I'm saving up for a new car** je fais des économies pour acheter une nouvelle voiture

save-as-you-earn N *Br Fin*

►► ***save-as-you-earn scheme*** = plan d'épargne à contributions mensuelles produisant des intérêts exonérés d'impôts

saveloy ['sævəlɔɪ] **N** cervelas *m*

saver ['seɪvə(r)] **N** *(person)* épargnant(e) *m,f*; **small savers** les petits épargnants

saving ['seɪvɪŋ] **N 1** *(thrift)* épargne *f*; **measures to encourage s.** des mesures pour encourager l'épargne **2** *(money saved)* économie *f*; **savings** économies *fpl*; *Econ* dépôts *mpl* d'épargne; **to make a s.** faire une économie; **we made a s. of £20 on the usual price** nous avons fait une économie de 20 livres sur le prix habituel **3** *(rescue ► of lives etc)* sauvetage *m*; *(► of person, souls)* salut *m*; **this was the s. of him** cela a été son salut

PREP *Formal* sauf, hormis; *Formal* **s. Your Grace** sauf le respect que je dois à Votre Excellence

►► ***savings account*** compte *m* (de caisse) d'épargne; ***savings bank*** caisse *f* d'épargne; *Am* ***savings bond*** bon *m* d'épargne; *Br* ***savings book*** livret *m* (de caisse) d'épargne; *Br* ***savings certificate*** bon *m* d'épargne; ***saving grace*** = bon côté qui rachète des défauts; **her sense of humour is her s. grace** on lui pardonne tout parce qu'elle a de l'humour; **the movie has one s. grace** une seule chose sauve le film; *Am* ***savings and loan association*** caisse *f* d'épargne logement; ***savings plan*** plan *m* d'épargne; *Br* ***savings stamp*** timbre-épargne *m*

saviour, *Am* **savior** ['seɪvjə(r)] **N** sauveur *m*; *Rel* **the S.** le Sauveur

savor, savory[1] *Am* = **savour, savoury**

savory[2] ['seɪvərɪ] **N** *Bot* sarriette *f*

savour, *Am* **savor** ['seɪvə(r)] **N 1** *(taste)* goût *m*, saveur *f*; **it has a s. of garlic** il y a un petit goût d'ail **2** *(interest, charm)* saveur *f*; **life had lost its s. fo**[r] **him** il avait perdu toute joie de vivre

VT *(taste)* goûter (à), déguster; *(enjoy ► food, ex*[perience]*, one's freedom)* savourer; **he savoure**[d] **the memory of his triumph** il savourait le souven[ir] de son triomphe

VI to s. of sth sentir qch; **it savours of heresy** cel[a] sent l'hérésie

savoury, *Am* **savory** ['seɪvərɪ] (*Br pl* **savourie**[s], *Am pl* **savories**) **ADJ 1** *(salty)* salé; *(spicy)* épicé; **s. biscuits** biscuits *mpl* salés **2** *(appetizing)* savou[reux], appétissant; **a s. meal** un repas savoureu[x] **3** *Formal (wholesome)* **it's not a very s. subject** c'es[t] un sujet peu ragoûtant; **he's not a very s. indiv**[i]**dual** c'est un individu peu recommandable; **on**[e] **of the less s. aspects of the affair** l'un des aspec[ts] les moins reluisants de l'affaire

N = petit plat salé servi soit comme hor[s] d'œuvre, soit en fin de repas après le dessert

Savoy [sə'vɔɪ] **N** *Geog* Savoie *f*; **in S.** en Savoie

ADJ savoyard

►► *Culin* ***savoy cabbage*** chou *m* frisé de Milan

savvy ['sævɪ] *Fam (compar* **savvier,** *superl* **savv**[iest]) **N** *(know-how)* savoir-faire[□] *m inv*; *(shrewd*[ness]) jugeote *f*, perspicacité[□] *f*; **to have n**[o] **technical/computer s.** être nul pour tout ce qu[i] est technique/en informatique

VI *Old-fashioned* **no s.** j'sais pas

ADJ *(well-informed)* calé, bien informé[□]; *(shrewd)* perspicace[□], astucieux[□]; **to be compu**[ter] **s.** être calé en informatique

saw [sɔː] *(Br pt* **sawed,** *pp* **sawed** *or* **sawn** [sɔːn], *Am pt & pp* **sawed)** *pt of* **see**

N 1 *(tool)* scie *f*; **to cut sth up with a s.** couper o[u] débiter qch à la scie; **metal s.** scie *f* à métaux *(saying)* dicton *m*

VT scier; **to s. a tree into logs** débiter un arbre e[n] rondins; **he sawed the table in half** il a scié l[a] table en deux; *Fig* **his arms sawed the air** il batta[it] l'air de ses bras; *Am Fam Hum* **to s. wood** *(snore* ronfler[□]

VI scier; **she sawed through the branch** elle a sci[é] la branche; *Fig* **he was sawing away at the cello** i[l] raclait le violoncelle

► **saw off VT SEP** scier, enlever à la scie

► **saw up VT SEP** scier en morceaux, débiter à l[a] scie

sawbones ['sɔːbəʊnz] *(pl inv or* **sawboneses)** *Fam* chirurgien[□] *m*

sawbuck ['sɔːbʌk] **N** *Am* **1** = **sawhorse 2** *($ 10* (billet *m* de) dix dollars *mpl*

sawdust ['sɔːdʌst] **N** sciure *f* (de bois)

sawfish ['sɔːfɪʃ] *(pl inv or* **sawfishes) N** *Ich* pois[son]-scie *m*

sawhorse ['sɔːhɔːs, *pl* -hɔːsɪz] **N** chevalet *m (pou*[r] *scier du bois)*, chèvre *f*

sawing ['sɔːɪŋ] **N** *(of wood)* sciage *m*; **s. up** débi[tage] *m*

sawmill ['sɔːmɪl] **N** scierie *f*

sawn [sɔːn] *Br pp of* **saw**

sawn-off ADJ *(truncated)* scié, coupé (à la scie

►► ***sawn-off shotgun*** carabine *f* à canon scié

sawyer ['sɔːjə(r)] **N** scieur *m*

sax [sæks] **N** *Fam (abbr* **saxophone)** saxo *m*

saxifrage ['sæksɪfreɪdʒ] **N** saxifrage *f*

Saxon ['sæksən] **N 1** *(person)* Saxon(onne) *m,f* *Ling* saxon *m*

ADJ saxon

Saxony ['sæksənɪ] **N** la Saxe

saxophone ['sæksəfəʊn] **N** saxophone *m*

saxophonist [*Br* sæk'sɒfənɪst, *Am* 'sæksəfəʊnɪs[t]] **N** saxophoniste *mf*

SAY [seɪ]

VT	
• dire **1–6**	• penser **5**
• indiquer **7**	• marquer **7, 8**
• exprimer **8**	
VI	
• dire	

(pt & pp **said** [sed], *3rd pers sing* **says** [sez])

VT 1 *(put into words)* dire; **to s. sth (to sb)** dire qc[h] (à qn); **to s. hello/goodbye to sb** dire bonjour/a[u] revoir à qn; **s. hello to them for me** dites-leur bon[jour]

jour de ma part; *Fig* **I think you can s. goodbye to your money** je crois que vous pouvez dire adieu à votre argent; **as I said yesterday/in my letter** comme je l'ai dit hier/dans ma lettre; **to s. yes/no** dire oui/non; **I wouldn't s. no!** je ne dis pas non!, ce n'est pas de refus!; **I wouldn't s. no to a cold drink** je prendrais volontiers *ou* bien une boisson fraîche; **to s. a prayer (for)** dire une prière (pour); **to s. one's prayers** faire sa prière; **I can't s. Russian names properly** je n'arrive pas à bien prononcer les noms russes; **I said to myself "let's wait a bit"** je me suis dit "attendons un peu"; **what did he s. about his plans?** qu'a-t-il dit de ses projets?; **have you said anything about it to him?** est-ce que vous lui en avez parlé?; **don't s. too much about our visit** ne parlez pas trop de notre visite; **the less said the better** moins nous parlerons, mieux cela vaudra; **what did you s.?** *(repeat what you said)* pardon?, qu'avez-vous dit?; *(in reply)* qu'avez-vous répondu?; **I have nothing to s.** *(gen)* je n'ai rien à dire; *(no comment)* je n'ai aucune déclaration à faire; **I have nothing more to s. on the matter** je n'ai rien à ajouter là-dessus; **nothing was said about going to Moscow** on n'a pas parlé d'aller *ou* il n'a pas été question d'aller à Moscou; **let's s. no more about it** n'en parlons plus; **can you s. that again?** pouvez-vous répéter ce que vous venez de dire?; **you can s. that again!** c'est le cas de le dire!, je ne vous le fais pas dire!; *Tel* **who shall I s. is calling?** c'est de la part de qui?; **s. what you mean** dites ce que vous avez à dire; **he didn't have a good word to s. about the plan** il n'a dit que du mal du projet; **he doesn't have a good word to s. about anybody** il n'a jamais rien de positif à dire sur personne; **what have you got to s. for yourself?** eh bien, expliquez-vous!; **he didn't have much to s. for himself** *(spoke little)* il n'avait pas grand-chose à dire; *(no excuses)* il n'avait pas de véritable excuse à donner; **he certainly has a lot to s. for himself** il n'a pas la langue dans la poche; **as you might s.** pour ainsi dire; **so saying, he walked out** sur ces mots, il est parti; **to s. nothing of the overheads…** sans parler des frais…; *Br* **just s. the word, you only have to s. (the word)** vous n'avez qu'un mot à dire; **having said that** ceci (étant) dit; **to s. one's piece** dire ce qu'on a à dire; **it goes without saying that we shall travel together** il va sans dire *ou* il va de soi que nous voyagerons ensemble; *Fam* **you said it!** tu l'as dit!, comme tu dis!; *Fam* **don't s. you've forgotten!** ne me dis pas que tu as oublié!; **s. no more** n'en dis pas plus; **enough said** *(I understand)* je vois; **well said!** bien dit!; **s. when** dis-moi stop; *Am* **s. what?** quoi?, hein?; **when all's said and done** tout compte fait, au bout du compte

2 *(with direct or indirect speech)* dire; **"not at all," she said** "pas du tout", dit-elle; **she says (that) the water's too cold** elle dit que l'eau est trop froide; **they said on the news that…** on a dit *ou* annoncé aux informations que… *+ indicative*

3 *(claim, allege)* dire; **you know what they s., no smoke without fire** tu sais ce qu'on dit, il n'y a pas de fumée sans feu; **as they s.** comme on dit; **it is said that no one will ever know the real story** on dit que personne ne saura jamais ce qui s'est vraiment passé; **I've heard it said that…** j'ai entendu dire que… *+ indicative*; **these fans are said to be very efficient** ces ventilateurs sont très efficaces, d'après ce qu'on dit; **he is said to be rich, they s. he is rich** on le dit riche, on dit qu'il est riche; **he is said to have emigrated** on dit qu'il a émigré

4 *(expressing personal opinion)* dire; **so he says, that's what he says** c'est ce qu'il dit; **who can s.?** qui sait?; **who can s. when he'll come?** qui sait quand il viendra?; **what can I say?** que voulez-vous que je vous dise?; **(you can) s. what you like, but I'm going** vous pouvez dire ce que vous voulez, moi je m'en vais; **I must s. she's been very helpful** je dois dire *ou* j'avoue qu'elle nous a beaucoup aidés; **well this is a fine time to arrive, I must s.!** en voilà une heure pour arriver!; **I'll s. this for him, he certainly tries hard** je dois reconnaître qu'il fait tout son possible; **you might as well s. we're all mad!** autant dire qu'on est tous fous!; **you don't mean to s. he's 86** vous n'allez pas me dire qu'il a 86 ans; **is he stupid? – I wouldn't s. that** est-ce qu'il est bête? – je n'irais pas jusque-là; **I should s. so** bien sûr que oui, je pense bien; **I should s. not!** bien sûr que non!; **if you s. so** si *ou* puisque tu le dis; **and so s. all of us** et nous sommes tous d'accord *ou* de cet avis; **there's no saying what will happen** impossible de prédire ce qui va arriver; **to s. the least** c'est le moins qu'on puisse dire; **it's rather dangerous, to s. the least** c'est plutôt dangereux, c'est le moins qu'on puisse dire; **I was surprised, not to s. astounded** j'étais surpris, pour ne pas dire stupéfait; **there's something to be said for the idea** l'idée a du bon; **there's not much to be said for the idea** l'idée ne vaut pas grand-chose; **there's a lot to be said for doing sport** il y a beaucoup d'avantages à faire du sport; **there is little to be said for beginning now** on n'a pas intérêt à commencer dès maintenant; **that's not saying much** ça ne veut pas dire grand-chose; **it doesn't s. much for his powers of observation** cela en dit long sur son sens de l'observation; **you're honest, I'll s. that for you** je dirais en votre faveur que vous êtes honnête; **that isn't saying much for him** ce n'est pas à son honneur; **it says a lot for his courage/about his real motives** cela en dit long sur son courage/ses intentions réelles; **the way you dress says something about you as a person** la manière dont les gens s'habillent est révélatrice de leur personnalité

5 *(think)* dire, penser; **what do you s.?** qu'en dites-vous?, qu'en pensez-vous?; **what will people s.?** que vont dire les gens?; **what do you s. we drive over** *or* **to driving over to see them?** que diriez-vous de prendre la voiture et d'aller les voir?; **what would you s. to a picnic?** que diriez-vous d'un pique-nique?, ça vous dit de faire un pique-nique?; **when would you s. would be the best time for us to leave?** quel serait le meilleur moment pour partir, à votre avis?; **to look at them, you wouldn't s. they were a day over 40** à les voir, on ne leur donnerait pas plus de 40 ans

6 *(suppose, assume)* **(let's) s. your plan doesn't work, what then?** admettons *ou* supposons que votre plan ne marche pas, qu'est-ce qui se passe?; **s. he doesn't arrive, who will take his place?** si jamais il n'arrive pas, qui prendra sa place?; **look at, s., Jane Austen or George Eliot…** prends Jane Austen ou George Eliot, par exemple…; **if I had, s., £100,000 to spend** si j'avais, mettons *ou* disons, 100000 livres à dépenser; **come tomorrow, s. after lunch** venez demain, disons *ou* mettons après le déjeuner; **shall we s. Sunday?** disons dimanche, d'accord?

7 *(indicate, register)* indiquer, marquer; **the clock says 10.40** la pendule indique 10 heures 40; **what does your watch s.?** quelle heure est-il à ta montre?; **the sign says 50 km** le panneau indique 50 km; **the gauge says 3.4** la jauge indique *ou* marque 3,4; **it says "shake well"** c'est marqué "bien agiter"; **the instructions s. (to) open it out of doors** dans le mode d'emploi, on dit qu'il faut l'ouvrir dehors; **it says in the newspaper that…** on dit dans le journal que… *+ indicative*; **the Bible says** *or* **it says in the Bible that…** il est écrit dans la Bible que… *+ indicative*

8 *(express ▸ of intonation, eyes)* exprimer, marquer; **his expression said everything** son expression était très éloquente *ou* en disait long; **that look says a lot** ce regard en dit long

9 *(mean)* **that is to s.** c'est-à-dire; **it's short, that's to s. about 20 pages** c'est court, ça fait dans les 20 pages; **that's not to s. I don't like it** cela ne veut pas dire que je ne l'aime pas

VI *(tell)* dire; **he won't s.** il ne veut pas le dire; **I can't s. exactly** je ne sais pas au juste; **it's not for me to s.** *(speak)* ce n'est pas à moi de le dire; *(decide)* ce n'est pas à moi de décider; **I can't s. fairer than that** je ne peux pas mieux dire; **so to s.** pour ainsi dire; **I s.!** *(expressing surprise)* eh bien!; *(expressing indignation)* dites donc!; *(to attract attention)* dites!; *Am* **s.!** dites donc!; **I mean to s.!** tout de même!, quand même!; **I'll s.!** et comment donc!; **you don't s.!** sans blague!, ça alors!

N to have a s. in sth avoir son mot à dire dans qch; **I had no s. in choosing the wallpaper** on ne m'a pas demandé mon avis pour le choix du papier peint; **I have no s. in the matter** je n'ai pas voix au chapitre; **we had little s. in the matter** on ne nous a pas vraiment demandé notre avis; **to have one's s.** dire ce qu'on a à dire; **now you've had your s., let me have mine** maintenant que vous avez dit ce que vous aviez à dire, laissez-moi parler

SAYE [ˌeseɪˌwaɪ'iː] **N** *Br Fin (abbr* **save-as-you-earn***)* = plan d'épargne à contributions mensuelles produisant des intérêts exonérés d'impôts

saying ['seɪɪŋ] **N** dicton *m*, proverbe *m*; **as the s. goes** *(proverb)* comme dit le proverbe; *(as we say)* comme on dit

say-so N *Br* **1** *(authorization)* **I'm not going without her s.** je n'irai pas sans qu'elle m'y autorise *ou* sans son accord; **you may open the box only on my s.** n'ouvrez *ou* vous ne pourrez ouvrir la boîte que lorsque je vous le dirai, n'ouvrez pas la boîte avant que je vous le dise **2** *(assertion)* **I won't believe it just on his s.** je ne le croirai pas parce qu'il l'a dit que j'y crois

S-bend N *Br* double virage *m*, virage *m* en S

SBU [ˌesbiː'juː] **N** *(abbr* **strategic business unit***)* DAS *m*, UAS *f*

SC[1] [ˌes'siː] **N** *Law (abbr* **Supreme Court***)* Cour *f* suprême *(des États-Unis)*

SC[2] *(written abbr* **South Carolina***)* Caroline *f* du Sud

scab [skæb] *(pt & pp* **scabbed**, *cont* **scabbing***)* **N 1** *Med (from cut, blister)* croûte *f*

2 *Bot & Vet* gale *f*

3 *Fam Pej (strikebreaker)* jaune *mf*

4 *Fam (cad)* crapule *f*, sale type *m*

VI 1 *Med* former une croûte **2** *Fam Pej (strikebreaker)* briser une grève▫, refuser de faire grève▫

▸scab over VI former une croûte

scabbard ['skæbəd] **N** *(for sword)* fourreau *m*; *(for dagger, knife)* gaine *f*, étui *m*

scabby ['skæbɪ] *(compar* **scabbier**, *superl* **scabbiest***)* **ADJ 1** *Med (skin)* croûteux, recouvert d'une croûte

2 *Vet (sheep etc)* galeux

3 *Fam Pej (mean ▸ person)* mesquin▫; *(▸ attitude)* moche

4 *Br Fam (shabby)* merdique, craignos *(inv)*; *(dirty)* cradingue, crado *(inv)*

scabies ['skeɪbiːz] **N** *(UNCOUNT) Med* gale *f*

scabious ['skeɪbɪəs] **ADJ** *Med* scabieux

N *Bot* scabieuse *f*

scabrous ['skeɪbrəs] **ADJ** *Literary* **1** *(joke, story)* scabreux, osé; *(subject)* scabreux, risqué **2** *(skin, surface)* rugueux, rêche

scaffold ['skæfəʊld] **N 1** *Constr* échafaudage *m* **2** *(for execution)* échafaud *m*; **to go to the s.** monter à l'échafaud

scaffolding ['skæfəldɪŋ] **N** *(framework)* échafaudage *m*

scag [skæg] **N** *Fam* **1** *Drugs slang (heroin)* héro *f*, blanche *f* **2** *Am (ugly woman)* boudin *m*, cageot *m*

scalawag ['skæləwæg] *Am* = **scallywag**

scald [skɔːld] **VT 1** *(hands, skin)* ébouillanter; **I scalded myself with the milk** je me suis ébouillanté avec le lait; **the hot tea scalded my tongue** le thé bouillant m'a brûlé la langue **2** *Culin (tomatoes)* ébouillanter; *(milk)* porter presque à ébullition; *(pot, container)* échauder, ébouillanter **3** *(sterilize)* stériliser

VI brûler

N brûlure *f (causée par un liquide, de la vapeur)*; **I got a nasty s.** je me suis bien ébouillanté

scalding ['skɔːldɪŋ] **ADJ 1** *(water)* bouillant; *(metal, tea, soup, tears)* brûlant **2** *(sun)* brûlant; *(heat)* suffocant, torride; *(weather)* très chaud, torride **3** *(criticism)* cinglant, acerbe

ADV s. hot *(coffee)* brûlant; *(weather)* torride

scale [skeɪl] **N 1** *(of model, drawing)* échelle *f*; **the sketch was drawn to s.** l'esquisse était à l'échelle; **the map is on a s. of 1 cm to 1 km** l'échelle de la carte est de 1 cm pour 1 km; **the s. of the map is 1 to 50,000** la carte est au 50 millième; **the drawing is out of s.** *or* **is not to s.** le croquis n'est pas à l'échelle

2 *(for measurement, evaluation)* échelle *f*; *(of thermometer)* échelle *f* (graduée), graduation *f*; *(of salaries, taxes)* échelle *f*, barème *m*; *(of values)* échelle *f*; **the social s.** l'échelle *f* sociale; **at the top of the s.** en haut de l'échelle; **to judge sth on a s. of one to ten** noter qch sur dix

3 *(extent)* ampleur *f*, étendue *f*; *(size)* importance *f*; **the sheer s. of the devastation** l'étendue *f* des dégâts; **the sheer s. of the problem/task** l'énormité *f* du problème/de la tâche; **to do sth on a large s.** faire qch sur une grande échelle; **on an industrial s.** à l'échelle industrielle; **economies of s.** économies *fpl* d'échelle

4 *Mus* gamme *f*; **to practise** *or* **to do one's scales** faire ses gammes; **the s. of D major** la gamme de ré majeur

5 *(of fish, reptile)* écaille *f*; *(of epidermis)* squame *f*; *Fig* **the scales fell from her eyes** les écailles lui sont tombées des yeux

6 *(in kettle, pipes)* tartre *m*, (dépôt *m*) calcaire *m*; *(on teeth)* tartre *m*

7 *(of paint, plaster, rust)* écaille *f*, écaillure *f*

8 *(scale pan)* plateau *m* (de balance)

9 *Am (for weighing)* pèse-personne *m*, balance *f*

VT 1 *(climb over ▸ wall, fence)* escalader

2 *(drawing)* dessiner à l'échelle

3 *(test)* graduer, pondérer

4 *(fish, paint)* écailler; *(teeth, pipes)* détartrer

VI *(paint, rust)* s'écailler; *(skin)* peler, se desquamer

• **scales NPL** *(for food)* balance *f*; *(for letters)* pèse-lettre *m*; *(in bathroom etc)* pèse-personne *m*; *(for babies)* pèse-bébé *m*; *(public)* bascule *f*; **a set** *or* **pair of scales** une balance à plateaux; **(a set** *or* **pair of) kitchen scales** une balance de cuisine

▸▸ ***scale drawing*** dessin *m* à l'échelle; ***scale model*** *(of car, plane)* modèle *m* réduit; *(of building, town centre)* maquette *f*

▸**scale down VT SEP 1** *(drawing)* réduire l'échelle de; *Typ (font)* réduire (la taille de) **2** *(figures, demands)* réduire, baisser, diminuer; **production is being scaled down** on a entrepris de réduire la production

▸**scale up VT SEP 1** *(drawing)* augmenter l'échelle de; *Typ (font)* agrandir **2** *(figures, demands)* réviser à la hausse, augmenter; **allowances were scaled up by 10 percent** les allocations ont été augmentées de 10 pour cent

scaling ['skeɪlɪŋ] **N 1** *(removal of incrustation ▸ of teeth)* détartrage *m*; *(▸ of boiler, pipes)* détartrage *m*, désincrustation *f* **2** *(deposit inside pipe, boiler, kettle)* tartre *m*, calcaire *m*; *(process of incrustation)* formation *f* du tartre, entartrage *m*

▸▸ ***scaling down*** réduction *f*, diminution *f*; *(proportionately)* réduction *f* proportionnelle; ***scaling up*** augmentation *f*

scallion ['skælɪən] **N** *Am & Ir (spring onion)* oignon *m* blanc; *Am (leek)* poireau *m*; *Am & Ir (shallot)* échalote *f*

scallop ['skɒləp] **VT 1** *Culin (fish, vegetable)* gratiner **2** *Sewing (edge, hem)* festonner

N 1 *Ich* coquille *f* Saint-Jacques **2** *Austr Culin* = croquette de pommes de terre frite

• **scallops NPL** *Sewing* festons *mpl*

scally ['skælɪ] *(pl* **scallies) N** *N Eng Fam* racaille *f*, lascar *m*

scallywag ['skælɪwæg], *Am* **scalawag** ['skæləwæg] **N 1** *Fam (rascal)* voyou *m*, coquin (e)□ *m,f*; **little s.** *(child)* petit(e) coquin(e) *m,f* **2** *Am Hist* = sudiste favorable à l'émancipation des Noirs (et par conséquent considéré comme un traître par les siens)

scalp [skælp] **N 1** *(top of head)* cuir *m* chevelu **2** *(Indian trophy)* scalp *m* **3** *Fig (trophy)* trophée *m*; *Hunt* trophée *m* de chasse

VT 1 *(person, animal)* scalper; *Hum (of hairdresser)* ratiboiser

2 *Am Fam (tickets)* = acheter pour revendre au noir; **to s. shares** *or* **securities** boursicoter

3 *Fam (cheat)* arnaquer; **to get scalped** se faire avoir *ou* arnaquer

4 *Am Fam (defeat)* battre à plate couture

scalpel ['skælpəl] **N** scalpel *m*

scalper ['skælpə(r)] **N** *Fam* **1** *Am (ticket tout)* revendeur(euse) *m,f* de tickets à la sauvette□ *(pour un concert, un match etc)* **2** *St Exch* spéculateur(trice) *m,f* à la journée□

scaly ['skeɪlɪ] *(compar* **scalier**, *superl* **scaliest) ADJ** *(creature)* écailleux; *(paint)* écaillé; *(skin)* squameux; *(pipe)* entartré

scam [skæm] **N** *Fam* arnaque *f*, escroquerie□ *f*

scammer ['skæmə(r)] **N** *Fam* arnaqueur(euse) *m,f*

scamp [skæmp] **N** *Fam (child)* garnement□ *m*, coquin(e)□ *m,f*; *(rogue)* fripouille *f*

scamper ['skæmpə(r)] **VI 1** *(mice)* trottiner; *(children)* gambader, galoper; **the kids scampered into the house/up the stairs** les gosses sont entrés dans la maison/ont monté l'escalier en courant; **the squirrel scampered up the tree** l'écureuil a grimpé à l'arbre en un clin d'œil **2** *Fam (work quickly)* **I positively scampered through the book** j'ai lu le livre à toute vitesse□

N trottinement *m*

▸**scamper away, scamper off VI** détaler, se sauver

scampi ['skæmpɪ] **N** *(UNCOUNT)* scampi *mpl*

scan [skæn] *(pt & pp* **scanned**, *cont* **scanning) VT 1** *(look carefully at)* scruter, fouiller du regard; *(read carefully)* lire attentivement; **we scanned the horizon** nous avons scruté l'horizon; **the troops scanned the sky for enemy planes** les soldats scrutaient *ou* observaient le ciel à la recherche d'avions ennemis; **I scanned her face for some reaction** j'ai scruté son visage pour y déceler une réaction

2 *(consult quickly ▸ report, notes)* lire en diagonale, parcourir rapidement; *(▸ magazine)* feuilleter; *(▸ screen, image)* balayer; *(▸ tape, memory)* lire; **he scans the local papers for bargains** il parcourt le journal local à la recherche de bonnes affaires

3 *Phys (spectrum)* balayer, parcourir; *(of radar, searchlight)* balayer

4 *Med* examiner au scanner *ou Offic* au scanographe, faire une scanographie de; *(using ultrasound)* faire une échographie à

5 *Electron & TV* balayer

6 *Literature* scander

7 *Comput* passer au scanner *ou* au scanneur

VI *Literature* se scander; **this line doesn't s.** ce vers est faux

N 1 *(look)* regard *m* appuyé; **after a quick s. around the room they left** ils examinèrent rapidement la pièce et s'en allèrent

2 *Med (examination ▸ by tomography)* examen *m* au scanner *ou Offic* au scanographe; *(▸ by ultrasound)* échographie *f*; **to have a s.** se faire faire un examen au scanner *ou Offic* au scanographe; *(ultrasound)* se faire faire une échographie

3 *Literature* scansion *f*

4 *Electron & TV* balayage *m*

5 *Comput* lecture *f* au scanner *ou* au scanneur

scandal ['skændəl] **N 1** *(disgrace)* scandale *m*; **the whole business is an absolute s.!** toute cette affaire est absolument scandaleuse *ou* est un véritable scandale!; **to cause** *or* **to create a s.** provoquer un scandale **2** *(UNCOUNT) (gossip)* ragots *mpl*; *(evil)* médisance *f*, médisances *fpl*, calomnie *f*; **to spread s. about sb** répandre des ragots sur le compte de qn; **this newspaper specializes in s.** c'est un journal à scandale

▸▸ *Press* ***scandal sheet*** journal *m* à scandale

scandalize, -ise ['skændəlaɪz] **VT** scandaliser, choquer; **he was scandalized by what she said** il a été scandalisé par ses propos

scandalmonger ['skændəlmʌŋgə(r)] **N** mauvaise langue *f*, colporteur(euse) *m,f* de ragots

scandalmongering ['skændəlmʌŋgərɪŋ] **N** *(UNCOUNT)* commérage *m*, médisance *f*

scandalous ['skændələs] **ADJ 1** *(conduct)* scandaleux, choquant; *(news, price)* scandaleux; **it's absolutely s.!** c'est un véritable scandale! **2** *(gossip)* calomnieux

scandalously ['skændələslɪ] **ADV 1** *(expensive, rich)* scandaleusement **2** *(behave)* de façon scandaleuse

Scandinavia [ˌskændɪ'neɪvɪə] **N** Scandinavie *f*

Scandinavian [ˌskændɪ'neɪvɪən] **N** *(person)* Scandinave *mf*

ADJ scandinave

scanner ['skænə(r)] **N 1** *Med* scanner *m*, *Offic* scanographe *m*; *(ultrasound)* échographe *m*

2 *Electron* scanner *m*

3 *(for radar)* antenne *f*

4 *Comput* scanner *m*, scanneur *m*

scanning ['skænɪŋ] **N 1** *(in prosody ▸ of verse)* scansion *f*

2 *(close examination)* examen *m* minutieux

3 *Electron & Rad* balayage *m*; *Med* examen *m* au scanner *ou Offic* au scanographe; *(with ultrasound)* échographie *f*; **radar s.** balayage *m* radar

4 *Comput* passage *m* au scanne(u)r, scannérisation *f*

5 *Mktg* veille *f* technologique

▸▸ ***scanning electron microscope*** microscope *m* électronique à balayage

scansion ['skænʃən] **N** *Literature* scansion *f*

scant [skænt] **ADJ** maigre; **to pay s. attention to sb/sth** ne prêter que peu d'attention à qn/qch; **she received s. praise** elle n'a reçu que de maigres louanges; **they showed s. regard for our feelings** ils ne se sont pas beaucoup souciés *ou* ils se sont peu souciés de ce que nous pouvions ressentir

scantily ['skæntɪlɪ] **ADV** *(furnished)* pauvrement, chichement; *(dressed)* légèrement; **s. clad** légèrement vêtue

scantiness ['skæntɪnɪs] **N** *(of meal)* frugalité *f*; *(of crops)* maigreur *f*; *(of knowledge)* insuffisance *f*; *(of dress)* légèreté *f*

scanty ['skæntɪ] *(compar* **scantier**, *superl* **scantiest) ADJ 1** *(small in number, quantity ▸ meal, crops)* maigre, peu abondant; *(▸ information, knowledge)* maigre, limité; *(▸ audience)* clairsemé; *(▸ praise, aid)* limité **2** *(brief ▸ clothing)* léger; **she was wearing only a s. negligee** elle ne portait qu'un négligé qui ne cachait pas grand-chose

scapegoat ['skeɪpgəʊt] **N** bouc *m* émissaire

scapegrace ['skeɪpgreɪs] **N** *Br* voyou *m*, vaurien(enne) *m,f*

scapula ['skæpjʊlə] *(pl* **scapulas** *or* **scapulae** [-liː]) **N** *Anat* omoplate *f*

scapular ['skæpjʊlə(r)] **ADJ** scapulaire

N scapulaire *m*

scar [skɑː(r)] *(pt & pp* **scarred**, *cont* **scarring) N 1** *(from wound, surgery)* cicatrice *f*; *(from deep cut on face)* balafre *f*; **to have acne scars** avoir des traces d'acné **2** *Fig (on land, painted surface, tree)* cicatrice *f*, marque *f*; *(emotional, psychological)* cicatrice *f*; **the mine was like an ugly s. on the landscape** la mine déparait terriblement le paysage; **he carried the (mental) scars for the rest of his life** il en est resté marqué à vie **3** *(rock)* rocher *m* escarpé; *(in river)* écueil *m*

VT 1 *(skin, face)* laisser une cicatrice sur; *(with knife etc)* balafrer; **his hands were badly scarred** il avait de profondes cicatrices sur les mains; **smallpox had scarred his face** il avait le visage grêlé par la variole **2** *Fig* marquer; **the paintwork was badly scarred** la peinture était tout éraflée; **to be scarred for life** *(person ▸ by experience etc)* être marqué à vie; **war-scarred** *(country etc)* dévasté par la guerre

VI *(form scar)* se cicatriser; *(leave scar)* laisser une cicatrice

▸▸ ***scar tissue*** tissu *m* cicatriciel

▸**scar over VI** *(form scar)* former une cicatrice; *(close up)* se cicatriser

scarab ['skærəb] **N 1** *Entom* **s. (beetle)** scarabée *m* **2** *(precious stone)* scarabée *m*

scarce [skeəs] **ADJ** *(rare)* rare; *(infrequent)* peu fréquent; *(in short supply)* peu abondant; **to become s.** se faire rare; **water is becoming s.** l'eau commence à manquer; **rain is s. in this region** il ne pleut pas souvent dans cette région; *Fam* **to make oneself s.** *(run away)* se sauver, décamper; *(get out)* débarrasser le plancher; **can you make yourself s. for half an hour?** peux-tu disparaître pendant une demi-heure?

ADV *Literary* à peine; **I could s. believe my eyes** j'en croyais à peine mes yeux

scarcely ['skeəslɪ] **ADV 1** *(no sooner)* à peine; **we had s. begun** *or* **s. had we begun when the bell rang** nous avions tout juste commencé quand *ou* à peine avions-nous commencé que la cloche a sonné **2** *(barely)* à peine, guère; **we s. saw her** nous l'avons à peine vue, nous ne l'avons guère vue; **he s. spoke to me** c'est tout juste s'il m'a adressé la parole; **she's s. more than a child** elle n'est encore qu'une enfant; **s. anybody** presque personne; **s. anything** presque rien; **I know s. any of those people** je ne connais pratiquement personne parmi ces gens *ou* pratiquement au-

:une de ces personnes; **he has s. any hair left** il ı'a presque plus de cheveux **3** *(indicating diffi- ·ulty)* à peine, tout juste; **I s. know where to begin** e ne sais pas trop par où commencer; **I can s. wait to meet her** j'ai hâte de la rencontrer; **I can ;. believe what you're saying** j'ai du mal à croire :e que vous dites

carcity ['skeəsɪtɪ] *(pl* **scarcities)** **N** *(rarity)* rareté *f*; *'lack)* manque *m*; *(shortage)* manque *m*, pénurie *f*

▸▸ ***scarcity value*** valeur *f* de rareté; **the book has a high s. value** ce livre vaut cher parce qu'il est pratiquement introuvable *ou* parce qu'il n'en existe que très peu d'exemplaires

care [skeə(r)] **VT** effrayer, faire peur à; **you'll s. her** vous allez lui faire peur *ou* l'effrayer; **the high costs scared them off the idea** les coûts élevés eur en ont fait abandonner l'idée; *Fam* **the movie scared me stiff!** le film m'a flanqué une de ces trousses!; *Fam* **to s. the wits** *or* **the living daylights** *or* **the life out of sb** flanquer une peur bleue *ou* une trouille pas possible à qn; *Fam* **he scared the hell** *or Vulg* **the shit out of me** il m'a foutu les etons

VI s'effrayer, prendre peur; **I don't s. easily** je ne suis pas peureux

N 1 *(fright)* peur *f*, frayeur *f*; **to give sb a s.** effrayer qn, faire peur à qn **2** *(alert)* alerte *f*; *(rumour)* bruit *m* alarmiste, rumeur *f*; **health s.** = inquiétudes concernant la santé publique; **the revelations about the contaminated meat have resulted in a food s.** les révélations sur la viande contaminée ont provoqué une vague de panique chez les consommateurs; **a takeover s.** des rumeurs *fpl* concernant une possible OPA; **a bomb/fire s.** une alerte à la bombe/au feu

COMP *(sensational)* alarmiste; *(frightening)* effrayant, qui fait peur

▸▸ ***scare tactics*** manœuvres *fpl* d'intimidation

scare away, scare off **VT SEP** *(bird, customer)* faire fuir

carecrow ['skeəkrəʊ] **N** *(for birds)* épouvantail *m*; *Fig (person* ▸ *thin)* squelette *m*; *(*▸ *badly dressed)* épouvantail *m*

cared ['skeəd] **ADJ** *(frightened)* effrayé; *(nervous)* craintif, peureux; **to be s. (of sth)** avoir peur (de qch); **he was s. to ask** il avait peur de demander; *Fam* **to be s. stiff** *or* **to death** avoir une peur bleue; *Fam* **I was s. out of my wits!** j'étais mort de peur!; **to run like a s. rabbit** courir comme un dératé

caredy cat ['skeədɪ-] **N** *Fam (in children's language)* froussard(e) *m,f*, poule *f* mouillée

caremonger ['skeəmʌŋgə(r)] **N** alarmiste *mf*

caremongering ['skeəmʌŋgərɪŋ] **N** alarmisme *m*

carf [skɑːf] *(pl* **scarfs** *or* **scarves** [skɑːvz]) **N** *(long)* écharpe *f*; *(headscarf, cravat)* foulard *m*

VT *Am Fam (eat)* bouffer, boulotter

carface ['skɑːfeɪs] **PR N** le Balafré

carification [ˌskærɪfɪ'keɪʃən] **N** *Agr & Med* scarification *f*

carify ['skeərɪfaɪ] *(pt & pp* **scarified)** **VT 1** *Agr & Med* scarifier **2** *(frighten)* donner la frousse à

carlatina [ˌskɑːlə'tiːnə] **N** *(UNCOUNT) Med* scarlatine *f*

carlet ['skɑːlət] **ADJ** *(gen)* écarlate; *(face* ▸ *from illness, effort)* cramoisi; *(*▸ *from shame)* écarlate, cramoisi

N écarlate *f*

▸▸ *Med* ***scarlet fever*** *(UNCOUNT)* scarlatine *f*; *Bot* ***scarlet pimpernel*** mouron *m* rouge; *Br Bot* ***scarlet runner*** haricot *m* (à rames); *Hum* ***scarlet woman*** femme *f* de mauvaise vie

carp [skɑːp] **N** *Geog (of hill)* escarpement *m*

carper ['skɑːpə(r)] **VI** *Br Fam* déguerpir□, se barrer, se tirer

CART [skɑːt] **N** *Elec (abbr* **Syndicat des Constructeurs d'Appareils Radiorécepteurs et Téléviseurs)**

▸▸ ***SCART cable*** câble *m* Péritel®; ***SCART plug*** prise *f* Péritel

carves [skɑːvz] *pl of* **scarf**

cary ['skeərɪ] *(compar* **scarier**, *superl* **scariest)** **ADJ** *Fam (frightening* ▸ *place, person)* effrayant□; *(*▸ *story)* qui donne le frisson□

scat [skæt] *(pt & pp* **scatted**, *cont* **scatting)** **VI** *Fam (go away)* se sauver, ficher le camp, se casser; **s.!** allez, ouste!, casse-toi!, dégage!

N *Mus* scat *m*

scathing ['skeɪðɪŋ] **ADJ** *(criticism, remark)* caustique, cinglant; **to give sb a s. look** foudroyer qn du regard; **he can be very s.** il sait se montrer acerbe *ou* cinglant; **the critics were s. about his new movie** les critiques ont été féroces à propos de son dernier film

scathingly ['skeɪðɪŋlɪ] **ADV** *(retort, criticize)* de manière cinglante; **she refers to him s. as "the toad"** elle l'appelle méchamment "le crapaud"

scatological [ˌskætə'lɒdʒɪkəl] **ADJ** scatologique

scatology [skæ'tɒlədʒɪ] **N** scatologie *f*

scatter ['skætə(r)] **VT 1** *(strew)* éparpiller, disperser; **don't s. your toys all over the room** n'éparpille pas tes jouets partout dans la pièce; **papers had been scattered all over the desk** le bureau était jonché *ou* couvert de papiers

2 *(spread)* répandre; *(sprinkle)* saupoudrer; **she scattered crumbs for the birds** elle a jeté des miettes de pain aux oiseaux; **to s. seeds** semer des graines à la volée

3 *(disperse* ▸ *crowd, mob)* disperser; *(*▸ *enemy)* mettre en fuite; *(*▸ *clouds)* dissiper, disperser; **my friends are scattered all over the world** mes amis sont dispersés aux quatre vents *ou* un peu partout dans le monde

4 *Phys (light)* disperser

VI 1 *(people, clouds)* se disperser; **they told us to s.** ils nous ont dit de partir **2** *(beads, papers)* s'éparpiller

N 1 *(of rice, bullets)* pluie *f* **2** *(in statistics)* dispersion *f*

▸▸ ***scatter bomb*** obus *m* à mitraille, shrapnel *m*, shrapnell *m*; ***scatter cushion*** petit coussin *m*; ***scatter rug*** petit tapis *m*, carpette *f*

scatterbrain ['skætəbreɪn] **N** tête *f* de linotte, étourdi(e) *m,f*

scatterbrained ['skætəbreɪnd] **ADJ** écervelé, étourdi

scattered ['skætəd] **ADJ 1** *(strewn)* éparpillé; **papers/toys lying s. all over the floor** des papiers/des jouets éparpillés par terre; **the table was s. with empty cups** il y avait des tasses vides éparpillées sur la table

2 *(sprinkled)* parsemé; **the tablecloth was s. with crumbs** la nappe était parsemée de miettes

3 *(dispersed* ▸ *population)* dispersé, disséminé; *(*▸ *clouds, villages, houses)* épars; *(*▸ *light)* diffus; *(*▸ *fortune)* dissipé; **she tried to collect her s. thoughts** elle essaya de mettre de l'ordre dans ses idées

4 *Am (scatterbrained)* écervelé, étourdi

▸▸ *Cin & TV* ***scattered light*** lumière *f* diffuse; *Met* ***scattered showers*** averses *fpl* éparses

scattering ['skætərɪŋ] **N 1** *(small number)* **a s. of followers** une poignée d'adeptes; **there was a s. of farms** il y avait quelques fermes çà et là **2** *(dispersion)* dispersion *f*

scattiness ['skætɪnɪs] **N** *Br Fam* étourderie□*f*

scatty ['skætɪ] *(compar* **scattier**, *superl* **scattiest)** **ADJ** *Br Fam* étourdi□, écervelé□

scavenge ['skævɪndʒ] **VI 1** *(bird, animal)* **to s. (for food)** chercher sa nourriture **2** *(person)* fouiller; **to s. in the dustbins** fouiller *ou* faire les poubelles

VT 1 *(material, metals)* récupérer; **he managed to s. a meal** il a finalement trouvé quelque chose à se mettre sous la dent **2** *(streets)* nettoyer

scavenger ['skævɪndʒə(r)] **N 1** *Zool (eating flesh)* charognard *m*; *(eating refuse)* animal *m* qui se nourrit d'ordures **2** *(salvager)* ramasseur(euse) *m,f* d'épaves; *(in rubbish)* pilleur(euse) *m,f* de poubelles **3** *Br (street cleaner)* éboueur *m*

▸▸ ***scavenger hunt*** ≃ chasse *f* au trésor

scenario [sɪ'nɑːrɪəʊ] *(pl* **scenarios)** **N** *Cin & Fig* scénario *m*

scene [siːn] **N 1** *Cin & Theat (in film)* scène *f*, séquence *f*; *(in play)* scène *f*; **the murder/love/balcony s.** la scène du meurtre/d'amour/du balcon; **Act IV s. 2** Acte IV scène 2; **to set the s.** planter le décor; **the s. is set** *or* **takes place in Bombay** la scène se passe *ou* l'action se déroule à Bombay; *Fig* **this set the s. for a major confrontation** ceci a jeté les bases d'une vaste confrontation

2 *Theat (scenery)* décor *m*; **scenes painted by...** décors par…; *also Fig* **behind the scenes** dans la coulisse, dans les coulisses

3 *(sphere of activity, milieu)* scène *f*, situation *f*; **the world political s.** la scène politique internationale; **she's a newcomer on** *or* **to the sports s.** c'est une nouvelle venue sur la scène sportive *ou* dans le monde du sport; **the drug s.** le monde de la drogue; **a change of s. will do you good** un changement d'air *ou* de décor vous fera du bien; *Fam* **hip-hop isn't really my s.** le hip-hop, ça n'est pas vraiment mon truc; **the gay s.** le milieu gay

4 *(place, spot)* lieu *m*, lieux *mpl*, endroit *m*; **the s. of the disaster** l'endroit *m* où s'est produit la catastrophe; **the s. of the crime** le lieu du crime; **to arrive** *or* **come on the s.** arriver sur les lieux *ou* sur place; **the police were soon on the s.** la police est rapidement arrivée sur les lieux *ou* sur place; **I was first on the s.** j'étais le premier présent *ou* le premier sur les lieux; *Mil* **s. of operations** théâtre *m* des opérations

5 *(image)* scène *f*, spectacle *m*; *(incident)* scène *f*, incident *m*; *(view)* spectacle *m*, perspective *f*, vue *f*; **scenes of horror/violence** scènes *fpl* d'horreur/de violence; **scenes from** *or* **of village life** scènes *fpl* de la vie villageoise; **there were some nasty scenes at the match** il y a eu des incidents violents lors du match

6 *Art* tableau *m*, scène *f*; **country/city scenes** scènes *fpl* champêtres/de ville

7 *(fuss, row)* scène *f*; **to make a s.** faire une scène; **to have a s. with sb** se disputer avec qn; **he made an awful s. about it** il en a fait toute une histoire

▸▸ *Theat* ***scene change*** changement *m* de décors; *Theat* ***scene designer*** décorateur(trice) *m,f* de théâtre; *Theat* ***scene painter*** décorateur(trice) *m,f* de théâtre

scenery ['siːnərɪ] **N** *(UNCOUNT)* **1** *(natural setting)* paysage *m*; **I was admiring the s.** j'admirais le paysage; **the s. round here is lovely** les paysages sont très beaux par ici; *Fig* **she needs a change of s.** elle a besoin de changer de décor *ou* d'air **2** *Theat* décor *m*, décors *mpl*

sceneshifter ['siːnʃɪftə(r)] **N** *Theat* machiniste *mf*

scenester ['siːnstə(r)] **N** = jeune qui adopte les stéréotypes vestimentaires et comportementaux d'un style donné

scenic ['siːnɪk] **ADJ 1** *(surroundings)* pittoresque; **let's take the s. route** prenons la route touristique; *Fig Hum* prenons le chemin des écoliers; **an area of great s. beauty** une région qui offre de très beaux panoramas **2** *Art & Theat* scénique

▸▸ *Theat* ***scenic cloth*** rideau *m* de fond scénique; *Theat* ***scenic design*** décoration *f* de théâtre, scénographie *f*; *Theat* ***scenic designer*** décorateur (trice) *m,f* de théâtre, scénographe *mf*; ***scenic railway*** *(for tourists)* petit train *m* (touristique); *(in fairground)* montagnes *fpl* russes

scent [sent] **N 1** *(smell)* parfum *m*, odeur *f*; **the s. of new-mown hay** l'odeur *f* du foin fraîchement fauché

2 *Hunt (of animal)* fumet *m*; *(of person)* odeur *f*; *(track)* trace *f*, piste *f*; **the hounds are on the s.** *or* **have picked up the s. of a fox** les chiens sont sur la trace d'un renard *ou* ont dépisté un renard; **they've lost the s.** ils ont perdu la piste; **to put** *or* **to throw sb off the s.** semer qn; **we're on the s. of a major scandal** nous flairons un gros scandale

3 *Br (perfume)* parfum *m*

4 *(sense of smell* ▸ *of dog)* odorat *m*, flair *m*

VT 1 *(smell* ▸ *prey)* flairer; *(detect* ▸ *danger, treachery)* flairer, subodorer; *Fig* **to s. blood** sentir que sa victime est affaiblie **2** *(perfume)* parfumer, embaumer

scented ['sentɪd] **ADJ** *(soap etc)* parfumé

scentless ['sentlɪs] **ADJ** *(odourless* ▸ *substance)* inodore; *(*▸ *flower)* sans parfum

scepter *Am* = **sceptre**

sceptic, *Am* **skeptic** ['skeptɪk] **ADJ** sceptique

N sceptique *mf*

sceptical, *Am* **skeptical** ['skeptɪkəl] **ADJ** sceptique

sceptically, *Am* **skeptically** ['skeptɪkəlɪ] **ADV** avec scepticisme

scepticism, *Am* **skepticism** ['skeptɪsɪzəm] **N** scepticisme *m*

sceptre, *Am* **scepter** ['septə(r)] **N** sceptre *m*

schedule [*Br* 'ʃedju:l, *Am* 'skedʒʊl] **N 1** *(programme)* programme *m*; *(calendar)* programme *m*, calendrier *m*; *(timetable)* programme *m*, emploi *m* du temps; *(for work)* planning *m*; *(plan)* prévisions *fpl*, plan *m*; **I have a busy s.** *(in general)* j'ai un emploi du temps chargé; *(over period)* j'ai un calendrier chargé; **everything went according to s.** tout s'est déroulé comme prévu; **I work to a very tight s.** mon emploi du temps est très chargé; **the work was carried out according to s.** le travail a été effectué selon les prévisions; **we are on s.** *or* **up to s.** nous sommes dans les temps; **our work is ahead of/behind s.** nous sommes en avance/en retard dans notre travail; **the bridge was opened on/ahead of s.** le pont a été ouvert à la date prévue/en avance sur la date prévue; **to draw up a s.** faire un planning; **to fall behind s.** prendre du retard sur les prévisions de travail

2 *(timetable ▸ for transport)* horaire *m*; **the train is on/is running behind s.** le train est à l'heure/a du retard

3 *(list ▸ of prices)* barème *m*; *(▸ of contents)* inventaire *m*; *(▸ of items)* nomenclature *f*; *(▸ of payments)* échéancier *m*

4 *Law (to law, articles of association etc)* annexe *f*, avenant *m*

VT 1 *(plan ▸ event)* prévoir, programmer; *(▸ appointment)* fixer; **the meeting was scheduled for three o'clock/Wednesday** la réunion était prévue pour trois heures/mercredi; **the building is scheduled for demolition** il est prévu que le bâtiment soit démoli; **she wasn't scheduled to arrive until Sunday** elle ne devait pas arriver *ou* il n'était pas prévu qu'elle arrive avant dimanche

2 *(period, work, series)* organiser; **to s. one's time** aménager *ou* organiser son temps; **our whole week is scheduled** notre programme *ou* emploi du temps pour cette semaine est déjà établi

3 *(topic, item)* inscrire; **it's scheduled as a topic for the next meeting** c'est inscrit à l'ordre du jour de la prochaine réunion

4 *Br Admin (monument)* classer

5 *Law (add as appendix)* ajouter en annexe

scheduled [*Br* 'ʃedju:ld, *Am* 'skedʒʊld] **ADJ 1** *(planned)* prévu; **at the s. time** à l'heure prévue; *TV* **we announce a change to our s. programmes** nous annonçons une modification de nos programmes

2 *(regular ▸ flight)* régulier; *(▸ stop, change)* habituel

3 *(official ▸ prices)* tarifé

4 *Br Admin* **the s. territories** la zone sterling

▸▸ *Br Admin* ***scheduled building*** bâtiment *m* classé monument historique

scheduler [*Br* 'ʃedju:lə(r), *Am* 'skedʒu:lər] **N** *Comput (package)* logiciel *m* de planification (de projets)

scheduling [*Br* 'ʃedju:lɪŋ, *Am* 'skedʒu:lɪŋ] **N** *TV & Rad* programmation *f*

schema ['ski:mə] *(pl* **schemata** [-mətə]) **N 1** *(diagram)* schéma *m* **2** *Phil & Psy* schème *m*

schematic [ski'mætɪk] **ADJ** schématique

scheme [ski:m] **N 1** *(plan)* plan *m*, projet *m*; **a s. for helping the homeless** un projet pour aider les sans-abri; **a s. for new investment** un plan *ou* projet pour de nouveaux investissements; **the s. of things** l'ordre *m* des choses; **where does he fit into the s. of things?** quel rôle joue-t-il dans cette affaire?; **where does mankind fit into the great** *or* **cosmic s. of things?** quelle est la place de l'humanité dans l'univers?

2 *(plot)* intrigue *f*, complot *m*; *(unscrupulous)* procédé *m* malhonnête; **their little s. didn't work** leur petit complot a échoué

3 *Br Admin* plan *m*, système *m*; **the firm has a profit-sharing/a pension s.** l'entreprise a un système de participation aux bénéfices/un régime de retraites complémentaires; **government unemployment schemes** plans *mpl* antichômage du gouvernement; **National Savings S.** ≃ Caisse *f* nationale d'épargne

4 *(arrangement)* disposition *f*, schéma *m*

VI intriguer, *Fam* magouiller; **to s. to do sth** projeter de faire qch; **they schemed against the general** ils ont comploté contre le général

VT combiner, manigancer

schemer ['ski:mə(r)] **N** intrigant(e) *m,f*; *(in conspiracy)* conspirateur(trice) *m,f*

scheming ['ski:mɪŋ] **N** *(UNCOUNT)* intrigues *fpl*, machinations *fpl*

ADJ intrigant, conspirateur

Schengen agreement ['ʃeŋən-] **N** *EU* accord *m* de Schengen

scherzo ['skeətsəʊ] *(pl* **scherzos** *or* **scherzi** [-tsi:]) **N** *Mus* scherzo *m*

schilling ['ʃɪlɪŋ] **N** *Formerly* schilling *m*

schism ['sɪzəm, 'skɪzəm] **N** schisme *m*; *Hist* **the Great S.** *(between the Eastern and Western churches)* le schisme d'Orient; *(within the Roman Catholic Church)* le grand schisme d'Occident

schismatic [sɪz'mætɪk, skɪz'mætɪk] **ADJ** schismatique

N schismatique *mf*

schist [ʃɪst] **N** *Geol* schiste *m*

▸▸ ***schist oil*** huile *f* de schiste

schizo ['skɪtsəʊ] *(pl* **schizos)** *Fam (abbr* **schizophrenic) ADJ** schizo; *Fig (mad)* cinglé

N schizo *mf*; *Fig (mad person)* cinglé(e) *m,f*

schizoid ['skɪtsɔɪd] **ADJ** schizoïde

N schizoïde *mf*

schizophrenia [ˌskɪtsə'fri:nɪə] **N** schizophrénie *f*; **to suffer from s.** être atteint de schizophrénie, être schizophrène

schizophrenic [ˌskɪtsə'frenɪk] **ADJ** schizophrène

N schizophrène *mf*

schlemiel, schlemihl [ʃlə'mi:l] **N** *esp Am very Fam* minable *mf*

schlep, schlepp [ʃlep] *(pt & pp* **schlepped,** *cont* **schlepping)** *esp Am Fam* **VT** trimbaler, trimballer; **I've got to s. all this stuff over to the office** il faut que je trimbal(l)e *ou* transbahute tous ces trucs au bureau

VI *(walk)* crapahuter; **I had to s. to the grocery store** il a fallu que je crapahute jusqu'à l'épicerie

N 1 *(person)* crétin(e) *m,f*, lourdaud(e)ᵅ *m,f* **2** *(journey)* trotte *f*; **it's a bit of a s. to the supermarket** ça fait une trotte jusqu'au supermarché

▸**schlep(p) about, schlep(p) around** *esp Am Fam* **VT INSEP to s. around the town** crapahuter en ville

VI crapahuter

schlock [ʃlɒk] *esp Am Fam* **N 1** *(junk)* camelote *f* **2** *(lazy person)* flemmard(e) *m,f*

ADJ *(worthless)* qui ne vaut pas un clou, nul; *(jewellery)* en toc

schlong [ʃlɒŋ] **N** *Am Vulg* queue *f*, bite *f*

schlub [ʃlʌb] **N** *Am Fam* andouille *f*, cruche *f*

schmaltz [ʃmɔ:lts] **N** *Fam* guimauveᵅ *f*

schmaltzy ['ʃmɔ:ltsɪ] *(compar* **schmaltzier,** *superl* **schmaltziest) ADJ** *Fam* à l'eau de roseᵅ, à la guimauveᵅ

schmo [ʃməʊ] *(pl* **schmoes) N** *Am Fam (unlucky person)* guignard(e) *m,f*; *(stupid person)* nul (nulle) *m,f*

schmooze [ʃmu:z] **VI** *Fam (chat)* bavarderᵅ, jaspiner, jacasser; *(at social gathering)* faire des mondanitésᵅ

schmuck [ʃmʌk] **N** *Am Fam* andouille *f*, courge *f*

schnaps, schnapps [ʃnæps] *(pl* **inv) N** schnaps *m*

schnook [ʃnʊk] **N** *Am Fam* poire *f*, pigeon *m*

schnozz [ʃnɒz], **schnozzle** ['ʃnɒzəl] **N** *Fam* pif *m*, tarin *m*, blair *m*

scholar ['skɒlə(r)] **N 1** *(academic)* érudit(e) *m,f*, savant(e) *m,f*; *(specialist)* spécialiste *mf*; *(intellectual)* intellectuel(elle) *m,f*; **an Egyptian s.** un spécialiste de l'Égypte; **Latin s.** latiniste *mf*; **I'm not much of a s.** je ne suis pas très savant **2** *(holder of grant)* boursier(ère) *m,f* **3** *Old-fashioned (pupil)* élève *mf*; **she's a poor/good s.** c'est une mauvaise/bonne élève

scholarly ['skɒləlɪ] **ADJ 1** *(person)* érudit, cultivé

2 *(article, work)* savant

3 *(approach)* rigoureux, scientifique

4 *(circle)* universitaire

scholarship ['skɒləʃɪp] **N 1** *Sch & Univ (grant* bourse *f* (d'études); **to win a s. to Stanford** obteni une bourse pour Stanford *(sur concours)* **2** *(knowledge)* savoir *m*, érudition *f*

▸▸ ***scholarship holder, scholarship student*** bour sier(ère) *m,f*

scholastic [skə'læstɪk] **ADJ 1** *(ability, record, sup plier)* scolaire; *(profession)* d'enseignant **2** *(philo sophy, approach, argument)* scolastique

N scolastique *m*

school [sku:l] **N 1** *(educational establishment* école *f*, établissement *m* scolaire; *(secondar school ▸ to age 15)* collège *m*; *(▸ 15 to 18)* lycée *m*; *(classes)* école *f*, classe *f*, classes *fpl*, cour *mpl*; **to go to s.** aller à l'école/au collège/au ly cée; **to be at** *or* **in s.** être à l'école *ou* en classe **to go back to s.** reprendre l'école; **what are you going to do when you leave s.?** qu'est-ce que t comptes faire quand tu auras quitté l'école *o* fini ta scolarité?; **I was at s. with him** j'étais e classe avec lui, c'était un de mes camarades d classe; **he's still at s.** il va encore à l'école; **there' no s. today** il n'y a pas (d')école *ou* il n'y a pa classe aujourd'hui; **s. starts at nine** *(primar* l'école *ou* la classe commence à neuf heure *(secondary)* les cours commencent à neuf heu res; **s. starts back next week** c'est la rentrée (sco laire *ou* des classes) la semaine prochaine; *Fig* **the s. of life** l'école *f* de la vie; *Fig* **I went to the s. o hard knocks** j'ai été à rude école

2 *(institute)* école *f*, académie *f*

3 *Univ (department)* département *m*, institut *m* *(faculty)* faculté *f*; *(college)* collège *m*; *Am (univer sity)* université *f*; **London S. of Economics** = institu d'études économiques de l'université de Lon dres; **she's at law s.** elle fait des études de droit elle fait son droit

4 *(of art, literature)* école *f*; *Fig* **a doctor of the ol s.** un médecin de la vieille école *ou* de la vieill garde; **the Florentine/classical s.** l'école floren tine/classique

5 *(training session)* stage *m*; **a two-day s. for doc tors** un stage de deux jours pour les médecins

6 *(in Oxford and Cambridge)* **schools** *(examina tion hall)* salle *f* d'examens; *(examinations)* exa mens *mpl* de la licence

7 *Hist* **the Schools** l'École *f*, la scolastique

8 *(of fish, porpoises)* banc *m*

COMP *(trip, doctor)* scolaire; **I'm not allowed t stay up late on s. nights** je n'ai pas le droit de m coucher tard quand il y a école le lendemain; *B* **to do the s. run** emmener les enfants à l'école *(tour de rôle)*

VT 1 *(train ▸ person)* entraîner; *(▸ animal)* dres ser; **to be schooled in monetary/military matter** être rompu aux questions monétaires/militai res; **she schooled herself to listen to what other said** elle a appris à écouter (ce que disent) le autres **2** *(send to school)* envoyer à l'école, scola riser

▸▸ ***school age*** âge *m* scolaire; ***school attendanc*** *(going to school)* scolarisation *f*; ***school boar*** conseil *m* d'établissement; ***school bus*** autobu *m* scolaire; ***school dinners*** repas *mpl* servis à l cantine (de l'école); ***school district*** = aux États Unis, autorité locale décisionnaire dans le do maine de l'enseignement primaire et secon daire; ***school fees*** frais *mpl* de scolarité; ***schoo friend*** camarade *mf* de classe *ou* d'école, *Fam* co pain (copine) *m,f* de classe *ou* d'école; *Br* ***schoo governor*** membre *m* du conseil de gestion d l'école; ***school holiday*** jour *m* de congé scolaire **tomorrow is a s. holiday** il n'y a pas école *o* classe *ou* cours demain; **during the s. holiday** pendant les vacances *ou* congés scolaire ***school hours*** heures *fpl* de classe *ou* d'école; **in s hours** pendant les heures de classe; **out of s hours** en dehors des heures de classe; ***school ma gazine*** journal *m* de l'école; ***school of medicine*** fa culté *f* de médecine; ***school of motoring*** auto école *f*, école *f* de conduite; ***school of musi (gen)*** école *f* de musique; *(superior level)* con servatoire *m*; ***school report*** bulletin *m* scolaire ***school of thought*** école *f* de pensée; *Fig* théori *f*; **one s. of thought argues that this is due to genet ic factors** il existe une théorie selon laquelle ce a une origine génétique; ***school tie*** = cravat propre à une école et faisant partie de l'uni forme; ***school uniform*** uniforme *m* scolaire

:chool year année *f* scolaire; **my s. years** ma sco-arité, mes années *fpl* d'école; **the s. year runs rom September to July** l'année scolaire dure de eptembre à juillet

choolboy ['sku:lbɔɪ] **N** écolier *m*; *(11 to 15)* col-égien *m*; *(15 to 18)* lycéen *m*
▸▸ ***schoolboy error*** erreur *f* stupide; ***schoolboy humour*** humour *m* de potache

choolchild ['sku:ltʃaɪld] *(pl* **schoolchildren** -tʃɪldrən]) **N** écolier(ère) *m,f*

chooldays ['sku:ldeɪz] **NPL** années *fpl* d'école; **n my s.** quand j'étais à l'école

choolfellow ['sku:lfeləʊ] **N** *Old-fashioned* ca-narade *m ou* copain *m* de classe

choolgirl ['sku:lgɜ:l] **N** écolière *f*; *(11 to 15)* col-égienne *f*; *(15 to 18)* lycéenne *f*; **she had the usual . crush on the gym teacher** comme toutes les fil-es de son âge, elle était tombée amoureuse de on prof de gym
▸▸ ***schoolgirl complexion*** teint *m* de jeune fille

choolhouse ['sku:lhaus, *pl* -hauzɪz] **N** école *f* (du village)

chooling ['sku:lɪŋ] **N 1** *(education)* instruction *f*, ducation *f*; *(enrolment at school)* scolarité *f*; **I aven't had much s.** je ne suis pas allé longtemps l'école, je ne suis pas très instruit; **s. is compul-ory** la scolarité est obligatoire **2** *(of horse)* dres-age *m*

choolkid ['sku:lkɪd] **N** *Fam* écolier(ère)□ *m,f*; **e's only a s.** ce n'est qu'un gosse

chool-leaving age [-'li:vɪŋ-] **N** fin *f* de la sco-arité obligatoire; **the s. was raised to 16** l'âge lé-gal de fin de scolarité a été porté à 16 ans

choolma'am, schoolmarm ['sku:lmɑ:m] **N** *'am* **1** *Hum (teacher)* maîtresse *f* d'école□ **2** *Br Pej 'prim woman)* bégueule *f*

choolmarmish ['sku:lmɑ:mɪʃ] **ADJ** *Br Fam Pej* **he's very s.** elle fait très maîtresse d'école□

choolmaster ['sku:lmɑ:stə(r)] **N** *Br (at primary school)* maître *m*, instituteur *m*; *(at secondary chool)* professeur *m*

choolmate ['sku:lmeɪt] **N** camarade *mf* d'école

choolmistress ['sku:lmɪstrɪs] **N** *Br (primary chool)* maîtresse *f*, institutrice *f*; *(secondary chool)* professeur *m*

choolroom ['sku:lrum] **N** (salle *f* de) classe *f*; *in private house)* salle *f* d'étude

choolteacher ['sku:lti:tʃə(r)] **N** *(at any level)* enseignant(e) *m,f*; *(at primary school)* institu-eur(trice) *m,f*; *(at secondary school)* professeur *n*

choolteaching ['sku:lti:tʃɪŋ] **N** enseignement *n*

choolyard ['sku:ljɑ:d] **N** *Am* cour *f* de récréa-ion

chooner ['sku:nə(r)] **N 1** *Naut* schooner *m*, goé-ette *f* **2** *Br & Austr (for sherry, beer)* grand verre *m*; **s. of sherry** un verre de xérès

chtuk [ʃtuk] **N** *Br Fam* **to be in s.** être dans le pé-rin, être dans la panade

chtup [ʃtʌp] *(pt & pp* **schtupped**, *cont* **schtup-ping)** **VT** *Am very Fam* baiser; **he's been schtupping his secretary for years** ça fait des années qu'il baise sa secrétaire

ciatic [saɪ'ætɪk] **ADJ** *Anat* sciatique
▸▸ ***sciatic nerve*** nerf *m* sciatique

ciatica [saɪ'ætɪkə] **N** *(UNCOUNT) Med* sciatique *f*

cience ['saɪəns] **N** *(UNCOUNT)* science *f*; **mod-ern s.** la science moderne; **she studied s.** elle a 'ait des études de science *ou* scientifiques; **I've always been interested in s.** j'ai toujours été inté-ressé par les sciences
COMP *(exam)* de science; *(teacher)* de science, de sciences; *(student)* en sciences; *(lab, subject)* scientifique
▸▸ ***science fiction*** science-fiction *f*; ***science park*** parc *m* scientifique

cientific [,saɪən'tɪfɪk] **ADJ 1** *(research, expedi-tion)* scientifique **2** *(precise, strict)* scientifique, rigoureux

cientifically [,saɪən'tɪfɪkəlɪ] **ADV** scientifique-ment, de manière scientifique; **s. speaking** d'un ou du point de vue scientifique

scientist ['saɪəntɪst] **N** *(worker)* scientifique *mf*; *(academic)* scientifique *mf*, savant(e) *m,f*

scientistic [,saɪən'tɪstɪk] **ADJ** *Pej* prétendument scientifique

Scientologist [,saɪən'tɒlədʒɪst] **N** scientologiste *mf*

Scientology® [,saɪən'tɒlədʒɪ] **N** *Rel* scientologie *f*

sci-fi ['saɪfaɪ] *Fam (abbr* **science fiction)** **N** SF *f*
ADJ de SF

Scillies ['sɪlɪz] = **Scilly Isles**

Scilly Isles ['sɪlɪ-] **NPL the S.** les îles *fpl* Sorlin-gues

scimitar ['sɪmɪtə(r)] **N** cimeterre *m*

scintillate ['sɪntɪleɪt] **VI** *(stars)* scintiller, briller; *Fig (person ▸ in conversation)* briller, être bril-lant; **to s. with wit** briller par son esprit, pétiller d'esprit

scintillating ['sɪntɪleɪtɪŋ] **ADJ** *(conversation, wit)* brillant, pétillant, étincelant; *(person, personal-ity)* brillant

scion ['saɪən] **N 1** *Literary (descendant)* descen-dant(e) *m,f* **2** *Bot* scion *m*

scissor ['sɪzə(r)] **VT** couper avec des ciseaux
• **scissors NPL (a pair of) scissors** (une paire de) ciseaux *mpl*
▸▸ *Orn* ***scissor bill*** bec-en-ciseaux *m*; *Sport* ***scis-sors hold*** ciseau *m*; *Sport* ***scissors jump*** saut *m* en ciseaux, ciseau *m*; *Sport* ***scissors kick*** ciseau *m*

sclerosis [sklə'rəusɪs] **N** *(UNCOUNT) Bot, Med & Fig* sclérose *f*

scoff [skɒf] **VI 1** *(mock)* se moquer, être mépri-sant; **they scoffed at my efforts/ideas** ils se sont moqués de mes efforts/idées; **don't s., I'm serious** ne te moque pas de moi, je parle sérieusement **2** *Fam (eat)* s'empiffrer
VT *Fam (eat)* bouffer, boulotter; **he scoffed the whole packet** il s'est enfilé tout le paquet
N 1 *(expression of mockery)* **we had a good s. at his expense** nous nous sommes bien moqués de lui **2** *Br Fam (food)* bouffe *f*, graille *f*

scoffing ['skɒfɪŋ] **N** moquerie *f*, sarcasme *m*
ADJ railleur, sarcastique

scold [skəʊld] **VT** gronder, réprimander; **we were scolded** *or* **we got scolded for giggling in class** on s'est fait gronder parce qu'on rigolait en classe; **she scolded him for being late** elle l'a grondé à cause de son retard
VI rouspéter
N *Old-fashioned* chipie *f*, mégère *f*

scolding ['skəʊldɪŋ] **N** gronderie *f*, gronderies *fpl*, réprimande *f*, réprimandes *fpl*; **to give sb a s.** gronder qn; **to get a s.** se faire gronder
ADJ *(tone)* de réprimande

scoliosis [,skɒlɪ'əʊsɪs] **N** scoliose *f*

scollop ['skɒləp] = **scallop**

sconce [skɒns] **N 1** *(with handle)* bougeoir *m* **2** *(on wall)* applique *f*

scone [skɒn] **N** scone *m (petit pain rond)*; **cheese s.** scone *m* au fromage

scoop [sku:p] **N 1** *Press* scoop *m*, exclusivité *f*; **to get** *or* **to make a s.** faire un scoop; **the paper got a s. on the story** le journal a publié la nouvelle en exclusivité
2 *(utensil, ladle ▸ for ice-cream, mashed potatoes)* cuillère *f* à boule; *(▸ for flour, grain)* pelle *f*; *(▸ for water)* écope *f*; *(on crane, dredger)* pelle *f*; *(on bulldozer)* lame *f*
3 *(amount scooped ▸ of ice-cream, potatoes)* boule *f*; *(▸ of flour, grain, earth, rocks)* pelletée *f*
4 *Naut (bailer)* épuisette *f*, écope *f*; *(of dredger)* godet *m*
5 *Br Fam (profit)* bénéfice *m* (important)□; **to make a s.** faire un gros bénéfice□
VT 1 *(take, measure, put)* prendre (avec une me-sure); *(serve)* servir (avec une cuillère); **we had to s. the water out of the barrel** nous avons dû vi-der le tonneau avec un récipient; **she scooped the grain out of the bucket** elle a pris le grain dans le seau à l'aide d'une mesure; **he scooped the potatoes onto my plate** il m'a servi des pom-mes de terre **2** *Fin (market)* s'emparer de; *(com-petitor)* devancer; **they scooped a big profit** ils ont ramassé un gros bénéfice; *Fig* **to s. the field** *or* **the pool** tout rafler **3** *Press (story)* publier en exclusivité; *(competitor)* publier avant, devan-cer
▸▸ *Fishing* ***scoop net*** drague *f*

▸ **scoop out VT SEP 1** *(take ▸ with scoop)* prendre (avec une cuillère); *(▸ with hands)* prendre (avec les mains) **2** *(hollow ▸ wood, earth)* creuser; *(empty, remove)* vider; **s. out the flesh from the grapefruit** évidez le pamplemousse

▸ **scoop up VT SEP 1** *(take, pick up ▸ in scoop)* prendre *ou* ramasser à l'aide d'une pelle/d'un récipient; *(▸ in hands)* prendre *ou* ramasser dans les mains; **the gangsters scooped the money up and jumped into the car** les gangsters ont ra-massé l'argent et ont sauté dans la voiture; **the helicopter scooped him up** l'hélicoptère le repê-cha **2** *(gather together)* entasser

scoot [sku:t] *Fam* **VI** se sauver, filer; **the children scooted across the fields/up the stairs** les enfants ont filé à travers champs/ont monté les esca-liers à toute vitesse□; **s.!** fichez le camp!, allez, ouste!
N *Br* **to make a s. for it** prendre ses jambes à son cou

scooter ['sku:tə(r)] **N 1** *(child's)* trottinette *f* **2** *(moped)* **(motor) s.** scooter *m*

scope [skəʊp] **N 1** *(range)* étendue *f*, portée *f*; *(limits)* limites *fpl*; **does the matter fall within the s. of the law?** est-ce que l'affaire tombe sous le coup de la loi?; **it is beyond the s. of this study/of my powers** cela dépasse le cadre de cette étude/ de mes compétences; **the book is too narrow in s.** le livre est d'une portée trop limitée
2 *(size, extent ▸ of change)* étendue *f*; *(▸ of under-taking)* étendue *f*, envergure *f*; **it's a venture of unusual s.** c'est une entreprise d'une envergure exceptionnelle
3 *(opportunity, room)* occasion *f*, possibilité *f*; **the guidelines leave a lot of s. for interpretation** les instructions laissent une grande place à l'in-terprétation; **there's plenty of s. for development/ for improvement** les possibilités de développe-ment/d'amélioration ne manquent pas; **there's little s. for people with your qualifications** il y a peu de possibilités pour des gens avec des qua-lifications telles que les vôtres
4 *Fam (telescope)* télescope□ *m*; *(microscope)* mi-croscope□ *m*; *(periscope)* périscope□ *m*
VT 1 *Med (examine)* examiner par endoscopie **2** *Am Fam (look at)* mater, reluquer; **he's at the beach scoping the babes** il est à la plage en train de mater les nanas; **did you s. that ring he was wearing?** t'as vu un peu la bague qu'il avait au doigt?

scorch [skɔ:tʃ] **VT 1** *(with iron ▸ clothing, linen)* roussir, brûler légèrement; *(with heat ▸ skin)* brûler; *(▸ meat)* brûler, carboniser; *(▸ wood-work)* brûler, marquer **2** *(grass, vegetation ▸ with sun)* roussir, dessécher; *(▸ with fire)* brûler
VI 1 *(linen)* roussir **2** *Br Fam (in car)* filer à toute allure; *(on bike)* pédaler comme un fou (folle) *ou* à fond de train; **we were soon scorching along at over 100 mph** ≃ nous filions bientôt à plus de 160 à l'heure
N *(on linen)* marque *f* de roussi; *(on hand, furni-ture)* brûlure *f*; **there's a s. (mark) on my shirt** ma chemise a été roussie; **the cigarette has left a s. (mark) on the table** la cigarette a fait une marque de brûlure sur la table

scorcher ['skɔ:tʃə(r)] **N** *Fam* **1** *(hot day)* journée *f* de forte chaleur□; **yesterday was a real s.** hier c'était une vraie fournaise **2** *(something exciting, fast etc)* **this film is a s.** ce film est absolument gé-nial; **she's a real s.** c'est une fille superbe□

scorching ['skɔ:tʃɪŋ] **ADJ 1** *(weather, tea, surface)* brûlant; **the sun is s.** il fait un soleil de plomb **2** *(criticism)* cinglant **3** *Fam (speed)* **the car does a s. 120 mph** ≃ la voiture file à 190 à l'heure
ADV s. hot *(water, drink, saucepan etc)* brûlant; *(day)* torride

SCORE [skɔ:(r)]

N	
• score **1**	• points **1, 2**
• note **1**	• avantage **2**
• titre **3**	• partition **4**
• entaille **5**	• rayure **5**
• vingtaine **6**	• compte **8**

VT	
• marquer **1**	• obtenir **1**
• érafler **2**	• noter **4**
VI	
• marquer un point/ but/*etc* **1**	• marquer les points **2**
• avoir du succès **3**	

N 1 *Sport* score *m*; *Cards* points *mpl*; *(in exam, test ▸ mark)* note *f*; *(▸ result)* résultat *m*; **the s. was five–nil** le score était de cinq à zéro; **after 20 minutes there was still no s.** après 20 minutes le score était toujours zéro à zéro; **to keep the s.** *Sport* tenir le score; *Cards & (in games)* compter *ou* marquer les points; *(on scorecard)* tenir la marque; **the final s.** *(gen)* le résultat final; *Sport* le score final; **what's the s.?** *(in game)* quel est le score?; *Fam Fig* qu'est-ce qui se passe?ᵒ; *Fam Fig* **to know the s.** connaître le topo, savoir à quoi s'en tenirᵒ
2 *Fig (advantage ▸ in debate etc)* avantage *m*, points *mpl*; **to make a s. off an opponent** marquer des points sur son adversaire
3 *(reason, motive)* sujet *m*, titre *m*; **don't worry on that s.** ne vous inquiétez pas à ce sujet; **on what s. was I turned down?** à quel titre *ou* sous quel prétexte ai-je été refusé?
4 *Mus* partition *f*; *Cin & Theat* musique *f*; **to follow the s.** suivre (sur) la partition
5 *(notch, deep cut)* entaille *f*; *(scratch)* rayure *f*; *Geol (in rock)* strie *f*
6 *(twenty)* vingtaine *f*; *Arch* **three s. and ten** soixante-dix
7 scores *(many)* beaucoup; **scores of people** beaucoup de gens; **motorbikes by the s.** un nombre incroyable de motos
8 *(debt, account)* compte *m*; *Fig* **to have an old s. to settle with sb** avoir un vieux compte à régler avec qn; **I prefer to forget old scores** je préfère oublier les vieilles histoires
VT 1 *Sport (goal, point, try)* marquer; *(in test, exam ▸ marks)* obtenir; **to s. five goals/50 points for one's team** marquer cinq buts/50 points pour son équipe; **she scored the highest mark** elle a obtenu *ou* eu la note la plus élevée; **to s. a hit** *(with bullet, arrow, bomb)* atteindre la cible; *(in fencing)* toucher; *Fig (of idea etc)* faire un tabac; *(of person)* faire des ravages; *Fig* **to s. a success** remporter un succès; *Fig* **he's always trying to s. points off me** il essaie toujours d'avoir le dessus avec moi
2 *(scratch)* érafler; *(cut a line in ▸ paper)* couper; *(▸ wood)* entailler; *(▸ ground)* tracer une raie sur; *(▸ pastry, meat)* inciser, faire des incisions dans; **she scored her name on the bench** elle grava son nom sur le banc; **water had scored grooves into the rock** l'eau avait creusé des rainures dans le rocher
3 *Mus (symphony, opera)* orchestrer; *Cin & Theat* composer la musique de
4 *Am (grade, mark ▸ test)* noter
5 *Fam Drugs slang (drugs)* acheterᵒ
VI 1 *Sport (team, player)* marquer; **the team didn't s.** l'équipe n'a pas marqué; **to s. high/low** *(in test)* obtenir un bon/mauvais score
2 *(keep the score)* marquer les points; **would you mind scoring for us?** vous voulez bien marquer les points pour nous?
3 *Fam (succeed)* avoir du succèsᵒ, réussirᵒ; **he certainly scores with the girls** il a du succès auprès des filles, c'est sûrᵒ; **this is where the new Renault really scores** c'est là que la nouvelle Renault est vraiment super; **he scores on looks but not much else** il est mignon mais ça s'arrête là
4 *Fam (sexually)* lever quelqu'un, emballer quelqu'un; **did you s.?** tu as réussi à lever une nana/un mec?
5 *Fam Drugs slang (get drugs)* acheter de la came
▸▸ *Ftbl* **score draw** match *m* nul *(où chaque équipe a marqué)*

▸**score off** **VT INSEP** *(win point in argument etc)* prendre l'avantage sur, marquer des points sur
VT SEP *(delete)* rayer, barrer; **s. his name off the list** rayez son nom de la liste

▸**score out, score through** **VT SEP** *Br* biffer, barrer

scoreboard ['skɔːbɔːd] **N** tableau *m* d'affichage *(du score)*

scorecard ['skɔːkɑːd] **N 1** *(for score ▸ in game)* fiche *f* de marques *ou* de score; *(▸ in golf)* carte *f* de parcours; *(▸ at shooting range)* carton *m* **2** *(list of players)* liste *f* des joueurs

scorer ['skɔːrə(r)] **N 1** *Ftbl (regularly)* buteur(euse) *m,f*; *(of goal)* marqueur(euse) *m,f*; **Henry was the s.** c'est Henry qui a marqué le but; **the team's top s.** le meilleur buteur de l'équipe **2** *(scorekeeper)* marqueur(euse) *m,f* **3** *(in test, exam)* **the highest s.** le candidat qui obtient le meilleur score

scoring ['skɔːrɪŋ] **N** *(UNCOUNT)* **1** *(of goals)* marquage *m* d'un but; *(number scored)* buts *mpl* (marqués); **to open the s.** ouvrir la marque
2 *Cards & (in games ▸ scorekeeping)* marquage *m* des points, marque *f*; *(▸ points scored)* points *mpl* marqués
3 *(scratching)* rayures *fpl*, éraflures *fpl*; *(notching)* entaille *f*, entailles *fpl*; *Geol* striage *m*
4 *Mus (orchestration)* orchestration *f*; *(arrangement)* arrangement *m*; *(composition)* écriture *f*

scorn [skɔːn] **N 1** *(contempt)* mépris *m*, dédain *m*; **I feel nothing but s. for them** ils ne m'inspirent que du mépris; **to pour s. on sth** rejeter qch avec mépris **2** *(object of derision)* (objet *m* de) risée *f*; **she was the s. of the whole school** elle était la risée de toute l'école
VT 1 *(be contemptuous of)* mépriser **2** *(reject ▸ advice, warning)* rejeter, refuser d'écouter; *(▸ idea)* rejeter; *(▸ help)* refuser, dédaigner; *Literary* **she scorned to answer** elle n'a pas daigné répondre

scornful ['skɔːnfʊl] **ADJ** dédaigneux, méprisant; **she's rather s. about** *or* **of my ideas** elle manifeste un certain mépris envers mes idées

scornfully ['skɔːnfʊlɪ] **ADV** avec mépris, dédaigneusement; **they looked at us s.** ils nous ont regardés avec dédain *ou* d'un air méprisant; **"of course not," he said s.** "bien sûr que non", dit-il d'un ton méprisant

Scorpio ['skɔːpɪəʊ] **N** *(pl* **Scorpios***)* **1** *Astron* Scorpion *m* **2** *Astrol* Scorpion *m*; **he's a S.** il est (du signe du) Scorpion
ADJ *Astrol* du Scorpion; **he's S.** il est (du signe du) Scorpion

scorpion ['skɔːpɪən] **N** *Entom* scorpion *m*
▸▸ *Ich* **scorpion fish** rascasse *f*, *Spec* scorpène *f*

Scot [skɒt] **N** Écossais(e) *m,f*; **the Scots** les Écossais *mpl*

Scotch [skɒtʃ] **N** *(whisky)* scotch *m*; **a glass of S.** un verre de scotch
NPL *esp Am (people)* **the S.** les Écossais *mpl*
ADJ écossais
▸▸ *Culin* **Scotch broth** = soupe écossaise à base de légumes et d'orge perlée; *Culin* **Scotch egg** = œuf dur entouré de chair à saucisse et enrobé de chapelure; **Scotch mist** bruine *f*; *Culin* **Scotch pancake** = crêpe épaisse, pancake *m*; **Scotch pine** pin *m* sylvestre; *Am* **Scotch tape®** Scotch® *m*; **Scotch terrier** scottish-terrier *m*, Scotch-terrier *m*; **Scotch whisky** scotch *m*, whisky *m* écossais

scotch [skɒtʃ] **VT 1** *(suppress ▸ revolt, strike)* mettre fin à, réprimer, étouffer; *(▸ rumour)* étouffer; **we'll have to s. that idea** il faudra abandonner cette idée **2** *(hamper ▸ plans)* entraver, contrecarrer **3** *(block ▸ wheel)* caler

Scotch-tape® **VT** scotcher

scot-free **ADJ** impuni; **they were let off s.** on les a relâchés sans les punir

Scotland ['skɒtlənd] **N** Écosse *f*
▸▸ *Br* **Scotland Yard** = ancien nom du siège de la police à Londres (aujourd'hui "New Scotland Yard"), ≃ Quai *m* des Orfèvres

Scots [skɒts] **N** anglais *m* d'Écosse
ADJ *(accent, law etc)* écossais
▸▸ **the Scots Guards** la Garde écossaise *(régiment de l'armée britannique)*; **Scots pine** pin *m* sylvestre

Scotsman ['skɒtsmən] *(pl* **Scotsmen** [-mən]*)* **N** Écossais *m*

Scotswoman ['skɒtswʊmən] *(pl* **Scotswomen** [-wɪmɪn]*)* **N** Écossaise *f*

Scott [skɒt] **EXCLAM** *Old-fashioned* **Great S.!** Grand Dieu!

Scotticism ['skɒtɪsɪzəm] **N** expression *f* propre à l'anglais d'Écosse

Scottie ['skɒtɪ] **N** *Fam* **S. (dog)** scottish-terrierᵒ *m*, Scotch-terrierᵒ *m*

Scottish ['skɒtɪʃ] **NPL** **the S.** les Écossais *mpl*
ADJ écossais; *Theat* **the S. play** *('Macbeth')* = e[…]pression utilisée pour éviter de désigner […] pièce de Shakespeare par son nom, le m[…] "Macbeth" étant censé porter malheur
▸▸ *Ling* **Scottish Gaelic** gaélique *m* d'Écosse, ers[…] *m*; *Pol* **the Scottish National Party** = parti ind[…]pendantiste écossais fondé en 1934; **the Scotti[…] Office** = ministère des Affaires écossaises, ba[…] à Édimbourg; **Scottish terrier** scottish-terrier […] Scotch-terrier *m*

SCOTTISH LAW

Le système juridique écossais, inspiré du droit romain, est différent du système anglais. Les lois édictées par le Parlement britannique ne s'appliquent pas toujours en Écosse, même si la plus haute instance judiciaire reste, comme en Angleterre, la Chambre des lords.

THE SCOTTISH PARLIAMENT

Le parlement écossais fut établi dans le cadre du projet de décentralisation du gouvernement travailliste et fut inauguré à Édimbourg en mai 1999. Les 129 membres du parlement écossais ("MSPs") siègent sous la houlette du "First Minister". Le parlement est pourvu d'une grande autonomie en matière de fiscalité mais ses pouvoirs législatifs sont néanmoins limités. Ainsi, il n'est pas habilité à légiférer dans certains domaines qui restent le privilège du parlement de Westminster, tels que la politique extérieure et la défense. Voir aussi l'encadré sur **Devolution**.

scoundrel ['skaʊndrəl] **N** bandit *m*, vaurie[…] (enne) *m,f*; *(child)* vilain(e) *m,f*, coquin(e) *m*[…]; **come here, you little s.!** viens ici, petit coquin […] vaurien!

scour ['skaʊə(r)] **VT 1** *(clean ▸ pan)* récurer; *(*[…] *metal surface)* décaper; *(▸ floor)* lessiver, frotte[…]; *(▸ tank)* vidanger, purger
2 *(scratch)* rayer
3 *(of water, erosion)* creuser
4 *(search ▸ area)* ratisser, fouiller; **the surroun[…]ing countryside was scoured for the missing girl** o[…] a ratissé *ou* fouillé la campagne environnan[…] pour retrouver la jeune fille disparue; **I'[…] scoured the whole library looking for her** j'[…] fouillé toute la bibliothèque pour la trouver
N **give the pans a good s.** récurez bien les cass[…]roles

scourer ['skaʊrə(r)] **N** *(metal)* tampon *m* à réc[…]rer; *(sponge)* éponge *f* à récurer

scourge [skɜːdʒ] **N 1** *(bane)* fléau *m*; **the s. […] war/of disease** le fléau de la guerre/de la mal[…]die; **pollution is the s. of the century** la pollutio[…] est le fléau de ce siècle **2** *(person)* peste *f* **3** *(whi[…])* fouet *m*
VT 1 *(afflict)* ravager **2** *(whip)* fouetter, flagelle[…]

scouring ['skaʊərɪŋ] **N** *(scrubbing ▸ of pan)* réc[…]rage *m*; *(▸ of metal surface)* décapage *m*
• **scourings** **NPL** résidu *m* (de récurage)
▸▸ **scouring pad** *(metal)* tampon *m* à récure[…] *(sponge)* éponge *f* à récurer; **scouring powd[…]** poudre *f* à récurer

Scouse [skaʊs] *Br Fam* **N 1** *(person)* = personn[…] originaire de Liverpool **2** *(dialect)* = dialecte d[…] la région de Liverpool
ADJ de Liverpoolᵒ

Scouser ['skaʊsə(r)] **N** *Br Fam* = personne orig[…]naire de Liverpool

scout [skaʊt] **N 1** *(boy)* scout *m*; *(girl)* scoute *f*; *A[…]* **he's a good s.** c'est un chouette *ou* brave type; **s[…] honour** parole *f* de scout
2 *Mil (searcher)* éclaireur *m*; *(watchman)* sen[…]nelle *f*, guetteur *m*; *(ship)* vedette *f*; *(aircraf[…])* avion *m* de reconnaissance
3 *(for players, models, dancers)* dénicheur(eus[…]) *m,f* de vedettes
4 *(search)* tour *m* de reconnaissance; **to have […] to take a s. around** (aller) reconnaître le terrai[…]; **to have a s. around for sth** chercher qch
5 *Br Aut (patrolman)* dépanneur *m*
6 *Br Univ (servant)* garçon *m* de service *(à O[…]ford)*

COMP *(knife, uniform)* (de) scout, d'éclaireur; **the movement** le mouvement scout, le scoutisme
VT *(area)* explorer; *Mil* reconnaître; **to s. (out) a** **rail** reconnaître une piste
VI partir en reconnaissance
▸▸ ***the Scout Association*** l'association *f* de scoutisme; ***scout camp*** camp *m* scout; *Mil* ***scout car*** scout-car *m*

scout about, scout around VI explorer les ieux; *Mil* partir en reconnaissance; **to s. about for an excuse** chercher un prétexte

couting ['skaʊtɪŋ] N **1** *(movement)* **s., S.** scoutisme *m* **2** *Mil* reconnaissance *f*

coutmaster ['skaʊtmɑːstə(r)] N chef *m* scout

cow [skaʊ] N *Naut* chaland *m*

cowl [skaʊl] N *(angry)* mine *f* renfrognée *ou* hargneuse, air *m* renfrogné; *(threatening)* air *m* menaçant; **"of course not," she said with a s.** "bien sûr que non", dit-elle d'un air renfrogné
VI *(angrily)* se renfrogner, faire la grimace; *(threateningly)* prendre un air menaçant; **to s. at sb** jeter un regard mauvais à qn

cowling ['skaʊlɪŋ] ADJ *(face)* renfrogné, hargneux; **he fell silent, a s. look on his face** il s'est tu, l'air renfrogné

crabble® ['skræbəl] N *(UNCOUNT)* Scrabble® *m*; **do you fancy a game of S.?** tu veux faire un Scrabble®?

crabble ['skræbəl] VI **1** *(search)* **she was scrabbling in the grass for the keys** elle cherchait les clés à tâtons dans l'herbe; **the man was scrabbling for a handhold on the cliff face** l'homme cherchait désespérément une prise sur la paroi de la falaise **2** *(scrape)* gratter **3** *(scuffle)* **to s. with sb for sth** lutter avec qn pour s'emparer de qch
N *(scramble)* **there was a wild s. for the food** les gens se ruèrent sur la nourriture

crag [skræg] *(pt & pp* **scragged**, *cont* **scragging)** N **1** *(person)* personne *f* très maigre; *(horse)* haridelle *f* **2** *Br Culin* collet *m (de mouton ou de veau)*
VT *(wring the neck of)* tordre le cou à
▸▸ *Br Culin* ***scrag end*** collet *m (de mouton ou de veau)*

craggy ['skrægɪ] *(compar* **scraggier**, *superl* **scraggiest)** ADJ **1** *(thin* ▸ *neck, person)* efflanqué, maigre, décharné; *(*▸ *horse, cat)* efflanqué **2** *(jagged)* déchiqueté; *(rock)* rugueux; *(branch)* noueux; *(tree)* rabougri

cram [skræm] *(pt & pp* **scrammed**, *cont* **scramming)** VI *Fam (get out)* ficher le camp, se casser; **s.!** du vent!, file!

cramble ['skræmbəl] VI **1** *(move hurriedly or with difficulty)* **they scrambled for shelter** ils se sont précipités pour se mettre à l'abri; **he scrambled to his feet** il s'est levé précipitamment; **to s. away** s'enfuir à toutes jambes; **to s. down** dégringoler; **to s. up** grimper avec difficulté; **to s. over rocks** escalader des rochers en s'aidant des mains; **the soldiers scrambled up the hill** les soldats ont escaladé la colline tant bien que mal
2 *(scrabble, fight)* **to s. for seats** se bousculer pour trouver une place assise, se ruer sur les places assises; **everyone was scrambling to get to the telephones** tout le monde se ruait vers les téléphones
3 *Aviat & Mil* décoller sur-le-champ
4 *Sport* **to go scrambling** faire du trial
5 *(in rock climbing)* grimper à quatre pattes
VT **1** *Rad & Tel (message)* brouiller; *(encode)* crypter
2 *(jumble)* mélanger
3 *Aviat & Mil (aircraft)* ordonner le décollage immédiat de
4 *Culin (eggs)* brouiller; **I'll s. some eggs** je vais faire des œufs brouillés
N **1** *(rush)* bousculade *f*, ruée *f*; **my glasses were broken in the s. to get out** mes lunettes ont été cassées dans la ruée vers la sortie; **there was a s. for seats** on s'est bousculé pour avoir une place assise, on s'est rué sur les places assises; *(for tickets)* on s'est arraché les places; **there was a s. for the door** tout le monde s'est rué vers la porte
2 *Sport (on motorbikes)* course *f* de trial
3 *Aviat & Mil* décollage *m* d'urgence
4 *(in rock climbing)* escalade *f*
▸▸ ***scrambled egg(s)*** *(food)* œufs *mpl* brouillés; *Fam Mil* = insigne d'officier porté sur la casquette ou l'épaulette

scrambler ['skræmbələ(r)] N *Rad & Tel* brouilleur *m*

scrambling ['skræmbəlɪŋ] N **1** *Br Sport* trial *m* **2** *TV* cryptage *m*

scran [skræn] N *Br Fam (food)* bouffe *f*, graille *f*

scrap [skræp] *(pt & pp* **scrapped**, *cont* **scrapping)** N **1** *(small piece* ▸ *of paper, cloth)* bout *m*; *(*▸ *of bread, cheese)* petit bout *m*; *(*▸ *of conversation)* bribe *f*; *(*▸ *for scrapbook)* image *f*; **he left a few scraps of poetry** il a laissé quelques vers; **scraps of news/of information** des bribes de nouvelles/d'informations; **there isn't a s. of truth in the story** il n'y a absolument rien de vrai dans cette histoire; **it didn't do me a s. of good** *(action)* cela ne m'a servi absolument à rien; *(medicine)* cela ne m'a fait aucun bien; **what I say won't make a s. of difference** ce que je dirai ne changera rien du tout **2** *(metal)* ferraille *f*; **we sold the car for s.** on a vendu la voiture à la ferraille *ou* à la casse **3** *Fam (fight)* bagarre ᵖ *f*, baston *m ou f*; **to get into** *or* **to have a s. with sb** se bagarrer avec qn ᵖ, se castagner avec qn
VT **1** *(discard* ▸ *shoes, furniture)* jeter; *(*▸ *idea, plans)* renoncer à, abandonner; *(*▸ *system)* abandonner, mettre au rancart; *(*▸ *machinery)* mettre au rebut *ou* au rancart; **you can s. the whole idea** vous pouvez laisser tomber *ou* abandonner cette idée **2** *(send for scrap* ▸ *car, ship)* envoyer *ou* mettre à la ferraille *ou* à la casse
VI *Fam (fight)* se bagarrer ᵖ, se castagner
• **scraps** NPL *(food)* restes *mpl*; *(fragments)* débris *mpl*
▸▸ ***scrap dealer*** Ferrailleur *m*; ***scrap iron*** ferraille *f*; *Br* ***scrap merchant*** ferrailleur *m*; ***scrap metal*** ferraille *f*; ***scrap metal dealer*** ferrailleur *m*; ***scrap paper*** (papier *m*) brouillon *m*; ***scrap value*** valeur *f* à la casse

scrapbook ['skræpbʊk] N *(for photos, press cuttings etc)* album *m*

scrape [skreɪp] N **1** *(action)* coup *m* de grattoir *ou* de racloir; *(wound on skin)* éraflure *f*; **just give the saucepan a quick s.** frotte *ou* gratte un peu la casserole; **he had a nasty s. on his knee** il avait une méchante éraflure au genou, il s'était bien éraflé le genou; **she had given the car a nasty s. on the side** elle avait fait une belle éraflure sur le côté de la voiture
2 *Fam (dilemma, trouble)* pétrin *m*; **to get into a s.** se mettre dans le pétrin; **now you've really got yourself into a s.!** vous voilà dans de beaux draps *ou* dans un sacré pétrin!; **you got me into this s., now get me out of it!** c'est vous qui m'avez mis dans ce pétrin, maintenant il faut me tirer de là!
3 *(sound)* grattement *m*, grincement *m*
4 *(thin layer)* mince couche *f*; **toast with a s. of butter** du pain grillé recouvert d'une mince couche de beurre
VT **1** *(clean* ▸ *boots, saucepan)* gratter, racler; *(*▸ *tools)* gratter, décaper; *(*▸ *vegetables, windows)* gratter; **s. the mud off your shoes** enlève *ou* gratte la boue de tes chaussures; **I spent the afternoon scraping the paint off the door** j'ai passé l'après-midi à gratter la peinture de la porte; **to s. sth clean/smooth** gratter qch pour qu'il soit propre/lisse; *Fig* **to s. (the bottom of) the barrel** *(looking for money)* racler les fonds de tiroir; *(be reduced to extremes)* être tombé bien bas; **you took him on? you must really be scraping the bottom of the barrel!** tu as embauché ce type-là? tu devais vraiment être coincé!
2 *(scratch* ▸ *paint, table, wood)* rayer; *(*▸ *skin, knee)* érafler; *(touch lightly)* effleurer, frôler; **I scraped my knee** je me suis éraflé le genou; **I just scraped the garage door as I drove in** j'ai effleuré la porte du garage en rentrant la voiture; **to s. the bottom** *(ship)* sillonner *ou* talonner le fond
3 *(drag)* traîner; **don't s. the chair across the floor like that** ne traîne pas la chaise par terre comme ça
4 *(achieve with difficulty)* **to s. a living** arriver tout juste à survivre, vivoter; **to s. a pass** *(in exam)* réussir de justesse
VI **1** *(rub)* frotter; *(rasp)* gratter; **the branches s. against the shutters** les branches frottent contre les volets; **the gardener scraped at the ground with a stick** le jardinier grattait la terre avec un bâton; **I heard the noise of his pen scraping across the paper** j'entendais le grattement de son stylo sur le papier
2 *(manage with difficulty)* **to s. home** *(win game, race)* gagner de justesse; **the ambulance just scraped past** l'ambulance est passée de justesse
3 *(economize)* faire des petites économies
4 *(be humble)* faire des courbettes *ou* des ronds de jambes

▸ **scrape along** VI *(financially)* se débrouiller, vivre tant bien que mal; **she had to s. along on a small pension** elle devait se débrouiller avec une petite retraite; **we'll s. along somehow** on va se débrouiller avec ce qu'on a

▸ **scrape by** VI *(financially)* se débrouiller; **I have just enough to s. by (on)** j'ai juste assez d'argent pour vivre

▸ **scrape in** VI *(in election)* être élu de justesse; *(in entering university)* entrer de justesse; *Sport (in qualifying)* se qualifier de justesse; **I just scraped in as the doors were closing** j'ai réussi à entrer juste au moment où les portes se fermaient

▸ **scrape off** VT SEP *(mud, paint)* enlever au grattoir *ou* en grattant; *(skin)* érafler; *Hum* **we had to s. him off the ground** il a fallu le ramasser à la petite cuillère

▸ **scrape out** VT SEP **1** *(saucepan)* récurer, racler; *(residue)* enlever en grattant *ou* raclant; **to s. out a mixing bowl** *(with spatula)* racler un bol avec une spatule; *(with finger)* racler un bol avec le doigt **2** *(hollow)* creuser

▸ **scrape through** VT INSEP *(exam)* réussir de justesse; *(doorway, gap)* passer (de justesse); **the government will probably just s. through the next election** le gouvernement va probablement l'emporter de justesse aux prochaines élections
VI *(in exam)* réussir de justesse; *(in election)* être élu *ou* l'emporter de justesse; *(through gap)* passer de justesse; *(financially)* se débrouiller tout juste

▸ **scrape together** VT SEP **1** *(two objects)* frotter l'un contre l'autre **2** *(into pile)* mettre en tas **3** *(collect* ▸ *supporters, signatures, money)* rassembler à grand-peine

▸ **scrape up** VT SEP **1** *(into pile* ▸ *leaves, stones)* mettre en tas **2** *(collect* ▸ *supporters, signatures, money)* rassembler à grand-peine

scraper ['skreɪpə(r)] N grattoir *m*; *(for muddy shoes)* décrottoir *m*

scrapheap ['skræphiːp] N **1** décharge *f*; **to throw sth on the s.** mettre qch à la ferraille *ou* au rebut **2** *Fig* rebut *m*; **to be thrown on** *or* **consigned to the s.** être mis au rebut; **he ended up on the s.** on l'a mis au rebut

scrapie ['skreɪpɪ] N *Vet* maladie *f* tremblante des moutons, tremblante *f*

scraping ['skreɪpɪŋ] ADJ *(sound)* de grattement
N **1** *(sound)* grattement *m*; **I could hear the sound of s.** j'ai entendu un grattement; **the s. of chalk on the blackboard** le crissement *ou* le grincement de la craie sur le tableau **2** *(thin layer)* mince couche *f*; **toast with a s. of butter** du pain grillé recouvert d'une mince couche de beurre
• **scrapings** NPL *(food)* déchets *mpl*, restes *mpl*; *(from paint, wood)* raclures *fpl*; **give the scrapings to the dogs** donnez les restes aux chiens

scrapman ['skræpmən] *(pl* **scrapmen** [-men]) N ferrailleur *m*, casseur *m*

scrappy ['skræpɪ] *(compar* **scrappier**, *superl* **scrappiest)** ADJ **1** *(disconnected* ▸ *speech, film, novel)* décousu; *(*▸ *work, performance)* inégal; **it was a rather s. second half** la deuxième mi-temps a été assez inégale **2** *Am Fam (quarrelsome)* bagarreur, chamailleur

scratch [skrætʃ] N **1** *(action* ▸ *to relieve itch)* grattement *m*; *(wound* ▸ *with fingernail)* coup *m* d'ongle; *(*▸ *with claw)* coup *m* de griffe; **to have a s.** se gratter; **could you give my back a s.?** tu peux me gratter le dos?
2 *(wound* ▸ *from thorns, nail)* égratignure *f*, écorchure *f*; *(*▸ *made by claw)* griffure *f*; *(mark* ▸ *on furniture)* rayure *f*, éraflure *f*; *(*▸ *on glass, record)* rayure *f*; **I've got a s. on my hand** je me suis égratigné la main; **her hands were covered in scratches** elle avait les mains tout écorchées *ou* couvertes d'égratignures; **we escaped without a**

s. on s'en est sorti sans une égratignure
3 *Golf* to play off s. être scratch
4 *(sound ▸ of pen on paper)* grincement *m*
5 *Am Fam (money)* fric *m*, pognon *m*, flouze *m*
6 *(idioms)* to start from s. partir de rien *ou* de zéro; *(restart)* repartir à zéro; to build a house from s. construire une maison de bout en bout; I learnt Italian from s. in six months j'ai appris l'italien en six mois en partant de zéro; to be up to s. être à la hauteur; her work still isn't up to s. son travail n'est toujours pas satisfaisant *ou* à la hauteur; their performance wasn't up to *or* didn't come up to s. leur performance n'était pas suffisante *ou* à la hauteur; we must get the team up to s. before April il faut mettre l'équipe à niveau avant avril
ADJ 1 *(team, meal)* improvisé 2 *Golf (player)* scratch *(inv)*, sans handicap
VT 1 *(rub ▸ itch, rash)* gratter; to s. one's head se gratter la tête; *Fig* you s. my back, and I'll s. yours donnant donnant
2 *(wound ▸ of cat, person)* griffer; (▸ *of thorn, nail)* égratigner, écorcher; the cat scratched my hand le chat m'a griffé la main; she scratched her hand on the brambles elle s'est écorché *ou* égratigné la main dans les ronces; he was badly scratched il était tout écorché
3 *(mark ▸ woodwork, marble)* rayer, érafler; (▸ *glass, record)* rayer; the paintwork's badly scratched la peinture est sérieusement éraflée; someone has scratched their initials on the tree quelqu'un a gravé ses initiales sur l'arbre; she quickly scratched a few notes on her pad elle griffonna rapidement quelques notes sur son calepin; *Fig* you've barely scratched the surface vous avez fait un travail très superficiel, vous n'avez qu'effleuré la question; *Fig* s. any patriot and you will invariably find a bigot si l'on gratte un peu, on trouve un fanatique derrière chaque patriote; *Br Fig* they s. a living selling secondhand books ils gagnent péniblement leur vie en vendant des livres d'occasion; to s. about *or* around for sth essayer de dénicher qch
4 *(of bird, animal ▸ ground)* gratter
5 *(irritate)* gratter; this wool scratches my skin cette laine me gratte la peau
6 *(cancel ▸ meeting, match)* annuler; *(withdraw)* to s. sb off *or* from a list rayer *ou* biffer qn d'une liste; to s. sb from a team exclure qn d'une équipe; *Horseracing* to s. a horse scratcher un cheval
7 *Am Pol (candidate)* rayer de la liste
VI 1 *(person, animal ▸ to relieve itch)* se gratter; stop scratching arrête de te gratter
2 *(bird ▸ in ground)* gratter; I could hear something scratching at the door j'entendais quelque chose gratter à la porte, j'entendais un grattement à la porte
3 *(cat)* griffer; *(brambles, nail)* griffer, écorcher; *(wool, new clothes)* gratter
4 *(pen etc)* grincer, gratter
5 *Sport (competitor)* déclarer forfait
6 *Mus (DJ)* scratcher
▸▸ *scratch mark (on hand)* égratignure *f*; *(on leather, furniture)* rayure *f*, éraflure *f*; *Am scratch paper* (papier *m*) brouillon *m*; *Am scratch sheet (for horse races)* journal *m* des courses; *Med scratch test* test *m* cutané

▸**scratch out** VT SEP *(word)* raturer; to s. sb's eyes out arracher les yeux à qn

▸**scratch together** VT SEP *Br (team)* réunir (difficilement); *(sum of money)* réunir *ou* rassembler (en raclant les fonds de tiroir)

scratchcard ['skrætʃkɑːd] N *(lottery card)* carte *f* à gratter

scratching ['skrætʃɪŋ] N 1 *(with fingernail)* coups *mpl* d'ongle; *(to relieve itch)* grattement *m* 2 *(damaging ▸ action)* rayage *m*; (▸ *result)* rayures *fpl* 3 *(sound)* grattement *m*; *(of pen nib)* grincement *m*; *(of record)* craquement(s) *m(pl)*

scratchpad ['skrætʃpæd] N *Am* bloc-notes *m*
▸▸ *Comput scratchpad memory* mémoire *f* bloc-notes

scratchy ['skrætʃɪ] *(compar* scratchier, *superl* scratchiest) ADJ 1 *(prickly ▸ jumper, blanket)* rêche, qui gratte; (▸ *bush)* piquant 2 *(pen ▸ messy)* qui gratte; (▸ *noisy)* qui grince *(sur le papier)* 3 *(record)* qui craque

scrawl [skrɔːl] N griffonnage *m*, gribouillage *m*; I can't read this s. je ne peux pas déchiffrer ce gribouillage; her signature is just a s. sa signature est totalement illisible
VT griffonner, gribouiller; she left me a scrawled note elle m'a laissé quelques mots griffonnés; someone has scrawled anti-war slogans on the walls quelqu'un a gribouillé des slogans pacifistes sur le mur
VI gribouiller

scrawny ['skrɔːnɪ] *(compar* scrawnier, *superl* scrawniest) ADJ 1 *(person, neck)* efflanqué, décharné; *(cat, chicken)* efflanqué 2 *(vegetation)* maigre

scream [skriːm] VI 1 *(shout ▸ once)* pousser un cri perçant *ou* aigu, hurler; (▸ *repeatedly)* pousser des cris aigus, hurler; *(baby)* crier, hurler; *(birds, animals)* crier; to s. at sb crier après qn; to s. in anger/with pain hurler de colère/de douleur; to s. in delight crier *ou* hurler de plaisir; she screamed for help elle cria à l'aide *ou* au secours; they were screaming with laughter ils se tordaient de rire, ils riaient aux éclats 2 *(tyres)* crisser; *(engine, siren)* hurler
VT 1 *(shout)* hurler; she just stood there screaming insults at me elle était là, à me couvrir d'insultes; she screamed herself hoarse elle cria jusqu'à en perdre la voix 2 *(order, answer)* hurler; "come here at once!" she screamed "viens ici tout de suite!" hurla-t-elle 3 *(newspaper)* étaler; headlines screamed the news of his defeat la nouvelle de sa défaite s'étalait en gros titres
N 1 *(cry)* cri *m* perçant, hurlement *m*; she gave a loud s. elle a poussé un hurlement; screams of laughter des éclats *mpl* de rire 2 *(of tyres)* crissement *m*; *(of sirens, engines)* hurlement *m* 3 *Fam (person)* he's an absolute s. il est vraiment tordant; you look a s. in that hat! vous êtes tordant avec ce chapeau!; it was a s. *(situation, event)* c'était tordant, c'était à se tordre de rire; the party was a s. on s'est amusés comme des fous à la soirée

screaming ['skriːmɪŋ] N *(UNCOUNT) (of person)* cris *mpl*, hurlements *mpl*; *(of birds, animals)* cris *mpl* perçants
ADJ *(fans)* qui crie, qui hurle; *(tyres)* qui crisse; *(sirens, jets)* qui hurle; *(need)* criant; he tends to dress in s. reds and greens il s'habille souvent de rouges et de verts criards
▸▸ *Fam screaming queen* grande folle *f*

screamingly ['skriːmɪŋlɪ] ADV *Fam* s. funny on ne peut plus drôle, à se tordre *ou* à mourir de rire

scree [skriː] N éboulis *m*, pierraille *f*

screech [skriːtʃ] VI 1 *(owl)* ululer, hululer, huer; *(gull)* crier, piailler; *(parrot)* crier; *(monkey)* hurler 2 *(person ▸ in high voice)* pousser des cris stridents *ou* perçants; (▸ *loudly)* hurler; *(singer)* crier, chanter d'une voix stridente 3 *(tyres)* crisser; *(brakes, machinery)* grincer (bruyamment); *(siren, jets)* hurler; the car screeched to a halt la voiture s'est arrêtée dans un crissement de pneus; the machine screeched to a stop la machine s'est arrêtée en grinçant; the car came screeching round the corner la voiture a pris le virage dans un crissement de pneus
VT *(order)* hurler, crier à tue-tête; "never!" she screeched "jamais!" dit-elle d'une voix stridente
N 1 *(of owl)* ululement *m*, hululement *m*; *(of gull)* cri *m*, piaillement *m*; *(of parrot)* cri *m*; *(of monkey)* hurlement *m*; the parrot gave a loud s. le perroquet a poussé un grand cri 2 *(of person)* cri *m* strident *ou* perçant; *(with pain, rage)* hurlement *m*; we heard screeches of laughter coming from next door on entendait des hurlements de rire qui venaient d'à côté; "never!" she said with a s. "jamais!" dit-elle d'une voix stridente 3 *(of tyres)* crissement *m*; *(of brakes)* grincement *m*; *(of sirens, jets)* hurlement *m*; we stopped with a s. of brakes/tyres on s'arrêta dans un grincement de freins/dans un crissement de pneus
▸▸ *Orn screech owl* chat-huant *m*, hulotte *f*

screeching ['skriːtʃɪŋ] ADJ *(laugh)* perçant, aiguë; *(tyres)* qui crissent
N *(UNCOUNT) (cries)* cris *mpl* perçants *ou* aigus; *(of tyres)* crissement *m*

screed [skriːd] N 1 *(essay, story)* longue dissertation *f*; *(letter)* longue lettre *f*; *(speech)* laïus *m*; he wrote screeds and screeds on the French Revolution il a écrit des pages et des pages *ou* des vo lumes sur la Révolution française 2 *Cons (level)* règle *f* à araser le béton; *(depth guide)* guide *m*; *(plaster)* plâtre *m* de ragrément *ou* d ragréage

screen [skriːn] N 1 *Cin, Phot & TV* écran *m*; stars c stage and s. des vedettes du théâtre et du cin éma; the book was adapted for the s. le livre été porté à l'écran; the big s. *(cinema)* le gran écran; the small s. *(television)* le petit écran
2 *(for protection ▸ in front of fire)* pare-étincelle *m inv*; (▸ *over window)* moustiquaire *f*; (▸ *again draught)* paravent *m*
3 *(for privacy)* paravent *m*; a s. of trees un ridea d'arbres; the rooms are divided by sliding screen les pièces sont séparées par des cloisons cou lissantes
4 *Fig (mask)* écran *m*, masque *m*; the shop wa just a s. for her criminal activities le magasi n'était qu'une couverture pour ses activités cr minelles
5 *(sieve)* tamis *m*, crible *m*; *Am (ventilation grill door)* grille *f* de ventilation
6 *(filter ▸ for employees, candidates)* filtre *n* crible *m*
7 *(in basketball)* écran *m*
8 *Comput* écran *m*; to work on s. travailler su écran; to bring up the next s. amener l'écran su vant
COMP *(star)* de cinéma
VT 1 *Cin & TV (film)* projeter, passer; *(show o television)* passer à l'écran
2 *(shelter, protect)* protéger; he screened his eye from the sun with his hand il a mis sa main devar ses yeux pour se protéger du soleil; they've trie to s. her from the harsh realities of life ils ont es sayé de la protéger des dures réalités de la vie
3 *(hide)* cacher, masquer; to s. sth from sight ca cher *ou* masquer qch aux regards
4 *(filter, check ▸ employees, applications, sus pects)* passer au crible; we s. all our security sta nous faisons une enquête préalable sur tous le candidats aux postes d'agent de sécurité; all ai lines now s. passengers systematically les compa gnies aériennes font maintenant passe systématiquement tous les passagers par u détecteur; the hospital screens thousands o women a year for breast cancer l'hôpital fait pas ser un test de dépistage du cancer du sein à de milliers de femmes tous les ans
5 *(sieve ▸ coal, dirt, grain)* cribler, passer a crible
▸▸ *Cin screen actor* acteur *m* de cinéma; *Cin & T screen adaptation* adaptation *f* à l'écran, scénar sation *f*; *Comput screen display* affichage *m*; *Ar screen door* porte *f* avec moustiquaire; *Compu screen dump* capture *f* d'écran; *Comput screen re fresh* actualisation *f ou* régénération *f* de l'écran *Cin screen rights* droits *mpl* d'adaptation l'écran; *Comput screen saver* économiseur *n* d'écran; *Cin screen test* bout *m* d'essai; *Aut scree wash* lave-glace *m*; *TV & Cin screen writing* écr ture *f* de scénarios

▸**screen off** VT SEP 1 *(put screens round ▸ patien* abriter derrière un paravent; (▸ *bed)* entoure de paravents 2 *(divide, separate ▸ with partitio* séparer par une cloison; (▸ *with curtain)* sépare par un rideau; (▸ *with folding screen)* séparer pa un paravent; the manager's office is screened of by a glass partition le bureau du directeur est sé paré par une cloison vitrée 3 *(hide ▸ with foldin screen)* cacher derrière un paravent; (▸ *with cu tain)* cacher derrière un rideau; (▸ *behind trees wall)* cacher; the house was screened off from th road by tall trees de grands arbres empêchaien de voir la maison depuis la route

▸**screen out** VT SEP filtrer, éliminer; this crear screens out UV rays cette crème protège des U cette crème absorbe *ou* filtre les UV

screening ['skriːnɪŋ] N 1 *Cin* projection *f* (e salle); *TV* passage *m* (à l'écran), diffusion *f*; whe the movie had its first s. quand le film est pass pour la première fois à l'écran
2 *(of applications, candidates)* tri *m*, sélection *(for security)* contrôle *m*; *Med (for disease)* test *r ou* tests *mpl* de dépistage; she went for cancer s elle est allée passer un test de dépistage d cancer; early s. dépistage *m* précoce

3 *(mesh)* grillage *m*

4 *(of coal, dirt, grain)* criblage *m*

▸▸ *Cin & TV* ***screening room*** salle *f* de projection

screen-oriented ADJ *Comput* orienté écran

screenplay ['skri:npleɪ] N scénario *m*

screenporch ['skri:npɔ:tʃ] N *Am* véranda *f (entourée d'une moustiquaire)*

screen-test VT faire faire un bout d'essai à; **she was screen-tested for the part** on lui a fait faire un bout d'essai pour le rôle

screenwriter ['skri:nraɪtə(r)] N *Cin* scénariste *mf*

screenwriting ['skri:nraɪtɪŋ] N *Cin* écriture *f* de scénarios

screw [skru:] N **1** *(for wood, in vice)* vis *f*; *(bolt)* boulon *m*; *Fig* **to turn the s.** *or* **screws** serrer la vis; *Fam* **to put the screws on sb** faire pression sur qn□; *Fam* **he has a s. loose** il lui manque une case

2 *(turn)* tour *m* de vis; **give it a couple more screws** donnez-lui encore un ou deux tours de vis

3 *(thread)* pas *m* de vis

4 *(propeller)* hélice *f*

5 *Br (of salt, tobacco)* cornet *m*; **a s. of paper** un cornet en papier

6 *Br Fam Crime slang (prison guard)* maton (onne) *m,f*

7 *Br Fam (salary)* salaire□*m*, paye□*f*; **he's on a good s.** il gagne plein de fric

8 *Vulg (sexual intercourse)* **to have a s.** baiser, s'envoyer en l'air; **she's a good s.** elle baise bien

VT **1** *(bolt, screw, lid on bottle)* visser; *(handle, parts)* fixer avec des vis; **to s. sth shut** fermer qch (en vissant); **to s. the lid on a bottle** visser le bouchon d'une bouteille; **s. it tight** vissez-le bien

2 *(crumple)* froisser, chiffonner

3 *(wrinkle ▸ face)* **he screwed his face into a grimace** une grimace lui tordit le visage

4 *Fam (obtain)* arracher□; **he managed to s. the money/the answer out of her** il a réussi à lui soutirer l'argent/la réponse□

5 *very Fam (con)* arnaquer; **we've been screwed!** on s'est fait arnaquer!; **they're out to s. you for every penny you've got** ils essayent de vous extorquer tout l'argent que vous avez□

6 *Vulg (have sex with ▸ of man)* baiser, troncher; *(▸ of woman)* baiser avec, s'envoyer

7 *very Fam (as invective)* **s. the expense!** et merde, je peux bien m'offrir ça!; **s. you!** va te faire foutre!

VI **1** *(bolt, lid)* se visser **2** *Vulg (have sex)* baiser, s'envoyer en l'air

▸▸ ***screw propeller*** hélice *f*; ***screw thread*** pas *m ou* filet *m* de vis; ***screw top*** couvercle *m* qui se visse; **the jar has a s. top** le couvercle du pot se visse

▸**screw around** VI **1** *Am very Fam (waste time)* glander, glandouiller; *(fool about)* déconner **2** *Vulg (sleep around)* baiser avec n'importe qui, coucher à droite à gauche

VT SEP *very Fam* **to s. sb around** *(treat badly)* se foutre de la gueule de qn; *(waste time of)* faire perdre son temps à qn□

▸**screw down** VT SEP visser

VI se visser

▸**screw off** VT SEP dévisser

VI se dévisser

▸**screw on** VT SEP visser; **the cupboard was screwed on to the wall** le placard était vissé au mur

VI se visser; **it screws on to the wall** ça se visse dans le mur

▸**screw up** VT SEP **1** *(tighten, fasten)* visser

2 *(crumple ▸ handkerchief, paper)* chiffonner, faire une boule de

3 *Br (eyes)* plisser; **she screwed up her eyes** elle plissa les yeux; **to s. up one's courage** prendre son courage à deux mains

4 *Fam (mess up ▸ plans, chances)* bousiller, foutre en l'air, faire foirer; **you've screwed everything up** tu as tout foutu en l'air

5 *Fam (person)* mettre dans tous ses états, déboussoler; **the divorce really screwed her up** le divorce l'a complètement perturbée□ *ou* déboussolée

VI **1** *(lid, nut etc)* se visser **2** *(eyes)* (se) plisser; **her face screwed up in distaste** *or* **disgust** elle fit une grimace de dégoût **3** *Fam (make a mess of something)* foirer, merder

screwball ['skru:bɔ:l] *Am Fam* N *(person)* cinglé(e) *m,f*, dingue *mf*

ADJ cinglé, dingue

▸▸ *Cin & TV* ***screwball comedy*** comédie *f* loufoque

screwdriver ['skru:draɪvə(r)] N **1** *(tool)* tournevis *m* **2** *(drink)* vodka-orange *f*

screwed [skru:d] ADJ *very Fam* **to be s.** *(in trouble)* être foutu

screw-loose ADJ *Am Fam* loufoque, loufedingue

screw-on ADJ *(earrings)* à vis; *Phot (lens)* détachable, mobile

screwy ['skru:ɪ] *(compar* **screwier**, *superl* **screwiest)** ADJ *Fam (person)* cinglé, dingue; *(situation)* bizarre□

scribble ['skrɪbəl] VT *(note, drawing)* gribouiller, griffonner; **she scribbled a few lines to her sister** elle griffonna quelques lignes à l'intention de sa sœur

VI gribouiller

N **1** *(act of scribbling)* gribouillis *m*, gribouillage *m*, griffonnage *m*; **I can't read this s.** je n'arrive pas à déchiffrer ce gribouillage; **what are all these scribbles?** qu'est-ce que c'est que tous ces gribouillis? **2** *(bad handwriting)* écriture *f* illisible, pattes *fpl* de mouche; **his handwriting is nothing but a s.** son écriture est illisible

▸**scribble down** VT SEP *(address, number)* griffonner, noter (rapidement)

scribbler ['skrɪbələ(r)] N *Br Pej (author)* écrivaillon *m*

scribbling ['skrɪbəlɪŋ] N gribouillis *m*, gribouillage *m*; *Fam* **scribblings** *(inferior writings)* écrits *mpl* médiocres□

▸▸ ***scribbling pad*** bloc-notes *m*

scribe [skraɪb] N scribe *m*

VT graver

scrimmage ['skrɪmɪdʒ] N **1** *(in American football)* mêlée *f*; **line of s.** ligne *f* de mêlée **2** *(brawl)* mêlée *f*, bagarre *f*

VI *Sport* faire une mêlée

VT *Sport (ball)* mettre dans la mêlée

scrimp [skrɪmp] VI lésiner; **she scrimps on food** elle lésine sur la nourriture; **to s. and save** économiser sur tout, se serrer la ceinture

scrip [skrɪp] N **1** *St Exch* titre *m* provisoire **2** *(of paper)* morceau *m*

▸▸ *St Exch* ***scrip certificate*** certificat *m* d'actions provisoire

script [skrɪpt] N **1** *(text)* script *m*, texte *m*; *Cin* script *m*

2 *(UNCOUNT) (handwriting)* script *m*, écriture *f* script; **to write in s.** écrire en script

3 *(lettering, characters)* écriture *f*, caractères *mpl*, lettres *fpl*; **Arabic s.** caractères *mpl* arabes, écriture *f* arabe; **in italic s.** en script

4 *(copy) & Law* original *m*; *Univ (answer paper)* copie *f* (d'examen)

VT *Cin* écrire le script de

▸▸ *Cin & TV* ***script girl*** scripte *f*, script girl *f*

scripted ['skrɪptɪd] ADJ *(speech, interview etc)* (dont le texte a été) écrit d'avance

scriptural ['skrɪptʃərəl] ADJ biblique

Scripture ['skrɪptʃə(r)] N **1** *(Christian)* Écriture *f* (sainte); **a reading from the Scriptures** une lecture biblique *ou* de la Bible; **a S. lesson** une leçon d'études bibliques **2** *(non-Christian)* **the Scriptures** les textes *mpl* sacrés

scriptwriter ['skrɪptraɪtə(r)] N scénariste *mf*

scriptwriting ['skrɪptraɪtɪŋ] N écriture *f* de scénarios, scénarisation *f*

scrofula ['skrɒfjʊlə] N *(UNCOUNT) Med* scrofule *f*

scrofulous ['skrɒfjʊləs] ADJ *Med* scrofuleux

scroll [skrəʊl] N **1** *(of paper, parchment)* rouleau *m*

2 *(manuscript)* manuscrit *m* (ancien)

3 *(on column, violin, woodwork)* volute *f*; *(in writing)* enjolivement *m*, arabesque *f*; *(in engraving etc)* cartouche *m (encadrant un titre)*

4 *Comput* défilement *m*

VT *Comput* faire défiler

VI *Comput* défiler

▸▸ *Comput* ***scroll bar*** barre *f* de défilement; *Comput* ***scroll box*** ascenseur *m*, cage *f*; *Comput* ***scroll button*** bouton *m* de défilement

▸**scroll down** VT INSEP *Comput* faire défiler un document vers le bas; **to s. down a page** passer à la page suivante

▸**scroll through** VT INSEP *Comput* faire défiler d'un bout à l'autre, parcourir

▸**scroll up** VT INSEP *Comput* **to s. up a document** faire défiler un document vers le haut; **to s. up a page** passer à la page précédente

scrolling ['skrəʊlɪŋ] N *Comput* défilement *m*

scrooge [skru:dʒ] N grippe-sou *m*, harpagon *m*

• **Scrooge** PR N = personnage de Dickens incarnant l'avarice

scrota ['skrəʊtə] *pl of* **scrotum**

scrotal ['skrəʊtəl] ADJ *Anat* scrotal

scrotum ['skrəʊtəm] *(pl* **scrotums** *or* **scrota** [-tə]) N *Anat* scrotum *m*

scrounge [skraʊndʒ] *Fam* VT *(sugar, pencil)* piquer, emprunter□; *(meal)* se faire offrir□; *(money)* se faire prêter□; **he tried to s. $10 off me** il a essayé de me taper de 10 dollars; **can I s. a cigarette off you?** je peux te taper *ou* te taxer une cigarette?

VI **to s. on** *or* **off sb** *(habitually)* vivre aux crochets de qn; **he's always scrounging off his friends** *(gen)* il tape toujours ses amis; *(for food, meals)* il fait toujours le pique-assiette chez ses amis

N **to be on the s.** *(for food)* venir quémander de quoi manger; *(for cigarette)* venir quémander une cigarette; **she's on the s. for a meal** elle veut se faire inviter à manger; **he's always on the s.** il vit toujours aux crochets des autres

scrounger ['skraʊndʒə(r)] N *Fam* pique-assiette *mf*, parasite□*m*; *(living off state benefits)* parasite□*m*

scrub [skrʌb] *(pt & pp* **scrubbed**, *cont* **scrubbing)** VT **1** *(clean, wash ▸ floor, carpet)* nettoyer à la brosse, frotter avec une brosse; *(▸ saucepan, sink)* frotter, récurer; *(▸ clothes, face, back)* frotter; *(▸ fingernails)* brosser; **to s. sth clean** nettoyer qch à fond, récurer qch; **s. yourself all over** frotte-toi bien partout; **have you scrubbed your hands clean?** est-ce que tu t'es bien nettoyé les mains? **2** *Fam (cancel ▸ order)* annuler□; *(▸ plans, holiday)* annuler□, laisser tomber□; *(recording, tape)* effacer□; **we'll have to s. dinner** il faudra qu'on se passe de dîner□ **3** *Tech (gas)* laver

VI **I spent the morning scrubbing** j'ai passé la matinée à frotter les planchers *ou* les sols

N **1** *(with brush)* coup *m* de brosse; **give the floor a good s.** frotte bien le plancher; **can you give my back a s.?** peux-tu me frotter le dos?

2 *(UNCOUNT) (vegetation)* broussailles *fpl*

3 *(cosmetic)* gommage *m*

4 *Austr Fam (wilderness)* cambrousse *f*

• **scrubs** NPL *Med* blouse *f* stérile

▸▸ *Am* ***scrub brush*** brosse *f* à récurer

▸**scrub away** VT SEP *(mark, mud)* faire partir en brossant

VI partir à la brosse

▸**scrub down** VT SEP *(wall, paintwork)* lessiver; *(horse)* bouchonner

▸**scrub off** = **scrub away**

▸**scrub out** VT SEP **1** *(dirt, stain)* faire partir à la brosse; *(bucket, tub)* nettoyer à la brosse; *(pan)* récurer; *(ears)* nettoyer, bien laver **2** *(erase ▸ graffiti, comment)* effacer; *(▸ name)* barrer, biffer

VI partir à la brosse

▸**scrub up** VI *Med (before operation)* se laver les mains

scrubber ['skrʌbə(r)] N **1** *(for saucepans)* tampon *m* à récurer **2** *Br very Fam Pej (woman)* pute *f*, salope *f*

scrubbing ['skrʌbɪŋ] N *(cleaning ▸ of saucepan)* récurage *m*; *(▸ with brush)* nettoyage *m* avec une brosse dure

▸▸ *Br* ***scrubbing brush*** brosse *f* à récurer

scrubland ['skrʌblænd] N maquis *m*, garrigue *f*

scruff [skrʌf] N **1** *Br Fam (untidy person)* individu *m* débraillé□ *ou* dépenaillé□ *ou* peu soigné□;

(ruffian) voyou□ *m*; **you look a real s.** tu es ficelé comme l'as de pique **2** *(idiom)* **by the s. of the neck** par la peau du cou

scruffily ['skrʌfɪlɪ] **ADV s. dressed** dépenaillé, mal habillé

scruffiness ['skrʌfɪnɪs] **N** *(in dress, appearance)* négligence *f*; *(of district)* état *m* de délabrement

scruffy ['skrʌfɪ] *(compar* **scruffier,** *superl* **scruffiest) ADJ** *(appearance)* négligé; *(clothes)* dépenaillé; *(hair)* ébouriffé; *(person)* débraillé, dépenaillé, peu soigné; *(building, area)* délabré, miteux; **he's a s. dresser** il s'habille mal

scrum [skrʌm] *(pt & pp* **scrummed,** *cont* **scrumming) N 1** *(in rugby)* mêlée *f* **2** *(brawl)* mêlée *f*, bousculade *f*; **there was a s. for tickets** les gens se sont bousculés pour obtenir des billets

VI former une mêlée

scrummage ['skrʌmɪdʒ] **N 1** *(in rugby)* mêlée *f* **2** *(brawl)* mêlée *f*, bousculade *f*

VI *(in rugby)* former une mêlée

scrummy ['skrʌmɪ] *(compar* **scrummier,** *superl* **scrummiest) ADJ** *Br Fam* délicieux□, super bon

scrump [skrʌmp] *Br Fam* **VI to go scrumping (for apples)** aller chaparder (des pommes)

VT *(apples)* chaparder

scrumptious ['skrʌmpʃəs] **ADJ** *Fam* délicieux□, succulent□

scrumpy ['skrʌmpɪ] **N** = cidre brut et sec fabriqué dans le sud-ouest de l'Angleterre

scrunch [skrʌntʃ] **VT** *(biscuit, apple)* croquer; *(snow, gravel)* faire craquer *ou* crisser; *(paper ▸ noisily)* froisser (bruyamment)

VI *(footsteps ▸ on gravel, snow)* craquer, faire un bruit de craquement; *(gravel, snow ▸ underfoot)* craquer, crisser

N *(of gravel, snow, paper)* craquement *m*, bruit *m* de craquement

▸**scrunch up VT SEP 1** *(crumple ▸ paper)* froisser; **he scrunched up his face in disgust** il a fait une grimace de dégoût **2** *Am (hunch)* **she was sitting with her shoulders scrunched up** elle était assise, les épaules rentrées

scrunch-dry *(pt & pp* **scrunch-dried) VT** *(hair)* sécher en froissant; **to s. one's hair** se sécher les cheveux en les froissant

scrunchie, scrunchy ['skrʌntʃɪ] *(pl* **scrunchies) N** chouchou *m (pour tenir les cheveux)*

scruple ['skru:pəl] **N** scrupule *m*; **he has no scruples** il n'a aucun scrupule; **to act without s.** agir sans scrupule

VI they don't s. to cheat ils n'ont aucun scrupule *ou* ils n'hésitent pas à tricher; **I would s. to steal even if I was starving** j'aurais scrupule à voler même si je mourais de faim

scrupulous ['skru:pjʊləs] **ADJ 1** *(meticulous)* scrupuleux, méticuleux; **they're rather s. about punctuality** ils tiennent beaucoup à la ponctualité; **he acted with s. honesty** il a agi avec une honnêteté irréprochable **2** *(conscientious)* scrupuleux

scrupulously ['skru:pjʊləslɪ] **ADV** *(meticulously)* scrupuleusement, parfaitement; *(honestly)* scrupuleusement, avec scrupule; **s. clean/honest** d'une propreté/honnêteté irréprochable; **s. punctual** parfaitement à l'heure

scrupulousness ['skru:pjʊləsnɪs] **N** *(quality)* esprit *m* scrupuleux

scrutineer [ˌskru:tɪ'nɪə(r)] **N** *Br Pol* scrutateur (trice) *m,f*

scrutinize, -ise ['skru:tɪnaɪz] **VT** scruter, examiner attentivement

scrutiny ['skru:tɪnɪ] *(pl* **scrutinies) N 1** *(examination)* examen *m* minutieux *ou* approfondi; *(watch)* surveillance *f*; *(gaze)* regard *m* insistant; **to be under s.** *(prisoners)* être sous surveillance; *(accounts, staff)* faire l'objet d'un contrôle; **to come under s.** être contrôlé; **her work does not stand up to close s.** son travail ne résiste pas à un examen minutieux **2** *Br Pol* deuxième pointage *m* (des suffrages)

SCSI ['skʌzɪ] **N** *Comput (abbr* **small computer systems interface)** SCSI *f*

▸▸ ***SCSI card*** carte *f* SCSI

scuba ['sku:bə] **N** scaphandre *m* autonome

▸▸ ***scuba dive*** plongée *f* sous-marine; ***scuba diver*** plongeur(euse) *m,f* sous-marin(e); ***scuba diving*** plongée *f* sous-marine; **to go s. diving** faire de la plongée sous-marine

scud [skʌd] *(pt & pp* **scudded,** *cont* **scudding) VI** glisser, filer; **clouds scudded across the sky** des nuages filaient dans le ciel; **two boats scudded across the lake** deux voiliers filaient sur le lac

scuff [skʌf] **VT 1** *(shoe, leather)* érafler, râper; **her shoes were all scuffed (up)** ses chaussures étaient toutes éraflées *ou* râpées **2** *(drag)* **to s. one's feet** marcher en traînant les pieds, traîner les pieds

VI marcher en traînant les pieds

N *(mark)* éraflure *f*; *(on floor)* rayure *f*

▸▸ ***scuff mark*** éraflure *f*; *(on floor)* rayure *f*

scuffle ['skʌfəl] **N** *(fight)* bagarre *f*, échauffourée *f*

VI 1 *(fight)* se bagarrer, se battre **2** *(with feet)* marcher en traînant les pieds; **they scuffled along the corridor** ils avançaient dans le couloir en traînant les pieds

scull [skʌl] **N 1** *(double paddle)* godille *f*; *(single oar)* aviron *m* **2** *(boat)* yole *f*

VT *(with double paddle)* godiller; *(with oars)* ramer

VI ramer en couple; **to go sculling** faire de l'aviron

scullery ['skʌlərɪ] *(pl* **sculleries) N** *Br* arrière-cuisine *f*

▸▸ *Br* ***scullery maid*** fille *f* de cuisine

sculpt [skʌlpt] **VT** sculpter

VI faire de la sculpture

sculptor ['skʌlptə(r)] **N** sculpteur *m*

sculptress ['skʌlptrɪs] **N** (femme *f*) sculpteur *mf*, sculptrice *f*

sculptural ['skʌlptʃərəl] **ADJ** sculptural

sculpture ['skʌlptʃə(r)] **N 1** *(art)* sculpture *f* **2** *(object)* sculpture *f*; **it's a beautiful (piece of) s.** c'est une très belle sculpture

VT sculpter; **she has finely sculptured features** elle a le visage très fin

VI faire de la sculpture

scum [skʌm] **N 1** *(on liquid, sea)* écume *f*; *(in bath)* (traînées *fpl* de) crasse *f*; *Metal* écume *f*, scories *fpl*; **to take the s. off** *(liquid)* écumer; *(bath)* nettoyer **2** *Fam (people)* rebut□ *m*, ordures *fpl*; **he's s.** c'est une ordure; **he's the s. of the earth** c'est le dernier des derniers; **they treated us like s.** on nous a traités comme des moins que rien *ou* des chiens

scumbag ['skʌmbæg] **N** *Fam (person)* salaud *m*, ordure *f*

scunner ['skʌnə(r)] *Scot* **N** *(dislike)* **to take a s. to sb/sth** prendre qn/qch en grippe

VT énerver□

scunnered ['skʌnəd] **ADJ** *Scot* **to be s. (with)** en avoir marre (de)

scupper ['skʌpə(r)] **VT** *Br* **1** *(ship)* saborder **2** *Fam (plans, attempt)* saborder□, faire capoter; **we're completely scuppered unless we can find the cash** on est finis si on ne trouve pas l'argent

N *Naut* dalot *m*

scurf [skɜ:f] **N** *(UNCOUNT) (dandruff)* pellicules *fpl*; *(on skin)* squames *fpl*; *(on plant)* lamelles *fpl*

scurfy ['skɜ:fɪ] *(compar* **scurfier,** *superl* **scurfiest) ADJ** *(scalp)* couvert de pellicules; *(skin)* squameux

scurrility [skʌ'rɪlɪtɪ] *(pl* **scurrilities) N 1** *(of remarks)* caractère *m* calomnieux *ou* outrageant; *(of action)* bassesse *f* **2** *(vulgarity)* grossièreté *f*

scurrilous ['skʌrɪləs] **ADJ** *(lying)* calomnieux, mensonger; *(insulting)* outrageant, ignoble; *(bitter)* fielleux; *(vulgar)* grossier, vulgaire

scurrilously ['skʌrɪləslɪ] **ADV** *(insultingly)* injurieusement; *(coarsely)* grossièrement

scurrilousness ['skʌrɪləsnɪs] = **scurrility**

scurry ['skʌrɪ] *(pt & pp* **scurried,** *pl* **scurries) VI** se précipiter, courir; **all the animals were scurrying for shelter** tous les animaux couraient pour se mettre à l'abri; **they scurried for the trees** ils se précipitèrent vers les arbres; **a sound of scurrying feet** un bruit de pas précipités

N 1 *(rush)* course *f* (précipitée), débandade *f*; **there was a s. for the door** tout le monde s'est rué vers la porte **2** *(sound ▸ of feet)* bruit *m* de pas précipités

▸**scurry away, scurry off VI** *(animal)* détaler; *(person)* décamper, prendre ses jambes à son cou

scurvy ['skɜ:vɪ] *(compar* **scurvier,** *superl* **scurviest) N** *(UNCOUNT) Med* scorbut *m*

ADJ *(trick)* honteux, ignoble

scutcheon ['skʌtʃən] = **escutcheon**

scuttle ['skʌtəl] **VI** *(run)* courir à pas précipités, se précipiter

VT 1 *(ship)* saborder; **the whole fleet was scuttled** toute la flotte a été sabordée **2** *(hopes)* ruiner; *(plans)* saborder, faire échouer

N 1 *(run)* course *f* précipitée, débandade *f*

2 (coal) s. seau *m* à charbon

3 *Naut* écoutille *f*

4 *Am (in ceiling, floor)* trappe *f*

▸**scuttle away, scuttle off VI** déguerpir, se sauver

scuttling ['skʌtəlɪŋ] **N** *(of ship)* sabordage *m*

scuzzy ['skʌzɪ] *(compar* **scuzzier,** *superl* **scuzziest) ADJ** *Fam* dégueulasse, cradingue

scythe [saɪð] **N** faux *f*

VT faucher

▸**scythe through VT INSEP** *(with a weapon)* faucher; **her stick scythed through the air** son bâton fendit l'air

SDI [ˌesdi:'aɪ] **N** *Mil (abbr* **Strategic Defense Initiative)** initiative *f* de défense stratégique

SDLP [ˌesdi:el'pi:] **N** *(abbr* **Social Democratic and Labour Party)** = parti politique d'Irlande du Nord

SDP [ˌesdi:'pi:] **N** *(abbr* **Social Democratic Party)** Parti *m* social démocrate

SE *(written abbr* **south-east)** S-E

SEA [ˌesi:'eɪ] **N** *EU (abbr* **Single European Act)** AUE *m*

sea [si:] **N 1** *(gen)* mer *f*; **by land and s.** par terre et par mer; **to travel by s.** voyager par mer *ou* par bateau; **the goods were sent by s.** les marchandises ont été expédiées par bateau; **we spent six months at s.** on a passé six mois en mer; **life at s.** la vie en mer *ou* de marin; **to swim in the s.** nager *ou* se baigner dans la mer; **to put (out) to s.** prendre la mer; **to go to s.** *(boat)* prendre la mer, *(sailor)* se faire marin; **to run away to s.** partir se faire marin; **to look out to s.** regarder vers le large; **the little boat was swept** *or* **washed out to s.** le petit bateau a été emporté vers le large; **across** *or* **over the s.** *or* **seas** outre-mer; **a heavy s., heavy seas** une grosse mer; *Br Fam* **to be at s.** *(be lost)* nager (complètement); *(be mixed-up)* être déboussolé *ou* désorienté□; **when it comes to computers, I'm all at s.** je ne connais strictement rien aux ordinateurs□; **he's been all at s. since his wife left him** il est complètement déboussolé depuis que sa femme l'a quitté; *Fam* **to find** *or* **to get one's s. legs** s'amariner□, s'habituer à la mer□

2 *(seaside)* bord *m* de la mer; **they live by** *or* **beside the s.** ils habitent au bord de la mer

3 *(large quantity ▸ of blood, mud)* mer *f*; *(▸ of problems, faces)* multitude *f*

▸▸ ***sea air*** air *m* marin *ou* de la mer; ***sea anchor*** ancre *f* flottante; *Zool* ***sea anemone*** anémone *f* de mer; *Ich* ***sea bass*** bar *m*, loup *m*; ***sea bathing*** *(UNCOUNT)* bains *mpl* de mer; ***sea battle*** bataille *f* navale; *Ich* ***sea bream*** daurade *f*, dorade *f*; ***sea breeze*** *(wind)* brise *f* marine; *(cocktail)* sea breeze *m*; ***sea captain*** capitaine *m* de la marine marchande; ***sea change*** changement *m* radical, profond changement *m*; *Naut* ***sea chest*** coffre *m* de marin *ou* de bord; *Zool* ***sea cow*** vache *f* marine, sirénien *m*; *Zool* ***sea crayfish*** langouste *f*; ***sea crossing*** traversée *f*; *Zool* ***sea cucumber*** concombre *m* de mer, bêche *f* de mer, holothurie *f*; ***sea dog*** **1** *Ich* roussette *f*, chien *m* de mer; *Zool (seal)* phoque *m* **2** *Literary or Hum (sailor)* (vieux) loup *m* de mer; *Orn* ***sea eagle*** aigle *m* des mers; *Zool* ***sea elephant*** éléphant *m* de mer; ***sea fight*** combat *m* naval; ***sea fish*** poisson *m* de mer; ***sea fishery*** pêche *f* maritime; ***sea fishing*** pêche *f* maritime; ***sea floor*** fond *m* de la mer; ***sea fog*** brouillard *m (en mer)*; ***sea god*** dieu *m* marin *ou* de la mer; ***sea green*** vert *m* glauque; *Zool* ***sea hare*** lièvre *m* marin, *Spec* aplysie *f*; *Bot* ***sea kale***

chou *m* marin, crambe *m*; **sea kayak** kayak *m* de mer; **sea lane** couloir *m* de navigation; **sea level** niveau *m* de la mer; **above/below s. level** au-dessus/au-dessous du niveau de la mer; *Zool* **sea lion** otarie *f*; *Scot* **sea loch** bras *m* de mer; *Br Mil* **Sea Lord** lord *m* de l'Amirauté; **sea mile** mille *m* marin; **sea mist** brume *f* marine; *Myth* **sea monster** monstre *m* marin; *Zool* **sea otter** loutre *f* de mer; *Ich* **sea perch** perche *f* de mer; **sea salt** sel *m* marin *ou* de mer; *Ich* **sea scorpion** chabot *m*, scorpion *m* de mer; **sea scout** scout *m* marin; *Zool & Myth* **sea serpent** serpent *m* de mer; **sea shanty** chanson *f* de marins; *Zool* **sea snake** serpent *m* marin; *Zool* **sea spider** araignée *f* de mer; **the Sea of Tranquillity** la mer de la Tranquillité; *Ich* **sea trout** truite *f* de mer; *Zool* **sea turtle** tortue *f* marine; *Zool* **sea urchin** oursin *m*; **sea view** vue *f* sur la mer; **sea wall** digue *f*; **sea water** eau *f* de mer

seabed ['siːbed] **N** fond *m* de la mer *ou* marin

seabird ['siːbɜːd] **N** oiseau *m* de mer

seaboard ['siːbɔːd] **N** *(coastline)* littoral *m*, côte *f*; *(coastal region)* bord *m* de la mer, région *f* côtière; **on the Atlantic s.** sur la côte atlantique

seaboots ['siːbuːts] **NPL** bottes *fpl* de marin *ou* de mer

seaborne ['siːbɔːn] **ADJ** *(trade)* maritime; *(goods, troops)* transporté par mer *ou* par bateau

seafarer ['siːfeərə(r)] **N** marin *m*

seafaring ['siːfeərɪŋ] **ADJ** *(nation)* maritime, de marins; *(life)* de marin

N vie *f* de marin

seafood ['siːfuːd] **N** *(UNCOUNT)* (poissons *mpl* et) fruits *mpl* de mer

seafront ['siːfrʌnt] **N** bord *m* de mer, front *m* de mer

seagoing ['siːgəʊɪŋ] **ADJ** *(trade, nation)* maritime; *(life)* de marin; **a s. man** un marin, un homme de mer; **a s. ship** un navire de haute mer, un (navire) long-courrier

sea-green **ADJ** vert glauque *(inv)*

seagull ['siːgʌl] **N** mouette *f*

seahorse ['siːhɔːs, *pl* -hɔːsɪz] **N** *Ich* hippocampe *m*

seal [siːl] **N 1** *Zool* phoque *m*

2 *(on document, letter)* sceau *m*; *(on bottle of wine)* cachet *m*; *(on crate)* plombage *m*; *(on battery, gas cylinder)* bande *f* de garantie; *(on meter)* plomb *m*; *Br Admin & Law* **given under my hand and s.** signé et scellé par moi; **to put one's s. to a document** apposer son sceau à un document; **does the project have her s. of approval?** est-ce qu'elle a approuvé le projet?; **to put** *or* **to set the s. on sth** *(confirm)* sceller qch; *(bring to end)* mettre fin à qch

3 *(UNCOUNT) Law (on door)* scellé *m*, scellés *mpl*; **under s.** sous scellés; *Fig* **under (the) s. of secrecy/of silence** ≃ sous le sceau du secret/du silence; *Rel* **under the s. of confession** *or* **of the confessional** dans le secret de la confession

4 *(tool)* sceau *m*, cachet *m*

5 *Com* label *m*

6 *(joint ▸ for engine, jar, sink)* joint *m* d'étanchéité; *(putty)* mastic *m*

7 *(stamp)* **Christmas s.** timbre *m* de Noël

VT 1 *(document)* apposer son sceau à, sceller; **sealed with a kiss** scellé d'un baiser; **sealed orders** des ordres scellés sous pli; *Fig* **her fate is sealed** son sort est réglé; *Fig* **they finally sealed the deal** ils ont enfin conclu l'affaire

2 *(close ▸ envelope, package)* cacheter, fermer; *(▸ with sticky tape)* coller, fermer; *(▸ jar)* sceller, fermer hermétiquement; *(▸ can)* souder; *(▸ tube, mineshaft)* sceller; *(window, door ▸ for insulation)* isoler; *Fig* **my lips are sealed** je ne dirai rien

3 *Law (door)* apposer des scellés sur; *(evidence)* mettre sous scellés; *(at customs ▸ goods)* (faire) sceller

4 *Culin (meat)* saisir

▸▸ *Com* **seal of quality** label *m* de qualité; **seal ring** chevalière *f*

▸ **seal in** **VT SEP** enfermer hermétiquement; **the flavour is sealed in by freeze-drying** le produit garde toute sa saveur grâce à la lyophilisation; **fry the meat at a high temperature to s. in the flavour** faites revenir la viande à feu vif afin de lui conserver toute sa saveur

▸ **seal off** **VT SEP** *(passage, road)* interdire l'accès de; *(entrance)* condamner; **the street had been sealed off** la rue avait été fermée (à la circulation)

▸ **seal up** **VT SEP** *(close ▸ envelope)* cacheter, fermer; *(▸ with sticky tape)* coller, fermer; *(▸ jar)* sceller, fermer hermétiquement; *(▸ can)* souder; *(▸ tube, mineshaft)* sceller; *(window, door ▸ for insulation)* isoler

sealant ['siːlənt] **N 1** *(paste, putty)* produit *m* d'étanchéité; *(paint)* enduit *m* étanche; *(for radiator)* anti-fuite *m* **2** *(joint)* joint *m* d'étanchéité

sealed [siːld] **ADJ** *(document)* scellé; *(envelope)* cacheté; *(orders)* scellé sous pli; *(jar)* fermé hermétiquement; *(mineshaft)* obturé, bouché; *(joint)* étanche

▸▸ *Austr* **sealed road** route *f* avec revêtement

sealer ['siːlə(r)] **N 1** *(hunter)* chasseur(euse) *m,f* de phoques; *(ship)* navire *m* équipé pour la chasse aux phoques **2** *(paint, varnish)* enduit *m*, première couche *f*

sealing ['siːlɪŋ] **N 1** *(hunting)* chasse *f* aux phoques; **to go s.** aller à la chasse aux phoques **2** *(of document)* cachetage *m*; *(of crate)* plombage *m*; *(of door)* scellage *m*; *(of shaft, mine)* fermeture *f*, obturation *f*

▸▸ **sealing wax** cire *f* à cacheter

sealskin ['siːlskɪn] **N** peau *f* de phoque

ADJ en peau de phoque

seam [siːm] **N 1** *(on garment, in stocking)* couture *f*; *(in airbed, bag)* couture *f*, joint *m*; *(weld)* soudure *f*; *(between planks)* joint *m*; **your coat is coming** *or* **falling apart at the seams** votre manteau se découd; **my suitcase was bulging** *or* **bursting at the seams** ma valise était pleine à craquer; *Fig* **the building was bursting at the seams** le bâtiment était plein à craquer; *Fig* **their marriage is coming** *or* **falling apart at the seams** leur couple bat de l'aile **2** *(of coal, ore)* filon *m*, veine *f*; *(in rocks)* couche *f*

VT *(garment)* faire une couture dans, coudre; *(plastic, metal, wood)* faire un joint à

seaman ['siːmən] *(pl* **seamen** [-mən]) **N 1** *(sailor)* marin *m* **2** *(in US Navy)* quartier-maître *m* de 2ème classe

▸▸ *Am* **seaman apprentice** matelot *m* en formation; *Am* **seaman recruit** matelot *m*

seamanship ['siːmənʃɪp] **N** *(UNCOUNT)* qualités *fpl* de marin

seamen ['siːmən] *pl of* **seaman**

seamless ['siːmlɪs] **ADJ 1** *(stocking)* sans couture; *(made from single piece of metal)* sans soudure **2** *Fig (changeover, whole)* continu; **a s. transition** une transition en douceur

seamlessly ['siːmlɪslɪ] **ADV** d'une façon cohérente *ou* homogène

seamstress ['semstrɪs] **N** couturière *f*

seamy ['siːmɪ] *(compar* **seamier**, *superl* **seamiest)** **ADJ** sordide, louche; **the s. side of life** le côté sordide de la vie

séance, seance ['seɪɑːns] **N 1** *(for raising spirits)* séance *f* de spiritisme **2** *(meeting)* séance *f*, réunion *f*

seaplane ['siːpleɪn] **N** hydravion *m*

seaport ['siːpɔːt] **N** port *m* maritime

sear [sɪə(r)] **VT 1** *(burn)* brûler; *(brand)* marquer au fer rouge; *Med* cautériser; **the scene seared itself on my memory** la scène est restée gravée *ou* marquée dans ma mémoire

2 *Culin (meat etc)* saisir

3 *(wither)* dessécher, flétrir

4 *Literary (harden ▸ heart, feelings)* endurcir

N *(burn)* (marque *f* de) brûlure *f*

ADJ *Literary* desséché, flétri

search [sɜːtʃ] **VT 1** *(look in ▸ room)* chercher (partout) dans; *(▸ pockets, drawers)* fouiller (dans), chercher dans; **we've searched the whole house for the keys** nous avons cherché dans toute la maison pour retrouver les clés; **she searched her bag for a comb** elle fouilla dans son sac à la recherche d'un peigne

2 *(of police, customs)* fouiller; *(with warrant)* perquisitionner, faire une perquisition dans; **the flat was searched for drugs** ils ont fouillé l'appartement à la recherche de drogue; **the spectators were searched before they were let in** les spectateurs ont été fouillés à l'entrée; **customs searched our luggage/our car** les douaniers ont fouillé nos bagages/notre voiture; *Fam* **s. me!** je n'en ai pas la moindre idée ☐!

3 *(examine, consult ▸ records)* chercher dans; *(▸ memory)* chercher dans, fouiller; *(▸ conscience)* sonder; *Comput (▸ file, directory)* rechercher dans; **I searched her face for some sign of emotion** j'ai cherché sur son visage des signes d'émotion; *Comput* **to s. and replace sth** rechercher et remplacer qch

VI chercher; **to s. for sth** chercher qch, rechercher qch; **to s. after the truth** rechercher la vérité; *Comput* **to s. for a file** rechercher un fichier; **searching** *(on computer screen)* recherche

N 1 *(gen)* recherche *f*, recherches *fpl*; **the s. for the missing climbers has been resumed** les recherches ont repris pour retrouver les alpinistes disparus; **helicopters made a s. for survivors** des hélicoptères ont fait *ou* effectué des recherches pour retrouver des survivants; **to make a s. through one's pockets/the drawers** fouiller (dans) ses poches/les tiroirs; **s. and rescue operation** opération *f* de recherche et secours **2** *(by police, customs ▸ of house, person, bags)* fouille *f*; *(▸ with warrant)* perquisition *f*; **the police made a thorough s. of the premises** la police a fouillé les locaux de fond en comble; **the s. unearthed a stockpile of arms** la fouille a permis de mettre à jour une cache d'armes **3** *Comput* recherche *f*; **to do a s.** faire une recherche; **to do a s. for sth** rechercher qch; **s. and replace** recherche et remplacement *m*

• **in search of** **PREP** à la recherche de; **in s. of the truth** à la recherche de la vérité; **I went in s. of a restaurant** je suis parti à la recherche d'un restaurant

▸▸ *Comput* **search engine** moteur *m* de recherche; **search party** équipe *f* de secours; **search warrant** mandat *m* de perquisition

▸ **search out** **VT SEP** *(look for)* rechercher; *(find)* trouver, dénicher

▸ **search through** **VT INSEP** *(drawer, pockets)* fouiller (dans); *(case, documents)* fouiller; *(records)* consulter, faire des recherches dans; *(memory)* fouiller, chercher dans

searchable ['sɜːtʃəbəl] interrogeable; **s. database** base *f* de données interrogeable

searcher ['sɜːtʃə(r)] **N** chercheur(euse) *m,f*; **300 searchers combed the woods** 300 personnes ont passé les bois au peigne fin

searching ['sɜːtʃɪŋ] **N** *(of suspect, house, ship etc)* fouille *f*; *(at customs)* visite *f*; *Law* perquisition *f*

ADJ 1 *(look, eyes)* pénétrant; **he gave me a s. look** il m'a lancé un regard pénétrant **2** *(examination)* rigoureux, minutieux

searchlight ['sɜːtʃlaɪt] **N** projecteur *m*; **to turn a s. on sth** braquer un projecteur sur qch; **in the s.** à la lumière des projecteurs

searing ['sɪərɪŋ] **ADJ 1** *(pain)* fulgurant; *(light)* éclatant, fulgurant **2** *(attack, criticism)* acerbe, impitoyable

seascape ['siːskeɪp] **N 1** *(view)* paysage *m* marin **2** *Art* marine *f*

seashell ['siːʃel] **N** coquillage *m*

seashore ['siːʃɔː(r)] **N** *(edge of sea)* rivage *m*, bord *m* de (la) mer; *(beach)* plage *f*

seasick ['siːsɪk] **ADJ** **to be s.** avoir le mal de mer

seasickness ['siːsɪknɪs] **N** mal *m* de mer

seaside ['siːsaɪd] **N** bord *m* de (la) mer; **we spent the afternoon at the s.** nous avons passé l'après-midi au bord de la mer *ou* à la mer; **we live by** *or* **at the s.** nous habitons au bord de la mer

COMP *(holiday, vacation)* au bord de la mer, à la mer; *(town, hotel)* au bord de la mer, de bord de mer

▸▸ *Br* **seaside landlady** = propriétaire d'une pension de famille au bord de la mer

season ['siːzən] **N 1** *(summer, winter etc)* saison *f* **2** *(for trade)* saison *f*; **the start of the tourist/of the holiday s.** le début de la saison touristique/des vacances; **at the height of the Christmas s.** en pleine période de Noël; **the low/high s.** la basse/haute saison; **in s.** en saison; **off s.** hors saison

3 *(for fruit, vegetables)* saison *f*; **strawberries are in/out of s.** les fraises sont/ne sont pas de saison, c'est/ce n'est pas la saison des fraises
4 *(for breeding)* époque *f*, période *f*; **to be in s.** *(animal)* être en chaleur
5 *(for sport, entertainment)* saison *f*; **the football s.** la saison de football
6 *(for show, actor)* saison *f*; **he did a s. at Brighton** il a fait la saison de Brighton; *Rad & TV* **a new s. of French drama** un nouveau cycle de pièces de théâtre français
7 *(for hunting)* saison *f*, période *f*; **the hunting/fishing s.** la saison de la chasse/de la pêche; **the start of the s.** *Hunt* l'ouverture *f* de la chasse; *Fishing* l'ouverture *f* de la pêche
8 *(Christmas)* **S.'s Greetings** *(on card)* Joyeux Noël et Bonne Année
9 *Literary (suitable moment)* moment *m* opportun; **in due s.** en temps voulu, au moment opportun
VT 1 *(food ▸ with seasoning)* assaisonner; *(▸ with spice)* épicer; *Fig* **his speech was seasoned with witty remarks** son discours était parsemé *ou* agrémenté de remarques spirituelles **2** *(timber)* (faire) sécher, laisser sécher; *(cask)* abreuver; *(wine)* mûrir **3** *Formal (moderate)* modérer, tempérer
▸▸ *season creep* décalage *m* des saisons *(dû au réchauffement climatique)*; ***season ticket*** (carte *f* d')abonnement *m*; **to take out a s. ticket** prendre un abonnement; ***season ticket holder*** abonné(e) *m,f*

seasonable ['si:zənəbəl] **ADJ 1** *(weather)* de saison **2** *(opportune)* à propos, opportun

seasonal ['si:zənəl] **ADJ** saisonnier
▸▸ *Econ* ***seasonal adjustment*** ajustement *m* saisonnier; ***seasonal affective disorder*** dépression *f* saisonnière; ***seasonal employment*** emploi *m* saisonnier; ***seasonal job*** emploi *m* saisonnier; ***seasonal unemployment*** chômage *m* saisonnier; ***seasonal variations*** variations *fpl* saisonnières; ***seasonal worker*** saisonnier(ère) *m,f*

seasonally ['si:zənəlɪ] **ADV** de façon saisonnière
▸▸ *Econ* ***seasonally adjusted index*** indice *m* corrigé des variations saisonnières; ***seasonally adjusted statistics*** statistiques *fpl* corrigées des variations saisonnières, statistiques *fpl* désaisonnalisées

seasoned ['si:zənd] **ADJ 1** *(food)* assaisonné, épicé; **highly s.** bien épicé *ou* relevé **2** *(wood)* desséché, séché; *(wine)* mûr **3** *(experienced)* expérimenté, chevronné, éprouvé; **a s. political campaigner** un(e) militant(e) politique chevronné(e); **a s. traveller** un(e) voyageur(euse) expérimenté(e)

seasoning ['si:zənɪŋ] **N 1** *(process ▸ of food)* assaisonnement *m* **2** *(process ▸ of wood)* séchage *m*; *(▸ of wine)* maturation *f*; *(▸ of cask)* abreuvage *m* **3** *(condiment)* assaisonnement *m*, condiment *m*

seat [si:t] **N 1** *(chair, stool)* siège *m*; *(on bicycle)* selle *f*; *(in car ▸ single)* siège *m*; *(▸ bench)* banquette *f*; *(on train, at table)* place *f*; *(of toilet)* lunette *f*, siège *m*; **take a s.** asseyez-vous, prenez un siège; **keep a s. for me** gardez-moi une place
2 *(accommodation, place ▸ in theatre, cinema, train)* place *f*; *(space to sit)* place *f* (assise); **I'd like to book two seats for tomorrow** je voudrais réserver deux places pour demain; **please take your seats** veuillez prendre *ou* gagner vos places; **there were no seats left** il n'y avait plus de places; **I couldn't find a s. on the train** je n'ai pas pu trouver de place (assise) dans le train
3 *(of trousers)* fond *m*; *(of chair)* siège *m*; *(buttocks)* derrière *m*; **they grabbed him by the s. of his pants** ils l'ont attrapé par le fond du pantalon; *Fam* **by the s. of one's pants** de justesse▫
4 *Pol* siège *m*; **he kept/lost his s.** il a été/il n'a pas été réélu; **she has a s. in Parliament** elle est députée; **he was elected to a s. on the council** *(municipal)* il a été élu conseiller municipal; *(commercial)* il a été élu au conseil; **the government has a 30-s. majority** le gouvernement a une majorité de 30 sièges
5 *(centre ▸ of commerce)* centre *m*; *Admin* siège *m*; *Med (of disease, infection)* foyer *m*; **the s. of government** le siège du gouvernement
6 *(manor)* **(country) s.** manoir *m*
7 *Horseriding* **to have a good s.** se tenir bien en selle, avoir une bonne assiette; **to lose one's s.** être désarçonné
VT 1 *(passengers, children)* faire asseoir; *(guests ▸ at table)* placer; **please be seated** veuillez vous asseoir; **please remain seated** restez *ou* veuillez rester assis **2** *(accommodate)* avoir des places assises pour; **the plane can s. 400** l'avion a une capacité de 400 personnes; **how many does the bus s.?** combien y a-t-il de places assises dans le bus?; **how many does the table s.?** combien de personnes peut-on asseoir autour de la table? **3** *(chair)* mettre un fond à; *(with straw)* rempailler; *(with cane)* canner
VI *(skirt, trousers)* se déformer (à l'arrière)
▸▸ *seat belt* ceinture *f* de sécurité

seatback ['si:tbæk] **N** dossier *m*

-seater ['si:tə(r)] **SUFF two/four-s. (car)** voiture *f* à deux/quatre places

seating ['si:tɪŋ] **N** *(UNCOUNT)* **1** *(seats)* sièges *mpl*; *(benches, pews)* bancs *mpl*; **the s. isn't very comfortable** les sièges ne sont pas très confortables
2 *(sitting accommodation)* places *fpl* (assises); **there's additional s. at the back** il y a des places (assises) supplémentaires au fond; **there's s. for 300 in the hall** il y a 300 places dans la salle; **there's s. for eight round this table** on peut asseoir huit personnes autour de cette table
3 *(plan)* affectation *f* des places; **who's in charge of the s.?** qui est chargé de placer les gens?
4 *(material ▸ cloth, canvas)* (tissu *m* du) siège *m*; *(▸ wicker)* cannage *m*
5 *Tech (of bearing)* logement *m*; *(of valve)* siège *m*
▸▸ *seating accommodation* nombre *m* de places assises; **the hall has s. accommodation for 800 people** la salle a une capacité de 800 places (assises); ***seating arrangements*** placement *m* *ou* disposition *f* des gens; ***seating capacity*** nombre *m* de places assises; **the theatre has a s. capacity of 500** il y a 500 places dans le théâtre; ***seating plan*** *(in theatre)* plan *m* de la disposition des places; *(at table)* plan *m* de table

SEATO ['si:təʊ] **N** *Formerly (abbr* **Southeast Asia Treaty Organization***)* OTASE *f*

seaward ['si:wəd] **ADJ** de (la) mer; **on the s. side** du côté de la mer
ADV vers la mer *ou* le large
▸▸ *seaward breeze* brise *f* de mer

seawater ['si:wɔ:tə(r)] **N** eau *f* de mer

seaway ['si:weɪ] **N** route *f* maritime

seaweed ['si:wi:d] **N** *(UNCOUNT)* algues *fpl*; **a piece of s.** une algue

seaworthiness ['si:wɜ:ðɪnɪs] **N** navigabilité *f*

seaworthy ['si:wɜ:ðɪ] **ADJ** *(boat)* en état de naviguer

sebaceous [sɪ'beɪʃəs] **ADJ** *Anat* sébacé

sebum ['si:bəm] **N** *Anat* sébum *m*

SEC [,esi:'si:] **N** *(abbr* **Securities and Exchange Commission***)* = commission américaine des opérations de Bourse, ≃ COB *f*

sec [sek] **N** *Fam (abbr* **second***)* seconde▫*f*, instant▫*m*; **in a s.!** une seconde!; **I'll only be a s.** j'en ai pour une seconde

secant ['si:kənt] *Math* **ADJ** sécant
N sécante *f*

secateurs [,sekə'tɜ:z] **NPL** *Br* **(pair of) s.** sécateur *m*

secede [sɪ'si:d] **VI** faire sécession, se séparer; **they voted to s. from the federation** ils ont voté en faveur de leur sécession de la fédération

secession [sɪ'seʃən] **N** sécession *f*, scission *f*

secessionist [sɪ'seʃənɪst] **ADJ** sécessionniste
N sécessionniste *mf*, séparatiste *mf*

seclude [sɪ'klu:d] **VT** éloigner du monde, isoler; **they are secluded from the world** ils sont retirés du monde; **she secludes herself from contact with society** elle se coupe de tout contact avec autrui

secluded [sɪ'klu:dɪd] **ADJ** *(village)* retiré, à l'écart; *(garden)* tranquille; **to live a s. life** mener une vie solitaire, vivre en reclus; **I tried to find a s. corner to read** j'ai essayé de trouver un coin tranquille pour lire

seclusion [sɪ'klu:ʒən] **N** *(isolation ▸ chosen)* solitude *f*, isolement *m*; *(▸ imposed)* isolement *m*; **he lives a life of total s.** il vit en solitaire *ou* retiré du monde

SECOND¹ ['sekənd]

> **N**
> • seconde **1–3, 6, 8** • second **4**
> • deuxième **4**
> **ADJ**
> • deuxième **1, 2** • second **1, 2**
> **ADV**
> • en seconde place **1** • deuxièmement **3**
> **VT**
> • appuyer
> **NPL**
> • articles de second choix **1** • rab **2**

N 1 *(unit of time)* seconde *f*; **the ambulance arrived within seconds** l'ambulance est arrivée en quelques secondes
2 *(instant)* seconde *f*, instant *m*; **I'll be with you in a s.** je serai à vous dans un instant; **I'll only be a s.** j'en ai seulement pour deux secondes; **just a o half a s.!** une seconde!
3 *Math & Astron* seconde *f*
4 *(in order)* second(e) *m,f*, deuxième *mf*; **I was the s. to arrive** je suis arrivé deuxième *ou* le deuxième; **to come a close s.** *(in race)* être battu de justesse
5 *(in duel)* témoin *m*, second *m*; *(in boxing)* soigneur *m*; **seconds out!** soigneurs hors du ring!
6 *Aut* seconde *f*; **in s.** en seconde
7 *Br Univ* **an upper/a lower s.** une licence avec mention bien/assez bien
8 *Mus* seconde *f*; **major/minor s.** seconde *f* majeure/mineure
ADJ 1 *(in series)* deuxième; *(of two)* second; **every s. person** une personne sur deux; **Charles the S.** Charles Deux *ou* II; **the s. of March** le deux mars; **for the s. time** pour la deuxième fois; **to be s. in command** *(in hierarchy)* être deuxième dans la hiérarchie; *Mil* commander en second; **he's s. in line for promotion** il sera le second à bénéficier d'une promotion; *Gram* **in the s. person singular/plural** à la deuxième personne du singulier/pluriel; **to take s. place** *(in race)* prendre la deuxième place; *(in exam)* être deuxième; **his wife took s. place to his career** sa femme venait après sa carrière; **and in the s. place…** *(in demonstration, argument)* et en deuxième lieu…; **it's s. nature to her** c'est une seconde nature chez elle; **he's s. only to his teacher as a violinist** en tant que violoniste, il n'y a que son professeur qui le surpasse *ou* qui lui soit supérieur; **as a goalkeeper, he's s. to none** comme gardien de but, il n'a pas son pareil; **her short stories are s. to none** ses nouvelles sont inégalées *ou* sans pareilles
2 *(another, additional)* deuxième, second, autre; **a s. Camus/Churchill** un nouveau Camus/Churchill; **he was given a s. chance** on lui a accordé une seconde chance; **you are unlikely to get a s. chance to join the team** il est peu probable que l'on vous propose à nouveau de faire partie de l'équipe; **to take a s. helping** se resservir; **would you like a s. helping?** en reprendrez-vous un peu?; **can I have a s. helping of meat?** est-ce que je peux reprendre de la viande?; **they have a s. home in France** ils ont une résidence secondaire en France; **France is my s. home** la France est ma seconde patrie; **I'd like a s. opinion** *(said by doctor)* je voudrais prendre l'avis d'un confrère; *(said by patient)* je voudrais consulter un autre médecin; **to have s. thoughts** avoir des doutes, hésiter; **are you having s. thoughts?** est-ce que vous hésitez?; **he left his family without a s. thought** il a quitté sa famille sans réfléchir *ou* sans se poser de questions; **on s.** *Br* **thought** *or Am* **thought I'd better go myself** réflexion faite il vaut mieux que j'y aille moi-même
ADV 1 *(in order)* en seconde place; **to come s.** *(in race)* arriver en seconde position; **she arrived s.** *(at party, meeting)* elle est arrivée la deuxième; **the horse came s. to Juniper's Lad** le cheval s'est classé deuxième derrière Juniper's Lad
2 *(with superlative adj)* **the s. largest/s. richest** le second par la taille/second par le revenu; **the s**

argest city in the world/in Portugal la deuxième ille du monde/du Portugal
3 *(secondly)* en second lieu, deuxièmement
VT *(motion)* appuyer; *(speaker)* appuyer la motion de; **I'll s. that!** je suis d'accord!

seconds NPL 1 *Com (goods)* articles *mpl* de second choix; *(crockery)* vaisselle *f* de second hoix
2 *Fam (of food)* rab *m*; **are there any seconds?** il y a du rab?
▸ ***second ballot*** deuxième tour *m*; ***second best*** N is-aller *m inv*; **I refuse to make do with s. best** je efuse de me contenter d'un pis-aller; **she knew he would never be more than s. best** *(in person's ffection)* elle savait qu'elle ne serait jamais plus u'un second choix; *(athlete)* elle savait qu'elle erait toujours deuxième ADV **to come off s. best** tre battu, se faire battre; *Pol* ***second chamber*** *gen)* deuxième chambre *f*; *(in UK)* Chambre *f* es lords; *(in US)* Sénat *m*; ***second childhood*** gâ-isme *m*, seconde enfance *f*; **he's in his s. child-ood** il est retombé en enfance; *Rail* ***second lass*** seconde *f* (classe *f*); *Rel* ***the Second Coming*** e second avènement du Messie; ***second cousin*** ousin(e) *m,f* issu(e) de germains; *Br* ***second elev-n*** *(in soccer, cricket)* équipe *f* de réserve *(dans le adre scolaire ou amateur)*; *Cin* ***second feature*** euxième film *m (d'un programme où figurent eux longs métrages)*; ***second floor*** *(in UK)* euxième étage *m*; *(in US)* premier étage *m*; *ut* ***second gear*** seconde *f*; *Am Sch* ***second grade*** = classe de primaire pour les 6–7 ans; *Sport* ***sec-nd half*** deuxième mi-temps *f inv*; ***second hand*** *of watch, clock)* aiguille *f* des secondes, trot-euse *f*; ***second language*** deuxième langue *f*; ***sec-nd lieutenant*** ≃ sous-lieutenant *m*; ***second name*** nom *m* de famille; *Naut* ***second officer*** (offi-ier *m* en) second *m*; *Br Parl* ***second reading*** *(of ill)* deuxième lecture *f*; ***second sight*** seconde u double vue *f*; **to have s. sight** avoir un don de ouble vue; *Sport* ***second team*** équipe *f* de ré-erve; ***second teeth*** deuxième dentition *f*, denti-ion *f* définitive; *Cin* ***second unit*** deuxième quipe *f*; *Mus* ***second violin*** deuxième violon *m*

econd[2] [sɪ'kɒnd] VT *Br (employee)* détacher, en-oyer en détachement; *Mil* détacher; **she was se-onded to the UN** elle a été détachée à l'ONU; **eter was seconded for service abroad** Peter a été nvoyé en détachement à l'étranger

econdary ['sekəndərɪ] *(pl* **secondaries)** ADJ 1 *gen) & Med* secondaire; *(minor)* secondaire, de eu d'importance; **the word has a s. meaning** le not a un sens secondaire; **this issue is of s. im-ortance** cette question est d'une importance econdaire; **any other considerations are s. to her wellbeing** son bien-être prime sur toute autre onsidération 2 *Sch* secondaire
N 1 *(deputy)* subordonné(e) *m,f*, adjoint(e) *m,f* 2 *Med (tumour)* tumeur *f* secondaire, métastase *f*
▸▸ ***secondary colour*** couleur *f* secondaire *ou* bi-aire; ***secondary education*** enseignement *m* se-ondaire *ou* du second degré; *Geol* ***secondary era*** (ère *f*) secondaire *m*; ***secondary market*** mar-hé *m* secondaire; *Br* ***secondary modern (school)*** = établissement secondaire d'enseignement énéral et technique, aujourd'hui remplacé ar la "comprehensive school"; *Br Ind* ***secondary icketing*** *(UNCOUNT)* piquets *mpl* de grève de olidarité; ***secondary product*** sous-produit *m*; ***econdary production*** production *f* manufactu-ée; *Transp* ***secondary road*** route *f* secondaire *ou* départementale; ***secondary school*** = établisse-ment secondaire; *Econ* ***secondary sector*** secteur *n* secondaire; *Ling* ***secondary stress*** accent *m* se-ondaire

econd-class ADJ 1 *Rail* de seconde (classe); **wo s. returns to Glasgow** deux allers (et) retours our Glasgow en seconde (classe); **a s. season icket** un abonnement de seconde
2 *(hotel)* de seconde catégorie
3 *(mail)* à tarif réduit *ou* lent
4 *(inferior)* de qualité inférieure
ADV 1 *Rail* en seconde (classe); **to travel s.** voya-er en seconde 2 *(for mail)* **to send a parcel s.** ex-édier un paquet en tarif réduit
▸▸ ***second-class citizen*** citoyen(enne) *m,f* de se-onde zone; **to be treated like a s. citizen** être raité comme un citoyen de seconde zone; *Br Univ* ***second-class honours degree*** ≃ licence *f* avec mention (assez) bien

second-degree ADJ
▸▸ ***second-degree burn*** brûlure *f* au deuxième degré; *Am Law* ***second-degree murder*** meurtre *m* sans préméditation

seconder ['sekəndə(r)] N 1 *(in debate* ▸ *of motion)* personne *f* qui appuie une motion 2 *(of candidate)* deuxième parrain *m*

second-generation ADJ *(immigrant, computer)* de la seconde génération

second-guess VT *Fam (before event)* essayer de prévoir *ou* d'anticiper[a]

second-hand ADJ 1 *(car, clothes, books)* d'occasion; **the s. market** le marché de l'occasion 2 *(information)* de seconde main
ADV 1 *(buy)* d'occasion 2 *(indirectly)* **I heard the news s.** j'ai appris la nouvelle indirectement
▸▸ ***second-hand dealer*** *(gen)* marchand(e) *m,f* d'articles d'occasion; *(in clothes)* fripier(ère) *m,f*; *(in books)* bouquiniste *mf*; ***second-hand shop*** magasin *m* d'articles d'occasion

second-in-command N *Mil* commandant *m* en second; *Naut* second *m*, officier *m* en second; *(in hierarchy)* second *m*, adjoint *m*

secondly ['sekəndlɪ] ADV deuxièmement, en deuxième lieu

secondment [sɪ'kɒndmənt] N *Br Formal* détachement *m*, affectation *f* provisoire; **to be on s.** *(teacher)* être en détachement; *(diplomat)* être en mission

second-rate ADJ *(goods, equipment)* de qualité inférieure; *(movie, book)* médiocre; *(politician, player)* médiocre, de second ordre

secrecy ['si:krəsɪ] N *(UNCOUNT)* secret *m*; **why all the s.?** pourquoi tous ces secrets?; **in the strictest s.** dans le plus grand secret

secret ['si:krɪt] N 1 *(information kept hidden)* secret *m*; **it's a s. between you and me** c'est un secret entre nous; **I have no secrets from her** je ne lui cache rien; **can you keep a s.?** pouvez-vous garder un secret?; **shall we let them into the s.?** est-ce qu'on va les mettre dans le secret *ou* dans la confidence?; **I'll tell you** *or* **I'll let you into a s.** je vais vous dire *ou* révéler un secret; **not many people were in on the s.** il n'y avait pas beaucoup de gens qui étaient dans la confidence *ou* au courant; **I make no s. of** *or* **about my humble origins** je ne cache pas mes origines modestes
2 *(explanation)* secret *m*; **the s. of his success** le secret de sa réussite; **the s. is to warm the dish first** le secret consiste à chauffer le plat d'abord
3 *(mystery)* secret *m*, mystère *m*; **the secrets of nature** les secrets *mpl ou* les mystères *mpl* de la nature; **these locks have** *or* **hold no s. for me** ces serrures n'ont pas de secret pour moi
ADJ 1 *(meeting, plan)* secret(ète); **to keep sth s.** tenir qch secret
2 *(personal)* secret(ète); **it's my s. belief that he doesn't really love her** je crois en mon for intérieur qu'il ne l'aime pas vraiment
3 *(hidden* ▸ *door)* caché, dérobé; *(*▸ *compartment, safe)* caché; *Literary* **the s. places of the heart** les plis et les replis du cœur
4 *(identity)* inconnu; **the flowers were from a s. admirer of hers** les fleurs venaient d'un admirateur inconnu
5 *(secluded* ▸ *beach, garden)* retiré, secret(ète)
• **in secret** ADV en secret, secrètement
▸▸ ***secret agent*** agent *m* secret; ***secret ballot*** vote *m* à bulletin secret; ***secret funds*** caisse *f* noire, fonds *mpl* secrets; ***secret police*** police *f* secrète; *Am* ***the Secret Service*** = service de protection des hauts fonctionnaires américains et de leurs familles; ***secret service*** *(government organization)* services *mpl* secrets

secretarial [,sekrə'teərɪəl] ADJ *(tasks)* de secrétaire, de secrétariat; **I have a part-time s. job** j'ai un travail de secrétaire à mi-temps; **I followed a s. course** j'ai pris des cours de secrétariat
▸▸ ***secretarial college, secretarial school*** école *f* de secrétariat; ***the secretarial staff*** le secrétariat; ***secretarial work*** travail *m* de secrétaire; **she does s. work** elle fait un travail de secrétariat *ou* de secrétaire

secretariat [,sekrə'teərɪət] N secrétariat *m*

secretary [*Br* 'sekrətərɪ, *Am* 'sekrə,terɪ] *(pl* **secretaries)** N 1 *(gen) & Com* secrétaire *mf* 2 *Pol (in UK* ▸ *minister)* ministre *m*; *(*▸ *non-elected official)* secrétaire *mf* d'État; *(in US)* secrétaire *mf* d'État 3 *(diplomat)* secrétaire *mf* d'ambassade
▸▸ *Am* ***Secretary of Agriculture*** ministre *m* de l'Agriculture; *Am* ***Secretary of Commerce*** ministre *m* du Commerce; *Am* ***Secretary of Defense*** ministre *m* de la Défense; *Am* ***Secretary of Education*** ≃ ministre *m* de l'Éducation nationale; *Am* ***Secretary of (the) Interior*** ministre *m* de l'Intérieur; *Am* ***Secretary of Labor*** ministre *m* du Travail; ***secretary of state*** *(in UK)* ministre *m*; *(in US)* secrétaire *mf* d'État, ≃ ministre *m* des Affaires étrangères; *Br* ***Secretary of State for Transport*** ministre *m* des Transports; *Am* ***Secretary of Transportation*** ministre *m* des Transports; *Am* ***Secretary of (the) Treasury*** ≃ ministre *m* de l'Économie et des Finances

secretary-general N secrétaire *mf* général(e)
▸▸ ***Secretary-General of the UN*** secrétaire *mf* général(e) de l'ONU

secrete [sɪ'kri:t] VT 1 *Biol & Physiol* sécréter 2 *Formal (hide)* cacher

secretion [sɪ'kri:ʃən] N 1 *Biol & Physiol* sécrétion *f* 2 *Formal (act of hiding)* action *f* de cacher

secretive ['si:krətɪv] ADJ *(nature)* secret(ète); *(behaviour)* cachottier; **she's very s. about her new job** elle ne dit pas grand-chose de son nouveau travail; **she's quite a s. person** c'est une personne assez secrète; **why are you being so s. about it?** pourquoi fais-tu tant de cachotteries là-dessus?

secretively ['si:krətɪvlɪ] ADV en cachette, secrètement

secretiveness ['si:krətɪvnɪs] N *(UNCOUNT)* *(of character)* réserve *f*; *(keeping secrets)* cachotteries *fpl*

secretly ['si:krɪtlɪ] ADV *(do, act)* en secret, secrètement; *(believe, think)* en son for intérieur, secrètement

sect [sekt] N secte *f*

sectarian [sek'teərɪən] N sectaire *mf*
ADJ sectaire
▸▸ ***sectarian killing*** assassinat *m* sectaire; ***sectarian violence*** violence *f* d'origine religieuse

> Note that, unlike the word **sectarian** in British English, the French word **sectaire** does not specifically refer to tensions between Catholics and Protestants.

sectarianism [sek'teərɪənɪzəm] N sectarisme *m*

> Note that, unlike the word **sectarianism** in British English, the French word **sectarisme** does not specifically refer to tensions between Catholics and Protestants.

section ['sekʃən] N 1 *(sector)* section *f*, partie *f*; **there has been snow over large sections of southern England** il a neigé sur une grande partie du sud de l'Angleterre; **the residential s. of the town** les quartiers résidentiels de la ville
2 *(division* ▸ *of company, staff, services, in orchestra)* section *f*; *(*▸ *in army)* groupe *m* de combat
3 *(component part* ▸ *of furniture)* élément *m*; *(*▸ *of tube)* section *f*; *(*▸ *of track, road)* section *f*, tronçon *m*; *Rail* section *f*; **the kitchen units/the shelves come in easy-to-assemble sections** les éléments de cuisine/les étagères se vendent en kit
4 *(subdivision* ▸ *of law)* article *m*; *(*▸ *of book, exam, text)* section *f*, partie *f*; *(of newspaper* ▸ *page)* page *f*; *(*▸ *pages)* pages *fpl*; *(of library)* section *f*; **the children's s.** la section pour enfants; **the sports/women's s.** les pages *fpl* des sports/réservées aux femmes
5 *(in department store)* rayon *m*; **furniture/children's s.** rayon *m* meubles/enfants
6 *Am Rail (train)* train *m* supplémentaire; *(sleeper)* compartiment-lits *m*
7 *(cut, cross-section* ▸ *drawing)* coupe *f*, section *f*; *Geom* section *f*; *(*▸ *for microscope)* coupe *f*, lamelle *f*
8 *Med* sectionnement *m*
9 *Am (land)* = division (administrative) d'un mille carré
VT 1 *(divide into sections)* sectionner 2 *Br (send to psychiatric hospital)* interner

▸▸ *Typ* **section mark** signe *m* de paragraphe; *Br* **Section 28** = article de loi, introduit en 1986 sous le gouvernement Thatcher et abrogé en 2003, qui interdisait aux enseignants d'aborder le thème de l'homosexualité dans les écoles

sectional ['sekʃənəl] **ADJ 1** *(furniture)* en kit **2** *(interests)* d'un groupe **3** *(drawing)* en coupe

sectionalism ['sekʃənəlɪzəm] **N** défense *f* des intérêts d'un groupe

sector ['sektə(r)] **N 1** *(area, realm)* secteur *m*, domaine *m*; *Econ* secteur *m*; *(part, subdivision)* secteur *m*, partie *f*; *Comput (of screen, disk)* secteur *m*; **the banking s.** le secteur bancaire; **whole sectors of society live below the poverty line** des catégories sociales entières vivent en dessous du seuil de pauvreté

2 *Mil* secteur *m*, zone *f*

3 *Geom* secteur *m*

4 *(for measuring)* compas *m* de proportion

VT *(gen)* diviser en secteurs; *Admin & Geog* sectoriser

secular ['sekjʊlə(r)] **ADJ 1** *(life, clergy)* séculier

2 *(education, school)* laïque

3 *(music, art)* profane

4 *(ancient)* séculaire

secularism ['sekjʊlərɪzəm] **N** laïcisme *m*

secularization, -isation [ˌsekjʊləraɪ'zeɪʃən] **N** sécularisation *f*; *(of education)* laïcisation *f*

secularize, -ise ['sekjʊləraɪz] **VT** séculariser; *(education)* laïciser

secure [sɪ'kjʊə(r)] **ADJ 1** *(protected)* sûr, en sécurité, en sûreté; **put the papers in a s. place** mettez les papiers en lieu sûr; **to be put in s. accommodation** être placé dans un centre d'éducation surveillée; **I feel s. from** *or* **against attack** je me sens à l'abri des attaques

2 *(guaranteed* ▸ *job)* sûr; *(*▸ *victory, future)* assuré; **a country must ensure its borders are s.** un pays doit assurer ses frontières *ou* faire en sorte que ses frontières soient sûres

3 *(calm, confident)* tranquille, sécurisé; **now she's married, she feels more s.** maintenant qu'elle est mariée, elle se sent plus sécurisée; **I was s. in the belief that all danger was past** j'étais intimement persuadé que tout danger était écarté

4 *(solid* ▸ *investment, base)* sûr; *(*▸ *foothold, grasp)* sûr, ferme; *(solidly fastened* ▸ *bolt, window)* bien fermé; *(*▸ *scaffolding, aerial)* solide, qui tient bien; *(*▸ *knot)* solide; **can you make the door/the rope s.?** pouvez-vous vous assurer que la porte est bien fermée/la corde est bien attachée?

VT 1 *Formal (obtain)* se procurer, obtenir; *(agreement)* obtenir; *(loan)* obtenir, se voir accorder; **to s. a majority** *(gen)* obtenir une majorité; *Pol* emporter la majorité; **to s. the release of sb** obtenir la libération de qn; **will it be possible to s. a hall for the debate?** serait-il possible de réserver une salle pour le débat?

2 *(fasten, fix* ▸ *rope)* attacher; *(*▸ *parcel)* ficeler; *(*▸ *ladder, aerial)* bien fixer; *(*▸ *window, lock)* bien fermer; *(*▸ *cargo)* arrimer; **the rope was secured around a rock** la corde était solidement attachée à un rocher; **s. the ladder against the wall first** assurez-vous d'abord que l'échelle est bien appuyée contre le mur; **doors and windows should be properly secured** les portes et les fenêtres doivent être bien fermées

3 *(guarantee* ▸ *future)* assurer; *(*▸ *debt, borrower)* garantir; **that secured his future with the company** cela a assuré son avenir dans l'entreprise

4 *(from danger)* préserver, protéger; **to s. a pass** *(in mountains)* garder un défilé; **we did everything we could to s. the boat against** *or* **from the storm** nous avons tout fait pour protéger le bateau contre la tempête

▸▸ *Comput* ***secure electronic transaction*** protocole *m* SET; ***secure tenancy*** location *f* assurée *ou* garantie; ***secure unit*** *(in psychiatric hospital)* quartier *m* de haute sécurité; *(in children's home)* section *f* surveillée; *Comput* ***secure Web site*** site *m* sécurisé

secured [sɪ'kjʊəd] **ADJ** *Fin (debt, loan)* garanti

▸▸ *Fin* ***secured loan*** prêt *m* garanti

securely [sɪ'kjʊəlɪ] **ADV 1** *(firmly)* fermement, solidement; **the door was s. fastened** la porte était bien fermée *ou* verrouillée **2** *(safely)* en sécurité, en sûreté; **put the jewels s. away** mettez les bijoux en lieu sûr; **he is s. behind bars** il est hors d'état de nuire

securitization, -isation [sɪˌkjʊərɪtaɪ'zeɪʃən] **N** *St Exch* titrisation *f*

securitize, -ise [sɪ'kjʊərɪtaɪz] **VT** *St Exch* titriser

security [sɪ'kjʊərətɪ] *(pl* **securities***)* **N 1** *(safety)* sécurité *f*; **national s.** la sécurité nationale; **the President's national s. advisers** les conseillers du président en matière de sécurité nationale; **they slipped through the s. net** ils sont passés au travers des mailles du filet des services de sécurité

2 *(police measures, protection etc)* sécurité *f*; **for reasons of s.** par mesure de *ou* pour des raisons de sécurité; **there was maximum s. for the President's visit** des mesures de sécurité exceptionnelles ont été prises pour la visite du président; **maximum s. wing** *(in prison)* quartier *m* de haute surveillance

3 *(assurance)* sécurité *f*; **job s.** sécurité *f* de l'emploi; **to have s. of tenure** *(in job)* être titulaire, avoir la sécurité de l'emploi; *(as tenant)* avoir un bail qui ne peut être résilié; **financial s.** sécurité *f* matérielle *ou* financière

4 *(guarantee)* garantie *f*, caution *f*; **what s. do you have for the loan?** quelle garantie avez-vous pour couvrir ce prêt?; **to give sth as s.** donner qch en cautionnement; **to lend money on s.** prêter de l'argent sur nantissement *ou* sur garantie; **have you anything to put up as s.?** qu'est-ce que vous pouvez fournir comme garantie?; **she gave her diamonds as s. for the loan** elle a donné ses diamants comme garantie pour le prêt; **loans without s.** prêts *mpl* sans garantie

5 *(guarantor)* garant(e) *m,f*; *Br* **to stand s. for sb** se porter garant de qn; **to stand s. for a loan** avaliser un prêt

6 *(department)* sécurité *f*; **please call s.** appelez la sécurité s'il vous plaît

7 *Comput* sécurité *f*

• **securities NPL** *Fin* titres *mpl*, actions *fpl*, valeurs *fpl*; **government securities** titres *mpl* d'État; **the securities market** le marché des valeurs

▸▸ ***security barrier*** barrière *f* Vauban; ***security blanket*** doudou *m*; *Psy* objet *m* transitionnel; *Admin & Mil* ***security clearance*** habilitation *f*; *(document)* laissez-passer *m inv*; ***security code*** code *m* confidentiel; ***Security Council*** Conseil *m* de sécurité; *Am* ***Securities and Exchange Commission*** = commission américaine des opérations de Bourse, ≃ COB *f*; ***security firm*** société *f* de gardiennage; ***security forces*** forces *fpl* de sécurité; ***security guard*** garde *m* (chargé de la sécurité); *(for armoured van)* convoyeur(euse) *m,f* de fonds; ***security leak*** = fuite de documents ou d'informations concernant la sécurité; *Fin* ***securities market*** marché *m* des titres *ou* des valeurs (mobilières); ***security measures*** mesures *fpl* de sécurité; ***security officer*** *(on ship)* officier *m* chargé de la sécurité; *(in firm)* employé(e) *m,f* chargé(e) de la sécurité; *(inspector)* inspecteur (trice) *m,f* de la sécurité; ***security police*** (services *mpl* de la) sûreté *f*; *Fin* ***securities portfolio*** portefeuille *m* de titres; ***security tag*** agrafe *f* antivol

security-coded ADJ *(radio)* codé, à code de sécurité

sedan [sɪ'dæn] **N 1** *Am (car)* berline *f* **2** *Hist (chair)* chaise *f* à porteurs

▸▸ *Hist* ***sedan chair*** chaise *f* à porteurs

sedate [sɪ'deɪt] **ADJ** *(person, manner)* calme, posé; *(behaviour)* calme, pondéré; **we strolled home at a s. pace** nous sommes rentrés chez nous sans hâte *ou* en flânant; **we live a very s. existence** nous menons une existence très calme

VT donner des sédatifs à; **he's heavily sedated** on lui a donné de fortes doses de calmants

sedately [sɪ'deɪtlɪ] **ADV** posément, calmement; **she walked s. back to her house** elle est revenue chez elle d'un pas lent *ou* tranquille

sedation [sɪ'deɪʃən] **N** sédation *f*; **under s.** sous calmants

sedative ['sedətɪv] **ADJ** calmant

N calmant *m*

sedentary ['sedəntərɪ] **ADJ** sédentaire

sedge [sedʒ] **N** *Bot* laîche *f*, carex *m*

▸▸ *Orn* ***sedge warbler*** phragmite *m* des joncs

sediment ['sedɪmənt] **N 1** *Geol* sédiment *m* **2** *(i... liquid)* sédiment *m*, dépôt *m*; *(in wine)* dépôt *m* lie *f*

VT déposer

VI se déposer

sedimentary [ˌsedɪ'mentərɪ] **ADJ** sédimentaire

sedimentation [ˌsedɪmen'teɪʃən] **N** sédimentation *f*

sedition [sɪ'dɪʃən] **N** sédition *f*

seditious [sɪ'dɪʃəs] **ADJ** séditieux

seduce [sɪ'dju:s] **VT 1** *(sexually)* séduire **2** *(attrac...)* séduire, attirer; *(draw)* entraîner; **she was seduced away from the company** on l'a persuadée de *ou* incitée à quitter la société

> Note that the most common meaning of the French verb **séduire** is **to charm** or **to appeal to**, depending on the context.

seducer [sɪ'dju:sə(r)] **N** séducteur(trice) *m,f*

seduction [sɪ'dʌkʃən] **N** séduction *f*

seductive [sɪ'dʌktɪv] **ADJ** *(person)* séduisant; *(personality)* séduisant, attrayant; *(voice, smile)* aguichant, séducteur; *(offer)* séduisant, alléchant

seductively [sɪ'dʌktɪvlɪ] **ADV** *(dress)* d'une manière séduisante; *(smile)* d'une manière enjôleuse

seductiveness [sɪ'dʌktɪvnɪs] **N** *(of person)* séduction *f*, charme *m*; *(of personality)* caractère *m* séduisant *ou* attrayant; *(of voice, smile)* caractère *m* aguichant *ou* séducteur; *(of offer)* caractère *m* séduisant *ou* alléchant

sedulous ['sedjʊləs] **ADJ** *Formal* diligent, persévérant

sedulously ['sedjʊləslɪ] **ADV** *Formal* assidûment, avec persévérance

SEE [si:]

VT
- voir **1–8, 10–15, 17–19, 21**
- recevoir **7**
- s'imaginer **12**
- connaître **18**
- consulter **4**
- rencontrer **5**
- comprendre **10**
- s'assurer **16**
- accompagner **20**

VI
- voir **1–5**
- comprendre **4**

(pt **saw** [sɔ:], *pp* **seen** [si:n]*)*

VT 1 *(perceive with eyes)* voir; **can you s. me?** est-ce que tu me vois?; **I can't s. a thing** je ne vois rien; **she could s. a light in the distance** elle voyait une lumière au loin; **he saw her talk** *or* **talking to the policeman** il l'a vue parler *ou* qui parlait au policier; **did anyone s. you take it?** est-ce que quelqu'un t'a vu le prendre?; **did you s. what happened?** avez-vous vu ce qui s'est passé?; **let me see your hands** fais-moi voir *ou* montre-moi tes mains; **now s. what you've done!** regarde ce que tu as fait!; **I s. her around a lot** je la croise assez souvent; **I don't want to be seen with him** je ne veux pas être vu *ou* qu'on me voie avec lui; **there wasn't a car to be seen** il n'y avait pas une seule voiture en vue; **the cathedral can be seen from a long way off** on voit la cathédrale de très loin; **nothing more was ever seen of her** on ne l'a plus jamais revue; **it has to be seen to be believed** il faut le voir pour le croire; **there's nothing there, you're seeing things!** il n'y a rien, tu as des hallucinations!; **I could s. what was going to happen (a mile off)** je le voyais venir (gros comme une maison); *Fam* **they saw you coming (a mile off)** ils t'ont vu arriver de loin; **could you s. your way (clear) to lending me £20?** est-ce que vous pourriez me prêter 20 livres?; **to s. the back** *or* **last of sth** en avoir fini avec qch; **I'll be glad to s. the back** *or* **last of her** je serai content d'être débarrassé d'elle; **if you've seen one, you've seen them all** quand tu en as vu un, tu les as tous vus; *Fam* **you ain't seen nothing yet!** tu n'as encore rien vu

2 *(watch* ▸ *movie, play, programme)* voir; **did you s. the match last night?** est-ce que tu as vu le match hier soir?

3 *(refer to* ▸ *page, chapter)* voir; **s. page 317** voir page 317; **s. above** voir plus haut; **s. (on) the back** voir au verso

4 *(consult* ▸ *doctor, lawyer)* consulter, voir; **you should s. a doctor** tu devrais voir *ou* consulter n médecin; **I'll be seeing my lawyer about this** je 'ais consulter mon avocat à ce sujet; **can I s. you or a minute in my office?** je peux vous voir un nstant dans mon bureau?; **I'd like to s. you on usiness** je voudrais vous parler affaires

5 *(meet by chance)* voir, rencontrer; **guess who I aw at the supermarket!** devine qui j'ai vu *ou* qui 'ai rencontré au supermarché!

6 *(visit ▸ person, place)* voir; **come round and s. ne sometime** passe me voir un de ces jours; **they ame to s. me in hospital** ils sont venus me voir à 'hôpital; **I've always wanted to s. China** j'ai touours voulu voir la Chine

7 *(receive a visit from)* recevoir, voir; **he's too ill to . anyone** il est trop malade pour voir qui que ce oit; **she can't s. you right now, she's busy** elle ne eut pas vous recevoir *ou* voir maintenant, elle st trop occupée

8 *(spend time with socially)* voir; **do you still s. the Browns?** est-ce que vous voyez toujours les Brown?; **we've seen quite a lot of them recently** ous les avons beaucoup vus dernièrement; **we s. less of them these days** nous les voyons noins en ce moment; **is he seeing anyone at the noment?** *(going out with)* est-ce qu'il sort avec quelqu'un en ce moment?

9 *Fam (saying goodbye)* **s. you!, (I'll) be seeing you!** salut!; **s. you later!** à tout à l'heure!; **s. you around!** à un de ces jours!; **s. you tomorrow!** à demain!; **s. you in London!** on se verra à Londres!

10 *(understand)* voir, comprendre; **I s. what you mean** je vois *ou* comprends ce que vous voulez dire; **I don't s. what's so funny!** je ne vois pas ce qu'il y a de si drôle!; **he can't s. the joke** il ne comprend pas la plaisanterie; **I can s. why you were worried** je comprends pourquoi vous étiez inquiet; **I can't s. that it matters** je ne vois pas quelle importance ça a

11 *(consider, view)* voir; **we s. things differently** nous ne voyons pas les choses de la même façon; **you'll s. things differently in the morning** demain tu verras les choses d'un autre œil; **that's how I s. it** c'est comme ça que je vois les choses; **as I s. it, it's the parents who are to blame** à mon avis, ce sont les parents qui sont responsables

12 *(envisage, picture)* voir, s'imaginer; **she just couldn't s. herself as a wife and mother** elle ne s'imaginait pas *ou* elle ne se voyait pas mariée et avec des enfants; **I can't s. them accepting this** je ne peux pas croire qu'ils vont accepter cela; **I can't s. it myself** je n'y crois pas trop; **they say this will be more efficient but I don't s. it** ils disent que cela sera plus efficace, mais je n'y crois pas; **I don't s. any chance of that** à mon avis c'est peu probable; **can I borrow the car? – I don't s. why not** est-ce que je peux prendre la voiture? – je n'y vois pas d'inconvénients; **will you finish in time? – I don't s. why not** vous aurez fini à temps? – il n'y a pas de raison; **what do you s. happening next?** d'après vous, qu'est-ce qui va se passer ensuite?; **how do you s. things developing?** comment est-ce que vous envisagez l'avenir?

13 *(try to find out)* voir; **I'll s. if I can fix it** je vais voir si je peux le réparer; **I'll s. what I can do** je vais voir ce que je peux faire; **go and s. if he's still asleep** va voir s'il dort encore

14 *(perceive)* voir; **I can't s. any improvement** je ne vois pas d'amélioration; **what can she possibly s. in him?** qu'est-ce qu'elle peut bien lui trouver?

15 *(discover, learn)* voir; **I'll be interested to s. how he gets on** je serais curieux de voir comment il se débrouillera; **I s. (that) he's getting married** j'ai appris qu'il allait se marier; **I saw it in the paper this morning** je l'ai vu *ou* lu ce matin dans le journal; **as we shall s. in a later chapter** comme nous le verrons dans un chapitre ultérieur

16 *(make sure)* s'assurer, veiller à; **s. that all the lights are out before you leave** assurez-vous que *ou* veillez à ce que toutes les lumières soient éteintes avant de partir; **I shall s. that he comes** je me charge de le faire venir; *Fam* **she'll s. you right** elle veillera à ce que tu ne manques de rien[□], elle prendra bien soin de toi[□]

17 *(inspect ▸ file, passport, ticket)* voir; **can I s. your ticket, sir?** puis-je voir votre ticket, Monsieur?

18 *(experience)* voir, connaître; **he thinks he's seen it all** il croit tout savoir; **most recruits never s. active service** la plupart des recrues ne voient jamais la guerre de près; **our car has seen better days** notre voiture a connu des jours meilleurs; **the city hasn't seen such crowds in decades** la ville n'a pas connu une foule pareille depuis des dizaines d'années; **the country saw many changes** le pays a connu de grands changements

19 *(witness)* voir; **they have seen their purchasing power halved** ils ont vu leur pouvoir d'achat diminuer de moitié; **last year saw an increase in profits** l'année dernière a vu une augmentation des bénéfices; **I never thought I'd s. the day when he'd admit he was wrong** je n'aurais jamais cru qu'un jour il admettrait avoir tort

20 *(accompany)* accompagner; **I'll s. you to the bus stop** je t'accompagne à *ou* jusqu'à l'arrêt du bus; **I'll s. you home** je te raccompagne chez toi; **s. Mr Smith to the door, please** veuillez raccompagner M. Smith jusqu'à la porte; **he saw her into a taxi/onto the train** il l'a mise dans un taxi/le train; **to s. sb across the road** aider qn à traverser la rue

21 *(in poker)* voir; **I'll s. you** je vous vois; **I'll s. your $10 and raise you 20** je vous suis à 10 dollars et je relance de 20

VI 1 *(perceive with eyes)* voir; **I can't s. without (my) glasses** je ne vois rien sans mes lunettes; **on a clear day you can s. as far as the coast** par temps clair on voit jusqu'à la mer; **cats can s. in the dark** les chats voient dans l'obscurité; **I haven't quite finished – so I s.** je n'ai pas tout à fait terminé – c'est ce que je vois; **to s. into the future** voir *ou* lire dans l'avenir; **she can't s. any further than the end of her nose** elle ne voit pas plus loin que le bout de son nez; **for all to s.** au vu et au su de tous

2 *(look)* voir; **can I s.?** je peux voir?; **let me s.!, let's s.!** fais voir!; **s. for yourself** voyez par vous-même; *Fam* **s.! I told you he wouldn't let us down** tu vois! je t'avais dit qu'il ne nous laisserait pas tomber

3 *(find out)* voir; **is that the baby crying? – I'll go and s.** c'est le bébé qu'on entend pleurer? – je vais voir; **you'll s.!** tu verras!; **we shall s.** nous verrons (bien); **we'll soon s.** on le saura vite; **we'll soon s. if…** on saura vite si…

4 *(understand)* voir, comprendre; **it makes no difference as far as I can s.** autant que je puisse en juger, ça ne change rien; **I was tired, you s., and…** j'étais fatigué, voyez-vous, et…; **I s.** je vois; *Fam* **I don't want any trouble, s.?** je ne veux pas d'histoires, OK?; *Fam Old-fashioned* **now s. here, young man!** écoutez-moi, jeune homme![□]

5 *(consider)* **let me** *or* **let's s.** voyons voir; **it was, let me s., in 1938** c'était, voyons (voir), en 1938; **Mum said you'd take us to the cinema – we'll s.** Maman a dit que tu nous amènerais au cinéma – on verra (ça)

N *Rel (of bishop)* siège *m* épiscopal, évêché *m*; *(of archbishop)* archevêché *m*

▸**see about VT INSEP 1** *(deal with)* s'occuper de; **I'll s. about making the reservations** je m'occuperai des réservations; **they're sending someone to s. about the gas** ils envoient quelqu'un pour vérifier le gaz **2** *(consider)* voir; **I'll s. about it** je verrai ça; **we'll have to s. about getting a new car** il va falloir songer à acheter une nouvelle voiture; *Fam* **they won't let us in – we'll (soon) s. about that!** ils ne veulent pas nous laisser entrer – c'est ce qu'on va voir!

▸**see in VT SEP 1** *(escort)* faire entrer **2** *(celebrate)* **to s. in the New Year** fêter le Nouvel An

VI voir à l'intérieur; **the curtains were drawn, so we couldn't s. in** les rideaux étaient tirés, nous ne pouvions pas voir à l'intérieur

▸**see off VT SEP 1** *(say goodbye to)* dire au revoir à; **she came to s. me off at the station** elle est venue à la gare me dire au revoir **2** *(chase away)* chasser; **s. him off!** *(to dog)* chasse-le! **3** *(repel ▸ attack)* repousser

▸**see out VT SEP 1** *(accompany to the door)* reconduire *ou* raccompagner à la porte; **can you s. yourself out?** pouvez-vous trouver la sortie tout seul?; **goodbye, I'll s. myself out** au revoir, ce n'est pas la peine de me raccompagner **2** *(stay or last until end of)* **we've got enough food to s. the week out** nous avons assez à manger pour tenir jusqu'à la fin de la semaine; **I don't think these boots will s. the winter out** je ne crois pas que ces bottes feront l'hiver; **he isn't expected to s. out the week** il y a peu de chances qu'il survive jusqu'à la fin de la semaine; **he'll s. us all out!** *(will survive us)* il nous enterrera tous! **3** *(celebrate)* **to s. out the Old Year** fêter le Nouvel An

▸**see through VT INSEP 1** *(window, fabric)* voir à travers

2 *(be wise to ▸ person)* percer à jour, voir dans le jeu de; *(▸ trick, scheme, behaviour)* ne pas se laisser tromper par; **I saw through him** je l'ai percé à jour, j'ai vu dans son jeu; **she saw through his apparent cheerfulness** elle ne s'est pas laissée tromper par *ou* elle n'a pas été dupe de son apparente bonne humeur; **I saw through their little game** j'ai vite compris leur petit jeu

VT SEP 1 *(bring to a successful end)* mener à bonne fin; **we can count on her to s. the job through** on peut compter sur elle pour mener l'affaire à bien

2 *(stay until end of)* **to s. a show/film through** assister à un spectacle/regarder un film jusqu'au bout

3 *(support, sustain)* **I've got enough money to s. me through the week** j'ai assez d'argent pour tenir jusqu'à la fin de la semaine; **£20 should s. me through (to Monday)** 20 livres devraient me suffire (jusqu'à lundi); **their love has seen them through many a crisis** leur amour les a aidés à surmonter de nombreuses crises; **her good humour will always s. her through any difficulties** sa bonne humeur lui permettra toujours de traverser les moments difficiles

▸**see to VT INSEP 1** *(look after)* s'occuper de; **I'll s. to the dinner** je m'occuperai du dîner; **I'll s. to it** je vais m'en occuper, je m'en charge; **s. to it that everything's ready by 5 p.m.** veillez à ce que tout soit prêt pour 17 heures; **she saw to it that our picnic was ruined** elle a fait en sorte de gâcher notre pique-nique **2** *(repair)* réparer; **you should get the brakes seen to** tu devrais faire réparer les freins

---

seed [siːd] **N 1** *Bot & Hort* graine *f*; *(UNCOUNT)* graines *fpl*, semence *f*; **grass s.** semence *f* pour gazon; **to go** *or* **to run to s.** *Hort* monter en graine; *Fig (physically)* se laisser aller, se décatir; *(mentally)* perdre ses facultés; **his mother has really gone to s. during the past year** sa mère a bien baissé au cours de l'année passée

2 *(in fruit, tomatoes)* pépin *m*

3 *(source)* germe *m*; **the seeds of doubt/of suspicion** les germes *mpl* du doute/de la suspicion

4 *Bible & Literary (offspring)* progéniture *f*; *(sperm)* semence *f*

5 *Sport* tête *f* de série; **the top seeds** les meilleurs joueurs *mpl* classés

VT 1 *Bot & Hort (garden, field)* ensemencer; *(plants)* planter; **seeded borders** bordures *fpl* ensemencées

2 *Met* **to s. clouds** ensemencer les nuages

3 *(take seeds from ▸ melon, grapes)* épépiner

4 *Sport* **he's seeded number 5** il est tête de série numéro 5; **seeded player** tête *f* de série

VI *(lettuce)* monter en graine; *(corn)* grener, grainer

▸▸ *Fin* ***seed capital*** capital *m* initial *ou* de départ, mise *f* de fonds initiale; *Br* ***seed merchant*** grainetier(ère) *m,f*; *Fin* ***seed money*** capital *m* initial *ou* de départ, mise *f* de fonds initiale; ***seed pearl*** perle *f* minuscule; ***seed pearls*** semence *f* de perles; ***seed potato*** pomme *f* de terre de semence; *Hort* ***seed tray*** terrine *f* à semis

seedcake [ˈsiːdkeɪk] **N** gâteau *m* aux graines de carvi

seediness [ˈsiːdɪnɪs] **N 1** *(appearance)* aspect *m* miteux *ou* minable **2** *Fam Old-fashioned (ill health)* mauvais état[□] *m*

seedless [ˈsiːdlɪs] **ADJ** sans pépins

seedling [ˈsiːdlɪŋ] **N** *(plant)* semis *m*, jeune plant *m*; *(tree)* jeune plant *m*

seedsman [ˈsiːdzmən] *(pl* **seedsmen** [-mən]) **N** grainetier *m*

seedy [ˈsiːdi] *(compar* **seedier**, *superl* **seediest)** **ADJ 1** *(person, hotel, clothes)* miteux, minable; *(area)* délabré; **the hotel was in the seediest part of town** l'hôtel était dans le quartier le plus délabré de la ville **2** *Fam (unwell)* patraque, mal fichu **3** *(fruit)* plein de pépins

seeing [ˈsiːɪŋ] **N** *(vision)* vue *f*, vision *f*; *Prov* **s. is believing** = il faut le voir pour le croire

CONJ vu que + *indicative*; *Fam* **s. (that** *or* **as how) no one came, we left** vu que *ou* étant donné que personne n'est venu, nous sommes partis; *Fam* **I decided not to encourage him, s. as how he was married** je décidai de ne pas l'encourager, puisqu'il était *ou* vu qu'il était marié
▸▸ *Am* ***seeing eye (dog)*** chien *m* d'aveugle

seeing-to N *Br Fam* **to give sb a good s.** *(beat up)* tabasser qn; *(have sex with)* faire passer qn à la casserole

seek [si:k] *(pt & pp* **sought** [sɔ:t]) VT **1** *(search for ▸ job, person, solution)* chercher, rechercher; **he constantly sought her approval** il cherchait constamment à obtenir son approbation; **he sought revenge on them** il a cherché à se venger d'eux; **we'd better s. help** il vaut mieux aller chercher de l'aide; **they sought shelter from the rain** ils ont cherché à se mettre à l'abri de la pluie; **to s. one's fortune** chercher fortune; **to s. re-election** chercher à se faire réélire; **gentleman, 50s, seeks mature woman…** *(in personal column)* homme, la cinquantaine, recherche femme mûre… **2** *(ask for ▸ advice, help)* demander, chercher; **I sought professional advice** j'ai demandé conseil à un professionnel, j'ai cherché conseil auprès d'un professionnel; **he sought my help** il m'a demandé de l'aide *ou* de l'aider **3** *(attempt)* **to s. to do sth** chercher à faire qch, tenter de faire qch; **we are seeking to improve housing conditions** nous nous efforçons d'améliorer *ou* nous cherchons à améliorer les conditions de logement
VI chercher; **to s. after sth** rechercher qch; *Bible* **s. and ye shall find** cherchez et vous trouverez
▸ **seek after** VT INSEP rechercher
▸ **seek out** VT SEP **1** *(go to see)* aller voir **2** *(search for)* chercher, rechercher; *(dig out)* dénicher

seeker ['si:kə(r)] N chercheur(euse) *m,f*; **a s. after truth** une personne qui recherche la vérité

SEEM [si:m]

- sembler **1, 4, 5**
- paraître **4, 6**
- avoir l'air **1, 2**

VI **1** *(with adjective)* sembler, avoir l'air; **he seems very nice** il a l'air très gentil; **you don't s. very pleased with the result** vous n'avez pas l'air ravi du résultat; **you s. (to be) lost** vous semblez (être) *ou* vous avez l'air (d'être) perdu; **things aren't always what they s. (to be)** les apparences sont parfois trompeuses; **the wind makes it s. colder than it is** on dirait qu'il fait plus froid à cause du vent; **her behaviour seemed perfectly normal to me** son comportement m'a semblé tout à fait normal; **how does the situation s. to you? – it seems hopeless** que pensez-vous de la situation? – elle me semble désespérée; **how did grandfather s. to you? – he seemed much older** comment as-tu trouvé grand-père? – j'ai trouvé qu'il avait beaucoup vieilli
2 *(with infinitive)* sembler, avoir l'air; **the door seemed to open by itself** la porte sembla s'ouvrir toute seule; **she seems to have recovered completely** elle a l'air d'être tout à fait remise; **he didn't s. to know, he seemed not to know** il n'avait pas l'air de savoir; **you s. to think you can do as you like here** vous avez l'air de croire que vous pouvez faire ce que vous voulez ici; **I s. to have heard his name somewhere** il me semble avoir entendu son nom quelque part; **I s. to sleep better with the window open** je crois que je dors mieux avec la fenêtre ouverte; **I s. to remember (that)…** je crois bien me souvenir que… + *indicative*; **I'm sorry, I s. to have forgotten your name** excusez-moi, je crois que j'ai oublié votre nom; **I seemed to be floating on a cloud** j'avais l'impression de flotter sur un nuage; **now, what seems to be the problem?** alors, quel est le problème?
3 *(with "can't", "couldn't")* **I can't s. to do it** je n'y arrive pas; **I can't s. to remember** je n'arrive pas à me souvenir
4 *(with noun, often with "like")* sembler, paraître; **he seems (like) a nice boy** il a l'air très sympathique *ou* d'un garçon charmant; **it seems (like) an excellent idea** cela me semble (être) une excellente idée; **after what seemed (like) ages, the doctor arrived** après une attente qui parut interminable, le médecin arriva; **it all seems (like) a long time ago now** ça me paraît loin maintenant; **it seems like only yesterday** il me semble que c'était hier
5 *(impersonal use)* sembler; **it seemed that** *or* **as if nothing could make her change her mind** il semblait que rien ne pourrait la faire changer d'avis; **it seemed as though I'd known her for years** j'avais l'impression de la connaître depuis des années; **it seems to be raining** on dirait qu'il pleut; **it seems like only yesterday** c'est comme si c'était hier; **it seems to me that…** il me semble que… + *indicative*, j'ai l'impression que… + *indicative*; **it seems to me there's no solution** j'ai l'impression qu'il n'y a pas de solution; **there seems to be some mistake** on dirait qu'il y a une erreur, il semble y avoir une erreur; **there doesn't s. (to be) much point in going on** je ne crois pas qu'il y ait *ou* j'ai l'impression qu'il n'y a pas grand intérêt à continuer; **we've been having a spot of bother – so it seems** *or* **would s.!** nous avons eu un petit problème – c'est ce qu'on dirait!
6 *(indicating that information is hearsay or second-hand)* paraître; **it seems over 200 people were killed** il paraît que plus de 200 personnes ont été tuées; **it would s. so** il paraît que oui; **it would s. not** il paraît que non, apparemment pas; **it seems** *or* **it would s. (that) he already knew** il semble *ou* il semblerait qu'il était déjà au courant

seeming ['si:mɪŋ] ADJ apparent; **her explanation soon resolved any s. contradictions in her story** ses précisions ne tardèrent pas à lever les apparentes contradictions de son récit

seemingly ['si:mɪŋlɪ] ADV **1** *(judging by appearances)* apparemment, en apparence **2** *(from reports)* à ce qu'il paraît; **s. so/not** il paraît que oui/non; **he s. never received the letter** à ce qu'il paraît, il n'a jamais reçu la lettre

seemliness ['si:mlɪnɪs] N **1** *(of behaviour)* bienséance *f* **2** *(of dress)* décence *f*

seemly ['si:mlɪ] *(compar* **seemlier**, *superl* **seemliest)** ADJ **1** *(behaviour)* convenable, bienséant; **it is not s. to ask personal questions** cela ne se fait pas de poser des questions personnelles **2** *(dress)* décent; **it was hardly the most s. attire for a supper party** ce n'était certainement pas la tenue la plus indiquée pour un dîner

seen [si:n] *pp of* **see**
ADJ *Sch* **a s. translation** une traduction préparée

seep [si:p] VI filtrer, s'infiltrer; **water was seeping through the cracks in the floor** l'eau s'infiltrait par *ou* filtrait à travers les fissures du sol

seepage ['si:pɪdʒ] N *(gradual ▸ process)* suintement *m*, infiltration *f*; *(▸ leak)* fuite *f*

seer ['sɪə(r)] N *Literary (man)* prophète *m*; *(woman)* prophétesse *f*

seersucker ['sɪəsʌkə(r)] N *Tex* coton *m* gaufré, seersucker *m*

seesaw ['si:sɔ:] N bascule *f*, tape-cul *m*
COMP *(motion)* de bascule
VI **1** *(play on a seesaw)* jouer à la bascule, faire du tape-cul **2** *(machine part etc)* basculer; *Fig (oscillate)* osciller

seethe [si:ð] VI **1** *(liquid, lava)* bouillir, bouillonner; *(sea)* bouillonner **2** *(with anger, indignation)* bouillir; **he was seething (with anger)** il bouillait de rage; **the country is currently seething with unrest** le mécontentement gronde en ce moment dans le pays **3** *(teem)* grouiller; **the streets seethed with shoppers** les rues grouillaient de gens qui faisaient leurs courses

seething ['si:ðɪŋ] ADJ **1** *(liquid, lava, sea)* bouillonnant **2** *(furious)* furieux **3** *(teeming)* grouillant; **a s. mass of people** une masse fourmillante de gens

see-through, *Am* **see-thru** ADJ transparent

segment N ['segmənt] **1** *(piece ▸ gen) & Anat & Geom* segment *m*; *(▸ of fruit)* quartier *m*
2 *(part ▸ of book, film, programme)* partie *f*
3 *Ling* segment *m*
4 *Mktg (of market, population)* segment *m*
VT [seg'ment] segmenter, diviser *ou* partager en segments
VI [seg'ment] se segmenter

segmentation [,segmen'teɪʃən] N segmentation *f*

segregate ['segrɪgeɪt] VT *(separate)* sépare *(isolate)* isoler; **he went to a school where th sexes were segregated** l'école qu'il a fréquenté n'était pas mixte; **the children were segregate into racial groups** les enfants ont été regroupé en fonction de leur race; **the sick were segre gated from the other villagers** les malade étaient tenus à l'écart des autres habitants d village

segregation [,segrɪ'geɪʃən] N **1** *Pol* ségrégatior **2** *(separation ▸ of sexes, patients)* séparation *f (in genetics)* division *f*

segregationist [,segrɪ'geɪʃənɪst] ADJ ségrég tionniste
N ségrégationniste *mf*

segue ['segweɪ] N *Mus* enchaînement *m*; *F* transition *f*
VI **one track neatly segued into the other** les mo ceaux s'enchaînaient parfaitement; *Fig* **summ segued into autumn** peu à peu, l'été fit place l'automne

seismic ['saɪzmɪk] ADJ sismique, séismique; *F (changes)* gigantesque; **an increase/a change of proportions** une augmentation/un changeme aux proportions gigantesques

seismograph ['saɪzməgrɑ:f] N sismographe *r* séismographe *m*

seismologist [saɪz'mɒlədʒɪst] N sismologue *m* séismologue *mf*

seismology [saɪz'mɒlədʒɪ] N sismologie *f*, séi mologie *f*

seize [si:z] VT **1** *(grasp)* attraper, saisir; *(in fis* saisir, empoigner; **my mother seized me by th arm/the collar** ma mère m'a attrapé par le bras le col; **she seized the rail to steady herself** ell s'agrippa à la rampe pour ne pas tomber; **h seized a knife** il s'empara d'un couteau; **to s. hol of sth** saisir *ou* attraper qch
2 *(by force)* s'emparer de, saisir; **to s. power** s'en parer du pouvoir; **the rebels have seized control c the radio station** les rebelles se sont emparés d la station de radio; **pirates seized the ship** des p rates se sont rendus maîtres du navire; **five ho tages were seized during the hold-up** les auteur du hold-up ont pris cinq otages
3 *(arrest ▸ terrorist, smuggler)* se saisir de, ap préhender, capturer; *(capture, confiscate ▸ co traband, arms)* se saisir de, saisir; *Law (propert* saisir; **all copies of the book were seized** tous le exemplaires du livre ont été saisis
4 *(opportunity)* saisir, sauter sur; **s. any opport nity that comes your way** saute sur la moindr occasion qui se présentera
5 *(understand ▸ meaning)* saisir; **he is quick to the implications** il saisit vite les implications
6 *(overcome)* saisir; **to be seized with fright** êtr saisi d'effroi; **to be seized with rage** avoir un ac cès de rage; **she was seized with a desire to trav** elle fut prise d'une envie irrésistible de voyage
VI *(mechanism)* se gripper
▸ **seize on** VT INSEP *(opportunity)* saisir, saute sur; *(excuse)* saisir; *(idea)* saisir, adopter
▸ **seize up** VI **1** *(machinery)* se gripper; **the brake seized up** les freins se sont grippés *ou* bloqués *(system)* se bloquer; **traffic in the centre has seize up completely** la circulation dans le centre es complètement bloquée **3** *(leg)* s'ankylose *(back)* se bloquer; *(heart)* s'arrêter
▸ **seize upon** = **seize on**

seizure ['si:ʒə(r)] N **1** *(of goods, property)* saisie *(of city, fortress)* prise *f*; *(of ship)* capture *f*; *(arres* arrestation *f*; **s. of power** prise *f* de pouvoir; **th police made a big arms s.** la police a saisi un im portant stock d'armes **2** *Med* crise *f*, attaque *also Fig* **to have a s.** avoir une attaque; *Fam* **he jus about had a s. when he found out!** il a failli fair une crise quand il a su!; **heart s.** crise *f* cardiaqu

seldom ['seldəm] ADV rarement; **I s. see her** je l vois rarement, je la vois peu; **he s. comes** il n vient que *ou* il vient rarement; **he s., if ever, visi his mother** il rend rarement, pour ne pas dire ja mais, visite à sa mère; **s. have I heard such nor sense** j'ai rarement entendu des bêtise pareilles

select [sɪ'lekt] VT **1** *(gen)* choisir; *(team)* sélec tionner; **you have been selected from among ou**

many customers vous avez été choisi parmi nos nombreux clients; **she hopes to be selected to play for Ireland** elle espère faire partie de la sélection qui jouera pour l'Irlande **2** *Comput* **s. "enter"** tapez "entrée"; **to s. an option** activer une option

ADJ 1 *(elite ▸ restaurant, neighbourhood)* chic, sélect; *(▸ club)* fermé, sélect; **the membership is very s.** les membres appartiennent à la haute société; **she invited a few s. friends** elle a invité quelques amis choisis; **only a s. few were informed** seuls quelques privilégiés furent informés **2** *(in quality ▸ goods)* de (premier) choix

▸▸ *Pol* ***select committee*** commission *f* d'enquête parlementaire

selected [sɪˈlektɪd] **ADJ** *(friends, poems)* choisi; *(customers)* privilégié; *(fruit, cuts of meat)* de (premier) choix; **before a s. audience** devant un public choisi

selection [sɪˈlekʃən] **N 1** *(act of choosing)* choix *m*, sélection *f*; *(of team)* sélection *f*; **to make a s.** faire un choix; **make your s. from among the books on the bottom shelf** faites votre choix parmi les livres de l'étagère du bas **2** *(range)* choix *m*; **a wide s.** un grand choix; **a narrow s.** un choix limité; **the restaurant offers an excellent s. of wines** ce restaurant propose un excellent choix de vins *ou* dispose d'une excellente carte des vins; **they don't have a very good s.** ils n'ont pas beaucoup de choix **3** *(of stories, music)* choix *m*, sélection *f*; **a s. of poems** *(in book)* des poèmes *mpl* choisis; *(for recital)* un choix de poèmes; **selections from Balzac** morceaux *mpl* choisis de Balzac

COMP *(committee, criteria)* de sélection

▸▸ ***selection box*** **1** *(of chocolates)* assortiment *m* de barres chocolatées **2** *Comput* rectangle *m* de sélection

selective [sɪˈlektɪv] **ADJ 1** *(gen)* sélectif; **we can't take them all, we have to be s.** on ne peut pas les emmener tous, il faut faire un choix; **you should be more s. in your choice of friends/in your reading** vous devriez choisir vos amis/vos lectures avec plus de discernement **2** *Electron* sélectif

▸▸ ***selective breeding*** élevage *m* sélectif; *Sch* ***selective entry*** sélection *f*; *Am Mil* ***selective service*** service *m* militaire obligatoire, conscription *f*; ***selective welfare*** allocations *fpl* sociales sélectives

selectively [sɪˈlektɪvlɪ] **ADV** sélectivement, de manière sélective

selectivity [ˌsɪlekˈtɪvətɪ] **N 1** *(choice)* discernement *m* **2** *Electron* sélectivité *f*

selectman [sɪˈlektmən] *(pl* **selectmen** [-men]) **N** *Am (in New England)* ≃ conseiller *m* municipal

selector [sɪˈlektə(r)] **N 1** *(gen) & Sport* sélectionneur(euse) *m,f* **2** *Tel & TV* sélecteur *m*

selenium [sɪˈliːnɪəm] **N** *Chem* sélénium *m*

self [self] *(pl* **selves** [selvz]) **N 1** *(individual)* **she's back to her old** *or* **usual s.** elle est redevenue elle-même *ou* comme avant; **she's only a shadow of her former s.** elle n'est plus que l'ombre d'elle-même; **he was his usual tactless s.** il a fait preuve de son manque de tact habituel; **they began to reveal their true selves** ils ont commencé à se montrer sous leur véritable jour

2 *Psy* moi *m*; **the conscious s.** le moi conscient

3 *(self-interest)* **all she thinks of is s., s., s.** elle ne pense qu'à sa petite personne

4 *(on cheque)* **pay s.** = mention portée sur un chèque libellé à son propre nom

self- [self] **PREF 1** *(of oneself)* de soi-même, auto-; **s.-accusation** autoaccusation *f*; **s.-admiration** narcissisme *m* **2** *(by oneself)* auto-, par soi-même; **s.-financing** qui s'autofinance **3** *(automatic)* auto-, automatique; **s.-checking** à contrôle automatique; **s.-lubricating** autolubrifiant; **s.-opening** à ouverture automatique

self-abasement **N** humiliation *f* de soi-même; *Rel* anéantissement *m*

self-abnegation **N** abnégation *f*, sacrifice *m* de soi

self-absorbed [-əbˈsɔːbd] **ADJ** égocentrique

self-abuse **N** *Pej* onanisme *m*, masturbation *f*

self-acting **ADJ** automatique

self-addressed [-əˈdrest] **ADJ send three s. (stamped) envelopes** envoyez trois enveloppes (timbrées) à votre adresse

self-adhesive **ADJ** autocollant, autoadhésif

self-adjusting **ADJ** à autoréglage, à réglage automatique

self-advertisement **N** = publicité qu'on se fait à soi-même; **to indulge in s.** aimer se faire de la publicité

self-advocacy **N** *esp Am Admin (of mentally handicapped person)* affirmation *f* de soi

self-aggrandizement, -isement **N** autoglorification *f*

self-analysis **N** autoanalyse *f*

self-apparent **ADJ** évident

self-appointed **ADJ** qui s'est nommé *ou* proclamé lui-même, autoproclamé; **she is our s. guide** elle a assumé d'elle-même le rôle de guide au sein de notre groupe

self-appraisal **N** auto-évaluation *f*

▸▸ ***self-appraisal scheme*** système *m* d'auto-évaluation

self-assembly **N the furniture is flat-packed for easy s.** les meubles sont emballés sous forme de kit pour faciliter le montage

ADJ *(furniture)* en kit

self-assertive **ADJ** sûr de soi

self-assertiveness **N** affirmation *f* de soi

self-assessment **N 1** *(gen)* auto-évaluation *f* **2** *Br (for taxes)* = système de déclaration des revenus pour le paiement des impôts, par opposition au prélèvement à la source

▸▸ *Br* ***self-assessment form*** formulaire *m* de déclaration de revenus

self-assurance **N** confiance *f* en soi, aplomb *m*; **she has plenty of s.** elle ne manque pas de confiance en elle

self-assured **ADJ** sûr de soi, plein d'assurance; **he's very s.** il est très sûr de lui

self-aware **ADJ** conscient de soi-même

self-awareness **N** conscience *f* de soi

self-belief **N** confiance *f* en soi; **to have s.** croire en soi-même

self-betterment **N** amélioration *f* de sa condition

self-catering **ADJ** *Br (apartment, accommodation)* indépendant *(avec cuisine)*; *(holiday)* dans un appartement/un logement indépendant

self-censorship **N** autocensure *f*; **to practise s.** s'autocensurer

self-centred, *Am* **self-centered** **ADJ** égocentrique

self-centredness, *Am* **self-centeredness** [-ˈsentədnɪs] **N** égocentrisme *m*

self-certification **N** *Br* = système dans lequel les employés n'ont pas besoin de certificat médical pour justifier d'une absence

self-check routine **N** *Comput* routine *f* d'autotest

self-clean **VI** s'autonettoyer

self-cleaning **ADJ** autonettoyant

self-coloured, *Am* **self-colored** **ADJ** uni

self-composed **ADJ** posé, calme

self-composure **N** calme *m*, sang-froid *m inv*; **to keep/to lose one's s.** garder/perdre son sang-froid

self-concept **N** image *f* de soi

self-confessed **ADJ** *(murderer, rapist)* qui reconnaît sa culpabilité; **he's a s. drug addict** il avoue lui-même qu'il se drogue

self-confidence **N** confiance *f* en soi, assurance *f*; **she is full of/she lacks s.** elle a une grande/elle manque de confiance en elle

self-confident **ADJ** sûr de soi, plein d'assurance

self-congratulation **N** autosatisfaction *f*

self-congratulatory **ADJ** satisfait de soi

self-conscious **ADJ 1** *(embarrassed)* timide, gêné; **to make sb feel s.** intimider qn; **he's very s. about his red hair** il fait un complexe à cause de ses cheveux roux; **I feel very s. in front of all these people** je me sens très mal à l'aise devant tous ces gens **2** *(style)* appuyé; **I find her writing too s.** je trouve son style un peu trop appuyé

self-consciously **ADV** timidement

self-consciousness **N** timidité *f*, gêne *f*

self-contained **ADJ 1** *(device)* autonome **2** *(flat)* indépendant **3** *(person)* réservé

self-contempt **N** mépris *m* de soi-même; **to be full of s.** se mépriser

self-contradictory **ADJ** qui se contredit; **your arguments are s.** vos arguments se contredisent

self-control **N** sang-froid *m inv*, maîtrise *f* de soi; **to lose one's s.** perdre son sang-froid; **to have no s.** ne pas savoir se maîtriser; **to regain one's s.** se ressaisir

self-controlled **ADJ** maître de soi

self-correcting [-kəˈrektɪŋ] **ADJ** à correction automatique, autocorrecteur

self-critical **ADJ** qui fait son autocritique; **to be s.** être critique envers soi-même; **you're too s.** tu es trop sévère avec toi-même

self-criticism **N** autocritique *f*

self-deceit, self-deception **N** aveuglement *m*; **it's pure s. on his part** il se fait des illusions

self-defeating [-dɪˈfiːtɪŋ] **ADJ** qui va à l'encontre du but recherché

self-defence, *Am* **self-defense** **N 1** *(physical)* autodéfense *f*; **the art of s.** l'art *m* de l'autodéfense; **a course in s.** un cours d'autodéfense *ou* de self-défense **2** *Law* légitime défense *f*; **to plead s.** plaider la légitime défense; **to act in s.** agir en état de légitime défense; **I shot him in s.** j'ai tiré sur lui en état de légitime défense

self-delusion **N** illusion *f*; **it is nothing but s. on her part** elle se fait des illusions

self-denial **N** abnégation *f*, sacrifice *m* de soi

self-denying [-dɪˈnaɪɪŋ] **ADJ** qui fait preuve d'abnégation; **a s. life** une vie de sacrifice

self-deprecation **N** *(ironic)* autodérision *f*; *(from sense of inferiority)* dénigrement *m* de soi-même

self-destruct **VI** s'autodétruire

ADJ *(mechanism)* autodestructeur

self-destruction **N 1** *(of spacecraft, missile)* autodestruction *f* **2** *Psy (of personality)* autodestruction *f* **3** *(suicide)* suicide *m*

self-destructive **ADJ** autodestructeur

self-determination **N** *Pol* autodétermination *f*

self-diagnosis **N** *Med* autodiagnostic *m*

self-diagnostic **ADJ** *Med* autodiagnostique

self-discipline **N** *(self-control)* maîtrise *f* de soi; *(good behaviour)* autodiscipline *f*

self-doubt **N** doute *m* de soi-même

self-drive **ADJ** *Br*

▸▸ ***self-drive car*** voiture *f* sans chauffeur

self-educated **ADJ** autodidacte

self-effacing **ADJ** modeste, effacé

self-employed **ADJ** indépendant, qui travaille à son compte

NPL the s. les travailleurs *mpl* indépendants

self-employment **N** travail *m* en indépendant *ou* à son propre compte

self-esteem **N** respect *m* de soi, amour-propre *m*; **to suffer from low s.** avoir peu d'estime de soi

self-evident **ADJ** évident, qui va de soi, qui saute aux yeux; **the truth is s.** la vérité saute aux yeux; **it's s. that neither side can win** il est évident qu'aucune des deux parties ne peut gagner

self-evidently **ADV** bien évidemment

self-examination **N** *(of conscience)* examen *m* de conscience; *(of breast, testicles)* autopalpation *f*

self-explanatory **ADJ** qui se passe d'explications, évident

self-expression **N** expression *f* libre

self-fertilization, -isation **N** *Biol* autofécondation *f*

self-fertilizing, -ising [-ˈfɜːtɪlaɪzɪŋ] **ADJ** *Biol* autofécondant

self-financing **N** autofinancement *m*

ADJ autofinancé

self-flagellation N *also Fig* autoflagellation *f*

self-fulfilling ADJ

▸▸ ***self-fulfilling prophecy*** = prophétie défaitiste qui se réalise

self-fulfilment, *Am* **self-fulfillment** N épanouissement *m*

self-funding ADJ qui s'autofinance

self-governing ADJ *Pol* autonome

self-government N *Pol* autonomie *f*

self-harm N automutilation *f*

VI s'automutiler

self-hatred N haine *f* de soi

self-help N autonomie *f*; *(in welfare)* entraide *f*

▸▸ ***self-help group*** groupe *m* d'entraide; ***self-help guide*** = guide pour apprendre à résoudre ses problèmes par soi-même

self-hypnosis N autohypnose *f*

self-ignition N *Aut* autoallumage *m*

self-image N image *f* de soi-même

self-importance N suffisance *f*

self-important ADJ vaniteux, suffisant

self-imposed [-ɪm'pəʊzd] ADJ que l'on s'impose à soi-même

▸▸ ***self-imposed exile*** exil *m* volontaire

self-improvement N perfectionnement *m* des connaissances personnelles

self-induction N *Elec* self-induction *f*, autoinduction *f*

self-indulgence N complaisance *f* envers soi-même, habitude *f* de ne rien se refuser

self-indulgent ADJ *(person)* qui ne se refuse rien; *(book, film)* complaisant

self-inflicted [-ɪn'flɪktɪd] ADJ que l'on s'inflige à soi-même, volontaire

self-interest N intérêt *m* personnel; **to act out of s.** agir par intérêt personnel

self-interested ADJ intéressé, qui agit par intérêt personnel

selfish ['selfɪʃ] ADJ égoïste; **you're acting out of purely s. motives** vous agissez par pur égoïsme

selfishly ['selfɪʃlɪ] ADV égoïstement

selfishness ['selfɪʃnɪs] N égoïsme *m*

self-justification N autojustification *f*

self-knowledge N connaissance *f* de soi

selfless ['selflɪs] ADJ altruiste, désintéressé

selflessness ['selflɪsnɪs] N altruisme *m*, désintéressement *m*

self-loading ADJ *(gun)* automatique

self-loathing N dégoût *m* de soi-même

self-locking ADJ à verrouillage automatique

self-love N narcissisme *m*, amour *m* de soi-même

self-made ADJ qui a réussi tout seul *ou* par ses propres moyens; **a s. man** un self-made-man

self-management N autogestion *f*

self-managing ADJ d'autogestion

self-mockery N autodérision *f*

self-mocking ADJ *(tone)* d'autodérision; *(remarks)* empreint d'autodérision

self-motivated ADJ capable de prendre des initiatives

self-motivation N motivation *f*

self-obsessed ADJ obsédé par soi-même

self-opinionated ADJ sûr de soi

self-perpetuating [-pə'petʃʊeɪtɪŋ] ADJ qui se perpétue

self-pity N apitoiement *m* sur son propre sort; **she's full of s.** elle s'apitoie beaucoup sur son sort; **to wallow in s.** s'apitoyer sur son propre sort

self-pitying ADJ qui s'apitoie sur son propre sort; **don't be so s.** cesse de t'apitoyer sur ton sort

self-pollination N *Bot* autopollinisation *f*, pollinisation *f* directe

self-portrait N *(in painting)* autoportrait *m*; *(in book)* portrait *m* de l'auteur par lui-même

self-possessed ADJ maître de soi, qui garde son sang-froid

self-possession N sang-froid *m inv*

self-praise N éloge *m* de soi-même

self-preservation N instinct *m* de conservation

self-proclaimed [-prə'kleɪmd] ADJ **he is the s. king of the ring** il s'est proclamé lui-même roi du ring; **she's a s. art critic** elle se proclame critique d'art

self-promoter N = personne qui se fait valoir

self-promoting ADJ = fait de se faire valoir

self-promotion N = fait de se faire valoir

self-propelled [-prə'peld], **self-propelling** [-prə'pelɪŋ] ADJ autopropulsé

self-publicist N **he is an accomplished s.** il sait soigner sa publicité

self-publishing N autoédition *f*, publication *f* à compte d'auteur

self-raising [-'reɪzɪŋ] ADJ *Br*

▸▸ ***self-raising flour*** farine *f* avec levure incorporée

self-regard N égoïsme *m*

self-regulating ADJ autorégulateur

self-regulation N autorégulation *f*

self-reliance N indépendance *f*

self-reliant ADJ indépendant; **you must learn to be more s.** tu dois apprendre à moins compter sur les autres

self-replicate VI s'autoreproduire

self-replicating [-'replɪkeɪtɪŋ] ADJ autoreproducteur

self-replication N autoreproduction *f*

self-respect N respect *m* de soi, amour-propre *m*

self-respecting ADJ qui se respecte; **no s. girl would be seen dead going out with him** une fille qui se respecte ne sortirait pour rien au monde avec lui

self-restraint N retenue *f*; **to exercise s.** se retenir; **with great s.** avec beaucoup de retenue

self-righteous ADJ suffisant

self-righteousness N suffisance *f*, *Formal* pharisaïsme *m*

self-righting [-'raɪtɪŋ] ADJ *(boat)* inchavirable

self-rule N *Pol* autonomie *f*

self-ruling ADJ *Pol* autonome

self-sacrifice N abnégation *f*; **there's no need for s.** vous n'avez pas besoin de vous sacrifier

self-same ADJ même, identique; *Fam* **the s. day I got the sack** le jour même j'ai été viré

self-satisfaction N suffisance *f*, contentement *m* de soi, fatuité *f*

self-satisfied ADJ *(person)* suffisant, content de soi; *(look, smile, attitude)* suffisant, satisfait; **she gave a s. smile** elle esquissa un sourire empreint de suffisance

self-sealing ADJ *(envelope)* autocollant, autoadhésif; *(tank)* à obturation automatique

self-seeking [-'siːkɪŋ] ADJ égoïste

self-service ADJ en self-service, en libre service

N *(restaurant)* self-service *m*; *(garage, shop)* libre-service *m*

▸▸ ***self-service restaurant*** self-service *m*; ***self-service shop*** libre-service *m*

self-serving ADJ intéressé

self-starter N **1** *Aut* starter *m* automatique **2** *(person)* personne *f* pleine d'initiative; **to be a s.** être autonome

self-styled [-'staɪld] ADJ prétendu, soi-disant *(inv)*; **he's a s. expert on the matter** il se prétend *ou* c'est un soi-disant expert en la matière

self-sufficiency N **1** *(of person ▸ independence)* indépendance *f* **2** *Econ (of nation, resources)* autosuffisance *f*; *Pol* **(economic) s.** autarcie *f*

self-sufficient ADJ **1** *(person ▸ independent)* indépendant **2** *(nation) Econ* autosuffisant; *Pol* autarcique; **s. in copper** autosuffisant en cuivre

self-supporting ADJ **1** *(financially)* indépendant **2** *(framework)* autoporteur, autoportant

self-tapping ADJ

▸▸ ***self-tapping screw*** vis *f* autotaraudeuse

self-taught ADJ autodidacte

self-test *Comput* N autotest *m*

VI s'autotester

▸▸ ***self-test program*** programme *m* d'autotest

self-timer N *Phot* retardateur *m*

self-willed ADJ têtu, obstiné

self-winding [-'waɪndɪŋ] ADJ *(watch)* qui n'a pas besoin d'être remonté, (à remontage) automatique

SELL [sel]

N
- vente **1**
- déception **2**

VT
- vendre **1**
- faire vendre **2**
- faire accepter **3**
- faire avaler **4**
- rouler **5**

VI
- se vendre **1**
- vendre **2**

(*pt & pp* **sold** [səʊld])

N **1** *Com* vente *f*

2 *Fam (disappointment)* déception□ *f*; *(hoax)* attrape-nigaud□ *m*

VT **1** *(goods)* vendre; **to s. sb sth** *or* **sth to sb** vendre qch à qn; **he sold me his car for $1,000** il m'a vendu sa voiture (pour) 1000 dollars; **stamps are now also sold in some shops** les timbres sont maintenant vendus aussi dans certains magasins; **he sells computers for a living** il gagne sa vie en vendant des ordinateurs; **a shop that sells clothes/furniture** un magasin de vêtements/meubles; **the book sold 50,000 copies, 50,000 copies of the book were sold** le livre s'est vendu à 50000 exemplaires; **to s. sth for cash** vendre qch au comptant; **to s. sth on credit** vendre qch à crédit; **to s. sth cheap** vendre qch à bas prix; **to s. sth at a loss** vendre qch à perte; **they s. the cassettes at £3 each** ils vendent les cassettes 3 livres pièce; **she was sold into slavery/prostitution** on l'a vendue comme esclave/prostituée; **she sold her body** *or* **herself to buy food** elle s'est prostituée pour acheter à manger; **they sold classified information to our competitors** ils ont vendu des renseignements confidentiels à nos concurrents; *Fig* **he'd s. his own grandmother for a pint of beer** il vendrait son âme pour une bière; *Fig* **to s. one's soul to the devil** vendre son âme au diable; *Hum* **I'd s. my soul for a holiday in the Caribbean** je ferais *ou* donnerais n'importe quoi pour passer des vacances aux Caraïbes; **to s. sb short** *(cheat)* rouler qn; *(belittle)* ne pas rendre justice à qn; **to s. oneself short** ne pas se montrer à sa juste valeur; **don't s. yourself short** il faut vous mettre en valeur; **I'm often accused of selling the country short** on m'accuse souvent de donner une mauvaise image du pays; *Fam* **we were sold a pup** *or* **a dud** *(cheated)* on nous a roulés; *(sold rubbish)* on nous a vendu de la camelote; *Fig* **to s. sb down the river** trahir qn

2 *(cause to be sold)* faire vendre; **what really sells newspapers is scandal** ce sont les scandales qui font vraiment vendre les journaux; **you need a star to s. the movie** *(to backers)* il faut une star dans la distribution du film pour intéresser les investisseurs potentiels; *(to the public)* il faut une star dans la distribution du film pour attirer le public

3 *(promote ▸ idea, image, policy)* faire accepter; **to s. an idea to the electorate** faire passer une idée auprès des électeurs; **as a politician, it is important to be able to s. yourself** les hommes politiques doivent savoir se mettre en valeur

4 *Fam (make believe ▸ story, excuse)* faire avaler; **she tried to s. me some story** *or* **line about running out of petrol** elle a essayé de me faire avaler une histoire de panne d'essence

5 *Fam (cheat, deceive)* rouler; **we've been sold!** on s'est fait avoir *ou* posséder!

VI **1** *(goods)* se vendre; **the record is selling well** le disque se vend bien; **the cakes s. for** *or* **at 70 pence each** les gâteaux se vendent (à) *ou* valent 70 pence pièce; **shares in the company are selling at 109 pence** les actions de cette compagnie s'échangent à 109 pence; **to s. like hot cakes** se vendre comme des petits pains

2 *(person, shop)* vendre; **sorry, I'm not interested in selling** désolé, je ne cherche pas à vendre; *St*

:xch **to s. short** vendre à découvert
▸ *Am* ***sell date*** date *f* limite de vente
sell forward *Fin* **VI** vendre à terme
VT SEP to s. sth forward vendre qch à terme
sell off VT SEP *(at reduced price)* solder; *(clear)* liquider; *(get cash)* vendre; *(privatize)* privatiser; **he house was sold off to pay debts** la maison a été vendue pour régler des créances; **they're elling the plates off at bargain prices** ils liquident es assiettes à des prix défiant toute concurrence
sell out VT SEP 1 *(usu passive) (concert, match)* **he match was sold out** le match s'est joué à guichets fermés; **the tickets are sold out** tous les billets ont été vendus **2** *(betray ▸ person, principles)* rahir **3** *St Exch* vendre, réaliser
VI 1 *Com (sell business)* vendre son commerce; *sell stock)* liquider (son stock); *(run out)* vendre u écouler tout le stock; **my father sold out and etired** mon père a vendu son affaire et a pris sa etraite; **he sold out to some Japanese investors** il a endu à des investisseurs japonais; **we've sold ut of sugar** nous n'avons plus de sucre, nous vons vendu *ou* écoulé tout notre stock de sure **2** *Fin (sell shares)* vendre ses parts; **to s. out o sb** vendre ses parts à qn **3** *(betray one's principles)* renier ses principes; **to s. out to the enemy** asser à l'ennemi; **the government were accused f selling out to terrorism** le gouvernement fut ccusé d'avoir traité avec les terroristes; **critics ccused the writer of selling out** les critiques ont ccusé l'écrivain d'avoir renié ses principes our plaire au plus grand nombre
sell up *Br* **VT SEP 1** *Fin & Law (goods)* opérer la vente forcée de, procéder à la liquidation de **2** *Com (business)* vendre, liquider
VI *(shopkeeper)* vendre son fonds de commerce u son affaire; *(businessman)* vendre son affaire; **he sold up and went to Canada** il a tout vendu et est parti au Canada

ell-by date N *Br* date *f* limite de vente; *Fig* **the TV programme/minister is past its/his s.** l'émission de télévision/le ministre a fait son temps
eller ['selə(r)] **N 1** *(person ▸ gen)* vendeur(euse) *n,f*; (▸ *merchant)* vendeur(euse) *m,f*, marchand (e) *m,f* **2** *(goods)* **these shoes are good/poor sellers** ces chaussures se vendent bien/mal; **it's one of our biggest sellers** c'est un des articles qui se vend le mieux
▸▸ ***seller's market*** *(for property)* marché *m* vendeur *ou* favorable aux vendeurs; *St Exch (for stocks, shares)* marché *m* à la hausse; *St Exch* ***seller's option*** prime *f* vendeur
elling ['selɪŋ] **N** vente *f*
▸▸ ***selling cost, selling costs*** frais *mpl* commerciaux; ***selling off, selling out*** *(of stock)* liquidation *f*; *St Exch (of stocks, shares)* (re)vente *f*; ***selling point*** avantage *m*, atout *m*, point *m* fort; ***selling price*** prix *m* de vente; ***selling rate*** *(of currency)* taux *m* de vente
ell-off N *(gen)* vente *f*; *St Exch (of stocks, shares)* (re)vente *f*
ellotape® ['seləteɪp] **N** *Br* Scotch® *m*, ruban *m* adhésif
ellotape ['seləteɪp] **VT** scotcher, coller avec du ruban adhésif
ell-out N 1 *Com* liquidation *f* **2** *(betrayal)* trahison *f*; *(capitulation)* capitulation *f* **3** *(play, concert etc)* **it was a s.** on a vendu tous les billets; **the match was a s.** le match s'est joué à guichets fermés
elvage, selvedge ['selvɪdʒ] **N** *Tex* lisière *f* *(d'un tissu)*
elves [selvz] *pl of* **self**
emantic [sɪ'mæntɪk] **ADJ** sémantique
emantically [sɪ'mæntɪkəlɪ] **ADV** du point de vue sémantique
emantics [sɪ'mæntɪks] **N** *(UNCOUNT)* sémantique *f*; **it's all a question of s.** tout dépend du sens que l'on donne aux mots
emaphore ['seməfɔː(r)] **N 1** *(UNCOUNT) (signals)* signaux *mpl* à bras; **in** *or* **by s.** par signaux à bras **2** *Rail & Naut* sémaphore *m*
VT transmettre par signaux à bras
emblance ['sembləns] **N** semblant *m*, apparence *f*; **a s. of order** un semblant d'ordre; **we need to show at least some s. of unity** nous devons au moins montrer un semblant d'unité

semen ['siːmən] **N** *(UNCOUNT)* sperme *m*, semence *f*
semester [sɪ'mestə(r)] **N** semestre *m*

> **SEMI-** PRÉFIXE
> • Le rôle le plus courant de ce préfixe est d'indiquer le CARACTÈRE PARTIEL d'une qualité ou d'un état. Dans ce sens il se traduit le plus souvent par **semi-**:
> **semiprecious** semi-précieux; **semiprofessional** semi-professionnel; **semi-transparent** demi-transparent, semi-transparent; **semiconscious** à demi *ou* moitié conscient; **a semi-automatic** une arme semi-automatique; **a semi-skilled worker** un travailleur spécialisé; **a semi-detached house** une maison jumelée.
> • Ce préfixe peut également véhiculer la notion de MOITIÉ EXACTE, comme dans les exemples suivants:
> **semicircular** demi-circulaire, semi-circulaire; **semifinal** demi-finale; **semitone** demi-ton; **semiquaver** double croche.
> Dans ce sens, **semi-** se traduit le plus souvent par **demi-**.
> • Ce préfixe s'emploie également pour indiquer qu'un événement se produit DEUX FOIS dans une période donnée:
> **a semi-annual publication** une publication semestrielle; **semimonthly/semiweekly meetings** des réunions bimensuelles/bihebdomadaires.

semi ['semɪ] **N** *Fam* **1** *Br (abbr* **semi-detached house)** maison *f* jumelée **2** *(abbr* **semifinal)** demi-finale *f* **3** *Am, Austr & NZ (abbr* **semitrailer)** semi *m*
semi- ['semɪ] **PREF 1** *(partly)* semi-, demi-; **in s.-darkness** dans la pénombre *ou* la semi-obscurité; **he's in s.-retirement** il est en semi-retraite **2** *(twice)* **s.-yearly** semestriel
semi-automatic ADJ semi-automatique
N arme *f* semi-automatique
semibreve ['semɪbriːv] **N** *Br Mus* ronde *f*
▸▸ ***semibreve rest*** pause *f*
semicircle ['semɪsɜːkəl] **N** demi-cercle *m*
semicircular [ˌsemɪ'sɜːkjʊlə(r)] **ADJ** demi-circulaire, semi-circulaire
semicolon [ˌsemɪ'kəʊlən] **N** point-virgule *m*
semiconductor [ˌsemɪkən'dʌktə(r)] **N** *Phys* semi-conducteur *m*
semiconscious [ˌsemɪ'kɒnʃəs] **ADJ** à demi *ou* moitié conscient; **she was only s.** *(losing consciousness)* elle avait pratiquement perdu connaissance; *(regaining consciousness)* elle n'avait pas encore tout à fait repris connaissance
semiconsciousness [ˌsemɪ'kɒnʃəsnɪs] **N in a state of s.** à demi conscient
semi-darkness N pénombre *f*, semi-obscurité *f*
semi-detached N maison *f* jumelée
▸▸ ***semi-detached house*** maison *f* jumelée
semi-documentary *(pl* **semi-documentaries)** **N** film *m* semi-documentaire
semifinal [ˌsemɪ'faɪnəl] **N** demi-finale *f*; **she lost in the semifinals** elle a perdu en demi-finale
semifinalist [ˌsemɪ'faɪnəlɪst] **N** demi-finaliste *mf*
semi-finished goods NPL *Ind* produits *mpl* semi-finis
semi-graphics N *Comput* semi-graphisme *m*
semiliterate [ˌsemɪ'lɪtərət] **ADJ** quasi analphabète
semi-manufactured product [-ˌmænjʊ'fæktʃəd-] **N** demi-produit *m*
semimonthly [ˌsemɪ'mʌnθlɪ] **ADJ** *Am (publication)* bimensuel
seminal ['semɪnəl] **ADJ 1** *Anat & Bot* séminal **2** *(important)* majeur, qui fait école; **she was a s. influence on his art** elle eut une influence majeure sur son art
▸▸ *Anat & Bot* ***seminal duct*** voie *f* séminale; *Anat & Bot* ***seminal fluid*** liquide *m* séminal; *Anat* ***seminal vesicle*** vésicule *f* séminale
seminar ['semɪnɑː(r)] **N 1** *(conference)* séminaire *m*, colloque *m* **2** *Univ (class)* séminaire *m*, travaux *mpl* dirigés
seminarist ['semɪnərɪst] **N** *Rel* séminariste *m*
seminary ['semɪnərɪ] *(pl* **seminaries)** **N** *Rel & Sch (for boys, priests)* séminaire *m*; *(for girls)* pensionnat *m* de jeunes filles
semi-obscurity N *(darkness)* pénombre *f*; *Fig* quasi-obscurité *f*
semi-official ADJ semi-officiel
semiological [ˌsemɪə'lɒdʒɪkəl] **ADJ** sémiologique
semiology [ˌsemɪ'ɒlədʒɪ] **N** sémiologie *f*
semiotic [ˌsemɪ'ɒtɪk] **ADJ** sémiotique
semiotician [ˌsemɪə'tɪʃən] **N** sémioticien(enne) *m,f*
semiotics [ˌsemɪ'ɒtɪks] **N** *(UNCOUNT)* sémiotique *f*
semiprecious ['semɪˌpreʃəs] **ADJ** semi-précieux
semi-public company N société *f* d'économie mixte
semiquaver ['semɪkweɪvə(r)] **N** *Br Mus* double croche *f*
semi-retired ADJ en préretraite progressive
semi-retirement N préretraite *f* progressive
semi-skilled ADJ *(worker)* spécialisé
semi-skimmed ADJ *(milk)* demi-écrémé
Semite ['siːmaɪt] **N** Sémite *mf*
Semitic [sɪ'mɪtɪk] **N** *Ling* langue *f* sémitique, sémitique *m*
ADJ sémite, sémitique
semitone ['semɪtəʊn] **N** *Mus* demi-ton *m*
semitrailer ['semɪtreɪlə(r)] **N** semi-remorque *m*
semitropical [ˌsemɪ'trɒpɪkəl] **ADJ** semi-tropical
semivowel ['semɪvaʊəl] **N** *Ling* semi-voyelle *f*
semolina [ˌsemə'liːnə] **N** semoule *f*
SEN [ˌesiː'en] **N** *Formerly (abbr* **State Enrolled Nurse)** aide-soignant(e) *m,f* diplômé(e)
Sen. *(written abbr* **Senator)** sénateur *m*
sen. *(written abbr* **senior)** *(in rank)* (de grade) supérieur; **John Brown s.** John Brown père
senate ['senɪt] **N 1** *Hist & Pol* sénat *m*; **the United States S.** le Sénat américain; **the French S.** le Sénat **2** *Univ* conseil *m* d'université
▸▸ ***Senate majority*** majorité *f* sénatoriale

> **THE SENATE**
> Le Sénat constitue, avec la Chambre des représentants, l'organe législatif américain. Il est composé de 100 membres (deux par État) élus directement par le peuple et qui occupent leur fonction pendant une période de six ans. Le Sénat a pour responsabilité d'approuver les nominations présidentielles, de ratifier les traités ainsi que tenir les audiences en cas de mise en accusation d'un élu.

senator ['senətə(r)] **N** sénateur *m*
senatorial [ˌsenə'tɔːrɪəl] **ADJ** sénatorial
SEND [send] *(pt & pp* **sent** [sent]) **VT 1** *(dispatch ▸ gen)* envoyer; (▸ *by post)* envoyer, expédier; **to s. sb a letter, to s. a letter to sb** envoyer une lettre à qn; **he sent (us) word that he would be delayed** il (nous) a fait savoir qu'il aurait du retard; **she sends her love** *or* **regards** elle vous envoie ses amitiés; **s. them our love** embrassez-les pour nous; **s. them our best wishes** faites-leur nos amitiés; **I sent my luggage by train** j'ai fait expédier *ou* envoyer mes bagages par le train; **images sent by satellite** images transmises par satellite; **to s. a message over the radio** envoyer un message radio; **it's like manna sent from heaven** c'est une véritable aubaine; **what will the future s. us?** que nous réserve l'avenir?; **we sent help to the refugees** nous avons envoyé des secours aux réfugiés; **they sent a car to fetch us** ils ont envoyé une voiture nous chercher
2 *(cause to go ▸ person)* envoyer; **the government sent an ambassador to Mexico** le gouvernement envoya un ambassadeur au Mexique; **I was sent**

to bed/to my room on m'a envoyé me coucher/dans ma chambre; **to s. sb home** *(from school)* renvoyer qn chez lui; *(from abroad)* rapatrier qn; *Ind (lay off)* mettre qn en chômage technique; **to s. sb to prison** envoyer qn en prison; **to s. sb to school** envoyer qn à l'école; **s. the children indoors** faites rentrer les enfants; **s. him to me** envoyez-le-moi; **s. him to my office** dites-lui de venir dans mon bureau, envoyez-le-moi; **she sent her daughter for the meat** *or* **to get the meat** elle a envoyé sa fille chercher la viande; **she sent her brother on an errand/with a message** elle a envoyé son frère faire une course/porter un message; **the dogs were sent after him** on lança les chiens à sa poursuite *ou* à ses trousses; **heavy smoking sent him to an early grave** il est mort prématurément parce qu'il fumait trop; *Fam* **to s. sb packing** *or* **about his business** envoyer promener qn, envoyer qn sur les roses; *Fig* **don't s. a boy to do a man's job** il faut que la personne soit à la mesure de la tâche

3 *(propel, cause to move)* envoyer; **he sent the ball over the heads of the spectators** il envoya le ballon par-dessus la tête des spectateurs; **the collision sent showers of sparks/clouds of smoke into the sky** la collision fit jaillir une gerbe d'étincelles/provoqua des nuages de fumée; **the sound sent shivers down my spine** le bruit m'a fait froid dans le dos; **I sent the cup flying** j'ai envoyé voler la tasse; **the blow sent me flying** le coup m'a envoyé rouler par terre; **a gust of wind sent the papers flying across the table** un coup de vent balaya les papiers qui se trouvaient sur la table; **a sudden storm sent us all running for shelter** un orage soudain nous força à courir nous mettre à l'abri; **to s. profits tumbling** faire chuter les bénéfices; **to s. prices sky-high** faire flamber les prix; **the news sent a murmur of excitement through the hall** la nouvelle provoqua un murmure d'agitation dans la salle

4 *(into a specific state)* rendre; **that sent him into fits of laughter** cela l'a fait éclater de rire; **the news sent them into a panic** les nouvelles les ont fait paniquer; **to s. sb into a rage** enrager qn; **to s. sb to sleep** endormir qn

5 *Fam Old-fashioned (thrill)* emballer; **his voice really sends me** sa voix me fait vraiment craquer

VI 1 *(send word)* **he sent to say he couldn't come** il nous a fait savoir qu'il ne pouvait pas venir

2 *(for information, equipment)* **we sent to Paris for a copy** nous avons demandé une copie à Paris

▸**send along VT SEP** envoyer; **s. him along!** envoyez-le-moi!

▸**send away VT SEP 1** *(letter, parcel)* expédier, mettre à la poste; **to s. a radio away to be repaired** expédier une radio chez le réparateur **2** *(dismiss ▸ person)* renvoyer, faire partir; **the children were sent away to school** les enfants furent mis en pension

VI to s. away for sth *(by post)* se faire envoyer qch; *(by catalogue)* commander qch; **s. away for your free copy now** demandez maintenant votre exemplaire gratuit

▸**send back VT SEP** *(return ▸ books, goods, food in restaurant)* renvoyer; **s. the chocolates back to the shop** renvoyez les chocolats au magasin; **we sent her back to fetch a coat** *or* **for a coat** nous l'avons renvoyée prendre un manteau

▸**send down VT SEP 1** *(person, lift)* faire descendre, envoyer en bas; **they sent me down to the cellar** ils m'ont fait descendre à la cave; **she was sent down to ask if they wanted coffee** on l'a envoyée en bas pour demander s'ils voulaient du café

2 *(cause to fall ▸ prices, temperature)* faire baisser, provoquer la baisse de

3 *Br Univ (student)* expulser, renvoyer

4 *Br Fam (to prison)* coffrer; **he was sent down for 20 years** il a écopé de 20 ans (de prison), il en a pris pour 20 ans

VI *(by message or messenger)* **to s. down for sth** (se) faire monter qch

▸**send for VT INSEP 1** *(doctor, taxi)* faire venir, appeler; *(mother, luggage)* faire venir; *(police)* appeler; *(help)* envoyer chercher; **we sent for another bottle** *(in hotel, restaurant)* on a demandé une autre bouteille; **we sent for a couple of pizzas** *(home delivery)* nous nous sommes fait livrer deux pizzas **2** *(by post)* se faire envoyer; *(by catalogue)* commander; *(catalogue, price list)* demander

▸**send in VT SEP 1** *(visitor)* faire entrer; *(troops, police)* envoyer **2** *(submit ▸ bill, report, form)* envoyer; *(▸ suggestions, resignation)* envoyer, soumettre; **why don't you s. your name in for the competition?** pourquoi ne pas vous inscrire au concours?; **to s. in a request** faire une demande; **please s. in a written application** veuillez envoyer une demande écrite; *(for job)* veuillez poser votre candidature par écrit

▸**send off VT SEP 1** *(by post)* expédier, mettre à la poste

2 *(person)* envoyer; **I sent him off home/upstairs** je l'ai envoyé chez lui/en haut; **they sent us off to bed/to get washed** ils nous ont envoyés nous coucher/nous laver; **they are sent off to school every morning** on les envoie à l'école tous les matins

3 *Sport* expulser

4 *also Fig* **to s. sb off (to sleep)** endormir qn

VI to s. off for sth *(by post)* se faire envoyer qch; *(by catalogue)* commander qch

▸**send on VT SEP 1** *(mail)* faire suivre; *(luggage)* expédier; **to s. a message on to sb** faire suivre un message à qn; **my luggage was sent on to New York** *(in advance)* on a expédié mes bagages à New York; *(by mistake)* mes bagages ont été expédiés à New York par erreur; **if you've forgotten anything, we'll s. it on** si vous avez oublié quelque chose, nous vous le renverrons **2** *(person)* **they sent us on ahead** *or* **in front** ils nous ont envoyés en éclaireurs; **we sent them on to find a hotel** nous les avons envoyés en éclaireurs pour trouver un hôtel **3** *Sport (player)* faire entrer (sur le terrain)

▸**send out VT SEP 1** *(by post ▸ invitations)* expédier, poster

2 *(messengers, search party)* envoyer, dépêcher; *(patrol)* envoyer; *(outside)* envoyer dehors; **we sent her out for coffee** nous l'avons envoyée chercher du café; **they sent me out to Burma** ils m'ont envoyé en Birmanie; **they sent out a car for us** ils ont envoyé une voiture nous chercher; **we sent them all out into the garden** on les a tous envoyés dans le jardin; **s. the children out to play** envoyez les enfants jouer dehors

3 *(transmit ▸ message, signal)* envoyer; **a call was sent out for Dr Bramley** on a fait appeler le Dr Bramley

4 *(produce, give out ▸ leaves)* produire; *(▸ light, heat)* émettre, répandre, diffuser; *(▸ fumes, smoke)* répandre; **the chimney/engine sent out billows of smoke** la cheminée/le moteur crachait des tourbillons de fumée

VI to s. out for coffee/sandwiches envoyer quelqu'un chercher du café/des sandwiches

▸**send up VT SEP 1** *(messenger, luggage, drinks)* faire monter; *(rocket, flare)* lancer; *(plane)* faire décoller; *(smoke)* répandre

2 *(raise ▸ price, pressure, temperature)* faire monter

3 *Br Fam (ridicule)* mettre en boîte, se moquer de[□]; *(parody)* parodier[□]

4 *Am Fam (to prison)* coffrer

sender ['sendə(r)] **N** expéditeur(trice) *m,f*; **return to s.** retour à l'expéditeur

sending ['sendɪŋ] **N** envoi *m*; **s. by rail** expédition *f* par chemin de fer

send-off N to give sb a s. dire au revoir à qn, souhaiter bon voyage à qn; **to give sb a big s.** venir nombreux pour dire au revoir à qn; **he was given a warm s. by all his colleagues** tous ses collègues sont venus lui faire des adieux chaleureux; **to give sb a good s.** *(funeral)* faire à qn de belles funérailles

send-up N *Br Fam* parodie[□] *f*

Senegal [ˌsenɪ'gɔːl] **N** Sénégal *m*

Senegalese [ˌsenɪgə'liːz] *(pl inv)* **NPL the S.** les Sénégalais *mpl*

N Sénégalais(e) *m,f*

ADJ sénégalais

senescence [sɪ'nesəns] **N** sénescence *f*

senile ['siːnaɪl] **ADJ** sénile

▸▸ ***senile decay*** dégénérescence *f* sénile; ***seni... dementia*** démence *f* sénile

senility [sɪ'nɪlətɪ] **N** sénilité *f*

senior ['siːnɪə(r)] **ADJ 1** *(in age)* plus âgé, aîné; *(... rank)* (de grade) supérieur; *(longer-serving)* plu... ancien; **he's two years s. to me** il est mon aîné d... deux ans; **I am s. to them** *(have higher position)* ... suis leur supérieur; *(have served longer)* j'ai plu... d'ancienneté qu'eux; **s. airport officials** la direc... tion de l'aéroport; **she holds a s. position in th... company** elle est haut placée dans la sociét... **George is the s. partner in our firm** George est l'a... socié principal de notre société

2 *Sch* **the s. boys/girls of the school** les garçon... *mpl*/filles *fpl* des grandes classes

N 1 *(older person)* aîné(e) *m,f*; **he is my s. by s... months, he is six months my s.** il a six mois de plu... que moi, il est de six mois mon aîné

2 *Am (senior citizen)* personne *f* âgée *ou* du tro... sième âge

3 *Am Sch* élève *mf* de terminale; *Univ* étudia... (e) *m,f* de licence

4 *Br Sch* **the seniors** ≃ les grands (grandes) *mp... fpl*

5 *(in hierarchy)* supérieur(e) *m,f*

• **Senior ADJ** *(in age)* **John Brown S.** John Brow... père

▸▸ *Br* ***senior aircraftman*** ≃ caporal *m*; *Am* ***senio... airman*** ≃ caporal-chef *m*; ***senior citizen*** pe... sonne *f* âgée *ou* du troisième âge; ***senior citizen... club*** club *m* du troisième âge; ***senior citizen's ra... pass*** ≃ Carte *f* Vermeil; ***senior civil servant*** adm... nistrateur(trice) *m,f* civil(e); ***senior clerk*** comm... *m* principal, chef *m* de bureau; *Br Univ* ***Senio... Common Room*** salle *f* des professeurs; ***senior ex... ecutive*** cadre *m* supérieur; ***senior government o... ficial*** haut(e) fonctionnaire *mf*; *Am* ***senior hig... school*** lycée *m*; ***(the) senior management*** la direc... tion; *Br Sch* ***senior master*** professeur *m* principa... ***senior officer*** officier *m* supérieur; ***senior partne...*** associé(e) *m,f* principal(e); *Br* ***Senior Service*** ma... rine *f*; *Am Sch & Univ* ***senior year*** dernière année

seniority [ˌsiːnɪ'ɒrɪtɪ] **N 1** *(in age)* priorité *f* d'âge... **he became chairman by virtue of s.** il est deven... président parce qu'il était le plus âgé *ou* l... doyen **2** *(in rank)* supériorité *f*; *(in length of se... vice)* ancienneté *f*; **to have s. over sb** être le supé... rieur de qn; **according to** *or* **by s.** en fonction d... *ou* à l'ancienneté

senna ['senə] **N** *Bot* séné *m*

▸▸ *Pharm* ***senna pods*** follicules *mpl* de séné

sensation [sen'seɪʃən] **N 1** *(UNCOUNT) (sensiti... ity)* sensation *f*; **the cold made me lose all s. in m... hands** le froid m'a complètement engourdi le... mains **2** *(impression)* impression *f*, sensation *f*; ... **had a strange s. in my leg** j'avais une drôle de sen... sation dans la jambe; **I had the s. of falling** j'avai... la sensation *ou* l'impression de tomber **3** *(excite... ment, success)* sensation *f*; **to cause** *or* **to be a s...** faire sensation; **the film was a s.** le film a fait sen... sation

sensational [sen'seɪʃənəl] **ADJ 1** *(causing a sen... sation)* sensationnel, qui fait sensation; **a s... story** une histoire sensationnelle; **a s. crime/tria...** un crime/procès qui fait sensation; **it was th... most s. event of the year** ce fut l'événement l... plus sensationnel de l'année **2** *(press, newspa... per, novel, film)* à sensation **3** *(wonderful)* formi... dable, sensationnel; **you look s.** tu es superbe... **that's s. news** c'est une nouvelle formidable *o...* sensationnelle

sensationalism [sen'seɪʃənəlɪzəm] **N 1** *(in press... novels etc)* sensationnalisme *m* **2** *Phil* sensation... nisme *m* **3** *Psy* sensualisme *m*

sensationalist [sen'seɪʃənəlɪst] **N** *(writer)* auteu... *m* à sensation; *(journalist)* journaliste *mf* qui fai... du sensationnel

ADJ *(article, style, journalism)* à sensation; **to b... s.** *(tabloids, reporting)* faire du sensationnel

sensationalize, -ise [sen'seɪʃənəlaɪz] **VT** *(event...* faire du sensationnel sur; **it's been so sensationa... lized that...** on a fait tant de sensationnel là... dessus que... + *indicative*

sensationally [sen'seɪʃənəlɪ] **ADV 1** *(describe... write)* d'une manière sensationnelle; **the inci... dent was s. reported in the tabloids** l'incident ...

été couvert dans la presse populaire à grand renfort de sensationnalisme **2** *(as intensifier ▸ beautiful, successful, popular)* extraordinairement; **we found this s. good restaurant** on a découvert un restaurant vraiment génial

SENSE [sens]

N	
• sens **1, 3, 5, 6**	• sensation **2**
• sentiment **2**	• notion **3**
• bon sens **4**	
VT	
• sentir **1**	
NPL	
• raison	

N 1 *(faculty)* sens *m*; **the five senses** les cinq sens *mpl*; **to have a keen s. of smell/hearing** avoir l'odorat fin/l'ouïe fine; **she seemed to have a sixth s.** elle semblait posséder un sixième sens; **to be in possession of all one's senses** jouir de toutes ses facultés; **to excite the senses** exciter les sens **2** *(sensation)* sensation *f*; *(feeling)* sentiment *m*; **a s. of pleasure/warmth** une sensation de plaisir/chaleur; **I felt a certain s. of pleasure** j'ai ressenti un certain plaisir; **a s. of achievement/injustice** un sentiment d'accomplissement/d'injustice; **I felt a s. of shame** je me suis senti honteux; **children need a s. of security** les enfants ont besoin de se sentir en sécurité **3** *(notion)* sens *m*, notion *f*; **she seems to have lost all s. of reality** elle semble avoir perdu le sens des réalités; **I lost all s. of time** j'ai perdu toute notion du temps; **to have a (good) s. of direction** avoir le sens de l'orientation; *Fig* **she lost her s. of direction when her husband died** elle s'est sentie complètement désorientée après la mort de son mari; **he has a good s. of humour** il a le sens de l'humour; **I try to teach them a s. of right and wrong** j'essaie de leur inculquer la notion du bien et du mal; **she acted out of a s. of duty/of responsibility** elle a agi par sens du devoir/des responsabilités; **they have no business s. at all** ils n'ont aucun sens des affaires; **he has an overdeveloped s. of his own importance** il est trop imbu de lui-même **4** *(practical wisdom)* bon sens *m*; **to show good s.** faire preuve de bon sens; **there's a lot of s. in what she says** il y a beaucoup de bon sens dans ce qu'elle dit, ce qu'elle dit est tout à fait sensé; **to have the (good) s. to do sth** avoir l'intelligence ou le bon sens de faire qch; **to have more s. than to do sth** avoir assez de bon sens pour ne pas faire qch; **they didn't even have enough s. to telephone** ils n'ont même pas eu l'idée de téléphoner **5** *(reason, rational quality)* sens *m*; **there's no s. in all of us going** cela ne rime à rien d'y aller tous; **I can't see any s.** *or* **the s. in continuing this discussion** je ne vois pas l'intérêt de continuer cette discussion; **to see s.** entendre raison; **to talk s.** dire des choses sensées; **oh, come on, talk s.!** voyons, ne dis pas n'importe quoi!; **to make s.** *(words)* avoir un sens; *(be logical)* tenir debout, être sensé; **can you make (any) s. of this message?** est-ce que vous arrivez à comprendre ce message?; **it makes no s.** ça n'a pas de sens; **it makes/doesn't make s. to wait** c'est une bonne idée/idiot d'attendre; **it makes more s. to do this first** c'est plus logique de commencer par cela; **that makes good s.** c'est logique, c'est une bonne idée; **it makes good political/business s. to…** il est bon sur le plan politique/commercial de… **6** *(meaning ▸ of word, expression)* sens *m*, signification *f*; *(▸ of text)* sens *m*; **don't take what I say in its literal s.** ne prenez pas ce que je dis au sens propre *ou* au pied de la lettre; **in every s. of the word** dans tous les sens du terme; **in the normal s. (of the word)** à proprement parler; **I got the general s.** j'ai saisi le sens général; **I think we have, in a very real s., grasped the problem** je crois que nous avons parfaitement saisi le problème; **this is not in any real s. a change of policy** ça ne représente pas du tout un changement de politique; **in a s.** dans un sens; **in no s.** en aucune manière; **in more senses than one** à plus d'un titre; **in the s. that…** en ce sens que…, dans le sens où…

VT 1 *(feel ▸ presence)* sentir; *(▸ danger, catastrophe)* pressentir; **I sensed something was wrong** j'ai senti que quelque chose n'allait pas; **I sensed as much** c'est bien l'impression *ou* le sentiment que j'avais; **I sensed her meaning** j'ai compris ce qu'elle voulait dire **2** *Electron* détecter; *Comput* lire

• **senses NPL** *(sanity, reason)* raison *f*; **to come to one's senses** *(become conscious)* reprendre connaissance; *(be reasonable)* revenir à la raison; **to take leave of one's senses** perdre la raison *ou* la tête; **to bring sb to his/her senses** ramener qn à la raison

▸▸ ***sense organ*** organe *m* sensoriel *ou* des sens

senseless ['senslɪs] **ADJ 1** *(pointless, futile)* insensé, absurde; **it's s. trying to persuade her** inutile d'essayer *ou* on perd son temps à essayer de la persuader; **a s. killing** un meurtre gratuit; **what a s. waste of time!** quelle perte de temps stupide! **2** *(unconscious)* sans connaissance; **to knock sb s.** assommer qn; **he fell s. to the floor** il est tombé par terre sans connaissance

senselessly ['senslɪslɪ] **ADV** stupidement, de façon absurde

senselessness ['senslɪsnɪs] **N** *(silliness)* manque *m* de bon sens, stupidité *f*; *(absurdity)* absurdité *f*

sensibility [ˌsensɪ'bɪlətɪ] (*pl* **sensibilities**) **N** *(physical or emotional)* sensibilité *f*; **he's a man of great s.** c'est un homme d'une grande sensibilité; **s. to pain** sensibilité à la douleur

• **sensibilities NPL** sensibilité *f*; **we must avoid offending our viewers' sensibilities** nous devons éviter de heurter la sensibilité de nos spectateurs

sensible ['sensɪbəl] **ADJ 1** *(reasonable ▸ choice)* judicieux, sensé; *(▸ reaction, person)* sensé, raisonnable; **it's a very s. idea** c'est une très bonne idée; **the most s. thing to do is to phone** la meilleure chose à faire, c'est de téléphoner; **it would be more s. to…** il serait plus raisonnable de…; **be s.** soyez raisonnable **2** *(practical ▸ clothes, shoes)* pratique; **you need s. walking shoes** il vous faut de bonnes chaussures de marche; **it's not a very s. swimsuit** ce maillot de bain n'est pas très pratique **3** *Formal (notable ▸ change, quantity, difference)* sensible, appréciable **4** *Formal or Literary (aware)* **I am s. of the fact that things have changed between us** j'ai conscience du fait que les choses ont changé entre nous

> Note that the French word **sensible** is a false friend and is almost never a translation for the English word **sensible**. It means **sensitive**.

sensibly ['sensɪblɪ] **ADV 1** *(reasonably)* raisonnablement; **they very s. decided to give up before someone got hurt** ils se sont montrés très raisonnables et ont décidé de renoncer avant que quelqu'un ne soit blessé; **to be s. dressed** porter des vêtements pratiques **2** *Formal (perceptibly)* sensiblement, perceptiblement

sensitive ['sensɪtɪv] **ADJ 1** *(eyes, skin)* sensible; **my eyes are very s. to bright light** j'ai les yeux très sensibles à la lumière vive; **special soaps for s. skin** savons spéciaux pour peaux sensibles *ou* délicates; **to be s. to the cold** *(person)* être frileux **2** *(emotionally)* sensible; **she's very s.** elle est très sensible; **to be s. to sth** être sensible à qch **3** *(aware)* sensibilisé; **the seminar made us more s. to the problem** le séminaire nous a sensibilisés au problème **4** *(touchy ▸ person)* susceptible; *(▸ age)* où l'on est susceptible; *(▸ public opinion)* sensible; **she's very s. about her height** elle n'aime pas qu'on lui parle de sa taille **5** *(issue, topic)* délicat, épineux; *(information)* confidentiel; **you're touching on a s. area** vous abordez un sujet délicat *ou* épineux; **avoid such politically s. issues** évitez des questions politiques aussi délicates **6** *(instrument)* sensible; *Phot (film)* sensible; *(paper)* sensibilisé; *Cin (film)* rapide **7** *St Exch (market)* instable

▸▸ *Bot* ***sensitive plant*** sensitive *f*

sensitively ['sensɪtɪvlɪ] **ADV** avec sensibilité

sensitiveness ['sensɪtɪvnɪs], **sensitivity** [ˌsensɪ'tɪvɪtɪ] **N** *(of person, skin, machine, instrument)* sensibilité *f*; *Phot* sensibilité *f*; *Cin* rapidité *f*; *(of question, issue)* caractère *m* délicat; *(of document, information)* caractère *m* confidentiel; *St Exch* instabilité *f*

sensitization, -isation [ˌsensɪtaɪ'zeɪʃən] **N** *Med & Phot* sensibilisation *f*

sensitize, -ise ['sensɪtaɪz] **VT** sensibiliser, rendre sensible

sensitizer, -iser ['sensɪtaɪzə(r)] **N** *Biol & Phot* sensibilisateur *m*

sensor ['sensə(r)] **N** détecteur *m*, capteur *m*

sensory ['sensərɪ] **ADJ** *(nerve, system)* sensoriel

▸▸ ***sensory deprivation*** isolation *f* sensorielle; ***sensory organs*** organes *mpl* des sens

sensual ['sensjʊəl] **ADJ** sensuel

> Attention: ne pas confondre avec **sensuous**.

sensualism ['sensjʊəlɪzəm] **N** *(gen)* sensualité *f*; *Phil* sensualisme *m*

sensualist ['sensjʊəlɪst] **N** *(gen)* personne *f* sensuelle; *Phil* sensualiste *mf*

sensuality [ˌsensjʊ'ælətɪ] **N** sensualité *f*

sensuous ['sensjʊəs] **ADJ** *(language, poetry)* très imagé; *(lips, person)* sensuel

> Attention: ne pas confondre avec **sensual**.

sensuously ['sensjʊəslɪ] **ADV** voluptueusement, sensuellement

sensuousness ['sensjʊəsnɪs] **N** volupté *f*

sent [sent] *pt & pp of* **send**

sentence ['sentəns] **N 1** *Gram* phrase *f* **2** *Law (conviction)* condamnation *f*, sentence *f*; *(period in prison)* peine *f*; **to pass s. on sb** prononcer une condamnation contre qn; **to pronounce s.** prononcer la sentence *ou* condamnation; **under s. of death** condamné à mort; **he got a five-year s. for burglary** il a été condamné à cinq ans de prison *ou* à une peine de cinq ans pour cambriolage; **while he was serving his s.** pendant qu'il purgeait sa peine

VT *Law* condamner; **to s. sb to life imprisonment** condamner qn à la prison à perpétuité

sententious [sen'tenʃəs] **ADJ** sentencieux, pompeux

sententiousness [sen'tenʃəsnɪs] **N** *(personality)* caractère *m* sentencieux; *(in speech)* ton *m* sentencieux

sentient ['sentɪənt] **ADJ** *Formal* doué de sensation

sentiment ['sentɪmənt] **N 1** *(feeling)* sentiment *m*; **your sentiments towards my sister** vos sentiments envers ma sœur, les sentiments que vous éprouvez pour ma sœur **2** *(opinion)* sentiment *m*, avis *m*, opinion *f*; **these are my sentiments** voilà mon sentiment *ou* mon opinion; **my sentiments exactly** je partage entièrement votre avis **3** *(sentimentality)* sentimentalité *f*; *(mawkishness)* sensiblerie *f*; **there's no place for s. in business matters** il n'y a pas de place pour les sentiments en affaires

sentimental [ˌsentɪ'mentəl] **ADJ** *also Pej* sentimental; **the photos have s. value** ces photos ont une valeur sentimentale; **to have a s. attachment to sth** être attaché à qch pour des raisons sentimentales; **to be s. about animals/children** se laisser attendrir par les animaux/les enfants

sentimentalism [ˌsentɪ'mentəlɪzəm] **N 1** *(of film, novel, image, attitude etc)* sentimentalisme *m*; *Pej* sensiblerie *f* **2** *Literature* sentimentalisme *m*

sentimentalist [ˌsentɪ'mentəlɪst] **N** sentimental (e) *m,f*

sentimentality [ˌsentɪmen'tælətɪ] (*pl* **sentimentalities**) **N** sentimentalité *f*; *Pej* sensiblerie *f*

sentimentalize, -ise [ˌsentɪ'mentəlaɪz] **VT** *(to others)* présenter de façon sentimentale; *(to oneself)* percevoir de façon sentimentale

VI faire du sentiment

sentimentally [ˌsentɪ'mentəlɪ] **ADV** *also Pej* sentimentalement, de manière sentimentale; **he spoke s. about his past** il a évoqué son passé avec émotion

sentinel ['sentɪnəl] **N** sentinelle *f*, factionnaire *m*; *also Fig* **to stand s. over sth** monter la garde devant qch

sentry ['sentrɪ] (*pl* **sentries**) **N** sentinelle *f*, factionnaire *m*; *also Fig* **to stand s. (over sth)** monter la garde (devant qch)

▸▸ ***sentry box*** guérite *f*; *Mil* ***sentry duty*** faction *f*; **to be on s. duty** être en *ou* de faction

Seoul [səʊl] N Séoul

sepal ['sepəl] N *Bot* sépale *m*

separable ['sepərəbəl] ADJ séparable

separate ADJ ['sepərət] **1** *(different, distinct ▸ category, meaning, issue)* distinct, à part; *(▸ incident, times, episodes)* différent; **that's quite a s. matter** ça, c'est une toute autre affaire; **the two issues are quite s.** les deux problèmes sont distincts; **they sleep in s. rooms** *(children)* ils ont chacun leur chambre; *(couple)* ils font chambre à part; **administration and finance are in s. departments** l'administration et les finances relèvent de services différents; **the canteen is s. from the main building** la cantine se trouve à l'extérieur du bâtiment principal; **begin each chapter on a s. page** commencez chaque chapitre sur une nouvelle page; **use a s. piece of paper** utilisez une feuille séparée; **I'd prefer them to come on s. days** je préférerais qu'ils viennent à des jours différents; **it happened on four s. occasions** cela s'est produit à quatre reprises; **she likes to keep her home life s. from the office** elle tient à ce que son travail n'empiète pas sur sa vie privée; **the peaches must be kept s. from the lemons** les pêches et les citrons ne doivent pas être mélangés; **he was kept s. from the other children** on le tenait à l'écart *ou* on l'isolait des autres enfants; **s. but equal** = doctrine en vigueur aux États-Unis de 1896 à 1954, selon laquelle la séparation entre Noirs et Blancs était licite du moment qu'ils bénéficiaient de services (éducation, transports etc) équivalents

2 *(independent ▸ entrance, living quarters)* indépendant, particulier; *(▸ existence, organization)* indépendant; **they lead very s. lives** ils mènent chacun leur vie; **they went their s. ways** *(after meeting)* ils sont partis chacun de leur côté; *Fig (in life)* chacun a suivi sa route

N ['sepərət] **1** *(in stereo)* élément *m* séparé **2** *Am (offprint)* tiré *m* à part

VT ['sepəreɪt] **1** *(divide, set apart)* séparer; *(detach ▸ parts, pieces)* séparer, détacher; **he stepped in to s. the fighting dogs** il est intervenu pour séparer les chiens qui se battaient; **the last three coaches will be separated from the rest of the train** les trois derniers wagons seront détachés du reste du train; **the Bosphorus separates Europe from Asia** le Bosphore sépare l'Europe de l'Asie; **the seriously ill were separated from the other patients** les malades gravement atteints étaient isolés des autres patients; **the records can be separated into four categories** les disques peuvent être divisés *ou* classés en quatre catégories

2 *(keep distinct)* séparer, distinguer; **to s. reality from myth** distinguer le mythe de la réalité, faire la distinction entre le mythe et la réalité

3 *Culin (milk)* écrémer; *(egg)* séparer; **s. the whites from the yolks** séparez les blancs des jaunes

VI ['sepəreɪt] **1** *(go different ways)* se quitter, se séparer; **they separated after the meeting** ils se sont quittés après la réunion

2 *(split up ▸ couple)* se séparer, rompre; *(▸ in boxing, duel)* rompre; *Pol (▸ party)* se scinder; **they separated on good terms** ils se sont séparés à l'amiable; **the party separated into various factions** le parti s'est scindé en diverses factions

3 *(come apart, divide ▸ liquid)* se séparer; *(▸ parts)* se séparer, se détacher, se diviser; **the boosters s. from the shuttle** les propulseurs auxiliaires se détachent de la navette; **the model separates into four parts** la maquette se divise en quatre parties

• **separates** NPL ['sepərəts] *(clothes)* coordonnés *mpl*

▸▸ ***separate peace*** paix *f* séparée; *Can* ***separate school*** ≃ école *f* libre

▸ **separate out** VT SEP séparer, trier

VI se séparer

separately ['sepərətlɪ] ADV **1** *(apart)* séparément, à part; **woollens must be washed s.** les lainages doivent être lavés séparément **2** *(individually)* séparément; **can we pay s.?** pouvons-nous payer séparément *ou* avoir des additions séparées?; **they don't sell yogurts s.** ils ne vendent pas les yaourts à l'unité

separation [ˌsepə'reɪʃən] N **1** *(division)* séparation *f*; **the s. of Church and State** la séparation de l'Église et de l'État; **her s. from her family caused her great heartache** sa séparation d'avec sa famille l'a beaucoup chagrinée **2** *(of couple)* séparation *f*

▸▸ *Law* ***separation agreement*** = accord par lequel les époux décident de suspendre leur droit et devoir de cohabitation; ***separation allowance*** *Mil* allocation *f* mensuelle *(versée par l'armée à la femme d'un soldat)*; *(alimony)* pension *f* alimentaire; *Pol* ***separation of powers*** séparation *f* des pouvoirs

separatism ['sepərətɪzəm] N séparatisme *m*

separatist ['sepərətɪst] ADJ séparatiste

N séparatiste *mf*

▸▸ ***separatist movement*** mouvement *m* séparatiste *ou* indépendantiste

separator ['sepəreɪtə(r)] N *(gen)* séparateur *m*; *Culin (for milk)* écrémeuse *f*

sepia ['si:pjə] N **1** *(pigment, print)* sépia *f* **2** *(fish)* seiche *f*

ADJ sépia *(inv)*

sepoy ['si:pɔɪ] N cipaye *m*

sepsis ['sepsɪs] N *Med* septicité *f*

Sept. *(written abbr* **September***)* sept

septa ['septə] *pl of* **septum**

September [sep'tembə(r)] N septembre *m*; *see also* **February**

septet [sep'tet] N *Mus* septuor *m*

septic ['septɪk] ADJ septique; *(wound)* infecté; **to go** *or* **to become s.** s'infecter; **I have a s. finger** j'ai une blessure infectée au doigt

▸▸ ***septic poisoning*** septicémie *f*; ***septic shock*** choc *m* septique; ***septic tank*** fosse *f* septique

septicaemia, *Am* **septicemia** [ˌseptɪ'si:mɪə] N *(UNCOUNT) Med* septicémie *f*

septuagenarian [ˌseptjʊədʒɪ'neərɪən] ADJ septuagénaire

N septuagénaire *mf*

Septuagesima [ˌseptjʊə'dʒesɪmə] N *Rel* septuagésime *f*

Septuagint ['septjʊədʒɪnt] N *Rel* **the S.** la version des Septante

septum ['septəm] *(pl* **septa** [-tə]*)* N *Anat* septum *m*

sepulcher *Am* = **sepulchre**

sepulchral [sɪ'pʌlkrəl] ADJ *(figure, voice)* sépulcral; *(atmosphere)* funèbre, lugubre; *(silence)* de mort

sepulchre, *Am* **sepulcher** ['sepəlkə(r)] N sépulcre *m*

sequel ['si:kwəl] N **1** *(result, aftermath)* conséquence *f*; *(to illness, war)* séquelles *fpl*; **as a s. to this event** à la suite de cet événement; **it was a decision that had an unfortunate s.** c'est une décision qui a eu des répercussions fâcheuses **2** *(to novel, movie etc)* suite *f*

sequelize, -ise ['si:kwəlaɪz] VT *esp Am (movie)* donner une suite à

sequence ['si:kwəns] N **1** *(order)* suite *f*, ordre *m*; **in s.** *(in order)* par ordre, en série; *(one after another)* l'un après l'autre; **numbered in s.** numérotés dans l'ordre; **in historical s.** par ordre chronologique; **the pages were out of s.** les pages n'étaient pas dans l'ordre; **he saw the episodes of the TV series out of s.** il a vu le feuilleton dans le désordre; **logical s.** ordre *m* logique

2 *(series)* série *f*; *(in cards)* séquence *f*; **the s. of events** le déroulement *ou* l'enchaînement *m* des événements

3 *Cin & Mus* séquence *f*; **dance s.** numéro *m* de danse

4 *Ling & Math* séquence *f*

5 *Biol & Chem* séquençage *m*

6 *Comput* séquence *f*

VT **1** *(order)* classer, ordonner **2** *Biol & Chem* séquencer **3** *Comput* mettre en séquence

▸▸ *Cin* ***sequence shot*** plan-séquence *m*; *Gram* ***sequence of tenses*** concordance *f* des temps

sequencer ['si:kwənsə(r)] N *Comput* séquenceur *m*

sequencing ['si:kwənsɪŋ] N **1** *Biol & Chem* séquençage *m* **2** *Comput* mise *f* en séquence

sequential [sɪ'kwenʃəl] ADJ **1** *Comput* séquentiel **2** *Formal (following)* subséquent; **a lower income is s. upon retirement** la retraite entraîn[e] une baisse de revenus

▸▸ *Comput* ***sequential access*** accès *m* séquentie[l]; *Comput* ***sequential processing*** traitement *m* sé[quentiel]; *Cin & TV* ***sequential shooting*** tourné[e] monté *m*

sequentially [sɪ'kwenʃəlɪ] ADV *(follow, happen)* séquentiellement

sequester [sɪ'kwestə(r)] VT **1** *Formal (set apart)* isoler, mettre à part **2** *Formal (shut away)* sé[questrer]; **he was sequestered in his office** il était a été séquestré dans son bureau; **to s. onesel[f] (from the world)** se retirer (du monde) **3** *La[w] (goods, property)* séquestrer, placer sous sé[questre]

sequestrate [sɪ'kwestreɪt] VT **1** *Law* séquestre[r], placer sous séquestre **2** *Formal (confiscate)* sai[sir]

sequestration [ˌsi:kwe'streɪʃən] N **1** *Law* mise sous séquestre **2** *Formal (confiscation)* saisie *f*; *Literary* retraite *f*, éloignement *m* du monde

▸▸ *Law* ***sequestration order*** ordonnance *f* d[e] mise sous séquestre

sequin ['si:kwɪn] N paillette *f*

sequined ['si:kwɪnd] ADJ pailleté, à paillettes

sequoia [sɪ'kwɔɪə] N *Bot* séquoia *m*

sera ['sɪərə] *pl of* **serum**

seraglio [se'rɑ:lɪəʊ] *(pl* **seraglios***)* N sérail *m*

seraph ['serəf] *(pl* **seraphs** *or* **seraphim** [-fɪm]*)* *Rel* séraphin *m*

seraphic [se'ræfɪk] ADJ *Literary* séraphique

seraphim ['serəfɪm] *pl of* **seraph**

Serb [sɜ:b] N Serbe *mf*

ADJ serbe

Serbia ['sɜ:bɪə] N Serbie *f*

Serbian ['sɜ:bɪən] N **1** *(person)* Serbe *mf* **2** *Lin[g]* serbe *m*

ADJ serbe

▸▸ ***Serbian Republic of Bosnia-Herzegovina*** Répu[blique] *f* serbe de Bosnie

Serbo-Croat, Serbo-Croatian [ˌsɜ:bəʊ-] N *(person)* Serbo-croate *mf* **2** *Ling* serbo-croate *m*

ADJ serbo-croate

sere [sɪə(r)] ADJ *Literary* flétri, desséché

serenade [ˌserə'neɪd] N sérénade *f*

VT *(sing)* chanter une sérénade à; *(play)* joue[r] une sérénade à; **she serenaded me to sleep** ell[e] m'a chanté une sérénade pour m'endormir

serendipitous [ˌserən'dɪpɪtəs] ADJ *Literary* for[tuit]

serendipity [ˌserən'dɪpɪtɪ] N *Literary* = don d[e] faire des trouvailles

serene [sɪ'ri:n] ADJ *(person, existence, sky, expres[sion])* serein; *(sea, lake)* calme; *Formal* **His/Her S[erene] Highness** Son Altesse Sérénissime

serenely [sɪ'ri:nlɪ] ADV sereinement, avec séré[nité]; **she was s. unaware of what was going on** ell[e] vivait dans la douce inconscience de ce qui s[e] passait autour d'elle; **"of course not," she an[swered] s.** "bien sûr que non", répondit-elle tran[quillement]

serenity [sɪ'renətɪ] N sérénité *f*

serf [sɜ:f] N *(male)* serf *m*; *(female)* serve *f*

serfdom ['sɜ:fdəm] N servage *m*

serge [sɜ:dʒ] *Tex* N serge *f*

COMP *(cloth, trousers)* de *ou* en serge; **a blue s[erge] suit** un costume de *ou* en serge bleue

sergeant ['sɑ:dʒənt] N **1** *(in infantry, air force)* ≃ sergent *m*; *(in artillery, armoured corps, cavalry)* ≃ maréchal *m* des logis **2** *(in police)* brigadier *m*

▸▸ ***sergeant major*** sergent-chef *m*

sergeant-at-arms N huissier *m* d'armes

serial ['sɪərɪəl] N **1** *Rad & TV* feuilleton *m*; *(in ma[gazine])* feuilleton *m*, roman-feuilleton *m*; **TV s[erial]** feuilleton *m* télévisé; **published in s. form** publi[é] sous forme de feuilleton **2** *(periodical)* pério[dique] *m*

ADJ **1** *(arranged in series)* en série; *(from series)* d'une série; *(forming series)* formant une série; **in s. order** en ordre sériel **2** *(music)* sériel **3** *Com[put] (processing, transmission, data)* série *(inv)*

▸▸ *Comput* ***serial access*** accès *m* séquentie[l]; *Comput* ***serial cable*** câble *m* série; *Comput* ***seria[l]*** *nterface* interface *f* série; ***serial killer*** tueur(euse) *n,f* en série; ***serial killings*** meurtres *mpl* en série; ***serial monogamist*** = personne qui a une succession de relations monogamiques; ***serial monogamy*** = succession de relations monogamiques; ***serial murderer*** tueur(euse) *m,f* en série; ***serial murders*** meurtres *mpl* en série; ***serial number*** *(of product, publication)* numéro *m* de série; *(of cheque, voucher)* numéro *m*; *(of soldier)* (numéro *n*) matricule *m*; *Comput* ***serial port*** port *m* série; ***serial printer*** imprimante *f* série; ***serial rights*** droits *mpl* de reproduction en feuilleton; ***serial writer*** feuilletoniste *mf*

erialization, -isation [ˌsɪərɪəlaɪˈzeɪʃən] **N** *(of book)* publication *f* en feuilleton; *(of play, film)* adaptation *f* en feuilleton

erialize, -ise [ˈsɪərɪəlaɪz] **VT** *(book)* publier en feuilleton; *(play, film)* adapter en feuilleton; **serialized in six parts** *(novel etc)* publié en six épisodes; *TV & Rad* diffusé en six parties; **it's being serialized in 'The Times'** ça sort en feuilleton dans le 'Times'

erially [ˈsɪərɪəlɪ] **ADV 1** *Math* en série **2** *Press (as series)* en feuilleton, sous forme de feuilleton; *(periodically)* périodiquement, sous forme de périodique

eriatim [ˌsɪərɪˈeɪtɪm] **ADV** *Formal* successivement, l'un après l'autre; **to examine the questions s.** examiner successivement les questions, examiner les questions l'une après l'autre

ericulture [ˈserɪkʌltʃə(r)] **N** sériciculture *f*

eries [ˈsɪəriːz] *(pl inv)* **N 1** *(set, group ▸ gen) & Chem & Geol* série *f*; *(sequence ▸ gen) & Math* séquence *f*, suite *f*; *Ling & Mus* série *f*, séquence *f*; **we drove through a s. of mining villages** on a traversé en voiture une série de villages miniers; **a whole s. of catastrophes** toute une série de catastrophes

2 *(of cars, clothes)* série *f*

3 *Rad & TV* série *f*; *(in magazine, newspaper)* série *f* d'articles; **a detective s.** une série policière; **TV s.** série *f* télévisée; **there's a s. of** *or* **about the life of the stars** il y a une série d'articles sur la vie des stars

4 *(collection ▸ of stamps, coins, books)* collection *f*, série *f*; **a new detective s.** une nouvelle série *ou* collection de romans policiers

5 *Elec* série *f*; **wired in s.** branché en série

6 *Sport* série *f* de matches

▸▸ *Elec* ***series connection*** montage *m* en série

eries-connected **ADJ** *Elec* monté en série

eries-wound motor [-waʊnd-] **N** *Elec* moteur *m* à enroulements série

erif [ˈserɪf] **N** *Typ* empattement *m*

eriocomic [ˌsɪərɪəʊˈkɒmɪk] **ADJ** tragicomique

erious [ˈsɪərɪəs] **ADJ 1** *(not frivolous ▸ suggestion, subject, writer, publication)* sérieux; *(▸ occasion)* solennel; **is that a s. offer?** c'est une offre sérieuse?; **she's not really a s. novelist** *(doesn't write real literature)* ce n'est pas un écrivain majeur; **she's a s. actress** *(cinema)* elle fait des films sérieux; *(theatre)* elle joue dans des pièces sérieuses; **the s. cinemagoer** le cinéphile averti; **the book is meant for the s. student of astronomy** le livre est destiné aux personnes qui possèdent déjà de solides connaissances en astronomie; **life is a s. business** la vie est une affaire sérieuse; **can I have a s. conversation with you?** est-ce qu'on peut parler sérieusement?

2 *(in speech, behaviour)* sérieux; **you can't be s.!** vous n'êtes pas sérieux!, vous plaisantez!; **I'm quite s.** je suis tout à fait sérieux, je ne plaisante absolument pas; **is he s. about emigrating?** est-ce qu'il envisage sérieusement d'émigrer?; **is she s. about Peter?** est-ce qu'elle tient vraiment à Peter?

3 *(thoughtful ▸ person, expression)* sérieux, plein de sérieux; *(▸ voice, tone)* sérieux, grave; *(careful ▸ examination)* sérieux, approfondi; *(▸ consideration)* sérieux, sincère; **don't look so s.** ne prends pas cet air sérieux; **to give s. thought** *or* **consideration to sth** songer sérieusement à qch

4 *(grave ▸ mistake, problem, illness, injury)* grave; *(▸ loss)* lourd; *(▸ doubt)* sérieux; **the situation is s.** la situation est préoccupante; **s. crime** délit *m* grave; **those are s. allegations** ce sont de graves accusations; **it poses a s. threat to airport security** cela constitue une menace sérieuse pour la sécurité des aéroports; *Med* **his condition is described as s.** son état est jugé préoccupant; **the fire caused s. damage to the hotel** l'incendie a causé d'importants dégâts à l'hôtel

5 *Fam (as intensifier)* **she makes s. money** elle gagne un fric fou; **they go in for some really s. drinking at the weekends** le week-end, qu'est-ce qu'ils descendent!; **that is one s. computer** c'est pas de la gnognotte, cet ordinateur

▸▸ *Br* ***serious crime squad*** brigade *f* criminelle; *Br* ***Serious Fraud Office*** ≃ Service *m* de la répression des fraudes; *Br* ***Serious Organised Crime Agency*** = organisme gouvernemental de lutte contre le crime organisé

seriously [ˈsɪərɪəslɪ] **ADV 1** *(earnestly)* sérieusement, avec sérieux; **to take sb/sth s.** prendre qn/qch au sérieux; **he takes himself too s.** il se prend trop au sérieux; **she is s. thinking of leaving him** elle pense *ou* songe sérieusement à le quitter; **think about it s. before you do anything** réfléchissez-y bien avant de faire quoi que ce soit; **s. though, what are you going to do?** sérieusement, qu'est-ce que vous allez faire?; **you can't s. expect me to believe that!** vous plaisantez, j'espère? **2** *(severely ▸ damage)* sérieusement, gravement; *(▸ ill)* gravement; *(▸ injured, wounded)* grièvement; *Mil* **the s. wounded** les grands blessés *mpl*; **she is s. worried about him** elle se fait énormément de souci à son sujet **3** *Fam (very)* **he's s. rich** il est méchamment riche, il est riche et pas qu'un peu; **she's getting s. fat** elle devient énorme[□]; **he was s. drunk** il était complètement soûl

serious-minded **ADJ** sérieux

seriousness [ˈsɪərɪəsnɪs] **N 1** *(of person, expression, intentions, occasion, writing)* sérieux *m*; *(of voice, manner)* (air *m*) sérieux *m*; **in all s.** sérieusement, en toute sincérité **2** *(of illness, situation, loss)* gravité *f*; *(of allegation)* sérieux *m*; *(of damage)* importance *f*, étendue *f*; **it is a matter of some s.** c'est une affaire assez sérieuse; **it will take some weeks to assess the s. of the damage** on ne pourra pas évaluer l'étendue *ou* l'ampleur des dégâts avant plusieurs semaines; **you don't seem aware of the s. of the problem** vous ne semblez pas avoir conscience de la gravité du problème

serjeant = **sergeant**

serjeant-at-arms = **sergeant-at-arms**

sermon [ˈsɜːmən] **N 1** *Rel* sermon *m*; **to give** *or* **to preach a s.** faire un sermon; *Bible* **the S. on the Mount** le Sermon sur la Montagne **2** *Fig Pej* sermon *m*, laïus *m*; **he gave me a s. on the evils of drink** il m'a fait un sermon sur les effets néfastes de l'alcool

sermonize, -ise [ˈsɜːmənaɪz] **VT** sermonner
VI faire des sermons, prêcher

sermonizing, -ising [ˈsɜːmənaɪzɪŋ] **N** *(UNCOUNT) Pej* prêchi-prêcha *m inv*

seroconversion [ˌsɪərəʊkənˈvɜːʃən] **N** *Med* séroconversion *f*

serogroup [ˈsɪərəʊgruːp] **N** *Med* sérogroupe *m*

seronegative [ˌsɪərəʊˈnegətɪv] **ADJ** *Med* séronégatif

seronegativity [ˌsɪərəʊnegəˈtɪvɪtɪ] **N** *Med* séronégativité *f*

seropositive [ˌsɪərəʊˈpɒzɪtɪv] **ADJ** *Med* séropositif

seropositivity [ˌsɪərəʊpɒzɪˈtɪvɪtɪ] **N** *Med* séropositivité *f*

serotonin [ˌserəˈtəʊnɪn] **N** *Biol & Chem* sérotonine *f*

serotype [ˈsɪərəʊtaɪp] **N** *Med* sérotype *m*

serous [ˈsɪərəs] **ADJ** séreux

serpent [ˈsɜːpənt] **N** serpent *m*

serpentine [ˈsɜːpəntaɪn] **ADJ** *Literary (winding)* sinueux, qui serpente

SERPS [sɜːps] **N** *Br (abbr* **State Earnings-Related Pension Scheme***)* = régime de retraite minimal en Grande-Bretagne

serrated [sɪˈreɪtɪd] **ADJ** *(edge)* en dents de scie, dentelé; *(knife, scissors, instrument)* cranté, en dents de scie

serration [sɪˈreɪʃən] **N** dentelure *f*

serried [ˈserɪd] **ADJ** serré; **in s. ranks** en rangs serrés

serum [ˈsɪərəm] *(pl* **serums** *or* **sera** [-rə]*)* **N** *Biol* sérum *m*

servant [ˈsɜːvənt] **N 1** *(in household)* domestique *mf*; *(maid)* bonne *f*, servante *f*; **I'm not your s.!** je ne suis pas ta bonne!; **a large staff of servants** une nombreuse domesticité **2** *(of God, of people)* serviteur *m*; **politicians are the servants of the community** les hommes politiques sont au service de la communauté **3** *Formal or Old-fashioned (in correspondence)* **your most obedient s.** votre très humble *ou* dévoué serviteur

▸▸ ***servant girl*** servante *f*, bonne *f*; ***servants' quarters*** appartements *mpl* des domestiques

serve [sɜːv] **VT 1** *(employer, monarch, country, God)* servir; **to have served one's country well** avoir bien servi sa patrie, *Literary* bien mériter de la patrie; **she has served the company well over the years** elle a bien servi la société pendant des années

2 *(in shop, restaurant ▸ customer)* servir; **to s. sb with sth** servir qch à qn; **are you being served?** est-ce qu'on s'occupe de vous?

3 *(provide ▸ with electricity, gas, water)* alimenter; *(▸ with transport service)* desservir; **the village is served with water from the local reservoir** le village est alimenté en eau depuis le réservoir voisin; **the town is well served with transport facilities** la ville est bien desservie par les transports en commun; **this train serves all stations south of Queensferry** ce train dessert toutes les gares au sud de Queensferry

4 *(food, drink)* servir; **dinner is served** le dîner est servi; **coffee is now being served in the lounge** le café est servi au salon; **they served me (with) some soup** ils m'ont servi de la soupe; **white wine should be served chilled** le vin blanc doit être servi très frais; **this recipe serves four** cette recette est prévue pour quatre personnes; *Rel* **to s. mass** servir la messe

5 *(be suitable for)* servir; **the plank served him as a desk** la planche lui servait de bureau; **this box will s. my purpose** cette boîte fera l'affaire; **when the box had served its purpose, he threw it away** quand il n'eut plus besoin de la boîte, il la jeta; **it serves no useful purpose** cela ne sert à rien de spécial

6 *(term, apprenticeship)* faire; **he has served two terms (of office) as president** il a rempli deux mandats présidentiels; **to s. one's apprenticeship as an electrician** faire son apprentissage d'électricien; **to s. one's time** *Mil* faire son service; *(prison sentence)* purger sa peine; **to s. time** faire de la prison; **she served four years for armed robbery** elle a fait quatre ans (de prison) pour vol à main armée

7 *Law (summons, warrant, writ)* notifier, remettre; **to s. sb with a summons, to s. a summons on sb** remettre une assignation à qn; **to s. sb with a writ, to s. a writ on sb** assigner qn en justice

8 *Sport* servir; **she served the ball into the net** son service a échoué dans le filet; **to s. an ace** faire un ace

9 *(idioms)* **it serves you right** c'est bien fait pour toi; **it serves them right for being so selfish!** ça leur apprendra à être si égoïstes!

VI 1 *(in shop or restaurant, at table)* servir; *(be in service ▸ maid, servant)* servir; **to s. at table** servir à table; **could you s., please?** pourriez-vous faire le service, s'il vous plaît?; **she served as Lady Greenmount's maid** elle était au service de Lady Greenmount

2 *(as soldier)* servir; **to s. in the army** servir dans l'armée; **he served as a corporal during the war** il a servi comme caporal pendant la guerre

3 *(in profession)* **he served as treasurer for several years** il a exercé les fonctions de trésorier pendant plusieurs années

4 *(on committee)* **she serves on the housing committee** elle est membre de la commission au logement

5 *(function, act ▸ as example, warning)* servir; **let that s. as a lesson to you!** que cela vous serve de leçon!; **the tragedy should s. as a reminder of the threat posed by nuclear power** cette tragédie devrait rappeler à tous la menace que représente l'énergie nucléaire; **this stone will s. to keep the door open** cette pierre servira à maintenir la porte ouverte; **their bedroom had to s. as a cloakroom for their guests** leur chambre a dû servir *ou* faire office de vestiaire pour leurs invités

6 *Sport* servir, être au service; **whose turn is it to s.?** c'est à qui de servir?; **Simmons to s.** au service, Simmons

7 *Rel* servir la messe

N *Sport* service *m*; **it's your s.** c'est à vous de servir; **to have a good s.** avoir un bon service

▸ **serve out** **VT SEP 1** *(food)* servir; *(provisions)* distribuer **2** *(period of time)* faire; **the president retired before he had served his term out** le président a pris sa retraite avant d'arriver à *ou* d'atteindre la fin de son mandat; **to s. out a prison sentence** purger une peine (de prison)

VI *Sport* sortir son service

▸ **serve up** **VT SEP** *(meal, food)* servir; *Fig (facts, information)* servir, débiter; **she serves up the same old excuse every time** elle ressort chaque fois la même excuse

server ['sɜːvə(r)] **N 1** *(at table)* serveur(euse) *m,f*

2 *Sport* serveur(euse) *m,f*

3 *Rel* servant *m* (d'autel)

4 *(utensil)* couvert *m* de service; **(set of) salad/fish servers** service *m* à salade/à poisson

5 *Comput* serveur *m*

▸▸ *Comput* ***server administrator*** administrateur *m* de serveur; ***server farm*** batterie *f* de serveurs, parc *m* de serveurs

SERVICE ['sɜːvɪs] **N 1** *(to friend, community, country, God)* service *m*; **in the s. of God/one's country** au service de Dieu/sa patrie; **he was rewarded for services rendered to industry/to his country** il a été récompensé pour services rendus à l'industrie/à son pays; **to require the services of a priest/of a doctor** avoir recours aux services d'un prêtre/d'un médecin; **many people gave their services free** beaucoup de gens donnaient des prestations bénévoles; **to offer one's services** proposer ses services; **for services rendered** pour services rendus; **at your s.** à votre service, à votre disposition; **to be of s. to sb** rendre service à qn, être utile à qn; **can I be of s. (to you)?** puis-je vous aider *ou* vous être utile?; *(in shop)* qu'y a-t-il pour votre service?; **she's always ready to be of s.** elle est très serviable, elle est toujours prête à rendre service; **the jug had to do s. as a teapot** le pichet a dû faire office de *ou* servir de théière; **to do sb a s.** rendre (un) service à qn; **he did me a great s. by not telling them** il m'a rendu un grand service en ne leur disant rien; **the car has given us/has seen good s.** la voiture nous a bien servi/a fait long usage

2 *(working order ▸ of machine)* service *m*; **to bring** *or* **to put a machine into s.** mettre une machine en service; **to come into s.** *(system, bridge)* entrer en service; **the cash dispenser is out of s. at the moment** le distributeur automatique de billets est hors service *ou* n'est pas en service en ce moment

3 *(employment ▸ in firm)* service *m*; **20 years' s. with the same company** 20 ans de service dans la même entreprise; **bonuses depend on length of s.** les primes sont versées en fonction de l'ancienneté

4 *Old-fashioned (as domestic servant)* service *m*; **to be in s.** être domestique; **to go into** *or* **to enter sb's s.** entrer au service de qn

5 *(in shop, hotel, restaurant)* service *m*; **the food was good but the s. was poor** on a bien mangé mais le service n'était pas à la hauteur; **you get fast s. in a supermarket** on est servi rapidement dans un supermarché; **10 percent s. included/not included** *(on bill, menu)* service 10 pour cent compris/non compris; **s. with a smile** *(slogan)* servi avec le sourire

6 *Mil* service *m*; **he saw active s. in Korea** il a servi en Corée, il a fait la campagne de Corée; **fit/unfit for s.** apte/inapte au service; *Naut* **s. afloat/ashore** service *m* à bord/à terre; **the services** les (différentes branches des) forces *fpl* armées; **their son is in the services** leur fils est dans les forces armées

7 *(department, scheme)* service *m*; **bus/train s.** service *m* d'autobus/de trains; **postal/telephone services** services *mpl* postaux/téléphoniques; **a new 24-hour banking s.** un nouveau service bancaire fonctionnant 24 heures sur 24; **a bus provides a s. between the two stations** un autobus assure la navette entre les deux gares

8 *Rel (Catholic)* service *m*, office *m*; *(Protestant)* service *m*, culte *m*; **to attend (a) s.** assister à l'office *ou* au culte

9 *(of car, machine ▸ upkeep)* entretien *m*; *(▸ overhaul)* révision *f*; **the car is due for its 20,000 mile s.** ≃ la voiture arrive à la révision des 32000 km

10 *(set of tableware)* service *m*

11 *Sport* service *m*; **Smith broke his opponent's s.** Smith a pris le service de son adversaire *ou* a fait le break

12 *Law (of summons, writ)* signification *f*, notification *f*

COMP 1 *(entrance, hatch, stairs)* de service

2 *Aut & Tech (manual, history, record)* d'entretien

3 *Mil (family, pay)* de militaire; *(conditions)* dans les forces armées

VT 1 *(overhaul ▸ central heating, car)* réviser; **to have one's car serviced** faire réviser sa voiture; **the car has been regularly serviced** la voiture a été régulièrement entretenue

2 *Fin (debt)* assurer le service de

3 *(supply needs of)* pourvoir aux besoins de

4 *Agr (of bull, stallion)* couvrir, servir

• **services** **NPL 1** *Br (on motorway)* aire *f* de service

2 *Com & Econ* services *mpl*; **goods and services** biens *mpl* et services *mpl*; **more and more people will be working in services** de plus en plus de gens travailleront dans le tertiaire

▸▸ *Am* ***service academy*** école *f* militaire; ***service agreement*** contrat *m* de service; ***service area*** *Aut (on motorway)* aire *f* de service; *TV & Rad* zone *f* desservie *ou* de réception; *Aut* ***service bay*** *(in garage)* zone *f* de travail; ***service bell*** *(in hotel)* sonnette *f (pour appeler un employé de l'hôtel)*; *Comput* ***service bureau*** société *f* de traitement à façon; *Austr & NZ* ***service bus*** autocar *m*; *Austr & NZ* ***service car*** autocar *m*; *Aviat* ***service ceiling*** plafond *m* de fonctionnement normal; *Am Aut* ***service center*** aire *f* de services *(au bord d'une autoroute)*; ***service charge*** service *m*; **they've forgotten to include the s. charge on the bill** ils ont oublié de facturer le service; ***service company*** entreprise *f* prestataire de services; ***service court*** *(in tennis)* rectangle *m* de service; ***service engineer*** technicien(enne) *m,f* de maintenance; ***service fault*** *(in tennis)* faute *f* de service; ***service fee*** prestation *f* de service; *Br* ***service flat*** appartement *m* dans une résidence hôtelière; ***service hatch*** passe-plat *m*; ***service industry*** industrie *f* de services; ***service life*** durée *f* de vie; *Br* ***service lift*** monte-charge *m*; ***service line*** *(in tennis)* ligne *f* de service; ***service mark*** marque *f* de service; *Mil* ***service personnel*** personnel *m* militaire; ***service provider*** *(person, company)* prestataire *m* de service(s); *Comput (for Internet)* fournisseur *m* d'accès; *Mil* ***service rifle*** fusil *m* réglementaire *ou* de l'armée; ***service road*** *(behind shops, factory)* = voie d'accès réservée aux livreurs; *(on motorway)* = voie d'accès réservée à l'entretien et aux services d'urgence; *Com & Econ* ***service sector*** secteur *m* tertiaire, tertiaire *m*; ***service station*** station-service *f*; *Mil* ***service vehicle*** véhicule *m* militaire *ou* de l'armée

serviceable ['sɜːvɪsəbəl] **ADJ 1** *(durable ▸ clothes, material)* qui fait de l'usage, qui résiste à l'usure; *(▸ machine, construction)* durable, solide

2 *(useful ▸ clothing, tool)* commode, pratique

3 *(usable)* utilisable, qui peut servir; **this coat is still s.** ce manteau peut encore servir

4 *(ready for use)* prêt à servir

serviced ['sɜːvɪst] **ADJ** avec service d'entretien

▸▸ ***serviced accommodation*** résidence *f* hôtelière; ***serviced apartment*** appartement *m* dans une résidence hôtelière

serviceman ['sɜːvɪsmən] *(pl* **servicemen** [-mən]) **N 1** *Mil* militaire *m* **2** *Am (mechanic)* dépanneur *m*

servicewoman ['sɜːvɪswʊmən] *(pl* **servicewomen** [-wɪmɪn]) **N** *Mil* femme *f* soldat

servicing ['sɜːvɪsɪŋ] **N 1** *(of heating, car)* entretien *m* **2** *(by transport)* desserte *f*; **the s. of an area by rail** la desserte d'une région par chemin de fer

serviette [ˌsɜːvɪ'et] **N** *Br* serviette *f* (de table)

▸▸ ***serviette ring*** rond *m* de serviette

servile ['sɜːvaɪl] **ADJ 1** *(person, behaviour)* servil[e] obséquieux; *(admiration, praise)* servile; *(cond[i]tion, task)* servile, d'esclave **2** *(imitation, transl[a]tion)* servile

servility [sɜː'vɪlətɪ] **N** servilité *f*

serving ['sɜːvɪŋ] **N 1** *(of drinks, meal)* service *m* *(helping)* portion *f*, part *f*

ADJ *Admin (member, chairman)* actuel, en exe[r]cice; **the longest-s. employee** l'employé ayant l[e] plus d'ancienneté; **the longest-s. monarch/prim[e] minister** le monarque/premier ministre qui es[t] resté le plus longtemps au pouvoir

▸▸ ***serving dish*** plat *m*, assiette *f* de service; *B[r]* ***serving hatch***, *Am* ***serving window*** passe-plat *m*

servitude ['sɜːvɪtjuːd] **N** servitude *f*; **in a state o[f] s.** en esclavage

servo ['sɜːvəʊ] *(pl* **servos)** *Tech* **ADJ** servo-

N *(mechanism)* servomécanisme *m*; *(motor)* se[r]vomoteur *m*

▸▸ *Aut* ***servo brake*** servofrein *m*

servo-assistance **N** *Tech* servo-assistance *f*

servocontrol [ˌsɜːvəʊkən'trəʊl] **N** *Tech* servo[-]commande *f*

servomechanism ['sɜːvəʊˌmekənɪzəm] **N** *Tec[h]* servomécanisme *m*

servomotor ['sɜːvəʊˌməʊtə(r)] **N** *Tech* servomo[-]teur *m*

servo-unit **N** *Tech* servomoteur *m*

sesame ['sesəmɪ] **N** sésame *m*; **open s.!** sésam[e] ouvre-toi!

▸▸ *Culin* ***sesame oil*** huile *f* de sésame; *Culin* ***ses[-]ame seed*** graine *f* de sésame

sesh [seʃ] **N** *Br Fam (abbr* **session)** **to have a drink[-]ing s.** se pinter; **we had a bit of a s. last night** o[n] s'en est donné hier soir

session ['seʃən] **N 1** *Admin, Law & Pol* séance session *f*; **this court is now in s.** l'audience est ou[-]verte; **the House is not in s. during the summe[r] months** la Chambre ne siège pas pendant le[s] mois d'été **2** *(interview, meeting, sitting)* séanc[e] *f*; *(for painter, photographer)* séance *f* de pose **morning/evening s.** *(at swimming pool etc)* séanc[e] *f* du matin/soir; **he had a long s. with his psychia[-]trist** il a eu un long entretien avec son psychia[-]tre; **we're having another s. tomorrow** *(working[)]* nous avons encore une séance de travail o[u] nous allons retravailler demain; *(negotiation[s,] discussion)* nous avons encore une séance (d[e]) négociations *ou* d'entretiens) demain; **a drink[-]ing s.** une beuverie **3** *Am & Scot Univ (term)* tri[-]mestre *m*; *(year)* année *f* universitaire; *A[m]* **school is in s.** on est en période scolaire

▸▸ ***session musician*** musicien(enne) *m,f* de stu[-]dio

SET® *Comput (written abbr* **secure electroni[c] transaction)** SET® *f*

SET [set]

N	
• jeu **1**	• série **1**
• ensemble **1, 3**	• cercle **2**
• appareil **4**	• poste **4**
• set **5**	• plateau **6**
• scène **6**	
ADJ	
• fixe **1**	• arrêté **2**
• figé **2**	• résolu **3**
• prêt **4**	
VT	
• mettre **1, 3, 4**	• poser **1, 3, 5, 9**
• situer **2**	• régler **3**
• fixer **6, 9**	• établir **6**
• faire prendre **8**	
VI	
• se coucher **1**	• prendre **2**
• se mettre **4**	

(pt & pp **set**, *cont* **setting)**

N 1 *(of tools, keys, golf clubs)* jeu *m*; *(of numbers names, instructions, stamps)* série *f*, *(of books* collection *f*, *(of furniture, facts, conditions, char[-]acteristics, data)* ensemble *m*; *(of cutlery, dishes glasses)* service *m*; *(of lingerie)* parure *f*, *(o[f] wheels)* train *m*; *(of events, decisions, questions* série *f*, suite *f*, *Comput (of characters, instructions* jeu *m*, ensemble *m*; **a s. of matching luggage** u[n] ensemble de valises assorties; **a s. of table/bed linen** une parure de table/de lit; **badminton/chess s.** jeu *m* de badminton/d'échecs; **they're playing with Damian's train s.** ils jouent avec le train électrique de Damian; **the cups/the chairs are sold in sets of six** les tasses/les chaises sont vendues par six; **I can't break up the s.** je ne peux pas les dépareiller; **they make a s.** ils vont ensemble; **to collect the (whole) s.** rassembler toute la collection, faire la collection; **he made me a duplicate s.** *(of keys)* il m'a fait un double des clés; *(of contact lenses)* il m'en a fait une autre paire; **a full s. of the encyclopedia** une encyclopédie complète; **a full s. of Tolstoy's works** les œuvres complètes de Tolstoï; **they've detected two sets of fingerprints** ils ont relevé deux séries d'empreintes digitales *ou* les empreintes digitales de deux personnes; **given another s. of circumstances, things might have turned out differently** dans d'autres circonstances, les choses auraient pu se passer différemment; **the first s. of reforms** la première série *ou* le premier train de réformes

2 *(social group)* cercle *m*, milieu *m*; **he's not in our s.** il n'appartient pas à notre cercle; **the riding/yachting s.** le monde *ou* milieu de l'équitation/du yachting; **the literary s.** les milieux *mpl* littéraires

3 *Math* ensemble *m*

4 *(electrical device)* appareil *m*; *(radio, TV)* poste *m*; **a colour TV s.** un poste de télévision *ou* un téléviseur couleur

5 *Sport* set *m*, manche *f*; **first s. to Miss Williams** set Williams

6 *Cin & TV* plateau *m*; *Theat (stage)* scène *f*; *(scenery)* décor *m*; **on (the) s.** *Cin & TV* sur le plateau; *Theat* sur scène

7 *(part of performance ▸ by singer, group)* **he'll be playing two sets tonight** il va jouer à deux reprises ce soir; **her second s. was livelier** la deuxième partie de son spectacle a été plus animée

8 *Br Sch* groupe *m* de niveau

9 *(for hair)* mise *f* en plis; **to have a s.** se faire faire une mise en plis

10 *(posture ▸ of shoulders, body)* position *f*, attitude *f*; *(▸ of head)* port *m*; **I could tell he was angry by the s. of his jaw** rien qu'à la façon dont il serrait les mâchoires, j'ai compris qu'il était en colère

11 *(direction ▸ of wind, current)* direction *f*; **suddenly the s. of the wind changed** le vent a tourné soudainement

12 *(of badger)* terrier *m*

ADJ 1 *(specified, prescribed ▸ rule, price, quantity, sum, wage)* fixe; **meals are at s. times** les repas sont servis à heures fixes; **there are no s. rules for raising children** il n'y a pas de règles toutes faites pour l'éducation des enfants; **the tasks must be done in the s. order** les tâches doivent être accomplies dans l'ordre prescrit; **with no s. purpose** sans but précis

2 *(fixed, rigid ▸ ideas, views)* arrêté; *(▸ smile, frown)* figé; **her day followed a s. routine** sa journée se déroulait selon un rituel immuable; **he has a s. way of doing it** il a sa méthode pour le faire; **to be s. in one's ways** avoir ses (petites) habitudes

3 *(intent, resolute)* résolu, déterminé; **to be s. on** *or* **upon sth** vouloir qch à tout prix; **I'm (dead) s. on finishing it tonight** je suis (absolument) déterminé à le finir ce soir; **he's dead s. against it** il s'y oppose formellement

4 *(ready, in position)* prêt; **are you (all) s. to go?** êtes-vous prêt à partir?

5 *(likely)* probablement; **house prices are s. to rise steeply** les prix de l'immobilier vont vraisemblablement monter en flèche

6 *Br Sch (book, subject)* au programme; **one of our s. books is 'Oliver Twist'** un des ouvrages au programme est 'Oliver Twist'

VT 1 *(put in specified place or position)* mettre, poser; **he s. his cases down on the platform** il posa ses valises sur le quai; **to s. sth before sb** *(dish, glass)* placer qch devant qn; *(proposal, plan)* présenter qch à qn; **she s. the steaming bowl before him** elle plaça le bol fumant devant lui; **to s. a proposal before the board** présenter un projet au conseil d'administration; **to s. sb on his/her feet again** remettre qn sur pied; **to s. a match to sth** mettre le feu à qch

2 *(usu passive) (locate, situate ▸ building, story)* situer; **the house is s. in large grounds** la maison est située dans un grand parc; **his eyes are s. too close together** ses yeux sont trop rapprochés; **the story is s. in Tokyo/in the 18th century** l'histoire se passe *ou* se déroule à Tokyo/au XVIIIème siècle

3 *(adjust ▸ clock, mechanism)* régler; *(▸ alarm)* mettre; *Comput (▸ tabs, format)* poser; **I s. my watch to New York time** j'ai réglé ma montre à l'heure de New York; **he's so punctual you can s. your watch by him!** il est si ponctuel qu'on peut régler sa montre sur lui!; **I've s. the alarm for six** j'ai mis le réveil à (sonner pour) six heures; **how do I s. the margins?** comment est-ce que je fais pour placer les marges?; **s. the timer for one hour** mettez le minuteur sur une heure; **first s. the control knob to the desired temperature** mettez tout d'abord le bouton de réglage sur la température voulue

4 *(fix into position)* mettre, fixer; *(jewel, diamond)* sertir, monter; **the handles are s. into the drawers** les poignées sont encastrées dans les tiroirs; **to s. a stake in the ground** enfoncer *ou* planter un pieu dans la terre; **metal bars had been s. in the concrete** des barres en métal avaient été fixées dans le béton; **the brooch was s. with pearls** la broche était sertie de perles; **the ruby was s. in a simple ring** le rubis était monté sur un simple anneau; *Med* **to s. a bone** réduire une fracture; *Fig* **his face was s. in a frown** son visage était figé dans une grimace renfrognée; **she s. her jaw and refused to budge** elle serra les dents et refusa de bouger; **we had s. ourselves to resist** nous étions déterminés à résister

5 *(lay, prepare in advance ▸ trap)* poser, tendre; **to s. the table** mettre le couvert *ou* la table; **to s. the table for two** mettre deux couverts; **s. an extra place at (the) table** rajoutez un couvert

6 *(establish ▸ date, price, schedule, terms)* fixer, déterminer; *(▸ rule, guideline, objective, target)* établir; *(▸ mood, precedent)* créer; **they still haven't s. a date for the party** ils n'ont toujours pas fixé de date pour la réception; **you've s. yourself a tough deadline** vous vous êtes fixé un délai très court; **they s. their own production targets** ils établissent *ou* fixent leurs propres objectifs de production; **to s. a value on sth** décider de la valeur de qch; *Fig* **they s. a high value on creativity** ils accordent une grande valeur à la créativité; **the price was s. at £500** le prix a été fixé à 500 livres; **how are exchange rates s.?** comment les taux de change sont-ils déterminés?; **to s. an age limit at…** fixer une limite d'âge à…; **to s. a new fashion** *or* **trend** lancer une nouvelle mode; **to s. a new world record** établir un nouveau record mondial; **to s. the tone for** *or* **of sth** donner le ton de qch

7 *(indicating change of state or activity)* **to s. sth alight** *or* **on fire** mettre le feu à qch; **it sets my nerves on edge** ça me crispe; *also Fig* **she s. me in the right direction** elle m'a mis sur la bonne voie; **to s. sb against sb** monter qn contre qn; **he/the incident s. the taxman on my trail** il/l'incident a mis le fisc sur ma piste; **to s. the dogs on sb** lâcher les chiens sur qn; **the incident s. the family against him** l'incident a monté la famille contre lui; **it will s. the country on the road to economic recovery** cela va mettre le pays sur la voie de la reprise économique; **his failure s. him thinking** son échec lui a donné à réfléchir; **the scandal will s. the whole town talking** le scandale va faire jaser toute la ville; **the wind s. the leaves dancing** le vent a fait frissonner les feuilles; **to s. a machine going** mettre une machine en marche

8 *(solidify ▸ yoghurt, jelly, concrete)* faire prendre; **pectin will help to s. the jam** la pectine aidera à épaissir la confiture

9 *(pose ▸ problem)* poser; *(assign ▸ task)* fixer; **the strikers' demands s. the management a difficult problem** les exigences des grévistes posent un problème difficile à la direction; **I s. them to work tidying the garden** je les ai mis au désherbage du jardin; **I've s. myself the task of writing to them regularly** je me suis fixé la tâche de leur écrire régulièrement

10 *Br Sch (exam)* composer, choisir les questions de; *(books, texts)* mettre au programme; **she s. the class a maths exercise** elle a donné un exercice de maths à la classe; **who sets the test questions?** qui choisit les questions de l'épreuve?

11 *(hair)* **to s. sb's hair** faire une mise en plis à qn; **I've just had my hair s.** je viens de me faire faire une mise en plis

12 *Typ (text, page)* composer; **to s. type** composer

13 *Mus (poem, words)* **to s. sth to music** mettre qch en musique

VI 1 *(sun, moon)* se coucher; **we saw the sun setting** nous avons vu le coucher du soleil

2 *(become firm ▸ glue, cement, plaster, jelly, yoghurt)* prendre; **her features had s. in an expression of determination** ses traits s'étaient durcis en une expression de très forte détermination

3 *(bone)* se ressouder

4 *(start)* se mettre; **he s. to work** il s'est mis au travail

5 *(wind, tide)* **the wind looks s. fair to the east** on dirait un vent d'ouest

▸▸ *Cin & TV* ***set decorator*** ensemblier *m*; *Theat, Cin & TV* ***set designer*** décorateur(trice) *m,f*; *Gram* ***set expression*** expression *f* figée; ***set figures*** *(in skating)* figures *fpl* imposées; *Cin & TV* ***set lighting*** éclairage *m* de plateau; ***set menu*** menu *m*; *Gram* ***set phrase*** expression *f* figée; ***set piece*** **1** *Art, Literature & Mus* morceau *m* de bravoure **2** *(of scenery)* élément *m* de décor **3** *Sport* combinaison *f* préparée *ou* calculée; *Sport* ***set point*** *(in tennis)* balle *f* de set; ***set square*** équerre *f (à dessiner)*; ***set task*** tâche *f* assignée; **to give sb a s. task to do** assigner à qn une tâche bien précise; *Math* ***set theory*** théorie *f* des ensembles

▸**set about** **VT INSEP 1** *(start ▸ task)* se mettre à; **she s. about changing the tyre** elle s'est mise à changer le pneu; **I didn't know how to s. about it** je ne savais pas comment m'y prendre **2** *(attack)* attaquer, s'en prendre à; **he s. about the mugger with his umbrella** il s'en est pris à son agresseur à coups de parapluie

▸**set against** **VT SEP 1** *(compare)* **to s. sth against sth** comparer qch à qch; **to s. the benefits against the costs** évaluer les bénéfices par rapport aux coûts **2** *Fin (offset)* **some of these expenses can be s. against tax** certaines de ces dépenses peuvent être déduites des impôts **3** *(friends, family)* monter contre; **religious differences have s. family against family** les différences religieuses ont monté les familles les unes contre les autres; **to s. oneself** *or* **one's face against sth** s'opposer résolument à qch

▸**set apart** **VT SEP 1** *(place separately ▸ object)* mettre à part *ou* de côté; **there was one deck chair s. slightly apart from the others** il y avait une chaise longue un peu à l'écart des autres; **they s. themselves apart** ils faisaient bande à part **2** *(distinguish)* distinguer (**from** de); **her talent sets her apart from the other students** son talent la distingue des autres étudiants

▸**set aside** **VT SEP 1** *(put down ▸ knitting, book)* poser; **could you s. aside your work for a while?** pouvez-vous laisser votre travail un moment?

2 *(reserve, keep ▸ time, place)* réserver; *(▸ money)* mettre de côté; *(▸ arable land)* mettre en friche; **I've s. tomorrow aside for house hunting** j'ai réservé la journée de demain pour chercher une maison; **can you s. the book aside for me?** pourriez-vous me mettre ce livre de côté?; **chop the onions and s. them aside** coupez les oignons et réservez-les

3 *(overlook, disregard)* mettre de côté, oublier, passer sur; **they s. their differences aside in order to work together** ils ont mis de côté leurs différences pour travailler ensemble

4 *(reject ▸ dogma, proposal, offer)* rejeter

5 *Law (annul ▸ contract, will)* annuler; *(▸ verdict, judgment)* casser

▸**set back** **VT SEP 1** *(situate towards the rear)* **the building is s. back slightly from the road** l'immeuble est un peu en retrait par rapport à la route **2** *(delay ▸ plans, progress)* retarder; **his illness s. him back a month in his work** sa maladie l'a retardé d'un mois dans son travail; **the news may s. him** *or* **his recovery back** la nouvelle risque de retarder sa guérison **3** *Fam (cost)* coûter à[□]; **the trip will s. her back a bit** le voyage va lui coûter cher

▸**set down** VT SEP **1** *(tray, bag etc)* poser
2 *Br (passenger)* déposer; **the bus sets you down in front of the station** le bus vous dépose devant la gare
3 *(note, record)* noter, inscrire; **try and s. your thoughts down on paper** essayez de mettre vos pensées par écrit
4 *(establish ▸ rule, condition)* établir, fixer; **the government has s. down a margin for pay increases** le gouvernement a fixé une fourchette pour les augmentations de salaire; **permissible levels of pollution are s. down in the regulations** les taux de pollution tolérés sont fixés dans les réglementations; **to s. sth down in writing** coucher qch par écrit

▸**set forth** VT SEP *Formal (expound ▸ plan, objections)* exposer, présenter; **the recommendations are s. forth in the last chapter** les recommandations sont détaillées *ou* énumérées dans le dernier chapitre
VI *Literary* partir, se mettre en route

▸**set in** VI *(problems)* survenir, surgir; *(disease)* se déclarer; *(winter)* commencer; *(night)* tomber; **if infection sets in** si la plaie s'infecte; **the bad weather has s. in for the winter** le mauvais temps s'est installé pour tout l'hiver; **panic s. in** *(began)* la panique éclata; *(lasted)* la panique s'installa
VT SEP *Sewing (sleeve)* monter

▸**set off** VT SEP **1** *(alarm)* déclencher; *(bomb)* faire exploser; *(fireworks)* faire partir
2 *(reaction, process, war)* déclencher, provoquer; **their offer s. off another round of talks** leur proposition a déclenché une autre série de négociations; **it s. her off on a long tirade against bureaucracy** cela eut pour effet de la lancer dans une longue tirade contre la bureaucratie; **to s. sb off laughing** faire rire qn; **this answer s. them off (laughing)** cette réponse a déclenché les rires; **one look at his face s. me off again** en le voyant, mon fou rire a repris de plus belle; **if you say anything it'll only s. him off (crying) again** si tu dis quoi que ce soit, il va se remettre à pleurer; **the smallest amount of pollen will s. her off** la moindre dose de pollen lui déclenche une réaction allergique; **don't mention Maradona or you'll s. him off again** surtout ne prononce pas le nom de Maradona sinon il va recommencer; *Fig* **to s. sb off on the wrong track** mettre qn sur une fausse piste
3 *(enhance)* mettre en valeur; **the vase sets off the flowers beautifully** le vase met vraiment les fleurs en valeur
4 *Fin (offset)* **some of these expenses can be s. off against tax** certaines de ces dépenses peuvent être déduites des impôts
VI partir, se mettre en route; **he s. off at a run** il est parti en courant; **I s. off to explore the town** je suis parti explorer la ville; **after lunch, we s. off again** après le déjeuner, nous avons repris la route

▸**set on** VT INSEP *(attack)* attaquer, s'en prendre à
VT SEP **1** *(cause to follow)* **to s. the police on the tracks of a thief** mettre la police aux trousses d'un voleur; **to s. sb on his/her way** mettre qn sur les rails **2** *(cause to attack)* **to s. a dog on sb** lâcher un chien sur qn

▸**set out** VT SEP **1** *(arrange ▸ chairs, game pieces)* disposer; *(▸ merchandise)* étaler; **the shopping centre is very well s. out** le centre commercial est très bien conçu **2** *(present ▸ ideas)* exposer, présenter; **the information is s. out in the table below** ces données sont présentées dans le tableau ci-dessous
VI **1** *(leave)* se mettre en route, partir; **just as he was setting out** au moment de son départ; **to s. out again** repartir; **to s. out in pursuit/in search of sb** se mettre à la poursuite/à la recherche de qn **2** *(undertake course of action)* **he has trouble finishing what he sets out to do** il a du mal à terminer ce qu'il entreprend; **I can't remember now what I s. out to do** je ne me souviens plus de ce que je voulais faire à l'origine; **they all s. out with the intention of changing the world** au début, ils veulent tous changer le monde; **she didn't deliberately s. out to annoy you** il n'était pas dans ses intentions de vous froisser; **his theory sets out to prove that…** sa théorie a pour objet de prouver que… + *indicative*

▸**set to** VI **1** *(begin work)* commencer, s'y mettre; **we s. to with a will** nous nous y sommes mis avec ardeur **2** *Fam (two people ▸ start arguing)* avoir une prise de bec; *(▸ start fighting)* en venir aux mains

▸**set up** VT SEP **1** *(install ▸ equipment, computer)* installer; *(▸ roadblock)* installer, disposer; *(▸ experiment)* préparer; **everything's s. up for the show** tout est préparé *ou* prêt pour le spectacle; **s. the chairs up in a circle** mettez *ou* disposez les chaises en cercle; **the equation sets up a relation between the two variables** l'équation établit un rapport entre les deux variables; **the system wasn't s. up to handle so many users** le système n'était pas conçu pour gérer autant d'usagers; **he s. the situation up so she couldn't refuse** il a arrangé la situation de telle manière qu'elle ne pouvait pas refuser
2 *(erect, build ▸ tent, furniture kit, crane)* monter; *(▸ shed, shelter)* construire; *(▸ monument, statue)* ériger; **to s. up camp** installer *ou* dresser le camp
3 *(start up, institute ▸ business, scholarship)* créer; *(▸ hospital, school)* fonder; *(▸ committee, task force)* constituer; *(▸ system of government, republic)* instaurer; *(▸ programme, review process, system)* mettre en place; *(▸ inquiry)* ouvrir; *(arrange ▸ dinner, meeting, appointment)* organiser; **to s. up house** *or* **home** s'installer; **they s. up house together** ils se sont mis en ménage; **to s. up a dialogue** entamer le dialogue; **you'll be in charge of setting up training programmes** vous serez responsable de la mise en place des programmes de formation; **the medical system s. up after the war** le système médical mis en place après la guerre
4 *(financially, in business ▸ person)* installer, établir; **he s. his son up in a dry-cleaning business** il a acheté à son fils une entreprise de nettoyage à sec; **she could finally s. herself up as an accountant** elle pouvait enfin s'installer comme comptable; **the money would s. him up for life** l'argent le mettrait à l'abri du besoin pour le restant de ses jours
5 *(provide)* **she can s. you up with a guide/the necessary papers** elle peut vous procurer un guide/les papiers qu'il vous faut; **I can s. you up with a girlfriend of mine** je peux te présenter à *ou* te faire rencontrer une de mes copines
6 *(restore energy to)* remonter, remettre sur pied; **have a brandy, that'll s. you up** prends un cognac, ça va te remonter
7 *Fam (frame)* monter un coup contre; **she claims she was s. up** elle prétend qu'elle est victime d'un coup monté
8 *Typ (text)* composer
VI s'installer, s'établir; **he's setting up in the fast-food business** il se lance dans la restauration rapide; **to s. up on one's own** *(business)* s'installer à son compte; *(home)* prendre son propre appartement/sa propre maison

▸**set upon** VT INSEP *(physically or verbally)* attaquer, s'en prendre à

setback ['setbæk] N revers *m*, échec *m*; *(minor)* contretemps *m*; *Fin & St Exch* tassement *m*, repli *m*; *Med* rechute *f*; **to suffer a s.** essuyer un revers; **the government has suffered a s. in its plans to change the legislation** le gouvernement a vu son projet de réforme compromis; **this has been a severe s. for the government** cela a constitué un grave revers *ou* échec pour le gouvernement

set-in ADJ *(sleeve)* rapporté

sett [set] N **1** *(for paving)* pavé *m* **2** *(of badger)* terrier *m* (de blaireau)

settee [se'tiː] N canapé *m*

setter ['setə(r)] N **1** *(dog)* setter *m* **2** *(of jewels)* sertisseur(euse) *m,f* **3** *Typ* compositeur(trice) *m,f*

setting ['setɪŋ] N **1** *(of sun, moon)* coucher *m*
2 *(situation, surroundings)* cadre *m*, décor *m*; *Theat* décor *m*; **the house is in a lovely country s.** la maison est située dans un très beau cadre campagnard; **they photographed the foxes in their natural s.** ils ont photographié les renards dans leur milieu naturel
3 *(position, level ▸ of machine, instrument)* réglage *m*; **try a higher s.** *(of oven, iron, microwave etc)* augmentez la température; **what s. was it on?** sur quoi était-elle réglée?
4 *Comput* **settings** paramètres *mpl*
5 *(for jewels)* monture *f*; *(process)* sertissage *m*
6 *(at table)* couvert *m*
7 *Mus (of poem, play)* mise *f* en musique; *(for instruments)* arrangement *m*, adaptation *f*; **s. for male voice** arrangement *m* pour voix d'homme
8 *(of fracture)* réduction *f*; *(in plaster)* plâtrage *m*
9 *(of jam)* prise *f*; *(of cement)* prise *f*, durcissement *m*
10 *Typ* composition *f*
▸▸ ***setting lotion*** lotion *f* pour mise en plis

SETTLE ['setəl]

VT
- régler **1, 3**
- fixer **2**
- installer **4**
- coloniser **5**
- calmer **6**

VI
- s'installer **1, 2**
- s'établir **1**
- se calmer **3**
- tenir **4**
- se poser **4**
- se tasser **5**

VT **1** *(solve ▸ question, issue)* régler; *(▸ dispute, quarrel, differences)* régler, trancher; **to s. a matter** régler une question; **the case was settled out of court** l'affaire a été réglée à l'amiable; **questions not yet settled** questions *fpl* en suspens; **to s. an old score** *or* **old scores** régler des comptes
2 *(determine, agree on ▸ date, price)* fixer; **have you settled where to go for the picnic?** avez-vous décidé d'un endroit pour le pique-nique?; **it was settled that I would go to boarding school** il fut convenu *ou* décidé que j'irais en pension; **you must s. that among yourselves** il va falloir que vous arrangiez cela entre vous; **nothing is settled yet** rien n'est encore décidé *ou* arrêté; **that's that settled then!** voilà une affaire réglée!; **that's settled then, I'll meet you at eight o'clock** alors c'est entendu *ou* convenu, on se retrouve à huit heures; **that settles it, the party's tomorrow!** c'est décidé, la fête aura lieu demain!; **that settles it, he's fired!** trop c'est trop, il est renvoyé!
3 *(pay ▸ debt, account, bill)* régler; **to s. a claim** *(insurance)* régler un litige
4 *(install)* installer; *(arrange, place ▸ on table, surface)* installer, poser (soigneusement); **when I'm settled, I'll write to you** quand je serai installé, je vous écrirai; **to s. oneself comfortably in an armchair** s'installer confortablement dans un fauteuil; **he settled the children for the night** il a mis les enfants au lit, il est allé coucher les enfants; **to get settled** s'installer (confortablement)
5 *(colonize)* coloniser; **Peru was settled by the Spanish** le Pérou a été colonisé par les Espagnols, les Espagnols se sont établis au Pérou
6 *(calm ▸ nerves, stomach)* calmer, apaiser; **this brandy will s. your nerves** ce cognac te calmera les nerfs; **give me something to s. my stomach** donnez-moi quelque chose pour l'estomac; **to s. sb's doubts** dissiper les doutes de qn; **the rain settled the dust** la pluie a fait retomber la poussière
7 *Law (money, allowance, estate)* constituer; **to s. an annuity on sb** constituer une rente à qn; **she settled all her money on her nephew** elle a légué toute sa fortune à son neveu; *Fig* **how are you settled for money at the moment?** est-ce que tu as suffisamment d'argent en ce moment?
VI **1** *(go to live ▸ gen)* s'installer, s'établir; *(▸ colonist)* s'établir; **she finally settled abroad** elle s'est finalement installée à l'étranger
2 *(install oneself ▸ in new home, bed)* s'installer; *(adapt ▸ to circumstances)* s'habituer; **she lived here a few years, but didn't s.** *(didn't stay)* elle a vécu ici quelques années, mais ne s'est pas installée définitivement; *(didn't adapt)* elle a vécu ici quelques années, mais ne s'est jamais habituée; **to s. in an armchair/for the night** s'installer dans un fauteuil/pour la nuit; **I couldn't s.** *(in bed)* je n'arrivais pas à m'endormir; **to s. to work/to do sth** se mettre sérieusement au travail/à faire qch; **he can't s. to anything** il n'arrive pas à se concentrer sur quoi que ce soit
3 *(become calm ▸ nerves, stomach, storm)* s'apaiser, se calmer; *(▸ situation)* s'arranger; **wait for things to s. before you do anything** attends que les choses se calment *ou* s'arrangent avant de faire quoi que ce soit; **the weather is settling** le temps se calme
4 *(come to rest ▸ snow)* tenir; *(▸ dust, sediment)* se

déposer; (▸ *liquid, beer*) reposer; (▸ *bird, insect, eyes*) se poser; **the snow began to s. (on the ground)** la neige commençait à tenir; **a fly settled on the butter** une mouche s'est posée sur le beurre; **let your dinner s. before you go out** prends le temps de digérer avant de sortir; **allow the mixture to s.** laissez reposer le mélange; *Com* **contents may s. during transport** *(on packaging)* le contenu risque de se tasser pendant le transport; **her gaze settled on the book** son regard se posa sur le livre; **an eerie calm settled over the village** un calme inquiétant retomba sur le village; **the cold settled on his chest** le rhume lui est tombé sur la poitrine

5 *(road, wall, foundations)* se tasser

6 *(financially)* **to s. with sb for sth** régler le prix de qch à qn; **can I s. with you tomorrow?** est-ce que je peux vous régler demain?

7 *Law* **to s. out of court** régler une affaire à l'amiable

N *(seat)* banquette *f* à haut dossier

▸ **settle down** **VI 1** *(in armchair, at desk)* s'installer; *(in new home)* s'installer, se fixer; *(at school, in job)* s'habituer, s'adapter; *(adopt steady lifestyle)* se ranger, s'assagir; **they settled down by the fire for the evening** ils se sont installés près du feu pour la soirée; **to s. down to watch television** s'installer (confortablement) devant la télévision; **it took the children some weeks to s. down in their new school** il a fallu plusieurs semaines aux enfants pour s'habituer à leur nouvelle école; **Susan is finding it hard to s. down to life in Paris** Susan a du mal à s'habituer *ou* à s'adapter à la vie parisienne; **they never s. down anywhere for long** ils ne se fixent jamais nulle part bien longtemps; **it's about time Tom got married and settled down** il est temps que Tom se marie et qu'il se range; **2** *(concentrate, apply oneself)* **to s. down to do sth** se mettre à faire qch; **to s. down to work** se mettre au travail; **I can't seem to s. down to anything these days** je n'arrive pas à me concentrer sur quoi que ce soit ces jours-ci **3** *(become calm* ▸ *excitement)* s'apaiser; (▸ *situation)* s'arranger; *(market)* se stabiliser; **things are settling down** *(calming down)* les choses sont en train de se calmer; *(becoming more definite)* les choses commencent à prendre tournure; **s. down, children!** calmez-vous, les enfants!, du calme, les enfants!

VT SEP *(person)* installer; **to s. oneself down in an armchair** s'installer (confortablement) dans un fauteuil; **she settled the patient/the baby down for the night** elle a installé le malade/le bébé pour la nuit

▸ **settle for** **VT INSEP** accepter, se contenter de; **I settled for £100** j'ai accepté 100 livres; **I insist on the best quality, I never s. for (anything) less** j'exige ce qu'il y a de mieux, je n'accepte jamais rien en dessous; **there was no wine left so they had to s. for beer** comme il ne restait plus de vin, ils durent se contenter de bière

▸ **settle in** **VI** *(at new house)* s'installer; *(at new school, job)* s'habituer, s'adapter; **once we're settled in, we'll invite you round** une fois que nous serons installés, nous t'inviterons; **it took him a while to s. in at his new school** il a mis un certain temps à s'habituer à sa nouvelle école

▸ **settle on** **VT INSEP** *(decide on)* décider de; **they've settled on Rome for their honeymoon** ils ont décidé d'aller passer leur lune de miel à Rome; **they've settled on a Volkswagen** ils se sont décidés pour une Volkswagen; **they settled on a compromise solution** ils ont finalement choisi le compromis

▸ **settle up** **VI** régler (la note); **I must s. up with the plumber** il faut que je règle le plombier; **can we s. up?** est-ce qu'on peut faire les comptes?

VT SEP régler

settled ['setəld] **ADJ 1** *(stable, unchanging* ▸ *person)* rangé, établi; (▸ *life)* stable, régulier; (▸ *habits)* régulier; **he's very s. in his ways** il est très routinier, il a ses petites habitudes; **she is s. in her job** elle est habituée à son emploi

2 *Met (calm)* beau (belle); **the weather will remain s.** le temps demeurera au beau fixe

3 *(inhabited)* peuplé; *(colonized)* colonisé

4 *(fixed* ▸ *population)* fixe, établi

5 *(account, bill)* réglé

settlement ['setəlmənt] **N 1** *(resolution* ▸ *of question, dispute)* règlement *m*, solution *f*; (▸ *of problem)* solution *f*

2 *(payment)* règlement *m*; **I enclose a cheque in s. of your account** veuillez trouver ci-joint un chèque en règlement de votre facture; **out-of-court s.** règlement *m* à l'amiable

3 *(agreement)* accord *m*; **to reach a s.** parvenir à *ou* conclure un accord; **marriage s.** contrat *m* de mariage

4 *(decision* ▸ *on details, date)* décision *f*; **s. of the final details will take some time** il faudra un certain temps pour régler les derniers détails

5 *Law (financial)* donation *f*; *(dowry)* dot *f*; *(of annuity)* constitution *f*; **to make a s. on sb** faire une donation à *ou* en faveur de qn

6 *(colony)* colonie *f*; *(village)* village *m*; *(dwellings)* habitations *fpl*

7 *(of people in a country)* établissement *m*, installation *f*; *(colonization)* colonisation *f*, peuplement *m*; **there were signs of human s.** il y avait des traces de présence humaine

8 *(of contents, road)* tassement *m*; *(of sediment)* dépôt *m*

▸▸ *St Exch* ***settlement day*** jour *m* de (la) liquidation; *Com* ***settlement discount*** remise *f* pour règlement rapide; *Com* ***settlement period*** délai *m* de règlement; *St Exch* ***settlement price*** cours *m* de résiliation; *St Exch* ***settlement value*** valeur *f* liquidative

settler ['setələ(r)] **N** colonisateur(trice) *m,f*, colon *m*

settling ['setəlɪŋ] **N** *(UNCOUNT)* **1** *(of question, problem, dispute)* règlement *m*

2 *(of account, debt)* règlement *m*

3 *(of contents)* tassement *m*

4 *(of country)* colonisation *f*

set-to *(pl* **set-tos)** **N** *Br Fam (fight)* bagarre▫*f*, baston *m ou f*; *(argument)* prise *f* de bec

set-top box **N** *TV* décodeur *m* numérique

set-up **N 1** *(arrangement, system)* organisation *f*, système *m*; **the project manager explained the s. to me** le chef de projet m'a expliqué comment les choses fonctionnaient *ou* étaient organisées; **what's the economic s. in these countries?** quel est le système économique de ces pays?; **you've got a nice s. here** vous êtes bien installé ici; **it's an odd s.** *(company)* c'est une drôle de boîte; *(marriage, relationship)* c'est un drôle de ménage; *(collection of people)* c'est une drôle d'équipe **2** *Fam (trap, trick)* coup *m* monté, machination▫*f* **3** *Comput* configuration *f*

▸▸ *Comput* ***set-up CD*** CD-ROM *m inv ou* cédérom *m* d'installation; ***set-up charge*** frais *mpl* d'inscription; *Acct* ***set-up costs*** frais *mpl* de lancement; ***set-up fee*** frais *mpl* d'inscription; *Comput* ***set-up program*** programme *m* d'installation

seven ['sevən] **N** *(number, numeral)* sept *m inv*

PRON sept

ADJ sept; *see also* **five**

▸▸ ***the seven deadly sins*** les sept péchés *mpl* capitaux; ***the seven seas*** toutes les mers *fpl* (du monde); **to sail the s. seas** parcourir les mers; ***the Seven Sisters*** *(US universities)* = groupe de sept universités prestigieuses du nord-est des États-Unis, qui étaient toutes, à l'origine, des établissements pour jeunes filles; *Astron* les Sept Sœurs; *Geog* = ensemble de sept falaises sur la côte sud de l'Angleterre; *(oil companies)* les sept sœurs, = nom donné à sept compagnies pétrolières parmi les plus importantes (Exxon, Shell, BP, Mobil, Chevron, Gulf, Texaco); *Hist* ***the Seven Years' War*** la guerre de Sept Ans

seven-bit character **N** *Comput* caractère *m* à sept bits

seven-bit data **N** *Comput* données *fpl* à sept bits

sevenfold ['sevənfəʊld] **ADJ** septuple

ADV au septuple; **profits have increased s.** les bénéfices ont été multipliés par sept

seventeen [ˌsevən'tiːn] **N** dix-sept *m inv*

PRON dix-sept

ADJ dix-sept; *see also* **five**

seventeenth [ˌsevən'tiːnθ] **N 1** *(fraction)* dix-septième *m* **2** *(in series)* dix-septième *mf* **3** *(of month)* dix-sept *m inv*

ADJ dix-septième

ADV dix-septièmement; *(in contest)* en dix-septième position, à la dix-septième place; *see also* **fifth**

seventh ['sevənθ] **N 1** *(fraction)* septième *m*

2 *(in series)* septième *mf*

3 *(of month)* sept *m inv*

4 *Mus* septième *f*

ADJ septième

ADV septièmement; *(in contest)* en septième position, à la septième place; *see also* **fifth**

▸▸ *Rel* ***Seventh Day Adventist*** adventiste *mf* du septième jour; *Am Sch* ***seventh grade*** = classe de lycée pour les 11–12 ans; ***seventh heaven*** le septième ciel; **to be in (one's) s. heaven** être au septième ciel

seventieth ['sevəntɪəθ] **N 1** *(fraction)* soixante-dixième *m* **2** *(in series)* soixante-dixième *mf*

ADJ soixante-dixième

ADV soixante-dixièmement; *(in contest)* en soixante-dixième position, à la soixante-dixième place; *see also* **fifth**

seventy ['sevəntɪ] *(pl* **seventies)** **N** soixante-dix *m inv*, *Belg & Suisse* septante *m inv*

PRON soixante-dix, *Belg & Suisse* septante

ADJ soixante-dix, *Belg & Suisse* septante

COMP **s.-one** soixante et onze; **s.-two** soixante-douze; **s.-nine** soixante-dix-neuf; **s.-first** soixante et onzième; **s.-second** soixante-douzième; *see also* **fifty**

sever ['sevə(r)] **VT 1** *(cut off* ▸ *rope, limb)* couper, trancher; **his hand was severed (at the wrist)** il a eu la main coupée (au poignet); **a severed head** une tête coupée; **the roadworks severed a water main** les travaux ont crevé une canalisation d'eau; **communications with outlying villages have been severed** les communications avec les villages isolés ont été rompues **2** *(cease* ▸ *relationship, connections, contact)* cesser, rompre; **she severed all ties with her family** elle a rompu tous les liens avec sa famille

VI se rompre, casser, céder; **the rope severed under the strain** la corde a cédé sous la tension

several ['sevərəl] **ADJ** plusieurs; **on s. occasions** à plusieurs occasions *ou* reprises; **s. thousand dollars** plusieurs milliers *mpl* de dollars

PRON plusieurs; **s. of my colleagues have left** plusieurs de mes collègues sont partis; **s. of us** plusieurs d'entre nous; **there are s. of them** ils sont plusieurs; **s. of us got together to organize a party** nous nous sommes mis à plusieurs pour organiser une soirée

ADJ *Law (separate)* distinct; **they went their s. ways** ils s'en allèrent, chacun de son côté

severally ['sevərəlɪ] **ADV** *Law* séparément, individuellement

severance ['sevərəns] **N** *(of relations)* rupture *f*, cessation *f*; *(of communications, contact)* interruption *f*, rupture *f*

▸▸ ***severance pay*** *(UNCOUNT)* indemnité *f ou* indemnités *fpl* de licenciement

severe [sɪ'vɪə(r)] **ADJ 1** *(harsh* ▸ *criticism, punishment, regulations)* sévère, dur; (▸ *conditions)* difficile, rigoureux; (▸ *winter, weather, climate)* rude, rigoureux; (▸ *competition)* rude, serré; *(strict* ▸ *tone, person)* sévère; **s. weather conditions** conditions *fpl* météorologiques très rudes; **she's too s. with her children** elle est trop dure avec ses enfants; **I gave them a s. telling-off** je les ai sévèrement grondés

2 *(serious* ▸ *illness, handicap)* grave, sérieux; (▸ *defeat)* grave; (▸ *pain)* vif, aigu(ë); **I've got s. backache/toothache** j'ai très mal au dos/une rage de dents; **to suffer s. losses** subir de lourdes pertes; **his death was a s. blow to them/to their chances** sa mort les a sérieusement ébranlés/a sérieusement compromis leurs chances; **it will be a s. test of our capabilities** cela mettra nos aptitudes à rude épreuve

3 *(austere* ▸ *style, dress, haircut)* sévère, strict; **the building has a certain s. beauty** l'édifice a une certaine beauté austère

4 *Br Fam (for emphasis)* sacré, vache (de); **he is a s. nuisance** c'est un sacré emmerdeur

severely [sɪ'vɪəlɪ] ADV **1** *(harshly ▸ punish, treat, criticize)* sévèrement, durement; *(strictly)* strictement, sévèrement; **don't judge them too s.** ne les jugez pas trop sévèrement *ou* avec trop de sévérité; **he spoke s. to them** il leur parla d'un ton sec

2 *(seriously ▸ ill, injured, disabled)* gravement, sérieusement; **to be s. handicapped** être gravement handicapé; **her patience was s. tried by his behaviour** sa patience a été durement éprouvée par son comportement

3 *(austerely)* d'une manière austère, sévèrement; **she dresses very s.** elle s'habille de manière très austère

4 *Br Fam (for emphasis)* sérieusement□, vachement; **you are s. annoying me!** tu me cours sérieusement sur le haricot!

severity [sɪ'verɪtɪ] N **1** *(harshness ▸ of judgment, treatment, punishment, criticism)* sévérité *f*, dureté *f*; *(▸ of climate)* rigueur *f*, dureté *f*; *(▸ of frost, cold)* intensité *f* **2** *(seriousness ▸ of illness, injury, handicap)* gravité *f*, sévérité *f* **3** *(austerity)* austérité *f*, sévérité *f*

Seville [sə'vɪl] N Séville

▸▸ ***Seville orange*** orange *f* amère, bigarade *f*

sew [səʊ] *(pt* **sewed**, *pp* **sewn** [səʊn] *or* **sewed)** VT coudre; **to s. a button on(to) a shirt** coudre *ou* recoudre un bouton sur une chemise; **she can't even s. a button on** elle ne sait même pas coudre un bouton; **you'll have to s. the pieces together again** il va falloir recoudre les pièces ensemble

VI coudre, faire de la couture

▸**sew up** VT SEP **1** *(tear, slit)* coudre, recoudre; *(seam)* faire; *Med (wound)* coudre, recoudre, suturer; *(hole)* raccommoder **2** *Fam Fig (arrange, settle ▸ contract)* régler□; *(▸ details)* régler□, mettre au point□; **the deal is all sewn up** l'affaire est dans le sac; **they've got the election all sewn up** l'élection est gagnée d'avance□

sewage ['suːɪdʒ] N *(UNCOUNT)* vidanges *fpl*, eaux *fpl* d'égout, eaux-vannes *fpl*

▸▸ ***sewage disposal*** évacuation *f* des eaux usées; ***sewage farm*** champ *m* d'épandage; ***sewage outlet*** émissaire *m* d'évacuation; ***sewage plant*** station *f* d'épuration; ***sewage system*** égouts *mpl*; ***sewage tanker*** camion-citerne *m*; ***sewage treatment plant*** station *f* d'épuration; ***sewage works*** champ *m* d'épandage

sewer[1] ['səʊə(r)] N *(person who sews)* couseur (euse) *m,f*; **to be a good s.** être bon (bonne) couturier(ère); **to be a bad s.** être mauvais(e) couturier(ère)

sewer[2] ['suːə(r)] N *(drain)* égout *m*; **open s.** égout *m* à ciel ouvert; *Fig* **s. of vice** cloaque *m* de vice; **he's got a mind like a s.** il a l'esprit mal placé

▸▸ *Zool* ***sewer rat*** (rat *m*) surmulot *m*, rat gris *ou* d'égout

sewerage ['suːərɪdʒ] N *(UNCOUNT)* **1** *(disposal)* évacuation *f* des eaux usées **2** *(system)* égouts *mpl*, réseau *m* d'égouts **3** *(sewage)* eaux *fpl* d'égout

sewermouth ['suːəmaʊθ] N *Am Fam* **to be a s.** jurer comme un charretier

sewing ['səʊɪŋ] N **1** *(activity)* couture *f*; **she likes s.** elle aime coudre *ou* la couture **2** *(piece of work)* couture *f*, ouvrage *m*; **what have I done with my s.?** où ai-je posé ma couture?

COMP *(cotton, thread)* à coudre; *(class)* de couture

▸▸ ***sewing basket*** boîte *f* à couture; ***sewing kit*** nécessaire *m* de couture; ***sewing machine*** machine *f* à coudre; ***sewing needle*** aiguille *f* à coudre

sewn [səʊn] *pp of* **sew**

sex [seks] N **1** *(gender)* sexe *m*; **the club is open to both sexes** le club est ouvert aux personnes des deux sexes **2** *(UNCOUNT) (sexual intercourse)* relations *fpl* sexuelles, rapports *mpl* (sexuels); **to have s. with sb** avoir des rapports (sexuels) *ou* faire l'amour avec qn **3** *(sexual activity)* sexe *m*; **that film is just full of s.** il n'y a que du sexe dans ce film; **all he ever thinks about is s.** c'est un obsédé (sexuel); **there is too much s. on TV** il y a trop de sexe à la télévision

COMP sexuel

VT *(animal)* déterminer le sexe de

▸▸ ***sex act*** acte *m* sexuel; ***sex addict*** dépendant(e) *m,f* sexuel(elle); ***sex addiction*** dépendance *f* sexuelle; ***sex aid*** gadget *m* érotique; ***sex appeal*** sex-appeal *m*; *Fam Pej* ***sex beast*** pervers(e) *m,f* (sexuel(elle))□; ***sex bomb*** bombe *f* sexuelle; ***sex change (operation)*** (opération *f* de) changement *m* de sexe; **to have a s. change (operation)** changer de sexe; ***sex chromosome*** chromosome *m* sexuel; ***sex crime*** délit *m* sexuel; ***sex discrimination*** discrimination *f* sexuelle; ***the Sex Discrimination Act*** = loi britannique de 1975 interdisant la discrimination sexuelle, notamment dans les domaines de l'emploi et de l'enseignement; ***sex drive*** pulsion *f* sexuelle, pulsions *fpl* sexuelles, libido *f*; **to have a low/high s. drive** avoir un appétit sexuel faible/élevé; ***sex education*** éducation *f* sexuelle; ***sex fiend*** maniaque *mf* sexuel(elle); *Fam* ***sex god*** apollon□*m*; *Fam* ***sex goddess*** bombe *f* sexuelle; ***sex hormone*** hormone *f* sexuelle; ***the sex industry*** l'industrie *f* du sexe; *Fam* ***sex kitten*** bombe *f* sexuelle; ***sex life*** vie *f* sexuelle; *Hum* **how's your s. life?** et ta vie amoureuse, comment ça va?; ***sex maniac*** obsédé(e) *m,f* sexuel(elle); ***sex object*** objet *m* sexuel; *Br* ***sex offence*** délit *m* sexuel; *Br* ***sex offender*** délinquant *m* sexuel; *Br* ***sex offenders' register*** registre *m* des délinquants sexuels; ***sex organ*** organe *m* sexuel; ***sex partner*** partenaire *mf* sexuel(elle); *Fam* ***sex pest*** obsédé *m (qui harcèle les femmes)*; ***sex scandal*** affaire *f* de mœurs, scandale *m* sexuel; ***sex scene*** scène *f* érotique; ***sex shop*** sex-shop *m*; ***sex symbol*** sex-symbol *m*; ***sex therapist*** sexologue *mf*; ***sex therapy*** sexothérapie *f*; ***sex tourism*** tourisme *m* sexuel; ***sex tourist*** touriste *mf* sexuel(elle); ***sex toy*** gadget *m* érotique; ***sex urge*** pulsion *f* sexuelle; ***sex worker*** = personne qui gagne de l'argent grâce à l'industrie du sexe; *(prostitute)* prostitué(e) *m,f*

▸**sex up** VT SEP **1** *(image, style)* rendre plus sexy; **that actress has really sexed up her look** l'actrice a adopté un look beaucoup plus sexy; **the company is trying to s. up the mobile phone** la société essaie de rendre les portables plus intéressants **2** *Fig (text, document, story)* enjoliver; **the government is accused of sexing up the report** on accuse le gouvernement d'avoir monté le rapport en épingle

sexagenarian [ˌseksədʒɪ'neərɪən] ADJ sexagénaire

N sexagénaire *mf*

sexed [sekst] ADJ *Biol & Zool* sexué; **to be highly s.** *(person)* avoir une forte libido

sexiness ['seksɪnɪs] N caractère *m* sexy; **the s. of her appearance** son air sexy; **they are all agreed on his s.** ils sont tous d'accord pour dire qu'il est sexy

sexism ['seksɪzəm] N sexisme *m*

sexist ['seksɪst] ADJ sexiste

N sexiste *mf*

sexless ['sekslɪs] ADJ **1** *Biol* asexué **2** *(person ▸ asexual)* asexué; *(▸ frigid)* frigide; **theirs is a s. marriage** ils sont mariés mais n'ont pas de rapports sexuels

sex-mad ADJ *Fam* **he's/she's s.** il/elle ne pense qu'à ça

sexologist [sek'sɒlədʒɪst] N sexologue *mf*

sexology [sek'sɒlədʒɪ] N sexologie *f*

sexploitation [ˌseksplɔɪ'teɪʃən] N exploitation *f* du sexe; **a s. movie** un film dont le propos se résume au sexe

sexploits ['seksplɔɪts] NPL *Fam Hum* aventures *fpl* sexuelles□

sexpot ['sekspɒt] N *Fam (woman)* femme *f* très sexy, bombe *f* sexuelle; *(man)* homme *m* très sexy

sex-starved ADJ *Hum* (sexuellement) frustré

sextant ['sekstənt] N sextant *m*

sextet [seks'tet] N sextuor *m*

sexton ['sekstən] N sacristain *m*, bedeau *m*

sextuple ['sekstjʊpəl] ADJ sextuple

N sextuple *m*

VI sextupler

VT sextupler

sextuplet ['sekstjʊplɪt] N **1** *(child)* sextuplé(e) *m,f* **2** *Mus* sextolet *m*

sexual ['sekʃʊəl] ADJ sexuel

▸▸ ***sexual abuse*** *(UNCOUNT)* sévices *mpl* sexuels; ***sexual assault*** agression *f* sexuelle; ***sexual attraction*** attirance *f* sexuelle; ***sexual discrimination*** discrimination *f* sexuelle, sexisme *m*; ***sexual equality*** égalité *f* entre les sexes; ***sexual harassment*** harcèlement *m* sexuel; ***sexual intercourse*** *(UNCOUNT)* rapports *mpl* sexuels; ***sexual liberation*** libération *f* sexuelle; ***sexual orientation*** tendances *fpl* sexuelles; ***sexual politics*** = (étude du) rôle respectif des hommes et des femmes dans la société; ***sexual reproduction*** reproduction *f* sexuelle; ***the sexual revolution*** la révolution sexuelle

sexuality [ˌsekʃʊ'ælɪtɪ] N sexualité *f*

sexually ['sekʃʊəlɪ] ADV sexuellement; **s. active** qui a une activité sexuelle; **to be s. assaulted** être victime d'une agression sexuelle

▸▸ *Med* ***sexually transmitted disease*** maladie sexuellement transmissible, *Can* maladie transmise sexuellement

sexy ['seksɪ] *(compar* **sexier**, *superl* **sexiest)** ADJ *Fam* **1** *(person)* sexy *(inv)*; *(book, film)* érotique□; **hi s.!** *(to man)* salut, beau gosse!; *(to woman)* salut, beauté! **2** *(product, idea, car)* branché

Seychelles [seɪ'ʃelz] NPL **the S.** les Seychelles *fpl*

sez [sez] *Fam* = **says**

SF [ˌes'ef] *(abbr* **science fiction)** N SF *f*

ADJ de SF

SFA [ˌesef'eɪ] N *(abbr* **Scottish Football Association)** Fédération *f* écossaise de football

SFO [ˌesef'əʊ] N *(abbr* **Serious Fraud Office)** = service britannique de la répression des fraudes

sfx [ˌesef'eks] N *Cin (abbr* **special effects)** effets *mpl* spéciaux

SGML [ˌesdʒiːˌem'el] N *Comput (abbr* **Standard Generalized Mark-up Language)** SGML *m*

SGP [ˌesdʒiː'piː] N *EU (abbr* **Stability and Growth Pact)** PSC *m*

Sgt *(written abbr* **sergeant)** Sgt

sh [ʃ] EXCLAM chut!

shabbily ['ʃæbɪlɪ] ADV **1** *(dressed, furnished)* pauvrement **2** *(behave, treat)* mesquinement, petitement; **I think she's been very s. treated** je trouve qu'on l'a traitée de manière très mesquine

shabbiness ['ʃæbɪnɪs] N **1** *(poor condition ▸ of dress, person)* aspect *m* misérable; *(▸ of house, street)* délabrement *m*; *(▸ of carpet, furniture, clothes)* mauvais état *m* **2** *(meanness ▸ of behaviour, treatment, trick)* mesquinerie *f*, petitesse **3** *(mediocrity ▸ of excuse, reasoning)* médiocrité

shabby ['ʃæbɪ] *(compar* **shabbier**, *superl* **shabbiest)** ADJ **1** *(clothes)* râpé, élimé; *(carpet, curtains)* usé, élimé; *(person)* pauvrement vêtu *(hotel, house, furniture)* miteux, minable; *(street, area)* misérable, miteux **2** *(mean ▸ behaviour, treatment)* mesquin, vil, bas; **that was a s. trick** c'était vraiment mesquin **3** *(mediocre ▸ excuse)* piètre; *(▸ reasoning)* médiocre

shabby-genteel ADJ désargenté mais digne

shack [ʃæk] N cabane *f*, case *f*, hutte *f*

▸**shack up** VI *Fam* **to s. up with sb** se mettre à la colle avec qn, s'installer avec qn□; **they've shacked up together** ils se sont mis à la colle

shackle ['ʃækəl] VT enchaîner, mettre aux fers; **he was shackled to the post** on l'a enchaîné au poteau; *Fig* **shackled by convention** entravé par les conventions

• **shackles** NPL chaînes *fpl*, fers *mpl*; *Fig* chaînes *fpl*, entraves *fpl*; *Fig* **the shackles of convention** le carcan des conventions sociales

shacktown ['ʃæktaʊn] N *Am Fam* bidonville□*m*

shade [ʃeɪd] N **1** *(shadow)* ombre *f*; *Art* ombre *f*, ombres *fpl*; **to sit in the s.** s'asseoir à l'ombre; **45 degrees in the s.** 45 degrés à l'ombre; **in the s. of a tree** à l'ombre d'un arbre; **these trees give plenty of s.** ces arbres font beaucoup d'ombre; **the use of light and s. in the painting** l'utilisation *f* des ombres et des lumières *ou* du clair-obscur dans le tableau; *Fig* **to put sb in the s.** éclipser qn; **his achievements really put mine in the s.** ses réalisations éclipsent vraiment les miennes

2 *(nuance ▸ of colour)* nuance *f*, ton *m*; *(▸ of meaning, opinion)* nuance *f*; **a different s. of green**

un ton de vert différent, une autre nuance de vert; **an attractive s. of blue** un joli bleu; **all shades of political opinion were represented** toutes les nuances politiques étaient représentées, tous les courants politiques étaient représentés; *Comput* **shades of grey** niveaux *mpl ou* tons *mpl* de gris

3 *(for lamp)* abat-jour *m inv*; *(for eyes)* visière *f*; *Am (blind ▸ on window)* store *m*; **to pull the shades (down)** baisser les stores

4 *Literary (spirit)* ombre *f*, fantôme *m*; *Myth* **the Shades** les Enfers *mpl*, le royaume des ombres

VT 1 *(screen ▸ eyes, face)* abriter; *(▸ place)* ombrager, donner de l'ombre à; *(of hat ▸ face)* obscurcir; **to s. one's eyes with one's hand** s'abriter les yeux de la main; **to s. sth from the sun** protéger qch du soleil **2** *(cover ▸ light, lightbulb)* masquer, voiler **3** *Art (painting)* ombrer; *(by hatching)* hachurer; **I've shaded the background green** j'ai coloré l'arrière-plan en vert

VI *(merge)* se dégrader, se fondre; **the blue shades into purple** le bleu se fond en violet; **these categories s. into one another** ces catégories se confondent

• **a shade ADV she's a s. better today** elle va un tout petit peu mieux aujourd'hui; **his books are just a s. too sentimental for me** ses livres sont un peu trop sentimentaux pour moi

• **shades NPL 1** *Literary (growing darkness)* **the shades of evening** les ombres *fpl* du soir **2** *Fam (sunglasses)* lunettes *fpl* de soleil□, lunettes *fpl* noires□ **3** *(reminder, echo)* échos *mpl*; **shades of Proust** des échos *mpl* proustiens; **there are shades of 1968** ça rappelle 1968

shadeband [ˈʃeɪdbænd] **N** *Aut* bande *f* pare-soleil

shaded [ˈʃeɪdɪd] **ADJ 1** *(path, corner)* ombragé; *(lamp)* à abat-jour **2** *Art (drawing)* ombré; *(area on diagram, map)* hachuré

shadeless [ˈʃeɪdlɪs] **ADJ** sans ombre

shadiness [ˈʃeɪdɪnɪs] **N 1** *(of place)* ombre *f*, ombrage *m* **2** *Fam (of behaviour, dealings)* caractère *m* louche *ou* suspect□

shading [ˈʃeɪdɪŋ] **N** *(UNCOUNT) Art (in painting)* ombres *fpl*; *(hatching)* hachure *f*, tramage *m*, hachures *fpl*; *Fig (difference)* nuance *f*

shadow [ˈʃædəʊ] **N 1** *(of figure, building)* ombre *f*; **to see a s. on a wall** voir une ombre sur un mur; **she's a s. of her former self** elle n'est plus que l'ombre d'elle-même; *Fig* **he's afraid of his own s.** il a peur de son ombre; *Fig* **to live in sb's s.** vivre dans l'ombre de qn; **to cast a s. on** *or* **over sth** projeter une ombre sur qch; *Fig* jeter une ombre sur qch

2 *(under eyes)* cerne *m*

3 *(shade)* ombre *f*, ombrage *m*; **in the s. of the trees/the mountain** à l'ombre des arbres/de la montagne; **in the s. of the doorway** dans l'ombre de la porte; **she was standing in (the) s.** elle se tenait dans l'ombre; **the gardens lie in s. now** les jardins sont maintenant à l'ombre

4 *(slightest bit)* ombre *f*; **without** *or* **beyond a** *or* **the s. of a doubt** sans l'ombre d'un doute

5 *(detective)* **I want a s. put on him** je veux qu'on le fasse suivre; **he managed to lose his s.** il a réussi à semer la personne qui l'avait pris en filature

6 *(companion)* ombre *f*; **he follows me everywhere like a s.** il me suit comme mon ombre, il ne me lâche pas d'une semelle

7 *Med (on lung)* voile *m*

VT 1 *(follow secretly)* filer, prendre en filature; **our job was to s. enemy submarines** nous étions chargés de suivre les sous-marins ennemis **2** *(observe at work)* observer, suivre; **she's shadowing a senior journalist for a month to get work experience** pendant un mois elle suit un journaliste expérimenté en train de travailler afin d'acquérir de l'expérience **3** *Literary (screen from light)* ombrager; **tall trees shadowed the pathway** de grands arbres ombrageaient le chemin

ADJ *Br Pol* **the S. Education Secretary/Defence Secretary** le porte-parole de l'opposition pour l'éducation/pour la défense nationale

• **shadows NPL** *Literary (darkness)* ombre *f*, ombres *fpl*, obscurité *f*

▸▸ *Br Pol* ***shadow cabinet*** cabinet *m* fantôme; ***shadow economy*** économie *f* parallèle; *Br Pol* ***shadow minister*** ministre *mf* fantôme; *Comput* ***shadow printing*** impression *f* ombrée; ***shadow puppet*** = silhouette découpée utilisée dans les spectacles d'ombres chinoises

THE SHADOW CABINET

En Grande-Bretagne, le "shadow cabinet" est composé de parlementaires de l'opposition qui deviendraient ministres si l'opposition accédait au pouvoir. Chaque ministre du gouvernement dispose de son homologue "fantôme" dans l'opposition (on parle de "shadow minister"), qui étudie les mêmes dossiers et se spécialise ainsi dans un domaine donné. Les ministres fantômes occupent les "frontbenches" de l'opposition à la Chambre des communes.

shadowing [ˈʃædəʊɪŋ] **N 1** *(tailing)* filature *f* **2** *(observing at work)* = fait de suivre et d'observer quelqu'un au travail afin d'acquérir de l'expérience

shadowy [ˈʃædəʊɪ] **ADJ 1** *(shady ▸ woods, path)* ombragé; **he looked into the s. depths** il scruta les profondeurs insondables **2** *(vague ▸ figure, outline)* vague, indistinct; *(▸ plan)* vague, imprécis

shady [ˈʃeɪdɪ] *(compar* **shadier**, *superl* **shadiest)** **ADJ 1** *(place)* ombragé **2** *Fam (person, behaviour)* louche, suspect□; *(dealings)* louche; **a s. character** un individu louche

shaft [ʃɑːft] **N 1** *(of spear)* hampe *f*; *(of feather)* tuyau *m*; *Archit (of column)* fût *m*

2 *(of axe, tool, golf club)* manche *m*

3 *(of cart, carriage)* brancard *m*, limon *m*; **to put a horse between the shafts** atteler un cheval

4 *Tech (for propeller, in machine)* arbre *m*, axe *m*

5 *(in mine)* puits *m*; *(of ventilator)* puits *m*, cheminée *f*; *(of lift)* cage *f*; **air** *or* **ventilation s.** puits *m* d'aérage, conduit *m* d'air

6 *(of light)* rayon *m*; *(of lightning)* éclair *m*; *Fig* **a s. of wit** un trait d'esprit

7 *Literary (arrow)* flèche *f*

8 *Vulg (penis)* chibre *m*, queue *f*

9 *Am very Fam (idiom)* **he got the s.** *(got shouted at)* il s'est fait engueuler; *(got fired)* il s'est fait virer; *(got cheated)* il s'est fait arnaquer

VT 1 *very Fam (cheat)* baiser, entuber; **to get shafted** se faire baiser *ou* entuber **2** *Br Vulg (have sex with)* baiser, tringler

shag [ʃæg] *(pt & pp* **shagged**, *cont* **shagging)** **N 1** *(of hair, wool)* toison *f*

2 *(tobacco)* tabac *m* (très fort)

3 *Orn* cormoran *m* huppé

4 *Br very Fam (sex)* baise *f*; **to have a s.** baiser, tirer un coup, s'envoyer en l'air; **to be a good s.** *(person)* être un bon coup

VT *Br very Fam (have sex with ▸ of man)* baiser, troncher; *(▸ of woman)* baiser avec, s'envoyer

VI *Br very Fam (have sex)* baiser, s'envoyer en l'air

▸▸ ***shag (pile) carpet*** moquette *f* à poils longs; ***shag tobacco*** tabac *m* (très fort)

▸ **shag out VT SEP** *Br Fam (exhaust)* crever; **I'm shagged out** je suis crevé

shagged [ʃægd] **ADJ** *Br Fam (exhausted)* crevé

shagger [ˈʃægə(r)] **N** *Br very Fam* baiseur *m*

shaggy [ˈʃægɪ] *(compar* **shaggier**, *superl* **shaggiest)** **ADJ** *(hair, beard)* hirsute, touffu; *(eyebrows)* hérissé, broussailleux; *(dog, pony)* à longs poils (rudes); *(carpet, rug)* à longs poils; **a s.-looking man** un homme hirsute

shah [ʃɑː] **N** chah *m*, shah *m*

shake [ʃeɪk] *(pt* **shook** [ʃʊk], *pp* **shaken** [ˈʃeɪkən]) **N 1** *(movement)* secousse *f*, ébranlement *m*; *(trembling ▸ of hand, voice etc)* tremblement *m*; **to give sb/sth a s.** secouer qn/qch; **she gave the thermometer a few shakes** elle secoua un peu le thermomètre; **to give oneself a s.** se secouer; **with a s. of his head** *(in refusal, in resignation, sympathy)* avec un hochement de tête; **with a s. in his voice** d'une voix tremblotante; **give him a s.** *(to waken)* secouez-le; **I feel like giving him a good s.** *(to stimulate)* j'ai une furieuse envie de le secouer; *Fam* **to have the shakes** avoir la tremblote

2 *Fam (moment)* instant□ *m*; **you go, I'll be there in a s.** *or* **a couple of shakes** vas-y, j'arrive dans un instant *ou* dans une seconde□; **in two shakes (of a lamb's tail)** en un clin d'œil□, en moins de deux

3 *Am Fam (earthquake)* tremblement *m* de terre□

4 *(drink)* milk-shake *m*; **a banana s.** un milk-shake à la banane

5 *Fam (idiom)* **it's/he's no great shakes** ça/il casse pas des briques, ça/il casse pas trois pattes à un canard; **he's no great shakes at painting** *or* **as a painter** il ne casse rien *ou* il casse pas des briques comme peintre

VT 1 *(rug, tablecloth, person)* secouer; *(bottle, cocktail, dice)* agiter; *(of earthquake, explosion)* ébranler, faire trembler; **he had to be shaken awake** on a dû le secouer pour le réveiller; **she shook me by the shoulders** elle m'a secoué par les épaules; **the wind shook the branches** le vent agitait les branches; **they shook the apples from the tree** ils secouèrent l'arbre pour (en) faire tomber les pommes; **he shook the gravel into the bag** il secouait le gravier pour le faire tomber dans le sac; **to s. sugar onto sth** saupoudrer qch de sucre; **to s. vinegar onto sth** asperger qch de vinaigre; **to s. salt/pepper onto sth** saler/poivrer qch; **s. well before use** *(on packaging)* bien agiter avant l'emploi; **the dog shook itself (dry)** le chien s'est ébroué (pour se sécher); **they shook themselves free** ils se sont libérés d'une secousse; **I can't seem to s. him out of his apathy** je n'arrive pas à le tirer de son apathie; **he shook his head** *(in refusal)* il a dit *ou* fait non de la tête; *(in resignation, sympathy)* il a hoché la tête; *Fam* **s. a leg!** secoue-toi!, remue-toi!

2 *(brandish)* brandir; **to s. one's finger at sb** *(in warning)* avertir qn en lui faisant signe du doigt; *(threateningly)* menacer qn du doigt; **he shook his fist at him** il l'a menacé du poing; *Br Fam* **he's won more awards than you can s. a stick at** on lui a décerné une flopée de prix

3 *(hand)* serrer; **to s. hands with sb, to s. sb's hand** serrer la main à qn; **they shook hands** ils se sont serré la main; **let me s. you by the hand** permettez-moi de vous serrer la main; **let's s. hands on the deal** serrons-nous la main pour sceller cet accord

4 *(upset ▸ faith, confidence, reputation)* ébranler; *(▸ person)* secouer, bouleverser; **that has shaken my faith in him** cela a ébranlé la confiance que j'avais en lui; **his beliefs would not be that easily shaken** ses convictions ne sauraient être ébranlées pour si peu; **the whole world was shaken by the news** le monde entier a été ébranlé par la nouvelle; **to feel shaken after a fall** se ressentir d'une chute; **I bet that shook him!** voilà qui a dû le secouer!

VI 1 *(ground, floor, house)* trembler, être ébranlé; *(leaves, branches)* trembler, être agité; **the whole house shook with the sound** la maison entière a été ébranlée par le bruit; **the whole building shook** *(after explosion etc)* tout le bâtiment a tremblé; **the child shook free of his captor** l'enfant a échappé à son ravisseur **2** *(with emotion ▸ voice)* trembler, frémir; *(▸ body, knees)* trembler; **her whole frame shook** elle tremblait de tous ses membres; **in a voice shaking with emotion** d'une voix émue *ou* tremblotante; **to s. with laughter** se tordre de rire; **to s. with fear/cold** trembler de peur/de froid; **to s. like a jelly** *or* **leaf** trembler comme une feuille; **his hands were shaking uncontrollably** il ne pouvait empêcher ses mains de trembler **3** *(in agreement)* **let's s. on it!** tope là!; **they shook on the deal** ils ont scellé leur accord par une poignée de main

▸ **shake down VT SEP 1** *(from tree)* faire tomber en secouant; **to s. cherries down from a tree** secouer un arbre pour en faire tomber les cerises **2** *(after fall)* **to s. oneself down** s'ébrouer, se secouer

3 *Am Fam* **to s. sb down** *(rob)* racketter qn□; *(blackmail)* faire chanter qn□

4 *Am Fam (search)* fouiller□, palper□

VI 1 *Fam (go to bed)* coucher□; **they had to s. down on the floor for the night** ils ont dû dormir *ou* coucher par terre **2** *Fam (adapt ▸ to new situation, job)* s'habituer□; **she's new to the job but she'll s. down soon enough** elle débute dans le métier mais elle s'y fera rapidement **3** *(contents of packet, bottle)* se tasser

▸ **shake off VT SEP 1** *(physically)* secouer; **to s. the sand/water off sth** secouer le sable/l'eau de qch **2** *(get rid of ▸ cold, pursuer, depression)* se débarrasser de; *(▸ habit)* se défaire de, se débarrasser de; **I can't s. him off** il ne me lâche pas d'une semelle; **she's always phoning me up, I can't s. her off** elle me téléphone sans cesse, je n'arrive pas à m'en débarrasser

▸ **shake out** VT SEP *(tablecloth, rug)* (bien) secouer; *(sail, flag)* déferler, déployer; *(bag)* vider en secouant; **he shook the coins out of the bag** il a fait tomber les pièces en secouant le sac; **he picked up his shoes and shook the sand out** il a ramassé ses chaussures et en a secoué le sable

▸ **shake up** VT SEP **1** *(physically ▸ pillow)* secouer, taper; *(▸ bottle)* agiter

2 *Fig (upset ▸ person)* secouer, bouleverser; **they were badly shaken up after the accident** ils ont été très secoués après l'accident

3 *(rouse ▸ person)* secouer; **he needs shaking up a bit** il a besoin qu'on le secoue un peu

4 *Fam (overhaul ▸ organization, company)* remanier□, réorganiser de fond en comble□

shakedown ['ʃeɪkdaʊn] N **1** *(bed)* lit *m* improvisé *ou* de fortune **2** *Am Fam (search)* fouille□*f* **3** *Am Fam (extortion)* racket□*m*, chantage□*m*

shaken ['ʃeɪkən] *pp of* **shake**

shaker ['ʃeɪkə(r)] N *(for cocktails)* shaker *m*; *(for salad)* panier *m* à salade; *(for dice)* cornet *m*

Shakers ['ʃeɪkəz] NPL *Rel* **the S.** les Shakers *mpl (secte protestante du XVIIIème siècle, aujourd'hui presque disparue, qui prêchait le célibat)*

Shakespearean, Shakespearian [ʃeɪks'pɪərɪən] ADJ shakespearien

shake-up N *Fam* **1** *(of company, organization)* remaniement□*m*, restructuration□*f* **2** *(emotional)* bouleversement□*m*

shakily ['ʃeɪkɪlɪ] ADV **1** *(unsteadily ▸ walk)* d'un pas chancelant *ou* mal assuré; *(▸ write)* d'une main tremblante; *(▸ speak)* d'une voix tremblante *ou* chevrotante **2** *(uncertainly)* d'une manière hésitante *ou* peu assurée; **she started s. then went on to win the game** au début, elle n'était pas très sûre d'elle, mais elle a fini par gagner la partie

shakiness ['ʃeɪkɪnɪs] N **1** *(unsteadiness ▸ of chair, table)* manque *m* de stabilité; *(▸ of foundations, building)* manque *m* de solidité; *(▸ of hand)* tremblement *m*; *(▸ of voice)* chevrotement *m*, tremblement *m* **2** *(weakness, uncertainty ▸ of health, memory, argument, faith)* faiblesse *f*; *(▸ of knowledge)* insuffisance *f*; *(▸ of position, authority)* fragilité *f*, précarité *f*; *(▸ of future)* incertitude *f*

shaking ['ʃeɪkɪŋ] N *Med* tremblement *m*

shako ['ʃækəʊ] *(pl* **shakos** *or* **shakoes)** N *Mil (headgear)* shako *m*, schako *m*

shaky ['ʃeɪkɪ] *(compar* **shakier**, *superl* **shakiest)** ADJ **1** *(unsteady ▸ chair, table)* branlant, peu solide; *(▸ ladder)* branlant, peu stable; *(▸ hand)* tremblant, tremblotant; *(▸ writing)* tremblé; *(▸ voice)* tremblotant, chevrotant; *(▸ steps)* chancelant; **he's a bit s. on his legs** il ne tient pas bien *ou* il n'est pas très solide sur ses jambes; **I'm still s. after my accident** je ne me suis pas encore complètement remis de mon accident; **to be based** *or* **built on s. foundations** avoir des bases chancelantes **2** *(uncertain, weak ▸ health, faith)* précaire, vacillant; *(▸ authority, regime)* incertain, chancelant; *(▸ future, finances)* incertain, précaire; *(▸ business)* incertain; **her memory is a bit s.** sa mémoire n'est pas très sûre; **my memories of the war are rather s.** mes souvenirs de la guerre sont assez vagues; **things got off to a s. start** les choses ont plutôt mal commencé; **my knowledge of German is a bit s.** mes notions d'allemand sont plutôt vagues

shale [ʃeɪl] N *Geol* argile *f* schisteuse, schiste *m* argileux

shall [ʃəl, *stressed* ʃæl]

> On trouve généralement **I/you/he/***etc* **shall** sous leurs formes contractées **I'll/you'll/he'll/***etc*. La forme négative correspondante est **shan't** que l'on écrira **shall not** dans des contextes formels.

MODAL AUX V **1** *(as future auxiliary)* **I s.** *or* **I'll come tomorrow** je viendrai demain; **I s. not** *or* **I shan't be able to come** je ne pourrai pas venir; **we s. have finished by tomorrow** nous aurons fini demain; **as we s. see** comme nous le verrons, comme nous allons le voir **2** *(in suggestions, questions)* **s. I open the window?** voulez-vous que j'ouvre la fenêtre?; **s. we go for a drive?** on va faire un tour en voiture?; **I'll shut that window, s. I?** je peux fermer cette fenêtre, si vous voulez; **we'll all go then, s. we?** dans ce cas, pourquoi n'y allons-nous pas tous?; **where s. we go?** où est-ce qu'on va aller? **3** *Formal (emphatic use)* **it s. be done** ce sera fait; *Bible* **thou shalt not kill** tu ne tueras point

shallot [ʃə'lɒt] N échalote *f*

shallow ['ʃæləʊ] ADJ **1** *(water, soil, dish, grave)* peu profond; **the s. end** *(of swimming pool)* le petit bain, *Can* la partie peu profonde **2** *(superficial ▸ person, mind, character)* superficiel, qui manque de profondeur; *(▸ conversation)* superficiel, futile; *(▸ argument)* superficiel **3** *(breathing)* superficiel

• **shallows** NPL bas-fond *m*, bas-fonds *mpl*, haut-fond *m*, hauts-fonds *mpl*

▸▸ *Cin & TV* ***shallow focus*** faible profondeur *f* de champ

shallowness ['ʃæləʊnɪs] N **1** *(of water, soil, dish)* faible profondeur *f* **2** *(of mind, character, sentiments)* manque *m* de profondeur; *(of person)* esprit *m* superficiel, manque *m* de profondeur; *(of talk, ideas)* futilité *f* **3** *(of breathing)* **the s. of his breathing** sa respiration *f* superficielle

shallow-rooted ADJ *(tree)* à enracinement superficiel

shalt [ʃælt] *Arch 2nd pers sing of* **shall**

shaly ['ʃeɪlɪ] ADJ schisteux

sham [ʃæm] *(pt & pp* **shammed**, *cont* **shamming)** N **1** *(pretence ▸ of sentiment, behaviour)* comédie *f*, farce *f*, faux-semblant *m*; **what he says is all s.** il n'y a rien de vrai dans ce qu'il dit; **her illness/grief is a s.** sa maladie/son chagrin n'est qu'une mascarade; **their marriage is a complete s.** leur mariage est une véritable farce **2** *(impostor ▸ person)* imposteur *m*; *(▸ organization)* imposture *f*

ADJ **1** *(pretended ▸ sentiment, illness)* faux (fausse), feint, simulé; *(▸ battle)* simulé **2** *(mock ▸ jewellery)* fantaisie *(inv)*, faux (fausse); **a s. election** un simulacre d'élections; **a s. peace** une paix de pacotille

VT feindre, simuler; **to s. illness** faire semblant d'être malade

VI faire semblant, jouer la comédie; **he's not really ill, he's only shamming** il n'est pas vraiment malade, il fait semblant

shaman ['ʃɑːmən] N chaman *m*

shamanism ['ʃɑːmənɪzəm] N chamanisme *m*

shamanistic [ʃɑːmə'nɪstɪk] ADJ chamanistique

shamateur ['ʃæmətɜː(r)] *Fam Sport* N = sportif prétendument amateur

ADJ *(competition, game, race)* = auquel participent des sportifs prétendument amateurs

shamble ['ʃæmbəl] VI **to s. (along)** marcher en traînant les pieds; **to s. in/out/past** entrer/sortir/passer en traînant les pieds; **he shambled up to them** il s'approcha d'eux d'un pas traînant

shambles ['ʃæmbəlz] N *Fam* **1** *(place)* désordre□*m*, foutoir *m*; **your room is a total s.!** quelle pagaille dans ta chambre!, ta chambre est un vrai foutoir!; **the house was in a s.** la maison était sens dessus dessous; **what a s.!** quelle pagaille! **2** *(department, company, accounts)* foutoir *m*; *(situation, event)* désastre□*m*; **his life is (in) a real s.** sa vie est un véritable désastre; **the evening was a s.** la soirée fut un vrai désastre; **what a s.!** quelle pagaille!, quel foutoir!

shambolic [ʃæm'bɒlɪk] ADJ *Br Fam* désordonné□

shame [ʃeɪm] N **1** *(feeling)* honte *f*, confusion *f*; **to my great s.** à ma grande honte; **he has no sense of s.** il n'a aucune honte; **to lose all sense of s.** perdre toute honte; **to have no s.** *(no scruples)* n'avoir aucune honte; **have you no s.?** vous n'avez pas honte? **2** *(disgrace, dishonour)* honte *f*; **to bring s. on one's family/country** déshonorer sa famille/sa patrie, couvrir sa famille/sa patrie de honte; **to put sb to s.** faire honte à qn; **she works so hard, she puts you to s.** elle vous ferait honte, tellement elle travaille; **the s. of it!** quelle honte!; **s. on him!** c'est honteux!, quelle honte!; *Literary* o*r Hum* **for s.!** c'est une honte! **3** *(pity)* dommage *m*; **it's a s.!** c'est dommage!; **what a s.!** quel dommage!; **it's a s. he can't come** c'est dommage qu'il ne puisse pas venir; **it would be a great s. if she missed it** ce serait vraiment dommage qu'elle ne le voie pas

VT *(disgrace ▸ family, country)* être la honte de, faire honte à, déshonorer; *(put to shame)* faire honte à; **their record on staff training shames other firms** ce qu'ils réalisent en matière de formation du personnel devrait faire honte aux autres entreprises; **it shames me to admit it** j'ai honte de l'avouer; **to s. sb into doing sth** oblige qn à faire qch en lui faisant honte; **she was shamed into admitting the truth** elle avait tellement honte qu'elle a dû avouer la vérité

shamefaced [ʃeɪm'feɪst] ADJ **1** *(ashamed)* honteux, penaud; **he was a bit s. about it** il en avait un peu honte **2** *(bashful)* timide, pudique; *(modest)* modeste

shamefacedly [ʃeɪm'feɪsɪdlɪ] ADV **1** *(looking ashamed)* d'un air honteux *ou* penaud; **he admitted, rather s., that it was his fault** il a reconnu d'un air plutôt penaud, que c'était (de) sa faute **2** *(bashfully)* timidement, avec pudeur; *(modestly)* modestement, avec modestie

shameful ['ʃeɪmfʊl] ADJ honteux, indigne; **it's s. to spread such rumours!** c'est honteux *ou* une honte de faire courir de telles rumeurs!; **it's a s. waste of talent** c'est un gaspillage de talent honteux *ou* scandaleux

shamefully ['ʃeɪmfʊlɪ] ADV honteusement, indignement; **she has been treated s.** elle a été traitée de façon honteuse; **they've been s. neglected** ils ont été honteusement négligés; **he was s. ignorant about the issue** son ignorance sur la question était honteuse

shamefulness ['ʃeɪmfʊlnɪs] N honte *f*, infamie *f*

shameless ['ʃeɪmlɪs] ADJ **1** *(without shame ▸ conduct)* effronté; *(▸ person)* effronté, sans vergogne; **that's a s. lie!** c'est un mensonge éhonté!; **they are quite s. about it!** ils ne s'en cachent pas! **2** *(immodest ▸ person)* sans pudeur, dévergondé; *(▸ conduct)* impudique; *Hum* ou *Old-fashioned* **a s. (little) hussy** une dévergondée

shamelessly ['ʃeɪmlɪslɪ] ADV **1** *(without shame ▸ abuse, exploit)* sans honte, sans vergogne; **to lie s.** mentir effrontément **2** *(immodestly)* avec impudeur; **they were walking about quite s. with nothing on** ils se promenaient tout nus sans la moindre gêne *ou* sans que ça ait l'air de les gêner

shamelessness ['ʃeɪmlɪsnɪs] N **1** *(lack of shame)* effronterie *f*, impudence *f* **2** *(sexual immodesty)* impudeur *f*; *(of conduct)* impudicité *f*

shaming ['ʃeɪmɪŋ] ADJ mortifiant, humiliant

shammy ['ʃæmɪ] *(pl* **shammies)** N *(leather)* peau *f* de chamois

▸▸ ***shammy leather*** peau *f* de chamois

shampoo [ʃæm'puː] *(pl* **shampoos**, *pt & pp* **shampooed)** N shampooing *m*, shampoing *m*; **s. and set** shampooing *m* (et) mise *f* en plis

VT *(person, animal)* faire un shampooing à; *(carpet)* shampouiner; **to s. one's hair** se faire un shampooing, se laver les cheveux; **to have one's hair shampooed** se faire faire un shampooing

shamrock ['ʃæmrɒk] N *Bot* trèfle *m* *(en tant qu'emblème de l'Irlande)*

shamus ['ʃeɪməs] N *Am Fam Old-fashioned (policeman)* flic *m*, poulet *m*; *(detective)* détective *m)* privé□*m*

shandy ['ʃændɪ] *(pl* **shandies)** N *Br* panaché *m*

Shanghai [ʃæŋ'haɪ] N Shanghai

shanghai [ʃæŋ'haɪ] VT **1** *Naut* embarquer de force *(comme matelot)* **2** *Fam Fig* **to s. sb into doing sth** forcer qn à faire qch□; **I was shanghaied into it** on m'a forcé la main

Shangri-la [ʃæŋgrɪ'lɑː] N paradis *m* terrestre

shank [ʃæŋk] N **1** *Anat* jambe *f*; *(of horse)* canon *m*; *Culin (of beef)* jarret *m* **2** *(stem ▸ of anchor)* verge *f*; *(▸ of key, rivet)* tige *f*; *Typ (▸ of letter)* corps *m*, tige *f* **3** *Am Fam (knife)* surin *m*, lame□*f*

shanks's pony, shanks's mare ['ʃæŋksɪz-] *Fam Hum* **to go on s.** aller pedibus *ou* à pattes

han't [ʃɑːnt] = **shall not**

hantung [ˌʃænˈtʌŋ] N *Tex* shantung *m*, chan-oung *m*

hanty [ˈʃæntɪ] (*pl* **shanties**) N **1** *(shack)* baraque *f*, cabane *f* **2** *(song)* chanson *f* de marins

►► *shanty town* bidonville *m*

HAPE [ʃeɪp] N *(abbr* **Supreme Headquarters Allied Powers Europe***)* SHAPE *m*

HAPE [ʃeɪp]

N
• forme **1–6** • silhouette **2**
VT
• façonner **1** • influencer **2**
• formuler **3**
VI
• prendre forme

N **1** *(outer form)* forme *f*; **what s. is it?** de quelle forme est-ce?; **the room was triangular in s.** la pièce était de forme triangulaire *ou* avait la forme d'un triangle; **in the s. of a heart** en forme de cœur; **the house is an odd s.** la maison a une drôle de forme; **they were the same s.** ils étaient de la même forme, ils avaient la même forme; **each pebble is a different s.** chaque caillou a une forme différente; **they come in all shapes and sizes** il y en a de toutes les formes et de toutes les tailles; **to change s.** changer de forme; **she moulded the clay into s.** elle façonna l'argile; **my hat was knocked out of s.** mon chapeau a été déformé; **my sweater has lost its s.** *or* **is out of s.** mon pull s'est déformé

2 *(figure, silhouette)* forme *f*, silhouette *f*; **vague shapes could be seen in the mist** on distinguait des formes vagues dans la brume

3 *(abstract form or structure)* forme *f*; **the s. of our society** la structure de notre société; **the new technologies have changed the s. of our lives** les nouvelles technologies ont changé la façon dont nous vivons; **the s. of things to come** ce qui nous attend, ce que l'avenir nous réserve; **to take s.** prendre forme *ou* tournure; **her plan was beginning to take s.** son projet commençait à se concrétiser *ou* à prendre forme; **to give s. to sth** donner forme à qch

4 *(guise)* forme *f*; **help eventually arrived in the s. of her parents** ce sont ses parents qui finirent par arriver pour lui prêter secours; **progress, in the s. of motorways/supermarkets** le progrès que représentent les autoroutes/les supermarchés; **he can't take alcohol in any s. or form** il ne supporte l'alcool sous aucune forme

5 *(condition)* forme *f*; **to be in good s.** *(person)* être en forme; *(business, economy)* marcher bien; **to be in bad s.** *(person)* ne pas être en forme; *(business, economy)* être mal en point; **I'm pretty out of s.** je ne suis pas très en forme; **I need to get (back) into s.** j'ai besoin de me remettre en forme; **the economy is in poor s. at the moment** l'économie est mal en point actuellement; **to keep oneself** *or* **to stay in s.** garder la forme, rester en forme; **what sort of s. was he in?** dans quel état était-il?, comment allait-il?; **she was in pretty bad s.** *(very ill, badly injured)* elle était mal en point *ou* dans un sale état; **he's in no s. to be doing this kind of work!** il n'est pas en état de faire ce genre de travail!; *Fam* **to knock** *or* **to lick sth into s.** mettre qch au point[□]; *Fam* **I'll soon knock** *or* **lick them into s.!** *(soldiers)* j'aurai vite fait de les dresser, moi!; *(team)* j'aurai vite fait de les remettre en forme, moi!

6 *(mould* ► *gen)* moule *m*; *(*► *for hats)* forme *f*

VT **1** *(mould* ► *clay)* façonner, modeler; *(*► *wood, stone)* façonner, tailler; **she shaped the clay into rectangular blocks** elle a façonné l'argile en blocs rectangulaires; **he shaped a pot from the wet clay** il a façonné un pot dans l'argile

2 *(influence* ► *events, life, future)* influencer, déterminer; **to s. sb's character** former *ou* façonner le caractère de qn; **the war shaped her perception of the army** la guerre a influencé sa perception de l'armée

3 *(plan* ► *essay)* faire le plan de; *(*► *excuse, explanation, statement)* formuler

VI *(develop* ► *plan)* prendre forme *ou* tournure; **things are shaping well** les choses se présentent bien *ou* prennent une bonne tournure; **how is he shaping as a teacher?** comment se débrouille-t-il dans l'enseignement?

► **shape up** VI **1** *(improve)* se secouer; **you'd better s. up, young man!** il est temps que tu te secoues, jeune homme!; *Fam* **s. up or ship out!** secouez-vous sinon c'est la porte! **2** *(get fit again)* retrouver la forme **3** *(progress, develop* ► *plans, situation)* prendre (une bonne) tournure; **the business is beginning to s. up** les affaires commencent à bien marcher; **our plans are shaping up nicely** nos projets prennent une bonne tournure; **the new team is shaping up well** la nouvelle équipe commence à bien fonctionner; **they are shaping up into a good orchestra** ils commencent à former un bon orchestre; **how is she shaping up as a translator?** comment se débrouille-t-elle *ou* comment s'en sort-elle en tant que traductrice?

shaped [ʃeɪpt] ADJ **1** *(wooden object)* façonné; *(metal object)* profilé **2** *(in descriptions)* **s. like a triangle** en forme de triangle

-shaped [ʃeɪpt] SUFF en forme de; **egg/crescent/heart-s.** en forme d'œuf/de croissant/de cœur

shapeless [ˈʃeɪplɪs] ADJ *(mass, garment, heap)* informe; **to become s.** se déformer

shapelessness [ˈʃeɪplɪsnɪs] N absence *f* de forme, aspect *m* informe

shapeliness [ˈʃeɪplɪnɪs] N *(of legs)* galbe *m*; *(of figure)* beauté *f*, belles proportions *fpl*

shapely [ˈʃeɪplɪ] *(compar* **shapelier**, *superl* **shapeliest***)* ADJ *(legs)* bien galbé, bien tourné; *(figure, woman)* bien fait; **a s. pair of legs** une belle paire de jambes

shaper [ˈʃeɪpə(r)] N façonneur(euse) *m,f*; **the s. of our destinies** celui qui dirige notre destin; **the s. of the plan** l'auteur *m* du projet

shapeshifter [ˈʃeɪpʃɪftə(r)] N = créature fantastique qui a le pouvoir de se métamorphoser

shaping [ˈʃeɪpɪŋ] N *(of block of stone)* façonnement *m*, façonnage *m*; **the s. of his character** le développement *ou* la formation de son caractère; **the s. of a policy** la conception d'une politique

shard [ʃɑːd] N *(of glass)* éclat *m*; *(of pottery)* tesson *m*

SHARE [ʃeə(r)]

N
• part **1, 2** • action **3**
VT
• partager **1–4** • avoir en commun **3**
VI
• partager

N **1** *(portion* ► *of property, cost, food, credit, blame)* part *f*; **divided into equal shares** divisé en parts égales; **there's your s.** voici votre part *ou* ce qui vous revient; **to pay one's s.** payer sa part *ou* quote-part *ou* son écot; **they went shares in the cost of the present** ils ont tous participé à l'achat du cadeau; **I went half shares with her** on a payé la moitié chacun; **he got his (fair) s. of the profits** il a eu sa part des bénéfices; **to have a s. in the profits** *(of employees)* participer aux bénéfices; **to have a s. in a business** être l'un des associés dans une affaire; **they've had their s. of misfortune** ils ont eu leur part de malheurs; **he's come in for his full s. of criticism** il a été beaucoup critiqué; **we've had more than our (fair) s. of rain this summer** nous avons eu plus que notre compte de pluie cet été

2 *(part, role* ► *in activity, work)* part *f*; **what was her s. in it all?** quel rôle a-t-elle joué dans tout cela?; **to do one's s. (of the work)** faire sa part (du travail); **he hasn't done his s.** il n'a pas fait sa part du travail; **to have a s. in doing sth** contribuer à faire qch; **she must have had a s. in his downfall** elle doit être pour quelque chose dans sa chute; **you had a s. in this** *(you are partly responsible)* vous y êtes pour quelque chose; *(you contributed)* votre participation a été importante

3 *Fin* action *f*; **to have shares in a company** détenir des actions dans une société; **to own 51 percent of the shares** détenir 51 pour cent du capital

VT **1** *(divide* ► *money, property, food, chores)* partager; **he shared the chocolate with his sister/among the children** il a partagé le chocolat avec sa sœur/entre les enfants; **responsibility is shared between the manager and his assistant** la responsabilité est partagée entre le directeur et son assistant; **they must s. the blame for the accident** ils doivent se partager la responsabilité de l'accident

2 *(use jointly* ► *tools, house, bed)* partager; **we shared a taxi home** nous avons partagé un taxi pour rentrer

3 *(have in common* ► *interest, opinion)* partager; *(*►*characteristic)* avoir en commun; *(*► *worry, sorrow)* partager, prendre part à, compatir à; **I s. your hope that war may be avoided** j'espère comme vous qu'on pourra éviter la guerre; **we s. the same name** nous avons le même nom

4 *(tell)* partager; **to s. one's ideas/impressions with sb** partager des idées/impressions avec qn; **he shares all his secrets with me** il me fait part de tous ses secrets; *Ironic* **thank you very much for sharing that with me!** c'est vachement intéressant ce que tu dis là!; **a problem shared is a problem halved** = cela soulage de parler de ses problèmes

VI partager; **he doesn't like sharing** il n'aime pas partager; **some children will have to s.** certains enfants devront partager; **to s. in** *(cost, work)* participer à, partager; *(profits)* participer *ou* être intéressé à; *(credit, responsibility)* partager; *(joy, sorrow)* partager, prendre part à; *(grief)* compatir à; **s. and s. alike** = à chacun sa part

►► *Fin* ***share account*** compte-titres *m*; *Fin* ***share capital*** capital-actions *m*; *Fin* ***share certificate*** certificat *m ou* titre *m* d'actions; *St Exch* ***share dealing*** opérations *fpl* de Bourse, négoce *m* de titres; *St Exch* ***share dividend*** dividende *m* d'action; ***share economy*** économie *f* d'actionnariat populaire; *St Exch* ***share fluctuation*** mouvement *m* des valeurs; *St Exch* ***share index*** indice *m* boursier; ***share issue*** émission *f* d'actions; ***share market*** marché *m* des valeurs mobilières; ***share option*** possibilité *f* d'acheter des actions; *Fin* ***share option scheme*** plan *m* de participation par achat d'actions; ***share owner*** détenteur(trice) *m, f* d'actions; ***share ownership*** actionnariat *m*; ***share point*** point *m* de part de marché; ***share portfolio*** portefeuille *m* d'actions; *St Exch* ***share prices*** cours *mpl* des actions; **s. prices have fallen** le cours des actions est tombé; *St Exch* ***share price index*** indice *m* des cours d'actions; *Fin* ***share savings account*** compte *m* d'épargne en actions; *St Exch* ***share splitting*** division *f ou* fractionnement *m* des actions; *St Exch* ***share swap*** échange *m* d'actions

► **share out** VT SEP partager, répartir; **the profits were shared out among them** ils se sont partagé les bénéfices

sharecropper [ˈʃeəkrɒpə(r)] N *Am* métayer(ère) *m,f*

sharecropping [ˈʃeəkrɒpɪŋ] N *Am* = système de métayage en usage dans le sud des États-Unis après la guerre de Sécession

shared [ʃeəd] ADJ *(experience, responsibility)* partagé; **a s. bathroom** une salle de bain commune

►► *Tel* ***shared line*** ligne *f* partagée, raccordement *m* collectif; *Pol* ***shared powers*** pouvoirs *mpl* partagés

shareholder [ˈʃeəhəʊldə(r)] N actionnaire *mf*; **the shareholders** l'actionnariat *m*, les actionnaires *mfpl*

►► *Acct* ***shareholders' funds*** haut *m* de bilan; ***shareholders' meeting*** réunion *f* d'actionnaires

shareholding [ˈʃeəhəʊldɪŋ] N *(shares)* participation *f*; *(share ownership)* actionnariat *m*

share-out N partage *m*, répartition *f*

sharepicker [ˈʃeəpɪkə(r)] N *Fin & St Exch* = personne qui sélectionne des actions pour établir un portefeuille

sharepicking [ˈʃeəpɪkɪŋ] N *Fin & St Exch* sélection *f* d'actions

shareware [ˈʃeəweə(r)] N *Comput* shareware *m*, partagiciel *m*, logiciel *m* contributif

sharing [ˈʃeərɪŋ] N *(of money, power)* partage *m*

shark [ʃɑːk] N **1** *Ich* requin *m*

2 *Fam Fig (swindler)* escroc[□] *m*, filou[□] *m*; *(predator* ► *in business)* requin[□] *m*

3 *Am Fam (genius)* génie[a] *m*; **to be a s. at sth** être calé en qch

4 *Am (at match)* revendeur(euse) *m,f* de billets à la sauvette

sharkskin [ˈʃɑːkskɪn] **N** peau *f* de requin

COMP en peau de requin

sharp [ʃɑːp] **ADJ 1** *(blade, scissors, razor)* affûté, bien aiguisé; *(knife)* tranchant, affilé; *(edge)* tranchant, coupant; *(point)* aigu(ë), acéré; *(teeth, thorn)* pointu; *(claw)* acéré; *(needle, pin ▸ for sewing)* pointu; *(▸ for pricking)* qui pique; *(pencil)* pointu, bien taillé; **these scissors are s.** ces ciseaux coupent bien; *Fig* **to be at the s. end** être en première ligne

2 *(features)* anguleux, tiré; *(nose)* pointu

3 *(clear ▸ photo, line, TV picture)* net; *(▸ contrast, distinction)* net, marqué

4 *(abrupt, sudden ▸ blow, bend, turn)* brusque; *(▸ rise, fall, change)* brusque, soudain; **the car made a s. turn** la voiture a tourné brusquement; **a s. rise/fall in prices** une forte hausse/baisse des prix

5 *(piercing ▸ wind, cold)* vif, pénétrant; **a s. frost** une forte gelée

6 *(intense ▸ pain, disappointment)* vif

7 *(sour, bitter ▸ taste, food)* âpre, piquant; *(apple)* acide; *(wine)* vert

8 *(harsh ▸ words, criticism)* mordant, cinglant; *(▸ reprimand)* sévère; *(▸ voice, tone)* âpre, acerbe; **some s. words were exchanged** on échangea quelques propos acerbes; **he can be very s. with customers** il lui arrive d'être très brusque avec les clients; **she has a s. tongue** elle a la langue bien affilée

9 *(keen ▸ eyesight)* perçant; *(▸ hearing, senses)* fin; *(in intellect, wit ▸ person)* vif; *(▸ child)* vif, éveillé; *(▸ judgment)* vif; **she is s. of hearing** elle a l'oreille *ou* l'ouïe fine; **he has a s. eye** il a le coup d'œil; **to have a s. eye for a bargain** savoir repérer une bonne affaire; **she has a very s. mind** elle a l'esprit très vif; **she was too s. for them** elle était trop maligne pour eux; **he's as s. as a needle** *(intelligent)* il est malin comme un singe; *(shrewd)* il est très perspicace, rien ne lui échappe

10 *(shrill ▸ sound, cry)* aigu(ë), perçant

11 *Mus* **C s.** do *m inv* dièse; **to be s.** *(singer)* chanter trop aigu; *(violinist)* jouer trop aigu

12 *Pej (unscrupulous ▸ trading, lawyer)* peu scrupuleux, malhonnête; **accused of s. practice** accusé de procédés indélicats *ou* malhonnêtes

13 *Fam (smart)* chicos, classe *(inv)*; **he's always been a s. dresser** il s'est toujours habillé très classe

ADV 1 *(precisely)* **at six o'clock s.** à six heures pile *ou* précises **2** *(in direction)* **turn s. left** tournez tout de suite à gauche; **the road turns s. left** la route tourne brusquement à gauche **3** *Mus (sing, play)* trop haut, faux **3** *Br Fam (idiom)* **look s. (about it)!** grouille-toi!, dépêche-toi![a]

N 1 *Mus* dièse *m* **2** *Am Fam (expert)* expert(e)[a] *m,f*

sharpen [ˈʃɑːpən] **VT 1** *(blade, knife, razor)* affiler, aiguiser, affûter; *(pencil)* tailler, *Can* affiler; *(stick)* tailler en pointe; **the cat sharpened its claws on the wood** le chat aiguisait ses griffes *ou* se faisait les griffes sur le bois

2 *(appetite, pain)* aviver, aiguiser; *(intelligence)* affiner; **the events sharpened my desire to travel** les événements ont accru mon désir de voyager; **you'll need to s. your wits** il va falloir te dégourdir

3 *(outline, image)* mettre au point, rendre plus net; *(contrast)* accentuer, rendre plus marqué

4 *Culin (sauce)* donner du piquant à

5 *Br Mus* diéser

VI *(tone, voice)* devenir plus vif *ou* âpre; *(pain)* s'aviver, devenir plus vif; *(appetite)* s'aiguiser; *(wind, cold)* devenir plus vif

sharpener [ˈʃɑːpənə(r)] **N** *(for knife ▸ machine)* aiguisoir *m* (à couteaux); *(▸ manual)* fusil *m* (à aiguiser); *(for pencil)* taille-crayon *m*

sharpening [ˈʃɑːpənɪŋ] **N** affilage *m*, aiguisage *m*, affûtage *m*

sharper [ˈʃɑːpə(r)] **N** escroc *m*; *Cards* tricheur (euse) *m,f* professionnel(elle)

sharp-eyed **ADJ** *(with good eyes)* qui a l'œil vif; *(with insight)* à qui rien n'échappe

sharply [ˈʃɑːplɪ] **ADV 1 s. pointed** *(knife)* pointu; *(pencil)* à pointe fine, taillé fin; *(nose, chin, shoes)* pointu

2 *(contrast, stand out)* nettement; *(differ)* nettement, clairement; **this contrasts s. with her usual behaviour** voilà qui change beaucoup de son comportement habituel; **to bring sth s. home, to bring sth s. into focus** faire apparaître qch de façon évidente

3 *(abruptly, suddenly ▸ curve, turn)* brusquement; *(▸ rise, fall, change)* brusquement, soudainement; **the car took the bend too s.** la voiture a pris le virage trop vite; **inflation has risen s. since May** l'inflation est montée en flèche depuis mai

4 *(harshly ▸ speak)* vivement, sèchement, de façon brusque; *(▸ criticize)* vivement, sévèrement; *(▸ reply, retort)* vertement, vivement; **she reprimanded him s. for being late** elle lui a fait de vifs reproches pour son retard; **I had to speak to her s. about her persistent lateness** j'ai dû lui faire des observations sévères au sujet de ses retards répétés

5 *(alertly ▸ listen)* attentivement

sharpness [ˈʃɑːpnɪs] **N 1** *(of blade, scissors, razor, knife)* tranchant *m*; *(of needle, pencil, thorn)* pointe *f* aiguë

2 *(of features)* aspect *m* anguleux

3 *(of outline, image, contrast)* netteté *f*

4 *(of bend, turn)* angle *m* brusque; *(of rise, fall, change)* soudaineté *f*

5 *(of wind, cold, frost)* âpreté *f*

6 *(of taste, smell)* piquant *m*, aigreur *f*; *(of pain)* vivacité *f*

7 *(of word, criticism, reprimand)* sévérité *f*; *(of tone, voice)* brusquerie *f*, âpreté *f*

8 *(of eyesight, hearing, senses)* finesse *f*, acuité *f*; *(of appetite, pain)* acuité *f*; *(of mind, intelligence)* finesse *f*, vivacité *f*; *(of irony, wit)* mordant *m*; **s. of vision** acuité *f* visuelle

sharpshooter [ˈʃɑːpʃuːtə(r)] **N** tireur(euse) *m,f* d'élite

sharp-sighted **ADJ** *(with good eyes)* qui a l'œil vif; *(perspicacious)* perspicace; *(observant)* observateur, à qui rien n'échappe

sharp-tongued [-ˈtʌŋd] **ADJ** caustique

sharp-witted [-ˈwɪtɪd] **ADJ** à l'esprit vif *ou* fin

shat [ʃæt] *pt & pp of* **shit**

shatter [ˈʃætə(r)] **VT 1** *(break ▸ glass, window, door)* fracasser; **a stone shattered the windscreen** un caillou a fait éclater le pare-brise; **the noise shattered my eardrums** le bruit m'a assourdi **2** *Fig (destroy ▸ career, health)* briser, ruiner; *(▸ nerves)* démolir, détraquer; *(▸ confidence, faith, hope)* démolir, détruire; **they were shattered by the news, the news shattered them** ils ont été complètement bouleversés par la nouvelle, la nouvelle les a complètement bouleversés

VI *(glass, vase, windscreen)* voler en éclats; **her whole world shattered** son univers tout entier s'est écroulé *ou* a été anéanti

shattering [ˈʃætərɪŋ] **ADJ 1** *(emotionally ▸ news, experience)* bouleversant; *(▸ revelation)* choquant; *(▸ disappointment)* fort, cruel **2** *(extreme ▸ defeat)* écrasant; **a s. blow** un coup violent; *Fig* un coup terrible **3** *Br Fam (exhausting)* crevant

shatterproof [ˈʃætəpruːf] **ADJ**

▸▸ ***shatterproof glass*** verre *m* sans éclats *ou* Securit®

shave [ʃeɪv] **VT 1** *(face, legs etc)* raser; **the barber shaved him** *or* **his face** le barbier l'a rasé *ou* lui a fait la barbe; **to s. one's legs/one's head** se raser les jambes/la tête **2** *(wood)* raboter; **can you s. a few millimetres off the bottom of the door?** pouvez-vous raboter le bas de la porte de quelques millimètres? **3** *(graze)* raser, frôler; **the car just shaved the garage door** la voiture n'a fait que frôler la porte du garage

VI se raser

N to have a s. se raser; **to give sb a s.** raser qn; *(of barber)* faire la barbe à qn

▸**shave off** **VT SEP to s. off one's beard/moustache/hair** se raser la barbe/la moustache/la tête; *Fig* **this has shaved a few points off the government's lead in the polls** cela a légèrement rogné l'avance du gouvernement dans les sor dages

shaven [ˈʃeɪvən] **ADJ** *(face, head)* rasé

shaver [ˈʃeɪvə(r)] **N** *(razor)* rasoir *m* (électrique)

▸▸ *Am* ***shaver outlet,*** *Br* ***shaver point*** prise *f* pou rasoir électrique

Shavian [ˈʃeɪvɪən] **ADJ** *(writings)* de George Be nard Shaw; *(style)* à la Shaw; *(society)* consacré Shaw

N partisan *m ou* disciple *mf* de George Bernar Shaw

shaving [ˈʃeɪvɪŋ] **N** *(act)* rasage *m*

COMP *(cream, foam)* à raser

• **shavings** **NPL** *(of wood)* copeaux *mpl*; *(c metal)* copeaux *mpl*, rognures *fpl*; *(of paper)* rc gnures *fpl*

▸▸ ***shaving brush*** blaireau *m*; ***shaving mirror*** mi roir *m* à raser; ***shaving soap*** savon *m* à barbe ***shaving stick*** (bâton *m* de) savon *m* à barbe

shawl [ʃɔːl] **N** châle *m*

she [ʃiː] **PRON 1** *(referring to woman, girl)* elle; **s.' tall** elle est grande; **s.'s a teacher/an engineer** ell est enseignante/ingénieur; **s.'s a very interestin woman** c'est une femme très intéressante; **SH can't do it** elle? elle ne peut pas le faire; *Forma* **s. who** *or* **whom he loves** celle qu'il aime **2** *(refer ring to boat, car, country)* **s.'s a fine ship** c'est u bateau magnifique; **s. can do over 120 mph** ≃ ell fait plus de 190 km à l'heure **3** *(referring to femal animal)* **s.'s a lovely dog** c'est une chienne ado rable

N *(referring to animal, baby)* **it's a s.** *(animal)* c'es une femelle; *(baby)* c'est une fille

she- [ʃiː] **PREF s.-bear** ourse *f*; **s.-wolf** louve *f*

sheaf [ʃiːf] *(pl* **sheaves** [ʃiːvz]*)* **N 1** *(of papers, let ters)* liasse *f* **2** *(of barley, corn)* gerbe *f*; *(of arrows* faisceau *m*

VT gerber, engerber

shear [ʃɪə(r)] *(pt* **sheared,** *pp* **sheared** *or* **shor** [ʃɔːn]*)* **VT 1** *(sheep, wool)* tondre; **her blonde lock had been shorn** on avait tondu ses boucles blon des; *Fig* **to be shorn of sth** être dépouillé de qch **he was shorn of all real power** il s'est vu dépouille de tout pouvoir véritable **2** *(metal)* couper (net) cisailler; **the girder had been shorn in two** la pou tre métallique avait été coupée en deux

VI céder

• **shears** **NPL** *(for gardening)* cisaille *f*; *(for sew ing)* grands ciseaux *mpl*; *(for sheep)* tondeuse *f*; **pair of shears** *(for gardening)* une paire de cisail les; *(for sewing)* une paire de grands ciseaux

▸**shear off** **VT SEP** *(wool, hair)* tondre; *(branch* couper, élaguer; *(something projecting)* coupe enlever; **the tail section of the car had bee sheared off on impact** la partie arrière de la voi ture avait été arrachée par le choc

VI *(part, branch)* se détacher; **the wing sheare right off** l'aile a été complètement arrachée

shearer [ˈʃɪərə(r)] **N** *(machine)* tondeuse *f* (à moutons); *(person)* tondeur(euse) *m,f* (de mou tons)

shearing [ˈʃɪərɪŋ] **N** *(process)* tonte *f*

• **shearings** **NPL shearings (of wool)** laine *f* ton due

sheath [ʃiːθ] *(pl* **sheaths** [ʃiːðz]*)* **N 1** *(scabbard case ▸ for sword)* fourreau *m*; *(▸ for dagger)* gain *f*; *(▸ for scissors, tool)* étui *m* **2** *(covering ▸ for ca ble)* gaine *f*; *Bot, Anat & Zool* gaine *f* **3** *Br (condom* préservatif *m*

▸▸ ***sheath dress*** (robe *f*) fourreau *m*; ***sheath knif*** couteau *m* à gaine

sheathe [ʃiːð] **VT 1** *(sword, dagger)* rengainer **the cat sheathed her claws** la chatte a rentré se griffes; *Literary* **to s. the sword** cesser les hostili tés, faire la paix **2** *(cable)* gainer; *(water pipe)* gai ner, mettre dans un manchon protecteur; *Fig* **she was sheathed from head to foot in black sati** elle était moulée dans du satin noir de la tête aux pieds

sheathing [ˈʃiːðɪŋ] **N** *(gen)* revêtement *m*; *(of ca ble)* gaine *f*

sheave [ʃiːv] **VT** gerber, engerber

sheaves [ʃiːvz] *pl of* **sheaf**

Sheba [ˈʃiːbə] **N** Saba; **the Queen of S.** la reine de Saba; *Ironic* **who do you think you are, the Queen of S.?** mais pour qui te prends-tu?

shebang [ʃɪˈbæŋ] **N** *Fam* **the whole s.** et tout le tremblement, et tout le bataclan

shed [ʃed] *(pt & pp* **shed**, *cont* **shedding**) **N 1** *(in garden)* abri *m*, remise *f*, resserre *f*; *(lean-to)* appentis *m* **2** *(barn)* grange *f*, hangar *m*; *(for trains, aircraft, vehicles)* hangar *m*; **bike s.** *(big)* hangar *m* à vélos; *(small)* remise *f* à vélos **3** *(in factory)* atelier *m*

VT 1 *(cast off ▸ leaves, petals) & St Exch* perdre; *(▸ skin, shell)* se dépouiller de; *(take off ▸ garments)* enlever; **the snake regularly sheds its skin** le serpent mue; **the dog has s. her hairs all over the carpet** la chienne a laissé des poils partout sur la moquette; **the trees are beginning to s. their leaves** les arbres commencent à perdre leurs feuilles; **oil stocks s. 1.4 percent yesterday** les valeurs pétrolières ont perdu 1,4 pour cent hier; **to s. one's clothes** se dépouiller de ses vêtements

2 *(get rid of ▸ inhibitions, beliefs)* se débarrasser de, se défaire de; *(▸ staff)* congédier; *(▸ jobs)* supprimer

3 *(tears, blood)* verser, répandre; *(weight)* perdre; **to s. bitter tears over sth** verser des larmes amères sur qch; **too much blood has been s. in the name of this cause** trop de sang a été versé au nom de cette cause

4 *Br (eject, lose)* déverser; **the truck s. its load on the by-pass** le camion a perdu son chargement sur la rocade; **the plane needs to s. 10 tons of fuel** l'avion doit larguer 10 tonnes de carburant

5 *(idiom)* **to s. light on** éclairer; *Fig* éclairer, éclaircir; **perhaps this will s. some new light on the situation** ça éclairera peut-être la situation d'un jour nouveau

she'd [ʃid, *stressed* ʃiːd] **1** = **she had 2 she would**

shedding [ˈʃedɪŋ] **N 1** *(of leaves, petals, hair)* perte *f*, chute *f*; *Elec* **load s.** délestage *m* **2** *(of blood)* effusion *f*

shedload [ˈʃedləʊd] **N** *Br Fam* **a s. of, shedloads of** une tapée de; **she earns a s.** *or* **shedloads of cash** elle se fait un fric fou

sheen [ʃiːn] **N** *(on satin, wood, hair, silk)* lustre *m*; *(on apple)* poli *m*; **the cello had a beautiful red s.** le violoncelle avait de magnifiques reflets rouges

sheep [ʃiːp] *(pl inv)* **N** mouton *m*; *(ewe)* brebis *f*; *Pej* **they're just a load of s.** ils se comportent comme des moutons (de Panurge) *ou* un troupeau de moutons; *Fig* **to separate** *or* **to sort out the s. from the goats** séparer le bon grain de l'ivraie

COMP *(farm, farming)* de moutons

▸▸ ***sheep farmer*** éleveur(euse) *m,f* de moutons; ***sheep pen*** parc *m* à moutons; ***sheep station*** grand élevage *m* de moutons

sheep-dip **N** bain *m* parasiticide (pour moutons)

sheepdog [ˈʃiːpdɒg] **N** chien *m* de berger

▸▸ ***sheepdog trials*** concours *m* de chiens de berger

sheepfold [ˈʃiːpfəʊld] **N** parc *m* à moutons, bergerie *f*

sheepish [ˈʃiːpɪʃ] **ADJ** penaud

sheepishly [ˈʃiːpɪʃlɪ] **ADV** d'un air penaud

sheepishness [ˈʃiːpɪʃnɪs] **N** air *m* penaud

sheep-shagger **N** *Br Vulg (Welsh person)* = terme injurieux désignant un Gallois; *(any rural person)* péquenaud(e) *m,f*

sheepskin [ˈʃiːpskɪn] **N 1** *Tex* peau *f* de mouton **2** *Am Fam (diploma)* parchemin *m*

COMP *(coat, rug)* en peau de mouton

▸▸ ***sheepskin jacket*** canadienne *f*, veste *f* en peau lainée

sheer [ʃɪə(r)] **ADJ 1** *(as intensifier)* pur; **it was s. coincidence** c'était une pure coïncidence; **the s. scale of the project was intimidating** l'envergure même du projet était impressionnante; **by s. accident** *or* **chance** tout à fait par hasard, par pur hasard; **out of** *or* **in s. boredom** par pur ennui; **in s. desperation** en désespoir de cause; **it was s. stupidity** c'était franchement stupide; **it's s. folly!** c'est de la folie pure! **2** *(steep ▸ cliff)* à pic, abrupt; **it's a s. 50-metre drop** cela descend à pic sur 50 mètres; **we came up against a s. wall of water** nous nous sommes trouvés devant un véritable mur d'eau **3** *Tex (stockings)* extra-fin; *(garment, fabric)* transparent

ADV à pic, abruptement

VI *Naut (ship)* faire une embardée

▸ **sheer away** **VI 1** *(ship)* larguer les amarres, prendre le large **2** *(animal, shy person)* filer, détaler; **to s. away from** éviter

sheesh [ʃiːʃ] **EXCLAM** *Fam (in surprise)* tiens!; *(in exasperation)* allez!

sheet [ʃiːt] **N 1** *(for bed)* drap *m*; *(for furniture)* housse *f*; *(shroud)* linceul *m*; *(tarpaulin)* bâche *f*; **to change the sheets (on a bed)** changer les draps (d'un lit); **to get between the sheets** se mettre au lit; *Fam* **what's he like between the sheets?** comment est-il au lit?

2 *(of paper, cardboard, plastic)* feuille *f*; *(of glass, metal)* feuille *f*, plaque *f*; *(of iron, steel)* tôle *f*, plaque *f*; **loose s.** feuille *f* volante; **a s. of newspaper** une feuille de journal; **the book is still in sheets** le livre n'a pas encore été relié; **order s.** bulletin *m* de commande

3 *(newspaper)* feuille *f*, journal *m*

4 *(of water, snow)* nappe *f*, étendue *f*; *(of rain)* rideau *m*, torrent *m*; *(of flames)* rideau *m*; **a s. of ice** une plaque de glace; *(on road)* une plaque de verglas; **the rain came down in sheets** il pleuvait des hallebardes *ou* à torrents

5 *Culin* **baking s.** plaque *f* de four *ou* à gâteaux

6 *Naut* écoute *f*; *Fam Fig* **to be three sheets to the wind** avoir du vent dans les voiles

VT *(figure, face)* draper, couvrir d'un drap; *(furniture)* couvrir de housses; *Fig* **sheeted (over) in snow** couvert de neige

▸▸ *Naut* ***sheet bend*** nœud *m* d'écoute; *Comput* ***sheet feed*** avancement *m* du papier; *Comput* ***sheet feeder*** bac *m* d'alimentation papier; ***sheet ice*** plaque *f* de glace; *(on road)* (plaque *f* de) verglas *m*; ***sheet lightning*** éclair *m* en nappe *ou* en nappes; ***sheet metal*** tôle *f*; ***sheet music*** *(UNCOUNT)* partitions *fpl*

▸ **sheet down** **VI** *(rain, snow)* tomber à torrents

sheet-fed **ADJ** *(printer)* feuille à feuille

sheeting [ˈʃiːtɪŋ] **N 1** *(cloth)* toile *f* pour draps **2** *(plastic, polythene)* feuillet *m*; *(metal)* feuille *f*, plaque *f*

sheik [ʃeɪk] **N** cheikh *m*

sheikdom [ˈʃeɪkdəm] **N** territoire *m* sous l'autorité d'un cheikh

sheikh, sheikhdom = **sheik, sheikdom**

sheila [ˈʃiːlə] **N** *Austr & NZ Fam* nana *f*

shekel [ˈʃekəl] **N** *(Israeli currency)* shekel *m*; *Bible* sicle *m*

• **shekels** **NPL** *esp Am Fam (money)* fric *m*, sous *mpl*

shelf [ʃelf] *(pl* **shelves** [ʃelvz]) **N 1** *(individual)* planche *f*, étagère *f*; *(as part of set, in fridge)* étagère *f*; *(short)* tablette *f*; *(in oven)* plaque *f*; *(in shop)* étagère *f*, rayon *m*; **(set of) shelves** étagère *f*; **to put up shelves/a s.** monter des étagères/une étagère; **to buy sth off the s.** acheter qch tout fait; **I bought the cakes off the s.** j'ai acheté les gâteaux tout faits; **to stay on the shelves** *(goods)* se vendre difficilement; *Fig* **to be left on the s.** *(woman)* rester vieille fille; *(man)* rester vieux garçon **2** *Geol* banc *m*, rebord *m*, saillie *f*; *(under sea)* écueil *m*, plate-forme *f*

▸▸ *Mktg* ***shelf facing*** facing *m*, frontale *f*; ***shelf filler*** *(person in supermarket)* réassortisseur(euse) *m,f*; *Com* ***shelf life*** durée *f* de conservation avant vente; **bread has a short s. life** le pain ne se conserve pas très longtemps; *Fig* **to have a short s. life** *(idea, pop group etc)* avoir une durée de vie courte; ***shelf mark*** *(of book)* cote *f*; *Com* ***shelf space*** linéaire *m*, rayonnage *m*; ***shelf stacker*** *(person in supermarket)* réassortisseur(euse) *m,f*

shell [ʃel] **N 1** *Biol (gen ▸ of egg, mollusc, nut)* coquille *f*; *(▸ of peas)* cosse *f*; *(▸ of crab, lobster, tortoise)* carapace *f*; *(empty ▸ on beach)* coquillage *m*; *also Fig* **to come out of one's s.** sortir de sa coquille; *also Fig* **to go back** *or* **to retire into one's s.** rentrer dans sa coquille; **to bring sb out of his/her s.** faire sortir qn de sa coquille **2** *(of building)* carcasse *f*; *(of car, ship, machine)* coque *f*; **he's just an empty s.** il n'est plus que l'ombre de lui-même **3** *Mil* obus *m*; *Am (cartridge)* cartouche *f*

COMP *(ornament, jewellery)* de *ou* en coquillages

VT 1 *(peas)* écosser, égrener; *(nut)* décortiquer, écaler; *(oyster)* ouvrir; *(prawn, crab)* décortiquer **2** *Mil* bombarder (d'obus)

▸▸ *Comput* ***shell program*** logiciel *m* shell; ***shell shock*** *(UNCOUNT)* syndrome *m* commotionnel; ***shell suit*** survêtement *m* *(en polyamide froissé et doublé)*

> When translating the English word **shell**, note that the French words **coquillage** and **coquille** are not interchangeable. **Coquillage** applies mostly to seashells, whereas **coquille** refers to the more general sense of a shell as the outer layer of something.

she'll [ʃiːl] = **she will**

▸ **shell out** *Fam* **VI** casquer; **to s. out for sth** casquer pour qch, payer qch; **I'm always shelling out** je suis toujours en train de casquer; **she had to s. out for new school uniforms** elle a dû casquer pour acheter de nouveaux uniformes scolaires

VT INSEP raquer; **I had to s. out £500** j'ai dû raquer 500 livres

shellac [ʃəˈlæk] *(pt & pp* **shellacked**, *cont* **shellacking**) **N** gomme-laque *f*

VT 1 *(varnish)* laquer **2** *Am Fam (defeat)* battre à plate(s) couture(s), écrabouiller

shellacking [ʃəˈlækɪŋ] **N** *Am Fam* **1** *(defeat)* raclée *f*, déculottée *f*; **to give sb a s.** battre qn à plate(s) couture(s), écrabouiller qn; **to take a s.** être battu à plates coutures, se faire écrabouiller **2** *(beating)* **to give sb a s.** tabasser qn, passer qn à tabac; **to take a s.** se faire tabasser, se faire passer à tabac

shelled [ʃeld] **ADJ** *(peas)* écossé, égrené; *(nut, shellfish)* décortiqué

shellfire [ˈʃelfaɪə(r)] **N** *(UNCOUNT)* tirs *mpl* d'obus; **to be under s.** subir des tirs d'obus; **we came under heavy s.** nous avons subi un pilonnage intensif

shellfish [ˈʃelfɪʃ] *(pl inv)* **N 1** *Zool (crab, lobster, shrimp)* crustacé *m*; *(mollusc)* coquillage *m* **2** *(UNCOUNT)* *Culin* fruits *mpl* de mer

shelling [ˈʃelɪŋ] **N** *Mil* pilonnage *m*

shell-shaped **ADJ** en forme de coquillage, conchoïde

shell-shocked [-ʃɒkt] **ADJ** commotionné *(après une explosion)*; **a s. soldier** un commotionné (de guerre); *Fig* **I'm still feeling pretty s. by it all** je suis encore sous le choc après toute cette histoire

shelter [ˈʃeltə(r)] **N 1** *(cover, protection)* abri *m*; **to take** *or* **to get under s.** se mettre à l'abri *ou* à couvert; **they took** *or* **sought s. from the rain under a tree** ils se sont abrités de la pluie *ou* mis à l'abri de la pluie sous un arbre; **we ran for s.** nous avons couru nous mettre à l'abri; **under the s. of the mountain** à l'abri de la montagne

2 *(accommodation)* asile *m*, abri *m*; **to give s. to sb** *(hide)* donner asile à *ou* cacher qn; *(accommodate)* héberger qn; **they gave us food and s.** ils nous ont offert le gîte et le couvert

3 *(enclosure ▸ gen)* abri *m*; *(▸ for sentry)* guérite *f*; **(bus) s.** Abribus® *m*

4 *(for homeless people, battered wives etc)* refuge *m*

VT 1 *(protect ▸ from rain, sun, bombs)* abriter; *(▸ from blame, suspicion)* protéger; **to s. sb from sth** protéger qn de qch; **the trees sheltered us from the wind** les arbres nous abritaient du vent; **her reputation sheltered her from any scandal** sa réputation lui évita le scandale; **we were sheltered from the rain/from danger** nous étions à l'abri de la pluie/du danger **2** *(give asylum to ▸ fugitive, refugee)* donner asile à, abriter; **the police suspected them of sheltering a murderer** la police les soupçonnait d'abriter un assassin

VI s'abriter, se mettre à l'abri; *(from bullets)* se mettre à couvert; **he sheltered from the rain in a shop doorway** il s'est abrité de la pluie *ou* il s'est mis à l'abri de la pluie dans l'entrée d'un magasin

sheltered [ˈʃeltəd] **ADJ 1** *(position, garden, cove, waters)* abrité **2** *(upbringing, life)* protégé; **to lead a s. life** vivre à l'abri des soucis **3** *(protected ▸ industry)* protégé *(de la concurrence)*; *(▸ work)* dans un centre pour handicapés

▸▸ ***sheltered accommodation, sheltered housing*** = logement dans une résidence pour personnes âgées ou handicapées; ***sheltered workshop*** = atelier pour personnes handicapées

shelve [ʃelv] **VT 1** *(put aside, suspend)* laisser en suspens; **the project was shelved for two years** le projet a été mis en veilleuse pendant deux ans; **the problem has been shelved** le problème reste en suspens **2** *(books ▸ in shop)* mettre sur les rayons; *(▸ at home)* mettre sur les étagères **3** *(wall, room ▸ in shop)* garnir de rayons; *(▸ at home)* garnir d'étagères

VI *(ground)* être en pente douce; **the land shelves down to the sea** le terrain descend en pente douce jusqu'à la mer

shelves [ʃelvz] *pl of* **shelf**

shelving ['ʃelvɪŋ] **N** *(UNCOUNT)* **1** *(in shop)* rayonnage *m*, rayonnages *mpl*; *(at home)* étagères *fpl* **2** *(suspension ▸ of plan, question etc)* mise *f* en attente *ou* en suspens

shemozzle [ʃɪ'mɒzəl] *esp Am Fam* **N 1** *(confusion)* bazar *m*, pagaille *f*, merdier *m* **2** *(fight)* chamaillerie *f*, bagarre□*f*

shenanigans [ʃɪ'nænɪgənz] **NPL** *Fam* **1** *(mischief)* malice□*f*, espièglerie□*f* **2** *(scheming, tricks)* manigances□*fpl*, combines *fpl*; **there have been some s. going on here** il s'est passé des choses pas très claires ici□

shepherd ['ʃepəd] **N 1** berger *m*, *Literary* pâtre *m* **2** *Rel & Literary* pasteur *m*, berger *m*; **the Good S.** le bon Pasteur *ou* Berger

VT 1 *(tourists, children)* guider, conduire; **the boys were shepherded onto the coach** on a fait entrer les garçons dans le car **2** *(sheep)* garder, surveiller; **he shepherded all the ewes into the fold** il a conduit toutes les brebis à la bergerie

▸▸ ***shepherd's crook*** bâton *m* de berger, houlette *f*; ***shepherd dog*** (chien *m* de) berger *m*; *Culin* ***shepherd's pie*** hachis *m* Parmentier, *Can* pâté *m* chinois; *Bot* ***shepherd's purse*** bourse-à-pasteur *f*

shepherdess [ʃepə'des] **N** bergère *f*

sherbet ['ʃɜːbət] **N 1** *Br (powder ▸ sweet)* poudre *f* acidulée; *(▸ for drink)* = poudre servant à préparer une boisson gazeuse **2** *Am (water ice)* sorbet *m*

sheriff ['ʃerɪf] **N 1** *Am (in Wild West and today)* shérif *m* **2** *Br Law (Crown officer)* shérif *m*, officier *m* de la Couronne **3** *Scot Law* ≃ juge *m* au tribunal de grande instance

▸▸ *Scot Law* ***sheriff court*** ≃ tribunal *m* de grande instance

sherry ['ʃerɪ] *(pl* **sherries***)* **N** sherry *m*, xérès *m*, vin *m* de Xérès

▸▸ ***sherry glass*** verre *m* à madère

she's [ʃiːz] **1** = **she has 2** = **she is**

Shetland ['ʃetlənd] **N the Shetlands** les (îles *fpl*) Shetland *fpl*

▸▸ ***the Shetland Islands, the Shetland Isles*** les (îles *fpl*) Shetland *fpl*; ***Shetland pony*** poney *m* des Shetland; ***Shetland wool*** laine *f* d'Écosse *ou* de Shetland

shew [ʃəʊ] *(pt* **shewed**, *pp* **shewn** [ʃəʊn] *or* **shewed***)* *Arch* = **show VT & VI**

Shia(h) ['ʃiːə] **N 1** *(religion)* chiisme *m* **2** *(Shiite)* **S. (Muslim)** chiite *mf*

ADJ chiite

shiatsu, shiatzu [ʃɪ'ætsuː] **N** shiatsu *m*

shibboleth ['ʃɪbəˌleθ] **N** *Bible* schibboleth *m*; *Fig (custom)* coutume *f* dépassée; *(tradition)* tradition *f* dépassée; *(idea)* idée *f* dépassée; *(catchword ▸ of party etc)* mot *m* d'ordre

shield [ʃiːld] **N 1** *(carried by soldier, warrior)* bouclier *m*

2 *Fig* bouclier *m*, paravent *m*; **to provide a s. against sth** protéger contre qch; **to use sb/sth as a s.** se servir de qn/qch comme bouclier

3 *Tech (on machine)* écran *m* de protection *ou* de sécurité; *(on nuclear reactor, spacecraft)* bouclier *m*; **sun s.** pare-soleil *m inv*

4 *(trophy)* trophée *m*

5 *(police badge)* plaque *f* de policier

6 *(in spray painting)* masque *m*, cache *m*

VT 1 *(protect)* protéger; **to s. sb from sth** protéger qn de *ou* contre qch; **to s. one's eyes** se protéger les yeux; **the police think he's trying to s. somebody** la police pense qu'il essaie de protéger quelqu'un; **she shielded him with her own body** elle lui a fait un bouclier *ou* rempart de son corps **2** *(in spray painting ▸ surfaces)* masquer

shift [ʃɪft] **N 1** *(change)* changement *m*; **a s. in position/opinion** un changement de position/d'avis; **there was a slight s. in the wind** le vent a légèrement tourné; *Pol* **a s. to the right/left** un glissement à droite/gauche; *Ling* **a s. in meaning** un glissement de sens; *Ling* **consonant/vowel s.** mutation *f* consonantique/vocalique

2 *(move)* déplacement *m*; **there's been a s. of population towards the towns** on a assisté à un déplacement de la population vers les villes

3 *Ind (work period)* poste *m*; *(group of workers)* équipe *f*, brigade *f*; **I'm on the night/morning s.** je suis dans l'équipe de nuit/du matin; **she works long shifts** elle fait de longues heures; **he's on eight-hour shifts** il fait les trois-huit; **to work shifts, to be on shifts** travailler en équipe, faire les trois-huit; **when does** *or* **do the morning s. arrive?** à quelle heure arrive l'équipe du matin?

4 *(turn, relay)* relais *m*; **to do sth in shifts** se relayer; **there was a lot of work so they did it in shifts** comme il y avait beaucoup de travail, ils se sont relayés (pour le faire); **I'm exhausted, can you take a s. at the wheel?** je suis épuisé, peux-tu me relayer au volant?

5 *Am Aut* **(gear) s.** *(lever)* levier *m* de (changement de) vitesse; *(action)* changement *m* de vitesse, *Can* bras *m* de vitesse

6 *(dress)* (robe *f*) fourreau *m*; *Old-fashioned (woman's slip)* combinaison *f*

7 *Comput (on keyboard)* touche *f* majuscule; **press s.** appuyer sur la touche majuscule; **an asterisk is s. 8** pour l'astérisque, il faut appuyer simultanément sur la touche majuscule et la touche 8

VT 1 *(move ▸ object)* déplacer, bouger; *(▸ part of body)* bouger, remuer; *Theat (scenery)* changer; **it took three strong men to s. the wardrobe** il a fallu trois hommes forts pour déplacer l'armoire; **the drawer's stuck, I can't s. it** le tiroir est coincé, je ne peux le faire bouger; *Fam* **s. yourself!** *(move)* pousse-toi!, bouge-toi!; *(hurry)* remue-toi!, grouille-toi!

2 *(transfer ▸ employee) (to new job, place of work)* muter; *(to new department)* affecter; *(▸ blame, responsibility)* rejeter; **they've shifted offices again** ils ont déménagé de nouveau; **he keeps getting shifted to a different job** on n'arrête pas de le muter; **they're trying to s. the blame onto me** ils essaient de rejeter la responsabilité sur moi; **the latest developments have shifted attention away from this area** les événements récents ont détourné l'attention de cette région; **they won't be shifted from their opinion** impossible de les faire changer d'avis; **to s. ground** *or* **one's position** changer de position

3 *(remove ▸ stain)* enlever, faire partir

4 *Am* **to s. gears** changer de vitesse

5 *Fam (sell)* écouler□, fourguer; **how can we s. this old stock?** comment écouler *ou* nous débarrasser de ces vieilles marchandises?□

VI 1 *(move)* se déplacer, bouger; **the cargo has shifted in the hold** la cargaison s'est déplacée dans la cale; **the table won't s., it's bolted to the floor** on ne peut pas bouger la table, elle est fixée au sol; **the anticyclone is expected to s. eastwards** l'anticyclone devrait se déplacer vers l'est; **she kept shifting from one foot to the other** elle n'arrêtait pas de se balancer d'un pied sur l'autre; **could you s.?** *(out of the way)* pouvez-vous dégager?

2 *(change, switch ▸ gen)* changer; *(▸ wind)* tourner; **their policy has shifted over the last week** leur politique a changé *ou* s'est modifiée au cours de la semaine; *Theat* **the scene shifts** la scène change; **in the second act the scene shifts to Venice** dans le deuxième acte, l'action se déroule à Venise; **he wouldn't s.** *(in negotiations etc)* il est resté ferme sur ses positions; *Am Aut* **to s. into fourth (gear)** passer en quatrième (vitesse)

3 *Br Fam (move quickly)* foncer; **this car can really s.!** cette voiture est un vrai bolide!

4 *(manage)* **to s. for oneself** se débrouiller tout seul; **she can** *or* **knows how to s. for herself** elle est débrouillarde

5 *(stain)* partir, s'enlever; **this stain won't s.** cette tache ne veut pas partir

6 *Br Fam (sell)* se vendre□; **those TVs just aren['t] shifting at all** ces télévisions ne se vendent pa[s] du tout

▸▸ *Comput* ***shift key*** touche *f* majuscule; *Compu[t]* ***shift lock*** touche *f* de blocage des majuscules; *Am Aut* ***shift stick*** levier *m* de (changement de) vitesse, *Can* bras *m* de vitesse; ***shift work*** travai[l] *m* en équipe; **she does s. work** elle fait les trois-huit; ***shift worker*** = personne qui fait les trois-huit

▸ **shift along, shift over, shift up VI** *Fam* s[e] pousser□; **can you s. along** *or* **over** *or* **up a bit?** t[u] peux te pousser un peu?

shift-click *Comput* **N** majuscule-clic *m*

VI faire un majuscule-clic

shiftily ['ʃɪftɪlɪ] **ADV** sournoisement

shiftiness ['ʃɪftɪnɪs] **N** sournoiserie *f*

shifting ['ʃɪftɪŋ] **ADJ** *(ideas, opinions)* chan[geant]; *(alliances)* instable; *(ground)* mouvant

▸▸ ***shifting sands*** sables *mpl* mouvants; *Fig* ter[rain] *m* mouvant

shiftless ['ʃɪftlɪs] **ADJ** *(lazy)* paresseux, fai[néant]; *(apathetic)* apathique, mou (molle); *(lacking initiative)* qui manque de ressource[s], peu débrouillard

shiftlessness ['ʃɪftlɪsnɪs] **N** *(laziness)* paresse *f*, fainéantise *f*; *(apathy)* apathie *f*, mollesse *f*; *(lack of initiative)* manque *m* de ressource *ou* d'initia[tive]

shifty ['ʃɪftɪ] *(compar* **shiftier**, *superl* **shiftiest***)* **AD[J]** *Fam (person)* louche□; *(eyes, look)* fuyant□; **h[e] looks a s. customer** il a l'air louche

Shiism ['ʃiːɪzəm] **N** *Rel* chiisme *m*

shiitake mushroom [ʃɪ'tækɪ-] **N** champignon *m* shiitake

Shiite ['ʃiːaɪt] *Rel* **N S. (Muslim)** chiite *mf*

ADJ chiite

shill [ʃɪl] **N** *esp Am Fam (encouraging buyers)* baron *m*, = complice d'un camelot qui attire le[s] clients par achats simulés; *(of gambler)* com[pè]re *m (d'un joueur professionnel)*

shillelagh [ʃɪ'leɪlɪ] **N** gourdin *m*

shilling ['ʃɪlɪŋ] **N** shilling *m (ancienne pièce bri[tannique valant 12 pence, soit un vingtième de livre)*

shilly-shally ['ʃɪlɪˌʃælɪ] *(pt & pp* **shilly-shallied***)* **V[I]** *Fam Pej* hésiter□, tergiverser□; **stop shilly-shally[ing] (around)!** décide-toi enfin!□

shilly-shallying ['ʃɪlɪˌʃælɪɪŋ] **N** *(UNCOUNT) Fam Pej* hésitations□*fpl*, valse-hésitation *f*; **after a lot of s. they eventually came to an agreement** après de longues hésitations *ou* une longue valse-hésitation, ils ont fini par se mettre d'accord

shimmer ['ʃɪmə(r)] **VI** *(light)* scintiller; *(sequins, jewellery, silk)* chatoyer, scintiller; *(water)* miroiter; **the sea shimmered in the moonlight, the moonlight shimmered on the sea** la mer miroitait au clair de lune

N *(of light)* scintillement *m*; *(of sequins, jewellery, silk)* chatoiement *m*, scintillement *m*; *(of water)* miroitement *m*; **the s. of the moon on the lake** les reflets *mpl* de la lune sur le lac

shimmering ['ʃɪmərɪŋ] **ADJ** *(light)* scintillant; *(sequins, jewellery, silk)* chatoyant; *(water)* miroitant

shimmy ['ʃɪmɪ] *(pl* **shimmies**, *pt & pp* **shimmied***)* **N 1** *(dance)* shimmy *m* **2** *Am Aut* shimmy *m*, flottement *m* des roues directrices

VI 1 *(dance)* danser le shimmy **2** *Am Aut* avoir du shimmy; **at speed it tends to s.** la direction a tendance à flotter à grande vitesse

shin [ʃɪn] *(pt & pp* **shinned**, *cont* **shinning***)* **N 1** *Ana[t]* tibia *m*; **she kicked him in the shins** elle lui a donné un coup de pied dans les tibias **2** *Culin (of beef)* gîte *m ou* gîte-gîte *m* (de bœuf); *(of veal)* jarret *m* (de veau)

VI grimper; **to s. (up) a lamp post** grimper à un réverbère; **I shinned down the drainpipe** je suis descendu le long de la gouttière

shinbone ['ʃɪnbəʊn] **N** tibia *m*

shindig ['ʃɪndɪg] **N** *Fam* **1** *(party)* (grande) fête□*f*; **to have a s.** faire la fiesta **2** *(fuss)* tapage□*m*, raffut *m*; **he kicked up a real s.** il a fait un sacré tapage

shindy ['ʃɪndɪ] (*pl* **shindies**) N *Fam* **1** *Br (din)* raffut *m*, ramdam *m*; **to kick up a s.** *(make a din)* faire du raffut *ou* du ramdam; **to kick up a s. about sth** *(protest loudly)* faire du raffut pour protester contre qch **2** *Am* = **shindig**

shine [ʃaɪn] (*pt & pp vt* **1** & vi **shone** [ʃɒn], *vt sense* **2** **shined**) VI **1** *(sun, moon, lamp, candle)* briller; *(surface, glass, hair)* briller, luire; **the sun/the moon was shining** le soleil/la lune brillait; **the sun was shining in my eyes** j'avais le soleil dans les yeux, le soleil m'éblouissait; **there was a light shining in the window** une lumière brillait à la fenêtre; **bright light shone from the window** une lumière vive brillait à la fenêtre; **his eyes shone with excitement** ses yeux brillaient *ou* son regard brillait d'émotion; **her face shone with joy** son visage rayonnait de joie; *very Fam* **stick it where the sun don't s.!** tu peux te le mettre où je pense! **2** *(excel)* briller; **John shines at sports** John est très bon en sport; **he doesn't s. in company** il ne brille pas en société

VT **1** *(focus)* braquer, diriger; **the guard shone his torch on the prisoner** le gardien a braqué sa lampe sur le prisonnier; **don't s. that lamp in my eyes** ne m'éblouis pas avec cette lampe **2** *(polish)* faire briller, faire reluire, astiquer

N **1** *(polished appearance)* éclat *m*, brillant *m*, lustre *m*; **to put a s. on sth, to give sth a s.** faire reluire *ou* briller qch; **to take the s. off sth** délustrer qch, ternir qch; *Fig* faire perdre de son éclat à qch; *Fam* **to take a s. to sb** *(take a liking to)* se prendre d'amitié pour qn□; *(get a crush on)* s'enticher de qn□ **2** *(polish)* polissage *m*; **your shoes need a s.** tes chaussures ont besoin d'un coup de brosse *ou* chiffon

shiner ['ʃaɪnə(r)] N *Fam (black eye)* coquard *m*, œil *m* au beurre noir

shingle ['ʃɪŋgəl] N **1** *(UNCOUNT) (pebbles)* galets *mpl* **2** *Constr (for roofing)* bardeau *m*, aisseau *m* **3** *Am (nameplate ▸ of doctor, lawyer etc)* plaque *f*

VT *(roof)* couvrir de bardeaux *ou* d'aisseaux

▸▸ ***shingle beach*** plage *f* de galets; ***shingle roof*** toit *m* en bardeaux

shingles ['ʃɪŋgəlz] N *(UNCOUNT) Med* zona *m*

shingly ['ʃɪŋgəlɪ] ADJ *(ground)* couvert de galets; *(beach)* de galets

shininess ['ʃaɪnɪnɪs] N éclat *m*, brillant *m*

shining ['ʃaɪnɪŋ] ADJ **1** *(gleaming ▸ glass, metal, shoes)* luisant, reluisant; *(▸ eyes)* brillant; *(▸ face)* rayonnant **2** *(outstanding)* éclatant, remarquable; **a s. example of bravery** un modèle de courage

shinny ['ʃɪnɪ] (*pt & pp* **shinnied**) *Am* = **shin** VI

Shintoism ['ʃɪntəʊɪzəm] N *Rel* shintoïsme *m*

shiny ['ʃaɪnɪ] (*compar* **shinier**, *superl* **shiniest**) ADJ **1** *(gleaming ▸ glass, metal, shoes)* luisant, reluisant; **my nose is s.** j'ai le nez qui brille **2** *(clothing ▸ with wear)* lustré; **s. at the elbows** lustré aux coudes

ship [ʃɪp] (*pt & pp* **shipped**, *cont* **shipping**) N **1** *Naut* navire *m*; *(smaller)* bateau *m*; *(esp warship)* bâtiment *m*; **aboard** *or* **on board s.** à bord; *Literary* **the good s. Calypso** la Calypso; **sailing s.** bateau *m* à voiles, voilier *m*; *Fam* **when my s. comes in** *or* **home** *(money)* quand je serai riche□, quand j'aurai fait fortune□; *(success)* quand j'aurai réussi dans la vie□; **the s. of the desert** le vaisseau du désert; **the s. of State** le char de l'État; *Fig* **to be like ships that pass in the night** *(lovers)* être des amants de passage; **these days we're like ships that pass in the night** ces temps-ci on ne fait que se croiser **2** *(airship)* dirigeable *m*; *(spaceship)* vaisseau *m* (spatial)

VT **1** *(send by ship)* expédier (par bateau *ou* par mer); *(carry by ship)* transporter (par bateau *ou* par mer); **we're having most of our luggage shipped** nous expédions la plupart de nos bagages par bateau **2** *(send by any means)* expédier; *(carry by any means)* transporter; **the goods will be shipped by train** *(sent)* les marchandises seront expédiées par le train; *(transported)* les marchandises seront transportées par chemin de fer **3** *(embark ▸ passengers, cargo)* embarquer

VI **1** *(passengers, crew)* embarquer, s'embarquer **2** *Com (product)* sortir de l'usine

▸▸ ***ship's biscuit*** biscuit *m* de mer; ***ship's boy*** mousse *m*; ***ship's chandler*** shipchandler *m*, marchand(e) *m,f* d'articles de marine; ***ship's company*** équipage *m*

▸ **ship off** VT SEP *Fam* expédier□; **we've shipped the kids off to their grandparents'** nous avons expédié les gosses chez leurs grands-parents

▸ **ship out** VT SEP *(send ▸ goods)* expédier; *(▸ troops etc)* envoyer

VI *esp Am Fam (leave)* mettre les voiles

-SHIP — SUFFIXE

Lorsqu'on l'ajoute à des noms, le suffixe **-ship** produit de nouveaux noms selon les schémas suivants:

- Il peut servir à former des noms représentant un CONCEPT lié au nom dont il est dérivé: **friendship** l'amitié; **relationship** les rapports, les relations; **membership** l'adhésion; **fellowship** la camaraderie; **they have established the authorship of the book** ils ont identifié l'auteur du livre.
- Il peut servir à former des noms désignant un POSTE dans une hiérarchie: **headship** poste de directeur *ou* de directrice; **professorship** chaire; **chairmanship** présidence; **to be elected to the premiership** être élu Premier ministre.
- Il peut également servir à véhiculer l'idée de DURÉE des notions indiquées ci-dessus: **during their friendship** pendant le temps qu'a duré leur amitié; **under the chairmanship of Mr Black** sous la présidence de M. Black.
- Employé avec un nom de personne pratiquant une activité, ce préfixe sert a véhiculer la notion de SAVOIR-FAIRE: **craftsmanship** la connaissance d'un *ou* du métier; **musicianship** don pour la musique; **horsemanship** talent de cavalier; **scholarship** l'érudition; **he showed great statesmanship in dealing with the problem** il a traité ce problème avec toute l'habileté d'un grand chef d'État.
- Il peut servir à véhiculer la notion de GROUPE SPÉCIFIQUE à partir du nom dont il est dérivé: **the magazine has a readership of 5,000** le magazine compte environ 5000 lecteurs; **our club has a large membership** notre club compte de nombreux adhérents *ou* membres.
- Enfin, il sert a créer des TITRES tels que **Your/Her Ladyship** Madame (la baronne/la vicomtesse/la comtesse); **Your/His Lordship** Monsieur (le baron/le vicomte/le comte).

shipboard ['ʃɪpbɔːd] ADJ *(romance, drama)* qui a lieu à bord d'un navire

shipbroker ['ʃɪpbrəʊkə(r)] N courtier *m* maritime

shipbuilder ['ʃɪpbɪldə(r)] N constructeur *m* de navires

shipbuilding ['ʃɪpbɪldɪŋ] N construction *f* navale; **the s. industry** (l'industrie *f* de) la construction navale

shipload ['ʃɪpləʊd] N cargaison *f*, fret *m*

shipmate ['ʃɪpmeɪt] N compagnon *m* de bord

shipment ['ʃɪpmənt] N **1** *(goods sent)* cargaison *f* **2** *(sending of goods)* expédition *f*; **the containers awaiting s.** les conteneurs prêts pour l'expédition

shipowner ['ʃɪpəʊnə(r)] N armateur *m*

shipped [ʃɪpt] ADJ embarqué

▸▸ *Com* ***shipped bill*** connaissement *m* embarqué; *Com* ***shipped weight*** poids *m* embarqué

shipper ['ʃɪpə(r)] N *(charterer)* affréteur *m*, chargeur *m*; *(transporter)* transporteur *m*; *(sender)* expéditeur(trice) *m,f*

shipping ['ʃɪpɪŋ] N *(UNCOUNT)* **1** *(ships)* navires *mpl*; *(traffic)* navigation *f*; **dangerous to s.** dangereux pour la navigation; **all s. has been warned to steer clear of the area** on a prévenu les navires qu'il fallait éviter le secteur **2** *(transport ▸ gen)* transport *m*; *(▸ by sea)* transport *m* maritime; **cost includes s.** le coût du transport est compris **3** *(loading)* chargement *m*, embarquement *m*

COMP *(line)* maritime, de navigation; *(sport, trade, intelligence)* maritime

▸▸ ***shipping agent*** agent *m* maritime; ***shipping charges*** frais *mpl* d'expédition; ***shipping clerk*** expéditionnaire *mf*; ***shipping company*** entreprise *f* de transport routier; ***shipping forecast*** météo *f ou* météorologie *f* marine; ***shipping lane*** couloir *m* de navigation; ***shipping office*** bureau *m* d'expédition

shipshape ['ʃɪpʃeɪp] ADJ en ordre, rangé; **let's try to get this place s.** essayons de mettre un peu d'ordre ici

shipwreck ['ʃɪprek] N **1** *(disaster at sea)* naufrage *m*; **they died in a s.** ils ont péri dans un naufrage **2** *(wrecked ship)* épave *f*

VT **1 they were shipwrecked on a desert island** ils ont échoué sur une île déserte **2** *Fig (ruin, spoil)* ruiner

shipwrecked ['ʃɪprekt] ADJ **to be s.** *(boat)* faire naufrage; *(crew, passenger)* être naufragé; **a s. sailor** un marin naufragé

shipwright ['ʃɪpraɪt] N *(company)* constructeur *m* de navires; *(worker)* ouvrier(ère) *m,f* de chantier naval

shipyard ['ʃɪpjɑːd] N chantier *m* naval; **hundreds of s. workers were sacked** des centaines d'ouvriers des chantiers navals ont été licenciés

shire ['ʃaɪə(r)] N *Br* **1** *(county)* comté *m* **2** (horse) shire *m*

• **Shires** NPL **the Shires** = les comtés (ruraux) du centre de l'Angleterre

▸▸ ***shire horse*** shire *m*

shirk [ʃɜːk] VT *(work, job, task)* éviter de faire, échapper à; *(duty)* se dérober à; *(problem, difficulty, question)* esquiver, éviter; **he always shirks doing the washing-up** il s'arrange toujours pour éviter de *ou* pour ne pas faire la vaisselle; **she doesn't s. her responsibilities** elle n'essaie pas de se dérober à ses responsabilités

VI tirer au flanc

shirker ['ʃɜːkə(r)] N tire-au-flanc *mf inv*

shirr [ʃɜː(r)] VT *Sewing* froncer

shirring ['ʃɜːrɪŋ] N *(UNCOUNT) Sewing* fronces *fpl*

shirt [ʃɜːt] N *(gen)* chemise *f*; *(footballer's, cyclist's etc)* maillot *m*; **s. collar/cuff** col *m*/manchette *f* de chemise; *Fam Fig* **keep your s. on!** ne vous énervez pas!□, du calme!□; *Br Fam Fig* **to put one's s. on sth** miser toute sa fortune sur qch□, miser jusqu'à son dernier centime sur qch□; *Fam Fig* **to lose one's s.** *(lose everything)* y laisser sa chemise, perdre tout ce qu'on a□; *Am (lose one's temper)* s'emporter□, prendre la mouche; *Fam Fig* **to take the s. off sb's back** faire cracher jusqu'à son dernier centime à qn; *Fam Fig* **he'd give you the s. off his back** il donnerait jusqu'à sa chemise

shirting ['ʃɜːtɪŋ] N shirting *m*, tissu *m* pour chemises

shirtlifter ['ʃɜːtlɪftə(r)] N *Br very Fam* tantouze *f*, tapette *f*, = terme injurieux désignant un homosexuel

shirtmaker ['ʃɜːtmeɪkə(r)] N chemisier *m (magasin)*

shirt-sleeved ADJ en manches *ou* bras de chemise

shirtsleeves ['ʃɜːtsliːvz] NPL **to be in (one's) s.** être en manches *ou* bras de chemise

shirt-tail N pan *m* de chemise

shirtwaister ['ʃɜːtˌweɪstə(r)], *Am* **shirtwaist** ['ʃɜːtweɪst] N robe *f* chemisier

shirty ['ʃɜːtɪ] (*compar* **shirtier**, *superl* **shirtiest**) ADJ *Br Fam* désagréable□; **don't get s. with me** ne te mets pas en rogne contre moi

shit [ʃɪt] (*pt & pp* **shat** [ʃæt], *cont* **shitting**) *very Fam* N **1** *(excrement)* merde *f*; **to** *Br* **have** *or Am* **take a s.** (aller) chier; **to have the shits** avoir la chiasse; **dog s.** merde *f* de chien; **tough s.!** tant pis pour ma/ta/sa/*etc* gueule!; **she thinks she's hot s.** elle ne se prend pas pour de la merde; **to kick** *or* **to beat** *or* **to knock the s. out of sb** casser la gueule à qn, défoncer la gueule à qn; **to scare the s. out of sb** foutre une trouille bleue à qn; **to bore the s. out of sb** faire crever qn d'ennui; **I don't give a s.** je m'en fous, j'en ai rien à foutre; **who gives a s.?** qu'est-ce que ça peut foutre?; **to treat sb like s.** traiter qn comme de la merde; **to be in the s.** être dans la merde; **to drop sb in the s.** foutre qn dans la merde; **when the s. hits the fan** quand nous serons dans la merde (jusqu'au cou); **to get one's s. together** se ressaisir◻; **to be up s. creek (without a paddle)** être dans une merde noire; *Vulg* **he thinks his s. doesn't stink** il se prend pas pour de la merde; **s. happens** ce sont des choses qui arrivent◻

2 *(UNCOUNT) (nonsense, rubbish)* conneries *fpl*; **I hate it when he starts on his anarchy s.** je déteste quand il se met à débiter ses conneries sur l'anarchie; **that's a load of s.!** c'est des conneries, tout ça!; **don't give me that s.!** arrête tes conneries!; **to talk s.** raconter des conneries; **he's full of s.** il dit que des conneries, il sait pas ce qu'il dit; **no s.!** sans déconner!, sans dec!

3 *(person)* ordure *f*, bâton *m* merdeux; **he's been a real s. to her** il s'est vraiment conduit en salaud avec elle

4 *Drugs slang (hashish)* shit *m*, hasch *m*, chichon *m*; *(heroin)* héro *f*, blanche *f*

5 *(anything)* **I can't see s.** j'y vois que dalle, j'y vois goutte; **he doesn't do s.** il en rame pas une, il en fout pas une rame

6 *(worthless things)* **to be a load of s.**, *Am* **to be the shits** être de la merde

7 *(useless things)* bordel *m*, foutoir *m*; **clear all that s. off your desk** vire-moi ce bordel de ton bureau

8 *(disgusting substance)* merde *f*, saloperie *f*; **I can't eat this s.** je peux pas bouffer cette merde

9 *(unfair treatment)* **to give sb s.** faire chier qn; **I don't need this s.!** j'ai pas envie de m'emmerder avec ce genre de conneries!

10 to feel/look like s. *(ill)* se sentir/avoir l'air patraque

VI 1 *(defecate)* chier **2 to s. on sb** *(treat badly)* traiter qn comme de la merde; *Br* **to s. on sb from a great height** *(treat badly)* traiter qn comme de la merde; *(defeat)* battre qn à plates coutures, écrabouiller qn **3** *Am (react with anger)* piquer une crise; *(react with surprise)* ne pas en revenir

VT 1 to s. oneself *(defecate, be scared)* chier dans son froc, *Can* chier dans ses culottes; *(react with anger)* piquer une crise; *(react with surprise)* ne pas en revenir; **to s. a brick** *or* **bricks** chier dans son froc, *Can* chier dans ses culottes **2** *Am* **to s. sb** *(lie to)* raconter des craques à qn; *(deceive)* se foutre de la gueule de qn

ADJ *(worthless)* merdique; **to feel s.** *(ill)* se sentir patraque; *(guilty)* se sentir coupable◻, avoir les boules *ou* les glandes; **I had a really s. time** j'en ai bavé; **he's a s. driver** il conduit comme un pied

ADV to be s. out of luck ne pas avoir de bol *ou* de pot

EXCLAM merde!

shite [ʃaɪt] *Br very Fam* **N 1** *(UNCOUNT) (excrement)* merde *f* **2** *(nonsense)* conneries *fpl*; **he's full of s.** il raconte que des conneries, il sait pas ce qu'il dit; **to talk s.** raconter des conneries, déconner; **that's s.!** n'importe quoi!◻; **don't believe that s.!** n'écoute pas ces conneries!

ADJ *(bad)* merdique; **to feel s.** *(ill)* se sentir patraque; *(guilty)* se sentir coupable◻, avoir les boules *ou* les glandes; **I had a really s. time** j'ai passé un moment dégueulasse; **he's a s. singer** il chante comme un pied

EXCLAM merde!

shit-faced **ADJ** *very Fam (drunk)* bourré, pété, beurré; *(on drugs)* défoncé, raide

shithead [ˈʃɪthed] **N** *very Fam (unpleasant person)* enfoiré(e) *m,f*

shithole [ˈʃɪthəʊl] **N** *very Fam (dirty place)* porcherie *f*, taudis◻ *m*; **this town's a complete s.** *(boring, ugly)* cette ville est un vrai trou

shit-hot **ADJ** *very Fam* vachement bon

shithouse [ˈʃɪthaʊs, *pl* -haʊzɪz] **N** *very Fam* chiottes *fpl*, gogues *mpl*; **built like a brick s.** bâti comme une armoire à glace◻

shitless [ˈʃɪtlɪs] **ADJ** *very Fam* **to be scared s.** avoir une trouille bleue, être mort de trouille; **to be bored s.** se faire chier à mort

shitload [ˈʃɪtləʊd] **N** *very Fam* **a s. (of)** une chiée (de)

shit-scared **ADJ** *very Fam* **to be s.** avoir une trouille bleue, être mort de trouille

shit-stirrer **N** *very Fam* fouteur(euse) *m,f* de merde

shitstorm [ˈʃɪtstɔːm] **N** *Am very Fam* foin *m*; **the announcement caused a hell of a s.** la déclaration a fait un sacré foin

shitty [ˈʃɪtɪ] *(compar* **shittier**, *superl* **shittiest)** **ADJ** *very Fam* **1** *(worthless)* merdique; **we stayed in a really s. hotel** nous sommes descendus dans un hôtel vraiment merdique **2** *(mean)* dégueulasse; **what a s. thing to do!** c'est dégueulasse de faire ça!; **to feel s.** *(ill)* se sentir patraque; *(guilty)* se sentir coupable◻, avoir les boules *ou* les glandes

shitweasel [ˈʃɪtwiːzəl] **N** *Am very Fam* ordure *f*, raclure *f*

shiv [ʃɪv] *(pt & pp* **shivved**, *cont* **shivving)** *Am Fam Crime slang* **N** *(knife)* surin *m*, lame◻ *f*

VT *(stab)* planter

shiver [ˈʃɪvə(r)] **VI 1** *(gen)* frissonner, trembler; *(with excitement)* frissonner, trembler; *(with cold, fever)* grelotter, trembler; **she shivered at the mention of his name** elle eut un frisson quand elle entendit son nom **2** *Naut (sail)* faseyer **3** *(splinter)* se fracasser, voler en éclats

VT *(break)* casser en morceaux; **s. me timbers!** = expression stéréotypée de marin, ≃ mille sabords!

N 1 *(from cold, fever, fear)* frisson *m*, tremblement *m*; *(from excitement)* frisson *m*; *Fam* **it gives me the shivers** ça me donne le frisson *ou* des frissons◻; **it sent cold shivers down my back** cela m'a fait froid dans le dos **2** *(fragment)* éclat *m*

shivering [ˈʃɪvərɪŋ] **ADJ** frissonnant; *(with cold, fever)* grelottant

N *(UNCOUNT) (gen)* frissonnement *m*; *(with cold, fever)* grelottement *m*

shivery [ˈʃɪvərɪ] **ADJ** *(from cold)* grelottant; *(frightened)* frissonnant, tremblant; *(feverish)* grelottant de fièvre; **to feel s.** avoir des frissons; **it gives you a s. feeling** cela donne le frisson

shoal [ʃəʊl] **N 1** *(of fish)* banc *m*

2 *Fig (large number)* foule *f*; **shoals of tourists** une foule de touristes

3 *(shallows)* haut-fond *m*

4 *(sandbar)* barre *f*; *(sandbank)* banc *m* de sable

shock [ʃɒk] **N 1** *(surprise)* choc *m*, surprise *f*; **she got a s. when she saw me again** ça lui a fait un choc de me revoir; **what a s. you gave me!** qu'est-ce que tu m'as fait peur!

2 *(upset)* choc *m*, coup *m*; **it's all been a bit of a s. for us** tous ces événements nous ont bouleversés; **the s. killed him** le choc l'a tué; **the news of his death came as a terrible s. to me** la nouvelle de sa mort a été un grand choc pour moi; **it came as a s. to the system to see her ex again after ten years** ça lui a fait un choc de revoir son ex au bout de dix ans; **getting up at six o'clock every morning came as a s. to the system** ça m'a fait un sacré changement de me lever à six heures tous les matins; *Fam Hum & Ironic* **s. horror!** l'horreur!; *Mil* **s. and awe** choc *m* et stupeur *f*

3 *Elec* décharge *f* (électrique); **to get a s.** recevoir *ou* prendre une décharge (électrique)

4 *(impact ▸ of armies, vehicles)* choc *m*, heurt *m*; *(vibration ▸ from explosion, earthquake)* secousse *f*

5 *Med* choc *m*; **to be in (a state of) s., to be suffering from s.** être en état de choc; **post-operative s.** choc *m* post-opératoire

6 *Fam (shock absorber)* amortisseur◻ *m*

7 *(mass)* **a s. of hair** une tignasse

COMP *(measures, argument, headline)* choc *(inv)*; *(attack)* surprise *(inv)*; *(tactics)* de choc; *(result, defeat, decision)* inattendu; **to use s. tactics** employer la manière forte

VT 1 *(surprise greatly)* stupéfier; *(upset)* bouleverser; **I was shocked to hear that she had left** j'ai été stupéfait d'apprendre qu'elle était partie; **she was deeply shocked by her daughter's death** elle a été profondément bouleversée par la mort de sa fille

2 *(offend, scandalize)* choquer, scandaliser; **his behaviour shocked them** son comportement les a choqués *ou* scandalisés; **she is easily shocked** elle se choque facilement; **I'm not easily shocked, but that book…** il en faut beaucoup pour me choquer, mais ce livre…

3 *(force)* **to s. sb into action** secouer qn pour qu'il/elle agisse; **to s. sb into doing sth** secouer qn jusqu'à ce qu'il/elle fasse qch; **the news reports shocked them out of their apathy** les bull tins d'information les ont fait sortir de leu torpeur

4 *Elec* donner une secousse *ou* un choc éle trique à

▸▸ ***shock absorber*** amortisseur *m*; *Am Fam* ***shoc jock*** = animateur ou animatrice de radio au to irrévérencieux et provocateur; ***shock therap shock treatment*** *Med* (traitement *m* par) électr choc *m*, sismothérapie *f*, *Fig* traitement *m* d choc; *Mil* ***shock troops*** troupes *fpl* de choc

shockable [ˈʃɒkəbəl] **ADJ he's easily/not easily** il se choque facilement/ne se choque pas fac lement

shocked [ʃɒkt] **ADJ 1** *(upset, distressed)* boul versé; *(stunned)* stupéfait; **there was a s. silen when…** il y eut un silence atterré lorsque… *(offended, scandalized)* choqué, scandalisé; **sh spoke in s. tones** elle parlait d'un ton scandalis

shocker [ˈʃɒkə(r)] **N** *Fam* **1** *(book)* livre *m* à se sation◻; *(film)* film *m* à sensation◻; *(news)* no velle *f* sensationnelle◻; *(play)* pièce *f* sensation◻; *(story)* histoire *f* sensationnelle◻ **that's a real s. of a story** cette histoire est vra ment choquante◻ **2** *(bad mistake)* faute énorme; *(in behaviour)* grosse bourde *f* **3** *Hu (atrocious person)* **you little s.!** petit monstre!

shocking [ˈʃɒkɪŋ] **ADJ 1** *(scandalous)* scand leux, choquant; **a s. price** un prix scandaleu **it's s. the way he behaves** son comportement es scandaleux, sa conduite est scandaleuse *(horrifying)* atroce, épouvantable; **a s. crime** u crime odieux *ou* atroce; **the s. truth about cond tions in our prisons** la terrible vérité sur les co ditions de vie dans nos prisons **3** *Fam (very ba* affreux◻, épouvantable◻; **you look s. today** tu a une mine affreuse aujourd'hui; **his room is in a state** sa chambre est dans un état épouvar table; **he's a s. actor** il est nul comme acteur

ADV *Fam* **it was raining something s.!** il fallait vo ce qu'il *ou* comme ça tombait!

▸▸ ***shocking pink*** rose *m* bonbon

shockingly [ˈʃɒkɪŋlɪ] **ADV 1** *(as intensifier)* a freusement, atrocement; **this whisky is s. exper sive** ce whisky est affreusement cher; **in s. ba taste** du dernier mauvais goût **2** *(extreme badly)* très mal, lamentablement; **he played on Saturday** il a très mal joué samedi **3** *(scar dalously ▸ behave)* scandaleusement; *(▸ trea* abominablement

shockproof [ˈʃɒkpruːf] **ADJ** résistant aux choc

shod [ʃɒd] *pt & pp of* **shoe**

shoddily [ˈʃɒdɪlɪ] **ADV 1** *(built, made)* mal *(meanly, pettily)* de façon mesquine; **they've trea ted you s.** ils ont été mesquins avec vous

shoddiness [ˈʃɒdɪnɪs] **N 1** *(poor quality)* mau vaise qualité *f* **2** *(meanness, pettiness)* mesquine rie *f*

shoddy [ˈʃɒdɪ] *(compar* **shoddier**, *superl* **shod diest)** **ADJ 1** *(of inferior quality)* de mauvaise qua lité; **s. workmanship** du travail mal fait; **a imitation** une piètre *ou* médiocre imitation *(mean, petty)* sale; **that's a s. trick to play on her** on lui a joué un sale tour!; **I want no part in tha s. affair** je ne veux pas être mêlé à cette sale a faire

shoe [ʃuː] *(pt & pp* **shod** [ʃɒd]) **N 1** *(gen)* chaussur *f*; **a pair of shoes** une paire de chaussures; **man's/woman's s.** une chaussure d'homme/d femme; **to take off one's shoes** enlever se chaussures, se déchausser; **to put on one's shoe** mettre ses chaussures, se chausser; **he wasn' wearing any shoes, he didn't have any shoes on** ne portait pas de chaussures; *Fig* **I wouldn't lik to be in his shoes** je n'aimerais pas être à s place; *Fig* **put yourself in my shoes** mettez-vou à ma place; *Fig* **to step into** *or* **to fill sb's shoe** prendre la place de qn, succéder à qn **2 (horse s.** fer *m* (à cheval)

VT 1 *(horse)* ferrer **2** *(usu passive) Literary (pe son)* chausser; **to be well shod** être bien chauss

▸▸ ***shoe box*** boîte *f* à chaussures; ***shoe cream*** c rage *m* en crème; ***shoe leather*** cuir *m* pou chaussures; **save your s. leather and take the bu** prenez l'autobus au lieu d'user vos souliers ***shoe polish*** cirage *m*; ***shoe repairer*** cordonnie (ère) *m,f*; ***shoe repairs*** cordonnerie *f*; ***shoe scrape*** gratte-pieds *m inv*; ***shoe shop*** magasin *m* de chaussures; **I was in the s. shop** j'étais chez le marchand de chaussures; ***shoe size*** pointure *f*

shoeblack ['ʃu:blæk] **N** *Old-fashioned* cireur (euse) *m,f* (de chaussures)

shoebrush ['ʃu:brʌʃ] **N** brosse *f* à chaussures

shoehorn ['ʃu:hɔ:n] **N** chausse-pied *m*
VT *Fig* **we can s. a few more in** on peut en faire tenir encore quelques-uns

shoeing ['ʃu:ɪŋ] **N** *(of horse)* ferrage *m*, ferrure *f*

shoelace ['ʃu:leɪs] **N** lacet *m* (de chaussures); **your s. is undone** ton lacet est défait

shoemaker ['ʃu:meɪkə(r)] **N** *(manufacturer)* fabricant(e) *m,f* de chaussures; *(who makes and sells shoes)* chausseur *m*; *(cobbler)* cordonnier (ère) *m,f*

shoemender ['ʃu:mendə(r)] **N** cordonnier(ère) *m,f*

shoe-polishing machine **N** machine *f* à cirer les chaussures

shoeshine ['ʃu:ʃaɪn] **N 1** *(action)* cirage *m*; **to get a s.** se faire cirer les chaussures **2** *Fam (boy)* (petit) cireur *m* (de chaussures)▫
▸▸ ***shoeshine boy*** (petit) cireur *m* (de chaussures)

shoestring ['ʃu:strɪŋ] **N 1** *Am (shoelace)* lacet *m* (de chaussure) **2** *Fam (idiom)* **on a s.** avec trois fois rien; **the film was made on a s.** c'est un film à très petit budget▫; **a s. budget** un petit budget▫

shogun ['ʃəʊgən] **N** shogoun *m*, shogun *m*

shogunal ['ʃəʊgənəl] **ADJ** shogounal, shogunal

shogunate ['ʃəʊgənət] **N** shogounat *m*, shogunat *m*

shone [ʃɒn] *pt & pp of* **shine**

shoo [ʃu:] *(pt & pp* **shooed)** **EXCLAM** *(to animal, children)* allez!, ouste!
VT chasser

▸ **shoo away, shoo off** **VT SEP** chasser

shoo-in **N** *Fam* **he's/she's a s.** il/elle gagnera à coup sûr▫; **it's a s.** c'est couru d'avance

shook [ʃʊk] *pt of* **shake**
N *Agr* gerbe *f*, botte *f*

shoot [ʃu:t] *(pt & pp* **shot** [ʃɒt]) **N 1** *Bot (young plant)* pousse *f*; *(offshoot)* rejet *m*, scion *m*; *(of vine)* sarment *m*
2 *Br Hunt (party)* partie *f* de chasse; *(land)* (terrain *m* de) chasse *f*; **he went on a pheasant s.** il est allé chasser le faisan
3 *Am (chute* ▸ *for coal, rubbish etc)* glissière *f*
4 *Cin* tournage *m*
5 *Phot* séance *f* photo, prise *f* de vues
6 *(shooting contest)* concours *m* de tir
7 *Mil* tir *m*
8 *Fam (idiom)* **the whole (bang) s.** tout le tremblement
VT 1 *(hit)* atteindre d'une balle; *(injure)* blesser par balle; *(kill)* tuer par balle; *(execute by firing squad)* fusiller; **she was shot in the arm/leg** elle a reçu une balle dans le bras/la jambe; **to s. sb through the head** tirer une balle dans la tête de qn; **she was shot through the heart** elle a été tuée d'une balle en plein cœur; **a man was shot (and killed) yesterday** un homme a été tué par balle hier; **they shot him (dead)** ils l'ont tué *ou* abattu; **to s. oneself** se tuer, se tirer une balle; *Fam* **to s. oneself in the foot** se desservir▫; *Fam Hum* **you'll get me shot** je vais me faire incendier à cause de toi
2 *(fire* ▸ *gun)* tirer un coup de; *(*▸ *bullet)* tirer; *(*▸ *arrow)* tirer, lancer, décocher; *(*▸ *rocket, dart, missile)* lancer; **they were shooting their rifles in the air** ils tiraient des coups de feu en l'air; *Fig* **to s. holes in sb's argument/case** démonter les arguments/la théorie de qn; **to s. questions at sb** bombarder *ou* mitrailler qn de questions; **to s. a glance at sb** lancer *ou* décocher un regard à qn; **she shot a shy smile at him** elle lui jeta un petit sourire timide
3 *(hunt)* chasser, tirer; **to s. grouse** chasser la grouse
4 *Cin* tourner; *Phot* prendre (en photo); **the movie was shot in Rome** le film a été tourné à Rome; **the photos were all shot in Paris** les photos ont toutes été prises à Paris; *TV & Cin* **to s. sound** effectuer une prise de son
5 *Sport & (games* ▸ *play)* jouer; *(*▸ *score)* marquer; **to s. pool** jouer au billard américain; **to s. a goal/basket** marquer un but/panier; *Golf* **he shot (a) 71 in the first round** il a fait 71 au premier tour
6 *(send)* envoyer; **the explosion shot debris high into the air** l'explosion a projeté des débris dans les airs; **to s. the ball into the net** envoyer le ballon dans les filets
7 *(go through* ▸ *rapids)* franchir; *Br (*▸ *traffic lights)* brûler; **the car shot the lights** la voiture a brûlé le feu rouge
8 *(bolt* ▸ *close)* fermer; *(*▸ *open)* ouvrir, tirer
9 *Fam (drugs)* se shooter à; **to s. heroin** se shooter à l'héroïne
10 *(idioms) Am Fam* **to s. the breeze** *or* **(the) bull** tailler une bavette, discuter le bout de gras; *Vulg* **to s. one's load** *or* **wad** *(ejaculate)* tirer son coup, décharger
VI 1 *(with gun)* tirer; **s.!** tirez!, feu!; **don't s.!** ne tirez pas!; **to s. at sb/sth** tirer sur qn/qch; **to s. on sight** tirer à vue; **to s. to kill** tirer pour tuer; **to s. into the air** tirer en l'air; *Fig* **to s. from the hip** parler franchement
2 *(hunt)* chasser; **to go shooting** aller à la chasse
3 *(go fast)* **to s. in/past** entrer/passer en trombe; **she shot across the road** elle a traversé la rue comme une flèche; **he shot ahead of the other runners** il a rapidement distancé les autres coureurs; **she shot along the corridor** elle a couru à toutes jambes le long du couloir; **the rabbit shot into its burrow** le lapin s'est précipité dans son terrier; **debris shot into the air** des débris ont été projetés en l'air; **Paul has shot ahead at school recently** Paul a fait d'énormes progrès à l'école ces derniers temps; **a violent pain shot up my leg** j'ai senti une violente douleur dans la jambe; **I've got pains shooting through my shoulder** j'ai des élancements dans l'épaule
4 *Cin* tourner; **s.!** moteur!, on tourne!; **we'll begin shooting next week** nous commencerons à tourner la semaine prochaine
5 *Sport* tirer, shooter
6 *Bot (sprout)* pousser; *(bud)* bourgeonner
7 *Fam (go ahead, speak)* **can I ask you something? – s.!** je peux te poser une question? – vas-y!▫
8 *Am* **to s. for** *or* **at** *(aim for)* viser
EXCLAM *Am Fam* zut!, mince!

▸ **shoot back** **VI 1** *(fire back)* riposter; **a sniper shot at them and they shot back at him** un tireur isolé leur a tiré dessus et ils ont riposté **2** *(return quickly)* revenir à toute vitesse
VT SEP *(retort)* répliquer, riposter; **the candidate shot back his answers** le candidat répondait du tac au tac

▸ **shoot down** **VT SEP** *(person, plane, helicopter)* abattre; *also Fig* **to s. sb/sth down in flames** descendre qn/qch en flammes; *Fam* **my proposal was shot down by the chairman** ma proposition a été démolie par le président

▸ **shoot off** **VT SEP 1** *(weapon)* tirer, décharger; **they shot off their rifles to celebrate their victory** ils ont tiré des coups de feu en l'air pour fêter la victoire; **she shot off a few rounds into the darkness** elle a tiré dans le noir **2** *(limb)* emporter, arracher **3** *very Fam (idiom)* **to s. one's mouth off** parler à tort et à travers▫; **I'd told him not to tell anyone but he had to go and s. his mouth off** je lui avais dit de n'en parler à personne mais il a fallu qu'il ouvre sa grande gueule; **don't go shooting your mouth off about it** ne va pas le gueuler sur les toits
VI 1 *(leave quickly)* s'enfuir à toutes jambes; **he shot off down the alley** il s'est enfui à toutes jambes dans la ruelle **2** *Vulg (ejaculate)* décharger

▸ **shoot out** **VT SEP 1** *(extend quickly* ▸ *sparks etc)* lancer; **the snake shot out its tongue** le serpent a dardé sa langue; **she shot out a hand** elle a étendu le bras d'un geste vif **2** *(use gun, destroy with gunshots* ▸ *light, window)* tirer dans; **the robbers tried to s. their way out** les voleurs tentèrent de se sauver en tirant des coups de feu; *Fam* **to s. it out (with sb)** s'expliquer (avec qn) à coups de revolver *ou* de fusil
VI *(emerge quickly* ▸ *water, flames)* jaillir; **the water shot out of the hose** l'eau a jailli du tuyau d'arrosage; **the car shot out in front of us** *(changed lanes)* la voiture a déboîté tout d'un coup devant nous; *(from another street)* la voiture a débouché devant nous

▸ **shoot through** **VI** *Br Fam (leave)* se tirer, mettre les bouts

▸ **shoot up** **VI 1** *(move skywards* ▸ *flame, geyser, lava)* jaillir; *(*▸ *rocket)* monter en flèche
2 *(increase* ▸ *inflation, price)* monter en flèche
3 *(grow* ▸ *plant)* pousser rapidement *ou* vite; *(*▸ *person)* grandir; **you've really shot up since I last saw you!** qu'est-ce que tu as grandi depuis que je t'ai vu la dernière fois!
4 *Fam (take drugs)* se shooter, se piquer
VT SEP 1 *Fam (with weapon)* **they shot up the saloon/town** ils ont terrorisé tout le monde dans le saloon/la ville en tirant plein de coups de feu; **he was badly shot up in the war** il a été sérieusement blessé à la guerre▫; **he's been shot up** il a reçu des balles (dans la peau) **2** *Fam (drug)* se faire un shoot de; *(habitually)* se shooter à, se piquer à

shoot-'em-up **N** *Fam* = film ou jeu vidéo ultraviolent

shooter ['ʃu:tə(r)] **N 1** *Fam (gun)* flingue *m*, feu *m* **2** *(drink)* = cocktail servi dans un petit verre

shooting ['ʃu:tɪŋ] **N 1** *(UNCOUNT) (firing)* coups *mpl* de feu, fusillade *f*; **we heard s.** nous avons entendu des coups de feu
2 *(incident)* fusillade *f*; *(killing)* meurtre *m*; **there have been several shootings in the area** plusieurs personnes ont été abattues dans le secteur
3 *(ability to shoot)* tir *m*; **he's useless at s.** il tire mal
4 *(sport* ▸ *at targets)* tir *m*; *Br (*▸ *at birds, animals)* chasse *f*; **I've done a lot of s.** j'ai beaucoup chassé
5 *Cin* tournage *m*; **s. starts next week on her new movie** le tournage de son nouveau film commence la semaine prochaine
COMP 1 *(with weapon)* **s. practice** entraînement *m* au tir **2** *Hunt* de chasse; **the s. season** la saison de la chasse
ADJ *(pain)* lancinant
▸▸ *Br Aut* ***shooting brake*** break *m*; ***shooting gallery*** **1** *(at fairground)* stand *m* de tir **2** *Am Fam Drugs slang (for buying drugs)* = lieu où l'on achète, vend et consomme de la drogue; ***shooting match*** concours *m* de tir; *Hunt* ***shooting party*** partie *f* de chasse; ***shooting range*** champ *m* de tir; *Cin* ***shooting script*** découpage *m*; ***shooting star*** étoile *f* filante

shoot-out **N** *Fam* fusillade▫*f*

shop [ʃɒp] *(pt & pp* **shopped**, *cont* **shopping)** **N 1** *Br (store)* magasin *m*; *(smaller)* boutique *f*; **she's gone out to the shops** elle est sortie faire des courses; **to have** *or* **to keep a s.** être propriétaire d'un magasin, tenir un magasin; **you can't get these in the shops** on ne les trouve pas en magasin; **at the baker's s.** à la boulangerie, chez le boulanger; **at the fruit s.** chez le marchand de fruits, chez le fruitier, à la fruiterie; **the new book should reach the shops in July** le nouveau livre devrait être en vente en juillet; **to set up s.** ouvrir un magasin; *Fig* s'établir, s'installer; **he's set up s. as a freelance translator** il s'est installé comme traducteur indépendant; *also Fig* **to shut up s.** fermer boutique; *Fam* **all over the s.** *(everywhere)* partout▫; *(in disorder)* en pagaille; *Fam* **my notes are all over the s.** c'est la pagaille dans mes notes; *Fam* **they're all over the s. on defence policy** leur politique de défense n'est absolument pas cohérente▫; *Fam Fig* **you've come to the wrong s.** vous vous trompez de porte; **to talk s.** parler boutique **2** *(shopping trip)* **to do one's weekly s.** faire les courses *ou* les achats de la semaine **3** *Br (workshop)* atelier *m*; **the repair/paint/assembly s.** l'atelier *m* de réparations/de peinture/de montage
VI *(for food, necessities)* faire les *ou* ses courses; *(for clothes, gifts etc)* faire les magasins, faire du shopping, *Can* magasiner; **I always s. at the local supermarket** je fais toujours mes courses *ou* mes achats au supermarché du coin; **to go shopping** faire des courses, courir les magasins; **I went shopping for a new dress** je suis allée faire les magasins *ou Can* magasiner pour m'acheter une nouvelle robe
VT *Br Fam (inform on)* dénoncer▫, balancer
▸▸ *Br* ***shop assistant*** vendeur(euse) *m,f* (de magasin), employé(e) *m,f* de magasin; ***shop floor***

(place) atelier *m*; ***the shop floor*** *(workers)* les ouvriers *mpl*; **he was on the s. floor for 22 years** il a travaillé 22 ans comme ouvrier; ***shop foreman*** chef *m* d'atelier; *Br* ***shop front*** devanture *f*; ***shop steward*** porte-parole *mf inv* des ouvriers, délégué(e) *m,f* syndical(e); ***shop window*** vitrine *f* (de magasin); *Fig* **a s. window for British exports** une vitrine pour les exportations britanniques

▸**shop around** **VI** comparer les prix; **I shopped around before opening a bank account** j'ai comparé plusieurs banques *ou* je me suis renseigné auprès de plusieurs banques avant d'ouvrir un compte; **our company is shopping around for new premises** notre société est à la recherche de nouveaux locaux

shopaholic [ˌʃɒpəˈhɒlɪk] **N he's a real s.** il adore faire les boutiques

shopfitter [ˈʃɒpfɪtə(r)] **N** *Br* décorateur(trice) *m,f* de magasins

shopgirl [ˈʃɒpgɜːl] **N** *Br Old-fashioned* vendeuse *f*

shopkeeper [ˈʃɒpkiːpə(r)] **N** *Br* commerçant(e) *m,f*

shoplifter [ˈʃɒplɪftə(r)] **N** voleur(euse) *m,f* à l'étalage

shoplifting [ˈʃɒplɪftɪŋ] **N** vol *m* à l'étalage

shopman [ˈʃɒpmən] *(pl* **shopmen** [-men]) **N** *Am* mécanicien *m (dans un atelier de réparations)*

shopper [ˈʃɒpə(r)] **N 1** *(person)* personne *f* qui fait ses courses; **the streets were crowded with Christmas shoppers** les rues étaient bondées de gens qui faisaient leurs courses pour Noël **2** *(shopping bag)* cabas *m*, sac *m* à provisions

shopping [ˈʃɒpɪŋ] **N** *(UNCOUNT)* **1** *(for food, necessities)* courses *fpl*; *(for clothes, gifts etc)* courses *fpl*, shopping *m*, *Can* magasinage *m*; **I do all the s.** c'est moi qui fais toutes les courses; **we're going into town to do some s.** nous allons en ville pour faire des courses *ou* pour faire le tour des magasins; **this area is good for s.** ce quartier est bon pour faire les courses; **to do a bit of s.** faire quelques (petites) courses *ou* emplettes; **to do one's Christmas s.** faire ses achats de Noël; **there is late-night s. on Thursdays** les magasins restent ouverts tard le jeudi **2** *(goods bought)* achats *mpl*, courses *fpl*, emplettes *fpl*; **there were bags of s. everywhere** il y avait des cabas remplis de provisions partout

COMP *(street, area)* commerçant; **my weekly s. trip** mes courses *fpl* hebdomadaires; **there are only three s. days to Christmas** il ne reste plus que trois jours pour faire les courses avant Noël

▸▸ ***shopping arcade*** galerie *f* marchande; ***shopping bag*** sac *m ou* filet *m* à provisions, cabas *m*; ***shopping basket*** panier *m* (à provisions); *Econ* panier *m* de la ménagère; *Comput (for Internet shopping)* caddie *m*; *Am* ***shopping cart*** chariot *m*, Caddie® *m*; *Comput (for Internet shopping)* caddie *m*; ***shopping centre*** centre *m* commercial; *TV* ***shopping channel*** chaîne *f* de téléachat; ***shopping list*** liste *f* des courses; *Am* ***shopping mall*** galerie *f* marchande; ***shopping plaza*** centre *m* commercial; *Br* ***shopping precinct*** centre *m* commercial; *Br* ***shopping trolley*** chariot *m*, Caddie® *m*

shopsoiled [ˈʃɒpsɔɪld] **ADJ** *Br also Fig* défraîchi

shoptalk [ˈʃɒptɔːk] **N all I ever hear from you is s.** tu ne fais que parler boutique *ou* travail

shopwalker [ˈʃɒpwɔːkə(r)] **N** *Br* = dans un grand magasin, personne chargée de renseigner les clients et de surveiller le travail des vendeurs

shopworn [ˈʃɒpwɔːn] **ADJ** *Am also Fig* défraîchi

shore [ʃɔː(r)] **N 1** *(edge, side ▸ of sea)* rivage *m*, bord *m*; *(▸ of lake, river)* rive *f*, rivage *m*, bord *m*; *(coast)* côte *f*, littoral *m*; **the shores of the Mediterranean** les rivages *mpl* de la Méditerranée **2** *(dry land)* terre *f*; **all the crew members are on s.** tous les membres de l'équipage sont à terre; **to go on s.** débarquer **3** *(prop)* étai *m*, étançon *m*

VT étayer, étançonner

• **shores** **NPL** *Literary (country)* rives *fpl*; **he was one of the first Europeans to set foot on these shores** il fut l'un des premiers Européens à poser le pied sur ces rives; **this bird is a rare visitor to these shores** on observe rarement cet oiseau dans nos contrées

▸▸ ***shore excursion*** excursion *f (lors d'une escale)*; ***shore leave*** permission *f* à terre

▸**shore up** **VT SEP** *Br* **1** *(prop up)* étayer, étançonner **2** *Fig* soutenir; **the army shored up the crumbling dictatorship** l'armée a maintenu au pouvoir la dictature qui s'effondrait; **the government must act to s. up the pound** le gouvernement doit prendre des mesures visant à soutenir la livre

shoreline [ˈʃɔːlaɪn] **N** littoral *m*

shoreward [ˈʃɔːwəd] **ADJ** *(near the shore)* près du rivage *ou* de la côte; *(facing the shore)* face au rivage *ou* à la côte

ADV vers le rivage *ou* la côte

shorewards [ˈʃɔːwədz] **ADV** vers le rivage *ou* la côte

shorn [ʃɔːn] *pp of* **shear**

ADJ 1 *(head, hair)* tondu **2** *Fig* **s. of** dépouillé de

SHORT [ʃɔːt]

N	
• court-métrage **1**	• alcool fort **2**
• court-circuit **3**	
ADJ	
• court **1, 3, 4**	• petit **2, 3**
• bref **4, 10**	• brusque **6, 7**
ADV	
• net **1**	
NPL	
• short	

N 1 *Cin* court-métrage *m*

2 *Br (drink)* alcool *m* fort

3 *Fam Elec* court-circuit ◻ *m*

ADJ 1 *(in length)* court; **her dress is too s./shorter than yours** sa robe est trop courte/plus courte que la tienne; **to have s. hair** avoir les cheveux courts; *Fam Fig* **to have sb by the s. hairs** *or Br* **by the s. and curlies** avoir qn à sa merci ◻, pouvoir faire ce qu'on veut de qn ◻; **to be s. in the leg** *(trousers)* être court; **it's s. in the arms** *(jacket)* les manches sont trop courtes; **skirts are getting shorter and shorter** les jupes raccourcissent de plus en plus *ou* sont de plus en plus courtes; **the editor made the article shorter by a few hundred words** le rédacteur a raccourci l'article de quelques centaines de mots; **a s. history of France** un précis d'histoire de France; **s. and to the point** bref et précis; **to be in s. trousers** être en culottes courtes; **s. back and sides** *(haircut)* coupe *f* dégagée sur la nuque et les oreilles

2 *(in height ▸ person)* petit, de petite taille; **he's s. and stocky** il est petit et râblé

3 *(in distance ▸ gen)* court; *(▸ walk)* petit, court; **what's the shortest way home?** quel est le chemin le plus court pour rentrer?; **we took the shortest route** nous avons pris le chemin le plus court; **to go for a s. walk** faire une petite promenade; **a few s. miles away** à quelques kilomètres de là à peine; **at s. range** à courte portée; **it's only a s. distance from here** ce n'est pas très loin (d'ici); **she lives a s. distance from the church** elle n'habite pas très loin de l'église; **they continued for a s. distance** ils ont poursuivi un peu leur chemin

4 *(not lasting long ▸ period, interval)* court, bref; **a s. stay** un court séjour; **you should take a s. holiday** vous devriez prendre quelques jours de vacances; **we've just got time for a s. game** nous avons juste le temps de faire une petite partie; **after a s. time** après un court intervalle *ou* un petit moment; **to have a s. memory** avoir la mémoire courte; **she was in London for a s. time** elle a passé quelque temps à Londres; **I met him a s. time** *or* **while later** je l'ai rencontré peu (de temps) après; **it's rather s. notice to invite them for tonight** c'est un peu juste pour les inviter ce soir; **time's getting s.** il ne reste plus beaucoup de temps; **a few s. hours/years ago** il y a à peine quelques heures/années; **the days are getting shorter** les jours raccourcissent; **to demand shorter hours/a shorter working week** exiger une réduction des heures de travail/une réduction du temps de travail hebdomadaire; **to be on s. time** faire des journées réduites; **she made a s. speech** elle a fait un court *ou* petit discours; **he read out a s. statement** il a lu une courte *ou* brève déclaration; **I'd just like to say a few s. words** j'aimerais dire quelques mots très brefs; **the s. answer is "no"** en deux mots, la réponse est "non"; **in s. order** en vitesse; **he dealt with the naughty children in s. order** il a eu vite fait de s'occuper de ces enfants désobéissants; **to be s. and sweet** être bref; **I'll keep it s. and sweet** je serai bref; *Ironic* **her stay with us was s. and sweet** heureusement, son séjour chez nous fut de courte durée; **in the s. run** à court terme

5 *(abbreviated)* **HF is s. for high frequency** HF est l'abréviation de haute fréquence; **Bill is s. for William** Bill est un diminutif de William

6 *(gruff)* brusque, sec (sèche); **Mary was very s. with me on the telephone** Mary a été très sèche avec moi au téléphone; **to have a s. temper** être irascible, s'emporter facilement

7 *(sudden ▸ sound, action)* brusque; **her breath came in s. gasps** elle avait le souffle court; **he gave a s. laugh** il eut un rire bref; **s., sharp shock** = punition sévère mais de courte durée; *Br* **s., sharp shock treatment** = régime pénal des années 80–90 où les jeunes délinquants étaient détenus pour une courte période dans des conditions très sévères destinées à décourager la récidive

8 *(lacking, insufficient)* **to give sb s. weight** ne pas donner le bon poids à qn; **money is s.** on manque d'argent, l'argent manque; **whisky is in s. supply** on manque *ou* on est à court de whisky; **it's 2 euros s.** il manque 2 euros; **I'm 5 euros s.** il me manque 5 euros; **to be s. of breath** *(in general)* avoir le souffle court; *(at the moment)* être hors d'haleine; **to be s. of staff** manquer de personnel; **I'm a bit s. (of money) at the moment** je suis un peu à court (d'argent) en ce moment; **he's a bit s. on imagination** il manque un peu d'imagination; *Fam Hum* **he's one sandwich s. of a picnic** il a une case vide

9 *Br (drink)* **a s. drink** un petit verre

10 *Ling* bref

11 *Fin & St Exch (sale, seller)* à découvert; **bills at s. date** billets *mpl ou* traites *fpl* à courte échéance

12 *(in betting ▸ odds)* faible

ADV 1 *(abruptly)* **to stop s.** s'arrêter net; **the driver stopped s. just in front of the child** le conducteur s'arrêta net juste devant l'enfant; **to stop s. of doing sth** se retenir de faire qch; **she stopped s. of actually calling him a liar** pour un peu, elle le traitait de menteur; **to pull** *or* **to bring sb up s.** couper qn dans son élan

2 *(idioms)* **to fall s. of** *(objective, target)* ne pas atteindre; *(expectations)* ne pas répondre à; **his winnings fell far s. of what he had expected** ses gains ont été bien moindres que ce à quoi il s'attendait; **to go s. of sth** manquer de qch; **my children never went s. (of anything)** mes enfants n'ont jamais manqué de rien; **I don't want you to go s.** je ne veux pas que tu manques de quoi que ce soit; **to run s. (of sth)** être à court (de qch); **we're running s. of fuel/sugar** nous sommes presque à court de carburant/de sucre; **time is running s.** le temps commence à manquer; *Br Fam* **to be taken** *or* **caught s.** être pris d'un besoin pressant ◻

3 *St Exch* **to buy s.** acheter à court terme; **to sell s.** vendre à découvert

VT *Elec* court-circuiter

VI *Elec* se mettre en court-circuit

• **for short** **ADV they call him Ben for s.** on l'appelle Ben pour faire plus court; **trinitrotoluene, or TNT for s.** le trinitrotoluène, ou TNT en abrégé

• **in short** **ADV** (en) bref

• **short of** **PREP 1** *(except)* sauf; **he would do anything s. of stealing** il ferait tout sauf voler; **nothing s. of a miracle can save him now** seul un miracle pourrait le sauver maintenant

2 *(less than)* **they were £50 s. of their target** il leur manquait 50 livres pour atteindre la somme qu'ils s'étaient fixée; **it is little s. of folly** c'est de la folie (pure); **it was nothing s. of a masterpiece** ce n'était rien moins qu'un chef-d'œuvre

• **shorts** **NPL** *(short trousers)* short *m*; *(underpants)* caleçon *m*; **a pair of shorts** un kaki

▸▸ *Fin & St Exch* ***short bills*** billets *mpl ou* traites *fpl* à courte échéance; ***short break*** *(holiday)* mini-séjour *m*; *Elec* ***short circuit*** court-circuit *m*; *Fin & St Exch* ***short investment*** investissement *m* à court terme; *Fin & St Exch* ***short loan*** prêt *m* à court terme; *Culin* ***short pastry*** pâte *f* brisée; *Fin* ***short payment*** moins-perçu *m*; *Fin & St Exch* ***short***

position position *f* vendeur, position *f* à découvert; *St Exch* ***short sale*** vente *f* à découvert; *Literature* ***short story*** nouvelle *f*; ***short tennis*** tennis *m* pour enfants; ***short ton*** tonne *f* (américaine), short ton *f*; *Ling* ***short vowel*** voyelle *f* brève; *Rad* ***short wave*** onde *f* courte; **on s. wave** sur ondes courtes

shortage [ˈʃɔːtɪdʒ] N *(of labour, resources, materials)* manque *m*, pénurie *f*; *(of money)* manque *m*; **a petrol s., a s. of petrol** une pénurie d'essence; **the housing/energy s.** la crise du logement/de l'énergie; **food s.** disette *f*, pénurie *f* de vivres; **there's no s. of good restaurants in this part of town** les bons restaurants ne manquent pas dans ce quartier

short-arse N *Br very Fam* rase-bitume *mf inv*, bas-du-cul *mf inv*

shortbread [ˈʃɔːtbred] N *Culin* sablé *m*
▸▸ *Br* ***shortbread biscuit*** sablé *m*

short-change VT **1** to s. sb ne pas rendre assez (de monnaie) à qn **2** *Fam (swindle)* rouler, escroquer

short-circuit VT *Elec & Fig* court-circuiter
VI *Elec* se mettre en court-circuit

shortcode [ˈʃɔːtkəʊd] N *Tel* code *m* abrégé
▸▸ ***shortcode dialling*** numérotation *f* abrégée

shortcoming [ˈʃɔːtkʌmɪŋ] N défaut *m*

shortcrust pastry [ˈʃɔːtkrʌst-] N *Culin* pâte *f* brisée

shortcut [ˈʃɔːtkʌt] N raccourci *m*; **to take a s.** prendre un raccourci; *Fig* **there are no shortcuts** il n'y a pas moyen d'aller plus vite
▸▸ *Comput* ***shortcut key*** touche *f* de raccourci

short-dated ADJ *Fin (bill)* à courte échéance; *(paper)* court

shorten [ˈʃɔːtən] VT **1** *(in length ▸ garment, string)* raccourcir; *(▸ text, article, speech)* raccourcir, abréger; **the name James is often shortened to Jim** Jim est un diminutif courant de James **2** *(in time)* écourter; **we had to s. our trip** nous avons dû écourter notre voyage; **the new railway line will s. the journey time to London** la nouvelle ligne de chemin de fer réduira le temps de trajet jusqu'à Londres
VI *(gen)* (se) raccourcir

shortening [ˈʃɔːtənɪŋ] N **1** *Culin* matière *f* grasse **2** *(of garment, string)* raccourcissement *m*; *(of text, speech)* raccourcissement *m*, abrègement *m*; *(of time, distance)* réduction *f*

shortfall [ˈʃɔːtfɔːl] N insuffisance *f*, manque *m*; **there's a s. of $100** il manque 100 dollars

short-focus lens N *Phot* objectif *m* à courte focale

short-haired ADJ *(person)* aux cheveux courts; *(animal)* à poil ras

shorthand [ˈʃɔːthænd] N sténographie *f*, sténo *f*; **to take notes in s.** prendre des notes en sténo; *Fig* **this term has become s. for corruption** ce terme est devenu synonyme de corruption
▸▸ ***shorthand typing*** sténodactylographie *f*; ***shorthand typist*** sténodactylo *mf*

shorthanded [ˌʃɔːtˈhændɪd] ADJ à court de personnel; **we're very s. at the moment** nous sommes vraiment à court *ou* nous manquons vraiment de personnel en ce moment

short-haul ADJ *(flight, route, aircraft)* court-courrier
▸▸ ***short-haul aircraft*** court-courrier *m*

shorthorn [ˈʃɔːthɔːn] N *Zool* shorthorn *m (race de bovins)*

shortish [ˈʃɔːtɪʃ] ADJ *(in length)* plutôt court; *(in height)* plutôt petit; *(in time)* plutôt court *ou* bref

short-legged ADJ aux jambes courtes

shortlist [ˈʃɔːtlɪst] *Br* N liste *f* de candidats présélectionnés
VT présélectionner; **five candidates have been shortlisted** cinq candidats ont été présélectionnés; **you've been shortlisted** on a retenu votre candidature

short-lived [-ˈlɪvd] ADJ *(gen)* de courte durée, éphémère, bref; *(animal, species)* éphémère

shortly [ˈʃɔːtlɪ] ADV **1** *(soon)* bientôt; *(in a couple of minutes)* sous peu; **I'll join you s.** je vous rejoindrai bientôt; **s. afterwards** peu (de temps) après **2** *(gruffly)* sèchement, brusquement

> Attention: ne pas confondre avec **briefly**.

shortness [ˈʃɔːtnɪs] N **1** *(in length)* manque *m* de longueur; *(in height)* petite taille *f* **2** *(in time, of speech, of essay)* brièveté *f* **3** *(abruptness)* brusquerie *f*

short-range ADJ **1** *(weapon)* de courte portée **2** *(prediction, outlook)* à court terme

shortsighted [ˌʃɔːtˈsaɪtɪd] ADJ **1** *(myopic)* myope **2** *Fig (person)* qui manque de perspicacité *ou* de prévoyance; *(plan, policy)* à courte vue; **I find their attitude extremely s.** je trouve qu'ils font preuve d'un manque total de prévoyance

shortsightedness [ˌʃɔːtˈsaɪtɪdnɪs] N **1** *(myopia)* myopie *f* **2** *Fig* myopie *f*, manque *m* de perspicacité *ou* de prévoyance

short-staffed [-ˈstɑːft] ADJ à court de personnel; **we're a bit s.** nous sommes un peu à court de *ou* nous manquons un peu de personnel

short-stay ADJ
▸▸ ***short-stay car park*** parking *m* courte durée; ***short-stay patient*** patient(e) *m,f* hospitalisé(e) pour une courte durée

short-tempered ADJ irascible, irritable

short-term ADJ *(solution, memory)* à court terme; *(contract)* de courte durée; *(prisoner)* qui purge une peine de prison de courte durée
▸▸ ***short-term borrowings*** emprunts *mpl* à court terme; ***short-term contract*** contrat *m* à courte durée; ***short-term loan*** prêt *m* à court terme; ***short-term planning*** planification *f* à court terme; ***short-term unemployment*** chômage *m* à court terme

short-termism [-ˈtɜːmɪzəm] N *Br* politique *f* du court terme

short-time N **to be on s.** être en chômage partiel
ADJ **to be on s. working** être en chômage partiel

short-wave ADJ *(radio)* à ondes courtes; *(programme, broadcasting)* sur ondes courtes

short-winded [-ˈwɪndɪd] ADJ au souffle court; **to be s.** manquer de souffle

shorty [ˈʃɔːtɪ] *(pl* **shorties***)* N *Fam* rase-bitume *mf inv*, bas-du-cul *mf*; **hey, s.!** hé, rase-bitume!

shot [ʃɒt] *pt & pp of* **shoot**
N **1** *(instance of firing)* coup *m* (de feu); **he fired four shots** il a tiré quatre coups de feu; **to have** *or* **to fire** *or* **to take a s. at sth** tirer sur qch; *also Fig* **a s. across the bows** un coup de semonce; *Fig* **it was a s. in the dark** j'ai/il a/*etc* dit ça au hasard; *Fam* **to do sth like a s.** *(speedily)* faire qch à tout berzingue; *(with no hesitation)* faire qch sans hésiter; *Fam* **the dog was off like a s.** le chien est parti comme une flèche; *Fam* **would you marry him? – like a s.!** est-ce que tu l'épouserais? – sans hésiter *ou* et comment!
2 *(sound of gun)* coup *m* de feu; **I was woken by a s.** j'ai été réveillé par un coup de feu
3 *(UNCOUNT) (shotgun pellets)* plomb *m*, plombs *mpl*
4 *(marksman)* tireur(euse) *m,f*, fusil *m*; **she's a good/poor s.** elle tire bien/mal
5 *Sport (at goal ▸ in football, hockey etc)* tir *m*; *(stroke ▸ in tennis, cricket, billiards etc)* coup *m*; *(throw ▸ in darts)* lancer *m*; **each player has three shots** chaque joueur joue trois fois; **good s.!** bien joué!; **to call the shots** mener le jeu
6 *Sport* **to put the s.** lancer le poids
7 *Phot* photo *f*; *Cin* plan *m*, prise *f* de vue; **you can get a good s. of the castle from here** d'ici vous prendrez bien le château
8 *Fam (try)* tentative *f*, essai *m*; **I'd like to have a s. at it** j'aimerais tenter le coup; **it's worth a s.** ça vaut le coup; **give it your best s.** fais pour le mieux
9 *Fam (injection)* piqûre *f*; **tetanus s.** piqûre *f* antitétanique; *Fig* **a s. in the arm** un coup de fouet
10 *(drink)* (petit) verre *m*; **a s. of vodka** un petit verre de vodka
ADJ **1** *Br (rid) Fam* **to get s. of sb/sth** se débarrasser de qn/qch; **I'll be glad to be s. of them** je serai content d'en être débarrassé; **I can't wait to be s. of this house** j'ai hâte de me débarrasser de cette maison **2** *(streaked)* strié; **her dress was of a deep red s. through with gold** sa robe était rouge foncé avec des stries dorées; *Fig* **the book is s. through with subtle irony** le livre est plein d'une ironie subtile **3** *esp Am Fam (exhausted)* épuisé, crevé; *(broken, spoilt)* fichu, bousillé; **my nerves are s.** je suis à bout de nerfs
▸▸ ***shot glass*** petit verre *m*; *Cin & TV* ***shot list*** liste *f* des prises de vue; *Sport* ***shot put*** lancer *m* du poids; *Sport* ***shot putter*** lanceur(euse) *m,f* de poids; *Sport* ***shot putting*** (lancer *m* du) poids *m*; *Tex* ***shot silk*** soie *f* changeante

shotgun [ˈʃɒtgʌn] N *(weapon)* fusil *m* de chasse
ADV *Am* **to ride s.** voyager comme passager
▸▸ ***shotgun wedding*** mariage *m* forcé *(lorsque la future mariée est enceinte)*

SHOULD [ʃʊd]

> La forme négative **should not** s'écrit **shouldn't** en forme contractée.

MODAL AUX V **1** *(indicating duty, necessity)* **I s. be working, not talking to you** je devrais être en train de travailler au lieu de parler avec vous; **papers s. not exceed ten pages** les devoirs ne devront pas dépasser dix pages; **you really s. call her, you know** tu devrais l'appeler, tu sais
2 *(indicating likelihood)* **they s. have arrived by now** ils devraient être arrivés maintenant; **I s. have finished the work yesterday** j'aurais dû finir ce travail hier; **the election results s. be out soon** on devrait bientôt connaître les résultats des élections
3 *(indicating what is acceptable, desirable etc)* **I s. never have married him** je n'aurais jamais dû l'épouser; **a present? oh, you shouldn't have!** un cadeau? vous n'auriez pas dû *ou* il ne fallait pas!; **you shouldn't laugh at him** vous avez tort de vous moquer de lui; **you s. have seen the state of the house!** si tu avais vu dans quel état était la maison!; **you s. hear the way he talks!** il faut voir comment il s'exprime!; **s. he tell her? – yes he s.** est-ce qu'il devrait le lui dire? – oui, sans aucun doute; **I'm very sorry – and so you s. be!** je suis vraiment désolé – il y a de quoi!; **why shouldn't I enjoy myself now and then?** pourquoi est-ce que je n'aurais pas le droit de m'amuser de temps en temps?; **I don't remember – well you s.** je ne m'en souviens pas – eh bien tu devrais; **I didn't want to, but he told me I s.** je ne voulais pas, mais il m'a dit que je devais le faire; **I s. perhaps say, at this point, that...** à ce stade, je devrais peut-être dire que... + *indicative*
4 *(forming conditional tense) (would)* **I s. like to meet your parents** j'aimerais rencontrer vos parents; **I shouldn't be surprised if they got married** cela ne m'étonnerait pas qu'ils se marient; **I s. say** *or* **think it costs about £50** je dirais que ça coûte dans les 50 livres; **I s. have thought the answer was obvious** j'aurais pensé que la réponse était évidente; **s. you be interested, I know a good hotel there** si cela vous intéresse, je connais un bon hôtel là-bas; **how s. I know?** comment voulez-vous que je le sache?; **I s. think so/not!** j'espère bien/bien que non!
5 *(were to ▸ indicating hypothesis, speculation)* **if I s. forget, s. I forget** si (jamais) j'oublie; **I'll be upstairs s. you need me** je serai en haut si (jamais) vous avez besoin de moi; **s. the occasion arise** le cas échéant
6 *(after "that" and in expressions of feeling, opinion etc)* **it's strange (that) she s. do that** c'est bizarre qu'elle fasse cela; **I'm anxious that she s. come** je tiens à ce qu'elle vienne
7 *(after "who" or "what") (expressing surprise)* **and who s. I meet but Betty!** et sur qui je tombe? Betty!
8 *Fam Ironic (needn't)* **he s. worry (about money), he owns half of Manhattan!** tu parles qu'il a des soucis d'argent, la moitié de Manhattan lui appartient!

shoulda [ˈʃʊdə] *Fam* = **should have**

shoulder [ˈʃəʊldə(r)] N **1** *(part of body, of garment)* épaule *f*; **he's got broad shoulders** il est large d'épaules; **round shoulders** dos *m* rond *ou* voûté; **she put an arm around my s.** elle mit son bras autour de mon épaule; **slung across** *or* **over the s.** *(bag, rifle etc)* en bandoulière; **you can carry it over your s.** tu peux le porter en bandoulière;

put a jacket over your shoulders mets une veste sur tes épaules; **I looked over my s.** j'ai jeté un coup d'œil derrière moi; **it's a heavy burden to place on his shoulders** c'est une lourde charge à mettre sur ses épaules; *Fig* **to cry on sb's s.** pleurer sur l'épaule de qn; **we all need a s. to cry on** nous avons tous besoin d'une épaule pour pleurer; **to have a good head on one's shoulders** avoir la tête sur les épaules; *Fig* **to put one's s. to the wheel** s'atteler à la tâche; **s. to s.** coude à coude

2 *Culin* épaule *f*; **s. of lamb** épaule *f* d'agneau

3 *(along road)* accotement *m*, bas-côté *m*

4 *(of hill, mountain)* replat *m*

VT 1 *(pick up)* charger sur son épaule; **she shouldered the heavy load** elle chargea le lourd fardeau sur son épaule; *Mil* **to s. arms** se mettre au port d'armes; *Mil* **s. arms!** portez armes! **2** *Fig (take on ▸ blame)* assumer; *(▸ responsibility)* endosser, assumer; *(▸ cost)* faire face à **3** *(push)* pousser (de l'épaule); **he shouldered me aside** il m'écarta d'un coup d'épaule; **I shouldered my way through the crowd** je me suis frayé un chemin à travers la foule (en jouant des épaules)

▸▸ ***shoulder bag*** sac *m* à bandoulière; ***shoulder belt*** ceinture *f* épaulière; ***shoulder blade*** omoplate *f*; *(of horse)* paleron *m*; *Mil* ***shoulder braid*** fourragère *f*; ***shoulder charge*** charge *f* épaule contre épaule; *Am Mil* ***shoulder loop*** patte *f* d'épaule, épaulette *f*; ***shoulder pad*** *(in garment)* épaulette *f (coussinet de rembourrage)*; *Sport* protège-épaule *m*; ***shoulder strap*** *(on dress, bra, accordion)* bretelle *f*; *(on bag)* bandoulière *f*; *Mil* patte *f* d'épaule, épaulette *f*; ***shoulder surfing*** = fait de regarder par-dessus l'épaule de quelqu'un qui tape son code confidentiel à un distributeur automatique ou son mot de passe sur un clavier d'ordinateur

shoulder-high ADJ qui arrive (jusqu')à l'épaule

ADV **to carry sb s.** porter qn en triomphe

shouldn't [ˈʃʊdənt] = **should not**

should've [ˈʃʊdəv] = **should have**

shout [ʃaʊt] **N 1** *(cry)* cri *m*, hurlement *m*; **I heard a s. of joy** j'ai entendu un cri de joie; *Fam* **give me a s. if you need a hand** appelle-moi si tu as besoin d'un coup de main **2** *Br & Austr Fam (round of drinks)* tournée□ *f*; **it's my s.** c'est ma tournée

VI *(cry out)* crier, hurler; **there's no need to s.** pas besoin de crier comme ça; **to s. at the top of one's voice** crier à tue-tête; **to s. (out) for help** appeler au secours; **he shouted (out) to her to be careful** il lui a crié de faire attention; **he shouted at me for being late** il a crié parce que j'étais en retard; **don't s. at me!** baisse le ton!; *Fig* **it's nothing to s. about** *(to boast about)* il n'y a pas de quoi se vanter; *Fam* **my new job is nothing to s. about** mon nouveau travail n'a rien de bien passionnant□

VT *(cry out)* crier; **the sergeant shouted (out) an order** le sergent hurla un ordre; **they shouted themselves hoarse** ils crièrent jusqu'à en perdre la voix

▸**shout down** VT SEP *(speaker)* empêcher de parler en criant; *(speech)* couvrir par des cris; **she was shouted down** les gens ont hurlé tellement fort qu'elle n'a pas pu parler

shouting [ˈʃaʊtɪŋ] **N** *(UNCOUNT)* cris *mpl*, vociférations *fpl*; *Fig* **it's all over bar the s.** l'affaire est dans le sac

▸▸ *Fam* ***shouting match*** prise *f* de bec, engueulade *f*

shouty [ˈʃaʊtɪ] *(compar* **shoutier**, *superl* **shoutiest)** ADJ *Fam (gen)* grande gueule; *(singer, music)* braillard

shove [ʃʌv] **VT 1** *(push)* pousser; *(push roughly)* pousser sans ménagement; *(insert, stick)* enfoncer; **he shoved me out of the way** il m'a écarté sans ménagement; **she shoved him down the stairs** elle l'a poussé dans les escaliers **2** *Fam (put hurriedly or carelessly)* mettre□, flanquer, ficher; **s. it in the drawer** fiche-le dans le tiroir; **s. a few good quotes in and it'll be fine** tu y ajoutes quelques citations bien choisies et ce sera parfait

VI 1 *(push)* pousser; *(jostle)* se bousculer; **people kept pushing and shoving** les gens n'arrêtaient pas de se bousculer; **she shoved past me** elle m'a bousculé en passant **2** *Br Fam (move up)* se pousser□; **s. up** *or* **over** *or* **along a bit** pousse-toi un peu

N *(push)* poussée *f*; **to give sb/sth a s.** pousser qn/qch; *Fig* **he's lazy, he just needs a little s.** il est paresseux, il a juste besoin qu'on le pousse un peu

▸**shove about, shove around** VT SEP *(jostle)* bousculer; *(mistreat)* malmener; **don't let him s. you about!** ne le laisse pas te marcher sur les pieds!

▸**shove off** VI **1** *Fam (go away)* se casser, se tirer; **s. off, I'm busy!** casse-toi, je suis occupé! **2** *(boat)* pousser au large

VT SEP *(boat)* pousser au large, déborder

shove-halfpenny N jeu *m* de palet de table

shovel [ˈʃʌvəl] *(Br pt & pp* **shovelled**, *cont* **shovelling**, *Am pt & pp* **shoveled**, *cont* **shoveling)** N pelle *f*; *(on excavating machine)* pelle *f*, godet *m*

VT *(coal, earth, sand)* pelleter; *(snow)* déblayer (à la pelle); **they shovelled the gravel onto the drive** avec une pelle, ils ont répandu les gravillons sur l'allée; *Fam* **to s. food into one's mouth** enfourner de la nourriture; *Fam* **he shovelled his meal down** il a englouti son repas

▸**shovel up** VT SEP ramasser *ou* entasser à la pelle

shoveler [ˈʃʌvələ(r)] N *Orn* souchet *m*

shovelful [ˈʃʌvəlfʊl] N pelletée *f*

SHOW [ʃəʊ]

N	
• démonstration **1**	• semblant **1**
• ostentation **1**	• spectacle **2**
• émission **2**	• exposition **3**
• foire **3**	• performance **5**
VT	
• montrer **1–3, 5, 6**	• présenter **1**
• exposer **1**	• faire preuve de **2**
• marquer **4**	• indiquer **4, 6**
• enregistrer **8**	• passer **9**
VI	
• se voir **1**	• passer **2**

(pt **showed**, *pp* **shown** [ʃəʊn])

N 1 *(demonstration, display)* démonstration *f*, manifestation *f*; *(pretence)* semblant *m*, simulacre *m*; *(ostentation)* ostentation *f*, parade *f*; **a s. of strength/unity** une démonstration de force/d'unité; **a s. of hands** un vote à main levée; **to make a s. of being angry** faire semblant *ou* faire mine d'être fâché; **to make a great s. of friendship** faire de grandes démonstrations d'amitié; **s. of generosity** affectation *f* de générosité; **it's all a s.** ce n'est qu'une façade; **the metal strips are just for s.** les bandes métalliques ont une fonction purement décorative

2 *Theat* spectacle *m*; *TV & Rad* émission *f*; **to go to a s.** aller au spectacle; **variety s.** émission *f* de variétés; **the s. must go on** le spectacle continue; *Fig* il faut continuer; *Fig* **let's get this s. on the road!** allez, c'est parti *ou* on y va!; **to make a s. of oneself** se donner en spectacle

3 *(exhibition)* exposition *f*; *(trade fair)* foire *f*, salon *m*; **have you been to the Picasso s.?** avez-vous visité l'exposition Picasso?; **to be on s.** être exposé; **I dislike most of the paintings on s.** je n'aime pas la plupart des tableaux exposés; **the agricultural/motor s.** le salon de l'agriculture/de l'auto

4 *Fam (business, affair)* affaire□ *f*; **she ran the whole s.** c'est elle qui s'est occupée de tout□

5 *(performance)* performance *f*, prestation *f*; **the team put up a good s.** l'équipe s'est bien défendue; **it's a pretty poor s. when your own mother forgets your birthday** c'est un peu triste que ta propre mère oublie ton anniversaire

VT 1 *(display, present ▸ gen)* montrer, faire voir; *(▸ passport, ticket)* présenter; *(exhibit ▸ work of art, prize, produce)* exposer; **to s. sth to sb, to s. sb sth** montrer qch à qn; **s. me your presents** faismoi voir *ou* montre-moi tes cadeaux; **you have to s. your ticket on the way in** il faut présenter son billet à l'entrée; **you're showing a lot of leg this evening!** tu es habillée bien court ce soir!; **a TV screen shows what's happening in the next room** un écran de télévision permet de voir ce qui se passe dans la pièce d'à côté; **some of the drawings have never been shown in Europe before** quelques-uns des dessins n'ont jamais été exposés en Europe auparavant; **this jacket/colour really shows the dirt** cette veste/couleur est vraiment salissante; **come out from behind there and s. yourself!** sortez de là-derrière et montrez-vous!; **if he ever shows himself** *or* **his face round here again, I'll kill him!** si jamais il se montre encore par ici, je le tue!; **to have sth to s. for one's money** en avoir pour son argent; **I had very little to s. for my efforts** mes efforts n'avaient donné que peu de résultats; **three months' work, and what have we got to s. for it?** trois mois de travail, et qu'est-ce que cela nous a rapporté?

2 *(reveal ▸ talent, affection, readiness, reluctance)* montrer, faire preuve de; **she never shows any emotion** elle ne laisse jamais paraître *ou* ne montre jamais ses sentiments; **to s. itself** *(emotion, tendency)* se manifester; **she showed herself to be a hard worker** elle s'est révélée *ou* avérée dure à la tâche; **to s. a preference for sth** manifester une préférence pour qch; **to s. a taste for sth** témoigner d'un goût pour qch; **they will be shown no mercy** ils seront traités sans merci; **the audience began to s. signs of restlessness** le public a commencé à s'agiter; **the situation is showing signs of improvement** la situation semble être en voie d'amélioration; **to s. one's age** faire son âge

3 *(prove)* montrer, démontrer, prouver; **first I shall s. that Greenham's theory cannot be correct** je démontrerai d'abord que la théorie de Greenham ne peut être juste; **it just shows the strength of public opposition to the plan** cela montre à quel point le public est opposé à ce projet; **it just goes to s. what you can do if you work hard** cela montre *ou* c'est la preuve de ce que l'on peut faire en travaillant dur; **which only** *or* **all goes to s. that...** ce qui prouve que... + *indicative*

4 *(register ▸ of instrument, dial, clock)* marquer, indiquer; **the thermometer shows a temperature of 20°C** le thermomètre indique 20°C

5 *(represent, depict)* montrer, représenter; **this photo shows him at the age of 17** cette photo le montre à l'âge de 17 ans

6 *(point out, demonstrate)* montrer, indiquer; **s. me how to do it** montrez-moi comment faire; **to s. (sb) the way** montrer le chemin (à qn); *Fig* **to s. the way** donner l'exemple; **the government has very much shown the way with its green policies** le gouvernement a bien donné l'exemple avec sa politique écologique; *Fam* **I'll s. you!** tu vas voir!

7 *(escort, accompany)* **let me s. you to your room** je vais vous montrer votre chambre; **will you s. this gentleman to the door?** veuillez reconduire Monsieur à la porte; **to s. sb into a room** introduire *ou* faire entrer qn dans une pièce

8 *(profit, loss)* enregistrer; **prices s. a 10 percent increase on last year** les prix sont en hausse *ou* ont augmenté de 10 pour cent par rapport à l'an dernier

9 *(put on ▸ film, TV programme)* passer; **the film has never been shown on television** le film n'est jamais passé à la télévision

10 *Comput (files, records)* afficher

VI 1 *(be visible ▸ gen)* se voir; *(▸ petticoat)* dépasser; **she doesn't like him, and it shows** elle ne l'aime pas, et ça se voit; **a patch of sky showed through a hole in the roof** on voyait un pan de ciel à travers un trou dans le toit; **she lets her feelings s. too much** elle laisse trop voir ses sentiments; **it shows in your face** cela se voit *ou* se lit sur votre visage; **their tiredness is beginning to s.** ils commencent à donner des signes de fatigue; **it doesn't s.** ça ne se voit pas, on ne dirait pas; **ah well, it just** *or* **all goes to s.!** eh oui, c'est la vie!; **she hasn't started to s. yet** *(of pregnant woman)* on ne voit pas encore qu'elle est enceinte

2 *(be on ▸ film, TV programme)* passer

3 *Fam (turn up)* arriver□, se pointer; *Br* **he didn't s.** il n'est pas venu□

▸▸ ***show house*** maison *f* témoin; ***show jumper*** *(rider)* cavalier(ère) *m,f (participant à des concours de saut d'obstacle)*; *(horse)* sauteur *m*; ***show jumping*** jumping *m*, concours *m* de saut d'obstacles; ***show reel*** film *m*/cassette *f* de démonstration; *Law* ***show trial*** procès *m* à grand spectacle

▸**show in** VT SEP faire entrer

▸ **show off** VT SEP **1** *(parade)* faire étalage de; **to s. off one's skill/culture** faire étalage de son savoir-faire/sa culture; **he only came to s. off his new car** il n'est venu que pour exhiber sa nouvelle voiture; **she came in to s. off her new baby** elle est venue faire admirer son nouveau-né **2** *(set off)* mettre en valeur; **wearing white shows off a tan** porter du blanc met le bronzage en valeur; **a coat that shows off the figure well** un manteau qui marque *ou* dessine bien la taille

VI faire l'intéressant(e), frimer; **to s. off in front of sb** chercher à épater qn; **stop showing off!** arrête de faire l'intéressant!; **you don't have to drive that fast, you're just showing off** tu n'as pas besoin de conduire aussi vite, tu fais juste l'intéressant

▸ **show out** VT SEP reconduire *ou* raccompagner (à la porte); **it's okay, I'll s. myself out** inutile de vous déranger, je saurai retrouver le chemin (tout seul)

▸ **show through** VT INSEP se voir à travers; **her pants showed through her trousers** sa culotte se voyait à travers son pantalon

VI se voir (à travers), transparaître; **the old paint still shows through** l'ancienne peinture se voit encore à travers; **her pants showed through under her dress** on voyait sa culotte au travers de sa robe

▸ **show up** VT SEP **1** *(unmask ▸ impostor)* démasquer; **the investigation showed him up for the coward he is** l'enquête a révélé sa lâcheté **2** *(draw attention to ▸ deficiency, defect)* faire apparaître, faire ressortir; **the poor results s. up the deficiencies in the training programme** les mauvais résultats font apparaître les défauts du programme de formation **3** *(embarrass)* faire honte à; *(deliberately humiliate)* humilier; **you're always showing me up in public** il faut toujours que tu me fasses honte en public

VI **1** *Fam (turn up, arrive)* arriver▫; **only two of our guests have shown up** seuls deux de nos invités sont arrivés; **to fail to s. up** ne pas se présenter▫ **2** *(be visible)* se voir, ressortir; **the dirt really shows up on a white carpet** la saleté ressort *ou* se voit vraiment sur une moquette blanche; **the difference is so slight it hardly shows up at all** la différence est si tellement minime qu'elle se remarque à peine

showbiz [ˈʃəʊbɪz] N *Fam* show-biz *m inv*, le monde *m* du spectacle▫; **she wants to get into s.** elle veut entrer dans le show-biz

showboat [ˈʃəʊbəʊt] N bateau-théâtre *m*

showbusiness [ˈʃəʊbɪznɪs] N show-business *m inv*, le monde *m* du spectacle

showcase [ˈʃəʊkeɪs] N vitrine *f*; *Fig* **a s. for British exports** une vitrine pour les exportations britanniques

ADJ *(role)* prestigieux; *(operation)* de prestige

VT *Com* exposer, présenter; *Fig* servir de vitrine à; **the exhibition will s. our new product range** nous présenterons notre nouvelle gamme de produits dans le cadre de l'exposition

showdown [ˈʃəʊdaʊn] N *(confrontation)* confrontation *f*, épreuve *f* de force

shower [ˈʃaʊə(r)] N **1** *(for washing)* douche *f*; **to have** *or* **to take a s.** prendre une douche; **he's in the s.** il est sous la douche

2 *Met* averse *f*; **scattered showers** averses *fpl* intermittentes; **a snow s.** une chute de neige

3 *(stream ▸ of confetti, gravel)* pluie *f*; *(▸ of sparks)* gerbe *f*; *(▸ of praise, abuse)* avalanche *f*; *(▸ of blows)* pluie *f*, volée *f*, grêle *f*

4 *Am (party)* = fête au cours de laquelle les invités offrent des cadeaux; **to have a baby s.** = faire une fête où les invités apporteront des cadeaux pour le bébé

VI **1** *(have a shower)* prendre une douche, se doucher **2** *(rain)* pleuvoir par averses; **it's started to s.** il a commencé à pleuvoir **3** *Fig (rain down)* pleuvoir

VT **passers-by were showered with broken glass** des passants ont été atteints par des éclats de verre; **they showered him with gifts, they showered gifts on him** ils l'ont comblé de cadeaux; **to s. sb with praise** encenser qn

▸▸ ***shower cabinet*** cabine *f* de douche; ***shower cap*** bonnet *m* de douche; ***shower curtain*** rideau *m* de douche; ***shower gel*** gel *m* de douche; ***shower head*** pomme *f* de douche; ***shower unit*** bloc-douche *m*

▸ **shower down** VI *(rocks)* tomber; *Fig (compliments, insults)* pleuvoir; **rocks showered down on us** des pierres s'abattirent sur nous

showerproof [ˈʃaʊəpruːf] ADJ imperméable

showery [ˈʃaʊərɪ] ADJ **the weather was s.** il pleuvait de façon intermittente; **it will be rather a s. day tomorrow** il y aura des averses demain

showground [ˈʃəʊgraʊnd] N parc *m* d'expositions

showily [ˈʃəʊɪlɪ] ADV de façon voyante *ou* ostentatoire

showiness [ˈʃəʊɪnɪs] N ostentation *f*; *(of jewellery)* clinquant *m*; *(of dress, decoration)* aspect *m* tapageur

showing [ˈʃəʊɪŋ] N **1** *(of paintings, sculpture)* exposition *f*; *(of film)* projection *f*, séance *f*; **a private s. of her new film** une projection privée de son nouveau film; **a midnight s.** une séance à minuit **2** *(performance)* performance *f*, prestation *f*; **on its present s. our party should win hands down** à en juger par ses performances actuelles, notre parti devrait gagner haut la main

showman [ˈʃəʊmən] (*pl* **showmen** [-mən]) N *Theat* metteur *m* en scène; *(in fairground)* forain *m*; *(circus manager)* propriétaire *m* de cirque; *Fig* **he's a real s.** il a vraiment le sens de la mise en scène

showmanship [ˈʃəʊmənʃɪp] N sens *m* de la mise en scène

showmen [ˈʃəʊmən] *pl of* **showman**

shown [ʃəʊn] *pp of* **show**

show-off N *Fam* frimeur(euse) *m,f*; **stop being such a s.!** arrête de frimer!

showpiece [ˈʃəʊpiːs] N **the s. of his collection** le joyau de sa collection; **the school had become a s. of educational excellence** l'école est devenue un modèle quant à la qualité de l'enseignement

showplace [ˈʃəʊpleɪs] N endroit *m* pittoresque, site *m* touristique

showring [ˈʃəʊrɪŋ] N *(at auction ▸ for horses, cattle)* arène *f* de vente; *(at equestrian event)* arène *f* de concours hippique

showroom [ˈʃəʊrʊm] N salle *f ou* salon *m* d'exposition; **the new model will be in the showrooms soon** le nouveau modèle sera bientôt chez votre concessionnaire; **a car in s. condition** une voiture à l'état neuf

show-stopping ADJ sensationnel

showy [ˈʃəʊɪ] (*compar* **showier**, *superl* **showiest**) ADJ voyant; *(jewellery)* clinquant; **he's a bit s. in the way he dresses** la façon dont il s'habille est un peu voyante

shrank [ʃræŋk] *pt of* **shrink**

shrapnel [ˈʃræpnəl] N **1** *(UNCOUNT) (fragments)* éclats *mpl* d'obus; *(shell)* shrapnel *m*; **a piece of s.** un éclat d'obus **2** *Fam (loose change)* mitraille *f*

▸▸ ***shrapnel wound*** blessure *f* provoquée par des éclats d'obus

shred [ʃred] (*pt & pp* **shredded**, *cont* **shredding**) N **1** *(of paper, fabric)* lambeau *m*; **in shreds** en lambeaux; *Fig* **his reputation was in shreds** sa réputation était ruinée; **to tear sth to shreds** déchirer qch en petits morceaux; *Fig* démolir qch; *Fig* **to tear sb to shreds** démolir qn **2** *(of truth, evidence)* parcelle *f*; **anyone with a s. of decency would have refused** n'importe qui ayant un minimum de décence aurait refusé

VT **1** *(tear up ▸ paper, fabric)* déchiqueter; **s. this document as soon as you have read it** détruisez ce document dès que vous l'aurez lu **2** *Culin* couper en lamelles; **shredded cabbage** chou *m* coupé en lamelles *ou* haché

shredder [ˈʃredə(r)] N *(for documents)* destructeur *m* de documents

shreddies [ˈʃredɪz] NPL *Fam (underwear)* calbute *m*, calcif *m*

shredding [ˈʃredɪŋ] N *(of paper, fabric)* déchiquetage *m*; *(of confidential documents)* destruction *f*

shrew [ʃruː] N **1** *Zool* musaraigne *f* **2** *Pej (woman)* mégère *f*, harpie *f*

shrewd [ʃruːd] ADJ *(person ▸ astute)* perspicace; *(▸ crafty)* astucieux, rusé, habile; *(judgment)* perspicace; **that was a s. move** c'était bien joué; **to make a s. guess** deviner juste; **a s. investment** un placement judicieux

shrewdly [ˈʃruːdlɪ] ADV *(act)* avec perspicacité *ou* sagacité; *(answer, guess)* astucieusement

shrewdness [ˈʃruːdnɪs] N *(astuteness)* perspicacité *f*; *(craftiness)* habileté *f*, ruse *f*

shrewish [ˈʃruːɪʃ] ADJ *(woman, character)* acariâtre, hargneux

shriek [ʃriːk] VI hurler, crier; **to s. with pain** pousser un cri de douleur; **to s. with laughter** hurler de rire

VT hurler, crier

N *(of person, animal)* cri *m* aigu *ou* perçant; **shrieks of joy** cris *mpl* joyeux; **shrieks of laughter** grands éclats *mpl* de rire

shrieking [ˈʃriːkɪŋ] N *(UNCOUNT)* cris *mpl* aigus *ou* perçants

shrift [ʃrɪft] N **to give sb short s.** envoyer promener qn; **I got short s. from him** il m'a envoyé promener

shrike [ʃraɪk] N *Orn* pie-grièche *f*

shrill [ʃrɪl] ADJ perçant, aigu(ë), strident

VI *(siren, whistle)* retentir

VT crier d'une voix perçante; **"cooee!" she shrilled** "coucou!" cria-t-elle d'une voix perçante

shrillness [ˈʃrɪlnɪs] N *(of voice)* ton *m* perçant *ou* aigu; *(of note, whistle)* stridence *f*

shrilly [ˈʃrɪlɪ] ADV *(say, sing)* d'une voix perçante *ou* aiguë; *(whistle)* d'une manière stridente

shrimp [ʃrɪmp] (*pl sense* **1** *Am* **inv**) N **1** *Zool* crevette *f* **2** *Fam Pej (small person)* minus *m*, avorton *m*

VI **to go shrimping** aller aux crevettes

▸▸ ***shrimp boat*** crevettier *m*; *Am* ***shrimp cocktail*** cocktail *m* de crevettes; ***shrimp net*** haveneau *m*

shrimping net [ˈʃrɪmpɪŋ-] N crevettier *m (filet)*

shrine [ʃraɪn] N **1** *(place of worship)* lieu *m* saint

2 *(container for relics)* reliquaire *m*

3 *(tomb)* tombe *f*, mausolée *m*

4 *Fig* haut lieu *m*; **a s. of learning** un haut lieu du savoir

shrink [ʃrɪŋk] (*pt* **shrank** [ʃræŋk], *pp* **shrunk** [ʃrʌŋk]) VI **1** *(garment, cloth)* rétrécir; *(timber)* se contracter; **to s. in the wash** rétrécir au lavage

2 *(grow smaller ▸ gen)* rétrécir, rapetisser; *(▸ economy)* se ralentir; *(▸ person)* rapetisser; *(▸ numbers, profits, savings)* diminuer, baisser; *(▸ business, trade)* se réduire; **the village seems to have shrunk** le village semble plus petit; **the number of candidates has shrunk alarmingly** le nombre de candidats a diminué de façon inquiétante; **my savings have shrunk (away) to nothing** mes économies ont complètement fondu

3 *(move backwards)* reculer; **they shrank (away** *or* **back) in horror** ils reculèrent, horrifiés; **to s. into oneself** se refermer *ou* se replier sur soi-même

4 *(shy away)* se dérober; *(hesitate)* répugner; **she shrank from the thought of meeting him again** l'idée de le revoir lui faisait peur

VT (faire) rétrécir; **old age had shrunk him** il s'était tassé avec l'âge

N *Fam Pej (psychiatrist, psychoanalyst)* psy *mf*

shrinkage [ˈʃrɪŋkɪdʒ] N *(UNCOUNT)* **1** *(of garment, cloth)* rétrécissement *m*; *(of timber)* retrait *m* **2** *(of economy)* ralentissement *m*; *(of numbers, profits, savings)* diminution *f*, réduction *f*; **allow for s.** tenir compte du rétrécissement **3** *Com (of goods in transit)* pertes *fpl*; *(through pilferage)* coulage *m*; *(through damage)* casse *f*

shrinking [ˈʃrɪŋkɪŋ] ADJ *(fearful)* craintif; *(shy)* timide

▸▸ ***shrinking violet*** = personne sensible et timide; **she's no s. violet** elle est loin d'être timide

shrink-wrap (*pt & pp* **shrink-wrapped**, *cont* **shrink-wrapping**) VT emballer sous film plastique

shrink-wrapped ADJ emballé sous film plastique

shrink-wrapping N **1** *(process)* emballage *m* sous film plastique **2** *(material)* film *m* plastique

shrivel [ˈʃrɪvəl] (*Br pt & pp* **shrivelled**, *cont* **shrivelling**, *Am pt & pp* **shriveled**, *cont* **shriveling**) VI *(fruit, vegetable)* se dessécher, se ratatiner; *(leaf)* se recroqueviller; *(flower, crops, face, skin)* se flétrir; *(meat, leather)* se racornir

VT *(fruit, vegetable)* dessécher, ratatiner; *(leaf)* dessécher; *(flower, crops)* flétrir; *(face, skin)* flétrir, rider, parcheminer; *(meat, leather)* racornir

▸ **shrivel up VI & VT SEP** = **shrivel**

shrivelled, *Am* **shriveled** [ˈʃrɪvəld] **ADJ** ratatiné

shroud [ʃraʊd] **N 1** *(burial sheet)* linceul *m*, suaire *m* **2** *Fig (covering)* voile *m*, linceul *m*; **a s. of mist/mystery** un voile de brume/mystère; *Literary* **under a s. of darkness** sous les voiles de la nuit **3** *(rope, cord* ▸ *for aerial, mast etc)* hauban *m*; *(*▸ *on parachute)* suspente *f*

VT 1 *(body)* ensevelir, envelopper dans un linceul *ou* suaire; **she always shrouds herself in voluminous black clothes** elle se drape toujours dans de grands vêtements noirs **2** *(obscure)* voiler, envelopper; **the town was shrouded in mist/darkness** la ville était noyée dans la brume/plongée dans l'obscurité; **its origins are shrouded in mystery** ses origines sont entourées de mystère

Shrovetide [ˈʃrəʊvtaɪd] **N** les jours *mpl* gras *(précédant le Carême)*

Shrove Tuesday [ʃrəʊv-] **N** Mardi *m* gras

shrub [ʃrʌb] **N** arbrisseau *m*, arbuste *m*

shrubbery [ˈʃrʌbərɪ] *(pl* **shrubberies***)* **N** *(shrub garden)* jardin *m* d'arbustes; *(scrubland)* maquis *m*

shrug [ʃrʌg] *(pt & pp* **shrugged**, *cont* **shrugging***)* **VT to s. one's shoulders** hausser les épaules

VI hausser les épaules

N 1 *(of shoulders)* haussement *m* d'épaules **2** *(garment)* boléro *m*

▸ **shrug off VT SEP** *(disregard)* dédaigner; **to s. off an illness** se débarrasser d'une maladie; **to s. off one's problems** faire abstraction de ses problèmes; **it's not a problem you can simply s. off** on ne peut pas faire simplement comme si le problème n'existait pas

shrunk [ʃrʌŋk] *pp of* **shrink**

shrunken [ˈʃrʌŋkən] **ADJ** *(garment, fabric)* rétréci; *(person, body)* ratatiné, rapetissé; *(head)* réduit; **s. with age** *(person)* tassé par l'âge

shtick [ʃtɪk] **N** *Am Fam (of comedian)* numéro ▫ *m*

shuck [ʃʌk] *Am* **N 1** *(pod)* cosse *f*; *(of nut)* écale *f*; *(of chestnut)* bogue *f*; *(of maize)* spathe *f*; *(of oyster, clam)* coquille *f* **2** *Fam (trick)* arnaque *f*

VT 1 *(beans, peas)* écosser; *(nuts)* écaler; *(chestnuts, maize)* éplucher; *(oysters, clams)* écailler **2** *Fam (discard)* se débarrasser de ▫; **to s. (off) one's clothes** se déshabiller ▫ **3** *Fam (tease)* faire marcher, mener en bateau; *(trick)* arnaquer

▸ **shuck off VT SEP** *Am (rid oneself of* ▸ *bad habit)* se défaire de ▫

shudder [ˈʃʌdə(r)] **N** *(of person)* frisson *m*, frémissement *m*; *(of engine)* vibration *f*; *Fam* **it gives me the shudders** j'en ai des frissons

VI 1 *(person)* frissonner, frémir, trembler; **I s. to think how much it must have cost!** je frémis rien que de penser au prix que ça a dû coûter!; **I wonder what they're doing now? – I s. to think!** je me demande ce qu'ils sont en train de faire – je n'ose même pas y penser! **2** *(vehicle, machine)* vibrer; *(stronger)* trépider; **the train shuddered to a halt** le train s'arrêta dans une secousse

shuffle [ˈʃʌfəl] **VI 1** *(walk)* traîner les pieds; **he was shuffling along** il marchait en traînant les pieds; **she shuffles round the house in her slippers** elle traîne dans la maison en pantoufles; **he shuffled shamefacedly into the room** il est entré tout penaud dans la pièce **2** *(fidget)* remuer, s'agiter; **the children were shuffling in their seats** les enfants s'agitaient sur leur chaise **3** *(in card games)* battre les cartes

VT 1 *(drag)* **to s. one's feet** *(when walking)* traîner les pieds; **he stood there shuffling his feet** il était là debout dansant d'un pied sur l'autre **2** *(move round* ▸ *belongings, papers)* remuer; **she was shuffling the papers on her desk** elle déplaçait les papiers qui se trouvaient sur son bureau **3** *(cards)* battre, brasser, mélanger

N 1 *(in walking)* pas *m* traînant; *(in dancing)* pas *mpl* glissés **2** *(of cards)* battage *m*; **let's give the cards a s.** on va battre *ou* mélanger les cartes

▸ **shuffle off VI** partir en traînant les pieds; **the badger shuffled off into the bushes** le blaireau disparut dans les buissons en trottinant

VT SEP *(responsibility)* se dérober à; **he shuffled the responsibility off on to me** il s'est déchargé de la responsabilité sur moi

shuffleboard [ˈʃʌfəlbɔːd] **N** jeu *m* de palet

shuffling [ˈʃʌflɪŋ] **ADJ** *(gait)* traînant

shufti, shufty [ˈʃʊftɪ] *(pl* **shufties***)* **N** *Br Fam* coup *m* d'œil ▫; **to have a s. at sth** jeter un coup d'œil à qch; **have a quick s. at this!** regarde un peu ça!

shun [ʃʌn] *(pt & pp* **shunned**, *cont* **shunning***)* **VT** fuir, éviter

shunt [ʃʌnt] **VT 1** *(move)* déplacer; **the neighbours upstairs were shunting furniture around** les voisins du dessus déplaçaient des meubles; **he just shunted me out of his way** il m'a poussé hors de son chemin **2** *Br Rail (move about)* manœuvrer; *(direct)* aiguiller; *(marshal)* trier; **the carriages had been shunted into a siding** les wagons avaient été mis sur une voie de garage **3** *Elec (circuit)* shunter, monter en dérivation; *(current)* dériver

VI 1 *Rail* manœuvrer **2** *(travel back and forth)* faire la navette; **I spent the day shunting back and forth between the two offices** j'ai passé ma journée à faire la navette entre les deux bureaux

N 1 *Rail* manœuvre *f* (de triage) **2** *Elec* shunt *m*, dérivation *f*

shunter [ˈʃʌntə(r)] **N** *Rail* locomotive *f* de manœuvre

shunting [ˈʃʌntɪŋ] **N** *(UNCOUNT)* **1** *Rail* manœuvres *fpl* (de triage) **2** *Elec* shuntage *m*, dérivation *f*

COMP *Rail (engine, track)* de manœuvre

▸▸ *Rail* ***shunting yard*** gare *f* de triage

shush [ʃʊʃ] **EXCLAM** chut!

VT he kept shushing us il n'arrêtait pas de nous dire de nous taire

shut [ʃʌt] *(pt & pp* **shut**, *cont* **shutting***)* **VT 1** *(close)* fermer; **s. your eyes!** fermez les yeux!; *Fig* **you shouldn't s. your eyes to the problem** vous ne devriez pas fermer les yeux sur le problème; **s. your books** refermez *ou* fermez vos livres; **please s. the door after you** veuillez fermer *ou* refermer la porte derrière vous; *Fam* **s. your mouth** *or* **face!, s. it!** ferme ton clapet!, la ferme! **2** *(trap)* **I s. my finger in the door** je me suis pris le doigt dans la porte

VI 1 *(door, window, container etc)* (se) fermer; **the door won't s.** la porte ne ferme pas; **the lid shuts very tightly** le couvercle ferme hermétiquement **2** *(shop, gallery etc)* fermer; **the post office shuts at 6 p.m.** la poste ferme à 18 heures

ADJ fermé; *Fam* **keep your mouth** *or* **trap s.!** ferme-la!, boucle-la!

▸ **shut away VT SEP** *(criminal, animal)* enfermer; *(precious objects)* mettre sous clé; **I s. myself away for two months to finish my novel** je me suis enfermé pendant deux mois pour terminer d'écrire mon roman

▸ **shut down VT SEP 1** *(store, factory, cinema)* fermer **2** *(machine, engine)* arrêter; *(computer)* éteindre

VI 1 *(store, factory, cinema)* fermer **2** *Comput (system)* s'arrêter

▸ **shut in VT SEP** enfermer; **he went to the bathroom and s. himself in** il est allé à la salle de bains et s'y est enfermé; **to feel s. in** avoir un sentiment d'étouffement

▸ **shut off VT SEP 1** *(cut off* ▸ *supplies, water, electricity)* couper; *(*▸ *radio, machine)* éteindre, arrêter; *(*▸ *light)* éteindre **2** *(isolate)* couper, isoler; **the village was s. off from the rest of the world** le village a été coupé du reste du monde; **she s. herself off from other people** elle s'isolait du reste des gens **3** *(block)* boucher; **that new building shuts off all our sunlight** ce nouvel immeuble nous cache la lumière du jour

VI se couper, s'arrêter; **it shuts off automatically** ça s'arrête automatiquement

▸ **shut out VT SEP 1** *(out of building, room)* **she s. us out** elle nous a enfermés dehors; **we got s. out** nous ne pouvions plus rentrer

2 *(exclude)* exclure; **he drew the curtains to s. out the light** il tira les rideaux pour empêcher la lu mière d'entrer; **she felt s. out from all decisior making** elle avait l'impression que toutes les dé cisions étaient prises sans qu'elle soit consulté **3** *(block out* ▸ *thought, feeling)* chasser (de so esprit)

4 *(turn off* ▸ *light)* éteindre

▸ **shut up VI 1** *Fam (be quiet)* la fermer, la boucle **s. up!** la ferme!, boucle-la!; **s. up and do you work** ferme-la et fais ton travail; **he never know when to s. up** il ne sait pas se taire ▫ *ou* la ferme quand il faut; **she hasn't s. up about her holida since she got back** elle n'a pas arrêté de parler d ses vacances depuis qu'elle est rentrée ▫ *(close)* fermer; **we decided to s. up early** nou avons décidé de fermer tôt

VT SEP 1 *(close* ▸ *shop, factory)* fermer **2** *(lock up* enfermer; **to s. oneself up** s'enfermer chez soi *Fam (silence)* **to s. sb up** clouer le bec à qn; **tha s. him up!** ça lui a cloué le bec!

VT INSEP *(idiom)* **to s. up shop** *(close shop at end o day)* fermer le magasin; *(close shop permanently* fermer boutique; *(theatre, factory)* fermer se portes

shutdown [ˈʃʌtdaʊn] **N 1** *(of shop, factory)* fer meture *f* définitive **2** *Comput* fermeture *f*, arrê *m* de fin de session

shut-eye N *Fam* **to get some s.** piquer un roupi lon, roupiller; **I need a bit of s.** il faut que je rou pille un peu

shut-in ADJ confiné, enfermé

shutoff [ˈʃʌtɒf] **N 1** *(device)* **the automatic s. didn' work** le dispositif d'arrêt automatique n'a pa fonctionné **2** *(action)* arrêt *m*

shutout [ˈʃʌtaʊt] **N 1** *Ind* lock-out *m inv* **2** *Sport* = match où l'on n'a laissé passer aucun but

shutter [ˈʃʌtə(r)] **N 1** *(on window)* volet *m* *(slatted)* persienne *f*; **to put up the shutters** *(ge* mettre les volets; *(on shop)* fermer boutique *Phot* obturateur *m*; **to release the s.** actionne l'obturateur

▸▸ *Phot* ***shutter release*** déclencheur *m* d'obtura teur; ***shutter speed*** vitesse *f* d'obturation

shuttered [ˈʃʌtəd] **ADJ** *(with shutters fitted)* à vo lets; *(with shutters closed)* aux volets fermés; **a the windows were tightly s.** les volets de toute les fenêtres étaient bien fermés

shuttering [ˈʃʌtərɪŋ] **N** *(for concrete)* coffrage *m*

shutting [ˈʃʌtɪŋ] **N** fermeture *f*

▸▸ ***shutting down*** **1** *(of shop, factory)* fermeture définitive **2** *(of computer)* fermeture *f*, arrêt *m* d fin de session

shuttle [ˈʃʌtəl] **N 1** *(vehicle, service)* navette **there is a s. (bus) service from the station to th stadium** il y a une navette d'autobus entre la gar et le stade **2** *(on weaving loom, sewing machine* navette *f* **3** *(shuttlecock)* volant *m (au badminton*

VI faire la navette; **he shuttles between New Yor and Chicago** il fait la navette entre New York e Chicago

VT a helicopter shuttled the injured to hospital u hélicoptère a fait la navette pour transporter le blessés à l'hôpital; **passengers are shuttled to th airport by bus** les passagers sont transportés e bus à l'aéroport

shuttlecock [ˈʃʌtəlkɒk] **N** volant *m (au badmin ton)*

shy [ʃaɪ] *(compar* **shyer** *or* **shier**, *superl* **shyest** *o* **shiest**, *pl* **shies**, *pt & pp* **shied***)* **ADJ 1** *(person* ▸ *timid)* timide; *(*▸ *ill at ease)* gêné, mal à l'aise; *(*▸ *unsociable)* sauvage; **she gave a s. smile** elle sou rit timidement; **he's s. of adults** il est timide ave les adultes; **to make sb s.** intimider qn; **most peo ple are s. of speaking in public** la plupart des gen ont peur de parler en public; **don't be s. of asking for more** n'hésitez pas à en redemander; **h fought s. of admitting his interest** il a fait tout c qu'il a pu pour ne pas avoir à admettre qu'il étai intéressé **2** *(animal, bird)* peureux **3** *Am (short lacking)* **to be s. of** manquer de, être à court de **we're $600 s. of making our goal** il nous manqu 600 dollars pour atteindre notre objectif

N *Br* **1** *(throw)* lancer *m*, jet *m*; **he took a s. at th pigeon with a stone** il a lancé une pierre sur l pigeon **2** *Old-fashioned (attempt)* essai *m*, tenta tive *f*; **she decided to have** *or* **to take a s. at skiing** elle a décidé d'essayer le ski

VI *(horse)* broncher
VT lancer, jeter
▸ **shy away from** VT INSEP **to s. away from sth/doing sth** éviter qch/de faire qch; **she shied away from talking to him** elle a évité de lui parler

Shylock [ˈʃaɪlɒk] N *Pej* usurier(ère) *m,f*

shyly [ˈʃaɪlɪ] ADV timidement

shyness [ˈʃaɪnɪs] N timidité *f*

shyster [ˈʃaɪstə(r)] N *esp Am Fam (crook)* escroc[□] *m*, filou[□] *m*; *(corrupt lawyer)* avocat *m* marron[□]; *(businessman)* homme *m* d'affaires véreux[□]

SI [ˌesˈaɪ] N *(abbr* **Système International***)* SI *m*
▸▸ ***SI unit*** unité *f* SI

si [siː] N *Mus* si *m inv*

Siam [ˌsaɪˈæm] N *Formerly* Siam *m*

Siamese [ˌsaɪəˈmiːz] *(pl* **inv***)* N **1** *(person)* Siamois(e) *m,f* **2** *Ling* siamois *m* **3** *(cat)* siamois *m*
ADJ siamois
▸▸ ***Siamese cat*** chat *m* siamois; ***Siamese twins*** *(male)* frères *mpl* siamois; *(female)* sœurs *fpl* siamoises; *Fam Fig* **they're like S. twins, those two!** c'est des vrais siamois, ces deux-là!

Siberia [saɪˈbɪərɪə] N Sibérie *f*

Siberian [saɪˈbɪərɪən] N Sibérien(enne) *m,f*
ADJ sibérien

sibilance [ˈsɪbɪləns] N *Ling* sifflement *m*

sibilant [ˈsɪbɪlənt] *Ling* ADJ sifflant
N sifflante *f*

sibling [ˈsɪblɪŋ] N *(brother)* frère *m*; *(sister)* sœur *f*; **all his siblings** tous ses frères et sœurs, *Spec* sa fratrie
▸▸ ***sibling rivalry*** rivalité *f* entre frères et sœurs

sibyl [ˈsɪbəl] N sibylle *f*

sibylline [ˈsɪbəlaɪn] ADJ sibyllin

sic [sɪk] ADV sic

siccative [ˈsɪkətɪv] N siccatif *m*

Sicilian [sɪˈsɪlɪən] N **1** *(person)* Sicilien(enne) *m,f* **2** *Ling* sicilien *m*
ADJ sicilien

Sicily [ˈsɪsɪlɪ] N Sicile *f*; **in S.** en Sicile

sick [sɪk] ADJ **1** *(unwell ▸ person, plant, animal)* malade; *(▸ state)* maladif; **to fall s.,** *Am* **to take s.,** *Am & Ir* **to get s.** tomber malade; *Am* **to look s.** avoir l'air malade; **my secretary is off s.** ma secrétaire est en congé de maladie; **s. people** les malades *mpl*; *Mil* **to report** *or Fam* **to go s.** se faire porter malade[□] *ou* pâle; *Fam* **are you s. in the head or something?** ça va pas la tête?; **to be s. with fear/worry** être malade de peur/d'inquiétude

2 *(nauseous)* **to be s.** vomir; **to feel s.** avoir envie de vomir *ou* mal au cœur; **I get s. at the sight of blood** la vue du sang me rend malade *ou* me soulève le cœur; **oysters make me s.** les huîtres me rendent malade; **you'll make yourself s. if you eat too fast** tu vas te rendre malade si tu manges trop vite; **I felt s. to my stomach** j'avais mal au cœur; *Fam* **to be s. as a dog** être malade comme un chien

3 *(fed up, disgusted)* écœuré, dégoûté; *Fam* **to be s. (and tired) of sb/sth** en avoir marre *ou* ras le bol de qn/qch; **I'm s. (and tired) of telling you!** j'en ai assez de te le répéter!; **it made him s. to think of all that waste** ça l'écœurait de penser à tout ce gâchis; **you make me s.!** tu m'écœures *ou* me dégoûtes!; **he was s. of living alone** il en avait assez de vivre seul; *Fam* **to be s. to death** *or* **s. of the sight of sb/sth** en avoir sa claque de qn/qch; *Br Fam* **I was as s. as a parrot!** j'en étais malade!; *Literary* **to be s. at heart** avoir la mort dans l'âme

4 *Fam (unwholesome)* malsain[□], pervers[□]; *(morbid ▸ humour)* malsain[□]; *(▸ joke)* macabre[□]; **that's the sickest thing I ever heard!** je n'ai jamais entendu quelque chose d'aussi écœurant![□]
NPL **the s.** les malades *mpl*
N *Br Fam (vomit)* vomi[□] *m*
▸▸ *(UNCOUNT)* ***sick benefit*** prestations *fpl* de l'assurance maladie; ***sick building syndrome*** syndrome *m* des bâtiments malsains, = syndrome comprenant des maux de tête, qu'on retrouve chez des personnes résidant ou travaillant dans des bâtiments équipés de la climatisation; *Br* ***sick headache*** migraine *f*; ***sick leave*** congé *m* (de) maladie; **to be (away) on s. leave** être en congé (de) maladie; *Br* ***sick note*** mot d'absence *(pour cause de maladie)*; *Br Mil* ***sick parade*** *(soldiers)* = ensemble des soldats se rendant à la consultation; *(time)* = heure à laquelle les soldats se rendent à la consultation; **to go on s. parade** se faire porter malade; ***sick pay*** indemnité *f* de maladie *(versée par l'employeur)*
▸ **sick up** VT SEP *Br Fam* dégueuler, vomir[□]

sicken [ˈsɪkən] VT **1** *(disgust, distress)* écœurer, dégoûter; **it sickened him to see them together** ça l'écœurait de les voir ensemble **2** *(make nauseous)* donner mal au cœur à, écœurer; *(make vomit)* faire vomir; **the smell sickens me** cette odeur me soulève le cœur *ou* me donne des haut-le-cœur
VI **1** *(fall ill ▸ person, animal)* tomber malade; *(▸ plant)* dépérir; *Br* **he's sickening for something** il couve quelque chose **2** *Literary (become weary)* se lasser; **she sickened of her idle life** elle se lassa de mener une vie désœuvrée

sickening [ˈsɪkənɪŋ] ADJ **1** *(nauseating ▸ smell, mess)* nauséabond, écœurant; *(▸ sight)* écœurant **2** *Fig (disgusting, distressing)* écœurant, répugnant; **it's s. the way the refugees are treated** c'est écœurant, la façon dont on traite les réfugiés; **he fell with a s. thud** il est tombé avec un bruit qui laissait présager le pire; *Hum* **she's so talented it's s.!** elle est si douée que c'en est écœurant!

sickeningly [ˈsɪkənɪŋlɪ] ADV **he's s. pious** il est d'une piété écœurante; *Hum* **she's s. successful** elle réussit si bien que c'en est écœurant

sickie [ˈsɪkɪ] N *Br, Austr & NZ Fam* **to take** *or* **to pull a s.** se faire porter pâle *(lorsqu'on est bien portant)*

sickle [ˈsɪkəl] N faucille *f*

sickliness [ˈsɪklɪnɪs] N **1** *(of person)* faiblesse *f*, fragilité *f*; *(of complexion)* pâleur *f* maladive **2** *(of food)* goût *m* écœurant

sickly [ˈsɪklɪ] *(compar* **sicklier**, *superl* **sickliest***)* ADJ **1** *(person)* chétif, maladif; *(complexion, pallor)* maladif; *(plant)* chétif; *(dawn, light, glare)* blafard; *(smile)* pâle **2** *(nauseating)* écœurant; *(sentimentality)* mièvre; **s. sweet** écœurant, douceâtre

sickness [ˈsɪknɪs] N **1** *(nausea)* nausée *f* **2** *(illness)* maladie *f*
▸▸ *Br* ***sickness benefit*** *(UNCOUNT)* prestations *fpl* de l'assurance maladie

sicko [ˈsɪkəʊ] *(pl* **sickos***)* *Fam* ADJ dérangé, malade
N malade *mf*, tordu(e) *m,f*

sickroom [ˈsɪkrʊm] N *(sickbay)* infirmerie *f*; *(in home)* chambre *f* de malade

SIDE [saɪd]

N
- côté **1–4, 6–8**
- face **3**
- bord **4**
- camp **8**
- parti **8**
- chaîne **12**
- flanc **1, 5**
- paroi **3**
- part **6**
- équipe **8**
- page **11**

ADJ
- latéral **1, 2**
- de côté **2**

VI
- prendre parti

N **1** *(part of body ▸ of person)* côté *m*; *(▸ of animal)* flanc *m*; **lie on your s.** couchez-vous sur le côté; **I've got a pain in my right/left s.** j'ai mal au côté droit/gauche; **I sat down/stood at** *or* **by his s.** je me suis assis/j'étais debout à ses côtés *ou* à côté de lui; **the child remained at her mother's s.** l'enfant restait à côté de sa mère; **she was called to the president's s.** elle a été appelée auprès du président; *Fig* **to get on sb's good/bad s.** s'attirer la sympathie/l'antipathie de qn

2 *(as opposed to top, bottom, front, back)* côté *m*; **lay the barrel on its s.** mettez le fût sur le côté; **her hair is cut short at the sides** ses cheveux sont coupés court sur les côtés; **there's a door at the s.** il y a une porte sur le côté

3 *(outer surface ▸ of cube, pyramid)* côté *m*, face *f*; *(inner surface ▸ of bathtub, cave, stomach)* paroi *f*; *(of flat object ▸ of biscuit, sheet of paper, cloth)* côté *m*; *(▸ of coin, record, tape)* côté *m*, face *f*; **the sides of the crate are lined with newspaper** l'intérieur de la caisse est recouvert de papier journal; **printed on one s. only** imprimé d'un seul côté; **write on both sides of the paper** écrivez recto verso; **grill for three minutes on each s.** passez au gril trois minutes de chaque côté; **this s. up** *(on packaging)* haut; **the right/wrong s. of the cloth** l'endroit *m*/l'envers *m* du tissu; **the under/upper s. of sth** le dessous/le dessus de qch; *Fig* **the other s. of the coin** *or* **picture** le revers de la médaille; *Fig* **to know which s. one's bread is buttered on** savoir où est son intérêt

4 *(edge ▸ of triangle, lawn)* côté *m*; *(▸ of road, pond, river, bed)* bord *m*; **there's a wall on three sides of the property** il y a un mur sur trois côtés du terrain; **she held on to the s. of the pool** elle s'accrochait au rebord de la piscine; **a wave washed him over the s. (of the ship)** une vague l'emporta par-dessus bord; **I sat on the s. of the bed** je me suis assis sur le bord du lit; **she was kneeling by the s. of the bed** elle était agenouillée à côté du lit

5 *(slope ▸ of mountain, hill, valley)* flanc *m*, versant *m*; **the village is set on the s. of a mountain** le village est situé sur le flanc d'une montagne

6 *(opposing part, away from centre)* côté *m*; **on the other s. of the room/wall** de l'autre côté de la pièce/du mur; **you're driving on the wrong s.!** vous conduisez du mauvais côté!; **on the left-/right-hand s.** à (main) gauche/droite; **on the south s.** du côté sud; **which s. of the bed do you sleep on?** de quel côté du lit dors-tu?; **she got in on the driver's s.** elle est montée côté conducteur; **the dark s. of the moon** la face cachée de la lune; **the Mexican s. of the border** le côté mexicain de la frontière; **the lamppost leaned to one s.** le réverbère penchait d'un côté; **he wore his hat on one s.** il portait son chapeau de côté; **move the bags to one s.** écartez *ou* poussez les sacs; **to jump to one s.** faire un bond de côté; **to put sth on** *or* **to one s.** mettre qch de côté; **to take sb on** *or* **to one s.** prendre qn à part; **to stand on** *or* **to one s.** se tenir à l'écart *ou* à part; **leaving that on one s. for the moment...** en laissant cela de côté pour l'instant...; **it's way on the other s. of town** c'est à l'autre bout de la ville; **on both sides** des deux côtés, de part et d'autre; **on every s., on all sides** de tous côtés, de toutes parts; **they were attacked on** *or* **from all sides** ils ont été attaqués de tous côtés *ou* de toutes parts; **from s. to s.** d'un côté à l'autre; **the ship rolled from s. to s.** le bateau roulait; **he's on the right/wrong s. of 40** il n'a pas encore/il a dépassé la quarantaine; **stay on the right s. of the law** restez dans la légalité; **he operates on the wrong s. of the law** il fait des affaires en marge de la loi; **to get on the wrong s. of sb** prendre qn à rebrousse-poil; **to get/keep on the right s. of sb** se mettre/rester bien avec qn; *esp Am* **to live on the right/wrong s. of the tracks** habiter un bon/mauvais quartier; *esp Am* **to come from the wrong s. of the tracks** être issu d'un milieu défavorisé; **there's no other hotel this s. of Reno** il n'y a pas d'autre hôtel entre ici et Reno; **these are the best beaches this s. of Hawaii** ce sont les meilleures plages après celles de Hawaii; **I can't see myself finishing the work this s. of Easter** je ne me vois pas finir ce travail d'ici Pâques; **it's a bit on the pricey/small s.** c'est un peu cher/petit

7 *(facet, aspect ▸ of problem, situation)* aspect *m*, côté *m*; *(▸ of person)* côté *m*; **to examine all sides of an issue** examiner un problème sous tous ses aspects; **there are many sides to her character** elle a bien des facettes à son caractère; **there are two sides to every argument** dans toute discussion il y a deux points de vue; **he's told me his s. of the story** il m'a donné sa version de l'affaire; **I could see the funny s. of the situation** je voyais le côté drôle de la situation; **I can't see the funny s. of that** je ne vois pas ce qu'il y a de drôle là-dedans; **he stressed the positive/humanitarian s.** il a souligné le côté positif/humanitaire; **he always looks on the gloomy s. of things** il voit tout en noir; **I've kept my s. of the deal** j'ai tenu mes engagements dans cette affaire; **she's very good at the practical s. of things** elle est excellente sur le plan pratique; **she has her good s.** elle a ses bons côtés; **to have a jealous s.** avoir un côté jaloux

8 *(group, faction)* côté *m*, camp *m*; *(team)* équipe *f*, *Pol (party)* parti *m*; **the winning s.** le camp des vainqueurs; **whose s. is he on?** de quel côté est-il?, dans quel camp est-il?; **he's on our s.** il est avec nous *ou* de notre côté; **they fought on our**

s. ils se sont battus à nos côtés; **which s. won the war?** qui a gagné la guerre?; **there is mistrust on both sides** il y a de la méfiance dans les deux camps; **there's still no concrete proposal on** *or* **from their s.** il n'y a toujours pas de proposition concrète de leur part; **to go over to the other s., to change sides** changer de camp; **luck is on our s.** la chance est avec nous; **time is on their s.** le temps joue en leur faveur; **he has youth on his s.** il a l'avantage de la jeunesse; **he really let the s. down** il nous/leur/*etc* a fait faux bond; **she tried to get the committee on her s.** elle a essayé de mettre le comité de son côté; **to take sides** prendre parti; **he took Tom's s. against me** il a pris le parti de Tom contre moi

9 *(line of descent)* **she's Polish on her mother's s.** sa mère est polonaise; **my grandmother on my mother's/father's s.** ma grand-mère maternelle/paternelle; **she gets her love for music from her mother's/father's s. of the family** elle tient son goût pour la musique du côté maternel/paternel de sa famille

10 *Culin* **s. of pork** demi-porc *m*; **s. of beef/lamb** quartier *m* de bœuf/d'agneau

11 *Br (page of text)* page *f*; **I wrote ten sides** j'ai écrit dix pages

12 *Br Fam (TV channel)* chaîne[□] *f*; **what's on the other s.?** qu'est-ce qu'il y a sur l'autre chaîne?

13 *Am (side order)* **a pork chop with a s. of fries** une côte de porc avec des frites *(servies à part)*

ADJ 1 *(situated on one side ▸ chapel, window)* latéral

2 *(directional ▸ view)* de côté, de profil; *(▸ elevation, kick)* latéral; *Sport* **to put s. spin on a ball** donner de l'effet à une balle

3 *(additional)* en plus; **would anyone like any s. orders?** *(in restaurant)* désirez-vous un plat d'accompagnement?; **I'd like a s. order of fries** je voudrais aussi des frites

VI to s. with sb se ranger *ou* se mettre du côté de qn, prendre parti pour qn; **it's in our interest to s. with the majority** nous avons intérêt à nous ranger du côté de la majorité; **they all sided against her** ils se sont tous mis contre elle

• on the side ADV to make a bit of money on the s. *(gen)* se faire un peu d'argent en plus *ou* supplémentaire; *(dishonestly)* se remplir les poches; **she's an artist but works as a taxi driver on the s.** elle est artiste mais elle fait le chauffeur de taxi pour arrondir ses fins de mois; **a hamburger with salad on the s.** un hamburger avec une salade; *Fam* **to have a bit on the s.** *(of man)* avoir une maîtresse[□]; *(of woman)* avoir un amant[□]

• side by side ADV côte à côte; **they were walking s. by s.** ils marchaient côte à côte; **to put two boxes s. by s.** mettre deux boîtes l'une à côté de l'autre; **the road and the river run s. by s.** la route longe la rivière; **we'll be working s. by s. with the Swiss on this project** nous travaillerons en étroite collaboration avec les Suisses sur ce projet

▸▸ ***side aisle*** *(in church)* bas-côté *m*; *Theat* allée *f* latérale; ***side chapel*** chapelle *f* latérale; ***side dish*** plat *m* d'accompagnement; *(of vegetables)* garniture *f*; ***side door*** porte *f* latérale; *Fig* **to enter a profession by the s. door** entrer dans une profession par la petite porte; ***side drum*** tambour *m*; ***side effect*** *(of drug)* effet *m* secondaire; *Fig* **consumers suffered the s. effects of inflation** les consommateurs ont subi les répercussions de l'inflation; ***side entrance*** entrée *f* latérale; ***side glance*** regard *m* oblique *ou* de côté; *Fig (allusion)* allusion *f*; ***side impact*** *(between vehicles)* choc *m* latéral; ***side issue*** question *f* secondaire; **the s. issues of a question** les à-côtés *mpl* d'une question; ***side panel*** *(of vehicle)* ridelle *f*; ***side plate*** petite assiette *f (que l'on met à gauche de chaque convive)*; ***side pocket*** poche *f* extérieure; ***side rail*** *(on bridge)* garde-fou *m*; *Naut* rambarde *f*; ***side road*** *(minor road ▸ in country)* route *f* secondaire; *(▸ in town)* petite rue *f*; *(road at right angles)* rue *f* transversale; ***side salad*** salade *f (pour accompagner un plat)*; ***side street*** *(minor street)* petite rue *f*; *(at right angles)* rue *f* transversale; ***side table*** petite table *f*; *(for dishes)* desserte *f*; *(beside bed)* table *f* de chevet

sideboard ['saɪdbɔːd] **N 1** *(for dishes)* buffet *m* bas **2** *Br* **sideboards** *(whiskers)* pattes *fpl*

sideburns ['saɪdbɜːnz] **NPL** pattes *fpl*

sidecar ['saɪdkɑː(r)] **N 1** *(of motorbike)* side-car *m* **2** *(drink)* side-car *m (cocktail composé de cognac, de cointreau et de jus de citron)*

-sided ['saɪdɪd] **SUFF three-/five-s.** à trois/cinq côtés; **a many-s. figure** une figure polygonale; **a steep-s. valley** une vallée encaissée

side-impact bar N *Aut* renfort *m* anti-impact latéral

sidekick ['saɪdkɪk] **N** *Fam* acolyte[□] *m*

sidelight ['saɪdlaɪt] **N 1** *Br Aut* feu *m* de position **2** *Constr (window)* fenêtre *f* latérale **3** *(information)* **to give sb a s. on sth** donner à qn un aperçu de qch

sideline ['saɪdlaɪn] **N 1** *Sport (gen)* ligne *f* de côté; *(touchline)* (ligne *f* de) touche *f*, ligne *f* de jeu; **to wait on the sidelines** *Sport* attendre sur la touche; *Fig* attendre dans les coulisses; **to watch from the sidelines** *Sport* regarder de la ligne de touche; *Fig* être là en spectateur; *Fig* **I prefer to stand on the sidelines** je préfère ne pas m'en mêler **2** *(job)* activité *f ou* occupation *f* secondaire; **he takes wedding photos as a s.** il fait des photos de mariage pour arrondir ses fins de mois **3** *Com (product line)* ligne *f* de produits secondaires; **they've made recycling a profitable s.** ils ont fait du recyclage une activité secondaire rentable; **it's only a s. for us** ce n'est pas notre spécialité

VT *Sport & Fig* mettre sur la touche; *Fig* **to be feeling sidelined** avoir l'impression d'avoir été laissé sur la touche

sidelong ['saɪdlɒŋ] **ADJ** oblique, de côté; **they exchanged s. glances** ils ont échangé un regard complice

ADV en oblique, de côté

sidereal [saɪ'dɪərɪəl] **ADJ** *Astron* sidéral

sidesaddle ['saɪdsædəl] **N** selle *f* de femme

ADV to ride s. monter en amazone

sideshow ['saɪdʃəʊ] **N 1** *(in fair ▸ booth)* stand *m*, baraque *f* foraine; *(▸ show)* attraction *f* **2** *(minor event)* détail *m*

sideslip ['saɪdslɪp] *(pt & pp* **sideslipped**, *cont* **sideslipping)** **N 1** *Aviat* glissade *f* sur l'aile **2** *Aut & Ski* dérapage *m*; **to go into s.** déraper

VI 1 *Aviat* glisser sur l'aile **2** *Aut & Ski* déraper

sidesman ['saɪdzmən] *(pl* **sidesmen** [-mən]) **N** *Br Rel* adjoint *m* du bedeau

sidesplitting ['saɪd,splɪtɪŋ] **ADJ** *Fam (story, joke)* tordant, bidonnant

sidesplittingly ['saɪdsplɪtɪŋlɪ] **ADV** *Fam* **s. funny** drôle à se tordre de rire

sidestep ['saɪdstep] *(pt & pp* **sidestepped**, *cont* **sidestepping)** **N** crochet *m*; *Sport* esquive *f*

VT 1 *(in football, rugby ▸ opponent, tackle)* crocheter; *(in boxing ▸ punch)* esquiver **2** *(issue, question)* éluder, éviter; *(difficulty)* esquiver; **he'll s. making any decision** il évitera de prendre quelque décision que ce soit; **they'll s. the regulations/the law** ils contourneront le règlement/la loi

VI 1 *(dodge)* esquiver **2** *(in skiing)* **to s. up a slope** monter une pente en escalier **3** *(be evasive)* rester évasif

sidestroke ['saɪdstrəʊk] **N** nage *f* indienne; **to swim s.** nager à l'indienne

sideswipe ['saɪdswaɪp] **N 1** *(blow ▸ glancing)* coup *m* oblique; *(▸ severe)* choc *m* latéral **2** *(remark)* allusion *f* désobligeante; **he took a few sideswipes at the project** il a fait quelques allusions désobligeantes sur le projet

VT *Am* faucher

sidetrack ['saɪdtræk] **VT** *(person ▸ in talk)* faire dévier de son sujet; *(▸ in activity)* distraire; *(enquiry, investigation)* détourner; **the speaker kept getting sidetracked** le conférencier s'écartait sans cesse de son sujet; **sorry, I got sidetracked for a moment** pardon, je m'égare; **he's easily sidetracked** il se laisse facilement distraire

sidewalk ['saɪdwɔːk] **N** *Am* trottoir *m*

▸▸ ***sidewalk artist*** artiste *mf* de rue *(qui dessine à la craie sur le trottoir)*; ***sidewalk café*** café *m* avec terrasse

sideways ['saɪdweɪz] **ADV** *(lean)* d'un côté; *(glance)* obliquement, de côté; *(walk)* en crabe; **to step s.** faire un pas de côté; **I was thrown s.** j'ai été projeté sur le côté; **the cup slid s.** la tasse glissa de côté; **now turn s.** maintenant mettez-vous de profil; *Fam* **the news really knocked him s.** *(astounded him)* la nouvelle l'a vraiment époustouflé; *(upset him)* la nouvelle l'a vraiment mis dans tous ses états

ADJ *(step)* de côté; *(look)* oblique, de côté; **the job is a s. move** c'est une mutation et non pas une promotion

sidewinder ['saɪdwaɪndə(r)] **N 1** *Am (blow)* grand coup *m* de poing **2** *Zool* crotale *m* cornu

siding ['saɪdɪŋ] **N** *Br Rail (in yard)* voie *f* de garage; *(off main track)* voie *f* d'évitement

sidle ['saɪdəl] **VI** se faufiler; **to s. up** *or* **over to sb** se glisser vers *ou* jusqu'à qn; **to s. in/out** entrer/sortir furtivement

SIDS [sɪdz] **N** *Med (abbr* **sudden infant death syndrome)** MSN *f*

siege [siːdʒ] **N** *Mil & Fig* siège *m*; **to lay s. to sth** assiéger qch; **to be under s.** être assiégé; **to raise a s.** lever le siège; **a state of s. has been declared** l'état de siège a été déclaré

COMP *(machine, warfare)* de siège; **to have a s. mentality** être toujours sur la défensive

Siena [sɪ'enə] **N** Sienne

sienna [sɪ'enə] **N 1** *(earth)* terre *f* de Sienne; **raw/burnt s.** terre *f* de Sienne naturelle/brûlée **2** *(colour)* ocre *m* brun

ADJ ocre brun *(inv)*

sierra [sɪ'erə] **N** sierra *f*

▸▸ ***Sierra Leone*** Sierra Leone *f*; ***Sierra Leonean*** Sierra-Léonais(e) *m,f* **ADJ** de la Sierra Leone; ***Sierra Nevada*** la Sierra Nevada

siesta [sɪ'estə] **N** sieste *f*; **to have** *or* **to take a s.** faire la sieste

sieve [sɪv] **N** *(gen)* tamis *m*; *(kitchen utensil)* passoire *f*; *(for gravel, seed, ore)* crible *m*; **I've got a memory** *or* **mind like a s.!** ma mémoire est une vraie passoire!

VT *(flour, sand, powder)* tamiser, passer au tamis; *(purée, soup)* passer; *(gravel, seed, ore)* cribler, passer au crible

sift [sɪft] **VT 1** *(ingredients, soil)* tamiser, passer au tamis; *(gravel, seed, ore)* cribler, passer au crible; **s. a little sugar onto the cakes** saupoudrez un peu de sucre sur les gâteaux **2** *(scrutinize ▸ evidence, proposal)* passer au crible; **the experts are sifting the facts** les experts passent les faits au crible **3** = **sift out**

VI 1 *(search)* fouiller; **they sifted through the Br rubbish** *or* **Am garbage/the ruins** ils fouillaient (dans) les ordures/les ruines **2** *(pass, filter)* filtrer; **I let the sand s. through my fingers** j'ai laissé le sable couler entre mes doigts

▸ sift out VT SEP 1 *(remove ▸ lumps, debris)* enlever (à l'aide d'un tamis/d'un crible) **2** *Fig (distinguish)* dégager, distinguer; **they sifted out the relevant information** ils n'ont retenu que les éléments intéressants

sifter ['sɪftə(r)] **N** *(sieve ▸ for flour, powder, soil)* tamis *m*; *(▸ for gravel, seed, ore)* crible *m*; *(shaker)* saupoudreuse *f*

sifting ['sɪftɪŋ] **N** *(of flour, powder, soil)* tamisage *m*; *(of gravel, seed, ore)* criblage *m*

sig [sɪg] **N** *Fam Typ (section of book)* cahier[□] *m*; *(mark)* signature[□] *f*

sigh [saɪ] **VI 1** *(gen)* soupirer, pousser un soupir; **to s. with relief** pousser un soupir de soulagement

2 *Literary (lament)* se lamenter; **to s. over sth** se lamenter sur qch

3 *Literary (grieve)* soupirer; **to s. for** *or* **over sb sth** soupirer pour qn/qch

4 *(wind)* murmurer

VT "it's so lovely here," she sighed "c'est tellement joli ici", soupira-t-elle

N soupir *m*; **to give** *or* **to heave a s. of relief** pousser un soupir de soulagement

sighing ['saɪɪŋ] **N** *(UNCOUNT) (of person)* soupirs *mpl*; *(of wind)* murmure *m*

SIGHT [saɪt]

N
- vue **1–3**
- curiosité **5**
- pagaille **7**
- spectacle **4**
- avis **6**
- viseur **8**

VT
- voir **1**
- viser **2**
- repérer **1**

N 1 *(faculty, sense)* vue *f*; **to have good/bad s.** avoir une bonne/mauvaise vue; **her s. is failing** sa vue baisse; **to lose/to recover one's s.** perdre/recouvrer la vue

2 *(act, instance of seeing)* vue *f*; **it was my first s. of the Pacific** c'était la première fois que je voyais le Pacifique; **at first s. the place seemed abandoned** à première vue, l'endroit avait l'air abandonné; **it was love at first s.** ce fut le coup de foudre; **do you believe in love at first s.?** est-ce que tu crois au coup de foudre?; **to catch s. of sb/sth** apercevoir *ou* entrevoir qn/qch; **to lose s. of sb/sth** perdre qn/qch de vue; *Fig* **we mustn't lose s. of the fact that...** il ne faut pas perdre de vue (le fait) que… + *indicative*; **I can't stand** *or* **bear the s. of him!** je ne le supporte pas!; **I can't stand the s. of blood** je ne supporte pas la vue du sang; **to know sb by s.** connaître qn de vue; **to buy sth s. unseen** acheter qch sans l'avoir vu; *Com* **we need to have s. of it first** il faut le voir d'abord; **he can play music at** *or Am* **by s.** il sait déchiffrer une partition; **to shoot at** *or* **on s.** tirer à vue; **payable at** *or Am* **on s.** payable à vue

3 *(range of vision)* (portée *f* de) vue *f*; **the plane was still in s.** l'avion était encore en vue; **there wasn't a taxi in s.** il n'y avait pas un (seul) taxi en vue; **there's still no end in s.** je n'en vois pas la fin; **keep that car/your goal in s.** ne perdez pas cette voiture/votre but de vue; **the mountains/runners came into s.** les montagnes/les coureurs sont apparues; **out of s.** *(invisible)* hors de vue; **I watched her until she was out of s.** je l'ai regardée jusqu'à ce qu'elle disparaisse de ma vue; **keep it out of s.** ne le montrez pas, cachez-le; **she never lets him out of her s.** elle ne le perd jamais de vue; **(get) out of my s.!** hors de ma vue!; **get that dog out of my s.!** faites disparaître ce chien!; **a peace settlement now seems within s.** un accord de paix semble maintenant possible; **it was impossible to get within s. of the accident** il était impossible de s'approcher du lieu de l'accident pour voir ce qui se passait; **he had to give up within s. of the summit** il a dû renoncer à quelques mètres du sommet; *Prov* **out of s., out of mind** loin des yeux, loin du cœur

4 *(spectacle)* spectacle *m*; **the cliffs were an impressive s.** les falaises étaient impressionnantes à voir; **beggars are a common s. on the streets** on voit beaucoup de mendiants dans les rues; **it was not a pretty s.** ça n'était pas beau à voir; **it was a s. for sore eyes** c'était un soulagement de voir ça; **you're a s. for sore eyes!** *(you're a welcome sight)* Dieu merci te voilà!; *(you look awful)* tu fais vraiment peine à voir!

5 *(tourist attraction)* curiosité *f*; **one of the sights of Rome** une des choses à voir à Rome; **to see the sights of the town** visiter la ville

6 *Literary (opinion, judgment)* avis *m*, opinion *f*; **in my father's s. she could do no wrong** aux yeux de mon père, elle était incapable de faire du mal

7 *Fam (mess)* pagaille *f*; *(ridiculously dressed person)* tableau *m*; **the kitchen was a s.!** quelle pagaille dans la cuisine!; **what a s. you are!, you look a s.!** *(wet, dirty)* te voilà dans un drôle d'état!; *(ridiculous)* de quoi tu as l'air comme ça!; **I must look a s.!** je ne dois pas être beau à voir!; **what a s.!** quel tableau!

8 *(aiming device)* viseur *m*; *(on mortar)* appareil *m* de pointage; **to take a s. on sth** viser qch; **to have sth in one's sights** avoir qch dans sa ligne de tir; *Fig* avoir qch en vue; *Fig* **to lower one's sights** viser moins haut; **to set one's sights on sth** viser qch; **to set one's sights on doing sth** avoir pour ambition de faire qch; **he's set his sights on becoming a doctor** son ambition est de devenir médecin; **she has her sights set on the presidency** elle vise la présidence

VT 1 *(see)* voir, apercevoir; *(spot)* repérer; **the clouds parted and we sighted the summit** les nuages se déchirèrent et nous aperçûmes le sommet; **a submarine was sighted** un sous-marin a été repéré

2 to s. one's gun *(aim)* viser; *(adjust sights of)* régler le viseur de son fusil; **he carefully sighted his pistol at the target** il visa soigneusement la cible avec son pistolet

• **a sight** **ADV** *Br Fam* beaucoup; **you'd earn a (damn) s. more money working in industry** votre salaire serait beaucoup plus important si vous travailliez dans l'industrie; **it's a (far) s. worse than before** c'est bien pire qu'avant

▸▸ *Fin* **sight bill** effet *m* à vue; *Tech* **sight check** contrôle *m* à vue, contrôle *m* visuel; *Fin* **sight deposit** dépôt *m* à vue; *Fin* **sight draft** traite *f* à vue; **sight gag** gag *m* visuel

sighted ['saɪtɪd] **ADJ** voyant; **partially s.** mal voyant

sighting ['saɪtɪŋ] **N** *(act of seeing)* **UFO sightings have increased** un nombre croissant de personnes déclarent avoir vu des ovnis; **several sightings of teal have been reported** on a vu des sarcelles à plusieurs reprises

sightless ['saɪtlɪs] **ADJ** *(blind)* aveugle

sightlessness ['saɪtlɪsnɪs] **N** cécité *f*

sightly ['saɪtlɪ] (*compar* **sightlier**, *superl* **sightliest**) **ADJ** agréable à regarder

sight-read [-riːd] (*pt & pp* **sight-read** [-red]) *Mus*
VI déchiffrer
VT déchiffrer

sight-reading **N** *Mus* déchiffrage *m*

sightsee ['saɪtsiː] **VI to go sightseeing** faire du tourisme; *(in town)* visiter la ville

sightseeing ['saɪtsiːɪŋ] **N** tourisme *m*; **to do some s.** faire du tourisme; *(in town)* visiter la ville

COMP I went on a s. tour of Rome j'ai fait une visite guidée de Rome

sightseer ['saɪtsiːə(r)] **N** touriste *mf*

SIGN [saɪn]

N
- signe **1, 2, 5–7**
- geste **2**
- panneau **4**
- enseigne **4**
- symbole **1**
- signal **3**
- écriteau **4**

VT
- signer **1**
- signaliser **3**
- engager **2**

VI
- signer **1**
- signer un contrat **2**

N 1 *(symbol ▸ gen)* signe *m*, symbole *m*; *Math, Mus & Ling* signe *m*; **this s. means "real leather"** ce symbole signifie "cuir véritable"; **plus/minus s.** signe *m* plus/moins

2 *(gesture, motion)* signe *m*; **to make a s. to sb** faire signe à qn; **to make a rude s.** faire un geste grossier; **she made a s. for me to enter** elle m'a fait signe d'entrer; **to make the s. of the cross** faire le signe de croix; **the victory s.** le signe de la victoire

3 *(arranged signal)* signal *m*; **a lighted lamp in the window is the s. that it's safe** une lampe allumée à la fenêtre signifie qu'il n'y a pas de danger; **when I give the s., run** à mon signal, courez

4 *(written notice ▸ gen)* panneau *m*; (▸ *smaller*) écriteau *m*; (▸ *on shop, bar, cinema etc*) enseigne *f*; **the signs are all in Arabic** tous les panneaux sont en arabe; **follow the signs for Manchester** suivre les panneaux indiquant Manchester; **traffic signs** panneaux *mpl* de signalisation; **stop s.** stop *m*; **a "for sale" s.** un écriteau "à vendre"

5 *(evidence, indication)* signe *m*, indice *m*; *Med* signe *m*; **his speech was interpreted as a s. of goodwill** on a interprété son discours comme un signe de bonne volonté; **as a s. of respect** en témoignage *ou* en signe de respect; **a distended belly is a s. of malnutrition** un ventre dilaté est un signe de sous-alimentation; **a red sunset is a s. of fair weather** un coucher de soleil rouge est signe qu'il fera beau; **it's a s. of the times** c'est un signe des temps; **it's a good s. if he's making jokes** c'est bon signe s'il fait des plaisanteries; **at the first s. of trouble, he goes to pieces** au premier petit problème, il craque; **were there any signs of a struggle?** y avait-il des traces de lutte?; **all the signs are that the economy is improving** tout laisse à penser que l'économie s'améliore; **the room showed signs of having been recently occupied** il était clair que la pièce avait récemment été occupée; **there's no s. of her changing her mind** rien n'indique qu'elle va changer d'avis; **there's no s. of the file anywhere** on ne trouve trace du dossier nulle part; **he gave no s. of having heard me** il n'a pas eu l'air de m'avoir entendu; **is there any s. of Amy yet?** est-ce qu'on a eu des nouvelles d'Amy?; **since then, he's given no s. of life** depuis lors, il n'a pas donné signe de vie; **there is little s. of progress in the negotiations** les négociations ne semblent pas avancer

6 *Astrol* signe *m*; **what s. are you?** de quel signe êtes-vous?

7 *Rel (manifestation)* signe *m*; **a s. from God** un signe de Dieu

VT 1 *(document, book)* signer; **s. your name here** signez ici; **here are the letters to be signed** voici les lettres à signer; **a signed Picasso lithograph** une lithographie signée par Picasso; **a signed photo** *(of a celebrity etc)* une photo dédicacée; **she signs herself "A.M. Hall"** elle signe "A.M. Hall"; **to s. a deal** passer un marché; **the deal will be signed and sealed tomorrow** l'affaire sera définitivement conclue demain; *Law* **signed, sealed and delivered in the presence of...** fait et signé en présence de…; *Fig* **you're signing your own death warrant** vous signez votre arrêt de mort

2 *(footballer, musician, band)* engager; **he's been signed for next season** il a été engagé pour la saison prochaine

3 *(provide with signs)* signaliser; **the museum is not very well signed** la signalisation du musée n'est pas très bonne

4 *(signal)* **to s. assent** faire signe que oui; **to s. sb to do sth** faire signe à qn de faire qch

VI 1 *(write name)* signer; **he signed with an X** il a signé d'une croix; **to s. on the dotted line** signer à l'endroit indiqué; *Fig* s'engager

2 *(footballer, musician, band)* signer un contrat; **he signed for United** il a signé avec United

3 *(signal)* **to s. to sb to do sth** faire signe à qn de faire qch

4 *(know sign language)* connaître la langue des signes; *(use sign language)* signer, communiquer en langue des signes *ou* par signes; **they were signing to each other** ils se parlaient par signes

▸▸ **sign language** *(UNCOUNT)* langue *f* des signes; **to speak in s. language** parler par signes; **sign painter** *(of lettering)* peintre *m* en lettres; *(of pub signs etc)* peintre *m* d'enseignes

▸ **sign away** **VT SEP** *(right, land, inheritance)* se désister de; *(independence)* renoncer à; *(power, control)* abandonner; **I felt I was signing away my freedom** j'avais l'impression qu'en signant je renonçais à ma liberté; **you're signing your life away** c'est comme si tu signais ton arrêt de mort

▸ **sign for** **VT INSEP 1** *(acknowledge receipt of)* **to s. for a delivery/a registered letter** signer un bon de livraison/le récépissé d'une lettre recommandée **2** *(undertake work on)* **she's signed for another series** elle s'est engagée à faire un autre feuilleton

▸ **sign in** **VI 1** *(at hotel)* remplir sa fiche (d'hôtel); *(in club)* signer le registre **2** *(worker)* pointer (en arrivant)

VT SEP 1 *(guest)* inscrire *(en faisant signer le registre)*; **I'm a member, so I can s. you in** je suis membre, donc je peux vous faire entrer **2** *(file, book)* rendre, retourner

▸ **sign off** **VI 1** *Rad & TV* terminer l'émission; **it's time to s. off for today** il est l'heure de nous quitter pour aujourd'hui **2** *(in letter)* **I'll s. off now** je vais conclure ici

▸ **sign on** **VI** *Br* **1** *(register as unemployed)* s'inscrire au chômage; **you have to s. on every two weeks** il faut pointer (au chômage) toutes les deux semaines **2** *(enrol)* s'inscrire; **she signed on for an evening class** elle s'est inscrite à des cours du soir **3** *Comput* ouvrir une session

VT SEP 1 *Br (enrol ▸ student, participant)* inscrire **2** *esp Am (recruit ▸ employee, staff)* embaucher

▸ **sign out** **VT SEP 1** *(file, car)* retirer (contre décharge); *(library book)* emprunter **2** *(hospital patient)* autoriser le départ de; **he signed himself out** il est parti sous sa propre responsabilité

VI *(guest)* signer le registre (en partant); *(worker)* pointer (en partant)

▸ **sign over** **VT SEP** transférer; **she signed the property over to her son** elle a transféré la propriété au nom de son fils

▸ **sign up** **VT SEP 1** *(employee)* embaucher; *Mil (recruit)* engager; *(player, musician)* engager **2** *(student, participant)* inscrire

VI 1 *(for job)* se faire embaucher; **he signed up as a crew member** il s'est fait embaucher comme membre d'équipage **2** *Mil (enlist)* s'engager; **to s.**

up for the Marines s'engager dans les marines 3 *(enrol)* s'inscrire; **she signed up for an evening class** elle s'est inscrite à des cours du soir

signal ['sɪgnəl] *(Br pt & pp* **signalled**, *cont* **signalling**, *Am pt & pp* **signaled**, *cont* **signaling)** **N 1** *(indication)* signal *m*; **to give sb the s. to do sth** donner à qn le signal de faire qch; **he'll give the s. to attack** il donnera le signal de l'attaque; **she gave the s. for us to leave** elle nous a donné le signal de départ; **you're sending all the wrong signals if you want her to realize you're attracted to her** si tu veux qu'elle comprenne qu'elle t'intéresse, tu t'y prends vraiment mal; **he's putting out a lot of confusing signals** son attitude n'est pas claire; **it was the first s. (that) the regime was weakening** c'était le premier signe de l'affaiblissement du régime; **the demonstration is a clear s. to the government to change its policy** la manifestation signifie clairement que le gouvernement doit changer de politique; **to send smoke signals** envoyer des signaux de fumée
2 *Rail* sémaphore *m*
3 *Rad, Tel & TV* signal *m*; **radio s.** signal *m* radio
COMP *Rad & Tel (strength, frequency)* de signal
ADJ *Formal* insigne; **you showed a s. lack of tact** vous avez fait preuve d'une maladresse insigne
VT 1 *(send signal to)* envoyer un signal à; **to s. sb** faire signe à qn; **he signalled the plane forward** il a fait signe au pilote d'avancer
2 *(indicate ▸ refusal)* indiquer, signaler; *(▸ malfunction)* signaler, avertir de; **the parachutist signalled his readiness to jump** le parachutiste fit signe qu'il était prêt à sauter; **the cyclist signalled a left turn** le cycliste a indiqué qu'il tournait à gauche
3 *(announce, mark ▸ beginning, end, change)* marquer; **the speech signalled a radical change in policy** le discours a marqué une réorientation politique radicale; **this signals the start of the rainy season** cela indique le début *ou* c'est le signe du début de la saison des pluies
VI 1 *(gesture)* faire des signes; **to s. to sb to do sth** faire signe à qn de faire qch; **he signalled for the bill** il a fait signe qu'il voulait l'addition; **she was signalling for us to stop** elle nous faisait signe de nous arrêter
2 *(send signal)* envoyer un signal
3 *Aut (with indicator)* mettre son clignotant; *(with arm)* indiquer de la main un changement de direction
►► *Naut* ***signal book*** code *m* international des signaux; *Rail* ***signal box*** poste *m* de signalisation; ***signal communications*** télécommunications *fpl*, transmissions *fpl*; ***signal flag*** *Mil* fanion *m* de signalisation; *Naut* pavillon *m* pour signaux; ***signal flare*** *(rocket)* fusée *f* éclairante; *(stationary)* feu *m* de Bengale; *Rad & Tel* ***signal lamp*** *(for making signals)* lampe *f ou* projecteur *m* de signalisation; *(serving as a signal)* (lampe *f*) témoin *m*; ***signal light*** *Naut* fanal *m*; *Mil* voyant *m* (lumineux); ***signal rocket*** fusée *f* de signalisation; *Am* ***signal tower*** poste *m* d'aiguillage

signalize, -ise ['sɪgnəlaɪz] **VT** signaler, faire remarquer

signaller, *Am* **signaler** ['sɪgnələ(r)] **N** signaleur *m*

signalling, *Am* **signaling** ['sɪgnəlɪŋ] **N** *(UNCOUNT)* **1** *Aviat, Aut, Naut & Rail* signalisation *f* **2** *(warning)* avertissement *m*; **the s. of any malfunction is automatic** toute défaillance est signalée par un dispositif automatique **3** *(of electronic message)* transmission *f*; **the satellite s. was interrupted** le satellite a cessé d'émettre des signaux
►► ***signalling flag*** *Naut* pavillon *m* de signalisation; *Mil* drapeau *m* de signalisation

signally ['sɪgnəlɪ] **ADV** *Formal* **they have s. failed to achieve their goal** ils n'ont manifestement pas pu atteindre leur but

signalman ['sɪgnəlmən] *(pl* **signalmen** [-mən]) **N** *Rail* aiguilleur *m*; *Mil & Naut* signaleur *m*

signatory ['sɪgnətərɪ] *(pl* **signatories)** **N** signataire *mf*
ADJ signataire

signature ['sɪgnətʃə(r)] **N 1** *(name)* signature *f*; **to put one's s. to sth** apposer sa signature sur qch; **his s. was on the letter** la lettre portait sa signature **2** *(signing)* signature *f*; **to witness a s.** signer comme témoin **3** *Typ (section of book)* cahier *m*; *(mark)* signature *f*
COMP Chanel and her s. two-piece suit Chanel et son fameux tailleur; **this seafood pasta is the chef's s. dish** ces pâtes aux fruits de mer sont la spécialité de ce cuisinier
►► ***signature book*** parapheur *m*; ***signature stamp*** griffe *f*; *Br Rad & TV* ***signature tune*** indicatif *m* (musical); *Fig* **the song became their s. tune** cette chanson est devenue leur indicatif

signboard ['saɪnbɔːd] **N** *(for notices)* panneau *m* d'affichage; *(for ads)* panneau *m* publicitaire; *(on shop, bar, cinema etc)* enseigne *f*

signet ['sɪgnɪt] **N** sceau *m*, cachet *m*
►► ***signet ring*** chevalière *f*; *Hist (for sealing)* anneau *m* sigillaire

significance [sɪg'nɪfɪkəns] **N 1** *(importance, impact)* importance *f*, portée *f*; **what happened? – nothing of any s.** qu'est-ce qui s'est passé? – rien d'important *ou* de spécial; **his decision is of no s. to our plans** sa décision n'aura aucune incidence sur nos projets **2** *(meaning)* signification *f*, sens *m*; **sounds take on a new s. at night** la nuit, les bruits se chargent d'un autre sens *ou* acquièrent une autre signification; **the stones have religious s. for the tribe** les pierres ont une signification religieuse pour la tribu **3** *(in statistics)* signification *f*

significant [sɪg'nɪfɪkənt] **ADJ 1** *(notable ▸ change, amount, damage)* important, considérable; *(▸ discovery, idea, event)* de grande portée; **no s. progress has been made** aucun progrès notable n'a été réalisé; **was anything s. decided at the meeting?** s'est-il décidé quelque chose d'important à la réunion? **2** *(meaningful, indicative ▸ look, pause)* significatif; **the government has made a small but s. gesture** le gouvernement a fait un geste petit mais significatif **3** *(in statistics)* significatif
►► ***significant other*** partenaire *mf (dans une relation affective)*; *Psy* = personne dont on se sent très proche

significantly [sɪg'nɪfɪkəntlɪ] **ADV 1** *(differ, change, increase)* considérablement, sensiblement; **his health has improved s.** sa santé s'est considérablement améliorée; **unemployment figures are not s. lower** le nombre de chômeurs n'a pas considérablement baissé; **there have been s. fewer problems** on a eu nettement moins de problèmes **2** *(nod, frown, wink)* de façon significative; **s., she arrived early** fait révélateur, elle est arrivée en avance **3** *(in statistics)* de manière significative

signification [ˌsɪgnɪfɪ'keɪʃən] **N** signification *f*

significative [sɪg'nɪfɪkətɪv] **ADJ** significatif

signify ['sɪgnɪfaɪ] *(pt & pp* **signified)** **VT 1** *(indicate, show)* signifier, indiquer; **she stood up, signifying that the interview was over** elle se leva, signifiant ainsi que l'entrevue était terminée; **the riots s. an urgent need for reform** les émeutes indiquent un besoin pressant de réforme **2** *(mean)* signifier, vouloir dire; **for him, socialism signified chaos** pour lui, le socialisme était synonyme de chaos
VI *Fam (be important)* être important❑; **it doesn't s.!** c'est sans importance!❑

signing ['saɪnɪŋ] **N 1** *(of document etc)* signature *f*; *(of deed)* passation *f*; *Com (of bill)* acceptation *f*; **a manager with s. authority** un fondé de pouvoir **2** *(sign language)* = traduction simultanée en langage des signes; **her s. is excellent** elle connaît très bien le langage des signes **3** *Ftbl (transfer)* transfert *m*; *(player)* recrue *f*; **Arsenal's newest s. will make his debut this Saturday** la nouvelle recrue d'Arsenal fera ses débuts samedi

signing-in **N** *(of employees)* pointage *m*

sign-off **N** *TV* annonce *f* de la fin des émissions

signpost ['saɪnpəʊst] **N 1** *(giving directions)* poteau *m* indicateur **2** *Fig (guide)* repère *m*; *(omen)* présage *m*
VT *(provide with signs)* signaliser, baliser; *also Fig (indicate)* indiquer; **the village is clearly signposted** le chemin du village est bien indiqué

signposting ['saɪnpəʊstɪŋ] **N** signalisation *f*, balisage *m*; *Fig* indications *fpl*

Sikh [siːk] *Rel* **N** Sikh *mf*
ADJ sikh

Sikhism ['siːkɪzəm] **N** *Rel* sikhisme *m*

silage ['saɪlɪdʒ] **N** *Agr* ensilage *m*

silence ['saɪləns] **N** silence *m*; **s.** *(sign)* défense de parler; **an explosion shattered the s. of the night** une explosion déchira le silence de la nuit; **there was a sudden s.** soudain, il y a eu un silence; **a s. fell between them** un silence s'installa entre eux; **to suffer in s.** souffrir en silence; **to pass sth over in s.** passer qch sous silence; **his s. on the issue/about his past intrigues me** le silence qu'il garde à ce sujet/sur son passé m'intrigue; **there's been complete s. from head office** le siège est resté totalement silencieux; **what's my s. worth to you?** combien êtes-vous disposé à payer pour acheter mon silence?; **to observe a minute's s.** observer une minute de silence; *Prov* **s. is golden** le silence est d'or
VT 1 *(person)* réduire au silence, faire taire; *(sound)* étouffer; *(guns)* faire taire; **she silenced the child with a look** d'un regard elle fit taire l'enfant **2** *(stifle ▸ opposition)* réduire au silence; *(▸ conscience, rumours, complaints)* faire taire; **dissidents cannot be silenced forever** on ne peut pas réduire les dissidents au silence *ou* faire taire les dissidents très longtemps

silencer ['saɪlənsə(r)] **N 1** *(on gun)* silencieux *m* **2** *Aut* pot *m* d'échappement, silencieux *m*

silent ['saɪlənt] **ADJ 1** *(saying nothing)* silencieux; **to fall s.** se taire; **to keep** *or* **to be s.** garder le silence, rester silencieux; *Fam* **to give sb the s. treatment** ne pas adresser la parole à qn❑
2 *(taciturn)* silencieux, taciturne; **he's the strong s. type** il est du genre fort et taciturne
3 *(unspoken ▸ prayer, emotion, reproach)* muet; **his mouth twisted in s. agony** sa bouche se tordit dans un cri de douleur muette
4 *(soundless ▸ room, forest)* silencieux, tranquille; *(▸ tread)* silencieux; *(▸ film)* muet; **the machines/the wind fell s.** le bruit des machines/du vent cessa; **as s. as the grave** muet comme la tombe
5 *Ling (letter)* muet
N *Cin* film *m* muet; **the silents** le (cinéma) muet
►► ***silent film*** film *m* muet; ***silent films*** *(genre)* le (cinéma) muet; ***silent majority*** majorité *f* silencieuse; ***silent movie*** film *m* muet; ***silent movies*** *(genre)* le (cinéma) muet; *Rel* ***silent order*** ordre *m* silencieux; *Am Com* ***silent partner*** (associé *m*) commanditaire *m*, bailleur *m* de fonds

silently ['saɪləntlɪ] **ADV** silencieusement

silex ['saɪleks] **N** silex *m*

silhouette [ˌsɪluː'et] **N** silhouette *f*; **I saw her s. at the window** j'ai aperçu sa silhouette à la fenêtre; **he could just see the church in s. against the sky** il ne voyait que la silhouette de l'église qui se découpait contre le ciel
VT *(usu passive)* **to be silhouetted against sth** se découper contre qch; **the tower was silhouetted against the sky** la tour se découpait sur le ciel

silica ['sɪlɪkə] **N** silice *f*
►► ***silica gel*** gel *m* de silice

silicate ['sɪlɪkɪt] **N** *Chem* silicate *m*

siliceous [sɪ'lɪʃəs] **ADJ** *Chem* siliceux

silicon ['sɪlɪkən] **N** *Chem* silicium *m*
►► ***silicon chip*** puce *f*; ***Silicon Glen*** = appellation formée sur le modèle de "Silicon Valley" ("glen" signifiant "vallée" en écossais), d'une région du centre de l'Écosse où sont concentrées un grand nombre de sociétés informatiques; ***Silicon Valley*** Silicon Valley *f (centre de l'industrie électronique américaine, situé en Californie)*; ***silicon wafer*** tranche *f* de silicium

silicone ['sɪlɪkəʊn] **N** *Chem* silicone *f*
►► ***silicone implant*** implant *m* mammaire en silicone

silicosis [ˌsɪlɪ'kəʊsɪs] **N** *(UNCOUNT)* *Med* silicose *f*

silk [sɪlk] **N 1** *(fabric)* soie *f*; *(thread)* fil *m* de soie **2** *Br Law (King's, Queen's Counsel)* conseiller *m* du roi/de la reine; *(collectively)* conseillers *mpl* du roi/de la reine; **to take s.** être nommé avocat de la couronne
COMP *(scarf, blouse etc)* de *ou* en soie
• **silks** **NPL** *(jockey's jacket)* casaque *f*; **Jo Burns, in**

the Graham (Stable) silks Jo Burns, portant les couleurs (de l'Écurie) Graham
▸▸ ***the silk industry*** l'industrie *f* de la soie; ***silk merchant*** marchand(e) *m,f* de soierie, soyeux *m*; ***the Silk Road*** la route de la soie; ***silk screen printing, silk screen process*** sérigraphie *f*; ***silk stocking*** bas *m* de soie; *Am Fam (aristocratic person)* aristocrate▫*mf*; *(wealthy person)* riche▫*mf*; ***silk trader*** marchand(e) *m,f* de soierie, soyeux *m*

silken ['sɪlkən] ADJ *Literary* **1** *(made of silk)* de *ou* en soie **2** *(like silk ▸ hair, cheek etc)* soyeux; *(▸ voice, tone)* doux (douce)

silkiness ['sɪlkɪnɪs] N **1** *(of fabric, hair, skin)* toucher *m* soyeux **2** *(of voice, tone)* douceur *f*

silkworm ['sɪlkwɜːm] N ver *m* à soie
▸▸ ***silkworm breeder*** sériciculteur(trice) *m,f*; ***silkworm breeding*** sériciculture *f*; ***silkworm farm*** magnanerie *f*; ***silkworm moth*** bombyx *m* du mûrier

silky ['sɪlkɪ] *(compar* **silkier**, *superl* **silkiest)** ADJ **1** *(like silk ▸ fabric, hair, cheek)* soyeux **2** *(suave ▸ tone, manner)* doux (douce) **3** *(made of silk)* de *ou* en soie

sill [sɪl] N **1** *(ledge ▸ gen)* rebord *m*; *(▸ of window)* rebord *m*, appui *m*; *(▸ of door)* seuil *m* **2** *Aut* marchepied *m*

sillabub = **syllabub**

silliness ['sɪlɪnɪs] N bêtise *f*, stupidité *f*; **no more s. from you!** arrête de faire l'idiot!

silly ['sɪlɪ] *(compar* **sillier**, *superl* **silliest**, *pl* **sillies)**
ADJ **1** *(foolish ▸ person)* bête, stupide; *(▸ quarrel, book, grin, question)* bête, stupide, idiot; *(infantile)* bébête; **that was a s. thing to say** c'était bête de dire ça; **I'll pay – don't be s.!** je vais payer – ah ça, pas question!; **don't do anything s.** ne fais pas de bêtises; **how s. of me!** que je suis bête!; **it was s. of me to ask** c'était idiot de ma part de demander ça; **you look s. in that hat** tu as l'air ridicule avec ce chapeau; **there was a new manager every week, it was** *or* **things were getting s.** il y avait un nouveau gérant chaque semaine, ça en devenait ridicule; *Br Fam Press* **the s. season** la période creuse▫*(pour les journalistes)* **2** *(comical ▸ mask, costume, voice)* comique, drôle; **we all wore s. hats** nous portions tous des chapeaux marrants
ADV *Fam (senseless)* **to laugh oneself s.** mourir de rire; **I was bored s.** je m'ennuyais à mourir; **he drank himself s.** il s'est complètement soûlé; **she's been worrying herself s.** elle est morte d'inquiétude
N *Fam* idiot(e)▫*m,f*; **don't be such a s.!** que tu es bête!

silly-billy *(pl* **silly-billies)** N *Br Fam* gros bêta (grosse bêtasse) *m,f*

silly-season story N *Br Fam Press* serpent *m* de mer

silly-willy *(pl* **silly-willies)** N *Am* = **silly-billy**

silo ['saɪləʊ] *(pl* **silos)** N *Agr & Mil* silo *m*

silt [sɪlt] N *Geol* limon *m*; *(mud)* vase *f*
▸ **silt up** VI *(with mud)* s'envaser; *(with sand)* s'ensabler
VT SEP *(of mud)* envaser; *(of sand)* ensabler

silting ['sɪltɪŋ] N **s. (up)** *(with mud)* envasement *m*; *(with sand)* ensablement *m*

silty ['sɪltɪ] *(compar* **siltier**, *superl* **siltiest)** ADJ limoneux

silver ['sɪlvə(r)] N **1** *(metal)* argent *m*
2 *(UNCOUNT) Br (coins)* pièces *fpl* (d'argent); **£5 in s.** 5 livres en argent, 5 livres en pièces *ou* en monnaie d'argent
3 *(UNCOUNT) (dishes)* argenterie *f*; *(cutlery ▸ gen)* couverts *mpl*; *(▸ made of silver)* argenterie *f*, couverts *mpl* en argent; **to clean the s.** nettoyer *ou* faire l'argenterie
4 *(colour)* (couleur *f*) argent *m*
5 *Sport (medal)* médaille *f* d'argent; **he's hoping to win the s.** il espère remporter la médaille d'argent
ADJ **1** *(of silver)* d'argent, en argent; **is your ring s.?** est-ce que votre bague est en argent?; **he was born with a s. spoon in his mouth** il est né coiffé **2** *(in colour)* argenté, argent *(inv)* **3** *(sound)* argentin; **she has a s. tongue** elle sait parler
VT **1** *(gen) & Fig* argenter; **the moon silvered the lake** la lune donnait au lac des reflets d'argent **2** *(mirror)* étamer
▸▸ ***silver birch*** bouleau *m* blanc; ***silver disc*** disque *m* d'argent; ***silver fir*** *(gen)* sapin *m* blanc *ou* pectiné; *(ornamental)* sapin *m* argenté; ***silver foil*** papier *m* d'aluminium; ***silver fox*** renard *m* argenté; *Ftbl* ***silver goal*** but *m* en argent; ***silver grey*** gris *m* argenté; ***silver jubilee*** (fête *f* du) vingt-cinquième anniversaire *m*; **the Queen's s. jubilee** le vingt-cinquième anniversaire de l'accession au trône de la reine; *Sport* ***silver medal*** médaille *f* d'argent; ***silver mine*** mine *f* d'argent; ***silver paper*** papier *m* d'argent; ***silver plate*** **1** *(coating)* plaquage *m* d'argent; **the cutlery is s. plate** les couverts sont en plaqué argent **2** *(tableware)* argenterie *f*; ***silver plating*** argentage *m*; *(layer)* argenture *f*; ***the silver screen*** le grand écran, le cinéma; **stars of the s. screen** stars *fpl* du grand écran; ***silver service*** *(in restaurant)* service *m* de grande classe; *esp Br* ***silver service waiter*** serveur *m* pour service au guéridon; *esp Br* ***silver service waitress*** serveuse *f* pour service au guéridon; *Fam Comput* ***silver surfer*** internaute *mf* âgé(e); ***silver wedding (anniversary)*** noces *fpl* d'argent

silverfish ['sɪlvəfɪʃ] *(pl inv or* **silverfishes)** N *Entom* poisson *m* d'argent, lépisme *m*

silver-haired ADJ aux cheveux argentés

silver-plate VT argenter

silver-plated [-'pleɪtɪd] ADJ argenté, plaqué argent; **s. tableware** argenterie *f*

silverside ['sɪlvəsaɪd] N *Br Culin* ≃ gîte *m* à la noix

silversmith ['sɪlvəsmɪθ] N orfèvre *m*

silverware ['sɪlvəweə(r)] N *(UNCOUNT)* **1** *(gen)* argenterie *f* **2** *Am (cutlery)* couverts *mpl*

silverwork ['sɪlvəwɜːk] N orfèvrerie *f*

silvery ['sɪlvərɪ] ADJ *(hair, fabric, cloud, water)* argenté; *(voice, sound)* argentin

SIM [sɪm] N *(abbr* **subscriber identity module)**
▸▸ ***SIM card*** *(in mobile phone)* carte *f* SIM

simian ['sɪmɪən] ADJ simien; *(ape-like)* simiesque
N simien *m*

similar ['sɪmɪlə(r)] ADJ *(showing resemblance)* similaire, semblable; **they're very s.** ils se ressemblent beaucoup; **other customers have had s. problems** d'autres clients ont eu des problèmes similaires *ou* analogues *ou* du même ordre; **they are very s. in content** leurs contenus sont pratiquement identiques; **your case is s. to mine** votre cas est semblable au mien; **it's an assembly s. to the US Senate** c'est une assemblée comparable au Sénat américain; **something s. happened to me** il m'est arrivé quelque chose de semblable

similarity [ˌsɪmɪ'lærətɪ] *(pl* **similarities)** N *(resemblance)* ressemblance *f*, similarité *f*; **there are points of s. in their strategies** leurs stratégies ont des points communs *ou* présentent des similitudes; **there the s. ends** c'est là que s'arrête la comparaison
• **similarities** NPL *(features in common)* ressemblances *fpl*, points *mpl* communs; **our similarities are more important than our differences** nos points communs sont plus importants que nos différends

similarly ['sɪmɪləlɪ] ADV **1** *(in a similar way)* d'une façon similaire; **other people were s. treated** d'autres personnes ont été traitées de la même manière **2** *(likewise)* de même; **s., it is obvious that...** de même, il est évident que... + *indicative*

simile ['sɪmɪlɪ] N *Literature* comparaison *f*

similitude [sɪ'mɪlɪtjuːd] N similitude *f*

SIMM [sɪm] N *Comput (abbr* **single in-line memory module)** SIMM *m*

simmer ['sɪmə(r)] VI **1** *(water, milk, sauce)* frémir; *(soup, stew, vegetables)* mijoter **2** *(smoulder ▸ violence, quarrel, discontent)* couver, fermenter; *(seethe ▸ with anger, excitement)* être en ébullition; **unrest is simmering in the big cities** des troubles couvent dans les grandes villes; **his anger simmered just below the surface** il bouillait de colère **3** *(be hot)* rôtir; *(when humid)* mijoter; **the city simmered in the heat** la ville était accablée par la canicule
VT *(water, milk, sauce)* laisser frémir; *(soup, stew, vegetables)* faire mijoter
N faible ébullition *f*
▸ **simmer down** VI *Fam (person)* se calmer▫; **s. down!** calme-toi!, du calme!

simnel cake ['sɪmnəl-] N *Br* = gâteau aux fruits confits, recouvert de pâte d'amandes ou fourré à la pâte d'amandes (mangé traditionnellement à Pâques)

simoleon [sɪ'məʊlɪən] N *Am Fam (dollar)* dollar▫ *m*

Simon ['saɪmən] PR N Simon
▸▸ ***Simon says*** *(game)* Jacques a dit *m*

simon crane ['saɪmən-] N *TV & Cin* grue *f* hydraulique

simony ['saɪmənɪ] N simonie *f*

simp [sɪmp] N *Am Fam Pej (abbr* **simpleton)** andouille *f*, crétin(e) *m,f*

simper ['sɪmpə(r)] VI minauder
VT **"of course, madam", he simpered** "bien sûr, chère Madame," dit-il en minaudant
N sourire *m* affecté; **"may I help you?" she said with a s.** "vous désirez?", dit-elle en minaudant

simpering ['sɪmpərɪŋ] N *(UNCOUNT)* minauderies *fpl*

simple ['sɪmpəl] ADJ **1** *(easy)* simple, facile; *(uncomplicated)* simple; **it's a s. operation** c'est une opération simple; **it's a s. meal to prepare** c'est un repas facile à préparer; **it would be simpler to do it myself** ce serait plus simple que je le fasse *ou* si je le faisais moi-même; **it should be a s. matter to change your ticket** tu ne devrais avoir aucun mal à changer ton billet; **to yearn for the s. life** aspirer au retour à la nature; **let's hear your story, then, but keep it s.** bon, racontez votre histoire, mais passez-moi les détails; **it's as s. as that** c'est aussi simple que ça
2 *(plain ▸ tastes, ceremony, life, style)* simple; **she wore a s. black dress** elle portait une robe noire toute simple; **let me explain in s. terms** *or* **language** laissez-moi vous expliquer ça en termes simples; **for the s. reason that...** pour la simple raison que... + *indicative*
3 *(unassuming)* simple, sans façons
4 *(naive)* simple, naïf; *(feeble-minded)* simple, niais; **he's a bit s.** il est un peu simplet
5 *(basic ▸ substance, fracture, sentence)* simple
▸▸ *Math* ***simple fraction*** fraction *f* ordinaire; *Med* ***simple fracture*** fracture *f* simple; *Gram* ***simple tense*** temps *m* simple

simple-hearted ADJ *(person)* candide, ouvert; *(wisdom, gesture)* simple, naturel

simple-minded ADJ *(naive)* naïf, simplet; *(feeble-minded)* simple d'esprit; **it's a very s. view of society** c'est une vision très simpliste de la société

simple-mindedness [-'maɪndɪdnɪs] N *(naivety)* naïveté *f*; *(feeble-mindedness)* simplicité *f* d'esprit

simpleness ['sɪmpəlnɪs] = **simplicity**

simpleton ['sɪmpəltən] N *Old-fashioned* nigaud (e) *m,f*

simplex ['sɪmpleks] ADJ *Comput & Tel* simplex *(inv)*, unidirectionnel
N *Comput & Tel* simplex *m*, transmission *f* unidirectionnelle; *Ling (sentence)* unité *f* proportionnelle; *(word)* mot *m* simple

simplicity [sɪm'plɪsətɪ] N **1** *(UNCOUNT) (candour)* candeur *f*, simplicité *f*; *(foolishness)* bêtise *f*, sottise *f* **2** *(UNCOUNT) (easiness)* simplicité *f*; **the instructions are s. itself** les instructions sont simples comme bonjour *ou* tout ce qu'il y a de plus simple

simplification [ˌsɪmplɪfɪ'keɪʃən] N simplification *f*

simplify ['sɪmplɪfaɪ] *(pt & pp* **simplified)** VT simplifier

simplistic [sɪm'plɪstɪk] ADJ simpliste

simply ['sɪmplɪ] ADV **1** *(in a simple way)* simplement, avec simplicité; **put s., it's a disaster** c'est tout simplement une catastrophe **2** *(just, only)* simplement, seulement; **it's not s. a matter of money** ce n'est pas une simple question d'argent; **I s. told her the truth** je lui ai tout simplement dit la vérité **3** *(as intensifier)* absolument; **I s. don't understand you** je ne vous comprends vraiment pas; **we s. must go now** il faut absolument que nous partions maintenant

simulacrum [ˌsɪmjʊˈleɪkrəm] *(pl* **simulacra** [-krə]) **N** *Formal or Literary* simulacre *m*, semblant *m*

simulate [ˈsɪmjʊleɪt] **VT 1** *(imitate ▸ blood, battle, sound)* simuler, imiter **2** *(feign ▸ pain, pleasure)* simuler, feindre **3** *Comput & Tech* simuler

simulation [ˌsɪmjʊˈleɪʃən] **N** simulation *f*
▸▸ *Comput* ***simulation model*** modèle *m* de simulation

simulator [ˈsɪmjʊleɪtə(r)] **N** simulateur *m*

simulcast [*Br* ˈsɪməlkɑːst, *Am* ˈsaɪməlkæst] **VT** diffuser simultanément à la télévision et à la radio
ADJ radiotélévisé
N émission *f* radiotélévisée

simultaneity [*Br* ˌsɪmltəˈniːətɪ, *Am* ˌsaɪmltəˈniːətɪ] **N** simultanéité *f*

simultaneous [*Br* ˌsɪməlˈteɪnɪəs, *Am* ˌsaɪməlˈteɪnɪəs] **ADJ** simultané
▸▸ ***simultaneous broadcast*** émission *f* diffusée simultanément, retransmission *f* simultanée; *Math* ***simultaneous equations*** système *m* d'équations simultanées; ***simultaneous translation*** traduction *f* simultanée

simultaneously [*Br* ˌsɪməlˈteɪnɪəslɪ, *Am* ˌsaɪməlˈteɪnɪəslɪ] **ADV** simultanément, en même temps

sin [sɪn] *(pt & pp* **sinned**, *cont* **sinning**) **N** péché *m*; **to commit a s.** pécher, commettre un péché; **sins of omission/commission** péchés *mpl* par omission/action; **it's a s. to tell a lie** mentir *ou* le mensonge est un péché; **it would be a s. to sell it** ce serait un crime de le vendre; *Hum* **for my sins, I'm the person in charge of all this** malheureusement pour moi, c'est moi le responsable de tout ça; *Rel or Hum* **to live in s.** vivre dans le péché
VI pécher; **to s. against sth** pécher contre qch; *Fig* **to be more sinned against than sinning** être plus victime que coupable
▸▸ *Fam Sport* ***sin bin*** banc *m* des pénalités*, prison *f*; *Hum* ***sin tax*** = appellation humoristique de la taxe sur l'alcool et le tabac

Sinai [ˈsaɪnaɪ] **N** *(region)* Sinaï *m*; **the S. (Desert)** le (désert du) Sinaï; **(Mount) S.** le (mont) Sinaï
▸▸ ***the Sinai Peninsula*** la presqu'île de Sinaï

since [sɪns] **PREP** depuis; **he has been talking about it s. yesterday/s. before Christmas** il en parle depuis hier/depuis avant Noël; **the fair has been held annually (ever) s. 1950** la foire a lieu chaque année depuis 1950; **she's the best soul singer s. Aretha Franklin** c'est la meilleure chanteuse de soul depuis Aretha Franklin; **how long is it s. their divorce?** ça fait combien de temps qu'ils ont divorcé?; **s. then** depuis lors; **that was in 1966, s. when the law has been altered** c'était en 1966 – depuis, la loi a été modifiée; **s. when have you been married?** depuis quand êtes-vous marié?; *Fam Ironic* **they really have changed – oh yes, s. when?** ils ont vraiment changé – ah oui, depuis quand?
CONJ 1 *(in time)* depuis que; **I've worn glasses s. I was six** je porte des lunettes depuis que j'ai six ans *ou* depuis l'âge de six ans; **how long has it been s. you last saw Hal?** ça fait combien de temps que tu n'as pas vu Hal?; **s. leaving New York, I...** depuis que j'ai quitté New York, je...; **it had been ten years s. I had seen him** cela faisait dix ans que je ne l'avais pas revu **2** *(expressing cause)* puisque, comme; **s. you don't want to go, I'll go by myself** puisque *ou* comme tu ne veux pas y aller, j'irai tout seul
ADV depuis; **she used to be his assistant, but she's s. been promoted** elle était son assistante, mais depuis elle a été promue; **I've never seen it/her s.** je ne l'ai jamais revu/revue depuis
• **ever since CONJ** depuis que; **ever s. she resigned, things have been getting worse** depuis qu'elle a démissionné *ou* depuis sa démission, les choses ont empiré **PREP** depuis; **ever s. that day he's been afraid of dogs** depuis ce jour-là, il a peur des chiens **ADV** depuis; **he arrived at nine o'clock and he's been sitting there ever s.** il est arrivé à nine heures et il est assis là depuis
• **long since ADV I've long s. forgotten why** il y a longtemps que j'ai oublié pourquoi

sincere [sɪnˈsɪə(r)] **ADJ** sincère; **please accept my s. apologies** veuillez accepter mes sincères excuses; **it is my s. belief that...** je crois sincèrement que... + *indicative*

sincerely [sɪnˈsɪəlɪ] **ADV** sincèrement; **I s. hope we can be friends** j'espère sincèrement que nous serons amis; *Br* **Yours s.**, *Am* **S. yours** je vous prie d'agréer, Monsieur/Madame, mes sentiments les meilleurs

sincerity [sɪnˈserətɪ] **N** sincérité *f*; **in all s., I must admit that...** en toute sincérité, je dois admettre que... + *indicative*

sine [saɪn] **N** *Math* sinus *m*

sinecure [ˈsaɪnɪˌkjʊə(r)] **N** sinécure *f*

sinew [ˈsɪnjuː] **N** *(tendon)* tendon *m*; *(muscle)* muscle *m*; *Literary (strength)* force *f*, forces *fpl*; **I will resist with every s. of my body** je résisterai de toutes mes forces

sinewy [ˈsɪnjuːɪ] **ADJ 1** *(muscular ▸ person, body, arm)* musclé; *(▸ neck, hands)* nerveux; *(with tendons)* tendineux **2** *(meat)* tendineux

sinful [ˈsɪnfʊl] **ADJ** *(deed, urge, thought)* coupable, honteux; *(world)* plein de péchés, souillé par le péché; **his s. ways** sa vie de pécheur; **s. man** pécheur *m*; **s. woman** pécheresse *f*; **she thought alcohol was s.** pour elle, boire de l'alcool était un péché; **it's downright s.!** c'est un vrai scandale!

sinfully [ˈsɪnfʊlɪ] **ADV** d'une façon coupable *ou* scandaleuse

sinfulness [ˈsɪnfʊlnɪs] **N** *(of deed, thought)* caractère *m* honteux; **a life of s.** une vie de péché

sing [sɪŋ] *(pt* **sang** [sæŋ], *pp* **sung** [sʌŋ]) **VI 1** *(person)* chanter **2** *(bird, kettle)* chanter; *(wind, arrow)* siffler; *(ears)* bourdonner, siffler; **the noise made my ears s.** ce bruit m'a fait bourdonner les oreilles **3** *Am Fam (confess, inform)* cracher, lâcher le morceau, se mettre à table; **somebody's been singing to our competitors** quelqu'un a vendu la mèche à *ou* tuyauté nos concurrents
VT 1 *(song, note, mass)* chanter; **to s. opera/jazz** chanter de l'opéra/du jazz; **who sings tenor?** qui est ténor?; **to s. sb to sleep** chanter pour endormir qn; *Fig* **now they're singing another** *or* **a different tune** ils ont changé de ton **2** *(laud)* célébrer, chanter; **to s. the praises of sb/sth** chanter *ou* célébrer les louanges de qn/qch
▸ **sing along VI** chanter (tous) ensemble *ou* en chœur; **to s. along to** *or* **with the radio** chanter en même temps que la radio
▸ **sing out VI 1** *(sing loudly)* chanter fort **2** *Fam (shout)* crier*; **when you're ready, s. out** quand tu seras prêt, fais-moi signe*
▸ **sing up VI** chanter plus fort; **s. up!** plus fort!

singable [ˈsɪŋəbəl] **ADJ** chantable

Singapore [ˌsɪŋəˈpɔː(r)] **N** Singapour

Singaporean [ˌsɪŋəˈpɔːrɪən] **N** Singapourien(enne) *m,f*
ADJ singapourien

singe [sɪndʒ] *(cont* **singeing**) **VT 1** *(gen)* brûler légèrement; *(shirt, fabric, paper)* roussir; **the lighter singed his moustache** il s'est brûlé la moustache avec le briquet **2** *Culin (carcass, chicken)* flamber, passer à la flamme
N *(burn)* brûlure *f* (légère); *(mark)* marque *f* de brûlure

singer [ˈsɪŋə(r)] **N** *(of songs)* chanteur(euse) *m,f*; **she's a jazz s.** elle est chanteuse de jazz; **I'm a terrible s.** je chante affreusement mal; **s. songwriter** auteur-compositeur-interprète *mf*

Singhalese = **Sinhalese**

singing [ˈsɪŋɪŋ] **N 1** *(of person, bird)* chant *m*; *(of kettle, wind)* sifflement *m*; *(in ears)* bourdonnement *m*, sifflement *m*; **the s. went on until dawn** on a chanté *ou* les chants ont continué jusqu'à l'aube **2** *(art)* chant *m*; **to study s.** étudier le chant; **her s. has improved** elle chante mieux
ADJ *(lesson, teacher, contest)* de chant; **she's got a fine s. voice** elle a une belle voix

SINGLE [ˈsɪŋgəl]

N	
• single **1**	• aller simple **2**
• chambre individuelle **3**	
ADJ	
• seul **1, 2**	• unique **1**
• simple **3**	• singulier **3**
• pour une personne **4**	• célibataire **5**

N 1 *(record)* 45 tours *m inv*, single *m*; *(CD, cassette)* single *m*
2 *Br (ticket ▸ for journey)* aller *m* simple; *Theat* **we only have singles left** il ne nous reste que des places séparées
3 *(hotel room)* chambre *f* pour une personne *ou* individuelle
4 *(usu pl) (money) Br* pièce *f* d'une livre; *Am* billet *m* d'un dollar
ADJ 1 *(sole)* seul, unique; **the room was lit by a s. lamp** la pièce était éclairée par une seule lampe; **the report comes in a s. volume** le rapport est publié en un (seul) volume; **I can't think of one s. reason why I should do it** je n'ai aucune raison de le faire; **there wasn't a s. person in the street** il n'y avait pas un chat dans la rue; **not a s. one of her friends came** pas un seul de ses amis *ou* aucun de ses amis n'est venu; **don't say a s. word** ne dites pas un (seul) mot
2 *(individual, considered separately)* **our s. most important resource is oil** notre principale ressource est le pétrole; **we sell s. items at a higher price per unit** le prix unitaire est plus élevé; **s. copies cost more** un exemplaire seul coûte plus cher; **in any s. year, average sales are ten million** sur une seule année, les ventes sont en moyenne de dix millions; **every s. day** tous les jours; **every s. time** chaque fois; **every s. apple** *or* **every s. one of the apples was rotten** toutes les pommes sans exception étaient pourries
3 *(not double ▸ flower, thickness)* simple; *(▸ combat)* singulier; **the score is still in s. figures** le score est toujours inférieur à dix
4 *(for one person ▸ bed)* à une place, pour une personne; *Naut (▸ cabin)* individuel; **a s. sheet** un drap pour un lit d'une personne
5 *(unmarried)* célibataire; **a s. man/woman** un/une célibataire; **the s. life seems to agree with you** la vie de célibataire a l'air de te convenir
6 *Br (one way)* **a s. ticket to Oxford** un aller (simple) pour Oxford; **the s. fare is £12** un aller simple coûte 12 livres
▸▸ *Br* ***single cream*** crème *f* (fraîche) liquide; ***single currency*** monnaie *f* unique; ***the Single European Act*** l'Acte *m* unique européen; ***the Single European Market*** le Marché unique (européen); ***single file*** file *f* indienne; **to walk in s. file** marcher en file indienne *ou* à la queue leu leu; *Br Univ* ***single honours*** = licence portant sur une seule matière; ***the Single Market*** le Marché unique (européen); ***single occupancy*** *(of hotel room)* occupation *f* par une seule personne; ***single parent*** *(gen)* père *m*/mère *f* célibataire; *Admin* parent *m* isolé; **he's a s. parent** c'est un père célibataire; ***single price*** prix *m* unique; ***single quotes*** guillemets *mpl*; ***single room*** chambre *f* pour une personne *ou* individuelle; ***single room supplement*** supplément *m* chambre individuelle; *Comput* ***single sheet feed*** alimentation *f* feuille à feuille; *Typ* ***single spacing*** interlignage *m* simple; ***single supplement*** supplément *m* chambre individuelle; *Comput* ***single user licence*** licence *f* individuelle d'utilisation; *Br* ***single yellow line*** = ligne jaune indiquant que le stationnement est autorisé à certaines heures
• **singles** *(pl* **inv**) **N 1** *Sport* simple *m*; **the men's, women's s. champion** le champion du simple messieurs/dames **2** *(unmarried people)* célibataires *mpl*; **a package holiday for s.** des vacances organisées pour célibataires **COMP** *(bar, club, magazine)* pour célibataires; **Tuesday is s. night** mardi, c'est la soirée pour célibataires
▸ **single out VT SEP** *(for attention, honour)* sélectionner, distinguer; **a few candidates were singled out for special praise** quelques candidats ont eu droit à des félicitations supplémentaires; **they were all guilty, so why s. anyone out?** ils étaient tous coupables, alors pourquoi accuser quelqu'un en particulier?

single-breasted [-ˈbrestɪd] **ADJ** *(jacket, coat)* droit

single-chamber **ADJ** *Pol* monocaméral

single-colour, *Am* **single-color** **ADJ** *Phot & Typ* en une couleur

single-column **ADJ** *Typ* à une colonne

single-cylinder **ADJ**
▸▸ *Aut* ***single-cylinder engine*** moteur *m* monocylindrique

single-decker [-ˈdekə(r)] N *Br* autobus *m* sans impériale
▸▸ ***single-decker bus*** autobus *m* sans impériale

single-density ADJ
▸▸ *Comput* ***single-density disk*** disquette *f* simple densité

single-drive ADJ *(computer)* à un seul lecteur de disquettes

single-engined [-ˈendʒɪnd] ADJ *(plane)* monomoteur

single-handed [-ˈhændɪd] ADV *(on one's own)* tout seul, sans aucune aide; **she's tripled our sales s.** elle a triplé nos ventes à elle toute seule
ADJ **1** *(unaided ▸ voyage)* en solitaire; **to be s.** être tout seul, n'avoir aucune aide **2** *(using one hand)* à une main

single-handedly [-ˈhændɪdlɪ] ADV **1** *(on one's own)* tout seul, sans l'aide de personne; **she was s. responsible for the firm's success** c'est grâce à elle seule que l'entreprise a réussi **2** *(with one hand)* d'une seule main

single-income ADJ *(family, couple)* à salaire unique

single-lane ADJ *(traffic)* à voie unique

single-lens ADJ *Phot*
▸▸ ***single-lens camera*** appareil photo *m* monoculaire; ***single-lens reflex*** reflex *m* à un objectif

single-minded ADJ résolu, acharné; **the s. pursuit of money** la poursuite acharnée de l'argent; **to be s. about sth** s'acharner sur qch; **he is s. in his efforts to block the project** il fait tout ce qu'il peut pour bloquer le projet

single-mindedly [-ˈmaɪndɪdlɪ] ADV avec acharnement

single-mindedness [-ˈmaɪndɪdnɪs] N résolution *f*, acharnement *m*

singleness [ˈsɪŋgəlnɪs] N **with s. of purpose** avec un seul but en vue; **his s. of purpose** sa détermination

single-parent family N famille *f* monoparentale

single-phase ADJ *(current)* monophasé

single-sex ADJ *Sch* non mixte

single-sided ADJ *Comput (disk)* à une seule face

single-spaced [-speɪst] ADJ *Typ* à interligne simple

singlet [ˈsɪŋglɪt] N *Br (undergarment)* maillot *m* de corps; *Sport* maillot *m*

singletasking [ˌsɪŋgəlˈtɑːskɪŋ] *Comput* N monotâche *m*
ADJ monotâche

singleton [ˈsɪŋgəltən] N **1** *Cards & Math* singleton *m* **2** *Br Fam (single person)* célibataire ▫ *mf*

single-track ADJ à voie unique

singly [ˈsɪŋglɪ] ADV **1** *(one at a time)* séparément **2** *(alone)* seul; **they arrived either in couples or s.** ils sont arrivés en couples ou seuls **3** *(individually ▸ packaged)* individuellement; **you can't buy them s.** vous ne pouvez pas les acheter à la pièce

singsong [ˈsɪŋsɒŋ] N *Br (singing)* chants *mpl* (en chœur); **let's have a s.** chantons tous ensemble *ou* en chœur
ADJ *(voice, accent)* chantant; **in a s. voice** d'une voix chantante

singular [ˈsɪŋgjʊlə(r)] ADJ **1** *(remarkable)* singulier; *(odd)* singulier, bizarre **2** *Gram* singulier
N *Gram* singulier *m*; **in the third person s.** à la troisième personne du singulier

singularity [ˌsɪŋgjʊˈlærətɪ] (*pl* **singularities**) N singularité *f*

singularize, -ise [ˈsɪŋgjʊləraɪz] VT **1** *(distinguish)* singulariser **2** *Gram* mettre au singulier

singularly [ˈsɪŋgjʊləlɪ] ADV singulièrement; **I was s. unimpressed** cela ne m'a vraiment pas impressionné

Sinhalese [ˌsɪnhəˈliːz] (*pl* inv *or* **Sinhaleses**) N **1** *(person)* Cinghalais(e) *m,f* **2** *Ling* cinghalais *m*
ADJ cinghalais

sinister [ˈsɪnɪstə(r)] ADJ *(ominous, evil)* sinistre

SINK [sɪŋk]

N	
• évier **1**	• lavabo **1**
VT	
• couler **1**	• faire échouer **2**
• oublier **3**	• enfoncer **4**
• creuser **5**	• investir **6**
VI	
• couler **1**	• sombrer **1, 6**
• s'enfoncer **2, 6, 7**	• baisser **3, 5**
• s'affaisser **3**	• s'écrouler **4**
• plonger **5**	

(*pt* **sank** [sæŋk], *pp* **sunk** [sʌŋk])
N **1** *(in kitchen)* évier *m*; *(in bathroom)* lavabo *m* **2** *(cesspool)* puisard *m*; *Fig* **a s. of sin and corruption** un cloaque du vice **3** *Geol* doline *f*
VT **1** *(boat, submarine)* couler, envoyer par le fond; *Fig* **to be sunk in thought** être plongé dans ses pensées
2 *(ruin ▸ plans)* faire échouer; **this latest scandal looks certain to s. him** ce dernier scandale va sûrement le couler; *Fam* **if they don't come we're sunk!** s'ils ne viennent pas, nous sommes fichus!
3 *(forget)* oublier; **he sank his troubles in drink** il noya ses soucis dans l'alcool
4 *(plunge, drive ▸ knife, spear, stake)* enfoncer; **they're sinking the piles for the jetty** ils sont en train de mettre en place les pilotis de la jetée; **the fishpond was a metal basin sunk in the ground** l'étang à poissons était un bassin en métal enfoncé dans le sol; **I sank my teeth into the peach** j'ai mordu dans la pêche; **the dog sank its teeth into my leg** le chien m'enfonça *ou* me planta ses crocs dans la jambe
5 *(dig, bore ▸ well, mine shaft)* creuser, forer
6 *(invest ▸ money)* mettre, investir; *(▸ extravagantly)* engloutir; **we sank a fortune into this company** nous avons englouti une fortune dans cette société
7 *Sport (score ▸ basket)* marquer; *(▸ putt)* réussir; **to s. the ball** *(in snooker)* couler la bille; *(in basketball)* réussir le tir *ou* le panier; *(in golf)* envoyer la balle dans le trou
8 *Fin (debt)* amortir
9 *Br Fam (drink down)* s'envoyer, siffler; **to s. a pint** s'envoyer une pinte de bière
VI **1** *(below surface ▸ boat)* couler, sombrer; *(▸ person, stone, log)* couler; **to s. like a stone** couler à pic; **the bottle sank slowly to the bottom of the pool** la bouteille a coulé lentement jusqu'au fond de la piscine; **the prow had not yet sunk beneath the surface** la proue n'était pas encore submergée; **to s. without (a) trace** disparaître sans laisser de trace; *Fig* tomber dans l'oubli; *Fig* **it was a case of s. or swim** il a bien fallu se débrouiller; **now it's up to them to s. or swim by themselves** à eux maintenant de se débrouiller comme ils peuvent
2 *(in mud, snow etc)* s'enfoncer; **at each step, I sank up to my knees in water** à chaque pas, je m'enfonçais dans l'eau jusqu'aux genoux; **to s. into quicksand** s'enliser dans des sables mouvants
3 *(subside ▸ level, water, flames)* baisser; *(▸ building, ground)* s'affaisser; **Venice is sinking** Venise est en train de s'affaisser; **the sun/moon is sinking** le soleil/la lune disparaît à l'horizon; **as I climbed, the valley sank out of sight** au fur et à mesure que je grimpais, la vallée disparaissait
4 *(sag, slump ▸ person)* s'affaler, s'écrouler; *(▸ hopes)* s'écrouler; **I sank back in my seat** je me suis enfoncé dans mon fauteuil; **her head sank back on the pillow** sa tête retomba sur l'oreiller; **he sank onto the bed** il s'est affalé *ou* il s'est laissé tomber sur le lit; **to s. to the ground** s'effondrer; **to s. to one's knees** tomber à genoux; **she sank down on her knees** elle tomba à genoux; **my heart** *or* **spirits sank when I saw I was too late** j'ai perdu courage en voyant que j'arrivais trop tard; **his heart sinks every time he gets a letter from her** il a un serrement de cœur chaque fois qu'il reçoit une lettre d'elle
5 *(decrease, diminish ▸ wages, rates, temperature)* baisser; *(more dramatically)* plonger, chuter; **you have sunk in my estimation** tu as baissé dans mon estime; **the dollar has sunk to half its former value** le dollar a perdu la moitié de sa valeur; **profits have sunk to an all-time low** les bénéfices sont au plus bas; **her voice had sunk to a whisper** *(purposefully)* elle s'était mise à chuchoter; *(weakly)* sa voix n'était plus qu'un murmure
6 *(slip, decline)* sombrer, s'enfoncer; **to s. into apathy/depression** sombrer dans l'apathie/dans la dépression; **he sank deeper into crime** il s'enfonça dans la délinquance; **the house sank into decay and ruin** la maison est tombée en ruines; **how could you s. so low?** comment as-tu pu tomber si bas?; **to s. to new depths** tomber plus bas; **the patient is sinking fast** le malade décline rapidement; **he has sunk into a coma** il est tombé dans le coma; **I sank into a deep sleep** j'ai sombré dans un sommeil profond
7 *(penetrate ▸ blade, arrow)* s'enfoncer; **I felt the dog's teeth s. into my arm** j'ai senti les crocs du chien s'enfoncer dans mon bras
▸▸ *Am* ***sink board*** égouttoir *m*; *Br* ***sink estate*** cité *f* dépotoir; ***sink school*** = école située dans une zone défavorisée, dont une grande proportion d'élèves sont en échec scolaire; ***sink tidy*** = rangement pour ustensiles sur un évier; ***sink unit*** bloc-évier *m*

▸ **sink in** VI **1** *(nail, blade)* s'enfoncer **2** *(soak ▸ varnish, cream)* pénétrer **3** *(register ▸ news)* être compris *ou* assimilé; **I heard what you said, but it didn't s. in at the time** je vous ai entendu, mais je n'ai pas vraiment saisi sur le moment; **I paused to let my words s. in** j'ai marqué une pause pour que mes paroles fassent leur effet; **it was beginning to s. in that things had changed** je commençais/il commençait/*etc* à comprendre que les choses avaient changé

sinker [ˈsɪŋkə(r)] N *(weight)* plomb *m (pour la pêche)*

sinkhole [ˈsɪŋkhəʊl] N *Geol* entonnoir *m*

sinking [ˈsɪŋkɪŋ] N **1** *(of ship ▸ accidental)* naufrage *m*; *(▸ deliberate)* torpillage *m* **2** *(of building, ground)* affaissement *m* **3** *Fin (of debt)* amortissement *m*
ADJ **I experienced that s. feeling you get when you've forgotten something** j'ai eu cette angoisse que l'on ressent quand on sait que l'on a oublié quelque chose; **I get that s. feeling every time I think about what happened** à chaque fois que je pense à ce qui s'est passé, j'ai l'estomac qui se serre
▸▸ *Fin* ***sinking fund*** caisse *f ou* fonds *mpl* d'amortissement

sinless [ˈsɪnlɪs] ADJ sans péché; *(pure)* innocent, pur

sinner [ˈsɪnə(r)] N pécheur(eresse) *m,f*

Sinn Féin [ʃɪnˈfeɪn] N le Sinn Féin *(faction politique de l'IRA)*

sinning [ˈsɪnɪŋ] N péché *m*

sinologist [saɪˈnɒlədʒɪst], **sinologue** [ˈsaɪnəlɒg] N sinologue *mf*

sinology [saɪˈnɒlədʒɪ] N sinologie *f*

sinuosity [ˌsɪnjʊˈɒsətɪ] N sinuosité *f*

sinuous [ˈsɪnjʊəs] ADJ *(road, neck, movement, reasoning)* sinueux; **he danced with s. grace** lorsqu'il dansait, son corps ondulait avec grâce

sinus [ˈsaɪnəs] N sinus *m*

sinusitis [ˌsaɪnəˈsaɪtɪs] N *(UNCOUNT) Med* sinusite *f*

Sioux [suː] (*pl* inv [suː, suːz]) N **1** *(person)* Sioux *mf inv* **2** *Ling* sioux *m*
ADJ sioux *(inv)*; **the S. Indians** les Sioux *mpl*

sip [sɪp] (*pt & pp* **sipped**, *cont* **sipping**) VT *(drink slowly)* boire à petites gorgées *ou* à petits coups; *(savour)* siroter
VI **to s. at sth** boire qch à petites gorgées; **he was at the bar, sipping at a cognac** il était au comptoir, sirotant un cognac
N petite gorgée *f*; **can I have a s.?** je peux goûter *ou* en boire un peu?; **she took a s. of wine** elle a bu une petite gorgée de vin

siphon [ˈsaɪfən] N siphon *m*
VT **1** *(liquid, petrol)* siphonner **2** *(money, resources)* transférer; *(illicitly)* détourner; **the money is siphoned from one account into another** l'argent est transféré d'un compte à un autre

▸ **siphon off** VT SEP **1** *(liquid, petrol)* siphonner **2** *(remove ▸ money)* absorber, éponger; *(divert illegally)* détourner; **the private sector is siphoning off the best graduates** le secteur privé absorbe les meilleurs diplômés; **the road will s. traffic off**

from the city centre la route va détourner une bonne partie de la circulation du centre-ville

SIPP [sɪp] **N** *Br (abbr* **self-invested personal pension**) plan *m* de retraite individuel

sir [sɜː(r)] **N 1** *(term of address)* **no, s.** non, Monsieur; *Mil (to officer)* non, mon général/mon colonel/*etc*; **Dear S.** *(in letter)* (Cher) Monsieur; **Dear Sirs** Messieurs; *Fam* **not for me, no s.!** *(emphatic)* pas pour moi, ça non *ou* pas question! **2** *(title of knight, baronet)* **S. Ian Hall** sir Ian Hall; **to be made a s.** être anobli **3** *Br Fam (male teacher)* **S.'s coming!** le maître arrive!❑

sire [ˈsaɪə(r)] **N 1** *(animal)* père *m* **2** *(term of address)* **no, s.** *(to king)* non, sire; *(to lord)* non, seigneur

VT *(of stallion, man)* engendrer

siren [ˈsaɪərən] **N 1** *(device)* sirène *f*; **ambulance/police s.** sirène *f* d'ambulance/de voiture de police **2** *Myth* sirène *f*; *Fig (temptress)* sirène *f*, femme *f* fatale

►► ***siren call, siren song*** chant *m* des sirènes; *Fig* attrait *m*, appât *m*; **who can resist the s. call of fame and wealth?** qui peut résister à l'attrait de la gloire et de la fortune?

sirloin [ˈsɜːlɔɪn] **N** aloyau *m*; **a s. steak** un bifteck dans l'aloyau

sirocco [sɪˈrɒkəʊ] *(pl* **siroccos**) **N** sirocco *m*, siroco *m*

sirup *Am* = **syrup**

sis [sɪs] **N** *Fam* frangine *f*, sœurette *f*

sisal [ˈsaɪsəl] **N** sisal *m*

ADJ en *ou* de sisal

sissy [ˈsɪsɪ] *(pl* **sissies**) *Fam* **N 1** *(coward)* poule *f* mouillée, peureux(euse)❑*m,f* **2** *(effeminate person)* **he's a real s.** c'est une vraie mauviette; **that's a game for sissies!** c'est un jeu de filles!

ADJ 1 *(cowardly)* peureux❑ **2** *(effeminate)* **don't be so s.** t'es une mauviette ou quoi?

sister [ˈsɪstə(r)] **N 1** *(member of family)* sœur *f*; **they're sisters** elles sont sœurs; **my big/little s.** ma grande/petite sœur

2 *(nun)* religieuse *f*, (bonne) sœur *f*; **no, S.** non, ma sœur; **S. Pauline** sœur Pauline; **S. of Mercy** sœur *f* de la Charité

3 *Br (nurse)* infirmière *f* en chef; **I'll have to ask S.** il faudra que je demande à l'infirmière en chef

4 *(fellow woman, feminist)* sœur *f*; *(term of address)* ma fille

5 *Am Fam (black woman)* = nom donné par les Noirs américains à une femme noire; *(term of address)* ma fille

ADJ *(publication, hotel)* qui appartient au même groupe; **s. state/party** pays *m*/parti *m* frère; **s. company** société *f* sœur

►► *Am* ***sister cities*** villes *fpl* jumelées; **to be a s. city with** être jumelé avec

sisterhood [ˈsɪstəhʊd] **N 1** *(group of women)* communauté *f* de femmes; *Rel* communauté *f* religieuse **2** *(solidarity)* solidarité *f* entre femmes

sister-in-law *(pl* **sisters-in-law**) **N** belle-sœur *f*

sisterly [ˈsɪstəlɪ] **ADJ** *(advice, devotion)* de sœur

Sistine Chapel [ˈsɪstiːn-] **N the S.** la chapelle Sixtine

Sisyphus [ˈsɪsɪfəs] **PR N** *Myth* Sisyphe; **the myth of S.** le mythe de Sisyphe

SIT [sɪt]

VT	
• asseoir **1**	• faire asseoir **2**
• passer **3**	
VI	
• s'asseoir **1**	• être assis **1**
• rester **1, 7**	• poser **2**
• être en séance **4**	• garder les enfants **5**
• être **6**	• se trouver **6**

(pt & pp **sat** [sæt], *cont* **sitting**)

VT 1 *(place)* asseoir, installer; **he sat the child in the pram/on his knee** il a assis l'enfant dans le landau/sur ses genoux

2 *(invite to be seated)* faire asseoir; **she sat me in the waiting room** elle m'a fait asseoir dans la salle d'attente

3 *Br (examination)* se présenter à, passer

VI 1 *(take a seat)* s'asseoir; *(be seated)* être assis; **she came and sat next to me** elle est venue s'asseoir à côté de moi; **s. in the back of the car** mettez-vous à l'arrière (de la voiture); **she was sitting reading** elle était assise à lire *ou* en train de lire; **where shall I s.?** où est-ce que je me mets?; **they were sitting at (the) table** ils étaient à table, ils étaient attablés; **we usually s. in the living room** nous sommes d'ordinaire dans le salon; **s. still!** tiens-toi *ou* reste tranquille!; **s.!** *(to dog)* assis!; **they sat over the meal for hours** ils sont restés à table pendant des heures; **to s. at home,** *Am* **to s. home** rester à la maison; **don't think I'm just going to s. and wait for you!** ne t'imagine pas que je vais rester là à t'attendre!; **he sits in front of the television all day** il passe toute la journée devant la télévision; *Fam* **s. tight, I'll be back in a moment** ne bouge pas, je reviens tout de suite; **we just have to s. tight and wait for things to get better** on ne peut qu'attendre patiemment que les choses s'arrangent

2 *Art & Phot (pose)* poser; **she sat for Modigliani** elle a posé pour Modigliani

3 *(be a member)* **to s. on a board** faire partie *ou* être membre d'un conseil d'administration; *Br Pol* **to s. in Parliament** = être député

4 *(be in session)* être en séance, siéger; **the council was still sitting at midnight** à minuit, le conseil siégeait toujours *ou* était toujours en séance; **the House sits for another two months** la session de la Chambre doit durer encore deux mois

5 *Fam (baby-sit)* **I'll ask Amy to s. for us** je demanderai à Amy de garder les enfants❑

6 *(be situated ► building)* être, se trouver; *(► vase)* être posé; **the houses s. nestled in a beautiful valley** les maisons sont nichées *ou* blotties dans une belle vallée; **a clock sat on the mantelpiece** une horloge était posée sur la cheminée; **your keys are sitting right in front of you** tes clés sont là, devant ton nez; **her mail sat in a pile on her desk** son courrier était empilé sur son bureau

7 *(remain inactive or unused)* rester; **the plane sat waiting on the runway** l'avion attendait sur la piste; **the letter sat unopened** la lettre n'avait pas été ouverte

8 *(fit ► coat, dress)* tomber; **the jacket sits well on you** la veste vous va parfaitement; *Fig* **age sits well on him** la maturité lui va bien; **the thought sat uneasily on my conscience** cette pensée me pesait sur la conscience

9 *(bird ► perch)* se percher, se poser; *(► brood)* couver; **they take turns sitting on the eggs** ils couvent les œufs à tour de rôle

► **sit about, sit around VI** rester à ne rien faire, traîner; **she just sits around (the house) all day** elle reste toute la journée à la maison à ne rien faire; **I'm not going to s. around waiting for you** je ne vais pas passer mon temps à t'attendre

► **sit back VI 1** *(relax)* s'installer confortablement; **to s. back (in an armchair)** se caler *ou* s'installer confortablement dans un fauteuil; **just s. back and close your eyes** installe-toi bien et ferme les yeux; **s. back and enjoy it** détends-toi et profites-en **2** *(refrain from intervening)* **I can't just s. back and watch!** je ne peux pas rester là à regarder sans rien faire!; **he just sits back and lets the others do the work** il regarde les autres travailler sans lever le petit doigt

► **sit down VT SEP** *(place ► person)* asseoir, installer; **he sat himself down beside me** il s'est assis à côté de moi; **s. yourself down and have a drink** asseyez-vous et prenez un verre

VI s'asseoir; **please s. down** asseyez-vous, je vous en prie; **to be sitting down** être assis; **I was just sitting down to work when the phone rang** j'étais sur le point de me mettre au travail quand le téléphone a sonné; **to s. down to a meal** se mettre à table pour un repas; **to s. down to a game of bridge** s'installer pour faire une partie de bridge; **I think we should s. down and talk about it** je crois qu'il faut qu'on en discute *ou* parle

► **sit in VI 1** *(attend)* assister (sans participer); **do you mind if I s. in for a while?** cela vous ennuie-t-il si je reste à écouter un moment?; **to s. in on a meeting/a class** assister à une réunion/un cours **2** *(replace)* **to s. in for sb** remplacer qn **3** *(hold a demonstration)* faire un sit-in

► **sit on VT INSEP** *Fam* **1** *(suppress, quash ► file, report)* garder le silence sur❑; *(► suggestion, proposal)* repousser❑, rejeter❑; **any new initiative is promptly sat on** on décourage rapidement toute nouvelle initiative❑ **2** *(take no action on)* ne pas s'occuper de❑; **his office has been sitting on those recommendations for months now** ça fait des mois que son bureau a ces recommandations sous le coude; **they mustn't s. on their one-goal lead** il ne faut pas qu'ils s'endorment sur leurs lauriers maintenant qu'ils ont un but d'avance

► **sit out VT SEP 1** *(endure)* attendre la fin de; **it was very boring but I sat it out** c'était très ennuyeux, mais je suis restée jusqu'au bout **2** *(not take part in)* **I think I'll s. the next one out** *(dance)* je crois que je ne vais pas danser la prochaine danse; *(in cards)* je crois que je ne jouerai pas la prochaine main

VI *(sit outside)* s'asseoir *ou* se mettre dehors; *(be seated outside)* être assis dehors

► **sit through VT INSEP** attendre la fin de; **he sat through the whole play** il est resté jusqu'à la fin de la pièce; **I can't bear to s. through another of his speeches** je ne supporterai pas un autre de ses discours; **we sat through dinner in silence** nous avons passé tout le dîner sans rien dire

► **sit up VI 1** *(raise oneself to sitting position)* s'asseoir; *(sit straight)* se redresser; **she was sitting up in bed reading** elle lisait, assise dans son lit; **the baby can s. up now** le bébé peut se tenir assis maintenant; **s. up straight!** redresse-toi!, tiens toi droit!; *Fig* **to make sb s. up** secouer qn, secouer les puces à qn; **the public began to s. up and take notice** le public a commencé à montrer un certain intérêt **2** *(not go to bed)* rester debout ne pas se coucher; **I sat up watching TV until 3 a.m.** j'ai regardé la télé jusqu'à trois heures du matin; **I'll s. up with her until the fever passes** je vais rester avec elle jusqu'à ce que sa fièvre tombe

VT SEP *(child, patient)* asseoir, redresser; **to s. sb up against a wall** adosser qn contre un mur

sitar [sɪˈtɑː(r)] **N** sitar *m ou f*

sitcom [ˈsɪtkɒm] **N** comédie *f* de situation, sitcom *m*

sit-down **N** *Fam (rest)* **I could do with a nice s.** j'aimerais bien m'asseoir un peu❑; **come and have a s.** viens t'asseoir❑

►► ***sit-down meal*** repas *m* pris à table; *Br* ***sit-down strike*** grève *f* sur le tas

site [saɪt] **N 1** *(piece of land)* terrain *m*; **the development project includes sites for small businesses** le projet immobilier prévoit des terrains pour de petites entreprises

2 *(place, location)* emplacement *m*, site *m*; **there's been a church on this s. for centuries** cela fait des siècles qu'il y a une église à cet endroit *ou* ici; **this forest has been the s. of several battles** cette forêt a été le théâtre de plusieurs batailles

3 *Constr* **(building) s.** chantier *m*; **helmets must be worn on (the) s.** le port du casque est obligatoire sur le chantier

4 *Archeol* site *m*

5 *Med (of pain)* siège *m*

6 *Comput (on Internet)* site *m*

COMP *Constr (office, inspection, visit)* de chantier

VT *(situate)* placer, situer

• **on site ADV** sur place

►► ***site manager*** chef *m* de chantier; *Comput* ***site map*** plan *m* de navigation; ***Site of Special Scientific Interest*** = site protégé présentant un intérêt particulier du point de vue de la faune, de la flore ou de la géologie

site-specific ADJ conçu pour un lieu particulier

sit-in N 1 *(demonstration)* sit-in *m inv*; **to stage** *or* **to hold a s.** faire un sit-in **2** *(strike)* grève *f* sur le tas

siting [ˈsaɪtɪŋ] **N the s. of the nuclear plant is highly controversial** le choix de l'emplacement de la centrale nucléaire provoque une vive controverse

sitter [ˈsɪtə(r)] **N 1** *(for children)* baby-sitter *mf*; **couldn't find a s. for the dog/house** je n'ai trouvé personne pour garder le chien/la maison

2 *Art (model)* modèle *m*

3 *(hen)* couveuse *f*

4 *Br Fam (easy chance)* coup *m* facile; **to miss a s.** rater un coup facile

itting ['sɪtɪŋ] **N 1** *(for meal)* service *m*; **first/second s.** premier/deuxième service *m*; **to serve 500 people in** *or* **at one s.** servir 500 personnes à la fois **2** *Art (for portrait)* séance *f* de pose; **to paint a portrait in three sittings** faire un portrait en trois séances **3** *(of assembly, committee, court)* séance *f*; **I read the book at** *or* **in one s.** j'ai lu le livre d'une traite
ADJ 1 *(seated)* assis; **in a s. position** en position assise **2** *(in office)* en exercice; **the s. member for Leeds** le député actuel de Leeds **3** *(hen)* en train de couver
▸▸ ***sitting duck*** *Fam (target)* cible *f* facile[▫]; *(victim)* proie *f* facile[▫], pigeon *m*; **old people are s. ducks for all sorts of confidence tricksters** les personnes âgées sont des proies faciles pour les escrocs en tous genres; *Br* ***sitting room*** salon *m*, salle *f* de séjour; *Br* ***sitting target*** cible *f* facile; *Br* ***sitting tenant*** locataire *mf* en place

ituate ['sɪtjʊeɪt] **VT** *Formal (in place)* situer, implanter; *(in context)* resituer

ituation [,sɪtjʊ'eɪʃən] **N 1** *(state of affairs)* situation *f*; **the s. at work/in China is getting worse** la situation au travail/en Chine ne s'arrange pas; **I've got myself into a ridiculous s.** je me suis mis dans une situation ridicule; **what would you do in my s.?** qu'est-ce que tu ferais à ma place *ou* dans ma situation?; **the firm's financial s. isn't good** la situation financière de la société n'est pas bonne; *Fam* **what's** *or* **how's the coffee s.?** combien nous reste-t-il de café?[▫]; **a crisis s.** une situation de crise; **the skills needed in an interview s.** les compétences dont on a besoin pour faire face à un entretien **2** *(job)* situation *f*, emploi *m*; **situations vacant/wanted** *(in newspaper)* offres *fpl*/demandes *fpl* d'emploi **3** *(location)* situation *f*, emplacement *m*
▸▸ *TV & Rad* ***situation comedy*** sitcom *m ou f*

it-up **N** *Sport* redressement *m* assis; **to do sit-ups** faire des abdominaux

it-upon **N** *Fam Old-fashioned* derrière *m*, postérieur *m*

ix [sɪks] **N 1** *(number, numeral)* six *m inv*; *Br* **to be at sixes and sevens** être sens dessus dessous; **I'm at sixes and sevens as to what to do** je ne sais absolument pas quoi faire; *Fam* **it's s. of one and half a dozen of the other, it's s. and half a dozen** c'est blanc bonnet et bonnet blanc, c'est kif-kif; *Br Fam Old-fashioned Sch* **to get s. of the best** se faire fouetter[▫] **2** *(ice hockey team)* équipe *f*; *(cub or brownie patrol)* patrouille *f* **3** *(in cricket)* six points *mpl*; **he scored five sixes** il a marqué cinq fois six points; *Br Fam Fig* **to knock sb for s.** *(person ▸ knock down)* étendre qn[▫]; *(▸ flabbergast)* abasourdir qn[▫]; *(enemy, opponent)* battre qn à plate(s) couture(s)
PRON six
ADJ six; *Fam* **to be s. feet under** être six pieds sous terre, manger les pissenlits par la racine; *see also* **five**
▸▸ ***the Six Counties*** (les six comtés *mpl* de) l'Irlande *f* du Nord; *Hist* ***the Six Day War*** la guerre des Six-Jours; *Sport* ***the Six Nations (Tournament)*** le Tournoi des Six Nations

ixfold ['sɪksfəʊld] **ADJ** sextuple
ADV au sextuple; **the population has increased s.** la population a sextuplé *ou* s'est multipliée par six

ix-foot **ADJ** *(beam)* de six pieds; **a s. bodyguard** ≃ un garde du corps d'un mètre quatre-vingts

ix-footer [-'fʊtə(r)] **N** *Fam* **both her sons are six-footers** ≃ ses deux fils mesurent plus d'un mètre quatre-vingts

ix-pack **N 1** *(of beer)* pack *m* de six; **he polishes off a couple of six-packs every night** il s'envoie une bonne douzaine de bières chaque soir; *Br Fam Hum* **he's one can short of a s.** il n'est pas très net **2** *Fam Hum (stomach muscles)* **to have a s.** avoir les abdos en tablette de chocolat; **he's got a great s.** il a des super abdos

ixpence ['sɪkspəns] **N 1** *(sum)* six pence *mpl* **2** *(coin)* pièce *f* de six pence

ixpenny ['sɪkspənɪ] **ADJ** *Old-fashioned (costing six pence)* qui coûte six pence; *(stamp)* de six pence
▸▸ ***sixpenny piece*** pièce *f* de six pence

sixpennyworth [sɪks'penɪwəθ] **N** *Old-fashioned* **to buy s. of chocolate** acheter pour six pence de chocolat

six-shooter **N** *Am Fam* pistolet *m* à six coups[▫], six-coups *m inv*

six-sided **ADJ** qui a six côtés, hexagonal

sixteen [sɪks'tiːn] **N** seize *m inv*; **she was sweet s.** c'était une jolie jeune fille de seize ans
PRON seize
ADJ seize; *see also* **five**

sixteenth [sɪks'tiːnθ] **N 1** *(fraction)* seizième *m* **2** *(in series)* seizième *mf* **3** *(of month)* seize *m inv*
ADJ seizième
ADV seizièmement; *(in contest)* en seizième position, à la seizième place; *see also* **fifth**
▸▸ *Am Mus* ***sixteenth note*** double croche *f*

sixth [sɪksθ] **N 1** *(fraction)* sixième *m*
2 *(in series)* sixième *mf*
3 *(of month)* six *m inv*
4 *Mus* sixte *f*
5 *Br Sch* **to be in the lower/upper s.** ≃ être en première/en terminale
ADJ sixième
ADV sixièmement; *(in contest)* en sixième position, à la sixième place; *see also* **fifth**
▸▸ *Br Sch* ***sixth form*** = classe terminale de l'enseignement secondaire en Angleterre et au pays de Galles, préparant aux "A levels", ≃ classes *fpl* de première et de terminale; *Br Sch* ***sixth form college*** = établissement préparant aux "A levels"; *Br Sch* ***sixth former*** = élève de première ou de terminale; **all the s. formers** tous les élèves de première et de terminale; *Am Sch* ***sixth grade*** = classe du primaire pour les 10–11 ans; ***sixth sense*** sixième sens *m*; **some s. sense told me she wouldn't come** j'avais l'intuition qu'elle ne viendrait pas

sixth-form **ADJ** *Br (student, teacher)* = de première ou de terminale

sixthly ['sɪksθlɪ] **ADV** sixièmement, en sixième lieu

sixtieth ['sɪkstɪəθ] **N 1** *(fraction)* soixantième *m* **2** *(in series)* soixantième *mf*
ADJ soixantième
ADV soixantièmement; *(in contest)* en soixantième position, à la soixantième place; *see also* **fifth**

sixty ['sɪkstɪ] **N** *(pl* **sixties***)* soixante *m inv*; **sixties pop music** la musique pop des années soixante
PRON soixante; **about s.** une soixantaine
ADJ soixante; *see also* **fifty**

sixty-four **ADJ** soixante-quatre; *Fam* **the s. thousand dollar question** la question cruciale[▫]
N soixante-quatre *m*

sixty-nine **N** *Fam (sexual position)* soixante-neuf *m*

sizable = **sizeable**

-size = **-sized**

size [saɪz] **N 1** *(gen)* taille *f*; *(of ball, tumour)* taille *f*, grosseur *f*; *(of region, desert, forest)* étendue *f*, superficie *f*; *(of carpet, machine, car)* dimensions *fpl*, taille *f*; *(of difficulty, operation, problem)* importance *f*, ampleur *f*; *(of debt, bill, sum)* montant *m*, importance *f*; *Comput (of file)* taille *f*; *(of font)* corps *m*, taille *f*; **the two rooms are the same s.** les deux pièces sont de la même taille *ou* ont les mêmes dimensions; **it's about the s. of a dinner plate** c'est à peu près de la taille d'une assiette; **the kitchen is the s. of a cupboard** la cuisine est grande comme un placard; **my garden is half the s. of hers** mon jardin fait la moitié du sien; **you should have seen the s. of the truck!** si tu avais vu la taille du camion!; **it's a city of some s.** c'est une ville assez importante; **the town has no hotels of any s.** la ville n'a pas d'hôtel important; **I was surprised by the s. of the bill** j'ai été étonné par le montant de la note; **we weren't expecting a crowd of this s.** nous ne nous attendions pas à une foule aussi nombreuse; **the crowd was steadily growing in s.** la foule grossissait à vue d'œil; **the budget will have to double in s.** le budget devra être multiplié par deux; **a block of marble one cubic metre in s.** un bloc de marbre d'un mètre cube; **the cupboards can be built to s.** les placards peuvent être construits sur mesure; *Fam* **that's about the s. of it!** en gros, c'est ça!
2 *(of clothes ▸ gen)* taille *f*; *(of shoes, gloves, hat)* pointure *f*, taille *f*; **what s. are you?, what s. do you take?** *(for clothes)* quelle taille faites-vous?; *(for shoes)* quelle est votre pointure?, vous chaussez du combien?; **I take (a) s. 40** je fais du 40; **I take a s. 5 shoe** ≃ je chausse du 38; **I need a s. larger/smaller** *(clothes)* il me faut la taille au-dessus/au-dessous; *(shoes)* il me faut la pointure au-dessus/au-dessous; **we've nothing in your s.** nous n'avons rien dans votre taille; **try this jacket on for s.** essayez cette veste pour voir si c'est votre taille; *Fam* **try this one for s.!** prends ça!
VT 1 *(sort)* trier selon la taille **2** *(make)* fabriquer aux dimensions voulues; **the clothing is sized for the American market** les vêtements sont faits pour le marché américain **3** *Comput* dimensionner
▸▸ *Comput* ***size box*** case *f* de dimensionnement; ***size zero*** taille *f* zéro

▸size up **VT SEP** *(stranger, rival)* jauger; *(problem, chances)* mesurer; **we all waited outside, sizing each other up** nous attendions tous dehors, nous observant les uns les autres; **she sized up the situation immediately** elle a tout de suite compris ce qui se passait

sizeable ['saɪzəbəl] **ADJ** *(piece, box, car)* assez grand; *(apple, egg, tumour)* assez gros (grosse); *(sum, income, quantity, crowd)* important; *(town)* assez important; *(error)* de taille; **they were elected by a s. majority** ils ont été élus à une assez large majorité

-sized [saɪzd] **SUFF** **medium-s.** de taille moyenne; **small and medium-s. businesses** petites et moyennes entreprises *fpl*, PME *fpl*; **a fair-s. crowd** une foule assez nombreuse

sizing ['saɪzɪŋ] **N** *(of clothes)* **s. varies in different shops/countries** les tailles varient selon les magasins/les pays

sizzle ['sɪzəl] **VI 1** *(sputter)* grésiller **2** *Fam (be hot)* **the city sizzled in the heat** la ville étouffait sous la chaleur[▫]
N grésillement *m*

sizzler ['sɪzlə(r)] **N** *Fam* journée *f* torride[▫]; **it's going to be a s.!** il va faire une chaleur torride aujourd'hui!

sizzling ['sɪzlɪŋ] **ADJ 1** *(sputtering)* grésillant **2** *Fam (hot)* brûlant[▫]
ADV *Fam* **s. hot** brûlant[▫]
N grésillement *m*

skank [skæŋk] **N** *Am Fam (ugly woman)* cageot *m*, boudin *m*

skanky ['skæŋkɪ] **ADJ** *Am Fam (ugly)* hyper moche; *(dirty)* crado

skate [skeɪt] *(pl sense* **2** *inv or* **skates***)* **N 1** *(ice skate)* patin *m* à glace; *(roller skate)* patin *m* à roulettes; *Br Fam* **to get** *or* **to put one's skates on** se magner, se grouiller **2** *Ich* raie *f*
VI 1 *(gen)* patiner; **to go skating** *(ice-skating)* faire du patin *ou* du patinage; *(roller-skating)* faire du patin à roulettes; **we used to s. to school** nous allions à l'école en patins à roulettes; *Fig* **to be skating on thin ice** être sur un terrain dangereux, avancer en terrain miné **2** *(slide ▸ person, pen, plate)* glisser; **his legs skated out from under him** ses jambes se sont dérobées sous lui

▸skate around, skate over **VT INSEP** *(problem, issue)* esquiver, éviter; **the book skates around** *or* **over his two divorces** le livre passe sous silence ses deux divorces

skateboard ['skeɪtbɔːd] **N** skateboard *m*, planche *f* à roulettes
VI faire du skate *ou* de la planche à roulettes

skateboarder ['skeɪtbɔːdə(r)] **N** skateur(euse) *m,f*; **a champion s.** un champion de skateboard

skateboarding ['skeɪtbɔːdɪŋ] **N** skate *m*; **to go s.** faire du skate

skatepark ['skeɪtpɑːk] **N** skatepark *m*

skater ['skeɪtə(r)] **N** *(on ice)* patineur(euse) *m,f*; *(on roller skates)* patineur(euse) *m,f* à roulettes; *(on skateboard)* skateur(euse) *m,f*

skating ['skeɪtɪŋ] **N** *(on ice)* patin *m* (à glace); *(on roller skates)* patin *m* (à roulettes)
ADJ de patinage
▸▸ ***skating rink*** *(for ice-skating)* patinoire *f*; *(for roller-skating)* piste *f* pour patin à roulettes

skean dhu [ˌski:ən'du:] **N** *Scot* = dague décorative que l'on porte dans la chaussette

skedaddle [skɪ'dædəl] **VI** *Fam* décamper, se tailler; **I'd better s.** il faut que je me sauve *ou* que je file

skeet shooting [ski:t-] **N** (tir *m* au) skeet *m*

skeezer ['ski:zə(r)] **N** *Am very Fam* **1** *(ugly woman)* cageot *m*, boudin *m* **2** *(promiscuous woman)* pouffiasse *f*, traînée *f*

skein [skeɪn] **N 1** *(of wool, silk)* écheveau *m* **2** *(flight ▸ of geese)* vol *m*

skeletal ['skelɪtəl] **ADJ** squelettique; *Fig (presentation, report)* sommaire

skeleton ['skelɪtən] **N 1** *Anat* squelette *m*; **he was little more than a s.** il n'avait plus que la peau sur les os; *Fig* **to have a s. in the** *Br* **cupboard** *or Am* **closet** avoir un squelette dans le placard

2 *Constr & Chem (structure)* squelette *m*

3 *(outline ▸ of book, report)* ébauche *f*, esquisse *f*; *(▸ of project, strategy, speech)* schéma *m*, grandes lignes *fpl*

4 *(sledge, sport)* skeleton *m*

COMP *(team)* (réduit au) minimum; **a s.** *Br* **staff** *or Am* **crew** des effectifs *mpl* réduits au minimum; **a s. train service** un service minimum de trains

▸▸ ***skeleton key*** passe-partout *m inv*, passe *m*

skeptic, skeptical *etc Am* = **sceptic, sceptical** *etc*

sketch [sketʃ] **N 1** *(drawing)* croquis *m*, esquisse *f*; **the map is only a s.** la carte n'est qu'un croquis

2 *(brief description)* résumé *m*; **a biographical s. of the author** une biographie succincte de l'auteur; *(on book jacket)* une notice bibliographique sur l'auteur

3 *(preliminary outline ▸ of book)* ébauche *f*; *(▸ of proposal, speech, campaign)* grandes lignes *fpl*; **give us a rough s. of your plan** donnez-nous un aperçu de ce que vous proposez

4 *Theat* sketch *m*

VT 1 *(person, scene)* faire un croquis *ou* une esquisse de, croquer, esquisser; *(line, composition, form)* esquisser, croquer; *(portrait, illustration)* faire (rapidement); **he began by sketching the foreground** il a commencé par esquisser *ou* croquer le premier plan **2** *(book)* ébaucher, esquisser; *(proposal, speech)* ébaucher, préparer dans les grandes lignes

▸sketch in VT SEP 1 *(provide ▸ background, main points)* indiquer; **Harry will s. a few more details in for you** Harry va vous donner encore quelques précisions **2** *(draw)* ajouter, dessiner

▸sketch out VT SEP 1 *(book)* ébaucher, esquisser; *(plan, speech)* ébaucher, préparer dans les grandes lignes; *(details, main points)* indiquer **2** *(draw)* ébaucher

sketchbook ['sketʃbʊk] **N** carnet *m* à dessins

sketchily ['sketʃɪlɪ] **ADV** *(describe, report)* sommairement; **his article is very s. researched** son article repose sur des recherches très superficielles

sketching ['sketʃɪŋ] **N** *(action)* action *f* de croquer *ou* d'esquisser; *(picture)* croquis *m*, esquisse *f*

▸▸ ***sketching block*** bloc *m* à croquis *ou* à dessins; ***sketching pad*** carnet *m* à dessins

sketchwriter ['sketʃraɪtə(r)] **N** auteur *m* de sketches comiques

sketchy ['sketʃɪ] (*compar* **sketchier**, *superl* **sketchiest**) **ADJ** *(description, account)* sommaire; *(research, work, knowledge)* superficiel; *(idea, notion)* vague; *(plan)* peu détaillé; **my memory of that day is very s.** mes souvenirs de cette journée sont très flous

skew [skju:] **VT** *(distort ▸ facts, results)* fausser; *(▸ idea, truth)* dénaturer; **it will s. the sample** *(in statistics)* ça va fausser l'échantillonnage; **this reform is skewed toward higher earners** cette réforme avantage ceux qui ont de gros revenus

VI obliquer, dévier de sa trajectoire; **the truck skewed across the intersection** le camion a traversé le carrefour en biais

ADJ *(crooked ▸ picture)* de travers; *(▸ pole)* penché

N *Br* **to be on the s.** être de travers

skewbald ['skju:bɔ:ld] **ADJ** pie *(inv)*

N cheval *m* pie

skewer ['skju:ə(r)] **N** *Culin* brochette *f*; *(larger)* broche *f*

VT *Culin (roast, duck)* embrocher; *(pieces of meat, mushrooms, tomatoes)* mettre en brochette; *Fig (person)* transpercer

skew-whiff *Br Fam* **ADJ** de traviole, de travers[□]

ADV de traviole, de travers[□]

ski [ski:] **N** *Sport* ski *m*; **a pair of skis** une paire de skis

VI faire du ski, skier; **to go skiing** *(activity)* faire du ski; *(on holiday)* partir aux sports d'hiver *ou* faire du ski; **they skied down the slope** ils descendirent la pente à ski

VT I've never skied the red run je n'ai jamais descendu la piste rouge

▸▸ ***ski instructor*** moniteur(trice) *m,f* de ski; ***ski jump*** *(ramp)* tremplin *m* de ski; ***ski jumping*** saut *m* à skis; ***ski lift*** *(gen)* remontée *f* mécanique; *(chair lift)* télésiège *m*; ***ski mask*** masque *m* de ski; ***ski pants*** fuseau *m*, pantalon *m* de ski; ***ski pass*** forfait *m* de remonte-pente; ***ski plane*** avion *m* à skis; ***ski pole*** bâton *m* de ski; ***ski resort*** station *f* de ski; ***ski run, ski slope*** piste *f* de ski; *Am* ***ski stick*** bâton *m* de ski; ***ski suit*** combinaison *f* de ski; ***ski tow*** téléski *m*; ***ski trail*** piste *f* de ski; ***ski wax*** fart *m* (pour skis)

skid [skɪd] (*pt & pp* **skidded**, *cont* **skidding**) **VI 1** *(on road ▸ driver, car, tyre)* déraper; *(wheel)* patiner; **the car skidded across the junction** la voiture a traversé le carrefour en dérapant; **to s. to a halt** s'arrêter en dérapant; **his glasses went skidding across the table** ses lunettes ont glissé jusqu'à l'autre bout de la table **2** *(slide ▸ person, object)* déraper, glisser; **I skidded on the wet floor** j'ai dérapé *ou* glissé sur le sol mouillé; **the plates skidded off the tray** les assiettes ont glissé du plateau

VT *(vehicle)* **he skidded the truck into the ditch** il a perdu le contrôle du camion qui est parti dans le fossé

N 1 *Aut (action)* dérapage *m*; **to go into a s.** partir en dérapage, déraper; **to get out of** *or* **to correct a s.** redresser *ou* contrôler un dérapage **2** *Fam Fig* **to put the skids on** *or* **under sb** mettre des bâtons dans les roues à qn; **to hit the skids** *(company, sales, prices)* dégringoler; **to be on the skids** *(company, marriage)* battre de l'aile

▸▸ ***skid mark*** *(on road)* trace *f* de pneus *(après un dérapage)*; *Fam Hum (on underpants, nappy)* trace *f*; *Am Fam* ***skid row*** bas-fonds *mpl* [□], quartier *m* mal famé[□]; **you'll end up on s. row!** tu es sur une mauvaise pente!

skid-lid **N** *Br Fam* casque *m* (de moto)[□]

skidpan ['skɪdpæn] **N** *Br* piste *f* d'entraînement au dérapage

skier ['ski:ə(r)] **N** skieur(euse) *m,f*

skiff [skɪf] **N** skiff *m*, yole *f*

skiing ['ski:ɪŋ] **N** ski *m (activité)*

COMP *(lessons, instructor, accident, clothes)* de ski; **to go on a s. holiday** partir aux sports d'hiver

skilful, *Am* **skillful** ['skɪlfʊl] **ADJ** habile, adroit; **she's very s. with the scissors** elle sait se servir d'une paire de ciseaux; **a s. move** une démarche habile

skilfully, *Am* **skillfully** ['skɪlfʊlɪ] **ADV** habilement, avec habileté, adroitement

skilfulness, *Am* **skillfulness** ['skɪlfʊlnɪs] **N** habileté *f*, adresse *f*

skill [skɪl] **N 1** *(ability)* compétence *f*, aptitude *f*; *(dexterity)* habileté *f*, adresse *f*; *(expertise)* savoir-faire *m inv*; **you don't need any special s.** ça ne demande aucune compétence précise; **with great s.** *(in manoeuvre)* avec une grande habileté; *(diplomacy)* avec un grand savoir-faire; *(dexterity)* avec beaucoup d'adresse; **his work shows s. and imagination** son travail est plein de talent et d'imagination **2** *(learned technique)* aptitude *f*, technique *f*; *(knowledge)* connaissances *fpl*; **management skills** techniques *fpl* de gestion; **language skills** aptitudes *fpl* linguistiques; **computer technology requires us to learn new skills** l'informatique nous oblige à acquérir de nouvelles compétences

skilled [skɪld] **ADJ 1** *Ind (engineer, worker, labour)* qualifié; *(task)* de spécialiste **2** *(experienced ▸ driver, negotiator)* habile, expérimenté; *(expert)* habile, expert; *(manually)* adroit; *(clever ▸ gesture)* habile, adroit; **s. in the art of public speaking** versé dans l'art oratoire, rompu aux techniques oratoires; **to be s. at doing sth** être doué pour faire qch

skillet ['skɪlɪt] **N** *Am* poêle *f* (à frire)

skillful, skillfully *etc Am* = **skilful, skilfully** *etc*

skillset ['skɪlset] **N** ensemble *m* de compétences

skim [skɪm] (*pt & pp* **skimmed**, *cont* **skimming**) **VT** *(milk)* écrémer; *(jam)* écumer; *(floating matter ▸ with skimmer)* écumer, enlever avec une écumoire; *(▸ with spatula)* enlever avec une spatule; **to s. the fat from the gravy** dégraisser la sauce; **to s. the cream from the milk** écrémer le lait

2 *(glide over ▸ surface)* effleurer, frôler; **the glider skimmed the tops of the trees** le planeur frôlait *ou* rasait la cime des arbres; **the stone skimmed the lake** la pierre a ricoché à la surface du lac; *Fig* **the book only skims the surface** le livre ne fait qu'effleurer *ou* que survoler la question

3 *(stone)* faire ricocher

4 *(read quickly ▸ letter, book)* parcourir, lire en diagonale; *(▸ magazine)* parcourir, feuilleter

5 *Fam* **to s. a credit card** = récupérer illégalement les données d'une carte bancaire lors d'une transaction grâce à un lecteur caché

6 *Com (market)* écrémer

VI to s. over the ground/across the waves *(bird)* raser le sol/les vagues; **to s. over** *or* **across the lake** *(stone)* faire des ricochets sur le lac

▸▸ *Am* ***skim milk*** lait *m* écrémé

▸skim off VT SEP 1 *(cream, froth)* enlever (avec une écumoire); *Fig* **the accounts department skims off the best recruits** la comptabilité récupère les meilleures recrues **2** *(steal ▸ money)* **he skimmed a little off the top for himself** il s'est un peu servi au passage

▸skim through VT INSEP *(letter, page)* parcourir, lire en diagonale; *(magazine)* feuilleter; **I only had time to s. through the report** je n'ai eu que le temps de lire le rapport en vitesse

skimmer ['skɪmə(r)] **N** *Culin* écumoire *f*

skimp [skɪmp] **VI** lésiner; **to s. on sth** lésiner sur qch; **the builders skimped on materials** les constructeurs ont lésiné sur les matériaux

VT *(resources, food)* économiser sur, lésiner sur; *(job)* faire à la va-vite

skimpily ['skɪmpɪlɪ] **ADV** *(furnished)* parcimonieusement; **s. made** *(garment)* étriqué; **s. dressed** légèrement vêtu

skimpiness ['skɪmpɪnɪs] **N** insuffisance *f*; *(of garment)* aspect *m* étriqué

skimpy ['skɪmpɪ] (*compar* **skimpier**, *superl* **skimpiest**) **ADJ 1** *(mean ▸ meal, offering, praise, thanks)* maigre, chiche **2** *(clothes, dress ▸ too small)* trop juste; *(▸ light)* léger; **a s. skirt** une jupe étriquée

skin [skɪn] (*pt & pp* **skinned**, *cont* **skinning**) **N 1** *(of person)* peau *f*; **to have dark/fair s.** avoir la peau brune/claire; **to have bad/good s.** avoir une vilaine/jolie peau; **I always wear cotton next to my s.** je porte toujours du coton sur la peau; **you're nothing but s. and bone** tu n'as que la peau et les os; **we're all human under the s.** au fond, nous sommes tous humains; **she escaped by the s. of her teeth** elle l'a échappé belle, elle s'en est tirée de justesse; **she nearly jumped out of her s.** elle a sauté au plafond; *Fam* **it's no s. off my nose** ça m'est égal[□], ce n'est pas mon problème[□]; *Fam* **he really gets under my s.** il me tape sur les nerfs celui-là; *Fam* **I've got her under my s.** je l'ai dans la peau; **to save one's s.** sauver sa peau; **to be soaked to the s.** être trempé jusqu'aux os

2 *(of animal)* peau *f*; **to cast** *or* **to shed its s.** *(snake)* muer; **a crocodile-s. handbag** un sac en crocodile

3 *(on fruit, vegetable, sausage)* peau *f*; *(on onion)* pelure *f*; **potatoes cooked in their skins** des pommes de terre en robe de chambre *ou* des champs

4 *(on milk, sauce, pudding)* peau *f*

5 *(of plane)* revêtement *m*; *(of building)* revêtement *m* extérieur; *(of drum)* peau *f*

6 *Fam (abbr* **skinhead***)* skinhead[□] *mf*, skin *mf*

7 *Br Fam (cigarette paper)* papier *m* à cigarette[□]

COMP *(cancer, disease, tone)* de la peau

VT 1 *(animal)* dépouiller, écorcher; *(vegetable)* éplucher; *Fig* **if I find him I'll s. him alive** si je le

trouve, je l'écorche vif; *Prov* **there's more than one way to s. a cat** = il y a bien des moyens d'arriver à ses fins **2** *(graze ▸ limb)* écorcher; **I skinned my knee** je me suis écorché le genou **3** *Fam (swindle)* arnaquer; *(rob)* plumer; **you've been skinned** tu t'es fait avoir *ou* arnaquer
▸▸ ***skin cream*** crème *f* pour la peau; ***skin diver*** plongeur(euse) *m,f*; ***skin diving*** plongée *f* sous-marine; *Fam* ***skin flick*** film *m* porno; *Fam* ***skin game*** arnaque *f*; ***skin graft*** greffe *f* de la peau; ***skin grafting*** greffage *m* de la peau; *Fam* ***skin mag*** revue *f* porno; ***skin patch*** timbre *m* transdermique; *Med* ***skin test*** cuti-réaction *f*

▸ **skin up** VI *Br Fam Drugs slang* rouler un joint

skin-deep ADJ superficiel; **beauty is only s.** la beauté n'est pas tout

skinflint ['skɪnflɪnt] N *Fam* radin(e) *m,f*

skinful ['skɪnfʊl] N *Br Fam* **to have had a s.** tenir une bonne cuite

skinhead ['skɪnhed] N skinhead *mf*

skinless ['skɪnlɪs] ADJ *(sausages)* sans peau

-skinned [skɪnd] SUFF à la peau…; **she's dark-s.** elle a la peau foncée

skinned [skɪnd] ADJ *(rabbit)* à qui on a enlevé la peau; **to keep one's eyes s.** ouvrir l'œil; **to keep one's eyes s. for sb/sth** guetter qn/qch; **I'll keep my eyes s. for one** j'en guette un

skinniness ['skɪnɪnɪs] N maigreur *f*; *(slenderness)* minceur *f*

skinny ['skɪnɪ] *(compar* **skinnier,** *superl* **skinniest)** N *Am Fam (inside information)* renseignements❑ *mpl*; **what's the s. on the situation?** est-ce qu'il y a du nouveau?❑
ADJ **1** *(person ▸ too thin)* maigre; *(slender)* mince; **she's a s. little thing** elle est petite et menue **2** *(sweater, T-shirt etc)* collant

skinny-dip *(pt & pp* **skinny-dipped,** *cont* **skinny-dipping)** VI *Fam* se baigner à poil

skinny-malinky [-mə'lɪŋkɪ] *(pl* **skinny-malinkies)** N *Fam* asperge *f*

skin-pop *(pt & pp* **skin-popped,** *cont* **skin-popping)** *Fam Drugs slang* VT *(drugs)* se piquer *ou* se shooter à
VI *(inject drugs)* se piquer, se shooter

skint [skɪnt] ADJ *Br Fam* fauché, raide

skin-tight ADJ *(clothing)* moulant

skip [skɪp] *(pt & pp* **skipped,** *cont* **skipping)** VI **1** *(with skipping rope)* sauter à la corde
2 *(jump)* sautiller; **he skipped out of the way** il s'est écarté d'un bond; **the children were skipping around in the garden** les enfants gambadaient dans le jardin; *Fig* **the book keeps skipping from one subject to another** le livre passe sans arrêt d'un sujet à l'autre
3 *Fam (go)* faire un saut, aller❑; **we skipped across to Paris for the weekend** on a fait un saut à Paris pour le week-end
VT **1** *(omit)* sauter, passer; **s. the details** passez les détails, épargnez-nous les détails; **let's s. the next chapter** sautons le chapitre suivant
2 *(miss ▸ meeting, meal)* sauter; *Sch (class)* sécher; **we decided to s. lunch** nous avons décidé de sauter le déjeuner *ou* de ne pas déjeuner; *Fam* **to s. bail** se dérober à la justice❑ *(alors qu'on jouit de la liberté provisoire)*; *Fig* **my heart skipped a beat** mon cœur s'est arrêté de battre pendant une seconde; *Fam* **s. it!** laisse tomber!
3 *Fam (leave)* fuir❑, quitter❑; **the thieves have skipped the country** les voleurs ont quitté le pays
4 *Comput (command)* sauter
N **1** *(jump)* (petit) saut *m*; **with a little s., she jumped over the rope** d'un bond léger, elle sauta par-dessus la corde **2** *Br (on lorry, for rubbish)* benne *f*

▸ **skip off** VI *Fam* **1** *(disappear)* décamper; **they skipped off without doing the washing up** ils ont décampé sans faire la vaisselle **2** *(go)* faire un saut; **we skipped off to Greece for a holiday** on est allés passer quelques jours de vacances en Grèce❑

▸ **skip over** VT INSEP *(omit)* sauter, passer

skipper ['skɪpə(r)] N **1** *(of ship, plane)* capitaine *m*; *(of yacht)* skipper *m* **2** *Sport* capitaine *m*, chef *m* d'équipe **3** *Fam (boss)* patron❑ *m*
VT **1** *(ship, plane)* commander, être le capitaine de; *(yacht)* skipper **2** *Sport (team)* être le capitaine de

skipping ['skɪpɪŋ] N saut *m* à la corde
▸▸ ***skipping rope*** corde *f* à sauter

skirl [skɜːl] VI *(emit a sound)* sonner; *(player)* jouer de la cornemuse
N son *m* (de la cornemuse)

skirmish ['skɜːmɪʃ] N *Mil* escarmouche *f*, échauffourée *f*; *Fig* escarmouche *f*, accrochage *m*; **I had a bit of a s. with the authorities** j'ai eu un différend avec les autorités
VI *Mil* s'engager dans une escarmouche; *Fig* **to s. with sb (over sth)** avoir un accrochage *ou* s'accrocher avec qn (au sujet de qch)

skirmisher ['skɜːmɪʃə(r)] N *Mil* tirailleur *m*

skirt [skɜːt] N **1** *(garment)* jupe *f*; *(part of coat)* pan *m*, basque *f*
2 *Tech* jupe *f*
3 *Br (cut of meat)* ≃ flanchet *m*
4 *(of hovercraft)* jupe *f*
5 *(UNCOUNT) Br Fam (women)* nanas *fpl*, gonzesses *fpl*; **a bit of s.** une nana, une gonzesse
VT **1** *(go around)* contourner; **the road skirts the mountain** la route contourne la montagne **2** *(avoid ▸ issue, problem)* éluder, esquiver
▸▸ ***skirt clearance*** jeu *m* à la jupe

▸ **skirt around,** *Br* **skirt round** VT INSEP = **skirt** VT

skirting (board) ['skɜːtɪŋ-] N *Br* plinthe *f*

skit [skɪt] N parodie *f*, satire *f*; **to do a s. on sth** parodier qch; **it's a s. on football commentators** c'est une parodie des commentateurs de football

skitter ['skɪtə(r)] VI **1** *(small animal)* trottiner; *(bird)* voleter; **the bird skittered over the ground** l'oiseau volait en rase-mottes **2** *(ricochet)* faire des ricochets; **the stone skittered across the lake** la pierre a fait des ricochets sur le lac

skittish ['skɪtɪʃ] ADJ **1** *(person ▸ playful)* espiègle; *(▸ frivolous)* frivole **2** *(horse)* ombrageux, difficile

skittishly ['skɪtɪʃlɪ] ADV **1** *(of person ▸ playfully)* avec espièglerie; *(▸ frivolously)* avec frivolité **2** *(of horse)* d'une manière ombrageuse

skittishness ['skɪtɪʃnɪs] N **1** *(of person ▸ playfulness)* espièglerie *f*; *(▸ frivolousness)* frivolité *f* **2** *(of horse)* caractère *m* ombrageux

skittle ['skɪtəl] N quille *f*
• **skittles** N (jeu *m* de) quilles *fpl*; **to play skittles** jouer aux quilles, faire une partie de quilles
▸▸ ***skittle alley*** piste *f* de jeu de quilles

skive [skaɪv] *Br Fam* VI *(avoid work)* tirer au flanc, tirer au cul; *Sch* sécher les cours
N *(easy job)* planque *f*; **she's taking PE because it's such a s.** elle a choisi éducation physique parce que c'est pépère

▸ **skive off** *Br Fam* VI se défiler, tirer au flanc, tirer au cul; *Sch* sécher les cours
VT INSEP **to s. off school** sécher les cours; **to s. off work** ne pas aller bosser

skiver ['skaɪvə(r)] N *Br Fam* tire-au-flanc *mf inv*, tire-au-cul *mf inv*

skiving ['skaɪvɪŋ] N *Br Fam* **there's too much s. round here** il y a trop de tire-au-flanc ici

skivvy ['skɪvɪ] *(pt & pp* **skivvied,** *pl* **skivvies)** VI *Br Fam* faire la boniche; **I won't s. for you** je ne vais pas vous servir de boniche
N *Br Fam Pej* bonne *f* à tout faire❑; **I'm not your s.** je ne suis pas ta boniche
• **skivvies** NPL *Am Fam (for women)* dessous❑ *mpl*; *(for men ▸ underwear)* sous-vêtements❑ *mpl*; *(▸ underpants)* calbute *m*, calcif *m*

skua ['skjuːə] N *Orn* skua *m*, labbe *m*

skulduggery [skʌl'dʌgərɪ] N *(UNCOUNT)* combines *fpl ou* manœuvres *fpl* douteuses

skulk [skʌlk] VI rôder; **there's somebody skulking (about) in the bushes** il y a quelqu'un qui se cache dans les buissons; **to s. away** *or* **off** s'éclipser

skull [skʌl] N crâne *m*; *Fam Fig* **can't you get it into your thick s. that she doesn't like you!** tu n'as toujours pas compris qu'elle ne t'aime pas!❑; *Fam* **to be out of one's s.** *(drunk)* être plein comme une barrique, être rond comme une queue de pelle; *Fam* **I was bored out of my s.** je crevais d'ennui
▸▸ ***skull and crossbones*** *(motif)* tête *f* de mort; *(flag)* pavillon *m* à tête de mort

skullcap ['skʌlkæp] N *(headgear)* calotte *f*

skunk [skʌŋk] *(pl sense* **1** *inv or* **skunks,** *pl sense* **2** **skunks)** N **1** *Zool* moufette *f*, mouffette *f*, sconse *m*, *Can* bête *f* puante; *(fur)* sconse *m* **2** *Fam (person)* canaille *f*, ordure *f* **3** *(UNCOUNT) Fam Drugs slang (type of cannabis)* skunk *m*

sky [skaɪ] *(pl* **skies,** *pt & pp* **skied)** N *(gen)* ciel *m*; **the s. went dark** le ciel s'est assombri; **smoke rose into the s.** de la fumée s'élevait dans le ciel; *Fam* **the s.'s the limit** tout est possible❑
VT *Sport (ball)* envoyer au ciel
• **skies** NPL *(climate)* cieux *mpl*; *(descriptive)* ciels *mpl*; **we spend the winter under sunnier skies** nous passons l'hiver sous des cieux plus cléments; **Turner is famous for his skies** Turner est renommé pour ses ciels
▸▸ ***sky blue*** bleu ciel *m*; *TV* ***sky cloth*** rideau *m* de fond; ***sky marshal*** = policier armé embarqué dans un avion de transport de passagers afin d'assurer la sécurité de ces derniers

sky-blue ADJ bleu ciel *(inv)*

skydiver ['skaɪdaɪvə(r)] N parachutiste *mf* (en chute libre)

skydiving ['skaɪdaɪvɪŋ] N saut *m* en chute libre

Skye [skaɪ] N (l'île *f* de) Skye *f*

skyjack ['skaɪdʒæk] VT *Fam (plane)* détourner❑

skyjacker ['skaɪdʒækə(r)] N *Fam* pirate *m* de l'air❑

skyjacking ['skaɪdʒækɪŋ] N *Fam* piraterie *f* aérienne❑

skylark ['skaɪlɑːk] N *Orn* alouette *f* des champs
VI *Fam Old-fashioned* faire le fou (la folle), chahuter

skylarking ['skaɪlɑːkɪŋ] N *Fam Old-fashioned* chahut *m*

skylight ['skaɪlaɪt] N lucarne *f*

skyline ['skaɪlaɪn] N *(horizon)* (ligne *f* d')horizon *m*; *(of city)* silhouette *f*; **it radically alters the s.** ça change radicalement le profil de la ville

Skype® [skaɪp] N *Comput & Tel* Skype® *m*

skyrocket ['skaɪrɒkɪt] N fusée *f*
VI *Fam (prices)* grimper en flèche❑

skyscape ['skaɪskeɪp] N *Art & Phot* ciel *m*

skyscraper ['skaɪskreɪpə(r)] N gratte-ciel *m inv*
▸▸ *Mktg* ***skyscraper ad*** skyscraper *m*

skywalk ['skaɪwɔːk] N passerelle *f* panoramique

skyway ['skaɪweɪ] N **1** *Aviat* couloir *m* aérien **2** *Am Aut* route *f* surélevée

skywriting ['skaɪraɪtɪŋ] N publicité *f* aérienne *(tracée dans le ciel par un avion)*

slab [slæb] *(pt & pp* **slabbed,** *cont* **slabbing)** N **1** *(block ▸ of stone, wood)* bloc *m*; *(flat)* plaque *f*, dalle *f*; *(for path)* pavé *m*; **the path was made of stone slabs** le chemin était pavé de pierres **2** *(piece ▸ of cake)* grosse tranche *f*; *(▸ of chocolate)* tablette *f*; *(▸ of meat)* pavé *m* **3** *(table, bench ▸ of butcher)* étal *m*; **on the s.** *(in mortuary)* sur la table d'autopsie; *(for operation)* sur la table d'opération
VT *(cut ▸ stone)* tailler en blocs; *(▸ log)* débiter

slack [slæk] ADJ **1** *(loose ▸ rope, wire)* lâche, insuffisamment tendu; *(▸ knot)* mal serré, desserré; *(▸ chain)* lâche; *(▸ grip)* faible; *(▸ handshake)* mou (molle); **the rope is very s.** la corde a du mou; **the chain is very s.** la chaîne n'est pas assez tendue
2 *(careless ▸ work)* négligé; *(▸ worker, student)* peu sérieux, peu consciencieux; **he's becoming very s. about his appearance/his work** il commence à négliger son apparence/son travail; **her work has become rather s. lately** il y a eu un certain laisser-aller dans son travail dernièrement
3 *(slow, weak ▸ demand)* faible; *(▸ business)* calme; **the s. season for tourists** la période creuse pour le tourisme; **business is s. at the moment** les affaires marchent au ralenti en ce moment
4 *(lax ▸ discipline, laws, control)* mou (molle), relâché; *(▸ parents)* négligent; **they're rather s. about discipline** ils sont plutôt laxistes
VI *(person ▸ become negligent)* se laisser aller; *(▸ in one's work, efforts)* se relâcher
N **1** *(in rope)* mou *m*; *(in cable, joint)* jeu *m*; *Naut*

(in cable) battant *m*; **to take up the s. in a rope** tendre une corde; **leave a bit of s.** laissez un peu de mou; *Am Fam Fig* **cut me some s.!** fiche-moi la paix! **2** *Fig (in economy)* secteurs *mpl* affaiblis; **to take up the s. in the economy** relancer les secteurs faibles de l'économie

• **slacks** NPL *Am* **(pair of) slacks** pantalon *m*

▸ **slack off, slack up** VI *Fam (slow down)* se laisser aller

slacken ['slækən] VT **1** *(loosen* ▸ *cable, rope)* détendre, relâcher; *(*▸ *reins)* relâcher; *(*▸ *grip, hold)* desserrer **2** *(reduce* ▸ *pressure, speed)* réduire, diminuer; *(*▸ *pace)* ralentir; **the train slackened speed** le train a ralenti

VI **1** *(rope, cable)* se relâcher; *(grip, hold)* se desserrer **2** *(lessen* ▸ *speed, demand, interest)* diminuer; *(*▸ *business)* ralentir; *(*▸ *wind)* diminuer de force; *(*▸ *standards)* baisser

▸ **slacken off** VT SEP **1** *(rope)* relâcher, donner du mou à **2** *(speed, pressure)* diminuer; *(efforts)* relâcher

VI **1** *(rope)* se relâcher **2** *(speed, demand)* diminuer

slackening ['slækənɪŋ] N *(in speed)* diminution *f*, réduction *f*; *(in interest)* diminution *f*; *(in demand)* affaiblissement *m*; *(in knot)* desserrement *m*; *(in rope)* relâchement *m*; *(in standards)* abaissement *m*; **a s. of speed** un ralentissement

slacker ['slækə(r)] N *Fam* fainéant(e) *m,f*, raté(e) *m,f*

slackly ['slæklɪ] ADV *(work)* négligemment, sans soin; *(hang)* mollement

slackness ['slæknɪs] N **1** *(of rope, wire)* mou *m* **2** *(in business)* ralentissement *m* **3** *(negligence)* négligence *f*, paresse *f*

slag [slæg] *(pt & pp* **slagged**, *cont* **slagging**) N **1** *(UNCOUNT) (waste* ▸ *from mine)* stériles *mpl*; *(*▸ *from foundry)* scories *fpl*, crasses *fpl*; *(*▸ *from volcano)* scories *fpl* volcaniques **2** *Br very Fam (promiscuous woman)* pouffiasse *f*, traînée *f*

VT *Br very Fam* **1** *(criticize)* débiner, éreinter, descendre en flammes **2** *(make fun of)* se foutre de

▸ **slag off** VT SEP *Br very Fam* **1** *(criticize)* débiner, éreinter, descendre en flammes **2** *(make fun of)* se foutre de

slagging ['slægɪŋ] N *Br very Fam* **to give sb a s.** *(criticize)* débiner *ou* éreinter qn, descendre qn en flammes; *(make fun of)* se foutre de qn

slaggy ['slægɪ] *(compar* **slaggier**, *superl* **slaggiest**) ADJ *Br Fam (tarty)* qui fait pute; **she looks really s. in all that make-up** elle fait vraiment pute avec tout son maquillage

slain [sleɪn] *pp of* **slay**

slake [sleɪk] VT **1** *Literary (thirst)* étancher; *(desire)* assouvir **2** *Chem (lime)* éteindre

slalom ['slɑːləm] N slalom *m*

VI slalomer, faire du slalom

slam [slæm] *(pt & pp* **slammed**, *cont* **slamming**) VT **1** *(close* ▸ *window, door)* claquer; *(*▸ *drawer)* fermer violemment; **to s. the door shut** claquer la porte; **I tried to explain but she slammed the door in my face** j'ai essayé de lui expliquer mais elle m'a claqué la porte au nez

2 *(bang)* **he slammed the books on the desk** il a posé bruyamment les livres sur le bureau; **he slammed the ball into the net** il a envoyé le ballon dans le filet d'un grand coup de pied

3 *Fam (defeat)* écraser; **our team got slammed** notre équipe a été battue à plate couture

4 *Fam (criticize)* éreinter, descendre en flammes; **to get slammed** se faire éreinter, se faire descendre en flammes

VI *(door, window)* claquer; **the door slammed shut** la porte a claqué

N *(of door, window)* claquement *m*; **give the door a good s.** claque la porte un bon coup; **I heard a loud s.** j'ai entendu un grand claquement

▸▸ *Am Sport* ***slam dunk*** smash *m* au panier

▸ **slam on** VT SEP **to s. on the brakes** freiner brutalement; **he slammed on a hat and stormed out** il enfonça un chapeau sur sa tête et sortit comme un ouragan

slammer ['slæmə(r)] N *Fam* **in the s.** *(in jail)* en taule, en cabane

slander ['slɑːndə(r)] VT *(gen)* calomnier, dire du mal de; *Law* diffamer

N *(gen)* calomnie *f*; *Law* diffamation *f*

slanderer ['slɑːndərə(r)] N *(gen)* calomniateur(trice) *m,f*; *Law* diffamateur(trice) *m,f*

slanderous ['slɑːndərəs] ADJ *(gen)* calomniateur; *Law* diffamatoire

slanderously ['slɑːndərəslɪ] ADV *(gen)* calomnieusement; *Law* de façon diffamatoire

slang [slæŋ] N argot *m*; **he uses a lot of s.** il emploie beaucoup de mots d'argot; **prison s.** argot *m* carcéral *ou* de prison

ADJ argotique, d'argot

VT *Br Fam* traiter de tous les noms□; **they started slanging each other in the street** ils commencèrent à se traiter de tous les noms dans la rue

slangily ['slæŋɪlɪ] ADV *(speak, express oneself)* en argot

slanging match ['slæŋɪŋ-] N *Br Fam* prise *f* de bec, engueulade *f*

slangy ['slæŋɪ] *(compar* **slangier**, *superl* **slangiest**) ADJ argotique

slant [slɑːnt] N **1** *(line)* ligne *f* oblique; *(slope)* inclinaison *f*; **the table has a s.** *or* **is on a s.** la table penche *ou* n'est pas d'aplomb **2** *(point of view)* perspective *f*, point *m* de vue; **his articles usually have an anti-government s.** il a tendance à critiquer le gouvernement dans ses articles; **to put a different s. on things** apporter une perspective différente sur les choses

VT **1** *(news, evidence)* présenter avec parti pris *ou* de manière peu objective; **the article was slanted** l'article était orienté **2** *(line, perspective)* incliner, faire pencher

VI *(line, handwriting)* pencher; *(ray of light)* passer obliquement

slant-eyed ADJ aux yeux bridés, qui a les yeux bridés

slanting ['slɑːntɪŋ] ADJ *(floor, table, roof)* en pente, incliné; *(writing)* penché; *(line)* oblique, penché

slantwise ['slɑːntwaɪz] ADV *(hang, fall)* en oblique, obliquement; *(write)* d'une écriture penchée

slap [slæp] *(pt & pp* **slapped**, *cont* **slapping**) VT **1** *(hit)* donner une claque à; **she slapped his face, she slapped him across the face** elle l'a giflé, elle lui a donné une gifle; **to s. sb on the back** *(for hiccups, in greeting)* donner à qn une tape dans le dos; *(in praise)* féliciter qn en lui donnant une tape dans le dos; **to s. sb's wrist** *or* **wrists, to s. sb on the wrist** *or* **wrists** taper sur les doigts de qn **2** *(put)* **just s. some paint over it** passe un coup de pinceau dessus

VI **the waves slapped against the harbour wall** les vagues battaient contre la digue

N **1** *(smack)* claque *f*; *(on face)* gifle *f*; *(on back)* tape *f* dans le dos; *(on wrist)* tape *f*; **they gave him a s. on the back** *(in praise)* ils lui ont donné une tape dans le dos pour le féliciter; **I got a s. in the face** j'ai reçu une gifle; *Fig* **it was a real s. in the face** ça m'a fait l'effet d'une gifle; **I got away with just a s. on the wrist** j'en ai été quitte pour une tape sur les doigts **2** *(noise)* **the s. of the waves against the side of the boat** le clapotis des vagues contre la coque **3** *Br Fam (make-up)* maquillage□ *m*

ADV *Fam* en plein□; **I ran s. into a tree** je suis rentré en plein *ou* tout droit dans un arbre□; **s. in the middle of the meeting** en plein *ou* au beau milieu de la réunion□

▸ **slap about, slap around** VT SEP battre

▸ **slap down** VT SEP **1** *(book, money)* poser bruyamment; **she slapped £1,000 down on the table** elle a jeté une liasse de 1000 livres sur la table **2** *Fam (suggestion)* rejeter□; *(person)* rembarrer

▸ **slap on** VT SEP **1** *(paint)* appliquer n'importe comment *ou* à la va-vite; *(jam, butter)* étaler généreusement; **s. some paint on the door** donne un coup de pinceau sur la porte; **hang on, I'll just s. some make-up on** attends, je vais juste me maquiller vite fait **2** *(tax, increase)* **they slapped on a 3 percent surcharge** ils ont mis une surtaxe de 3 pour cent

slapdash ['slæpdæʃ] ADV à la va-vite, sans soin n'importe comment

ADJ *(work)* fait n'importe comment *ou* à la va-vite; *(person)* négligent; **he's very s. in everything he does** il fait tout un peu n'importe comment *ou* à la va-vite

slaphappy ['slæp,hæpɪ] ADJ *Fam* relax

slaphead ['slæphed] N *Br Fam* chauve□ *m*, crâne *m* d'œuf; **he's a total s.** il n'a pas un poil sur le caillou, il a une casquette en peau de fesse

slapper ['slæpə(r)] N *Br Fam (promiscuous woman)* pouffiasse *f*, traînée *f*, salope *f*

slapping ['slæpɪŋ] N *(UNCOUNT) (blows)* claques *fpl*, gifles *fpl*

slapstick ['slæpstɪk] N grosse farce *f*, bouffonnerie *f*

ADJ *(humour)* bouffon

▸▸ ***slapstick comedy*** comédie *f* bouffonne

slap-up ADJ *Br Fam* **a s. meal** un repas de derrière les fagots; **he invited me out for a s. lunch** il m'a invité à déjeuner dans un restaurant chic□

slash [slæʃ] VT **1** *(cut* ▸ *gen)* taillader; *(*▸ *face)* balafrer; **he slashed my arm with a knife** il m'a tailladé le bras avec un couteau; **the bus seats had been slashed by vandals** les sièges du bus avaient été lacérés par des vandales; **he slashed his way through the jungle** il s'est taillé *ou* frayé un chemin à travers la jungle à coups de couteau

2 *(hit* ▸ *with whip)* frapper, cingler; *(*▸ *with stick)* battre; **she slashed the bushes with a stick** elle donnait des coups de bâton dans les buissons

3 *Am (verbally)* critiquer violemment; **she slashed the government in her speech** elle a violemment critiqué le gouvernement dans son discours

4 *(prices)* casser; *(cost, taxes, unemployment)* réduire considérablement; **prices slashed!** *(sign)* prix cassés!; **prices have been slashed by 40 per cent** les prix ont été réduits de 40 pour cent

VI **to s. at sb with a knife** donner des coups de couteau en direction de qn; **he slashed at the bushes with a stick** il donna des coups de bâton dans les buissons; **they slashed through the undergrowth** ils se sont taillés un chemin dans les sous-bois

N **1** *(with knife)* coup *m* de couteau; *(with sword)* coup *m* d'épée; *(with whip)* coup *m* de fouet; *(with stick)* coup *m* de bâton

2 *(cut)* entaille *f*; *(on face)* balafre *f*

3 *Sewing* crevé *m*

4 *Typ & Comput* (barre *f*) oblique *f*

5 *Br Fam (idioms)* **to have a s.** pisser

slashing ['slæʃɪŋ] ADJ *(attack, criticism)* cinglant

N *(severe criticism)* critique *f* acerbe

slat [slæt] N *(in blinds, louvre)* lamelle *f*; *(wooden)* latte *f*

slate [sleɪt] N **1** *Constr & Sch* ardoise *f*; *Br Fam Fig* **put it on the s.** mettez-le sur mon compte□; *Br Fam* **to have a s. loose** *(person)* avoir une case de vide, avoir une araignée au plafond **2** *Am Pol* liste *f* provisoire de candidats; **the Republicans have a full s.** les Républicains présentent des candidats dans toutes les circonscriptions **3** *(colour)* gris ardoise *m inv*

COMP *(mine)* d'ardoise; *(roof)* en ardoise *ou* ardoises, d'ardoise; *(industry)* ardoisier; **s. pencil** crayon *m* d'ardoise; **s. quarry** carrière *f* d'ardoise ardoisière *f*

ADJ *(in colour)* gris ardoise *(inv)*

VT **1** *(cover* ▸ *roof)* couvrir d'ardoises

2 *Am Pol* proposer *(un candidat)*; **Magee is slated for President** Magee a été choisi comme candidat aux élections présidentielles

3 *Am (expect)* prévoir; **we're slating a full house** nous comptons faire salle comble; **she was slated for a gold medal/for victory** *(destined)* elle devait remporter une médaille d'or/la victoire

4 *Br Fam (criticize)* éreinter, descendre en flammes; **his latest novel was slated by the critics** les critiques ont descendu son dernier roman

▸▸ ***slate blue*** bleu ardoise *m inv*; ***slate grey*** gris ardoise *m inv*

slate-blue ADJ bleu ardoise *(inv)*

slate-coloured, *Am* **slate-colored** ADJ ardoise *(inv)*

slate-grey ADJ gris ardoise *(inv)*

slater ['sleɪtə(r)] **N** *(roofer)* couvreur *m*

slating ['sleɪtɪŋ] **N 1** *(UNCOUNT) Constr (of roof)* couverture *f*; *(material)* ardoises *fpl* **2** *Br Fam (reprimand)* savon *m*; *(severe criticism)* critique *f* acerbe□; **the play got a s. in the press** la pièce a été éreintée par la presse

slatted ['slætɪd] **ADJ** à lattes

slattern ['slætən] **N** souillon *f*

slatternly ['slætənlɪ] **ADJ** *(woman)* mal soigné; *(habit, dress)* négligé

slaty ['sleɪtɪ] (*compar* **slatier**, *superl* **slatiest**) **ADJ** *(in colour)* ardoise *(inv)*; *(in appearance, texture)* qui ressemble à l'ardoise

slaughter ['slɔːtə(r)] **VT 1** *(kill ▸ animal)* abattre, tuer; *(▸ people)* massacrer, tuer (sauvagement) **2** *Fam Fig (defeat ▸ team, opponent)* écrabouiller, battre à plates coutures□

N *(of animal)* abattage *m*; *(of people)* massacre *m*, tuerie *f*

slaughtered ['slɔːtəd] **ADJ** *Br Fam (drunk)* bourré, beurré, pété

slaughterer ['slɔːtərə(r)] **N** *(in abattoir)* abatteur *m*, tueur *m (dans un abattoir)*; *(murderer)* meurtrier(ère) *m,f*; *(in massacre)* massacreur(euse) *m,f*

slaughterhouse ['slɔːtəhaus, *pl* -hauzɪz] **N** abattoir *m*

slaughtering ['slɔːtərɪŋ] **N 1** *(of animals)* abattage *m* **2** *(of people)* carnage *m*, massacre *m*, boucherie *f*

Slav [slɑːv] **ADJ** slave

N Slave *mf*

slave [sleɪv] **N** *also Fig* esclave *mf*; **to be a s. to fashion** être esclave de la mode; **he's a s. to drink** il est prisonnier de l'alcool; *Fam Hum* **what did your last s. die of?** je ne suis pas ta bonne!

VI travailler comme un esclave *ou* un forçat, trimer; **I've been slaving over a hot stove all morning** j'ai travaillé comme un forçat à la cuisine toute la matinée; **they slaved to get their house finished in time** ils ont travaillé comme des forçats pour terminer leur maison à temps

▸▸ ***slave cylinder*** cylindre *m* récepteur; ***slave driver*** meneur *m* d'esclaves; *Fig* négrier *m*; ***slave labour*** *(work)* travail *m* fait par des esclaves; *Fig* travail *m* de forçat; **the Great Wall was built by s. labour** la Grande Muraille a été construite par des esclaves; **I'm not working there any more, it's s. labour** je ne travaillerai plus pour eux, c'est le *ou* un vrai bagne; ***slave ship*** négrier *m (bateau)*; ***slave trade*** commerce *m* des esclaves; *(of Africans)* traite *f* des Noirs; ***slave trader*** marchand *m* d'esclaves, négrier *m*

▸ slave away VI *(work hard)* trimer (**over** *or* **at** sur)

slaver[1] ['sleɪvə(r)] **N 1** *(trader)* marchand *m* d'esclaves **2** *(ship)* (vaisseau *m*) négrier *m*

slaver[2] ['slævə(r)] **VI** *(dribble)* baver; **the dog was slavering at the mouth** le chien bavait

N 1 *(saliva)* bave *f* **2** *Literary (flattery)* flatterie *f* grossière, flagornerie *f*

slavery ['sleɪvərɪ] **N** esclavage *m*; **to be sold into s.** être vendu comme esclave; **to reduce to s.** *(person)* réduire en esclavage; *(a people)* asservir; **this work is sheer s.** ce travail est un véritable esclavage

Slavic ['slɑːvɪk] = **Slavonic**

slavish ['sleɪvɪʃ] **ADJ** *(mentality, habits)* d'esclave; *(devotion)* servile; *(imitation)* sans aucune originalité, servile

slavishly ['sleɪvɪʃlɪ] **ADV** *(work)* comme un forçat; *(copy, worship)* servilement

slavishness ['sleɪvɪʃnɪs] **N** servilité *f*

Slavonic [slə'vɒnɪk] **N** *Ling* slave *m*

ADJ slave

slaw [slɔː] **N** *Am* salade *f* de chou cru

slay [sleɪ] (*pt* **slew** [sluː], *pp* **slain** [sleɪn]) **VT 1** *(kill)* tuer **2** *Br Fam (impress)* impressionner□; *(amuse)* faire mourir de rire; *Ironic* **you s. me!** tu es impayable!

slayer ['sleɪə(r)] **N** *Literary* tueur(euse) *m,f*

slaying ['sleɪɪŋ] **N** *Literary (killing ▸ of dragon)* destruction *f*; *(▸ of person)* meurtre *m*; *esp Am Journ (murder)* assassinat *m*, meurtre *m*

sleaze [sliːz] *Fam* **N 1** *(squalidness)* aspect *m* miteux□, caractère *m* sordide□ **2** *(pornography)* porno *m* **3** *(corruption)* corruption□*f*; **it's the s. factor that led to the government's downfall** ce sont les affaires de corruption dans lesquelles le gouvernement a été impliqué qui en ont provoqué la chute

sleazebag ['sliːzbæg], **sleazeball** ['sliːzbɔːl] **N** *Fam* **1** *(despicable person)* ordure *f*, raclure *f* **2** *(repulsive man)* gros dégueulasse *m*

sleaziness ['sliːzɪnɪs] **N** *Fam* sordide□*m*

sleazo ['sliːzəʊ] (*pl* **sleazos**) **N** *Fam* personne *f* louche□

sleazy ['sliːzɪ] (*compar* **sleazier**, *superl* **sleaziest**) **ADJ** *Fam (squalid)* miteux□, sordide□; *(disreputable)* mal famé□; *(person)* louche□

sled [sled] (*pt & pp* **sledded**, *cont* **sledding**) *Am* **N 1** *(for fun or sport)* luge *f* **2** *(pulled by animals)* traîneau *m*

VI 1 *(for fun or sport)* faire de la luge; **to go sledding** faire de la luge; **children were sledding down the slope** des enfants descendaient la pente sur une *ou* en luge **2** *(pulled by animals)* faire du traîneau

▸▸ ***sled dog*** chien *m* de traîneau; ***sled race*** course *f* de traîneaux

sledge [sledʒ] *Br* **N 1** *(for fun or sport)* luge *f* **2** *(pulled by animals)* traîneau *m*

VI 1 *(for fun or sport)* faire de la luge; **to go sledging** faire de la luge; **children were sledging down the slope** des enfants descendaient la pente sur une *ou* en luge **2** *(pulled by animals)* faire du traîneau

sledgehammer ['sledʒhæmə(r)] **N** *(tool)* masse *f*; *Fig* **a s. blow** un coup très violent; *Fig* **to use a s. to crack a walnut** employer les grands moyens (pour régler un problème mineur)

sleek [sliːk] **ADJ 1** *(fur, hair)* luisant, lustré, lisse; *(feathers)* brillant, luisant **2** *(person ▸ in appearance)* soigné, tiré à quatre épingles; *(▸ in manner)* onctueux, doucereux **3** *(vehicle, plane)* aux lignes pures; **the car has very s. lines** cette voiture a une très belle ligne; **a s. black limousine** une limousine d'un noir brillant

sleekly ['sliːklɪ] **ADV 1** *(glossily)* **its fur shone s.** il/elle avait le poil luisant **2** *(elegantly ▸ dress)* élégamment, avec chic **3** *(unctuously ▸ behave)* onctueusement, doucereusement

sleekness ['sliːknɪs] **N 1** *(of fur, hair, feathers)* brillant *m*, luisant *m* **2** *(of person ▸ in appearance)* chic *m*, élégance *f*; *(▸ in manner)* onctuosité *f* **3** *(of vehicle, plane)* pureté *f* de lignes, ligne *f* aérodynamique

SLEEP [sliːp]

N	
• sommeil **1**	• somme **2**
• chassie **3**	
VI	
• dormir **1**	• coucher **2**
• passer la nuit **2**	• rêvasser **3**

(*pt & pp* **slept** [slept])

N 1 *(rest)* sommeil *m*; **to turn over in one's s.** se retourner dans son sommeil; **to talk in one's s.** parler en dormant *ou* dans son sommeil; **to walk in one's s.** être somnambule; **she walked in her s. last night** elle a fait une crise de somnambulisme *ou* a marché en dormant la nuit dernière; **to be in a deep s.** dormir profondément; **to have a good (night's) s.** bien dormir; **you need (to get) a good night's s.** il te faut une bonne nuit de sommeil; **I only had two hours' s.** je n'ai dormi que deux heures; **I need my s.** j'ai besoin de beaucoup de sommeil; **I couldn't get to s.** je n'arrivais pas à m'endormir; **to go to s.** s'endormir; **to go** *or* **to get back to s.** se rendormir; **my legs have gone to s.** *(numb)* j'ai les jambes engourdies; *(tingling)* j'ai des fourmis dans les jambes; **to read oneself to s.** lire pour s'endormir; **to sing a child to s.** chanter une berceuse à un enfant; **I won't lose any s. over it** cela ne va pas m'empêcher de dormir; **to put to s.** endormir; *Euph (horse, dog)* piquer; **to send sb to s.** endormir qn; *Fig (bore)* endormir qn, assommer qn

2 *(nap)* **to have a s.** faire un somme; **the children usually have a s. in the afternoon** en général les enfants font la sieste l'après-midi

3 *(substance in eyes)* chassie *f*; **to rub the s. out of one's eyes** se frotter les yeux *(au réveil)*

VT 1 *(accommodate)* **the house sleeps four** on peut coucher à quatre dans cette maison

2 *Literary* **to s. the s. of the just** dormir du sommeil du juste

VI 1 *(rest)* dormir; **s. well** *or* **tight!** bonne nuit!; **did you s. well?** avez-vous bien dormi?; **to s. (for) six hours** dormir six heures; **he can't s. for thinking about it** il n'en dort pas; **to s. late** faire la grasse matinée; **to s. soundly** dormir profondément *ou* à poings fermés; **to s. like a log** dormir comme une souche *ou* comme un loir, dormir à poings fermés

2 *(spend night)* coucher, passer la nuit; **can I s. at your place?** est-ce que je peux coucher *ou* dormir chez vous?; **to s. on the floor** coucher *ou* dormir par terre; **the bed had not been slept in** le lit n'avait pas été défait; **where did you s. last night?** où est-ce que tu as passé la nuit?; **to s. rough** coucher sur la dure

3 *(daydream)* rêvasser, rêver; **Walsh is sleeping at the back of the class as usual** Walsh rêvasse au fond de la classe, comme d'habitude

4 *Comput* être en veille; **to put a notebook to s.** mettre un portable en veille

▸▸ *Comput* ***sleep mode*** veille *f*

▸ sleep around VI *Fam* coucher à droite et à gauche

▸ sleep away VT SEP he slept the night away il a dormi toute la nuit; **he sleeps the day away** il passe toute la journée à dormir

▸ sleep in VI *(lie in ▸ voluntarily)* faire la grasse matinée; *(▸ involuntarily)* se lever en retard, ne pas se réveiller (à l'heure)

▸ sleep off VT SEP *(hangover, fatigue)* dormir pour faire passer *ou* se remettre de; **he's sleeping off the effects of the journey** il dort pour se remettre de la fatigue du voyage; *Fam* **he's sleeping it off** il cuve son vin

▸ sleep out VI *(away from home)* découcher; *(in the open air)* coucher à la belle étoile; *(in tent)* coucher sous la tente

▸ sleep together VI coucher ensemble

▸ sleep with VT INSEP coucher avec

---

sleeper ['sliːpə(r)] **N 1** *(sleeping person)* dormeur(euse) *m,f*; **to be a light/heavy s.** avoir le sommeil léger/lourd; **a late s.** un (une) couche-tard

2 *(train)* train-couchettes *m*; *(sleeping car)* wagon-lit *m*, voiture-lit *f*; *(berth)* couchette *f*; **I took the s. to Rome** je suis allé à Rome en train-couchettes

3 *Am (sofa bed)* canapé-lit *m*

4 *Br Rail (track support)* traverse *f*, *Can* dormant *m*

5 *(spy)* agent *m* dormant *ou* en sommeil

6 *(earring)* dormeuse *f*

7 *Fam (unexpected success)* révélation□*f*

▸▸ ***sleeper cell*** cellule *f* (terroriste) dormante *ou* en sommeil

sleepily ['sliːpɪlɪ] **ADV** *(look)* d'un air endormi; *(speak)* d'un ton endormi; **she wandered s. into the kitchen** elle est arrivée à moitié endormie dans la cuisine; **a village nestled s. in the hills** un village blotti tranquillement contre les collines

sleepiness ['sliːpɪnɪs] **N** *(of person)* envie *f* de dormir; *(of town)* torpeur *f*

sleeping ['sliːpɪŋ] **ADJ** dormant, endormi; *Prov* **let s. dogs lie** ne réveillez pas le chat qui dort

N sommeil *m*; **the house has s. accommodation for ten** c'est une maison où dix personnes peuvent dormir; **what are the s. arrangements?** et pour dormir, comment on fait?; **she was a bit vague about the s. arrangements** elle est restée vague concernant les lits

▸▸ ***sleeping bag*** sac *m* de couchage; *Rail & Naut* ***sleeping berth*** couchette *f*; *Rail* ***sleeping car, sleeping carriage*** wagon-lit *m*; *Fig* ***sleeping giant*** = pays ou organisation dont le très fort potentiel reste inexploité; *Br Com* ***sleeping partner*** (associé *m*) commanditaire *m*, bailleur *m* de fonds; ***sleeping pill*** somnifère *m*; *Br* ***sleeping policeman*** casse-vitesse *m inv*, ralentisseur *m*; ***sleeping quarters*** chambres *fpl* à coucher; *Mil* chambrées *fpl*; *Sch* dortoir *m*; ***sleeping sickness*** maladie *f* du sommeil; *Am* ***sleeping suit*** grenouillère *f*; ***sleeping tablet*** somnifère *m*

sleepless ['sli:plɪs] ADJ **1** *(without sleep)* sans sommeil; **I had** *or* **spent a s. night** j'ai passé une nuit blanche, je n'ai pas fermé l'œil de la nuit **2** *Literary (person)* qui ne peut trouver le sommeil; **s. vigilance** vigilance *f* sans faille

sleeplessly ['sli:plɪslɪ] ADV sans pouvoir dormir

sleeplessness ['sli:plɪsnɪs] N *(UNCOUNT)* insomnie *f*, insomnies *fpl*

sleepsuit ['sli:psu:t] N grenouillère *f*

sleepwalk ['sli:pwɔ:k] VI être somnambule; **he's sleepwalking** il marche en dormant; **I sleepwalked last night** j'ai eu une crise de somnambulisme la nuit dernière; *Fig* **we are sleepwalking into disaster** nous allons tout droit à la catastrophe sans nous en rendre compte

sleepwalker ['sli:pwɔ:kə(r)] N somnambule *mf*

sleepwalking ['sli:pwɔ:kɪŋ] N somnambulisme *m*

sleepy ['sli:pɪ] *(compar* **sleepier**, *superl* **sleepiest)** ADJ **1** *(person)* qui a envie de dormir, somnolent; **I'm** *or* **I feel s.** j'ai sommeil, j'ai envie de dormir; **to make sb (feel) s.** endormir qn; **s. look** air *m* endormi **2** *(town)* plongé dans la torpeur

sleepyhead ['sli:pɪhed] N *Fam* **come on, s., it's time for bed!** allez, va au lit, tu dors debout!□; **wake up, s.!** debout, paresseux/paresseuse!

sleet [sli:t] N **1** *(icy rain)* neige *f* fondue *(tombant du ciel)* **2** *Am (ice)* verglas *m*

VI **it's sleeting** il tombe de la neige fondue

sleeve [sli:v] N **1** *(of garment)* manche *f*; **short s.** manche *f* courte; *Fig* **to have** *or* **to keep something up one's s.** avoir plus d'un tour dans son sac; **he's got a surprise up his s.** il nous/leur/*etc* réserve une surprise; **I wonder what else she's got up her s.** je me demande ce qu'elle nous/leur/*etc* réserve encore comme surprise **2** *Tech (tube)* manchon *m*; *(lining)* chemise *f*, fourreau *m* **3** *Br (for record)* pochette *f*

▸▸ ***sleeve board*** jeannette *f*; ***sleeve hole*** *(in clothing)* emmanchure *f*; *Br* ***sleeve notes*** = texte figurant au dos des pochettes de disques

-sleeved [sli:vd] SUFF à manches…; **short/long-s.** à manches courtes/longues

sleeveless ['sli:vlɪs] ADJ sans manches

sleigh [sleɪ] N traîneau *m*

VI se promener en traîneau, aller en traîneau

▸▸ ***sleigh bell*** grelot *m* (de traîneau); ***sleigh ride*** promenade *f* en traîneau

sleight of hand ['slaɪt-] N *(skill)* dextérité *f*; *(trick)* tour *m* de passe-passe; **by s.** par un tour de passe-passe

slender ['slendə(r)] ADJ **1** *(slim* ▸ *figure)* mince, svelte; *(*▸ *fingers, waist, neck, stem)* fin **2** *(limited* ▸ *resources)* faible, maigre, limité; *(*▸ *majority, margin)* étroit, faible; *(*▸ *hope, chance)* maigre, faible; *(*▸ *knowledge)* faible, limité; **there is a very s. chance that…** il y a une chance très faible que… + *subjunctive*; *Euph* **he's a person of s. means** il ne roule pas sur l'or

slenderize, -ise ['slendəraɪz] *Am Fam* VI maigrir□, mincir□

VT mincir□, amincir□

slenderly ['slendəlɪ] ADV **s. built** svelte, mince

slenderness ['slendənɪs] N **1** *(of figure)* minceur *f*, sveltesse *f*; *(of neck, waist, fingers)* finesse *f* **2** *(of resources)* insuffisance *f*; *(of hope, majority, margin)* faiblesse *f*

slept [slept] *pt & pp of* **sleep**

sleuth [slu:θ] *Fam Hum* N (fin) limier *m*, détective□*m*

VI enquêter□

sleuthhound ['slu:θhaʊnd] N **1** *Fam Hum (detective)* (fin) limier *m*, détective□*m* **2** *(dog)* limier *m*

S level N *Br* = examen de niveau supérieur au "A level" que passent les élèves les plus doués, généralement en même temps que ce dernier

slew [slu:] *pt of* **slay**

VI **1** *(pivot)* pivoter, se retourner; **he slewed round in his chair** il a pivoté sur sa chaise **2** *(vehicle* ▸ *skid)* déraper; *(*▸ *turn)* virer; *(*▸ *turn right round)* faire un tête-à-queue; **the car slewed into the ditch** la voiture a dérapé et a fini dans le fossé

VT **1** *(twist)* faire tourner *ou* pivoter **2** *(vehicle)* faire déraper; **he slewed the car around** il a fait un tête-à-queue

N **1** *Fam (large number)* **a s. of, slews of** un tas de; **a whole s. of photographers** un tas de photographes **2** *(of vehicle* ▸ *turn)* virage *m*; *(*▸ *180-degree turn)* tête-à-queue *m inv*

slice [slaɪs] N **1** *(of bread, meat, cake, cheese)* tranche *f*; *(of pizza)* part *f*; *(round* ▸ *of lemon, sausage, carrot, onion etc)* rondelle *f*; **to cut sth into slices** *(bread, meat, cake, cheese)* couper qch (en tranches); *(pizza)* couper qch (en parts); *(lemon, sausage, carrot, onion etc)* couper qch (en rondelles); **he cut himself a large s. of bread** il s'est coupé une grande tranche de pain

2 *Fig (share, percentage)* part *f*, partie *f*; **a large s. of my income goes on rent** une bonne partie de mes revenus est absorbée par le loyer; **a s. of the profits** une part des bénéfices; *Fam* **they were all very keen to get a s. of the action** tout le monde voulait participer□

3 *(utensil)* pelle *f*, spatule *f*; **cake s.** pelle *f* à gâteau

4 *(in golf)* slice *m*; *(in tennis)* balle *f* coupée; **she puts a lot of s. on her serve** elle slice beaucoup ses balles au service

5 *Culin* **apple s.** tartelette *f* aux pommes

VT **1** *(cut into pieces* ▸ *cake, bread, ham)* couper (en tranches); *(*▸ *pizza)* couper (en parts); *(*▸ *sausage, carrot, courgette)* couper (en rondelles); *Am Fam* **any way you s. it** il n'y a pas à tortiller

2 *(cut)* couper, trancher; **to s. sth in two** *or* **in half** couper qch en deux; **to s. sth open** ouvrir qch en le coupant

3 *(in golf)* slicer; *(in tennis)* couper

VI *(knife)* couper; *(bread)* se couper; **this bread doesn't s. very easily** ce pain n'est pas très facile à couper; **the knife sliced into the flesh** le couteau a pénétré dans la chair

▸**slice off** VT SEP *(branch)* couper; **to s. off the tip of one's finger** se trancher le bout du doigt; **s. me off some ham/cheese** coupe-moi une tranche de jambon/fromage

▸**slice through** VT INSEP **1** *(cut* ▸ *rope, cable)* couper (net), trancher; *Fig* **he sliced through the red tape** il a éliminé toute la paperasserie d'un seul coup **2** *(go, move)* traverser (rapidement), fendre; **the boat sliced through the water** le bateau fendait l'eau; **the arrow sliced through the air** la flèche fendit l'air; **the river slices through the city** la rivière coupe la ville en deux; **to s. through the enemy lines** transpercer les lignes adverses

▸**slice up** VT SEP *(cake, ham, bread)* couper (en tranches); *(pizza)* couper (en parts); *(sausage, carrot, courgette)* couper (en rondelles)

sliced [slaɪst] ADJ *(cake, ham, bread)* en tranches; *(pizza)* découpée en parts; *(banana, sausage, carrot, courgette)* en rondelles

▸▸ ***sliced bread*** pain *m* (coupé) en tranches; *Fam* **it's the best thing since s. bread** c'est ce qu'on a fait de mieux depuis l'invention du fil à couper le beurre□

slicer ['slaɪsə(r)] N *(gen)* machine *f* à trancher; *(for bread)* machine *f* à couper le pain; *(for meat)* machine *f* à couper la viande; *(for salami, ham)* coupe-jambon *m inv*

slick [slɪk] ADJ **1** *Pej (glib)* qui a du bagout; *(in manner)* doucereux; *(in content)* superficiel; **he always has a s. answer** il a toujours réponse à tout; **the explanation was rather too s.** l'explication était trop bonne (pour être vraie)

2 *(smoothly efficient)* habile; **she made a s. gear change** elle effectua un changement de vitesse en souplesse; **a s. campaign** une campagne astucieuse; **a s. take-over** un rachat rondement mené

3 *(smart)* chic, tiré à quatre épingles; *(style, magazine)* beau (belle); **you're looking very s.** tu fais très chic

4 *(hair)* lisse, lissé, luisant

5 *Am (slippery)* glissant; **the road was s. with ice/mud** le verglas/la boue avait rendu la chaussée glissante

6 *Am (cunning)* malin(igne), rusé

N *(oil spill* ▸ *on sea)* nappe *f* de pétrole; *(*▸ *on beach)* marée *f* noire

▸**slick back** VT SEP **to s. back one's hair** se lisser les cheveux en arrière

▸**slick down** VT SEP **to s. one's hair down** se lisser les cheveux

▸**slick up** *Am Fam* VT SEP *(appearance)* mettre en valeur□; *(house, room)* astiquer□, faire reluire□; **to s. oneself up** se pomponner□

VI *(dress smartly)* se pomponner□

slicker ['slɪkə(r)] N **1** *(person)* **(city) s.** homme *m* de finance habile, *Pej* requin *m* **2** *Am (raincoat)* imperméable *m*; *(oilskin)* ciré *m*

slickly ['slɪklɪ] ADV **1** *(skilfully)* habilement; *(perform)* brillamment **2** *Pej (say, reply)* doucereusement **3 his hair shone s.** il avait les cheveux luisants

slickness ['slɪknɪs] N **1** *(of hair)* brillant *m*, luisant *m* **2** *Pej (in speech)* bagout *m*; *(in manner)* caractère *m* doucereux; *(in style)* brillance *f* (apparente) **3** *(skill)* habileté *f*, adresse *f*

slide [slaɪd] *(pt & pp* **slid** [slɪd]) VI **1** *(on ice, slippery surface)* glisser; **he slid on the ice** il a glissé sur la glace; **he slid down the banisters** il a descendu l'escalier en glissant sur la rampe; **the dish slid off the table/onto the floor** le plat a glissé de la table/sur le sol; **tears slid down her face** des larmes roulèrent sur son visage

2 *(move quietly)* se glisser; **she slid into/out of the room** elle s'est glissée dans la pièce/hors de la pièce; **the car slid away into the dark** la voiture s'enfonça dans l'obscurité; **the door slid open/shut** la porte s'est ouverte/fermée en glissant

3 *(go gradually)* glisser; **the sheet music slid (down) behind the piano** la partition a glissé derrière le piano; **the country was sliding into anarchy** le pays glissait vers l'anarchie; **he's sliding into bad habits** il est en train de prendre de mauvaises habitudes; **to let things s.** laisser les choses aller à la dérive

4 *Tech (between runners etc)* coulisser

5 *(prices, value)* baisser

VT faire glisser, glisser; **I slid the book into my pocket** j'ai glissé le livre dans ma poche; **he slid the door open/shut** il a ouvert/fermé la porte en la faisant coulisser; **s. the lid into place** faites glisser le couvercle à sa place; **she slid the money across the table** elle fit glisser l'argent sur la table

N **1** *(in playground)* toboggan *m*; *(on ice, snow)* glissoire *f*; **(escape) s.** *(of plane)* toboggan *m* d'évacuation

2 *(act of sliding)* glissade *f*; **to go into a s.** faire une glissade

3 *(landslide)* glissement *m* de terrain; **a mud s.** une coulée de boue; **a rock s.** un éboulement

4 *(fall* ▸ *in prices)* baisse *f*, chute *f*; **the stock exchange is on a downward s.** la Bourse est en baisse; **the s. in standards** la dégradation des valeurs; **the alarming s. of the economy** le dérapage alarmant de l'économie; **this began his s. into despair** c'est alors qu'il commença à sombrer dans le désespoir

5 *Phot* diapositive *f*, diapo *f*

6 *(for microscope)* porte-objet *m*; *(what is on the slide)* préparation *f*

7 *Br (for hair)* barrette *f*

8 *(of machine, trombone)* coulisse *f*; *(of slide guitar)* slide *m*; *(of slide rule)* coulisseau *m*, réglette *f*

▸▸ *Am* ***slide fastener*** fermeture *f* à glissière, fermeture *f* Éclair®; ***slide guitar*** slide guitar *f*; ***slide projector*** projecteur *m* de diapositives; ***slide rule*** règle *f* à calcul; ***slide show*** diaporama *m*; *Comput* diaporama *m*, projection *f* de diapositives; ***slide trombone*** trombone *m* à coulisse

▸**slide down** VI *(go down by sliding)* descendre en glissant

VT INSEP *(go down by sliding)* descendre en glissant; **to s. down the banisters** glisser le long de la rampe; **it's sliding down the charts** il perd des places au hit-parade

▸**slide off** VI **1** *(lid)* s'enlever en glissant; **this part slides off easily** il suffit de faire coulisser cette pièce pour l'enlever **2** *(fall)* glisser; **the book keeps sliding off** le livre n'arrête pas de glisser **3** *(sneak away)* s'en aller discrètement, s'éclipser; **she slid off to the bar in the interval** elle s'est éclipsée à l'entracte pour aller au bar

▸**slide out** VI **1** *(come out by sliding)* sortir (en glissant) **2** *(sneak outside)* se glisser dehors

VT SEP *(drawers, battery)* enlever en faisant glisser

slide out of VT INSEP *(evade)* se sortir de; **I'd like to see him s. out of that one** j'aimerais bien voir comment il va se tirer d'affaire

liding ['slaɪdɪŋ] ADJ *(part)* qui glisse; *(movement)* glissant; *(door)* coulissant; *(panel)* mobile
N glissement *m*
▸▸ *Aut* ***sliding roof*** toit *m* ouvrant; ***sliding scale*** *(for salaries)* échelle *f* mobile; *(for prices)* barème *m* des prix; *(for tax)* barème *m* des impôts; *Aut* ***sliding seat*** siège *m* réglable *ou* mobile

liding-scale taxation N impôt *m* dégressif

light [slaɪt] ADJ **1** *(minor ▸ error, movement)* petit; *(▸ increase, improvement, cut, graze)* léger; *(▸ difference)* petit, léger; **a s. accident** un petit incident; **there's a s. drizzle/wind** il y a un peu de crachin/de vent; **the difference is only very s., there's only a very s. difference** la différence est minime, il n'y a qu'une très légère différence; **he has a s. accent** il a un léger accent; **she has a s. temperature** elle a un peu de température; **there's a s. chance of some sunshine tomorrow** il y a une petite chance qu'il fasse beau demain **2** *(in superlative)* **it makes not the slightest bit of difference** ça ne change absolument rien; **I haven't the slightest idea** je n'en ai pas la moindre idée; **he gets angry at the slightest thing** il se fâche pour un rien; **they haven't the slightest chance of winning** ils n'ont pas la moindre chance *ou* la plus petite chance de l'emporter; **not in the slightest** pas le moins du monde, pas du tout; **they weren't (in) the slightest bit interested, they weren't interested in the slightest** ils n'étaient pas le moins du monde intéressés **3** *(person ▸ slender)* menu, mince; *(▸ frail)* frêle; *(structure)* fragile, frêle
VT *(snub)* manquer d'égards envers; *(insult)* insulter; *(offend)* froisser, blesser; **she felt slighted** elle a été blessée *ou* froissée; **to s. sb's memory** faire affront à la mémoire de qn
N *(snub)* manque *m* d'égards; *(insult)* insulte *f*; *(offence)* affront *m*; **it's a s. on her reputation** c'est un affront à sa réputation

lighting ['slaɪtɪŋ] ADJ offensant, désobligeant

lightingly ['slaɪtɪŋlɪ] ADV *(behave)* d'une manière désobligeante; **to speak s. of sb** faire des remarques désobligeantes sur qn

lightly ['slaɪtlɪ] ADV **1** *(a little)* un peu, légèrement; **s. better** légèrement mieux, un peu mieux; **a s. higher number** un chiffre un peu plus élevé; *Br* **I felt ever so s. ridiculous** je me suis senti légèrement ridicule **2** *(slenderly)* **s. built** menu, mince

lightness ['slaɪtnɪs] N **1** *(of number, increase)* caractère *m* insignifiant *ou* négligeable; *(of difference)* petitesse *f*; *(of damage)* insignifiance *f* **2** *(frailty, of build)* minceur *f*

lim [slɪm] *(compar* **slimmer**, *superl* **slimmest**, *pt & pp* **slimmed**, *cont* **slimming***)* ADJ **1** *(person, waist, figure)* mince, svelte; *(wrist)* fin, délicat; **tall and s.** élancé; **to keep s.** rester mince **2** *(book, wallet)* mince **3** *(faint, feeble ▸ hope, chance)* faible, minime; *(▸ pretext)* mince, piètre, dérisoire; **they have only a s. chance of winning the next election** ils n'ont que de faibles chances de gagner les prochaines élections
VI *(get thin)* maigrir, mincir; *(diet)* faire *ou* suivre un régime
VT *(of diet, exercise)* faire maigrir

slim down VT SEP **1** *(of diet)* faire maigrir; *(of clothes)* amincir **2** *Fig (industry)* dégraisser; *(workforce)* réduire; *(ambitions, plans)* limiter, réduire; *(design, car)* épurer, alléger; **the company is slimming down its electronics operation** la société réduit ses activités dans le domaine de l'électronique; **a slimmed-down version of the old model** une version épurée de l'ancien modèle
VI **1** *(person ▸ get thin)* maigrir; *(▸ diet)* suivre un régime **2** *(company, army etc)* diminuer de taille

lime [slaɪm] N **1** *(sticky substance)* substance *f* gluante *ou* poisseuse; *(from snail, slug)* bave *f*; *(mud)* vase *f* **2** *Fam (person)* ordure *f*

limebag ['slaɪmbæg], **slimeball** ['slaɪmbɔːl] N *Fam (despicable person)* ordure *f*, raclure *f*; *(repulsive man)* gros dégueulasse *m*

liminess ['slaɪmɪnɪs] N **1** *(muddiness)* état *m* vaseux **2** *Fam (servility)* servilité[a] *f*, obséquiosité[a] *f*

slimly ['slɪmlɪ] ADV **s. built** svelte

slimmer ['slɪmə(r)] N = personne qui suit un régime (amaigrissant)

slimming ['slɪmɪŋ] N amaigrissement *m*; **s. can be bad for you** les régimes amaigrissants ne sont pas toujours bons pour la santé
ADJ **1** *(diet)* amaigrissant; *(cream, product)* amincissant; *(exercises)* pour maigrir; *(meal)* à faible teneur en calories **2** *(flattering ▸ dress, suit, colour)* amincissant
▸▸ ***slimming club*** centre *m* d'amaigrissement; ***slimming pill*** pilule *f* amaigrissante

slimness ['slɪmnɪs] N **1** *(of person, waist, figure)* minceur *f*, sveltesse *f*; *(of wrist, ankle)* minceur *f*, finesse *f*, délicatesse *f*; *(of book)* minceur *f* **2** *(of chances, hopes)* faiblesse *f*

slimy ['slaɪmɪ] *(compar* **slimier**, *superl* **slimiest***)* ADJ **1** *(with mud)* vaseux, boueux; *(with oil, secretion)* gluant, visqueux; *(wall)* suintant; **the frog felt all s.** la grenouille était toute visqueuse; **the slug left a s. trail** la limace laissa une traînée visqueuse **2** *Br Fam (person)* mielleux[a]; *(manners)* doucereux[a], obséquieux[a]

sling [slɪŋ] *(pt & pp* **slung** [slʌŋ]*)* VT **1** *(fling)* jeter, lancer; **the children were slinging stones at the statue** les enfants lançaient des pierres sur la statue; **she slung the case into the back of the car** elle a jeté la valise à l'arrière de la voiture; *Br Fam* **if he's not careful, he'll get slung off the course** s'il ne fait pas attention, il se fera virer du cours; *Fig* **to s. mud at sb** couvrir qn de boue; **they were slinging insults at each other** ils se lançaient des insultes; *Fam* **to s. one's hook** mettre les bouts, ficher le camp **2** *(lift, hang ▸ load)* hisser; *Naut* élinguer; **the hammock was slung between two trees** le hamac était suspendu *ou* accroché entre deux arbres; **the soldiers wore rifles slung across** *or* **over their shoulders** les soldats portaient des fusils en bandoulière; **he slung his jacket over his shoulder** il a jeté sa veste par-dessus son épaule
N **1** *Br (for broken arm)* écharpe *f*; **she had her arm in a s.** elle avait le bras en écharpe
2 *(for baby)* porte-bébé *m*
3 *(for loads) & Naut* élingue *f*; *(for removal men)* corde *f*, courroie *f*; *(for rifle)* bretelle *f*
4 *(weapon)* fronde *f*; *(toy)* lance-pierres *m inv*

▸**sling out** VT SEP *Br Fam (person)* flanquer *ou* ficher à la porte; *(rubbish, magazines etc)* bazarder, balancer; **he was slung out on his ear** il a été fichu à la porte, on l'a fichu dehors

▸**sling up** VT SEP *Fam* suspendre[a], accrocher[a]

slingback ['slɪŋbæk] N *Br* chaussure *f* à talon découvert

slingshot ['slɪŋʃɒt] N *Am* lance-pierres *m inv*

slink [slɪŋk] *(pt & pp* **slunk** [slʌŋk]*)* VI **to s. in/out** entrer/sortir furtivement; **she slunk into the room** elle s'est glissée discrètement dans la pièce; **to s. off** *or* **away** s'éclipser

slinkily ['slɪŋkɪlɪ] ADV *Fam (walk)* d'une démarche ondoyante[a]; *(dress)* d'une manière sexy; **she sidled s. up to him** elle s'est dirigée vers lui en roulant des hanches

slinking ['slɪŋkɪŋ] ADJ *(look)* furtif
N **s. off** *or* **away** départ *m* furtif; **s. in** entrée *f* furtive

slinky ['slɪŋkɪ] *(compar* **slinkier**, *superl* **slinkiest***)* ADJ *Fam (figure)* svelte[a], mince[a]; *(manner)* aguichant[a]; *(dress)* moulant[a]; *(walk)* ondoyant[a], chaloupé[a]

SLIP [slɪp] N *Comput (abbr* **serial line Internet protocol***)* protocole *m* SLIP

SLIP [slɪp]

N	
• bout de papier **1**	• bon **1**
• fiche **1**	• glissade **2**
• erreur **3**	• bévue **3**
• étourderie **3**	• écart **3**
• éboulis **4**	• combinaison **5**
VT	
• glisser **1, 4**	• lâcher **3**
VI	
• glisser **1, 2**	• s'ébouler **1**
• se glisser **3**	• baisser **4**

(pt & pp **slipped**, *cont* **slipping***)*
N **1** *(piece of paper)* bout *m* de papier; *(coupon)* bon *m*; *(docket)* fiche *f*; **s. of paper** bout *m* de papier; *Com* **delivery s.** bordereau *m* de livraison
2 *(on ice, banana skin)* glissade *f*
3 *(mistake)* erreur *f*; *(blunder)* bévue *f*; *(careless oversight)* étourderie *f*; *(moral)* écart *m*, faute *f* légère; **s. of the tongue/pen** lapsus *m*
4 *(landslide)* éboulis *m*, éboulement *m*
5 *(petticoat ▸ full length)* combinaison *f*, fond *m* de robe; *(▸ skirt)* jupon *m*
6 *(usu pl) Naut* cale *f*; **the Queen Helen is still on the slips** le Queen Helen est toujours en cale sèche
7 *(idioms) Br* **a (mere) s. of a girl** une petite jeune, une gamine; **to give sb the s.** fausser compagnie à qn
VT **1** *(give or put discreetly)* glisser; **to s. sb a note** glisser un mot à qn; **to s. a letter into sb's hand/pocket** glisser une lettre dans la main/la poche de qn; **she slipped the jigsaw piece into place** elle a fait glisser le morceau de puzzle à sa place; **I slipped my arm round her waist** j'ai glissé mon bras autour de sa taille; **to s. sth into the conversation** glisser qch dans la conversation; **to s. the bolt (home)** pousser le verrou à fond
2 *(escape)* **it slipped my mind** ça m'est sorti de la tête; **her name has completely slipped my memory** j'ai complètement oublié son nom
3 *(release) Br* **he slipped the dog's lead** il a lâché la laisse du chien; *Br* **the dog slipped its lead** le chien s'est dégagé de sa laisse; *Naut* **to s. anchor/a cable** filer l'ancre/un câble
4 *Knitting* **to s. a stitch** glisser une maille
5 *Med* **to have slipped a disc, to have a slipped disc** avoir une hernie discale
VI **1** *(slide ▸ gen)* glisser; *(▸ knot)* couler, courir; *(▸ earth)* s'ébouler; **I slipped on the ice** j'ai glissé sur une plaque de verglas; **the knife slipped and cut my finger** le couteau a glissé et je me suis coupé le doigt; **my hand slipped** ma main a glissé; **the cup slipped out of my hands** la tasse m'a glissé des mains; **she let the sand s. through her fingers** elle laissa le sable glisser entre ses doigts; *Fig* **the prize slipped from her grasp** *or* **from her fingers** le prix lui a échappé; **somehow, the kidnappers slipped through our fingers** je ne sais comment les ravisseurs nous ont filé entre les doigts; **money just slips through his fingers** l'argent lui file entre les doigts
2 *(go gradually)* glisser; **the patient slipped into a coma** le patient a glissé *ou* s'est enfoncé peu à peu dans le coma; **to s. into bad habits** prendre de mauvaises habitudes
3 *(go quickly, smoothly etc)* se glisser; **to s. into bed** se glisser dans son lit; **she slipped quietly into the room** elle s'est glissée discrètement dans la pièce; **some misprints have slipped into the text** des coquilles se sont glissées dans le texte; **the thieves managed to s. through the road blocks** les voleurs ont réussi à passer à travers les barrages routiers; **why don't you s. round the back?** pourquoi ne passez-vous pas par derrière?; **we slipped through the rush hour traffic** on s'est faufilés dans les embouteillages des heures de pointe; **I'll s. into something cooler** je vais enfiler *ou* mettre quelque chose de plus léger
4 *(go down ▸ prices)* baisser; **prices have slipped (by) 10 percent** les prix ont baissé de 10 pour cent
5 *Fam (be less efficient)* **you're slipping!** dis donc, tu baisses!; **I must be slipping!** je crois que je perds mes capacités!
6 *(idioms)* **to let s.** *(opportunity)* laisser passer *ou* échapper; *(word)* lâcher, laisser échapper; **she let (it) s. that she was selling her house** elle a laissé échapper qu'elle vendait sa maison; **he let his guard s.** il a baissé sa garde; **don't let your concentration s.** ne relâche pas ta concentration
▸▸ *Br* ***slip road*** bretelle *f* d'accès; *Typ* ***slip sheet*** feuille *f* intercalaire

Note that the French noun **slip** is a false friend and is never a translation for the English word **slip**. It means **underpants** or **briefs**.

▸**slip away** VI *(person)* s'éclipser, partir discrètement; *(moment)* passer; *(boat)* s'éloigner doucement; **I felt my life slipping away** j'avais l'impression que ma vie me glissait entre les doigts; **control was slipping away from her** elle perdait peu à peu son emprise; **the patient was slipping away** le malade s'éteignait doucement

▸**slip back** VI *(car)* glisser (en arrière); *(person)* revenir discrètement; **she slipped back for a sweater** elle est retournée chercher un pullover; **he slipped back into a coma** il est retombé dans le coma; **he slipped back into his old habits** il est retombé dans ses vieilles habitudes

▸**slip by** VI *(time)* passer; *(person)* se faufiler; **I slipped by without being noticed** je me suis faufilé sans qu'on me remarque; *Fig* **you shouldn't let this chance s. by** tu ne devrais pas laisser passer cette chance

▸**slip down** VI *(fall ▸ picture, car, socks, skirt)* glisser; **this whisky slips down very nicely** ce whisky descend tout seul

▸**slip in** VT SEP *(moving part)* faire glisser à sa place; *(quotation, word)* glisser, placer; **she slipped in several references to...** elle a placé plusieurs allusions à...

VI *(person)* entrer discrètement *ou* sans se faire remarquer; *(boat)* entrer lentement; **I just slipped in for five minutes** je n'ai fait qu'entrer *ou* je suis juste passé cinq minutes; **some misprints have slipped in** des coquilles se sont glissées dans le texte

▸**slip off** VT SEP *(remove ▸ coat, hat)* enlever, ôter; *(▸ shoe, ring, sock)* enlever; *(▸ top, lid)* faire glisser pour ouvrir

VI **1** *(go away)* s'éclipser **2** *(fall ▸ bottle, hat, book)* glisser (et tomber)

▸**slip on** VT SEP *(dress, ring, coat)* mettre, enfiler; *(lid)* mettre *ou* remettre (en faisant glisser)

▸**slip out** VI **1** *(leave unseen ▸ person)* sortir discrètement, s'esquiver **2** *(escape ▸ animal, child)* s'échapper; **the soap slipped out of my hands** le savon m'a glissé des mains; **the word slipped out before he could stop himself** le mot lui a échappé; **it just slipped out!** ça m'a échappé! **3** *(go out)* sortir (un instant); **I'm just slipping out for a few minutes** je m'éclipse quelques minutes, je reviens dans une minute; **I'll s. out and buy some milk** je sors juste acheter du lait

▸**slip past** VI *(time)* passer; *(person)* se faufiler; **I managed to s. past unseen** j'ai réussi à passer discrètement

▸**slip through** VI *(person)* passer sans se faire remarquer; *(mistake)* passer inaperçu

▸**slip up** VI *Fam* faire une gaffe

slipcase ['slɪpkeɪs] N *(for single volume)* étui *m*; *(for several volumes, for records)* coffret *m*

slipcover ['slɪpkʌvə(r)] N *Am* **1** *(for furniture)* housse *f* **2** = **slipcase**

slipknot ['slɪpnɒt] N nœud *m* coulant

slip-on ADJ *(shoe)* sans lacets

N **1** *(shoe)* chaussure *f* sans lacets **2** *Am (sweater)* pull-over *m*

slipover ['slɪpəʊvə(r)] N débardeur *m (vêtement)*

slippage ['slɪpɪdʒ] N *(in targeting)* retard *m (par rapport aux prévisions)*; *(in standards)* baisse *f*; **there's too much s.** *(loss of time)* on perd de plus en plus de temps

slipped disc [slɪpt-] N *Med* hernie *f* discale

slipper ['slɪpə(r)] N chausson *m*, pantoufle *f*; *(with no back)* mule *f*; *(for dancing)* escarpin *m*

slipperiness ['slɪpərɪnɪs] N **1** *(of surface, soap)* caractère *m* glissant; **the s. of the road/floor** l'état *m* glissant de la route/du sol **2** *(of person ▸ evasiveness)* caractère *m* insaisissable *ou* fuyant; *(▸ unreliability)* nature *f* peu fiable

slippery ['slɪpərɪ] ADJ **1** *(surface, soap)* glissant; **the path is s.** le chemin est glissant; **it's s. (underfoot)** ça glisse; *Fig* **to be on s. ground** être sur un terrain glissant; *Fig* **we're on the s. slope to bankruptcy** nous allons droit à la faillite **2** *Fam (person ▸ evasive)* fuyant□; *(▸ unreliable)* sur qui on ne peut pas compter□; **he's as s. as an eel** il glisse comme une *ou* est aussi insaisissable qu'une anguille

slippy ['slɪpɪ] *(compar* **slippier**, *superl* **slippiest)** ADJ *Fam* **1** *(slippery)* glissant□ **2** *Br (fast)* **you'll have to be pretty s. about it** il va falloir que tu fasses ficelle; **look s.!** grouille-toi!

slipshod ['slɪpʃɒd] ADJ *(appearance)* négligé, débraillé; *(style)* peu soigné, négligé; *(work)* négligé, mal fait

slipstream ['slɪpstriːm] N *(of car, boat)* sillage *m*; *(of plane)* souffle *m ou* vent *m* de l'hélice; *Fig* **to be dragged along in sb's s.** se laisser entraîner par qn

VT *(driver, cyclist)* rester dans le sillage de

slip-up N *Fam* bévue□*f*, gaffe *f*; **there's been a s.** quelqu'un a fait une gaffe; **to make a s.** faire une gaffe

slipway ['slɪpweɪ] N *Naut (for repairs)* cale *f* de construction; *(for launching)* cale *f* de lancement

slit [slɪt] *(pt & pp* **slit**, *cont* **slitting)** N *(narrow opening)* fente *f*; *(cut)* incision *f*; *(for shooting through)* meurtrière *f*; **the skirt has a s. at the back** la jupe a une fente *ou* est fendue dans le dos

VT *(split)* fendre; *(cut)* inciser, couper; **the skirt was s. up the side** la jupe était fendue sur le côté; **the mattress had been s. open** le matelas avait été éventré; **to s. sb's throat** égorger qn; **she s. her wrists** elle s'est ouvert les veines

ADJ *(skirt)* fendu; *(eyes)* bridé

▸▸ ***slit pocket*** poche *f* fendue

slither ['slɪðə(r)] VI **1** *(snake, worm)* ramper, onduler **2** *(car, person ▸ slide)* glisser, patiner; *(▸ skid)* déraper; **the car slithered on a patch of oil** la voiture a dérapé sur une flaque d'huile; **I slithered down the tree/drainpipe** je me suis laissé glisser le long de l'arbre/de la gouttière

sliver ['slɪvə(r)] N **1** *(of glass, wood)* éclat *m* **2** *(small slice)* tranche *f* fine

Sloane [sləʊn] N *Br Fam* ≃ jeune femme *f* BCBG

▸▸ ***Sloane Ranger*** ≃ jeune femme *f* BCBG

Sloaney ['sləʊnɪ] ADJ *Br Fam* ≃ BCBG *(inv)*

slob [slɒb] N *Fam (dirty)* souillon *mf*; *(lazy)* flemmard(e) *m,f*; **big fat s.** gros lard *m*

slobber ['slɒbə(r)] VI **1** *(dribble)* baver; **to s. over** baver sur; **the baby has slobbered all over the book** le bébé a bavé partout sur le livre **2** *Fam Fig* **to s. over** *(person, possession, pet)* baver d'admiration devant

N **1** *(dribble)* bave *f* **2** *Pej (behaviour)* sensiblerie *f*

sloe [sləʊ] N *(berry)* prunelle *f*; *(tree)* prunellier *m*

▸▸ ***sloe gin*** gin *m* à la prunelle

slog [slɒg] *(pt & pp* **slogged**, *cont* **slogging)** *Fam* N **1** *(hard task)* boulot *m* pénible; *(effort)* (gros) effort□*m*; **it was a real s. to finish in time** on a dû bosser comme des malades pour finir à temps; **what a s.!** quelle corvée!□; **it was a s. teaching them history** leur enseigner l'histoire n'était pas une mince affaire□; **this book is a hard s.** ce livre est vraiment dur à lire□; **it's been a long hard s. for her to get where she is** elle en a bavé pour arriver là où elle est; **it was quite a s. getting up that hill** on en a bavé pour monter cette côte

2 *Br (hit)* grand coup□*m*; **he gave the ball an almighty s.** il a frappé la balle de toutes ses forces□

VI **1** *(work hard)* trimer, bosser; **do we really have to s. through all this paperwork?** est-ce qu'il est indispensable de se farcir toute cette paperasse?

2 *(walk, go)* avancer péniblement□; **he slogged (along) through the snow** il avançait péniblement dans la neige; **we slogged slowly up the hill** nous avons gravi la côte à pas lents□

VT **1** *(move)* **we slogged our way through the snow** nous nous sommes péniblement frayé un chemin dans la neige□; **he slogged his way through the text** il a déchiffré le texte avec grande difficulté□

2 *Br (hit ▸ ball)* donner un grand coup dans□; *(▸ person)* cogner sur□; **to s. it out** *(fight)* se tabasser; *(argue)* s'enguirlander

▸**slog along** VI *Fam (keep walking)* marcher d'un pas lourd *ou* péniblement□

▸**slog away** VI *Fam (keep working, trying)* trimer

▸**slog away at** VT INSEP *Fam* **1** *(work hard at)* **to s. away (at sth)** travailler comme un dingue (à qch); **she spent all weekend slogging away at that report** elle a passé tout le week-end à trimer sur ce rapport **2** *(keep hitting)* continuer à frapper□

▸**slog on** VI *Fam* **1** = **slog along 2** *(keep working)* continuer à trimer

slogan ['sləʊgən] N slogan *m*

slogger ['slɒgə(r)] N *Br Fam* **1** *(in boxing, cricke*
cogneur□*m* **2** *(hard worker)* bûcheur(euse) *m,f*

slo-mo ['sləʊməʊ] ADJ *Fam (abbr* **slow-motion)** a
ralenti□

sloop [sluːp] N *Naut* sloop *m*

slop [slɒp] *(pt & pp* **slopped**, *cont* **slopping)** V
(spill) renverser; *(overflow)* déborder; **the te
slopped into the saucer/onto the tablecloth** le th
s'est renversé dans la soucoupe/sur la nappe

VT renverser; **he slopped soup onto the tableclot**
il a renversé *ou* répandu de la soupe sur l
nappe; **don't s. water all over the floor** ne ren
verse pas d'eau par terre

N **1 s., slops** *(liquid waste ▸ for pigs)* pâtée *f*; *(
from tea, coffee)* fond *m* de tasse; *Pej (tasteles
food)* mixture *f* **2** *(UNCOUNT) Fam (sentimenta
ity)* bêtises *fpl* à l'eau de rose

▸▸ *Br* ***slop basin*** vide-tasses *m inv*; ***slop bucke
slop pail*** *(gen)* seau *m* (à ordures); *(in prison)* sea
m hygiénique; *(for pigs)* seau *m* à pâtée

▸**slop about, slop around** VI **1** *(liquid)* clapo
ter **2** *(paddle)* patauger **3** *Fam (be lazy)* traînasse

VT SEP *(paint)* éclabousser; *(tea)* renverser

VT INSEP *Fam* **he slops about the house doin
nothing** il traîne à la maison à ne rien faire□

▸**slop out** VI *(prisoner)* vider les seaux hygién
ques

▸**slop over** VI *(spill)* se renverser; *(overflow)* dé
border

VT SEP renverser, répandre

slope [sləʊp] N **1** *(incline ▸ of roof)* inclinaison
pente *f*; *(▸ of ground)* pente *f*; **the house is built o
a s.** la maison a été construite sur une pente; *M
rifle at the s. fusil sur l'épaule **2** *(hill ▸ up)* côte
montée *f*; *(▸ down)* pente *f*, descente *f*; *(mour
tainside)* versant *m*, flanc *m*; **tea is grown on th
higher slopes** on cultive le thé plus haut sur le
versants de la montagne; **on the slopes of Mour
Fuji** sur les versants du mont Fuji; **halfway down
up the s.** à mi-pente **3** *(for skiing)* piste *f*

VI *(roof)* être en pente *ou* incliné; *(writing, pic
ture)* pencher; **to s. forward/backward** *(writing*
pencher à droite/à gauche; **the beach slope
gently to the sea** la plage descendait en pent
douce vers la mer; **the football pitch slopes fror
left to right** le terrain de foot descend vers l
droite; **the ground slopes up to the house** le ter
rain monte en pente vers la maison; **the tabl
slopes** la table penche *ou* n'est pas droite

VT incliner; *Mil* **to s. arms** mettre l'arme su
l'épaule; **s. arms!** arme sur l'épaule!

▸**slope off** VI *Fam* filer

sloping ['sləʊpɪŋ] ADJ *(table, roof)* en pente, in
cliné; *(writing)* penché; *(shoulders)* tombant

sloppily ['slɒpɪlɪ] ADV **1** *(work)* sans soin; *(dress*
de façon négligée **2** *Br Fam (sentimentally)* ave
sensiblerie□

sloppiness ['slɒpɪnɪs] N **1** *(of work)* manque *r*
de soin *ou* de sérieux; *(in dress)* négligence *.*
manque *m* de soin; *(of thought)* flou *m*, manqu
m de précision **2** *Fam (sentimentality)* sensible
rie□*f*, mièvrerie□*f*

slopping out ['slɒpɪŋ-] N *(in prison)* vidange
des seaux hygiéniques

sloppy ['slɒpɪ] *(compar* **sloppier**, *superl* **sloppies**
ADJ **1** *(untidy ▸ appearance)* négligé, débraillé
(careless ▸ work) bâclé, négligé; *(▸ worker)* négl
gent; *(▸ writing)* peu soigné; *(▸ thinking)* flou
vague, imprécis; **he has a very s. way of speakin**
il s'exprime d'une manière peu élégante **2** *Far
(loose ▸ garment)* large□, lâche□ **3** *Fam (sent
mental ▸ person, letter)* sentimental□; *(▸ book
film)* à l'eau de rose□; **stop all that s. talk!** arrêt
de faire du sentiment!□

▸▸ *Fam* ***sloppy joe*** **1** *Br (sweater)* gros pull□*m*
Am (hamburger) hamburger□*m*

slosh [slɒʃ] VT **1** *(spill)* renverser, répandre **2** *Far
(pour ▸ onto floor)* répandre□; *(▸ into glass
bucket)* verser□; *(apply ▸ paint, glue)* flanque
she sloshed whitewash on *or* **over the wall** elle
barbouillé le mur de blanc de chaux□ **3** *Br Far
(hit)* flanquer un coup de poing à

VI **1** *(liquid ▸ spill)* se répandre; *(▸ move arounc*
clapoter; **the juice sloshed all over the tableclot**
le jus s'est renversé partout sur la nappe; **wate
sloshed over the edge** l'eau a débordé **2** *(move ▸ i*

'quid, mud) patauger; **we sloshed through the** **nud** on a pataugé dans la boue
ONOMAT plouf

slosh about, slosh around VI *(liquid)* clapo-er; *(person)* patauger

oshed [slɒʃt] **ADJ** *Fam* bourré, pété, beurré; **to** **et s.** prendre une cuite

ot [slɒt] *(pt & pp* **slotted,** *cont* **slotting)** **N 1** *(open-ng ▸ for coins, papers)* fente *f*; *(groove, in screw* *ead)* rainure *f*; **put the coin in the s.** mettez la ièce dans la fente
2 *(in schedule, timetable)* créneau *m*; *Rad & TV* réneau *m*, tranche *f ou* plage *f* horaire; **we could** **ut the new series in the 7.30 s.** on pourrait caser *u* placer le nouveau feuilleton dans le créneau e 19h30; **we've missed our s. for take-off** nous vons raté notre créneau de décollage
3 *(job opening)* créneau *m*
4 *Aviat (in aerofoil)* fente *f*
5 *Comput* emplacement *m*
VT 1 *(insert)* emboîter; **s. this bit in here** *(in ma-hine, model)* introduisez cette pièce ici; *(in jig-aw)* posez *ou* mettez cette pièce ici **2** *(find time* *r, fit)* insérer, faire rentrer; **she managed to s. me** **nto her timetable** elle a réussi à me réserver un noment *ou* à me caser dans son emploi du emps
VI 1 *(fit ▸ part)* rentrer, s'encastrer, s'emboîter; **he tape slots into the recorder here** c'est ici qu'on ntroduit la cassette dans le magnétophone; **the** **lade slots into the handle** la lame rentre dans le nanche **2** *(in timetable, schedule)* rentrer, s'insé-er; **where do we s. into the scheme?** où interve-ons-nous dans le projet?
▸▸ ***slot machine*** *(for vending)* distributeur *m* (au-omatique); *(for gambling)* machine *f* à sous; *Br* ***lot meter*** compteur *m* à pièces

slot in VT SEP *(into schedule)* faire rentrer; *(pa-ient, customer etc)* caser; **she just slots me in** **vhen it suits her** elle n'est disponible pour moi ue quand ça l'arrange; **when can you s. me in?** uand pouvez-vous me caser *ou* trouver un mo-nent pour moi?
VI *(part)* s'emboîter, s'encastrer; *(programme)* s'insérer; **she slotted into the department well** lle s'est bien intégrée au service

slot together VT SEP emboîter, encastrer; **s.** **hese two parts together** emboîtez ces deux piè-es l'une dans l'autre
VI s'emboîter, s'encastrer; **the two parts s. to-ether** les deux pièces s'emboîtent l'une dans autre

oth [sləʊθ] **N 1** *(laziness)* paresse *f* **2** *Zool* pares-eux *m*

othful ['sləʊθfʊl] **ADJ** paresseux

othfully ['sləʊθfʊlɪ] **ADV** paresseusement, vec indolence

othfulness ['sləʊθfʊlnɪs] **N** paresse *f*

ot-in card **N** *Comput* carte *f* enfichable

ouch [slaʊtʃ] **VI** *(hold oneself badly)* être avachi; *walk badly)* avoir une démarche mollasse; **she** **vas slouching against the wall** elle était noncha-amment adossée au mur; **stop slouching!** re-resse-toi!; **to s. in/out** entrer/sortir en traînant es pieds
VT to s. one's shoulders rentrer les épaules
N 1 *(way of walking)* démarche *f* mollasse; *(de-ortment)* allure *f* avachie *ou* molle; **s. of the** **houlders** épaules *fpl* tombantes; **to have a s.** voir le dos voûté **2** *Fam (person)* **he's no s.** ce est pas un empoté
▸▸ ***slouch hat*** chapeau *m* à larges bords

slouch about, slouch around VI se traîner; *at home, in front of television)* traînasser

ough[1] [slaʊ] **N** *(mud pool)* bourbier *m*; *swamp)* marécage *m*; *Literary* **to sink into a s. of** **loom/despair** sombrer dans la mélancolie/le ésespoir; *Literary* **the S. of Despond** le plus pro-ond désespoir

ough[2] [slʌf] **N 1** *(skin ▸ of snake)* dépouille *f*, nue *f*; *Med* escarre *f* **2** *Cards* carte *f* défaussée
VT to s. its skin *(reptile, insect)* muer

slough off VT SEP **to s. off its skin** *(reptile, insect)* nuer; *Fig* **to s. off one's worries** chasser ses idées oires
VI *(scab)* se détacher, tomber

Slovak ['sləʊvæk] **N 1** *(person)* Slovaque *mf* **2** *Ling* slovaque *m*
ADJ slovaque

Slovakia [slə'vækɪə] **N** Slovaquie *f*

Slovakian [slə'vækɪən] **N** Slovaque *mf*
ADJ slovaque

sloven ['slʌvən] **N 1** *(untidy person)* mal soigné(e) *m,f*; *(woman)* souillon *f* **2** *Old-fashioned (careless worker)* saboteur(euse) *m,f*

Slovene ['sləʊviːn] **N 1** *(person)* Slovène *mf* **2** *Ling* slovène *m*
ADJ slovène

Slovenia [slə'viːnɪə] **N** Slovénie *f*

Slovenian [slə'viːnɪən] **N** Slovène *mf*
ADJ slovène

slovenliness ['slʌvənlɪnɪs] **N** *(of dress)* négligé *m*, débraillé *m*; *(of habits)* laisser-aller *m inv*; *(of work)* manque *m* de soin

slovenly ['slʌvənlɪ] **ADJ** *(appearance)* négligé, débraillé; *(habits)* relâché; *(work)* peu soigné; *(style, expression)* relâché, négligé; **he's often s. in appearance** il fait souvent négligé; **done in a s. way** fait sans soin

SLOW [sləʊ]

ADJ
- lent **1, 3**
- calme **2**
- ennuyeux **4**
- qui retarde **5**

ADV
- lentement

VT
- ralentir

ADJ 1 *(not fast ▸ movements, runner, speed, service, traffic)* lent; **he's a s. worker** il travaille lentement; **it's s. work** c'est un travail qui n'avance pas vite *ou* de longue haleine; **to make s. progress** *(in work, on foot)* avancer lentement; **it was s. going, the going was s.** ça n'avançait pas; **a s. dance** un slow; **with s. steps** d'un pas lent; **we had a pain-fully s. journey** le voyage a duré un temps fou; **the pace of life is s.** on vit au ralenti; **you're very s. today** tu es très lent aujourd'hui; **you were a bit s. there** là, tu t'es laissé prendre de vitesse; **the fog was s. to clear** le brouillard a mis long-temps à se dissiper; **he was rather s. to make up** *or* **in making up his mind** il a mis assez longtemps à se décider; **she wasn't s. to offer her help/in ac-cepting the cheque** elle ne se fit pas prier pour proposer son aide/pour accepter le chèque; **she's very s. to anger** il lui en faut beaucoup pour se mettre en colère; **the company was s. to get off the ground** la société a été lente à démarrer; *Br* **to be s. off the mark** *(to start)* être lent à démar-rer; *(to understand)* être dur à la détente; *Prov* **s. and steady wins the race** rien ne sert de courir, il faut partir à point
2 *(slack ▸ business, market)* calme; **business is s.** les affaires ne marchent pas fort; **s. economic growth** une faible croissance économique
3 *(intellectually)* lent; **he's a s. learner/reader** il apprend/lit lentement
4 *(dull ▸ evening, film, party)* ennuyeux
5 *(clock)* qui retarde; **your watch is (half an hour) s.** ta montre retarde (d'une demi-heure)
6 *Culin* **bake in a s. oven** faire cuire à four doux
7 *Sport (green, court, surface)* lourd
8 *Am Fam* **to do a s. burn** sentir la colère monter▫
ADV lentement; **go a bit slower** ralentissez un peu; **the clock is going** *or* **running s.** l'horloge prend du retard; *Ind* **to go s.** faire une grève per-lée; **s.** *(road marking)* ralentir; *Naut* **s. ahead/ astern!** en avant/arrière doucement!
VT ralentir; **the mud slowed our progress** la boue nous a ralentis; **I slowed the horse to a trot** j'ai mis le cheval au trot
▸▸ *Culin* ***slow burner*** feu *m* doux; ***slow cooker*** mi-joteuse *f*; *Anat & Bot* ***slow growth*** croissance *f* lente; *Br* ***slow handclap*** applaudissements *mpl* rythmés *(pour montrer sa désapprobation)*; **they gave him the s. handclap** ≃ ils l'ont sifflé; ***the slow lane*** *(when driving on left)* la file de gauche; *(when driving on right)* la file de droite; ***slow match*** mèche *f* à combustion lente; *Cin & TV* ***slow motion*** ralenti *m*; **in s. motion** au ralenti; *Mus* ***slow movement*** mouvement *m* lent; *Phys* ***slow neutron*** neutron *m* lent; *Sport* ***slow pitch*** slow pitch *m (sport proche du softball)*; *Tech* ***slow running*** ralenti *m*; ***slow train*** omnibus *m*; *Med* ***slow virus*** virus *m* lent

▸**slow down, slow up** VT SEP ralentir; **produc-tion is slowed down during the winter** pendant l'hiver, la production tourne au ralenti; **I'll only s. you down** je vais vous retarder
VI *(driver, train, speed)* ralentir; *Fig (person)* ra-lentir (le rythme); **if he doesn't s. down he'll have a heart attack** s'il ne ralentit pas le rythme il va faire une crise cardiaque; **s. down!** moins vite!; **growth slowed down in the second quarter** il y a eu une diminution *ou* un ralentissement de la croissance au cours du deuxième trimestre

---

slow-burning **ADJ** *(fuse, fuel)* à combustion lente; *Fig* **s. anger** colère *f* froide

slowcoach ['sləʊkəʊtʃ] **N** *Br Fam (in moving)* lambin(e) *m,f*, traînard(e) *m,f*; *(in thought)* ba-lourd(e) *m,f*, lourdaud(e) *m,f*; **come on, s.!** allez, du nerf!

slow-cook VT mitonner, mijoter

slowdown ['sləʊdaʊn] **N 1** *Am (go-slow)* grève *f* perlée **2** *(of economy)* ralentissement *m* **(in** de**)**

slow-growing **ADJ 1** *(plant)* à pousse lente **2** *(business, industry)* qui se développe lentement; *(economy)* à croissance lente

slowing ['sləʊɪŋ] **N s. (down** *or* **up)** ralentisse-ment *m*

slowly ['sləʊlɪ] **ADV 1** *(not fast)* lentement; **could you walk/speak more s.?** pouvez-vous marcher/ parler moins vite?; **the time/morning has gone very s.** le temps/la matinée a passé très lente-ment; **to cook sth s.** faire cuire qch à feu doux; **s. but surely** lentement mais sûrement **2** *(grad-ually)* peu à peu

slow-moving **ADJ** *(person, car, queue, river)* lent; *(film, play, plot)* dont l'action est lente; *(market)* stagnant

slowness ['sləʊnɪs] **N 1** *(of progress, reaction, ser-vice, traffic)* lenteur *f*; *(of plot, play, film)* lenteur *f*, manque *m* d'action
2 *(of intellect)* lenteur *f* (d'esprit)
3 *(of trading, market)* stagnation *f*
4 *(of watch, clock)* retard *m*

slowpoke ['sləʊpəʊk] *Am Fam* = **slowcoach**

slow-release **ADJ** *Med (medicine)* à libération prolongée; *Agr (fertilizer)* à action lente

slow-witted [-'wɪtɪd] **ADJ** lent

slowworm ['sləʊwɜːm] **N** orvet *m*

SLR [ˌesel'ɑː(r)] **N** *Phot (abbr* **single-lens reflex)** re-flex *m* à un objectif

sludge [slʌdʒ] **N** *(UNCOUNT)* **1** *(mud)* boue *f*, vase *f*; *(snow)* neige *f* fondue **2** *(sediment)* dépôt *m*, boue *f*; *(in engine)* cambouis *m* **3** *(sewage)* **(sewage) s.** vidanges *fpl*

sludgy ['slʌdʒɪ] *(compar* **sludgier,** *superl* **sludgi-est)** **ADJ 1** *(muddy)* vaseux **2** *(sediment)* boueux **3** *(sea)* plein de glaçons

slug [slʌg] *(pt & pp* **slugged,** *cont* **slugging)** **N 1** *Zool* limace *f*
2 *Fam Fig (lazy person)* mollusque *m*
3 *Typ (of metal)* lingot *m*
4 *Am (token)* jeton *m*
5 *Fam (blow)* beigne *f*
6 *Fam (of drink)* coup *m*; *(mouthful)* goulée *f*, lampée *f*; **to take a s. of whisky** boire une lampée de whisky
7 *Fam (bullet)* pruneau *m*, bastos *f*
VT *Fam* **1** *(hit)* frapper (fort)▫, cogner▫; **he was slugged over the head with a rubber cosh** il a reçu un coup de matraque en caoutchouc sur la tête▫ **2** *(idiom)* **to s. it out** *(fight)* se bastonner, se castagner; *(argue)* s'enguirlander
▸▸ ***slug pellet*** pastille *f* anti-limace

slugfest ['slʌgfest] **N** *Am Fam* **1** *Boxing* combat▫ *m* **2** *(fight)* baston *m ou f*, castagne *f*

sluggard ['slʌgəd] **N** *Literary* paresseux(euse) *m,f*, fainéant(e) *m,f*

sluggish ['slʌgɪʃ] **ADJ 1** *(person, day ▸ lazy)* pa-resseux, *Fam* flemmard; *(▸ not energetic)* léthar-gique **2** *(mind)* lent, engourdi; *(response, attempt, engine)* mou (molle); *(river, pulse)* lent, paresseux; *(market)* stagnant; *(sales)* médiocre; *(organization, bureaucracy)* lourd; **at a s. pace** au ralenti; **trading is always rather s. on Mondays** les affaires ne marchent jamais très bien *ou* très fort le lundi; **the engine is very s. in the mornings** le moteur est très lent à démarrer le matin

sluggishly ['slʌgɪʃlɪ] **ADV 1** *(lazily)* paresseusement; *(lethargically)* mollement **2** *(slowly)* lentement; **the market reacted s.** la Bourse a réagi faiblement; **the car started s.** la voiture a démarré avec difficulté

sluggishness ['slʌgɪʃnɪs] **N 1** *(of person ▸ laziness)* paresse *f*, *Fam* flemme *f*; *(▸ lethargy)* mollesse *f* **2** *(of mind, reaction, pulse, market)* lenteur *f*; *(of growth)* faiblesse *f*, lenteur *f*; *(of engine)* mollesse *f*; *(of organization, bureaucracy)* lourdeur *f*

sluice [slu:s] **N 1** *(lock)* écluse *f*; *(gate)* porte *f ou* vanne *f* d'écluse; *(channel)* canal *m* à vannes
2 *(UNCOUNT) (lock water)* eaux *fpl* retenues par la vanne
3 *(in hospital)* égout *m*
4 *(wash)* **to give sth a s. (down)** laver qch à grande eau; **to give sb a s. (down)** asperger qn d'eau
VT *(wash)* laver à grande eau; *Mining (ore)* laver
▸▸ *sluice gate, sluice valve* porte *f ou* vanne *f* d'écluse

▸sluice down VT SEP *(wash down)* laver à grande eau; **to s. oneself down with cold water** s'asperger d'eau fraîche; **we sluiced down the meal with cheap red wine** on a arrosé le repas d'un petit vin rouge

▸sluice out VT SEP 1 *Tech (release ▸ water from reservoir)* laisser échapper (par les vannes) **2** *(rinse ▸ cup, pot etc)* rincer; **to s. out one's mouth** se rincer la bouche; **they sluiced out the stable** ils ont lavé l'écurie à grande eau
VI *(water ▸ flow out in great quantity)* couler à flots

sluiceway ['slu:sweɪ] **N** canal *m* à vannes

slum [slʌm] *(pt & pp* **slummed**, *cont* **slumming)** **N** *also Fig (house)* taudis *m*; *(district)* quartier *m* pauvre, bas quartiers *mpl*
VT *Fam Hum* **to s. it** *(live in substandard conditions)* renoncer au luxe auquel on est habitué[□]; *(when socializing)* s'encanailler
VI *Fam Hum* **we're slumming tonight** on va s'encanailler ce soir
▸▸ *Br* ***slum clearance*** rénovation *f ou* aménagement *m* des quartiers insalubres; ***slum dwelling*** taudis *m*; ***slum landlord*** marchand *m* de sommeil

slumber ['slʌmbə(r)] *Literary* **N** sommeil *m* (profond); **deep in s.** plongé dans un sommeil profond; **her s. was** *or* **her slumbers were interrupted by...** son sommeil a été interrompu par...; *Fig* **the country had finally awoken from its slumbers** le pays était enfin sorti de sa torpeur
VI sommeiller
▸▸ *Am* ***slumber party*** soirée *f* entre copines *(au cours de laquelle on regarde des films, on discute et on dort dans la même pièce)*

slumlord ['slʌmlɔ:d] **N** marchand *m* de sommeil

slummy ['slʌmɪ] *(compar* **slummier**, *superl* **slummiest)** **ADJ** *(area, house, lifestyle)* sordide, misérable; **the s. area of town** les bas quartiers *mpl*

slump [slʌmp] **N 1** *(in attendance, figures, popularity)* chute *f*, forte baisse *f*, baisse *f* soudaine; **there has been a s. in investment** les investissements sont en forte baisse; **a s. in prices/demand** une forte baisse des prix/de la demande **2** *Econ (depression)* crise *f* économique; *(recession)* récession *f*; *St Exch* effondrement *m* (des cours), krach *m* (boursier) **3** *Am Sport* passage *m* à vide
VI 1 *(person)* s'écrouler, s'effondrer; **she slumped into an armchair** elle s'est effondrée dans un fauteuil **2** *(shoulders)* **her shoulders s.** elle a les épaules tombantes; **her shoulders slumped when she heard the bad news** elle eut l'air complètement abattue quand elle entendit la nouvelle **3** *(business, prices, market)* s'effondrer; *(morale, attendance)* baisser soudainement
VT *(usu passive)* **to be slumped in an armchair** être affalé *ou* affaissé dans un fauteuil; **he was slumped over the wheel** *(in car)* il était affaissé sur le volant

slumpflation [slʌmp'fleɪʃən] **N** *Econ* = forte récession accompagnée d'une inflation des prix et des salaires

slung [slʌŋ] *pt & pp of* **sling**

slunk [slʌŋk] *pt & pp of* **slink**

slur [slɜ:(r)] *(pt & pp* **slurred**, *cont* **slurring)** **N 1** *(insult)* insulte *f*, affront *m*; *(on reputation)* tache *f*; **a racial s.** une insulte raciste; **it's a s. on his character** c'est une tache à sa réputation; **to cast a s. on sb** porter atteinte à la réputation de qn **2** *(in speech)* mauvaise articulation *f*; **in a drunken s.** de la voix traînante d'un ivrogne; **to speak with a s.** mal articuler; *(as result of stroke etc)* parler d'une voix traînante **3** *Mus (sign)* liaison *f*; *(passage)* coulé *m*
VT 1 *(speech, words)* mal articuler **2** *(denigrate)* dénigrer **3** *Mus (two notes)* lier; *(passage)* couler
VI *(speak indistinctly)* mal articuler ses mots, manger la moitié de ses mots; **his speech slurred** ses paroles étaient indistinctes

slurp [slɜ:p] **VI** *(when drinking)* faire du bruit en buvant; *(when eating)* faire du bruit en mangeant
VT to s. sth boire/manger qch en faisant du bruit
N a loud s. un lapement bruyant; *Fam* **can I have a quick s. of your tea?** je peux boire une gorgée de ton thé?[□]

▸slurp up VT SEP *(soup)* avaler en faisant du bruit

slush [slʌʃ] **N 1** *(snow)* neige *f* fondue; *(mud)* gadoue *f* **2** *Fam (sentimentality)* sensiblerie[□] *f*
▸▸ *slush fund* caisse *f* noire *(servant généralement au paiement des pots-de-vin)*; *Fam* ***slush money*** dessous-de-table[□] *mpl*

slushy ['slʌʃɪ] *(compar* **slushier**, *superl* **slushiest)** **ADJ 1** *(snow)* fondu; *(ground)* détrempé; *(path)* couvert de neige fondue **2** *Fam (film, book)* à l'eau de rose[□]; *(person)* fleur bleue[□] *(inv)*

slut [slʌt] **N** *Pej* **1** *(slovenly woman)* souillon *f* **2** *(promiscuous woman)* salope *f*, pouffiasse *f*, traînée *f*; *(prostitute)* pute *f*

sluttish ['slʌtɪʃ] **ADJ** *Pej* **1** *(dirty)* sale; **to lead a s. existence** vivre salement **2** *(morals)* dépravé; *(behaviour)* débauché, dépravé; **a s. woman** une débauchée

sluttishness ['slʌtɪʃnɪs] **N** *Pej* **1** *(dirtiness)* saleté *f* **2** *(promiscuity)* conduite *f* débauchée *ou* dépravée

slutty ['slʌtɪ] *(compar* **sluttier**, *superl* **sluttiest)** **ADJ** *Pej (promiscuous)* coucheuse; *(appearance, behaviour)* qui fait pute; **to look s.** *(person)* avoir l'air d'une pute

sly [slaɪ] *(compar* **slyer** *or* **slier**, *superl* **slyest** *or* **sliest)** **ADJ 1** *(cunning, knowing)* rusé; **he's a s. (old) devil** *or* **dog** c'est un fin renard; **he gave me a s. look/smile** il m'a regardé/souri d'un air rusé
2 *(deceitful ▸ person)* sournois; *(▸ behaviour)* déloyal; *(▸ trick)* malhonnête
3 *(mischievous)* malin(igne), espiègle
4 *(secretive)* dissimulé; **he's a s. one!** c'est un petit cachottier!
N *Fam* **on the s.** en douce

slyboots ['slaɪbu:ts] **N** *Br Fam* petit(e) malin (igne) *m,f*

slyly ['slaɪlɪ] **ADV 1** *(cunningly)* de façon rusée, avec ruse
2 *(deceitfully)* sournoisement
3 *(mischievously)* avec espièglerie, de façon espiègle
4 *(secretly)* discrètement

slyness ['slaɪnɪs] **N 1** *(cunning)* ruse *f*
2 *(deceitfulness)* sournoiserie *f*
3 *(mischief)* espièglerie *f*
4 *(secrecy)* dissimulation *f*

smack [smæk] **N 1** *(slap ▸ gen)* grande tape *f*, claque *f*; *(▸ on face)* gifle *f*; *(▸ on bottom)* fessée *f*; **to give sb a s. in the face** gifler qn; **to give sb a s. on the bottom** donner une claque sur les fesses à qn; *Fig* **a s. in the face** *or* **eye** une gifle, une rebuffade; **give the ball a good s.** donne un grand coup dans le ballon
2 *(sound)* bruit *m* sec; *(of whip)* claquement *m*; **with a s. of his lips** avec un claquement de langue; **there was a resounding s. as the bat hit the ball** la batte heurta la balle avec un claquement sonore
3 *(slight taste)* léger *ou* petit goût *m*; *Culin* soupçon *m*; *Fig* **the s. of hypocrisy** une nuance d'hypocrisie
4 *(boat)* smack *m*, sémaque *m*
5 *Fam (kiss)* gros baiser[□] *m*; **to give sb a s. on the lips** embrasser qn bruyamment sur les lèvres[□]
6 *Br Fam (try)* **to have a s. at doing sth** essayer de faire qch[□]; **I'll have a s. at it** je vais essayer
7 *Fam Drugs slang (heroin)* héro *f*, blanche *f*
VT *(person ▸ gen)* donner une grande tape à, donner une claque à; *(▸ in face)* donner une gifle à, gifler; *(▸ on bottom)* donner une claque sur les fesses à; **to s. sb's face** *or* **sb in the face** gifler qn, donner une gifle à qn; **to s. sb's bottom** *(as punishment)* donner la fessée à qn; *(in play)* donner une tape sur les fesses à qn; **she smacked the book down on the table** elle posa le livre sur la table avec un claquement sonore; **to s. one's lips** se lécher les babines
VI *also Fig* **to s. of sth** sentir qch; **the whole thing smacks of corruption** tout ça, ça sent la corruption
ADV 1 *(forcefully)* en plein; **she went s. into a wall** elle est rentrée en plein dans un mur; **he caught him s. on the chin** il l'a frappé en plein sur le menton; **she kissed him s. on the lips** elle l'a embrassé en plein sur la bouche **2** *(exactly)* en plein; **s.** *or Am Fam* **s. dab in the middle** en plein milieu[□], au beau milieu[□]; **we arrived s.** *or Am Fam* **s. dab in the middle of the meeting** nous sommes arrivés au beau milieu de la réunion

smacker ['smækə(r)] *Fam* **1** *(kiss)* gros baiser[□] **2** *(pound)* livre[□] *f*; *(dollar)* dollar[□] *m*; **50 smackers** 50 livres *fpl*/dollars *mpl*

smacking ['smækɪŋ] **N** fessée *f*; **to give sb a s.** donner une fessée à qn

small [smɔ:l] **ADJ 1** *(in size)* petit; **s. children** les jeunes enfants *mpl*; **s. child** *(young)* enfant *mf* en bas âge, petit(e) enfant *mf*; *(small in size)* enfant *mf* de petite taille; **a s. coffee** une petite tasse (de café); *Euph* **the smallest room** le petit coin; **the s. screen** le petit écran; **s. sizes** les petites tailles *fpl*; **to get** *or* **to grow smaller** devenir plus petit, diminuer; **to make smaller** *(hole)* réduire; **the new wallpaper makes the room look smaller** le nouveau papier peint rapetisse la pièce; **to make oneself s.** se faire tout petit
2 *(in number ▸ crowd, family, population)* peu nombreux; *(in quantity ▸ dose, amount, percentage)* petit, faible; *(▸ resources)* faible; *(▸ supply)* petit; *(▸ salary, sum)* petit, modeste; *(▸ helping)* petit, peu copieux; *(▸ meal)* léger; **the audience was very s.** l'assistance était très peu nombreuse, il y avait très peu de monde; **the smallest possible number of guests** le moins d'invités possible; **in s. numbers** en petit nombre; **to get** *or* **to grow smaller** diminuer, décroître; **the problems don't get any smaller** les problèmes ne vont pas (en) s'amenuisant; **to make smaller** *(income)* diminuer; *(staff)* réduire
3 *(in scale, range)* petit; *(minor)* petit, mineur; **down to the smallest details** jusqu'aux moindres détails; **a s. voice** une petite voix; **it's no s. achievement** c'est une réussite non négligeable; **it makes not the smallest difference** ça ne fait pas la moindre différence; **there's the s. matter of the £150 you still owe me** il reste ce petit problème des 150 livres que tu me dois; **I like to be able to help in a s. way** j'aime me sentir utile; **I do some acting, in a s. way** je fais un peu de théâtre; **in her own s. way she had made a worthwhile contribution** dans la limite de ses moyens, elle avait apporté une pierre à l'édifice; *Fam* **it's** *Br* **s. beer** *or Am* **s. potatoes** c'est de la petite bière; *Fam* **we're very** *Br* **s. beer** *or Am* **s. potatoes in the advertising world** nous ne représentons pas grand-chose dans le monde de la publicité[□]
4 *(petty)* petit, mesquin; **I felt very s.** *(ashamed)* je n'étais pas fier; *(humiliated)* je me suis senti très humilié; **to make sb look** *or* **feel s.** humilier qn, rabaisser qn; **they've got s. minds** ce sont des esprits mesquins
ADV *(chop)* menu, fin; *(write)* petit; **to cut sth up** couper qch en tout petits morceaux; **to roll sth up s.** *(lengthways)* rouler qch bien serré; *(in ball)* rouler qch en petite boule; **the cat curled itself up s.** le chat s'est roulé en boule; **to think** voir petit
N 1 *(small part)* **s. of the back** creux *m ou* chute *f* des reins; **I have a pain in the s. of my back** j'ai mal aux reins *ou* au creux des reins; **he took her by the s. of the waist** il l'a prise par la taille **2** *(size*

petite taille *f*; **this T-shirt's a s.** ce tee-shirt est une petite taille

• **smalls** NPL *Fam Hum* sous-vêtements *mpl*; **to wash one's smalls** faire sa petite lessive

►► ***small ad*** petite annonce *f*; ***small arms*** armes *fpl* portatives; **the sound of s. arms fire** des tirs *mpl* d'arme portative; ***small business*** *(firm)* petite entreprise *f*, PME *f*; *(shop)* petit commerce *m*; ***small businessman*** petit entrepreneur *m ou* patron *m*; *Typ & Comput* ***small capitals, small caps*** petites capitales *fpl*; ***small change*** petite monnaie *f*; *Aut* ***small end*** *(of connecting rod)* pied *m*; ***small fry*** menu fretin *m*; **he's** *Br* **s. fry** *or Am* **a s. fry** il ne compte pas; ***small hours*** petit matin *m*; **in the s. hours** au petit matin; *Anat* ***small intestine*** intestin *m* grêle; *Fin* ***small investor*** petit porteur *m*; ***small letter*** (lettre *f*) minuscule *f*; **in s. letters** en (lettres) minuscules; ***small print*** petits caractères *mpl*; **make sure you read the s. print before you sign** lisez bien ce qui est écrit en petits caractères avant de signer; ***small scale*** petite échelle *f*; **on a s. scale** sur une petite échelle; ***small talk*** *(UNCOUNT)* banalités *fpl*; **to make s. talk** échanger des banalités; **to make s. talk with sb** faire la conversation à qn; **I'm no good at s. talk** je ne sais pas faire la conversation; *Typ* ***small type*** petits corps *mpl*

smallholder ['smɔːlhəʊldə(r)] N *Br* petit exploitant *m*

smallholding ['smɔːlhəʊldɪŋ] N *Br* petite exploitation *f*

smallish ['smɔːlɪʃ] ADJ *(gen)* assez petit; *(income)* assez modeste; *(family)* assez peu nombreux

small-minded ADJ *(attitude, person)* mesquin

smallness ['smɔːlnɪs] N **1** *(of child)* petite taille *f*; *(of hand, room)* petitesse *f*; *(of salary, fee)* modicité *f*; *(of extent)* caractère *m* limité **2** *(pettiness)* **the s. of his mind** sa mesquinerie

smallpox ['smɔːlpɒks] N variole *f*; **a s. case** un cas de variole

small-scale ADJ *(replica, model)* à taille réduite, réduit; *(map, operation)* à petite échelle; **a s. event** un événement de peu d'importance

►► *Comput* ***small-scale integration*** intégration *f* à petite échelle

small-time ADJ peu important, de petite envergure; **a s. thief/crook** un petit voleur/escroc

small-town ADJ provincial; **a s. attitude** une mentalité provinciale

►► ***small-town America*** l'Amérique *f* profonde; ***small-town gossip*** *(UNCOUNT)* commérages *mpl* de quartier; ***small-town rivalries*** rivalités *fpl* de clocher

►**smarm down** VT SEP *Br Fam* **to s. down one's hair** se brillantiner les cheveux

smarminess ['smɑːmɪnɪs] N *Br Fam Pej* caractère *m* doucereux *ou* mielleux; **his s. gets on my nerves** son côté mielleux me tape sur les nerfs

smarmy ['smɑːmɪ] *(compar* **smarmier**, *superl* **smarmiest**) ADJ *Br Fam Pej (toadying)* lèche-bottes *(inv)*; *(obsequious)* doucereux, mielleux

smart [smɑːt] ADJ **1** *Br (elegant* ► *person, clothes, hotel)* chic, élégant; *(attractive)* coquet, pimpant; **she's a s. dresser** elle s'habille avec beaucoup de chic; **to make oneself look s.** se faire beau (belle); *(for interview etc)* bien s'habiller; **you look very s. in your new suit** vous avez beaucoup d'allure avec votre nouveau costume; **the s. set** les gens *mpl* chics, le beau monde

2 *(clever)* habile, intelligent; *(shrewd, resourceful)* malin(igne); *(quick-thinking)* à l'esprit vif; **he's a s. lad** il n'est pas bête; **it isn't s. to break the law** ce n'est pas malin de ne pas respecter la loi; **it was s. of her to think of it** c'était futé de sa part d'y penser; **she was too s. for them** elle était trop maligne *ou* futée pour eux; **don't try to be s. with me** n'essaie pas de faire le malin avec moi; **that wasn't very s., was it?** ce n'était pas très malin, tu ne trouves pas?; **s. businesswoman** femme *f* d'affaires habile; **a s. move** une sage décision; *Fam* **he's a s. one** c'est un malin

3 *(cheeky)* impertinent, audacieux; **don't get s. with me!** n'essaie pas de jouer au plus malin avec moi!

4 *(quick)* vif, prompt; **a s. pace** une allure vive; **that was s. work!** voilà du travail rapide!, voilà qui a été vite fait!; **look s.!** grouille-toi!; **a s. slap across the face** une bonne gifle; **give the top a s. tap** donnez une bonne tape sur le dessus

5 *Comput* intelligent

6 *(bomb, weapon)* intelligent

VI **1** *(eyes, wound)* picoter, brûler; **her eyes were smarting** elle avait les yeux qui piquaient; **the onion made her eyes s.** les oignons lui piquaient les yeux *ou* la faisaient pleurer; **my face was still smarting from the blow** le visage me cuisait encore du coup que j'avais reçu **2** *(person)* être piqué au vif; **he's still smarting from the insult** il n'a toujours pas digéré l'insulte

ADV *(quickly* ► *walk)* vivement, à vive allure; *(*► *act)* vivement, promptement

N *(pain)* douleur *f* cuisante; *Fig* effet *m* cinglant

• **smarts** NPL *Am Fam (intelligence)* intelligence *f*; **to have smarts** en avoir dans le ciboulot

►► *Fam* ***smart alec, smart aleck*** petit(e) malin (igne) *m,f*; ***smart card*** carte *f* à puce; ***smart card reader*** lecteur *m* de cartes à puce *ou* de cartes à mémoire; ***smart drug*** psychotrope *m*; ***smart missile*** missile *m* guidé *ou* téléguidé; *Fin* ***smart money*** placement *m* astucieux; *Fam* **all the s. money is on him to win the presidency** tous les spécialistes le donnent comme favori aux élections présidentielles; *Comput* ***smart quotes*** = conversion automatique des guillemets saisis au clavier en guillemets typographiques; ***smart sanctions*** sanctions *fpl* ciblées

smartarse ['smɑːtɑːs], *Am* **smartass** ['smɑːtæs] *very Fam* N petit(e) malin(igne) *m,f*

ADJ *(reply, comment)* sarcastique

smarten ['smɑːtən] VT **1** *(improve appearance)* **to s. (the appearance of) sth** arranger qch; **to s. oneself** se faire beau (belle) **2** *Br (speed up)* **to s. one's pace** accélérer l'allure

►**smarten up** VI **1** *(improve appearance* ► *person)* se faire beau (belle); *(*► *restaurant)* devenir plus chic, être retapé; *(*► *town, street)* devenir plus pimpant; **I went upstairs to s. up** je suis monté me faire beau **2** *Fam (improve)* se reprendre

VT SEP **1** *(person)* pomponner; *(room, house, town)* arranger, rendre plus élégant; **a coat of paint would help s. the restaurant/the car up** une couche de peinture et le restaurant/la voiture aurait déjà meilleure allure; **to s. oneself up** se faire beau (belle), soigner son apparence

2 *(production)* accélérer

3 *Fam (improve)* **you'd better s. up your ideas** *or* **your act!** tu ferais bien de te reprendre!; *(to lazy person)* tu ferais bien de te secouer!

4 *Am Fam (realize what is happening)* **s. up!** ouvre les yeux!, cesse de faire l'imbécile!

smarting ['smɑːtɪŋ] ADJ *(pain, eyes)* brûlant

N douleur *f* cuisante

smartish ['smɑːtɪʃ] ADV *Br Fam* vite fait, en vitesse; **you'd better get ready pretty s.** tu ferais mieux de te préparer vite fait

smartness ['smɑːtnɪs] N **1** *Br (elegance* ► *of appearance, dress, style)* allure *f*, chic *m*, élégance *f* **2** *(cleverness)* intelligence *f*, habileté *f*; *(shrewdness)* astuce *f*, vivacité *f* (d'esprit); *(ingenuity)* débrouillardise *f* **3** *(quickness* ► *of pace)* rapidité *f*; *(*► *of reply, behaviour)* promptitude *f*, rapidité *f*

smarty ['smɑːtɪ] *(pl* **smarties**), **smarty-pants** *(pl* **inv**) N *Fam* (Monsieur/Madame/Mademoiselle) je-sais-tout *mf inv*, petit(e) malin(igne) *m,f*; **OK, s., show me how to do it** allez, vas-y, montre-moi comment faire puisque tu es si malin

smash [smæʃ] N **1** *(noise* ► *of breaking)* fracas *m*; **with a loud s.** avec un grand fracas; **the vase fell with a s.** le vase s'est fracassé en tombant

2 *(blow)* coup *m ou* choc *m* violent; **forearm s.** manchette *f*; **a s. on the head** un coup violent sur la tête

3 *Fam (collision)* collision *f*; *(accident)* accident *m*; *(pile-up)* carambolage *m*, télescopage *m*; **a five-car s.** un carambolage de cinq voitures

4 *(collapse* ► *of business, market)* débâcle *f* (financière), effondrement *m* (financier); *St Exch* krach *m*, effondrement *m* des cours; *(bankruptcy)* faillite *f*

5 *(in tennis, badminton, table-tennis)* smash *m*

6 *Fam (success)* succès *m* bœuf; **it was a s.** ça a fait un tabac

7 *Am (drink)* = boisson composée d'une liqueur, de menthe, de sucre et d'eau gazeuse

ONOMAT patatras

ADV **to go** *or* **to run s. into a wall** heurter un mur avec violence, rentrer en plein dans un mur

VT **1** *(break* ► *cup, window)* casser, briser; **to s. sth to pieces** briser qch en morceaux; **I've smashed my glasses** j'ai cassé mes lunettes; **to s. sth open** *(box, crate)* ouvrir qch d'un grand coup; **to s. the door open** enfoncer la porte; **he smashed his head open on a rock** il s'est ouvert la tête en heurtant un rocher

2 *(crash, hit)* écraser; **he smashed his fist (down) on the table** il écrasa son poing sur la table; **she smashed him over the head with a chair** elle lui a cassé une chaise sur la tête; **they smashed their way in** ils sont entrés par effraction *(en enfonçant la porte ou la fenêtre)*; **the raft was smashed against the rocks** le radeau s'est fracassé contre *ou* sur les rochers; **he smashed the ball into the back of the net** *(in football)* d'un tir terrible, il a envoyé le ballon au fond des filets

3 *(in tennis, badminton, table-tennis)* **to s. the ball** faire un smash, smasher; **he smashed the ball into the net** il a envoyé son smash dans le filet

4 *(destroy* ► *gen)* briser; *(*► *resistance, opposition)* briser, écraser; *(*► *opponent, record)* pulvériser; **to s. a drugs ring** démanteler un réseau de trafiquants de drogue

5 *Phys (atom)* désintégrer

VI *(break, crash)* se briser, se casser; **to s. into bits** se briser en mille morceaux; **the car smashed into the lamppost** la voiture s'est écrasée contre le réverbère

►► ***smash hit*** *(song, record)* gros succès *m*; **this record is a s. hit in America** ce disque fait fureur *ou* connaît un succès fou en Amérique

►**smash down** VT SEP *(door)* défoncer

►**smash in** VT SEP *(door, window)* enfoncer, défoncer; *(safe)* forcer; *Fam* **to s. sb's face in** casser la figure *ou* la gueule à qn; **I'll s. your face in** je te casse la gueule

►**smash up** VT SEP *(furniture)* casser, démolir; *(room, shop)* tout casser *ou* démolir dans; *(car)* démolir; **they smashed the place up in revenge** ils ont tout démoli pour se venger

smash-and-grab (raid) N *Br* pillage *m* de vitrine; **the jewels were stolen in a s.** des cambrioleurs ont brisé la vitrine et se sont enfuis avec les bijoux

smashed [smæʃt] ADJ *Fam (drunk)* bourré, pété, beurré; *(on drugs)* raide, défoncé; **to get s.** *(drunk)* se bourrer; *(on drugs)* se défoncer

smasher ['smæʃə(r)] N *Br Fam* **1** *(person)* **she's a real s.** *(in appearance)* c'est un vrai canon; *(in character)* elle est vraiment sensass **2** *(object)* **it's a real s.!** c'est sensass!

smashing ['smæʃɪŋ] ADJ *Br Fam* super *(inv)*, génial, géant; **it was a s. party!** ça a été une soirée du tonnerre!; **we had a s. time!** on s'est super bien amusés!; **she's a s. girl** c'est une fille super

smash-up N *(accident)* accident *m*; *(collision)* carambolage *m*, télescopage *m*; **five cars were involved in the s.** cinq voitures se sont télescopées

smattering ['smætərɪŋ] N *(of knowledge)* notions *fpl* vagues; *(of people, things)* poignée *f*, petit nombre *m*; **they only have a s. of grammar** ils n'ont que quelques vagues notions de grammaire; **she has a s. of Italian** elle a quelques notions d'italien, elle sait un peu d'italien; **there was the usual s. of artists at the party** comme toujours, il y avait un petit groupe d'artistes à la réception

SME [ˌesem'iː] N *(abbr* **small and medium-sized enterprise**) PME *f*

smear [smɪə(r)] N **1** *(mark* ► *on glass, mirror, wall)* trace *f*, tache *f*; *(longer)* traînée *f*; *(of ink)* pâté *m*, bavure *f*; **smears of blood/paint** des traînées *fpl* de sang/de peinture **2** *(defamation)* diffamation *f*; *(spoken)* calomnie *f*; **a s. on sb's integrity/reputation** une atteinte à l'honneur/à la réputation de qn; **to use s. tactics** avoir recours à la calomnie **3** *Med* frottis *m*, prélèvement *m*

VT 1 *(spread ▸ butter, oil)* étaler; *(coat)* barbouiller; **to s. sth with grease, to s. grease on sth** étaler de la graisse sur qch; **she smeared the dish with butter** elle a beurré le plat; **to s. paint/chocolate on one's face** se barbouiller le visage de peinture/de chocolat; **they smeared red paint everywhere** ils ont tout barbouillé de peinture rouge

2 *(smudge)* **the ink on the page was smeared** l'encre a coulé sur la page; **the rain has smeared the address** la pluie a en partie effacé l'adresse; **don't s. the wet paint/varnish** ne faites pas de taches de peinture/de vernis; **the walls were smeared with blood** les murs étaient tout maculés de sang; **the mirror was smeared with fingermarks** il y avait des traces de doigts sur la glace

3 *(defame ▸ person)* diffamer; *(verbally)* calomnier; *(▸ person's reputation)* salir; **an attempt to s. the prime minister** une tentative de diffamation du premier ministre

4 *Am Fam (defeat easily)* battre à plates coutures❑

VI *(paint)* couler; *(ink)* baver

▸▸ ***smear campaign*** campagne *f* de diffamation *ou* dénigrement; *Med* ***smear test*** frottis *m* (vaginal), *Can* test *m* de Papanicolaou

smeary ['smɪərɪ] **ADJ** *(stained)* taché, barbouillé; *(windows, mirror)* sale

smell [smel] *(Br pt & pp* **smelled** *or* **smelt** [smelt], *Am pt & pp* **smelled**) **VT 1** *(notice an odour of)* sentir; **to s. gas** sentir le gaz, *Am* sentir le gaz *ou* l'essence; **I can s. (something) burning** (je trouve que) ça sent le brûlé; **she smelt** *or* **she could s. alcohol on his breath** elle s'aperçut que son haleine sentait l'alcool

2 *Fig (sense ▸ trouble, danger)* flairer, pressentir; **to s. a rat** flairer quelque chose de louche

3 *(sniff at ▸ food)* sentir, renifler; *(▸ flower)* sentir, humer; *(of dog)* flairer, renifler; **she smelt the cream to see if it was fresh** elle a senti la crème pour voir si elle était fraîche

VI 1 *(have odour)* sentir; **to s. good** *or* **sweet** sentir bon; **to s. bad** sentir mauvais; **it smells musty** ça sent le renfermé; **that soup smells delicious!** cette soupe sent délicieusement bon!; **what does it s. of** *or* **like?** qu'est-ce que ça sent?; **it smells of lavender** ça sent la lavande; **it smells like lavender** on dirait de la lavande; *Fig* **to s. of treachery/hypocrisy** sentir la trahison/l'hypocrisie; *Fam* **to s. fishy** sembler louche❑

2 *(have bad odour)* sentir (mauvais); **it smells (awful) in here!** ça pue ici!; **his breath smells** il a mauvaise haleine; **the dog smells** le chien sent mauvais *ou* pue

3 *(perceive odour)* **he can't s.** il n'a pas d'odorat

N 1 *(sense ▸ of person)* odorat *m*; *(▸ of animal)* odorat *m*, flair *m*; **he has no sense of s.** il n'a pas d'odorat; **I've lost my sense of s.** j'ai perdu l'odorat; **to have a keen sense of s.** avoir le nez fin; *(dog etc)* avoir beaucoup de flair

2 *(odour)* odeur *f*; *(of flowers, fruit)* parfum *m*; *(bad odour)* mauvaise odeur *f*; *(stench)* puanteur *f*; **there's a bad s.** ça sent mauvais; **what's that s.?** quelle est cette odeur?; **there's a strong s. of gas in here** il y a une forte odeur de gaz ici; **there was a s. of burning in the kitchen** il y avait une odeur de brûlé dans la cuisine; **there was a lovely s. of lavender** ça sentait bon la lavande; **it has no s.** ça n'a pas d'odeur; **what an awful s.!** qu'est-ce que ça sent mauvais!; *Fig* **the s. of defeat/fear** l'odeur *f* de la défaite/de la peur; *Fig* **I don't like the s. of this at all** ça ne me plaît pas du tout, c'est louche

3 *(sniff)* **to have** *or* **take a s. of sth** sentir qch, renifler qch; **have a s. of this** sentez-moi ça

▸**smell out VT SEP 1** *(of dog)* dénicher en flairant; *Fig (of person)* découvrir, dépister; *(secret, conspiracy)* découvrir **2 his cigarettes are smelling the office out** ses cigarettes empestent *ou* empuantissent le bureau

smelliness ['smelɪnɪs] **N** mauvaise odeur *f*; *(stench)* puanteur *f*

smelling salts ['smelɪŋ-] **NPL** sels *mpl*

smelly ['smelɪ] *(compar* **smellier**, *superl* **smelliest**) **ADJ 1** *(person, socks etc)* qui sent mauvais, qui pue; **it's awfully s. in here** ça sent horriblement mauvais *ou* ça pue ici; **to have s. feet** sentir des pieds **2** *Fam Pej (unpleasant)* dégueulasse; **you can stuff your s. homework!** tes devoirs, tu peux te les mettre où je pense!; **I hate my s. sister** je déteste ma cruche de sœur

smelt [smelt] *(pl* **inv** *or* **smelts**) *pt & pp of* **smell**

N *Ich* éperlan *m*

VT *Metal (ore)* fondre; *(metal)* extraire par fusion

smelter ['smeltə(r)] **N** *Metal* haut-fourneau *m*

smelting ['smeltɪŋ] **N** *(of ore)* fonte *f*, fusion *f*; *(of metal)* extraction *f* par fusion

▸▸ ***smelting works*** fonderie *f*

SMI [,esem'aɪ] **N** *(abbr* **small and medium-sized industry**) PMI *f*

smidgen, smidgin ['smɪdʒɪn] **N** *Fam* **just a s.** juste un petit peu❑; **a s. of** un tout petit peu de

smile [smaɪl] **N** sourire *m*; **"of course," he said with a s.** "bien sûr", dit-il en souriant; **he has a nice s.** il a un joli sourire; **come on, give us a s.!** allez, faisnous un sourire!; **she gave me a friendly little s.** elle m'a adressé un petit sourire amical; **to have a s. on one's face** avoir le sourire; **take that s. off your face!** arrête de sourire comme ça!; **that'll take** *or* **wipe the s. off his face!** cela va lui faire passer l'envie de sourire!; **to be all smiles** être tout souriant *ou* tout sourire; *(as a pretence)* elle était tout sucre tout miel

VI sourire; **to s. at sb** sourire à qn; **s. (please)!** *(for photograph)* souriez!; **to s. to oneself** sourire pour soi; **she smiled at his awkwardness** sa maladresse l'a fait sourire; **keep smiling!** gardez le sourire!; **he always comes up smiling** il garde toujours le sourire; **she smiled back (at him)** elle lui rendit son sourire; *Fig* **fortune smiled on him** la fortune lui sourit; *Literary* **to s. in the face of adversity** faire contre mauvaise fortune bon cœur

VT to s. one's approval exprimer son approbation par un sourire; **to s. one's thanks** remercier d'un sourire; **she smiled a sad s.** elle eut un sourire triste

smiley ['smaɪlɪ] **N** *Comput* souriant *m*, émoticon *m*, *Can* binette *f*

smiling ['smaɪlɪŋ] **ADJ** souriant

smilingly ['smaɪlɪŋlɪ] **ADV** en souriant, avec un sourire

smirch [smɜːtʃ] *Literary* **VT 1** *(stain)* salir, souiller **2** *Fig (name, reputation)* salir, ternir

N tache *f*, salissure *f*, souillure *f*

smirk [smɜːk] **VI** *(smugly)* sourire d'un air suffisant *ou* avec suffisance; *(foolishly)* sourire bêtement

N *(smug)* petit sourire *m* satisfait *ou* suffisant; *(foolish)* sourire *m* bête

smite [smaɪt] **VT** *(pt* **smote** [sməʊt], *pp* **smitten** ['smɪtən]) **1** *Arch or Literary (strike ▸ object)* frapper; *(▸ enemy)* abattre **2 to be smitten with blindness** être frappé de cécité; **to be smitten with remorse** être pris de remords; **to be smitten with a desire to do sth** être pris d'un *ou* du désir de faire qch **3** *Bible (punish)* châtier

▸**smite down VT SEP** *Arch or Literary* abattre

smith [smɪθ] **N** forgeron *m*; *(who shoes horses)* maréchal-ferrant *m*

smithereens [,smɪðə'riːnz] **NPL** morceaux *mpl*; **to smash sth to s.** briser qch en mille morceaux; **the house was blown to s. in the explosion** la maison a été complètement soufflée par l'explosion

Smithsonian Institution [smɪθ'səʊnɪən-] **N** = complexe culturel à Washington

smithy ['smɪðɪ] *(pl* **smithies**) **N** forge *f*; *(blacksmith's workshop)* (atelier *m* de) maréchalerie *f*

smitten ['smɪtən] *pp of* **smite**

ADJ he's really s. (with that girl) il est vraiment très épris (de cette fille)

smock [smɒk] **N** *(loose garment)* blouse *f*, sarrau *m*; *(maternity wear ▸ blouse)* tunique *f* de grossesse; *(▸ dress)* robe *f* de grossesse

VT *Sewing* faire des smocks à

smocking ['smɒkɪŋ] **N** *(UNCOUNT)* smocks *mpl*

smog [smɒg] **N** smog *m*

smoke [sməʊk] **N 1** *(from fire, cigarette)* fumée *f*; **to go up in s.** *(building)* brûler; *Fig (plans)* partir *ou* s'en aller en fumée; *Fam* **he had s. coming out of his ears** *(was angry)* ses yeux lançaient des éclairs❑; *Prov* **there's no s. without fire** il n'y a pas de fumée sans feu; *Fam Fig* **it's all s. and mirrors** ce n'est qu'une illusion

2 *(act of smoking)* **to have a s.** fumer; **I went outside for a s.** je suis sorti fumer une cigarette

3 *Fam (cigarette)* clope *m ou f*; *(cigar)* cigare❑*m*; **have you got any smokes?** t'as des clopes?

4 *Fam Drugs slang (cannabis cigarette)* joint *m*; *(cannabis)* chichon *m*, shit *m*

5 *Br Fam* **the (Big) S.** *(any big city)* la grande ville❑; *(London)* Londres❑

VI 1 *(fireplace, chimney, lamp)* fumer; **the horses flanks were smoking** les chevaux étaient tout fumants **2** *(person)* fumer; **do you s.?** (est-ce que vous fumez?; **do you mind if I s.?** ça vous gêne si je fume?; *Fam* **to s. like a chimney** fumer comme un pompier *ou* un sapeur

VT 1 *(cigarette, pipe, opium etc)* fumer; **to s. a pipe** fumer la pipe; **to s. 20 a day** fumer 20 cigarettes par jour

2 *Culin (fish, meat)* fumer

3 *(glass)* fumer

4 *(fumigate ▸ plants, greenhouse, room)* soumettre à des fumigations

▸▸ ***smoke alarm*** détecteur *m* de fumée; ***smoke bomb*** bombe *f* fumigène; ***smoke detector*** détecteur *m* de fumée; ***smoke hood*** hotte *f* (aspirante); *Am* ***smoke shop*** tabac *m*; ***smoke signal*** signal *m* de fumée

▸**smoke out VT SEP 1** *(fugitive, animal)* enfumer; *Fig (traitor, bandits)* débusquer; *(conspiracy, plot)* découvrir **2** *(room)* enfumer **3** *(finish)* **my pipe is smoked out** j'ai fini ma pipe

smoked [sməʊkt] **ADJ** fumé

▸▸ ***smoked glass*** verre *m* fumé; ***smoked salmon*** saumon *m* fumé

smoke-filled [-fɪld] **ADJ** enfumé; *Fig* **in s. rooms** dans les salles du pouvoir

smokeless ['sməʊklɪs] **ADJ**

▸▸ ***smokeless fuel*** combustible *m* non polluant; ***smokeless zone*** = zone dans laquelle seul l'usage de combustibles non polluants est autorisé

smoker ['sməʊkə(r)] **N 1** *(person)* fumeur(euse) *m,f*; **cigarette/pipe s.** fumeur(euse) *m,f* de cigarettes/pipe; **heavy s.** gros (grosse) fumeur(euse) *m,f*; **to have a s.'s cough** avoir une toux de fumeur **2** *(train compartment)* compartiment *m* fumeurs

smokestack ['sməʊkstæk] **N** cheminée *f*

▸▸ ***smokestack industry*** industrie *f* lourde

smoking ['sməʊkɪŋ] **ADJ** fumant, qui fume; **s. or non-s.?** fumeurs ou non-fumeurs?

N 1 *(of tobacco ▸ habit)* tabagisme *m*; **s. can damage your health** fumer nuit à votre santé; **I've given up s.** j'ai arrêté de fumer; **no s.** *(sign)* défense de fumer; **s. can cause cancer** le tabac peut provoquer le cancer **2** *Culin (of meat, fish)* fumage *m*

▸▸ ***smoking area*** zone *f* fumeurs; ***smoking ban*** interdiction *f* de fumer; ***smoking carriage*** voiture fumeurs; ***smoking compartment*** compartiment *m* fumeurs; *Fig* ***smoking gun*** *(clue)* indice *m* flagrant; ***smoking jacket*** veste *f* d'intérieur; ***smoking room*** fumoir *m (pour fumeurs)*

SMOKING BAN

En 2004, une loi interdisant de fumer dans les lieux de travail et les lieux publics est entrée en vigueur en République d'Irlande. Cette loi concerne également les bars, les clubs et les restaurants, où elle vise à protéger le personnel travaillant dans ce type d'établissement des effets nocifs de la fumée. La même interdiction est entrée en application en Écosse en mars 2006 et a été étendue au reste du Royaume-Uni en 2007. Cette loi a créé toute une polémique; certains de ses détracteurs l'accusaient en effet d'aller à l'encontre des libertés civiques et de nombreux tenanciers de pub craignaient de voir fuir leur clientèle. Il est encore tôt pour juger des effets de cette nouvelle loi mais force est de reconnaître qu'elle a été bien accueillie en Irlande.

smoky ['sməʊkɪ] *(compar* **smokier**, *superl* **smokiest**) **ADJ 1** *(atmosphere, room)* enfumé

2 *(chimney, lamp, fire)* qui fume

3 *(ceiling, wall)* noirci par la fumée

4 *(taste)* de fumée; *(food)* qui sent le fumé, qui a un goût de fumé

5 *(in colour)* **s. blue** gris bleu *(inv)*

▸▸ ***smoky grey*** gris fumée *m inv*; *Geol* ***smoky quartz*** quartz *m* fumé

smolder, smoldering *Am* = **smoulder, smouldering**

smooch [smu:tʃ] *Fam* **N 1 to have a s.** *(kiss)* se bécoter; *(cuddle)* se peloter **2** *Br* **to have a s.** *(dance)* danser joue contre joue

VI 1 *(kiss)* se bécoter; *(cuddle)* se peloter **2** *Br (dance)* danser joue contre joue

smoochy [smu:tʃɪ] *(compar* **smoochier,** *superl* **smoochiest) ADJ** *Fam (music)* sentimental, tendre

smooth [smu:ð] **ADJ 1** *(surface)* lisse; *(pebble, stone)* lisse, poli; *(skin)* lisse, doux (douce); *(chin* ▸ *close-shaven)* rasé de près; *(*▸ *beardless)* glabre, lisse; *(hair, fabric, road)* lisse; *(sea, water)* calme; **this razor gives a s. shave** ce rasoir vous rase de près; **the steps were worn s.** les marches étaient devenues lisses; **the stone had been washed** *or* **worn s. by the sea** la pierre avait été polie par la mer; *Br Fam* **as s. as a baby's bottom** *(skin, face)* doux comme une peau de bébé

2 *(comfortable* ▸ *ride, flight)* confortable; *(*▸ *take-off, landing)* en douceur; **they had a s. crossing** la traversée a été calme

3 *(trouble-free* ▸ *life, course of events)* paisible, calme; *(*▸ *journey)* sans anicroches; *(*▸ *organization)* qui marche bien; *(rhythm, style)* fluide; **to get off to a s. start** bien démarrer; **to make things s. for sb** faciliter les choses pour qn; **the s. running of the department** le bon fonctionnement du service; **the bill had a s. passage through Parliament** le projet de loi a été voté sans problèmes au Parlement

4 *Culin (in texture)* onctueux, homogène; *(in taste)* moelleux

5 *Pej (slick, suave)* doucereux, onctueux, suave; *Fam* **he's a s. operator** il sait y faire; **to be a s. talker, to have a s. tongue** être beau parleur

VT 1 *(tablecloth, skirt)* défroisser; *(hair, feathers)* lisser; *(wood)* rendre lisse, planer; **to s. one's brow** dérider son front; *Fig* **to s. the way for sb, to s. sb's path** aplanir les difficultés pour qn

2 *(rub* ▸ *oil, cream)* masser; **to s. oil into one's skin** mettre de l'huile sur sa peau *(en massant doucement)*

3 *(polish)* lisser, polir

4 *(features, lines)* lisser

N 1 to give one's hair a s. lisser ses cheveux, se lisser les cheveux; **to give sth a s. down with sandpaper** égaliser qch avec du papier de verre **2** *(smooth part)* partie *f* lisse; *(smooth surface)* surface *f* unie

▸▸ *Anat* ***smooth muscle*** muscle *m* lisse, muscle *m* viscéral; *Zool* ***smooth snake*** coronelle *f*

▸ **smooth away VT SEP** *(problems, fears)* faire oublier

▸ **smooth back VT SEP** *(hair)* lisser en arrière; *(sheet)* rabattre en lissant

▸ **smooth down VT SEP** *(hair, feathers)* lisser; *(sheets, dress)* lisser, défroisser; *(wood)* planer, aplanir

▸ **smooth off VT SEP** *(angle)* adoucir

▸ **smooth out VT SEP** *(clothes, sheet, map, piece of paper)* lisser, défroisser; *(crease, pleat, wrinkle)* faire disparaître (en lissant); *Fig (difficulties, obstacles)* aplanir, faire disparaître

▸ **smooth over VT SEP 1** *(gravel, sand)* rendre lisse (en ratissant); *(soil)* aplanir, égaliser **2** *Fig (difficulties, obstacles)* aplanir; **to s. things over** *(embarrassing situation)* arranger les choses

smoothbore ['smu:ðbɔ:(r)] *Mil* **ADJ** à canon lisse

N fusil *m* non rayé

smoothie ['smu:ðɪ] **N 1** *Fam (smooth talker)* individu *m* mielleux; **he's a real s.** *(in manner)* il roule les mécaniques; *(in speech)* c'est vraiment un beau parleur **2** *(drink)* = boisson à base de jus de fruit mélangé à du yaourt ou à du lait

smoothly ['smu:ðlɪ] **ADV 1** *(easily, steadily* ▸ *operate, drive, move)* sans à-coups, en douceur; **to run s.** *(engine)* tourner bien; *(operation, meeting)* marcher comme sur des roulettes; **things are not going very s. between them** ça ne va pas très bien entre eux; **the journey went s.** le voyage s'est déroulé sans anicroches; **the interview went quite s. until I...** l'entretien s'est bien passé jusqu'à ce que je... **2** *(gently* ▸ *rise, fall)* doucement, en douceur; **the plane took off s.** l'avion a décollé en douceur **3** *Pej (talk)* doucereusement; *(behave)* (trop) suavement

smoothness ['smu:ðnɪs] **N 1** *(of surface)* égalité *f*, aspect *m* uni *ou* lisse; *(of fabric, skin, hair)* douceur *f*; *(of road)* surface *f* lisse; *(of sea)* calme *m*; *(of stone)* aspect *m* lisse *ou* poli; *(of tyre)* aspect *m* lisse; **she has a wonderful s. of touch on the piano** elle a un merveilleux doigté au piano

2 *(of flow, breathing, pace, supply)* régularité *f*; *(of engine, machine)* bon fonctionnement *m*; *(of life, course of events)* caractère *m* paisible *ou* serein; *Fig (of temperament)* calme *m*, sérénité *f*; **the operation was carried out with great s.** l'opération s'est déroulée sans accroc *ou* heurt

3 *Culin (of texture)* onctuosité *f*; *(of taste)* moelleux *m*

4 *(of voice)* douceur *f*

5 *Pej (suaveness)* caractère *m* doucereux *ou* mielleux, onctuosité *f*

smooth-running ADJ *(machine)* qui fonctionne bien *ou* sans à-coups; *(engine)* qui tourne bien; *(business, organization)* qui marche bien; *(plan, operation)* qui se déroule bien

smooth-spoken ADJ doucereux, mielleux

smooth-talk VT don't let him s. you ne te laisse pas enjôler par lui; **she was smooth-talked into accepting the job** ils l'ont convaincue d'accepter le travail à force de belles paroles; **let's see if he can s. his way out of this one** voyons s'il est assez beau parleur pour se sortir de ce pétrin

smooth-talking ADJ doucereux, mielleux

smooth-tongued ADJ doucereux, mielleux

smoothy *(pl* **smoothies)** = **smoothie**

smote [sməʊt] *pt of* **smite**

smother ['smʌðə(r)] **VT 1** *(suppress* ▸ *fire, flames)* étouffer; *(*▸ *sound)* étouffer, amortir; *(*▸ *cry)* étouffer, retenir; *(*▸ *emotions, laughter, yawn)* réprimer; *(*▸ *scandal, criticism, opposition)* étouffer

2 *(suffocate* ▸ *person)* étouffer; **she felt smothered by her mother** elle se sentait étouffée par sa mère

3 *(cover)* couvrir, recouvrir; **strawberries smothered in** *or* **with cream** des fraises *fpl* couvertes de crème; **she was smothered in furs** elle était emmitouflée dans des fourrures

4 *(overwhelm* ▸ *with kindness, love)* combler; **to s. sb with kisses** couvrir *ou* dévorer qn de baisers; **to s. sb with attention** être aux petits soins pour qn

VI *(person)* étouffer

smothered ['smʌðəd] **ADJ** *(cry)* sourd, étouffé; *(sound)* étouffé

smother-love N *Fam* amour *m* étouffant d'une mère

smoulder, *Am* **smolder** ['sməʊldə(r)] **VI 1** *(fire* ▸ *before flames)* couver; *(*▸ *after burning)* fumer **2** *(feeling, rebellion)* couver; **her eyes smouldered with passion** son regard brûlait de désir

smouldering, *Am* **smoldering** ['sməʊldərɪŋ] **ADJ** *(fire, anger, passion, jealousy)* qui couve; *(embers, ruins)* fumant; *(eyes)* de braise

SMS [ˌesem'es] *Tel* **N** *(abbr* **short message service)** service *m* SMS

VT to S. sb envoyer un SMS à qn

SMTP [ˌesem,ti:'pi:] **N** *Comput (abbr* **Simple Mail Transfer Protocol)** protocole *m* SMTP

smudge [smʌdʒ] **N** *(on face, clothes, surface)* (petite) tache *f*; *(of make-up)* traînée *f*; *(on page of print)* bavure *f*; **you've got a s. on your chin** tu as du noir sur le menton; **the ship was just a s. on the horizon** le navire n'était plus qu'une tache à l'horizon

VT *(face, hands)* salir; *(clothes, surface)* tacher, salir; *(ink)* répandre; *(writing)* étaler; *(eye make-up)* faire couler; **you've made me s. my lipstick** à cause de toi je me suis mis du rouge à lèvres partout

VI *(ink, make-up)* faire des taches; *(print)* être maculé; *(wet paint)* s'étaler

smudgy ['smʌdʒɪ] *(compar* **smudgier,** *superl* **smudgiest) ADJ** *(make-up, ink)* étalé; *(print, page)* maculé; *(writing)* à demi effacé; *(face)* sali, taché; *(outline)* estompé, brouillé

smug [smʌg] *(compar* **smugger,** *superl* **smuggest) ADJ** *Pej (person)* content de soi, suffisant; *(attitude, manner, voice)* suffisant; **he has a s. look** il a un air suffisant, il a l'air content de lui; **stop looking so s.** arrête de te croire supérieur; **he's so s.!** ce qu'il peut être suffisant *ou* content de sa petite personne!

smuggle ['smʌgəl] **VT** *(contraband)* passer en contrebande; *(into prison* ▸ *mail, arms)* introduire clandestinement; **to s. sth through customs** passer qch en fraude à la douane; **to s. sb into a country** faire entrer qn clandestinement dans un pays; **to s. sb out of a country** faire sortir qn clandestinement d'un pays; **the terrorists were smuggled over the border** les terroristes ont passé la frontière clandestinement; **he managed to s. a knife into the prison** il a réussi à faire entrer *ou* passer clandestinement un couteau dans la prison; **they are suspected of smuggling arms/heroin** on les soupçonne de trafic d'armes/d'héroïne; *Fig* **to s. sth into a room** apporter qch subrepticement dans une pièce

VI faire de la contrebande

▸ **smuggle in VT SEP** *(on a large scale* ▸ *drugs, arms)* faire entrer *ou* passer en contrebande; *(as tourist* ▸ *cigarettes, alcohol)* introduire en fraude; *(into prison, classroom)* introduire clandestinement

▸ **smuggle out VT SEP** *(arms, drugs)* faire sortir en contrebande; *(when coming through customs)* faire sortir en fraude; *(from prison, classroom)* faire sortir clandestinement

smuggler ['smʌglə(r)] **N** contrebandier(ère) *m,f*

smuggling ['smʌglɪŋ] **N** *(of drugs, arms etc)* trafic *m*, contrebande *f*; *(when coming through customs)* fraude *f*

▸▸ ***smuggling operation*** opération *f* de contrebande

smugly ['smʌglɪ] **ADV** *(say)* d'un ton suffisant, avec suffisance; *(look, smile)* d'un air suffisant, avec suffisance

smugness ['smʌgnɪs] **N** suffisance *f*

smut [smʌt] **N 1** *(UNCOUNT) (obscenity)* cochonneries *fpl*; *(pornography)* porno *m*; **to talk s.** dire des cochonneries; **that book's/film's just s.** il n'y a que des cochonneries dans ce livre/film **2** *Br (speck of dirt)* poussière *f*; *(smudge of soot)* tache *f* de suie; **you've got a s. on your cheek** tu as de la suie sur la joue; **I've got a s. in my eye** j'ai une poussière dans l'œil **3** *Agr* charbon *m ou* nielle *f* du blé

smuttiness ['smʌtɪnɪs] **N** obscénité *f*

smutty ['smʌtɪ] *(compar* **smuttier,** *superl* **smuttiest) ADJ 1** *(obscene)* cochon; *(pornographic)* porno; **a book full of s. stories** un livre plein d'histoires cochonnes **2** *(dirty* ▸ *hands, face, surface)* sali, noirci

snack [snæk] **N 1** *(light meal)* casse-croûte *m inv*, en-cas *m inv*; **to have a s.** casser la croûte, manger un morceau; **if you eat too many snacks between meals...** si vous grignotez (trop) entre les repas...; **to have a s. lunch** déjeuner sur le pouce **2** *(usu pl) (appetizer* ▸ *crisps, peanuts etc)* amuse-gueule *m*

VI manger entre les repas; **I've been snacking on chocolates all day** j'ai passé la journée à grignoter des chocolats

▸▸ ***snack bar*** snack *m*, snack-bar *m*; ***snack food*** *(UNCOUNT)* amuse-gueules *mpl*

snaffle ['snæfəl] **VT 1** *Br Fam (get)* rafler; *(steal)* piquer, faucher; **who's snaffled my pen?** qui est-ce qui m'a piqué mon stylo? **2** *Horseriding* mettre un bridon à

N *Horseriding* mors *m* brisé, bridon *m*

▸▸ *Horseriding* ***snaffle bit*** mors *m* brisé, bridon *m*

▸ **snaffle up VT SEP** *Br Fam (bargains, cakes, prizes etc)* rafler

snafu ['snæfu:] *Fam* **ADJ** en pagaille, bordélique

VT *Am* mettre la pagaille *ou* le bordel dans

N *(confused situation)* pagaille *f*, bordel *m*; *(blunder)* grosse gaffe *f*

snag [snæg] *(pt & pp* **snagged,** *cont* **snagging) N 1** *(problem)* problème *m*, hic *m*; **to come across** *or* **to run into a s.** tomber sur un hic *ou* sur un os; **there are several snags in your plan** il y a plusieurs choses qui clochent dans ton projet; **that's the s.!** voilà le hic!; **the only s. is that you have to pay first** le seul problème, c'est qu'il faut payer d'abord

2 *(tear ▸ in garment)* accroc *m*; *(▸ in stocking)* fil *m* tiré

3 *(sharp protuberance)* aspérité *f*; *(tree stump)* chicot *m*; **I caught my dress on a s.** j'ai fait un accroc à ma robe

4 *Austr Fam (sausage)* saucisse□*f*

VT 1 *(tear ▸ cloth, garment)* faire un accroc à, déchirer; **she snagged her stocking on the brambles** elle a accroché son bas *ou* fait un accroc à son bas dans les ronces **2** *Am Fam (obtain)* dégoter; **I managed to s. a great prize in the raffle** j'ai réussi à décrocher un super lot à la tombola

VI s'accrocher; **the rope snagged on the ledge** la corde s'est trouvée coincée sur le rebord

snail [sneɪl] **N** escargot *m*; **at a s.'s pace** *(move)* comme un escargot; *(change, progress)* très lentement

▸▸ *Aut* ***snail cam*** came *f* en colimaçon; *Fam Hum* ***snail mail*** courrier *m* escargot, = courrier postal

snake [sneɪk] **N 1** *(reptile)* serpent *m* **2** *(person)* vipère *f*; **he's a real s.** c'est un faux jeton; **a s. in the grass** un faux jeton **3** *Econ* serpent *m* (monétaire)

VI serpenter, *Literary* sinuer; **the smoke snaked upwards** une volute de fumée s'élevait vers le ciel

VT the river/road snakes its way down to the sea le fleuve serpente/la route descend en lacets jusqu'à la mer

▸▸ ***snake charmer*** charmeur(euse) *m,f* de serpent; ***snake oil*** remède *m* de charlatan; *Am Fig* ***snake pit*** fosse *f* aux serpents, nid *m* de vipères

snakebite ['sneɪkbaɪt] **N 1** *(wound)* morsure *f* de serpent **2** *Fam (drink)* = boisson comprenant une mesure de bière et une mesure de cidre

snakeskin ['sneɪkskɪn] **N** peau *f* de serpent

COMP *(shoes, handbag)* en (peau de) serpent

snap [snæp] *(pt & pp* **snapped,** *cont* **snapping) N 1** *(of whip)* claquement *m*; *(of something breaking, opening, closing)* bruit *m* sec; **with a s. of his fingers** en claquant des doigts; **to open/to close sth with a s.** ouvrir/refermer qch d'un coup sec; **the branch broke with a s.** la branche a cassé avec un bruit sec

2 *(of jaws)* **to make a s. at sb/sth** essayer de mordre qn/qch; **the dog made a s. at the bone** le chien a essayé de happer l'os

3 *Fam (photo)* photo□*f*, instantané□*m*; **to take a s. of sb** prendre qn en photo; **holiday snaps** photos *fpl* de vacances

4 *Br Cards* ≃ bataille *f*; **to play s.** ≃ jouer à la bataille

5 *Met* **a cold s., a s. of cold weather** une vague de froid

6 *Fam (effort)* effort□*m*; *(energy)* énergie□*f*; **put some s. into it!** allez, mettez-y un peu de nerf!

7 *Am Fam (easy task)* **it's a s.!** c'est simple comme bonjour!

8 *Culin* biscuit *m*, petit gâteau *m* sec

9 *(clasp, fastener)* fermoir *m*; *(press stud)* bouton-pression *m*

10 *NEng Fam (food)* bouffe *f*

11 *(in American football)* remise *f* directe

ADJ 1 *(vote)* éclair; *(reaction)* immédiat; *(judgment)* irréfléchi, hâtif; **she made a s. decision to go to Paris** elle décida tout à coup d'aller à Paris; **the President made a s. decision to send troops** le Président décida immédiatement d'envoyer des troupes; **to call a s. election** procéder à une élection surprise **2** *Am Fam (easy)* facile□

VT 1 *(break)* casser net; **to s. sth in two** *or* **in half** casser qch en deux d'un coup sec

2 *(crack ▸ whip, fingers, rubber band)* faire claquer; **she snapped her case shut** elle ferma sa valise d'un coup sec; **she only needs to s. her fingers and he comes running** il lui suffit de claquer des doigts pour qu'il arrive en courant; **to s. one's fingers at sb** *(to gain attention)* faire claquer ses doigts pour attirer l'attention de qn; *(mockingly)* faire la nique à qn

3 *(say brusquely)* dire d'un ton sec *ou* brusque; **to s. an order at sb** lancer un ordre à qn d'un ton sec

4 *(seize ▸ gen)* saisir; *(▸ of dog)* happer; **she snapped the letter out of my hand** elle m'a arraché la lettre des mains

5 *Fam (photograph)* prendre une photo de□

VI 1 *(break ▸ branch)* se casser net *ou* avec un bruit sec, craquer; *(▸ elastic band)* claquer; *(▸ rope)* se casser, rompre; **to s. in two** se casser net

2 *(make cracking sound ▸ whip, fingers, jaw)* claquer; **to s. open/shut** s'ouvrir/se fermer avec un bruit sec *ou* avec un claquement; *Fam* **s. to it!** grouille-toi!, magne-toi!

3 *Fig (person, nerves)* craquer

4 *(speak brusquely)* **to s. at sb** parler à qn d'un ton sec; **there's no need to s.!** tu n'as pas besoin de me/lui/*etc* parler sur ce ton-là!

5 *(try to bite)* **to s. at** chercher à *ou* essayer de mordre; **the dog snapped at his ankles** le chien essayait de lui mordre les chevilles; **the fish snapped at the bait** les poissons cherchaient à happer l'appât; *Fig* **the taxmen were beginning to s. at his heels** les impôts commençaient à le talonner

6 *Fam (take photos)* **tourists snapping away with their cameras** des touristes qui n'arrêtent pas de prendre des photos□

EXCLAM *Br* **1** *Cards* **s.!** ≃ bataille! **2** *Fam (in identical situation)* **s.!** tiens!□, quelle coïncidence!□; **my mother's a teacher – s., so's mine!** ma mère est prof – tiens! la mienne aussi!

ADV to go s. casser net

▸▸ *Am* ***snap bean*** haricot *m* vert; ***snap fastener*** *(press stud)* bouton-pression *m*, pression *f*; *(clasp ▸ on handbag, necklace)* fermoir *m* (à pression)

▸**snap back VI 1** *(trigger, elastic)* revenir brusquement **2** *(reply brusquely)* répondre d'un ton sec

▸**snap off VT SEP** casser; *Fam Fig* **to s. sb's head off** envoyer promener qn

VI (se) casser net

▸**snap out VT SEP** *(question)* poser d'un ton sec; *(order, warning)* lancer brutalement

VI to s. out of *(out of depression, mood, trance)* se sortir de, se tirer de; *(out of temper)* dominer, maîtriser; **s. out of it!** *(out of depression)* secoue-toi!; *(out of bad temper)* arrête de t'énerver comme ça!

▸**snap up VT SEP 1** *(of dog, fish)* happer, attraper **2** *(bargain, offer, opportunity)* sauter sur, se jeter sur; **the books were snapped up in no time** les livres sont partis *ou* se sont vendus en un rien de temps; **the cakes/the best bargains were soon snapped up** les gâteaux sont partis/les meilleures affaires sont parties très vite **3** *Am Fam (idiom)* **s. it up!** dépêchons!

snapdragon ['snæpdrægən] **N** *Bot* muflier *m*, gueule-de-loup *f*

snapper ['snæpə(r)] *(pl* **inv** *or* **snappers) N** *Ich* vivaneau *m*

snappily ['snæpɪlɪ] **ADV 1** *(dress)* avec chic **2** *(act, converse)* vivement; *(work)* vite, sans traîner; *(reply)* d'un ton brusque

snappish ['snæpɪʃ] **ADJ** *(dog)* hargneux, toujours prêt à mordre; *(person)* hargneux; *(voice)* mordant, cassant; *(reply)* brusque, cassant, sec (sèche); **she's in a very s. mood today** elle n'est pas à prendre avec des pincettes aujourd'hui

snappishly ['snæpɪʃlɪ] **ADV** *(reply)* d'un ton hargneux

snappishness ['snæpɪʃnɪs] **N** hargne *f*

snappy ['snæpɪ] *(compar* **snappier,** *superl* **snappiest) ADJ 1** *(fashionable)* **she's a s. dresser** elle sait s'habiller **2** *(lively ▸ pace, rhythm)* vif, entraînant; *(▸ dialogue, debate)* plein d'entrain, vivant; *(▸ style, slogan)* qui a du punch; *(▸ reply)* bien envoyé; *Fam* **make it s.!** grouille-toi!, et que ça saute! **3** *(unfriendly ▸ person)* hargneux; *(▸ answer)* brusque; *(▸ voice)* cassant; **you're a bit s. today!** tu es de mauvais poil aujourd'hui!; **a s. little dog** un petit roquet

snapshot ['snæpʃɒt] **N 1** *Phot* instantané *m* **2** *Fig* portrait *m*; **the film is a s. of life in postwar London** le film est un portrait du Londres d'après-guerre

snare [sneə(r)] **N 1** *(in hunting)* lacet *m*, collet *m*; *Fig* piège *m*, traquenard *m*; **to lay** *or* **set a s.** *(for animal)* poser un collet; *Fig* tendre un piège; **to be caught in a s.** *(animal)* être pris au lacet; *Fig (person)* être pris au piège; *Literary* **the snares of love** les pièges *mpl* de l'amour **2** *Mus* caisse *f* claire

VT *(bird)* prendre au filet; *(animal)* prendre au collet *ou* au lacet; *Fig (person)* prendre au piège

▸▸ *Mus* ***snare drum*** caisse *f* claire

snarl [snɑːl] **VI 1** *(dog)* gronder, grogner; *(tiger)* feuler; *(person)* gronder; **the dog snarled at me as I walked past** le chien a grogné quand je suis passé; **the lions snarled at their tamer** les lions rugissaient contre leur dompteur; **there's no need to s. at me!** tu n'as pas besoin de prendre ce ton hargneux pour me parler! **2** *(thread, rope, hair)* s'emmêler; *(traffic)* se bloquer; *(plan, programme)* cafouiller

VT 1 *(of person)* lancer d'une voix rageuse, rugir; **to s. a reply** répondre d'une voix rageuse; **"go away!" he snarled** "va-t'en!", gronda-t-il **2** *(thread, rope, hair)* enchevêtrer, emmêler; **your hair is all snarled** tu as les cheveux tout emmêlés; **the wool is all snarled** la laine est tout enchevêtrée

N 1 *(sound)* grognement *m*, grondement *m*; *(of tiger)* feulement *m*; **to give a s.** *(dog)* pousser un grognement; *(tiger)* feuler; *(person)* gronder; **she answered him with a s.** elle lui a répondu d'un ton hargneux **2** *(tangle ▸ in thread, wool, hair)* nœud *m*, nœuds *mpl*; **caught in a s. of traffic** pris dans un embouteillage *ou* un bouchon

▸**snarl up VI** *(thread, rope, hair)* s'emmêler; *Br (traffic)* se bloquer; *(plan, programme)* cafouiller

VT SEP *(usu passive)* **1** *(thread, rope, hair)* emmêler, enchevêtrer; **to get snarled up** s'emmêler, s'enchevêtrer **2** *Br (traffic)* bloquer, coincer; *(plans)* faire cafouiller; **the traffic gets snarled up at the traffic lights** la circulation bouchonne aux feux; **the postal service is completely snarled up** le service des postes est complètement bloqué

snarling ['snɑːlɪŋ] **ADJ** grondant, grognant

N *(sound)* grondement *m*, grognement *m*

snarl-up N *Br (of traffic)* bouchon *m*, embouteillage *m*; *(of plans)* cafouillage *m*

snatch [snætʃ] **VT 1** *(seize ▸ bag, money)* saisir; *(▸ opportunity)* saisir, sauter sur; **to s. sth from sb** arracher qch à qn; **to s. sth from sb's hands** arracher qch des mains de qn; **a boy on a motorbike snatched her bag** un garçon en moto lui a arraché son sac; **his mother snatched him out of the path of the bus** sa mère l'a attrapé par le bras pour l'empêcher d'être renversé par le bus

2 *(manage to get ▸ meal, drink)* avaler à la hâte; *(▸ holiday, rest)* réussir à avoir; **to s. some sleep** réussir à dormir un peu; **I was only able to s. a sandwich** j'ai juste eu le temps d'avaler un sandwich; **to s. a glance at sb** lancer un coup d'œil furtif à qn

3 *(steal ▸ gen)* voler; *(▸ kiss)* voler, dérober; *(▸ victory)* décrocher; **she had her bag snatched** on lui a volé son sac

4 *(kidnap)* kidnapper

5 *(in weightlifting)* arracher

VI don't s.! *(to child ▸ from hand)* prends-le doucement!

N 1 *(grab)* geste *m* vif de la main *(pour attraper qch)*; **to make a s. at sth** essayer de saisir *ou* d'attraper qch

2 *Br Fam (robbery)* vol *m* à l'arraché□; **bag s.** vol *m* (de sac) à l'arraché; **to carry out a wages/jewellery s.** voler la paye/des bijoux□

3 *(kidnapping)* kidnapping *m*

4 *(fragment ▸ of conversation)* fragment *m*, bribes *fpl*; *(▸ of song, music)* fragment *m*, mesure *f*; *(▸ of poetry)* fragment *m*, vers *m*; **she could only catch a few snatches of their conversation/the song** elle ne put saisir que quelques bribes de leur conversation/quelques mesures de la chanson

5 *(short period)* courte période *f*; **to sleep in snatches** dormir par intervalles *ou* de façon intermittente; **to work in snatches** travailler par à-coups

6 *(in weightlifting)* arraché *m*

7 *Vulg (woman's genitals)* cramouille *f*, chatte *f*

▸▸ *Br* ***snatch squad*** = groupe de policiers chargé d'arrêter les meneurs (lors d'une manifestation)

▸**snatch at VT INSEP** *(try to grab)* essayer de saisir *ou* d'attraper; *Fig* **to s. at an opportunity** saisir une occasion (au vol)

▸**snatch away VT SEP** *(letter, plate etc)* arracher, enlever d'un geste vif; *(hope)* ôter, enlever; **to s. sth away from sb** arracher qch à qn; **victory was**

snatched away from them in the last minute la victoire leur a été soufflée à la dernière minute

▸**snatch up** VT SEP ramasser vite *ou* vivement *ou* d'un seul coup; **she snatched up her child** elle a saisi *ou* empoigné son enfant

snazzy ['snæzɪ] *(compar* **snazzier**, *superl* **snazziest**) ADJ *Fam* chicos *(inv)*, classe *(inv)*; **she's a s. dresser** elle s'habille avec chic□, elle est toujours bien sapée; **he's got a s. new suit** il s'est acheté un nouveau costume drôlement chic

sneak [sniːk] *(Br pt & pp* **sneaked**, *Am pt & pp* **sneaked** *or* **snuck** [snʌk]) VI **1** *(verb of movement)* se glisser, se faufiler; *(furtively)* se glisser furtivement; *(quietly)* se glisser à pas feutrés *ou* sans faire de bruit; *(secretly)* se glisser sans se faire remarquer; **to s. up/down the stairs** monter/descendre l'escalier furtivement; **to s. into/out of a room** entrer dans une pièce/sortir d'une pièce à pas feutrés; **he sneaked into her bedroom** il s'est glissé *ou* faufilé dans sa chambre; **we sneaked in at the back** nous nous sommes glissés dans le fond discrètement *ou* sans nous faire remarquer; **they sneaked into the cinema without paying** ils se sont introduits dans le cinéma sans payer; **we managed to s. past the guards/window** nous avons réussi à passer devant les gardes/la fenêtre sans nous faire remarquer

2 *Fam (tell tales)* cafter, cafarder; **to s. on sb** cafter qn, cafarder qn

VT **1** *(give ▸ letter, message)* glisser en douce *ou* sans se faire remarquer; **they sneaked the money to her** ils lui ont glissé l'argent en douce; **the visitor managed to s. him a knife** le visiteur réussit à lui glisser un couteau sans se faire remarquer; **she sneaked her boyfriend into her bedroom** elle fit entrer son petit ami en douce dans sa chambre

2 *(take)* enlever, prendre; **he sneaked the keys from her pocket** il a pris les clés dans sa poche sans qu'elle s'en aperçoive; **to s. a look at sth** lancer *ou* jeter un coup d'œil furtif à qch

3 *Fam (steal)* chiper, piquer, faucher

N **1** *Fam (devious person)* faux jeton *m* **2** *Br Fam (tell-tale)* cafardeur(euse) *m,f*, mouchard(e) *m,f* **3** *Am Fam* **sneaks** *(sneakers)* baskets□*fpl*

ADJ *(attack)* furtif

▸▸ ***sneak preview*** avant-première *f* privée; **I was given a s. preview of the new film** j'ai pu voir le nouveau film en avant-première; *Br* ***sneak thief*** chapardeur(euse) *m,f*

▸**sneak about, sneak around** VI *(move furtively)* rôder

▸**sneak away, sneak off** VI se défiler, s'esquiver

sneaker ['sniːkə(r)] N *Am* (chaussure *f* de) tennis *m ou f*, basket *f*

sneaking ['sniːkɪŋ] ADJ *(feeling, respect)* inavoué, secret(ète); **she had a s. suspicion that he was guilty** quelque chose lui disait qu'il était coupable; **she felt a s. admiration for him** elle ne pouvait (pas) s'empêcher de l'admirer; **I had a s. feeling that he was right** quelque chose me disait qu'il avait raison

sneaky ['sniːkɪ] *(compar* **sneakier**, *superl* **sneakiest**) ADJ *(person)* sournois; *(action)* fait en cachette, fait à la dérobée; **I caught him having a s. cigarette** je l'ai surpris en train de fumer une cigarette en cachette

sneer [snɪə(r)] VI ricaner, sourire avec mépris *ou* d'un air méprisant; **don't s.** ne sois pas si méprisant; **to s. at sb/sth** se moquer de qn/qch

N *(facial expression)* ricanement *m*, rictus *m*; *(remark)* raillerie *f*, sarcasme *m*; **"who do you think you are?" he said with a s.** "pour qui est-ce que tu te prends?", dit-il en ricanant *ou* ricana-t-il

sneerer ['snɪərə(r)] N ricaneur(euse) *m,f*, moqueur(euse) *m,f*

sneering ['snɪərɪŋ] ADJ ricaneur, méprisant

N *(UNCOUNT)* ricanement *m*, ricanements *mpl*

sneeringly ['snɪərɪŋlɪ] ADV *(look)* d'un air ricaneur, en ricanant; *(say)* d'un ton ricaneur, en ricanant

sneeze [sniːz] N éternuement *m*

VI éternuer; *Fam Fig* **an offer not to be sneezed at** une proposition qui n'est pas à dédaigner□*ou* sur laquelle il ne faut pas cracher

sneezing ['sniːzɪŋ] N *(UNCOUNT)* éternuement *m*; **his s. irritates me** ses éternuements m'agacent

▸▸ ***sneezing fit*** crise *f* d'éternuements; ***sneezing powder*** poudre *f* à éternuer

snick [snɪk] N **1** *(notch)* petite entaille *f*, encoche *f*; **to make a s. in sth** faire une entaille *ou* une encoche à qch **2** *(in cricket)* = coup (de batte) qui fait dévier la balle

VT **1** *(cloth, wood)* faire une petite entaille *ou* une encoche dans **2** *(in cricket ▸ ball)* couper

snicker ['snɪkə(r)] N **1** *(snigger)* ricanement *m* **2** *(of horse)* (petit) hennissement *m*

VI **1** *(snigger)* ricaner; **to s. at sb** se moquer de qn **2** *(horse)* hennir doucement

snide [snaɪd] ADJ *(sarcastic)* narquois, railleur; *(unfriendly)* inamical; **I've had enough of your s. remarks!** j'en ai assez de tes sarcasmes!; **a s. dig at his colleagues** une remarque désobligeante sur ses collègues

sniff [snɪf] VI **1** *(from cold, crying etc)* renifler **2** *(disdainfully)* faire la grimace *ou* la moue

VT **1** *(smell ▸ food, soap)* renifler, sentir l'odeur de; *(▸ rose, perfume)* humer, sentir l'odeur de; *(of dog)* renifler, flairer **2** *(inhale ▸ air)* humer, respirer; *(▸ smelling salts)* respirer; *(▸ cocaine)* sniffer, priser; *(▸ snuff)* priser; *(▸ glue)* respirer, sniffer **3** *(say disdainfully)* dire d'un air méprisant *ou* dédaigneux; **"it's not my cup," she sniffed** "ce n'est pas ma tasse", fit-elle d'un air méprisant

N *(gen)* reniflement *m*; **to give a s.** renifler; *(scornfully)* faire la grimace *ou* la moue; **"I've no idea," she said with a scornful s.** "je n'en ai aucune idée", dit-elle d'un air dédaigneux; **to have** *or* **to take a s. of sth** renifler *ou* flairer qch; **take a s. of this meat/this perfume** renifle-moi cette viande/ce parfum; *Fam* **one s. of that stuff is enough to knock you out** une bouffée de ce truc et tu tombes raide

▸**sniff at** VT INSEP **1 to s. at sth** *(of person)* renifler qch; *(of dog)* renifler *ou* flairer qch **2** *Fig* faire la grimace *ou* la moue devant; **their offer is not to be sniffed at** leur offre n'est pas à dédaigner

▸**sniff out** VT SEP *(of dog)* découvrir en reniflant *ou* en flairant; *(of person ▸ criminal)* découvrir, dépister; *(▸ secret)* découvrir

sniffer ['snɪfə(r)] N *(person ▸ gen)* renifleur(euse) *m,f*; **cocaine s.** = personne qui sniffe de la cocaïne

▸▸ ***sniffer dog*** chien *m* policier *(dressé pour le dépistage de la drogue ou des explosifs)*

sniffle ['snɪfəl] VI *(sniff)* renifler; *(have runny nose)* avoir le nez qui coule

N *(sniff)* (léger) reniflement *m*; *(cold)* petit rhume *m* de cerveau; *Fam* **to have the sniffles** avoir le nez qui coule□

sniffy ['snɪfɪ] *(compar* **sniffier**, *superl* **sniffiest**) ADJ *Fam* méprisant□, dédaigneux□; **to be s. about sth** faire le dédaigneux devant qch

snifter ['snɪftə(r)] N **1** *Br Fam (drink)* petit verre *m* (d'alcool)□; **fancy a s.?** tu prends un petit verre? **2** *Am (glass)* verre *m* à dégustation

snigger ['snɪgə(r)] VI ricaner, rire dans sa barbe; **to s. at** *(appearance)* se moquer de, ricaner à la vue de; **he sniggered at this suggestion** il a ricané en entendant cette suggestion

N ricanement *m*; **to give a s.** ricaner

sniggering ['snɪgərɪŋ] N *(UNCOUNT)* ricanements *mpl*

ADJ ricaneur

snip [snɪp] *(pt & pp* **snipped**, *cont* **snipping**) N **1** *(cut)* petit coup *m (de ciseaux etc)*, petite entaille *f ou* incision *f*; *Br Fam* **to have the s.** *(vasectomy)* se faire faire une vasectomie□

2 *(sound)* clic *m*; **he could hear the s. of scissors** il entendait le clic-clac de ciseaux

3 *(small piece ▸ of cloth, paper)* petit bout *m*; *(▸ of hair)* mèche *f* (coupée)

4 *Br Fam (bargain)* affaire□*f*, occase *f*

5 *Br Fam (cinch)* **it's a s.!** c'est du gâteau!, c'est simple comme bonjour!

VT couper *(en donnant de petits coups de ciseaux)*

VI **he was snipping at the hedge** il coupait la haie

▸**snip off** VT SEP couper *ou* enlever (à petits coups de ciseaux)

snipe [snaɪp] *(pl* **inv**) N *Orn* bécassine *f*

VI *(shoot)* tirer (d'une position cachée); **to s. at sb** tirer sur qn; *Fig (criticize)* critiquer qn par en-dessous

sniper ['snaɪpə(r)] N tireur *m* embusqué *ou* isolé; **killed by a s.'s bullet** abattu par un tireur (embusqué)

sniping ['snaɪpɪŋ] N *Mil* tir *m* d'embuscade; *Fig* critique *f* sournoise (**at sb** de qn)

ADJ *(criticism, remarks)* sournois

snippet ['snɪpɪt] N *(of material, paper)* petit bout *m*; *(of conversation, information)* bribe *f*; **a s. of news** une petite nouvelle

snit [snɪt] N *Am Fam* **to be in a s.** être fumasse *ou* furibard

snitch [snɪtʃ] *Fam* N **1** *(telltale)* cafard(e) *m,f*, cafteur(euse) *m,f* **2** *Br (nose)* blair *m*, tarin *m*

VI *(tell tales)* cafter, cafarder; **to s. on sb** cafter qn, cafarder qn

VT *(steal)* chiper, piquer, faucher

snivel ['snɪvəl] *(Br pt & pp* **snivelled**, *cont* **snivelling**, *Am pt & pp* **sniveled**, *cont* **sniveling**) VI *(whine)* pleurnicher; *(sniff because of cold)* renifler (continuellement); *(have runny nose)* avoir le nez qui coule; **stop snivelling!** *(crying)* arrête de pleurnicher comme ça!; *(sniffing)* arrête de renifler comme ça!

VT **"it wasn't my fault," he snivelled** "ce n'était pas de ma faute", fit-il en pleurnichant

N *(sniffing)* reniflement *m*, reniflements *mpl*; *(tears)* pleurnichements *mpl*; **to have a s.** pleurnicher

sniveller, *Am* **sniveler** ['snɪvələ(r)] N pleurnicheur(euse) *m,f*, pleurnichard(e) *m,f*

snivelling, *Am* **sniveling** ['snɪvəlɪŋ] ADJ pleurnicheur, larmoyant; **shut up, you s. little wretch!** tais-toi, espèce de pleurnicheur!

N *(UNCOUNT) (crying)* pleurnicheries *fpl*; *(sniffing because of cold)* reniflements *mpl*; **stop your s.!** *(tears)* arrête de pleurnicher comme ça!; *(sniffing)* arrête de renifler comme ça!

snob [snɒb] N snob *mf*; **she's an awful s./a bit of a s.** elle est terriblement/un peu snob; **to be an intellectual/a literary s.** être un snob intellectuel/en matière de littérature; **reverse** *or Br* **inverted s.** = personne d'origine modeste qui affiche un mépris pour les valeurs bourgeoises

snobbery ['snɒbərɪ] N snobisme *m*; **reverse** *or Br* **inverted s.** snobisme *m* à rebours; **intellectual s.** snobisme *m* intellectuel

snobbish ['snɒbɪʃ] ADJ snob

snobbishness ['snɒbɪʃnɪs] N snobisme *m*

snog [snɒg] *(pt & pp* **snogged**, *cont* **snogging**) *Br Fam* VI se bécoter, se rouler des pelles *ou* des patins

VT bécoter, rouler des pelles *ou* des patins à

N **to have a s.** se bécoter, se rouler des pelles *ou* des patins

snogging ['snɒgɪŋ] N *Br Fam* **there was a lot of s. going on** ça se bécotait dans tous les coins

snood [snuːd] N *(for hair)* résille *f*

snook [snuːk] N *(gesture)* pied *m* de nez; *Fam also Fig* **to cock a s. at sb** faire un pied de nez à qn

snooker ['snuːkə(r)] N **1** *(game)* = billard qui se joue avec 22 boules **2** *(shot)* snooker *m*

VT **1** *Br Fam (thwart)* mettre dans de beaux draps *ou* dans le pétrin, mettre dans l'embarras□; **if that doesn't work, we're snookered!** si ça marche pas, on est dans de beaux draps *ou* dans le pétrin! **2** *Am Fam (trick)* arnaquer, avoir; **they've got us snookered!** ils nous ont eus! **3** *(in game of snooker)* = mettre dans une position difficile en faisant un snooker

snoop [snuːp] *Fam* VI fourrer son nez dans les affaires des autres; **someone has been snooping about in my room** quelqu'un est venu fouiner dans ma chambre; **to s. on sb** espionner qn□; **he's always snooping around** il est toujours à se mêler des affaires des autres□*ou* de ce qui ne le regarde pas□

N **1** *(search)* **to have a s. around** fouiller, fouiner; **she had a good s. around the house** elle a fouillé *ou* fureté partout dans la maison **2** *(nosy person)* fouineur(euse) *m,f*

snooper ['snuːpə(r)] N *Pej* fouineur(euse) *m,f*

snoot [snuːt] N *Fam (nose)* blair *m*, tarin *m*, pif *m*

snooty ['snu:tɪ] (*compar* **snootier**, *superl* **snootiest**) **ADJ** *Fam (person)* bêcheur; *(restaurant)* snob; **she's very s.** c'est une bêcheuse

snooze [snu:z] **N 1** *Fam (nap)* petit somme▫ *m*, roupillon *m*; **to have a s.** faire un petit somme▫, piquer un roupillon; *(in afternoon)* faire la sieste▫ **2** *(on alarm clock)* (position *f*) sommeil *m*

VI *Fam* sommeiller▫, piquer un roupillon; *(in afternoon)* faire la sieste▫

►► ***snooze button*** bouton *m* de veille; ***snooze position*** *(on alarm clock)* (position *f*) sommeil *m*

snoozefest ['snu:zfest] **N** *Fam* **that history lecture was a total s.** ce cours d'histoire était hyper rasoir

snore [snɔ:(r)] **VI** ronfler

N ronflement *m*

snorer ['snɔ:rə(r)] **N** ronfleur(euse) *m,f*

snoring ['snɔ:rɪŋ] **N** *(UNCOUNT)* ronflement *m*, ronflements *mpl*

snorkel ['snɔ:kəl] (*Br pt & pp* **snorkelled**, *cont* **snorkelling**, *Am pt & pp* **snorkeled**, *cont* **snorkeling**) **N** *(of swimmer)* tuba *m*; *(on submarine)* schnorchel *m*, schnorkel *m*

VI nager sous l'eau *(avec un tuba)*

snort [snɔ:t] **VI 1** *(horse)* s'ébrouer; *(pig)* grogner; *(bull)* renâcler **2** *(person ► in anger)* grogner, ronchonner; **to s. with laughter** s'étouffer *ou* pouffer de rire; **he snorted in disbelief** il eut un petit grognement incrédule

VT 1 *(angrily)* grogner; *(laughingly)* dire en pouffant de rire; **"nonsense!" he snorted** "c'est absurde!", grommela-t-il **2** *Fam Drugs slang (cocaine)* sniffer

N 1 *(of bull, horse)* ébrouement *m*; *(of person)* grognement *m*; **the horse gave a loud s.** le cheval s'ébroua bruyamment; **he gave a s. of contempt** il poussa un grognement de mépris; **he gave a s. of laughter** il pouffa de rire **2** *Fam (drink)* petit verre *m* (d'alcool)▫ **3** *Fam Drugs slang (of drug)* **to have a s.** se faire une ligne

snorter ['snɔ:tə(r)] **N** *Br Fam* **1** *(as intensifier)* **her second serve was a s.** son deuxième service a été terrible; **a s. of a problem** un vrai casse-tête, un sacré problème; **he wrote them a real s. of a letter** il leur a écrit une vraie lettre d'engueulade **2** *(drink)* petit verre *m* (d'alcool)▫; **to have a s.** prendre un petit verre

snot [snɒt] **N** *Fam* **1** *(mucus)* morve▫ *f*; **2** *(person)* morveux(euse) *m,f*; **you pathetic little s.!** pauvre petit morveux!

►► ***snot rag*** tire-jus *m inv*, tire-moelle *m inv*

snotty ['snɒtɪ] (*compar* **snottier**, *superl* **snottiest**) **ADJ** *Fam* **1** *(nose, handkerchief)* morveux▫, plein de morve▫; *(face, child)* morveux▫ **2** *(haughty)* bêcheur, prétentiard; *(insolent)* insolent▫; **one of those incredibly s. officials** un de ces officiels qui pètent plus haut que leur cul

snout [snaʊt] **N 1** *(of pig)* groin *m*, museau *m*; *(of other animal)* museau *m*; *Fam Fig* **to have/get one's s. in the trough** avoir/prendre sa part du gâteau▫

2 *(projection)* saillie *f*; *(of gun)* canon *m*

3 *Fam Hum (nose)* pif *m*

4 *Br very Fam (cigarette)* sèche *f*, clope *m ou f*; *(tobacco)* tabac▫ *m*, foin *m*

5 *Br Fam (informer)* mouchard(e) *m,f*, indic *m*

snow [snəʊ] **N 1** *(gen)* neige *f*; **heavy s. is forecast** la météo prévoit d'abondantes chutes de neige; **the roads are covered with s.** les routes sont enneigées **2** *Fig (on screen)* neige *f* **3** *Fam Drugs slang (cocaine)* coco *f*, neige *f*; *(heroin crystals)* cristaux *mpl* d'héroïne▫

VI neiger; **it's snowing** il neige

VT *Am Fam (persuade)* **to s. sb into doing sth** baratiner qn pour qu'il fasse qch; **she snowed him into giving her the money** elle l'a embobiné pour qu'il lui donne l'argent

►► ***snow blindness*** cécité *f* des neiges; ***snow blower*** chasse-neige *m inv* à soufflerie; *Aut* ***snow chains*** chaînes *fpl* (à neige); ***snow cover*** couverture *f* neigeuse; ***snow fence*** pare-neige *m inv*; *Orn* ***snow goose*** oie *f* des neiges; ***snow hole*** *(in mountaineering)* trou *m* de neige; *Am Fam* ***snow job*** baratin *m*; **to give sb a s. job** baratiner qn, rouler qn dans la farine; ***snow leopard*** léopard *m* des neiges, once *f*; *Am* ***snow pea*** mange-tout *m inv*; ***snow route*** = artère sur laquelle il est interdit de stationner par temps de neige; ***snow scooter*** scooter *m* des neiges, motoski *m*, *Can* motoneige *f*; ***snow tyre*** pneu *m* neige

► **snow in VT SEP** **to be snowed in** être bloqué par la neige

► **snow under VT SEP** *Fig* **to be snowed under with work** être débordé *ou* complètement submergé de travail; **they're snowed under with applications/offers** ils ont reçu une avalanche de demandes/d'offres

► **snow up VT SEP** **to be snowed up** *(house, village, family)* être bloqué par la neige; *(road)* être complètement enneigé

snowball ['snəʊbɔ:l] **N 1** *(made of snow)* boule *f* de neige, *Can* balle *f* de neige; *Fam* **he hasn't a s.'s chance in hell** il n'a pas l'ombre d'une chance▫ **2** *(cocktail)* snowball *m (advokaat allongé de limonade)*

VI *Fig* faire boule de neige

►► ***snowball effect*** effet *m* boule de neige; ***snowball fight*** bataille *f* de boules de neige; **they had a s. fight** ils ont fait une bataille de boules de neige

snowbank ['snəʊbæŋk] **N** congère *f*

snowbike ['snəʊbaɪk] **N** motoski *m*

snowboard ['snəʊbɔ:d] **N** snowboard *m*, surf *m* des neiges

snowboarder ['snəʊbɔ:də(r)] **N** snowboarder *m*, snowboardeur(euse) *m,f*, surfeur(euse) *m,f* des neiges

snowboarding ['snəʊbɔ:dɪŋ] **N** snowboard *m*; **to go s.** faire du snowboard

snow-boot **N** après-ski *m*

snowbound ['snəʊbaʊnd] **ADJ** *(person, house, village)* bloqué par la neige; *(road)* enneigé

snowcap ['snəʊkæp] **N** sommet *m* couronné de neige

snow-capped [-kæpt] **ADJ** couronné de neige

snowdome ['snəʊdəʊm] **N 1** *(ornament)* boule *f* à neige **2** *(for skiing, snowboarding)* centre *m* de ski couvert

snowdrift ['snəʊdrɪft] **N** congère *f*

snowdrop ['snəʊdrɒp] **N** *Bot* perce-neige *m inv ou f inv*

snowfall ['snəʊfɔ:l] **N 1** *(snow shower)* chute *f* de neige **2** *(amount)* enneigement *m*

snowfield ['snəʊfi:ld] **N** champ *m* de neige

snowflake ['snəʊfleɪk] **N** *(of snow)* flocon *m* de neige

snowglobe ['snəʊgləʊb] **N** boule *f* à neige

snowline ['snəʊlaɪn] **N** limite *f* des neiges éternelles

snowman ['snəʊmæn] (*pl* **snowmen** [-men]) **N** bonhomme *m* de neige

snowmobile ['snəʊməbi:l] **N** scooter *m* des neiges, motoski *m*, *Can* motoneige *f*

snowpark ['snəʊpɑ:k] **N** snowpark *m*

snowplough, *Am* **snowplow** ['snəʊplaʊ] **N 1** *(vehicle, implement)* chasse-neige *m inv* **2** *(in skiing)* chasse-neige *m inv*

VI *(in skiing)* faire du chasse-neige

snowshoe ['snəʊʃu:] **N** raquette *f (pour marcher sur la neige)*

snowstorm ['snəʊstɔ:m] **N** tempête *f* de neige

snowsuit ['snəʊsu:t] **N** combinaison *f* de ski

snow-white **ADJ 1** *(in colour)* blanc (blanche) comme neige **2** *Fig* pur, innocent

snowy ['snəʊɪ] (*compar* **snowier**, *superl* **snowiest**) **ADJ 1** *(weather, region etc)* neigeux; *(countryside, roads etc)* enneigé, couvert *ou* recouvert de neige; *(day)* de neige; **a s. Christmas** un Noël enneigé **2** *Fig (hair, beard)* de neige; *(sheets, tablecloth)* blanc (blanche) comme neige

►► *Orn* ***snowy owl*** chouette *f* blanche, harfang *m*

SNP [,esen'pi:] **N** *(abbr* **Scottish National Party***)* = parti indépendantiste écossais fondé en 1934

snub [snʌb] (*pt & pp* **snubbed**, *cont* **snubbing**) **N** rebuffade *f*

VT *(person)* snober; *(offer, suggestion)* repousser (dédaigneusement); **to be snubbed** essuyer une rebuffade

ADJ *(nose)* retroussé

snub-nosed **ADJ** au nez retroussé

►► ***snub-nosed revolver*** revolver *m* au canon court

snuck [snʌk] *Am pt & pp of* **sneak**

snuff [snʌf] **N** tabac *m* à priser; **to take s.** priser; **a pinch of s.** une prise (de tabac)

VT 1 *(candle)* moucher

2 *Am Fam (murder)* buter, refroidir, zigouiller

3 *(sniff)* renifler, flairer

4 *Fam (idiom)* **to s. it** *(die)* calancher, passer l'arme à gauche

►► *Fam* ***snuff film***, ***snuff movie*** snuff movie *m*, = film pornographique au cours duquel un participant est réellement assassiné

► **snuff out VT SEP** *(candle)* éteindre, moucher *Fig (hope)* ôter, supprimer; *(rebellion)* étouffer *(enthusiasm)* briser

snuffbox ['snʌfbɒks] **N** tabatière *f (pour tabac à priser)*

snuffer ['snʌfə(r)] **N** *(candle)* **s.** éteignoir *m*

• **snuffers** **NPL** mouchettes *fpl*

snuffle ['snʌfəl] **VI 1** *(sniffle)* renifler **2** *(in speech)* parler du nez, nasiller

VT dire *ou* prononcer d'une voix nasillarde

N 1 *(sniffle)* reniflement *m*; **to have the snuffles** être un peu enrhumé **2** *(in speech)* voix *f* nasillarde; **to speak in a s.** parler d'une voix nasillarde

snug [snʌg] (*compar* **snugger**, *superl* **snuggest**) **ADJ 1** *(warm and cosy ► bed, room)* douillet (bien) confortable; *(►sleeping bag, jacket)* douillet, bien chaud; **a s. little house** une petite maison confortable; **it's very s. in this room** on est bien *ou* il fait bon dans cette pièce; **I wish I was home and s. in bed** j'aimerais être bien au chaud dans mon lit; *Fam* **to be (as) s. as a bug in a rug** être bien au chaud▫ **2** *(clothing)* bien ajusté; **it's a s. fit** *(clothing)* c'est bien ajusté; *(machine part etc)* ça s'emboîte parfaitement; **it's a bit of a s. fit, it's a bit too s.** *(too tight ► clothing)* c'est un peu trop serré **3** *(harbour)* bien abrité; *(hideout)* sûr

N *Br (in pub)* petite arrière-salle *f*

snuggery ['snʌgərɪ] (*pl* **snuggeries**) **N** *Br* petite pièce *f* douillette; *(in pub)* petite arrière-salle *f*

snuggle ['snʌgəl] **VI** se blottir, se pelotonner; **a village snuggling in the valley** un village niché dans la vallée

VT *(child, kitten)* serrer contre soi, câliner

N câlin *m*; **to have a s.** (se) faire un câlin

► **snuggle down VI** se blottir, se pelotonner; **to s. down under the blankets** s'enfouir sous les couvertures; **she snuggled down beside her mum** elle s'est blottie contre sa maman

► **snuggle up VI** **to s. up to sb** se blottir *ou* se serrer contre qn; **to s. up with a good book** s'installer bien confortablement avec un bon livre

snugly ['snʌglɪ] **ADV 1** *(cosily)* douillettement, confortablement; *(warmly)* bien au chaud; **soon they were settled s. by the fire** ils se retrouvèrent bientôt réunis autour d'un bon feu **2** *(in fit)* **the skirt fits s.** la jupe est très ajustée; **the two parts fit together s.** les deux pièces s'emboîtent parfaitement

So. **1** *(written abbr* **South***)* S **2** *(written abbr* **Southern***)* S

SO¹ [səʊ]

ADV	
• si **1, 2**	• tellement **1**
• aussi **2, 5**	• ainsi **6**
CONJ	
• donc **1**	• alors **1, 4–6**
• pour que **2**	• de même **3**

ADV 1 *(to such an extent ► before adjective or adverb)* si, tellement; *(► with verb)* tellement; **it's so easy** c'est si *ou* tellement facile; **I'm so glad to see you** ça me fait tellement plaisir *ou* je suis si content de te voir; **she makes me so angry** elle a le don de me mettre en colère; **I've never been so surprised in all my life** jamais de ma vie je n'avais eu une surprise pareille *ou* une telle surprise; **I have never seen so beautiful a sight** je n'ai jamais rien vu d'aussi beau; **she was so shocked (that) she couldn't speak** elle était tellement choquée qu'elle ne pouvait pas parler; **the problem was so complex (that) it baffled even the experts** l

roblème était si *ou* tellement complexe que ıême les experts ne comprenaient pas; **he's so ch that he doesn't know what he's worth** il est ri-he au point d'ignorer le montant de sa fortune; **ne so detests him that she won't even speak to m** elle le hait au point de refuser *ou* elle le dé-ste tellement qu'elle refuse de lui parler; **he as upset, so much so that he cried** il était boule-ersé, à tel point qu'il en a pleuré; **would you be kind as to carry my case?** auriez-vous l'amabi-té *ou* la gentillesse de porter ma valise?; **is it so ery hard to say you're sorry?** est-ce si difficile de emander pardon?; **you mustn't worry so** il ne ıut pas te faire du souci comme ça; **I loved her (much)** je l'aimais tant; **you do exaggerate so!** exagères tellement!; **I wish he wouldn't go on** j'aimerais qu'il arrête de radoter

2 *(in negative comparisons)* si, aussi; **I'm not so ure** je n'en suis pas si sûr; **it's not so bad, there's nly a small stain** ça n'est pas si grave que ça, il y a qu'une petite tache; **the young and the not young** les jeunes et les moins jeunes; **he's not handsome as his father/as all that** il n'est pas ussi beau que son père/si beau que ça; **he was not so ill (that) he couldn't go out** il n'était as malade au point de ne pas pouvoir sortir; **ne wouldn't be so stupid as to do that** elle ne se-ıit pas bête au point de faire cela, elle ne serait as assez bête pour faire cela

3 *(indicating an unspecified size, amount)* **the able is about so high/wide** la table est haute/ ırge comme ça à peu près; **a little girl so high** ne petite fille grande comme ça

4 *(referring to previous statement, question, word c)* **I believe/think/suppose so** je crois/pense/ ıppose (que oui); **I don't believe/think so** je ne rois/pense pas; **I don't suppose so** je suppose ue non; **he's clever – do you think so?** il est intel-gent – vous trouvez?; **I hope so** *(answering uestion)* j'espère que oui; *(agreeing)* j'espère ien, je l'espère; **I'm afraid so** j'en ai bien peur, je crains; **who says so?** qui dit ça?; **I told you so!** je ous l'avais bien dit!; **if so** si oui; **how/why so?** omment/pourquoi cela?; **perhaps so** peut-être ien; **quite so** tout à fait, exactement; **so I be-eve/see** c'est ce que je crois/vois; **so I've been old/he said** c'est ce qu'on m'a dit/qu'il a dit; **is he really ill? – so it seems** elle est donc vraiment ıalade? – à ce qu'il paraît; **I'm not very organ-ed – so I see!** je ne suis pas très organisé – c'est e que je vois!; **is that so?** vraiment?; **that is so** est vrai, c'est exact; **if that is so** si c'est le cas, il en est ainsi; **that being so** *(as this is the case)* uisqu'il en est ainsi; *(should this prove the case)* ans ces conditions; **isn't that Jane over there? – hy, so it is!** ce ne serait pas Jane là-bas? – mais (c'est elle)!; **he was told to leave the room and id so immediately** on lui a ordonné de quitter la ièce et il l'a fait immédiatement; **she was furi-us and understandably/and justifiably so** elle tait furieuse et ça se comprend/et c'est nor-ıal; **the same only more so** tout autant sinon lus; **he's very sorry – so he should be!** il est déso-é – c'est la moindre des choses *ou* j'espère ien!; **he thinks he can do it – so he can** il pense u'il peut le faire – en effet il le peut; **so help me od!** que Dieu me vienne en aide!; *Arch or Hum* **be it!** soit!, qu'il en soit ainsi!; *Fam* **I can so!** si, peux!ᵅ; *Fam* **I didn't say that! – you did so!** je ai pas dit ça! – si, tu l'as dit!ᵅ

5 *(likewise)* aussi; **we arrived early and so did he** ous sommes arrivés tôt et lui aussi; **if he can do , then so can I** s'il peut le faire, alors moi aussi; **ny shoes are Italian and so is my shirt** mes chaus-ures sont italiennes et ma chemise aussi

6 *(like this, in such a way)* ainsi; **hold the pen (like) o** tenez le stylo ainsi *ou* comme ceci; **any prod-ct so labelled is guaranteed lead-free** tous les roduits portant cette étiquette sont garantis ans plomb; **the laptop computer is so called be-ause...** l'ordinateur lap-top tient son nom e...; **the helmet is so constructed as to absorb ıost of the impact** le casque est conçu de façon amortir le choc; **it (just) so happens that...** il se rouve (justement) que... + *indicative*; **she likes verything (to be) just so** elle aime que tout soit arfait; **it has to be positioned just so or it won't go** ı il faut le mettre comme ça sinon ça n'entre pas

CONJ 1 *(therefore)* donc, alors; **the door was open, so I went in** la porte était ouverte, alors je suis entré; **she has a bad temper, so be careful** elle a mauvais caractère, donc faites attention

2 *(indicating purpose)* pour que + *subjunctive*, afin que + *subjunctive*; **give me some money so I can buy some sweets** donne-moi de l'argent pour que je puisse acheter des bonbons

3 *(in the same way)* de même; **as 3 is to 6, so 6 is to 12** le rapport entre 6 et 12 est le même qu'entre 3 et 6; **as he has lived so will he die** il mourra comme il a vécu

4 *(introductory remark)* **so then she left** alors elle est partie; **and so we come to the next question** et maintenant nous en venons à la question sui-vante; **so what's the problem?** alors, qu'est-ce qui ne va pas?; **so we can't go after all** donc nous ne pouvons plus y aller; **so, what do we do?** eh bien, qu'est-ce qu'on fait?

5 *(in exclamations)* alors; **so you're Anna's bro-ther!** alors (comme ça) vous êtes le frère d'An-na?; **so there you are!** vous voilà donc!; **so publish it!** eh bien *ou* alors allez-y, publiez-le!; *esp Am* **so long!** au revoir!

6 *(introducing a concession)* et alors; **so it costs a lot of money, we can afford it** ça coûte cher, et alors? on peut se le permettre; **so?** et alors?, et après?; **he'll be angry – so what?** il va se fâcher! – qu'est-ce que ça peut (me) faire *ou* et alors?; **so what if she does find out?** qu'est-ce que ça peut faire si elle s'en rend compte?

• **or so ADV** environ, à peu près; **it costs £5 or so** ça coûte environ 5 livres; **there were 30 or so people** il y avait 30 personnes environ *ou* à peu près, il y avait une trentaine de personnes

• **so as CONJ** *Fam* pour queᵅ + *subjunctive*, afin queᵅ + *subjunctive*; **give me some money so as I can buy some sweets** donne-moi de l'argent pour que je puisse acheter des bonbons

• **so as to CONJ** pour, afin de; **she went to bed early so as not to be tired the next day** elle s'est couchée tôt afin de *ou* pour ne pas être fatiguée le lendemain

• **so that CONJ 1** *(in order that)* pour que + *sub-junctive*, afin que + *subjunctive*; **they tied him up so that he couldn't escape** ils l'ont attaché afin qu'il *ou* pour qu'il ne s'échappe pas; **I took a taxi so that I wouldn't be late** j'ai pris un taxi pour *ou* afin de ne pas être en retard

2 *(with the result that)* si bien que + *indicative*, de façon à ce que + *indicative*; **she didn't eat enough, so that in the end she fell ill** elle ne mangeait pas assez, de telle sorte *ou* si bien qu'elle a fini par tomber malade; **the crates had fallen over so that we couldn't get past** comme les caisses étaient tombées, nous n'avons pas pu passer

• **so to speak, so to say ADV** pour ainsi dire

---

so[2] **N** *Mus* sol *m inv*

soak [səʊk] **VT 1** *(washing, food)* faire *ou* laisser tremper; **he soaked the shirts in warm water** il a fait tremper les chemises dans de l'eau chaude; **s. the prunes overnight** laisser tremper les pru-neaux toute la nuit; **to s. oneself (in the bath)** faire trempette dans la baignoire

2 *(drench ▸ person, dog etc)* tremper; **I got soaked waiting in the rain** je me suis fait tremper en at-tendant sous la pluie

3 *Fig (immerse)* imprégner; **to s. oneself in the history of a period** se plonger dans *ou* s'impré-gner de l'histoire d'une époque

4 *Fam (exploit ▸ by swindling)* rouler, arnaquer; *(▸ through taxation)* faire casquer; **to s. the rich** faire casquer les riches

VI *(washing)* tremper; **he put the washing (in) to s.** il a mis le linge à tremper; **to s. in the bath** faire trempette dans la baignoire

N 1 *(in water)* trempage *m*; **these shirts need a good s.** il faut laisser *ou* bien faire tremper ces chemises; **I had a nice long s. in the bath** je suis resté longtemps plongé dans un bon bain **2** *Fam (heavy drinker)* **(old) s.** soûlard(e) *m,f*, po-chard(e) *m,f*

▸ **soak in VI 1** *(water)* pénétrer, s'infiltrer **2** *Fam Fig (comment, news)* faire son effetᵅ; **she told me what happened, but it hasn't soaked in yet** elle m'a dit ce qui s'est passé, mais je n'ai pas encore vraiment bien comprisᵅ

▸ **soak through VI** *(liquid)* filtrer au travers, s'in-filtrer

▸ **soak up VT SEP 1** *(absorb)* absorber; **we spent a week soaking up the sun** nous avons passé une semaine à lézarder *ou* à nous faire dorer au so-leil; **to s. up the atmosphere** s'imprégner de l'at-mosphère; **they come to Europe to s. up the culture** ils viennent en Europe pour s'imbiber de culture **2** *Fam Hum (drink)* **he can really s. it up** il peut vraiment boire comme un trou

soaked [səʊkt] **ADJ** trempé; *(ground)* détrempé; *Fig (immersed)* imprégné; **to be s. through** *or* **to the skin** être trempé jusqu'aux os; **his shirt was s. with** *or* **in blood/sweat** sa chemise était maculée de sang/trempée de sueur

soaking ['səʊkɪŋ] **ADJ** trempé; **I'm s. (wet)!** je suis trempé jusqu'aux os!

N 1 *(gen)* trempage *m*; **these clothes need a good s.** il faut laisser tremper ces vêtements **2** *Fam (in rain)* **to get a s.** se faire tremperᵅ *ou* saucer **3** *Fam (financial loss)* perte *f* financièreᵅ; **we got a real s. on the stock market** on a vraiment beaucoup perdu à la Bourseᵅ

▸▸ ***soaking solution*** *(for contact lenses)* solution *f* de trempage

so-and-so *(pl* **so-and-sos)** **N** *Fam* **1** *(referring to stranger)* untel *m*, unetelle *f*; **Mr s.** Monsieur Un-tel; **Mrs s.** Madame Unetelle **2** *(annoying person)* **you little s.!** espèce de petit minable!; **the old s.!** *(angry)* le salaud!; *(admiring, surprised)* le bou-gre!; **you greedy old s.!** espèce de gourmand!

soap [səʊp] **N** *(UNCOUNT)* **1** *(gen)* savon *m*

2 *Fam (flattery)* flagornerieᵅ*f*, flatterie(s)ᵅ*f(pl)*

3 *Fam Rad & TV* soap operaᵅ*m*, feuilleton *m* (populaire)ᵅ

4 *Am Fam (idiom)* **no s.!** des clous!, des nèfles!

VT savonner

▸▸ ***soap bubble*** bulle *f* de savon; *Rad & TV* ***soap opera*** feuilleton *m* (populaire), soap opera *m*; ***soap powder*** lessive *f* (en poudre), poudre *f* à la-ver; ***soap star*** vedette *f* de soap opera

> **SOAP OPERAS**
>
> Les "soap operas" (ou "soaps") (feuilletons télévisés ou radiophoniques) sont une véri-table institution en Grande-Bretagne. Les premiers furent diffusés à la radio dans les années 1940 et 1950 – le feuilleton radio-phonique The Archers est diffusé par la BBC depuis 1951. Les feuilletons télévisés les plus connus sont Coronation Street (dont l'action se situe dans le Nord de l'An-gleterre, diffusé depuis 1960) et EastEnders (diffusé sur BBC1 depuis le milieu des an-nées 80) qui suit la vie de personnages de l'East End londonien. Certains soap operas venus de l'étranger ont également du suc-cès auprès du public, notamment les feuil-letons australiens Neighbours et Home and Away. Les vedettes de soap operas acquièrent souvent le statut de célébrités nationales; les tabloïds et les magazines de presse people sont très friands de toute anecdote les concernant. Le terme "soap opera" (littéralement "opéra-savon") est d'origine américaine. Il s'explique par le fait qu'au départ ces feuilletons diffusés pen-dant la journée pour un public presque uni-quement composé de femmes au foyer étaient financés par des marques de déter-gents.

▸ **soap down VT SEP** savonner; **to s. oneself down** se savonner

soapbox ['səʊpbɒks] **N 1** *(container)* caisse *f* à sa-von; *Fig (for speaker)* tribune *f* improvisée *ou* de fortune; *Fig* **to get up on a s.** faire un discours im-provisé, haranguer les foules; *Fig* **get off your s.!** ne monte pas sur tes grands chevaux! **2** *(go-kart)* chariot *m*, ≃ kart *m (sans moteur)*

COMP *Pej (oratory)* de démagogue; **he's just a s. orator** ce n'est qu'un harangueur

soapdish ['səʊpdɪʃ] **N** porte-savon *m*

soap-dodger N *Br Fam Hum (man)* mec *m* cra-dingue; *(woman)* bonne femme *f* cradingue

soapflakes ['səʊpfleɪks] **NPL** paillettes *fpl* de sa-von, savon *m* en paillettes

soapiness ['səʊpɪnɪs] **N** caractère *m* savonneux

soapstone ['səʊpstəʊn] **N** stéatite *f*

soapsuds ['səʊpsʌdz] **NPL** *(foam)* mousse *f* de savon; *(soapy water)* eau *f* savonneuse

soapy ['səʊpɪ] *(compar* **soapier,** *superl* **soapiest)** **ADJ 1** *(water, hands, surface)* savonneux; *(taste)* de savon **2** *Fam Fig (person, manner, voice)* onctueux□, mielleux□

soar [sɔː(r)] **VI 1** *(bird, plane ▸ rise)* monter en flèche; *(▸ glide)* planer *(en utilisant les courants ascendants)*; *(flames)* jaillir; **to s. into the sky** *or* **the air** *(bird, balloon etc)* s'élever dans les airs; **the ball soared over the fence/our heads** le ballon s'est envolé au-dessus de la clôture/de nos têtes; **the jet soared above us** l'avion est monté en flèche au-dessus de nous
2 *(spire)* s'élancer vers le ciel; *(mountain)* s'élever vers le ciel; **the mountain seemed to s. into the clouds** la montagne paraissait s'élancer dans les nuages
3 *(temperature, profits, prices etc)* grimper en flèche; *(suddenly)* faire un bond
4 *(spirits)* remonter en flèche; *(hopes)* grandir démesurément; *(reputation)* monter en flèche
5 *(sound, music)* s'élever

soaring ['sɔːrɪŋ] **ADJ 1** *(bird, glider)* qui s'élève dans le ciel; *(spire, tower)* qui s'élance vers le ciel; *(mountain)* qui s'élève vers le ciel; **the s. flight of the eagle** le vol majestueux de l'aigle **2** *(prices, inflation)* qui monte *ou* qui grimpe en flèche; *(hopes, reputation)* grandissant
N *(of bird)* essor *m*, élan *m*; *(of plane)* envol *m*; *(of prices)* envolée *f*, explosion *f*

sob¹, SOB [ˌesəʊ'biː] **N** *Am very Fam (abbr* **son of a bitch)** salaud *m*, fils *m* de pute

sob² [sɒb] *(pt & pp* **sobbed,** *cont* **sobbing)** **N** sanglot *m*; **"it wasn't me," he said with a s.** "ce n'est pas moi", dit-il en sanglotant; **with a s. in her voice** la voix étouffée par un sanglot
VI sangloter
VT to s. oneself to sleep s'endormir à force de sangloter *ou* en sanglotant; **"I can't remember," he sobbed** "je ne me rappelle pas", dit-il en sanglotant
▸▸ *Am Fam* ***sob sister*** = journaliste qui fait le courrier du cœur; *Fam Pej* ***sob story*** histoire *f* larmoyante□, histoire *f* à vous fendre le cœur□; **he told us some s. story about his deprived childhood** il a cherché à nous apitoyer en nous parlant de son enfance malheureuse□; *Fam Pej* ***sob stuff*** sensiblerie□*f*, mélo *m*

▸**sob out VT SEP** raconter en sanglotant; **to s. one's heart out** sangloter de tout son corps, pleurer à gros sanglots

sobbing ['sɒbɪŋ] **N** *(UNCOUNT)* sanglots *mpl*; **stop your s.** arrête de sangloter
ADJ sanglotant

sober ['səʊbə(r)] **ADJ 1** *(not drunk)* **are you sure he was s.?** tu es sûr qu'il n'avait pas bu?; **he's never s.** il est toujours ivre; **to be as s. as a judge** *(serious)* être sérieux comme un pape; *(temperate)* être sobre comme un chameau
2 *(sobered up)* dessoûlé; **wait until he's s. again** attends qu'il dessoûle
3 *(moderate ▸ person)* sérieux, posé, sensé; *(▸ attitude, account, opinion)* modéré, mesuré; *(▸ manner)* sérieux, posé
4 *(serious, solemn ▸ atmosphere, occasion)* solennel, plein de solennité; *(▸ expression)* grave, plein de gravité; *(▸ voice)* grave, empreint de gravité; *(▸ reminder)* solennel; **you're in (a) s. mood** vous êtes d'humeur bien solennelle
5 *(subdued ▸ colour, clothing)* discret(ète), sobre; **he was wearing a s. blue tie** il portait une cravate d'un bleu sobre; **of s. appearance** d'aspect sobre
6 *(plain ▸ fact, reality)* (tout) simple; *(▸ truth)* simple, tout nu; *(▸ tastes)* simple, sobre; **the s. fact is...** le fait est que... + *indicative*
VT *(calm)* calmer, assagir

▸**sober down VI** *(calm down)* se calmer, s'assagir
VT SEP *(calm)* calmer, assagir

▸**sober up VI** dessoûler
VT SEP dessoûler

sobering ['səʊbərɪŋ] **ADJ it's a s. thought** cela donne à réfléchir; **what she said had a s. effect on everyone** ce qu'elle a dit donnait à réfléchir à tous

sober-minded ADJ *(serious)* sérieux, réfléchi

soberness ['səʊbənɪs] **N 1** *(non-drunkenness)* sobriété *f* **2** *(of style, dress, character)* sobriété *f*; *(seriousness)* sérieux *m*

sobersides ['səʊbəsaɪdz] **N** *Br Fam* **he's a real s.** c'est un vrai bonnet de nuit

sobriety [səʊ'braɪətɪ] **N 1** *(non-drunkenness)* sobriété *f*
2 *(moderation ▸ of person)* sobriété *f*, sérieux *m*; *(▸ of opinion, judgement)* mesure *f*, modération *f*; *(▸ of manner, style, tastes)* sobriété *f*
3 *(solemnity ▸ of occasion)* solennité *f*; *(▸ of voice)* ton *m* solennel *ou* grave; *(▸ of mood)* sobriété *f*
4 *(of colour, dress)* sobriété *f*

Soc [sɒk] **N** *(abbr* **Society)** ≃ club *m* *(abréviation utilisée dans la langue parlée notamment par les étudiants pour désigner les différents clubs universitaires)*

SOCA ['səʊkə] **N** *Br (abbr* **Serious Organised Crime Agency)** = organisme gouvernemental de lutte contre le crime organisé

so-called [-kɔːld] **ADJ 1** *(supposed)* soi-disant *(inv)*, prétendu; **his s. aunt** sa soi-disant tante; **s. social workers** des soi-disant assistants *mpl* sociaux; **her s. boudoir** son boudoir, comme elle l'appelle; **s. progress** de prétendus progrès *mpl* **2** *(so named)* appelé ainsi, ainsi nommé; **the s. temperate zone** la zone dite tempérée

soccer ['sɒkə(r)] **N** football *m*, foot *m*
COMP *(pitch, match, team)* de football, de foot; *(supporter)* d'une équipe de foot
▸▸ ***soccer hooligans*** hooligans *mpl (lors de matchs de football)*; ***soccer player*** footballeur (euse) *m,f*

sociability [ˌsəʊʃə'bɪlətɪ] **N** sociabilité *f*

sociable ['səʊʃəbəl] **ADJ 1** *(enjoying company)* sociable, qui aime la compagnie (des gens); *(friendly)* sociable, amical; *(evening)* amical, convivial; **try to be more s.** *(go out more)* essaie de sortir un peu et de rencontrer des gens; *(mix more)* essaie d'être un peu plus sociable; **I had a drink with them to be s.** j'ai pris un verre avec eux pour me montrer sociable; **I'm not in a s. mood** je ne suis pas d'humeur sociable, je n'ai pas envie de voir du monde **2** *(in sociology) & Zool* sociable
N *Am* fête *f*

sociably ['səʊʃəblɪ] **ADV** *(behave)* de manière sociable, amicalement; *(say)* amicalement

social ['səʊʃəl] **ADJ 1** *(background, behaviour, conditions, reform, tradition)* social; *(phenomenon)* social, de société; **to bow to s. pressures** se plier aux pressions sociales; **they are our s. equals** ils sont de même condition sociale que nous; *Hum* **it's s. death to wear such clothes there** plus personne ne te connaît si tu t'habilles comme ça pour y aller; **they move in high** *or* **the best s. circles** ils évoluent dans les hautes sphères de la société
2 *(in society ▸ activities)* mondain; *(leisure)* de loisir *ou* loisirs; **his life is one mad s. whirl** il mène une vie mondaine insensée
3 *(evening, function)* amical; **it was the s. event of the year** c'était l'événement mondain de l'année; **to pay someone a s. call** faire à quelqu'un une visite amicale
4 *Zool* social; **man is a s. animal** l'homme est un animal social
N soirée *f* (dansante)
▸▸ ***social anthropologist*** spécialiste *mf* d'anthropologie sociale; ***social anthropology*** anthropologie *f* sociale; ***social behaviourism*** béhaviorisme *m* social; ***social benefits*** prestations *fpl* sociales; *EU* ***the Social Chapter*** le volet social *(du traité de Maastricht)*; *EU* ***Social Charter*** Charte *f* sociale; ***social class*** classe *f* sociale; ***social cleansing*** = élimination ou expulsion des éléments indésirables de la société; ***social climber*** arriviste *mf*; ***social climbing*** arrivisme *m*; ***social club*** club *m*; ***social conscience*** conscience *f* sociale; **to have a s. conscience** avoir conscience des problèmes sociaux; ***social contract*** contrat *m* social; ***social democracy*** **1** *(system)* social-démocratie *f* *(country)* démocratie *f* socialiste; **we live in a s. democracy** nous vivons dans une démocra[tie] socialiste; ***social democrat*** social(e)-démocra[te] *m,f*; ***social democratic*** social-démocrate; ***Soc[ial] Democratic and Labour Party*** = parti travaillis[te] d'Irlande du Nord; ***Social Democratic Party*** Pa[rti] *m* social-démocrate; ***social disease*** *(gen)* malad[ie] *f* provoquée par des facteurs socio-écono[mi]ques; *Euph (venereal)* maladie *f* vénérienne; ***s[o]cial drinker*** = personne qui ne boit d'alcool qu'[en] société; **he's purely a s. drinker** il ne boit pas se[ul,] il boit seulement en société *ou* en compagni[e;] ***social drinking*** = consommation d'alcool lors [de] réunions entre amis; ***social engineering*** manip[u]lation *f* des structures sociales; ***social enterpri[se]*** entreprise *f* d'économie sociale; ***social fund*** caisse *f* d'aide sociale; ***social graces*** bonnes m[a]nières *fpl*; ***social historian*** spécialiste *mf* d'hi[s]toire sociale; ***social history*** histoire *f* social[e;] ***social housing*** logements *mpl* sociaux; ***social [in]surance*** *(UNCOUNT)* prestations *fpl* sociales; ***s[o]cial integration*** insertion *f* *ou* intégration sociale; ***social justice*** justice *f* sociale; ***social li[fe]*** vie *f* mondaine; **to have a busy s. life** sortir bea[u]coup; **he doesn't have much of a s. life** il ne so[rt] pas beaucoup; **work is getting in the way of r[ny] s. life** j'ai trop de travail pour pouvoir sort[ir;] **there isn't much of a s. life in this town** les ge[ns] ne sortent pas beaucoup dans cette ville, il [ne] se passe rien dans cette ville; ***social mobility*** m[o]bilité *f* sociale; ***social networking*** = fait de constituer un réseau social; *Comput* ***social n[et]working site*** site *m* de réseaux sociaux; ***social [or]der*** ordre *m* social; ***social outcast*** paria *m*; ***soc[ial] ownership*** propriété *f* collective; ***social positi[on]*** rang *m* dans la société; ***social psychology*** ps[y]chologie *f* sociale, psychosociologie *f*; ***soc[ial] realism*** réalisme *m* social; *Am* ***Social Register*** Bottin® *m* mondain; ***social rights*** droits *mpl* s[o]ciaux; ***social science*** sciences *fpl* humaines; ***s[o]cial scientist*** spécialiste *mf* des scienc[es] humaines; ***social secretary*** *(of organization)* = s[e]crétaire chargé d'organiser les événemen[ts] mondains; *(personal secretary)* secrétaire particulier(ère); ***social security*** *(UNCOUNT)* *(gen)* prestations *fpl* sociales; **to be on s. securi[ty]** toucher une aide sociale **2** *Br (money paid to u[n]employed)* ≃ allocations *fpl* de chômage; *Am* ***S[o]cial Security Administration*** ≃ Sécurité *f* social[e;] ***social security benefits*** prestations *fpl* sociale[s;] ***social security contribution*** prélèvement *m* s[o]cial; *Am* ***social security number*** numéro *m* de S[é]curité sociale; ***social security system*** régime *m* [de] Sécurité sociale; ***social services*** services *mpl* s[o]ciaux; ***social skills*** = manière de se comporter [en] société; **to have good/poor s. skills** être à l'ais[e/] ne pas être à l'aise en société; **he has no s. ski[lls]** il ne sait pas comment se comporter en sociét[é;] *Comput* ***social software*** logiciel *m* social, logic[iel] *m* relationnel; ***social spending*** *(UNCOUNT)* d[é]penses *fpl* sociales; ***social structure*** structur[e] sociale; ***social studies*** sciences *fpl* sociales; ***s[o]cial unrest*** *(UNCOUNT)* *(discontent)* malaise social; *(disorder)* troubles *mpl* sociaux; ***soc[ial] welfare*** protection *f* sociale; ***social welfare sy[s]tem*** système *m* *ou* régime *m* de protection s[o]ciale; ***social work*** assistance *f* sociale, travail social; ***social worker*** assistant(e) *m,f* social(e), travailleur(euse) *m,f* social(e)

socialism ['səʊʃəlɪzəm] **N** socialisme *m*

socialist ['səʊʃəlɪst] **ADJ** socialiste
N socialiste *mf*
▸▸ ***socialist economy*** économie *f* socialiste; *Art [&] Literature* ***Socialist Realism*** réalisme *m* socialist[e]

socialite ['səʊʃəlaɪt] **N** mondain(e) *m,f*, pe[r]sonne *f* qui fréquente la haute société; **she's famous s.** elle est connue pour fréquenter bea[u]coup la haute société

socialize, -ise ['səʊʃəlaɪz] **VI** *(go out)* sortir, fr[é]quenter des gens; *(make friends)* se faire d[es] amis; **to s. with sb** fréquenter qn; **she used to s[ocialize a] lot when she was at college** elle sortait beauco[up] quand elle était étudiante; **he finds it difficult [to] s.** il a du mal à lier connaissance, il est très p[eu] sociable
VT *Pol & Psy* socialiser
▸▸ *Am* ***socialized medicine*** médecine *f* socialis[ée]

ocially [ˈsəʊʃəlɪ] ADV socialement; **s. acceptable behaviour** comportement *m* socialement acceptable; **we've never met s.** on ne s'est jamais rencontrés en société; **I saw her s. for a while, but nothing beyond that** je l'ai vaguement fréquentée pendant un temps, mais rien de plus; **to be s. inadequate** ne pas être doué pour les relations avec les gens; **s. inferior** socialement inférieur; **s. disadvantaged** défavorisé

ociety [səˈsaɪətɪ] *(pl* **societies***)* N **1** *(social community)* société *f*; **it is a danger to s.** cela constitue un danger pour la société; **woman's place in s.** la place de la femme dans la société

2 *(nation, group)* société *f*; **primitive/industrial societies** des sociétés *fpl* primitives/industrielles; **Western s.** la société occidentale

3 *(fashionable circles)* **(high) s.** la haute société, le (beau *ou* grand) monde; **to make one's debut in s.** faire ses débuts dans le monde

4 *Literary (company)* société *f*, compagnie *f*; **to avoid the s. of sb** éviter la société de qn; **in polite s.** dans la bonne société *ou* le (beau) monde

5 *(association, club)* société *f*, association *f*; *(for sports)* club *m*, association *f*; *Sch & Univ (for debating, study etc)* société *f*; **charitable s.** œuvre *f* de charité, association *f* caritative

COMP *(gossip, news, wedding)* mondain; *(hostess)* de soirées mondaines; **a s. man/woman** un homme/une femme du monde, un mondain/une mondaine; *Press* **the s. column** la chronique mondaine

►► ***the Society of Friends*** la Société des Amis *(les Quakers)*; ***the Society of Jesus*** la Compagnie de Jésus; ***the Society for the Protection of the Unborn Child*** = ligue américaine contre l'avortement

> Note that the French word **société** is also used as a translation for the English words **company** and **firm**.

ociocultural [ˌsəʊsɪəʊˈkʌltʃərəl] ADJ socioculturel

ocioeconomic [ˈsəʊsɪəʊˌiːkəˈnɒmɪk] ADJ socio-économique

►► *Mktg* ***socioeconomic classification*** classification *f* socioprofessionnelle; ***socioeconomic group*** groupe *m* socio-économique

ociolinguistic [ˌsəʊsɪəʊlɪŋˈgwɪstɪk] ADJ sociolinguistique

ociolinguistics [ˌsəʊsɪəʊlɪŋˈgwɪstɪks] N *(UNCOUNT)* sociolinguistique *f*

ociological [ˌsəʊsɪəˈlɒdʒɪkəl] ADJ sociologique

ociologist [ˌsəʊsɪˈɒlədʒɪst] N sociologue *mf*

ociology [ˌsəʊsɪˈɒlədʒɪ] N sociologie *f*

ociometry [ˌsəʊsɪˈɒmɪtrɪ] N sociométrie *f*

ociopath [ˌsəʊsɪəʊˈpæθ] N sociopathe *mf*

ocioprofessional [ˌsəʊsɪəʊprəˈfeʃənəl] ADJ socioprofessionnel

►► ***socioprofessional group*** catégorie *f* socioprofessionnelle, CSP *f*

ock [sɒk] N **1** *(garment)* chaussette *f*; *Fam* **it'll knock your socks off!** tu vas tomber à la renverse!; *Fam* **to pull one's socks up** se secouer (les puces); *Br Fam* **to put a s. in it** la fermer, la boucler

2 *(insole)* semelle *f* (intérieure)

3 *Aviat & Met* **(wind) s.** manche *f* à air

4 *Fam (blow)* beigne *f*, châtaigne *f*; **she gave him a s. in the face** elle lui a filé une beigne; **I got a s. on the jaw** j'ai pris une beigne

VT *Fam (hit)* filer une beigne *ou* une châtaigne à; **she socked him in the face** elle lui a filé une beigne dans la tronche; **they socked me over the head with a cosh** ils m'ont flanqué un coup de matraque sur la tête; **s. it to him!, s. him one!** fous-lui une beigne!, cogne-le!; *Fig* **s. it to them!** vas-y, montre-leur ce que tu sais faire!, vas-y, donne le maximum!; **s. it to me, then!** allez, accouche!

ocket [ˈsɒkɪt] N **1** *Elec (for bulb)* douille *f*; *Br (in wall)* prise *f* (de courant)

2 *Tech* cavité *f*; *(in carpentry)* mortaise *f*; **it fits into a s.** ça s'emboîte dans un support prévu à cet effet

3 *Comput (slot)* prise *f* (femelle); *(on Internet)* socket *f*, port *m*

4 *Anat (of arm, hipbone)* cavité *f* articulaire; *(of tooth)* alvéole *f*; *(of eye)* orbite *f*; **her arm was pulled out of its s.** elle a eu l'épaule luxée; *Fig* **her eyes almost popped** *or* **jumped out of their sockets** les yeux lui en sont presque sortis de la tête

►► ***socket joint*** **1** *(in carpentry)* joint *m* à rotule **2** *Anat* énarthrose *f*; ***socket set*** coffret *m* de douilles; ***socket wrench*** clef *f* à douille

Socrates [ˈsɒkrətiːz] PR N Socrate

Socratic [sɒˈkrætɪk] ADJ socratique

►► ***Socratic irony*** ironie *f* socratique

sod [sɒd] *(pt & pp* **sodded**, *cont* **sodding***)* N **1** *Br very Fam (obnoxious person)* enfoiré(e) *m,f*, con (conne) *m,f*; **the stupid s.!** tu parles d'un enfoiré!; **you (rotten) s.!** espèce de saligaud!; **he's a real s.!** c'est un salopard!

2 *Br very Fam (fellow)* bougre *m*, con *m*; **poor s.** le pauvre con

3 *Br very Fam (difficult or unpleasant thing)* saloperie *f*; **it's a s. of a job** c'est un boulot vraiment chiant; **these screws are real sods to get out** ces vis sont vraiment emmerdantes *ou* chiantes à enlever

4 *Br very Fam* **s. all** que dalle; **they do s. all all day** ils n'en fichent pas une rame de la journée; **s. all money** pas d'argent du tout; **there's s. all to eat** il y a que dalle à bouffer; **they've got s. all hope of winning** ils n'ont pas une putain de chance de gagner

5 *(of turf)* motte *f* (de gazon); *(earth and grass)* terre *f*; *(lawn)* gazon *m*; **to cut** *or* **turn the first s.** donner le premier coup de bêche; **under the s.** *(buried)* enterré

VT *Br very Fam* **s. it!** merde!; **s. him!** qu'il aille se faire foutre!; **s. the expense, let's just go!** tant pis si ça coûte cher, allons-y!

►► *Br Fam* ***Sod's law*** la loi de l'emmerdement maximum; **that's S.'s law!** c'est la poisse!

►**sod off** VI *Br very Fam* foutre le camp, dégager; **s. off!** fous le camp!, dégage!

soda [ˈsəʊdə] N **1** *Chem* soude *f* **2** *(fizzy water)* eau *f* de Seltz; **a whisky and s.** un whisky soda **3** *Am (soft drink)* soda *m*

►► *Br* ***soda biscuit*** = biscuit sec à la levure chimique; ***soda bread*** pain *m* à la levure chimique; *Am* ***soda cracker*** = biscuit sec à la levure chimique; *Am* ***soda fountain*** **1** *(café)* ≃ café *m*; *(counter)* buvette *f (où sont servis des sodas)* **2** *(device)* siphon *m* (d'eau de Seltz); *Am Fam* ***soda jerk*** serveur(euse) *m,f (de soda)*; *Am* ***soda pop*** boisson *f* gazeuse; ***soda siphon*** siphon *m* (d'eau de Seltz); ***soda water*** eau *f* de Seltz

sodden [ˈsɒdən] ADJ *(ground)* détrempé; *(clothes)* trempé; *Fig* **to be s. with drink** être abruti par l'alcool

sodding [ˈsɒdɪŋ] *Br very Fam* ADJ *(for emphasis)* sacré, foutu; **get that s. dog out of here!** fous-moi cette saleté de clébard dehors!; **s. hell!** merde alors!; **I lost my s. umbrella** j'ai perdu ce foutu parapluie

ADV *(for emphasis)* vachement; **you can s. well do it yourself!** démerde-toi tout seul pour le faire!; **don't be so s. lazy!** ce que tu peux être flemmard!

sodium [ˈsəʊdɪəm] N sodium *m*

►► ***sodium bicarbonate*** bicarbonate *m* de soude; ***sodium carbonate*** carbonate *m* de sodium, soude *f*; ***sodium chloride*** chlorure *m* de sodium; ***sodium hydroxide*** hydroxyde *m* de sodium; ***sodium lamp*** lampe *f* à vapeur de sodium; ***sodium nitrate*** nitrate *m* de sodium

Sodom [ˈsɒdəm] N Sodome; **S. and Gomorrah** Sodome et Gomorrhe

sodomite [ˈsɒdəmaɪt] N sodomite *m*

sodomize, -ise [ˈsɒdəmaɪz] VT sodomiser

sodomy [ˈsɒdəmɪ] N sodomie *f*

sofa [ˈsəʊfə] N sofa *m*, canapé *m*

►► ***sofa bed*** canapé-lit *m*

SOFT [sɒft]

ADJ
- doux **1, 4, 5, 7, 8, 13, 16–18**
- moelleux **2**
- tendre **3, 8**
- léger **4**
- indulgent **9**
- modéré **14**
- mou **2, 10**
- souple **1**
- ramolli **2**
- gras **3**
- estompé **6**
- facile **13**
- faible **15**

ADV
- doucement **1**

ADJ **1** *(to touch ► skin, hands, wool, fur)* doux (douce); *(► leather)* souple; *(► material, hair)* doux (douce), soyeux; **as s. as velvet/as a baby's bottom** doux comme du velours/comme une peau de bébé; **s. to the touch** doux au toucher; **to become s.** *or* **softer, to get s.** *or* **softer** *(skin)* s'adoucir; *(leather)* s'assouplir; **the cream will make your hands/the leather s.** la crème t'adoucira les mains/assouplira le cuir

2 *(yielding, not firm ► bed, mattress, pillow)* moelleux; *(► collar, ground, snow)* mou (molle); *(► butter)* mou (molle), ramolli; *(► muscles, body)* ramolli, avachi, flasque; *(too yielding ► bed, mattress)* mou (molle); **a nice s. bed** un lit moelleux; **the butter has gone s.** le beurre s'est ramolli; **mix to a s. paste** mélanger jusqu'à obtention d'une pâte molle; **these chocolates have s. centres** ces chocolats sont mous à l'intérieur; *Horseracing* **the going is s.** le terrain est mou; **the brakes are s.** il y a du mou dans les freins

3 *(malleable ► metal, wood, stone)* tendre; *(► pencil)* gras (grasse), tendre

4 *(quiet, not harsh ► voice, music)* doux (douce); *(► sound, accent)* doux (douce), léger; *(► tap, cough)* petit, léger; *(► step)* feutré; **"yes," he said in a s. whisper/voice** "oui", murmura-t-il doucement/dit-il d'une voix douce

5 *(muted ► colour, glow)* doux (douce), *(► shade)* doux (douce), pastel *(inv)*; *(► light, lighting)* doux (douce), tamisé

6 *(blurred ► outline)* estompé, flou

7 *(gentle, mild ► breeze, rain, words)* doux (douce); *(► expression, eyes)* doux (douce), tendre; *(► curve, shadow)* doux (douce); *(► climate, weather)* doux (douce), clément; **she suits a softer hairstyle** ce qui lui va bien, c'est une coiffure plus souple

8 *(kind ► person)* doux (douce), tendre; **to have a s. heart** avoir le cœur tendre; **to have a s. nature** être doux de nature

9 *(lenient)* indulgent; **you're too s. with the boy** vous êtes trop indulgent avec le garçon; **to be s. on sb** se montrer indulgent envers qn, faire preuve d'indulgence envers qn; **to be s. on terrorism** faire preuve de laxisme envers le terrorisme

10 *(weak ► physically)* mou (molle); **the boy's too s.** ce garçon n'a pas de caractère; **you're getting s.** tu te ramollis; **city life has made you s.** la vie citadine t'a ramolli

11 *Fam (stupid)* **he's going s. in his old age** il devient gâteux en vieillissant; **you must be s. in the head!** ça va pas, non?; **don't be s.** arrête de dire des bêtises

12 *(fond) Fam* **to be s. on sb** avoir le béguin pour qn; **to have a s. spot for sb** avoir un faible pour qn

13 *(easy ► life)* doux (douce), tranquille, facile; *(► job)* facile; *Fam* **to have a s. time of it** se la couler douce; **to take the s. option** opter pour la solution de facilité

14 *(moderate)* modéré; *Pol* **the s. left/right** la gauche/droite modérée; **to take a s. line on sth** adopter une ligne modérée sur qch; *(compromise)* adopter une politique de compromis sur qch

15 *Econ & Fin (currency)* faible; *(market)* faible, lourd

16 *(water)* doux (douce)

17 *Ling (consonant)* doux (douce)

18 *(drug)* doux (douce)

ADV **1** *Literary (softly)* doucement

2 *Fam* **don't talk s.!** ne sois pas idiot!

►► ***soft cheese*** fromage *m* à pâte molle; ***soft coal*** houille *f* grasse; *Com* ***soft commodities*** biens *mpl* non durables; ***soft contact lenses*** lentilles *fpl* souples; *Comput* ***soft copy*** visualisation *f* sur écran; ***soft drink*** boisson *f* non alcoolisée; *Phot* ***soft focus*** flou *m* artistique, point *m* diffus; ***soft fruit*** *(UNCOUNT)* ≃ fruits *mpl* rouges; *Br* ***soft furnishings*** tissus *mpl* d'ameublement; *Br* ***soft goods*** tissus *mpl*, textiles *mpl*; *Comput* ***soft hyphen*** césure *f* automatique, tiret *m* conditionnel; *Chem* ***soft iron*** fer *m* doux; *Comput* ***soft key*** touche *f* programmable; *also Fig* ***soft landing*** atterrissage *m* en douceur; *Am Pol* ***soft line*** ligne *f* de conduite modérée; *Econ & Fin* ***soft loan*** prêt *m* avantageux *ou* à des conditions avantageuses; *Anat* ***soft palate*** voile *m* du palais; ***soft pedal*** *(on piano)* pédale *f* douce, sourdine *f*; ***soft porn*** pornographie *f* peu explicite, *Fam* soft *m*; ***soft-porn film*** film *m* érotique; ***soft-porn magazine*** revue *f* de charme; ***soft-porn magazines*** presse *f* de charme; *Comput* ***soft return*** saut *m* de ligne automatique; ***the soft sciences*** ≃ les sciences *fpl* humaines; *Comput* ***soft sectoring*** formatage *m* logiciel; *Com* ***soft sell*** = méthodes de vente non agressives; **she has a flair for the s. sell** elle a le don de *ou* pour circonvenir ses clients; ***soft shoulder*** *(on road)* accotement *m* non stabilisé; ***soft skills*** qualités *fpl* humaines *(dans un cadre professionnel)*; ***soft soap*** **1** *Med* savon *m* vert **2** *(UNCOUNT) Fam (flattery)* flagornerie□*f*, flatterie□*f*, flatteries□*fpl*; ***soft target*** cible *f* facile; *Anat* ***soft tissue*** parties *fpl* charnues; *Fam* ***soft top*** (voiture *f*) décapotable□*f*; *Br Fam* ***soft touch*** bonne poire *f*; **he's a real s. touch** *(easily fooled)* il est vraiment bonne poire; *(for money)* il se laisse facilement taper; ***soft toy*** (jouet *m* en) peluche *f*; ***soft verge*** *(on road)* accotement *m* non stabilisé

softback ['sɒftbæk] **N** (livre *m* de) poche *m*
▸▸ ***softback version*** version *f* poche

softball ['sɒftbɔːl] **N 1** *(game)* = sorte de base-ball joué sur un terrain plus petit et avec une balle moins dure, *Can* balle *f* molle **2** *(ball)* = balle utilisée au "softball" (plus grande et plus molle qu'une balle de base-ball)

soft-boiled **ADJ**
▸▸ ***soft-boiled egg*** œuf *m* (à la) coque

soft-centre, *Am* **soft-center** **N** *(chocolate)* chocolat *m* fourré

soft-centred, *Am* **soft-centered** **ADJ** *(chocolate)* fourré; *(sweet)* mou (molle); *(person)* au cœur tendre; *(film)* à l'eau de rose

soft-core **ADJ** *(pornography)* soft *(inv)*

soft-cover **ADJ** broché

soften ['sɒfən] **VT 1** *(butter, ground, wax)* ramollir; *(skin, water)* adoucir; *(cloth, wool, leather)* assouplir; **centuries of erosion had softened the stone** des siècles d'érosion avaient rendu la pierre tendre
2 *(voice, tone)* adoucir, radoucir; *(colour, light, sound)* adoucir, atténuer; **to s. one's voice** *(make less strident)* parler d'une voix plus douce; *(make quieter)* parler moins fort
3 *(make less strict)* assouplir; **he has softened his stance on vegetarianism** son attitude envers le végétarisme est plus modérée qu'avant
4 *(lessen* ▸ *pain, emotion)* soulager, adoucir, atténuer; *(*▸ *shock, effect, impact)* adoucir, amoindrir; *(*▸ *opposition, resistance)* réduire, amoindrir; *also Fig* **to s. the blow** amortir le choc
VI 1 *(butter, ground, wax)* se ramollir; *(skin)* s'adoucir; *(cloth, wool, leather)* s'assouplir
2 *(become gentler* ▸ *eyes, expression, voice)* s'adoucir; *(*▸ *breeze, rain)* s'atténuer; *(*▸ *lighting, colour)* s'atténuer, s'adoucir; *(*▸ *angle, outline)* s'adoucir, s'estomper
3 *(become friendlier, more receptive)* **to s. towards sb** se montrer plus indulgent envers qn; **their attitude towards immigration has softened noticeably** leur position par rapport à l'immigration est nettement plus tolérante

▸**soften up** **VT SEP 1** *Fam (make amenable* ▸ *gen)* attendrir□, rendre plus souple□; *(*▸ *by persuasion)* amadouer□; *(*▸ *aggressively)* intimider□; **they tried to s. us up with champagne lunches** ils ont essayé de nous amadouer à coups de déjeuners au champagne **2** *Mil* affaiblir **3** *(make softer* ▸ *butter, ground, wax)* ramollir; *(*▸ *skin)* adoucir; *(*▸ *cloth, wool, leather)* assouplir
VI 1 *(ground)* devenir mou (molle), se ramollir; *(butter, wax)* se ramollir; *(leather)* s'assouplir; *(skin)* s'adoucir **2** *(become gentler* ▸ *person, voice)* s'adoucir

softener ['sɒfənə(r)] **N 1** *(for water)* adoucisseur *m* (d'eau); *(for fabric)* assouplissant *m* (textile) **2** *Fam (bribe)* pot-de-vin□*m*

softening ['sɒfənɪŋ] **N** *(of butter, ground, wax)* ramollissement *m*; *(of cloth, wool, leather)* assouplissement *m*, adoucissement *m*; *(of attitude, expression, voice)* adoucissement *m*; *(of colours, contrasts)* atténuation *f*; **there has been no s. of attitude on the part of the management** la direction n'a pas modéré son attitude; *Med* **s. of the brain** ramollissement *m* cérébral

soft-faced hammer [-feɪst-] **N** maillet *m*

soft-focus **ADJ**
▸▸ ***soft-focus lens*** objectif *m* pour créer des effets de flou

soft-headed **ADJ** *Fam (weak-minded)* faible d'esprit□; *(silly)* bête, idiot□

softhearted [ˌsɒft'hɑːtɪd] **ADJ** (au cœur) tendre; **he's too s.** il a trop de cœur

softie ['sɒftɪ] **N** *Fam* **1** *(weak person)* mauviette *f*, mollasson(onne) *m,f*; *(coward)* poule *f* mouillée, dégonflé(e) *m,f* **2** *(gentle person)* bonne pâte *f*; **he's just a big s. really** au fond, c'est un grand sentimental

softly ['sɒftlɪ] **ADV 1** *(quietly* ▸ *breathe, say)* doucement; *(*▸ *move, walk)* à pas feutrés, (tout) doucement **2** *(gently* ▸ *blow, touch)* doucement, légèrement **3** *(fondly* ▸ *smile, look)* tendrement, avec tendresse

softly-softly *Br* **ADV** tout doucement, avec prudence
ADJ prudent; **try a s. approach** allez-y doucement

softness ['sɒftnɪs] **N 1** *(to touch* ▸ *of skin, hands, hair)* douceur *f*; *(*▸ *of fabric, wool, fur, pillow)* douceur *f*, moelleux *m*; *(*▸ *of leather)* souplesse *f*
2 *(to pressure* ▸ *of bed, ground, snow, butter)* mollesse *f*; *(*▸ *of collar)* souplesse *f*; *(*▸ *of wood)* tendreté *f*
3 *(gentleness* ▸ *of breeze, weather, voice, music)* douceur *f*; *(*▸ *of expression, manner)* douceur *f*, gentillesse *f*; *(*▸ *of eyes, light, colour)* douceur *f*; *(*▸ *of outline, curve)* flou *m*, douceur *f*
4 *(kindness* ▸ *of person)* douceur *f*; *(*▸ *of heart)* tendresse *f*; *(indulgence)* indulgence *f*
5 *(weakness* ▸ *of character, person)* mollesse *f*
6 *(easiness* ▸ *of life)* douceur *f*; *(*▸ *of job)* facilité *f*
7 *Fam (silliness)* niaiserie□*f*, stupidité□*f*

soft-pedal **VI 1** *Mus* mettre la sourdine **2** *Fig* **to s. on reforms** ralentir le rythme des réformes
VT *Fig* glisser sur, atténuer

soft-sectored [-'sektəd] **ADJ** *Comput (disk)* formaté par programme, à secteurs logiciels

soft-soap **VT** *Fam* passer de la pommade à

soft-spoken **ADJ** à la voix douce; **to be s.** avoir la voix douce

soft-top **ADJ** décapotable

software ['sɒftweə(r)] **N** *Comput* logiciel *m*, software *m*; **a piece of s.** un logiciel
▸▸ ***software company*** éditeur *m* de logiciels; ***software developer*** développeur(euse) *m,f*; ***software engineer*** ingénieur *m* développement logiciel; ***software engineering*** ingénierie *f* logicielle; ***software house*** éditeur *m* de logiciel; ***software package*** logiciel *m*; ***software piracy*** piratage *m* de logiciels; ***software platform*** plate-forme *f* logicielle; ***software producer*** éditeur *m* de logiciels; ***software tool*** outil *m* logiciel; ***software writer*** concepteur *m* de logiciel

software-compatible **ADJ** compatible du point de vue logiciel

softwood ['sɒftwʊd] **N** bois *m* tendre, *Can* bois *m* mou
COMP en bois tendre, *Can* en bois mou

softy *(pl* **softies)** = **softie**

SOGAT ['səʊgæt] **N** *Br (abbr* **Society of Graphical and Allied Trades)** = syndicat britannique des métiers du graphisme

soggy ['sɒgɪ] *(compar* **soggier,** *superl* **soggiest)** **ADJ** *(ground)* détrempé, imbibé d'eau; *(clothes, shoes)* trempé; *(bread, cake)* mou (molle); *(rice)* trop cuit, collant

soh [səʊ] **N** *Mus* sol *m*

soil [sɔɪl] **N 1** *(earth)* terre *f*; **to work the s.** travailler la terre
2 *(type of earth)* terre *f*, sol *m*; **good farming s.** de la bonne terre agricole; **sandy/clay soils** sols *mpl* sablonneux/argileux, terres *fpl* sablonneuses/argileuses
3 *Fig (land)* terre *f*, sol *m*; **his native s.** sa terre natale; **on Irish s.** sur le sol irlandais
4 *(UNCOUNT) (excrement)* excréments *mpl*, ordures *fpl*; *(sewage)* vidange *f*
VT 1 *(dirty* ▸ *clothes, linen, paper)* salir, souiller; **she refused to s. her hands with such work** elle a refusé de se salir les mains avec ce genre de travail **2** *Fig (reputation)* salir, souiller, entacher
VI *(clothes, material)* se salir; **these covers s. easily** ces housses sont salissantes
▸▸ ***the Soil Association*** = organisation britannique de normalisation des produits issus de l'agriculture biologique; ***soil erosion*** érosion du sol; *Geog* ***soil horizon*** horizon *m*; ***soil pipe*** tuyau *m* de chute unique; *Geog* ***soil profile*** profil *m* de sol, profil *m* pédologique; ***soil science*** science *f* du sol

soiled [sɔɪld] **ADJ** *(dressings)* usagé; *(bedlinen)* souillé; *(goods)* défraîchi; **if it's s. the shop won't exchange it** si c'est sale la boutique ne fera pas l'échange; **some slightly s. items at reduced prices** des articles *mpl* légèrement salis à prix réduits

soirée ['swɑːreɪ] **N** soirée *f*

sojourn ['sɒdʒɜːn] *Literary* **N** séjour *m*
VI séjourner

sol [sɒl] **N** *Mus* sol *m inv*

solace ['sɒləs] *Literary* **N** consolation *f*, réconfort *m*; **he found s. in religion** il a trouvé un réconfort dans la religion
VT *(person)* consoler, réconforter

sola of exchange ['səʊlə-] **N** *Fin* seule *f* de change

solar ['səʊlə(r)] **ADJ 1** *(of, concerning the sun* ▸ *heat, radiation)* solaire, du soleil; *(*▸ *cycle, year)* solaire **2** *(using the sun's power* ▸ *energy, heating)* solaire
▸▸ ***solar battery*** batterie *f* solaire; ***solar cell*** pile solaire, photopile *f*; ***solar eclipse*** éclipse *f* solaire; ***solar flare*** éruption *f* solaire; ***solar furnace*** four *m* solaire; ***solar panel*** panneau *m* solaire; *Anat* ***solar plexus*** plexus *m* solaire; ***solar power*** énergie *f* solaire; ***solar radiation*** rayonnement *m* solaire; ***solar system*** système *m* solaire; ***solar tile*** tuile solaire; ***solar wind*** vent *m* solaire

solarium [sə'leərɪəm] *(pl* **solariums** *or* **solaria** [-rɪə]) **N** solarium *m*

solar-powered [-'paʊəd] **ADJ** à énergie solaire

sold [səʊld] *pt & pp of* **sell**
ADJ 1 *Com* vendu **2** *Fam Fig* **to be s. on sb/sth** être emballé par qn/qch; **he's really s. on her** il est vraiment entiché *ou* toqué d'elle

• **sold out** **ADJ 1** *(goods)* épuisé; **s. out** *(sign* ▸ *for play, concert)* complet; **the concert was completely s. out** tous les billets pour le concert ont été vendus **2** *(stockist)* **we're s. out of bread** nous avons vendu tout le pain, il ne reste plus de pain

solder ['səʊldə(r)] **VT** souder; **to s. a wire to a contact** souder un fil à un plot
N soudure *f*, métal *m* d'apport; **brazing s.** soudure *f* au laiton, brasure *f*; **soft s.** soudure *f* à l'étain, brasure *f* tendre

soldering ['səʊldərɪŋ] **N** soudure *f*
▸▸ ***soldering iron*** fer *m* à souder

soldier ['səʊldʒə(r)] **N 1** *(gen)* soldat *m*, militaire *m*; **to become a s.** se faire soldat, entrer dans l'armée; **to play (at) soldiers** *(children)* jouer aux soldats *ou* à la guerre; *Pej (country, adults)* jouer à la guerre *ou* à la guéguerre; *Mil* **old s.** vétéran *m* **2** *(strip of bread)* mouillette *f*
VI être soldat, servir dans l'armée
▸▸ ***soldier ant*** (fourmi *f*) soldat *m*; ***soldier of fortune*** soldat *m* de fortune

▸**soldier on** **VI** *Br* continuer *ou* persévérer (malgré tout); **despite the freezing conditions they soldiered on** ils ont persévéré en dépit d'un froid glacial; **I'll s. on with this for another half hour** je vais encore m'escrimer là-dessus pendant une demi-heure

soldiering ['səʊldʒərɪŋ] **N** carrière *f ou* vie *f* (de) militaire; **to go s.** partir à l'armée *ou* à la guerre; **their love of s.** leur amour de la vie militaire; **after many years' s.** après avoir servi pendant de nombreuses années dans l'armée

soldierlike ['səʊldʒəlaɪk], **soldierly** ['səʊldʒəl-] **ADJ** *(act, behaviour)* de soldat; *(appearance, manner, bearing)* militaire

soldiery ['səʊldʒərɪ] **N** *Old-fashioned* **1** *(soldiers collectively)* soldats *mpl*, militaires *mpl* **2** *(profession)* métier *m* de soldat

sole [səʊl] (*pl sense* 3 inv *or* soles) ADJ 1 (*only*) seul, unique; **the s. survivor** le seul survivant 2 (*exclusive*) exclusif; **to have s. rights on sth** avoir l'exclusivité des droits sur qch; **to have s. responsibility for sth** être entièrement responsable de qch

N 1 (*of foot*) plante *f* 2 (*of shoe, sock*) semelle *f* 3 *Ich* sole *f*

VT ressemeler; **to have one's shoes soled** faire ressemeler ses chaussures

▸▸ ***sole agency*** représentation *f* exclusive; ***sole agent*** agent *m* exclusif; **to be s. agent for Mitsubishi** avoir la représentation exclusive de Mitsubishi; *Com* ***sole dealer*** concessionnaire *mf* exclusif(ive); ***sole owner*** propriétaire *mf* unique; ***sole right*** droit *m* exclusif; *Br Com* ***sole trader*** entreprise *f* individuelle *ou* unipersonnelle

solecism ['sɒlɪsɪzəm] N 1 *Gram* solécisme *m* 2 *Formal* (*social error*) manque *m* de savoir-vivre

solely ['səʊllɪ] ADV 1 (*only*) seulement, uniquement 2 (*entirely*) entièrement; **to be s. responsible for sth** être entièrement responsable de qch

solemn ['sɒləm] ADJ 1 (*grave, serious*) sérieux, grave, solennel; **a s. face** un visage grave *ou* solennel

2 (*sombre*) sobre; **a s. grey suit** un costume gris sobre

3 (*formal* ▸ *agreement, promise*) solennel; **a s. oath** un serment solennel

4 (*grand* ▸ *occasion, music*) solennel

▸▸ ***solemn mass*** grand-messe *f*, messe *f* solennelle

solemness ['sɒləmnɪs] N sérieux *m*, gravité *f*

solemnity [sə'lemnətɪ] (*pl* **solemnities**) N 1 (*serious nature*) sérieux *m*, gravité *f* 2 (*formality*) solennité *f*; *Law* (*of agreement, promise*) solennité *f*; **she was received with great s.** elle fut accueillie très solennellement 3 (*usu pl*) *Literary* (*solemn event*) solennité *f*; **the Easter solemnities** les solennités *fpl* de Pâques

solemnization, -isation [ˌsɒləmnaɪ'zeɪʃən] N *Literary* (*gen*) solennisation *f*; (*of marriage*) célébration *f*

solemnize, -ise ['sɒləmnaɪz] VT *Literary* (*gen*) solenniser; (*marriage*) célébrer

solemnly ['sɒləmlɪ] ADV 1 (*seriously, gravely*) gravement, solennellement; **"it's time I left," he said s.** "il est temps que je parte", dit-il d'un ton grave; **she s. believes that what she did was right** elle croit fermement que ce qu'elle a fait était juste 2 (*formally*) solennellement; **they s. swore to avenge their brother's death** ils jurèrent solennellement de venger la mort de leur frère 3 (*grandly*) solennellement, avec solennité

solenoid ['səʊlənɔɪd] N *Elec* solénoïde *m*

▸▸ ***solenoid switch*** contacteur *m* à solénoïde

sol-fa [ˌsɒl'fɑː] N *Mus* solfège *m*

solicit [sə'lɪsɪt] VT 1 (*business, support, information*) solliciter; (*opinion*) demander 2 (*of prostitute*) racoler

VI (*prostitute*) racoler

solicitation [səˌlɪsɪ'teɪʃən] N sollicitation *f*

soliciting [sə'lɪsɪtɪŋ] N (*by prostitute*) racolage *m*

solicitor [sə'lɪsɪtə(r)] N 1 *Br Law* (*for drawing up documents, conveyancing*) ≃ notaire *m*; (*for court work, divorce cases*) avocat(e) *m,f* 2 *Am Admin* = conseil juridique d'une municipalité 3 (*person who solicits*) solliciteur(euse) *m,f*; *Am* **caution, unofficial solicitors** (*sign*) attention aux démarcheurs non autorisés

▸▸ ***solicitor general*** 1 (*in UK*) conseil *m* juridique de la Couronne 2 (*in US*) représentant(e) *m,f* du gouvernement (*auprès de la Cour suprême*)

solicitous [sə'lɪsɪtəs] ADJ (*showing consideration, concern*) plein de sollicitude; (*eager, attentive*) empressé; (*anxious*) soucieux; **he was most s. about your future happiness** il était extrêmement soucieux de votre avenir et de votre bonheur

solicitously [sə'lɪsɪtəslɪ] ADV (*with consideration, concern*) avec sollicitude; (*eagerly, attentively*) avec empressement; (*anxiously*) avec inquiétude

solicitousness [sə'lɪsɪtəsnɪs], **solicitude** [sə'lɪsɪtjuːd] N (*consideration, concern*) sollicitude *f*; (*eagerness, attentiveness*) empressement *m*; (*anxiety*) souci *m*, préoccupation *f*

solid ['sɒlɪd] ADJ 1 (*not liquid or gas*) solide; **a s. body** un corps solide; **frozen s.** complètement gelé; **the fat had set s.** la graisse était complètement figée; **she can't eat s. food** elle ne peut pas absorber d'aliments solides

2 (*of one substance*) massif; **her necklace is s. gold** son collier est en or massif; **s. oak furniture** meubles *mpl* en chêne massif; **they dug until they reached s. rock** ils ont creusé jusqu'à ce qu'ils atteignent la roche compacte; **caves hollowed out of s. rock** des grottes *fpl* creusées à même la roche

3 (*not hollow*) plein; **s. tyres** pneus *mpl* pleins

4 (*unbroken, continuous*) continu; **a s. yellow line** une ligne jaune continue; **I worked for eight s. hours** *or* **eight hours s.** j'ai travaillé sans arrêt pendant huit heures, j'ai travaillé huit heures d'affilée; **we had two s. weeks of rain** nous avons eu deux semaines de pluie ininterrompue

5 *Am* (*of one colour*) uni; **the walls were painted a s. green** les murs étaient peints en vert uni

6 (*dense, compact*) dense, compact; **knead it until it forms a s. mass** travailler jusqu'à ce que cela forme une masse compacte; **the streets were a s. mass of people** les rues étaient noires de monde; **the concert hall was packed s.** la salle de concert était bondée

7 (*powerful* ▸ *blow*) puissant; **I gave him a s. punch to the jaw** je lui ai assené un violent coup de poing sur la mâchoire

8 (*sturdy, sound* ▸ *structure, understanding, relationship*) solide; (▸ *evidence, argument*) solide, irréfutable; (▸ *advice*) valable, sûr; **a man of s. build** un homme bien charpenté; **I have very s. reasons for believing the opposite** j'ai de solides raisons de croire le contraire; **we need somebody with some s. experience in the field** nous avons besoin de quelqu'un qui possède une solide expérience de travail sur le terrain; **he's a good s. worker** c'est un bon travailleur; **to be on s. ground** être sur la terre ferme; *Fig* être en terrain sûr

9 (*respectable, worthy*) respectable, honorable; **the s. citizens of this town** les respectables citoyens *mpl* de cette ville

10 *Pol* (*firm*) massif; (*unanimous*) unanime; **we have the s. support of the electorate** nous avons le soutien massif des électeurs; **the south is s. for the Christian Democrats** le sud soutient massivement les démocrates-chrétiens; **the strike was 100 percent s.** la grève était totale

11 *Am Fam* (*excellent*) génial, super (*inv*)

N *Geom & Phys* solide *m*

ADV *Am Fam* (*absolutely*) absolument[□]; **I s. gotta do it!** il faut absolument que je le fasse!

• **solids** NPL 1 (*solid food*) aliments *mpl* solides; **I can't eat solids** je ne peux pas absorber d'aliments solides 2 *Chem* particules *fpl* solides; **milk solids** extrait *m* du lait

▸▸ *Math* ***solid angle*** angle *m* solide; *Math* ***solid figure*** solide *m*; ***solid fuel*** combustible *m* solide; *Math* ***solid geometry*** géométrie *f* des solides

solidarity [ˌsɒlɪ'dærətɪ] N solidarité *f*; **they went on strike in s. with the miners** ils ont fait grève par solidarité avec les mineurs

▸▸ ***solidarity strike*** grève *f* de solidarité

solidification [səˌlɪdɪfɪ'keɪʃən] N solidification *f*

solidify [sə'lɪdɪfaɪ] (*pt & pp* **solidified**) VI 1 (*liquid, gas*) se solidifier 2 (*system, opinion*) se consolider

VT 1 (*liquid, gas*) solidifier 2 (*system, opinion*) consolider

solidity [sə'lɪdətɪ] N solidité *f*

solidly ['sɒlɪdlɪ] ADV 1 (*sturdily*) solidement; **the town hall stands s. in the middle of the square** la mairie est solidement plantée au milieu de la place; **to be s. built** (*person*) avoir une forte carrure

2 (*thoroughly*) très, tout à fait; **a s. established reputation** une réputation solidement établie

3 (*massively*) massivement, en masse; **Massachusetts voted s. for the Democrats** l'État du Massachussetts a voté massivement *ou* en masse pour les démocrates

4 (*continuously*) sans arrêt; **I worked s. for five hours** j'ai travaillé sans interruption pendant cinq heures

solid-state ADJ 1 *Phys* des solides 2 *Electron* à semi-conducteurs

solidus ['sɒlɪdəs] (*pl* **solidi** [-daɪ]) N *Typ* barre *f* oblique

soliloquize, -ise [sə'lɪləkwaɪz] VI soliloquer, monologuer

soliloquy [sə'lɪləkwɪ] (*pl* **soliloquies**) N soliloque *m*, monologue *m*

solitaire [ˌsɒlɪ'teə(r)] N 1 (*pegboard*) solitaire *m* 2 *Am* (*card game*) réussite *f*, patience *f*; **to play s.** faire des réussites *ou* des patiences 3 (*gem*) solitaire *m*

solitary ['sɒlɪtərɪ] (*pl* **solitaries**) ADJ 1 (*alone* ▸ *person, life, activity*) solitaire

2 (*single*) seul, unique; **a s. tree on the horizon** un seul arbre à l'horizon; **can you give me one s. reason why I should go?** peux-tu me donner une seule raison d'y aller?

3 (*remote* ▸ *place*) retiré, isolé

4 (*empty of people*) vide, désert; **the s. streets of the suburbs** les rues *fpl* désertes de la banlieue

N 1 *Fam* (*solitary confinement*) isolement *m* cellulaire[□] 2 (*person*) solitaire *mf*

▸▸ ***solitary confinement*** isolement *m* cellulaire[□]

solitude ['sɒlɪtjuːd] N (*feeling*) solitude *f*; **to live in s.** vivre dans la solitude

solo ['səʊləʊ] (*pl* **solos**) N 1 *Mus* solo *m*; **he played a violin/drum s.** il a joué un solo de violon/de batterie 2 (*flight*) vol *m* solo 3 (*card game*) solo *m* (*variante du whist*)

ADJ 1 *Mus* solo; **she plays s. violin** elle est soliste de violon, elle est violon solo 2 (*unaided*) en solitaire; **a s. act** un one-man-show; **her first s. flight** son premier vol en solo

ADV 1 *Mus* en solo 2 (*unaided*) seul, en solitaire, en solo; **to fly s.** voler en solo

▸▸ ***solo album*** album *m* solo; ***solo whist*** solo *m* (*variante du whist*)

soloist ['səʊləʊɪst] N soliste *mf*

Solomon ['sɒləmən] PR N *Bible* Salomon

▸▸ ***the Solomon Islands*** les îles *fpl* Salomon

solstice ['sɒlstɪs] N solstice *m*; **the winter/summer s.** le solstice d'hiver/d'été

solubility [ˌsɒljʊ'bɪlətɪ] N solubilité *f*

soluble ['sɒljʊbəl] ADJ 1 (*substance*) soluble 2 (*problem*) soluble

solution [sə'luːʃən] N 1 (*answer* ▸ *to problem, equation, mystery*) solution *f*; **a political s. to the conflict** une solution politique au conflit 2 (*act of solving* ▸ *of problem, equation, mystery*) résolution *f*; **our main aim should be the rapid s. of the problem** notre principal objectif devrait être de résoudre rapidement le problème 3 *Chem & Pharm* solution *f*; **salt in s.** sel *m* en solution

solvable ['sɒlvəbəl] ADJ soluble

> Note that the French adjective **solvable** is a false friend and is never a translation for the English adjective **solvable**. It means **financially solvent.**

solve [sɒlv] VT (*equation*) résoudre; (*problem*) résoudre, trouver la solution de; (*crime, mystery*) élucider; **I couldn't s. a single clue in the 'Times' crossword** je n'ai pas réussi à trouver une seule définition dans les mots croisés du 'Times'

solvency ['sɒlvənsɪ] N solvabilité *f*

solvent ['sɒlvənt] ADJ 1 (*financially*) solvable 2 (*substance, liquid*) dissolvant

N solvant *m*, dissolvant *m*

▸▸ ***solvent abuse*** usage *m* de solvants hallucinogènes; ***solvent abuser*** toxicomane *mf* utilisant des solvants hallucinogènes

Somali [sə'mɑːlɪ] N 1 (*person*) Somalien(enne) *m,f* 2 *Ling* somali *m*

ADJ somalien

Somalia [sə'mɑːlɪə] N Somalie *f*

Somaliland [sə'mɑːlɪlænd] N Somalie *f*

somatic [sə'mætɪk] ADJ somatique

▸▸ *Biol* ***somatic cell*** cellule somatique

sombre, *Am* **somber** ['sɒmbə(r)] ADJ 1 (*dark* ▸ *colour, place*) sombre 2 (*grave, grim* ▸ *outlook, person, day*) sombre, morne; **what are you looking so s. about?** pourquoi cet air si sombre?; **a s.**

episode in the history of Europe un épisode sombre dans l'histoire de l'Europe

sombrely, *Am* **somberly** ['sɒmbəlɪ] **ADV** sombrement

sombrero [sɒm'breərəʊ] (*pl* **sombreros**) **N** sombrero *m*

SOME [sʌm]

ADJ
- du, de la, de l', des **1**
- certains **2**
- un certain **3**
- quelques **3**

PRON
- quelques-uns **1, 2**
- en **1**
- certains **2**

ADV
- quelque **1**
- environ **1**
- un peu **2**

ADJ 1 *(a quantity of)* du, de la, de l'; *(a number of)* des; **don't forget to buy s. cheese/beer/garlic** n'oublie pas d'acheter du fromage/de la bière/de l'ail; **I ate s. fruit** j'ai mangé des fruits; **let me give you s. advice** laissez-moi vous donner un conseil; **we've invited s. friends round** nous avons invité des amis à la maison; **s. red flowers** des fleurs *fpl* rouges; **s. pretty flowers** de *ou* des jolies fleurs *fpl*; **I met s. old friends last night** j'ai rencontré de *ou* des vieux amis hier soir

2 *(not all, certain)* certains *mpl*, certaines *fpl*; **s. wine/software is very expensive** certains vins/logiciels coûtent très cher; **s. petrol still contains lead** il existe encore de l'essence avec plomb; **s. employees like the new system, others don't** certains employés aiment le nouveau système, d'autres pas; **s. people say...** certains disent..., il y en a *ou* il y a des gens qui disent...; **s. cars shouldn't be allowed on the road** il y a des voitures qu'on ne devrait pas laisser circuler

3 *(a considerable amount of)* un certain, une certaine; *(a considerable number of)* quelques *mfpl*; **I haven't been abroad for s. time** ça fait un certain temps que je ne suis pas allé à l'étranger; **it happened (quite) s. time ago** ça s'est passé il y a (bien) longtemps; **it will be s. time before it's finished** ça va prendre un certain temps *ou* un moment avant que ça soit fini; **it's s. distance from here** c'est assez loin d'ici; **the money should go s. way towards compensating them** l'argent devrait les dédommager dans une certaine mesure; **at s. length** assez longuement; **not without s. opposition** non sans rencontrer une certaine opposition; **it happened s. years/months ago** ça s'est passé il y a quelques années/mois

4 *(a small amount or number of)* **you might have shown s. gratitude!** tu aurais pu faire preuve d'un peu de gratitude(, quand même)!; **I felt s. uneasiness** je ressentais quelque inquiétude; **you must have s. idea of how much it will cost** vous devez avoir une petite idée de combien ça va coûter; **I hope I've been of s. help to you** j'espère que je vous ai un peu aidé; **in s. measure, to s. degree** jusqu'à un certain point, dans une certaine mesure; **I'm glad s. people understand me!** je suis content qu'il y ait quand même des gens qui me comprennent!

5 *(unknown, unspecified)* **we must find s. alternative** il faut que nous trouvions une autre solution; **he's gone to s. town in the north** il est parti dans une ville quelque part dans le nord; **she works for s. publishing company** elle travaille pour je ne sais quelle maison d'édition; **s. fool left the door open** un imbécile a laissé la porte ouverte; **s. book or other** un livre quelconque; **I'll get even with them s. day!** je me vengerai d'eux un de ces jours *ou* un jour ou l'autre!; **come back s. other time** revenez un autre jour

6 *Fam (expressing scorn, irritation)* **did you go to the party? – s. party!** est-ce que tu es allé à la fête? – tu parles d'une fête!; **s. hope we've got of winning!** comme si on avait la moindre chance de gagner!$^{\square}$; **s. people!** il y a des gens, je vous assure!

7 *Fam (expressing admiration, approval)* **that was s. party!** ça c'était une fête!; **(that was) s. storm!** quelle tempête!$^{\square}$; **that was s. meal!** ce que nous avons bien mangé!; **she's s. girl!** c'est une fille formidable!; **he's s. tennis player!** c'est un sacré tennisman!

PRON 1 *(an unspecified number or amount* ▸ *as subject)* quelques-uns *mpl*, quelques-unes *fpl*, certains *mpl*, certaines *fpl*; *(*▸ *as object)* en; **s. are plain and s. are patterned** certains sont unis et certains ont des motifs; **they went off, s. one way, s. another** ils se sont dispersés, les uns d'un côté, les autres de l'autre; **s. say it wasn't an accident** certains disent *ou* il y a des gens qui disent que ce n'était pas un accident; **I've got too much cake, do you want s.?** j'ai trop de gâteau, en voulez-vous un peu?; **can I have s. more?** est-ce que je peux en reprendre?; **I have s. more** *(I have some left)* j'en ai encore; *(I have some others)* j'en ai d'autres; **where are the envelopes? – there are s. in my drawer** où sont les enveloppes? – il y en a dans mon tiroir; **he wants the lot and then s.** il veut tout et puis le reste

2 *(not all)* **s. of the snow had melted** une partie de la neige avait fondu; **s. of the time** une partie du temps; **I only believe s. of what I read in the papers** je ne crois pas tout ce que je lis dans les journaux; **s. of the most beautiful scenery in the world is in Australia** certains des plus beaux paysages du monde se trouvent en Australie; **I've seen s. of her films** j'ai vu quelques-uns *ou* certains de ses films; **if you need pencils, take s. of these/mine** si vous avez besoin de crayons à papier, prenez quelques-uns de ceux-ci/des miens; **do you want s. or all of them?** en voulez-vous quelques-uns ou les voulez-vous tous?; **s. of us/them** certains d'entre nous/eux; **s. of my friends** certains de mes amis; **s. of the guests had already left** quelques invités étaient déjà partis

ADV 1 *(approximately)* quelque, environ; **it's s. 50 kilometres from London** c'est à environ 50 kilomètres *ou* c'est à une cinquantaine de kilomètres de Londres; **s. 500 people** quelque 500 personnes; **s. 30 pounds** une trentaine de livres, quelque 30 livres; **s. 15 minutes** un bon quart d'heure; **s. few minutes ago** il y a quelques minutes

2 *Am Fam (a little)* un peu$^{\square}$; *(a lot)* beaucoup$^{\square}$, pas mal; **I need to rest up s.** j'ai besoin de me reposer un peu; **admit it, you like her s.!** avoue-le, tu l'aimes bien!$^{\square}$

somebody ['sʌmbədɪ] **PRON 1** *(an unspecified person)* quelqu'un; **s. else** quelqu'un d'autre; **s. big/small** quelqu'un de grand/de petit; **they're looking for s. with a lot of experience** ils cherchent quelqu'un qui ait beaucoup d'expérience; **he's not s. you can trust** ce n'est pas quelqu'un en qui on peut avoir confiance; **there's s. on the phone for you** on vous demande au téléphone; **s.'s at the door, there's s. at the door** on a frappé; **we need s. a bit taller/who speaks Russian** il nous faut quelqu'un d'un peu plus grand/qui parle russe; **s. has left their/his/her umbrella behind** quelqu'un a oublié son parapluie; **is this s.'s wallet?** est-ce que ce portefeuille est à quelqu'un?; **s. or other** quelqu'un, je ne sais qui **2** *(an important person)* **he's (a) s.** c'est un personnage, ce n'est pas le premier venu; **you really think you're s., don't you?** tu te crois vraiment quelqu'un, n'est-ce pas?

someday ['sʌmdeɪ] **ADV** un jour (ou l'autre), un de ces jours

somehow ['sʌmhaʊ] **ADV 1** *(in some way)* d'une manière ou d'une autre, d'une façon ou d'une autre; **don't worry, we'll manage s. (or other)** ne t'inquiète pas, nous nous débrouillerons d'une façon ou d'une autre; **she'd s. (or other) managed to lock herself in** elle avait trouvé moyen de s'enfermer **2** *(for some reason)* pour une raison ou pour une autre, je ne sais pas trop pourquoi; **s. I'm not surprised he didn't come** je ne sais pas trop pourquoi, mais cela ne m'étonne pas qu'il ne soit pas venu

someone ['sʌmwʌn] = **somebody 1**

someplace ['sʌmpleɪs] *Am* = **somewhere 1**

somersault ['sʌməsɔːlt] **N 1** *(on ground or accidentally)* culbute *f*; *(in air)* saut *m* périlleux; *(by car)* tonneau *m*; **to turn** *or* **do a s.** *(on ground or accidentally)* faire la culbute; *(in air)* faire un saut périlleux; *(car)* faire un tonneau **2** *esp Am (of opinion)* volte-face *f*

VI *(on ground or accidentally)* faire la culbute; *(in air)* faire un saut périlleux/des sauts périlleux; *(car)* faire un tonneau/des tonneaux; **the car somersaulted twice** la voiture a fait deux tonneaux

SOMETHING ['sʌmθɪŋ] **PRON 1** *(an unspecified object, event, action etc)* quelque chose; **there must be s. going on** il doit se passer quelque chose; **I've got s. in my eye** j'ai quelque chose dans l'œil; **I've thought of s.** j'ai eu une idée; **don't just stand there, do s.!** ne reste pas là, fais quelque chose!; **s. else** quelque chose d'autre, autre chose; **s. or other** quelque chose; **s. big/small** quelque chose de grand/de petit; **I've done/said s. stupid** j'ai fait/dit une bêtise; **was it s. I said?** est-ce que j'ai dit quelque chose (qu'il ne fallait pas)?; **I've got a feeling there's s. wrong** j'ai le sentiment que quelque chose ne va pas; **there's s. wrong with the ship's computer** l'ordinateur de bord ne marche pas bien; **take s. to read on the train** prenez quelque chose à lire *ou* prenez de quoi lire dans le train; **he gave them s. to eat/drink** il leur a donné à manger/boire; **would you like s. to eat?** voulez-vous manger quelque chose?; **s. to live for** une raison de vivre; **to have s. to cry/be annoyed about** avoir une bonne raison de pleurer/se fâcher; **a film with s. for everybody** un film qui peut plaire à tout le monde; **they all want s. for nothing** ils veulent tous avoir tout pour rien; **there's s. about him/in the way he talks that reminds me of Gary** il y a quelque chose chez lui/dans sa façon de parler qui me rappelle Gary; **she's s. in the City/in insurance** elle travaille dans la finance/dans les assurances; **she slipped the head waiter a little s.** elle a glissé un petit pourboire au maître d'hôtel; **I've brought you a little s.** je vous ai apporté un petit quelque chose *ou* une bricole; **I'm sure she's got s. going with him** je suis sûr qu'il y a quelque chose entre elle et lui; **to be** *or* **have s. to do with sth** avoir un rapport avec qch; **I don't know what it means, I think it's got s. to do with nuclear physics** je ne sais pas ce que ça veut dire, je crois que ça a (quelque chose) à voir avec la physique nucléaire; **I'm sure the weather has s. to do with it** je suis sûre que le temps y est pour quelque chose *ou* que ça a un rapport avec le temps

2 *(thing of significance, value etc)* **to make s. of oneself** *or* **one's life** faire quelque chose de sa vie; **at least they've replied to my letter, that's s.** au moins ils ont répondu à ma lettre, c'est toujours *ou* déjà ça; **there must be s. in** *ou* **to all these rumours** il doit y avoir quelque chose de vrai dans toutes ces rumeurs; **there's s. in her plan** son projet mérite considération; **there's s. in what you say** il y a du vrai dans ce que vous dites; **I think you've got s. there** ce n'est pas bête ce que vous dites là; **that new singer has got s.** ce nouveau chanteur n'est pas mal; **he's got a certain s.** il a un petit quelque chose; *Fam* **that was quite s.!, that was s. else!** c'était vraiment quelque chose!; *Fam* **he really is s. else!** *(wonderful)* il est vraiment génial!; *(exasperating)* il est pas possible!; *Fam* **well, isn't that s.?** et bien, ça alors!; *Fam* **it was really s. to see those kids dancing!** c'était quelque chose de voir ces gosses danser!; *Fam* **the new model is really s.** le nouveau modèle est sensationnel

3 *(replacing forgotten amount, word, name etc)* **the battle took place in 1840 s.** la bataille a eu lieu dans les années 1840; **he's 40 s.** il a dans les 40 ans; **it cost £7 s.** ça a coûté sept livres et quelques; **her friend, Maisie s. (or other)** son amie, Maisie quelque chose

ADV 1 *(a little)* un peu; **s. over a month's salary** un peu plus d'un mois de salaire; **temperatures were s. under what we expected** les températures étaient un peu en-dessous de ce que nous attendions; **s. in the region of $10,000** quelque chose comme 10 000 dollars; **an increase of s. between 10 and 15 percent** une augmentation de 10 à 15 pour cent

2 *Fam (as intensifier)* **s. rotten** *or* **awful** *or* **terrible** vachement; **it hurts s. awful** ça fait vachement mal; **he was screaming s. terrible** il gueulait comme un putois; **he fancies her s. rotten** il est dingue d'elle

• **something like** **PREP 1** *(rather similar to)* **it looks s. like a grapefruit** ça ressemble un peu à un pamplemousse; **now that's s. like it!** c'est déjà mieux!

2 *(roughly)* environ; **it's s. like 5 metres long/wide**

;a fait quelque chose comme 5 mètres de long/ arge; **it costs s. like £500** ça coûte quelque chose :omme *ou* dans les 500 livres
• **something of** ADV *(rather)* **he's s. of an expert n the field** c'est en quelque sorte un expert dans :e domaine; **she became s. of a legend** elle est de- venue une sorte de légende; **she's s. of a miser** elle est un peu *ou* quelque peu avare; **how they lo it remains s. of a mystery** comment ils s'y pren- nent, ça c'est un mystère
• **or something** ADV **would you like a cup of tea or s.?** veux-tu une tasse de thé, ou autre chose?; **she must be ill or s.** elle doit être malade ou quelque chose dans ce genre-là; **are you deaf or s.?** tu es sourd ou quoi?

ometime ['sʌmtaɪm] ADV **1** *(in future)* un jour ou l'autre), un de ces jours; **you must come and see us s.** il faut que vous veniez nous voir un de ces jours; **I hope we'll meet again s. soon** j'espère que nous nous reverrons bientôt; **you'll have to ace up to it s. or other** un jour ou l'autre il faudra bien voir les choses en face; **her baby is due s. in May** elle attend son bébé pour le mois de mai; **s. after/before next April** après le mois/d'ici au mois d'avril; **s. next year** dans le courant de l'an- née prochaine **2** *(in past)* **she phoned s. last week** elle a téléphoné (dans le courant de) la semaine dernière; **the last time I saw him was s. in August** la dernière fois que je l'ai vu, c'était en août; **it happened s. before/after the Second World War** ça s'est passé avant/après la Seconde Guerre mondiale; **s. around 1920** vers 1920; **s. between 1927 and 1931** entre 1927 et 1931
ADJ **1** *(former)* ancien; **Mrs Evans, the club's s. president** l'ancienne présidente du club, Mme Evans **2** *Am (occasional)* intermittent; **he was a baseball player and s. golfer** il jouait au base-ball et parfois au golf; *Fam* **it's very much a s. thing** c'est très épisodique

> Attention: ne pas confondre avec **sometimes**.

ometimes ['sʌmtaɪmz] ADV quelquefois, par- fois; **I s. think that it's a waste of time** parfois je me dis que c'est une perte de temps; **you can be so irritating s.!** qu'est-ce que tu peux être aga- çant quelquefois!; **s. they're friendly, s. (they're) not** tantôt ils sont aimables, tantôt (ils ne le sont) pas

> Attention: ne pas confondre avec **sometime**.

omewhat ['sʌmwɒt] ADV quelque peu, un peu; **I was s. disappointed** j'ai été quelque peu dé- çu; **everybody came, s. to my surprise** tout le monde est venu, ce qui n'a pas été sans me sur- prendre; **it was s. of a failure** c'était plutôt un échec

omewhere ['sʌmweə(r)] ADV **1** *(indicating an unspecified place)* quelque part; **s. in the drawer/ on the desk** quelque part dans le tiroir/sur le bu- reau; **s. in the world** quelque part (dans le monde); **s. in France** quelque part en France; **s. near us** pas bien loin de nous; **she's s. around** elle est quelque part par là, elle n'est pas loin; **let's go s. else** allons ailleurs *ou* autre part; **but it's got to be s. or other!** mais il doit bien être quelque part!; **I read s. that it can be fatal** j'ai lu quelque part que ça peut être mortel; **I'm looking for s. to stay** je cherche un endroit où loger; **I need s. quiet to work** j'ai besoin d'un endroit calme pour travailler; **she's found s. more comfortable to sit** elle a trouvé un siège plus confortable; **now we're getting s.!** nous arrivons enfin à quelque chose! **2** *(approximately)* environ; **she earns s. around $2,000 a month** elle gagne quelque chose comme 2000 dollars par mois; **s. between five and six hundred people were there** il y avait entre cinq et six cents personnes; **he must be s. in his forties** il doit avoir entre quarante et cinquante ans

omnambulism [sɒm'næmbjʊlɪzəm] N som- nambulisme *m*

omnambulist [sɒm'næmbjʊlɪst] N somnam- bule *mf*

omniferous [sɒm'nɪfərəs] ADJ soporifique, omnifère

omnolence ['sɒmnələns] N somnolence *f*

omnolent ['sɒmnələnt] ADJ somnolent

son[1] [sʌn] N **1** *(family member)* fils *m*; **she's got two sons** elle a deux fils *ou* garçons; *Fig* **the sons of Ireland** les fils *mpl* de l'Irlande; **s. and heir** héri- tier *m* **2** *Fam (term of address)* fiston *m*
• **Son** N *Rel* Fils *m*; **the S. of God** le Fils de Dieu; **the S. of Man** le Fils de l'Homme

son[2] [sɔʊn] N *Mus* son *m*

sonar ['səʊnɑː(r)] N sonar *m*

sonata [sə'nɑːtə] N sonate *f*; **piano/violin s.** so- nate *f* pour piano/violon

sonatina [ˌsɒnə'tiːnə] N sonatine *f*

sonde [sɒnd] N *Astron & Met* sonde *f*

son et lumière [ˌsɒneɪ'luːmjeə(r)] N spectacle *m* son et lumière, son et lumière *m*

song [sɒŋ] N **1** *(piece of music with words)* chan- son *f*; **I'll sing you a s.** je vais vous chanter une chanson; **give us a s.** chante-nous quelque chose; **a s. and dance act** un numéro de comédie musicale; **it was going for a s.** ça se vendait pour une bouchée de pain *ou* trois fois rien; *Literary* **with a s. in one's heart** la joie au cœur, le cœur léger; *Br Fam* **to make a s. and dance about sth** faire toute une histoire pour qch; *Br Fam* **to be on s.** être en super forme **2** *(songs collectively, act of singing)* chanson *f*; **an anthology of British s.** une anthologie de la chanson britannique; **they all burst into s.** ils se sont tous mis à chanter; **we raised our voice in s.** nous avons entonné une chanson à pleins poumons **3** *(of birds, insects)* chant *m*
►► ***song cycle*** cycle *m* de chansons; *Bible* ***the Song of Songs, the Song of Solomon*** le Cantique des cantiques; ***song thrush*** grive *f* musicienne

songbird ['sɒŋbɜːd] N oiseau *m* chanteur

songster ['sɒŋstə(r)] N **1** *(person)* chanteur (euse) *m,f* **2** *Literary (bird)* oiseau *m* chanteur

songstress ['sɒŋstrɪs] N *Literary* chanteuse *f*

songwriter ['sɒŋˌraɪtə(r)] N *(of lyrics)* parolier (ère) *m,f*; *(of music)* compositeur(trice) *m,f*; *(of lyrics and music)* auteur-compositeur *m*

sonic ['sɒnɪk] ADJ **1** *(involving, producing sound)* acoustique **2** *(concerning speed of sound)* so- nique
• **sonics** N acoustique *f*
►► ***sonic bang*** bang *m*; ***sonic barrier*** mur *m* du son; ***sonic boom*** bang *m*

son-in-law *(pl* **sons-in-law***)* N gendre *m*, beau- fils *m*

sonnet ['sɒnɪt] N sonnet *m*

sonny ['sʌnɪ] N *Fam* fiston *m*; **come here, s. (boy** *or* **Jim)** viens-là, fiston

son-of-a-bitch *(pl* **sons-of-bitches***)* *Am very Fam* N **1** *(man)* fils *m* de pute; **you old s., how are you doing?** comment ça va, enfoiré? **2** *(object)* saloperie *f*; **this s. is too heavy to carry** cette salo- perie est trop lourde à porter
EXCLAM putain!

son-of-a-gun *(pl* **sons-of-guns***)* *Am Fam* N sa- laud *m*; **hey there, you old s.!** salut, vieux bandit!
EXCLAM putain!

sonority [sə'nɒrətɪ] N sonorité *f*

sonorous ['sɒnərəs] ADJ **1** *(resonant)* sonore **2** *(grandiloquent* ► *tone, language)* grandiloquent

> Note that the French adjective **sonore** only applies to sounds.

sonorously ['sɒnərəslɪ] ADV **1** *(speak, sing)* d'une voix sonore; *(echo, crash)* avec un bruit re- tentissant **2** *Pej (declare, announce)* de manière grandiloquente

sonorousness ['sɒnərəsnɪs] N sonorité *f*; *Pej (of tone, language)* grandiloquence *f*

soon [suːn] ADV **1** *(in a short time)* bientôt, sous peu; **(I'll) see you/speak to you s.!** à bientôt!; **write s.!** écris-moi vite!; **I'll be back s.** je serai vite de retour; **a burglar can s. open a lock like that** un cambrioleur a vite fait d'ouvrir une serrure comme celle-ci; **she phoned s. after you'd left** elle a téléphoné peu après ton départ; **s. after** peu après; **s. after four** (un) peu après quatre heu- res; **it will s. be three years since...** voici bientôt trois ans que... + *indicative*, cela fera bientôt trois ans que... + *indicative*; **they were s. making friends** ils se sont bien vite fait des amis **2** *(early)* tôt; **oh dear, I spoke too s.!** mince, j'ai parlé trop tôt!; **it's too s. to make any predictions** il est trop tôt pour se prononcer; **how s. can you finish it?** pour quand pouvez-vous le terminer?; **the po- lice have arrived, and not a moment too s.** les poli- ciers sont arrivés, et ce n'est pas trop tôt
• **as soon as** CONJ dès que + *indicative*, aussitôt que + *indicative*; **as s. as possible** dès *ou* aussitôt que possible; **phone me as s. as you hear anything** téléphonez-moi dès que vous aurez des nouvel- les; **he came as s. as he could** il est venu dès *ou* aussitôt qu'il a pu
• **(just) as soon** ADV **I'd (just) as s. go by boat as by plane** j'aimerais autant *ou* mieux y aller en bateau qu'en avion; **do you want to come with us? – I'd just as s. not, if you don't mind** veux-tu venir avec nous? – j'aimerais autant *ou* mieux pas, si ça ne t'ennuie pas; **I'd just as s. he came tomorrow** j'aimerais autant *ou* mieux qu'il vienne demain; **I'd as s. die as do that!** plutôt mourir que de faire ça!

sooner ['suːnə(r)] ADV *(compar of* **soon***)* **1** *(earlier)* plus tôt; **the s. the better** le plus tôt sera le mieux; **the s. it's over the s. we can leave** plus tôt ce sera fini, plus tôt nous pourrons partir; **no s. said than done!** aussitôt dit, aussitôt fait!; **no s. had I sat down than...** je venais juste de m'asseoir quand...; **s. or later** tôt ou tard; **the problem should be dealt with s. rather than later** il faut faire face au problème le plus tôt possible **2** *(indicat- ing preference)* **shall we go out tonight? – I'd s. not** si on sortait ce soir? – j'aimerais mieux pas; **I'd s. die than go through that again!** plutôt mourir que de revivre ça!; **someone will have to do it – s. you than me!** quelqu'un devra le faire – il vaudrait mieux que ce soit vous, plutôt que moi!

soot [sʊt] N suie *f*

sooth [suːθ] N *Arch* **in s.** en vérité

soothe [suːð] VT **1** *(calm, placate)* calmer, apai- ser; *(the mind)* tranquilliser; **to s. sb's anger** apai- ser la colère de qn **2** *(relieve* ► *pain)* calmer, soulager; **this will s. your sore throat** ça va soula- ger votre mal de gorge
► **soothe down** VT SEP *(make less angry, worried* ► *person)* calmer

soothing ['suːðɪŋ] ADJ **1** *(music, words, voice)* apaisant; *(atmosphere, presence)* rassurant; **the music had a s. effect on them** la musique les a cal- més; **the chairman made the usual s. noises** le pré- sident a fait son laïus habituel pour calmer les esprits **2** *(lotion, ointment)* apaisant, calmant

soothingly ['suːðɪŋlɪ] ADV *(gen)* d'une manière apaisante *ou* rassurante; *(say, speak)* d'un ton apaisant *ou* tranquillisant

soothsayer ['suːθˌseɪə(r)] N devin *m*, devine- resse *f*

soothsaying ['suːθˌseɪɪŋ] N divination *f*

sooty ['sʊtɪ] *(compar* **sootier**, *superl* **sootiest***)* ADJ **1** *(dirty)* couvert de suie, noir de suie **2** *(dark)* **s. (black)** noir comme de la suie **3** *(deposit)* de suie

sop [sɒp] N **1** *(concession)* **as a s. to his conscience** pour soulager sa conscience; **they threw in the measure as a s. to the ecologists** ils ont ajouté cette mesure pour amadouer les écologistes; **she said it as a s. to their pride/feelings** elle l'a dit pour flatter leur amour-propre/pour ménager leur sensibilité **2** *Fam (weak person)* mauviette *f*
• **sops** NPL *Culin* pain *m* trempé
► **sop up** VT SEP *(absorb)* absorber; *(mop up)* éponger; **he sopped up the sauce in his plate with a piece of bread** il a essuyé la sauce qu'il y avait dans son assiette avec un morceau de pain

soph [sɒf] N *Am Fam (abbr* **sophomore***)* étudiant (e) *m,f* de deuxième année

sophism ['sɒfɪzəm] N sophisme *m*

sophist ['sɒfɪst] N *(false reasoner)* sophiste *mf*
• **Sophist** N *Phil* sophiste *m*

sophistic [sə'fɪstɪk], **sophistical** [sə'fɪstɪkəl] ADJ sophistique, captieux

sophisticate [sə'fɪstɪkeɪt] N personne *f* raffinée; **New York sophisticates** la bonne société new-yor- kaise

sophisticated [sə'fɪstɪkeɪtɪd] ADJ **1** *(person, manner, tastes* ► *refined)* raffiné; *(*► *chic)* chic, élégant; *(*► *well-informed)* bien informé; *(*► *ma- ture)* mûr; *(style)* recherché; **they used to think it was s. to smoke** ils croyaient que ça faisait chic de fumer; **our more s. readers** nos lecteurs les plus avertis; **the electorate has become too s. to believe that promise** l'électorat est désormais trop bien informé *ou* trop averti pour croire à cette promesse **2** *(argument, novel, film ▸ subtle)* subtil; *(▸ complicated)* complexe **3** *(machine, system, technology ▸ advanced)* sophistiqué, perfectionné

sophistication [sə,fɪstɪ'keɪʃən] **N 1** *(of person, manners, tastes ▸ refinement)* raffinement *m*; *(▸ chic)* chic *m*, élégance *f*; *(▸ maturity)* maturité *f*; **lack of s.** *(unworldliness)* simplicité *f*; *(lack of polish)* manque *m* de raffinement; **the growing s. of cinema audiences** le fait que le public de cinéma est de plus en plus averti **2** *(of argument, novel, film ▸ subtlety)* subtilité *f*; *(▸ complexity)* complexité *f* **3** *(of system, technology)* sophistication *f*, degré *m* de perfectionnement *m*

sophistry ['sɒfɪstrɪ] *(pl* **sophistries***)* **N 1** *(argumentation)* sophistique *f* **2** *(argument)* sophisme *m*

Sophocles ['sɒfəkli:z] **PR N** Sophocle

sophomore ['sɒfəmɔ:(r)] **N** *Am* étudiant(e) *m,f* de seconde année; **in my s. year** lorsque j'étais en seconde année

soporific [,sɒpə'rɪfɪk] **ADJ** soporifique
N soporifique *m*, somnifère *m*

soppiness ['sɒpɪnɪs] **N** *Br Fam (sentimentality)* sentimentalisme□ *m*, sensiblerie□ *f*

sopping ['sɒpɪŋ] **ADJ & ADV** *Fam* **s. (wet)** *(person)* trempé (jusqu'aux os)□; *(shirt, cloth)* détrempé□

soppy ['sɒpɪ] *(compar* **soppier**, *superl* **soppiest***)* **ADJ** *Br Fam* **1** *(sentimental ▸ person)* sentimental□, fleur bleue□ *(inv)*; *(▸ story, picture)* sentimental□, à l'eau de rose□ **2** *(silly)* nigaud, bébête **3** *(in love)* **to be s. about sb** avoir le béguin pour qn

soprano [sə'prɑ:nəʊ] *(pl* **sopranos** *or* **soprani** [-ni:]*)* **N** *(singer)* soprano *mf*; *(voice, part, instrument)* soprano *m*; **to sing s.** avoir une voix de soprano
ADJ *(voice, part)* de soprano; *(music)* pour soprano
▸▸ ***soprano saxophone*** saxophone *m* soprano

sorb [sɔ:b] **N** *(fruit)* sorbe *f*; *(tree)* sorbier *m*

sorbet ['sɔ:beɪ] **N** *Br* sorbet *m*

sorbitol ['sɔ:bɪtɒl] **N** sorbitol *m*

sorcerer ['sɔ:sərə(r)] **N** sorcier *m*

sorceress ['sɔ:sərɪs] **N** sorcière *f*

sorcery ['sɔ:sərɪ] *(pl* **sorceries***)* **N** sorcellerie *f*

sordid ['sɔ:dɪd] **ADJ 1** *(dirty, wretched)* sordide, misérable **2** *(base, loathsome)* sordide, infâme, vil; **they've got s. little minds** ce sont des esprits mesquins et sordides; **a s. affair** une affaire sordide; **I'll spare you the s. details** je vous épargnerai les détails sordides

sordidly ['sɔ:dɪdlɪ] **ADV** sordidement

sordidness ['sɔ:dɪdnɪs] **N** *(gen)* sordidité *f*; *(of business, motives)* bassesse *f*

sore [sɔ:(r)] **ADJ 1** *(aching ▸ gen)* douloureux, endolori; *(▸ eyes, gums)* irrité; **we stopped to rest our s. feet** nous nous sommes arrêtés pour reposer nos pieds endoloris; **I'm s. all over** j'ai mal partout; **I've a s. throat** j'ai mal à la gorge; **my arms/legs are s.** j'ai mal aux bras/jambes, mes bras/jambes me font mal; **don't touch me there, it's s.** ne me touche pas là, ça fait mal; **where is it s.?** où as-tu mal?; *Fig* **it's a s. point with her** elle est très sensible sur ce point *ou* là-dessus **2** *Am Fam (angry)* en boule; *(resentful)* vexé□, amer□; **are you still s. at me?** est-ce que tu es toujours en boule contre moi?; **he got s.** il s'est mis en boule; **he's s. because they left him out of the team** il est vexé parce qu'ils l'ont laissé en dehors de l'équipe **3** *Literary (great)* grand; **in s. distress** dans une grande détresse; **to be in s. need of sth** avoir grand besoin de qch
N plaie *f*; **open sores** des plaies *fpl* ouvertes
ADV *Arch* grandement; **they were s. afraid** ils éprouvèrent une grande frayeur

sorehead ['sɔ:hed] **N** *Am Fam* ronchon(onne) *m, f*, grincheux(euse) *m,f*

sorely ['sɔ:lɪ] **ADV 1** *(as intensifier)* grandement; **the house is s. in need of a new coat of paint** la maison a grandement *ou* bien besoin d'être repeinte; **we are s. pressed for time** nous manquons cruellement de temps; **she will be s. missed** elle nous manquera cruellement; **I was s. tempted to accept her offer** j'ai été très tenté d'accepter sa proposition **2** *Literary (painfully)* **s. wounded** grièvement blessé

soreness ['sɔ:nɪs] **N** douleur *f*

sorghum ['sɔ:gəm] **N** *Bot* sorgho *m*

sorrel ['sɒrəl] **N 1** *Bot & Culin* oseille *f* **2** *(colour)* roux *m*, brun rouge *m* **3** *(horse)* alezan *m* clair
ADJ *(gen)* roux (rousse); *(horse)* alezan clair *(inv)*

sorrow ['sɒrəʊ] **N** chagrin *m*, peine *f*, tristesse *f*; *(stronger)* affliction *f*, douleur *f*; **I am writing to express my s. at your sad loss** je vous écris pour vous faire part de la tristesse que j'ai éprouvée en apprenant votre deuil; **to our great s.** à notre grand regret; **more in s. than in anger** avec plus de tristesse que de colère; **his son's failure was a great s. to him** l'échec de son fils lui a fait *ou* causé beaucoup de peine; **life is full of joys and sorrows** la vie est faite de joies et de peines
VI *Literary* éprouver du chagrin *ou* de la peine; **he is still sorrowing over his son's death** il pleure encore la mort de son fils

sorrowful ['sɒrəfʊl] **ADJ** *(person)* triste; *(look, smile)* affligé

sorrowfully ['sɒrəfəlɪ] **ADV** tristement

sorrowing ['sɒrəʊɪŋ] **ADJ** attristé, affligé

SORRY ['sɒrɪ] *(compar* **sorrier**, *superl* **sorriest***)*

• désolé **1, 3**	• excusez-moi **1**
• pardon **1**	• navré **3**
• triste **5**	

ADJ 1 *(in apologies)* désolé; **I'm s. we won't be able to fetch you** je regrette que *ou* je suis désolé que nous ne puissions venir vous chercher; **(I'm) s. to have bothered you** (je suis) désolé *ou* excusez-moi de vous avoir dérangé; **I'm so** *or* **very** *or* **terribly s.** je suis vraiment navré; **ouch, that's my foot! – (I'm) s.!** aïe! mon pied! – je suis désolé *ou* excusez-moi!; **(I'm) s. about the mess** excusez le désordre; **I'm s. about the mix-up** excusez-moi pour la confusion; **I'm s., but that's absolute rubbish!** désolé, mais c'est vraiment n'importe quoi!; **s. to interrupt you but you're wanted on the phone** excusez-moi de vous interrompre mais on vous demande au téléphone; **s. about forgetting your birthday** désolé d'avoir oublié ton anniversaire; **he said he was s.** il a présenté ses excuses; **say (you're) s. to the lady** demande pardon à la dame; **what's the time? – s.?** quelle heure est-il? – pardon? *ou* comment?; **they're coming on Tuesday, s., Thursday** ils viennent mardi, pardon, jeudi
2 *(regretful)* **to be s.** regretter; **I'm s. I ever came here!** je regrette d'être venu ici!; **I'm only s. we couldn't have stayed longer** je regrette que nous n'ayons pas pu rester plus longtemps; **I'm s. to say there's little we can do** malheureusement, nous ne pouvons pas faire grand-chose; **we are s. to inform you that...** nous avons le regret *ou* nous sommes au regret de vous informer que... + *indicative*; **you'll be s. for this** tu le regretteras; **you won't be s.** tu ne le regretteras pas; **I'll make him s. (that) he ever came here** je lui ferai regretter d'être venu ici
3 *(expressing sympathy)* désolé, navré, peiné; **I was s. to hear about your father's death** j'ai été désolé *ou* peiné *ou* navré d'apprendre la mort de votre père
4 *(expressing pity)* **to be** *or* **to feel s. for sb** plaindre qn; **there's no need to feel s. for them** ils ne sont pas à plaindre; **she felt s. for him and gave him a pound** elle eut pitié de lui et lui donna une livre; **to be** *or* **to feel s. for oneself** s'apitoyer sur soi-même *ou* sur son propre sort; **stop feeling s. for yourself!** arrête un peu de t'apitoyer sur ton propre sort!
5 *(pitiful, wretched)* triste, piteux; **to cut a s. figure** faire triste *ou* piètre figure; **they were a s. sight after the match** ils étaient dans un triste état après le match; **the garden was in a s. state** le jardin était en piteux état *ou* dans un triste état; **it's a s. state of affairs** c'est bien triste; **the whole s. tale** toute cette malheureuse affaire

sorry-ass, sorry-assed **ADJ** *Am very Fam (inferior, contemptible)* à la con

SORT [sɔ:t]

N	
• sorte **1**	• espèce **1**
• genre **1**	• tri **3**
VT	
• classer **1**	• trier **1**
• répartir **1**	• séparer **1**
VI	
• (se) trier	

N 1 *(kind, type)* sorte *f*, espèce *f*, genre *m*; *(bran* marque *f*; **a hat with a s. of veil** un chapeau ave une sorte *ou* une espèce *ou* un genre de voil **it's a strange s. of film** c'est un drôle de film; **it's different s. of problem** c'est un autre type de pr blème; **the trees formed a s. of arch** les arbres fo maient comme une arche; **I think that he's som s. of specialist** *or* **that he's a specialist of some s.** crois que c'est un genre de spécialiste; **she's n the s. (of woman) to let you down** elle n'est pas c genre à vous laisser tomber; **this** *or Fam* **these of people** les gens de cette espèce, ces gens-là **know your s.!** les gens de ton espèce, je le connais!; **there's too much of this s. of thing goir on** il se passe trop de choses de ce genre; **goo luck, and all that s. of thing!** bonne chance, tout et tout!; **what s. of fish are we having** qu'est-ce qu'on mange comme poisson?; **wh s. of dog is that?** qu'est-ce que c'est comme chie *ou* comme race de chien?; **what s. of woman she?** quel genre de femme est-ce?; **what s. day did you have?** comment s'est passée ta jou née?; **that's my s. of holiday** voilà des vacance comme je les aime; **all sorts of people** des ger de toutes sortes; **you get all sorts at these parti** on rencontre toutes sortes de gens dans ces sc rées; **there are all sorts of materials to choose fro** on peut choisir parmi toutes sortes de mat riaux; **I've heard all sorts of good things abo you** j'ai entendu dire beaucoup de bien de vou **to be out of sorts** *(a little unwell)* ne pas être dar son assiette; *(in a bad mood)* être de mauvais humeur; **something of the s.** *or* **of that s.** quelqu chose de pareil *ou* de semblable *ou* dans c genre-là; **I said nothing of the s.!** je n'ai rien d de pareil *ou* de tel!; **you were drunk last night – was nothing of the s.!** tu étais ivre hier soir – a solument pas! *ou* mais pas du tout!; *Prov* **it tak all sorts (to make a world)** il faut de tout pour fai un monde
2 *Fam (person)* **she's a good** *or* **decent s.** *(your woman)* c'est une brave fille; *(older woman)* c'e une brave femme; **he's not a bad s.** ce n'est pas mauvais cheval
3 *(gen) & Comput (▸ putting in order)* tri *m*; **th program will do an alphabetical s.** le programm exécutera un tri alphabétique; **s. routine** routir *f* de tri; *Fam* **I've had a s. through all the wint clothes** j'ai trié tous les vêtements d'hiver□
VT 1 *(classify)* classer, trier; *(divide up)* réparti *(separate)* séparer; *Comput* trier; **to s. mail** trier courrier; **they were sorting the shirts according t colour** ils triaient les chemises selon leur co leur; **s. the letters into urgent and less urgent** re partissez les lettres entre celles qui so urgentes et celles qui le sont moins; **help me the good fruit from the bad** aidez-moi à sépar les bons fruits des mauvais; *Comput* **to s. sth ascending/descending order** trier qch par ord croissant/décroissant
2 *(organize)* = **sort out**
VI *Comput (arrange in list)* trier; *(file, data)* s trier

• **of sorts, of a sort** **ADV** **they served us char pagne of sorts** *or* **of a s.** ils nous ont servi une e pèce de champagne; **a peace/solution of sorts** u semblant de paix/de solution; **they live in home of sorts** ils habitent dans une maison, on peut appeler ça une maison

• **sort of** **ADV** *Fam* **I s. of expected it to rain** m'attendais un peu à ce qu'il pleuve□; **I'm s. glad that I missed them** je suis plutôt content d les avoir ratés; **it's s. of big and round** c'est du genr grand et rond; **it's s. of heavy** c'est un peu lour c'est plutôt lourd□; **he s. of apologized** d'une ce taine façon, il s'est excusé□; **did you hit him? – we s. of** tu l'as frappé? – en quelque sorte, oui□
▸▸ *Banking* ***sort code*** code *m* guichet

▸ **sort out VT SEP 1** *(separate)* séparer; **to s. out the foreign stamps from the British ones** séparer les timbres étrangers des timbres britanniques
2 *(select and set aside)* trier; **we've already sorted out the likely candidates from the rest** nous avons déjà trié les candidats intéressants (et les autres)
3 *(tidy up, put in order ▸ papers, clothes, room, cupboard)* ranger; *(▸ finances, ideas)* mettre en ordre; **give me a few minutes to get (myself) sorted out** *or* **to s. myself out** donnez-moi quelques minutes pour m'organiser; **she needs to get her personal life sorted out** il faut qu'elle règle ses problèmes personnels
4 *(settle, resolve ▸ problem, dispute)* régler, résoudre; **they still haven't sorted out the mistake in my tax form** ils n'ont toujours pas réglé cette erreur dans ma feuille d'impôts; **everything's sorted out now** tout est arrangé *ou* réglé maintenant; **things will s. themselves out in the end** les choses finiront par s'arranger; *Fam* **two aspirins ought to s. out that headache** deux aspirines devraient avoir raison de ce mal de tête▫
5 *(establish, clarify)* **have you sorted out how to do it?** est-ce que tu as trouvé le moyen de le faire?; **I'm trying to s. out what's been going on** j'essaie de savoir *ou* de comprendre ce qui s'est passé; **you've got to s. out your priorities** il faut que tu définisses ce qui prime pour toi
6 *(arrange)* arranger, fixer; **I'll go and s. the tickets out** je vais m'occuper des billets; **to s. out the details** faire le nécessaire; **to s. out a room for sb** préparer une chambre pour qn
7 *Br Fam (solve the problems of ▸ person)* **he's very depressed, you should try to s. him out** il est très déprimé, tu devrais essayer de l'aider à s'en sortir▫; **she needs time to s. herself out** il lui faut du temps pour régler ses problèmes▫
8 *Br Fam (punish)* régler son compte à▫
sort through VT INSEP trier; **I've been sorting through the old magazines** j'ai trié les vieux magazines

sorta ['sɔːtə] *Fam* = **sort of**

sorted ['sɔːtɪd] *Br Fam* **ADJ to be s.** *(psychologically)* être équilibré▫, être bien dans ses baskets *ou* dans sa peau; *(have everything one needs)* être paré▫; **to be s. for sth** disposer de qch▫
EXCLAM super!, génial!

sorter ['sɔːtə(r)] **N 1** *(person)* trieur(euse) *m,f*; **letter s.** employé(e) *m,f* au tri postal **2** *(machine ▸ gen)* trieur *m*; *(▸ for punched cards)* trieuse *f*

sortie ['sɔːtiː] **N** *Mil* sortie *f*; *Hum* **I sometimes make the odd s. to the pub/shops** de temps en temps je fais un petit tour dans les pubs/magasins

sorting ['sɔːtɪŋ] **N** tri *m*
▸▸ *Banking* ***sorting code*** code *m* guichet; ***sorting office*** centre *m* de tri; *Comput* ***sorting routine*** routine *f* de tri

SOS [ˌesəʊ'es] **N** *(abbr* **save our souls)** SOS *m*; **to send out an S.** lancer un SOS; **we received an S. call** *or* **message** nous avons reçu un SOS; *Fig* **relief organizations are sending out an S. for food and clothing** les organisations d'aide demandent d'urgence de la nourriture et des vêtements

so-so ADJ *Fam* pas fameux; *(in health)* comme ci comme ça, couci-couça; **the film was only s.** le film n'était pas fameux

sot [sɒt] **N** *Literary* ivrogne(esse) *m,f*

Note that the French word **sot** is a false friend and is never a translation for the English word **sot**. It means **fool**.

sottish ['sɒtɪʃ] **ADJ** *Literary* sot (sotte), stupide, abruti

sotto voce [ˌsɒtəʊ'vəʊtʃɪ] **ADV 1** *(gen)* à voix basse **2** *Mus* sotto voce

soufflé ['suːfleɪ] **N** soufflé *m*; **cheese/chocolate s.** soufflé *m* au fromage/au chocolat
▸▸ ***soufflé dish*** moule *m* à soufflé

sough [saʊ] *Literary* **VI** murmurer, susurrer
N murmure *m*, susurrement *m (du vent)*

sought [sɔːt] *pt & pp of* **seek**

sought-after ADJ recherché

soul [səʊl] **N 1** *Rel* âme *f*; **God rest his s.!** que Dieu ait son âme!; *Old-fashioned* **upon my s.!** grands dieux!; *Fig* **it's good for the s.** *(character-forming)* ça forme le caractère; *(makes a person feel better)* c'est bon pour le moral
2 *(emotional depth)* profondeur *f*; **it was a polished performance, but it lacked s.** c'était une prestation impeccable, mais sans âme; **you've got no s.!** tu n'as pas de cœur!
3 *(leading figure)* âme *f*; **she was the s. of the early feminist movement** elle était l'âme du mouvement féministe à ses débuts
4 *(perfect example)* modèle *m*; **the s. of discretion** la discrétion même *ou* personnifiée
5 *(person)* personne *f*, âme *f*; **poor old s.!** le (la) pauvre!; **without meeting a (living) s.** sans rencontrer âme qui vive; **there wasn't a s. in the streets** il n'y avait pas âme qui vive dans les rues; **I didn't know a s. at the party** je ne connaissais personne à la réception; **I won't tell a s.** je ne le dirai à personne; **she's a happy s.** elle a un tempérament heureux *ou* optimiste; *Literary* **a town of 20,000 souls** une ville de 20 000 âmes
6 *(music)* (musique *f*) soul *f*, soul music *f*; **a s. singer** un(e) chanteur(euse) *m,f* de soul
ADJ *Am Old-fashioned* = caractéristique de la culture des Noirs américains
▸▸ *Am Fam* ***soul brother*** = nom que les Noirs américains donnent aux hommes noirs; *Fam* ***soul food*** cuisine *f* afroaméricaine▫; ***soul music*** musique *f* soul, soul music *f*; *Am Fam* ***soul sister*** = nom que les Noirs américains donnent aux femmes noires

soul-destroying [-dɪ'strɔɪɪŋ] **ADJ** *(job)* abrutissant; *(situation, place)* déprimant

soulful ['səʊlfʊl] **ADJ** *(song, performance, sigh)* émouvant, attendrissant; *(look, eyes)* mélancolique

soulfully ['səʊlfəlɪ] **ADV** *(sing, perform, sigh)* de façon émouvante *ou* attendrissante; *(look)* d'un air mélancolique

soulless ['səʊllɪs] **ADJ 1** *(inhuman ▸ place)* inhumain, sans âme; *(▸ work)* abrutissant **2** *(heartless)* sans cœur, insensible

soullessly ['səʊllɪslɪ] **ADV** sans émotion; **the house had been s. renovated** on avait rénové la maison sans aucune sensibilité

soullessness ['səʊllɪsnɪs] **N 1** *(of building)* côté *m* inhumain; **the s. of my surroundings** le cadre inhumain qui m'entoure **2** *(of person)* manque *m* de sensibilité

soulmate ['səʊlmeɪt] **N** âme *f* sœur

soul-searching N introspection *f*; **after much s. she decided to leave** après mûre réflexion *ou* après avoir mûrement réfléchi, elle décida de partir

soul-stirring ADJ (profondément) émouvant

SOUND [saʊnd]

N
- bruit **1**
- son **1–4**
- musique **5**
- sonde **7, 8**

ADJ
- solide **1, 3**
- en bon état **1**
- sain **1, 2**
- en bonne santé **2**
- sensé **3**
- valable **3**
- bon **3, 4**
- profond **5**

COMP
- sonore

ADV
- profondément

VT
- sonner **1**
- prononcer **2**
- ausculter **3**
- sonder **3–5**

VI
- sonner **1**
- résonner **1**
- retentir **1**
- se prononcer **2**
- sembler **3**

N 1 *(noise ▸ of footsteps, thunder, conversation)* bruit *m*; *(▸ of voice, musical instrument)* son *m*; **I was woken by the s. of voices/laughter** j'ai été réveillé par un bruit de voix/par des éclats de rires; **a scratching s.** un grattement; **don't make a s.!** surtout ne faites pas de bruit!; **they tiptoed out without (making) a s.** ils sont sortis sur la pointe des pieds sans faire de bruit; **there was not a s. to be heard** on n'entendait pas le moindre bruit; **within (the) s. of the church bells** à portée du son des cloches de l'église
2 *Phys* son *m*; **the speed of s.** la vitesse du son
3 *Ling* son *m*; **the English vowel sounds** les sons *mpl* vocaliques de l'anglais
4 *Rad & TV* son *m*; **to turn the s. up/down** monter/baisser le son *ou* volume
5 *(type of music)* style *m* de musique, musique *f*; **the Liverpool s.** la musique de Liverpool; **a brand new s. has hit the charts** un son complètement nouveau a fait son entrée au hit-parade
6 *(impression, idea)* **I don't like the s. of these new measures** ces nouvelles mesures ne me disent rien qui vaille; **it's pretty easy by the s. of it** ça a l'air assez facile; **he's angry by the s. of it** on dirait bien qu'il est fâché
7 *Med (probe)* sonde *f*
8 *Naut (sounding line)* (ligne *f* de) sonde *f*
9 *Geog (channel)* détroit *m*, bras *m* de mer
ADJ 1 *(structure, building, wall ▸ sturdy)* solide; *(▸ in good condition)* en bon état, sain; **built on s. foundations** construit sur des fondations solides
2 *(healthy ▸ person)* en bonne santé; *(▸ body, mind, limbs)* sain; **to be of s. mind** être sain d'esprit; **s. in body and mind** sain de corps et d'esprit; **to be as s. as a bell** être en parfaite santé
3 *(solid, well-founded ▸ advice, idea, strategy)* sensé, judicieux; *(▸ argument, claim)* valable, fondé, solide; *(▸ reason)* valable; *(▸ basis, knowledge)* solide; *(▸ manager, musician, lawyer etc)* compétent, fiable; *(▸ investment)* sûr; *(▸ company, business)* solide; **to show s. judgment** faire preuve de jugement; **do you think that was a s. move?** croyez-vous que c'était une décision judicieuse; **my knowledge of German history isn't too s.** mes connaissances en ce qui concerne l'histoire de l'Allemagne laissent à désirer; **his grammar's pretty s.** il a de bonnes bases en grammaire; **Crawford seems a s. enough chap** Crawford semble être quelqu'un en qui on peut avoir confiance; **is she politically s.?** ses convictions politiques sont-elles solides?; **ecologically s. legislation** législation *f* juste du point de vue écologique; **s. financial position** situation *f* financière saine
4 *(severe ▸ defeat)* total; *(▸ hiding)* bon
5 *(deep ▸ sleep)* profond; **I'm a very s. sleeper** j'ai le sommeil profond
COMP *(level, recording)* sonore; *(broadcasting)* radiophonique; *Ling (change)* phonologique
ADV to be s. asleep dormir profondément *ou* à poings fermés
VT 1 *(bell)* sonner; *(wind instrument)* sonner de; **the huntsman sounded his horn** le chasseur sonna du cor; **the driver behind me sounded his horn** le conducteur derrière moi a klaxonné; *also Fig* **to s. the alarm** sonner *ou* donner l'alarme; **the bugler sounded the reveille** le clairon sonna le réveil; **to s. a warning** lancer un avertissement
2 *(pronounce)* prononcer; **the "p" isn't sounded** le "p" ne se prononce pas
3 *Med (chest, lungs)* ausculter; *(cavity, passage)* sonder
4 *Naut* sonder
5 *(person)* sonder; **to s. public opinion** sonder l'opinion publique; **I'll try to s. their feelings on the matter** j'essaierai de connaître leur sentiment à cet égard
VI 1 *(make a sound)* sonner, résonner, retentir; **it sounds hollow if you tap it** ça sonne creux lorsqu'on tape dessus; **their voices sounded very loud in the empty house** leurs voix résonnaient bruyamment dans la maison vide; **sirens sounded in the streets** des sirènes retentissaient dans les rues; **if the alarm sounds, run** si vous entendez l'alarme, enfuyez-vous
2 *Br (be pronounced)* se prononcer
3 *(seem)* sembler, paraître; **he sounded sad** il semblait triste; **he sounded bored** il semblait s'ennuyer; **the name sounded French** le nom avait l'air d'être *ou* sonnait français; **she sounds French** elle a l'air d'être française; **it doesn't s. very interesting to me** ça ne m'a pas l'air très intéressant; **"attractive four-bedroomed house", how does that s.?** "belle maison avec quatre chambres à coucher", qu'est-ce que tu en penses?; **(that) sounds like a good idea** ça semble être une bonne idée; **two weeks in Crete, that sounds nice!** deux semaines en Crète, pas mal du tout!; **it sounds like Mozart** on dirait du Mozart; **you s. as though** *or* **as if** *or* **like you've got a cold** on dirait que tu es

enrhumé; **it sounds to me as though they don't want to do it** j'ai l'impression qu'ils ne veulent pas le faire; **it doesn't s. to me as though they want to do it** je n'ai pas l'impression qu'ils veuillent le faire; **you s. just like your brother on the phone** tu as la même voix que ton frère *ou* on dirait vraiment ton frère au téléphone; **that sounds like the postman now** je crois entendre le facteur

• **sounds** NPL *Fam (music)* zizique *f*, zicmu *f*

▸▸ ***sound archives*** phonothèque *f*; **a recording from the BBC s. archives** un enregistrement qui vient des archives de la BBC; ***sound barrier*** mur *m* du son; **to break the s. barrier** franchir le mur du son; *Mus* ***sound box*** caisse *f* de résonance; ***sound camera*** caméra *f* sonore; *Comput* ***sound card*** carte *f* son; ***sound check*** soundcheck *m*; *Cin, TV & Rad* ***sound crew*** équipe *f* du son; ***sound designer*** concepteur(trice) *m,f* sonore; ***sound director*** directeur(trice) *m,f* du son; ***sound editing*** montage *m* sonore; ***sound editor*** monteur *m* son; ***sound effects*** bruitage *m*; ***sound effects library*** sonothèque *f*; *Rad* ***sound effects person*** bruiteur(euse) *m,f*; ***sound engineer*** ingénieur *m* du son; ***sound fade*** fondu *m* sonore; ***sound film*** film *m* sonore; ***sound hole*** *(of violin, viola etc)* ouïe *f*, esse *f*; *(of guitar, lute etc)* rosace *f*, rose *f*; ***sound man*** preneur *m* de son, opérateur *m* du son; ***sound mix*** mixage *m*; ***sound mixer*** table *f ou* console *f* de mixage; ***sound mixing*** mixage *m* sonore; ***sound montage*** montage *m* sonore; ***sound plot*** = liste des sons et bruitages nécessaires pour la production d'une pièce de théâtre ou radiophonique; ***sound quality*** qualité *f* du son, qualité *f* sonore; ***sound recordist*** preneur *m* de son; ***sound reel*** bande *f* son; *Ling* ***sound shift*** mutation *f* phonologique; ***sound stage*** studio *m* insonorisé; ***sound studio*** auditorium *m ou* studio *m* d'enregistrement; ***sound system*** *(hi-fi)* chaîne *f* hifi; *(PA system)* sonorisation *f*; ***sound technician*** preneur *m* de son, opérateur *m* du son; ***sound wave*** onde *f* sonore

▸ **sound off** VI *Fam* **1** *(declare one's opinions)* crier son opinion sur tous les toits; *(complain)* râler; **he's always sounding off about the management** il est toujours à râler contre la direction; **to s. off at sb** *(angrily)* passer un savon à qn **2** *(boast)* se vanter▫

▸ **sound out** VT SEP *(person, public opinion)* sonder

---

soundbite ['saʊndbaɪt] N petite phrase *f (prononcée par un homme politique à la radio ou à la télévision pour frapper les esprits)*

sounder ['saʊndə(r)] N *Naut* sondeur *m*

sounding ['saʊndɪŋ] N **1** *Aviat, Met & Naut (measuring)* sondage *m* **2** *(of bell, horn)* son *m*; **wait for the s. of the alarm** attendez le signal d'alarme *ou* que le signal d'alarme retentisse; *Mil* **the s. of the retreat** le signal de la retraite

• **soundings** NPL *(investigations)* sondages *mpl*; **to take soundings** faire des sondages

▸▸ ***sounding board*** **1** *(over pulpit, rostrum)* abat-voix *m inv* **2** *Fig (person)* **she uses her assistants as a s. board for any new ideas** elle essaie toutes ses nouvelles idées sur ses assistants **3** *(of piano, violin)* table *f* d'harmonie; *(of organ)* tamis *m*; ***sounding lead*** (plomb *m* de) sonde *f*; ***sounding line*** sonde *f*

soundless ['saʊndlɪs] ADJ **1** *(silent)* silencieux **2** *Literary (deep)* insondable

soundlessly ['saʊndlɪslɪ] ADV *(silently)* silencieusement, sans bruit

soundly ['saʊndlɪ] ADV **1** *(deeply ▸ sleep)* profondément, à poings fermés; **we can all sleep s. in our beds now that we know that the murderer has been caught** nous pouvons tous dormir sur nos deux oreilles maintenant que nous savons que le meurtrier a été arrêté

2 *(sensibly ▸ advise, argue)* judicieusement, avec bon sens

3 *(safely ▸ invest)* de façon sûre, sans risque *ou* risques

4 *(competently ▸ work, run)* avec compétence

5 *(thoroughly)* **to be s. beaten** *(defeated)* être battu à plates coutures; **he deserves to be s. thrashed** il mérite une bonne correction

soundness ['saʊndnɪs] N **1** *(of body, mind)* santé *f*, équilibre *m*; *(of health)* robustesse *f* **2** *(of building, structure)* solidité *f*; *(of business, financial situation)* solvabilité *f*; *(of decision, advice)* sagesse *f*; *(of argument, reasoning)* justesse *f*

soundproof ['saʊndpruːf] ADJ insonorisé
VT insonoriser

soundproofing ['saʊndpruːfɪŋ] N *(UNCOUNT) (act, process)* insonorisation *f*; *(material)* matériau *m* isolant *ou* insonore

soundtrack ['saʊndtræk] N bande *f* sonore; **s. (album)** bande *f* originale

soup [suːp] N *Culin* soupe *f*; *(thin or blended)* soupe *f*, potage *m*; *(smooth and creamy)* velouté *m*; **onion/fish/leek s.** soupe *f* à l'oignon/de poisson/aux poireaux; **cream of mushroom s.** velouté *m* de champignons; *Fam* **to be in the s.** être dans le pétrin *ou* dans la panade

▸▸ ***soup kitchen*** soupe *f* populaire; ***soup ladle*** louche *f*; ***soup plate*** assiette *f* creuse *ou* à soupe; ***soup spoon*** cuillère *f ou* cuiller *f* à soupe; ***soup tureen*** soupière *f*

▸ **soup up** VT SEP *Fam (engine)* gonfler; *(car)* gonfler le moteur de; *(machine, computer program)* perfectionner▫

soupçon ['suːpsɒn] N *Formal or Hum* soupçon *m*, pointe *f*

souped-up [suːpt-] ADJ *Fam (engine)* gonflé, poussé; *(car)* au moteur gonflé *ou* poussé; *(machine, computer program)* perfectionné▫; **a s. version of the previous model** une version plus performante du modèle précédent▫

sour ['saʊə(r)] ADJ **1** *(flavour, taste)* aigre; *(wine)* suret, verjuté

2 *(rancid ▸ milk)* tourné, aigre; *(▸ breath)* fétide; **the milk has gone** *or* **turned s.** le lait a tourné

3 *(disagreeable ▸ person, character, mood)* aigre, revêche, hargneux; *(▸ look)* hargneux; *(▸ comment, tone)* aigre, acerbe

4 *(wrong, awry)* **to go** *or* **to turn s.** mal tourner; **their marriage went s.** leur mariage a tourné au vinaigre

5 *(too acidic ▸ soil)* trop acide

VI **1** *(wine)* surir, s'aigrir; *(milk)* tourner, aigrir **2** *(person, character)* s'aigrir; *(relationship)* se dégrader, tourner au vinaigre; *(situation)* mal tourner

VT **1** *(milk, wine)* aigrir **2** *(person, character)* aigrir; *(relationship)* gâter, empoisonner; *(situation)* gâter; **the experience soured his view of life** cette expérience l'a aigri

▸▸ ***sour cherry*** *(fruit)* cerise *f* acide; *(tree)* cerisier *m* acide; ***sour cream*** crème *f* aigre; ***sour grapes*** dépit *m*; **it was just s. grapes that made her say that** elle a simplement dit ça par rancœur *ou* dépit; ***sour mash*** = pâte spéciale utilisée dans la fabrication de certains whiskies américains

source [sɔːs] N **1** *(gen)* source *f*; **a good s. of vitamin C** une bonne source de vitamine C; **they have traced the s. of the power cut** ils ont découvert l'origine de la panne de courant; **energy sources** sources *fpl* d'énergie; **at s.** à la source; *Med* **s. of infection** foyer *m* d'infection **2** *(of information)* source *f*; **I have it from a good s.** je le sais *ou* tiens de source sûre; **the journalist refused to name his sources** le journaliste a refusé de nommer ses sources; **according to reliable sources war is imminent** selon des sources sûres *ou* bien informées, la guerre est imminente **3** *(of river)* source *f*

VT **1** *Com (products)* s'approvisionner en, se fournir en; **to be sourced from** provenir de **2** *(give source of)* **the quotations are sourced in footnotes** la source des citations figure dans les notes en bas de page

▸▸ *Comput* ***source code*** code *m* source; *Comput* ***source disk*** *(hard)* disque *m* source; *(floppy)* disquette *f* source; *Comput* ***source document*** document *m* de base, document *m* source; *Comput* ***source file*** fichier *m* source; ***source language*** **1** *Ling* langue *f* source **2** *Comput* langage *m* source; ***source material, source materials*** *(documents)* documentation *f*; *Comput* ***source program*** programme *m* source; *Comput* ***source text*** texte *m* de départ

sourdough ['saʊədəʊ] N *Am* levain *m*

▸▸ *Culin* ***sourdough bread*** pain *m* au levain

sourface ['saʊəfeɪs] N *Fam (ill-tempered person)* grincheux(euse)▫ *m,f*; *(kill-joy)* rabat-joie▫ *m inv*

sour-faced ADJ à la mine revêche; **what are you looking so s. about?** pourquoi cet air maussade *ou* cette mine revêche?

sourly ['saʊəlɪ] ADV aigrement, avec aigreur

sourness ['saʊənɪs] N **1** *(of flavour, taste)* aigreur *f*, acidité *f*; *(of milk)* aigreur *f* **2** *(of person, character, mood)* aigreur *f*; *(of speech, comment)* ton *m* aigre

sourpuss ['saʊəpʊs] N *Fam (ill-tempered person)* grincheux(euse)▫ *m,f*; *(kill-joy)* rabat-joie▫ *m in*

sousaphone ['suːzəfəʊn] N *Mus* sousaphone *m*

sous chef ['suːʃef] N second *m*, assistant *m* du chef de cuisine

souse [saʊs] VT **1** *Culin (in vinegar)* (faire) mariner dans du vinaigre; *(in brine)* (faire) mariner dans de la saumure **2** *(immerse)* immerger, plonger; *(drench)* tremper; **he soused himself with cold water** il s'aspergea abondamment d'eau froide

N *Culin (vinegar)* marinade *f* de vinaigre; *(brine)* saumure *f*

soused [saʊst] ADJ **1** *Culin* mariné **2** *Fam (drunk)* bourré, pété; **to get s.** se soûler

▸▸ *Culin* ***soused herrings*** harengs *mpl* marinés

south [saʊθ] N **1** *Geog* sud *m*; **in the s.** au sud dans le sud; **the region to the s. of Edinburgh** la région au sud d'Édimbourg; **two miles to the s.** trois kilomètres au sud; **look towards the s.** regardez vers le sud; **I was born in the s.** je suis né dans le Sud; **in the S. of India** dans le sud de l'Inde; **in the S. of France** dans le Midi (de la France); **the wind is in the s.** le vent est au sud; **the wind is coming from the s.** le vent vient ou souffle du sud; *Hist* **the S.** *(of United States)* le Sud, les États *mpl* du Sud **2** *Cards* sud *m*

ADJ **1** *Geog* sud *(inv)*, du sud, méridional; *(country, state)* du Sud; *(wall)* exposé au sud; **the s. coast** la côte sud; **in s. London** dans le sud de Londres; **in S. India** en Inde du Sud; **the S. Atlantic/Pacific** l'Atlantique *m*/le Pacifique Sud; **the S. Sea** les mers *fpl* du Sud; **the S. Bank** = complexe su la rive sud de la Tamise réunissant des salles de concert, des théâtres et des musées **2** *(wind)* du sud, du sud

ADV au sud; *(travel)* vers le sud, en direction du sud; **the living room faces s.** la salle de séjour est exposée au sud; **the path heads (due) s.** le chemin va *ou* mène (droit) vers le sud; **walk s. until you come to a main road** marchez vers le sud jusqu'à ce que vous arriviez à une route principale; **I drove s. for two hours** j'ai roulé pendant deux heures en direction du sud; **we're going s. for our holidays** nous allons passer nos vacances dans le Sud; **I travelled s.** je suis allée vers le sud; **to sail s.** naviguer cap sur le sud; **it's 20 miles s. of Birmingham** c'est à 32 kilomètres au sud de Birmingham; **they live down s.** ils habitent dans le Sud; **s. by east/west** sud-quart-sud-est/-ouest; **further s.** plus au sud

▸▸ ***South Africa*** l'Afrique *f* du Sud; ***South African*** N Sud-Africain(e) *m,f* ADJ sud-africain, d'Afrique du Sud; ***South America*** l'Amérique *f* du Sud; ***South American*** N Sud-Américain(e) *m,f* ADJ sud-américain, d'Amérique du Sud; ***South Australia*** l'Australie-Méridionale *f*; *Geog* ***South Carolina*** la Caroline du Sud; *Geog* ***South Dakota*** le Dakota du Sud; ***South Korea*** la Corée du Sud; ***South Korean*** N Sud-Coréen(enne) *m,f*, Coréen(enne) *m* du Sud ADJ sud-coréen; ***South Pole*** le pôle Sud; ***South Sea Islands*** l'Océanie *f*; ***South Vietnam*** le Viêt-nam du Sud; ***South Vietnamese*** N Sud-Vietnamien(enne) *m,f*; **the S. Vietnamese** les Sud-Vietnamiens *mpl* ADJ sud-vietnamien

southbound ['saʊθbaʊnd] ADJ *(traffic)* en direction du sud; *(lane)* du sud; *(road)* vers le sud; **traffic is subject to delays** la circulation est ralentie dans le sens sud; *Br* **the s. carriageway of the motorway is closed** l'axe sud de l'autoroute est fermé (à la circulation); **there's a jam on the s. carriageway** il y a un bouchon en direction du sud

southeast ['saʊθiːst] N sud-est *m*; **in the s. of England** dans le sud-est de l'Angleterre

ADJ **1** *Geog* sud-est *(inv)*, du sud-est; **in s. England** dans le sud-est de l'Angleterre **2** *(wind)* de sud-est, du sud-est

ADV au sud-est; *(travel)* vers le sud-est, en direction du sud-est; **it's 50 miles s. of Liverpool** c'est 80 kilomètres au sud-est de Liverpool

►► **Southeast Asia** Asie *f* du Sud-Est; **Southeast Asia Treaty Organization** Organisation *f* du traité de l'Asie du Sud-Est

southeaster [saʊθ'iːstə(r)] N vent *m* de *ou* du sud-est

southeasterly [saʊθ'iːstəlɪ] (*pl* **southeasterlies**) ADJ **1** *Geog* sud-est *(inv)*, du sud-est; **to travel in a s. direction** aller vers le sud-est; *Naut* **to steer a s. course** faire route vers le sud-est; *(when setting out)* mettre le cap au sud-est **2** *(wind)* de sud-est, du sud-est

ADV vers le sud-est, en direction du sud-est

N vent *m* de *ou* du sud-est

southeastern [saʊθ'iːstən] ADJ sud-est *(inv)*, du sud-est; *(wind)* de sud-est, du sud-est; **the s. suburbs** la banlieue sud-est

southerly ['sʌðəlɪ] (*pl* **southerlies**) ADJ **1** *Geog* sud *(inv)*, du sud; **in a s. direction** vers le sud; **the most s. point of the United States** le point situé le plus au sud des États-Unis; **a room with a s. aspect** une pièce exposée au sud *ou* au midi; *Naut* **to steer a s. course** faire route vers le sud; *(when setting out)* mettre le cap au sud **2** *(wind)* de sud, du sud

ADV vers le sud, en direction du sud

N vent *m* de *ou* du sud

southern ['sʌðən] ADJ **1** *Geog* sud *(inv)*, du sud, méridional; **he has a s. accent** il a un accent du sud; *(in France)* il a l'accent méridional; **the s. wing of the castle** l'aile *f* sud du château; **in s. India** dans le sud de l'Inde; **the s. hemisphere** l'hémisphère *m* sud *ou* austral **2** *(wind)* de sud, du sud **3** *Hist (in American Civil War)* sudiste

►► **southern Africa** l'Afrique *f* australe; *Astron* **the Southern Cross** la Croix du Sud; **southern Europe** l'Europe *f* méridionale, l'Europe *f* du Sud; **Southern Ireland** l'Irlande *f* du Sud; **southern lights** aurore *f* australe; **the Southern States** = les États du sud-est des États-Unis, au sud de la ligne Mason-Dixon

southerner, southerner ['sʌðənə(r)] N *(gen)* habitant(e) *m,f* du sud; *(in continental Europe)* méridional(e) *m,f*; **she's a s.** elle vient du sud

south-facing ADJ *(house, wall)* (exposé) au sud *ou* au midi

southpaw ['saʊθpɔː] *Am Fam* N gaucher(ère)ᵔ *m,f*

ADJ gaucherᵔ

south-south-east N sud-sud-est *m*

ADJ **1** *Geog* sud-sud-est *(inv)*, du sud-sud-est **2** *(wind)* de *ou* du sud-sud-est

ADV au sud-sud-est; *(travel)* vers le sud-sud-est, en direction du sud-sud-est

south-south-west N sud-sud-ouest *m*

ADJ **1** *Geog* sud-sud-ouest *(inv)*, du sud-sud-ouest **2** *(wind)* de *ou* du sud-sud-ouest

ADV au sud-sud-ouest; *(travel)* vers le sud-sud-ouest, en direction du sud-sud-ouest

southward ['saʊθwəd] ADJ vers le sud, en direction du sud

ADV vers le sud, en direction du sud; **to sail s.** naviguer cap sur le sud

N sud *m*

southwards ['saʊθwədz] ADV vers le sud, en direction du sud; **to sail s.** naviguer cap sur le sud

southwest ['saʊθwest] N sud-ouest *m*; **in the s. of the United States** dans le sud-ouest des États-Unis

ADJ **1** *Geog* sud-ouest *(inv)*, du sud-ouest; **in s. Scotland** dans le sud-ouest de l'Écosse **2** *(wind)* de sud-ouest, du sud-ouest

ADV au sud-ouest; *(travel)* vers le sud-ouest, en direction du sud-ouest; **it's s. of London** c'est au sud-ouest de Londres

south-wester [saʊθ'westə(r)] N vent *m* de *ou* du sud-ouest

southwesterly [saʊθ'westəlɪ](*pl* **southwesterlies**) ADJ **1** *Geog* sud-ouest *(inv)*, du sud-ouest; **in a s. direction** vers le sud-ouest; *Naut* **to steer a s. course** faire route vers le sud-ouest; *(when setting out)* mettre le cap au sud-ouest **2** *(wind)* de sud-ouest, du sud-ouest

ADV vers le sud-ouest, en direction du sud-ouest

N vent *m* de *ou* du sud-ouest; *Naut* suroît *m*

southwestern [saʊθ'westən] ADJ sud-ouest *(inv)*, du sud-ouest; **the s. States** *(of USA)* les États *mpl* du sud-ouest; **the s. frontier** la frontière sud-ouest

souvenir [ˌsuːvə'nɪə(r)] N souvenir *m (objet)*

►► **souvenir shop** boutique *f* de souvenirs

> Note that the French word **souvenir** also means **memory**.

sovereign ['sɒvrɪn] N **1** *(monarch)* souverain(e) *m,f* **2** *(coin)* souverain *m (pièce d'or de la valeur d'une livre)*

ADJ *Pol (state, territory, immunity)* souverain; *(powers)* souverain, suprême; *(rights)* de souveraineté; **the s. good** le bien souverain; **Parliament remains s.** le Parlement reste souverain

sovereignty ['sɒvrɪntɪ] (*pl* **sovereignties**) N souveraineté *f*; **with no loss of s.** sans perte de souveraineté

soviet ['səʊvɪət] N *(council)* soviet *m*

• **Soviet** N *(inhabitant)* Soviétique *mf* ADJ soviétique; *Formerly* **the Union of S. Socialist Republics** l'Union *f* des républiques socialistes soviétiques

►► *Hist* **the Soviet Bloc** le bloc soviétique; *Formerly* **Soviet Russia** la Russie soviétique; *Formerly* **the Soviet Union** l'Union *f* soviétique

sovietization, -isation [ˌsəʊvɪətaɪ'zeɪʃən] N soviétisation *f*

sow[1] [səʊ] (*pt* **sowed**, *pp* **sowed** *or* **sown** [səʊn], *cont* **sowing**) VT **1** *(seed, crop)* semer; *(field)* ensemencer **2** *Fig* semer; **to s. discord/terror** semer la discorde/la terreur; **he sowed (the seeds of) doubt in their minds** il a semé le doute dans leur esprit; **it was at this time that the seeds of the Industrial Revolution were sown** c'est à cette époque que remontent les origines de la révolution industrielle; *Prov* **s. the wind and reap the whirlwind** qui sème le vent récolte la tempête

VI semer; *Bible* **as you s. so shall you reap** comme tu auras semé tu moissonneras

sow[2] [saʊ] N *(pig)* truie *f*; *(wild pig)* laie *f*

sower ['səʊə(r)] N *(person)* semeur(euse) *m,f*; *(machine)* semoir *m*

sowing ['səʊɪŋ] N **1** *(act)* ensemencement *m* **2** *(UNCOUNT) (work, period, seed)* semailles *fpl*

sown [səʊn] *pp of* **sow**[1]

sox [sɒks] NPL *Am Fam* chaussettesᵔ *fpl*

soy [sɔɪ] N *(sauce)* sauce *f* de soja

►► **soy sauce** sauce *f* de soja

soya ['sɔɪə] N soja *m*

►► *Br* **soya bean** graine *f* de soja; **soya flour** farine *f* de soja; **soya milk** lait *m* de soja

soybean ['sɔɪbiːn] N *Am* graine *f* de soja

sozzled ['sɒzəld] ADJ *Br Fam* bourré, beurré

SP [ˌes'piː] N *Horseracing* (*abbr* **starting price**) cote *f* au départ; *Br Fam Fig* **to give sb the SP (on)** mettre qn au parfum (à propos de *ou* concernant)

spa [spɑː] N **1** *(resort)* station *f* thermale

2 *(spring)* source *f* minérale

3 *(whirlpool bath)* bain *m* à remous

4 *(health club)* centre *m* de fitness, centre *m* de remise en forme

►► **spa town** ville *f* d'eau, station *f* thermale

space [speɪs] N **1** *Astron & Phys* espace *m*; **the first man in s.** le premier homme dans l'espace; **she sat staring into s.** elle était assise, le regard perdu dans le vide

2 *(room)* espace *m*, place *f*; **there's too much wasted s. in this kitchen** il y a trop de place perdue *ou* d'espace inutilisé dans cette cuisine; **to take up a lot of s.** prendre *ou* occuper beaucoup de place; **he cleared a** *or* **some s. on his desk for the tray** il a fait un peu de place sur son bureau pour le plateau; **can you make s. for one more?** pouvez-vous faire de la place pour une personne de plus?; **the author devotes a lot of s. to philosophical speculations** l'auteur fait une large part aux spéculations philosophiques; *Fig* **I need some s.** j'ai besoin de liberté; **to invade sb's personal s.** empiéter sur l'espace vital de qn

3 *(volume, area, distance)* espace *m*; **open spaces** *(green)* espaces *mpl* verts; *(not built on)* étendues *fpl* non bâties; **wide open spaces** grands espaces *mpl*; **there are at least five pubs in the s. of a few hundred yards** il y a au moins cinq pubs sur quelques centaines de mètres

4 *(gap)* espace *m*, place *f*; *(on page, official form)* espace *m*, case *f*; *Typ (gap between words)* espace *m*, blanc *m*; *(blank type)* espace *m*; **there's barely any s. between the houses** il n'y a pratiquement pas d'espace entre les maisons; **leave a s. for the teacher's comments** laissez un espace pour les remarques du professeur; **please add any further details in the s. provided** veuillez ajouter tout détail supplémentaire dans la case prévue à cet effet

5 *(period of time, interval)* intervalle *m*, espace *m* (de temps), période *f*; **in** *or* **within the s. of six months** en (l'espace de) six mois; **over a s. of several years** sur une période de plusieurs années; **it'll all be over in a very short s. of time** tout sera fini dans très peu de temps *ou* d'ici peu

6 *(seat, place)* place *f*

COMP *(programme, research)* spatial

VT = **space out**

►► **the space age** l'ère *f* spatiale; **space bar** *(on keyboard)* barre *f* d'espacement; **space blanket** couverture *f* de survie; *Fam* **space cadet** allumé(e) *m,f*; **space capsule** capsule *f* spatiale; **space flight** vol *m ou* voyage *m* spatial; **space heater** radiateur *m*; **space helmet** casque *m* d'astronaute; **space opera** space opera *m*; **space platform** station *f* spatiale *ou* orbitale; **space probe** sonde *f* spatiale; **space race** course *f* pour la suprématie dans l'espace; **space rocket** fusée *f* spatiale *ou* interplanétaire; *Typ* **space rule** filet *m* maigre; **space shot** lancement *m* spatial; **space shuttle** navette *f* spatiale; **space sickness** mal *m* de l'espace; **space station** station *f* spatiale *ou* orbitale; **space tourism** tourisme *m* spatial; **space travel** voyages *mpl* dans l'espace, *Spec* astronautique *f*

►**space out** VT SEP **1** *(in space)* espacer; **evenly spaced out** régulièrement espacés; **s. yourselves out a bit more** écartez-vous un peu plus les uns des autres **2** *(in time)* échelonner, espacer; **spaced out over a period of ten years** échelonné sur une période de dix ans

space-age ADJ **1** *(of the period of space exploration)* de l'ère spatiale **2** *(futuristic)* futuriste

spacecraft ['speɪskrɑːft] (*pl* **inv**) N vaisseau *m* spatial

spacelab ['speɪslæb] N laboratoire *m* spatial

spaceman ['speɪsmæn] (*pl* **spacemen** [-men]) N *(gen)* spationaute *m*, astronaute *m*; *(Russian)* cosmonaute *m*

spacer ['speɪsə(r)] N *Tech* pièce *f* d'écartement

space-saving ADJ qui fait gagner de la place

spaceship ['speɪsʃɪp] N vaisseau *m* spatial habité

space-time N *Phys* espace-temps *m*

►► **space-time continuum** continuum *m* espace-temps *ou* spatio-temporel

spacewalk ['speɪswɔːk] N marche *f* dans l'espace

VI marcher dans l'espace

spacewoman ['speɪsˌwʊmən] (*pl* **spacewomen** [-ˈwɪmɪn]) N *(gen)* spationaute *f*, astronaute *f*; *(Russian)* cosmonaute *f*

spacing ['speɪsɪŋ] N **1** *(of text on page* ► *horizontal)* espacement *m*; *(*► *vertical)* interligne *m*; **typed in single/double s.** tapé avec interligne simple/double **2** *(between trees, columns, buildings etc)* espacement *m*, écart *m*

spacious ['speɪʃəs] ADJ *(house, room, office)* spacieux, grand; *(park, property)* étendu, grand

spaciousness ['speɪʃəsnɪs] N grandeur *f*, dimensions *fpl* spacieuses

Spackle® ['spækəl] N *Am* enduit *m* de colmatage de fissures

spackle ['spækəl] VT *Am* passer à l'enduit de colmatage de fissures

spade [speɪd] N **1** *(tool)* bêche *f*; **to call a s. a s.** appeler un chat un chat; *Fam* **to have sth in spades** avoir des tonnes de qch; **and you've got it in spades** et tu en as à revendre **2** *(in cards)* pique *m*; **my partner played a s.** mon partenaire a joué pique; **the ace/ten of spades** l'as *m*/le dix de pique **3** *Fam (black man)* nègre *m*, bamboula *m*, = terme injurieux désignant un Noir; *(black woman)* négresse *f*, = terme injurieux désignant une Noire

spadeful ['speɪdfʊl] N pelletée *f*

spadework ['speɪdwɜːk] **N** travail *m* de préparation *ou* de déblayage

spag bol [ˌspæg'bɒl] **N** *Br Fam (abbr* **spaghetti bolognese***)* spaghettis *mpl* (à la) bolognaise◻

spaghetti [spə'getɪ] **N** *(UNCOUNT)* **1** *Culin* spaghetti *mpl*, spaghettis *mpl* **2** *Fam Fig (cables, wires)* enchevêtrement◻*m (de fils, de câbles)*

►► ***spaghetti bolognese*** spaghettis *mpl* (à la) bolognaise; ***Spaghetti Junction*** = surnom d'un échangeur sur l'autoroute M6 au nord de Birmingham; ***spaghetti western*** western-spaghetti *m*

Spain [speɪn] **N** Espagne *f*

Spam® [spæm] **N** = pâté de jambon en conserve

spam [spæm] *Comput* **N** *(UNCOUNT)* spams *mpl*, messages *mpl* publicitaires, pourriels *mpl*

VI envoyer des spams *ou* des messages publicitaires *ou* des pourriels en masse

spammer ['spæmə(r)] **N** *Comput* spammeur *m*, = personne qui envoie des messages publicitaires en masse

spamming ['spæmɪŋ] **N** *Comput* spamming *m*, = envoi de spams *ou* de messages publicitaires en masse

span [spæn] *(pt & pp* **spanned***, cont* **spanning***)* **N 1** *(duration)* durée *f*, laps *m* de temps; **a short attention s.** une capacité d'attention limitée; **his work covers a s. of twenty-odd years** son œuvre s'étend sur une vingtaine d'années

2 *(range)* gamme *f*; **we cover only a limited s. of subjects** nous ne couvrons qu'un nombre restreint de sujets

3 *(of hands, arms, wings)* envergure *f*

4 *(of bridge)* travée *f*; *(of arch, dome, girder)* portée *f*

5 *(unit of measurement)* empan *m*

6 *(matched pair* ► *of horses, oxen)* paire *f*

VT 1 *(encompass, stretch over* ► *in time, extent)* couvrir, embrasser; **her career spanned more than 50 years** sa carrière s'étend sur plus de 50 ans; **her knowledge spans a wide range of subjects** ses connaissances couvrent une grande variété de sujets **2** *(cross* ► *river, ditch etc)* enjamber, traverser; **a modern bridge now spans the valley** un pont moderne enjambe maintenant la vallée **3** *(build bridge over)* jeter un pont sur; **once the river had been spanned** une fois qu'on a eu construit un pont pour traverser la rivière

spangle ['spæŋgəl] **N** paillette *f*

VT pailleter, décorer de paillettes; **spangled with gold** pailleté d'or; **stars spangled the night sky** le ciel était semé d'étoiles

Spaniard ['spænjəd] **N** Espagnol(e) *m,f*

spaniel ['spænjəl] **N** épagneul *m*

Spanish ['spænɪʃ] **ADJ** espagnol

N *Ling* espagnol *m*

NPL the S. les Espagnols *mpl*

►► ***Spanish America*** Amérique *f* hispanophone; ***the Spanish Armada*** l'Invincible Armada *f*; ***the Spanish Civil War*** la guerre (civile) d'Espagne; ***Spanish fly* 1** *(insect)* cantharide *f*, mouche *f* d'Espagne **2** *(product)* poudre *f* de cantharide; ***Spanish guitar*** guitare *f* classique; ***the Spanish Inquisition*** l'Inquisition *f* espagnole; ***the Spanish Main*** la mer des Caraïbes; ***Spanish omelette*** omelette *f* à l'espagnole; ***Spanish onion*** oignon *m* d'Espagne

Spanish-American N 1 *(in the US)* Hispanique *mf* **2** *(in Latin America)* Hispano-Américain(e) *m,f*

ADJ 1 *(in the US)* hispanique **2** *(in Latin America)* hispano-américain

►► *Am Hist* ***the Spanish-American War*** la guerre hispano-américaine

Spanish-speaking ADJ hispanophone

spank [spæŋk] **VT** donner une fessée à, fesser

VI *(go at a lively pace)* **to be** *or* **to go spanking along** aller bon train *ou* à bonne allure

N tape *f* sur les fesses; **to give a child a s.** donner une tape sur les fesses à un enfant

spanking ['spæŋkɪŋ] **N** fessée *f*; **to give sb a s.** donner une fessée à qn

ADJ 1 *Fam (excellent)* épatant; **in s. condition** en excellent état◻ **2** *(brisk)* vif; **a s. breeze** une bonne brise; **to go at a s. pace** aller bon train *ou* à bonne allure

ADV *Fam* **s. new** flambant neuf; **s. clean** propre comme un sou neuf

spanner ['spænə(r)] **N** clé *f*, clef *f (outil)*; **to throw** *or* **to put a s. in the works** poser des problèmes; **that's put a s. in the works** ça a tout chamboulé

spar [spɑː(r)] *(pt & pp* **sparred***, cont* **sparring***)* **VI 1** *Sport (in boxing* ► *train)* s'entraîner (avec un sparring-partner); *(*► *test out opponent)* faire des feintes *(pour tester son adversaire)*; **they sparred with each other for a few rounds** ils boxèrent amicalement durant quelques rounds **2** *(argue)* se disputer

N 1 *(pole* ► *gen)* poteau *m*, mât *m*; *Naut* espar *m* **2** *Aviat* longeron *m* **3** *Miner* spath *m*

SPARE [speə(r)]

N	
• pièce de rechange **1**	• roue de secours **1**
ADJ	
• disponible **1**	• libre **1**
• de réserve **1**	• de rechange **1**
• en plus **1**	• maigre **2**
• austère **3**	
VT	
• accorder **1**	• se passer de **1**
• épargner **2, 3**	• ménager **4**

N 1 *(spare part)* pièce *f* de rechange; *(wheel)* roue *f* de secours; *(tyre)* pneu *m* de rechange; **I've lost my pencil, have you got a s.?** j'ai perdu mon crayon, en as-tu un à me prêter?

2 *(in ten-pin bowling)* honneur *m* simple; **to get** *or* **to score a s.** réussir un honneur simple

ADJ 1 *(free, not in use)* disponible, libre; *(kept in reserve)* de réserve, de rechange; *(extra, surplus)* en plus, de trop, en trop; **take a s. pullover** prenez un pull de rechange; **have you got a s. piece of paper?** est-ce que tu as une feuille de papier à me prêter?; **have you got any s. cash on you?** est-ce que tu peux me prêter de l'argent?; **with the s. cash they bought a table** avec l'argent qui leur restait ils ont acheté une table; **I've got two s. tickets for the match** j'ai deux billets en plus *ou* en trop pour le match; **you can stay here if you want, we have a s. bed** tu peux rester ici si tu veux, nous avons un lit pour toi; **there are plenty of s. seats at the back** il y a de nombreuses places libres au fond; **call in next time you have a s. moment** passez la prochaine fois que vous aurez un moment de libre; *Fam* **I'll have some more cake if there's any going s.** je vais reprendre du gâteau s'il en reste◻

2 *(lean)* maigre, sec (sèche)

3 *(austere* ► *style, decor)* austère; *(frugal* ► *meal)* frugal

4 *Br Fam (mad)* **to go s.** péter les plombs, péter une durite; **to drive sb s.** rendre qn chèvre, faire tourner qn en bourrique

VT 1 *(make available, give)* accorder, consacrer; *(do without)* se passer de; **Mr Austen can s. you a few minutes this afternoon** M. Austen peut vous consacrer quelques minutes cet après-midi; **come and see us if you can s. the time** venez nous voir si vous avez le temps; **I can't s. the time to finish it** je n'ai pas le temps de le finir; **s. a thought for their poor parents!** pensez un peu à leurs pauvres parents!; **can you s. (me) a few pounds?** vous n'auriez pas quelques livres (à me passer)?; **I'm afraid we can't s. anyone at the moment** je regrette mais nous ne pouvons nous passer de personne *ou* nous avons besoin de tout le monde en ce moment; **young people with money to s.** des jeunes qui ont de l'argent à dépenser; **to have nothing to s.** n'avoir que le strict nécessaire, ne rien avoir de superflu; **there is room to s.** la place ne manque pas; **I've got no time to s.** je n'ai pas le temps; **to have no time to s. for sb/sth** ne pas avoir de temps à consacrer à qn/qch; **do you have a few minutes to s.?** avez-vous quelques minutes de libres *ou* devant vous?; **we got to the airport with over an hour to s.** nous sommes arrivés à l'aéroport avec plus d'une heure d'avance; **I caught the train with just a few seconds to s.** à quelques secondes près je ratais le train

2 *(refrain from harming, punishing, destroying)* épargner; **a few villages were miraculously spared** par miracle, quelques villages furent épargnés; **the report spared no one** le rapport ne ménageait personne; **to s. sb's life** épargner la vie de qn; **s me!** *(don't kill me)* de grâce!, épargnez-moi! *(don't expose me to that etc)* par pitié, pas ça!; **to s. sb's feelings** ménager les sentiments de qn; **to s. sb's blushes** épargner qn

3 *(save* ► *trouble, suffering)* épargner, éviter; **to s. sb the trouble of doing sth** éviter à qn la peine de faire qch; **you could have spared yourself/u the trouble** vous auriez pu vous/nous évite cette peine; **she was spared further distress b the judge's intervention** l'intervention du juge mit fin à ses tortures; **he was spared the shame of a public trial** la honte d'un procès public lui a été épargnée; **s. me the details!** épargne-moi les détails!; **I'll s. you the rest** je vous fais grâce du reste

4 *(economize)* ménager; **they spared no expense on the celebrations** ils n'ont rien reculé devant aucune dépense pour les fêtes; **the first prize is a real luxury trip, with no expense spared** le premier prix est un voyage de rêve pour lequel on n'a pas regardé à la dépense; **we shall s. no effort to push the plan through** nous ne ménagerons pas nos efforts pour faire accepter le projet; *Prov* **s. the rod and spoil the child** qui aime bien châtie bien

►► ***spare part*** pièce *f* de rechange, pièce *f* détachée; ***spare rib*** travers *m* de porc; **barbecue s. rib** travers *mpl* de porc grillés sauce barbecue; ***spare room*** chambre *f* d'amis; ***spare time*** temps *m* libre; **what do you do in your s. time?** que faites-vous pendant votre temps libre *ou* pendant vos moments de loisirs?; *Br* ***spare tyre***, *Am* ***spare tire* 1** *Aut* pneu *m* de secours *ou* de rechange **2** *Fam Hum (roll of fat)* pneu *m* de secours, bourrelet *m* de graisse; **to get a s. tyre** prendre de l'embonpoint; *Br* ***spare wheel*** roue *f* de secours

sparing ['speərɪŋ] **ADJ 1** *(economical* ► *person)* économe; **she's very s. with her compliments praise** elle est très avare de compliments/louanges; **they were s. in their efforts to help us** ils ne se sont pas donnés beaucoup de mal pour nous aider **2** *(meagre* ► *quantity)* limité, modéré; *(*► *use)* modéré, économe; **to make s. use of sth** utiliser qch avec parcimonie *ou* modération

sparingly ['speərɪŋlɪ] **ADV** *(eat)* frugalement *(drink, use)* avec modération; *(praise)* chichement, avec parcimonie; **they should be watered often but s.** il faudrait les arroser souvent mais avec modération

spark [spɑːk] **VI 1** *(produce sparks* ► *gen)* jeter des étincelles **2** *Aut (spark plug, ignition system)* allumer *(par étincelle)*

VT = spark off

N 1 *(from flame, electricity)* étincelle *f*; *Fig* **whenever they meet the sparks fly** chaque fois qu'ils se rencontrent, ça fait des étincelles; **they strike sparks off each other** ils se stimulent mutuellement **2** *(flash, trace* ► *of excitement, wit)* étincelle *f*, lueur *f*; *(*► *of interest, enthusiasm)* lueur *f*; **his eyes retained a s. of life** il restait une lueur de vie dans ses yeux

• **sparks N** *Br Fam (electrician)* électricien(enne)◻*m,f*; *Fam Old-fashioned Naut & Aviat (radio operator)* radio◻*m*

►► *Elec* ***spark coil*** bobine *f* d'allumage; *Aut* ***spark gap*** écartement *m* des électrodes; *Aut* ***spark plug*** bougie *f*; ***spark plug spanner*** clé *f* à bougie

►**spark off VT SEP** *(trigger* ► *interest, argument)* susciter, provoquer; **the incident was the catalyst that sparked the revolution** c'est l'incident qui a déclenché la révolution; **the news sparked off an intense debate** la nouvelle déclencha un débat animé

sparkle ['spɑːkəl] **VI 1** *(jewel, frost, glass, star)* étinceler, scintiller; *(sea, lake)* étinceler, miroiter; *(eyes)* étinceler, pétiller **2** *(person)* briller *(conversation)* être brillant **3** *(wine, cider, mineral water)* pétiller

N 1 *(of jewel, frost, glass, star)* scintillement *m (of sea, lake)* étincellement *m*, miroitement *m (of eyes)* éclat *m*; **she has a s. in her eye** elle a des yeux pétillants **2** *(of person, conversation, wit, performance)* éclat *m*; **he's lost his s.** il a perdu sa joie de vivre; **if the s. has gone out of your marriage...** si la magie a disparu de votre mariage...

sparkler ['spɑːklə(r)] **N 1** *(firework)* cierge *m* magique **2** *Fam (diamond)* diam *m*

sparkling ['spɑːklɪŋ] ADJ **1** *(jewel, frost, glass, star)* étincelant, scintillant; *(sea, lake)* étincelant, miroitant; *(eyes)* étincelant, pétillant **2** *(person, conversation, wit, performance)* brillant **3** *(soft drink, mineral water)* gazeux, pétillant
ADV **s. clean/white** d'une propreté/blancheur éclatante
▸▸ ***sparkling wine*** vin *m* mousseux

sparkly ['spɑːklɪ] ADJ *(jewel, dress)* scintillant

sparring ['spɑːrɪŋ] N *(UNCOUNT) Boxing* entraînement *m*; *(arguing)* échanges *mpl* verbaux; **it was just a little good-natured s.** *(verbal)* ce n'était qu'une petite bagarre amicale
▸▸ ***sparring match*** *Boxing* combat *m* d'entraînement; *Fig* discussion *f* animée; ***sparring partner*** *Boxing* sparring-partner *m*; *Fig* adversaire *m*

sparrow ['spærəʊ] N moineau *m*

sparrowhawk ['spærəʊhɔːk] N *Orn* **(Eurasian) s.** épervier *m*; **American s.** faucon *m* des moineaux

sparse [spɑːs] ADJ *(trees, vegetation, population)* clairsemé, épars; *(crowd, audience)* clairsemé; **s. hair** cheveux *mpl* rares *ou* clairsemés; **the s. furnishings in the room** le peu de meubles qu'il y avait dans la pièce

sparsely ['spɑːslɪ] ADV *(wooded, populated)* peu; **the room was s. furnished** la pièce contenait peu de meubles; **it grows only s. in the north** ça ne pousse pas beaucoup dans le nord

sparseness ['spɑːsnɪs] N *(of population)* faible densité *f*; *(of hair, vegetation)* manque *m*

Sparta ['spɑːtə] N Sparte

spartan ['spɑːtən] ADJ *Fig (lifestyle)* spartiate; *(meal)* frugal; **s. living conditions** des conditions *fpl* de vie spartiates
• **Spartan** *Hist* N Spartiate *mf* ADJ spartiate

spasm ['spæzəm] N **1** *(muscular contraction)* spasme *m* **2** *(fit)* accès *m*; **a s. of anger/pain** un accès de colère/de douleur; **he had a s. of coughing** il a eu une quinte de toux; **she went into spasms of laughter** elle a été prise d'une crise de fou rire; *Br* **I tend to work in spasms** j'ai tendance à travailler de façon irrégulière

spasmodic [spæz'mɒdɪk] ADJ **1** *(intermittent)* intermittent, irrégulier **2** *Med (pain, contraction)* spasmodique

spasmodically [spæz'mɒdɪkəlɪ] ADV de façon intermittente, par à-coups

spastic ['spæstɪk] N **1** *Med (gen)* handicapé(e) *m,f* (moteur); *(person affected by spasms)* spasmophile *mf* **2** *very Fam (clumsy person)* gol *mf*, gogol *mf*
ADJ **1** *Med (gen)* handicapé (moteur); *(affected by spasms)* spasmophile **2** *very Fam (clumsy)* empoté, gourde

spat [spæt] *pt & pp of* **spit**
N **1** *(on shoe)* guêtre *f* **2** *Fam (quarrel)* prise *f* de bec **3** *(shellfish)* naissain *m*

spate [speɪt] N **1** *(of letters, visitors)* avalanche *f*; *(of abuse, insults)* torrent *m*; **a s. of murders/burglaries** une série de meurtres/cambriolages **2** *Br (flood)* crue *f*; **the river was in s.** le fleuve était en crue; *Fig* **to interrupt sb in full s.** interrompre qn en plein discours

spatial ['speɪʃəl] ADJ spatial
▸▸ ***spatial awareness, spatial intelligence*** perception *f* de l'espace

spatiotemporal [ˌspeɪʃɪəʊ'tempərəl] ADJ spatio-temporel

spatter ['spætə(r)] VT *(splash)* éclabousser; **he spattered ink on** *or* **over the table** il a fait des éclaboussures d'encre sur la table; **the car spattered me with mud, the car spattered mud over me** l'auto m'a éclaboussé *ou* aspergé de boue; **the wall was spattered with grease** le mur était couvert d'éclaboussures *ou* tout éclaboussé de graisse
VI *(liquid)* gicler; *(oil)* crépiter; **rain spattered on the windowpane** la pluie crépitait sur la vitre
N *(on garment)* éclaboussure *f*, éclaboussures *fpl*; *(sound* ▸ *of rain, oil, applause)* crépitement *m*

spattered ['spætəd] SUFF **blood/mud/oil-s.** couvert d'éclaboussures de sang/de boue/d'huile

spatula ['spætjʊlə] N **1** *Culin* spatule *f* **2** *Med* abaisse-langue *m inv*, spatule *f*

spavin ['spævɪn] N *Vet* éparvin *m*, épervin *m*

spawn [spɔːn] N *(UNCOUNT)* **1** *Zool (of frogs, fish)* œufs *mpl*, frai *m* **2** *Bot (of mushrooms)* mycélium *m* **3** *Fig Pej (offspring)* progéniture *f*
VT **1** *Zool* pondre **2** *Fig (produce)* engendrer, donner naissance à; **the organization/movement spawned various offshoots** l'organisation/le mouvement a donné naissance à plusieurs ramifications
VI *Zool* frayer

spawning ['spɔːnɪŋ] N *Zool* frai *m*
▸▸ ***spawning ground*** frayère *f*; ***spawning season*** frai *m*

spay [speɪ] VT *Vet* castrer

spaz, spazz [spæz] N *Fam* **1** *(spastic)* infirme ᵔ*mf*, = terme injurieux désignant un handicapé moteur **2** *(idiot)* crétin(e) *m,f*, idiot(e)ᵔ*m,f*
▸ **spaz out, spazz out** VI *Fam* faire le con

> SUFFIXE
> **-SPEAK**
> Les mots contenant ce suffixe sont construits sur le modèle du terme **newspeak**. Ce terme, apparu pour la première fois sous la plume de George Orwell dans son roman *1984* (paru en 1949), désignait le langage délibérément ambigu des politiciens et des bureaucrates.
> On emploie aujourd'hui le suffixe **-speak** pour véhiculer la notion de jargon lié à une activité donnée ou parlé par un groupe de personnes particulier.
> Parmi les termes passés dans la langue citons **computer-speak** langage *ou* jargon de l'informatique; **psycho-speak** jargon psychologique *ou* des psychologues. Un autre terme, plus proche de l'original créé par Orwell est **double-speak**, mot qui désigne des propos ambigus ou équivoques.
> Parmi les créations plus récentes, mentionnons **oil-speak** le jargon de l'industrie pétrolière; **consultant-speak** le jargon des consultants en entreprise; **luvvie-speak** le jargon des acteurs de théâtre.

SPEAK [spiːk] *(pt* **spoke** [spəʊk], *pp* **spoken** ['spəʊkən]) VT **1** *(say, pronounce)* dire, prononcer; **the baby spoke his first words** le bébé a dit ses premiers mots; **to s. one's mind** dire ce qu'on pense; **she spoke my name in her sleep** elle a prononcé mon nom dans son sommeil; **he didn't s. a word** il n'a pas dit un mot; **without a word being spoken** sans qu'un mot ne soit prononcé; **to s. the truth** dire la vérité; **his silence speaks volumes** son silence en dit long
2 *(language)* parler; **he doesn't s. a word of Greek** il ne parle pas un mot de grec; **English spoken** *(sign)* ici on parle anglais; *Fig* **we just don't s. the same language** nous ne parlons pas le même langage, c'est tout
VI **1** *(talk)* parler; **to s. to** *or esp Am* **with sb** parler à *ou* avec qn; **to s. about** *or* **of sth** parler de qch; **to s. to sb about sth** parler à qn de qch; **I'll s. to her about it** je lui en parlerai; **to s. in a whisper** chuchoter; **s. to me!** dites(-moi) quelque chose!; **don't s. to your mother like that!** ne parle pas à ta mère sur ce ton!; **it seems I spoke too soon** on dirait que j'ai parlé un peu vite; **s. now or forever hold your peace** parlez maintenant ou gardez le silence pour toujours; **she isn't speaking to me** elle ne me parle plus; **she hasn't spoken to me since** elle ne m'a pas adressé la parole depuis; **they're not speaking (to each other)** ils ne s'adressent pas *ou* plus la parole; **isn't it about time you two started speaking again?** est-ce que vous ne devriez pas faire la paix?; **I know them by sight but not to s. to** je ne les connais que de vue; **are you on speaking terms with them?** *(do you know them?)* tu les connais?; *(are you reconciled with them?)* vous vous parlez?; **we're no longer on speaking terms** nous ne nous parlons plus; **speaking of which** justement, à ce propos; **generally speaking** en général; **personally speaking** en ce qui me concerne, quant à moi; **financially/legally speaking** financièrement/légalement parlant, du point de vue financier/légal; **speaking as a politician** en tant qu'homme politique; **you shouldn't s. ill of the dead** tu ne devrais pas dire du mal des morts; **he always speaks well/highly of you** il dit toujours du bien/beaucoup de bien de vous
2 *(on telephone)* parler; **who's speaking?** *(gen)* qui est à l'appareil?; *(on switchboard)* c'est de la part de qui?; **Kate Smith speaking** Kate Smith à l'appareil, c'est Kate Smith; **may I s. to Kate? – speaking** puis-je parler à Kate? – c'est moi; **I'm speaking from Australia** j'appelle d'Australie
3 *(in debate, meeting etc* ▸ *make a speech)* faire un discours, parler; *(*▸ *intervene)* prendre la parole, parler; **he began to s.** il a pris la parole; **she got up to s.** elle s'est levée pour parler; **the chair called upon Mrs Fox to s.** le président a demandé à Mme Fox de prendre la parole; **he was invited to s. to us on** *or* **about Chile** il a été invité à venir nous parler du Chili; **to s. to** *or* **on a motion** soutenir une motion; **to s. from the floor** intervenir dans un débat
4 *Fig (give an impression)* **his paintings s. of terrible loneliness** ses peintures expriment une immense solitude; **the gift speaks well of her concern for old people** son don témoigne de l'intérêt qu'elle porte aux personnes âgées; **this speaks of large-scale corruption** c'est le signe d'une corruption à grande échelle
• **not to speak of** PREP sans parler de; **his plays are hugely popular, not to s. of his many novels** ses pièces sont extrêmement populaires, sans parler de ses nombreux romans
• **so to speak** ADV pour ainsi dire
• **to speak of** ADV **there's no wind/mail to s. of** il n'y a presque pas de vent/de courrier

▸ **speak against** VT INSEP *(motion, bill, proposal)* se prononcer contre; **she spoke passionately against the practice** elle a condamné cette pratique avec virulence

▸ **speak for** VT INSEP **1** *(speak on behalf of)* parler au nom de, parler pour; *(speak in support of)* parler en faveur de, plaider pour; **I'm sure I s. for everyone when I say...** je suis sûr que j'exprime la pensée générale lorsque je dis...; **speaking for myself** pour ma part, en ce qui me concerne; **let her s. for herself!** laisse-la s'exprimer!; **he is old enough to s. for himself** *(ask for something)* il est assez grand pour le demander tout seul; *(say something)* il est assez grand pour le dire lui-même; *Fam* **s. for yourself!** parle pour toi!; *Fig* **the facts s. for themselves** les faits parlent d'eux-mêmes **2 to be spoken for** *(to be reserved)* être réservé; *(person* ▸ *gen)* ne pas être libre; *(*▸ *at dance)* être accompagné; *(*▸ *have girlfriend, boyfriend)* avoir un(e) petit(e) ami(e); *(*▸ *have wife, husband)* être marié; **she's already spoken for** elle est déjà prise

▸ **speak out** VI parler franchement, ne pas mâcher ses mots; **don't be afraid to s. out** n'aie pas peur de parler franchement *ou* de dire ce que tu penses; **to s. out for sth** parler en faveur de qch; **to s. out against sth** s'élever contre qch

▸ **speak up** VI **1** *(louder)* parler plus fort; *(more clearly)* parler plus clairement **2** *(be frank)* parler franchement; **to s. up for sb** parler en faveur de qn, défendre les intérêts de qn; **why didn't you s. up?** pourquoi n'avez-vous rien dit?

speakeasy ['spiːkˌiːzɪ] *(pl* **speakeasies)** N *Am* bar *m* clandestin *(pendant la prohibition)*

speaker ['spiːkə(r)] N **1** *(gen)* celui *m*/celle *f* qui parle; *(in discussion)* interlocuteur(trice) *m,f*; *(in public)* orateur(trice) *m,f*; *(during debate, at conference)* intervenant(e) *m,f*; **she's a good s.** elle sait parler *ou* s'exprimer en public
2 *Ling* locuteur(trice) *m,f*; **native speakers of English** ceux dont la langue maternelle est l'anglais; **Spanish s.** hispanophone *mf*; **my parents are Welsh speakers** mes parents sont galloisants *ou* parlent (le) gallois; **there are very few surviving speakers of the language** il reste très peu de personnes qui parlent cette langue
3 *Pol* speaker *m*, président(e) *m,f* de l'assemblée; **the S. (of the House of Commons)** = le président de la Chambre des communes; **the S. of the House** = le président de la Chambre des représentants américaine
4 *(loudspeaker)* haut-parleur *m*; *(in stereo system)* enceinte *f*, baffle *m*

speakerphone ['spi:kəfəʊn] **N** téléphone *m* avec haut-parleur; **he was on s.** on entendait ce qu'il disait au haut-parleur

speaking ['spi:kɪŋ] **ADJ 1** *(involving speech)* **do you have a s. part in the play?** est-ce que vous avez du texte?; **she has a good s. voice** elle a une belle voix **2** *(which speaks ▸ robot, machine, doll)* parlant

N art *m* de parler

▸▸ *Br* ***speaking clock*** horloge *f* parlante; *Cin, Theat & TV* ***speaking role*** rôle *m* parlant; ***speaking tube*** tuyau *m* acoustique

-speaking ['spi:kɪŋ] **SUFF 1** *(person)* **they're both German/Spanish-s.** ils sont tous deux germanophones/hispanophones; **a child of Polish-s. parents** un enfant dont les parents sont de langue *ou* d'origine polonaise **2** *(country)* **French/English-s. countries** les pays *mpl* francophones/anglophones; **the Arab-s. world** le monde arabophone

spear [spɪə(r)] **N 1** *(weapon)* lance *f*; *(harpoon)* harpon *m* **2** *(of asparagus, broccoli etc)* pointe *f*

VT 1 *(enemy)* transpercer d'un coup de lance; *(fish)* harponner **2** *(food)* piquer; **he speared a piece of meat with his fork/on a skewer** il a piqué un morceau de viande avec sa fourchette/enfilé un morceau de viande sur une brochette

▸▸ ***spear fishing*** pêche *f ou* chasse *f* (sous-marine) au harpon

spearhead ['spɪəhed] **N** *also Fig* fer *m* de lance

VT *(attack)* être le fer de lance de; *(campaign, movement)* mener, être à la tête de

spearmint ['spɪəmɪnt] **N 1** *(plant)* menthe *f* verte; *(flavour)* menthe *f* **2** *(sweet)* bonbon *m* à la menthe

ADJ *(flavour)* de menthe; *(toothpaste, chewing gum)* à la menthe

spec [spek] **N 1** *(abbr* **specification***)* spécifications *fpl* **2** *Br Fam (idiom)* **on s.** au hasard[□]; **he bought the car on s.** il a risqué le coup en achetant la voiture

speccy ['spekɪ] *Br Fam* **N** binoclard(e) *m,f*

ADJ binoclard

special ['speʃəl] **ADJ 1** *(exceptional, particular ▸ offer, friend, occasion, ability)* spécial; *(▸ reason, effort, pleasure)* particulier; **pay s. attention to the details** faites particulièrement attention aux détails; **this is a very s. moment for me** c'est un moment particulièrement important pour moi; **as a s. treat** *(present)* comme cadeau; *(outing)* pour vous faire plaisir; **I'll do it as a s. favour to you** je le ferai, mais c'est bien pour toi *ou* parce que c'est toi; **it's a s. case** c'est un cas particulier *ou* à part; **a s. feature of the church is its Gothic belltower** le clocher gothique de l'église est l'un de ses traits distinctifs; **a s. feature** *(in newspaper)* un article spécial; *(on TV)* une émission spéciale; **they put on a s. train for the match** ils ont prévu un train supplémentaire pour le match; **what did you do last night? – nothing s.** qu'as-tu fait hier soir? – rien de spécial; **the food was OK but nothing s.** la nourriture était assez bonne mais elle n'avait rien d'exceptionnel; **I'm going to cook something s. for dinner tonight** ce soir, je vais cuisiner quelque chose qui sorte de l'ordinaire; **what's so s. about this car?** qu'est-ce que cette voiture a de si extraordinaire?; **to get s. treatment** bénéficier d'un traitement de faveur

2 *(specific ▸ need, problem)* spécial, particulier; *(▸ equipment)* spécial; *(▸ adviser)* particulier; **s. characteristic** particularité *f*; **you need s. permission** il vous faut une autorisation spéciale; **by s. permission of the Lyme museum** avec l'aimable autorisation du musée Lyme; **she has a s. interest in Italian art** elle s'intéresse beaucoup à *ou* porte un intérêt tout particulier à l'art italien; **children with s. needs** enfants ayant des difficultés d'apprentissage

3 *(valued)* cher; **this house is very s. to me** cette maison m'est très chère; **you're very s. to me** je tiens beaucoup à toi; **a s. relationship** des rapports *mpl* privilégiés; *Pol* **the s. relationship** = relations d'amitié entre les USA et la Grande-Bretagne; **a present for a s. person** un cadeau pour un être cher

N 1 *(train)* train *m* supplémentaire; *(bus)* car *m* supplémentaire; **they put on a football/holiday s.** ils ont mis un train/car supplémentaire pour le match de football/les départs en vacances **2** *(in restaurant)* spécialité *f*; **the chef's/the house s.** la spécialité du chef/de la maison; **today's s.** le plat du jour

3 *TV* émission *f* spéciale; *Journ (issue)* numéro *m* spécial; *(feature)* article *m* spécial

4 *Br (police officer)* auxiliaire *mf* de police

5 *Am Com* offre *f* spéciale; **sugar is on s. today** le sucre est en promotion aujourd'hui

▸▸ ***special agent*** *(spy etc)* agent *m* secret; ***Special Air Service*** = commando d'intervention spéciale de l'armée britannique; ***Special Branch*** = service de police britannique chargé des crimes contre la sûreté de l'État, ≃ Renseignements *mpl* généraux; *Br* ***special constable*** auxiliaire *mf* de police; *Journ* ***special correspondent*** envoyé(e) *m,f* spécial(e); ***special delivery*** = service postal britannique garantissant la distribution du courrier sous 24 heures; **to send sth s. delivery** envoyer qch en exprès; *Fin* ***special drawing rights*** droits *mpl* de tirage spéciaux; ***special education*** enseignement *m* spécialisé; *Cin & TV* ***special effects*** effets *mpl* spéciaux; ***special feature*** *(on DVD)* bonus *m*; *Comput* ***special interest group*** groupe *m* d'intérêt; ***special interest holidays*** vacances *fpl* à thème; *Br* ***special licence*** dispense *f* de bans; **to be married by s. licence** se marier avec dispense de bans; ***special needs*** besoins *mpl* (éducatifs) particuliers; **a child with s. needs** un enfant à besoins (éducatifs) particuliers; ***special needs school*** établissement *m* spécialisé *(pour enfants ayant des besoins éducatifs particuliers)*; ***special offer*** promotion *f*; **to be on s. offer** être en promotion; ***special pleading*** *(gen)* argument *m* spécieux; *Law* plaidoyer *m* partial; *Pol* ***special powers*** pouvoirs *mpl* extraordinaires; *Br* ***special school*** établissement *m* d'enseignement spécialisé *(pour enfants handicapés ou inadaptés)*

> Note that the French adjective **spécial** also means **peculiar, odd**.

specialist ['speʃəlɪst] **N 1** *(gen) & Med* spécialiste *mf*; **she's a heart s.** elle est cardiologue; **he's a s. in rare books** c'est un spécialiste en livres rares **2** *Am Mil* officier *m* technicien

ADJ *(skills, vocabulary, knowledge)* spécialisé, de spécialiste; *(writing, publication)* pour spécialistes; *(bookshop, dictionary)* spécialisé; **it's a s. job** c'est un travail de spécialiste; **to seek s. advice** demander conseil à *ou* consulter un spécialiste

▸▸ *TV* ***specialist channel*** chaîne *f* thématique; ***specialist press*** presse *f* spécialisée; *Com* ***specialist retailer*** détaillant(e) *m,f* spécialisé(e); ***specialist teacher*** professeur *m* spécialisé; **she's a s. maths teacher** elle n'enseigne que *ou* enseigne uniquement les maths

speciality [ˌspeʃɪ'ælətɪ] *(pl* **specialities***)*, *Am* **specialty** ['speʃəltɪ] *(pl* **specialties***)* **N 1** *(service, product)* spécialité *f*; **he made a s. of croissants** il s'est spécialisé dans les croissants; **our s. is electronic components** nous nous spécialisons *ou* nous sommes spécialisés dans les composants électroniques **2** *(of academic)* domaine *m* de spécialité; **her s. is Chinese history** c'est une spécialiste de l'histoire chinoise; **what's his s.?** dans quel domaine est-ce qu'il s'est spécialisé?

specialization, -isation [ˌspeʃəlaɪ'zeɪʃən] **N** spécialisation *f*; **his s. is computers** il est spécialisé en informatique

specialize, -ise ['speʃəlaɪz] **VI** *(company, restaurant, student)* se spécialiser; **to s. in sth** se spécialiser en *ou* dans qch

specialized, -ised ['speʃəlaɪzd] **ADJ** spécialisé; **we need somebody with s. knowledge** il nous faut un spécialiste

specially ['speʃəlɪ] **ADV 1** *(particularly)* spécialement, particulièrement, surtout; **she was s. interested in old cars** elle s'intéressait (tout) particulièrement *ou* surtout aux vieilles voitures; **I would s. like to hear that song** j'aimerais beaucoup écouter cette chanson; **do you want to come? – not s.** (est-ce que) tu veux venir? – pas spécialement; **she s. requested a non-smoking seat** elle a bien spécifié qu'elle voulait un siège non-fumeurs **2** *(on purpose, specifically)* exprès, spécialement; **I made your favourite meal s.** j'ai fait exprès ton repas préféré; **the coat was s. made for him** le manteau a été fait tout spécialement pour lui; **we've driven 500 miles s. to see you** nous avons fait 800 kilomètres spécialement pour venir te voir

> Attention: ne pas confondre avec **especially**.

specialty ['speʃltɪ] *(pl* **specialties***)* **N 1** *Am* = **speciality 2** *Law* contrat *m* sous seing privé

specie ['spi:ʃi:] **N** *(UNCOUNT) (coins)* espèces *fpl* numéraire *m*; **in s.** en espèces, en numéraire; *Fig* de manière identique

species ['spi:ʃi:z] *(pl* **inv***)* **N 1** *Biol* espèce *f*; **the human s.** l'espèce *f* humaine **2** *Fig* espèce *f*; **an unusual s. of politician** un homme politique d'une espèce rare

specific [spə'sɪfɪk] **ADJ 1** *(precise)* précis; **I gave him s. instructions** je lui ai donné des instructions précises; **could you please be a little** *or* **a bit more s.?** pourriez-vous être un peu plus précis? **2** *(particular ▸ gen)* particulier, précis; *(▸ role problem, conditions, needs)* spécifique, particulier; **in this s. case** dans ce cas précis *ou* particulier; **give me a s. example** donnez-moi un exemple précis; **what did he say? – nothing s** qu'a-t-il dit? – rien de précis *ou* de particulier; **s. to** spécifique à, propre à

N *Med* (remède *m*) spécifique *m*; **insulin is a s. for diabetes** l'insuline est le médicament spécifique pour le diabète

• specifics NPL détails *mpl*

▸▸ *Phys* ***specific gravity*** densité *f*

specifically [spə'sɪfɪklɪ] **ADV 1** *(precisely)* précisément, de façon précise; *(clearly)* clairement expressément; *(explicitly)* explicitement; **your name was mentioned s.** votre nom a été mentionné explicitement; **his book does not s. say what happened** son livre ne dit pas clairement *ou* ne précise pas ce qui s'est passé; **I s. asked to speak to Mr Myers** j'avais bien spécifié *ou* précisé que je voulais parler à M. Myers **2** *(particularly)* particulièrement; *(specially)* spécialement *(purposely)* exprès, expressément; **our kitchens are s. designed for the modern family** nos cuisines sont (tout) spécialement conçues pour la famille moderne; **it's not a s. British problem** ce n'est pas un problème spécifiquement britannique **we were s. forbidden to...** il nous était expressément défendu de...

specification [ˌspesɪfɪ'keɪʃən] **N 1** *(often pl) (in contract ▸ of machine, building materials etc)* spécifications *fpl*; *(▸ for technical project, including work schedule)* cahier *m* des charges; **made (according) to s.** construit en fonction de spécifications techniques; **standard specifications** normes *fpl* de qualité **2** *(stipulation)* spécification *f*, précision *f*; **there was no s. as to age** l'âge n'était pas précisé **3** *Comput* spécifications *fpl*

specificity [ˌspesɪ'fɪsətɪ] *(pl* **specificities***)* **N** spécificité *f*

specify ['spesɪfaɪ] *(pt & pp* **specified***)* **VT** spécifier, préciser; **the rules s. a five-minute break** le règlement spécifie une pause de cinq minutes; **unless otherwise specified** sauf indication contraire; **on a specified date** à une date précise

specimen ['spesɪmən] **N 1** *(sample ▸ of work handwriting)* spécimen *m*; *(▸ of blood)* prélèvement *m*; *(▸ of urine)* échantillon *m* **2** *(single example)* spécimen *m*; **this butterfly is a superb s.** ce papillon est un superbe spécimen; **a fine s. of Gothic architecture** un bel exemple d'architecture gothique; **the finest specimens in his collection** les plus belles pièces de sa collection **3** *Fam Pej (person)* spécimen *m*; **he's a peculiar s.** c'est un drôle de spécimen

COMP *(page, letter, reply)* spécimen; **they will ask you for a s. signature** ils vous demanderont un exemplaire de votre signature

▸▸ ***specimen bottle*** flacon-échantillon *m*; ***specimen copy*** spécimen *m (livre, magazine)*

specious ['spi:ʃəs] **ADJ** *(argument, reasoning)* spécieux; *(appearance)* trompeur

speciousness ['spi:ʃəsnɪs] **N** caractère *m* spécieux

speck [spek] **N 1** *(of dust, dirt)* grain *m*; *(in eye)* poussière *f*; **there wasn't a s. of dust anywhere** il n'y avait pas le moindre grain de poussière *(stain, mark ▸ gen)* petite tache *f*; *(▸ on skin, fruit)* ache *f*, tavelure *f*; (▸ *of blood*) petite tache *f*; **I** **eep seeing black specks in front of my eyes** j'ai ouvent des taches noires devant les yeux **3** *dot* ▸ *on horizon, from height*) point *m* noir; **from** **he top of the tower, the people looked like mere** **pecks** vus du haut de la tour, les gens avaient air de minuscules points noirs

VT *(usu passive)* tacheter

peckle ['spekəl] **N** moucheture *f*

VT tacheter, moucheter; **speckled with yellow** acheté *ou* moucheté de jaune

peckled ['spekəld] **ADJ** *(egg)* tacheté, mou-cheté; *(plumage)* grivelé; *(hen)* tacheté

pecs [speks] **NPL** *Fam* (*abbr* **spectacles**) carreaux *npl*, hublots *mpl*

pectacle ['spektəkəl] **N 1** *(sight)* spectacle *m*; **he was a sorry** *or* **sad s.** il était triste à voir; **to make a . of oneself** se donner en spectacle **2** *Cin, Theat & TV* superproduction *f*

pectacled ['spektəkəld] **ADJ** *(gen) & Zool* à lunettes

pectacles ['spektəkəlz] **NPL** lunettes *fpl*; **a pair of s.** une paire de lunettes

pectacular [spek'tækjʊlə(r)] **ADJ** *(event, defeat, result, success, view)* spectaculaire; **there has been a s. rise in house prices** le prix des maisons a fait un bond spectaculaire

N *Cin, Theat & TV* superproduction *f*

pectacularly [spek'tækjʊləlɪ] **ADV** *(big, beautiful)* extraordinairement; **it went s. wrong** ça s'est vraiment très mal passé; **the movie was s. successful** le film a eu un succès monstre; **the government has failed s. in its effort to combat unemployment** le gouvernement a échoué lamentablement dans sa tentative de lutte contre le chômage

pectate [spek'teɪt] **VI** = être présent en tant que spectateur

pectator [spek'teɪtə(r)] **N** spectateur(trice) *m,f*; **we don't want any spectators** nous ne voulons pas qu'on nous regarde

▸▸ ***spectator sport*** sport *m* grand public; **swimming is not a very good s. sport** la natation n'est pas un sport très intéressant à regarder; *Fig* **television has turned war into a s. sport** la télévision a transformé la guerre en spectacle

pecter *Am* = **spectre**

pectral ['spektrəl] **ADJ 1** *Phys (analysis, band, colour, density)* spectral **2** *(ghostly)* fantomatique, spectral

▸▸ *Phys* ***spectral range*** domaine *m* spectral

pectre, *Am* **specter** ['spektə(r)] **N** spectre *m*; *Fig* **the s. of war/famine** *(threat)* le spectre de la guerre/la famine; **to be the s. at the feast** jeter une ombre au tableau

pectrogram ['spektrəgræm] **N** spectrogramme *m*

pectrograph ['spektrəgrɑːf] **N** spectrographe *m*

pectrometer [spek'trɒmɪtə(r)] **N** spectromètre *m*

pectroscope ['spektrəskəʊp] **N** spectroscope *m*

pectroscopy [spek'trɒskəpɪ] (*pl* **spectroscopies**) **N** spectroscopie *f*

pectrum ['spektrəm] (*pl* **spectrums** *or* **spectra** [-trə]) **N 1** *Phys* spectre *m*; **the colours of the s.** les couleurs *fpl* spectrales *ou* du spectre **2** *Fig* *(range)* gamme *f*; **right across the s.** sur toute la gamme; **we've covered the whole s. of opinion** nous avons couvert tous les secteurs d'opinion; **people across the political s.** des représentants de toutes les tendances politiques

▸▸ ***spectrum analysis*** analyse *f* spectrale

peculate ['spekjʊleɪt] **VI 1** *(wonder)* s'interroger, se poser des questions; *(make suppositions)* faire des suppositions; *Phil* spéculer; **we can only s.** nous ne pouvons que faire des suppositions; **the press is speculating about the future of the present government** la presse s'interroge sur l'avenir du gouvernement actuel **2** *Com & Fin* spéculer; **to s. on the stock market** spéculer *ou* jouer en Bourse

peculation [ˌspekjʊ'leɪʃən] **N 1** *(UNCOUNT)* *(supposition, conjecture)* conjecture *f*, conjecture(s) *f(pl)*, supposition(s) *f(pl)*; *Phil* spéculation *f*; **it's pure s.** ce n'est qu'une conjecture *ou* supposition; **there's been a lot of s. about her motives** tout le monde s'est demandé quels étaient ses motifs; **the affair has been the subject of intense s. in the press** l'affaire a donné lieu à toutes sortes de conjectures dans la presse **2** *(guess)* supposition *f*, conjecture *f* **3** *Com & Fin* spéculation *f*; **s. in oil** spéculation *f* sur le pétrole

speculative ['spekjʊlətɪv] **ADJ** spéculatif

▸▸ *Fin & St Exch* ***speculative buying*** achats *mpl* spéculatifs; ***speculative securities*** valeurs *fpl* spéculatives; ***speculative selling*** vente *f* spéculative; ***speculative shares*** valeurs *fpl* spéculatives

speculatively ['spekjʊlətɪvlɪ] **ADV** *(suggest, argue)* à titre d'hypothèse; *(invest)* spéculativement

speculator ['spekjʊleɪtə(r)] **N** *Com & Fin* spéculateur(trice) *m,f*

speculum ['spekjʊləm] (*pl* **speculums** *or* **specula** [-lə]) **N** *Med* spéculum *m*; *Opt* miroir *m*, réflecteur *m*

sped [sped] *pt & pp of* **speed**

speech [spiːtʃ] **N 1** *(faculty)* parole *f*, *(spoken language)* parole *f*, langage *m* parlé; **to express oneself in s.** s'exprimer oralement *ou* par la parole; **things which people say in everyday s.** des choses que les gens disent dans la langue de tous les jours

2 *(manner of speaking)* façon *f* de parler, langage *m*; *(elocution)* élocution *f*, articulation *f*; **his s. was slurred** il bafouillait; **her s. grew hesitant** son élocution devenait hésitante

3 *(dialect, language)* parler *m*, langage *m*; **the s. of the islanders/local fishermen** le parler des habitants de l'île/des pêcheurs du coin

4 *(talk)* discours *m*, *Formal* allocution *f*; *(shorter, more informal)* speech *m*; **to make a s. on** *or* **about sth** faire *ou* prononcer un discours sur qch; **s.! s.!** un discours! un discours!

5 *Theat* tirade *f*

▸▸ *Ling* ***speech act*** acte *m* de parole; ***speech bubble*** bulle *f*; *Ling* ***speech community*** communauté *f* linguistique; *Br Sch* ***speech day*** distribution *f* des prix; **on s. day** le jour de la distribution des prix; ***speech defect*** défaut *m* de prononciation, *Spec* trouble *f* du langage; ***speech impediment*** défaut *m* d'élocution *ou* de prononciation; ***speech pattern*** schéma *m* linguistique; *Comput* ***speech recognition*** reconnaissance *f* de la parole; *Ling* ***speech sound*** phone *m*, son *m* linguistique; *Rad* ***speech station*** station *f* de radio à vocation culturelle; ***speech synthesizer*** synthétiseur *m* de parole; ***speech therapist*** orthophoniste *mf*, *Belg & Suisse* logopède *mf*; ***speech therapy*** orthophonie *f*

> SPEECH DAY
>
> À la fin de l'année scolaire en Grande-Bretagne, certaines écoles invitent une personnalité à prononcer un discours et à distribuer des prix.

speechify ['spiːtʃɪfaɪ] (*pt & pp* **speechified**) **VI** *Pej* discourir, faire de beaux discours

speechifying ['spiːtʃɪfaɪɪŋ] **N** *Pej* beaux discours *mpl*, laïus *m*

speechless ['spiːtʃlɪs] **ADJ** *(with amazement, disbelief)* muet, interloqué; *(with rage, joy)* muet; **she was s. with admiration** elle était muette d'admiration; **to leave sb s.** laisser qn sans voix; *Fam* **I'm s.!** je ne sais pas quoi dire!▫, les bras m'en tombent!

speechlessly ['spiːtʃlɪslɪ] **ADV** d'un air interdit *ou* interloqué

speechwriter ['spiːtʃˌraɪtə(r)] **N** = personne qui écrit des discours; **she's the mayor's s.** c'est elle qui écrit les discours du maire

speed [spiːd] (*pt & pp vi sense* **1 sped** [sped], *vi sense* **2 speeded**, *vt* **sped** [sped] *or* **speeded**) **N 1** *(rate, pace* ▸ *of car, progress, reaction, work)* vitesse *f*; **I was driving** *or* **going at a s. of 65 mph** ≃ je roulais à 100 km/h; **to do a s. of 100 km/h** faire du 100 km/h; **at (a) great** *or* **high s.** à toute vitesse, à grande vitesse; **at top** *or* **full s.** *(drive)* à toute vitesse *ou* allure; *(work)* très vite, en quatrième vitesse; **at the s. of light/sound** à la vitesse de la lumière/du son; **typing/shorthand s.** nombre *m* de mots-minute en dactylo/en sténo; *Literary* **to make all s.** faire diligence, se hâter; *Fam* **to be up to s. on sth** être au courant de qch▫; *Fam* **to bring sb up to s. on sth** mettre qn au courant de qch▫

2 *(rapid rate)* vitesse *f*, rapidité *f*; **the s. with which she learnt/the building was completed** la vitesse à laquelle elle a appris/le bâtiment a été terminé; *Br* **I hate having to work at s.** j'ai horreur de devoir travailler vite; *Br* **the actress delivered her lines at s.** l'actrice a débité son texte à toute allure; **to pick up/to lose s.** prendre/perdre de la vitesse

3 *(gear* ▸ *of car, bicycle)* vitesse *f*; **a 10-s. racer** un vélo de course à 10 vitesses

4 *Phot (of film)* rapidité *f*, sensibilité *f*; *(of shutter)* vitesse *f*; *(of lens)* luminosité *f*

5 *Fam Drugs slang (amphetamines)* amphets *fpl*, speed *m*

6 *Comput* vitesse *f*; **32 s. CD-ROM drive** lecteur *m* de CD-ROM 32 x

VI 1 *(go fast)* aller à toute allure; **we sped across the field** nous avons traversé le champ à toute allure; **I saw her speeding down the street** je l'ai vue descendre la rue à toute allure; **he sped away** il est parti à toute vitesse, il a pris ses jambes à son cou; **time seems to s. by** le temps passe comme un éclair; **the torpedo sped through the water** la torpille se déplaçait dans l'eau à toute vitesse **2** *Aut (exceed speed limit)* faire des excès de vitesse, rouler trop vite **3** *Fam Drugs slang* **to be speeding** *(have taken amphetamines)* être sous amphets, speeder

VT *(person)* **to s. sb on his way** souhaiter bon voyage à qn; **I gave him a drink to s. him on his way** je lui ai offert quelque chose pour la route; *Arch* **God s. (you)!** (que) Dieu vous garde!

▸▸ ***speed bump*** casse-vitesse *m*, ralentisseur *m*; ***speed camera*** radar *m*; ***speed chess*** échecs *mpl* rapides; *Am Fam* ***speed cop*** motard *m* (de la police); ***speed dating*** speed dating *m*, = soirées de rencontre dont chaque participant dispose d'un temps limité pour s'entretenir avec tous les autres; *Am Fam* ***speed demon*** mordu(e) *m,f* de vitesse; *Tel* ***speed dial*** numérotation *f* abrégée; *Am Fam* ***speed freak*** *(drug addict)* drogué(e) *m,f* aux amphétamines▫; ***speed gun*** radar *m* à main; ***speed limit*** limitation *f* de vitesse; **the s. limit is 60** la vitesse est limitée à 60; *Br, Austr & NZ Fam* ***speed merchant*** mordu(e) *m,f* de vitesse; *Sport* ***speed skating*** patinage *m* de vitesse; ***speed trap*** contrôle *m* de vitesse

▸ **speed along VI** *(in car, on bike)* rouler vite, *Fam* foncer; *(walk)* marcher vite; *(run)* courir vite; **the work is speeding along** le travail avance à bonne allure

VT SEP *(work)* faire avancer *ou* progresser en vitesse

▸ **speed off VI** *(on foot, in car)* partir à toute allure

VT SEP they sped him off to hospital ils l'ont transporté à l'hôpital à toute vitesse

▸ **speed up VI** *(gen)* aller plus vite; *(driver)* rouler plus vite; *(worker)* travailler plus vite; *(machine, film)* accélérer

VT SEP *(worker)* faire travailler plus vite; *(person)* faire aller plus vite; *(work)* activer, accélérer; *(pace)* presser; *(production)* accélérer, augmenter; *(reaction, film)* accélérer

speedball ['spiːdbɔːl] **N** *Fam Drugs slang* speedball *m (mélange d'héroïne et de cocaïne)*

speedboat ['spiːdbəʊt] **N** vedette *f* (rapide); *(with outboard engine)* hors-bord *m inv*

speedfreak ['spiːdfriːk] **N to be a s.** consommer beaucoup d'amphets

speedily ['spiːdɪlɪ] **ADV** *(quickly)* vite, rapidement; *(promptly)* promptement, sans tarder; *(soon)* bientôt

speediness ['spiːdɪnɪs] **N** rapidité *f*

speeding ['spiːdɪŋ] **N** *Aut* excès *m* de vitesse; **I was stopped for s.** j'ai été arrêté pour excès de vitesse

▸▸ ***speeding fine*** contravention *f* pour excès de vitesse; ***speeding ticket*** P-V *m* pour excès de vitesse; ***speeding up*** accélération *f*

speedo ['spi:dəʊ] *(pl* **speedos)** N *Br Fam* compteur *m* de vitesse

speedometer [spɪ'dɒmɪtə(r)] N compteur *m* de vitesse

speedster ['spi:dstə(r)] N *(car)* bolide *m*; *(driver)* fou (folle) *m,f* du volant, *Pej* chauffard *m*

speed-up N accélération *f*

speedway ['spi:dweɪ] N **1** *(racing)* speedway *m* **2** *Am (track)* piste *f* de vitesse pour motos **3** *Am (expressway)* voie *f* express *ou* rapide

speedwell ['spi:dwel] N *Bot* véronique *f*

Speedwriting® ['spi:d,raɪtɪŋ] N sténo *f* alphabétique

speedy ['spi:dɪ] *(compar* **speedier,** *superl* **speediest)** ADJ **1** *(rapid)* rapide; *(prompt)* prompt; **her help brought a s. end to the dispute** son aide a permis de mettre rapidement fin au différend; **to wish sb a s. recovery** souhaiter à qn un prompt rétablissement **2** *(car)* rapide, nerveux

speleologist [,spi:lɪ'ɒlədʒɪst] N spéléologue *mf*

speleology [,spi:lɪ'ɒlədʒɪ] N spéléologie *f*

spell [spel] *(Br pt & pp* **spelt** [spelt] *or* **spelled,** *Am pt & pp* **spelled)** VT **1** *(write)* écrire, orthographier; *(aloud)* épeler; **they've spelt my name wrong** ils ont mal écrit mon nom; **his name is spelt J-O-N** son nom s'écrit J-O-N; **how do you s. it?** comment est-ce que ça s'écrit?; **she spells Maud with an "e"** elle écrit Maud avec un "e"; **shall I s. my name for you?** voulez-vous que j'épelle mon nom?

2 *(of letters)* former, donner; **C-O-U-G-H spells "cough"** C-O-U-G-H donnent "cough"

3 *Fig (mean)* signifier; **her discovery could s. success for our business** sa découverte pourrait être très profitable à notre entreprise

4 *Am (worker, colleague)* relayer

VI **to learn to s.** apprendre l'orthographe; **she can't s. very well** elle n'est pas très bonne en orthographe

N **1** *(period)* (courte) période *f*; **during the cold s.** pendant la vague de froid; **we're in for a s. of wet weather** le temps se met à la pluie; **scattered showers and sunny spells** des averses locales et des éclaircies; **she did** *or* **had a s. as a reporter** elle a été journaliste pendant un certain temps; **it's his second s. in prison** c'est son deuxième séjour en prison; **he had a dizzy s.** il a été pris de vertige

2 *(of duty etc)* tour *m*; **do you want me to take** *or* **to do a s. at the wheel?** voulez-vous que je vous relaie au volant *ou* que je conduise un peu?

3 *(magic words)* formule *f* magique, incantation *f*; **she muttered a s.** elle marmonna une incantation

4 *(enchantment)* charme *m*, sort *m*, sortilège *m*; **to cast** *or* **to put a s. on sb** jeter un sort *ou* un charme à qn, ensorceler *ou* envoûter qn; **to break the s.** rompre le charme; *also Fig* **to be under sb's s.** être sous le charme de qn

▸**spell out** VT SEP **1** *(read out letter by letter)* épeler; *(decipher)* déchiffrer **2** *(make explicit)* expliquer bien clairement; **she spelt out in detail what the scheme would cost** elle a expliqué en détail quel serait le coût du projet; **do I have to s. it out for you?** est-ce qu'il faut que je mette les points sur les i?

spellbinder ['spel,baɪndə(r)] N **1** *(speaker)* orateur(trice) *m,f* fascinant(e) **2** *(fascinating thing)* **her latest novel is a s.** son dernier roman est un enchantement; **the match was a s.** le match a tenu tout le monde en haleine

spellbinding ['spel,baɪndɪŋ] ADJ ensorcelant, envoûtant

spellbound ['spelbaʊnd] ADJ *(spectator, audience)* captivé, envoûté; **the children listened s.** les enfants écoutaient, captivés; **the movie held me s. from start to finish** le film m'a tenu en haleine *ou* m'a captivé du début jusqu'à la fin

spellcheck ['speltʃek] *Comput* N correction *f* orthographique; **to do** *or* **run a s. on a document** effectuer la correction orthographique sur un document

VT faire la vérification orthographique de

spellchecker ['spel,tʃekə(r)] N *Comput* correcteur *m* orthographique *ou* d'orthographe

spellchecking ['spel,tʃekɪŋ] N *Comput* correction *f* orthographique *ou* d'orthographe

speller ['spelə(r)] N **1** *(person)* **he's a good/bad s.** il est bon/mauvais en orthographe **2** *(book)* livre *m* d'orthographe

spelling ['spelɪŋ] N **1** *(word formation)* orthographe *f*; **what is the s. of this word?** quelle est l'orthographe de *ou* comment s'écrit ce mot? **2** *(ability to spell)* orthographe *f*; **his s. is awful** il est nul en orthographe; **he's good/bad at s.** il est bon/mauvais en orthographe

COMP *(error, test, book)* d'orthographe; *(pronunciation)* orthographique

▸▸ *Am* ***spelling bee*** concours *m* d'orthographe; *Comput* ***spelling checker*** correcteur *m* orthographique *ou* d'orthographe; ***spelling mistake*** faute *f* d'orthographe

spelt [spelt] *Br pt & pp of* **spell**

N *Bot* épeautre *m*

spend [spend] *(pt & pp* **spent** [spent]) VT **1** *(money, fortune)* dépenser; **to s. money on** *(food, clothes)* dépenser de l'argent en; *(house, car)* dépenser de l'argent pour, consacrer de l'argent à; **how much do you s. on the children's clothes?** combien (d'argent) dépensez-vous pour habiller vos enfants?; **he spends most of his pocket money on (buying) records** la plus grande partie de son argent de poche passe dans l'achat de disques; **I consider it money well spent** je considère que c'est un bon investissement; **without spending a penny** sans dépenser un centime, sans bourse délier; *Br Fam Euph* **to s. a penny** aller au petit coin

2 *(time* ▸ *pass)* passer; *(*▸ *devote)* consacrer; **to s. time on sth/on doing sth** passer du temps sur qch/à faire qch; **she spent the whole afternoon reading** elle a passé tout l'après-midi à lire; **I spent three hours on the job** le travail m'a pris *ou* demandé trois heures; **how do you s. your weekends?** qu'est-ce que tu fais le week-end?; **I spent a lot of time and effort on this** j'y ai consacré beaucoup de temps et d'efforts; **she spent her life helping the underprivileged** elle a consacré sa vie à aider les défavorisés

3 *(exhaust, use up* ▸ *one's strength, ammunition)* épuiser; **the gale had spent itself** le vent avait fini par tomber

VI dépenser, faire des dépenses

N *Br (allocated money)* allocation *f*, dépenses *fpl*; **we must increase our marketing s.** nous devons augmenter le budget marketing

spendable ['spendəbəl] ADJ

▸▸ ***spendable income*** revenu *m* dépensable

spender ['spendə(r)] N dépensier(ère) *m,f*; **she's a big s.** elle est très dépensière

spending ['spendɪŋ] N *(UNCOUNT)* dépenses *fpl*; **a cut in defence s.** une réduction du budget de la défense; **we went on a s. spree** nous avons fait des folies, nous avons dépensé des sommes folles

▸▸ ***spending cuts*** réductions *fpl* des dépenses; ***spending money*** argent *m* de poche; ***spending power*** pouvoir *m* d'achat; ***spending review*** examen *m* des dépenses

spendthrift ['spendθrɪft] N dépensier(ère) *m,f*; **she's a terrible s.** elle est terriblement dépensière, elle jette l'argent par les fenêtres

ADJ dépensier

spent [spent] *pt & pp of* **spend**

ADJ **1** *(used up* ▸ *fuel, bullet, match)* utilisé; *(*▸ *cartridge)* brûlé; **the party is a s. force in politics** le parti n'a plus l'influence qu'il avait en politique; **her courage was s.** elle n'avait plus de courage; **her strength/energy was all but s.** elle n'avait presque plus de forces/d'énergie **2** *(tired out)* épuisé; **he was completely s.** il était épuisé *ou* à bout

sperm [spɜ:m] *(pl inv or* **sperms)** N **1** *(cell)* spermatozoïde *m* **2** *(liquid)* sperme *m*

▸▸ ***sperm bank*** banque *f* de sperme; *Biol* ***sperm cell*** spermatozoïde *m*; ***sperm count*** nombre *m* de spermatozoïdes; **to have a low s. count** avoir un nombre de spermatozoïdes peu élevé; ***sperm oil*** blanc *m* de baleine, spermaceti *m*; *Zool* ***sperm whale*** cachalot *m*

spermaceti [,spɜ:mə'setɪ] N blanc *m* de baleine, spermaceti *m*

spermatozoon [,spɜ:mətəʊ'zəʊɒn] *(pl* **spermatozoa** [-'zəʊə]) N spermatozoïde *m*

spermicidal [,spɜ:mɪ'saɪdəl] ADJ spermicide

▸▸ ***spermicidal cream*** crème *f* spermicid ***spermicidal jelly*** gelée *f* spermicide

spermicide ['spɜ:mɪsaɪd] N spermicide *m*

spew [spju:] VT *Fam* dégueuler, gerber; **to s. on guts up** rendre tripes et boyaux

VI **1** *Fam (vomit)* dégueuler, gerber **2** *Fig (po out)* gicler; **the acid spewed everywhere** l'acide giclé partout

N *Fam* vomi *m*, dégueulis *m*

▸**spew forth, spew out** *Literary* VI vomir

VT SEP vomir

▸**spew up** *Fam* VI dégueuler, gerber

VT SEP dégueuler, gerber

sphagnum ['sfægnəm] N *Bot* sphaigne *f*

▸▸ ***sphagnum moss*** sphaigne *f*

sphere [sfɪə(r)] N **1** *(globe)* sphère *f*; *Literary (s* cieux *mpl*; **the heavenly s.** la sphère céleste **2** *(of interest, activity)* sphère *f*, domaine *m*; **her s. activity** *(professional)* son domaine d'activi *(personal)* sa sphère d'activité; **it's not my s.** n'est pas de mon domaine, cela ne relève p de mes compétences; **the question is outsi the committee's s.** la question ne relève pas d compétences du comité; **s. of influence** sphèr d'influence; **in the public s.** *(in industry)* dans domaine public; *(in politics)* dans la vie po tique

spherical ['sferɪkəl], **spheric** ['sferɪk] ADJ sph rique

▸▸ ***spherical geometry*** géométrie *f* sphériqu ***spherical trigonometry*** trigonométrie *f* sphériq

spheroid ['sfɪərɔɪd] N sphéroïde *m*

sphincter ['sfɪŋktə(r)] N sphincter *m*

Sphinx [sfɪŋks] N *Myth* **the S.** le Sphinx

sphinx-like ADJ de sphinx; *(smile)* énigm tique

spic [spɪk] N *Am very Fam* métèque *mf*, = tern injurieux désignant une personne d'origine la no-américaine

spice [spaɪs] N **1** *Culin* épice *f*; **it needs more s.** n'est pas assez épicé *ou* relevé; **mixed s.** *(U COUNT)* épices *fpl* mélangées **2** *Fig* piquant sel *m*; **it added a bit of s. to our routine** ça a ajou un peu de piquant à *ou* ça a pimenté notre trai train quotidien

VT **1** *Culin* épicer, parfumer; **spiced with nutm** parfumé à la muscade **2** *Fig* pimenter, corse **the story is spiced with political anecdotes** l'hi toire est pimentée d'anecdotes politiques

▸▸ ***spice cake*** gâteau *m* aux épices; ***spice ra*** étagère *f* ou présentoir *m* à épices

spiciness ['spaɪsɪnɪs] N **1** *(of food)* goût *m* épic *ou* relevé **2** *Fig (of story, adventure)* piquant *m*

spick = **spic**

spick-and-span ADJ *Fam (room)* nickel, ir peccable; *(appearance)* tiré à quatre épingles

spicy ['spaɪsɪ] *(compar* **spicier,** *superl* **spiciest)** A **1** *(food)* épicé **2** *Fig (story, adventure)* piquar corsé

spider ['spaɪdə(r)] N **1** *Entom* araignée *f*

2 *Br (for luggage)* araignée *f* (à bagages)

3 *Am Culin* poêle *f* (à trépied)

4 *(snooker rest)* râteau *m*

▸▸ ***spider crab*** araignée *f* (de mer); ***spider monk*** singe *m* araignée; ***spider plant*** chlorophytum ***spider's web*** toile *f* d'araignée

spiderman ['spaɪdəmæn] *(pl* **spidermen** [-men]) *Br Fam* = ouvrier travaillant sur de hautes con tructions

spidery ['spaɪdərɪ] ADJ *(in shape)* en forn d'araignée; *(finger)* long (longue) et mince; **handwriting** pattes *fpl* de mouches

spiel [ʃpi:l, spi:l] *Fam* N baratin *m*, speech *m*; *(salesperson)* boniment *m*; **he gave me some about having been held up at the airport** il m'a se vi tout un baratin comme quoi il avait é bloqué à l'aéroport

VI baratiner

▸**spiel off** VT SEP *Am Fam (recite)* débiter

spiffing ['spɪfɪŋ] ADJ *Br Fam Old-fashioned* ép tant

spigot ['spɪgət] N **1** *(in cask)* fausset *m* **2** *(part tap)* clé *f* **3** *Am (tap)* robinet *m* (extérieur)

pike [spaɪk] VT **1** *(shoes, railings)* garnir de pointes
2 *(impale)* transpercer
3 *Fam (drink)* corser□; **my coffee was spiked with brandy** mon café était arrosé de cognac□
4 *(thwart ▸ affair)* faire avorter; *(▸ plan)* contrecarrer, entraver; *Mil & Hist (canon, guns)* enclouer; *Fig* **to s. sb's guns** priver qn de ses moyens d'action, mettre qn hors d'action
5 *Press (story)* rejeter
VI *(in volleyball)* smasher
N **1** *(on railings, shoe, helmet)* pointe *f*; *(on barbed wire)* piquant *m*; *(on cactus)* épine *f*; *(on tyre)* clou *m*; *(for paper)* pique-notes *m inv*; *Press* **the story was put on the s.** l'article a été rejeté
2 *(peak ▸ on graph)* pointe *f*
3 *Am (sharp increase)* forte augmentation *f* (in de)
4 *(nail)* gros clou *m*
5 *(antler)* dague *f*
6 *(in volleyball)* smash *m*
7 *Bot* épi *m*
8 *Fam Drugs slang (hypodermic needle)* shooteuse *f*, pompe *f*
• **spikes** NPL *Fam (shoes)* chaussures *fpl* à pointes□
▸▸ ***spike heels*** (chaussures *fpl* à) talons *mpl* aiguilles

spiked [spaɪkt] ADJ *(railings)* garni *ou* hérissé de pointes; *(shoes)* à pointes; *(tyre)* clouté, à clous

spikenard ['spaɪknɑːd] N *Bot* nard *m* (indien)

spiky ['spaɪkɪ] *(compar* **spikier**, *superl* **spikiest)** ADJ **1** *(branch, railings)* garni *ou* hérissé de pointes; *(writing)* pointu; **s. hair** *(sticking up, tousled)* cheveux *mpl* en épis; *(as hairstyle)* cheveux *mpl* hérissés **2** *Br Fam (bad-tempered)* chatouilleux□, ombrageux□

spill [spɪl] *(Br pt & pp* **spilt** [spɪlt] *or* **spilled**, *Am pt & pp* **spilled)** VT **1** *(liquid, salt etc)* renverser, répandre; **she spilt coffee down** *or* **over her dress** elle a renversé du café sur sa robe; **try to carry the bucket upstairs without spilling any water** essaie de monter le seau sans renverser d'eau; **she spilt the contents of her handbag onto the bed** elle vida (le contenu de) son sac à main sur le lit
2 *Fam Fig (secret)* dévoiler□; **to s. the beans** vendre la mèche
3 *(blood)* verser, faire couler; **not a drop of blood was spilled** pas une goutte de sang n'a été versée
4 *(person)* **he was spilled from his motorbike** il est tombé de sa moto; **the rider was spilled into the stream** le cavalier a été projeté dans le ruisseau
VI **1** *(liquid, salt etc)* se renverser, se répandre **2** *(crowd)* se déverser; **the huge crowd spilled into the square** l'immense foule se répandit *ou* se déversa sur la place
N **1** *(spillage ▸ of liquid)* renversement *m* **2** *(fall ▸ from horse, bike)* chute *f*, culbute *f*; **to take a s.** faire la culbute **3** *(for fire)* allume-feu *m*
▸ **spill out** VT SEP **1** *(contents, liquid)* renverser, répandre **2** *Fig (secret)* dévoiler, révéler; **he got drunk and spilled out all his problems** il a bu et s'est mis à parler de tous ses problèmes
VI **1** *(contents, liquid)* se renverser, se répandre; **the water spilt out onto the floor** l'eau s'est renversée par terre **2** *Fig (crowd)* se déverser, s'échapper; **the commuters spilled out of the train** un flot de banlieusards s'est échappé du train
▸ **spill over** VI **1** *(liquid)* déborder, se répandre; **the tea spilled over into the saucer** le thé a débordé dans la soucoupe **2** *Fig (overflow)* se déverser, déborder; **the city's population has spilled over into the surrounding villages** les habitants de la ville ont envahi les villages environnants; **the conflict could s. over into neighbouring countries** le conflit risquerait de s'étendre aux pays voisins; **her work spills over into her family life** son travail empiète sur sa vie familiale

spillage ['spɪlɪdʒ] N *(act of spilling)* renversement *m*, fait *m* de renverser; *(liquid spilt)* liquide *m* renversé; **we managed to avoid too much s.** nous avons réussi à ne pas trop en renverser; **there's been a diesel s. on the M25** un chargement de gasoil s'est renversé sur la M25

spillover ['spɪl,əʊvə(r)] N **1** *(act of spilling)* renversement *m*; *(quantity spilt)* quantité *f* renversée **2** *(excess)* excédent *m*

spillway ['spɪlweɪ] N déversoir *m*

spilt [spɪlt] *Br pt & pp of* **spill**

spin [spɪn] *(pt & pp* **spun** [spʌn], *cont* **spinning)** N **1** *(rotation)* tournoiement *m*; *Aviat* vrille *f*; **give the wheel a s.** faites tourner la roue; **the plane went into a s.** *(accidentally)* l'avion a fait une chute en vrille; *(in aerobatics)* l'avion a effectué une descente en vrille; **the car went into a s.** la voiture a fait un tête-à-queue
2 *(in spin-dryer)* essorage *m*; **long/short s.** essorage *m* complet/court; **to give sth a s.** essorer qch; **give the washing a quick s.** donne un petit coup d'essorage au linge
3 *Fam (panic)* **to be in a (flat) s.** être dans tous ses états; **the news sent him into a s.** la nouvelle l'a complètement paniqué□; **the office was thrown into a (flat) s. by the arrival of the boss** les employés se sont affolés en voyant arriver le patron□
4 *Sport (on ball)* effet *m*; **to put s. on a ball** donner de l'effet à une balle; **there was a lot of s. on that ball** il y avait beaucoup d'effet dans cette balle
5 *Fam (on information)* **to put the right s. on a story** présenter une affaire sous un angle favorable□; **the government put its own s. on the situation** le gouvernement a présenté la situation sous un angle qui lui convenait□; **this government is all s. and no substance** ce gouvernement est très fort pour le bavardage mais n'a aucun programme réel□
6 *Fam (ride ▸ in car)* tour□ *m*, balade□ *f*; **to go for a s.** faire une (petite) balade en voiture
7 *Fam (try)* **to give sth a s.** essayer *ou* tenter qch□; **would you like to give the car a s.?** voulez-vous essayer la voiture?
8 *Austr Fam (luck)* coup *m* de chance; *(bad luck)* malchance□ *f*
VT **1** *(cause to rotate ▸ wheel, chair)* faire tourner; *(▸ top)* lancer, faire tournoyer; *Sport (▸ ball)* donner de l'effet à; **to s. the wheel** *(in casino)* faire tourner la roue; *(in car)* braquer; **to s. a coin** jouer à pile ou face
2 *(yarn, glass)* filer; *(thread)* fabriquer
3 *(of spider, silkworm)* tisser
4 *(invent ▸ tale)* inventer, débiter; **she spun some yarn about the buses being on strike** elle a prétexté que les bus étaient en grève
5 *(in spin-dryer)* essorer
6 *Fam (present in a good light ▸ image, information, event)* présenter sous un angle favorable□
VI **1** *(rotate ▸ planet, wheel)* tourner (sur soi-même); *(▸ skater, top)* tournoyer, tourner; *Sport (▸ ball)* tournoyer; **it spins on its axis** il tourne sur son axe *ou* sur lui-même; **the skater/ballerina spun on one foot** le patineur/la ballerine virevolta sur un pied; **the room seemed to be spinning (around me)** la pièce semblait tourner autour de moi; **the wheels were spinning in the mud** les roues patinaient dans la boue; **to s. out of control** *(plane)* tomber en vrille; *(car)* faire un tête-à-queue
2 *Fig (grow dizzy)* tourner; **my head's spinning** j'ai la tête qui (me) tourne; **these figures make your head s.** ces chiffres vous donnent le tournis *ou* le vertige; **his mind was spinning from the recent events** les derniers événements lui donnaient le vertige
3 *(spinner)* filer; *(spider)* tisser sa toile
4 *(in spin-dryer)* essorer; **put the clothes in to s.** mets le linge à essorer
5 *(travel fast)* **we were spinning along at a hundred** on filait à cent à l'heure
6 *Fishing* **to s. for pike** pêcher le brochet à la cuiller *ou* cuillère
7 *Fam (spin doctor)* présenter les choses sous un angle favorable□
▸▸ *Sport* ***spin bowler*** = lanceur qui donne de l'effet à la balle; *Fam Pej Pol* ***spin doctor*** = chargé des relations publiques d'un parti politique
▸ **spin out** VT SEP *(story, idea)* délayer; *(discussion)* faire durer; *(supplies, money)* faire durer, économiser
▸ **spin round** *Br* VI **1** *(planet, wheel)* tourner (sur soi-même); *(skater, top)* tournoyer, tourner **2** *(face in opposite direction)* se retourner; **she spun round and faced me** elle se retourna vivement vers moi
VT SEP *(wheel)* faire tourner; *(dancer, top)* faire tourner *ou* tournoyer

spina bifida [,spaɪnə'bɪfɪdə] N *Med* spina-bifida *m inv*

spinach ['spɪnɪdʒ] N *(UNCOUNT)* épinards *mpl*

spinal ['spaɪnəl] ADJ *(nerve, muscle)* spinal; *(ligament, disc)* vertébral; **a s. injury** une blessure à la colonne vertébrale
▸▸ ***spinal anaesthesia*** anesthésie *f* rachidienne, rachianesthésie *f*; ***spinal column*** colonne *f* vertébrale; ***spinal cord*** moelle *f* épinière; ***spinal fluid*** liquide *m* céphalo-rachidien; ***spinal tap*** ponction *f* lombaire

spindle ['spɪndəl] N **1** *(for spinning ▸ by hand)* fuseau *m*; *(▸ by machine)* broche *f* **2** *Tech* broche *f*, axe *m*; *(in motor, lathe)* arbre *m*; *(of valve)* tige *f*

spindleshanks ['spɪndəl,ʃæŋks] N *(man)* grand échalas *m*

spindly ['spɪndlɪ] *(compar* **spindlier**, *superl* **spindliest)** ADJ *(legs)* grêle; *(body)* chétif, maigrichon; *(tree)* grêle; *(plant)* étiolé

spindrift ['spɪndrɪft] N *(UNCOUNT)* embruns *mpl*

spin-dry VT essorer

spin-dryer N essoreuse *f*

spin-drying N essorage *m*

spine [spaɪn] N **1** *Anat* colonne *f* vertébrale; *Zool* épine *f* dorsale
2 *(prickle ▸ of hedgehog)* piquant *m*; *(▸ of plant, rose)* épine *f*
3 *(of book)* dos *m*
4 *(of hill)* crête *f*
5 *Am (courage)* résolution *f*, volonté *f*

spine-chiller N *(book)* livre *m* d'horreur; *(film)* film *m* d'épouvante; **that story is a real s.** c'est une histoire à vous glacer le sang

spine-chilling ADJ à vous glacer le sang, terrifiant

spineless ['spaɪnlɪs] ADJ **1** *(weak)* mou (molle); *(cowardly)* lâche **2** *Zool* invertébré **3** *Bot* sans épines

spinelessness ['spaɪnlɪsnɪs] N lâcheté *f*

spinet [spɪ'net] N *Mus* épinette *f*

spinnaker ['spɪnəkə(r)] N *Naut* spinnaker *m*, spi *m*

spinner ['spɪnə(r)] N **1** *Tex (person)* fileur(euse) *m,f*
2 *(in fishing)* cuiller *f*, cuillère *f*
3 *(spin-dryer)* essoreuse *f*
4 *Br Sport (bowler in cricket)* = lanceur qui donne de l'effet à une balle; *(ball)* = balle qui a de l'effet; **to bowl a s.** lancer une balle avec de l'effet
5 *Fam Pej Pol (spin doctor)* = chargé des relations publiques d'un parti politique

spinneret ['spɪnəret] N *Entom & Tex* filière *f*

spinney ['spɪnɪ] N *Br* bosquet *m*, boqueteau *m*, petit bois *m*

spinning ['spɪnɪŋ] N **1** *Tex (by hand)* filage *m*; *(by machine)* filature *f* **2** *(in fishing)* pêche *f* à la cuiller *ou* cuillère **3** *(exercise)* spinning *m*
ADJ *(rotating)* tournant, qui tourne
▸▸ ***spinning jenny*** jenny *f*; ***spinning mill*** filature *f*; ***spinning top*** toupie *f*; ***spinning wheel*** rouet *m*

spin-off N **1** *(by-product)* retombée *f*, produit *m* dérivé; **the spin-offs from research into nuclear physics** les retombées des recherches en physique nucléaire **2** *(work derived from another)* **the book is a s. from the TV series** le roman est tiré de la série télévisée; **the TV series gave rise to a number of spin-offs** la série télévisée a donné lieu à plusieurs produits dérivés
▸▸ *Mktg* ***spin-off product*** produit *m* dérivé

spinster ['spɪnstə(r)] N *Admin & Law* célibataire *f*, *Pej* vieille fille *f*

spinsterhood ['spɪnstəhʊd] N célibat *m (pour une femme)*

spiny ['spaɪnɪ] *(compar* **spinier**, *superl* **spiniest)** ADJ épineux, couvert d'épines
▸▸ *Zool* ***spiny anteater*** échidné *m*; *Zool* ***spiny lobster*** langouste *f*

spiracle ['spaɪrəkəl] N *Zool (in insect)* stigmate *m*; *(in whale)* évent *m*, spiracle *m*; *(in fish)* ouïe *f*

spiral ['spaɪərəl] *(Br pt & pp* **spiralled**, *cont* **spiralling**, *Am pt & pp* **spiraled**, *cont* **spiraling)** N **1** *(gen) & Econ & Geom* spirale *f*; **in a s.** en spirale; **a s. of**

smoke rose into the sky une volute de fumée s'éleva dans le ciel; **the wage-price s.** la spirale des prix et des salaires **2** *Aviat* vrille *f*
ADJ *(motif, shell, curve)* en (forme de) spirale; *(descent, spring)* en spirale; **the plane went into a s. descent** l'avion amorça une descente en vrille
VI **1** *(in flight ▸ plane)* vriller; *(▸ bird)* voler en spirale; *(in shape ▸ smoke, stairs)* monter en spirale **2** *(prices, inflation)* s'envoler, monter en flèche; **to s. downwards** chuter
▸▸ ***spiral binding*** reliure *f* à spirale; *Astron* ***spiral galaxy*** galaxie *f* spirale; ***spiral staircase*** escalier *m* en colimaçon

▸**spiral down** VI *(plane)* descendre en vrille; *(leaf, feather)* tomber en tourbillonnant

▸**spiral up** VI *(plane, smoke)* monter en spirale; *(prices)* monter en flèche

spirally ['spaɪərəlɪ] ADV *(gen)* en spirale; *Aviat* en vrille

spire ['spaɪə(r)] N **1** *Archit* flèche *f* **2** *(of blade of grass)* tige *f*; *(of mountain, tree)* cime *f*

spirit ['spɪrɪt] N **1** *(non-physical part of being, soul)* esprit *m*; **the poor in s.** les pauvres d'esprit; **the s. is willing but the flesh is weak** l'esprit est prompt mais la chair est faible; **he is with us in s.** il est avec nous en pensée *ou* par la pensée
2 *(supernatural being)* esprit *m*; **she is possessed by spirits** elle est possédée par des esprits; **to call up the spirits of the dead** évoquer les âmes des morts; **evil spirits** esprits *mpl* malins; **the s. world** le monde des esprits
3 *(person)* esprit *m*, âme *f*; **he is a generous s.** il a une âme généreuse, c'est une bonne âme; **he is a courageous s.** il est courageux; **he is a leading s. in the movement** il est l'un de ceux qui donnent son impulsion au mouvement
4 *(attitude, mood)* esprit *m*; **the s. of the age** l'esprit *m ou* le génie de l'époque; **to do sth in a s. of fun** faire qch pour s'amuser; **you mustn't do it in a s. of vengeance** il ne faut pas le faire par esprit de vengeance; **to take sth in the right/wrong s.** prendre qch bien/mal; **he took it in the s. in which it was intended** il l'a pris comme il fallait; **to have the party s.** avoir envie de s'amuser; **to enter into the s. of things** *(at party)* se mettre au diapason; *(in work)* participer de bon cœur; *Fam* **that's the s.!** voilà comment il faut réagir!ᵕ, à la bonne heure!
5 *(deep meaning)* esprit *m*, génie *m*; **the s. of the law** l'esprit *m* de la loi; **you haven't understood the s. of the poem** vous n'avez pas saisi l'esprit du poème
6 *(energy)* énergie *f*, entrain *m*; *(courage)* courage *m*; *(character)* caractère *m*; **to do sth with s.** faire quelque chose avec entrain; **he replied with s.** il a répondu énergiquement; **they sang with s.** ils ont chanté avec entrain; **a man of s.** un homme de caractère; **he is entirely lacking in s.** il est complètement amorphe; **to show s.** montrer du caractère *ou* du courage; **to have s.** avoir de l'allant; **his s. was broken** il avait perdu courage
7 *Br (alcoholic drink)* alcool *m*, spiritueux *m*; **wines and spirits** vins *mpl* et spiritueux *mpl*; **I prefer beer to spirits** je préfère la bière aux spiritueux; **brandy is my favourite s.** le cognac est mon alcool préféré; **taxes on spirits have increased** les taxes sur les spiritueux ont augmenté
8 *Chem* essence *f*, sel *m*
VT *(move secretly)* **they spirited her in/out by a side door** ils l'ont fait entrer/sortir discrètement par une porte dérobée; **he seems to have been spirited into thin air** il semble avoir disparu comme par enchantement; **to s. sth in/out** introduire/sortir discrètement qch
• **spirits** NPL *(mood, mental state)* humeur *f*, état *m* d'esprit; *(morale)* moral *m*; **to be in good spirits** être de bonne humeur, avoir le moral; **to feel out of spirits** avoir le cafard; **to be in high spirits** être de très bonne humeur, avoir le moral au beau fixe; **to be in low spirits** être déprimé; **you must keep your spirits up** il faut garder le moral, il ne faut pas vous laisser abattre; **my spirits rose at the thought** mon moral est remonté rien que d'y penser; **to raise sb's spirits** remonter le moral à qn
▸▸ ***spirit gum*** colle *f* gomme; *Br* ***spirit lamp*** lampe *f* à alcool; ***spirit level*** niveau *m* à bulle; ***spirit stove*** réchaud *m* à alcool; ***spirit varnish*** vernis *m* à alcool; ***spirit of wine, spirits of wine*** esprit-de-vin *m*

▸**spirit away, spirit off** VT SEP *(carry off secretly)* faire disparaître (comme par enchantement); *(steal)* escamoter, subtiliser

spirited ['spɪrɪtɪd] ADJ **1** *(lively ▸ person)* vif, plein d'entrain; *(▸ horse)* fougueux; *(▸ manner, reply, argument)* vif; *(▸ music, rhythm, dance)* entraînant; **to give a s. performance** *(musician)* jouer avec brio *ou* avec verve; *(team, player)* jouer avec brio **2** *(courageous ▸ person, action, decision, defence)* courageux; **to put up a s. resistance** résister courageusement, opposer une résistance courageuse; **he's a s. young fellow** il ne manque pas de courage, ce petit

spiritless ['spɪrɪtlɪs] ADJ *(lifeless)* sans vie, sans entrain, apathique; *(depressed)* démoralisé, déprimé; *(cowardly)* lâche

spiritual ['spɪrɪtʃʊəl] ADJ **1** *(relating to the spirit)* spirituel; **a very s. man** un homme d'une grande spiritualité; **a s. heir** un successeur spirituel; **China is her s. home** elle se sent chez elle en Chine; **his s. home is probably 18th century Holland** c'est probablement dans la Hollande du XVIIIème siècle qu'il se sentirait le plus à l'aise **2** *(religious, sacred)* religieux, sacré
N *(song)* (negro) spiritual *m*
▸▸ ***spiritual adviser*** conseiller(ère) *m,f* spirituel (elle); ***spiritual life*** vie *f* spirituelle

spiritualism ['spɪrɪtʃʊəlɪzəm] N *Rel* spiritisme *m*; *Phil* spiritualisme *m*

spiritualist ['spɪrɪtʃʊəlɪst] ADJ *Rel* spirite; *Phil* spiritualiste
N *Rel* spirite *mf*; *Phil* spiritualiste *mf*

spirituality [ˌspɪrɪtʃʊ'ælətɪ] N spiritualité *f*

spiritually ['spɪrɪtʃʊəlɪ] ADV spirituellement

spirituous ['spɪrɪtʃʊəs] ADJ *Formal* spiritueux, alcoolique
▸▸ ***spirituous liquor*** alcool *m* fort, spiritueux *m*

spirt = **spurt**

spit [spɪt] *(pt & pp* **spit** *or* **spat** [spæt], *cont* **spitting)**
VI **1** *(in anger, contempt)* cracher; **to s. at sb** cracher sur qn; **to s. in sb's face** cracher à la figure de qn; **she spat at him** elle lui a craché dessus
2 *(while talking)* postillonner, envoyer des postillons
3 *(fire)* crépiter; *(hot fat)* sauter, grésiller
4 *(idiom)* **it's spitting (with rain)** il bruine, il pleut légèrement
VT **1** *also Fig (blood, flames, venom, words)* cracher **2** *Culin (put on a spit)* embrocher, mettre à la broche
N **1** *(UNCOUNT) (spittle ▸ in mouth)* salive *f*; *(▸ spat out)* crachat *m*; *(▸ ejected while speaking)* postillon *m*; *(act of spitting)* crachement *m*; *Mil* **s. and polish** astiquage *m*; *Br Fam* **it's a bit of a s. and sawdust pub** c'est un pub sans prétentionsᵕ
2 *Br Fam (likeness)* **to be the (very) s. of sb** être le portrait craché de qn; **he's the s. of his dad** c'est son père tout craché
3 *(of insects)* écume *f* printanière, crachat *m* de coucou
4 *Culin* broche *f*
5 *Geog* pointe *f*, langue *f* de terre
6 *Hort (spade's depth)* **to dig the ground three spits deep** creuser la terre à une profondeur de trois fers de bêche
7 *(idiom)* **there was just a s. of rain** il n'est tombé que quelques gouttes de pluie
▸▸ *Am* ***spit curl*** accroche-cœur *m*; ***spit roast*** rôti *m* à la broche

▸**spit out** VT SEP *(food, medicine)* cracher, recracher; *(words, invective)* cracher; **"you're fired!" he spat out** "vous êtes viré!" lança-t-il; *Fam* **come on, spit it out!** allez, accouche!

▸**spit up** VT SEP *(blood, food)* cracher

spite [spaɪt] N *(pique)* dépit *m*; *(malice)* méchanceté *f*, malveillance *f*; **to do sth out of s.** *(out of pique)* faire qch par dépit; *(maliciously)* faire qch par pure méchanceté; **he broke her toy out of pure** *or* **sheer s.** il a cassé son jouet par pure méchanceté envers elle
VT contrarier, vexer
• **in spite of** PREP en dépit de, malgré; **he went out in s. of my advice** il est sorti en dépit de mes conseils; **in s. of myself** malgré moi; **in s. of th fact that we have every chance of winning** bie que nous ayons toutes les chances de gagner

spiteful ['spaɪtfʊl] ADJ *(person, remark, chara ter)* malveillant; *(because of a grudge)* rancunie vindicatif; **that was a s. thing to say** c'était mé chant de dire ça; **to have a s. tongue** avoir un langue de vipère

spitefully ['spaɪtfʊlɪ] ADV par dépit, par mé chanceté, méchamment

spitefulness ['spaɪtfʊlnɪs] N méchanceté malveillance *f*; *(because of grudge)* rancœur *f*

spitfire ['spɪtfaɪə(r)] N *(person)* furie *f*

spitting ['spɪtɪŋ] N **no s.** *(sign)* défense de cra cher; *Fam* **he was within s. distance of me** il éta à deux pas de moiᵕ; *Fam* **he's the s. image of h father** c'est son père tout craché

spittle ['spɪtəl] N *(saliva ▸ of person)* salive *f*; *(▸ o floor)* crachat *m*; *(▸ of dog)* bave *f*

spittoon [spɪ'tu:n] N crachoir *m*

spitz [spɪts] N *(dog)* loulou *m*

spiv [spɪv] N *Br Fam* filou *m*

spivvy ['spɪvɪ] *(compar* **spivvier**, *superl* **spivvies** ADJ *Br Fam (appearance, clothes)* tape-à-l'œ *(inv)*, tapageurᵕ; **do I look a bit s. in this?** n'ai-j pas l'air un peu filou avec ça?

splash [splæʃ] VT **1** *(with water, mud)* éclabous ser; **the bus splashed us with mud** *or* **splashe mud over us** le bus nous a éclaboussés de boue **to s. water at one another** se jeter de l'eau; **sh splashed wine on** *or* **over her dress** elle a écla boussé sa robe de vin; **I splashed my face wit cold water** *or* **cold water onto my face** je me su aspergé le visage d'eau froide *ou* avec de l'ea froide; **he splashed his way across the river** il a tra versé la rivière en pataugeant
2 *(pour carelessly)* répandre; **I splashed disinfec ant round the sink** j'ai aspergé le tour de l'évier d désinfectant
3 *(daub)* barbouiller; **he splashed whitewash o the wall** il a barbouillé le mur au blanc de chau
4 *Press* étaler; **the story was splashed across th front page** l'affaire était étalée à la une des jou naux
VI **1** *(rain, liquid)* faire des éclaboussures *(waves ▸ gen)* clapoter; *(▸ more violently)* se br ser; **the paint splashed on my trousers** la peintur a éclaboussé mon pantalon; **heavy drops of rai splashed on the ground** de grosses gouttes d pluie s'écrasaient sur le sol **2** *(walk, run etc)* pa tauger, barboter; **we splashed across the strear** nous avons traversé le ruisseau en pataugean **he splashed through the mud/puddles** il a travers la boue/les flaques d'eau en pataugeant
N **1** *(noise)* plouf *m*; **the ball made a loud s.** le ba lon a fait un grand plouf; **he fell/jumped in with s.** il est tombé/il a sauté dedans avec un gran plouf
2 *(of mud, paint)* éclaboussure *f*; *(of colour, ligh* tache *f*; **to give sth a s. of colour** donner une tou che de couleur à qch; **splashes of white** des ta ches blanches
3 *(small quantity ▸ of liquid)* goutte *f*; **would yo like a s. of soda in your whisky?** voulez-vous u peu de soda dans votre whisky?; **just a s. of lem onade, please** juste une goutte de limonade, s' vous plaît
4 *Fam Fig (sensation)* sensationᵕ *f*; **to make a s** faire sensation; **his arrival caused a bit of a s.** so arrivée n'est pas passée inaperçueᵕ
ADV **to go/to fall s. into the water** entrer/tombe dans l'eau en faisant plouf
▸▸ ***splash headline*** manchette *f*; *Comput* ***splas screen*** splash screen *m*

▸**splash about, splash around** VI *(duck, swim mer)* barboter
VT SEP *(liquid)* faire jaillir, faire gicler; *(mone* dépenser sans compter

▸**splash down** VI *(spaceship)* amerrir

▸**splash out** *Fam* VI *(spend)* faire des folies; **to s out on sth** se payer qch
VT INSEP *(money)* claquer; **she splashed out a lo of money on a camera** elle a claqué un argent fo pour s'acheter un appareil photo

▸**splash up** VI *(liquid, mud etc)* gicler
VT SEP *(liquid, mud etc)* faire gicler

splashdown ['splæʃdaʊn] **N** *(of spaceship)* amerrissage *m*

splat [splæt] **N** floc *m*
ADV to go s. faire floc

splatter ['splætə(r)] **VT** éclabousser; **splattered with mud/blood** éclaboussé de boue/sang
VI *(rain)* crépiter; *(mud)* éclabousser; **the tomato splattered against the wall** la tomate a giclé sur le mur
N 1 *(mark ▸ of mud, ink)* éclaboussure *f* **2** *(sound of rain)* crépitement *m*
▸ *Fam* ***splatter movie*** = film violent et sanglant

splay [spleɪ] **VT** *(fingers, legs)* écarter; *(feet)* tourner en dehors
VI *(fingers, legs)* s'écarter; *(feet)* se tourner en dehors

splay out = **splay**

splayfooted [ˌspleɪ'fʊtɪd] **ADJ** *(person)* aux pieds plats; *(horse)* panard

spleen [spli:n] **N 1** *Anat* rate *f* **2** *(bad temper)* humeur *f* noire, mauvaise humeur *f*; **to vent one's s. on sb/sth** décharger sa mauvaise humeur *ou* sa bile sur qn/qch **3** *Arch or Literary (melancholy)* spleen *m*

splendid ['splendɪd] **ADJ 1** *(beautiful, imposing ▸ dress, setting, decor)* splendide, superbe, magnifique **2** *(very good ▸ idea, meal)* excellent, magnifique; *(▸ work)* excellent, superbe; **I think he's a s. cook** je trouve que c'est un excellent cuisinier; **a policy of s. isolation** une politique isolationniste; *Fig* **the statue stands in s. isolation looking down on the park** la statue domine le parc, solitaire et majestueuse; **we had a s. time on holiday** nous avons passé d'excellentes vacances; **how s. for you!** mais c'est formidable pour vous!
EXCLAM excellent!, parfait!

splendidly ['splendɪdlɪ] **ADV 1** *(dress, decorate, furnish)* magnifiquement, superbement; *(entertain)* somptueusement; **he was s. turned out in military uniform** il était vraiment superbe en uniforme militaire **2** *(perform)* superbement; **you acted s.!** tu as été merveilleux!; **the children behaved s.** les enfants ont été des anges; **my work is going s.** mon travail avance à merveille

splendiferous [ˌsplen'dɪfərəs] **ADJ** *Fam Hum* épatant, mirobolant

splendour, *Am* **splendor** ['splendə(r)] **N** splendeur *f*; **the mountains in all their s.** les montagnes dans toute leur splendeur; **to live in s.** mener grand train; **the splendours of the Scottish Highlands/India** les beautés *fpl* des Highlands/de l'Inde

splice [splaɪs] **VT 1** *(join)* **to s. (together)** *(film, tape)* coller; *Naut (rope, cable)* épisser; *Carp (pieces of wood)* enter; **to s. one piece of tape onto another** coller un morceau de bande sur un autre; **to s. the mainbrace** *Naut* border l'artimon; *Fig (dans la marine)* avoir droit à une double ration de rhum; *Fam Fig* boire un coup **2** *Br Fam (marry)* **to get spliced** se maquer
N *(in tape, film)* collure *f*; *Naut (in rope)* épissure *f*; *Carp (in wood)* enture *f*

splicer ['splaɪsə(r)] **N** colleuse *f*

splicing ['splaɪsɪŋ] **N** *(of film, magnetic tape)* collage *m*; *Naut (of rope, cable)* épissage *m*; *Carp (of two pieces of wood)* enture *f*
▸ ***splicing table*** table *f* de montage (de films); ***splicing tape*** ruban *m* de collage; ***splicing unit*** presse *f* à coller

spliff [splɪf] **N** *Fam Drugs slang* pétard *m*, joint *m*

splint [splɪnt] **N** *Med* éclisse *f*, attelle *f*; **to put a limb in splints** éclisser un membre; **her arm was in a s.** *or* **in splints** elle avait le bras dans une attelle
VT éclisser, mettre dans une attelle

splinter ['splɪntə(r)] **N** *(of glass, wood)* éclat *m*; *(of bone)* esquille *f*; *(in foot, finger)* écharde *f*
VT *(glass, windscreen, bone)* briser *(en formant des éclats)*; *(wood)* fendre en éclats
VI *(glass, windscreen, bone)* se briser *(en formant des éclats)*; *(marble, wood)* se fendre *(en formant des éclats)*; *(political party)* se scinder, se fractionner
▸ ***splinter group*** groupe *m* dissident *ou* scissionniste

splinterproof ['splɪntəpru:f] **ADJ** *(glass)* se brisant sans éclats

split [splɪt] *(pt & pp* **split**, *cont* **splitting) N 1** *(in wood)* fissure *f*, fente *f*; *(in rock ▸ gen)* fissure *f*; *(▸ deeper)* crevasse *f*; *(in skin)* gerçure *f*; *(in garment ▸ on purpose)* fente *f*; *(▸ tear)* déchirure *f*; **there is a long s. in the wood** le bois est fendu sur une bonne longueur
2 *(division)* division *f*; *(separation)* séparation *f*; *(quarrel)* rupture *f*; *Pol* scission *f*, schisme *m*; *Rel* schisme *m*; *(gap)* fossé *m*, écart *m*; **a s. in the ranks** une division dans les rangs; **there was a three-way s. in the voting** les votes étaient répartis en trois groupes; **a deep s. within the party** un schisme profond au sein du parti; **the s. between rich and poor nations** l'écart entre les pays riches et les pays pauvres
3 *(share)* part *f*; **they suggested a two-way s. of the profits** ils ont proposé de partager les bénéfices en deux parts égales
4 *Culin* coupe *f* glacée
ADJ *(lip, skirt)* fendu; **he works a s. shift** sa journée de travail est divisée en deux tranches horaires
VT 1 *(cleave ▸ wood, stone)* fendre; *(▸ slate)* cliver; **the lightning s. the oak right down the middle** la foudre a fendu le chêne en plein milieu; **karate experts can s. bricks with their bare hands** les karatékas sont capables de casser des briques à main nue; **to s. sth in two** *or* **in half** casser *ou* fendre qch en deux; **to s. sth open** ouvrir qch *(en le coupant en deux ou en le fendant)*; **he s. his head open on the concrete** il s'est fendu le crâne sur le béton; **they s. open the mattress in their search for drugs** ils ont éventré le matelas à la recherche de stupéfiants; *Phys* **to s. the atom** fissionner l'atome; *Fam* **to s. one's sides (laughing)** se tenir les côtes (de rire)
2 *(tear)* déchirer; **the plastic sheet had been s. right down the middle** la bâche en plastique avait été fendue en plein milieu; **I've s. my trousers** j'ai déchiré mon pantalon
3 *(separate into groups ▸ family)* diviser; *Pol (▸ party)* diviser, créer *ou* provoquer une scission dans; **we were s. into two groups** on nous a divisés en deux groupes; **the committee is s. on this issue** le comité est divisé sur cette question; **to s. the vote** disperser les voix; **the vote was s. down the middle** les deux camps avaient obtenu exactement le même nombre de voix; **we were s. 30–70** on était 30 pour cent d'un côté et 70 pour cent de l'autre; *Am Pol* **to s. one's ticket** panacher son bulletin de vote
4 *(divide and share ▸ profits)* (se) partager, (se) répartir; *(▸ bill)* (se) partager; *Fin (▸ stocks)* faire une redistribution de; **they decided to s. the work between them** ils ont décidé de se partager le travail; **to s. the profits four ways** diviser les bénéfices en quatre; **you can't s. it in three** on ne peut pas le diviser en trois; **to s. a bottle** partager une bouteille; **to s. the difference** *(share out)* partager la différence; *(compromise)* couper la poire en deux
5 *Gram* **to s. an infinitive** = intercaler un adverbe ou une expression adverbiale entre "to" et le verbe
6 *Comput (file, image)* découper
VI 1 *(break ▸ wood, slate)* se fendre, éclater; **the ship s. in two** le navire s'est brisé (en deux); *Fig* **my head is splitting** j'ai un mal de tête atroce
2 *(tear ▸ fabric)* se déchirer; *(▸ seam)* craquer; **the bag s. open** le sac s'est déchiré; **her dress s. right down the back** le dos de sa robe s'est déchiré de haut en bas
3 *(divide ▸ gen)* se diviser; *(▸ political party)* se scinder; *(▸ road, railway)* se diviser, bifurquer; **the hikers s. into three groups** les randonneurs se sont divisés en trois groupes; **the committee s. down the middle on the issue** le comité s'est divisé en deux clans sur la question
4 *(separate ▸ couple)* se séparer; *(▸ family, group)* s'éparpiller, se disperser; **she has s. with her old school friends** elle ne voit plus ses anciennes camarades de classe
5 *Fam (leave)* se casser, mettre les bouts; **let's s.!** on se casse!
• **splits NPL** *Br* **to do the splits**, *Am* **to do splits** faire le grand écart
▸▸ ***split cane*** osier *m*; *Fin* ***split capital investment trust*** SICAV *f* mixte; *Sport* ***split decision*** *(in boxing)* victoire *f*, décision *f* aux points; ***split end*** fourche *f*; **I tend to get s. ends** j'ai des cheveux qui ont tendance à fourcher; *Gram* ***split infinitive*** = infinitif où un adverbe ou une expression adverbiale est intercalé entre "to" et le verbe; ***split pea*** pois *m* cassé; ***split personality*** double personnalité *f*, dédoublement *m* de la personnalité; **he has a s. personality** il souffre d'un dédoublement de personnalité; *Br* ***split pin*** goupille *f* fendue; ***split ring*** bague *f* à fente; *Cin & Comput* ***split screen*** écran *m* divisé; ***split second*** fraction *f* de seconde; **in a s. second** en une fraction de seconde; **it only took a s. second** cela n'a demandé qu'une fraction de seconde; *Am Pol* ***split ticket*** panachage *m*

▸ **split off VT SEP 1** *(break, cut ▸ branch, piece)* enlever (en fendant) **2** *(person, group)* séparer; **our branch was s. off from the parent company** notre succursale a été séparée de la maison mère
VI 1 *(branch, splinter)* se détacher; **a large rock s. off from the cliff** un gros rocher s'est détaché de la falaise **2** *(separate ▸ person, group)* se séparer; **we s. off (from the others) to visit the museum** nous avons quitté les autres pour visiter le musée; **a radical movement s. off from the main party** un mouvement radical s'est détaché du gros du parti

▸ **split on VT INSEP** *Br Fam (inform on)* vendre, moucharder; **he s. on his friend to the police** il a donné son ami à la police

▸ **split up VT SEP 1** *(wood)* fendre; *(cake)* couper en morceaux **2** *(divide ▸ loot, profits)* partager; *(▸ work)* répartir; **let's s. the work up between us** répartissons-nous le travail; **the teaching syllabus is s. up into several chapters** le programme d'enseignement est divisé en plusieurs chapitres; *Chem* **to s. up a compound into its elements** dédoubler un composé en ses éléments **3** *(couple, people fighting)* séparer; *(disperse)* disperser; **the police s. up the meeting/crowd** la police a mis fin à la réunion/dispersé la foule
VI 1 *(wood, marble)* se fendre; *(ship)* se briser **2** *(couple)* se séparer, rompre; *(friends)* rompre, se brouiller; *(meeting, members)* se disperser; *Pol* se diviser, se scinder; **to s. up with sb** rompre avec qn; **the band s. up in 1992** le groupe s'est séparé en 1992; **the search party s. up into three groups** l'équipe de secours s'est divisée en trois groupes

split-level ADJ *(house, flat)* à deux niveaux
▸▸ ***split-level cooker*** cuisinière *f* à éléments de cuisson séparés

split-second ADJ *(timing, reaction)* au quart de seconde

splitter ['splɪtə(r)] **N** *Aut* **s. (box)** doubleur *m* de gamme

splitting ['splɪtɪŋ] **N 1** *(of wood, marble)* fendage *m*; *Phys* **the s. of the atom** la fission de l'atome
2 *(of fabric, seams)* déchirure *f*
3 *(division)* division *f*
4 *(sharing)* partage *m*
ADJ I have a s. headache j'ai un mal de tête atroce
▸▸ ***splitting up* 1** *(of wood)* fendage *m* **2** *(division)* division *f* **3** *(of two people)* séparation *f*; *(of political party)* scission *f*

split-up N *(gen)* rupture *f*, séparation *f*; *Pol* scission *f*

splodge [splɒdʒ], **splotch** [splɒtʃ] *Br Fam* **N 1** *(splash ▸ of paint, ink)* éclaboussure❑ *f*, tache❑ *f*; *(▸ of colour)* tache❑ *f* **2** *(dollop ▸ of cream, of jam)* grosse cuillerée❑ *f*
VT *(stain)* éclabousser❑, barbouiller❑ (**with** de); **he splodged a great lump of cream on top** il balança une grosse cuillerée de chantilly par-dessus
VI s'étaler❑, faire des pâtés❑

splurge [splɜ:dʒ] *Fam* **N 1** *(spending spree)* folie❑ *f*, folles dépenses❑ *fpl*; **I went on** *or* **I had a s. and bought a fur coat** j'ai fait une folie, je me suis acheté un manteau de fourrure **2** *(display)* flafla *m*, tralala *m*; **the book came out in a s. of publicity** la sortie du livre a été accompagnée d'un grand battage publicitaire; **a great s. of colour** une débauche de couleur❑
VT *(spend)* dépenser❑; *(waste)* dissiper❑; **she splurged her savings on a set of encyclopedias** toutes ses économies ont été englouties par l'achat d'une encyclopédie❑

▸ **splurge out** VI faire une folie *ou* des folies; **to s. out on sth** se payer qch

splutter ['splʌtə(r)] **VI 1** *(spit ▸ speaker)* postillonner; *(▸ flames, fat)* crépiter, grésiller; *(▸ pen, ink)* cracher **2** *(stutter ▸ speaker)* bredouiller; *(▸ engine)* tousser, avoir des ratés; **she was spluttering with rage** elle bredouillait de rage; **the engine spluttered and died** le moteur toussa et s'arrêta

VT *(protest, apology, thanks)* bredouiller, balbutier, bafouiller

N 1 *(spitting ▸ in speech)* crachotement *m*; *(▸ of fat, flames)* crépitement *m*, grésillement *m* **2** *(stutter ▸ in speech)* bredouillement *m*, balbutiement *m*; *(▸ of engine)* toussotement *m*

spoil [spɔɪl] *(pt & pp* **spoilt** [spɔɪlt] *or* **spoiled)** **VT 1** *(make less attractive or enjoyable)* gâter, gâcher; **our holiday was spoilt by the wet weather** le temps pluvieux a gâché nos vacances; **you've spoilt everything by your foolish behaviour** tu as tout gâché avec ton comportement stupide; **don't s. the ending for me** ne me raconte pas la fin, ça va tout gâcher; **the dinner was spoilt because they were late** le dîner a été gâché par leur retard; **to s. sb's appetite** couper l'appétit *ou* la faim à qn; **if you eat those chocolates, you'll s. your appetite for dinner** si tu manges ces chocolats, tu n'auras plus faim *ou* plus d'appétit à l'heure du dîner

2 *(damage ▸ goods, objects)* abîmer, endommager; **to get spoilt** *or* **spoiled** s'abîmer; **I spoilt my eyesight by reading in the dark** je me suis abîmé la vue *ou* les yeux en lisant dans la pénombre

3 *(pamper)* gâter; *Fam* **she's spoilt rotten** elle est super gâtée; **to s. oneself** s'offrir une petite folie

4 *Pol (ballot paper)* rendre nul

VI *(fruit, food)* se gâter, s'abîmer; *(in store, hold of ship)* s'avarier, devenir avarié

N *(UNCOUNT)* **1** = **shindig spoils 2** *(earth, diggings)* déblai *m*, déblais *mpl*

• **spoils NPL 1** *(loot)* butin *m*, dépouilles *fpl*; *(profit)* bénéfices *mpl*, profits *mpl*; *(prize)* prix *m*; **he made off with the spoils** il s'est enfui avec le butin; *Fig* **to claim one's share of the spoils** demander sa part du gâteau; **the spoils of war** les dépouilles *fpl* de la guerre **2** *Am Pol Pej* assiette *f* au beurre

▸▸ *Am Pol Pej* ***spoils system*** système *m* des dépouilles, assiette *f* au beurre

spoilage ['spɔɪlɪdʒ] **N** *(UNCOUNT) (damage)* détérioration *f*; *(spoilt matter)* déchets *mpl*

spoiler ['spɔɪlə(r)] **N 1** *Aut* becquet *m*; *Aviat* aérofrein *m* **2** *(person)* empêcheur(euse) *m,f* de tourner en rond; *(candidate)* = candidat qui se présente dans le seul but de compromettre les chances d'un autre candidat **3** *Journ* = tactique utilisée pour s'approprier le scoop d'un journal rival

▸▸ *Mktg* ***spoiler campaign*** = campagne lancée par une entreprise pour minimiser l'impact d'une campagne publicitaire menée par une société concurrente

spoilsport ['spɔɪlspɔːt] **N** trouble-fête *mf inv*, rabat-joie *mf inv*; **don't be a s.!** ne joue pas les trouble-fête *ou* les rabat-joie!

spoke [spəʊk] *pt of* **speak**

N *(in wheel)* rayon *m*; *(in ladder)* barreau *m*, échelon *m*; *(on ship's wheel)* manette *f*; *Br Fig* **to put a s. in sb's wheel** mettre des bâtons dans les roues à qn

spoken ['spəʊkən] *pp of* **speak**

ADJ *(dialogue)* parlé, oral; **the s. word** la parole; **s. language** langue *f* parlée; **she's better at the s. language** elle est meilleure à l'oral

spoken-voice ADJ *(record)* parlé

spokeshave ['spəʊkʃeɪv] **N** vastringue *f*

spokesman ['spəʊksmən] *(pl* **spokesmen** [-mən]) **N** porte-parole *m inv*; **a government s., a s. for the government** un porte-parole du gouvernement

spokesperson ['spəʊks,pɜːsən] *(pl* **spokespersons** *or* **spokespeople** [-'piːpəl]) **N** porte-parole *m inv*

spokeswoman ['spəʊks,wʊmən] *(pl* **spokeswomen** [-'wɪmɪn]) **N** porte-parole *m inv (femme)*

spoliation [,spəʊlɪ'eɪʃən] **N** *(plundering)* spoliation *f*, pillage *m*

spondaic [spɒn'deɪɪk] **ADJ** *(in prosody)* spondaïque

spondee ['spɒndiː] **N** *(in prosody)* spondée *m*

spondulicks, spondulix [spɒn'djuːlɪks] **NPL** *Fam* fric *m*, pognon *m*, flouze *m*

sponge [spʌndʒ] **N 1** *Zool* éponge *f*

2 *(for cleaning, washing)* éponge *f*; **I gave the table a s.** j'ai passé un coup d'éponge sur la table; *Fig* **to throw in the s.** jeter l'éponge

3 *Fam Pej (scrounger)* parasite▫ *m*

4 *Br (cake)* gâteau *m* de Savoie; **jam/cream s.** gâteau *m* de Savoie fourré à la confiture/à la crème

VT 1 *(wipe ▸ table, window)* donner un coup d'éponge à; *(▸ wound, body, spilt liquid)* éponger; **she sponged his face** elle lui a épongé le visage; **can you s. the milk off the table?** peux-tu éponger le lait renversé sur la table? **2** *Fam (cadge ▸ food, money)* taper; **I sponged £20 off** *or* **from him** je l'ai tapé de 20 livres; **can I s. a cigarette off you?** est-ce que je peux te taper une cigarette?; **she sponged a meal off her friends** elle s'est fait inviter à manger par ses amis▫

VI *Fam (cadge)* jouer au parasite▫; **to s. on** *or* **from sb** vivre aux crochets de qn▫; **she's always sponging** c'est un vrai parasite; **too many people s. off the state** trop de gens vivent aux crochets de l'État

▸▸ *Br* ***sponge bag*** trousse *f ou* sac *m* de toilette; ***sponge bath*** toilette *f* à l'éponge; ***sponge cake*** biscuit *m* de Savoie, génoise *f*, *Can* gâteau *m* éponge; *Br* ***sponge finger*** boudoir *m (biscuit)*; ***sponge pudding*** = dessert chaud fait avec une pâte de gâteau de Savoie; ***sponge rubber*** mousse *f*, caoutchouc *m* Mousse®

▸ **sponge down VT SEP** éponger, laver à l'éponge; **he sponged himself down** il s'est lavé avec une éponge

▸ **sponge up VT SEP** *(liquid)* éponger

sponger ['spʌndʒə(r)] **N** *Fam Pej (gén)* parasite▫ *m*, *(for meals)* pique-assiette *mf*

sponginess ['spʌndʒɪnɪs] **N** *(gen)* spongiosité *f*; *(of cake, pastry)* moelleux *m*; *(of road surface)* caractère *m* mou; *(of soles)* souplesse *f*

spongy ['spʌndʒɪ] *(compar* **spongier**, *superl* **spongiest) ADJ** *(gen)* spongieux; *(cake, pastry)* moelleux; *(road surface)* mou; *(soles)* souple

sponsor ['spɒnsə(r)] **N 1** *Com & Sport (of sportsman, team, tournament)* sponsor *m*; *(of film, TV programme)* sponsor *m*, commanditaire *m*; *(of artist, musician)* commanditaire *m*, mécène *m*; *(of student, studies)* parrain *m*; *(for charity)* donateur(trice) *m,f*; **he's looking for sponsors for his Channel swim** *(financial backers)* il cherche des sponsors pour financer sa traversée de la Manche à la nage; *(charitable donations)* il cherche des gens qui accepteront de faire une donation aux bonnes œuvres s'il réussit sa traversée de la Manche à la nage; **to act as s. for sb** sponsoriser qn

2 *(of would-be club member ▸ man)* parrain *m*; *(▸ woman)* marraine *f*; *(guarantor ▸ for loan)* répondant(e) *m,f*, garant(e) *m,f*; *(backer ▸ for business)* parrain *m*, bailleur *m* de fonds; **he was the s. of the proposal** c'est lui qui a lancé la proposition; **her uncle stood (as) s. to her** *(for loan)* son oncle a été son répondant; *(for business)* son oncle l'a parrainée

3 *Am (of godchild ▸ man)* parrain *m*; *(▸ woman)* marraine *f*; **to stand s. to a child** *(at baptism)* tenir un enfant sur les fonts (baptismaux)

VT 1 *Com & Sport* sponsoriser; *Rad & TV (programme)* sponsoriser, parrainer; *(concert, exhibition)* parrainer, commanditer; *(studies, student)* parrainer; **our firm sponsored her to the tune of £10,000** notre firme l'a sponsorisée pour un montant de 10 000 livres

2 *(for charity)* **I sponsored him to swim 10 miles** je me suis engagé à lui donner de l'argent (pour des œuvres charitables) s'il faisait *ou* parcourait 10 milles à la nage

3 *(appeal, proposal)* présenter; *(would-be club member)* parrainer; *(loan, borrower)* se porter garant de; *(firm)* patronner; *Pol* **to s. a bill** présenter un projet de loi

4 *(godchild)* être le parrain/la marraine de

▸▸ ***sponsored walk*** = marche parrainée

SPONSORED EVENT

La Grande-Bretagne compte de très nombreuses organisations caritatives ("charities") œuvrant pour des causes aussi diverses que la recherche médicale, l'aide à l'enfance défavorisée ou l'établissement de centres pour animaux abandonnés. L'un des moyens employés pour rassembler des fonds est de s'engager auprès d'autres gens (généralement des amis, voisins et collègues de travail) à accomplir une épreuve en échange d'une somme d'argent déterminée. Il peut s'agir d'épreuves physiques ("sponsored walk", "sponsored swim") ou de défis saugrenus, tels que se rendre au bureau en pyjama ou bien encore garder le silence pendant toute une journée ("sponsored silence"). Des "sponsored events" sont également organisés par des écoles et des clubs sportifs afin d'obtenir de l'argent pour acheter du matériel.

sponsoring ['spɒnsərɪŋ] **N 1** *Com & Sport* spo[…]soring *m*, parrainage *m* **2** *(of appeal, proposa[…])* présentation *f*; *(of would-be club member, god[…]child)* parrainage *m*; *(of loan, borrower)* cautio[…]nement *m*

sponsorship ['spɒnsəʃɪp] **N 1** *Com & Sport* spo[…]soring *m*, parrainage *m*; **under the s. of** sous parrainage de **2** *(of appeal, proposal)* présent[…]tion *f*; *Pol (of bill)* proposition *f*, présentation *(of would-be club member, godchild)* parrainag[…] *m*; *(of loan, borrower)* cautionnement *m*

▸▸ ***sponsorship agreement*** contrat *m* de spons[…]ring; ***sponsorship deal*** contrat *m* de sponsoring

spontaneity [,spɒntə'neɪətɪ] **N** spontanéité *f*

spontaneous [spɒn'teɪnɪəs] **ADJ** spontané

▸▸ ***spontaneous combustion*** combustion *f* spo[…]tanée

spontaneously [spɒn'teɪnɪəslɪ] **ADV** spontan[…]ment

spoof [spuːf] *Fam* **N 1** *(mockery)* satire▫*f*, par[…]die▫*f*; **it's a s. on horror films** c'est une parod[…] des films d'horreur **2** *(trick)* blague▫*f*, canula[…] *m*; **the whole thing was just a s.** c'était un simp[…] canular du début à la fin

ADJ faux▫, fait par plaisanterie▫; **a s. horr[…] movie/documentary** une parodie de film d'ho[…]reur/de documentaire▫; **he sent around a memo about redundancies** il a fait passer une c[…]culaire bidon *ou* une fausse circulaire parla[…] de licenciements

VI *Comput* usurper des adresses IP

VT 1 *(book, style)* parodier▫; *(person)* faire ma[…]cher **2** *Comput (computer user)* usurper l'adres[…] IP de; *(e-mail address)* usurper

spoofing [spuːfɪŋ] **N** *Comput* usurpation d'adresse IP

spook [spuːk] **N 1** *(ghost)* fantôme *m* **2** *Am Fa[…] (spy)* barbouze *mf* **3** *Am very Fam (black man)* n[…]gre *m*, bamboula *m*, = terme injurieux dé[…]gnant un Noir; *(black woman)* négresse *f*, terme injurieux désignant une Noire

VT *Fam* **1** *(startle)* foutre la trouille à; *(frighte[…] disturb)* donner la chair de poule à▫ **2** *(haun[…])* hanter▫

spooky ['spuːkɪ] *(compar* **spookier**, *superl* **spoo[…]est) ADJ** *Fam* **1** *(atmosphere)* qui donne la chair […] poule▫, qui fait froid dans le dos▫; *(person)* […]nistre▫; **it's s. here at night** c'est sinistre ici le so[…] **2** *Am (skittish)* peureux▫ **3** *(odd)* bizarre▫

spool [spuːl] **N** *(of film, tape, thread)* bobine *f*; *([…] fishing)* tambour *m*; *(of wire)* rouleau *m*; *(of se[…]ing machine, weaving machine)* cannette *f*; *(ri[…]bon)* **s.** *(for typewriter)* bobine *f* du ruban

VT *(gen)* bobiner; *Comput* spouler

spooler ['spuːlə(r)] **N** *Comput* spouleur *m*, pilo[…] *m* de mise en file d'attente

spoon [spuːn] **N 1** *(utensil)* cuiller *f*, cuillère *f*

2 *(quantity)* cuillerée *f*; **add two spoons of sug[…]** ajoutez deux cuillerées de sucre

3 *Fishing* cuiller *f*, cuillère *f*

4 *(in golf)* spoon *m*

VT *(food ▸ serve)* servir à l'aide d'une cuiller; *([…] transfer)* verser à l'aide d'une cuiller; **to s. t[…] cream from** *or* **off the milk** enlever la crème […]

ait avec une cuiller; **he spooned the ice cream nto a bowl** il a servi la glace dans un bol (avec ıne cuiller); **she spooned the porridge into his nouth** elle lui a fait manger la bouillie avec une uiller
VI *Fam Old-fashioned* se faire des mamours

spoon out VT SEP *(serve)* servir à l'aide d'une :uiller *ou* cuillère; *(transfer)* verser à l'aide d'une :uiller *ou* cuillère

spoon up VT SEP *(eat)* manger avec une cuiller *ou* cuillère; *(clear up)* ramasser avec une cuiller *ou* cuillère

poonbill ['spu:nbɪl] N *Orn* spatule *f*

poonerism ['spu:nərɪzəm] N contrepèterie *f*

poon-feed VT 1 *(child, sick person)* nourrir à la :uiller *ou* cuillère 2 *Fig* **to s. sb** mâcher le travail ı qn

poonful ['spu:nfʊl] N cuillerée *f*

poor [spɔ:(r)] N trace *f*, traces *fpl*, empreintes *pl*

poradic [spəˈrædɪk] ADJ sporadique; **s. fighting** les combats *mpl* sporadiques; **s. violence** des ac:ès *mpl* de violence sporadiques; **s. showers** des ıverses *fpl* éparses

poradically [spəˈrædɪklɪ] ADV sporadiquement; **to work s.** travailler par à-coups

pore [spɔ:(r)] N *Biol* spore *f*

porran ['spɒrən] N = aumônière en cuir parfois ıgrémentée de fourrure, portée sur le devant du kilt

port [spɔ:t] N 1 *(physical exercise)* sport *m*; **she does a lot of s.** elle fait beaucoup de sport, elle est très sportive; **you shouldn't mix s. and politics** :u ne devrais pas mélanger sport et politique; **I hated s.** *or* **sports at school** je détestais le sport *ou* les sports à l'école; **the s. of kings** *(horse racing)* les courses *fpl* de chevaux
2 *Literary (hunting)* chasse *f*; *(fishing)* pêche *f*; **to have good s.** *(in hunting)* faire bonne chasse; *(in fishing)* faire bonne pêche *ou* bonne prise
3 *Literary (fun)* amusement *m*, divertissement *m*; **to say sth in s.** dire qch pour rire *ou* en plaisantant; **it's great s. flying these remote-controlled planes** c'est très amusant de faire voler ces avions radio-guidés; **to make s. of sb/sth** se moquer de qn/qch, tourner qn/qch en ridicule
4 *Fam (friendly person ▸ male)* chic type *m*; *(▸ female)* chic fille *f*; **he's a real s.** c'est vraiment un chic type; **go on, be a s.!** allez, sois sympa!
5 *(good loser)* **to be a (good) s.** être beau joueur; **they're not very good sports** ils sont plutôt mauvais joueurs
6 *(gambler)* joueur(euse) *m,f*; *(high flyer)* bon vivant *m*
7 *Austr & NZ Fam (fellow)* pote *m*, vieux *m*
8 *Old-fashioned (term of address)* **hallo, old s.!** bonjour, mon vieux!
9 *Biol* variété *f* anormale
VT *(wear)* porter, arborer; **he was sporting a tartan jacket/a yellow carnation** il portait une veste tartan/arborait un œillet jaune
VI 1 *Literary (amuse oneself)* batifoler, s'ébattre 2 *Biol (plants, animals)* produire une variété anormale
• **sports** NPL *(athletics meeting)* meeting *m* d'athlétisme; *(competition)* compétition *f* sportive; **the school sports** la compétition sportive scolaire COMP *(equipment, programme, reporter)* sportif; *(fan)* de sport
▸▸ ***sports bag*** sac *m* de sport; ***sports bar*** = bar où l'on passe des cassettes vidéo d'événements sportifs, où l'on suit certains matches en direct à la télévision etc; ***sports bra*** soutien-gorge *m* de sport; ***sports car*** voiture *f* de sport; ***sports centre*** complexe *m ou* centre *m* sportif, *Suisse* halle *f* de gymnase; ***sports club*** club *m* de sport; *Am* ***sports coat*** veste *f* sport; ***sports commentary*** commentaire *m* sportif; ***sports commentator*** commentateur(trice) *m,f* sportif(ive); ***sports correspondent*** journaliste *mf* sportif(ive); *Br Sch* ***sports day*** = réunion sportive annuelle où les parents sont invités; ***sports desk*** service *m* des sports; ***sports editor*** rédacteur *m* en chef sportif; ***sports facilities*** installations *fpl* sportives; ***sports ground*** terrain *m* de sport *ou* de jeux; ***sports hall*** salle *f* de sport, gymnase *m*, *Suisse* halle *f* de gymnase; ***sports jacket***, *Am* ***sport jacket*** veste *f* sport; ***sports journalism*** journalisme *m* sportif; ***sports journalist*** journaliste *mf* sportif(ive); *Br Pol* ***Sports Minister*** ministre *m* des Sports; ***sports page*** *(of newspaper)* page *f* des sports; ***sports press*** presse *f* sportive; ***sports reporter*** journaliste *mf* sportif (ive); *TV etc* ***sports results*** résultats *mpl* sportifs; *Aut* ***sports saloon*** berline *f* sport; *Am* ***sports scholarship*** = bourse pour les élèves qui sont bons en sport; ***sports science*** sciences *fpl* du sport; ***sports shoe*** training *m*; ***sports shop*** magasin *m* de sport

sporting ['spɔ:tɪŋ] ADJ 1 *Sport (fixtures, interests)* sportif 2 *(friendly, generous ▸ behaviour)* chic *(inv)*; **it's very s. of you** c'est très chic de votre part 3 *(fairly good ▸ chance)* assez bon; **we're in with a s. chance (of winning)** on a une assez bonne chance de gagner
▸▸ ***sporting event*** manifestation *f* sportive; ***sporting man/woman*** *(horseracing enthusiast)* turfiste *mf*

sportingly ['spɔ:tɪŋlɪ] ADV (très) sportivement

sportive ['spɔ:tɪv] ADJ *Literary* folâtre, badin

sportscast ['spɔ:tskɑ:st] N *Am* émission *f* sportive

sportscaster ['spɔ:tsˌkɑ:stə(r)] N *Am* reporter *m* sportif

sportsman ['spɔ:tsmən] *(pl* **sportsmen** [-mən]) N 1 *(player of sport)* sportif *m* 2 *(in attitude, approach)* **he's a real s.** *(plays fair)* il a l'esprit sportif; *(good loser)* il est beau joueur

sportsmanlike ['spɔ:tsmənlaɪk] ADJ sportif; **in a s. way** sportivement

sportsmanship ['spɔ:tsmənʃɪp] N sportivité *f*, esprit *m* sportif

sportsperson ['spɔ:tsˌpɜ:sən] *(pl* **sportspeople** [-ˈpi:pəl]) N sportif(ive) *m,f*

sportswear ['spɔ:tsweə(r)] N *(UNCOUNT)* vêtements *mpl* de sport

sportswoman ['spɔ:tsˌwʊmən] *(pl* **sportswomen** [-ˈwɪmɪn]) N *(player)* sportive *f*

sporty ['spɔ:tɪ] *(compar* **sportier**, *superl* **sportiest)** ADJ 1 *(person)* sportif; *(garment)* de sport 2 *(car)* de sport

SPOT [spɒt]

N	
• pois **1**	• tache **1–4**
• point **1**	• éclaboussure **2**
• bouton **3**	• goutte **5**
• pincée **5**	• endroit **6**
• site **6**	• poste **8**
• numéro **10**	• spot **10, 11**
VT	
• repérer **1**	• trouver **1**
• tacheter **2**	• tacher **2**
VI	
• se tacher **1**	

(pt & pp **spotted**, *cont* **spotting)**
N 1 *(dot ▸ on material, clothes)* pois *m*; *(▸ on leopard, giraffe)* tache *f*, moucheture *f*; *(▸ on dice, playing card)* point *m*; **a tie with red spots** une cravate à pois rouges; **I've got spots before my eyes** j'ai des points lumineux *ou* des taches devant les yeux; **the carnations brought a s. of colour into the church** les œillets apportaient une tache de couleur dans l'église
2 *(stain, unwanted mark)* tache *f*; *(on fruit)* tache *f*, tavelure *f*; *(splash)* éclaboussure *f*; **a dirty s.** une tache, une salissure; **there are some spots of mould on the jam** il y a des taches de moisissure sur la confiture; **how did you get these spots of blood on your shirt?** d'où viennent ces taches de sang sur ta chemise?
3 *(pimple)* bouton *m*; *(freckle)* tache *f* de son *ou* de rousseur; **I've got a s. on my chin** j'ai un bouton sur le menton; **to come out in spots** avoir une éruption de boutons; **to suffer from spots** souffrir d'acné
4 *(blemish ▸ on character)* tache *f*, souillure *f*; **there isn't a s. on his reputation** sa réputation est sans tache
5 *Fam (small amount ▸ of liquid)* goutte *f*; *(▸ of salt)* pincée *f*; *(▸ of irony, humour)* pointe *f*, soupçon *m*; **would you like cream in your coffee? – just a s.** voulez-vous de la crème dans votre café? – juste un soupçon; **a s. of whisky** une larme de whisky; **there were a few spots of rain** il est tombé quelques gouttes (de pluie); **to do a s. of work** faire un peu de travail; **she hardly did a s. of work** elle n'a quasiment rien fait; **I'm having a s. of bother with the neighbours** j'ai quelques ennuis *ou* problèmes avec les voisins; **I could do with a s. of sleep** un petit somme me ferait du bien; **do you want a s. of supper?** veux-tu manger un morceau?
6 *(place)* endroit *m*, coin *m*; *(site)* site *m*; *(on body)* endroit *m*, point *m*; **this is a peaceful s.** c'est un endroit très tranquille; **this is the exact s. where the market cross was situated** c'est l'endroit exact où se trouvait la croix du marché; **X marks the s.** *(of crime etc)* la croix indique le lieu; **a tender** *or* **sore s.** un point sensible; **to find sb's weak s.** trouver le défaut dans la cuirasse de qn, trouver le point faible de qn; **that hits the s.!** ça fait du bien!
7 *(aspect, feature, moment)* **the only bright s. of the week** le seul bon moment de la semaine
8 *(position, job)* poste *m*, position *f*
9 *(difficult situation) Fam* **to be in a s.** être dans le pétrin; *Fam* **we're in a bit of a (tight) s.** nous sommes dans le pétrin *ou* dans de beaux draps; **to put sb on the s.** *(put in difficult position)* mettre qn dans une situation difficile; *(force to answer difficult questions)* mettre qn en mauvaise posture *(en posant des questions difficiles)*
10 *Rad & TV (for artist, interviewee)* numéro *m*; *(news item)* brève *f*; *(advertisement)* spot *m* publicitaire; **he got a s. on the Larry King show** *(as singer, comedian)* il a fait un numéro dans le show de Larry King; *(interview)* il s'est fait interviewer *ou* il est passé dans le show de Larry King; **advertising s.** message *m ou* spot *m* publicitaire
11 *(spotlight ▸ in home etc)* spot *m*; *Theat & Cin* projecteur *m*
12 *(in billiards, snooker)* mouche *f*
COMP *(random ▸ count, test)* fait à l'improviste
VT 1 *(notice ▸ friend, object)* repérer, apercevoir; *(▸ talent, mistake)* trouver, déceler; *Horseracing etc (winner)* prédire, repérer; *Mil* repérer, observer; **I could s. him a mile off** je pourrais le repérer à des kilomètres; **I spotted her in the crowd** je l'ai repérée au milieu de la foule; **she was spotted in the pub** on l'a vue au pub; **to s. sb doing sth** apercevoir qn en train de faire qch; **to s. an opportunity** repérer une occasion; **I'd never have spotted it** je ne l'aurais jamais remarqué; **well spotted!** bien vu!
2 *(mark with spots)* tacheter; *(stain)* tacher; **the wall is spotted with mildew** le mur est taché *ou* piqué d'humidité; **the rain spotted the pavement** des gouttes de pluie formaient des taches sur le trottoir
3 *Am (opponent)* accorder un avantage à; **he spotted his opponent ten points** il a cédé *ou* concédé dix points à son adversaire
4 *Am (remove ▸ stain)* enlever; **a chemical for spotting clothes** un produit pour détacher les vêtements
5 *Am Fam (lend)* prêter; **can somebody s. me ten dollars?** est-ce que quelqu'un peut me prêter dix dollars?
VI 1 *(garment, carpet)* se tacher, se salir
2 *(rain)* **it's spotting (with rain)** il tombe quelques gouttes de pluie
3 *Mil* servir d'observateur
• **on the spot** ADV *(at once)* sur-le-champ; *(at the scene)* sur les lieux, sur place; **the police are on the s.** la police est sur les lieux; **he was killed on the s.** il a été tué sur le coup; **to be fined on the s.** recevoir une amende sur-le-champ; **to have sb on the s.** *(reporter, representative, agent)* avoir qn sur place; **the doctor arrived on the s. in five minutes** le docteur est arrivé sur les lieux en cinq minutes; **to run on the s.** courir sur place
▸▸ *Fin* ***spot buying*** achat *m* au comptant; *Br* ***spot cash*** argent *m* liquide; ***spot check*** *(investigation)* contrôle *m* surprise; *(for quality)* contrôle *m* par sondage; *(by customs)* fouille *f* au hasard; *Comput & Typ* ***spot colour*** couleur *f* (du nuancier) Pantone®; *St Exch* ***spot deal*** opération *f ou* transaction *f* au comptant; *Geog* ***spot height*** altitude *f*; *Fin* ***spot market*** marché *m* au comptant; *Fin* ***spot price*** cours *m* spot; *Fin* ***spot rate*** cours *m* à vue, cours *m* spot; *Fin* ***spot trading*** négociations

fpl au comptant; *St Exch* **spot transaction** opération *f ou* transaction *f* au comptant

spot-check **VT** contrôler au hasard; *(for quality)* contrôler par sondage; *(without notice)* faire des contrôles surprises de; **athletes are regularly spot-checked for anabolic steroids** on effectue souvent des contrôles surprises sur les athlètes pour détecter les anabolisants

spotless ['spɒtlɪs] **ADJ** *(gen)* impeccable; *(character)* sans tache

spotlessly ['spɒtlɪslɪ] **ADV s. clean** reluisant de propreté, d'une propreté impeccable

spotlessness ['spɒtlɪsnɪs] **N** propreté *f*

spotlight ['spɒtlaɪt] *(pt & pp* **spotlit** [-lɪt]) **N 1** *(in theatre ▸ device)* spot *m*, projecteur *m*; *(▸ beam)* lumière *f* de projecteur; *also Fig* **in the s.** sous le feu *ou* la lumière des projecteurs; **to turn the s. on sb** braquer les projecteurs sur qn; *Fig* mettre qn en vedette; **the s. was on her** les projecteurs étaient braqués sur elle; *Fig (she was in the limelight)* elle était en vedette; *(she was the focus of unwelcome media attention)* elle était sur la sellette **2** *(lamp ▸ in home, on car)* spot *m*

VT 1 *Theat* diriger les projecteurs sur **2** *Fig (personality, talent)* mettre en vedette; *(pinpoint ▸ flaws, changes)* mettre en lumière, mettre le doigt sur

spotlighting ['spɒtlaɪtɪŋ] **N** éclairage *m* à effet

spot-on *Br Fam* **ADJ 1** *(correct ▸ measurement)* pile, très précis[□]; *(▸ guess)* en plein dans le mille; **his answer was s.** sa réponse était parfaitement exacte *ou* correcte[□]; **his remark was s.** sa remarque était vachement bien vue[□] **2** *(perfect)* parfait[□]

ADV *(guess)* en plein dans le mille; **he timed it s.** il a calculé son coup à la seconde près[□]

spotter ['spɒtə(r)] **N 1** *(observer)* observateur (trice) *m,f*; *(lookout)* dénicheur(euse) *m,f* **2** *Br (enthusiast)* **train/plane s.** passionné(e) *m,f* de trains/d'avions

COMP *(plane)* d'observation

spotting ['spɒtɪŋ] **N train/plane s.** repérage *m* de trains/d'avions

spotty ['spɒtɪ] *(compar* **spottier**, *superl* **spottiest**)

ADJ 1 *(pimply ▸ face, person)* couvert de boutons, boutonneux; **a s. adolescent** un adolescent boutonneux

2 *(covered with spots ▸ wallpaper)* piqué *ou* taché d'humidité; *(▸ mirror)* piqueté, piqué; *(stained)* taché

3 *(patterned ▸ fabric, tie)* à pois

4 *(patchy)* irrégulier; **a s. performance** une représentation inégale

spot-weld **VT** souder par points

N soudure *f* par points

spot-welding **N** soudure *f* par points

spousal ['spaʊzəl] **ADJ** *Law* **s. right** = droit de l'époux d'hériter les biens de son conjoint; **s. support** pension *f* alimentaire

spouse [spaʊs] **N** *Formal* époux (épouse) *m,f*; *Admin & Law* conjoint(e) *m,f*

spout [spaʊt] **N 1** *(of teapot, kettle, carton)* bec *m* verseur; *(of watering can)* tuyau *m*; *(of tap)* brise-jet *m inv*; *(of pump)* dégorgeoir *m*; *(of gutter)* gargouille *f*; *(of pipe)* embout *m* **2** *(of water ▸ from fountain, geyser)* jet *m*; *(▸ from whale)* jet *m*, souffle *m* d'eau; *(of flame)* colonne *f*; *(of lava)* jet *m*; **a s. of boiling water** un jet d'eau bouillante **3** *Br Fam (idiom)* **to be up the s.** *(ruined)* être fichu *ou* foutu; *(pregnant)* être en cloque; **our plans are up the s.** nos projets sont tombés à l'eau; **now we're really up the s.** maintenant nous sommes vraiment dans de beaux draps *ou* dans le pétrin; **that's our holidays up the s.** on peut faire une croix sur nos vacances[□]

VI 1 *(water, oil)* jaillir; *(whale)* souffler; **water spouted out of the pipe** de l'eau jaillit du tuyau **2** *Fam Pej (talk)* dégoiser; **he's always spouting (on) about politics** il est toujours à dégoiser sur la politique

VT 1 *(water, oil)* faire jaillir un jet de; *(fire, smoke)* vomir, émettre un jet de **2** *Fam Pej (words, poetry)* débiter, sortir[□]

▸**spout out** **VI** *(water, lava)* jaillir, sortir en giclant; **the liquid was spouting out of the barrel** le liquide sortait du tonneau en giclant, le liquide jaillissait du tonneau

VT SEP 1 *(liquid)* faire jaillir un jet de; *(lava)* cracher; **the pipe spouted out water** de l'eau jaillissait du tuyau **2** *Fam Fig (utter ▸ statistics, poetry, quotations)* débiter

sprain [spreɪn] **VT** *(joint ▸ gen)* se fouler; *(▸ more seriously)* se faire une entorse à; *(muscle)* s'étirer; **she has sprained her ankle** *or* **has a sprained ankle** elle s'est foulé la cheville; *(more serious)* elle s'est fait une entorse à la cheville

N foulure *f*; *(more serious)* entorse *f*

sprang [spræŋ] *pt of* **spring**

sprat [spræt] **N** *Ich* sprat *m*; *Fig* **it's a s. to catch a mackerel** c'est un bien petit sacrifice pour un grand gain

sprawl [sprɔːl] **VI 1** *(be sitting, lying)* être affalé *ou* vautré; *(sit down, lie down)* s'affaler, se laisser tomber; **she was sprawling in the armchair/on the bed** elle était avachie dans le fauteuil/vautrée sur le lit; **the blow sent him sprawling** le coup l'a fait tomber de tout son long **2** *(spread ▸ gen)* s'étaler, s'étendre; *(▸ plant)* s'étendre, se déployer; **the new industrial estate is beginning to s. into the countryside** la nouvelle zone industrielle commence à grignoter *ou* envahir la campagne; **her signature sprawled across half the page** sa signature s'étalait sur la moitié de la page

VT *(usu passive)* **she was sprawled in the armchair/on the pavement** elle était vautrée dans le fauteuil/étendue de tout son long sur le trottoir

N 1 *(position)* position *f* affalée; **he lay in an ungainly s.** il était étendu de tout son long de façon peu élégante **2** *(of city)* étendue *f*; **suburban s.** *(suburb)* banlieue *f* tentaculaire; **an urban s.** une agglomération

sprawling ['sprɔːlɪŋ] **ADJ** *(body)* affalé; *(suburbs, metropolis)* tentaculaire; **s. handwriting** écriture *f* irrégulière et étalée

spray [spreɪ] **VT 1** *(treat ▸ crops, garden, tree)* faire des pulvérisations sur, traiter; *(▸ field)* pulvériser; *(▸ house plant)* arroser au vaporisateur; *(sprinkle ▸ road)* asperger; **to s. one's hair** se laquer les cheveux; **she sprayed her hairstyle in place** elle s'est mis de la laque pour faire tenir sa coiffure; **to s. a plant with insecticide** pulvériser de l'insecticide sur une plante; **I got sprayed with cold water** je me suis fait arroser *ou* asperger d'eau froide; *Fig* **they sprayed the bar with bullets/with machine-gun fire** ils arrosèrent le bar de balles/de rafales de mitrailleuses

2 *(apply ▸ water, perfume)* vaporiser; *(▸ paint, insecticide)* pulvériser; *(▸ coat of paint, fixer)* mettre, appliquer; *(▸ graffiti, slogan)* écrire, tracer (à la bombe); **she sprayed perfume behind her ears** elle se vaporisa du parfum derrière les oreilles; **they sprayed water on the flames** ils vaporisèrent de l'eau sur les flammes; **she sprayed air freshener around the room** elle vaporisa du désodorisant dans la pièce; **three layers of paint are sprayed onto the metal** on passe trois couches de peinture au pistolet sur le métal; **a slogan sprayed on a wall** un slogan écrit à la bombe sur un mur

VI 1 *(liquid)* jaillir; **the water sprayed (out) over** *or* **onto the road** l'eau a jailli sur la route; **water sprayed up in our faces** de l'eau éclaboussait nos visages

2 *(against crop disease)* pulvériser, faire des pulvérisations

N 1 *(droplets)* fines gouttelettes *fpl*; *(from sea)* embruns *mpl*; **the liquid comes out in a fine s.** le liquide est pulvérisé

2 *(container ▸ for aerosol)* bombe *f*, aérosol *m*; *(▸ for perfume)* atomiseur *m*; *(▸ for cleaning fluids, water, lotion)* vaporisateur *m*; **this deodorant is a s.** ce déodorant est un aérosol; **throat s.** vaporisateur *m* pour la gorge

3 *(act of spraying ▸ of crops)* pulvérisation *f*; *(▸ against infestation)* traitement *m* (par pulvérisation); *(▸ of aerosol product)* coup *m* de bombe; **to give sth a s.** *(fields, roses etc)* pulvériser qch; *(walls etc)* peindre qch au pistolet; *(hair)* mettre du spray *ou* de la laque sur qch

4 *Fig (of bullets)* grêle *f*; **the welding sent up sprays** *or* **a s. of bright sparks** la soudure faisait voler des gerbes d'étincelles

5 *(cut branch)* branche *f*; **forsythia sprays** bra[nches] *fpl* de forsythia

6 *(bouquet)* (petit) bouquet *m*

7 *(brooch)* aigrette *f*

COMP *(insecticide, deodorant)* en aérosol; *Br Fa[m]* **he took the car in for a s. job** il a amené la voitu[re] au garage pour la faire repeindre[□]

▸▸ **spray can** *(for aerosol)* bombe *f*, aérosol *[m]*; *(refillable)* vaporisateur *m*; **spray gun** *(for pai[nt])* pistolet *m* (à peinture); **spray paint** peinture *f* [en] bombe; **a can of s. paint** une bombe de peintu[re]

sprayer ['spreɪə(r)] **N 1** *(container ▸ for perfum[e])* atomiseur *m*; *(spray gun)* pistolet *m* (à peinture); *(nozzle)* buse *f* **2** *Agr (machine)* pulvérisateur; *(plane)* avion-pulvérisateur *m* **3** *(person)* arr[o]seur(euse) *m,f*

spread [spred] *(pt & pp* **spread**) **N 1** *(diffusio[n], growth ▸ of epidemic, fire)* propagation *f*, pr[o]gression *f*; *(▸ of technology, idea)* diffusion *f*, d[is]sémination *f*; *(▸ of religion)* propagation *f*; **th[ey] are trying to prevent the s. of unrest to other citi[es]** ils essaient d'empêcher les troubles d'atteind[re] *ou* de gagner d'autres villes

2 *(range ▸ of ages, interests)* gamme *f*, éventa[il] *m*; **s. in interest rates** différentiel *m* de taux d'int[é]rêt; **the commission represented a broad s. [of] opinion** la commission représentait un lar[ge] éventail d'opinions

3 *(of wings)* envergure *f*

4 *(of land)* étendue *f*

5 *(period)* période *f*; **growth occurred over a s. [of] several years** la croissance s'étala sur une p[é]riode de plusieurs années

6 *(cover ▸ for bed)* couvre-lit *m*; *(tableclot[h])* nappe *f*; *(dustcover)* housse *f*

7 *Culin (paste)* pâte *f* à tartiner; *(jam)* confiture; *(butter substitute)* ≃ margarine *f*; **salmon [s.]** beurre *m* de saumon; **chocolate s.** chocolat *m* [à] tartiner

8 *Press & Typ (two pages)* double page *f*; *(tw[o-]page advertisement)* double page *f* publicitair[e]; **the event was given a good s.** l'événement a é[té] largement couvert par la presse

9 *Fam (meal)* festin[□] *m*; **the hotel lays on a dece[nt] s.** l'hôtel propose des repas tout à fait conven[a]bles[□]; **cold s.** repas *m* froid[□]

10 *Am Fam (farm)* ferme[□] *f*; *(ranch)* ranch[□] *m*

11 *St Exch* spread *m*

ADJ 1 *(arms, fingers, legs)* écarté **2** *Ling (vowe[l])* non arrondi

VT 1 *(apply ▸ paint, jam, icing, plaster, glue)* ét[a]ler; *(▸ asphalt)* répandre; *(▸ manure)* épandre; **I [s.] mustard on the ham, I s. the ham with mustard** j'[ai] étalé de la moutarde sur le jambon; **he s. butt[er] on a slice of toast** *or* **a slice of toast with butter** il tartiné de beurre une tranche de pain grillé; **[to] s. ointment on a burn** appliquer *ou* mettre de [la] pommade sur une brûlure

2 *(open out, unfold ▸ wings, sails)* étendre, d[é]ployer; *(▸ arms, legs, fingers)* écarter; *(▸ ma[p], napkin, blanket)* étaler; *(▸ rug)* étendre; *(▸ fa[n])* ouvrir; **he s. his handkerchief over his face** il étal[a] son mouchoir sur son visage; **she lay on her bac[k], her arms s.** elle était allongée sur le dos, les bra[s] écartés; **a bird with its wings s.** un oiseau aux a[iles] déployées; *Fig* **it's time you s. your wings** il e[st] temps que vous voliez de vos propres ailes

3 *(disseminate ▸ disease, fire)* propager, répa[n]dre; *(▸ news, idea, faith)* propager; *(▸ rumour)* r[é]pandre, faire courir; *(▸ lies)* colporter; *(▸ terro[r], panic)* répandre; **the wind will s. the fire to th[e] fields** le vent va propager l'incendie jusque dan[s] les champs; **trade helped to s. the new technolog[y] to Asia** le commerce a facilité la diffusion *ou* dissémination de cette nouvelle technologi[e] en Asie; **the attack is at noon, s. the word!** l'a[t]taque est pour midi, faites passer *ou* passez [le] mot!; **to s. the gospel** prêcher *ou* répandr[e] l'Évangile; *Fig* répandre la bonne parole

4 *(distribute over an area ▸ photos, cards, posse[s]sions)* étaler; *(sand, straw)* répandre; **her hair wa[s] s. over the pillow** ses cheveux s'étalaient s[ur] l'oreiller; **we s. the contents of the bag over th[e] floor** nous étalâmes le contenu du sac sur [le] sol; **the floor was s. with straw** le sol était reco[u]vert de paille; **take your shoes off, you're sprea[d]ing dirt everywhere!** enlève tes chaussures, t[u] salis tout!; **the explosion had s. debris over a larg[e]**

area l'explosion avait dispersé des débris sur une grande superficie; **their troops are s. too thinly to be effective** leurs troupes sont trop dispersées pour être efficaces; *Fig* **to s. oneself too thinly** se disperser

5 *(space out over a period of time)* échelonner, étaler; **the tourist season is now s. over six months** la saison touristique s'étale maintenant sur six mois; **the payments are s. over several months** les paiements sont échelonnés *ou* étalés *ou* répartis sur plusieurs mois

6 *(divide up ▸ tax burden, work load)* répartir; **a policy designed to s. wealth more evenly** une mesure qui vise à distribuer plus équitablement les richesses

7 *Mus (chord)* arpéger

VI 1 *(stain)* s'élargir; *(disease, fame, suburb)* s'étendre; *(fire, desert, flood)* gagner du terrain, s'étendre; *(rumour, ideas, faith, terror, crime, suspicion)* se répandre; **panic s. through the crowd** la panique a envahi *ou* gagné la foule; **the epidemic is spreading to other regions** l'épidémie gagne de nouvelles régions; **the cancer had s. through her whole body** le cancer s'était généralisé; **the flood waters have s. across** *or* **over the whole plain** l'inondation a gagné toute la plaine; **the species s. throughout Africa** l'espèce s'est répandue à travers toute l'Afrique

2 *(extend ▸ over a period of time, a range of subjects)* s'étendre; **their correspondence spreads over 20 years** leur correspondance s'étend sur 20 ans

3 *(butter, glue)* s'étaler; **the icing should s. easily** le glaçage devrait s'étaler facilement

4 *St Exch* spéculer sur les différentiels de cours

▸▸ ***spread betting*** = système de paris portant sur le résultat d'un événement sportif ou autre, où les gains sont proportionnels à la justesse des prédictions, selon une fourchette de résultats préétablie; ***spread eagle*** **1** *Her* aigle *f* éployée **2** *(in skating)* grand aigle *m*; **to do a s. eagle** faire un grand aigle

▸**spread about, spread around** **VT SEP** *(rumour)* répandre; **have you been spreading it about that I...?** est-ce que tu as été raconter partout que je...?

▸**spread out** **VT SEP 1** *(disperse)* disperser, éparpiller; **the buildings are s. out among the trees** les bâtiments sont dispersés parmi les arbres; **the runners are now s. out (along the course)** les coureurs sont maintenant éparpillés le long du parcours; **the population is very s. out** la population est très dispersée; **in a city as s. out as Los Angeles** dans une ville aussi étendue que Los Angeles

2 *(space out in time ▸ deliveries, payments)* échelonner; **to s. out over several financial years** étaler sur plusieurs exercices; **to s. out the losses over five years** répartir les pertes sur cinq ans

3 *(open out, unfold ▸ wings)* étendre, déployer; *(▸ arms, legs, fingers)* écarter; *(▸ map, napkin, blanket)* étaler; *(▸ rug)* étendre; *(▸ fan)* ouvrir; *(lay out ▸ photos, cards, possessions)* étaler; **she lay on her back, her arms s. out** elle était allongée sur le dos, les bras écartés; **a bird with its wings s. out** un oiseau aux ailes déployées; **to spread oneself out** *(on sofa etc)* s'étendre, s'allonger; **the plain lay s. out in front of us** la plaine s'étalait *ou* se déployait devant nous; **their troops are s. out too thinly to be effective** leurs troupes sont trop dispersées pour être efficaces

VI 1 *(town, forest)* s'étendre

2 *(disperse)* se disperser; *(in formation)* se déployer; **the search party had s. out through the woods** l'équipe de secours s'était déployée à travers les bois

3 *(open out ▸ sail)* se déployer, se gonfler

4 *(make oneself at ease)* s'installer confortablement; **I need an office where I can s. out** j'ai besoin d'un bureau où je puisse étaler mes affaires

spread-eagled [-'iːgəld] **ADJ** bras et jambes écartés; **the police had him s. against the wall** les policiers l'ont plaqué contre le mur, bras et jambes écartés; **sunbathers lay s. on the sand** des baigneurs étaient étalés sur le sable

spreader ['spredə(r)] **N 1** *Agr & Tech (for fertilizer, manure, asphalt)* épandeur *m*, épandeuse *f*; *(for putty, plaster etc)* spatule *f* **2** *(person ▸ of idea)* propagateur(trice) *m,f*; *(▸ of news)* rapporteur (euse) *m,f*; *(▸ of rumour)* colporteur(euse) *m,f*, propagateur(trice) *m,f*

spreading ['spredɪŋ] **ADJ a s. waistline** une taille qui s'épaissit; **under a s. chestnut tree** sous un châtaignier à la belle ramure

N 1 *(of paint, jam, glue)* étalement *m*; *(of asphalt)* répandage *m*; *(of manure)* épandage *m*; *(of ointment)* application *f*

2 *(of wings, sails)* déploiement *m*

3 *(of disease, fire, news, rumours, ideas)* propagation *f*; *(of lies)* colportage *m*

4 *(over time ▸ of payments)* échelonnement *m*

5 *(division ▸ of burden, work load)* répartition *f*

6 *Mus* arpègement *m*

spreadsheet ['spredʃiːt] **N** *Comput (document)* feuille *f* de calcul; *(software)* tableur *m*

spree [spriː] **N** fête *f*; **to go/to be on a s.** faire la fête; **her drinking/gambling sprees** les périodes où elle boit/joue; **to go on a shopping s.** faire des folies dans les magasins; **killing s.** accès *m* de folie meurtrière

sprig [sprɪg] **N** brin *m*

sprightliness ['spraɪtlɪnɪs] **N** *(of person)* vivacité *f*, vitalité *f*; *(of tune)* gaieté *f*

sprightly ['spraɪtlɪ] *(compar* **sprightlier**, *superl* **sprightliest)** **ADJ** *(person)* alerte, fringant; *(step)* vif; *(tune, whistle)* gai; **he's a s. 80-year-old** c'est un alerte octogénaire

spring [sprɪŋ] *(pt* **sprang** [spræŋ] *or* **sprung** [sprʌŋ], *pp* **sprung)** **N 1** *(season)* printemps *m*; **in (the) s.** au printemps; **s. is here!** c'est le printemps!

2 *(device, coil)* ressort *m*; *Aut* **the springs** la suspension

3 *(natural source)* source *f*; **hot** *or* **thermal s.** source *f* thermale

4 *(leap)* bond *m*, saut *m*; **he made a sudden s. for the knife** tout à coup, il bondit pour s'emparer du couteau

5 *(resilience)* élasticité *f*; **the diving board has plenty of s.** le plongeoir est très élastique; **the mattress has no s. left** le matelas n'a plus de ressort; **the news put a s. in her step** la nouvelle l'a rendue toute guillerette; **he set out with a s. in his step** il est parti d'un pas alerte

COMP 1 *(flowers, weather, colours)* printanier, de printemps; **his new s. collection** sa nouvelle collection de printemps **2** *(mattress)* à ressorts **3** *(water)* de source

VI 1 *(leap)* bondir, sauter; **to s. to one's feet** se lever vivement *ou* d'un bond; **to s. at** bondir *ou* se jeter sur; **the cat sprang at the bird** le chat bondit sur l'oiseau; **she sprang back in horror** elle recula d'un bond, horrifiée; **the couple sprang apart** le couple se sépara hâtivement; **the bus stopped and she sprang off** le bus s'arrêta et elle descendit d'un bond; **he sprang ashore** il sauta à terre; **the car sprang forward** la voiture fit un bond en avant; **springing out of the armchair** bondissant du fauteuil; **to s. to attention** bondir au garde-à-vous

2 *(be released)* **to s. shut/open** se fermer/s'ouvrir brusquement; **the branch sprang back** la branche s'est redressée d'un coup

3 *Fig* **the police sprang into action** les forces de l'ordre passèrent rapidement à l'action; **the engine sprang to** *or* **into life** le moteur s'est mis soudain en marche *ou* a brusquement démarré; **she sprang to his defence** elle a vivement pris sa défense; **the issue has made the town s. to life** l'affaire a galvanisé la ville; **new towns/companies have sprung into existence** des villes nouvelles/ de nouvelles sociétés ont surgi d'on ne sait où *ou* sont soudain apparues; **to s. to the rescue** se précipiter pour porter secours; **tears sprang to his eyes** les larmes lui sont montées *ou* venues aux yeux; **just say the first thing which springs to mind** dites simplement la première chose qui vous vient à l'esprit; **you didn't notice anything strange? – nothing that springs to mind** vous n'avez rien remarqué d'anormal? – rien qui me frappe particulièrement; **he sprang to fame overnight** il est devenu célèbre du jour au lendemain; *Fam* **where did you s. from?** d'où est-ce que tu sors?

4 *(originate)* **to s. from** venir de, provenir de; **their conservatism springs from fear** leur conservatisme vient de ce qu'ils ont peur

5 *(plank ▸ warp)* gauchir, se gondoler; *(▸ crack)* se fendre

6 *Am Fam (pay)* **to s. for sth** casquer pour qch

VT 1 *(trap)* déclencher; *(mine)* faire sauter; *(bolt)* fermer; **the mousetrap had been sprung but it was empty** la souricière avait fonctionné, mais elle était vide

2 *(car)* munir de ressorts; **sprung carriage** voiture *f* suspendue

3 *(make known ▸ decision, news)* annoncer de but en blanc *ou* à brûle-pourpoint; **I hate to have to s. it on you like this** cela m'embête d'avoir à vous l'annoncer de but en blanc comme ça; **he doesn't like people springing surprises on him** il n'aime pas les surprises *ou* qu'on lui réserve des surprises; **to s. a question on sb** poser une question à qn de but en blanc

4 *(develop)* **to s. a leak** *(boat)* commencer à prendre l'eau; *(tank, pipe)* commencer à fuir; **the radiator has sprung a leak** il y a une fuite dans le radiateur

5 *(jump over ▸ hedge, brook)* sauter

6 *(plank ▸ warp)* gauchir, gondoler; *(▸ crack)* fendre

7 *Hunt (game)* lever

8 *Fam (prisoner)* faire évader□; **the gang sprung him from prison with a helicopter** le gang l'a fait évader de prison en hélicoptère

▸▸ *Br* ***spring balance*** peson *m* à ressort; ***the Spring Bank Holiday*** = le dernier lundi de mai, jour férié en Grande-Bretagne; ***spring binding*** reliure *f* à ressort; ***spring chicken*** **1** *Am Culin* poulet *m (à rôtir)* **2** *(young person)* **he's no s. chicken** il n'est plus tout jeune, il n'est plus de la première jeunesse; ***spring fever*** excitation *f*; **to have s. fever** *(gen)* être tout excité; *(be in love)* être amoureux; ***spring greens*** choux *mpl* précoces; ***spring lock*** serrure *f* à fermeture automatique; *Br* ***spring onion*** petit oignon *m*; ***spring roll*** rouleau *m* de printemps; *Sch & Univ* ***spring term*** ≃ dernier trimestre *m*; ***spring tide*** grande marée *f*; *(at equinox)* marée *f* d'équinoxe (de printemps); ***spring water*** eau *f* de source

▸**spring up** **VI 1** *(get up)* se lever d'un bond

2 *(move upwards)* bondir, rebondir; **the lid sprang up** le couvercle s'est ouvert brusquement; **several hands sprang up** plusieurs mains se sont levées

3 *(grow in size, height)* pousser; **hasn't Lisa sprung up this year!** comme Lisa a grandi cette année!

4 *(appear ▸ towns, factories)* surgir, pousser comme des champignons; *(▸ doubt, suspicion, rumour, friendship)* naître; *(▸ difficulty, threat)* surgir; *(▸ breeze)* se lever brusquement; **new companies are springing up every day** de nouvelles entreprises apparaissent chaque jour; **an argument/friendship sprang up between them** une querelle éclata/une amitié naquit entre eux

springboard ['sprɪŋbɔːd] **N** *Sport & Fig* tremplin *m*; **the job is a s. for ministerial office** ce poste est un tremplin pour un portefeuille ministériel

springbok ['sprɪŋbɒk] *(pl* **inv** *or* **springboks)**, **springbuck** ['sprɪŋbʌk] *(pl* **inv** *or* **springbucks)** **N** *Zool* springbok *m*

spring-clean **VI** faire un nettoyage de printemps

VT nettoyer de fond en comble

N nettoyage *m* de printemps; **to give the house a s.** nettoyer la maison de fond en comble; *Fig* **the accounting department needs a s.** le service comptabilité a besoin d'un bon coup de balai

spring-cleaning **N** nettoyage *m* de printemps

springe [sprɪndʒ] **N** *(snare)* collet *m*

springer ['sprɪŋə(r)] **N 1** *(dog)* springer *m* **2** *Archit (stone)* sommier *m*; *(impost)* imposte *f*

▸▸ ***springer spaniel*** springer *m*

springform tin, *Am* **springform pan** ['sprɪŋ ˌfɔːm-] **N** *Culin* moule *m* à charnière

springiness ['sprɪŋɪnɪs] **N** *(of spring)* effet *m* de ressort; *(of hair)* gonflant *m*; *(of mattress)* élasticité *f*; *(of turf, ground)* souplesse *f*

springing ['sprɪŋɪŋ] **ADJ 1 a s. step** un pas dansant **2** *Her* élancé

springless ['sprɪŋlɪs] **ADJ** *Tech* sans ressort(s)

springlike ['sprɪŋlaɪk] **ADJ** *(gen)* de printemps; *(dress)* printanier

spring-loaded **ADJ** à ressort

springtide ['sprɪŋtaɪd] **N** *Literary* printemps *m*

springtime ['sprɪŋtaɪm] **N** printemps *m*

springy ['sprɪŋɪ] (*compar* **springier**, *superl* **springiest**) ADJ *(mattress, diving board)* élastique; *(step)* souple, élastique; *(floor)* souple; *(moss, carpet)* moelleux; *(hair)* dru

sprinkle ['sprɪŋkəl] VT 1 *(with salt, sugar, spices, breadcrumbs, talc)* saupoudrer (**with** de); *(with parsley, raisins)* parsemer (**with** de); *(with liquid)* arroser légèrement (**with** de); **I sprinkled sugar on** *or* **over my cereal, I sprinkled my cereal with sugar** j'ai saupoudré mes céréales de sucre; **s. with grated cheese** recouvrez de fromage râpé; **he sprinkled sawdust on the floor** il a répandu de la sciure par terre; **to s. water on sth** *or* **sth with water** asperger qch d'eau; **he sprinkled vinegar on** *or* **over his chips** il mit un peu de vinaigre sur ses frites 2 *(usu passive) (strew, dot)* parsemer, semer; **the sky was sprinkled with stars** le ciel était parsemé d'étoiles; **the fields were sprinkled with snow** les champs étaient tachetés de neige; **his hair was sprinkled with grey** ses cheveux étaient légèrement grisonnants; **a speech sprinkled with metaphors** un discours émaillé de métaphores; **a few policemen were sprinkled among the crowd** quelques policiers étaient disséminés dans la foule

VI *(rain)* tomber des gouttes

N 1 *(rain)* petite pluie *f*; **I felt a s. (of rain)** j'ai senti quelques gouttes (de pluie) 2 = **sprinkling**

sprinkler ['sprɪŋklə(r)] N 1 *Agr & Hort* arroseur *m* (automatique)

2 *(fire-extinguishing device)* sprinkler *m*

3 *(for sugar)* saupoudreuse *f*

4 *(for holy water)* goupillon *m*, aspersoir *m*

►► ***sprinkler head*** *(of shower)* pommeau *m*; *(of watering can)* pomme *f*; *(buried in ground)* arroseur *m*; ***sprinkler system*** installation *f* d'extinction automatique d'incendie, installation *f* sprinkler; ***sprinkler truck*** arroseuse *f*

sprinkling ['sprɪŋklɪŋ] N 1 *(action ► with sugar etc)* saupoudrage *m*; *(► with water)* arrosage *m* léger; *Rel* **s. of holy water** aspergès *m*, aspersion *f* 2 *(small quantity)* petite quantité *f*; *(pinch)* pincée *f*; **it was a male audience with a s. of women** c'était une assistance masculine avec quelques rares femmes; **with a liberal s. of literary references** avec moult références littéraires données ici et là; **there was a s. of grey in her hair** elle avait quelques cheveux gris

sprint [sprɪnt] N *Sport (dash)* sprint *m*; *(race)* course *f* de vitesse, sprint *m*; **he was beaten in the finishing s.** il a été battu au sprint final; **the 60-metre s.** le 60 mètres; **to break into** *or* **to put on a s.** piquer un sprint

VI sprinter; **I was good at sprinting** j'étais bon dans les courses de vitesse; **the little boy sprinted off** le petit garçon s'élança à toutes jambes; **he sprinted after her** il a couru derrière elle à toute vitesse; **I had to s. for the bus** j'ai dû courir *ou Fam* piquer un sprint pour attraper le bus

►► ***sprint finish*** sprint *m*; **there was a s. finish** il y a eu un sprint à l'arrivée; **he has a good s. finish** il est très rapide dans les sprints (de fin de course)

sprinter ['sprɪntə(r)] N sprinter *m*

sprite [spraɪt] N *Myth (male)* lutin *m*, farfadet *m*; *(female)* nymphe *f*; **water s.** naïade *f*

sprocket ['sprɒkɪt] N 1 *(wheel)* pignon *m* 2 *(cog)* dent *f* (de pignon)

►► ***sprocket hole*** *(for film)* perforation *f*

sprog [sprɒg] N *Br Fam* 1 *(child)* gosse *mf*, môme *mf* 2 *Mil (novice)* bleu *m*

sprout [spraʊt] N 1 *(on plant, from ground)* pousse *f*; *(from bean, potato)* germe *m*, *Belg* jet *m*; **alfalfa sprouts** germes *mpl* de luzerne 2 **(Brussels) sprouts** choux *mpl* de Bruxelles

VI 1 *(germinate ► bean, seed, onion)* germer, *Belg* jeter 2 *(grow ► plant, leaves, hair)* pousser; **he had hair sprouting from his ears** des touffes de poils lui sortaient des oreilles 3 *(appear)* apparaître, surgir; **satellite dishes have sprouted on all the rooftops** des antennes paraboliques ont surgi sur tous les toits

VT 1 *(grow ► leaves)* pousser, produire; *(► beard)* se laisser pousser; **some lizards can s. new tails** la queue de certains lézards repousse; *Fam* **to s. a moustache** se laisser pousser la moustache 2 *(germinate ► seeds, beans, lentils)* faire germer

►**sprout up** VI 1 *(grow ► grass, wheat, plant)* pousser, pointer; *(► person)* pousser 2 *(appear ► towns, factories)* pousser comme des champignons, surgir; *(► new community, sect)* surgir, naître; **a tented city had sprouted up overnight** une ville de toile avait poussé *ou* surgi pendant la nuit

spruce [spru:s] (*pl* **inv**) N *Bot* épicéa *m*; *(timber)* épinette *f*

ADJ *(person, car, building, town)* pimpant; *(haircut)* net; *(garment)* impeccable; **s. white curtains** des rideaux blancs impeccables; **she looked very s. in her uniform** elle était toute pimpante dans son uniforme

►**spruce up** VT SEP *(car, building, town)* donner un coup de neuf à; *(paintwork)* refaire; *(child)* faire beau (belle); **a coat of paint will s. the room up** une couche de peinture rafraîchira la pièce; **his image needs sprucing up** son image de marque a besoin d'être rafraîchie; **to s. oneself up, to get spruced up** se faire beau; **he was all spruced up** il était tiré à quatre épingles, il était sur son trente et un

spruceness ['spru:snɪs] N *(of person)* mise *f* soignée; *(of house, room)* propreté *f*

sprung [sprʌŋ] *pt & pp of* **spring**

ADJ *(mattress)* à ressorts

►► *Literature* ***sprung rhythm*** = mètre heurté proche du rythme naturel de la parole

spry [spraɪ] (*compar* **sprier** *or* **spryer**, *superl* **spriest** *or* **spryest**) ADJ *(person)* alerte, leste

spud [spʌd] N 1 *Fam (potato)* patate *f* 2 *(gardening tool)* sarcloir *m*

spume [spju:m] N *Literary* écume *f*

spun [spʌn] *pt & pp of* **spin**

ADJ filé; **her hair was like s. gold** elle avait des cheveux d'or

►► ***spun glass*** verre *m* filé; ***spun silk*** schappe *f*; *Culin* ***spun sugar*** sucre *m* filé; ***spun yarn*** bitord *m*

spunk [spʌŋk] N 1 *Fam (pluck)* cran *m*, nerf *m*; **show some s.!** un peu de nerf, voyons! 2 *Br Vulg (semen)* foutre *m*

spunky ['spʌŋkɪ] (*compar* **spunkier**, *superl* **spunkiest**) ADJ *Fam (courageous ► person)* plein de cran, qui a du cran; *(► retort, fight)* courageux

spur [spɜ:(r)] (*pt & pp* **spurred**, *cont* **spurring**) N 1 *Horseriding* éperon *m*; **to dig in one's spurs** piquer des éperons; *Hist* **to win one's spurs** gagner son épée de chevalier; *Fig* faire ses preuves

2 *Fig (stimulation)* aiguillon *m*; **the s. of competition** l'aiguillon de la concurrence; **easy credit is a s. to consumption** le crédit facile pousse *ou* incite à la consommation; **on the s. of the moment** sans réfléchir

3 *Geog (ridge)* éperon *m*, saillie *f*

4 *Rail (siding)* voie *f* latérale *ou* de garage; *(branch line)* embranchement *m*; **the warehouse is served by a s. line** l'entrepôt est desservi par un embranchement

5 *(on motorway)* bretelle *f*

6 *(breakwater)* brise-lames *m inv*, digue *f*

7 *Bot & Zool* éperon *m*; *(on gamecock)* ergot *m*

VT 1 *(horse)* éperonner 2 *Fig* inciter; **her words spurred me into action** ses paroles m'ont incité à agir

►**spur on** VT SEP 1 *(horse)* éperonner 2 *Fig* éperonner, aiguillonner; **their shouts spurred us on** leurs cris nous aiguillonnaient *ou* encourageaient; **to s. sb on to do sth** inciter *ou* pousser qn à faire qch

spurge [spɜ:dʒ] N *Bot* euphorbe *f*

►► ***spurge laurel*** daphné *m*

spurious ['spjʊərɪəs] ADJ 1 *(false ► gen)* faux (fausse); *(► comparison, argument, reason, objection, distinction)* spécieux; **your claim is a s. one** votre revendication est sans fondement 2 *(pretended ► enthusiasm, sympathy)* simulé; *(► flattery, compliment)* hypocrite 3 *(of doubtful origin ► text)* apocryphe

spuriously ['spjʊərɪəslɪ] ADV faussement

spuriousness ['spjʊərɪəsnɪs] N 1 *(gen)* fausseté *f*; *(of comparison, argument, reason, distinction)* non-validité *f* 2 *(of enthusiasm, sympathy)* fausseté *f* 3 *(of text)* caractère *m* apocryphe

spurn [spɜ:n] VT *(gen)* dédaigner, mépriser; *(suitor)* éconduire, rejeter; **those who s. tradition** ceux qui dédaignent les traditions; **a spurned lover** un amoureux éconduit

spurt [spɜ:t] VI 1 *(water, blood)* jaillir, gicler; *(flames, steam)* jaillir; **beer spurted (out) from the can** la bière a giclé de la boîte; **the milk spurted into the pail** le lait gicla dans le seau; **some lemon juice spurted into my eye** j'ai reçu une giclée de jus de citron dans l'œil 2 *(dash ► runner, cyclist)* sprinter, piquer un sprint; **he spurted past us** nous a dépassés comme une flèche; **the car spurted through the maze of streets** la voiture fil à travers le dédale de rues

VT *(gush ► of pierced container)* laisser jailli; *(spit ► of gun, chimney)* cracher; **his wound spurted blood** le sang gicla *ou* jaillit de sa blessure; **we spurted each other with water** nous nous sommes mutuellement aspergés d'eau; **the pipe spurted water everywhere** de l'eau jaillissait du tuyau; **the pen spurted ink onto the carpet** l'encre jaillit du stylo et tacha la moquette

N 1 *(of steam, water, flame)* jaillissement *m*; *(of blood, juice)* giclée *f*; **the water came out of the tap in spurts** l'eau jaillit du robinet par à-coups; **a s. of machine gun fire** une rafale de mitrailleus 2 *(dash)* accélération *f*; *(at work)* coup *m* de collier; *(revival)* regain *m*; *(flash ► of temper, jealousy, sympathy)* sursaut *m*; **to put on a s.** *(while running, cycling)* piquer un sprint; *(while working)* donner un coup de collier; **after a brief s. of economic growth** après un bref regain de croissance économique; **her inspiration came in spurts** l'inspiration lui venait par à-coups

►**spurt out** VI = **spurt** VI 1

Sputnik ['spʊtnɪk] N Spoutnik *m*

sputter ['spʌtə(r)] VI 1 *(motor)* toussoter, crachoter; *(fire, candle)* crépiter; *(meat on grill)* grésiller; **the engine sputtered to a halt** le moteur s'arrêta dans un toussotement 2 *(stutter)* bredouiller, bafouiller; **he sputtered angrily** il bredouillait de colère 3 *(spit ► gen)* crachoter; *(► when talking)* postillonner

VT *(apology, curses)* bredouiller, bafouiller

N 1 *(of motor)* toussotement *m*, hoquet *m*; *(of fire, candle)* crépitement *m*; **the engine gave a final s.** le moteur toussa une dernière fois 2 *(stuttering)* bredouillement *m*; **"go away!" he said with a s.** "va-t'en!", bredouilla-t-il

►**sputter out** VI *(candle, enthusiasm, anger)* s'éteindre

sputum ['spju:təm] (*pl* **sputa** [-tə]) N *Med* crachat *m*, expectoration *f*

spy [spaɪ] (*pl* **spies**, *pt & pp* **spied**) N espion(onne) *m,f*

COMP *(novel, film, scandal)* d'espionnage; *(network)* d'espions

VI *(engage in espionage)* faire de l'espionnage; **accused of spying for the enemy** accusé d'espionnage au profit de l'ennemi

VT *Literary (notice)* apercevoir; *(make out)* discerner; **he spied someone running away** il a aperçu quelqu'un qui se sauvait; **I s. with my little eye something beginning with... T!** *(in guessing game)* je vois quelque chose qui commence par T, devine ce que c'est

►► ***spy camera*** caméra *f* espionne; ***spy plane*** avion-espion *m*; ***spy ring*** réseau *m* d'espions; ***spy satellite*** satellite *m* espion

►**spy out** VT SEP *(someone's methods, designs)* chercher à découvrir (subrepticement); *(landing sites)* repérer; *also Fig* **to s. out the land** reconnaître le terrain

spyglass ['spaɪglɑ:s] N longue-vue *f*

spyhole ['spaɪhəʊl] N judas *m*

spying ['spaɪɪŋ] N *(gen) & Ind* espionnage *m*

spyware ['spaɪweə(r)] N *Comput* logiciel *m* espion

Sq. *(written abbr* **Square**) *(in addresses)* ≃ Place

sq. ft. *(written abbr* **square foot/feet**) pied(s) carré(s)

SQL [,eskju:'el] N *Comput (abbr* **structured query language**) SQL *m*

►► ***SQL engine*** processeur *m* SQL

Sqn. Ldr. *Br Mil (written abbr* **Squadron Leader**) ≃ commandant *m*, *Belg & Can* ≃ major *m*

squab [skwɒb] (*pl* **inv** *or* **squabs**) N *Orn* pigeonneau *m*

quabble ['skwɒbəl] **VI** se disputer, se quereller **N** dispute *f*, querelle *f*

quabbler ['skwɒbələ(r)] **N** querelleur(euse) *m*, chamailleur(euse) *m,f*

quabbling ['skwɒbəlɪŋ] **N** *(UNCOUNT)* chamailleries *fpl*, disputes *fpl*

quad [skwɒd] **N 1** *(group ▸ gen)* équipe *f*, escouade *f*; *Sport* **the England football s.** l'équipe anglaise de football **2** *Mil* escouade *f*, section *f* *(of police detachment)* brigade *f*
▸ **squad car** voiture *f* de patrouille de police

quaddie, squaddy ['skwɒdɪ] *(pl* **squaddies***)* **N** *Br Fam* bidasse *m*, troufion *m*

quadron ['skwɒdrən] **N** *(in air force)* escadron *m*; *(in navy ▸ small)* escadrille *f*; *(▸ large)* escadre *f*; *(in armoured regiment, cavalry)* escadron *m*
▸ *Br* **squadron leader** *(in air force)* ≃ commandant *m*, *Belg & Can* ≃ major *m*

qualid ['skwɒlɪd] **ADJ** sordide

qualidly ['skwɒlɪdlɪ] **ADV** de façon sordide

qualidness ['skwɒlɪdnɪs] **N** *(sordid conditions)* conditions *fpl* sordides; *(filth)* saleté *f* repoussante

quall [skwɔːl] **N 1** *Met (storm)* bourrasque *f*, rafale *f*; *Naut* grain *m*; *(rain shower)* grain *m*; **snow squalls** bourrasques *fpl* de neige **2** *(argument)* dispute *f* **3** *(bawling)* braillement *m*
VI 1 *(bawl)* brailler; **he could hear squalling children** il entendait brailler des enfants **2** *Naut* **it was squalling** on a pris un grain
VT "no!" he squalled "non!", brailla-t-il

qualling ['skwɔːlɪŋ] **ADJ** braillard
N braillements *mpl*

qually ['skwɔːlɪ] *(compar* **squallier**, *superl* **squalliest***)* **ADJ** *(wind)* qui souffle par *ou* en rafales; *(rain)* qui tombe en rafales; **there will be s. showers in the morning** il y aura des averses en rafales dans la matinée

qualor ['skwɒlə(r)] **N** *(UNCOUNT) (sordid conditions)* conditions *fpl* sordides; *(filth)* saleté *f* repoussante; **to live in s.** vivre dans des conditions sordides *ou* dans une misère noire

quander ['skwɒndə(r)] **VT** *(resources, time, money)* gaspiller; *(fortune, inheritance)* dissiper; *(opportunity)* gâcher, passer à côté de; **huge sums were squandered on unworkable schemes** les sommes énormes ont été dépensées en pure perte pour des projets irréalisables

quandering ['skwɒndərɪŋ] **N** *(of resources, time, money)* gaspillage *m*; *(of fortune, inheritance)* dissipation *f*; *(of opportunity)* fait *m* de gâcher *ou* de passer à côté de

QUARE [skweə(r)]

N	
• carré **1, 2, 5**	• case **3**
• place **4**	• square **4**
• équerre **6**	• ringard **7**
ADJ	
• carré **1, 2**	• à angle droit **3**
• honnête **4**	• net **5**
• équilibré **6**	• quitte **6**
• ringard **7**	
ADV	
• en plein **3**	• honnêtement **4**
VT	
• mettre droit **1**	• carrer **1, 2**
• élever au carré **2**	• concilier **3**
• régler **4**	• arranger **6**
VI	
• coïncider	

N 1 *(shape ▸ gen) & Geom* carré *m*; **she arranged the pebbles in a s.** elle a disposé les cailloux en carré; **he folded the napkin into a neat s.** il a plié la serviette en un carré bien net; **cut the cake into squares** coupez le gâteau en carrés; *Fam* **to be on the s.** être réglo; *Fam* **I'm telling you this on the s.** je vous le dis carrément
2 *(square object ▸ gen)* carré *m*; *(▸ tile)* carreau *m*; **a silk s.** un carré de soie; **a s. of chocolate** un carré *ou* morceau de chocolat; **a bathroom in grey and white squares** une salle de bains avec un carrelage gris et blanc
3 *(square space ▸ in matrix, crossword, board game)* case *f*; **to divide a map into squares** quadriller une carte; **locate s. D4 on the map** trouvez la case D4 sur la carte; *Fig* **we're back at** *or* **to s. one** nous voilà revenus à la case départ; **I had to start from s. one again** j'ai dû repartir à zéro
4 *(in town, village ▸ with streets)* place *f*; *(▸ with gardens)* square *m*; *Mil (parade ground)* place *f* d'armes; **barrack s.** cour *f* de caserne; **the town s.** la place, la grand-place
5 *Math (of number)* carré *m*
6 *Math & Tech (instrument)* équerre *f*; **to cut sth on the s.** couper qch à angles droits; **out of s.** qui n'est pas d'équerre
7 *Fam Pej (person)* ringard(e) *m,f*; **he's such a s.!** qu'est-ce qu'il est ringard!
ADJ 1 *(in shape ▸ field, box, building, face)* carré; **a tall man with s. shoulders** un homme grand aux épaules carrées; *Fig* **to be a s. peg in a round hole** ne pas être à sa place; *Hum* **you'll get s. eyes if you keep watching TV all day** tu vas t'abîmer les yeux à force de regarder la télé
2 *(metre, mile, inch etc)* carré; **10 s. kilometres** 10 kilomètres carrés; **the room is 5 metres s.** la pièce fait 5 mètres sur 5
3 *(right-angled)* à angle droit; **a s. corner** un angle droit; **the shelves aren't s.** les étagères ne sont pas droites; **s. with** *or* **to** *(at right angles)* à angle droit avec; *(parallel)* parallèle à
4 *(fair, honest)* honnête, correct; **to be s. with sb** être honnête *ou* correct avec qn; **to give sb a s. deal** agir correctement avec qn; **the farmers aren't getting a s. deal** les perdants dans l'affaire, ce sont les agriculteurs
5 *(blunt ▸ denial, refusal)* net, catégorique; **he won't give me a s. answer** il refuse de me donner une réponse claire et nette
6 *(even, balanced ▸ accounts, books)* équilibré; **to be s. with sb** être quitte envers qn; **they are (all) s.** *(financially)* ils sont quittes; *(in competition)* ils sont à égalité; **to get s. with sb** *(get revenge)* régler son compte à qn; *(settle debts)* être quitte envers qn; **did you get things s. with Julia?** est-ce que tu as pu arranger les choses avec Julia?
7 *Fam (old-fashioned)* ringard
8 *(proper)* **I haven't had a s. meal in days** ça fait plusieurs jours que je n'ai pas fait de vrai repas;
ADV 1 *(at right angles)* **she set the box s. with** *or* **to the edge of the paper** elle a aligné la boîte sur les bords de la feuille de papier
2 *(parallel)* **the house stands s. to the street** la maison est parallèle à la rue
3 *(directly)* **s. in the middle** en plein milieu; **he hit the ball s. in the middle of the racket** il frappa la balle avec le milieu de sa raquette; **she looked him s. in the face/eyes** elle le regarda bien en face/droit dans les yeux; **the blow landed s. on his nose** il a reçu le coup en plein sur le nez
4 *(honestly)* honnêtement
VT 1 *(make square ▸ pile of paper)* mettre droit, aligner; *(▸ stone)* carrer; *(▸ log)* équarrir; *(▸ shoulders)* redresser; **it's like trying to s. the circle** c'est la quadrature du cercle
2 *Math* carrer, élever au carré; **three squared is nine** trois au carré égale neuf
3 *(reconcile)* concilier; **how do you s. your wealth with being a socialist?** comment arrivez-vous à concilier votre richesse avec vos idées socialistes?; **I couldn't s. the story with the image I had of him** je n'arrivais pas à faire coïncider cette histoire avec l'image que j'avais de lui
4 *(settle ▸ account, bill)* régler; *(▸ debt)* acquitter; *(▸ books)* balancer, mettre en ordre; **to s. accounts with sb** *(pay money owed)* régler (ses comptes avec) qn; *(get revenge)* régler son compte à qn
5 *Sport* **his goal squared the match** son but a mis les équipes à égalité
6 *(arrange)* arranger; **can you s. it with the committee?** pourriez-vous arranger cela avec le comité?; **how do you s. it with your conscience?** comment arrangez-vous cela avec votre conscience?
7 *Fam (bribe)* soudoyer[□]
VI cadrer, coïncider; **his story doesn't s. with the facts** son histoire ne cadre *ou* ne coïncide pas avec les faits; **her figures/results don't s. with mine** ses chiffres/résultats ne cadrent pas avec les miens
▸▸ *Sport* **square ball** passe *f* latérale; **square bracket** crochet *m*; **in s. brackets** entre crochets; **square dance** quadrille *m*, *Can* danse *f* carrée; **square dancing** quadrille *m* américain, *Can* danse *f* carrée; **there'll be s. dancing at the saloon tonight** on va danser au saloon ce soir; *Am* **square knot** nœud *m* plat; **square leg** *(in cricket)* = chasseur situé derrière le batteur; **square measure** mesure *f* de surface *ou* de superficie; **the Square Mile** = la City de Londres *(dont la superficie fait environ un mile carré)*; **square number** carré *m*; **square pass** passe *f* latérale; *Naut* **square rigger** navire *m* gréé en carré; **square root** racine *f* carrée; *Am Fam* **square shooter** personne *f* franche[□]; *Electron* **square wave** onde *f* carrée *ou* rectangulaire
▸ **square away VT SEP** *Am Fam* régler[□], mettre en ordre[□]; **did you get everything squared away?** est-ce que tu as pu tout régler?
▸ **square off VT SEP 1** *(piece of paper, terrain)* quadriller **2** *(stick, log)* mettre d'équerre, équarrir
VI *(opponents, boxers)* se mettre en garde
▸ **square up VT SEP** *(make square ▸ end of plank)* mettre d'équerre, équarrir
VI 1 *(settle debt)* faire les comptes; **to s. up with sb** régler ses comptes avec qn **2** *(opponents, boxers)* se mettre en garde

---

square-bashing **N** *(UNCOUNT) Br Fam Mil slang* exercice[□] *m*

square-built **ADJ** *(person)* aux épaules carrées; *(short and sturdy)* trapu; *(building)* carré

square-headed **ADJ** à tête carrée

squarely ['skweəlɪ] **ADV 1** *(firmly)* fermement, carrément; *(directly)* en plein; **s. opposed to** fermement opposé à; **we must confront the dilemma s.** nous devons affronter ce dilemme avec fermeté; **to look sb s. in the eye** regarder qn droit dans les yeux; **s. in the middle** en plein milieu; **the blow landed s. on his nose** il a reçu le coup en plein sur le nez **2** *(honestly)* honnêtement; **to deal s. with sb** agir avec qn de façon honnête

squareness ['skweənɪs] **N 1** *(shape)* forme *f* carrée **2** *Fam (of person, views)* conservatisme[□] *m*

square-shouldered [-'ʃəʊldəd] **ADJ** aux épaules carrées

square-toed **ADJ** *(shoes)* à bout carré

squaring ['skweərɪŋ] **N 1** *(of account)* règlement *m* **2 the s. of the circle** la quadrature du cercle

squash [skwɒʃ] **VT 1** *(crush)* écraser; **you're squashing me!** tu m'écrases!; **I was squashed between two large ladies** j'étais serré *ou* coincé entre deux grosses dames; **we were squashed in like sardines** nous étions serrés comme des sardines
2 *(cram, stuff)* fourrer; **she squashed the laundry down in the bag** elle a tassé le linge dans le sac; **I squashed another sweater into my rucksack** j'ai pu faire entrer un pull supplémentaire dans mon sac à dos
3 *(silence, repress ▸ person)* remettre à sa place; *(▸ objection)* écarter; *(▸ suggestion)* repousser; *(▸ argument)* réfuter; *(▸ hopes)* réduire à néant; *(▸ rumour)* mettre fin à; *(▸ rebellion)* réprimer; **she squashed him with a look** elle l'a foudroyé du regard
VI 1 *(push ▸ people)* s'entasser; **all seven of us managed to s. into her car** on a réussi à s'entasser à sept dans sa voiture **2** *(fruit, package)* s'écraser
N 1 *(crush of people)* cohue *f*; **with five of us it'll be a bit of a s.** à cinq, nous serons un peu serrés
2 *Sport* squash *m*
3 *Br (drink)* **lemon/orange s.** sirop *m* de citron/d'orange
4 *(vegetable)* courge *f*
COMP *Sport (ball, court, champion, racket)* de squash
▸▸ *Old-fashioned* **squash hat** chapeau *m* mou; *Br* **squash rackets** *(game)* squash *m*
▸ **squash up VI** *(people)* se serrer (les uns contre les autres), s'entasser
VT SEP écraser

squashy ['skwɒʃɪ] *(compar* **squashier**, *superl* **squashiest***)* **ADJ** *(fruit, package)* mou (molle); *(cushion, sofa)* moelleux; *(ground)* spongieux

squat [skwɒt] *(pt & pp* **squatted**, *cont* **squatting**, *compar* **squatter**, *superl* **squattest***)* **VI 1** *(crouch ▸ person)* s'accroupir; *(▸ animal)* se tapir; **we ate squatting (down) on our haunches** nous avons mangé accroupis **2** *(occupy building)* vivre dans un squat; **they're allowed to s. in abandoned**

buildings on leur permet de squatter dans des immeubles abandonnés

N 1 *(building)* squat *m*; *(action)* squat *m*, occupation *f* de logements vides **2** *(crouch)* accroupissement *m* **3** *Am very Fam (nothing)* que dalle

ADJ *(person, figure)* trapu; *(building)* trapu, massif; **he had short, s. legs** il avait des petites jambes trapues

▸▸ ***squat thrust*** = exercice de musculation des jambes effectué accroupi

squatter ['skwɒtə(r)] **N 1** *(unlawful occupier)* squatter *m*; **there are s. settlements all round the town** il y a des communautés de squatters un peu partout autour de la ville **2** *Austr (rancher)* squatter *m*, éleveur *m*

squaw [skwɔ:] **N** *(American Indian)* squaw *f*

squawk [skwɔ:k] **VI 1** *(bird)* criailler; *(person)* brailler **2** *Fam (complain)* criailler□, râler

VT "let go of me!" she squawked "lâchez-moi!", brailla-t-elle

N 1 *(of bird)* criaillement *m*, cri *m*; *(of person)* cri *m* rauque; **to let out** *or* **to give a s.** pousser un cri rauque; *Fig* **the measure raised squawks of protest from the oil industry** cette mesure a suscité de vives protestations au sein de l'industrie pétrolière **2** *Am Fam (complaint)* plainte□*f*; **what's your s.?** c'est quoi ton problème?

▸▸ *Am Fam* ***squawk box*** *(loudspeaker)* haut-parleur□*m*; *(intercom)* interphone□*m*; *(telephone)* bigophone *m*

squeak [skwi:k] **VI 1** *(floorboard, chalk, wheel, machine part)* grincer; *(animal)* piauler, piailler; *(person)* glapir; *(shoes)* crisser; *(toy)* couiner; **she squeaked with delight** elle poussa un cri de joie **2** *Fam (succeed narrowly)* **the team squeaked into the finals** l'équipe s'est qualifiée de justesse pour la finale□; **they squeaked past Canada to become the biggest wheat producer** ils ont dépassé le Canada de justesse pour devenir le plus grand producteur de blé□

VT "who, me?" he squeaked "qui? moi?", glapit-il

N 1 *(of floorboard, chalk, wheel, machine part)* grincement *m*; *(of animal)* piaillement *m*; *(of person)* petit cri *m* aigu, glapissement *m*; *(of shoes)* crissement *m*; *(of toy)* couinement *m*; **to let out** *or* **to give a s. of pleasure** pousser un petit cri de plaisir; **don't let me hear one more s. out of you!** et que je ne t'entende plus! **2** *(idiom)* **that was a narrow s.!** on l'a échappé belle!

squeaking ['skwi:kɪŋ] **N** *(of floorboard, chalk, wheel, machine part)* grincement *m*; *(of animal)* piaillement *m*, piaillements *mpl*; *(of person)* petits cris *mpl* aigus, glapissements *mpl*; *(of shoes)* crissement *m*; *(of toy)* couinement *m*

squeaky ['skwi:kɪ] *(compar* **squeakier**, *superl* **squeakiest)** **ADJ** *(floorboard, bed, hinge)* grinçant; *(voice)* aigu(ë); *(toy)* qui couine; *Fam* **s. clean** *(hands, hair)* extrêmement propre□; *(image, reputation)* sans tache□; **a shampoo that leaves your hair s. clean** un shampooing qui donne à vos cheveux une propreté impeccable□

squeal [skwi:l] **VI 1** *(person, animal)* pousser un cri perçant; *(tyres, brakes)* crisser; *(pig)* couiner; **to s. with pain** pousser un cri de douleur; **to s. with laughter** hurler de rire; **the car squealed around the corner** la voiture prit le virage dans un crissement de pneus; **he was squealing like a stuck pig** il criait comme un cochon qu'on égorge **2** *very Fam (inform)* moucharder; **to s. on sb** balancer *ou* moucharder qn **3** *Fam (complain)* protester□, jeter les hauts cris□

VT "ouch!" she squealed "aïe!", cria-t-elle

N *(of person, animal)* cri *m* perçant; *(of tyres, brakes)* crissement *m*; **he gave a s. of delight** il poussa un cri de joie

squealer ['skwi:lə(r)] **N** *very Fam (informer)* mouchard(e) *m,f*, indic *mf*

squealing ['skwi:lɪŋ] **N** *(of person)* cris *mpl* aigus; *(of tyres, brakes)* crissement *m*

squeamish ['skwi:mɪʃ] **ADJ 1** *(oversensitive)* trop émotif, impressionnable; **it makes me feel s.** ça me donne mal au cœur; **I'm very s. about the sight of blood** je ne supporte pas la vue du sang; **she's s. about physical violence** elle ne supporte pas les scènes de violence; **he was too s. even to taste it** il n'a même pas eu le courage d'y goûter; **don't be so s.** ne fais pas le délicat; **he wasn't s. about evicting them in the middle of winter** il n'a eu aucun scrupule à les expulser en plein hiver **2** *(prudish)* prude

NPL the s. les âmes *fpl* sensibles, les petites natures *fpl*; **this film is not for the s.** ce film n'est pas conseillé aux âmes sensibles

squeamishness ['skwi:mɪʃnɪs] **N 1** *(oversensitivity)* trop grande émotivité *f*; **her s. about mice/spiders** sa peur des souris/araignées; **because of his s. about violence** du fait qu'il ne supportait pas la violence; **because of his s. about seafood** parce qu'il a horreur des fruits de mer **2** *(prudishness)* pruderie *f*

squeegee ['skwi:dʒi:] **N 1** *(with rubber blade)* raclette *f*; *(sponge mop)* balai-éponge *m*; *Phot (roller)* rouleau *m (en caoutchouc)* **2** *(person)* = personne qui lave les pare-brises

VT *(window)* passer une raclette sur, laver avec une raclette

squeeze [skwi:z] **N 1** *(pressure, grip)* pression *f*; *(handshake)* poignée *f* de main; *(hug)* étreinte *f*; **to give sth a s.** *(toothpaste, lemon)* presser qch; *(cloth)* essorer qch; **he gave my hand a reassuring s.** il a serré ma main pour me rassurer; **to give sb a s.** serrer qn dans ses bras; *Fam* **to put the s. on sb** faire pression sur qn□

2 *(crush of people)* cohue *f*; **it was a tight s.** *(in vehicle, room)* on était très serré; *(through opening)* on est passé de justesse

3 *(small amount* ▸ *of liquid)* quelques gouttes *fpl*; **a s. of lemon** quelques gouttes de citron; **a s. of toothpaste** un peu de dentifrice

4 *Econ & Fin (on profits, wages)* baisse *f* (**on** de); **(credit) s.** resserrement *m* du crédit; **a s. on jobs** des suppressions *fpl* d'emploi; **since her husband lost his job, they've really been feeling the s.** depuis que son mari a perdu son emploi, ils ont de sérieux problèmes d'argent

5 *(in bridge)* squeeze *m*

6 *Fam* **(main) s.** *(boyfriend)* mec *m*, Jules *m*; *(girlfriend)* nana *f*, gonzesse *f*

VT 1 *(press* ▸ *tube, sponge, pimple)* presser; *(*▸ *cloth)* essorer; *(*▸ *trigger)* presser sur, appuyer sur; *(*▸ *package)* palper; *(*▸ *hand, shoulder)* serrer; **she squeezed her knees together** elle serra les genoux; **I kept my eyes squeezed tight shut** j'ai gardé les yeux bien fermés; **to s. the life out of sb** étouffer qn

2 *(extract, press out* ▸ *liquid)* exprimer; *(*▸ *paste, glue)* faire sortir; *Fig (money, information)* soutirer; **I squeezed a dab of cream onto my nose** je me suis mis un peu de crème sur le nez; **a glass of freshly squeezed orange juice** une orange pressée; **to s. the juice out of a lemon** extraire le jus d'un citron; **to s. the water out of a sponge** essorer une éponge; **to s. the air out of** *or* **from sth** faire sortir l'air de qch en appuyant dessus; **you won't s. another penny out of me!** tu n'auras pas un sou de plus!; **they want to s. more concessions from the EU** ils veulent forcer l'Union européenne à faire de nouvelles concessions

3 *(cram, force)* faire entrer (avec difficulté); **I can't s. another thing into my suitcase** je ne peux plus rien faire entrer dans ma valise; **they're squeezing more and more circuits onto microchips** ils réussissent à mettre de plus en plus de circuits sur les puces; **she squeezed the ring onto her finger** elle enfila la bague avec difficulté; **he squeezed his way under the fence** il s'est glissé *ou* faufilé sous le grillage; **20 men were squeezed into one small cell** 20 hommes étaient entassés dans une petite cellule

4 *(constrain* ▸ *profits, budget)* réduire; *(*▸ *taxpayer, workers)* pressurer; **universities are being squeezed by the cuts** les réductions (de budget) mettent les universités en difficulté; **the British car industry has been squeezed by foreign competition** l'industrie automobile britannique subit la pression de la concurrence étrangère; *Fam* **I'm a bit squeezed for time/money** question temps/argent, je suis un peu juste

5 *(in bridge)* squeezer

VI I squeezed as hard as I could j'ai serré aussi fort que j'ai pu; **the lorry managed to s. between the posts** le camion a réussi à passer de justesse entre les poteaux; **I squeezed into the crowded room** j'ai réussi à me glisser dans la salle bondée; **they all squeezed onto the bus** ils se sont tous entassés dans le bus; **can you s. into that parking space?** y a-t-il assez de place pour te garer là?; **try and s. into these trousers** essayez de rentrer dans c[e] pantalon; **it was possible just to s. under the wi[re]** il était tout juste possible de se glisser sous le [fil] de fer

▸ **squeeze out VT SEP 1** *(sponge, wet clothes)* e[s]sorer **2** *(liquid)* exprimer; *Tech (plastic)* extrude[r]; **I squeezed out the last of the glue** j'ai fini le tub[e] de colle; **she gently squeezed the splinter out** e[n] pressant doucement, elle a fait sortir l'échard[e] **3** *(get rid of* ▸ *candidate, competitor)* évince[r]; **they're trying to s. me out** ils essaient de se d[é]barrasser de moi; **we were squeezed out by a Ge[r]man firm** une société allemande nous [a] devancés d'une courte tête; **the Japanese a[re] squeezing them out of the market** ils sont en tra[in] de se faire évincer du marché par les Japonais

▸ **squeeze through VI** se faufiler, se glisser

VT INSEP to s. through a narrow window se gliss[er] par une fenêtre étroite

▸ **squeeze up VI** se serrer, se pousser; **s. up a b[it] so Jane can sit down** serrez-vous un peu pour qu[e] Jane puisse s'asseoir

squeezebox ['skwi:zbɒks] **N** *Fam (accordio[n])* accordéon□*m*, piano *m* à bretelles; *(concertin[a])* concertina□*m*

squeezer ['skwi:zə(r)] **N** *Culin* presse-agrum[es] *m inv*

squelch [skweltʃ] **VI 1** *(walk* ▸ *in wet terrain)* p[a]tauger; *(*▸ *with wet shoes)* marcher les pie[ds] trempés; **I squelched across the field** j'ai travers[é] le champ en pataugeant; **he squelched into th[e] kitchen** il entra dans la cuisine avec les pie[ds] trempés **2** *(make noise* ▸ *mud)* clapoter; **I hea[rd] something soft s. beneath my foot** j'ai entend[u] quelque chose de mou s'écraser sous mon pie[d]; **the water squelched in his shoes** l'eau gargouilla[it] dans ses chaussures

VT 1 *(crush)* écraser **2** *Fam (rumour)* étouffer; *(person)* clouer le bec à

N *(noise)* clapotement *m*; **I heard the s. of tyres** [in] **mud** j'ai entendu le bruit des pneus dans la bou[e]

squib [skwɪb] **N 1** *(firecracker)* pétard *m* **2** *(pie[ce] of satire)* pamphlet *m*

squid [skwɪd] *(pl* **inv** *or* **squids)** **N** *Zool* cal(a)m[ar] *m*, encornet *m*

squiffy ['skwɪfɪ] *(compar* **squiffier**, *superl* **squi[f]fiest)** **ADJ** *Br Fam Old-fashioned* éméché, pom[]pette

squiggle ['skwɪgəl] **N 1** *(scrawl, doodle)* gr[i]bouillis *m* **2** *(wavy line, mark)* ligne *f* ondulé[e]; **something had left squiggles in the sand** quelqu[e] chose avait laissé des traces sinueuses sur [le] sable

VI 1 *(scrawl, doodle)* gribouiller, faire des gr[i]bouillages **2** *(twist* ▸ *road, lines)* sinuer, serpe[n]ter; *(*▸ *worm)* se tortiller

squiggly ['skwɪglɪ] **ADJ** pas droit, ondulé

squillion ['skwɪlɪən] **N** *Br Fam Hum* **squillions (o[f])** une foultitude (de), une ribambelle (de)

squint [skwɪnt] **N 1** *Med* strabisme *m*; **to have a** [s]**.** loucher **2** *Fam (glimpse)* coup *m* d'œil□; **have** [a] **take a s. at this!** vise-moi un peu ça!

ADJ 1 *(eyes)* louche **2** *Fam (crooked)* de traviole

VI 1 *Med* loucher **2** *(half-close eyes)* plisser le[s] yeux; **they're all squinting because of the sun** i[ls] font tous la grimace à cause du soleil; **h[e] squinted at the photo** *(with difficulty)* il regard[a] la photo en plissant les yeux; *(quickly)* il jeta u[n] coup d'œil à la photo; *(sidelong)* il regarda [la] photo du coin de l'œil

squint-eyed ADJ 1 *Fam (cross-eyed)* qui lo[u]che□, bigleux **2** *(sidelong)* de côté

squinting ['skwɪntɪŋ] **N** strabisme *m*

squire ['skwaɪə(r)] **N 1** *Br (landowner)* propri[é]taire *m* terriens, ≃ châtelain *m*; **he's the village** [s]**.** c'est le propriétaire du plus grand domaine d[u] coin; **S. Greaves** le squire Greaves **2** *(for knigh[t])* écuyer *m* **3** *Br Fam (term of address)* **evening, s**[.] bonsoir, chef!

VT *Old-fashioned (woman)* escorter, accomp[a]gner

squirearchy ['skwaɪərɑ:kɪ] *(pl* **squirearchies)** [N] propriétaires *mpl* terriens, ≃ châtelains *m[pl]*; **the island's planters form a s.** les planteurs d[e] l'île forment une petite noblesse terrienne

quirm [skwɜ:m] **VI 1** *(wriggle)* se tortiller; **he squirmed out of my grasp** il a échappé à mon étreinte en se tortillant; **she squirmed with impatience** elle était tellement impatiente qu'elle ne tenait plus en place **2** *(be ill-at-ease)* être gêné, être très mal à l'aise; *(be ashamed)* avoir honte; **to s. with embarrassment** être mort de honte; **I still s. when I remember how I treated her** j'ai encore honte quand je pense à la manière dont je l'ai traitée; **his speech was so bad it made me s.** son discours était si mauvais que j'en ai eu honte pour lui

VT to s. one's way out of a situation se sortir d'une situation; **to s. one's way out of one's commitments** se défiler de ses obligations

quirrel [*Br* 'skwɪrəl, *Am* 'skwɜ:rəl] (*Br pt & pp* **squirrelled,** *cont* **squirrelling,** *Am pt & pp* **squirreled,** *cont* **squirreling**) **N 1** *Zool* écureuil *m* **2** *Fig (hoarder)* **she's a real s.** c'est une vraie fourmi

squirrel away VT SEP *(hoard, store)* engranger; *(hide)* cacher; **he's got a fortune squirrelled away in various Swiss banks** il a amassé une fortune dans plusieurs banques suisses

quirrelly ['skwɜ:rəlɪ] **ADJ** *Am Fam (eccentric)* loufedingue

quirt [skwɜ:t] **VT** *(liquid)* faire gicler; *(mustard, ketchup, washing-up liquid)* faire jaillir; **s. some oil on the hinges** mettez quelques gouttes d'huile sur les gonds; **they were squirting each other with water, they were squirting water at each other** ils s'aspergeaient d'eau mutuellement; **he squirted some soda water into his whisky** il versa une rasade d'eau de Seltz dans son whisky; **she squirted perfume on her wrists** elle se vaporisa du parfum sur les poignets

VI *(juice, blood, ink)* gicler; *(water)* jaillir; **juice squirted onto my shirt** le jus a giclé sur ma chemise; **the milk squirted (out) into the pail** le lait giclait dans le seau

N 1 *(of juice, ink)* giclée *f*; *(of water)* jet *m*; *(of mustard, ketchup, washing-up liquid)* dose *f*; *(of oil, perfume)* quelques gouttes *fpl* **2** *Fam Pej (person)* minus *m*; *(short person)* avorton *m*, demi-portion *f*; *(child)* mioche *mf*; **get lost, you little s.!** va donc, eh minus!

►► *Am* ***squirt gun*** pistolet *m* à eau

quish [skwɪʃ] *Fam* **VT** *(crush)* écrabouiller; **he squished his nose against the glass** il a écrasé son nez contre la vitre[□]; **the cake got all squished** le gâteau était complètement écrabouillé

VI 1 *Am (squash* ► *insect, fruit)* s'écrabouiller **2** *(squelch)* clapoter[□]; **the mud squished between my toes** la boue s'infiltrait entre mes orteils[□]

quishy ['skwɪʃɪ] (*compar* **squishier,** *superl* **squishiest**) **ADJ** *Fam (fruit, wax)* mou (molle)[□]; *(chocolate)* ramolli[□]; *(ground)* boueux[□]

quit [skwɪt] *Br Fam* **N 1** *(person)* minus *m* **2** *(UNCOUNT) (nonsense)* bêtises[□] *fpl*, conneries *fpl*

NPL the squits *(diarrhoea)* la courante

r 1 *(written abbr* **senior)** **Ralph Todd Sr** Ralph Todd père **2** *(written abbr* **sister)** sœur *f*

RAM ['esræm] **N** *Comput (abbr* **static random access memory)** mémoire *f* vive statique

ri Lanka [ˌsri:'læŋkə] **N** Sri Lanka *m*

ri Lankan [ˌsri:'læŋkən] **N** Sri Lankais(e) *m,f*

ADJ sri lankais

RN [ˌesɑ:'ren] **N** *Br (abbr* **State Registered Nurse)** infirmier(ère) *m,f* diplômé(e) *(remplacé en 1992 par "Registered Nurse")*

S [ˌes'es] **N 1** *Naut (abbr* **steamship)** = initiales précédant le nom des navires de la marine marchande; **the SS Norfolk** le Norfolk **2** *(abbr* **Schutzstaffel)** **the SS** les SS; **an SS officer** un officier SS

SL [ˌeses'el] **N** *Comput (abbr* **secure sockets layer)** protocole *m* SSL

SN [ˌeses'en] **N** *Am (abbr* **social security number)** numéro *m* de Sécurité sociale

SSI [ˌeses,es'aɪ, ˌtrɪpəles'aɪ] **N** *Br (abbr* **Site of Special Scientific Interest)** = en Grande-Bretagne, site déclaré d'intérêt scientifique

t 1 *(written abbr* **saint)** St, Ste **2** *(written abbr* **street)** rue *f*

t *(written abbr* **stone)** *(unit of weight)* ≃ 6 kg

tab [stæb] (*pt & pp* **stabbed,** *cont* **stabbing**) **VT 1** *(injure* ► *with knife)* donner un coup de couteau à, poignarder; *(*► *with bayonet)* blesser d'un coup de baïonnette; *(*► *with spear)* blesser avec une lance; **he stabbed me in the arm** il me donna un coup de couteau dans le bras; **they were stabbed to death** ils ont été tués à coups de couteau; **to s. sb in the back** poignarder qn dans le dos; *Fig* trahir qn

2 *(thrust, jab)* planter; **she stabbed the needle into my arm** elle planta l'aiguille dans mon bras; **I stabbed myself in the thumb with a pin** je me suis enfoncé une épingle dans le pouce; **I stabbed my finger in his eye** je lui ai enfoncé mon doigt dans l'œil; **I stabbed a turnip with my fork** j'ai piqué un navet avec ma fourchette

VI he stabbed at the map with his finger il frappa la carte du doigt; **she stabbed frantically at the different control buttons** elle poussa frénétiquement les différents boutons de contrôle; **he stabbed at the leaves with his walking stick** il piquait les feuilles de la pointe de sa canne

N 1 *(with dagger)* coup *m* de poignard; *(with knife)* coup *m* de couteau; **she felt the s. of the needle in her finger** elle a senti la piqûre de l'aiguille dans son doigt; **s. wound** blessure *f* par arme blanche; **a man was rushed to hospital with s. wounds** un homme blessé à coups de couteau a été transporté d'urgence à l'hôpital; **it was a s. in the back** c'était un véritable coup de poignard dans le dos

2 *Literary (of neon, colour)* éclat *m*; **a s. of lightning** un éclair

3 *(sensation)* **s. of pain** élancement *m*; **I felt a s. of doubt** l'espace d'un instant je fus saisi par le doute; **I felt a s. of envy** je sentis un pincement de jalousie

4 *Fam (try)* **to have** *or* **to make** *or* **to take a s. at sth/doing sth** s'essayer à qch[□]/à faire qch[□]; **I'll have a s.** je vais essayer

stabbing ['stæbɪŋ] **N** *(knife attack)* agression *f* (à l'arme blanche); **there was a s. in the pub last night** quelqu'un s'est fait poignarder au pub hier soir; **there were two fatal stabbings at the football match** deux personnes ont été tuées à coups de couteau au match de football; **the number of stabbings has increased** le nombre d'attaques à l'arme blanche est en hausse

ADJ *(pain)* lancinant

stability [stə'bɪlətɪ] **N** stabilité *f*; **a period of political s.** une période de stabilité politique; **it will undermine the s. of their marriage** cela va ébranler leur mariage; **his mental s.** son équilibre mental

►► *EU* ***stability pact*** pacte *m* de stabilité

stabilization, -isation [ˌsteɪbəlaɪ'zeɪʃən] **N** stabilisation *f*

►► *Fin* ***stabilization fund*** fonds *m* de stabilisation; *Fin* ***stabilization plan*** plan *m* d'assainissement

stabilize, -ise ['steɪbəlaɪz] **VT** stabiliser

VI se stabiliser

stabilizer, -iser ['steɪbəlaɪzə(r)] **N 1** *Aviat, Aut, Naut & Elec & (on bicycle)* stabilisateur *m*; *Fig* **the measure is intended to act as an economic s.** cette mesure a pour but de stabiliser l'économie **2** *Chem (in food)* stabilisateur *m*, stabilisant *m*

stabilizing, -ising ['steɪbəlaɪzɪŋ] **ADJ** stabilisateur; **to have** *or* **to exert a s. effect on prices** exercer une action stabilisatrice sur les prix; **her new job had a s. effect on her** son nouvel emploi a eu un effet stabilisateur *ou* équilibrant sur elle

►► ***stabilizing agent*** *(in foodstuffs)* agent *m* stabilisant; ***stabilizing policy*** politique *f* de stabilité

stable ['steɪbəl] **ADJ 1** *(steady, permanent* ► *gen)* stable; *(*► *marriage)* solide; **the patient's condition is s.** l'état du malade est stationnaire; **he never had a s. family life** il n'a jamais eu de vie de famille stable **2** *(person, personality)* stable, équilibré; **he's not s.** il n'est pas équilibré, il est instable **3** *Chem & Phys* stable

N 1 *(building)* écurie *f*; **riding s.** *or* **stables** centre *m* d'équitation **2** *(group* ► *of racehorses, sportspeople)* écurie *f*; *(*► *of authors, actors)* équipe *f*; *(*► *of companies, businesses)* groupe *m*

VT *(take to stable)* mettre à l'écurie; **her horse is stabled at Dixon's** son cheval est en pension chez Dixon; **we can s. three horses** nous avons de la place pour trois chevaux

►► ***stable boy*** valet *m* d'écurie, lad *m*; ***stable door*** porte *f* d'écurie, porte *f* à deux vantaux *ou* battants; *Fig* **to shut** *or* **to lock the s. door after the horse has bolted** réagir trop tard, arriver après la bataille; ***stable girl*** valet *m* d'écurie *(fille)*; ***stable lad*** lad *m*

> Note that the French word **étable** is a false friend and is never a translation for the English word **stable**. It means **cowshed**.

stabling ['steɪbəlɪŋ] **N** *(UNCOUNT)* **1** *(of horses)* logement *m* dans une écurie **2** *(space in stables)* **we have plenty of s.** nous ne manquons pas de place aux écuries; **we supply s. for 40 horses** nous pouvons accueillir 40 chevaux

staccato [stə'kɑ:təʊ] (*pl* **staccatos**) **ADJ 1** *Mus (note)* piqué; *(passage)* joué en staccato **2** *(noise, rhythm)* saccadé; **in a s. voice** d'une voix saccadée

ADV *Mus* staccato

N *Mus* staccato *m*; **she replied in a rapid s.** elle répondit d'un ton rapide et saccadé

►► *Mus* ***staccato mark*** trait *m* vertical

stache [stæʃ] **N** *Am Fam (abbr* **mustache)** bacchantes *fpl*, moustagache *f*

stack [stæk] **N 1** *(pile)* tas *m*, pile *f*; **a huge s. of books** une pile énorme de livres

2 *Fam (large quantity)* tas *m*; **stacks of…** des tas de…; **I've written a s. of** *or* **stacks of postcards** j'ai écrit un tas de cartes postales; **we've got stacks of time** on a largement le temps; **she has stacks of money** elle est bourrée de fric

3 *Agr (of hay, straw)* meule *f*

4 *(chimney) & (of locomotive)* cheminée *f*

5 *Aviat* avions *mpl* en attente, empilage *m*; **the s. is 20 planes high** il y a 20 avions qui attendent le feu vert de la tour de contrôle pour atterrir

6 *Comput (file)* pile *f*

7 *Mil (of rifles)* faisceau *m*

8 *(in library)* **the s.** *or* **stacks** les rayons *mpl*

9 *(idiom) Am Fam* **to blow one's s.** exploser, piquer une crise

VT 1 *(pile* ► *chairs, boxes etc)* empiler; **oil cans were stacked in pyramids** des bidons d'huile étaient empilés en pyramide

2 *Agr (hay)* mettre en meule *ou* meules

3 *(fill* ► *room, shelf)* remplir; **his desk was stacked high with files** des piles de dossiers s'entassaient sur son bureau

4 *Comput* empiler

5 *Aviat (planes)* mettre en attente (à altitudes échelonnées)

6 *(fix, rig* ► *committee)* remplir de ses partisans; **to s. the cards** *or* **the deck** truquer les cartes; *Fig* **he's playing with a stacked deck** *(in his favour)* les dés sont pipés en sa faveur; *(against him)* les dés sont pipés contre lui; *Fig* **the cards** *or* **the odds are stacked against us** nous sommes dans une mauvaise situation; **a woman in this profession starts with the cards stacked against her** dans ce métier les femmes partent avec un handicap; **the election system is heavily stacked against the smaller parties** ce mode de scrutin défavorise fortement les petits partis

VI s'empiler

• **stacks ADV** *Br Fam* vachement; **it's stacks easier** c'est vachement plus facile

▸ **stack up VT SEP** *(pile up)* empiler

VI 1 *Am Fam (add up, work out)* **I don't like the way things are stacking up** je n'aime pas la tournure que prennent les événements[□]; **I wanted someone honest and dynamic and that's how Jan stacks up** je voulais quelqu'un d'honnête et de dynamique et Jan fait parfaitement l'affaire[□] **2** *(compare)* se comparer; **our product stacks up well against theirs** notre produit soutient bien la comparaison avec le leur; **how does he s. up against** *or* **with the other candidates?** que vaut-il comparé aux autres candidats?

stacker ['stækə(r)] **N** *(worker)* manutentionnaire *mf*; *(pallet truck)* transpalette *m*

stacking chairs ['stækɪŋ-] **NPL** chaises *fpl* superposables

stadium ['steɪdjəm] (*pl* **stadiums** *or* **stadia** [-djə]) **N** stade *m*

staff [stɑ:f] (*pl senses* **3 & 4 staffs** *or* **staves** [stɑ:vz]) **N 1** *(work force)* personnel *m*; *(teachers)* professeurs *mpl*, personnel *m* enseignant; **the com-**

pany has a s. of 50 l'effectif de la société est de 50 personnes; **we have ten lawyers on the s.** notre personnel comprend dix avocats; **is he s.** *or* **a member of s.?** est-ce qu'il fait partie du personnel?; **s. only** *(sign)* réservé au personnel; **s./student ratio** taux *m* d'encadrement, rapport *m* entre le nombre de professeurs et le nombre d'étudiants

2 *Mil & Pol* état-major *m*; **she was asked to join the President's campaign s.** on lui a demandé de faire partie de l'état-major de campagne du Président

3 *(rod)* bâton *m*; *(flagpole)* mât *m*; *(of banner, lance)* hampe *f*; *(for shepherd)* houlette *f*; *(for bishop)* crosse *f*, bâton *m* pastoral; *Br (in surveying)* jalon *m*; *Fig (support)* soutien *m*; **the s. of life** *(bread)* l'aliment de base; *Fig* le pain et le sel de la vie

4 *Mus* portée *f*; **treble s.** portée *f* en clé de sol

COMP *(canteen, outing etc)* du personnel

VT *(usu passive)* pourvoir en personnel; **the branch is staffed by** *or* **with competent people** le personnel de la succursale est compétent; **the office is only staffed between the hours of 2 and 4 pm** il y a quelqu'un au bureau de 14h à 16h seulement; **the committee is completely staffed by volunteers** le comité est entièrement composé de bénévoles

►► ***staff association*** ≃ comité *m* d'entreprise; *Mil* ***staff college*** école *f* supérieure de guerre; *Mil* ***staff corporal*** ≃ sergent-major *m*; ***staff manager*** chef *m* du personnel; *Br* ***staff nurse*** infirmier (ère) *m,f* diplômé(e); *Mil* ***staff officer*** officier *m* d'état-major; ***staff retention*** rétention *f* du personnel; *Mil* ***staff sergeant*** *Br* ≃ sergent-chef *m*; *Am* ≃ sergent *m*; ***staff training*** formation *f* du personnel; ***staff turnover*** roulement *m* du personnel

staffer ['stɑːfə(r)] **N 1** *Journ* rédacteur(trice) *m,f*, membre *m* de la rédaction **2** *Am (staff member)* membre *m* du personnel

staffing ['stɑːfɪŋ] **N** *(recruiting)* recrutement *m*; **the delay is due to s. difficulties** le retard est dû à des problèmes de recrutement

►► ***staffing arrangements*** organisation *f* du personnel; ***staffing levels*** effectifs *mpl*; ***staffing policy*** politique *f* de recrutement du personnel

Staffs *(written abbr* **Staffordshire***)* Staffordshire *m*

stag [stæg] *(pl* **inv** *or* **stags***)* **N 1** *(animal)* cerf *m* **2** *Br St Exch* loup *m*

ADJ *(event ► for men)* entre hommes

ADV *Am Fam* **to go s.** sortir en célibataire

►► *Entom* ***stag beetle*** cerf-volant *m*, *Spec* lucane *m*; *Fam* ***stag film*** film *m* porno; ***stag night, stag party*** *(gen)* soirée *f* entre hommes; **we're having** *or* **holding a s. night for Bob** *(before wedding day)* nous enterrons la vie de garçon de Bob

STAGE [steɪdʒ]

N
- stade **1**
- étape **1**
- théâtre **2**
- étage **4, 6**
- phase **1**
- scène **2**
- plate-forme **3**
- diligence **5**

VT
- monter **1, 2**
- organiser **2**
- mettre en scène **1**

N 1 *(period, phase ► of development, career etc)* stade *m*; *(► of illness, negotiations, project, process)* stade *m*, phase *f*; *(► of journey, life)* étape *f*; **larval s.** stade *m* larvaire; **the first/final s. of the project** la première/dernière phase du projet; **the next s. in computer technology** le stade suivant *ou* l'étape suivante du développement de l'informatique; **at this s.** à ce stade; **at this s. of the negotiations, I won't venture to comment** à ce stade des négociations, je m'interdirai tout commentaire; **at one s. it looked like he was going to win** à un moment donné il avait l'air parti pour gagner; **we'll deal with that at a later s.** nous nous en occuperons plus tard; **at a later s. in his life** plus tard dans la vie; **the conflict is still in its early stages** le conflit n'en est encore qu'à ses débuts; **s. by s.** étape par étape; **to do sth by** *or* **in stages** faire qch par étapes; **the changes were instituted in stages** les changements ont été introduits progressivement; **we travelled to Lisbon in (easy) stages** nous avons voyagé jusqu'à Lisbonne par (petites) étapes

2 *Theat (place)* scène *f*; **the s.** *(profession, activity)* le théâtre; **on s.** sur scène; **s. right/left** côté jardin/cour; **to go on s.** monter sur (la) scène; **to go on the s.** *(as career)* monter sur les planches, faire du théâtre; **he first appeared on the s. in 1920** il a commencé à faire du théâtre en 1920; **to write for the s.** écrire pour la scène; **she was the first to bring the play to the London s.** elle a été la première à monter cette pièce sur la scène londonienne; *Fig* **the political s.** la scène politique; **on the s. of world events** sur la scène internationale; **his concerns always take centre s.** ses soucis à lui doivent toujours passer avant tout; **to set the s. for sth** préparer le terrain pour qch

3 *(platform ► gen)* plate-forme *f*; *(► for speaker, presenter)* estrade *f*; *(► on microscope)* platine *f*; *(scaffolding)* échafaudage *m*

4 *Astron* étage *m*; **a three-s. satellite launcher** un lanceur spatial à trois étages

5 *(stagecoach)* diligence *f*

6 *Electron (circuit part)* étage *m*

COMP *(version)* pour le théâtre; **a s. Irishman** une caricature d'Irlandais; **she has great s. presence** elle a énormément de présence sur scène

VT 1 *Theat (put on ► play)* monter, mettre en scène; **it's the first time the play has been staged** c'est la première fois qu'on monte cette pièce; **Macbeth was very well staged** la mise en scène de Macbeth était très réussie; **the company is staging plays in parks this summer** la troupe joue dans les parcs cet été

2 *(organize, hold ► ceremony, demonstration, festival, robbery)* organiser; *(► coup)* monter; *(fake ► accident)* monter, manigancer; **to s. a hijacking** détourner un avion; **to s. a diversion** créer une *ou* faire diversion; **she staged her entrance for maximum effect** elle prépara son entrée de façon à faire le plus d'effet possible; **the handshake was staged for the TV cameras** la poignée de main était une mise en scène destinée aux caméras de télévision

►► ***stage design*** décoration *f* de théâtre, scénographie *f*; ***stage designer*** décorateur(trice) *m,f* de théâtre, scénographe *mf*; ***stage direction*** indication *f* scénique; ***stage diving*** stage diving *m*, = fait de se jeter dans la foule depuis la scène; ***stage door*** entrée *f* des artistes; ***stage effect*** effet *m* scénique; ***stage fright*** trac *m*; **to have s. fright** avoir le trac, être pris de trac; ***stage manager*** régisseur *m*; ***stage name*** nom *m* de scène; ***stage play*** pièce *f* de théâtre; ***stage school*** cours *m* de théâtre; ***stage set*** décor *m*; ***stage show*** pièce *f* de théâtre; ***stage whisper*** aparté *m*; **"it's midnight," he announced in a loud s. whisper** "il est minuit", chuchota-t-il, suffisamment fort pour que tout le monde l'entende

> Note that the French word **stage** is a false friend and is never a translation for the English word **stage**. It means **training course**.

stagecoach ['steɪdʒkəʊtʃ] **N** diligence *f*

stagecraft ['steɪdʒkrɑːft] **N** *(of playwright)* maîtrise *f* de l'écriture théâtrale; *(of director)* maîtrise *f* de la mise en scène; *(of actor)* maîtrise *f* du jeu

stagehand ['steɪdʒhænd] **N** *Theat* machiniste *mf*

stage-manage **VT 1** *Theat (play, production)* s'occuper de la régie sur **2** *(press conference, appearance)* orchestrer, mettre en scène; **her arrival at the airport was stage-managed to generate publicity** son arrivée à l'aéroport a été une vraie mise en scène publicitaire; **the unrest was stage-managed to coincide with the summit meeting** les troubles ont été orchestrés de manière à coïncider avec le sommet

stager ['steɪdʒə(r)] **N** *(veteran)* **old s.** vieux *m* de la vieille

stagestruck ['steɪdʒstrʌk] **ADJ** possédé par le démon du théâtre, qui rêve de faire du théâtre

stagey *Am* = **stagy**

stagflation [stæg'fleɪʃən] **N** stagflation *f*

stagger ['stægə(r)] **VI** *(totter ► person, horse)* chanceler, tituber; **to s. out** sortir en chancelant *ou* titubant; **I staggered over to the chair** je me suis dirigé vers la chaise d'un pas chancelant; **I staggered under the weight** je titubais sous [le] poids; **we staggered into bed at 3 o'clock in t[he] morning** nous nous sommes écroulés sur n[os] lits à 3 heures du matin

VT 1 *(usu passive) (payments)* échelonner; *(ho[li]days)* étaler; **they plan to bring in staggered wo[rk]ing hours** ils ont l'intention de mettre en pla[ce] un système d'échelonnement des heures de t[ra]vail **2** *(usu passive) (astound)* **to be staggered** ê[tre] atterré, être stupéfait; **I was staggered to learn his decision** j'ai été stupéfait d'apprendre sa [dé]cision

N *(totter)* pas *m* chancelant; **he got up with a s.** [il] s'est levé en chancelant

• **staggers N** *(in diver)* ivresse *f* des profo[n]deurs; **(blind) staggers** *(in sheep)* tournis cœnurose *f*; *(in horses)* vertigo *m*

staggered ['stægəd] **ADJ** *(amazed)* atterré, st[u]péfait

►► ***staggered junction*** carrefour *m* décalé; ***sta[g]gered payments*** paiements *mpl* échelonn[és]; *Sport* ***staggered start*** *(on oval track)* départ *m* d[é]calé

staggering ['stægərɪŋ] **ADJ** *(news, amount)* st[u]péfiant, ahurissant; *(problems)* énorme; *Fig* **was a s. blow** ce fut un sacré coup; **the price t[ag] is a s. $500,000** ça vaut la somme astronomiq[ue] de 500 000 dollars

N 1 *(of vacations)* étalement *m*; *(of paymen[ts])* échelonnement *m* **2** *(unsteady gait)* démarch[e] chancelante

staghorn ['stæghɔːn] **N** bois *mpl* de cerf

staghunt ['stæghʌnt], **staghunting** ['stæ[g]ˌhʌntɪŋ] **N** chasse *f* au cerf

staging ['steɪdʒɪŋ] **N 1** *Theat (of play)* mise *f* [en] scène **2** *(scaffolding)* échafaudage *m*; *(shelvin[g])* rayonnage *f* **3** *Astron* largage *m (d'un étage de [fu]sée)*

►► *Mil* ***staging area, staging point*** lieu *m* de ra[s]semblement; *Br* ***staging post*** lieu *m ou* point de ravitaillement; *Aviat* escale *f* aérienne; *H[ist] (for coaches)* relais *m* (de diligences)

stagnant ['stægnənt] **ADJ 1** *(water, pond ► st[ill])* stagnant; *(► stale)* croupissant; *(air ► still)* co[n]finé; *(► stale)* qui sent le renfermé **2** *(econom[y], trade, career)* stagnant; *(society)* statique, en st[a]gnation

stagnate [stæg'neɪt] **VI 1** *(water ► be still)* st[a]gner; *(► be stale)* croupir **2** *(economy, trade, ca[r]eer)* stagner; *(person)* croupir; **he stagnated in t[he] same job for years** il a croupi dans le même em[]ploi pendant des années

stagnation [stæg'neɪʃən] **N** stagnation *f*

stagy, Am stagey ['steɪdʒɪ] *(compar* **stagi[er],** *superl* **stagiest***)* **ADJ** théâtral; **she's very s.** elle [a] des manières très théâtrales

staid [steɪd] **ADJ** *(person)* rangé; *(colours)* sobr[e] discret(ète); *(job)* très ordinaire; **a man of [...] habits** un homme rangé; **a s. and simple life** ur[e] vie simple et rangée; **the party was all very s.** [la] soirée fut sans surprises *ou* très banale

staidness ['steɪdnɪs] **N** sobriété *f*

stain [steɪn] **N 1** *(mark, spot)* tache *f*; **coffee/i[nk] stains** taches *fpl* de café/d'encre; **to leave a [s.]** laisser une tache **2** *Fig (on character)* tache *f*; **[it] was a s. on his reputation** cela a entaché sa rép[u]tation **3** *(colour, dye)* teinte *f*, teinture *f*; **a wood [s.]** une teinture pour bois; **oak/mahogany s.** tein[ture] chêne/acajou

VT 1 *(soil, mark)* tacher; **the sink was stained wi[th] rust** l'évier était taché de rouille; **smoking stai[ns] your teeth** le tabac jaunit les dents; *also Fig* **h[is] hands are stained with blood** il a du sang sur l[es] mains **2** *(character, reputation)* tacher, entache[r,] ternir **3** *(colour, dye ► wood)* teindre; *(► glass, c[ells], specimen)* colorer

VI 1 *(mark ► wine, oil etc)* tacher **2** *(becom[e] marked ► cloth)* se tacher; **silk stains easily** la so[ie] se tache facilement *ou* est salissante

►► ***stain remover*** détachant *m*

stained-glass ADJ

►► ***stained-glass window*** vitrail *m*

staining ['steɪnɪŋ] **N** *(of wood)* teinture *f*

stainless ['steɪnlɪs] **ADJ 1** *(rust-resistant)* inox[y]dable **2** *Fig* sans tache, pur; **a s. reputation** ur[e] réputation sans tache

▸ *stainless steel* N acier *m* inoxydable, Inox® *m* OMP en acier inoxydable, en Inox®

air [steə(r)] **N 1** *(step)* marche *f*; **the bottom s.** la remière marche **2** *(staircase)* escalier *m*

stairs NPL *(stairway)* escalier *m*, escaliers *mpl*; **slipped on the stairs** j'ai glissé dans l'escalier; **to un up/down the stairs** monter/descendre les es-aliers en courant; **at the top of the stairs** en aut de l'escalier; **at the bottom** *or* **the foot of 1e stairs** en bas *ou* au pied de l'escalier; **we assed on the stairs** on s'est croisés dans les es-aliers; *Br* **above/below stairs** chez les patrons/ ›s domestiques

▸ *stair carpet* tapis *m* d'escalier

aircase ['steəkeɪs] N escalier *m*

airway ['steəweɪ] N escalier *m*

airwell ['steəwel] N cage *f* d'escalier

ake [steɪk] **N 1** *(post, pole)* pieu *m*; *(in surveying)* iquet *m*, jalon *m*; *(for plant)* tuteur *m*; *(for vine)* chalas *m*; *(for tethering animal, for tent)* piquet *i*; *(for execution)* poteau *m*; **to die** *or* **to be burned t the s.** mourir sur le bûcher; **she went to the s. or her beliefs** ses convictions l'ont menée au ûcher; *Am* **to (pull) up stakes** *(leave place, job)* aire ses valises; *(leave one's home)* déménager

2 *(in gambling)* enjeu *m*, mise *f*; **to lose one's s.** erdre sa mise; **the stakes are too high for me** enjeu est trop important pour moi; *also Fig* **to lay for high stakes** jouer gros jeu; **to raise the takes** augmenter la mise; *Fig* faire monter les nchères

3 *(interest, share)* intérêt *m*, part *f*; *(investment)* ıvestissement *m*, investissements *mpl*; *(share-olding)* participation *f*; **she has a 10% s. in the ompany** elle a une participation de 10% dans ı société, elle détient 10% du capital de la so-iété; **the company has a big s. in nuclear energy** ı société a misé gros sur *ou* a fait de gros inves-ssements dans le nucléaire; **we all have a s. in he education of the young** l'éducation des jeu-es nous concerne tous

4 *Am (savings)* (petit) pécule *m*, bas *m* de laine

VT 1 *(bet ▸ sum of money, valuables)* jouer, miser; *ig (▸ reputation)* jouer, risquer; **he staked $10 on irdy** il a joué *ou* misé *ou* mis 10 dollars sur Birdy; **e had staked everything** *or* **his all on getting the ›b** il avait tout misé sur l'acceptation de sa can-idature; **I'd s. my all** *or* **my life on it** j'en mettrais a main au feu

2 *Am (aid financially)* financer; **he is staking the ewspaper for half a million dollars** il investit un emi-million de dollars dans le journal; *Fam* **an you s. me for a new suit?** est-ce que tu peux ı'avancer de quoi m'acheter un nouveau cos-ume□?

3 *(fasten ▸ boat, animal)* attacher à un piquet; *▸ tent)* attacher avec des piquets; *(▸ plant)* tu-eurer; *(▸ vine)* échalasser

4 *(mark out ▸ piece of land)* jalonner, piqueter; *in surveying ▸ line, road)* jalonner; **to s. one's laim to a territory** revendiquer un territoire *(en › délimitant avec des piquets)*; **she has staked her laim to a place in the history of our country** elle ıérite une place d'honneur dans l'histoire de otre pays

at stake ADJ **to be at s.** être en jeu; **what** *or* **how nuch is at s.?** quels sont les enjeux?, qu'est-ce ui est en jeu?; **our honour is at s.** il y va de notre onneur, notre honneur est en jeu; **there are ves at s.!** il y a des vies en jeu!; **she has a lot at s.** lle joue gros jeu, elle risque gros

stakes NPL *(horse race)* course *f* de chevaux; *orize)* prix *m*; *Horseracing* **the Bingham Stakes** le 'rix de Bingham; *Fig* **she hasn't got much going or her in the beauty/personality stakes** elle n'est ›as particulièrement gâtée physiquement/ ôté caractère

stake off VT SEP = **stake out**

stake out VT SEP **1** *(delimit ▸ area, piece of land)* élimiter (avec des piquets); *(▸ boundary, line)* ıarquer, jalonner; *Fig (▸ sphere of influence)* dé-inir; *(▸ market)* se tailler; *(▸ job, research field)* 'approprier **2** *(keep watch on)* mettre sous sur-eillance, surveiller; **they've got the house taked out** ils surveillent la maison

takeholder ['steɪk,həʊldə(r)] **N** *(for bets)* dépo-itaire *mf* des enjeux; *(for property)* dépositaire *mf* d'enjeux; *(in enterprise, business)* partie *f* pre-nante

▸▸ *stakeholder pension* = système de retraite ac-cessible aux salariés (notamment ceux qui ont de faibles revenus) ne bénéficiant pas d'une re-traite complémentaire; *stakeholder society* = terme popularisé par Tony Blair, qui désigne un type de société où chaque citoyen a un rôle à jouer car il y va de son propre intérêt

stakeout ['steɪkaʊt] **N** *Am (activity)* surveillance *f*; *(place)* locaux *mpl* sous surveillance; **to be on s.** effectuer une surveillance

staking ['steɪkɪŋ] **N 1** *(marking off ▸ of piece of land)* jalonnement *m*, piquetage *m* **2** *(support ▸ of plants)* tuteurage *m*; *(▸ of vine)* échalassage *m*

stalactite ['stæləktaɪt] N stalactite *f*

stalagmite ['stæləgmaɪt] N stalagmite *f*

stale [steɪl] **ADJ 1** *(bread, cake)* rassis, sec (sè-che); *(chocolate, cigarette)* vieux (vieille); *(cheese ▸ hard)* desséché; *(▸ mouldy)* moisi; *(fizzy drink)* éventé, plat; *(air ▸ foul)* vicié; *(▸ confined)* con-finé; **the car smelt of s. cigarette smoke** la voiture sentait le tabac froid; **s. breath** haleine *f* fétide; **to go s.** *(bread, cake)* (se) rassir; *(chocolate, cigar-ette)* perdre son goût; *(cheese)* se dessécher; *(fizzy drink)* s'éventer

2 *(idea, plot, joke)* éculé, rebattu; *(discovery, news)* éventé, dépassé; *(pleasure)* émoussé, qui n'a plus de goût; *(beauty)* fané, défraîchi; *Fin (market)* lourd, plat; **his arguments were s. and unconvincing** ses arguments étaient éculés et peu convaincants

3 *(person, relationship)* **he's getting s. in that job** il s'encroûte dans ce poste; **to go s.** *(athlete etc)* se surentraîner; *(actor, musician etc)* perdre son inspiration; **her marriage had gone s.** son bon-heur conjugal s'était fané

4 *Law (warrant)* périmé; *(debt)* impayable

VI *Literary (novelty, place, activity)* perdre son charme

▸▸ *Fin stale cheque* chèque *m* prescrit

stalemate ['steɪlmeɪt] **N 1** *(in chess)* pat *m*; **the game ended in s.** la partie s'est terminée par un pat **2** *(deadlock)* impasse *f*; **the nuclear arms s.** l'impasse de la course aux armements nucléai-res; **the argument ended in (a) s.** la discussion s'est terminée dans une impasse; **the announce-ment broke the s. in the negotiations** l'annonce a fait sortir les négociations de l'impasse

VT *(usu passive) (in chess ▸ opponent)* faire pat à; **Black is stalemated** les Noirs sont pat; *Fig* **the ne-gotiations were stalemated** les négociations étaient dans l'impasse

staleness ['steɪlnɪs] **N** *(of food, air)* manque *m* de fraîcheur; *(of information, joke etc)* manque *m* de nouveauté

Stalinism ['stɑːlɪnɪzəm] N stalinisme *m*

Stalinist ['stɑːlɪnɪst] ADJ stalinien

N stalinien(enne) *m,f*

stalk [stɔːk] **N 1** *Bot (of flower, plant)* tige *f*; *(of cab-bage, cauliflower)* trognon *m*; *(of fruit)* queue *f*; *(of wheat, corn)* chaume *m*; *(of bunch of grapes)* rafle *f*, râpe *f* **2** *Zool* pédoncule *m*; *Fam* **his eyes stood out on stalks** il avait les yeux qui lui sor-taient de la tête **3** *(gen ▸ long object)* tige *f*

VT 1 *(game, fugitive etc)* traquer; *(of private de-tective)* filer; *(of obsessive fan etc)* suivre en per-manence *(de façon obsessionnelle)* **2** *(prowl about in)* rôder dans; **to s. the woods/the bush on foot** *(gen)* battre les bois/la brousse à pied; *Hunt* faire une battue dans les bois/la brousse **3** *Literary (of disease, terror)* régner dans, rôder dans; **hunger stalked the countryside** la faim ré-gnait dans les campagnes

VI 1 *(person)* **she stalked out angrily/in disgust** elle sortit d'un air furieux/dégoûté; **he was stalk-ing up and down the deck** il arpentait le pont **2** *(prowl ▸ tiger, animal)* rôder; *(hunt)* chasser; **a stalking lion** un lion en chasse; *Literary* **famine stalked through the land** la famine régnait dans le pays

stalker ['stɔːkə(r)] **N 1** *(criminal)* = criminel sui-vant sa victime à la trace; *(obsessive fan etc)* = admirateur obsessionnel qui suit une personne en permanence **2** *(hunter)* chasseur *m* à l'appro-che

stalking ['stɔːkɪŋ] **N 1** *(in hunting)* chasse *f* à l'ap-proche **2** *(form of harassment)* = forme de harcè-lement qui consiste à suivre quelqu'un en permanence

▸▸ *stalking horse* *Hunt* cheval *m* d'abri; *Fig (pre-text)* prétexte *m*; *Pol* **we'll use him as a s. horse** on va s'en servir comme d'un candidat bidon

stall [stɔːl] **N 1** *(at market)* étal *m*, éventaire *m*; *(at fair, exhibition)* stand *m*; **I bought some peaches at a fruit s.** j'ai acheté des pêches chez un mar-chand de fruits; *Br* **flower s.** *(on street)* kiosque *m* de fleuriste

2 *(for animal)* stalle *f*; *Horseracing* **(starting) stalls** stalles *fpl* de départ

3 *(cubicle)* cabine *f*

4 *(in church)* stalle *f*

5 *Br Cin & Theat* orchestre *m*, fauteuil *m* d'or-chestre; **the stalls** l'orchestre *m*; **a seat in the stalls** un fauteuil d'orchestre

6 *Am (in parking lot)* emplacement *m (de par-king)*

7 *(for finger)* doigtier *m*

8 *Aviat* décrochage *m*; *Aut* calage *m (du moteur)*; **the aircraft went into a s.** l'avion a décroché

9 *(delaying tactic)* manœuvre *f* dilatoire; *(pre-text)* prétexte *m*

VI 1 *(motor, vehicle, driver)* caler; *(plane)* décro-cher; *(pilot)* faire décrocher son avion **2** *(delay)* **to s. for time** essayer de gagner du temps; **I can s. for another month** je peux essayer de gagner du temps pendant encore un mois; **I think they're stalling on the loan until we make more conces-sions** je crois qu'ils vont retarder le prêt jusqu'à ce que nous leur fassions davantage de conces-sions

VT 1 *(motor, vehicle)* caler; *(plane)* faire décro-cher **2** *(delay ▸ sale, decision)* retarder; *(▸ person)* faire attendre; **try to s. him (off)!** essayez de ga-gner du temps!; **I'll s. her in the lobby while you grab a taxi** je la retiendrai dans le hall le temps que tu sautes dans un taxi; **the project/his career is stalled** le projet/sa carrière est au point mort; **we managed to s. the enemy's advance** nous avons réussi à retarder la progression de l'enne-mi **3** *(animal)* mettre à l'étable

stall-feed **VT** *(pt & pp* **stall-fed** [-fed]) *(cattle)* en-graisser à l'étable

stallholder ['stɔːl,həʊldə(r)] **N** *Br (in market)* marchand(e) *m,f* de *ou* des quatre-saisons; *(in fair)* forain(e) *m,f*; *(in exhibition)* exposant(e) *m,f*

stalling ['stɔːlɪŋ] **N** *(UNCOUNT)* atermoiements *mpl*, manœuvres *fpl* dilatoires

▸▸ *stalling tactic* manœuvre *f* dilatoire

stallion ['stælɪən] **N 1** *(horse)* étalon *m* **2** *Fam (man)* étalon *m*

stalwart ['stɔːlwət] **ADJ** *(person)* robuste; *(citi-zen, fighter)* vaillant, brave; *(work, worker)* exemplaire; **he was a s. supporter of the England team** c'était un supporter inconditionnel de l'équipe d'Angleterre; **they put up a s. defence** ils se sont défendus d'arrache-pied

N fidèle *mf*; **the party stalwarts** les fidèles du par-ti

stamen ['steɪmən] *(pl* **stamens** *or* **stamina** ['stæmɪ-nə]) **N** *Bot* étamine *f*

stamina ['stæmɪnə] **N** *(physical)* résistance *f*, en-durance *f*; *(mental)* force *f* intérieure, résistance *f*; *Sport* **to build up one's s.** développer son endu-rance; **she has more s. than he does** elle est plus résistante que lui

stammer ['stæmə(r)] **VI** *(through fear, excitement)* balbutier, bégayer; *(through speech defect)* bé-gayer, être bègue

VT bredouiller, bégayer; **I managed to s. (out) an apology** j'ai réussi à bredouiller des excuses

N *(through fear, excitement)* balbutiement *m*, bé-gaiement *m*; *(through speech defect)* bégaiement *m*; **to have a s.** bégayer, être bègue

stammerer ['stæmərə(r)] N bègue *mf*

stammering ['stæmərɪŋ] **N** *(through fear, excite-ment)* bégaiement *m*, balbutiement *m*; *(speech defect)* bégaiement *m*

stamp [stæmp] **N 1** *(on letter, document)* timbre *m*; **(postage) s.** timbre *m*, timbre-poste *m*; **fiscal** *or* **revenue s.** timbre *m* fiscal; **television (licence) s.** timbre *m* pour la redevance; *Br* **(national insur-**

ance) s. cotisation *f* de sécurité sociale

2 *(device for marking ▸ rubber)* tampon *m*, timbre *m*; *(▸ for metal)* poinçon *m*; *(▸ for leather)* fer *m*; **signature s.** griffe *f*

3 *(mark, impression ▸ in passport, library book etc)* cachet *m*, tampon *m*; *(▸ on metal)* poinçon *m*; *(▸ on leather)* motif *m*; *(▸ on antique)* estampille *f*; *(postmark)* cachet *m* (d'oblitération de la poste); **he has an Israeli s. in his passport** il a un tampon de la douane israélienne sur son passeport; *Fig* **s. of approval** approbation *f*, aval *m*

4 *(distinctive trait)* marque *f*, empreinte *f*; **a work which bears the s. of genius** une œuvre qui porte l'empreinte du génie; **his story had the s. of authenticity** son histoire semblait authentique; **poverty has left its s. on him** la pauvreté a laissé son empreinte sur lui *ou* l'a marqué de son sceau

5 *(type, ilk, class)* genre *m*, *Pej* acabit *m*; *(calibre)* trempe *f*; **we need more teachers of his s.** nous avons besoin de plus d'enseignants de sa trempe

6 *(noise ▸ of boots)* bruit *m* (de bottes); *(▸ of audience)* trépignement *m*; **"no!" he cried with an angry s. of his foot** "non!", cria-t-il en tapant rageusement du pied

COMP *(collection)* de timbres, de timbres-poste

VT 1 *(envelope, letter)* timbrer, affranchir

2 *(mark ▸ document)* tamponner; **he stamped the firm's name on each document** il a tamponné le nom de la société sur chaque document; **incoming mail is stamped with the date received** la date de réception est tamponnée sur le courrier qui arrive; **the machine stamps the time on your ticket** la machine marque *ou* poinçonne l'heure sur votre ticket; **it's stamped "fragile"** c'est marqué "fragile"

3 *(imprint ▸ leather, metal)* estamper; **the belt has a stamped design** la ceinture porte un motif estampé; **a design is stamped on the butter** un dessin est imprimé dans le beurre

4 *(affect, mark ▸ society, person)* marquer; **as editor she stamped her personality on the magazine** comme rédactrice en chef, elle a marqué la revue du sceau de sa personnalité

5 *(characterize, brand)* étiqueter; **recent events have stamped the president as indecisive** le président a été taxé d'indécision au vu des derniers événements; **her actions stamped her as a pacifist in the eyes of the public** son comportement lui a valu une réputation de pacifiste

6 *(foot)* **she stamped her foot in anger** furieuse, elle tapa du pied; **the audience were stamping their feet and booing** la salle trépignait et sifflait; **they were stamping their feet to keep warm** ils sautillaient sur place pour se réchauffer; **he stamped the snow off his boots** il a tapé du pied pour enlever la neige de ses bottes

VI 1 *(in one place ▸ person)* taper du pied; *(▸ audience)* trépigner; *(▸ horse)* piaffer **2** *(walk)* **to s. in/out** *(noisily)* entrer/sortir bruyamment; *(angrily)* entrer/sortir en colère; **he stamped up the stairs** il monta l'escalier d'un pas lourd; **they were stamping about** *or* **around to keep warm** ils sautillaient sur place pour se réchauffer

▸▸ *stamp album* album *m* de timbres *ou* de timbres-poste; ***stamp book*** *(of postage stamps)* carnet *m* de timbres *ou* de timbres-poste; *(for trading stamps)* carnet *m* pour coller les vignettes-épargne; ***stamp collecting*** philatélie *f*; ***stamp collector*** collectionneur(euse) *m,f* de timbres *ou* de timbres-poste, philatéliste *mf*; *Law* ***stamp duty*** droit *m* de timbre, timbre *m* fiscal; ***stamp hinge*** charnière *f*; ***stamp machine*** distributeur *m* automatique de timbres *ou* de timbres-poste

▸stamp on VT INSEP 1 *(step on ▸ cockroach, worm)* écraser (avec le talon); **I stamped on his fingers** je lui ai marché sur les doigts; **he stamped on the rotten plank and it broke** il a tapé du pied sur la planche pourrie et elle s'est cassée **2** *Fig (rebellion)* écraser; *(dissent, protest)* étouffer; *(proposal)* repousser

▸stamp out VT SEP 1 *(fire)* éteindre avec les pieds *ou* en piétinant **2** *(end ▸ disease, crime, corruption, abuse)* éradiquer; *(▸ strike, movement, rebellion)* réprimer; *(▸ dissent, protest)* étouffer **3** *(hole)* découper (à l'emporte-pièce); *(medal)* frapper; *(pattern)* estamper

stamped [stæmpt] **ADJ** *(letter, envelope)* timbré; **send a s. addressed envelope** envoyez une enveloppe timbrée à votre adresse

stampede [stæm'pi:d] **N 1** *(of animals)* fuite *f*, débandade *f* **2** *(of people ▸ flight)* sauve-qui-peut *m inv*, débandade *f*; *(▸ rush)* ruée *f*; **several people were injured in the s.** plusieurs personnes ont été blessées dans la panique; **there was a s. for seats** il y a eu une ruée vers *ou* sur les sièges; **there's been a s. to buy up the share issue** les acheteurs se sont précipités *ou* se sont jetés sur la souscription

VI *(flee)* s'enfuir (pris d'affolement); *(rush)* se ruer, se précipiter; **the cattle stampeded across the river** pris d'affolement, le bétail a traversé la rivière; **shoppers stampeded for the sales counters** les clients se sont rués *ou* se sont précipités vers les rayons des soldes; **the children came stampeding along the corridor** les enfants se sont rués dans le couloir

VT 1 *(animals)* faire fuir; *(crowd)* semer la panique dans **2** *(pressurize)* forcer la main à; **to s. a nation into war** précipiter un peuple dans la guerre; **to s. sb into doing sth** presser qn de faire qch, bousculer qn pour qu'il fasse qch; **I don't want to s. you into (making) a decision** je ne veux pas te bousculer dans ta décision; **don't let yourself be stampeded into anything** ne vous laissez pas forcer la main

stamping ['stæmpɪŋ] **N 1** *(of letters, parcels)* affranchissement *m*, timbrage *m* **2** *(in metalwork)* estampage *m*, étampage *m*; *(item)* pièce *f* estampée **3** *(with feet)* piétinement *m*, trépignement *m*

▸▸ *Fam* ***stamping ground*** lieu *m* favori; **this was one of my old s. grounds** j'y allais tout le temps; ***stamping out*** *(of disease, crime, corruption, abuse)* éradication *f*; *(of strike, movement, rebellion)* répression *f*; *(of dissent, protest)* étouffement *m*; ***stamping press*** estampeuse *f*

stance [stæns] **N 1** *(physical posture)* posture *f*; **she altered her s. slightly** elle changea légèrement de position; **he took up a boxer's s.** il adopta la position d'un boxeur; **he took up his usual s. in front of the fire** il s'est planté devant le feu à sa place habituelle; *Sport* **widen your s.** écartez les jambes **2** *(attitude)* position *f*; **to adopt** *or* **to take a tough s. on sth** adopter *ou* prendre une position ferme sur qch

stanch [stɑ:ntʃ] *Am* = **staunch VT**

stanchion ['stænʃən] **N 1** *(post)* étai *m*, étançon *m*; *(in window)* montant *m* **2** *(for cow)* attache *f*

STAND [stænd]

N	
• stand **1**	• étal **1**
• kiosque **1**	• support **2**
• plate-forme **3**	• tribune **3, 4**
• barre **6**	• position **7**
• résistance **8**	
VT	
• mettre **1**	• poser **1**
• supporter **2–4**	
VI	
• se lever **1**	• être debout **2, 3**
• être **2, 5, 6**	• se tenir **2**
• reposer **4, 7**	• se trouver **5**
• rester **7**	• rester valable **8**
• mesurer **9**	• se classer **10**
• se présenter **13**	• s'arrêter **14**

(pt & pp **stood** [stʊd]*)*

N 1 *(stall, booth ▸ at exhibition, trade fair)* stand *m*; *(▸ in market)* étal *m*, éventaire *m*; *(kiosk)* kiosque *m*; **a shooting s.** un stand de tir; **newspaper s.** kiosque *m* (à journaux)

2 *(frame, support ▸ gen)* support *m*; *(▸ for lamp, sink)* pied *m*; *(▸ on bicycle, motorbike)* béquille *f*; *(▸ for pipes, guns)* râtelier *m*; *Com (▸ for magazines, sunglasses)* présentoir *m*; *(lectern)* lutrin *m*; **bicycle s.** *(in street)* râtelier *m* à bicyclettes; **plate s.** support *m* à assiette, présentoir *m*

3 *(platform ▸ gen)* plate-forme *f*; *(▸ for speaker)* tribune *f*; *(pulpit)* chaire *f*

4 *(in sports ground)* tribune *f*; **the stands roared** un rugissement s'éleva des tribunes *ou* des gradins

5 *(for taxis)* **(taxi) s.** station *f* de taxis

6 *(in courtroom)* barre *f*; **the first witness took the s.** le premier témoin est venu à la barre
7 *(position, stance)* position *f*; **to take a s. on s**
prendre position sur qch; **what's your s. on t**
issue? quelle est votre position sur la questio
he refuses to take a s. il refuse de prendre po
tion
8 *Mil & Fig (defensive effort)* résistance *f*, opp
sition *f*; **to make a s.** résister; **to make a s. agai**
an abuse s'opposer résolument à un abus; *H*
Custer's last s. la dernière bataille de Custer
9 *(of trees)* bosquet *m*, futaie *f*; *(of crop)* récol
sur pied; **a fine s. of corn** un beau champ de blé
s. of bamboo un massif de bambous
VT 1 *(set, place)* mettre, poser; **he stood the b**
on a chair il a mis le garçon debout sur u
chaise; **she stood her umbrella in the corner** e
a mis son parapluie dans le coin; **to s. sth**
(its) end mettre qch debout; **help me s. the be**
stead against the wall aide-moi à dresser le so
mier *ou* mettre le sommier debout contre le m
2 *(endure, withstand)* supporter; **his he**
couldn't s. the shock son cœur n'a pas résisté
ou n'a pas supporté le choc; **it will s. high te**
peratures without cracking cela peut résiste
ou supporter des températures élevées sans
fissurer; **how much weight can the bridge s.?** qu
poids le pont peut-il supporter?; **wool carpet**
can s. a lot of hard wear les moquettes en lai
sont très résistantes; **he certainly doesn't s. co**
parison with Bogart il n'est absolument pas po
sible de le comparer avec Bogart; **their figur**
don't s. close inspection leurs chiffres ne résiste
pas à un examen sérieux
3 *(put up with, bear ▸ toothache, cold)* support
(▸ behaviour) supporter, tolérer; **I can't s. it a**
longer! je n'en peux plus!; **how can you s. worki**
with him? comment est-ce que vous faites po
ou comment arrivez-vous à travailler avec lu
I've had as much as I can s. of your griping! j'en
assez de tes jérémiades!; **if there's one thin**
can't s., it's hypocrisy s'il y a quelque chose q
je ne supporte pas, c'est bien l'hypocrisie; **I ca**
s. (the sight of) him! je ne peux pas le supporte
je ne peux pas le voir en peinture!; **she can't**
Wagner/smokers elle ne peut pas suppor
Wagner/les fumeurs; **he can't s. flying** il déte
prendre l'avion
4 *Fam (do with, need)* supporter□, avoir beso
de□; **oil company profits could certainly s. a c**
une diminution de leurs bénéfices ne ferait a
cun mal aux compagnies pétrolières; **he could**
a bath! un bain ne lui ferait pas de mal!; *Am* **cou**
I s. a drink! je prendrais bien un petit verre!
5 *(perform duty of)* remplir la fonction de; **to**
witness for sb *(at marriage)* être le témoin de q
6 *Fam (treat to)* **to s. sb a meal** payer un repa
qn; *Br* **I'll s. you a drink,** *Am* **I'll s. you to a drink**
t'offre un verre
7 *(idiom)* **to s. a chance (of doing sth)** avoir
bonnes chances (de faire qch); **you don't s.**
chance! vous n'avez pas la moindre chanc
the plans s. little chance of being approved les p
jets ont peu de chances d'être approuvés
VI 1 *(rise to one's feet)* se lever, se mettre debo
he refused to s. for the national anthem il a refu
de se lever pendant l'hymne national
2 *(be on one's feet)* être debout, se tenir debo
(in a specified location, posture) être, se tenir; **I'**
been standing all day je suis resté debout toute
journée; **I had to s. all the way** j'ai dû voyager d
bout pendant tout le trajet; **she was so tired s**
could hardly s. elle était si fatiguée qu'elle av
du mal à tenir debout *ou* sur ses jambes; **I do**
mind standing ça ne me gêne pas de rester d
bout; **don't s. near the edge** ne restez pas pr
du bord; **don't just s. there, do something!** ne re
tez pas là à ne rien faire!; **s. clear!** écartez-vou
I saw her standing at the window je l'ai vue (d
bout) à la fenêtre; **a man stood in the doorw**
un homme se tenait à la porte; **do you see th**
man standing over there? vous voyez cet hom
là-bas?; **where should I s.? – beside Yvonne**
dois-je me mettre? – à côté d'Yvonne; **I'll**
standing outside the theatre j'attendrai devant
théâtre; **small groups of men stood talking**
street corners des hommes discutaient par p
tits groupes au coin des rues; **he was standi**
at the bar il était debout au comptoir; **is there**
chair I can s. on? y a-t-il une chaise sur laquelle

puisse monter?; **they were standing a little way off** ils se tenaient un peu à l'écart; **excuse me, you're standing on my foot** excusez-moi, vous me marchez sur le pied; *Am* **to s. in line** faire la queue; *Sch* **s. in the corner!** au coin!; **to s. upright** *or* **erect** se tenir droit; **he was so nervous he couldn't s. still** il était si nerveux qu'il ne tenait pas en place; **I stood perfectly still, hoping they wouldn't see me** je me suis figé sur place en espérant qu'ils ne me verraient pas; **s. still!** ne bougez pas!, ne bougez plus!; **s. with your feet apart** écartez les pieds; **the heron was standing on one leg** le héron se tenait debout sur une patte; **to s. on tiptoe** se tenir sur la pointe des pieds; **s. and deliver!** la bourse ou la vie!; *Fig* **to s. on one's own two feet** se débrouiller tout seul; *Fig* **he left the others standing** *(gen)* il était de loin le meilleur; *(in race)* il a laissé les autres sur place

3 *(be upright ▸ post, target etc)* être debout; **not a stone (of the building) was left standing** le bâtiment était complètement détruit; **the house is still standing** la maison tient toujours debout; **the aqueduct has stood for centuries** l'aqueduc est là depuis des siècles; **the wheat stood high** les blés étaient hauts

4 *(be supported, be mounted)* reposer; **the coffin stood on trestles** le cercueil reposait sur des tréteaux; **the house stands on solid foundations** la maison repose *ou* est bâtie sur des fondations solides

5 *(be located ▸ building, tree, statue)* se trouver; *(▸ clock, vase, lamp)* être, être posé; **this is where the city gates once stood** c'est ici qu'autrefois se dressaient les portes de la ville; **the piano stood in the centre of the room** le piano était au centre *ou* occupait le centre de la pièce; **the bottles stood in rows of five** les bouteilles étaient disposées en rangées de cinq; **do you see the lorry standing next to my car?** vous voyez le camion qui est à côté de ma voiture?; **a wardrobe stood against one wall** il y avait une armoire contre un mur

6 *(indicating current state of affairs, situation)* être; **how do things s.?** où en est la situation?; **how do we s.?** *(in work etc)* où en sommes-nous?; *(financially)* où en sont nos comptes?; **I'd like to know where I s. with you** j'aimerais savoir où en sont les choses entre nous; **I don't know where I s.** j'ignore quelle est ma situation *ou* ma position; **you never know how** *or* **where you s. with her** on ne sait jamais sur quel pied danser avec elle; **as things s., as matters s.** telles que les choses se présentent; **he's dissatisfied with the contract as it stands** il n'est pas satisfait du contrat tel qu'il a été rédigé; **just print the text as it stands** imprimez le texte tel quel; **he stands accused of rape** il est accusé de viol; **she stands alone in advocating this approach** elle est la seule à préconiser cette approche; **I s. corrected** je reconnais m'être trompé *ou* mon erreur; **the doors stood wide open** les portes étaient grandes ouvertes; **I've got a taxi standing ready** j'ai un taxi qui attend; **the police are standing ready to intervene** la police se tient prête à intervenir; **the party stands united behind him** le parti est uni derrière lui; **to s. at** *(gauge, barometer)* indiquer; *(score)* être de; *(unemployment)* avoir atteint; **their turnover now stands at three million pounds** leur chiffre d'affaires atteint désormais les trois millions de livres; **the exchange rate stands at 2 dollars to the pound** le taux de change est de 2 dollars pour une livre; **we're standing right behind you** nous sommes avec vous; **nothing stood between her and victory** rien ne pouvait désormais l'empêcher de gagner; **it's the only thing standing between us and financial disaster** c'est la seule chose qui nous empêche de sombrer dans un désastre financier; **to s. in need of...** avoir besoin de...; **he stands in danger of losing his job** il risque de perdre son emploi; **I stood lost in admiration** j'en suis resté béat d'admiration; **to s. in sb's way** bloquer le passage à qn; *Fig* **don't s. in my way!** n'essaie pas de m'en empêcher!; **nothing stands in our way now** maintenant, la voie est libre; **if you want to leave school I'm not going to s. in your way** si tu veux quitter l'école, je ne m'y opposerai pas; **it's his lack of experience that stands in his way** c'est son manque d'expérience qui le handicape; **her pride is the only thing standing in the way of their reconciliation** son orgueil est le seul obstacle à leur réconciliation

7 *(remain)* rester; *(be left undisturbed ▸ marinade, dough)* reposer; *(▸ tea)* infuser; **the machines stood idle** les machines étaient arrêtées; **the houses stood empty awaiting demolition** les maisons, vidées de leurs occupants, attendaient d'être démolies; **time stood still** le temps semblait s'être arrêté; **the car has been standing in the garage for a year** ça fait un an que la voiture n'a pas bougé du garage; **I've decided to let my flight reservation s.** j'ai décidé de ne pas changer ma réservation d'avion; **the champion stands unbeaten** le champion reste invaincu; **his theory stood unchallenged for a decade** pendant dix ans, personne n'a remis en cause sa théorie; **the government will s. or fall on the outcome of this vote** le maintien ou la chute du gouvernement dépend du résultat de ce vote; **united we s., divided we fall** l'union fait la force

8 *(be valid, effective ▸ offer, law, verdict)* rester valable; *(▸ decision)* rester inchangé; **my invitation still stands** vous êtes toujours invité; **even with this new plan, our objection still stands** ce nouveau projet ne remet pas en cause notre objection première; **the bet stands** le pari tient; **what you said last week, does that still s.?** et ce que tu as dit la semaine dernière, ça tient toujours?

9 *(measure ▸ person, tree)* mesurer; **she stands 5 feet in her stocking feet** elle mesure moins de 1,50 m pieds nus; **the building stands ten storeys high** l'immeuble compte dix étages

10 *(rank)* se classer, compter; *Am* **she stands first/last in her class** elle est la première/la dernière de sa classe; **I know she stands high in your opinion** je sais que tu as une très bonne opinion d'elle; **for price and quality, it stands high on my list** en ce qui concerne le prix et la qualité, je le range *ou* le compte parmi les meilleurs

11 *(on issue)* **how** *or* **where does he s. on the nuclear issue?** quelle est sa position *ou* son point de vue sur la question du nucléaire?; **you ought to tell them where you s.** vous devriez leur faire part de votre position

12 *(be likely)* **to s. to lose** risquer de perdre; **to s. to win** avoir des chances de gagner; **they s. to make a huge profit on the deal** ils ont des chances de faire un bénéfice énorme dans cette affaire; **no one stands to gain from a quarrel like this** personne n'a rien à gagner d'une telle querelle

13 *Br (run in election)* se présenter, être candidat; **she stood for Waltham** elle a été candidate à la circonscription de Waltham; **will he s. for re-election?** va-t-il se représenter aux élections?; **she's standing as an independent** elle se présente en tant que candidate indépendante

14 *Am (stop)* s'arrêter *(pour un court instant)*

15 *Am (pay)* payer la tournée; **you're standing** c'est ta tournée

▸stand about, stand around VI rester là; **we stood about** *or* **around waiting for the flight announcement** nous restions là à attendre que le vol soit annoncé; **the prisoners stood about** *or* **around in small groups** les prisonniers se tenaient par petits groupes; **after Mass, the men s. about** *or* **around in the square** après la messe, les hommes s'attardent sur la place; **I can't afford to pay people to s. around all day doing nothing** je n'ai pas les moyens de payer les gens à ne rien faire; **I'm not just going to s. about waiting for you to make up your mind!** je n'ai pas l'intention de rester là à attendre que tu te décides!

▸stand aside VI *(move aside)* s'écarter; **he politely stood aside to let us pass** il s'écarta *ou* s'effaça poliment pour nous laisser passer; *Fig* **to s. aside in favour of sb** *(gen)* laisser la voie libre à qn; *Pol* se désister en faveur de qn

▸stand back VI **1** *(move back)* reculer, s'écarter; **s. back from the doors!** écartez-vous des portes!; **she stood back to look at herself in the mirror** elle recula pour se regarder dans la glace; **the painting is better if you s. back from it** le tableau est mieux si vous prenez du recul **2** *(be set back)* être en retrait *ou* à l'écart; **the house stands back from the road** la maison est en retrait (de la route) **3** *(take mental distance)* prendre du recul

▸stand by VT INSEP **1** *(support ▸ person)* soutenir; **I'll s. by you through thick and thin** je te soutiendrai *ou* je resterai à tes côtés quoi qu'il arrive **2** *(adhere to ▸ promise, word)* tenir; *(▸ decision, offer)* s'en tenir à; **to s. by an agreement** respecter un accord; **I s. by what I said/my original analysis of the situation** je m'en tiens à ce que j'ai dit/ma première analyse de la situation

VI **1** *(not intervene)* rester là (sans rien faire *ou* sans intervenir); **how could you just s. by and watch them mistreat that poor dog?** comment as-tu pu rester là à les regarder maltraiter ce pauvre chien (sans intervenir)?; **I stood by helplessly while they searched the room** je restais là, impuissant, pendant qu'ils fouillaient la pièce **2** *(be ready ▸ person)* être *ou* se tenir prêt; *(▸ vehicle)* être prêt; *(▸ army, embassy)* être en état d'alerte; **the police were standing by to disperse the crowd** la police se tenait prête à disperser la foule; **we have an oxygen machine standing by** nous avons une machine à oxygène prête en cas d'urgence; **s. by!** attention!; *Naut* paré!, attention!; *Aviat* **s. by for takeoff** préparez-vous pour le décollage; *Rad* **s. by to receive** prenez l'écoute; *Mil* **standing by for orders!** à vos ordres!

▸stand down VI **1** *Br Pol (withdraw)* se désister; *(resign)* démissionner; **will he s. down in favour of a younger candidate?** va-t-il se désister en faveur d'un candidat plus jeune? **2** *(leave witness box)* quitter la barre; **you may s. down, Mr Simms** vous pouvez quitter la barre, M. Simms **3** *Mil (troops)* être déconsigné *(en fin d'alerte)*; **s. down!** *(after drill)* rompez (les rangs)!

VT SEP *(workers)* licencier

▸stand for VT INSEP **1** *(represent)* représenter; **what does DNA s. for?** que veut dire l'abréviation ADN?; **the R stands for Ryan** le R signifie Ryan; **the dove stands for peace** la colombe symbolise la paix; **we want our name to s. for quality and efficiency** nous voulons que notre nom soit synonyme de qualité et d'efficacité; **she supports the values and ideas the party once stood for** elle soutient les valeurs et les idées qui furent autrefois celles du parti; **I detest everything that they s. for!** je déteste tout ce qu'ils représentent! **2** *(tolerate)* tolérer, supporter; *(allow)* permettre; **I'm not going to s. for it!** je ne le tolérerai *ou* permettrai pas!

▸stand in VI assurer le remplacement; **to s. in for sb** remplacer qn; *Cin* doubler qn

▸stand off VT SEP *Br (workers)* mettre en chômage technique

VT INSEP *Naut (coast, island)* croiser au large de

VI **1** *(move away)* s'écarter **2** *Naut (take up position)* croiser; *(sail away)* mettre le cap au large

▸stand out VI **1** *(protrude ▸ vein)* saillir; *(▸ ledge)* faire saillie, avancer; **the veins in his neck stood out** les veines de son cou saillaient *ou* étaient gonflées **2** *(be clearly visible ▸ colour, typeface)* ressortir, se détacher; *(▸ in silhouette)* se découper; **the pink stands out against the green background** le rose ressort *ou* se détache sur le fond vert; **the masts stood out against the sky** les mâts se découpaient *ou* se dessinaient contre le ciel; **the name on the truck stood out clearly** le nom sur le camion était bien visible; **she stands out in a crowd** on la remarque dans la foule; *Fig* **I don't like to s. out in a crowd** je n'aime pas me singulariser; **this one book stands out from all his others** ce livre-ci surclasse tous ses autres livres; **there is no one issue which stands out as being more important than the others** il n'y a pas une question qui soit plus importante que les autres; **the qualities that s. out in his work** les qualités marquantes de son œuvre; **she stands out above all the rest** elle surpasse *ou* surclasse tous les autres; **the day stands out in my memory** cette journée est marquée d'une pierre blanche dans ma mémoire; *Fam* **that stands out a mile!** *(is very obvious)* ça se voit comme le nez au milieu de la figure! **3** *(resist, hold out)* tenir bon, tenir, résister; **they won't be able to s. out for long** ils ne pourront pas tenir *ou* résister longtemps; **to s. out against** *(attack, enemy)* résister à; *(change, tax increase)* s'opposer avec détermination à; **to s. out for sth** revendiquer qch

▸stand over VT INSEP *(watch over)* surveiller; **I can't work with someone standing over me** je ne peux pas travailler quand quelqu'un regarde par-dessus mon épaule; **she stood over him until he'd eaten every last bit** elle ne l'a pas lâché avant qu'il ait mangé la dernière miette

VT SEP *Br (postpone)* remettre (à plus tard); **I'd prefer to s. this discussion over until we have more information** je préférerais remettre cette discussion jusqu'à ce que nous disposions de plus amples renseignements

VI *Br* être remis (à plus tard); **we have two items standing over from the last meeting** il nous reste deux points à régler depuis la dernière réunion

▸**stand to** *Mil* **VT SEP** mettre en état d'alerte

VI se mettre en état d'alerte; **s. to!** à vos postes!

▸**stand together VI** être *ou* rester solidaire

▸**stand up VT SEP 1** *(set upright ▸ chair, bottle)* mettre debout; **they stood the prisoner up against a tree** ils ont adossé le prisonnier à un arbre; **s. the ladder up against the wall** mettez *ou* appuyez l'échelle contre le mur; **to s. a child up (again)** (re) mettre un enfant sur ses pieds **2** *Fam (fail to meet)* poser un lapin à; **I was stood up twice in a row** on m'a posé un lapin deux fois de suite

VI 1 *(rise to one's feet)* se lever, se mettre debout; **she stood up to offer me her seat** elle se leva pour m'offrir sa place; **s. up!** levez-vous!, debout!; *Fig* **to s. up and be counted** avoir le courage de ses opinions

2 *(be upright)* être debout; **I can't get the candle to s. up straight** je n'arrive pas à faire tenir la bougie droite

3 *(last)* tenir, résister; **how is that repair job standing up?** est-ce que cette réparation tient toujours?

4 *(be valid ▸ argument, claim)* être valable, tenir debout; **his evidence won't s. up in court** son témoignage ne sera pas valable en justice

▸**stand up for VT INSEP** défendre; **to s. up for oneself** se défendre

▸**stand up to VT INSEP to s. up to sth** résister à qch; **to s. up to sb** tenir tête à *ou* faire face à qn; **he's too weak to s. up to her** il est trop faible pour lui tenir tête; **she had a hard time standing up to their criticism** ça ne lui a pas été facile de faire face à leurs critiques; **it won't s. up to that sort of treatment** ça ne résistera pas à ce genre de traitement

---

stand-alone *Comput* **ADJ** *(system)* autonome; **it has s. capability** ça peut fonctionner de façon autonome

N poste *m* autonome

▸▸ ***stand-alone computer*** ordinateur *m* autonome

standard ['stændəd] **N 1** *(level of quality)* niveau *m*; *(criterion)* critère *m*; **to have high/low standards** *(person)* être exigeant/ne pas être exigeant; *(school)* exiger un bon niveau/ne pas exiger un bon niveau; **he sets high standards for himself** il est très exigeant avec lui-même; **a high s. of playing/academic achievement** un niveau de jeu/de réussite scolaire élevé; **your work isn't up to s.** *or* **is below s.** votre travail laisse à désirer; **to be up to/below s.** être du/en dessous du niveau requis; **most of the goods are** *or* **come up to s.** la plupart des marchandises sont de qualité satisfaisante; **she's an Olympic s. swimmer** c'est une nageuse de niveau olympique; **it's a difficult task by any s.** *or* **by anybody's standards** c'est indiscutablement une tâche difficile; **we apply the same standards to all candidates** nous jugeons tous les candidats selon les mêmes critères; **we don't have the same aesthetic standards** nous n'avons pas les mêmes valeurs esthétiques

2 *(official specification, norm)* norme *f*; **to set quality standards for a product** fixer des normes de qualité pour un produit; **to comply with** *or* **to meet government standards** être conforme aux normes établies par le gouvernement; **their salaries are low by European standards** leurs salaires sont bas par rapport aux salaires européens; **high safety standards** des règles de sécurité très strictes; **standards and practices** normes et usages

3 *(moral principle)* principe *m*; **I won't do it! I have my standards!** je ne le ferai pas! j'ai des principes!; **to have high moral standards** avoir de grands principes moraux

4 *(for measures, currency ▸ model)* étalon *m*; *(in coins ▸ proportion)* titre *m*

5 *(tune)* classique *m*; **a jazz s.** un classique du jazz, un standard

6 *Am (car)* **I can't drive a s.** je ne sais conduire que les voitures à boîte de vitesse automatique

7 *(flag)* étendard *m*; *(of sovereign, noble)* bannière *f*; *Naut* pavillon *m*; *Fig* **under the s. of Liberty** sous l'étendard de la liberté

8 *(support ▸ pole)* poteau *m*; (▸ *for flag)* mât *m*; (▸ *for lamp)* pied *m*; (▸ *for power-line)* pylône *m*

9 *Br (lamp)* lampadaire *m* (de salon)

10 *Agr & Hort (fruit tree)* haute-tige *f*

11 *Br Old-fashioned (class)* classe *f*

ADJ 1 *(ordinary, regular ▸ gen)* normal; (▸ *model, size)* standard; **catalytic converters are now s. features** les pots catalytiques sont désormais la norme; **headrests are s.** *or* **are fitted as s.** les appuis-têtes sont montés en série; **the s. return fare is $500** l'aller-retour au tarif normal coûte 500 dollars; **what's the s. tip?** que laisse-t-on normalement comme pourboire?; **there's a s. procedure for reporting accidents** il y a une procédure bien établie pour signaler les accidents; **it was just a s. hotel room** c'était une chambre d'hôtel ordinaire; **the cooking is fairly s.** la cuisine n'a rien de sensationnel; **she has a s. speech for such occasions** elle a un discours tout prêt pour ce genre d'occasions; **one of his s. jokes** une de ses plaisanteries habituelles

2 *(measure ▸ metre, kilogramme etc)* étalon *(inv)*

3 *(text, work)* classique, de base; **the s. works in English poetry** les ouvrages classiques de la poésie anglaise; **it's the s. work on the Reformation** c'est l'ouvrage de base sur la Réforme

4 *Ling (pronunciation, spelling etc)* standard

5 *Agr & Hort (fruit tree, shrub)* à haute tige

▸▸ ***standard bearer*** *(of cause)* porte-drapeau *m*; *(of political party)* chef *m* de file; *(of flag)* porte-étendard *m*; ***standard deviation*** *(in statistics)* écart-type *m*; ***standard document*** document *m* type; ***standard English*** l'anglais *m* standard; ***standard error*** *(in statistics)* écart-type *m*; *Rail* ***standard gauge*** voie *f* normale, écartement *m* normal; *Am Aut* ***standard gear shift*** changement *m* de vitesse manuel; *Scot Sch* ***Standard grade*** = premier examen de fin de scolarité en Écosse, équivalent du GCSE anglais; *Br* ***standard lamp*** lampadaire *m* (de salon); *Econ* ***standard of living*** niveau *m* de vie; ***standard operating procedure*** = marche à suivre normale; ***standard practice*** pratique *f* courante; *Law* ***standard of proof*** standard *m* de preuve; ***standard rate*** *(of tax)* taux *m* standard; *Bot* ***standard rose*** rose *f* tige; ***standard time*** heure *f* légale

standardization, -isation [ˌstændədaɪ'zeɪʃən] **N 1** *(gen)* standardisation *f*; *(of dimensions, terms etc)* normalisation *f* **2** *Tech (verification)* étalonnage *m*

standardize, -ise ['stændədaɪz] **VT 1** *(gen)* standardiser; *(dimensions, products, terms)* normaliser **2** *Tech (verify)* étalonner

▸▸ ***standardized parts*** pièces *fpl* standardisées *ou* standard

standby ['stændbaɪ] *(pl* **standbys***)* **ADJ 1** *(equipment, provisions etc)* de réserve; *(generator)* de secours; **to be on s. duty** *(doctor)* être de garde *ou* d'astreinte; *(flight personnel, emergency repairman)* être d'astreinte; *(troops, police, firemen)* être prêt à intervenir; **the s. team can take over operations within an hour** l'équipe de secours est prête à prendre le contrôle des opérations en moins d'une heure **2** *Aviat (ticket, fare)* stand-by *(inv)*; *(passenger)* stand-by *(inv)*, en attente

N 1 *(substitute ▸ person)* remplaçant(e) *m,f*; *Theat (understudy)* doublure *f*; **to be on s.** *(doctor)* être de garde *ou* d'astreinte; *(flight personnel, emergency repairman)* être d'astreinte; *(troops, police, firemen)* être prêt à intervenir; **we have a repair crew on s.** nous avons une équipe de dépannage prête à intervenir en cas de besoin; **make sure you have a s.** *(tool, piece of equipment)* vérifiez que vous en avez un/une de secours; *(person)* assurez-vous que vous pouvez vous faire remplacer; **eggs are a great s. in the kitchen** il est toujours bon d'avoir des œufs dans une cuisine; **that story is an old s. of his** cette histoire lui a beaucoup servi **2** *Aviat (system)* stand-by *m inv*; *(passenger)* (passager(ère) *m,f)* stand-by *m inv*; **to be on s.** *(passenger)* être en stand-by *ou* sur la liste d'attente

▸▸ *Aviat* ***standby list*** liste *f* d'attente; *Compu* ***standby mode*** veille *f*; **in s. mode** en veille

standee [stæn'di:] **N** *Am (in theatre)* = spectateu qui n'a pas de place assise; *(in public transport* passager(ère) *m,f* debout

stand-in N *(gen)* remplaçant(e) *m,f*; *Cin (fo lighting check)* doublure *f*; *(stunt person)* casca deur(euse) *m,f*; *Theat (understudy)* doublure *f* **she asked him to go as her s.** elle lui a demandé de la remplacer

ADJ *(gen)* remplaçant; *(office worker)* intéri maire; *(teacher)* suppléant, qui fait des rempla cements; **we'll need s. staff during the summe** nous aurons besoin d'intérimaires pendan l'été; **I can't find a s. speaker for tomorrow's sessio** je ne trouve personne qui puisse remplacer le conférencier prévu pour demain

standing ['stændɪŋ] **ADJ 1** *(upright ▸ position person, object)* debout *(inv)*

2 *(grain, timber)* sur pied

3 *(stagnant ▸ water)* stagnant

4 *(permanent ▸ army, offer etc)* permanent; (▸ *claim)* de longue date; **it's a s. joke with us** c'es une vieille plaisanterie entre nous; **you have a s. invitation** tu peux venir chez moi/nous quanc tu veux

N 1 *(reputation)* réputation *f*; *(status)* standing *m* **a man of your s. needs to be more careful** ur homme de votre standing se doit d'être plus prudent; **an economist of considerable s.** un éco nomiste de grand renom *ou* très réputé; **people of lower/higher social s.** des gens d'une positior sociale moins/plus élevée; **they are a family o some s. in the community** c'est une famille qu jouit d'une certaine position dans la commu nauté; **the scandal has damaged the company's s in the eyes of the public** le scandale a nui à la ré putation de la société auprès du public

2 *(ranking)* rang *m*, place *f*; *Sch & Sport (orderec list)* classement *m*; **her s. in the opinion polls is a its lowest yet** sa cote de popularité dans les son dages est au plus bas; **what's their s. in the league table?** quel est leur classement dans le cham pionnat?

3 *(duration)* durée *f*; **of long s.** de longue date; **o 15 years' s.** *(collaboration, feud)* qui dure depuis 15 ans; *(treaty, account)* qui existe depuis 15 ans; *(friend, member)* depuis 15 ans; **an employee of 10 years' s.** un salarié qui a 10 ans d'ancienneté dans l'entreprise

4 *Am Aut* **no s.** *(sign)* arrêt interdit

▸▸ ***standing charges*** *(on bill)* frais *mpl* d'abonne ment; ***standing committee*** comité *m* permanent *Agr* ***standing crop*** récolte *f* sur pied; *Sport* ***stand ing jump*** saut *m* à pieds joints; *Am* ***standing lamp*** lampadaire *m* (de salon); *Br Banking* ***standing order*** virement *m* automatique; **to pay by s. orde** payer par prélèvement (bancaire) automa tique; **I get paid by s. order** je reçois mon salaire par virement bancaire; *Br Pol* ***standing orders*** rè glement *m* intérieur *(d'une assemblée délibéra tive)*; ***standing ovation*** ovation *f*; **to get a s ovation** se faire ovationner; ***standing places*** pla ces *fpl* debout; ***standing room*** places *fpl* debout **it was s. room only on the train** il n'y avait plus de places assises dans le train; **it was s. room only a the meeting** la salle était pleine à craquer lors de la réunion; *Sport* ***standing start*** départ *m* debout *Aut* départ *m* arrêté; **it reaches 100 mph in 40 sec onds from a s. start** ≃ elle atteint les 160 km/h er 40 secondes départ arrêté; ***standing stone*** pierre *f* levée; *Phys* ***standing wave*** onde *f* stationnaire

standoff ['stændɒf] **N 1** *Pol (inconclusive clash* affrontement *m* indécis; *(deadlock)* impasse *f* **their debate ended in a s.** leur débat n'a rier donné; **the s. over the budget is making Wall Stree nervous** l'impasse dans laquelle se trouve le budget inquiète Wall Street **2** *Br (in rugby)* dem *m* d'ouverture

▸▸ *Br* ***standoff half*** *(in rugby)* demi *m* d'ouverture

standoffish [ˌstænd'ɒfɪʃ] **ADJ** distant, froid

standoffishness [ˌstænd'ɒfɪʃnɪs] **N** raideur *f* réserve *f*

standout ['stændaʊt] **N his article was a real s.** sor article sortait vraiment du lot; **the second book i**

the series is the s. le deuxième tome de la série est celui qui ressort (par rapport aux autres)

standpipe ['stændpaɪp] **N** *(in street ▸ for fire brigade)* bouche *f* d'incendie; *(▸ for public)* point *m* d'alimentation en eau de secours

standpoint ['stændpɔɪnt] **N** point *m* de vue; **try to see the situation from her s.** essayez de voir la situation de son point de vue à elle; **from a late 20th-century s.** dans une perspective de fin de XXème siècle

standstill ['stændstɪl] **N** arrêt *m*; **to come to a s.** *(vehicle, person)* s'immobiliser; *(talks, work etc)* piétiner; **to bring to a s.** *(vehicle, person)* arrêter; *(talks, traffic)* paralyser; **to be at a s.** *(talks, career)* être au point mort; *(traffic)* être paralysé; *(economy)* piétiner, stagner
▸▸ *Fin* ***standstill agreement*** moratoire *m*

stand-up **N** *(comedy)* spectacle *m* comique; **to do s.** faire des spectacles comiques
ADJ 1 *(collar)* droit; *(meal)* (pris) debout; **a s. fight** *(physical)* une bagarre en règle; *(verbal)* une discussion violente **2** *Am Fam (decent)* bien
▸▸ ***stand-up comic, stand-up comedian*** comique *mf (qui se produit seul en scène)*; ***stand-up comedy*** spectacles *mpl* comiques; *Am* ***stand-up counter, stand-up diner*** buvette *f*

stank [stæŋk] *pt of* **stink**

Stanley knife® ['stænlɪ-] **N** cutter *m*

stannic ['stænɪk] **ADJ** *Chem* stannique

stanza ['stænzə] **N 1** *(in poetry)* strophe *f* **2** *Am Sport* période *f*

staphylococcus [ˌstæfɪləʊ'kɒkəs] *(pl* **staphylococci** [-'kɒksaɪ]) **N** staphylocoque *m*

staple ['steɪpəl] **N 1** *(for paper)* agrafe *f*
2 *(for wire)* cavalier *m*, crampillon *m*
3 *(foodstuff)* aliment *m ou* denrée *f* de base; **kitchen** *or* **household staples** provisions *fpl* de base; **staples are being rationed** en ce moment, les produits de première nécessité sont rationnés
4 *Com & Econ (item)* article *m* de base; *(raw material)* matière *f* première
5 *(constituent)* partie *f* intégrante; **divorce cases are a s. of his law practice** son cabinet s'occupe essentiellement de divorces; **sex scandals are a s. of the tabloid press** la presse à sensation se nourrit des scandales sexuels
6 *Tex* fibre *f* artificielle à filer
VT *(paper, upholstery etc)* agrafer; **s. the sheets together** agrafez les feuilles; **posters were stapled on** *or* **onto** *or* **to the walls** des posters étaient agrafés aux murs
ADJ *(food, products)* de base; *(export, crop)* principal; **a s. diet of rice and beans** un régime à base de riz et de haricots; **for young children, milk is the s. diet** pour les jeunes enfants, le lait est l'aliment de base; *Fig* **the s. diet of these TV channels consists of soap operas** les programmes de ces chaînes de télévision sont essentiellement constitués de feuilletons; **their s. commodity is cotton** le coton est leur produit de base; **tanks are a s. feature of conventional warfare** les tanks sont un des éléments de base de la guerre conventionnelle
▸▸ ***staple gun*** agrafeuse *f* (professionnelle); ***staple remover*** arrache-agrafes *m inv*

stapler ['steɪplə(r)] **N** agrafeuse *f* (de bureau)

stapling ['steɪplɪŋ] **N** *(of paper, upholstery)* fixation *f* à l'aide d'agrafes, agrafage *m*

star [stɑː(r)] *(pt & pp* **starred**, *cont* **starring) N 1** *(in sky)* étoile *f*; **to sleep (out) under the stars** dormir ou coucher à la belle étoile; **the morning/evening s.** l'étoile *f* du matin/du soir; **to have stars in one's eyes** être sur un petit nuage; *Fig* **to see stars** voir trente-six chandelles; *Fig* **to reach for the stars** essayer d'atteindre les sommets
2 *(symbol of fate, luck)* étoile *f*; *Astrol* astre *m*, étoile *f*; **his s. is rising** son étoile brille chaque jour davantage; **his s. is on the wane** son étoile pâlit; **to be born under a lucky s.** être né sous une bonne étoile; **I thanked my (lucky) stars I wasn't chosen** j'ai remercié le ciel de ne pas avoir été choisi; **the influence of the stars** l'influence des astres; *Fam* **what do my stars say today?** que dit mon horoscope aujourd'hui?; **it's written in the stars** c'est le destin
3 *(figure, emblem)* étoile *f*, *Sch* bon point *m*; **the restaurant has gained another s.** le restaurant s'est vu décerner une étoile supplémentaire; **the S. of David** l'étoile *f* de David; **the Stars and Stripes** la bannière étoilée *(le drapeau américain)*
4 *(asterisk)* astérisque *m*
5 *(celebrity)* vedette *f*, star *f*; **she was an up-and-coming rock s.** elle était en train de devenir une grande star du rock; **he's a rising s. in the Labour party** il est en train de devenir un personnage important du parti travailliste; **to be the s. of the class** être la vedette de la classe
6 *(blaze ▸ on animal)* étoile *f*
7 *Br Fam (kind, helpful person)* **I've managed to fix your computer for you – oh, thanks, you're a s.!** j'ai réparé ton ordinateur – oh, merci, tu es un ange!
COMP 1 *Cin & Theat* **the s. attraction of tonight's show** la principale attraction du spectacle de ce soir; **to get s. billing** être en tête d'affiche; **to give sb s. billing** mettre qn en tête d'affiche **2** *(salesman, pupil etc)* meilleur; **he's our s. witness** c'est notre témoin-vedette *ou* notre témoin principal **3** *Comput* **in a s. configuration** connecté en étoile
VT 1 *Cin & Theat* avoir comme *ou* pour vedette; **the play starred David Caffrey** la pièce avait pour vedette David Caffrey; **'Casablanca', starring Humphrey Bogart and Ingrid Bergman** 'Casablanca', avec Humphrey Bogart et Ingrid Bergman (dans les rôles principaux) **2** *(mark with asterisk)* marquer d'un astérisque
VI *Cin & Theat* être la vedette; **who starred with Redford in 'The Sting'?** qui jouait avec Redford dans 'L'Arnaque'?; **'Othello', with Laurence Olivier starring in the title role** 'Othello', avec Laurence Olivier dans le rôle principal; **he's starring in a new TV serial** il est la vedette d'un nouveau feuilleton télévisé; **he starred as a gangster** il avait un rôle de gangster
▸▸ ***star anise*** anis *m* étoilé; *Elec* ***star connection*** couplage *m* en étoile; ***star fruit*** carambole *f*; ***star jump*** *(exercise)* = saut avec extension latérale des membres; *Comput* ***star network*** réseau *m* en étoile; *Comput* ***star point*** point *m* neutre; ***star ruby*** rubis *m* étoilé; ***star sapphire*** saphir *m* étoilé; *Mil* ***star shell*** obus *m* éclairant; ***star sign*** signe *m* (du zodiaque); *Comput* ***star structure*** structure *f* en étoile; ***star system* 1** *Cin & Theat* star-system *m* **2** *Astron* système *m* stellaire; ***star turn*** numéro *m* de premier ordre; *Fam (of performance, conference, evening)* clou *m*

starboard ['stɑːbəd] **N** *Naut* tribord *m*; *Aviat* tribord *m*, droite *f*; **on the s. side, to s.** à tribord; **vessel to s.!** navire par tribord!
ADJ *Naut (rail, lights)* de tribord; *Aviat (door, wing)* droit, de tribord

starch [stɑːtʃ] **N 1** *(for laundry)* amidon *m*, empois *m*
2 *(in cereals)* amidon *m*; *(in root vegetables)* fécule *f*; **try and avoid s.** *or* **starches** essayez d'éviter les féculents
3 *(UNCOUNT) Fam (formality)* manières *fpl* guindées
4 *Am (idiom)* **to take the s. out of sb** *(critic, bully)* rabattre le caquet à qn
VT empeser, amidonner

starched [stɑːtʃt] **ADJ** amidonné

starchy ['stɑːtʃɪ] *(compar* **starchier**, *superl* **starchiest) ADJ 1** *(diet)* riche en féculents; *(taste)* farineux **2** *Pej (person)* guindé, compassé; **he's so s.!** on dirait qu'il a avalé son parapluie!
▸▸ ***starchy foods*** féculents *mpl*

star-crossed **ADJ** *Literary* maudit par le sort

stardom ['stɑːdəm] **N** célébrité *f*, vedettariat *m*; **to rise to s.** devenir célèbre, devenir une vedette; **she has been groomed for s.** on l'a façonnée pour en faire une vedette

stardust ['stɑːdʌst] **N** *(UNCOUNT) (illusions)* chimères *fpl*, illusions *fpl*; *(sentimentality)* sentimentalité *f*; **to have s. in one's eyes** *(be deluded)* être en proie aux chimères; *(be a romantic)* être très fleur bleue

stare [steə(r)] **VI** regarder (fixement); **to s. at sb/sth** regarder qn/qch fixement; **it's rude to s.!** ça ne se fait pas de regarder les gens comme ça!; **stop it, people are staring!** arrête, les gens nous regardent!; **I stared into his eyes** je l'ai regardé dans le blanc des yeux; **she stared at me in disbelief** elle m'a regardé avec des yeux incrédules; **he stared straight ahead** il regardait fixement devant lui; **she sat staring into the distance** elle était assise, le regard perdu (au loin); **I stared out of the train window** j'ai regardé longuement par la fenêtre du train
VT 1 *(intimidate)* **to s. sb into silence** faire taire qn en le fixant du regard; **her steely eyes stared him into submission** son regard d'acier l'a réduit à l'obéissance **2** *(idiom)* **the answer is staring you in the face!** mais la réponse saute aux yeux!; **I'd looked everywhere for my keys and there they were staring me in the face** j'avais cherché mes clefs partout alors qu'elles étaient là sous mon nez; **failure was staring us in the face** nous courions à l'échec
N regard *m* (fixe); **to give sb a hostile/an incredulous s.** fixer qn d'un regard hostile/incrédule
▸ **stare out,** *Am* **stare down** **VT SEP** faire baisser les yeux à

starfish ['stɑːfɪʃ] *(pl* **inv** *or* **starfishes) N** *Zool* étoile *f* de mer

stargaze ['stɑːgeɪz] **VI 1** *(watch)* observer les étoiles **2** *(daydream)* rêvasser

stargazer ['stɑːˌgeɪzə(r)] **N 1** *(astronomer)* astronome *mf*; *(astrologer)* astrologue *mf* **2** *(daydreamer)* rêveur(euse) *m,f*, rêvasseur(euse) *m,f*

stargazing ['stɑːˌgeɪzɪŋ] **N 1** *(astronomy)* observation *f* des étoiles; *(astrology)* astrologie *f* **2** *(UNCOUNT) (daydreaming)* rêveries *fpl*, rêvasseries *fpl*

staring ['steərɪŋ] **ADJ** *(bystanders)* curieux; **to have s. eyes** *(fixed)* avoir les yeux fixes; *(wide-open)* avoir les yeux écarquillés; *(blank)* avoir les yeux vides
ADV *see* **stark**

stark [stɑːk] **ADJ 1** *(bare, grim ▸ landscape, scene)* désolé; *(▸ branches, hills, crag)* nu; *(▸ room, façade)* austère; *(▸ silhouette)* net; **in the s. light of day** à la lumière crue du jour; **the chimneys rose in s. relief against the sky** les cheminées se découpaient nettement contre le ciel; **the s. simplicity of the shapes** l'austère dépouillement des formes; **the s. beauty of the landscape** la beauté âpre du paysage **2** *(blunt ▸ description, statement)* cru, sans ambages; *(▸ refusal, denial)* catégorique; *(harsh ▸ words)* dur; **the s. realities of war** les dures réalités de la guerre; **those are the s. facts** ce sont les faits tels qu'ils sont; **the s. realism of her book** le réalisme cru de son livre **3** *(utter ▸ brutality, terror)* absolu; *(▸ madness)* pur; **in s. poverty** dans la misère absolue *ou* la plus noire; **their foreign policy success is in s. contrast to the failure of their domestic policies** la réussite de leur politique étrangère contraste nettement avec l'échec de leur politique intérieure
ADV complètement; *Fam* **s. raving** *or* **staring mad** complètement dingue; **s. naked** tout nu

starkers ['stɑːkəz] *Br Fam* **ADJ** à poil
ADV à poil

starkness ['stɑːknɪs] **N** *(of landscape, scene)* désolation *f*; *(of branches, hills, crag)* nudité *f*; *(of room, façade)* austérité *f*; *(of light)* crudité *f*; *(of life, reality)* dureté *f*; **the s. of the author's style** le style dépouillé de l'auteur; **a mirror offset the s. of the bare walls** une glace adoucissait l'austérité des murs nus

starless ['stɑːlɪs] **ADJ** *(sky, night)* sans étoiles

starlet ['stɑːlɪt] **N** starlette *f*

starlight ['stɑːlaɪt] **N** lumière *f* des étoiles; **by s.** à *ou* sous la lumière des étoiles

starling ['stɑːlɪŋ] **N** *Orn* étourneau *m*, sansonnet *m*

starlit ['stɑːlɪt] **ADJ** *(night)* étoilé; *(landscape, beach, sea)* illuminé par les étoiles, baigné par la lumière des étoiles

star-of-Bethlehem **N** *Bot* étoile *f* de Bethléem

starred [stɑːd] **ADJ** *Typ (asterisked)* marqué d'un astérisque

starry ['stɑːrɪ] *(compar* **starrier**, *superl* **starriest) ADJ 1** *(adorned with stars)* étoilé; **a s. night** une nuit étoilée **2** *(sparkling)* étincelant, brillant; **a s. diadem** un diadème étincelant **3** *Literary Fig (lofty)* élevé; **the s. heights of Mount Olympus** les hauteurs infinies de l'Olympe

starry-eyed ADJ *(idealistic)* idéaliste; *(naive)* naïf, ingénu; *(dreamy)* rêveur, dans la lune; **the children stood s. in front of the Christmas tree** les enfants se tenaient devant le sapin de Noël, émerveillés; **there's nothing s. about her** elle a vraiment les pieds sur terre

star-spangled [-'spæŋgəld] ADJ *(flag)* étoilé; *(sky)* semé *ou* parsemé d'étoiles

▸▸ ***the Star-Spangled Banner*** *(flag)* la bannière étoilée; *(national anthem)* l'hymne *m* national des États-Unis

START [stɑːt]

N
- commencement **1**
- début **1**
- départ **1, 2**
- avance **3**
- sursaut **4**

VT
- commencer **1**
- amorcer **1**
- déclencher **2**
- faire **3**
- démarrer **4**
- mettre en marche **4**
- entamer **5**
- créer **6**
- installer **7**

VI
- commencer **1, 3**
- débuter **2**
- démarrer **4, 6**
- se mettre en marche **4**
- partir **5**
- sursauter **7**
- bondir **7**

N 1 *(beginning* ▸ *gen)* commencement *m*, début *m*; *(*▸ *of inquiry)* ouverture *f*; *(of journey, race)* départ *m*; **the s. of the school year** la rentrée scolaire; **the s. of the footpath is marked by an arrow** le début du sentier est signalé par une flèche; **£5 isn't much, but it's a s.** 5 livres ce n'est pas grand-chose, mais c'est un début; **I've cleaned the kitchen – well, it's a s.** j'ai nettoyé la cuisine – eh bien, c'est déjà ça; **things are off to a bad/good s.** ça commence mal/bien, c'est mal/bien parti; **my new boss and I didn't get off to a very good s.** dès le début, mes rapports avec mon nouveau patron ont été un peu difficiles; **it was a good/bad s. to the day** la journée commençait bien/mal; **to get a good s. in life** prendre un bon départ dans la vie *ou* l'existence; **we want an education that will give our children a good s.** nous voulons une éducation qui donne à nos enfants des bases solides; **the programme will give ex-prisoners a fresh** *or* **new s. (in life)** le programme va donner aux anciens détenus une seconde chance (dans la vie); **to make a s.** *(gen)* commencer; *(begin journey)* se mettre en route; **to make** *or* **to get an early s.** *(gen)* commencer de bonne heure; *(on journey)* partir de bonne heure; **to make a s. on sth** commencer qch; **I've made a good s. on my Christmas shopping** j'ai déjà fait une bonne partie de mes achats de Noël; **I was lonely at the s.** au début je me sentais seule; **at the s. of the war** au début de la guerre; **at the very s.** au tout début; **(right) from the s.** dès le début *ou* commencement; **the trip was a disaster from s. to finish** le voyage a été un désastre d'un bout à l'autre; **I laughed from s. to finish** j'ai ri du début à la fin; **the project was ill-conceived from s. to finish** le projet était mal conçu de bout en bout

2 *Sport (departure line)* (ligne *f* de) départ *m*; *(signal)* signal *m* de départ; **they are lined up for** *or* **at the s.** ils sont sur la ligne de départ; **where's the s. of the rally?** où est le départ du rallye?

3 *(lead, advance)* avance *f*; **she has two hours' s.** *or* **a two-hour s. on us** elle a une avance de deux heures sur nous; **he gave him 20 metres' s.** *or* **a 20-metre s.** il lui a accordé une avance de 20 mètres; **our research gives us a s. over our competitors** nos recherches nous donnent de l'avance sur nos concurrents; **to have a s. on sb** être en avance sur qn

4 *(jump)* sursaut *m*; **she woke up with a s.** elle s'est réveillée en sursaut; **with a s., I recognized my own handwriting** j'ai eu un sursaut quand j'ai reconnu ma propre écriture; **he gave a s.** il a tressailli, il a sursauté; **to give sb a s.** faire sursauter *ou* tressaillir qn

VT 1 *(begin* ▸ *gen)* commencer; *(*▸ *climb, descent)* amorcer; **I've started the first chapter** *(write)* j'ai commencé (à écrire) le premier chapitre; *(read)* j'ai commencé (à lire) le premier chapitre; **to s. doing** *or* **to do sth** commencer à *ou* se mettre à faire qch; **it's starting to rain** il commence à pleuvoir; **she started driving** *or* **to drive again a month after her accident** elle a recommencé à conduire *ou* elle s'est remise à conduire un mois après son accident; **to s. school** *(for the first time)* commencer l'école; *(after holidays)* rentrer à *ou* reprendre l'école; **she started her speech with a quotation from the Bible** elle a commencé son discours par une citation de la Bible; **they started the year with a deficit** ils ont commencé l'année avec un déficit; **he started work at 16** il a commencé à travailler à 16 ans; **when do you s. your new job?** quand commencez-vous votre nouveau travail?; **he started life as a delivery boy** il débuta dans la vie comme garçon livreur; **go ahead and s. lunch without me** allez-y, vous pouvez commencer (à déjeuner) sans moi; **I like to finish anything I s.** j'aime aller au bout de tout ce que j'entreprends; **to get started** *(person* ▸ *on task)* commencer, s'y mettre; *(*▸ *on journey)* partir, se mettre en route; *(*▸ *in career)* débuter, démarrer; **I got started on the dishes** j'ai commencé la vaisselle; **shall we get started on the washing-up?** si on attaquait la vaisselle?; **to help sb get started in life** aider qn à démarrer dans la vie; **let's get started!** allons-y!; **once he gets started there's no stopping him** une fois lancé, il n'y a pas moyen de l'arrêter; **I need a coffee to get me started in the morning** j'ai besoin d'un café pour commencer la journée

2 *(initiate, instigate* ▸ *reaction, revolution, process)* déclencher; *(*▸ *fashion)* lancer; *(*▸ *violence)* déclencher, provoquer; *(*▸ *conversation, discussion)* engager, amorcer; *(*▸ *rumour)* faire naître; **her article started the controversy** son article a été à l'origine de la controverse; **to s. legal proceedings** engager une action en justice; **which side started the war?** quel camp a déclenché la guerre?; **you started it** c'est toi qui as commencé; **it wasn't me who started the quarrel/the fight!** ce n'est pas moi qui ai commencé la dispute/la bagarre!; **to s. a fire** *(in fireplace)* allumer le feu; *(campfire)* faire du feu; *(by accident, bomb)* mettre le feu; **the fire was started by arsonists** l'incendie a été allumé par des pyromanes; *Fam* **are you trying to s. something?** tu cherches la bagarre, ou quoi?

3 *(cause to do* ▸ *person)* faire; **it started her (off) crying/laughing** cela l'a fait pleurer/rire; **I'll s. a team (working) on it right away** je vais mettre une équipe là-dessus tout de suite; **if you s. him on this subject he will never stop** si vous le lancez sur ce sujet il ne tarira pas

4 *(set in motion* ▸ *motor, car)* (faire) démarrer, mettre en marche; *(*▸ *machine, device)* mettre en marche; *(*▸ *meal)* mettre en route; **how do I s. the tape (going)?** comment est-ce que je dois faire pour mettre le magnétophone en marche?; **I couldn't get the car started** je n'ai pas réussi à faire démarrer la voiture; **to s. the printer again, press this key** pour remettre en marche l'imprimante, appuyez sur cette touche

5 *(begin using* ▸ *bottle, pack)* entamer

6 *(establish, found* ▸ *business, school, political party, newspaper)* créer, fonder; *(*▸ *restaurant, shop)* ouvrir; *(*▸ *social programme)* créer, instaurer; **to s. a family** fonder un foyer

7 *(person* ▸ *in business, work)* installer, établir; **he started his son in the family business** il a fait entrer son fils dans l'entreprise familiale; **his election success started him on his political career** son succès aux élections l'a lancé dans sa carrière d'homme politique; **they s. new pilots on domestic flights** ils font débuter les nouveaux pilotes sur les vols intérieurs

8 *Sport* **to s. the race** donner le signal du départ; **the referee blew his whistle to s. the match** l'arbitre siffla pour signaler le début du match

9 *Hunt (flush out* ▸ *hare, stag)* lever

VI 1 *(begin)* commencer; **the movie starts at 8 o'clock** le film commence à 20 heures; **school starts on 5 September** la rentrée a lieu *ou* les cours reprennent le 5 septembre; **our problems are just starting** nos ennuis ne font que commencer; **before the New Year/the rainy season starts** avant le début de l'année prochaine/de la saison des pluies; **before the cold weather starts** avant qu'il ne commence à faire froid; **starting (from) next week** à partir de la semaine prochaine; **to s. again** *or* **afresh** recommencer; **to s. all over again, to s. again from scratch** recommencer à zéro; **calm down and s. at the beginning** calmez-vous et commencez par le commencement; **I didn't know where to s.** je ne savais pas par quel bout commencer; **she started with a joke/by introducing everyone** elle a commencé par une plaisanterie/par faire les présentations; **I'd like to s. by saying how pleased I am to be here tonight** j'aimerais commencer par vous dire à quel point je suis heureux d'être parmi vous ce soir; **the book starts with a quotation** le livre commence par une citation; **I'll have the soup to s. (with)** pour commencer, je prendrai du potage; **to s. as one means to go on** donner la mesure dès le début; **isn't it time you got a job? don't YOU s.!** il serait peut-être temps que tu trouves du travail – tu ne vas pas t'y mettre, toi aussi!

2 *(in career, job)* débuter; **she started in personnel/as an assistant** elle a débuté au service du personnel/comme assistante; **have you been working here long? – no, I've just started** vous travaillez ici depuis longtemps? – non, je viens de commencer; **I s. on $500 a week** je débute à 500 dollars par semaine; **gymnasts have to s. young** les gymnastes doivent commencer jeunes

3 *(in space* ▸ *desert, fields, slope, street)* commencer; *(*▸ *river)* prendre sa source; **there's an arrow where the path starts** il y a une flèche qui indique le début du sentier; **the bus route starts at the station** la ligne de bus commence à la gare; **where does the tunnel s.?** où est l'entrée du tunnel?

4 *(car, motor)* démarrer, se mettre en marche; **the engines started with a roar** les moteurs ont démarré en vrombissant; **why won't the car s.** pourquoi la voiture ne veut-elle pas démarrer?

5 *(set off* ▸ *person, convoy)* partir, se mettre en route; *(*▸ *train)* s'ébranler; **the tour starts at or from the town hall** la visite part de la mairie; **I'll have to s. for the airport soon** il va bientôt falloir que je parte pour l'aéroport; **we s. tomorrow** nous partons demain; **the train was starting across** *or* **over the bridge** le train commençait à traverser le pont *ou* s'engageait sur le pont; **she started along the path** elle s'engagea sur le sentier; *Sport* **only four horses started** quatre chevaux seulement ont pris le départ

6 *(prices)* démarrer; **houses here s. at $100,000** ici, le prix des maisons démarre à 100 000 dollars; **return fares s. from £299** on trouve des billets aller retour à partir de 299 livres

7 *(jump involuntarily* ▸ *person)* sursauter; *(*▸ *horse)* tressaillir, faire un soubresaut; *(jump up)* bondir; **he started in surprise** il a tressailli de surprise; **she started from her chair** elle bondit de sa chaise

8 *(gush)* jaillir, gicler; **tears started to his eyes** les larmes lui sont montées aux yeux

• **for a start** ADV pour commencer, d'abord

• **for starts** ADV *Am Fam* pour commencer, d'abord

• **to start with** ADV **1** *(firstly)* pour commencer, d'abord; **to s. with, my name isn't Jo** pour commencer *ou* d'abord, je ne m'appelle pas Jo

2 *(in the beginning)* au début; **there were only six members to s. with** il n'y avait que six membres au début; **she was an architect to s. with, then journalist** elle a d'abord été architecte, puis journaliste

▸▸ *Comput* ***start bit*** bit *m* de départ; *Comput* ***start button*** *(in Windows)* bouton *m* Démarrer; *Comput* ***start code*** code *m* de départ; *Cin* ***start leader*** amorce *f* de début

▸ **start in on** VT INSEP s'attaquer à; **once he starts in on liberty and democracy, there's no stopping him** une fois qu'il est lancé sur le sujet de la liberté et de la démocratie, il n'y a plus moyen de l'arrêter; *Fam* **to s. in on sb** s'en prendre à qn, tomber à bras raccourcis sur qn

▸ **start off** VT SEP **1** *(begin* ▸ *book, meeting, show)* commencer **2** *(person* ▸ *on task, in business)* **here's some wool to s. you off** voici de la laine pour commencer; **he lent us a couple of thousand pounds to s. us off** il nous a prêté quelques milliers de livres pour nous aider à démarrer; **the pianist played a few bars to s. them off** le pianiste a joué quelques mesures d'introduction **3** *(set off)* déclencher; **what started the alarm off** u'est-ce qui a déclenché l'alarme?; **if you mention it it'll only s. her off again** n'en parle pas, sinon elle va recommencer; **to s. sb off laughing/ rying** faire rire/pleurer qn; **the baby's crying gain, what started him off this time?** le bébé s'est emis à pleurer, qu'est-ce qu'il a cette fois?; **dad's nally calmed down, don't you s. him off again** pa-a s'est enfin calmé, ne va pas l'énerver

VI 1 *(leave)* partir, se mettre en route; **he started ff at a run** il est parti en courant; **when do you s. ff on your trip?** quand est-ce que vous partez n voyage? **2** *(begin ▸ speech, film)* commencer; **starts off with a description of the town** ça commence par une description de la ville; **she tarted off by talking about…** elle commença en arlant de…; **the interview started off badly/well** entretien a mal/bien commencé; **I started off greeing with him** au début, j'étais d'accord avec ui **3** *(in life, career)* débuter; **he started off as a ashier** il a débuté comme caissier; **she started ff as a Catholic** elle était catholique à l'origine; **ou're starting off with all the advantages** vous artez avec tous les avantages

start on VT INSEP 1 *(begin ▸ essay, meal)* commencer; *(▸ task, dishes)* se mettre à; *(▸ new bot-'e, pack)* entamer; **they had already started on heir dessert** ils avaient déjà commencé à manger *ou* entamé leur dessert; **after they'd searched he car they started on the luggage** après avoir ouillé la voiture, ils sont passés aux bagages **2** *ttack, berate)* s'en prendre à

start out VI 1 *(begin journey)* partir, se mettre n route **2** *(begin career)* débuter; **he started out s a cashier** il a débuté comme caissier; **she tarted out as a Catholic** elle était catholique à origine; **he started out in business with his wife's oney** il s'est lancé dans les affaires avec l'argent de sa femme; **when she started out there vere only a few women lawyers** quand elle a ommencé sa carrière, il y avait très peu de emmes avocats **3** *(intend)* **he started out to write novel** au départ il voulait écrire un roman

start over *Am* **VI** recommencer (depuis le début)

VT SEP recommencer (depuis le début)

start up VT SEP 1 *(establish, found ▸ business, chool, political party)* créer, fonder; *(▸ restaur-nt, shop)* ouvrir **2** *(set in motion ▸ car, motor)* aire démarrer; *(▸ machine)* mettre en marche; *▸ computer)* mettre en route; *(▸ program)* lancer, démarrer

VI 1 *(guns, music, noise, band)* commencer; *vind)* se lever; **the applause started up again** les pplaudissements ont repris **2** *(car, motor)* démarrer, se mettre en marche; *(machine)* se mettre en marche; *(computer, program)* se mettre en oute **3** *(set up business)* se lancer, s'installer, 'établir; **he decided to s. up by himself** il a décidé e se mettre à son compte

tarter ['stɑːtə(r)] **N 1** *Aut (motor, button)* démareur *m*; *(on motorbike)* kick *m*, démarreur *m* au ied

2 *(runner, horse)* partant *m*; *(in relay race)* premier(ère) coureur(euse) *m,f*; **to be a slow s.** *gen) & Sport* être lent à démarrer

3 *Sport (official)* starter *m*, juge *m* de départ; **to e under s.'s orders** *(in horseracing)* attendre le signal du starter

4 *(fermenting agent)* ferment *m*; **yoghurt s.** ferment *m* lactique pour yaourt

5 *Br (first course of meal)* hors-d'œuvre *m inv*; **for tarters** *(in meal)* comme hors-d'œuvre; *Fig* pour ommencer; **that was just for starters** ce n'était u'un hors-d'œuvre

6 *Am Fam (house)* première maison ᵅ*f (achetée ar un individu ou un couple)*

▸ *Br* ***starter flat*** = appartement convenant à eux qui achètent pour la première fois; ***starter ome*** première maison *f (achetée par un individu u un couple)*; ***starter motor*** démarreur *m*; ***starter ack*** kit *m* de base; *Comput (for Internet)* kit *m* de onnexion; *Am* ***starter set*** *(dishes)* service *m* our six

Note that the most common meaning of the French word **starter** is **choke** (in an engine).

tarting ['stɑːtɪŋ] **N 1** *(beginning)* commencement *m*; **who wants to be responsible for the s. of a nuclear war?** qui veut assumer la responsabilité du déclenchement d'une guerre nucléaire? **2** *(of business etc)* mise *f* en route *ou* en train **3** *(of engine etc)* mise *f* en marche, démarrage *m*; *(of machine)* lancement *m*

ADJ initial; **the s. line-up** la composition initiale de l'équipe

▸▸ ***starting block*** *(in athletics)* starting-block *m*; *(for swimmers)* plot *m* de départ; ***starting gate*** *Horseracing* starting-gate *f*; *(for skier)* porte *f* de départ; ***starting grid*** *(in motor racing)* grille *f* de départ; *Br Aut* ***starting handle*** manivelle *f*; *Sport* ***starting line*** ligne *f* de départ; *Tech* ***starting motor*** moteur *m* de démarrage; ***starting pistol*** pistolet *m* du starter; ***starting point*** point *m* de départ; *Sport* ***starting post*** ligne *f* de départ; ***starting price*** *(gen)* prix *m* initial; *Horseracing* cote *f* au départ; *(at auction)* mise *f* à prix, prix *m* d'appel; *Br* ***starting rate*** *(of income tax)* = taux d'imposition le plus bas du barème de l'impôt sur le revenu; ***starting salary*** salaire *m* d'embauche; ***starting signal*** signal *m* de *ou* du départ; *Horseracing* ***starting stalls*** stalles *fpl* de départ; ***starting up*** *(of business etc)* mise *f* en route *ou* en train; *(of engine)* mise *f* en marche, démarrage *m*; *(of machine)* lancement *m*

starting-rate ADJ *Br (taxpayer)* = qui paie l'impôt sur le revenu à son taux le plus bas

startle ['stɑːtəl] **VT** *(person ▸ surprise)* surprendre, étonner; *(▸ frighten, alarm)* faire peur à, alarmer; *(▸ cause to jump)* faire sursauter; *(animal, bird, fish)* effaroucher; **I didn't mean to s. you** je ne voulais pas vous faire peur; **it startled me** *or* **I was startled to see how much he had aged** j'ai été surpris *ou* ç'a été un choc pour moi de voir à quel point il avait vieilli; **the noise startled him out of his reverie** le bruit l'a brusquement tiré de ses rêveries

VI s'effaroucher

startled ['stɑːtəld] **ADJ** *(person)* étonné; *(expression, shout, glance)* de surprise; *(animal)* effarouché; **there was a s. silence** il y a eu un silence étonné; **the s. waiter dropped the tray** le serveur, surpris, a laissé tomber son plateau

startling ['stɑːtlɪŋ] **ADJ** étonnant, surprenant; *(contrast, resemblance)* saisissant; **s. green eyes** des yeux d'un vert saisissant

start-up N 1 *Comput* démarrage *m* **2** *(of new business)* ouverture *f*, lancement *m*; **there have been 500 start-ups this year** il y a eu 500 créations d'entreprises cette année **3** *(Internet company)* start-up *f*, jeune pousse *f*

▸▸ *Fin* ***start-up capital*** capital *m* initial, capital *m* de départ; *Fin* ***start-up costs*** frais *mpl* d'établissement; *Comput* ***start-up disk*** disquette *f* de démarrage; ***start-up loan*** prêt *m* initial; *Comput* ***start-up screen*** écran *m* d'accueil

starvation [stɑː'veɪʃən] **N** famine *f*; **to die of** *or* **from s.** mourir de faim

▸▸ ***starvation diet*** ration *f* de famine; *Fig* régime *m* draconien; **the prisoners subsisted on a s. diet of rice and water** les prisonniers devaient se contenter de riz et d'eau; ***starvation wages*** salaire *m* de famine *ou* de misère; **they pay s. wages** ce sont des affameurs

starve [stɑːv] **VI** *(suffer)* souffrir de la faim, être affamé; **to s. (to death)** *(die)* mourir de faim; *Fam* **I'm starving!** je meurs de faim!

VT 1 *(cause to suffer)* affamer; **he starved himself to feed his child** il s'est privé de nourriture pour donner à manger à son enfant; *Fam* **I'm starved!** je meurs de faim!; **the garrison was starved into surrender** la garnison affamée a fini par se rendre **2** *(cause to die)* laisser mourir de faim; **they were prepared to s. themselves to death rather than give in** ils étaient prêts à se laisser mourir de faim plutôt que de capituler **3** *(deprive)* priver; **the libraries have been starved of funds** les bibliothèques manquent cruellement de subventions; **to be starved of affection** être privé d'affection; **the inhabitants were starved of news** les habitants étaient privés d'informations

▸**starve out VT SEP** *(rebels, inmates)* affamer, réduire par la faim; *(animal)* obliger à sortir en l'affamant

starving ['stɑːvɪŋ] **ADJ** affamé; *Fam* **I've got four s. kids to feed!** j'ai quatre gosses affamés à nourrir!; **think of all the s. people in the world** pense à tous ces gens qui meurent de faim dans le monde

stash [stæʃ] *Fam* **VT 1** *(hide)* planquer; **it was stashed under the bed** c'était planqué sous le lit; **he's got a lot of money stashed (away) somewhere** il a plein de fric planqué quelque part **2** *(put away)* rangerᵅ; **let me s. my things** attends que je ramasse mon bazar

N 1 *(reserve)* réserveᵅ*f*; **a s. of money** un magot; **the police found a big s. of guns/of cocaine** la police a découvert une importante cache d'armesᵅ/un important stock de cocaïneᵅ **2** *(hiding place)* planque *f*; *(hidden supply)* provisionᵅ*f*; **the police found his s. under the floorboards** *(of drugs)* la police a trouvé sa réserve de drogue planquée sous le plancher

▸**stash away VT SEP = stash VT**

stasis ['steɪsɪs] *(pl* **stases** [-siːz]) **N 1** *Med* stase *f* **2** *(equilibrium)* équilibre *m*, repos *m*; *(stagnation)* stagnation *f*

STATE [steɪt]

N	
• état **1**	• État **2, 3**
• apparat **4**	
ADJ	
• d'État, de l'État **1, 2**	• public **1**
• national **1**	• officiel **3**
VT	
• déclarer	• formuler

N 1 *(condition)* état *m*; **the country is in a s. of war/ shock** le pays est en état de guerre/choc; **a s. of confusion prevailed** la confusion régnait; **he was in a s. of confusion** il ne savait plus où il en était; **he was in a s. of panic** il a été pris de panique; **the married s.** le mariage; **the single s.** le célibat; **chlorine in its gaseous/liquid s.** le chlore à l'état gazeux/liquide; **to be in a good/bad s.** *(road, carpet, car)* être en bon/mauvais état; *(person, economy, friendship)* aller bien/mal; **the house was in a good/poor s. of repair** la maison était en bon/mauvais état; **to be in a terrible s.** *(person ▸ emotionally)* être dans tous ses états; *(▸ physically)* être dans un état lamentable; *(room, papers)* être sens dessus dessous; **she was in no (fit) s. to make a decision** elle était hors d'état de *ou* elle n'était pas en état de prendre une décision; **the car's not in a s. to be driven** la voiture n'est pas en état de rouler; **what's the current s. of play?** où en sont-ils?; **what's the current s. of play on the project?** où en est le projet?; *Fam* **to get into a s.** se mettre dans tous ses états; **there's no need to get into such a s. about it** ce n'est pas la peine de te mettre dans un état pareil

2 *Pol (nation, body politic)* État *m*; **the head of s.** le chef de l'État; **heads of s.** chefs *mpl* d'État; **the separation of (the) Church and (the) S.** la séparation de l'Église et de l'État

3 *(in US, Australia, India etc ▸ political division)* État *m*; *Fam* **the States** les États-Unisᵅ, les US; **the S. of Ohio** l'État *m* de l'Ohio

4 *(pomp)* apparat *m*, pompe *f*; **he was in his robes of s.** il était en costume d'apparat

ADJ 1 *(government ▸ secret)* d'État; *(▸ subsidy, intervention)* de l'État; *(▸ airline, funeral)* national

2 *Am (not federal ▸ legislature, policy, law)* de l'État; **the s. capital** la capitale de l'État; **a s. university** une université d'État *ou* publique; **the Michigan S. team** l'équipe de l'État du Michigan; **a s. park** un parc régional; *Am* **to turn s.'s evidence** *or* **s.'s witness** = témoigner contre ses complices en échange d'une remise de peine

3 *(official, ceremonious ▸ ball, dinner, visit)* officiel; *(▸ coach, carriage)* d'apparat; **s. occasion** cérémonie *f* officielle; **the S. Opening of Parliament** = l'ouverture officielle du Parlement britannique en présence du souverain

VT *(utter, say)* déclarer; *(express, formulate ▸ intentions)* déclarer; *(▸ demands)* formuler; *(▸ proposition, problem, conclusions, views)* énoncer, formuler; *(▸ conditions)* poser; **I have already stated my position on that issue** j'ai déjà fait connaître ma position à ce sujet; **I have stated my opinion** j'ai donné mon opinion; **the regulations clearly s. that daily checks must be made** le règlement dit *ou* indique clairement que des vérifications quotidiennes doivent être effectuées; **please s. salary expectations** veuillez indiquer le salaire souhaité; **s. your name and address** donnez vos nom, prénoms et adresse; **the man refused to s. his business** l'homme a refusé d'expliquer ce qu'il voulait; **as stated above** comme indiqué plus haut; **s. the figure as a percentage** exprimez *ou* indiquez le chiffre en pourcentage; **to s. one's case** présenter ses arguments; *Law* **to s. the case for the defence/the prosecution** présenter le dossier de la défense/de l'accusation

• **State** N *Am (department)* le Département d'État

• **in state** ADV en grand apparat, en grande pompe; **to travel in s.** voyager en grand apparat; **to dine in s.** dîner en grande pompe; **to lie in s.** être exposé solennellement; **to live in s.** mener grand train

►► ***state of affairs*** circonstances *fpl* actuelles; **nothing can be done in the present s. of affairs** vu les circonstances actuelles, on ne peut rien faire; **this is an appalling s. of affairs** c'est une situation épouvantable; *Ironic* **this is a fine s. of affairs!** c'est du propre!; ***state apartments*** appartements *mpl* de parade; ***state of the art*** *(of procedures, systems)* ce qui se fait de mieux; **the s. of the art in linguistics** l'état actuel des connaissances en linguistique; ***state attorney*** procureur *m*; *Am* ***state bank*** banque *f* de dépôt *(agréée par un État)*; ***state buildings*** bâtiments *mpl* publics; ***state capitalism*** capitalisme *m* d'État; ***state church*** église *f* d'État; ***state control*** contrôle *m* étatique; *(doctrine)* étatisme *m*; **to be put** *or* **placed under s. control** être nationalisé; **s. control of the means of communication** nationalisation *f* des moyens de communication; *Am* ***State Department*** ministère *m* des Affaires étrangères; ***state of emergency*** état *m* d'urgence; **a s. of emergency has been declared** l'état d'urgence a été déclaré; *Br* ***State Enrolled Nurse*** aide-soignant(e) *m,f* diplômé(e); *Hist* ***States General*** États *mpl* généraux; ***state government*** gouvernement *m* d'État; *Am* ***state line*** frontière *f* entre États; *Am* ***state lottery*** loterie *f* d'État; ***state of mind*** état *m* d'esprit; **in your present s. of mind** dans l'état d'esprit qui est le vôtre; **is he in a better s. of mind?** est-ce qu'il est dans de meilleures dispositions?; ***state monopoly*** monopole *m* d'État; ***state occasion*** cérémonie *f* officielle; ***state paper*** imprimé *m* officiel; ***state pension*** pension *f* de l'État; ***state planning*** planification *f* nationale; ***state police*** police *f* de l'État; *Am* ***state prison*** prison *f* d'État *(pour les longues peines)*; *Br* ***State Registered Nurse*** infirmier(ère) *m,f* diplômé(e) *(remplacé en 1992 par "Registered Nurse")*; ***state revenue*** recettes *fpl* publiques; *Br* ***state school*** école *f* publique; *Br* ***state sector*** secteur *m* public; ***state of siege*** état *m* de siège; ***state socialism*** socialisme *m* d'État; ***the state system*** *(education)* le public, l'enseignement *m* public; *Am* ***state trooper*** ≃ gendarme *m*; *Am* ***State of the Union address, State of the Union message*** discours *m* sur l'état de l'Union; *Pol* ***state visit*** visite *f* officielle; **he's on a s. visit to Japan** il est en visite officielle *ou* voyage officiel au Japon

STATE OF THE UNION ADDRESS

Ce discours radiotélévisé, dans lequel le président des États-Unis dresse le bilan de son programme et en définit les orientations, est prononcé devant le Congrès. L'allocution présidentielle a lieu tous les ans en janvier.

statecraft ['steɪtkrɑːft] N *(skill ► in politics)* habileté *f* politique; *(► in diplomacy)* (art *m* de la) diplomatie *f*

Statehouse ['steɪthaʊs] N = siège de l'assemblée législative d'un État aux États-Unis

stateless ['steɪtlɪs] ADJ apatride

►► ***stateless person*** apatride *mf*; ***stateless society*** société *f* sans État

statelessness ['steɪtlɪsnɪs] N apatridie *f*

stateliness ['steɪtlɪnɪs] N *(of ceremony, building, monument)* majesté *f*, grandeur *f*; *(of person, bearing)* dignité *f*

stately ['steɪtlɪ] *(compar* **statelier**, *superl* **stateliest)** ADJ *(ceremony, building)* majestueux, imposant; *(person, bearing)* noble, plein de dignité

►► ***stately home*** = château ou manoir à la campagne, généralement ouvert au public

statement ['steɪtmənt] N **1** *(declaration ► gen)* déclaration *f*; *(► to the press)* communiqué *m*; **a written/policy s.** une déclaration écrite/de principe; **to put out** *or* **to issue** *or* **to make a s. about sth** émettre un communiqué concernant qch; **a s. to the effect that...** une déclaration selon laquelle...; *Fig* **the film is making a s.** il y a un message dans ce film; *Fig* **someone who wears jeans to a wedding reception is making a s.** quelqu'un qui va à un mariage en jeans veut faire comprendre quelque chose

2 *(act of stating ► of theory, opinions, policy, aims)* exposition *f*; *(► of problem)* exposé *m*, formulation *f*; *(► of facts, details)* exposé *m*, compte-rendu *m*; **to call him a thief is nothing more than a s. of fact** le traiter de voleur est une simple constatation

3 *Law* déposition *f*; **to make a s. to the police** faire une déposition dans un commissariat de police; **to take sb's s.** prendre la déposition de qn; **a sworn s.** une déposition faite sous serment

4 *Com, Fin & Banking* relevé *m*; *(of expenses, sales figures)* état *m*

5 *Ling* affirmation *f*

6 *Comput* instruction *f*

►► *Acct* ***statement of account*** état *m ou* relevé *m* de compte; *Com, Fin & Banking* ***statement of affairs*** *(in bankruptcy)* bilan *m* de liquidation; *Acct* ***statement of assets and liabilities*** relevé *m* des dettes actives et passives; *Law* ***statement of claim*** demande *f* introductive d'instance; *Acct* ***statement of expenses*** état *m ou* relevé *m* des dépenses

state-of-the-art ADJ *(design, device)* de pointe; **the method incorporates s. technology** la méthode utilise des techniques de pointe; *Fam* **it's s.** c'est ce qui se fait de mieux❑, c'est du dernier cri❑

stateroom ['steɪtrʊm] N **1** *(in ship)* cabine *f* de grand luxe; *Am (in railway coach)* compartiment *m* privé **2** *(in public building)* salon *m* (de réception)

stateside ['steɪtsaɪd] *Am Fam* ADJ **1** *(in the United States)* aux États-Unis❑ **2** *(of the United States)* des États-Unis❑

ADV aux États-Unis❑, ≃ au pays; **he has a wife s.** il a une épouse au pays

statesman ['steɪtsmən] *(pl* **statesmen** [-mən]) N homme *m* d'État

statesmanlike ['steɪtsmənlaɪk] ADJ *(protest, reply)* diplomatique; *(solution)* de grande envergure; *(caution)* pondéré

statesmanship ['steɪtsmənʃɪp] N qualités *fpl* d'homme d'État; **he showed great s. in dealing with the problem** il a traité ce problème avec toute l'habileté d'un grand chef d'État

state-wide *Am* ADJ *(support, protest, celebration)* dans tout l'État; **the epidemic/our distribution is s.** l'épidémie/notre réseau de distribution s'étend à tout l'État

ADV dans tout l'État; **better schools are needed s.** on a besoin de meilleures écoles dans tout l'État

static ['stætɪk] ADJ **1** *(stationary, unchanging)* stationnaire, stable; **prices are fairly s. just now** les prix sont relativement stables en ce moment; **the situation remains s.** la situation reste inchangée **2** *Elec* statique

N *(UNCOUNT)* **1** *Rad & Tel* parasites *mpl* **2** *Elec* électricité *f* statique; **you get a lot of s. from nylon carpets** les moquettes en nylon produisent beaucoup d'électricité statique **3** *Am Fam (aggravation, criticism)* **to give sb s. about** *or* **over sth** passer un savon à qn à propos de qch; **to get a lot of s. (about** *or* **over) sth** se faire enguirlander (pour qch)

►► *Elec* ***static electricity*** électricité *f* statique; *Comput* ***static RAM*** mémoire *f* vive statique; *TV & Cin* ***static shot*** plan *m* fixe

statics ['stætɪks] N *(UNCOUNT) Phys* statique *f*

statin ['stætɪn] N *Pharm* statine *f*

station ['steɪʃən] N **1** *(for trains)* gare *f*; *(underground)* station *f* (de métro); **I'll meet you at Brighton s.** je vous retrouverai à la gare de Brighton

2 *(establishment, building)* station *f*, poste *m*; **must ask you to accompany me to the s.** je do vous demander de m'accompagner au commi sariat

3 *Mil (gen ► position)* poste *m*; **to take up one's** prendre position; **action** *or* **battle stations!** à v postes!

4 *Mil (base)* poste *m*, base *f*; *Br* **airforce s.** base aérienne

5 *Rad & TV (broadcasting organization)* station *(channel)* chaîne *f*; **commercial radio s.** station *f* c radio commerciale, radio *f* commerciale; *Rad* **change stations** changer de fréquence *ou* de st tion

6 *(social rank)* rang *m*, condition *f*, situation **they tend to forget their true s. in life** ils ont te dance à oublier leur véritable position social **to marry below one's s.** faire une mésalliance; **marry above one's s.** se marier au-dessus de condition sociale

7 *Comput* station *f*

8 *Rel* **the Stations of the Cross** le chemin de Cro

9 *Austr & NZ (farm)* = ferme (et ses dépenda ces)

COMP *(buffet, platform etc)* de gare

VT **1** *(position)* placer, poster; **police were st tioned at all the exits** des policiers étaient post à toutes les issues **2** *Mil (garrison)* **British troo stationed in Germany** les troupes britanniqu stationnées en Allemagne

►► *Am* ***station break*** pause *f* publicitaire, pag de publicité; *Rad* ***station director*** directeur(tric *m,f* d'antenne; *Am* ***station house*** *(police statio* poste *m* de police, commissariat *m*; *(fire statio* caserne *f* de pompiers; *TV* ***station identificati*** habillage *m* chaîne; *Rail* ***station manager*** chef de gare; *Rad* ***station signal*** indicatif *m* (de l'éme teur); *Am Aut* ***station wagon*** break *m*

stationary ['steɪʃnərɪ] ADJ **1** *(not moving)* st tionnaire; **he hit a s. vehicle** il a heurté un véh cule à l'arrêt *ou* en stationnement **2** *(fixed)* fix

►► *Tech* ***stationary engine*** moteur *m* fixe; *Met* ***st tionary front*** front *m* stationnaire; *Mil* ***stationa target*** cible *f* fixe; *Phys* ***stationary wave*** onde stationnaire

Attention: ne pas confondre avec **stationery**.

stationer ['steɪʃnə(r)] N *Br* papetier(ère) *m,f*; **s (shop)** papeterie *f*; **at the s.'s** à la papeterie

stationery ['steɪʃnərɪ] N *(in general)* papeterie *(writing paper)* papier *m* à lettres; **a letter writte on hotel s.** une lettre écrite sur le papier à en-tê d'un hôtel; **school/office s.** fournitures *fpl* scola res/de bureau

►► *BrAdmin* ***the Stationery Office*** = maison d'é tion britannique publiant les documents a prouvés par le Parlement, les ministères autres organismes officiels, ≃ l'Imprimerie nationale

Attention: ne pas confondre avec **stationary**.

statism ['steɪtɪzəm] N étatisme *m*

statist ['steɪtɪst] ADJ étatiste

statistic [stə'tɪstɪk] N chiffre *m*, statistique *f*; **th particular s. is certain to embarrass the gover ment** ces chiffres *ou* statistiques vont sûreme embarrasser le gouvernement; **he may be ju another s. to the police, but he was my brother** n'est peut-être qu'une statistique de plus pour police, mais il s'agissait de mon frère

statistical [stə'tɪstɪkəl] ADJ *(analysis, data, tec nique)* statistique; *(error)* de statistique; **it's a certainty** c'est statistiquement certain; **mechanism** mécanique *f* statistique

►► ***statistical indicator*** indicateur *m* statistiqu ***statistical inference*** inférence *f* statistique

statistically [stə'tɪstɪklɪ] ADV statistiquement

statistician [ˌstætɪ'stɪʃən] N statisticien(enn *m,f*

statistics [stə'tɪstɪks] N *(UNCOUNT) (scienc* statistique *f*

NPL **1** *(figures)* statistiques *fpl*, chiffres *mpl* **2** *Fa (of woman)* mensurations❑ *fpl*

stator ['steɪtə(r)] N stator *m*

statuary ['stætʃʊərɪ] N *(UNCOUNT) Form (statues collectively)* statues *fpl*; *(art)* statuaire *f*

ADJ statuaire
▸ *statuary marble* marbre *m* statuaire

atue ['stætʃu:] N statue *f*; **the S. of Liberty** la statue de la Liberté

atuesque [ˌstætjʊ'esk] ADJ sculptural; **a s. woman** une femme d'une beauté sculpturale

atuette [ˌstætjʊ'et] N statuette *f*

ature ['stætʃə(r)] N **1** *(height)* stature *f*, taille *f*; **e is rather short in** *or* **of s.** il est plutôt petit **2** *greatness)* envergure *f*, calibre *m*; **he doesn't ave the s. to be prime minister** il n'a pas l'envergure d'un premier ministre; **a mathematician of onsiderable s.** un mathématicien d'une très rande envergure

atus [*Br* 'steɪtəs, *Am* 'stætəs] N **1** *(position* ▸ *in ociety, hierarchy etc)* rang *m*, position *f*, situaon *f*; **what's your s. in the company?** quelle est otre position dans l'entreprise?; **she quickly chieved celebrity s.** elle est vite devenue une cébrité

2 *(prestige)* prestige *m*, standing *m*; **living here efinitely confers a certain s.** le fait de vivre ici onfère indéniablement un certain standing u prestige

3 *(legal or official standing)* statut *m*; **legal s.** statut *m* légal

4 *(general state or situation)* état *m*, situation *f*, ondition *f*; **their financial s. is under investigation** n enquête sur leur situation financière

5 *Med* **HIV-positive s.** séropositivité *f*

COMP *(car, club)* de prestige, prestigieux

▸ *Comput* ***status bar*** barre *f* d'état; *Comput* ***status box*** zone *f* d'état; ***status enquiry*** *(about creditorthiness)* prise *f* de renseignements sur la olvabilité; ***status enquiry department*** service *m* es renseignements commerciaux; *Comput* ***status line*** ligne *f* d'état; *Comput* ***status printout*** *(of rinter)* impression *f* des paramètres de l'impriante; ***status quo*** statu quo *m*; **to maintain** *or* **to reserve the s. quo** maintenir le statu quo; *Comut* ***status report*** état *m* du projet; ***status symbol*** arque *f* de prestige

atute ['stætju:t] N **1** *Law* loi *f*; *Br Pol (act)* acte *m* u Parlement **2** *(of club, company, university)* rèle *f*; **the statutes** le règlement, les statuts *mpl*

▸ *Br* ***statute book*** code *m* (des lois), recueil *m* e lois; **the new law is not yet on the s. book** la ouvelle loi n'est pas encore entrée en vigueur; ***tatute law*** droit *m* écrit; ***statute of limitations*** loi *f* e prescription, prescription *f* légale; **the s. of mitations in this country is ten years** dans ce ays, il y a prescription de dix ans

atutory ['stætjʊtrɪ] ADJ **1** *(regulations)* statuaire; *(duties, penalty)* statutaire, juridique; *(holiay)* légal; *(offence)* prévu par la loi; *(price ontrols, income policy)* obligatoire **2** *Br (token)* **he s. woman** la femme-alibi *(présente pour que oit respectée la réglementation sur l'égalité des exes)*

▸ ***statutory company*** entreprise *f* de service pulic; ***statutory damages*** dommages *mpl* et intéêts *mpl* octroyés par la loi; ***statutory declaration*** ttestation *f*; ***statutory instrument*** acte *m* réglementaire; ***statutory law*** droit *m* écrit; *Br* ***statutory aternity pay*** = indemnités versées par l'emloyeur à une employée en congé de maternité; *r* ***statutory paternity pay*** = indemnités versées ar l'employeur, pour un maximum de deux senaines, à un employé qui vient d'avoir un enant; *Am* ***statutory rape*** détournement *m* de nineur; ***statutory rights*** droits *mpl* statutaires; *r* ***statutory sick pay*** = indemnité de maladie verée par l'employeur

taunch [stɔ:ntʃ] ADJ *(loyal)* loyal, dévoué; *(unwerving)* constant, inébranlable; **he's my taunchest ally** c'est mon allié le plus sûr; **a s. atholic** un(e) catholique à tout crin; **a s. socialist** n(e) socialiste convaincu(e)

VT *(liquid, blood)* étancher; *(flow)* arrêter, endiuer

taunchly ['stɔ:ntʃlɪ] ADV *(loyally)* loyalement, vec dévouement; *(unswervingly)* avec contance, fermement; **their house is in a s. Republican area** ils habitent un quartier résolument épublicain

taunchness ['stɔ:ntʃnɪs] N *(loyalty)* loyauté *f*, lévouement *m*; *(firmness)* constance *f*, fermeté *f*

stave [steɪv] *(pt & pp* **staved** *or* **stove** [stəʊv]) N **1** *Mus* portée *f* **2** *(stanza)* strophe *f* **3** *(part of barrel)* douve *f*, douelle *f*

VT *Scot (finger, toe)* se faire une entorse à

▸**stave in** VT SEP enfoncer, défoncer

▸**stave off** VT SEP *(defeat)* retarder; *(worry, danger)* écarter; *(disaster, threat)* conjurer; *(misery, hunger, thirst)* tromper; *(questions)* éluder; **to s. off a cold** éviter un rhume

staves [steɪvz] *pl of* **staff, stave**

STAY [steɪ]

N	
• séjour **1**	• étai **3, 4**
VT	
• aller jusqu'au bout de **1**	• arrêter **2**
• retarder **2**	• étayer **3**
VI	
• rester **1, 2**	• loger **2**

N **1** *(sojourn)* séjour *m*; **enjoy your s.!** bon séjour!; **an overnight s. in hospital** une nuit d'hospitalisation

2 *Law (suspension)* suspension *f*

3 *(support, prop)* étai *m*, support *m*, soutien *m*

4 *(cable, wire* ▸ *for mast, flagpole etc)* étai *m*, hauban *m*

5 *(in corset)* baleine *f*

VT **1** *(last out)* aller jusqu'au bout de, tenir jusqu'à la fin de; *Sport & Fig* **to s. the distance** tenir la distance; **to s. the course** *Sport* finir la course; *Fig* tenir jusqu'au bout

2 *(stop)* arrêter, enrayer; *(delay)* retarder; **to s. sb's hand** retenir qn; **to s. one's hand** se retenir; *Law* **to s. judgment/proceedings** surseoir au jugement/aux poursuites

3 *(prop up* ▸ *wall)* étayer; *(secure with cables* ▸ *mast)* haubaner

VI **1** *(remain)* rester; **to s. still** rester tranquille; **to s. at home** rester à la maison *ou* chez soi; **to s. in bed** rester au lit; *(when ill)* garder le lit; **s. here** *or Fam* **s. put until I come back** restez ici *ou* ne bougez pas jusqu'à ce que je revienne; *Fam* **I'll s. put, I'm staying put** j'y suis, j'y reste; **s.!** *(to dog)* pas bouger!; **I can't s. long, I've got a train to catch** je ne peux pas rester longtemps, j'ai un train à prendre; **would you like to s. for** *or* **to dinner?** voulez-vous rester dîner?; **I don't want to s. in the same job all my life** je ne veux pas faire le même travail toute ma vie; **to s. awake all night** rester éveillé toute la nuit, ne pas dormir de la nuit; **it stays dark here until at least 10 o'clock in the morning** ici, il ne fait pas jour avant 10 heures du matin; **the weather stayed fine/wet all week** le temps est resté au beau/à la pluie toute la semaine; **if the weather stays like this** si le temps se maintient; **let's try and s. calm** essayons de rester calmes; **she managed to s. ahead of the others** elle a réussi à conserver son avance sur les autres; **digital cameras have come to s.** *or* **are here to s.** le numérique fait désormais partie de notre quotidien

2 *(reside temporarily* ▸ *in hotel, with friends)* loger; *(*▸ *in a city)* rester; **how long are you staying in New York?** combien de temps restez-vous à New York?; **we decided to s. an extra week** nous avons décidé de rester une semaine de plus *ou* de prolonger notre séjour d'une semaine; **I always s. at the same hotel** je descends toujours au *ou* je loge toujours dans le même hôtel; **to look for a place to s.** chercher un endroit où loger; **she's staying with friends** elle loge chez des amis; **he has come to s. (for a few days/weeks)** il est venu passer quelques jours/semaines chez nous; **I like having people to s.** j'aime bien avoir des gens chez moi; **you can s. here for the night, you can s. the night here** tu peux coucher ici cette nuit *ou* passer la nuit ici

3 *Literary (stop, pause)* s'arrêter

4 *Scot (live)* habiter, demeurer

• **stays** NPL corset *m*

▸▸ *Law* ***stay of execution*** ordonnance *f* à surseoir (à un jugement), sursis *m*; *Fig* sursis; *Law* ***stay of proceedings*** suspension *f* d'instances; ***stay stitch*** point *m* d'arrêt

▸**stay away** VI *(not go)* ne pas aller; *(not come)* ne pas venir; *(not approach)* ne pas approcher; **she stayed away from school last week** elle n'est pas allée à l'école la semaine dernière; **people are staying away from the beaches** les plages sont désertées en ce moment; **to s. away from danger** se tenir à l'écart du danger; **you can play outside but s. away from the road** tu peux jouer dehors mais ne va pas sur la route; **s. away from my sister!** ne t'approche pas de ma sœur!

▸**stay behind** VI rester; **I'll s. behind to clear up** je vais rester pour ranger; **a few pupils stayed behind to talk to the teacher** quelques élèves sont restés (après le cours) pour parler au professeur

▸**stay down** VI **1** *(gen)* rester en bas; *(remain crouched)* rester accroupi; *(remain lying)* rester couché; *(remain under water)* rester sous l'eau

2 *(hair, lid)* tenir en place

3 *Br Sch* redoubler; **she had to s. down a year** elle a dû redoubler

4 *(food)* **I do eat, but nothing will s. down** je mange, mais je ne peux rien garder

▸**stay in** VI **1** *(stay at home)* rester à la maison, ne pas sortir; *(stay indoors)* rester à l'intérieur, ne pas sortir **2** *(be kept in after school)* être consigné, être en retenue **3** *(not fall out)* rester en place, tenir; **I can't get this nail to s. in** je n'arrive pas à faire tenir ce clou

▸**stay off** VT INSEP **1** *(keep away from* ▸ *main roads, private property)* éviter, ne pas passer par; *(*▸ *alcohol, drugs)* ne pas prendre, éviter; **s. off the whisky!** pas de whisky! **2** *(not attend* ▸ *school, work)* ne pas aller à

VI *(bad weather)* ne pas arriver; **we're hoping the rain will s. off a little longer** nous espérons que la pluie attendra encore un peu

▸**stay on** VI **1** *(not leave)* rester; **more pupils are staying on at school after the age of 16** de plus en plus d'élèves poursuivent leur scolarité au-delà de l'âge de 16 ans; **he's staying on in the firm as product manager** il va rester dans l'entreprise en tant que chef de produit **2** *(remain in place* ▸ *hat, wig)* tenir *ou* rester en place; *(sticker, handle)* tenir

▸**stay out** VI **1** *(not come home)* ne pas rentrer; *(remain outside)* rester dehors; **she stayed out all night** elle n'est pas rentrée de la nuit; **to s. out late** rentrer tard; **get out and s. out!** sors d'ici et ne t'avise pas de revenir! **2** *(remain on strike)* rester en grève; **the miners stayed out for nearly a year** la grève des mineurs a duré près d'un an **3** *(not get involved)* ne pas se mêler (**of** de); **s. out of this!** ne te mêle pas de ça!

▸**stay over** VI **1** *(not leave)* prolonger son séjour, rester plus longtemps; **we decided to s. over until the weekend** nous avons décidé de prolonger notre séjour jusqu'au week-end **2** *(stay the night)* passer la nuit; **do you want to s. over?** veux-tu passer la nuit ici?

▸**stay up** VI **1** *(not go to bed)* veiller, ne pas se coucher; **don't s. up too late** ne veillez pas *ou* ne vous couchez pas trop tard; **we stayed up all night talking** nous sommes restés à parler toute la nuit; **my parents always s. up until I get home** mes parents attendent toujours que je sois rentré pour aller se coucher **2** *(remain in place* ▸ *building, mast)* rester debout; *(*▸ *shelf, socks, trousers)* tenir; *(*▸ *pictures, decorations)* rester en place

stay-at-home *Fam Pej* N pantouflard(e) *m,f*

ADJ pantouflard, popote *(inv)*

▸▸ ***stay-at-home mother*** mère *f* au foyer

stayer ['steɪə(r)] N **1** *Sport (runner)* coureur(euse) *m,f* de fond; *(cyclist)* stayer *m*; *(horse)* stayer *m*, cheval *m* qui a du fond **2** *(person who perseveres)* personne *f* persévérante; **she's a real s.** elle va jusqu'au bout de ce qu'elle entreprend

staying power ['steɪɪŋ-] N résistance *f*, endurance *f*

STD [ˌesti:'di:] N **1** *Br Tel (abbr* **subscriber trunk dialling)** automatique *m* (interurbain) **2** *(abbr* **sexually transmitted disease)** MST *f*

▸▸ ***STD code*** indicatif *m* de zone

stead [sted] N *Br Formal* **in sb's s.** à la place de qn; **he asked me to go in his s.** il m'a demandé d'y aller à sa place; **to stand sb in good s.** rendre grand service *ou* être très utile à qn

steadfast ['stedfɑ:st] **ADJ 1** *(unswerving)* constant, inébranlable; *(loyal)* loyal, dévoué; **to be s. in one's support of sb** apporter un soutien inconditionnel à qn **2** *(steady ▸ stare, gaze)* fixe

steadfastly ['stedfɑ:stlɪ] **ADV** avec constance, fermement; **she has s. refused to identify her sources** elle a toujours refusé de désigner ses sources

steadfastness ['stedfɑ:stnɪs] **N** constance *f*, fermeté *f*; **they showed great s. of purpose** ils ont fait preuve d'une grande ténacité *ou* persévérance

Steadicam® ['stedɪkæm] **N** *TV & Cin* Steadicam® *m*

▸▸ *Steadicam® operator* opérateur *m* Steadicam®

steadily ['stedɪlɪ] **ADV 1** *(at regular rate ▸ increase, decline)* régulièrement, progressivement; *(▸ breathe)* régulièrement; **to work s. at sth** travailler assidûment à qch **2** *(non-stop ▸ rain)* sans interruption, sans cesse; **her health grew s. worse** sa santé s'est progressivement détériorée **3** *(firmly ▸ stand)* planté *ou* campé sur ses jambes; *(▸ walk)* d'un pas ferme; *(▸ gaze)* fixement, sans détourner les yeux; **she looked at him s.** elle l'a fixé du regard, elle l'a regardé fixement

steadiness ['stedɪnɪs] **N 1** *(regularity ▸ of growth, increase, decline, speed, pace, pulse)* régularité *f*
2 *(firmness, stability ▸ of ladder, boat, relationship, market)* stabilité *f*; *(▸ of structure, desk, chair)* stabilité *f*, solidité *f*; *(▸ of hand)* sûreté *f*
3 *(firmness ▸ of voice)* fermeté *f*; *(▸ of gaze)* fixité *f*; *(▸ of nerves)* solidité *f*
4 *(reliability ▸ of person)* sérieux *m*

steady ['stedɪ] *(compar* **steadier**, *superl* **steadiest**, *pl* **steadies**, *pt & pp* **steadied**) **ADJ 1** *(regular, constant ▸ growth, increase, decline)* régulier, progressif; *(▸ speed, pace)* régulier, constant; *(▸ demand)* suivi; *(▸ pulse)* régulier, égal; *(▸ work)* stable; *(▸ income)* régulier; *(▸ rain)* persistant; **inflation remains at a s. 5 percent** l'inflation s'est stabilisée à 5 pour cent; **to drive at a s. 90** rouler constamment à 90; **he's never been able to hold down a s. job** il n'a jamais pu garder un emploi stable; **I've got several boyfriends but no one s.** j'ai des flirts, mais pas de petit ami attitré; **he has a s. girlfriend** il sort avec la même copine depuis longtemps
2 *(firm, stable ▸ ladder, boat, relationship, market)* stable; *(▸ structure, desk, chair)* solide, stable; **hold the ladder s. for me** tiens-moi l'échelle; **to have a s. hand** avoir la main sûre; **to be s. on one's feet** *or* **legs** être d'aplomb sur ses jambes
3 *(calm ▸ voice)* ferme; *(▸ gaze)* fixe; *(▸ nerves)* solide
4 *(reliable ▸ person)* sérieux
ADV to go s. with sb sortir avec qn; **are Diana and Paul going s.?** c'est sérieux entre Diana et Paul?
N *Fam* petit(e) ami(e) *m,f*
EXCLAM *Br* **s. (on)!** *(be careful)* attention!; *(calm down)* du calme!; **s.! you almost knocked me over!** eh! doucement! tu as failli me faire tomber!
VT 1 *(stabilize)* stabiliser; *(hold in place)* maintenir, retenir; **I reached out to s. the vase** j'ai tendu le bras pour retenir le vase; **he almost fell off, but he managed to s. himself** il a failli tomber, mais il a réussi à se rattraper; **she rested her elbows on the wall to s. the camera** elle appuya ses coudes sur le mur pour que l'appareil photo ne bouge pas **2** *(calm)* calmer; **drink this, it'll s. your nerves** bois ça, ça te calmera (les nerfs); **marriage has steadied him** le mariage lui a donné un certain équilibre
VI *(boat, prices, stock market)* se stabiliser; *(pulse, breathing)* devenir régulier; *(person ▸ regain balance)* retrouver son équilibre; *(▸ calm down)* se calmer
▸▸ *Phys* ***steady state theory*** théorie *f* de l'état *ou* de l'univers stationnaire

steak [steɪk] **N 1** *(for frying, grilling)* steak *m*, bifteck *m*; **s. and chips** steak frites *m* **2** *(for stews, casseroles)* bœuf *m* à braiser; *Br* **s. and kidney pie** = tourte à la viande et aux rognons cuite au four; *Br* **s. and kidney pudding** = tourte à la viande et aux rognons cuite à la vapeur **3** *(cut ▸ of veal, turkey)* escalope *f*; *(▸ of other meat)* tranche *f*; *(▸ of fish)* tranche *f*, darne *f*
▸▸ *steak knife* couteau *m* à steak *ou* à viande; ***steak tartare*** steak *m* tartare

steakhouse ['steɪkhaʊs, *pl* -haʊzɪz] **N** grill *m*, grill-room *m*

steal [sti:l] *(pt* **stole** [stəʊl], *pp* **stolen** ['stəʊlən]) **VT 1** *(money, property)* voler; **to s. sth from sb** voler qch à qn; **he stole money from her purse** il a volé de l'argent dans son porte-monnaie; **I've had my purse stolen** on m'a volé mon porte-monnaie; **several paintings have been stolen from the museum** plusieurs tableaux ont été volés au musée; **they've stolen my idea!** ils ont volé mon idée! **2** *Fig (time)* voler, prendre; *(attention, affection)* détourner; **to s. sb's heart** séduire qn; **to s. a kiss** voler un baiser; **to s. all the credit for sth** s'attribuer tout le mérite de qch; **may I s. a few moments of your precious time?** pouvez-vous m'accorder quelques instants de votre temps si précieux?; **to s. a glance at sb** jeter un regard furtif à qn; *Br* **to s. a march on sb** prendre qn de vitesse, couper l'herbe sous le pied à qn; **to s. the show from sb** ravir la vedette à qn; **he really stole the show with that act of his!** son numéro a été le clou du spectacle!; **to s. sb's thunder** éclipser qn
VI 1 *(commit theft)* voler; **he was caught stealing** il a été pris en train de voler; *Bible* **thou shalt not s.** tu ne voleras point **2** *(move secretively)* **to s. in/out** entrer/sortir à pas furtifs *ou* feutrés; **to s. into a room** se glisser *ou* se faufiler dans une pièce; **she stole up on me from behind** elle s'est approchée de moi par derrière sans faire de bruit; *Fig Literary* **shadows began to s. across the courtyard** des ombres commencèrent à envahir la cour; *Literary* **a strange sadness stole over me** une étrange tristesse m'envahit
N 1 *Fam (bargain)* affaire *f*; **it was a s.** c'était une bonne affaire **2** *Sport (in basketball)* récupération *f* du ballon

stealing ['sti:lɪŋ] **N** vol *m*

stealth [stelθ] **N 1** *(of animal)* ruse *f* **2** *(UNCOUNT) (underhandedness)* moyens *mpl* détournés; **the documents were obtained by s.** nous nous sommes procuré les documents en cachette *ou* par des moyens détournés
▸▸ *stealth bomber, stealth plane* avion *m* furtif; ***stealth tax*** = mesure visant à augmenter les recettes du gouvernement par un moyen détourné, afin d'éviter une hausse directe et visible des impôts qui mécontenterait les citoyens

stealthily ['stelθɪlɪ] **ADV** furtivement, subrepticement, en catimini

stealthiness ['stelθɪnɪs] **N** *(of action etc)* caractère *m* furtif; *(of person)* manières *fpl* furtives; **his s. in defaming his rivals** la ruse avec laquelle il parvenait à diffamer ses rivaux

stealthy ['stelθɪ] *(compar* **stealthier**, *superl* **stealthiest**) **ADJ** furtif

steam [sti:m] **N 1** *(vapour)* vapeur *f*; *(condensation)* buée *f*; **she wiped the s. from the mirror** elle essuya la buée sur la glace **2** *Tech & Rail (as power)* vapeur *f*; **to run on** *or* **to work by s.** marcher à la vapeur; **at full s.** à toute vapeur, à pleine vitesse; **full s. ahead!** en avant toute!; **to do sth under one's own s.** faire qch par ses propres moyens; **to get up** *or* **to pick up s.** *(vehicle)* prendre de la vitesse; *(campaign)* être lancé; **the battle against drugs is finally picking up s.** la lutte contre la drogue est enfin bien lancée; *Fam* **to let off s.** se défouler; *Fam* **to run out of s.** s'essouffler[□], s'épuiser[□]
COMP *(boiler, locomotive etc)* à vapeur
VT 1 *(unstick with steam)* **s. the stamps off the envelope** passez l'enveloppe à la vapeur pour décoller les timbres; **to s. open an envelope** décacheter une enveloppe à la vapeur **2** *Culin* (faire) cuire à la vapeur
VI 1 *(give off steam ▸ soup, kettle, wet clothes)* fumer **2** *(cook in steam)* cuire à la vapeur **3** *(go ▸ train, ship)* **the train steamed into/out of the station** le train entra en gare/quitta la gare; **the liner steamed into the harbour** le paquebot entra dans le port; *Fig* **my brother steamed on ahead** mon frère filait devant; *Fig* **she steamed into/out of the room** elle est entrée dans/sortie de la pièce comme une furie
▸▸ *steam bath* bain *m* de vapeur; ***steam coal*** charbon *m* à vapeur, houille *f* de chaudière; ***steam cooking*** cuisson *f* à la vapeur; ***steam e gine*** *Tech* moteur *m* à vapeur; *Rail* locomotive vapeur; ***steam heat*** chaleur *f* fournie par la v peur; ***steam iron*** fer *m* (à repasser) à vapeur; *Te* ***steam jacket*** enveloppe *f* de cylindre, chemise de vapeur; ***steam point*** point *m* d'ébullitio ***steam power*** vapeur *f*; *Br Fam Old-fashion* ***steam radio*** *(broadcasting)* ≃ la bonne vieille r dio *(par opposition à la télévision)*; *(set)* poste de radio antédiluvien; *Am* ***steam shovel*** bulld zer *m*; ***steam turbine*** turbine *f* à vapeur; ***stea whistle*** sifflet *m* à vapeur

▸ steam up VI *(window, glasses)* s'embuer, couvrir de buée
VT SEP 1 *(window, glasses)* embuer **2** *Am Fam (i furiate)* **to s. sb up** mettre qn en pétard *ou* e boule

steamboat ['sti:mbəʊt] **N** bateau *m* à vapeu vapeur *m*

steamed [sti:md] **ADJ** *(fish, vegetables etc)* à vapeur
▸▸ *steamed pudding* = pudding cuit au bai marie

steamer ['sti:mə(r)] **N 1** *Naut* bateau *m* à vapeu vapeur *m* **2** *Culin (pan)* marmite *f* à vapeur; *(ba ket inside pan)* panier *m* de cuisson à la vapeu

steaming ['sti:mɪŋ] **ADJ 1** *(very hot)* fumant **2** *A Fam (angry)* en pétard, en boule **3** *Br Fam (drun* complètement bourré *ou* pété
ADV s. hot fumant; *Br Fam* **s. drunk** complèt ment bourré *ou* pété
N 1 *Culin* cuisson *f* à la vapeur **2** *Fam Crime slar* = vol de sacs à main pratiqué en bande, da les endroits publics aux heures de grande a fluence

steamroller ['sti:mˌrəʊlə(r)] **N** rouleau *m* co presseur; *Fig* **to use s. tactics** employer la tec nique du rouleau compresseur
VT 1 *(road)* cylindrer **2** *Fig (crush ▸ oppositio obstacle)* écraser **3** *Fig (force)* **to s. a bill throug Parliament** = faire passer une loi à la Chamb sans tenir compte de l'opposition; **to s. sb in doing sth** forcer qn à faire qch

steamship ['sti:mʃɪp] **N** navire *m* à vapeur, v peur *m*

steamy ['sti:mɪ] *(compar* **steamier**, *supe* **steamiest**) **ADJ 1** *(room)* plein de vapeur; *(wi dow, mirror)* embué **2** *Fam (erotic)* chaud, sexy

steed [sti:d] **N** *Literary* coursier *m*

steel [sti:l] **N 1** *(iron alloy)* acier *m*; **a grip/a will s.** une poigne/une volonté de fer
2 *(steel industry)* industrie *f* sidérurgique, sid rurgie *f*; **the nationalization of s.** la nationalis tion de l'industrie sidérurgique
3 *(for sharpening knives)* aiguisoir *m*
4 *Literary (sword)* fer *m*
COMP *(plant)* sidérurgique; *(strike)* des sidéru gistes
ADJ *(helmet, cutlery etc)* en acier
VT 1 *Br (harden)* **to s. oneself against sth** se cuira ser contre qch; **s. yourself for a terrible orde** préparez-vous à affronter une rude épreuve; **had steeled myself for the worst** je m'étais pr paré au pire **2** *Metal* aciérer
▸▸ *Mus* ***steel band*** steel band *m*; ***steel blue*** bleu acier; ***steel grey*** gris *m* acier; ***steel guitar*** ste guitar *f*; ***the steel industry*** la sidérurgie; ***ste manufacturer*** sidérurgiste *mf*; ***steel mill*** aciérie ***steel wool*** paille *f* de fer

steelclad ['sti:lklæd] **ADJ** *(gen)* couvert *ou* revêt d'acier; *Literary (knight)* bardé de fer

steel-plated **ADJ** cuirassé

steelwork ['sti:lwɜ:k] **N** *(UNCOUNT) Tech* tôl ries *fpl*; **constructional s.** profilés *mpl* pour con tructions

steelworker ['sti:lˌwɜ:kə(r)] **N** sidérurgiste *mf*

steelworks ['sti:lwɜ:ks] *(pl* **inv**) **N** aciérie *f*, usin *f* sidérurgique

steely ['sti:lɪ] **ADJ 1** *(in colour)* d'acier, gris aci *(inv)* **2** *(strong ▸ determination, will)* de fer; *(look)* d'acier
▸▸ *steely blue* bleu *m* acier *(inv)*

steelyard ['sti:ljɑ:d] **N** balance *f* romaine

steely-blue **ADJ** bleu acier *(inv)*

steep [stiːp] ADJ 1 *(hill)* raide, abrupt, escarpé; *(slope)* fort, raide; *(cliff)* abrupt; *(road, path)* raide, escarpé; *(staircase)* raide; **it's a s. climb to the village** la montée est raide pour arriver au village; **the plane went into a s. dive** l'avion se mit à piquer du nez
2 *(increase, fall)* fort; **a s. drop in share prices** une forte chute du prix des actions
3 *Fam (fee, price)* excessif□, élevé□; **the prices are a bit s.** l'addition est plutôt salée
4 *Fam (unreasonable)* **it's a bit s. asking us to do all that work by Friday** c'est un peu fort *ou* un peu raide de nous demander de faire tout ce travail pour vendredi
VT *(soak)* (faire) tremper; *Culin* (faire) macérer, (faire) mariner; **s. the onions in vinegar** faites macérer les oignons dans du vinaigre; *Fig* **I want to s. myself in the atmosphere of the place** je veux m'imprégner de l'atmosphère de l'endroit
VI *(gen)* tremper; *Culin* macérer, mariner

steepen [ˈstiːpən] VI 1 *(slope, road, path)* devenir plus raide *ou* escarpé; **the climb steepened as we neared the top** la pente devenait de plus en plus raide à mesure que nous approchions du sommet 2 *(increase ▸ inflation, rate)* croître

steeple [ˈstiːpəl] N *(bell tower)* clocher *m*; *(spire)* flèche *f* (de clocher)

steeplechase [ˈstiːpəltʃeɪs] N *(in horseracing, athletics)* steeple *m*, steeple-chase *m*

steeplechaser [ˈstiːpəlˌtʃeɪsə(r)] N 1 *(jockey)* jockey *m* de steeple *ou* steeple-chase 2 *(runner)* coureur(euse) *m,f* de steeple *ou* steeple-chase

steeplechasing [ˈstiːpəlˌtʃeɪsɪŋ] N *(in horseracing, athletics)* steeple-chases *mpl*

steeplejack [ˈstiːpəldʒæk] N *Br* = réparateur de clochers et de cheminées

steeply [ˈstiːplɪ] ADV en pente raide, à pic; **the path climbs s.** le chemin monte en pente raide; **a s. sloping field leads down to the lake** un champ descend en pente raide jusqu'au lac; **costs are rising s.** les coûts montent en flèche

steepness [ˈstiːpnɪs] N 1 *(of climb, road, staircase)* raideur *f* 2 *(of price rise)* importance *f*

steer [stɪə(r)] VT 1 *(car)* conduire; **the lorry was surprisingly easy to s.** le camion était étonnamment facile à conduire; **she steered the car into the garage/out onto the main road** elle a rentré la voiture au garage/conduit jusqu'à la route principale
2 *Naut (boat)* gouverner, barrer; **to s. a course for** mettre le cap sur; *Fig* **to s. a middle course** trouver un compromis; *Fig* **it's a dangerous course you're steering** vous vous engagez sur un terrain dangereux; **steered course** route *f* au compas *ou* apparente
3 *(person)* guider, diriger; **she steered me over to a sofa** elle m'a guidé vers un canapé; **try to s. him away from the bar** essayez de l'éloigner du bar
4 *(conversation, project etc)* diriger; **I tried to s. the conversation round to/away from the subject** j'ai essayé d'amener la conversation sur le sujet/de détourner la conversation du sujet; **she successfully steered the company through the crisis** elle a réussi à sortir la société de la crise; **to s. a bill through Parliament** réussir à faire voter un projet de loi par le Parlement
VI 1 *(driver)* conduire; **I steered carefully into the garage** j'ai manœuvré avec soin pour entrer dans le garage; **she steered smoothly round the bend** elle prit le virage en douceur
2 *Naut (helmsman)* gouverner, barrer; *(boat)* se diriger; **the ferry was steering for Dover** le ferry se dirigeait vers Douvres; **s. for that buoy** mettez le cap sur cette bouée; **to s. clear of sb/sth** éviter qn/qch; **s. clear of her husband, he's a real bore** évite son mari, c'est un vrai raseur
3 *(car)* **this car steers very well/badly** cette voiture a une excellente/très mauvaise direction; **a taxi steered out of a side street** un taxi a débouché d'une rue latérale
N 1 *Agr* bœuf *m* 2 *Am Fam (piece of advice)* conseil□ *m*; *(tip)* tuyau *m*

steerage [ˈstɪərɪdʒ] N *Naut* 1 *Old-fashioned (accommodation)* entrepont *m*; **s. passengers** passagers *mpl* d'entrepont 2 *(steering)* conduite *f*, pilotage *m*

steerageway [ˈstɪərɪdʒˌweɪ] N *Naut* vitesse *f* acquise, *Spec* erre *f*; **to get up/to lose s.** augmenter/diminuer l'erre

steering [ˈstɪərɪŋ] N 1 *Aut (apparatus, mechanism)* direction *f*; *(manner of driving)* conduite *f* 2 *Naut* conduite *f*, pilotage *m*
COMP *Aut (arm, lever)* de direction
►► *Aut* ***steering box*** boîtier *m* de direction; ***steering column*** colonne *f* de direction; *Br* ***steering committee*** comité *m* directeur; *Aviat & Aut* ***steering gear*** mécanisme *m* de direction; *Naut* appareil *m* à gouverner; *Aut* ***steering lock*** *(turning circle)* rayon *m* de braquage; *(antitheft device)* antivol *m* de direction; ***steering rod*** bielle *f* de direction; ***steering wheel*** *Aut* volant *m*; *Naut* roue *f* du gouvernail, barre *f*; *Aut* ***steering wheel cover*** housse *f* de volant

steersman [ˈstɪəzmən] N (*pl* **steersmen** [-mən]) timonier *m*, barreur *m*

stellar [ˈstelə(r)] ADJ 1 *Astron* stellaire 2 *Fig (outstanding)* éblouissant; **the singer gave a s. performance** la prestation de la chanteuse a été éblouissante

stem [stem] (*pt & pp* **stemmed**, *cont* **stemming**) N 1 *Bot (of plant, tree)* tige *f*; *(of fruit, leaf)* queue *f*
2 *(of glass)* pied *m*
3 *(of tobacco pipe)* tuyau *m*
4 *Ling (of word)* radical *m*
5 *Tech (in lock, watch, valve)* tige *f*; **winding s.** tige *f* de remontoir
6 *(vertical stroke ▸ of letter)* hampe *f*; *(▸ of musical note)* queue *f*
7 *Naut (timber, structure)* étrave *f*; *(forward section)* proue *f*; **from s. to stern** de l'étrave à l'étambot; *Fig* **the party is split from s. to stern on this issue** le parti est totalement divisé sur cette question
8 *Bible (family, stock)* souche *f*
9 *Sport (in skiing)* stem(m) *m*; **s. Christie/parallel** stem(m) *m* christie/parallèle
VT 1 *(check, stop ▸ flow, spread, bleeding)* arrêter, endiguer; *(▸ blood)* étancher; *(▸ river, flood)* endiguer, contenir; **the government has taken new measures to s. the flow of capital abroad** le gouvernement a pris de nouvelles mesures pour arrêter la fuite des capitaux à l'étranger; **to s. the rise in unemployment/crime** enrayer la montée du chômage/de la criminalité; **they are trying to s. the tide of protest** ils essaient d'endiguer le nombre croissant de protestations 2 *Sport* **to s. one's skis** faire un stem(m)
VI 1 *(derive)* **to s. from** avoir pour cause, être le résultat de; **all her difficulties s. from her insecure childhood** tous ses problèmes ont pour cause une enfance difficile 2 *Sport (in skiing)* faire du stem(m)
►► *Biol* ***stem cell*** cellule *f* souche; ***stem ginger*** gingembre *m* confit; ***stem glass*** verre *m* à pied; ***stem turn*** *(in skiing)* stem(m) *m*

stemmed [stemd] ADJ *(glass)* à pied

stemware [ˈstemweə(r)] N *Am (glasses)* verres *mpl*

stench [stentʃ] N puanteur *f*, odeur *f* nauséabonde; *Fig* **the s. of decay** l'odeur nauséabonde de la putréfaction

stencil [ˈstensəl] (*Br pt & pp* **stencilled**, *cont* **stencilling**, *Am pt & pp* **stenciled**, *cont* **stenciling**) N 1 *(for typing)* stencil *m* 2 *(template)* pochoir *m* 3 *(pattern ▸ drawn)* dessin *m* au pochoir; *(▸ painted)* peinture *f* au pochoir
VT *(draw)* dessiner au pochoir; *(paint)* peindre au pochoir

Sten gun [sten-] N mitraillette *f* légère

stenographer [stəˈnɒgrəfə(r)] N *Am* sténographe *mf*

stenography [stəˈnɒgrəfɪ] N sténographie *f*

Stenotype® [ˈstenəʊtaɪp] N sténotype *f*

stenotypist [ˈstenəʊˌtaɪpɪst] N sténotypiste *mf*

stenotypy [ˈstenətaɪpɪ] N sténotypie *f*

stentorian [stenˈtɔːrɪən] ADJ *Literary (voice)* de stentor

STEP [step]

N
- pas **1, 2, 4**
- mesure **2**
- étape **3**
- marche **5**
- seconde **6**
- step **7**

VT
- mesurer **1**
- échelonner **2**

VI
- faire un pas **1**
- marcher **1, 2**

(*pt & pp* **stepped**, *cont* **stepping**)
N 1 *(pace)* pas *m*; **with quick steps** d'un pas rapide; **to take two steps forwards/backwards** faire deux pas en avant/en arrière; **I grew wearier with every s. I took** je m'épuisais un peu plus à chaque pas (que je faisais); **I heard her s.** *or* **steps on the stairs** j'ai entendu (le bruit de) ses pas dans l'escalier; **he was following a few steps behind me** il me suivait à quelques pas; **it's only a (short) s. to the shops** les magasins sont à deux pas d'ici; **within a few steps of the house** à quelques pas de la maison; **watch** *or* **mind your s.!** faites attention où vous mettez les pieds!; *Fig* faites attention!
2 *(move, action)* pas *m*; *(measure)* mesure *f*, disposition *f*; **it's a great s. forward for mankind** c'est un grand pas en avant pour l'humanité; **our first s. will be to cut costs** notre première mesure sera de réduire les coûts; **to take steps to do sth** prendre des mesures pour faire qch; **what steps have you taken?** quelles mesures avez-vous prises?; **it's only a short s. from what you are suggesting to an outright ban** entre ce que vous suggérez et une interdiction absolue, il n'y a qu'un pas; **it's a s. in the right direction** c'est un pas dans la bonne direction; **this promotion is a big s. up for me** cette promotion est un grand pas en avant pour moi; **we are still one s. ahead of our competitors** nous conservons une petite avance sur nos concurrents
3 *(stage)* étape *f*; **the different steps in the manufacturing process** les différentes étapes du processus de fabrication; **the next s. is to...** l'étape suivante consiste à...; **we'll support you every s. of the way** nous vous soutiendrons à fond *ou* sur toute la ligne; **they fought us every s. of the way** ils nous ont combattus sans répit *ou* sur chaque point; **one s. at a time** petit à petit; **s. by s.** petit à petit
4 *(in marching, dancing)* pas *m*; **a minuet s.** un pas de menuet; **in s.** au pas; **to march in s.** marcher au pas; **to be out of s.** ne pas être en cadence; **they were walking out of s.** ils ne marchaient pas en cadence; **to break s.** rompre le pas; **to change s.** changer de pas; **to fall into s. with sb** s'aligner sur le pas de qn; *Fig* se ranger à l'avis de qn; **he fell into s. beside me** arrivé à ma hauteur, il régla son pas sur le mien; **to keep (in) s.** marcher au pas; **do try and keep s.!** *(in dancing)* essaie donc de danser en mesure!; **to be in s. with the times/with public opinion** être au diapason de son temps/de l'opinion publique; **to be out of s. with the times/with public opinion** être déphasé par rapport à son époque/à l'opinion publique; **supply has got out of s. with demand** l'offre ne correspond plus à la demande
5 *(stair ▸ gen)* marche *f*; *(▸ into bus, train etc)* marche-pied *m*; **a flight of steps** *(indoors)* un escalier; *(outdoors)* un perron; **the church steps** le perron de l'église; **mind the s.** *(sign)* attention à la marche; **to cut steps** *(in mountaineering)* tailler des marches
6 *Am Mus (interval)* seconde *f*
7 *(aerobics)* step *m*; **I go to s. twice a week** je vais à un cours de step deux fois par semaine
VT 1 *(measure out)* mesurer
2 *(space out)* échelonner
VI 1 *(take a single step)* faire un pas; *(walk, go)* marcher, aller; **s. this way, please** par ici, je vous prie; **s. inside!** entrez!; **he carefully stepped round the sleeping dog** il contourna précautionneusement le chien endormi; **I stepped onto/off the train** je suis monté dans le/descendu du train; **she stepped lightly over the ditch** elle enjamba le fossé lestement; *Fig* **to s. out of line** s'écarter du droit chemin
2 *(put one's foot down, tread)* marcher; **to s. on sb's foot** marcher sur le pied de qn; **I stepped on a banana skin/in a puddle** j'ai marché sur une peau de banane/dans une flaque d'eau; *Fam* **s. on it!** appuie sur le champignon!
• **steps** NPL *Br (stepladder)* **(pair of) steps** escabeau *m*

►► ***step aerobics*** step *m*; *Comput & Typ* ***step effect*** escalier *m*

► **step aside** VI **1** *(move to one side)* s'écarter, s'effacer **2** *(quit position, job)* se retirer, se désister; **he stepped aside in favour of a younger person** il a cédé la place à quelqu'un de plus jeune

► **step back** VI **1** reculer, faire un pas en arrière **2** *Fig* prendre du recul; **we don't have time to s. back and figure out what it all means** nous n'avons pas le temps de prendre du recul pour essayer de comprendre tout cela

► **step down** VT SEP *Elec (voltage)* abaisser

VI **1** *(descend)* descendre (**from** de) **2** *(quit position, job)* se retirer, se désister; **he stepped down in favour of a younger person** il a cédé la place à quelqu'un de plus jeune; **he has stepped down as managing director** il a démissionné de son poste de directeur général

► **step forward** VI faire un pas en avant; *Fig (make oneself known)* se manifester; *(volunteer)* se porter volontaire

► **step in** VI **1** *(enter)* entrer **2** *(intervene)* intervenir

► **step out** VI **1** *(go out of doors)* sortir **2** *(walk faster)* presser le pas **3** *Am Old-fashioned* **to be stepping out with sb** sortir avec qn

► **step up** VT SEP **1** *(increase ► output, pace)* augmenter, accroître; *(► activity, efforts)* intensifier **2** *Elec (voltage)* augmenter

VI s'approcher; **to s. up to sb/sth** s'approcher de qn/qch; **s. up!, s. up!, come and see…** approchez! approchez! venez voir…; **he stepped up onto the platform** il est monté sur le podium

---

stepbrother ['step,brʌðə(r)] N demi-frère *m (fils du beau-père ou de la belle-mère)*

step-by-step ADV *(gradually)* pas à pas, petit à petit

ADJ *(point by point)* **a s. guide to buying your own house** *(title)* acheter une maison: guide détaillé

stepchild ['step,tʃaɪld] *(pl* **stepchildren** [-'tʃɪldrən]*)* N beau-fils (belle-fille) *m,f (fils ou fille du conjoint)*

stepdaughter ['step,dɔːtə(r)] N belle-fille *f (fille du conjoint)*

stepfather ['step,fɑːðə(r)] N beau-père *m (conjoint de la mère)*

stepladder ['step,lædə(r)] N escabeau *m*

stepmother ['step,mʌðə(r)] N belle-mère *f (conjointe du père)*

steppe [step] N steppe *f*

stepper ['stepə(r)] N *(gym equipment)* stepper *m*

►► *Elec* ***stepper motor*** moteur *m* pas-à-pas

stepping-stone ['stepɪŋ-] N pierre *f* de gué; *Fig* tremplin *m*; **a s. to a new career** un tremplin pour (se lancer dans) une nouvelle carrière

stepping up N **1** *(of output, pace)* augmentation *f*; *(of activity, efforts)* intensification *f* **2** *Elec (of voltage)* augmentation *f*

stepsister ['step,sɪstə(r)] N demi-sœur *f (fille du beau-père ou de la belle-mère)*

stepson ['stepsʌn] N beau-fils *m (fils du conjoint)*

stereo ['sterɪəʊ] *(pl* **stereos***)* N **1** *(stereo sound)* stéréo *f*; **broadcast in s.** retransmis en stéréo **2** *(hi-fi system)* chaîne *f* (stéréo); **I need a new s.** il me faudrait une nouvelle chaîne

ADJ *(cassette, record, record player)* stéréo *(inv)*; *(recording, broadcast)* en stéréo

►► ***stereo signal*** signal *m* stéréo; ***stereo sound*** son *m* stéréo; ***stereo system*** chaîne *f* stéréo; ***stereo transmitter*** émetteur *m* stéréo

stereophonic [,sterɪə'fɒnɪk] ADJ stéréophonique

stereoscope ['sterɪəʊskəʊp] N stéréoscope *m*

stereoscopic [,sterɪə'skɒpɪk] ADJ stéréoscopique

stereotype ['sterɪətaɪp] N **1** *(idea, trait, convention)* stéréotype *m*; **they don't really conform to our s. of what Americans are like** ils ne correspondent pas vraiment au stéréotype que nous avons des Américains **2** *Typ* cliché *m*

VT **1** *(person, role)* stéréotyper **2** *Typ* clicher

stereotyped ['sterɪəʊtaɪpt] ADJ stéréotypé; **the film is full of very s. images of women** dans ce film, les personnages de femmes sont très stéréotypés *ou* les femmes ont des rôles très stéréotypés

stereotypical [,sterɪəʊ'tɪpɪkəl] ADJ stéréotypé

stereotyping ['sterɪəʊ,taɪpɪŋ] N **we want to avoid sexual s.** nous voulons éviter les stéréotypes sexuels

sterile ['steraɪl] ADJ stérile

sterility [ste'rɪlətɪ] N stérilité *f*

sterilization, -isation [,sterəlaɪ'zeɪʃən] N stérilisation *f*

sterilize, -ise ['sterəlaɪz] VT stériliser

sterilizer, -iser ['sterəlaɪzə(r)] N stérilisateur *m*

sterilizing, -ising ['sterəlaɪzɪŋ] N stérilisation *f*

►► ***sterilizing tablets*** comprimés *mpl* purificateurs d'eau

sterling ['stɜːlɪŋ] N **1** *(currency)* sterling *m inv*; **to pay in s.** payer en livres sterling; **twenty thousand pounds s.** vingt mille livres sterling **2** *(standard)* titre *m* **3** *(silverware)* argenterie *f*

COMP *(reserves, balances)* en sterling; *(traveller's cheques)* en livres sterling

ADJ **1** *(metal)* fin **2** *Formal (first-class)* excellent, de premier ordre; **a s. fighter** un combattant inlassable

►► ***sterling area*** zone *f* sterling; ***sterling bloc*** bloc *m* sterling; ***sterling qualities*** qualités *fpl* solides; ***sterling silver*** argent *m* fin; **a s. silver spoon** une cuillère en argent

stern [stɜːn] ADJ **1** *(strict, harsh ► person, measure)* sévère, strict; *(► appearance)* sévère, austère; *(► discipline, punishment)* sévère, rigoureux; *(► look, rebuke)* sévère, dur; *(► warning)* solennel, grave **2** *(robust)* solide, robuste; **his wife is made of sterner stuff** sa femme est d'une autre trempe

N *Naut* arrière *m*, poupe *f*

►► *Naut* ***stern post*** étambot *m*; ***stern sheets*** chambre *f* (d'embarcation)

sternly ['stɜːnlɪ] ADV sévèrement

sternness ['stɜːnnɪs] N sévérité *f*

sternum ['stɜːnəm] *(pl* **sternums** *or* **sterna** [-nə]*)* N *Anat* sternum *m*

steroid ['stɪərɔɪd] N stéroïde *m*; **the doctor put him on a course of steroids** le médecin lui a prescrit *ou* donné un traitement stéroïdien

stertorous ['stɜːtərəs] ADJ *Literary* stertoreux, ronflant

stet [stet] *Typ* N *(on proof)* bon, à maintenir

VT maintenir

stethoscope ['steθəskəʊp] N stéthoscope *m*

Stetson® ['stetsən] N Stetson® *m*, chapeau *m* de cow-boy

stevedore ['stiːvədɔː(r)] N *Am* docker *m*, débardeur *m*

VI travailler comme docker *ou* débardeur

stew[1] [stjuː] N *Culin* ragoût *m*; **lamb/vegetable s.** ragoût *m* d'agneau/de légumes; *Br Fam* **to be in a s.** *(bothered)* être dans tous ses états; *(in a mess)* être dans de beaux draps *ou* dans le pétrin

VT *(meat)* préparer en ragoût, cuire (en ragoût); *(fruit)* (faire) cuire en compote

VI **1** *Culin (meat)* cuire en ragoût, mijoter; *(fruit)* cuire; **leave the meat to s. for at least two hours** laissez mijoter la viande pendant deux bonnes heures; *Br Fam* **to let sb s. (in his/her own juice)** laisser cuire *ou* mijoter qn dans son jus

2 *(tea)* infuser trop longtemps

3 *(worry)* **to s. over sth** ruminer qch; **don't just sit there and s.** ne reste pas là assis à ruminer

4 *Br Fam (person)* **to be stewing** crever de chaleur; **it's stewing in here** il fait une chaleur à crever ici

stew[2] N *Am Fam (abbr* **stewardess***)* hôtesse *f* de l'air

steward ['stjʊəd] N **1** *(on aeroplane, ship)* steward *m*

2 *(at race, sports event)* commissaire *m*

3 *(at dance, social event)* organisateur(trice) *m,f*; *(at meeting, demonstration)* membre *m* du service d'ordre

4 *(of property)* intendant(e) *m,f*; *(of estate, finances)* régisseur(euse) *m,f*; *(in college)* économe *mf*

►► *Br* ***steward's enquiry*** enquête *f* des commissaires

stewardess ['stjʊədɪs] N hôtesse *f*

stewardship ['stjʊədʃɪp] N intendance *f*, économat *m*; *Fig* **under his s. the situation improved markedly** quand il était responsable, les choses s'étaient nettement améliorées

stewed [stjuːd] ADJ **1** *Culin* **we had s. lamb for supper** au dîner, nous avons mangé un ragoût d'agneau **2** *(tea)* trop infusé **3** *Fam (drunk)* bourré, cuité; **to get s.** se cuiter; **s. to the gills** rond comme une queue de pelle, pété à mort

►► ***stewed fruit*** compote *f* de fruits; ***stewed meat*** ragoût *m*

stewing ['stjuːɪŋ] N *(of meat)* préparation *f* en ragoût, cuisson *f* (en ragoût); *(of fruit)* cuisson *f* en compote

►► ***stewing beef*** bœuf *m* à braiser; ***stewing pan*** (grande) casserole *f*; ***stewing pears*** poires *fpl* à cuire; *Br* ***stewing steak*** bœuf *m* à braiser

stewpan ['stjuːpæn] N (grande) casserole *f*

stewpot ['stjuːpɒt] N cocotte *f*, fait-tout *m inv*

St. Ex. *(written abbr* **stock exchange***)* Bourse *f*

STI [,estiː'aɪ] N *(abbr* **sexually transmitted infection***)* IST *f*

STICK [stɪk]

N	
• bâton **1–3**	• canne **1**
• baguette **1**	• morceau **2**
• crosse **3**	• meuble **4**
• critiques **5**	• levier de vitesse **6**
VT	
• planter **1**	• enfoncer **1**
• mettre **2**	• fixer **3**
• coller **4**	• supporter **6**
VI	
• se planter **1**	• coller **2**
• se coincer **3**	• rester **4**
NPL	
• cambrousse	

(pt & pp **stuck** [stʌk]*)*

N **1** *(piece of wood)* bâton *m*; *(for kindling)* bout *m* de bois; *(twig)* petite branche *f*, brindille *f*; *(walking stick)* canne *f*, bâton *m*; *(for plants)* rame *f*, tuteur *m*; *(drumstick)* baguette *f*; *(for lollipop)* bâton *m*; **gather some sticks, we'll make a fire** ramassez du bois, on fera du feu; **she had legs like sticks** elle avait des jambes comme des allumettes; **I'm going to take a s. to that boy one day!** un jour je vais donner une bonne correction à ce garçon!; *Fig* **the threat of redundancy has become a s. with which industry beats the unions** pour le patronat, la menace du licenciement est devenue une arme contre les syndicats; **his behaviour became a s. to beat him with** son comportement s'est retourné contre lui; **to get (hold of) the wrong end of the s.** mal comprendre, comprendre de travers; **to get the short** *or* **dirty end of the s.** être mal loti; **she got the short** *or* **dirty end of the s. as usual** c'est tombé sur elle comme d'habitude; *Prov* **sticks and stones may break my bones (but words will never hurt me)** la bave du crapaud n'atteint pas la blanche colombe

2 *(piece ► of chalk)* bâton *m*, morceau *m*; *(► of cinnamon, incense, liquorice, dynamite)* bâton *m*; *(► of charcoal)* morceau *m*; *(► of chewing gum)* tablette *f*; *(► of glue, deodorant)* bâton *m*, stick *m*; *(► of celery)* branche *f*; *(► of rhubarb)* tige *f*

3 *Sport (in lacrosse)* crosse *f*; *(in hockey)* crosse *f*, stick *m*; *(ski pole)* bâton *m* (de ski); *(baseball bat)* batte *f*; *(billiard cue)* queue *f* de billard; *(in pick-up-sticks)* bâton *m*, bâtonnet *m*, jonchet *m*

4 *Br Fam (furniture)* meuble *m*; **a few sticks (of furniture)** quelques meubles

5 *(UNCOUNT) Br Fam (criticism)* critiques *fpl*; **to take a lot of s.** *(to be criticized)* se faire éreinter *ou* démolir; *(to be mocked)* se faire chambrer *ou* charrier; **to give sb s. (for sth)** *(criticize)* éreinter *ou* démolir qn (à cause de qch); *(laugh at)* chambrer *ou* charrier qn (à cause de qch); **the police got a lot of s. from the press** la police s'est fait éreinter *ou* démolir par la presse; **he got a lot of s. from his friends about his new hairstyle** ses amis l'ont bien chambré *ou* charrié avec sa nouvelle coupe

6 *esp Am Fam (joystick)* manche *m* à balai; *(gear lever)* levier *m* de vitesse

7 *Mil (cluster ► of bombs)* chapelet *m*; *(► of parachutists)* stick *m*

3 *Br Fam Old-fashioned (person)* type *m*; **a dry old** un pince-sans-rire; **she's not a bad old s., she's a ice old s.** elle est plutôt sympa
9 *Fam (glue)* colle❑*f*; *(stickiness)* pouvoir *m* dhésif❑
10 *Am Fam (cannabis cigarette)* stick *m*
11 *Br very Fam* **to be up the s.** *(pregnant)* être en loque
VT 1 *(jab, stab ▸ spear, nail, knife)* planter, enfoncer; *(▸ needle)* piquer, planter; *(▸ pole, shovel)* lanter; *(▸ elbow, gun)* enfoncer; **he stuck his fork nto a potato** il a planté sa fourchette dans une omme de terre; **don't s. drawing pins in the wall** e plantez pas de punaises dans le mur; **there vere maps with coloured pins stuck in them** il y vait des cartes avec des épingles de couleur; **ham stuck with cloves** un jambon piqué de lous de girofle; **watch out! you almost stuck your mbrella in my eye!** fais attention! tu as failli n'enfoncer ton parapluie dans l'œil!; **he stuck his lbow in my ribs** il m'a enfoncé son coude dans es côtes; **s. the skewer through the chicken** enfiez le poulet sur la broche, embrochez le poulet
2 *(put)* mettre; *(insert)* insérer, mettre; *Fam (put asually)* mettre❑, coller; **s. the candles in the olders** mettez les bougies dans les bougeoirs; **e stuck a rose in his lapel** il s'est mis une rose à a boutonnière; **she stuck the cork in the bottle** lle a enfoncé le bouchon dans le goulot de la outeille; **here, s. this under the chair leg** tenez, alez la chaise avec ça; **he stuck his foot in the oor** il glissa son pied dans l'entrebâillement le la porte; **he stood there with a cigar stuck in is mouth/with his hands stuck in his pockets** il tait planté là, un cigare entre les dents/les nains enfoncées dans les poches; **she stuck her ead into the office/out of the window** elle a assé la tête dans le bureau/par la fenêtre; **I ad to s. my fingers down my throat** il a fallu que e me mette les doigts dans la bouche; *Fam* **mix it ll together and s. it in the oven** mélange bien et nets-le au four❑; *Fam* **s. it in your pocket** colle ça ans ta poche; *Fam* **can you s. my name on the st?** tu peux ajouter mon nom sur la liste?❑; *very am* **you can s. your job/money!** ton boulot/fric, u peux te le mettre où je pense!; *very Fam* **s. it!** a te faire voir!
3 *(fasten)* fixer; *(pin up)* punaiser; **she stuck the room head on the handle** elle a fixé la brosse à alai au manche; **it was stuck on the notice-board vith tacks** c'était punaisé au tableau d'affichage
4 *(with adhesive)* coller; **to s. a stamp on an envelope** coller un timbre sur une enveloppe; **help ne s. this vase together** aide-moi à recoller le ase; **he had posters stuck to the walls with Sellotape** il avait scotché des posters aux murs; **s. no ills** *(sign)* défense d'afficher
5 *(kill ▸ pig)* égorger
6 *Br Fam (tolerate)* supporter❑; **I can't s. him** je eux pas l'encadrer; **I don't know how you've tuck it for so long** je ne sais pas comment tu as ait pour supporter ça si longtemps; **I'm amazed he stuck a term, let alone three years** je suis tonné qu'elle ait tenu (le coup) un trimestre, t à plus forte raison trois ans
7 *Fam (with chore, burden)* **to s. sb with a fine/the lame** coller une amende/faire endosser la resonsabilité❑ à qn
8 *Am Fam (give injection to)* faire une piqûre à❑, iquer❑
VI 1 *(be embedded ▸ arrow, dart, spear)* se planer; **the point was sticking through the lining** la ointe avait percé la doublure; **don't leave the pade sticking in the ground** ne laisse pas la pelle lantée dans le sol; **they had straw sticking in heir hair** ils avaient des brins de paille dans les heveux
2 *(attach, adhere ▸ wet clothes, bandage, chewing gum)* coller; *(▸ gummed label, stamp)* tenir, coller; *(▸ burr)* s'accrocher; **the dough stuck to my fingers** la pâte collait à mes doigts; **the damp has made the stamps s. together** l'humidité a collé es timbres les uns aux autres; **the dust will s. to the wet varnish** la poussière va coller sur le vernis frais; **her shirt stuck to her back** elle avait la hemise collée au dos; **a butterfly had stuck to the flypaper** un papillon était venu se coller au apier tue-mouches; **these badges s. to any surface** ces autocollants adhèrent sur toutes les surfaces; **food won't s. to these pans** ces casseroles n'attachent pas; **the noodles had got all stuck together** les nouilles avaient collé *ou* étaient toutes collées
3 *(become jammed, wedged ▸ mechanism, drawer, key)* se coincer, se bloquer; **the lorry stuck fast in the mud** le camion s'est complètement enlisé dans la boue; **a fishbone stuck in my throat** j'avais une arête (de poisson) coincée dans la gorge; *Fig* **it stuck in my throat** ça m'est resté en travers de la gorge; **having to ask him for a loan really sticks in my throat** ça me coûte vraiment d'avoir à lui demander de me prêter de l'argent; **the words stuck in his throat** les mots lui restèrent dans la gorge
4 *(remain, keep)* rester; **they called him Boney as a child and the name stuck** quand il était petit, on le surnommait Boney et le nom lui est resté; **she has the kind of face that sticks in your memory** elle a un visage qu'on n'oublie pas *ou* dont on se souvient; **dates just never s. in my head** je n'ai vraiment pas la mémoire des dates
5 *Fam (be upheld)* **to make the charge** *or* **charges s.** prouver la culpabilité de qn❑; **the important thing now is to make the agreement s.** ce qui compte maintenant, c'est de faire respecter l'accord❑
6 *(in card games)* **(I) s.** j'arrête, je ne veux pas d'autre carte; **the dealer must s. on** *or* **with seventeen** le donneur doit s'arrêter à dix-sept
• **sticks NPL** *Fam* **the sticks** la cambrousse; **they live out in the sticks** ils habitent en pleine cambrousse
▸▸ ***stick deodorant*** déodorant *m* en stick; ***stick figure*** personnage *m* stylisé; ***stick insect*** phasme *m*; *Am Aut* ***stick shift*** levier *m* de vitesse; **I don't know how to drive a s. shift** je ne sais pas conduire une voiture à vitesses manuelles

▸ **stick around VI** *Fam (stay)* rester (dans les parages); *(wait)* attendre❑; **s. around if you want, she'll be back in a little while** tu peux rester si tu veux, elle ne va pas tarder à rentrer; **I'm not sticking around a moment longer!** je n'attendrai pas une minute de plus!

▸ **stick at VT INSEP 1** *Br (persevere)* **to s. at it** persévérer **2** *(stop)* **to s. at nothing** ne reculer *ou* n'hésiter devant rien; **she'll s. at nothing to get her way** elle ne reculera devant rien pour parvenir à ses fins

▸ **stick by VT INSEP 1** *(person)* soutenir; **don't worry, I'll always s. by you** sois tranquille, je serai toujours là pour te soutenir **2** *(one's decision)* s'en tenir à; **I s. by what I said** je maintiens ce que j'ai dit

▸ **stick down VT SEP 1** *(flap, envelope)* coller **2** *Br Fam (note down)* noter❑; *(scribble)* griffonner❑ **3** *Fam (place)* coller; **he stuck the plate down in front of me** il a collé l'assiette devant moi
VI *(flap, envelope)* (se) coller

▸ **stick in VT SEP 1** *(nail, knife, spear)* planter, enfoncer; *(needle)* piquer, enfoncer; *(pole, shovel)* enfoncer, planter; **he stuck the knife all the way in** il a enfoncé le couteau jusqu'au bout *ou* jusqu'à la garde **2** *(insert ▸ coin, bank card, key)* insérer; *(▸ electric plug)* brancher; *(▸ cork, sink plug)* enfoncer; *(▸ word, sentence)* ajouter; **I stuck my hand in to test the water temperature** j'ai plongé la main pour vérifier la température de l'eau; **he stuck his head in through the door** il passa la tête par la porte **3** *(glue in)* coller
VI 1 *(dart, arrow, spear)* se planter; **the last dart failed to s. in** la dernière fléchette n'est pas restée plantée **2** *Fam (persevere)* **s. in there!** tenez bon!

▸ **stick on VT SEP 1** *(fasten on ▸ gummed badge, label, stamp)* coller; *(▸ china handle)* recoller; *(▸ broom head)* fixer **2** *Fam (jacket, boots)* enfiler❑; **he hurriedly stuck a hat on** il s'est collé en vitesse un chapeau sur la tête
VI coller, se coller; **the stamp won't s. on** le timbre ne colle pas; **the patch sticks on when ironed** la pièce se colle au tissu quand on la repasse

▸ **stick out VT SEP 1** *(extend ▸ hand, leg)* tendre, allonger; *(▸ feelers, head)* sortir; **to s. one's tongue out (at sb)** tirer la langue (à qn); **he stuck his foot out to trip me up** il a allongé la jambe pour me faire un croche-pied; **I opened the window and stuck my head out** j'ai ouvert la fenêtre et j'ai passé la tête au dehors; **to s. one's chest out** bomber le torse; **to s. out one's lower lip** faire la moue **2** *Fam (persevere)* **to s. it out** tenir le coup jusqu'au bout
VI 1 *(protrude ▸ nail, splinter)* sortir; *(▸ teeth)* avancer; *(▸ plant, shoot)* pointer; *(▸ ledge, balcony)* être en saillie; **his belly stuck out over his belt** son ventre débordait au-dessus de sa ceinture; **her ears s. out** elle a les oreilles décollées; **her teeth s. out** elle a les dents qui avancent; **my feet stuck out over the end of the bed** mes pieds dépassaient du lit; **the front of the car stuck out of the garage** l'avant de la voiture dépassait du garage; **his ticket was sticking out of his pocket** son billet sortait *ou* dépassait de sa poche; **only her head was sticking out of the water** seule sa tête sortait *ou* émergeait de l'eau **2** *(be noticeable ▸ colour)* ressortir; **the red Mercedes really sticks out** on ne voit que la Mercedes rouge; **I don't like to s. out in a crowd** je n'aime pas me singulariser *ou* me faire remarquer; **it's her accent that makes her s. out** c'est à cause de son accent qu'on la remarque; **it sticks out a mile** c'est clair comme le jour

▸ **stick out for VT INSEP** s'obstiner à vouloir, exiger; **the union is sticking out for a five percent rise** le syndicat continue à revendiquer une augmentation de cinq pour cent

▸ **stick to VT INSEP 1** *(keep to ▸ schedule)* tenir, respecter; *(▸ plan)* tenir; **I can never s. to diets** je n'arrive jamais à suivre un régime longtemps; **we must s. to our plan** nous devons continuer à suivre notre plan; **once I make a decision I s. to it** une fois que j'ai pris une décision, je m'y tiens *ou* je n'en démords pas; **to s. to one's word** *or* **promises** tenir (sa) parole; **to s. to one's principles** rester fidèle à ses principes
2 *(continue to affirm)* maintenir; **she's still sticking to her story** elle maintient ce qu'elle a dit; **that's my story and I'm sticking to it** c'est ma version et je m'y tiens
3 *(restrict oneself to)* s'en tenir à; **s. to the point!** ne vous éloignez pas du sujet!, tenez-vous en au sujet!; **can we s. to the business in hand?** peut-être pourrions-nous revenir au sujet qui nous occupe?; **to s. to the text** serrer le texte de près; **the author would be better off sticking to journalism** l'auteur ferait mieux de se cantonner au journalisme
4 *(not leave)* **to s. to one's post** rester à son poste; **he sticks to his room** il ne sort pas de sa chambre; **s. to the main road** suivez la route principale
5 *(stay near)* **s. close to the house** restez près de la maison; **his bodyguards s. close to him at all times** ses gardes du corps l'accompagnent partout *ou* ne le quittent jamais d'une semelle; **to s. to sb like glue** se cramponner *ou* s'accrocher à qn, coller qn

▸ **stick together VT SEP** coller (ensemble)
VI 1 *(pages etc)* être collé (ensemble) **2** *(stay together ▸ people)* rester ensemble; *Fig* se serrer les coudes; **we'd better s. together** il vaut mieux que nous restions ensemble, il vaut mieux ne pas nous séparer; *Fig* **we'll get through this bad patch if we s. together** on sortira de cette mauvaise passe si on se serre les coudes

▸ **stick up VT SEP 1** *(sign, notice, poster)* afficher; *(postcard)* coller; *(with drawing pins)* punaiser **2** *(raise ▸ pole)* dresser; **s. the target back up** redressez la cible; **to s. one's hand up** lever la main; *Fam* **s. 'em up!** haut les mains! **3** *Fam (rob ▸ person, bank, supermarket)* braquer
VI *(point upwards ▸ tower, antenna)* se dresser; *(▸ plant shoots)* pointer; **I saw a chimney sticking up in the distance** j'ai vu une cheminée qui se dressait au loin; **a branch was sticking up out of the water** une branche sortait de l'eau; **his hair's sticking up** il est ébouriffé

▸ **stick up for VT INSEP to s. up for sb** prendre la défense *ou* le parti de qn; **s. up for yourself!** ne te laisse pas faire!; **she can s. up herself** elle peut se défendre toute seule; **he has trouble sticking up for himself/his rights** il a du mal à défendre ses intérêts/à faire valoir ses droits

▸ **stick with VT INSEP 1** *(activity, subject)* s'en tenir à, persister dans; **now I've started the job, I'm going to s. with it** maintenant que j'ai commencé ce travail, je ne le lâche pas; **I'm sticking with my**

old car for now je garde ma vieille voiture pour le moment **2** *Fam (person)* **s. with me, kid, and you'll be all right** reste avec moi, petit, et tout ira bien

sticker ['stɪkə(r)] **N 1** *(adhesive label)* autocollant *m* **2** *Fam (determined person)* **she's a s.** elle est persévérante⁻, elle va au bout de ce qu'elle entreprend⁻
▸▸ *Mktg* ***sticker price*** prix *m* affiché, prix *m* à la vente

stickiness ['stɪkɪnɪs] **N 1** *(of substance, surface, jamjar)* caractère *m* gluant *ou* poisseux; **the s. of his hands** ses mains poisseuses **2** *(of weather, climate)* moiteur *f*, humidité *f*

sticking ['stɪkɪŋ] **ADJ**
▸▸ *Br* ***sticking plaster*** pansement *m* adhésif, sparadrap *m*; *Fig* ***sticking point*** point *m* de désaccord, point *m* de friction

stick-in-the-mud **N** *Fam (fogey)* vieux croûton *m*; *(killjoy)* rabat-joie *m inv*; **don't be such a s.!** ne sois pas rabat-joie!

stickleback ['stɪkəlbæk] **N** *Ich* épinoche *f (de rivière)*

stickler ['stɪklə(r)] **N to be a s. for** *(regulations, discipline, good manners)* être à cheval sur; *(tradition, routine)* insister sur

stick-on **ADJ** autocollant

stick-up **N** *Fam* braquage *m*, hold-up *m*; **this is a s.!** c'est un hold-up!

stickweed ['stɪkwi:d] **N** *Bot* jacobée *f*

sticky ['stɪkɪ] *(compar* **stickier**, *superl* **stickiest)** **ADJ 1** *(adhesive)* adhésif, gommé
2 *(tacky, gluey ▸ hands, fingers)* collant, poisseux; *(▸ substance, surface, jamjar)* gluant, poisseux; **his mouth was all s. with jam** il avait la bouche poisseuse de confiture; **to have s. fingers** avoir les doigts collants *ou* poisseux; *Fig* être porté sur la fauche
3 *(sweaty)* moite
4 *(humid ▸ weather)* moite, humide; **it was a hot, s. afternoon** c'était un après-midi chaud et moite
5 *Fam (awkward ▸ situation)* difficile⁻, délicat⁻; *Br* **to be (batting) on a s. wicket** être dans une situation difficile⁻; *Br* **to come to a s. end** mal finir⁻
6 *Fam Comput (site, advert)* qui attire de nombreux utilisateurs⁻
▸▸ *Fam* ***sticky bun*** petit pain *m* sucré; ***sticky label*** étiquette *f* autocollante, étiquette *f* gommée; ***sticky tape*** ruban *m* adhésif; ***sticky toffee pudding*** = pudding au caramel cuit à la vapeur

stickybeak ['stɪkɪbi:k] *Austr & NZ Fam* **N** fouineur(euse) *m,f*, fouinard(e) *m,f*
VI fouiner, fureter

stiff [stɪf] **ADJ 1** *(rigid)* raide, rigide; **s. paper/cardboard** papier *m*/carton *m* rigide; **a s. brush** une brosse à poils durs; **as s. as a poker** raide comme un piquet; **to keep a s. upper lip** garder son flegme
2 *(thick, difficult to stir)* ferme, consistant; **beat the mixture until it is s.** battez jusqu'à obtention d'une pâte consistante; **beat the egg whites until s.** battre les blancs en neige jusqu'à ce qu'ils soient (bien) fermes
3 *(difficult to move)* dur; **this door handle is very s.** cette poignée de porte est très dure; **the drawers have got a bit s.** les tiroirs sont devenus un peu durs à ouvrir
4 *(aching)* courbaturé, raide; **I'm still s. after playing squash the other day** j'ai encore des courbatures d'avoir joué au squash l'autre jour; **to have a s. back** avoir mal au dos; **to have a s. neck** avoir un *ou* le torticolis
5 *(over-formal ▸ smile, welcome)* froid; *(▸ person, manners, behaviour)* froid, guindé; *(▸ style)* guindé
6 *(difficult)* dur, ardu; **to face s. competition** avoir affaire à forte concurrence; **it will be a s. match** la partie sera dure
7 *(severe)* sévère; **a s. sentence** une condamnation sévère, une lourde condamnation; **I sent them a s. letter** je leur ai envoyé une lettre bien sentie
8 *(strong ▸ breeze, drink)* fort; **you need a s. drink** tu as besoin d'un remontant; **she poured herself a s. whisky** elle s'est versé un whisky bien tassé
9 *(high ▸ price, bill)* élevé
10 *(determined ▸ resistance, opposition)* tenace, acharné; *(▸ resolve)* ferme, inébranlable
11 *Br Fam (full)* plein (à craquer); **the place was s. with men in suits** l'endroit était plein de mecs en costume
12 *Am Fam (drunk)* bourré, rond, beurré
ADV *Fam* **to be bored s.** mourir d'ennui⁻; **to be worried/scared s.** être mort d'inquiétude/de peur; **I was frozen s.** j'étais frigorifié
N 1 *Fam (corpse)* macchabée *m* **2** *Br Fam (failure)* bide *m* **3** *Am Fam (tramp)* clodo *mf*

stiffen ['stɪfən] **VT 1** *(paper, fabric)* raidir, renforcer
2 *(thicken ▸ batter, paste, concrete)* donner de la consistance à; *(▸ sauce)* lier
3 *(make painful ▸ arm, leg, muscle)* courbaturer; **his joints had become stiffened by arthritis** ses articulations s'étaient raidies à cause de l'arthrite
4 *(strengthen ▸ resistance, resolve)* renforcer
VI 1 *(harden ▸ paper, fabric)* devenir raide *ou* rigide
2 *(tense, stop moving)* se raidir; **everybody in the room suddenly stiffened** tout à coup, tout le monde dans la pièce retint son souffle *ou* s'immobilisa
3 *(thicken ▸ batter, paste, concrete)* épaissir, devenir ferme; *(▸ sauce)* se lier
4 *(become hard to move ▸ hinge, handle, door)* se coincer
5 *(start to ache)* s'ankyloser
6 *(strengthen ▸ resistance, resolve)* se renforcer; *(▸ breeze)* forcir

stiffener ['stɪfənə(r)] **N 1** *(in collar)* baleine *f* **2** *Br Fam (drink)* remontant⁻*m*

stiffening ['stɪfənɪŋ] **N** renforcement *m*

stiffly ['stɪflɪ] **ADV 1** *(rigidly)* **s. starched** très empesé *ou* amidonné; **he stood s. to attention** il se tenait au garde-à-vous, très raide **2** *(painfully ▸ walk, bend)* avec raideur **3** *(coldly ▸ smile, greet)* froidement, d'un air distant

stiff-necked **ADJ** qui a le torticolis; *Fig* opiniâtre, entêté, intraitable

stiffness ['stɪfnɪs] **N 1** *(of paper, fabric)* raideur *f*, rigidité *f*
2 *(of batter, paste, concrete)* consistance *f*, fermeté *f*
3 *(of hinge, handle, door)* dureté *f*
4 *(of joints, limbs)* raideur *f*, courbatures *fpl*
5 *(of manners, smile, welcome)* froideur *f*, distance *f*; *(of style)* caractère *m* guindé
6 *(difficulty ▸ of exam, competition)* difficulté *f*, dureté *f*
7 *(severity ▸ of sentence, warning)* sévérité *f*
8 *(determination ▸ of resistance)* ténacité *f*, acharnement *m*; *(▸ of resolve)* fermeté *f*

stiffy ['stɪfɪ] *(pl* **stiffies)** **N** *Br very Fam (erection)* **to have a s.** bander; **to get a s.** se mettre à bander

stifle ['staɪfəl] **VT 1** *(suppress ▸ resistance, creativity, progress)* réprimer, étouffer; *(▸ tears, anger, emotion)* réprimer; **to s. a cough** réprimer une envie de tousser; **I tried to s. my laughter/a yawn** j'ai essayé de ne pas rire/bâiller **2** *(suffocate)* étouffer, suffoquer
VI étouffer, suffoquer

stifled ['staɪfəld] **ADJ** *(cry)* étouffé; **with a s. voice** d'une voix éteinte

stifling ['staɪflɪŋ] **ADJ** suffocant, étouffant; **open the window, it's s. in here!** ouvre la fenêtre, on étouffe ici!; **it was a s. hot day** il faisait une chaleur étouffante

stigma ['stɪgmə] *(pl* **stigmas** *or* **stigmata** [stɪg'mɑ:tə]) **N 1** *(social disgrace)* honte *f*; **the s. attached to having been in prison** l'opprobe qui ne quitte pas ceux qui ont fait de la prison; **there is no longer any s. in being a single mother** il n'y a plus de honte à être mère célibataire **2** *Zool* stigma *m* **3** *Bot & Med* stigmate *m*

stigmata [stɪg'mɑ:tə] **NPL** *Rel* stigmates *mpl*

stigmatic [stɪg'mætɪk] **ADJ** *Opt (lens)* stigmatique, anastigmate, anastigmatique
N *Rel* stigmatisé(e) *m,f*

stigmatize, -ise ['stɪgmətaɪz] **VT** stigmatiser

stile [staɪl] **N 1** *(over fence)* échalier *m* **2** *(turnstile)* tourniquet *m*

stiletto [stɪ'letəʊ] *(pl* **stilettos)** **N 1** *(heel)* talon *m* aiguille **2** *(knife)* stylet *m* **3** *(for sewing, leatherwork)* poinçon *m*
• **stilettos** **NPL** (chaussures *fpl* à) talons *mpl* a guilles
▸▸ ***stiletto heel*** talon *m* aiguille

still¹ [stɪl] **ADV 1** *(as of this moment)* encore, tou jours; **he's s. here** il est encore *ou* toujours ici; **he s. not here** il n'est toujours pas là; **we're s. waitin for the repairman to come** nous attendons tou jours que le réparateur vienne; **there's s. a bit c cake left** il reste encore un morceau de gâteau **the worst was s. to come** le pire n'était pas encor arrivé; **I s. have 50 euros** il me reste 50 euros, j' encore 50 euros; **I s. can't see what was wron with my suggestion** je ne vois toujours pas e quoi ma suggestion était mauvaise **2** *(all th same)* quand même; **it's certainly difficult, but it s. better than my last job** c'est difficile, c'est sû mais c'est quand même mieux que mon derni emploi; **it's a shame we lost – s., it was a goo game** (c'est) dommage que nous ayons perdu quand même, c'était un bon match **3** *(with com paratives) (even)* encore; **s. more/less** encor plus/moins; **s. further, further s.** encore plu loin; **the sea was getting s. rougher** la mer éta de plus en plus agitée

still² **ADJ 1** *(motionless ▸ person, air, surface)* im mobile; **her eyes were never s.** ses yeux ne re taient jamais immobiles; **be s.!** arrête d remuer!; *Prov* **s. waters run deep** méfie-toi d l'eau qui dort **2** *(calm)* calme, tranquille; *(quie* silencieux; **a s. night** une nuit calme **3** *(not fizz* plat
ADV sans bouger; **stand s.!** ne bougez pas!; **m heart stood s.** mon cœur a cessé de battr **they're so excited they can't sit s.** ils sont telle ment excités qu'ils ne peuvent pas rester e place; **try to hold the camera s.** essaie de ne pa bouger l'appareil photo
VT *Literary* **1** *(silence)* faire taire; **the voices of pr test had been stilled** on avait fait taire les contes tataires **2** *(allay ▸ doubts, fears)* apaiser, calme
N 1 *Literary (silence)* silence *m*; **in the s. of th night** dans le silence de la nuit **2** *Cin* photo *f* (d plateau) **3** *(apparatus)* alambic *m*
▸▸ ***still life*** nature *f* morte; ***still photograph*** photographe *mf* de plateau

stillbirth ['stɪlbɜ:θ] **N** *(birth)* mort *f* à la nais sance; *(fœtus)* enfant *mf* mort-né(e); **the numbe of stillbirths** la mortinatalité

stillborn ['stɪlbɔ:n] **ADJ 1** *Med* mort-né **2** *Fi (idea, plan)* avorté

stillness ['stɪlnɪs] **N 1** *(motionlessness)* immob lité *f* **2** *(calm)* tranquillité *f*, paix *f*

stilt [stɪlt] **N 1** *(for walking)* échasse *f*; **to walk o stilts** marcher sur des échasses **2** *Archit* pilotis *n*

stilted ['stɪltɪd] **ADJ** *(speech, writing, perso* guindé, emprunté; *(discussion)* qui manque d naturel

Stilton® ['stɪltən] **N** stilton *m*, fromage *m* de Sti ton

stimulant ['stɪmjʊlənt] **N** stimulant *m*; **deval ation acts as a s. to exports** la dévaluation stimu les exportations
ADJ stimulant

stimulate ['stɪmjʊleɪt] **VT 1** *(person, enthusiasm* stimuler; *(mind, appetite etc)* aiguiser; *Ind (pro duction)* encourager, activer; **the bracing sea a stimulated me** l'air de la mer m'a revigoré; **to sb to do sth** inciter *ou* encourager qn à fair qch; **sexually stimulated** excité (sexuellement) *Med (organ)* stimuler

stimulating ['stɪmjʊleɪtɪŋ] **ADJ 1** *(medicin drug)* stimulant **2** *(work, conversation, exper ence)* stimulant, enrichissant; **intellectually s.** ir tellectuellement stimulant

stimulation [,stɪmjʊ'leɪʃən] **N 1** *(of person)* st mulation *f* **2** *(stimulus)* stimulant *m*

stimulative ['stɪmjʊlətɪv] **ADJ** stimulant
N stimulant *m*

stimulus ['stɪmjʊləs] *(pl* **stimuli** [-laɪ, -li:]) **N 1** *(ir centive)* stimulant *m*, incitation *f*; **her exampl will be a powerful s. to others** son exemple ser un stimulant extrêmement efficace pour d'au tres **2** *Physiol* stimulus *m*
▸▸ ***stimulus response*** réponse *f* stimulée

sting [stɪŋ] *(pt & pp* **stung** [stʌŋ]) **VT 1** *(of insec nettle, scorpion)* piquer; *(of smoke)* piquer, brû r; *(of vinegar, acid, disinfectant)* brûler; *(of whip, ain)* cingler; **the smoke stung my eyes** la fumée e brûlait *ou* me piquait les yeux; **a bee stung er finger** *or* **stung her on the finger** une abeille i a piqué le doigt

2 *(of remark, joke, criticism)* piquer (au vif), bles-er; **she was stung by their sharp criticisms** leurs ritiques acérées l'ont piquée au vif; **to s. sb into ction** inciter *ou* pousser qn à agir; **our comments ight s. them into doing something** nos remarques les inciteront peut-être à faire quelque hose

3 *Fam (swindle)* arnaquer, refaire; **to get stung** e faire arnaquer, se faire refaire; **they stung im for a hundred quid** ils l'ont arnaqué *ou* refait e cent livres

VI 1 *(insect, nettle, scorpion)* piquer; *(vinegar, cid, disinfectant)* brûler, piquer; *(whip, rain)* cin-ler; **this is going to s. a bit** ça va faire un peu mal *(eyes, skin)* piquer, brûler; **my eyes are stinging** i les yeux qui piquent

N 1 *(organ ▸ of bee, wasp, scorpion)* aiguillon *m*, ard *m*; *(▸ of nettle)* poil *m* (urticant); *Br* **there's a in the tail** il y a une mauvaise surprise à la fin; **s remarks often have a s. in the tail** ses remarques sont rarement innocentes; **to take the s. ut of sth** rendre qch moins douloureux, adou-r qch

2 *(wound, pain, mark ▸ from insect, nettle, scor-ion)* piqûre *f*; *(▸ from vinegar, acid, disinfectant)* rûlure *f*; *(▸ from whip)* douleur *f* cinglante

3 *Fam (swindle)* arnaque *f*

4 *Am Fam (police operation)* coup *m* monté *(dans cadre d'une opération de police)*

ingily ['stɪndʒɪlɪ] **ADV** *(give, serve out, behave)* hichement

inginess ['stɪndʒɪnɪs] **N** *(of person, behaviour)* varice *f*, pingrerie *f*; *(of amount, helping)* insuf-sance *f*

inging ['stɪŋɪŋ] **ADJ 1** *(wound, pain)* cuisant; *bite, eyes)* qui pique; *(lash, rain)* cinglant **2** *(re-ark, joke, criticism)* cinglant, mordant

▸ ***stinging nettle*** ortie *f*

ingray ['stɪŋreɪ] **N** *Ich* pastenague *f*

ingy ['stɪndʒɪ] **ADJ** *Fam (person)* radin; *(amount, elping)* misérable□; **he's too s. with his money** il st trop radin; **they're never s. about food** ils ne ésinent jamais sur la nourriture□

ink [stɪŋk] *(pt* **stank** [stæŋk], *pp* **stunk** [stʌŋk]) **VI 1** *mell)* puer, empester; **the room stank of cigar-tte smoke** la pièce puait *ou* empestait la fumée e cigarette; **it stinks in here** ça pue ici; *Fam Fig* **o s. of money** puer le fric; **the whole business tinks of corruption** tout ça sent la corruption à lein nez **2** *Fam (be bad)* être nul, craindre; **what o you think of my plan? – it stinks!** qu'est-ce que ı penses de mon projet? -- il est nul!; **this town tinks!** cette ville est pourrie!

N 1 *(stench)* puanteur *f*, odeur *f* nauséabonde; *am* **what a s.!** qu'est-ce que ça pue! **2** *Fam (fuss)* oin *m*; **to raise** *or* **to make** *or Br* **to kick up a s. about sth)** faire toute un foin (de qch)

▸ ***stink bomb*** boule *f* puante; *Am Entom* ***stink ug*** punaise *f*

stink out VT SEP *Fam (room, place)* empester□

inker ['stɪŋkə(r)] **N** *Fam* **1** *(person)* peau *f* de va-he, ordure *f* **2** *(unpleasant, difficult thing)* **to be a** être vachement dur, être coton; **today's cross-ord's a s.** les mots croisés d'aujourd'hui sont achement durs; **I've got a s. of a cold** j'ai un hume carabiné **3** *(worthless thing)* **to be a s.** être ul, être merdique

inkhorn ['stɪŋkhɔːn] **N** *Bot* phallus *m* impu-ique, satyre *m* puant

inking ['stɪŋkɪŋ] **ADJ 1** *(smelly)* puant, nauséa-ond **2** *Fam (as intensifier)* **I'm tired of seeing this mess all the time!** j'en ai assez de voir tout le emps cette pagaille *ou* ce bazar!; **I've got a s. old** j'ai un rhume carabiné **3** *Fam (worthless)* nerdique, nul

ADV *Fam* vachement; **to be s. drunk** être soûl omme un cochon; **to be s. rich** être plein aux s, *Pej* puer le fric

inko ['stɪŋkəʊ] **ADJ** *Am Fam (drunk)* pété, ourré, fait

inkpot ['stɪŋkpɒt] **N** *Fam Old-fashioned (un-leasant person)* salaud *m*, salope *f*

stint [stɪnt] **N 1** *(period of work)* période *f* de travail; *(share of work)* part *f* de travail; **she did a s. in Africa/as a teacher** elle a travaillé pendant un certain temps en Afrique/comme professeur; **she had a two-year s. in the army** elle a fait deux ans dans l'armée; **I'll take** *or* **I'll do another s. at the wheel** je vais reprendre le volant **2** *Formal (limitation)* **without s.** *(spend)* sans compter; *(give)* généreusement; *(work)* inlassablement

VT *Br* **1** *(skimp on)* lésiner sur; **don't s. the cream** ne lésine pas sur la crème **2** *(deprive)* priver; **he's incapable of stinting himself of anything** il est incapable de se priver de quoi que ce soit

VI *Br* **to s. on sth** lésiner sur qch

stipend ['staɪpend] **N** traitement *m*, appointements *mpl*

stipendiary [staɪ'pendjərɪ] *(pl* **stipendiaries**) **ADJ** *(work, person)* rémunéré; *Law* **s. magistrate** magistrat *m* professionnel *(rémunéré)*

N *(clergyman)* = prêtre percevant un traitement; *Law (magistrate)* magistrat *m* professionnel *(rémunéré)*

stipple ['stɪpəl] **VT 1** *(apply ▸ paint)* appliquer par petites touches **2** *(mark ▸ cement, wet paint)* granuler

stipulate ['stɪpjʊleɪt] **VT** stipuler; **the contract stipulates that the work must be finished by March** le contrat stipule que le travail doit être terminé d'ici le mois de mars

stipulation [ˌstɪpjʊ'leɪʃən] **N** stipulation *f*; **they accepted, but with the s. that the time limit be extended** ils ont accepté sous réserve que les délais soient prolongés

stir [stɜː(r)] *(pt & pp* **stirred**, *cont* **stirring**) **VT 1** *(mix)* remuer, tourner; **your tea is sugared but not stirred** ton thé est sucré mais il faut le remuer; **s. the flour into the sauce** incorporez la farine à la sauce en remuant

2 *(move)* agiter, remuer; **a light breeze stirred the leaves** une brise légère agitait les feuilles; *Br Fam* **s. yourself** *or* **your stumps, it's time to go!** grouille-toi, il est l'heure de partir!

3 *(touch)* émouvoir; **his story has stirred us deeply** son histoire nous a profondément émus

4 *(rouse, excite)* éveiller, exciter; **to s. sb's curiosity/sympathy** éveiller la curiosité/sympathie de qn; **to s. sb into action** pousser qn à agir

5 *Br Fam* **to s. it** *(cause trouble)* semer la zizanie

VI 1 *(move ▸ person)* bouger, remuer; *(▸ leaves)* remuer; **I shan't s. from my bed until midday** je ne bougerai pas de mon lit avant midi; **the audience were stirring in their seats** les spectateurs s'agitaient dans leur fauteuil

2 *(awaken, be roused ▸ feeling, anger)* s'éveiller

3 *Fam (cause trouble)* semer la zizanie

N 1 *(act of mixing)* **to give sth a s.** remuer qch; **the sauce needs a s.** il faudrait remuer la sauce

2 *(commotion)* émoi *m*, agitation *f*; **to cause** *or* **to create** *or* **to make quite a s.** soulever un vif émoi, faire grand bruit; **there was a big s. about** *or* **over the unemployment figures** les chiffres du chômage ont soulevé un vif émoi

3 *(movement)* mouvement *m*; **a s. of excitement** un frisson d'excitation

4 *Fam (prison)* taule *f*, placard *m*, cabane *f*; **in s.** en taule, en cabane, à l'ombre; **s. crazy** cinglé *(à force d'être en prison)*

▸ **stir up VT SEP 1** *(disturb ▸ dust, mud)* soulever **2** *(incite, provoke ▸ trouble)* provoquer; *(▸ emotions)* exciter, attiser; *(▸ dissent)* fomenter; *(▸ memories)* réveiller; *(▸ crowd, followers)* ameuter; **he likes stirring it** *or* **things up** il aime provoquer **3** *Literary (fire)* attiser, tisonner

stir-fry *(pt & pp* **stir-fried**, *pl* **stir-fries**) **VT** faire sauter à feu vif *(tout en remuant)*

ADJ sauté; **s. pork** porc sauté

N sauté *m*

stirrer ['stɜːrə(r)] **N 1** *Fam (troublemaker)* fouteur (euse) *m,f* de merde **2** *Culin (implement)* fouet *m*

stirring ['stɜːrɪŋ] **ADJ** *(music, song)* entraînant; *(story)* excitant, passionnant; *(speech)* vibrant; **it's s. stuff** c'est passionnant

N he felt vague stirrings of guilt il éprouva un vague sentiment de culpabilité; **the first stirrings of what was to become the Romantic movement** les premières manifestations de ce qui allait devenir le mouvement romantique

stirrup ['stɪrəp] **N** *Horseriding* étrier *m*; **to put one's feet in the stirrups** chausser les étriers

• **stirrups NPL** *Med* étriers *mpl*

▸▸ ***stirrup cup*** coup *m* de l'étrier; ***stirrup leather*** étrivière *f*; ***stirrup pump*** seau-pompe *m*

stitch [stɪtʃ] **N 1** *(in sewing)* point *m*; *(in knitting, crochet)* maille *f*; **to make/drop a s.** faire/sauter une maille; **to pick up a s.** reprendre une maille; *Fam* **I didn't have a s. (of clothing) on** j'étais nu comme un ver, *Hum* j'étais dans le plus simple appareil□; *Prov* **a s. in time saves nine** un point à temps en vaut cent

2 *Med* point *m* de suture; **she had to have ten stitches in her face** il a fallu lui faire dix points de suture au visage; **I'm having my stitches (taken) out tomorrow** on m'ôte les points demain

3 *(pain)* point *m* de côté; **to get a s.** attraper un point de côté

4 *Fam (idioms)* **to be in stitches** se tenir les côtes (de rire), être plié de rire; **to have sb in stitches** faire rire qn aux larmes□

VT 1 *(material, shirt, hem)* coudre; **he stitched the button back on his shirt** il a recousu son bouton de chemise **2** *Med* suturer **3** *(in bookbinding)* brocher

▸ **stitch down VT SEP** rabattre

▸ **stitch up VT SEP 1** *(material, shirt, hem)* coudre **2** *Med* suturer **3** *Fam (deal)* conclure□ **4** *Br Fam (frame)* **to s. sb up** monter un coup contre qn

stitching ['stɪtʃɪŋ] **N 1** *(in sewing)* couture *f*; *(ornamental)* broderie *f*; **the s.'s coming undone** la couture se défait **2** *Med* suture *f* **3** *(in bookbinding)* brochage *m*

St John Ambulance, St John's Ambulance N = organisme bénévole de secours d'urgence en Grande-Bretagne

stoat [stəʊt] **N** *Zool* hermine *f (brune)*

stoater ['stəʊtə(r)] **N** *Scot Fam* **1** *(excellent thing)* **what a s. of a goal!** quel but d'enfer!; **we had a s. of an idea** on a eu une idée géniale **2** *(beautiful person)* canon *m*; **his new girlfriend's a wee s.!** sa nouvelle copine est canon!

stochastic [stɒ'kæstɪk] **ADJ** stochastique

stock [stɒk] **N 1** *(supply)* réserve *f*, provision *f*, stock *m*; *Com & Ind* stock *m*; **we got in a s. of food** nous avons fait tout un stock de nourriture; **huge stocks of nuclear weapons** d'énormes stocks d'armes nucléaires; **she always has a wonderful s. of funny stories** elle a toujours un tas d'histoires drôles en réserve; **in s.** en stock, en magasin; **to keep sth in s.** stocker qch; **out of s.** épuisé; **I'm afraid we're out of s.** je regrette, nous n'en avons plus en stock; **while stocks last** jusqu'à épuisement des stocks; **to take s.** faire l'inventaire, *Fig* faire le point; **we took s. of the situation** nous avons fait le point de la situation

2 *(total amount)* parc *m*; **the housing s.** le parc de logements

3 *(usu pl) St Exch (gen)* valeur *f* mobilière; *(share)* action *f*; *(bond)* obligation *f*; **mining stocks are falling** les actions minières sont en baisse; **to invest in stocks and shares** investir dans des actions et obligations *ou* en portefeuille

4 *Fin (equity)* capital *m*; **he already owns 27% of the company's s.** il possède déjà 27 % du capital de la société

5 *Fig (value, credit)* cote *f*; **the Prime Minister's s. is rising/falling** la cote du Premier ministre est en hausse/en baisse; **to put s. in sth** faire (grand) cas de qch

6 *(descent, ancestry)* souche *f*, lignée *f*; **of peasant/noble s.** de souche paysanne/noble

7 *Agr (animals)* cheptel *m*

8 *Culin* bouillon *m*; **beef/chicken/vegetable s.** bouillon *m* de bœuf/poulet/légumes

9 *(handle, butt ▸ of gun, plough)* fût *m*; *(▸ of whip)* manche *m*; *(▸ of fishing rod)* gaule *f*

10 *Bot* giroflée *f*

11 *(tree trunk)* tronc *m*; *(tree stump)* souche *f*

12 *Hort (stem receiving graft)* porte-greffe *m*, sujet *m*; *(plant from which graft is taken)* plante *f* mère *(sur laquelle on prélève un greffon)*

13 *(in card games, dominoes)* talon *m*, pioche *f*

14 *Theat* répertoire *m*

15 *(neckcloth)* lavallière *f*, foulard *m*; **riding s.** col-cravate *m*

16 *Naut (of anchor)* jas *m*

VT 1 *Com (have in stock)* avoir (en stock), vendre; **I'm afraid we don't s. that item any more** je regrette, mais nous ne vendons plus *ou* nous ne faisons plus cet article; **we s. all leading makes of furniture** nous faisons toutes les grandes marques de meubles **2** *(supply)* approvisionner; *(fill)* remplir; **they have a well stocked cellar** ils ont une cave bien approvisionnée; **we stocked the fridge with food** nous avons rempli le frigo de nourriture **3** *(stream, lake)* empoissonner; *(farm)* monter en bétail

ADJ 1 *(common, typical ▸ phrase, expression)* tout fait; *(▸ question, answer, excuse)* classique; **he has three s. speeches** il a, en tout et pour tout, trois discours qu'il ressort périodiquement **2** *Com (kept in stock)* en stock; *(widely available)* courant; **the sale of s. goods** la liquidation du stock; **available in all s. sizes** disponible dans toutes les tailles courantes **3** *Theat (play)* du répertoire

• **stocks** **NPL 1** *(instrument of punishment)* pilori *m*; **sentenced to the stocks** condamné au pilori **2** *Naut (frame)* cale *f*; **on the stocks** en chantier

▸▸ ***stock car* 1** *Aut* stock-car *m* **2** *Am Rail* wagon *m* à bestiaux; ***stock car racing*** (courses *fpl* de) stock-car *m*; *Am* ***stock certificate*** titre *m*; *Fin* ***stock check*** contrôle *m* des stocks; ***stock clearance*** liquidation *f* de stock; *Am* ***stock company* 1** *Fin* société *f* anonyme par actions **2** *Theat* troupe *f* à demeure *(dans une ville)*; ***stock control*** contrôle *m* des stocks; *Culin* ***stock cube*** bouillon *m* Kub®; *Orn* ***stock dove*** petit ramier *m*, colombin *m*; ***stock exchange*** Bourse *f*; **he lost a fortune on the s. exchange** il a perdu une fortune à la Bourse; ***stock exchange dealer*** opérateur(trice) *m,f* boursier(ère); ***stock farm*** élevage *m* (de bétail); ***stock farmer*** éleveur *m*; ***stock farming*** élevage *m* (de bétail) *(activité)*; *Cin & TV* ***stock footage*** séquences *fpl* d'archives; ***stock index*** indice *m* de la Bourse; ***stock in hand*** marchandises *fpl* en stock, marchandises *fpl* en magasin; ***stock market*** Bourse *f* (des valeurs), marché *m* financier; **he lost a fortune on the s. market** il a perdu une fortune à la Bourse; **the London s. market is rising** la Bourse de Londres est en hausse; ***stock market boom*** envolée *f* du marché boursier; ***stock market bubble*** bulle *f* boursière; ***stock market crash*** krach *m* boursier; ***stock market forecast*** prévision *f* boursière; ***stock market price*** cours *m* de la Bourse; ***stock market value*** valeur en Bourse; *Am* ***stock saddle*** selle *f* de cow-boy; *TV* ***stock shot*** image *f ou* document *m* d'archives; *Com* ***stock take*** inventaire *m* des stocks

▸ **stock up** **VI** s'approvisionner; **to s. up on** *or* **with sth** s'approvisionner en qch

VT SEP approvisionner, garnir

stockade [stɒ'keɪd] **N 1** *(enclosure)* palissade *f* **2** *Am Mil (prison)* prison *f* (militaire)

VT palissader

stockboy ['stɒkbɔɪ] **N** magasinier *m*

stockbroker ['stɒk,brəʊkə(r)] **N** agent *m* de change

▸▸ *Br Fam* ***the stockbroker belt*** la banlieue aisée▫

stockbroking ['stɒk,brəʊkɪŋ] **N** commerce *m* des valeurs en Bourse; **a s. firm** *or* **company** une société de Bourse

▸▸ ***stockbroking firm*** société *f* de Bourse

stockfish ['stɒkfɪʃ] *(pl inv or* **stockfishes***)* **N** stockfisch *m*, poisson *m* séché, merluche *f*

stockgirl ['stɒkgɜːl] **N** magasinière *f*

stockholder ['stɒk,həʊldə(r)] **N** actionnaire *mf*

▸▸ ***stockholder's equity*** capitaux *mpl ou* fonds *mpl* propres, avoir *m* des actionnaires

stockily ['stɒkɪlɪ] **ADV s. built** trapu, râblé

stockiness ['stɒkɪnɪs] **N** aspect *m* trapu *ou* râblé

stocking ['stɒkɪŋ] **N 1** *(for women)* bas *m*; **silk stockings** bas *mpl* de soie **2** *Old-fashioned (sock)* bas *m* de laine; **in one's s. feet** sans chaussures, en chaussettes, *Can* en pied de bas

▸▸ ***stocking filler*** = petit cadeau destiné à remplir le "Christmas stocking" à Noël; ***stocking mask*** bas *m (utilisé par un bandit masqué)*; ***stocking stitch*** point *m* de jersey

stockist ['stɒkɪst] **N** stockiste *mf*

stockjobber ['stɒk,dʒɒbə(r)] **N** *St Exch* **1** *Br Formerly* = intermédiaire en Bourse qui traite directement avec les agents de change et non avec le public (cette fonction n'existe plus depuis 1987) **2** *Am Pej* agent *m* de change

stockkeeper ['stɒk,kiːpə(r)] **N 1** *(cowherd)* vacher(ère) *m,f*, bouvier(ère) *m,f* **2** *Am (storekeeper)* magasinier(ère) *m,f*

stockkeeping ['stɒk,kiːpɪŋ] **N** tenue *f* des stocks

stockman ['stɒkmən] *(pl* **stockmen** [-mən]*)* **N 1** *(cowherd)* vacher *m*, bouvier *m*; *(breeder)* éleveur *m* (de bétail) **2** *Am (warehouseman)* magasinier *m*

stockpicker ['stɒk,pɪkə(r)] **N** *Fin & St Exch* = personne qui sélectionne des actions pour établir un portefeuille

stockpicking ['stɒk,pɪkɪŋ] **N** *(UNCOUNT) Fin & St Exch* sélection *f* d'actions

stockpile ['stɒkpaɪl] **N** stock *m*, réserve *f*

VT *(goods)* stocker, constituer un stock de; *(weapons)* amasser, accumuler

VI faire des stocks

stockpiling ['stɒkpaɪlɪŋ] **N** stockage *m (de nourriture, d'armes etc)*; **to accuse sb of s.** *(food)* accuser qn de faire des réserves de nourriture; *(weapon)* accuser qn de faire des réserves d'armes

stockpot ['stɒkpɒt] **N** marmite *f (pour le bouillon)*

stockroom ['stɒkrum] **N** magasin *m*, réserve *f*

stock-still **ADV** (complètement) immobile; **she was standing s. in the middle of the road** elle se tenait complètement immobile au milieu de la route

stocktaking ['stɒk,teɪkɪŋ] **N 1** *Com* inventaire *m*; **closed for s.** *(sign)* fermé pour inventaire **2** *Fig* **to do some s.** faire le point

stocky ['stɒkɪ] *(compar* **stockier**, *superl* **stockiest***)* **ADJ** trapu, râblé

stockyard ['stɒkjɑːd] **N** parc *m* à bestiaux

stodge [stɒdʒ] **N** *(UNCOUNT) Br Fam* **1** *(food)* trucs *mpl* bourratifs, étouffe-chrétien *m inv*; **the canteen food is pure s.** ce qu'on mange à la cantine est vraiment bourratif **2** *(writing)* littérature *f* indigeste▫

stodgy ['stɒdʒɪ] *(compar* **stodgier**, *superl* **stodgiest***)* **ADJ** *Fam* **1** *(food, meal)* bourratif **2** *(style)* lourd▫, indigeste▫ **3** *(person, manners, ideas)* guindé▫

stogie, stogy ['stəʊgɪ] *(pl* **stogies***)* **N** *Am Fam* cigare *m* bon marché

stoic ['stəʊɪk] **ADJ** stoïque

N stoïque *mf*

• **Stoic** **N** *Phil* stoïcien(enne) *m,f*

stoical ['stəʊɪkəl] **ADJ** stoïque

stoically ['stəʊɪklɪ] **ADV** stoïquement, avec stoïcisme

stoicism ['stəʊɪsɪzəm] **N** stoïcisme *m*

• **Stoicism** **N** *Phil* stoïcisme *m*

stoke [stəʊk] **VT 1** *(fire, furnace)* alimenter, entretenir; *(locomotive, boiler)* chauffer **2** *Fig (emotions, feelings, anger)* entretenir, alimenter

▸ **stoke up** **VI 1** *(put fuel on ▸ fire)* alimenter le feu; *(▸ furnace)* alimenter la chaudière **2** *Br Fam (fill one's stomach)* s'empiffrer; **I stoked up on pasta** je me suis s'empiffré de pâtes

VT SEP = **stoke**

stoker ['stəʊkə(r)] **N** chauffeur *m*, chargeur *m (d'un four, d'une chaudière etc)*

STOL [stɒl] **N** *(abbr* **short takeoff and landing***) (system)* décollage *m* et atterrissage *m* courts; *(aircraft)* ADAC *m*

stole [stəʊl] *pt of* **steal**

N 1 *(shawl)* étole *f*, écharpe *f*; **mink s.** étole *f* de *ou* en vison **2** *Rel* étole *f*

stolen ['stəʊlən] *pp of* **steal**

ADJ *(goods, car)* volé; **a s. kiss** un baiser volé

stolid ['stɒlɪd] **ADJ** flegmatique, impassible

stolidity [stɒ'lɪdətɪ] **N** flegme *m*, impassibilité *f*

stolidly ['stɒlɪdlɪ] **ADV** flegmatiquement, avec flegme, de manière impassible

stolidness ['stɒlɪdnɪs] **N** flegme *m*

stoma ['stəʊmə] *(pl* **stomata** [-mətə]*)* **N** stomate *m*

stomach ['stʌmək] **N 1** *(organ)* estomac *m*; **t[o] have an upset s.** avoir l'estomac barbouillé; **I can'[t] work on an empty s.** je ne peux pas travailler l'es[tomac] vide; **to have a pain in one's s.** avoir mal [à] l'estomac; *(lower)* avoir mal au ventre; **the sigh[t] was enough to turn your s.** le spectacle avait d[e] quoi vous soulever le cœur; **an army marches o[n] its s.** une armée ne peut pas se battre l'estoma[c] vide **2** *(region of body)* ventre *m*; **he has a fat s.** il [a] du ventre; **lie on your s.** couchez-vous sur le ven[tre] **3** *(usu neg) (desire, appetite)* envie *f*, goût *m*; **she has no s. for spicy food** elle supporte mal l[a] cuisine épicée; **I've no s. for his vulgar jokes thi[s] evening** je n'ai aucune envie d'écouter ses pla[i]santeries vulgaires ce soir

COMP *(infection)* de l'estomac, gastrique; *(ulce[r], operation)* à l'estomac; *(pain)* à l'estomac, a[u] ventre

VT *Fam* **1** *(tolerate ▸ person)* blairer, encaisse[r]; *(▸ thing)* encaisser; **I can't s. the way he looks a[t] me** il a une façon de me regarder qui me dé[] becte; **I just can't s. the thought of him being m[y] boss** je ne peux vraiment pas encaisser l'idé[e] qu'il soit mon patron **2** *(digest)* digérer; **I can't [] too much rich food** je ne digère pas bien la cu[i]sine riche

▸▸ *Med* ***stomach cancer*** cancer *m* de l'estoma[c]; ***stomach pump*** pompe *f* stomacale; ***stoma[ch] stapling*** agrafage *m* de l'estomac

stomach-ache **N** mal *m* de ventre; **to have (a)** avoir mal au ventre; **don't eat so much, you'll g[et] (a) s.** ne mange pas tant, ça va te donner mal a[u] ventre

stomp [stɒmp] *Fam* **VI** marcher d'un pas lourd▫; **he stomped out of the room** il est sorti de la pièc[e] d'un pas lourd

N 1 *(tread)* pas *m* lourd▫ **2** *(dance)* = jazz que l'o[n] danse en frappant du pied pour marquer [le] rythme

VT *Am Fam (defeat)* flanquer une peignée *ou* un[e] déculottée à

stomping ground ['stɒmpɪŋ-] **N** lieu *m* de pré[]dilection; **this was one of my old stompin[g] grounds** j'y allais tout le temps

stone [stəʊn] *(pl senses* **1** *to* **6 stones**, *pl sense* **7 in** *or* **stones***)* **N 1** *(material)* pierre *f*; **the houses ar[e] built of s.** les maisons sont en pierre; *Fig* **are yo[u] made of s.?** n'as-tu donc pas de cœur?; *Fig* **a hea[rt] of s.** un cœur de pierre

2 *(piece of rock)* pierre *f*, caillou *m*; *(on beach)* g[a]let *m*; **they threw stones at me** ils m'ont lancé de[s] pierres; **to fall like a s.** tomber comme une pierr[e]; **we will leave no s. unturned to find the culpri[t]** nous remuerons ciel et terre pour retrouver le[s] coupables; **it's within a s.'s throw of the countr[y]side** c'est à deux pas de la campagne

3 *(memorial)* stèle *f*, pierre *f*

4 *(gem)* pierre *f*

5 *Med* calcul *m*; **he has a s. in his kidney** il a u[n] calcul rénal

6 *(in fruit)* noyau *m*

7 *(unit of weight)* ≃ 6 kg; **she weighs about 8 s.** [e]**stones** elle pèse dans les 50 kilos

8 *(colour)* gris *m* mastic

ADJ 1 *(made of stone)* de *ou* en pierre; **a s. jar** u[n] pot de grès **2** *(in colour)* mastic *(inv)* **3** *Am Fa[m] (absolute, real)* vrai▫, total▫; **this is turning in[to] a s. drag!** ça devient vraiment galère!

VT 1 *(fruit, olive)* dénoyauter **2** *(person, car)* jet[er] des pierres sur, bombarder de pierres; *(as pu[n]ishment)* lapider **3** *Br Fam (idiom)* **s. the crows!, [s.] me!** mince alors!

▸▸ ***Stone Age*** âge *m* de (la) pierre; ***stone axe*** h[a]che *f* de pierre; ***stone circle*** cromlech *m*; *Br* ***sto[ne] fruit*** fruit *m* à noyau; *Zool* ***stone marten*** fouine; ***stone saw*** scie *f* à pierre *ou* de carrier

Stone-Age **ADJ** *(man, dwelling, weapon)* d[e] l'âge de (la) pierre

stone-blind **ADJ** complètement aveugle

stone-broke = **stony-broke**

stonechat ['stəʊntʃæt] **N** *Orn* traquet *m* (pâtre)

stone-cold **ADJ** complètement froid

ADV *Fam* **s. sober** pas du tout soûl

stonecrop ['stəʊnkrɒp] **N** orpin *m*

stoned [stəʊnd] **ADJ 1** *Fam (on drugs)* raide, d[é]foncé; **to get s.** se défoncer **2** *Fam Old-fashione[d] (drunk)* bourré, schlass **3** *(fruit)* dénoyauté

one-dead ADJ raide mort
ADV raide mort; **the blow killed him s.** le coup l'a ıé instantanément; *Fig* **to kill a proposal s.** soner le glas d'une proposition

one-deaf ADJ complètement sourd

one-ground ADJ moulu à la pierre

onemason ['stəʊn,meɪsən] N tailleur *m* de ierre

oner ['stəʊnə(r)] N *Fam Drugs slang* adepte *mf* e la fumette

onewall [,stəʊn'wɔːl] VI **1** *(obstruct discussion)* ıonopoliser la parole *(pour empêcher les autres e parler)*; *(avoid questions)* donner des réponses évasives **2** *Sport (in cricket)* jouer très pruemment, bétonner
VT *Parl* bloquer, faire barrage à

onewalling [,stəʊn'wɔːlɪŋ] N **1** *Sport (in cricket)* ɜu *m* défensif **2** *Parl* obstructionnisme *m*

oneware ['stəʊnweə(r)] N (poterie *f* en) grès *m*

onewashed ['stəʊnwɒʃt] ADJ *(jeans, denim)* élavé *(avant l'achat)*

onework ['stəʊnwɜːk] N *(UNCOUNT)* maçonerie *f*, ouvrage *m* en pierre

onily ['stəʊnɪlɪ] ADV froidement; **to look at sb s.** egarder qn froidement

oniness ['stəʊnɪnɪs] N **1** *(of soil, land)* nature *f* ierreuse **2** *(of heart)* dureté *f*; *(of look)* froideur *f*

oning ['stəʊnɪŋ] N *(of person)* lapidation *f*

onker ['stɒŋkə(r)] N *Br Fam* **what a s. of a goal!** uel but d'enfer!; **their latest album's a complete .** leur dernier album est absolument génial!

onking ['stɒŋkɪŋ] ADJ *Br Fam* super, génial, 'enfer; **he scored a s. goal** il a marqué un but enfer

ony ['stəʊnɪ] *(compar* **stonier**, *superl* **stoniest)** DJ **1** *(covered with stones* ▸ *ground, soil, road, and)* pierreux, caillouteux, rocailleux; *(*▸ *each)* de galets; *Fig* **his requests fell on s. ground** es revendications n'ont rien donné **2** *(stone-like* ▸ *texture, feel)* pierreux **3** *(unfeeling* ▸ *gen)* insenible; *(*▸ *reception)* froid; *(*▸ *look, silence)* glacial; **s. heart** un cœur de pierre

ony-broke ADJ *Br Fam* fauché (comme les lés), raide

ony-faced [-'feɪst] ADJ au visage impassible

ony-hearted ADJ au cœur de pierre; **he's s.** il un cœur de pierre

ood [stʊd] *pt & pp of* **stand**

ooge [stuːdʒ] N **1** *Fam Pej (lackey)* larbin *m* **2** *heat (straight man)* faire-valoir *m inv* **3** *Fam dupe)* pigeon *m*, poire *f*
VI *Theat* **to s. for a comedian** servir de faire-valoir un comique

ook [stʊk] N moyette *f*
VT moyetter

ool [stuːl] N **1** *(seat)* tabouret *m*; *Br* **to fall beween two stools** être assis entre deux chaises *Med* selle *f* **3** *Hort (tree stump)* souche *f*; *(shoot)* ejet *m* de souche; *(base of plant)* pied *m* de lante
▸▸ *Fam* **stool pigeon** indic *mf*, mouchard(e) *m,f*

oop [stuːp] VI **1** *(bend down)* se baisser, se pencher; **she stooped to pick up her pen** elle se baissa u se pencha pour ramasser son stylo
2 *(stand, walk with a stoop)* avoir le dos voûté; **he was beginning to s.** il commençait à se voûter
3 *(abase oneself)* s'abaisser; **I can't believe he tooped to lying** je n'arrive pas à croire qu'il se oit abaissé à mentir; **she would s. to anything** lle est prête à toutes les bassesses
4 *(condescend)* daigner; **she wouldn't s. to doing the dirty work herself** elle ne s'abaisserait pas à aire elle-même le sale travail
VT baisser, pencher, incliner; **he stooped his head to go through the door** il a baissé la tête our passer la porte
N **1** *(of person)* **to walk with** *or* **to have a s.** avoir le dos voûté **2** *Am (veranda)* véranda *f*, porche *m*

ooping ['stuːpɪŋ] ADJ *(back, shoulders, figure)* voûté

tooze [stuːz] VI *Br Fam Fin* = spéculer sur les offres spéciales proposées par les sociétés de cartes de crédit

stoozing ['stuːzɪŋ] N *Br Fam Fin* = fait de spéculer sur les offres spéciales proposées par les sociétés de cartes de crédit

STOP [stɒp]

N	
• arrêt **1–3, 6**	• gare **1**
• station **1**	• pause **2**
VT	
• arrêter **1, 3, 4, 6**	• cesser **1**
• empêcher **2**	• interrompre **4**
• couper **4**	• mettre fin à **5**
• retenir **7**	• boucher **9**
VI	
• s'arrêter **1, 2**	• cesser **2**

(pt & pp **stopped**, *cont* **stopping)**
N **1** *(stopping place* ▸ *for buses)* arrêt *m*; *(*▸ *for trains)* gare *f*; *(*▸ *for underground)* station *f*; **we get off at the next s.** nous descendons au prochain arrêt
2 *(break* ▸ *in journey, process)* arrêt *m*, halte *f*; *(*▸ *in work)* pause *f*; *Aviat & Naut* escale *f*; **ten minutes' s., a ten-minute s.** dix minutes d'arrêt; **to make a s.** *(gen)* s'arrêter; *(of plane, boat)* faire escale; **we made several stops to pick up passengers** nous nous sommes arrêtés à plusieurs reprises pour prendre des passagers; **we travelled/worked all day without a s.** nous avons voyagé/travaillé toute la journée sans nous arrêter; **our first s. was Brussels** nous avons fait une première halte à Bruxelles; **let's have a s. for lunch** faisons une pause pour le déjeuner
3 *(standstill)* arrêt *m*; **to come to a s.** s'arrêter; **to bring sth to a s.** arrêter qch; **to be at a s.** être arrêté
4 *(end)* **to put a s. to sth** mettre fin *ou* un terme à qch
5 *Br (full stop)* point *m*; *(in telegrams)* stop *m*
6 *Sport (save)* arrêt *m*
7 *(on organ* ▸ *pipes)* jeu *m* (d'orgue); *(*▸ *knob)* registre *m* (d'orgue); *Fig* **to pull out all the stops (to do sth)** remuer ciel et terre (pour faire qch)
8 *(plug, stopper)* bouchon *m*
9 *(blocking device* ▸ *gen)* butoir *m*; *(*▸ *for drawer)* butée *f*; *(*▸ *on typewriter)* taquet *m*
10 *Phot* diaphragme *m*
11 *Ling* occlusive *f*
12 *(in bridge)* contrôle *m*; **to have a s. in hearts** avoir un contrôle à cœur
COMP *(button, mechanism, signal)* d'arrêt
VT **1** *(cease, finish)* arrêter, cesser; **to s. doing** arrêter *ou* cesser de faire; **you should s. smoking** tu devrais arrêter de fumer; **he never stops talking** il n'arrête pas de parler, il parle sans cesse; **I wish they'd s. that noise!** j'aimerais qu'ils arrêtent ce bruit!; **she stopped work when she got married** elle a arrêté de travailler quand elle s'est mariée; **s. it!** *(to naughty child)* ça suffit!, assez!; **s. it, that hurts!** arrête, ça fait mal!
2 *(prevent)* empêcher; **to s. sb (from) doing sth** empêcher qn de faire qch; **it's too late to s. the meeting from taking place** il est trop tard pour empêcher la réunion d'avoir lieu; **she's made up her mind and there's nothing we can do to s. her** elle a pris sa décision et nous ne pouvons rien faire pour l'arrêter; **what's stopping you?** qu'est-ce qui vous retient?, qu'est-ce qui vous en empêche?; **I couldn't s. myself** je n'ai pas pu m'en empêcher
3 *(cause to halt* ▸ *person, car, machine)* arrêter; **this lever stops the motor** ce levier arrête le moteur; **a policeman stopped the traffic** un agent arrêta la circulation; **we could do nothing to s. the bleeding** nous ne pouvions rien faire pour arrêter l'hémorragie; **a woman stopped me to ask the way to the station** une femme m'a arrêté pour me demander le chemin de la gare; **the sound of voices stopped him short** *or* **stopped him in his tracks** un bruit de voix le fit s'arrêter net; *Fam* **to s. a bullet** se prendre une balle; **s. thief!** au voleur!
4 *(interrupt* ▸ *activity, production)* interrompre, arrêter; *(cut off* ▸ *electricity, gas, water)* couper; *(suspend* ▸ *grant, payment, subscription)* suspendre; **once he starts talking about the war there's no stopping him** une fois qu'il commence à parler de la guerre, on ne peut plus l'arrêter; **the referee stopped the fight in the third round** l'arbitre a arrêté le combat à la troisième reprise; **I forgot to s. the newspaper** j'ai oublié de faire suspendre mon abonnement au journal; **his father threatened to s. his allowance** son père menaça de lui couper les vivres; *Mil* **all leave is stopped** toutes les troupes sont consignées, toutes les permissions sont suspendues; **to s. a cheque** faire opposition à un chèque
5 *(put an end to* ▸ *abuse, rumours)* mettre fin à, faire cesser; **dumping nuclear waste should be stopped** il faut qu'on arrête de jeter n'importe où les déchets nucléaires; **it ought to be stopped** il faut que cela cesse
6 *(arrest)* arrêter
7 *Br (withhold* ▸ *sum of money, salary)* retenir; **the money will be stopped out of your wages** la somme sera retenue sur votre salaire; **he had £10 a week stopped out of his wages** on lui retenait 10 livres par semaine sur son salaire
8 *Sport (check* ▸ *blow)* parer; *Boxing (defeat* ▸ *opponent)* mettre un adversaire K.O.
9 *(block, fill* ▸ *hole)* boucher; **to s. one's ears** se boucher les oreilles; **to s. a gap** *(around door etc)* boucher un espace; *Fig* combler une lacune
10 *(fill* ▸ *tooth)* plomber
11 *Hort* pincer
12 *Mus (string)* presser; *(wind instrument)* boucher les trous de
VI **1** *(halt, pause* ▸ *person, vehicle, machine)* s'arrêter; **to s. to do** s'arrêter pour faire; **my watch has stopped** ma montre s'est *ou* est arrêtée; **does the bus s. near the church?** le bus s'arrête-t-il près de l'église?; **we can s. for tea on the way** nous pouvons nous arrêter en chemin pour prendre le thé; **we drove from London to Edinburgh without stopping** nous avons roulé de Londres à Édimbourg d'une traite; *Naut* **to s. at a port** faire escale à *ou* dans un port; **I used to play football but I stopped last year** je jouais au football mais j'ai arrêté l'année dernière; **she doesn't know where** *or* **when to s.** elle ne sait pas s'arrêter; **she did not s. at that** elle ne s'en tint pas là; **they'll s. at nothing to get what they want** ils ne reculeront devant rien pour obtenir ce qu'ils veulent; **we don't have time to s. and think** nous n'avons pas le temps de nous arrêter pour réfléchir; **to s. dead in one's tracks, to s. short** s'arrêter net; **she began talking then stopped short** elle commença à parler puis s'arrêta net *ou* brusquement; **they stopped short of actually harming him** ils ne lui ont pas fait de mal, mais il s'en est fallu de peu
2 *(come to an end)* cesser, s'arrêter, se terminer; **the rain has stopped** la pluie s'est arrêtée; **wait for the music to s.** attendez que la musique s'arrête; **the road stops a few miles east of Alice Springs** la route se termine à quelques kilomètres à l'est d'Alice Springs; **the matter will not s. there** l'affaire n'en restera *ou* demeurera pas là
3 *Br Fam (stay)* rester[□]; *(reside)* loger[□]; **I'm late, I can't s.** je suis en retard, je ne peux pas rester; **we've got friends stopping with us** nous avons des amis chez nous en ce moment; **which hotel did you s. at?** dans quel hôtel êtes-vous descendus[□]?
▸▸ *Phot* **stop bath** bain *m* d'arrêt; *Comput* **stop bit** bit *m* d'arrêt; *Comput* **stop code** code *m* d'arrêt; *Cin & TV* **stop frame** arrêt *m* sur image; **stop payment** opposition *f (à un chèque)*; *Br* **stop press** N nouvelles *fpl* de dernière minute; **'s. press!'** 'dernière minute' ADJ de dernière heure *ou* minute; **stop sign** (signal *m* de) stop *m*; **stop valve** soupape *f ou* robinet *m* d'arrêt

▸ **stop away** VI *Br Fam* rester absent[□]

▸ **stop by** VI *Fam* passer[□]; **you must s. by and see us next time you're in London** il faut que vous passiez nous voir la prochaine fois que vous venez à Londres; **I'll s. by at the chemist's on my way home** je passerai à la pharmacie en rentrant

▸ **stop down** VT SEP *Phot* diaphragmer
VI **1** *Phot* réduire l'ouverture **2** *Br Fam (gen)* rester en bas[□]; *Sch* **to s. down a year** redoubler une année

▸ **stop in** VI *Fam* **1** *Br (stay at home)* ne pas sortir[□], rester à la maison[□] **2** *(visit)* passer[□]; **to s. in to see sb** passer voir qn

▸ **stop off** VI s'arrêter, faire une halte; **they're stopping off at Bali for a couple of days on their**

way home au retour ils font étape à Bali pour quelques jours

▸**stop out** VI *Br Fam* ne pas rentrer□; **to s. out all night** découcher□, ne pas rentrer de toute la nuit; **to s. out (till) late** rentrer tard

▸**stop over** VI *(gen)* s'arrêter, faire une halte; *Aviat & Naut* faire escale

▸**stop up** VT SEP *(block ▸ hole)* boucher; *(▸ pipe)* obstruer, obturer

VI *Br Fam* ne pas se coucher□, veiller□; **to s. up late** veiller tard; **to s. up all night** veiller toute la nuit

---

stopcock ['stɒpkɒk] N *Br* robinet *m* d'arrêt

stopgap ['stɒpgæp] N *Br* bouche-trou *m*

ADJ de remplacement; **a s. measure** un palliatif

stop-go ADJ

▸▸ *Br Econ* ***stop-go policy*** politique *f* économique en dents de scie *(alternant arrêt de la croissance et mesures de relance)*, politique *f* du stop-and-go

stoplight ['stɒplaɪt] N **1** *(traffic light)* feu *m* rouge **2** *Br (brake-light)* stop *m*

stop-limit order N *St Exch* ordre *m* stop à cours limité

stop-list N *Banking (for lost cheques)* liste *f* de chèques volés ou perdus

stop-motion photography N prise *f* de vues image par image

stop-off N halte *f*, courte halte *f*

stopover ['stɒp,əʊvə(r)] N *(gen)* halte *f*; *(on flight)* escale *f*

stoppage ['stɒpɪdʒ] N **1** *(strike)* grève *f*, arrêt *m* de travail

2 *Br (sum deducted)* retenue *f*; **my wages are a lot less after stoppages** après les retenues, il ne reste plus grand-chose de mon salaire

3 *(halting, stopping)* arrêt *m*, interruption *f*; *Ftbl* arrêt *m* de jeu

4 *(blockage)* obstruction *f*; *Med* occlusion *f*

▸▸ *Sport* ***stoppage time*** arrêts *mpl* de jeu

stopper ['stɒpə(r)] N **1** *(for bottle, jar)* bouchon *m*; *(for sink)* bouchon *m*, bonde *f*; *(for pipe)* obturateur *m*; *(on syringe)* embout *m* de piston; **I can't get the s. out of the jar/back in the jar** je n'arrive pas à déboucher/à reboucher le bocal **2** *Ftbl* stoppeur *m* **3** *(in bridge)* arrêt *m*; **to have a s. in clubs** avoir un arrêt à trèfle

VT boucher, fermer

stopping ['stɒpɪŋ] N **1** *(coming or bringing to a halt)* arrêt *m* **2** *(blocking)* obturation *f*; **the s. (up) of a leak** le colmatage d'une fuite **3** *(cancellation ▸ of payment, leave etc)* suspension *f*; *(▸ of service)* suppression *f*; *(▸ of cheque)* opposition *f*

ADJ *(place)* où l'on s'arrête

▸▸ *Aut* ***stopping distance*** distance *f* d'arrêt; *Br* ***stopping train*** omnibus *m*

stopwatch ['stɒpwɒtʃ] N chronomètre *m*

storage ['stɔːrɪdʒ] N **1** *(putting into store)* entreposage *m*, emmagasinage *m*, stockage *m*; *(keeping, conservation)* stockage *m*; **our furniture is in s.** nos meubles sont au garde-meubles

2 *Comput* (mise *f* en) mémoire *f*

3 *(costs)* frais *mpl* de stockage *ou* d'emmagasinage, (frais *mpl* de) magasinage *m*

4 *(available space ▸ in store, for storing)* espace *m* disponible; *(▸ of business)* entrepôts *mpl*, magasins *mpl*

COMP **1** *(charges)* de stockage, d'emmagasinage, de magasinage **2** *Comput* de mémoire

▸▸ ***storage battery*** accumulateur *m*, batterie *f* secondaire; *Comput* ***storage capacity*** capacité *f* de stockage; ***storage card*** carte *f* à mémoire; ***storage cell*** accumulateur *m*, batterie *f* secondaire; *Comput* ***storage device*** dispositif *m* de stockage; *Br* ***storage heater*** radiateur *m* à accumulation; *Br* ***storage heating*** chauffage *m* par accumulation; *Comput* ***storage medium*** support *m* de stockage; ***storage room*** *(small)* cagibi *m*; *(larger)* débarras *m*; ***storage space*** espace *m* de rangement; **there is additional s. space for luggage in the rack above your head** vous pouvez également déposer vos bagages dans les casiers au-dessus de vos têtes; *Br* ***storage radiator*** radiateur *m* à accumulation; ***storage tank*** *(for fuel)* réservoir *m* (de stockage); *(for rainwater)* citerne *f*; ***storage unit*** meuble *m* de rangement

store [stɔː(r)] N **1** *(large shop)* grand magasin *m*; *Am (shop)* magasin *m*; *Am* **candy s.** confiserie *f*

2 *(stock ▸ of goods)* stock *m*, réserve *f*, provision *f*; *(▸ of food)* provision *f*; *(▸ of facts, jokes, patience, knowledge)* réserve *f*; *(▸ of wisdom)* fonds *m*; **we should get in** *or* **lay in a s. of coal** nous devrions faire provision de charbon

3 *(place ▸ warehouse)* entrepôt *m*, dépôt *m*; *(▸ in office, home, shop)* réserve *f*; *(▸ in factory)* magasin *m*, réserve *f*; *Br* **goods in s.** marchandises *fpl* en entrepôt; **furniture s.** garde-meubles *m inv*

4 *Comput (memory)* mémoire *f*

5 *(value)* **to lay** *or* **to put** *or* **to set great s. by sth** faire grand cas de qch; **I don't set much s. by his advice** je ne fais pas grand cas de ses conseils

COMP *Am (store-bought ▸ gen)* de commerce; *(▸ clothes)* de confection; **a s. cake** un gâteau de pâtisserie

VT **1** *(put away, put in store ▸ goods, food)* emmagasiner, entreposer; *(▸ grain, crop)* engranger; *(▸ heat)* accumuler, emmagasiner; *(▸ electricity)* accumuler; *(▸ files, documents)* classer; *(▸ facts, ideas)* engranger, enregistrer dans sa mémoire; **we stored our furniture at my mother's house** nous avons laissé *ou* mis nos meubles chez ma mère

2 *(keep)* conserver, stocker; **s. in a cool place** *(on packaging)* à conserver au frais

3 *(fill with provisions)* approvisionner; **he stored the larder with enough tinned goods to last the winter** il a rempli le placard avec assez de boîtes de conserve pour passer l'hiver

4 *Comput* stocker

VI *(goods)* **these goods don't s. well** ces produits ne se conservent pas bien

• **stores** NPL *(provisions)* provisions *fpl*; **the expedition's stores are running low** l'expédition commence à manquer de provisions

• **in store** ADV **they had a surprise in s. for her** ils lui avaient réservé une surprise; **who knows what the future has in s.?** qui sait ce que l'avenir nous réserve?; **if only we'd realized all the problems that were in s. for us** si seulement nous nous étions rendu compte de tous les problèmes qui nous attendaient

▸▸ *Mktg* ***store brand*** marque *f* de magasin; ***store card*** carte *f* de crédit *(d'un grand magasin)*; ***store cupboard*** placard *m* de rangement; ***store detective*** vigile *m (dans un magasin)*; ***store manager*** chef *m* de magasin; *Am* ***store window*** vitrine *f*, devanture *f*

▸**store away** VT SEP garder en réserve; **he stored away the joke for future use** il a noté la blague en se disant qu'il la replacerait

▸**store up** VT SEP *(goods, food)* emmagasiner; *(heat, electricity)* accumuler; *(memories, emotions)* accumuler; **he's just storing up trouble for himself by keeping silent** en ne disant rien, il ne fait que se préparer des ennuis

store-bought ADJ *(gen)* de commerce; *(clothes)* de confection; **a s. cake** un gâteau de pâtisserie

storefront ['stɔːfrʌnt] N *Am* devanture *f* de magasin

storehouse ['stɔːhaʊs, *pl* -haʊzɪz] N **1** *(warehouse)* magasin *m*, entrepôt *m*, dépôt *m* **2** *Fig (of information, memories)* mine *f*

storekeeper ['stɔː,kiːpə(r)] N **1** *(in warehouse)* magasinier(ère) *m,f* **2** *Am (shopkeeper)* commerçant(e) *m,f*

storeman ['stɔːmən] *(pl* **storemen** [-mən]) N *Br* manutentionnaire *m*

storeroom ['stɔːrʊm] N **1** *(in office, shop)* réserve *f*; *(in factory)* magasin *m*, réserve *f*; *(in home)* débarras *m* **2** *Naut* soute *f*, magasin *m*

-storey, -storeyed ['stɔːrɪd] SUFF **a single-s./five-s. building** un bâtiment à un étage/à cinq étages

storey *(pl* **storeys**), *Am* **story** *(pl* **stories**) ['stɔːrɪ] N étage *m*; **a four-s. building** un immeuble de quatre étages

Attention: ne pas confondre avec **story**.

storing ['stɔːrɪŋ] N **1** *(of goods, food)* emmagasinage *m*, entreposage *m*; *(of grain, crop)* engrangement *m*; *(of heat)* accumulation *f*, emmagasinage *m*; *(of electricity)* accumulation *f*; *(of files, documents)* archivage *m*

2 *(keeping)* conservation *f*, stockage *m*

3 *(filling with provisions)* approvisionnement

4 *Comput* stockage *m*

stork [stɔːk] N *Orn* cigogne *f*; **young s.** cigognea

m

storm [stɔːm] N **1** *Met* tempête *f*; *(thunderstorm)* orage *m*; *(on Beaufort scale)* tempête *f*; *Br* **it w a s. in a teacup** ce fut une tempête dans un ver d'eau

2 *Fig (furore)* tempête *f*, ouragan *m*; *(roar)* tempête *f*; **the arms deal caused a political s.** la vent d'armes a déclenché un véritable scandale p litique; **to go down a s.** faire un tabac, faire u malheur; **a s. of protest** une tempête de prote tations; **a s. of criticism** une marée de condar nations

3 *Mil* **to take by s.** prendre d'assaut; *Fig* **the sho took Broadway by s.** le spectacle a connu un su cès foudroyant à Broadway

VI **1** *(go angrily)* **to s. in/out** entrer/sortir comm un ouragan; **she stormed off without saying word** elle est partie furieuse, sans dire un mo **she was storming about the place like a ma woman** elle se démenait dans la pièce comm une folle

2 *Mil* donner ou livrer l'assaut; **th enemy stormed through our defences** l'enner donna l'assaut et franchit nos lignes de défens

VT prendre d'assaut; **the troops stormed the ra parts** les troupes ont pris d'assaut les remparts

▸▸ *Am* ***storm cellar*** abri *m* contre les cyclone ***storm centre*** *Met* œil *m* de la tempête *ou* du c clone; *Fig* centre *m* de l'agitation, point *m* n vralgique; ***storm cloud*** *Met* nuage *m* d'orage; *F* nuage *m* menaçant; **the s. clouds of war we gathering** le danger *ou* la menace d'une guer grandissait; ***storm cone*** cône *m* de tempêt ***storm damage*** dommages *mpl ou* dégâts *mpl* ca sés par l'orage *ou* la tempête; *Am* ***storm do*** porte *f* extérieure *(qui double la porte de la ma son pour éviter les courants d'air)*; ***storm dra*** égout *m* pluvial; ***storm lantern*** lampe *f* tempêt *Orn* ***storm petrel*** pétrel-tempête *m*; ***storm sew*** égout *m* pluvial; ***storm trooper*** membre *m* d troupes d'assaut; ***storm troops*** troupes *fpl* d'as saut; ***storm warning*** avis *m* de tempête; ***stor window*** contre-fenêtre *f*

stormbound ['stɔːmbaʊnd] ADJ bloqué p l'orage *ou* la tempête

storming ['stɔːmɪŋ] N *(attack)* assaut *m*; *(ca ture)* prise *f* (d'assaut); *Hist* **the s. of the Bastil** la prise de la Bastille

stormy ['stɔːmɪ] *(compar* **stormier**, *supe* **stormiest**) ADJ **1** *(weather)* orageux, d'orag *(sea)* houleux, démonté; **it was a s. day** il faisa un temps orageux **2** *Fig (relationship)* orageu *(debate)* houleux; *(look)* furieux; *(career, life)* t multueux, mouvementé

▸▸ *Orn* ***stormy petrel*** pétrel-tempête *m*

story ['stɔːrɪ] *(pl* **stories**) N **1** *(tale, work of fiction spoken)* histoire *f*; *(▸ written)* histoire *f*, conte *Literature (short story)* nouvelle *f*; **to tell sb a s.** r conter une histoire à qn; **ghost/murder s.** hi toire *f* de fantômes/de meurtre; **fairy s.** conte de fées; **this is a true s.** c'est une histoire vrai **there is a s. that…, the s. goes that…** on racon que…; **there's a s. behind** *or* **attached to every hibit in the museum** chacune des pièces du m sée a sa propre histoire

2 *(plot)* intrigue *f*, scénario *m*; **the s. of the film very complicated** l'intrigue du film est très co pliquée; **the s. is set in wartime London** l'histoi se passe à Londres, pendant la guerre

3 *(account)* histoire *f*; **let me tell you my side the s.** laisse-moi te donner ma version de l'hi toire; *Hum* **well, that's my s. and I'm sticking to** c'est la version officielle; **the witness change his s.** le témoin est revenu sur sa version d faits; **but that's another s.** mais ça, c'est une aut histoire; **that's not the whole s., that's only part the s.** mais ce n'est pas tout; **it's always the sam old s., it's the old, old s.** c'est toujours la mêm histoire *ou* chanson; **these bruises tell their ow s.** ces meurtrissures en disent long; **it's a long** c'est toute une histoire, c'est une longue hi toire; **to** *Br* **cut** *or Am* **make a long s. short** enf bref

4 *(history)* histoire *f*; **his life s.** l'histoire de sa vie; *Hum* **that's the s. of my life!** ça m'arrive tout le temps!

5 *Euph (lie)* histoire *f*; **are you telling stories again?** est-ce que tu racontes encore des histoires?

6 *(rumour)* rumeur *f*, bruit *m*; **there's a s. going about that they're getting divorced** le bruit court qu'ils vont divorcer; **or so the s. goes** c'est du moins ce que l'on raconte

7 *Press (article)* article *m*; *(event, affair)* affaire *f*; **here's a front-page s. about** *or* **on the riots** il y a un article en première page sur les émeutes; **all the papers ran** *or* **carried the s.** tous les journaux en ont parlé; **have you been following this corruption s.?** est-ce que vous avez suivi cette affaire de corruption?; **the s. broke just after the morning papers had gone to press** on a appris la nouvelle juste après la mise sous presse des journaux du matin

8 *Am* = **storey**

Attention: ne pas confondre avec **storey**.

storyboard ['stɔːrɪbɔːd] **N** story-board *m*, *Offic* scénarimage *m*

storybook ['stɔːrɪbʊk] **N** livre *m* de contes
ADJ a s. ending une fin digne d'un conte de fées; **a s. romance** une idylle de conte de fées; **a s. castle** un château de conte de fées

storyline ['stɔːrɪlaɪn] **N** *(of book)* intrigue *f*; *(of film)* intrigue *f*, scénario *m*; **it was quite hard to follow the s.** j'ai/il a/*etc* eu du mal à suivre le fil de l'histoire; **his novels always have a strong s.** l'intrigue de ses romans est toujours passionnante

storyteller ['stɔːrɪˌtelə(r)] **N 1** *(narrator)* conteur (euse) *m,f*; **to be a good/bad s.** être bon/mauvais conteur **2** *Euph (liar)* menteur(euse) *m,f*

storytelling ['stɔːrɪtelɪŋ] **N 1** *(art)* art *m* de conter; **to be good at s.** avoir l'art de raconter les histoires **2** *Euph (telling lies)* mensonges *mpl*

stoup [stuːp] **N** *Rel* bénitier *m*

stout [staʊt] **ADJ 1** *(corpulent)* corpulent, fort; **to grow s.** prendre de l'embonpoint
2 *(strong ▸ stick)* solide; *(▸ structure, material)* solide, robuste; *(sturdy)* costaud *m*; **a pair of s. walking shoes** une paire de chaussures de marche solides *ou* robustes
3 *(firm, resolute ▸ resistance, opposition, enemy)* acharné; *(▸ support, supporter)* fidèle, loyal
4 *(brave)* vaillant, courageux; **a s. heart** un cœur vaillant
N stout *m*, bière *f* brune forte

stouthearted [ˌstaʊt'hɑːtɪd] **ADJ** vaillant, courageux

stoutly ['staʊtlɪ] **ADV 1** *(firmly, resolutely ▸ resist, defend, oppose)* avec acharnement; *(▸ support)* fidèlement, loyalement; **she still s. maintains she was in the right** elle continue à prétendre dur comme fer qu'elle avait raison **2** *(bravely)* vaillamment, courageusement **3** *(solidly)* solidement, robustement; **s. built houses** des maisons solides

stoutness ['staʊtnɪs] **N 1** *(corpulence)* corpulence *f*, embonpoint *m* **2** *(solidity, strength ▸ of structure, materials)* solidité *f*, robustesse *f* **3** *(firmness, resolution ▸ of resistance, defence, opposition)* acharnement *m*; *(▸ of support, supporter)* fidélité *f*, loyauté *f*

stove [stəʊv] *pt & pp of* **stave**
N 1 *(for heating)* poêle *m* **2** *(cooker ▸ gen)* cuisinière *f*; *(▸ portable)* réchaud *m*; *(kitchen range)* fourneau *m* **3** *Ind (kiln)* four *m*, étuve *f*
▸▸ ***stove enamel*** laque *f ou* vernis *m* à cuire

stovepipe ['stəʊvpaɪp] **N 1** *(on stove)* tuyau *m* de poêle **2** *Fam* **s. (hat)** tuyau *m* de poêle

stow [stəʊ] **VT 1** *(store)* ranger, stocker; *(in warehouse)* emmagasiner; *Naut (cargo)* arrimer; *(equipment, sails)* ranger; **he stowed the keys behind the clock** *(hid)* il a caché les clés derrière la pendule; *(hurriedly)* il a fait disparaître les clés derrière la pendule **2** *(pack, fill)* remplir **3** *Br very Fam (idiom)* **s. it!** *(stop)* ça suffit!; *(shut up)* la ferme!

▸ **stow away VI** *(on ship, plane)* s'embarquer clandestinement, être passager clandestin
VT SEP 1 = **stow 2** *Br Fam (food)* enfourner; **he can certainly s. it away!** qu'est-ce qu'il descend!

stowage ['stəʊɪdʒ] **N 1** *(of goods ▸ in warehouse)* emmagasinage *m*; *Naut (▸ on ship)* arrimage *m*; *(cost)* frais *mpl* d'arrimage **2** *(capacity ▸ gen)* espace *m* utile *ou* de rangement; *(▸ in warehouse)* espace *m* d'emmagasinage; *(▸ on ship)* espace *m* d'arrimage

stowaway ['stəʊəweɪ] **N** passager(ère) *m,f* clandestin(e)

strabismus [strə'bɪzməs] **N** *Opt* strabisme *m*

straddle ['strædəl] **VT 1** *(sit astride of ▸ horse, bicycle)* chevaucher; *(▸ wall, chair)* se mettre à califourchon sur; *(mount ▸ horse, bicycle)* enfourcher; *(step over ▸ ditch, obstacle)* enjamber
2 *(span, spread over)* enjamber; **the bridge straddles the river** le pont enjambe la rivière; **the park straddles the state line** le parc est à cheval sur la frontière entre les États; **a company that straddles two continents** une entreprise qui a des intérêts dans deux continents
3 *Mil (target)* encadrer
4 *Am Fam* **to s. the fence** *(be noncommittal)* ne pas prendre position[□]; **you can't s. the fence** vous devez prendre position
VI *Am Fam Fig (sit on the fence)* ne pas prendre position[□]

strafe [strɑːf] **VT** *(with machine guns)* mitrailler en rase-mottes; *(with bombs)* bombarder (à faible altitude)

straggle ['strægəl] **VI 1** *(spread in long line ▸ roots, creeper, branches)* pousser de façon désordonnée; *(be scattered ▸ trees, houses)* être disséminé; *(hang untidily ▸ hair)* pendre lamentablement; **vines straggled over the fence** la vigne envahissait la clôture; **the suburbs straggled on for miles along the railway line** la banlieue s'étendait sur des kilomètres le long de la voie ferrée **2** *(linger)* traîner, traînasser; **she was straggling behind all the others** elle traînassait derrière tous les autres; **to s. in/out** entrer/sortir de manière dispersée *ou* par petits groupes

straggler ['stræglə(r)] **N 1** *(lingerer)* traînard(e) *m,f*; *(in race)* retardataire *mf* **2** *Bot* gourmand *m*

straggling ['stræglɪŋ] **ADJ** *(vine, plant)* maigre, (qui pousse) tout en longueur; *(houses, trees)* épars, éparpillé; *(village, street)* tout en longueur; *(beard)* épars; **to have s. hair** avoir les cheveux fins et ternes

straggly ['stræglɪ] **ADJ** *(hair)* fins et ternes; *(beard)* épars; *(roots)* long (longue) et mince; **a s. line of refugees** une file désordonnée de réfugiés

STRAIGHT [streɪt]

N	
• ligne droite **1**	
ADJ	
• droit **1–3, 7**	• raide **1**
• honnête **3**	• franc **3**
• clair **4**	• en ordre **5**
• quitte **6**	• direct **7**
• pur **8**	• consécutif **9**
• sérieux **11, 12**	• hétéro **13**
• clean **14**	
ADV	
• droit **1–3**	• directement **3, 4**
• franchement **5**	

N 1 *(on racetrack, railway track)* ligne *f* droite; **the final** *or* **home s.** la dernière ligne droite; *Fig* **we're on the home s. now** nous sommes dans la dernière ligne droite; **to keep to the s. and narrow** rester dans le droit chemin
2 *(level)* **to be out of s.** être de biais *ou* de travers; **to cut a material on the s.** couper une étoffe de droit fil
3 *(in poker)* quinte *f*
4 *Fam (heterosexual)* hétéro *mf*
5 *Fam (conventional person)* personne *f* conventionnelle *ou* sérieuse[□]; **don't be such a s.!** sois pas si sérieux!
6 *Fam Drugs slang (cigarette)* clope *f (par opposition à une cigarette de haschisch)*
ADJ 1 *(not curved ▸ line, road, nose)* droit; *(▸ hair)* raide; *Math* **a s. line** une (ligne) droite; **in a s. line** en ligne droite; **to have a s. back** avoir le dos bien droit, se tenir bien droit; **keep your back s.** tiens-toi droit, redresse-toi; *Fig* **to play with** *or* **to keep a s. bat** se conduire honorablement
2 *(level, upright)* droit; **the picture isn't s.** le tableau n'est pas droit *ou* est de travers; **is my tie s.?** est-ce que ma cravate est droite?; **to put** *or* **to set s.** *(picture)* remettre d'aplomb, redresser; *(hat, tie)* ajuster; **hold** *or* **keep the tray s.** tenez le plateau bien droit
3 *(honest ▸ person)* honnête, droit; *(frank ▸ person, answer)* franc (franche); **s. as a die** d'une droiture *ou* honnêteté absolue; **he's always been s. in his dealings with me** il a toujours été honnête avec moi; **to be s. with sb** être franc avec qn; **are you being s. with me?** est-ce que tu joues franc jeu avec moi?; **to give sb a s. answer** répondre franchement à qn; **to have a s. talk about sth** parler franchement de qch; **at the meeting he did some s. talking** il n'a pas mâché ses mots à la réunion; **it's time we did some s. talking** il faut qu'on parle, tous les deux; *Am Fam* **a s. shooter** une personne franche[□]; *Am Fam* **a s. arrow** *(man)* un brave type; *(woman)* une brave femme
4 *(correct, clear)* clair; **to put** *or* **to set the record s.** mettre les choses au clair; **just to set the record s.** pour que ce soit bien clair; **I'd like to get things s. before I leave** je voudrais mettre les choses au clair avant de partir; **let's get this s., he left at two o'clock?** mettons les choses au clair, il est parti à deux heures?; **have you put her s.?** as-tu mis les choses au point avec elle?; **you ought to put her s. about what he's (really) like** tu devrais lui dire comment il est vraiment; **now just you get this s.!** mets-toi bien ceci dans la tête!, qu'on se mette bien d'accord sur ce point!
5 *(tidy, in order ▸ room, desk, accounts)* en ordre; **to put** *or* **to set s.** *(room, house)* mettre en ordre, mettre de l'ordre dans; *(affairs, accounts)* mettre de l'ordre dans; **put your desk s.** rangez votre bureau
6 *(quits)* quitte; **here's the £5 I owe you, now we're s.** voilà les 5 livres que je te dois, maintenant nous sommes quittes
7 *(direct)* droit, direct; *Boxing* **he hit him a s. left/right** il lui a porté un direct du gauche/du droit; *Am* **to vote a s. ticket** voter pour une liste sans panachage
8 *(pure, utter)* pur; **it's just s. prejudice** ce sont des préjugés, tout simplement; **it's just s. propaganda** c'est de la propagande pure et simple
9 *(consecutive)* consécutif, de suite; **to have three s. wins** gagner trois fois de suite *ou* d'affilée; *Sport* **he won in s. sets** *(best of three sets)* il a gagné en deux sets; *(best of five sets)* il a gagné en trois sets; **we worked for three s. days** nous avons travaillé trois jours d'affilée; **he got s. As all term** il n'a eu que de très bonnes notes tout le semestre; **a s. flush** *(in poker)* une quinte flush
10 *(neat ▸ whisky, vodka)* sec (sèche)
11 *(serious)* sérieux; **to keep a s. face** garder son sérieux; **it's the first s. role she's played in years** c'est son premier rôle sérieux depuis des années
12 *Fam (conventional)* conventionnel[□], sérieux[□]
13 *Fam (heterosexual)* hétéro
14 *Fam* **to be s.** *(not criminal)* être rangé des voitures; *(not on drugs)* être clean
15 *Aut (cylinders)* en ligne; **a s. eight engine** un moteur huit cylindres en ligne
16 *Geom (angle)* plat
17 *Am Fam (true)* vrai[□]; **this is the s. story of what happened** voici comment ça s'est vraiment passé
ADV 1 *(in a straight line)* droit, en ligne droite; **try and walk s.!** essaie de marcher droit!; **the rocket shot s. up** la fusée est montée à la verticale *ou* en ligne droite; **to shoot s.** viser juste; *Fam* **to go s.** *(criminal)* se ranger des voitures
2 *(upright ▸ walk, sit, stand)* (bien) droit; **sit up s.!** tiens-toi droit *ou* redresse-toi (sur ta chaise)!
3 *(directly)* (tout) droit, directement; **he looked me s. in the face/in the eye** il me regarda bien en face/droit dans les yeux; **to drink s. from the bottle** boire à (même) la bouteille; **it's s. across the road** c'est juste en face; **the car came s. at me** la voiture a foncé droit sur moi; **the ball went s.**

through the window la balle est passée par la fenêtre; **the knife went s. through my arm** le couteau m'a transpercé le bras; **we drove s. through Nantes** nous avons traversé Nantes sans nous arrêter; **to read a book s. through** *(from beginning to end)* lire un livre d'un bout à l'autre; *(without stopping)* lire un livre d'une traite; **he looked s. through me** il m'a regardé sans me voir; **s. ahead** tout droit; **where's the crossroads? – it's s. ahead** où se trouve le carrefour? – c'est tout droit devant vous; **he looked s. ahead** il regarda droit devant lui; **s. on** tout droit; **go s. on till you come to a roundabout** continuez tout droit jusqu'à ce que vous arriviez à un rond-point; **at the roundabout go s. over** au rond-point allez tout droit; **to come s. out with sth** dire qch tout net

4 *(without delay)* directement; **come s. home after the concert!** rentre à la maison tout de suite après le concert!; **go s. to bed!** va tout de suite te coucher!; **I'll be s. back** je reviens directement; **they mostly go s. from school to university** pour la plupart, ils passent directement du lycée à l'université; **to come s. to the point** aller droit au fait; **to get s. on with one's work** se mettre directement au travail; **s. away** immédiatement, aussitôt, tout de suite; *Fam* **s. off** tout de suite❑

5 *(frankly, honestly)* franchement, carrément; **I told him s. (out) what I thought of him** je lui ai dit franchement ce que je pensais de lui; **to play s.** jouer franc jeu; *Fam* **to let sb have it s.** dire son fait à qn❑; *Fam* **I'm giving it to you s.** je vous le dis tout net❑; *Br Fam* **s. up?** sans blague?; **s. up!** sans blague!, je t'assure!

6 *(clearly)* **I can't see s.** je ne vois pas bien; **I can't think s.** je n'ai pas les idées claires

7 *(neat, unmixed)* **to drink whisky s.** boire son whisky sec

8 *(conventionally)* **to play (it) s.** *Theat* jouer de façon classique; *Mus* suivre la partition

▸▸ *Theat* ***straight actor*** acteur(trice) *m,f* sérieux (euse); *Theat* ***straight actress*** actrice *f* sérieuse; *Theat* ***straight man*** *(of comedian)* faire-valoir *m inv*; *Theat* ***straight part*** rôle *m* sérieux; *Am* ***straight razor*** rasoir *m* à main; ***straight theatre*** le théâtre traditionnel; *Am Pol* ***straight ticket*** liste *f* non panachée

straightaway [ˌstreɪtəˈweɪ] **ADV** tout de suite, sur-le-champ

ADJ *Am* droit

N *Am* ligne *f* droite

straight-edged **ADJ** *(blade)* à tranchant droit

straighten [ˈstreɪtən] **VT 1** *(remove bend or twist from ▸ line, wire)* redresser; *(▸ nail)* redresser, défausser; *(▸ wheel)* redresser, dévoiler; *(▸ hair)* défriser **2** *(adjust ▸ picture)* redresser, remettre d'aplomb; *(▸ tie, hat)* redresser, ajuster; *(▸ hem)* arrondir, rectifier; **she straightened her back** *or* **shoulders** elle se redressa; **he had his nose straightened** il s'est fait redresser le nez **3** *(tidy ▸ room, papers)* ranger, mettre de l'ordre dans; *(organize ▸ affairs, accounts)* mettre en ordre, mettre de l'ordre dans; **s. your desk before you leave** rangez votre bureau avant de partir

VI *(person)* se dresser, se redresser; *(plant)* pousser droit; *(hair)* devenir raide; *(road)* devenir droit

▸**straighten out** **VT SEP 1** *(nail, wire)* redresser; **he straightened out the crumpled bedclothes** il a remis les draps en place **2** *(situation)* débrouiller, arranger; *(problem)* résoudre; *(mess, confusion)* mettre de l'ordre dans, débrouiller; **don't worry, things will s. themselves out** ne t'en fais pas, les choses vont s'arranger **3** *Fam* **to s. sb out** *(help)* remettre qn dans la bonne voie❑; *(punish)* remettre qn à sa place❑; **I'll soon s. her out!** je vais lui apprendre!

VI *(road)* devenir droit; *(plant)* pousser droit; *(hair)* devenir raide

▸**straighten up** **VI** *(person)* se dresser, se redresser; *(plant)* pousser droit

VT SEP *(room, papers)* ranger, mettre de l'ordre dans; *(affairs)* mettre de l'ordre dans, mettre en ordre

straight-faced **ADJ** qui garde son sérieux, impassible

straightforward [ˌstreɪtˈfɔːwəd] **ADJ 1** *(direct ▸ person)* direct, franc (franche); *(▸ explanation)* franc (franche); *(▸ account)* très clair; **to give a s. answer to a question** répondre franchement *ou* sans détours à une question; **it's impossible to get a s. answer out of her** il est impossible d'obtenir d'elle une réponse nette et précise **2** *(easy, simple ▸ task, problem)* simple, facile; *(▸ instructions)* clair; **it was all quite s.** ce n'était pas compliqué du tout **3** *(pure, utter)* pur; **it's s. elitism** c'est de l'élitisme pur et simple

straightforwardly [ˌstreɪtˈfɔːwədlɪ] **ADV 1** *(honestly ▸ act, behave)* avec franchise; *(▸ answer)* franchement, sans détour **2** *(without complications)* simplement; **it can be assembled s. enough** le montage est assez facile; **the meeting did not go off quite as s. as hoped** la réunion ne s'est pas passée aussi bien qu'on l'avait espéré

straightforwardness [ˌstreɪtˈfɔːwədnɪs] **N 1** *(directness ▸ of person)* franchise *f* **2** *(simplicity ▸ of matter, question)* simplicité *f*

straight-line **ADJ** *Econ & Fin* constant

▸▸ *Acct* ***straight-line depreciation*** amortissement *m* linéaire

straightness [ˈstreɪtnɪs] **N 1** *(of line)* rectitude *f* **2** *(of conduct)* droiture *f*, rectitude *f*

straight-to-video **ADJ** *(movie)* sorti directement sur cassette vidéo

strain [streɪn] **N 1** *Tech (pressure)* pression *f*; *(tension)* tension *f*; *(pull)* traction *f*; *(weight)* poids *m*; **the weight put too much s. on the rope** le poids a exercé une trop forte tension sur la corde; **to collapse under the s.** *(bridge, animal)* s'effondrer sous le poids; **I took most of the s.** c'est moi qui ai fourni le plus gros effort; **the girder can't take the s.** la poutre ne peut pas supporter cette pression; *Fig* **the war is putting a great s. on the country's resources** la guerre grève sérieusement les ressources du pays

2 *(mental or physical effort)* (grand) effort *m*; *(overwork)* surmenage *m*; *(tiredness)* (grande) fatigue *f*; *(stress)* stress *m*, tension *f ou* fatigue *f* nerveuse; **he's beginning to feel/show the s.** il commence à sentir la fatigue/à donner des signes de fatigue; **I've been under great physical s.** je me suis surmené; **it was quite a s. for me to have to stand** j'ai trouvé très fatigant de devoir rester debout; **the situation has put our family under a great deal of s.** la situation a mis notre famille à rude épreuve; **he can't take the s. any more** il ne peut plus supporter cette situation stressante; **it's a terrible s. on her nerves** ses nerfs sont mis à rude épreuve; **they've been under a lot of s. recently** leurs nerfs ont été mis à rude épreuve ces derniers temps; **I couldn't stand the s. of commuting** je trouvais trop épuisant de prendre les transports en commun tous les matins

3 *Med (of muscle)* froissement *m*; *(sprain ▸ of ankle, wrist)* entorse *f*; **to give one's back a s.** se donner un tour de reins

4 *(breed, variety ▸ of animal, insect)* race *f*; *(▸ of virus, bacteria)* souche *f*; *(▸ of plant, grain)* variété *f*

5 *(style)* genre *m*, style *m*; **his other books are all very much in the same s.** ses autres livres sont tout à fait dans le même genre *ou* dans le même style *ou* dans le même esprit

6 *(streak, tendency)* fond *m*, tendance *f*; **there is a s. of madness in the family** il y a une prédisposition à la folie dans la famille; **there's a strong s. of fantasy in his novels** il y a une grande part de rêve dans ses romans

VT 1 *(rope, cable, girder)* tendre (fortement); *Fig (resources, economy, budget)* grever; *(patience)* mettre à l'épreuve, abuser de; *(friendship, relationship)* mettre à l'épreuve, mettre à rude épreuve; **to be strained to breaking point** être tendu au point de se rompre; **this new expense is straining our income to the limit** nos revenus nous permettent tout juste cette dépense supplémentaire

2 *(force ▸ voice)* forcer; **he strained his ears to hear what they were saying** il tendit l'oreille pour entendre ce qu'ils disaient; **to s. one's eyes to see sth** plisser les yeux pour mieux voir qch; **to s. every nerve** *or* **sinew to do sth** s'efforcer de faire qch

3 *(hurt, damage ▸ eyes)* fatiguer; **you'll s. your eyes** tu vas te fatiguer les yeux; **to s. a muscle** se froisser un muscle; **I have to be careful not to s. my heart** il faut que je veille à ménager mon cœur; **to s. one's back** se donner un tour de rein[s]; **I've strained my arm** je me suis froissé un musc[le] du bras; **to s. oneself** *(by gymnastics, lifting)* s[e] froisser un muscle; *(by overwork)* se surmene[r]; **mind you don't s. yourself lifting that suitcase** a[ttention] de ne pas te faire mal en soulevant cet[te] valise; *Ironic* **don't s. yourself!** surtout ne te fat[igue] pas!

4 *(distort ▸ meaning)* forcer; *(▸ word)* forcer [le] sens de; **it would be straining the truth to call th[is] play a masterpiece** dire que cette pièce est u[n] chef-d'œuvre serait exagéré

5 *Culin (soup, milk)* passer; *(vegetables)* (faire) égoutter

6 *Tech (deform ▸ part)* déformer

VI 1 *(pull)* tirer fort; *(push)* pousser fort; **she wa[s] straining at the door** *(pulling)* elle tirait sur [la] porte de toutes ses forces; *(pushing)* elle pous[sait] (sur) la porte de toutes ses forces; **to s. at [a] rope/at the oars** tirer sur une corde/sur les ra[mes]; **the dog strained at the leash** le chien tira[it] sur sa laisse; *Fig* **to be straining at the leash** pia[ffer] d'impatience; **she strained under the weigh[t]** elle ployait sous la charge

2 *(strive)* s'efforcer, faire beaucoup d'efforts; **t[o] s. to do sth** s'efforcer de faire qch; **I strained t[o] understand/hear what they were saying** je m[e] suis efforcé de comprendre/d'entendre ce qu'i[ls] disaient; **he tends to s. after effect** il a tendance [à] vouloir se faire remarquer

3 *(be under tension ▸ rope, cable)* se tendre; *([▸] beam)* fatiguer, travailler; *(become deformed)* gauchir, se fausser

4 *(liquid)* filtrer (**through** à travers)

• **strains** **NPL** *(of music)* accents *mpl*, accord[s] *mpl*; **the crowd rose to the strains of the nationa[l] anthem** le public s'est levé aux accents d[e] l'hymne national

strained [streɪnd] **ADJ 1** *(forced ▸ manner, laugh)* forcé, contraint; *(▸ voice)* forcé; *(▸ language, style, interpretation)* forcé, exagéré; **she gave m[e] a s. smile** elle m'adressa un sourire contraint *o[u]* forcé

2 *(tense ▸ atmosphere, relations, person)* tendu

3 *(sprained ▸ ankle, limb)* foulé; *(▸ muscle)* froissé; **to have a s. shoulder** s'être froissé u[n] muscle à l'épaule; **to have a s. neck** avoir un tort[i]colis

4 *(tired ▸ eyes)* fatigué; **his eyes looked s.** il ava[it] l'air d'avoir les yeux fatigués

5 *Culin (liquid)* filtré; *(soup)* passé; *(vegetables)* égoutté; *(baby food)* en purée

strainer [ˈstreɪnə(r)] **N** passoire *f*

strait [streɪt] **N** *Geog* **s., straits** détroit *m*

• **straits** **NPL** *(difficulties)* gêne *f*, situation *f* fâ[cheuse]; **to be in financial straits** avoir des ennu[is] financiers *ou* des problèmes d'argent

▸▸ ***the Straits of Dover*** le pas de Calais; ***the Stra[its] of Gibraltar*** le détroit de Gibraltar

straitened [ˈstreɪtənd] **ADJ** **in s. circumstance[s]** dans le besoin *ou* la gêne

straitjacket [ˈstreɪtˌdʒækɪt] **N** camisole *f* d[e] force; *Fig* **a financial s.** un carcan financier

VT *Fig* gêner, entraver; **to be straitjacketed by lack of investment/by censorship** être bloqué pa[r] le manque d'investissement/par la censure

straitlaced [ˌstreɪtˈleɪst] **ADJ** collet monté *(inv)*

strand [strænd] **N 1** *(of thread, string, wire)* bri[n] *m*, toron *m*; *(of cotton)* brin *m*; **a s. of hair** une mè[che] de cheveux **2** *(in argument, plot, sequence)* f[il] *m*; **the main s. of the narrative** le fil conducteu[r] (du récit) **3** *Ir or Literary (beach)* plage *f*; *(shore)* grève *f*, rivage *m*

VT 1 *(ship, whale)* échouer; **the ship was strande[d] on a mudbank** le bateau s'est échoué sur un ban[c] de vase **2** *(usu passive)* **to be stranded** *(person, vehicle)* rester en plan *ou* coincé; **she was strande[d] in Seville with no money** elle s'est retrouvée coin[cée] à Séville sans un sou vaillant; **we were le[ft] stranded with no way of getting home** on est res[tés] en plan sans aucun moyen de rentrer che[z] nous

stranded [ˈstrændɪd] **ADJ** *(person, car)* bloqué; **the s. holidaymakers camped out in the airport** le[s] vacanciers, ne pouvant pas partir, campèrent [à] l'aéroport

trange [streɪndʒ] **ADJ 1** *(odd)* étrange, bizarre; ɔeculiar) singulier, insolite; **it's s. that he should e so late** c'est bizarre *ou* étrange qu'il ait tant de etard; **she has some s. ideas** elle a des idées bi- arres *ou* de drôles d'idées; **s. beasts** bêtes *fpl* antastiques; **it was s. to see her in a dress** ça fai- ait bizarre *ou* drôle de la voir en robe; **it feels s. o be back in Scotland again** cela me fait bizarre l'être de retour en Écosse; **s. to say, I've never een there** chose curieuse *ou* étrange, je n'y suis ɪmais allé; **s. as it may seem** aussi étrange que ela paraisse *ou* puisse paraître; **truth is stranger han fiction** la vérité dépasse la fiction
2 *(unfamiliar)* inconnu; **to find oneself in s. sur- oundings** se trouver dans un endroit inconnu; **I voke up to find a s. man in my room** lorsque je me uis réveillé il y avait un inconnu dans ma hambre; **I can never sleep in a s. bed** je n'arrive as à dormir quand je ne suis pas dans mon lit
3 *(unaccustomed)* **he is still s. to city life** il n'est as encore accoutumé à *ou* il n'a pas encore habitude de la vie citadine
4 *(unwell)* bizarre; **to look/to feel s.** avoir l'air/se entir bizarre
5 *Phys (matter, particle)* étrange

trangely ['streɪndʒlɪ] **ADV** étrangement, bizar- ement; **s. enough, I never saw him again** chose urieuse *ou* chose étrange, je ne l'ai jamais re- u; **her face was s. familiar to him** son visage lui était singulièrement familier

trangeness ['streɪndʒnɪs] **N** *(of person, situ- ation)* étrangeté *f*, bizarrerie *f*, singularité *f*

tranger ['streɪndʒə(r)] **N 1** *(unknown person)* in- onnu(e) *m,f*; **never talk to strangers** ne parle ja- nais à des inconnus; **we are complete strangers** ɪous ne nous sommes jamais rencontrés; **a per- ect s.** un parfait inconnu; **she has become a s. to ɪer own family** elle est devenue une étrangère ɔour sa propre famille; **you've become quite a s. ound here** on ne vous voit plus beaucoup par ici *ɔu* dans les parages; **don't be a s.!** donne des ɪouvelles!; *Hum* **hello s.!** tiens, un revenant! **2** *person from elsewhere)* étranger(ère) *m,f*; **I'm a s. here myself** je ne suis pas d'ici non plus; **little s.** *(newborn baby)* nouveau-né(e) *m,f* je demande e huis clos! **3** *(novice)* novice *mf*; **I am not exactly a s. to jazz** je ne suis pas complètement ignorant en matière de jazz; **he is no s. to loneliness/mis- fortune** il sait ce qu'est la solitude/le malheur; **no s. to controversy, he...** étant habitué aux polé- miques, il...
►► ***Strangers' Gallery*** = la tribune du public à la Chambre des communes et à la Chambre des ords

Attention: ne pas confondre avec **foreigner**.

trangle ['stræŋgəl] **VT 1** *(person, animal)* étran- gler; **I could cheerfully have strangled that child** ce n'est pas l'envie qui me manquait d'étrangler cet enfant **2** *Fig (opposition, growth, originality)* étrangler, étouffer

trangled ['stræŋgəld] **ADJ** *(cry, sob)* étranglé, étouffé; *(voice)* étranglé

tranglehold ['stræŋgəlhəʊld] **N** *(grip around throat)* étranglement *m*, étouffement *m*, stran- gulation *f*; *(in wrestling)* étranglement *m*; *also Fig* **to have a s. on sb** tenir qn à la gorge; *Fig* **to have a s. on sth** avoir la mainmise sur qch; **they have a s. on the government** ils tiennent le gou- vernement à leur merci; **superstition still retains a s. on the country** l'emprise des superstitions sur le pays est toujours très forte; **to have a s. on the market/economy** jouir d'un monopole sur le mar- ché/l'économie

trangler ['stræŋglə(r)] **N** étrangleur(euse) *m,f*

trangling ['stræŋglɪŋ] **N 1** *(killing)* étrangle- ment *m*, strangulation *f*; *Fig (of opposition, pro- test, originality)* étranglement *m*, étouffement *m* **2** *(case)* **there has been yet another s.** une nou- velle victime a été étranglée; **that brings to five the number of stranglings** cela porte à cinq le nombre de personnes étranglées

trangulate ['stræŋgjʊleɪt] **VT 1** *Med* étrangler **2** = **strangle**

trangulation [ˌstræŋgjʊ'leɪʃən] **N** strangula- tion *f*; **the victim died of s.** la victime est morte étranglée; *Fig* **economic s.** asphyxie *f* écono- mique

strap [stræp] *(pt & pp* **strapped**, *cont* **strapping)** **N 1** *(belt ► of leather)* courroie *f*, sangle *f*, lanière *f*; *(► of cloth, metal)* sangle *f*, bande *f*
2 *(for carrying ► of bag, harness)* sangle *f*; *(► of shoulder bag or camera)* bandoulière *f*; *(fastening ► for dress, bra)* bretelle *f*; *(► for hat, bonnet)* bride *f*; *(► for helmet)* attache *f*; *(► for sandal)* lanière *f*; *(► under trouser leg)* sous-pied *m*; *(► for watch)* bracelet *m*
3 *(as punishment)* **to give sb the s.** administrer à qn une correction (à coups de ceinture); **to get the s.** recevoir une correction (à coups de cein- ture)
4 *(on bus, underground)* poignée *f*
5 *(for razor)* cuir *m* (à rasoir)
6 *Tech* lien *m*
VT attacher *(avec une sangle)*; **she had a knife strapped to her leg** elle portait un couteau atta- ché à sa jambe

►**strap down VT SEP** sangler, attacher avec une sangle *ou* une courroie

►**strap in VT SEP** *(in car)* attacher la ceinture (de sécurité) de; *(child ► in high chair, pram)* attacher avec un harnais *ou* avec une ceinture; **he strapped himself into the driving seat** il s'est ins- tallé au volant et a attaché sa ceinture de sécu- rité; **are you strapped in?** as-tu mis ta ceinture?

►**strap up VT SEP** *(suitcase, parcel)* sangler; *Br (limbs, ribs)* mettre un bandage à, bander

straphang ['stræphæŋ] **VI** *Br Fam* voyager de- bout□ *(en se tenant à la courroie ou à la poignée, dans les transports en commun)*

straphanger ['stræphæŋə(r)] **N** *Br Fam* voyageur (euse) *m,f* debout□ *(qui se tient à la courroie ou à la poignée, dans les transports en commun)*

strapless ['stræplɪs] **ADJ** *(dress, bra etc)* sans bre- telles
►► ***strapless top*** bustier *m*

strapline ['stræplaɪn] **N** *Press* sous-titre *m*

strapped [stræpt] **ADJ** *Fam* **1** *(lacking money)* **to be s. (for cash)** être fauché, ne pas avoir un rond **2** *Am (armed)* armé□, chargé

strapping ['stræpɪŋ] **ADJ** *Fam* costaud; **s. fellow** grand gaillard; **a fine s. girl** un beau brin de fille

strata ['strɑːtə] *pl of* **stratum**

stratagem ['strætədʒəm] **N** stratagème *m*

strategic [strə'tiːdʒɪk] **ADJ** stratégique; **we de- cided on a s. withdrawal of our troops** nous avons décidé d'opérer un repli stratégique de nos troupes
►► ***strategic business plan*** plan *m* stratégique d'entreprise; ***strategic business unit*** domaine *m* d'activité stratégique; *Mil* ***Strategic Defense Ini- tiative*** initiative *f* de défense stratégique; ***stra- tegic management*** gestion *f* stratégique; ***strategic planning*** planification *f* stratégique; ***strategic re- view*** revue *f* stratégique;

strategically [strə'tiːdʒɪklɪ] **ADV** stratégique- ment, du point de vue de la stratégie; **s. placed** *(country, town)* situé à un endroit stratégique; *Hum (object)* placé à un endroit stratégique

strategist ['strætɪdʒɪst] **N** stratège *m*

strategy ['strætɪdʒɪ] *(pl* **strategies)** **N** *(gen) & Mil* stratégie *f*; **marketing strategies** stratégies *fpl* de marketing

stratification [ˌstrætɪfɪ'keɪʃən] **N** stratification *f*

stratified ['strætɪfaɪd] **ADJ** stratifié
►► ***stratified sample*** échantillon *m* stratifié; ***stratified sampling*** échantillonnage *m* stratifié

stratify ['strætɪfaɪ] *(pt & pp* **stratified)** **VT** stratifier
VI se stratifier

stratosphere ['strætəˌsfɪə(r)] **N** stratosphère *f*

stratum ['strɑːtəm] *(pl* **strata** [-tə]) **N 1** *Geol* strate *f*, couche *f* **2** *Fig* couche *f*; **the various strata of so- ciety** les différentes couches de la société

straw [strɔː] **N 1** *Agr* paille *f*; *Br Fig* **man of s.** homme *m* de paille **2** *(for drinking)* paille *f*; **to drink sth through a s.** boire qch avec une paille **3** *(idioms)* **to catch** *or* **to clutch at a s.** *or* **at straws** se raccrocher désespérément à la moindre lueur d'espoir; **you're just grasping at straws** vous vous raccrochez à de faux espoirs; **to draw** *or* **to get the short s.** être tiré au sort, être de corvée; **a s. in the wind** un aperçu (de ce que l'avenir nous réserve); **that's the last s.** *or* **the s. that breaks the camel's back** c'est la goutte d'eau qui fait débor- der le vase; **it's the last s.!** ça c'est le comble *ou* le bouquet!; *Fam* **it's not worth a s.** ça ne vaut pas un clou
COMP *(gen)* de *ou* en paille; *(roof)* en paille, en chaume
►► *Am* ***straw boss*** homme *m* de terrain; ***straw hat*** chapeau *m* de paille; *Am Fig* ***straw man*** homme *m* de paille; ***straw mat*** paillasson *m*; ***straw mat- tress*** paillasse *f*; ***straw poll***, *Am* ***straw vote*** *(vote)* vote *m* blanc; *(opinion poll)* sondage *m* d'opinion

strawberry ['strɔːbərɪ] *(pl* **strawberries)** **N** *(fruit)* fraise *f*; *(plant)* fraisier *m*; **wild s.**, *Am* **field s.** fraise des bois
COMP *(jam)* de fraises; *(tart)* aux fraises; *(ice cream)* à la fraise
►► ***strawberry bed*** planche *f ou* plant *m* de frai- siers; ***strawberry blonde*** **ADJ** blond vénitien *(inv)* **N** blonde *f* qui tire sur le roux; ***strawberry field*** fraiseraie *f*; ***strawberry mark*** tache *f* de vin, envie *f*; ***strawberry tree*** arbousier *m*, arbre *m* aux frai- ses

STRAWBERRIES AND CREAM

En Grande-Bretagne, les fraises à la crème sont traditionnellement consommées lors de certaines manifestations en plein air, no- tamment au tournoi de tennis de Wimble- don.

straw-coloured, *Am* **straw-colored** **ADJ** (couleur) paille *(inv)*

stray [streɪ] **VI 1** *(child, animal)* s'égarer; **some sheep had strayed onto the railway line** des mou- tons s'étaient aventurés sur la ligne de chemin de fer; **the children strayed (away) from the rest of the group** les enfants se sont écartés du groupe; **the plane had strayed off course** l'avion s'était écarté de sa route; **we strayed into what must have been the red light area** nous nous som- mes retrouvés dans ce qui devait être le quar- tier des prostituées; *also Fig* **to s. from the fold** s'écarter du troupeau; **to s. (away) from the right path** faire fausse route; *Fig* s'écarter du droit chemin **2** *(speaker, writer)* s'éloigner du sujet; **but I am straying from the point** mais je m'écarte du sujet **3** *(thoughts)* errer, vagabonder; **her thoughts strayed (back) to her days in Japan** elle se mit à penser à sa vie au Japon
N *(dog)* chien *m* errant *ou* perdu; *(cat)* chat *m* errant *ou* perdu; *(cow, sheep)* animal *m* égaré; *(child)* enfant *m* perdu *ou* abandonné; **she set up a home for strays** elle a ouvert un centre pour recueillir les chiens et les chats perdus
ADJ 1 *(lost ► dog, cat)* perdu, errant; *(► cow, sheep)* égaré; *(► child)* perdu, abandonné **2** *(ran- dom ► bullet)* perdu; *(► thought)* vagabond; *(► memory)* fugitif; **she pushed back a few s. curls** elle repoussa quelques mèches folles *ou* rebelles **3** *(occasional ► car, boat)* isolé, rare; **a few s. cars drove by** quelques rares voitures passaient par là
• **strays** **NPL** *Rad & Tel* parasites *mpl*, friture *f*

streak [striːk] **N 1** *(smear ► of blood)* filet *m*; *(► of dirt, ink, paint)* traînée *f*; *(line, stripe ► of light)* trait *m*, rai *m*; *(► of ore)* filon *m*, veine *f*; *(► in mar- ble)* veine *f*; **there were a few streaks of cloud in an otherwise blue sky** il y avait quelques traînées nuageuses dans le ciel bleu; **the first streaks of dawn** les premières lueurs de l'aube; **black wings with white streaks** des ailes noires avec des traî- nées blanches; **the carpet has green streaks** la moquette est striée de vert; **her hair has grey streaks in it** elle a des cheveux gris; **to have blond streaks put in one's hair** se faire faire des mèches blondes; **streaks of lightning lit up the sky** des éclairs zébraient le ciel; **they drove past like a s. of lightning** leur voiture est passée comme un éclair
2 *(of luck)* période *f*; **I've had a s. of (good) luck** j'ai eu de la chance; **he's hit a winning s., he's on a winning s.** *(in gambling)* la chance lui sourit; *(good deal)* il tient un bon filon; **to be on a losing s.** *(in gambling) & Fig* être dans une mauvaise passe; **he's just had a s. of bad luck lately** il vient d'essuyer toute une série de revers
3 *(tendency, trace)* côté *m*; **he has a mean s.** *or* **a s.**

of meanness in him il a un côté mesquin; **there was a s. of cowardice in him** il avait un côté lâche; **there has always been a s. of madness in the family** il y a toujours eu une prédisposition à la folie dans la famille

4 *Fam (naked dash)* **to do a s.** = traverser un lieu public nu en courant

VT *(smear)* tacher; *(stripe)* strier, zébrer; **the wall was streaked with paint** il y avait des traînées de peinture sur le mur; **her hands were streaked with blue ink** elle avait des taches d'encre bleue sur les mains; **the mirror was streaked with finger marks** il y avait des traces de doigts sur le miroir; **their cheeks were streaked with tears** leurs joues étaient couvertes de larmes; **marble streaked with red** du marbre strié de rouge; **fur streaked with black** pelage rayé de noir; **her hair is streaked with grey** *(natural)* elle a des cheveux gris; *(artificial)* elle s'est fait des mèches grises; **she's had her hair streaked** elle s'est fait faire des mèches

VI 1 *(go quickly)* **to s. in/out** entrer/sortir comme un éclair; **to s. off** partir à toute allure; **to s. past** passer en trombe **2** *(run naked)* = traverser un lieu public nu en courant; **he was arrested for streaking** ≃ il a été arrêté pour exhibitionnisme

streaker ['stri:kə(r)] **N** = personne nue qui traverse un lieu public en courant

streaking ['stri:kɪŋ] **N 1** *(streaks)* raies *fpl*, rayures *fpl*, bandes *fpl*; *(in hairdressing)* effet *m* de mèches **2** *Fam* = pratique consistant à traverser un lieu public nu en courant

streaky ['stri:kɪ] *(compar* **streakier**, *superl* **streakiest**) **ADJ 1** *(colour, surface)* marbré, zébré, jaspé; *(rock, marble)* veiné; *(glass, window)* couvert de traînées; **s. pattern** stries *fpl*, zébrures *fpl*; **her make-up had gone s.** son maquillage avait dégouliné **2** *Culin (meat)* entrelardé, persillé **3** *Am (person)* agité, énervé

►► *Br Culin* ***streaky bacon*** bacon *m* entrelardé

stream [stri:m] **N 1** *(brook)* ruisseau *m*; **mountain s.** torrent *m*

2 *(current)* courant *m*; **to go with the s.** aller au fil de l'eau; *Fig* suivre le courant *ou* le mouvement; *also Fig* **to go against the s.** aller à contre-courant

3 *(flow ► of liquid)* flot *m*, jet *m*; *(► of air)* courant *m*; *(► of blood, lava)* ruisseau *m*, flot *m*, cascade *f*, torrent *m*; *(► of people, traffic)* flot *m*, défilé *m* (continu); *(► of tears)* ruisseau *m*, torrent *m*; **a s. of water shot out of the tap** l'eau jaillit à flot du robinet; **a red hot s. of lava flowed down the mountain** une coulée de lave incandescente descendait le flanc de la montagne; **there was a continuous s. of visitors** il y avait un défilé continu *ou* ininterrompu de visiteurs; **streams of wellwishers have been arriving all day** des flots de sympathisants sont arrivés tout au long de la journée; **we've received a steady s. of applications** nous avons reçu un flot incessant de candidatures; **she unleashed a s. of insults** elle lâcha un torrent d'injures

4 *Ind & Tech* **to be on/off s.** être en service/hors service; **to come on s.** être mis en service

5 *Br Sch* classe *f* de niveau; **we're in the top s.** nous sommes dans la section forte

VI 1 *(flow ► water, tears)* ruisseler, couler à flots; *(► blood)* ruisseler; **the wall was streaming with condensation, condensation streamed down the wall** la condensation ruisselait le long du mur; **tears streamed down her face** des larmes ruisselaient sur son visage; **the onions made her eyes s.** les oignons l'ont fait pleurer; **sunlight streamed into the room** le soleil entra à flots dans la pièce

2 *(flutter)* flotter, voleter; **flags were streaming in the wind** des drapeaux flottaient au vent; **her long hair streamed (out) behind her** ses longs cheveux flottaient derrière elle

3 *(people, traffic)* **to s. in/out** entrer/sortir à flots; **cars streamed out of the city in their thousands** des milliers de voitures sortaient de la ville en un flot ininterrompu; **I watched as the demonstrators streamed past** je regardai passer les flots de manifestants

VT 1 *(flow with)* **to s. blood/tears** ruisseler de sang/de larmes **2** *Br Sch* répartir en groupes de niveau

►► *Literature* ***stream of consciousness*** monologue *m* intérieur; **a s. of consciousness novel** un roman qui utilise la technique du monologue intérieur

streamer ['stri:mə(r)] **N 1** *(decoration)* serpentin *m* **2** *(banner)* banderole *f*; *(pennant)* flamme *f* **3** *Journ* manchette *f*

streaming ['stri:mɪŋ] **ADJ** *(surface, window, windscreen)* ruisselant; *Br* **I've got a s. cold** j'ai attrapé un gros rhume

N 1 *Br Sch* répartition *f* en classes de niveau **2** *Comput* streaming *m*

streamline ['stri:mlaɪn] **VT 1** *Aut & Aviat* donner un profil aérodynamique à, caréner **2** *Econ & Ind (company, production)* rationaliser; *(industry)* dégraisser, restructurer

streamlined ['stri:mlaɪnd] **ADJ 1** *Aut & Aviat* aérodynamique; *Naut (ship)* hydrodynamique; *Zool (fish, animal)* à la forme hydrodynamique **2** *Fig (building)* aux contours harmonieux; *(kitchen, bathroom)* aux lignes épurées; *(figure)* svelte **3** *Econ & Ind (company, production)* rationalisé; *(industry)* dégraissé, restructuré

streamlining ['stri:mlaɪnɪŋ] **N 1** *Aut & Aviat* carénage *m* **2** *Econ & Ind (of company, production)* rationalisation *f*; *(of industry)* dégraissage *m*, restructuration *f*

street [stri:t] **N** rue *f*; *Br* **in** *or Am* **on a s.** dans une rue; **a s. of houses** une rue résidentielle; **the whole s. knows about it** toute la rue est au courant; **to put** *or* **to turn sb out into the s.** mettre qn à la rue; **to be on the s.** *or* **streets** *(as prostitute)* faire le trottoir; *(homeless person)* être à la rue; **to take to the streets** *(protestors)* descendre dans la rue; **to walk the streets** *(as prostitute)* faire le trottoir *ou Fam* le tapin; *(from idleness)* battre le pavé, flâner dans les rues; *(in search)* faire les rues; **they walked the streets looking for her** ils ont parcouru la ville à pied à sa recherche; *Hum* **that'll keep him off the streets!** ça l'empêchera de faire des bêtises!; **that's right up his s.!** *(competence)* c'est tout à fait son rayon *ou* dans ses cordes!; *(interest)* c'est tout à fait son truc!

COMP *(noises)* de la rue; *(musician)* des rues

• **streets ADV** *Fam* **to be streets ahead of sb** dépasser qn de loin

►► *Br Old-fashioned* ***street Arab*** gamin(e) *m,f ou* gosse *mf* des rues; ***street art*** peintures *fpl* murales *(dans la rue)*; ***street atlas*** plan *m* de la ville; *Br* ***street café*** café *m* avec terrasse; **we had breakfast at a s. café** nous avons pris le petit déjeuner à la terrasse d'un café; ***street cleaner*** *(person)* balayeur(euse) *m,f*; *(machine)* balayeuse *f*; *Fam* ***street cred, street credibility*** image *f* cool *ou* branchée; **she thinks that the leather jacket gives her more s. cred** elle trouve que son blouson en cuir fait très branché *ou* lui donne l'air encore plus cool; **this won't do much for my s. cred** ça va craindre pour mon image de marque; ***street cry*** cri *m* de colporteur; **the s. cries of old Paris** le cri des colporteurs du vieux Paris; ***street dance*** street dance *m ou f*; *St Exch* ***street dealing*** transactions *fpl* hors Bourse; ***street directory*** plan *m* de la ville; ***street door*** porte *f* (qui donne) sur la rue, porte *f* d'entrée; ***street fighting*** combats *mpl* de rue; ***street furniture*** mobilier *m* urbain; ***street guide*** plan *m* de la ville; *Am Sport* ***street hockey*** hockey *m* sur roulettes; ***street interview*** micro-trottoir *m*; ***street level*** rez-de-chaussée *m inv*; **below s. level** au sous-sol; ***street lighting*** éclairage *m* public; **the s. lighting comes on at sunset** on allume la lumière dans les rues au coucher du soleil; ***street map*** plan *m* de la ville; ***street market*** marché *m* en plein air *ou* à ciel ouvert; *St Exch* marché *m* hors Bourse; ***street musician*** musicien(enne) *m,f* des rues; ***street party*** = fête de rue organisée pour célébrer un événement; ***street person*** SDF *mf*; ***street plan*** plan *m* de la ville; ***street price*** *St Exch* cours *m* hors Bourse; *(of drugs)* prix *m* à la revente; ***street sweeper*** *(person)* balayeur(euse) *m,f*; *(machine)* balayeuse *f*; ***street theatre*** théâtre *m* de rue *ou* de foire; ***street trader*** marchand(e) *m,f* ambulant(e); ***street trading*** vente *f* ambulante; ***street value*** *(of drugs)* valeur *f* marchande; *Am* ***street vendor*** marchand(e) *m,f* ambulant(e)

streetcar ['stri:tkɑ:(r)] **N** *Am* tramway *m*

streetwalker ['stri:t,wɔ:kə(r)] **N** *Old-fashioned* prostituée *f*; **to be a s.** faire le trottoir

streetwise ['stri:t,waɪz] **ADJ** *Fam* dégourdi

strength [streŋθ] **N 1** *(UNCOUNT) (physic*
power ► of person, animal, muscle) force *f*, pui
sance *f*; *(health)* forces *fpl*; **she doesn't know h**
own s. elle ne connaît pas sa force; **his s. faile**
him ses forces l'ont trahi *ou* abandonné; **I haven**
the s. to lift these boxes je n'ai pas assez de forc
ou je ne suis pas assez fort pour soulever ce
cartons; **to lose s.** perdre des forces, s'affaibli
by sheer s. de force; **with all my s.** de toutes me
forces; **to get one's s. back** reprendre des *ou* r
couvrer ses forces; **to go from s. to s.** *(sick perso*
aller de mieux en mieux; *Fig (business)* être e
plein essor

2 *(of faith, opinion, resolution)* force *f*, fermeté
(of emotion, feeling, music, art) force *f*; **s. of cha**
acter force *f* de caractère; **s. of purpose** résol
tion *f*; **they have great s. of purpose** ils sont trè
déterminés; **s. of will** volonté *f*; **I haven't the s.**
start again je n'ai pas le courage de recommer
cer; **give me s.!** pitié!

3 *(intensity ► of earthquake, wind)* force *f*, inte
sité *f*; *(► of current, light)* intensité *f*; *(► of soun*
voice, lens, magnet) force *f*, puissance *f*

4 *(strong point, asset)* force *f*, point *m* fort; **h**
ambition is her main s. son ambition fait l'esse
tiel de sa force; **it's one of their strengths** c'est u
de leurs points forts

5 *(solidity) & Fig (of claim, position, relationshi*
solidité *f*; *(vigour ► of argument, protest)* force
vigueur *f*; *Fin (► of currency, economy)* solidité
to argue from a position of s. être en position d
force; **the dollar has gained/fallen in s.** le doll
s'est consolidé/a chuté

6 *(of alcohol)* teneur *f* en alcool; *(of solution)*
tre *m*; *(of coffee, tobacco)* force *f*; **solution at full s**
full-s. solution solution *f* concentrée

7 *(UNCOUNT) (numbers)* effectif *m*, effecti
mpl; **the office staff is below** *or* **under s.** il nou
manque du personnel de bureau; **we're at full**
nos effectifs sont au complet; **the protesto**
turned up in s. les manifestants sont venus e
force *ou* en grand nombre

• **on the strength of PREP** en vertu de, sur
foi de; **to do sth on the s. of what one has been to**
faire qch en se fiant à *ou* en s'appuyant sur c
qu'on vous a dit; **he was accepted on the s. of h**
excellent record il a été accepté grâce à ses e
cellents antécédents

strengthen ['streŋθən] **VT 1** *(physically ► bod*
muscle) fortifier, raffermir; *(► person)* fortifie
tonifier; *(► voice)* renforcer; *(improve ► eyesigh*
hearing) améliorer; *also Fig* **to s. one's grip** *or* **ho**
on sth resserrer son emprise sur qch

2 *(reinforce ► firm, nation)* renforcer; *(► fe*
emotion, effect) renforcer, intensifier; *(► belie*
argument) renforcer; *(► link, friendship)* renfo
cer, fortifier; *(morally ► person)* fortifier; **the d**
cision strengthened my resolve la décision n'a fa
que renforcer ma détermination

3 *(foundation, structure)* renforcer, consolide
(material) renforcer

4 *Fin (currency, economy)* consolider, raffermir

VI 1 *(physically ► body)* se fortifier, se raffermi
(► voice) devenir plus fort; *(► grip)* se resserrer
(increase ► influence, effect, desire) augmente
s'intensifier; *(► wind)* forcir; *(► current)* augme
ter, se renforcer; *(► friendship, character, resolve*
se renforcer, se fortifier **3** *Fin (prices, market)* s
consolider, se raffermir

strengthening ['streŋθənɪŋ] **N 1** *(physical ►*
body, muscle) raffermissement *m*; *(► of voice*
renforcement *m*; *(► of hold, grip)* resserreme
m

2 *(increase ► of emotion, effect, desire)* renforce
ment *m*, augmentation *f*, intensification *f*; *(r*
inforcement ► of character, friendship, positio
wind, current) renforcement *m*

3 *(of structure, building)* renforcement *m*, co
solidation *f*; *(of material)* renforcement *m*

4 *Fin* consolidation *f*

ADJ fortifiant, remontant; *Med* tonifiant; **to hav**
a s. effect on sb fortifier qn

strenuous ['strenjʊəs] **ADJ 1** *(physically ► acti*
ity, exercise, sport) ardu; **it was a long, s. climb** c
fut une ascension longue et ardue; **I'm not a**
lowed to do anything s. je ne dois pas me fat
guer; **she leads a s. life** elle mène une v
stressante **2** *(vigorous ► opposition, suppor*
acharné, énergique; *(► protest)* vigoureu

ergique; (▸ *opponent, supporter*) zélé, très ac- **to make s. efforts to do sth** faire des efforts narnés pour faire qch; **he is a s. campaigner civil rights** il milite avec acharnement pour droits civils

enuously ['strenjʊəslɪ] **ADV 1** *(play, swim, rk)* en se dépensant beaucoup, en faisant de)s efforts **2** *(fight, oppose, resist)* avec achar- ment, énergiquement

enuousness ['strenjʊəsnɪs] **N 1** *(of activity, rk)* dureté *f (de l'effort physique exigé)* **2** *(of op- sition)* acharnement *m*

ep throat [strep-] **N** *esp Am Fam* = gorge at- nte d'une infection streptococcique☐

eptococcal [ˌstreptəˈkɒkəl], **streptococcic** reptəˈkɒksɪk] **ADJ** *Med* streptococcique

eptococcus [ˌstreptəˈkɒkəs] *(pl* **streptococci** ɒksaɪ]) **N** *Med* streptocoque *m*

eptomycin [ˌstreptəˈmaɪsɪn] **N** streptomy- e *f*

ess [stres] **N 1** *(nervous tension)* stress *m*, ten- n *f* nerveuse; **to suffer from s.** être stressé; **to under s.** *(person)* être stressé; *(relationship)* e tendu; **she's been under a lot of s. lately** elle té très stressée ces derniers temps; **how does react under s.?** comment réagit-il sous le ess *ou* sous la pression?; **it puts our relation- p under s.** ça crée des tensions dans nos rela- ns; **the stresses and strains of city life** le stress la vie urbaine; **I always work better under s.** je vaille toujours mieux quand je suis sous ession

Constr & Tech contrainte *f*, tension *f*; **to be in s.** *eam, girder)* être sous contrainte; **there is too ch s. on the foundations** la contrainte que su- ssent les fondations est trop forte; **can the gir- rs take the s.?** est-ce que les poutres peuvent utenir la charge *ou* la tension?

(emphasis) insistance *f*; **to lay s. on sth** *(fact, int, detail)* insister sur qch, souligner qch; *ualities, values, manners)* insister sur qch, met- l'accent sur qch

Ling (gen) accentuation *f*; *(accent on syllable)* cent *m* (tonique); *(accented syllable)* syllabe *f* centuée; **the s. is** *or* **falls on the third syllable** ccent tombe sur la troisième syllabe; **there three stresses in the sentence** il y a trois sylla- s accentuées dans la phrase

Mus accent *m*

T 1 *(emphasize* ▸ *fact, point, detail)* insister sur, re ressortir, souligner; (▸ *value, qualities)* in- ter sur, mettre l'accent sur; **this point cannot stressed enough** on ne saurait trop insister ce point; **she stressed that no decision had en taken** elle a insisté sur *ou* souligné le fait 'aucune décision n'avait été prise **2** *(in phon- cs, poetry, music)* accentuer **3** *Constr & Tech ructure, foundation)* mettre sous tension *ou* charge; *(concrete, metal)* solliciter

Fam stresser

Med ***stress fracture*** fracture *f* de surmenage; ***ess management*** gestion *f* du stress; *Ling* ***stress rk*** marque *f* d'accent

essed [strest] **ADJ 1** *(person)* stressé, tendu; *lationship)* tendu **2** *(syllable, word)* accentué

essed-out **ADJ** *Fam* stressé

essful ['stresfʊl] **ADJ** *(lifestyle, job, conditions)* essant; *(moments)* de stress; **to lead a s. life** ener une vie très stressante

'ess-related **ADJ** dû au stress

stress-related illness maladie *f* due au stress

etch [stretʃ] **N 1** *(expanse* ▸ *of land, water)* endue *f*; **this s. of the road is particularly danger- s in the winter** cette partie de la route est très ngereuse en hiver; **a new s. of road/motorway** nouveau tronçon de route/d'autoroute; **it's a ely s. of river/scenery** cette partie de la rivière/ paysage est magnifique; *Horseracing & Fig* **to into the final** *or* **finishing** *or* **home s.** entamer la rnière ligne droite

(period of time) période *f*; **for a long s. of time** ndant longtemps; **for long stretches at a time ere was nothing to do** il n'y avait rien à faire ndant de longues périodes; **to do a s. of ten ars in the army** passer dix ans dans l'armée; *m* **he did a s. in Dartmoor** il a fait de la taule à Dartmoor; *Fam* **he was given a five-year s.** *(in prison)* il a écopé de cinq ans

3 *(act of stretching)* étirement *m*; **he stood up, yawned and had a s.** il se leva, bâilla et s'étira; **to give one's legs a s.** se dégourdir les jambes; *Mus* **s. of the fingers** *(at the piano)* écart *m* des doigts; **by no s. of the imagination** même en faisant un gros effort d'imagination; **he's the better writer by a long s.** c'est de loin le meilleur écrivain; **not by a long s.!** loin de là!

4 *(elasticity)* élasticité *f*; **there isn't much s. in these gloves** ces gants ne sont pas très souples; **there's a lot of s. in these stockings** ces bas sont très élastiques *ou* s'étirent facilement

ADJ *Tex (material)* élastique, Stretch® *(inv)*; *(cover)* extensible

VT 1 *(pull tight)* tendre; **s. the rope tight** tendez bien la corde; **a cable was stretched across the ra- vine** on avait tendu un câble à travers le ravin; **they stretched a net over the pit** ils ont tendu un filet au-dessus de la fosse; *Art* **to s. the canvas on the frame** tendre la toile sur le châssis

2 *(pull longer or wider* ▸ *elastic)* étirer; (▸ *spring)* tendre; (▸ *garment, shoes)* élargir; **to s. sth out of shape** déformer qch; **don't pull your socks like that, you'll s. them** ne tire pas sur tes chaussettes comme ça, tu vas les déformer

3 *(extend, reach to full length)* étendre; **s. your arms upwards** tendez les bras vers le haut; **he stretched his arm through the broken window** il al- longea le bras à travers le carreau cassé; **if I s. up my hand I can reach the ceiling** si je tends la main je peux toucher le plafond; **to s. one's neck to see sth** tendre le cou pour voir qch; **to s. oneself** s'éti- rer; **to s. one's legs** étirer ses jambes; *Fam Fig* se dégourdir les jambes; **the bird stretched its wings** l'oiseau déploya ses ailes; *Fig* **to s. one's wings** *(become more independent)* voler de ses propres ailes; *(seek out new challenges)* aller de l'avant

4 *(force, bend* ▸ *meaning)* forcer; (▸ *rules)* tour- ner, contourner, faire une entorse à; (▸ *prin- ciple)* faire une entorse à; (▸ *imagination)* faire un gros effort de; **you're really stretching my pa- tience** ma patience a des limites; **to s. the truth** exagérer; **that's stretching it a bit!** il ne faut pas exagérer!; **it would be stretching a point to call him a diplomat** dire qu'il est diplomate serait exagérer *ou* aller un peu loin; **I suppose we could s. a point and let him stay** je suppose qu'on pour- rait faire une entorse au règlement et lui per- mettre de rester

5 *(budget, income, resources, supplies* ▸ *get the most from)* tirer le maximum de; (▸ *overload)* surcharger, mettre à rude épreuve; **our re- sources are stretched to the limit** nos ressources sont exploitées *ou* utilisées au maximum; **I can't s. my income that far** mon salaire ne me permet pas de faire de telles dépenses; **we should be able to s. the food until the weekend** nous de- vrions pouvoir faire durer les provisions jus- qu'au week-end; **our staff are really stretched today** le personnel travaille à la limite de ses possibilités aujourd'hui; **to be fully stretched** *(machine, engine)* tourner à plein régime; *(fac- tory, economy)* fonctionner à plein régime; *(re- sources, services)* être sollicité à fond; *(person, staff)* faire son maximum; **the job won't s. you enough** le travail ne sera pas assez stimulant pour vous

6 *(ligament, muscle)* étirer

VI 1 *(be elastic)* s'étirer; *(become longer)* s'allon- ger; *(become wider)* s'élargir; **this fabric tends to s.** ce tissu a tendance à s'étirer; **the shoes will s. with wear** vos chaussures vont se faire *ou* s'élar- gir à l'usage; **my pullover has stretched out of shape** mon pull s'est déformé

2 *(person, animal* ▸ *from tiredness)* s'étirer; (▸ *on ground, bed)* s'étendre, s'allonger; (▸ *to reach something)* tendre la main; **he had to s. to reach it** *(reach out)* il a dû tendre le bras pour l'attein- dre; *(stand on tiptoe)* il a dû se mettre sur la pointe des pieds pour l'atteindre; **she stretched across me to get the salt** elle a passé le bras de- vant moi pour attraper le sel; **can you s. over and get me the paper?** pouvez-vous tendre le bras et me passer le journal?; **he stretched up to touch the cupboard** il s'est mis sur la pointe des pieds pour atteindre le placard

3 *(spread, extend* ▸ *in space, time)* s'étendre; **the forest stretches as far as the eye can see** la forêt s'étend à perte de vue; **the road stretches away into the distance** la route s'étend au lointain; **the road stretched across 500 miles of desert** ≃ la route parcourait 800 km de désert; **minutes stretched into hours** les minutes devenaient des heures; **our powers don't s. as far as you imagine** nos pouvoirs ne sont pas aussi étendus que vous l'imaginez

4 *(money, resources)* **my salary won't s. to a new car** mon salaire ne me permet pas d'acheter une nouvelle voiture; **my resources won't s. to that** mes moyens (pécuniaires) ne vont pas jusque-là

• **at a stretch** **ADV 1** *(in a row)* d'affilée; **we worked for five hours at a s.** nous avons travaillé cinq heures d'affilée **2** *(with much effort)* à la li- mite, à la rigueur; **we could fit six people in the car at a s.** à la rigueur, on pourrait tenir à six dans la voiture

• **at full stretch** **ADV** **to be at full s.** *(factory, ma- chine)* fonctionner à plein régime *ou* à plein ren- dement; *(person)* se donner à fond, faire son maximum; **we were working at full s.** nous tra- vaillions d'arrache-pied

▸▸ ***stretch class*** cours *m* de stretching; ***stretch fabric*** Stretch® *m*; ***stretch limo*** limousine *f* à la carrosserie allongée

▸ **stretch out** **VT SEP 1** *(pull tight)* tendre; **the sheets had been stretched out on the line to dry** on avait étendu les draps sur le fil à linge pour qu'ils sèchent; **the plastic sheet was stretched out on the lawn** la bâche en plastique était étalée sur la pelouse

2 *(extend, spread* ▸ *arms, legs)* allonger, étendre; (▸ *hand)* tendre; (▸ *wings)* déployer; **she stretched out her hand towards him/for the cup** elle tendit la main vers lui/pour prendre la tasse; **she lay stretched out in front of the televi- sion** elle était allongée par terre devant la télé- vision

3 *(prolong* ▸ *interview, meeting)* prolonger, faire durer; (▸ *account)* allonger; **she has to s. her the- sis out a bit for publication** il faut qu'elle étoffe un peu sa thèse pour la publier

4 *(make last* ▸ *supplies, income)* faire durer

VI 1 *(person, animal)* s'étendre, s'allonger; **they stretched out on the lawn in the sun** ils se sont al- longés au soleil sur la pelouse **2** *(forest, country- side)* s'étendre; *(prospects, season)* s'étendre, s'étaler; **a nice long holiday stretched out before them** ils avaient de longues vacances devant eux

stretcher ['stretʃə(r)] **N 1** *Med* brancard *m*, ci- vière *f*; **he was carried off on a s.** on l'a emmené sur une civière *ou* un brancard

2 *(for shoes)* tendeur *m*, forme *f*; *(for gloves)* ou- vre-gant *m*; *(in umbrella)* baleine *f*; *Art & Sewing (for canvas)* cadre *m*, châssis *m*

3 *Constr (brick, stone)* panneresse *f*, carreau *m*

4 *(crossbar* ▸ *in structure)* traverse *f*, tirant *m*; (▸ *on chair)* barreau *m*, bâton *m*

▸▸ ***stretcher case*** = blessé ou malade ayant be- soin d'être porté sur un brancard; *Hum* **I was practically a s. case by the time the parents got home** je ne tenais plus debout *ou* j'étais bon pour l'hôpital quand les parents sont rentrés; ***stretcher party*** détachement *m* de brancardiers

▸ **stretcher off** **VT SEP** *Sport* **to s. sb off** emmener sur une civière *ou* un brancard

stretching ['stretʃɪŋ] **N 1** *Sport (warm-up)* étire- ment *m* (musculaire) **2** *Fig* **s. of the rules** entorse *f* au règlement

stretchy ['stretʃɪ] *(compar* **stretchier,** *superl* **stretchiest)** **ADJ** élastique, extensible

strew [struː] *(pt* **strewed,** *pp* **strewn** [struːn] *or* **strewed)** **VT** *Literary* **1** *(cover* ▸ *ground, floor, path)* joncher, parsemer; (▸ *table)* joncher; **the path was strewn with leaves/litter** l'allée était jonchée de feuilles/de détritus **2** *(scatter* ▸ *seeds, flowers, leaves)* répandre, éparpiller; *(throw* ▸ *toys, papers)* éparpiller, jeter; (▸ *debris)* éparpiller, disséminer; **they strewed sand on the floor** ils ont répandu du sable sur le sol; **wreckage was strewn all over the road** il y avait des débris par- tout sur la route; **references to classical literature are strewn throughout his work** son œuvre est émaillée de références à la littérature classique

strewth [struːθ] **EXCLAM** *Br & Austr Fam* mince alors!

striated [straɪ'eɪtɪd] **ADJ** strié

stricken ['strɪkən] **ADJ** *Formal* **1** *(ill)* malade; *(wounded)* blessé; *(damaged, troubled)* ravagé, dévasté; **our s. industry** notre industrie dévastée; **the s. vessel** le vaisseau en détresse *ou* naufragé; **the s. city** la ville sinistrée; **the s. army retreated** l'armée défaite battit en retraite **2** *(afflicted ▸ person, voice, look)* affligé; **s. by** *or* **with blindness** frappé de cécité; **s. by** *or* **with polio** atteint de polio; **they were s. with grief/fear** ils étaient accablés de chagrin/transis de peur

strict [strɪkt] **ADJ 1** *(severe, stern ▸ person, discipline)* strict, sévère; *(inflexible ▸ principles)* strict, rigoureux; *(▸ deadline)* strict; *(▸ belief, code, rules)* strict, rigide; *(▸ Catholic, Muslim etc)* de stricte obédience; **you must be very s. with him** il faut être très strict avec lui; **they belong to a s. religious sect** ils appartiennent à une secte religieuse très stricte; **she's a s. vegetarian** c'est une végétarienne pure et dure; **I gave s. orders not to be disturbed** j'ai formellement ordonné qu'on ne me dérange pas; **I'm on a s. diet** je suis un régime très strict **2** *(exact, precise ▸ meaning, interpretation)* strict; **the s. minimum** le strict minimum; **in the s. sense of the word** au sens strict du terme; **the s. truth** la stricte vérité **3** *(absolute ▸ accuracy, hygiene)* strict, absolu; **he told me in the strictest confidence** il me l'a dit à titre strictement confidentiel; **in s. secrecy** dans le plus grand secret

strictly ['strɪktlɪ] **ADV 1** *(severely ▸ act, treat)* strictement, avec sévérité; **the children were very s. brought up** les enfants ont reçu une éducation extrêmement stricte **2** *(exactly ▸ interpret, translate)* fidèlement, exactement; **s. speaking** à strictement *ou* à proprement parler **3** *(absolutely, rigorously)* strictement, absolument; **what you say is not s. accurate** ce que vous dites n'est pas tout à fait exact; **s. confidential** strictement confidentiel; **the rules must be s. observed** le règlement doit être scrupuleusement observé; **to adhere s. to one's diet** suivre scrupuleusement son régime; **s. forbidden** *or* **prohibited** formellement interdit; **smoking s. forbidden** *(sign)* défense absolue de fumer

strictness ['strɪktnɪs] **N 1** *(severity ▸ of person, rules, diet)* sévérité *f*; **their s. in applying the rules** la rigueur avec laquelle ils appliquent le règlement **2** *(exactness ▸ of interpretation)* exactitude *f*, rigueur *f*

stricture ['strɪktʃə(r)] **N** *Formal* **1** *(criticism)* critique *f* sévère; **to pass s. on sb/sth** critiquer qn/qch sévèrement **2** *(restriction)* restriction *f* **3** *Med* striction *f*, sténose *f*

stride [straɪd] *(pt* **strode** [strəʊd], *pp* **stridden** ['strɪdən]) **N 1** *(step)* grand pas *m*, enjambée *f*; *(when running)* foulée *f*; **to take big** *or* **long strides** faire de grandes enjambées; **to shorten/lengthen one's s.** ralentir/allonger le pas; **he crossed the threshold in** *or* **with one s.** il a franchi le seuil d'une seule enjambée; **to get into** *or Am* **hit one's s.** trouver son rythme; *Am* **to be caught off s.** être pris au dépourvu; **to take sth in one's s.** *or Am* **in s.** *(do easily)* faire qch sans le moindre effort; *(not be disconcerted by)* ne pas se laisser troubler par qch; **he took all their criticisms in his s.** leurs critiques n'ont pas semblé le déranger; **they've always taken exams in their s.** ils ont toujours réussi leurs examens facilement; **she takes everything in her s.** elle ne se laisse jamais démonter *ou* abattre; **to put sb off their s.** faire perdre le rythme à qn **2** *Fig (progress)* **to make great strides** faire de grands progrès, avancer à pas de géant; **he is making great strides in German** il fait de grands progrès en allemand; **he is making great strides with his research** sa recherche avance à grands pas

VI marcher à grands pas *ou* à grandes enjambées; **to s. away/in/out** s'éloigner/entrer/sortir à grands pas; **he came striding over** *or* **up to them** il avança vers eux à grands pas; **she strode away across the fields** elle s'éloigna à travers les champs à grands pas; **he strode up and down the room** il arpentait la pièce

VT *(streets, fields, deck)* arpenter

● **strides NPL** *Br & Austr Fam (trousers)* bénard *m*, bène *m*

stridency ['straɪdənsɪ] **N** stridence *f*; *(of demand, protest)* véhémence *f*

strident ['straɪdənt] **ADJ** strident; *(colour)* criard; *(demand, protest)* véhément

stridently ['straɪdəntlɪ] **ADV** *(call, cry, sing)* d'une voix stridente; *(sound, ring)* en faisant un bruit strident; *(demand, protest)* avec véhémence, à grands cris

strife [straɪf] **N** *(UNCOUNT) Formal (conflict)* dissensions *fpl*; *(struggles)* luttes *fpl*; *(quarrels)* querelles *fpl*; **a period of political s.** une période marquée par des dissensions politiques; **industrial s.** conflits *mpl* sociaux; **sectarian s.** luttes *fpl* sectaires

STRIKE [straɪk]

N
- grève **1**
- attaque **2**
- découverte **4**
- coup **6**
- strike **7, 8**
- raid **2**
- escadre **3**
- sonnerie **5**
- bruit **6**

VT
- frapper **1, 3–5, 14**
- atteindre **1**
- sonner **6**
- conclure **8**
- découvrir **12**
- attaquer **17**
- toucher **1**
- heurter **2**
- jouer **7**
- rendre **10**
- rayer **16**

VI
- frapper **1**
- faire grève **3**
- se produire **5**
- ferrer **8**
- attaquer **2**
- sonner **4**
- marquer **7**

(pt & pp **struck** [strʌk], *cont* **striking**)

N 1 *Ind* grève *f*; **to go on s.** se mettre en *ou* faire grève; **to be (out) on s.** être en grève; **to threaten s. action** menacer de faire *ou* de se mettre en grève; **railway s.** grève *f* des chemins de fer; **teachers' s.** grève *f* des enseignants; **postal** *or* **post office s.** grève *f* des postes

2 *Mil* raid *m*, attaque *f*; *(by bird of prey, snake)* attaque *f*; **to carry out air strikes against** *or* **on enemy bases** lancer des raids aériens contre des bases ennemies; **retaliatory s.** raid *m* de représailles; *(nuclear)* deuxième frappe *f*

3 *Aviat & Mil (planes)* escadre *f (d'avions participant à un raid)*

4 *Petr & Mining (discovery)* découverte *f*; **a gold s.** la découverte d'un gisement d'or; **the recent oil strikes in the North Sea** la découverte récente de gisements de pétrole en mer du Nord; **it was a lucky s.** c'était un coup de chance

5 *(of clock ▸ chime, mechanism)* sonnerie *f*

6 *(act or instance of hitting)* coup *m*; *(sound)* bruit *m*; **the s. of iron on iron** le bruit du fer qui frappe le fer; **he adjusted the s. of the keys on the platen roll** il a réglé la frappe des caractères contre le cylindre

7 *(in baseball)* strike *m*; *Am Fig (black mark)* mauvais point *m*; *Fig* **he has two strikes against him** il est mal parti; *Fig* **being too young was another s. against her** le fait d'être trop jeune constituait un handicap supplémentaire pour elle

8 *(in bowling)* honneur *m* double, strike *m*; **to get** *or* **to score a s.** réussir un honneur double, faire un strike

9 *Fishing (by fisherman)* ferrage *m*; *(by fish)* touche *f*

COMP 1 *(committee, movement)* de grève

2 *Mil (mission)* d'intervention, d'attaque; *(aircraft)* d'assaut

VT 1 *(hit ▸ gen)* frapper; *(▸ of bullet, torpedo, bomb)* toucher, atteindre; **he struck me with his fist** il m'a donné un coup de poing; **the chairman struck the table with his gavel** le président donna un coup de marteau sur la table; **she took the vase and struck him on** *or* **over the head** elle saisit le vase et lui donna un coup sur la tête; **she struck him across the face** elle lui a donné une gifle; **a wave struck the side of the boat** une vague a heurté le côté du bateau; **the arrow struck the target** la flèche a atteint la cible; **he was struck by a piece of shrapnel** il a été touché par *ou* il a reçu un éclat de grenade; **to be struck by lightning** être frappé par la foudre, être foudroyé; **who struck the first blow?** qui a porté le prem coup?, qui a frappé le premier?; **he struck the tree a mighty blow with the axe** il a donné grand coup de hache dans l'arbre; **the tra struck the post a glancing blow** la remorque a p cuté le poteau en passant; *Fig* **to s. a blow democracy/women's rights** *(law, event)* faire p gresser la démocratie/les droits de la femr *(person, group)* marquer des points en fav de la démocratie/des droits des femmes

2 *(bump into, collide with)* heurter, cogner; **foot struck the bar on his first jump** son pie heurté la barre lors de son premier saut; **she and struck her head on** *or* **against the kerb** elle s cogné la tête contre le bord du trottoir en tc bant; **the Volvo struck the bus head on** la Volv heurté le bus de plein fouet; *Naut* **we've str ground!** nous avons touché (le fond)!

3 *(afflict ▸ of drought, disease, worry, regret)* fr per; *(▸ of storm, hurricane, disaster, wave of lence)* s'abattre sur, frapper; **an earthqu struck the city** un tremblement de terre a frap la ville; **I was struck by** *or* **with doubts** j'ai été p de doute, le doute s'est emparé de moi

4 *(occur to)* frapper; **only later did it s. me as usual** ce n'est que plus tard que j'ai trouvé ça que cela m'a paru bizarre; **it suddenly struck how little had changed** il a soudain pris c science du fait que peu de choses avai changé; **it strikes me as useless/as the perfect** ça me semble *ou* paraît inutile/être le cade idéal; **he strikes me as (being) sincere** il me pa sincère; **it doesn't s. me as being the best course action** il ne me semble pas que ce soit la m leure voie à suivre

5 *(impress)* frapper, impressionner; **the f thing that struck me was his pallor** la premi chose qui m'a frappé, c'était sa pâleur; **how she s. you?** quelle impression vous a-t-elle fai quel effet vous a-t-elle fait?; **how did Tokyo film s. you?** comment avez-vous trouvé Tok le film?; **we can eat here and meet them la how does that s. you?** on peut manger ici et retrouver plus tard, qu'en penses-tu?; **I was v struck** *Br* **with** *or Am* **by the garden** le jardin m'a énormément; **I wasn't very struck** *Br* **with** *or Am* **his wife** sa femme ne m'a pas fait une grande pression

6 *(chime)* sonner; **the church clock struck f** l'horloge de l'église a sonné cinq heures; **it v striking midnight as we left** minuit sonnait qua nous partîmes

7 *(play ▸ note, chord)* jouer; **to s. a false note** faire une fausse note; *Fig (speech)* sonner fa **his presence/his words struck a gloomy note** présence a/ses paroles ont mis une note de t tesse; **the report strikes an optimistic note/a n of warning for the future** le rapport est très o miste/très alarmant pour l'avenir; **does it s chord?** est-ce que cela te rappelle *ou* dit quelc chose?; **her description of company life will chord with many managers** beaucoup de cad se reconnaîtront dans sa description de la en entreprise

8 *(arrive at, reach ▸ deal, treaty, agreeme* conclure; **to s. a bargain** conclure un marché; **s. a bargain with you** je te propose un marché; **not easy to s. a balance between too much and little freedom** il n'est pas facile de trouver équilibre *ou* de trouver le juste milieu entre t et pas assez de liberté

9 *(cause a feeling of)* **to s. fear** *or* **terror into** remplir qn d'effroi

10 *(cause to become)* rendre; **to s. sb blind/du** rendre qn aveugle/muet; **the news struck speechless with horror** nous sommes res muets d'horreur en apprenant la nouvell **was struck dumb by the sheer cheek of the m** je suis resté muet devant le culot de homme!; **a stray bullet struck him dead** il a tué par une balle perdue; **she was struck d by a heart attack** elle a été foudroyée par u crise cardiaque; **God s. me dead if I lie!** je j que c'est la vérité!

11 *(ignite ▸ match)* frotter, allumer; *(▸ spa* faire jaillir; **he struck a match** *or* **a light** il a fro une allumette; *Br Fam Old-fashioned* **s. a lig** nom de Dieu!

12 *(discover ▸ gold)* découvrir; *(▸ oil, wa*

rouver; *(path)* tomber sur, découvrir; *Fam Br* **to s. it lucky,** *Am* **to s. it rich** *(make material gain)* trouver le filon; *(be lucky)* avoir de la veine
13 *(adopt ▸ attitude)* adopter; **he struck an attitude of wounded righteousness** il a pris un air de dignité offensée
14 *(mint ▸ coin, medal)* frapper
15 *(take down ▸ tent)* démonter; *Naut (▸ sail)* amener, baisser; **to s. camp** lever le camp; *Naut* **to s. the flag** *or* **the colours** amener les couleurs; *Theat* **to s. the set** démonter le décor
16 *(delete ▸ name, remark, person)* rayer; *(▸ from professional register)* radier; **that remark must be struck** *or Am* **stricken from the record** cette remarque doit être retirée du procès-verbal
17 *(attack)* attaquer
18 *Am (go on strike at)* **the union is striking four of the company's plants** le syndicat a déclenché des grèves dans quatre des usines de la société; **students are striking their classes** les étudiants font la grève des cours
19 *Bot* **to s. roots** prendre racine
VI 1 *(hit)* frapper; **she struck at me with her umbrella** elle essaya de me frapper avec son parapluie; **to s. home** *(blow)* porter; *(missile, remark)* faire mouche; *Fam* **to s. lucky** avoir de la veine; *Prov* **s. while the iron is hot** il faut battre le fer pendant qu'il est chaud
2 *(attack ▸ gen)* attaquer; *(▸ snake)* mordre; *(▸ wild animal)* sauter *ou* bondir sur sa proie; *(▸ bird of prey)* fondre *ou* s'abattre sur sa proie; **the bombers struck at dawn** les bombardiers attaquèrent à l'aube; **the murderer has struck again** l'assassin a encore frappé; **these are measures which s. at the root/heart of the problem** voici des mesures qui attaquent le problème à la racine/qui s'attaquent au cœur du problème; **this latest incident strikes right at the heart of government policy** ce dernier incident remet complètement en cause la politique gouvernementale
3 *Ind* faire grève; **they're striking for more pay** ils font grève pour obtenir une augmentation de salaire
4 *(chime)* sonner; **midnight had already struck** minuit avait déjà sonné
5 *(happen suddenly ▸ illness, disaster, earthquake)* survenir, se produire, arriver; **we were travelling quietly along when disaster struck** nous roulions tranquillement lorsque la catastrophe s'est produite; **the first tremors struck at 3 a.m.** les premières secousses sont survenues à 3 heures du matin
6 *(travel, head)* **to s. across country** prendre à travers champs; **they then struck west** ils sont ensuite partis vers l'ouest
7 *Sport (score)* marquer
8 *Fishing (fisherman)* ferrer; *(fish)* mordre (à l'hameçon)
9 *(of cutting)* prendre (racine)
▸▸ strike ballot = vote avant que les syndicats ne décident d'une grève; *Ins* **strike force** *(nuclear capacity)* force *f* de frappe; *(of police, soldiers ▸ squad)* détachement *m ou* brigade *f* d'intervention; *(▸ larger force)* force *f* d'intervention; **strike fund** = caisse de prévoyance permettant d'aider les grévistes; **strike pay** salaire *m* de gréviste *(versé par le syndicat ou par un fonds de solidarité)*
strike back VI 1 *(retaliate)* se venger; *Mil* contre-attaquer; **the government struck back at its critics** le gouvernement a répondu à ceux qui le critiquaient **2** *Sport (score in response)* marquer à son tour
strike down VT SEP foudroyer, terrasser; *Fig* **struck down by disease** terrassé par la maladie
strike off VT SEP 1 *(delete, remove ▸ from list)* rayer, barrer; *(▸ from professional register)* radier; **to be struck off** *(doctor, solicitor)* être radié **2** *(sever)* couper **3** *Typ* tirer
VI *(go)* **to s. off to the left** prendre à gauche; **we struck off into the forest** nous sommes entrés *ou* avons pénétré dans la forêt
strike on VT INSEP *Br (solution, right answer)* trouver (par hasard), tomber sur; *(plan)* trouver; *(idea)* avoir
strike out VT SEP 1 *(cross out)* rayer, barrer **2** *(in baseball)* éliminer
VI 1 *(set up on one's own)* s'établir à son compte
2 *(go)* **she struck out across the fields** elle prit à travers champs; *Fig* **they decided to s. out into a new direction** ils ont décidé de prendre une nouvelle direction
3 *(swim)* **we struck out for the shore** nous avons commencé à nager en direction de la côte
4 *(aim a blow)* frapper; **she struck out at him** elle essaya de le frapper; *Fig* elle s'en est prise à lui
5 *(in baseball)* être éliminé
▸ strike up VT INSEP 1 *(start)* **to s. up a conversation with sb** engager la conversation avec qn; **they immediately struck up a conversation** ils sont immédiatement entrés en conversation; **to s. up an acquaintance/a friendship with sb** lier connaissance/se lier d'amitié avec qn **2** *Mus (start playing)* commencer à jouer; **the band struck up the national anthem** l'orchestre commença à jouer l'hymne national *ou* entonna les premières mesures de l'hymne national
VI *(musician, orchestra)* commencer à jouer; *(music)* commencer

strikebound [ˈstraɪkˌbaʊnd] **ADJ** *(factory, department)* paralysé par une *ou* la grève; *(industry, country)* paralysé par des grèves
strikebreaker [ˈstraɪkˌbreɪkə(r)] **N** briseur(euse) *m,f* de grève
strike-out mode N *Comput* mode *m* barré
striker [ˈstraɪkə(r)] **N 1** *Ind* gréviste *mf* **2** *Ftbl* buteur *m* **3** *(device ▸ on clock)* marteau *m*; *(▸ in gun)* percuteur *m*
strike-thru mode N *Comput* mode *m* barré
striking [ˈstraɪkɪŋ] **ADJ 1** *(remarkable ▸ sight, contrast, resemblance, beauty)* frappant, saisissant; **he cut a s. figure** il avait une allure impressionnante; **a s. example of Baroque architecture** un très bel exemple d'architecture baroque
2 *(clock)* qui sonne les heures
3 *Mil (force)* d'intervention
4 *Ind* en grève
5 *(idiom)* **within s. distance** à proximité; **she lives within s. distance of London** elle habite tout près de Londres; **they came within s. distance of finding a solution** ils ont failli trouvé *ou* presque trouvé une solution
N 1 *(of clock)* sonnerie *f* (des heures) **2** *(of coins)* frappe *f*
▸▸ striking mechanism sonnerie *f* (des heures); **striking off** *(of name)* suppression *f*; *(of lawyer, doctor)* radiation *f*
strikingly [ˈstraɪkɪŋlɪ] **ADV** remarquablement; **a s. beautiful woman** une femme d'une beauté saisissante; **it was s. obvious to everyone but me** c'était une évidence pour tout le monde sauf pour moi
Strimmer® [ˈstrɪmə(r)] **N** débroussailleuse *f* (à fil)
Strine [straɪn] **N** *Hum* l'anglais *m* australien
string [strɪŋ] *(pt & pp* **strung** [strʌŋ]) **N 1** *(gen ▸ for parcel)* ficelle *f*; *(▸ on apron, pyjamas)* cordon *m*; *(▸ for puppet)* ficelle *f*, fil *m*; **a piece of s.** un bout *ou* un morceau de ficelle; *Fig* **how long will the work take? – how long is a piece of s.?** est-ce que ce travail prendra longtemps? – comment le savoir?; *Fam* **to have sb on a s.** mener qn par le bout du nez; **to keep sb on a s.** *(in uncertainty)* laisser qn dans l'incertitude; *(keep control over)* tenir qn en laisse; **he pulls the strings** c'est lui qui tire les ficelles; *Fam* **to pull strings for sb** *(obtain favours)* user de son influence *ou* faire jouer ses relations pour aider qn▫; *(get job, promotion)* pistonner qn; **somebody pulled strings to get him the job** il a eu le poste par piston; *Fam* **no strings attached** sans condition *ou* conditions▫; **there are no strings attached** cela n'engage à rien
2 *(for bow, tennis racket, musical instrument)* corde *f*; *Mus* **the strings** les cordes; **to have more than one/a second s. to one's bow** avoir plus d'une/une seconde corde à son arc
3 *(row, chain ▸ of pearls)* rang *m*, collier *m*; *(▸ of onions, sausages)* chapelet *m*; *(▸ of visitors, cars)* file *f*; **s. of beads** collier *m*; *Rel* chapelet *m*; **a s. of islands** un chapelet d'îles; **she owns a s. of shops** elle est propriétaire d'une chaîne de magasins; **a s. of race horses** une écurie de course
4 *(series ▸ of successes, defeats)* série *f*; *(▸ of lies, insults)* kyrielle *f*, chapelet *m*; **he has a whole s. of letters after his name** il a toute une kyrielle de diplômes
5 *Comput & Ling* chaîne *f*; *Math* séquence *f*
6 *Bot* fil *m*
COMP 1 *Mus (band, instrument, orchestra)* à cordes **2** *(made of string)* de *ou* en ficelle
VT 1 *(guitar, violin)* monter, mettre des cordes à; *(racket)* corder; *(bow)* mettre une corde à
2 *(beads, pearls)* enfiler
3 *(hang)* suspendre; *(stretch)* tendre; **Christmas lights had been strung across the street** des décorations de Noël avaient été suspendues en travers de la rue; **he strung the chain across the gateway** il a tendu *ou* attaché la chaîne en travers de l'entrée
4 *Culin (beans)* enlever les fils de
▸▸ string bag filet *m* à provisions; **string band** orchestre *m* à cordes; **string bass** contrebasse *f*; **string bean 1** *(vegetable)* haricot *m* vert **2** *Am Fam (person)* grande perche *f*, asperge *f*; **string player** = musicien qui joue d'un instrument à cordes; **string quartet** quatuor *m* à cordes; **string section** les cordes *fpl*; **string tie** = cordon noué autour du cou et orné d'une boucle; *Comput* **string variable** variable *f* alphanumérique; **string vest** tricot *m* de corps à grosses mailles
▸ string along *Fam* **VI 1** *(tag along)* suivre (les autres)▫; **do you mind if I s. along?** est-ce que ça vous gêne si je viens avec vous *ou* si je vous accompagne?▫ **2** *(agree)* **to s. along with sb** se ranger à l'avis de qn▫; **he always strings along with everybody else** il est toujours d'accord avec tout le monde▫
VT SEP *(person)* faire marcher
▸ string out VT SEP 1 *(washing, lamps)* suspendre (sur une corde); **lights were strung out along the runway** des lumières s'échelonnaient le long de la piste; **armed guards were strung out along the route** des gardes armés avaient été postés tout le long du parcours **2** *(in time)* **to s. sth out** faire durer qch; **the TV series was strung out over six weeks** le feuilleton (de) télé a traîné pendant six semaines
▸ string up VT SEP 1 *(lights)* suspendre; *(washing)* étendre **2** *Fam (hang ▸ person)* pendre▫; *Fig* **I could s. her up!** je lui tordrais bien le cou!
stringboard [ˈstrɪŋbɔːd] **N** *Constr* limon *m* (d'escalier)
stringed [strɪŋd] **ADJ** *(instrument)* à cordes
stringency [ˈstrɪndʒənsɪ] **N 1** *(severity)* rigueur *f*, sévérité *f* **2** *Econ & Fin* austérité *f*; **there is a need for financial s.** des mesures d'austérité s'imposent
stringent [ˈstrɪndʒənt] **N 1** *(rules)* rigoureux, strict, sévère; *(measures, conditions)* rigoureux, draconien **2** *Econ & Fin (market)* tendu
stringently [ˈstrɪndʒəntlɪ] **ADV** rigoureusement, strictement
stringer [ˈstrɪŋə(r)] **N 1** *Press* reporter *m* local **2** *Constr (timber)* poutre *f* de renforcement; *(metal)* serre *f*
stringing [ˈstrɪŋɪŋ] **N** *(act ▸ of violin)* montage *m*; *(▸ of racket)* cordage *m*; *(▸ of bow)* bandage *m*
stringpiece [ˈstrɪŋpiːs] **N** *Constr* longrine *f*
string-puller [-ˈpʊlə(r)] **N** = personne qui fait jouer ses relations
stringy [ˈstrɪŋɪ] *(compar* **stringier,** *superl* **stringiest) ADJ 1** *(meat, vegetable)* filandreux, fibreux; *(cooked cheese)* qui file; *(liquid)* visqueux **2** *(long ▸ plant)* (qui pousse) tout en longueur; *(▸ build, limbs)* filiforme
strip [strɪp] *(pt & pp* **stripped,** *cont* **stripping) N 1** *(of paper, material, carpet)* bande *f*; *(of metal)* bande *f*, ruban *m*; *(of land)* bande *f*, langue *f*; **there was a thin s. of light under the door** il y avait un mince rai de lumière sous la porte; **each house had a s. of grass in front of it** il y avait une bande de gazon devant chaque maison; **a narrow s. of water** *(sea)* un étroit bras de mer; *(river)* un étroit ruban de rivière; **she cut the dough/material into strips** elle coupa la pâte en lamelles/le tissu en bandes; **to tear sth into strips** déchirer qch en bandes; *Fig* **to tear sb off a s.** sonner les cloches à qn
2 *Am (street with businesses)* avenue *f* commerçante; **the S., Sunset S.** = artère de Las Vegas où se trouvent tous les casinos
3 *Aviat* piste *f*
4 *(light)* **neon s.** néon *m*, tube *m* (au) néon
5 *Sport* tenue *f*, **the Liverpool s.** la tenue *ou* les

couleurs de l'équipe de Liverpool

6 *(striptease)* strip-tease *m*; **to do a s.** faire un strip-tease

7 *(cartoons)* bande *f* dessinée, BD *f*

VT 1 *(undress)* déshabiller, dévêtir; **they were stripped to the waist** ils étaient torse nu, ils étaient nus jusqu'à la ceinture; **to s. sb naked** déshabiller qn (complètement)

2 *(remove everything from ▸ tree)* dépouiller, dénuder; *(▸ house, room)* vider; *(▸ door, furniture)* décaper; *(▸ wire)* dénuder; **to s. a tree (of its bark)** écorcer un arbre; **the walls need to be stripped first** *(of wallpaper)* il faut d'abord enlever *ou* arracher le papier peint; *(of paint)* il faut d'abord décaper les murs; **to s. a bed** défaire un lit; **thieves have stripped the house bare** les cambrioleurs ont complètement vidé la maison; **the windows had been stripped of their curtains** on avait enlevé les rideaux des fenêtres; **the liner is to be completely stripped and refitted** le paquebot doit être refait de fond en comble

3 *(remove ▸ gen)* enlever; *(▸ paint)* décaper; **we stripped the wallpaper from the walls** nous avons arraché le papier peint des murs; **the birds have stripped the cherries from the trees** les oiseaux ont fait des ravages dans les cerisiers; **the storm stripped the leaves off the trees** la tempête a dépouillé les arbres de leurs feuilles; **the years of suffering had stripped away all pretence** les années de souffrance avaient effacé toute trace d'affectation

4 *(deprive)* dépouiller, démunir; **to s. sb of their privileges/possessions** dépouiller qn de ses privilèges/biens; **he was stripped of his rank/title** on lui a retiré son grade/titre

5 *(dismantle ▸ engine, gun)* démonter

6 *Tech (screw, bolt)* arracher le filet de; *(gear)* arracher les dents de

7 *Com (sell off ▸ assets)* revendre

VI 1 *(undress)* se déshabiller, se dévêtir; **to s. to the waist** se mettre torse nu **2** *(do a striptease)* faire un strip-tease

▸▸ *Br* **strip cartoon** bande *f* dessinée; **strip club** boîte *f* de strip-tease; **strip cropping** *(UNCOUNT)* culture *f* en bande *(pour limiter l'érosion)*; **strip farming 1** *Hist* système *m* des openfields **2** *Agr* culture *f* en bande *(pour limiter l'érosion)*; *Fam* **strip joint** boîte *f* de strip-tease; *Br* **strip light** néon *m*, tube *m* (au) néon; *Br* **strip lighting** éclairage *m* fluorescent *ou* au néon; *Metal* **strip mill** démouleur *m*; *esp Am* **strip mining** extraction *f* à ciel ouvert; **strip poker** strip-poker *m*; **strip search** fouille *f* corporelle *(la personne fouillée devant se déshabiller)*; **strip show** (spectacle *m* de) strip-tease *m*

▸**strip down VT SEP 1** *(bed)* défaire (complètement); *(wallpaper)* arracher, enlever; *(door, furniture)* décaper; **to s. the walls down** *(remove wallpaper)* arracher *ou* enlever le papier peint des murs; *(remove paint)* décaper les murs; *Fig* **the text has been stripped down to its bare essentials** le texte a été réduit à l'essentiel **2** *(dismantle ▸ engine, mechanism)* démonter

VI se déshabiller; **he stripped down to his underpants** il s'est déshabillé, ne gardant que son slip

▸**strip off VT SEP** *(gen)* enlever, arracher; *(clothes, shirt)* enlever; *(paint)* décaper; *(wallpaper)* décoller; **to s. the leaves off a tree** dépouiller un arbre de ses feuilles; **to s. the bark off a tree** écorcer un arbre

VI se déshabiller, se mettre nu

stripe [straɪp] **N 1** *(on animal)* rayure *f*, zébrure *f*; *(on material, shirt)* raie *f*, rayure *f*; *(on car)* filet *m*; **black with orange stripes** noir avec des rayures orange

2 *Mil* galon *m*, chevron *m*; **to get/to lose one's stripes** gagner/perdre ses galons

3 *(kind)* genre *m*; **they are of the same political s.** ils partagent les mêmes idées politiques, ils appartiennent à la même famille politique

4 *(lash)* coup *m* de fouet; *(mark)* marque *f* d'un coup de fouet

VT rayer, marquer de rayures

striped [straɪpt] **ADJ** *(animal)* tigré, zébré; *(material, shirt, pattern)* rayé, à rayures; **s. with blue** avec des rayures bleues

stripling ['strɪplɪŋ] **N** *Literary or Hum* tout jeune homme *m*

strippagram ['strɪpəgræm] **N** = message qu'on envoie par l'intermédiaire d'une personne qui fait un strip-tease

stripped-down ADJ

▸▸ **stripped-down version** version *f* simplifiée

stripper ['strɪpə(r)] **N 1** *(in strip club)* strip-teaseuse *f*; **(male) s.** strip-teaseur *m* **2** *(for paint)* décapant *m*

strip-search VT to s. sb fouiller qn après l'avoir fait se déshabiller; **he was strip-searched by prison warders** des gardiens de prison lui ont fait subir une fouille corporelle *ou* l'ont fouillé après l'avoir fait se déshabiller

striptease ['strɪpti:z] **N** strip-tease *m*

▸▸ **striptease artist** strip-teaseur(euse) *m,f*

stripy ['straɪpɪ] *(compar* **stripier**, *superl* **stripiest)** **ADJ** *(material, shirt, pattern)* rayé, à rayures; *Zool* tigré, zébré

strive [straɪv] *(pt* **strove** [strəʊv], *pp* **striven** ['strɪvən]) **VT** *Formal or Literary* **1** *(attempt)* **to s. to do sth** s'évertuer à *ou* s'acharner à faire qch; **to s. after** *or* **for sth** faire tout son possible pour obtenir qch, s'efforcer d'obtenir qch; **to s. for effect** chercher à faire de l'effet **2** *(struggle)* lutter, se battre; **to s. against misfortune** lutter *ou* se battre contre la malchance; **all her life she strove for success/recognition** toute sa vie, elle s'est battue pour réussir/être reconnue

strobe [strəʊb] **N 1** *(lighting)* lumière *f* stroboscopique **2** *(stroboscope)* stroboscope *m*

▸▸ **strobe lighting** lumière *f* stroboscopique

stroboscope ['strəʊbəskəʊp] **N** stroboscope *m*

strode [strəʊd] *pt of* **stride**

stroke [strəʊk] **N 1** *(blow, flick)* coup *m*; **with a s. of the brush** d'un coup de pinceau; **with a s. of the pen** d'un trait de plume; **a s. of lightning** un coup de foudre; **they were given 50 strokes** ils ont reçu 50 coups de fouet

2 *Sport (in golf, tennis, cricket, billiards)* coup *m*; *(in swimming ▸ movement)* mouvement *m* des bras; *(▸ style)* nage *f*; *(in rowing ▸ movement)* coup *m* d'aviron; *(▸ technique)* nage *f*; **the Oxford team rowed at 25 strokes to the minute** l'équipe d'Oxford ramait à une cadence de 25 coups à la minute; **to keep s.** garder la cadence; *also Fig* **to set the s.** donner la cadence; **to put sb off their s.** *(in rowing)* faire perdre sa cadence *ou* son rythme à qn; *(in golf)* faire manquer son coup à; *Fig* faire perdre tous ses moyens à qn; **to be off one's s.** ne pas être au mieux de sa forme

3 *(mark ▸ from pen, pencil)* trait *m*; *(▸ from brush)* trait *m*, touche *f*; *(on letters, figures)* barre *f*; *Typ (oblique dash)* barre *f* oblique; **written with thick/thin strokes** écrit d'une écriture appuyée/fine; *Br* **225 s. 62** 225 barre oblique 62

4 *(piece, example ▸ of luck)* coup *m*; *(▸ of genius, wit)* trait *m*; **a s. of luck** un coup de chance; **by a s. of luck, she had remembered to take the key** par chance, elle avait pensé à prendre la clé; **it was a s. of brilliance!** c'était un coup de génie!; *Br* **she didn't do a s. (of work) all day** elle n'a rien fait de la journée

5 *(of clock, bell)* coup *m*; **on the s. of midnight** sur le coup de minuit; **on the s. of 6** à 6 heures sonnantes *ou* tapantes; **he arrived on the s.** il est arrivé à l'heure exacte *ou* précise

6 *Med* attaque *f* (d'apoplexie); **to have a s.** avoir une attaque

7 *(oarsman)* chef *m* de nage; **to row s.** être chef de nage, donner la nage

8 *Tech (of piston)* course *f*; **two-/four-s. engine** un moteur à deux/quatre temps

9 *(caress)* caresse *f*; **she gave the cat a s.** elle a caressé le chat

VT 1 *(caress)* caresser; **he stroked her hand** il lui caressait la main; **to s. sb's ego** caresser qn dans le sens du poil

2 *(in rowing)* **to s. a boat** être chef de nage, donner la nage

3 *Sport (ball)* frapper

4 *Am Fam (flatter)* passer de la pommade à

VI *(in rowing)* être chef de nage, donner la nage

• **at a stroke, at one stroke ADV** d'un seul coup

▸▸ **stroke play** *(in golf)* partie *f* par coups; **stroke rate** *(in rowing)* cadence *f* de nage

stroll [strəʊl] **VI** se balader, flâner; **to s. in/out past** entrer/sortir/passer sans se presser; **w strolled round the shops** nous avons fait un peti tour dans les magasins; **she strolled in an hou late and didn't even say sorry** elle est arrivée tran quillement avec une heure de retard et ne s'es même pas excusée

VT to s. the streets se promener dans les rues

N petit tour *m*, petite promenade *f*; **to go for a s** aller faire un tour *ou* une petite promenade

stroller ['strəʊlə(r)] **N 1** *(walker)* promeneu (euse) *m,f*, flâneur(euse) *m,f* **2** *Am & Austr (pusl chair)* poussette *f*

strolling ['strəʊlɪŋ] **ADJ** *(musician, minstrel)* am bulant

▸▸ **strolling player** comédien(enne) *m,f* ambu lant(e); **a troupe of s. players** une troupe ambu lante

STRONG [strɒŋ]

- fort **1–3, 5, 6, 10, 11**
- solide **1, 2, 4, 9**
- ferme **2, 9**
- sérieux **4, 6**
- robuste **1**
- puissant **2**
- énergique **2**
- grossier **7**

(compar **stronger** ['strɒŋgə(r)], *superl* **stronges** ['strɒŋgɪst])

ADJ 1 *(sturdy ▸ person, animal, constitution, arms* fort, robuste; *(▸ building)* solide; *(▸ cloth, mater ial)* solide, résistant; *(▸ shoes, table)* solide, ro buste; *(in health ▸ person)* robuste; *(▸ hear* solide, robuste; *(▸ eyesight)* bon; **he's not very s** *(not muscular)* il n'est pas très fort; *(not healthy)* n'est pas très robuste; *Fam* **you need a s. stomacl to eat this junk** il faut avoir un estomac en béto pour manger des cochonneries pareilles; **you'** **need a s. stomach to go and watch that movie** faut avoir l'estomac bien accroché pour alle voir ce film; **he'll be able to go out once he's s again** il pourra sortir quand il aura repris des for ces; **to be as s. as a horse** *(powerful)* être for comme un Turc *ou* un bœuf; *(in good health* avoir une santé de fer

2 *(in degree, force, intensity ▸ sea current, winc light, lens, voice)* fort, puissant; *(▸ magnet)* puis sant; *(▸ current)* intense; *Mus (▸ beat)* fort; *(▸ conviction, belief)* ferme, fort, profond; *(▸ pro test, support)* énergique, vigoureux; *(▸ meas ures)* énergique, draconien; *(▸ desire imagination, interest)* vif; *(▸ colour)* vif, fort; *(▸ character, personality)* fort, bien trempé; *(▸ fee ings)* intense, fort; *(▸ nerves)* solide; **the wind i growing stronger** le vent forcit; **there is a s. elem ent of suspense in the story** il y a beaucoup d suspense dans cette histoire; **it's my s. suit** *(i cards)* c'est ma couleur forte; *Fig* c'est mon for *Fig* **tact isn't her s. suit** *or* **point** le tact n'est pas so (point) fort; **what are his s. points?** quels sont se points forts?; **he is a s. believer in discipline** il es de ceux qui croient fermement à la discipline **she is a s. supporter of the government** elle sou tient le gouvernement avec ferveur; **to exert s. influence on sb** exercer beaucoup d'influenc *ou* une forte influence sur qn; **she has a s. person ality, she's a s. character** elle a une forte person nalité; **I have s. feelings on** *or* **about the deat penalty** *(against)* je suis absolument contre l peine de mort; *(for)* je suis tout à fait pour l peine de mort; **I have no s. feelings** *or* **views on way or the other** cela m'est égal; **he had a s. sens of guilt** il éprouvait un fort sentiment de culpa bilité; **to have a s. will** avoir de la volonté; **you' have to be s. now** *(when consoling or encouraging* il va falloir être courageux maintenant; **you'v got to be s. and say "no"** il faut être ferme et dir "non"

3 *(striking ▸ contrast, impression)* fort, frappan marquant; *(▸ accent)* fort; **to bear a s. resem blance to sb** ressembler beaucoup *ou* fortemer à qn; **his speech made a s. impression on them** so discours les a fortement impressionnés *ou* a e un profond effet sur eux; **there is a s. chance** *c* **probability that he will win** il y a de fortes chan ces pour qu'il gagne

4 *(solid ▸ argument, evidence)* solide, sérieu **we have s. reasons to believe them innocent** nou avons de bonnes *ou* sérieuses raisons de croir qu'ils sont innocents; **they have a s. case** ils on de bons arguments; **there's s. evidence that h**

committed suicide tout porte à croire qu'il s'est suicidé; to be in a s. position être dans une position de force; we're in a s. bargaining position nous sommes bien placés ou en position de force pour négocier

5 (in taste, smell) fort; I like s. coffee j'aime le café fort ou corsé; this whisky is s. stuff ce whisky est fort; there's a s. smell of gas in here il y a une forte odeur de gaz ici

6 (in ability ▸ student, team) fort; (▸ candidate, contender) sérieux; he is a s. contender for the presidency il a de fortes chances de remporter l'élection présidentielle; he's a s. candidate for the post il a le profil idéal pour le poste; she is particularly s. in science subjects elle est particulièrement forte dans les matières scientifiques; the film was s. on style but weak on content le film était très bon du point de vue de la forme mais pas du tout du point de vue du contenu

7 (tough, harsh ▸ words) grossier; to use s. language dire des grossièretés, tenir des propos grossiers; I wrote him a s. letter je lui ai écrit une lettre bien sentie; she gave us her opinion in s. terms elle nous a dit ce qu'elle pensait sans mâcher ses mots; his latest film is s. stuff son dernier film est vraiment dur

8 (in number) an army 5,000 s. une armée forte de 5000 hommes; the marchers were 400 s. les manifestants étaient au nombre de 400

9 Com & Econ (currency, price) solide; (market) ferme; the dollar has got stronger le dollar s'est raffermi

10 Phys s. force, s. interaction interaction f forte

11 Gram (verb, form) fort

ADV Fam to be going s. (person) être toujours solide□ ou toujours d'attaque; (party) battre son plein; (machine, car) fonctionner toujours bien□; (business, economy) être florissant□, prospérer□; he's 80 years old and still going s. il a 80 ans et toujours bon pied bon œil; the favourite was going s. as they turned into the home straight le favori marchait fort quand les chevaux ont entamé la dernière ligne droite□; to come on s. (insist) insister lourdement□; (make a pass) faire des avances□; that's coming it a bit s.! vous y allez un peu fort!, vous exagérez!

strong-arm VT Fam faire violence à□; to s. sb into doing sth forcer la main à qn pour qu'il fasse qch□

stronghold ['strɒŋhəʊld] N 1 Mil forteresse f, fort m 2 Fig bastion m, fief m; a Conservative Party s. un bastion ou fief du parti conservateur

strongly ['strɒŋlɪ] ADV 1 (greatly ▸ regret) vivement, profondément; (▸ impress, attract) fortement, vivement; the kitchen smelt s. of bleach il y avait une forte odeur de Javel dans la cuisine; to be s. in favour of sth être fortement en faveur ou chaud partisan de qch; I s. advise you to accept je vous conseille vivement d'accepter; I am s. tempted to say yes j'ai très envie de dire oui; I s. disagree with you je ne suis pas du tout d'accord avec vous; the report was s. critical of the hospital le rapport était extrêmement critique à l'égard de l'hôpital; he s. resembles his mother il ressemble beaucoup à sa mère 2 (firmly ▸ believe, support) fermement; (forcefully ▸ attack, defend, protest) énergiquement, vigoureusement, avec force; (▸ emphasize) fortement; a s. worded protest une lettre de protestation énergique; I feel very s. about the matter c'est un sujet ou une affaire qui me tient beaucoup à cœur; I don't feel s. about it je n'ai pas d'opinion particulière à ce sujet 3 (sturdily ▸ constructed) solidement; s. built (person) costaud, bien bâti; (wall, structure) solide, bien construit

strongman ['strɒŋmæn] (pl strongmen [-men]) N (in circus, fair) hercule m (de foire); Fig (powerful man) homme m fort

strong-minded ADJ résolu, déterminé; she is very s. elle sait ce qu'elle veut

strong-mindedness [-'maɪndɪdnɪs] N force f de caractère, résolution f

strongroom ['strɒŋruːm] N Br (in castle, house) chambre f forte; (in bank) chambre f forte, salle f des coffres

strong-willed [-'wɪld] ADJ volontaire, résolu, tenace

strontium ['strɒntɪəm] N Chem strontium m; s. 90 strontium 90

strop [strɒp] (pt & pp stropped, cont stropping) N 1 (for razor) cuir m (à rasoir) 2 Br Fam to be in a s. être mal luné, être de mauvais poil

VT (razor) repasser sur le cuir

strophe ['strəʊfɪ] N strophe f

stroppiness ['strɒpɪnɪs] N Br Fam (insolence) insolence□ f; I'm fed up with his constant s. (bad temper) j'en ai marre de ses humeurs

stroppy ['strɒpɪ] (compar stroppier, superl stroppiest) ADJ Br Fam (bad-tempered) mal luné, de mauvais poil; (insolent) insolent□; there's no need to get s.! tu n'as pas besoin de monter sur tes grands chevaux!

strove [strəʊv] pt of strive

struck [strʌk] pt & pp of strike

ADJ Am (industry) bloqué pour cause de grève; (factory) fermé pour cause de grève

structural ['strʌktʃərəl] ADJ 1 (gen) structural; (change, problem) structurel, de structure; (unemployment) structurel; Ling (analysis) structural, structurel 2 Constr (fault, steel, iron) de construction; (damage, alterations) de structure

▸▸ structural engineer ingénieur m civil; structural engineering génie m civil; Chem structural formula formule f de constitution; structural linguistics (UNCOUNT) linguistique f structurale; structural psychology psychologie f structurale

structuralism ['strʌktʃərəlɪzəm] N structuralisme m

structurally ['strʌktʃərəlɪ] ADV 1 (gen) du point de vue de la structure; s. similar de structure semblable; the book is s. well written le livre est bien structuré ou construit 2 Constr du point de vue de la construction; the building is s. sound le bâtiment est de construction solide

structure ['strʌktʃə(r)] N 1 (composition, framework) structure f 2 (building) construction f, bâtisse f; the scaffolding was a flimsy-looking s. l'échafaudage était une construction d'apparence fragile; Fig the social s. l'édifice social

VT structurer

structured ['strʌktʃəd] ADJ structuré

▸▸ Comput structured query language langage m d'interrogation structuré

struggle ['strʌgəl] N (gen) lutte f; (physical fight) bagarre f, lutte f; armed s. lutte f armée; he got hurt in the s. il a été blessé dans la bagarre; there was evidence of a s. il y avait des traces de lutte; the rebels put up a fierce s. les rebelles ont opposé une vive résistance; they surrendered without a s. ils se sont rendus sans opposer de résistance; it was a s. to convince him on a eu du mal à le convaincre; life is a s. la vie est un combat; there was a bitter s. for leadership of the party les candidats à la direction du parti se sont livré une lutte acharnée; it's a bit of a s. to manage on one income ce n'est pas facile de s'en sortir avec un seul salaire; it was a s. for him to climb the ten flights of stairs il a eu de la peine à monter les dix étages à pied; it'll be a s. but I think we'll make it ce sera difficile ou dur, mais je crois que nous y arriverons

VI 1 (fight) lutter, se battre; she struggled with her attacker elle a lutté contre ou s'est battue avec son agresseur; to s. with one's conscience se débattre avec sa conscience; he struggled violently when they tried to force him into the car il s'est violemment débattu quand ils ont essayé de le pousser dans la voiture; she was struggling with her umbrella elle se débattait avec son parapluie

2 (try hard, strive) lutter, s'efforcer, se démener; I struggled to open the door je me suis démené pour ouvrir la porte; he struggled with the lock il s'est battu avec la serrure; she struggled to control her temper elle avait du mal à garder son calme; we're struggling to meet their deadlines nous faisons tout notre possible pour finir dans les délais; she had to s. to make ends meet elle a eu du mal à joindre les deux bouts; many companies are struggling (financially) beaucoup d'entreprises ont du mal ou sont en difficulté

3 (expressing movement) he struggled back up onto the ledge il remonta avec peine ou avec difficulté sur la corniche; he struggled into his clothes il enfila ses habits avec peine; she struggled through the undergrowth elle s'est péniblement frayé un chemin à travers les broussailles; to s. to one's feet (old person) se lever avec difficulté ou avec peine; (in fight) se relever péniblement; to s. up a hill (person) gravir péniblement une colline; (car) peiner dans une côte

struggling ['strʌglɪŋ] ADJ (hard up ▸ painter, writer etc) qui tire le diable par la queue, qui a du mal à joindre les deux bouts

strum [strʌm] (pt & pp strummed, cont strumming) VT (guitar) jouer de; to s. a tune on the guitar jouer un petit air à la guitare

VI (guitarist) jouer; she started strumming on her guitar elle commença à jouer sur sa guitare

N (on guitar) he gave the guitar a s. il a gratté les cordes de la guitare

strumming ['strʌmɪŋ] N (on guitar) raclement m

strumpet ['strʌmpɪt] N Arch or Hum catin f

strung [strʌŋ] pt & pp of string

ADJ (guitar, piano) muni de cordes, monté; (tennis racket) cordé

strung-out ADJ Fam 1 Drugs slang to be s. (addicted) être accroché ou accro; (high) être shooté, planer; (suffering withdrawal symptoms) être en manque; to get s. se défoncer 2 (uptight) crispé□, tendu□

strung-up ADJ Fam tendu□, nerveux□; she's all s. about her exams elle est très tendue à la perspective de ses examens; don't get s. about it! ne te mets pas dans tous tes états!

strut [strʌt] (pt & pp strutted, cont strutting) N 1 (support ▸ for roof, wall) étrésillon m, étançon m, contrefiche f; (▸ for building) étai m, support m; (▸ between uprights) entretoise f, traverse f; (▸ for beam) jambe f de force; (▸ in plane wing, model) support m; metal s. support m métallique 2 (crossbar ▸ of chair, ladder) barreau m 3 (gait) démarche f fière

VI to s. (about or around) plastronner, se pavaner; he strutted about the room il arpentait la pièce en se pavanant

VT Am Fam to s. one's stuff frimer

strychnine ['strɪkniːn] N strychnine f

stub [stʌb] (pt & pp stubbed, cont stubbing) N 1 (stump ▸ of tree) chicot m, souche f; (▸ of pencil) bout m; (▸ of tail) moignon m; (▸ of cigarette) mégot m; an ashtray full of cigarette stubs un cendrier plein de mégots 2 (counterfoil ▸ of cheque) souche f, talon m; (▸ of ticket) talon m

VT to s. one's toe/foot se cogner le doigt de pied/le pied; he stubbed his toe against the kerb il a buté contre le bord du trottoir

▸▸ stub axle essieu m à chapes fermées

▸ **stub out** VT SEP (cigarette) écraser

stubble ['stʌbəl] N 1 Agr chaume m 2 (on chin) barbe f de plusieurs jours

▸▸ stubble burning action f de brûler le chaume; stubble field chaume m

stubbly ['stʌblɪ] (compar stubblier, superl stubbliest) ADJ 1 (chin, face) mal rasé; (beard) de plusieurs jours; (hair) en brosse 2 (field) couvert de chaume

stubborn ['stʌbən] ADJ 1 (determined ▸ person) têtu, obstiné; (▸ animal) rétif, récalcitrant; (▸ opposition) obstiné, acharné; (▸ refusal, insistence) obstiné; she maintained a s. silence elle garda obstinément le silence ou s'obstina à ne rien dire 2 (resistant ▸ cold, cough, symptoms) persistant, opiniâtre; (▸ stain) récalcitrant, rebelle

stubbornly ['stʌbənlɪ] ADV obstinément, opiniâtrement; he s. insisted on doing it himself il s'obstina à le faire lui-même

stubbornness ['stʌbənnɪs] N (of person) entêtement m, obstination f, opiniâtreté f; (of resistance) acharnement m

stubby ['stʌbɪ] (compar stubbier, superl stubbiest, pl stubbies) ADJ (finger) boudiné, court et épais (aisse); (tail) très court, tronqué; (person) trapu; a s. pencil un petit bout de crayon

N Austr Fam (bottle of beer) canette f (de bière)

stucco ['stʌkəʊ] (pl stuccos or stuccoes) N stuc m

COMP (ceiling, wall, façade) de ou en stuc, stuqué

VT stuquer

▸▸ stucco work (act, process) stucage m; (result) stuc m

stuck [stʌk] *pt & pp of* **stick**

ADJ 1 *(jammed ▸ window, mechanism)* coincé, bloqué; *(▸ vehicle, lift)* bloqué; **he got his hand s. inside the jar** il s'est pris *ou* coincé la main dans le pot; **the wheel is s. fast** la roue est complètement coincée; **to get s. in the mud** s'embourber; **to get s. in the sand** s'enliser; **to be** *or* **to get s. in traffic** être coincé *ou* bloqué dans les embouteillages; *(stranded)* coincé, bloqué; **they were** *or* **they got s. at the airport overnight** ils sont restés bloqués *ou* ils ont dû passer toute la nuit à l'aéroport

2 *(in difficulty)* **if you get s. go on to the next question** si tu sèches, passe à la question suivante; **he's never s. for an answer** il a toujours réponse à tout; **to be s. for money** être à court d'argent

3 *(in an unpleasant situation, trapped)* coincé; **to be s. in a boring/dead-end job** avoir un boulot ennuyeux/sans avenir

4 *Fam (lumbered)* **to get** *or* **to be s. with sth** se retrouver avec qch sur les bras; **I always get s. with the washing-up** je me retrouve toujours avec la vaisselle sur les bras, c'est toujours moi qui dois me taper la vaisselle; **he was s. with the nickname "Teddy"** le surnom de "Teddy" lui est resté; **it's not a very good car but we're s. with it** ce n'est pas génial comme voiture, mais on n'a pas le choix

5 *Fam (fond, keen)* **to be s. on sb** en pincer pour qn; **I'm not exactly s. on the idea** je ne peux pas dire que l'idée m'emballe vraiment

6 *Br Fam (idioms)* **to get s. into sb** *(physically, verbally)* rentrer dans le lard à qn; **to get s. into sth** *(book, work, meal)* attaquer qch; **he got s. into his work** il s'est mis au travail ᵕ; **get s. in!** attaque!

stuck-up **ADJ** *Fam* bêcheur, snob; **she's very s.** elle s'y croit vraiment

stud [stʌd] *(pt & pp* **studded**, *cont* **studding**) **N 1** *(nail, spike)* clou *m (à grosse tête)*; *(decorative)* clou *m (décoratif)*; *(on shoe)* clou *m (à souliers)*, caboche *f*; *(on belt)* clou *m*; *Br (on football boots, track shoes)* crampon *m*; *(on tyre)* clou *m*

2 *(earring)* clou *m* d'oreille

3 *(on roadway)* catadioptre *m*

4 *(on shirt)* bouton *m (servant à fermer un col, un plastron etc)*

5 *Tech (screw)* goujon *m*; *(pin, pivot)* tourillon *m*; *(lug)* ergot *m*

6 *Constr (upright timber)* latte *f*, montant *m*

7 *(on chain)* étai *m*

8 *(reproduction)* monte *f*; **animals kept for s.** animaux destinés à la monte; **to put a stallion (out) to s.** mener un étalon à la monte; **to be at s.** saillir

9 *(stud farm)* haras *m*

10 *(stallion)* étalon *m*

11 *Fam (man)* étalon *m*; *(promiscuous man)* tombeur *m*

12 *Am* stud-poker *m (variété de poker où certaines cartes sont exposées)*

VT 1 *(shoes, belt)* clouter; *(door, chest)* clouter, garnir de clous; *Fig* **stars studded the night sky** le ciel était parsemé d'étoiles **2** *Constr* latter

▸▸ ***stud earring*** clou *m* d'oreille; ***stud farm*** haras *m*; ***stud fastener*** pression *f (bouton)*; ***stud mare*** (jument *f*) poulinière *f*; *Am Fam* ***stud muffin*** super beau mec *m*; ***stud poker*** stud-poker *m (variété de poker où certaines cartes sont exposées)*

studbook [ˈstʌdbʊk] **N** stud-book *m*

student [ˈstjuːdənt] **N** *Univ* étudiant(e) *m,f*; *Sch* élève *mf*, lycéen(enne) *m,f*; **she's a biology s.** *or* **a s. of biology** elle étudie la biologie *ou* est étudiante en biologie; **a good s.** *Sch* un bon élève; *Univ* un bon étudiant; *Fig* **students of human nature/Middle Eastern politics will know that...** ceux qui s'intéressent à la nature humaine/à la politique au Moyen-Orient sauront que...

COMP *(life)* d'étudiant, estudiantin; *(hall of residence, canteen)* universitaire; *(participation) Univ* étudiant; *Sch* des élèves; *(power)* étudiant; *(protest) Univ* d'étudiants, étudiant; *Sch* d'élèves, de lycéens; *(attitudes) Univ* des étudiants; *Sch* des élèves

▸▸ ***student adviser*** conseiller(ère) *m,f* pédagogique; ***student body*** *Univ* étudiants *mpl* inscrits; *Sch* élèves *mpl* inscrits; ***student card*** carte *f* d'étudiant; *Br* ***student flat*** appartement *m* d'étudiants; ***student grant*** bourse *f* (d'études); ***student hostel*** résidence *f* universitaire; ***student house*** maison *f* d'étudiants; *Am* ***student lamp*** lampe *f* de bureau; ***student loan*** = prêt bancaire pour étudiants; ***student nurse*** élève *mf* infirmier (ère); ***student teacher*** *(in primary school)* instituteur(trice) *m,f* stagiaire; *(in secondary school)* professeur *m* stagiaire; ***students' union*** *(trade union)* syndicat *m ou* union *f* des étudiants; *(premises)* ≃ foyer *m* des étudiants

> **STUDENTS' UNION**
>
> Dans les universités britanniques et américaines, on appelle "students' union" à la fois le syndicat et les locaux où il se trouve. Le syndicat est chargé de défendre les intérêts des étudiants, sert de centre d'information et de conseil en matière de logement, de santé et de financement, et organise des événements culturels et des activités.

studhorse [ˈstʌdhɔːs, *pl* -hɔːsɪz] **N** étalon *m*

studied [ˈstʌdɪd] **ADJ 1** *(ease, politeness, indifference)* étudié; *(insult, rudeness, negligence)* délibéré; *(elegance)* recherché; *(manner, pose)* étudié, affecté; **he wore a look of s. boredom** il affichait l'ennui **2** *Literary (of person)* instruit, versé (**in** dans)

studio [ˈstjuːdɪəʊ] *(pl* **studios**) **N** *(of artist, photographer)* atelier *m*, studio *m*; *Rad & TV* studio *m*; *(for dance, exercise)* studio *m*; **recording s.** studio *m* d'enregistrement

▸▸ *Am* ***studio apartment*** studio *m*; ***studio audience*** public *m (présent lors de la diffusion ou de l'enregistrement d'une émission)*; ***studio couch*** canapé-lit *m*, canapé *m* convertible; *Br* ***studio flat*** studio *m*; *TV* ***studio monitor*** écran *m* de contrôle studio; ***studio portrait*** portrait *m* photographique; *Cin* ***the studio system*** l'hégémonie *f* des grands studios (hollywoodiens)

studious [ˈstjuːdɪəs] **ADJ 1** *(diligent ▸ person)* studieux, appliqué **2** *(painstaking ▸ attention, effort)* soutenu **3** *(deliberate ▸ indifference)* délibéré, voulu; **because of his s. avoidance of the topic** parce qu'il évitait soigneusement le sujet

studiously [ˈstjuːdɪəslɪ] **ADV 1** *(diligently ▸ prepare, work, examine)* minutieusement, soigneusement **2** *(deliberately)* d'une manière calculée *ou* délibérée; **s. indifferent** d'une indifférence feinte; **she s. ignored him** elle s'ingéniait à ignorer sa présence

studiousness [ˈstjuːdɪəsnɪs] **N 1** *(eagerness to study)* application *f* (à l'étude), assiduité *f* **2** *(carefulness)* empressement *m*, zèle *m* (**in doing sth** à faire qch)

study [ˈstʌdɪ] *(pt & pp* **studied**, *pl* **studies**) **VT 1** *(gen) & Sch & Univ* étudier; **she's studying medicine/history** elle fait des études de médecine/d'histoire, elle est étudiante en médecine/histoire **2** *(examine ▸ plan, evidence, situation)* étudier, examiner; *(observe ▸ expression, reactions)* étudier, observer attentivement; *(▸ stars)* observer

VI *(gen)* étudier; *Sch & Univ* étudier, faire ses études; **she's studying to be an architect** elle fait des études pour devenir architecte *ou* des études d'architecture; **he's studying for a degree in history** il étudie dans le but d'obtenir un diplôme d'histoire; **where's Brian? – he's upstairs studying** où est Brian? – il travaille en haut; **to s. for an exam** préparer un examen; **I studied under her at university** je suivais ses cours à l'université

N 1 *(academic work, acquisition of knowledge)* étude *f*; **she devotes most evenings to s.** elle passe la plupart de ses soirées à étudier; **he sets aside one day a week for s.** il consacre un jour par semaine à ses études

2 *(investigation)* étude *f* (**of** de); *(report)* étude *f*, rapport *m*; **the plan is under s.** le projet est à l'étude *f*; **I've made an extensive s. of animal behaviour** j'ai fait une étude approfondie du comportement animal; **scientific studies have shown that...** des études *ou* des recherches scientifiques ont montré que...

3 *(room)* bureau *m*, cabinet *m* de travail

4 *Art, Mus & Phot* étude *f*; **a s. in black** une étude en noir; *Fig Literary* **her face was a s.** il fallait voir son visage

COMP *(hour, room)* d'étude

• **studies** **NPL** *Sch & Univ* études *fpl*; **how are your studies going?** comment vont vos études?

▸▸ ***study group*** groupe *m* de travail *ou* d'étud *Am* ***study hall*** *(place)* salle *f* d'étude; *(perio* heure *f* d'étude; ***study period*** heure *f* de perma nence *ou* d'étude; **we have a s. period on Monda mornings** nous avons une heure d'étude le lun matin; ***study tour, study trip*** voyage *m* d'études

STUFF [stʌf]

> **N**
> • choses **1** • substance **1**
> • bêtises **2** • affaires **3**
> • étoffe **4, 5**
>
> **VT**
> • bourrer **1** • farcir **1**
> • fourrer **2** • boucher **4**
> • empailler **5**

N *(UNCOUNT)* **1** *Fam (indefinite sense ▸ thing* choses ᵕ *fpl*, trucs *mpl*; *(▸ substance)* substance *f*, matière ᵕ *f*; **what's that sticky s. in the sin** qu'est-ce que c'est que ce truc gluant dar l'évier?; **here's some s. to put on that burn** voi de quoi soigner cette brûlure; **his pockets are a ways full of all kinds of s.** il a toujours un tas c trucs dans les poches; **he writes some good s.** écrit de bons trucs; **there was some s. abo unions on the news** ils ont dit un truc sur les sy dicats aux informations; **it's made of tomato and onions and s.** il y a des tomates, des oignor et des trucs comme ça; **they go climbing and sa ing and s. like that** ils font de l'escalade, de voile et des trucs du même genre; **this materi is good s.** c'est un bon tissu *ou* du tissu de bonr qualité ᵕ; **I used to drink whisky but now I neve touch the s.** avant, je buvais du whisky, ma maintenant je n'y touche plus ᵕ; **no thanks, can't stand the s.** non merci, j'ai horreur de ç **this mustard is strong s.** cette moutarde est fort **the book is strong s.** *(sexually explicit)* ce liv n'est pas à mettre entre toutes les mains *(hard-hitting)* ce livre est dur ᵕ

2 *Fam Pej (rubbish, nonsense)* bêtises ᵕ *fpl*, sott ses ᵕ *fpl*; **s. and nonsense!** balivernes!; **don't giv me all that s. about the British Empire!** passe-m le topo débile sur l'empire britannique!; **yo don't believe all that s. about ghosts, do you?** vou ne croyez tout de même pas à toutes ces bêtise sur les fantômes?; **do you call that s. art/musi** vous appelez ça de l'art/de la musique? ᵕ

3 *Fam (possessions)* affaires ᵕ *fpl*; *(equipment)* a faires ᵕ *fpl*, matériel ᵕ *m*; **clear all that s. off th table!** enlève tout ce bazar de sur la table!; **hav you packed all your s.?** est-ce que tu as fini c faire tes bagages? ᵕ; **where's my shaving/fishir s.?** où est mon matériel de rasage/de pêche?

4 *(essence)* étoffe *f*; **he's the s. that heroes ar made of** il est de l'étoffe dont sont faits les héro *Literary* **the very s. of life** l'essence *f* même de vie; **the very s. of melodrama** ce dont on fait le mélodrames

5 *(fabric)* étoffe *f* (de laine)

6 *Fam (drugs)* came *f*

7 *Br Fam (woman)* **she's a nice bit of s., she's hot** elle est vraiment bien balancée, elle est cano **he was there with his bit of s.** il était là avec s petite copine

8 *Am Sport (spin)* effet *m*

9 *Fam (idioms)* **to do one's s.** faire ce qu'on a faire ᵕ; **get out there and do your s.!** allez, fais c que tu as à faire *ou* à toi de jouer!; **that's the s** c'est ça!, allez-y!, parfait!; **good s.!** bien! ᵕ; **know one's s.** s'y connaître ᵕ, connaître son a faire ᵕ; **I don't give a s.!** rien à fiche!

VT 1 *(fill ▸ gen)* bourrer (**with** de); *(▸ cushio armchair)* rembourrer; *Culin* farcir; **stuffed wi sausage meat** farci de chair à saucisse; **stuffe with foam** rembourré de mousse; **their house stuffed with souvenirs from India** leur maison e bourrée de souvenirs d'Inde; **her pockets a stuffed with sweets** elle a les poches bourrée de bonbons, elle a des bonbons plein les po ches; **his teachers stuffed his head with a load c political nonsense** ses professeurs lui ont bour le crâne d'un tas d'idées politiques fausses; **h head is stuffed with useless information** elle a l tête farcie de renseignements inutiles

2 *(shove)* fourrer; **he stuffed the papers into h pocket** il a fourré les papiers dans sa poche

3 *Fam (expressing anger, rejection etc)* **he told me I could s. my report** il m'a dit qu'il se foutait pas mal de mon rapport; **I've had enough, he can s. his job!** j'en ai marre! son boulot il peut se le mettre où je pense!; **s. it!** et puis merde!; *very Fam* **get stuffed!, s. you!** va te faire foutre!

4 *(plug ▸ gap)* boucher; **the hole had been stuffed with paper** le trou avait été bouché avec du papier

5 *(in taxidermy ▸ animal, bird)* empailler

6 *Fam (with food)* **to s. oneself** *or* **one's face** se goinfrer, s'empiffrer; **to s. oneself with cake** s'empiffrer de gâteau; **I'm stuffed** je n'ai plus faim▫

7 *Am Pol* **to s. the ballot box** *(fill with false ballot papers)* remplir les urnes de faux bulletins de vote; *(rig election)* truquer les élections

8 *Fam (defeat)* écrabouiller, ficher une déculottée à, battre à plates coutures▫

▸**stuff up** VT SEP *(block)* boucher; **my nose is all stuffed up, I'm all stuffed up** j'ai le nez complètement bouché

---

stuffed [stʌft] ADJ **1** *Culin* farci

2 *(chair, cushion)* rembourré

3 *(owl, fox, rabbit etc)* empaillé

4 *Br & Austr Fam (in trouble)* cuit, fichu; **if that cheque doesn't arrive soon, we're s.** si ce chèque n'arrive pas bientôt, on est cuits

▸▸ ***stuffed animal*** *(mounted)* animal *m* empaillé; *Am (toy)* peluche *f*; ***stuffed shirt*** prétentieux (euse) *m,f*; **he's a real s. shirt** il est vraiment prétentieux

stuffing [ˈstʌfɪŋ] N **1** *(for furniture, toys)* rembourrage *m*, bourre *f*; *(for clothes)* rembourrage *m*; *(in taxidermy)* paille *f*; **horsehair s.** matelassure *f* de crin; *Fam* **to knock the s. out of sb** *(defeat heavily)* mettre la pâtée à qn; *(of blow, attacker, illness)* mettre qn KO; **the news of his death really knocked the s. out of me** ça m'a fait un sacré coup d'apprendre qu'il était mort **2** *Culin* farce *f*

stuffy [ˈstʌfɪ] *(compar* **stuffier**, *superl* **stuffiest)** ADJ **1** *(room)* mal aéré, mal ventilé, qui sent le renfermé; **it's a bit s. in here** *(stale)* ça sent le renfermé ici; *(stifling)* on manque d'air *ou* on étouffe ici

2 *Pej (person ▸ prim)* collet monté *(inv)*; *(▸ old-fashioned)* vieux jeu *(inv)*; *(atmosphere, reception)* guindé; **don't be so s.!** *(shocked)* il n'y a pas de quoi être scandalisé!; *(prim)* ne sois pas si prude!; *(old-fashioned)* ne sois pas si vieux jeu!

3 *(dull ▸ book, subject, lecture)* ennuyeux

4 *(nose)* bouché

stultify [ˈstʌltɪfaɪ] *(pt & pp* **stultified)** VT *(make stupid)* abrutir; *(stifle ▸ creativity, talent)* étouffer

stultifying [ˈstʌltɪfaɪɪŋ] ADJ *(work)* abrutissant, assommant; *(atmosphere)* abrutissant, débilitant; **their policies have had a s. effect on the country's economy** leur politique a paralysé *ou* étouffé l'économie du pays

stumble [ˈstʌmbəl] VI **1** *(person)* trébucher, faire un faux pas; *(horse)* broncher, faire un faux pas; **she stumbled and fell** elle trébucha et tomba; **he stumbled against me** il a trébuché et m'a heurté; **he stumbled over the toys in the hall** il a trébuché sur les jouets dans le couloir; **to s. along/in/out** avancer/entrer/sortir en trébuchant; **they stumbled, exhausted, over the finishing line** ils ont franchi la ligne d'arrivée en titubant de fatigue; **he was stumbling about in the dark** il avançait en trébuchant dans le noir **2** *(in speech)* trébucher; **to s. over a long word** trébucher sur un mot long; **he managed to s. through his lecture** c'est d'une voix mal assurée qu'il a finalement prononcé son cours

N **1** *(in walking)* faux pas *m* **2** *(in speech)* **she read the poem without a s.** elle a lu le poème sans se tromper *ou* sans se reprendre une seule fois

▸**stumble across, stumble on, stumble upon** VT INSEP **1** *(meet)* rencontrer par hasard, tomber sur **2** *(discover)* trouver par hasard, tomber sur

stumblebum [ˈstʌmbəlbʌm] N *Am Fam* **1** *(drunken vagrant)* clodo *mf* alcoolo **2** *(clumsy, incompetent person)* manche *m*

stumbling [ˈstʌmblɪŋ] ADJ *(speech)* hésitant; **she took her first s. steps** elle a fait ses premiers pas

▸▸ ***stumbling block*** pierre *f* d'achoppement

stump [stʌmp] N **1** *(of tree)* chicot *m*, souche *f*

2 *(of limb, tail)* moignon *m*; *(of tooth)* chicot *m*; *(of pencil, blade, candle)* (petit) bout *m*

3 *Am Pol* estrade *f (d'un orateur politique)*; **to be/go on the s.** faire une tournée électorale

4 *Art* estompe *f*

5 *(in cricket)* piquet *m*

VT **1** *Fam (bewilder)* laisser perplexe▫, déconcerter▫; *(with question)* coller; **I'm stumped** *(don't know answer)* je sèche; *(don't know what to do)* je ne sais pas quoi faire▫; **the question had them stumped** la question les a laissés sans voix▫; **she's stumped for an answer** *(in quiz)* elle ne connaît pas la réponse▫; *(for solution)* elle ne trouve pas de solution▫; **it stumps me how anybody could be so silly!** que quelqu'un puisse être aussi bête, ça me dépasse!▫**2** *Am Pol (constituency, state)* faire une tournée électorale dans

VI **1** *(walk heavily)* marcher d'un pas lourd; **to s. in/out** *(heavily)* entrer/sortir d'un pas lourd **2** *Am Pol* faire une tournée électorale

● **stumps** NPL *Fam (legs)* quilles *fpl*

▸**stump up** *Br Fam* VI casquer, raquer (**for** pour); **come on, s. up!** allez, raque!; **I had to s. up for the taxi** c'est moi qui ai dû payer le taxi▫

VT SEP *(money)* cracher, aligner, casquer; *(deposit)* payer▫

stumpy [ˈstʌmpɪ] *(compar* **stumpier**, *superl* **stumpiest)** ADJ *(person)* boulot(otte), courtaud; *(arms, legs)* court et épais(aisse); *(tail)* tronqué

stun [stʌn] *(pt & pp* **stunned**, *cont* **stunning)** VT **1** *(knock out)* assommer **2** *Fig (astonish)* abasourdir, stupéfier

▸▸ ***stun grenade*** grenade *f* incapacitante; ***stun gun*** fusil *m* hypodermique

stung [stʌŋ] *pt & pp of* **sting**

stunner [ˈstʌnə(r)] N *Br Fam (person)* canon *m*; *(thing)* bijou *m*; **his new car's a s.!** sa nouvelle voiture est un vrai bijou!; **that was a s. of a goal!** c'était un but magnifique!

stunning [ˈstʌnɪŋ] ADJ **1** *(blow)* étourdissant; *Fig* **this has dealt a s. blow to the party** ceci a porté un coup terrible au parti **2** *(astounding ▸ news, event)* stupéfiant, renversant, sidérant; *(beautiful ▸ dress, car)* fantastique; *(▸ woman, figure)* superbe; **she looked s. in a black velvet dress** elle était superbe dans sa robe de velours noir; **the film wasn't exactly s.** le film n'avait rien de bien sensationnel

stunningly [ˈstʌnɪŋlɪ] ADV remarquablement, incroyablement; **s. beautiful** d'une beauté éblouissante

stunt [stʌnt] N **1** *(feat)* tour *m* de force, exploit *m* spectaculaire; *(in plane)* acrobatie *f* (aérienne)

2 *(by stunt man)* cascade *f*; **to do a s.** *(in plane)* faire des acrobaties; *(stunt man)* faire une cascade; **to do one's own stunts** *(actor, actress)* ne pas se faire doubler dans les scènes dangereuses

3 *(trick)* truc *m*; *(hoax)* farce *f*, canular *m*; *(done to attract publicity)* coup *m* de pub; **to pull a s.** faire un canular *ou* une farce; **it's just a s. to raise money** ce n'est qu'un truc *ou* une combine pour se faire de l'argent

4 *(plant)* plante *f* chétive *ou* rabougrie; *(animal)* = animal dont la croissance a été freinée

VT *(impede ▸ growth, development)* retarder; *(▸ person)* freiner *ou* retarder la croissance de; *(▸ intelligence)* freiner le développement de

▸▸ ***stunts coordinator*** coordinateur(trice) *m,f* des cascades; ***stunt double*** doublure *f* pour les cascades; ***stunt driver*** conducteur(trice) *m,f* cascadeur(euse); ***stunt driving*** cascades *fpl* automobiles; *Aviat* ***stunt flying*** vol *m* acrobatique; ***stunt man*** cascadeur *m*; ***stunt pilot*** pilote *m* de voltige aérienne, voltigeur *m*; ***stunt woman*** cascadeuse *f*

stunted [ˈstʌntɪd] ADJ *(person)* chétif; *(plant)* chétif, rabougri; *(growth, intelligence)* retardé

stupe [stuːp] N **1** *Am Fam* andouille *f*, crétin(e) *m,f* **2** *Med* compresse *f*

stupefaction [ˌstjuːpɪˈfækʃən] N stupéfaction *f*, stupeur *f*

stupefy [ˈstjuːpɪfaɪ] *(pt & pp* **stupefied)** VT **1** *(of alcohol, drugs, tiredness)* abrutir; *(of blow)* assommer, étourdir **2** *(astound)* stupéfier, abasourdir

stupefying [ˈstjuːpɪfaɪɪŋ] ADJ stupéfiant

stupendous [stjuːˈpendəs] ADJ *(amount, achievement, talent)* extraordinaire, prodigieux; *(event)* prodigieux, extraordinaire; *(book, film)* extraordinaire

stupendously [stjuːˈpendəslɪ] ADV prodigieusement, formidablement

stupid [ˈstjuːpɪd] ADJ **1** *(foolish)* idiot; **he's always saying/doing s. things** il dit/fait sans arrêt des bêtises; **I was s. enough to go and apologize** j'ai eu la sottise d'aller *ou* j'ai été assez bête pour aller m'excuser; **he's s. enough to believe you** il est assez bête pour vous croire; **stop being so s.!** arrête de faire l'idiot *ou* l'imbécile!; **how s. of me!** que je suis bête!; **what a s. place to put it!** c'est idiot de l'avoir mis là!; **I'm not s., you know!** je ne suis pas idiot quand même! **2** *Literary (from alcohol, drugs, sleep)* abruti, hébété; *(from blow)* étourdi; **he was still s. from** *or* **with sleep** il était encore abruti de sommeil; **to drink oneself s.** s'abrutir d'alcool **3** *Fam (wretched, confounded)* maudit, fichu; **where did I put that s. hammer?** où est-ce que j'ai mis ce maudit marteau?

N *Fam* bêta(asse) *m,f*, idiot(e)▫*mf*; **I'm only joking, s.!** je plaisante, gros bêta!

stupidity [stjuːˈpɪdətɪ] *(pl* **stupidities)** N stupidité *f*, bêtise *f*, sottise *f*

stupidly [ˈstjuːpɪdlɪ] ADV stupidement, bêtement; **I s. forgot to phone them** je suis bête, j'ai oublié de leur téléphoner

stupor [ˈstjuːpə(r)] N stupeur *f*, abrutissement *m*; **to be in a drunken s.** être abruti par l'alcool

sturdily [ˈstɜːdɪlɪ] ADV **1** *(solidly)* solidement, robustement; **to be s. built** *(person)* être costaud *ou* bien bâti; *(toys, furniture, equipment)* être solide; *(house)* être de construction solide, être robuste **2** *(firmly ▸ deny, refuse, oppose)* énergiquement, vigoureusement

sturdiness [ˈstɜːdɪnɪs] N **1** *(solidity)* solidité *f*, robustesse *f* **2** *(firmness)* fermeté *f*; **with great s. of purpose** avec une grande résolution

sturdy [ˈstɜːdɪ] *(compar* **sturdier**, *superl* **sturdiest)** ADJ **1** *(robust ▸ person)* robuste, vigoureux; *(▸ limbs)* robuste; *(▸ table, tree, shoes)* robuste, solide **2** *(firm ▸ denial, defence, opposition, support)* énergique, vigoureux; *(▸ voice)* ferme

sturgeon [ˈstɜːdʒən] *(pl* **inv)** N *Ich* esturgeon *m*

stutter [ˈstʌtə(r)] N bégaiement *m*; **to speak with a** *or* **to have a s.** bégayer, être bègue

VI bégayer; *Fig* **the engine stuttered into life** le moteur toussa avant de démarrer

VT **to s. (out)** bégayer, bredouiller

stutterer [ˈstʌtərə(r)] N bègue *mf*

stuttering [ˈstʌtərɪŋ] N bégaiement *m*

ADJ bègue, qui bégaie

sty [staɪ] *(pl* **sties)** N **1** *(for pigs)* porcherie *f* **2** = **stye**

stye [staɪ] N orgelet *m*, compère-loriot *m*

Stygian [ˈstɪdʒɪən] ADJ *Literary* ténébreux, sombre

▸▸ ***Stygian gloom*** ténèbres *fpl* impénétrables *ou* insondables

style [staɪl] N **1** *(manner)* style *m*, manière *f*; *Art, Literature & Mus* style *m*; **in the s. of Vermeer** dans le style de Vermeer; **s. of life** mode *m* de vie; **I don't like his s. of dressing** je n'aime pas sa façon de s'habiller; **written in the s. of a 1940s thriller** écrit dans le style du roman policier des années 1940; **they've adopted a new management s.** *(approach)* ils ont adopté un nouveau style de gestion; **the meal was prepared in authentic Japanese s.** le repas a été préparé dans la plus pure tradition japonaise; **you've got to admire his s.!** *(way of doing things)* on ne peut qu'admirer la façon dont il s'y prend!

2 *(fashion ▸ in clothes)* mode *f*; *(model, design)* modèle *m*; **to be dressed in the latest s.** être habillé à la dernière mode; **all the latest styles** tous les derniers modèles; **this winter's styles** les modèles de cet hiver; **the boots come in two styles** ces bottes existent en deux modèles

3 *(elegance, sophistication ▸ of person)* allure *f*, chic *m*; *(▸ of dress, picture, building, film)* style *m*; **she's got real s.** elle a vraiment de l'allure *ou* du chic; **she does everything with great s.** elle fait tout avec beaucoup de style; **to live in s.** mener grand train, vivre dans le luxe; **he likes to do**

things in s. il aime faire bien les choses; **they were dressed in s.** ils étaient habillés avec beaucoup de chic; **they made their entrance in great s.** ils ont fait une entrée très remarquée; **they drove off in s. in a fleet of limousines** ils sont partis en grande pompe dans un cortège de limousines

4 *(type)* genre *m*; **I wouldn't have thought cheating was your s.** je n'aurais jamais pensé que c'était ton genre de tricher; **I don't like his s.** je n'aime pas son genre; **that's the s.!** c'est ça!, bravo!

5 *(of calendar)* **February 12 old/new s.** le 12 février vieux/nouveau style

6 *Typ (in editing)* style *m*; **house s.** style *m* de la maison

7 *Br Formal (title)* titre *m*

8 *Bot* style *m*

VT 1 *(call)* appeler, désigner; **she styles herself "countess"** elle se fait appeler "comtesse" **2** *(design ► dress, jewel, house)* créer, dessiner; **dress styled by Dior** robe créée par Dior; **to s. sb's hair** coiffer qn; **styled for comfort and elegance** conçu pour le confort et l'élégance

►► ***style bar*** *(place)* bar *m* chic; *Comput* barre *f* de style; *Comput* ***style sheet*** feuille *f* de style

styling ['staɪlɪŋ] **N** *(of dress)* forme *f*, ligne *f*; *(of hair)* coupe *f*; *(of car)* ligne *f*

►► ***styling brush*** brosse *f* coiffante; ***styling gel*** gel *m* coiffant; ***styling mousse*** mousse *f* coiffante

stylish ['staɪlɪʃ] **ADJ** *(person)* élégant, chic *(inv)*; *(clothes, hotel, neighbourhood)* élégant, chic *(inv)*; *(book, film)* qui a du style

stylishly ['staɪlɪʃlɪ] **ADV** *(dress)* avec chic, avec allure, élégamment; *(live)* élégamment; *(travel)* dans le luxe; *(write)* avec style *ou* élégance

stylishness ['staɪlɪʃnɪs] **N** chic *m*, élégance *f*; *(of prose)* élégance *f*

stylist ['staɪlɪst] **N 1** *(designer ► for clothes)* styliste *mf* (de mode), modéliste *mf*; *(► for cars, furniture)* styliste *mf*; **(hair) s.** coiffeur(euse) *m,f* **2** *Art & Literature* styliste *mf*

stylistic [staɪ'lɪstɪk] **ADJ** *Art, Literature & Ling* stylistique

stylistically [staɪ'lɪstɪklɪ] **ADV** d'un point de vue stylistique

stylistics [staɪ'lɪstɪks] **N** *(UNCOUNT)* stylistique *f*

stylization, -isation [ˌstaɪəlaɪ'zeɪʃən] **N** stylisation *f*

stylize, -ise ['staɪəlaɪz] **VT** styliser

stylus ['staɪləs] *(pl* **styluses** *or* **styli** [-laɪ]) **N** *(on record player)* pointe *f* de lecture; *(made of sapphire)* saphir *m*; *(made of diamond)* diamant *m*; *(tool)* style *m*, stylet *m*; *(of PDA)* stylet *m*

stymie ['staɪmɪ] **VT 1** *(in golf)* barrer le trou à **2** *Br Fam Fig (person)* coincer; *(plan)* ficher en l'air; **to be stymied** être coincé *ou* dans une impasse□

N *(in golf)* trou *m* barré; *Fig* obstacle *m*, entrave *f*

styptic ['stɪptɪk] **ADJ** styptique

N styptique *m*

►► ***styptic pencil*** crayon *m* hémostatique

suasion ['sweɪʒən] **N** *Formal* persuasion *f*; **to subject sb to moral s.** agir sur la conscience de qn

suave [swɑːv] **ADJ 1** *(polite, charming)* poli, *Literary* urbain; *Pej (smooth)* doucereux, mielleux, onctueux; **he's a bit too s. for my liking** je le trouve un peu trop doucereux **2** *(elegant)* élégant, chic

> Note that the French word **suave** is a false friend and is almost never a translation for the English word **suave**. It is used to describe something that appeals to the senses in a pleasant way.

suavely ['swɑːvlɪ] **ADV 1** *(politely, charmingly)* poliment; *Pej (smoothly)* mielleusement **2** *(elegantly)* avec élégance

suaveness ['swɑːvnɪs], **suavity** ['swɑːvətɪ] **N 1** *(politeness, charm)* politesse *f*; *Pej* manières *fpl* doucereuses **2** *(elegance)* élégance *f*

> **PRÉFIXE**
>
> **SUB-**
>
> • Le préfixe **sub-** peut signifier AU-DESSOUS DE et ce dans differents contextes. Dans ce sens il se traduit le plus souvent par **sous-** ou **sub-**:
>
> **subsoil** sous-sol; **subcutaneous** sous-cutané; **sub-zero temperatures** températures au-dessous de zéro; **subsonic flight** vol subsonique; **subaqua club** club de plongée sous-marine.
>
> Il est également possible de créer des combinaisons plus complexes telles que:
>
> **to run a sub-four-minute mile** courir le mile en moins de quatre minutes; **a sub-ten-thousand-pound deal** une transaction de moins de mille livres.
>
> • **Sub-** véhicule aussi l'idée de MOINDRE IMPORTANCE dans une hiérarchie ou un ordre donné. Dans ce sens il se traduit généralement par **sous-**:
>
> **subcontractor** sous-traitant; **subdeacon** sous-diacre; **subcommittee** sous-comité, sous-commission; **subcontinent** sous-continent; **subplot** intrigue secondaire.
>
> • **Sub-** peut également signaler qu'une chose est une PARTIE D'UN ENSEMBLE; les traductions sont alors variables en fonction du contexte:
>
> **subculture** subculture; **to subdivide** subdiviser; **to sublet** sous-louer; **subtotal** total partiel; **subpopulation** sous-population.
>
> • **Sub-** peut également exprimer l'idée d'INFÉRIORITÉ et de MÉDIOCRITÉ comme dans les exemples suivants:
>
> **substandard work** un travail en dessous du niveau requis; **to live in subhuman conditions** vivre dans des conditions inhumaines.
>
> Il peut se combiner avec des noms de personne pour indiquer que ce dont on parle est inférieur au point de référence:
>
> **he writes in a sub-Dickens style** son style est celui d'un sous-Dickens; **the film has a sub-Chaplinesque quality** le film rappelle Chaplin mais en moins bien.

sub [sʌb] *(pt & pp* **subbed**) *Fam* **N 1** *(subscription ► to club, union etc)* cotisation□*f*; **to pay one's subs** payer sa cotisation

2 *Sport (substitute)* remplaçant(e)□*m,f*

3 *Naut (submarine)* sous-marin□*m*

4 *Br Journ (subeditor)* secrétaire *mf* de rédaction□

5 *Am & Ir (substitute teacher)* suppléant(e)□*m,f*

6 *Br (small loan)* prêt□*m*; **to give sb a s.** dépanner qn; **to get a s.** se faire dépanner

7 *(sandwich)* = grand sandwich mixte de forme allongée

VI 1 *(substitute)* **to s. for sb** remplacer qn□ **2** *Br Journ (subedit)* travailler comme secrétaire de rédaction□

VT 1 *Journ (article)* mettre au point□, corriger□ **2** *Br (lend)* **to s. sb sth** dépanner qn de qch□; **can you s. me a fiver?** tu peux me dépanner de cinq livres?

sub-account **N** *Acct* sous-compte *m*

subagent [ˌsʌb'eɪdʒənt] **N** sous-agent *m*

subalpine [ˌsʌb'ælpaɪn] **ADJ** subalpin

subaltern ['sʌbəltən] **N 1** *Br Mil* = officier de l'armée de terre d'un rang inférieur à celui de capitaine **2** *(subordinate ► gen)* subalterne *mf*, subordonné(e) *m,f*

ADJ subalterne

sub-aqua [-'ækwə] **ADJ** sous-marin, subaquatique

►► ***sub-aqua diving*** plongée *f* sous-marine

subatomic [ˌsʌbə'tɒmɪk] **ADJ** subatomique

►► *Phys* ***subatomic particle*** particule *f* subatomique

subbed [sʌbd] **ADJ** *Journ* corrigé

sub-branch **N** *Biol* sous-embranchement *m*

subclass ['sʌbklɑːs] **N** sous-classe *f*

subclause ['sʌbklɔːz] **N** *Law (of contract)* paragraphe *m*

subcommittee ['sʌbkəˌmɪtɪ] **N** sous-comité *m*, sous-commission *f*

subconscious [ˌsʌb'kɒnʃəs] **ADJ** subconscient; **the s. mind** le subconscient

N subconscient *m*

subconsciously [ˌsʌb'kɒnʃəslɪ] **ADV** d'une ma nière subconsciente, inconsciemment

subcontinent [ˌsʌb'kɒntɪnənt] **N** sous-conti nent *m*; **the (Indian) S.** le sous-continent indien

subcontract **VT** [ˌsʌbkən'trækt] *(pass on)* (faire sous-traiter; **they s. some of the work (out) t local firms** ils sous-traitent une partie du travai à des entreprises locales

VI [ˌsʌbkən'trækt] travailler en sous-traitance **they have a lot of small companies who s. for the** beaucoup de petites sociétés travaillent pou eux en sous-traitance

N [ˌsʌb'kɒntrækt] (contrat *m* de) sous-traitance *f*

subcontracting [ˌsʌbkən'træktɪŋ] **ADJ** sous traitant

►► ***subcontracting firm*** sous-traitant *m*

subcontractor [ˌsʌbkən'træktə(r)] **N** sous-trai tant *m*

subculture ['sʌbˌkʌltʃə(r)] **N 1** *(gen & sociologic al)* subculture *f* **2** *Biol* culture *f* repiquée *ou* se condaire

subcutaneous [ˌsʌbkjuː'teɪnɪəs] **ADJ** *Anat* sous cutané

subdeacon [ˌsʌb'diːkən] **N** sous-diacre *m*

subdirectory ['sʌbˌdɪrektərɪ] *(pl* **subdirectories** **N** *Comput* sous-répertoire *m*

subdivide [ˌsʌbdɪ'vaɪd] **VT** subdiviser

VI se subdiviser

subdivision [ˌsʌbdɪ'vɪʒən] **N** subdivision *f*

subdominant [ˌsʌb'dɒmɪnənt] **N** *Biol & Mu* sous-dominante *f*

subdue [səb'djuː] **VT 1** *(country, tribe, rebels)* sou mettre; *(rebellion)* réprimer **2** *(feelings, passions* refréner, réfréner, maîtriser; *(fears, anxiety* apaiser

subdued [səb'djuːd] **ADJ 1** *(person ► gen)* silen cieux; *(► quieter than usual)* inhabituellemen calme; *(mood)* sombre; *(emotion, feeling)* conte nu; *(audience)* peu enthousiaste; **you're very s. what's the matter?** vous n'êtes pas très bavard qu'est-ce qui ne va pas?; **it was rather a s. gather ing** ce fut un rassemblement plutôt sombre **2** *(voice, sound)* bas; *(conversation)* à voix basse **3** *(light, lighting)* tamisé, atténué; *(colours)* sobre

subedit [ˌsʌb'edɪt] *Br* **VT** corriger, préparer pou l'impression

VI travailler comme secrétaire de rédaction

subediting [ˌsʌb'edɪtɪŋ] **N** *Br* mise *f* au point correction *f*

subeditor [ˌsʌb'edɪtə(r)] **N** *Br* secrétaire *mf* d rédaction

subfamily ['sʌbˌfæməlɪ] *(pl* **subfamilies**) **N** sous famille *f*

subfolder ['sʌbˌfəʊldə(r)] **N** *Comput* sous dossier *m*

subframe ['sʌbˌfreɪm] **N** *Aut* faux-châssis *m inv*

subfusc ['sʌbˌfʌsk] **N** *Br* tenue *f* universitaire *(e particulier à Oxford)*

ADJ *Literary (dark)* sombre; *(dusky)* bistre *(inv)*

subgenre ['sʌbˌʒɑ̃rə] **N** sous-genre *m*

subgenus [ˌsʌb'dʒiːnəs] *(pl* **subgenuses** *or* **sub genera** [-'dʒenərə]) **N** sous-genre *m*

subgroup ['sʌbˌgruːp] **N** sous-groupe *m*

subhead ['sʌbhed], **subheading** ['sʌbˌhedɪŋ] **N** *(title)* sous-titre *m*; *(division)* paragraphe *m*

subhuman [ˌsʌb'hjuːmən] **ADJ** *(intelligence, spe cies)* inférieur à celui/celle des humains; *(crime* brutal, bestial; **to live in s. conditions** vivre dan des conditions terribles *ou* inhumaines

N sous-homme *m*

subject **N** ['sʌbdʒɪkt] **1** *(topic)* sujet *m*; **on the s. o** au sujet de, à propos de; **this will be the s. of m next lecture** ma prochaine conférence porter sur ce sujet; **to wander from the s.** s'écarter d sujet, faire une digression; **let's come** *or* **get bac to the s.** revenons à nos moutons; **don't try an change the s.** n'essaie pas de changer de suje *ou* de détourner la conversation; **let's drop th s.** parlons d'autre chose; **while we're on the s.** (ce) propos; **while we're on the s. of holiday** puisque nous parlons de vacances

2 *(of legal case, contract)* objet *m*; *(in letters an memos)* **s.: recruitment of new staff** objet: recru tement de personnel

3 *Art, Literature & Phot* sujet *m*
4 *Gram & Phil* sujet *m*
5 *Sch & Univ* matière *f*, discipline *f*; *(field)* domaine *m*; **she's taking exams in four subjects** elle passe des examens dans quatre matières; **I was always better at science subjects** j'ai toujours été plus fort en sciences; **it's not really my s.** ce n'est pas vraiment mon domaine; **that would be a good s. for a PhD thesis** ce serait un bon sujet pour une thèse de doctorat
6 *Pol (of monarch)* sujet(ette) *m,f*; **she is a British s.** c'est une ressortissante britannique; **foreign subjects** ressortissants *mpl* étrangers
7 *Med & Psy (of test)* sujet *m*; **subjects were tested for their reactions** on a testé la réaction des sujets
8 *(cause)* objet *m*; **he was the s. of much comment** il a été l'objet de nombreux commentaires
9 *Comput (of e-mail message)* objet *m*
ADJ ['sʌbdʒɪkt] **1** *(subordinate ▸ people, country)* assujetti, soumis; **they are s. to my authority** ils sont placés sous mon autorité, ils dépendent de moi; **we are all s. to the rule of law** nous sommes tous soumis à la loi; **s. states** États *mpl* dépendants **2** *(liable, prone)* **s. to** sujet à; **s. to attack** exposé à l'attaque; **to be s. to violent changes of mood/fits of jealousy** être sujet à de brusques sautes d'humeur/des crises de jalousie; **the terms are s. to alteration without notice** les termes peuvent être modifiés sans préavis; **s. to tax** imposable, assujetti à l'impôt; **the price is s. to a handling charge** les frais de manutention sont en sus; **all trains will be s. to delay** des retards sont à prévoir sur toutes les lignes
VT [sʌb'dʒekt] **1** *(country, people)* soumettre, assujettir **2** *(expose)* **to s. to** soumettre à; **to s. sb/sth to an examination** faire subir un examen à qn/qch, soumettre qn/qch à un examen; **the material was subjected to intense heat** le matériau a été soumis *ou* exposé à une température très élevée; **I refuse to s. anyone to such indignities** je refuse de faire subir de tels affronts à qui que ce soit; **their plans were subjected to much criticism** leurs projets ont fait l'objet de nombreuses critiques
• **subject to PREP** ['sʌbdʒɪkt] *(save for)* sous réserve de, sauf; *(conditional upon)* à condition de; **these are the rules, s. to revision** voici le règlement, sous réserve de modification; **s. to your passing the exam** à condition de réussir *ou* à condition que vous réussissiez l'examen; **it's all s. to her approval** tout est subordonné à son approbation
▸▸ ***subject catalogue*** fichier *m* par matières; ***subject index*** index *m* des matières; ***subject matter*** *(topic)* sujet *m*, thème *m*; *(substance)* substance *f*, contenu *m*

subjection [səb'dʒekʃən] **N 1** *(act of subjecting)* assujettissement *m* **2** *(state of being subjected)* sujétion *f*, assujettissement *m*, soumission *f*; **they live in (a state of) complete s.** ils vivent dans la soumission la plus totale

subjective [səb'dʒektɪv] **ADJ 1** *(viewpoint, argument, criticism)* subjectif **2** *Gram (pronoun, case)* sujet; *(genitive)* subjectif **3** *Med (symptom)* subjectif
N *Gram* (cas *m*) sujet *m*, nominatif *m*
▸▸ *Cin & TV* ***subjective time*** temps *m* subjectif

subjectively [səb'dʒektɪvlɪ] **ADV** subjectivement

subjectivism [səb'dʒektɪvɪzəm] **N** subjectivisme *m*

subjectivity [ˌsʌbdʒek'tɪvətɪ] **N** subjectivité *f*

subjoin [ˌsʌb'dʒɔɪn] **VT** adjoindre

sub judice [-'dʒuːdɪsɪ] **ADJ** *Law* en instance, pendant; **I cannot comment on a case which is still s.** je ne peux faire aucun commentaire sur une affaire qui est encore en cours de jugement

subjugate ['sʌbdʒʊgeɪt] **VT 1** *(people, tribe, country)* assujettir, soumettre; *(rebels)* soumettre **2** *(feelings)* dompter; *(reaction)* réprimer

subjugation [ˌsʌbdʒʊ'geɪʃən] **N** soumission *f*, assujettissement *m*

subjunctive [səb'dʒʌŋktɪv] **ADJ** subjonctif
N subjonctif *m*; **in the s.** au subjonctif; **some verbs always take the s.** certains verbes sont toujours suivis du subjonctif
▸▸ ***subjunctive mood*** mode *m* subjonctif

sublease **N** [ˌsʌb'liːs] sous-location *f*
VT [ˌsʌb'liːs] sous-louer

sublessee [ˌsʌble'siː] **N** sous-locataire *mf*

sublessor [ˌsʌble'sɔː(r)] **N** sous-bailleur(eresse) *m,f*

sublet *(pt & pp* **sublet**, *cont* **subletting)** **N** [ˌsʌb'let] sous-location *f*
VT [ˌsʌb'let] sous-louer

subletter ['sʌbˌletə(r)] **N** sous-bailleur(eresse) *m,f*

subletting ['sʌbˌletɪŋ] **N** sous-location *f*

sublieutenant [ˌsʌbluː'tenənt, *Br* ˌsʌblef'tenənt] **N** *(in navy)* ≃ enseigne *m* de vaisseau première/deuxième classe, *Can* ≃ sous-lieutenant *m*

sublimate **VT** ['sʌblɪmeɪt] *(gen) & Chem* sublimer
N ['sʌblɪmət] *Chem* sublimé *m*

sublimation [ˌsʌblɪ'meɪʃən] **N** sublimation *f*

sublime [sə'blaɪm] **ADJ 1** *(noble, inspiring)* sublime **2** *Fam (very good)* génial, sensationnel; **you look s.** tu es superbe **3** *(utter ▸ disregard, contempt, ignorance)* suprême, souverain
N the s. le sublime; **from the s. to the ridiculous** du sublime au grotesque
VT *Chem* sublimer

sublimely [sə'blaɪmlɪ] **ADV 1** *(extremely)* **s. beautiful** d'une beauté sublime **2** *(utterly)* complètement, totalement; **they were s. unaware of the danger** ils étaient totalement inconscients du danger

subliminal [ˌsʌb'lɪmɪnəl] **ADJ** subliminaire, subliminal
▸▸ ***subliminal advertising*** publicité *f* subliminale *ou* invisible

sublimity [sə'blɪmətɪ] **N** sublimité *f*

submachine gun [ˌsʌbmə'ʃiːn-] **N** mitraillette *f*

submarine [ˌsʌbmə'riːn] **N 1** *Naut* sous-marin *m* **2** *(sandwich)* = grand sandwich mixte de forme allongée
ADJ *(cable, volcano)* sous-marin
▸▸ ***submarine pen*** abri *m* pour sous-marins; ***submarine sandwich*** = grand sandwich mixte de forme allongée

submariner [ˌsʌb'mærɪnə(r)] **N** sous-marinier *m*

sub-market **N** sous-marché *m*

submediant [ˌsʌb'miːdjənt] **N** sus-dominante *f*, sixte *f*

submenu [ˌsʌb'menjuː] **N** *Comput* sous-menu *m*

submerge [səb'mɜːdʒ] **VT 1** *(plunge)* submerger, immerger; *Fig* **to s. oneself in work** se plonger dans le travail **2** *(flood)* submerger, inonder; **the flood waters had submerged the fields** les eaux en crue avaient inondé les champs; **the rocks were soon submerged by the tide** les rochers furent bientôt recouverts par la marée
VI *(submarine)* plonger

submerged [səb'mɜːdʒd] **ADJ** *(field etc)* submergé; *(submarine)* en plongée; *(reef, volcano)* sous-marin; *Fig* **s. in work** submergé de travail, qui croule sous le travail

submergence [səb'mɜːdʒəns] **N** submersion *f*

submersible [səb'mɜːsəbəl] **ADJ** submersible
N submersible *m*

submersion [səb'mɜːʃən] **N 1** *(in liquid)* immersion *f*; *(of submarine)* plongée *f* **2** *(flooding)* inondation *f*

submission [səb'mɪʃən] **N 1** *(yielding)* soumission *f*; **to beat/starve sb into s.** réduire qn par la violence/la famine
2 *(submissiveness)* soumission *f*, docilité *f*
3 *(referral ▸ gen)* soumission *f*; *Law (of case)* renvoi *m*; **after s. of the project to the coordinating committee** après soumission du projet au comité de coordination
4 *(proposition, argument ▸ gen)* thèse *f*; *Law* plaidoirie *f*; **her s. is that...** elle soutient que...; **in my s., the defendant is lying** je soutiens que l'accusé ment
5 *(in wrestling)* soumission *f*

submissive [səb'mɪsɪv] **ADJ** soumis

submissively [səb'mɪsɪvlɪ] **ADV** *(behave, confess, accept)* docilement; *(yield, react)* avec résignation

submissiveness [səb'mɪsɪvnɪs] **N** soumission *f*, docilité *f*

submit [səb'mɪt] *(pt & pp* **submitted**, *cont* **submitting)** **VI 1** *(surrender)* se rendre, se soumettre **2** *Fig* se soumettre, se plier; **to s. to authority** se soumettre à l'autorité; **we shall never s. to such demands** nous n'accéderons jamais à de telles exigences; **to s. to one's fate** accepter son destin
VT 1 *(present)* soumettre; **to s. sth for sb's approval/for sb's inspection** soumettre *ou* présenter qch à l'approbation/à l'inspection de qn; **to s. proof of identity** présenter des pièces d'identité; **all proposals must be submitted to the coordinating committee** toutes les propositions doivent être soumises au comité de coordination; *Law* **I s. that...** je soutiens *ou* je maintiens que... **2** *(yield)* **to s. oneself to sb/sth** se soumettre à qn/qch

subnormal [ˌsʌb'nɔːməl] **ADJ 1** *(person)* arriéré; **educationally s. children** des enfants arriérés *(du point de vue scolaire)* **2** *(temperatures)* au-dessous de la normale

suborder ['sʌbˌɔːdə(r)] **N** *Biol* sous-ordre *m*

subordinate **N** [sə'bɔːdɪnət] subordonné(e) *m,f*, subalterne *mf*
ADJ [sə'bɔːdɪnət] **1** *(in rank, hierarchy)* subalterne; **he is s. to the duty officer** son grade est inférieur à celui de l'officier de permanence; **of s. rank** de rang subalterne **2** *(secondary)* subordonné, accessoire; **but that is s. to the main problem** mais c'est secondaire par rapport au problème principal **3** *Gram* subordonné
VT [sə'bɔːdɪneɪt] subordonner
▸▸ *Gram* ***subordinate clause*** (proposition *f*) subordonnée *f*

subordination [səˌbɔːdɪ'neɪʃən] **N** subordination *f*

suborn [sə'bɔːn] **VT** *Law* suborner

suborning [sə'bɔːnɪŋ] **N** *Law* subornation *f*

subplot ['sʌbˌplɒt] **N** intrigue *f* secondaire

subpoena, *Am* **subpena** [sə'piːnə] **N** citation *f* *(à comparaître en qualité de témoin)*, assignation *f*
VT citer *(à comparaître en qualité de témoin)*

sub-postmaster **N** *Br* receveur *m* *(dans un petit bureau de poste local)*

sub-postmistress **N** *Br* receveuse *f* *(dans un petit bureau de poste local)*

sub-post office **N** *Br* petit bureau *m* de poste local

sub-prefect **N** *Admin* sous-préfet *m*

subprime ['sʌbpraɪm] **ADJ** *Fin* **s. loans** subprimes *fpl*; **s. mortgage** prêt *m* hypothécaire à risque; **s. crisis** crise *f* des subprimes

subprogram ['sʌbˌprəʊgræm] **N** *Comput* sous-programme *m*

subroutine ['sʌbruːˌtiːn] **N** *Comput* sous-programme *m*

subscribe [səb'skraɪb] **VI 1** *(to magazine, service, telephone system, ISP)* s'abonner, être abonné; **to s. to a newspaper** *(become a subscriber)* s'abonner à un journal; *(be a subscriber)* être abonné à un journal **2** *(to loan, fund, campaign, share issue)* souscrire; **to s. to a charity** faire des dons à une œuvre de charité **3 to s. to** *(opinion, belief)* souscrire à
VT 1 *(money)* verser; *(donate)* donner, faire don de; **she subscribed £800 to the election fund** elle a donné 800 livres à la caisse électorale **2** *Formal (write ▸ one's name, signature)* apposer; *(sign ▸ document)* signer

subscriber [səb'skraɪbə(r)] **N 1** *(to magazine, service, telephone system, ISP)* abonné(e) *m,f*; **telephone s.** abonné(e) *m,f* du *ou* au téléphone
2 *(to fund, campaign, share issue)* souscripteur(trice) *m,f*; **subscribers to various charities** les personnes qui ont fait des dons à diverses œuvres de charité
3 *(to opinion, belief)* partisan *m*, adepte *mf*
4 *(of new company)* signataire *mf* des statuts
▸▸ *Br* ***subscriber trunk dialling*** automatique *m*

subscript ['sʌbskrɪpt] *Comput, Math & Typ*
N indice *m*
ADJ en indice

subscription [səb'skrɪpʃən] **N 1** *(to magazine, service, telephone system, ISP)* abonnement *m*; **to cancel a s.** résilier un abonnement; **to take out a s. to a magazine** s'abonner à un magazine **2** *(to fund, campaign, share issue)* souscription *f*,

Br (to club, organization) cotisation *f* **3** *(to opinion, belief)* adhésion *f*

►► *TV* ***subscription channel*** chaîne *f* payante, chaîne *f* à péage; ***subscription charges*** tarifs *mpl* d'abonnement; ***subscription fee*** frais *mpl* d'inscription; *(for share purchase)* droit *m* de souscription; ***subscription renewal*** réabonnement *m*; *Am, Austr & NZ* ***subscription television*** chaînes *fpl* à péage

subsection [ˈsʌbˌsekʃən] **N** *(of text, contract etc)* article *m*, paragraphe *m*

subsequent [ˈsʌbsɪkwənt] **ADJ 1** *(next)* suivant, ultérieur; **the s. days** les jours *mpl* suivants; **at a s. meeting** au cours d'une séance ultérieure; **to await s. events** attendre de connaître la suite des événements; **s. generations** les générations *fpl* suivantes; **s. to 1880** après 1880; **s. to this** par la suite **2** *(consequent)* conséquent, consécutif

subsequently [ˈsʌbsɪkwəntlɪ] **ADV** par la suite, ultérieurement

subservience [səbˈsɜːvjəns] **N 1** *(servility)* servilité *f* **2** *(subjugation)* asservissement *m*; **s. to a foreign power** asservissement *m* à une puissance étrangère

subservient [səbˈsɜːvjənt] **ADJ 1** *(servile)* servile, *Pej* obséquieux **2** *(subjugated)* asservi; **they are totally s. to the town council** ils sont totalement dépendants de la municipalité **3** *(secondary)* secondaire, accessoire

subset [ˈsʌbset] **N** sous-ensemble *m*

subside [səbˈsaɪd] **VI 1** *(abate ► shooting, laughter)* cesser; *(► storm, rage, pain)* se calmer; *(recede ► water)* se retirer, baisser; *(► danger)* s'éloigner **2** *(sink ► house, land)* s'affaisser; *(► wall, foundations)* se tasser; *(settle ► sediment)* se déposer

subsidence [səbˈsaɪdəns, ˈsʌbsɪdəns] **N** *(of house, land)* affaissement *m*; *(of wall, foundations)* tassement *m*; **road liable to s.** *(sign)* ≃ chaussée déformée

subsidiarity [sʌbˌsɪdɪˈærɪtɪ] **N** subsidiarité *f*

subsidiary [səbˈsɪdjərɪ] *(pl* **subsidiaries***)* **ADJ** *(supplementary)* supplémentaire, complémentaire; *(secondary ► question, reason)* subsidiaire; *(► idea, action)* accessoire

N *Com* filiale *f*

►► ***subsidiary account*** sous-compte *m*; ***subsidiary company*** filiale *f*

subsidize, -ise [ˈsʌbsɪdaɪz] **VT** subventionner; **to be subsidized by the State** recevoir une subvention de *ou* être subventionné par l'État; **why should I carry on subsidizing you?** je ne vois pas pourquoi je continuerais à te donner de l'argent!

subsidy [ˈsʌbsɪdɪ] *(pl* **subsidies***)* **N** subvention *f*; **government s.** subvention *f* de l'État; **export subsidies** primes *fpl* à l'exportation

subsist [səbˈsɪst] **VI 1** *(remain in existence)* subsister; **custom that still subsists** coutume qui existe *ou* subsiste encore (de nos jours) **2** *(stay alive)* **to s. on sth** vivre de qch; **they have just enough to s. on** ils ont tout juste de quoi subsister

subsistence [səbˈsɪstəns] **N** subsistance *f*, existence *f*; **means of s.** moyens *mpl* d'existence

COMP *(wage)* à peine suffisant pour vivre; *(economy)* de subsistance; **to live at s. level** avoir tout juste de quoi vivre

►► *Br* ***subsistence allowance*** acompte *m* *(perçu avant l'engagement définitif)*; *(expenses)* frais *mpl* (de subsistance); *Agr* ***subsistence crop*** culture *f* de subsistance; ***subsistence farming*** agriculture *f* de subsistance

subsoil [ˈsʌbsɔɪl] **N** *Geol* sous-sol *m*

subsonic [ˌsʌbˈsɒnɪk] **ADJ** subsonique

subspecies [ˈsʌbˌspiːʃiːz] *(pl* **inv***)* **N** sous-espèce *f*

substance [ˈsʌbstəns] **N 1** *(matter)* substance *f*; **tobacco contains harmful substances** le tabac contient des substances nocives; **illegal substances** stupéfiants *mpl*

2 *(solidity)* solidité *f*; **it seemed to have as little s. as a ghost** cela semblait aussi immatériel qu'un fantôme

3 *(essential part, gist)* essentiel *m*, substance *f*; *(basis)* fond *m*; **that's the s. of what he said** voilà en substance ce qu'il a dit; **the s. of the charges** l'essentiel *m* de l'inculpation; **the s. of the case** le fond de l'affaire; **I agree in s.** je suis d'accord sur le fond

4 *(significance, weight)* étoffe *f*, poids *m*; **these developments add s. to our hypothesis** ces développements donnent davantage de poids à notre hypothèse; **their claim lacks s.** leur revendication est sans fondement *ou* n'est pas fondée

5 *(wealth)* richesses *fpl*; *(power)* pouvoir *m*; *(influence)* influence *f*; **a woman of s.** *(rich)* une femme riche *ou* aisée; *(powerful)* une femme puissante; *(influential)* une femme influente

• **in substance ADV** *(generally)* en gros, en substance; *(basically)* à la base, au fond; *(in brief)* en substance, en somme

►► ***substance abuse*** abus *m* de stupéfiants

substandard [ˌsʌbˈstændəd] **ADJ 1** *(work, output)* médiocre, en dessous des niveaux requis; *(meal, merchandise)* de qualité inférieure; **they live in s. housing** ils habitent des logements insalubres **2** *Ling* non conforme à la norme

substantial [səbˈstænʃəl] **ADJ 1** *(considerable)* considérable, important; *Law (damages)* élevé; **for a s. sum** pour une somme importante; **s. differences remain** il reste des divergences importantes; **a s. number of teachers were there** il y avait de nombreux professeurs

2 *(nourishing ► food)* nourrissant; *(► meal)* solide, copieux, substantiel

3 *(convincing ► argument, evidence)* solide, convaincant

4 *(real, tangible)* réel, substantiel; *Phil* substantiel

5 *(house ► large)* grand; *(► solidly built)* solide

6 *(rich)* riche, aisé; *(powerful)* puissant; *(influential)* influent; *(well-established)* solide, bien établi; **a s. company** une société solidement implantée

> Attention: ne pas confondre avec **substantive.**

substantially [səbˈstænʃəlɪ] **ADV 1** *(considerably)* considérablement; **taxes have been cut s.** les impôts ont été considérablement réduits **2** *(generally)* en gros, en grande partie; *(fundamentally)* fondamentalement, au fond; **it is s. correct** c'est en grande partie correct; **the text is s. unaltered** le texte est dans l'ensemble *ou* pour l'essentiel resté inchangé **3** *(solidly)* solidement; **s. built** solide

substantiate [səbˈstænʃɪeɪt] **VT** confirmer, apporter *ou* fournir des preuves à l'appui de; **he had no evidence to s. his accusation** il n'avait aucune preuve pour appuyer son accusation

substantiation [səbˌstænʃɪˈeɪʃən] **N** *(UNCOUNT) (proof)* preuve *f*; *(reason)* bien-fondé *m*, justification *f*; **do you have any s. for your allegations?** pouvez-vous fournir des preuves de ce que vous avancez?

substantival [ˌsʌbstənˈtaɪvəl] **ADJ** *Gram* substantif

substantive ADJ [sʌbˈstæntɪv] **1** *(real, important)* substantiel; *(permanent ► rank)* permanent; *(independent ► means, resources)* indépendant **2** *Gram* nominal

N [ˈsʌbstəntɪv] *Gram* substantif *m*

►► *Law* ***substantive law*** droit *m* positif

> Attention: ne pas confondre avec **substantial.**

substantively [səbˈstæntɪvlɪ] **ADV** *(considerably)* substantiellement, considérablement

substation [ˈsʌbˌsteɪʃən] **N** sous-station *f*

substitute [ˈsʌbstɪtjuːt] **N 1** *(person)* remplaçant(e) *m,f*, suppléant(e) *m,f*; *Sport* remplaçant(e) *m,f* **2** *(thing ► gen)* produit *m* de remplacement *ou* de substitution; *(► foodstuff, drug)* succédané *m*; **we'll have to find a s. for it** il faut que nous trouvions quelque chose pour le remplacer; **use a low-fat s. instead of butter** utilisez un produit à faible teneur en matière grasse à la place du beurre; **coffee s.** ersatz *m ou* succédané *m* de café; **sugar s.** édulcorant *m* de synthèse; **there's no s. for real coffee** rien ne vaut le vrai café; **tapes are a poor s. for live music** les cassettes ne valent pas la musique live **3** *Gram* terme *m* suppléant

ADJ remplaçant; **a s. goalkeeper** un gardien de but remplaçant; **it'll do as a s. cork** ça fera offi[ce] de bouchon

VT *(gen)* substituer, remplacer; *Sport* rempl[a]cer; **to s. sth for sth** substituer qch à qch; **marg[ar]ine may be substituted for butter** on pe[ut] remplacer le beurre par de la margarine, [on] peut utiliser de la margarine au lieu du beurr[e]

VI to s. for sb/sth remplacer qn/qch

►► *Am, Austr & Ir* ***substitute teacher*** suppléant(e) *m,f*

substitution [ˌsʌbstɪˈtjuːʃən] **N** *(gen)* remplac[e]ment *m*, substitution *f*; *Sport* remplacement [*m*]; **the s. of man-made fibres for cotton** le fait d'av[oir] remplacé le coton par des fibres synthétique[s]

substratum [ˌsʌbˈstrɑːtəm] *(pl* **substrata** [-tə]*)* [**N 1**] *(infrastructure, base)* fond *m* **2** *Geol (underlyi[ng] formation)* substratum *m*; *(subsoil)* sous-sol *m*; *Ling* substrat *m*

substring [ˈsʌbstrɪŋ] **N** *Comput* sous-chaîne *f*

substructure [ˈsʌbˌstrʌktʃə(r)] **N** *Constr* infra[s]tructure *f*; **various substructures make up the org[a]nization** l'organisation se compose de plusieu[rs] services distincts

subsume [səbˈsjuːm] **VT** subsumer

subsystem [ˈsʌbˌsɪstəm] **N** sous-système *m*

subtenancy [ˌsʌbˈtenənsɪ] *(pl* **subtenancies***)* [**N**] sous-location *f*

subtenant [ˌsʌbˈtenənt] **N** sous-locataire *mf*

subtend [səbˈtend] **VT** sous-tendre

subterfuge [ˈsʌbtəfjuːdʒ] **N** subterfuge *m*

subterranean [ˌsʌbtəˈreɪnɪən] **ADJ** souterrain; **forces were at work** des forces secrètes étaien[t à] l'œuvre

subtext [ˈsʌbˌtekst] **N** *(of book, film, situatio[n])* message *m* sous-jacent; **if you pay attention the s. of the minister's speech you will see that** si vous lisez le discours du ministre entre les [li]gnes, vous verrez que…

subtitle [ˈsʌbˌtaɪtəl] *Cin, Literature & Press* [**N**] sous-titre *m*; **a film with English subtitles** un fi[lm] sous-titré en anglais

VT sous-titrer

subtitled [ˈsʌbˌtaɪtəld] **ADJ** sous-titré, avec sou[s-]titrage

subtitler [ˈsʌbˌtaɪtələ(r)] **N** *Cin* sous-titreur(eus[e]) *m,f*

subtitling [ˈsʌbˌtaɪtəlɪŋ] **N** sous-titrage *m*

subtle [ˈsʌtəl] **ADJ** subtil; **s. distinction** distincti[on] *f* ténue *ou* subtile; **s. irony** fine ironie *f*, ironi[e] subtile; **there's a very s. difference between the[m]** il y a une très légère différence entre eux; **shades of green and blue** des nuances subtil[es] de vert et de bleu; **a s. form of propaganda/bla[ck]mail** une forme insidieuse de propagande/[de] chantage; **you're not very s., are you?** la subtili[té] n'est vraiment pas ton fort!

subtlety [ˈsʌtəltɪ] *(pl* **subtleties***)* **N 1** *(subtle natu[re] ► of style, mind, film, argument, flavour)* subtilit[é] **2** *(detail, distinction)* subtilité *f*

subtly [ˈsʌtlɪ] **ADV** subtilement; **the atmospher[e in] his expression had s. altered** l'atmosphère/[son] expression avait changé insensiblement; **s. d[if]ferent** légèrement différent

subtonic [ˌsʌbˈtɒnɪk] **N** sous-tonique *f*

subtotal [ˈsʌbˌtəʊtəl] **N** total *m* partiel

subtract [səbˈtrækt] **VT** soustraire, retrancher; **52 from 110** ôtez *ou* retranchez *ou* soustrayez [52] de 110

subtraction [səbˈtrækʃən] **N** soustraction *f*

subtropical [ˌsʌbˈtrɒpɪkəl] **ADJ** subtropical

subtype [ˈsʌbtaɪp] **N** sous-classe *f*

suburb [ˈsʌbɜːb] **N** banlieue *f*, *Old-fashioned* fa[u]bourg *m*; **the London s. of Eltham** Eltham, dans [la] banlieue de Londres; **the suburbs stretch f[or] miles** la banlieue s'étend sur des kilomètres; **the suburbs** en banlieue; **the outer suburbs** [la] grande banlieue; **the inner suburbs** la banlie[ue] proche

suburban [səˈbɜːbən] **ADJ 1** *(house, street, ra[il]way, dweller)* de banlieue; *(population, growt[h])* de banlieue, suburbain **2** *Pej (mentality, outlo[ok])* (de) petit-bourgeois

suburbanite [səˈbɜːbənaɪt] **N** banlieusard(e) *m,f*

suburbia [sə'bɜːbɪə] N la banlieue; **in s.** en banlieue

subvention [səb'venʃən] N subvention *f*

subversion [səb'vɜːʃən] N subversion *f*

subversive [səb'vɜːsɪv] ADJ subversif

N élément *m* subversif; **a group of subversives** un groupe subversif

subvert [səb'vɜːt] VT **1** *(undermine ▸ society, state, institution)* subvertir **2** *(corrupt ▸ individual)* corrompre

subway ['sʌbweɪ] N **1** *Br (pedestrian underpass)* passage *m* souterrain **2** *Am (railway)* métro *m*; **it's quicker by s.** c'est plus rapide en métro

subwoofer [ˌsʌb'wʊfə(r)] N caisson *m* de graves, subwoofer *m*

sub-zero ADJ au-dessous de zéro

succeed [sək'siːd] VI **1** *(do well)* réussir, avoir du succès; **we all want to s. in life** nous voulons tous réussir dans la vie; **to s. in business/in publishing** réussir dans les affaires/l'édition; **he succeeds in everything he does** il réussit tout ce qu'il entreprend, tout lui réussit; *Prov* **nothing succeeds like success** = un succès en entraîne un autre

2 *(manage successfully)* réussir; **to s. in doing sth** réussir *ou* parvenir *ou* arriver à faire qch; **he succeeded only in confusing things further** il n'a réussi qu'à compliquer davantage les choses; *Prov* **if at first you don't s., try again** = si vous ne réussissez pas du premier coup, recommencez

3 *(work out)* réussir; **the first attack did not s.** la première offensive a échoué

4 *(follow on)* succéder; **to s. to the throne** monter sur le trône

VT *(of person)* succéder à, prendre la suite de; *(of event, thing)* succéder à, suivre; **I succeeded him as editor** je lui ai succédé au poste de rédacteur; **as month succeeded month** au fur et à mesure que les mois passaient

succeeding [sək'siːdɪŋ] ADJ **1** *(subsequent)* suivant, qui suit; **we met several times during the s. weeks** nous nous sommes vus plusieurs fois pendant les semaines qui ont suivi; **each s. year** chaque année qui passe **2** *(future)* futur, à venir; **s. generations will right these wrongs** les générations à venir redresseront ces torts

success [sək'ses] N réussite *f*, succès *m*; **her s. in the elections** sa victoire aux élections; **his s. in the exam** son succès à l'examen; **to meet with** *or* **to achieve s.** réussir; **I wish you every s.** je vous souhaite beaucoup de succès; **I had no s. in trying to persuade them** je n'ai pas réussi à les convaincre; **I tried to convince them, but without s.** j'ai essayé de les convaincre, mais sans succès; **to make a s. of sth** mener qch à bien; **she made a great s. of her career** elle a bien réussi dans son métier; **I haven't had much s. in finding work** mes recherches pour un emploi n'ont pas donné grand-chose; **to be a s.** *(go well, work out well etc)* réussir, être réussi, être un succès; *(be popular ▸ movie, book etc)* être un succès; *(▸ party, cake)* être une réussite, être réussi; **their record was a great s.** leur disque a eu un succès fou; **you were a great s. at the party** tu as eu beaucoup de succès à la fête

COMP *(rate)* de réussite, de succès

▸▸ *Fin & Law* ***success fee*** rémunération *f* au résultat; ***success story*** réussite *f*

successful [sək'sesfʊl] ADJ **1** *(resulting in success ▸ attempt, effort, plan)* qui réussit; *(▸ negotiations)* fructueux; *(▸ outcome)* heureux; *(▸ performance, mission, partnership)* réussi; **were you s.?** avez-vous réussi?; **s. candidates will be notified officially** les candidats reçus en seront informés par voie officielle; **she was not s. in her application for the post** sa candidature à ce poste n'a pas été retenue; **I was s. in convincing them** j'ai réussi *ou* je suis arrivé *ou* je suis parvenu à les convaincre; **she brought the project to a s. conclusion** elle a mené le projet à bien **2** *(thriving ▸ singer, record, author, book, play)* à succès; *(▸ businessman)* qui a réussi; *(▸ life, career)* réussi; **their first record was very s.** leur premier disque a eu un succès fou; **she's a s. businesswoman** elle a réussi dans les affaires; **she's s. in everything she does** tout lui réussit, elle réussit tout ce qu'elle entreprend

successfully [sək'sesfʊlɪ] ADV avec succès; **to do sth s.** réussir à faire qch; **we managed to tackle the problem s.** nous avons trouvé une solution satisfaisante au problème; **students who s. complete the course are awarded a certificate** les étudiants qui parviennent au terme du stage reçoivent un certificat

succession [sək'seʃən] N **1** *(series)* succession *f*, suite *f*; **a s. of visitors** une succession *ou* une suite de visiteurs; **we won three years in s.** nous avons gagné trois ans de suite; **for five years in s.** pendant cinq années consécutives *ou* cinq ans de suite; **she made three phone calls in s.** elle a passé trois coups de fil de suite; **the fireworks went off in quick** *or* **rapid s.** les feux d'artifice sont partis les uns après les autres; **he got several promotions in rapid s.** il a eu plusieurs promotions coup sur coup; **they fired questions at him in rapid s.** ils l'ont soumis à un feu roulant de questions; **a s. of gains and losses** une succession de gains et de pertes **2** *(ascension to power)* succession *f*; **his s. to the post** sa succession au poste; **she's first in s. (to the throne)** elle occupe la première place dans l'ordre de succession (au trône); **at the time of his s. to the throne** au moment de son accession au trône **3** *Law (descendants)* descendance *f*; *(heirs)* héritiers *mpl*

successive [sək'sesɪv] ADJ *(attempts, generations)* successif; *(days, years)* consécutif

successively [sək'sesɪvlɪ] ADV *(in turn)* successivement, tour à tour, l'un/l'une après l'autre

successor [sək'sesə(r)] N **1** *(replacement)* successeur *m*; **I'm her s. to the position** je suis son successeur à ce poste; **I'm to be his s.** c'est moi qui dois lui succéder; **she's the s. to the throne** c'est l'héritière de la couronne **2** *(heir)* héritier(ère) *m,f*

succinct [sək'sɪŋkt] ADJ succinct, concis

succinctly [sək'sɪŋktlɪ] ADV succinctement, avec concision

succinctness [sək'sɪŋktnɪs] N concision *f*

succour, *Am* **succor** ['sʌkə(r)] N secours *m*, aide *f*

VT secourir, aider

succulence ['sʌkjʊləns] N succulence *f*

succulent ['sʌkjʊlənt] ADJ **1** *(tasty)* succulent **2** *Bot* succulent

N plante *f* grasse

succumb [sə'kʌm] VI **1** *(yield)* succomber, céder; **don't s. to temptation!** ne succombez pas à la tentation!; **he succumbed to her charm** il a succombé à son charme **2** *(die)* succomber, mourir; **he succumbed to cancer** il est mort d'un cancer; **he finally succumbed** il a finalement succombé

SUCH [sʌtʃ] ADJ & PREDET **1** *(of the same specified kind)* tel, pareil; **s. a song** une telle chanson, une chanson pareille *ou* de ce genre; **s. songs** de telles chansons, des chansons pareilles *ou* de ce genre; **in s. weather** par un temps pareil; **in s. cases** en pareils cas; **how can you tell s. lies?** comment peux-tu raconter de tels mensonges *ou* des mensonges pareils?; **no s. place exists** un tel endroit n'existe pas; **on s. an occasion** pour l'occasion; **we had s. a case last year** nous avons eu un cas semblable l'année dernière; **have you ever heard s. a thing?** avez-vous jamais entendu une chose pareille?; **you wouldn't have s. a thing as a corkscrew, would you?** vous n'auriez pas un tire-bouchon, par hasard?; **s. a thing is unheard-of** ce genre de chose est sans précédent; **I said no s. thing!** je n'ai rien dit de tel *ou* de la sorte!; **you'll do no s. thing!** il n'en est pas question!; **there is no s. thing** cela n'existe pas; **there is no s. thing as magic** la magie n'existe pas; **they called her Jane or some s. thing** ils l'ont baptisée Jane ou quelque chose de ce genre *ou* dans ce style; **he said he didn't have enough money or some s. excuse** son excuse était qu'il n'avait pas assez d'argent, ou quelque chose de ce genre *ou* dans ce style; **we will take s. steps as are considered necessary** nous prendrons toutes les mesures nécessaires; **I'm not s. a fool as to believe him!** je ne suis pas assez bête pour le croire!; **until s. time as is convenient to me** jusqu'à ce que cela me convienne; **s. money as we have** le peu d'argent que nous avons; **their timetable is s. that we never see them** leur emploi du temps est tel que nous ne les voyons jamais; **she works in s. a way that we can't keep up** elle travaille de telle façon que nous ne pouvons pas suivre; **she arranges things in s. a way that she is free on Saturdays** elle s'arrange de manière à être libre le samedi

2 *(as intensifier)* tel; **my accounts are in s. a mess!** mes comptes sont dans un de ces états!; **he is s. a liar** il est tellement menteur, c'est un tel menteur; **she has s. courage!** elle a un de ces courages!; **it's s. a pity you can't come!** c'est tellement dommage que vous ne puissiez pas venir!; **you gave me s. a scare!** tu m'as fait une de ces peurs!; **s. tall buildings** des immeubles aussi hauts; **s. a handsome man** un si bel homme; **she has s. a nice voice!** elle a une si jolie voix!; **we had s. a good time** on s'est tellement amusés; **it's been s. a long time since I've seen her** ça fait si longtemps que je ne l'ai pas vue; **I didn't realize it was s. a long way** je ne me rendais pas compte que c'était si loin; **her grief was s. that we feared for her sanity** son chagrin était tel que nous craignions pour sa santé mentale; **he was in s. pain that he fainted** il souffrait tellement qu'il s'est évanoui

PRON **s. is the power of the media** voilà ce que peuvent faire les médias; **s. was the result** voilà quel était le résultat; **s. is not my intention** ce n'est pas là mon intention; **s. is life!** c'est la vie!

• **and such** ADV et d'autres choses de ce genre *ou* de la sorte; **he enjoys cakes, ice cream and s.** il mange avec plaisir des gâteaux, des glaces et autres choses de ce genre; **detective stories, thrillers and s.** des policiers, des romans à suspense et d'autres livres de ce genre *ou* de la sorte

• **as such** ADV *(strictly speaking)* en soi; *(in that capacity)* en tant que tel, à ce titre; **she doesn't get a salary as s.** elle n'a pas de véritable salaire *ou* pas de salaire à proprement parler; **the text as s. is fine but…** le texte en soi est bien mais…; **have they offered you more money? – well, not as s.** vous ont-ils proposé plus d'argent? – pas véritablement; **they are not opposed to privatization as s.** ils ne sont pas opposés à la privatisation en soi *ou* à proprement parler; **she's an adult and as s. she has rights** elle est majeure et en tant que telle elle a des droits

• **such and such** PREDET tel; **on s. and s. a date** à telle date; **on s. and s. a day in s. and s. a place** tel jour à tel endroit

• **such as** PREP tel que, comme; **a country s. as Germany** un pays tel que *ou* comme l'Allemagne; **films s. as Fellini's** les films tels que ceux de Fellini; **books s. as these** *or* **s. books as these are always useful** les livres de ce genre sont toujours utiles; **I can think of lots of reasons – s. as?** je vois beaucoup de raisons – comme quoi par exemple?

• **such as it is** ADV **and this is my study, s. as it is** et voici ce que j'appelle mon bureau; **I'll give you my opinion, s. as it is** je vais vous donner mon avis, prenez-le pour ce qu'il vaut; **you're welcome to use my notes, s. as they are** je te prêterai mes notes avec plaisir, elles valent ce qu'elles valent

suchlike ['sʌtʃlaɪk] *Fam* ADJ semblable, pareil; **and other s. dishes** et d'autres plats du même genre

PRON **frogs, toads and s.** les grenouilles, les crapauds et autres animaux (du même genre)

suck [sʌk] VT **1** *(with mouth)* sucer; *(drink, sweets)* sucer, suçoter; *(mother's milk)* téter; *(pipe)* tirer sur; *(not smoking)* sucer; **to s. one's thumb** sucer son pouce; **he sucked the end of his pencil thoughtfully** il suçait pensivement le bout de son crayon; **she was sucking orange juice through a straw** elle sirotait du jus d'orange avec une paille; **he was sucking a sweet** il suçait un bonbon; **to s. poison out of a wound** extraire le poison d'une blessure en la suçant; **to s. sb dry** prendre jusqu'à son dernier sou à qn **2** *(pull)* aspirer; **the dust is sucked into the bag** la poussière est aspirée dans le sac; **the whirlpool sucked him to the bottom** le tourbillon l'a entraîné au fond; *Fig* **we found ourselves sucked into an argument** nous nous sommes trouvés entraînés dans une dispute **3** *Am Fam* **to s. face** se rouler des pelles *ou* des patins

VI **1** *(with mouth)* **to s. at** *or* **on sth** sucer *ou* suçoter qch; **the child was sucking at her breast** l'enfant têtait son sein **2** *Fam (be bad)* craindre, être nul *ou* merdique; **this town sucks!** cette ville est merdique!; **this bar/movie sucks** ce bar/film est vraiment nul; **this sucks, let's do something else** c'est nul, si on faisait autre chose?; **I've got to work all weekend – that sucks!** il faut que je travaille tout le week-end – ça craint! **3** *Fam Old-fashioned (idiom)* **(ya boo) sucks to you!** va te faire voir!

N 1 *(act of sucking ▸ gen)* **to have a s. at sth** sucer *ou* suçoter qch; **he took a long s. on his cigar** il tira longuement sur son cigare **2** *(act of sucking ▸ at breast)* tétée *f*; **to give s.** donner le sein, allaiter **3** *(force)* aspiration *f*

▸ **suck down** **VT SEP** *(of sea, quicksand, whirlpool)* engloutir

▸ **suck in** **VT SEP** *(with mouth)* sucer; *(draw in by vacuum)* aspirer; *(of air pump)* aspirer; *(in vortex)* engloutir; *(cheeks)* creuser; *(knowledge)* absorber; **to get sucked in (to sth)** *(to conspiracy, plot etc)* se laisser entraîner (dans qch)

▸ **suck off** **VT SEP** *Vulg* **to s. sb off** sucer qn, tailler une pipe à qn

▸ **suck up** **VT SEP** *(of person)* aspirer, sucer; *(of vacuum cleaner, pump)* aspirer; *(of porous surface)* absorber

VI *Fam* **to s. up to sb** faire de la lèche à qn, cirer les pompes à qn

sucker ['sʌkə(r)] **N 1** *Fam (dupe)* pigeon *m*, gogo *m*; **he's a real s.** c'est un vrai pigeon; **I'm a s. for chocolate** je ne sais pas résister au chocolat, je raffole du chocolat; *Am* **you've been played for a s.** vous vous êtes fait rouler *ou* pigeonner; **OK, s., you asked for it** OK, mec, tu l'auras voulu

2 *Br (suction cup or pad)* ventouse *f*; **there are rubber suckers on the end of the arrows** il y a des ventouses au bout des flèches

3 *Zool (of insect)* suçoir *m*; *(of octopus, leech)* ventouse *f*

4 *Bot* drageon *m*

5 *Am (lollipop)* sucette *f*

6 *Am Fam (object)* truc *m*, machin *m*, bitoniau *m*; **what's this s. for?** à quoi ça sert, ce truc?

VT 1 *Hort* enlever les drageons de **2** *Am Fam (dupe)* refaire, pigeonner; **she suckered him out of $300** elle l'a refait de 300 dollars

VI *Bot (plant)* drageonner

sucking ['sʌkɪŋ] **N** *(of baby)* succion *f*; *(of pump)* aspiration *f*

▸▸ ***sucking pig*** cochon *m* de lait

suckle ['sʌkəl] **VT 1** *(child)* allaiter, donner le sein à; *(animal)* allaiter **2** *Fig (raise)* élever

VI téter

suckling ['sʌklɪŋ] **N 1** *(child)* nourrisson *m*, enfant *m* encore au sein; *(animal)* animal *m* qui tète **2** *(act)* allaitement *m*

▸▸ ***suckling pig*** cochon *m* de lait

sucrose ['su:krəʊz] **N** saccharose *m*

suction ['sʌkʃən] **N** succion *f*, aspiration *f*; **it adheres by s.** ça fait ventouse

▸▸ ***suction cup, suction pad*** ventouse *f*; ***suction pump*** pompe *f* aspirante; ***suction valve*** clapet *m ou* soupape *f* d'aspiration

Sudan [su:'dɑ:n] **N (the) S.** Soudan *m*

Sudanese [ˌsu:də'ni:z] *(pl inv)* **N** Soudanais(e) *m*, *f*

ADJ soudanais

sudden ['sʌdən] **ADJ** *(gen)* soudain, subit; *(movement)* brusque; **there was a s. bend in the road** soudain il y a eu un virage; **she had a s. change of heart** elle a soudainement *ou* subitement changé d'avis; **this is all very s.!** c'est plutôt inattendu!

• **all of a sudden** **ADV** soudain, subitement, tout d'un coup; **I feel very cold all of a s.** j'ai très froid tout d'un coup

▸▸ ***sudden death*** mort *f* subite; *(games) & Sport* = jeu pour partager les ex aequo (où le premier point perdu, le premier but concédé etc, entraîne l'élimination immédiate); ***sudden infant death syndrome*** mort *f* subite du nourrisson

suddenly ['sʌdənlɪ] **ADV** soudainement, subitement; **he died s. in the night** il est mort subitement dans la nuit; **s. it started to rain** tout à coup il s'est mis à pleuvoir

suddenness ['sʌdənnɪs] **N** soudaineté *f*, caractère *m* subit *ou* imprévu; **the s. of the attack surprised us** la soudaineté de l'attaque nous a surpris

sudoku [su'dəʊku:] **N** sudoku *m*

suds [sʌdz] **NPL 1** *(foam)* mousse *f*; *(soapy water)* eau *f* savonneuse **2** *Am Fam (beer)* bière ▫*f*

sue [su:] **VT** *Law* poursuivre en justice, intenter un procès à; **to s. sb for** *or* **over sth** poursuivre qn en justice pour qch; **he sued the factory for damages** il a poursuivi l'usine pour obtenir des dommages et intérêts; **to be sued for damages/libel** être poursuivi en dommages-intérêts/en diffamation; **she's suing him for divorce** elle a entamé une procédure de divorce

VI 1 *Law* intenter un procès, engager des poursuites; **she threatened to s. for libel** elle a menacé d'intenter un procès en diffamation; **he's suing for divorce** il a entamé une procédure de divorce **2** *Formal (solicit)* **to s. for** solliciter; *Pol* **to s. for peace** demander la paix

suede [sweɪd] **N** daim *m*, *Spec* suède *m*

COMP *(jacket, purse, shoes)* en *ou* de daim; *(leather)* suédé

suet ['su:ɪt] **N** graisse *f* de rognon

▸▸ ***suet pudding*** = sorte de pudding sucré ou salé à base de farine et de graisse de bœuf

Suez ['su:ɪz] **N** Suez

▸▸ ***the Suez Canal*** le canal de Suez; ***the Suez crisis*** l'affaire *f* du canal de Suez

suffer ['sʌfə(r)] **VI 1** *(feel pain)* souffrir; **to s. in silence** souffrir en silence; **he drank too much and suffered for it next day** il a trop bu et, le lendemain, il a payé ses excès; *Fig* **I'll make you s. for this!** tu vas me payer ça!, je te revaudrai ça!

2 *(be ill, afflicted)* **to s. from** *(serious disease)* souffrir de; *(cold, headache)* avoir; **to s. from rheumatism** souffrir de *ou* avoir des rhumatismes; **to s. from diabetes** être diabétique; **he's still suffering from the effects of the anaesthetic** il ne s'est pas encore tout à fait remis des suites de l'anesthésie; **to s. from a speech defect** avoir un défaut de prononciation; **they're still suffering from shock** ils sont encore sous le choc; **she suffers from an inferiority complex** elle fait un complexe d'infériorité

3 *(be affected)* souffrir; **it's the children who s. in a marriage break-up** ce sont les enfants qui souffrent lors d'une séparation; **there was a fall in investment and the company's profits suffered** les investissements ont baissé et les bénéfices s'en sont ressenti; **the low-paid will be the first to s.** les petits salaires seront les premiers touchés; **the schools s. from a lack of funding** les établissements scolaires manquent de crédits; **she became severely depressed and her work began to s.** elle a sombré dans la dépression et son travail a commencé à s'en ressentir; **her health is suffering under all this stress** sa santé se ressent de tout ce stress

VT 1 *(experience ▸ thirst)* souffrir de; *(▸ hardship)* souffrir, subir; *(▸ loss, indignity, consequence)* subir; **she suffered a lot of pain** elle a beaucoup souffert; *Fam* **I suffered agonies!** j'ai souffert le martyre!; **our scheme has suffered a serious setback** notre projet a subi *ou* essuyé un grave revers; **you'll have to s. the consequences** vous devrez en subir les conséquences; **his popularity suffered a decline** sa cote de popularité a baissé

2 *(stand, put up with)* tolérer, supporter; **I won't s. him another minute** je ne le supporterai pas une minute de plus; **he doesn't s. fools gladly** il ne supporte pas les imbéciles

3 *Literary (allow)* permettre, *Literary* souffrir; **to s. sb to do sth** souffrir que qn fasse qch; *Bible* **s. the little children to come unto me** laissez venir à moi les petits enfants

sufferance ['sʌfərəns] **N** *(tolerance)* tolérance *f*; **on s.** par tolérance; **remember you are only here on s.** n'oubliez pas que votre présence ici n'est que tolérée *ou* est tout juste tolérée

sufferer ['sʌfərə(r)] **N** malade *mf*, victime *f*; **sufferers from heart disease** les personnes *fpl* cardiaques; **polio s.** polio *mf*; **good news for arthritis sufferers** une bonne nouvelle pour les personnes sujettes à l'arthrite *ou* qui souffrent d'arthrite

suffering ['sʌfərɪŋ] **N** souffrance *f*, souffranc *fpl*; **war causes great s.** la guerre est cause d nombreuses souffrances

ADJ souffrant, qui souffre

suffice [sə'faɪs] **VI** *Formal* suffire, être suffisar **will some bread and soup s.?** du pain et de soupe seront-ils suffisants?; **s. it to say (tha she's overjoyed** inutile de dire qu'elle est ravie

VT suffire à, satisfaire; **empty promises will not him** il ne se contentera pas de vaines promess

sufficiency [sə'fɪʃənsɪ] *(pl* **sufficiencies***)* **N** qua tité *f* suffisante; **the country already had a s. of c** le pays avait déjà suffisamment de pétrole *ou c* pétrole en quantité suffisante

sufficient [sə'fɪʃənt] **ADJ 1** *(gen)* suffisant; **there s. food for everyone** il y a assez *ou* suffisamme à manger pour tout le monde; **have you had s. eat?** avez-vous mangé à votre faim?; **one lig will be s.** une lampe suffira; **three will be quite for our needs** trois nous suffiront amplement; **I me know in s. time so that I can...** prévenez-m suffisamment à l'avance pour que je puisse... **we don't have s. evidence to convict them** nou ne disposons pas d'assez de preuves pour l inculper **2** *Phil* suffisant; **a s. condition** une co dition suffisante

sufficiently [sə'fɪʃəntlɪ] **ADV** suffisamment, a sez; **it's s. strong to withstand your weight** c'e assez solide pour supporter votre poids; **a large quantity** une quantité suffisante

suffix ['sʌfɪks] **N** suffixe *m*

VT suffixer

suffocate ['sʌfəkeɪt] **VI 1** *(die)* s'étouffer, s'a phyxier **2** *(be hot, lack fresh air)* suffoquer, étou fer; **open the window, I'm suffocating!** ouvre fenêtre, j'étouffe! **3** *Fig (with anger, emotion et* s'étouffer, suffoquer

VT 1 *(kill)* suffoquer, étouffer, asphyxier **2** *F (repress, inhibit)* étouffer, suffoquer

suffocating ['sʌfəkeɪtɪŋ] **ADJ 1** *(heat, room)* su focant, étouffant; *(smoke, fumes)* asphyxian suffocant; **it's s. (in) here** on étouffe ici **2** *F* étouffant

suffocation [ˌsʌfə'keɪʃən] **N** suffocation étouffement *m*, asphyxie *f*; **to die from s.** mou asphyxié

suffragan ['sʌfrəgən] **N s. (bishop)** (évêque *n* suffragant *m*

ADJ suffragant

suffrage ['sʌfrɪdʒ] **N 1** *(right to vote)* droit *m* c suffrage *ou* de vote; **universal s.** suffrage *m* ur versel; **women's s.** le droit de vote pour les fer mes **2** *Formal (vote)* suffrage *m*, vote *m*

suffragette [ˌsʌfrə'dʒet] **N** suffragette *f*

suffuse [sə'fju:z] **VT** *(usu passive)* se répand sur, baigner; **suffused with light** inondé de l mière; **the sky was suffused with red** le ciel éta tout empourpré

sugar ['ʃʊgə(r)] **N 1** *(gen) & Chem* sucre *m*; **ho many sugars?** combien de sucres?; **I don't take** je ne prends pas de sucre **2** *Fam (term of addres* chéri(e) *m,f* **3** *Fam* **she's found herself a s. dadc** elle s'est trouvé un vieux friqué qui l'entretien **I've no intention of being your s. daddy** je n'ai pa l'intention de t'entretenir▫

VT sucrer; *Fig* **to s. the pill (for sb)** dorer la pilu (à qn); **to s. one's legs** *(remove unwanted hair fron* s'épiler les jambes au sucre

EXCLAM *Fam* miel!, punaise!

▸▸ ***sugar almond*** dragée *f*; *Br* ***sugar basin*** sucri *m*; ***sugar beet*** betterave *f* sucrière *ou* à sucr ***sugar bowl*** sucrier *m*; ***sugar candy*** sucre *m* canc ***sugar cane*** canne *f* à sucre; ***sugar cube*** morcea *m* de sucre; ***sugar lump*** morceau *m* de sucr ***sugar maple*** érable *m* à sucre; ***sugar pea*** mang tout *m inv*; ***sugar shaker*** saupoudreuse *f* (à s cre); *Br* ***sugar soap*** décapant *m* alcalin po peintures; *Culin* ***sugar syrup*** sirop *m* de sucr ***sugar tongs*** pince *f* à sucre

sugar-coat **VT** enrober de sucre; *Fig (unplea ant measure)* faire passer; *(bad news)* présent de façon diplomatique

sugar-coated [-'kəʊtɪd] **ADJ** enrobé de sucre

▸▸ ***sugar-coated almonds*** dragées *fpl*; ***sugar-co ted pill*** comprimé *m* dragéifié

sugar-free **ADJ** sans sucre

sugaring ['ʃʊgərɪŋ] N épilation *f* au sucre

sugarloaf ['ʃʊgələʊf] (*pl* **sugarloaves** [-ləʊvz]) N pain *m* de sucre
▸▸ ***Sugarloaf Mountain*** le Pain de Sucre

sugarplum ['ʃʊgəplʌm] N *(candied plum)* prune *f* confite; *(boiled sweet)* bonbon *m*

sugary ['ʃʊgərɪ] ADJ **1** *(drink, food)* (très) sucré; *(taste)* sucré **2** *(manner, tone)* mielleux, doucereux; **s. sentimentality** mièvrerie *f*

suggest [sə'dʒest] VT **1** *(propose, put forward)* suggérer, proposer; **I s. (that) we do nothing for the moment** je suggère *ou* je propose que nous ne fassions rien pour l'instant; **he suggested that the meeting be held next Tuesday** il a proposé de fixer la réunion à mardi prochain; **a solution suggested itself to me** une solution m'est venue à l'esprit; **this, I s., is how it happened** voici, à mon avis, comment c'est arrivé
2 *(recommend)* suggérer, recommander; **who do you s. for the job?** qui suggérez-vous pour cette tâche?
3 *(imply, insinuate)* suggérer; **just what are you suggesting?** que voulez-vous dire par là?, qu'allez-vous insinuer là?; **are you suggesting that I might be wrong?** suggérez-vous que je pourrais avoir tort?
4 *(indicate, point to)* suggérer, laisser supposer; **which suggests that it was an accident** ce qui semblerait indiquer qu'il s'agissait d'un accident; **the marks in the sand s. a person of about…** les traces sur le sable indiquent la présence d'une personne d'environ…
5 *(evoke)* suggérer, évoquer; **what does this picture s. to you?** qu'est-ce que ce tableau évoque pour vous?, à quoi ce tableau vous fait-il penser?

suggestible [sə'dʒestəbəl] ADJ *Psy* suggestible

suggestion [sə'dʒestʃən] N **1** *(proposal)* suggestion *f*, proposition *f*; **may I make a s.?** puis-je faire une suggestion?; **if nobody has any other suggestions, we'll move on** si personne n'a rien d'autre à suggérer *ou* à proposer, nous allons passer à autre chose; **we are always open to suggestions** toute suggestion est la bienvenue; **serving s.** *(on packaging)* suggestion *f* de présentation
2 *(recommendation)* conseil *m*, recommandation *f*; **at her doctor's s. she stayed in bed** suivant le conseil de son médecin, elle est restée au lit; **their s. is that we stop work immediately** ils proposent que nous arrêtions le travail immédiatement
3 *(indication)* indication *f*; **her expression gave no s. of what she was really thinking** son expression ne donnait aucune indication sur *ou* ne laissait rien paraître de ce qu'elle pensait vraiment
4 *(trace, hint)* soupçon *m*, trace *f*; **with just a s. of irony** avec un soupçon d'ironie
5 *(implication)* suggestion *f*, implication *f*; **there is no s. of negligence on their part** rien ne laisse penser qu'il y ait eu négligence de leur part
6 *Psy* suggestion *f*; **the power of s.** le pouvoir de suggestion
▸▸ ***suggestion box*** boîte *f* à idées

suggestive [sə'dʒestɪv] ADJ **1** *(indicative, evocative)* suggestif; **his sculptures are s. of natural forms** ses sculptures rappellent *ou* évoquent des formes naturelles **2** *(erotic ▸ lyrics, dance, pose)* suggestif; *(▸ joke)* grivois

suggestively [sə'dʒestɪvlɪ] ADV de façon suggestive

suggestiveness [sə'dʒestɪvnɪs] N *(of picture etc)* caractère *m* suggestif

suicidal [suːɪ'saɪdəl] ADJ suicidaire; **s. tendencies** des tendances *fpl* suicidaires; **I was feeling s.** j'avais envie de me tuer; **to stop now would be s.** ce serait du suicide de s'arrêter maintenant

suicide ['suːɪsaɪd] N *(act)* suicide *m*; *(person)* suicidé(e) *m,f*; **to commit s.** se suicider; **there were several attempted suicides** il y a eu plusieurs tentatives de suicide; **privatization would be financial s.** la privatisation représenterait un véritable suicide financier
COMP *(mission, plane, squad)* suicide; *(attempt, bid)* de suicide
▸▸ ***suicide attack*** attentat-suicide *m*; ***suicide bomber*** auteur *m* d'un attentat-suicide à la bombe; ***suicide note*** lettre *f* *(que l'on laisse quand on se suicide)*; ***suicide pact*** = accord de suicide collectif entre deux ou plusieurs personnes; ***suicide watch*** = surveillance renforcée pour détenu(e) suicidaire consistant à multiplier les rondes; **to be on (a) s. watch** faire l'objet d'une surveillance renforcée pour éviter toute tentative de suicide

suit [suːt] N **1** *(outfit ▸ for men)* costume *m*, complet *m*; *(▸ for women)* tailleur *m*; *(▸ for particular activity)* combinaison *f*; **he came in a s. and tie** il est venu en costume-cravate; **two-piece/three-piece s.** complet *m* deux/trois pièces; **the workers wear protective suits** les ouvriers portent des combinaisons de protection; **s. of clothes** tenue *f*; **s. of armour** armure *f* complète; *Fig Pej* **the men in grey suits** les bureaucrates *mpl*
2 *(complete set)* jeu *m*; **a s. of sails** un jeu de voiles
3 *(in card games)* couleur *f*; **long** *or* **strong s.** couleur *f* forte; *Fig* **generosity is not his strong s.** la générosité n'est pas vraiment son (point) fort; **to follow s.** fournir à la couleur (demandée); *Fig* en faire autant, faire de même
4 *Law (lawsuit)* action *f*, procès *m*; **to bring** *or* **to file a s. against sb** intenter un procès à qn, poursuivre qn en justice; **criminal s.** action *f* au pénal
5 *Formal (appeal)* requête *f*, pétition *f*; *Literary (courtship)* cour *f*; **to pay s. to sb** faire la cour à qn
6 *Fam Pej (person)* employé(e) *m,f* de bureau[□] *(en costume ou tailleur)*
VT **1** *(be becoming to ▸ of clothes, colour)* aller à; **black really suits her** le noir lui va à merveille
2 *(be satisfactory or convenient to)* convenir à, arranger; **Tuesday suits me best** c'est mardi qui me convient *ou* qui m'arrange le mieux; **their relaxed approach suits me fine** leur attitude décontractée me convient parfaitement *ou* tout à fait; *Fam* **s. yourself!** faites ce qui vous chante!, faites comme vous voudrez![□]
3 *(agree with)* convenir à, aller à, réussir à; **life in the country obviously suits her** de toute évidence, la vie à la campagne lui convient *ou* lui réussit
4 *(be appropriate)* convenir à, aller à, être fait pour; **clothes to s. all tastes** des vêtements pour tous les goûts; **the role suits her perfectly** le rôle lui va comme un gant; **he is not suited to be a doctor** il n'est pas fait pour être médecin; **they are suited to each other, they s. each other** ils sont faits l'un pour l'autre
5 *(adapt)* adapter, approprier; **he tries to s. his act to his audience** il essaie d'adapter son numéro à son public; **to s. the action to the word** joindre le geste à la parole
6 *Am (dress in suit)* vêtir d'un costume; **his followers were suited in black** ses disciples étaient vêtus d'un costume noir
VI *(be satisfactory)* convenir, aller; **will that date s.?** cette date vous convient-elle *ou* est-elle à votre convenance?
▸▸ ***suit carrier*** housse *f* (pour costume)

suitability [ˌsuːtə'bɪlɪtɪ] N *(of clothing)* caractère *m* approprié; *(of behaviour, arrangements)* caractère *m* convenable; *(of act, remark)* à-propos *m*, pertinence *f*; *(of time, place)* opportunité *f*; **they doubt his s. for the post** ils ne sont pas sûrs qu'il soit fait *ou* qu'il ait les qualités requises pour ce poste; **they're worried about the film's s. for younger audiences** ils ont peur que le film ne convienne pas à un public jeune; **we need to assess the s. of the accommodation** il nous faut vérifier si le logement convient

suitable ['suːtəbəl] ADJ **1** *(convenient)* approprié, adéquat; **will that day be s. for you?** cette date-là vous convient-elle?; **the most s. date** la date qui conviendra le mieux **2** *(appropriate ▸ gen)* qui convient; *(▸ clothing)* approprié, adéquat; *(▸ behaviour)* convenable; *(▸ act, remark, expression)* approprié, pertinent; *(▸ time, place)* propice; **s. for all occasions** qui convient dans toutes les occasions; **not s. for children** *(on packaging)* réservé aux adultes; **this is hardly a s. time for a heart-to-heart** ce n'est pas vraiment le bon moment pour se parler à cœur ouvert; **the most s. candidate for the post** le candidat le plus apte à occuper ce poste; **the house is not s. for a large family** la maison ne conviendrait pas à une famille nombreuse; **he's not s. for our Christine** ce n'est pas l'homme qu'il faut à notre Christine; **the stage was not considered a s. career for a woman** le théâtre n'était pas considéré comme un métier convenable pour une femme

suitably ['suːtəblɪ] ADV *(dress)* de façon appropriée; *(behave)* convenablement, comme il faut; **s. matched** bien assortis; **he was s. equipped for his trip** il était convenablement équipé pour son voyage; **I tried to look s. surprised** j'ai essayé d'avoir l'air surpris, comme il se devait; **he was s. impressed** il a été plutôt impressionné

suitcase ['suːtkeɪs] N valise *f*; **I've been living out of a s. for weeks** ça fait des semaines que je n'ai pas défait mes valises; **she'd been travelling around, living out of a s.** elle avait voyagé un peu partout sans jamais vraiment s'installer

suite [swiːt] N **1** *(rooms)* suite *f*, appartement *m*; **a s. of rooms** une enfilade de pièces
2 *(furniture)* mobilier *m*; **bedroom s.** chambre *f* à coucher
3 *Mus* suite *f*; **a cello s.** une suite pour violoncelle
4 *(staff, followers)* suite *f*
5 *Comput (of software)* suite *f* logicielle, ensemble *m* logiciel

suiting ['suːtɪŋ] N tissu *m* de confection

suitor ['suːtə(r)] N **1** *Old-fashioned (wooer)* amoureux *m*, soupirant *m* **2** *Law* plaignant(e) *m,f*

sulfa, sulphate *etc Am* = **sulpha, sulphate** *etc*

sulk [sʌlk] VI bouder, faire la tête; **there's no need to s.!** (ce n'est) pas la peine de faire la tête!
N bouderie *f*; **to have a s.** *or* **(a fit of) the sulks** bouder, faire la tête

sulkily ['sʌlkɪlɪ] ADV *(act)* en boudant, d'un air maussade; *(answer)* d'un ton maussade

sulkiness ['sʌlkɪnɪs] N *(mood)* bouderie *f*, humeur *f* maussade; *(temperament)* caractère *m* boudeur *ou* maussade

sulking ['sʌlkɪŋ] N bouderie *f*

sulky ['sʌlkɪ] (*compar* **sulkier**, *superl* **sulkiest**, *pl* **sulkies**) ADJ *(person, mood)* boudeur, maussade; **now, don't go all s. on me!** allez, pas la peine de me faire la tête!
N sulky *m*

sullen ['sʌlən] ADJ **1** *(person, behaviour, appearance, remark)* maussade, renfrogné **2** *(clouds)* menaçant

sullenly ['sʌlənlɪ] ADV *(behave)* d'un air maussade *ou* renfrogné; *(answer, say, refuse)* d'un ton maussade; *(agree, obey)* de mauvaise grâce, à contrecœur

sullenness ['sʌlənnɪs] N *(temperament)* humeur *f* maussade; *(of appearance)* air *m* renfrogné

sullied ['sʌlɪd] ADJ *Formal (dirty)* souillé; *(reputation)* terni

sully ['sʌlɪ] (*pt & pp* **sullied**) VT *Formal* **1** *(dirty)* souiller **2** *Fig (reputation)* ternir

sulpha, *Am* **sulfa** ['sʌlfə] N *Pharm* sulfamide *m*
▸▸ ***sulpha drug*** sulfamide *m*

sulphate, *Am* **sulfate** ['sʌlfeɪt] N sulfate *m*; **copper/zinc s.** sulfate *m* de cuivre/de zinc

sulphide, *Am* **sulfide** ['sʌlfaɪd] N sulfure *m*; **to treat sth with s.** sulfurer qch

sulphonamide, *Am* **sulfonamide** [sʌl'fɒnəmaɪd] N sulfonamide *m*, sulfamide *m*

sulphur, *Am* **sulfur** ['sʌlfə(r)] N soufre *m*
▸▸ ***sulphur dioxide*** dioxyde *m* de soufre, anhydride *m* sulfureux

sulphureous, *Am* **sulfureous** [sʌl'fjʊərɪəs] ADJ sulfureux; *(coloured)* couleur de soufre *(inv)*, soufré

sulphuric, *Am* **sulfuric** [sʌl'fjʊərɪk] ADJ sulfurique
▸▸ ***sulphuric acid*** acide *m* sulfurique

sulphurous, *Am* **sulfurous** ['sʌlfərəs] ADJ *also Fig* sulfureux

sultan ['sʌltən] N sultan *m*

sultana [səl'tɑːnə] N **1** *Br (raisin)* raisin *m* de Smyrne **2** *(woman)* sultane *f*
▸▸ ***sultana cake*** gâteau *m* aux raisins de Smyrne

sultanate ['sʌltənət] N sultanat *m*

sultriness ['sʌltrɪnɪs] N **1** *(of weather)* chaleur *f* étouffante; **the s. of the weather** le temps lourd **2** *(sensuality)* sensualité *f*

sultry ['sʌltrɪ] (*compar* **sultrier**, *superl* **sultriest**) ADJ **1** *(weather)* lourd; *(heat)* étouffant, suffocant

2 *(person, look, smile)* sensuel; *(voice)* chaud, sensuel

sum [sʌm] *(pt & pp* **summed,** *cont* **summing)** **N 1** *(amount of money)* somme *f*; **it's going to cost us a considerable s. (of money)** ça va nous coûter beaucoup d'argent *ou* très cher

2 *(total)* total *m*, somme *f*; **the whole is greater than the s. of its parts** l'ensemble est encore meilleur que la somme des éléments qui le compose

3 *(arithmetical operation)* calcul *m*; *Br* **to do sums** faire du calcul; *Br* **he's very weak at sums** il est très faible en calcul; **I tried to do the s. in my head** j'ai essayé de faire le calcul de tête; *Fig* **they've really got their sums right** ils ont bien calculé leur coup

4 *(gist)* somme *f*; **in s.** en somme, somme toute; **the s. and substance of her argument** les grandes lignes de son raisonnement

VT *(add)* additionner, faire le total de; *(calculate)* calculer

►► *Fin* ***sum payable*** charge *f* à payer; ***sum total*** totalité *f*, somme *f* totale; **the report contains the s. total of research in the field** ce rapport contient tous les résultats de la recherche en ce domaine; **that is the s. total of our knowledge** voilà à quoi se résume tout ce que nous savons; **is that the s. total of what you've done today?** c'est tout ce que vous avez fait aujourd'hui?

►**sum up** **VT SEP 1** *(summarize)* résumer, récapituler; **one word sums the matter up** un mot suffit à résumer la question; *Law* **to s. up the case** *or* **the evidence** *(judge)* résumer les débats **2** *(size up)* jauger; **he summed us up immediately** il nous a jaugés *ou* classés sur-le-champ; **I summed up the situation at a glance** un simple coup d'œil m'a suffi pour jauger la situation

VI *(gen)* récapituler, faire un résumé; *Law (judge)* résumer; **to s. up I will say that...** en résumé je dirai que...; **in summing up the judge said...** dans son résumé, le juge a dit...

summarily [ˈsʌmərəlɪ] **ADV** sommairement; **they were s. dismissed without any explanation** on les a sommairement *ou* tout simplement congédiés sans plus d'explications

summarize, -ise [ˈsʌməraɪz] **VT** résumer

summary [ˈsʌmərɪ] *(pl* **summaries) N 1** *(synopsis* ► *of argument, situation)* résumé *m*, récapitulation *f*; *(*► *of book, film)* résumé *m*; **he gave us a brief s. of the situation** il nous a fait un bref résumé de la situation; **there is a news s. every hour** il y a un court bulletin d'information toutes les heures; **here is a brief news s.** et maintenant le rappel des titres **2** *(written list)* sommaire *m*, résumé *m*; *Fin (of accounts)* relevé *m*

ADJ *(gen) & Law* sommaire

►► ***summary dismissal*** renvoi *m* sommaire; ***summary judgment*** jugement *m* en référé; ***summary offence*** infraction *f* mineure, délit *m*

summation [sʌˈmeɪʃən] **N 1** *(addition)* addition *f*; *(sum)* somme *f*, total *m* **2** *(summary)* récapitulation *f*, résumé *m*; **the book is a s. of her life's work** ce livre constitue une récapitulation de l'œuvre de sa vie

summer [ˈsʌmə(r)] **N 1** *(season)* été *m*; **in (the) s.** en été; **in the s. of 1942** pendant *ou* au cours de l'été 1942; **a s.** *or* **s.'s day** un jour d'été; **they spend every s. at the seaside** ils passent tous leurs étés au bord de la mer; **we've had a good s.** *(good weather)* on a eu un bel été; *(profitable tourist season)* la saison était bonne **2** *Literary (year of age)* **a youth of 15 summers** un jeune homme de 15 printemps **3** *Fig (high point)* apogée *m*

COMP *(clothes, residence, day)* d'été; *(heat, sports)* estival; **the s. holidays** *(gen)* les vacances *fpl* d'été; *Sch* les grandes vacances *fpl*

VI passer l'été

VT *(cattle, sheep)* estiver

►► *Am* ***summer camp*** colonie *f* de vacances; *Am* ***summer house*** maison *f* de campagne; *Br* ***summer pudding*** = pudding composé d'une compote de fruits rouges recouverte de pain; ***summer resort*** station *f* estivale; ***summer school*** université *f* d'été; ***summer solstice*** solstice *m* d'été; *Am* ***summer squash*** courgette *f* jaune; ***summer term*** troisième trimestre *m*; *Admin* ***summer time*** *(by clock)* heure *f* d'été

summerhouse [ˈsʌməhaʊs, *pl* -haʊzɪz] **N** *Br* pavillon *m* (de jardin)

summertime [ˈsʌmətaɪm] **N** *(season)* été *m*; **in the s.** en été

summery [ˈsʌmərɪ] **ADJ** d'été; **s. weather** un temps d'été *ou* estival; **you look very s. in that dress** cette robe te donne un petit air estival

summing-up [ˈsʌmɪŋ-] *(pl* **summings-up) N** *(gen)* résumé *m*, récapitulation *f*; *Law* résumé *m*

summit [ˈsʌmɪt] **N 1** *(peak* ► *of mountain)* sommet *m*, cime *f*; *(*► *of glory, happiness, power)* apogée *m*, summum *m* **2** *Pol (meeting)* sommet *m*

COMP *(talks, agreement)* au sommet

►► ***summit conference*** (conférence *f* au) sommet *m*

summiteer [ˌsʌmɪˈtɪə(r)] **N** *Pol* participant(e) *m,f* à un sommet

summon [ˈsʌmən] **VT 1** *(send for* ► *person)* appeler, faire venir; *(*► *help)* appeler à, requérir; **they were summoned to the headmaster's office** ils ont été convoqués au bureau du directeur

2 *(convene)* convoquer; **to s. a meeting** convoquer une réunion

3 *Law* citer, assigner; **to s. sb to appear in court** citer qn en justice; **the court summoned her as a witness** la cour l'a citée comme témoin; **s. the next witness!** *(in courtroom)* faites entrer le témoin suivant

4 *(muster* ► *strength)* rassembler, faire appel à; **he couldn't s. enough courage to ask her out** il n'a pas trouvé le courage nécessaire pour lui demander de sortir avec lui

5 *Formal (order)* sommer, ordonner à; **she summoned us in/up** elle nous a sommés *ou* ordonné d'entrer/de monter

►**summon up** **VT SEP 1** *(courage, strength)* rassembler, faire appel à; **she summoned up her courage to ask him** elle a pris son courage à deux mains pour lui poser la question; **I'll be there if I can s. up the energy** j'y serai si j'arrive à rassembler suffisamment d'énergie

2 *(help, support)* réunir, faire appel à; **I can't s. up much interest in this plan** je n'arrive pas à m'intéresser beaucoup à ce projet

3 *(memories, thoughts)* évoquer

4 *(spirits)* invoquer

summons [ˈsʌmənz] *(pl* **summonses) N 1** *Law* citation *f*, assignation *f*; **he received** *or* **got a s. for speeding** il a reçu une citation à comparaître en justice pour excès de vitesse; **to take out a s. against sb** faire assigner qn en justice **2** *(gen)* convocation *f*

VT *Law* citer *ou* assigner (à comparaître); **she was summonsed to testify** elle a été citée à comparaître en tant que témoin

sump [sʌmp] **N 1** *Tech* puisard *m*; *Br Aut* carter *m* **2** *(cesspool)* fosse *f* d'aisances

►► *Br* ***sump oil*** huile *f* de carter

sumptuous [ˈsʌmptʃʊəs] **ADJ** somptueux

sumptuously [ˈsʌmptʃʊəslɪ] **ADV** somptueusement

sumptuousness [ˈsʌmptʃʊəsnɪs] **N** somptuosité *f*

Sun. *(written abbr* **Sunday)** dim.

sun [sʌn] *(pt & pp* **sunned,** *cont* **sunning) N** soleil *m*; **the s. is shining** le soleil brille, il y a du soleil; **the s. is rising/setting** le soleil se lève/se couche; **rising/setting s.** soleil *m* levant/couchant; **the s. is in my eyes** j'ai le soleil dans les yeux; **I can't stay in the s. for very long** je ne peux pas rester très longtemps au soleil; **let's get out of the s.** mettons-nous à l'abri du soleil; **she's caught the s.** elle a pris des couleurs; **the living room gets the s. in the afternoon** le salon est ensoleillé l'après-midi; **to take the s.** prendre le soleil; **to take a photograph into the s.** prendre une photo à contre-jour; **a place in the s.** une place au soleil; **I've tried everything under the s.** j'ai tout essayé; **she called him all the names under the s.** elle l'a traité de tous les noms; **every species/subject under the s.** toutes les espèces existantes/tous les sujets possibles; *Hist* **the S. King** le Roi-Soleil

VT to s. oneself *(person)* prendre le soleil, se faire bronzer; *(animal)* se chauffer au soleil

►► ***sun block*** écran *m* total; ***sun cream*** crème *f* solaire; ***sun dance*** danse *f* du soleil; ***sun deck*** *(of house)* véranda *f*, terrasse *f*; *Naut* pont *m* supérieur, pont-promenade *m*; ***sun god*** dieu *m* solaire, dieu-soleil *m*; ***sun lotion*** lait *m* solaire; *Br* ***sun lounge*** solarium *m*; *Am* ***sun parlor, sun porch*** solarium *m*; ***sun protection factor*** indice *m* de protection solaire; *Br* ***Sun reader*** = lecteur du 'Sun' (typique de la droite populaire); ***sun visor*** *(on cap, for eyes)* visière *f*; *Aut* pare-soleil *m inv*

sunbaked [ˈsʌnbeɪkt] **ADJ** desséché par le soleil

sunbathe [ˈsʌnbeɪð] **VI** prendre un bain de soleil, se faire bronzer

N *Br* bain *m* de soleil

sunbather [ˈsʌnbeɪðə(r)] **N** = personne qui prend un bain de soleil; **hundreds of sunbathers converged on the beach** des centaines de gens se dirigeaient vers la plage pour aller s'étendre au soleil

sunbathing [ˈsʌnbeɪðɪŋ] **N** *(UNCOUNT)* bain *mpl* de soleil

sunbeam [ˈsʌnbiːm] **N** rayon *m* de soleil

sunbed [ˈsʌnbed] **N** *(in garden, on beach)* (fauteuil *m*) relax *m*; *(with tanning lamps)* lit *m* à ultraviolets

sunblind [ˈsʌnblaɪnd] **N** *Br* store *m*

sunburn [ˈsʌnbɜːn] **N** coup *m* de soleil

sunburnt [ˈsʌnbɜːnt], **sunburned** [ˈsʌnbɜːnd] **ADJ** brûlé par le soleil; **I get s. easily** j'attrape facilement des coups de soleil

sunburst [ˈsʌnbɜːst] **N 1** *(through clouds)* éclaircie *f* **2** *(pattern)* soleil *m*; *(brooch)* broche *f* en forme de soleil; **a s. clock** une pendule soleil

sundae [ˈsʌndeɪ] **N** = coupe de glace aux fruits et à la crème chantilly

Sunday [ˈsʌndɪ] **N 1** *(day)* dimanche *m* **2** *Br (newspaper)* **the Sundays** les journaux *mpl* du dimanche

COMP *(clothes, newspaper, driver)* du dimanche; *(peace, rest, mass)* dominical; **the S. roast** *or* **joint** le rôti du dimanche; *see also* **Friday**

►► ***Sunday best*** vêtements *mpl* du dimanche; **to put on one's S. best** s'habiller en dimanche, s'endimancher; **they were dressed in their S. best** ils étaient tout endimanchés, ils avaient mis leurs vêtements du dimanche; ***Sunday opening*** = ouverture des magasins le dimanche; ***Sunday school*** ≃ catéchisme *m*; ***Sunday school teacher*** catéchiste *mf*, personne *f* qui fait le catéchisme; ***Sunday supplement*** = supplément joint à un journal du dimanche; ***Sunday trading*** = ouverture des magasins le dimanche

> **SUNDAY PAPERS**
>
> La lecture des journaux du dimanche constitue une sorte de rituel pour de nombreux Britanniques. Les journaux du dimanche sont très volumineux; ils comprennent de nombreux suppléments sur des sujets tels que le sport, la mode, les voyages et les arts, et sont souvent accompagnés d'un magazine en couleurs. Ils coûtent plus cher que les journaux vendus en semaine. Certains journaux du dimanche sont des éditions dominicales de quotidiens paraissant en semaine (c'est le cas de 'The Sunday Times' et de 'The Independent on Sunday' par exemple) tandis que d'autres, comme 'The Observer', paraissent uniquement le dimanche.

sunder [ˈsʌndə(r)] **VT** *Arch* séparer, briser

sundial [ˈsʌndaɪəl] **N** cadran *m* solaire

sundown [ˈsʌndaʊn] **N** coucher *m* du soleil; **at s.** au coucher du soleil

sundowner [ˈsʌndaʊnə(r)] **N** *Fam (drink)* verre *m* *(qu'on prend le soir)*

sundrenched [ˈsʌndrentʃt] **ADJ** inondé de soleil

sun-dried **ADJ** séché au soleil

sundry [ˈsʌndrɪ] **ADJ** divers, différent; **on s. occasions** à diverses reprises

PRON all and s. were having a good time tout le monde s'amusait bien; **she told all and s. about it** elle l'a raconté à qui voulait l'entendre

• **sundries** **NPL** *(items)* articles *mpl* divers; *(costs)* frais *mpl* divers

►► *Acct* ***sundry expenses*** frais *mpl* divers

unfish ['sʌnfɪʃ] *(pl* **inv** *or* **sunfishes)** N *Ich (sea-water)* poisson-lune *m*, môle *f*; *(freshwater)* poisson-lune *m*

unflower ['sʌnˌflaʊə(r)] N tournesol *m*
COMP *(oil, seed)* de tournesol

ung [sʌŋ] *pp of* **sing**
▸▸ ***sung mass*** messe *f* chantée

unglasses ['sʌnˌglɑːsɪz] NPL lunettes *fpl* de soleil, *Belg* lunettes *fpl* solaires

ungun ['sʌngʌn] N *TV & Cin* sun-gun *m*, éclairage *m* sur batterie

unhat ['sʌnhæt] N chapeau *m* de soleil

unk [sʌŋk] *pp of* **sink**
ADJ *Fam* fichu; **if she catches us, we're s.** si elle nous surprend, on est fichus
▸▸ ***sunk fence*** saut-de-loup *m*

unken ['sʌŋkən] ADJ **1** *(boat, rock)* submergé; *(garden)* en contrebas; *(bathtub)* encastré (au ras du sol) **2** *(hollow ▸ cheeks)* creux, affaissé; *(▸ eyes)* creux

unless ['sʌnlɪs] ADJ sans soleil

unlight ['sʌnlaɪt] N (lumière *f* du) soleil *m*; **in the s.** au soleil

unlit ['sʌnlɪt] ADJ ensoleillé

unni ['sʌnɪ] N **1** *(religion)* sunnisme *m* **2** *(person)* sunnite *mf*
▸▸ ***Sunni Muslim*** N musulman(e) *m,f* sunnite ADJ sunnite

unnies ['sʌnɪz] NPL *Fam (abbr* **sunglasses)** lunettes *fpl* de soleil[□]

unniness ['sʌnɪnɪs] N *(of place)* ensoleillement *m*; *Fig* **the s. of her disposition** sa gaieté

unnite ['sʌnaɪt] ADJ sunnite
N sunnite *mf*

unny ['sʌnɪ] *(compar* **sunnier**, *superl* **sunniest)**
ADJ **1** *(day, place etc)* ensoleillé; *(building)* qui reçoit beaucoup de soleil; *(side of street or building)* exposé au soleil; **it's a s. day, it's s.** il fait (du) soleil *ou* beau; *Met* **s. intervals** *or* **periods** éclaircies *fpl* **2** *Fig (cheerful ▸ disposition)* joyeux, heureux; *(▸ smile)* radieux, rayonnant; **to look on the s. side (of things)** voir le bon côté des choses; *Br* **he's on the s. side of sixty** il n'a pas encore la soixantaine

unray ['sʌnreɪ] N rayon *m* de soleil, rayon solaire
▸▸ *Br* ***sunray lamp*** lampe *f* à rayons ultraviolets; *(for tanning)* lampe *f* à bronzer; ***sunray pleats*** plissé *m* soleil; *Med* ***sunray treatment*** héliothérapie *f*

unrise ['sʌnraɪz] N lever *m* du soleil; **at s.** au lever du soleil; **to get up at s.** se lever avec le soleil; **s. is about 6 o'clock** le soleil se lève vers 6 h
▸▸ ***sunrise industry*** industrie *f* de pointe

unroof ['sʌnruːf] N toit *m* ouvrant

unset ['sʌnset] N coucher *m* du soleil; **at s.** au coucher du soleil; **s. is about 6 o'clock** le soleil se couche vers 18 h; **it was a beautiful s.** le coucher de soleil était magnifique; *Literary* **the s. of life/of an empire** le déclin de la vie/d'un empire
▸▸ ***sunset clause*** clause *f* de temporarisation; ***sunset industry*** industrie *f* déclinante; *Am* ***sunset law*** = loi en vigueur dans la plupart des États américains, selon laquelle les programmes mis en place par le gouvernement doivent être régulièrement réévalués

unshade ['sʌnʃeɪd] N *(lady's parasol)* ombrelle *f*; *(for table)* parasol *m*; *(on cap)* visière *f*

unshine ['sʌnʃaɪn] N **1** *(sunlight)* (lumière *f* du) soleil *m*; **in the s.** au soleil; **we generally get at least 150 hours of s. in July** en général, nous avons au moins 150 heures d'ensoleillement en juillet; *Fig* **his visit brought a little s. into our lives** sa visite a apporté un peu de soleil dans notre vie **2** *Br Fam (term of address)* chéri(e) *m,f*; **watch it, s.!** fais gaffe, mon coco!
▸▸ ***sunshine roof*** toit *m* ouvrant

un-soaked ADJ *(beach)* inondé de soleil

unspot ['sʌnspɒt] N **1** *(on sun)* tache *f* solaire **2** *Fam (holiday resort)* station *f* estivale[□]; **it's our favourite winter s.** c'est là que nous préférons aller prendre du soleil pendant nos vacances d'hiver[□]

unstroke ['sʌnstrəʊk] N *(UNCOUNT)* insolation *f*; **to have/to get s.** avoir/attraper une insolation

suntan ['sʌntæn] N bronzage *m*; **to have a s.** être bronzé; **to get a s.** se faire bronzer, bronzer; **where did you get that lovely s.?** d'où est-ce que tu viens pour être bronzé comme ça?
COMP *(cream, lotion, oil)* solaire, de bronzage

suntanned ['sʌntænd] ADJ bronzé

suntrap ['sʌntræp] N coin *m* abrité et très ensoleillé; **the garden is a real s.** le jardin est toujours très ensoleillé

sun-up N *Am* lever *m* du soleil; **at s.** au lever du soleil

sun-worship N culte *m* du Soleil

sun-worshipper N **1** *Rel* adorateur(trice) *m,f* du Soleil **2** *Fig* fanatique *mf* du bronzage

sup [sʌp] *(pt & pp* **supped**, *cont* **supping)** VI *Arch (have supper)* souper; **they supped on** *or* **off some leftovers** ils ont soupé de quelques restes
VT boire à petites gorgées
N petite gorgée *f*
▸ **sup up** VT SEP *(drink up)* finir
VI finir son verre

> **SUPER-** PRÉFIXE
>
> • Le préfixe **super-** sert à indiquer le CARACTÈRE EXTRÊME de quelque chose, en ce qui concerne la taille ou l'intensité. La traduction est le plus souvent **super-** ou **sur-**.
> **supermarket** supermarché; **superabundance** surabondance; **supertanker** supertanker; **superconductor** supraconducteur; **supercomputer** superordinateur; **supertax** surtaxe; **supersonic** supersonique; **supernova** supernova; **a supercharged engine** un moteur suralimenté.
>
> • Sur le modèle du mot **superman**, le préfixe **super-** peut aussi venir s'ajouter à des noms pour en indiquer le CARACTÈRE REMARQUABLE :
> **superstar** superstar; **supermodel** supermodel; **supermum** maman de choc; **supergrass** indic de choc; **superpower** superpuissance, supergrand.
>
> • **Super-** peut également signifier:
> (i) AU-DESSUS DE OU PAR-DESSUS : **superstructure** superstructure; **to superimpose** superposer.
> (ii) AU-DELÀ DE : **supernatural** surnaturel; **superhuman** surhumain.

super ['suːpə(r)] ADJ **1** *Fam (wonderful)* super *(inv)*, formidable; **it was a s. party!** c'était génial comme fête! **2** *(superior)* supérieur, super; **they're developing a new sort of s. hydrogen bomb** ils sont en train de mettre au point une nouvelle superbombe H
EXCLAM *Fam* super!, formidable!
N **1** *Am (petrol)* super *m*, supercarburant *m* **2** *Fam (police superintendent)* ≃ commissaire *m* (de police) **3** *Am Fam (in apartment block)* gardien(enne)[□] *m,f*, concierge[□] *mf*
ADV *Fam (very)* super, hyper; **his family is s. rich** sa famille est hyper riche
▸▸ *Am* ***the Super Bowl*** le Superbowl *(finale du championnat des États-Unis de football américain)*; *Cin* ***Super 8*** super-8; ***Super League*** *(in rugby league)* = ligue de rugby composée des meilleures équipes britanniques; ***super Tuesday*** super mardi *m*, super Tuesday *m*, = premier mardi du mois de mars, jour le plus important des élections primaires aux États-Unis

superable ['suːpərəbəl] ADJ surmontable

superabundance [ˌsuːpərə'bʌndəns] N surabondance *f*

superabundant [ˌsuːpərə'bʌndənt] ADJ surabondant

superabundantly [ˌsuːpərə'bʌndəntlɪ] ADV surabondamment

superannuate [ˌsuːpər'ænjʊeɪt] VT **1** *(person)* mettre à la retraite **2** *(object)* mettre au rebut

superannuated [ˌsuːpər'ænjʊeɪtɪd] ADJ **1** *(person)* à la retraite, retraité **2** *(object)* suranné, désuet(ète)

superannuation [ˌsuːpərˌænjʊ'eɪʃən] N *Br* **1** *(act of retiring)* mise *f* à la retraite **2** *(pension)* pension *f* de retraite **3** *(contribution)* versement *m ou* cotisation *f* pour la retraite
▸▸ ***superannuation fund*** caisse *f* de retraite

superb [suː'pɜːb] ADJ superbe, magnifique

superbly [suː'pɜːblɪ] ADV superbement, magnifiquement; **she performed s.** elle a merveilleusement bien joué

superbug ['suːpəˌbʌg] N infection *f* nosocomiale à bactéries multi-résistantes

supercar ['suːpəkɑː(r)] N supercar *f*

supercargo ['suːpəˌkɑːgəʊ] *(pl* **supercargoes)** N subrécargue *m*

supercasino ['suːpəkə'siːnəʊ] N casino *m* géant

supercharge ['suːpətʃɑːdʒ] VT **1** *Tech (engine)* surcomprimer, suralimenter **2** *Fig (atmosphere)* électriser, galvaniser, survolter

supercharger ['suːpətʃɑːdʒə(r)] N compresseur *m*

supercilious [ˌsuːpə'sɪlɪəs] ADJ hautain, arrogant, dédaigneux

superciliously [ˌsuːpə'sɪlɪəslɪ] ADV *(act)* d'un air hautain, avec arrogance *ou* dédain; *(speak)* d'un ton hautain, avec arrogance *ou* dédain

superciliousness [ˌsuːpə'sɪlɪəsnɪs] N hauteur *f*, arrogance *f*, dédain *m*

superconductor [ˌsuːpəkən'dʌktə(r)] N supraconducteur *m*

supercooling ['suːpəˌkuːlɪŋ] N surfusion *f*

supercritical [ˌsuːpə'krɪtɪkəl] ADJ *Nucl* supercritique, surcritique

super-duper [-'duːpə(r)] ADJ *Fam* super, superchouette

superego [ˌsuːpər'iːgəʊ] *(pl* **superegos)** N *Psy* surmoi *m*

superelevation [ˌsuːpərelɪ'veɪʃən] N *(of road)* dévers *m*

supererogation [ˌsuːpəˌrerə'geɪʃən] N surérogation *f*

superficial [ˌsuːpə'fɪʃəl] ADJ *(knowledge)* superficiel; *(differences)* superficiel, insignifiant; *(person)* superficiel, frivole, léger; *(wound)* superficiel, léger

superficiality ['suːpəˌfɪʃɪ'ælətɪ] N caractère *m* superficiel, manque *m* de profondeur

superficially [ˌsuːpə'fɪʃəlɪ] ADV superficiellement

superfine ['suːpəfaɪn] ADJ *(quality, product)* extra-fin, superfin, surfin; *(analysis)* très fin; *(distinction, detail)* subtil

superfluity [ˌsuːpə'fluːɪtɪ] N **1** *(superfluousness)* caractère *m* superflu **2** *(excess)* surabondance *f*; **a s. of details** une surabondance de détails

superfluous [suː'pɜːflʊəs] ADJ superflu; **it is s. to say…** (il est) inutile de *ou* il va sans dire…; **I'm starting to feel a bit s.** je commence à me sentir un peu de trop ici

superfluously [suː'pɜːflʊəslɪ] ADV de manière superflue, inutilement

superfluousness [suː'pɜːflʊəsnɪs] N superfluité *f*

superfood ['suːpəfuːd] N superaliment *m*, = aliment exceptionnellement bon pour la santé

superglue® ['suːpəgluː] N Super glue® *f*
VT coller à la Super glue®

supergrass ['suːpəgrɑːs] N *Br Fam Crime slang* indic *m* de choc

superhighway ['suːpəˌhaɪweɪ] N **1** *Am Aut* autoroute *f* **2** *Comput* autoroute *f*

superhuman [ˌsuːpə'hjuːmən] ADJ surhumain

superimpose [ˌsuːpərɪm'pəʊz] VT superposer; **to s. sth on sth** superposer qch à qch; **superimposed photos** des photos en surimpression; *Fig* **a Western culture superimposed on an indigenous one** une culture occidentale venue se superposer à une culture indigène

superimposition [ˌsuːpərɪmpə'zɪʃən] N superposition *f*; *Phot & Cin* surimpression *f*

superinfection [ˌsuːpərɪn'fekʃən] N *Med* superinfection *f*

superintend [ˌsuːpərɪn'tend] VT **1** *(oversee ▸ activity)* surveiller; *(▸ person)* surveiller, avoir l'œil sur **2** *(run ▸ office, institution)* diriger

superintendence [ˌsuːpərɪn'tendəns] N **1** *(overseeing)* surveillance *f* **2** *(running)* direction *f*

superintendent [ˌsuːpərɪn'tendənt] N **1** *(of institution)* directeur(trice) *m,f*, *(of department, of-*

fice) chef *m* **2** *(of police)* ≃ commissaire *m* (de police) **3** *Am (of apartment block)* gardien(enne) *m,f*, concierge *mf*

superior [suːˈpɪərɪə(r)] **ADJ 1** *(better, greater)* supérieur; **a s. wine** un vin de qualité supérieure; **s. to** supérieur à; **the book is vastly s. to the film** le livre est bien meilleur que le film; **s. in number to** supérieur en nombre à, numériquement supérieur à; **the enemy troops were s. in numbers** les troupes ennemies étaient en plus grand nombre *ou* supérieures en nombre
2 *(senior ▸ officer, position)* supérieur; **s. to** supérieur à, au-dessus de
3 *Pej (supercilious)* suffisant, hautain; **with a s. smile** avec un sourire suffisant *ou* condescendant; **in a s. voice** d'un ton suffisant *ou* supérieur; **she feels s.** elle se croit supérieure
4 *(upper)* supérieur; **the s. limbs** les membres *mpl* supérieurs
5 *Typ (letter, number)* supérieur, suscrit
6 *Biol* supérieur; **the s. mammals** les mammifères *mpl* supérieurs
N supérieur(e) *m,f*
▸▸ *Law* ***superior court*** ≃ tribunal *m* de grande instance, *Can* Cour *f* supérieure; *Astron* ***superior planet*** planète *f* supérieure

superiority [suːˌpɪərɪˈɒrətɪ] **N 1** *(higher amount, worth)* supériorité *f*; **their s. in numbers** leur supériorité numérique; **the s. of this brand to** *or* **over all the others** la supériorité de cette marque par rapport à toutes les autres **2** *Pej (arrogance)* supériorité *f*, arrogance *f*
▸▸ *Psy* ***superiority complex*** complexe *m* de supériorité

superlative [suːˈpɜːlətɪv] **ADJ 1** *(outstanding ▸ quality, skill, performance)* sans pareil; *(▸ performer, athlete)* sans pareil, inégalé **2** *(overwhelming ▸ indifference, ignorance, joy)* suprême **3** *Gram* superlatif
N superlatif *m*; **in the s.** au superlatif; *Fig* **she always speaks in superlatives** elle a tendance à tout exagérer

superlatively [suːˈpɜːlətɪvlɪ] **ADV** au plus haut degré, exceptionnellement; **a s. good candidate** un candidat exceptionnel; **she is s. efficient** elle est on ne peut plus efficace

superman [ˈsuːpəmæn] *(pl* **supermen** [-men]) **N** *Phil (gen)* surhomme *m*; *(gen)* superman *m*
• **Superman PR N** *(comic book hero)* Superman

supermarket [ˈsuːpəˌmɑːkɪt] **N** supermarché *m*
▸▸ ***supermarket bank*** = banque qui appartient à une chaîne de supermarchés; ***supermarket trolley*** caddie *m*

supermini [ˈsuːpəmɪnɪ] **N** *Aut* citadine *f*

supermodel [ˈsuːpəmɒdəl] **N** supermodel *m*

supernatural [ˌsuːpəˈnætʃərəl] **ADJ** surnaturel
N surnaturel *m*

supernaturally [ˌsuːpəˈnætʃərəlɪ] **ADV** de manière surnaturelle

supernova [ˌsuːpəˈnəʊvə] *(pl* **supernovas** *or* **supernovae** [-viː]) **N** supernova *f*

supernumerary [ˌsuːpəˈnjuːmərərɪ] *(pl* **supernumeraries**) **ADJ** *(extra)* surnuméraire; *(superfluous)* superflu
N surnuméraire *m*; *Cin & TV* figurant(e) *m,f*

superphosphate [ˌsuːpəˈfɒsfeɪt] **N** superphosphate *m*

superpose [ˌsuːpəˈpəʊz] **VT** superposer; **to s. sth on sth** superposer qch à qch

superpower [ˈsuːpəˌpaʊə(r)] **N** superpuissance *f*, supergrand *m*
▸▸ ***superpower talks*** négociations *fpl* entre les superpuissances

superscript [ˈsuːpəskrɪpt] **N** exposant *m*
ADJ en exposant

superscription [ˌsuːpəˈskrɪpʃən] **N** *(gen)* inscription *f*; *(heading on document)* en-tête *m*

supersede [ˌsuːpəˈsiːd] **VT** *(person ▸ get rid of)* supplanter, détrôner; *(▸ replace)* succéder à, remplacer; *(object)* remplacer; **she superseded him as director** elle lui a succédé *ou* elle l'a remplacé à la direction; **this price list supersedes all previous ones** ce tarif remplace et annule les précédents; **the RWQ20 has long been superseded by smaller models** la RWQ20 a depuis longtemps été supplantée par des modèles plus petits; **superseded methods** méthodes *fpl* périmées

supersensitive [ˌsuːpəˈsensɪtɪv] **ADJ** hypersensible

supersonic [ˌsuːpəˈsɒnɪk] **ADJ** supersonique
▸▸ ***supersonic bang, supersonic boom*** bang *m* (supersonique)

superstar [ˈsuːpəstɑː(r)] **N** superstar *f*

superstition [ˌsuːpəˈstɪʃən] **N** superstition *f*

superstitious [ˌsuːpəˈstɪʃəs] **ADJ** superstitieux; **to be s. about sth** être superstitieux au sujet de qch

superstitiously [ˌsuːpəˈstɪʃəslɪ] **ADV** superstitieusement

superstore [ˈsuːpəstɔː(r)] **N** hypermarché *m*, grande surface *f*

superstructure [ˈsuːpəˌstrʌktʃə(r)] **N** superstructure *f*

supertanker [ˈsuːpəˌtæŋkə(r)] **N** supertanker *m*, superpétrolier *m*

supertax [ˈsuːpətæks] **N** surtaxe *f*

supertonic [ˌsuːpəˈtɒnɪk] **N** sus-tonique *f*

superuser [ˈsuːpəjuːzə(r)] **N** *Comput* gros utilisateur *m*

supervene [ˌsuːpəˈviːn] **VI** survenir

supervention [ˌsuːpəˈvenʃən] **N** *Formal* survenue *f*

supervise [ˈsuːpəvaɪz] **VT 1** *(oversee ▸ activity, exam)* surveiller; *(▸ child, staff)* surveiller, avoir l'œil sur **2** *(run ▸ office, workshop)* diriger
VI surveiller

supervision [ˌsuːpəˈvɪʒən] **N 1** *(of person, activity)* surveillance *f*, contrôle *m*; **the children must be under the s. of qualified staff at all times** les enfants doivent être sous la surveillance de personnel qualifié à tout moment; **translated under the s. of the author** traduit sous la direction de l'auteur **2** *(of office)* direction *f*
▸▸ *Law* ***supervision order*** = nomination par un tribunal pour enfants d'un travailleur social chargé d'assurer la tutelle d'un enfant

supervisor [ˈsuːpəvaɪzə(r)] **N** *(gen)* surveillant(e) *m,f*; *Com (of department)* chef *m* de rayon; *Sch & Univ (at exam)* surveillant(e) *m,f*; *Univ (of thesis)* directeur(trice) *m,f* de thèse; *(of research)* directeur(trice) *m,f* de recherches

supervisory [ˈsuːpəvaɪzərɪ] **ADJ** de surveillance; **in a s. role** *or* **capacity** à titre de surveillant

superwoman [ˈsuːpəˌwʊmən] *(pl* **superwomen** [-ˈwɪmɪn]) **N** superwoman *f*

supine [ˈsuːpaɪn] **N** *Gram* supin *m*
ADJ 1 *(on one's back)* couché *ou* étendu sur le dos; **she was lying s., she was in a s. position** elle était couchée sur le dos **2** *Fig (passive)* indolent, mou (molle), passif

supper [ˈsʌpə(r)] **N** *(evening meal)* dîner *m*; *(late-night snack)* souper *m*; **to have** *or* **to eat s.** dîner; *(late at night)* souper; **we had steak for s.** nous avons mangé du steak au dîner/souper; **I'll raise his salary but I intend to make him sing for his s.!** je vais lui accorder une augmentation, mais c'est donnant donnant!
▸▸ *Am* ***supper club*** = boîte de nuit qui fait aussi restaurant

suppertime [ˈsʌpətaɪm] **N** *(in evening)* heure *f* du *ou* de dîner; *(later at night)* heure *f* du *ou* de souper; **at s.** à l'heure du dîner/souper

supplant [səˈplɑːnt] **VT** *(person)* supplanter, évincer; *(thing)* supplanter, remplacer

supple [ˈsʌpəl] **ADJ** souple; **to become s.** s'assouplir

supplement N [ˈsʌplɪmənt] **1** *(additional amount ▸ paid)* supplément *m*; *(▸ received)* complément *m*; **a small s. to my income** un petit supplément à mes revenus; **a s. is charged for occupying a single room** il y a un supplément à payer pour les chambres à un lit; **food s.** complément *m* alimentaire **2** *Press* supplément *m*; **they have produced a s. to the encyclopedia** ils ont sorti un supplément à l'encyclopédie **3** *Br Admin (allowance)* allocation *f*
VT [ˈsʌplɪment] *(increase)* augmenter; *(complete)* compléter; **I work nights to s. my income** j'augmente mes revenus en travaillant la nuit; **he supplements his diet with vitamins** il complèt son régime en prenant des vitamines

supplementary [ˌsʌplɪˈmentərɪ] **ADJ 1** *(ger* complémentaire, additionnel; **s. to** en plus d **may I ask a s. question?** puis-je poser encore un question? **2** *Geom (angle)* supplémentaire
▸▸ *Formerly* ***supplementary benefit*** = allocatio versée par l'État à ceux qui ont les plus faible revenus; ***supplementary income*** revenus *mpl* ar nexes

suppleness [ˈsʌpəlnɪs] **N** souplesse *f*

suppliant [ˈsʌplɪənt] **ADJ** suppliant
N suppliant(e) *m,f*

supplicant [ˈsʌplɪkənt] **N** suppliant(e) *m,f*

supplicate [ˈsʌplɪkeɪt] *Literary or Formal* **VT** sup plier, implorer; **to s. sb to do sth** supplier qn d faire qch
VI to s. for forgiveness/mercy implorer le pa don/la pitié

supplicating [ˈsʌplɪkeɪtɪŋ] **ADJ** suppliant, d supplication

supplication [ˌsʌplɪˈkeɪʃən] **N** supplication *f*; **h knelt in s.** il supplia à genoux

supplier [səˈplaɪə(r)] **N** *Com* fournisseur(euse *m,f*
▸▸ ***supplier code*** code *m* fournisseur; *Acct* ***sup plier credit*** crédit-fournisseur *m*

supply[1] [səˈplaɪ] *(pt & pp* **supplied**, *pl* **supplies**) **V 1** *(provide ▸ goods, services)* fournir; **to s. sth to s** fournir qch à qn; **to s. electricity/water to a tow** alimenter une ville en électricité/eau; **cows s milk** les vachent donnent du lait
2 *(provide sth to ▸ person, institution, city)* fou nir, approvisionner; *Mil* ravitailler, approvision ner; **to s. sb with sth** fournir qch à q approvisionner qn en qch; **the farm keeps us sup plied with eggs and milk** grâce à la ferme nou avons toujours des œufs et du lait; **I supplie him with the details/the information** je lui ai fou ni les détails/les informations; **the arteries that s the brain** les artères qui amènent le sang au ce veau
3 *(equip)* munir; **all toys are supplied with batte ies** des piles sont fournies avec tous les jouets
4 *(make good ▸ deficiency)* suppléer à; *(▸ omis sion)* réparer, compenser; *(satisfy ▸ need)* ré pondre à
N 1 *(stock)* provision *f*, réserve *f*; **the nation's s. o oil** les réserves *fpl* nationales de pétrole; **we'r getting in** *or* **laying in a s. of coal** nous faison des provisions de charbon, nous nous approvi sionnons en charbon; **to get in a fresh s. of st** renouveler sa provision de *ou* se réapprovision ner en qch; **water is in short s. in the southeast** o manque d'eau dans le Sud-Est
2 *(provision ▸ of goods, equipment)* fourniture *(▸ of fuel)* alimentation *f*; *Mil* ravitaillement *n* approvisionnement *m*; **the domestic hot water s** l'alimentation *f* domestique en eau chaude **they won a contract for the s. of 10,000 compute to schools** ils ont obtenu un contrat pour la fou niture de 10 000 ordinateurs à des établisse ments scolaires
3 *Econ* offre *f*; **s. and demand** l'offre *f* et la de mande
4 *Br (clergyman, secretary, teacher)* remplaçar (e) *m,f*, suppléant(e) *m,f*; **to be on s.** faire de remplacements *ou* des suppléances
COMP 1 *(convoy, train, truck, route)* de ravitaille ment **2** *(secretary)* intérimaire; *(clergyman)* sup pléant
• **supplies NPL** *(gen)* provisions *fpl*; *(of food)* v vres *mpl*; *Mil* subsistances *fpl*, approvisionne ments *mpl*; **our supplies are running low** no provisions seront bientôt épuisées, nous com mençons à manquer de provisions; **office sup plies** fournitures *fpl* de bureau
▸▸ *Com* ***supply chain*** chaîne *f* logistique; *Mil* ***sup ply lines*** lignes *fpl* de ravitaillement; ***supply pip*** *(for fuel)* conduite *f* d'arrivée du combustible ***supply ship*** ravitailleur *m*; *Br* ***supply teacher*** rem plaçant(e) *m,f*, *Br* ***supply teaching*** remplace ments *mpl*

> Note that the French verb **supplier** is a false friend and is never a translation for the English verb **to supply**. It means **to implore, to beg**.

upply[2] ['sʌplɪ] ADV souplement, avec souplesse

upport [sə'pɔːt] N **1** *(backing)* soutien *m*, appui *m*; **s. for the Socialist Party is declining** le parti socialiste est en baisse *ou* en perte de vitesse; **the rebels have little s.** les rebelles bénéficient d'un soutien limité; **there is widespread s. for the government/these policies** le gouvernement bénéficie/ces politiques bénéficient d'un très large soutien; **he's trying to drum up** *or* **to mobilize s. for his scheme** il essaie d'obtenir du soutien pour son projet; **to give** *or* **to lend one's s. to sth** appuyer *ou* soutenir qch; **she gave us her full s.** elle nous a pleinement appuyés; **to speak in s. of a motion** appuyer une motion; **they are striking in s. of the miners** ils font grève par solidarité avec les mineurs; **a collection in s. of the homeless** une quête au profit des sans-abri

2 *(assistance, encouragement)* appui *m*, aide *f*; **a mutual s. scheme** un système d'entraide; **she gave me the emotional s. I needed** elle m'a apporté le soutien affectif dont j'avais besoin

3 *(funding)* appui *m*, soutien *m*; **they depend on the government for financial s.** ils sont subventionnés par le gouvernement; **with (financial) s. from the council** avec l'appui *ou* le soutien (financier) du conseil; **what are your means of s.?** quelles sont vos sources de revenus?; **she is their only means of s.** ils n'ont qu'elle pour les faire vivre

4 *(holding up)* soutien *m*; **I was holding his arm for s.** je m'appuyais sur son bras; **this bra gives good s.** ce soutien-gorge maintient bien la poitrine

5 *(person)* soutien *m*; **she's been a great s. to me** elle m'a été d'un grand soutien; **she is the s. of the family** *(financially)* c'est elle qui fait vivre la famille

6 *(supporting structure, prop)* appui *m*; *Constr & Tech* support *m*; *Med (bandage)* bandage *m* de maintien

7 *(substantiation, corroboration)* corroboration *f*; **in s. of her theory** à l'appui de *ou* pour corroborer sa théorie; **the investigation found no s. for this view** l'enquête n'a rien trouvé pour corroborer ce point de vue

8 *Am Econ (subsidy)* subvention *f*; **farm supports** subventions *fpl* agricoles

9 *Cin (supporting actor)* second rôle *m*; *Mus* groupe *m* en première partie

COMP **1** *(troops, unit)* de soutien **2** *(hose, stockings)* de maintien; *(bandage)* de soutien **3** *Constr & Tech (structure, device, frame)* de soutien

VT **1** *(back ▸ action, campaign, person)* soutenir, appuyer; *(▸ cause, idea)* être pour, soutenir; *Mil (troops)* soutenir; *Sport (team)* être pour; *(actively)* être supporter de; *(assist ▸ person)* soutenir, aider; **she supports the Labour Party** elle est pour *ou* elle soutient le parti travailliste; **I can't s. their action** je ne peux pas approuver leur action; **we s. her in her decision** nous approuvons sa décision; **the Democrats will s. the bill** les Démocrates seront pour *ou* appuieront le projet de loi; **the mayor, supported by the clergy** le maire, avec le soutien du clergé; **he supports Tottenham** c'est un supporter de Tottenham; *Cin & Theat* **supported by a superb cast** avec une distribution superbe

2 *(hold up)* supporter, soutenir; **the pillars that s. the ceiling** les piliers qui soutiennent le plafond; **her legs were too weak to s. her** ses jambes étaient trop faibles pour la porter; **he supported himself on a stick/my arm** il s'appuyait sur un bâton/mon bras; **she held on to the table to s. herself** elle s'agrippa à la table pour ne pas tomber

3 *(provide for financially ▸ person)* subvenir aux besoins de; *(▸ campaign, project)* aider financièrement; **she has three children to s.** elle a trois enfants à charge; **she earns enough to s. herself** elle gagne assez pour subvenir à ses propres besoins; **he supports himself by teaching** il gagne sa vie en enseignant; **his parents supported him through college** ses parents ont financé ses études; **the theatre is supported by contributions** le théâtre est financé par des contributions

4 *(sustain)* faire vivre; **the land has supported four generations of tribespeople** cette terre a fait vivre la tribu pendant quatre générations; **the atmosphere on the planet could not s. life** l'atmosphère de la planète ne permettrait pas le développement d'êtres vivants

5 *(substantiate, give weight to)* appuyer, confirmer, donner du poids à; **there is no evidence to s. his claim** il n'y a aucune preuve pour appuyer ses dires

6 *Fin (price, currency)* soutenir

7 *Comput (file format, device, technology)* permettre l'utilisation de, supporter; **this package is supported by all workstations** ce progiciel peut être utilisé sur tous les postes de travail

8 *(endure)* supporter, tolérer

▸▸ ***support band*** groupe *m* en première partie; **who was the s. band?** qui est-ce qu'il y avait en première partie?; ***support group*** **1** *(for therapy)* groupe *m* de soutien **2** *(at concert)* groupe *m* en première partie; *Comput* ***support line*** assistance *f* technique téléphonique; ***support price*** prix *m* de soutien; *Admin* ***support services*** services *mpl* d'assistance technique; ***support socks*** chaussettes *fpl* de contention; ***support staff*** personnel *m* de soutien *ou* des services généraux; ***support tights*** collants *mpl* de contention; *Naut* ***support vessel*** bâtiment *m* de soutien

> Note that the English verb **to support** only translates **supporter** when it means **to hold up**. The most common meaning of the French verb **supporter** is **to bear, to withstand**.

supportable [sə'pɔːtəbəl] ADJ *Formal* supportable

supporter [sə'pɔːtə(r)] N **1** *Constr & Tech (device)* soutien *m*, support *m* **2** *(advocate, follower ▸ of cause, opinion)* adepte *mf*, partisan *m*; *(▸ of political party)* partisan *m*; *Sport* supporter *m*, supporteur(trice) *m,f*; **he's a Liverpool s.** c'est un supporter de Liverpool

supporting [sə'pɔːtɪŋ] ADJ **1** *Constr & Tech (pillar, structure)* d'appui, de soutènement; *(wall)* porteur **2** *Cin & Theat (role)* secondaire, de second plan; *(actor)* qui a un rôle secondaire *ou* de second plan; **with a s. cast of thousands** avec des milliers de figurants **3** *(substantiating)* qui confirme, qui soutient; **do you have any s. evidence?** avez-vous des preuves à l'appui?

▸▸ *Constr* ***supporting beam*** sommier *m*; ***supporting film, supporting programme*** = film qui passe en première partie de la séance

supportive [sə'pɔːtɪv] ADJ *(person)* qui est d'un grand soutien; *(attitude)* de soutien; **my parents have always been very s.** mes parents m'ont toujours été d'un grand soutien

▸▸ *Med* ***supportive therapy*** thérapie *f* de soutien

supportiveness [sə'pɔːtɪvnɪs] N soutien *m*, appui *m*

suppose [sə'pəʊz] VT **1** *(assume)* supposer; **I s. it's too far to go and see them now** je suppose que c'est trop loin pour qu'on aille les voir maintenant; **if we s. it is worth £5** si nous supposons que cela vaut 5 livres; *Math* **s. x equals y** soit x égal à y; **I s. you think that's funny!** je suppose que vous trouvez ça drôle!; **let's s. (that)...** supposons que...

2 *(think, believe)* penser, croire; **do you s. he'll do it?** pensez-vous *ou* croyez-vous qu'il le fera?; **I s. so** *(affirmative response)* je suppose que oui; *(expressing reluctance)* oui, peut-être; **I s. not, I don't s. so** je ne (le) pense pas; **I don't s. he'll agree** ça m'étonnerait qu'il soit d'accord, je ne pense pas qu'il sera d'accord; **you don't s. anything's happened to them, do you?** tu ne penses pas qu'il leur est arrivé quelque chose?; **I don't s. you'd have time to read this, would you?** tu n'as pas le temps de lire ceci, je suppose?; **and who do you s. I met in the shop?** et devine qui j'ai rencontré dans le magasin!

3 *(imply)* supposer; **that theory supposes a balanced budget** cette théorie suppose un budget équilibré

VI supposer, imaginer; **he's gone, I s.?** il est parti, je suppose *ou* j'imagine?; **there were, I s., about fifty people there** il y avait, je dirais, une cinquantaine de personnes

CONJ si; **s. they see you?** et s'ils vous voyaient?; **s. we wait and see?** et si on attendait pour voir?; **s. I'm right and she DOES come?** mettons *ou* supposons que j'aie raison et qu'elle vienne?

supposed [sə'pəʊzd] ADJ **1** *(presumed)* présumé, supposé; *(alleged)* prétendu; **the s. author of this poem** l'auteur présumé de ce poème; *Pej* **all these s. experts** tous ces prétendus experts **2** *(meant)* **to be s. to do sth** être censé faire qch; **there is s. to be a well in the garden** on dit qu'il y a un puits dans le jardin; **she was s. to be at work** elle était censée être à son travail; **what's that switch s. to do?** à quoi sert cet interrupteur?; **how am I s. to know?** comment est-ce que je saurais *ou* suis censé savoir, moi?; **you're not s. to do that!** tu ne devrais pas faire ça!; **the computer's not s. to make a noise like that** l'ordinateur ne devrait pas faire un tel bruit; **how am I s. to work in conditions like these!** comment veut-on que je travaille dans de telles conditions!; **what's that s. to mean?** qu'est-ce que tu veux dire par là?; **we're not s. to use dictionaries** nous n'avons pas le droit de nous servir de dictionnaires; **this restaurant is s. to be very good** il paraît que ce restaurant est excellent; **you're s. to be my friend!** je te croyais mon ami!

supposedly [sə'pəʊzɪdlɪ] ADV soi-disant; **she s. went to get help** elle est soi-disant allée chercher de l'aide

supposition [ˌsʌpə'zɪʃən] N supposition *f*, hypothèse *f*; **his theory was pure s.** sa théorie n'était qu'une hypothèse; **on the s. that your mother agrees** dans l'hypothèse où votre mère serait d'accord, à supposer que votre mère soit d'accord

suppositious [ˌsʌpə'zɪʃəs], **supposititious** [səˌpɒzɪ'tɪʃəs] ADJ *Formal* **1** *(hypothetical)* hypothétique **2** *(fraudulent)* faux (fausse)

suppository [sə'pɒzɪtrɪ] *(pl* **suppositories***)* N suppositoire *m*

suppress [sə'pres] VT **1** *(put an end to)* supprimer, mettre fin à; **the new regime suppressed all forms of dissent** le nouveau régime a mis fin *ou* un terme à toute forme de dissidence

2 *(withhold)* supprimer, faire disparaître; *(conceal)* supprimer, cacher; **to s. evidence** faire disparaître des preuves; **to s. the truth/a scandal** étouffer la vérité/un scandale

3 *(withdraw from publication)* supprimer, interdire; **the government has suppressed the report** le gouvernement a interdit la parution du rapport

4 *(delete)* supprimer, retrancher; **the judge ordered that the controversial passages should be suppressed** le juge ordonna la suppression des passages controversés

5 *(inhibit ▸ growth, weeds)* supprimer, empêcher

6 *(hold back, repress ▸ anger, yawn, smile)* réprimer; *(▸ tears)* retenir, refouler; *(▸ feelings, desires)* étouffer, refouler; **to s. a cough** réprimer *ou* retenir son envie de tousser; **to s. a sneeze** se retenir pour ne pas éternuer; **she suppressed a smile** elle réprima un sourire

7 *Psy* refouler

8 *Electron & Rad* antiparasiter

> Note that the French verb **supprimer** is a false friend and is not always a translation for the English verb **to suppress**. Its most common meaning is **to cancel, to abolish**.

suppressed [sə'prest] ADJ *(emotion)* étouffé, refoulé; *(anger)* refoulé; *Psy (sexuality)* refoulé; **s. excitement** agitation *f* contenue

suppression [sə'preʃən] N **1** *(ending ▸ of rebellion, demonstration)* suppression *f*, répression *f*; *(▸ of rights)* suppression *f*, abolition *f*; *(▸ of a law, decree)* abrogation *f*

2 *(concealment ▸ of evidence, information)* suppression *f*, dissimulation *f*; *(▸ of scandal)* étouffement *m*

3 *(non-publication ▸ of document, report)* suppression *f*, interdiction *f*; *(▸ of part of text)* suppression *f*

4 *(holding back ▸ of feelings, thoughts)* refoulement *m*

5 *Psy* refoulement *m*

6 *Electron & Rad* antiparasitage *m*

suppressor [sə'presə(r)] N *Elec* dispositif *m* antiparasite *(inv)*

▸▸ *Elec* ***suppressor grid*** grille *f* d'arrêt

suppurate [ˈsʌpjʊreɪt] **VI** suppurer; **a suppurating wound** une plaie suppurante

suppuration [ˌsʌpjʊˈreɪʃən] **N** suppuration *f*

supranational [ˌsu:prəˈnæʃənəl] **ADJ** supranational

suprarenal [ˌsu:prəˈri:nəl] **ADJ** *Anat* surrénal
►► ***suprarenal gland*** glande *f* surrénale

suprastate [ˌsu:prəˈsteɪt] **ADJ** superétatique

supremacist [sʊˈpreməsɪst] **N** = personne qui croit en la suprématie d'un groupe; **they are white supremacists** ils croient en la suprématie de la race blanche

supremacy [sʊˈpreməsɪ] **N 1** *(dominance)* suprématie *f*, domination *f*; **each nation tried to gain s. over the other** chaque nation essayait d'avoir la suprématie sur l'autre **2** *(superiority)* suprématie *f*; **they believe in the s. of their methods over all others** ils croient leurs méthodes supérieures à *ou* meilleures que toutes les autres

supreme **ADJ 1** *(highest in rank, authority)* suprême; **the S. Commander of Allied Forces** le commandant suprême *ou* le commandant en chef des Forces alliées **2** *(great, outstanding)* extrême; **a s. effort** un effort suprême; **she handles politicians with s. skill** elle sait parfaitement s'y prendre avec les hommes politiques; **it would be an act of s. folly to do that now** ce serait de la folie pure de faire ça maintenant; **to make the s. sacrifice** sacrifier sa vie, faire le sacrifice de sa vie
►► *Rel* ***the Supreme Being*** l'Être *m* suprême; *Am Law* ***the Supreme Court*** la Cour suprême *(des États-Unis)*

supremely [sʊˈpri:mlɪ] **ADV** suprêmement, extrêmement

supremo [sʊˈpri:məʊ] *(pl* **supremos***)* **N** *Br Fam* (grand) chef *m*

Supt. *(written abbr* **superintendent***)* ≃ commissaire *m* (de police)

surcharge [ˈsɜ:tʃɑ:dʒ] **N 1** *(extra duty, tax)* surtaxe *f*; **a 7 percent import s.** une surtaxe de 7 pour cent sur les importations **2** *(extra cost)* supplément *m*; **there is a s. for the express train** il faut payer un supplément pour le train rapide **3** *(overprinting* ► *on postage stamp)* surcharge *f*
VT 1 *(charge extra duty or tax on)* surtaxer **2** *(charge a supplement to)* faire payer un supplément à **3** *(overprint* ► *postage stamp)* surcharger

surd [sɜ:d] **N 1** *Ling* sourde *f* **2** *Math* équation *f* irrationnelle

SURE [ʃʊə(r)] **ADJ 1** *(convinced, positive)* sûr, certain; **are you s. of the facts?** êtes-vous sûr *ou* certain des faits?; **I'm not s. you're right** je ne suis pas sûr *ou* certain que vous ayez raison; **I'm not s. when they're coming/what he wants** je ne sais pas au juste quand ils doivent venir/ce qu'il veut; **I'm s. of it** j'en suis sûr *ou* certain; **I can't be s., but I think it was 2 o'clock** je n'en suis pas tout à fait sûr, mais je pense qu'il était 2 heures; **he's not s. whether he's going to come or not** il n'est pas sûr de venir; **she isn't s. of** *or* **about her feelings for him** elle n'est pas sûre de ses sentiments pour lui; **you seem convinced, but I'm not so s.** tu sembles convaincu, mais moi j'ai des doutes; **I wouldn't be so s. about that!** ça, ça m'étonnerait!; **he'll win, I'm s.** il gagnera, j'en suis sûr; **I'm s. I've been here before** je suis sûr d'être déjà venu ici; **what makes you so s.?, how can you be so s.?** qu'est-ce qui te fait dire ça?; **I don't know, I'm s.** ma foi, je ne sais pas
2 *(confident, assured)* sûr; **is he someone we can be s. of?** est-ce quelqu'un de sûr?; **you can be s. of good service in this restaurant** dans ce restaurant, vous êtes sûr d'être bien servi; **to be s. of oneself** être sûr de soi, avoir confiance en soi
3 *(definite, certain)* sûr, certain; **one thing is s., he won't be back in a hurry!** une chose est sûre *ou* certaine, il ne va pas revenir de sitôt!; **we're s. to meet again** nous nous reverrons sûrement; **they're s. to get caught** ils vont sûrement se faire prendre; **the play is s. to be a success** la pièce va certainement avoir du succès; **it's a s. thing** c'est dans la poche; *esp Am Fam* **s. thing!** d'accord!; **be s. to go to bed early** il faut que tu te couches tôt; **be s. not to lose it, be s. that you don't lose it** prenez garde de ne pas le perdre; **we made s. that no one was listening** nous nous sommes assurés *ou* nous avons vérifié que personne n'écoutait; **I'll just go and make s.** je vais vérifier; **it is his job to make s. that everyone is satisfied** c'est lui qui veille à ce que tout le monde soit satisfait; **make s. you don't lose your ticket** prends garde à ne pas perdre ton billet; **make s. you've turned off the gas** vérifie que tu as éteint le gaz
4 *(firm, steady)* sûr; **with a s. hand** d'une main sûre; *Fig* **a s. grasp of the subject** des connaissances solides en la matière
5 *(reliable, safe* ► *method, remedy, judgment)* sûr; *(*► *profit, success)* assuré; **insomnia is a s. sign of depression** l'insomnie est un signe incontestable de dépression; **it's a s. bet he'll be late** il y a tout à parier qu'il sera en retard
ADV 1 *Fam (of course)* bien sûr□; **can I borrow your car? – s. (you can)!** (est-ce que) je peux emprunter ta voiture? – bien sûr (que oui)!
2 *esp Am Fam (really)* drôlement, rudement; **she s. can cook!** elle cuisine drôlement bien!; **it s. was difficult** c'était vraiment *ou* bien difficile; **are you hungry? – I s. am!** as-tu faim? – plutôt *ou* et comment!; **I s. as hell do object!** et comment que je proteste!
3 *(as intensifier)* **(as) s. as** aussi sûr que; **as s. as I'm standing here (today), as s. as fate, as s. as eggs are** *or Fam* **is eggs** aussi sûr que deux et deux font quatre
4 *Ir Fam* **s., he's a terrible liar** c'est un grand menteur□; **s., he doesn't know anything** il n'y connaît rien□
5 *Am Fam (you're welcome)* **s.!** de rien!□, il n'y a pas de quoi!□
• **for sure** **ADV I'll give it to you tomorrow for s.** je te le donnerai demain sans faute; **one thing's for s., I'm not staying here!** une chose est sûre, je ne reste pas ici!; **she won't come, that's for s.** elle ne viendra pas, c'est certain; **I think he's single but I can't say for s.** je crois qu'il est célibataire, mais je ne peux pas l'affirmer
• **sure enough** **ADV** effectivement, en effet; **she said she'd ring and s. enough she did** elle a dit qu'elle appellerait, et c'est ce qu'elle a fait; **no, it's whisky s. enough** non, c'est bien du whisky
• **to be sure** **ADV to be s., his offer is well-intentioned** certes, son offre est bien intentionnée

surefooted [ˈʃʊəˌfʊtɪd] **ADJ** au pied sûr; **to be s.** avoir le pied sûr; *Fig* **the Prime Minister gave a s. performance in the debate** le Premier ministre a fait une très bonne prestation lors du débat

surely [ˈʃʊəlɪ] **ADV 1** *(used to express surprise, incredulity, to contradict)* quand même, tout de même; **they s. can't have forgotten** ils n'ont pas pu oublier, quand même; **you're s. not suggesting it was my fault?** vous n'insinuez tout de même pas que c'était de ma faute?; **s. you must be joking!** vous plaisantez, j'espère?; **s. he didn't say that** il n'a pas pu dire ça; **the real figures are a lot higher, s.?** mais les chiffres sont en fait beaucoup plus élevés, non?; **it's all gone – s. not?** il n'y en a plus – c'est pas vrai!
2 *(undoubtedly, assuredly)* sûrement, sans (aucun) doute; **they will s. succeed** ils réussiront sûrement
3 *(steadily)* sûrement; **things are improving slowly but s.** les choses s'améliorent lentement mais sûrement
4 *(of course)* bien sûr, certainement; **would you give me a hand? – s.!** peux-tu me donner un coup de main? – bien sûr *ou* certainement!

sureness [ˈʃʊənɪs] **N 1** *(certainty)* certitude *f* **2** *(assurance)* assurance *f* **3** *(steadiness)* sûreté *f*; *(accuracy)* justesse *f*, précision *f*; **he handled the problem with great s. of touch** il a réglé le problème avec beaucoup de doigté

surety [ˈʃʊərətɪ] *(pl* **sureties***)* **N 1** *(guarantor)* garant(e) *m,f*, caution *f*; **to act as** *or* **to stand s. (for sb)** se porter garant (de qn) **2** *(collateral)* caution *f*, sûreté *f*

surf [sɜ:f] **N** *(UNCOUNT)* **1** *(waves)* vagues *fpl* (déferlantes), ressac *m*; **the s. crashed against the rocks** les vagues venaient s'écraser contre les rochers; **to ride the s.** faire du surf **2** *(foam)* écume *f*
VT *Comput* **to s. the Net** naviguer sur l'Internet
VI 1 *(on surfboard)* surfer, faire du surf; **he goes surfing every weekend** il fait du surf tous les week-ends **2** *Fam (on outside of train)* = s'accrocher à la paroi extérieure ou au toit d'un train

surface [ˈsɜ:fɪs] **N 1** *(exterior, top)* surface *f*; **the submarine/diver came to the s.** le sous-marin/plongeur fit surface; **the miners who work on the s.** les mineurs qui travaillent à la surface; *Fig* **all the old tensions came** *or* **rose to the s. when they met** toutes les vieilles discordes ont refait surface quand ils se sont revus
2 *(flat area)* surface *f*
3 *(covering layer)* revêtement *m*; **the pan has a non-stick s.** la poêle a une surface antiadhésive *ou* qui n'attache pas; **road s.** revêtement *m*
4 *(outward appearance)* surface *f*, extérieur *m*, dehors *m*; **on the s. she seems nice enough** au premier abord elle paraît assez sympathique; **his politeness is only on the s.** sa politesse est toute de surface; **there was a feeling of anxiety lying beneath** *or* **below the s.** on sentait une angoisse sous-jacente; **the discussion hardly scratched the s. of the problem** le problème a à peine été abordé dans la discussion
5 *Geom (area)* surface *f*, superficie *f*; **s. of revolution** surface *f* de révolution *ou* de rotation
VI 1 *(submarine, diver, whale)* faire surface, monter à la surface; *(return to surface)* refaire surface, remonter à la surface **2** *(become manifest)* apparaître, se manifester; **he surfaced again after many years of obscurity** il a réapparu après être resté dans l'ombre pendant de nombreuses années; **rumours like this tend to s. every so often** ce type de rumeur a tendance à refaire surface de temps à autre **3** *Fam (get up)* se lever□, émerger; **he didn't s. till 11 o'clock** il n'a pas émergé avant 11 heures
VT *(put a surface on* ► *road)* revêtir; *(*► *paper)* calandrer; **the track is surfaced with cement** la piste est revêtue de ciment
ADJ 1 *(superficial)* superficiel; **a s. scratch** une égratignure superficielle, une légère égratignure; *Fig* **his enthusiasm is purely s.** son enthousiasme n'est que superficiel **2** *(exterior)* de surface; **s. finish** *(of metal)* état *m* de surface, finissage *m*; **s. measurements** superficie *f* **3** *Mining (workers)* de surface, au jour; *(work)* à la surface au jour; *Mil (forces)* au sol; *(fleet)* de surface
►► ***surface area*** surface *f*, superficie *f*; *Ling* ***surface grammar*** grammaire *f* de surface; ***surface mail*** *(by land)* courrier *m* par voie de terre; *(by sea)* courrier *m* par voie maritime; ***surface noise*** bruit *m* de surface; ***surface speed*** *(of submarine)* vitesse *f* en surface; ***surface structure*** structure superficielle *ou* de surface; ***surface tension*** tension *f* superficielle; ***surface transport*** transport *m* terrestre et/ou maritime; **by s. transport** par voie de terre et/ou maritime

surface-mounted **ADJ** *Comput (chip)* monté en surface

surface-to-air **ADJ** sol-air *(inv)*

surface-to-surface **ADJ** sol-sol *(inv)*

surfacing [ˈsɜ:fɪsɪŋ] **N** *Constr* revêtement *m*

surfboard [ˈsɜ:fbɔ:d] **N** (planche *f* de) surf *m*

surfboarder [ˈsɜ:fbɔ:də(r)] **N** surfeur(euse) *m,f*

surfeit [ˈsɜ:fɪt] **N** *Formal (excess)* excès *m*, surabondance *f*; **we had a s. of pasta when we were on holiday in Rome** nous nous sommes gavés de pâtes pendant nos vacances à Rome; **there is a s. of imported goods** il y a trop d'importations
VT rassasier; **to s. oneself with sth** se gorger de qch jusqu'à s'en dégoûter

surfer [ˈsɜ:fə(r)] **N 1** *(in sea)* surfeur(euse) *m,f* **2** *(on Internet)* internaute *mf*

surfie [ˈsɜ:fi] **N** *Austr Fam* surfeur(euse)□ *m,f*

surfing [ˈsɜ:fɪŋ] **N 1** *(in sea)* surf *m*; **to go s.** faire du surf **2** *(on Internet)* navigation *f*

surfrider [ˈsɜ:fˌraɪdə(r)] **N** surfeur(euse) *m,f*

surge [sɜ:dʒ] **N 1** *(increase* ► *of activity)* augmentation *f*, poussée *f*; *(*► *of emotion)* vague *f*, accès *m*; *Elec* surtension *f*; **a big s. in demand** une forte augmentation de la demande; **a s. of pain/pity** un accès de douleur/de pitié; **he felt a s. of pride at the sight of his son** la fierté l'envahit en regardant son fils; **I felt a s. of hatred** j'ai senti la haine monter en moi **2** *(rush, stampede)* ruée *f*; **there was a sudden s. for the exit** tout à coup les gens se sont rués vers la sortie; **the demonstrator made a s. forward and broke through the police**

cordon les manifestants se ruèrent en avant et le cordon de police céda **3** *Naut* houle *f*

VI 1 *(well up ▸ emotion)* monter; **I felt anger/hope/despair s. in me** j'ai senti la colère/l'espoir/le désespoir monter en moi **2** *(rush ▸ crowd)* se ruer, déferler; *(▸ water)* couler à flots *ou* à torrents; *(▸ waves)* déferler; **the demonstrators surged forward** les manifestants se ruèrent en avant; **the gates of the stadium opened and the fans surged in/out** les portes du stade s'ouvrirent et des flots de spectateurs s'y engouffrèrent/en sortirent; **water surged through the breach in the dam** des torrents *ou* trombes d'eau jaillirent de la brèche dans le barrage **3** *Elec* subir une brusque pointe de tension

▸ **surge up VI** = **surge VI 1**

surgeon ['sɜːdʒən] **N** chirurgien(enne) *m,f*

▸▸ ***surgeon general*** *Mil* médecin-général *m*; *Am Admin* chef *m* des services de santé; ***surgeon's knot*** nœud *m* de chirurgien, nœud *m* chirurgical

surgery ['sɜːdʒərɪ] (*pl* **surgeries**) **N 1** *(UNCOUNT) (field of medicine)* chirurgie *f*; **to study s.** étudier la chirurgie

2 *(UNCOUNT) (surgical treatment)* intervention *f* chirurgicale, interventions *fpl* chirurgicales; **he'll need s.** il faudra l'opérer; **minor/major s. might be necessary** une intervention chirurgicale mineure/importante pourrait s'avérer nécessaire; **to perform s. on sb** opérer qn; **to have brain/heart s.** se faire opérer du cerveau/du cœur; **the patient is undergoing s.** le malade est au bloc opératoire

3 *Br (consulting room)* cabinet *m* médical *ou* de consultation; *(building)* centre *m* médical; *(consultation)* consultation *f*; **Doctor Jones doesn't take s. on Fridays** le Dr Jones ne consulte pas le vendredi; **can I come to the s. tomorrow?** puis-je venir au cabinet *ou* à la consultation demain?; **s. hours** heures *fpl* de consultation

4 *Br Pol* permanence *f*; **our MP holds a s. on Saturdays** notre député tient une permanence le samedi

> Note that the French word **chirurgie** only has a medical sense.

surgical ['sɜːdʒɪkəl] **ADJ 1** *(operation, treatment)* chirurgical; *(manual, treatise)* de chirurgie; *(instrument, mask)* chirurgical, de chirurgien; *(methods, shock)* opératoire **2** *(appliance, boot, stocking)* orthopédique

▸▸ ***surgical collar*** minerve *f*; ***surgical dressing*** pansement *m*; *Br* ***surgical spirit*** alcool *m* à 90 (degrés); *Mil* ***surgical strike*** frappe *f* chirurgicale

surging ['sɜːdʒɪŋ] **ADJ** *(crowd, waves)* déferlant; *(water)* qui coule à flots *ou* à torrents

surliness ['sɜːlɪnɪs] **N** *(character)* caractère *m* hargneux *ou* grincheux; *(mood)* humeur *f* hargneuse *ou* grincheuse

surly ['sɜːlɪ] (*compar* **surlier**, *superl* **surliest**) **ADJ** *(ill-tempered)* hargneux, grincheux

surmise [sɜː'maɪz] **VT** conjecturer, présumer; **I can only s. what the circumstances were** je ne puis que conjecturer quelles étaient les circonstances; **I surmised that he was lying** je me suis douté qu'il mentait

N *Formal* conjecture *f*, supposition *f*; **your conclusion is pure s.** votre conclusion est entièrement hypothétique

surmount [sɜː'maʊnt] **VT 1** *(triumph over)* surmonter, vaincre **2** *Formal (cap, top)* surmonter; **the building is surmounted by a large dome** le bâtiment est surmonté d'un grand dôme

surmountable [sɜː'maʊntəbəl] **ADJ** surmontable

surname ['sɜːneɪm] **N** *Br* nom *m* (de famille); **s. and Christian name** nom *m* et prénom *m*

> Note that the French word **surnom** is a false friend and is never a translation for the English word **surname**. It means **nickname**.

surpass [sə'pɑːs] **VT 1** *(outdo, outshine)* surpasser; *also Ironic* **you've surpassed yourselves** vous vous êtes surpassés **2** *(go beyond)* surpasser, dépasser; **that kind of behaviour surpasses my understanding** ce genre de comportement me dépasse; **the result surpassed all our expectations** le résultat dépassa toutes nos espérances

surpassing [sə'pɑːsɪŋ] **ADJ** *Literary* sans égal; **a woman of s. beauty** une femme d'une beauté sans égale *ou* inégalable

surplice ['sɜːplɪs] **N** surplis *m*

surplus ['sɜːpləs] **N 1** *(overabundance)* surplus *m*, excédent *m*; **a labour s.** un surplus de main-d'œuvre; **Japan's trade s.** l'excédent *m* commercial du Japon **2** *(UNCOUNT) (old military clothes)* surplus *mpl*; **an army s. overcoat** un manteau des surplus de l'armée; **an army s. store** un magasin de surplus de l'armée **3** *Fin (in accounting)* boni *m*

ADJ 1 *(gen)* en surplus, en trop; **pour off any s. liquid** enlevez tout excédent de liquide; **to be s. to requirements** excéder les besoins **2** *Com & Econ* en surplus, excédentaire; **they export their s. agricultural produce** ils exportent leurs surplus agricoles

▸▸ ***surplus population*** population *f* excédentaire; *Com & Econ* ***surplus production*** production *f* excédentaire; *Com* ***surplus stock*** stocks *mpl* excédentaires, surplus *m*

surprise [sə'praɪz] **N 1** *(unexpected event, experience etc)* surprise *f*; **it was a s. to see her there** ce fut une surprise de la voir là; **what a lovely s.!** quelle merveilleuse surprise!; **her death came as no s.** sa mort n'a surpris personne; **his resignation came as a s. to everyone** sa démission a surpris tout le monde; **to give sb a s.** faire une surprise à qn; **it was no s. to learn that he had a criminal record** il n'y avait rien d'étonnant à ce qu'il ait un casier judiciaire; **you're in for (a bit of) a s.!** tu vas être surpris!, tu vas avoir une (sacrée) surprise! **2** *(astonishment)* surprise *f*, étonnement *m*; **much to my s., she agreed** à ma grande surprise *ou* à mon grand étonnement, elle accepta; **her announcement caused some s.** sa déclaration a provoqué un certain étonnement; **he looked at me in s.** il me regarda d'un air surpris *ou* étonné **3** *(catching unawares)* surprise *f*; **to take sb by s.** surprendre qn, prendre qn au dépourvu; **their arrival took me by s.** leur arrivée m'a pris au dépourvu; **the soldiers took the enemy by s.** les soldats ont pris l'ennemi par surprise

COMP *(attack, present, victory)* surprise; *(announcement)* inattendu

VT 1 *(amaze)* surprendre, étonner; **it surprised me that they didn't give her the job** j'ai été surpris *ou* étonné qu'ils ne l'aient pas embauchée; **shall we s. her?** si on lui faisait une surprise?; **it wouldn't s. me if they lost** ça ne m'étonnerait pas *ou* je ne serais pas surpris qu'ils perdent; *Ironic* **go on, s. me!** vas-y, annonce! **2** *(catch unawares)* surprendre; **the burglar was surprised by the police** le cambrioleur fut surpris par la police

EXCLAM s.(, s.)! coucou!

▸▸ ***surprise party*** = fête organisée pour quelqu'un sans qu'il ou elle le sache; ***surprise visit*** visite *f* surprise; **the Prime Minister made a s. visit to Ireland** le Premier ministre a fait une visite surprise en Irlande

surprised [sə'praɪzd] **ADJ** surpris, étonné; **she was s. to learn that she had got the job** elle a été surprise d'apprendre qu'on allait l'embaucher; **don't be s. if she doesn't come** ne vous étonnez pas si elle ne vient pas; **I wouldn't** *or* **I shoudn't be s. if they'd forgotten** cela ne m'étonnerait pas qu'ils aient oublié; **I'm s. by** *or* **at his reaction** sa réaction me surprend *ou* m'étonne; **I'm s. at you!** tu m'étonnes!; **it looks easy but you'd be s.** ça semble facile mais ne vous y fiez pas

surprising [sə'praɪzɪŋ] **ADJ** surprenant, étonnant; **it's s. (that) she left so early** il est surprenant *ou* étonnant qu'elle soit partie si tôt; **it's not at all** *or* **not in the least s.** cela n'a rien d'étonnant; **that's s. coming from him** (venant) de sa part, c'est surprenant

surprisingly [sə'praɪzɪŋlɪ] **ADV** étonnamment; **for a ten-year-old, she's s. mature** elle est vraiment très mûre pour une fille de dix ans; **s. (enough), he managed to win** chose surprenante *ou* étonnante, il a quand même gagné; **not s., the play sold out** toutes les places ont été louées, ce qui n'a rien d'étonnant

surreal [sə'rɪəl] **ADJ 1** *(strange, dreamlike)* étrange, onirique **2** *Art & Literature* surréaliste

N the s. le surréel

surrealism [sə'rɪəlɪzəm] **N** *Art & Literature* surréalisme *m*

surrealist [sə'rɪəlɪst] *Art & Literature* **ADJ** surréaliste

N surréaliste *mf*

surrealistic [səˌrɪəl'ɪstɪk] **ADJ 1** *Art & Literature* surréaliste **2** *Fig* surréel, surréaliste

surrealistically [səˌrɪə'lɪstɪkəlɪ] **ADV** d'une manière *ou* dans un style surréaliste

surrender [sə'rendə(r)] **VI 1** *Mil (capitulate)* se rendre, capituler; **they surrendered to the enemy** ils se rendirent à *ou* ils capitulèrent devant l'ennemi **2** *(give oneself up)* se livrer; **after 16 hours the hijackers surrendered to the police** au bout de 16 heures, les pirates de l'air se sont livrés à la police **3** *Fig (abandon oneself)* se livrer, s'abandonner; **to s. to temptation** se livrer *ou* s'abandonner à la tentation

VT 1 *(city, position)* livrer; *(relinquish ▸ possessions, territory)* céder, rendre; *(▸ one's seat)* céder, laisser; *(▸ arms)* rendre, livrer; *(▸ claim, authority, freedom, rights)* renoncer à; *(▸ hopes)* abandonner; **to s. oneself to sth** se livrer *ou* s'abandonner à qch **2** *(hand in ▸ ticket, coupon)* remettre **3** *Ins (policy)* racheter

N 1 *(capitulation)* reddition *f*, capitulation *f*; **no s.!** nous ne nous rendrons pas!; **the town was starved into s.** la famine a obligé la ville à capituler; **the government's s. to the unions** la capitulation du gouvernement devant les syndicats **2** *(relinquishing ▸ of possessions, territory)* cession *f*; *(▸ of arms)* remise *f*; *(▸ of claim, authority, freedom, rights)* renonciation *f*, abdication *f*; *(▸ of hopes)* abandon *m* **3** *Ins (of policy)* rachat *m*

▸▸ *Ins* ***surrender value*** valeur *f* de rachat

surreptitious [ˌsʌrəp'tɪʃəs] **ADJ** furtif, clandestin, *Literary* subreptice

surreptitiously [ˌsʌrəp'tɪʃəslɪ] **ADV** furtivement, à la dérobée, *Literary* subrepticement

surreptitiousness [ˌsʌrəp'tɪʃəsnɪs] **N** caractère *m* furtif *ou Literary* subreptice

surrogacy ['sʌrəgəsɪ] **N** maternité *f* de substitution

▸▸ ***surrogacy laws*** législation *f* sur la maternité de substitution

surrogate ['sʌrəgeɪt] **N 1** *Formal (substitute ▸ person)* remplaçant(e) *m,f*, substitut *m*; *(▸ thing)* succédané *m*

2 *Psy* substitut *m*

3 *Am Law* magistrat *m* de droit civil *(juridiction locale)*

4 *Br Rel* évêque *m* auxiliaire

ADJ de substitution, de remplacement; **they served as s. parents to her** ils ont en quelque sorte remplacé ses parents

▸▸ ***surrogate mother*** *Psy* substitut *m* maternel; *Med* mère *f* porteuse

surround [sə'raʊnd] **VT 1** *(gen)* entourer; **the garden is surrounded by a brick wall** le jardin est entouré d'un mur en briques; **the president surrounded himself with advisers** le président s'est entouré de conseillers; **there is a great deal of controversy surrounding the budget cuts** il y a une vive controverse autour des réductions budgétaires **2** *(of troops, police, enemy)* encercler, cerner

N *Br (border, edging)* bordure *f*

▸▸ *TV & Comput* ***surround sound*** son *m* 3D

surrounding [sə'raʊndɪŋ] **ADJ** environnant; **there's a lovely view of the s. countryside** il y a une belle vue sur le paysage alentour

• **surroundings NPL 1** *(of town, city)* alentours *mpl*, environs *mpl* **2** *(setting)* cadre *m*, décor *m*; **it's a pleasure to be in such lovely surroundings** c'est un vrai plaisir de se trouver dans un cadre aussi joli **3** *(environment)* environnement *m*, milieu *m*; **she's indifferent to her surroundings** elle est indifférente à son environnement; **to be in familiar surroundings** être en pays de connaissance

surtax ['sɜːtæks] **N** surtaxe *f*; *(on income)* = surtaxe progressive sur le revenu

surtitle ['sɜːtaɪtəl] **N** surtitre *m*

surtitled ['sɜːtaɪtəld] **ADJ** surtitré

surveillance [sɜː'veɪləns] **N** surveillance *f*; **to keep sb under constant s.** garder qn sous surveillance continue; **the house is under police s.** la maison est surveillée par la police

survey VT [sə'veɪ] **1** *(contemplate)* contempler; *(inspect)* inspecter, examiner; *(review)* passer en revue; **we sat surveying the view** nous étions assis à contempler le paysage

2 *(make a study of)* dresser le bilan de, étudier; **the report surveys the current state of manufacturing industry in Britain** le rapport dresse le bilan de l'industrie manufacturière en Grande-Bretagne

3 *(poll)* sonder; **65 percent of women surveyed were opposed to the measure** 65 pour cent des femmes interrogées étaient contre cette mesure

4 *(land)* arpenter, relever, faire un relèvement de

5 *Br (house)* expertiser, faire une expertise de; **always have a house independently surveyed before buying** il faut toujours faire faire une expertise indépendante avant d'acheter une maison

N ['sɜːveɪ] **1** *(study, investigation)* étude *f*, enquête *f*; **they carried out a s. of retail prices** ils ont fait une enquête sur les prix au détail

2 *(overview)* vue *f* d'ensemble; **the exhibition offers a comprehensive s. of contemporary British art** l'exposition présente une vision d'ensemble de l'art contemporain britannique

3 *(poll)* sondage *m*

4 *(of land)* relèvement *m*, levé *m*; **aerial s.** levé *m* aérien

5 *Br (of house)* expertise *f*; **to have a s. done** faire faire une expertise

> Note that the French verb **surveiller** is a false friend and is never a translation for the English verb **to survey**. Its most common meaning is **to supervise, to keep an eye on**.

surveying [sə'veɪɪŋ] N **1** *(measuring ▸ of land)* arpentage *m*, levé *m* **2** *Br (examination ▸ of buildings)* examen *m*

▸▸ ***surveying instruments*** instruments *mpl* topographiques

surveyor [sə'veɪə(r)] N **1** *(of land)* arpenteur *m*, géomètre *m* **2** *Br (of buildings)* géomètre-expert *m*; **the council s. declared the building unsafe** l'expert envoyé par la mairie déclara l'immeuble dangereux

> Note that the French word **surveillant** is a false friend and is never a translation for the English word **surveyor**. Its most common meaning is **supervisor**.

survivability [sə,vaɪvə'bɪlɪtɪ] N survivabilité *f*

survivable [sə'vaɪvəbəl] ADJ **a s. attack** une attaque à laquelle on peut survivre; **the conditions were not s.** il était impossible de survivre dans de telles conditions

survival [sə'vaɪvəl] N **1** *(remaining alive)* survie *f*; **what are their chances of s.?** quelles sont leurs chances de survie?; *also Fig* **the s. of the fittest** la survie du plus apte **2** *(relic, remnant)* survivance *f*, vestige *m*; **the custom is a s. from the Victorian era** cette coutume remonte à l'époque victorienne

COMP *(course)* de survie

▸▸ ***survival bag*** sac *m* de couchage de survie; ***survival kit*** équipement *m* de survie

survivalism [sə'vaɪvəlɪzəm] N = entraînement en vue de la survie en cas de catastrophe

survivalist [sə'vaɪvəlɪst] N = personne qui s'entraîne à la survie en cas de catastrophe

survive [sə'vaɪv] VI **1** *(remain alive)* survivre **2** *(cope, pull through)* **how can they s. on such low wages?** comment font-ils pour vivre *ou* pour subsister avec des salaires si bas?; **he earned just enough to s. on** il gagnait tout juste de quoi survivre; **those toys wouldn't s. two minutes with our kids** ces jouets ne survivraient pas plus de deux minutes avec nos gamins; *Fam* **it'll be awful, I don't know how I'll s.!** ça va être horrible, je ne sais pas comment je vais m'en sortir!; *Fam* **don't worry, I'll s.!** ne t'inquiète pas, je n'en mourrai pas! **3** *(remain, be left)* subsister; **only a dozen of his letters have survived** il ne subsiste *ou* reste qu'une douzaine de ses lettres

VT **1** *(live through)* survivre à, réchapper à *ou* de; **few of the soldiers survived the battle** peu de soldats ont survécu à la bataille; **we thought he'd never s. the shock** nous pensions qu'il ne se remettrait jamais du choc

2 *(cope with, get through)* supporter; **she survived the death of her father better than expected** elle a surmonté la mort de son père mieux que prévu; **I never thought I'd s. the evening!** jamais je n'aurais cru que je tiendrais jusqu'à la fin de la soirée!

3 *(outlive, outlast)* survivre à; **she survived her husband by 20 years** elle a survécu 20 ans à son mari; **she is survived by two daughters** elle laisse deux filles

4 *(withstand)* survivre à, résister à; **her beauty has survived the passage of time** sa beauté a résisté au temps

surviving [sə'vaɪvɪŋ] ADJ survivant; **his only s. son** son seul fils encore en vie; **the longest s. whale in captivity** la baleine qui vit depuis le plus longtemps en captivité

survivor [sə'vaɪvə(r)] N **1** *(of accident, attack, earthquake)* survivant(e) *m,f*, rescapé(e) *m,f*; **the survivors of the death camps** les rescapés *mpl* des camps de la mort; **there are no reports of any survivors** aucun survivant n'a été signalé; **she'll be all right, she's a born s.** elle s'en sortira, elle est solide **2** *Law* survivant(e) *m,f*

susceptibility [sə,septə'bɪlətɪ] *(pl* **susceptibilities)** N **1** *(predisposition ▸ to an illness, a disease)* prédisposition *f*; **she has a s. to respiratory complaints** elle a une prédisposition aux infections respiratoires

2 *(vulnerability)* sensibilité *f*; **his s. to flattery** sa sensibilité à la flatterie

3 *Formal (sensitivity)* sensibilité *f*, émotivité *f*

4 *Phys* susceptibilité *f*

• **susceptibilities** NPL *(feelings)* sentiments *mpl*, susceptibilité *f*; **try to spare their susceptibilities** essayez de ménager leur susceptibilité

susceptible [sə'septəbəl] ADJ **1** *(prone ▸ to illness, disease)* prédisposé; **I'm very s. to colds** je m'enrhume très facilement

2 *(responsive)* sensible; **the management is s. to pressure from the staff** la direction est sensible aux pressions du personnel; **the virus is not s. to treatment** le virus ne répond pas au traitement

3 *Formal (sensitive, emotional)* sensible, émotif

4 *Formal (capable)* susceptible; **her decisions are s. of modification** ses décisions sont susceptibles d'être modifiées

suspect VT [sə'spekt] **1** *(presume, imagine)* soupçonner, se douter de; **I suspected there would be trouble** je me doutais qu'il y aurait des problèmes; **I suspected as much!** je m'en doutais!; **what happened, I s., is that they had an argument** ce qui s'est passé, j'imagine, c'est qu'ils se sont disputés

2 *(have intuition of)* soupçonner; **to s. foul play** soupçonner quelque chose de louche; **does your husband s. anything?** est-ce que ton mari se doute de quelque chose?; **I never suspected it for a moment** je n'avais pas le moindre soupçon, je ne m'en suis jamais douté

3 *(mistrust)* douter de, se méfier de; **to s. sb's motives** avoir des doutes sur les intentions de qn

4 *(person ▸ of wrongdoing)* soupçonner, suspecter; **to be suspected of sth** être soupçonné de qch; **to s. sb of sth/of doing sth** soupçonner qn de qch/d'avoir fait qch

N ['sʌspekt] *(of crime, wrongdoing)* suspect(e) *m,f*

ADJ ['sʌspekt] suspect; **his views on apartheid are rather s.** ses vues sur l'apartheid sont plutôt douteuses

suspected [sə'spektɪd] ADJ présumé; **a s. terrorist** un terroriste présumé; **he's undergoing tests for a s. tumour** on est en train de lui faire des analyses pour s'assurer qu'il ne s'agit pas d'une tumeur

suspend [sə'spend] VT **1** *(hang)* suspendre; **suspended from the ceiling/in the air** suspendu au plafond/en l'air; **particles of radioactive dust were suspended in the atmosphere** des particules radioactives étaient en suspension dans l'atmosphère

2 *(discontinue)* suspendre; *(withdraw ▸ permit, licence)* retirer (provisoirement), suspendre; **bus services have been suspended** le service des autobus a été suspendu *ou* interrompu

3 *(defer)* suspendre, reporter; **to s. judgment** suspendre son jugement; **the commission decided to s. its decision** la commission décida de surseoir à sa décision; **to s. one's disbelief** faire taire son incrédulité

4 *(exclude temporarily ▸ official, member, sportsman)* suspendre; *(▸ worker)* suspendre, mettre à pied; *(▸ pupil, student)* exclure provisoirement; **suspended for six months** suspendu pendant six mois; **two pupils have been suspended from school for smoking** deux élèves surpris à fumer font l'objet d'un renvoi provisoire; *Admin* **suspended on full pay** suspendu sans suppression de traitement; *Mil* suspendu sans suppression de solde

suspended [sə'spendɪd] ADJ *(gen)* suspendu; *(particles)* en suspension

▸▸ ***suspended animation*** *(natural state)* hibernation *f*; *(induced state)* hibernation *f* artificielle *(after accident, trauma)* syncope *f*, arrêt *m* momentané des fonctions; **to be in a state of s. animation** *(animal)* être en hibernation; *(person)* avoir une syncope; **the scheme is in a state of s. animation** le projet est en suspens; *Law* ***suspended sentence*** condamnation *f* avec sursis **she got a three-month s. sentence** elle a été condamnée à trois mois de prison avec sursis

suspender [sə'spendə(r)] N *Br (for stockings)* jarretelle *f*; *(for socks)* fixe-chaussette *m*

• **suspenders** NPL *Am (for trousers)* bretelles *fpl*

▸▸ *Br* ***suspender belt*** porte-jarretelles *m inv*

suspense [sə'spens] N **1** *(anticipation)* incertitude *f*; **to keep** *or* **to leave sb in s.** laisser qn dans l'incertitude; **to put sb out of (their) s.** mettre fin à l'incertitude de qn; *Fam* **the s. is killing me!** quel suspense!❑**2** *(in films, literature)* suspense *m* **3** *Admin & Law* **in s.** en suspens; **the question remains in s.** la question reste posée *ou* en suspens

▸▸ *Fin* ***suspense account*** compte *m* d'ordre

suspension [sə'spenʃən] N **1** *(interruption)* suspension *f*; *(withdrawal)* suspension *f*, retrait *m* (provisoire); **the s. of hostilities/payments** la suspension des hostilités/des paiements

2 *(temporary dismissal ▸ from office, political party, club, team)* suspension *f*; *(▸ from job)* suspension *f*, mise *f* à pied; *(▸ from school, university)* exclusion *f* provisoire

3 *Aut & Tech* suspension *f*; **independent s.** suspension *f* à roues indépendantes

4 *Chem* suspension *f*; **in s.** en suspension

▸▸ ***suspension bridge*** pont *m* suspendu; ***suspension cable*** câble *m* porteur; ***suspension file*** hamac *m*, dossier *m* suspendu; *Typ & Gram* ***suspension points*** points *mpl* de suspension

suspensory [sə'spensərɪ] ADJ **1** *Anat* suspenseur **2** *Med (bandage, sling)* de soutien

suspicion [sə'spɪʃən] N **1** *(presumption of guilt, mistrust)* soupçon *m*, suspicion *f*; **her neighbours' strange behaviour aroused her s.** *or* **suspicions** le comportement étrange de ses voisins éveilla ses soupçons; **to be above** *or* **beyond s.** être au-dessus de tout soupçon; **I have my suspicions about this fellow** j'ai des doutes sur cet individu; **the new boss was regarded with s.** on considérait le nouveau patron avec méfiance; **to be under s.** être soupçonné; *Law* **he was arrested on s. of drug trafficking** il a été arrêté parce qu'on le soupçonnait de trafic de drogue **2** *(notion, feeling)* soupçon *m*; **I had a growing s. that he wasn't telling the truth** je soupçonnais de plus en plus qu'il ne disait pas la vérité; **I had a (sneaking) s. you'd be here** j'avais comme un pressentiment que tu serais là **3** *(trace, hint)* soupçon *m*, pointe *f*

suspicious [sə'spɪʃəs] ADJ **1** *(distrustful)* méfiant, soupçonneux; **his strange behaviour made us s.** son comportement étrange a éveillé nos soupçons *ou* notre méfiance; **she became s. when he refused to give his name** elle a commencé à se méfier quand il a refusé de donner son nom; **I'm s. of his motives** je me méfie de ses intentions; **she gave him a s. look** elle lui jeta un regard méfiant **2** *(suspect)* suspect; **there are a lot of s.-looking characters in this pub** il y a beaucoup d'individus suspects dans ce pub; **it is s.**

hat she didn't phone the police le fait qu'elle n'a as téléphoné à la police est suspect

uspiciously [sə'spɪʃəslɪ] ADV **1** *(distrustfully)* avec méfiance, soupçonneusement **2** *(strangely)* de façon suspecte; **police saw a man acting s.** a police a vu un homme qui se comportait de açon suspecte; **she was s. keen to leave** son empressement à partir était suspect; **it looks s. like malaria** ça ressemble étrangement au paludisme; **it sounded s. as though she had lost it** on aurait dit qu'elle l'avait perdu

uspiciousness [sə'spɪʃəsnɪs] N **1** *(distrust)* méfiance *f* **2** *(suspect nature)* caractère *m* suspect

uss[1] [sʌs] VT *Br Fam (work out)* découvrir⁻; *(realize)* se rendre compte de⁻; **I soon sussed what he was up to** j'ai vite compris son petit manège; **I haven't got her sussed yet** je l'ai pas encore vraiment cernée; **I haven't got this computer sussed yet** j'ai pas encore pigé comment fonctionne cet ordinateur

uss[2] [sʌs] ADJ *Br & Austr Fam (abbr* **suspicious***)* louche⁻; **he says he's working late but it all seems a bit s. to me** il dit qu'il doit rester tard au travail mais ça m'a l'air un peu louche

▸ **suss out** VT SEP *Br Fam* **1 to s. sth out** *(work out)* découvrir qch⁻; *(realize)* se rendre compte de qch⁻; **I couldn't s. out how the modem worked** j'ai pas pigé comment le modem fonctionnait; **I haven't sussed out his motives yet** j'ai toujours pas pigé ses motivations; **we have to s. out the best places to go at night** il faut qu'on repère les endroits où sortir le soir⁻ **2** *(person)* saisir le caractère de⁻; **I've got him sussed out** je sais à qui j'ai affaire⁻; **I can't quite s. her out** c'est quelqu'un que j'ai du mal à cerner⁻

ussed [sʌst] ADJ *Fam (astute)* rusé⁻, malin (igne)⁻

ustain [sə'steɪn] VT **1** *(maintain, keep up* ▸ *conversation)* entretenir; *(*▸ *effort, attack, pressure)* soutenir, maintenir; *(*▸ *someone's interest)* maintenir; **if the present level of economic growth is sustained** si le niveau actuel de croissance économique est maintenu

2 *(support physically)* soutenir, supporter; **steel girders s. the weight of the bridge** le pont est soutenu par des poutres en acier

3 *(support morally)* soutenir; **it was only their belief in God that sustained them** seule leur croyance en Dieu les a soutenus

4 *Mus (note)* tenir, soutenir

5 *(nourish)* nourrir; **they had only dried fruit and water to s. them** ils n'avaient que des fruits secs et de l'eau pour subsister; **one meal a day is not enough to s. you** l'homme a besoin pour vivre de plus d'un repas par jour; **a planet capable of sustaining life** une planète capable de maintenir la vie

6 *(suffer* ▸ *damage)* subir; *(*▸ *defeat, loss)* subir, essuyer; **to s. an injury** recevoir une blessure, être blessé; **the man sustained a serious blow to the head** l'homme a été grièvement atteint à la tête

7 *(withstand)* supporter; **her fragile condition will not s. another shock** étant donné la fragilité de son état, elle ne supportera pas un nouveau choc

8 *Law (accept as valid)* admettre; **objection sustained** objection admise; **the court sustained her claim** le tribunal lui accorda gain de cause

9 *(corroborate* ▸ *assertion, theory, charge)* corroborer

ustainable [səs'teɪnəbəl] ADJ **1** *(development, agriculture, politics)* viable, durable **2** *(energy, resources)* renouvelable

ustained [sə'steɪnd] ADJ *(effort, attack)* soutenu; *(discussion, applause)* prolongé

ustaining [sə'steɪnɪŋ] ADJ nourrissant, nutritif
▸▸ *Mus* ***sustaining pedal*** pédale *f* forte

ustenance ['sʌstɪnəns] N **1** *(nourishment)* valeur *f* nutritive; **there is little s. in such foods** de tels aliments ont peu de valeur nutritive *ou* sont peu nourrissants; **stale bread provided her only form of s.** elle se nourrissait uniquement de pain rassis; *Fig* **his neighbours provided moral s. during the crisis** ses voisins l'ont soutenu moralement pendant la crise **2** *(means of subsistence)* subsistance *f*; **they could not derive s. from the land** ils ne pouvaient pas vivre de la terre

suttee ['sʌti:] N *(tradition)* sati *m inv*; *(widow)* sati *f inv*

suture ['su:tʃə(r)] N **1** *Med* point *m* de suture **2** *Anat & Bot* suture *f*
VT *Med* suturer

SUV [ˌesju:'vi:] N *Am (abbr* **sport utility vehicle***)* 4 x 4 *m*

suzerain ['su:zəreɪn] N **1** *Hist* suzerain(e) *m,f* **2** *Pol (state)* État *m* dominant
ADJ **1** *Hist* suzerain **2** *Pol (state, power)* dominant
▸▸ ***suzerain lord*** suzerain *m*

suzerainty ['su:zərəntɪ] N **1** *(power)* suzeraineté *f*, dominance *f*; **under the s. of** sous la suzeraineté de **2** *Hist (domain)* suzeraineté *f*

svelte [svelt] ADJ svelte

Svengali [ˌsveŋ'gɑ:lɪ] N manipulateur *m*

SVGA [ˌesvi:dʒi:'eɪ] N *Comput (abbr* **super video graphics array***)* SVGA *m*
▸▸ ***SVGA monitor*** moniteur *m* SVGA

SW 1 *(written abbr* **short wave***)* OC **2** *(written abbr* **south-west***)* S-O

swab [swɒb] *(pt & pp* **swabbed**, *cont* **swabbing***)* N **1** *Med (cotton)* tampon *m*; *(specimen)* prélèvement *m* **2** *(mop)* serpillière *f* **3** *(brush for firearms)* écouvillon *m*
VT **1** *Med (clean)* nettoyer (avec un tampon) **2** *(mop)* laver; **to s. down the decks** laver le pont

▸ **swab out** VT SEP *Mil (firearm)* écouvillonner; *Med (wound)* nettoyer avec un tampon

swacked [swækt] ADJ *Am Fam (drunk)* bourré, fait

swaddle ['swɒdəl] VT **1** *(wrap)* envelopper, emmitoufler; **her head was swaddled in bandages** elle avait la tête enveloppée de pansements **2** *Arch (baby)* emmailloter

swaddling clothes ['swɒdlɪŋ-] NPL *Arch or Bible* maillot *m*, langes *mpl*; **the infant was wrapped in s.** le nourrisson était emmailloté

swag [swæg] *Fam* N **1** *Br (booty)* butin⁻*m* **2** *Austr & NZ (bundle)* baluchon *m*, balluchon *m*; **to go on the s.** vagabonder⁻

swagger ['swægə(r)] VI **1** *(strut)* se pavaner; **he swaggered into/out of the room** il entra dans/sortit de la pièce en se pavanant **2** *(boast)* se vanter, fanfaronner, plastronner
N *(manner)* air *m* arrogant; *(walk)* démarche *f* arrogante; **he entered the room with a s.** il entra dans la pièce en se pavanant
▸▸ ***swagger cane, swagger stick*** *(gen)* badine *f*, canne *f*; *Mil* bâton *m* (d'officier)

swaggering ['swægərɪŋ] ADJ *(gait, attitude)* arrogant; *(person)* fanfaron, bravache
N *(proud gait)* démarche *f ou* allure *f* arrogante; *(boasting)* vantardise *f*

swagman ['swægmæn] *(pl* **swagmen** [-men]*)* N *Austr & NZ Fam* clochard⁻*m*

Swahili [swɑ:'hi:lɪ] N **1** *Ling* swahili *m*, souahéli *m* **2** *(person)* Swahili(e) *m,f*, Souahéli(e) *m,f*
ADJ swahili, souahéli

swain [sweɪn] N *Arch (young man)* jeune homme *m* de la campagne; *(lover)* soupirant *m*

SWALK [swɔ:k] N *Fam (abbr* **sealed with a loving kiss***)* ≃ doux baisers *(écrit sur une enveloppe contenant une lettre d'amour)*

swallow ['swɒləʊ] VT **1** *(food, drink, medicine)* avaler; **he almost swallowed his tongue** il a failli avaler sa langue

2 *Fam (believe)* avaler⁻, croire⁻; **she swallowed the story whole** elle a avalé *ou* cru toute l'histoire; **he'll s. anything** il avalerait n'importe quoi; **I find it hard to s.** j'ai du mal à avaler ça

3 *(accept unprotestingly)* avaler, accepter; **I find it hard to s.** je trouve ça un peu raide; **I'm not going to s. that sort of treatment** pas question que j'accepte d'être traité de cette façon

4 *(repress)* ravaler; **to s. one's anger/disappointment** ravaler sa colère/sa déception; **he had to s. his pride** il a dû ravaler sa fierté

5 *(retract)* **to s. one's words** ravaler ses paroles

6 *(absorb)* engloutir; **they were soon swallowed by the crowd** la foule eut tôt fait de les engloutir; **I wished the ground would open up and s. me** j'aurais voulu être à six pieds sous terre

VI avaler, déglutir; **it hurts when I s.** j'ai mal quand j'avale; **she swallowed hard and continued her speech** elle avala sa salive et poursuivit son discours

N **1** *(action)* gorgée *f*; **she took a long s. of champagne** elle prit *ou* but une grande gorgée de champagne; **he finished his drink with one s.** il finit sa boisson d'un trait *ou* d'un seul coup **2** *Orn* hirondelle *f*; *Prov* **one s. doesn't make a summer** une hirondelle ne fait pas le printemps
▸▸ *Br* ***swallow dive*** saut *m* de l'ange

▸ **swallow down** VT SEP = **swallow** VT **1**

▸ **swallow up** VT SEP engloutir; **the Baltic States were swallowed up by the Soviet Union** les pays Baltes ont été engloutis par l'Union soviétique; **they were soon swallowed up in the mist** ils furent bientôt noyés dans la brume; **they were swallowed up in the crowd** ils ont disparu dans la foule

swallow-dive VI *Br* faire le saut de l'ange

swallowtail ['swɒləʊteɪl] N **1** *(forked tail)* queue *f* fourchue **2** *Fam Old-fashioned (coat)* queue-de-morue *f* **3** *Entom* **s. (butterfly)** machaon *m*

swallow-tailed ADJ **1** *(bird)* à queue fourchue **2** *(coat)* à queue de morue

swam [swæm] *pt of* **swim**

swamp [swɒmp] N marais *m*, marécage *m*
VT **1** *(flood)* inonder; *(cause to sink)* submerger **2** *(overwhelm)* inonder, submerger; **she was swamped with calls** elle a été submergée d'appels; **we're swamped (with work) at the office at the moment** nous sommes débordés de travail au bureau en ce moment
▸▸ *Am* ***swamp buggy*** *(boat)* hydroglisseur *m*; *(tractor)* tracteur *m* amphibie; *Am* ***swamp fever*** *(malaria)* paludisme *m*, malaria *f*

swampy ['swɒmpɪ] *(compar* **swampier**, *superl* **swampiest***)* ADJ marécageux

swan [swɒn] *(pt & pp* **swanned**, *cont* **swanning***)* N cygne *m*; **the S. of Avon** = surnom donné à Shakespeare
VI *Br Fam* **they spent a year swanning round Europe** ils ont passé une année à se balader en Europe; **where's he swanning off to now?** où est-ce qu'il va encore traîner?; **he came swanning into the office at ten o'clock** il est arrivé au bureau comme si de rien n'était à dix heures⁻; **don't think you can come swanning back just when you feel like it** ne crois pas que tu peux revenir les mains dans les poches quand tu en as envie
▸▸ *Am* ***swan dive*** saut *m* de l'ange; ***swan neck*** col-de-cygne *m*

swank [swæŋk] *Fam* N *Br* **1** *(boasting)* frime *f*; **ignore him, it's all s.** ne fais pas attention à lui, tout ça c'est de la frime **2** *(boastful person)* frimeur(euse) *m,f* **3** *Am (luxury)* luxe⁻*m*, chic⁻*m*; **it's got lots of s.!** ça a une de ces classes!
VI se vanter⁻, frimer
ADJ **1** *(chic)* classe *(inv)*, chicos **2** *(boastful)* frimeur

swanky ['swæŋkɪ] *(compar* **swankier**, *superl* **swankiest***)* ADJ *Fam* **1** *(chic)* classe *(inv)*, chicos **2** *(boastful)* frimeur

swan-necked ADJ *Br* **1** *(person)* au cou de cygne **2** *(object)* en col-de-cygne

swannery ['swɒnərɪ] *(pl* **swanneries***)* N réserve *f* de cygnes

swansdown ['swɒnzdaʊn] N **1** *(feathers)* duvet *m* de cygne **2** *Tex* molleton *m*

swap [swɒp] *(pt & pp* **swapped**, *cont* **swapping***)* VT **1** *(possessions, places)* échanger; **to s. sth for sth** échanger qch contre qch; **I'll s. my coat for yours, I'll s. coats with you** échangeons nos manteaux; **(I'll) s. you!** je te l'échange!; **they've swapped places** ils ont échangé leurs places; **he swapped places with his sister** il a échangé sa place contre celle de sa sœur; **I wouldn't s. places with him for love nor money** je ne voudrais être à sa place pour rien au monde; **I'd s. jobs with him any day!** j'échangerais mon travail contre le sien sans hésiter!; **as soon as the music stops, everybody s. partners** dès que la musique s'arrête, tout le monde change de cavalier **2** *(ideas, opinions, stories)* échanger; **they swapped insults over the garden fence** ils échangèrent des insultes par-dessus la clôture du jardin **3** *St Exch* swaper

VI échanger, faire un échange *ou* un troc; **I'll s. with you** on échangera, on fera un échange

N 1 *(exchange)* troc *m*, échange *m*; **to do a s.** faire un troc *ou* un échange; **it's a good s.** c'est un échange avantageux; **I gave her my bicycle as a s. for hers** je lui ai donné mon vélo en échange du sien **2** *(duplicate ▸ stamp in collection etc)* double *m* **3** *St Exch* swap *m*, échange *m* financier

▸▸ *Am* ***swap meet*** foire *f* au troc; *St Exch* ***swap option*** option *f* sur swap de taux d'intérêt; ***swap shop*** foire *f* au troc, magasin *m* de troc

SWAPO ['swɑːpəʊ] **N** *(abbr* **South West Africa People's Organization***)* SWAPO *f*

sward [swɔːd] **N** *Arch or Literary* gazon *m*, pelouse *f*

swarm [swɔːm] **N 1** *(of bees)* essaim *m*; *(of ants)* colonie *f* **2** *Fig (of people)* essaim *m*, nuée *f*, masse *f*; **surrounded by a s. of admirers** entouré d'une foule d'admirateurs

VI 1 *(bees)* essaimer

2 *Fig (place)* fourmiller, grouiller; **the streets were swarming with people** les rues grouillaient de monde

3 *Fig (people)* affluer; **the crowd swarmed in/out** la foule s'est engouffrée à l'intérieur/est sortie en masse; **bargain-hunters swarmed into the department store** les chercheurs d'occasions envahirent le grand magasin; **children were swarming round the ice-cream van** les enfants s'agglutinaient autour du camion du marchand de glaces

4 *(climb)* grimper (lestement); **she swarmed up the tree** elle grimpa lestement à l'arbre

swarming ['swɔːmɪŋ] **N** *(in beekeeping)* essaimage *m*

swarthiness ['swɔːðɪnɪs] **N** teint *m* basané

swarthy ['swɔːðɪ] *(compar* **swarthier**, *superl* **swarthiest***)* **ADJ** basané; **he has a s. complexion** il a le teint basané

swash [swɒʃ] **N** *(splash)* clapotis *m*

VI clapoter

swashbuckler ['swɒʃˌbʌklə(r)] **N 1** *(adventurer)* aventurier(ère) *m,f*; *(swaggerer)* fier-à-bras *m*, matamore *m* **2** *(film)* film *m* de cape et d'épée; *(novel)* roman *m* de cape et d'épée

swashbuckling ['swɒʃˌbʌklɪŋ] **ADJ** *(person)* fanfaron; *(film, story)* de cape et d'épée

swashplate ['swɒʃpleɪt] **N** *Aut* plateau *m* oscillant

swastika ['swɒstɪkə] **N** *Antiq* svastika *m*; *(Nazi)* croix *f* gammée

swat[1] [swɒt] *(pt & pp* **swatted**, *cont* **swatting***)* **VT 1** *(insect)* écraser **2** *Fam (slap)* frapper[□]

N 1 *(device)* tapette *f* **2** *(swipe)* **he took a s. at the mosquito** il essaya d'écraser le moustique

swat[2] = **swot**

swath [swɔːθ] = **swathe N**

swathe [sweɪð] **VT 1** *(bind)* envelopper, emmailloter; **his head was swathed in bandages** sa tête était enveloppée de pansements; **she lay in bed swathed in blankets** elle était dans son lit, enveloppée *ou* emmitouflée dans des couvertures **2** *(envelop)* envelopper; **swathed in mist** enveloppé de brume

N 1 *Agr* andain *m* **2** *(strip of land)* bande *f* de terre; **the army cut a s. through the town** l'armée a tout détruit sur son passage dans la ville; **the new motorway cuts a s. through the countryside** la nouvelle autoroute coupe à travers la campagne; **she cut a s. through the opposition** elle a fait des ravages dans les rangs de l'opposition **3** *(strip of cloth)* lanière *f*

sway [sweɪ] **VI 1** *(pylon, bridge)* se balancer, osciller; *(tree)* s'agiter; *(bus, train)* pencher; *(boat)* rouler; *(person ▸ deliberately)* se balancer; *(▸ from tiredness, drink)* chanceler, tituber; **the poplars swayed in the wind** les peupliers étaient agités par le vent; **they were swaying to the music** ils se balançaient au rythme de la musique; **to s. from side to side** se balancer de droite à gauche; **to s. to and fro** se balancer d'avant en arrière **2** *(vacillate)* vaciller, hésiter; *(incline, tend)* pencher; **to s. towards conservatism** pencher vers le conservatisme

VT 1 *(pylon)* (faire) balancer, faire osciller; *(tree)* agiter; *(hips)* rouler, balancer; **they started swaying their bodies in time to the music** ils ont commencé à se balancer au rythme de la musique **2** *(influence)* influencer; **to s. sb from his/her course** détourner qn de ses projets; **to refuse to be swayed** refuser de se laisser influencer; **don't be swayed by his charm** ne te laisse pas influencer par son charme

N 1 *(rocking ▸ gen)* balancement *m*; *(▸ of a boat)* roulis *m* **2** *(influence)* influence *f*, emprise *f*, empire *m*; **under her s.** sous son empire, sous son influence; **to hold s. over sb/sth** avoir de l'influence *ou* de l'emprise sur qn/qch; **the economic theories that hold s. today** les théories économiques qui ont cours aujourd'hui

swaying ['sweɪɪŋ] **ADJ** qui se balance, qui oscille; **s. motion** balancement *m*, mouvement *m* de va-et-vient

N *(motion)* balancement *m*, mouvement *m* de va-et-vient; *(of bridge, pylon)* balancement *m*, oscillation *f*; *(of boat, car)* roulis *m*; *(of person ▸ deliberate)* balancement *m*; *(▸ from tiredness, drink)* vacillement *m*

Swazi ['swɑːzɪ] **N** Swazi *mf*

Swaziland ['swɑːzɪlænd] **N** Swaziland *m*

swear [sweə(r)] *(pt* **swore** [swɔː(r)], *pp* **sworn** [swɔːn]*)* **VI 1** *(curse)* jurer; **to s. at sb** injurier qn; **they started swearing at each other** ils ont commencé à se traiter de tous les noms *ou* à s'injurier; **don't s. in front of the children** ne dis pas de gros mots devant les enfants; **to s. like a trooper** jurer comme un charretier **2** *(vow, take an oath)* jurer; **he swore on the Bible** il jura sur la Bible; **I can't s. to its authenticity** je ne peux pas jurer de son authenticité; **I would s. to it** j'en jurerais; **I wouldn't s. to it, but I think it was him** je n'en jurerais pas, mais je crois que c'était lui; **I s. I'll never do it again!** je jure de ne plus jamais recommencer!; **he swears he's never seen her before** il jure qu'il ne l'a jamais vue; **it wasn't me, I s.!** ce n'était pas moi, je le jure!; **they swore to defend the family honour** ils jurèrent de défendre l'honneur de la famille

VT 1 *(pledge, vow)* **to s. an oath** prêter serment; **to s. allegiance to the Crown** jurer allégeance à la couronne **2** *(make pledge)* **to s. sb to secrecy** faire jurer à qn de garder le secret

▸▸ *Br* ***swear box*** boîte *f* à gros mots *(dans laquelle on est censé mettre, en guise de punition, une pièce de monnaie à chaque fois que l'on jure)*

▸ **swear by VT INSEP 1** *(invoke)* jurer par; **to s. by all that one holds sacred** jurer sur tout ce qu'on a de plus sacré **2** *(have confidence in)* **she swears by that old sewing machine of hers** elle ne jure que par sa vieille machine à coudre; **you should try honey and hot milk for your cold, my mother swears by it** pour ton rhume, tu devrais essayer du miel dans du lait chaud, ma mère ne jure que par ça

▸ **swear in VT SEP** *(witness, president)* faire prêter serment à, *Formal* assermenter

▸ **swear off VT INSEP** *Fam* renoncer à[□]; **he has sworn off drinking** il a renoncé à l'alcool *ou* arrêté de boire

swearing ['sweərɪŋ] **N 1** *(use of swearwords)* jurons *mpl*, gros mots *mpl*; **there's too much s. on television** il y a trop de grossièretés à la télévision **2** *Law* **after the s. in of the jury** après que le jury eut prêté serment

swearword ['sweəwɜːd] **N** grossièreté *f*, juron *m*, gros mot *m*

sweat [swet] *(Br pt & pp* **sweated**, *Am pt & pp* **sweat** *or* **sweated***)* **N 1** *(perspiration)* sueur *f*, transpiration *f*; **I woke up covered in s.** je me suis réveillé en nage *ou* couvert de sueur *ou* tout en sueur; **the s. was pouring off him** il dégoulinait de sueur; **to break out in** *or* **to come out in a cold s.** avoir des sueurs froides; **she earned it by the s. of her brow** elle l'a gagné à la sueur de son front

2 *Fam (unpleasant task)* corvée[□] *f*; *Br* **picking strawberries is a real s.** la cueillette des fraises est une vraie corvée; **can you give me a hand? – no s.!** peux-tu me donner un coup de main? – pas de problème!

3 *Br Fam (anxious state)* **to work oneself (up) into a s. (about sth)** se faire du mauvais sang (au sujet de qch); **there's no need to get into a s. about it!** pas la peine de te mettre dans des états pareils!

4 *(on wall, surface)* suintement *m*

5 *Br Fam Old-fashioned* **(old) s.** *(old soldier)* vieu soldat *m*; *(experienced worker)* vieux routier *m*

6 *Am (sweatshirt)* sweat *m*

VI 1 *(perspire)* suer, transpirer; **the effort mac him s.** l'effort l'a mis en sueur; **she was sweatir profusely** elle suait à grosses gouttes; *Fam* **to like a pig** suer comme un bœuf

2 *Fig (work hard, suffer)* suer; **my mother sweate over a hot stove from morning till night** ma mè suait sur ses fourneaux du matin jusqu'au soi **I'll make them s. for this!** ils vont me le payer **she's sweating over her homework** elle est en tra de suer sur ses devoirs

3 *Fam (worry)* se faire de la bile, se faire un san d'encre; **I was sweating in case he found out wh I'd done** j'avais la trouille qu'il découvre ce qu j'avais fait; **I'm going to leave him to s. for a whi** je vais le laisser mijoter un peu

4 *(ooze ▸ walls, surface)* suer, suinter; *(▸ chees* suer

VT 1 *(cause to perspire)* faire suer *ou* transpire **the doctor recommended sweating the patient** médecin recommanda de faire transpirer malade

2 *(exude) Fig* **to s. blood** suer sang et eau; *Fam* **s. buckets** suer comme un bœuf

3 *Am Fam (extort)* **we sweated the informatic out of him** on lui a fait cracher le morceau

4 *Culin* faire suer

▸▸ *Anat* ***sweat duct*** conduit *m* sudorifère; ***swe gland*** glande *f* sudoripare; ***sweat suit*** survêt ment *m*, jogging *m*

▸ **sweat off VT SEP** éliminer; **you should do som exercise to s. off those excess pounds** tu devra faire un peu d'exercice pour éliminer ces kilo superflus

▸ **sweat out VT SEP 1** *(illness)* **stay in bed and try s. out the cold** restez au lit et essayez de transp rer pour faire partir votre rhume **2** *(idiom)* **to s. out** prendre son mal en patience, tenir jusqu'à bout; **leave him to s. it out** laissez-le se débrou ler tout seul

sweatband ['swetbænd] **N 1** *Sport (headbanc* bandeau *m*; *(wristband)* poignet *m* **2** *(in a ha* cuir *m* intérieur

sweated ['swetɪd] **ADJ**

▸▸ ***sweated labour*** *(staff)* main-d'œuvre *f* exploitée; *(work)* exploitation *f*

sweater ['swetə(r)] **N** pull *m*, pull-over *m*

▸▸ ***sweater dress*** robe-pull *f*

sweatiness ['swetɪnɪs] **N** moiteur *f*

sweating ['swetɪŋ] **N** transpiration *f*, *Spec* suda tion *f*

sweatpants ['swetpænts] **NPL** pantalon *m* d survêtement

sweatshirt ['swetʃɜːt] **N** sweat-shirt *m*

sweatshop ['swetʃɒp] **N** ≃ atelier *m* clandestir *Fig Hum* **it's a real s. here** c'est le bagne ici

sweaty ['swetɪ] *(compar* **sweatier**, *superl* **sweat est***)* **ADJ 1** *(person)* (tout) en sueur; *(hands)* moite *(feet)* qui transpire; *(clothing)* trempé de sueu **he's got s. feet** il transpire des pieds; **his uniforr smelt s.** son uniforme sentait la sueur

2 *(weather, place)* d'une chaleur humide *o* moite; **she went back into the s. workshop** elle re plongea dans la chaleur humide de l'atelier

3 *(cheese)* qui sue

4 *(activity)* qui fait transpirer; **it was a hard, s climb** l'ascension était rude et donnait chaud

Swede [swiːd] **N** Suédois(e) *m,f*

swede [swiːd] **N** *Br* rutabaga *m*, chou-navet *m*

Sweden ['swiːdən] **N** Suède *f*

Swedish ['swiːdɪʃ] **NPL the S.** les Suédois *mpl*

N *(language)* suédois *m*

ADJ suédois

sweep [swiːp] *(pt & pp* **swept** [swept]*)* **N 1** *(with brush)* coup *m* de balai; **the room needs a good s** la pièce aurait besoin d'un bon coup de balai

2 *(movement)* **with a s. of her arm** d'un gest large; **with a s. of his sword/scythe** d'un gran coup d'épée/de faux; **to make a wide s. to take bend** prendre du champ pour effectuer un vi rage; **in** *or* **at one s.** d'un seul coup

3 *(curved line, area)* (grande) courbe *f*, étendu *f*, *Archit (of arch)* courbure *f*; **a vast s. of woodlan**

ne vaste étendue de forêt; **from where we tood, we could see the whole s. of the bay** de là ù nous étions, nous voyions toute (l'étendue e) la baie

4 *(range ▸ of gun, telescope)* champ *m*; *(▸ of lighthouse)* balayage *m*, portée *f*; *(▸ of wings)* envergure *f*; *(▸ of knowledge)* étendue *f*; **the members f the commission represent a broad s. of opinion** es membres de la commission représentent un arge éventail d'opinions

5 *(search)* fouille *f*; *Mil (reconnaissance)* reconnaissance *f*; *Mil (attack)* attaque *f*; **police made a rugs s. on the university** la police a ratissé l'université à la recherche de drogues; **the rescue arty made a s. of the area** l'équipe de secours a atissé les environs *ou* passé les environs au eigne fin; **to make a s. for mines** chercher des nines

6 *(chimney sweep)* ramoneur *m*

7 *Fam (sweepstake)* sweepstake ▫ *m*

8 *Electron (by electron beam)* balayage *m*

9 *(rapid flow ▸ of river)* course *f ou* flot *m* rapide

VT 1 *(with a brush ▸ room, street, dust, leaves)* balayer; *(▸ chimney)* ramoner; **to s. the floor** balayer le sol; **the steps had been swept clean** uelqu'un avait balayé l'escalier; **she swept the eaves from the path into a pile** elle balaya les euilles du chemin et les mit en tas; **I swept the roken glass into the dustpan** j'ai poussé le verre assé dans la pelle avec le balai; *Br Fig* **to s. sth nder the carpet** *or* **the rug** tirer le rideau sur qch

2 *(with hand)* **he angrily swept the papers off the esk** d'un geste furieux, il balaya les papiers de essus le bureau; **she swept the coins off the able into her handbag** elle a fait glisser les pièces de la table dans son sac à main

3 *(of wind, tide, crowd etc)* **her dress sweeps the round** sa robe balaie le sol; **a storm swept the own** un orage ravagea la ville; **the wind swept is hat into the river** le vent a fait tomber son chaeau dans la rivière; **the small boat was swept ut to sea** le petit bateau a été emporté vers le arge; **three fishermen were swept overboard** un aquet de mer emporta trois pêcheurs; *Fig* **the ictorious army swept all before it** l'armée victoeuse a tout balayé sur son passage; **he was wept to power on a wave of popular discontent** il été porté au pouvoir par une vague de mécontentement populaire; **he swept her off to Paris for he weekend** il l'a emmenée en week-end à Paris; **o be swept off one's feet** *(fall in love)* tomber fou moureux; *(be filled with enthusiasm)* être enhousiasmé; **to s. the board** rafler tous les prix; **he German athletes swept the board at the Olymics** les athlètes allemands ont remporté toutes es médailles aux jeux Olympiques

4 *(spread through ▸ of fire, epidemic, rumour, beef)* gagner; **a new craze is sweeping America** une ouvelle mode fait fureur aux États-Unis; **a vave of fear swept the city** une vague de peur agna la ville; **the flu epidemic which swept Europe in 1919** l'épidémie de grippe qui sévit en Europe en 1919

5 *(scan, survey)* parcourir; **her eyes swept the orizon/the room** elle parcourut l'horizon/la ièce des yeux; **to s. the horizon with a telescope** arcourir *ou* balayer l'horizon avec un télescoe; **searchlights continually s. the open ground utside the prison camp** des projecteurs parcourent *ou* balayent sans cesse le terrain qui enoure la prison

6 *(win easily)* gagner *ou* remporter haut la main; **he Popular Democratic Party swept the polls** le arti démocratique populaire a fait un raz-denarée aux élections; *Am Sport* **she swept the ournament** elle a gagné le tournoi sans concéder une seule partie

7 *Naut (mines, sea, channel)* draguer; **the port as been swept for mines** le port a été dragué

VI 1 *(with a brush)* balayer

2 *(move quickly, powerfully)* **harsh winds swept cross the bleak steppes** un vent violent balayait es mornes steppes; **the beam swept across the ea** le faisceau lumineux balaya la mer; **I vatched storm clouds sweeping across the sky** je egardais des nuages orageux filer dans le ciel; **hurricane swept through the town** un ouragan a évasté la ville; **a wave of nationalism swept hrough the country** une vague de nationalisme a déferlé sur le pays; **a wave of panic swept over him** une vague de panique le submergea; **the planes swept low over the town** les avions passèrent en rase-mottes au-dessus de la ville; **the fire swept through the forest** l'incendie a ravagé la forêt

3 *(move confidently, proudly)* **he swept into the room** il entra majestueusement dans la pièce; **she swept past me without even a glance** elle passa majestueusement à côté de moi sans même m'adresser un regard

4 *(stretch ▸ land)* s'étendre; **the rolling prairies s. away into the distance** les prairies ondoyantes se perdent dans le lointain; **the fields s. down to the lake** les prairies descendent en pente douce jusqu'au lac; **the river sweeps round in a wide curve** le fleuve décrit une large courbe

5 *Naut* **to s. for mines** draguer, déminer

▸▸ ***sweep hand*** trotteuse *f*

▸ **sweep along** VT SEP *(of wind, tide, crowd)* emporter, entraîner; **we were swept along by a tide of nationalism** nous avons été balayés par une vague nationaliste

▸ **sweep aside** VT SEP **1** *(object, person)* écarter **2** *(advice, objection)* repousser, rejeter; *(obstacle, opposition)* écarter

▸ **sweep away** VT SEP **1** *(dust, snow)* balayer **2** *(of wind, tide, crowd)* emporter, entraîner; **three bathers were swept away by a huge wave** trois baigneurs ont été emportés par une énorme vague

▸ **sweep by** VI *(car)* passer à toute vitesse; *(person ▸ majestically)* passer majestueusement; *(▸ disdainfully)* passer dédaigneusement

▸ **sweep down** VI **1** *(steps)* descendre; **hills sweeping down to the sea** des collines qui descendent vers la mer **2** *(attack)* **the enemy swept down on us** l'ennemi s'abattit *ou* fonça sur nous

▸ **sweep out** VT SEP *(clean ▸ room)* balayer

▸ **sweep past** = **sweep by**

▸ **sweep up** VT SEP *(dust, leaves)* balayer; **she swept up the pieces of glass** elle balaya les morceaux de verre; **with her hair swept up into a chignon** avec ses cheveux relevés en chignon; **she swept up her two babies and left** en toute hâte, elle prit ses deux bébés dans ses bras et partit

VI 1 *(clean up)* balayer **2** *(approach)* **she swept up to me** *(majestically)* elle s'approcha de moi d'un pas majestueux; *(angrily)* elle s'approcha de moi d'un pas furieux; **the car swept up to the main entrance** *(quickly)* la voiture s'approcha à toute allure de l'entrée principale; *(impressively)* la voiture s'approcha à une allure majestueuse de l'entrée principale

sweepback ['swi:pbæk] **N** flèche *f* (arrière)

sweeper ['swi:pə(r)] **N 1** *(person)* balayeur(euse) *m,f* **2** *(device ▸ for streets)* balayeuse *f*; *(▸ for carpets)* balai *m* mécanique **3** *Ftbl* libero *m*

sweeping ['swi:pɪŋ] **ADJ 1** *(wide ▸ movement, curve)* large; **with a s. gesture** d'un geste large, d'un grand geste; **a s. view** une vue panoramique

2 *(indiscriminate)* **a s. generalization** *or* **statement** une généralisation excessive; **he makes s. statements about the European mentality** il fait des généralisations abusives *ou* hâtives sur la mentalité européenne

3 *(significant, large ▸ amount)* considérable; **s. budget cuts** des coupes *fpl* sombres dans le budget; **the opposition has made s. gains** l'opposition a énormément progressé

4 *(far-reaching ▸ measure, change)* de grande portée, de grande envergure; **s. reforms** des réformes *fpl* de grande envergure

• **sweepings** NPL balayures *fpl*

sweepingly ['swi:pɪŋlɪ] **ADV** *(describe, criticize)* de façon trop générale *ou* hâtive

sweepstake ['swi:psteɪk] **N** sweepstake *m*

sweet [swi:t] **ADJ 1** *(in taste)* sucré; *(wine)* moelleux; **to taste s., to have a s. taste** être sucré, avoir un goût sucré; **to have a s. tooth** être un bec sucré, adorer les *ou* être friand de sucreries

2 *(fresh, clean ▸ air)* doux (douce); *(▸ breath)* frais (fraîche); *(▸ water)* pur

3 *(fragrant ▸ smell)* agréable, suave; **the roses smell so s.!** les roses sentent si bon!; *Fig* **to enjoy the s. smell of success** goûter à l'ivresse du succès

4 *(musical ▸ sound, voice)* mélodieux; *(▸ words)* doux (douce); **to whisper s. nothings (in sb's ear)** murmurer des mots d'amour (à l'oreille de qn), *Old-fashioned* conter fleurette (à qn)

5 *(pleasant, satisfactory ▸ emotion, feeling, success)* doux (douce); **revenge is s.** la vengeance est douce

6 *(kind, generous)* gentil; **a s. old lady** une vieille dame charmante; **it was very s. of you** c'était très gentil de votre part; **how s. of her to phone!** comme elle est gentille d'avoir téléphoné!; *Br* **to keep sb s.** cultiver les bonnes grâces de qn

7 *(attractive, cute)* mignon, adorable; **what a s. little baby** quel adorable bébé!; **a s. little dress** une gentille petite robe, une petite robe exquise

8 *Br Fam Old-fashioned* **to be s. on sb** *(in love)* avoir le béguin pour qn

9 *Fam (as intensifier)* **he'll please his own s. self, he'll go his own s. way** il n'en fera qu'à sa tête; **she'll come in her own s. time** elle viendra quand ça lui chantera; *Br very Fam* **s. FA** que dalle

N 1 *Br (piece of confectionery)* bonbon *m*; **I don't really like sweets** je n'aime pas beaucoup les sucreries **2** *Br (dessert)* dessert *m*; **what's for s.?** qu'est-ce qu'il y a comme dessert? **3** *(term of address)* **my s.** mon (ma) chéri(e)

EXCLAM *Fam* cool!, génial!

▸▸ *Bot* ***sweet cherry*** merisier *m*; *Bot* ***sweet chestnut*** marron *m*; ***sweet cider*** *Am* jus *m* de pomme *(non fermenté)*; *Br* cidre *m* doux; *Bot* ***sweet pea*** pois *m* de senteur; ***sweet pepper*** poivron *m*; ***sweet potato*** patate *f* douce; *Br* ***sweet shop*** confiserie *f*; *Fam* ***sweet talk*** *(UNCOUNT)* flatteries ▫ *fpl*, paroles *fpl* mielleuses ▫; *Bot* ***sweet william*** œillet *m* de poète

sweetbread ['swi:tbred] **N** *Culin (thymus)* ris *m*; *(pancreas)* pancréas *m*

sweetcorn ['swi:tkɔ:n] **N** maïs *m* doux

sweeten ['swi:tən] **VT 1** *(food, drink)* sucrer; **sweetened with honey** sucré avec du miel

2 *(mollify, soften)* **to s. (up)** amadouer, enjôler; **she tried to s. him (up) by taking him out to dinner** elle a essayé de l'amadouer en l'emmenant dîner au restaurant; **their remarks did nothing to s. my temper** leurs remarques n'ont rien fait pour apaiser ma colère

3 *Fam (bribe)* graisser la patte à; **how much would it cost to s. (up) the committee?** combien ça coûterait de graisser la patte au comité?

4 *(make more attractive ▸ task)* adoucir; *(▸ offer)* améliorer

5 *(improve the odour of ▸ air)* parfumer, embaumer; *(▸ breath)* purifier

sweetener ['swi:tənə(r)] **N 1** *(for food, drink)* édulcorant *m*, sucrette *f*; **artificial sweeteners** édulcorants *mpl* artificiels **2** *Br Fam (present)* cadeau ▫ *m*; *(bribe)* pot-de-vin ▫ *m*; **they gave him a bigger office as a s.** ils lui ont donné un plus grand bureau pour l'amadouer ▫; **the government was accused of offering the company sweeteners** on a accusé le gouvernement de donner des pots-de-vin à la compagnie

sweetening ['swi:tənɪŋ] **N** *(UNCOUNT)* **1** *(substance)* édulcorant *m*, édulcorants *mpl* **2** *(process ▸ of wine)* sucrage *m*; *(▸ of water)* adoucissement *m*

sweetheart ['swi:thɑ:t] **N 1** *(lover)* petit(e) ami(e) *m,f*; **they're sweethearts** ils sont amoureux; **they were childhood sweethearts** ils s'aimaient *ou* ils étaient amoureux quand ils étaient enfants **2** *(term of address)* mon (ma) chéri(e)

▸▸ *Ind* ***sweetheart agreement*** = accord entre un employeur et des dirigeants syndicaux dont les termes sont favorables aux deux parties mais pas aux travailleurs concernés

sweetie ['swi:tɪ] **N** *Fam* **1** *(darling)* chéri(e) *m,f*, chou *m*; **he's a real s.** il est vraiment adorable; **what's the matter, s.?** qu'est-ce qu'il y a, mon chou? **2** *Br (sweet)* bonbon ▫ *m*

sweetish ['swi:tɪʃ] **ADJ** sucré; *(unpleasantly)* douceâtre

sweetly ['swi:tlɪ] **ADV 1** *(pleasantly, kindly)* gentiment; *(cutely)* d'un air mignon; **she smiled at him s.** elle lui sourit gentiment; **the child smiled at them s.** l'enfant leur adressa un joli sourire **2**

(smoothly) sans à-coups; *(accurately)* avec précision; **the engine was running s.** le moteur ronronnait; *Br* **he's starting to hit the ball more s.** il commence à frapper la balle avec plus de précision **3** *(musically)* harmonieusement, mélodieusement; **she sings very s.** elle a une voix très mélodieuse

sweetmeat ['swi:tmi:t] **N** *Old-fashioned or Literary* friandise *f*

sweetness ['swi:tnɪs] **N 1** *(in taste)* goût *m* sucré; *(of wine)* (goût *m*) moelleux *m*
2 *(freshness ▸ of air)* douceur *f*; *(▸ of breath)* fraîcheur *f*; *(▸ of water)* pureté *f*
3 *(fragrance)* parfum *m*
4 *(musicality ▸ of sound)* son *m* mélodieux; *(▸ of voice, words)* douceur *f*
5 *(pleasure, satisfaction)* douceur *f*; **the s. of revenge** le plaisir (exquis) de la vengeance
6 *(kindness, generosity)* gentillesse *f*; **she's all s. and light** elle est on ne peut plus gentille

sweet-scented **ADJ** parfumé

sweet-talk **VT** *Fam* embobiner; **don't try to s. me!** n'essaie pas de m'embobiner!; **she sweet-talked him into doing it** elle l'a si bien embobiné qu'il a fini par le faire

sweet-tempered **ADJ** doux (douce), agréable

swell [swel] (*pt* **swelled**, *pp* **swelled** *or* **swollen** ['swəʊlən]) **VI 1** *(distend ▸ wood, pulses etc)* gonfler; *(▸ part of body)* enfler, gonfler; **the damp has made the wood s.** l'humidité a fait gonfler le bois; *Fig* **her heart swelled with joy/pride** son cœur s'est gonflé de joie/d'orgueil
2 *(increase)* augmenter; **the crowd swelled to nearly two hundred** la foule grossit et il y eut bientôt près de deux cents personnes
3 *(well up ▸ emotion)* monter, surgir; **I felt anger s. in me** je sentais la colère monter en moi
4 *(rise ▸ sea, tide)* monter; *(▸ river)* se gonfler, grossir
5 *(grow louder)* s'enfler; **the music swelled to its climax** la musique atteignit alors son point culminant
VT 1 *(distend)* gonfler; **the wind swelled the sails** le vent gonfla les voiles; **her eyes were swollen with tears** ses yeux étaient pleins de larmes **2** *(increase)* augmenter, grossir; **she asked her friends to come along to s. the numbers** elle a demandé à ses amis de venir pour qu'il y ait plus de monde; **to s. the ranks of the unemployed** venir grossir les rangs des chômeurs **3** *(cause to rise)* gonfler, grossir; **the rivers had been swollen by torrential rains** les cours d'eau avaient été gonflés *ou* grossis par des pluies torrentielles
N 1 *Naut* houle *f*; **there was a deep** *or* **heavy s.** il y avait une forte houle
2 *(bulge)* gonflement *m*
3 *(increase)* augmentation *f*; *Mus* crescendo *m*
4 *Mus (device)* soufflet *m*
5 *Am Fam Old-fashioned (big shot)* gros bonnet *m*; *(dandy)* dandy *m*, gandin *m*; *(rich person)* personne *f* huppée, rupin *m*
ADJ *Am Fam Old-fashioned (great)* super, chouette; **she's a s. girl** c'est une chic fille; **we had a s. time** on s'est super bien amusés
EXCLAM *Am Fam Old-fashioned* super!
▸▸ *Mus* ***swell box*** boîte *f* expressive

▸swell out **VI** (se) gonfler
VT SEP gonfler

▸swell up = **swell VI 1**

swell-headed **ADJ** *Fam* suffisant[□], qui a la grosse tête

swelling ['swelɪŋ] **N 1** *Med* enflure *f*, gonflement *m*; **they gave her something to relieve the s.** ils lui ont donné quelque chose pour que ça désenfle; **there was some s. around the ankle** la cheville était un peu enflée **2** *(increase)* augmentation *f*, grossissement *m*
ADJ *(increasing)* croissant; **the s. numbers of the unemployed** le nombre croissant des chômeurs

swelter ['sweltə(r)] **VI** *(feel too hot)* étouffer de chaleur; *(sweat)* suer à grosses gouttes, être en nage

sweltering ['sweltərɪŋ] **ADJ** *(day, heat)* étouffant, oppressant; **it was simply s. in the kitchen** il faisait une chaleur vraiment étouffante dans la cuisine

swept [swept] *pt & pp of* **sweep**

sweptwing ['sweptwɪŋ] **ADJ** *Aviat (aircraft)* à ailes en flèche

swerve [swɜ:v] **VI 1** *(car, driver, ship)* faire une embardée; *(ball)* dévier; *(aeroplane, bird, runner)* virer; **the cyclist was swerving in and out of the traffic** le cycliste zigzaguait entre les voitures; **the car swerved to the left/towards us/round the corner/off the road** la voiture fit une embardée vers la gauche/vira pour foncer droit vers nous/prit le virage brusquement/fit une embardée et quitta la chaussée **2** *Fig (budge, deviate)* dévier; **she'll never s. from her resolve** rien ne la détournera de sa résolution
VT *(vehicle)* faire virer; *(ball)* faire dévier; **she swerved the car to the left** elle donna un coup de volant vers la gauche
N *(by car, driver, ship)* embardée *f*; *(by aeroplane, bird, runner, ball)* déviation *f*

SWIFT [swɪft] **N** *Banking* (*abbr* **Society for Worldwide Interbank Financial Telecommunication**) = société internationale de télécommunications financières interbanques
▸▸ ***SWIFT transfer*** virement *m* SWIFT

swift [swɪft] **ADJ 1** *(fast)* rapide; *Literary* **s. of foot** leste, rapide à la course; *Br Fam* **let's stop here for a s. half** arrêtons-nous ici pour boire un coup en vitesse **2** *(prompt)* prompt, rapide; **s. to react** prompt à réagir; **she received a s. reply** elle reçut une réponse immédiate; **the government was s. to deny the rumours** le gouvernement fut prompt à démentir les rumeurs; **she took s. revenge** elle n'a pas tardé à se venger **3** *Am Fam (clever)* malin (igne)[□]; **that was a real s. move** c'était bien joué
N *Orn* martinet *m*; *(Apus apus)* martinet *m* noir

swift-flowing **ADJ** *(river)* au cours rapide

swift-footed **ADJ** *Literary* leste, véloce

swiftly ['swɪftlɪ] **ADV 1** *(quickly)* rapidement, vite; **the meeting moved s. to its conclusion** la réunion se termina rapidement; **moving s. along!** passons! **2** *(promptly)* promptement, rapidement; **they reacted s. to the threat** ils réagirent promptement à la menace

swiftness ['swɪftnɪs] **N 1** *(speed)* rapidité *f* **2** *(promptness)* promptitude *f*, rapidité *f*; **the ambulance arrived with remarkable s.** l'ambulance arriva avec une rapidité remarquable

swig [swɪg] (*pt & pp* **swigged**, *cont* **swigging**) *Fam*
VT lamper, siffler
N lampée *f*, coup *m*; **he took a s. of whisky** il a bu une lampée *ou* gorgée[□] de whisky; **have a s. of this** bois un coup de ça; **he took a long s. at his bottle** il porta sa bouteille à sa bouche et but un grand coup

▸swig down **VT SEP** *Fam* vider d'un trait[□], siffler

swill [swɪl] **VT 1** *Br (wash)* laver à grande eau; **he swilled the floor (down)** il a lavé le sol à grande eau; **go and s. the glass under the tap** va passer le verre sous le robinet **2** *Fam (drink)* écluser
N 1 *(for pigs)* pâtée *f* **2** *(wash)* lavage *m* à grande eau; **to give sth a s. out** laver *ou* rincer qch à grande eau

▸swill out **VT SEP** *esp Br (rinse)* laver à grande eau; **to s. out a basin** rincer une cuvette à grande eau

swim [swɪm] (*pt* **swam** [swæm], *pp* **swum** [swʌm], *cont* **swimming**) **VI 1** *(fish, animal)* nager; *(person ▸ gen)* nager; *(▸ for amusement)* nager, se baigner; *(▸ for sport)* nager, faire de la natation; **to go swimming** *(gen)* (aller) se baigner; *(in swimming pool)* aller à la piscine; **to s. for one's country** faire partie de l'équipe nationale de natation; **we went swimming in the lake** nous sommes allés nous baigner dans le lac; **I can't s.!** je ne sais pas nager!; **the lake was too cold to s. in** le lac était trop froid pour qu'on s'y baigne; **to s. across a river** traverser une rivière à la nage; **she swam away from/back to the shore** elle quitta/regagna la rive à la nage; **he managed to s. to safety** il a réussi à se sauver en nageant; **the raft sank and they had to s. for it** le radeau a coulé et ils ont été obligés de nager; *also Fig* **to s. against the tide** nager à contre-courant
2 *(be soaked)* nager, baigner; **the salad was swimming in oil** la salade baignait dans l'huile; **the kitchen floor was swimming with water** le sol de la cuisine était inondé
3 *(spin)* **my head is swimming** j'ai la tête q
tourne; **everything swam before my eyes** to
semblait tourner autour de moi
VT 1 *(river, lake etc)* traverser à la nage
2 *(a stroke)* nager; **can you s. butterfly?** est-
que tu sais nager le papillon?
3 *(distance)* nager; **she swam ten lengths** elle
fait dix longueurs
4 *(animal)* **they swam their horses across the riv**
ils ont fait traverser la rivière à leurs chevaux
la nage)
N 1 *(for leisure)* baignade *f*, *(for exercise)* nage
to go for a s. *(gen)* (aller) se baigner; *(in swir
ming pool)* aller à la piscine; **he had his mornir
s.** il s'est baigné comme tous les matins; **I feel li
a s.** j'ai envie d'aller me baigner; **did you have
nice s.?** *(for leisure)* tu t'es bien baigné?; *(for exe
cise)* tu as bien nagé?; **it's a good 20-minute s. o
to the island** il faut 20 bonnes minutes pour a
teindre l'île à la nage **2** *Fam Fig* **to be in the s. (
things)** être dans le coup
▸▸ ***swim bladder*** vessie *f* natatoire

swimmer ['swɪmə(r)] **N** *(gen)* nageur(euse) *m
(for leisure)* baigneur(euse) *m,f*; **he's an excelle
s.** c'est un excellent nageur, il nage très bien

swimming ['swɪmɪŋ] **N** *(gen)* nage *f*, *Sport* nat
tion *f*; **her doctor advised her to take up s.** son m
decin lui a conseillé la natation; **no s.** *(sig*
baignade interdite
COMP *(lesson, classes)* de natation
▸▸ *Br* ***swimming bath, swimming baths*** piscine
swimming cap bonnet *m* de bain; *Br* ***swimmi
costume*** maillot *m* de bain; ***swimming instruct***
maître-nageur *m*; ***swimming pool*** piscine
swimming trunks maillot *m ou* slip *m* de bain

swimmingly ['swɪmɪŋlɪ] **ADV** *Br Fam* à me
veille[□]; **your mother and I are getting on s.** no
nous entendons à merveille, ta mère et mc
everything's going s. tout marche comme s
des roulettes

swimsuit ['swɪmsu:t] **N** maillot *m* de bain

swimwear ['swɪmweə(r)] **N** *(UNCOUNT)* ma
lots *mpl* de bain

swindle ['swɪndəl] **VT** escroquer; **to s. sb out
sth** escroquer qch à qn; **they were swindled o
of all their savings** on leur a escroqué tout
leurs économies
N escroquerie *f*, vol *m*; **it's a real s.** c'est une vé
table escroquerie

swindler ['swɪndlə(r)] **N** escroc *m*

swine [swaɪn] (*pl sense* **1 inv**, *pl sense* **2 inv
swines**) **N 1** *Literary (pig)* porc *m*, pourceau *m*
Br Fam (unpleasant person) salaud *m*; **he's a la
s.!** c'est une grosse feignasse!; **you (filthy) s.!** e
pèce de fumier!; **it's a s. of a job** c'est un sale bo
lot
▸▸ ***swine fever*** peste *f* porcine

swineherd ['swaɪnhɜ:d] **N** porcher(ère) *m,f*

swing [swɪŋ] (*pt & pp* **swung** [swʌŋ]) **N 1** *(to-an
fro movement, sway ▸ gen)* balancement *m*; *(▸
pendulum)* oscillation *f*; **with a s. of his arm** en b
lançant son bras; **the s. of her hips** le balanc
ment de ses hanches
2 *(arc described)* arc *m*, courbe *f*; **the plane cam
round in a wide s.** l'avion décrivit une grand
courbe
3 *(swipe, attempt to hit)* (grand) coup *m*; **I took
s. at him** je lui ai décoché un coup de poing; **h
took a s. at the ball** il essaya de frapper la balle
4 *(hanging seat)* balançoire *f*; **they're playing o
the swings** ils jouent sur les balançoires; *Br* **wh
you lose on the swings you gain on the roun
abouts** ce que l'on perd d'un côté, on le récupè
de l'autre; *Br* **it's swings and roundabouts really** e
fait, on perd d'un côté ce qu'on gagne de l'autr
5 *(in public opinion, voting)* revirement *m*; *(
prices, market)* fluctuation *f*; **his mood swings a
very unpredictable** ses sautes d'humeur sont trè
imprévisibles; *St Exch* **the upward/downward
of the market** la fluctuation du marché vers
haut/le bas; **a sudden s. in public opinion** un rev
rement inattendu de l'opinion publique; **th
party needs a 10 percent s. to win the election**
parti a besoin d'un revirement d'opinion de 1
pour cent pour gagner aux élections
6 *(in boxing, golf)* swing *m*
7 *(rhythm ▸ gen)* rythme *m*; *Mus (style of jaz*

wing *m*; **a s. band** un orchestre de swing; **the s.** **ra** l'époque *f* du swing

8 *Am Pol (tour)* tournée *f*; **on his s. around the cir-** **le, the President visited 35 States** pendant sa ournée électorale, le Président a visité 35 États

9 *Fam (idioms)* **to get into the s. of things** se met-re dans le bain; **it'll be a lot easier once you've got** **nto the s. of things** ce sera beaucoup plus facile ne fois que tu seras dans le bain; **to go with a s.** *music)* être très rythmé *ou* entraînant□; *(party)* swinguer; *(business)* marcher très bien□

VT 1 *(cause to sway)* balancer; **she was swinging** **er umbrella as she walked** elle marchait en ba-ançant son parapluie; **he walked along swinging** **is arms** il marchait en balançant les bras; **to s.** **ne's hips** balancer les *ou* rouler des hanches; *ig* **to s. the lead** tirer au flanc

2 *(move from one place to another, in a curve)* **she** **wung her bag onto the back seat** elle jeta son sac ur le siège arrière; **the crane swung the cargo** **nto the wharf** la grue pivota pour déposer la argaison sur le quai; **I swung myself (up) into** **he saddle** j'ai sauté en selle; **she swung the door** **hut** elle ferma la porte; **he swung the axe in a** **wide arc** il leva la hache avec un large mouve-ment du bras; **she swung the bat at the ball** elle ssaya de frapper la balle avec sa batte; **I swung** **he club at him** j'ai essayé de le frapper avec le gourdin; **to s. the ball** *(in cricket)* faire dévier la alle en l'air

3 *(suspend ▸ hammock)* suspendre, pendre, ac-rocher

4 *(turn ▸ steering wheel)* (faire) tourner; *(▸ ve-icle)* faire virer; **the helmsman swung the wheel** **o port** le timonier fit tourner la roue à bâbord; **I** **wung the lorry through 180°** j'ai pris le virage à 180° (avec le camion)

5 *(cause to change)* **to s. the voters** faire changer es électeurs d'opinion; **that swung the decision** **our way/against us** cela a influencé la décision inale en notre faveur/en notre défaveur; **the ac-** **ident swung public opinion against the company** 'accident a provoqué un revirement de l'opi-ion contre la compagnie

6 *Fam (manage, pull off)* **to s. sth** réussir *ou* arri-ver à faire qch□; **I think I should be able to s. it** je rois pouvoir me débrouiller□; **to s. it so that...** *arrange things)* arranger les choses de manière à ce) que... + *subjunctive*

7 *Mus (tune)* interpréter en swing; *Fam* **he can** **eally s. it** il a vraiment le swing

VI 1 *(sway, move to and fro ▸ gen)* se balancer; *(▸* *endulum)* osciller; *(hang, be suspended)* pen-dre, être suspendu; **to s. to and fro** se balancer; **he shop sign was swinging (to and fro) in the wind** 'enseigne de magasin ballottait au vent; **he** **walked along with his arms swinging** il marchait en balançant les bras; **swinging from a cord** sus-endu à une corde; **a long rope swung from the** **eiling** une longue corde pendait du plafond; **he door swung open/shut** la porte s'est ouverte/ s'est refermée; *Fam Fig* **to s. both ways** *(be bisex-ual)* marcher à voile et à vapeur

2 *(move along, around)* **to s. from tree to tree** se alancer d'arbre en arbre; **to s. into the saddle** auter à cheval *ou* en selle; **they came swinging** **down the street** ils ont descendu la rue d'un pas ythmé; *Fig* **to s. into action** passer à l'action

3 *(make a turn)* virer; **the car swung left** la voiture vira à gauche; **the lorry swung through the gate** le amion vira pour franchir le portail; **the road** **swings east** la route oblique vers l'est

4 *(change opinion, mood etc)* virer; **the country** **has swung to the left** le pays a viré à gauche; **she swings between depression and elation** elle passe de la dépression à l'exultation

5 *Fam (be hanged)* être pendu□; **he'll s. for this!** il sera pendu pour ça!; *Fig* il le paiera!

6 *(hit out, aim a blow)* essayer de frapper; **I** **swung at him** je lui ai décoché un coup de poing; **he swung wildly at the ball** il essaya désespéré-ment de frapper la balle; *Fam* **to s. for sb** essayer d'en coller une à qn

7 *Fam (musician)* swinguer; *(music)* swinguer, avoir du swing; **the saxophonist really swings!** il swingue, ce saxo!

8 *Fam Old-fashioned (be modern, fashionable)* être dans le vent; **he was there in the sixties, when** **London was really swinging** il était là dans les an-nées soixante, quand ça bougeait à Londres

9 *Fam (be lively)* chauffer; **the party was begin-ning to s.** la fête commençait à être très animée□

10 *Fam (try hard)* **he's in there swinging** il fait ce qu'il peut□; **I'm in there swinging for you** je fais tout ce que je peux pour toi□

11 *Fam (exchange sexual partners)* faire de l'échangisme□

• in full swing **ADJ** **the party was in full s.** la fête battait son plein; **production is in full s.** on pro-duit à plein rendement; **once it's in full s., the pro-ject will require more people** une fois lancé, il faudra plus de gens sur le projet

▸▸ ***swing bridge*** pont *m* tournant; ***swing door*** porte *f* battante; *Am Fam* ***swing shift*** *(work period)* = poste de 16 heures à minuit; *(team)* = équipe qui travaille de 16 heures à minuit; *Am Pol* ***swing State*** État *m* en balance; *Am Pol* ***swing voter*** électeur(trice) *m,f* indécis(e)

▸ swing out **VI** *(car, driver)* faire un écart; *(from side road)* déboucher; **the car in front swung out** **to overtake** la voiture de devant a déboîté pour doubler

▸ swing round **VT SEP** *(vehicle)* faire virer; *(per-son)* faire tourner; **he swung the car round the cor-ner** il a tourné au coin; **he swung the car right** **round** il a fait un tête-à-queue; **he swung her** **round** il la fit tourner; *Fig* **to swing sb round** convaincre qn

VI *(turn round ▸ person)* se retourner, faire volte-face; *(▸ crane)* tourner, pivoter; *Fig (public opin-ion, person)* faire volte-face; **the car swung right** **round** la voiture a fait un tête-à-queue

swingeing ['swɪndʒɪŋ] **ADJ** *Br (increase, drop)* énorme; *(cuts)* draconien; *(blow)* violent; *(criti-cism, condemnation)* sévère; *(victory, defeat)* écrasant

swinger ['swɪŋə(r)] **N** *Fam* **1** *Old-fashioned (fash-ionable person)* branché(e) *m,f*; *(sociable person)* fêtard(e) *m,f* **2** *(promiscuous person)* débau-ché(e)□*m,f*; *(who swaps sexual partners)* échan-giste□*mf*

swinging ['swɪŋɪŋ] **ADJ 1** *(swaying)* qui se ba-lance; *(pivoting)* tournant, pivotant; **with s. arms** les bras ballants **2** *(rhythmic ▸ gen)* rythmé, en-traînant; *(▸ jazz)* qui swingue **3** *Fam Old-fash-ioned (fashionable)* in *(inv)*; **the s. sixties** les folles années soixante

▸▸ *Austr* ***swinging voter*** électeur(trice) *m,f* indé-cis(e)

swingometer [swɪŋ'ɒmɪtə(r)] **N** *Br* indicateur *m* de tendances *(lors de la diffusion télévisée des ré-sultats d'élections législatives)*

swing-wing **ADJ** à géométrie variable

N avion *m* à géométrie variable

swinish ['swaɪnɪʃ] **ADJ** *Fam* sale, pas sympa; **that** **was a s. trick!** c'était pas sympa!

swipe [swaɪp] **VI** **he swiped at the fly with his** **newspaper** il donna un grand coup de journal pour frapper la mouche; **she swiped at the ball** **and missed** elle donna un grand coup pour frap-per la balle et la manqua

VT 1 *(hit)* donner un coup à; **I managed to s. my-self in the eye** j'ai réussi à me donner un coup dans l'œil **2** *Fam (steal)* piquer, chouraver; **who's** **swiped my pen?** qui m'a piqué *ou* chouravé mon stylo? **3** *(card)* passer; *(credit card)* passer (au fer à repasser)

N (grand) coup *m*; **to take a s. at sth** donner un grand coup pour frapper qch; *Fig (criticize)* tirer à boulets rouges sur qch

▸▸ ***swipe card*** badge *m*

▸ swipe in **VI** entrer en utilisant son badge

▸ swipe out **VI** sortir en utilisant son badge

swirl [swɜːl] **VI** tourbillonner, tournoyer; **the** **water swirled beneath us** l'eau tourbillonnait au-dessous de nous

VT faire tourbillonner *ou* tournoyer; **a sudden** **wind swirled the leaves around** une brusque bourrasque fit tournoyer *ou* tourbillonner les feuilles; **s. a bit of water round the sink** rince un peu le lavabo; **the raft was swirled downstream** le radeau a été emporté dans le tourbillon du cou-rant; **he swirled her round the dance floor** il la fit tournoyer autour de la piste (de danse)

N tourbillon *m*; *(of water)* remous *m*; *(of cream)* spirale *f*

swirling ['swɜːlɪŋ] **ADJ** tourbillonnant, tour-noyant

swish [swɪʃ] **VI** *(whip)* siffler; *(leaves, wind)* chuinter, *Literary* bruire; *(fabric, skirt)* froufrou-ter; *(water)* murmurer; **the curtains swished** **open/shut** les rideaux s'ouvrirent/se refermè-rent en froufroutant

VT **the horse swished its tail** le cheval donna un coup de queue

N 1 *(sound ▸ of fabric, skirt)* froufroutement *m*, froissement *m*; *(▸ of leaves, wind)* bruissement *m*; *(▸ of water)* murmure *m*; *(of scythe)* crisse-ment *m* **2** *(movement)* **the cow flicked the flies** **away with a s. of its tail** la vache chassa les mou-ches d'un coup de queue **3** *Am Fam (effeminate homosexual)* folle *f*, = terme injurieux désignant un homosexuel

ADJ *Fam* **1** *Br (smart)* classe *(inv)*, chicos **2** *Am (ef-feminate)* chochotte

swishy ['swɪʃɪ] *(compar* **swishier**, *superl* **swishiest)** *Fam* **1** *Br (smart)* classe *(inv)*, chicos **2** *Am (effemi-nate)* chochotte

Swiss [swɪs] *(pl* **inv)** **NPL** **the S.** les Suisses *mpl*

N *(man)* Suisse *m*; *(woman)* Suissesse *f*, Suisse *f*

ADJ *(gen)* suisse; *(government)* helvétique

▸▸ ***Swiss army knife*** couteau *m* suisse; ***Swiss bank account*** compte *m* en Suisse; ***Swiss chard*** bette *f*, blette *f*; ***Swiss cheese*** emmental *m*; ***Swiss cheese plant*** monstera *m*; ***Swiss franc*** franc *m* suisse; ***Swiss Guard*** *(papal bodyguard)* garde *f* (pontificale) suisse; *Hist (in France)* membre *m* des troupes suisses; **the S. Guard** *(papal body-guards)* la garde (pontificale) suisse; *Hist (in France)* les troupes *fpl* suisses; ***Swiss roll*** (gâteau *m*) roulé *m*; *Am* ***Swiss steak*** = bifteck fariné et braisé

Swiss-French **N 1** *Ling* suisse *m* romand **2** *(per-son)* Suisse *mf* romand(e)

ADJ suisse romand

Swiss-German **N 1** *Ling* suisse *m* allemand *ou* alémanique **2** *(person)* Suisse *mf* allemand(e)

ADJ suisse allemand *ou* alémanique

switch [swɪtʃ] **N 1** *Elec (for light)* interrupteur *m*; *(on radio, television)* bouton *m*; *Tech & Tel* com-mutateur *m*; **is the s. on/off?** est-ce que c'est al-lumé/éteint?

2 *(change ▸ gen)* changement *m*; *(▸ of opinion, attitude)* revirement *m*; **the s. to the new equip-ment went very smoothly** on s'est très bien adap-tés au nouveau matériel; **a sudden s. in foreign** **policy** un subit revirement de la politique étran-gère; **to make the s. from gas to electricity** passer du gaz à l'électricité

3 *(swap, trade)* échange *m*

4 *Am Rail* **switches** *(points)* aiguillage *m*

5 *(stick)* baguette *f*, badine *f*; *(riding crop)* crava-che *f*

6 *(hairpiece)* postiche *m*

7 *Zool (hair on tail)* fouet *m* de la queue

VT 1 *(change)* changer de; *(exchange)* échanger; **he switched subjects after two years at university** il a changé de filière après deux ans d'univer-sité; **the two employees asked to s. jobs** les deux employés ont demandé à échanger leurs pos-tes; **to s. places with sb** échanger sa place avec qn; **can I s. it for another one?** puis-je l'échanger contre un autre?; **he's been switched to another** **department** il a été muté dans un autre service

2 *(transfer ▸ allegiance, attention)* transférer; *(di-vert ▸ conversation)* orienter, détourner; **she** **switched her attention back to the speaker** elle re-porta son attention sur le conférencier; **I tried to** **s. the discussion to something less controversial** j'ai essayé d'orienter la discussion vers un sujet moins épineux

3 *Elec, Rad & TV (circuit)* commuter; **to s. chan-nels/frequencies** changer de chaîne/de fré-quence

4 *Am Rail* aiguiller; **the freight train was switched** **to another track** le train de marchandises fut ai-guillé sur une autre voie

5 *(hit with stick)* donner un coup de baguette à; **to s. its tail** *(cow)* battre l'air de sa queue

VI changer; **she started studying medicine but** **switched to architecture** elle a commencé par étudier la médecine, mais elle a changé pour faire architecture; **I'd like to s. to another topic** j'aimerais changer de sujet; **can I s. to another**

channel? est-ce que je peux changer de chaîne?; **we've switched to another brand** nous avons changé de marque; **they've switched to American equipment** ils ont adopté du matériel américain; **to s. (from gas) to electricity** passer (du gaz) à l'électricité; **he switches effortlessly from one language to another** il passe d'une langue à une autre avec une grande aisance

▸**switch back** VI *(revert to)* **we switched back to gas** nous sommes revenus au gaz

▸**switch off** VT SEP *Br (light)* éteindre; *(electrical appliance)* éteindre, arrêter; **don't forget to s. the light off when you leave** n'oublie pas d'éteindre la lumière en partant; **the radio switches itself off** la radio s'éteint *ou* s'arrête automatiquement; **they've switched off the power** ils ont coupé le courant; *Aut* **to s. off the ignition** *or* **engine** couper le contact, arrêter le moteur

VI **1** *Br (go off ▸ light)* s'éteindre; *(▸ electrical appliance)* s'éteindre, s'arrêter; **how do you get the oven to s. off?** comment tu éteins le four? **2** *Br (TV viewer, radio listener)* éteindre le poste **3** *Fam (stop paying attention)* décrocher

▸**switch on** VT SEP **1** *(light, heating, oven, TV, radio)* allumer; *(engine, washing machine, vacuum cleaner)* mettre en marche; **could you s. on the light?** pourrais-tu allumer (la lumière)?; **the power isn't switched on** il n'y a pas de courant; *Aut* **to s. on the ignition** mettre le contact **2** *Fig* **to s. on the charm** faire du charme; **to s. on the tears** pleurer sur commande; *Fam* **they switched me on to new ideas** ils m'ont initié aux idées nouvelles

VI **1** *(light, heating, oven, TV, radio)* s'allumer; *(engine, washing machine, vacuum cleaner)* se mettre en marche; **the lights s. on and off automatically** les lumières s'allument et s'éteignent automatiquement **2** *(TV viewer, radio listener)* allumer le poste

▸**switch over** VI **1** = **switch**

VI **2** *TV* changer de chaîne; *Rad* changer de station

▸**switch round** VT SEP changer de place, déplacer; **why don't we switch the desks round?** et si on changeait les bureaux de place?; **he switched the glasses round when she wasn't looking** il échangea les verres pendant qu'elle ne regardait pas; **the manager has switched the team round again** l'entraîneur a encore changé la composition de l'équipe

VI *(two people)* changer de place; **she's switched round with her brother** elle a changé de place avec son frère

switchback [ˈswɪtʃbæk] N **1** *(road)* route *f* en lacets **2** *Br (rollercoaster)* montagnes *fpl* russes

ADJ **a s. road** une route accidentée et sinueuse

switchblade [ˈswɪtʃbleɪd] N *Am* (couteau *m* à) cran *m* d'arrêt

switchboard [ˈswɪtʃbɔːd] N **1** *Tel* central *m* (téléphonique); *(in hotel, office)* standard *m* **2** *Elec* tableau *m*

▸▸ ***switchboard line*** ligne *f* principale; ***switchboard operator*** standardiste *mf*

switched [swɪtʃt] ADJ

▸▸ ***switched line*** *(in datacomms)* ligne *f* commutée; *Comput* ***switched network*** réseau *m* commuté

switched-on ADJ *Fam* **1** *(fashionable)* dans le vent, in *(inv)* **2** *(bright)* à l'esprit vif

switchman [ˈswɪtʃmən] *(pl* **switchmen** [-mən]*)* N *Am* aiguilleur *m*

Switzerland [ˈswɪtsələnd] N Suisse *f*; **French-/Italian-speaking S.** la Suisse romande/italienne; **German-speaking S.** la Suisse allemande *ou* alémanique

swivel [ˈswɪvəl] *(Br pt & pp* **swivelled**, *cont* **swivelling**, *Am pt & pp* **swiveled**, *cont* **swiveling***)* N **1** *(gen)* pivot *m*; *(for gun)* tourillon *m* **2** *(in rowing)* dame *f* de nage

COMP *(lamp)* pivotant, tournant

VI pivoter, tourner; **his eyes swivelled back to the screen** ses yeux se tournèrent à nouveau vers l'écran

VT faire pivoter

▸▸ ***swivel arm*** bras *m* pivotant; ***swivel base*** socle *m* pivotant; ***swivel chair*** chaise *f* pivotante; *(with arms)* fauteuil *m* pivotant; ***swivel joint*** (joint *m* à) rotule *f*; *Aut* ***swivel pin*** pivot *m* central

▸**swivel round** VI *(turn)* pivoter, tourner; **to s. round on one's heels** pivoter sur ses talons; **she swivelled round in her chair** elle pivota sur sa chaise

VT SEP faire pivoter

swivelling, *Am* **swiveling** [ˈswɪvəlɪŋ] ADJ pivotant, mobile

swiz, swizz [swɪz] N *Br Fam* arnaque *f*; **what a s.!** c'est du vol!

swizzle [ˈswɪzəl] N **1** *Br Fam (swizz)* arnaque *f* **2** *Am (cocktail)* cocktail *m (préparé dans un verre mélangeur)*

▸▸ ***swizzle stick*** cuillère *f* à cocktails

swollen [ˈswəʊlən] *pp of* **swell**

ADJ **1** *(part of body)* enflé, gonflé; **her ankle was badly s.** sa cheville était très enflée; **his face was s.** il avait le visage enflé *ou* bouffi; **starving children with s. abdomens** des enfants affamés au ventre ballonné; **her eyes were red and s. with crying** elle avait les yeux rouges et gonflés à force de pleurer; *Fam Fig* **to have a s. head** avoir la grosse tête **2** *(sails)* bombé, gonflé; *(lake, river)* en crue

swollen-headed ADJ *Br Fam* qui a la grosse tête

swoon [swuːn] VI **1** *(become ecstatic)* se pâmer, tomber en pâmoison; **he used to make all the young girls s.** il fut un temps où toutes les jeunes filles se pâmaient devant lui **2** *Old-fashioned (faint)* s'évanouir, *Literary* se pâmer

N pâmoison *f*; **to fall to the ground in a s.** tomber par terre en pâmoison

swoop [swuːp] VI **1** *(dive ▸ bird)* s'abattre, fondre; *(▸ aircraft)* piquer, descendre en piqué; **the helicopter swooped low over the battlefield** l'hélicoptère descendit en piqué au-dessus du champ de bataille **2** *(make a raid ▸ police, troops etc)* faire une descente; **the police swooped on the nightclub** la police a fait une descente dans la boîte de nuit

N **1** *(dive ▸ by bird, aircraft)* descente *f* en piqué **2** *(raid ▸ by police, troops etc)* descente *f*; **a dawn s.** une descente à l'aube; **15 arrested in drugs s.** 15 personnes arrêtées dans une opération antidrogue **3** *(idiom)* **in one fell s.** d'un seul coup

swoosh [swʊʃ] *Fam* VI *(water)* bruire; *(wind)* siffler; **the express train swooshed past** le rapide est passé à toute vitesse; **the waves swooshed over the deck** les vagues déferlaient sur le pont; **you could hear the liquid swooshing around in the tank** on entendait le liquide clapoter dans le réservoir

N *(of water)* bruissement *m*; *(of wind)* sifflement *m*

VT **he swooshed it down the loo** il l'a fait disparaître dans les toilettes; **she then swooshed it out with clean water** elle l'a ensuite rincé à grande eau; **s. the detergent all over the stain** répandre le détergent généreusement sur la tache

swop *(pt & pp* **swopped**, *cont* **swopping***)* = **swap**

sword [sɔːd] N épée *f*; *Mil & Naut* sabre *m*; **to draw one's s.** tirer son épée, dégainer; **they fought with swords** ils se sont battus à l'épée; **all the prisoners were put to the s.** tous les prisonniers furent passés au fil de l'épée; *Fam* **a s. and sandals movie** un péplum; **the s. of justice** le glaive de la justice; *Prov* **those that live by the s. shall die by the s.** quiconque se sert de l'épée périra par l'épée; *Fig* **to turn swords into ploughshares** faire la paix, se réconcilier

COMP *(blow, handle, wound)* d'épée

▸▸ ***the Sword of Damocles*** l'épée *f* de Damoclès; ***sword dance*** danse *f* du sabre; ***sword swallower*** avaleur(euse) *m,f* de sabres

swordbearer [ˈsɔːdˌbeərə(r)] N *(in ceremony)* = officier qui porte le glaive

swordbelt [ˈsɔːdbelt] N ceinturon *m*

sword-fight N *(between two people)* duel *m* (à l'épée); *(between several people)* bataille *f* à l'épée

swordfish [ˈsɔːdfɪʃ] *(pl* inv *or* **swordfishes***)* N *Ich* espadon *m*, poisson-épée *m*

swordplay [ˈsɔːdpleɪ] N *(UNCOUNT) (skill)* maniement *m* de l'épée; *(activity)* escrime *f*; **the last scene consisted of s.** la dernière scène était une scène de combats à l'épée

swordsman [ˈsɔːdzmən] *(pl* **swordsmen** [-mən]*)* N épéiste *m*, lame *f (personne)*; **he's a fine s.** c'es[t] une fine lame

swordsmanship [ˈsɔːdzmənʃɪp] N manieme[nt] *m* de l'épée; **we admired her s.** nous admirâme[s] sa façon de manier l'épée

swordstick [ˈsɔːdstɪk] N canne-épée *f*, canne armée

swore [swɔː(r)] *pt of* **swear**

sworn [swɔːn] *pp of* **swear**

ADJ **1** *Law (declaration)* fait sous serment; *(evidence)* donné sous serment; **a s. statement** un[e] déposition faite sous serment **2** *(committed ▸ enemy)* juré; *(▸ friend)* indéfectible

SWOT [swɒt] N *Mktg (abbr* **strengths, weaknesse[s,] opportunities, threats***)* forces, faiblesses, oppo[r]tunités et menaces *fpl*

▸▸ ***SWOT analysis*** analyse *f* des forces, faibles[ses,] opportunités et menaces

swot [swɒt] *(pt & pp* **swotted**, *cont* **swotting***)* *B[r] Fam* VI bûcher, potasser; **to s. for an exam** bûche[r] *ou* potasser un examen

N *Pej* bachoteur(euse) *m,f*

▸**swot up** *Br Fam* VI bûcher, potasser; **to s. up o[n] sth** bûcher *ou* potasser qch

VT SEP bûcher, potasser

swotting [ˈswɒtɪŋ] N *Br Fam* bachotage *m*; **I'[ll] have to do some s. to pass my exam** il va fallo[ir] que je bûche *ou* que je potasse pour réuss[ir] mon examen

swum [swʌm] *pp of* **swim**

swung [swʌŋ] *pt & pp of* **swing**

▸▸ *Typ* ***swung dash*** tilde *m*

sybarite [ˈsɪbəraɪt] N sybarite *mf*

sybaritic [ˌsɪbəˈrɪtɪk] ADJ sybarite

sycamore [ˈsɪkəmɔː(r)] N **1** *Br* sycomore *m*, fau[x] platane *m* **2** *Am* platane *m*

sycophancy [ˈsɪkəfənsɪ] N flagornerie *f*

sycophant [ˈsɪkəfænt] N flagorneur(euse) *m,f*

sycophantic [ˌsɪkəˈfæntɪk] ADJ *(person)* flatteu[r,] flagorneur; *(behaviour)* de flagorneur; *(approv[al,] praise)* obséquieux

syllabic [sɪˈlæbɪk] ADJ syllabique

syllabication [sɪˌlæbɪˈkeɪʃən], **syllabificatio[n]** [sɪˌlæbɪfɪˈkeɪʃən] N syllabation *f*

syllabify [sɪˈlæbɪfaɪ] *(pt & pp* **syllabified***)* VT dé[-]composer en syllabes

syllable [ˈsɪləbəl] N syllabe *f*; **I had to explain it t[o] him in words of one s.** j'ai dû le lui expliquer e[n] termes simples

syllabub [ˈsɪləbʌb] N *Br (dessert)* (crème *f*) sa[]bayon *m*

syllabus [ˈsɪləbəs] *(pl* **syllabuses** *or* **syllabi** [-baɪ]*)* N *Sch & Univ* programme *m* (d'enseignement); **d[o] you know what's on the s.?** savez-vous ce qu'il y a[] au programme?

syllogism [ˈsɪlədʒɪzəm] N syllogisme *m*

syllogistic [ˌsɪləˈdʒɪstɪk] ADJ syllogistique

sylph [sɪlf] N **1** *(mythical being)* sylphe *m* **2** *Li[t]erary (slender woman)* sylphide *f*

sylphlike [ˈsɪlflaɪk] ADJ *Literary (figure)* gracile de sylphe; *(woman)* gracieuse; *Hum* **you're loo[k]ing positively s., my dear** tu es une vraie sylphide ma chère

sylvan [ˈsɪlvən] ADJ *Literary* sylvestre

symbiosis [ˌsɪmbɪˈəʊsɪs] N *also Fig* symbiose *f*; **i[n] s.** en symbiose

symbiotic [ˌsɪmbɪˈɒtɪk] ADJ *also Fig* symbio[]tique; **a s. relationship** une association symbio[]tique

symbol [ˈsɪmbəl] N symbole *m*

symbolic [sɪmˈbɒlɪk] ADJ symbolique

▸▸ ***symbolic logic*** logique *f* symbolique

symbolically [sɪmˈbɒlɪklɪ] ADV symbolique[]ment

symbolism [ˈsɪmbəlɪzəm] N symbolisme *m*

symbolist [ˈsɪmbəlɪst] ADJ symboliste

N symboliste *mf*

symbolization, -isation [ˌsɪmbəlaɪˈzeɪʃən] N symbolisation *f*

symbolize, -ise ['sɪmbəlaɪz] VT symboliser

symmetrical [sɪ'metrɪkəl] ADJ symétrique

symmetrically [sɪ'metrɪkəlɪ] ADV symétriquement

symmetry ['sɪmətrɪ] (*pl* **symmetries**) N symétrie *f*

sympathetic [,sɪmpə'θetɪk] ADJ **1** *(compassionate)* compatissant; **s. words** des paroles compatissantes *ou* de sympathie; **they weren't very s.** ils ne se sont pas montrés très compatissants
2 *(well-disposed)* bien disposé; *(understanding)* compréhensif; **the public is generally s. to** *or* **towards the strikers** l'opinion publique est dans l'ensemble bien disposée envers les grévistes; **she spoke to a s. audience** elle s'adressa à un auditoire bienveillant; **the town council was s. to our grievances** la municipalité a accueilli nos revendications avec compréhension
3 *(congenial, likeable)* sympathique, agréable
4 *Physiol* sympathique; **the s. nervous system** le système nerveux sympathique, le sympathique
5 *Phys (vibration)* dû à la résonance
►► ***sympathetic magic*** magie *f* sympathique; *Mus* ***sympathetic string*** corde *f* qui vibre par résonance

> Note that the French word **sympathique** is a false friend and is rarely a translation for the English word **sympathetic**. It means **kind, friendly**.

sympathetically [,sɪmpə'θetɪklɪ] ADV **1** *(compassionately)* avec compassion; **he patted me s. on the hand** il me donna une petite tape sur la main en signe de compassion *ou* de sympathie
2 *(with approval)* avec bienveillance; **she received his request s.** elle reçut sa requête avec bienveillance
3 *Physiol* par sympathie
4 *Phys (vibrate)* par résonance

sympathize, -ise ['sɪmpəθaɪz] VI **1** *(feel compassion)* sympathiser, compatir; **we all sympathized with him when his wife left** nous avons tous compati à son malheur quand sa femme est partie; **poor Emma, I really s. with her!** cette pauvre Emma, je la plains vraiment! **2** *(feel understanding)* **he could not s. with their feelings** il ne pouvait pas comprendre leurs sentiments; **we understand and s. with their point of view** nous comprenons et partageons leur point de vue **3** *(favour, support)* sympathiser; **certain heads of state openly sympathized with the terrorists** certains chefs d'État sympathisaient ouvertement avec les terroristes

> Note that the French verb **sympathiser avec** is a false friend and is almost never a translation for the English verb **to sympathize with**. It means **to be friendly with**.

sympathizer, -iser ['sɪmpəθaɪzə(r)] N **1** *(comforter)* **she received many cards from sympathizers after her husband's death** elle a reçu de nombreuses cartes de condoléances après la mort de son mari **2** *(supporter)* sympathisant(e) *m,f*; **she was suspected of being a communist s.** elle était soupçonnée d'être sympathisante communiste

sympathy ['sɪmpəθɪ] (*pl* **sympathies**) N **1** *(compassion)* compassion *f*; **to have** *or* **to feel s. for sb** éprouver de la compassion envers qn; **he showed no s. for the children** il n'a fait preuve d'aucune compassion envers les enfants; **her tears were only a means of gaining s.** elle ne pleurait que pour qu'on s'attendrisse sur elle; **you have my deepest sympathies** toutes mes condoléances; **our sympathies are with the families of the dead** nous compatissons avec les familles des victimes; **if you do catch a cold don't expect any s. from me!** si tu attrapes un rhume, ne compte pas sur moi pour te plaindre! **2** *(approval, support)* soutien *m*; **the audience was clearly not in s. with the speaker** il était évident que le public ne partageait pas les sentiments de l'orateur; **she has strong left-wing sympathies** elle est très à gauche; **I have no s. for** *or* **with terrorism** je désapprouve tout à fait le terrorisme; **to come out in s. (with sb)** faire grève par solidarité (avec qn) **3** *(affinity)* sympathie *f*; **there was a strong bond of s. between them** ils étaient liés par une forte sympathie
►► ***sympathy card*** carte *f* de condoléances; ***sympathy strike*** grève *f* de solidarité

> Note that the French word **sympathie** is a false friend and is rarely a translation for the English noun **sympathy**. It is usually used to convey the idea of liking somebody.

symphonic [sɪm'fɒnɪk] ADJ symphonique; **a s. poem** un poème symphonique

symphony ['sɪmfənɪ] (*pl* **symphonies**) N **1** *(composition)* symphonie *f*; *Fig* **the landscape was a s. of browns and greens** le paysage était une symphonie de bruns et de verts **2** *Am (orchestra)* orchestre *m* symphonique
COMP *(concert, orchestra)* symphonique

symposium [sɪm'pəʊzɪəm] (*pl* **symposiums** *or* **symposia** [-zɪə]) N symposium *m*, colloque *m*

symptom ['sɪmptəm] N *Med & Fig* symptôme *m*; **to show symptoms of fatigue** donner des signes de fatigue

symptomatic [,sɪmptə'mætɪk] ADJ *Med & Fig* symptomatique

symptomless ['sɪmptɪmlɪs] ADJ *(disease)* asymptomatique

synagogue ['sɪnəgɒg] N synagogue *f*

synapse ['saɪnæps], **synapsis** [sɪ'næpsɪs] N synapse *f*

sync, synch [sɪŋk] N *Fam (abbr* **synchronization***)* synchronisation ᵒ*f*; **to be in/out of s.** être/ne pas être synchro; **the engine is a bit out of s.** le moteur ne tourne pas très rond ᵒ

synchromarketing [,sɪŋkrəʊ'mɑːkətɪŋ] N synchromarketing *m*

synchromesh ['sɪŋkrəʊmeʃ] N synchroniseur *m*
►► ***synchromesh gearbox*** boîte *f* de vitesses à synchroniseur

synchronic [sɪŋ'krɒnɪk] ADJ synchronique

synchronism ['sɪŋkrənɪzəm] N synchronisme *m*

synchronization, -isation [,sɪŋkrənaɪ'zeɪʃən] N synchronisation *f*

synchronize, -ise ['sɪŋkrənaɪz] VT *(watches, actions, movements, events)* synchroniser; *Elec (generators)* coupler en phase
VI être synchronisé; **the chimes of the clocks synchronized perfectly** les carillons des horloges étaient parfaitement synchronisés

synchronized, -ised ['sɪŋkrənaɪzd] ADJ synchronisé
►► ***synchronized sound*** son *m* synchrone; ***synchronized swimming*** natation *f* synchronisée

synchronizer, -iser ['sɪŋkrənaɪzə(r)] N synchronisateur *m*

synchronous ['sɪŋkrənəs] ADJ synchrone

syncline ['sɪŋklaɪn] N synclinal *m*

syncopate ['sɪŋkəpeɪt] VT *Mus* syncoper

syncopation [,sɪŋkə'peɪʃən] N *Mus* syncope *f*

syncope ['sɪŋkəpɪ] N *Ling & Med* syncope *f*

syncretic [sɪŋ'kretɪk] ADJ syncrétique

syncretism ['sɪŋkrɪtɪzəm] N syncrétisme *m*

syndic ['sɪndɪk] N syndic *m*

syndicalism ['sɪndɪkəlɪzəm] N *(doctrine)* syndicalisme *m* révolutionnaire

syndicalist ['sɪndɪkəlɪst] N syndicaliste *mf* révolutionnaire
ADJ de syndicalisme révolutionnaire

syndicate N ['sɪndɪkət] **1** *Com & Fin* groupement *m*, syndicat *m*; **the loan was underwritten by a s. of banks** le prêt était garanti par un consortium bancaire; **a s. of British and French companies** un groupement de sociétés françaises et britanniques **2** *(of organized crime)* association *f*; **crime syndicates** associations *fpl* de grand banditisme **3** *Journ* agence *f* de presse *(qui vend des articles, des photos etc à plusieurs journaux pour publication simultanée)*
VT ['sɪndɪkeɪt] **1** *Com & Fin (loan)* syndiquer **2** *Journ* publier simultanément dans plusieurs journaux; *Am Rad* vendre à plusieurs stations; *Am TV* vendre à plusieurs chaînes; **the photograph was syndicated in all the local newspapers** la photographie a été publiée dans toute la presse régionale; **a syndicated TV news programme** des informations *fpl* télévisées reprises par plusieurs chaînes
VI ['sɪndɪkeɪt] *(form a syndicate)* former un groupement *ou* syndicat
►► ***syndicated loan*** prêt *m* en participation

syndication [,sɪndɪ'keɪʃən] N *Journ (of article)* publication *f* simultanée dans plusieurs journaux
►► ***syndication agency*** agence *f* de presse

syndrome ['sɪndrəʊm] N syndrome *m*

synectics [sɪ'nektɪks] N *(UNCOUNT)* synectique *f*

synergism ['sɪnədʒɪzəm] = **synergy**

synergy ['sɪnədʒɪ] (*pl* **synergies**) N *Biol & Fig* synergie *f*

synod ['sɪnəd] N **1** *Rel* synode *m*; **the General S.** le conseil d'administration de l'Église anglicane **2** *(council)* assemblée *f*, convention *f*

synonym ['sɪnənɪm] N synonyme *m*

synonymous [sɪ'nɒnɪməs] ADJ *also Fig* synonyme; **success is not always s. with merit** le succès n'est pas toujours synonyme de mérite

synonymously [sɪ'nɒnɪməslɪ] ADV *(use a word)* comme synonyme (**with** de); **these two words can be used s.** ces deux mots peuvent être employés comme synonymes

synonymy [sɪ'nɒnɪmɪ] N synonymie *f*

synopsis [sɪ'nɒpsɪs] (*pl* **synopses** [-siːz]) N *(gen)* résumé *m*; *(of a film)* synopsis *m*

synoptic [sɪ'nɒptɪk] ADJ synoptique
►► ***the Synoptic Gospels*** les Évangiles *mpl* synoptiques, les synoptiques *mpl*

synovia [saɪ'nəʊvɪə] N *Anat* synovie *f*

synovial [saɪ'nəʊvɪəl] ADJ *Anat* synovial
►► ***synovial fluid*** liquide *m* synovial; ***synovial membrane*** membrane *f* synoviale

syntactic [sɪn'tæktɪk], **syntactical** [sɪn'tæktɪkəl] ADJ syntaxique

syntax ['sɪntæks] N syntaxe *f*
►► *Comput* ***syntax error*** erreur *f* de syntaxe

synthesis ['sɪnθəsɪs] (*pl* **syntheses** [-siːz]) N synthèse *f*

synthesize, -ise ['sɪnθəsaɪz] VT **1** *Biol & Chem (produce by synthesis)* synthétiser **2** *(amalgamate, fuse)* synthétiser **3** *Mus* synthétiser

synthesizer, -iser ['sɪnθəsaɪzə(r)] N synthétiseur *m*; **voice s.** synthétiseur *m* de voix

synthetic [sɪn'θetɪk] ADJ **1** *(artificial, electronically produced)* synthétique; **research on s. speech** les recherches sur la parole synthétique **2** *Fig Pej (food)* qui a un goût chimique; **the sauce tasted a bit s.** la sauce avait un goût un peu chimique **3** *Ling* synthétique
N produit *m* synthétique
• **synthetics** NPL fibres *fpl* synthétiques
►► ***synthetic drug*** drogue *f* de synthèse; ***synthetic fibre*** fibre *f* synthétique; ***synthetic image*** image *f* de synthèse; ***synthetic rubber*** caoutchouc *m* synthétique

synthetically [sɪn'θetɪkəlɪ] ADV synthétiquement

syph [sɪf] N *Fam* syphilis ᵒ*f*

syphilis ['sɪfɪlɪs] N *(UNCOUNT)* syphilis *f*

syphilitic [,sɪfɪ'lɪtɪk] ADJ syphilitique
N syphilitique *mf*

syphon = **siphon**

Syria ['sɪrɪə] N Syrie *f*

Syrian ['sɪrɪən] N Syrien(enne) *m,f*
ADJ syrien

syringe [sɪ'rɪndʒ] N seringue *f*
VT seringuer; **to have one's ears syringed** se faire déboucher les oreilles *(avec une seringue)*

syrup, *Am* **sirup** ['sɪrəp] N **1** *(sweetened liquid)* sirop *m*; **peaches in s.** pêches *fpl* au sirop
2 *(Br* **golden) s.** mélasse *f* raffinée
3 *Pharm* sirop *m*
4 *Pej (sentimentality)* douceur *f* affectée
►► ***syrup of figs*** sirop *m* de figues *(utilisé comme laxatif)*

syrupy ['sɪrəpɪ] ADJ **1** *(viscous)* sirupeux **2** *Pej (sentimental)* sirupeux, à l'eau de rose

SYSOP ['sɪsɒp] N *Comput (abbr* **Systems Operator***)* sysop *m*, opérateur *m* système

system ['sɪstəm] N **1** *(organization, structure)* système *m*; **the Social Security s.** le système des prestations sociales; **they live in a democratic/totalitarian s.** ils vivent dans un système démocratique/totalitaire

2 *(method)* système *m*; **a new s. of sorting mail** un nouveau système pour trier le courrier

3 *Anat* système *m*; **the muscular s.** le système musculaire

4 *(orderliness)* méthode *f*; **you need some s. in the way you work** vous devriez être plus systématique *ou* méthodique dans votre travail

5 *(human body)* organisme *m*; **bad for the s.** nuisible à l'organisme; **it's a bit of a shock to the s.** ça fait un choc; *Fig* **to get sth out of one's s.** se débarrasser de qch; **she can't get him out of her s.** elle n'arrive pas à l'oublier

6 *(equipment, device, devices)* **the electrical s. needs to be replaced** l'installation électrique a besoin d'être remplacée; **a fault in the cooling s.** un défaut dans le circuit de refroidissement

7 *(network)* réseau *m*; **the rail/river/road s.** le réseau ferroviaire/fluvial/routier

8 *Comput* système *m*

9 *(established order)* **the s.** le système; *Fam* **you can't beat** *or* **buck the s.** on ne peut rien contre le système

10 *Geol* système *m*

▸▸ *Comput* ***systems analysis*** analyse *f* des systèmes; *Comput* ***systems analyst*** analyste-programmeur(euse) *m,f*; *Comput* ***systems board*** carte *f* système; *Archit* ***system building*** préfabrication *f*; *Comput* ***system bus*** bus *m* système; *Comput* ***system crash*** panne *f* du système; *Comput* ***system date*** date *f* système; *Comput* ***system disk*** disque *f* système; *Comput* ***systems engineer*** ingénieur *m* système; *Comput* ***systems engineering*** ingénierie *f* des systèmes; *Comput* ***system error*** erreur *f* système; *Comput* ***system failure*** panne *f* du système; *Comput* ***system file*** fichier *m* système; *Comput* ***system folder*** dossier *m* système; *Comput* ***systems management*** direction *f* systématisée; *Comput* ***systems operator*** sysop *m*, opérateur *m* système; *Comput* ***system privilege*** privilège *m* d'accès au système; *Comput* ***system program*** programme *m* système; *Comput* ***system prompt*** invite *f* du système, message *m* d'attente du système; *Comput* ***system software*** logiciel *m* d'exploitation, logiciel *m* système

systematic [ˌsɪstəˈmætɪk] **ADJ** systématique

systematically [ˌsɪstəˈmætɪklɪ] **ADV** systématiquement

systematization, -isation [ˌsɪstɪmətaɪˈzeɪʃən] **N** systématisation *f*

systematize, -ise [ˈsɪstəmətaɪz] **VT** systématiser

systemic [sɪsˈtemɪk] **ADJ** systémique

systemization, -isation [ˌsɪstəmaɪˈzeɪʃən] **N** systématisation *f*

systemize, -ise [ˈsɪstəmaɪz] **VT** systématiser

T, t [tiː] **N 1** *(letter)* T, t *m inv*; **two t's** deux t; **T for Tommy** ≃ T comme Thérèse **2** *(idiom)* **to a T** parfaitement, à merveille; **you've described him to a T** vous l'avez parfaitement décrit; **that's her to a T** c'est tout à fait elle; **the jacket fits/suits her to a T** la veste lui va à merveille

TA [ˌtiːˈeɪ] **N 1** *Br Mil* (*abbr* **Territorial Army**) = force armée constituée de réservistes volontaires **2** *Am & Can Univ* (*abbr* **teaching assistant**) = étudiant de deuxième cycle qui assure quelques heures de cours en échange d'une bourse d'études

ta [tɑː] **EXCLAM** *Br Fam* merci!

TAB [tæb] **N** *Med* (*abbr* **typhoid-paratyphoid A and B**) (vaccin *m*) TAB *m*; **he's had a T. injection** on lui a fait le TAB

tab [tæb] *(pt & pp* **tabbed**, *cont* **tabbing**) **N 1** *(on garment* ▸ *flap)* patte *f*; (▸ *loop)* attache *f*; *(over ear)* oreillette *f*; *(on shoelaces)* ferret *m*

2 *(tag* ▸ *on clothing, luggage)* étiquette *f*; (▸ *on file, dictionary)* onglet *m*; *Fig* **to keep tabs on sb/sth** avoir qn/qch à l'œil, avoir l'œil sur qn/qch; **I'll keep tabs on how the case progresses** je vais surveiller l'évolution de cette affaire

3 *(bill* ▸ *gen)* note *f*; (▸ *in bar, restaurant)* addition *f*; *also Fig* **to pick up the t.** payer l'addition *ou* la note

4 *Br Fam (cigarette)* clope *f*, tige *f*

5 *Fam Drugs slang (of LSD)* buvard *m*

6 *Comput* tabulation *f*; **to set tabs (at)** régler *ou* positionner les tabulateurs (à)

VT *Comput (text)* mettre en colonnes (avec des tabulations)

▸▸ *Comput* ***tab key*** touche *f* de tabulation; ***tab stop*** taquet *m* de tabulation

tabard [ˈtæbəd] **N** tabard *m*, tabar *m*

Tabasco® [təˈbæskəʊ] **N** Tabasco® *m*

tabbouleh [tæˈbuːleɪ] **N** *Culin* taboulé *m*

tabby [ˈtæbɪ] *(pl* **tabbies**) **N** chat (chatte) *m,f* tigré(e)

ADJ tigré

▸▸ ***tabby cat*** chat (chatte) *m,f* tigré(e)

tab-delimited **ADJ** *Comput* délimité par des tabulations

tabernacle [ˈtæbənækəl] **N 1** *Bible & Rel (tent, receptacle)* tabernacle *m* **2** *(place of worship)* temple *m*

table [ˈteɪbəl] **N 1** *(furniture)* table *f*; **to get round the negotiating t.** s'asseoir à la table des négociations; **to set** *or Br* **to lay the t.** mettre *ou* dresser la table *ou* le couvert; *Formal* **to be at t.** être à table; **to be (sitting) at the breakfast/dinner t.** être à table pour le petit déjeuner/(le) dîner; **may I leave the t.?** puis-je sortir de table *ou* quitter la table?; *Fam* **to drink sb under the t.** mieux tenir l'alcool que qn; *Fam* **I could drink you under the t.!** je te parie que je peux boire plus que toi!; *Fam* **two drinks and I'm under the t.** deux verres et je suis complètement paf!

2 *(people seated)* table *f*, tablée *f*; **my uncle kept the whole t. amused** mon oncle a diverti toute la tablée; **we were seated with a t. of card players** nous étions assis à une table de joueurs de cartes

3 *Formal (food)* **she keeps an excellent t.** elle a une excellente table; **the restaurant has a hot and cold t.** le restaurant propose des plats chauds et des plats froids

4 *Tech (of machine)* table *f*; *Mus (of violin)* table *f* d'harmonie

5 *(list)* liste *f*; *(chart)* table *f*, tableau *m*; *(of fares, prices)* tableau *m*, barème *m*; *Comput* tableau *m*; **the results are set out in the following t.** les résultats sont donnés dans le tableau suivant

6 *Sport* classement *m*; **our team came bottom in the t.** notre équipe s'est classée dernière *ou* était dernière au classement

7 *Sch* **(multiplication) t.** table *f* (de multiplication); **we have to learn our 4 times t.** il faut qu'on apprenne la table de 4

8 *(slab* ▸ *of stone, marble)* plaque *f*

9 *Geog* plateau *m*

10 *(idioms)* **to put** *or* **to lay sth on the t.** mettre qch sur la table; **we will not negotiate until they put a better offer on the t.** nous ne négocierons pas tant qu'ils ne mettront pas une meilleure offre sur la table; **he offered me £100 under the t.** il m'a offert 100 livres en dessous-de-table

COMP de table

VT 1 *Br Parl (submit* ▸ *bill, motion)* présenter

2 *Am Parl (postpone* ▸ *bill, motion)* ajourner, reporter; **the bill has been tabled** la discussion du projet de loi a été reportée

3 *(tabulate)* présenter sous forme de tableau; *(classify)* classifier

4 *(schedule)* prévoir, fixer; **the discussion is tabled for 4 o'clock** la discussion est prévue *ou* a été fixée à 4 heures

▸▸ ***table of contents*** table *f* des matières; ***table dancing*** table dancing *m*, danse *f* aux tables; ***table football*** baby-foot *m*; ***table knife*** couteau *m* de table; ***table lamp*** petite lampe *f*; ***table leg*** pied *m* de table; ***table linen*** linge *m* de table; ***table manners*** manière *f* de se tenir à table; **he has terrible/excellent t. manners** il se tient très mal/très bien à table; *Geog* ***Table Mountain*** la montagne de la Table; ***table napkin*** serviette *f* de table; ***table runner*** chemin *m* de table; ***table salt*** sel *m* de table, sel *m* fin; ***table top*** dessus *m* de table; ***table wine*** vin *m* de table

tableau [ˈtæbləʊ] *(pl* **tableaus** *or* **tableaux** [-bləʊz]) **N** tableau *m*

tablecloth [ˈteɪbəlklɒθ] **N** nappe *f*

table-hop **VI** *Am* = aller de table en table dans un restaurant ou une réception, pour montrer qu'on a des relations

tableland [ˈteɪbəllænd] **N** *Geog* plateau *m*

table-rapping **N** *(in spiritualism)* = coups frappés sur un guéridon, attribués à un esprit frappeur

tablespoon [ˈteɪbəlspuːn] **N** *(for serving)* grande cuillère *f*, cuillère *f* à soupe; *(as measure)* grande cuillerée *f*, cuillerée *f* à soupe

tablespoonful [ˈteɪbəlˌspuːnful] **N** grande cuillerée *f*, cuillerée *f* à soupe

tablet [ˈtæblɪt] **N 1** *(for writing* ▸ *stone, wax etc)* tablette *f*; (▸ *pad)* bloc-notes *m*

2 *(pill)* comprimé *m*, cachet *m*

3 *Br (of chocolate)* tablette *f*; *(of soap)* savonnette *f*

4 *(plaque)* plaque *f* (commémorative)

5 *Comput* tablette *f*

6 *Scot (sweet)* fondant *m* au caramel

table-tennis **N** tennis *m* de table, ping-pong *m*

▸▸ ***table-tennis ball*** balle *f* de ping-pong; *Br* ***table-tennis bat****, Am* ***table-tennis paddle*** raquette *f* de ping-pong; ***table-tennis player*** joueur(euse) *m,f* de ping-pong, pongiste *mf*

tableware [ˈteɪbəlweə(r)] **N** vaisselle *f*

tabloid [ˈtæblɔɪd] **N** *(format)* tabloïd *m*; *(newspaper)* tabloïde *m*; **the tabloids** les journaux à sensation

ADJ in t. form condensé, en résumé

▸▸ ***tabloid format*** format *m* tabloïd; ***tabloid newspaper*** tabloïde *m*; ***tabloid press*** presse *f* à sensation; ***tabloid television, tabloid TV*** émissions *fpl* à sensation

> **TABLOIDS**
>
> Dans les pays anglo-saxons, le format tabloïd est caractéristique de la presse populaire, bien que certains journaux de qualité aient récemment adopté le même format (voir aussi l'encadré à **broadsheet**). En Grande-Bretagne, les plus connus des "tabloids" sont le 'Sun', le 'Daily Mirror', le 'Daily Mail' et le 'Daily Express'. Ces journaux sont très influents en Grande-Bretagne – le 'Sun' affiche ainsi les plus grands tirages de la presse britannique. Les "tabloids" privilégient tout particulièrement les histoires à scandale et à sensation, ce qui a suscité un débat sur le code de conduite de la presse et sur la législation à mettre en place pour protéger la vie privée.

tabloidese [ˌtæblɔɪˈdiːz] **N** style *m* tabloïde

taboo [təˈbuː] *(pl* **taboos**) **ADJ** *(subject, word)* tabou

N tabou *m*

VT proscrire, interdire

tabular [ˈtæbjʊlə(r)] **ADJ** *(statistics, figures)* tabulaire; **in t. form** sous forme de tableau

▸▸ ***tabular ledger*** grand livre *m* (à colonnes)

tabulate [ˈtæbjʊleɪt] **VT 1** *(in table form)* mettre sous forme de table *ou* tableau; *(in columns)* mettre en colonnes **2** *(classify)* classifier

tabulation [ˌtæbjʊˈleɪʃən] **N 1** *(in tables)* présentation *f ou* disposition *f* en tables; *(in columns)* disposition *f* en colonnes **2** *(classification)* classification *f*

tabulator [ˈtæbjʊleɪtə(r)] **N** *Comput* tabulation *f*

▸▸ ***tabulator key*** touche *f* de tabulation

tacheometer [ˌtækɪˈɒmɪtə(r)] **N** tachéomètre *m*

tachistoscope [təˈkɪstəˌskəʊp] **N** tachistoscope *m*

tachograph [ˈtækəgrɑːf] **N** tachygraphe *m*

tachometer [tæˈkɒmɪtə(r)] **N** tachymètre *m*

tachycardia [ˌtækɪˈkɑːdɪə] **N** *Med* tachycardie *f*

tachycardiac [ˌtækɪˈkɑːdɪk] **ADJ** *Med* tachycardique

tachymeter [tæˈkɪmɪtə(r)] **N** tachéomètre *m*

tacit [ˈtæsɪt] **ADJ** tacite, implicite; **t. approval** accord *m* tacite; **t. knowledge** connaissances *fpl* implicites

tacitly [ˈtæsɪtlɪ] **ADV** tacitement

taciturn [ˈtæsɪtɜːn] **ADJ** taciturne, qui parle peu

taciturnity [ˌtæsɪˈtɜːnɪtɪ] **N** taciturnité *f*

tack [tæk] **N 1** *(nail)* pointe *f*; *(for carpeting, upholstery)* semence *f*; *(for poster, notice etc)* punaise *f*

2 *Br Sewing* point *m* de bâti; **to take out the tacks** retirer le bâti

3 *Naut (course)* bordée *f*, bord *m*; **to make** *or* **to set a t.** courir *ou* tirer une bordée; **to be on a starboard/port t.** être tribord/bâbord amures; *Fig* **to be on the right t.** être sur la bonne voie; *Fig* **to be on the wrong t.** faire fausse route; *Fig* **he went off on a quite different t.** il est parti sur une toute autre piste; *Fig* **let's try another t.** essayons une autre tactique, changeons de tactique; *Fig* **she changed t. in mid-conversation** elle changea de sujet en pleine conversation

4 *Fam (tacky things)* trucs *mpl* de mauvais goût; **her house is full of t.** sa maison est pleine de trucs de mauvais goût

VT 1 *(carpet)* clouer **2** *Sewing* faufiler, bâtir

VI *Naut* faire *ou* courir *ou* tirer une bordée, louvoyer

tackiness ['tækɪnɪs] **N 1** *(of paint, glue, substance)* **because of the t. of the paint/glue** parce que la peinture n'est pas encore sèche/la colle est encore poisseuse **2** *Fam (shabbiness ▸ of shop, neighbourhood etc)* apparence *f* minable **3** *Fam (vulgarity ▸ of remark, joke etc)* goût *m* douteux◻; *(of clothes)* aspect *m* ringard; *(jewellery, decor)* kitsch *m inv*; *(of person)* vulgarité◻*f*

tacking ['tækɪŋ] **N** *Sewing* bâti *m*, faufilage *m*; **you'll have to take out the t.** il va falloir enlever le faufilage

▸▸ *tacking stitch* point *m* de bâti; ***tacking thread*** fil *m* à bâtir, faufil *m*

tackle ['tækəl] **VT 1** *(task, problem)* s'attaquer à; *(question, subject)* s'attaquer à, aborder; **I'm going to t. 'War and Peace' during the holidays** je vais attaquer 'Guerre et paix' pendant les vacances; **he tackled an enormous plate of chips** il attaqua une énorme assiettée de frites

2 *(confront)* interroger; **I tackled him on** *or* **about his stand on abortion** je l'ai interrogé sur sa prise de position sur l'avortement; **I'll t. her about the extra cost** je lui toucherai un mot *ou* je lui parlerai du coût supplémentaire

3 *(in football, hockey)* tacler; *(in rugby, American football)* plaquer; *Fig (assailant, bank robber)* saisir, empoigner

VI *(in football, hockey)* faire un tacle; *(in rugby, American football)* faire un plaquage

N 1 *(equipment)* attirail *m*, matériel *m*; **fishing t.** matériel *m ou* articles *mpl* de pêche

2 *(ropes and pulleys)* appareil *m ou* appareils *mpl* de levage; *(hoist)* palan *m*; **under ship's t.** sous palan

3 *(challenge ▸ in football, hockey)* tacle *m*; *(▸ in rugby, American football)* plaquage *m*, placage *m*; **good t.!** bien taclé!

4 *(player ▸ in American football)* plaqueur *m*

5 *Br Fam Hum* **(wedding) t.** *(man's genitals)* service *m* trois pièces, bijoux *mpl* de famille

tackler ['tæklə(r)] **N** *(in football, hockey)* tacleur (euse) *m,f*; *(in rugby, American football)* plaqueur(euse) *m,f*

tackling ['tæklɪŋ] **N** *(UNCOUNT)* **1** *(in football, hockey)* tacle *m*; *(in rugby, American football)* plaquage *m*, placage *m* **2** *(of problem, job)* manière *f* d'aborder

tacky ['tækɪ] *(compar* **tackier**, *superl* **tackiest)** **ADJ 1** *(sticky)* collant, poisseux; *(paint)* pas encore sec (sèche); **wait until the glue is t.** attendez que la colle ait commencé à prendre **2** *Fam (shoddy)* minable, moche **3** *Fam (vulgar ▸ clothes)* ringard; *(▸ jewellery, decor)* kitsch *inv*; *(▸ person)* beauf, vulgaire◻; *(▸ remark, joke)* de mauvais goût◻

taco ['tækəʊ] *(pl* **tacos)** **N** *Culin* taco *m (crêpe mexicaine farcie et frite)*

tact [tækt] **N** tact *m*, diplomatie *f*, doigté *m*

tactful ['tæktfʊl] **ADJ** *(person)* plein de tact, qui fait preuve de tact; *(answer, remark, suggestion)* plein de tact; *(inquiry)* discret(ète); *(behaviour)* qui fait preuve de tact *ou* de délicatesse; **that wasn't a very t. thing to say** ce n'était pas très diplomatique de dire ça; **try to be more t.** essaie de faire preuve de plus de tact; **they gave us a t. hint** ils nous ont fait discrètement comprendre

tactfully ['tæktfʊlɪ] **ADV** avec tact *ou* délicatesse; **I t. refrained from asking him** par tact *ou* délicatesse, je me suis retenu de lui poser la question

tactfulness ['tæktfʊlnɪs] = **tact**

tactic ['tæktɪk] **N** tactique *f*

• tactics NPL *Mil & Sport* tactique *f*

tactical ['tæktɪkəl] **ADJ 1** *(gen)* tactique **2** *(shrewd)* adroit; **a purely t. manoeuvre** une manœuvre purement diplomatique

▸▸ *tactical mistake* erreur *f* tactique; ***tactical vote*** vote *m* utile; ***tactical voter*** = personne qui fait un vote utile; ***tactical voting*** vote *m* utile; **there has been a lot of t. voting** beaucoup de gens ont voté utile

tactically ['tæktɪklɪ] **ADV** du point de vue tactique; **to vote t.** voter utile

tactician [tæk'tɪʃən] **N** tacticien(enne) *m,f*

tactile ['tæktaɪl] **ADJ** tactile

tactless ['tæktlɪs] **ADJ** *(person)* dépourvu de tact, qui manque de doigté; *(answer)* indiscret(ète), peu diplomatique; **what a t. thing to say/to do!** il faut vraiment manquer de tact pour dire/faire une chose pareille!; **how t. of him!** quel manque de tact de sa part!

tactlessly ['tæktlɪslɪ] **ADV** sans tact; **she asked him rather t. about his first wife** elle lui a posé des questions sur sa première femme, ce qui n'était pas très délicat de sa part

tad [tæd] **N** *Fam* **1** *(small bit)* **a t.** un peu◻; **it's a t. expensive** c'est un chouia trop cher; **I think you're exaggerating a t.** je crois que t'exagères un tantinet **2** *esp Am (boy)* mioche *m*, gamin *m*

tadger ['tædʒə(r)] **N** *Br very Fam (penis)* chipolata *f*

tadpole ['tædpəʊl] **N** *Zool* têtard *m*

Tadzhik [tɑ:dʒɪk, tɑ:'dʒi:k], **Tadzhiki** [tɑ:'dʒi:kɪ] **N 1** *(person)* Tadjik *mf* **2** *(language)* tadjik *m*

ADJ tadjik

COMP *(embassy, history)* du Tadjikistan; *(teacher)* de tadjik

Tadzhikistan [tɑ:,dʒɪkɪ'stɑ:n] **N** Tadjikistan *m*

taffeta ['tæfɪtə] **N** taffetas *m*

ADJ *(dress)* en taffetas

taffrail ['tæfreɪl] **N** *Naut* lisse *f* de couronnement, rambarde *f* arrière

Taffy ['tæfɪ] *(pl* **Taffies)** **N** *Fam* = nom péjoratif ou humoristique désignant un Gallois

taffy ['tæfɪ] *(pl* **taffies)** **N** *Am* caramel *m* (au beurre)

▸▸ *taffy apple* pomme *f* d'amour

tag [tæg] *(pt & pp* **tagged**, *cont* **tagging)** **N 1** *(label ▸ on clothes, suitcase)* étiquette *f*; *(▸ on file)* onglet *m*; **(price) t.** étiquette *f* de prix; **(name) t.** *(gen)* étiquette *f (où est marqué le nom)*; *(for dog, soldier)* plaque *f* d'identité

2 *(on shoelace)* ferret *m*

3 *(on jacket, coat ▸ for hanging)* patte *f*

4 *(for offender)* bracelet *m* électronique *(permettant de localiser les délinquants en liberté surveillée)*

5 *(graffiti)* tag *m*

6 *Am (licence plate)* plaque *f* minéralogique

7 *(quotation)* citation *f*; *(cliché)* cliché *m*, lieu *m* commun; *(catchword)* slogan *m*; **a Latin t.** une citation latine

8 *(epithet, nickname)* surnom *m*

9 *Gram* question-tag *f*

10 *(game)* chat *m*; **to play t.** jouer à chat

11 *Comput (code)* balise *f*

VT 1 *(label ▸ package, article, garment)* étiqueter; *(▸ animal)* marquer; *(▸ file)* mettre un onglet à

2 *Fig (▸ person)* étiqueter; **he was tagged as a trouble-maker** il a été classé parmi les agitateurs

3 *(offender)* mettre un bracelet électronique à

4 *Am (follow)* suivre; *(of detective)* filer

5 *Am (for traffic offence ▸ vehicle)* coller une contravention sur; *(▸ person)* mettre une contravention à

6 *(leave graffiti on)* faire des graffiti sur

7 *(in game of tag)* toucher

8 *Comput* baliser

▸▸ *Am* ***tag end*** *(oddment ▸ of cloth, thread)* bout *m*; *(▸ of goods)* restes *mpl*; *(end ▸ of performance, day)* fin *f*; ***tag line*** *(in play)* mot *m* de la fin; *(in poem)* dernier vers *m*; *(of entertainer)* slogan *m*; *Journ* chute *f*; *Gram* ***tag question*** question-tag *f*

▸ tag along VI suivre; **to t. along with sb** *(follow)* suivre qn; *(accompany)* aller *ou* venir avec qn; **do you mind if I t. along?** ça vous gêne si je viens?; **she tagged along behind the others** *(followed)* elle suivit les autres; *(lagged behind)* elle était à la traîne derrière les autres

▸ tag on VT SEP ajouter

VI *Fam* **to t. on to sb** suivre qn partout◻; **to t. on behind sb** traîner derrière qn◻

Tagalog [tə'gɑ:lɒg] **N 1** *(person)* Tagal *mf* **2** *Ling* tagalog *m*, tagal *m*

tagboard ['tægbɔ:d] **N** carton *m* pour étiquettes

tagliatelle [,tæljə'telɪ] **N** *Culin* tagliatelles *fpl*

Tahiti [tɑ:'hi:tɪ] **N** Tahiti

Tahitian [tɑ:'hi:ʃən] **N** Tahitien(enne) *m,f*

ADJ tahitien

tai chi [taɪ'tʃi:] **N** tai chi *m*

taiga ['taɪgə] **N** *Geog* taïga *f*

tail [teɪl] **N 1** *(of animal)* queue *f*; *Fig* **with one's t between one's legs** la queue basse, la queue entre les jambes; **to be on sb's t.** suivre qn de près; **the detective was still on his t.** le détective le filait toujours; *Fam* **the car was right on my t.** la voiture me collait au derrière *ou* aux fesses; **to turn t and run** prendre ses jambes à son cou; **it's a case of the t. wagging the dog** c'est le monde à l'envers; **the t. of the hostages is wagging the dog o[f] foreign policy** le problème des otages décide de la politique étrangère

2 *(of kite, comet, aircraft)* queue *f*; *(of musica[l] note)* queue *f*

3 *(of coat)* basque *f*; *(of dress)* traîne *f*; *(of shir[t])* pan *m*

4 *(end ▸ of storm)* queue *f*; *(▸ of procession)* fin *f*, queue *f*; *(▸ of queue)* bout *m*

5 *Fam (follower ▸ police officer, detective)* = personne qui file; **to put a t. on sb** faire filer qn◻; **we've got a t.** quelqu'un nous file◻, nous sommes suivis◻

6 *Fam (buttocks)* fesses◻*fpl*; **he worked his t. off** il s'est vraiment décarcassé

7 *(UNCOUNT) very Fam* **a bit of t.** *(woman)* une gonzesse; **he's looking for some t.** il cherche une femme à se mettre sur le bout

VT 1 *Fam (follow)* filocher, filer le train à **2** *(animal)* couper la queue à

• tails NPL *Fam (tailcoat)* queue *f* de pie◻ **ADV** *(o[f] coin)* **it's tails!** (c'est) pile!

▸▸ *Aviat* ***tail assembly*** dérive *f*; ***tail end*** *(of storm, season, meeting, story)* fin *f*; *(of cloth)* bout *m*; *(o[f] procession)* queue *f*, fin *f*; ***tail feather*** penne *f*; *Au[t]* ***tail lamp*** feu *m* arrière; *Am Aut* ***tail pipe*** tuyau *m* d'échappement; *Aviat* ***tail section*** arrière *m*

▸ tail away VI *(sound)* s'affaiblir, décroître; *(interest, enthusiasm, support)* diminuer petit à petit; *(book)* se terminer en queue de poisson; *(competitors in race)* s'espacer

▸ tail back VI *Br (traffic)* être arrêté, former un bouchon; *(demonstration, runners)* s'égrener, s'espacer; **the line of cars tailed back for 10 mile[s]** ≃ la file de voitures s'étendait sur 16 km

▸ tail off VI *(quality)* baisser; *(numbers)* diminuer, baisser; *(voice)* devenir inaudible; *(story)* se terminer en queue de poisson

tailback ['teɪlbæk] **N** *Br* bouchon *m* (de circulation)

tailboard ['teɪlbɔ:d] **N** hayon *m (de camion)*

-tailed [teɪld] **SUFF** **short-/long-t.** à queue courte/longue

tailender [teɪl'endə(r)] **N** *(in race)* dernier(ère) *m,f*

tailgate ['teɪlgeɪt] *Aut* **N** hayon *m*

VT coller au pare-chocs de

tailhopping ['teɪl,hɒpɪŋ] **N** *Ski* ruade *f*

tailings ['teɪlɪŋz] **NPL** *(from mining)* déchets *mp[l]*

taillight ['teɪllaɪt] **N** *Aut* feu *m* arrière

tailor ['teɪlə(r)] **N** tailleur *m*

VT 1 *(garment)* faire sur mesure **2** *Fig* **to t. sth t[o]** *(person, needs, requirements ▸ adapt)* adapter qch à; *(▸ conceptualize)* concevoir qch pour; **the car has been tailored for the American marke[t]** la voiture a été modifiée pour le marché américain; **the kitchen was tailored to our needs** la cu

ine a été faite spécialement pour nous *ou* :onçue en fonction de nos besoins
▸▸ ***tailor's chalk*** craie *f* de tailleur; ***tailor's dummy*** nannequin *m*; *Fig Pej* **he looks like a t.'s dummy** il ɛst tout endimanché

ailoring ['teɪlərɪŋ] **N 1** *(profession)* métier *m* de ailleur **2** *(work)* ouvrage *m* de tailleur

ailor-made **ADJ** *(specially made* ▸ *clothes, ›quipment)* (fait) sur mesure; *(very suitable)* comme) fait exprès; **top players have their ackets t. for them** les joueurs de haut niveau ›nt des raquettes faites sur mesure; **the job ould have been t. for her** on dirait que le poste ɛst taillé pour elle

ailpiece ['teɪlpi:s] **N 1** *(addition* ▸ *to speech)* ajout *m*; *(*▸ *to document)* appendice *m*; *(*▸ *to let-er)* post-scriptum *m inv* **2** *Mus* cordier *m (d'un ›iolon)* **3** *Typ* cul-de-lampe *m*

ailplane ['teɪlpleɪn] **N** *Aviat* stabilisateur *m*

ailrace ['teɪlreɪs] **N** *(for mill)* bief *m* d'aval

ailshaft ['teɪlʃɑ:ft] **N** *Aut* arbre *m* de sortie

ailskid ['teɪlskɪd] **N** *Aviat* béquille *f* de queue

ailspin ['teɪlspɪn] **N** *Aviat* vrille *f*; **to be in a t.** vril-er; *Fig (economy, business)* être en dégringo-ade; *(person)* paniquer, s'affoler

ailwind ['teɪlwɪnd] **N** vent *m* arrière

aint [teɪnt] **VT 1** *(minds, morals)* corrompre, souiller; *(person)* salir la réputation de; *(reputa-ion)* salir; **his personal life is tainted with scandal** sa vie privée fait beaucoup de scandale **2** *(food)* gâter; *(air)* polluer, vicier; *(water)* polluer, infec-er
N 1 *(infection)* infection *f*; *(contamination)* con-amination *f*; *(decay)* décomposition *f* **2** *Fig (of sin, corruption)* tache *f*, souillure *f*

ainted ['teɪntɪd] **ADJ 1** *(morals)* corrompu, dé-ɔravé; *(reputation)* terni, sali; *(money)* sale **2** *(food)* gâté; *(meat)* avarié; *(air)* vicié, pollué; *(water)* infecté, pollué; *(blood)* impur

aiwan [,taɪ'wɑ:n] **N** Taïwan

aiwanese [,taɪwə'ni:z] **N** Taïwanais(e) *m,f*
ADJ taïwanais

ajik = **Tadzhik**

ajikistan = **Tadzhikistan**

AKE [teɪk]

VT
- prendre **A1, 2, B1, 3–5, C2, D1, 2, E1, F1, G1, 2, 4, H1, 2, I1, 3, 4, 6, 7, 15, 18**
- porter **B1**
- mener **B2**
- conduire **C1**
- recevoir **D3**
- croire **F2**
- supporter **F4**
- supposer **G3**
- contenir **I5**
- passer **I9**

VI
- prendre **1–3**

N
- prise **1**
- prise de vue **2**
- enregistrement **2**

(pt **took** [tʊk], *pp* **taken** ['teɪkən])

VT A. 1 *(get hold of)* prendre; *(seize)* prendre, sai-sir; **let me t. your coat** donnez-moi votre man-teau; **she took the book from him** elle lui a pris le livre; **to t. sb's hand** prendre qn par la main; **she took his arm** elle lui a pris le bras; **Peter took her in his arms** Peter l'a prise dans ses bras; **the wolf took its prey by the throat** le loup a saisi sa proie à la gorge

2 *(get control of, capture* ▸ *person)* prendre, cap-turer; *(*▸ *fish, game)* prendre, attraper; *Mil (*▸ *town, area)* prendre, s'emparer de; **to t. sb prison-er** faire qn prisonnier; **to t. sb alive** prendre *ou* capturer qn vivant; **I took his queen with my rook** *(in chess)* j'ai pris sa reine avec ma tour; **to t. con-trol of a situation** prendre une situation en main; **we took our courage in both hands** nous avons pris notre courage à deux mains; **you're taking your life in your hands doing that** c'est ta vie que tu risques en faisant cela; **to t. the lead in sth** *(in competition)* prendre la tête de qch; *(set example)* être le premier à faire qch

B. 1 *(carry from one place to another)* porter, ap-porter; *(carry along, have in one's possession)* prendre, emporter; **she took her mother a cup of tea** elle a apporté une tasse de thé à sa mère; **he took the map with him** il a emporté la carte; **she took some towels up(stairs)/down(stairs)** elle a monté/descendu des serviettes; **don't forget to t. your camera** n'oubliez pas (de prendre) votre appareil photo; *Fig* **the committee wanted to t. the matter further** le comité voulait mener l'af-faire plus loin; **you can't t. it with you** *(money when you die)* tu ne l'emporteras pas avec toi dans la tombe

2 *(person* ▸ *lead)* mener, emmener; *(*▸ *accom-pany)* accompagner; **her father takes her to school** son père l'emmène à l'école; **could you t. me home?** pourriez-vous me ramener *ou* me rac-compagner?; **to t. sb across the road** faire traver-ser la rue à qn; **may I t. you to dinner?** puis-je vous inviter à dîner *ou* vous emmener dîner?; **he offered to t. them to work in the car** il leur a proposé de les emmener au bureau en voiture *ou* de les conduire au bureau; **to t. oneself to bed** aller se coucher; **please t. me with you** em-mène-moi, s'il te plaît; *Hum* **I can't t. you any-where** tu n'es pas sortable; **the estate agent took them over the house** l'agent immobilier leur a fait visiter la maison; **he took her round the museum** il lui a fait visiter le musée; **she used to t. me along to meetings** (avant,) elle m'emmenait aux réu-nions; **this road will t. you to the station** cette route vous mènera *ou* vous conduira à la gare; **I don't want to t. you out of your way** je ne veux pas vous faire faire un détour; **her job took her all over Africa** son travail l'a fait voyager dans toute l'Afrique; **that's what first took me to Portugal** c'est ce qui m'a amené au Portugal; **whatever took him there?** qu'allait-il faire là-bas?; **the record took her to number one in the charts** le disque lui a permis d'être première au hit-parade

3 *(obtain from specified place)* prendre, tirer; *(re-move from specified place)* prendre, enlever; **she took a handkerchief from her pocket** elle a sorti un mouchoir de sa poche; **I took a chocolate from the box** j'ai pris un chocolat dans la boîte; **t. a book from the shelf** prenez un livre sur l'étagère; **t. your feet off the table** enlève tes pieds de la table; **he took the saucepan off the heat** il a ôté *ou* retiré la casserole du feu

4 *(appropriate, steal)* prendre, voler; **to t. sth from sb** prendre qch à qn; **someone's taken my wallet** on a pris mon portefeuille; **his article is taken directly from my book** le texte de son art-icle est tiré directement de mon livre

5 *(draw, derive)* prendre, tirer; **a passage taken from a book** un passage extrait d'un livre; **a phrase taken from Latin** une expression emprun-tée au latin; **the title is taken from the Bible** le titre vient de la Bible

C. 1 *(of bus, car, train etc)* conduire, transporter; **the ambulance took him to hospital** l'ambulance l'a transporté à l'hôpital; **this bus will t. you to the theatre** ce bus vous conduira au théâtre; **will this train t. me to Cambridge?** est-ce que ce train va à *ou* passe par Cambridge?

2 *(bus, car, plane, train)* prendre; *(road)* prendre, suivre; *Am* **t. a right** prenez à droite

D. 1 *(have* ▸ *attitude, bath, holiday)* prendre; *(make* ▸ *nap, trip, walk)* faire; *(*▸ *decision)* pren-dre; **she took a quick look at him** elle a jeté un ra-pide coup d'œil sur lui; *Am Fam* **let's t. five** soufflons cinq minutes□; **he took a flying leap** il a bondi; *Am Vulg* **to t. a shit** *or* **a dump** chier; *Arch or Literary* **to t. a wife** prendre femme

2 *Phot* **to t. a photo** *or* **a picture** prendre une pho-to; **she took his picture** *or* **a picture of him** elle l'a pris en photo; **we had our picture taken** nous nous sommes fait photographier *ou* prendre en photo; *Fam* **he takes a good photo** *(is photogenic)* il est photogénique□

3 *(receive, get)* recevoir; *(earn, win* ▸ *prize)* rem-porter, obtenir; *(*▸ *degree, diploma)* obtenir, avoir; **he took the blow on his arm** il a pris le coup sur le bras; **you can t. the call in my office** vous pouvez prendre l'appel dans mon bureau; **the bookstore takes about $3,000 a day** la librairie fait à peu près 3000 dollars (de recette) par jour; **how much does he t. home a month?** quel est son salaire mensuel net?; **their team took the match** leur équipe a gagné *ou* remporté le match

E. 1 *(assume, undertake)* prendre; **to t. the blame for sth** prendre la responsabilité de qch; **you'll have to t. the consequences** c'est vous qui en su-birez les conséquences; **she takes all the credit for our success** elle s'attribue tout le mérite de notre réussite; **I t. responsibility for their safety** je me charge de leur sécurité

2 *(commit oneself to)* **he took my side in the argu-ment** il a pris parti pour moi dans la dispute; **the boy took an oath** *or* **a vow to avenge his family** le garçon a fait serment *ou* a juré de venger sa fa-mille; *Am* **to t. the Fifth (Amendment)** invoquer le Cinquième Amendement *(pour refuser de ré-pondre)*

3 *(allow oneself)* **may I t. the liberty of inviting you to dinner?** puis-je me permettre de vous inviter à dîner?; **he took the opportunity to thank them** *or* **of thanking them** il a profité de l'occasion pour les remercier

F. 1 *(accept* ▸ *job, gift, payment)* prendre, accep-ter; *(*▸ *cheque, bet)* accepter; **the doctor only takes private patients** le docteur ne prend pas les patients du service public; **the owner won't t. less than $100 for it** le propriétaire en veut au moins 100 dollars; **does this machine t. pound coins?** cette machine accepte-t-elle les pièces d'une livre?; **to t. a bribe** se laisser acheter *ou* corrompre; **you'll have to t. me as I am** il faut me prendre comme je suis; **t. things as they come** prenez les choses comme elles viennent; **I won't t. "no" for an answer** pas question de refu-ser; **it's my last offer, (you can) t. it or leave it** c'est ma dernière offre, c'est à prendre ou à laisser; **I'll t. it from here** je prends la suite; **I'll t. it from there** je verrai à ce moment-là

2 *(accept as valid)* croire; **to t. sb's advice** suivre les conseils de qn; **t. it from me, he's a crook** croyez-moi, c'est un escroc

3 *(deal with)* **let's t. things one at a time** prenons les choses une par une; **the mayor took their questions calmly** le maire a entendu leurs ques-tions avec calme; **how did she t. the questioning?** comment a-t-elle réagi à *ou* pris l'interroga-toire?; **they took the news well** *or* **in their stride** ils ont plutôt bien pris la nouvelle; **to t. sth badly** prendre mal qch; *Fam* **to t. it** *or* **things easy** se la couler douce; *Fam* **t. it easy!** *(don't get angry)* du calme!□

4 *(bear, endure* ▸ *pain, heat, pressure, criticism)* supporter; *(*▸ *damage, loss)* subir; **don't t. any nonsense!** ne te laisse pas faire!; **your father won't t. any nonsense** ton père ne plaisante pas avec ce genre de choses; **she can t. it** elle tiendra le coup; *esp Am* **I'm not taking any!** je ne marche pas!; **we couldn't t. any more** on n'en pouvait plus; **I can't t. much more of this** je commence à en avoir assez, je ne vais pas supporter cela bien longtemps; **I find his constant sarcasm rather hard to t.** je trouve ses sarcasmes perpétuels dif-ficiles à supporter; **I won't t. this lying down** je ne vais pas accepter ça sans rien dire; **those shoes have taken a lot of punishment** ces chaussures en ont vu de toutes les couleurs; **to t. heavy loads** *(crane, engine etc)* supporter de lourdes charges; **it won't t. your weight** ça ne supportera pas ton poids

5 *(experience, feel)* **to t. fright** prendre peur; **to t. an interest in sb/sth** s'intéresser à qn/qch; **don't t. offence** ne vous vexez pas, ne vous offensez pas; **no offence taken** il n'y a pas de mal; **we t. pleasure in travelling** nous prenons plaisir à voyager; **she takes pride in her work** elle est fière de ce qu'elle fait; **to t. pride in one's appearance** prendre soin de sa personne

G. 1 *(consider, look at)* prendre, considérer; **t. Ein-stein (for example)** prenons (l'exemple d')Eins-tein; **t. the case of Colombia** prenons le cas de la Colombie; **taking everything into consideration** tout bien considéré; **to t. sb/sth seriously** pren-dre qn/qch au sérieux

2 *(consider as)* **do you t. me for an idiot?** vous me prenez pour un idiot?; **what do you t. me for?** pour qui me prenez-vous?; **I took you for an Eng-lishman** je vous croyais anglais; **he took me for somebody else** il m'a pris pour quelqu'un d'autre; **to t. the news as** *or* **to be true** tenir la nouvelle pour vraie; **how old do you t. her to be?** quel âge est-ce que tu lui donnes?

3 *(suppose, presume)* supposer, présumer; **I t. it you're his mother** je suppose que vous êtes sa mère

4 *(interpret, understand)* prendre, comprendre; **we never know how to t. his jokes** on ne sait jamais comment prendre ses plaisanteries; **don't t. that literally** ne le prenez pas au pied de la lettre; **he didn't t. my meaning** il ne comprenait pas ce que je voulais dire

H.1 *(require)* prendre, demander; **how long will it t. to get there?** combien de temps faudra-t-il pour y aller?; **the flight takes three hours** le vol dure trois heures; **it will t. you ten minutes** vous en avez pour dix minutes; **it took him a minute to understand** il a mis une minute avant de comprendre; **it took us longer than I expected** cela nous a pris plus de temps que je ne pensais; **it takes time to learn a language** il faut du temps pour apprendre une langue; **what kind of batteries does it t.?** quelle sorte de piles faut-il?; **my car takes unleaded** ma voiture roule au sans-plomb; **he took a bit of coaxing before he accepted** il a fallu le pousser un peu pour qu'il accepte; **it took four people to stop the brawl** ils ont dû se mettre à quatre pour arrêter la bagarre; **it takes courage to admit one's mistakes** il faut du courage pour admettre ses erreurs; **one glance was all it took** un regard a suffi; **the job took some doing** la tâche n'a pas été facile; **that will t. some explaining** voilà qui va demander des explications; **to have what it takes to do/to be sth** avoir les qualités nécessaires pour faire/être qch; **we need someone with leadership qualities – she has what it takes** il nous faut quelqu'un qui ait des qualités de dirigeant – ce n'est pas ce qui lui manque; *Fam* **he's so lazy – it takes one to know one!** il est vraiment paresseux – tu peux parler!

2 *Gram* **"falloir" takes the subjunctive** "falloir" est suivi du subjonctif; **noun that takes an "s" in the plural** nom qui prend un "s" au pluriel

I.1 *(food, drink etc)* prendre; **do you t. milk in your coffee?** prenez-vous du lait dans votre café?; **how do you t. your coffee?** qu'est-ce que tu prends dans ton café?; **I invited him to t. tea** je l'ai invité à prendre le thé; **she refused to t. any food** elle a refusé de manger (quoi que ce soit); **to t. drugs** se droguer; **how many pills has he taken?** combien de comprimés a-t-il pris *ou* absorbé?; **not to be taken internally** *(on packaging)* (à) usage externe; **to be taken twice a day** *(on packaging)* à prendre deux fois par jour; **to t. the air** prendre l'air

2 *(wear)* faire, porter; **she takes a size 10** elle prend du 38; **what size shoe do you t.?** quelle est votre pointure?

3 *(pick out, choose)* prendre, choisir; *(buy)* prendre, acheter; *(rent)* prendre, louer; **I'll t. it** je le prends; **what newspaper do you t.?** quel journal prenez-vous?

4 *(occupy ▸ chair, seat)* prendre, s'asseoir sur; **t. a seat** asseyez-vous; **t. your seats!** prenez vos places!; **is this seat taken?** cette place est-elle occupée *ou* prise?

5 *(hold ▸ of container, building etc)* contenir, avoir une capacité de; **this bus takes fifty passengers** c'est un car de cinquante places

6 *(ascertain, find out)* prendre; **to t. sb's pulse/temperature** prendre le pouls/la température de qn; **to t. a reading from a meter** lire *ou* relever un compteur

7 *(write down ▸ notes, letter)* prendre; **he took a note of her address** il a noté son adresse

8 *(subtract)* soustraire, déduire; **they took 10 percent off the price** ils ont baissé le prix de 10 pour cent; **t. 4 from 9 and you have 5** ôtez 4 de 9, il reste 5

9 *Sch & Univ (exam)* passer, se présenter à; *(course)* prendre, suivre; **I took Latin and Greek at A level** ≃ j'ai pris latin et grec au bac; **she took her degree last year** elle a obtenu son diplôme l'an dernier; **she takes us for maths** on l'a en maths

10 *(be in charge of)* *Rel* **to t. a service** célébrer un office; **the assistant director took the rehearsals** l'assistant réalisateur s'est occupé des répétitions

11 *(contract, develop)* **to t. a chill, to t. cold** prendre froid; **to t. sick, to be taken ill** tomber malade; **she took an instant dislike to him** elle l'a tout de suite pris en aversion

12 *(direct, aim)* **she took a swipe at him** elle a voulu le gifler; *Ftbl* **to t. a penalty** tirer un penalty

13 *(refer)* **he took the matter to his boss** il a soumis la question à son patron; *Law* **they intend to t. the case to the High Court** ils ont l'intention d'en appeler à la Cour suprême

14 *(have recourse to)* **t. the scissors to it** vas-y avec les ciseaux; **his father took a stick to him** son père lui a donné des coups de bâton; *Law* **they took legal proceedings against him** ils lui ont intenté un procès

15 *(catch unawares)* prendre, surprendre; **to t. sb by surprise** *or* **off guard** surprendre qn, prendre qn au dépourvu; **his death took us by surprise** sa mort nous a surpris

16 *(negotiate ▸ obstacle)* franchir, sauter; *(▸ bend in road)* prendre, négocier

17 *Fam (deceive, cheat)* avoir, rouler; **they took him for every penny (he was worth)** ils lui ont pris jusqu'à son dernier sou

18 *Arch or Literary (have sex with)* prendre

VI 1 *(work, have desired effect)* prendre; **did the dye t.?** est-ce que la teinture a pris?; **it was too cold for the seeds to t.** il faisait trop froid pour que les graines germent

2 *(become popular)* prendre, avoir du succès

3 *(fish)* prendre, mordre

N 1 *(capture)* prise *f*

2 *Cin, Phot & TV* prise *f* de vue; *Rad* enregistrement *m*, prise *f* de son; *(of record etc)* enregistrement *m*

3 *(interpretation)* interprétation *f*; **what's your t. on her attitude?** comment est-ce que tu interprètes son attitude?

4 *Am Fam (takings)* recette□*f*; *(share)* part□*f*; **to be on the t.** toucher des pots-de-vin□, palper

▸ **take aback** VT SEP *(astonish)* étonner, ébahir; *(disconcert)* déconcerter; **her question took him aback** sa question l'a déconcerté; **I was taken aback by the news** la nouvelle m'a beaucoup surpris

▸ **take after** VT INSEP ressembler à, tenir de; **she takes after her mother in looks** physiquement, elle tient de sa mère

▸ **take apart** VT SEP **1** *(dismantle)* démonter; *Fig* **they took the room apart looking for evidence** ils ont mis la pièce sens dessus dessous pour trouver des preuves **2** *(criticize)* critiquer

▸ **take away** VT SEP **1** *(remove)* enlever, retirer; **take that knife away from him** enlevez-lui ce couteau; **they took away his pension** ils lui ont retiré sa pension; **they took their daughter away from the club** ils ont retiré leur fille du club; **his work took him away from his family for long periods** son travail le tenait éloigné de sa famille pendant de longues périodes; *Euph* **the police took his father away** son père a été arrêté par la police; **it takes away the fun** ça gâche tout **2** *(carry away ▸ object)* emporter; *(▸ person)* emmener; *Br* **sandwiches to t. away** *(sign)* sandwiches à emporter; **not to be taken away** *(in library)* à consulter sur place **3** *Math* soustraire, retrancher; **nine t. away six is three** neuf moins six font trois

▸ **take back** VT SEP **1** *(after absence, departure)* reprendre; **she took her husband back** elle a accepté que son mari revienne vivre avec elle; **the factory took back the workers** l'usine a repris les ouvriers

2 *(gift, unsold goods, sale item etc)* reprendre

3 *(return)* rapporter; *(accompany)* raccompagner; **take it back to the shop** rapporte-le au magasin; **he took her back home** il l'a raccompagnée *ou* ramenée chez elle

4 *(retract, withdraw)* retirer, reprendre; **I t. back everything I said** je retire tout ce que j'ai dit; **all right, I t. it back!** d'accord, je n'ai rien dit!

5 *(remind of the past)* **that takes me back to my childhood** ça me rappelle mon enfance; **it takes you back a bit, doesn't it?** ça ne nous rajeunit pas tout ça, hein?

6 *Typ* transférer à la ligne précédente

▸ **take down** VT SEP **1** *(carry, lead downstairs ▸ object)* descendre; *(▸ person)* faire descendre; **the lift took us down to the fourth floor** l'ascenseur nous a amenés au quatrième étage

2 *(lower)* descendre; **she took the book down from the shelf** elle a pris le livre sur l'étagère; **can you help me t. the curtains down?** peux-tu m'aider à décrocher les rideaux?; **she took his picture down from the wall** elle a enlevé sa photo du mur; **he took his trousers down** il a baissé s[…] pantalon

3 *(note)* prendre, noter; **he took down the regi[…] tration number** il a relevé le numéro d'immat[…] culation; **to t. down a letter in shorthar[…]** prendre une lettre en sténo

4 *(dismantle ▸ scaffolding, circus tent)* démonte[…]

▸ **take in** VT SEP **1** *(lead ▸ person)* faire entre[…] *(carry ▸ washing, harvest etc)* rentrer

2 *(bring into one's home ▸ person)* héberger; *(▸ boarder)* prendre; *(▸ orphan, stray animal)* r[…] cueillir; **she takes in ironing** elle fait du repa[…] sage à domicile

3 *(place in custody)* **the police took him in** la p[…] lice l'a mis *ou* placé en garde à vue

4 *(air, water, food etc)* **she can only t. in food intr[…] venously** on ne peut la nourrir que par intrave[…] neuse; **whales t. in air through their blowhole** l[…] baleines respirent par l'évent

5 *(understand, perceive)* saisir, comprendre; **[…] was sitting taking it all in** il était là, assis, éco[…] tant tout ce qui se disait; **he didn't t. in the re[…] implications of her announcement** il n'a pas sai[…] les véritables implications de sa déclaration[…] **can't t. in the fact that I've won** je n'arrive pas croire que j'ai gagné; **she took in the situation a glance** elle a compris la situation en un cl[…] d'œil

6 *(make smaller ▸ garment)* reprendre; *(▸ in kn[…] ting)* diminuer; **to t. in the slack on a rope** tend[…] *ou* retendre une corde; *Naut* **to t. in a sail** cargu[…] *ou* serrer une voile

7 *(cover ▸ several countries etc)* comprendre, e[…] glober; *(▸ questions, possibilities)* embrasser; **t[…] tour takes in all the important towns** l'excursic[…] passe par toutes les villes importantes

8 *(attend, go to)* aller à; **to t. in a show** aller a[…] théâtre; **they took in the sights in Rome** ils ont fa[…] le tour des sites touristiques à Rome

9 *Fam (cheat, deceive)* tromper□, rouler; **don't b[…] taken in by him** ne vous laissez pas rouler par lu[…] **I'm not going to be taken in by your lies** je ne su[…] pas dupe de tes mensonges□; **he was complete[…] taken in** il marchait complètement

▸ **take off** VT SEP **1** *(remove ▸ clothing, lid, mak[…] up, tag)* enlever; **the boy took his clothes off** […] garçon a enlevé ses vêtements *ou* s'est désh[…] billé; **she took her glasses off** elle a enlevé ses l[…] nettes; **t. the phone off the hook** laisse[…] téléphone décroché; **to t. sb off a list** rayer q[…] d'une liste; **the surgeon had to t. her leg off** le ch[…] rurgien a dû l'amputer de la jambe; *Aut* **to t. o[…] the brake** desserrer le frein (à main); *Fig* **he didn[…] t. his eyes off her all night** il ne l'a pas quittée de[…] yeux de la soirée; **I tried to t. her mind off h[…] troubles** j'ai essayé de lui changer les idées *o[…]* de la distraire de ses ennuis; *Fam* **his retiremer[…] has taken ten years off him** sa retraite l'a rajeu[…] de dix ans□; **to t. sth off sb's hands** débarrass[…] qn de qch; **I'll t. the baby off your hands for a fe[…] hours** je vais garder le bébé pendant quelque[…] heures, ça te libérera

2 *(deduct)* déduire, rabattre; **the teacher too[…] one point off her grade** le professeur lui a reti[…] un point; **the manager took 10 percent off th[…] price** le directeur a baissé le prix de 10 pour cer[…]

3 *(lead away)* emmener; **the murderer was take[…] off to jail** on a emmené l'assassin en prison; **h[…] friend took her off to dinner** son ami l'a emmené[…] dîner; **she took herself off to Italy** elle est part[…] en Italie; **to t. the passengers off** *(by boat from ship)* débarquer les passagers; **the injured ma[…] was taken off the ship by helicopter** le blessé été évacué du bateau par hélicoptère

4 *(time)* **to t. some time off** prendre un congé; **t.[…] few days off** prenez quelques jours de vacance[…] *ou* de congé; **she takes Thursdays off** elle ne tra[…] vaille pas le jeudi

5 *Fam (copy)* imiter□; *(mimic)* imiter□, singer

6 *(discontinue ▸ train, bus etc)* supprimer; *(▸ show, programme)* annuler

VI 1 *(aeroplane)* décoller; **they took off for** *or* **t[…] Heathrow** ils se sont envolés pour Heathrow[…] *Fam (person ▸ depart)* partir□; *(hurriedly)* se ba[…] rer, se tirer; **he took off without telling us** il e[…] parti sans nous avertir **3** *Fam (become success[…] ful)* décoller

▸ **take on** VT SEP **1** *(accept, undertake)* prendre[…] accepter; **to t. on the responsibility for sth** s[…]

:harger de qch; **don't t. on more than you can han-** **dle** ne vous surchargez pas; **she took it on herself** **o tell him** elle a pris sur elle de le lui dire; **he took** **he job on** *(position)* il a accepté le poste; *(task)* il ;'est mis au travail; **to t. on a bet** accepter un pari **2** *(contend with, fight against)* lutter *ou* se battre :ontre; *(compete against)* jouer contre; **the** **unions took on the government** les syndicats se ont attaqués *ou* s'en sont pris au gouverne- nent; **I wouldn't like to t. him on** je n'aimerais pas avoir affaire à lui; **he took us on at poker** il ıous a défiés au poker **3** *(acquire, assume)* prendre, revêtir; **her face** **ook on a worried look** elle a pris un air inquiet; **he word takes on another meaning** le mot prend ıne autre signification **4** *(load)* prendre, embarquer **5** *(hire)* embaucher, engager

VI *Br Fam (fret, carry on)* s'en faire; **don't t. on so!** ıe t'en fais pas!

take out VT SEP 1 *(remove ▸ object)* prendre, sortir; *(▸ stain)* ôter, enlever; *(extract ▸ tooth)* ar- acher; **t. the cheese out of the fridge** sors le fro- nage du frigo; **he took the knife out of his pocket** l a sorti le couteau de sa poche; **t. your hands** **out of your pockets** enlève les mains de tes po- :hes; **they took their children out of school** ils ont retiré leurs enfants de l'école; *Med* **to t. out sb's** **appendix/tonsils** enlever l'appendice/les amyg- dales à qn; *Fig* **to t. the food out of sb's mouth** re- irer le pain de la bouche de qn **2** *(carry, lead outside ▸ object)* sortir; *(▸ person)* aire sortir; *(escort)* emmener; **to t. sb out to din- ner/to the movies** emmener qn dîner/au ci- néma; **would you t. the dog out?** tu veux bien sortir le chien *ou* aller promener le chien? **3** *(food)* emporter; *Am* **sandwiches to t. out** *(sign)* sandwiches à emporter **4** *(obtain ▸ subscription)* prendre; *(▸ insurance policy)* souscrire à, prendre; *(▸ licence)* se procu- rer; *(▸ patent)* prendre; **to t. out a mortgage** faire un emprunt immobilier **5** *Fam (destroy ▸ factory, town)* détruire; **to t. sb out** *(kill)* buter qn, zigouiller qn, refroidir qn; **the planes took the factory out by bombing** les avions ont détruit l'usine (en la bombardant) **6** *(idioms)* **to t. sb out of himself/herself** changer les idées à qn; *Fam* **working as an interpreter takes a lot out of you** le travail d'interprète est épuisant; *Fam* **the operation really took it out of him** l'opération l'a mis à plat; *Fam* **it takes the fun out of it** ça gâche tout; *Fam* **to t. it out on sb** s'en prendre à qn; *Fam* **he took his anger out on his wife** il a passé sa colère sur sa femme; *Fam* **don't t. it out on me!** ne t'en prends pas à moi!

take over VT SEP 1 *(assume responsibility of)* re- prendre; **he wants his daughter to t. over the busi- ness** il veut que sa fille reprenne l'affaire; **she took over my classes** elle a pris la suite de mes cours; **will you be taking over his job?** est-ce que vous allez le remplacer (dans ses fonctions)? **2** *(gain control of, invade)* s'emparer de; **the mili- tary took over the country** l'armée a pris le pou- voir; **she takes the place over** *(by being bossy etc)* elle joue les despotes; **fast-food restaurants have taken over Paris** les fast-foods *ou Can* restau- rants-minute ont envahi Paris **3** *Fin (buy out)* absorber, racheter; **they were taken over by a Japanese firm** ils ont été rachetés par une entreprise japonaise **4** *(carry across)* apporter; *(escort across)* emme- ner; **the boat took us over to Seattle** le bateau nous a emmenés jusqu'à Seattle **5** *Typ* transférer à la ligne suivante

VI 1 *(as replacement)* **who will t. over now that the mayor has stepped down?** qui va prendre la re- lève maintenant que le maire a donné sa démis- sion?; **I'll t. over when he leaves** je le remplacerai quand il partira; **will he allow her to t. over?** va-t-il lui céder la place?; **DVDs have taken over from videos** le DVD a remplacé la cassette vidéo **2** *(army, dictator)* prendre le pouvoir

take to VT INSEP 1 *(have a liking for ▸ person)* se prendre d'amitié *ou* de sympathie pour, prendre en amitié; *(▸ activity, game)* prendre goût à; **we took to one another at once** nous avons tout de suite sympathisé; **she didn't t. to him** il ne lui a pas plu; **we've really taken to golf** nous avons vraiment pris goût au golf **2** *(acquire as a habit)* se mettre à; **to t. to drink** *or* **to the bottle** se met- tre à boire; **to t. to doing sth** se mettre à faire qch; **she took to wearing black** elle s'est mise à s'habil- ler en noir **3** *(make for, head for)* **he's taken to his bed with the flu** il est alité avec la grippe; **the rebels took to the hills** les insurgés se sont réfu- giés dans les collines; **to t. to the road** prendre la route

▸ **take up VT SEP 1** *(carry, lead upstairs ▸ object)* monter; *(▸ person)* faire monter; **the lift took us up to the 25th floor** l'ascenseur nous a amenés au 25ème étage **2** *(pick up ▸ object)* ramasser, prendre; *(▸ pas- senger)* prendre; *(▸ paving stones, railway tracks)* enlever; **she took up the notes from the table** elle a ramassé *ou* pris les notes sur la table; **they're taking up the street** la rue est en travaux; **we fi- nally took up the carpet** nous avons enfin enlevé la moquette **3** *(absorb)* absorber **4** *(shorten)* raccourcir; **to t. up the slack in a rope** retendre *ou* tendre une corde **5** *(fill, occupy ▸ space)* prendre, tenir; *(▸ time)* prendre, demander; **this table takes up too much room** cette table prend trop de place *ou* est trop encombrante; **moving house took up the whole day** le déménagement a pris toute la journée; **her work takes up all her attention** son travail l'ab- sorbe complètement **6** *(begin, become interested in ▸ activity, hobby)* se mettre à; *(▸ job)* prendre; *(▸ career)* commencer, embrasser; **when did you t. up Greek?** quand est- ce que tu t'es mis au grec?; **I've taken up garden- ing** je me suis mis au jardinage **7** *(continue, resume)* reprendre, continuer; **I took up the story where Susan had left off** j'ai re- pris l'histoire là où Susan l'avait laissée; **she took up her knitting again** elle a repris son tricot **8** *(adopt ▸ attitude)* prendre, adopter; *(▸ method)* adopter; *(▸ place, position)* prendre; *(▸ idea)* adopter; **they took up residence in town** ils se sont installés en ville; **to t. up one's duties** entrer en fonctions **9** *(accept ▸ offer)* accepter; *(▸ advice, suggestion)* suivre; *(▸ challenge)* relever **10** *(discuss)* discuter, parler de; *(bring up)* abor- der; **t. it up with the boss** parlez-en au patron

VI reprendre, continuer

takeaway ['teɪkəweɪ] **N** *Br & NZ (shop)* = bou- tique de plats à emporter; *(food)* plat *m* à em- porter; **Chinese t.** *(shop)* traiteur *m* chinois; *(meal)* repas *m* chinois à emporter

▸▸ ***takeaway food*** plats *mpl* à emporter; ***take- away restaurant*** = restaurant qui fait des plats à emporter

take-home pay N salaire *m* net *(après impôts et déductions sociales)*

taken ['teɪkən] *pp of* **take**

ADJ 1 *(seat)* pris, occupé **2 to be t. with sb/sth** *(impressed)* être impressionné par qn/qch; *(interested)* s'intéresser à qn/qch; **they were quite t. with the performance** l'interprétation leur a beaucoup plu

take-off N 1 *Aviat* décollage *m* **2** *(of high-jumper, long-jumper)* appel *m* **3** *(imitation)* imitation *f*, caricature *f*; **he did a clever t. of the prime minister** il a fait une très bonne imitation du premier ministre **4** *Econ* décollage *m* économique

takeout ['teɪkaut] **N** *Am (shop)* = boutique de plats à emporter; *(food)* plat *m* à emporter

takeover ['teɪk,əuvə(r)] **N** *(of power, of govern- ment)* prise *f* de pouvoir; *(of company)* prise *f* de contrôle, rachat *m*

▸▸ *Fin* ***takeover bid*** offre *f* publique d'achat, OPA *f*; **to be the subject of a t. bid** être l'objet d'une OPA; **to make** *or* **to launch a t. bid (for)** faire *ou* lancer une OPA (sur)

taker ['teɪkə(r)] **N** *(buyer)* acheteur(euse) *m,f*, preneur(euse) *m,f*; *(of suggestion, offer)* preneur (euse) *m,f*; **there were no takers** personne n'en voulait; **any takers?** y a-t-il des preneurs?

take-up N *(of benefits)* réclamation *f*; **there has been a 75 percent t. rate for the new benefit** 75 pour cent des gens concernés par la nouvelle allocation l'ont effectivement demandée; **t. has been poor** la demande a été faible

▸▸ ***take-up point*** *(of clutch)* point *m* de prise; *Tech* ***take-up reel*** bobine *f* enrouleuse; *Tech* ***take-up spool*** bobine *f* réceptrice

taking ['teɪkɪŋ] **ADJ** *Old-fashioned (attractive)* en- gageant, séduisant

N *(of city, power)* prise *f*; *(of criminal)* arrestation *f*; *(of blood, sample)* prélèvement *m*; **the apples are there for the t.** prenez (donc) une pomme, elles sont là pour ça; **the money/job is his for the t.** il n'a qu'à accepter l'argent/le poste

• **takings NPL** *Br Com* recette *f*; **the day's takings** la recette de la journée

talc [tælk] **N** talc *m*

talcum powder ['tælkəm-] **N** talc *m*

tale [teɪl] **N 1** *(story)* conte *m*, histoire *f*; *(legend)* histoire *f*, légende *f*; *(account)* récit *m*; **to tell a t.** raconter une histoire; **he told them the t. of his escape** il leur a raconté son évasion *ou* fait le ré- cit de son évasion; **the astronaut lived/didn't live to tell the t.** l'astronaute a survécu/n'a pas survé- cu pour raconter ce qui s'est passé; **his face told the t. of his sufferings** ses traits en disaient long sur ses souffrances **2** *(gossip)* histoires *fpl*; **to tell tales** *(inform)* cafter, rapporter; **to tell tales on sb** raconter des histoires sur le compte de qn; **she's been telling tales to the teacher again** elle est en- core allée cafter *ou* rapporter à la maîtresse; *Fig* **to tell tales out of school** *(be indiscreet)* être in- discret, trop parler

talebearer ['teɪl,beərə(r)] **N** *Literary* rapporteur (euse) *m,f*

talent ['tælənt] **N 1** *(gift)* talent *m*, don *m*; **she has great musical t.** elle est très douée pour la mu- sique, elle a un grand don pour la musique; **you have quite a t. for sewing** tu es assez doué pour la *ou* en couture; **it's just one of my many hidden talents** c'est un de mes nombreux talents cachés; **you have a t. for saying the wrong thing** tu as le don pour dire ce qu'il ne faut pas **2** *(talented person)* talent *m*; **she is one of our most promising young talents** c'est un de nos jeunes talents les plus prometteurs **3** *Br Fam (attractive men)* beaux mecs *mpl*; *(attractive women)* belles na- nas *fpl*; **he's out chatting up the local t.** il est en train de draguer les minettes du coin; **it's an OK bar, but there's not much t.** c'est pas mal comme bar, mais question mecs/nanas, ça casse pas des briques

▸▸ ***talent scout, talent spotter*** *(for films)* déni- cheur(euse) *m,f* de vedettes; *(for sport)* déni- cheur(euse) *m,f* de futurs grands joueurs

talented ['tæləntɪd] **ADJ** talentueux, doué; **she's a t. musician** c'est une musicienne de talent; **she's really t.** elle a beaucoup de talent

tale-telling N rapportage *m*

Taliban ['tælɪbæn] **N** taliban *m*

talisman ['tælɪzmən] *(pl* **talismans) N** talisman *m*

TALK [tɔːk]

VI
- parler **1, 3**
- discuter **1**
- s'entretenir **1**
- causer **2**

VT
- parler **1, 2**

N
- conversation **1**
- discussion **1, 4**
- causette **1**
- entretien **1**
- exposé **2**
- paroles **3**
- racontars **5**

NPL
- négociations

VI 1 *(speak)* parler; *(discuss)* discuter; *(confer)* s'entretenir; **to t. to sb** parler à qn; **to t. with sb** parler *ou* s'entretenir avec qn; **to t. of** *or* **about sth** parler de qch; **we sat talking together** nous sommes restés à discuter *ou* à bavarder; **she didn't t. to me all evening** elle ne m'a pas dit un mot de la soirée; **to t. in signs/riddles** parler par signes/par énigmes; **they were talking in Chinese** ils parlaient en chinois; **that's no way to t.!** en voilà des façons de parler!; **they no longer t. to each other** ils ne se parlent plus, ils ne s'adres- sent plus la parole; **who do you think you're talk- ing to?** non, mais à qui croyez-vous parler?; **don't you t. to me like that!** je t'interdis de me par- ler sur ce ton!; **to t. to oneself** parler tout seul; **he**

likes to hear himself t. il s'écoute parler; **I'll t. to you about it tomorrow morning** *(converse)* je vous en parlerai demain matin; *(as threat)* j'aurai deux mots à vous dire à ce sujet demain matin; **it's no use talking to him, he never listens!** on perd son temps avec lui, il n'écoute jamais!; **to t. of this and that** parler de la pluie et du beau temps *ou* de choses et d'autres; **talking of Switzerland, have you ever been skiing?** à propos de la Suisse, vous avez déjà fait du ski?; **they talked of little else** ils n'ont parlé que de cela; **he's always talking big** c'est un beau parleur; **now you're talking!** voilà, c'est beaucoup mieux!; **you can t.!, look who's talking!, you're a fine one to t.!** tu peux parler, toi!; **it's easy for you to t., you've never had a gun in your back!** c'est facile à dire *ou* tu as beau jeu de dire ça, on ne t'a jamais braqué un pistolet dans le dos!; **t. about luck!** *(admiring)* qu'est-ce qu'il a comme chance!, quel veinard!; *(complaining)* tu parles d'une veine! **t. about lucky!** tu parles d'un coup de bol!; **to t. through** *Fam* **one's hat** *or* **the back of one's neck** *or* **one's backside** *or Vulg* **one's arse** dire des bêtises▫ *ou* n'importe quoi▫

2 *(chat)* causer, bavarder; *(gossip)* jaser; **you know how people t.** les gens sont tellement bavards

3 *(reveal secrets)* parler; **to make sb t.** faire parler qn; **we have ways of making people t.** on a les moyens de faire parler les gens

VT 1 *(language)* parler; **t. sense!** ne dis pas de sottises!, ne dis pas n'importe quoi!; **now you're talking sense** vous dites enfin des choses sensées; **to t. (some) sense into sb** faire entendre raison à qn; **stop talking rubbish** *or* **nonsense!** arrête de dire des bêtises!; *Am Fam* **to t. the t.** avoir la langue bien pendue; *esp Am Fam* **he can t. the t. but can he walk the walk?** est-ce qu'il est aussi doué pour agir que pour parler?▫

2 *(discuss)* parler; **to t. business/politics** parler affaires/politique; **to t. shop** parler boutique

N 1 *(conversation)* conversation *f*; *(discussion)* discussion *f*; *(chat)* causette *f*, causerie *f*; *(formal)* entretien *m*; **to have a t. with sb about sth** parler de qch avec qn, s'entretenir avec qn de qch; **I'll have a t. with him about it** je lui en parlerai; **we had a long t.** nous avons eu une longue discussion; **can we have a little t.?** je peux vous parler deux minutes?; **that's fighting t.!** c'est un défi!

2 *(speech, lecture)* exposé *m*; **to give a t. on** *or* **about sth** faire un exposé sur qch; **there was a series of radio talks on modern Japan** il y a eu à la radio une série d'émissions où des gens venaient parler du Japon moderne

3 *(UNCOUNT) (noise of talking)* paroles *fpl*, propos *mpl*; **there is a lot of t. in the background** il y a beaucoup de bruit *ou* de gens qui parlent

4 *(speculative)* discussion *f*, rumeur *f*; **most of the t. was about the new road** il a surtout été question de *ou* on a surtout parlé de la nouvelle route; **there's some t. of building a concert hall** *(discussion)* il est question *ou* on parle de construire une salle de concert; *(rumour)* le bruit court qu'on va construire une salle de concert; **there has been t. of it** on en a parlé, il en a été question; **enough of this idle t.!** assez parlé!; **he's all t.** tout ce qu'il dit, c'est du vent

5 *(UNCOUNT) (gossip)* racontars *mpl*, bavardages *mpl*; **it's only t.** ce sont des racontars, tout ça; **their behaviour is causing a lot of t.** leur conduite fait jaser; **it's/she's the t. of the town** on ne parle que de ça/que d'elle

• **talks NPL** *(negotiations)* négociations *fpl*, pourparlers *mpl*; *(conference)* conférence *f*; **peace talks** des pourparlers *mpl* sur la paix

►► ***talk show*** causerie *f* (radiodiffusée/télévisée), talk-show *m*

▸**talk away VI** passer le temps à parler, parler sans arrêt; **they were still talking away at 3 a.m.** ils étaient encore en grande conversation à 3 heures du matin

VT SEP to t. the night away passer la nuit à parler

▸**talk back VI** *(insolently)* répondre; **to t. back to sb** répondre (insolemment) à qn; **don't you t. back to me!** ne me réponds pas (comme ça)!

▸**talk down VT SEP 1** *(silence)* **to t. sb down** réduire qn au silence (en parlant plus fort que lui/qu'elle/*etc*) **2** *(aircraft)* faire atterrir par radio-contrôle **3** *(would-be suicide)* **the police managed to t. him down from the roof** la police a réussi à le convaincre de redescendre du toit

VI to t. down to sb parler à qn comme à un enfant

▸**talk out VT SEP 1** *(problem, disagreement)* débattre de, discuter de; **they managed to t. out the problem** à force de discussions, ils sont arrivés à trouver une solution au problème **2** *Pol* **to t. out a bill** = prolonger la discussion d'un projet de loi jusqu'à ce qu'il soit trop tard pour le voter avant la clôture de la séance

▸**talk over VT SEP** discuter *ou* débattre de; **let's t. it over** discutons-en, parlons-en; **we'll have to t. the problem over** il va falloir que l'on parle de ce problème; **to t. things over** discuter

▸**talk round VT SEP** *(convince)* persuader, convaincre; **to t. sb round to one's way of thinking** amener qn à sa façon de penser *ou* à son point de vue; **I'm sure she can be talked round** je suis sûr qu'on peut la convaincre

VT INSEP *(problem)* tourner autour de; **I'm tired of just talking round the subject** j'en ai assez de tourner autour de la question

▸**talk up VT SEP** vanter les mérites de, faire de la publicité pour; **to t. up sb's chances** surestimer les chances de qn; **the Chancellor is trying to t. up the economy** le Chancelier s'est montré optimiste pour tenter de redynamiser l'économie

---

talkathon ['tɔːkəθɒn] **N** *Am Hum (in Congress, on television etc)* débat-marathon *m*

talkative ['tɔːkətɪv] **ADJ** bavard, loquace

talkativeness ['tɔːkətɪvnɪs] **N** volubilité *f*, loquacité *f*

talk-back N *TV & Rad* émetteur-récepteur *m*

talker ['tɔːkə(r)] **N** *(speaker)* causeur(euse) *m,f*, bavard(e) *m,f*; **she's a real t.** c'est une grande bavarde, c'est un vrai moulin à paroles; **he's not much of a t.** il n'est jamais été très bavard; **he's a brilliant t.** c'est un beau parleur; **he's a fast t.** *(gen)* il parle vite; *Com* il a du bagout

talkie ['tɔːkɪ] **N** *Fam Old-fashioned* film *m* parlant▫

talking ['tɔːkɪŋ] **N** *(UNCOUNT)* conversation *f*, propos *mpl*; **he did all the t.** il était le seul à parler; **let me do the t.** laisse-moi parler; **no t., please!** pas de bavardage!

ADJ *(bird)* qui parle

►► ***talking book*** livre *m* enregistré; ***talking film*** film *m* parlant; *TV* ***talking head*** *(presenter)* présentateur(trice) *m,f* de télévision *(dont on ne voit que la tête et les épaules)*; *Hum or Pej (interviewee)* = expert qui s'exprime à la télévision; ***talking movie, talking picture*** film *m* parlant; ***talking point*** sujet *m* de conversation *ou* de discussion; *Br* ***talking shop*** lieu *m* de palabres; **the United Nations is accused of being a t. shop** on accuse les Nations Unies de ne faire que de la parlotte

talking-to N *Fam* savon *m*; **to give sb a t.** passer un savon à qn; **he needs a good t.** il a besoin qu'on lui passe un bon savon

talktime ['tɔːktaɪm] **N** *Tel* autonomie *f*

talky ['tɔːkɪ] *(compar* **talkier**, *superl* **talkiest)** **ADJ** *Am (film, novel)* où il y a beaucoup de dialogues, qui manque d'action

tall [tɔːl] **ADJ 1** *(person)* grand, de grande taille; **how t. are you?** combien mesurez-vous?; **I'm 6 feet t.** ≃ je mesure *ou* fais 1 mètre 80; **my sister is taller than me** ma sœur est plus grande que moi; **she's grown a lot taller** elle a beaucoup grandi **2** *(building)* haut, élevé; *(tree)* grand, haut; *(grass)* haut; **how t. is that tree?** quelle est la hauteur de cet arbre?; **it's at least 80 feet t.** ≃ il fait au moins 25 mètres de haut **3** *(idioms) Hum* **he's t., dark and handsome** c'est un beau ténébreux; **a t.** *Br* **story** *or Am* **tale** une histoire invraisemblable *ou* abracadabrante, une histoire à dormir debout; **that's a t. order** c'est beaucoup demander

ADV *Fig* **to walk** *or* **stand t.** marcher la tête haute

►► ***tall ship*** grand voilier *m*

tallboy ['tɔːlbɔɪ] **N** *(furniture)* (grande) commode *f*

Tallin, Tallinn ['tælɪn] **N** Tallinn

tallness ['tɔːlnɪs] **N** *(of person)* (grande) taille *(of tree, building, grass)* hauteur *f*

tallow ['tæləʊ] **N** suif *m*

►► ***tallow candle*** chandelle *f*

tally ['tælɪ] *(pl* **tallies**, *pt & pp* **tallied)** **N 1** *(recor*... compte *m*, enregistrement *m*; *Com* pointage *r*... *Am Sport (score)* score *m*; **to keep a t. of name**... pointer des noms sur une liste; **to keep a t. o**... **the score** compter les points **2** *(counterfoil* ▸ ... *cheque, ticket)* talon *m*; *(duplicate)* contreparti... *f*, double *m*

VT 1 *(record)* pointer **2** *(count up)* compter

VI correspondre; **I couldn't make the figures t.** j... ne pouvais faire concorder les chiffres; **you**... **story must t. with mine** il faut que ta version de... faits concorde avec la mienne

tally-ho *(pl* **tally-hos)** **EXCLAM** taïaut!, tayaut!

N cri *m* de taïaut

Talmud ['tælmʊd] **N** Talmud *m*

Talmudic [tæl'mʊdɪk] **ADJ** talmudique

Talmudist ['tælmʊdɪst] **N** Talmudiste *m*

talon ['tælən] **N** *(of hawk, eagle)* serre *f*; *(of tige*... *lion)* griffe *f*; *Fig (of person)* griffe *f*

tamable = **tameable**

tamarind ['tæmərɪnd] **N** *(fruit)* tamarin *m*; *(tre*... tamarinier *m*

tamarisk ['tæmərɪsk] **N** *Bot* tamaris *m*, tamarix *r*...

tambour ['tæmˌbʊə(r)] **N 1** *Sewing* tambour *n*... métier *m* à broder **2** *Archit & Mus* tambour *m*

tambourine [ˌtæmbə'riːn] **N** tambour *m* d... basque, tambourin *m*

tame [teɪm] **ADJ 1** *(as pet* ▸ *hamster, rabbit)* appr... voisé, domestiqué; *(normally wild* ▸ *bear, hawk*... apprivoisé; *(in circus* ▸ *lion, tiger)* dompté; **th**... **deer had become very t.** les cerfs n'étaient plu... du tout farouches; *Hum* **I'll ask our t. Frenchma**... **if he knows what it means** je vais demander à no... tre Français de service s'il sait ce que cela veu... dire **2** *(insipid, weak)* fade, insipide; **it was a ver**... **t. party** cette soirée n'était vraiment pas très fo... lichonne; **the government's measures were con**... **sidered rather t.** les mesures gouvernementale... ont été jugées plutôt modérées

VT 1 *(as pet* ▸ *hamster, rabbit)* apprivoiser, do... mestiquer; *(normally wild* ▸ *bear, hawk)* appri... voiser; *(in circus* ▸ *lion, tiger)* dompter **2** *(perso*... mater, soumettre; *(natural forces)* apprivoiser... *(passions)* dominer; *(plant, wilderness)* cultiver

tameable ['teɪməbəl] **ADJ** *(hawk, bear, rabbi*... apprivoisable; *(lion, tiger)* domptable

tamely ['teɪmlɪ] **ADV** *(submit)* docilement, san... résistance; *(end)* platement, de manière ins... pide; *(write)* de manière fade, platement

tamer ['teɪmə(r)] **N** dompteur(euse) *m,f*

Tamil ['tæmɪl] **N 1** *(person)* Tamoul(e) *m,f* **2** *Lin*... tamoul *m*

ADJ tamoul

►► ***the Tamil Tigers*** les Tigres *mpl* tamouls

taming ['teɪmɪŋ] **N** *(of hawk, bear, rabbit)* appri... voisement *m*; *(of lions, tigers)* domptage *m*, dres... sage *m*

tammy ['tæmɪ] *(pl* **tammies)** **N** *Fam (cap)* béret *n*... écossais▫

tam-o'-shanter [tæmə'ʃæntə(r)] **N** béret *n*... écossais

tamp [tæmp] **VT** *(earth)* tasser, damer; *(pipe*... bourrer; *(tobacco)* tasser; *(for blasting* ▸ *dri*... *hole)* bourrer (à l'argile/au sable)

▸**tamp down VT SEP** *(earth)* tasser, damer; *(gu*... *powder, tobacco)* tasser

Tampax® ['tæmpæks] **N** tampon *m*

tamper ['tæmpə(r)] **N 1** *(person)* borreur *m* **2**... *(tool)* dame *f* à fouler **3** *Phys* réflecteur *m* de neu... trons

▸**tamper with VT INSEP** *(meddle with* ▸ *brakes*... *machinery)* trafiquer; *(*▸ *lock)* essayer de force... *ou* crocheter, fausser; *(*▸ *possessions)* touche... à; *(falsify* ▸ *records, accounts, evidence)* falsifie... altérer; **someone has been tampering with m**... **papers** on a touché à mes papiers; **the TV ha**... **been tampered with** quelqu'un a déréglé la télé... vision

tampon [ˈtæmpɒn] **N** *Med* tampon *m*; *(for menstrual use)* tampon *m* (périodique *ou* hygiénique)

tan [tæn] *(pt & pp* **tanned**, *cont* **tanning**) **N 1** *(from sun)* bronzage *m*; **I got a good t. in the mountains** j'ai bien bronzé à la montagne; **to have a t.** être bronzé *ou* hâlé; **to lose one's t.** perdre son bronzage **2** *Math* tangente *f*
VT 1 *(leather, skins)* tanner; *Fam Fig* **to t. sb's hide** rosser qn **2** *(of sun)* bronzer, brunir
VI bronzer; **I t. easily** je bronze facilement
ADJ 1 *(colour)* brun roux *(inv)*, brun clair *(inv)*; *(leather)* jaune **2** *Am (tanned)* bronzé
▸▸ ***tan line*** marque *f* de bronzage

tanager [ˈtænədʒə(r)] **N** *Orn* tangara *m*

tandem [ˈtændəm] **N 1** *(carriage)* tandem *m*; **to harness two horses in t.** atteler deux chevaux en tandem *ou* en flèche; *Fig* **to work in t.** travailler en tandem *ou* en collaboration **2** *(bike)* tandem *m*
ADV to ride t. rouler en tandem

tang [tæŋ] **N 1** *(taste)* goût *m* (fort); **the t. of oranges** le goût acide des oranges; **the t. of mustard** le goût fort de la moutarde
2 *(smell)* odeur *f* forte; **the t. of the sea** l'odeur *f* forte de la mer; **the t. of the morning air** l'air *m* vif du matin
3 *(hint* ▸ *of irony)* pointe *f*
4 *(of knife, sword)* soie *f*

tangent [ˈtændʒənt] **N** *Geom* tangente *f*; **to be at a t.** former une tangente; *Fig* **to go off at** *or* **on a t.** partir dans une digression

tangential [tænˈdʒenʃəl] **ADJ** *Geom* tangentiel; *Fig* **that is t. to the main issue** étant donné le sujet, ceci est secondaire

tangerine [ˌtændʒəˈriːn] **N 1** *(fruit)* mandarine *f*; *(tree)* mandarinier *m* **2** *(colour)* mandarine *f*
ADJ *(in colour)* mandarine *(inv)*

tangibility [ˌtændʒəˈbɪlətɪ] **N** tangibilité *f*

tangible [ˈtændʒəbəl] **ADJ 1** *(palpable)* tangible; *(real, substantial)* tangible, réel; **the t. world** le monde sensible; **t. proof** des preuves *fpl* tangibles; **it made no t. difference** ça n'a pas changé grand-chose **2** *Law (property)* corporel
▸▸ *Fin* ***tangible assets*** actif *m* corporel, valeurs *fpl* matérielles; *Fin* ***tangible fixed assets*** immobilisations *fpl* corporelles

tangibly [ˈtændʒəblɪ] **ADV** tangiblement, manifestement, de manière tangible

Tangier [tænˈdʒɪə(r)] **N** Tanger

tanginess [ˈtæŋɪnɪs] **N** *(in taste)* goût *m* fort; *(in smell)* odeur *f* forte

tangle [ˈtæŋgəl] **N 1** *(of wire, string, branches, weeds)* enchevêtrement *m*; **to get into a t.** *(wires, string, hair)* s'emmêler; **a t. of hair** des cheveux *mpl* emmêlés; **a t. of creepers** un enchevêtrement de lianes
2 *(muddle)* fouillis *m*, confusion *f*; **a legal t.** une affaire compliquée *ou* embrouillée du point de vue juridique; **to get into a t.** *(person)* s'empêtrer, s'embrouiller; *(records, figures)* s'embrouiller; **I get into a t. with figures/tax returns** je m'embrouille dans les chiffres/déclarations d'impôts; **the accounts are in a bit of a t.** les comptes sont un peu embrouillés; **her private life is in a terrible t.** sa vie privée est un véritable sac de nœuds
3 *(disagreement)* accrochage *m*, différend *m*; **they got into a t. over the new salary scales** ils ont eu un différend au sujet de la nouvelle échelle des salaires; **I had a t. with the social security officials** j'ai eu des mots *ou* maille à partir avec les employés de la sécurité sociale
VT *(wire, wool)* emmêler; *(figures)* embrouiller; **to get tangled** *(string)* s'emmêler; *(situation)* s'embrouiller
VI 1 *(wire, hair)* s'emmêler
2 *Fam (disagree)* avoir un différend ▫, avoir un accrochage; **you'd better not t. with her** il vaut mieux éviter de se frotter à elle; **they tangled over who should pay for the meal** ils se sont disputés pour savoir qui allait payer le repas ▫

▸ **tangle up VT SEP 1** *(make confused* ▸ *threads)* emmêler, enchevêtrer; (▸ *hair)* emmêler; (▸ *question)* embrouiller; **to get tangled up** *(threads, wire)* s'emmêler; **to get tangled up in sth** *(of person* ▸ *in ropes, net, brambles)* s'empêtrer dans qch; (▸ *in barbed wire)* se prendre dans qch; *(of string)* s'emmêler *ou* s'enchevêtrer dans qch; **she had got tangled up in some barbed wire** elle était prise dans des barbelés; **the threads were all tangled up** les fils étaient emmêlés *ou* enchevêtrés **2** *(involve)* **he got himself tangled up in the Smith case** il s'est retrouvé impliqué dans l'affaire Smith; **they got tangled up in something dishonest** ils ont été mêlés à une affaire malhonnête

tangled [ˈtæŋgəld] **ADJ 1** *(string, wool)* emmêlé; *(creepers)* enchevêtré; *(undergrowth)* touffu; *(hair)* emmêlé **2** *(complex* ▸ *story, excuse)* embrouillé; (▸ *love life)* complexe

tango [ˈtæŋgəʊ] *(pl* **tangos**) **N** tango *m*
VI danser le tango

tangy [ˈtæŋɪ] *(compar* **tangier**, *superl* **tangiest**) **ADJ** *(in taste)* qui a un goût fort; *(in smell)* qui a une odeur forte

tank [tæŋk] **N 1** *(container* ▸ *for liquid, gas)* réservoir *m*, cuve *f*, citerne *f*; (▸ *for rainwater)* citerne *f*, bac *m*; (▸ *for transport)* réservoir *m*, citerne *f*; *(barrel)* tonneau *m*, cuve *f*; *Aut* **(fuel** *or Br* **petrol) t.** réservoir *m* (d'essence); **(fish) t.** aquarium *m* **2** *Mil* tank *m*, char *m* d'assaut; **the tanks** les blindés *mpl*; *Fam Fig* **to be built like a t.** être une armoire à glace **3** *Ind* (▸ *for processing)* cuve *f*
COMP *Mil* de char/chars d'assaut
VT stocker *ou* mettre en réservoir
VI *Fam* **1** *(crash, collapse)* dégringoler; **the stock-market tanked** les cours de la Bourse ont dégringolé **2** *(do badly)* **the film tanked at the box office** le film a fait un bide
▸▸ ***tank car*** wagon-citerne *m*; ***tank commander*** commandant *m* de char; ***tank engine*** locomotive *f* tender, machine *f* tender; ***tank regiment*** régiment *m* de chars (d'assaut); ***tank top*** débardeur *m*, pull *m* sans manches; ***tank trap*** piège *m* à chars; ***tank truck*** camion-citerne *m*; ***tank warfare*** guerre *f* combattue à l'aide de chars

▸ **tank along VI** *Fam (driver, vehicle)* foncer

▸ **tank up** *Br* **VI** *Aut (fill fuel tank)* faire le plein d'essence
VT SEP *Fam (usu passive)* **to get tanked up** *(drunk)* prendre une cuite; **to be tanked up** être bourré *ou* pété

tankard [ˈtæŋkəd] **N** chope *f*

tanker [ˈtæŋkə(r)] **N** *(lorry)* camion-citerne *m*; *(ship)* bateau-citerne *m*, navire-citerne *m*; *(plane)* avion-ravitailleur *m*; *Naut* **(oil) t.** pétrolier *m*
▸▸ *Br* ***tanker lorry***, *Am* ***tanker truck*** camion-citerne *m*

tankini [tænˈkiːnɪ] **N** maillot *m* brassière, tankini *m*

tanned [tænd] **ADJ 1** *(person)* bronzé; *(face, complexion)* bronzé, hâlé **2** *(leather)* tanné

tanner [ˈtænə(r)] **N 1** *(of leather)* tanneur(euse) *m,f* **2** *Br Fam (coin)* = ancienne pièce de six pence

tannery [ˈtænərɪ] *(pl* **tanneries**) **N** tannerie *f*

tannic [ˈtænɪk] **ADJ** tannique

tannin [ˈtænɪn] **N** tanin *m*, tannin *m*

tanning [ˈtænɪŋ] **N 1** *(of skin)* bronzage *m* **2** *(of hides)* tannage *m* **3** *Fam Fig (beating)* raclée *f*; **to give sb a t.** rosser qn
▸▸ ***tanning booth*** cabine *f* de bronzage; ***tanning cream*** *(self-tanning)* crème *f* autobronzante; *(for natural tan)* crème *f* solaire; ***tanning salon, tanning studio*** centre *m* de bronzage

Tannoy® [ˈtænɔɪ] **N** *Br* système *m* de haut-parleurs; **the delay was announced over the T.** le retard fut annoncé par haut-parleur

tansy [ˈtænzɪ] *(pl* **tansies**) **N** *Bot* tanaisie *f*, herbe *f* aux coqs

tantalize, -ise [ˈtæntəlaɪz] **VT** tourmenter, taquiner

tantalizing, -ising [ˈtæntəˌlaɪzɪŋ] **ADJ** *(woman)* provocant, aguichant; *(smell)* alléchant, appétissant; *(hint, possibility)* tentant

tantalizingly, -isingly [ˈtæntəˌlaɪzɪŋlɪ] **ADV victory was t. close** nous étions si près de la victoire que c'en était frustrant; **the cool water was t. near** cette eau fraîche à proximité était un véritable supplice

tantamount [ˈtæntəmaʊnt] **tantamount to PREP** équivalent à; **his statement was t. to an admission of guilt** sa déclaration équivalait à un aveu; **that's t. to saying I'm a liar** cela revient à dire que je mens

Tantra, tantra [ˈtæntrə] **N** tantra *m*

Tantric, tantric [ˈtæntrɪk] **ADJ** tantrique
▸▸ ***Tantric sex*** sexe *m* tantrique

Tantrism [ˈtæntrɪzəm] **N** tantrisme *m*

tantrum [ˈtæntrəm] **N** crise *f* de colère *ou* de rage; **to have** *or* **to throw a t.** piquer une crise

Tanzania [ˌtænzəˈnɪə] **N** Tanzanie *f*

Tanzanian [ˌtænzəˈnɪən] **N** Tanzanien(enne) *m,f*
ADJ tanzanien
COMP *(embassy)* de Tanzanie; *(history)* de la Tanzanie

Taoism [ˈtaʊɪzəm] **N** taoïsme *m*

Taoist [ˈtaʊɪst] **ADJ** taoïste
N taoïste *mf*

tap [tæp] *(pt & pp* **tapped**, *cont* **tapping**) **VT 1** *(strike)* taper légèrement, tapoter; **someone tapped me on the shoulder** quelqu'un m'a tapé sur l'épaule; **she was tapping her fingers on the table** elle pianotait *ou* tapotait sur la table; **he tapped his foot to the rhythm** il marquait le rythme en tapant du pied
2 *(barrel, cask)* mettre en perce, percer; *(gas, water main)* faire un branchement sur; *(watercourse)* capter; *(tree)* inciser; *(pine tree)* gemmer; *(wine)* tirer; **the trees were tapped for their gum** on a incisé les arbres pour en recueillir la résine
3 *(exploit* ▸ *resources, market)* exploiter; (▸ *talent, service)* faire appel à, tirer profit de; (▸ *capital)* drainer; **we must t. all the resources we have** nous devons puiser dans toutes nos ressources; **to t. sb for information** soutirer des informations à qn; *Fam* **he tapped me for £15** il m'a tapé de 15 livres
4 *Tel (conversation)* écouter; **to t. sb's line** *or* **phone** mettre qn sur (table d')écoute; **the phones are tapped** les téléphones sont sur écoute
5 *Tech (bolt, nut)* tarauder, fileter
VI *(knock)* tapoter, taper légèrement; **to t. at the door** frapper doucement à la porte; **to t. on the table** tapoter sur la table; **the woodpeckers are tapping on the bark** les piverts donnent des coups de bec sur l'écorce
N 1 *(for water, gas)* robinet *m*; *(on barrel)* robinet *m*, chantepleure *f*; *(plug)* bonde *f*; **to turn a t. on/off** ouvrir/fermer un robinet; **to leave the t. running** laisser le robinet ouvert; **on t.** *(beer)* en fût; *Fam Fig (money, person, supply)* toujours disponible ▫; **they seem to have funds on t.** ils semblent avoir des fonds toujours disponibles
2 *(blow)* petit coup *m*, petite tape *f*; **to give sb a t. on the shoulder** donner une petite tape sur l'épaule à qn
3 *(on shoe)* fer *m*
4 *(dancing)* claquettes *fpl*; **to do** *or* **to dance t.** faire des claquettes
5 *Tech* **(screw) t.** taraud *m*
6 *Tel* **to put a t. on sb's phone** mettre (le téléphone de) qn sur écoute; **who authorized the t.?** qui a autorisé la mise sur écoute?
7 *Fin* = valeur du Trésor mise aux enchères; **long/medium/short t.** = valeurs émises à un prix déterminé par l'État à long/moyen/court terme
▸▸ ***tap dance*** claquettes *fpl (danse)*; ***tap dancer*** danseur(euse) *m,f* de claquettes; ***tap dancing*** *(UNCOUNT)* claquettes *fpl (danse)*; ***tap shoes*** claquettes *fpl (chaussures)*; ***tap water*** eau *f* du robinet

▸ **tap out VT SEP 1** *(plug)* sortir à petits coups; *(pipe)* vider, débourrer **2** *(code, rhythm)* taper; **to t. out a message** *(in morse code)* émettre un message

tape [teɪp] **N 1** *(strip)* bande *f*, ruban *m*; *Sewing* ruban *m*, ganse *f*; *Med* sparadrap *m*; **to cut the t.** *(at ceremony)* couper le ruban
2 *(for recording)* bande *f* (magnétique); *Comput* bande *f*; *(cassette)* cassette *f*; *(recording)* enregistrement *m*; **on t.** sur bande, enregistré; **to get** *or* **put sth on t.** enregistrer qch; **I've got it on t.** je l'ai en cassette
3 *Sport* fil *m* d'arrivée; **to breast the t.** franchir la ligne d'arrivée
4 *(for measuring)* mètre *m* (à ruban)
VT 1 *(record)* enregistrer

2 *(fasten ▸ package)* attacher avec du ruban adhésif; *(stick)* scotcher; **the address was taped to the suitcase** l'adresse était scotchée sur la valise

3 *Am (bandage)* bander

4 *Br Fam (idiom)* **she's got him taped** elle sait ce qu'il vaut□; **we have the situation taped** on a la situation bien en main□

▸▸ *Comput* ***tape backup*** sauvegarde *f* sur bande; *Comput* ***tape backup system*** système *m* de sauvegarde sur bande; *Comput* ***tape backup unit*** unité *f* de sauvegarde sur bande; ***tape cleaner*** nettoyeur *m* de tête, produit *m* de nettoyage de tête; ***tape deck*** platine *f* de magnétophone; ***tape drive*** dérouleur *m* de bande (magnétique), lecteur *m* de bande (magnétique); ***tape head*** tête *f* de lecture; ***tape machine*** téléscripteur *m*, téléimprimeur *m*; ***tape measure*** mètre *m* (ruban), centimètre *m*; ***taped music*** musique *f* enregistrée; *Comput* ***tape reader*** lecteur *m* de bande; ***tape recorder*** magnétophone *m*, lecteur *m* de cassettes; ***tape recording*** enregistrement *m* (sur bande magnétique); *Comput* ***tape streamer*** streamer *m*; ***tape transport*** mécanisme *m* d'entraînement *(d'une bande magnétique)*; *Comput* ***tape unit*** unité *f* de bande

▸**tape up** VT SEP **1** *(fasten ▸ parcel)* attacher avec du ruban adhésif; *(close ▸ letterbox, hole)* fermer avec du ruban adhésif **2** *Am (bandage up)* bander

taper ['teɪpə(r)] VT *(column, trouser leg, plane wing)* fuseler; *(stick, shape, table leg)* effiler, tailler en pointe

VI *(column, trouser leg, plane wing)* être fuselé; *(stick, shape, table leg)* se terminer en pointe, s'effiler; *(finger)* être effilé; **it tapers to a point** c'est taillé en pointe

N **1** *(candle)* = longue bougie fine; *Rel* cierge *m* **2** *(for lighting candle, fire)* allume-feu *m inv*

▸**taper off** VT SEP effiler, tailler en pointe

VI **1** *(shape)* se terminer en fuseau *ou* en pointe **2** *(noise)* diminuer progressivement, décroître, s'affaiblir; *(conversation)* tomber; *(level of interest, activity)* décroître progressivement; **street crime shows signs of tapering off** tout laisse à penser que les agressions sont en baisse

tape-record [-rɪ'kɔːd] VT enregistrer (sur bande magnétique)

tapered ['teɪpəd] ADJ *(column, trousers, plane wing)* en fuseau; *(stick, candle)* en pointe, pointu; *(table leg)* fuselé; *(finger)* effilé

tapering ['teɪpərɪŋ] ADJ **1** = **tapered 2** *Fin (rate)* dégressif

tapestry ['tæpɪstrɪ] *(pl* **tapestries***)* N tapisserie *f*; *Fig* **it's all part of life's rich t.** ça fait partie de la vie

tapeworm ['teɪpwɜːm] N ténia *m*, ver *m* solitaire

tapioca [,tæpɪ'əʊkə] N tapioca *m*

tapir ['teɪpə(r)] *(pl* **inv** *or* **tapirs***)* N *Zool* tapir *m*

tapped [tæpt] ADJ **1** *Elec (coil, transformer)* à prises **2** *Tech (bolt, nut)* taraudé, fileté **3** *Am Fam* **t. out** *(exhausted)* crevé

tappet ['tæpɪt] N *Tech* **(valve) t.** poussoir *m* (de soupape), taquet *m*

tapping ['tæpɪŋ] N **1** *(knocking)* petits coups *mpl*; *(with hand)* tapotement *m*

2 *Tel* **(telephone) t.** écoutes *fpl* (de communications téléphoniques)

3 *(exploitation)* exploitation *f*; **t. of natural resources** exploitation *f* des ressources naturelles

4 *(of barrel, cask)* mise *f* en perce, perçage *m*; *(of gas, water main)* branchement *m*; *(of watercourse)* captage *m*; *(of tree)* incision *f*; *(of pine tree)* gemmage *m*; *(of wine)* tirage *m*

5 *Tech (of bolt, nut)* taraudage *m*

taproom ['tæprum] N *Br* salle *f (d'un café)*, bar *m*

taproot ['tæpruːt] N *Bot* racine *f* pivotante

tar [tɑː(r)] *(pt & pp* **tarred**, *cont* **tarring***)* N **1** *(in cigarettes)* goudron *m*; *(on road)* goudron *m*, bitume *m* **2** *Fam (sailor)* matelot□*m*, loup *m* de mer

VT *(gen)* goudronner; *(road)* bitumer, goudronner; *Naut* goudronner; **to t. and feather sb** couvrir qn de goudron et de plumes; *Fig* **we're all tarred with the same brush** ou nous a tous mis dans le même panier *ou* sac

ta-ra [tə'rɑː] EXCLAM *Br Fam* salut!, ciao!

tarantella [,tærən'telə] N tarentelle *f*

tarantula [tə'ræntjʊlə] *(pl* **tarantulas** *or* **tarantulae** [-liː]*)* N *Entom* tarentule *f*

tardily ['tɑːdɪlɪ] ADV *Formal or Literary* **1** *(late)* tardivement **2** *(slowly)* lentement

tardiness ['tɑːdɪnɪs] N *Formal or Literary* **1** *(lateness)* retard *m* **2** *(slowness)* lenteur *f*

tardy ['tɑːdɪ] *(compar* **tardier**, *superl* **tardiest***)* ADJ **1** *Am Sch* en retard **2** *Formal or Literary (late)* tardif; *(slow)* lent, nonchalant

tare [teə(r)] N **1** *(weight)* tare *f*, poids *m* à vide **2** *Bible* **tares** ivraie *f*

target ['tɑːgɪt] *(pt & pp* **targeted**, *cont* **targeting***)* N *(for archery, shooting)* cible *f*; *Mil* cible *f*, but *m*; *Electron & Phys* cible *f*; *(objective)* cible *f*, objectif *m*; **the t. of criticism/jokes** la cible de critiques/plaisanteries; **an easy t.** une cible facile; **to be on t.** *(missile)* suivre la trajectoire prévue; *(plans)* se dérouler comme prévu; *(productivity)* atteindre les objectifs prévus; **to meet production/sales targets** atteindre les objectifs de production/de vente

COMP *(date, amount)* prévu; **my t. weight is 63 kg** je me suis fixé le poids idéal de 63 kg, mon poids idéal est (de) 63 kg

VT **1** *(aim at ▸ enemy troops, city etc)* prendre pour cible, viser; *(▸ market)* cibler **2** *(aim ▸ missile)* diriger; *(of funds, resources, benefits)* viser, être destiné à; *(of advertisement, advertising campaign)* viser; **the benefits are targeted at one-parent families** les allocations visent les *ou* sont destinées aux familles monoparentales; **the programme is targeted at 18- to 25-year-olds** l'émission s'adresse aux 18 à 25 ans *ou* vise les jeunes de 18 à 25 ans

▸▸ *Mil* ***target area*** zone *f* cible; *Mktg* ***target audience*** audience *f* cible; *Mktg* ***target buyer*** acheteur(euse) *m,f* cible; *Fin* ***target company*** société *f* opéable; *Mktg* ***target consumer*** consommateur (trice) *m,f* cible; *Mktg* ***target cost*** coût *m* ciblé; *Comput* ***target disk*** *(hard)* disque *m* cible; *(floppy)* disquette *f* cible; *Comput* ***target drive*** unité *f* de destination; ***target figures*** chiffres *mpl* prévus; *Comput* ***target file*** fichier *m* de destination; *Mktg* ***target group*** groupe *m* cible; ***target language*** langue *f* cible, langue *f* d'arrivée; *Mktg* ***target market*** marché *m* cible; *Mktg* ***target marketing*** marketing *m* ciblé; *Mktg* ***target population*** population *f* cible; *Mil* ***target practice*** *(UNCOUNT)* exercices *mpl* de tir; *Mktg* ***target price*** prix *m* d'équilibre; *Mktg* ***target pricing*** fixation *f* du prix en fonction de l'objectif; ***target readership*** lectorat *m* cible; ***target setting*** arrêt *m* des objectifs

targeted ['tɑːgɪtɪd] ADJ ciblé

targeting ['tɑːgɪtɪŋ] N **1** *(setting targets)* détermination *f* d'objectifs **2** *Mktg* ciblage *m* **3** *(of funds, resources, benefits)* ciblage *m*; **we need better t. of resources** il nous faut mieux cibler les ressources

tariff ['tærɪf] N **1** *(at customs)* tarif *m* douanier **2** *(list of prices)* tarif *m*, tableau *m* des prix **3** *Br (rate ▸ of gas, electricity)* tarif *m*

COMP tarifaire

▸▸ ***tariff agreement*** accord *m* tarifaire; ***tariff barrier*** barrière *f* douanière *ou* tarifaire; ***tariff laws*** lois *fpl* tarifaires; ***tariff wall*** barrière *f* douanière *ou* tarifaire

tarmac® ['tɑːmæk] *(pt & pp* **tarmacked**, *cont* **tarmacking***)* *Br* N **1** *(on road)* tarmacadam *m*, macadam *m* **2** *(at airport ▸ runway)* piste *f*; *(▸ apron)* aire *f* de stationnement, piste *f* d'envol; **the plane had to wait for half an hour on the t.** l'avion a dû attendre une demi-heure sur l'aire de stationnement

VT macadamiser, goudronner

tarn [tɑːn] N petit lac *m* de montagne

tarnish ['tɑːnɪʃ] VT **1** *(metal)* ternir; *(mirror)* ternir, désargenter **2** *(reputation)* ternir, salir

VI se ternir

N ternissure *f*

tarnishing ['tɑːnɪʃɪŋ] N *(of metal)* ternissure *f*; **this led to the t. of his reputation** cela a terni sa réputation

tarot ['tærəʊ] N *(UNCOUNT)* tarot *m*, tarots *mpl*

▸▸ ***tarot card*** carte *f* de tarot

tarp [tɑːp] N *Fam* bâche□*f*

tarpaulin [tɑː'pɔːlɪn] N bâche *f*; *Naut* prélart *m*

tarragon ['tærəgən] N estragon *m*

COMP *(sauce, vinegar)* à l'estragon

tarry[1] ['tærɪ] *(pt & pp* **tarried***)* VI *Literary (delay)* s'attarder, tarder; *(remain)* rester, demeurer

tarry[2] ['tɑːrɪ] *(compar* **tarrier**, *superl* **tarriest***)* ADJ **1** *(made of tar)* goudronneux, bitumineux **2** *(covered or stained with tar)* couvert de goudron

tarsus ['tɑːsəs] *(pl* **tarsi** [-saɪ]*)* N *Anat* tarse *m*

tart [tɑːt] N **1** *Culin* tarte *f*; *(small)* tartelette *f* **2** *Br very Fam (prostitute)* pute *f*; *(promiscuous woman)* salope *f*, pute *f*; *(any woman)* gonzesse *f*; **(you silly t.!** espèce d'andouille!; *Fam Hum* **she's a t. with a heart** elle fait un peu vulgos mais elle est gentille

ADJ **1** *(sour ▸ fruit)* acide; *(▸ taste)* aigre, acide **2** *(remark)* acerbe, caustique

▸**tart up** VT SEP *Br Fam (house, room, restaurant)* retaper, rénover□; **to t. oneself up, to get tarted up** se pomponner; **it's just a tarted up version of the old model** ce n'est qu'une version enjolivée de l'ancien modèle□

tartan ['tɑːtən] N *(design)* tartan *m*; *(fabric)* tartan *m*, tissu *m* écossais

COMP *(skirt, trousers)* en tissu écossais; *(pattern)* tartan

tartar ['tɑːtə(r)] N **1** *(on teeth)* tartre *m* **2** *Br (fear some person)* tyran *m*

• **Tartar** = **Tatar**

▸▸ ***tartar sauce*** sauce *f* tartare

tartare sauce ['tɑːtə-] N sauce *f* tartare

tartaric [tɑː'tærɪk] ADJ *Chem* tartrique

▸▸ ***tartaric acid*** acide *m* tartrique

tartly ['tɑːtlɪ] ADV *(say)* avec aigreur, de manière acerbe

tartness ['tɑːtnɪs] N *(of fruit, wine, tone, remark)* aigreur *f*, acidité *f*

tarty ['tɑːtɪ] *(compar* **tartier**, *superl* **tartiest***)* ADJ *Br very Fam (person, clothes)* qui fait pute; **to look t.** *(person)* avoir l'air d'une pute

tash [tæʃ] N *Br Fam (abrév* **moustache***)* moustache□*f*, bacchantes *fpl*

task [tɑːsk] N *(chore)* tâche *f*, besogne *f*; *(job)* tâche *f*, travail *m*; *Sch* devoir *m*; *Comput* tâche *f*; **to set sb a t.** imposer une tâche à qn; **convincing them will be no easy t.** les convaincre ne sera pas chose facile; **to take sb to t. (for sth/for doing sth)** réprimander qn (pour qch/pour avoir fait qch), prendre qn à partie (pour qch/pour avoir fait qch)

VT *(entrust)* **to t. sb with sth/with doing sth** charger qn de qch/de faire qch; **to be tasked with sth/doing sth** être chargé de qch/de faire qch

▸▸ ***task force*** *(to investigate)* commission *f*; *(to do special job)* groupe *m* de travail; *Mil* corps *m* expéditionnaire

taskbar ['tɑːskbɑː(r)] N *Comput* barre *f* des tâches

taskmaster ['tɑːsk,mɑːstə(r)] N tyran *m*; **he's a hard t.** il mène la vie dure à ses subordonnés, c'est un véritable négrier

Tasmania [tæz'meɪnjə] N Tasmanie *f*

Tasmanian [tæz'meɪnjən] N Tasmanien(enne) *m,f*

ADJ tasmanien

▸▸ *Zool* ***Tasmanian devil*** diable *m* de Tasmanie

tassel ['tæsəl] *(Br pt & pp* **tasselled**, *cont* **tasselling**, *Am pt & pp* **tasseled**, *cont* **tasseling***)* N *(on clothing, furnishing)* gland *m*

VT garnir de glands

tasselled, *Am* **tasseled** ['tæsəld] ADJ à glands, orné de glands

TASTE [teɪst]

N
- goût **1, 2, 4, 5**
- saveur **2**
- bouchée **3**
- goutte **3**
- aperçu **6**

VT
- sentir **1**
- goûter (à) **2, 4**
- manger **3**
- boire **3**

VI
- avoir un goût

N **1** *(sense)* goût *m*; **to lose one's sense of t.** perdre le goût, *Spec* être atteint d'agueusie; **to be sweet/salty to the t.** avoir un goût sucré/salé

2 *(flavour)* goût *m*, saveur *f*; **these apples have a**

ovely/strange t.** ces pommes sont délicieuses/nt un drôle de goût; **this cheese doesn't have much t.** ce fromage n'a pas beaucoup de goût u est assez fade; **the cake has a t. of almonds/a urnt t.** le gâteau a un goût d'amandes/de brûlé; **dd sugar to t.** ajouter du sucre à volonté; **to ave a bad t. in the mouth** *(food)* laisser un mauvais goût dans la bouche; *Fig* laisser un mauvais souvenir *ou* un goût amer
3 *(small amount ▸ of food)* bouchée *f*; *(▸ of drink)* outte *f*; **can I have a t. of the chocolate cake?** est-e que je peux goûter au gâteau au chocolat?
4 *(liking, preference)* goût *m*, penchant *m*; **to ave simple/expensive tastes** avoir des goûts simples/de luxe; **to develop a t. for sth** prendre goût qch; **to have a t. for sth** avoir un penchant *ou* un aible pour qch; **it's a matter of t.** c'est (une) affaire de goût; **musical/artistic tastes** goûts *mpl* musicaux/artistiques; **I don't share his t. in music** e ne partage pas ses goûts en (matière de) musique, nous n'avons pas les mêmes goûts en matière de) musique; **is it to your t.?** est-ce à votre goût?, est-ce que cela vous convient?, cela ous plaît?
5 *(discernment)* goût *m*; **to have good t.** avoir du oût, avoir bon goût; **they have no t.** ils n'ont aucun goût; **she has good t. in clothes** elle s'habille vec goût; **they don't have much t. when it comes o art** en matière d'art, ils n'ont pas beaucoup de oût; **the joke was in extremely bad t.** la plaisanterie était de très mauvais goût
6 *(experience)* aperçu *m*; *(sample)* échantillon *n*; **to have a t. of freedom/happiness** avoir un perçu de la liberté/du bonheur; **the sweet t. of uccess** les joies *fpl ou* les délices *fpl* de la réussite; **he's already had a t. of prison life** il a déjà tâté u goûté de la prison; **the experience gave me a t. f life in the army** l'expérience m'a donné un perçu de la vie militaire; **a t. of things to come** n avant-goût de l'avenir
VT 1 *(flavour, ingredient)* sentir (le goût de); **can ou t. the brandy in it?** est-ce que vous sentez le goût du) cognac?
2 *(sample, try)* goûter à; *(for quality)* goûter; **have ou tasted the sauce?** avez-vous goûté (à) la auce?; **to t. (the) wine** *(in restaurant)* goûter le in; *(in vineyard)* déguster le vin
3 *(eat)* manger; *(drink)* boire; **I've never tasted ysters before** je n'ai jamais mangé d'huîtres; **ou don't often get a chance to t. such good wine** n n'a pas souvent l'occasion de boire un aussi on vin
4 *(experience ▸ happiness, success)* goûter, onnaître
VI *(food)* **to t. good/bad** avoir bon/mauvais oût; **to t. salty** avoir un goût salé; **to t. funny** voir un drôle de goût; **it tastes like chicken** cela un goût de poulet; **to t. of sth** avoir le *ou* un oût de qch; **it doesn't t. of anything** cela n'a aucun goût
▸▸ ***taste bud*** papille *f* gustative

asteful ['teɪstfʊl] **ADJ** *(decoration, work of art, remark, action)* de bon goût; *(clothing)* de bon oût, élégant

astefully ['teɪstfʊlɪ] **ADV** avec goût

astefulness ['teɪstfʊlnɪs] **N** *(of decoration, work f art, remark, action)* bon goût *m*; *(of clothing)* chic *m*, élégance *f*

asteless ['teɪstlɪs] **ADJ 1** *(food)* fade, insipide, ans goût; *(medicine)* qui n'a aucun goût **2** *(remark)* de mauvais goût; *(decoration, outfit)* de mauvais goût, qui manque de goût

astelessly ['teɪstlɪslɪ] **ADV** *(decorated, dressed)* ans goût

astelessness ['teɪstlɪsnɪs] **N 1** *(of food)* fadeur *f*, manque *m* de saveur *ou* de goût; *(of medicine)* bsence *f* de goût **2** *(of remark)* mauvais goût *n*; *(in decoration, clothes)* manque *m* de goût, mauvais goût *m*

aster ['teɪstə(r)] **N 1** *(person)* dégustateur(trice) *n,f* **2** *(foretaste)* **this is just a t. (of what's to come)** ceci n'est qu'un avant-goût (de ce qui va suivre)

-TASTIC — SUFFIXE

Il s'agit d'un suffixe de registre familier assez récent dérivé de l'adjectif **fantastic** et qui véhicule la notion d'EXCELLENCE du terme auquel il est accolé. Ainsi a **poptastic concert** est un excellent concert de musique pop. Ce suffixe se rencontre souvent dans les publicités et dans les magazines qui s'adressent aux jeunes et à tous les passionnés du monde des célébrités. Parmi les termes nouvellement créés, citons :
it was a celebtastic party c'était une soirée pleine de célébrités; **the Star Trek convention was geektastic** le congrès StarTrek a attiré plein de ringards.

tastiness ['teɪstɪnɪs] **N** saveur *f* agréable, bon goût *m*

tasting ['teɪstɪŋ] **N** dégustation *f*

tasty ['teɪstɪ] *(compar* **tastier**, *superl* **tastiest)** **ADJ 1** *(flavour)* savoureux, délicieux; *(dish)* qui a bon goût **2** *Br Fam (attractive)* bien foutu, bien balancé

TAT ['tiːeɪ'tiː] **N** *Psy & Mktg (abbr* **thematic apperception test)** TAT *m*

tat [tæt] **N** *(UNCOUNT) Br Fam Pej (clothes)* fripes *fpl*; *(goods)* camelote *f*

ta-ta [tæ'tɑː] **EXCLAM** *Br Fam* au revoir!▫, salut!

Tatar ['tɑːtə(r)] **N 1** *(person)* Tatar(e) *m,f* **2** *Ling* tatar *m*
ADJ tatar

Tatary ['tɑːtərɪ] **N** Tatarie *f*

tater ['teɪtə(r)] **N** *Fam (potato)* patate *f*

tattered ['tætəd] **ADJ** *(clothes)* en lambeaux, en loques; *(page, book)* en lambeaux, en morceaux, tout déchiré; *(person)* en haillons, loqueteux; *(reputation)* en miettes, ruiné

tatters ['tætəz] **NPL to be in t.** *(clothes)* être en lambeaux *ou* en loques; *Fig* **her reputation is in t.** sa réputation est ruinée

tattie ['tætɪ] **N** *esp Scot Fam (potato)* patate *f*

tattle ['tætəl] *Fam* **VI** *(chatter)* jaser▫, cancaner; *(tell secrets)* rapporter▫
N *(UNCOUNT) (gossiping)* commérages *mpl*, cancans *mpl*

tattler ['tætlə(r)] **N** *Fam* commère *f*, bavard (e)▫*m,f*

tattle-tale = **telltale N**

tattoo [tə'tuː] *(pl* **tattoos)** **N 1** *(on skin)* tatouage *m*; **to get a t.** se faire faire un tatouage; **he had tattoos across his chest** il avait la poitrine tatouée **2** *Mil (signal)* retraite *f*; *(ceremony, parade)* parade *f* militaire; **to sound the t.** sonner la retraite **3** *(on drums)* battements *mpl*; **to beat a t. on the drums** battre le tambour
VI tatouer
VT tatouer
▸▸ ***tattoo parlour*** boutique *f* de tatouages

tattooing [tə'tuːɪŋ] **N** tatouage *m*

tattooist [tə'tuːɪst] **N** tatoueur(euse) *m,f*

tatty ['tætɪ] *(compar* **tattier**, *superl* **tattiest)** **ADJ** *Br Fam (clothes)* fatigué▫, défraîchi▫; *(person)* défraîchi▫, miteux; *(house)* délabré▫, en mauvais état▫; *(book)* écorné▫, en mauvais état▫

taught [tɔːt] *pt & pp of* **teach**

taunt [tɔːnt] **VT** railler, tourner en ridicule, persifler; **to t. sb with sth** railler qn à propos de qch
N raillerie *f*, sarcasme *m*

taunting ['tɔːntɪŋ] **N** *(UNCOUNT)* railleries *fpl*, sarcasmes *mpl*
ADJ railleur, sarcastique

tauntingly ['tɔːntɪŋlɪ] **ADV** d'un ton railleur *ou* persifleur

taurine ['tɔːriːn] **N** *Biol & Chem* taurine *f*

Taurus ['tɔːrəs] **N 1** *Astron* Taureau *m* **2** *Astrol* Taureau *m*; **he's a T.** il est (du signe du) Taureau
ADJ *Astrol* du Taureau; **he's T.** il est (du signe du) Taureau

taut [tɔːt] **ADJ** *(rope, cable)* tendu, raide; *(situation)* tendu

tauten ['tɔːtən] **VT** *(rope, cable etc)* tendre, raidir
VI se tendre

tautness ['tɔːtnɪs] **N** tension *f*, raideur *f*

tautological [,tɔːtə'lɒdʒɪkəl] **ADJ** tautologique, pléonastique

tautology [tɔː'tɒlədʒɪ] *(pl* **tautologies)** **N** tautologie *f*, pléonasme *m*

tavern ['tævən] **N** auberge *f*, taverne *f*

tawdriness ['tɔːdrɪnɪs] **N** *(of clothes)* aspect *m* tapageur *ou* voyant; *(of jewellery)* clinquant *m*; *(of goods)* mauvaise qualité *f*; *(of motives, situation)* bassesse *f*, indignité *f*; **there was a t. about everything in the hotel** tout dans l'hôtel était d'un luxe tapageur

tawdry ['tɔːdrɪ] *(compar* **tawdrier**, *superl* **tawdriest)** **ADJ** *(clothes)* voyant et de mauvaise qualité; *(jewellery)* clinquant; *(goods)* de mauvaise qualité; *(motives, situation)* bas, indigne

tawny ['tɔːnɪ] *(compar* **tawnier**, *superl* **tawniest)** **ADJ** *(colour)* fauve
▸▸ *Orn* ***tawny owl*** chouette *f* hulotte; ***tawny port*** = porto qui a jauni dans le fût

tax [tæks] **N 1** *(on income)* contributions *fpl*; *Admin & Fin* impôt *m*; **to levy** *or* **to collect taxes** lever *ou* percevoir des impôts; **most of my income goes in t.** la plus grande partie de mes revenus va aux impôts; **I don't pay much t.** je ne paie pas beaucoup d'impôts; **I paid over $5,000 in t.** j'ai payé plus de 5000 dollars d'impôts; **to be liable to t.** être assujetti à l'impôt; **after t.** net, après impôt; **before t.** avant impôt
2 *(on goods, services, imports)* taxe *f*; **to levy** *or* **to put a 10 percent t. on sth** frapper qch d'une taxe de 10 pour cent, imposer *ou* taxer qch à 10 pour cent; **there is a high t. on whisky** le whisky est fortement taxé; **free of t.** exempt *ou* exonéré de taxe; **a t. on books/knowledge** une taxe sur les livres/le savoir; **liable to t.** assujetti à l'impôt; **before t.** hors taxe; **exclusive of t.** hors taxe
3 *Fig (strain)* épreuve *f*; **it was a t. on his strength/nerves** ça l'a beaucoup éprouvé (physiquement/psychologiquement)
VT 1 *(person, company)* imposer, frapper d'un impôt; *(goods)* taxer, frapper d'une taxe; **the rich will be more heavily taxed** les riches seront plus lourdement imposés *ou* payeront plus d'impôts; **luxury goods are taxed at 28 percent** les articles de luxe sont taxés à 28 pour cent *ou* font l'objet d'une taxe de 28 pour cent; **we're being taxed out of existence** on nous accable d'impôts
2 *Br* **to t. one's car** acheter la vignette (automobile)
3 *Fig (strain ▸ patience, resources)* mettre à l'épreuve; *(▸ strength, nerves)* éprouver
4 *Literary (accuse)* **to t. sb with sth** accuser *ou* taxer qn de qch; **to t. sb with doing sth** accuser qn d'avoir fait qch
▸▸ ***tax adjustment*** redressement *m* fiscal *ou* d'impôt; ***tax allowance*** abattement *m* fiscal, déduction *f* fiscale; ***tax assessment*** avis *m* d'imposition, fixation *f* de l'impôt; ***tax audit*** vérification *f* fiscale; ***tax authorities*** administration *f* fiscale; ***tax avoidance*** optimisation *f ou* évasion *f* fiscale, *Can* évitement *m* fiscal; ***tax band*** tranche *f* d'imposition; ***tax base*** assiette *f* fiscale; ***tax benefit*** avantage *m* fiscal; ***tax bracket*** tranche *f ou* fourchette *f* d'imposition; ***tax break*** réduction *f* d'impôt, allègement *m* fiscal; ***tax burden*** pression *f* fiscale, poids *m* de la fiscalité; ***tax ceiling*** plafond *m* fiscal *ou* de l'impôt; ***tax centre*** centre *m* des impôts, CDI *m*; ***tax clearance*** quitus *m* fiscal; ***tax code*** barème *m* fiscal; ***tax collection*** recouvrement *m ou* perception *f* d'impôts; ***tax collector*** percepteur *m* d'impôt, receveur *m* des contributions; ***tax consultant*** conseiller(ère) *m,f* fiscal(e), conseil *m* fiscal; ***tax credit*** aide *f* fiscale, avoir *m* fiscal; ***tax cut*** baisse *f ou* réduction *f* des impôts; ***tax deduction*** prélèvement *m* fiscal, déduction *f* fiscale; ***tax deduction at source*** perception *f* à la source; *Br* ***tax disc*** vignette *f* (automobile); *Am* ***tax dollars*** argent *m* du contribuable; ***tax evasion*** fraude *f ou* évasion *f* fiscale; ***tax exemption*** exonération *f ou* exemption *f* d'impôt; ***tax exile*** = personne qui réside à l'étranger pour minimiser la responsabilité fiscale; ***tax form*** feuille *f ou* déclaration *f* d'impôts; ***tax fraud*** fraude *f* fiscale; *EU* ***tax harmonization*** harmonisation *f* fiscale; ***tax haven*** paradis *m* fiscal; ***tax holiday*** période *f* de grâce *(accordée pour le paiement des impôts)*; ***tax impact*** incidence *f* fiscale; ***tax incentive*** incitation *f* fiscale, avantage *m* fiscal; ***tax inspection*** contrôle *m* fiscal; ***tax inspector*** inspecteur(trice) *m,f* des contributions directes *ou* des impôts; ***tax law*** droit *m* fiscal; ***tax liability*** *(of person)* assujetissement *m* à l'impôt; *(of goods, product)* exigibilité *f* de l'impôt; ***tax loophole*** échappatoire *f* fiscale; ***tax loss*** défi-

cit *m* fiscal reportable; ***tax office*** centre *m* des impôts; ***tax official*** agent *m* du fisc; ***tax rate*** taux *m* d'imposition; ***tax rebate*** dégrèvement *m* fiscal; ***tax reduction*** abattement *m* fiscal; ***tax refund*** *(of income tax)* restitution *f* d'impôts; *(on goods)* détaxe *f*; ***tax regime*** régime *m* fiscal; ***tax relief*** *(UNCOUNT)* dégrèvement *m* fiscal; ***tax return*** déclaration *f* de revenu, feuille *f* d'impôt; ***tax revenue*** recettes *fpl ou* rentrées *fpl* fiscales; ***tax roll*** rôle *m* d'impôt *ou* des contributions; ***tax shelter*** avantage *m* fiscal; ***tax shield*** protection *f* fiscale; ***tax stamp*** timbre *m* fiscal; ***tax system*** régime *m* fiscal *ou* d'imposition; ***tax threshold*** minimum *m* imposable, seuil *m* d'imposition; ***tax wrapper*** = moyen de mettre ses investissements à l'abri du fisc; ***tax write-off*** *(expense)* dépense *f* déductible des impôts; *(loss)* perte *f* déductible des impôts; ***tax year*** année *f* fiscale *ou* d'imposition *(qui commence en avril en Grande-Bretagne)*

taxable ['tæksəbəl] **ADJ** *(land)* imposable; *(goods)* taxable
►► ***taxable base*** base *f* d'imposition; ***taxable income*** revenu *m* imposable, assiette *f* fiscale *ou* de l'impôt; ***taxable profit*** bénéfice *m* fiscal *ou* imposable; ***taxable transaction*** opération *f* imposable

taxation [tæk'seɪʃən] **N** *(UNCOUNT)* **1** *(of goods)* taxation *f*; *(of companies, people)* imposition *f*, prélèvement *m* fiscal; **t. at source** prélèvement *m* de l'impôt à la source, imposition *f* à la source **2** *(taxes)* impôts *mpl*, contributions *fpl*
COMP *(system)* fiscal

tax-deductible **ADJ** déductible des impôts, sujet à un dégrèvement d'impôts

tax-exempt **ADJ** *(goods)* exonéré de taxes, non taxé; *(income)* exonéré d'impôts

tax-free **ADJ** *(goods)* exonéré de taxes, non taxé; *(interest)* exonéré d'impôts, exempt d'impôts; *(income)* exonéré d'impôts
►► ***tax-free shop*** boutique *f* hors taxes; ***tax-free shopping*** achats *mpl* hors taxes

taxi ['tæksɪ] *(pl* **taxis** *or* **taxies**, *pt & pp* **taxied**, *cont* **taxiing) N** taxi *m*; **to take a t.** prendre un taxi; **to hail a t.** héler un taxi
VI *(aircraft)* se déplacer au sol; **the plane taxied across the tarmac** l'avion traversa lentement l'aire de stationnement
VT *(carry passengers)* transporter en taxi
►► ***taxi driver*** chauffeur *m* de taxi; ***taxi fare*** *(gen)* tarif *m* de taxi; *(cost of journey)* coût *m* du taxi, prix *m* de la course (en taxi); **can you pay the t. fare?** pouvez-vous régler *ou* payer le taxi?; ***taxi rank***, *Am* ***taxi stand*** station *f* de taxis

taxicab ['tæksɪkæb] **N** taxi *m*

taxidermist ['tæksɪˌdɜːmɪst] **N** empailleur(euse) *m,f*, taxidermiste *mf*, naturaliste *mf*

taxidermy ['tæksɪˌdɜːmɪ] **N** empaillage *m*, taxidermie *f*, naturalisation *f* des animaux

taximeter ['tæksɪˌmiːtə(r)] **N** taximètre *m*, compteur *m* (de taxi)

taxing ['tæksɪŋ] **ADJ** *(problem, time)* difficile; *(climb)* ardu

taxiplane ['tæksɪpleɪn] **N** avion-taxi *m*

taxonomic [ˌtæksə'nɒmɪk] **ADJ** taxinomique

taxonomy [tæk'sɒnəmɪ] *(pl* **taxonomies**) **N** taxinomie *f*

taxpayer ['tæksˌpeɪə(r)] **N** contribuable *mf*

TB [ˌtiː'biː] **N** *(abbr* **tuberculosis**) tuberculose *f*

T-bar **N** *(for skiers)* téléski *m*, remonte-pente *m*

T-bone (steak) **N** steak *m* dans l'aloyau *(sur l'os)*

tbs., tbsp. *(written abbr* **tablespoon(ful)**) cs

TCP® [ˌtiːsiː'piː] **N** *Br (abbr* **trichlorophonoxyacetic acid**) = désinfectant utilisé pour nettoyer des petites plaies ou pour se gargariser

TCP/IP [ˌtiːsiːpiːˌaɪ'piː] **N** *Comput (abbr* **transmission control protocol/Internet protocol**) TCP-IP

TD [ˌtiː'diː] **N 1** *(abbr* **Treasury Department**) ministère *m* des Finances **2** *Ir Pol (abbr* **Teachta Dála**) ≃ député(e) *m,f*

tea [tiː] **N 1** *(drink, leaves)* thé *m*; **a cup of t.** une tasse de thé; **two teas and a coffee, please** deux thés et un café, s'il vous plaît; **not for all the t. in China** pour rien au monde **2** *(afternoon snack)* thé *m*; *Scot, NEng & Ir (evening meal)* repas *m* du soir; **to ask sb to t.** inviter qn à prendre le thé
3 *(infusion)* infusion *f*, tisane *f*
4 *(plant)* thé *m*
►► *Br* ***tea boy*** = jeune employé chargé de préparer le thé pour ses collègues; ***tea bread*** *(UNCOUNT)* ≃ cake *m*; *Br* ***tea break*** pause *f* pour prendre le thé, pause-thé *f*; ***tea caddy*** boîte *f* à thé; ***tea chest*** caisse *f* (à thé); *Br* ***tea cloth*** torchon *m* (à vaisselle); *Br* ***tea cosy*** cosy *m*; ***tea dance*** thé *m* dansant; ***tea garden*** *(garden)* = jardin de restaurant qui fait salon de thé; *(plantation)* plantation *f* de thé; *Br* ***tea lady*** = dame qui prépare ou sert le thé pour les employés d'une entreprise; ***tea party*** *(for adults)* thé *m*; *(for children)* goûter *m*; ***tea plant*** arbre *m* à thé, théier *m*; ***tea plantation*** plantation *f* de thé; ***tea planter*** planteur *m* de thé; ***tea rose*** rose thé *f*; ***tea service, tea set*** service *m* à thé; *Br* ***tea shop*** salon *m* de thé; ***tea strainer*** passoire *f* à thé, passe-thé *m inv*; ***tea table*** table *f* (mise) pour le thé, table *f* à thé; *Br* ***tea towel*** torchon *m* (à vaisselle); ***tea tray*** plateau *m* à thé; *Br* ***tea trolley*** table *f* roulante *(pour servir le thé)*; ***tea urn*** fontaine *f* à thé

teacake ['tiːkeɪk] **N** = petite brioche

teach [tiːtʃ] *(pt & pp* **taught** [tɔːt]) **VT 1** *(gen)* apprendre; **to t. sb sth** *or* **sth to sb** apprendre qch à qn; **she taught herself knitting/French** elle a appris à tricoter/elle a appris le français toute seule; **you can't t. them anything!** ils savent tout!, ils n'ont plus rien à apprendre!; **to t. sb (how) to do sth** apprendre à qn à faire qch; **she taught them to play the piano** elle leur a appris à jouer du piano; **they taught us what to do in emergencies** ils nous ont appris *ou* montré ce qu'il fallait faire en cas d'urgence; **didn't anyone ever t. you not to interrupt people?** on ne t'a jamais dit *ou* appris qu'il ne faut pas couper la parole aux gens?; **I'll t. you to be rude to your elders!** *(as threat)* je vais t'apprendre à être insolent envers les aînés!; **that'll t. you (not) to go off on your own** ça t'apprendra à t'en aller toute seule; **that'll t. you (a lesson)!** ça t'apprendra!, c'est bien fait pour toi!; *Fam* **to t. sb a thing or two** dégourdir qn ☐; *Br Prov* **you can't t. your grandmother to suck eggs** on n'apprend pas à un vieux singe à faire la grimace **2** *Sch (physics, history etc)* enseigner, être professeur de; *(pupils, class)* faire cours à; **she teaches geography** elle enseigne la géographie, elle est professeur de géographie; **I've been teaching 3B since Christmas** j'ai la 3B depuis Noël, je fais cours à la 3B depuis Noël; *Am* **to t. school** être enseignant
VI *(as profession)* être enseignant, enseigner; *(give lessons)* faire cours; **I started teaching in 1980** j'ai commencé à enseigner *ou* je suis entré dans l'enseignement en 1980; **she spent the morning teaching** elle a fait cours toute la matinée

teachable ['tiːtʃəbəl] **ADJ** *(subject)* que l'on peut enseigner, susceptible d'être enseigné; *(children)* à qui on peut apprendre quelque chose

teacher ['tiːtʃə(r)] **N** *(in primary school)* instituteur(trice) *m,f*, maître (maîtresse) *m,f*; *(in secondary school)* professeur *m*, enseignant(e) *m,f*; *(in special school)* éducateur(trice) *m,f*; **French/history t.** professeur *m* de français/d'histoire; **t.-pupil ratio** taux *m* d'encadrement
►► *Am* ***teacher's college*** centre *m* de formation pédagogique, ≃ école *f* normale; ***teacher's pet*** chouchou(oute) *m,f* du professeur; *Br* ***teacher training*** formation *f* pédagogique des enseignants; **to do one's t. training** suivre une formation pédagogique; *Br* ***teacher training college*** centre *m* de formation pédagogique, ≃ école *f* normale

teach-in **N** séminaire *m*

teaching ['tiːtʃɪŋ] **N 1** *(profession)* enseignement *m*; **to go into t.** entrer dans l'enseignement, devenir enseignant(e) **2** *(action)* enseignement *m*; **chemistry/history t.** l'enseignement *m* de la chimie/de l'histoire **3** *(UNCOUNT) (hours taught)* heures *fpl* d'enseignement, (heures *fpl* de) cours *mpl*; **she only does a few hours' t. a week** elle ne donne *ou* n'a que quelques heures de cours par semaine
COMP *(staff)* enseignant; **the t. profession** *(teachers)* le corps enseignant
• **teachings** **NPL** *(of leader, church)* enseignements *mpl*
►► ***teaching aid*** matériel *m* pédagogique; ***teaching assistant*** *Br Sch* assistant(e) *m,f* scolaire; *Am & Can Univ* = étudiant de deuxième cycle qui assure quelques heures de cours en échange d'une bourse d'étude; ***teaching hospital*** centre *m* hospitalo-universitaire, CHU *m*; *Br* ***teaching practice*** *(UNCOUNT)* stage *m* pédagogique *(pour futurs enseignants)*

Teachta Dála ['tʃɒxtə'dɔːlə] **N** *Pol* ≃ député(e) *m,f (du Parlement irlandais)*

teacup ['tiːkʌp] **N** tasse *f* à thé

teacupful ['tiːkʌpˌfʊl] **N** tasse *f* à thé *(mesure)*; **three teacupfuls of milk** trois tasses de lait

teak [tiːk] **N** teck *m*, tek *m*
COMP en teck

teal [tiːl] *(pl* **inv** *or* **teals**) **N** *Orn* sarcelle *f* d'hiver

tealight ['tiːlaɪt] **N** bougie *f* chauffe-plat

team [tiːm] **N 1** *(of players, workers)* équipe *f*; **medical/basketball t.** équipe *f* médicale/de basket-ball; **he's one of the t.** il fait partie de l'équipe **2** *(of horses, oxen etc)* attelage *m*
VT 1 *(workers, players)* mettre en équipe; *(horses, oxen etc)* atteler; **I was teamed with my brother** j'ai fait équipe avec mon frère **2** *(colour, garments)* assortir, harmoniser
COMP **a t. effort** un travail d'équipe
►► ***team building*** création *f* d'un esprit d'équipe, team-building *m*; ***team game*** jeu *m* d'équipe; ***team leader*** chef *m* d'équipe; ***team mate*** coéquipier(ère) *m,f*; ***team member*** équipier(ère) *m,f*; ***team player*** *(in sports)* = joueur qui a l'esprit d'équipe; *(employee)* = personne qui a l'esprit d'équipe; *Fig* **to be a (good) t. player** avoir l'esprit d'équipe; **he's not much of a t. player** il n'a pas l'esprit d'équipe; *Sport* ***team sheet*** liste *f* des joueurs; ***team spirit*** esprit *m* d'équipe
▸ **team up** **VT SEP** *(workers, players)* mettre en équipe; *(horses, oxen etc)* atteler; **we're often teamed up (together)** on fait souvent équipe (ensemble)
VI *(workers)* faire équipe, travailler en collaboration; **to t. up with sb** faire équipe avec qn; **the two villages teamed up to put on the show** les deux villages ont collaboré pour monter le spectacle

team-building **COMP** *(activity, course, weekend)* de team-building

teamster ['tiːmstə(r)] **N** *Am* routier *m*, camionneur *m*

teamwork ['tiːmwɜːk] **N** travail *m* d'équipe

teapot ['tiːpɒt] **N** théière *f*

TEAR[1] [teə(r)]

VT	
• déchirer **1, 2, 4**	• froisser **2**
• arracher **3, 5**	
VI	
• se déchirer **1**	• se précipiter **2**
N	
• déchirure	

(pt **tore** [tɔː(r)], *pp* **torn** [tɔːn])
VT 1 *(rip ▸ page, material)* déchirer; *(▸ clothes)* déchirer, faire un accroc à; *(▸ flesh)* déchirer, arracher; **I tore my jacket on a nail** j'ai fait un accroc à ma veste avec un clou; **he tore a hole in the paper** il a fait un trou dans le papier; **t. along the dotted line** *(on form)* détacher suivant le pointillé; **the dog was tearing the meat from a bone** le chien déchiquetait la viande d'un os; **her heart was torn by grief/remorse** elle était déchirée par la douleur/le remords; **she tore open the letter** elle ouvrit l'enveloppe en la déchirant, elle déchira l'enveloppe; **to t. sth in two** *or* **in half** déchirer qch en deux; *also Fig* **to t. one's hair** s'arracher les cheveux; **to t. sth to pieces** *(document, banknote etc)* déchirer qch en mille morceaux; **the fox was torn to pieces by the hounds** le renard a été déchiqueté *ou* mis en pièces par la meute; **to be torn to shreds** être en lambeaux; **to t. sth to shreds** mettre qch en lambeaux; *Fig* **the critics tore the film to shreds** *or* **pieces** les critiques ont éreinté le film; *Fig* **to t. sb to shreds** *or* **pieces** mettre qn en pièces, écharper qn

2 *(muscle, ligament)* froisser, déchirer
3 *(grab, snatch)* arracher; **he tore the cheque from** *or* **out of my hand** il m'a arraché le chèque des mains
4 *Fig (divide)* tirailler, déchirer; **I'm torn between going and staying** je suis tiraillé entre le désir de partir et celui de rester, j'hésite entre partir et rester; **the country had been torn by civil war for 30 years** ça faisait 30 ans que le pays était déchiré par la guerre civile
5 *Fig (separate)* arracher; **sorry to t. you from your reading, but I need your help** je regrette de vous arracher à votre lecture, mais j'ai besoin de votre aide; *Fam Br* **that's torn it,** *Am* **that tears it** c'est le bouquet, il ne manquait plus que cela
VI 1 *(paper, cloth)* se déchirer; **this cloth tears easily** ce tissu se déchire facilement
2 *(as verb of movement)* **to t. after sb** se précipiter *ou* se lancer à la poursuite de qn; **to t. along** *(runner)* courir à toute allure; *(car)* filer à toute allure; **the children were tearing around the playground** les enfants couraient de tous les côtés dans la cour de récréation
3 *(hurry)* **to t. through a job** faire un travail à toute vitesse; **he tore through the book/the report** il a lu le livre/le rapport très rapidement
N *(in paper, cloth)* déchirure *f*; *(in clothes)* déchirure *f*, accroc *m*; **this page has a t. in it** cette page est déchirée

tear away VT SEP 1 *(remove ▸ wallpaper)* arracher, enlever; *Fig (▸ gloss, façade)* enlever 2 *(from activity)* arracher; **to t. sb away from sth** arracher qn à qch; **I just couldn't t. myself away** je ne pouvais tout simplement pas me décider à partir; **surely you can t. yourself away from your work for ten minutes?** tu peux quand même laisser ton travail dix minutes!

tear down VT SEP 1 *(remove ▸ poster)* arracher 2 *(demolish ▸ building)* démolir; *Fig (▸ argument)* démolir, mettre par terre

tear into VT INSEP 1 *(attack, rush at)* se précipiter sur; **the boxers tore into each other** les boxeurs se sont jetés l'un sur l'autre 2 *Fam (reprimand)* enguirlander, passer un savon à; *(criticize)* taper sur, descendre (en flèche); **he really tore into me over my exam results** il m'a bien engueulé au sujet de mes résultats d'examen; **the critics have really torn into his latest film** les critiques ont complètement descendu son dernier film 3 *(bite into ▸ of teeth, knife)* s'enfoncer dans

tear off VT SEP *(tape, wrapper)* arracher, enlever en arrachant; *(along perforations)* détacher; *(clothing)* retirer *ou* enlever rapidement; *Br Fam* **to t. sb off a strip, to t. a strip off sb** passer un savon à qn, enguirlander qn

tear out VT SEP *(page)* arracher; *(coupon, cheque)* détacher; *also Fig* **to t. one's hair out** s'arracher les cheveux

tear up VT SEP 1 *(paper, letter)* déchirer (en morceaux); *Fig (agreement, contract)* déchirer 2 *(pull up ▸ fence, weeds, surface)* arracher; *(▸ tree)* déraciner

tear² [tɪə(r)] N *(from eye)* larme *f*; **to be in tears** être en larmes; **to burst into tears** fondre en larmes; **to shed tears** verser des larmes; **I shed no tears over her resignation** sa démission ne m'a pas ému outre mesure *ou* ne m'a pas arraché de larmes; **to shed tears of joy** pleurer de joie, verser des larmes de joie; **he had tears** *or* **there were tears in his eyes** il avait les larmes aux yeux; **to be on the verge of tears, to be near to tears** être au bord des larmes; **to be moved to tears** être ému aux larmes; *Fig* **to be bored to tears** s'ennuyer à mourir
▸▸ ***tear duct*** canal *m* lacrymal; ***tear gas*** gaz *m* lacrymogène

tearaway ['teərə,weɪ] N *Br Fam* casse-cou *mf inv*

teardrop ['tɪədrɒp] N larme *f*

tearful ['tɪəfʊl] ADJ 1 *(emotional ▸ departure, occasion)* larmoyant; *(▸ story, account)* larmoyant, à faire pleurer; **they said a t. goodbye** ils se sont dit au revoir en pleurant 2 *(person)* en larmes, qui pleure; *(face)* en larmes; *(voice)* larmoyant; **I'm feeling a bit t.** j'ai envie de pleurer

tearfully ['tɪəfʊlɪ] ADV en pleurant, les larmes aux yeux

tearing ['teərɪŋ] N déchirement *m*
ADJ 1 **a t. sound** *(from paper)* un bruit de déchirement; *(from stitching)* un (bruit de) craquement 2 *Br (as intensifier)* **to be in a t. hurry** être terriblement pressé

tearjerker ['tɪə,dʒɜːkə(r)] N *Fam* **the film/the book is a real t.** c'est un film/un livre à faire pleurer[□]

tearless ['tɪəlɪs] ADJ sans larmes

tear-off ['teərɒf] ADJ *(label)* perforé; *(reply slip)* détachable
▸▸ *Comput* ***tear-off menu*** menu *m* flottant

tearoom ['tiːruːm] N salon *m* de thé

tearstained ['tɪəsteɪnd] ADJ barbouillé de larmes

tease [tiːz] VT 1 *(person)* taquiner; *(sexually)* allumer; *(animal)* tourmenter; **to t. sb about sth** taquiner qn à propos de qch
2 *(fabric)* peigner; *(wool)* peigner, carder
3 *(coax)* **he teased the wire through the slot** à force de patience, il a réussi à faire passer le fil dans la fente; **he teased the engine into life** à force de patience, il a réussi à faire démarrer le moteur
4 *Am (hair)* crêper
VI faire des taquineries; **I'm only teasing** c'est pour rire
N *Fam (person)* taquin(e)[□] *m,f*; *(sexually)* allumeuse *f*; **don't be such a t.!** ne sois pas si taquin!

▸ **tease out** VT SEP 1 *(wool, hair)* démêler 2 *(information, facts)* faire ressortir; **to t. out a problem** débrouiller *ou* démêler un problème, tirer un problème au clair

teasel ['tiːzəl] N *Bot* cardère *f*

teaser ['tiːzə(r)] N *Fam* 1 *(person)* taquin(e)[□] *m,f* 2 *(problem)* problème *m* difficile[□], colle *f* 3 *Mktg* aguiche[□] *f*
▸▸ *Mktg* ***teaser ad*** aguiche[□] *f*; *Mktg* ***teaser advertising (technique)*** aguichage *m*, teasing *m*; *Mktg* ***teaser campaign*** campagne *f* teasing[□]

teasing ['tiːzɪŋ] N *(UNCOUNT) (tormenting)* taquineries *fpl*
ADJ taquin

teasingly ['tiːzɪŋlɪ] ADV *(in order to tease)* pour (me/te/*etc*) taquiner, par taquinerie

teaspoon ['tiːspuːn] N *(spoon, measure)* cuiller *f ou* cuillère *f* à café

teaspoonful ['tiːspuːn,fʊl] ADJ cuiller *f ou* cuillère *f* à café *(mesure)*

teat [tiːt] N 1 *(on breast)* mamelon *m*, bout *m* de sein; *(of animal)* tétine *f*, tette *f*; *(for milking)* trayon *m* 2 *Br (on bottle)* tétine *f*; *(dummy)* tétine *f*, sucette *f*

teatime ['tiːtaɪm] N l'heure *f* du thé

teazel = **teasel**

tech [tek] N *Br Fam Sch (abbr* **technical college***)* ≃ IUT[□] *m*

techie ['tekɪ] N *Fam* = terme péjoratif ou humoristique désignant un informaticien

technical ['teknɪkəl] ADJ 1 *(gen) & Tech* technique; **don't get too t.** n'emploie pas de termes trop techniques 2 *(according to rules)* technique; **for t. reasons** pour des raisons d'ordre technique; *Law* **the judgment was quashed on a t. point** le jugement a été cassé pour vice de forme *ou* de procédure; *Fig* **it's a purely t. point** ce n'est qu'un point de détail
▸▸ ***technical college*** ≃ IUT *m*; *St Exch* ***technical correction*** correction *f* d'un cours en Bourse; ***technical drawing*** dessin *m* industriel; ***technical education*** enseignement *m* technique; *Br* ***technical hitch*** incident *m* technique; *Law* ***technical offence*** quasi-délit *m*; ***technical school*** ≃ collège *m* technique, ≃ lycée *m* d'enseignement professionnel; *Comput* ***technical support*** support *m* technique; ***technical term*** terme *m* technique; ***technical writing*** rédaction *f* technique

technicality [,teknɪ'kælətɪ] *(pl* **technicalities***)* N 1 *(technical nature)* technicité *f* 2 *(formal detail)* détail *m ou* considération *f* (d'ordre) technique; *(technical term)* terme *m* technique; **it's only a t.** ce n'est qu'un détail technique; *Law* **to lose one's case on a t.** perdre un procès pour vice de forme

technically ['teknɪklɪ] ADV 1 *(on a technical level)* sur un plan technique; *(in technical terms)* en termes techniques; **t., it shouldn't be able to fly** d'un point de vue technique, il ne devrait pas pouvoir voler; **t. advanced** de pointe, sophistiqué, avancé sur le plan technique 2 *(in theory)* en théorie, en principe; **t., I'm in charge** théoriquement, c'est moi le responsable

technician [tek'nɪʃən] N technicien(enne) *m,f*

Technicolor® ['teknɪ,kʌlə(r)] N Technicolor® *m*; **in (glorious) T.** en Technicolor®
ADJ en Technicolor®

technique [tek'niːk] N technique *f*

techno ['teknəʊ] N *Mus* techno *f*

technobabble ['teknəʊ,bæbəl] N jargon *m* technique

technocracy [tek'nɒkrəsɪ] *(pl* **technocracies***)* N technocratie *f*

technocrat ['teknəkræt] N technocrate *mf*

technological [,teknə'lɒdʒɪkəl] ADJ technologique

technologist [tek'nɒlədʒɪst] N technologue *mf*, technologiste *mf*

technology [tek'nɒlədʒɪ] *(pl* **technologies***)* N technologie *f*; **the latest t.** la technologie de pointe *ou* la plus avancée
▸▸ ***technology transfer*** transfert *m* de technologie

technophobia [,teknəʊ'fəʊbɪə] N technophobie *f*

tectonic [tek'tɒnɪk] ADJ tectonique
• **tectonics** N *(UNCOUNT)* tectonique *f*

tedder ['tedə(r)] N *Agr (machine)* faneuse *f*; *(person)* faneur(euse) *m,f*

teddy ['tedɪ] *(pl* **teddies***)* N 1 *(toy)* ours *m* en peluche 2 *(garment)* teddy *m*
▸▸ ***teddy bear*** ours *m* en peluche; *Br* ***teddy boy*** ≃ blouson *m* noir *(personne)*

tedious ['tiːdɪəs] ADJ *(activity, work)* ennuyeux, fastidieux; *(time)* ennuyeux; *(journey)* fatigant, pénible; *(person)* pénible; **it's a very t. job** c'est un travail très fastidieux *ou* pénible; **as he explained in t. detail** comme il l'a expliqué en de fastidieux détails

tediously ['tiːdɪəslɪ] ADV péniblement; *(monotonously)* de façon monotone, fastidieusement

tediousness ['tiːdɪəsnɪs] N *(of job, life)* ennui *m*, monotonie *f*

tee [tiː] *Golf* N *(peg)* tee *m*; *(area)* tertre *m ou* point *m* de départ; **the 17th t.** le départ du 17ème trou
VT placer sur le tee
▸▸ ***tee peg*** tee *m*; ***tee shirt*** tee-shirt *m*, t-shirt *m*

▸ **tee off** VI *Golf* jouer sa balle *ou* partir du tee *(du tertre de départ)*; *Fig* commencer, démarrer
VT SEP *Am Fam (annoy)* agacer[□], casser les pieds à; **he really tees me off with his arrogance** son arrogance m'énerve vraiment[□]; **I'm teed off** j'en ai ras le bol *ou* marre

▸ **tee up** VT SEP 1 *Golf* **to t. up the ball** placer la balle sur le tee 2 *Fig* **to t. up a deal** préparer le terrain pour obtenir un contrat; **to t. up a job for sb** apporter un travail à qn sur un plateau
VI *Golf* placer la balle sur le tee

teem [tiːm] VI 1 *(be crowded)* grouiller, fourmiller; **the streets were teeming (with people)** les rues grouillaient (de monde); **the river is teeming with fish** la rivière grouille de poissons 2 *(rain)* **the rain was teeming down** la pluie tombait à verse; **it's absolutely teeming (with rain)** il pleut à verse *ou* à torrents

teeming ['tiːmɪŋ] ADJ 1 *(streets)* grouillant de monde; *(crowds, shoppers)* grouillant, fourmillant; *(ants, insects etc)* grouillant 2 *(rain)* battant, torrentiel

teen [tiːn] ADJ *(teenage ▸ fashion, magazine)* pour adolescents *ou* jeunes
N *(teenager)* jeune *mf (entre 13 et 19 ans)*, adolescent(e) *m,f*
▸▸ ***teen idol*** idole *f* des jeunes

teenage ['tiːneɪdʒ] ADJ *(boy, girl)* jeune, adolescent; *(habits, activities)* d'adolescents; *(fashion, magazine)* pour les jeunes *ou* adolescents; **the t. years** l'adolescence *f*
▸▸ ***teenage acne*** acné *f* juvénile; ***teenage movie*** film *m* pour adolescents

teenager ['tiːnˌeɪdʒə(r)] N jeune *mf (entre 13 et 19 ans)*, adolescent(e) *m,f*

teens [tiːnz] NPL 1 *(age)* adolescence *f (entre 13 et 19 ans)*; **she's in her t.** c'est une adolescente **2** *(numbers)* = les chiffres entre 13 et 19

teenybopper ['tiːnɪˌbɒpə(r)] N *Fam* petite minette *f*

teeny-weeny [ˌtiːnɪ'wiːnɪ], *Am* **teeny-tiny** [ˌtiːnɪ'taɪnɪ] ADJ *Fam* tout petit[□], minuscule[□]

teeter ['tiːtə(r)] VI *(person)* chanceler; *(pile, object)* vaciller, être sur le point de tomber; *Fig* **to t. on the brink of sth** être au bord de qch, friser qch
N jeu *m* de bascule

teeth [tiːθ] *pl of* **tooth**

teethe [tiːð] VI faire *ou* percer ses premières dents; **to be teething** commencer à faire ses dents

teething ['tiːðɪŋ] N poussée *f* dentaire, dentition *f*
▸▸ ***teething ring*** anneau *m* de dentition; ***teething troubles*** douleurs *fpl* provoquées par la poussée des dents; *Fig* difficultés *fpl* initiales *ou* de départ

teetotal [tiː'təʊtəl] ADJ *(person)* qui ne boit jamais d'alcool; *(organization)* antialcoolique

teetotalism [tiː'təʊtəlɪzəm] N abstention *f* de toute boisson alcoolisée

teetotaller, *Am* **teetotaler** [tiː'təʊtlə(r)] N = personne qui ne boit jamais d'alcool

TEFL ['tefəl] N *(abbr* **Teaching (of) English as a Foreign Language**) enseignement *m* de l'anglais langue étrangère

tegument ['tegjʊmənt] N tégument *m*

Tehran, Teheran [ˌteə'rɑːn] N Téhéran

tel. *(written abbr* **telephone**) tél

telebanking ['telɪˌbæŋkɪŋ] N télébanque *f*

telecast ['telɪkɑːst] N émission *f* de télévision, programme *m* télédiffusé
VT diffuser, téléviser

telecaster ['telɪˌkɑːstə(r)] N *(broadcaster)* téléaste *mf*; *(broadcasting company)* société *f* de télédiffusion

telecine [ˌtelɪ'sɪnɪ] N télécinéma *m*

telecom ['telɪkɒm] N *(UNCOUNT) (abbr* **telecommunications**) télécoms *fpl*

telecommunications ['telɪkəˌmjuːnɪ'keɪʃənz] N télécommunications *fpl*
▸▸ ***telecommunications engineer*** technicien *m* des télécommunications; ***telecommunications industry*** industrie *f* des télécommunications; ***telecommunications link*** liaison *f* de télécommunications; ***telecommunications media*** médias *mpl* de télécommunication; ***telecommunications network*** réseau *m* de télécommunications; ***telecommunications satellite*** satellite *m* de télécommunications

telecommute ['telɪkəmjuːt] VI faire du télétravail, télétravailler

telecommuter ['telɪkəˌmjuːtə(r)] N télétravailleur(euse) *m,f*

telecommuting ['telɪkəˌmjuːtɪŋ] N télétravail *m*

telecoms ['telɪkɒmz] = **telecom**

teleconference ['telɪˌkɒnfərəns] N téléconférence *f*

teleconferencing ['telɪˌkɒnfərənsɪŋ] N téléconférence *f*

telefilm ['telɪfɪlm] N téléfilm *m*

telegenic [ˌtelɪ'dʒenɪk] ADJ télégénique

telegram ['telɪgræm] N télégramme *m*; *(in press, diplomacy)* dépêche *f*; **by t.** par télégramme

telegraph ['telɪgrɑːf] N 1 *(system)* télégraphe *m* **2** *(telegram)* télégramme *m*
COMP *(service, wire)* télégraphique
VT 1 *(news)* télégraphier; *(money)* télégraphier, envoyer par télégramme; **she telegraphed us to say she couldn't come** elle nous a télégraphié *ou* envoyé un télégramme pour dire qu'elle ne pouvait pas venir **2** *Sport* **to t. a punch/pass** téléphoner un coup/une passe
VI télégraphier; **he telegraphed to say he'd be late** il a télégraphié *ou* envoyé un télégramme pour dire qu'il serait en retard
▸▸ ***telegraph pole, telegraph post*** poteau *m* télégraphique

telegrapher [tɪ'legrəfə(r)] N télégraphiste *mf*

telegraphese [ˌtelɪgrɑː'fiːz] N langage *m ou* style *m* télégraphique

telegraphic [ˌtelɪ'græfɪk] ADJ télégraphique
▸▸ ***telegraphic payment*** paiement *m* télégraphique; ***telegraphic transfer*** transfert *m* télégraphique

telegraphist [tɪ'legrəfɪst] N télégraphiste *mf*

telegraphy [tɪ'legrəfɪ] N télégraphie *f*

telejector ['telɪdʒektə(r)] N *TV* projecteur *m* de télévision

telekinesis [ˌtelɪkaɪ'niːsɪs] N télékinésie *f*

telemarket ['telɪˌmɑːkɪt] N *Mktg* télémarché *m*

telemarketing ['telɪˌmɑːkɪtɪŋ] N *Mktg* télémarketing *m*

telematics [ˌtelɪ'mætɪks] N *(UNCOUNT)* télématique *f*

Telemessage® ['telɪˌmesɪdʒ] N *Br* télégramme *m (transmis par télex ou par téléphone)*

telemeter [tɪ'lemɪtə(r)] N télémètre *m*

teleological [ˌtelɪə'lɒdʒɪkəl] ADJ *Phil* téléologique

teleology [ˌtelɪ'ɒlədʒɪ] N *Phil* téléologie *f*

telepathic [ˌtelɪ'pæθɪk] ADJ *(person)* télépathe; *(message, means)* télépathique; **tell me, I'm not t.!** dis-le moi, je ne suis pas médium!

telepathically [ˌtelɪ'pæθɪkəlɪ] ADV *(communicate)* par télépathie

telepathy [tɪ'lepəθɪ] N télépathie *f*, transmission *f* de pensée

telepayment ['telɪˌpeɪmənt] N télépaiement *m*

telephone ['telɪfəʊn] N 1 *(for communication)* téléphone *m*; **to be on the t.** *(be talking)* être au téléphone, téléphoner; *(be subscriber)* avoir le téléphone, être abonné au téléphone; **the boss is on the t. for you** le patron te demande au téléphone; **you're wanted on the t.** on vous demande au téléphone; **to answer the t.** répondre au téléphone; **to order sth over the** *or* **by t.** commander qch par téléphone **2** *Am (game)* téléphone *m* arabe
COMP *(receiver)* de téléphone; *(message)* téléphonique; *(charges)* téléphonique, de téléphone; *(service)* des télécommunications; **to have a good t. manner** savoir bien parler au téléphone
VT *(person)* téléphoner à, appeler (au téléphone); *(place)* téléphoner à, appeler; *(news, message, invitation)* téléphoner, envoyer par téléphone; **I'll t. him later** je lui téléphonerai *ou* je l'appellerai plus tard; **to t. the United States/home** téléphoner aux États-Unis/chez soi
VI *(call)* téléphoner, appeler; *(be on phone)* être au téléphone; **he telephoned to say he'd be late** il a téléphoné *ou* appelé pour dire qu'il serait en retard
▸▸ ***telephone banking*** opérations *fpl* bancaires par téléphone, banque *f* à domicile; ***telephone bill*** facture *f* de téléphone; ***telephone book*** annuaire *m* (téléphonique); ***telephone booking*** réservation *f* par téléphone; ***telephone booth,*** *Br* ***telephone box*** cabine *f* téléphonique; ***telephone call*** appel *m* téléphonique, coup *m* de téléphone; *Mktg* ***telephone canvassing*** prospection *f* téléphonique, démarchage *m* à distance, télédémarchage *m*; ***telephone code*** indicatif *m*; ***telephone conversation*** entretien *m* téléphonique; ***telephone directory*** annuaire *m* (téléphonique); ***telephone exchange*** central *m* téléphonique; *Mktg* ***telephone follow-up*** relance *f* téléphonique; ***telephone interview*** entretien *m* téléphonique, entretien *m* par téléphone; ***telephone jack*** fiche *f* téléphonique; *Br* ***telephone kiosk*** cabine *f* téléphonique; ***telephone line*** ligne *f* téléphonique; ***telephone link*** liaison *f* téléphonique; ***telephone number*** numéro *m* de téléphone; ***telephone operator*** téléphoniste *mf*, standardiste *mf*; ***telephone order*** commande *f* téléphonique *ou* par téléphone; *Mktg* ***telephone prospecting*** télédémarchage *m*, démarchage *m* à distance; ***telephone sales*** ventes *fpl* par téléphone, téléventes *fpl*; ***telephone salesman*** télévendeur *m*, télé-acteur *m*; ***telephone saleswoman*** télévendeuse *f*, télé-actrice *f*; ***tel[...] phone selling*** vente *f* par téléphone, télévente; ***telephone subscriber*** abonné(e) *m,f* du tél[...]phone; ***telephone survey*** enquête *f* téléph[...]nique, enquête *f* par téléphone; ***telephon[...] switchboard*** standard *m* téléphonique

telephonic [ˌtelɪ'fɒnɪk] ADJ téléphonique

telephonist [tɪ'lefənɪst] N *Br* standardiste *m[...]* téléphoniste *mf*

telephony [tɪ'lefənɪ] N téléphonie *f*

telephotography [ˌtelɪfə'tɒgrəfɪ] N téléphot[...]graphie *f*

telephoto lens [ˌtelɪ'fəʊtəʊ-] N téléobjectif *m*

teleplay ['telɪpleɪ] N scénario *m* de téléfilm

teleprinter ['telɪˌprɪntə(r)] N *Br* téléscripteur *[...]* téléimprimeur *m*

teleprocessing [ˌtelɪ'prəʊsesɪŋ] N *Comput* tél[...] gestion *f*

Teleprompter® ['telɪˌprɒmptə(r)] N téléprom[...]teur *m*, télésouffleur *m*

telesales ['telɪseɪlz] N *Mktg* vente *f* par tél[...] phone, télévente *f*
▸▸ ***telesales operator*** téléopérateur(trice) *m,f*

telescope ['telɪskəʊp] N télescope *m*, longu[...] vue *f*; *Astron* télescope *m*, lunette *f* astrono[...]mique
VT 1 *(make collapse* ▸ *parts)* emboîter **2** *F[...] (shorten, condense* ▸ *parts, report)* condense[...] abréger
VI 1 *(collapse* ▸ *parts)* s'emboîter **2** *(railway ca[...]riages)* se télescoper; **the carriages telescope[...] into each other** les wagons se sont télescopés

telescopic [ˌtelɪ'skɒpɪk] ADJ *(aerial)* télesc[...]pique; *(umbrella)* pliant
▸▸ ***telescopic lens*** téléobjectif *m*; ***telescopic sig[...]*** lunette *f*

teleselling [ˌtelɪ'selɪŋ] N *Mktg* vente *f* par télé[...] phone

teleshopping ['telɪˌʃɒpɪŋ] N *Mktg* achats *mpl* [...] domicile, téléachat *m*

teletex ['telɪteks] N Télétex® *m*

teletext ['telɪtekst] N télétexte *m*, vidéographie diffusée

telethon ['telɪθɒn] N téléthon *m*

Teletype® ['telɪtaɪp] N Télétype® *m*

teletypewriter [ˌtelɪ'taɪpraɪtə(r)] N *Am* télé[...]scripteur *m*, téléimprimeur *m*

televangelism [ˌtelɪ'vændʒəlɪzəm] N = prêch[...] évangéliste à la télévision

televangelist [ˌtelɪ'vændʒəlɪst] N = évangélist[...] qui prêche à la télévision

televiewer ['telɪvjuːə(r)] N téléspectateur(trice) *m,f*

televise ['telɪvaɪz] VT téléviser

television ['telɪˌvɪʒən] N 1 *(system, broadcast[...])* télévision *f*; **to watch t.** regarder la télévisio[...] **we don't watch much t.** on ne regarde pas so[...]vent la télévision; **to go on t.** passer à la télév[...]sion; **to work in t.** travailler à la télévision; **a fil[...] made for t.** un téléfilm; **it makes/doesn't mak[...] good t.** ça a/n'a pas un bon impact télévisuel *(set)* téléviseur *m*, (poste *m* de) télévision *f*; **[...] saw her on (the) t.** je l'ai vue à la télévision; **[...] turn the t. up/down** monter le son de/baisser l[...] son de la télévision; **to turn the t. on/off** allume[...] éteindre la télévision; **is there anything good o[...] t. tonight?** qu'est-ce qu'il y a de bien à la télév[...]sion ce soir?; **colour/black-and-white t.** télévisio[...] *f* (en) couleur/(en) noir et blanc
COMP *(station, screen)* de télévision; *(picture)* t[...]lévisé; *(satellite)* de télédiffusion; **to make a t. a[...]pearance** passer à la télévision
▸▸ ***television advertisement*** publicité *f* télévisée; ***television advertising*** publicité *f* télévisée; ***telev[...]sion audience*** *(reached by advertising)* audience télévisuelle; ***television broadcaster*** télédiffuseu[...] *m*; ***television broadcasting*** télédiffusion *f*; ***telev[...]sion broadcasting network*** réseau *m* de télédistr[...]bution; ***television camera*** caméra *f* (d[...] télévision); ***television campaign*** campagne *f* télé[...]visuelle; ***television channel*** chaîne *f* de télév[...]sion; ***television commercial*** spot *m*; ***televisio[...] crew*** équipe *f* de télévision; ***television dram[...]*** drame *m* télévisé; ***television engineer*** réparateu[...]

n de télévisions; ***television film*** téléfilm *m*, film *m* ›our la télévision; ***television guide*** journal *m* de élévision; ***television interview*** interview *f* télévi-ée *ou* à la télévision; ***television journalism*** jour-ıalisme *m* de télévision; ***television journalist*** ɔurnaliste *mf* de télévision; *Br* ***television licence*** *fee)* redevance *f*; *(document)* quittance *f* de télé-ision; ***television lounge*** salle *f* de télévision; ***tele-vision movie*** téléfilm *m*, film *m* pour la élévision; ***television network*** réseau *m* télévi-uel; ***television news*** journal *m* télévisé, JT *m*; ***tele-vision news reporter*** reporteur *m* d'images; ***elevision personality*** vedette *f* de la télévision; ***elevision programme*** émission *f* de télévision, ›rogramme *m* télévisé; ***television receiver*** récep-eur *m* de télévision; ***television report*** reportage *n* télévisé; ***television reporter*** téléreporter *m*; ***elevision rights*** droits *mpl* de télédiffusion; ***tele-vision room*** salle *f* de télévision; ***television series*** érie *f* télévisée; ***television set*** téléviseur *m*, poste *m* de) télévision *f*; ***television show*** specta-le *m* télévisé; ***television sponsoring*** parrainage-élévision *m*; ***television studio*** studio *m* de télévi-ion; ***television tie-in*** **1** *(film)* = téléfilm tiré d'un ivre ou d'un film; *(series)* = série télévisée tirée l'un livre ou d'un film **2** *(at conference, public event)* retransmission *f*; **there will be a t. tie-in at he conference** la conférence sera retransmise à a télévision; ***television tube*** tube *m* cathodique; ***elevision viewer*** téléspectateur(trice) *m,f*; *Mktg* ***elevision viewing panel*** panel *m* de téléspecta-eurs

elevisual [ˌtelɪˈvɪʒʊəl] **ADJ** télévisuel

elework [ˈtelɪˌwɜːk] **VI** travailler chez soi; **I'm eleworking today** je travaille chez moi aujour-l'hui

eleworking [ˈtelɪˌwɜːkɪŋ] **N** télétravail *m*

elewriting [ˈtelɪˌraɪtɪŋ] **N** téléécriture *f*

elex [ˈteleks] **N** télex *m*; **to send sth by t.** télexer ɪch

VT envoyer par télex, télexer

►► ***telex operator*** télexiste *mf*; ***telex transfer*** vire-nent *m* par télex

ELL [tel]

VT
- dire à **1–3, 7**
- raconter **4**
- dire **4–6**
- voir **9**
- comprendre **9**
- expliquer à **2**
- annoncer **4**
- distinguer **8**
- savoir **9**

VI
- dire **1**
- se faire sentir **3**
- savoir **2**

pt & pp **told** [təʊld])

VT 1 *(inform)* dire à; **to t. sb sth** dire qch à qn; **I old him the answer/what I thought** je lui ai dit la éponse/ce que je pensais; **to t. sb about** *or Lit-erary* **of sth** dire qch à qn, parler à qn de qch; **I old her about the new restaurant** je lui ai parlé lu nouveau restaurant; **she wrote to t. me of her father's death** elle m'a écrit pour m'annoncer a mort de son père; **they told me (that) they would be late** ils m'ont dit qu'ils seraient en re-ard; **I'm pleased to t. you you've won** j'ai le plaisir le vous informer *ou* annoncer que vous avez gagné; **are you telling me (that) you spent £50 on THAT?** tu ne vas pas me dire que tu as payé 50 ivres pour ça?; **let me t. you how pleased I am** aissez-moi vous dire *ou* permettez-moi de vous lire à quel point je suis heureux; **it's not easy, let me t. you!** ce n'est pas facile, je t'assure *ou* je te le lis!; **we are told that there is little hope** on nous lit qu'il y a peu d'espoir; **it's just as I told you** c'est exactement ce que je t'avais dit; **I'm told he's coming tomorrow** j'ai entendu dire *ou* on m'a dit qu'il venait demain; **so I've been told** c'est ce qu'on m'a dit; **it doesn't t. us much** cela ne nous en dit pas très long, cela ne nous apprend pas grand-chose; **can you t. me the time/your name?** pouvez-vous me dire l'heure (qu'il est)/votre nom?; **I know, Dennis told me** je sais, Dennis me 'a dit; **a little bird told me!** c'est mon petit doigt qui me l'a dit!

2 *(explain to)* expliquer à, dire à; **this brochure tells me all I need to know** cette brochure m'ex-plique tout ce que j'ai besoin de savoir; **I told him what to do in case of an emergency** je lui ai dit *ou* expliqué ce qu'il fallait faire en cas d'ur-gence; **did you t. them how to get here?** leur as-tu expliqué comment se rendre ici?; **can you t. me the way to the station/to Oxford?** pouvez-vous m'indiquer le chemin de la gare/la route d'Oxford?; **do you want me to t. you again?** vou-lez-vous que je vous le redise *ou* répète?; **who can t. me the best way to make omelettes?** qui peut me dire *ou* m'expliquer la meilleure façon de faire des omelettes?; **I can't t. you how pleased I am** je ne saurais vous dire combien je suis con-tent; **if I've told you once, I've told you a thousand times!** je te l'ai dit cent fois!; **(I'll) t. you what, let's play cards** j'ai une idée, on n'a qu'à jouer aux car-tes

3 *(instruct, order)* **to t. sb to do sth** dire à qn de faire qch; **you can't t. me what to do!** tu n'as pas à me dire ce que je dois faire!; **do as you're told!** fais ce qu'on te dit!; **t. her to wait outside** dites-lui d'attendre dehors; **I told them not to interrupt** je leur ai dit de ne pas interrompre; **I thought I told you not to run?** je croyais t'avoir interdit *ou* dé-fendu de courir?; **I told you no!** je t'ai dit non!; **he didn't need to be told twice!** il ne s'est pas fait prier!, je n'ai pas eu besoin de lui dire deux fois!

4 *(recount ► story, joke)* raconter; *(► news)* an-noncer; *(► secret)* dire, raconter; **to t. sb about sth** parler à qn de qch, parler de qch à qn, racon-ter qch à qn; **to t. sb about sb** parler à qn de qn, parler de qn à qn; **t. them about** *or* **of your life as an explorer** racontez-leur votre vie d'explora-teur; **t. me what you know about it** dites-moi ce que vous en savez; **I'll t. you what happened** je vais vous raconter ce qui est arrivé; **could you t. me a little about yourself?** pourriez-vous me par-ler un peu de vous-même?; **what does this t. us about his character?** qu'est-ce que cela nous ap-prend sur son caractère?; **I told myself it didn't matter** je me suis dit que cela n'avait pas d'im-portance; **I could t. you a thing or two about his role in it** je pourrais vous en dire long sur son rôle dans tout cela; **don't t. me you got lost!** ne me dites pas que vous vous êtes perdu!; **don't t. me, let me guess!** ne me dites rien, laissez-moi deviner!; *Fam* **t. it like it is!** n'ayez pas peur de dire la vérité!ᵁ; **to hear t. that...** entendre dire que... + *indicative*

5 *(recite)* **to t. one's beads** dire *ou* égrener son chapelet

6 *(utter ► truth, lie)* dire, raconter; **to t. sb the truth** dire la vérité à qn; **to t. lies** mentir, dire des mensonges; *Fig* **I t. a lie!** je me trompe!

7 *(assure)* dire à, assurer; **didn't I t. you?, I told you so!, what did I t. you!** je vous l'avais bien dit!; **let me t. you!** *(believe me)* je vous assure!, croyez-moi!; *(as threat)* tenez-vous-le pour dit!; **I can t. you!** c'est moi qui vous le dis!; *Fam* **you're telling me!, t. me about it!** à qui le dis-tu!

8 *(distinguish)* distinguer; **to t. right from wrong** distinguer le bien du mal; **you can hardly t. the difference between them** on voit *ou* distingue à peine la différence entre eux; **you can t. him by his voice** on le reconnaît à sa voix; **she can't t. the time** elle ne sait pas lire l'heure

9 *(see)* voir; *(know)* savoir; *(understand)* com-prendre; **you could t. he was disappointed** on voyait bien qu'il était déçu; **no one could t. whether the good weather would last** personne ne pouvait dire si le beau temps allait durer; **I can t. it from the look in your eyes** ça se lit dans tes yeux; **there's no telling what he might do next/how he'll react** (il est) impossible de dire ce qu'il est susceptible de faire ensuite/com-ment il réagira

VI 1 *(reveal)* **that would be telling!** ce serait trahir un secret!; **I won't t.** je ne dirai rien à personne; **time will t.** qui vivra verra, le temps nous le dira

2 *(know)* savoir; **how can I t.?** comment le sau-rais-je?; **who can t.?** qui peut savoir?, qui sait?; **you never can t.** on ne sait jamais; **it's difficult** *or* **hard to t.** c'est difficile à dire; **it's too early to t.** il est trop tôt pour se prononcer

3 *(have effect)* se faire sentir, avoir de l'in-fluence; **her age is beginning to t.** elle commence à accuser son âge; **the strain is beginning to t.** la tension commence à se faire sentir

4 *Literary (story, book)* **to t. of sth** raconter qch; **the first volume tells of the postwar period** le pre-mier volume raconte la période d'après-guerre; **I've heard t. of phantom ships** j'ai entendu parler de navires fantômes

5 *Literary (bear witness)* **to t. of** témoigner de; **the scars told of his reckless life** ses cicatrices té-moignaient de sa vie mouvementée

► **tell apart VT SEP** distinguer (entre); **I couldn't t. the twins apart** je ne pouvais pas distinguer les jumeaux l'un de l'autre

► **tell off VT SEP** *(scold)* réprimander, gronder; **to t. sb off for doing sth** gronder *ou* réprimander qn pour avoir fait qch

► **tell on VT INSEP 1** *(denounce)* dénoncer; **don't t. on me** ne me dénonce pas **2** *(have effect on)* se faire sentir sur, produire un effet sur; **her age is telling on her** elle accuse son âge; **the strain soon began to t. on her health** la tension ne tarda pas à avoir un effet néfaste sur sa santé

teller [ˈtelə(r)] **N 1** *(in bank)* **(bank) t.** caissier(ère) *m,f*, guichetier(ère) *m,f* **2** *Pol (of votes)* scrutateur (trice) *m,f* **3** *(of story)* **(story) t.** conteur(euse) *m,f*, narrateur(trice) *m,f*

telling [ˈtelɪŋ] **ADJ 1** *(effective ► style)* efficace; *(► account)* saisissant; *(► remark, argument)* qui porte; **it was a t. blow** le coup fut bien asséné, le coup porta **2** *(revealing ► smile, figures, evi-dence)* révélateur, éloquent; **a t. look** un regard qui en dit long; **her remarks were very t.** ses re-marques étaient très révélatrices

N récit *m*, narration *f*; **the story is long in the t.** l'histoire est longue à raconter

telltale [ˈtelteɪl] **N** *Br (person)* rapporteur(euse) *m,f*, cafteur(euse) *m,f*

ADJ *(marks)* révélateur; *(look, blush, nod)* élo-quent; **a t. sign** un signe révélateur

tellurium [teˈlʊərɪəm] **N** *Chem* tellure *m*

telly [ˈtelɪ] *(pl* **tellies) N** *Br Fam* télé *f*; **on (the) t.** à la télé

►► ***telly addict*** drogué(e) *m,f* de la télé

Telnet [ˈtelnet] **N** *Comput* Telnet *m*

temerity [tɪˈmerətɪ] **N** témérité *f*, audace *f*; **he had the t. to suggest I had lied** il a eu l'audace *ou* le front d'insinuer que j'avais menti

temp [temp] **N** *(abbr* **temporary employee)** intéri-maire *mf*

ADJ to do t. work faire de l'intérim

VI faire de l'intérim

temper [ˈtempə(r)] **N 1** *(character)* caractère *m*, tempérament *m*; **to have an even t.** être d'un tem-pérament calme *ou* d'humeur égale; **to have a quick** *or* **hot t.** se mettre facilement en colère; **he's got a foul** *or* **an awful t.** il a mauvais carac-tère

2 *(patience)* patience *f*; *(calm)* calme *m*, sang-froid *m inv*; **do try and keep your t.** essayez donc de garder votre calme *ou* sang-froid, essayez donc de vous maîtriser; **to lose one's t.** perdre patience, se mettre en colère; **to lose one's t. with sb** s'emporter contre qn

3 *(mood)* humeur *f*; *(bad mood)* (crise *f* de) co-lère *f*, mauvaise humeur *f*; **to be in a (bad) t.** être de mauvaise humeur; **to fly into a t.** piquer une colère

4 *Metal* trempe *f*

VT 1 *(moderate ► passions)* modérer, tempérer; *(►pain, suffering)* atténuer; **justice tempered with mercy** la justice tempérée de pitié **2** *Metal* trem-per **3** *(piano)* accorder par tempérament

EXCLAM *Fam* **t.(, t.)!** on se calme!, du calme!

►► ***temper tantrum*** crise *f* de colère; **to have** *or* **to throw a t. tantrum** piquer une colère

tempera [ˈtempərə] **N** *(paint)* tempera *f*, dé-trempe *f*

►► ***tempera painting*** détrempe *f*

temperament [ˈtempərəmənt] **N** *(character)* tempérament *m*, nature *f*; *(moodiness)* humeur *f* changeante *ou* lunatique

temperamental [ˌtempərəˈmentəl] **ADJ 1** *(moody ► person)* capricieux, lunatique **2** *(un-predictable ► animal, machine)* capricieux; **his knee has been a bit t. since his accident** son genou lui joue des tours depuis son accident **3** *(relating to character)* du tempérament, de la personna-lité; **he has a t. aversion to conflict/hard work** fon-damentalement, il déteste les conflits/le travail

temperamentally [ˌtempərəˈmentəlɪ] ADV de par son caractère; **they were t. unsuited** *(couple)* leurs caractères étaient incompatibles; **she's t. unsuited to this sort of work** elle n'est pas de nature à *ou* elle n'a pas le caractère pour faire ce genre de travail

temperance [ˈtempərəns] N 1 *(moderation)* modération *f*, sobriété *f* 2 *(abstinence from alcohol)* tempérance *f*
►► ***temperance hotel*** = hôtel où l'on ne sert pas de boissons alcoolisées; ***temperance movement*** mouvement *m* antialcoolique; ***temperance society*** société *f* de tempérance, ligue *f* antialcoolique

temperate [ˈtempərət] ADJ 1 *(climate)* tempéré 2 *(moderate ► person)* modéré, mesuré; *(► character, appetite)* modéré; *(► reaction, criticism)* modéré, sobre

temperature [ˈtemprətʃə(r)] N 1 *Med* température *f*; **to have** *or* **to run a t.** avoir de la température *ou* de la fièvre; **she has a t. of 39°C** elle a 39° de fièvre; **to take sb's t.** prendre la température de qn; *Fig* **to take the t. of a situation** prendre le pouls d'une situation; **her contribution certainly raised the t. of the debate** son intervention a sans aucun doute fait monter le ton du débat 2 *Met & Phys* température *f*; **a drop in t.** une baisse de température; **the t. fell overnight** la température a baissé du jour au lendemain; **temperatures will be in the low twenties** il fera un peu plus de vingt degrés
►► ***temperature chart*** feuille *f* de température; ***temperature gauge*** indicateur *m* de température; ***temperature sensor*** capteur *m* de température

tempered [ˈtempəd] ADJ *(steel)* trempé

-tempered [ˈtempəd] SUFF **good-/bad-t.** de bonne/mauvaise humeur; **an even-t. person** une personne d'humeur égale

tempest [ˈtempɪst] N *Literary* tempête *f*, orage *m*

tempestuous [temˈpestjʊəs] ADJ 1 *(weather)* de tempête; *(sea)* tumultueux, *Literary* tempétueux 2 *(person)* impétueux, fougueux; *(meeting)* agité; *(relationship)* tumultueux; *(argument)* violent

tempestuously [temˈpestjʊəslɪ] ADV 1 *Literary* **the winds blew t. outside** un vent tempétueux soufflait au dehors 2 *(violently ► to argue etc)* violemment

tempestuousness [temˈpestjʊəsnɪs] N 1 *(of weather, sea)* violence *f* 2 *(of person)* impétuosité *f*, fougue *f*; *(of meeting)* caractère *m* orageux; *(of relationship)* violence *f*; *(of crowd)* turbulence *f*, agitation *f*

temping [ˈtempɪŋ] N intérim *m*; **to do some t.** faire de l'intérim
►► ***temping agency*** société *f* d'intérim

Templar [ˈtemplə(r)] N *Hist (in crusades)* **Knight T.** chevalier *m* du Temple, templier *m*

template [ˈtemplɪt] N 1 *Tech* gabarit *m*, calibre *m*, patron *m* 2 *Comput (for keyboard)* réglette *f*; *(for program)* modèle *m*; *(for DTP document)* gabarit *m*

temple [ˈtempəl] N 1 *Rel* temple *m* 2 *Anat* tempe *f*

tempo [ˈtempəʊ] *(pl* **tempos** *or* **tempi** [-piː]) N tempo *m*

temporal[1] [ˈtempərəl] ADJ 1 *(gen) & Gram* temporel 2 *(secular)* temporel, séculier

temporal[2] ADJ *Anat* temporal

temporarily [*Br* ˈtempərərəlɪ, *Am* ˌtempəˈrerəlɪ] ADV *(provisionally)* provisoirement; *(for a time)* temporairement; **we were t. delayed** nous avons été un peu retardés

temporary [*Br* ˈtempərərɪ, *Am* ˈtempərerɪ] ADJ *(accommodation, solution, powers)* temporaire, provisoire; *(employee, employment)* temporaire, intérimaire; *(improvement)* passager, momentané; *(relief)* passager; **on a t. basis** à titre temporaire; **he suffered t. hearing loss** il a eu une perte momentanée de l'ouïe; **this will at least give you t. relief** cela vous soulagera pendant un moment
►► ***temporary contract*** *(for employment)* contrat *m* de mission d'intérim, contrat *m* temporaire; *Comput* ***temporary file*** fichier *m* temporaire; ***temporary replacement*** suppléance *f*; *Am Law* ***temporary restraining order*** injonction *f* du tribunal; ***temporary surface*** *(of road)* revêtement *m* provisoire; ***temporary tattoo*** tatouage *m* éphémère

temporize, -ise [ˈtempəraɪz] VI *Formal* temporiser, chercher à gagner du temps

tempt [tempt] VT *(entice)* tenter, donner envie à; *(seduce)* tenter, séduire; *(attract)* attirer, tenter; **to t. sb to do sth** *or* **into doing sth** donner à qn l'envie de faire qch; **did you hit him? – no, but I was sorely tempted** tu l'as frappé? – non, mais ce n'est pas l'envie qui m'en manquait; **I'm tempted to accept their offer** je suis tenté d'accepter leur proposition; **a rival company tried to t. him away** une entreprise rivale a essayé de le débaucher en lui faisant une offre alléchante; **the mild weather tempted us into the garden** le temps doux nous a incités à aller au jardin; *Hum* **don't t. me!** n'essayez pas de me tenter!, ne me tentez pas!; **can I t. you to another sandwich?** je peux vous proposer encore un sandwich?, vous voulez encore un sandwich?; **to t. fate** *or* **Providence** tenter le sort *ou* le diable

temptation [tempˈteɪʃən] N tentation *f*; **to put t. in sb's way** exposer qn à la tentation; **it's a great t.** c'est très tentant; **to give in to t.** céder *ou* succomber à la tentation; **to resist t.** résister à la tentation; *Bible* **lead us not into t.** ne nous soumets pas à la tentation

tempter [ˈtemptə(r)] N tentateur(trice) *m,f*

tempting [ˈtemptɪŋ] ADJ *(offer)* tentant, attrayant; *(smell, meal)* appétissant

temptingly [ˈtemptɪŋlɪ] ADV d'une manière tentante; **the grapes glistened t. in their bowl** les grappes dans le plat étaient brillantes et appétissantes; **the cool water beckoned t.** l'eau fraîche donnait envie de se baigner

temptress [ˈtemptrɪs] N *Literary or Hum* tentatrice *f*

ten [ten] N *(number, numeral)* dix *m inv*; **tens of thousands of refugees** des dizaines *fpl* de milliers de réfugiés; **t. to one** *(in ratio, bets)* dix contre un; **it's t. to one we won't sell anything** je te parie que nous ne vendrons rien; *Fig* **they're t. a penny** il y en a à la pelle
PRON dix; **about t.** une dizaine
ADJ dix; **about t. people** une dizaine de personnes; *see also* **five**
►► *Bible* ***the Ten Commandments*** les dix commandements *mpl*

tenable [ˈtenəbəl] ADJ 1 *(argument, position)* défendable, soutenable 2 *(post)* que l'on occupe, auquel on est nommé; **the appointment is t. for a five-year period** on est nommé à ce poste pour cinq ans

tenacious [tɪˈneɪʃəs] ADJ 1 *(persistent ► person)* tenace, résolu; *(► prejudice, tradition)* tenace; *(► opposition)* tenace, acharné; *(► stain)* tenace 2 *(firm ► grip)* ferme, solide 3 *(long-lasting ► memory)* excellent

tenaciously [tɪˈneɪʃəslɪ] ADV avec ténacité, obstinément

tenaciousness [tɪˈneɪʃəsnɪs], **tenacity** [tɪˈnæsətɪ] N 1 *(of person)* ténacité *f*; *(of opposition)* acharnement *m*; *(of tradition)* ténacité *f* 2 *(of stain)* ténacité *f*

tenancy [ˈtenənsɪ] *(pl* **tenancies**) N 1 *(of house, land)* location *f*; **to take up the t. on a house** prendre une maison en location 2 *(period)* **(period of) t.** (période *f* de) location *f*; **during my t. of the house** quand j'étais locataire de la maison 3 *(property)* **a council t.** un logement appartenant à la municipalité, ≃ une HLM
►► ***tenancy agreement*** contrat *m* de location

tenant [ˈtenənt] N locataire *mf*; **t. for life** usufruitier(ère) *m,f*
VT habiter comme locataire, louer; **only half the farms were still tenanted** il n'y avait de locataires que dans la moitié des fermes
►► ***tenant farmer*** métayer(ère) *m,f*; ***tenant farming*** métayage *m*; ***tenant rights*** droits *mpl* du locataire

tenantry [ˈtenəntrɪ] *(pl* **tenantries**) N *Agr* ensemble *m* des métayers *ou* locataires

tench [tenʃ] *(pl* **inv**) N *Ich* tanche *f*

tend [tend] VI 1 *(be inclined)* **to t. to** avoir te dance à, tendre à; **he does t. to take himself se iously** il a vraiment tendance à se prendre a sérieux; **some people like that kind of film, but I not to** il y a des gens qui aiment ce genre de filn moi (je n'aime) pas trop; **I t. to think (that) politi is a waste of time** j'ai tendance à penser que politique est une perte de temps; **that does t. t be the case** c'est souvent le cas
2 *(colour)* **red tending to orange** rouge tirant su l'orange
3 *(go, move)* tendre; **his writings t. to** *or* **towar exoticism** ses écrits tendent vers l'exotisme
4 *(look after)* **she tended to his every wish** elle l a passé tous ses caprices, elle a fait ses quat volontés; **to t. to one's business/one's guests** s'oc cuper de ses affaires/ses invités; **to t. to sb wounds** panser *ou* soigner les blessures de qn
VT *(take care of ► sheep)* garder; *(► the sick wounded)* soigner; *(► garden)* entretenir, s'occu per de; **to t. sb's wounds** panser *ou* soigner le blessures de qn

tendency [ˈtendənsɪ] *(pl* **tendencies**) N 1 *(incli ation)* tendance *f*; **he has a t. to forget things** il tendance à tout oublier; **she has a natural t. to towards laziness** elle est d'un naturel paresseu **suicidal tendencies** des tendances suicidaires *(trend)* tendance *f*; **a growing t. towards conser atism** une tendance de plus en plus marqué vers le conservatisme

tendentious [tenˈdenʃəs] ADJ tendancieux

tendentiously [tenˈdenʃəslɪ] ADV tendancieu sement

tendentiousness [tenˈdenʃəsnɪs] N caractè *m* tendancieux

tender [ˈtendə(r)] ADJ 1 *(affectionate ► perso* tendre, affectueux, doux (douce); *(► hear smile, words, look)* tendre; *(► memories)* dou (douce); **they bade each other a t. farewell** ils s sont fait de tendres adieux; *Ironic* **I leave him t your t. mercies** je l'abandonne à vos soins
2 *(sensitive ► skin)* délicat, fragile; *(sore)* se sible, douloureux; **my knee is still t.** mon geno me fait encore mal; *Fig* **to touch sb on a t. sp** toucher le point sensible de qn
3 *(meat, vegetables)* tendre
4 *Literary (innocent ► age, youth)* tendre; **sh gave her first concert at the t. age of six** elle donné son premier concert alors qu'elle n'ava que six ans; **to be of t. years** être d'âge tendre
VT 1 *(resignation)* donner; *(apologies)* présente *(thanks)* offrir; *(bid, offer)* faire 2 *(money, far* tendre; **to t. sth to sb** tendre qch à qn
VI faire une soumission; **to t. for a contract** fai une soumission pour une adjudication, sou missionner une adjudication
N 1 *(statement of charges)* soumission *f*; **to mak** *or* **to put in a t. for sth** soumissionner *ou* faire un soumission pour qch; **to invite tenders for a jo to put a job out to t.** mettre un travail en adjud cation; **by t.** par voie d'adjudication; **a call for** un appel d'offres 2 *Rail* tender *m* 3 *Naut (shuttl* navette *f*; *(supply boat)* ravitailleur *m*
►► ***tender document*** dossier *m* d'appel d'offre ***tender form*** formule *f* de soumission; ***tender pr posal*** soumission *f* d'offre

tenderer [ˈtendərə(r)] N *Com* soumissionnai *mf*; **the successful t.** l'adjudicataire *mf*

tenderfoot [ˈtendəfʊt] *(pl* **tenderfoots** *or* **tende feet** [-fiːt]) N 1 *(beginner)* novice *mf*, nouvea (elle) *m,f* 2 *Am Fam (newcomer)* nouveau(elle venu(e)□ *m,f*

tenderhearted [ˌtendəˈhɑːtɪd] ADJ au cœ tendre, compatissant

tenderheartedness [ˌtendəˈhɑːtɪdnɪs] N com passion *f*

tenderize, -ise [ˈtendəraɪz] VT attendrir

tenderizer, -iser [ˈtendəraɪzə(r)] N attendrisse *m*

tenderloin [ˈtendəlɔɪn] N *(meat)* filet *m*

tenderly [ˈtendəlɪ] ADV tendrement, avec ten dresse

tenderness [ˈtendənɪs] N 1 *(of person, feeling* tendresse *f*, affection *f*; **she feels a certain t. f the old man** elle éprouve une certaine tendress pour ce vieux monsieur 2 *(of skin)* sensibilité *(of plant)* fragilité *f*; *(soreness)* sensibilité *f* **3** *(of meat, vegetables)* tendreté *f*

endinitis [ˌtendɪˈnaɪtəs] **N** *Med* tendinite *f*

endon [ˈtendən] **N** tendon *m*

endril [ˈtendrəl] **N 1** *Bot* vrille *f*, cirre *m* **2** *(of hair)* boucle *f*

enement [ˈtenəmənt] **N 1** *Am & Scot (block of flats)* immeuble *m* (ancien) **2** *(slum)* taudis *m*

►► *Am & Scot* ***tenement building*** immeuble *m* (ancien)

enet [ˈtenɪt] **N** *(principle)* principe *m*, dogme *m*; *(belief)* croyance *f*

enfold [ˈtenfəʊld] **ADV** dix fois autant *ou* plus, au décuple; **to increase t.** décupler

ADJ a t. increase in applications dix fois plus de demandes

en-gallon hat N chapeau *m* de cowboy

enner [ˈtenə(r)] **N** *Fam Br (ten-pound note)* billet *m* de dix livres□; *Am (ten-dollar note)* billet *m* de dix dollars□; *Br (sum)* dix livres□*fpl*

ennis [ˈtenɪs] **N** tennis *m*; **to play t.** jouer au tennis

►► ***tennis ball*** balle *f* de tennis; ***tennis club*** club *m* de tennis; ***tennis court*** court *m* de tennis; ***tennis elbow*** *(UNCOUNT)* tennis-elbow *m*, synovite *f* du coude; ***tennis player*** joueur(euse) *m,f* de tennis; ***tennis racket, tennis racquet*** raquette *f* de tennis; ***tennis shoe*** chaussure *f* de tennis, tennis *m ou f*

enon [ˈtenən] **N** *Carp* tenon *m*

enor [ˈtenə(r)] **N 1** *(general sense ► of conversation)* sens *m* général, teneur *f*; *(► of letter)* contenu *m*, teneur *f*

2 *(general flow ► of events)* cours *m*, marche *f*; **the even t. of their life** le cours paisible de leur vie

3 *Mus* ténor *m*

4 *Fin (of bill)* (terme *m* d')échéance *f*

COMP *Mus (part, voice)* de ténor; *(aria)* pour (voix de) ténor

ADV to sing t. avoir une voix de *ou* être ténor

►► ***tenor clef*** clé *f* d'ut quatrième ligne; ***tenor saxophone*** saxophone *m* ténor

enpence [ˈtenpəns] **N** *Br (amount)* dix pence *mpl*; *(coin)* pièce *f* de dix pence

enpenny [ˈtenpənɪ] **ADJ** *Br* de *ou* à dix pence

enpin bowling [ˈtenpɪn-] **N** *Br* bowling *m*; **to go t.** aller faire du bowling, aller au bowling

enpins [ˈtenpɪnz] **N** *Am* bowling *m*

ense [tens] **ADJ 1** *(person, situation, atmosphere)* tendu; *(smile)* crispé; **her voice was t. with emotion** elle avait la voix étranglée par l'émotion; **we spent several t. hours waiting for news** nous avons passé plusieurs heures à attendre des nouvelles dans un état de tension nerveuse; **things are getting t. in the war zone** la situation devient tendue dans la zone de combat **2** *(muscles, rope, spring)* tendu; **to become t.** se tendre

VT *(muscle)* tendre, bander; **to t. oneself** se raidir

N *Gram* temps *m*

▸ **tense up VI** *(muscle)* se tendre, se raidir; *(person)* se crisper, devenir tendu

VT SEP *(person)* rendre nerveux; **she's all tensed up** elle est vraiment tendue

tensely [ˈtenslɪ] **ADV** *(move, react)* de façon tendue; *(speak)* d'une voix tendue; **they waited t. for the doctor to arrive** ils ont attendu le médecin dans un état de grande tension nerveuse; **we watched t. as he approached the door** le regard tendu, nous le regardâmes s'approcher de la porte

tenseness [ˈtensnɪs] **N** tension *f*

tensile [ˈtensaɪl] **ADJ** *Tech* extensible, élastique

►► ***tensile load*** charge *f* de traction; ***tensile strength*** résistance *f* à la tension, limite *f* élastique à la tension; ***tensile stress*** force *f* de tension

tension [ˈtenʃən] **N 1** *(of person, situation, voice)* tension *f*

2 *(of muscle, rope, spring)* tension *f*; *Phys (of fluid)* tension *f*, force *f* élastique

3 *Elec* tension *f*, voltage *m*

4 *Tech* tension *f*, (force *f* de) traction *f*; **in t.** en traction

VT tendre

►► ***tension headache*** mal *m* de tête dû à la tension nerveuse

tent [tent] **N** *(for camping)* tente *f*; **to put up** *or* **to pitch a t.** monter une tente

►► *Br* ***tent peg*** piquet *m* de tente; ***tent pole*** mât *m* de tente; *Am* ***tent stake*** piquet *m* de tente

tentacle [ˈtentəkəl] **N** tentacule *m*

tentative [ˈtentətɪv] **ADJ 1** *(provisional)* provisoire; *(preliminary)* préliminaire; *(experimental)* expérimental; **our plans are only t.** nos projets ne sont pas définitifs **2** *(uncertain ► smile)* timide; *(► person)* indécis, hésitant; *(► steps)* hésitant

tentatively [ˈtentətɪvlɪ] **ADV 1** *(suggest)* provisoirement; *(act)* à titre d'essai **2** *(smile)* timidement; *(walk)* d'un pas hésitant

tenterhooks [ˈtentəhʊks] **NPL** *Tex* clous *mpl* à crochet; *Fig* **to be on t.** être sur des charbons ardents; **to keep sb on t.** tenir qn en haleine

tenth [tenθ] **N 1** *(fraction)* dixième *m*

2 *(in series)* dixième *mf*

3 *(of month)* dix *m inv*

4 *Mus* dixième *f*

ADJ dixième

ADV dixièmement; *(in contest)* en dixième position, à la dixième place; *see also* **fifth**

►► *Am Sch* ***tenth grade*** = classe de lycée pour les 14–15 ans

tenting [ˈtentɪŋ] **N** toile *f* de tente

tenuous [ˈtenjʊəs] **ADJ 1** *(flimsy ► link, relationship)* précaire, fragile; *(► evidence)* mince, faible; *(► argument)* faible **2** *(precarious ► existence)* précaire

tenuously [ˈtenjʊəslɪ] **ADV** de manière ténue *ou* précaire

tenuousness [ˈtenjʊəsnɪs] **N 1** *(of link, relationship)* fragilité *f*, précarité *f*; *(of evidence)* minceur *f*, faiblesse *f*; *(of argument)* faiblesse *f* **2** *(of existence)* précarité *f*

tenure [ˈtenjə(r)] **N 1** *Hist (of land, property)* bail *m*

2 *(of post)* occupation *f*; **during his t. as chairman** pendant qu'il occupait le poste de président *ou* était président; *Am Univ* **to have t.** être titulaire

tepee [ˈtiːpiː] **N** tipi *m*

tepid [ˈtepɪd] **ADJ 1** *(water)* tiède **2** *(welcome, thanks)* tiède, réservé

tepidly [ˈtepɪdlɪ] **ADV** tièdement

tepidness [ˈtepɪdnɪs] **N** tiédeur *f*

tequila [tɪˈkiːlə] **N** tequila *f*

►► ***tequila slammer*** tequila *f* bang bang; ***tequila sunrise*** tequila *f* sunrise

tercentenary [ˌtɜːsenˈtiːnərɪ] *(pl* **tercentenaries***)*, *esp Am* **tercentennial** [ˌtɜːsenˈtenɪəl] **N** tricentenaire *m*

ADJ du tricentenaire

tercet [ˈtɜːsɪt] **N** tercet *m*

TERM [tɜːm]

N	
• terme **1, 5, 6**	• trimestre **2**
• session **3**	• mandat **3**
• peine **4**	• échéance **7**
VT	
• appeler	
NPL	
• conditions **1, 3**	• termes **1, 4**
• tarifs **3**	• accord **5**

N 1 *(period, end of period)* terme *m*; *(of pregnancy)* terme *m*; **in the long/short t.** à long/court terme; **to reach (full) t.** *(pregnancy)* arriver *ou* être à terme; **to set** *or* **put a t. to sth** mettre fin *ou* un terme à qch

2 *Br Sch & Univ* trimestre *m*; **in** *or* **during t. (time)** pendant le trimestre; **autumn t.** trimestre *m* d'automne, premier trimestre *m*

3 *Law & Pol (of court, parliament)* session *f*; *(of elected official)* mandat *m*; **the president is elected for a four-year t.** le président est élu pour (une période *ou* une durée de) quatre ans; **during my t. of office** *(gen)* pendant que j'étais en fonction; *Pol* pendant mon mandat

4 *(in prison)* peine *f*; **t. of imprisonment** peine *f* de prison; **to serve one's t.** purger sa peine

5 *(word, expression)* terme *m*; **medical/legal t.** terme *m* médical/juridique; **she spoke of you in very flattering terms** elle a parlé de vous en (des) termes très flatteurs; **she told him what she thought in no uncertain terms** elle lui a dit carrément ce qu'elle pensait

6 *Math & (in logic)* terme *m*

7 *Fin (of bill of exchange)* (terme *m* d')échéance *f*

VT appeler, nommer; **I wouldn't t. it a scientific book exactly** je ne dirais pas vraiment que c'est un livre scientifique

• **terms NPL 1** *(conditions ► of employment)* conditions *fpl*; *(► of agreement, contract)* termes *mpl*; **under the terms of the agreement** selon les termes de l'accord; *Law* **terms and conditions of sale/of employment** conditions *fpl* de vente/d'emploi; **what are the inquiry's terms of reference?** quelles sont les attributions *ou* quel est le mandat de la commission d'enquête?; **what are your terms?** quelles sont vos conditions?; **she would only accept on her own terms** elle n'était disposée à accepter qu'après avoir posé ses conditions; **not on any terms** à aucun prix, à aucune condition

2 *(perspective)* **we must think in less ambitious terms** il faut voir moins grand; **he refuses to consider the question in international terms** il refuse d'envisager la question d'un point de vue international; **in financial terms** financièrement parlant, en matière de finance

3 *(rates, tariffs)* conditions *fpl*, tarifs *mpl*; **we offer easy terms** nous proposons des facilités de paiement; **special terms for families** tarifs *mpl* spéciaux pour les familles

4 *(relations)* **to be on good terms with sb** être en bons termes avec qn; **we remained on friendly terms** nos relations sont restées amicales; **on equal terms** d'égal à égal; **they're no longer on speaking terms** ils ne se parlent plus

5 *(agreement)* accord *m*; **to make terms** *or* **to come to terms with sb** arriver à *ou* conclure un accord avec qn

6 *(acceptance)* **to come to terms with sth** se résigner à qch, arriver à accepter qch; **she'll have to come to terms with her problems eventually** tôt ou tard elle devra faire face à ses problèmes

• **in terms of PREP** en ce qui concerne, pour ce qui est de; **in terms of profits, we're doing well** pour ce qui est des bénéfices, tout va bien; **I was thinking more in terms of a Jaguar** je pensais plutôt à une Jaguar

►► *Fin* ***term bill*** effet *m* à terme; *Fin* ***terms of credit*** conditions *fpl* de crédit; *Fin* ***term day*** (jour *m* du) terme *m*; *Fin* ***term deposit*** dépôt *m* à terme; *Fin* ***term draft*** traite *f* à terme; *Fin* ***terms of exchange*** termes *mpl* d'échange; ***term insurance*** assurance *f* à terme; *Fin* ***term loan*** *(money lent)* prêt *m* à terme (fixe); *(money borrowed)* emprunt *m* à terme (fixe); ***term of notice*** période *f* de préavis; *Am Sch & Univ* ***term paper*** dissertation *f* trimestrielle; ***terms of payment*** modalités *fpl* de paiement, conditions *fpl ou* termes *mpl* de paiement; *Econ* ***terms of trade*** termes *mpl* de l'échange

termagant [ˈtɜːməgənt] **N** mégère *f*, harpie *f*

terminal [ˈtɜːmɪnəl] **ADJ 1** *(final)* terminal **2** *Med (patient)* en phase terminale; *(disease ► incurable)* incurable; *(► in its last stages)* dans sa *ou* en phase terminale; **I'm afraid it's t.** je crains que vous ne soyez/qu'il ne soit/*etc* condamné; **he has t. cancer** il a un cancer en phase terminale; *Fig* **an industry in t. decline** une industrie irrémédiablement en déclin; *Hum* **I think I'm suffering from t. boredom** je crois que je vais mourir d'ennui

N 1 *(for bus, underground)* terminus *m*; *(at airport)* terminal *m*, aérogare *f*; **t. B** aérogare *ou* terminal B

2 *Petr (platform)* terminal *m*

3 *Comput* (poste *m*) terminal *m*

4 *Elec (of battery)* borne *f*

►► *Fin* ***terminal charges*** charges *fpl* terminales; *Comput* ***terminal emulation*** émulation *f* de terminal; *Comput* ***terminal emulator*** émulateur *m* de terminal; *Acct* ***terminal loss*** perte *f* finale; *St Exch* ***terminal market*** marché *m* à terme; *Fin* ***terminal price*** cours *m* du livrable; *Comput* ***terminal server*** serveur *m* de terminaux; *Rail* ***terminal station*** terminus *m*; ***terminal velocity*** vitesse *f* limite; *Elec* ***terminal voltage*** tension *f* aux bornes

terminally [ˈtɜːmɪnəlɪ] **ADV to be t. ill** être condamné; **the t. ill** les malades *mpl* condamnés

terminate [ˈtɜːmɪneɪt] **VT 1** *(end ▸ project, work)* terminer; *(▸ employment)* mettre fin *ou* un terme à; *(▸ contract)* résilier, mettre fin *ou* un terme à; *(▸ pregnancy)* interrompre **2** *Fam (kill)* descendre

VI 1 *(end)* se terminer; **the row terminated in** *or* **with her resignation** la dispute s'est terminée par sa démission **2** *Rail* **this train terminates at Glasgow** ce train ne va pas plus loin que Glasgow; **this train terminates here** terminus du train!

termination [ˌtɜːmɪˈneɪʃən] **N 1** *(end ▸ gen)* fin *f*; *(▸ of contract)* résiliation *f*; *(▸ of relations, dealings etc)* cessation *f* **2** *(abortion)* interruption *f* (volontaire) de grossesse, IVG *f* **3** *Ling* terminaison *f*, désinence *f*

terminator [ˈtɜːmɪneɪtə(r)] **N** *Comput (of chain)* terminateur *m*

terminological [ˌtɜːmɪnəˈlɒdʒɪkəl] **ADJ** terminologique

terminologist [ˌtɜːmɪˈnɒlədʒɪst] **N** terminologue *mf*

terminology [ˌtɜːmɪˈnɒlədʒɪ] (*pl* **terminologies**) **N** terminologie *f*

terminus [ˈtɜːmɪnəs] (*pl* **terminuses** *or* **termini** [-naɪ]) **N** terminus *m*

termite [ˈtɜːmaɪt] **N** *Entom* termite *m*, fourmi *f* blanche

tern [tɜːn] **N** *Orn* sterne *f*

ternary [ˈtɜːnərɪ] **ADJ** ternaire

Terr. *Br (written abbr* **terrace***)* ≃ rue *f*

terrace [ˈterəs] **N 1** *Agr & Geol* terrasse *f* **2** *(patio)* terrasse *f* **3** *Br (row of houses)* = rangée de maisons attenantes et identiques; *(house)* = maison faisant partie d'une "terrace"

VT *Agr* cultiver en terrasses

• **terraces NPL** *Br Sport* gradins *mpl*; **on the terraces** dans les gradins

> **TERRACE**
>
> Ce mot désigne une rangée de maisons à un ou deux étages. À l'origine, les "terraced houses" étaient surtout des logements ouvriers (équivalents des corons) construits à proximité d'usines ou de mines de charbon.

terraced [ˈterəst] **ADJ** *(garden)* en terrasses; *(hillside)* cultivé en terrasses

▸▸ *Br* ***terraced house*** = maison située dans une rangée de maisons attenantes et identiques; **t. houses** maisons *fpl* alignées

terracotta [ˌterəˈkɒtə] **N 1** *(earthenware)* terre *f* cuite **2** *(colour)* ocre *m* brun

ADJ *(colour)* ocre brun *(inv)*

COMP *(pottery)* en terre cuite

terra firma [ˌterəˈfɜːmə] **N** *Literary or Hum* terre *f* ferme; **on t.** sur la terre ferme

terrain [teˈreɪn] **N** terrain *m*

terrapin [ˈterəpɪn] **N** *Zool* tortue *f* d'eau douce

terrarium [təˈreərɪəm] **N** *(for plants)* mini-serre *f*; *(for reptiles)* terrarium *m*

terrestrial [təˈrestrɪəl] **ADJ** terrestre

N terrien(enne) *m,f*

▸▸ ***terrestrial broadcaster*** diffuseur *m* hertzien; ***terrestrial broadcasting*** diffusion *f* hertzienne *ou* terrestre; ***terrestrial channel*** chaîne *f* hertzienne; ***terrestrial television*** diffusion *f* hertzienne *ou* terrestre

terrible [ˈterəbəl] **ADJ 1** *(severe, serious ▸ accident, shock, injury)* terrible; *(▸ weather)* affreux, épouvantable; *(▸ pain)* terrible, affreux, atroce; *(▸ storm, heat)* terrible, épouvantable; **I have a t. headache** j'ai un mal de tête affreux; **it caused t. damage** cela a provoqué d'importants dégâts; **it was a t. blow** ce fut un coup terrible **2** *(very bad ▸ experience, dream)* affreux; *(▸ food, smell)* épouvantable; *(▸ conditions, poverty)* épouvantable, effroyable; **to feel t.** *(ill)* se sentir très mal; *(guilty)* s'en vouloir beaucoup, avoir des remords; **I feel t. about the whole situation** je m'en veux beaucoup pour tout ce qui s'est passé; **I'm t. at maths** je suis nul en math; **the food was a t. disappointment** on a été terriblement déçus par la nourriture **3** *(for emphasis)* **it's a t. shame!** c'est vraiment dommage!; **he's a t. gossip** *(gossips a lot)* c'est un sacré bavard

terribly [ˈterəblɪ] **ADV 1** *(as intensifier)* terriblement, extrêmement; **I'm t. sorry** je suis vraiment désolé; **she'll be t. disappointed** elle sera terriblement déçue; **that's t. kind of you** c'est vraiment très gentil de votre part, vous êtes vraiment trop aimable; **it must have hurt (you) t.** *(physically)* cela a dû vous faire terriblement mal; *(mentally)* cela a dû vous faire énormément de peine **2** *(very badly)* affreusement mal, terriblement mal; **she dresses/plays t. (badly)** elle s'habille/joue affreusement mal; **the economy has performed t.** les résultats économiques sont désastreux

terrier [ˈterɪə(r)] **N** terrier *m (chien)*; *Fig* **he's a real t.** il n'abandonne jamais

terrific [təˈrɪfɪk] **ADJ 1** *(extreme, intense ▸ noise, crash)* épouvantable, effroyable; *(▸ speed)* fou (folle); *(▸ heat)* terrible, épouvantable; **it must have come as a t. shock (to you)** cela a dû vous faire un choc terrible **2** *Fam (superb)* terrible, génial, super; **you look t. in that dress** cette robe te va super bien

terrifically [təˈrɪfɪkəlɪ] **ADV** *Fam* **1** *(extremely, enormously)* extrêmement, très **2** *(very well)* merveilleusement (bien)

terrified [ˈterɪfaɪd] **ADJ** terrifié; **to be t. of sb/sth** avoir une peur bleue *ou* avoir très peur de qn/qch; **to be t. (that…)** être terrifié *ou* mort de peur (à l'idée que… + *subjunctive*); **I was absolutely t.** j'étais complètement terrifié *ou* complètement terrorisé

terrify [ˈterɪfaɪ] (*pt & pp* **terrified**) **VT** terrifier, effrayer

terrifying [ˈterɪfaɪɪŋ] **ADJ** *(dream)* terrifiant; *(person)* terrible, épouvantable; *(weaker use)* terrifiant, effroyable

terrifyingly [ˈterɪfaɪɪŋlɪ] **ADV** de façon terrifiante *ou* effroyable

terrine [teˈriːn] **N** terrine *f*

territorial [ˌterɪˈtɔːrɪəl] **ADJ 1** *(possessions, tax, claim etc)* territorial **2** *(instinct)* territorial; **cats are very t. (animals)** les chats sont des animaux farouchement attachés à leur territoire; *Fig* **they're very t. about their part of the office** ils considèrent leur partie du bureau comme leur territoire exclusif

N territorial *m*; *Br Mil* **the Territorials** = force armée constituée de réservistes volontaires

▸▸ *Br Mil* ***Territorial Army*** = force armée constituée de réservistes volontaires; ***territorial waters*** eaux *fpl* territoriales

territoriality [ˌterɪtɔːrɪˈælɪtɪ] **N** territorialité *f*

territory [ˈterətrɪ] (*pl* **territories**) **N** *(area)* territoire *m*; *(of salesperson)* territoire *m*, région *f*; *(of knowledge)* domaine *m*; *Fig* **this will be familiar t. for his readers** le lecteur se retrouvera en terrain familier; **to be on familiar t.** être en terrain connu; **it goes with the t.** *(goes with the job)* cela fait partie du travail

terror [ˈterə(r)] **N 1** *(fear)* terreur *f*, épouvante *f*; **to be** *or* **to go in t. of one's life** craindre pour sa vie; **to be in a state of t.** être terrorisé *ou* terrifié; **there was a look of t. on her face** elle avait l'air terrorisée; **to be** *or* **to live in t. of sb** avoir une peur bleue de qn; **to have a t. of sth/of doing sth** avoir extrêmement peur *ou* la terreur de qch/de faire qch

2 *(frightening event or aspect)* terreur *f*; **the terrors of the night** les terreurs *fpl* de la nuit

3 *(terrorism)* terreur *f*; **campaign of t.** campagne *f* terroriste *ou* de terreur

4 *Fam (person)* terreur *f*; **he was the t. of the countryside** c'était la terreur du pays; **you little t.!** petite terreur, va!

terrorism [ˈterərɪzəm] **N** terrorisme *m*

terrorist [ˈterərɪst] **N** terroriste *mf*

ADJ *(bomb)* de terroriste; *(campaign, attack, group)* terroriste

terrorize, -ise [ˈterəraɪz] **VT** terroriser

terror-stricken, terror-struck ADJ épouvanté, saisi de terreur

terry (towelling) [ˈterɪ-] **N** tissu-éponge *m*

COMP *(nappy, bathrobe)* en tissu-éponge

terse [tɜːs] **ADJ** *(concise)* concis, succinct; *(laconic)* laconique; *(abrupt)* brusque, sec (sèche)

tersely [ˈtɜːslɪ] **ADV** *(concisely)* avec concision *(laconically)* laconiquement; *(abruptly)* brusquement, sèchement

terseness [ˈtɜːsnɪs] **N** *(concision)* concision *f*; *(laconicism)* laconisme *m*; *(abruptness)* brusquerie

tertiary [ˈtɜːʃərɪ] **ADJ** *(gen) & Ind* tertiaire; *(education)* postscolaire, supérieur

▸▸ ***tertiary employment*** activité *f* tertiaire; ***tetiary sector*** secteur *m* tertiaire

Terylene® [ˈterəliːn] **N** Térylène® *m*, ≃ Tergal®

ADJ en Térylène®, ≃ en Tergal®

TESL [ˈtesəl] **N** *(abbr* **Teaching (of) English as a Seond Language***)* enseignement *m* de l'anglais langue seconde

TESOL [ˈtiːsɒl] **N** *(abbr* **Teaching English to Speakeof Other Languages***)* enseignement *m* de l'anglais aux étrangers *ou* comme langue étrangèr

TESSA [ˈtesə] **N** *(abbr* **tax-exempt special saving account***)* = en Grande-Bretagne, plan d'épargn exonéré d'impôt

TEST [test]

> **N**
> - test **1–5** • contrôle **1, 3**
> - examen **2**
>
> **VT**
> - tester **1, 3** • analyser **2, 6**
> - examiner **2** • essayer **3**
> - vérifier **4** • contrôler **4**
> - mesurer **5** • évaluer **5**
> - éprouver **7**

N 1 *(examination ▸ gen)* test *m*; *Sch* contrôle *n* interrogation *f*; **to pass a t.** réussir à un examen **biology t.** interrogation *f* de biologie; **to take** *or* **to sit a t.** passer un examen; **I'm taking m (driving) t. tomorrow** je passe mon permis (d conduire) demain; **did you pass your (driving) t.** avez-vous été reçu au permis (de conduire)?

2 *Med (of blood, urine)* test *m*, analyse *f*; *(of eye hearing)* examen *m*; **to undergo tests** subir de tests *ou* examens; **to have a blood t.** faire fair une analyse de sang; **to have an eye t.** se fair examiner la vue

3 *(trial ▸ of equipment, machine)* test *m*, essai *n* épreuve *f*; *(▸ of quality)* contrôle *m*; *Mktg (▸ of r action, popularity)* évaluation *f*; **to carry out test on sth** effectuer des tests sur qch; **all new drug undergo clinical tests** tous les nouveaux médica ments subissent des tests cliniques; **to be on** être testé *ou* à l'essai; **to put sth to the t.** teste qch, faire l'essai de qch

4 *(of character, endurance, resolve)* test *m*; **a goo t. of character** un bon test de personnalité, u bon moyen de tester la personnalité; **to put s to the t.** éprouver qn, mettre qn à l'épreuve; **h courage was really put to the t.** son courage fu sérieusement mis à l'épreuve *ou* éprouvé; **it the first major t. for the Prime Minister** c'est la pre mière fois que le Premier ministre est réelle ment mis à l'épreuve; *also Fig* **t. of strengt** épreuve *f* de force; **to stand the t. of time** dure résister à l'épreuve du temps; **her books have ce tainly stood the t. of time** ses livres n'ont pas pri une ride

5 *(measure)* test *m*; **it's a t. of union solidarity** c'es un test de la solidarité syndicale; **the by-electio will be a good t. of public opinion** l'élection pa tielle représentera un bon test de l'opinion pu blique

6 *Br Sport* test-match *m*

COMP d'essai

VT 1 *(examine ▸ ability, knowledge, intelligence* tester, mesurer; *Sch (▸ pupils)* tester, contrôle les connaissances de; **she was tested on he knowledge of plants** on a testé *ou* vérifié se connaissances botaniques

2 *Med (blood, urine)* analyser, faire une analys de; *(sight, hearing)* examiner; **to have one's eye tested** se faire examiner la vue; *Fig* **you nee your eyes tested** *or Br* **testing!** il faut mettre de lunettes!; **to t. sb for Aids** faire subir le test de dé pistage du sida à qn

3 *(try out ▸ prototype, car)* essayer, faire l'essa de; *(▸ product)* essayer; *(▸ weapon, procedure* tester; *(▸ drug)* tester, expérimenter; **none o our products is tested on animals** nos produits n sont pas testés sur les animaux

4 *(check ▸ batteries, pressure, suspension)* vériɪer, contrôler
5 *(measure ▸ reaction, popularity)* mesurer, évaɪer; *Mktg (▸ quality)* contrôler; **the day of action** ɪ**ill t. union solidarity** la journée d'action permetra de mesurer *ou* d'évaluer la solidarité syndiale
6 *(analyse ▸ soil)* analyser, faire des prélèvenents dans; *(▸ water)* analyser; **the water was** ɘ**sted for phosphates** on a analysé l'eau pour en ɪéterminer le taux de phosphates; *Fig* **to t. the** ɪ**vater** tâter le terrain
7 *(tax ▸ machinery, driver, patience)* éprouver, nettre à l'épreuve; **to t. sb to the limit** pousser ɪn à bout *ou* à la dernière extrémité; **to t. sb's pa**ɪ**ence to the limit** mettre la patience de qn à rude preuve
ɪ**VI 1** *(make examination)* **to t. for Aids** procéder à ɪn test de dépistage du sida; **to t. for the** ɪ**resence of gas** rechercher la présence de gaz
2 *(show test result)* **she tested positive for Aids** son ɘst de dépistage du sida s'est révélé positif
3 *Rad & Tel* **testing, testing!** un, deux, trois!
ɪ▸ ***test area*** région *f* test; ***test ban*** interdiction *f* ɪes essais nucléaires; ***test ban treaty*** traité *m* de ɪrohibition des essais nucléaires; ***test bench*** ɪanc *m* d'essai; *Br TV* ***test card*** mire *f*; *Law* ***test*** ɪ***ase*** affaire *f* qui fait jurisprudence; ***test certifi***ɪ***ate*** certificat *m* d'essai; *TV* ***test chart*** mire *f* (de églage); *Mktg* ***test city*** ville *f* test; ***test drive*** essai ɪ sur route; **to go for a t. drive** essayer une voiure; *Aviat* ***test flight*** vol *m* d'essai; ***test market*** ɪarché-test *m*, marché *m* témoin; *Br* ***test match*** ɪatch *m* international, test-match *m*; *Br Sch* ***test*** ɪ***aper*** interrogation *f* écrite; *Am TV* ***test pattern*** ɪire *f* (de réglage); *Mus* ***test piece*** morceau *m* imɪosé *ou* de concours; ***test pilot*** pilote *m* d'essai; ɪ***est run*** essai *m*; ***test shot*** lancement *m* d'essai; ɪ***est signal*** signal *m* de mesure; ***test site*** site *m* téɪoin; *Aut* ***test track*** piste *f* d'essai; ***test tube*** ɪprouvette *f*

ɪ**test out VT SEP 1** *(idea, theory)* tester **2** *(protoɪype, product)* essayer, mettre à l'essai

---

ɘ**stament** ['testəmənt] **N 1** *Law* testament *m*; **to** ɪ**ake one's (last will and) t.** tester, faire son testaɪent **2** *(tribute)* preuve *f*, témoignage *m*; **the vic**ɪ**ory was a t. to her bravery** cette victoire a été le émoignage de son courage **3** *Bible* testament ɪ; **the Old/New T.** le Nouveau/l'Ancien Testaɪent

ɘ**stamentary** [ˌtestə'mentərɪ] **ADJ** testamentaire

ɘ**state** ['testeɪt] **ADJ to die t.** mourir en ayant ɪissé un testament *ou* testé

ɘ**stator** [te'steɪtə(r)] **N** *Law* testateur *m*

ɘ**st-bed N** banc *m* d'essai *ou* d'épreuve

ɘ**st-drive N** *(of car)* essai *m* de conduite
VT *(car)* essayer

ɘ**ster** ['testə(r)] **N 1** *(person)* contrôleur(euse) *m*, vérificateur(trice) *m,f*; *(machine)* appareil *m* de ɪontrôle *ou* de vérification **2** *(sample ▸ of makeɪp, perfume)* échantillon *m*

ɘ**stes** ['testi:z] *pl of* **testis**

ɘ**st-fly** *(pt* **test-flew**, *pp* **test-flown) VT to t. a** ɪ**lane** faire le vol d'essai d'un avion

ɘ**sticle** ['testɪkəl] **N** testicule *m*

ɘ**stify** ['testɪfaɪ] *(pt & pp* **testified) VT 1** *(affirm, ɪtate)* déclarer, affirmer; *Law* déclarer sous serɪent, attester, témoigner; **I can t. that she re**ɪ**mained at home** je peux attester qu'elle est ɪestée à la maison **2** *Literary (demonstrate, prove)* émoigner de; **this work testifies his deep know**ɪ**edge of the subject** cet œuvre témoigne de sa ɪrofonde connaissance du sujet
VI *(be witness)* porter témoignage, témoigner; ɪ**o t. for/against sb** témoigner en faveur de/ ɪontre qn; **I can t. to her honesty** je peux attester ɪu témoigner de son honnêteté

ɘ**stily** ['testɪlɪ] **ADV** d'un ton irrité

ɘ**stimonial** [ˌtestɪ'məʊnɪəl] **N 1** *(certificate)* atestation *f*; *(reference ▸ gen)* (lettre *f* de) recomɪandation *f*; *(▸ given by company, manager)* ɪéférences *fpl* **2** *(tribute)* témoignage *m* d'estime **3** *Br Sport (match)* jubilé *m*
ADJ qui porte témoignage; **they organized a t.** ɪ**inner for him** ils ont organisé un dîner en son ɪonneur
▸▸ *Mktg* ***testimonial advertising*** témoignage *m*, publicité *f* testimoniale; *Br* ***testimonial match*** jubilé *m*

testimony [*Br* 'testɪmənɪ, *Am* 'testəməʊnɪ] *(pl* **testimonies) N 1** *(statement)* déclaration *f*; *Law* témoignage *m*, déposition *f*; **to call sb in t.** appeler qn en témoignage **2** *(sign, proof)* témoignage *m*; **to bear t. to sth** témoigner de qch; **the monument is a lasting t. to** *or* **of his genius** ce monument est le témoignage vivant de son génie; *Law* **in t. whereof** en foi de quoi

testing ['testɪŋ] **ADJ** *(problem, time, experience etc)* difficile, éprouvant
N 1 *(of product, machine, vehicle)* (mise *f* à l')essai *m*; *(of quality)* contrôle *m* **2** *Med (of sight, hearing)* examen *m*; *(of blood, urine)* analyse *f*; *(of reaction)* mesure *f*; *(of drug, cosmetic)* expérimentation *f* **3** *(of intelligence, knowledge, skills)* évaluation *f*; *(of candidate)* évaluation *f*, examen *m*
▸▸ ***testing ground*** terrain *m* d'essai; **Scotland was often used as a t. ground for new government policies** le gouvernement utilisait souvent l'Écosse pour tester ses nouvelles mesures politiques; ***testing laboratory*** laboratoire *m* d'essai de produits

testis ['testɪs] *(pl* **testes** [-ti:z]) **N** *Anat* testicule *m*

test-market VT tester sur le marché

testosterone [te'stɒstərəʊn] **N** testostérone *f*

test-tube ADJ de laboratoire
▸▸ ***test-tube baby*** bébé-éprouvette *m*

testy ['testɪ] *(compar* **testier**, *superl* **testiest) ADJ** irritable, grincheux

tetanus ['tetənəs] **N** tétanos *m*
COMP *(vaccination, injection)* antitétanique

tetchily ['tetʃɪlɪ] **ADV** d'un ton irrité

tetchiness ['tetʃɪnɪs] **N** irritabilité *f*

tetchy ['tetʃɪ] *(compar* **tetchier**, *superl* **tetchiest) ADJ** grincheux, irascible

tête-à-tête [ˌteɪtɑ:'teɪt] **N** (conversation *f* en) tête-à-tête *m inv*
ADJ en tête-à-tête

tether ['teðə(r)] **N** *(for horse)* longe *f*, attache *f*; **to be at the end of one's t.** *(unable to cope, depressed)* être au bout du rouleau; *(exasperated)* être à bout de patience
VT *(horse)* attacher

tetrachloride [ˌtetrə'klɔ:raɪd] **N** *Chem* tétrachlorure *m*

tetragon ['tetrəgən] **N** quadrilatère *m*

tetragonal [te'trægənəl] **ADJ** quadrilatère

tetrahedron [ˌtetrə'hi:drən] *(pl* **tetrahedrons** *or* **tetrahedra** [-drə]) **N** tétraèdre *m*

tetrameter [te'træmɪtə(r)] **N** *Literature* tétramètre *m*

Teutonic [tju:'tɒnɪk] **ADJ** teuton

Tex *(written abbr* **Texas)** Texas *m*

Texan ['teksən] **N** Texan(e) *m,f*
ADJ texan

Texas ['teksəs] **N** le Texas

Tex-Mex [ˌteks'meks] **ADJ** *Culin* tex-mex *(inv)*

text [tekst] **N** *(gen) & Comput* texte *m*; *Tel (text message)* texto *m*, SMS *m*
VT *(send text message to)* envoyer un texto *ou* un SMS à
VI *(send text messages)* envoyer des textos *ou* des SMS
▸▸ *Comput & Typ* ***text area*** empasement *m*; *Comput* ***text block*** bloc *m* de texte; *Comput* ***text box*** encadré *m* texte; *Comput* ***text buffer*** mémoire *f* tampon de texte; ***text editing*** édition *f* de texte, mise *f* en forme de texte; *Comput* ***text editor*** éditeur *m* de texte; *Comput* ***text field*** champ *m* de text; *Comput* ***text file*** fichier *m* texte; *Comput* ***text layout*** disposition *f* de texte; ***text message*** texto *m*, SMS *m*; *Comput* ***text mode*** mode *m* texte; *Comput* ***text processing*** traitement *m* de texte; *Comput* ***text processor*** (unité *f* de) traitement *m* de texte; *Typ & Comput* ***text wrap*** texte *m* en habillage

textbook ['tekstbʊk] **N** *(gen) & Sch* manuel *m*
COMP *(typical)* typique; *(ideal)* parfait, idéal; **it's a t. case** c'est un exemple classique *ou* typique; **a t. example (of)** un exemple parfait *ou* typique (de)
▸▸ ***textbook definition*** définition *f* classique

textile ['tekstaɪl] **N** textile *m*
COMP *(industry)* textile

texting ['tekstɪŋ] **N** *(sending text messages)* envoi *m* de textos *ou* de SMS

text-message VT envoyer un texto *ou* un SMS à

text-size ADJ *(newspaper)* plein format

textspeak ['tekstspi:k] **N** = langue des SMS

textual ['tekstjʊəl] **ADJ** textuel, de texte
▸▸ ***textual analysis*** analyse *f* de texte; ***textual error*** erreur *f* dans le texte

textually ['tekstjʊəlɪ] **ADV** *(in written form)* à l'écrit; *(in the text)* dans le texte

texture ['tekstʃə(r)] **N 1** *(of fabric)* tissage *m*; *(of leather, wood, paper, skin, stone)* grain *m*; **the paper is grainy in t.** le papier est de texture granuleuse **2** *(of food, soil)* texture *f*, consistance *f*; *(of writing)* structure *f*, texture *f*; **music is part of the t. of their lives** la musique fait partie intégrante de leur vie

TFT [ˌti:ef'ti:] **N** *Electron (abbr* **thin film transistor)** transistor *m* en couche mince

TGWU [ˌti:dʒi:ˌdʌbəlju:'ju:] **N** *Ind (abbr* **Transport and General Workers' Union)** = le plus grand syndicat interprofessionnel britannique

Thai [taɪ] *(pl* **inv** *or* **Thais) N 1** *(person)* Thaï *mf*, Thaïlandais(e) *m,f* **2** *(language)* thaï *m*
ADJ thaï, thaïlandais
COMP *(embassy)* de Thaïlande; *(history)* de la Thaïlande; *(teacher)* de thaï

Thailand ['taɪlænd] **N** Thaïlande *f*

thalassotherapy [ˌθæləsəʊ'θerəpɪ] **N** thalassothérapie *f*

thalidomide [θə'lɪdəmaɪd] **N** *Pharm* thalidomide *f*
▸▸ ***thalidomide baby*** = bébé victime de la thalidomide

Thames [temz] **N the (River) T.** la Tamise
▸▸ ***the Thames Valley*** la vallée de la Tamise

than [ðæn, *unstressed* ðən] **CONJ 1** *(after comparative adj, adv)* que; **he plays tennis better t. I do** il joue au tennis mieux que moi; **it's quicker by train t. by bus** ça va plus vite en train qu'en bus; **I was more disappointed t. angry** j'étais plus déçu que fâché
2 *(following negative clause)* **no sooner had he finished speaking t. everyone made for the door** à peine avait-il fini de parler que tout le monde s'est précipité vers la porte; **there's nothing worse t. spending the holidays on your own** rien n'est pire que de passer les vacances tout seul
3 *(with "rather", "sooner")* **I'd do anything rather t. have to see him** je ferais n'importe quoi plutôt que d'être obligé de le voir; **I'd prefer to stay here rather t. go out, I'd rather** *or* **sooner stay here t. go out** je préférerais rester ici que de sortir
4 *Am (after "different")* **he is different t. he used to be** il n'est plus le même
PREP 1 *(after comparative adj, adv)* que; **he plays tennis better t. me** *or* **I** il joue au tennis mieux que moi; **the cedars are older t. the oaks** les cèdres sont plus vieux que les chênes
2 *(indicating quantity, number)* de; **more/fewer t. 15 people** plus/moins de 15 personnes; **I've been invited more t. once** j'ai été invité plus d'une fois; **there are more policemen t. demonstrators** il y a plus de policiers que de manifestants
3 *(after "other" in negative clauses)* **we have no sizes other t. 40 or 42** nous n'avons pas d'autres tailles que 40 ou 42; **it was none other t. the Prime Minister who launched the appeal** c'est le Premier ministre en personne *ou* lui-même qui a lancé l'appel
4 *Am (after "different")* **she has different tastes t. yours** elle a des goûts différents des vôtres

thane [θeɪn] **N** *Hist* thane *m*, ≃ baron *m*

thank [θæŋk] **VT 1** *(in gratitude)* remercier; **to t. sb for sth** remercier qn de *ou* pour qch; **to t. sb for doing sth** remercier qn d'avoir fait qch; **she thanked us for coming** elle nous remercia d'être venus; **I can't t. you enough for what you've done** je ne sais comment vous remercier pour ce que vous avez fait pour moi; **you have your father to t. for that** tu peux dire merci à ton père pour ça, c'est à ton père que tu dois ça; *Ironic* **you have only yourself to t. for that!** c'est à toi seul qu'il faut t'en prendre!; **you won't t. me for it** vous allez m'en vouloir; **t. God** *or* **goodness!** Dieu merci!; **t. heaven** *or* **heavens you're safe!** Dieu merci vous êtes sain et sauf! **2** *(as request)* **I'll t. you to mind your own business!** je te prie de t'occuper de ce qui te regarde!

• **thanks** **NPL 1** *(gen)* remerciements *mpl*; **give her my thanks for the flowers** remerciez-la de ma part pour les fleurs; **(many) thanks for all your help** merci (beaucoup) pour toute votre aide; *Admin* **received with thanks** pour acquit **2** *Rel* louange *f*, grâce *f*; **to give thanks to God** rendre grâce à Dieu **EXCLAM** merci; **thanks a lot, thanks very much** merci beaucoup, merci bien; **thanks a million** merci mille fois; **thanks for coming** merci d'être venu; **no thanks!** (non) merci!; *Ironic* **thanks for nothing!** je te remercie!

• **thanks to** **PREP** grâce à; **thanks to you, we saved a lot of money** grâce à vous, nous avons économisé beaucoup d'argent; **thanks to you, we lost the contract** à cause de vous, nous avons perdu le contrat; **no thanks to you!** ce n'est sûrement pas grâce à vous!

thankful ['θæŋkfʊl] **ADJ** reconnaissant, content; **to be t. to sb for sth** être reconnaissant à qn de qch, *esp Formal* savoir gré à qn de qch; **I was t. to get away** j'étais content de pouvoir partir; **she was just t. (that) no one recognized her** elle s'estimait surtout heureuse que personne ne l'ait reconnue; **you should be t. for what you've got** tu devrais t'estimer heureux de ce que tu as

thankfully ['θæŋkfʊlɪ] **ADV 1** *(with gratitude)* avec reconnaissance *ou* gratitude **2** *(with relief)* avec soulagement **3** *(fortunately)* heureusement

thankfulness ['θæŋkfʊlnɪs] **N** gratitude *f*, reconnaissance *f*

thankless ['θæŋklɪs] **ADJ** *(task, person)* ingrat

Thanksgiving ['θæŋks,gɪvɪŋ] **N T. (Day)** *Am* = fête nationale américaine célébrée le quatrième jeudi de novembre; *Can* Action *f* de grâces *(célébrée au Canada le deuxième lundi d'octobre)*

THANKSGIVING

Aux États-Unis, "Thanksgiving" commémore, le quatrième jeudi de novembre, l'installation des premiers colons en Amérique. Ceux-ci remercièrent Dieu de leur avoir permis de survivre dans des conditions difficiles et primitives. Le dîner en famille qui a généralement lieu à cette occasion est traditionnellement composé d'une dinde servie avec une sauce aux canneberges accompagnée de patates douces, et se termine par une tarte au potiron.

thanksgiving ['θæŋks,gɪvɪŋ] **N** action *f* de grâce

THAT

DEM PRON
• ce **1** • cela **1**
• ça **1** • celui-là **2**
• celui **3**

DEM ADJ
• ce **1** • ce…-là **2**

ADV
• si **1, 2** • aussi **1**
• tellement **2**

REL PRON
• qui **1** • que **2**
• lequel **3** • où **4**

CONJ
• que **1** • pour que **2**

(*pl* **those** [ðəʊz])

DEMONSTRATIVE PRON [ðæt] **1** *(thing indicated ▸ subject)* ce, cela, ça; *(▸ object)* cela, ça; **give me t.** donnez-moi ça; **after/before t.** après/avant cela; **what's t.?** qu'est-ce que c'est que ça?; **who's t.?** *(gen)* qui est-ce?; *(on phone)* qui est à l'appareil?; **t.'s Mr Thomas** c'est M. Thomas; **is t. you, Susan?** c'est toi, Susan?; **is t. all you've got to eat?** c'est tout ce que vous avez à manger?; **what did she mean by t.?** qu'est-ce qu'elle voulait dire par là?; **those are my things** ce sont mes affaires; **those are my parents** voilà mes parents; **t. is what he told me** c'est *ou* voilà ce qu'il m'a dit; **t. is where I live** c'est là que j'habite; **t. was three months ago** il y a trois mois de cela; **t.'s strange** c'est bizarre; **so THAT'S how it works!** c'est donc comme ça que ça marche!; **so THAT'S settled** bon, ça c'est réglé *ou* voilà qui est réglé; **t.'s as may be** peut-être bien; *Fam* **it's not as hot as (all) t.!** il ne fait pas si chaud que ça!; **so it's come to t.** voilà donc où nous en sommes (arrivés); **if it comes to t., you can always leave** si ça en arrive là, vous pouvez toujours partir; **t.'s a good boy!** en voilà un gentil petit garçon!; **t.'s all** c'est tout, voilà tout; **t.'s all we need!** il ne manquait plus que ça!; **t.'s enough (of t.)!** ça suffit!; **t.'s it!** *(finished)* c'est fini!; *(correct)* c'est ça!; **t.'s it for today!** ce sera tout pour aujourd'hui!; **t.'s life!** c'est la vie!; **t.'s more like it!** voilà qui est déjà mieux!; **well, t.'s t.!** eh bien voilà!; **I said "no" and t.'s t.!** j'ai dit "non", un point c'est tout!; **t.'s the government all over** *or* **for you!** c'est bien l'administration ça!; *Fam* **good stuff, t.!** ah c'est bon ça!

2 *(in contrast to "this")* celui-là (celle-là) *m,f*; **those** ceux-là (celles-là) *mpl,fpl*; **this is an ash, t. is an oak** ceci est un frêne et ça, c'est un chêne; **which book do you prefer, this or t.?** quel livre préférez-vous, celui-ci ou celui-là?; **I'd like some flowers, but not those!** j'aimerais des fleurs, mais pas celles-là!

3 *(used when giving further information)* celui (celle) *m,f*; **those** ceux (celles) *mpl,fpl*; **there are those who believe t.…** il y a des gens qui croient que…; **I'm not one of those who…** je ne suis pas du genre à *ou* de ceux qui…; **a sound like t. of a baby crying** un bruit comme celui que fait un bébé qui pleure; **the symptoms sound like those of malaria** les symptômes ressemblent à ceux du paludisme; **he spoke with those concerned** il a parlé à ceux qui sont concernés

DEMONSTRATIVE ADJ [ðæt] **1** *(the one indicated)* ce (cette); **those** ces; **t. man** cet homme; **those questions** ces questions; **at t. moment** à ce moment-là; **t. day** ce jour-là; **in those days** en ce temps-là, à cette époque; **we all agree on t. point** nous sommes tous d'accord là-dessus; **did you hear about t. fire?** as-tu entendu parler de cet incendie?; **do you remember t. play we saw?** tu te rappelles cette pièce que nous avons vue?; **how's t. son of yours?** comment va ton fils?; *Pej* **if I get hold of t. son of yours!** si je mets la main sur ton sacré fils!; **t. fool of a gardener** cet imbécile de jardinier; **they rode off into the sunset, it was t. kind of film** ils se sont éloignés vers le soleil couchant, c'était ce genre de film, tu vois?

2 *(in contrast to "this")* ce…-là (cette…-là); **those** ces…-là; **t. house over there** e cette *ou* la maison là-bas; **t. one** celui-là (celle-là) *m,f*; **choose between this restaurant and t. one** choisissez entre ce restaurant et l'autre; *Fam* **t. there table**-là ▫

ADV [ðæt] **1** *(so)* si, aussi; **can you run t. fast?** pouvez-vous courir aussi vite que ça?; **he's not (all) t. good-looking** il n'est pas si beau que ça; **there's a pile of papers on my desk t. high!** il y a une pile de papiers haute comme ça sur mon bureau!; **I don't go there t. often** *(not much)* je n'y vais pas très souvent; **I don't go there THAT often** je n'y vais pas aussi souvent que ça

2 *Fam (with result clause)* si ▫, tellement ▫; **he was t. weak he couldn't stand** il était tellement affaibli qu'il ne tenait plus debout

RELATIVE PRON [ðət]

On peut omettre le pronom relatif **that** sauf s'il est en position sujet.

1 *(subject of verb)* qui; **the conclusions t. emerge from this** les conclusions qui en ressortent; **nothing t. matters** rien d'important

2 *(object or complement of verb)* que; **the house t. Miles built** la maison que Miles a construite; **is this the best t. you can do?** est-ce que c'est ce que vous pouvez faire de mieux?; **fool t. I am, I agreed** imbécile que je suis, j'ai accepté

3 *(object of preposition)* lequel (laquelle) *m,f*; **the box t. I put it in** le carton dans lequel je l'ai mis; **the songs t. I was thinking of** *or* **about** les chansons auxquelles je pensais; **the woman/the film t. we're talking about** la femme/le film dont nous parlons; **not t. I know of** pas que je sache

4 *(when)* où; **the week t. he was sick** la semain[e] où il était malade

CONJ [ðət]

Sauf dans la langue soutenue, la conjonctio[n] **that** est souvent omise.

1 *(gen)* que; **I said t. I had read it** j'ai dit que [je] l'avais lu; **it's natural t. you should be nervous** c'e[st] normal que vous soyez nerveux; **it's not t. sh[e] isn't friendly** ce n'est pas qu'elle ne soit pas am[i]cale; **I'll see to it t. everything is ready** je veiller[ai] à ce que tout soit prêt; **it was so dark t. I cou[ld] barely see** il faisait si noir que je voyais à pein[e]; *Formal* **t. he is capable has already been proven** il [a] déjà prouvé qu'il était capable; *Formal* **t. I shou[ld] live to see the day when…** *(expressing incredulit[y])* je n'aurais jamais cru qu'un jour…

2 *Arch or Literary (in order that)* afin que, po[ur] que; **he died t. we might live** il est mort pour qu[e] nous puissions vivre

• **and (all) that** **ADV** *Fam (and so on)* et tout l[e] bastringue; **it was a very posh do, waiters in whi[te] gloves and (all) t.** c'était très classe, avec des se[r]veurs en gants blancs et tout le bastringue; **sh[e] went on about friendship and (all) t.** elle parla [d']amitié et tout ce qui s'ensuit

• **at that** **ADV 1** *(what's more)* en plus; **it's a fo[r]gery and a pretty poor one at t.** c'est une copie [et] une mauvaise en plus

2 *Fam (indicating agreement)* en fait ▫; **perhap[s] we're not so badly off at t.** en fait, on n'est peu[t-] être pas tellement à plaindre

3 *(then)* à ce moment-là; **at t., he paused** à c[e] moment-là, il a marqué un temps d'arrêt

• **like that** **ADJ 1** *(indicating character or attitud[e])* comme ça; **she's like t., she never says thank yo[u]** elle est comme ça, elle ne dit jamais merci; **don['t] be like t.** ne soyez pas comme ça

2 *(close, intimate)* comme les deux doigts de [la] main; **the two of them are like t.** ils sont comm[e] les deux doigts de la main **ADV** *(in that wa[y])* comme ça; **stop looking at me like t.!** arrête d[e] me regarder comme ça!

• **not that** **CONJ** **if he refuses, not t. he will, there an alternative?** s'il refuse, même si cela e[st] peu probable, est-ce qu'il y a une autre sol[u]tion?; **he's already left, not t. it matters** il est dé[jà] parti, encore que ce soit sans importance

• **that is (to say)** **ADV** enfin; **I work at the ho[s]pital, as a receptionist t. is, not as a nurse** je tr[a]vaille à l'hôpital, enfin à la réception, pa[s] comme infirmière; **I'd like to ask you somethin[g] t. is, if you've got a minute** j'aimerais vous pos[er] une question, enfin, si vous avez un instant

• **that way** **ADV 1** *(in that manner)* de cette fa[-]çon; **what makes him act t. way?** qu'est-ce qui [le] pousse à agir comme ça?; **t. way you'll only mak[e] things worse** de cette façon, tu ne feras qu'emp[i]rer les choses

2 *Fam (in that respect)* **she's funny t. way** c'est so[n] côté bizarre; **I didn't know he was t. way incline[d]** je ne connaissais pas ce côté-là de lui

• **with that** **ADV** là-dessus; **with t., she left** s[ur] ce *ou* là-dessus, elle est partie

thatch [θætʃ] **N 1** *Constr* chaume *m* **2** *Br Fam F[ig] (hair)* tignasse *f*; **a t. of blonde hair** une crinièr[e] blonde

COMP *(roof)* de *ou* en chaume

VT *(roof)* couvrir de chaume

thatcher ['θætʃə(r)] **N** couvreur *m* en chaume

Thatcherism ['θætʃərɪzəm] **N** *Pol* thatchérism[e] *m*

Thatcherite ['θætʃəraɪt] **N** partisan *m* du tha[t]chérisme

ADJ *(policy, view)* thatchérien

that's = **that is**

thaw [θɔː] **VI 1** *(ice, snow)* fondre; *(river, lake)* d[é]geler; **it's beginning to t.** il commence à dégele[r]

2 *(frozen food)* dégeler, se décongeler

3 *(get warmer ▸ person, hands)* se réchauffer

4 *Fig (person, relations)* se dégeler, être plus d[é]tendu; **she seems to finally be thawing towards m[e]** elle semble enfin perdre sa réserve *ou* sa fro[i]deur à mon égard

VT 1 *(ice, snow)* faire dégeler *ou* fondre **2** *(froze[n] food)* dégeler, décongeler ɴ 1 *Met* dégel *m* 2 *Pol* détente *f*, dégel *m*; *Fig* **a t. in** **elations** un dégel *ou* une détente des relations

thaw out VT SEP 1 *(frozen food)* décongeler, égeler 2 *(feet, hands)* réchauffer; **come and** **ıaw yourself out in the sitting room** venez vous échauffer au salon 3 *Fig (make relaxed ▸ person)* égeler, mettre à l'aise

VI 1 *(frozen food)* se décongeler 2 *(hands, feet)* e réchauffer; **I'm beginning to t. out now** je comıence à me réchauffer maintenant 3 *Fig (beome relaxed)* se dégeler, perdre sa froideur *ou* éserve

ıawing ['θɔːɪŋ] N *(of river, lake)* dégel *m*; *(of* *ıow, ice)* fonte *f*; *(of frozen food)* décongélation *Fig* **a t. in relations** un dégel *ou* une détente des elations

ıe [*before consonant sounds* ðə, *before vowel* *ounds* ðɪ, *stressed* ðiː] DEF ART 1 *(singular)* le (la); *ılural)* les; **t. blue dress is t. prettiest** la robe leue est la plus jolie; **t. dead/poor** les morts *ıpl*/pauvres *mpl*; **t. French/Germans** les Français *ıpl*/Allemands *mpl*; **I can't do t. impossible** je ne eux pas faire l'impossible; **translated from t.** **atin** traduit du latin; **she's giving up her job – t.** **voman's mad!** elle quitte son emploi – c'est une olle!

2 *(with names, titles)* **t. Smiths/Martins** les Smith/ Iartin; **Alexander t. Great** Alexandre le Grand; **lizabeth t. First** Élisabeth Première

3 *(with numbers, dates etc)* **Monday June t. tenth** **r t. tenth of June** le lundi 10 juin; **on t. Monday he** **ell ill** le lundi il est tombé malade; **t. 80s** *(decade)* es années 80; **t. temperature was in t. 80s** il faiait environ 25°C; **t. 1820s** les années 1820 à 830; **t. summer of 1946** l'été 1946; **t. second from** **left** le second en partant de la gauche

4 *(in prices, quantities)* **tomatoes are 40p t. pound** es tomates sont à 40 pence la livre; **t. car does 40** **ıiles to t. gallon** la voiture consomme 7 litres ux 100

5 *(with comparatives)* **t. more t. better** plus il y en , mieux c'est; **t. less said t. better** moins on en arlera, mieux cela vaudra; **t. sooner t. better** le lus tôt sera le mieux

6 *(stressed form)* **t. Olympics are THE event this** **vinter** les jeux Olympiques sont l'événement à e pas manquer cet hiver; **do you mean THE John** **ving?** vous voulez dire le célèbre John Irving?

7 *(enough ▸ singular)* le (la); *(▸ plural)* les; **I** **aven't t. time/money to do it** je n'ai pas le temps e/l'argent pour le faire

8 *(instead of possessive adj)* **she took him by t.** **and** elle l'a pris par la main; *Fam* **how's t. wife/** **amily?** comment va la femme/la famille?; *Fam* **vell, how's t. throat then?** eh bien, et cette gorge?

ıeatre, *Am* **theater** ['θɪətə(r)] N 1 *(building)* héâtre *m*; **to go to the t.** aller au théâtre

2 *(drama)* théâtre *m*, art *m* dramatique; *(plays in* *eneral)* théâtre *m*; *(profession)* théâtre *m*; **Greek/** **ıodern t.** le théâtre grec/moderne; **I've been in** **he t. for over 30 years** je fais du théâtre depuis lus de 30 ans

3 *(hall)* salle *f* de spectacle; *(for lectures)* salle *f* e conférences; *Univ* amphithéâtre *m*

4 *Med* **(operating) t.** salle *f* d'opération; **she's in** **the) t.** *(doctor)* elle est en salle d'opération; *(paent)* elle est sur la table d'opération

5 *Fig (for important event)* théâtre *m*

COMP 1 *(programme, tickets)* de théâtre; *(manger)* de théâtre 2 *Med (staff, nurse)* de salle l'opération; *(routine, job)* dans la salle d'opéraion

▸▸ ***theatre bill*** affiche *f* de théâtre; ***theatre company*** troupe *f* de théâtre, compagnie *f* théâtrale; ***heatre critic*** critique *mf* théâtral(e) *ou* de théâre; *Press* ***theatre review*** critique *f* théâtrale; ***theıtre in the round*** théâtre *m* en rond; *Mil* ***theatre of*** ***var*** théâtre *m* des hostilités; ***theatre workshop*** telier *m* de théâtre

ıeatregoer, *Am* **theatergoer** ['θɪətəˌɡəʊə(r)] amateur *m* de théâtre; **they're regular theatre-** **oers** ils vont régulièrement au théâtre

ıeatregoing, *Am* **theatergoing** ['θɪətə ɡəʊɪŋ] ADJ **the t. public** ceux qui vont au théâtre N fréquentation *f* des théâtres

ıeatrical [θɪ'ætrɪkəl] ADJ 1 *Theat (performance,* *eason)* théâtral 2 *Fig (exaggerated ▸ gesture, be-* *aviour)* théâtral, affecté

• **theatricals** NPL 1 *Theat* théâtre *m* d'amateur 2 *Fig* cinéma *m*, comédie *f*; **I'm fed up with all her** **theatricals** j'en ai assez de son cinéma

theatrically [θɪ'ætrɪkəlɪ] ADV théâtralement

thee [ðiː] PRON *Bible & Arch* te; *(after prep)* toi; **we** **beseech t.** nous te supplions

theft [θeft] N vol *m*; **to be charged with t.** être inculpé de vol

their [ðeə(r), *unstressed* ðə(r)] ADJ *(singular)* leur; *(plural)* leurs; **t. car** leur voiture; **t. clothes** leurs vêtements; **t. father and mother** leur père et leur mère, leurs père et mère; **t. eyes are blue** ils ont les yeux bleus; **somebody's left t. umbrella behind** quelqu'un a oublié son parapluie; **a house of t.** **own** leur propre maison, une maison à eux; **nobody in t. right mind would do such a thing!** personne de sensé ne ferait une chose pareille!

theirs [ðeəz] PRON 1 *(gen ▸ singular)* le leur (la leur) *m,f*; *(▸ plural)* les leurs *mfpl*; **our car is sturdier than t.** notre voiture est plus solide que la leur; **a friend of t.** un ami à eux/elles, un de leurs amis; **I can't stand that dog of t.** je ne supporte pas leur sacré chien; **is this yours or t.?** est-ce que ceci est à vous ou à eux?; **if anyone hasn't** **got t., they can use mine** si quelqu'un n'a pas le sien, il pourra utiliser le mien 2 *Fam (their house, flat ▸ gen)* chez eux□; *(▸ female household)* chez elles□

theism ['θiːɪzəm] N *Rel* théisme *m*

theist ['θiːɪst] *Rel* ADJ théiste
N théiste *mf*

theistic [θiː'ɪstɪk] ADJ *Rel* théiste

them [ðem, *unstressed* ðəm] PRON 1 *(direct object)* les; **I met t. last week** je les ai rencontrés la semaine dernière

2 *(indirect object)* leur; **we bought t. some flowers** nous leur avons acheté des fleurs

3 *(after preposition)* **it's for t.** c'est pour eux; **the** **yacht belongs to t.** le yacht leur appartient; **both** **of t. are wool** ils sont tous les deux en laine; **she's** **brighter than t.** elle est plus intelligente qu'eux; **neither of t. is happy** ils ne sont heureux ni l'un ni l'autre; **I don't want any of t.** je n'en veux aucun; **a** **few of t. seemed interested** quelques-uns d'entre eux semblaient intéressés; **all of t. came** ils sont tous venus; **most of t. are busy** la plupart d'entre eux sont occupés; **it was good of t. to come** c'était gentil de leur part *ou* à eux de venir

4 *Fam (as indefinite pronoun)* **when anyone comes** **she says to t....** quand quelqu'un vient elle lui dit...□

ADJ *Fam (those)* ces; **t. shoes/kids** ces bouquins/ gamins

thematic [θɪ'mætɪk] ADJ thématique

theme [θiːm] N 1 *(subject, topic)* thème *m*, sujet *m* 2 *Mus* thème *m*; **t. and variations** thème *m* et variations *fpl* 3 *Gram & Ling* thème *m*

▸▸ ***theme bar*** bar *m* à thème; ***theme music*** *Rad & TV (of programme)* générique *m*; *Cin (in film)* thème *m* principal de la musique d'un/du film; ***theme park*** parc *m* à thème; ***theme pub*** bar *m* à thème; ***theme song*** *(from film)* chanson *f* (de film); *Am (signature tune)* indicatif *m*; ***theme tune*** *(from film)* musique *f* (de film); *Br (signature tune)* indicatif *m*

themed [θiːmd] ADJ *(pub, restaurant)* à thème; **t.** **evening, t. night** soirée *f* thématique

themselves [ðəm'selvz] PRON 1 *(reflexive use)* **they hurt t.** ils se sont fait mal; **the girls enjoyed** **t.** les filles se sont bien amusées; **the children** **could see t. in the mirror** les enfants se voyaient dans la glace

2 *(emphatic use)* eux-mêmes (elles-mêmes) *mpl,fpl*; **they painted the house t.** ils ont peint la maison eux-mêmes; **they came by t.** ils sont venus tout seuls

3 *(referring to things)* eux-mêmes (elles-mêmes) *mpl,fpl*; **the boxes t. aren't very heavy** les boîtes (en) elles-mêmes ne sont pas très lourdes; **the** **details in t. are not important** ce ne sont pas les détails en eux-mêmes qui sont importants

4 *Fam (indefinite use)* **if anybody hurts t.** si quelqu'un se fait mal□

then [ðen] ADV 1 *(at a particular time)* alors, à ce moment-là; *(in distant past)* à l'époque, à cette époque, à cette époque-là; **we were very young** **t.** nous étions très jeunes à l'époque; **we can talk** **about it t.** nous pourrons en parler à ce moment-là; **Marilyn, or Norma Jean as she t. was known** Marilyn, ou Norma Jean comme elle s'appelait alors; **by t.** *(in future)* d'ici là; *(in past)* entretemps; **from t. on** à partir de ce moment-là; **since** **t.** depuis (lors); **until t.** *(in future)* jusque-là; *(in past)* jusqu'alors, jusqu'à ce moment-là

2 *(afterwards, next)* puis, ensuite; **we went shop-** **ping, t. we had lunch** nous avons fait des courses, puis nous avons déjeuné; **on the left the church,** **t. a few old houses** à gauche l'église, puis *ou* ensuite quelques vieilles maisons

3 *(so, in that case)* donc, alors; **what do you sug-** **gest, t.?** qu'est-ce que vous suggérez alors?; **I'll** **see you at 6, t.** bon, je te retrouve à 6 heures alors; **right t., anyone for more tea?** bon alors, quelqu'un veut encore du thé?; **if... t....** si... alors...; **if x equals 10 t. y...** si x égale 10 alors y...; **if it's not in my bag, t. look in the cupboard** si ce n'est pas dans mon sac, regarde dans le placard

4 *(also)* et puis; **t. there's Peter to invite** et puis il faut inviter Peter

5 *(therefore)* donc; **its significance, t., is twofold** sa signification, donc, est double

ADJ d'alors, de l'époque; **the t. head of depart-** **ment** le chef du département d'alors *ou* de l'époque

• **then again** ADV **and t. again, you may prefer to** **forget it** mais enfin peut-être que vous préférez ne plus y penser; **but t. again, no one can be sure** mais après tout, on ne sait jamais

thence [ðens] ADV *Literary or Formal* 1 *(from that place)* de là, de ce lieu, de ce lieu-là 2 *(from that time)* depuis lors 3 *(therefore)* par conséquent

thenceforth [ˌðens'fɔːθ], **thenceforward** [ˌðens'fɔːwəd] ADV *Literary or Formal* dès lors, désormais

theocracy [θɪ'ɒkrəsɪ] *(pl* **theocracies***)* N théocratie *f*

theocratic [ˌθɪə'krætɪk] ADJ théocratique

theodolite [θɪ'ɒdəlaɪt] N théodolite *m*

theologian [ˌθɪə'ləʊdʒən] N théologien(enne) *m,f*

theological [ˌθɪə'lɒdʒɪkəl] ADJ théologique
▸▸ ***theological college*** séminaire *m*

theologically [ˌθɪə'lɒdʒɪkəlɪ] ADV théologiquement; *(from a theological point of view)* d'un point de vue théologique

theology [θɪ'ɒlədʒɪ] *(pl* **theologies***)* N théologie *f*

theorem ['θɪərəm] N théorème *m*

theoretical [ˌθɪə'retɪkəl] ADJ théorique

theoretically [ˌθɪə'retɪkəlɪ] ADV théoriquement, en principe

theoretician [ˌθɪərə'tɪʃən] N théoricien(enne) *m,f*

theorist ['θɪərɪst] N théoricien(enne) *m,f*

theorize, -ise ['θɪəˌraɪz] VI *(speculate)* théoriser, faire des théories; **analysts have theorized about** **the reasons for this** les analystes ont émis toutes sortes de théories pour expliquer cela; **it's no** **use theorizing, we have to make a decision** ça ne sert à rien de faire de grandes théories, il faut qu'on prenne une décision

VT **scientists theorized that the space probe would** **disintegrate** les scientifiques émirent l'hypothèse que la sonde spatiale se désintègrerait

theorizing, -ising ['θɪəˌraɪzɪŋ] N théorisation *f*

theory ['θɪərɪ] *(pl* **theories***)* N 1 *(hypothesis)* théorie *f*; **I have a t. about his disappearance** j'ai mon idée sur sa disparition; **the t. of evolution/relativ-** **ity** la théorie de l'évolution/de la relativité 2 *(principles, rules)* théorie *f*; **musical t.** théorie *f* musicale

• **in theory** ADV en théorie, théoriquement, en principe

theosophical [ˌθɪə'sɒfɪkəl] ADJ théosophique

theosophist [θɪ'ɒsəfɪst] N théosophe *mf*

theosophy [θɪ'ɒsəfɪ] N théosophie *f*

therapeutic [ˌθerə'pjuːtɪk] ADJ thérapeutique; *Fig* **she finds gardening t.** elle trouve que le jardinage lui fait beaucoup de bien

▸▸ *Med* ***therapeutic cloning*** clonage *m* thérapeutique

therapeutically [ˌθerəˈpjuːtɪklɪ] ADV **used t.** utilisé comme thérapeutique

therapeutics [ˌθerəˈpjuːtɪks] N *(UNCOUNT) Med* thérapeutique *f*

therapist [ˈθerəpɪst] N thérapeute *mf*

therapy [ˈθerəpɪ] *(pl* **therapies**) N thérapie *f*; **to go for** *or* **to be in t.** suivre une thérapie

THERE [ðeə(r), *unstressed* ðə(r)]

> ADV
> • là **1–4** • y **1**
> PRON
> • il (il y a)
> EXCLAM
> • voilà **1–3**

ADV **1** *(in or to a particular place)* là, y; **they aren't t.** ils ne sont pas là, ils n'y sont pas; **we never go t.** nous n'y allons jamais; **we're t.!** nous voilà arrivés!; **who's t.?** qui est là?; **is Margot t.?** est-ce que Margot est là?; **see that woman t.?** tu vois cette femme là-bas?; **so t. we were/I was** donc, on était/j'étais là; **she got t. in the end** *(reached a place)* elle a fini par arriver; *(completed a task)* elle a fini par y arriver; **put it t.** mets-le là; *(shake my hand)* serre-moi la main; **she just sat/stood t.** elle était assise/debout là; **move along t., please!** circulez, s'il vous plaît; **we go to Paris and from t. to Rome** nous allons à Paris et de là à Rome; **here and t.** çà et là; **t. it is** le voilà; **it's around t. somewhere** c'est quelque part par là; **back t.** là-bas; **in t.** là-dedans; **on t.** là-dessus; **over t.** là-bas; **under t.** là-dessous; **that car t.** cette voiture-là; **those cars t.** ces voitures-là; *Fam Fig* **I've been t.** je suis passé par là, j'ai connu ça

2 *(available)* là; **it's t. if you need it** c'est là si tu en as besoin; **she's always t. for me** elle est toujours là quand j'ai besoin d'elle

3 *(in existence)* là; **I couldn't believe he was really t.** je n'arrivais pas à croire qu'il était vraiment là

4 *(on or at a particular point)* là; **we disagree t., t. we disagree** nous ne sommes pas d'accord là-dessus; **t.'s** *or* **t. lies the difficulty** voilà le problème, le problème est là; **you're right t.** là vous avez raison; **let's leave it t.** restons-en là; **we'll stop t. for today** nous nous arrêterons là pour aujourd'hui; **could I just stop you t.?** puis-je vous interrompre ici?; **as for the food, I've no complaints t.** pour ce qui est de la nourriture, là je n'ai pas à me plaindre; *Fam* **you've got me t.!** là, je ne sais pas quoi vous répondre *ou* dire!ᵓ

5 *(drawing attention to someone or something)* **hello** *or* **hi t.!** salut!; **hey t.!** hep, vous là-bas!; **t. they are!** les voilà!; **t. you go again!** ça y est, vous recommencez!; **t. she goes, complaining again!** voilà qu'elle recommence à se plaindre!; **t.'s the bell, I must be going** tiens ça sonne, je dois partir; *Ironic* **t.'s gratitude for you** c'est beau la reconnaissance!; **now finish your homework, t.'s a good boy** maintenant sois un grand garçon et finis tes devoirs

6 *(idiom)* **he's not all t.** *(stupid)* il n'a pas toute sa tête; *(senile)* il n'a plus toute sa tête

PRON **t. is** *(used before singular noun)* il y a; **t. are** *(used before plural noun)* il y a; **t. was/were** il y avait; **t. will be** il y aura; **t. is** *or* **t.'s a book on the table** il y a un livre sur la table; **t. are some books on the table** il y a des livres sur la table; **t. isn't any** il n'y en a pas; **t.'s a bus coming** il y a un bus qui arrive; **well, t.'s that girl I was telling you about…** il y a bien cette fille dont je t'ai parlé…; **what happens if t.'s a change of plan?** qu'est-ce qui se passe si on change d'idée?; **t. must have been a mistake** il a dû y avoir une erreur; **t. was once a king** il était *ou* il y avait une fois un roi; **t. was singing and dancing** on a chanté et dansé; **t. were some pieces missing** il manquait des pièces; **t. weren't any more, were t.?** il n'en restait pas, si?; **t.'s one slice left** il reste une tranche; **t. are** *or Fam* **t.'s two slices left** il reste deux tranches; **t.'s nothing we can do to help them** on ne peut rien faire pour les aider; **t.'s no stopping her** rien ne peut l'arrêter; **t.'s no knowing what he'll do next** il est impossible de prévoir ce qu'il fera ensuite; **t. comes a time when you have to slow down** il arrive un moment où il faut ralentir le rythme; **t. remain several points to be resolved** il reste plusieurs problèmes à résoudre

EXCLAM **1** *(soothing)* **t. now, don't cry!** allons *ou* là! ne pleure pas!; **t., that wasn't so bad, was it?** voilà, ça n'était pas si terrible que ça, si?; **t., t.!** allez!

2 *(aggressive)* **t., now you've made me lose count!** et voilà, tu m'as fait perdre le compte!

3 *(finishing task)* **t. (now), that's done!** là! voilà qui est fait!

• **so there** EXCLAM voilà!

• **there again** ADV après tout; **but t. again, no one really knows** mais après tout, personne ne sait vraiment

• **there and back** ADV **it will take you about an hour t. and back** l'aller et retour vous prendra à peu près une heure

• **there and then, then and there** ADV sur-le-champ; **I decided t. and then to have no more to do with him** j'ai tout de suite décidé de ne plus avoir affaire à lui

• **there you are, there you go** ADV **1** *(never mind)* **it wasn't the ideal solution, but t. you are** *or* **go** ce n'était pas l'idéal, mais enfin *ou* mais qu'est-ce que vous voulez

2 *(it's done)* **just press the button and t. you are** *or* **go!** vous n'avez qu'à appuyer sur le bouton et ça y est!

3 *(I told you so)* voilà, ça y est

4 *(here you are)* tenez, voilà

thereabouts [ˈðeərəbaʊts], *Am* **thereabout** [ˈðeərəbaʊt] ADV **1** *(indicating place)* par là, dans les environs, pas loin; **somewhere t.** quelque part par là

2 *(indicating quantity, weight)* à peu près, environ

3 *(indicating price)* environ; **£10 or t.** 10 livres environ

4 *(indicating time)* aux alentours de; **at 10 p.m. or t.** aux alentours de 22 heures, vers 10 heures du soir

thereafter [ˌðeərˈɑːftə(r)] ADV *Formal* **1** *(subsequently)* par la suite **2** *(below)* ci-dessous

thereby [ˌðeəˈbaɪ] ADV **1** *Formal* de ce fait, ainsi **2** *(idiom)* **t. hangs a tale!** c'est une longue histoire!

therefore [ˈðeəfɔː(r)] ADV donc, par conséquent; **I think, t. I am** je pense, donc je suis

therefrom [ˌðeəˈfrɒm] ADV *Arch or Formal* de là

therein [ˌðeərˈɪn] ADV *Law or Formal* **1** *(within)* à l'intérieur; **the box and all that is contained t.** la boîte et son contenu **2** *(in that respect)* là; **t. lies the difficulty** là est la difficulté

thereof [ˌðeərˈɒv] ADV *Arch or Formal* de cela, en; **all citizens of the republic are subject to the laws t.** tous les citoyens de la république doivent se soumettre aux lois de celle-ci

there's = **there is**

thereto [ˌðeəˈtuː] ADV *Law or Formal* **the letter attached t.** la lettre ci-jointe; **a copy of the Bill and the amendments t.** une copie du projet de loi et de ses amendements

thereupon [ˌðeərəˈpɒn] ADV **1** *Formal (then)* sur ce **2** *Law or Formal (on that subject)* à ce sujet, là-dessus

therewith [ˌðeəˈwɪð] ADV *Law (with)* avec cela; *(in addition)* en outre

therm [θɜːm] N *Br* ≃ 1,055 x 10^8 joules *(unité de chaleur)*

thermal [ˈθɜːməl] ADJ **1** *Phys (energy, insulation)* thermique; *(conductor, unit)* thermique, de chaleur **2** *(stream)* thermal **3** *(underwear)* en Thermolactyl®

N *Aviat & Met* thermique *m*, ascendance *f* thermique

• **thermals** NPL *(thermal underwear)* sous-vêtements *mpl* en Thermolactyl®

▸▸ ***thermal baths*** thermes *mpl*; ***thermal imager*** caméra *f* thermique; ***thermal imaging*** thermographie *f*; *Comput* ***thermal paper*** papier *m* thermique *ou* thermosensible; *Comput* ***thermal printer*** imprimante *f* thermique *ou* thermoélectrique; ***thermal reactor*** réacteur *m* thermique; ***thermal springs*** eaux *fpl ou* sources *fpl* thermales

thermic [ˈθɜːmɪk] ADJ *Phys* thermique

thermionic [ˌθɜːmɪˈɒnɪk] ADJ *Phys* thermoïonique, thermoélectronique

thermistor [θɜːˈmɪstə(r)] N thermistor *m*

thermocouple [ˈθɜːməʊkʌpəl] N thermocoup[le] *m*

thermodynamic [ˌθɜːməʊdaɪˈnæmɪk] ADJ the[r]modynamique

thermoelectric [ˌθɜːməʊɪˈlektrɪk], **therm[o]electrical** [ˌθɜːməʊɪˈlektrɪkəl] ADJ thermoéle[c]trique

thermoluminescence [θɜːməʊˌluːmɪˈnesən] N thermoluminescence *f*

thermometer [θəˈmɒmɪtə(r)] N thermomètre

thermonuclear [ˌθɜːməʊˈnjuːklɪə(r)] ADJ the[r]monucléaire

thermopile [ˈθɜːməʊpaɪl] N thermopile *f*

thermoplastic [ˌθɜːməʊˈplæstɪk] ADJ therm[o]plastique

N thermoplastique *m*

Thermos® [ˈθɜːmɒs] N Thermos® *m ou f*

▸▸ ***Thermos® flask*** (bouteille *f*) Thermos® *m o[u]* *f*

thermostat [ˈθɜːməʊstæt] N thermostat *m*

thermostatic [ˌθɜːməʊˈstætɪk] ADJ thermost[a]tique

thermostatically [ˌθɜːməʊˈstætɪkəlɪ] ADV **t. co[n]trolled** contrôlé par thermostat

thesaurus [θɪˈsɔːrəs] *(pl* **thesauri** [-raɪ] *or* **th[e]sauruses** [-sɪz]) N **1** *(book of synonyms)* ≃ dictio[n]naire *m* analogique **2** *Comput* thésaurus *m*

these [ðiːz] *pl of* **this**

thesis [ˈθiːsɪs] *(pl* **theses** [-siːz]) N *(gen) & Un[iv]* thèse *f*

thesp [θesp] N *Br Fam* acteur(trice)ᵓ *m,f*

thespian [ˈθespɪən] *Formal or Hum* ADJ drama[]tique, de théâtre

N acteur(trice) *m,f*

they [ðeɪ] PRON **1** *(subject)* ils (elles) *mpl,fp[l]*; *(stressed form)* eux (elles) *mpl,fpl*; **t.'ve left** i[ls] sont partis; **THEY bought the flowers** ce sont eu[x] qui ont acheté les fleurs; **oh, there t. are!** ah, le[s] voilà!; **t. say that she married him for his money** o[n] prétend qu'elle l'a épousé pour son argent **2** *Fa[m] (after indefinite pronoun or to replace "he/she")* **n[o]body ever admits t.'re wrong** on ne veut jama[is] reconnaître qu'on a tort; **each candidate must b[e] told that t. should…** chaque candidat doit êt[re] informé qu'il doit…

they'd [ðeɪd] **1** = **they had 2** = **they would**

they'll [ðeɪl] = **they will**

they're [ðeə(r)] = **they are**

they've [ðeɪv] = **they have**

THG [ˌtiːeɪtʃˈdʒiː] N *Chem (abbr* **tetrahydrogest[ri]none)** THG *m*

thiamin [ˈθaɪəmɪn], **thiamine** [ˈθaɪəmiːn] N thi[a]mine *f*

thick [θɪk] ADJ **1** *(wall, slice, writing)* épa[is] (aisse), gros (grosse); *(print)* gras (grasse); *(lip[s])* épais(aisse), charnu; *(shoes, boots)* gro[s] (grosse); **the boots have a t. fur lining** les botte[s] sont doublées de fourrure épaisse; **the sno[w] was t. on the ground** il y avait une épaisse co[u]che de neige sur le sol; **the boards are 20 cm** les planches ont une épaisseur de 20 cm, le[s] planches font 20 cm d'épaisseur; *Br Fam* **to giv[e] sb a t. ear** donner une gifle à qn

2 *(hair)* épais(aisse); *(beard, eyebrows)* épa[is] (aisse), touffu; *(grass, forest, crowd)* épa[is] (aisse), dense; *(carpet)* épais(aisse)

3 *(soup, cream, sauce)* épais(aisse); **to become** [or] **to get t.** épaissir

4 *(fog, smoke)* épais(aisse), dense; *(cloud[s])* épais(aisse); *(darkness, night)* profond; *Fam* **m[y] head feels a bit t. this morning** j'ai un peu mal a[u] crâne *ou* aux cheveux ce matin

5 *(covered, full)* **the shelves were t. with dust** l[es] étagères étaient recouvertes d'une épaiss[e] couche de poussière; **the air was t. with smo[ke]** *(from smokers)* la pièce était enfumée; *(from fir[e]* *guns)* l'air était empli d'une épaisse fumée; **th[e] streets were t. with police** les rues étaient plein[es] de policiers

6 *(voice ▸ with emotion)* voilé; *(▸ after late nigh[t] drinking)* pâteux; **in a voice t. with emotion** d'un[e] voix voilée par l'émotion

7 *(accent)* fort, prononcé

8 *Fam (intimate)* intimeᵓ, très liéᵓ; **those tw[o]**

are as t. as thieves ces deux-là s'entendent comme larrons en foire

9 *Br Fam (stupid)* bête□, débile; **to be as t. as two short planks** être bête comme ses pieds *ou* bête à manger du foin; **will you get that into your t. skull!** tu vas te mettre ça dans la tête, oui ou non?

10 *Br Fam (unreasonable)* **that's a bit t.!** c'est un peu fort!; **it's a bit t. expecting us to take them to the airport!** ils exagèrent de compter sur nous pour les conduire à l'aéroport!□

ADV *(spread)* en couche épaisse; *(cut)* en tranches épaisses, en grosses tranches; **the snow lay t. on the ground** il y avait une épaisse couche de neige sur le sol; **the grass grows t. at the bottom of the hill** l'herbe pousse dru en bas de la colline; **arrows started falling t. and fast around them** les flèches pleuvaient (dru) autour d'eux; **phone calls began to come in t. and fast** il y eut une avalanche de coups de téléphone; **the questions came t. and fast** les questions fusaient; *Fam* **to lay it on t.** exagérer□, en rajouter

N to stick *or* **to stay with sb through t. and thin** rester fidèle à qn contre vents et marées *ou* quoi qu'il arrive

• **in the thick of PREP** au milieu *ou* cœur de, en plein, en plein milieu de; **in the t. of the battle** en plein milieu *ou* au plus fort de la bataille; **in the t. of the discussion** en pleine discussion; **he's really in the t. of it** *(dispute, activity)* il est vraiment dans le feu de l'action; **we soon found ourselves in the t. of things** nous nous sommes vite retrouvés au cœur de l'action

hicken ['θɪkən] **VI 1** *(fog, clouds, smoke)* s'épaissir, devenir plus épais(aisse); *(bushes, forest)* s'épaissir

2 *(sauce)* épaissir; *(jam, custard)* durcir

3 *(crowd)* grossir

4 *(mystery)* s'épaissir; **the plot thickens** les choses se compliquent *ou* se corsent, l'histoire se corse

VT *(sauce, soup)* épaissir

hickener ['θɪkənə(r)] **N** *(for sauce, soup)* liant *m*; *(for oil, paint)* épaississant *m*

hickening ['θɪkənɪŋ] **N** *(of fog, clouds, smoke)* épaississement *m*; *(of sauce)* liaison *f*

ADJ *(agent)* épaississant; *(process)* d'épaississement

hicket ['θɪkɪt] **N** fourré *m*

hickhead ['θɪkhed] **N** *Fam* bêta(asse) *m,f*, andouille *f*

hickheaded [ˌθɪk'hedɪd] **ADJ** *Fam* obtus□, bouché

hickie ['θɪkɪ] **N** *Br Fam* bêta(asse) *m,f*, andouille *f*

hick-lipped ADJ aux lèvres épaisses *ou* charnues, lippu

hickly ['θɪklɪ] **ADV 1** *(spread)* en couche épaisse; *(cut)* en tranches épaisses; **the windows were t. covered in** *or* **with ice** les vitres étaient recouvertes d'une épaisse couche de givre; **t. buttered toast** pain grillé avec une épaisse couche de beurre; **t. carpeted rooms** des pièces au sol couvert de moquette épaisse **2** *(densely)* dru; **to grow t.** *(vegetation, beard)* pousser dru; **t. wooded** très boisé; **the snow fell t.** la neige tombait dru **3** *(speak)* d'une voix rauque *ou* pâteuse

hickness ['θɪknɪs] **N 1** *(of wall, snow, layer)* épaisseur *f*; *(of string, bolt)* épaisseur *f*, grosseur *f*

2 *(of beard, hair)* épaisseur *f*, abondance *f*; *(of lips)* épaisseur *f*

3 *(of fog, smoke, forest)* épaisseur *f*, densité *f*

4 *(layer ▸ of paper etc)* couche *f*

hicko ['θɪkəʊ] *(pl* **thickos***)* **N** *Br Fam* bêta(asse) *m*, *f*, andouille *f*

hickset [ˌθɪk'set] **ADJ** trapu, costaud

hick-skinned ADJ peu sensible, qui a la peau dure

hick-sliced ADJ *(bread)* coupé en tranches épaisses

hief [θi:f] *(pl* **thieves** [θi:vz]*)* **N** voleur(euse) *m,f*, **stop t.!** au voleur!; **like a t. in the night** *(leave, depart)* comme un voleur

▸▸ ***thieves' kitchen*** repaire *m* de brigands

hieve [θi:v] **VT** voler

VI voler

thieves [θi:vz] *pl of* **thief**

thieving ['θi:vɪŋ] **ADJ** voleur; *Fam* **keep your t. hands off!** pas touche!, bas les pattes!

N *(UNCOUNT)* vol *m*, vols *mpl*

thigh [θaɪ] **N** cuisse *f*

thighbone ['θaɪbəʊn] **N** fémur *m*

thigh-length ADJ *(dress, coat)* qui descend jusqu'à mi-cuisse

▸▸ ***thigh-length boots*** cuissardes *fpl*

thimble ['θɪmbəl] **N** dé *m* à coudre

thimbleful ['θɪmbəlfʊl] **N** *Fig (of liquid)* doigt *m*, goutte *f*

thin [θɪn] *(compar* **thinner**, *superl* **thinnest**, *pt & pp* **thinned**, *cont* **thinning***)* **ADJ 1** *(layer, wire)* mince, fin; *(wall)* mince, peu épais(aisse); *(person ▸ skinny)* maigre; *(▸ lean)* mince; *(leg, neck)* maigre; *(lips, book)* mince; *(clothing, blanket)* léger, fin; *(carpet)* ras; *(crowd)* peu nombreux, épars; **to become** *or* **to get** *or* **to grow t.** *(person)* maigrir; **he's as t. as a** *Br* **rake** *or Am* **rail** il est maigre comme un clou *ou* sec comme un coup de trique; **it's the t. end of the wedge** cela ne fait que commencer et ne présage rien de bon; **the move appears to be the t. end of the wedge of eventual privatisation** cette mesure est vraisemblablement le prélude à une privatisation à venir; **cheap hotels are t. on the ground** les hôtels bon marché sont rares

2 *(sparse ▸ beard, hair)* clairsemé; **he's getting a bit t. on top** il commence à perdre ses cheveux, il se dégarnit

3 *(in consistency ▸ soup, sauce)* clair; *(▸ cream)* liquide; *(▸ paint, ink)* délayé, dilué; *(▸ blood)* appauvri, anémié

4 *(smoke, clouds, mist)* léger; *(air)* raréfié; **to grow** *or* **become thinner** *(air)* se raréfier; *(ozone layer)* diminuer, s'amincir; **she seemed to vanish into t. air** elle semblait s'être volatilisée

5 *(feeble, lame ▸ excuse, argument)* mince, peu convaincant; *(▸ joke, plot, majority)* faible; **the report is rather t. on facts** le rapport ne présente pas beaucoup de faits concrets

6 *(profits)* maigre; **to have a t. time of it** *(go through difficult time)* traverser une période difficile; *(not enjoy oneself)* s'ennuyer, s'embêter; **there are t. times ahead for the coal industry** une période de vaches maigres s'annonce pour l'industrie houillère

7 *(voice)* grêle; *(smile)* petit

ADV *(spread)* en fine couche, en couche mince; *(cut)* en tranches minces *ou* fines

VT *(sauce, soup)* allonger, délayer, éclaircir

VI *(crowd)* s'éclaircir, se disperser; *(fog)* se lever, devenir moins dense *ou* épais(aisse); *(smoke)* devenir moins dense *ou* épais(aisse); *(population)* se réduire; **his hair is thinning** il perd ses cheveux

▸**thin down VT SEP** *(sauce, soup)* allonger, éclaircir, délayer; *(paint)* délayer, diluer

VI *(person)* maigrir

▸**thin out VT SEP** *(plants)* éclaircir; *(hair)* éclaircir, désépaissir

VI *(crowd)* se disperser; *(population)* se réduire, diminuer; *(fog)* se lever

thine [ðaɪn] *Bible or Arch* **POSSESSIVE ADJ** *(with singular possession)* ton (ta); *(with plural possession)* tes

PRON *(replacing singular possession)* le tien (la tienne) *m,f*; *(replacing plural possession)* les tiens (les tiennes) *mpl, fpl*; **for thee and t.** pour toi et les tiens

THING [θɪŋ]

N
- chose **A1, 2, B1–4**
- créature **A4**
- question **B2**
- mode **C4**
- objet **A1**
- idée **B1**
- idéal **C3**

NPL
- effets **1**
- choses **2–4**
- affaires **1**

N A. 1 *(object, item)* chose *f*, objet *m*; **what's that yellow t. on the floor?** qu'est-ce que c'est que ce truc jaune par terre?; **what's that t. for?** à quoi ça sert, ça?; **what's this knob t. for?** à quoi sert cette espèce de bouton?; **where's my hat? I can't find the t. anywhere** où est mon chapeau? je ne le trouve nulle part; **the only t. I could hear was a dripping tap** la seule chose que j'entendais c'était un robinet qui fuyait; **any idea how to work this t.?** tu sais comment ça marche?; **I had to rewrite the whole t.** j'ai dû tout réécrire; **the t. he loves most is his pipe** ce qu'il aime le plus, c'est sa pipe; **I need a few things from the shop** j'ai besoin de faire quelques courses; **he likes making things with his hands** il est très manuel; **I must be seeing things** je dois avoir des visions; **I must be hearing things** je dois rêver, j'entends des voix; **they were treated as things not people** on les traitait comme des choses, pas comme des êtres humains

2 *(activity, event)* chose *f*; **he likes things like gardening** il aime le jardinage et les choses dans ce goût-là; *Fam* **she's still into this art t. in a big way** elle est encore très branchée art; **the t. to do is to pretend you're asleep** vous n'avez qu'à faire semblant de dormir; **the first t. to do is (to) ring the police** la première chose à faire, c'est d'appeler la police; **the only t. left is to…** il ne reste plus qu'à…; **the next t. on the agenda** le point suivant à l'ordre du jour; **it's the best t. to do** c'est ce qu'il y a de mieux à faire; **that was a silly t. to do!** ce n'était pas la chose à faire!; **how could you do such a t.?** comment avez-vous pu faire une chose pareille?; **I have lots of things to do** j'ai des tas de choses à faire; **she certainly gets things done** avec elle, ça ne traîne pas

3 *(in negative clauses)* **I don't know a t. about algebra** je n'y connais absolument rien en algèbre; **not a t. was overlooked** pas un détail n'a été négligé; **I didn't understand a t.** je n'ai rien compris; **I couldn't do a t. to help** je n'ai rien pu faire pour me rendre utile; **it doesn't mean a t. to me** *(I don't understand it at all)* je n'y comprends (absolument) rien; *(it isn't at all familiar to me)* ça ne me dit absolument rien; *(it doesn't concern me at all)* ça ne me concerne pas; **I haven't got a t. to wear** je n'ai rien à me mettre sur le dos

4 *(creature, being)* créature *f*, être *m*; **there wasn't a living t. around** il n'y avait pas âme qui vive; **what a sweet little t.!** quel amour!; **she's a dear old t.** c'est une charmante petite vieille; **you silly t.** espèce d'idiot; **poor t.!** *(said about somebody)* le/la pauvre!; *(said to somebody)* mon/ma pauvre!; *(animal)* (la) pauvre bête!

B. 1 *(idea, notion)* idée *f*, chose *f*; **the best t. would be to ask them** le mieux serait de leur demander; **it's a good t. (for you) no one knew** heureusement (pour vous) que personne ne savait; **to be on to a good t.** être sur une bonne affaire; **to know a t. or two about sth** s'y connaître en qch; **I could show him a t. or two about hang gliding** je pourrais lui apprendre une ou deux petites choses en deltaplane

2 *(matter, question)* chose *f*, question *f*; **the t. is, we can't really afford it** le problème, c'est qu'on n'a pas vraiment les moyens; **the main t. is to succeed** ce qui importe, c'est de réussir; **the t. to remember is that…** ce dont il faut se souvenir est que…; **it's one t. to talk but quite another to act** parler est une chose, agir en est une autre; **and another t.** en plus; **we talked of one t. and another** nous avons parlé de choses et d'autres; **what with one t. and another, I haven't had time** avec tout ce qu'il y avait à faire, je n'ai pas eu le temps; **if it's not one t., it's another, it's one t. after another** ça ne s'arrête jamais

3 *(remark)* **that's not a very nice t. to say** ce n'est pas très gentil de dire ça; **she said some nasty things about him** elle a dit des méchancetés sur lui; **how can you say such a t.?** comment pouvez-vous dire une chose pareille?; **I said no such t.!** je n'ai rien dit de tel!; **I said the first t. that came into my head** j'ai dit la première chose qui m'est venue à l'esprit

4 *(quality, characteristic)* chose *f*; **one of the things I like about her is her sense of humour** une des choses que j'aime chez elle, c'est son sens de l'humour

C. 1 *Fam (strong feeling)* **to have a t. about sb/sth** *(like)* avoir un faible pour qn/qch□; *(dislike)* avoir horreur de qn/qch□; **he has a t. about red hair** *(likes)* il adore les cheveux roux□; *(dislikes)* il a quelque chose contre les cheveux roux□; **it's a bit of a t. with me** *(like)* j'aime assez ça□; *(dislike)* c'est ma bête noire

2 *Fam (interest)* **it's not really my t.** ce n'est pas vraiment mon truc; **he went off to the States to do his own t.** il est parti aux États-Unis vivre sa vie[◻]

3 *(what is needed, required)* idéal *m*; **that's just the t., that's the very t.** c'est juste ce qu'il faut; **hot cocoa is just the t. on a winter's night** un chocolat chaud, c'est l'idéal les soirs d'hiver; **that's the very t. for my bad back!** c'est juste ce dont j'avais besoin pour mon mal de dos!

4 *(fashion)* mode *f*; **it's the latest t. in swimwear** c'est la dernière mode en matière de maillots de bain; **it's quite the t.** c'est très à la mode; **a t. of the past** une chose du passé

5 *(fuss)* **to make a big t. about** *or* **out of sth** faire (tout) un plat de qch; **there's no need to make a big t. out of it!** ce n'est pas la peine d'en faire tout un plat *ou* toute une montagne!

6 *Fam (relationship)* **to have a t. with sb** avoir une liaison avec qn[◻]

7 *Fam (penis)* chose *f*

• **things** NPL **1** *(belongings)* effets *mpl*, affaires *fpl*; *(clothes)* affaires *fpl*; *(equipment)* affaires *fpl*, attirail *m*; *(tools)* outils *mpl*, ustensiles *mpl*; **put your things away** ramassez vos affaires; **take your wet things off** enlevez vos affaires humides; **have you brought your fishing/swimming things?** avez-vous apporté votre attirail de pêche/vos affaires de piscine?; **have you washed the breakfast things?** as-tu fait la vaisselle du petit déjeuner?; **to pack (up) one's things** faire ses valises

2 *(situation, circumstances)* choses *fpl*; *Fam* **how's** *or* **how are things?** comment ça va?; **things are getting better** les choses vont mieux; **things are going badly** ça va mal; **things began to get rather dangerous** les choses ont commencé à devenir assez dangereuses; **I feel rather out of things** je n'ai pas l'impression d'être vraiment dans le bain; **you take things too seriously** vous prenez les choses trop au sérieux; **I need time to think things over** j'ai besoin de temps pour réfléchir; **as things are** *or* **stand** dans l'état actuel des choses; **things being what they are** les choses étant ce qu'elles sont; **it's just one of those things** ce sont des choses qui arrivent

3 *(specific aspect of life)* choses *fpl*; **she's interested in all things French** elle s'intéresse à tout ce qui est français; **she wants to be an airline pilot of all things!** elle veut être pilote de ligne, non mais vraiment!

4 *(facts, actions etc)* choses *fpl*; **they did terrible things to their prisoners** ils ont fait des choses atroces à leurs prisonniers; **I've heard good things about his work** on dit du bien de son travail

• **for one thing** ADV (tout) d'abord; **for one t.... and for another t.** (tout) d'abord... et puis; **well for one t., we can't afford it** pour commencer, nous n'en avons pas les moyens

---

thingumabob [ˈθɪŋəmɪbɒb], **thingumajig** [ˈθɪŋəmɪdʒɪg], **thingummy** [ˈθɪŋəmɪ], **thingy** [ˈθɪŋɪ] N *Fam (person)* Bidule *mf*, Machin(e) *m,f*; *(thing)* truc *m*, machin *m*; **have you seen the thingy for the food processor?** tu as vu le machin du robot de cuisine?; **I saw thingy who you used to work with last week** la semaine dernière, j'ai vu Machin-Chose avec qui tu travaillais dans le temps

---

THINK [θɪŋk]

VI
- penser **1, 2, 4**
- réfléchir **2**
- croire **4**
- raisonner **1**
- (s')imaginer **3**

VT
- penser à **1, 5**
- penser **2, 6**
- juger **3**
- (s')imaginer **4**
- s'attendre à **6**
- réfléchir à **1**
- croire **2**
- considérer **3**
- se rappeler **5**

(pt & pp **thought** [θɔːt]*)*

VI **1** *(reason)* penser, raisonner; **to t. for oneself** se faire ses propres opinions; **sorry, I wasn't thinking clearly** *or* **straight** désolé, je n'avais pas les idées claires; **to t. aloud** penser tout haut; *Fam* **to t. big** voir les choses en grand[◻]; **t. big!** sois ambitieux![◻]; **to t. on one's feet** réfléchir vite; **you couldn't hear yourself t.** il n'était pas possible de se concentrer

2 *(ponder, reflect)* penser, réfléchir; **he thought for a moment** il a réfléchi un instant; **she doesn't say much but she thinks a lot** elle ne dit pas grand-chose, mais elle n'en pense pas moins; **t. before you speak** réfléchissez avant de parler; **t. again!** *(reconsider)* repensez-y!; *(guess)* vous n'y êtes pas, réfléchissez donc!; **let me t.** laisse-moi réfléchir; **t. carefully before deciding** réfléchissez bien avant de vous décider; **I thought hard** j'ai beaucoup réfléchi; **I thought twice before accepting** j'ai réfléchi à deux fois avant d'accepter; **to act without thinking** agir sans réfléchir; **I'm sorry, I wasn't thinking** désolé, je l'ai fait/dit sans réfléchir; **it makes you t.** ça vous fait réfléchir

3 *(imagine)* (s')imaginer; **if you t. I'd lend you my car again...** si tu t'imagines que je te prêterai encore ma voiture...; **just t.!** imaginez(-vous) un peu!; **just t., you might have married him!** imagine(-toi) que tu aurais pu l'épouser!

4 *(believe, have as opinion)* penser, croire; **she thinks as I do** elle pense comme moi; **to her way of thinking** à son avis; **it's a lot harder than I thought** c'est beaucoup plus difficile que je ne croyais

VT **1** *(ponder, reflect on)* penser à, réfléchir à; **he was thinking what they could do next** il se demandait ce qu'ils allaient pouvoir faire ensuite; **I'm thinking how to go about it** je me demande comment il faudrait s'y prendre; **I was just thinking how ironic it all is** je pensais simplement à l'ironie de la chose; **I kept thinking "why me?"** je n'arrêtais pas de me dire: pourquoi moi?; **to t. deep/evil thoughts** avoir des pensées profondes/de mauvaises pensées

2 *(believe)* penser, croire; **I t. so** je crois; **I don't t. so, I t. not** je ne crois pas; **he's a crook – I thought so** *or* **I thought as much** c'est un escroc – je m'en doutais; **I should t. so!** je crois bien!; **do you t. they'll agree? – I should t. so** croyez-vous qu'ils accepteront? – je pense que oui; **he's going to apologize – I should t. so (too)!** il va s'excuser – j'espère bien!; **I shouldn't t. so** je ne crois pas; **I t. you mean Johnson, not Boswell** je crois que tu veux dire Johnson, pas Boswell; **she didn't t. he would actually leave** elle ne pensait pas qu'il partirait vraiment; **she thinks you should leave town** elle croit que tu devrais quitter la ville; **they asked me what I thought** ils m'ont demandé mon avis; **he wants cream walls – what do you t.?** il veut des murs crème – qu'est-ce que tu en penses?; **I thought I heard a noise** j'ai cru *ou* il m'a semblé entendre un bruit; **it's expensive, don't you t.?** c'est cher, tu ne trouves pas?; *Fam* **oh, he's so honest, I don't t.!** honnête, mon œil, oui!; **I don't know what to t.** je ne sais pas quoi penser; **he thinks he knows everything** il croit tout savoir; **she thinks she's talented** elle se croit *ou* se trouve douée; **that's what you t.!** tu te fais des illusions!; **what will people t.?** qu'en dira-t-on?, qu'est-ce que les gens vont penser?; **it is thought that...** on suppose que... + *indicative*; **anyone would t. he owned the place** on croirait que c'est lui le propriétaire; **(just) who does he t. he is?** (mais) pour qui se prend-il?; **you always t. the best/the worst of everyone** vous avez toujours une très bonne/mauvaise opinion de tout le monde

3 *(judge, consider)* juger, considérer; **you must t. me very nosy** vous devez me trouver très curieux; **everyone thought he was mad** on le tenait pour fou; **she is thought to be one of the best** on dit qu'elle fait partie des meilleurs; **if you t. it necessary** si vous le jugez nécessaire; **I hardly t. it likely that...** il me semble peu probable que... + *subjunctive*

4 *(imagine)* (s')imaginer; **I can't t. why he refused** je ne vois vraiment pas pourquoi il a refusé; **you'd t. she'd be pleased** elle devrait être contente; **who'd have thought he'd become president!** qui aurait dit qu'il serait un jour président!; **who'd have thought it!** qui l'eût cru!; **just t. what we can do with all that money!** imaginez ce qu'on peut faire avec tout cet argent!; **I can't t. what you mean** je n'arrive pas à comprendre *ou* voir ce que vous voulez dire; **and to t. she did it all by herself** et dire *ou* quand on pense qu'elle a fait cela toute seule

5 *(remember)* penser à, se rappeler; **I can't t. what his name is** je n'arrive pas à me rappele[r] son nom, son nom m'échappe; **to t. to do st[h]** penser à faire qch; **they didn't t. to invite her** il[s] n'ont pas pensé à l'inviter

6 *(expect)* penser, s'attendre à; **I don't t. she'[ll] come** je ne pense pas qu'elle viendra *ou* vienne; **I little thought I would see him again** je ne m'atten[] dais guère à le revoir

7 *(have as intention)* **I t. I'll go for a walk** je croi[s] que je vais aller me promener; *esp Literary* **I onl[y] thought to help you** ma seule pensée était d[e] vous aider

8 *(in requests)* **do you t. you could help me?** pour[]riez-vous m'aider?

9 *Fam (have as main concern)* **the company i[s] thinking expansion** le maître mot dans la société c'est expansion[◻]

N **to have a t.** réfléchir; **we've had a t. about i[t]** nous y avons réfléchi; **I'll have another t. abou[t] it** je vais encore y réfléchir; *Fam* **you've got an[other] other t. coming!** tu te fais des illusions!

►► *think tank* groupe *m* de réflexion

► **think about** VT INSEP **1** *(ponder, reflect on)* **to [t.] about sth/doing sth** penser à qch/à faire qch; **what are you thinking about?** à quoi pensez[-]vous?; **we were just thinking about the holiday[s]** nous pensions justement aux vacances; **I'v[e] thought about your proposal** j'ai réfléchi à votr[e] proposition; **it's not a bad idea, if you t. about i[t]** ce n'est pas une mauvaise idée, si tu réfléchi[s] bien; **that's worth thinking about** cela mérite ré[]flexion; **she's thinking about starting a busines[s]** elle pense à *ou* envisage de monter une affaire; **we'll t. about it** nous allons y penser *ou* réfléchir; **she has a lot to t. about just now** elle est trè[s] préoccupée en ce moment; **there's so much to t. about when you buy a house** il y a tant de chose[s] à prendre en considération quand on achète une maison; **the conference gave us much to t. about** la conférence nous a donné matière à ré[]flexion; **I'll give you something to t. about!** je vai[s] te donner de quoi réfléchir! **2** *(consider seriously)* penser à; **all he thinks about is money** il n'y a qu[e] l'argent qui l'intéresse; **I've got my family/futur[e] to t. about** il faut que je pense à ma famille/mo[n] avenir **3** *(have opinion about)* penser de; **what d[o] you t. about him?** que pensez-vous de lui?; **wha[t] do you t. about it?** qu'en pensez-vous?

► **think back** VI **to t. back to sth** se rappeler qch; **t. back to that night** essayez de vous souvenir d[e] *ou* vous rappeler cette nuit-là; **when I t. bac[k]** quand j'y repense

► **think of** VT INSEP **1** *(have as tentative plan)* pen[]ser à, envisager de; **she's thinking of starting [a] business** elle pense à *ou* envisage de monte[r] une affaire; **what were you thinking of givin[g] her?** que pensais-tu lui donner?

2 *(have in mind)* penser à; **we're thinking of yo[u]** nous pensons à toi; **I was thinking of how muc[h] times have changed** je songeais combien le temps ont changé; **whatever were you thinkin[g] of?** où avais-tu la tête?; **come to t. of it, that's no[t] a bad idea** à la réflexion, ce n'est pas une mau[]vaise idée; **we wouldn't t. of letting our daughte[r] travel alone** il ne nous viendrait pas à l'esprit d[e] laisser notre fille voyager seule; **I couldn't t. of it** c'est impossible!

3 *(remember)* penser à, se rappeler; **he couldn't t. of the name** il ne se rappelait pas le nom, le nor[m] ne lui venait pas; **that makes me t. of my child[]hood** ça me rappelle mon enfance

4 *(come up with* ► *idea, solution)* **she's the on[e] who thought of double-checking** it c'est elle qui [a] eu l'idée de le vérifier; **try every method you can t. of** essayez toutes les méthodes que vous puis[]siez imaginer; **I thought of the answer** j'ai trouv[é] la réponse; **I've just thought of something, she'[ll] be out** j'avais oublié *ou* je viens de me rappele[r] elle ne sera pas là; **I've just thought of somethin[g] else** il y a autre chose, ce n'est pas tout; **I'd neve[r] have thought of that** je n'y aurais jamais pensé; **why didn't you phone? – I didn't t. of it** pourquo[i] n'avez-vous pas téléphoné? – je n'y ai pa[s] pensé; **whatever will they t. of next?** qu'est-c[e] qu'ils vont bien pouvoir trouver ensuite?; **t. of [a] number between 1 and 10** pensez à un chiffre en[]tre 1 et 10; **I thought better of it** je me suis ravisé; **to t. better of sb for doing sth** estimer qn davan[]tage d'avoir *ou* pour avoir fait qch; **he though[t]**

nothing of leaving the baby alone for hours at a time il trouvait (ça) normal de laisser le bébé seul pendant des heures; **thank you – t. nothing of it!** merci – mais je vous en prie *ou* mais c'est tout naturel!

5 *(judge, have as opinion)* **what do you t. of the new teacher?** comment trouvez-vous le *ou* que pensez-vous du nouveau professeur?; **what do you t. of it?** qu'en pensez-vous?; **she thinks very highly** *or* **well of him** elle a une très haute opinion de lui; **he thinks of himself as an artist** il se prend pour un artiste; **to t. a great deal of oneself, to t. too much of oneself** avoir une haute idée de soi-même *ou* de sa personne; **as a doctor she is very well thought of** elle est très respectée en tant que médecin; **I hope you won't t. badly of me if I refuse** j'espère que vous ne m'en voudrez pas si je refuse; **I don't t. much of that idea** cette idée ne me dit pas grand-chose; **I told her what I thought of her** je lui ai dit son fait

6 *(imagine)* penser à, imaginer; **I always thought of her as being blonde** je la croyais blonde; **just t. of it, me as president!** imaginez un peu: moi président!, vous m'imaginez président?; **when I t. of what might have happened!** quand je pense à ce qui aurait pu arriver!

7 *(take into consideration)* penser à, considérer; **I have my family to t. of** il faut que je pense à ma famille; **she never thinks of anyone but herself** elle ne pense qu'à elle-même; **he never thinks of her** il n'a aucun égard *ou* aucune considération pour elle; **you never t. of the expense** tu ne regardes jamais à la dépense; **t. of how much it will cost!** pense un peu à ce que ça va coûter!; **you can't t. of everything** on ne peut pas penser à tout

▸**think out** VT SEP *(plan)* élaborer, préparer; *(problem)* bien étudier *ou* examiner; *(solution)* bien étudier; **it needs thinking out** cela demande mûre réflexion; **he likes to t. things out for himself** il aime juger des choses par lui-même; **a well-thought-out plan** un projet bien conçu *ou* ficelé

▸**think over** VT SEP bien examiner, bien réfléchir à; **we'll have to t. it over** il va falloir que nous y réfléchissions; **t. the offer over carefully** réfléchissez bien à cette proposition; **on thinking things over we've decided not to sell the house** réflexion faite, on a décidé de ne pas vendre la maison

▸**think through** VT SEP *(plan etc)* bien considérer; **the scheme has not been properly thought through** le plan n'a pas été considéré suffisamment en détail

▸**think up** VT SEP *(excuse, plan, solution)* trouver

thinkable [ˈθɪŋkəbəl] ADJ pensable, concevable, imaginable; **it is scarcely** *or* **barely t. that...** il est difficilement concevable *ou* imaginable que... *+ subjunctive*

thinker [ˈθɪŋkə(r)] N penseur(euse) *m,f*

thinking [ˈθɪŋkɪŋ] ADJ *(person)* pensant, rationnel, qui réfléchit; **it's the t. man's answer to pulp fiction** c'est un roman de hall de gare en plus intelligent; *Br Fam Hum* **the t. man's/woman's crumpet** la petite préférée/le petit préféré des intellos; *Fam Fig* **to put on one's t. cap** se mettre à réfléchir[□], cogiter[□]

N **1** *(act)* pensée *f*, pensées *fpl*, réflexion *f*; **I've done some serious t. about the situation** j'ai bien *ou* sérieusement *ou* mûrement réfléchi à la situation; **his life was saved thanks to the nurses' quick t.** la réaction rapide des infirmières lui a sauvé la vie **2** *(opinion, judgment)* point *m* de vue, opinion *f*, opinions *fpl*; **my t. on disarmament has changed** mes opinions sur le désarmement ont changé; **she finally came round to my way of t.** elle s'est finalement ralliée à mon point de vue; **to his way of t. it was wrong** pour lui, ce n'était pas bien

▸▸ *Aut* ***thinking distance*** temps *m* de réaction

thin-lipped ADJ aux lèvres minces

thinly [ˈθɪnlɪ] ADV *(spread)* en couche mince; *(cut)* en fines tranches; **a t. disguised insult** une insulte à peine voilée; **the area is t. populated** la région n'est pas très peuplée

thinner [ˈθɪnə(r)] *compar of* **thin**

N *(solvent)* diluant *m*

thinness [ˈθɪnnɪs] N **1** *(of layer)* minceur *f*, finesse *f*; *(of wall)* minceur *f*, faible épaisseur *f*; *(of person* ▸ *skinniness)* maigreur *f*; *(*▸ *leanness)* minceur *f*; *(of lips)* minceur *f*; *(of wire)* finesse *f*; *(of clothing, blanket, carpet)* légèreté *f*, finesse *f*

2 *(of beard, hair)* finesse *f*, rareté *f*

3 *(of excuse)* faiblesse *f*, insuffisance *f*; *(of joke, storyline, plot)* faiblesse *f*; **because of the t. of their majority** à cause de leur faible majorité

4 *(of air)* raréfaction *f*

thinning [ˈθɪnɪŋ] ADJ **his t. hair** ses cheveux qui commencent à se clairsemer

▸▸ ***thinning agent*** diluant *m*

thin-skinned ADJ *Fig* susceptible

thin-sliced ADJ *(bread)* coupé en tranches fines, finement coupé

third [θɜːd] N **1** *(fraction)* tiers *m*

2 *(in series)* troisième *mf*

3 *(of month)* trois *m inv*

4 *Mus* tierce *f*

5 *Aut* troisième *f*; **in t.** en troisième

6 *Br Univ* ≃ licence *f* sans mention

ADJ troisième; **t. time lucky** la troisième fois sera la bonne

ADV troisièmement; *(in contest)* en troisième position, à la troisième place; *see also* **fifth**

▸▸ ***third base*** *(in baseball)* troisième but *m*; *Fam* ***third degree*** interrogatoire *m* serré[□]; **to get the t. degree** subir un interrogatoire; **to give sb the t. degree** *(torture)* passer qn à tabac; *(interrogate)* cuisiner qn; ***third finger*** majeur *m*; *Aut* ***third gear*** troisième vitesse *f*; *Am Sch* ***third grade*** = classe du primaire pour les 7–8 ans, *Can* 3ème année; ***third party*** tierce personne *f*, tiers *m*; *Gram* ***third person*** troisième personne *f*; **in the t. person** à la troisième personne; *Fin* ***third quarter*** *(of financial year)* troisième trimestre *m*; *Hist* ***the Third Reich*** le Troisième Reich; ***the Third World*** le tiers-monde

third-class ADJ *Br Univ (degree)* sans mention

third-degree burn N brûlure *f* au troisième degré

third-generation ADJ *Comput & Tel* de troisième génération, 3G

thirdly [ˈθɜːdlɪ] ADV troisièmement, en troisième lieu, tertio

third-rate ADJ de qualité inférieure

Third-World ADJ du tiers-monde

thirst [θɜːst] N *also Fig* soif *f*; **all that hard work has given me a t.** ça m'a donné soif de travailler dur comme ça; **to have a t. for knowledge/adventure** avoir soif de connaissances/d'aventure

VI *also Fig* **to t. for sth** avoir soif de qch; **he was thirsting for a beer** il avait envie d'une bière; **thirsting for revenge** assoiffé de vengeance; **to t. for knowledge** être avide de connaissances

thirstily [ˈθɜːstɪlɪ] ADV avidement

thirsty [ˈθɜːstɪ] *(compar* **thirstier**, *superl* **thirstiest***)* ADJ **1** *(wanting a drink)* qui a soif, assoiffé; **to be** *or* **to feel t.** avoir soif; **salted peanuts make you t.** les cacahuètes salées donnent soif; **it's t. work** ça donne soif **2** *Fig (for knowledge, adventure)* assoiffé; **to be t. for** avoir soif de, être assoiffé de; **she was t. for revenge** elle était assoiffée de vengeance **3** *(plant)* qui a besoin de beaucoup d'eau; *(soil)* desséché

thirteen [ˌθɜːˈtiːn] N treize *m inv*

PRON treize

ADJ treize; *see also* **five**

thirteenth [ˌθɜːˈtiːnθ] N **1** *(fraction)* treizième *m* **2** *(in series)* treizième *mf* **3** *(of month)* treize *m inv*

ADJ treizième

ADV treizièmement; *(in contest)* en treizième position, à la treizième place; *see also* **fifth**

thirtieth [ˈθɜːtɪəθ] N **1** *(fraction)* trentième *m* **2** *(in series)* trentième *mf* **3** *(of month)* trente *m inv*

ADJ trentième

ADV trentièmement; *(in contest)* en trentième position, à la trentième place; *see also* **fifth**

thirty [ˈθɜːtɪ] *(pl* **thirties***)* N trente *m inv*

PRON trente; **about t.** une trentaine

ADJ trente; *see also* **fifty**

thirty-second ADJ *Am Mus*

▸▸ ***thirty-second note*** triple croche *f*; ***thirty-second rest*** huitième *m* de soupir

thirty-three N *(record)* trente-trois tours *m inv*

thirty-year rule N *Br Pol* règle *f* des trente ans

THIS [ðɪs]

> **DEM PRON**
> • ceci **1** • ce **1**
> • celui-ci **2**
> **DEM ADJ**
> • ce **1** • ce…-ci **2**
> **ADV**
> • aussi • si

(pl **these** [ðiːz]*)*

DEMONSTRATIVE PRON **1** *(person, situation, statement, thing indicated* ▸ *subject)* ceci, ce; *(*▸ *object)* ce; **what's t.?** qu'est-ce que c'est (que ça)?; **who's t.?** *(gen)* qui est-ce?; *(on phone)* qui est à l'appareil?; **t. is for you** tiens, c'est pour toi; **t. is Mr Smith speaking** *(on phone)* M. Smith à l'appareil, c'est M. Smith; **t. is my mother** *(in introduction)* je vous présente ma mère; *(in picture)* c'est ma mère; **these are my children** voici mes enfants; **these are things we cannot do without** ce sont des choses dont on ne peut se passer; **t. is the place I was talking about** c'est *ou* voici l'endroit dont je parlais; **t. is terrible** c'est affreux; **t. is where I live** c'est ici que j'habite; **listen to t.** écoutez bien ceci; **eat/drink some of t.** mangez-/buvez-en un peu; **what's t. I hear about your leaving?** on me dit que vous partez?; **what's all t.?** *(these objects)* qu'est-ce que c'est que tout ça?; *(what's happening?)* qu'est-ce qu'il y a?, qu'est-ce qui se passe?; **it was like t.** voici comment les choses se sont passées; **do it like t.** voici comment il faut faire; **I didn't want it to end like t.** je ne voulais pas que ça finisse *ou* se termine comme ça; **that it should come to t.** qu'on en arrive là; **and there's no way she could live with you? – well, t. is it** et elle ne pourrait pas vivre avec toi? – non, justement; **t. is it, the moment we've all been waiting for!** nous y voilà, c'est le moment que nous attendons tous!; **I'll tell you t....** je vais te dire une chose…; **after/before t.** après/avant ça; **at t., he left the room** là-dessus *ou* sur ce, il a quitté la pièce; **to talk about t. and that** bavarder de choses et d'autres; **they sat chatting about t., that and the other** ils étaient là, assis, à bavarder de choses et d'autres; **it's always John t. and John that** c'est John par-ci, John par-là

2 *(contrasted with "that")* celui-ci (celle-ci) *m,f*; **these** ceux-ci (celles-ci) *mpl, fpl*; **t. is a rose, that is a peony** ceci est une rose, ça c'est une pivoine; **I want these, not those!** je veux ceux-ci, pas ceux-là!; **is t. more expensive than that?** celui-ci est-il plus cher que celui-là?

DEMONSTRATIVE ADJ **1** *(referring to a particular person, idea, time or thing)* ce (cette); **these** ces; **t. man** cet homme; **these ideas** ces idées; **t. plan of yours won't work** votre projet ne marchera pas; **t. book you wanted** le livre que vous vouliez; **t. way please** par ici, s'il vous plaît; **t. funny little man came up to me** un petit bonhomme à l'air bizarre est venu vers moi; **there were these two Germans...** il y avait ces deux Allemands…; **who's t. friend of yours?** c'est qui, cet ami?; *Fam* **t. here bike** ce vélo-ci[□]; **t. morning** ce matin; **by t. time tomorrow he'll be gone** demain à cette heure-ci, il sera parti; **t. time last week** la semaine dernière à la même heure; **t. time next year** l'année prochaine à la même époque; **t. coming week** la semaine prochaine *ou* qui vient; **saving money isn't easy these days** faire des économies n'est pas facile aujourd'hui *ou* de nos jours; **he's worked hard these last two months** il a beaucoup travaillé ces deux derniers mois; **I've been watching you t. past hour** ça fait une heure *ou* voici une heure que je vous regarde; **what are you doing t. Christmas?** qu'est-ce que vous faites pour Noël cette année?

2 *(contrasted with "that")* ce …-ci (cette …-ci); **these** ces …-ci; **t. table over here** cette table-ci; **which do you prefer, t. one or that one?** lequel tu préfères, celui-ci ou celui-là?; **t. dress is cheaper than that one** cette robe-ci est moins chère que celle-là *ou* que l'autre; **people ran t. way and that** les gens couraient dans tous les sens

ADV aussi, si; **it was t. high** c'était haut comme ça; **we've come t. far, we might as well go on** *(on* *journey)* nous sommes venus jusqu'ici, alors autant continuer; *(on project)* maintenant que nous en sommes là, autant continuer

thistle ['θɪsəl] **N** chardon *m*

thistledown ['θɪsəldaʊn] **N** duvet *m* de chardon

thither ['ðɪðə(r)] **ADV** *Formal or Literary* là

tho, tho' = **though**

> **-THON**
> *voir* **-ATHON**

thong [θɒŋ] **N 1** *(strip ▸ of leather, rubber)* lanière *f* **2** *(underwear)* cache-sexe *m*; *(swimwear)* tanga *m*

• **thongs NPL** *Am & Austr (flip-flops)* tongs *fpl*

thoracic [θɔː'ræsɪk] **ADJ** thoracique

thorax ['θɔːræks] *(pl* **thoraxes** *or* **thoraces** [-rəsiːz]) **N** thorax *m*

thorn [θɔːn] **N 1** *(prickle)* épine *f*; *Fig* **it's a t. in his side** *or* **flesh** c'est une source d'irritation constante pour lui, c'est sa bête noire **2** *(tree, shrub)* arbuste *m* épineux

thornback ['θɔːnbæk] **N** *Ich* raie *f* bouclée

thornbush ['θɔːnbʊʃ] **N** buisson *m* épineux

thornless ['θɔːnlɪs] **ADJ** sans épines

thorny ['θɔːnɪ] *(compar* **thornier**, *superl* **thorniest) ADJ** *also Fig* épineux

thorough ['θʌrə] **ADJ 1** *(complete ▸ inspection, research)* minutieux, approfondi; **to give sth a t. clean** nettoyer qch à fond; **she has a t. knowledge of her subject** elle a une connaissance parfaite de son sujet, elle connaît son sujet à fond *ou* sur le bout des doigts; **she was subjected to a t. cross-examination** elle a subi un contre-interrogatoire minutieux; **it needs a t. revision** il faut réviser ça en profondeur **2** *(meticulous ▸ work, worker)* minutieux; **he did a very t. job** il a fait un travail très minutieux **3** *(as intensifier)* absolu, complet(ète); **the man is a t. scoundrel!** c'est une crapule finie!; **it's a t. nuisance!** c'est vraiment très embêtant!

thoroughbred ['θʌrəbred] **ADJ** *(horse)* pur-sang *(inv)*; *(animal ▸ gen)* de race

N 1 *(horse)* pur-sang *m inv*; *(animal ▸ gen)* bête *f* de race **2** *(person)* **she's a t.** elle a de la classe, elle est racée

thoroughfare ['θʌrəfeə(r)] **N** voie *f* de communication; **one of the main thoroughfares of the town** une des rues principales *ou* une des artères de la ville; **no t.** *(no entry)* passage interdit; *(cul-de-sac)* voie sans issue

thoroughgoing ['θʌrəˌgəʊɪŋ] **ADJ** *(search, investigation)* minutieux, approfondi, complet (ète); **he's a t. nuisance** il est vraiment pénible

thoroughly ['θʌrəlɪ] **ADV 1** *(minutely, in detail ▸ search)* à fond, de fond en comble; *(▸ examine)* à fond, minutieusement; **the carpet has been t. cleaned** le tapis a été nettoyé à fond; **read the questions t.** lisez très attentivement les questions **2** *(as intensifier)* tout à fait, absolument; **to be t. bored** s'ennuyer mortellement; **I t. agree** je suis tout à fait d'accord

thoroughness ['θʌrənɪs] **N** minutie *f*; **the t. of his knowledge** ses connaissances très complètes; **the t. of his work** la minutie qu'il apporte à son travail

those [ðəʊz] *pl of* **that**

thou¹ [ðaʊ] **PRON** *NEng or Arch or Literary* tu; *(stressed form)* toi

thou² [θaʊ] *(pl* **inv** *or* **thous) N** *Fam (abbr* **thousand)** mille▫ *m inv*

though [ðəʊ] **CONJ** bien que + *subjunctive*, quoique + *subjunctive*; **t. young, she's very mature** bien qu'elle soit jeune *ou* quoique jeune, elle est très mûre; **t. it's a difficult language, I intend to persevere** bien que ce soit une langue difficile, j'ai l'intention de persévérer; **he enjoyed the company t. not the food** il appréciait les gens avec qui il était mais pas ce qu'il mangeait; **kind t. she was, we never really got on** malgré sa gentillesse, nous ne nous sommes jamais très bien entendus; **it's an excellent book, t. I say so myself** c'est un très bon livre, sans fausse modestie; **strange t. it may seem** aussi étrange que cela puisse paraître

ADV pourtant; **he's a difficult man; I like him t.** il n'est pas facile à vivre; pourtant je l'aime bien; **it's nice, t., isn't it?** c'est joli quand même, tu ne trouves pas?; *Fam* **did she t.!** elle a dit/fait cela?▫

thought [θɔːt] *pt & pp of* **think**

N 1 *(UNCOUNT) (reflection)* pensée *f*, réflexion *f*; **to give a problem much** *or* **a lot of t.** bien réfléchir à un problème; **after much t.** après mûre réflexion, après avoir mûrement réfléchi; **we gave some t. to the matter** nous avons réfléchi à la question; **this problem needs careful t.** nous devons bien réfléchir à ce problème; **she was lost** *or* **deep in t.** elle était plongée dans ses pensées **2** *(consideration)* considération *f*, pensée *f*; **I haven't given it a t.** je n'y ai pas pensé; **don't give it another t.** n'y pensez plus; **my thoughts were elsewhere** j'avais l'esprit ailleurs; **my thoughts went back to the time I had spent in Tunisia** j'ai repensé au temps où j'étais en Tunisie; **she accepted the job with no t. of her family** elle a accepté le travail sans tenir compte de sa famille; **he had no t. for his own safety** il ne pensait pas à sa propre sécurité; **our thoughts are with you** nos pensées vous accompagnent

3 *(idea, notion)* idée *f*, pensée *f*; **happy t.** heureuse idée *f*; **dark** *or* **gloomy thoughts** idées *fpl* noires; **the t. occurred to me that you might like to come** l'idée m'est venue *ou* je me suis dit que cela vous ferait peut-être plaisir de venir; **the mere** *or* **very t. of it makes me feel ill** rien que d'y penser, ça me rend malade; **that's a t.!** ça, c'est une idée!; **what an awful t.!** quelle horreur!; **what a kind t.!** quelle aimable attention!

4 *(intention)* idée *f*, intention *f*; **her one t. was to reach the top** sa seule idée était d'atteindre le sommet; **I have no t. of resigning** je n'ai pas l'intention de démissionner; **I had to give up all t.** *or* **thoughts of finishing on time** j'ai dû finalement renoncer à l'idée de terminer à temps; **you must give up all t.** *or* **thoughts of seeing him** il faut renoncer à le voir, il ne faut plus penser à le voir; **it's the t. that counts** c'est l'intention qui compte

5 *(opinion)* opinion *f*, avis *m*; **we'd like your thoughts on the matter** nous aimerions savoir ce que vous en pensez

6 *(UNCOUNT) (doctrine, ideology)* pensée *f*; **political t.** la pensée politique

thoughtful ['θɔːtfʊl] **ADJ 1** *(considerate, kind)* prévenant, attentionné; **it was a t. gesture** c'était un geste plein de délicatesse; **be more t. next time** pensez un peu plus aux autres la prochaine fois; **it was very t. of them to send the flowers** c'est très gentil de leur part d'avoir envoyé les fleurs **2** *(pensive)* pensif **3** *(reasoned ▸ decision, remark, essay)* réfléchi; *(▸ study)* sérieux

thoughtfully ['θɔːtfʊlɪ] **ADV 1** *(considerately, kindly)* avec prévenance *ou* délicatesse, gentiment **2** *(pensively)* pensivement **3** *(with careful thought)* d'une manière réfléchie

thoughtfulness ['θɔːtfʊlnɪs] **N 1** *(kindness)* prévenance *f*, délicatesse *f*, gentillesse *f* **2** *(pensiveness)* air *m* pensif

thoughtless ['θɔːtlɪs] **ADJ 1** *(inconsiderate ▸ person)* qui manque d'égards pour autrui, qui se soucie peu des autres; *(▸ act, behaviour)* qui dénote un manque d'égards *ou* de considération pour autrui; *(▸ remark)* indélicat; **it was t. of me** ce n'était pas très délicat de ma part; **what a t. thing to do!** quel manque de délicatesse! **2** *(hasty, rash ▸ person)* irréfléchi; *(▸ action, remark)* irréfléchi, inconsidéré

thoughtlessly ['θɔːtlɪslɪ] **ADV 1** *(without consideration)* sans aucun égard, sans aucune considération; **to treat sb t.** manquer d'égards envers qn; **she had t. thrown out all their notes** elle avait jeté toutes leurs notes sans s'inquiéter de savoir s'ils pouvaient en avoir besoin **2** *(without forethought)* sans réfléchir

thoughtlessness ['θɔːtlɪsnɪs] **N** *(UNCOUNT)* **1** *(lack of consideration)* manque *m* d'égards *ou* de prévenance **2** *(lack of forethought)* irréflexion *f*, étourderie *f*

thought-provoking **ADJ** qui pousse à la réflexion, stimulant

thousand ['θaʊzənd] **ADJ** mille; **a t. years** mille ans, un millénaire; **five t. people** cinq mille personnes; **I've got a t. and one things to ask you/to do** j'ai mille choses à vous demander/à faire

N mille *m inv*; **in the year two t.** en l'an deux mille; **thousands of people** des milliers de personnes; **how many people were there? – about a t.** combien de gens étaient là? – un millier

▸▸ ***Thousand Island dressing*** = sauce à base de mayonnaise, de ketchup et de cornichons hachés

thousandfold ['θaʊzəndfəʊld] **ADJ** multiplié par mille

ADV mille fois autant

thousandth ['θaʊzəntθ] **ADJ** millième

N 1 *(fraction)* millième *m* **2** *(in series)* millième *mf*

thraldom, *Am* **thralldom** ['θrɔːldəm] **N** *Formal* servitude *f*, esclavage *m*

thrall [θrɔːl] **N** *Formal* servitude *f*, esclavage *m*; **to be in t. to sb** être l'esclave de qn; *Fig* être sous l'emprise de qn; **to be in t. to sth** être l'esclave de qch; **the government are in t. to big business** le gouvernement est inféodé aux grandes entreprises; *Fig* **to hold sb in t.** fasciner qn

thrash [θræʃ] **VT 1** *(as a punishment)* rouer de coups, rosser; *Fam (defeat)* battre à plate(s) couture(s); **he thrashed the hedge with a stick** il donna des grands coups de bâton dans la haie; *Fam* **Liverpool thrashed Arsenal** Liverpool a battu Arsenal à plate(s) couture(s); **to t. sb soundly** *(as punishment)* donner une bonne raclée à qn; *Fam (defeat)* battre qn à plate(s) couture(s) **2** *(move vigorously)* **to t. one's arms/legs** agiter violemment les bras/jambes; **the dolphin thrashed its tail and disappeared** le dauphin donna de grands coups de queue et disparut

VI *(move violently)* se débattre; **a sea of thrashing limbs** une mer de bras et de jambes qui s'agitaient; **the waves thrashed against the rocks/boat** les vagues battaient violemment contre les rochers/le bateau

▸ **thrash about, thrash around VI** *(person, fish)* se débattre; **she was thrashing about in bed** elle se débattait dans le lit; **he thrashed about to free himself** il se débattait pour se libérer

VT SEP *(stick)* agiter; **to t. one's arms and legs about** se débattre des mains et des pieds

▸ **thrash out VT SEP** *(problem)* débattre de; *(agreement)* finir par trouver

thrashing ['θræʃɪŋ] **N 1** *(beating)* volée *f*, *(punishment)* correction *f*; **to give sb a t.** donner une volée à qn; *(as a punishment)* donner une bonne correction à qn; **to get a t.** prendre une volée **2** *Fam (defeat)* déculottée *f*, raclée *f*; **to give sb a t.** battre qn à plate(s) couture(s)

thread [θred] **N 1** *Sewing & Med* fil *m*; **gold t.** fil *m* d'or; *Fig* **his life hung by a t.** sa vie ne tenait qu'à un fil

2 *Fig (of water, smoke)* filet *m*; *(of light)* mince rayon *m*; *(of story, argument)* fil *m*; **it's difficult to follow the t. of her argument** il est difficile de suivre le fil de ses idées; **she gradually began to pick up the threads of her life again** elle a lentement commencé à reconstruire sa vie

3 *Tech (of screw)* pas *m*, filetage *m*

4 *Comput (in newsgroup)* fil *m* de discussion

VT 1 *(needle, beads, cotton)* enfiler; **she threaded the needle** elle a enfilé l'aiguille; **you have to t. the elastic through the loops** il faut enfiler *ou* faire passer l'élastique dans les boucles; *Fig* **her hair was threaded with grey** elle avait quelques fils blancs dans les cheveux, *Literary* ses cheveux étaient semés de fils d'argent; **she threaded her way through the crowd/market** elle s'est faufilée parmi la foule/à travers le marché **2** *Tech (screw)* tarauder, fileter

VI *(needle, cotton)* s'enfiler; **the tape threads through the slot** la bande passe dans la fente

• **threads NPL** *Fam (clothes)* fringues *fpl*

▸▸ ***thread mark*** filigrane *m (des billets de banque)*

threadbare ['θredbeə(r)] **ADJ 1** *(carpet, clothing)* usé, râpé; **he lived a t. existence** il menait une existence miséreuse **2** *(joke, excuse, argument)* usé, rebattu

threadworm ['θredwɜːm] **N** oxyure *m*

threat [θret] **N** *also Fig* menace *f*; **to make threats against sb** proférer des menaces contre qn; **they got what they wanted by threats** ils ont obtenu ce qu'ils voulaient par la menace; **terrorist attacks are a constant t. to our security** les attentats teroristes représentent une menace constante pour notre sécurité; **political unrest poses a t. to peace in the area** l'agitation politique menace la paix dans la région; **the country lives under (the) t. of war** le pays vit sous la menace de la guerre

hreaten ['θretən] VT **1** *(make threats against ▸ person)* menacer; **to t. to do sth** menacer de faire qch; **he threatened her with a gun** il l'a menacée avec un pistolet; **he started threatening me** il s'est mit menaçant, il s'est mis à me menacer; **we were threatened with the sack** on nous a menacés de licenciement **2** *(of danger, unpleasant event)* menacer; **the species is threatened with extinction** l'espèce est menacée *ou* en voie de disparition; **our jobs are threatened** nos emplois sont menacés; **it's threatening to rain/to snow** la pluie/la neige menace **3** *(be a danger for ▸ society, tranquillity)* menacer, être une menace pour

VI *(danger, storm)* menacer

hreatening ['θretənɪŋ] ADJ *(danger, sky, storm, person)* menaçant; *(letter)* de menaces; *(look, gesture)* menaçant, de menace

hreateningly ['θretənɪŋlɪ] ADV *(behave, move)* de manière menaçante, d'un air menaçant; *(say)* d'un ton *ou* sur un ton menaçant

hree [θri:] N *(number, numeral)* trois *m inv*

PRON trois

ADJ trois; *see also* **five**

hree-button mouse N *Comput* souris *f* à trois boutons

hree-colour, three-coloured, *Am* **three-color, three-colored** ADJ tricolore; *Phot* trichrome

▸▸ ***three-colour printing*** impression *f* en trois couleurs *ou* en trichromie, trichromie *f*; ***three-colour process*** trichromie *f*

hree-cornered ADJ triangulaire

▸▸ ***three-cornered discussion*** débat *m* à trois; ***three-cornered hat*** tricorne *m*

hree-course ADJ *(meal)* à trois plats

-D, three-D ADJ **1** *(figure, drawing)* à trois dimensions, tridimensionnel; *(film)* en relief; *(image)* en trois dimensions **2** *(character ▸ in book, play etc)* qui semble réel

hree-dimensional = **3-D**

hreefold ['θri:fəʊld] ADJ triple; **a t. increase in the membership figures** une augmentation au triple du nombre d'adhérents

ADV trois fois autant; **to increase t.** tripler

hree-four time N *Mus* mesure *f* à trois temps,trois-quatre *m inv*

G [,θri:'dʒi:] ADJ *Comput & Tel* 3G

hree-handed ADJ

▸▸ *Cards etc* ***three-handed game*** partie *f* à trois

hree-legged ADJ *(stool, table)* à trois pieds; *(animal)* à trois pattes

▸▸ ***three-legged race*** = course où les participants courent par deux, la jambe gauche de l'un attachée à la droite de l'autre

hree-line whip N *Br Pol* = convocation urgente d'un député par un "whip" à un vote lors d'une séance parlementaire

hreepence ['θrepəns, 'θrʌpəns] N *Br* trois (anciens) pence *mpl*

hreepenny ['θrepənɪ, 'θrʌpənɪ] *Br* ADJ à *ou* de trois pence

▸▸ ***threepenny bit, threepenny piece*** = ancienne pièce de trois pence

hree-piece ADJ

▸▸ *Mus* ***three-piece band*** trio *m*; ***three-piece suit*** (costume *m*) trois-pièces *m inv*; *Br* ***three-piece suite*** salon *m* trois pièces *(canapé et deux fauteuils)*

hree-pin ADJ

▸▸ ***three-pin plug*** prise *f* à trois fiches; ***three-pin socket*** prise *f* à trois douilles

hree-ply N *(wool)* laine *f* à trois fils; *(wood)* contreplaqué *m (à trois épaisseurs)*

ADJ *(wool)* à trois fils; *(rope)* à trois brins; *(tissue)* triple; *(wood)* à trois épaisseurs

hree-point ADJ

▸▸ *Aviat* ***three-point landing*** atterrissage *m* trois points; *Aut* ***three-point turn*** demi-tour *m* en trois manœuvres

three-quarter ADJ *(sleeve)* trois-quarts *(inv)*; *(portrait)* de trois-quarts; **t. (length) jacket** veste *f* trois-quarts; **t. (length) trousers** pantacourt *m*

N *(in rugby)* trois-quart *m inv*

▸▸ ***three-quarter back*** *(in rugby)* trois-quart *m inv*; ***three-quarter line*** *(in rugby)* ligne *f* des trois-quarts

three-quarters NPL trois quarts *mpl*

ADV aux trois quarts; **the tank is t. full** le réservoir est aux trois quarts plein

threequel ['θri:kwəl] N = troisième film d'une série

three-ring circus N *Am* cirque *m* à trois pistes; *Fig* **it's a real t.** c'est un véritable cirque

threescore [,θri:'skɔ:(r)] *Literary* ADJ soixante; **t. years and ten** soixante-dix ans

N soixante *m*

threesome ['θri:səm] N **1** *(group)* groupe *m* de trois personnes; **we went as a t.** nous y sommes allés à trois **2** *(match, game)* partie *f* à trois; **she came along to make up a t.** elle est venue pour que nous soyons trois (joueurs) **3** *Fam (for sex)* partouze *f* à trois

three-speed ADJ à trois vitesses

▸▸ ***three-speed gearbox*** boîte *f* trois vitesses

three-storey, three-storeyed, *Am* **three-story, three-storied** ADJ *(house)* à trois étages

three-way ADJ *(discussion, conversation)* à trois; *(division)* en trois; *(switch)* à trois voies *ou* directions

▸▸ *Br Pol* ***three-way marginal*** = circonscription où trois candidats ont d'égales chances de succès

three-wheeled vehicle N trois-roues *m*

three-wheeler N *(tricycle)* tricycle *m*; *(car)* voiture *f* à trois roues

thresh [θreʃ] VT *(corn, wheat)* battre

thresher ['θreʃə(r)] N **1** *Agr (person)* batteur (euse) *m,f* **2** *Agr (machine)* batteuse *f*

threshing ['θreʃɪŋ] N battage *m*

▸▸ ***threshing machine*** batteuse *f*

threshold ['θreʃhəʊld] N **1** *(doorway)* seuil *m*, pas *m* de la porte; **to cross the t.** franchir le seuil

2 *Fig* seuil *m*, début *m*; **on the t. of** *(era, new century, millennium)* au seuil de, à la veille de; **we are on the t. of new discoveries** nous sommes sur le point de faire de nouvelles découvertes

3 *Econ & Fin* limite *f*, seuil *m*; **the government has raised tax thresholds** le gouvernement a relevé les tranches de l'impôt

4 *Anat & Psy* seuil *m*; **to have a high/low pain t.** avoir un seuil de tolérance à la douleur élevé/peu élevé; **to have a low boredom t.** être prédisposé à l'ennui, s'ennuyer facilement

▸▸ *Fin* ***threshold price*** prix *m* du seuil; *Br Econ* ***threshold (wage) agreement*** accord *m* d'indexation des salaires sur les prix; *Br Econ* ***threshold (wage) policy*** politique *f* d'indexation des salaires sur les prix

threw [θru:] *pt of* **throw**

thrice [θraɪs] ADV *Literary or Arch* trois fois

thrift [θrɪft] N **1** *(care with money)* économie *f*, esprit *m* d'économie **2** *Am (savings bank)* caisse *f* d'épargne

▸▸ *Am* ***thrift institution*** caisse *f* d'épargne; *Am* ***thrift store*** = magasin vendant des articles d'occasion au profit d'œuvres charitables

thriftily ['θrɪftɪlɪ] ADV avec économie; *(live)* frugalement

thriftiness ['θrɪftɪnɪs] N sens *m* de l'économie

thriftless ['θrɪftlɪs] ADJ dépensier, peu économe

thriftlessness ['θrɪftlɪsnɪs] N tendance *f* au gaspillage

thrifty ['θrɪftɪ] *(compar* **thriftier**, *superl* **thriftiest***)* ADJ économe, peu dépensier

thrill [θrɪl] N *(feeling of excitement)* frisson *m*; *(exciting experience, event)* sensation *f*, (vive) émotion *f*; **he felt a t. of anticipation** un délicieux frisson le parcourut à l'idée du plaisir qui l'attendait; **it was a real t. to meet the president** j'ai ressenti une grande émotion à rencontrer le président; **the film gave the audience plenty of thrills** le film a procuré aux spectateurs beaucoup de sensations fortes; **the touch of his hand sent a t. through her** le contact de sa main la fit frissonner de plaisir; **he gets a t. out of gambling/driving fast** le jeu/la vitesse lui procure des sensations fortes; **they got quite a t. out of the experience** ils ont été ravis *ou* enchantés de l'expérience; **the t. of the chase** le frisson de la poursuite; *Fam* **all the thrills and spills of the circus/the hunt** tous les frissons que procure le cirque/la chasse□

VT *(person)* ravir, transporter de joie; *(audience)* électriser; **the news thrilled her** la nouvelle l'a ravie; *(stronger)* la nouvelle l'a transportée de joie; **the magician thrilled the audience with his tricks** le prestidigitateur a électrisé les spectateurs avec ses tours; **a novel/film that will t. you** un roman/film qui vous passionnera

VI *(with joy)* tressaillir, frissonner; **I thrilled at the sight** à la vue de ce spectacle, j'ai ressenti une vive émotion

thrilled [θrɪld] ADJ ravi; **she's thrilled with her new car** elle est ravie de sa nouvelle voiture; *Fam* **to be thrilled to bits** être aux anges

thriller ['θrɪlə(r)] N *(film)* thriller *m*, film *m* à suspense; *(book)* thriller *m*, roman *m* à suspense

thrilling ['θrɪlɪŋ] ADJ *(adventure, film, story)* palpitant, passionnant; *(speech)* exaltant; **what a t. experience!** quelle expérience excitante!

thrive [θraɪv] *(pt* **thrived** *or* **throve** [θrəʊv], *pp* **thrived** *or* **thriven** ['θrɪvən]) VI **1** *(plant)* pousser (bien); *(child)* grandir, se développer; *(adult)* se porter bien, respirer la santé; **the plants t. in peaty soil** les plantes poussent bien dans un sol tourbeux; **young children t. on affection** les enfants ont besoin d'affection pour s'épanouir; **some people t. on stress** il y a certaines personnes à qui le stress réussit; **do I like it? I t. on it!** si j'aime ça? j'adore! **2** *(business, company)* prospérer, être florissant; *(businessman)* prospérer, réussir

thriving ['θraɪvɪŋ] ADJ **1** *(person)* florissant de santé, vigoureux; *(animal)* vigoureux; *(plant)* robuste, vigoureux **2** *(business, company)* prospère, florissant; *(businessman)* prospère

throat [θrəʊt] N gorge *f*; **the back of the t.** le fond de la gorge, l'arrière-gorge *f*; **to have a sore t.** avoir mal à la gorge; **to cut sb's t.** couper la gorge à qn, égorger qn; *Hum* **get this drink/medicine down your t.!** avalez-moi cette boisson/ce médicament!; **he grabbed him by the t.** il l'a pris à la gorge; **to clear one's t.** s'éclaircir la voix; **they're always at each other's throats** ils sont toujours en train de se battre; *Fam* **she's always jumping down my t.** elle est toujours à me crier dessus; *Fam* **he never misses the chance to ram** *or* **to shove his success down my t.** il ne manque jamais une occasion de me rebattre les oreilles avec sa réussite

▸▸ *Med* ***throat infection*** angine *f*; *Pharm* ***throat lozenge*** pastille *f* pour la gorge

throatiness ['θrəʊtɪnɪs] N **the t. of his voice** sa voix rauque

throaty ['θrəʊtɪ] *(compar* **throatier**, *superl* **throatiest***)* ADJ *(voice, whisper, laugh, cough)* rauque

throb [θrɒb] *(pt & pp* **throbbed**, *cont* **throbbing***)* VI **1** *(music)* vibrer; *(drums)* battre (rythmiquement); *(engine, machine)* vrombir, vibrer; **a city throbbing with activity** une ville palpitante d'activité **2** *(heart)* battre fort, palpiter **3** *(with pain)* lanciner; **my head is throbbing** j'ai très mal à la tête; **my finger still throbs where I hit it** j'ai encore des élancements dans le doigt là où je l'ai cogné

N **1** *(of music, drums)* rythme *m*, battement(s) *m(pl)* rythmique(s); *(of engine, machine)* vibration(s) *f(pl)*, vrombissement(s) *m(pl)* **2** *(of heart)* battement(s) *m(pl)*, pulsation(s) *f(pl)* **3** *(of pain)* élancement *m*

throbbing ['θrɒbɪŋ] ADJ **1** *(rhythm)* battant; *(drum)* qui bat rythmiquement; *(engine, machine)* vibrant, vrombissant **2** *(heart)* battant, palpitant **3** *(pain)* lancinant

throes [θrəʊz] **in the throes of** PREP **in the t. of war/illness** en proie à la guerre/la maladie; **to be in the t. of doing sth** être en train de faire qch; **they are in the t. of moving house** ils sont en plein déménagement

thrombosis [θrɒm'bəʊsɪs] *(pl* **thromboses** [-si:z]) N *Med* thrombose *f*, thromboses *fpl*

throne [θrəʊn] **N** trône *m*; **to come to** *or* **ascend** *or* **mount the t.** monter sur le trône, accéder au trône; **the heir to the t.** l'héritier *m* au trône; **on the t.** sur le trône; *Euph* **to be on the t.** *(on the toilet)* être là où le roi va seul
▸▸ ***throne room*** salle *f* du trône

throng [θrɒŋ] **N** foule *f*, multitude *f*; **throngs of people** une foule de gens
VT demonstrators thronged the streets des manifestants se pressaient dans les rues; **the shops were thronged with people** les magasins grouillaient de monde *ou* étaient bondés
VI affluer, se presser; **crowds of people thronged towards the stadium** les gens se dirigeaient en masse vers le stade

thronging ['θrɒŋɪŋ] **ADJ a t. mass** une foule grouillante

throttle ['θrɒtəl] **N** *(of car)* accélérateur *m*; *(of motorcycle)* poignée *f* d'accélération *ou* des gaz; *(of aircraft)* commande *f* des gaz; **to open/to close the t.** mettre/réduire les gaz; **at full t.** (à) pleins gaz
VT 1 *(strangle)* étrangler; **I could t. you!** je pourrais t'étrangler! **2** *(engine)* mettre au ralenti
▸▸ ***throttle cable*** câble *m* d'accélération; ***throttle valve*** papillon *m* des gaz, soupape *f* d'étranglement

▸**throttle back, throttle down VI** *(slow engine)* mettre le moteur au ralenti; *(cut, close off fuel)* couper *ou* fermer les gaz; **the pilot/rider gradually throttled back** le pilote/motard coupa les gaz progressivement
VT SEP *(engine)* mettre au ralenti

THROUGH [θruː]

PREP
- à travers **1–3**
- dans **2**
- à **4**
- par **5**
- grâce à **5**
- à cause de **6**

ADV
- au travers **1**
- jusqu'au bout **2**
- directement **3**
- complètement **4**

ADJ
- direct **1**
- en transit **1**
- fini **2**

PREP 1 *(from one end or side to the other of)* à travers; **to walk t. the streets** se promener dans *ou* à travers les rues; **they drove t. the countryside** ils ont roulé à travers la campagne; **we travelled t. America** nous avons parcouru les États-Unis; **he swam quickly t. the water** il nageait rapidement; **the river flows t. a deep valley** le fleuve traverse une vallée profonde; **to go t. a tunnel** passer dans un tunnel; **the bullet went straight t. his shoulder** la balle lui a traversé l'épaule de part en part; **we went t. a door** nous avons passé une porte; **water poured t. the hole** l'eau coulait par le trou; **he could see her t. the window** il pouvait la voir par la fenêtre; **can you see t. it?** est-ce que tu peux voir au travers?; **I can't see much t. the fog** je ne vois pas grand-chose à travers le brouillard; **what can you see t. the telescope?** qu'est-ce que vous voyez dans *ou* à travers le télescope?; **I could hear them t. the wall** je les entendais à travers le mur; **she couldn't feel anything t. her gloves** elle ne sentait rien à travers ses gants; **a shiver ran t. him** il fut parcouru d'un frisson; **he drove t. a red light** il a brûlé un feu rouge; *also Fig* **to slip t. the net** passer à travers les mailles du filet; **he goes t. his money very quickly** l'argent lui brûle les doigts; **she ate her way t. a whole box of chocolates** elle a mangé toute une boîte de chocolats
2 *(in)* dans, à travers; **he got a bullet t. the leg** une balle lui a traversé la jambe; **she was shot t. the heart** on lui a tiré une balle dans le cœur; **the bull had a ring t. its nose** le taureau avait un anneau dans le nez; **to make a hole t. sth** percer un trou à travers qch
3 *(from beginning to end of)* à travers; **t. the ages** à travers les âges; **all t. his life** durant *ou* pendant toute sa vie; **halfway t. the performance** à la moitié *ou* au milieu de la représentation; **I'm halfway t. this book** j'ai lu la moitié de ce livre; **she has lived t. some difficult times** elle a connu *ou* traversé des moments difficiles; *Fam* **he's been t. it** *or* **t. a lot** il en a bavé, il en a vu de dures; **we had to sit t. a boring lecture** nous avons dû rester à écouter une conférence ennuyeuse; **I slept t. the storm** l'orage ne m'a pas réveillé; **will he live t. the night?** passera-t-il la nuit?; **the war lasted all t. 1914 to 1918** la guerre a duré de 1914 jusqu'en 1918; **she maintained her dignity t. it all** elle a toujours gardé sa dignité
4 *Am (to, until)* **80 t. 100** de 80 à 100; **Monday t. Friday** de lundi à vendredi, du lundi au vendredi; **April t. July** d'avril jusqu'en juillet, d'avril à juillet
5 *(by means of)* par, grâce à; **I sent it t. the post** je l'ai envoyé par la poste; **she can only be contacted t. her secretary** on ne peut la contacter que par l'intermédiaire de sa secrétaire; **I met a lot of people t. him** il m'a fait rencontrer beaucoup de gens; **she was interviewed t. an interpreter** on l'a interviewée par l'intermédiaire d'un interprète; **change must be achieved t. peaceful means** le changement doit être obtenu par des moyens pacifiques
6 *(because of)* à cause de; **t. no fault of his own, he lost his job** il a perdu son emploi sans que ce soit de sa faute; **t. ignorance** par ignorance; **it all came about t. a misunderstanding** tout est arrivé à cause d'un malentendu; **t. failing to lock the door…** pour n'avoir pas fermé la porte à clé…
ADV 1 *(from one end or side to the other)* **please go t. into the lounge** passez dans le salon, s'il vous plaît; **I couldn't get t.** je ne pouvais pas passer; **we shoved our way t.** nous nous sommes frayé un chemin en poussant; **the police let us t.** la police nous a laissés passer; **the rain was coming t.** la pluie passait au travers; **the nail had gone right t.** le clou était passé au travers
2 *(from beginning to end)* **I slept t. until 8 o'clock** j'ai dormi (sans me réveiller) jusqu'à 8 heures; **I slept the whole night t.** j'ai dormi d'un trait jusqu'au matin; **I saw the film all the way t.** j'ai vu le film jusqu'au bout; **I read the letter t.** j'ai lu la lettre jusqu'au bout; **I left halfway t.** je suis parti au milieu; **England are t. to the semi-final** l'Angleterre s'est qualifiée pour *ou* jouera la demi-finale
3 *(directly)* **the train goes t. to Paris without stopping** le train va directement à Paris *ou* est sans arrêt jusqu'à Paris; **to book t. to Paris** prendre un billet direct pour Paris; **can you get a bus right t. to the port?** est-ce qu'il y a un bus direct pour le port?
4 *(completely)* **to be wet t.** être complètement trempé; **she's an aristocrat t. and t.** c'est une aristocrate jusqu'au bout des ongles
5 *Tel* **can you put me t. to Elaine/to extension 363?** pouvez-vous me passer Elaine/le poste 363?; **I'm putting you t. now** je vous passe votre correspondant *ou* communication; **I tried ringing him, but I couldn't get t.** j'ai essayé de l'appeler mais je n'ai pas réussi à l'avoir; **you're t. now** vous êtes en ligne
ADJ 1 *(direct* ▸ *train, ticket)* direct; *(traffic)* en transit, de passage; **all t. passengers must remain seated** tous les passagers en transit doivent garder leur place; **a t. train to London** un train direct pour Londres; *Br* **no t. road,** *Am* **not a t. street** *(sign)* voie sans issue
2 *(finished)* **are you t.?** avez-vous fini?, c'est fini?; **he's t. with his work at last** il a enfin terminé tout son travail; **I'll be t. reading the newspaper in a minute** j'aurai fini de lire le journal dans un instant; **I'm t. with smoking** la cigarette, c'est fini; **she's t. with him** elle en a eu assez de lui; **we're t.** c'est fini entre nous

throughout [θruː'aʊt] **PREP 1** *(in space)* partout dans; **t. the world** dans le monde entier, partout dans le monde; **t. Europe** à travers *ou* dans toute l'Europe, partout en Europe **2** *(in time)* **t. the year** pendant toute l'année; **t. my life** (durant) toute ma vie
ADV 1 *(everywhere)* partout; **the house has been repainted t.** la maison a été entièrement repeinte **2** *(all the time)* (pendant) tout le temps; **she remained silent t.** elle est restée silencieuse du début jusqu'à la fin

throughput ['θruːpʊt] **N** *Comput* capacité *f* de traitement

throughway = **thruway**

throve [θrəʊv] *pt of* **thrive**

THROW [θrəʊ]

VT
- lancer **1, 5**
- jeter **1, 2, 5**
- projeter **3, 5**
- plonger **4**
- déconcerter **6**

VI
- lancer

N
- jet **1**
- lancer **1**
- coup **2**
- tour **2**

(*pt* **threw** [θruː], *pp* **thrown** [θrəʊn])
VT 1 *(stone)* lancer, jeter; *(ball)* lancer; *Spo* *(discus, javelin etc)* lancer; *(dice)* jeter; *(coal ont* *fire)* mettre; **t. me the ball, t. the ball to me** lance moi le ballon; **he threw the ball over the wall** il lancé *ou* envoyé le ballon par-dessus le mur **could you t. me my lighter?** peux-tu me lance mon briquet?; **she threw the serviette into th bin** elle a jeté la serviette à la poubelle; **he threw his jacket over a chair** il a jeté sa veste sur un chaise; **to t. a sheet over sth** couvrir qch d'u drap; **she threw a few clothes into a suitcase** ell a jeté quelques affaires dans une valise; **I threw some cold water on my face** je me suis aspergé l figure avec de l'eau froide; **the rioters threw stones at the police** les manifestants ont lanc *ou* jeté des pierres sur les policiers; **he threw two sixes** *(with dice)* il a jeté deux six; **to t. sb int prison** *or* **jail** jeter qn en prison; **to t. sb to the lion** jeter qn aux lions; *Fig* jeter qn en pâture
2 *(opponent, rider)* jeter (par *ou* à terre); **his op ponent threw him to the ground** *(in fight)* son ad versaire l'a jeté à terre; *(in wrestling match)* so adversaire l'a envoyé au sol *ou* au tapis; **th horse threw him** le cheval le désarçonna *ou* le je ta à terre
3 *(with force, violence)* projeter; **she was throw clear** *(in car accident)* elle a été éjectée; **to t. ope** ouvrir en grand *ou* tout grand; **she threw ope the door/windows** elle a ouvert la porte/les fe nêtres en grand; *Fig* **the House of Commons ha been thrown open to the television cameras** l Chambre des communes a été ouverte aux ca méras de télévision; **he threw himself at her fee** il s'est jeté à ses pieds; **she threw herself at hir** *(attacked)* elle s'est jetée *ou* s'est ruée sur lui; *(a lover)* elle s'est jetée sur lui *ou* à sa tête; *Fig* **h threw himself on the mercy of the king** il s'en es remis au bon vouloir du roi
4 *(plunge)* plonger; **the news threw them int confusion/a panic** les nouvelles les ont plongé dans l'embarras/les ont affolés; **the scandal ha thrown the country into confusion** le scandale semé la confusion dans le pays; **to t. oneself int one's work** se plonger dans son travail
5 *(direct, aim* ▸ *look, glance)* jeter, lancer; *(*▸ *ac cusation, reproach)* lancer, envoyer; *(*▸ *punch* lancer, porter; *(cast* ▸ *light, shadows)* projeter **to t. a question at sb** poser une question brûle-pourpoint à qn; **don't t. that one at me don't t. that in my face!** ne me faites pas ce repro che!, ne me jetez pas ça à la figure!; *Theat* **to t one's voice** projeter sa voix; *Constr* **to t. a bridg over a river** jeter un pont sur une rivière
6 *(confuse)* désarçonner, dérouter, déconce ter; **that question really threw me!** cette questio m'a vraiment désarçonné!, je ne savais vra ment pas quoi répondre à cette question!; **was completely thrown for a few seconds** je su resté tout interdit pendant quelques secondes
7 *(activate* ▸ *switch, lever, clutch)* actionner
8 *Sport (race, match)* perdre délibérément
9 to t. a pot *(potter)* tourner un vase
VI she can t. a hundred metres elle est capable d lancer à cent mètres; **I can't t. straight** je n'arriv pas à lancer droit
N 1 *(of ball, javelin)* jet *m*, lancer *m*; *(of dice)* lar cer *m*; **his whole fortune depended on a single t. c the dice** toute sa fortune dépendait d'un seu coup de dés; *Sport* **a free t.** un lancer franc; **tha was a good t.!** vous avez bien visé!
2 *Fam (go, turn)* coup[□] *m*, tour[□] *m*; **10p a t.** 1 pence le coup; **at £20 a t. I can't afford it** à 20 vres chaque fois, je ne peux pas me l'offrir[□]
3 *(cover)* couverture *f*; *(piece of fabric)* jeté *m* d fauteuil *ou* de canapé

throw about, throw around VT SEP **1** *(toss)* ancer; *(scatter)* jeter, éparpiller; **the boys were hrowing a ball about** les garçons jouaient à la alle; **don't t. your toys about like that** ne lance as tes jouets comme ça; **to t. one's money about** aspiller son argent; **to be thrown about** être allotté **2** *(move violently)* **to t. oneself about** agiter, se débattre; **she was throwing her arms bout wildly** elle agitait frénétiquement les bras

throw aside VT SEP *(unwanted object)* rejeter, aisser de côté; *(friend, work)* laisser tomber, aisser de côté; *(idea, suggestion)* rejeter, reousser; *(prejudices, fears, hatred etc)* se débarasser de

throw away VT SEP **1** *(old clothes, rubbish)* jeter *Fig (waste ▸ advantage, opportunity, talents)* aspiller, gâcher; *(▸ affection, friendship)* perre; **don't t. your money away on expensive toys** e gaspille pas ton argent à acheter des jouets oûteux; **you're throwing away your only chance f happiness** vous êtes en train de gâcher votre eule chance de bonheur; **to t. away one's life** *waste)* gâcher sa vie; *(sacrifice for nothing)* se sarifier inutilement; **don't t. yourself away on a vaster like him** ne gâche pas ta vie pour un bon rien pareil **3** *Theat (line, remark)* laisser tomber

throw back VT SEP **1** *(gen)* relancer, renvoyer; *ish)* rejeter (à l'eau); *Fig (image, light)* réfléchir, envoyer; *(heat)* réverbérer; **she threw his words f love back at him** elle lui a jeté tous ses mots 'amour à la tête; *Fig* **to t. sth back in sb's face** jeter ch à la figure de qn

2 *(hair, head)* rejeter en arrière; *(shoulders)* reresser, jeter en arrière

3 *(curtains)* ouvrir; *(shutters)* repousser, ouvrir out grand; *(bedclothes)* repousser

4 *(idiom) (force to rely on)* **we were thrown back n our own resources** on a dû se rabattre sur nos ropres ressources

throw down VT SEP **1** *(to lower level)* jeter; **can ou t. the towel down to me?** pouvez-vous me ancer la serviette?; **she threw her bag down on he floor** elle a jeté son sac par terre; **to t. oneself own on the ground/on one's knees** se jeter par erre/à genoux; **he threw his cards down on the able** il a jeté ses cartes sur la table **2** *(weapons)* eter, déposer **3** *Fig (challenge)* lancer **3** *Br Fam idiom)* **it's throwing it down** *(raining)* il pleut à erse[□], il tombe des cordes

throw in VT SEP **1** *(into box, cupboard etc)* jeter; *through window)* jeter, lancer; *also Fig* **to t. in the owel** jeter l'éponge; *also Fig* **to t. in one's hand** bandonner la partie

2 *(interject ▸ remark, suggestion)* placer; **she hrew in a few comments about housing problems** lle a placé quelques remarques sur les problèmes de logement

3 *(include)* **breakfast is thrown in** le petit déjeuer est compris; **with a special trip to Stockholm hrown in** avec en prime une excursion à Stockolm

4 *Sport (ball)* remettre en jeu

throw off VT SEP **1** *(discard ▸ clothes)* enlever *ou* ter (à la hâte); *(▸ mask, disguise)* jeter

2 *(get rid of ▸ habit, inhibition)* se défaire de, se ébarrasser de; *(▸ burden)* se libérer de, se dé-arrasser de; *(▸ cold, infection)* se débarrasser e

3 *(elude ▸ pursuer)* perdre, semer; **he managed to the dogs off the trail** il a réussi à dépister les hiens

4 *(write hastily ▸ poem etc)* composer au pied evé

throw on VT SEP *(clothes)* enfiler *ou* passer (à la âte); **she threw on some make-up** elle s'est maquillée à la hâte

throw out VT SEP **1** *(rubbish, unwanted items)* eter, mettre au rebut

2 *(eject ▸ from building)* mettre à la porte, jeter ehors; *(▸ from night club)* jeter dehors, vider; *evict ▸ from accommodation)* expulser; *(expel ▸ om school, army)* renvoyer, expulser; **we were hrown out of our jobs** on s'est fait mettre à la orte

3 *(reject ▸ bill, proposal)* rejeter, repousser

4 *(extend ▸ arms, leg)* tendre, étendre; **to t. out ne's chest** bomber le torse

5 *(make ▸ remark, suggestion)* émettre, laisser tomber; **to t. out a challenge** lancer un défi

6 *(disturb ▸ person)* déconcerter, désorienter; *(upset ▸ calculation, results)* fausser

7 *(emit ▸ light)* émettre, diffuser; *(▸ smoke, heat)* émettre, répandre

▸ **throw over** VT SEP *Fam (girlfriend, boyfriend)* quitter[□], laisser tomber[□]; *(plan)* abandonner[□], renoncer à[□]

▸ **throw together** VT SEP **1** *Fam (make quickly ▸ equipment, table)* fabriquer à la hâte[□], bricoler; **he managed to t. a meal together** il a réussi à improviser un repas[□]; **the film looks as if it's been thrown together** le film semble bâclé; **she threw the report together the night before** elle a rédigé le rapport en vitesse la veille au soir[□] **2** *(gather)* rassembler à la hâte; **she threw a few things together and called a taxi** elle a jeté quelques affaires dans un sac et a appelé un taxi **3** *(by accident)* réunir par hasard; **Fate had thrown them together** le destin les avait réunis

▸ **throw up** VT SEP **1** *(above one's head)* jeter *ou* lancer en l'air; **can you t. me up my towel?** peux-tu me lancer ma serviette?; **they threw their hats up into the air** ils ont lancé leur chapeau en l'air; **she threw up her hands in horror** elle a levé les bras en signe d'horreur

2 *(produce ▸ problem)* produire, créer; *(▸ evidence)* mettre à jour; *(▸ dust, dirt)* soulever; *(▸ artist)* produire; **the discussion threw up some new ideas** la discussion a amené de nouvelles idées

3 *(abandon ▸ career, studies)* abandonner, laisser tomber; *(▸ chance, opportunity)* laisser passer, gaspiller

4 *Pej (construct ▸ building)* construire *ou* bâtir en moins de deux

5 *Fam (vomit)* dégobiller

VI *Fam* vomir[□], rendre

---

throwaway ['θrəʊəˌweɪ] ADJ *(line, remark)* fait comme par hasard *ou* comme si de rien n'était; **it was just a t. remark** il a/elle a/*etc* dit ça comme ça; **we live in a t. culture** *or* **society** nous vivons dans une société de gaspillage

N **1** *(bottle)* bouteille *f* sans consigne; *(container)* emballage *m* perdu *ou* jetable **2** *Am (handbill)* prospectus *m*

COMP *(bottle, carton etc)* jetable, à jeter, à usage unique

throwback ['θrəʊbæk] N **1** *(anthropological) & Biol* régression *f* atavique; **he's a t. to his great-grandfather** il a hérité (des caractéristiques) de son arrière-grand-père **2** *(of fashion, custom)* **those new hats are a t. to the 1930s** ces nouveaux chapeaux marquent un retour aux années 30 *ou* sont inspirés des années 30

thrower ['θrəʊə(r)] N lanceur(euse) *m,f*

throw-in N *Ftbl* rentrée *f* en touche

thrown [θrəʊn] *pp of* **throw**

thru *Am* = **through**

thrum [θrʌm] VI **1** *(engine, machine)* vibrer, vrombir; *(rain)* tambouriner **2** *(guitarist)* gratter les cordes; **to t. on a guitar** gratter de la guitare

VT **1** *(repeat)* réciter *ou* répéter d'une manière monotone **2** *(guitar)* gratter de, taquiner; **to t. a tune on the guitar** racler un air sur la guitare

thrush [θrʌʃ] N **1** *Orn* grive *f* **2** *(UNCOUNT) Med (oral)* muguet *m*; *(vaginal)* mycose *f*, candidose *f*

thrust [θrʌst] *(pt & pp* **thrust***)* VT **1** *(push, shove ▸ finger)* enfoncer; *(▸ handkerchief)* fourrer; *(▸ knife)* plonger, planter, enfoncer; **he t. his finger/elbow into my ribs** il m'a enfoncé le doigt/le coude dans les côtes; **I t. the stick into the jar** j'ai plongé le bâton dans le pot; **to t. one's hands into one's pockets** enfoncer *ou* fourrer les mains dans ses poches; **he t. her into the cell** il l'a poussée violemment dans la cellule; **she t. the money towards him** elle a brusquement poussé l'argent vers lui; **she t. the money into his hands** elle lui a fourré l'argent dans les mains; **I had a gun t. at me** on m'a mis un revolver sous le nez; **she t. me to the front** elle m'a poussé devant; **to t. one's way through the crowd/to the front** se frayer un chemin à travers la foule/pour être devant **2** *(force ▸ responsibility, fame)* imposer; **the job was t. upon me** on m'a imposé ce travail; **to be t. into a position of responsibility** être parachuté à un poste à responsabilités; **he was t. into the limelight** il a été mis en vedette; **to t. oneself on** *or* **upon sb** imposer sa présence à qn, s'imposer à qn

VI **1** *(push)* **he t. past her** *(rudely)* il l'a bousculée en passant devant elle; *(quickly)* il est passé devant elle comme une flèche; *Fig* **towers thrusting upwards into the sky** des tours qui s'élancent vers le ciel **2** *Fencing* allonger *ou* porter une botte; **he t. at him with a knife** il a essayé de lui donner un coup de couteau

N **1** *(lunge)* poussée *f*; *(stab)* coup *m*; **with a single t. of his sword** d'un seul coup d'épée

2 *Fig (remark)* pointe *f*; **a few well-aimed thrusts at the opposition parties** quelques pointes bien senties contre les partis de l'opposition

3 *(UNCOUNT) (force ▸ of engine)* poussée *f*; *Fig (drive)* dynamisme *m*, élan *m*

4 *(of argument, story)* sens *m*, idée *f*; *(of policy)* idée *f* directrice; *(of research)* aspect *m* principal; **the main t. of her argument** l'idée maîtresse de son raisonnement

▸ **thrust aside** VT SEP *(person, thing)* écarter brusquement; *(suggestion)* écarter *ou* rejeter brusquement

▸ **thrust forward** VT SEP pousser en avant brusquement; **to t. oneself forward** se frayer un chemin; *Fig* se mettre en avant

▸ **thrust out** VT SEP **1** *(arm, leg)* allonger brusquement; *(hand)* tendre brusquement; *(chin)* projeter en avant; **to t. out one's chest** bomber la poitrine; **to t. one's way out** se frayer un chemin pour sortir **2** *(eject)* pousser dehors

thruster ['θrʌstə(r)] N **1** *Astron (rocket)* micropropulseur *m* **2** *(dynamic person)* personne *f* dynamique *ou* plein d'allant; *Pej (pushy person)* arriviste *mf*

thrusting ['θrʌstɪŋ] ADJ *Br (dynamic)* dynamique, entreprenant, plein d'entrain; *Pej (pushy)* qui se fait valoir, qui se met en avant

thruway ['θruːweɪ] N *Am* ≃ autoroute *f (à cinq ou six voies)*

thud [θʌd] *(pt & pp* **thudded**, *cont* **thudding***)* VI **1** *(make noise ▸ gen)* faire un bruit sourd; *(▸ falling object)* tomber en faisant un bruit sourd; **we could hear the cannon thudding in the distance** on entendait gronder les canons au loin **2** *(walk or run heavily)* **to t. across/in/past** traverser/entrer/passer à pas pesants; **his feet went thudding along the corridor** ses pas résonnaient sourdement dans le couloir; **we could hear people thudding about in the flat above** on entendait les gens du dessus marcher à pas lourds **3** *(heart)* battre fort

N bruit *m* sourd

thug [θʌg] N *(hooligan)* voyou *m*; *(brutal person)* brute *f*

thumb [θʌm] N pouce *m*; *Fig* **to be under sb's t.** être sous la coupe de qn; **his mother's really got him under her t.** sa mère a vraiment de l'emprise sur lui *ou* en fait vraiment ce qu'elle veut; **to be all (fingers and) thumbs** être maladroit; **to stick out like a sore t.** *(be obvious)* crever les yeux; *(be obtrusive)* faire tache

VT **1** *(book, magazine)* feuilleter, tourner les pages de; *(pages)* tourner; **the catalogue has been well thumbed** les pages du catalogue sont bien écornées **2** *(hitch)* **to t. a** *Br* **lift** *or Am* **ride** faire du stop *ou* de l'auto-stop; **they thumbed a lift to Exeter** ils sont allés à Exeter en stop; **she thumbed a lift from a passing motorist** elle a réussi à se faire prendre en stop par une voiture qui passait **3** *(idiom)* **to t. one's nose at sb** faire un pied de nez à qn

VI *Am Fam* faire du stop *ou* de l'auto-stop

▸▸ ***thumb index*** répertoire *m* à onglets

thumb-indexed ADJ *(book)* à onglets

thumbnail ['θʌmneɪl] N **1** *(on finger)* ongle *m* du pouce **2** *Comput* vignette *f*

▸▸ ***thumbnail sketch*** *(of plan)* aperçu *m*, croquis *m* rapide; *(of personality)* bref portrait *m*

thumbprint ['θʌmprɪnt] N empreinte *f* du pouce

thumbscrew ['θʌmskruː] N **1** *Tech* vis *f* à papillon *ou* à ailettes **2** *(instrument of torture)* = instrument de torture servant à écraser les pouces des prisonniers

thumbstall ['θʌmstɔːl] N poucier *m*

thumbtack ['θʌmtæk] N *Am* punaise *f*

thump [θʌmp] VT donner un coup de poing à, frapper d'un coup de poing; **he thumped me in the stomach/on the head** il m'a donné un coup de poing à l'estomac/à la tête; **to t. sb on the back** donner une grande tape dans le dos à qn; **he thumped his fist on the table** il a frappé du poing sur la table

VI **1** *(bang)* cogner; **he thumped on the door/wall** il a cogné à la porte/contre le mur; **she was thumping away on the piano** elle tapait sur le piano comme une sourde; **my heart was thumping with fear/excitement** la peur/l'émotion me faisait battre le cœur **2** *(run or walk heavily)* **to t. in/out/past** entrer/sortir/passer à pas lourds; **heavy boots thumped up the stairs** on entendait de lourds bruits de bottes dans l'escalier

N **1** *(blow ▸ gen)* coup *m*; *(▸ with fist)* coup *m* de poing; *(▸ with stick)* coup *m* de bâton; **to give sb a t.** assener un coup de poing à qn **2** *(sound)* bruit *m* sourd

ADV *Fam* **to go t.** faire boum

▸ **thump out** VT SEP **to t. out a tune on the piano** marteler un air au piano

thumping ['θʌmpɪŋ] *Br Fam* ADJ *(success)* énorme, immense, phénoménal; *(difference)* énorme

ADV *Old-fashioned (as intensifier)* **a t. great meal** un repas énorme; **a t. big lie** un gros mensonge

thunder ['θʌndə(r)] N **1** *Met* tonnerre *m*; **clap of t.** coup *m* de tonnerre; **there was a lot of t. last night** il a beaucoup tonné la nuit dernière; **there's t. in the air** le temps est à l'orage; **to be as black as t.** *(angry)* être dans une colère noire; **his voice was like t.** il avait une voix de tonnerre **2** *(of applause, guns)* tonnerre *m*; *(of engine, traffic)* bruit *m* de tonnerre; *(of hooves)* fracas *m*; **we could hear the t. of the waves crashing on the rocks below** on entendait le fracas des vagues qui s'écrasaient sur les rochers en contre-bas

VI **1** *Met* tonner; **it's thundering** il tonne, ça tonne **2** *(guns, waves)* tonner, gronder; *(hooves)* retentir; **a train thundered past** un train est passé dans un grondement de tonnerre **3** *(shout)* **to t. at sb/ against sth** tonner contre qn/contre qch

VT *(order, threat)* lancer d'une voix tonitruante *ou* tonnante; **"damn them!" he thundered** "qu'ils aillent au diable!" tonna-t-il; **the audience thundered their delight** *(applauded)* le public manifesta son plaisir par un tonnerre d'applaudissements

thunderbolt ['θʌndəbəʊlt] N *Met* foudre *m*; *Fig* coup *m* de tonnerre; **the news came like a t.** cette nouvelle m'a/l'a/*etc* stupéfait

thunderclap ['θʌndəklæp] N coup *m* de tonnerre

thundercloud ['θʌndəklaʊd] N *Met* nuage *m* orageux; *Fig* nuage *m* noir

thundering ['θʌndərɪŋ] *Br Fam Old-fashioned* ADJ **1** *(terrible)* **to be in a t. temper** *or* **rage** être dans une colère noire *ou* hors de soi; **it's a t. nuisance!** quelle barbe! **2** *(superb ▸ success)* foudroyant, phénoménal

thunderous ['θʌndərəs] ADJ *(shouts, noise)* retentissant; **there was t. applause** il y eut un tonnerre d'applaudissements

thunderstorm ['θʌndəstɔːm] N orage *m*

thunderstruck ['θʌndəstrʌk] ADJ foudroyé, abasourdi

thunderthighs ['θʌndəθaɪz] N *Fam Hum* = femme aux grosses cuisses

thundery ['θʌndərɪ] ADJ orageux; **t. weather is forecast** la météo prévoit de l'orage; **a t. shower** une averse accompagnée de tonnere

Thur. *(written abbr* **Thursday***)* jeu

thurible ['θjʊərɪbəl] N encensoir *m*

Thurs. *(written abbr* **Thursday***)* jeu

Thursday ['θɜːzdɪ] N jeudi *m*; *see also* **Friday**

thus [ðʌs] ADV *(so)* ainsi, donc; *(as a result)* ainsi, par conséquent; *(in this way)* ainsi; **t. far** *(in present)* jusqu'ici; *(in past)* jusque-là; **it was ever t.** il en a toujours été ainsi

thwack [θwæk] N **1** *(blow)* grand coup *m*; *(slap)* claque *f* **2** *(sound)* claquement *m*, coup *m* sec

VT donner un coup sec à; *(slap ▸ person)* gifler; **the player thwacked the ball into the crowd** *(footballer)* le joueur envoya la balle dans le public d'un vigoureux coup de pied; *(with racket)* le jouer envoya la balle dans le public

thwart [θwɔːt] VT *(plan)* contrecarrer, contrarier; *(plot, scheme)* déjouer; *(person ▸ in efforts)* contrarier les efforts de; *(▸ in plans)* contrarier les projets de; *(▸ in attempts)* déjouer les tentatives de; **I was thwarted in my attempts to leave the country** j'ai tenté vainement de quitter le pays, toutes les tentatives que j'ai faites pour quitter le pays ont échoué

thy [ðaɪ] ADJ *NEng or Arch or Literary (singular)* ton (ta); *(plural)* tes

thyme [taɪm] N thym *m*

thymus ['θaɪməs] *(pl* **thymuses** *or* **thymi** [-maɪ]) N *Anat* thymus *m*

thyristor [θaɪ'rɪstə(r)] N *Elec* thyristor *m*

thyroid ['θaɪrɔɪd] *Anat* N thyroïde *f*

ADJ thyroïde

thyself [ðaɪ'self] PRON *NEng or Arch or Literary (reflexive)* te; *(intensifier)* toi-même

tiara [tɪ'ɑːrə] N *(gen)* diadème *m*; *Rel* tiare *f*

Tiber ['taɪbə(r)] N **the (River) T.** le Tibre

Tiberius [taɪ'bɪərɪəs] PR N Tibère

Tibet [tɪ'bet] N le Tibet

Tibetan [tɪ'betən] N **1** *(person)* Tibétain(e) *m,f* **2** *Ling* tibétain *m*

ADJ tibétain

tibia ['tɪbɪə] *(pl* **tibias** *or* **tibiae** [-bɪiː]) N *Anat* tibia *m*

tic [tɪk] N *(nervous)* **t.** tic *m* (nerveux)

tich [tɪtʃ] N *Br Fam (person)* microbe *m*; **he's a real t.** il est haut comme trois pommes

tichy ['tɪtʃɪ] ADJ *Br Fam* minuscule, tout petit

tick [tɪk] VI *(clock, time-bomb)* faire tic-tac; *Fig* **I wonder what makes him t.** *(what motivates him)* je me demande ce qui le motive; *(what goes on in his mind)* je me demande ce qui se passe dans sa tête

VT *Br (mark ▸ name, item)* cocher, pointer; *(▸ box, answer)* cocher; *Sch (▸ as correct)* marquer juste

N **1** *(of clock)* tic-tac *m*

2 *Br Fam (moment)* instant *m*; **just a t.!** un instant!; **I'll be ready in a t./in a couple of ticks** je serai prêt dans une seconde/en moins de deux

3 *Br (mark)* coche *f*; **to put a t. against sth** cocher qch

4 *Entom* tique *f*

5 *Br Fam (credit)* crédit *m*; **to buy sth on t.** acheter qch à crédit

▸ **tick away** VI **1** *(clock)* faire tic-tac; *(taximeter)* tourner **2** *(time)* passer; **the minutes ticked away** les minutes passaient

▸ **tick off** VT SEP **1** *(name, item)* cocher

2 *Fig (count ▸ reasons, chapters)* compter, énumérer; **he ticked off the EU countries on his fingers** il compta les pays de l'Union européenne sur ses doigts

3 *Br Fam (scold)* attraper, passer un savon à; **she got ticked off for being late** elle s'est fait attraper pour être arrivée en retard

4 *Am Fam (annoy)* prendre la tête à; **to be ticked off (with)** en avoir marre (de)

▸ **tick over** VI **1** *Br (car engine)* tourner au ralenti **2** *Fig (business, production)* tourner doucement; **everything's ticking over nicely** tout tourne bien; **it keeps my brain ticking over** ça fait travailler ma cervelle

ticker ['tɪkə(r)] N **1** *Am (printer)* téléscripteur *m*, téléimprimeur *m* **2** *Fam (heart)* palpitant *m*, cœur *m* **3** *Fam (watch)* tocante *f*, toquante *f*

ticket ['tɪkɪt] N **1** *(for travel ▸ on coach, plane, train)* billet *m*; *(▸ on bus, underground)* billet *m*, ticket *m*; *(for entry ▸ to cinema, theatre, match)* billet *m*; *(▸ to car park)* ticket *m* (de parking); *(for membership ▸ of library)* carte *f*; **to buy a t.** prendre *ou* acheter un billet

2 *(receipt ▸ in shop)* ticket *m* (de caisse), reçu *m*; *(▸ for left-luggage, cloakroom)* ticket *m* (de consigne); *(▸ from pawnshop)* reconnaissance *f*

3 *(label)* étiquette *f*

4 *Aut (fine)* P-V *m*, contravention *f*, amende *f*; **give sb a t.** mettre un P-V *ou* une contravention qn; **to get a t.** avoir un P-V

5 *Am Pol (platform)* programme *m*; *(list)* liste **he fought the election on a Democratic t.** il a bas son programme électoral sur les principes d Parti démocrate; **to run on a presidential t.** êtr candidat à la vice-présidence

6 *Fam (idiom)* **that's (just) the t.!** voilà exact ment ce qu'il faut!

VT **1** *(label)* étiqueter

2 *(earmark)* désigner, destiner

3 *Am (issue with a ticket)* donner un billet à; **I' ticketed on the 7.30 flight** j'ai un billet pour le v de 7 heures 30

4 *Am (issue with a parking ticket)* mettre un P-V

▸▸ ***ticket agency*** *Theat* agence *f* de spectacle *Rail* agence *f* de voyages; ***ticket barrier*** portillo *m* automatique; *Rail* ***ticket collector*** contrôle (euse) *m,f*, *Belg* accompagnateur(trice) *m,f* d train; *Br* ***ticket desk*** guichet *m*; ***ticket holder*** pe sonne *f* munie d'un billet; *Br Rail* ***ticket inspect*** contrôleur(euse) *m,f*, *Belg* accompagnate (trice) *m,f* de train; *Br* ***ticket machine*** distribute *m* de tickets, billetterie *f* automatique; ***ticket o fice*** bureau *m* de vente des billets, guichet *m*; *A* ***ticket scalper*** revendeur(euse) *m,f* de billets *(s le marché noir)*; *Am Pol* ***ticket splitting*** panachag *m*; *Am* ***ticket taker*** contrôleur(euse) *m,f*; *Br* ***tick tout*** revendeur(euse) *m,f* de billets *(sur le marc noir)*; ***ticket window*** guichet *m*

ticketing ['tɪkɪtɪŋ] N *(issuing of tickets)* billetter *f*

ticketless ['tɪkɪtlɪs] ADJ

▸▸ *Aviat* ***ticketless travel*** = vol avec reçu de pai ment tenant lieu de billet

ticking ['tɪkɪŋ] N *(of clock)* tic-tac *m*

▸▸ *Br Fam* ***ticking off*** engueulade *f*; **to give sb a off** enguirlander qn, tirer les oreilles à qn; **sh got a t. off for being late** elle s'est fait enguirla der parce qu'elle était en retard

tickle ['tɪkəl] VT **1** *(by touching)* chatouiller; **dor t. my feet!** ne me chatouille pas les pieds!; **to sb in the ribs/under the chin** chatouiller les côte le menton à qn; **the blanket tickled her nose** couverture lui chatouillait le nez **2** *Fig (curiosit vanity)* chatouiller; **to t. the palate** *(of food, win* chatouiller le palais **3** *Fig (amuse)* amuser, fair rire; *(please)* faire plaisir à; **she was really tickle by the news** *(amused)* la nouvelle l'a vraime amusée; *(pleased)* la nouvelle lui a vraiment fa plaisir; **this idea tickled her fancy** cette idée lui plu *ou* l'a séduite; **to be tickled pink** *or* **to deat** être ravi *ou* aux anges; **he was tickled pink at b coming a grandfather** il était ravi de deven grand-père

VI *(person, blanket)* chatouiller; *(beard)* pique **that tickles!** ça chatouille!

N *(on body)* chatouillement *m*; *(in throat)* pico tement *m*, chatouillement *m*; **to give sb a t.** cha touiller qn, faire des chatouilles à qn; **I've got a awful t. in my throat** j'ai des picotements vra ment désagréables dans la gorge

tickler ['tɪklə(r)] N *Fam (question)* colle *f*; *(prol lem)* casse-tête *m inv*; *(situation)* situation *f* dél cate *ou* épineuse

tickling ['tɪklɪŋ] N *(UNCOUNT) (of person)* ch touilles *fpl*; *(of blanket)* picotement *m*

ADJ *(throat)* qui gratouille *ou* picote; *(coug* d'irritation, qui gratte la gorge; **a t. sensatio** une sensation de picotement

ticklish ['tɪklɪʃ] ADJ **1** *(person, feet)* chatouilleu *(sensation)* de chatouillement **2** *Fam (touch* chatouilleux; **she's very t. about certain subjec** il y a des sujets qu'il ne faut pas aborder ave elle **3** *Fam (delicate ▸ situation, topic)* délicat épineux; *(▸ moment)* crucial; *(▸ negotiation* délicat

tickly ['tɪklɪ] ADJ *(sensation)* de chatouillis; *(bla ket)* qui chatouille; *(beard)* qui pique; **a t. thro** une irritation dans la gorge

tick-tack-toe, tic-tac-toe N *Am (game)* mo pion *m*

tidal ['taɪdəl] ADJ *(estuary, river)* qui a des marée *(current, cycle, force)* de la marée

▸▸ ***tidal basin*** bassin *m* à flot; ***tidal energy, tid power*** énergie *f* marémotrice; ***tidal wave*** raz-d narée *m inv*; *Fig (of sympathy, enthusiasm, emo-ion)* vague *f*

idbit ['tɪdbɪt] *Am* = **titbit**

iddledywink ['tɪdəldɪwɪŋk], **tiddledywinks** 'tɪdəldɪwɪŋks] *Am* = **tiddlywink, tiddlywinks**

iddler ['tɪdlə(r)] **N** *Fam* **1** *(fish)* petit poisson ᵒ*m*; *minnow)* fretin ᵒ*m*; *(stickleback)* épinoche ᵒ*f* **2** *Br child)* mioche *mf*

iddly ['tɪdlɪ] *(compar* **tiddlier**, *superl* **tiddliest)** **ADJ** *Br Fam* **1** *(tiny)* tout petit ᵒ, minuscule ᵒ **2** *(tipsy)* éméché, paf

iddlywink ['tɪdlɪwɪŋk], *Am* **tiddledywink** ['-idəldɪwɪŋk] **N** pion *m* (du jeu de puce)

• tiddlywinks, *Am* **tiddledywinks N** jeu *m* de puce

ide [taɪd] **N 1** *(of sea)* marée *f*; **at high/low t.** à narée haute/basse; **high t. is at 17.29** la mer est naute à 17 heures 29, la marée haute est à 17 neures 29; **the raft was swept out to sea on the t.** a marée a emporté le radeau au large **2** *Fig (of opinion)* courant *m*; *(of discontent, indignation)* vague *f*; *(of events)* cours *m*, marche *f*; **the t. has turned** la chance a tourné; *Fig* **the t. had turned against them** les événements se sont retournés contre eux; **the rising t. of discontent** la vague croissante du mécontentement; **attempts to turn back the t. of progress/secularization** des efforts pour renverser la marche du progrès/de la sécularisation

►► ***tide race*** courant *m* de marée rapide; ***tide table*** échelle *f ou* table *f* des marées, almanach *m* (des marées)

tide over VT SEP dépanner; **to t. sb over a difficult patch** dépanner qn qui se trouve en difficulté; **here's £20 to t. you over until Monday** voici 20 livres pour vous dépanner jusqu'à lundi

idemark ['taɪdmɑːk] **N 1** *(on shore)* laisse *f* de haute mer **2** *Fig Hum (round bath, neck)* traînée *f* de crasse

idewater ['taɪd,wɔːtə(r)] **N** *(UNCOUNT)* **1** *Br (water)* (eaux *fpl* de) marée *f* **2** *Am (land)* côte *f* (baignée par des eaux de marée)

ideway ['taɪdweɪ] **N** *(channel)* lit *m* de la marée; *(part of river)* estuaire *m*, aber *m*

idily ['taɪdɪlɪ] **ADV** *(pack, fold)* soigneusement, avec soin; **her hair was tied back t.** ses cheveux étaient soigneusement attachés; **put your books/clothes away t.** range bien tes livres/habits

idiness ['taɪdɪnɪs] **N 1** *(of room, house, desk, drawer)* ordre *m*; *(of garden)* bon entretien *m*; *(of town)* propreté *f* **2** *(of appearance)* aspect *m* soigné **3** *(of person)* goût *m* de l'ordre; *(of work, exercise book)* propreté *f*; *(of writing)* netteté *f*

idings ['taɪdɪŋz] **NPL** *Arch or Literary* nouvelles *fpl*

idy ['taɪdɪ] *(compar* **tidier**, *superl* **tidiest**, *pl* **tidies**, *pt & pp* **tidied)** **ADJ 1** *(room, house, desk, drawer)* bien rangé, en ordre; *(garden)* bien entretenu; *(town)* propre; **he keeps his flat very t.** il tient son appartement bien rangé; **can't you make the room a bit tidier?** tu ne peux pas mettre un peu (plus) d'ordre dans cette pièce?

2 *(in appearance ► person, clothes, hair)* soigné

3 *(work, writing)* soigné, net

4 *(in character ► person)* ordonné, méthodique; **she has a very t. mind** elle a l'esprit très méthodique

5 *Fam (sum, profit)* joli, coquet

N *(receptacle)* vide-poches *m inv*

VT *(room)* ranger, mettre de l'ordre dans; *(desk, clothes, objects)* ranger; **to t. one's hair** se recoiffer; **t. those books into a cupboard** range ces livres dans un placard

tidy away VT SEP ranger, ramasser

tidy up VI 1 *(in room)* tout ranger; **after the last guests had gone she was left to t. up** elle a dû tout remettre en ordre *ou* tout ranger après le départ des derniers invités **2** *(in appearance)* s'arranger; **you'd better t. up before they arrive** tu ferais mieux de t'arranger un peu avant qu'ils arrivent

VT SEP *(room, clothes)* ranger, mettre de l'ordre dans; *(desk)* ranger; **to t. oneself up** s'arranger; **t. your things up** *(make tidy)* range tes affaires; *(put away)* range *ou* ramasse tes affaires

tidy-out N *Fam* **to have a t.** *(make tidy)* faire du (grand) rangement ᵒ; *(clear out)* faire le rangement par le vide ᵒ; **we gave the room a good t.** on a rangé la pièce de fond en comble ᵒ

tidy-up N *Fam* **to have a t.** faire du rangement ᵒ; **we'll have to give the place a t. before the guests arrive** il va falloir mettre de l'ordre ᵒ *ou* faire du rangement dans la maison avant l'arrivée des invités

TIE [taɪ]

> **N**
> - cravate **1**
> - lien **3**
> - égalité **5**
> - match **6**
> - attache **2, 3**
> - entrave **4**
> - match nul **5**
>
> **VT**
> - attacher **1, 2**
>
> **VI**
> - s'attacher **1**
> - être à égalité **2**

(cont **tying)**

N 1 *(necktie)* cravate *f*

2 *(fastener ► gen)* attache *f*; *(► on apron)* cordon *m*; *(► on shoes)* lacet *m*

3 *(bond, link)* lien *m*, attache *f*; **emotional ties** liens *mpl* affectifs; **family ties** liens *mpl* de parenté *ou* familiaux; **there are strong ties between the two countries** les deux pays entretiennent d'étroites relations; **he has no ties to the place** il n'y a rien qui l'attache à cet endroit

4 *(restriction)* entrave *f*; **pets/young children can be a t.** les animaux/les jeunes enfants peuvent être une entrave

5 *Sport (draw)* égalité *f*; *(drawn match)* match *m* nul; *(in competition)* = compétition dont les gagnants sont ex aequo; *Pol* égalité *f* de voix; **the match ended in a t.** les deux équipes ont fait match nul; **it was a t. for first/second place** il y avait deux premiers/seconds ex aequo; **the election resulted in a t.** les candidats ont obtenu le même nombre de voix *ou* étaient à égalité des voix

6 *Ftbl (match)* match *m*; **a European cup t.** un match de la coupe européenne

7 *Am Rail* traverse *f*, *Can* dormant *m*

8 *Constr* tirant *m*

VT 1 *(with string, rope ► parcel)* attacher, ficeler; **they tied him to a tree** il l'ont attaché *ou* ligoté à un arbre; **his hands and feet were tied** ses mains et ses pieds étaient ligotés

2 *(necktie, scarf, shoelaces)* attacher, nouer; **to t. one's shoelaces** attacher *ou* nouer ses lacets (de chaussures); **to t. a scarf round one's neck** nouer une écharpe autour de son cou; **she tied the ribbon in a bow** elle a fait un nœud au ruban; **she tied a bow/a ribbon in her hair** elle s'est mis un nœud/un ruban dans les cheveux; **to t. a knot in sth, to t. sth in a knot** faire un nœud à qch

3 *(confine ► of responsibility, job etc)* **she's tied to the house** *(unable to get out)* elle est clouée à la maison; *(kept busy)* la maison l'accapare beaucoup; **the job keeps me very much tied to my desk** mon travail m'oblige à passer beaucoup de temps devant mon bureau; **they're tied to** *or* **by the conditions of the contract** ils sont liés par les conditions du contrat

4 *(link)* **to be tied to** avoir un lien avec

VI 1 *(apron, shoelace etc)* s'attacher, se nouer; **the dress ties at the back** la robe s'attache par derrière

2 *(draw ► players)* être à égalité; *(► in match)* faire match nul; *(► in exam, competition)* être ex aequo; *(► in election)* obtenir le même score *ou* nombre de voix; **they tied for third place in the competition** ils étaient troisième ex aequo au concours

►► *Constr* ***tie beam*** longrine *f*; ***tie clasp, tie clip*** fixe-cravate *m*; ***tie pin*** épingle *f* de cravate; ***tie rack*** porte-cravates *m inv*; *Am* ***tie tack*** fixe-cravate *m*

► tie back VT SEP *(hair)* attacher (en arrière); *(curtains, plant)* attacher

► tie down VT SEP 1 *(with string, rope ► person, object)* attacher **2** *Fig (restrict)* accaparer; **she doesn't want to feel tied down** elle ne veut pas perdre sa liberté; **children can really t. you down** il arrive que les enfants vous accaparent totalement; **I'd rather not be tied down to a specific time** je préférerais qu'on ne fixe pas une heure précise

► tie in VI 1 *(be connected)* être lié *ou* en rapport; **everything seems to t. in** tout semble se tenir; **this ties in with what I said before** cela rejoint ce que j'ai dit avant **2** *(correspond)* correspondre, concorder; **the evidence doesn't t. in with the facts** les indices dont nous disposons ne correspondent pas aux faits *ou* ne cadrent pas avec les faits

VT SEP how is this tied in with your previous experiments? quel est le lien *ou* le rapport avec vos expériences antérieures?; **she's trying to t. her work experience in with her research** elle essaie de faire coïncider son expérience professionnelle et ses recherches

► tie on VT SEP 1 *(attach)* attacher, nouer **2** *Am Fam* **to t. one on** *(get drunk)* prendre une cuite, se cuiter

► tie up VT SEP 1 *(parcel, papers)* ficeler; *(plant, animal)* attacher; *(prisoner)* attacher, ligoter; *(boat)* attacher, arrimer; *(shoelace, hair)* nouer, attacher

2 *(usu passive) (money, supplies)* immobiliser; **her inheritance is tied up until her 21st birthday** elle ne peut toucher à son héritage avant son 21ème anniversaire

3 *(connect ► company, organization)* lier par des accords

4 *(complete, finalize ► deal)* conclure; *(► terms of contract)* fixer; **I'd like to get everything tied up before the holidays** je voudrais arriver à tout régler avant les vacances; **there are still a few loose ends to t. up** il y a encore quelques points de détail à régler

5 *(impede ► traffic)* bloquer; *(► progress, production)* freiner, entraver

VI 1 *(be connected)* être lié; **how does this t. up with the Chicago gang killings?** quel est le rapport avec les assassinats du gang de Chicago?; **it's all beginning to t. up** tout commence à s'expliquer **2** *Naut* accoster

tiebreak ['taɪbreɪk], **tiebreaker** ['taɪbreɪkə(r)] **N** *(in tennis)* tie-break *m*; *(in game, contest)* épreuve *f* subsidiaire; *(in quiz)* question *f* subsidiaire

tied [taɪd] **ADJ 1** *Sport* **to be t.** *(players)* être à égalité; *(game)* être nul **2** *(person ► by obligation, duties)* pris, occupé; **he doesn't want to feel t.** il ne veut pas s'engager; **she isn't t. by any family obligations** elle n'a *ou* elle n'est tenue par aucune obligation familiale

►► *Fin* ***tied agent*** agent *m* lié; *Pol* ***tied aid*** aide *f* liée; *Fin* ***tied loan*** prêt *m* conditionnel *ou* à condition

tied up ADJ 1 *(busy)* **to be t.** être occupé *ou* pris; **she's t. with the children every Wednesday** elle est prise par les enfants tous les mercredis; **I'll be t. all weekend writing these wretched reports** je vais devoir passer tout le week-end à rédiger ces maudits rapports **2 to be t. with sth** *(connected)* être lié à qch; **it's t. with the increase in the interest rate** c'est lié à l'augmentation des taux d'intérêt

tie-dye VT teindre en nouant *(pour obtenir une teinture non uniforme)*

tie-in N 1 *(connection)* lien *m*, rapport *m* **2** *Am Com (sale)* vente *f* par lots; *(items)* lot *m* **3** *(film from book)* = film tiré d'un livre; *(book from film, TV series)* = livre tiré d'un film *ou* d'un feuilleton; **there may be a film t.** on pourrait en tirer un film

►► ***tie-in promotion*** promotion *f* collective

tie-on ADJ *(label)* à œillet

tier [tɪə(r)] **N 1** *(row of seats ► in theatre, stadium)* gradin *m*, rangée *f*; *(level)* étage *m*; **to arrange seats in tiers** disposer des sièges en gradins **2** *Admin* échelon *m*, niveau *m*; **a five-t. system** un système à cinq niveaux; **a two-t. education system/health service** un système éducatif/de santé à deux vitesses **3** *(of cake)* étage *m*; **a three-t. wedding cake** un gâteau de mariage à trois étages

VT *(seating)* disposer en gradins

tiered [tɪəd] **ADJ** *(seating)* en gradins; *(system)* à plusieurs niveaux; **three-t. cake** pièce montée *f* à trois étages; **three-t. stand** *(for cakes etc)* étagère *f* à trois tablettes; **a t. dress/skirt** une robe/jupe à volants

tie-rod N *Aut* tirant *m*

Tierra del Fuego [tɪˌerədel'fweɪgəʊ] N Terre de Feu *f*

tie-up N **1** *(connection)* lien *m*, rapport *m*

2 *Com (merger)* (absorption-)fusion *f*, unification *f*; *(joint venture)* coentreprise *f*, joint-venture *m*

3 *Am (stoppage)* arrêt *m*, interruption *f*

4 *Am (traffic jam)* embouteillage *m*, bouchon *m*

TIF [ˌtiːaɪ'ef] N *Rail (abbr* **transport international ferroviaire)** TIF *m*

TIFF [tɪf] N *Comput (abbr* **Tagged Image File Format)** format *m* TIFF

tiff [tɪf] N *Br Fam* prise *f* de bec; **a lover's t.** une dispute d'amoureux

tiffin ['tɪfɪn] N *Br Old-fashioned* repas *m* de midi *(dans l'Inde coloniale)*

tig [tɪg] N (jeu *m* du) chat *m*; **to play t.** jouer à chat

tiger ['taɪgə(r)] N **1** *(animal)* tigre *m*; **to fight like a t.** se battre comme un tigre; **to have a t. by the tail** se trouver pris dans une situation dont on n'est plus maître **2** *Fam (keen, energetic person)* **easy, t.!** hé là, on se calme!

►► ***tiger cub*** petit *m* du tigre; ***tiger economy*** = pays à l'économie très performante; **the (Asian) t. economies** les dragons *mpl ou* les tigres *mpl* asiatiques; ***tiger lily*** lis *m* tigré; ***tiger prawn*** crevette *f* tigrée

tiger's-eye N *(stone)* œil-de-tigre *m*

tight [taɪt] ADJ **1** *(garment, footwear)* serré, étroit; **these shoes are a bit t.** ces chaussures sont un peu trop serrées; **it's a t. fit** c'est trop serré *ou* juste; **a t. skirt** *(too small)* une jupe trop serrée; *(close-fitting)* une jupe moulante; **my tie is too t.** ma cravate est trop serrée

2 *(stiff* ► *drawer, door)* dur à ouvrir; *(*► *tap)* dur à tourner; *(*► *lid)* dur à enlever; *(*► *screw)* serré; *(constricted)* pesant; **I've got a t. feeling across my chest** j'ai comme un poids sur la poitrine; **it was a t. squeeze but we got everyone in** on a eu du mal mais on a réussi à faire entrer tout le monde; *Fig* **to be in a t. corner** *or* **spot** être dans une situation difficile

3 *(taut* ► *rope)* raide, tendu; *(*► *bow)* tendu; *(*► *net, knitting, knot)* serré; *(*► *skin)* tiré; *(*► *group)* serré; **her face looked t. and drawn** elle avait les traits tirés; **they marched in t. formation** ils marchaient en ordre serré

4 *(firm)* **to keep a t. hold** *or* **grasp on sth** bien tenir qch; **she kept a t. hold on the rail** elle s'agrippait à la balustrade; *Fig* **she kept a t. hold on the expenses** elle surveillait les dépenses de près; **you should keep a tighter rein on the children/your emotions** il faudrait surveiller les enfants de plus près/mieux maîtriser vos émotions

5 *(sharp* ► *bend, turn)* brusque; **we had to make a t. turn to avoid the car** nous avons dû effectuer un virage serré pour éviter la voiture

6 *(strict* ► *control, restrictions)* strict, sévère; *(*► *security)* strict; **to run a t. ship** mener son monde à la baguette

7 *(limited* ► *budget, credit)* serré, resserré; **to work on a t. budget** travailler avec un budget serré; **money is a bit t.** *or* **things are a bit t. at the moment** l'argent manque un peu en ce moment

8 *(close* ► *competition)* serré; **it should be a t. finish** *(in race)* l'arrivée devrait être serrée

9 *(busy* ► *schedule)* serré, chargé; **it was t. but I made it in time** c'était juste, mais je suis arrivé à temps

10 *Fam (mean)* radin, pingre; **he's very t. with his money** il est très près de ses sous

11 *Fam (drunk)* pompette; **he gets t. on one glass of wine** un verre de vin suffit à le soûler

ADV *(close, fasten)* bien; **packed t.** *(bag)* bien rempli *ou* plein; *(pub, room)* bondé; **hold t.!** tenez-vous bien!, accrochez-vous bien!; **she held the rabbit t. in her arms** elle serrait le lapin dans ses bras; **pull the thread t.** tirez *ou* tendez bien le fil; **it needs to be turned/screwed t.** il faut le serrer/le visser à fond

• **tights** NPL **(pair of) tights** collant *m*, collants *mpl*

tight-arsed [-'ɑːst], *Am* **tight-assed** [-'æst] ADJ *very Fam (uptight)* coincé, constipé

tighten ['taɪtən] VT **1** *(belt, strap)* resserrer; **he tightened his grasp on the rail** il agrippa plus fermement la balustrade; **to t. one's belt** resserrer sa ceinture; *Fig* se serrer la ceinture; *Fig* **the army/government has tightened its grip on the region** l'armée/le gouvernement a renforcé son emprise sur la région **2** *(nut, screw)* serrer, bien visser; *(knot)* serrer **3** *(control, security, regulations)* renforcer; *(credit)* resserrer

VI **1** *(grip)* **her grasp tightened on my arm** elle serra mon bras plus fort

2 *(nut, screw, knot)* se resserrer

3 *(control, security, regulation)* être renforcé; *(credit)* se resserrer

4 *(throat, stomach)* se nouer; **her lips tightened** elle serra les lèvres

►**tighten up** VT SEP **1** *(nut, screw)* resserrer **2** *(control, security, regulation, blockade)* renforcer; **the law on drug peddling has been tightened up** la loi sur le trafic de drogue a été renforcée

tightening ['taɪtənɪŋ] N *(of screw, credit)* resserrement *m*; *(of control, regulation, blockade)* renforcement *m*; **he felt a t. in his throat** il sentit sa gorge se nouer

tight-fisted [-'fɪstɪd] ADJ *Fam* radin, pingre

tight-fitting ADJ *(skirt, trousers)* moulant; *(suit, joint)* bien ajusté; *(lid)* qui ferme bien

tight-knit ADJ *(community, family)* (très) uni

tight-lipped [-'lɪpt] ADJ **he sat t. and pale** il était assis, pâle et muet; **she sat in t. silence** elle se tenait assise, sans desserrer les dents

tightly ['taɪtlɪ] ADV **1** *(firmly* ► *hold, fit, screw)* (bien) serré; *(*► *seal, shut)* hermétiquement; **he held his daughter t. to him** il serrait sa fille tout contre lui; **hold on t.** tenez-vous *ou* accrochez-vous bien; **make sure the lid fits t.** vérifiez que le couvercle est bien fermé; **the cases were t. sealed** les caisses étaient bien scellées *ou* hermétiquement fermées; **her eyes were t. shut** elle avait les yeux bien fermés; **news is t. controlled** les informations sont soumises à un contrôle rigoureux **2** *(densely)* **the lecture hall was t. packed** l'amphithéâtre était bondé *ou* plein à craquer

tightness ['taɪtnɪs] N **1** *(of garment, shoes)* étroitesse *f*

2 *(stiffness* ► *of drawer, screw, tap)* dureté *f*

3 *(firmness* ► *of grip, embrace)* force *f*; **he felt a sudden t. in his throat** il sentit soudain sa gorge se nouer; **he felt a sudden t. in his chest** *(physical)* il ressentit soudain une douleur dans la poitrine; *(emotional)* il sentit soudain son cœur se serrer

4 *(strictness* ► *of control, regulation)* rigueur *f*, sévérité *f*; *(*► *of security)* rigueur *f*

tightrope ['taɪtrəʊp] N corde *f* raide; **to walk the t.** marcher sur la corde raide; *Fig* **she's walking a political t.** elle s'est aventurée sur un terrain politique glissant *ou* dangereux

►► ***tightrope walker*** funambule *mf*

tightwad ['taɪtwɒd] N *Am Fam Pej* radin(e) *m,f*; **he's a real t.** il est vraiment grippe-sou

tigress ['taɪgrɪs] N *Zool & Fig* tigresse *f*

Tigris ['taɪgrɪs] N **the (River) T.** le Tigre

tike = **tyke**

tilde ['tɪldə] N *Ling* tilde *m*

tile [taɪl] N *(for roof)* tuile *f*; *(for wall, floor)* carreau *m*; *Br Fam* **to have a night (out) on the tiles** faire la noce

VT **1** *(roof)* couvrir de tuiles; *(floor, wall)* carreler **2** *Comput (windows)* afficher en mosaïque

tiled [taɪld] ADJ *(floor, wall, room)* carrelé; *(roof)* de *ou* en tuiles

tiling ['taɪlɪŋ] N *(UNCOUNT)* **1** *(putting on tiles* ► *on roof)* pose *f* des tuiles; *(*► *on floor, wall)* carrelage *m* **2** *(tiles* ► *on roof)* tuiles *fpl*; *(*► *on floor, wall)* carrelage *m*, carreaux *mpl*

till[1] [tɪl] N *(cash register)* caisse *f* (enregistreuse); *(drawer)* tiroir-caisse *m*; *Fig* **to be caught with one's fingers** *or* **hands in the t.** être pris en flagrant délit *ou* la main dans le sac

VT *Agr (land)* labourer

►► ***till receipt*** ticket *m* de caisse

till[2] CONJ & PREP = **until**

tillage ['tɪlɪdʒ] N **1** *(act)* labour *m*, labourage *m* **2** *(land)* labour *m*, pièce *f* labourée

tiller ['tɪlə(r)] N *Naut* barre *f*, gouvernail *m*

tilt [tɪlt] VT *(lean)* pencher, incliner; **to t. one's chair (back)** se balancer sur sa chaise; **he tilted his head to one side** il pencha *ou* inclina la tête sur le côté; **to t. one's head back** renverser la tête en arrière; **her hat was tilted over one eye** son chapeau était penché sur le côté; *Fig* **this may t. the odds in our favour** cela peut faire pencher la balance de notre côté

VI **1** *(lean* ► *person)* se pencher, s'incliner; *(*► *building, picture etc)* pencher; **to t. backwards/forwards** pencher vers l'arrière/l'avant; **don't t. back on your chair** ne te balance pas sur ta chaise **2** *Hist (joust)* jouter; **to t. at sb** diriger un coup de lance contre qn; *Fig* lancer des piques à qn; *Fig* **to t. at windmills** se battre contre des moulins à vent

N **1** *(angle)* inclinaison *f*, *(slope)* pente *f*; **the room has a definite t. to it** la pièce penche nettement; **she wore her hat at a t.** elle portait son chapeau incliné; **I'm sure that picture's on a t.** je suis sûr que le tableau penche **2** *Hist (joust)* joute *f* *(thrust)* coup *m* de lance; *Fig* **to have a t. at sb** s'en prendre à qn, décocher des pointes à qn

• **full tilt** ADV à toute vitesse, **he ran full t. into her** il lui est rentré en plein dedans

►**tilt over** VI **1** *(slant)* pencher **2** *(overturn)* se renverser, basculer

tilted ['tɪltɪd] ADJ incliné, penché

tilth [tɪlθ] N *(act of tilling)* labourage *m*; *(soil)* terre *f* arable

tilting ['tɪltɪŋ] ADJ **1** *(at an angle)* incliné, penché **2** *(able to be tilted)* inclinable

N *Hist (jousting)* joute *f*

►► ***tilting train*** train *m* pendulaire

timber ['tɪmbə(r)] N **1** *(wood* ► *for building work)* bois *m* de construction *ou* de charpente; *(*► *for carpentry)* bois *m* de menuiserie **2** *(UNCOUNT) (trees)* arbres *mpl*, bois *m*; **to fell t.** abattre *ou* couper des arbres; **land under t.** terre *f* boisée; **standing t.** bois *m* sur pied **3** *(beam)* madrier *m*, poutre *f*; *(on ship)* membrure *f*

COMP *(roof, fence)* en bois

VT *(tunnel)* boiser

EXCLAM attention!

►► *Br* ***timber merchant*** marchand *m* de bois; ***timber trade*** commerce *m* du bois

timbered ['tɪmbəd] ADJ *(region, land)* boisé; *(house)* en bois

timbering ['tɪmbərɪŋ] N **1** *(of region)* boisage *m*; *(of mine shaft)* boisage *m*, cuvelage *m*

timberwork ['tɪmbəwɜːk] N structure *f* en bois

timbre ['tæmbrə, 'tɪmbə(r)] N *Ling & Mus* timbre *m*

Timbuktu [ˌtɪmbʌk'tuː] N Tombouctou

TIME [taɪm]

N
- temps **1–5, 13, 15**
- heure **6, 7, 13, 14**
- fois **11**
- fin **18**
- durée **5**
- moment **9, 10**
- époque **15**
- mesure **20**

VT
- chronométrer **1**
- choisir le moment de **3**
- fixer (l'heure de) **2**
- régler **4**

N **1** *(continuous stretch of time)* temps *m*; **as t. goes by** avec le temps; **the price has gone up over t.** le prix a augmenté avec le temps; **it's only a matter** *or* **a question of t.** ce n'est qu'une question de temps; **these things take t.** cela ne se fait pas du jour au lendemain; **to have t. on one's hands** *or* **t. to spare** avoir du temps; **t. hangs heavy on his hands** le temps lui pèse, il trouve le temps long; **since the dawn of t.** depuis la nuit des temps; **t. flies** le temps passe vite; **doesn't t. fly!** comme le temps passe vite!; **t. heals all wounds** le temps guérit tout; **only t. will tell** seul l'avenir nous le dira; **it's a race against t.** c'est une course contre la montre; **they're working against t. to save her** ils ne disposent que de très peu de temps pour la sauver; **t. is on our side** le temps joue en notre faveur; **t. is money** le temps, c'est de l'argent

2 *(period of time spent on particular activity)* temps *m*; **there's no t. to lose** il n'y a pas de temps à perdre; **he lost no t. in telling me** il s'est empressé de me le dire; **to make up for lost t.** rattraper le temps perdu; **to make good/poor t.** doin sth mettre peu de temps/longtemps à faire qch; passed the t. reading j'ai passé mon temps à lire; ake your t. prenez votre temps; take your t. over t prenez le temps qu'il faudra; it took me all my t. ust to get here! avec le temps que j'ai mis pour arriver ici!; you took your t. about it! tu en as mis du temps!; she took the t. to explain it to us elle a pris le temps de nous l'expliquer; she made the t. to read the report elle a pris le temps de lire le rapport; I can always make t. for you pour vous, e suis toujours là; I spend half/all my t. cleaning up je passe la moitié de/tout mon temps à faire e ménage; half the t. he doesn't know what he's doing la moitié du temps il ne sait pas ce qu'il fait; most of the t. la plupart du temps; he was ill part *or* some of the t. il a été malade une partie du temps; it rained part *or* some of the t. il a plu par moments; I start in three weeks' t. je commence dans trois semaines; they'll have finished the project in three weeks' t. ils auront terminé le projet dans trois semaines; all in good t.! chaque chose en son temps!; I'll finish it in my own good t. je le finirai quand bon me semblera; in no t. (at all), in next to no t. en un rien de temps, en moins de rien

3 *(available period of time)* temps *m*; I haven't (the) t. to do the shopping je n'ai pas le temps de faire les courses; I've no t. for gossip je n'ai pas de temps à perdre en bavardages; he has no t. for sycophants/for laziness il n'a pas de temps à perdre avec les flatteurs/les paresseux; my t. is my own mon temps m'appartient; my t. is not my own je ne suis pas libre de mon temps; we've just got t. to catch the train on a juste le temps d'attraper le train; that doesn't leave them much t. to get ready cela ne leur laisse guère de temps pour se préparer; you'll have to find the t. to see her il faut que tu trouves le temps de la voir; you have plenty of t. to finish it vous avez largement le temps de le finir; we've got plenty of t. *or* all the t. in the world nous avons tout le temps

4 *(while)* temps *m*; after a t. après un (certain) temps; a long t. longtemps; a long t. ago il y a longtemps; it's a long t. since we've been out for a meal ça fait longtemps que nous ne sommes pas sortis dîner; she's been dreaming of this for a long t. now voilà longtemps qu'elle en rêve; he waited for a long t. il a attendu longtemps; I worked for a long t. as a translator j'ai travaillé (pendant) longtemps comme traducteur; it'll be a long t. before I do that again je ne suis pas près de recommencer, je ne recommencerai pas de si tôt *ou* de sitôt; the car takes a long t. to warm up la voiture met longtemps à chauffer; you took a long t.! tu en as mis du temps!, il t'en a fallu du temps!; *Fam* long t. no see! ça faisait longtemps!; a short t. peu de temps; after a short t. peu (de temps) après; a short t. before their wedding peu avant leur mariage; for a short t. pendant quelque temps; after some t. au bout de quelque temps, après un certain temps; some t. after their trip quelque temps après leur voyage; some t. ago il y a quelque temps; for some t. (to come) pendant quelque temps; it's the best film I've seen for some t. c'est le meilleur film que j'aie vu depuis un moment; it will take (quite) some t. to repair il va falloir pas mal de temps pour le réparer; all this t. pendant tout ce temps

5 *(time taken or required to do something)* temps *m*, durée *f*; the cooking t. is two hours le temps de cuisson est de deux heures; the winner's t. was under four minutes le gagnant a fait un temps de moins de quatre minutes; it takes t. cela prend du temps; she finished in half the t. it took me to finish elle a mis deux fois moins de temps que moi pour finir

6 *(by clock)* heure *f*; what t. is it?, what's the t.? quelle heure est-il?; what t. do you make it? quelle heure avez-vous?; do you have the t.? vous avez l'heure?; have you got the right t. on you? avez-vous l'heure juste?; the t. is twenty past three il est trois heures vingt; what t. are we leaving? à quelle heure partons-nous?; do you know how to tell the t.? est-ce que tu sais lire l'heure?; could you tell me the t.? pourriez-vous me dire l'heure (qu'il est)?; have you seen the t.? avez-vous vu l'heure?; I looked at the t. j'ai regardé l'heure; this old watch still keeps good t. cette vieille montre est toujours à l'heure *ou* exacte; at this t. of day à cette heure de la journée; we'll have to keep an eye on the t. il faudra surveiller l'heure; it is almost t. to leave/for my bus il est presque l'heure de partir/de mon bus; it's t. I was going il est temps que je parte; it's dinner t., it's t. for dinner c'est l'heure de dîner; there you are, it's about t.! te voilà, ce n'est pas trop tôt!; I wouldn't give him the t. of day je ne lui dirais même pas bonjour; to pass the t. of day with sb échanger quelques mots avec qn

7 *(system)* local t. heure *f* locale; it's 5 o'clock Tokyo t. il est 5 heures, heure de Tokyo

8 *(schedule)* is the bus running to t.? est-ce que le bus est à l'heure?; within the required t. dans les délais requis

9 *(particular point in time)* moment *m*; at that t. I was in Madrid à ce moment-là, j'étais à Madrid *ou* j'étais alors à Madrid; I worked for her at one t. à un moment donné j'ai travaillé pour elle; at the present t. en ce moment, à présent; at the t. of delivery au moment de la livraison; at a later t. plus tard; at a given t. à un moment donné; at any one t. à la fois; there's room for 15 people at any one t. il y a de la place pour 15 personnes à la fois; an inconvenient t. un moment inopportun; there are times when I could scream il y a des moments où j'ai envie de hurler; at the best of times même quand tout va bien; even at the best of times he is not that patient même dans ses bons moments il n'est pas particulièrement patient; at no t. did I agree to that je n'ai jamais donné mon accord pour cela; by the t. you get this... le temps que tu reçoives ceci…, quand tu auras reçu ceci…; by that t. it will be too late à ce moment-là il sera trop tard; by that t. we'll all be dead d'ici là nous serons tous morts; by this t. next week d'ici une semaine, dans une semaine; this t. next week la semaine prochaine à cette heure-ci; this t. last week il y a exactement une semaine; in between times entre-temps; some t. next month dans le courant du mois prochain; until such t. as I hear from them jusqu'à ce que *ou* en attendant que j'aie de leurs nouvelles

10 *(suitable moment)* moment *m*; this is no t. for you to leave ce n'est pas le moment de partir; now is the t. to invest c'est maintenant qu'il faut investir; when the t. comes le moment venu, quand le moment sera venu; the t. has come to make a stand c'est le moment d'avoir le courage de ses opinions; the t. for talking is past ce n'est plus le moment de parler; it's about t. we taught her a lesson il est grand temps que nous lui donnions une bonne leçon; there's no t. like the present *(let's do it now)* faisons-le maintenant; there's a t. and a place for everything il y a un temps et un lieu pour *ou* à tout

11 *(occasion, instance)* fois *f*; this t. cette fois-ci; each *or* every t. chaque fois; she succeeds every t. elle réussit à chaque fois; the last t. he came la dernière fois qu'il est venu; the t. before la fois précédente *ou* d'avant; another *or* some other t. une autre fois; I called her three times je l'ai appelée trois fois; many times bien des fois, très souvent; many a t. I've wondered... je me suis demandé plus d'une *ou* bien des fois…; several times plusieurs fois; it costs 15 cents a t. ça coûte 15 cents à chaque fois; the one t. I'm winning, he wants to stop playing pour une fois que je gagne, il veut arrêter de jouer; nine times out of ten the machine doesn't work neuf fois sur dix la machine ne marche pas; we'll have to decide some t. or other tôt ou tard *ou* un jour ou l'autre il va falloir nous décider; do you remember that t. we went to Germany? tu te rappelles la fois où nous sommes allés en Allemagne?; there's always a first t. il y a un début à tout; I've told you a hundred times! je te l'ai dit vingt *ou* cent fois!; give me a good detective story every t.! rien ne vaut un bon roman policier!

12 *(experience)* to have a good t. bien s'amuser; she's had a terrible t. of it elle a beaucoup souffert; I had the t. of my life jamais je ne me suis si bien *ou* autant amusé; it was a difficult t. for all of us c'était une période difficile pour nous tous; to give sb a hard *or* rough *or* tough t. en faire voir de dures à qn, en faire voir de toutes les couleurs à qn; what a t. I had with him! *(fun)* qu'est-ce que j'ai pu m'amuser avec lui!; *(trouble)* qu'est-ce qu'il m'en a fait voir!

13 *(hours of work)* to put in t. faire des heures (de travail); to work part/full t. travailler à temps partiel/à plein temps; *Br* in company t., *Am* on company t. pendant les heures de travail; *Br* in your own t., *Am* on your own t. pendant votre temps libre, en dehors des heures de travail

14 *(hourly wages)* we pay t. and a half on weekends nous payons les heures du week-end une fois et demie le tarif normal; overtime is paid at double t. les heures supplémentaires sont payées *ou* comptées double

15 *(usu plural) (era)* époque *f*, temps *m*; in Victorian times à l'époque victorienne; in the t. of Henry IV à l'époque d'Henri IV, du temps d'Henri IV; in times past, in former times autrefois, jadis; in times to come à l'avenir; at one t., things were different autrefois *ou* dans le temps les choses étaient différentes; in happier times en un *ou* des temps plus heureux; in t. *or* times of need/war en temps de pénurie/de guerre; t. was when doctors made house calls il fut un temps où les médecins faisaient des visites à domicile; those were happy times! c'était le bon (vieux) temps!; times are hard les temps sont durs; in our t. de nos jours; the times we live in l'époque *f* où nous vivons; in my t.... de mon temps…; she was a good singer in her t. en son temps, c'était une bonne chanteuse; very advanced for its t. très en avance sur son temps *ou* sur l'époque; to be ahead of *or* before one's t. être en avance sur son époque *ou* sur son temps; to be behind the times être en retard sur son époque *ou* sur son temps; to keep up with the times vivre avec son temps; to move with the times évoluer avec son temps; times have changed autres temps, autres mœurs

16 *(lifetime)* I've heard some odd things in my t.! j'en ai entendu, des choses, dans ma vie!; at my t. of life à mon âge; that was before your t. *(birth)* vous n'étiez pas encore né; *(arrival)* vous n'étiez pas encore là; her t. has come *(childbirth)* elle arrive à son terme; *(death)* son heure est venue *ou* a sonné; *(success)* son heure est venue; he died before his t. il est mort avant l'âge

17 *(season)* it's hot for the t. of year il fait chaud pour la saison

18 *(end of period)* fin *f*; t.'s up *(on exam, visit)* c'est l'heure; *(on meter, telephone)* le temps est écoulé; *Br* t. (gentlemen), please! *(in pub)* on ferme!; *Sport* the referee called t. l'arbitre a sifflé la fin du match

19 *Fam (in prison)* to do t. faire de la taule; he's serving t. for murder il est en taule pour meurtre

20 *Mus (tempo)* mesure *f*; *(note value)* valeur *f (d'une note)*; to keep t., to be in t. être en mesure; he beat t. with his foot il battait *ou* marquait la mesure du pied; in triple *or* three-part t. à trois temps

21 *Rad & TV* espace *m*; to buy/to sell t. on television acheter/vendre de l'espace publicitaire à la télévision

VT 1 *(on clock ▸ runner, worker, race)* chronométrer; they timed her at four minutes a mile ils l'ont chronométrée *ou* ils ont chronométré son temps à quatre minutes au mille; t. how long she takes to finish regardez combien de temps elle met pour finir; he timed his speech to last 20 minutes il a fait en sorte que son discours dure 20 minutes

2 *(schedule)* fixer *ou* prévoir (l'heure de); *Phot (exposure)* calculer

3 *(choose right moment for)* choisir *ou* calculer le moment de; she timed her entrance well elle a bien choisi le moment pour faire son entrée; your remark was perfectly/badly timed votre observation est venue au bon/au mauvais moment

4 *(synchronize)* régler, ajuster; she tried to t. her steps to the music elle essayait de régler ses pas sur la musique

• **times** NPL *(indicating degree)* fois *f*; she's ten times cleverer than *or* as clever as he is elle est dix fois plus intelligente que lui; he ate four times as much cake as I did il a mangé quatre fois plus de gâteau que moi PREP *Math* 3 times 2 is 6 3 fois 2 font *ou* égalent 6; 1 times 6 is 6 une fois six fait *ou* égale six

• **ahead of time** ADV en avance; I'm ten minutes ahead of t. j'ai dix minutes d'avance

• **all the time** ADV he talked all the t. we were at lunch il a parlé pendant tout le déjeuner; he's been watching us all the t. il n'a pas cessé de nous regarder; **I knew it all the t.** je le savais depuis le début

• **any time** ADV n'importe quand; **come over any t.** venez quand vous voulez; **you're welcome any t.** vous serez toujours le bienvenu; **thanks for all your help – any t.** merci de votre aide – de rien

• **at a time** ADV **for days at a t.** pendant des journées entières, des journées durant; **to do two things at a t.** faire deux choses à la fois; **take one book at a t.** prenez les livres un par un *ou* un (seul) livre à la fois; **she ran up the stairs two at a t.** elle a monté les marches quatre à quatre

• **at all times** ADV à tous moments

• **at any time** ADV à toute heure; **hot meals at any t.** repas chauds à toute heure; **at any t. of the day or night** à n'importe quelle heure du jour ou de la nuit; **he could die at any t.** il peut mourir d'un moment à l'autre; **if at any t....** si à l'occasion...

• **at the same time** ADV **1** *(simultaneously)* en même temps; **they all spoke at the same t.** ils se sont mis à parler tous en même temps

2 *(yet)* en même temps; **she was pleased but at the same t. a bit concerned** elle était contente mais en même temps un peu inquiète

3 *(nevertheless)* pourtant, cependant; **at the same t., we must not forget...** pourtant *ou* cependant, il ne faut pas oublier...

• **at the time** ADV **at the t. of their wedding** au moment de leur mariage; **I didn't pay much attention at the t.** sur le moment, je n'ai pas fait vraiment attention

• **at times** ADV parfois, par moments

• **behind time** ADV en retard; **we're a bit behind t.** nous sommes légèrement en retard

• **for a time** ADV pendant un (certain) temps

• **for all time** ADV pour toujours

• **for the time being** ADV pour le moment

• **from time to time** ADV de temps en temps, de temps à autre

• **in time** ADV **1** *(eventually)* **she'll come to her senses in t.** elle finira par revenir à la raison

2 *(not too late)* **let me know in (good) t.** prévenez-moi (bien) à l'avance; **she arrived in t. for the play** elle est arrivée à l'heure pour la pièce; **you're just in t. to greet our guests** tu arrives juste à temps pour accueillir nos invités; **I'll be back in t. for the film** je serai de retour à temps pour le film

3 *Mus* en mesure

• **in (next to) no time, in no time at all** ADV en un rien de temps

• **of all time** ADV de tous les temps

• **on time** ADV à l'heure; **to run on t.** *(trains etc)* être à l'heure; **she arrived right on t.** elle est arrivée juste à l'heure

• **out of time** ADV *Mus* **he got out of t.** il a perdu la mesure

• **time after time, time and (time) again** ADV maintes et maintes fois

• **time off** N temps *m* libre; **what do you do in your t. off?** qu'est-ce que vous faites de votre temps libre?

• **time out** N **1** *Sport* temps *m* mort; *(in chess match)* temps *m* de repos; *Sport* **to take t. out** faire un temps mort

2 *(break)* **I took t. out to travel** *(from work)* je me suis mis en congé pour voyager; *(from studies)* j'ai interrompu mes études pour voyager; **she took t. out to read the report** elle a pris le temps de lire le rapport

►► *St Exch* **time bargain** marché *m* à terme; *Fin* **time bill** traite *f* à terme; *also Fig* **time bomb** bombe *f* à retardement; *Fig* **a demographic t. bomb** une situation démographique qui menace d'exploser; *Fig* **they're sitting on a t. bomb** ils sont assis sur un volcan; **time capsule** capsule *f* témoin *(qui doit servir de témoignage historique aux générations futures)*; *Ind* **time card** carte *f ou* fiche *f* de pointage; **time chart** *(showing time zones)* carte *f* des fuseaux horaires; *(showing events)* table *f* d'événements historiques; *(showing planning)* calendrier *m*, planning *m*; **time check** *(on radio)* rappel *m* de l'heure; *(in cycling, skiing, motor racing)* contrôle *m* du temps intermédiaire; *Ind* **time clock** pointeuse *f*; **time code** code *m* temporel; **time delay** retard *m*, délai *m*; **time of departure** heure *f* de départ; **time difference** décalage *m* horaire; *Fin* **time draft** traite *f* à terme; **time exposure** *(of film)* (temps *m* de) pose *f*; *(photograph)* photo *f* prise en pose; **time frame** délai *m*; **what's our t. frame?** de combien de temps disposons-nous?; **time lag** *(delay)* décalage *m* dans le temps; *(in time zones)* décalage *m* horaire; **time lapse** intervalle *m*, laps *m* de temps; **time limit** *(gen)* délai *m*, date *f* limite; *Law* délai *m* de forclusion; **we'll have to set ourselves a t. limit for the work** il va falloir nous imposer un délai pour finir ce travail; **the work must be completed within the t. limit** le travail doit être terminé avant la date limite; **time machine** machine *f* à voyager dans le temps; **time management** gestion *f* du temps de travail; *Phot* **time release** déclencheur *m* automatique; **time sheet** feuille *f* d'heures; *Rad* **time signal** signal *m ou* top *m* horaire; *Mus* **time signature** indication *f* de la mesure; *Comput* **time slice** tranche *f* de temps; *Comput* **time slicing** temps *m* partagé; **time slot** créneau *m ou* tranche *f* horaire; **time switch** *(for oven, heating)* minuteur *m*; *(for lighting)* minuterie *f*; **time travel** voyage *m* dans le temps; **time traveller** personne *f* qui voyage dans le temps; *Sport* **time trial** course *f* contre la montre, contre-la-montre *m inv*; *Tel* **time unit** unité *f*; **time value** *Mus* valeur *f (d'une note)*; *Fin* valeur *f* temporelle; **time warp** *(in science fiction)* faille *f* spatio-temporelle; **it's like living in a t. warp** c'est comme si on vivait hors du temps; **the house/company seems to be caught in a 19th-century t. warp** la maison/la société semble ne pas avoir changé depuis le XIXème siècle; **time zone** fuseau *m* horaire

---

time-consuming ADJ *(task, work, activity)* qui prend beaucoup de temps

time-honoured, *Am* **time-honored** [-ˈɒnəd] ADJ consacré (par l'usage)

timekeeper [ˈtaɪmˌkiːpə(r)] N **1** *(watch)* montre *f*; *(clock)* horloge *f*; *(stopwatch)* chronomètre *m*; **this watch is a good t.** cette montre est toujours à l'heure

2 *(supervisor)* pointeau *m*

3 *(employee, friend)* **he's a good t.** il est toujours à l'heure, il est toujours très ponctuel; **he's a bad t.** il n'est jamais à l'heure

4 *Sport (official)* chronométreur(euse) *m,f* officiel(elle)

timekeeping [ˈtaɪmˌkiːpɪŋ] N **1** *(of employee)* ponctualité *f*; **bad t.** manque *m* de ponctualité, non-respect *m* des horaires **2** *Sport etc (calculation of time)* chronométrage *m*

time-lapse N *Cin* accéléré *m*

►► **time-lapse photography** accéléré *m*

timeless [ˈtaɪmlɪs] ADJ éternel, hors du temps, intemporel

timeliness [ˈtaɪmlɪnɪs] N *(of remark)* à-propos *m*, opportunité *f*; *(of visit)* opportunité *f*

timely [ˈtaɪmlɪ] *(compar* **timelier**, *superl* **timeliest**) ADJ *(remark, intervention, warning)* qui tombe à point nommé, opportun; *(visit)* opportun; **he made a t. escape** il s'est échappé juste à temps

timepiece [ˈtaɪmpiːs] N *Formal or Old-fashioned (watch)* montre *f*; *(clock)* horloge *f*, pendule *f*

timer [ˈtaɪmə(r)] N **1** *Culin* minuteur *m*; **(egg) t.** sablier *m*, compte-minutes *m inv*

2 *(counter)* compteur *m*

3 *(for lighting)* minuterie *f*

4 *(stopwatch)* chronomètre *m*

5 *Sport (official)* chronométreur(euse) *m,f*

6 *Aut* distributeur *m* d'allumage

7 *(on time bomb)* minuterie *f*

time-saving ADJ *(device, method)* qui économise *ou* fait gagner du temps

N gain *m* de temps

timescale [ˈtaɪmskeɪl] N période *f* (de temps); **the overall t.** la durée totale; **what sort of t. were you thinking of?** *(for completing the job, being absent from work etc)* de combien de temps allez-vous avoir besoin?; **the t. of a novel** la période sur laquelle s'échelonne un roman

time-sensitive ADJ qui requiert un minutage très précis

time-served [-sɜːvd] ADJ *(toolmaker etc)* qui a fait son apprentissage

time-server N **1** *(opportunist)* opportuniste *mf*

2 *(employee)* tire-au-flanc *m inv*

time-serving ADJ opportuniste

N opportunisme *m*

time-share N **to buy a t. in a flat** acheter un ap[partement] en multipropriété

ADJ *(flat, villa)* en multipropriété

time-sharing N *(of flat, villa)* multipropriété

timespan [ˈtaɪmspæn] N intervalle *m* de temps

timetable [ˈtaɪmˌteɪbəl] N **1** *(for transport)* ho[raire] *m* **2** *(schedule)* emploi *m* du temps **3** *(cale[ndar])* calendrier *m*; **exam t.** dates *fpl ou* calendri[er] *m* des examens

VT *(meeting* ► *during day)* fixer une heure pou[r]; (► *during week, month)* fixer une date pour; *Sc[h] (classes, course)* établir un emploi du temp[s] pour; **the train is timetabled to arrive at six o'clo[ck]** l'arrivée du train est prévue à six heures; **h[is] visit is timetabled to coincide with the celebratio[ns]** sa visite est prévue pour coïncider avec les fe[s]tivités

timewaster [ˈtaɪmˌweɪstə(r)] N fainéant(e) *m,[f]*; **no timewasters please** *(in advertisement)* pas s[é]rieux s'abstenir

timewasting [ˈtaɪmˌweɪstɪŋ] N perte *f* de temp[s]

timework [ˈtaɪmwɜːk] N *(hourly)* travail *m* payé [à] l'heure; *(daily)* travail *m* payé à la journée; **to b[e] on t.** *(hourly)* être payé *ou* travailler à l'heur[e]; *(daily)* être payé *ou* travailler à la journée

timeworn [ˈtaɪmwɔːn] ADJ *(object)* usé par l[e] temps, vétuste; *Fig (idea, phrase)* rebattu, écul[é]

timid [ˈtɪmɪd] ADJ timide

timidity [tɪˈmɪdətɪ] N timidité *f*

timidly [ˈtɪmɪdlɪ] ADV timidement

timing [ˈtaɪmɪŋ] N **1** *(of actor)* minutage *m* (d[u] débit); *(of musician)* sens *m* du rythme; *(of tenn[is] player)* timing *m*; *(of stunt driver)* synchronisa[tion] *f*; **cooking such a big meal requires careful** pour préparer un si grand repas, il faut organ[i]ser son temps avec soin; **that was good t.!** voi[là] qui était bien calculé!; **he has no sense of t.** *(… what is suitable)* il n'a aucun sens de l'à-propos

2 *(chosen moment* ► *of operation, visit)* momen[t] *m* choisi; **they're still discussing the t. of the ele[c]tion** ils sont encore en train de discuter de [la] date des élections; **the t. of the statement was u[n]fortunate** cette déclaration est vraiment tom[bée] à un très mauvais moment

3 *Sport* chronométrage *m*

4 *Aut* réglage *m* de l'allumage

timorous [ˈtɪmərəs] ADJ timoré, craintif

timorously [ˈtɪmərəslɪ] ADV craintivement

timpani [ˈtɪmpənɪ] NPL *Mus* timbales *fpl*

timpanist [ˈtɪmpənɪst] N *Mus* timbalier *m*

tin [tɪn] *(pt & pp* **tinned**, *cont* **tinning**) N **1** *(meta[l])* étain *m*; **t. (plate)** fer-blanc *m*

2 *Br (can)* boîte *f* (en fer-blanc); *(containin[g] food)* boîte *f* de conserve; **tins of beans/of foo[d]** des boîtes *fpl* de haricots/de conserve; **a t. o[f] paint** un pot de peinture

3 *(for storing)* boîte *f* en fer; **biscuit t.** boîte *f* [à] biscuits

4 *Br (for cooking meat)* plat *m*; *(for cooking brea[d], cakes etc)* moule *m*

ADJ *(made of tin)* en étain; *(made of tinplate)* e[n] fer-blanc; *(box)* en fer; *(roof)* en tôle

VT *Br (food)* mettre en conserve *ou* en boîte

►► **tin can** boîte *f* (en fer-blanc); **tin god 1** *(pett[y] dictator)* petit chef *m*, chefaillon *m*; **he's nothin[g] but a little t. god** il est très imbu de sa personn[e], il se croit sorti de la cuisse de Jupiter **2** *(object o[f] veneration)* idole *f* de pacotille; *Br* **tin hat** casqu[e] *m* (militaire); **tin mine** mine *f* d'étain; *Br* **tin ope[ner]** ouvre-boîte *m*, ouvre-boîtes *m inv*; **Tin Pa[n] Alley** = le monde de la musique populaire; **t[in] soldier** soldat *m* de plomb; **tin whistle** flûtiau *m*, pipeau *m*

tincture [ˈtɪŋktʃə(r)] N **1** *Chem & Pharm* teinture

2 *(colour, tint)* teinte *f*, nuance *f*

VT *also Fig* teinter

tinder [ˈtɪndə(r)] N *(UNCOUNT) (in tinderbo[x])* amadou *m*; *(dry wood)* petit bois *m*; *(dry gras[s])* herbes *fpl* sèches; *Fig* **his words were t. to th[e] mob's fury** ses paroles ont eu un effet incen[…]diaire sur la foule en colère

tinderbox ['tɪndəbɒks] **N 1** *(lighter)* briquet *m* à amadou **2** *(dry place)* endroit *m* sec **3** *Fig (explosive situation)* poudrière *f*, situation *f* explosive

tine [taɪn] **N** *(of fork)* dent *f*; *(of antler)* andouiller *m*

tinfoil ['tɪnfɔɪl] **N** *Br* papier *m* d'aluminium

ting [tɪŋ] **ONOMAT** ding
VI tinter
VT faire tinter

ting-a-ling **ONOMAT** *(of phone, doorbell, bike)* dring-dring
N dring-dring *m*

inge [tɪndʒ] **N** teinte *f*, nuance *f*; **a t. of irony** une pointe *ou* une note d'ironie
VT teinter; **sky tinged with pink** ciel teinté de rose; *Fig* **her smile was tinged with sadness** son sourire était empreint de tristesse

ingle ['tɪŋgəl] **VI 1** *(with heat, cold ▸ ears, cheeks, hands)* fourmiller, picoter; **the cold wind made my face t.** le vent froid me piquait le visage; **his cheeks were tingling** les joues lui picotaient; **my whole body was tingling** j'avais des picotements *ou* des fourmis dans tout le corps; **2** *(with excitement, pleasure)* frissonner, frémir; **she was tingling with excitement** elle tremblait d'excitation; **the insult left me tingling with indignation** l'insulte me fit frémir d'indignation
N 1 *(stinging)* picotements *mpl*, fourmillements *mpl* **2** *(thrill)* frisson *m*, frémissement *m*; **he felt a t. of excitement** il sentit un frisson d'excitation le parcourir

ingling ['tɪŋglɪŋ] **N** *(stinging)* picotement *m*, fourmillement *m*; *(from excitement)* frisson *m*, frémissement *m*
ADJ *(sensation)* de picotement, de fourmillement

ingly ['tɪŋglɪ] **ADJ** *(sensation)* de picotement, de fourmillement; **my fingers have gone all t.** j'ai des fourmis dans les doigts; **the cold shower made me (feel) t. all over** la douche froide m'a fouetté le sang

iniess ['taɪmɪnɪs] **N** petitesse *f* (extrême)

inker ['tɪŋkə(r)] **N 1** *(pot mender)* rétameur *m* (ambulant); *(gipsy)* romanichel(elle) *m,f*; *Fam* **I don't give a t.'s cuss** je m'en fiche comme de ma première chemise!; *Fam* **it's not worth a t.'s cuss** ça vaut des clopinettes **2** *Br Fam (child)* voyou *m*, garnement *m*; **you little t.!** petit garnement! **3** *(act of tinkering)* bricolage *m*
VI **to t. about** bricoler; **he's forever tinkering with the radio** *(fiddling with it)* il n'arrête pas de tripoter la radio; *(repairing it)* il passe des heures à rafistoler le poste de radio; **who's been tinkering with the thermostat?** qui a touché au thermostat?; **someone has tinkered with this report** quelqu'un a trafiqué ce rapport; **so far you've only been tinkering with the problem** pour l'instant, tu n'as fait qu'effleurer le problème

inkle ['tɪŋkəl] **VI 1** *(bell)* tinter **2** *Fam (urinate)* faire pipi
VT *(small bell)* faire tinter
N 1 *(ring)* tintement *m*; **I heard the t. of a bell** j'ai entendu tinter une sonnette **2** *Br Fam (phone call)* **to give sb a t.** donner *ou* passer un coup de fil à qn **3** *Br Fam (act of urinating)* **to go for a t.** aller faire pipi

inkling ['tɪŋklɪŋ] **N** tintement *m*
ADJ *(bell)* qui tinte; *(water)* qui murmure

inned [tɪnd] **ADJ** *Br (preserved in tins)* en boîte, en conserve
▸▸ ***tinned food*** conserves *fpl*

innitus [tɪ'naɪtəs] **N** *(UNCOUNT) Med* acouphène *m*

inny ['tɪnɪ] *(compar* **tinnier**, *superl* **tinniest)** **ADJ 1** *(sound)* métallique, de casserole; *(music)* grêle **2** *Fam (poor quality ▸ radio, car)* de camelote, de quatre sous

inpot ['tɪnpɒt] **ADJ** *Br Fam* **1** *(worthless ▸ car, machine)* qui ne vaut rien□ **2** *(insignificant, hopeless)* médiocre□; **a t. regime/dictator** un régime/un dictateur de pacotille; **a t. frontier town** une petite ville frontalière sans importance□

insel ['tɪnsəl] *(Br pt & pp* **tinselled**, *cont* **tinselling**, *Am pt & pp* **tinseled**, *cont* **tinseling)** **N** *(UNCOUNT)* **1** *(for Christmas tree)* guirlandes *fpl* de Noël **2** *Fig* clinquant *m*
▸▸ *Hum Pej* ***Tinsel Town*** = surnom donné à Hollywood

tinsmith ['tɪnsmɪθ] **N** étameur *m*, ferblantier *m*

tint [tɪnt] **N 1** *(colour, shade)* teinte *f*, nuance *f*; **red with a blue t.** rouge avec une nuance de bleu **2** *(hair dye)* shampooing *m* colorant **3** *(in engraving, printing)* hachure *f*, hachures *fpl*
VT teinter; **blue-tinted walls** des murs bleutés; **tinted lenses** verres *mpl* teintés; **to t. one's hair** se faire un shampooing colorant

tintack ['tɪntæk] **N** clou *m* de tapissier, semence *f*

tinting ['tɪntɪŋ] **N** coloration *f*

tintinnabulation ['tɪntɪ,næbjʊ'leɪʃən] **N** *Literary* tintamarre *m*

tiny ['taɪnɪ] *(compar* **tinier**, *superl* **tiniest)** **ADJ** tout petit, minuscule; **a t. bit** un tout petit peu; **the meat is a t. bit overdone** la viande est un tantinet trop cuite

tip [tɪp] *(pt & pp* **tipped**, *cont* **tipping)** **N 1** *(extremity ▸ of ear, finger, nose)* bout *m*; *(▸ of tongue)* bout *m*, pointe *f*; *(▸ of cigarette, wing)* bout *m*; *(▸ of blade, knife, fork)* pointe *f*; **on the tips of one's toes** sur la pointe des pieds; **from t. to toe** de la tête aux pieds; **his name is on the t. of my tongue** j'ai son nom sur le bout de la langue
2 *(of island, peninsula)* extrémité *f*, pointe *f*; *Fig* **it's just the t. of the iceberg** ce n'est que la partie émergée de l'iceberg
3 *(cap ▸ on walking stick, umbrella)* embout *m*; *(▸ on snooker cue)* procédé *m*; **steel t.** *(of shoe)* bout *m* ferré
4 *Br (dump ▸ for rubbish)* décharge *f*, dépôt *m* d'ordures; *(▸ for coal)* terril *m*; *Fam Fig* **your room is a real t.!** quel bazar, ta chambre!; *Fam Fig* **the house is a bit of a t.** la maison est un vrai dépotoir
5 *(hint ▸ for stock market, race)* tuyau *m*; *(advice)* conseil *m*; **to give sb a t.** *(for race)* donner un tuyau à qn; *(for repairs, procedure)* donner un tuyau *ou* un conseil à qn; **to take a t. from sb** suivre le conseil de qn; **any tips for the 4.30?** avez-vous un tuyau pour la course de 16h30?; **Orlando's my t.** je pense qu'Orlando va gagner; **'Handy Tips for Successful Gardening'** *(book title)* 'Comment réussir votre jardin'
6 *(money)* pourboire *m*; **to give sb a t.** donner un pourboire à qn
VT 1 *(cane)* mettre un embout à; *(snooker cue)* mettre un procédé à; **arrows tipped with poison** des flèches empoisonnées
2 *(tilt, lean)* incliner, pencher; **she tipped her head to one side** elle a penché la tête sur le côté; **to t. one's hat to sb** saluer qn d'un coup de chapeau; **to t. one's hat over one's eyes** rabattre son chapeau sur ses yeux; **the boxer tipped the scales at 80 kg** le boxeur pesait 80 kg; *Fig* **to t. the scales in sb's favour** faire pencher la balance en faveur de qn; **the election tipped the balance of power** avec les élections, l'équilibre des forces politiques a été inversé
3 *(upset, overturn)* renverser, faire chavirer; **I was tipped off my stool/into the water** on m'a fait tomber de mon tabouret/dans l'eau
4 *Br (empty, pour)* verser; *(unload)* déverser, décharger; **she tipped the sugar into the bowl** elle a versé *ou* vidé le sucre dans le bol; **the lorry tipped the rubbish into the field** le camion a déchargé *ou* déversé les déchets dans le champ
5 *(winning horse)* pronostiquer; **Orlando is tipped for the 2.30** *or* **to win the 2.30** Orlando est donné gagnant dans la course de 14h30; **he tipped the winner** il a pronostiqué *ou* donné le cheval gagnant; *Fig* **you've tipped a winner there** vous avez trouvé un bon filon; **he's tipped to be the next president** *or* **as the next president** on prédit *ou* pronostique qu'il sera le prochain président
6 *(porter, waiter)* donner un pourboire à; **she tipped him £1** elle lui a donné une livre de pourboire
VI 1 *Br (tilt)* incliner, pencher; **to t. to the left** pencher à gauche
2 *Br (overturn)* basculer, se renverser
3 *Br (dump rubbish)* **no tipping** *(sign)* défense de déposer des ordures
4 *(give money)* laisser un pourboire; **how much do you usually t.?** combien de pourboire laissez-vous habituellement?

▸ **tip off** **VT SEP** avertir, prévenir; **the police had been tipped off about the robbery** la police avait été avertie que le hold-up aurait lieu

▸ **tip out** **VT SEP** *Br* **1** *(empty ▸ liquid, small objects)* vider, verser; *(▸ rubbish, larger objects)* déverser, décharger; **t. the tea out into the sink** vide *ou* verse le thé dans l'évier; **she tipped the coins out into my hand** elle a fait tomber les pièces dans ma main **2** *(overturn, toss)* faire basculer; **we were tipped out of the cart into the water** on nous a fait basculer de la charrette pour nous faire tomber dans l'eau

▸ **tip over** **VI 1** *(tilt)* pencher **2** *(overturn ▸ boat)* chavirer, se renverser
VT SEP faire basculer, renverser

▸ **tip up** **VI 1** *(cinema seat)* se rabattre; *(bunk, plank, cart)* basculer; **the table tipped up when I sat on it** la table a basculé quand je me suis assis dessus **2** *(bucket, cup, vase)* se renverser
VT SEP 1 *(seat, table)* faire basculer, rabattre **2** *(upside down ▸ bottle, barrel)* renverser

tip-off **N** *Fam* **to give sb a t.** *(hint)* filer un tuyau à qn; *(warning)* avertir qn□, prévenir qn□; **a t. to the police led to his arrest** quelqu'un l'a donné *ou* dénoncé à la police

tipped [tɪpt] **ADJ 1 t. with felt/steel** à bout feutré/ferré **2** *(cigarettes)* (à) bout filtre *(inv)*

-tipped [tɪpt] **SUFF** à bout…; **steel-/felt-t.** à bout ferré/feutré; **a felt-t. pen** un crayon-feutre, un feutre

tipper ['tɪpə(r)] **N 1** *(truck)* camion *m* à benne (basculante) **2** *(tipping device)* benne *f* (basculante) **3** *(customer)* **he's a generous t.** il laisse toujours de bons pourboires
▸▸ ***tipper truck*** camion *m* à benne (basculante)

tippet ['tɪpɪt] **N** *(cape ▸ gen)* pèlerine *f*; *(▸ of fur)* étole *f*

Tipp-Ex ['tɪpeks] **N** *Br* correcteur *m* liquide, Tipp-Ex® *m*

▸ **Tipp-Ex® out** **VT SEP** effacer (avec du Tipp-Ex®)

tipping ['tɪpɪŋ] **ADJ** *(wagon etc)* basculant, à bascule
N *(giving money)* distribution *f* de pourboires; *(system)* (système *m* des) pourboires *mpl*
▸▸ ***tipping point*** point *m* de bascule

tipple ['tɪpəl] **VI** *Fam* picoler
N 1 *Fam (drink)* **he likes a t. now and then** il aime boire un coup de temps à autre; **what's your t.?** qu'est-ce que vous prenez?□ **2** *Mining (device)* culbuteur *m*; *(place ▸ for loading)* aire *f* de chargement; *(▸ for unloading)* aire *f* de déchargement

tippler ['tɪplə(r)] **N** *Fam* picoleur(euse) *m,f*

tippy-toe ['tɪpɪ-] *Am* = **tiptoe**

tipsily ['tɪpsɪlɪ] **ADV** *Fam* **he got t. to his feet** il s'est levé en titubant□

tipsiness ['tɪpsɪnɪs] **N** *Fam* (légère) ivresse□*f*

tipstaff ['tɪpstɑːf] **N** *Br Law* huissier *m*

tipster ['tɪpstə(r)] **N** *(racing)* **t.** pronostiqueur (euse) *m,f*

tipsy ['tɪpsɪ] *(compar* **tipsier**, *superl* **tipsiest)** **ADJ** *Fam* éméché, pompette; **to get t.** se griser

tiptoe ['tɪptəʊ] **N** **on t.** sur la pointe des pieds
VI marcher sur la pointe des pieds; **to t. in/out** entrer/sortir sur la pointe des pieds; **he tiptoed downstairs** il est descendu sur la pointe des pieds *ou* sans faire de bruit

tip-top **ADJ** *Fam* de premier ordre□, de toute première qualité□; **in t. condition** en excellent état□

tip-up **ADJ**
▸▸ ***tip-up seat*** *(in cinema, theatre)* siège *m* rabattable, strapontin *m*; *(in metro)* strapontin *m*; *Br* ***tip-up truck*** camion *m* à benne (basculante)

TIR [,tiːaɪ'ɑː(r)] **N** *Transp (abbr* **transports internationaux routiers)** TIR *m*

tirade [taɪ'reɪd] **N** diatribe *f*; **a t. of abuse** une bordée d'injures; **he launched into a long t. against bureaucrats** il s'est lancé dans une longue diatribe contre les bureaucrates

tire[1] ['taɪə(r)] **VI 1** *(become exhausted)* se fatiguer; **she tires easily** elle est vite fatiguée **2** *(become bored)* se fatiguer, se lasser; **he soon tired of**

her/of her company il se lassa vite d'elle/de sa compagnie; **he never tires of talking about the war** il ne se lasse jamais de parler de la guerre

VT1 *(exhaust)* fatiguer **2** *(bore)* fatiguer, lasser

tire[2] *Am* = **tyre**

▸ **tire out** **VT SEP** épuiser, éreinter; **the long walk had tired us all out** cette longue marche nous avait tous épuisés; **I'm tired out!** je n'en peux plus!

tired ['taɪəd] **ADJ 1** *(exhausted)* fatigué; **to feel t.** se sentir fatigué; **to get t.** se fatiguer; **the walk made me t.** la marche m'a fatigué; **my eyes are t.** j'ai les yeux fatigués

2 *(fed up)* fatigué, las; **to be t. of sb/sth** en avoir assez de qn/qch; **I'm t. of their excuses** j'en ai assez de leurs excuses; **I'm t. of telling them** j'en ai assez de le leur répéter; **she soon got t. of him** elle se fatigua *ou* se lassa vite de lui; **the children make me t. with their constant whining** les enfants me fatiguent avec leur pleurnicheries continuelles

3 *(hackneyed)* rebattu

4 *Fig (old* ▸ *skin)* desséché; *(*▸ *upholstery, springs, car)* fatigué

tiredly ['taɪədlɪ] **ADV** *(say)* d'une voix lasse; *(move, walk)* avec lassitude

tiredness ['taɪədnɪs] **N 1** *(exhaustion)* fatigue *f* **2** *(tedium)* fatigue *f*, lassitude *f*

tireless ['taɪəlɪs] **ADJ** *(person)* infatigable, inlassable; *(effort, campaign)* soutenu; *(energy)* inépuisable

tirelessly ['taɪəlɪslɪ] **ADV** infatigablement, inlassablement, sans ménager ses efforts

tiresome ['taɪəsəm] **ADJ** *(irritating)* agaçant, ennuyeux; *(boring)* assommant, ennuyeux; **how t.!** que c'est ennuyeux!

> Attention: ne pas confondre avec **tiring**, qui se rapporte le plus souvent à la fatigue physique.

tiring ['taɪərɪŋ] **ADJ** fatigant

> Attention: ne pas confondre avec **tiresome**, qui signifie **ennuyeux**.

tiro = **tyro**

'tis [tɪz] *Literary, Fam or Ir* = **it is**

tissue ['tɪʃuː] **N 1** *Anat & Bot* tissu *m* **2** *Tex* voile *m*; *Fig* **a t. of lies** un tissu de mensonges **3** *(paper handkerchief)* mouchoir *m* en papier; *(toilet paper)* papier *m* hygiénique

▸▸ ***tissue paper*** papier *m* de soie

> Note that the French word **tissu** also means **fabric**.

tit [tɪt] **N 1** *Orn* mésange *f*

2 *very Fam (breast)* nichon *m*, robert *m*; *Br* **to get on sb's tits** courir sur le haricot à qn, taper sur les nerfs à qn

3 *Br very Fam Pej (person)* con (conne) *m,f*; **I felt a right t.** je me suis senti tout con

4 *(idiom)* **it's t. for tat!** c'est un prêté pour un rendu!

▸▸ *very Fam* ***tit tape*** = ruban adhésif empêchant une robe ou un haut décolleté de glisser

Titan ['taɪtən] **N** *Astron* Titan *m*; *Myth* Titan *m*; *Fig* **a T. of the motor industry** un géant de l'industrie automobile

titanic [taɪ'tænɪk] **ADJ** *(huge)* titanesque, colossal

titanium [taɪ'teɪnɪəm] **N** *Chem* titane *m*

titbit ['tɪtbɪt], *Am* **tidbit** ['tɪdbɪt] **N 1** *Culin* bon morceau *m*, morceau *m* de choix **2** *(of information, scandal)* détail *m* croustillant; **t. of gossip** potin *m*, racontar *m*

titch = **tich**

titchy = **tichy**

tit-for-tat **ADJ** *(killing, expulsions etc)* fait en représailles *ou* en riposte

tithe [taɪð] **N 1** *Hist* dîme *f*; **to pay tithes** payer la dîme **2** *(percentage of income)* = montant équivalant à un dixième du revenu, versé par les membres de certaines Églises

VT 1 *Hist* lever la dîme sur **2** *(income)* = verser à l'Église

Titian ['tɪʃən] **PR N** (le) Titien

titillate ['tɪtɪleɪt] **VT** titiller

VI titiller les sens

titillating ['tɪtɪˌleɪtɪŋ] **ADJ** titillant

titillation [ˌtɪtɪ'leɪʃən] **N** titillation *f*

titivate ['tɪtɪveɪt] *Fam Hum* **VI** se bichonner, se pomponner

VT to t. oneself se bichonner, se pomponner

title ['taɪtəl] **N 1** *(indicating rank, status)* titre *m*; **he has the t. of Chief Executive Officer** son titre officiel est directeur général; **to give sb a t.** donner un titre à qn, titrer qn; **to have a t.** *(nobleman)* avoir un titre de noblesse, être titré

2 *(nickname)* surnom *m*; **she earned the t. "the Iron Lady"** on l'a surnommée "la Dame de Fer"

3 *(of book, film, play, song)* titre *m*; *(of newspaper article)* titre *m*, intitulé *m*

4 *Typ (book)* titre *m*

5 *Sport* titre *m*; **to win the t.** remporter le titre; **to hold the t.** détenir le titre

6 *Law* droit *m*, titre *m*

COMP *(music)* de générique

VT *(book, chapter, film)* intituler

• **titles** **NPL** *Cin & TV (credits)* générique *m*

▸▸ *Comput* **title bar** barre *f* de titre; *Law* **title deed** titre *m* de propriété; *Boxing* **title fight** combat *m* comptant pour le titre; ***title page*** page *f* de titre; ***title role*** rôle-titre *m*; ***title track*** morceau *m* qui donne son titre à l'album; *Typ* ***title verso*** verso *m* de la page de titre

titled ['taɪtəld] **ADJ** *(person, family)* titré

titleholder ['taɪtəlˌhəʊldə(r)] **N** détenteur(trice) *m,f* du titre; *Sport* tenant(e) *m,f* du titre

titler ['taɪtələ(r)] **N** *Cin* titreur(euse) *m,f*

titrate [*Br* 'taɪtreɪt, *Am* taɪ'treɪt] **VT** *Chem* titrer

titter ['tɪtə(r)] **VI** rire bêtement *ou* sottement, glousser

N petit rire *m* bête *ou* sot, gloussement *m*

tittering ['tɪtərɪŋ] **N** *(UNCOUNT)* petits rires *mpl*

tittie = **titty**

tittle ['tɪtəl] **N** *Typ* signe *m* diacritique, iota *m*

tittle-tattle [-'tætəl] **N** *(UNCOUNT)* potins *mpl*, cancans *mpl*

VI jaser, cancaner

titty ['tɪtɪ] **N** *very Fam* **1** *(breast)* nichon *m*, robert *m* **2** **tough t.!** dur! dur!

▸▸ ***titty bar*** club *m* de strip-tease

titular ['tɪtjʊlə(r)] **ADJ** nominal

TiVo® ['tiːvəʊ] **N** TiVo® *m*

tizz [tɪz], **tizzy** ['tɪzɪ] **N** *Fam* panique *f*; **to be in a t.** être dans tous ses états, ne pas savoir où donner de la tête; **don't get into a t. about it** ne t'affole pas pour ça

T-junction **N** *Br* intersection *f* en T

TLC [ˌtiːel'siː] **N** *Fam (abbr* **tender loving care**) affection *f*; **she just needs a bit of T.** elle a juste besoin d'un peu d'affection

TNT [ˌtiːen'tiː] **N** *Chem (abbr* **trinitrotoluene**) TNT *m*

TO [tuː, *unstressed* tə]

• à **A1–3, 5, B2, D1, 8, 12**	• en **A3**
• jusqu'à **A4, B2**	• contre **A5**
• pour **C6, 7, D2**	• de **D9**

PREP A. 1 *(indicating direction)* **to go to school/the cinema** aller à l'école/au cinéma; **he climbed to the top** il est monté jusqu'au sommet *ou* jusqu'en haut; **she ran to where her mother was sitting** elle a couru (jusqu')à l'endroit où sa mère était assise; **we've been to it before** nous y sommes déjà allés; **the vase fell to the ground** le vase est tombé par *ou* à terre; **I invited them to dinner** je les ai invités à dîner; **let's go to Susan's** allons chez Susan; **to go to the doctor** *or* **doctor's** aller chez le médecin; **he pointed to the door** il a pointé son doigt vers la porte; **the road to the south** la route du sud; **our house is a mile to the south** notre maison est à un mile au sud; **it's 12 miles to the nearest town** *(from here)* nous sommes à 12 miles de la ville la plus proche; *(from there)* c'est à 12 miles de la ville la plus proche; **what's the best way to the station?** quel est le meilleur chemin pour aller à la gare?; **she turned his photograph to the wall** elle a retourné sa photo contre le mur; **I sat with my back to her** j'étais assis lui tournant le dos

2 *(indicating location, position)* à; **she lives ne[xt] door to us** elle habite à côté de chez nous; **[t]o one side** d'un côté; **to leave sth to one side** laiss[er] qch de côté; **to the left/right** à gauche/droit[e]; **the rooms to the back** les chambres de derrière

3 *(with geographical names)* **to Madrid** à Madri[d]; **to Le Havre** au Havre; **to France** en France; **[to] Japan** au Japon; **to the United States** aux État[s-]Unis; **I'm off to Paris** je pars à *ou* pour Paris; **th[e] road to Chicago** la route de Chicago; **on the wa[y] to Milan** en allant à Milan, sur la route de Mila[n]; **planes to and from Europe** les vols à destinatio[n] et en provenance de l'Europe

4 *(indicating age, amount or level reached)* ju[s]qu'à; **the snow came (up) to her knees** la neige l[ui] arrivait aux genoux; **unemployment is up [to] nearly 9 percent** le (taux de) chômage attei[nt] presque les 9 pour cent; **they cut expenses dow[n] to a minimum** ils ont réduit les frais au minimu[m]; **she can count (up) to one hundred** elle sa[it] compter jusqu'à cent; **it's accurate to the mil[li]metre** c'est exact au millimètre près; **it weighs [8] to 9 pounds** ça pèse entre 8 et 9 livres; **modera[te] to cool temperatures** des températures douce[s] ou fraîches; **to live to a great age** vivre jusqu'à un âge avancé

5 *(so as to make contact with)* à, contre; **sh[e] pinned the brooch to her dress** elle a épinglé [la] broche sur sa robe; **he clutched the baby to h[is] chest** il a serré l'enfant contre lui

B. 1 *(before the specified hour or date)* **it's ten mi[n]utes to three** il est trois heures moins dix; **we le[ft] at (a) quarter to six** nous sommes partis à s[ix] heures moins le quart; **it's twenty to** il est moi[ns] vingt; **how long is it to dinner?** on dîne dans co[m]bien de temps?; **there are only two weeks [to] Christmas** il ne reste que deux semaines ava[nt] Noël

2 *(up to and including)* (jusqu')à; **from Tuesda[y] night to Thursday morning** du mardi soir (jusqu')au jeudi matin; **from morning to night** du mati[n] au soir; **from March to June** de mars (jusqu')[en] juin; **it was three years ago to the day since I sa[w] her last** il y a trois ans jour pour jour que je l'[ai] vue pour la dernière fois; **to this day** jusqu'à c[e] jour, jusqu'à aujourd'hui; **from day to day** de jou[r] en jour; **I do everything from scrubbing the flo[or] to keeping the books** je fais absolument tout, de[-]puis le ménage jusqu'à la comptabilité

C. 1 *(before infinitive)* **to talk** parler; **to open** o[u]vrir; **to answer** répondre

2 *(after verb)* **she lived to be a hundred** elle a véc[u] jusqu'à cent ans; **we are to complete the work b[y] Monday** nous devons finir le travail pour lund[i]; **she went on to become a brilliant guitarist** elle e[st] ensuite devenue une excellente guitariste; **I fi[]nally accepted, (only) to find that they ha[d] changed their mind** lorsque je me suis décidé [à] accepter, ils avaient changé d'avis; **she turne[d] round to find him standing right in front of he[r]** lorsqu'elle s'est retournée, elle s'est retrouvé[e] nez à nez avec lui; **he left the house never to re[]turn to it again** il quitta la maison pour ne plus revenir; **you can leave if you want to** vous pouve[z] partir si vous voulez; **why? – because I told you t[o]** pourquoi? – parce que je t'ai dit de le faire; **yo[u] ought to** vous devriez le faire; **we shall have to** [il] le faudra bien, nous serons bien obligés

3 *(after noun)* **I have a lot to do** j'ai beaucoup [à] faire; **I have a letter to write** j'ai une lettre à écrir[e]; **that's no reason to leave** ce n'est pas une raiso[n] pour partir; **the first to complain** le premier à s[e] plaindre; **the house to be sold** la maison à ver[n]dre; **he isn't one to forget his friends** il n'est pa[s] homme à oublier ses amis

4 *(after adjective)* **I'm happy/sad to see her go** j[e] suis content/triste de la voir partir; **difficult/eas[y] to do** difficile/facile à faire; **it was strange to se[e] her again** c'était bizarre de la revoir; **she's to[o] proud to apologize** elle est trop fière pour s'excu[]ser; **he's old enough to understand** il est asse[z] grand pour comprendre

5 *(after "how", "which", "where" etc)* **do you kno[w] where to go?** savez-vous où aller?; **he told m[e] how to get there** il m'a dit comment y aller; **ca[n] you tell me when to get off?** pourriez-vous m[e] dire quand je dois descendre?; **she can't decid[e] whether to go or not** elle n'arrive pas à décide[r] si elle va y aller ou non

5 *(indicating purpose)* pour; **I did it to annoy her** je l'ai fait exprès pour l'énerver; **to answer that question, we must...** pour répondre à cette question, il nous faut...
7 *(introducing statement)* pour; **to be honest/frank** pour être honnête/franc; **to put it another way** en d'autres termes
8 *(in exclamations)* **oh, to be in France!** ah, si je pouvais être en France!; **and to think I nearly married him!** quand je pense que j'ai failli l'épouser!
9 *(in headlines)* **unions to strike** les syndicats s'apprêtent à déclencher la grève; **Russia to negotiate with Baltic States** la Russie va négocier avec les pays Baltes
D. 1 *(indicating intended recipient, owner)* à; **I showed the picture to her** je lui ai montré la photo; **I showed it to her** je le lui ai montré; **show it to her** montrez-le-lui; **the person I spoke to** la personne à qui j'ai parlé; **be kind to him/to animals** soyez gentil avec lui/bon envers les animaux; **what's it to him?** qu'est-ce que cela peut lui faire?; **did you have a room to yourself?** avais-tu une chambre à toi *ou* pour toi tout seul?; **I said to myself** je me suis dit; **he is known to the police** il est connu de la police
2 *(in the opinion of)* pour; **$20 is a lot of money to some people** il y a des gens pour qui 20 dollars représentent beaucoup d'argent; **it sounds suspicious to me** cela me semble bizarre; **it didn't make sense to him** ça n'avait aucun sens pour lui
3 *(indicating intention)* **with a view to clarifying matters** dans l'intention d'éclaircir la situation; **it's all to no purpose** tout cela ne sert à rien *ou* est en vain
4 *(indicating resulting state)* **the light changed to red** le feu est passé au rouge; **(much) to my relief/surprise/delight** à mon grand soulagement/mon grand étonnement/ma grande joie; **she rose rapidly to power** elle est arrivée au pouvoir très rapidement; **she sang the baby to sleep** elle a chanté jusqu'à ce que le bébé s'endorme
5 *(as regards)* **the answer to your question** la réponse à votre question; **a hazard to your health** un danger pour votre santé; **what's your reaction to all this?** comment réagissez-vous à tout ça?; **that's all there is to it** c'est aussi simple que ça; **there's nothing to it** il n'y a rien de plus simple; **there's nothing** *or* **there isn't a lot to these cameras** ils ne sont pas bien compliqués, ces appareils photos; *Com* **to translating annual report: $300** *(on bill)* traduction du rapport annuel: 300 dollars; **to services rendered** *(on bill)* pour services rendus
6 *(indicating composition or proportion)* **there are 16 ounces to a pound** il y a 16 onces dans une livre; **there are 2 dollars to the pound** une livre vaut 2 dollars; **there are 25 chocolates to a box** il y a 25 chocolats dans chaque *ou* par boîte; **one cup of sugar to every three cups of fruit** une tasse de sucre pour trois tasses de fruits; **three is to six as six is to twelve** trois est à six ce que six est à douze; **Milan beat Madrid by 4 (points) to 3** Milan a battu Madrid 4 (points) à 3; **I'll bet 100 to 1** je parierais 100 contre 1; **the odds are 1000 to 1 against it happening again** il y a 1 chance sur 1000 que cela se produise à nouveau; **the vote was 6 to 3** il y avait 6 voix contre 3
7 *(per)* **how many miles do you get to the gallon?** ≃ vous faites combien de litres au cent?
8 *(indicating comparison)* **inferior to** inférieur à; **they compare her to Callas** on la compare à (la) Callas; **that's nothing (compared) to what I've seen** ce n'est rien à côté de ce que j'ai vu; **inflation is nothing (compared) to last year** l'inflation n'est rien à côté de *ou* en comparaison de l'année dernière; **to prefer sth to sth** préférer qch à qch
9 *(of)* de; **the key to this door** la clé de cette porte; **he's secretary to the director/to the committee** c'est le secrétaire du directeur/du comité; **the French ambassador to Algeria** l'ambassadeur français en Algérie; **ambassador to the King of Thailand** ambassadeur auprès du roi de Thaïlande; **Susan, sister to Mary** Susan, sœur de Mary; **he's been like a father to me** il est comme un père pour moi
10 *(in accordance with)* **to his way of thinking, to his mind** à son avis; **to hear him talk, you'd think he was an expert** à l'entendre parler, on croirait que c'est un expert; **the climate is not to my liking** le climat ne me plaît pas; **she made out a cheque to the amount of £15** elle a fait un chèque de 15 livres
11 *(indicating accompaniment, simultaneity)* **we danced to live music** nous avons dansé sur la musique d'un orchestre; **in time to the music** en mesure avec la musique
12 *(in honour of)* à; **let's drink to his health** buvons à sa santé; **(here's) to your health!** à la vôtre!; **(here's) to the bride!** à la mariée!; **to my family** *(in dedication)* à ma famille; **a monument to the war dead** un monument aux morts
E. 1 *(indicating addition)* **add flour to the list** ajoutez de la farine sur la liste; **add 3 to 6** additionnez 3 et 6, ajoutez 3 à 6
2 *Math* **to the power...** à la puissance...; **2 to the 3rd power, 2 to the 3rd** 2 (à la) puissance 3
ADV 1 *(closed)* fermé; **the wind blew the door to** un coup de vent a fermé la porte
2 *(back to consciousness)* **to come to** revenir à soi, reprendre connaissance
3 *Naut* **to bring a ship to** mettre un bateau en panne
• **to and fro** ADV **to go to and fro** aller et venir, se promener de long en large; *(shuttle bus etc)* faire la navette; **to swing to and fro** se balancer d'avant en arrière

---

toad [təʊd] N 1 *(animal)* crapaud *m* 2 *Fam Fig* *(man)* sale bonhomme *m*, crapule▫*f*; *(woman)* sale bonne femme, crapule▫*f*; **you lying t.!** sale menteur!

toad-in-the-hole N *Br Culin* = plat composé de saucisses cuites au four dans une sorte de pâte à crêpes

toadstool ['təʊdstu:l] N champignon *m* (vénéneux)

toady ['təʊdɪ] *(pl* **toadies**, *pt & pp* **toadied**) *Pej* N flatteur(euse) *m,f*
VI être flatteur; **to t. to sb** passer de la pommade à qn

to-and-fro ADJ **a t. movement** un mouvement de va-et-vient

toast [təʊst] N 1 *(bread)* pain *m* grillé; **a piece** *or* **slice of t.** une tartine grillée, un toast; **three slices** *or Br* **rounds of t.** trois tartines grillées; **don't burn the t.** ne brûle pas le pain; **cheese/sardines on t.** fromage fondu/sardines sur du pain grillé; **as warm as t.** bien chaud 2 *(drink)* toast *m*; **to drink a t. to sb** porter un toast à qn, boire à la santé de qn; **we drank a t. to their success/future happiness** on a bu à leur succès/bonheur futur; **to propose a t. (to sb)** porter un toast (à qn); **she was the t. of the town** elle était la coqueluche de la ville 3 *Fam* **to be t.** *(in trouble)* être foutu; *(exhausted)* être naze *ou* crevé; **if Mum finds out, you're t.** si Maman s'en rend compte, t'es mort *ou* foutu!
VT 1 *(grill)* griller; *Fig* **he was toasting himself/his feet by the fire** il se chauffait/il se rôtissait les pieds devant la cheminée 2 *(drink to* ▸ *person)* porter un toast à, boire à la santé de; *(*▸ *success, win)* arroser; **to t. sb's health** boire à la santé de qn
VI *(bread)* griller; **it toasts well** ça fait du bon pain grillé
▸▸ *Br* **toast rack** porte-toasts *m inv*

toaster ['təʊstə(r)] N grille-pain *m inv* (électrique), toaster *m*

toastie ['təʊstɪ] N *Fam* sandwich *m* grillé▫

toasting fork ['təʊstɪŋ-] N fourchette *f* à griller le pain

toasty ['təʊstɪ] *(compar* **toastier**, *superl* **toastiest**, *pl* **toasties**) *Fam* ADJ *(warm)* **it's t. in here** il fait bon ici▫, on est bien au chaud ici▫
N *(sandwich)* sandwich *m* grillé▫

tobacco [tə'bækəʊ] *(pl* **tobaccos**) N 1 *(for smoking)* tabac *m* 2 *Bot (plant)* (pied *m* de) tabac *m*
COMP *(leaf, plantation, smoke)* de tabac; *(industry)* du tabac
▸▸ *Bot* **tobacco plant** pied *m* de tabac *m*; **tobacco pouch** blague *f* à tabac; **tobacco tin** boîte *f* à tabac, tabatière *f*

tobacconist [tə'bækənɪst] N marchand(e) *m,f* de tabac, buraliste *mf*; *(shop)* (bureau *m* de) tabac *m*
▸▸ **tobacconist's shop** bureau *m* de tabac

Tobin tax ['təʊbɪn-] N *Econ* taxe *f* Tobin

toboggan [tə'bɒgən] N luge *f*
COMP *(race)* de luge
VI 1 *(person)* faire de la luge; **they tobogganed down the slope** ils ont descendu la pente en luge
2 *Am (prices, sales)* dégringoler
▸▸ **toboggan run** piste *f* de luge

> Note that the French word **toboggan** is a false friend. Its most common meaning is **slide** (in a playground).

tobogganing [tə'bɒgənɪŋ] N luge *f*; **to go t.** faire de la luge

toby jug ['təʊbɪ-] N = tasse ou cruche en forme d'homme assis portant un tricorne et fumant la pipe

tocsin ['tɒksɪn] N tocsin *m*

tod [tɒd] N *Br Fam* *(rhyming slang* **Tod Sloan** = **own) to be on one's t.** être tout seul▫

today [tə'deɪ] ADV aujourd'hui; **she's arriving a week t.** elle arrive aujourd'hui en huit; **they arrived a week ago t.** ils sont arrivés il y a huit jours; **they've been here a week t.** ils sont là depuis exactement une semaine; **he died five years ago t.** cela fait cinq ans aujourd'hui qu'il est mort; **many new bands are here t. and gone tomorrow** beaucoup de groupes disparaissent aussi vite qu'ils sont apparus
N aujourd'hui *m*; **what's t.'s date?** quelle est la date d'aujourd'hui?; **what day is it t.?** quel jour est-on (aujourd'hui)?; **t. is** *Br* **17 March** *or Am* **March 17** aujourd'hui, on est le 17 mars; **it's Monday t.** on est lundi aujourd'hui; **a week from t.** dans une semaine aujourd'hui; **three weeks from t.** dans trois semaines; **as from t.** à partir d'aujourd'hui; **have you seen t.'s paper?** as-tu vu le journal d'aujourd'hui?; **the youth of t., t.'s youth** la jeunesse d'aujourd'hui; **t.'s the day!** c'est le grand jour!

toddle ['tɒdəl] VI 1 *(start to walk* ▸ *child)* faire ses premiers pas; *(walk unsteadily)* marcher d'un pas chancelant; **he's just started to t.** il vient de commencer à marcher; **he managed to t. across the room** il a réussi à faire quelques pas dans la pièce 2 *Fam (go)* aller▫; *(stroll)* se balader▫; *(go away)* s'en aller▫, partir▫; **she toddled along after him** elle trottinait derrière lui; **could you just t. down to the shops for me?** pourrais-tu faire une ou deux courses pour moi?▫
N *Fam* **I'm just going for a t.** je vais faire un tour *ou* une balade
▸ **toddle off** VI *Fam (go)* aller▫; *(go away)* s'en aller▫, partir bien gentiment; **he toddled off to the pub** il est allé au bistrot

toddler ['tɒdlə(r)] N tout(e) petit(e) *m,f (qui fait ses premiers pas)*; **he's just a t.** il est encore tout petit

toddy ['tɒdɪ] *(pl* **toddies**) N *(drink)* **(hot) t.** ≃ grog *m*

todger ['tɒdʒə(r)] N *Br very Fam (penis)* chipolata *f*

to-die-for ADJ *Fam* craquant

to-do N *Fam (fuss)* remue-ménage *m inv*, tohu-bohu *m inv*; **she made a great t. about it** elle en a fait tout un plat; **there was a great t. over her wedding** son mariage a fait grand bruit; **what a t.!** quelle affaire!, quelle histoire!
▸▸ **to-do list** liste *f* de choses à faire

toe [təʊ] N 1 *Anat* orteil *m*, doigt *m* de pied; **big/little t.** gros/petit orteil *m*; **to stand on one's toes** se dresser sur la pointe des pieds; *also Fig* **to step** *or* **to tread on sb's toes** marcher sur les pieds de qn; *Fig* **she kept us on our toes** elle ne nous laissait aucun répit 2 *(of sock, shoe)* bout *m*; **there's a hole in the t.** le bout est troué; *Fig* **the t. of Italy** le bout de l'Italie
VT 1 *(ball)* toucher du bout du pied 2 *(idioms)* **to t. the line** *or Am* **mark** se mettre au pas, obtempérer; *Pol* **to t. the party line** s'aligner sur le *ou* suivre la ligne du parti
▸▸ **toe clip** cale-pied *m*; **toe loop** *(in figure skating)* boucle *f* piquée

toecap ['təʊkæp] N bout *m* renforcé *(de soulier)*; **steel t.** bout *m* ferré

-toed [təʊd] SUFF **six-t.** à six orteils; **square-/pointed-t.** *(shoes)* à bouts carrés/pointus

toehold ['təʊhəʊld] N prise *f* de pied; **to get** *or* **to gain a t.** *(climber)* trouver une prise (pour le pied); *Fig* prendre pied, s'implanter; *Fig* **the company now has a t. in the foreign market** l'entreprise a désormais un pied sur le marché étranger

toe-in N *Aut* pincement *m* des roues avant

toenail ['təʊneɪl] N *(on foot)* ongle *m* de pied

toe-out N *Aut* ouverture *f*, pincement *m* négatif

toe-piece N *(of ski)* butée *f*

toerag ['təʊræg] N *Br very Fam Pej* ordure *f*

toff [tɒf] N *Br Fam Pej* rupin(e) *m,f*

toffee ['tɒfɪ] *Br* N caramel *m* (au beurre); *Fam* **he can't dance for t.** il danse comme un pied; *Fam* **I can't speak Italian for t.** je suis incapable de parler italien

COMP *(yogurt, ice cream)* au caramel

►► ***toffee apple*** pomme *f* d'amour *(confiserie)*

toffee-nosed ADJ *Br Fam Pej* bêcheur, snob

tofu ['təʊfu:] N *Culin* tofu *m inv*

tog [tɒg] *(pt & pp* **togged**, *cont* **togging***)* N *Br (measurement of warmth)* = unité servant à mesurer l'indice d'isolation thermique d'une couette

• **togs** NPL *Fam (clothes)* fringues *fpl*; *Sport* affaires *fpl*

► **tog out, tog up** VT SEP *Fam* nipper, fringuer; **she was all togged up in her best clothes** elle était super sapée; **they were all togged out for the match** ils s'étaient tous mis en tenue pour le match

toga ['təʊgə] N toge *f*

together [tə'geðə(r)] ADV **1** *(with each other)* ensemble; **we went shopping t.** nous sommes allés faire des courses ensemble; **are you t.?** êtes-vous ensemble?; **they get on well t.** ils s'entendent bien; **we're all in this t.!** on est tous logés à la même enseigne!; **those colours go well t.** ces couleurs vont bien ensemble; **the family will all be t. at Christmas** la famille sera réunie à Noël; **they're back t.** ils sont de nouveau ensemble

2 *(jointly)* **she's cleverer than both of them put t.** elle est plus intelligente qu'eux deux réunis; **even taken t., their efforts don't amount to much** même si on les considère dans leur ensemble, leurs efforts ne représentent pas grand-chose; **t. we can change things** ensemble, nous pouvons changer les choses

3 *(indicating proximity)* **tie the two ribbons t.** attachez les deux rubans l'un à l'autre; **we were crowded t. into the room** on nous a tous entassés dans la pièce; **they were bound t. by their beliefs** leurs convictions les unissaient

4 *(at the same time)* à la fois, en même temps, ensemble; **all t. now!** *(pull)* tous ensemble!, ho hisse!; *(sing, recite)* tous ensemble *ou* en chœur!

5 *(consecutively)* **for ten hours t.** pendant dix heures d'affilée *ou* de suite

ADJ *Fam (person)* équilibré, bien dans sa peau; **the band weren't very t.** *(didn't play in unison)* le groupe ne jouait pas vraiment ensemble

• **together with** CONJ *(as well as)* ainsi que; *(at the same time as)* en même temps que; **t. with the French, the Swedes objected** les Suédois émirent une objection, de même que les Français; **pick up a leaflet t. with an entry form** prenez un imprimé et une feuille d'inscription

togetherness [tə'geðənɪs] N *(unity)* unité *f*; *(solidarity)* solidarité *f*; *(comradeship)* camaraderie *f*; **the feeling of t. generated by a family Christmas** ce sentiment de chaleureuse communion que l'on ressent lors des Noëls passés en famille

toggle ['tɒgəl] N **1** *(peg)* cheville *f* **2** *Sewing* olive *f*, bouton *m* de duffle-coat

VI *Comput* basculer; **to t. between two applications** alterner entre deux applications

►► *Tech* ***toggle joint*** genouillère *f*; *Comput* ***toggle key*** touche *f* à bascule; ***toggle switch*** *Elec* interrupteur *m* à bascule; *Comput* commande *f* à bascule

Togo ['təʊgəʊ] N le Togo

Togolese [,təʊgə'li:z] *(pl* **inv***)* N Togolais(e) *m,f*

ADJ togolais

COMP *(embassy, history)* du Togo

toil [tɔɪl] VI **1** *(labour)* travailler dur, peiner; **he toiled over his essay for weeks** il a peiné *ou* il a sué sur sa dissertation pendant des semaines **2** *(as verb of movement)* avancer péniblement; **they toiled up the hill on their bikes/on foot** ils montèrent péniblement la colline à vélo/à pied; **they toiled on over the rough ground** ils poursuivirent péniblement leur chemin sur le terrain accidenté **3** *(make difficult progress)* **to be toiling** peiner; **I'm toiling to finish this drink as it is** j'ai déjà assez de mal à finir ce verre

VT **he toiled his way through a mass of papers** il a dû laborieusement lire tout un tas de documents

N labeur *m*, travail *m* (pénible)

toiler ['tɔɪlə(r)] N travailleur(euse) *m,f*

toilet ['tɔɪlɪt] N **1** *(lavatory)* toilettes *fpl*; **to go to the t.** aller aux toilettes *ou* aux cabinets; **he's still in** *or Fam* **on the t.** il est encore aux toilettes; **the t. won't flush** la chasse d'eau ne marche pas; **he threw it down the t.** il l'a jeté dans les toilettes; **Public Toilets** *(sign)* Toilettes, W-C Publics **2** *Formal or Old-fashioned (washing and dressing)* toilette *f*; **to make** *or* **perform one's t.** faire sa toilette; **to be at one's t.** être à sa toilette **3** *Fam* **to go down the t.** *(plan, career, work)* être foutu en l'air; **that's our holidays down the t.!** on peut faire une croix sur nos vacances!

►► ***toilet bag*** trousse *f* de toilette; ***toilet block*** bloc *m* sanitaire; ***toilet bowl*** cuvette *f* (de W-C); ***toilet humour*** humour *m* scatologique; ***toilet paper*** papier *m* hygiénique; ***toilet roll*** *(roll)* rouleau *m* de papier hygiénique; *(paper)* papier *m* hygiénique; ***toilet roll holder*** porte-papier *m inv*; ***toilet seat*** siège *m* des cabinets *ou* W-C *ou* toilettes; ***toilet soap*** savon *m* de toilette; ***toilet tank*** réservoir *m* de chasse d'eau; ***toilet tissue*** papier *m* hygiénique; ***toilet training*** apprentissage *m* de la propreté *(pour un enfant)*; ***toilet water*** eau *f* de toilette

toiletries ['tɔɪlɪtrɪz] NPL articles *mpl* de toilette

toilet-trained ADJ propre

toils [tɔɪlz] NPL *Literary* rets *mpl*, filets *mpl*

toilsome ['tɔɪlsəm] ADJ pénible, laborieux

to-ing and fro-ing [,tu:ɪŋən'frəʊɪŋ] N *(UNCOUNT) Fam* allées et venues *fpl*

Tokay [təʊ'kaɪ] N *(wine)* tokay *m*, tokaj *m*

toke [təʊk] *Fam* N *(of cigarette, joint)* taffe *f*; **to take a t. (on)** prendre une taffe (de)

VI **to t. on a cigarette/joint** prendre une taffe d'une cigarette/d'un joint

token ['təʊkən] N **1** *(of affection, appreciation, esteem etc)* marque *f*, témoignage *m*; **as a t. of** *or* **in t. of my gratitude** en témoignage *ou* en gage de ma reconnaissance; **as a t. of our love** en gage de notre amour

2 *(souvenir, gift)* souvenir *m*; **we'd like you to accept this little t. to remind you of your visit** nous aimerions que vous acceptiez ce petit cadeau en souvenir de votre visite

3 *(for machine)* jeton *m*

4 *(voucher)* bon *m*

5 *(indication)* signe *m*; **in t.** *or* **as a t. of sincerity** en signe *ou* en témoignage de bonne foi

6 *Ling* occurrence *f*

ADJ *(gesture, effort)* symbolique, pour la forme; *(increase, protest)* symbolique, de pure forme; **a t. black person/t. woman** un Noir/une femme qui est là pour la forme; **they only pay a t. rent** ils ne paient qu'un loyer symbolique; **to put up a t. resistance** opposer une résistance symbolique

• **by the same token** ADV de même, pareillement

►► ***token payment*** paiement *m* symbolique (d'intérêts); *Comput* ***token ring*** anneau *m* à jeton; *Comput* ***token ring network*** réseau *m* en anneau à jeton; ***token strike*** grève *f* symbolique *ou* d'avertissement; ***token vote*** vote *m* symbolique

tokenism ['təʊkənɪzəm] N = pratique qui consiste à nommer un ou deux membres d'une minorité (femmes, Noirs etc) pour donner l'impression d'une libéralisation; **the appointment of a woman to the board was nothing but t.** ils ont nommé une femme au conseil d'administration uniquement pour la forme

Tokyo ['təʊkjəʊ] N Tokyo

told [təʊld] *pt & pp of* **tell**

Toledo [tɒ'leɪdəʊ] N Tolède

tolerable ['tɒlərəbəl] ADJ **1** *(pain, situation, b[ehaviour])* tolérable; *(standard)* admissible **2** *(n[ot]* *too bad)* pas trop mal, passable

tolerably ['tɒlərəblɪ] ADV passablement; **s[he]** **performed t. (well)** elle n'a pas trop mal joué; **I[']m** **t. well** je me porte assez bien; **they were** **pleased with the results** ils étaient assez co[n]tents des résultats

tolerance ['tɒlərəns] N **1** *(of behaviour, belie[fs],* *opinions)* tolérance *f*; **they showed great t.** ils o[nt] fait preuve de beaucoup de tolérance, ils o[nt] été très tolérants; **religious/racial t.** tolérance religieuse/raciale **2** *Physiol & Med (to alcoho[l])* tolérance *f*; *(to cold)* résistance *f*, tolérance *f*; **develop (a) t. to a drug** développer une accout[u]mance à un médicament; **they have little t.** **cold** ils ont peu de résistance au froid **3** *Tech* t[o]lérance *f*; **a t. of a thousandth of a millimetre** un[e] tolérance d'un millième de millimètre

tolerant ['tɒlərənt] ADJ tolérant; **he's not very** **of others** il n'est pas très tolérant envers les a[u]tres; **she's not very t. of criticism** elle ne suppor[te] pas bien les critiques; *Phys* **t. to heat/cold** rés[is]tant à la chaleur/au froid

tolerantly ['tɒlərəntlɪ] ADV avec tolérance

tolerate ['tɒləreɪt] VT **1** *(permit)* tolérer **2** *(put u[p]* *with* ► *person, behaviour)* supporter; *(withstand* *drug, cold, climate, medical treatment)* supporte[r]

toleration [,tɒlə'reɪʃən] N tolérance *f*

toll [təʊl] N **1** *(on bridge, road)* péage *m*

2 *(of victims)* nombre *m* de victimes; *(of casu[al]ties)* nombre *m* de blessés; *(of deaths)* nombre de morts; **the epidemic took a heavy t. of** *or* **amo[ng]** **the population** l'épidémie a fait beaucoup d[e] morts *ou* de victimes parmi la population; **t[he]** **years have taken their t.** les années ont laiss[é] leurs traces; **her illness took its t. on her fami[ly]** sa maladie a ébranlé sa famille

3 *(of bell)* sonnerie *f*

4 *Am & NZ Tel* frais *mpl* d'interurbain

VT *(bell)* sonner; **to t. sb's death** sonner le gl[as] pour qn; **the church clock tolled midday** l'horlog[e] de l'église a sonné midi

VI *(bell)* sonner; **to t. for the dead** sonner po[ur] les morts

►► ***toll bar*** barrière *f* (de péage); ***toll bridge*** po[nt] *m* à péage; *Am & NZ Tel* ***toll call*** communicatio[n] interurbaine; ***toll charge*** **1** *(for bridge)* (coût du) péage *m* **2** *NZ Tel* tarif *m* interurbain; ***toll st[a]tion*** *(on motorway, bridge)* gare *f* de péage

toll-free ADV *Am* **to call t.** appeler un numé[ro] vert *ou Can* sans frais

►► ***toll-free number*** ≃ numéro *m* vert

tolling ['təʊlɪŋ] N *(of bell)* tintement *m*; *(fo[r]* *death)* glas *m*

tollroad ['təʊlrəʊd] N route *f* à péage

tollway ['təʊlweɪ] N *Am* autoroute *f* à péage

Tom [tɒm] PR N **any** *or* **every T., Dick or Harry** n'im[porte] qui, le premier venu

►► ***Tom Collins*** *(drink)* Tom Collins *m (boisso[n]* *glacée au gin et au jus de citron)*

tom [tɒm] N *(cat)* matou *m*

tomahawk ['tɒməhɔ:k] N tomahawk *m*

tomato [*Br* tə'mɑ:təʊ, *Am* tə'meɪtəʊ] *(pl* **tomatoe[s]***)* N tomate *f*

COMP *(salad, soup, juice)* de tomates

►► ***tomato ketchup*** ketchup *m*; ***tomato pla[nt]*** (pied *m* de) tomate *f*; ***tomato purée*** concentré [*m*] *ou* purée *f* de tomates; ***tomato sauce*** sauce *f* t[o]mate; *(ketchup)* ketchup *m*

tomb [tu:m] N tombeau *m*, tombe *f*

tombac ['tɒmbæk] N *Metal* tombac *m*

tombola [tɒm'bəʊlə] N *Br* tombola *f*

tomboy ['tɒmbɔɪ] N garçon *m* manqué

tomboyish ['tɒmbɔɪɪʃ] ADJ de garçon manqu[é], garçonnier

tombstone ['tu:mstəʊn] N pierre *f* tombale

tombstoning ['tu:mstəʊnɪŋ] N = pratique qu[i] consiste à sauter dans l'eau depuis un poin[t] élevé (falaise ou digue d'un port par exemple)

tomcat ['tɒmkæt] N chat *m*, matou *m*

► **tomcat around** VI *Am Fam* courir les filles

tome [təʊm] N gros volume *m*

omfool [ˌtɒm'fuːl] *Fam* N imbécile *mf*
ADJ imbécile

omfoolery [tɒm'fuːlərɪ] N *(UNCOUNT) Fam words, behaviour)* bêtises *fpl*

ommyrot ['tɒmɪrɒt] N *(UNCOUNT) Br Fam Old-ashioned* balivernes *fpl*, bêtises *fpl*; **t.!** mon eil!

omography [tə'mɒgrəfɪ] N *Med* tomographie *f*

omorrow [tə'mɒrəʊ] ADV demain; **t. morning/ vening** demain matin/soir; **see you t.!** à de-nain!; **a week t.** dans une semaine demain; **they rrived a week ago t.** ça fera huit jours demain u'ils sont arrivés; **they will have been here a veek t.** ça fera huit jours demain qu'ils sont là
N **1** *(the day after today)* demain *m*; **what's t.'s late?** le combien serons-nous demain?; **what ay is it** *or* **will it be t.?** quel jour serons-nous de-nain?; **t. is** *or* **will be** *Br* **17 March** *or Am* **March 17 emain,** on sera le 17 mars; **t. is Monday** demain, 'est lundi; **a week from t.** dans une semaine de-nain; **three weeks from t.** dans trois semaines emain; **the day after t.** après-demain, dans eux jours; **t. never comes** demain n'arrive ja-nais; **t. is another day** demain il fera jour; *Prov* **ever put off till t. what you can do today** il ne faut as remettre au lendemain ce que l'on peut aire le jour même **2** *Fig (future)* demain *m*; **we ook forward to a bright t.** nous espérons des len-emains qui chantent; **t.'s world** le monde de emain; *Fam* **he spends money like there was no** il dépense sans se soucier du lendemain *ou* ans souci du lendemain

omtit ['tɒmtɪt] N *Orn* mésange *f*

om-tom N tam-tam *m*

on [tʌn] N **1** *(weight)* tonne *f*; *Br* **(long) t.** tonne *f* ongue (= 1016 kg); *Am* **(short** *or* **net) t.** tonne *f* ourte (= 907 kg); **(metric) t.** tonne *f* (métrique) = 1000 kg); *Naut* **(register) t.** tonneau *m*; **a 35-t. rry** un 35 tonnes; *Fam* **this suitcase weighs a t.!** ette valise pèse une tonne! **2** *Fam (100 mph)* vi-esse *f* de cent milles à l'heure; *(score of 100)* ent *m*; *(£100)* cent livres *fpl*; **to do a t.** *(vehicle, river)* faire du cent milles à l'heure
tons NPL *Fam (lots)* **tons of money** des tas *mpl* u des tonnes *fpl* d'argent; **tons of people** des tas *pl* de gens; **tons better** beaucoup mieux

onal ['təʊnəl] ADJ tonal

onality [tə'nælətɪ] *(pl* **tonalities)** N *Mus* tonalité *f*

one [təʊn] N **1** *(way of speaking)* ton *m* (de la oix); **don't (you) speak to me in that t. (of voice)!** e me parle pas sur ce ton!; **I don't like your t.!** je aime pas votre ton!; **it was the t. of the letter I idn't like** c'est le ton de cette lettre qui ne m'a as plu; **I knew by the t. of his voice** j'ai compris u ton *ou* timbre de sa voix; **he spoke to me in soft ones** *or* **in a soft t.** il m'a parlé d'une voix douce
2 *(sound ▸ of voice, musical instrument)* sonorité *(▸ of singer)* timbre *m* (de la voix); **the rich bass ones of his voice** la richesse de sa voix dans les ns graves; **the stereo has an excellent t.** la sté-o a une excellente sonorité
3 *Mus (interval)* ton *m*
4 *Ling* ton *m*; **rising/falling t.** ton *m* ascendant/ escendant
5 *Tel* tonalité *f*; **please speak after the t.** veuillez arler après le signal sonore
6 *(control ▸ of amplifier, radio)* tonalité *f*
7 *(shade)* ton *m*; **in matching tones of red and gold** ans des tons rouge et or assortis; **soft blue ones** des tons bleu pastel
8 *(style, atmosphere ▸ of poem, article)* ton *m*; **to et the t.** donner le ton; **to give a serious t. to a scussion** donner un ton sérieux à une discus-on
9 *(classiness)* chic *m*, classe *f*; **it lowers/raises the of the neighbourhood** cela rabaisse/rehausse standing du quartier; *Hum* **you always have to wer the t. with your filthy comments!** il faut tou-urs que tu abaisses le niveau de la conversa-on avec tes grossièretés!
10 *Physiol (of muscle, nerves)* tonus *m*
11 *Am Mus (note)* note *f*
VI *(colour)* s'harmoniser; **the wallpaper doesn't t. ell with the carpet** le papier peint n'est pas bien ssorti à la moquette
VT *(body, muscles)* tonifier
▸▸ *tone arm* bras *m* de lecture; *tone colour* timbre *m*; *tone control* bouton *m* de tonalité; *tone deafness* manque *m* d'oreille; *Ling tone language* langue *f* à tons; *Mus tone poem* poème *m* symphonique

▸ **tone down** VT SEP **1** *(colour, contrast)* adoucir **2** *(sound, voice)* atténuer, baisser **3** *(moderate ▸ language, statement, views)* tempérer, modérer; *(▸ effect)* adoucir, atténuer; **his article had to be toned down for publication** son article a dû être édulcoré avant d'être publié

▸ **tone in** VI s'harmoniser, s'assortir; **the curtains t. in well with the carpet** les rideaux sont bien dans le ton du tapis

▸ **tone up** VT SEP *(body, muscles)* tonifier
VI *(body, muscles)* se tonifier

tone-deaf ADJ **to be t.** ne pas avoir d'oreille

toneless ['təʊnlɪs] ADJ *(voice)* blanc (blanche), sans timbre; *(colour)* terne

tonelessly ['təʊnlɪslɪ] ADV *(say, speak)* d'une voix blanche

toner ['təʊnə(r)] N **1** *(for hair)* colorant *m*; *(for skin)* lotion *f* tonique **2** *Phot & Comput* toner *m*, encre *f*
▸▸ *toner cartridge* cartouche *f* de toner

Tonga ['tɒŋgə] N Tonga *fpl*

Tongan ['tɒŋgən] N **1** *(person)* Tongan(e) *m,f* **2** *(language)* tongan *m*
ADJ tongan
COMP *(embassy, history)* de Tonga; *(teacher)* de tongan

tongs [tɒŋz] NPL **(pair of) t.** pinces *fpl*; *(for hair)* fer *m* à friser; **fire t.** pincettes *fpl*; **(sugar) t.** pince *f* (à sucre)

tongue [tʌŋ] N **1** *Anat* langue *f*; **to put** *or* **to stick one's t. out (at sb)** tirer la langue (à qn); *Fig* **his t. was practically hanging out** *(in eagerness)* il en salivait littéralement; *(in thirst)* il était pratiquement mort de soif
2 *Fig (for speech)* langue *f*; **to lose/to find one's t.** perdre/retrouver sa langue; **hold your t.!** tenez votre langue!, taisez-vous!; *Br* **I can't get my t. round his name** je n'arrive pas à prononcer correctement son nom; **to have a sharp t.** avoir la langue acérée; **she has a quick t.** elle n'a pas sa langue dans sa poche; **tongues will wag** les langues iront bon train, ça va jaser; **the news set tongues wagging** la nouvelle a fait jaser (les gens); **t. in cheek** ironiquement; **she said it t. in cheek** *or* **with her t. in her cheek** elle l'a dit avec une ironie voilée, il ne faut pas prendre au sérieux ce qu'elle a dit
3 *Formal or Literary (language)* langue *f*; *Rel* **to speak in tongues** avoir le don des langues
4 *(UNCOUNT) Culin* langue *f* (de bœuf)
5 *(of shoe)* languette *f*; *(of bell)* battant *m*; *(of buckle)* ardillon *m*; *Tech* langue *f*, languette *f*
6 *(of flame, land, sea)* langue *f*
VT *Mus (note)* détacher; *(phrase)* détacher les notes de
▸▸ *Med Am tongue depressor, Br tongue spatula* abaisse-langue *m*

tongue-and-groove *Carp* N *(joint, edge)* assemblage *m* à languette; *(wood)* lattes *fpl* à languette
VT *(boards, slats)* pratiquer des languettes et des rainures sur
▸▸ *tongue-and-groove joint* assemblage *m* à languette

tongue-in-cheek ADJ *(remark, article)* ironique

tongue-lashing N *Fam* **to give sb a t.** sonner les cloches à qn

tongue-tied ADJ *Fig* muet; **she was completely t.** elle semblait avoir perdu sa langue

tonguing ['tʌŋɪŋ] N *Mus* coup *m* de langue

tonic ['tɒnɪk] N **1** *Med* tonique *m*, fortifiant *m*; *Fig* **the news was a t. to us all** la nouvelle nous a remonté le moral à tous; **it's a t. to see you looking so happy** ça me fait du bien *ou* me remonte le moral de te voir si heureux; **he's a t.** il vous remonte le moral, il est stimulant
2 *(cosmetic)* lotion *f* tonique; **hair t.** lotion *f* capillaire
3 *(drink)* ≃ Schweppes® *m*
4 *Mus* tonique *f*
5 *Ling* syllabe *f* tonique *ou* accentuée
ADJ **1** *Med* tonique; **the t. effect of sea air** l'effet *m* tonique *ou* vivifiant de l'air marin **2** *Ling* tonique
▸▸ *Mus tonic sol-fa* solfège *m*; *Physiol tonic spasm* convulsion *f* tonique; *tonic water* ≃ Schweppes® *m*; *tonic wine* vin *m* tonique

tonicity [tə'nɪsətɪ] N *(gen)* tonicité *f*, *Physiol* tonus *m*

tonight [tə'naɪt] N *(this evening)* ce soir; *(this night)* cette nuit; **in t.'s newspaper** dans le journal de ce soir; **t.'s the night** c'est le grand soir
ADV *(this evening)* ce soir; *(this night)* cette nuit

toning ['təʊnɪŋ] N *Phot* virage *m*
▸▸ *toning lotion* lotion *f* tonifiante

tonnage ['tʌnɪdʒ] N **1** *(total weight)* poids *m* total **2** *(capacity ▸ of ship)* tonnage *m*, jauge *f*; *(▸ of port)* tonnage *m*
▸▸ *tonnage certificate* certificat *m* de jaugeage

tonne [tʌn] N tonne *f* (métrique)

tonsil ['tɒnsəl] N *(usu pl)* amygdale *f*; **your tonsils are inflamed** vous avez une inflammation des amygdales; **to have one's tonsils out** se faire opérer des amygdales

tonsillectomy [ˌtɒnsɪ'lektəmɪ] *(pl* **tonsillectomies)** N *Med* amygdalectomie *f*

tonsillitis [ˌtɒnsɪ'laɪtɪs] N *(UNCOUNT)* angine *f*, *Spec* amygdalite *f*; **to have t.** avoir une angine *ou Spec* une amygdalite

tonsure ['tɒnʃə(r)] N tonsure *f*
VT tonsurer

tontine [tɒn'tiːn] N *Fin* tontine *f*

ton-up boy N *Br Old-fashioned Fam* fou *m* de moto

tonus ['təʊnəs] N *Physiol* tonus *m*

too [tuː] ADV **1** *(as well)* aussi, également; **I like Thai food – I do t.** *or* **me t.** j'aime la cuisine thaïlandaise – moi aussi; **he's a professor t.** *(as well as something else)* il est également professeur; *(as well as someone else)* lui aussi est professeur; **stylistically, t., they are similar** du point de vue du style également, ils se ressemblent
2 *(excessively)* trop; **it's t. difficult** c'est trop difficile; **t. difficult a job** un travail trop difficile; **she works t. hard** elle travaille trop; **I have one apple t. many** j'ai une pomme de trop; **that's t. bad** c'est vraiment dommage; *Ironic* tant pis!; **t. little money** trop peu d'argent; **t. few people** trop peu de gens; **50p t. much** 50 pence de trop; **she's t. tired to go out** elle est trop fatiguée pour sortir; **all t. soon we had to go home** très vite, nous avons dû rentrer; **you're t. kind** vous êtes trop aimable; **I know her all** *or* **only t. well** je ne la connais que trop
3 *(with negatives)* trop; **the first ski slope wasn't t. bad** la première descente n'était pas trop difficile; **I wasn't t. happy about it** ça ne me réjouissait pas trop; **she hasn't been t. well** elle ne va pas trop bien depuis quelque temps
4 *(moreover)* en outre, en plus; **he's so silly! – and a grown man t.!** qu'est-ce qu'il peut être bête! – et il en a passé l'âge en plus!
5 *(for emphasis)* **and quite right t.!** tu as/il a/*etc* bien fait!; **about time t.!** ce n'est pas trop tôt!; **I should think so t.!** j'espère bien!; **t. true!** ça, c'est vrai!
6 *Am (indeed)* **you didn't do your homework – I did t.!** tu n'as pas fait tes devoirs – si!; **you will t. behave!** si, tu vas être sage!

toodle-oo [ˌtuːdəl'uː], **toodle-pip** [ˌtuːdəl'pɪp] EXCLAM *Br Fam Old-fashioned* salut!

took [tʊk] *pt of* **take**

tool [tuːl] N **1** *(instrument)* outil *m*; **set of tools** outillage *m*; **the tools of the trade** les instruments *mpl* de travail; **the computer has become an essential t. for most businesses** l'ordinateur est devenu un outil essentiel pour la plupart des entreprises; **to down tools** cesser le travail, se mettre en grève, débrayer
2 *Fig (means, instrument)* instrument *m*; **to use sb as a t.** utiliser qn; **he was nothing but a t. of the government** *(dupe)* il n'était que le jouet *ou* l'instrument du gouvernement
3 *very Fam (penis)* engin *m*
4 *Br very Fam Crime slang (gun)* flingue *m*
VT *(decorate ▸ wood)* travailler, façonner; *(▸ stone)* sculpter; *(▸ book cover)* ciseler; **tooled leather** cuir *m* repoussé

VI *Fam* rouler□ *(en voiture)*; **I was tooling along at 30 mph** je roulais peinardement à 50 km/h
►► *Comput* **tool bar** barre *m* d'outils; ***tool rack*** râtelier *m* à outils
▸**tool up** **VI** s'équiper
VT SEP 1 *(equip with tools)* outiller, équiper **2** *Br very Fam Crime slang* **to be tooled up** *(carrying weapons)* être armé□

toolbox ['tu:lbɒks] *(pl* **toolboxes***)* **N** boîte *f* à outils

tooling ['tu:lɪŋ] **N** *(decoration* ► *on wood)* façonnage *m*; *(*► *on leather)* repoussé *m*; *(*► *on stone)* ciselure *f*

toolmaker ['tu:lˌmeɪkə(r)] **N** outilleur *m*

toolmaking ['tu:lˌmeɪkɪŋ] **N** fabrication *f* d'outils

tooltip ['tu:ltɪp] **N** *Comput* infobulle *f*

toon [tu:n] **N** *Am Fam (cartoon)* dessin *m* animé

toot [tu:t] **VI 1** *(car)* klaxonner; *(train)* siffler **2** *Fam (sniff cocaine)* sniffer de la coke
VT 1 **to t. a horn/a trumpet** sonner du cor/de la trompette; *Aut* **he tooted his horn** il a klaxonné *ou* donné un coup de Klaxon **2** *Fam (cocaine)* sniffer
N 1 *(sound)* appel *m*; **the tugboat gave a t.** le remorqueur a donné un coup de sirène; *Aut* **a t. of the horn** un coup de Klaxon **2** *Fam (of cocaine)* prise *f* de coke

tooth [tu:θ] *(pl* **teeth***)* **N 1** *Anat* dent *f*; **a set of teeth** une denture, une dentition; **a false t.** une fausse dent; **a set of false teeth** un dentier; **to have a t. out** se faire arracher une dent; **to have good/bad teeth** avoir de bonnes/mauvaises dents; *also Fig* **to bare** *or* **to show one's teeth** montrer les dents; **to have no teeth** être édenté; *Fig* manquer de force; **the amendment will give the law some teeth** l'amendement renforcera quelque peu le pouvoir de la loi
2 *(of comb, file, cog, saw)* dent *f*
3 *(idioms) Fam* **to be fed up** *or* **sick to the back teeth (with sb/sth)** en avoir plein le dos *ou* ras le bol (de qn/qch); **armed to the teeth** armé jusqu'aux dents; **to fight t. and nail** se battre bec et ongles; *Fig* **to cut one's teeth on sth** se faire les dents sur qch; **to get one's teeth into sth** se mettre à fond à qch; **she needs something to get her teeth into** elle a besoin de quelque chose qui la mobilise; *Fam* **it was a real kick in the teeth** ça m'a fichu un sacré coup; *Fig* **to set sb's teeth on edge** faire grincer qn des dents; **she's a bit long in the t.** elle n'est plus toute jeune
VI *(cogwheels)* s'engrener
• **in the teeth of** **PREP** malgré; **he acted in the teeth of fierce opposition** il a agi malgré une opposition farouche
►► ***tooth decay*** carie *f* dentaire; ***the tooth fairy*** ≃ la petite souris; ***tooth glass*** verre *m* à dents; ***tooth mug*** verre *m* à dents; ***tooth powder*** poudre *f* dentifrice

toothache ['tu:θeɪk] **N** mal *m* de dents; **to have t.** *or Am* **a t.** avoir mal aux dents

toothbrush ['tu:θbrʌʃ] *(pl* **toothbrushes***)* **N** brosse *f* à dents

toothed [tu:θt] **ADJ** *(wheel)* denté

toothless ['tu:θlɪs] **ADJ 1** *(person)* édenté, sans dents **2** *Fig* sans pouvoir *ou* influence; **the committee has been criticized for being t.** on a reproché son impuissance à la commission

toothpaste ['tu:θpeɪst] **N** dentifrice *m*, pâte *f* dentifrice; **a tube of t.** un tube de dentifrice

toothpick ['tu:θpɪk] **N** cure-dents *m inv*

toothsome ['tu:θsəm] **ADJ** *Literary or Hum* **1** *(food)* appétissant **2** *(person)* séduisant

toothy ['tu:θɪ] *(compar* **toothier***, superl* **toothiest***)* **ADJ** *Fam* **a t. grin** un sourire tout en dents
►► ***toothy pegs*** *(in children's language)* dents□ *fpl*

tooting ['tu:tɪŋ] **N** *(UNCOUNT) Aut* coups *mpl* de Klaxon

tootle ['tu:təl] *Fam* **VI 1** *(on musical instrument)* jouer un petit air; **he was tootling on a recorder** il jouait un petit air sur sa flûte **2** *Br (drive)* **we were tootling along quite nicely until the tyre burst** nous suivions notre petit bonhomme de chemin lorsque le pneu a éclaté; **I'm going to t. into town this afternoon** je vais aller faire un petit tour en ville cet après-midi; **well, I'll t. along now** bon, je vais me mettre en route
N 1 *(on musical instrument)* petit air *m* **2** *Br (drive)* petit tour *m* en voiture

toots [tʊts] **N** *Fam (term of address)* chéri(e)□ *m,f*

tootsie ['tʊtsɪ], **tootsy** *(pl* **tootsies***)* **N** *Fam (in children's language* ► *foot)* pied□ *m*, peton *m*; *(*► *toe)* doigt *m* de pied□, orteil□ *m*

TOP [tɒp]

N	
• haut **1, 8**	• sommet **1**
• dessus **2**	• couvercle **4**
VT	
• couvrir **1**	• dépasser **3**
• être en tête de **4**	
ADJ	
• du dessus **1**	• du haut **1**
• premier **2**	

(pt & pp **topped***, cont* **topping***)*
N 1 *(highest point)* haut *m*, sommet *m*; *(of tree)* sommet *m*, cime *f*; **t. of the milk** crème *f* du lait; **at the t. of the stairs/tree** en haut de l'escalier/ l'arbre; **he searched the house from t. to bottom** il a fouillé la maison de fond en comble; *Br* **from t. to toe** de la tête aux pieds; **she filled the jar right to the t.** elle a rempli le bocal à ras bord; **the page number is at the t. of the page** la numérotation se trouve en haut de la page; *St Exch* **to buy at the t. and sell at the bottom** acheter au plus haut et vendre au plus bas
2 *(surface)* dessus *m*, surface *f*; **he's getting thin on t.** il commence à se dégarnir; **just put it on t.** mets-le sur le dessus; **a cake with a cherry on t.** un gâteau avec une cerise dessus
3 *(end)* **at the t. of the street** au bout de la rue; **at the t. of the garden** au fond du jardin
4 *(cap, lid)* couvercle *m*; **where's the t. to my pen?** où est le capuchon de mon stylo?; **bottle t.** *(screw-on)* bouchon *m* (de bouteille); *(on beer bottle)* capsule *f* (de bouteille)
5 *(highest degree)* **he is at the t. of his form** il est au meilleur de sa forme; **at the t. of one's voice** à tue-tête
6 *(most important position) Br* **at the t. of the table** à la place d'honneur; **she's t. of her class** elle est première de sa classe; **someone who has reached the t. in their profession** quelqu'un qui est arrivé en haut de l'échelle dans sa profession; **it went right to the t.** *(complaint, request etc)* cela est remonté jusqu'au sommet; *Theat* **to be (at the) t. of the bill** être en tête d'affiche; **to reach the t. of the tree** arriver en haut de l'échelle; **it's tough at the t.!** c'est la rançon de la gloire!; **this car is the t. of the range** c'est une voiture haut de gamme; *Ir* **t. of the morning!** bien le bonjour!
7 *Br Aut (fourth gear)* quatrième *f*; *(fifth gear)* cinquième *f*; **she changed into t.** elle a enclenché la quatrième/la cinquième; **in t.** en quatrième/ cinquième
8 *(garment)* haut *m*, top *m*; **does this t. go with my skirt?** est-ce que ce haut va avec ma jupe?
9 *(beginning)* **play it again from the t.** reprends au début; **let's take it from the t.** commençons par le commencement
10 *(toy)* toupie *f*; **to spin a t.** lancer *ou* fouetter une toupie; *Br* **to sleep like a t.** dormir comme un loir
11 *(idioms)* **to come out on t.** avoir le dessus; *Br Fam* **he doesn't have much up t.** il n'est pas très futé; **the soldiers went over the t.** les soldats sont montés à l'assaut; *Fam* **to blow one's t.** piquer une crise, exploser
VT 1 *(form top of)* couvrir, recouvrir; **a cake topped with chocolate** un gâteau recouvert de chocolat; **snow topped the mountains** les sommets (des montagnes) étaient recouverts de neige
2 *Br (trim)* écimer, étêter; **she was topping the carrots** elle coupait les fanes des carottes; **to t. and tail gooseberries** équeuter des groseilles
3 *(exceed)* dépasser; **he topped her offer** il a renchéri sur son offre; **his score tops the world record** avec ce score, il bat le record du monde; **his story topped them all** son histoire était la meilleure de toutes; **and to t. it all** et pour comble (de malheur), et en plus de tout cela; *Br* **that tops the lot!** ça, c'est le bouquet!
4 *(be at the top of)* **the book topped the best-seller list** ce livre est arrivé en tête des best-sellers; **she topped the polls in the last election** aux dernières élections, elle est arrivée en tête de scrutin; **topping the bill tonight we have...** le clou de cette soirée est...; **to t. the charts** *(record, singer)* être à la première place *ou* en tête des hit-parades
5 *Br Fam (kill)* buter, zigouiller; **to t. oneself** se suicider□, se foutre en l'air
ADJ 1 *(highest)* du dessus, du haut, d'en haut; **t. floor** *or* **storey** le dernier étage; **the t. shelf** l'étagère du haut; **the t. button of her dress** le premier bouton de sa robe; **in the t. right-hand corner** dans le coin en haut à droite; **the t. speed of this car is 150 mph** la vitesse maximum de cette voiture est de 240 km/h; **to travel at t. speed** *(plane, train etc)* aller à sa vitesse maximale; **to be on t. form** être en pleine forme; *Br Fam* **the t. brass** officiers *mpl* supérieurs□, les gros bonnets *m*; *Fam* **to pay t. dollar** *or Br* **whack for sth** payer q au prix fort□; *Br Fam* **I can offer you £20 t.** wha je vous en donne 20 livres, c'est mon dern prix□
2 *(best, major)* premier; **she got the t. mark came t. in history** elle a eu la meilleure note histoire; **the t. people** *(prominent people)* les ge *mpl* en vue; *(in an organization)* les gros bonn *mpl*; **the country's t. ten companies** les dix prem res sociétés du pays; **one of the world's t. players** un des dix meilleurs joueurs mondia **t. management** la direction générale; *Br Far* **family right out of the t. drawer** une famille de haute
3 *Br Fam* super *inv*; **we had a t. night out** o passé une super soirée
• **on top of** **PREP** sur; **suddenly the lorry was o of him** d'un seul coup, il a réalisé que le cami lui arrivait dessus; **we're living on t. of each ot** nous vivons les uns sur les autres; *Fig* **on t. everything else** pour couronner le tout; **it's j one thing on t. of another** ça n'arrête pas; **do worry, I'm on t. of things** ne t'inquiète pas, je m' sors très bien; **it's all getting on t. of him** il est c passé par les événements; **to feel on t. of t world** avoir la forme
►► *Fam* ***top banana*** *(person)* huile *f*, gros bonn *m*, grosse légume *f*; *Br* ***top boots*** bottes *fpl* ha tes; *Br* ***top copy*** original *m*; *Fam* ***top dog*** chef **he's t. dog around here** c'est lui qui comman ici; *Br* ***top gear*** vitesse *f* supérieure; ***top hat*** (cl peau *m*) haut-de-forme *m*; *Comput & Typ* ***top m gin*** marge *f* du haut *ou* supérieure *ou* de tête; ***t pupil*** premier(ère) *m,f* de la classe; ***top rate tax)*** taux *m* maximum; *Sport* ***top scorer*** (g meilleur(e) marqueur(euse) *m,f*; *Ftbl* meille (e) buteur(euse) *m,f*; ***top table*** *(at wedding)* ta *f* d'honneur; ***top ten*** = hit parade des dix me leures ventes de disques pop et rock
▸**top off** **VT SEP 1** *Br (conclude)* terminer, courc ner; **and to t. off a miserable day, it started to r** et pour conclure cette triste journée, il s'est m à pleuvoir; **topped off with a cherry** garni d'u cerise **2** *Am (fill to top)* remplir
▸**top out** **VT INSEP** *(building)* fêter l'achèveme de
▸**top up** *Br* **VT SEP** *(add more to* ► *glass etc)* re plir; *(*► *mobile phone)* recharger le compte c **can I t. up your drink** *or* **t. you up?** encore u goutte?; *Aut* **to t. up the tank** faire le plein; *A* **to t. up the battery** ajouter de l'eau dans la batt rie; **the government tops up the rest** *(pays the b ance)* le gouvernement met l'argent qui manq *ou* rajoute la différence
VI *Aut (with petrol)* faire le plein

topaz ['təʊpæz] **N** topaze *f*; **a t. bracelet** un brac let de topazes

top-bracket **ADJ** de première catégorie

topcoat ['tɒpkəʊt] **N 1** *(clothing)* pardessus manteau *m* **2** *(of paint)* couche *f* de finition

top-down **ADJ** hiérarchisé; *(manageme* contrôlé par le haut

top-drawer **ADJ** *Br Fam* de tout premier rang **he's a t. musician** c'est un musicien de haute v lée□

top-dress **VT** *Agr* fumer en surface

tope [təʊp] **VI** *Arch or Literary* boire

topee ['təʊpi:] **N** *Br* casque *m* colonial *(des Ind*

toper ['təʊpə(r)] **N** *Literary* alcoolique *mf*, buve (euse) *m,f*

p-flight ADJ de premier ordre

p-heavy ADJ 1 *(unbalanced)* trop lourd du aut, déséquilibré 2 *Fig (company, organization with too many senior staff)* où il y a trop de ca-res; (▸ *over-capitalized)* surcapitalisé 3 *Fam ig-breasted)* **to be t.** avoir de gros seins◻

p-hole ADJ *Br Fam Old-fashioned* épatant, rmidable◻

pi ['təupɪ] *(pl* **topis**) = **topee**

pic ['tɒpɪk] N *(theme)* sujet *m*, thème *m*; **to-ght's t. for debate is unemployment** le débat de e soir porte sur le chômage

pical ['tɒpɪkəl] ADJ 1 *(current)* actuel; **a t. ques-on** une question d'actualité; **matters of t. inter-st** des questions *fpl* d'actualité; **it's very t.** c'est ut à fait d'actualité; **a few t. references in the xt** quelques références à l'actualité dans le xte 2 *Med (remedy)* topique, à usage local

picality [ˌtɒpɪ'kælɪtɪ] *(pl* **topicalities**) N actua-té *f*

pically ['tɒpɪklɪ] ADV *(write, speak)* sur des èmes d'actualité

pknot ['tɒpnɒt] N *(of hair)* chignon *m*; *(of rib-ons)* ornement *m* fait de rubans; *(of feathers)* ai-rette *f*

pless ['tɒplɪs] ADJ *(sunbather, dancer)* aux eins nus; **to go t.** ne pas porter de haut
▸ ***topless bar*** bar *m* topless

p-level ADJ de très haut niveau

pline ['tɒplaɪn] VT *Cin* jouer le rôle principal e

p-loader N *(washing machine)* machine *f* à ver à chargement par le haut

pmast ['tɒpmɑːst] N *Naut* mât *m* de hune

pmost ['tɒpməust] ADJ le plus haut, le plus levé

p-notch ADJ *Fam* excellent◻

p-of-the-range ADJ haut de gamme

pographer [tə'pɒgrəfə(r)] N topographe *mf*

pographic [ˌtɒpə'græfɪk], **topographical** tɒpə'græfɪkəl] ADJ topographique

pographically [ˌtɒpə'græfɪkəlɪ] ADV topo-raphiquement

pography [tə'pɒgrəfɪ] *(pl* **topographies**) N to-ographie *f*

pologic [ˌtɒpə'lɒdʒɪk], **topological** [ˌtɒpə'-dʒɪkəl] ADJ topologique

pology [tə'pɒlədʒɪ] N topologie *f*

opped [tɒpt] SUFF *Literary* **cloud-t. peaks** som-nets *mpl* couronnés de nuages; **ivory-t. walking tick** canne *f* à pommeau d'ivoire

pper ['tɒpə(r)] N *Br Fam (top hat)* (chapeau *m*) aut-de-forme◻ *m*

pping ['tɒpɪŋ] N dessus *m*; *Culin (for dessert, izza etc)* garniture *f*; **ice-cream with raspberry t.** lace recouverte d'un coulis de framboises; **he dish has a cheese and breadcrumb t.** le plat st garni de fromage et de chapelure
ADJ *Br Fam Old-fashioned* épatant, formidable◻

pple ['tɒpəl] VI *(fall)* basculer; *(totter)* vaciller; **he whole pile toppled over** toute la pile s'est ef-ondrée; **he toppled over backwards** il a perdu équilibre et est tombé en arrière; **he toppled nto the pool/over the edge of the cliff** il a culbuté ans la piscine/par-dessus la falaise
VT 1 *(cause to fall)* faire tomber, faire basculer 2 *ig* renverser; **the scandal almost toppled the gov-rnment** ce scandale a failli faire tomber le gou-ernement

p-quality ADJ de qualité supérieure

p-ranking ADJ de premier rang, haut placé; **t. official** un haut fonctionnaire

ps [tɒps] *Fam* N *Old-fashioned* **it's the t.!** c'est ath!
ADV *Fam (at the most)* maxi; **it'll cost a fiver t.** ça oûtera cinq livres maxi *ou* à tout casser

psail ['tɒpsəl, 'tɒpseɪl] N *Naut* hunier *m*

p-secret ADJ top secret *(inv)*, ultraconfiden-iel

p-security ADJ de haute sécurité
▸ ***top-security prison*** ≃ quartier *m* de haute sé-urité

top-shelf ADJ *Br*
▸▸ ***top-shelf magazines*** revue *f* érotique

topside ['tɒpsaɪd] N *Br (of beef)* tende-de-tran-che *m*
• **topsides** NPL *Naut* accastillage *m*

topsoil ['tɒpsɔɪl] N terre *f* superficielle, couche *f* arable

topsy-turvy [ˌtɒpsɪ'tɜːvɪ] ADJ sens dessus des-sous; **a t. world** le monde à l'envers
ADV **the war turned their lives t.** la guerre a bou-leversé leur vie

top-up N *Br* **can I give you a t.?** je vous ressers?, encore une goutte?
▸▸ *Br* ***top-up card*** *(for mobile phone)* recharge *f*; *Br Univ* ***top-up fees*** = frais de scolarité complé-mentaires déterminés par chaque université, venant s'ajouter aux frais fixes payés par tous les étudiants britanniques; *Fin* ***top-up finance*** fonds *m* complémentaire; *Fin* ***top-up loan*** prêt *m* complémentaire

toque [təuk] N *(brimless hat)* toque *f*; *Can (knitted hat)* bonnet *m*

tor [tɔː(r)] N colline *f* rocailleuse *(notamment dans le sud-ouest de l'Angleterre)*

torch [tɔːtʃ] *(pl* **torches**) N 1 *Br (electric)* lampe *f* de poche 2 *(flaming stick)* torche *f*, flambeau *m*; **to put a t. to sth** mettre le feu à qch; *Fig* **to carry a t. for sb** en pincer pour qn 3 *Tech (for welding, soldering)* chalumeau *m*
VT mettre le feu à
▸▸ ***torch song*** chanson *f* d'amour triste

torchbearer ['tɔːtʃˌbeərə(r)] N porteur(euse) *m,f* de flambeau

torchlight ['tɔːtʃlaɪt] N lumière *f* de flambeau *ou* de torche; *Br (of electric torch)* lumière *f* d'une/de la torche électrique; **by t.** à la lueur des flam-beaux; *Br (electric torch)* à la lumière d'une tor-che électrique
▸▸ ***torchlight procession*** retraite *f* aux flambeaux

tore [tɔː(r)] *pt of* **tear**[1]

toreador ['tɒrɪədɔː(r)] N torero *m*, toréador *m*
▸▸ ***toreador pants*** pantalon *m* corsaire

torment N ['tɔːment] 1 *(suffering)* supplice *m*, *Literary* tourment *m*; **to be in t.** être au supplice; **to suffer t.** souffrir le martyre 2 *(ordeal)* rude épreuve *f* 3 *(pest)* démon *m*; **that child is a real t.** cet enfant est vraiment insupportable
VT [tɔː'ment] 1 *(cause pain to)* torturer; **tormented by doubt** harcelé de doutes 2 *(harass)* tourmen-ter, harceler; **stop tormenting your sister!** laisse ta sœur tranquille!

tormentor [tɔː'mentə(r)] N persécuteur(trice) *m,f*, bourreau *m*

torn [tɔːn] *pp of* **tear**[1]

tornado [tɔː'neɪdəu] *(pl* **tornados** *or* **tornadoes**) N *(storm)* tornade *f*; *Fig (person, thing)* ouragan *m*

Toronto [tə'rɒntəu] N Toronto

torpedo [tɔː'piːdəu] *(pl* **torpedoes**, *pt & pp* **torpe-doed**) N 1 *Mil* torpille *f* 2 *Am (firework)* pétard *m* 3 *Ich (fish)* (poisson *m*) torpille *f*
VT 1 *Mil* torpiller 2 *Fig (destroy* ▸ *plan)* faire échouer, torpiller
▸▸ ***torpedo boat*** torpilleur *m*, vedette *f* lance-torpilles; ***torpedo tube*** tube *m* lance-torpilles

torpid ['tɔːpɪd] ADJ *Formal* léthargique; **a t. mind** un esprit engourdi

torpor ['tɔːpə(r)] N *Formal* torpeur *f*, léthargie *f*, engourdissement *m*

torque [tɔːk] N 1 *(rotational force) Tech* moment *m* de torsion; *Aut* couple *m* moteur 2 *Hist (collar)* torque *m* 3 *(necklace)* collier *m* ras de cou
▸▸ ***torque converter*** convertisseur *m* de couple; ***torque wrench*** clé *f* dynamométrique

torqued [tɔːkt] ADJ *Am Fam* 1 *(angry)* furibard, furax 2 *(drunk)* bourré, fait

torrent ['tɒrənt] N 1 *(of liquid)* torrent *m*; **the rain came down in torrents** il pleuvait à torrents *ou* à verse 2 *(of emotion, abuse etc)* torrent *m*; **a t. of insults** un torrent *ou* flot d'injures

torrential [tə'renʃəl] ADJ torrentiel; **we've had t. rain all week** il y a eu des pluies torrentielles toute la semaine

torrid ['tɒrɪd] ADJ 1 *(hot)* torride; *Geog* **the t. zone** la zone intertropicale 2 *(passionate)* passionné, ardent, torride

torsion ['tɔːʃən] N torsion *f*
▸▸ ***torsion balance*** balance *f* de torsion; ***torsion bar*** barre *f* de torsion

torso ['tɔːsəu] *(pl* **torsos**) N *(human)* torse *m*; *(sculpture)* buste *m*

tort [tɔːt] N *Law* délit *m*, préjudice *m*
▸▸ ***tort lawyer, torts lawyer*** avocat(e) *m,f* spécia-lisé(e) en responsabilité civile

tortoise ['tɔːtəs] N tortue *f*

tortoiseshell ['tɔːtəsʃel] N 1 *(substance)* écaille *f* (de tortue) 2 *(cat)* chat *m* écaille de tortue 3 *(butterfly)* vanesse *f*
ADJ 1 *(comb, ornament)* en écaille 2 *(cat)* écaille de tortue *(inv)*

tortuous ['tɔːtjuəs] ADJ 1 *(path)* tortueux, si-nueux 2 *(argument, piece of writing)* contourné, tarabiscoté; *(mind)* tortueux, retors

tortuously ['tɔːtjuəslɪ] ADV tortueusement, de manière tortueuse

tortuousness ['tɔːtjuəsnɪs] N *(of path, thinking etc)* caractère *m* tortueux

torture ['tɔːtʃə(r)] N 1 *(cruelty)* torture *f*, supplice *m*; **to be subjected to t.** être torturé, subir des tor-tures; **instruments of t.** instruments *mpl* de tor-ture 2 *Fig* torture *f*, tourment *m*; **wearing these shoes is t.** c'est un vrai supplice de porter ces chaussures; **the waiting was sheer t.!** cette at-tente fut un vrai supplice!
VT 1 *(inflict pain on)* torturer 2 *Fig (torment)* tor-turer; **tortured by remorse** tenaillé par le re-mords 3 *Fig (distort)* **she tortures the Spanish language** elle écorche la langue espagnole; **to t. a song** massacrer une chanson
▸▸ ***torture chamber*** chambre *f* de torture

torturer ['tɔːtʃərə(r)] N tortionnaire *mf*, bour-reau *m*

Tory ['tɔːrɪ] *(pl* **Tories**) N *Pol* tory *m*, membre *m* du parti conservateur
ADJ *(party, MP)* tory, conservateur

Toryism ['tɔːrɪɪzəm] N *Pol* torysme *m*

tosh [tɒʃ] *Br Fam* N foutaises *fpl*; **that's a load of t.!** c'est des foutaises!
EXCLAM n'importe quoi!

toss [tɒs] VT 1 *(throw)* lancer, jeter; **she tossed him the ball** elle lui a lancé la balle; **the horse nearly tossed its rider into the ditch** le cheval a failli faire tomber son cavalier dans le fossé; **he was tossed by the bull** le taureau l'a projeté en l'air; *Br* **to t. pancakes** faire sauter des crêpes; **to t. a coin** jouer à pile ou face; **she tossed back her head with a laugh** elle rejeta la tête en arrière en riant; **who's going to pay? – I'll t. you for it** qui va payer? – décidons-le à pile ou face
2 *Culin* mélanger; **to t. a salad** remuer *ou* retour-ner une salade; **t. the carrots in butter** ajoutez du beurre et mélangez aux carottes
VI s'agiter; **I tossed and turned all night** je me suis tourné et retourné dans mon lit toute la nuit; **the trees were tossing in the wind** le vent secouait les arbres; **to pitch and t.** *(boat)* tanguer; **shall we t. for it?** on joue à pile ou face?
N 1 *(throw* ▸ *gen)* lancer *m*, lancement *m*; (▸ *of a coin)* coup *m* de pile ou face; *Sport* tirage *m* au sort; **to win/to lose the t.** gagner/perdre à pile ou face; **our team won the t.** notre équipe a gagné au tirage au sort; *Br* **to argue the t.** ergo-ter, chicaner; *Br Fam* **I don't give a t.** je m'en fiche; *Br Fam* **who gives a t.?** qu'est-ce que ça peut fou-tre?
2 *(of head)* mouvement *m* brusque
3 *(fall from horse)* chute *f*; **to take a t.** être désar-çonné, faire une chute

▸ **toss about, toss around** VT SEP 1 *(rock, buffet)* ballotter, secouer; **the boat was tossed about by the waves** les vagues faisaient tanguer le ba-teau 2 *(ball)* lancer; *Fig* **they were tossing ideas about** ils lançaient toutes sortes d'idées; **figures of £5,000 were being tossed around** on avançait allègrement des chiffres de l'ordre de 5000 li-vres
VI s'agiter

▸ **toss off** VT SEP 1 *(task, essay, article)* expédier; **to t. off a letter** écrire une lettre au pied levé 2 *(drink)* boire d'un coup, lamper **3** *Br very Fam (masturbate)* **to t. sb off** branler qn; **to t. oneself off** se branler

VI *Br very Fam (masturbate)* se branler

▸ **toss up** **VT SEP** lancer, jeter; **she tossed the ball up into the air** elle a lancé le ballon en l'air

VI jouer à pile ou face

tosser ['tɒsə(r)] **N** *Br very Fam* tache *f*, branque *m*

tossing ['tɒsɪŋ] **N** *(UNCOUNT) (of boat)* ballottement *m*

toss-up **N 1** *(with coin)* coup *m* de pile ou face; **in the event of a tie the winner will be decided by a t.** en cas d'égalité, on tirera à pile ou face pour désigner le gagnant **2** *Fam* **in the end it was a t. between Majorca and Rhodes** finalement, nous avons dû choisir entre Majorque et Rhodes□; **it's a t. which is best** il est impossible de dire quel est le meilleur□

tot [tɒt] *(pt & pp* **totted**, *cont* **totting**) **N 1** *(child)* petit(e) enfant□*mf*; **tiny tots** les tout petits□*mpl* **2** *Br (of alcohol)* goutte *f*; **a t. of rum** un petit verre de rhum

▸ **tot up** *Br* **VT SEP** additionner; **I'll t. up your bill** je vais vous faire l'addition

VI **that tots up to £3** ça fait 3 livres en tout

total ['təʊtəl] *(Br pt & pp* **totalled**, *cont* **totalling**, *Am pt & pp* **totaled**, *cont* **totaling**) **ADJ 1** *(amount, number)* total; **the t. gains/losses** le total des profits/pertes; **the t. cost** le coût total **2** *(as intensifier)* complet(ète); **t. silence** un silence absolu; **we are in t. disagreement** nous ne sommes pas d'accord du tout; **that's t. nonsense!** c'est complètement absurde!; **he was a t. stranger to me** je ne le connaissais ni d'Ève ni d'Adam

N total *m*; **there are a t. of thirteen inspectors in the whole country** au total, il y a treize inspecteurs dans tout le pays; **she wrote a t. of ten books** elle a écrit dix livres en tout; **that comes to a t. of £2** ça fait 2 livres en tout; **a t. of 102 hours/people** un total de 102 heures/personnes; **the t. payable** le total à payer

VT 1 *(add up)* additionner, faire le total de **2** *(amount to)* s'élever à; **the groceries t. £10** la note d'épicerie s'élève à 10 livres; **the collection totalled 50 cars** cette collection comptait 50 voitures en tout **3** *Am Fam (wreck)* démolir□; **he totaled his car** sa voiture est bonne pour la casse

● **in total** **ADV** au total; **there are 300 students in t.** au total, il y a 300 étudiants

▸▸ *Fin* ***total annual expenses*** consommations *fpl* de l'exercice; *Fin* ***total assets*** total *m* de l'actif; *Astron* ***total eclipse*** éclipse *f* totale; *Fin* ***total gross income*** revenu *m* brut global; *Fin* ***total liabilities*** total *m* du passif; *Fin* ***total loss*** perte *f* totale; *Fin* ***total net income*** revenu *m* net global; ***total recall*** mémoire *f* très précise; **to have t. recall of sth** avoir un souvenir très précis de qch, se souvenir de qch dans les moindres détails; *Fin* ***total sales*** chiffre *m* d'affaires global

totalitarian [ˌtəʊtælɪ'teərɪən] **ADJ** totalitaire

▸▸ ***totalitarian regime*** régime *m* totalitaire

totalitarianism [ˌtəʊtælɪ'teərɪənɪzəm] **N** totalitarisme *m*

totality [təʊ'tælətɪ] *(pl* **totalities**) **N 1** *(completeness, complete amount)* totalité *f*; **in its t.** dans sa totalité, intégralement **2** *Astron* occultation *f* totale

totalizator, -isator ['təʊtəlaɪzeɪtə(r)] **N** *Br (in betting)* pari *m* mutuel

totalize, -ise ['təʊtəlaɪz] **VT** totaliser, additionner

totalling, *Am* **totaling** ['təʊtəlɪŋ] **N** totalisation *f*

totally ['təʊtəlɪ] **ADV 1** *(completely)* totalement, entièrement, complètement; **do you agree? – yes, t.** êtes-vous d'accord? – oui, tout à fait **2** *(expressing agreement)* absolument **3** *Am Fam (a lot)* vachement; **I don't smoke but my parents t. smoke** moi je fume pas, mais mes parents fument vachement

tote[1] [təʊt] **N** *(bag)* grand sac *m*, fourre-tout *m inv*

VT *Fam* trimballer; **I've been toting that thing around all day** j'ai trimballé ce truc toute la journée; **he was toting a gun** il avait un fusil sur lui

▸▸ ***tote bag*** grand sac *m*, fourre-tout *m inv*

tote[2] **N** *Br Horseracing (abbr* **totalizator**) pari *m* mutuel

▸▸ ***tote board*** tableau *m* électronique

totem ['təʊtəm] **N** totem *m*

▸▸ ***totem pole*** mât *m* totémique

totemic [təʊ'temɪk] **ADJ** totémique

totemism ['təʊtəˌmɪzəm] **N** totémisme *m*

t'other, tother ['tʌðə(r)] *Br Fam or Hum* = **the other**

totter ['tɒtə(r)] **VI 1** *(person)* chanceler, tituber; *(pile, vase)* chanceler; **he tottered down the stairs** il descendit les escaliers en chancelant; **the child tottered into/out of the room** l'enfant est entré dans/sorti de la pièce d'un pas mal assuré **2** *Fig (government, company)* chanceler, être dans une mauvaise passe

N vacillement *m*; *(gait)* démarche *f* titubante *ou* chancelante; **with a t.** d'un pas chancelant, en chancelant

tottering ['tɒtərɪŋ], **tottery** ['tɒtərɪ] **ADJ** chancelant; *(building)* branlant; *(government)* chancelant, déstabilisé; **with t. steps** en titubant

totty ['tɒtɪ] **N** *Br Fam (attractive women)* belles nanas *fpl*, belles gonzesses *fpl*

toucan ['tuːkən] **N** *Orn* toucan *m*

▸▸ *Br* ***toucan crossing*** passage *m* piétons-vélos

TOUCH [tʌtʃ]

N
- toucher **1, 2, 8**
- effleurement **2**
- coup **5**
- contact **2, 7**
- touche **3, 9**
- pointe **6**

VT
- toucher **1, 5, 7**
- jouxter **3**
- concerner **7**
- toucher à **2, 4**
- émouvoir **5**

VI
- se toucher **1, 2**

(pl **touches**)

N 1 *(sense)* toucher *m*; **sense of t.** sens *m* du toucher; **soft to the t.** doux au toucher

2 *(physical contact)* toucher *m*, contact *m*; *(light brushing)* effleurement *m*, frôlement *m*; **she felt the t. of his hand** elle a senti le frôlement de sa main; **she felt a t. on her shoulder** elle sentit qu'on lui touchait l'épaule; **the machine works at the t. of a button** il suffit de toucher un bouton pour mettre en marche cet appareil

3 *(style)* touche *f*; **the pianist has a light t.** ce pianiste a le toucher léger; *Fig* **to give sth a personal t.** ajouter une note personnelle à qch; **to have the right t. with sb/sth** savoir s'y prendre avec qn/qch; **the house needed a woman's t.** il manquait dans cette maison une présence féminine; **the cook has lost his t.** le cuisinier a perdu la main

4 *(detail)* **to put the final** *or* **finishing touches to sth** apporter la touche finale à qch; **that logo in the bottom corner is a nice t.** c'est une bonne idée d'avoir mis ce logo dans le coin en bas

5 *(slight mark)* coup *m*; **with a t. of the pen** d'un coup de stylo; **to add a few touches to a picture** faire quelques retouches à un tableau

6 *(small amount, hint)* pointe *f*, note *f*; **a t. of garlic** une pointe *ou* un soupçon d'ail; **a t. of madness** un grain de folie; **there's a t. of spring in the air** ça sent le printemps; **he answered with a t. of bitterness** il a répondu avec une pointe d'amertume; **I've got a t. of flu** je suis un peu grippé, j'ai une petite grippe; **to add a t. of class to sth** rendre qch plus distingué; **there was a t. too much pepper in the soup** le potage était un petit peu trop poivré

7 *(contact)* **to be/to keep in t. with sb** être/rester en contact avec qn; **I'll be in t.!** je te contacterai!; **keep** *or* **stay in t.!** donne-nous de tes nouvelles!; **to get in t. with sb** contacter qn; **you can get in t. with me at this address** vous pouvez me joindre à cette adresse; **he put me in t. with the director** il m'a mis en relation avec le directeur; **she is** *or* **keeps in t. with current events** elle se tient au courant de l'actualité; **I am out of t. with her now** je ne suis plus en contact avec elle; **she is out of t. with politics** elle ne suit plus l'actualité politique; **they lost t. long ago** ils se sont perdus de vue il y a longtemps; **he has lost t. with reality** il a perdu le sens des réalités; **the President has lost t. with the electorate** le Président a perdu le contact av son électorat

8 *(of an instrument)* toucher *m*; *(of a typewrit* frappe *f*; **a keyboard with a light t.** un clavie frappe légère

9 *Sport* touche *f*; **to kick the ball into t.** mettre ballon en touche; **the ball landed in t.** le ball est sorti en touche; *Fig* **to kick sth into t.** mett qch au rencart

10 *(idiom) Fam* **to be an easy** *or* **soft t.** être un geon *ou* une poire

VT 1 *(make contact with)* toucher; **to t. lightly** fr ler, effleurer; **to t. sb on the shoulder** toucher qr l'épaule; **she touched it with her foot** elle l'a to ché du pied; **he loved to t. her hair** il adorait caresser les cheveux; **he touched his hat to h** il a porté la main à son chapeau pour la salu **since they met, her feet haven't touched t ground** depuis leur rencontre, elle est sur nuage; **can you t. the bottom?** as-tu pied?; **t boat touched land** le bateau a accosté; **the la can't t. him** la loi ne peut rien contre lui

2 *(handle)* toucher à; **don't t. her things** ne d rangez pas ses affaires; **I didn't t. it!** je n'y ai p touché!; **don't t. anything until I get home** ne to chez à rien avant mon retour; **he swears he nev touched her** il jure qu'il ne l'a jamais touchée; **r body will t. him these days** personne ne veut pl rien avoir à faire avec lui; **if it's against the la we won't t. it** si c'est illégal, nous ne nous en m lerons pas

3 *(adjoin)* jouxter; **Alaska touches Canada** l'Ala ka et le Canada sont limitrophes

4 *(usu neg) (eat, drink)* toucher à; **I never t. me** je ne mange jamais de viande; **she didn't t. h vegetables** elle n'a pas touché aux légumes

5 *(move emotionally)* émouvoir, toucher; **he w very touched by her generosity** il a été très touc par sa générosité; **his remark touched a (ra nerve** sa réflexion a touché un point sensib *Br* **to t. sb to the quick** toucher qn au vif

6 *(damage)* **fruit touched by frost** fruits abîm par le gel; **the fire didn't t. the pictures** l'incend a épargné les tableaux; **the war didn't t. this ar** cette région a été épargnée par la guerre

7 *(concern)* concerner, toucher; **the proble touches us all** ce problème nous concerne tou

8 *(usu neg) Fam (rival)* valoir□, égaler□; **nothi can t. butter for cooking** rien ne vaut la cuisine a beurre; **no professor can t. him** c'est un profe seur sans égal□

9 *Am (dial)* **t. 645** faites le 645

10 *(idiom) Fam* **to t. sb for a loan** taper qn; **to t. for a fiver** taper qn de cinq livres

VI 1 *(be in contact)* se toucher

2 *(adjoin* ▸ *properties, areas)* se toucher, êt contigus

3 *(handle)* **do not t.!** *(sign)* défense de toucher

4 *Naut* **the ship touches at Hong Kong** le navi fait escale à Hong Kong

▸▸ *Am* ***touch football*** = sorte de football sans t cles; ***touch hole*** *(in cannon)* lumière *f*; ***touch judg*** *(in rugby)* juge *m* de touche; ***touch kick*** *(in rugb* coup *m* de pied en touche; ***touch screen*** écran tactile; ***touch screen computer*** ordinateur *m* écran tactile

▸ **touch down** **VI 1** *(aeroplane, spacecraft* ▸ *c land)* atterrir; *(*▸ *on sea)* amerrir **2** *(in rugby)* ma quer un essai

VT SEP *(in rugby)* **to t. the ball down** marquer u essai

▸ **touch off** **VT SEP** *(explosive)* faire explose faire détoner; *Fig* déclencher, provoquer; **th ruling touched off widespread rioting** cette déc sion a provoqué une vague d'émeutes

▸ **touch on** **VT INSEP** aborder; **his speech bare touched on the problem of unemployment** son di cours a à peine effleuré le problème du ch mage

▸ **touch up** **VT SEP 1** *(painting, photograph)* fai des retouches à, retoucher; *(paintwork)* refair **to t. up one's make-up** rafraîchir son maquillag **2** *Br very Fam (sexually)* peloter; **to t. oneself up** s toucher

touch-and-go **ADJ** **a t. situation** une situatic dont l'issue est incertaine; **it was t. with him** revient de loin; **it was t. whether we'd make it time** nous avons bien failli ne pas arriver mps; **right up to the minute they signed it was t.** squ'au moment où ils ont signé, rien n'était sûr

ouchdown ['tʌtʃdaʊn] **N 1** *(on land)* atterrissage *m*; *(on sea)* amerrissage *m* **2** *(in American ootball)* essai *m*

uché ['tu:ʃeɪ] **EXCLAM 1** *(in fencing)* touché! **2** *g* très juste!

uched [tʌtʃt] **ADJ 1** *(with gratitude)* touché; **she as t. by his thoughtfulness** elle était touchée par a délicatesse **2** *Br Fam (mad)* toqué, timbré, ingle

uchiness ['tʌtʃɪnɪs] **N** susceptibilité *f*

uching ['tʌtʃɪŋ] **ADJ** touchant, émouvant

PREP *Literary* touchant

N t. is not allowed, no t.! il est défendu de toucher

uchingly ['tʌtʃɪŋlɪ] **ADV** d'une manière touchante

uchline ['tʌtʃlaɪn] **N** *Sport* ligne *f* de touche

uchpaper ['tʌtʃ,peɪpə(r)] **N** papier *m* nitraté

uch-sensitive ADJ *Comput (screen)* tactile; *key, switch)* à effleurement

uchstone ['tʌtʃstəʊn] **N** *Miner & Fig* pierre *f* de ouche

uch-tone ADJ

▸ ***touch-tone telephone*** téléphone *m* à touches

uch-type VI taper au toucher

uch-typing N dactylographie *f* au toucher

uch-up N *Art & Phot* retouche *f*; *(of object)* restauration *f*

uchwood ['tʌtʃwʊd] **N** amadou *m*

uchy ['tʌtʃɪ] *(compar* **touchier**, *superl* **touchiest)** **ADJ 1** *(oversensitive)* susceptible, ombrageux; **he's t. about her weight** elle est susceptible *ou* chatouilleuse sur la question de son poids; **he's ery t.** il se froisse *ou* se vexe pour un rien **2** *matter, situation)* délicat, épineux

uchy-feely [-'fi:lɪ] **ADJ** *Pej* qui affectionne les contacts physiques

ough [tʌf] **ADJ 1** *(resilient ▸ person)* solide, résistant, robuste; *(▸ meat)* dur, coriace; *(▸ animal, plant)* résistant, robuste; *(▸ substance, fabric)* solide, résistant; **you have to be t. to make it here** il faut être solide pour s'en tirer ici; **she's t. enough to win** elle a assez d'endurance pour gagner; *Br* **he's as t. as old boots** il est coriace; **this steak is as t. as old boots** ce n'est pas du bifteck, c'est de la semelle

2 *(difficult)* dur, pénible; **a t. problem** un problème épineux; **it's t. on him** c'est un coup dur pour lui; **she made it t. for him** elle lui a mené la vie dure; **I gave them a t. time** je leur en ai fait voir de toutes les couleurs; **they had a t. time when their parents died** ils en ont connu de dures quand leurs parents sont morts; **it's t. work** c'est un travail pénible; **she had a t. life** elle n'a pas eu une vie facile; **Wall Street is a t. environment** Wall Street est un milieu très dur

3 *(severe)* sévère; *(resolute)* dur, inflexible; **a t. economic policy** une politique économique draconienne; **to get t. with sb** se montrer dur avec qn; **the boss takes a t. line with people who are late** le patron ne plaisante pas avec les retardataires; *Fam* **he's a t. cookie** il n'est pas commode; *Fam* **they're t. customers** ce sont des durs à cuire

4 *(rough, hardened)* dur; **a t. criminal** un criminel endurci; *Fam* **a real t. guy** un vrai dur

5 *Fam (unfortunate)* malheureux[□]; **that's really t.** a, c'est vraiment vache; **it's t. for him, great for us** c'est dur pour lui, mais génial pour nous; **t. luck!** pas de pot!

ADV *Fam* **to talk/act t.** jouer au dur

VT *(idiom) Fam* **to t. it out** tenir bon

N *Fam* dur(e) *m,f*

▸▸ ***tough love*** = attitude stricte adoptée vis-à-vis d'un drogué, d'un alcoolique etc, dans le but de l'aider à se désaccoutumer

oughen ['tʌfən] **VT** *(metal, leather)* rendre plus solide, renforcer; *(person)* endurcir; *(conditions)* rendre plus sévère

VI *(metal, glass, leather)* durcir; *(person)* s'endurcir

toughen up VT SEP & VI = toughen

oughie ['tʌfɪ] **N** *Fam (person)* dur(e) *m,f*; *(problem)* casse-tête *m*; **question 5 was a real t.** la question 5 était une horreur

toughly ['tʌflɪ] **ADV** *(fight)* avec acharnement, âprement; *(speak)* durement, sans ménagement

toughness ['tʌfnɪs] **N 1** *(of fabric, glass, leather)* solidité *f*; *(of meat)* dureté *f*; *(of metal)* ténacité *f*, résistance *f* **2** *(of job)* difficulté *f*; *(of struggle)* acharnement *m*, âpreté *f* **3** *(of character ▸ strength)* force *f*, résistance *f*; *(▸ hardness)* dureté *f*; *(▸ severity)* inflexibilité *f*, sévérité *f*

toupee ['tu:peɪ] **N** postiche *m*

tour [tʊə(r)] **N 1** *(trip)* voyage *m*; **to go on a t. of the Highlands** partir en voyage dans les Highlands; **we're going on a t. of Eastern Europe** nous allons visiter les pays de l'Est; **she's on a walking t. in Wales** elle fait une randonnée à pied dans le pays de Galles; **they're off on a world t.** ils sont partis faire le tour du monde

2 *(of a building)* visite *f*; **we went on a t. of the factory** nous avons visité l'usine; **would you like a t. of the garden?** voulez-vous que je vous fasse visiter le jardin?

3 *(by entertainer, band, sports team)* tournée *f*; **the dance company is on t.** la troupe de danseurs est en tournée; **to go on t.** faire une tournée; **she's taking the play on t.** elle donne la pièce en tournée

4 *Sport (circuit)* circuit *m*

5 *(in cycling)* tour *m*; **the T. de France** le Tour de France

VT 1 *(visit)* visiter; **they're touring Italy** ils visitent l'Italie, ils font du tourisme en Italie **2** *(of entertainer, band, sports team)* faire une tournée dans; **the orchestra is touring the provinces** l'orchestre est en tournée en province

VI 1 *(tourist)* voyager, faire du tourisme; **we're just touring around** nous ne faisons que visiter la région; **we decided to t. through the Loire Valley** nous avons décidé de visiter la Vallée de la Loire **2** *(entertainer, band, sports team)* être en tournée; **we go touring every summer** nous partons en tournée tous les étés

▸▸ ***tour brochure*** brochure *f ou* catalogue *m* de voyages; ***tour bus*** car *m* de tournée, car *m* aménagé pour les tournées; *Am* ***tour conductor, tour director*** *(courier)* accompagnateur(trice) *m,f*; *Mil* ***tour of duty*** service *m*; ***tour de force*** tour *m* de force; ***tour group*** groupe *m* (de touristes); ***tour guide*** *(person)* guide *mf*; *(book)* guide *m* touristique; ***tour of inspection*** tournée *f* d'inspection; ***tour leader***, *Am* ***tour manager*** accompagnateur (trice) *m,f*; ***tour operator*** *(travel agency)* tour-opérateur *m*, voyagiste *m*; *(bus company)* compagnie *f* de cars *(qui organise des voyages)*; ***tour package*** forfait *m* voyage

tourer ['tʊərə(r)] **N** voiture *f* de tourisme

touring ['tʊərɪŋ] **ADJ we had a t. holiday in the North of Italy** pour nos vacances nous avons visité le Nord de l'Italie

N *(UNCOUNT)* tourisme *m*, voyages *mpl* touristiques; **to do some t.** faire du tourisme

▸▸ ***touring bicycle*** vélo *m* de randonnée; ***touring car*** voiture *f* de tourisme; *Theat* ***touring company*** *(permanently)* troupe *f* ambulante; *(temporarily)* troupe *f* en tournée; *Sport* ***touring party*** équipe *f* en tournée

tourism ['tʊərɪzəm] **N** tourisme *m*

tourism-generated ADJ généré par le tourisme

tourist ['tʊərɪst] **N** touriste *mf*; *Sport* **the tourists** les visiteurs *mpl*

COMP *(agency, centre)* de tourisme; *(information, ticket)* touristique; *(restaurant, pub)* pour touristes

▸▸ ***tourist area*** zone *f* touristique; ***tourist attraction*** attrait *m ou* attraction *f ou* site *m* touristique; ***tourist board*** comité *m* du tourisme; *Br* ***tourist class*** classe *f* touriste; ***tourist destination*** destination *f* touristique; ***tourist guide*** *(book)* guide *m* touristique; *(person)* guide *mf* (touristique); ***tourist industry*** industrie *f* touristique; ***tourist (information) centre, tourist (information) office*** office *m* de tourisme, syndicat *m* d'initiative; ***tourist route*** itinéraire *m* touristique; ***tourist season*** saison *f* touristique; ***tourist trade*** tourisme *m*; **the country relies on its t. trade** le pays vit du tourisme; ***tourist traffic*** flot *m* des touristes; ***tourist trap*** attrape-touristes *m inv*; ***tourist visa*** visa *m* de touriste

touristic [tʊə'rɪstɪk] **ADJ** touristique

touristy ['tʊərɪstɪ] **ADJ** *Fam Pej* trop touristique[□]

tournament ['tɔ:nəmənt] **N** tournoi *m*

tourniquet ['tʊənɪkeɪ] **N** garrot *m*, tourniquet *m*

tousle ['taʊzəl] **VT** *(hair)* ébouriffer; *(clothes)* friper, froisser

tout [taʊt] *Br* **N 1 (ticket) t.** revendeur(euse) *m,f* de billets *(au marché noir)* **2** *(in racing)* vendeur (euse) *m,f* de tuyaux

VT 1 *(peddle ▸ tickets)* revendre *(au marché noir)*; *(▸ goods)* vendre *(en vantant sa marchandise)*; **the cries of the market traders touting their wares** les cris des marchands essayant de racoler *ou* raccrocher les clients; **she had touted her article around all the newspapers** elle avait fait le tour de tous les journaux pour essayer de placer son article **2** *(promote)* **he is being touted as a future prime minister** on veut faire de lui un futur premier ministre

VI salesmen touting for custom des vendeurs qui essaient d'attirer les clients; **they've been touting around for work/business** ils essayaient de trouver du travail/de se constituer une clientèle

tow [təʊ] **VT** tirer; *(boat)* remorquer, touer; *(car)* remorquer; *(barge)* haler; **the ship was towed out of harbour** le navire a été remorqué hors du port; **they were towing a trailer** leur voiture tirait une remorque

N 1 *(action)* remorquage *m*; *(vehicle)* véhicule *m* en remorque; **to be** *Br* **on** *or Am* **under t.** être en remorque; **to give sb/sth a t.** remorquer qn/qch; **he took my car in t.** il a pris ma voiture en remorque; *Fam* **he always has his family in t.** il trimbale toujours toute sa famille avec lui **2** *Tex* filasse *f*, étoupe *f*

▸▸ *Am* ***tow truck*** dépanneuse *f*

▸ **tow away VT SEP** remorquer, prendre en remorque; *(of police)* emmener à la fourrière; **you'll get towed away** tu vas te retrouver à la fourrière

towage ['təʊɪdʒ] **N** *(UNCOUNT) (act)* remorquage *m*; *(fee)* frais *mpl* de remorquage

towards [tə'wɔ:dz], *esp Am* **toward** [tə'wɔ:d] **PREP 1** *(in the direction of)* dans la direction de, vers; **he turned t. her** il s'est tourné vers elle; **we headed t. Chicago** nous avons pris la direction de Chicago; **she was standing with her back t. him** elle lui tournait le dos; *Fig* **the negotiations are a first step t. peace** les négociations sont un premier pas sur le chemin de la paix; **they are working t. a solution** ils cherchent une solution

2 *(indicating attitude)* envers; **she's very hostile t. me** elle est très hostile à mon égard; **the public's attitude t. crime** l'attitude de l'opinion publique face à la criminalité; **his feelings t. her** ses sentiments pour elle, les sentiments qu'il éprouve pour elle

3 *(as contribution to)* pour; **the money is going t. a new car** l'argent contribuera à l'achat d'une nouvelle voiture; **I'll give you something t. your expenses** je vous donnerai quelque chose pour payer une partie de vos frais

4 *(near ▸ in time)* vers; *(▸ in space)* près de; **t. the end of his life** vers *ou* sur la fin de sa vie; **t. the middle** vers le milieu

towbar ['təʊbɑ:(r)] **N** barre *f* de remorquage

towel ['taʊəl] *(Br pt & pp* **towelled**, *cont* **towelling**, *Am pt & pp* **toweled** *or* **towelled**, *cont* **toweling** *or* **towelling)** **N** serviette *f* (de toilette); *(for hands)* essuie-mains *m inv*; *(for glasses)* essuie-verres *m inv*; **(***Br* **tea** *or Am* **dish) t.** torchon *m* à vaisselle

VT frotter avec une serviette; **to t. oneself dry** *or* **down** s'essuyer *ou* se sécher avec une serviette

▸▸ *Am* ***towel bar, towel rack***, *Br* ***towel rail*** porte-serviettes *m inv*; ***towel ring*** porte-serviettes *m inv*

towelhead ['taʊəlhed] **N** *Fam (Arab)* raton *m*, bicot *m*, = terme injurieux désignant un Arabe

towelling, *Am* **toweling** ['taʊəlɪŋ] **N 1** *(material)* tissu *m* éponge **2** *(drying)* **to give sb a t. (down)** frictionner qn avec une serviette

COMP *(robe, top)* en tissu éponge

tower ['taʊə(r)] **N 1** *(building)* tour *f*; **church t.** clocher *m*; *Fig* **he's a t. of strength** c'est un roc; **you've been a t. of strength to me** ton soutien m'a été précieux **2** *Comput* boîtier *m* vertical, tour *f* **3** *(for camera)* échafaudage *m* pour caméra

VI **to t. above** *or* **over sth** dominer qch; **he towered above** *or* **over me** j'étais tout petit à côté de lui; *Fig* **she towers above** *or* **over her contemporaries** elle domine de loin ses contemporains
▸▸ ***the Tower of Babel*** la tour de Babel; *Br* ***tower block*** tour *f* d'habitation; ***tower crane*** grue *f* à pylône; ***the Tower of London*** la Tour de Londres; *Comput* ***tower system*** système *m* à boîtier vertical, système *m* à tour

towering ['taʊərɪŋ] ADJ **1** *(very high ▸ skyscraper, tree, statue)* très haut, imposant; *(▸ person)* très grand; *(▸ ambitions)* sans bornes; **a t. great figure of a man** un géant **2** *(excessive)* démesuré; **in a t. rage** dans une colère noire

tow-headed ADJ *Br* aux cheveux (blond) filasse

towing ['təʊɪŋ] N remorque *f*, remorquage *m*, touage *m*; *(from towpath)* halage *m*
▸▸ ***towing charge*** (droit *m ou* frais *mpl* de) remorquage *m*; ***towing rod*** barre *f* de remorquage; ***towing rope*** câble *m* de remorquage; ***towing weight*** charge *f* remorquable; *Admin* ***towing zone*** zone *f* de touage

towline ['təʊlaɪn] N câble *m* de remorque; *(to towpath)* câble *m* de halage

town [taʊn] N **1** *(urban area)* ville *f*; **a country t.** une ville de province; **she's going into t.** elle va en ville; **he's out of t. this week** il n'est pas là *ou* il est en déplacement cette semaine; *Am* **we're from out of t.** nous ne sommes pas d'ici; **the best pizzas in t.** les meilleures pizzas de la ville; **t. and gown** = expression désignant collectivement les habitants et les étudiants de certaines villes universitaires et soulignant les différences de culture entre les deux milieux
2 *(main shopping or business area)* centre-ville *m*; **to go into t.** aller en ville; **I work in t.** je travaille en ville; *Fam* **they went out on the t. last night** hier soir, ils ont fait une virée en ville; *Fam* **to have a night (out) on the t.** faire la noce *ou* la java en ville; *Fam* **to go to t.** *(make great effort)* se mettre en quatre; *Fam* **they really went to t. on the stadium** pour le stade ils n'ont pas fait les choses à moitié *ou* ils ont vraiment mis le paquet
▸▸ ***town centre*** centre-ville *m*; *Hist* ***town clerk*** secrétaire *mf* de mairie; ***town council*** conseil *m* municipal; ***town councillor*** conseiller(ère) *m,f* municipal(e); ***town crier*** garde-champêtre *m*; *Br* ***town dweller*** citadin(e) *m,f*; ***town gas*** gaz *m* de ville; ***town hall*** hôtel *m* de ville, mairie *f*; ***town house*** *(gen)* maison *f* en ville; *(aristocratic mansion)* ≃ hôtel *m* particulier; *Am (semi-detached house)* maison *f* mitoyenne (en ville); *Am* ***town meeting*** = assemblée générale des habitants d'une ville; ***town planner*** urbaniste *mf*; ***town planning*** urbanisme *m*

townee, townie ['taʊnɪ] N *Fam Pej* citadin (e)ᵖ *m,f*, rat *m* des villes

townsfolk ['taʊnzfəʊk] NPL citadins *mpl*

township ['taʊnʃɪp] N **1** *(gen)* commune *f*
2 *(in South Africa)* township *f*
3 *Br Hist* = division d'une paroisse
4 *(in Canada, US)* canton *m*
5 *(in Australia)* petite agglomération *f*

townsman ['taʊnzmən] (*pl* **townsmen** [-mən]) N citadin *m*; **my fellow townsmen** mes concitoyens

townspeople ['taʊnz,piːpəl] NPL citadins *mpl*

townswoman ['taʊnz,wʊmən] (*pl* **townswomen** [-'wɪmɪn]) N habitante *f* de la ville, citadine *f*

towny (*pl* **townies**) = **townee**

towpath ['təʊpɑːθ, *pl* -pɑːðz] N chemin *m* de halage

towrope ['təʊrəʊp] N câble *m* de remorque; *(to towpath)* câble *m* de halage

tow-start N **to give sb a t.** faire démarrer qn en remorque

toxaemia, *Am* **toxemia** [tɒk'siːmɪə] N *Med* toxémie *f*

toxic ['tɒksɪk] ADJ toxique
▸▸ *Med* ***toxic shock syndrome*** syndrome *m* du choc toxique; ***toxic waste*** déchets *mpl ou* rejets *mpl* toxiques

toxicological [,tɒksɪkə'lɒdʒɪkəl] ADJ toxicologique

toxicologist [,tɒksɪ'kɒlədʒɪst] N toxicologue *mf*

toxicology [,tɒksɪ'kɒlədʒɪ] N toxicologie *f*

toxin ['tɒksɪn] N toxine *f*

toy [tɔɪ] N jouet *m*; *Fam Fig* **to throw one's toys out of the pram** faire un caprice, piquer une colère
COMP **1** *(car, train)* miniature **2** *(box, chest, drawer)* à jouets
▸▸ ***toy dog*** chien *m* nain; ***toy poodle*** caniche *m* nain; ***toy shop*** magasin *m* de jouets; ***toy soldier*** soldat *m* de plomb; ***toy theatre*** théâtre *m* de marionnettes; ***toy trumpet*** trompette *f* d'enfant

▸ **toy with** VT INSEP jouer avec; **to t. with one's food** manger du bout des dents; **she toyed with the idea of going home** elle jouait avec l'idée de rentrer chez elle; **he was toying with her affections** il jouait avec ses sentiments

tpi *Comput* (*written abbr* **tracks per inch**) pistes *fpl* par pouce

TQC [,tiːkjuː'siː] N (*abbr* **total quality control**) QG *f*

TQM [,tiːkjuː'em] N (*abbr* **total quality management**) gestion *f* de la QG

trace [treɪs] N **1** *(sign)* trace *f*; **to disappear** *or* **to sink without t.** disparaître sans laisser de traces; **there is no t. of it now** il n'en reste plus aucune trace; **we've lost all t. of her** nous ignorons ce qu'elle est devenue
2 *(small amount)* trace *f*, **traces of cocaine were found in his blood** l'analyse de son sang a révélé des traces de cocaïne; **without a t. of fear** sans la moindre peur
3 *(trail)* trace *f* de pas, piste *f*; *Am (path)* piste *f*, sentier *m*
4 *(drawing)* tracé *m*
5 *Tech* **a radar t.** la trace d'un spot
6 *(harness)* trait *m*; **in the traces** attelé; *Fig* **to kick over the traces** *(person ▸ rebel)* ruer dans les brancards; *(▸ break free)* s'émanciper
VT **1** *(follow trail of)* suivre la trace de; *(track down ▸ object)* retrouver; **she traced him as far as New York** elle a suivi sa piste jusqu'à New York; **I can't t. any reference to that letter** je ne trouve aucune mention de cette lettre; **we eventually traced the problem to a computer error** nous avons finalement découvert que le problème était dû à une erreur de l'ordinateur
2 *(follow development of)* suivre; **the film traces the rise to power of a gangland boss** ce film relate l'ascension d'un chef de gang
3 *(mark outline of)* tracer, dessiner; *(with tracing paper)* décalquer; **he traced (out) a map in the sand with his finger** avec son doigt, il a dessiné un plan sur le sable
▸▸ ***trace element*** élément *m* trace, oligoélément *m*; ***trace fossil*** trace *f* fossile

▸ **trace back** VT SEP **to t. sth back to its source** retrouver l'origine de qch; **she can t. her ancestry back to the 15th century** sa famille remonte au XVème siècle; **he traced the rumour back to her** il a découvert qu'elle était à l'origine de cette rumeur; **the cause of the epidemic was traced back to an infected water supply** on a découvert que l'épidémie était due à la contamination de l'alimentation en eau
VI *Am* **1** *(go back)* **to t. back to** remonter à; **his family traces back to the Norman Conquest** sa famille remonte à la conquête de l'Angleterre par les Normands **2** *(be due to)* être dû à

tracer ['treɪsə(r)] N **1** *(person)* traceur(euse) *m,f*; *(device)* traçoir *m* **2** *Chem* traceur *m*
▸▸ ***tracer bullet*** balle *f* traçante

tracery ['treɪsərɪ] (*pl* **traceries**) N **1** *(design)* filigrane *m*, dentelles *fpl*; *(on leaf, insect wing)* nervures *fpl* **2** *Archit* réseau *m*

trachea [trə'kiːə] (*pl* **tracheae** [-'kiːiː] *or* **tracheas**) N trachée *f*

tracheal [trə'kiːəl] ADJ *Anat* trachéal

tracheostomy [,trækɪ'ɒstəmɪ] (*pl* **tracheostomies**) N *Med* trachéostomie *f*

trachoma [trə'kəʊmə] N *Med* trachome *m*

tracing ['treɪsɪŋ] N *(process)* calquage *m*; *(result)* calque *m*
▸▸ ***tracing paper*** papier-calque *m inv*, papier *m* à décalquer

track [træk] N **1** *(path, route)* chemin *m*, sentier *m*; *(of planet, star, aeroplane)* trajectoire *f*; **a mountain t.** un sentier de montagne; **a farm t.** un chemin de campagne; *Fig* **to be on the right t.** être sur la bonne voie; *Fig* **he's on the wrong** [t.] il fait fausse route; *Fam* **you're way off t.!** tu [es] complètement à côté de la plaque!
2 *Sport (for running)* piste *f*; *Br* **motor-racing t.** a[u]todrome *m*; **t. and field events** épreuves *f*[pl] d'athlétisme
3 *Rail* voie *f*, rails *mpl*; **the train jumped the trac**[k] le train a déraillé *ou* a quitté les rails; *esp Am* [**to**] **live on the right/wrong side of the tracks** habit[er] un bon/mauvais quartier; *esp Am* **to come fro**[m] **the wrong side of the tracks** être issu d'un milie[u] défavorisé
4 *(mark, trail)* trace *f*, piste *f*; *(of animal, perso*[n]*)* piste *f*; *(of boat)* sillage *m*; **to be on sb's t.** *or* **trac**[ks] être sur la piste de qn; **the terrorists had covere**[d] **their tracks well** les terroristes n'avaient p[as] laissé de traces; **that should throw them off** [the] **t.** avec ça, je devrais arriver à les semer; **to kee**[p] **t. of suivre; it's hard to keep t. of her, she mov**[es] **around so much** il est difficile de rester en co[n]tact avec elle, elle bouge tout le temps; **we li**[ke] **to keep t. of current events** nous aimons nous t[e]nir au courant de l'actualité; **we'll have to keep** [**t.**] **of the time!** il ne faudra pas oublier l'heure[!] **don't lose t. of those files** n'égarez pas ces do[s]siers; **I lost t. of them years ago** j'ai perdu le co[n]tact avec eux *ou* je les ai perdus de vue il y a d[es] années; **she lost all t. of time** elle a perdu tou[te] notion du temps; **he lost t. of what he was sayir**[g] il a perdu le fil de ce qu'il disait; *Fam* **to ma**[ke] **tracks** mettre les voiles
5 *(on CD, LP, tape)* morceau *m*; *Comput (of dis*[k]*)* piste *f*; *Comput* **tracks per inch** pistes *fpl* p[ar] pouce
6 *Aut (of tracked vehicle)* chenille *f*; *(tyre trea*[d]*)* chape *f*; *(space between wheels)* écartement *m*
7 *Am Sch* classe *f* de niveau
8 *Fam Drugs slang* trace *f* de piqûre
VT **1** *(follow ▸ animal)* suivre à la trace, filer; *(*[▸]* rocket)* suivre la trajectoire de; *(▸ criminal)* tr[a]quer **2** *Am* **don't t. mud into the house!** ne traîn[e] pas de boue dans la maison!
VI **1** *(stylus)* suivre le sillon **2** *(with camera)* fai[re] un traveling *ou* travelling
▸▸ *Aut* ***track arm*** bras *m* de direction; *Sport* ***tra***[***ck***] ***event*** épreuve *f* sur piste; *Am Sport* ***track me***[***et***] rencontre *f* d'athlétisme; *Sport* ***track racing*** *(U*[*N*]*COUNT)* courses *fpl* sur piste; *Sport & Fig* ***tra***[***ck***] ***record*** *(past record, career to date)* antécéden[ts] *mpl*; *(list of achievements)* palmarès *m*; **she has** [**a**] **good t. record** elle a fait ses preuves; **he doesr**[**n't**] **have a very good t. record for punctuality** il n'e[st] pas réputé pour sa ponctualité; **a company wi**[**th**] **a good/poor t. record in winning export orde**[**rs**] une entreprise avec un bon/mauvais palmarè[s] sur le plan des commandes à l'exportatio[n]; **given the government's t. record in the field of cu**[**t**]**ting benefits** vu les antécédents du gouvern[e]ment en matière de réduction des prestatio[ns] sociales; *Br Aut* ***track rod*** biellette *f* de conn[e]xion; *Sport* ***track shoe*** chaussure *f* d'athlétism[e]; *Sport* ***track star*** star *f* de l'athlétisme; *Am Sch* ***tra***[***ck***] ***system*** = répartition des élèves en sections s[e]lon leurs aptitudes; ***track vehicle*** véhicule *m* ch[e]nillé

▸ **track down** VT SEP retrouver, localiser; *(an*[i]*mal, criminal)* traquer et capturer

trackball ['trækbɔːl] N *Comput* boule *f* de com[]mande, trackball *m ou f*

tracked [trækt] ADJ *(vehicle)* chenillé, à cheni[l]les

tracker ['trækə(r)] N **1** *(person ▸ gen)* poursuiva[nt]*(e) m,f*; *(▸ in hunting)* traqueur(euse) *m,f* **2** *(d*[*e*]*vice)* appareil *m* de poursuite **3** *TV* machinist[e] *m* de travelling
▸▸ ***tracker dog*** chien *m* policier; *St Exch* ***track***[***er***] ***fund*** fonds *m* indiciel *ou* à gestion indicielle

tracking ['trækɪŋ] N **1** *(following)* poursuite *f*; *(*[*of*] *missile)* repérage *m* **2** *Am Sch* = répartition de[s] élèves en sections selon leurs aptitudes
COMP *(radar, satellite)* de poursuite
▸▸ *Cin & TV* ***tracking shot*** traveling *m*, travellin[g] *m*; *Astron* ***tracking station*** station *f* d'observatio[n]

tracklayer ['træk,leɪə(r)] N *Am* poseur *m* de rail[s]

tracklaying ['træk,leɪɪŋ] ADJ *(vehicle)* à chenille[s]

trackless ['træklɪs] ADJ **1** *(forest)* sans chemin[s], sans sentiers **2** *(vehicle)* sans chenilles

ackpad ['trækpæd] N *Comput* tablette *f* tactile

acksuit ['træksu:t] N survêtement *m*

act [trækt] N **1** *(pamphlet)* tract *m* **2** *(large area)* tendue *f*; *Am (housing estate)* lotissement *m*; *ining* gisement *m*; **a t. house** un pavillon **3** *Anat* **espiratory/digestive t.** appareil *m* respiratoire/igestif

actable ['træktəbəl] ADJ *(person, animal)* accommodant; *(material)* malléable; *(problem)* soluble, facile à résoudre

action ['trækʃən] N **1** *Tech* traction *f*; **electric/team t.** traction *f* électrique/à vapeur **2** *Med* **to e in t.** être en extension

▸ **traction cable** câble *m* tracteur; *Aut* **traction ontrol** contrôle *m* de traction; **traction engine** locomotive *f*; **traction wheels** roues *fpl* motrices

active ['træktɪv] ADJ *Tech* tractif

▸ **tractive force** effort *m* de traction

actor ['træktə(r)] N *(on farm)* tracteur *m*; *Tech* locomobile *f*

▸ *Comput* **tractor feed** dispositif *m* d'entraînement à picots; **tractor holes** *(on tractor wheel)* ous *mpl* à ergots; **tractor pin** *(in tractor wheel)* rgot *m* de tracteur; **tractor wheel** *(on printer etc)* oue *f* d'entraînement

actor-trailer N *Am* semi-remorque *m*

ad [træd] *Fam* ADJ traditionnel[a]

N *Mus* jazz *m* traditionnel des années 30[a]

▸ *Mus* **trad jazz** jazz *m* traditionnel des années 0[a]

adable ['treɪdəbəl] ADJ *Econ & St Exch* négoiable

ade [treɪd] N **1** *(UNCOUNT) Com* commerce *m*, ffaires *fpl*; **the clothing t.** la confection, l'industie *f* de la confection; **she is in the tea t.** elle est ans le commerce du thé, elle est négociante n thé; **t. is brisk** les affaires vont bien; **to do a ood** *or* **roaring t.** faire des affaires en or; **it's ood for t.** cela fait marcher le commerce; **doestic/foreign t.** commerce *m* intérieur/extéieur; **retail/wholesale t.** commerce *m* de détail/ e gros

2 *(illicit dealings)* trafic *m*; **the drug t.** le trafic de rogue

3 *(vocation, occupation)* métier *m*; **she is an elecrician by t.** elle est électricienne de son métier *u* de son état; **to be in the t.** être du métier; **as we ay in the t.** comme on dit dans le métier; **open to embers of the t. only** pour les membres de la rofession seulement

4 *(exchange)* échange *m*; **to do a t.** faire un change; **fair t.** échange *m* équitable

5 *(regular customers)* clientèle *f*

6 *Am (transaction)* marché *m*, affaire *f*

VT *(exchange)* échanger, troquer; **he traded a VD for a comic** il a échangé *ou* troqué un DVD ontre une BD; **they traded insults over the dinner able** ils ont échangé des insultes pendant le îner

VI **1** *(businessman, country)* faire du commerce, ommercer; **he trades in clothing** il est négociant n confection, il est dans la confection; **what ame do you t. under?** quel est votre raison sociale?; **to t. at a loss** vendre à perte; **to t. with sb** voir ou entretenir des relations commerciales vec qn; **they stopped trading with Iran** ils ont arêté toute relation commerciale avec l'Iran

2 *Am (private individual)* faire ses achats; **to t. at r with** faire ses courses à *ou* chez

3 *Fin (shares, commodity, currency)* se négocier, échanger (**at** à); **corn is trading at £25** le maïs se égocie à 25 livres

trades NPL *(winds)* alizés *mpl*

▸ **trade agreement** accord *m* commercial; **trade llowance** remise *f* entre professionnels; **trade ssociation** association *f* professionnelle; **trade alance** balance *f* commerciale; **trade ban** interdiction *f* de commerce; **trade barriers** barrières *pl* douanières; **trade body** syndicat *m* professionnel; *Acct* **trade credit** crédit *m* fournisseur *u* commercial; **trade cycle** cycle *m* de commerialisation; *Acct* **trade debt** dettes *fpl* d'exploitaion; **trade deficit** balance *f* commerciale éficitaire, déficit *m* extérieur *ou* commercial; *r* **the Trade Descriptions Act** = loi qui empêche a publicité mensongère; **trade directory** anuaire *m* de commerce; **trade discount** *(to customer)* escompte *m* commercial *ou* d'usage; *(to retailer)* escompte *m* professionnel, remise *f* professionnelle; **trade embargo** embargo *m* commercial; **trade exhibition** foire-exposition *f*, exposition *f* commerciale; *Br* **trade fair** foire *f* commerciale, salon *m*; **trade figures** chiffre *m* d'affaires; **trade gap** déficit *m* commercial; **trade journal** journal *m* professionnel, revue *f* professionnelle; **trade mission** mission *f* commerciale; **trade name** *(of product)* nom *m* de marque; *(of firm)* raison *f* commerciale; **trade paper** revue *f* spécialisée; *Br Aut* **trade plate** plaque *f* d'immatriculation provisoire; **trade policy** politique *f* commerciale; **trade press** presse *f* spécialisée *ou* professionnelle; **trade price** *Com* prix *m* marchand; *St Exch* prix *m* de négociation; **trade publication** revue *f* spécialisée *ou* professionnelle; **trade register** registre *m* du commerce; **trade route** route *f* commerciale; **trade secret** secret *m* de fabrique; *Hum* **she won't tell me her recipe, she says it's a t. secret!** elle ne veut pas me donner sa recette, elle dit que c'est un secret!; **trade show** salon *m* (professionnel); **trade(s) union** syndicat *m*; **to join a t.** *or* **trades union** se syndiquer; **the workers formed a t.** *or* **trades union** les ouvriers ont formé un syndicat; **I am in the t.** *or* **trades union** je suis syndiqué, j'appartiens au syndicat; *Br* **the Trades Union Congress** = la Confédération des syndicats britanniques; **trade(s) unionism** syndicalisme *m*; **trade(s) unionist** syndicaliste *mf*; **trade union tariff** tarif *m* syndical; **trade wind** alizé *m*

▸ **trade down** VI **1** *St Exch* acheter des valeurs basses **2** *(car owner)* changer pour un modèle moins cher

▸ **trade in** VT SEP **I traded my television/car in for a new one** ils ont repris mon vieux téléviseur/ma vieille voiture quand j'ai acheté le nouveau/la nouvelle

▸ **trade off** VT SEP *(exchange)* échanger, troquer; *(as a compromise)* accepter en compensation; **to t. sth off against sth** laisser *ou* abandonner qch pour qch; **they have traded off quality against speed** ils ont fait primer la rapidité sur la qualité

VI *Am* **they t. off every year for first place** ils sont premiers chacun leur tour tous les ans

▸ **trade on** VT INSEP exploiter, profiter de; **he trades on her gullibility** il profite de sa crédulité

▸ **trade up** VI **1** *St Exch* acheter des valeurs hautes **2** *(car owner)* changer pour un modèle plus cher

tradeable ['treɪdəbəl] ADJ *Econ & St Exch* négociable

traded option ['treɪdɪd-] N *St Exch* option *f* négociable, option *f* cotée

trade-in N reprise *f*; **will he accept a t.?** acceptera-t-il la reprise?; **they took my old refrigerator as a t.** ils ont repris mon vieux réfrigérateur

▸▸ **trade-in allowance** (valeur *f* de) reprise *f*; **trade-in facility** facilité *f* de reprise; **trade-in price** prix *m* à la reprise; **trade-in value** valeur *f* de reprise

trademark ['treɪdmɑ:k] N marque *f* (de fabrique); *Fig* signe *m* caractéristique; *Fig* **these close-up shots are her t.** ces gros-plans sont sa marque *ou* sa signature; *Fig* **his t. moustache** ses fameuses moustaches

VT *(product ▸ label)* apposer une marque sur; *(▸ register)* déposer

trade-off N *(exchange)* échange *m*; *(compromise)* compromis *m*; **there's always a t. between speed and accuracy** il faut toujours faire un compromis entre la vitesse et la précision

trader ['treɪdə(r)] N **1** *(gen)* commerçant(e) *m,f*, marchand(e) *m,f*; *(on large scale)* négociant(e) *m,f* **2** *(ship)* navire *m* marchand *ou* de commerce **3** *St Exch* opérateur(trice) *m,f*

tradesman ['treɪdzmən] *(pl* **tradesmen** [-mən]) N **1** *(trader)* commerçant *m*, marchand *m* **2** *(skilled workman)* ouvrier *m* qualifié

▸▸ **tradesman's entrance** entrée *f* de service *ou* des fournisseurs; *Br Vulg (anus)* entrée *f* de service

trade-weighted index N *Econ* indice *m* pondéré par le commerce extérieur

trading ['treɪdɪŋ] N *(buying and selling)* commerce *m*, négoce *m*; *(illicit dealing)* trafic *m*; **t. on the Stock Exchange was heavy** le volume de transactions à la Bourse était important

COMP *(partner)* commercial

▸▸ *Acct* **trading account** compte *m* d'exploitation générale; **trading bank** banque *f* commerciale; **trading capital** capital *m* engagé *ou* de roulement; **trading company** société *f* commerciale; *St Exch* **trading day** jour *m* de Bourse; *Br* **trading estate** zone *f* artisanale et commerciale; *St Exch* **trading floor** corbeille *f*, parquet *m*; **trading hours** heures *fpl* d'ouverture; *St Exch* horaires *fpl* des criées; **trading licence** carte *f* de commerce; **trading loss** perte *f*; **t. losses for the past year were heavy** les pertes subies pour l'exercice de l'année écoulée ont été lourdes; **trading nation** nation *f* commerçante; *Am* **trading post** *(store)* comptoir *m* commercial; *St Exch* parquet *m*, corbeille *f*; *Com* **trading profit** bénéfice(s) *m(pl)* d'exploitation; *St Exch* **trading rate** cours *m*; **trading results** résultats *mpl* de l'exercice; *St Exch* **trading room** salle *f* des changes *ou* des marchés; *St Exch* **trading session** séance *f* boursière; **trading stamp** timbre-prime *m*, vignette-épargne *f*; **trading standards** normes *fpl* de conformité; **trading year** année *f* d'exploitation, exercice *m*

tradition [trə'dɪʃən] N tradition *f*, coutume *f*; **it's in the best t. of New Year's Eve parties** c'est dans la plus pure tradition des réveillons du Nouvel An; **t. has it that...** la tradition veut que...; **a comedian in the t. of Chaplin** un comédien dans la lignée de Chaplin; **to break with t.** rompre avec la tradition

traditional [trə'dɪʃənəl] ADJ traditionnel; **it is t. to sing 'Auld Lang Syne' at New Year** il est de tradition de chanter 'Auld Lang Syne' au Nouvel An

▸▸ **traditional dress** costume *m* traditionnel

traditionalism [trə'dɪʃənəlɪzəm] N traditionalisme *m*

traditionalist [trə'dɪʃənəlɪst] N traditionaliste *mf*

ADJ traditionaliste

traditionally [trə'dɪʃənəlɪ] ADV traditionnellement

traduce [trə'dju:s] VT *Formal (malign)* calomnier, diffamer

traffic ['træfɪk] *(pt & pp* **trafficked**, *cont* **trafficking**) N **1** *(on roads)* circulation *f*; *(rail, air, maritime)* trafic *m*; **the t. is heavy/light** la circulation est dense/fluide; **t. is building up** la circulation augmente; **there is a great deal of t. on the roads** les routes sont encombrées; **watch out for t. when crossing!** (fais) attention aux voitures en traversant!; **road closed to heavy t.** route interdite aux poids lourds; **eastbound t.** circulation *f* ouest-est; **the cyclist weaved through the t.** le cycliste se faufila entre les voitures; *Fig* **the resort experiences heavy ski t. in winter** il y a beaucoup de skieurs en hiver dans cette station

2 *Com* commerce *m*; *(illicit)* trafic *m*; *Am (customers)* clientèle *f*; **the t. in arms/drugs** le trafic des armes/de drogue

3 *Br (dealings)* échange *m*; **you should have no t. with these people** évitez d'avoir affaire à ces gens

VI **to t. in** faire le commerce de; **organizations trafficking in arms/drugs** des organisations spécialisées dans le trafic d'armes/de drogue; *Fig* **reporters who t. in human misery** journalistes qui exploitent la misère humaine

▸▸ **traffic calming** contrôle *m* de la circulation; *Am* **traffic circle** rond-point *m*, sens *m* giratoire; **traffic cone** cône *m* de signalisation (pour la circulation routière); **traffic control** régulation *f* de la circulation; *Aviat, Naut & Rail* contrôle *m* du trafic; *Aviat* **traffic controller** contrôleur(euse) *m,f* de la navigation aérienne, aiguilleur *m* du ciel; *Aviat* **traffic control tower** tour *f* de contrôle; *Am Fam* **traffic cop** agent *m* de la circulation[a]; *Am* **traffic court** = tribunal chargé des infractions au code de la route; **traffic island** refuge *m*; *Br* **traffic jam** embouteillage *m*, bouchon *m*; **traffic lights** feu *m* de signalisation; **the t. lights are (at) green** le feu est (au) vert; **carry on to the next set of t. lights** continuez jusqu'aux prochains feux; **traffic offence** infraction *f* au code de la route; **traffic offender** contravenant *m* au code de la route; **traffic patrol** patrouille *f* de la circulation (routière); *Aviat* ***traffic pattern*** couloir *m ou* position *f* d'approche; ***traffic police*** *(for speeding, safety)* police *f* de la route; *(on point duty)* agents *mpl* de la circulation; ***traffic policeman*** agent *m* de police; *(on point duty)* agent *m* de la circulation; ***traffic sign*** panneau *m* de signalisation, poteau *m* indicateur; ***traffic signal*** feu *m* de signalisation; *Am* ***traffic violation*** infraction *f* au code de la route; *Br* ***traffic warden*** contractuel (elle) *m,f*

trafficator ['træfɪkeɪtə(r)] **N** *Br Old-fashioned* flèche *f* de direction

trafficker ['træfɪkə(r)] **N** trafiquant(e) *m,f*; **drug t.** trafiquant *m* de drogue

tragedian [trə'dʒiːdɪən] **N** *(author)* auteur *m* tragique; *(actor)* tragédien *m*

tragedienne [trə,dʒiːdɪ'en] **N** tragédienne *f*

tragedy ['trædʒədɪ] *(pl* **tragedies***)* **N** *(gen) & Theat* tragédie *f*; **to make a t. out of sth** prendre qch au tragique; **it's a t. that this should happen to her** c'est tragique que ça lui arrive à elle

tragic ['trædʒɪk] **ADJ** tragique

▸▸ ***tragic actor*** tragédien *m*; ***tragic actress*** tragédienne *f*; ***tragic hero*** héros *m* tragique; ***tragic irony*** ironie *f* tragique

tragically ['trædʒɪkəlɪ] **ADV** tragiquement; **the trip went t. wrong** le voyage a tourné au drame; **he died at a t. early age** c'est tragique qu'il soit mort si jeune

tragicomedy [,trædʒɪ'kɒmədɪ] *(pl* **tragicomedies***)* **N** tragi-comédie *f*

tragicomic [,trædʒɪ'kɒmɪk] **ADJ** tragi-comique

tragus ['treɪgəs] *(pl* **tragi** [-gaɪ]*)* **N** *Anat & Zool* oreillon *m*

trail [treɪl] **N 1** *(path)* sentier *m*, chemin *m*; *(through jungle)* piste *f*; *Fig* **he hit the campaign t.** il est parti en campagne (électorale)

2 *(traces of passage)* piste *f*, trace *f*; **to be on the t. of sb/sth** être sur la piste de qn/qch; **the police were on his t.** la police était sur sa trace; **the t. was cold by then** la piste était déjà froide; **a false t.** une fausse piste; **the storm left a t. of destruction** l'orage a tout détruit sur son passage; *Fig* **she leaves a t. of broken hearts behind her** elle laisse beaucoup de cœurs brisés derrière elle

3 *(of blood, smoke)* traînée *f*; *(of comet)* queue *f*

4 *(of gun)* crosse *f ou* flèche *f* d'affût

VT 1 *(follow)* suivre, filer; *(track)* suivre la piste de; *(animal, criminal)* traquer

2 *(drag behind, tow)* traîner; *(boat, trailer)* tirer, remorquer; **she trailed her hand in the water** elle laissait traîner sa main dans l'eau; **he was trailing a sack of coal behind him** il traînait *ou* tirait un sac de charbon derrière lui; *Fig* **to t. one's coat** chercher la bagarre

3 *(lag behind)* être en arrière par rapport à; **he trails all his classmates** il est en retard par rapport aux autres élèves

4 *(gun)* porter à la main

5 *Cin, Rad & TV (advertise ▸ film, programme)* annoncer *(en diffusant un extrait)*

VI 1 *(long garment)* traîner; *(plant)* ramper; **smoke trailed from the chimney** de la fumée sortait de la cheminée; **your skirt is trailing (on the ground)** votre jupe traîne (par terre)

2 *(move slowly)* traîner; **the prisoners trailed slowly past** les prisonniers passaient lentement à la queue leu leu; *Sport* **he trailed in last** il est arrivé bon dernier

3 *(lag behind)* être à la traîne; **he's trailing in the polls** il est à la traîne dans les sondages; **our team is trailing at the bottom of the league** notre équipe se traîne en fin de classement

4 *(follow)* suivre, filer; **with five children trailing behind her** avec cinq enfants dans son sillage

▸▸ ***trail bike*** moto *f* de cross; ***trail mix*** = mélange de cacahuètes et de fruits secs; *Fishing* ***trail net*** traîne *f*, chalut *m*, traîneau *m*

▸ **trail away VI** s'estomper; **his voice trailed away to a whisper** sa voix ne fut plus qu'un murmure

▸ **trail off VI** s'estomper; **he trailed off in mid sentence** il n'a pas terminé sa phrase

trailblazer ['treɪl,bleɪzə(r)] **N** *Fig* pionnier(ère) *m,f*

trailblazing ['treɪl,bleɪzɪŋ] **ADJ** de pionnier

trailer ['treɪlə(r)] **N 1** *Aut* remorque *f*; *Am (mobile home)* camping-car *m* **2** *Br Cin & TV* bande-annonce *f*; *Rad* aperçu *m* **3** *(end of film roll)* amorce *f*

▸▸ *Am* ***trailer court*** = terrain aménagé pour les camping-cars; *Am* ***trailer hitch*** timon *m* de remorque; *Am* ***trailer home*** caravane *f*; *Am* ***trailer park*** = terrain aménagé pour les camping-cars; ***trailer tent*** tente *f* remorque; *Am Fam Pej* ***trailer trash*** prolos *mpl (qui vivent dans des caravanes)*

trailer-truck N *Am* semi-remorque *f*

trailing ['treɪlɪŋ] **ADJ** *(long garment)* traînant; *(plant)* rampant

▸▸ *Aut* ***trailing arm*** bras *m* tiré; *Aviat* ***trailing edge*** *(of wing)* bord *m* de fuite; *Aut* ***trailing shoe*** segment *m* secondaire; *Comput* ***trailing spaces*** espaces *mpl* à droite; *Comput* ***trailing zeroes*** zéros *mpl* à droite

train [treɪn] **N 1** *(on railway)* train *m*; *(on underground)* métro *m*, rame *f*; **to go by t.** prendre le train, aller en train; **the 5 o'clock t.** le train de 5 heures; **the Cardiff t., the t. to Cardiff** le train de Cardiff; **I met a friend on the t.** j'ai rencontré un ami dans le train; **to transport goods by t.** transporter des marchandises par voie ferrée *ou* rail; **to the trains** *(sign)* accès aux quais

2 *(procession ▸ of vehicles)* file *f*, cortège *m*; *(▸ of mules)* file *f*; *(▸ of camels)* caravane *f*; *Mil* convoi *m*; *(retinue)* suite *f*, équipage *m*; *Mil* équipage *m*; **the famine brought disease in its t.** la maladie succéda à la famine; **the evils that follow in the t. of war** les maux que la guerre engendre

3 *(of dress)* traîne *f*

4 *(connected sequence)* suite *f*, série *f*; **in an unbroken t.** en succession ininterrompue; **a t. of events** une suite d'événements; **a t. of thought** un enchaînement d'idées; **my remark interrupted her t. of thought** ma remarque a interrompu le fil de sa pensée *ou* ses pensées; **to follow sb's t. of thought** suivre le raisonnement de qn

5 *Tech* train *m*; **t. of gears** train *m* d'engrenage

6 *Formal (progress)* **in t.** en marche; **to set sth in t.** mettre qch en marche

7 *(fuse)* amorce *f*; *(of gunpowder)* traînée *f* (de poudre)

COMP *(dispute, strike)* des cheminots, des chemins de fer; *(reservation, ticket)* de train; **there is a good t. service to the city** la ville est bien desservie par le train; **there is an hourly t. service** il y a des trains toutes les heures

VT 1 *(employee, soldier)* former; *(voice)* travailler; *(ear)* exercer; *(animal)* dresser; *(mind)* former; *Sport* entraîner; **to t. sb in a trade** apprendre un métier à qn, préparer qn à un métier; **she was trained in economics** elle a reçu une formation d'économiste; **he was trained at Sandhurst** il a fait ses classes à Sandhurst; **to t. sb to use sth** apprendre à qn à utiliser qch; **he has been trained in the use of explosives** il a été formé au maniement des explosifs; **the dogs have been trained to detect explosives** les chiens ont été dressés pour détecter les explosifs

2 *(direct, aim)* braquer; **he trained his gun on us** il a braqué son arme sur nous

3 *(plant ▸ by pruning)* tailler; *(▸ by tying)* palisser; *(climbing plant)* diriger, faire grimper

4 *Fam* **we trained it down to the South of France** nous sommes allés en train jusque dans le Midi de la France▫

VI 1 *(do professional training)* recevoir une formation; **I trained as a translator** j'ai reçu une formation de traducteur; **she's training as a teacher** elle suit une formation pédagogique; **where did you t.?** où avez-vous reçu votre formation? **2** *Sport* s'entraîner, se préparer

▸▸ ***train set*** train *m* électrique; ***train station*** gare *f (de chemin de fer)*; ***train surfing*** = pratique dangereuse qui consiste pour des jeunes à sauter sur le marche-pied d'un train qui démarre et sauter à nouveau sur le quai quand le train arrive au bout du quai

▸ **train up VT SEP** former

trained [treɪnd] **ADJ 1** *(person)* compétent, qualifié; *(engineer)* breveté, diplômé; *(nurse, translator)* diplômé, qualifié; **he's not t. for this job** il n'est pas qualifié *ou* n'a pas la formation requise pour ce poste; **we need a well-t. employee** il nous faut quelqu'un qui ait une bonne formation; *Hum* **she has her boss well t.!** elle a bien dressé son patron!; **a t. eye** un œil exercé; **a t. ear** une oreille exercée; **he has a t. voice** il a travaillé sa voix *(animal)* dressé; **a t. parrot** un perroquet savan[t]; **a well-t. horse** un cheval bien dressé

trainee [treɪ'niː] **N** stagiaire *mf*; **sales t.** stagiai[re] *mf* de vente

ADJ stagiaire, en stage; *(in trades)* en apprenti[s]sage; **t. computer programmer** élève *mf* progran[n]meur(euse); **t. journalist** journaliste *mf* stagiai[re]

traineeship [treɪ'niːʃɪp] **N** stage *m*

trainer ['treɪnə(r)] **N 1** *Sport* entraîneur(euse) *m*[,f] **2** *(of animal)* dresseur(euse) *m,f*; *(of racehorse[s])* entraîneur(euse) *m,f*; *(of lion)* dompteur(eus[e]) *m,f*

3 *Aviat (simulator)* simulateur *m*; *(aircraft)* avio[n]-école *m*

4 *Br (shoe)* chaussure *f* de sport

▸▸ ***trainer aircraft*** avion-école *m*

training ['treɪnɪŋ] **N 1** *(of employee)* formation *(of soldier)* instruction *f*; *(of animal)* dressage *m*; **he is a carpenter by t.** il est menuisier de form[a]tion; **I have had some business t.** j'ai suivi une p[e]tite formation commerciale; *Mil* **to do one's bas[ic] t.** faire ses classes; *Fig* **it's good t. for when you' a parent** ça vous prépare pour quand vous aur[ez] des enfants **2** *Sport* entraînement *m*, prépara[]tion *f*; **to be in t.** être en cours d'entraîneme[nt] *ou* de préparation; **I'm out of t.** j'ai perdu [la] forme; **to be in t. for sth** s'entraîner pour *ou* s[e] préparer à qch

▸▸ *Mil* ***training base*** base *f* école; ***training cam[p]*** camp *m* d'entraînement; *Mil* base *f* école; ***trai[n]ing centre*** centre *m* de formation; ***training colle[ge]*** école *f* spécialisée *ou* professionnelle; ***trainir[g] course*** stage *m* de formation; ***training manual*** m[a]nuel *m* d'utilisation *ou* d'instruction; ***trainir[g] period*** stage *m*, stage *m* de formation; ***trainir[g] programme*** programme *m* de formation; ***trainir[g] scheme*** plan *m* de formation; ***training session*** e[n]traînement *m*; ***training ship*** navire-école *m*; ***training shoes*** chaussures *fpl* de sport; ***trainir[g] video*** vidéo *f* d'entraînement; *Am* ***training whee[ls]*** stabilisateurs *mpl*

trainload ['treɪnləʊd] **N t. of coal** train *m* charg[é] de houille; **t. of tourists** train *m* plein de touri[s]tes; **they were arriving by the t.** ils arrivaient p[ar] trains entiers

trainspotter ['treɪn,spɒtə(r)] **N** *Br* **1** *(who not[es] train numbers)* = amateur de trains dont la pa[s]sion consiste à relever les numéros des loc[o]motives **2** *Fam (unfashionable person)* ringard(e) *m,f*

trainspotting ['treɪn,spɒtɪŋ] **N** *Br* = activi[té] consistant à relever les numéros des locomo[ti]ves

traipse [treɪps] *Fam* **VI we all traipsed off to th[e] shops** nous sommes tous partis traîner dans le[s] magasins; **she came traipsing in** elle est entrée e[n] traînassant; **to t. about** *or* **around** se balader, v[a]drouiller; **they traipsed from one museum to a[n]other** ils ont fait tous les musées; **we had to t. a[ll] the way back to the station** il a fallu qu'on se re[]tape tout le trajet jusqu'à la gare

N longue promenade▫ *f*; **it's quite a t.** ça fait un[e] trotte

trait [treɪt] **N** trait *m*

traitor ['treɪtə(r)] **N** traître *mf*; **a t. to his countr[y]** un traître envers son pays; **you're a t. to yo[ur] country/to the cause** vous trahissez votre pay[s]/la cause; **he turned t.** *(gen)* il s'est mis à trahi[r]; *(soldier, spy)* il est passé *ou* s'est vendu à l'enne[]mi

traitorous ['treɪtərəs] **ADJ** *Formal* traître, perfid[e]

traitorously ['treɪtərəslɪ] **ADV** *Formal* traîtreuse[]ment

traitress ['treɪtrɪs] **N** traîtresse *f*

trajectory [trə'dʒektərɪ] *(pl* **trajectories***)* **N** traje[c]toire *f*

TRAM [træm] **N** *Comput (abbr* **transputer modul[e]***)* module *m* de transputer

tram [træm] **N** *Br* **1** *(in street)* tram *m*, tramway *m*; **to go by t.** prendre le tram; **the trams** *(system)* réseau des tramways; **to work on the trams** tr[a]vailler dans les tramways **2** *(in mine)* berline benne *f* roulante

▸▸ ***tram driver*** conducteur(trice) *m,f* de tram[]way

amcar ['træmkɑː(r)] N *Br* tram *m*, tramway *m*

amline ['træmlaɪn] N *Br (rails)* voie *f* de tram-ay; *(route)* ligne *f* de tramway

tramlines NPL **1** *(in tennis, badminton)* lignes *f* de côté **2** *Fam Drugs slang (on arm)* traces *fpl* piquouses

ammel ['træməl] *(Br pt & pp* **trammelled,** *cont* **ammelling,** *Am pt & pp* **trammeled,** *cont* **trammel-g)** VT *also Fig* entraver

1 *Literary (hindrance)* **the trammels of society/utine** les entraves *fpl* de la société/de la rou-e **2** *Fishing* tramail *m*, trémail *m*

amp [træmp] N **1** *(vagabond)* clochard(e) *m,f*, *d-fashioned* chemineau *m*

(sound) bruit *m* de pas; **I could hear the t. of ldiers' feet** j'entendais le pas lourd des soldats *(long walk)* randonnée *f* (à pied), promenade **t's a long t. into town** il y a un bon bout de che-in à faire jusqu'à la ville

(ship) **t. (steamer)** tramp *m*

Fam Pej (promiscuous woman) traînée *f*

1 *(hike)* marcher, se promener; **we tramped ong in silence for a while** nous avons poursuivi tre chemin en silence pendant un moment **2** *alk heavily)* marcher d'un pas lourd; **to t. up d down** faire les cent pas; **to t. on sth** piétiner écraser qch; **I wish you'd stop tramping on my ot!** j'aimerais bien que tu arrêtes de m'écraser pied!

T parcourir; **he tramped the streets in search of ork** il a battu le pavé pour trouver du travail

ample ['træmpəl] VT piétiner, fouler aux pieds; *g (somebody's feelings)* bafouer; **the crowd ampled the man to death** l'homme est mort pié-ié par la foule

I marcher d'un pas lourd

(action) piétinement *m*; *(sound)* bruit *m* de pas

ampoline ['træmpəliːn] N trampoline *m*

I faire du trampoline

amway ['træmweɪ] N *Br (rails)* voie *f* de tram-ay; *(route)* ligne *f* de tramway

ance [trɑːns] N transe *f*; *Med* catalepsie *f*; **to go to fall into a t.** entrer en transe; *Med* tomber en atalepsie; **he put me into a t.** il m'a hypnotisé, il 'a fait entrer en transe; **he's been wandering ound in a t. ever since his wife left him** il erre en anse *ou* dans un état de transe depuis que sa mme l'a quitté

anche [trɑːntʃ] N *(of loan, payment, shares)* anche *f*

annie, tranny ['trænɪ] *(pl* **trannies)** N *Br Fam* **1** *d-fashioned (transistor radio)* transistor□*m* **2** *ansvestite)* travelo *m*

anquil ['træŋkwɪl] ADJ tranquille, paisible

anquillity, *Am* **tranquility** [træŋ'kwɪlɪtɪ] N anquillité *f*, calme *m*

anquillize, -ise, *Am* **tranquilize** ['træŋkwɪ ɪz] VT calmer, apaiser; *Med* mettre sous tran-illisants

anquillizer, -iser, *Am* **tranquilizer** ['-æŋkwɪˌlaɪzə(r)] N tranquillisant *m*, calmant *m*

ansact [træn'zækt] VT traiter, régler; **to t. busi-ess with sb** faire des affaires avec qn; **the deal as successfully transacted** l'affaire a été conclue ec brio

ansaction [træn'zækʃən] N **1** *Com & Fin* tran-action *f*; *St Exch* opération *f*; **cash t.** transaction en liquide; **cash transactions have increased** les ouvements d'espèces ont augmenté **2** *(act of ansacting)* conduite *f*, gestion *f*; **t. of business ill continue as normal** la conduite des affaires poursuivra comme à l'accoutumée **3** *Comput* ouvement *m*

transactions NPL *(proceedings of organiza-n)* travaux *mpl*; *(minutes)* actes *mpl*

▸ *St Exch* **transaction costs** frais *mpl* de Bourse

ansalpine [ˌtrænz'ælpaɪn] ADJ transalpin

ansantarctic [ˌtrænzænt'ɑːktɪk] ADJ transan-rctique

ansatlantic [ˌtrænzət'læntɪk] ADJ transatlan-que

▸ *transatlantic carrier* transporteur *m* trans-lantique

ansaxle ['trænzæksəl] N *Aut* boîte-pont *f*

transceiver [træn'siːvə(r)] N émetteur-récepteur *m*

transcend [træn'send] VT **1** *(go beyond)* transcender, dépasser; *Phil & Rel* transcender; **the issue transcends party loyalties** le problème dépasse les clivages partisans **2** *(surpass)* surpasser

transcendence [træn'sendəns], **transcendency** [træn'sendənsɪ] N transcendance *f*

transcendent [træn'sendənt] ADJ transcendant

transcendental [ˌtrænsen'dentəl] ADJ transcendantal

▸▸ ***transcendental meditation*** méditation *f* transcendantale; *Math* ***transcendental number*** nombre *m* transcendant

transcendentalism [ˌtrænsen'dentəlɪzəm] N *Phil* transcendantalisme *m*

transcoder [trænz'kəʊdə(r)] N *TV* transcodeur *m*

transcontinental ['trænzˌkɒntɪ'nentəl] ADJ transcontinental

transcribe [træn'skraɪb] VT **1** *(write out)* copier, transcrire; *(shorthand)* traduire; *Acct* **to t. entries** transcrire des écritures

2 *Mus (for another instrument)* transcrire

3 *TV (record)* enregistrer; *(broadcast)* retransmettre en différé

4 *Comput (data)* transcrire

transcript ['trænskrɪpt] N transcription *f*; *Am Sch* livret *m* scolaire; *Am Univ* = liste officielle des notes obtenues dans chaque matière

transcription [træn'skrɪpʃən] N transcription *f*

transdermal [ˌtræns'dɜːməl] ADJ transdermique

▸▸ ***transdermal patch*** timbre *m* autocollant transdermique

transducer [trænz'djuːsə(r)] N transducteur *m*

transect [træn'sekt] VT sectionner transversalement

transept ['trænsept] N transept *m*

trans fat, trans fatty acid ['træns-] N *Biol & Chem* acide *m* gras trans

transfer VT [træns'fɜː(r)] **1** *(move)* transférer; *(employee, civil servant)* transférer, muter; *(soldier)* muter; *Br (player)* transférer; *(passenger)* transférer, transborder; *(object, goods)* transférer, transporter; **can this ticket be transferred to another airline?** peut-on utiliser ce billet d'avion sur une autre compagnie?

2 *Fin & Banking (money)* virer; **I transferred the funds to my bank account** j'ai fait virer l'argent sur mon compte bancaire

3 *(convey* ▸ *property, ownership)* transmettre, transférer, *Law* faire cession de, céder; *(*▸ *power, responsibility)* passer; **she will t. the rights over to him** elle va lui céder *ou* passer les droits

4 *Tel* **I'm transferring you now** *(operator)* je vous mets en communication; *Br* **I'd like to t. the charges** je voudrais téléphoner en PCV; *Br* **transferred charge call** communication *f* en PCV

5 *(displace* ▸ *design, picture)* reporter, décalquer; **to t. a design from one surface to another** décalquer un dessin d'un support sur un autre; *Fig* **she transferred her affection/allegiance to him** elle a reporté son affection/sa fidélité sur lui

VI [træns'fɜː(r)] **1** *(move)* être transféré; *(employee, civil servant)* être muté *ou* transféré; *(soldier)* être muté; *Br (player)* être transféré; *Am* **she transferred to another school** elle a changé d'école; **I'm transferring to history** je me réoriente en histoire

2 *(change mode of transport)* être transféré *ou* transbordé; **they had to t. to a train** ils ont dû changer et prendre le train

N ['trænsfɜː(r)] **1** *(gen)* transfert *m*; *(of employee, civil servant)* mutation *f*; *(of passenger)* transfert *m*, transbordement *m*; *Br (of player)* transfert *m*; *(of goods, objects)* transfert *m*, transport *m*; **he has asked for a t.** il a demandé son transfert *ou* à être muté; *Br (player)* il a demandé son transfert

2 *Fin & Banking (of funds, capital)* virement *m*, transfert *m*

3 *Law* transmission *f*, cession *f*; **t. of ownership from sb to sb** transfert *m ou* translation *f* de propriété de qn à qn

4 *Br (design, picture)* décalcomanie *f*; *(rub-on)* autocollant *m*; *(sew-on)* décalque *m*

5 *(change of mode of travel)* transfert *m*; *(at airport, train station)* correspondance *f*; **free t.** transfert *m* gratuit

6 *(ticket)* billet *m* de correspondance

7 *Comput (of data)* transfert *m*

8 *St Exch (of shares)* transfert *m*; *(document)* (feuille *f* de) transfert *m*

▸▸ ***transfer advice*** avis *m* de virement; ***transfer bus*** navette *f*; *Br Tel* ***transfer charge call*** communication *f* en PCV; ***transfer cheque*** chèque *m* de virement; *Law* ***transfer deed*** acte *m* de cession; ***transfer desk*** *(at airport)* guichet *m* de transit; ***transfer fee*** **1** *Br Sport* indemnité *f* de transfert **2** *Fin* frais *mpl* de transfert; *Br Sport* ***transfer list*** liste *f* des joueurs transférables; *Br* ***transfer lounge*** *(at airport)* salle *f* de transit; ***transfer order*** ordre *m ou* mandat *m* de virement; *Br* ***transfer passenger*** *(between flights)* voyageur(euse) *m,f* en transit; *Pol* ***transfer of power*** passation *f* de pouvoir; *Comput* ***transfer rate*** taux *m* de transfert; *Biol* ***transfer RNA*** ARN *m* de transfert; *Comput* ***transfer speed*** vitesse *f* de transfert; *Br* ***transfer tax*** droits *mpl* de succession; *(between living persons)* droit *m* de mutation; ***transfer ticket*** billet *m* de correspondance

transferable [træns'fɜːrəbəl] ADJ transmissible, transférable; *Law* cessible; **this ticket is not t.** ce billet est strictement personnel

▸▸ ***transferable credit*** crédit *m* transférable; ***transferable document*** document *m* transmissible; ***transferable securities*** valeurs *fpl* négociables *ou* mobilières; ***transferable share*** action *f* au porteur; ***transferable skills*** compétences *fpl* transférables; ***transferable vote*** = voix pouvant se reporter sur un autre candidat

transferee [ˌtrænsfɜː'riː] N *Law & Fin* cessionnaire *mf*, bénéficiaire *mf*

transference ['trænsfərəns] N *(gen) & Psy* transfert *m*; *(of employee, civil servant)* mutation *f*; *(of money)* virement *m*; *(of power)* passation *f*; *(of ownership)* transfert *m ou* translation *f* de propriété

transfiguration [ˌtrænsfɪgə'reɪʃən] N transfiguration *f*; *Rel* **the T.** la Transfiguration

transfigure [træns'fɪgə(r)] VT transfigurer

transfix [træns'fɪks] VT transpercer; *Fig* pétrifier; **to be transfixed with fear** être paralysé par la peur; **she stood transfixed** elle est restée clouée sur place

transform [træns'fɔːm] VT **1** *(change* ▸ *gen)* transformer; **to t. sth into sth** transformer qch en qch **2** *Elec* transformer; *Chem, Math & Phys* transformer, convertir **3** *Ling* transformer

transformation [ˌtrænsfə'meɪʃən] N **1** *(change)* transformation *f*, métamorphose *f* **2** *Elec, Math, Chem & Phys* transformation *f* **3** *Ling* transformation *f*

transformational grammar [ˌtrænsfə'meɪʃənəl-] N *Ling* grammaire *f* transformationnelle

transformer [træns'fɔːmə(r)] N *Elec* transformateur *m*

▸▸ ***transformer station*** station *f* de transformation; ***transformer unit*** bloc *m* transformateur

transfuse [træns'fjuːz] VT *(gen) & Med* transfuser; *Literary* **in a voice transfused with emotion** d'une voix emplie d'émotion

transfusion [træns'fjuːʒən] N *(gen) & Med* transfusion *f*; **they gave him a t.** ils lui ont fait une transfusion

transgender [ˌtræns'dʒendə(r)] N transsexuel (elle) *m,f*

transgendered [ˌtræns'dʒendəd] ADJ transsexuel

transgene ['trænsdʒiːn] N *Biol* transgène *m*

transgenic [ˌtrænz'dʒenɪk] ADJ transgénique

▸▸ ***transgenic animal*** animal *m* transgénique

transgress [trænz'gres] *Formal* VT *(law etc)* transgresser, enfreindre

VI enfreindre la loi; *(sin)* pécher

transgression [trænz'greʃən] N *Formal (of law etc)* transgression *f*, infraction *f* (**of** à); *(sin)* péché *m*

transgressor [trænz'gresə(r)] N *Formal (of law etc)* transgresseur *m*; *(sinner)* pécheur(eresse) *m,f*

tranship = **transship**

transhipment = **transshipment**

transience ['trænzɪəns], **transiency** ['trænzɪənsɪ] N *(temporariness)* caractère *m* transitoire *ou* passager; *(fleetingness)* caractère *m* éphémère

transient ['trænzɪənt] ADJ *(temporary)* transitoire, passager; *(fleeting)* éphémère
N *(person)* voyageur(euse) *m,f* en transit

transire [træn'saɪə(r)] N *Com* passavant *m*, laissez-passer *m inv*

transistor [træn'zɪstə(r)] N transistor *m*
▸▸ ***transistor radio*** transistor *m*

transistorize, -ise [træn'zɪstəraɪz] VT transistoriser
▸▸ ***transistorized circuit*** circuit *m* à transistors

transit ['trænsɪt] N **1** *(of goods, passengers)* transit *m*; **in t.** en transit; **goods lost in t.** marchandises *fpl* égarées pendant le transport **2** *Astron* passage *m*
COMP *(goods, passengers)* en transit; *(documents, port)* de transit
VT **1** *(goods, passengers)* transiter **2** *Astron* passer sur
▸▸ *Am* ***transit authority*** régie *f* des transports (en commun); ***transit bill*** passavant *m*; ***transit camp*** camp *m* de transit; ***transit duty*** droit *m* de transit; ***transit hotel*** hôtel *m* de passage *ou* de transit; ***transit lounge*** salle *f* de transit; ***transit visa*** visa *m* de transit

transition [træn'zɪʃən] N transition *f*, passage *m*; **the t. from childhood to maturity** le passage de l'enfance à l'âge adulte
COMP *(period)* de transition
▸▸ ***transition economy*** économie *f* de transition; *Chem* ***transition element*** élément *m* de transition

transitional [træn'zɪʃənəl] ADJ de transition, transitoire

transitive ['trænzɪtɪv] ADJ *Gram* transitif

transitively ['trænzɪtɪvlɪ] ADV *Gram* transitivement

transitory ['trænzɪtərɪ] ADJ transitoire, passager

translatable [træns'leɪtəbəl] ADJ traduisible

translate [træns'leɪt] VT **1** *(word, text, book)* traduire; **to t. sth from Spanish into English** traduire qch de l'espagnol en anglais; **it can be translated as...** on peut le traduire par...; **translated into Fahrenheit** exprimé *ou* converti en Fahrenheit; **we can now t. these figures into a graph** nous pouvons maintenant traduire ces chiffres en un graphe; **to t. ideas into action** traduire des idées en actes **2** *Rel (transfer ▸ cleric, relics)* transférer; *(convey to heaven)* ravir
VI **1** *(word, text, book)* se traduire; **it doesn't t.** c'est intraduisible; *Fig* **how does that t. into economic reality?** comment est-ce que ça se traduit sur le plan économique? **2** *(person)* traduire; **she translates for the EU** elle fait des traductions pour l'Union européenne

translation [træns'leɪʃən] N **1** *(of word, text, book)* traduction *f*; *Sch* version *f*; **to read sth in t.** lire une traduction de qch; **the book is a t. from (the) Chinese** le livre est traduit du chinois; **the text loses something in (the) t.** le texte perd quelque chose à la traduction **2** *Rel (of cleric, relics)* translation *f*; *(conveying to heaven)* ravissement *m*
▸▸ ***translation agency*** bureau *m ou* agence *f* de traduction; ***translation company*** cabinet *m ou* société *f* de traduction; *Comput* ***translation table*** table *f* de traduction

translator [træns'leɪtə(r)] N traducteur(trice) *m,f*

transliterate [trænz'lɪtəreɪt] VT translitérer, translittérer

transliteration [ˌtrænzlɪtə'reɪʃən] N translitération *f*, translittération *f*

translucence [trænz'luːsəns] N translucidité *f*

translucent [trænz'luːsənt] ADJ translucide, diaphane

transmigrate [ˌtrænzmaɪ'greɪt] VI *(soul)* transmigrer; *(people)* émigrer

transmigration [ˌtrænzmaɪ'greɪʃən] N *(of souls)* transmigration *f*; *(of people)* émigration *f*

transmissible [trænz'mɪsəbəl] ADJ transmissible

transmission [trænz'mɪʃən] N **1** *(gen)* transmission *f*; *Tel* transmission *f*, émission *f*; *TV & Rad (of programme)* diffusion *f* **2** *Aut* transmission *f*
▸▸ ***transmission brake*** frein *m* sur transmission; ***transmission rate*** débit *m* de transmission; ***transmission shaft*** arbre *m* de transmission; ***transmission speed*** vitesse *f* de transmission

transmit [trænz'mɪt] *(pt & pp* **transmitted**, *cont* **transmitting**) VT *(gen)* transmettre; *Tel* transmettre, émettre; *TV & Rad (programme)* diffuser
VI *Rad, Tel & TV* émettre, diffuser

transmitter [trænz'mɪtə(r)] N transmetteur *m*; *Rad & TV* émetteur *m*; *(in telephone)* microphone *m* (téléphonique)
▸▸ *Tel & Rad* ***transmitter receiver*** émetteur-récepteur *m*; *TV & Rad* ***transmitter van*** car *m* de transmission

transmogrify [trænz'mɒgrɪfaɪ] *(pt & pp* **transmogrified**) VT *Hum* métamorphoser, changer

transmutation [ˌtrænzmjuː'teɪʃən] N transmutation *f*

transmute [trænz'mjuːt] VT transmuer, transmuter; **the process transmutes the metal into gold** le processus transforme *ou* transmute le métal en or

transom ['trænsəm] N **1** *(in window)* petit bois *m* horizontal; *(above door)* traverse *f* d'imposte **2** *Am (fanlight)* imposte *f* (semi-circulaire)
▸▸ *Am* ***transom window*** imposte *f* (semi-circulaire)

transparency [træns'pærənsɪ] *(pl* **transparencies**) N **1** *(quality)* transparence *f* **2** *(for overhead projector)* transparent *m*; *esp Br (slide)* diapositive *f*

transparent [træns'pærənt] ADJ transparent

transparently [træns'pærəntlɪ] ADV *(obviously)* de toute évidence; **that's t. obvious** c'est clair comme de l'eau de roche

transpiration [ˌtrænspɪ'reɪʃən] N *Bot & Physiol* transpiration *f*

transpire [træn'spaɪə(r)] VI **1** *(be discovered, turn out)* apparaître; **it transpired that he had been embezzling funds** on a appris *ou* on s'est aperçu qu'il avait détourné des fonds **2** *(happen)* se passer, arriver; **the events that transpired later that day** les événements intervenus plus tard dans la journée **3** *Bot & Physiol* transpirer
VT *Bot (water, vapour)* dégager

> Note that the French verb **transpirer** is a false friend. Its most common meaning is **to sweat.**

transplant VT [træns'plɑːnt] **1** *Bot (plant)* transplanter; *(seedling)* repiquer **2** *Med (organ)* greffer, transplanter; *(tissue)* greffer **3** *(population)* transplanter
N ['trænsˌplɑːnt] *Med (organ)* transplant *m*; *(tissue, operation)* greffe *f*; **she's had a kidney t.** on lui a fait une greffe du rein; **she's had a heart t.** on lui a greffé un cœur

transplantation [ˌtrænsplɑːn'teɪʃən] N **1** *Bot (of plant)* transplantation *f*; *(of seedling)* repiquage *m* **2** *Med (of organ)* transplantation *f* **3** *Fig (of people)* transplantation *f*

transponder [træn'spɒndə(r)] N transpondeur *m*

transport N ['trænspɔːt] **1** (UNCOUNT) *Br (system)* transport *m*, transports *mpl*
2 *(means)* moyen *m* de transport *ou* de locomotion; *Br Fam* **have you got t. for tonight?** tu as un moyen de locomotion pour ce soir?
3 *(of goods)* transport *m*
4 *Literary (of joy)* transport *m*; *(of anger)* accès *m*; **he went into transports of delight** il fut transporté de joie
VT [træn'spɔːt] transporter
▸▸ ***transport allowance*** prime *f* de transport; *Br* ***transport café*** ≃ routier *m (restaurant)*; ***transport company*** entreprise *f ou* société *f* de transport; ***transport costs*** frais *mpl* de transport; ***transport cover*** garantie *f* transport; ***transport document*** titre *m ou* document *m* de transport; ***transport facilities*** moyens *mpl* de transport; ***transport museum*** musée *m* des transports; ***transport plane*** avion *m* de transport; *Br* ***transport police*** = service d'ordre des chemins de fer; ***transport s[hip]*** navire *m* de transport

transportable [træn'spɔːtəbəl] ADJ transp[or]table

transportation [ˌtrænspɔː'teɪʃən] N **1** *Am (tra[nsport])* transport *m*; **public t.** transports *mpl* p[u]blics; **t. system** système *m* des transports **2** *[(of] criminals)* transportation *f*
▸▸ *Am* ***transportation desk*** *(in hotel)* bureau *m* [des] voyages; *Am* ***transportation insurance*** assuran[ce] *f* transport

transporter [træn'spɔːtə(r)] N **1** *Mil (for troops, lorry)* camion *m* de transport; *(▸ ship)* navire [*m*] de transport; *(for tanks)* camion *m* porte-cha[rs]; *(for cars ▸ lorry)* camion *m* pour transport d'a[u]tomobiles; *(▸ train)* wagon *m* pour transp[ort] d'automobiles
▸▸ ***transporter bridge*** pont *m* transbordeur

transpose [træns'pəʊz] VT transposer

transposition [ˌtrænspə'zɪʃən] N transpositio[n]

transputer [træns'pjuːtə(r)] N *Comput* transp[u]ter *m*

transsexual [træns'sekʃʊəl] N transsexuel(el[le]) *m,f*

transsexuality [trænsˌsekʃʊ'ælɪtɪ] N tran[s]sexualisme *m*

transship [træns'ʃɪp] *(pt & pp* **transshipped**, *c[ont]* **transshipping**) VT transborder

transshipment [træns'ʃɪpmənt] N transbord[e]ment *m*

Trans-Siberian ['trænz-] ADJ **the T. (Railway)** Transsibérien

transubstantiation ['trænsəbˌstænʃɪ'eɪʃən] *Rel* transsubstantiation *f*

Transvaal ['trænzvɑːl] N Transvaal *m*

transversal [ˌtrænz'vɜːsəl] ADJ transversal
N *Geom* transversale *f*

transversally [ˌtrænz'vɜːsəlɪ] ADV transversal[e]ment

transverse ['trænzvɜːs] ADJ *(beam, line)* tran[s]versal; *Anat* transverse
N *(gen)* partie *f* transversale; *Geom* axe *m* tran[s]versal *(d'une hyperbole)*
▸▸ *Constr* ***transverse beam*** traverse *f*; *Aut* ***tra[nsverse] engine*** moteur *m* transversal; *Geom* ***tra[ns]verse line*** transversale *f*; *Phys* ***transverse wa[ve]*** onde *f* transversale

transversely [ˌtrænz'vɜːslɪ] ADV transversa[le]ment

transvestism [trænz'vestɪzəm] N travestisme transvestisme *m*

transvestite [trænz'vestaɪt] N travesti(e) *m,f*

trap [træp] *(pt & pp* **trapped**, *cont* **trapping**) N *(snare)* piège *m*; *(dug in ground)* trappe *f*; *(g[in] trap)* collet *m*; **to set** *or* **to lay a t. (for sth)** tend[re] un piège (à qch); **the badger was caught in a t.** blaireau était pris dans un piège
2 *Fig* piège *m*, traquenard *m*; **to set** *or* **to lay a[…] for sb** tendre un piège à qn; **they fell into the t.** sont tombés dans le piège; **the poverty t.** piège de la pauvreté
3 *Tech (for water, oil etc)* collecteur *m*; *(in dra[in])* siphon *m*
4 *(in dog racing)* box *m* de départ; *(for trapsho[ot]ing)* ball-trap *m*
5 *Golf* bunker *m* (de sable)
6 *(carriage)* cabriolet *m*, charrette *f* anglaise
7 *(trapdoor)* trappe *f*
8 *very Fam (mouth)* gueule *f*, clapet *m*; **shut yo[ur] t.!** ta gueule!, ferme-la!; **you would have to […] and open your big t.!** il a fallu que tu ouvres grande gueule!; **to keep one's t. shut** la ferme[r], la boucler
VT **1** *(animal)* prendre au piège, piéger
2 *Fig (person)* piéger; **now you're trapped!** mai[n]tenant vous êtes piégé *ou* pris!; **to t. sb into sa[y]ing sth** faire dire qch à qn en usant de ruse; **[…] trapped me into thinking I was safe** il m'a pié[gé] en me faisant croire que j'étais hors de dange[r]; **we got trapped into going** on s'est fait piéger on a dû y aller
3 *(immobilize, catch)* bloquer, immobilise[r]; *Sport (ball)* bloquer; **they were trapped** *or* **th[ey] got trapped in the lift** ils ont été bloqués *ou* coi[n]cés dans l'ascenseur; **we were trapped by the […]**

oming tide on a été surpris par la marée montante; **I trapped my leg** *or* **my leg got trapped under the table** je me suis coincé la jambe *ou* j'avais la jambe coincée sous la table; **she trapped her fingers in the door** elle s'est pris les doigts dans la porte; **they were trapped in the rubble** ils étaient coincés *ou* immobilisés sous les décombres; **to feel trapped** *(in relationship)* se sentir coincé
4 *(hold back ▸ water, gas)* retenir; **there's a grid to** **dead leaves** il y a une grille pour retenir les feuilles mortes

apeze [trəˈpiːz] **N** trapèze *m (de cirque)*
▸ ***trapeze artist*** trapéziste *mf*

apezium [trəˈpiːzɪəm] *(pl* **trapeziums** *or* **trapezia** [-zɪə]) **N** *Geom Br (with no parallel sides)* trapèze *m*; *Am (with two parallel sides)* quadrilatère trapézoïdal

apezoid [ˈtræpɪzɔɪd] **N** *Geom Br* quadrilatère *m* trapézoïdal; *Am* trapèze *m*

apper [ˈtræpə(r)] **N** trappeur *m*

appings [ˈtræpɪŋz] **NPL 1** *(accessories)* ornements *mpl*; **the trappings of power** les signes *mpl* extérieurs du pouvoir **2** *(harness)* harnachement *m*, carapaçon *m*

appist [ˈtræpɪst] **N** trappiste *m*
COMP *(monk, monastery)* de la Trappe

apshooting [ˈtræpˌʃuːtɪŋ] **N** ball-trap *m*; **to go** faire du ball-trap

ash [træʃ] **N** *(UNCOUNT)* **1** *(nonsense)* bêtises *fpl*, âneries *fpl*; **he talks/writes a lot of t.** il dit/écrit beaucoup d'âneries; **what utter t.!** c'est vraiment n'importe quoi!; **how can you watch that t.?** comment peux-tu regarder de telles nullités *ou* idioties?
2 *(goods, objects)* camelote *f*
3 *Am (waste)* ordures *fpl*; **to put something in the** mettre qch à la poubelle
4 *Fam (people)* racaille *f*; **they're just t.** c'est de la racaille
5 *Am Comput* poubelle *f*
VT *Fam* **1** *(reject)* jeter, bazarder; **they trashed all my ideas** ils ont rejeté toutes mes idées
2 *(criticize)* débiner, éreinter, démolir
3 *(vandalize)* foutre en l'air, bousiller
4 *Am Sport (opponent)* démolir
▸▸ *Am* ***trash bag*** sac *m* poubelle; *Am* ***trash barrel*** (grande) poubelle *f*; *Am* ***trash heap*** tas *m* d'ordures; *Am Comput* ***trash icon*** icône *f* de la corbeille; ***trash TV*** télé-poubelle *f*

ashcan [ˈtræʃkæn] **N** *Am* poubelle *f*

ashed [træʃt] **ADJ** *Fam (drunk)* rond, fait, bourré; *(on drugs)* défoncé, raide

ashy [ˈtræʃɪ] *(compar* **trashier**, *superl* **trashiest**) **ADJ** *(goods)* de pacotille; *(magazine, book)* de quatre sous; *(idea, article)* qui ne vaut rien; *(programme)* lamentable, au-dessous de tout; *(style, appearance)* vulgaire

auma [*Br* ˈtrɔːmə, *Am* ˈtraʊmə] *(pl* **traumas** *or* **traumata** [-mətə]) **N** *(gen) & Psy* traumatisme *m*, *Spec* trauma *m*; *Med* traumatisme *m*

aumatic [*Br* trɔːˈmætɪk, *Am* traʊˈmætɪk] **ADJ** *(gen) & Psy* traumatisant; *Med* traumatique

aumatism [*Br* ˈtrɔːmətɪzəm, *Am* ˈtraʊmətɪzəm] **N** traumatisme *m*

aumatize, -ise [*Br* ˈtrɔːmətaɪz, *Am* ˈtraʊmətaɪz] **VT** traumatiser

avail [ˈtræveɪl] *Arch or Literary* **N 1** *(work)* labeur *m* **2** *(in childbirth)* douleurs *fpl* de l'enfantement, travail *m*
• **travails** **NPL** *(hardship)* vicissitudes *fpl*

avel [ˈtrævəl] *(Br pt & pp* **travelled**, *cont* **travelling**, *Am pt & pp* **traveled**, *cont* **traveling**) **VI 1** *(journey)* voyager; *(journey around)* faire des voyages; **to t. by air/car** voyager en avion/en voiture; **they travelled to Greece by boat** ils sont allés en Grèce en bateau; **to t. round the world** faire le tour du monde; **she's travelling (about** *or* **around) somewhere in Asia** elle est en voyage quelque part en Asie; **we travelled across France by train** nous avons traversé la France en train; **they've travelled far and wide** ils ont voyagé partout dans le monde; **to t. light** voyager avec peu de bagages; **to t. back** revenir, rentrer; **let's t. back in time to 1940** retournons en 1940
2 *Com* être représentant(e) *m,f* de commerce; *Br* **he travels in confectionery** il est représentant en confiserie
3 *(go, move ▸ person)* aller; *(▸ vehicle, train)* aller, rouler; *(▸ piston, shuttle)* se déplacer; *(▸ light, sound)* se propager; **the train travelled at high speed through the countryside** le train roulait à toute vitesse à travers la campagne; **we were travelling at an average speed of 60 mph** ≃ on faisait du 96 km/h de moyenne; **the signals t. along different routes** les signaux suivent des trajets différents; **the components t. along a conveyor belt** les pièces détachées sont transportées sur un tapis roulant
4 *Fam (go very fast)* rouler (très) vite; **we were really travelling** on roulait vraiment très vite; **this car certainly travels!** elle bombe, cette voiture!
5 *Fig (thoughts, mind)* **my mind travelled back to last June** mes pensées m'ont ramené au mois de juin dernier
6 *(news, rumour)* se répandre, se propager, circuler; **news travels fast** les nouvelles vont vite
7 *(food)* supporter le voyage; *(humour)* bien passer les frontières
8 *(in basketball)* marcher
VT 1 *(distance)* faire, parcourir; **I travelled 50 miles to get here** j'ai fait 80 km pour venir ici **2** *(area, road)* parcourir; **we travelled the country from west to east** on a parcouru *ou* traversé le pays d'ouest en est
N *(UNCOUNT) (journeys)* voyage *m*, voyages *mpl*; **t. broadens the mind** les voyages ouvrent l'esprit; **I've done a lot of foreign t.** j'ai beaucoup voyagé à l'étranger; **t. was slower in those days** on voyageait plus lentement à cette époque; **what do you spend on t.?** à combien vous reviennent vos déplacements?
COMP *(guide, brochure)* touristique
• **travels** **NPL** *(journeys)* voyages *mpl*; *(comings and goings)* allées et venues *fpl*; **I met them on my travels in China** je les ai rencontrés au cours de mes voyages en Chine
▸▸ ***travel agency*** agence *f* de voyages; ***travel agent*** agent *m* de voyages; ***travel agent's*** agence *f* de voyages; ***travel allowance*** indemnité *f* de déplacement; ***travel book*** récit *m* de voyages; ***travel bureau*** agence *f* de voyages; ***travel company*** voyagiste *m*; ***travel documents*** documents *mpl* de voyage; ***travel expenses*** frais *mpl* de déplacement; ***travel insurance*** assurance-voyage *f*; **to take out t. insurance** prendre une assurance-voyage; ***travel literature*** documentation *f* touristique; ***travel programme*** *(travelogue)* émission *f* sur les voyages; ***travel rug*** plaid *m*; *Br* ***travel sickness*** mal *m* des transports; ***travel writer*** auteur *m* de récits de voyage

travelator [ˈtrævəleɪtə(r)] **N** tapis *m ou* trottoir *m* roulant

travelled, *Am* **traveled** [ˈtrævəld] **ADJ 1** *(person)* qui a beaucoup voyagé; **he's a well-t. man** il a beaucoup voyagé **2** *(road, path)* fréquenté; **this is a much t. road** c'est une route très fréquentée

traveller, *Am* **traveler** [ˈtrævələ(r)] **N 1** *(gen)* voyageur(euse) *m,f*; **I'm not a good t.** je supporte mal les voyages **2** *(salesman)* voyageur(euse) *m,f* de commerce **3** *(gipsy)* bohémien(enne) *m,f*
▸▸ ***traveller's cheque*** chèque *m* de voyage, traveller's cheque *m*

travelling, *Am* **traveling** [ˈtrævəlɪŋ] **N** *(UNCOUNT)* **1** *(gen)* voyage *m*, voyages *mpl*; **to do a lot of t.** beaucoup voyager; **there isn't a lot of t. in this job** on ne voyage pas beaucoup dans ce travail **2** *(in basketball)* marché *m*
ADJ *(companion, bag)* de voyage; *(preacher, musician)* itinérant; *(crane)* mobile
▸▸ ***travelling allowance*** indemnité *f* de déplacement; ***travelling circus*** cirque *m* forain; ***travelling clock*** réveil *m* de voyage; ***travelling expenses*** frais *mpl* de déplacement; ***travelling library*** ≃ bibliobus *m*; ***travelling people*** gens *mpl* du voyage; *Br* ***travelling rug*** plaid *m*; ***travelling salesman*** représentant *m ou* voyageur *m* de commerce; ***travelling scholarship*** bourse *f* de voyage; *Cin* ***travelling shot*** prise *f* de vue en travelling, plan *m* travelling

travelogue, *Am* **travelog** [ˈtrævəlɒg] **N** *(lecture, book)* récit *m* de voyage; *(film)* film *m* de voyage

travel-sick **ADJ** *Br* **to be t.** *(in car)* avoir mal au cœur en voiture, avoir le mal de la route; *(in boat)* avoir le mal de mer; *(in plane)* avoir le mal de l'air; **to get t.** souffrir du mal des transports, être malade en voyage

travel-size **ADJ** *(shampoo etc)* de voyage

travel-stained **ADJ** sali par le voyage *ou* les voyages

travel-weary **ADJ** fatigué par le voyage *ou* les voyages

traverse [ˈtrævəs, trəˈvɜːs] **VT** *Formal (go over)* traverser
VI *(in climbing, skiing)* faire une traversée, traverser
N 1 *(beam)* traverse *f*
2 *Geom* (ligne *f*) transversale *f*; *(in surveying)* cheminement *m*
3 *(in mountaineering, skiing ▸ across face of escarpment)* vire *f*
4 *(gallery)* galerie *f* transversale

travesty [ˈtrævəstɪ] *(pl* **travesties**, *pt & pp* **travestied**) **N** *(parody)* parodie *f*, pastiche *m*; *Pej (mockery, pretence)* simulacre *m*, parodie *f*; **the trial was a t. of justice** le procès n'était qu'un simulacre de justice, c'était une parodie de procès
VT *(justice)* bafouer
▸▸ *Theat* ***travesty role*** rôle *m* travesti

trawl [trɔːl] **N 1** *Fishing (net)* chalut *m* **2** *(search)* recherche *f*; **to do a t. through the Internet** faire une recherche *ou* des recherches sur Internet
VI 1 *Fishing* pêcher au chalut; **to t. for herring** pêcher le hareng au chalut **2** *(search)* chercher; **to t. for information** chercher des renseignements, aller à la pêche (aux renseignements)
VT *(net)* traîner, tirer; *(sea)* pêcher dans; *Fig* **she trawled the small-ads for bargains** elle épluchait les petites annonces à la recherche de bonnes affaires; **he trawled the singles bars** il écumait les bars pour célibataires
▸▸ *Fishing* ***trawl line*** palangre *f*; *Fishing* ***trawl net*** chalut *m*

trawler [ˈtrɔːlə(r)] **N** *(boat, fisherman)* chalutier *m*

trawlerman [ˈtrɔːləmən] *(pl* **trawlermen** [-mən]) **N** chalutier *m*

trawling [ˈtrɔːlɪŋ] **N** *Fishing* pêche *f* au chalut, chalutage *m*

tray [treɪ] **N 1** *(for carrying)* plateau *m*; *(for selling ice cream etc)* éventaire *m*; **a t. of sandwiches** un plateau de sandwichs **2** *(for papers)* casier *m* (de rangement); *(for mail)* corbeille *f*; *(of printer)* bac *m*; **in/out t.** *(for mail)* corbeille *f* arrivée/départ **3** *(in box of chocolates)* supports *mpl* alvéolés

traycloth [ˈtreɪklɒθ] **N** napperon *m* (de plateau)

treacherous [ˈtretʃərəs] **ADJ 1** *(disloyal ▸ ally)* traître, perfide; *Fig (memory)* infidèle **2** *(dangerous ▸ water, current, ice)* traître; **the roads are t.** les routes sont très glissantes

treacherously [ˈtretʃərəslɪ] **ADV** *(act)* traîtreusement; **the currents are t. strong** les courants sont traîtres tellement ils sont forts

treachery [ˈtretʃərɪ] *(pl* **treacheries**) **N** perfidie *f*, traîtrise *f*

treacle [ˈtriːkəl] **N** *Br (molasses)* mélasse *f*; *(golden syrup)* mélasse *f* raffinée
▸▸ ***treacle pudding*** pudding *m* à la mélasse; ***treacle tart*** tarte *f* à la mélasse

treacly [ˈtriːklɪ] **ADJ** *(sweet)* sirupeux; *Fig (sentimental)* mièvre, sirupeux

tread [tred] *(pt* **trod** [trɒd], *pp* **trod** *or* **trodden** [ˈtrɒdən]) **VT 1** *(walk)* **a path had been trodden through the grass** les pas des marcheurs avaient tracé un chemin dans l'herbe; **she trod the streets looking for him** elle a battu le pavé *ou* parcouru la ville à sa recherche; *Theat* **to t. the boards** monter sur les planches
2 *(trample)* fouler; **to t. grapes** fouler du raisin; **to t. sth underfoot** fouler qch aux pieds, piétiner qch; **to t. water** nager sur place; *Fig* faire du surplace
3 *(stamp)* enfoncer, écraser; **she trod the cigarette into the sand** elle a écrasé du pied le mégot dans le sable; **to t. mud/dirt into the carpet** mettre de la boue/de la terre sur le tapis (avec ses chaussures); **don't t. the crumbs into the carpet** ne piétinez pas les miettes sur la moquette
VI 1 *(walk)* marcher; **to t. lightly** marcher d'un pas léger; *Fig* **to t. carefully** *or* **warily** y aller doucement *ou* avec précaution

2 *(step)* **to t. on sth** *(accidentally)* marcher sur qch; *(deliberately)* marcher (exprès) sur qch; **I must have trodden in something** j'ai dû marcher sur *ou* dans quelque chose; **he trod on my foot** il m'a marché sur le pied; *Fig* **to t. on sb's heels** talonner qn, suivre qn de près; *also Fig* **to t. on sb's toes** marcher sur les pieds de qn

N 1 *(footstep)* pas *m*; *(sound of steps)* bruit *m* de pas; **to walk with a heavy t.** marcher d'un pas lourd; **she could hear the measured t. of his footsteps** elle entendait le bruit régulier de ses pas

2 *(of stairs)* marche *f*, *Spec* giron *m*

3 *(of shoe)* semelle *f*; *(of tyre ▸ depth)* bande *f* de roulement, chape *f*; *(▸ pattern)* sculptures *fpl*; **there's no t. left** *(on shoe)* la semelle est usée; *(on tyre)* le pneu est lisse

▸ **tread down VT SEP** tasser (du pied)

treading ['tredɪŋ] **N** *(of grapes)* foulage *m*

treadle ['tredəl] **N** pédale *f* *(sur un tour ou sur une machine à coudre)*

treadmill ['tredmɪl] **N 1** *Hist (gen)* = roue ou manège mus par un homme; *(driven by horse)* trépigneuse *f*; *Fig* **the same old t.** le train-train quotidien **2** *(in gym)* tapis *m* de jogging, tapis *m* de course

treason ['tri:zən] **N** trahison *f*; **to commit t.** commettre un acte de trahison; **high t.** haute trahison *f*

treasonable ['tri:zənəbəl] **ADJ** *(action, statement)* qui constitue une trahison

treasure ['treʒə(r)] **N 1** *(valuables)* trésor *m* **2** *(art)* joyau *m*, trésor *m*; **the museum has many treasures of Renaissance art** le musée contient de nombreux joyaux de la Renaissance **3** *Fam (person)* trésor *m*, ange *m*; **come here, my little t.** viens là, mon (petit) trésor; **she's a real t.** *(cleaning lady, servant etc)* c'est une vrai perle

VT 1 *(friendship, possession)* tenir beaucoup à **2** *(gift)* garder précieusement, être très attaché à; *(memory)* conserver précieusement, *Formal* chérir; *(moment)* chérir

▸▸ ***treasure house*** *(museum)* trésor *m* *(lieu)*; *(room, library)* mine *f*, trésor *m*; *Fig* **she's a t. house of information** c'est un puits de science *ou* une mine de renseignements; ***treasure hunt*** chasse *f* au trésor; *Law* ***treasure trove*** trésor *m* *(qu'on a découvert)*; *Fig* **the museum is a real t. trove** le musée est une véritable caverne d'Ali-Baba; **the book was a t. trove of anecdotes** le livre était une mine d'anecdotes

treasurer ['treʒərə(r)] **N 1** *(of club)* trésorier(ère) *m,f* **2** *Am (of company)* directeur(trice) *m,f* financier(ère)

treasury ['treʒərɪ] *(pl* **treasuries***)* **N 1** *(building)* trésorerie *f* **2** *Fig (of information)* mine *f*; *(of poems)* recueil *m* **3** *Admin (funds)* trésor *m* (public); **the T.** *(government department)* la Trésorerie, ≃ le ministère des Finances; *Am* **Secretary/Department of the T.** ≃ ministre *m*/ministère *m* des Finances

▸▸ *Fin* ***Treasury bill, Treasury bond*** certificat *m* de trésorerie, ≃ bon *m* du Trésor; *Am* ***Treasury Department*** ≃ ministère *m* des Finances; *Br* ***Treasury Minister*** ≃ ministre *m* des Finances; *Fin* ***Treasury note*** billet *m* de trésorerie; *Am* ***Treasury Secretary*** ≃ ministre *m* des Finances

treat [tri:t] **VT 1** *(deal with)* traiter; **to t. sb well** bien traiter qn; **to t. sb badly** mal traiter qn, ne pas bien traiter qn; **he treats them with contempt** il est méprisant envers eux; **teachers expect to be treated with respect by their pupils** les professeurs exigent que leurs élèves se conduisent respectueusement envers eux; **you shouldn't t. them like children** vous ne devriez pas les traiter comme des enfants; **you t. this place like a hotel!** ce n'est pas un hôtel ici!

2 *(handle ▸ substance, object)* utiliser, se servir de; *(▸ claim, request)* traiter; **the weedkiller needs to be treated with great care** il faut se servir du désherbant avec beaucoup de précaution

3 *(consider ▸ problem, question)* traiter, considérer; **the whole episode was treated as a joke** on a pris *ou* on a considéré tout cet épisode comme une plaisanterie; **she treated the subject rather superficially** elle a traité le sujet assez superficiellement

4 *Med (patient, illness)* soigner, traiter; **she's being treated for cancer** on la soigne pour un cancer

5 *(fruit, timber, crops)* traiter; **the land has been treated with fertilizer** la terre a été traitée aux engrais

6 *(buy)* **to t. sb to sth** offrir *ou* payer qch à qn; **I treated myself to a new coat** je me suis offert *ou* payé un manteau neuf; **go on, t. yourself!** vas-y, gâte-toi *ou* fais-toi plaisir!; *Ironic* **they were treated to a graphic description of her symptoms** ils ont eu droit à une description de ses symptômes dans tous les détails

VI *Formal* **1 to t. of** *(deal with)* traiter de; **the book treats of love** le livre traite de l'amour **2** *(negotiate)* **to t. with sb** traiter avec qn; **to t. with the enemy** pactiser avec l'ennemi

N 1 *(on special occasion ▸ enjoyment)* gâterie *f*, (petit) plaisir *m*; *(▸ surprise)* surprise *f*; *(▸ present)* cadeau *m*; *(▸ outing)* sortie *f*; **as a special t. we went to the planetarium** on nous a offert tout spécialement une visite au planétarium; **these chocolates are a real t.** ces chocolats sont un véritable délice *ou* un vrai régal; **I've got a t. for you** j'ai une bonne surprise pour toi; **to give oneself a t.** s'offrir un petit plaisir, se faire plaisir; **let's give her a t.** faisons-lui un petit plaisir, gâtons-la un peu; **this is my t.** c'est moi qui offre *ou* régale

2 *(pleasure)* plaisir *m*; **it's a t. for us to see you looking so happy** cela nous fait vraiment plaisir *ou* pour nous c'est une grande joie de vous voir si heureuse

• **a treat ADV** *Br Fam* à merveille; **the idea worked a t.** l'idée a marché à merveille; **to go down a t.** être très apprécié

treatise ['tri:tɪs] **N** traité *m*; **a t. on racism** un traité sur le racisme

treatment ['tri:tmənt] **N 1** *(of person)* traitement *m*; **we complained of ill t.** nous nous sommes plaints d'avoir été mal traités; **they gave him preferential t.** ils lui ont accordé un traitement préférentiel *ou* de faveur; **I got very good t.** on m'a très bien traité; *Fam* **to give sb the (full) t.** *(treat well)* traiter qn avec tous les égards; *(beat up)* rosser qn

2 *(UNCOUNT) Med* soins *mpl*, traitement *m*; **she was sent to Madrid for t.** on l'a envoyée se faire soigner à Madrid; **to receive/to undergo t.** recevoir/suivre un traitement; **is he responding to t.?** est-ce qu'il réagit au traitement?; **no doctor has the right to refuse t.** aucun médecin n'a le droit de refuser ses soins à un malade; **cancer t.** traitement *m* du cancer; **X-ray t.** traitement *m* par rayons X

3 *(of subject)* traitement *m*, façon *f* de traiter; **Cézanne's t. of colour** la façon dont Cézanne traite les couleurs

4 *(of crops, timber)* traitement *m*

5 *(chemical)* produit *m* chimique

6 *Cin* traitement *m*

treaty ['tri:tɪ] *(pl* **treaties***)* **N 1** *Pol* traité *m*; **to sign a t. (with sb)** signer *ou* conclure un traité (avec qn); **there is a t. between the two countries** les deux pays sont liés par traité **2** *Law (between individuals)* accord *m*; *(contract)* contrat *m*; **they sold the property by private t.** ils ont vendu la propriété par accord privé

▸▸ ***the Treaty on European Union*** le traité sur l'Union européenne; *Hist* ***the Treaty of Rome*** le traité de Rome; *Hist* ***the Treaty of Versailles*** le traité de Versailles

treble ['trebəl] **ADJ 1** *(triple)* triple; *Br* **my phone number is seven zero t. four** mon numéro de téléphone est le soixante-dix, quatre cent quarante-quatre **2** *Mus (voice)* de soprano; *(part)* pour voix de soprano

N 1 *Mus (part, singer)* soprano *m* **2** *(UNCOUNT) (in hi-fi)* aigus *mpl*

VT tripler

VI tripler

ADV trois fois plus; **t. the number** le triple; **t. the amount** trois fois plus; *Mus* **to sing t.** chanter dans un registre de soprano

▸▸ *Br* ***treble chance*** = méthode de pari en football; *Mus* ***treble clef*** clef *f* de sol

trebly ['treblɪ] **ADV** triplement, trois fois plus; **t. difficult** trois fois plus difficile

tree [tri:] **N 1** *Bot* arbre *m*; *Bible* **the T. of Knowledge/Life** l'arbre *m* de la science du bien et du mal/de vie; *Fig* **to be at the top of the t.** être au sommet; *Fig* **to get to the top of the t.** arriver au sommet de sa profession; *Am Fam* **to be up a** [t.] être dans une impasse; *Fam* **to be out of one's t.** *(mad)* être cinglé *ou* givré; *(drunk)* être rond *ou* rétamé *ou* bourré; *(on drugs)* être défoncé *ou* raide; *Fam* **money doesn't grow on trees!** l'argent ne pousse pas sur les arbres!; *Fam* **good plumbers don't grow on trees** les bons plombiers ne courent pas les rues

2 *(diagram)* **t. (diagram)** représentation *f* en arbre *ou* arborescente, arborescence *f*

3 *(for shoes)* embauchoir *m*, forme *f*

4 *(of saddle)* arçon *m*

VT 1 *(hunter, animal)* forcer *ou* obliger à se réfugier dans un arbre **2** *Am Fam Fig (trap)* piéger

▸▸ *Bot* ***tree fern*** fougère *f* arborescente; *Zo* ***tree frog*** rainette *f*; *Pej* ***tree hugger*** écologiste fanatique; ***tree line*** limite *f* des arbres; ***tree ri***[ng] cercle *m* d'arbres; *Orn* ***tree sparrow*** (moineau *m*) friquet *m*; *Comput* ***tree structure*** arborescence *f*, structure *f* arborescente; ***tree surge***[on] arboriculteur(trice) *m,f* *(qui s'occupe de soigner et d'élaguer les arbres)*; ***tree surgery*** arboriculture *(traitement des arbres malades)*; ***tree trunk*** tronc *m* d'arbre

treehouse ['tri:haʊs, *pl* -haʊzɪz] **N** = caba[ne] construite dans un arbre

treeless ['tri:lɪs] **ADJ** sans arbres, dénudé

treetop ['tri:tɒp] **N** cime *f* *ou* haut *m* *ou* faîte *m* d'un arbre; **in the treetops** au faîte *ou* au somm[et] des arbres; *Aviat* **to skim the treetops** voler en rase-mottes

trefoil ['trefɔɪl] **N** *Archit & Bot* trèfle *m*

trek [trek] *(pt & pp* **trekked**, *cont* **trekking***)* **N** *(walk)* marche *f*; *(hike)* randonnée *f*; **to go on a** [t.] faire une marche/une randonnée; **a long t.** un trajet long et pénible *(à pied)*; **it was a real t. to get here** ç'a été une véritable expédition pour arriver ici; **it's a bit of a t. to the shops** ça fait une trotte jusqu'aux magasins *ou* pour aller aux magasins **2** *SAfr Hist* voyage *m* en char à bœufs

VI 1 *(walk)* avancer avec peine; *(hike)* faire de randonnée; *Fig (drag oneself)* se traîner; **we ha[d] to t. across fields to get here** il a fallu passer à travers champs pour arriver ici; **they trekked all th[e] way out here to see us** ils ont fait tout ce chemin pour venir nous voir; **I can't be bothered to t. over to the supermarket again** je n'ai pas le courage de refaire tout ce chemin jusqu'au supermarché **2** *SAfr Hist* voyager en char à bœufs

trekking ['trekɪŋ] **N** *(as holiday activity)* randonnée *f*, trekking *m*; **I went on a t. holiday in Nepal** j'ai été faire de la randonnée au Népal pour mes vacances

trellis ['trelɪs] **N** treillage *m*, treillis *m*

VT *(wood strips)* faire un treillage de; *(plan[t])* treillager

trelliswork ['trelɪs,wɜ:k] **N** treillage *m*

tremble ['trembəl] **VI 1** *(person ▸ with cold)* trembler, frissonner; *(▸ with fear, excitement, rag[e])* trembler, frémir; *(hands)* trembler; **to t. with fe[ar]** trembler de peur; **to t. like a leaf** trembler comme une feuille

2 *(voice ▸ from emotion)* trembler, vibrer; *(▸ from fear)* trembler; *(▸ from infirmity, old age)* trembler, chevroter; **her voice trembled with emotio[n]** sa voix tremblait d'émotion

3 *(bridge, house, ground)* trembler; *(engine)* vibrer

4 *Fig (be anxious)* frémir; **she trembled at th[e] thought** elle frémissait à cette seule pensée; **h[e] trembled for their safety** il tremblait pour eux; **where are they? – I t. to think!** où sont-ils? – [je] n'ose y penser!

N 1 *(from fear)* tremblement *m*; *(from excitemen[t], rage)* frémissement *m*; *(from cold)* frissonnement *m*; *Fam* **to be all of a t.** être tout tremblan[t]

2 *(in voice)* frémissement *m*, frisson *m*

trembling ['tremblɪŋ] **ADJ 1** *(body ▸ with col[d])* frissonnant, grelottant; *(▸ in fear, excitemen[t])* frémissant, tremblant; *(hands)* tremblant *(voice ▸ with emotion)* vibrant; *(▸ with fear)* tremblant; *(▸ because of old age)* chevrotant; **with a [t.] voice** *(speaker)* d'une *ou* la voix tremblante *(singer)* d'une *ou* la voix chevrotante

N *(from cold)* tremblement *m*, frissonnement *m*

(from fear) tremblement *m*, frémissement *m*; **in fear and t.** tout tremblant

▸▸ *Bot* ***trembling poplar*** (peuplier *m*) tremble *m*

tremendous [trɪ'mendəs] ADJ **1** *(number, amount)* énorme, très grand; *(cost, speed)* très élevé, vertigineux; *(building, arch)* énorme; *(height)* vertigineux, très grand; *(undertaking)* énorme, monumental; *(admiration, disappointment, pride)* très grand, extrême; *(crash, noise)* terrible, épouvantable; **the fair was a t. success** la foire a été une très grande réussite; **there's been a t. improvement in her work** son travail s'est énormément amélioré; **there was a t. crowd** il y avait un monde fou *ou* une foule énorme; **you've been a t. help** vous m'avez été d'une aide précieuse **2** *(wonderful)* sensationnel, formidable; **I had a t. time** je me suis amusé comme un fou; **she looks t. in black** elle a beaucoup d'allure en noir

tremendously [trɪ'mendəslɪ] ADV *(as intensifier)* extrêmement; **we heard a t. loud explosion** on a entendu une formidable explosion; **we enjoyed it t.** cela nous a énormément plu; **I'm not t. keen on his plays** je n'aime pas vraiment ses pièces

tremolo ['tremələʊ] *(pl* **tremolos***)* N *Mus* trémolo *m*

▸▸ ***tremolo arm*** = levier sur une guitare électrique qui sert à varier le ton d'une note

tremor ['tremə(r)] N **1** *Geol* secousse *f* (sismique) **2** *(in voice)* frémissement *m*, frisson *m*, tremblement *m* **3** *(of fear, thrill)* frisson *m*; **a t. of anticipation ran through the audience** à l'idée de ce qui allait suivre, la salle fut parcourue d'un frisson

tremulous ['tremjʊləs] ADJ *Literary* **1** *(with fear)* tremblant; *(with excitement, nervousness)* frémissant; *(handwriting)* tremblé; **he was t. with emotion/fear** il tremblait d'émotion/de peur; **her voice was t. with joy** sa voix vibrait de joie **2** *(timid* ▸ *person, manner)* timide, craintif; *(*▸ *animal)* craintif, effarouché; *(*▸ *smile)* timide

tremulously ['tremjʊləslɪ] ADV *Literary* **1** *(with fear, emotion)* en tremblant; **to sing/to answer t.** chanter/répondre d'une voix tremblante **2** *(timidly)* timidement, craintivement

trench [trentʃ] N *(gen)* & *Constr* & *Mil* tranchée *f*; *(ditch)* fossé *m*; **life in the trenches** la vie dans les tranchées; **my grandfather fought in the trenches** mon grand-père a fait la guerre des tranchées

VT *(field)* creuser une tranchée *ou* des tranchées dans; *Mil* retrancher

VI creuser une tranchée *ou* des tranchées

▸▸ ***trench coat*** trench-coat *m*; *Med* ***trench fever*** rickettsiose *f*; *Med* ***trench foot*** = gelure au pied due au froid ou à l'humidité; *Mil* ***trench mortar*** engin *m ou* pièce *f* de tranchée; ***trench warfare*** guerre *f* de tranchées

trenchant ['trentʃənt] ADJ incisif, tranchant

trencher ['trentʃə(r)] N tranchoir *m*

trencherman ['trentʃəmən] *(pl* **trenchermen** [-mən]*)* N *Literary or Hum* gros mangeur *m*; **he's a good/great t.** il a un bon coup de fourchette

trend [trend] N *(tendency)* tendance *f*; *(fashion)* mode *f*; **the t. is towards shorter skirts** la tendance est aux jupes plus courtes; **there is a t. away from going abroad for holidays** on a tendance à délaisser les vacances à l'étranger; **house prices are on an upward t. again** le prix des maisons est de nouveau à la hausse; **if present trends continue** si les tendances actuelles se poursuivent; **the t. of events** le cours *ou* la tournure des événements; **the latest trends** la dernière mode; **to set a/the t.** *(style)* donner un/le ton; *(fashion)* lancer une/la mode

VI *(extend* ▸ *mountain range)* s'étendre; *(veer* ▸ *coastline)* s'incliner; *(turn* ▸ *prices, opinion)* s'orienter

▸▸ *Mktg* ***trend analysis*** analyse *f* des tendances

trendiness ['trendɪnɪs] N *Br Fam* côté *m* branché *ou* à la mode; **the t. of his haircut/views** sa coupe *f*/ses idées *fpl* à la mode; **the t. of the decor** le décor branché

trendsetter ['trend,setə(r)] N *(person* ▸ *in style)* personne *f* qui donne le ton; *(*▸ *in fashion)* personne *f* qui lance une mode

trendsetting ['trend,setɪŋ] ADJ *(person)* qui lance une mode; *(idea, garment)* d'avant-garde

N lancement *m* d'une mode

trendspotter ['trend,spɒtə(r)] N tendanceur *m*, = personne employée par une société commerciale pour identifier les nouvelles tendances de la mode telles qu'elles apparaissent dans la rue, les bars etc

trendy ['trendɪ] *(compar* **trendier**, *superl* **trendiest**, *pl* **trendies***)* *Br Fam* ADJ *(music, appearance, clothes)* branché; *(ideas, place, resort)* à la mode, branché; **he's a very t. dresser** il est toujours habillé à la dernière mode

N *Pej* branché(e) *m,f*

▸▸ *Pej* ***trendy lefty*** intello *mf* de gauche

trepan [trɪ'pæn] *(pt & pp* **trepanned**, *cont* **trepanning***)* *Med* VT trépaner

N trépan *m*

trepanning [trɪ'pænɪŋ] N *Med* trépanation *f*

trepidation [,trepɪ'deɪʃən] N **1** *(alarm)* appréhension *f*; **with great t.** avec une vive appréhension; **he stood there in t. before the headmaster** il se tenait tout tremblant devant le directeur de l'école **2** *(excitement)* agitation *f*

trespass ['trespəs] VI **1** *(on property)* pénétrer sans autorisation *ou* s'introduire dans une propriété privée; *Law* se rendre coupable d'une violation de propriété; **you're trespassing** vous êtes sur une propriété privée; **to t. on sb's land** s'introduire *ou* entrer sans autorisation dans une propriété privée; **no trespassing** *(sign)* défense d'entrer, propriété privée **2** *Fig (encroach)* **I don't want to t. on your time/hospitality** je ne veux pas abuser de votre temps/hospitalité; **he's trespassing on my area of responsibility** il empiète sur mon terrain; **to t. on sb's rights** violer *ou* enfreindre les droits de qn **3** *Bible* **to t. against sb** offenser qn; **as we forgive those that t. against us** comme nous pardonnons à ceux qui nous ont offensés; **to t. against the law** enfreindre la loi (divine)

N **1** *(UNCOUNT)* entrée *f* non autorisée; *Law* violation *f* de propriété; **to commit t.** s'introduire dans une propriété privée **2** *Bible* péché *m*; **forgive us our trespasses** pardonne-nous nos offenses

> Note that the French verb **trépasser** is a false friend and is never a translation for the English verb **to trespass**. It means **to die**.

trespasser ['trespəsə(r)] N *Law* intrus(e) *m,f* *(dans une propriété privée)*; **trespassers will be prosecuted** *(sign)* défense d'entrer sous peine de poursuites

trespassing ['trespəsɪŋ] N *(on someone's land)* violation *f* de propriété (foncière); **no t.** *(sign)* défense d'entrer

tress [tres] N *Literary* **a t. (of hair)** une mèche *ou* une boucle de cheveux; **her golden tresses** sa blonde chevelure *f*

trestle ['tresəl] N **1** *(for table)* tréteau *m* **2** *Constr* chevalet *m*

▸▸ ***trestle bridge*** pont *m* sur chevalets; ***trestle table*** table *f* à tréteaux

trews [truːz] NPL *Scot Old-fashioned* pantalon *m* en tissu écossais

triad ['traɪæd] N **1** *(group of three)* triade *f*

2 *(Chinese secret society)* triade *f*

3 *Mus* accord *m* parfait

4 *Chem (element)* élément *m* trivalent; *(atom)* atome *m* trivalent; *(ion)* ion *m* trivalent

trial ['traɪəl] N **1** *Law* procès *m*; **he pleaded guilty at the t.** il a plaidé coupable à son procès *ou* devant le tribunal; **to be** *or* **to go on t. for sth, to stand t. for sth** passer en jugement *ou* en justice pour qch; **he was put on** *or* **sent for t. for murder** il a été jugé pour meurtre; **to bring sb to t.** faire passer *ou* traduire qn en justice; **his case comes up for t. in September** son affaire passe en jugement en septembre; **famous trials** causes *fpl* célèbres

2 *(test)* essai *m*; *(for a drug, a process)* test *m*; **to give sth a t.** mettre qch à l'essai, essayer qch; **to be on t.** être à l'essai; **give her a month's t. before you take her on** prenez-la un mois à l'essai avant de l'embaucher; **it was a t. of strength** c'était une épreuve de force; **by t. and error** par tâtonnements, de façon empirique

3 *(hardship, adversity)* épreuve *f*; **the trials of married life** les vicissitudes *fpl* de la vie conjugale; **after all your trials and tribulations** après tout ce que vous avez dû souffrir; **her arthritis was a great t. to her** son arthrite l'a beaucoup fait souffrir; **he's always been a t. to his parents** il a toujours donné du souci à ses parents

4 *(competition)* concours *m*; *(for selection* ▸ *match)* match *m* de sélection; *(*▸ *race)* épreuve *f* de sélection

ADJ *(test* ▸ *flight)* d'essai; *(*▸ *marriage)* à l'essai; **on a t. basis** à titre d'essai

VT *(new product)* tester

• **trials** NPL *(competition)* concours *m*; *(for selection* ▸ *match)* match *m* de sélection; *(*▸ *race)* épreuve *f* de sélection

▸▸ *Acct* ***trial balance*** balance *f* d'inventaire; *also Fig* ***trial balloon*** ballon *m* d'essai; ***trial court*** tribunal *m* de première instance; *Sport* ***trial game*** match *m* de sélection; ***trial judge*** ≃ juge *m* d'instance; ***trial jury*** jury *m*; ***trial by jury*** jugement *m* par jury; *Am Law* ***trial lawyer*** avocat(e) *m,f*; ***trial offer*** offre *f* d'essai; *Mktg* ***trial order*** commande *f* d'essai; ***trial period*** période *f* d'essai; **to be on a t. period** *(of employee)* être en période d'essai; ***trial run*** essai *m*; **to give sth a t. run** essayer qch, faire un essai avec qch; **we'll have a t. run before we record** on fera un essai avant d'enregistrer; ***trial separation*** séparation *f* à l'essai

trialcohol [traɪ'ælkəhɒl] N *Med* trialcool *m*

triangle ['traɪæŋgəl] N **1** *Geom* triangle *m* **2** *Am (set square)* équerre *f* **3** *Mus* triangle *m*

triangular [traɪ'æŋgjʊlə(r)] ADJ triangulaire

triangulate [traɪ'æŋgjʊleɪt] VT **1** *Geom* diviser en triangles **2** *Geog (region)* trianguler

triangulation [traɪ,æŋgjʊ'leɪʃən] N triangulation *f*

▸▸ ***triangulation station*** point *m* géodésique

triathlon [traɪ'æθlɒn] N triathlon *m*

tribal ['traɪbəl] ADJ *(society, system)* tribal; *(warfare)* tribal, entre tribus; *(people)* qui vit en tribu; *(leader)* de tribu; *(loyalty)* à la tribu

tribalism ['traɪbəlɪzəm] N tribalisme *m*

tribalistic [,traɪbə'lɪstɪk] ADJ tribal

tri-band ['traɪbænd] ADJ *Tel* tri-bande

tribe [traɪb] N **1** *(gen)* tribu *f*; **the twelve tribes of Israel** les douze tribus *fpl* d'Israël **2** *Fam Fig* tribu *f*, smala *f*

tribesman ['traɪbzmən] *(pl* **tribesmen** [-mən]*)* N membre *m* d'une tribu; *(of particular tribe)* membre *m* de la tribu

tribulation [,trɪbjʊ'leɪʃən] N *Literary* affliction *f*, tourment *m*; **in times of t.** en temps de malheurs

tribunal [traɪ'bjuːnəl] N *(gen)* & *Law* tribunal *m*; *Fig* **the t. of public opinion** le jugement de l'opinion publique

▸▸ ***tribunal of inquiry*** commission *f* d'enquête

tribune ['trɪbjuːn] N **1** *Antiq* tribun *m* **2** *(platform)* tribune *f*; *Fig* **the newspaper provides a t. for the views of young people** le journal offre une tribune à des jeunes pour faire connaître leurs points de vue

tributary ['trɪbjʊtrɪ] *(pl* **tributaries***)* N **1** *(ruler, state)* tributaire *m* **2** *Geog (stream)* affluent *m*

ADJ tributaire

tribute ['trɪbjuːt] N **1** *(mark of respect)* hommage *m*; **to pay t. to sb** rendre hommage à qn; **to pay a last t. to sb** rendre à qn les derniers devoirs; **we stood in silent t.** nous lui avons rendu un hommage silencieux **2** *(indication of efficiency)* témoignage *m*; **it is a t. to their organizational skills that everything went so smoothly** si tout a si bien marché, c'est grâce à leurs qualités d'organisateurs **3** *Hist & Pol* tribut *m*

▸▸ ***tribute band*** = groupe qui joue uniquement des reprises d'un groupe très connu, dont il imite l'apparence et la façon de jouer

trice [traɪs] N *(moment)* **in a t.** en un clin d'œil, en un rien de temps

tricentenary [,traɪsen'tiːnərɪ], *esp Am* **tricentennial** [,traɪsen'tenɪəl] ADJ tricentenaire; *(celebrations)* du tricentenaire

N tricentenaire *m*

triceps ['traɪseps] *(pl* **tricepses** [-sɪz]*)* N triceps *m*

triceratops [traɪ'serətɒps] N tricératops *m*

trichinosis [,trɪkɪ'nəʊsɪs] N *Med* trichinose *f*

trick [trɪk] N 1 *(deception, ruse)* ruse *f*, astuce *f*; **it's just a t. to get you to open the door** c'est une ruse *ou* une astuce pour vous amener à ouvrir la porte; **a t. of the light** un effet d'optique

2 *(joke, prank)* tour *m*, farce *f*, blague *f*; **to play a t. on sb** faire une farce *ou* jouer un tour à qn; **my eyes must have been playing tricks on me** *or* **playing me tricks** mes yeux ont dû me jouer des tours, j'ai dû avoir la berlue; **what a dirty** *or* **mean** *or* **nasty t. to play!** quel sale tour!; **"t. or treat"** "une gâterie ou une farce" *(phrase rituelle des enfants déguisés qui vont de maison en maison pour demander des bonbons le soir de Halloween)*

3 *(usu pl) (silly behaviour)* bêtise *f*; **none of your tricks!** et pas de bêtises, hein!; **he's up to his old tricks again** il fait encore des siennes

4 *(knack)* truc *m*, astuce *f*; *(in conjuring, performance)* tour *m*; **there, that should do the t.** voilà, ça fera l'affaire; **he knows a t. or two** il a plus d'un tour dans son sac, c'est un malin; **to teach a dog tricks** apprendre des tours à un chien; **she still has a few tricks up her sleeve** il lui reste plus d'un tour dans son sac; **she doesn't miss a t.** rien ne lui échappe; **the tricks of the trade** les trucs *mpl ou* les astuces *fpl* du métier

5 *(habit)* habitude *f*, manie *f*; *(particularity)* particularité *f*; *(gift)* don *m*; *(mannerism)* manie *f*, tic *m*; **he has a t. of turning up at mealtimes** il a le chic pour arriver à l'heure des repas

6 *(in card games)* pli *m*, levée *f*; **to make** *or* **to take a t.** faire un pli *ou* une levée

7 *Am very Fam (prostitute's client)* micheton *m*; **to turn a t.** faire une passe

8 *(idiom) Fam* **how's tricks?** comment va?, quoi de neuf?

ADJ 1 *(for jokes)* d'attrape, faux (fausse), de farces et attrapes; **t. soap** savon *m* d'attrape, faux savon *m* 2 *(deceptive ▸ lighting)* truqué 3 *Am (weak ▸ knee)* faible; *(▸ leg)* boiteux

VT *(deceive)* tromper, rouler; *(swindle)* escroquer; *(catch out)* attraper; **you've been tricked!** vous vous êtes fait rouler!; **to t. sb into doing sth** amener qn à faire qch en usant de ruse; **I was tricked into leaving** on a manœuvré pour me faire partir; **to t. sb out of sth** *(of opportunity etc)* frustrer qn de qch; *(of money, inheritance)* escroquer qch à qn

▸▸ ***trick cyclist*** *(in circus)* cycliste *mf* acrobate; *Br Fam (psychiatrist)* psy *mf*; ***trick photograph*** photo *f* truquée; ***trick photography*** trucages *mpl*; ***trick question*** question-piège *f*

▸ **trick out, trick up** VT SEP *Literary* parer; **they were tricked out to look like circus performers** ils étaient déguisés en artistes de cirque; **she was tricked out in all her finery** elle était parée de ses plus beaux atours, elle était sur son trente et un

trickery [ˈtrɪkərɪ] N ruse *f*, supercherie *f*; **through** *or* **by t.** par la ruse

trickiness [ˈtrɪkɪnɪs] N *(of job, problem, negotiations)* difficulté *f*; *(of situation)* délicatesse *f*

trickle [ˈtrɪkəl] VI 1 *(liquid)* couler goutte à goutte; **rainwater trickled from the gutters** un mince filet d'eau de pluie s'échappait des gouttières; **water trickled down the window pane** un filet d'eau coulait *ou* dégoulinait le long de la vitre; **tears trickled down his face** les larmes coulaient *ou* dégoulinaient sur son visage

2 *Fig* **information began to t. out from behind enemy lines** les informations commencèrent à filtrer depuis l'arrière des lignes ennemies; **news is beginning to t. through** *or* **out from the devastated area** on commence à recevoir peu à peu des nouvelles de la région sinistrée; **cars began to t. over the border** la circulation a repris progressivement à la frontière; **the ball trickled into the goal** le ballon roula tranquillement dans les buts

VT 1 *(liquid)* faire couler goutte à goutte; **he trickled a few drops of milk into the flour** il a versé quelques gouttes de lait dans la farine; **she trickled some oil out of the can** elle a versé un peu d'huile de la boîte

2 *(sand, salt)* faire glisser *ou* couler; **to t. sand through one's fingers** faire glisser *ou* couler du sable entre ses doigts

N 1 *(liquid)* filet *m*; **the flow from the spring dwindled to a t.** la source ne laissait plus échapper qu'un mince filet d'eau; **there was only a t. of water from the tap** un maigre filet d'eau coulait du robinet

2 *Fig* **a t. of applications began to come in** les candidatures commencèrent à arriver au compte-gouttes; **there was only a t. of visitors** il n'y avait que quelques rares visiteurs, les visiteurs étaient rares

▸▸ ***trickle charger*** chargeur *m* à régime lent

trickster [ˈtrɪkstə(r)] N *(swindler)* filou *m*, escroc *m*

tricky [ˈtrɪkɪ] *(compar* **trickier**, *superl* **trickiest)** ADJ 1 *(complex, delicate ▸ job, situation, negotiations)* difficile, délicat; *(▸ problem)* épineux, difficile 2 *(sly ▸ person)* rusé, fourbe

tricolour, *Am* **tricolor** [ˈtrɪkələ(r)] N drapeau *m* tricolore

tricorn, tricorne [ˈtraɪkɔːn] ADJ **t. hat** tricorne *m*
N tricorne *m*

tricuspid [traɪˈkʌspɪd] ADJ tricuspide

tricycle [ˈtraɪsɪkəl] N tricycle *m*
VI faire du tricycle

trident [ˈtraɪdənt] N trident *m*
• **Trident** N *Mil* Trident *m*
COMP *(missile, submarine)* Trident *(inv)*

tried [traɪd] *pt & pp of* **try**

triennial [traɪˈenɪəl] ADJ triennal; *Bot* trisannuel
N 1 *(anniversary)* troisième anniversaire *m* 2 *(period)* période *f* de trois ans 3 *Bot* plante *f* trisannuelle

triennially [traɪˈenɪəlɪ] ADV tous les trois ans

trier [ˈtraɪə(r)] N **to be a t.** être persévérant; **he's a real t.** il ne se laisse jamais décourager

trifle [ˈtraɪfəl] N 1 *(unimportant thing, small amount)* bagatelle *f*, broutille *f*, rien *m*; **don't waste your time on trifles** ne perdez pas votre temps à des bagatelles; **they quarrel over trifles** il se disputent pour un oui pour un non *ou* pour un rien; **I bought it for a t.** je l'ai acheté pour une bouchée de pain *ou* pour trois fois rien; **£100 is a mere t. to them** 100 livres, c'est peu de chose pour eux 2 *Culin* = dessert où alternent une couche de génoise imbibée d'alcool et de fruits en gelée et une couche de crème anglaise, le tout recouvert de chantilly

• **a trifle** ADV un peu, un tantinet; **a t. too wide/too short** un tantinet trop large/trop court; **it's a t. easier than it was** c'est un peu *ou* un rien plus facile qu'avant

▸ **trifle with** VT INSEP **to t. with sb's affections** jouer avec les sentiments de qn; **he's not a man to be trifled with** avec lui, on ne plaisante pas

trifling [ˈtraɪflɪŋ] ADJ insignifiant; **that's a t. matter** ce n'est qu'une bagatelle *ou* une broutille; *Ironic* **the t. sum of 1000 pounds** la bagatelle de 1000 livres

triforium [traɪˈfɔːrɪəm] *(pl* **triforia** [-rɪə]) N triforium *m*

trigger [ˈtrɪgə(r)] N 1 *(in gun)* gâchette *f*, détente *f*; **to pull** *or* **to squeeze the t.** appuyer sur la gâchette; **he's fast** *or* **quick on the t.** il tire vite; *Fig* il réagit vite 2 *Fig (initiator)* déclenchement *m*; **the strike was the t. for nationwide protests** la grève a donné le signal d'un mouvement de contestation dans tout le pays

VT *(mechanism, explosion, reaction)* déclencher; *(revolution, protest)* déclencher, provoquer, soulever

▸▸ ***trigger action*** déclenchement *m*; ***trigger finger*** index *m (avec lequel on appuie sur la gâchette)*

▸ **trigger off** VT SEP = **trigger** VT

trigonometric [ˌtrɪgənəˈmetrɪk], **trigonometrical** [ˌtrɪgənəˈmetrɪkəl] ADJ trigonométrique

trigonometrically [ˌtrɪgənəˈmetrɪkəlɪ] ADV trigonométriquement

trigonometry [ˌtrɪgəˈnɒmətrɪ] N trigonométrie *f*

trike [traɪk] N *Fam* tricycle *m*

trilateral [ˌtraɪˈlætərəl] ADJ trilatéral, à trois côtés

trilby [ˈtrɪlbɪ] N *Br (hat)* (chapeau *m* en) feutre *m*
▸▸ ***trilby hat*** chapeau *m* en feutre

trilingual [traɪˈlɪŋgwəl] ADJ trilingue

trill [trɪl] N *Mus & Orn* trille *m*; *Ling* consonne *f* roulée
VI triller, faire des trilles
VT 1 *(note, word)* triller; **"I'm up here," she trilled** "je suis en haut", dit-elle d'une voix flûtée 2 *Ling (consonant)* rouler

trillion [ˈtrɪljən] N *Br* trillion *m*; *Am* billion *m*; **trillions of stars** des milliards *mpl* d'étoiles

trilogy [ˈtrɪlədʒɪ] *(pl* **trilogies)** N trilogie *f*

trim [trɪm] *(compar* **trimmer**, *superl* **trimmest**, *pt & pp* **trimmed**, *cont* **trimming)** ADJ 1 *(neat ▸ appearance)* net, soigné; *(▸ person)* d'apparence soignée; *(▸ garden, flowerbed)* bien entretenu; *(▸ ship)* en bon ordre 2 *(svelte ▸ figure)* svelte, mince 3 *(fit)* en bonne santé, en forme

VT 1 *(cut ▸ roses)* tailler, couper; *(▸ hair, nails)* couper; *(▸ beard)* tailler; *(▸ candle wick)* tailler, moucher; *(▸ paper, photo)* rogner; **to t. one's nails** se couper les ongles; **I had my hair trimmed** je me suis fait raccourcir les cheveux; **t. the frayed edges off** égalisez les bords du tissu

2 *(edge)* orner, garnir; *(decorate)* décorer; **a hat trimmed with fur** un chapeau bordé *ou* orné de fourrure; **the collar was trimmed with lace** le col était bordé *ou* garni de dentelle; **we trimmed the Christmas tree with tinsel** on a décoré le sapin de Noël avec des guirlandes

3 *Aviat & Naut (plane, ship)* équilibrer; *(sails)* régler; *Fig* **to t. one's sails** réviser son jugement

4 *(cut back ▸ budget, costs)* réduire, limiter; **they were able to t. several thousand pounds from the budget** ils ont pu réduire le budget de plusieurs milliers de livres

5 *Comput (database)* supprimer les espaces blancs inutiles de

N 1 *(neat state)* **to be in good t.** être en bon état; **the garden doesn't look in very good t.** le jardin a l'air un peu à l'abandon

2 *(fit condition ▸ of person)* **to get in** *or* **into t.** se remettre en forme; **are you in (good) t. for the match?** êtes-vous en forme pour le match?; **in fighting t.** prêt pour le combat

3 *(cut)* coupe *f*, taille *f*; *(of hair etc)* coupe *f* d'entretien; **she gave the hedge a t.** elle a taillé la haie; **she gave her nails a t.** elle s'est coupé les ongles; **to have a t.** *(at hairdresser's)* se faire raccourcir les cheveux; **just a t., please** vous me les raccourcissez juste un peu, s'il vous plaît

4 *(UNCOUNT) (moulding, decoration)* moulures *fpl*; *(on car)* aménagement *m* intérieur, finitions *fpl* intérieures; *(on dress)* garniture *f*; *Am (in shop window)* composition *f* d'étalage; *Aut* **interior t.** finitions *fpl* intérieures, garnissage *m*; **seat t.** habillage *m* des sièges

5 *Naut (of sails)* orientation *f*, réglage *m*

6 *Cin* coupe *f*

▸▸ ***trim track, trim trail*** parcours-santé *m*

▸ **trim down** VT SEP 1 *(wick)* tailler, moucher 2 *(budget, costs)* réduire
VI *(spend less)* réduire ses dépenses; *(shed staff)* réduire ses effectifs

▸ **trim off** VT SEP *(edge)* enlever, couper; *(hair)* couper; *(branch)* tailler; *(jagged edges)* ébarber; **t. the fat off the meat** enlevez le gras de la viande

trimaran [ˈtraɪməræn] N trimaran *m*

trimester [traɪˈmestə(r)] N 1 *Am* trimestre *m* 2 *(gen)* trois mois *mpl*

trimmer [ˈtrɪmə(r)] N 1 *(for timber)* trancheuse *(pour le bois)*; *(in papermaking, bookbinding etc)* massicot *m*; **(hedge) t.** taille-haie *m* 2 *Pej (person)* opportuniste *mf*

trimming [ˈtrɪmɪŋ] N 1 *Sewing* parement *m*; *(lace, ribbon)* passement *m*; **trimmings** *(on garment etc)* passementerie *f*

2 *Culin* garniture *f*, accompagnement *m*; **turkey with all the trimmings** la dinde avec sa garniture habituelle; *Fig* **with all the trimmings** avec tout le tralala

3 *(accessory)* accessoire *m*

4 *Am Fam (defeat)* raclée *f*; **to get a t.** prendre une raclée, se faire battre à plate(s) couture(s)

5 *(cutting ▸ of hedges, trees)* taille *f*; *(▸ of edges of book)* ébarbage *m*, rognage *m*

6 *(reduction ▸ of expenses etc)* réduction *f*

• **trimmings** NPL *(scraps)* chutes *fpl*, rognures *fpl*

trimness [ˈtrɪmnɪs] N *(of person, garden, thing)* aspect *m* soigné; *(of figure)* sveltesse *f*

Trinidad ['trɪnɪdæd] N (l'île *f* de) la Trinité *f*

trinity ['trɪnɪtɪ] (*pl* **trinities**) N *Formal or Literary* trio *m*, groupe *m* de trois

• **Trinity** N *Rel* **1** *(union)* **the T.** la Trinité **2** *(feast)* (la fête de) la Trinité

▸▸ ***Trinity Sunday*** (la fête de) la Trinité; *Univ* ***Trinity term*** troisième trimestre *m* (universitaire) *(à Oxford, Cambridge et au Trinity College de Dublin)*

trinket ['trɪŋkɪt] N *(bauble)* bibelot *m*, babiole *f*; *(jewel)* colifichet *m*; *(on bracelet)* breloque *f*

trinomial [traɪ'nəʊmɪəl] N trinôme *m*
ADJ à trois termes

trio ['triːəʊ] (*pl* **trios**) N **1** *Mus* trio *m (morceau)* **2** *(group)* trio *m*, groupe *m* de trois; *Mus* trio *m (joueurs)*

trip [trɪp] (*pt & pp* **tripped**, *cont* **tripping**) N **1** *(journey)* voyage *m*; **to go on a t.** faire un voyage, partir en voyage; **he's away on a business t.** il est parti en voyage d'affaires; **we went on a long bus t.** on a fait un long voyage en bus; **I had to make three trips into town** j'ai dû aller trois fois en ville *ou* faire trois voyages en ville; **to make a t. to the dentist's** aller chez le dentiste

2 *(excursion)* promenade *f*, excursion *f*; *(outing)* promenade *f*, sortie *f*; **we had a lovely t. to Devon** nous avons fait une très belle promenade dans le Devon; **she took the children on a t. to the seaside** elle a emmené les enfants en promenade au bord de la mer; **school t.** voyage *m* scolaire

3 *(stumble)* faux pas *m*; *Sport (foul)* croc-en-jambe *m*, croche-pied *m*

4 *very Fam Drugs slang* trip *m*; **an LSD t.** un trip au LSD; **to have a bad t.** faire un mauvais trip

5 *Fig (experience)* **he seems to be on some kind of nostalgia t.** il semble être en pleine crise de nostalgie; **to be on a guilt t.** culpabiliser; **to be on a power t.** être en plein trip mégalo; **to be on an ego t.** se faire mousser

VT **1** *(person ▸ make stumble)* faire trébucher; *(▸ make fall)* faire tomber; *(intentionally)* faire un croche-pied *ou* un croc-en-jambe à **2** *(switch, alarm)* déclencher **3** *(idiom) Hum* **to t. the light fantastic** danser

VI **1** *(stumble)* trébucher; **she tripped on** *or* **over the wire** elle s'est pris le pied dans le fil; **I tripped on a pile of books** j'ai buté contre *ou* trébuché sur une pile de livres **2** *(step lightly)* **to t. in/out** entrer/sortir d'un pas léger; **she tripped down the lane** elle descendit le chemin d'un pas léger; *Fig* **her name doesn't exactly t. off the tongue** son nom n'est pas très facile à prononcer **3** *very Fam Drugs slang* faire un trip, triper; **to t. on acid** faire un trip à l'acide

▸▸ *Aut* ***trip recorder*** compteur *m* journalier, totalisateur *m* partiel; ***trip switch*** interrupteur *m*

▸ **trip over** VI trébucher, faire un faux pas
VT INSEP buter sur *ou* contre, trébucher sur *ou* contre; *Fig* **you can't go anywhere here without tripping over celebrities** par ici on ne peut pas faire un pas sans se heurter à une célébrité

▸ **trip up** VT SEP **1** *(cause to fall)* faire trébucher; *(deliberately)* faire un croche-pied à **2** *(trap)* désarçonner
VI **1** *(fall)* trébucher; **I tripped up on a stone** j'ai trébuché *ou* buté contre une pierre **2** *(make a mistake)* gaffer, faire une gaffe; **I tripped up badly there** j'ai fait une grosse gaffe, là

tripartite [,traɪ'pɑːtaɪt] ADJ *(division, agreement)* tripartite, triparti

tripe [traɪp] N *(UNCOUNT)* **1** *Culin* tripes *fpl* **2** *Fam (nonsense)* foutaises *fpl*, conneries *fpl*; **don't talk t.!** dis pas n'importe quoi!, raconte pas de conneries!; **what a load of t.!** n'importe quoi!; **the film is absolute t.!** il vaut pas un clou, ce film!

triphammer ['trɪp,hæmə(r)] N marteau *m* à bascule

triphase ['traɪfeɪz] ADJ *Elec* triphasé

triphthong ['trɪfθɒŋ] N triphtongue *f*

triplane ['traɪpleɪn] N triplan *m*

triple ['trɪpəl] ADJ **1** *(in three parts)* triple; **the organization serves a t. purpose** le but de l'organisation est triple; **in t. time** à trois temps **2** *(treble)* triple; **a t. brandy** un triple cognac; **a t. murder** un triple meurtre; **t. the usual amount** trois fois la dose habituelle

N triple *m*
VT tripler
VI tripler

▸▸ *Hist* ***the Triple Alliance*** *(1668)* la Triple Alliance; *(1882–1914)* la Triple-Alliance, la Triplice; ***triple glazing*** triple vitrage *m*; ***triple jump*** triple saut *m*; *Phys* ***triple point*** point *m* triple

triplet ['trɪplɪt] N **1** *(child)* triplé(e) *m,f*; **triplets** des triplé(e)s *mpl, fpl* **2** *Mus* triolet *m*; *Literature* tercet *m*

triplex ['trɪpleks] ADJ *(triple)* triple
N *Am (apartment)* triplex *m*

triplicate ADJ ['trɪplɪkət] en trois exemplaires, en triple exemplaire
N ['trɪplɪkət] **1** *(document)* **in t.** en trois exemplaires, en triple exemplaire **2** *(third copy)* triplicata *m*
VT ['trɪplɪkeɪt] multiplier par trois, tripler

triply ['trɪplɪ] ADV triplement

tripod ['traɪpɒd] N trépied *m*

Tripoli ['trɪpəlɪ] N Tripoli

tripos ['traɪpɒs] N = examen de licence ("BA") à l'université de Cambridge

tripper ['trɪpə(r)] N *Br (on day trip)* excursionniste *mf*; *(on holiday)* vacancier(ère) *m,f*

trippy ['trɪpɪ] ADJ *Fam* psychédélique

triptych ['trɪptɪk] N triptyque *m*

trireme ['traɪriːm] N trirème *f*, trière *f*

trisect [traɪ'sekt] VT diviser en trois parties égales

trisomy ['traɪsəʊmɪ] N *Med* trisomie *f*
▸▸ ***trisomy 21*** trisomie *f* 21

trisyllabic [,traɪsɪ'læbɪk] ADJ trisyllabique, trisyllabe

trisyllable [,traɪ'sɪləbəl] N trisyllabe *m*

trite [traɪt] ADJ *(theme, picture)* banal; **t. remarks** banalités *fpl*, lieux *mpl* communs; **I know it sounds a bit t., but I do care** je sais que ça peut paraître banal de dire ça, mais vraiment je me sens concernée

tritely ['traɪtlɪ] ADV banalement

triteness ['traɪtnɪs] N banalité *f*

tritium ['trɪtɪəm] N *Chem* tritium *m*

triton N **1** ['traɪtən] *Zool* triton *m* **2** ['traɪtɒn] *Phys* triton *m*

• **Triton** ['traɪtən] PR N *Myth* Triton

triturate ['trɪtjʊreɪt] VT triturer

trituration [,trɪtjʊ'reɪʃən] N trituration *f*

triumph ['traɪəmf] N **1** *(jubilation)* (sentiment *m* de) triomphe *m*; **to return in t.** rentrer triomphalement; **a look of t.** un air triomphant **2** *(victory)* victoire *f*, triomphe *m*; *(success)* triomphe *m*, (grande) réussite *f*; **the musical was an absolute t.** la comédie musicale a été *ou* a fait un véritable triomphe; **the t. of reason over passion** le triomphe de la raison sur la passion; **the agreement will be seen as a personal t. for the President** cet accord sera considéré comme un triomphe personnel pour le président **3** *(in ancient Rome)* triomphe *m*

VI triompher; **to t. over difficulties/a disability** triompher des difficultés/d'une infirmité, vaincre les difficultés/une infirmité

triumphal [traɪ'ʌmfəl] ADJ triomphal
▸▸ *Archit* ***triumphal arch*** arc *m* de triomphe; ***triumphal procession*** triomphe *m*

triumphant [traɪ'ʌmfənt] ADJ *(team)* victorieux, triomphant; *(return)* triomphal; *(cheer, smile)* de triomphe, triomphant; *(success)* triomphal

triumphantly [traɪ'ʌmfəntlɪ] ADV *(march)* en triomphe, triomphalement; *(cheer, smile)* triomphalement; *(announce)* d'un ton triomphant, triomphalement; *(look)* d'un air triomphant, triomphalement

triumvirate [traɪ'ʌmvɪrət] N triumvirat *m*

triune ['traɪjuːn] ADJ *Rel* trin

trivet ['trɪvɪt] N *(when cooking)* trépied *m*, chevrette *f*; *(for table)* dessous-de-plat *m inv*

trivia ['trɪvɪə] NPL *(trifles)* bagatelles *fpl*, futilités *fpl*; *(details)* détails *mpl*; **the t. of everyday life** les petites choses de la vie quotidienne; **he has an amazing memory for t.** il a une mémoire remarquable pour les choses sans importance

trivial ['trɪvɪəl] ADJ **1** *(insignificant ▸ sum, reason)* insignifiant, dérisoire; **it's only a t. offence** ce n'est qu'une peccadille, c'est sans gravité **2** *(pointless ▸ discussion, question)* sans intérêt, insignifiant **3** *(banal ▸ story, conversation)* banal

> Note that the French word **trivial** is a false friend. It means **vulgar, coarse.**

triviality [,trɪvɪ'ælətɪ] (*pl* **trivialities**) N **1** *(of sum)* insignifiance *f*, caractère *m* insignifiant; *(of discussion)* insignifiance *f*, caractère *m* oiseux; *(of film)* banalité *f* **2** *(trifle)* futilité *f*, bagatelle *f*; **don't waste your time on trivialities** ne perdez pas votre temps à des bagatelles

trivialization, -isation [,trɪvɪəlaɪ'zeɪʃən] N banalisation *f*

trivialize, -ise ['trɪvɪəlaɪz] VT *(make insignificant)* banaliser, dévaloriser; **her work's very important to her, don't t. it** son travail est très important pour elle, ne le dévalorisez pas; **the tabloids t. even the most important events** la presse populaire banalise même les événements les plus importants

trochaic [trəʊ'keɪɪk] ADJ trochaïque

trochee ['trəʊkiː] N trochée *m*

trod [trɒd] *pt & pp of* **tread**

trodden ['trɒdən] *pp of* **tread**

trog [trɒg] (*pt & pp* **trogged**, *cont* **trogging**) VI *Br Fam* se traîner

trogloditic [,trɒglə'dɪtɪk] ADJ troglodytique

troglodyte ['trɒglədaɪt] N troglodyte *m*

troika ['trɔɪkə] N troïka *f*

troilism ['trɔɪlɪzəm] N triolisme *m*

Trojan ['trəʊdʒən] ADJ troyen
N Troyen(enne) *m,f*; **to work like a T.** travailler comme un forçat

▸▸ *Hist & Fig* ***Trojan Horse*** cheval *m* de Troie; ***Trojan War*** guerre *f* de Troie

troll [trəʊl] N **1** *(goblin)* troll *m* **2** *Fam Comput (message, person)* troll *m* **3** *Br Fam Pej (ugly person)* mocheté *f*

VI **1** *Fishing* pêcher à la traîne; **to t. for mackerel/pike** pêcher le maquereau/le brochet à la traîne **2** *Br Fam (stroll)* se balader **3** *Fam Comput* troller

trolley ['trɒlɪ] N **1** *(handcart)* chariot *m*; *(two-wheeled)* diable *m*; *(for child)* poussette *f*; *Br (in supermarket)* chariot *m*, caddie® *m*; *(in restaurant)* chariot *m*; **(dinner** *or* **tea) t.** table *f* roulante; **drinks t.** chariot *m* à boissons; *Br Fam* **to be off one's t.** être cinglé

2 *(on rails ▸ in mine)* wagonnet *m*, benne *f*
3 *Elec (for tram)* trolley *m*
4 *Am (tram)* tramway *m*, tram *m*

▸▸ *Am* ***trolley car*** tramway *m*, tram *m*

trolleybus ['trɒlɪbʌs] N trolleybus *m*, trolley *m*

trolleyed, trollied ['trɒlɪd] ADJ *Br Fam* bourré, pété, beurré

trolling ['trəʊlɪŋ] N *Fishing* pêche *f* à la traîne

trollop ['trɒləp] N *Old-fashioned Pej (prostitute)* catin *f*; *(slut)* souillon *f*

trombone [trɒm'bəʊn] N trombone *m (instrument)*

trombonist [trɒm'bəʊnɪst] N tromboniste *mf*, trombone *m (musicien)*

troop [truːp] N *(band ▸ of schoolchildren)* bande *f*, groupe *m*; *(▸ of scouts)* troupe *f*; *(▸ of animals)* troupe *f*; *Mil (of cavalry, artillery)* escadron *m*

VI **to t. by** *or* **past** passer en troupe; **to t. in/out** entrer/sortir en troupe; **the children trooped back to school** les enfants sont repartis à l'école en bande

VT *Br Mil* **to t. the colour** faire le salut au drapeau

• **troops** NPL *(gen) & Mil* troupes *fpl*

▸▸ ***troop carrier*** *(ship)* transport *m* de troupes; *(plane)* avion *m* de transport militaire; *(vehicle)* véhicule *m* de transport de troupes; ***troop train*** train *m* militaire; *Mil* ***troop transport*** transport *m* de troupes

trooper ['truːpə(r)] N **1** *(soldier)* soldat *m* de cavalerie; *Fam Fig* **he's a real t.** il répond toujours présent à l'appel, on peut toujours compter sur lui **2** *Am & Austr (mounted policeman)* membre *m* de la police montée; **(state) t.** ≃ gendarme *m* **3** *Br Mil (ship)* transport *m* de troupes

trooping ['truːpɪŋ] N *Br* t. **(of) the colour** salut *m* au drapeau; **T. the Colour** = défilé de régiments ayant lieu chaque année le jour officiel de l'anniversaire de la reine d'Angleterre

troopship ['truːpʃɪp] N navire *m* de transport

trophic ['trɒfɪk] ADJ trophique

trophy ['trəʊfɪ] (*pl* **trophies**) N trophée *m*
►► *Hum Pej* ***trophy wife*** = épouse considérée comme un signe extérieur de réussite sociale

tropic ['trɒpɪk] N tropique *m*
• **tropics** NPL **the tropics** les tropiques *mpl*; **in the tropics** sous les tropiques
►► ***the Tropic of Cancer*** le tropique du Cancer; ***the Tropic of Capricorn*** le tropique du Capricorne

tropical ['trɒpɪkəl] ADJ *(region)* des tropiques, tropical; *(weather, forest, medicine)* tropical
►► ***tropical rainforest*** forêt *f* tropicale humide

tropism ['trəʊpɪzəm] N tropisme *m*

troposphere ['trɒpəsfɪə(r)] N troposphère *f*

Trot [trɒt] N *Fam Pej Pol* (*abbr* **Trotskyist**) trotskiste*mf*

trot [trɒt] (*pt & pp* **trotted**, *cont* **trotting**) N **1** *(of horse)* trot *m*; **to set off at a t.** partir au trot; **to go at a t.** aller au trot, trotter
2 *(of person)* **he went off at a t.** il est parti au pas de course
3 *(ride)* promenade *f* à cheval; *Fam (run)* petite course*f*; **to go for a t.** *(on horseback)* aller faire une promenade à cheval; *Fam (on foot)* aller faire une balade; *Br Fam* **on the t.** *(busy)* affairé; *(in succession)* d'affilée, de suite; **they kept me on the t. all afternoon** ils m'ont fait courir tout l'après-midi; **he conducted ten interviews on the t.** il a fait dix interviews d'affilée *ou* de suite
4 *Am Fam (crib)* antisèche *f*
VI **1** *(horse, rider)* trotter; **he trotted up to us** il est venu vers nous au trot **2** *(on foot)* **to t. in/out/past** entrer/sortir/passer en courant; **can you t. down to the shops for me?** peux-tu faire un saut pour moi jusqu'aux magasins?
VT *(horse)* faire trotter
• **trots** NPL *Br Fam* courante *f*; **to have the trots** avoir la courante
▸**trot out** VT SEP *Br Fam (excuse, information)* débiter; *(story, list)* débiter, réciter

troth [trəʊθ] N *Arch* **by my t.!** ma foi!, pardieu!

Trotskyism ['trɒtskɪɪzəm] N trotskisme *m*

Trotskyite ['trɒtskɪaɪt] ADJ trotskiste
N trotskiste *mf*

trotter ['trɒtə(r)] N **1** *(horse)* trotteur(euse) *m,f* **2** *Culin* **pig's trotters** pieds *mpl* de porc

troubadour ['truːbədɔː(r)] N troubadour *m*

TROUBLE ['trʌbəl]

N	
• ennui(s) **1, 2, 5, 6, 8**	• problème(s) **1, 4–6, 8**
• difficultés **2**	• peine **3**
• mal **2, 3**	• troubles **7**
• défaut **4**	
VT	
• inquiéter **1**	• troubler **1, 5**
• gêner **2**	• déranger **3, 4**
VI	
• se déranger **1**	• se faire du souci **2**

N **1** *(UNCOUNT) (conflict)* ennuis *mpl*, problèmes *mpl*; *(discord)* discorde *f*; **to be in t.** avoir des ennuis; **you're really in t. now!** tu es dans de beaux draps *ou* te voilà bien maintenant!; **I've never been in t. with the police** je n'ai jamais eu d'ennuis *ou* d'histoires avec la police; **to get into t.** s'attirer des ennuis, se faire attraper; **to get into t. with the police** avoir affaire à la police; **her sharp tongue often gets her into t.** sa causticité lui attire souvent des ennuis; **he got into t. for stealing apples** il s'est fait attraper pour avoir volé des pommes; **he got his friends into t.** il a causé des ennuis à ses amis; **to get sb out of t.** tirer qn d'affaire; **to keep out of t.** éviter les ennuis; **to keep sb out of t.** éviter des ennuis à qn; **he's just looking** *or* **asking for t.** il cherche les ennuis; **it's asking for t. driving without insurance** on cherche les histoires quand on conduit sans assurance; **she caused a lot of t. between them** elle a semé la discorde entre eux; **this means t.** ça va mal se passer; **there'll be t. if he finds out** je vais/tu vas/on va/*etc* avoir des ennuis s'il s'en rend compte
2 *(UNCOUNT) (difficulties, problems)* difficultés *fpl*, ennuis *mpl*, mal *m*; **to make** *or* **to create t. for sb** causer des ennuis à qn; **to make t. for oneself** se créer des ennuis; **he's given his parents a lot of t.** *(hard time)* il a donné du fil à retordre à ses parents; *(worry)* il a donné beaucoup de soucis à ses parents; **this machine's been** *or* **given nothing but t.** cette machine ne m'a/ne nous a apporté que des problèmes; **my eyes have been giving me some t.** mes yeux me donnent quelques soucis; **what's the t.?** qu'est-ce qu'il y a?, quel est le problème?; **you'll have t. with him** il va vous causer des difficultés *ou* des ennuis; **to have t. (in) doing sth** avoir du mal *ou* des difficultés à faire qch; **to be in/to get into t.** *(climber, swimmer, business)* être/se trouver en difficulté; *Br Euph* **to get a girl into t.** mettre une fille dans une position intéressante; *Fam* **he's got woman/she's got man t.** ça ne va pas très bien pour lui/elle côté cœur
3 *(inconvenience, bother)* mal *m*, peine *f*; **to go** *or* **to put oneself to the t. to do** *or* **of doing sth** prendre *ou* se donner la peine de faire qch; **to go** *or* **to put oneself to a lot of t. to do** *or* **doing sth** se donner beaucoup de mal *ou* de peine pour faire qch; **you shouldn't have gone to all this t.** il ne fallait pas vous donner tout ce mal *ou* tant de peine; **I went to a lot of t. for nothing** je me suis donné beaucoup de mal pour rien; **I hope we're not putting you to too much t.** j'espère que nous ne vous donnons pas trop de mal; **he didn't even take the t. to read the instructions** il ne s'est même pas donné *ou* il n'a même pas pris la peine de lire les instructions; **I don't want to be any t.** je ne veux pas vous déranger; **if it's no t.** si ça ne vous dérange pas; **it's no t. (at all)** cela ne me dérange pas (du tout); **nothing is too much t. for her** elle se donne vraiment beaucoup de mal; **it's not worth the t., it's more t. than it's worth** cela n'en vaut pas la peine, le jeu n'en vaut pas la chandelle
4 *(drawback)* problème *m*, défaut *m*; **the only t. with your solution is that it's expensive** ta solution n'a qu'un défaut, c'est qu'elle revient cher; **the t. is that no one understands him** l'ennui *ou* le problème, c'est que personne ne le comprend; **that's the t.** c'est ça le problème
5 *(UNCOUNT) (mechanical failure)* ennuis *mpl*, problèmes *mpl*; **I'm having a bit of engine t.** j'ai des problèmes de moteur; **they've had t. with the new dishwasher, the new dishwasher has given them t.** ils ont eu des problèmes avec leur nouveau lave-vaisselle; **have you found out what the t. is?** avez-vous trouvé d'où vient la panne?; **what seems to be the t.?** qu'est-ce qui ne va pas?
6 *(worry, woe)* ennui *m*, souci *m*, problème *m*; **money troubles** ennuis *mpl* d'argent; **at last your troubles are over** enfin vos soucis sont terminés; **her troubles are not at an end yet** elle n'est pas encore au bout de ses peines; *Fam* **here comes t.!** tiens, voilà les ennuis qui arrivent!
7 *(UNCOUNT) (friction)* troubles *mpl*, conflits *mpl*; *(disorder, disturbance)* troubles *mpl*, désordres *mpl*; **the t. began when the police arrived** l'agitation a commencé quand la police est arrivée; **industrial** *or* **labour troubles** conflits *mpl* sociaux; **there will be t.** il va y avoir du grabuge; **there was t. on the pitch/on the terraces** il y a eu des histoires sur le terrain/dans les gradins
8 *(UNCOUNT) Med* ennuis *mpl*, problèmes *mpl*; **I have kidney/back t.** j'ai des ennuis rénaux/des problèmes de dos; **stomach t.** troubles *mpl* digestifs; **to have heart t.** être malade du cœur
VT **1** *(worry)* inquiéter; *(upset)* troubler; **he didn't want to t. her with bad news** il ne voulait pas l'inquiéter en lui annonçant de mauvaises nouvelles; **don't let it t. you!** que cela ne vous inquiète pas!, ne vous tourmentez pas à ce sujet!; **nothing seems to t. him** il ne s'en fait jamais, il ne se fait jamais de souci; **her conscience was troubling her** elle avait des problèmes de conscience
2 *(cause pain to)* gêner; **his back is troubling him** il a des problèmes de dos; **how long has this cough been troubling you?** depuis combien de temps souffrez-vous de cette toux?; **she's often troubled by nightmares** elle est sujette aux cauchemars
3 *(bother, disturb)* déranger; **I won't t. you with the details just now** je vous ferai grâce des *ou* épargnerai les détails pour l'instant; **he didn't even t. himself to phone** il ne s'est même pas donné la peine de téléphoner; **don't t. yourse**[lf] ne vous dérangez pas!; *Ironic* ne vous dérang[ez] surtout pas!
4 *(in polite phrases)* déranger; **can I t. you to ope**[n] **the window?** est-ce que je peux vous demand[er] d'ouvrir la fenêtre?; **I'm sorry to t. you, but coul**[d I] **have the newspaper?** excusez-moi de vous d[é]ranger, mais puis-je avoir le journal?; **may I** [t.] **you for a light/the salt?** puis-je vous demand[er] du feu/le sel?
5 *Literary (disturb* ▸ *water)* troubler
VI **1** *(bother)* se déranger; **don't t. to do the was**[h]**ing-up now** ne faites pas la vaisselle maint[e]nant, ce n'est pas la peine
2 *(worry)* se faire du souci, s'en faire; **don't** [t.] **about it** ne vous faites pas de souci *ou* ne vo[us] en faites pas (pour ça)
• **Troubles** NPL **the Troubles** = le conflit po[li]tique en Irlande du Nord
►► ***trouble spot*** point *m* chaud *ou* de conflit

troubled ['trʌbəld] ADJ **1** *(worried* ▸ *mind, loo*[k]*)* inquiet(ète), préoccupé; **he seems t. about som**[e]**thing** il semble préoccupé par quelque chos[e]; **he's got a t. conscience** il n'a pas la conscien[ce] tranquille **2** *(disturbed* ▸ *sleep, night, breathin*[g]*)* agité; *(*▸ *water)* troublé; *(*▸ *person)* tourment[é]; *(turbulent* ▸ *marriage, life)* agité, mouvement[é]; **we live in t. times** nous vivons une époque tro[u]blée *ou* agitée
►► *Fig* ***troubled waters*** eaux *fpl* troubles; **the waters of Middle Eastern politics** les troubles *m*[pl] politiques qui agitent le Moyen-Orien[t]; *(stronger)* la tourmente politique au Moye[n-]Orient

trouble-free ADJ *(journey, equipment)* sa[ns] problème, sans histoires; *(period of time, vis*[it]*)* sans histoires; *(life)* sans soucis, sans histoire[s]; *(industry)* sans grèves

troublemaker ['trʌbəl,meɪkə(r)] N provocate[ur] (trice) *m,f*

troubleshooter ['trʌbəl,ʃuːtə(r)] N **1** *(in crisi*[s]*)* expert *m (appelé en cas de crise)*; *Ind & Pol (in co*[n]*flict)* médiateur(trice) *m,f* **2** *(mechanic)* dépa[n]neur(euse) *m,f*

troubleshooting ['trʌbəl,ʃuːtɪŋ] N **1** *(in crisi*[s]*)* médiation *f* **2** *(gen) & Comput (in mechanism)* d[é]pannage *m*

troublesome ['trʌbəlsəm] ADJ **1** *(annoying* ▸ *person, cough)* gênant, pénible; **he was always t. child** il a toujours été un enfant difficile **2** *(diff*[i]*cult* ▸ *situation)* difficile; *(*▸ *request)* gênant, em[]barrassant; *(*▸ *job)* difficile, pénible

troubling ['trʌbəlɪŋ] ADJ *(news etc)* inquiétant

troublous ['trʌbləs] ADJ *Literary* agité

trough [trɒf] N **1** *(for animals* ▸ *drinking)* abre[u]voir *m*; *(*▸ *eating)* auge *f*
2 *(depression* ▸ *in land)* dépression *f*; *(*▸ *betwee*[n] *waves)* creux *m*
3 *Met* dépression *f*, zone *f* dépressionnaire; **a** [t.] **of low pressure** une zone de basse pression
4 *(on graph, in cycle)* creux *m*; *Fin* creux *m*, d[é]pression *f*
5 *(gutter)* gouttière *f*; *(channel)* chenal *m*

trounce [traʊns] VT *(defeat)* écraser, battre plate(s) couture(s); **to get trounced** être battu plates coutures

trouncing ['traʊnsɪŋ] N **we gave Rovers a real** [t.] nous avons écrasé les Rovers, nous avons batt[u] les Rovers à plate(s) couture(s)

troupe [truːp] N *Theat* troupe *f*

trouper ['truːpə(r)] N acteur(trice) *m,f (de thé*[â]*tre)*; **he's an old t.** c'est un vieux de la vieille

trousered ['traʊzəd] ADJ *Br Fam (very drun*[k]*)* rond comme une queue de pelle, plein comm[e] une barrique

trousers ['traʊzəz] NPL *Br* pantalon *m*; **(a pair o**[f]**) t.** un pantalon; **I need some new t.** il me faut u[n] pantalon neuf; *Fig* **she wears the t.** c'est elle qu[i] porte la culotte; *Fam* **to be caught with one's** [t.] **down** être pris au dépourvu
►► *Br* ***trouser press*** presse *f* à pantalons; *Br* ***tro***[u]***ser suit*** tailleur-pantalon *m*

trousseau ['truːsəʊ] (*pl* **trousseaus** *or* **trousseau**[x] [-əʊz]) N trousseau *m (de jeune mariée)*

trout [traʊt] (*pl* **inv** *or* **trouts**) N truite *f*; *Fa*[m] *(woman)* **(old) t.** vieille bique *f*

▸ *trout farm* élevage *m* de truites; *trout fishing* pêche à la truite; *Fam Hum trout pout* lèvres *fpl* collagène

ove [trəʊv] N *see* **treasure**

owel ['traʊəl] N *(for garden)* déplantoir *m*; *(for ment, plaster)* truelle *f*; *Fam Fig* **to lay it on with a** en faire trop

oy [trɔɪ] N Troie

oy [trɔɪ] N **t. (weight)** troy *m*, troy-weight *m*

uancy ['tru:ənsɪ] N absentéisme *m* (scolaire); **ey were punished for t.** ils ont été punis pour oir manqué l'école

uant ['tru:ənt] N élève *mf* absentéiste; **to play t.** ire l'école buissonnière manquer les cours

Note that the French word **truand** is a false friend. It means **crook**.

uce [tru:s] N trêve *f*; **to call a t.** conclure *ou* établir une trêve; *Fig* faire la paix

uck [trʌk] N **1** *esp Am (lorry)* camion *m*; **the eep were taken away by t.** les moutons ont été nmenés *ou* transportés en camion

Br (open lorry) camion *m* à plate-forme; *(van)* amionnette *f*

Br Rail wagon *m* ouvert, truck *m*; **cattle t.** fourgon *m* à bestiaux

(UNCOUNT) (dealings) **to have no t. with sb/sth** fuser d'avoir quoi que ce soit à voir avec qn/ch; **they refused to have any t. with him** ils ont fusé d'avoir affaire à lui

(UNCOUNT) Am (produce) produits *mpl* maîchers

(barter) troc *m*, échange *m*

T *Am (goods, animals)* camionner, transporter ar *ou* en camion

I *Am* aller *ou* rouler en camion; **keep on truckg!** bon courage!

▸ *esp Am* ***truck driver*** camionneur *m*, (chauffeur *m*) routier *m*; *Am* ***truck farm*** jardin *m* maraîcher; *Am* ***truck farmer*** maraîcher(ère) *m,f*; *Am* ***truck farming*** culture *f* maraîchère; *Am* ***truck garden*** jardin *m* maraîcher; *Am* ***truck gardener*** maraîcher(ère) *m,f*; *Am* ***truck gardening*** maraîchage *m*; *Am* ***truck stop*** (relais *m*) routier *m*

ucking ['trʌkɪŋ] N *Am* camionnage *m*, transport *m* par camion

▸ *Am* ***trucking company*** entreprise *f* de transports routiers

uckle ['trʌkəl] N *(of cheese)* ≃ meule *f*

I *Literary* **to t. to sb** s'abaisser *ou* s'humilier devant qn

▸ ***truckle bed*** lit *m* gigogne

uculence ['trʌkjʊləns], **truculency** ['trʌkjʊlənsɪ] N agressivité *f*

uculent ['trʌkjʊlənt] ADJ belliqueux, agressif

Note that the French word **truculent** is a false friend. It means **colourful** or **vivid**.

uculently ['trʌkjʊləntlɪ] ADV agressivement

udge [trʌdʒ] VI marcher péniblement *ou* en aînant les pieds; **we trudged wearily along the ath** nous avons marché *ou* avancé péniblement le long du chemin; **the prisoners trudged ast** les prisonniers passaient en traînant les eds; **she trudged home through the snow** elle entra chez elle en marchant péniblement dans neige; **we trudged from shop to shop** nous ous sommes traînés de magasin en magasin

VT **to t. the streets** se traîner de rue en rue

N marche *f* pénible; **they began the long t. up the ill** ils ont entrepris la longue ascension de la olline

ue [tru:] ADJ **1** *(factual ▸ statement, story)* vrai, éridique; *(▸ account, description)* exact, véridique; **it's a t. story** c'est une histoire vraie; **the adventures of a Second World War spy** les aventures véridiques d'un espion pendant la euxième Guerre mondiale; **is it t. that they ere lovers?** c'est vrai qu'ils étaient amants?; **is t. about Michael?** c'est vrai ce qu'on dit à propos de Michael?; **it is not t. that he has disappeared** ce n'est pas vrai qu'il a disparu; **I can't elieve it's t.** je n'arrive pas à le croire; **can it be ?** est-ce possible?; **he's a complete idiot – (that's) , but he's very lovable** il est complètement idiot – ça c'est vrai, mais il est très sympathique; **the same is** *or* **holds t. for many people** il en va de même pour *ou* c'est vrai pour beaucoup de gens; **to come t.** *(dream)* se réaliser; *(prophecy)* se réaliser, se vérifier; **too t.!** c'est vrai ce que vous dites!, ah oui alors!; *Fam* **he's so stingy it's not t.!** ce n'est pas possible d'être aussi radin!

2 *(precise, exact ▸ measurement)* exact, juste; *Mus (▸ note, voice)* juste; *(▸ copy)* conforme; *Constr (wall)* vertical, d'aplomb; *(beam)* droit; **he's not a genius in the t. sense of the word** ce n'est pas un génie au vrai sens du terme; *also Fig* **his aim is t.** il vise juste

3 *(genuine ▸ friendship, feelings)* vrai, véritable, authentique; *(▸ friend, love)* vrai, véritable; *(real, actual ▸ nature, motive)* réel, véritable; **she was a t. democrat** c'était une démocrate dans l'âme; **he's a t. Irishman** *(conforms to stereotype)* il est bien irlandais; *(by birth)* c'est un Irlandais, un vrai; **a story of t. love** l'histoire d'un grand amour; **to find t. love** trouver le grand amour; **to get a t. idea of the situation** se faire une idée juste de la situation; **it's not a t. amphibian** ce n'est pas vraiment un amphibien; **spoken like a t. soldier!** voilà qui est bien dit!

4 *(faithful ▸ lover)* fidèle; *(▸ portrait)* fidèle, exact; **a t. likeness** une ressemblance parfaite; **to be t. to sb** être fidèle à *ou* loyal envers qn; **to be t. to oneself** être fidèle à soi-même; **to be t. to one's ideals/principles** être fidèle à ses idéaux/principes; **she was t. to her word** elle a tenu parole; **t. to life** *(story, situation)* qui correspond bien à la réalité; **the painting is very t. to life** le tableau est très ressemblant; **to be** *or* **to run t. to type** être typique; **she was an accountant, and t. to type she...** elle était comptable, et bien entendu elle...; **t. to form, he arrived half an hour late** fidèle à son habitude *ou* comme à son habitude, il est arrivé avec une demi-heure de retard

ADV **1** *(aim, shoot, sing)* juste; **it doesn't ring t.** cela sonne faux **2** *Literary (truly)* **tell me t.** dites-moi la vérité; **love me t.** aime-moi fidèlement

VT aligner, ajuster

• **out of true** ADJ *Br (wall)* hors d'aplomb; *(beam)* tordu; *(wheel)* voilé; *(axle)* faussé; *(painting)* de travers

▸▸ ***true north*** vrai nord *m*, nord *m* géographique

true-blue ADJ **1** *(loyal)* loyal **2** *esp Br Pol* conservateur, tory; **t. Tories** des fidèles *mpl* du parti conservateur

trueborn ['tru:ˌbɔ:n] ADJ véritable, authentique; **a t. Englishman** un vrai Anglais d'Angleterre

true-false ADJ

▸▸ ***true-false test*** = questionnaire auquel on répond par "vrai" ou "faux"

truffle ['trʌfəl] N truffe *f*; **chocolate truffles** truffes *fpl* au chocolat

trug [trʌg] N *Br* corbeille *f* de jardinier

truism ['tru:ɪzəm] N truisme *m*, lapalissade *f*; **it is a t. that...** c'est un lieu commun de dire que... + *indicative*

truly ['tru:lɪ] ADV **1** *Formal (really)* vraiment, réellement; **I'm t. sorry for what I've done** je suis vraiment navré de ce que j'ai fait; **they t. believe they'll succeed** ils croient réellement qu'ils vont réussir; **t. it was the last thing on my mind** je vous assure que j'étais loin de penser à ça; **tell me t. now, do you want the job?** maintenant, dites-moi sincèrement, voulez-vous ce travail? **2** *(as intensifier)* vraiment, absolument; **it was a t. awful film** c'était absolument épouvantable comme film; **the meal was t. delicious** le repas était vraiment délicieux **3** *esp Am (in letter-writing) Am* **yours t., Kathryn Schmidt** je vous prie d'agréer, Monsieur *ou* Madame, l'expression de mes sentiments respectueux, Kathryn Schmidt; *Fam Hum* **yours t.** *(myself)* mézigue

trump [trʌmp] N **1** *(in cards)* atout *m*; *Fig* atout *m*, carte *f* maîtresse; **to play a t.** jouer (un) atout; **what's trumps?** quel est l'atout?; **diamonds are trumps** (c'est) atout carreau; **the six of trumps** le six d'atout; **no t.** sans-atout *m inv*; **to hold all the trumps** avoir tous les atouts dans son jeu *ou* en main; *Br* **to turn up** *or* **to come up trumps** sauver la situation **2** *Bible (trumpet)* trompette *f*; **the last t.** la trompette du Jugement dernier **3** *Br Fam (gas)* pet *m*, prout *m*

VT **1** *(card)* couper, jouer atout sur; *(trick)* remporter avec un atout **2** *(outdo ▸ remark, action)* renchérir sur

VI *Br Fam (break wind)* péter, lâcher *ou* larguer une caisse

▸▸ *also Fig* ***trump card*** atout *m*; *Fig* **to play one's t. card** jouer ses atouts

▸ **trump up** VT SEP *(invent ▸ excuse)* forger *ou* inventer de toutes pièces; **to t. up a charge against sb** forger une accusation contre qn

trumpery ['trʌmpərɪ] *Literary* N *(UNCOUNT)* **1** *(nonsense)* bêtises *fpl* **2** *(trinkets)* pacotille *f*

ADJ **1** *(flashy)* tapageur, criard **2** *(worthless)* sans valeur, insignifiant

trumpet ['trʌmpɪt] N **1** *(instrument)* trompette *f*; **Armstrong is on t.** Armstrong est à la trompette

2 *(trumpeter)* trompettiste *mf*; *(in military band)* trompette *f*

3 *(of elephant)* barrissement *m*

4 *(hearing aid)* **(ear) t.** cornet *m* acoustique

VI *(elephant)* barrir

VT *(secret, news)* claironner; **there's no need to t. it abroad** il n'est pas nécessaire de le crier sur les toits; **the government's much trumpeted land reforms** la réforme agraire annoncée à grand renfort de publicité par le gouvernement

▸▸ *Mus* ***trumpet call*** sonnerie *f* de trompette; *Fig (appeal)* appel *m*; *Fig* **a t. call to liberty** un appel vibrant à la liberté; *Mil* ***trumpet major*** trompette-major *m*; ***trumpet voluntary*** solo *m* pour trompette et orgue *(joué en prélude à une cérémonie religieuse)*

trumpeter ['trʌmpɪtə(r)] N *(musician)* trompettiste *mf*; *(in orchestra)* trompette *m*

trumpeting ['trʌmpɪtɪŋ] N **1** *(of elephant)* barrissement *m*, barrissements *mpl* **2** *Mus* coup *m ou* coups *mpl* de trompette

truncate [trʌŋ'keɪt] VT *(gen) & Comput* tronquer

truncated [trʌŋ'keɪtɪd] ADJ *(body, text)* tronqué; *(meeting, journey)* écourté

▸▸ *Geom* ***truncated cone*** cône *m* tronqué

truncheon ['trʌntʃən] N matraque *f*

VT matraquer

trundle ['trʌndəl] VI *(heavy equipment, wheelbarrow)* avancer *ou* rouler lentement; *(person)* aller *ou* avancer tranquillement; **to t. in/out/past** entrer/sortir/passer tranquillement; **the lorry trundled slowly along** le camion avançait lentement; *Br Hum* **do you fancy trundling down to the pub?** ça vous dit d'aller faire un tour au pub?

VT *(push)* pousser (avec effort); *(pull)* traîner (avec effort); *(wheel)* faire rouler bruyamment; **he trundled the trolley along behind him** il traînait le chariot derrière lui

N *Fam Hum (walk)* balade *f*

▸ **trundle out** VT SEP *(old bicycle, theory etc)* ressortir

trunk [trʌŋk] N **1** *(of tree, body)* tronc *m*

2 *(of elephant)* trompe *f*

3 *(case)* malle *f*; *(metal)* cantine *f*

4 *Am Aut* coffre *m*

• **trunks** NPL *(for swimming)* maillot *m ou* slip *m* de bain; *(underwear)* slip *m* (d'homme)

▸▸ *Br Old-fashioned* ***trunk call*** appel *m* interurbain; ***trunk line*** **1** *Old-fashioned Tel* inter *m*, interurbain *m* **2** *Rail* grande ligne *f*; *Br* ***trunk road*** (route *f*) nationale *f*; ***trunk roads*** grandes routes *fpl*

trunnion ['trʌnjən] N tourillon *m*

truss [trʌs] VT **1** *(prisoner, animal)* ligoter; *(poultry)* trousser; *(hay)* botteler **2** *Constr* armer, renforcer

N **1** *(of hay)* botte *f*; *(of fruit)* grappe *f* **2** *Constr* ferme *f* **3** *Med* bandage *m* herniaire

▸▸ ***truss bridge*** pont *m* à fermes

▸ **truss up** VT SEP *(prisoner)* ligoter; *(poultry)* trousser; **trussed up like a chicken** ficelé comme un poulet

trust [trʌst] VT **1** *(have confidence in ▸ person)* faire confiance à, avoir confiance en; *(▸ method, feelings, intuition)* faire confiance à, se fier à; *(▸ judgment, memory, instincts)* se fier à; **you can t. me** vous pouvez me faire confiance *ou* avoir confiance en moi; **she's not to be trusted** *(not trustworthy)* on ne peut pas lui faire confiance; *(unreliable)* on ne peut pas se fier à elle; **can we t. his account of events?** peut-on se fier à sa version des faits?; **to t. sb to do sth** faire confiance à qn *ou* compter sur qn pour faire qch; **we're trusting you to save the company** nous comptons sur vous pour sauver la société; **I can't t. him to do the job properly** je ne peux pas compter sur lui pour faire le travail correctement; *Hum* **t. Mark to put his foot in it!** pour mettre les pieds dans le plat, on peut faire confiance à Mark!; **t. you!** cela ne m'étonne pas de toi!; **I wouldn't t. her as far as I could throw her!** je ne lui ferais absolument pas confiance!

2 *(entrust)* **to t. sb with sth** confier qch à qn; **I don't t. you with money** je ne te confierais pas mon argent

3 *Formal (suppose)* supposer; *(hope)* espérer; **I t. (that) everyone enjoyed themselves** j'espère que tout le monde s'est bien amusé; **I t. not** j'espère que non

VI 1 *(believe)* **to t. in God** croire en Dieu **2** *(have confidence)* **I want someone I can t. in** il me faut une personne de confiance; **to t. to luck** s'en remettre à la chance

N 1 *(confidence, faith)* confiance *f*, foi *f*; **to betray sb's t.** trahir la confiance de qn; **to place** *or* **to put one's t. in sb** placer *ou* mettre sa confiance en qn; **to place** *or* **to put one's t. in sth** avoir confiance en qch, se fier à qch; **to take sth on t.** prendre *ou* accepter qch en toute confiance *ou* les yeux fermés; **you can't take everything he says on t.** on ne peut pas croire sur parole tout ce qu'il dit; **I bought the machine on t.** j'ai acheté la machine les yeux fermés; **the garage lent me the car on t.** au garage on m'a prêté la voiture parce qu'on me fait confiance

2 *(responsibility)* responsabilité *f*; **he has a position of t.** il a un poste de confiance *ou* à responsabilités

3 *(care)* charge *f*; **to give** *or* **to place sth into sb's t.** confier qch aux soins de qn

4 *Fin & Law (group of trustees)* administrateurs *mpl*; *(investment)* fidéicommis *m*; **the scholarship is run by a t.** la gestion de la bourse (d'études) a été confiée à un groupe d'administrateurs; **to set up a t. for sb** instituer un fidéicommis pour qn; **the money was held in t. until her 18th birthday** l'argent a été administré par fidéicommis jusqu'à ses 18 ans

5 *(cartel)* trust *m*, cartel *m*

►► *Fin* ***trust account*** compte *m* en fidéicommis; *Fin* ***trust company*** société *f* fiduciaire; *Fin* ***trust fund*** fonds *m* en fidéicommis; ***trust hospital*** = hôpital britannique ayant opté pour l'autogestion mais qui reçoit toujours son budget de l'État; ***trust territory*** territoire *m* sous tutelle

trustafarian [ˌtrʌstəˈfeərɪən] **N** *Br Fam* = jeune Anglais blanc de milieu relativement aisé qui cultive une image rasta

trustbusting [ˈtrʌstˌbʌstɪŋ] **N** *Am* démantèlement *m* des trusts

trusted [ˈtrʌstɪd] **ADJ** *(method)* éprouvé; *(figures)* fiable; **he's a t. friend** c'est un ami en qui j'ai entièrement confiance

►► *Comput* ***trusted third party*** *(for Internet transactions)* tierce partie *f* de confiance

trustee [trʌsˈtiː] **N 1** *Fin & Law* fidéicommissaire *m*; *(proxy)* mandataire *mf*, fondé(e) *m,f* de pouvoir; *(for minor)* curateur(trice) *m,f*; *(in bankruptcy)* syndic *m* **2** *Admin (of museum, charity, company, life assurance policy)* administrateur (trice) *m,f*; **board of trustees** conseil *m* d'administration

trusteeship [ˌtrʌsˈtiːʃɪp] **N 1** *Fin & Law* fidéicommis *m*; *(for minor)* curatelle *f* **2** *Admin* poste *m* d'administrateur; **she accepted the t.** elle a accepté d'être administratrice **3** *Pol (of territory)* tutelle *f*

trustful [ˈtrʌstfʊl] = **trusting**

trustfully [ˈtrʌstfʊlɪ] **ADV** avec confiance

trusting [ˈtrʌstɪŋ] **ADJ** *(nature, person)* qui a confiance; *(look)* confiant; **he's too t. of people** il fait trop confiance aux gens

trustingly [ˈtrʌstɪŋlɪ] **ADV** en toute confiance; **he looked at me t.** il m'a lancé un regard confiant

trustworthiness [ˈtrʌstˌwɜːðɪnɪs] **N 1** *(reliability ► of person)* loyauté *f*, sérieux *m*; *(► of information, source, report, figures)* fiabilité **2** *(honesty)* honnêteté *f*

trustworthy [ˈtrʌstˌwɜːðɪ] **ADJ 1** *(reliable ► person)* sur qui on peut compter, à qui on peut faire confiance; *(► information, source)* sûr, fiable; *(► report, figures)* fiable **2** *(honest)* honnête

trusty [ˈtrʌstɪ] *(compar* **trustier**, *superl* **trustiest)** **ADJ** *Arch or Hum (steed, sword)* loyal, fidèle; *Hum* **my t. typewriter** ma bonne vieille machine à écrire

truth [truːθ, *pl* truːðz] **N 1** *(true facts)* vérité *f*; **I then discovered the t. about Neil** j'ai alors découvert la vérité sur Neil; **there's some t. in what he says** il y a du vrai dans ce qu'il dit; **there is no t. in the rumour** il n'y a rien de vrai dans cette rumeur; **the t. of the matter is I really don't care any more** la vérité c'est que maintenant je m'en fiche vraiment; **...and that's the t.** ...et voilà la vérité; **to tell the t.** dire la vérité; **to tell (you) the t.** à vrai dire, à dire vrai; *Literary* **t. to tell, if t. be told** à dire vrai; **t. is the first casualty (of war)** toute guerre s'accompagne de son cortège de mensonges; *Law* **the t., the whole t., and nothing but the t.** la vérité, toute la vérité, rien que la vérité; *Prov* **(the) t. will out** = la vérité finit toujours par se savoir **2** *(fact, piece of information)* vérité *f*; **he learned some important truths about himself** on lui a dit ses quatre vérités; **universal truths** vérités *fpl* universelles

• **in truth ADV** en vérité

►► ***truth drug*** sérum *m* de vérité; *Math & (in logic)* ***truth set*** = ensemble qui n'a pas de solution unique; ***truth table*** table *f ou* matrice *f* de vérité

truthful [ˈtruːθfʊl] **ADJ** *(person)* qui dit la vérité; *(character)* honnête; *(article, statement)* fidèle à la réalité, vrai; *(story)* véridique, vrai; *(portrait)* fidèle

truthfully [ˈtruːθfʊlɪ] **ADV** *(answer, speak)* honnêtement, sans mentir; *(portray)* fidèlement

truthfulness [ˈtruːθfʊlnɪs] **N** *(of person)* honnêteté *f*; *(of portrait)* fidélité *f*; *(of story, statement)* véracité *f*

TRY [traɪ]

VT	
• essayer **1–6**	• goûter à **3**
• juger **7**	• éprouver **8**
VI	
• essayer	
N	
• essai **1–3**	• tentative **1**

(pt & pp **tried**, *pl* **tries)**

VT 1 *(attempt)* essayer; **to t. an experiment** tenter une expérience; **to t. to do** *or* **doing sth** essayer *ou* tâcher de faire qch, chercher à faire qch; **she tried not to think about it** elle essaya de ne pas y penser *ou* d'éviter d'y penser; **I tried hard to understand** j'ai tout fait pour essayer de comprendre, j'ai vraiment cherché à comprendre; **to t. one's best** *or* **hardest** faire de son mieux; **he tried his best to explain** il a essayé d'expliquer de son mieux; **I'm willing to t. anything once!** je suis prêt à tout essayer au moins une fois!; **I'd like to see you t. it!** je voudrais bien t'y voir!; **it's trying to rain** on dirait qu'il va pleuvoir; *Fam* **and don't t. any funny business!** et pas d'entourloupe!; **just you t. it!** *(as threat)* essaie un peu pour voir!

2 *(test ► method, approach, car)* essayer; **have you tried acupuncture?** avez-vous essayé l'acupuncture?; **tried and tested** *(remedy, method, friend)* éprouvé, qui a fait ses preuves; **he has been tried and found wanting** il ne s'est pas montré à la hauteur; *Fam* **(just) t. me!** essaie toujours!; **to t. one's strength against sb** se mesurer à qn; **to t. one's luck (at sth)** tenter sa chance (à qch)

3 *(sample ► recipe, wine)* essayer, goûter à; *(► clothes, product)* essayer; **t. it, you'll like it** essayez *ou* goûtez-y donc, vous aimerez; **t. this for size** *(garment)* essayez ceci pour voir la taille; *(shoe)* essayez ceci pour voir la pointure; *Fig* essayez ceci pour voir si ça va

4 *(attempt to open ► door, window)* essayer

5 *Tel* essayer; **t. the number again** refaites le numéro; *Fam* **t. him later** essayez de le rappeler plus tard

6 *(visit)* essayer; **I've tried six shops already** j'ai déjà essayé six magasins; **t. Jane** *(ask)* demande à Jane; **he tried the embassy first** il a d'abord e[…] sayé l'ambassade

7 *Law (person, case)* juger; **he was tried for m[…] der** il a été jugé pour meurtre

8 *(tax, strain ► patience)* éprouver, mettre […] l'épreuve; *Hum* **these things are sent to t. us!** c'[…] le ciel qui nous envoie ces épreuves!; **it's e[…] ough to t. the patience of a saint** même un an[…] n'aurait pas la patience; *Literary or Hum* **to […] sorely tried** être durement éprouvé

VI essayer; **to t. and do sth** essayer de faire qc[…] **t. again** refaites un essai, recommencez; **we c[…] but t.** on peut toujours essayer; **you can do it […] you t.** quand on veut, on peut; **just (you) t.!** e[…] saie un peu pour voir!; **I'd like to see you t.!** *(a[…] swer to threat, challenge)* je voudrais bien […] voir!; **...and she wasn't even trying** ...et elle l'a f[…] sans le moindre effort

N 1 *(attempt)* essai *m*, tentative *f*; **to have a t. […] sth/at doing sth** essayer qch/de faire qch; **go[…] t.!** bel effort!; **it's worth a t.** cela vaut la pei[…] d'essayer; **I managed it at the first t.** j'ai réussi […] premier coup; **can I have a t.?** (est-ce que) […] peux essayer?; **he had several tries at openi[…] the box** il a essayé plusieurs fois d'ouvrir la bo[…]

2 *(test, turn)* essai *m*; **to give sth a t.** essayer qc[…] **do you want a t. on my bike?** veux-tu essayer m[…] vélo?

3 *Sport (in rugby)* essai *m*; **to score a t.** marqu[…] un essai; *Sport* **the t. scorer** celui qui a marq[…] l'essai

►► *Tech* ***try square*** équerre *f* de menuisi[…] équerre *f* à chapeau

► **try for VT INSEP** *(attempt to obtain)* tâcher d'o[…] tenir; **to t. for a job** poser sa candidature à […] emploi; **he's trying for (a place at) music schoo[…]** essaie d'obtenir une place à l'école de musiqu[…] **she's trying for the record/a gold medal** elle essa[…] de battre le record/décrocher une médai[…] d'or; **they're trying for a baby** ils essaient d'av[…] un enfant

► **try on VT SEP 1** *(garment)* essayer; **t. it on for si[…]** essayez-le pour voir la taille **2** *Br Fam (idiom)* **t. it on with sb** essayer de voir jusqu'où on pe[…] pousser qn[□]; *(flirt)* essayer de flirter avec q[…] *(attempt to deceive)* essayer d'embobiner qn; *(a[…] tempt to seduce)* faire des avances à qn[□]; *(t[…] someone's tolerance)* faire le coup à qn; **do[…] you t. anything on with me!** *(gen)* ne fais pas […] malin avec moi!; *(flirt)* n'essaie pas de flir[…] avec moi!

► **try out VT SEP** *(new car, bicycle)* essayer, fa[…] un essai avec; *(method, chemical, recipe)* e[…] sayer; *(employee)* mettre à l'essai; **to t. sth o[…] on sb** essayer *ou* expérimenter qch sur qn

VI *Am* **to t. out for a team** faire un essai pour faire engager dans une équipe

trying [ˈtraɪɪŋ] **ADJ** *(experience)* pénible, épro[…] vant; *(journey, job)* ennuyeux, pénible; *(pers[…]* fatigant, pénible; **he had a very t. time** *(moment[…]* a passé un moment très difficile; *(period)* il a v[…] cu une période très difficile; *(experience)* il a v[…] cu une expérience très pénible *ou* éprouvant[…]

try-on N *Br Fam* **it's a t.** c'est du bluff

try-out N essai *m*; *Am Theat* audition *f*, *Sp[…]* épreuve *f* de sélection

tryst [trɪst] **N** *Literary* rendez-vous *m* galant

tsar [zɑː(r)] **N** tsar *m*, tzar *m*, czar *m*

tsarevitch [ˈzɑːrəvɪtʃ] **N** tsarévitch *m*, tzarévit[…] *m*

tsarina [zɑːˈriːnə] **N** tsarine *f*, tzarine *f*

tsarist [ˈzɑːrɪst] **ADJ** tsariste

N tsariste *mf*

tsetse fly [ˈtsetsɪ-] **N** *Entom* (mouche *f*) tsé-ts[…]

T-shaped ADJ en forme de T

T-shirt N tee-shirt *m*, t-shirt *m*; *Hum* **been the[…] done that, got the T.** je connais déjà

tsp. *(written abbr* **teaspoon(ful))** cc

TSS [ˌtiːesˈes] **N** *Med (abbr* **toxic shock syndrom[…]** SCT *m*

T-stop N *Phot* diaphragme *m*

TT [ˌtiːˈtiː] **ADJ** *(abbr* **teetotal)** qui ne boit jama[…] d'alcool

N *Sport (abbr* **Tourist Trophy)** **the TT races** = co[…] ses de moto sur l'île de Man

TL [ˌtiːtiːˈel] ADJ *Phot (abbr* **through the lens)**
▸ ***TTL flash*** flash *m* TTL; ***TTL measurement*** mesure *f* TTL *ou* à travers l'objectif

TP [ˌtiːtiːˈpiː] N *Comput (abbr* **trusted third party)** *(for Internet transactions)* TPC *f*

ub [tʌb] N **1** *(container ▸ for liquid)* cuve *f*, bac *m*; *(▸ for flowers)* bac *m*; *(▸ for washing clothes)* baquet *m*; *(▸ in washing machine)* cuve *f*
2 *(contents ▸ of washing powder)* baril *m*; *(▸ of wine, beer)* tonneau *m*; *(▸ of ice cream, yoghurt)* pot *m*
3 *Fam (bathtub)* **a hot t.** *(bath)* un bain chaud□; **he's in the t.** il prend un bain□
4 *Fam (boat)* rafiot *m*

uba [ˈtjuːbə] N tuba *m*

ubby [ˈtʌbɪ] *(compar* **tubbier**, *superl* **tubbiest)** ADJ *Fam* dodu, rondelet

ube [tjuːb] N **1** *(pipe)* tube *m*; **he was fed through a t.** on l'a nourri à la sonde
2 *Anat* tube *m*, canal *m*
3 *(of glue, toothpaste, paint)* tube *m*
4 *(in tyre)* **(inner) t.** chambre *f* à air
5 *Fam (television)* **what's on the t. tonight?** qu'est-ce qu'il y a à la télé ce soir?; **(cathode-ray) t.** tube *m* (cathodique)
6 *Br (underground)* **the t.** le métro londonien; **to go by t., to take the t.** aller en métro, prendre le métro
7 *Fam (idioms)* **to go down the tubes** tomber à l'eau; **he watched his marriage/life's work go down the tubes** il a vu son mariage/le travail de toute une vie tourner en eau de boudin; **that's £500 down the tubes** ça fait 500 livres de foutus en l'air
COMP *(map, station)* de métro
▸ *Br* ***tube dress*** robe *f* tube

ube-feeding N *Med* gavage *m*

ubeless [ˈtjuːblɪs] ADJ
▸▸ *Br* ***tubeless tyre*** pneu *m* sans chambre (à air)

uber [ˈtjuːbə(r)] N *Anat & Bot* tubercule *m*

ubercle [ˈtjuːbəkəl] N *Med* tubercule *m*
▸ *Biol & Med* ***tubercle bacillus*** bacille *f* de Koch

ubercular [tjuːˈbɜːkjʊlə(r)] ADJ *Med* tuberculeux

uberculin [tjuːˈbɜːkjʊlɪn] N *Med* tuberculine *f*

uberculin-tested [-ˈtestɪd] ADJ *Med & Vet (cow)* tuberculinisé, tuberculiné
▸ ***tuberculin-tested milk*** ≃ lait *m* certifié

uberculin-testing N *Med & Vet* tuberculination *f*

uberculosis [tjuːˌbɜːkjʊˈləʊsɪs] N *Med (UNCOUNT)* tuberculose *f*; **he has t.** il a la tuberculose, il est tuberculeux

uberculous [tjuːˈbɜːkjʊləs] ADJ *Med* tuberculeux

ubful [ˈtʌbfʊl] N cuvée *f*, plein baquet *m*

ubing [ˈtjuːbɪŋ] N *(UNCOUNT)* tubes *mpl*, tuyaux *mpl*; **a piece of plastic t.** un tube en plastique

ub-thumper [-θʌmpə(r)] N *Br Fam* orateur *(trice) m,f* démagogue□

ubular [ˈtjuːbjʊlə(r)] ADJ *(furniture, shape)* tubulaire
▸▸ *Mus* ***tubular bells*** carillon *m* d'orchestre

UC [ˌtiːjuːˈsiː] N *Br Ind (abbr* **Trades Union Congress)** = confédération des syndicats britanniques; **the T. annual conference** le congrès annuel des syndicats

uck [tʌk] VT **1** *(shirt)* rentrer; *(sheet)* rentrer, border; **he tucked his shirt into his trousers** il rentra sa chemise dans son pantalon; **she tucked the sheets under the mattress** elle borda le lit **2** *(put)* mettre; *(slip)* glisser; **she tucked the book under the bedclothes** elle glissa le livre sous les draps; **he had a newspaper tucked under his arm** il avait un journal sous le bras; **she tucked her hair behind her ears** elle ramena ses cheveux derrière les oreilles; **his mother came to t. him into bed** sa mère est venue le border dans son lit
N **1** *Sewing* rempli *m*; **to put** *or* **to make a t. in sth** faire un rempli dans qch **2** *(in diving)* plongeon *m* groupé **3** *Br Fam (food)* boustifaille *f*
▸▸ *Br Sch* ***tuck box*** gamelle *f (d'écolier)*; ***tuck position*** *(in skiing)* œuf *m*; *Br Sch* ***tuck shop*** = petite boutique où les écoliers achètent bonbons, gâteaux etc

▸ **tuck away** VT SEP **1** *(hide)* cacher; *(put)* mettre, ranger; **the house was tucked away in the hills** la maison était cachée dans les collines **2** *Fam (food)* s'enfiler, avaler; **she really can t. it away!** *(eat a lot)* qu'est-ce qu'elle peut bouffer!

▸ **tuck in** VT SEP **1** *(shirt, stomach)* rentrer **2** *(child)* border
VI *Fam (eat)* **we tucked in to a lovely meal** nous avons attaqué un excellent repas; **don't wait for me, t. in!** ne m'attendez pas, attaquez!

▸ **tuck up** VT SEP **1** *(person)* border (dans son lit); **all the children were safely tucked up in bed** les enfants étaient tous bien bordés dans leur lit **2** *(skirt, sleeves)* remonter; *(hair)* rentrer **3** *(legs)* replier, rentrer

tucker [ˈtʌkə(r)] N **1** *(on dress)* fichu *m* **2** *Austr & NZ Fam (food)* bouffe *f*
VT *Am Fam (exhaust)* crever; **you look tuckered out!** tu as l'air complètement crevé!

tuck-in N *Br Fam* **we had a great t.** on a super bien bouffé

Tudor [ˈtjuːdə(r)] ADJ *(family, period)* des Tudor; *(monarch, architecture)* Tudor *(inv)*
N Tudor *m inv*, membre *m* de la famille des Tudor

Tue., Tues. *(written abbr* **Tuesday)** mar

Tuesday [ˈtjuːzdɪ] N mardi *m*; *see also* **Friday**

tufa [ˈtjuːfə] N tuf *m* calcaire

tuft [tʌft] N **1** *(of hair, grass)* touffe *f*; **t. of bristles** *(in paint etc brush)* loquet *m* de soies **2** *Orn* **t. (of feathers)** huppe *f*, aigrette *f*

tufted [ˈtʌftɪd] ADJ **1** *(bird)* huppé **2** *(grass)* en touffe *ou* touffes **3** *(carpet)* tufté
▸▸ *Orn* ***tufted duck*** (fuligule *f*) morillon *m*

tug [tʌg] *(pt & pp* **tugged**, *cont* **tugging)** N **1** *(pull)* petit coup *m*; **to give sth a t.** tirer sur qch d'un coup sec; **give the rope a t., will you?** tire un peu sur la corde, tu veux?; **he felt a t. at his sleeve** il sentit qu'on le tirait par la manche **2** *Naut* remorqueur *m*
VT **1** *(handle, sleeve)* tirer sur; *(load)* tirer, traîner **2** *Naut* remorquer
VI **to t. at** *or* **on sth** tirer sur qch; *Fig* **the music tugged at her heartstrings** cette musique l'émouvait

tugboat [ˈtʌgbəʊt] N remorqueur *m*

tuition [tjuːˈɪʃən] N *(UNCOUNT)* **1** *Br (instruction)* cours *mpl*; **I give t. in Spanish** je donne des cours d'espagnol **2** *Univ (fees)* frais *mpl* de scolarité
▸▸ *Univ* ***tuition fees*** frais *mpl* de scolarité

tulip [ˈtjuːlɪp] N tulipe *f*
▸▸ ***tulip glass*** (verre *m*) tulipe *f*; ***tulip tree*** tulipier *m*

tulle [tjuːl] N *Tex* tulle *m*

tum [tʌm] N *Br Fam* ventre□*m*

tumble [ˈtʌmbəl] VI **1** *(fall ▸ person)* tomber, faire une chute; *(▸ ball, objects)* tomber; **he tumbled down the stairs** il a dégringolé *ou* il est tombé dans l'escalier; **the bottles came tumbling off the shelf** les bouteilles ont dégringolé *ou* sont tombées de l'étagère; **to t. into bed** se jeter dans son lit; **to t. out of bed** tomber du lit; **they were tumbling over one another** ils se bousculaient
2 *(collapse ▸ prices)* dégringoler, s'effondrer; **the Chancellor's resignation sent share prices tumbling** la démission du ministre des Finances a fait dégringoler *ou* chuter le cours des actions
3 *(rush)* se précipiter; **the children tumbled into the kitchen** les enfants se ruèrent *ou* se précipitèrent dans la cuisine; **they came tumbling after me** ils se sont lancés à ma poursuite
4 *(perform somersaults)* faire des cabrioles *ou* des culbutes
VT *(knock, push ▸ person)* renverser, faire tomber *ou* dégringoler; **she tumbled me into the pool** elle m'a fait tomber dans la piscine; **she tumbled the books onto the table** elle a fait tomber les livres sur la table
N *(fall)* chute *f*, culbute *f*, roulé-boulé *m*; *(somersault)* culbute *f*, cabrioles *fpl*; **he had a bad t. on the ice** il a fait une mauvaise chute sur la glace; **to take a t.** faire une chute *ou* une culbute; **share prices took a t. today** le prix des actions s'est effondré aujourd'hui; **they had a t. in the hay** ils ont batifolé dans le foin, ils se sont roulés dans le foin

▸ **tumble about** VI *(children)* gambader, batifoler; *(acrobat)* faire des cabrioles; *(swimmer)* s'ébattre; *(water)* clapoter
VT SEP mettre en désordre; **the waves tumbled us about** nous étions ballotés par les vagues

▸ **tumble down** VI *(person)* faire une culbute, dégringoler; *(pile)* dégringoler; *(wall, building)* s'effondrer; **the whole building came tumbling down** tout l'édifice s'est effondré *ou* écroulé

▸ **tumble out** VI **1** *(person ▸ from tree, loft)* dégringoler; *(▸ from bus, car)* se jeter, sauter; *(possessions, contents)* tomber (en vrac); **the apples tumbled out of her basket** les pommes ont roulé de son panier; **he tumbled out of bed at midday** il est tombé du lit à midi; **the van doors flew open and the children came tumbling out** les portes de la camionnette se sont ouvertes et les enfants se sont rués à l'extérieur **2** *(news, confession)* s'échapper; **all their secrets came tumbling out** ils ont déballé tous leurs secrets
VT SEP faire tomber en vrac *ou* en tas

▸ **tumble to** VT INSEP *Br Fam (fact, secret, joke)* piger, saisir; **I finally tumbled to their little game** j'ai enfin compris leur petit manège

tumbledown [ˈtʌmbəldaʊn] ADJ en ruines, délabré

tumble-drier N sèche-linge *m inv*

tumble-dry VT faire sécher dans le sèche-linge

tumbler [ˈtʌmblə(r)] N **1** *(glass)* verre *m* (droit); *(beaker)* gobelet *m*, timbale *f*; **a t. of orange (juice)** un verre de jus d'orange
2 *(acrobat)* acrobate *mf*
3 *(in lock)* gorge *f* (de serrure)
4 *(tumble-drier)* sèche-linge *m inv*
▸▸ ***tumbler switch*** interrupteur *m* à bascule

tumblerful [ˈtʌmbləfʊl] N plein verre *m* (**of** de)

tumbleweed [ˈtʌmbəlwiːd] N = espèce d'amarante (qui, en séchant, casse et est emportée par le vent)

tumbrel [ˈtʌmbrəl], **tumbril** [ˈtʌmbrɪl] N tombereau *m*

tumefaction [ˌtjuːmɪˈfækʃən] N tuméfaction *f*

tumefy [ˈtjuːmɪfaɪ] VT tuméfier
VI se tuméfier

tumescent [tjuːˈmesənt] ADJ tumescent

tumid [ˈtjuːmɪd] ADJ **1** *Med* tuméfié **2** *Literary (style)* ampoulé, boursouflé

tummy [ˈtʌmɪ] *Fam* N ventre□*m*; **to have (a) t. ache** avoir mal au ventre
▸▸ *Br* ***tummy button*** nombril□*m*; ***tummy tuck*** abdominoplastie□*f*; **to have a t. tuck** se faire faire une abdominoplastie

tumour, *Am* **tumor** [ˈtjuːmə(r)] N *Med* tumeur *f*

tumuli [ˈtjuːmjʊlaɪ] *pl of* **tumulus**

tumult [ˈtjuːmʌlt] N **1** *(noise)* tumulte *m*; *(agitation)* tumulte *m*, agitation *f*; **in (a) t.** *(auditorium, meeting)* tumultueux; *(person, feeling)* en émoi **2** *Formal or Literary (of feelings)* émoi *m*

tumultuous [tjuːˈmʌltjʊəs] ADJ *(crowd, noise)* tumultueux; *(applause)* frénétique; *(period)* mouvementé, agité; **he got a t. welcome** il a reçu un accueil enthousiaste

tumultuously [tjuːˈmʌltjʊəslɪ] ADV tumultueusement; *(applaud)* frénétiquement

tumulus [ˈtjuːmjʊləs] *(pl* **tumuli** [-laɪ]) N tumulus *m*

tun [tʌn] N fût *m*, tonneau *m*

tuna [ˈtjuːnə] N thon *m*
▸▸ ***tuna fish*** thon *m*

tundra [ˈtʌndrə] N toundra *f*

tune [tjuːn] N *(melody)* air *m*, mélodie *f*; **give us a t. on the mouth organ** joue-nous un petit air d'harmonica; **the band played some old Irish tunes** l'orchestre joua de vieilles mélodies irlandaises; **they marched to the t. of the Marseillaise** ils défilèrent aux accents de la Marseillaise; **it's got no t. to it** ça manque de mélodie, ce n'est pas mélodieux; *Br Fam Fig* **to call the t.** faire la loi; *Fig* **to change one's t.** changer de discours
VT **1** *(musical instrument)* accorder; **the strings are tuned to the key of G** les cordes sont en sol **2** *(regulate ▸ engine, machine)* mettre au point, régler **3** *(radio, television)* régler; **the radio is tuned to BBC7** la radio est réglée sur BBC7; **we can't t.**

our TV to Channel 5 nous ne pouvons pas capter Channel 5 sur notre télé; **stay tuned!** restez à l'écoute!

• **in tune** ADJ *(instrument)* accordé, juste; *(singer)* qui chante juste; **the violins are not in t. with the piano** les violons ne sont pas accordés avec le piano; *Fig* **to be in t. with** être en accord avec ADV juste; **to play/to sing in t.** jouer/chanter juste

• **out of tune** ADJ *(instrument)* faux (fausse), désaccordé; *(singer)* qui chante faux; *Fig* **to be out of t. with** être en désaccord avec ADV faux; **to play/to sing out of t.** jouer/chanter faux

• **to the tune of** PREP **they were given grants to the t. of £100,000** on leur a accordé des subventions qui s'élevaient à 100 000 livres

▸ **tune in** VI *Rad & TV* se mettre à l'écoute; **don't forget to t. in again tomorrow** n'oubliez pas de nous rejoindre *ou* de vous mettre à l'écoute demain; **I tuned in to Radio Ultra** je me suis mis sur Radio Ultra

VT SEP **1** *(radio, television)* régler sur **2** *Fam Fig* **to be tuned in to sth** être branché sur qch

▸ **tune up** VI *Mus (player)* accorder son instrument; *(orchestra)* accorder ses instruments

VT SEP **1** *Mus* accorder **2** *Aut* mettre au point, régler

tuned-in [tju:nd-] ADJ *Fam (aware)* branché; **she's very t. to other people's needs** elle est toujours consciente des besoins des gens

tuneful ['tju:nfʊl] ADJ *(song, voice)* mélodieux; *(singer)* à la voix mélodieuse

tunefully ['tju:nfʊlɪ] ADV mélodieusement

tunefulness ['tju:nfʊlnɪs] N qualité *f* mélodieuse

tuneless ['tju:nlɪs] ADJ peu mélodieux, discordant

tuner ['tju:nə(r)] N **1** *(of piano)* accordeur(euse) *m,f* **2** *Rad & TV* tuner *m*, *Spec* syntonisateur *m*

▸▸ ***tuner amplifier*** ampli-tuner *m*

tune-up N *Aut* réglage *m*, mise *f* au point; **to have a t.** faire faire une mise au point *ou* un réglage

tungsten ['tʌŋstən] N *Chem* tungstène *m*

▸▸ ***tungsten carbide*** carbure *m* de tungstène; ***tungsten steel*** acier *m* au tungstène

tungsten-halogen N *Chem* tungstène-halogène *m*

▸▸ ***tungsten-halogen lamp*** lampe *f* tungstène-halogène, lampe *f* au tungstène

tunic ['tju:nɪk] N *(gen) & Bot* tunique *f*

tuning ['tju:nɪŋ] N **1** *Mus* accord *m* **2** *Rad & TV* réglage *m* **3** *Aut* réglage *m*, mise *f* au point

▸▸ ***tuning fork*** diapason *m*; ***tuning hammer*** accordoir *m*, clef *f* d'accordeur; ***tuning key*** accordoir *m*; ***tuning knob*** bouton *m* de réglage

Tunisia [tju:'nɪzɪə] N Tunisie *f*

Tunisian [tju:'nɪzɪən] N Tunisien(enne) *m,f*

ADJ tunisien

COMP *(embassy)* de Tunisie; *(history)* de la Tunisie

tunnel ['tʌnəl] *(Br pt & pp* **tunnelled**, *cont* **tunnelling**, *Am pt & pp* **tunneled**, *cont* **tunneling**) N *(gen) & Rail* tunnel *m*; *Mining* galerie *f*; *(of mole, badger)* galerie *f*; **to make** *or* **to dig a t.** *(gen)* percer *ou* creuser un tunnel; *Mining* percer *ou* creuser une galerie; **to drive a t. through a mountain** percer un tunnel à travers *ou* sous une montagne

VT *(hole, passage)* creuser, percer; **the prisoners tunnelled their way to freedom** les prisonniers se sont évadés en creusant un tunnel

VI *(person)* creuser *ou* percer un tunnel *ou* des tunnels; *(badger, mole)* creuser une galerie *ou* des galeries; **they tunnelled into the mountain** *Constr* ils ont percé un tunnel dans la montagne; *Mining* ils ont percé une galerie dans la montagne

▸▸ ***tunnel vision*** *Opt* rétrécissement *m* du champ visuel; *Fig* esprit *m* borné; *Fig* **to have t. vision** avoir des vues étroites, voir les choses par le petit bout de la lorgnette

tunnelling, *Am* **tunneling** ['tʌnəlɪŋ] N percement *m* d'un tunnel/de tunnels

▸▸ ***tunnelling equipment*** équipement *m* pour le percement d'un tunnel; ***tunnelling machine*** foreuse *f*

tunny ['tʌnɪ] = **tuna**

tuppence ['tʌpəns] N *Br* deux pence *mpl*; *Fam* **the picture isn't worth t.** *(in price)* le tableau ne vaut pas un rond *ou* ne vaut rien; *(in quality)* le tableau ne vaut pas un clou; *Fam* **I don't care t. for your opinion** je me fiche pas mal de votre opinion *ou* de ce que vous pensez

tuppenny ['tʌpnɪ] ADJ *Br* de *ou* à deux pence

turban ['tɜ:bən] N turban *m*

turbid ['tɜ:bɪd] ADJ turbide, trouble

turbidity [tɜ:'bɪdɪtɪ], **turbidness** ['tɜ:bɪdnɪs] N état *m* trouble, turbidité *f*

turbine ['tɜ:baɪn] N turbine *f*; **gas/steam t.** turbine *f* à gaz/à vapeur

turbo ['tɜ:bəʊ] *(pl* **turbos**) N **1** *Aut* turbo *m* **2** *(turbine)* turbine *f*

▸▸ *Comput* ***turbo button*** bouton *m* de turbo; *Aut* ***turbo diesel*** turbodiesel *m*; *Aut* ***turbo diesel engine*** moteur *m* turbodiesel

turbocharged ['tɜ:bəʊtʃɑ:dʒd] ADJ turbo *(inv)*

turbocharger ['tɜ:bəʊtʃɑ:dʒə(r)] N turbocompresseur *m*

turboelectric [,tɜ:bəʊɪ'lektrɪk] ADJ turboélectrique

turbofan ['tɜ:bəʊfæn] ADJ

▸▸ ***turbofan engine*** turboventilateur *m*, turbofan *m*

turbogenerator [,tɜ:bəʊ'dʒenəreɪtə(r)] N turbogénérateur *m*

turbojet [,tɜ:bəʊ'dʒet] N *(engine)* turboréacteur *m*; *(plane)* avion *m* à turboréacteur

turbomarketing ['tɜ:bəʊ,mɑ:kɪtɪŋ] N *Mktg* turbo-marketing *m*

turboprop [,tɜ:bəʊ'prɒp] N *(engine)* turbopropulseur *m*; *(plane)* avion *m* à turbopropulseur

turbosupercharger [,tɜ:bəʊ'su:pə,tʃɑ:dʒə(r)] N turbocompresseur *m* de suralimentation

turbot ['tɜ:bət] *(pl* **inv** *or* **turbots**) N *Ich* turbot *m*

turbulence ['tɜ:bjʊləns] N **1** *(unrest)* turbulence *f*, agitation *f* **2** *(in air)* turbulence *f*; *(in sea)* agitation *f* **3** *Phys* turbulence *f*

turbulent ['tɜ:bjʊlənt] ADJ *(crowd, period, emotions)* tumultueux; *(sea)* agité

turbulently ['tɜ:bjʊləntlɪ] ADV *(gen)* d'une manière turbulente; *(flow)* en bouillonnant

turd [tɜ:d] N *very Fam* **1** *(excrement)* merde *f* **2** *(person)* ordure *f*

tureen [tə'ri:n] N soupière *f*

turf [tɜ:f] *(pl* **turfs** *or* **turves** [tɜ:vz]) N **1** *(grass)* gazon *m*

2 *(sod)* motte *f* de gazon

3 *Sport* turf *m*; **to follow the t.** être turfiste

4 *Ir (peat)* tourbe *f*

5 *Am Fam (field of expertise, authority)* domaine *m*; **that's not my t.** c'est pas mon rayon

6 *Fam (of gang)* territoire *m* réservé, chasse *f* gardée

VT **1** *(with grass)* **to t. (over)** gazonner **2** *Br Fam (throw)* balancer, flanquer, jeter

COMP *(fire)* de tourbe

▸▸ *Br Formal* ***turf accountant*** bookmaker *m*; ***turf war*** conflit *m* pour le contrôle d'un territoire

▸ **turf out** VT SEP *Br Fam (eject, evict ▸ person)* virer, flanquer à la porte; *(remove ▸ furniture, possessions)* sortir, enlever; *(throw away ▸ rubbish)* bazarder; **he turfed everything out of the cupboard** il a tout sorti du placard, il a bazardé tout ce qu'il y avait dans le placard; **he was turfed out of the club** il s'est fait virer *ou* vider du club

turgid ['tɜ:dʒɪd] ADJ **1** *(style, prose)* ampoulé, boursouflé **2** *Med* enflé, gonflé

turgidly ['tɜ:dʒɪdlɪ] ADV *(written etc)* dans un style ampoulé *ou* boursouflé

Turin [tjʊə'rɪn] N Turin

▸▸ ***the Turin Shroud*** le saint suaire

Turk [tɜ:k] N Turc (Turque) *m,f*

Turkey ['tɜ:kɪ] N Turquie *f*

turkey ['tɜ:kɪ] *(pl* **inv** *or* **turkeys**) N **1** *(bird ▸ cock)* dindon *m*; *(▸ hen)* dinde *f*

2 *Culin* dinde *f*

3 *Am Fam (person)* crétin(e) *m,f*, andouille *f*, courge *f*

4 *Am Fam (unsuccessful film, book)* bide *m*; *Theat* four *m*

5 *Fam (idioms) Am* **to talk t.** *(get down to busines[s])* passer aux choses sérieuses; *(speak frank[ly])* parler franc; **it's like turkeys voting for Christm[as]** c'est le monde à l'envers

▸▸ ***turkey buzzard*** vautour *m* aura; ***turkey co[ck]*** dindon *m*; *Fam Fig* crâneur(euse) *m,f*; ***turk[ey] hen*** dinde *f*; ***Turkey red*** rouge *m* d'Andrinop[le], rouge *m* turc; *Am* ***turkey shoot*** partie *f* de chas[se] au dindon; *Am Fig* **it was a real t. shoot** c'éta[it] gagné d'avance

Turkish ['tɜ:kɪʃ] N *(language)* turc *m*

ADJ turc

COMP *(embassy)* de Turquie; *(history)* de la Tu[r]quie; *(teacher)* de turc

▸▸ ***Turkish bath*** bain *m* turc; ***Turkish coffee*** café turc; ***Turkish delight*** loukoum *m*; ***Turkish tow[el]*** serviette *f* éponge

Turkmenistan [,tɜ:kmenɪ'stɑ:n] N Turkménista[n] *m*

turmeric ['tɜ:mərɪk] N curcuma *m*, safran *m* d[es] Indes

turmoil ['tɜ:mɔɪl] N **1** *(confusion)* agitation [*f*], trouble *m*, chaos *m*; **the country was in t.** le pa[ys] était en ébullition *ou* en effervescence **2** *(em[o]tional)* trouble *m*, émoi *m*; **her mind was in (a)** elle était dans le désarroi, la confusion régna[it] dans son esprit

TURN [tɜ:n]

VT
- tourner **A1, B1, 4, C4**
- faire tourner **A1**
- retourner **B1**
- changer **C1**
- faire devenir **C1**

VI
- tourner **1–3, 6**
- se tourner **1**
- se retourner **2**
- devenir **4**
- se changer **5**

N
- tour **1, 4, 6, 7, 10**
- tournant **2, 3**
- virage **2, 3**
- tournure **4**

VT **A. 1** *(cause to rotate, move round)* tourne[r]; *(shaft, axle)* faire tourner, faire pivoter; *(direc[t])* diriger; **she turned the key in the lock** *(to lock)* el[le] a donné un tour de clé (à la porte), elle a ferm[é] la porte à clé; *(to unlock)* elle a ouvert la por[te] avec la clé; **t. the wheel all the way round** fait[es] faire un tour complet à la roue; *Aut* **to t. th[e] (steering) wheel** tourner le volant; **t. the knob [to] the right** tournez le bouton vers la droite; **t. th[e] knob to "record"** mettez le bouton en positio[n] "enregistrer"; **she turned the oven to its highe[st] setting** elle a allumé *ou* mis le four à la tempér[a]ture maximum; **she turned her chair towards th[e] window** elle a tourné sa chaise face à la fenêtr[e]; **he turned the car into the drive** il a engagé la vo[i]ture dans l'allée; **we turned our steps homewa[rd]** nous avons dirigé nos pas vers la maison; **t. yo[ur] head this way** tournez la tête de ce côté

2 *Fig (change orientation of)* **she turned the co[n]versation to sport** elle a orienté la conversatio[n] vers le sport; **he would not be turned from his d[e]cision to resign** il n'y a pas eu moyen de le fai[re] revenir sur sa décision de démissionner; **you'v[e] turned my whole family against me** vous ave[z] monté toute ma famille contre moi; **we turne[d] his joke against him** nous avons retourné la pla[i]santerie contre lui; **let's t. our attention to th[e] matter in hand** occupons-nous de l'affaire e[n] question; **she turned her attention to the proble[m]** elle s'est concentrée sur le problème; **to t. one['s] thoughts to God** tourner ses pensées vers Die[u]; **to t. one's back on sb** tourner le dos à qn; **sh[e] looked at the letter the minute his back was turne[d]** dès qu'il a eu le dos tourné, elle a jeté un cou[p] d'œil à la lettre; **she turned her back on her frien[ds]** elle a tourné le dos à ses amis; **to t. one's back o[n] the past** tourner la page, tourner le dos a[u] passé; **she was so pretty that she turned hea[ds] wherever she went** elle était si jolie que tout [le] monde se retournait sur son passage; **succes[s] had not turned his head** la réussite ne lui ava[it] pas tourné la tête, il ne s'était pas laissé gris[er] par la réussite; **all their compliments had turne[d] her head** tous leurs compliments lui étaien[t] montés à la tête *ou* lui avaient tourné la tête; [**to**] **t. the tables on sb** reprendre l'avantage sur q[n]; *Fig* **now the tables are turned** maintenant les r[ô]les sont renversés

. 1 *(flip over ▸ page)* tourner; *(▸ collar, mattress, ausages, soil, hay)* retourner; **the very thought of ood turns my stomach** l'idée même de manger ne soulève le cœur; **to t. sth on its head** bouleerser qch, mettre qch sens dessus dessous; **reent events have turned the situation on its head** es événements récents ont retourné la situaion

2 *(send away)* **he turned the beggar from his door** a chassé le mendiant; **they turned the poachers ff their land** ils ont chassé les braconniers de eurs terres

3 *(release, let loose)* **he turned the cattle into the ield** il a fait rentrer le bétail dans le champ

4 *(go round ▸ corner)* tourner

5 *(reach ▸ in age, time)* passer, franchir; **I had just urned 20** je venais d'avoir 20 ans; **she's turned 30** lle a 30 ans passés, elle a dépassé le cap de la rentaine; **it has only just turned four o'clock** il est uatre heures passées de quelques secondes

6 *(do, perform)* faire; **the skater turned a circle on he ice** la patineuse a décrit un cercle sur la lace; **to t. a cartwheel** faire la roue

7 *(ankle)* tordre; **I've turned my ankle** je me suis ordu la cheville

. **1** *(transform, change)* changer, transformer; *make)* faire devenir, rendre; **to t. sth into sth** ransformer *ou* changer qch en qch; **she turned he remark into a joke** elle a tourné la remarque n plaisanterie; **they're turning the book into a ilm** ils adaptent le livre pour l'écran; *St Exch* **ou should t. your shares into cash** vous devriez éaliser vos actions; **time had turned the pages ellow** le temps avait jauni les pages

2 *(make bad, affect)* **the lemon juice turned the nilk (sour)** le jus de citron a fait tourner le lait

3 *Am Com (goods)* promouvoir la vente de; *money)* gagner; **to t. a good profit** faire de gros énéfices; **he turns an honest penny** il gagne sa ie honnêtement; *Fam* **he was out to t. a fast buck** l cherchait à gagner *ou* faire du fric facilement

4 *Tech (shape)* tourner, façonner au tour; **a wellurned leg** une jambe bien faite; *Fig* **to t. a phrase** aire des phrases

VI 1 *(move round ▸ handle, key, wheel)* tourner; *▸ shaft)* tourner, pivoter; *(▸ person)* se tourner; **o t. on an axis** tourner autour d'un axe; **the crane urned (through) 180°** la grue a pivoté de 180°; **he key won't t.** la clé ne tourne pas; **he turned ight round** il a fait volte-face; **they turned towards me** ils se sont tournés vers moi *ou* de non côté; **they turned from the gruesome sight** ls se sont détournés de cet horrible spectacle

2 *(flip over ▸ page)* tourner; *(▸ car, person, ship)* se retourner; *Fig* **the smell made my stomach t.** odeur m'a soulevé le cœur

3 *(change direction ▸ person)* tourner; *(▸ vehicle)* ourner, virer; *(▸ luck, wind)* tourner, changer; *▸ river, road)* faire un coude; *(▸ tide)* changer de direction; **t. (to the) right** *(walking)* tournez à droite; *(driving)* tournez *ou* prenez à droite; *Mil* **ight t.!** à droite!; **we turned towards town** nous ommes dirigés vers la ville; **he turned (round) and went back** il a fait demi-tour et est revenu sur ses pas; **the road turns south** la route ourne vers le sud; **the car turned into our street** a voiture a tourné dans notre rue; **we turned onto the main road** nous nous sommes engagés dans *ou* nous avons pris la grand-route; **we turned off the main road** nous avons quitté la grand-route; *Fig* **I don't know where** *or* **which way to t.** je ne sais plus quoi faire; *Fam Fig* **she's not for turning** elle ne changera pas d'avis

4 *(with adj or noun complement) (become)* devenir; **it's turning cold** il commence à faire froid; **the weather's turned bad** le temps s'est gâté; **the argument turned nasty** la dispute s'est envenimée; **she turned angry when he refused** elle s'est mise en colère quand il a refusé; **to t. red/blue** virer au rouge/bleu; **he turned red** il a rougi; **a lawyer turned politician** un avocat devenu homme politique; **the whole family turned Muslim** toute la famille s'est convertie à l'islam

5 *(transform)* se changer, se transformer; **the pumpkin turned into a carriage** la citrouille s'est transformée en carrosse; **the rain turned to snow** a pluie s'est transformée en neige; **the little girl had turned into a young woman** la petite fille était devenue une jeune femme; **their love turned to hate** leur amour se changea en haine *ou* fit place à la haine

6 *(leaf)* tourner, jaunir; *(milk)* tourner; **the weather has turned** le temps a changé

N 1 *(revolution, rotation)* tour *m*; **he gave the handle a t.** il a tourné la poignée; **give the screw another t.** donnez un autre tour de vis; **with a t. of the wrist** avec un tour de poignet

2 *(change of course, direction)* tournant *m*; *(in skiing)* virage *m*; **to make a right t.** *(walking)* tourner à droite; *(driving)* tourner *ou* prendre à droite; **take the second t. on the right** prenez la deuxième à droite; **no right t.** *(sign)* défense de tourner à droite; *Fig* **at every t.** à tout instant, à tout bout de champ

3 *(bend, curve in road)* virage *m*, tournant *m*; **there is a sharp t. to the left** la route fait un brusque virage *ou* tourne brusquement à gauche

4 *(change in state, nature)* tour *m*, tournure *f*; **the conversation took a new t.** la conversation a pris une nouvelle tournure; **it was an unexpected t. of events** les événements ont pris une tournure imprévue; **things took a t. for the worse/better** les choses se sont aggravées/améliorées; **the patient took a t. for the worse/better** l'état du malade s'est aggravé/amélioré; **the situation took a tragic t.** la situation a tourné au tragique

5 *(time of change)* **at the t. of the year** vers la fin de l'année; **at the t. of the century** au tournant du siècle

6 *(in game, order, queue)* tour *m*; **it's my t.** c'est à moi, c'est mon tour; **whose t. is it?** *(in queue)* (c'est) à qui le tour?; *(in game)* c'est à qui de jouer?; **it's his t. to do the dishes** c'est à lui *ou* c'est son tour de faire la vaisselle; **you'll have to wait your t.** il faudra attendre ton tour; **they laughed and cried by turns** ils passaient tour à tour du rire aux larmes; **to take it in turns to do sth** faire qch à tour de rôle; **let's take it in turns to drive** relayons-nous au volant; **we took turns sleeping on the floor** nous avons dormi par terre à tour de rôle; **t. and t. about** à tour de rôle

7 *(action, deed)* **to do sb a good/bad t.** rendre service/jouer un mauvais tour à qn; **I've done my good t. for the day** j'ai fait ma bonne action de la journée; *Prov* **one good t. deserves another** = un service en vaut un autre, un service rendu en appelle un autre

8 *Fam (attack of illness)* crise *f*, attaque *f*; **she had one of her (funny) turns this morning** elle a eu une de ses crises ce matin

9 *Fam (shock)* **you gave me quite a t.!** tu m'as fait une sacrée peur!, tu m'as fait une de ces peurs!; **it gave me such a t.!** j'ai eu une de ces peurs!

10 *Old-fashioned (short trip, ride, walk)* tour *m*; **let's go for** *or* **take a t. in the garden** allons faire un tour dans le jardin

11 *(tendency, style)* **to have an optimistic t. of mind** être optimiste de nature *ou* d'un naturel optimiste; **he has a strange t. of mind** il a une drôle de mentalité; **to have a good t. of speed** rouler vite; **t. of phrase** tournure *f ou* tour *m* de phrase; **she has a witty t. of phrase** elle est très spirituelle *ou* pleine d'esprit

12 *(purpose, requirement)* exigence *f*, besoin *m*; **this book has served its t.** ce livre a fait son temps

13 *Mus* doublé *m*

14 *BrTheat* numéro *m*; **a comedy t.** un numéro de comédie

15 *Br Culin* **done to a t.** cuit à point; *Fam Hum (tanned)* tout bronzé

• **in turn** ADV **she interviewed each of us in t.** elle a eu un entretien avec chacun de nous l'un après l'autre; **I told Sarah and she in t. told Paul** je l'ai dit à Sarah qui, à son tour, l'a dit à Paul; **I worked in t. as a waiter, an actor and a teacher** j'ai travaillé successivement *ou* tour à tour comme serveur, acteur et enseignant

• **on the turn** ADJ **to be on the t.** être sur le point de changer; **the tide is on the t.** c'est le changement de marée; *Fig* le vent tourne; **the milk is on the t.** le lait commence à tourner

• **out of turn** ADV **don't play out of t.** attends ton tour pour jouer; *Fig* **to speak out of t.** faire des remarques déplacées, parler mal à propos

▸▸ ***turn of duty*** *(gen)* tour *m* de service; *Mil* tour *m* de garde; *Am* ***turn signal*** clignotant *m*, *Belg* clignoteur *m*, *Suisse* signofil(e) *m*; *Am* ***turn signal lever*** (manette *f* de) clignotant *m*

▸ **turn against** VT INSEP se retourner contre, s'en prendre à

▸ **turn around** = **turn round**

▸ **turn aside** VI *(move to one side)* s'écarter; *also Fig (move away)* se détourner; **she turned aside to blow her nose** elle se détourna pour se moucher

VT SEP *also Fig* écarter, détourner

▸ **turn away** VT SEP **1** *(avert)* détourner; **she turned her head away from him** elle s'est détournée de lui **2** *(reject ▸ person)* renvoyer; *(stronger)* chasser; **the college turned away hundreds of applicants** l'université a refusé des centaines de candidats; **to t. people away** *(in theatre etc)* refuser du monde; **we've been turning business away** nous avons refusé du travail

VI se détourner; **he turned away from them in anger** en *ou* de colère, il leur a tourné le dos

▸ **turn back** VI **1** *(return ▸ person)* revenir, rebrousser chemin; *(▸ vehicle)* faire demi-tour; **my mind is made up, there is no turning back** ma décision est prise, je ne reviendrai pas dessus **2** *(go back in book)* **t. back to chapter one** revenez *ou* retournez au premier chapitre

VT SEP 1 *(force to return)* faire faire demi-tour à; *(refugee)* refouler **2** *(fold ▸ collar, sheet)* rabattre; *(▸ sleeves)* remonter, retrousser; *(▸ corner of page)* corner **3** *(idiom)* **to t. the clock back** remonter dans le temps, revenir en arrière

▸ **turn down** VT SEP **1** *(heating, lighting, sound)* baisser **2** *(fold ▸ sheet)* rabattre, retourner; *(▸ collar)* rabattre; **to t. down the corner of a page** corner une page; **to t. down the bed** ouvrir le lit **3** *(reject ▸ offer, request, suitor)* rejeter, repousser; *(▸ candidate, job)* refuser; **they offered him a job but he turned them down** ils lui ont proposé un emploi mais il a rejeté leur offre; *Fam* **she turned me down flat** elle m'a envoyé balader

VI *(move downwards)* tourner vers le bas; **the corners of his mouth turned down** il a fait la moue *ou* une grimace désapprobatrice

▸ **turn in** VT SEP **1** *(return, give in ▸ borrowed article, equipment, piece of work)* rendre, rapporter; **they turned the thief in** *(took him to the police)* ils ont livré le voleur à la police; *(informed on him)* ils ont dénoncé le voleur à la police **2** *(fold in)* **t. in the edges** rentrez les bords **3** *(produce)* **the actor turned in a good performance** l'acteur a très bien joué; **the company turned in record profits** l'entreprise a fait des bénéfices record

VI 1 *(feet, toes)* **my toes t. in** j'ai les pieds en dedans

2 *(go through entrance off road etc)* **he turned in at the gate** arrivé à la porte, il est entré

3 *Fam (go to bed)* se coucher[□]

4 *(idiom)* **to t. in on oneself** se replier sur soi-même

▸ **turn off** VT SEP **1** *(switch off ▸ light)* éteindre; *(▸ heater, radio, television)* éteindre, fermer; *(cut off at mains)* couper; *(tap)* fermer; **she turned the ignition/engine off** elle a coupé le contact/arrêté le moteur **2** *Fam (fail to interest)* rebuter[□]; *(sexually)* couper l'envie à; *(repulse)* débecter; **her superior attitude really turns me off** son air suffisant me rebute

VI 1 *(leave road)* tourner; **we turned off at junction 5** nous avons pris la sortie d'autoroute 5 **2** *(switch off)* s'éteindre

▸ **turn on** VT SEP **1** *(switch on ▸ electricity, heating, light, radio, television)* allumer; *(▸ engine)* mettre en marche; *(▸ water)* faire couler; *(▸ tap)* ouvrir; *(open at mains)* ouvrir; *Fig* **she can t. on the charm/the tears whenever necessary** elle sait faire du charme/pleurer quand il le faut **2** *Fam (person ▸ interest)* intéresser[□]; *(▸ sexually)* exciter; *(▸ introduce to drugs)* initier à la drogue[□]; **to be turned on** *(sexually)* être excité; **the movie didn't t. me on at all** le film ne m'a vraiment pas emballé; **he turned us on to this new pianist** il nous a fait découvrir ce nouveau pianiste

VT INSEP 1 *(attack)* attaquer; **his colleagues turned on him and accused him of stealing** ses collègues s'en sont pris à lui et l'ont accusé de vol **2** *(depend, hinge on)* dépendre de, reposer sur; **the whole case turned on** *or* **upon this detail** toute l'affaire reposait sur ce détail; **everything turns on**

whether he continues as president tout dépend s'il reste président ou non

VI **1** *(switch on)* s'allumer **2** *(take drugs)* se droguer

▸ **turn out** VT SEP **1** *(switch off ▸ light)* éteindre; *(▸ gas)* éteindre, couper

2 *(point outwards)* **she turns her toes out when she walks** elle marche en canard

3 *(dismiss, expel)* mettre à la porte; *(tenant)* expulser, déloger; **he was turned out of his job** il a été renvoyé

4 *(empty ▸ container, pockets)* retourner, vider; *(▸ contents)* vider; *(▸ jelly)* verser; **t. the cake out onto a plate** démoulez le gâteau sur une assiette

5 *Br (clean)* nettoyer à fond; **to t. out a room** faire une pièce à fond

6 *(produce)* produire, fabriquer; **he turns out a book a year** il écrit un livre par an; **few schools t. out the kind of people we need** peu d'écoles forment le type de gens qu'il nous faut

7 *(police, troops)* envoyer; **t. out the guard!** faites sortir la garde!

8 *(usu passive) (dress)* habiller; **nicely** *or* **smartly turned out** élégant; **he was turned out in a suit and a tie** il portait un costume-cravate

VI **1** *(show up)* venir, arriver; *Mil (guard)* (aller) prendre la faction; *(troops)* aller au rassemblement; **thousands turned out for the concert** des milliers de gens sont venus *ou* ont assisté au concert; **the doctor had to t. out in the middle of the night** le docteur a dû se déplacer au milieu de la nuit

2 *(car, person)* sortir, partir; **the car turned out of the car park** la voiture est sortie du parking

3 *(point outwards)* **my feet t. out** j'ai les pieds en canard *ou* en dehors

4 *(prove)* se révéler, s'avérer; **his statement turned out to be false** sa déclaration s'est révélée fausse; **her story turned out to be true** ce qu'elle a raconté était vrai; **he turned out to be a scoundrel** il s'est révélé être un vaurien, on s'est rendu compte que c'était un vaurien; **it turns out that...** il se trouve que... + *indicative*

5 *(end up)* **I don't know how it turned out** je ne sais pas comment cela a fini; **how did the cake t. out?** le gâteau était-il réussi?; **the story turned out happily** l'histoire s'est bien terminée *ou* a bien fini; **the evening turned out badly** la soirée a mal tourné; **everything will t. out fine** tout va s'arranger *ou* ira bien; **as it turns out, he needn't have worried** en l'occurrence *ou* en fin de compte, ce n'était pas la peine de se faire du souci

6 *Br Fam (get out of bed)* se lever□, sortir du lit□

▸ **turn over** VT SEP **1** *(playing card, mattress, person, stone)* retourner; *(page)* tourner; *(vehicle)* retourner; *(boat)* faire chavirer; **I was turning over the pages of the magazine** je feuilletais la revue; *Fig* **to t. over a new leaf** s'acheter une conduite; *Agr* **to t. over the soil** retourner la terre

2 *(consider)* réfléchir à *ou* sur; **I was turning the idea over in my mind** je tournais et retournais *ou* ruminais l'idée dans ma tête

3 *(hand over, transfer)* rendre, remettre; **he turned the responsibility over to his deputy** il s'est déchargé de la responsabilité sur son adjoint; **to t. sb over to the authorities** livrer qn aux autorités

4 *(change)* transformer, changer; **he's turning the land over to cattle farming** il reconvertit sa terre dans l'élevage du bétail

5 *Com* **the store turns over £10,000 a week** la boutique fait un chiffre d'affaires de 10000 livres par semaine

6 *(search through)* fouiller

7 *Br Fam (rob ▸ person)* voler□, dévaliser□; *(▸ store)* dévaliser□; *(▸ house)* cambrioler□

VI **1** *(roll over ▸ person)* se retourner; *(▸ vehicle)* se retourner, faire un tonneau; *(▸ boat)* se retourner, chavirer

2 *(engine)* commencer à tourner

3 *(when reading)* tourner; **please t. over** *(in letter)* TSVP

4 *TV (change channel)* changer de chaîne

▸ **turn round** VI *Br* **1** *(rotate ▸ person)* se retourner; *(▸ object)* tourner; **the dancers turned round and round** les danseurs tournaient *ou* tournoyaient (sur eux-mêmes) **2** *(face opposite direction ▸ person)* faire volte-face, faire demi-tour; *(▸ vehicle)* faire demi-tour; *Fig* **she turned round and accused us of stealing** elle s'est retournée contre nous et nous a accusés de vol

VT SEP **1** *(rotate ▸ head)* tourner; *(▸ object, person)* tourner, retourner; *(▸ vehicle)* faire faire demi-tour à; **could you t. the car round please?** tu peux faire demi-tour, s'il te plaît?

2 *(quantity of work)* traiter

3 *(change nature of)* **to t. a situation round** renverser une situation; *Com* **to t. a company round** sauver une entreprise de la faillite

4 *(sentence, idea)* retourner

▸ **turn up** VT SEP **1** *(heat, lighting, radio, TV)* mettre plus fort; **to turn the sound up** augmenter *ou* monter le volume; **she turned the oven up** elle a mis *ou* réglé le four plus fort, elle a augmenté la température du four; *Br very Fam* **turn it up!** la ferme!

2 *(find, unearth)* découvrir, dénicher; *(buried object)* déterrer; **her research turned up some interesting new facts** sa recherche a révélé de nouveaux détails intéressants

3 *(point upwards)* remonter, relever; **she has a turned-up nose** elle a le nez retroussé

4 *(collar)* relever; *(trousers)* remonter; *(sleeve)* retrousser, remonter; *(in order to shorten)* raccourcir en faisant un ourlet

5 *(uncover ▸ card)* retourner

VI **1** *(appear)* apparaître; *(arrive)* arriver; **she turned up at my office this morning** elle s'est présentée à mon bureau ce matin; **he'll t. up again one of these days** il reviendra bien un de ces jours; **I'll take the first job that turns up** je prendrai le premier poste qui se présentera **2** *(be found)* être trouvé *ou* retrouvé; **her bag turned up eventually** elle a fini par retrouver son sac **3** *(happen)* se passer, arriver; **don't worry, something will t. up** ne t'en fais pas, tu finiras par trouver quelque chose; **until something better turns up** en attendant mieux

---

turnabout ['tɜːnəbaʊt] N *(reversal ▸ of fortunes)* retournement *m*, renversement *m*; *(▸ of opinions)* revirement *m*

turnaround ['tɜːnəraʊnd] N **1** *(of passenger ship, plane)* temps *m* nécessaire au débarquement et à l'embarquement (de nouveaux passagers); *(for freight)* temps *m* nécessaire au déchargement et au chargement (d'une nouvelle cargaison)

2 *(time taken to complete round trip)* temps *m* de rotation

3 *Comput* temps *m* de rotation

4 *(reversal ▸ of fortunes)* retournement *m*, renversement *m*; *(▸ of opinions)* revirement *m*

▸▸ ***turnaround time*** **1** *(for job)* temps *m* d'exécution **2** = **turnaround 1–3**

turncoat ['tɜːnkəʊt] N renégat(e) *m,f*, transfuge *mf*

turndown ['tɜːndaʊn] ADJ *(collar)* rabattu; *(edge)* à rabattre

turned-up ADJ *(collar etc)* relevé; *(nose)* retroussé

turner ['tɜːnə(r)] N **1** *(lathe operator)* tourneur *m* **2** *Am (gymnast)* gymnaste *mf*

turnery ['tɜːnərɪ] *(pl* **turneries***)* N atelier *m* de tournage

turning ['tɜːnɪŋ] N **1** *Br (side road)* route *f* transversale; *(side street)* rue *f* transversale, petite rue *f*; **take the third t. on the right** prenez la troisième à droite

2 *Br (bend ▸ in road)* virage *m*; *(▸ in river, staircase)* coude *m*; *(fork)* embranchement *m*, carrefour *m*

3 the t. of the tide le changement *ou* renversement de la marée; *Fig* le renversement de tendances

4 *Ind* tournage *m*

▸▸ *Br Aut* ***turning circle*** rayon *m* de braquage; ***turning point*** *(decisive moment)* moment *m* décisif; *(change)* tournant *m*; **1989 marked a t. point in my career** l'année 1989 marqua un tournant dans ma carrière; **it was a t. point in her life** ce fut un tournant dans sa vie; *Am* ***turning radius*** rayon *m* de braquage

turnip ['tɜːnɪp] N navet *m*

turnkey ['tɜːnkiː] N *Arch (jailer)* geôlier(ère) *m,f*

ADJ *Constr (project, factory, plant)* clés en main

▸▸ *Comput* ***turnkey system*** système *m* clés en main

turn-off N **1** *(road)* sortie *f* (de route), route *f* transversale, embranchement *m* **2** *Fam* **it's a real t.** *(gen)* c'est vraiment à vous dégoûter; *(sexual)* ça vous coupe vraiment l'envie

turn-of-the-century ADJ du début du siècle; **t. London** le Londres du début du siècle

turn-on N *Fam* **what a t.!** c'est excitant!; **he finds leather a t.** il trouve le cuir excitant, le cuir l'excite

turnout ['tɜːnaʊt] N **1** *(attendance ▸ at meeting, concert)* assistance *f*; *Pol (at election)* (taux *m* de) participation *f*; **there was a good t.** *(gen)* il y avait beaucoup de monde, beaucoup de gens sont venus; *Pol* il y avait un fort taux de participation; **low turnouts at elections** faible participation *f* aux élections **2** *(dress)* mise *f*, tenue *f* **3** *Am Aut* refuge *m (pour se laisser doubler)*

turnover ['tɜːn,əʊvə(r)] N **1** *Br Fin (of company)* chiffre *m* d'affaires; *(of capital)* rotation *f*; **his t. is £100,000 per annum** il fait 100 000 livres de chiffre d'affaires par an

2 *(of staff, tenants)* renouvellement *m*; **the (staff) t. there is very high** le taux de renouvellement du personnel y est très élevé; **there is a high t. of tenants** les locataires changent souvent

3 *Am (of stock)* vitesse *f* de rotation, écoulement *m*; *(of shares)* mouvement *m*; **computer magazines have a high t.** les revues d'informatique se vendent bien

4 *Culin* **apple t.** chausson *m* aux pommes

5 *Sport (in basketball, American football)* perte *f* de balle

▸▸ *Com* ***turnover rate*** taux *m* de rotation; *Fin* ***turnover tax*** impôt *m ou* taxe *f* sur le chiffre d'affaires

turnpike ['tɜːnpaɪk] N **1** *(barrier)* barrière *f* de péage **2** *Am (road)* autoroute *f* à péage

turnround ['tɜːnraʊnd] *esp Br* = **turnaround**

turnstile ['tɜːnstaɪl] N tourniquet *m (barrière)*

turntable ['tɜːn,teɪbəl] N **1** *(on record player)* platine *f* **2** *Rail* plaque *f* tournante **3** *(on microscope)* platine *f*

▸▸ ***turntable ladder*** échelle *f* pivotante *(des pompiers)*

turn-up N *Br* **1** *(on trousers)* revers *m* **2** *Fam (surprise)* surprise□*f*; **that's a t. for the book** *or* **books** c'est une sacrée surprise

turpentine ['tɜːpəntaɪn] N *(UNCOUNT) Br* (essence *f* de) térébenthine *f*

▸▸ ***turpentine substitute*** white-spirit *m*

turpitude ['tɜːpɪtjuːd] N turpitude *f*

turps [tɜːps] N *(UNCOUNT) Br Fam* (essence *f* de) térébenthine□*f*

turquoise ['tɜːkwɔɪz] N **1** *(gem)* turquoise *f* **2** *(colour)* turquoise *m inv*

ADJ **1** *(bracelet, ring)* de *ou* en turquoise **2** *(in colour)* turquoise *(inv)*

turret ['tʌrɪt] N *Archit, Mil & Tech* tourelle *f*

▸▸ *Mil* ***turret gun*** canon *m* de tourelle; *Tech* ***turret lathe*** tour *m* revolver

turreted ['tʌrɪtɪd], **turriculated** [tə'rɪkjuleɪtɪd] ADJ *Archit (castle)* à tourelles

turtle ['tɜːtəl] N **1** *(in sea)* tortue *f* marine; *Am (on land)* tortue *f* **2** *Comput* tortue *f* **3** *(idiom)* **to turn t.** se renverser

▸▸ *Culin* ***turtle soup*** consommé *m* à la tortue

turves [tɜːvz] *pl of* **turf**

Tuscan ['tʌskən] N **1** *(person)* Toscan(e) *m,f* **2** *Ling* toscan *m*

ADJ toscan

Tuscany ['tʌskənɪ] N Toscane *f*

tush[1] [tʊʃ] N *Am Fam (buttocks)* fesses *fpl*

tush[2] [tʌʃ] EXCLAM *Old-fashioned* bah!, taratata

tusk [tʌsk] N *(of elephant, boar)* défense *f*

tusker ['tʌskə(r)] N *(elephant)* éléphant *m (adulte)*; *(boar)* sanglier *m (adulte)*

tussle ['tʌsəl] N **1** *(scuffle)* mêlée *f*, bagarre *f*; **to have a t. with sb** se battre contre qn, en venir aux mains avec qn **2** *(struggle)* lutte *f*; **it was quite a t. to get him to agree** il a fallu pas mal lutter *ou* faire des pieds et des mains pour qu'il accepte **3** *(quarrel)* dispute *f*; **to have a t. with sb** se disputer avec qn

VI *(scuffle, fight)* se battre; **I tussled with her for he ball** je me suis battu avec elle pour avoir la alle, on s'est disputé la balle; **the kids were tusling over the toy** les gosses se disputaient le ouet

ussock ['tʌsək] **N** touffe *f* d'herbe

ut [tʌt] *(pt & pp* **tutted**, *cont* **tutting)** **EXCLAM t.!, t.-.!** *(in disapproval)* allons donc!; *(in annoyance)* ut!

VI *(in disapproval)* pousser une exclamation ésapprobatrice; *(in annoyance)* exprimer son nécontentement; **she tutted with disapproval** lle eut une exclamation désapprobatrice

utelage ['tju:tɪlɪdʒ] **N** *Formal* tutelle *f*; **under his t.** ous sa tutelle

utelary ['tju:tɪlərɪ] **ADJ** *Formal* tutélaire

utor ['tju:tə(r)] **N 1** *(teacher)* professeur *m* particulier; *(full-time)* précepteur(trice) *m,f*; **piano t.** professeur *m* de piano; **she has a private German** . elle prend des cours particuliers avec un proesseur d'allemand **2** *Br Univ (teacher)* directeur trice) *m,f* d'études; *Br Sch* professeur *m* princial *(surtout dans les écoles privées)*

VT 1 *(instruct)* donner des cours (particuliers) à; **m tutoring her in maths** je lui donne des cours articuliers de maths **2** *Br Univ* diriger les études le

VI *(teacher)* donner des cours particuliers

utorial [tju:'tɔ:rɪəl] **N 1** *Univ* (séance *f* de) traaux *mpl* dirigés, TD *mpl*; **a maths t.** des TD *mpl* le maths **2** *Comput* didacticiel *m*

ADJ *(duties)* de directeur d'études; **t. work** traaux *mpl* dirigés; **the t. system** = le système d'enignement où les étudiants sont supervisés ar un directeur d'études

▸▸ *Comput* ***tutorial program*** didacticiel *m*

utti frutti [ˌtu:tɪ'fru:tɪ] *(pl* **tutti fruttis)** **N** plombières *f*, tutti frutti *m*

ADJ *(ice cream, flavour)* tutti frutti *(inv)*

ut-tut = **tut**

utu ['tu:tu:] **N** tutu *m*

u-whit tu-whoo [tə'wɪttə'wu:] **ONOMAT** houou

ux [tʌks] **N** *Fam (abbr* **tuxedo)** smoking▫ *m*

uxedo [tʌk'si:dəʊ] *(pl* **tuxedos)** **N** *Am* smoking *m*

V¹ [ˌti:'vi:] *(abbr* **television)** **N** TV *f*

COMP *(programme, set)* de télé; *(star)* de la télé

▸▸ ***TV advertisement*** publicité *f* télévisée; ***TV advertising*** publicité *f* télévisée; ***TV campaign*** campagne *f* télévisuelle; ***TV commercial*** spot *m*; ***TV dinner*** plateau-repas *m*, repas *m* tout prêt *ou* prêt à consommer *(que l'on mange devant la télé)*; ***TV movie*** téléfilm *m*

V² **N** *Fam (abbr* **transvestite)** travelo *m*

VP [ˌti:vi:'pi:] **N** *Culin (abbr* **textured vegetable protein)** protéine *f* végétale texturée

waddle ['twɒdəl] **N** *(UNCOUNT) Br Fam* bêtises *fpl*, âneries *fpl*, imbécillités▫ *fpl*; **what a load of t.!** n'importe quoi!; **to talk t.** dire *ou* débiter des bêises *ou* des âneries

wain [tweɪn] **N** *Literary* **the t.** les deux; **never or ne'er the t. shall meet** *(gen)* les deux sont inconciiables; *(of people)* les deux ne pourront jamais se mettre d'accord

wang [twæŋ] **N 1** *(of wire, guitar)* son *m* de corde pincée **2** *(in voice)* ton *m* nasillard; **she speaks with a t.** elle parle du nez, elle nasille **3** *(accent)* accent *m*; **he has a slight Australian t.** il a un léger accent australien

VT *(string instrument)* pincer les cordes de

VI *(arrow, bow, wire)* vibrer; **the arrow twanged through the air** la flèche a traversé l'air en vibrant

twas [twɒz] *Literary or Fam* = **it was**

wat [twæt] **N** *very Fam* **1** *(woman's genitals)* chatte *f*, chagatte *f* **2** *(person)* tache *f*, taré(e) *m,f*

weak [twi:k] **VT 1** *(twist* ▸ *ear, nose)* tordre (doucement), pincer; *(pull)* tirer (sur) **2** *Aut* mettre au point; *Fig (text)* apporter quelques petites modifications à, mettre au point; *Comput* peaufiner, mettre au point

N (petit) coup *m* sec; **he gave my ear a t.** il m'a tiré l'oreille

wee [twi:] **ADJ** *Br Fam Pej (person)* chichiteux; *(idea, sentiment)* mièvre▫; *(village, decor)* cucul *(inv)*

tweed [twi:d] **N** *(cloth)* tweed *m*

COMP *(jacket, skirt)* de tweed, en tweed

• **tweeds** **NPL** *(clothes)* vêtements *mpl* de *ou* en tweed; *(suit)* costume *m* de *ou* en tweed; **a smart lady in tweeds** une femme élégante en tailleur de tweed

tweedy ['twi:dɪ] *(compar* **tweedier**, *superl* **tweediest)** **ADJ 1** *(fabric)* qui ressemble au tweed **2** *Pej (man)* qui a le genre gentleman-farmer; *(woman)* qui fait bourgeoise de campagne

'tween [twi:n] *Literary* = **between**

tween [twi:n] = **tweenager**

tweenager ['twi:nˌeɪdʒə(r)] **N** *Fam* = terme utilisé par les professionnels de la vente pour désigner les enfants de 7 à 12 ans envisagés comme consommateurs

tweet [twi:t] **N** pépiement *m*

ONOMAT cui-cui

VI pépier

tweeter ['twi:tə(r)] **N** tweeter *m*, haut-parleur *m* d'aigus

tweezers ['twi:zəz] **NPL (pair of) t.** pince *f* à épiler

twelfth [twelfθ] **N 1** *(fraction)* douzième *m*
2 *(in series)* douzième *mf*
3 *(of month)* douze *m inv*
4 *Mus* douzième *f*

ADJ douzième

ADV douzièmement; *(in contest)* en douzième position, à la douzième place; *see also* **fifth**

▸▸ *Am Sch* ***twelfth grade*** = classe de lycée pour les 17–18 ans, ≃ (classe *f* de) terminale *f*; ***twelfth man (in cricket)*** joueur *m* de réserve; ***Twelfth Night*** la fête des Rois

twelve [twelv] **N** *(number, numeral)* douze *m inv*

PRON douze; **about t.** une douzaine

ADJ douze; **about t. people** une douzaine de personnes; *see also* **five**

twelvemonth ['twelvmʌnθ] **N** *Br Arch or Literary* année *f*, an *m*

twelve-tone **ADJ** *Mus* dodécaphonique

▸▸ ***twelve-tone system*** dodécaphonisme *m*

twentieth ['twentɪəθ] **N 1** *(fraction)* vingtième *m* **2** *(in series)* vingtième *mf* **3** *(of month)* vingt *m inv*

ADJ vingtième; *see also* **fifth**

twenty ['twentɪ] **N** *(pl* **twenties)** vingt *m inv*

PRON vingt; **about t.** une vingtaine

ADJ vingt; *see also* **fifty**

twenty-first **N** *(birthday)* vingt-et-unième anniversaire *m*

TWENTY-FIRST BIRTHDAY

En Grande-Bretagne, l'âge de la majorité est passé de 21 ans à 18 ans en 1970. Néanmoins, le vingt-et-unième anniversaire a conservé sa signification symbolique et reste une étape toute aussi importante – voire plus importante – que les 18 ans. Traditionnellement, l'on dit qu'à 21 ans on reçoit la clé de la porte de la maison ("to get the key to the door") et c'est pourquoi les cartes célébrant le vingt-et-unième anniversaire (ainsi que les gâteaux préparés à cette occasion) représentent le plus souvent une clé.

twenty-four **ADJ a t.-hour petrol station** une station-service ouverte jour et nuit *ou* vingt-quatre heures sur vingt-quatre; **open t. hours a day** ouvert vingt-quatre heures sur vingt-quatre

▸▸ ***twenty-four-hour clock*** = indication de l'heure selon un système qui va de 0 à 24; ***twenty-four-hour service*** service *m* vingt-quatre heures sur vingt-quatre *ou* jour et nuit

twenty-four/seven **ADV** *Fam* sans arrêt▫

twenty-one **N** *(pontoon)* vingt-et-un *m inv (jeu)*

twenty-twenty vision **N to have t.** avoir dix dixièmes à chaque œil

'twere [twɜ:(r)] *Literary or Fam* = **it were**

twerp [twɜ:p] **N** *Br Fam* courge *f*, nouille *f*

twice [twaɪs] **ADV 1** *(with noun)* deux fois; **t. 3 is 6** deux fois 3 font 6 **2** *(with verb)* deux fois; **I've already told you t.** je te l'ai déjà dit deux fois, je te l'ai déjà répété; **they didn't need to be asked** *or* **told t.** ils ne se sont pas fait prier, ils ne se le sont pas fait dire deux fois; **to think t. before doing sth** y regarder *ou* réfléchir à deux fois avant de faire qch; **to think t. before saying sth** réfléchir avant de parler; **she didn't have to think t. before accepting** elle a accepté sans hésiter **3** *(with adjective or adverb)* **t. weekly/daily** deux fois par semaine/jour; **she can run t. as fast as me** elle court deux fois plus vite que moi; **it's t. as good** c'est deux fois mieux; **t. as much time/as many apples** deux fois plus de temps/de pommes

PREDET deux fois; **t. a day** deux fois par jour; **t. the price** deux fois plus cher; **he's almost t. your height** il est presque deux fois plus grand que vous; **he's t. the man you are!** il vaut deux fois mieux que toi!

twiddle ['twɪdəl] **VT** *(knob, dial)* tourner, manier; *(moustache)* tripoter, jouer avec; *also Fig* **to t. one's thumbs** se tourner les pouces

VI to t. with the knob tourner le bouton; **to t. with the radio** jouer avec la radio; **she sat there twiddling with a ruler** elle était assise là à jouer avec une règle

N give the knob a t. tournez le bouton

twig [twɪg] *(pt & pp* **twigged**, *cont* **twigging)** **VI** *Br Fam (understand)* piger

VT *Br Fam (understand)* piger

N *(for fire)* brindille *f*; *(on tree)* petite branche *f*

twilight ['twaɪlaɪt] **N 1** *(in evening)* crépuscule *m*; *(in morning)* aube *f*; **at t.** *(evening)* au crépuscule; *(morning)* à l'aube **2** *(half-light)* pénombre *f*, obscurité *f*, demi-jour *m*; **I could hardly see you in the t.** je vous voyais à peine dans la pénombre **3** *Fig (last stages, end)* crépuscule *m*; **in the t. of his life** au crépuscule de sa vie

ADJ the t. hours le crépuscule; **a t. world** un monde nébuleux; **his t. years** les dernières années *fpl* de sa vie

▸▸ ***twilight zone*** *(in city)* quartier *m* délabré *(qui entoure un quartier commercial)*; *(in ocean)* zone *f* crépusculaire; *Fig* zone *f* d'ombre, zone *f* floue

'twill [twɪl] *Literary or Fam* = **it will**

twill [twɪl] **N** sergé *m*

twin [twɪn] *(pt & pp* **twinned**, *cont* **twinning)** **N** jumeau(elle) *m,f*; **she gave birth to twins** elle a donné naissance à des jumeaux

ADJ 1 *(child, sibling)* **they have t. boys/girls** ils ont des jumeaux/des jumelles; **my t. sister** ma sœur jumelle **2** *(dual* ▸ *spires, hills)* double, jumeau; *(*▸ *aims)* double; **the t. towers overlooking the bay** les deux tours qui surplombent la baie

VT *(town)* jumeler; **our town is twinned with Hamburg** notre ville est jumelée avec Hambourg

▸▸ ***twin beds*** lits *m* jumeaux; *Am Fam* ***twin bill*** *Cin* = séance avec deux longs métrages à la suite; *TV* = programmation de deux longs métrages à la suite; *Med* ***twin birth*** accouchement *m* de jumeaux; ***twin camshaft*** double arbre *m* à cames; ***twin carburettor*** carburateur *m* double-corps; ***twin cylinder*** **N** moteur *m* à deux cylindres **ADJ** à deux cylindres; ***twin room*** chambre *f* à deux lits; ***twin town*** ville *f* jumelée *ou* jumelle; ***twin tub*** machine *f* à laver à deux tambours

twin-bedded [-'bedɪd] **ADJ** *(room)* à deux lits

twin-cam **N** double arbre *m* à cames

twine [twaɪn] **VT 1** *(wind* ▸ *hair, string)* entortiller, enrouler; **she twined the rope round a post** elle enroula la corde autour d'un poteau; **the honeysuckle had twined itself around the tree** le chèvrefeuille s'était enroulé autour de l'arbre **2** *(weave)* tresser

VI 1 *(stem, ivy)* s'enrouler; **the honeysuckle had twined around the tree** le chèvrefeuille s'était enroulé autour de l'arbre **2** *(path, river)* serpenter

N *(UNCOUNT)* (grosse) ficelle *f*

twin-engined [-'endʒɪnd] **ADJ** bimoteur

twinge [twɪndʒ] **N 1** *(of guilt, shame)* sentiment *m*; *(of jealousy, regret, envy)* pointe *f*; **to have** *or* **to feel a t. of remorse** éprouver un certain remords; **he watched her leave with a t. of sadness** il la regarda partir avec (une certaine) tristesse **2** *(of pain)* élancement *m*, tiraillement *m*; **she felt a t. in her back** elle ressentit une petite douleur dans le dos

twining ['twaɪnɪŋ] **ADJ** *(plant)* volubile

twinjet ['twɪndʒet] **N** biréacteur *m*

twinkle ['twɪŋkəl] **VI 1** *(star, diamond)* briller, scintiller **2** *(eyes)* briller, pétiller; **her eyes twinkled with excitement** ses yeux brillaient d'excitation

N 1 *(of star, diamond, light)* scintillement *m* **2** *(in*

eye) pétillement *m*; **he had a mischievous t. in his eye** il avait les yeux pétillants de malice; *Hum* **when you were just a t. in your father's eye** bien avant que tu ne fasses ton entrée dans le monde; **in a t. (of an eye)** en un clin d'œil

twinkling ['twɪŋklɪŋ] **ADJ 1** *(star, gem, sea)* scintillant, brillant **2** *(eyes)* pétillant, brillant **3** *Fig (feet)* agile

N 1 *(of star, light, gem)* scintillement *m* **2** *(in eyes)* pétillement *m*; **in the t. of an eye** en un clin d'œil

twinky ['twɪŋkɪ] *(pl* **twinkies***)* **N** *Am Fam (homosexual)* homo *m*

twinning ['twɪnɪŋ] **N** *(of towns)* jumelage *m*

twinset ['twɪnˌset] **N** twin set *m*; *Br Fam Pej* **she's a bit t. and pearls** ≃ elle fait un peu foulard Hermès et collier de perles, elle fait plutôt BCBG

twirl [twɜːl] **VT 1** *(spin ▸ stick, parasol, lasso)* faire tournoyer; *(handle)* tourner; **she twirled the stick (round) in the air** elle jeta le bâton en l'air en le faisant tournoyer **2** *(twist ▸ moustache, hair)* tortiller, friser

VI *(dancer, lasso)* tournoyer; **she twirled round to face us** elle se tourna pour nous faire face, elle fit volte-face vers nous

N 1 *(whirl ▸ of body, stick)* tournoiement *m*; *(pirouette)* pirouette *f*; **I gave the top/wheel a t.** j'ai fait tourner la toupie/la roue; **to do a t.** tourner sur soi-même, faire une pirouette **2** *(written flourish)* fioriture *f*

TWIST [twɪst]

> **VT**
> - tourner **1–3**
> - tordre **1, 4**
> - tresser **2**
> - enrouler **2**
> - déformer **5**
>
> **VI**
> - serpenter **1**
> - s'enrouler **2**
> - se tortiller **3**
> - se tordre **4**
>
> **N**
> - tour **1, 5**
> - torsion **1**
> - tournant **2**
> - virage **2**
> - twist **6**

VT 1 *(turn ▸ round and round)* tourner; *(▸ round axis)* tourner, visser; *(▸ tightly)* tordre; **try twisting the dial to the left** essaie de tourner le cadran vers la gauche; **you have to t. the lid off** il faut dévisser le couvercle dans le sens des aiguilles d'une montre; **she twisted her hankie nervously** elle tordait nerveusement son mouchoir; **he twisted the wire into the shape of a dog** il a tordu le fil pour lui donner la forme d'un chien; **the railings were twisted out of shape** les grilles étaient toutes tordues

2 *(twine)* tresser, entortiller; *(wind)* enrouler, tourner; **she twisted her hair into a bun** elle s'est coiffée en chignon, elle a torsadé ses cheveux pour faire un chignon; **the seat belt got twisted** la ceinture (de sécurité) s'est entortillée; **the wires got twisted** les fils se sont entortillés; **he twisted the threads into a rope** il a tressé *ou* torsadé les fils pour en faire une corde

3 *(body, part of body)* tourner; **I twisted my head (round) to the left** j'ai tourné la tête vers la gauche; *Fig* **her face was twisted with pain** ses traits étaient tordus par la douleur, la douleur lui tordait le visage; **to t. sb's arm** tordre le bras à qn; *Fig* forcer la main à qn; **if you t. his arm, he'll agree to go** si tu insistes un peu, il voudra bien y aller

4 *(sprain ▸ ankle, wrist)* tordre, fouler; **I've twisted my ankle** je me suis tordu *ou* foulé la cheville; **I seem to have twisted my neck** je crois que j'ai attrapé un torticolis

5 *(distort ▸ words)* déformer; *(▸ argument)* déformer, fausser; **don't t. the facts to suit your argument** ne déformez pas les faits pour étayer votre argument

6 *Br Fam (cheat, swindle)* arnaquer; **I've been twisted** je me suis fait avoir

VI 1 *(road, stream)* serpenter; **the path twisted and turned through the forest** le chemin zigzaguait à travers la forêt

2 *(become twined)* s'enrouler; **the ivy twisted round the tree** le lierre s'enroulait autour de l'arbre

3 *(body, part of body)* se tortiller; **he twisted and turned to get himself free** il s'est tortillé tant qu'il a pu pour se dégager; **his mouth twisted into a smile** il eut un rictus

4 *(be sprained ▸ ankle)* se tordre, se fouler; *(▸ knee)* se tordre

5 *(dance)* twister

6 *(in pontoon)* **t.!** encore une carte!

N 1 *(turn, twirl)* tour *m*, torsion *f*; **to give sth a t.** *(dial, handle, lid)* (faire) tourner qch; *(wire)* tordre qch; **with a t. of the wrist** en un tour de main; **there's a t. in the tape** la bande est entortillée; **to get (oneself) into a t. about sth** *(get angry)* se fâcher *ou* s'énerver au sujet de qch; *(get upset)* prendre qch au tragique, se mettre dans tous ses états à cause de qch

2 *(in road)* tournant *m*, virage *m*; *(in river)* coude *m*; *(in staircase)* tournant *m*; *Fig (in thinking)* détour *m*; **the road has many twists and turns** la route a beaucoup de tournants et de virages *ou* fait de nombreux tours et détours; **it's difficult to follow the twists and turns of his argument/of government policy** il est difficile de suivre les méandres de son argumentation/de la politique gouvernementale

3 *(coil ▸ of tobacco)* rouleau *m*; *(▸ of paper)* tortillon *m*

4 *Culin* **a t. of lemon** un zeste de citron

5 *(in story, plot)* tour *m*; **the film has an exciting t. at the end** le film se termine par un coup de théâtre passionnant; **there is an ironic t. to the story** l'histoire comporte un tour ironique; **the book gives a new t. to the old story** le livre donne une nouvelle tournure *ou* un tour nouveau à cette vieille histoire; **by a strange t. of fate, we met again years later in Zimbabwe** par un hasard extraordinaire *ou* un caprice du destin, nous nous sommes retrouvés au Zimbabwe des années après

6 *(dance)* twist *m*; **to do** *or* **to dance the t.** twister

7 *Br Fam (cheat)* arnaque *f*; **it's a real t.!** c'est vraiment de l'arnaque *ou* du vol!; **what a t.!** on s'est bien fait avoir!

8 *Br Fam (idiom)* **to be completely round the t.** être complètement dingue *ou* cinglé; **to go round the t.** devenir dingue *ou* cinglé, perdre la boule; **to drive sb round the t.** rendre qn chèvre *ou* dingue

▸▸ ***twist grip*** *(accelerator)* poignée *f* d'accélération; *(gear change)* poignée *f* de changement de vitesses

▸ **twist off VT SEP** *(lid)* dévisser; *(cork)* enlever en tournant; *(branch)* enlever *ou* arracher en tordant

VI *(cap, lid)* se dévisser

▸ **twist round** *Br* **VT SEP** *(rope, tape)* enrouler; *(lid)* visser; *(handle)* (faire) tourner; *(swivel chair)* faire tourner *ou* pivoter; *(hat, head)* tourner; **I twisted myself round on my chair** je me suis retourné sur ma chaise

VI 1 *(person)* se retourner **2** *(strap, rope)* s'entortiller; *(swivel chair)* pivoter **3** *(path)* serpenter, zigzaguer

▸ **twist up VT SEP** *(threads, wires)* enrouler, emmêler

VI 1 *(threads, wires)* s'emmêler, s'enchevêtrer **2** *(smoke)* monter en volutes

twisted ['twɪstɪd] **ADJ 1** *(piece of metal)* tordu; *(piece of string)* entortillé; **the t. wreckage of the plane/car** l'épave *f* tordue de l'avion/de la voiture

2 *(personality, smile)* tordu; *(mind)* tordu, mal tourné

3 *(logic, argument)* faux (fausse), tordu; **by a kind of t. logic** selon une sorte de logique tordue

4 *(dishonest)* malhonnête; *(politician, lawyer, businessman)* malhonnête, véreux

5 *Fam (crazy)* tordu

▸▸ *Archit* ***twisted pillar*** colonne *f* torse

twisted-pair cable N câble *m* en paire torsadée

twister ['twɪstə(r)] **N** *Fam* **1** *Br (crook)* arnaqueur (euse) *m,f* **2** *(tornado)* tornade *f*

twisting ['twɪstɪŋ] **ADJ** *(path)* tortueux

twisty ['twɪstɪ] **ADJ** *(road, river)* sinueux, qui serpente

twit [twɪt] *(pt & pp* **twitted**, *cont* **twitting***)* **N** *Br Fam (idiot)* courge *f*, nouille *f*; **you silly t.!** espèce d'idiot *ou* de crétin!

VT *Old-fashioned (tease)* taquiner; **they twitted him about his hat** ils l'ont taquiné sur *ou* à propos de son chapeau

twitch [twɪtʃ] **VI** *(jerk ▸ once)* avoir un mouve ment convulsif; *(▸ habitually)* avoir un tic *(muscle)* se contracter convulsivement; **h hands twitched nervously** ses mains se contrac taient nerveusement; **his right eye twitches** il un tic à l'œil droit

VT *(ears, nose)* remuer, bouger; *(curtain, rope)* t rer d'un coup sec, donner un coup sec à; **to t. i tail** *(of cat)* remuer la queue; **she twitched m sleeve** elle tira ma manche d'un petit coup sec **she twitched the scarf out of my hands** elle m'arra cha l'écharpe des mains

N 1 *(nervous tic)* tic *m*; *(muscular spasm)* spasm *m*; **to have a (nervous) t.** avoir un tic (nerveux) *(tweak, pull ▸ on hair, rope)* coup *m* sec, saccad *f*; **a t. of the whip** un petit coup de fouet

twitcher ['twɪtʃə(r)] **N** *Fam Pej* dingue *mf* d'orn thologie

twitter ['twɪtə(r)] **VI 1** *(bird)* gazouiller, pépier *Pej (person ▸ chatter)* jacasser; **she's always twi tering (on) about her daughter** elle ne parle qu de sa fille

N 1 *(of bird)* gazouillement *m*, pépiement *m* *Pej (of person)* bavardage *m* **3** *Fam (agitation)* éta *m* d'agitation; **to be all of a** *or* **in a t. about s** être dans tous ses états *ou* sens dessus dessou à cause de qch

twittering ['twɪtərɪŋ] **ADJ** *(bird)* gazouillant; *P (person, voice)* piaillant

N *(of bird)* gazouillement *m*; *Pej (talk)* jacasse ment *m*

'twixt [twɪkst] *Literary* = **betwixt**

two [tuː] **N** *(pl* **twos***)* **1** *(number, numeral)* deux *inv*; **to cut sth in t.** couper qch en deux; **in twos, by t.** deux par deux; **in twos and threes** par (grou pes de) deux ou trois; **t. at a time** deux à la fois *(idioms)* **to put t. and t. together** faire le rappo (entre deux choses) et tirer ses conclusions **they're t. of a kind** ils sont du même genre, ils s ressemblent tous les deux; **that makes t. of u** vous n'êtes pas le seul, moi c'est pareil; **t.'s com pany, three's a crowd** deux ça va, trois c'est trop **she blames him but it takes t. to tango** elle dit qu c'est de sa faute à lui, mais ils ont tous les deu leur part de responsabilité

PRON deux

ADJ deux; *see also* **five**

2.5G [ˌtuːpɔɪntfaɪvˈdʒiː] **ADJ** *Comput & Tel* 2.5G

two-bit ADJ *Am Fam Pej* de pacotille

two-colour, two-coloured, *Am* **two-colo two-colored ADJ** de deux couleurs, bicolore *Phot* bicolore

▸▸ ***two-colour printing*** impression *f* en deu couleurs *ou* en bichromie, bichromie *f*; ***two colour process*** bichromie *f*

two-dimensional ADJ 1 *(figure, drawing)* deux dimensions **2** *(character ▸ in book, pla etc)* sans profondeur, simpliste

two-door ADJ *(car)* à deux portes

two-edged ADJ *(sword, policy, argument)* double tranchant

two-faced ADJ hypocrite

twofold ['tuːfəʊld] **ADJ** double; **their aims are** ils ont deux objectifs *ou* un objectif double **there has been a t. increase in attendance** le nom bre de personnes présentes a doublé

ADV *(increase)* au double; **prices have risen t.** le prix ont doublé

two-four time N *Mus* mesure *f* à deux temps deux-quatre *m inv*

2G [ˌtuːˈdʒiː] **ADJ** *Comput & Tel* 2G

two-handed ADJ 1 *(tool)* à deux poignées *(saw)* à deux mains, forestière; *(sword)* à deu mains **2** *(game)* qui se joue à deux, pour deu joueurs **3** *(in tennis)* à deux mains; **a t. backhan** un revers à deux mains

two-hander N *Theat* pièce *f* pour deux ac teurs; *Cin* film *m* à deux personnages

two-headed ADJ bicéphale; *Her (eagle)* dou ble, à deux têtes

two-horse ADJ *(carriage)* à deux chevaux; *E Fig* **a t. race** une épreuve/élection qui ne com prend que deux concurrents

two-legged ADJ bipède

vo-line whip N *Br Pol* = convocation d'un éputé par un "whip" à un débat ou à un vote rs d'une séance parlementaire

vonk [twɒŋk] N *Fam (fool)* andouille *f*, cruche *f*, oche *f*

vo-party ADJ *Pol (coalition, system)* biparti, partite

vopence ['tʌpəns] N *Br* deux (anciens) pence *pl*; *Fam* **I don't give t. for what he thinks** je me oque bien *ou* je me fiche pas mal de ce qu'il ense

vopenny ['tʌpnɪ] ADJ *Br* à *ou* de deux pence; *m Fig (worthless)* de quatre sous, qui ne vaut as un clou

▸ ***twopenny bit, twopenny piece*** = ancienne ièce de deux pence

vopenny-halfpenny ADJ *Fam* qui ne vaut as un clou; *(solicitor, system)* à la gomme

vo-phase ADJ *Elec* diphasé, biphasé

vo-piece ADJ en deux parties; **t. suit** *(man's)* ɔstume *m* deux-pièces; *(woman's)* tailleur *m*; **swimming costume** (maillot *m* de bain) deux-ièces *m*

N *(bikini)* deux-pièces *m*; *(man's suit)* costume *m* eux-pièces; *(woman's suit)* tailleur *m*

vo-pin ADJ

▸ *Elec* ***two-pin plug*** prise *f* à deux fiches; ***two-in socket*** prise *f* à deux douilles

vo-ply N *(wool)* laine *f* à deux fils; *(wood)* ɔntreplaqué *m (à deux épaisseurs)*

ADJ *(wool)* à deux fils; *(rope)* à deux brins; *(tis-ue)* double, à double épaisseur; *(wood)* à deux paisseurs

vo-seater ADJ à deux places

N *(plane)* avion *m* à deux places; *(car)* voiture *f* à eux places

vo-sided ADJ **1** *(problem)* qui a deux aspects; *rgument)* discutable, qui comporte deux oints de vue **2** *(copy)* en recto-verso

vosome ['tu:səm] N **1** *(pair)* paire *f*; *(of friends c)* couple *m* **2** *(match, game)* partie *f* à deux

vo-speed ADJ *also Fig* à deux vitesses

▸ ***two-speed economy*** économie *f* à deux vites-es; ***two-speed Europe*** Europe *f* à deux vitesses; ***wo-speed wiper*** essuie-glace *m* à deux vitesses

vo-star ADJ **1** *(restaurant, hotel)* deux étoiles **2** *(petrol)* ordinaire

N *Br (petrol)* (essence *f*) ordinaire *m*

vo-step N *(dance, music)* pas *m* de deux

vo-storey, two-storeyed, *Am* **two-story, wo-storied** ADJ *(house)* à deux étages

vo-stroke ADJ *Br (engine)* à deux temps

vo-tier ADJ *(cake)* à deux étages; *(manage-ent structure)* à deux niveaux; *(education sys-m, health service)* à deux vitesses

vo-time VT *Fam (lover)* tromper▫, être infi-èle à▫

vo-timer N *Fam* personne *f* infidèle▫

vo-timing ADJ *Fam* infidèle▫; **you t. bastard!** spèce de salaud!

vo-tone ADJ *(in colour)* à deux tons; *(in sound)* e deux tons

would [twʊd] *Literary or Fam* = **it would**

vo-way ADJ *(traffic, trade)* dans les deux sens; *street)* à double sens; *(agreement, process)* bila-éral; **a relationship has got to be a t. thing** en amour omme en amitié, il faut savoir prendre et donner

▸ ***two-way mirror*** glace *f* sans tain; *Tel* ***two-way adio*** émetteur-récepteur *m*; *Elec* ***two-way switch*** a-et-vient *m inv*

vo-wheeler N *(motorbike)* deux-roues *m*; *(bi-ycle)* bicyclette *f*, deux-roues *m*

coon [taɪ'ku:n] N homme *m* d'affaires impor-ant, magnat *m*; **oil/newspaper t.** magnat *m* du étrole/de la presse

tyke [taɪk] N *Fam* **1** *(dog)* chien *m* bâtard▫ **2** *(child)* morveux(euse) *m,f*, môme *mf* **3** *Br (coarse person)* lourdaud(e) *m,f*

tympanum ['tɪmpənəm] *(pl* **tympana** [-nə] *or* **tympanums)** N **1** *Anat, Archit & Zool* tympan *m* **2** *Mus* tymbale *f*

type [taɪp] N **1** *(gen) & Biol* **blood/hair t.** type *m* sanguin/de cheveux

2 *(sort, kind)* sorte *f*, genre *m*, espèce *f*; *(make ▸ of coffee, shampoo etc)* marque *f*; *(model ▸ of car, plane, equipment etc)* modèle *m*; **what t. of washing powder do you use?** quelle (marque de) lessive utilisez-vous?; **what t. of car do you drive?** qu'est-ce que vous avez comme voiture?, quel modèle de voiture avez-vous?

3 *(referring to person)* genre *m*, type *m*; **she's not that t. (of person)** ce n'est pas son genre; **she's not the t. to gossip** elle n'est pas du genre à faire des commérages; **he's not my t.** ce n'est pas mon genre *ou* type (d'homme); **men of his t.** les hommes de son genre *ou* son espèce; **I know his/their t.** je connais les gens de son espèce/de leur espèce, je connais le genre; **she's one of those sporty types** elle est du genre sportif

4 *(typical example)* type *m*, exemple *m*

5 *(UNCOUNT) Typ (single character)* caractère *m*; *(block of print)* caractères *mpl* (d'imprimerie); **to set t.** composer

VT **1** *(of typist)* taper (à la machine), dactylographier; **to t. sth into a computer** saisir qch à l'ordinateur; **to t. a letter** taper une lettre **2** *Med (blood sample)* classifier

VI *(typist)* taper (à la machine); **I can only t. with two fingers** je ne tape qu'avec deux doigts

▸▸ *Biol* ***type genus*** genre *m* type; *Typ* ***type height*** hauteur *f* de caractère; ***type library*** typothèque *f*; *Typ* ***type size*** taille *f* des caractères, corps *m*

▸**type in** VT SEP taper

▸**type out** VT SEP **1** *(letter)* taper (à la machine) **2** *(error)* effacer (à la machine)

▸**type up** VT SEP *(report, notes)* taper (à la machine)

typecase ['taɪpkeɪs] N *Typ* casse *f*

typecast ['taɪpkɑ:st] *(pt & pp* **typecast)** VT *(actor)* enfermer dans le rôle de; **she was being t. as a dumb blonde** elle était cantonnée aux rôles de blondes écervelées; **he is always t. as a villain** on lui fait toujours jouer des rôles de bandit

typed [taɪpt] ADJ dactylographié, écrit à la machine

typeface ['taɪpfeɪs] N **1** *Typ (printing surface)* œil *m* du caractère **2** *Typ (type family)* famille *f* de caractères; *Comput* police *f* (de caractères); **try another t.** essaie avec un autre caractère

typescript ['taɪpskrɪpt] N texte *m* dactylographié, tapuscrit *m*

typeset ['taɪpset] *(pt & pp* **typeset,** *cont* **typesetting)** VT *Typ* composer

typesetter ['taɪpˌsetə(r)] N *Typ (worker)* compositeur(trice) *m,f*; *(company)* compositeur *m*; *(machine)* linotype® *f*; *Comput (in DTP)* photocomposeuse *f*

typesetting ['taɪpˌsetɪŋ] N *Typ* composition *f*

▸▸ ***typesetting machine*** machine *f* à composer

typewriter ['taɪpˌraɪtə(r)] N machine *f* à écrire

COMP *(ribbon)* de machine à écrire; *(rubber)* pour machine à écrire

typewriting ['taɪpˌraɪtɪŋ] N dactylographie *f*

typewritten ['taɪpˌrɪtən] ADJ dactylographié, tapé à la machine

typhoid ['taɪfɔɪd] N *(UNCOUNT)* typhoïde *f*

COMP *(injection)* antityphoïdique; *(symptoms)* de la typhoïde

▸▸ ***typhoid bacillus*** bacille *m* typhoïdique; ***typhoid fever*** (fièvre *f*) typhoïde *f*; *Am* **typhoid Mary** source *f* d'un fléau

typhoon [taɪ'fu:n] N typhon *m*

typhus ['taɪfəs] N typhus *m*

▸▸ ***typhus fever*** typhus *m*

typical ['tɪpɪkəl] ADJ typique, caractéristique; **such behaviour is t. of young people nowadays** un tel comportement est typique *ou* caractéristique des jeunes d'aujourd'hui; **it was t. of him to offer to pay** c'était bien son genre de proposer de payer; **it's a t. example of Aztec pottery** c'est un exemple type de poterie aztèque; **in a t. day you can earn £300** en une journée normale vous pouvez gagner 300 livres; **the t. American** l'Américain *m* typique *ou* type; *Pej* **that's t. of her!** c'est bien d'elle!; **your letter took six days to get here – t.!** ta lettre a mis six jours pour arriver – ça c'est typique! *ou* ça ne m'étonne pas!; **he said with t. self-deprecation** dit-il avec son humilité habituelle

typically ['tɪpɪklɪ] ADV **1** *(normally)* d'habitude; **it was a t. sunny day** c'était une journée ensoleillée, comme d'habitude **2** *(characteristically)* typiquement; **she's t. English** elle est typiquement anglaise, c'est l'Anglaise type *ou* typique; **a group of t. noisy schoolboys** un groupe de lycéens bruyants comme le sont tous les lycéens; **t., she changed her mind at the last minute** comme à son habitude, elle a changé d'avis au dernier moment; **employees t. work a 40-hour week** les employés travaillent en moyenne 40 heures par semaine

typify ['tɪpɪfaɪ] *(pt & pp* **typified)** VT **1** *(be typical of)* être typique *ou* caractéristique de **2** *(embody, symbolize)* symboliser, être le type même de; **she typifies the modern career woman** c'est le type même de la femme moderne qui poursuit une carrière

typing ['taɪpɪŋ] N **1** *(typing work)* **he had 10 pages of t. to do** il avait 10 pages à taper *ou* dactylographier **2** *(typescript)* tapuscrit *m*, texte *m* dactylographié **3** *(skill)* dactylo *f*, dactylographie *f*

▸▸ ***typing error*** faute *f* de frappe; ***typing paper*** papier *m* machine; ***typing pool*** bureau *m ou* pool *m* des dactylos; ***typing skills*** compétences *fpl* en dactylographie; ***typing speed*** vitesse *f* de frappe; **I have a t. speed of 30 words a minute** je tape 30 mots à la minute

typist ['taɪpɪst] N dactylo *mf*, dactylographe *mf*

typo ['taɪpəʊ] *(pl* **typos)** N *Fam (in typescript)* faute *f* de frappe▫; *(in printed text)* coquille▫ *f*

typographer [taɪ'pɒgrəfə(r)] N typographe *mf*

typographic [ˌtaɪpə'græfɪk], **typographical** [ˌtaɪpə'græfɪkəl] ADJ typographique

typographically [ˌtaɪpə'græfɪkəlɪ] ADV typographiquement

typography [taɪ'pɒgrəfɪ] N typographie *f*

typosquatting ['taɪpəʊˌskwɒtɪŋ] N *Comput* typosquatting *m*

tyrannical [tɪ'rænɪkəl] ADJ tyrannique

tyrannically [tɪ'rænɪkəlɪ] ADV tyranniquement, avec tyrannie

tyrannize, -ise ['tɪrənaɪz] VT tyranniser

tyranny ['tɪrənɪ] *(pl* **tyrannies)** N tyrannie *f*

tyrant ['taɪrənt] N tyran *m*; **to be a domestic t.** être un tyran domestique

tyre, *Am* **tire** ['taɪə(r)] N pneu *m*

▸▸ ***tyre chain*** chaîne *f* (de pneu); ***tyre fitter*** monteur *m* de pneus; ***tyre gauge*** manomètre *m (pour pneus)*; ***tyre iron, tyre lever*** démonte-pneu *m*; ***tyre pressure*** pression *f* des pneus; ***tyre pump*** pompe *f* (pour gonfler les pneus); ***tyre valve*** valve *f* de gonflage

tyro ['taɪrəʊ] *(pl* **tyros)** N *Formal* débutant(e) *m,f*, novice *mf*

Tyrol [tɪ'rəʊl] N Tyrol *m*

Tyrolean [tɪrə'lɪən], **Tyrolese** [ˌtɪrə'li:z] N Tyrolien(enne) *m,f*

ADJ tyrolien

▸▸ ***Tyrolean hat*** chapeau *m* tyrolien

tzar, tzarevitch *etc* = **tsar, tsarevitch** *etc*

T-zone N zones *fpl* grasses du visage *(front, nez, menton)*

U¹, u [ju:] **N** *(letter)* U, u *m inv*; **two u's** deux u

ADJ *Br Fam Old-fashioned (upper-class ▸ expression, activity)* distingué; **U/non-U language** langage *m* distingué/vulgaire

U² [ju:] **N** *Cin (abbr* **universal***)* = désigne un film tous publics en Grande-Bretagne

UAE [ju:eɪ'i:] **N** *(abbr* **United Arab Emirates***)* EAU *mpl*

U-bend **N 1** *(in pipe)* coude *m*; *(under sink)* siphon *m* **2** *Br (in road)* virage *m* en épingle à cheveux

UB40 [ju:bi:'fɔ:tɪ] **N** *Br Formerly (abbr* **unemployment benefit form 40***) (card)* = carte de pointage pour bénéficier de l'allocation de chômage; *Fam (person)* chômeur(euse) *m,f*

ubiquitous [ju:'bɪkwɪtəs] **ADJ** *(gen)* omniprésent, que l'on trouve partout; *(person)* doué d'ubiquité, omniprésent

ubiquity [ju:'bɪkwətɪ] **N** ubiquité *f*, omniprésence *f*

U-boat **N** sous-marin *m* allemand

U-bolt **N** agrafe *f* filetée, étrier *m*

UCAS ['ju:kæs] **N** *Br (abbr* **University and College Admissions Service***)* = organisme centralisant les demandes d'inscription dans les universités britanniques

UCITS [ju:si:aɪ,ti:'es] **N** *Fin (abbr* **undertakings for collective investment in transferables***)* OPCVM *m*

UDA [ju:di:'eɪ] **N** *(abbr* **Ulster Defence Association***)* = organisation paramilitaire protestante d'Irlande du Nord, déclarée hors la loi en 1992

udder ['ʌdə(r)] **N** mamelle *f*, pis *m*

UDI [ju:di:'aɪ] **N** *(abbr* **Unilateral Declaration of Independence***)* = déclaration unilatérale d'indépendance

UDR [ju:di:'ɑ:(r)] **N** *Br Formerly (abbr* **Ulster Defence Regiment***)* = ancien régiment de réservistes d'Irlande du Nord qui fait aujourd'hui partie du "Royal Irish Regiment"

UEFA [ju:'eɪfə] **N** *Ftbl (abbr* **Union of European Football Associations***)* UEFA *f*

UFO [ju:ef'əʊ, 'ju:fəʊ] **N** *(abbr* **unidentified flying object***)* OVNI *m*, ovni *m*

ufologist [ju:'fɒlədʒɪst] **N** spécialiste *mf* d'ufologie

ufology [ju:'fɒlədʒɪ] **N** ufologie *f*

Uganda [ju:'gændə] **N** Ouganda *m*

Ugandan [ju:'gændən] **N** Ougandais(e) *m,f*

ADJ ougandais

COMP *(embassy)* d'Ouganda; *(history)* de l'Ouganda

ugh [ʌg] **EXCLAM** beurk!, berk!, pouah!

ugli® ['ʌglɪ] *(pl* **uglis** *or* **uglies***)* **N u. (fruit)** tangelo *m*

uglify ['ʌglɪfaɪ] *(pt & pp* **uglified***)* **VT** *Fam (city, building)* enlaidir

ugliness ['ʌglɪnɪs] **N** laideur *f*

ugly ['ʌglɪ] *(compar* **uglier**, *superl* **ugliest***)* **ADJ 1** *(in appearance ▸ person, face, building)* laid; **it was an u. sight** ce n'était pas beau à voir; **as u. as sin** laid à faire peur; *(person)* laid comme un pou **2** *(unpleasant, nasty ▸ habit)* sale, désagréable; *(▸ behaviour)* répugnant; *(▸ quarrel)* mauvais; *(▸ clouds, weather)* vilain, sale; *(▸ bruise, wound, scar)* vilain, méchant; *(▸ rumour, word)* vilain; *(▸ situation)* fâcheux, mauvais; **there were some u. scenes** il y a eu du vilain; **he was in an u. mood** il était d'une humeur massacrante, il était de très mauvaise humeur; **she gave me an u. look** elle m'a regardé d'un sale œil; **he's an u. customer** c'est un sale individu; **to turn** *or* **to get u.** *(situation)* dégénérer, mal tourner

▸▸ ***ugly duckling*** vilain petit canard *m*; ***Ugly Sisters*** = les sœurs de Cendrillon, personnages de la "pantomime" anglaise

U-haul® ['ju:hɔ:l] **N** *Am* = camion ou caravane de location servant aux déménagements

▸▸ ***U-haul truck*** = camion de location servant aux déménagements

UHF [ju:eɪtʃ'ef] **N** *(abbr* **ultra-high frequency***)* UHF *f*

uh-huh [ʌ'hʌ] **EXCLAM** *Fam* **u.!** *(as conversation filler)* ah ah!; *(in assent)* oui oui!, OK!; **u.?** *(in question)* ah ha?; *(in surprise)* ah bon?, ah ouais?

UHT [ju:eɪtʃ'ti:] **ADJ** *(abbr* **ultra-heat-treated***)* UHT

UK [,ju:'keɪ] *(abbr* **United Kingdom***)* **N** Royaume-Uni *m*

COMP du Royaume-Uni

ukelele = **ukulele**

UKIP ['ju:kɪp] **N** *Br Pol (abbr* **UK Independence Party***)* = parti politique britannique qui prône le retrait du Royaume-Uni de l'Union européenne

Ukraine [ju:'kreɪn] **N (the) U.** Ukraine *f*

Ukrainian [ju:'kreɪnjən] **N 1** *(person)* Ukrainien(enne) *m,f* **2** *(language)* ukrainien *m*

ADJ ukrainien

COMP *(embassy)* d'Ukraine; *(history)* de l'Ukraine; *(teacher)* d'ukrainien

ukulele [ju:kə'leɪlɪ] **N** guitare *f* hawaïenne, ukulélé *m*

ulcer ['ʌlsə(r)] **N 1** *Med (in stomach)* ulcère *m*; *(in mouth)* aphte *m* **2** *Fig* plaie *f*

ulcerate ['ʌlsəreɪt] *Med* **VT** ulcérer

VI s'ulcérer

ulceration [,ʌlsə'reɪʃən] **N** *Med* ulcération *f*

ulcerative ['ʌlsərətɪv] **ADJ** *Med* ulcératif

ulcerous ['ʌlsərəs] **ADJ 1** *(ulcerated)* ulcéreux **2** *(causing ulcers)* ulcératif

ullage ['ʌlɪdʒ] **N 1** *(in transport)* = quantité de liquide perdue par évaporation ou par des fuites au cours du transport **2** *(in wine bottle)* = espace entre le bouchon et le vin

ulna ['ʌlnə] *(pl* **ulnae** [-ni:] *or* **ulnas***)* **N** cubitus *m*

Ulster ['ʌlstə(r)] **N 1** *(province)* Ulster *m* **2** *(Northern Ireland)* Irlande *f* du Nord, Ulster *m*

▸▸ ***Ulster Unionists*** = parti politique essentiellement protestant, favorable au maintien de l'Irlande du Nord au sein du Royaume-Uni

Ulsterman ['ʌlstəmən] *(pl* **Ulstermen** [-mən]*)* **N** Ulstérien *m*, habitant *m* de l'Irlande du Nord

Ulsterwoman ['ʌlstə,wʊmən] *(pl* **Ulsterwomen** [-'wɪmɪn]*)* **N** Ulstérienne *f*, habitante *f* de l'Irlande du Nord

ult *Old-fashioned (written abbr* **ultimo***)* du mois dernier

ulterior [ʌl'tɪərɪə(r)] **ADJ** *(hidden, secret)* secret (ète), dissimulé

▸▸ ***ulterior motive*** arrière-pensée *f*

ultimate ['ʌltɪmət] **ADJ 1** *(eventual, final ▸ am-tion, power, responsibility)* ultime; *(▸ cost, de-tination, objective)* ultime, final; *(▸ solutio-decision, answer)* final, définitif; **her tragic illne- and u. death deprived the world of a great artist** mort survenue à l'issue d'une tragique malad- a privé le monde d'une grande artiste; **they ▸ gard nuclear weapons as the u. deterrent** ils con- dèrent les armes nucléaires comme l'ultim- moyen de dissuasion

2 *(basic, fundamental ▸ cause)* fondament- premier; *(▸ truth)* fondamental, élémentai- **the u. constituents of matter** les constituants fo- damentaux de la matière; **the u. meaning of l-** le sens fondamental de la vie

3 *(extreme, supreme ▸ authority, insult)* suprêm- *(▸ cruelty, stupidity)* suprême, extrême; **it's th- idea of the u. holiday** c'est leur conception d- vacances idéales; **the u. sound system** la me- leure sono qui soit; **the u. sacrifice** le sacrifice s- prême

4 *(furthest)* le plus éloigné; **the u. origins of ma- kind** les origines premières de l'homme

N comble *m*, summum *m*; **the u. in comfort** summum du confort; **the u. in hi-fi** le nec plus - tra de la hi-fi

ultimately ['ʌltɪmətlɪ] **ADV 1** *(eventually, final-* finalement, en fin de compte, à la fin; *(lat-* par la suite; **a solution will u. be found** on fini- bien par trouver une solution; **u. there will - peace** tôt ou tard, il y aura la paix **2** *(basical-* en dernière analyse, en fin de compte; **u., t- problem is a shortage of money** en dernière an- lyse, le problème est lié à un manque d'argen- **responsibility u. lies with you** en fin de comp- c'est vous qui êtes responsable

ultimatum [,ʌltɪ'meɪtəm] *(pl* **ultimatums** *or* **ul-mata** [-tə]*)* **N** ultimatum *m*; **to give** *or* **to issue - to deliver an u. to sb** adresser un ultimatum à -

ultimo ['ʌltɪməʊ] **ADV** *Old-fashioned* du mois de- nier; **the 16th u.** le 16 du mois dernier

PRÉFIX-

ULTRA-

- Dans un contexte technique, **ultra-** signifie AU-DELÀ DE. On emploie le même préfixe en français :

  ultrasound ultrason; **ultramicroscopic** ultramicroscopique; **ultramontane** ultramontain; **ultraviolet rays** rayons ultraviolets.

- Dans l'usage courant, le préfixe **ultra-** signifie EXTRÊMEMENT. Dans la plupart des cas, la traduction est **ultra-**, et parfois **hyper-**:

  ultrasensitive ultrasensible; **ultramodern** ultramoderne; **ultraconservative** ultraconservateur; **ultra-fashionable** ultra-chic; **ultraclean** hyper-propre; **ultra-trendy** hyper-branché; **the ultraleft** l'extrême gauche.

ultra- ['ʌltrə] **PREF** ultra-, hyper-; *Fam* **u.-tren-** hyper-branché; **u.-right-wing** d'extrême droit- **u.-bright** ultralumineux

ultra-fashionable **ADJ** ultra-chic

ultra-high frequency **N** ultra haute fr- quence *f*

ultraleft [,ʌltrə'left] *Pol* **ADJ** d'extrême gauche

N extrême gauche *f*

tramarine [ˌʌltrəmə'riːn] N bleu *m* outremer
DJ bleu outremer *(inv)*

tramodern [ˌʌltrə'mɒdən] **ADJ** ultramoderne

tramontane [ˌʌltrə'mɒnteɪn] *Geog & Rel* **ADJ** tramontain
ultramontain(e) *m,f*

tranationalist [ˌʌltrə'næʃənəlɪst] **N** ultranaɔnaliste *mf*
DJ ultranationaliste

taright [ˌʌltrə'raɪt] *Pol* **ADJ** d'extrême droite
extrême droite *f*

trasensitive [ˌʌltrə'sensɪtɪv] **ADJ** ultrasensible

trashort [ˌʌltrə'ʃɔːt] **ADJ** ultracourt
► *Rad* ***ultrashort wave*** onde *f* ultracourte

trasonic [ˌʌltrə'sɒnɪk] **ADJ** ultrasonique

ultrasonics **N** *(UNCOUNT)* science *f* des ulasons

trasonographer [ˌʌltrəsə'nɒgrəfə(r)] **N** *Med* chographiste *mf*

trasound ['ʌltrəsaʊnd] **N** ultrason *m*
► *Med* ***ultrasound scan*** échographie *f*

traviolet [ˌʌltrə'vaɪələt] **ADJ** ultraviolet
ultraviolet *m*
► ***ultraviolet rays*** rayons *mpl* ultraviolets; *Med* ***traviolet treatment*** traitement *m* aux (rayons) traviolets

tra vires [-'vaɪəriːz] **ADJ** au-delà des pouvoirs, tra-vires
ADV au-delà des pouvoirs; **to act u.** commettre n excès de pouvoir

ulate ['juːljʊleɪt] **VI** *Formal (owl)* ululer, hulu-r; *(wolf, dog)* hurler

ulation [juːljʊ'leɪʃən] **N** *Formal (of owl)* ululeent *m*, hululement *m*; *(of wolf, dog)* hurlement

ysses [juː'lɪsiːz] **PR N** Ulysse

m [ʌm] *(pt & pp* **ummed**, *cont* **umming**) *Fam* **EXLAM** euh
VI dire euh; **to um and ah** tergiverser, hésiter; **e's always umming and ahing** il n'arrive jamais à e décider

mber ['ʌmbə(r)] **ADJ** *(colour, paint)* terre d'ombre *(inv)*
N *(clay)* terre *f* d'ombre *ou* de Sienne

mbilical [ʌm'bɪlɪkəl, ʌmbɪ'laɪkəl] **ADJ** ombilical
► *Anat* ***umbilical cord*** cordon *m* ombilical

mbilicus [ʌm'bɪlɪkəs, ʌmbɪ'laɪkəs] *(pl* **umbilici** saɪ]) **N** *Anat* ombilic *m*, nombril *m*

mbrage ['ʌmbrɪdʒ] **N** *(offence)* **to take u. at sth** rendre ombrage de qch, s'offenser de qch

mbrella [ʌm'brelə] **N 1** *(device)* parapluie *m*; **to ut up** *or* **open an u.** ouvrir un parapluie; **to put own** *or* **to close an u.** fermer un parapluie
2 *Fig (protection, cover)* protection *f*; **under the u. f the United Nations** sous la protection des Naons Unies
3 *Mil* écran *m ou* rideau *m* de protection
4 *(of jellyfish)* ombrelle *f*
5 *Am Fam Mil slang (parachute)* parachute□ *m*, épin *m*
COMP *(term)* général
► ***umbrella committee*** comité *m* de coordinaon; ***umbrella group, umbrella organization*** orgaisation *f* qui en regroupe plusieurs autres; ***mbrella stand*** porte-parapluies *m inv*; ***umbrella ree*** magnolia *m* parasol

> Note that the French word **ombrelle** is a false friend. It means **sunshade**.

mbria ['ʌmbrɪə] **N** Ombrie *f*

mbrian ['ʌmbrɪən] **N** Ombrien(enne) *m,f*
ADJ ombrien

mlaut ['ʊmlaʊt] **N** *(in Germanic languages)* umaut *m*, inflexion *f* vocalique; *(diaeresis)* tréma *m*

mph [hm] **EXCLAM** *(in disbelief, displeasure)* um!, hmm!

mpire ['ʌmpaɪə(r)] **N** arbitre *m*
VT *(match, contest)* arbitrer
VI servir d'arbitre, être arbitre

mpteen [ˌʌmp'tiːn] *Fam* **ADJ** je ne sais combien e, des tas de; **she's got u. dresses** elle a je ne sais ombien de robes *ou* des tas de robes; **I've told ou u. times** je te l'ai dit trente-six fois *ou* cent ɔis; **u. people** des dizaines de gens, des tas de ens
PRON there were u. of them il y en avait des tas *ou* je ne sais combien

umpteenth [ˌʌmp'tiːnθ] **ADJ** *Fam* énième, nième; **for the u. time** pour la nième fois

UMTS [juːemtiː'es] **N** *Tel (abbr* **Universal Mobile Telecommunications Services**) UMTS *m*

> **UN-** — PRÉFIXE
>
> • Le préfixe **un-** est un préfixe de NÉGATION extrêmement générateur qui peut s'ajouter à un nombre incalculable d'adjectifs, de verbes et d'adverbes.
> Il se traduit différemment selon les cas :
> (i) **in-** :
> **unbelievable** incroyable, **unacceptable** inacceptable, **uncertain** incertain, **uncertainty** incertitude, **unusual** inhabituel
> (ii) **dé-** :
> **unpleasant** déplaisant, **to undo** défaire, **to untie** détacher, **to unbalance** déséquilibrer
> (iii) **non** :
> **unaccompanied** non accompagné, **unauthorized** non autorisé, **uncensored** non censuré, **unelected** non élu
> (iv) **sans** :
> **unleaded** sans plomb, **unaided** sans aide, **unpretentious** sans prétention, **unimportant** sans importance
> (v) **peu** :
> **unfriendly** peu aimable, **unattractive** peu attirant, **unappetizing** peu appétissant, **unmanly** peu viril, **unprofessional** peu professionnel
> • Souvent le français doit recourir a une périphrase :
> **unpredictably** de façon imprévisible
> **undignified** qui manque de dignité
> **unethical** contraire à l'éthique
> **unladylike** indigne d'une jeune fille bien élevée
> **unsurprisingly, he refused** il a refusé, ce qui n'a rien de surprenant.
> • **Un-** est également capable de produire des concepts tels que **un-American** ou **un-British** comme dans l'exemple :
> **that's a very un-British thing to do** on ne s'attend pas à ce genre de chose de la part d'un Britannique.

UN [juː'en] *(abbr* **United Nations**) **N the UN** l'ONU *f*, l'Onu *f*
COMP de l'ONU
►► ***UN peacekeeping forces*** les casques *mpl* bleus; ***UN resolution*** résolution *f* de l'ONU; ***UN Secretary-General*** secrétaire *mf* général(e) de l'ONU

'un [ʌn] **PRON** *Fam* **he's only a young 'un** ce n'est qu'un petit gars; **the little 'uns** les petiots *mpl*; **he's a bad 'un** c'est un sale type

unabashed [ˌʌnə'bæʃt] **ADJ 1** *(undeterred)* nullement décontenancé *ou* déconcerté, imperturbable; **she was quite u. by the criticism** elle ne se laissa pas intimider *ou* elle ne fut nullement décontenancée par les critiques; **to carry on u.** continuer sans se démonter *ou* décontenancer **2** *(unashamed)* sans honte, qui n'a pas honte

unabashedly [ˌʌnə'bæʃɪdlɪ] **ADV 1** *(without being discouraged)* sans se laisser décontenancer, sans se démonter **2** *(unashamedly)* sans aucune honte

unabated [ˌʌnə'beɪtɪd] **ADV** *(undiminished)* sans diminuer; **the storm/the noise continued u. for most of the night** la tempête/le bruit a continué sans répit pendant une grande partie de la nuit
ADJ non diminué; **their enthusiasm was u.** leur enthousiasme ne diminuait pas, ils montraient toujours autant d'enthousiasme

unabbreviated [ˌʌnə'briːvɪeɪtɪd] **ADJ** *(word)* sans abréviation; **in its u. form** sous sa forme non abrégée, en toutes lettres

unable [ˌʌn'eɪbəl] **ADJ to be u. to do sth** *(gen)* ne pas pouvoir faire qch; *(not know how to)* ne pas savoir faire qch; *(be incapable of)* être incapable de faire qch; *(not be in a position to)* ne pas être en mesure de faire qch; *(be prevented from)* être dans l'impossibilité de faire qch; **children who are u. to read/swim** les enfants qui ne savent pas lire/nager; **he seems totally u. to understand** il semble tout à fait incapable de comprendre; **he was u. to pay** il n'était pas en mesure de payer; **unfortunately I'm u. to come** malheureusement, je ne peux pas venir *ou* il m'est impossible de venir

unabridged [ˌʌnə'brɪdʒd] **ADJ** *(text, version, edition)* intégral; **the film is u.** le film est dans sa version intégrale

unabsorbed cost ['ʌnəbzɔːbd-] **N** *Fin* coût *m* non-absorbé

unaccented [ˌʌnək'sentɪd], **unaccentuated** [ˌʌnək'sentjʊeɪtɪd] **ADJ** *Ling (syllable)* non accentué, atone; *Mus* **u. beat** temps *m* faible

unacceptable [ˌʌnək'septəbəl] **ADJ 1** *(intolerable* ► *violence, behaviour)* inadmissible, intolérable; *(*► *language)* inacceptable; **it is u. that anyone should have to** *or* **for anyone to have to sleep rough** il est inadmissible que des gens soient obligés de coucher dehors; **the u. face of capitalism** la face honteuse du capitalisme **2** *(gift, proposal)* inacceptable

unacceptably [ˌʌnək'septəblɪ] **ADV** *(noisy, rude)* à un point inacceptable *ou* inadmissible; **the film was u. violent** le film était d'une violence inacceptable

unaccommodating [ˌʌnə'kɒmədeɪtɪŋ] **ADJ** *(person)* peu accommodant

unaccompanied [ˌʌnə'kʌmpənɪd] **ADJ 1** *(child, traveller)* non accompagné, seul; *(baggage)* non accompagné; **u. by an adult** non accompagné par un adulte **2** *Mus (singing)* sans accompagnement, a capella; *(singer)* non accompagné, a capella; *(song)* sans accompagnement; *(choir)* a capella; **for u. violin** pour violon seul

unaccomplished [ˌʌnə'kʌmplɪʃt] **ADJ 1** *(incomplete* ► *task)* inachevé, inaccompli **2** *(unfulfilled* ► *wish, plan)* non réalisé, non accompli **3** *(untalented* ► *actor, player)* sans grand talent, médiocre; *(*► *performance)* médiocre

unaccountable [ˌʌnə'kaʊntəbəl] **ADJ 1** *(inexplicable* ► *disappearance, reason)* inexplicable **2** *(not accountable)* qui n'a de comptes à rendre à personne; **to be u. to sb** ne pas avoir à répondre devant qn, ne pas avoir de comptes à rendre à qn; **representatives who are u. to the general public** les représentants qui ne sont pas responsables devant la population

unaccountably [ˌʌnə'kaʊntəblɪ] **ADV** inexplicablement, de manière inexplicable; **she was u. delayed** elle a été retardée sans que l'on sache (trop) pourquoi

unaccounted [ˌʌnə'kaʊntɪd] **unaccounted for ADJ 1** *(money)* qui manque; **there is still a lot of money u. for** il manque encore beaucoup d'argent; **these 60 pounds are u. for in the balance sheet** ces 60 livres ne figurent pas au bilan **2** *(person)* qui manque, qui a disparu; *(plane)* qui n'est pas rentré; **by nightfall, two children were still u. for** à la tombée de la nuit, il manquait encore deux enfants

unaccustomed [ˌʌnə'kʌstəmd] **ADJ 1** *(not used to* ► *person)* **he is u. to wearing a tie** il n'a pas l'habitude de mettre des cravates; **u. as I am to public speaking** bien que je n'aie guère l'habitude de prendre la parole en public **2** *(unusual, uncharacteristic* ► *rudeness, light-heartedness)* inhabituel, inaccoutumé

unacknowledged [ˌʌnək'nɒlɪdʒd] **ADJ 1** *(unrecognized* ► *truth, fact)* non reconnu; *(*► *qualities, discovery)* non reconnu, méconnu; **he's an u. genius** c'est un génie méconnu **2** *(ignored* ► *letter)* resté sans réponse; **you shouldn't let his letter go u.** tu ne devrais pas laisser sa lettre sans réponse

unacquainted [ˌʌnə'kweɪntɪd] **ADJ to be u. with sb/sth** ne pas connaître qn/qch; **we are not u. with pressure** nous n'ignorons pas ce que c'est que le stress

unadapted [ˌʌnə'dæptɪd] **ADJ** mal adapté, peu adapté (**to** à)

unaddressed [ˌʌnə'drest] **ADJ** *(letter, parcel, envelope)* sans adresse, qui ne porte pas d'adresse

unadopted [ˌʌnə'dɒptɪd] **ADJ 1** *Br (road)* non pris en charge *ou* entretenu par la commune **2** *(reso-*

lution, bill) non adopté, rejeté **3** *(child)* qui n'est pas adopté

unadorned [ˌʌnəˈdɔːnd] **ADJ** *(undecorated)* sans ornement, naturel, simple; *esp Literary* **her u. beauty** sa beauté sans parure *ou* sans fard; **the u. truth** la vérité pure *ou* toute nue

unadulterated [ˌʌnəˈdʌltəreɪtɪd] **ADJ 1** *(milk, flour)* pur, naturel; *(wine)* non frelaté **2** *(pleasure, joy)* pur (et simple), parfait; **the u. truth** la vérité pure et simple; **u. by Western influences** non corrompu par les influences occidentales; **it's u. rubbish!** c'est de la pure bêtise!

unadventurous [ˌʌnədˈventʃərəs] **ADJ** *(person)* qui ne prend pas de risques, qui manque d'audace; *(lifestyle)* conventionnel, banal; *(performance)* terne; *(holiday)* banal; **she is an u. cook** c'est une cuisinière qui manque d'imagination

unadventurously [ˌʌnədˈventʃərəslɪ] **ADV** *(produced, designed)* peu audacieusement; *(decide, choose)* sans prendre de risques; **we very u. chose beige carpets again** nous n'avons pas pris de risques et avons encore choisi des moquettes beiges

unadvertised [ˌʌnˈædvətaɪzd] **ADJ** *(job)* non affiché, pour lequel il n'y a pas eu d'annonce; *(meeting, visit)* discret(ète), sans publicité

unadvisable [ˌʌnədˈvaɪzəbəl] **ADJ** imprudent, à déconseiller; **it is u. for her to travel** les voyages lui sont déconseillés, il vaut mieux qu'elle évite de voyager

unadvised [ˌʌnədˈvaɪzd] **ADJ** *(unwise)* imprudent

unaesthetic, *Am* **unesthetic** [ˌʌniːsˈθetɪk] **ADJ** inesthétique

unaffected [ˌʌnəˈfektɪd] **ADJ 1** *(resistant)* non affecté, qui résiste; **u. by cold** qui n'est pas affecté par le *ou* qui résiste au froid; **u. by heat** qui résiste à la chaleur

2 *(unchanged, unaltered)* qui n'est pas touché *ou* affecté; **we were u. by the war** nous n'avons pas été affectés *ou* touchés par la guerre; **children cannot remain u. by TV violence** il est impossible que les enfants ne soient pas affectés *ou* marqués par la violence qu'ils voient à la télé; **there's snow almost everywhere, but the northwest is u.** il y a de la neige presque partout, mais le nord-ouest n'est pas touché

3 *(indifferent)* indifférent, insensible; **he seems quite u. by his loss** sa perte ne semble pas l'émouvoir, sa perte n'a pas du tout l'air de le toucher

4 *(natural ▸ person, manners, character)* simple, naturel, sans affectation; *(▸ style)* simple, sans recherche

unaffectedly [ˌʌnəˈfektɪdlɪ] **ADV** *(speak, behave)* sans affectation; *(write, dress)* simplement, sans recherche

unaffiliated [ˌʌnəˈfɪlɪeɪtɪd] **ADJ** *(unions)* indépendant

unaffordable [ˌʌnəˈfɔːdəbəl] **ADJ** inabordable

unafraid [ˌʌnəˈfreɪd] **ADJ** sans peur, qui n'a pas peur; **he was quite u.** il n'avait pas du tout peur

unaided [ˌʌnˈeɪdɪd] **ADJ** sans aide (extérieure); **it is his own u. work** c'est un travail qu'il a fait tout seul *ou* sans l'aide de personne

ADV *(work)* tout seul, sans être aidé; **he did it u.** il l'a fait tout seul *ou* à lui seul

unaired [ˌʌnˈeəd] **ADJ 1** *(room)* non aéré **2** *(opinions)* non exprimé

unalike [ˌʌnəˈlaɪk] **ADJ** différent, peu ressemblant; **the two sisters are quite u.** les deux sœurs ne se ressemblent pas du tout, les deux sœurs sont très différentes

unalleviated [ˌʌnəˈliːvɪeɪtɪd] **ADJ** sans répit; **u. boredom** ennui *m* mortel

unallocated [ˌʌnˈæləkeɪtɪd] **ADJ** *(rooms, places)* non assigné; *(money, grants)* non alloué

unallotted [ˌʌnəˈlɒtɪd] **ADJ** *St Exch (shares)* non réparti

unalloyed [ˌʌnəˈlɔɪd] **ADJ 1** *Literary (joy, enthusiasm)* sans mélange, parfait **2** *(metal)* pur, sans alliage

unalterable [ˌʌnˈɔːltərəbəl] **ADJ** *(fact)* immuable; *(decision)* irrévocable; *(truth)* certain, immuable

unalterably [ˌʌnˈɔːltərəblɪ] **ADV** immuablement

unaltered [ˌʌnˈɔːltəd] **ADJ** inchangé, non modifié; **the original building remains u.** le bâtiment d'origine reste tel quel *ou* n'a pas subi de modifications

unambiguous [ˌʌnæmˈbɪɡjʊəs] **ADJ** *(wording, rule)* non ambigu, non équivoque; *(thinking)* clair

unambiguously [ˌʌnæmˈbɪɡjʊəslɪ] **ADV** sans ambiguïté, sans équivoque

unambitious [ˌʌnæmˈbɪʃəs] **ADJ** sans ambition, peu ambitieux

un-American **ADJ 1** *(uncharacteristic)* peu américain; **it's very u.** ce n'est pas du tout américain **2** *(anti-American)* antiaméricain

unamused [ˌʌnəˈmjuːzd] **ADJ** qui n'est pas amusé; **she was distinctly u.** visiblement, cela ne l'amusait pas

unanimity [juːnəˈnɪmətɪ] **N** unanimité *f*; **there must be u. on the issue** il faut qu'il y ait unanimité à ce sujet

unanimous [juːˈnænɪməs] **ADJ** unanime; **passed by a u. vote** voté à l'unanimité; **we must give him our u. support** il faut que nous soyons unanimes à le soutenir; **the audience was u. in its approval** le public a approuvé à l'unanimité; **to reach a u. decision** se prononcer à l'unanimité

unanimously [juːˈnænɪməslɪ] **ADV** *(decide, agree)* à l'unanimité, unanimement; *(vote)* à l'unanimité

unannounced [ˌʌnəˈnaʊnst] **ADJ** *(arrival, event)* inattendu

ADV *(unexpectedly)* de manière inattendue, sans se faire annoncer; *(suddenly)* subitement; **he turned up u.** il est arrivé à l'improviste

unanswerable [ˌʌnˈɑːnsərəbəl] **ADJ 1** *(impossible ▸ question, problem)* auquel il est impossible de répondre **2** *(irrefutable ▸ argument, logic)* irréfutable, incontestable

unanswered [ˌʌnˈɑːnsəd] **ADJ 1** *(question)* qui reste sans réponse; *(prayer)* inexaucé; **my main argument was left u.** on n'a toujours pas réfuté mon argument principal; *Law* **an u. charge** une accusation non réfutée *ou* irréfutée **2** *(unsolved ▸ mystery, puzzle)* non résolu **3** *(letter, question)* (resté) sans réponse; **I have six u. letters to deal with** il y a six lettres auxquelles je n'ai pas encore répondu; **I had to leave two questions u.** j'ai dû laisser deux questions sans réponse

ADV to go u. rester sans réponse

unapologetic [ˌʌnəpɒləˈdʒetɪk] **ADJ he's an u. royalist/admirer of Hitler** il ne se cache pas d'être royaliste/d'être un admirateur d'Hitler; **they're u. about it** ils estiment qu'il n'ont pas à s'excuser

unappealing [ˌʌnəˈpiːlɪŋ] **ADJ** peu attrayant, peu attirant

unappeased [ˌʌnəˈpiːzd] **ADJ** *Literary (hunger, desire)* inassouvi; *(pain)* inapaisé

unappetizing, -ising [ˌʌnˈæpɪtaɪzɪŋ] **ADJ** peu appétissant

unappreciated [ˌʌnəˈpriːʃɪeɪtɪd] **ADJ** *(person, talents)* méconnu, incompris; *(efforts, kindness)* non apprécié, qui n'est pas apprécié

ADV her efforts go u. le mal qu'elle se donne n'est pas apprécié à sa juste valeur

unappreciative [ˌʌnəˈpriːʃɪətɪv] **ADJ** *(audience)* froid, indifférent; **to be u. of sth** être indifférent à qch

unapproachable [ˌʌnəˈprəʊtʃəbəl] **ADJ 1** *(person)* inabordable, d'un abord difficile **2** *(place)* inaccessible, inabordable; **u. by road** inaccessible par la route

unappropriated [ˌʌnəˈprəʊprɪeɪtɪd] **ADJ** *Fin (money)* inutilisé, disponible

▸▸ ***unappropriated profits*** bénéfices *mpl* non distribués

unarguable [ˌʌnˈɑːɡjʊəbəl] **ADJ** incontestable

unarguably [ˌʌnˈɑːɡjʊəblɪ] **ADV** incontestablement

unarmed [ˌʌnˈɑːmd] **ADJ 1** *(person, vehicle)* sans armes, non armé; **I'm not going in there u.** je n'entre pas là-dedans sans arme **2** *Bot & Zool* sans épines, inerme

▸▸ ***unarmed combat*** combat *m* à mains nues

unashamed [ˌʌnəˈʃeɪmd] **ADJ** *(curiosity, gaze)* sans gêne; *(greed, lie, hypocrisy)* effronté, sans scrupule; *(person)* sans honte; **to be u. abo[ut] doing sth** ne pas avoir honte de faire qch; **[he] was quite u. about** *or* **of his huge wealth** il ne cachait pas de son immense richesse, il étal[ait] son immense richesse sans vergogne *ou* sa[ns] pudeur

unashamedly [ˌʌnəˈʃeɪmɪdlɪ] **ADV** *(brazen[ly])* sans honte, sans scrupule; *(openly)* sans hon[te,] sans se cacher; **George was u. in favour of t[he] war** George se déclarait ouvertement en fave[ur] de la guerre; **she lied quite u.** elle mentait abs[o]lument sans vergogne, c'était une menteu[se] tout à fait éhontée; **he is u. greedy** il est d'u[ne] gourmandise éhontée

unasked [ˌʌnˈɑːskt] **ADJ** *(question)* que l'on [n'a] pas posé; **the central question is still u.** la que[s]tion essentielle reste à poser

ADV he came u. il est venu sans avoir été invi[té;] **they did the job u.** ils ont fait le travail sans qu'[on] le leur ait demandé *ou* spontanément

unasked-for **ADJ** *(gift)* spontané, qu'on n'a p[as] demandé; *(advice)* non sollicité

unaspirated [ˌʌnˈæspɪreɪtɪd] **ADJ** *Ling* non a[s]piré

unassailable [ˌʌnəˈseɪləbəl] **ADJ** *(fort, city)* i[m]prenable, inébranlable; *(certainty, belief)* in[é]branlable; *(reputation)* inattaquable; *(argume[nt,] reason)* inattaquable, irréfutable; **to be in an [u.] position** être dans une position inattaquable

unassigned [ˌʌnəˈsaɪnd] **ADJ** *(office, room ▸ [...] person)* non attribué; *(▸ for purpose)* non affec[té;] *(task)* non assigné

unassimilated [ˌʌnəˈsɪmɪleɪtɪd] **ADJ** inassimi[lé;] **u. knowledge** connaissances *fpl* mal assimilée[s]

unassisted [ˌʌnəˈsɪstɪd] **ADV** sans aide, tout se[ul]

ADJ to be u. ne pas être aidé

unassuming [ˌʌnəˈsjuːmɪŋ] **ADJ** modeste, sa[ns] prétention(s)

unassumingly [ˌʌnəˈsjuːmɪŋlɪ] **ADV** modes[te]ment, sans prétention(s)

unattached [ˌʌnəˈtætʃt] **ADJ 1** *(unconnected ▸ building, part, group)* indépendant **2** *(wire)* à [dé]tacher sôi-même **3** *(not in relationship)* lib[re,] sans attaches

unattainable [ˌʌnəˈteɪnəbəl] **ADJ** *(goal, pla[ce])* inaccessible

unattended [ˌʌnəˈtendɪd] **ADJ 1** *(vehicle, lu[g]gage)* laissé sans surveillance; **do not leave sm[all] children u.** ne laissez pas de jeunes enfants sa[ns] surveillance *ou* tout seuls; **do not leave lugga[ge] u.** ne laissez pas vos bagages sans surveillan[ce] **2** *(person)* sans escorte, seul; **I can't even go [to] the toilet u.** je ne peux même pas aller aux to[i]lettes seul; **don't leave the guests u. (to)** ne nég[li]gez pas les invités, occupez-vous des invités

unattractive [ˌʌnəˈtræktɪv] **ADJ** *(room, wa[ll]paper, decor)* peu attrayant, assez laid; *(smi[le,] face, person)* peu attirant, dépourvu de charm[e;] *(habit)* peu attrayant, désagréable, déplaisan[t;] *(personality)* déplaisant, peu sympathiqu[e;] *(prospect)* désagréable, peu attrayant, pe[u] agréable

unaudited [ˌʌnˈɔːdɪtɪd] **ADJ** *(accounts)* non vé[ri]fié

unauthenticated [ˌʌnɔːˈθentɪkeɪtɪd] **ADJ** *(stor[y])* non vérifié; *(painting, handwriting)* non authe[n]tifié; *(evidence)* non établi

unauthorized, -ised [ˌʌnˈɔːθəraɪzd] **ADJ** *(a[b]sence, entry)* non autorisé, fait sans autorisatio[n]

▸▸ *Comput* ***unauthorized access*** accès *m* non a[u]torisé

unavailability [ˌʌnəveɪləˈbɪlɪtɪ] **N** indisponib[i]lité *f*

unavailable [ˌʌnəˈveɪləbəl] **ADJ** *(person)* indi[s]ponible, qui n'est pas libre; *(resources)* indisp[o]nible, qu'on ne peut se procurer; **the book is [u.]** *(in library, bookshop)* le livre n'est pas disp[o]nible; *(from publisher)* le livre est épuisé; **Mr F[ox] is u.** M. Fox n'est pas disponible *ou* libre; **the mi[n]ister was u. for comment** le ministre s'est refusé [à] tout commentaire

unavailing [ˌʌnəˈveɪlɪŋ] **ADJ** *(effort, attemp[t])* vain, inutile; *(method)* inefficace

unavailingly [ˌʌnəˈveɪlɪŋlɪ] **ADV** en vain, sa[ns] succès

navenged [ˌʌnəˈvendʒd] **ADV it won't go u.** cela e restera pas impuni; **the u. death of his sister** la nort de sa sœur qui n'a pas été vengée

navoidable [ˌʌnəˈvɔɪdəbəl] **ADJ** *(accident, 'elay)* inévitable; **it is u. that...** il est inévitable ue…+ *subjunctive*

▸ *Fin* ***unavoidable costs*** coûts *mpl* induits

navoidably [ˌʌnəˈvɔɪdəblɪ] **ADV** *(happen)* iné-itablement; *(detain)* malencontreusement; **I vas u. delayed** j'ai été retardé malgré moi *ou* our des raisons indépendantes de ma volonté

naware [ˌʌnəˈweə(r)] **ADJ** *(ignorant)* incon-cient, qui ignore; **to be u. of** *(facts)* ignorer, ne as être au courant de; *(danger)* être incon-cient de, ne pas avoir conscience de; **I was u. hat they had arrived** j'ignorais *ou* je ne savais as qu'ils étaient arrivés; **her husband was to-ally u. of what was going on** son mari ne se ren-ait absolument pas compte de ce qui se assait; **he continued u. of what was happening** a continué, ignorant de ce qui se passait *ou* ans savoir ce qui se passait; **she is politically u.** lle n'a aucune conscience politique, elle gnore tout de la politique; **we are not u. of the eed for reform** nous avons conscience de la né-essité d'une réforme

nawares [ˌʌnəˈweəz] **ADV 1** *(by surprise)* au dé-ourvu, à l'improviste; **to catch** *or* **to take sb u.** rendre qn à l'improviste *ou* au dépourvu; **the hotographer caught us u.** le photographe nous pris sans que nous nous en rendions compte *u* à notre insu **2** *(unknowingly)* inconsciem-nent **3** *(by accident)* par mégarde, par inadver-ance

nbalance [ˌʌnˈbæləns] **VT** déséquilibrer

N déséquilibre *m*

nbalanced [ˌʌnˈbælənst] **ADJ 1** *(load)* mal équi-ibré

2 *(person, mind)* déséquilibré, désaxé

3 *(reporting)* tendancieux, partial

4 *Acct (account)* non soldé

nbandage [ˌʌnˈbændɪdʒ] **VT** *(wound)* déban-ler

nbankable [ˌʌnˈbæŋkəbəl] **ADJ** *Fin (bill, paper)* on bancable

nbaptized, -ised [ˌʌnbæpˈtaɪzd] **ADJ** non aptisé

nbar [ˌʌnˈbɑː(r)] *(pt & pp* **unbarred**, *cont* **unbar-ing) VT** *(door, gate)* enlever la barre de

nbearable [ˌʌnˈbeərəbəl] **ADJ** insupportable

nbearably [ˌʌnˈbeərəblɪ] **ADV** insupportable-nent; **he is u. conceited** il est d'une vanité insup-ortable; **it's u. hot** il fait une chaleur nsupportable

nbeatable [ˌʌnˈbiːtəbəl] **ADJ** *(champion, prices)* mbattable; **it's u. value for money** le rapport qua-ité-prix est imbattable

nbeaten [ˌʌnˈbiːtən] **ADJ** *(fighter, team)* invain-u; *(record, price)* non battu; **the record has re-nained u. for 20 years** le record n'a pas été battu lepuis 20 ans

nbecoming [ˌʌnbɪˈkʌmɪŋ] **ADJ 1** *(garment, col-ur, hat)* peu seyant, qui ne va pas; **that coat is ather u.** ce manteau ne lui/te/*etc* va pas **2** *(be-aviour)* malséant

nbeknown [ˌʌnbɪˈnəʊn], **unbeknownst** ˌʌnbɪˈnəʊnst] **ADV u. to** à l'insu de; **u. to him** à son nsu, sans qu'il le sache

nbelief [ˌʌnbɪˈliːf] **N 1** *(incredulity)* incrédulité *f* **2** *Rel* incroyance *f*

nbelievable [ˌʌnbɪˈliːvəbəl] **ADJ 1** *(extraordin-ry)* incroyable; **it's u. that they should want to narry so young** il est incroyable *ou* je n'arrive as à croire qu'ils veuillent se marier si jeunes; **she has an u. number of clothes** elle a une quan-ité incroyable de vêtements **2** *(implausible)* in-royable, invraisemblable; **his story was totally u.** son histoire était totalement incroyable *ou* à lormir debout

nbelievably [ˌʌnbɪˈliːvəblɪ] **ADV 1** *(extraordin-rily)* incroyablement, extraordinairement; **u. beautiful/cruel** d'une beauté/cruauté in-royable *ou* extraordinaire; **u., he agreed** aussi ncroyable que cela puisse paraître, il a ac-cepté **2** *(implausibly)* invraisemblablement, in-croyablement

unbeliever [ˌʌnbɪˈliːvə(r)] **N** *Rel* incroyant(e) *m,f*

unbelieving [ˌʌnbɪˈliːvɪŋ] **ADJ** *(gen)* incrédule, sceptique; *Rel* incroyant

unbelievingly [ˌʌnbɪˈliːvɪŋlɪ] **ADV** *(look, speak)* d'un air incrédule

unbend [ˌʌnˈbend] *(pt & pp* **unbent** [-ˈbent]) **VT** *(fork, wire)* redresser, détordre

VI *(relax)* se détendre

unbending [ˌʌnˈbendɪŋ] **ADJ** *(will, attitude)* in-transigeant, inflexible; **she remained u. on the is-sue** elle est restée intransigeante sur la question; **his u. puritanism** son puritanisme ri-gide

unbiased, unbiassed [ˌʌnˈbaɪəst] **ADJ** impar-tial

unbidden [ˌʌnˈbɪdən] **ADV** *Literary* spontané-ment, sans que l'on demande; **she did it u.** elle l'a fait de son propre chef *ou* sans qu'on le lui ait demandé; **she entered u.** elle est entrée sans y avoir été invitée; **the thought came u. to my mind** l'idée m'est venue spontanément

unbind [ˌʌnˈbaɪnd] *(pt & pp* **unbound** [-ˈbaʊnd]) **VT** *(prisoner)* délier; *(bandage)* défaire, dérouler

unbleached [ˌʌnˈbliːtʃt] **ADJ** *(fabric)* écru

unblemished [ˌʌnˈblemɪʃt] **ADJ** *(purity, skin, col-our, reputation)* sans tache, sans défaut; **an u. record** un parcours sans faute

unblinking [ˌʌnˈblɪŋkɪŋ] **ADJ** *(impassive)* impas-sible; *(fearless)* impassible, imperturbable; **she stared at me with u. eyes** elle me regarda fixe-ment *ou* sans ciller

unblock [ˌʌnˈblɒk] **VT** *(sink, pipe)* déboucher; *(road, path, traffic jam)* dégager

unblushing [ˌʌnˈblʌʃɪŋ] **ADJ** éhonté

unblushingly [ˌʌnˈblʌʃɪŋlɪ] **ADV** sans rougir

unbolt [ˌʌnˈbəʊlt] **VT** *(door)* déverrouiller, tirer le verrou de; *(scaffolding)* déboulonner

unbonded warehouse [ˌʌnˈbɒndɪd-] **N** entre-pôt *m* fictif

unborn [ˌʌnˈbɔːn] **ADJ** *(child)* qui n'est pas encore né

unbosom [ˌʌnˈbʊzəm] **VT** *Literary (secret, emo-tions)* confesser; **to u. oneself to sb** ouvrir son cœur à qn, se confier à qn

unbound [ˌʌnˈbaʊnd] *pt & pp of* **unbind**

ADJ 1 *(prisoner, hands)* non lié **2** *(book, period-ical)* non relié

unbounded [ˌʌnˈbaʊndɪd] **ADJ** *(gratitude, admir-ation)* illimité, sans borne; *(pride, greed)* déme-suré

unbowed [ˌʌnˈbaʊd] **ADJ** insoumis, invaincu; **they stood with their heads u.** ils étaient debout, la tête haute

unbranded [ˌʌnˈbrændɪd] **ADJ** *Mktg* sans marque

unbreakable [ˌʌnˈbreɪkəbəl] **ADJ 1** *(crockery)* in-cassable **2** *(habit)* dont on ne peut pas se débar-rasser **3** *(promise)* sacré; *(will, spirit)* inébranlable, que l'on ne peut briser

unbreathable [ˌʌnˈbriːðəbəl] **ADJ** *(air)* irrespi-rable

unbribable [ˌʌnˈbraɪbəbəl] **ADJ** incorruptible

unbridled [ˌʌnˈbraɪdəld] **ADJ** *(horse)* débridé, sans bride; *(anger, greed)* sans retenue, effréné; *(passion, enthusiasm)* débridé

unbroken [ˌʌnˈbrəʊkən] **ADJ 1** *(line)* continu; *(surface, expanse)* continu, ininterrompu; *(sleep, tradition, peace)* ininterrompu; **the peace re-mained u. for ten years** la paix n'a pas été trou-blée pendant dix ans

2 *(crockery, eggs)* intact, non cassé; *(fastening, seal)* intact, non brisé; *(record)* non battu

3 *Fig (promise)* tenu, non rompu; *(rules)* tou-jours observé *ou* respecté; **despite all her troubles, her spirit remains u.** malgré tous ses en-nuis, elle garde le moral *ou* elle ne se laisse pas abattre

4 *(horse)* indompté

unbrotherly [ˌʌnˈbrʌðəlɪ] **ADJ** peu fraternel

unbuckle [ˌʌnˈbʌkəl] **VT** *(belt)* déboucler, dégra-fer; *(shoe)* défaire la boucle de

unbuilt [ʌnˈbɪlt, ˈʌnbɪlt] **ADJ** *(ground, plot)* vague, non construit

unbundle [ˌʌnˈbʌndəl] **VT 1** *Com (company)* dé-grouper; *(products, services)* détailler, tarifer sé-parément **2** *Comput* décompresser

unbundling [ˌʌnˈbʌndəlɪŋ] **N 1** *Com (of company)* dégroupage *m*; *(of products, services)* tarification *f* séparée **2** *Comput* décompression *f*

unburden [ˌʌnˈbɜːdən] **VT 1** *Formal* décharger (d'un fardeau); **can I u. you of your bags?** puis-je vous décharger de vos sacs? **2** *Fig (heart)* livrer, épancher, soulager; *(grief, guilt)* se décharger de; *(conscience, soul)* soulager; **to u. oneself to sb** se confier à qn, s'épancher auprès de qn; **she unburdened her heart to me** elle s'est confiée à moi, elle m'a ouvert son cœur

unburied [ˌʌnˈberɪd] **ADJ** non enterré, non en-seveli

unbusinesslike [ˌʌnˈbɪznɪslaɪk] **ADJ** *(person)* peu commerçant, qui n'a pas le sens des affai-res; *(procedure, handling)* peu professionnel; **to conduct one's affairs in an u. way** mal mener ses affaires

unbutton [ˌʌnˈbʌtən] **VT** *(shirt, jacket)* débou-tonner

VI *Fam Fig* se déboutonner

unbuttoned [ˌʌnˈbʌtənd] **ADJ** *Fam (relaxed)* dé-contracté

uncallable [ˌʌnˈkɔːləbəl] **ADJ** *Fin (bond)* non remboursable

uncalled [ˌʌnˈkɔːld] **ADJ** *Fin (capital)* non appelé

uncalled-for **ADJ** *(rudeness, outburst, rebuke)* qui n'est pas nécessaire, injustifié; *(remark)* mal à propos, déplacé; **that was quite u.!** c'était tout à fait injustifié!

uncannily [ˌʌnˈkænɪlɪ] **ADV** *(accurate, familiar)* étrangement; *(quiet)* mystérieusement, étran-gement

uncanny [ˌʌnˈkænɪ] *(compar* **uncannier**, *superl* **uncanniest) ADJ 1** *(strange* ▸ *accuracy, likeness, ability)* troublant, étrange; **it's u. how you always know what I'm thinking** c'est curieux *ou* bizarre ce don que tu as de toujours savoir ce que je pense **2** *(eerie* ▸ *place)* sinistre, qui donne le fris-son; *(*▸ *noise)* mystérieux, sinistre; *(*▸ *atmos-phere)* étrange, sinistre

uncared-for [ˌʌnˈkeəd-] **ADJ** *(appearance)* né-gligé, peu soigné; *(house, bicycle)* négligé, (laissé) à l'abandon; *(child)* laissé à l'abandon, délaissé

uncaring [ˌʌnˈkeərɪŋ] **ADJ** *(unfeeling)* insensible, dur

uncarpeted [ˌʌnˈkɑːpɪtɪd] **ADJ** sans tapis, sans moquette

uncashed [ˌʌnˈkæʃt] **ADJ** non encaissé

uncatalogued [ˌʌnˈkætəlɒgd] **ADJ** qui n'est pas catalogué

unceasing [ˌʌnˈsiːsɪŋ] **ADJ** incessant, continuel

unceasingly [ˌʌnˈsiːsɪŋlɪ] **ADV** sans cesse, continuellement

uncensored [ˌʌnˈsensəd] **ADJ** *(correspondance)* non censuré; *(text)* non expurgé, non censuré

unceremonious [ˈʌnˌserɪˈməʊnɪəs] **ADJ 1** *(abrupt)* brusque; **after his u. departure from poli-tics** après qu'il eut peu glorieusement aban-donné la politique **2** *(without ceremony)* sans façon; **his u. dismissal** son brusque renvoi

unceremoniously [ˈʌnˌserɪˈməʊnɪəslɪ] **ADV 1** *(abruptly)* avec brusquerie, brusquement **2** *(without ceremony)* sans cérémonie; **they were pushed u. into the back of the police van** on les a poussés brutalement à l'arrière de la voiture cellulaire

uncertain [ˌʌnˈsɜːtən] **ADJ 1** *(unsure)* incertain; **we were u. whether to continue** *or* **whether we should continue** nous ne savions pas trop si nous devions continuer; **they were u. how to begin** ils ne savaient pas trop comment commencer; **I feel u. about him** j'ai des doutes à son sujet; **to be u. about sth** être inquiet au sujet de *ou* incer-tain de qch

2 *(unpredictable* ▸ *result, outcome)* incertain, aléatoire; *(*▸ *weather)* incertain; **it's u. whether we'll succeed or not** il n'est pas sûr *ou* certain que nous réussissions; **in no u. terms** en termes on ne peut plus clairs, sans mâcher ses mots **3** *(unknown)* inconnu, incertain; **the cause of her death is still u.** la cause de sa mort reste inconnue, on ignore encore la cause de sa mort **4** *(unsteady ▸ voice, steps)* hésitant, mal assuré **5** *(undecided ▸ plans)* incertain, pas sûr

uncertainly [ˌʌnˈsɜːtənlɪ] **ADV** avec hésitation, d'une manière hésitante

uncertainty [ˌʌnˈsɜːtəntɪ] *(pl* **uncertainties***)* **N** incertitude *f*, doute *m*; **to be in a state of u.** être dans le doute; **I am in some u. as to whether I should tell him** je ne sais pas trop *ou* je ne suis pas trop sûre si je dois le lui dire ou non; **there's still some u. as to what was actually said** il reste quelque incertitude sur ce qui s'est réellement dit; **to remove any u.** pour dissiper toute équivoque; **financial uncertainties** incertitudes *fpl* financières
▸▸ *Phys* ***uncertainty principle*** principe *m* d'incertitude *ou* d'indétermination de Heisenberg

uncertified [ˌʌnˈsɜːtɪfaɪd] **ADJ** *(copy)* non certifié; *(doctor, teacher)* non diplômé
▸▸ *Am* ***uncertified teacher*** ≃ maître *m* auxiliaire

unchain [ˌʌnˈtʃeɪn] **VT** *(door, dog)* enlever *ou* défaire les chaînes de, désenchaîner; *(emotions)* déchaîner

unchallengeable [ˌʌnˈtʃælɪndʒəbəl] **ADJ** *(argument)* irréfutable; *(right)* incontestable; *Law (evidence, proof)* irrécusable; **to be in an u. position** *(runner, team, politician etc)* être hors d'atteinte

unchallenged [ˌʌnˈtʃælɪndʒd] **ADJ 1** *(authority, leader)* incontesté, indiscuté; *(version)* non contesté; **his position/his authority remains u.** sa position/son autorité reste incontestée **2** *Law (witness)* non récusé; *(evidence)* non contesté
ADV 1 *(unquestioned)* sans discussion, sans protestation; **her decisions always go u.** ses décisions ne sont jamais contestées *ou* discutées; **that remark cannot go u.** on ne peut pas laisser passer cette remarque sans protester **2** *(unchecked)* sans rencontrer d'opposition; **he walked into the army base u.** il est entré dans la base militaire sans être interpellé *ou* sans rencontrer d'opposition

unchangeable [ˌʌnˈtʃeɪndʒəbəl] **ADJ** immuable, invariable

unchanged [ˌʌnˈtʃeɪndʒd] **ADJ** inchangé; *Med* **his condition remains u.** son état est stationnaire

unchanging [ˌʌnˈtʃeɪndʒɪŋ] **ADJ** invariable, immuable

uncharacteristic [ˈʌnˌkærəktəˈrɪstɪk] **ADJ** peu caractéristique, peu typique; **it's u. of him** cela ne lui ressemble pas; **it's u. for her to make a mistake like that** ce n'est pas dans son habitude de faire une erreur pareille

uncharacteristically [ˈʌnˌkærəktəˈrɪstɪkəlɪ] **ADV** d'une façon peu caractéristique

uncharitable [ˌʌnˈtʃærɪtəbəl] **ADJ** *(unkind)* peu charitable, peu indulgent

uncharted [ˌʌnˈtʃɑːtɪd] **ADJ 1** *(unmapped ▸ region, forest, ocean)* dont on n'a pas dressé la carte; *(not on map)* qui n'est pas sur la carte **2** *Fig* **we're moving into u. waters** nous faisons un saut dans l'inconnu; **we're sailing in u. waters** nous ne savons pas où nous allons

unchaste [ˌʌnˈtʃeɪst] **ADJ** *Literary* impudique, non chaste

unchastened [ˌʌnˈtʃeɪsənd] **ADJ** *(person)* aucunement repentant, nullement assagi; **he was u. by his experience** son expérience n'a rien rabattu de ses prétentions

unchecked [ˌʌnˈtʃekt] **ADJ 1** *(unrestricted ▸ growth, expansion, tendency)* non maîtrisé; *(anger, instinct)* non réprimé, auquel on laisse libre cours **2** *(unverified ▸ source, figures)* non vérifié; *(proofs)* non relu
ADV 1 *(grow, expand)* continuellement, sans arrêt; *(continue)* impunément, sans opposition; **such rudeness can't go u.** on ne peut pas laisser passer une telle impolitesse *ou* grossièreté; **the growth of industry continued u.** la croissance industrielle s'est poursuivie de façon constante **2** *(advance)* sans rencontrer d'opposition

unchivalrous [ˌʌnˈʃɪvəlrəs] **ADJ** peu galant, discourtois

UNCHR [juːensiːeɪtʃˈɑː(r)] **N** *(abbr* **United Nations Commission on Human Rights***)* CDH *f*

unchristian [ˌʌnˈkrɪstʃən] **ADJ 1** *Rel* peu chrétien **2** *Fig* barbare; **this is an u. hour to phone someone!** ce n'est pas une heure pour téléphoner aux gens!

uncircumcised [ˌʌnˈsɜːkəmsaɪzd] **ADJ** incirconcis

uncivil [ˌʌnˈsɪvəl] **ADJ** impoli, grossier; **to be u. to sb** être impoli envers *ou* à l'égard de qn

uncivilized, -ised [ˌʌnˈsɪvɪlaɪzd] **ADJ 1** *(people, tribe)* non civilisé **2** *(primitive, barbaric ▸ behaviour, conditions)* barbare; *(▸ people)* barbare, inculte; **it's very u. of him to keep us waiting like this** ce n'est pas correct de sa part de nous faire attendre comme ça **3** *Fig (ridiculous)* impossible, extraordinaire; **the plane arrives at the u. hour of 4 a.m.** l'avion arrive à une heure indue, 4 heures du matin

unclaimed [ˌʌnˈkleɪmd] **ADJ** *(property, reward, dividend)* non réclamé; *(rights)* non revendiqué

unclasp [ˌʌnˈklɑːsp] **VT** *(hands)* ouvrir; *(bracelet)* dégrafer, défaire

unclassifiable [ˌʌnklæsɪˈfaɪəbəl] **ADJ** inclassable

unclassified [ˌʌnˈklæsɪfaɪd] **ADJ 1** *(not sorted ▸ books, papers)* non classé **2** *Br (road)* non classé **3** *(information)* non secret

uncle [ˈʌŋkəl] **N** *(relative)* oncle *m*; **hello, U.** bonjour mon oncle, bonjour tonton; **U. Peter** l'oncle Peter, tonton Peter; *Am Fam* **to cry** *or* **to say u.** s'avouer vaincu, se rendre
▸▸ ***Uncle Sam*** l'Oncle *m* Sam *(personnification des États-Unis)*; *Am very Fam Pej* **Uncle Tom** = Noir qui se comporte de façon obséquieuse avec les Blancs

unclean [ˌʌnˈkliːn] **ADJ 1** *(dirty ▸ water, habits)* sale **2** *Rel* impur; **to feel u.** se sentir souillé

unclear [ˌʌnˈklɪə(r)] **ADJ 1** *(confused, ambiguous ▸ thinking, purpose, reason)* pas clair, pas évident; **the instructions were u.** les instructions n'étaient pas claires; **I'm still u. about what exactly I have to do** je ne sais pas encore très bien ce que je dois faire exactement **2** *(uncertain ▸ future, outcome)* incertain; **it is now u. whether the talks will take place or not** nous ne savons plus très bien si la conférence va avoir lieu **3** *(indistinct ▸ sound, speech)* indistinct, inaudible; *(▸ outline)* flou

uncleared [ˌʌnˈklɪəd] **ADJ 1** *(ground)* non défriché **2** *Fin (debt)* non liquidé; *(cheque)* non compensé, non crédité **3** *(goods)* non dédouané

unclench [ˌʌnˈklentʃ] **VT** *(fist, teeth)* desserrer

unclimbable [ˌʌnˈklaɪməbəl] **ADJ** *(mountain)* impossible à escalader

unclimbed [ˌʌnˈklaɪmd] **ADJ** *(mountain, peak)* invaincu

uncloak [ˌʌnˈkləʊk] **VT** *(mystery)* dévoiler; *(plans)* découvrir; *(impostor)* démasquer

unclog [ˌʌnˈklɒg] *(pt & pp* **unclogged**, *cont* **unclogging***)* **VT** *(drain)* déboucher; *(wheel, machine)* débloquer

unclothed [ˌʌnˈkləʊðd] **ADJ** dévêtu, nu

unclouded [ˌʌnˈklaʊdɪd] **ADJ 1** *(sky)* dégagé, sans nuages; *Fig (thinking)* limpide; *(mind, vision)* clair; **a future u. by financial worries** un avenir sans soucis financiers **2** *(liquid)* clair, limpide

uncluttered [ˌʌnˈklʌtəd] **ADJ** *(room)* dépouillé, simple; *(style of writing)* sobre; *(design)* dépouillé; *(mind, thinking)* clair, net; **the diagram should be neat and u.** le diagramme devrait être net et concis

unco [ˈʌŋkəʊ] **ADV** *Scot Arch* très

uncoil [ˌʌnˈkɔɪl] **VT** dérouler
VI se dérouler

uncollectable [ˌʌnkəˈlektəbəl] **ADJ** *(tax)* non percevable

uncollected [ˌʌnkəˈlektɪd] **ADJ** *(luggage)* non réclamé; *(tax)* non perçu

uncoloured, *Am* uncolored [ʌnˈkʌləd] **ADJ** non coloré; *Fig* **an u. account of sth** un rapport impartial sur qch

uncombed [ˌʌnˈkəʊmd] **ADJ** *(hair)* mal peign ébouriffé; *(wool)* non peigné

uncomely [ˌʌnˈkʌmlɪ] **ADJ** peu joli

uncomfortable [ˌʌnˈkʌmftəbəl] **ADJ 1** *(phy ically ▸ chair, bed, clothes)* inconfortable, pe confortable; *(▸ position)* inconfortable, pe commode; **this chair is very u.** cette chaise n'es pas du tout confortable, on est très mal sur cett chaise; **I feel most u. perched on this stool** je n me sens pas du tout à l'aise perché sur ce tabou ret **2** *Fig (awkward, uneasy ▸ person)* mal à l'aise gêné; *(difficult, embarrassing ▸ situation, truth* difficile, gênant; *(unpleasant)* désagréable; **I fe u. about the whole thing** je me sens mal à l'ais avec tout ça; **to make sb (feel) u.** mettre qn ma à l'aise; **to make life** *or* **things (very) u. for sb** crée des ennuis à qn; **I'd feel u. (about) asking my pa ents for money** ça me gênerait de demander d l'argent à mes parents; **it's a very u. feeling, know ing you could easily have been killed** c'est un ser timent très déplaisant de savoir que tu aura très bien pu mourir; **there was an u. silence** il eut un silence gêné

uncomfortably [ˌʌnˈkʌmftəblɪ] **ADV 1** *(lie, si stand)* inconfortablement, peu confortable ment; *(dressed)* mal, inconfortablement **2** *(ur pleasantly ▸ heavy, hot)* désagréablement; **h came u. close to discovering the truth** il a été dar gereusement près de découvrir la vérité; **I was aware of him watching me** j'étais désagréable ment conscient du fait qu'il me regardait **3** *(ur easily)* avec gêne; **he shifted u. in his seat** bougeait avec embarras sur son siège

uncommitted [ˌʌnkəˈmɪtɪd] **ADJ** *(person, litera ture)* non engagé; **he remains politically u.** il rest neutre politiquement; **an u. relationship** une re lation libre

uncommon [ˌʌnˈkɒmən] **ADJ 1** *(rare, unusual disease, species)* rare, peu commun; **it's not u. fo the heating to break down** il n'est pas rare que l chauffage soit en panne **2** *Formal (exceptiona* singulier, extraordinaire; **a child of u. abilities** u enfant aux dons singuliers

uncommonly [ˌʌnˈkɒmənlɪ] **ADV 1** *(rarely)* rare ment, inhabituellement **2** *Formal (exceptionall ▸ clever, cold, polite)* singulièrement, exception nellement; **he took an u. long time over it** il a mi exceptionnellement longtemps à le faire

uncommunicative [ˌʌnkəˈmjuːnɪkətɪv] **ADJ** pe communicatif, taciturne; **to be u. about sth** s montrer réservé sur qch

uncomplaining [ˌʌnkəmˈpleɪnɪŋ] **ADJ** qui ne s plaint pas; **he has a calm and u. wife** il a un femme calme et résignée

uncomplainingly [ˌʌnkəmˈpleɪnɪŋlɪ] **ADV** san se plaindre

uncomplicated [ˌʌnˈkɒmplɪkeɪtɪd] **ADJ** pe compliqué, simple

uncomplimentary [ˈʌnˌkɒmplɪˈmentərɪ] **AD** peu flatteur; **he was very u. about you** ce qu'il dit de vous était loin d'être flatteur

uncomprehending [ˈʌnˌkɒmprɪˈhendɪŋ] **AD** qui ne comprend pas; **to give sb an u. look** rega der qn sans comprendre; **in u. amazement** ahur

uncomprehendingly [ˈʌnˌkɒmprɪˈhendɪŋl **ADV** sans comprendre

uncompromising [ˌʌnˈkɒmprəmaɪzɪŋ] **AD** *(rigid ▸ attitude, behaviour)* rigide, intransi geant, inflexible; *(committed ▸ person)* convain cu, ardent; **a man of u. principles** un homme au principes très stricts; **we took an u. stance on th** nous avons adopté une position inflexible à c sujet

uncompromisingly [ˌʌnˈkɒmprəmaɪzɪŋlɪ] **AD** sans concession, de manière intransigeante **u. honest** d'une honnêteté absolue

unconcealed [ˌʌnkənˈsiːld] **ADJ** *(joy, anger)* évi dent, non dissimulé

unconcern [ˌʌnkənˈsɜːn] **N 1** *(indifference)* indif férence *f*; **your u. for others/for danger** ton indif férence envers les autres/au danger **2** *(calm* sang-froid *m inv*; **she continued with apparent u** elle poursuivit avec un sang-froid apparent

unconcerned [ˌʌnkənˈsɜːnd] **ADJ 1** *(unworried calm)* qui ne s'inquiète pas, insouciant; **h seemed quite u. about the exam/her health** il n emblait pas du tout s'inquiéter pour l'examen/ our sa santé **2** *(uninterested)* indifférent; **she's u. vith political matters** elle est indifférente aux questions politiques

nconcernedly [ˌʌnkən'sɜːnɪdlɪ] **ADV 1** *(calmly)* sans s'inquiéter, sans se laisser troubler **2** *(uninterestedly)* avec indifférence *ou* insouciance

nconditional [ˌʌnkən'dɪʃənəl] **ADJ** *(support, ubmission)* inconditionnel, sans condition
▸▸ *Law* ***unconditional discharge*** libération *f* inconditionnelle; ***unconditional surrender*** reddition *f* inconditionnelle

nconditionally [ˌʌnkən'dɪʃənəlɪ] **ADV** *(accept, urrender)* inconditionnellement, sans condition

nconfirmed [ˌʌnkən'fɜːmd] **ADJ** non confirmé; **he report remains u.** la nouvelle n'a pas encore té confirmée

ncongenial [ˌʌnkən'dʒiːnɪəl] **ADJ** *(surroundngs, atmosphere, work)* peu agréable; *(person)* antipathique; *(climate)* peu favorable (**to** à)

nconnected [ˌʌnkə'nektɪd] **ADJ** *(unrelated* ▸ *acts, incidents)* sans rapport; *(*▸ *ideas, thoughts)* sans suite, décousu; **the riot was u. with food prices** l'émeute n'avait pas de rapport *ou* était sans rapport avec les prix alimentaires; **the wo events are totally u.** les deux événements n'ont aucun rapport entre eux; **the two incidents are not u.** les deux incidents ne sont pas sans ien

nconquerable [ˌʌn'kɒŋkərəbəl] **ADJ** *(opponnt, mountain)* invincible; *(obstacle, problem)* insurmontable; *(instinct, will)* irrépressible

nconquered [ˌʌn'kɒŋkəd] **ADJ** *(nation, terriory)* qui n'a pas été conquis; *(mountain)* invaincu

nconscionable [ˌʌn'kɒnʃənəbəl] **ADJ** *Formal* **1** *liar)* sans scrupules **2** *(demand)* déraisonnable; *time)* extraordinaire

nconscious [ˌʌn'kɒnʃəs] **ADJ 1** *(in coma)* sans connaissance; *(in faint)* évanoui, sans connaissance; **to knock sb u.** assommer qn; **he lay u. for five days** il est resté sans connaissance pendant cinq jours
2 *(unaware)* inconscient; **to be u. of doing sth** ne pas se rendre compte qu'on fait qch; **to be u. of sth** ne pas avoir conscience de qch, ne pas se rendre compte de qch; **they are u. of the fact** ils n'en sont pas conscients
3 *(unintentional)* inconscient, involontaire; **it was an u. pun** c'était un jeu de mots involontaire; **there was an u. bias in his selection of candidates** il y avait un parti pris involontaire dans son choix de candidats
4 *Psy (motives)* inconscient; **the u. mind** l'inconscient *m*
N *Psy* **the u.** l'inconscient *m*

nconsciously [ˌʌn'kɒnʃəslɪ] **ADV** inconsciemment, sans s'en rendre compte

nconsciousness [ˌʌn'kɒnʃəsnɪs] **N** *(UNCOUNT)* **1** *Med (coma)* perte *f* de connaissance; *(fainting)* évanouissement *m*; **in a state of u.** sans connaissance **2** *(lack of awareness)* inconscience *f*

nconsecrated [ˌʌn'kɒnsɪkreɪtɪd] **ADJ** non consacré

nconsidered [ˌʌnkən'sɪdəd] **ADJ 1** *(thought, acion)* irréfléchi **2** *Formal (object)* sans importance

nconsolidated [ˌʌnkən'sɒlɪdeɪtɪd] **ADJ** *Fin (debt)* non consolidé

nconstitutional [ˌʌnkɒnstɪ'tjuːʃənəl] **ADJ** inconstitutionnel

nconstitutionally [ˌʌnkɒnstɪ'tjuːʃənəlɪ] **ADV** inconstitutionnellement

nconstrained [ˌʌnkən'streɪnd] **ADJ** *(feelings)* sans contrainte, non contraint; *(action)* spontané; *(manner)* aisé; **he is u. by inhibitions** les inhibitions ne l'arrêtent pas; **u. laughter** hilarité *f* débordante

nconsummated [ˌʌn'kɒnsəmeɪtɪd] **ADJ** *(mariage)* non consommé

ncontaminated [ˌʌnkən'tæmɪneɪtɪd] **ADJ** non contaminé

uncontested [ˌʌnkən'testɪd] **ADJ** *(position, authority)* non disputé, incontesté; *Pol* **the seat was u.** il n'y avait qu'un candidat pour le siège

uncontrollable [ˌʌnkən'trəʊləbəl] **ADJ 1** *(fear, desire, urge)* irrésistible, irrépressible; *(stammer)* que l'on ne peut maîtriser *ou* contrôler; **to be seized by u. laughter/anger** être pris d'un fou rire/d'un accès de colère; **I had an u. urge to slap her** j'ai eu une envie irrépressible de la gifler **2** *(animal)* indomptable; *(child)* impossible à discipliner **3** *(inflation)* qui ne peut être freiné, galopant

uncontrollably [ˌʌnkən'trəʊləblɪ] **ADV 1** *(helplessly)* irrésistiblement; **he was laughing u.** il avait le fou rire; **I shook u.** je tremblais sans pouvoir m'arrêter **2** *(out of control)* **the boat rocked u.** on n'arrivait pas à maîtriser le tangage du bateau **3** *(fall, rise)* irrésistiblement

uncontrolled [ˌʌnkən'trəʊld] **ADJ 1** *(unrestricted* ▸ *fall, rise)* effréné, incontrôlé; *(*▸ *population growth)* non contrôlé; *(*▸ *anger, emotion)* incontrôlé, non retenu; **inflation cannot remain u.** l'inflation ne peut demeurer incontrôlée; **scenes of u. violence** des scènes de violence incontrôlée *ou* d'une extrême violence **2** *(unverified* ▸ *experiment)* non contrôlé

uncontroversial ['ʌnˌkɒntrə'vɜːʃəl] **ADJ** qui ne prête pas à controverse, incontestable

unconventional [ˌʌnkən'venʃənəl] **ADJ** non conformiste

unconventionally [ˌʌnkən'venʃənəlɪ] **ADV** *(live, think)* d'une manière originale *ou* peu conventionnelle; *(dress)* d'une manière originale

unconvinced [ˌʌnkən'vɪnst] **ADJ** incrédule, sceptique; **I'm u.** je ne suis pas convaincu, je reste sceptique; **to be/to remain u. by sth** être/rester sceptique à l'égard de qch

unconvincing [ˌʌnkən'vɪnsɪŋ] **ADJ** peu convaincant

unconvincingly [ˌʌnkən'vɪnsɪŋlɪ] **ADV** *(argue, lie)* d'un ton *ou* d'une manière peu convaincante, peu vraisemblablement

uncooked [ˌʌn'kʊkt] **ADJ** non cuit, cru

uncool [ˌʌn'kuːl] **ADJ** *Fam* **1** *(unfashionable, unsophisticated)* ringard; **it's a really u. place** c'est vraiment ringard comme endroit; **what an u. thing to do!** c'est vraiment nul de faire un truc pareil! **2** *(not allowed, not accepted)* mal vu□; **I think it's a bit u. to smoke in here** je pense pas que ça soit très bien vu de fumer ici **3** *(upset)* **she was a bit u. about me moving in with them** elle tenait pas trop à ce que je m'installe chez eux

uncooperative [ˌʌnkəʊ'ɒpərətɪv] **ADJ** peu coopératif

uncooperatively [ˌʌnkəʊ'ɒpərətɪvlɪ] **ADV** de manière peu coopérative

uncooperativeness [ˌʌnkəʊ'ɒpərətɪvnɪs] **N** manque *m* de coopération

uncoordinated [ˌʌnkəʊ'ɔːdɪneɪtɪd] **ADJ 1** *(movements)* mal coordonné; **her hand and eye movements are u.** les mouvements de ses yeux et de ses mains ne sont pas coordonnés **2** *(clumsy)* maladroit **3** *(unorganized* ▸ *efforts, attack, undertaking)* qui manque de coordination, mal organisé

uncork [ˌʌn'kɔːk] **VT** *(bottle)* déboucher; *Fig (emotions)* déchaîner

uncorrected [ˌʌnkə'rektɪd] **ADJ** *(exercise, proof)* non corrigé; *(error)* non rectifié *ou* corrigé

uncorroborated [ˌʌnkə'rɒbəreɪtɪd] **ADJ** non corroboré

uncorrupted [ˌʌnkə'rʌptɪd] **ADJ** *(person)* non corrompu

uncountable [ˌʌn'kaʊntəbəl] **ADJ 1** *(numberless)* incalculable, innombrable **2** *Gram* indénombrable, non comptable

uncountably [ʌn'kaʊntəblɪ] **ADV** *Gram* de façon indénombrable

uncounted [ˌʌn'kaʊntɪd] **ADJ 1** *(not counted)* non compté **2** *Literary (numberless)* incalculable, innombrable

uncouple [ˌʌn'kʌpəl] **VT 1** *(engine)* découpler; *(carriage)* dételer; *(cart, trailer)* détacher **2** *Hunt* découpler

uncouth [ˌʌn'kuːθ] **ADJ** grossier, fruste

uncover [ˌʌn'kʌvə(r)] **VT 1** *(furniture, swimming pool)* découvrir; *(saucepan)* enlever le couvercle de **2** *(evidence, plot, conspiracy)* découvrir **3** *Chess (piece)* découvrir, dégarnir

uncovered [ˌʌn'kʌvəd] **ADJ 1** *(without a cover)* découvert; **food should not be left u.** la nourriture ne doit pas rester à l'air **2** *Fin* sans couverture; *(purchase, sale)* à découvert; *(cheque)* sans provision
▸▸ *Fin* ***uncovered advance*** avance *f* à découvert

uncreasable [ˌʌn'kriːsəbəl] **ADJ** *(fabric)* infroissable

uncritical [ˌʌn'krɪtɪkəl] **ADJ** *(naïve)* dépourvu d'esprit critique, non critique; *(unquestioning)* inconditionnel; *(audience)* peu exigeant; **to be u. of sb/sth** ne faire preuve d'aucun sens *ou* esprit critique à l'égard de qn/qch

uncross [ˌʌn'krɒs] **VT** décroiser

uncrossed [ˌʌn'krɒst] **ADJ 1** *(cheque)* non barré **2** *(legs)* décroisé

uncrowded [ˌʌn'kraʊdɪd] **ADJ** *(beach, streets)* où il n'y a pas trop de monde; *(road)* peu encombré

uncrowned [ˌʌn'kraʊnd] **ADJ** sans couronne, non couronné; **the u. king of rock 'n' roll** le roi sans couronne du rock'n'roll

uncrunch [ˌʌn'krʌntʃ] **VT** *Comput* décompresser, décompacter

uncrushable [ˌʌn'krʌʃəbəl] **ADJ** *(fabric)* infroissable

UNCTAD ['ʌŋktæd] **N** *(abbr* **United Nations Conference on Trade and Development***)* CNUCED *f*

unction ['ʌŋkʃən] **N 1** *Rel* onction *f* **2** *Formal (unctuousness)* manières *fpl* onctueuses

unctuous ['ʌŋktjʊəs] **ADJ** *Formal* mielleux, onctueux

unctuously ['ʌŋktjʊəslɪ] **ADV** *Formal* mielleusement, onctueusement

unctuousness ['ʌŋktjʊəsnɪs] **N** *(UNCOUNT) Formal* manières *fpl* mielleuses *ou* onctueuses

uncultivated [ˌʌn'kʌltɪveɪtɪd] **ADJ 1** *(land)* inculte, en friche **2** *(person)* inculte; *(manners, accent, speech)* qui manque de raffinement

uncultured [ˌʌn'kʌltʃəd] **ADJ** *(person)* inculte; *(manners, accent, speech)* qui manque de raffinement

uncurbed [ˌʌn'kɜːbd] **ADJ** *(authority)* sans restriction; *(passion)* déchaîné; **if these tendencies are allowed to go u.** si on ne met pas un frein à ces tendances

uncurl [ˌʌn'kɜːl] **VT** *(rope)* dérouler; *(body, toes)* étirer; **to u. oneself** s'étirer
VI *(leaf)* s'ouvrir; *(cat)* s'étirer; *(snake)* se dérouler

uncut [ˌʌn'kʌt] **ADJ 1** *(hair, nails)* non coupé; *(hedge, stone)* non taillé; *(diamond)* non taillé, brut; *(corn, wheat)* non récolté, sur pied; *(pages)* non rogné **2** *(uncensored* ▸ *film, text)* intégral, sans coupures; **the u. version** la version longue **3** *(drugs)* pur

undamaged [ˌʌn'dæmɪdʒd] **ADJ 1** *(car, contents, merchandise, building, roof)* indemne, intact, non endommagé **2** *Fig (reputation)* intact

undamped [ˌʌn'dæmpt] **ADJ 1** *(enthusiasm, feelings)* intact, non affaibli **2** *(piano string)* non étouffé

undated [ˌʌn'deɪtɪd] **ADJ** non daté, sans date

undaunted [ˌʌn'dɔːntɪd] **ADJ 1** *(not discouraged)* qui ne se laisse pas décourager *ou* démonter; **she was u. by their criticism** leurs critiques ne la décourageaient pas; **he carried on u.** il a continué sans se laisser décourager **2** *(fearless)* sans peur

undeceive [ˌʌndɪ'siːv] **VT** *Literary* détromper

undecided [ˌʌndɪ'saɪdɪd] **ADJ** *(person, issue)* indécis; *(outcome)* incertain; **to be u. about sth** être indécis à propos de qch; **he is u. whether to stay or go** il n'a pas décidé s'il restera ou s'il partira; **the matter is still u.** *(not settled)* la question n'a pas encore été tranchée; *(not yet decided)* aucune décision n'a encore été prise à ce sujet

undeclared [ˌʌndɪ'kleəd] **ADJ** *(goods, income, war)* non déclaré; *(love)* non avoué

undefeated [ˌʌndɪ'fiːtɪd] **ADJ** invaincu

undefended [ˌʌndɪˈfendɪd] **ADJ 1** *Mil (fort, town)* sans défense **2** *Law (lawsuit)* où on ne présente pas de défense

undefiled [ˌʌndɪˈfaɪld] **ADJ** sans souillure, immaculé; **u. by any contact with Western society** non corrompu par la civilisation occidentale

undefinable [ˌʌndɪˈfaɪnəbəl] **ADJ** indéfinissable, impossible à définir

undefined [ˌʌndɪˈfaɪnd] **ADJ** *(term etc)* non défini; *(vague ▸ feeling etc)* indéterminé, vague

undelete [ˌʌndɪˈliːt] **VT** *Comput* restaurer

undelivered [ˌʌndɪˈlɪvəd] **ADJ** *(letter)* non remis, non distribué; **if u. please return to sender** en cas de non-distribution, prière de retourner à l'expéditeur

undemanding [ˌʌndɪˈmɑːndɪŋ] **ADJ** *(person)* facile à vivre, qui n'est pas exigeant; *(work)* simple, qui n'est pas astreignant

undemocratic [ˈʌnˌdeməʊˈkrætɪk] **ADJ** antidémocratique, peu démocratique

undemonstrative [ˌʌndɪˈmɒnstrətɪv] **ADJ** réservé, peu démonstratif

undeniable [ˌʌndɪˈnaɪəbəl] **ADJ** indéniable, incontestable

undeniably [ˌʌndɪˈnaɪəblɪ] **ADV** *(true)* incontestablement, indiscutablement; **he's u. a very clever man** c'est incontestablement un homme très intelligent

undenominational [ˈʌndɪˌnɒmɪˈneɪʃənəl] **ADJ** non confessionnel

undependable [ˌʌndɪˈpendəbəl] **ADJ** *(machine, trains, person)* peu fiable

UNDER [ˈʌndə(r)]

PREP
- sous **1, 4–7, 11**
- au-dessous de **2**
- conformément à **8**
- moins de **2**
- sous le poids de **3**
- en cours de **9**

ADV
- dessous **1**

PREP 1 *(beneath, below)* sous; **I can't see anything u. it** je ne vois rien (en) dessous; **put it u. that** mettez-le là-dessous; **he wore a white shirt u. his jacket** il portait une chemise blanche sous sa veste; **he pulled a wallet from u. his jersey** il a sorti un portefeuille de sous son pull; **he was carrying a paper u. his arm** il portait un journal sous le bras; **stand u. my umbrella** mettez-vous sous mon parapluie; **to be born u. Aries/Leo** être né sous le signe du Bélier/du Lion; **it can only be seen u. a microscope** on ne peut le voir qu'au microscope; **you have to crawl u. it** il faut ramper dessous; **she was swimming u. water/u. the bridge** elle nageait sous l'eau/sous le pont; **it's unlucky to walk u. a ladder** ça porte malheur de passer sous une échelle

2 *(less than)* moins de, au-dessous de; **u. £7,000** moins de 7000 livres; **everything is u. £5** tout est à moins de 5 livres; **is she u. 16?** est-ce qu'elle a moins de 16 ans?; **children u. ten** les enfants au-dessous *ou* de moins de dix ans; **in u. ten minutes** en moins de dix minutes

3 *(weighed down by)* sous le poids de; **he staggered u. his heavy load** il chancelait sous le poids de son lourd chargement; *Fig* **to sink u. the weight of one's debts** sombrer sous le poids de ses dettes

4 *(indicating conditions or circumstances)* sous, dans; **we had to work u. appalling conditions** on a dû travailler dans des conditions épouvantables; **she was murdered u. strange circumstances** elle a été tuée dans d'étranges circonstances; **u. the circumstances** vu les circonstances

5 *(subject to)* sous; **u. duress/threat** sous la contrainte/la menace

6 *Med* sous; **u. sedation/treatment** sous calmants/traitement

7 *(directed, governed by)* sous (la direction de); **he studied u. Fox** il a été l'élève de Fox; **she has two assistants u. her** elle a deux assistants sous ses ordres; *Mus* **the Bristol Chamber Orchestra u. Martin Davenport** l'orchestre de (musique de) chambre de Bristol sous la direction de Martin Davenport; **I served u. General White** j'ai servi sous le général White; **the book describes Uganda u. Amin** le livre décrit l'Ouganda sous (le régime d')Amin Dada; **to come u. (the authority of) the Home Office** relever du ministère de l'Intérieur; **u. her management, the firm prospered** sous sa direction, l'entreprise a prospéré

8 *(according to)* conformément à, en vertu de, selon; **u. the new law, all this will change** avec la nouvelle loi, tout cela va changer; **u. the new law, elections will be held every four years** en vertu de *ou* selon la nouvelle loi, les élections auront lieu tous les quatre ans; **u. the Emergency Powers Act** conformément à la loi instituant l'état d'urgence; **u. this system, the President has little real power** dans ce système, le Président a peu de pouvoir véritable; **u. (the terms of) his will/the agreement** selon (les termes de) son testament/l'accord

9 *(in the process of)* en cours de; **u. construction** en cours de construction; **the matter is u. consideration/discussion** on est en train d'étudier/de discuter la question

10 *Agr* **u. wheat/barley** en blé/orge

11 *(in classification)* **you'll find the book u. philosophy** vous trouverez le livre sous la rubrique philosophie; **you'll find my number u. Magee** vous trouverez mon numéro sous Magee; **she writes u. the name of Heidi Croft** elle écrit sous le nom de Heidi Croft; **few singers perform u. their own name** peu de chanteurs gardent leur vrai nom

ADV 1 *(below ground, water, door etc)* **to slide** *or* **to slip u.** se glisser dessous; **to pass u.** passer dessous; **to stay u.** *(under water)* rester sous l'eau

2 *Med (anaesthetized)* sous l'effet de l'anesthésie

3 *(less ▸ in age, price)* **you have to be 16 or u. to enter** il faut avoir 16 ans ou moins pour se présenter; **items at £20 and u.** des articles à 20 livres et au-dessous

UNDER- PRÉFIXE

La traduction du préfixe **under-** est bien souvent **sous-**, mais parfois il est nécessaire d'avoir recours à une périphrase.

• Employé avec des verbes et leurs dérivés, **under-** signifie INSUFFISAMMENT :

to underestimate sous-estimer; **under-employed** sous-employé; **underpaid** sous-payé; **the underdevelopment of a country** le sous-développement d'un pays; **an under-exposed photo** une photo sous-exposée; **undercooked** pas assez cuit; **underdressed** habillé de façon trop décontractée/habillé trop léger; **underrehearsed** insuffisamment répété; **understaffed** qui manque de personnel; **to underachieve** ne pas obtenir les résultats escomptés.

• **Under-** signifie également AU-DESSOUS DE :

undergarments sous-vêtements; **underpass** passage souterrain; **underfoot** sous les pieds; **underskirt** jupon; **underwater** sous-marin; **the under-60s** les moins de 60 ans; **he serves underarm** il sert par en dessous; **to undercut someone** vendre moins cher que quelqu'un.

• Lorsqu'il est question d'un travail ou d'une fonction, le préfixe **under-** indique un RANG INFÉRIEUR et se traduit généralement par **sous-** :

undersecretary of state sous-secrétaire d'État; **the underclass** le sous-prolétariat.

underachieve [ˌʌndərəˈtʃiːv] **VI** ne pas obtenir les résultats escomptés; **he constantly under-achieves** il n'obtient jamais les résultats dont il est capable

underachiever [ˌʌndərəˈtʃiːvə(r)] **N** *(gen)* = personne ou élève qui n'obtient pas les résultats escomptés; **he's always been an u.** il a toujours été en deçà de ses possibilités

under-age **ADJ** *(person)* mineur

▸▸ ***under-age drinking*** consommation *f* d'alcool par les mineurs; ***under-age sex*** rapports *mpl* sexuels avant l'âge légal

underarm [ˈʌndərɑːm] **ADV** *Sport (bowl, hit, serve)* (par) en dessous

ADJ 1 *(deodorant)* pour les aisselles; *(hair)* sous les bras *ou* les aisselles **2** *Sport (bowl, throw, serve)* par en dessous

underbelly [ˈʌndəˌbelɪ] *(pl* **underbellies***)* **N 1** *(o... animal)* bas-ventre *m* **2** *Fig* point *m* faible; **th... soft u. of society** le point faible de la société

underbid [ˌʌndəˈbɪd] *(pt & pp* **underbid**, *cor...* **underbidding***)* **N** *Cards (in bridge)* annonce *f* au dessous de sa force

VT 1 *Com* **to u. sb** faire des soumissions *ou* offri... des conditions plus avantageuses que qn **2** *Cards (in bridge)* **to u. one's hand** annoncer au dessous de sa force

VI 1 *Cards (in bridge)* annoncer au-dessous de sa force **2** *(in auction)* ne pas offrir assez, faire un... enchère insuffisamment élevée

underblanket [ˈʌndəˌblæŋkɪt] **N** protège-mate... las *m*; *(waterproof)* alaise *f*

underbody [ˈʌndəˌbɒdɪ] *(pl* **underbodies***)* **N 1** *(o... animal)* ventre *m* **2** *(of car)* dessous *m* de caisse

underborrow [ˌʌndəˈbɒrəʊ] **VI** *Fin (company...)* ne pas emprunter assez

underborrowed [ˌʌndəˈbɒrəʊd] **ADJ** *Fin (com... pany)* sous-endetté

underborrowing [ˌʌndəˈbɒrəʊɪŋ] **N** *Fin (c... company)* sous-endettement *m*

underbrush [ˈʌndəbrʌʃ] **N** *(UNCOUNT) Am...* sous-bois *m*, broussailles *fpl*

undercapitalization, -isation [ˈʌnd... ˌkæpɪtəlaɪˈzeɪʃən] **N** *Econ* sous-capitalisation *f*

undercapitalized, -ised [ˌʌndəˈkæpɪtəlaɪzd...] **ADJ** *(entrepreneur, company)* sous-capitalisé

undercarriage [ˈʌndəˌkærɪdʒ] **N** *(of aeroplane...)* train *m* d'atterrissage; *(of vehicle)* châssis *m*

undercharge [ˌʌndəˈtʃɑːdʒ] **VT** *(customer)* fair... payer insuffisamment *ou* moins cher à; **I wa... undercharged** on m'a fait payer moins cher, o... ne m'a pas fait payer le prix indiqué; **she unde... charged him by £6** elle lui a fait payer 6 livres d... moins que le prix

underclass [ˈʌndəklɑːs] **N the u.** le sous-proléta... riat, les exclus *mpl*

undercloth [ˈʌndəklɒθ] **N** *(on table)* sous-napp... *f*

underclothes [ˈʌndəkləʊðz] **NPL** sous-vête... ments *mpl*; *(for women)* lingerie *f*, dessous *mpl*

undercoat [ˈʌndəkəʊt] **N** *(of paint)* sous-couch... *f*; *(of anti-rust treatment)* couche *f* d'antirouille

VT *(with paint)* poser une sous-couche su... *(with anti-rust treatment)* poser une couche d'an... tirouille sur

underconsumption [ˌʌndəkənˈsʌmpʃən] ... *Econ* sous-consommation *f*

undercook [ˌʌndəˈkʊk] **VT** ne pas assez cuire... **the potatoes were undercooked** les pommes d... terre n'étaient pas assez cuites *ou* n'avaient pa... cuit assez longtemps

undercover [ˈʌndəˌkʌvə(r)] **ADJ** *(methods, work...)* secret(ète), clandestin

ADV clandestinement

▸▸ ***undercover agent*** agent *m* secret

undercurrent [ˈʌndəˌkʌrənt] **N 1** *(in sea)* cou... rant *m* sous-marin; *(in river)* courant *m* **2** *Fi... (feeling)* sentiment *m* sous-jacent; **there was a... u. of hostility throughout the discussion** il y eu... une hostilité sous-jacente tout au long de la dis... cussion

undercut *(pt & pp* **undercut**, *cont* **undercutting***)* **VT** [ˌʌndəˈkʌt] **1** *Com (competitor)* vendre moin... cher que; *(prices)* casser **2** *(undermine ▸ efforts... principle)* amoindrir **3** *Sport (ball)* lifter

N [ˈʌndəkʌt] **1** *Sport* lift *m* **2** *Culin (meat)* (morcea... *m* de) filet *m*

underdeveloped [ˌʌndədɪˈveləpt] **ADJ 1** *(coun... try, society)* sous-développé; *(area)* insuffisam... ment mis en valeur; *(resources)* sous-exploité

2 *(stunted ▸ foetus, plant)* qui n'est pas complè... tement développé *ou* formé; *(▸ child)* peu déve... loppé; *(▸ muscle)* pas assez développé

3 *Fig (argument, idea)* insuffisamment déve... loppé *ou* exposé

4 *Phot (film, print)* insuffisamment développé

underdog [ˈʌndədɒg] **N the u.** *(in fight, contest...)* celui (celle) *m,f* qui risque de perdre *ou* qui par... perdant(e); *(in society)* le laissé-pour-compt... (la laissée-pour-compte) *m,f*, l'opprimé(e) *m,f*... **he's always been one to side with the u.** il pren... toujours le parti du perdant; **the underdogs wo...**

2 ceux qui étaient donnés perdants d'avance ıt gagné 5 à 2

ıderdone [ˌʌndəˈdʌn] ADJ *(accidentally)* pas ·sez cuit; *(deliberately ▸ meat)* saignant; *vegetable, cake)* pas trop cuit

ıderdrawers [ˈʌndəˌdrɔːz] NPL *Am* caleçon *m* ˈhomme)

ıderdressed [ˌʌndəˈdrest] ADJ *(too lightly)* op légèrement vêtu; *(too informally)* habillé op sport; **I feel really u. in these jeans** avec ce an, je me trouve très mal habillé pour la cir- ınstance

ıderemployed [ˌʌndərɪmˈplɔɪd] ADJ *(worker, ·uipment)* sous-employé; *(resources)* sous- xploité; **he feels u.** il trouve qu'il n'a pas assez travail

ıderemployment [ˌʌndərɪmˈplɔɪmənt] N *(of orkers)* sous-emploi *m*; *(of resources)* sous- xploitation *f*

ıderestimate VT [ˌʌndəˈrestɪmeɪt] *(size, ·ength)* sous-estimer; *(person, value)* sous-esti- er, mésestimer

N [ˌʌndəˈrestɪmət] sous-estimation *f*

ıderexpose [ˌʌndərɪkˈspəʊz] VT **1** *Phot (print, ˈm)* sous-exposer **2** *(underpublicize ▸ person, ˈm, event)* ne pas faire assez de publicité pour

ıderexposed [ˈʌndərɪkˈspəʊzd] ADJ *Phot* sous- xposé

ıderexposure [ˌʌndərɪkˈspəʊʒə(r)] N **1** *Phot ıck of exposure)* sous-exposition *f*; *(photo, ·int)* photo *f* sous-exposée **2** *(to publicity)* anque *m* de publicité; **the campaign suffered om u. in the media** la campagne a souffert d'un anque de publicité dans les médias **3** *(social)* **to other children may inhibit development** le anque de contact avec d'autres enfants peut einer le développement

ıderfed [ˌʌndəˈfed] ADJ *(person)* sous- imenté

ıderfeeding [ˌʌndəˈfiːdɪŋ] N sous-alimenta- on *f*

ıderfelt [ˈʌndəfelt] N thibaude *f*

ıderfinance [ˌʌndəˈfaɪnæns] VT financer in- ıffisamment

ıderfloor [ˈʌndəflɔː(r)] ADJ *(pipes, wiring)* qui trouve sous le plancher

▸ ***underfloor heating*** chauffage *m* par le sol

ıderfoot [ˌʌndəˈfʊt] ADV sous les pieds; **the ·ass is wet u.** l'herbe est humide; **I felt the gravel unch u.** j'ai senti les graviers crisser sous mes ieds; *also Fig* **to trample sb/sth u.** *(of person)* fou- r qn/qch aux pieds; *(of animal)* piétiner qn/ ch

ıderfunded [ˌʌndəˈfʌndɪd] ADJ *(gen)* qui ne spose pas de fonds suffisants; *Fin* sous-capi- ılisé

ıderfunding [ˌʌndəˈfʌndɪŋ] N *(gen)* finance- ·ent *m* insuffisant; *Fin* sous-capitalisation *f*

ıder-gardener N aide-jardinier(ère) *m,f*

ıdergarment [ˈʌndəˌgɑːmənt] N sous-vête- ·ent *m*

ıdergo [ˌʌndəˈgəʊ] *(pt* **underwent** [-ˈwent], *pp* **ıdergone** [-ˈgɒn]) VT **1** *(experience ▸ change)* su- ır; *(▸ hardship)* subir, éprouver **2** *(test, trials)* subir, passer; *(training)* suivre **3** *(be subject to)* subir; **the building/the system is ndergoing modernization** l'immeuble/le sys- ·me est en cours de modernisation **4** *Med* **to u. an operation** subir une intervention hirurgicale; **to u. treatment** suivre un traite- ·ent

ıdergrad [ˈʌndəgræd] N *Fam* étudiant(e) *m,f ·ui prépare une licence)*

ıdergraduate [ˌʌndəˈgrædʒʊət] N étudiant(e) *·,f (qui prépare une licence)*; **she was an u. at Man- ıester** elle était en licence à Manchester

ADJ *(circles, life)* estudiantin, étudiant; *(course)* our les étudiants de licence; *(accommodation, ·ant)* pour étudiants; *(humour)* d'étudiant

▸ ***undergraduate student*** étudiant(e) *m,f* en li- ence

ıderground ADJ [ˈʌndəgraʊnd] **1** *(subterra- ·ean ▸ explosion, pipe, lake, cable)* souterrain; *(▸ car park)* en sous-sol, souterrain **2** *(secret)* se- ·ret(ète), clandestin; **they joined an u. movement** *(clandestine)* ils sont entrés dans un mouvement clandestin; *(resistance)* ils sont entrés dans un mouvement de résistance; **the u. press** la presse clandestine **3** *(unofficial ▸ literature, theatre)* d'avant-garde, underground *(inv)*; *(▸ institutions)* parallèle

N [ˈʌndəgraʊnd] **1** *Mil & Pol (resistance)* résistance *f*; *(secret army)* armée *f* secrète **2** *Art, Mus & Theat* avant-garde *f*, underground *m inv* **3** *Br (railway)* métro *m*; **to go by u.** aller en métro; **the London u.** le métro de Londres *ou* londonien

ADV [ˌʌndəˈgraʊnd] **1** *(below surface)* sous (la) terre **2** *(in hiding)* **to go u.** passer dans la clandestinité, prendre le maquis

▸▸ ***underground economy*** économie *f* souterraine; ***underground railway*** métro *m*; ***underground station*** station *f* de métro; ***underground train*** rame *f* de métro

undergrowth [ˈʌndəgrəʊθ] N *(UNCOUNT)* sous-bois *m*; *(scrub)* broussailles *fpl*

underhand [ˌʌndəˈhænd] ADJ **1** *(action)* en dessous, en sous-main; *(person)* sournois; **in an u. way** sournoisement **2** *Sport* par en dessous

ADV sournoisement

underhanded [ˌʌndəˈhændɪd] ADJ **1** = **underhand 2** *(shorthanded)* qui manque de personnel

underhandedly [ˌʌndəˈhændɪdlɪ] ADV en dessous, sournoisement

underinsured [ˌʌndərɪnˈʃɔːd] ADJ sous-assuré

underinvestment [ˌʌndərɪnˈvestmənt] N insuffisance *f* d'investissement

underlaid [ˌʌndəˈleɪd] *pt & pp of* **underlay**

underlain [ˌʌndəˈleɪn] *pp of* **underlie**

underlay [ˌʌndəˈleɪ] *pt of* **underlie**

VT [ˌʌndəˈleɪ] *(pt & pp* **underlaid** [-ˈleɪd]) *(carpet)* doubler

N [ˈʌndəleɪ] *(felt)* thibaude *f*; *(foam)* doublure *f*

underlie [ˌʌndəˈlaɪ] *(pt* **underlay** [-ˈleɪ], *pp* **underlain** [-ˈleɪn]) VT sous-tendre, être à la base de

underline [ˌʌndəˈlaɪn] VT *also Fig* souligner

underling [ˈʌndəlɪŋ] N *Pej* subalterne *mf*, sous-fifre *m*

underlining [ˌʌndəˈlaɪnɪŋ] N soulignage *m*

underlying [ˌʌndəˈlaɪɪŋ] ADJ sous-jacent

▸▸ *Fin* ***underlying asset*** actif *m* sous-jacent; *Fin* ***underlying security*** titre *m* sous-jacent

undermanager [ˈʌndəˌmænɪdʒə(r)] N sous-chef *m*, sous-directeur(trice) *m,f*

undermanned [ˌʌndəˈmænd] ADJ qui manque de main-d'œuvre; *Naut* qui manque d'hommes d'équipage

undermanning [ˌʌndəˈmænɪŋ] N manque *m ou* pénurie *f* de main-d'œuvre; *Naut* manque *m* d'hommes d'équipage

undermentioned [ˌʌndəˈmenʃənd] ADJ *Formal* ci-dessous (mentionné)

undermine [ˌʌndəˈmaɪn] VT **1** *(cliff, coast, wall)* miner, saper **2** *(authority, person, principle)* saper; *(health)* user; *(confidence)* ébranler; **to u. the foundations of society** attaquer les bases de la société; **to u. democracy** fragiliser la démocratie; **stop undermining me!** arrête de me rabaisser!

undermost [ˈʌndəməʊst] ADJ *(in heap)* le dernier, le plus bas; *(in depth)* le plus profond *ou* bas

ADV tout en bas

underneath [ˌʌndəˈniːθ] PREP sous, au-dessous de, en dessous de; **the cat slipped u. the fence** le chat s'est glissé *ou* est passé sous *ou* par-dessous le grillage; **she was wearing two pullovers u. her coat** elle portait deux pullovers sous son manteau; **the noise was coming from u. the floorboards** le bruit venait de sous le plancher

ADV **1** *(in space)* (en) dessous, au-dessous; **I've got a jumper on u.** j'ai un pull dessous **2** *(within oneself)* **he smiled, but u. he felt afraid/helpless** il a souri, mais dans le fond *ou* en son for intérieur il avait peur/il se sentait impuissant

N dessous *m*; **what's written on the u.?** qu'est-ce qui est écrit sur le dessous?

ADJ de dessous, d'en dessous

undernourished [ˌʌndəˈnʌrɪʃt] ADJ sous-alimenté

undernourishment [ˌʌndəˈnʌrɪʃmənt] N sous-alimentation *f*

underpaid [ˌʌndəˈpeɪd] *pt & pp of* **underpay**

ADJ sous-payé

underpants [ˈʌndəpænts] NPL **1** *(for men)* slip *m (d'homme)*; **a pair of u.** un slip, un caleçon **2** *Am (for women)* culotte *f*

underpart [ˈʌndəpɑːt] N *Zool (underside)* dessous *m*, partie *f* inférieure

• **underparts** NPL *(abdomen)* ventre *m*

underpass [ˈʌndəpɑːs] N **1** *(subway)* passage *m* souterrain **2** *(road)* route *f* inférieure

underpay [ˌʌndəˈpeɪ] *(pt & pp* **underpaid** [-ˈpeɪd]) VT sous-payer

underperform [ˌʌndəpəˈfɔːm] VI rester en deçà de ses possibilités; *St Exch (shares)* avoir un cours trop bas

underpin [ˌʌndəˈpɪn] *(pt & pp* **underpinned,** *cont* **underpinning**) VT *also Fig* soutenir, étayer; **the principles which u. Marxism-Leninism** les principes de base du marxisme-léninisme

underpinning [ˌʌndəˈpɪnɪŋ] N soutien *m*, étayage *m*

underplay [ˌʌndəˈpleɪ] VT **1** *(minimize ▸ importance)* minimiser; *(▸ event)* réduire *ou* minimiser l'importance de; **to u. one's hand** *(in cards)* jouer volontairement une petite carte; *Fig* cacher son jeu **2** *Theat (role)* jouer avec retenue

VI *(in cards)* jouer volontairement une petite carte

underpopulated [ˌʌndəˈpɒpjʊleɪtɪd] ADJ sous-peuplé

underprice [ˌʌndəˈpraɪs] VT mettre en vente au-dessous de sa valeur réelle

underpriced [ˌʌndəˈpraɪst] ADJ très bon marché (par rapport à sa valeur réelle); **at £15.99 it's definitely u.** à 15,99 livres c'est vraiment donné

underpricing [ˌʌndəˈpraɪsɪŋ] N fixation *f* de prix trop bas

underprivileged [ˌʌndəˈprɪvɪlɪdʒd] ADJ *(person, social class)* défavorisé, déshérité

NPL **the u.** les défavorisés *mpl*

underproduce [ˌʌndəprəˈdjuːs] VT produire insuffisamment de

VI produire insuffisamment

underproduction [ˌʌndəprəˈdʌkʃən] N sous-production *f*

underqualified [ˌʌndəˈkwɒlɪfaɪd] ADJ sous-qualifié

underrate [ˌʌndəˈreɪt] VT sous-estimer

underrepresent [ˌʌndərepriˈzent] VT minimiser, ne pas donner assez d'importance à

underrepresentation [ˈʌndəˌreprɪzenˈteɪʃən] N *(gen) & Pol* sous-représentation *f*

underrepresented [ˌʌndərepriˈzentɪd] ADJ *(gen) & Pol* sous-représenté

underscore VT [ˌʌndəˈskɔː(r)] *also Fig* souligner

N [ˈʌndəskɔː(r)] *Typ (effect)* soulignage *m*, soulignement *m*; *(character)* trait *m* bas; **g u. brown at xmail dot com** *(in e-mail addresses)* g underscore brown, arobase, xmail, point com

undersea [ˈʌndəsiː] ADJ sous-marin

ADV sous la mer

underseal [ˈʌndəsiːl] *Br Aut* N **1** *(product)* produit *m* antirouille **2** *(act, result)* couche *f* antirouille

VT traiter contre la rouille

underseasoned [ˌʌndəˈsiːzənd] ADJ *(food)* fade

undersecretary [ˌʌndəˈsekrətərɪ] *(pl* **undersecretaries**) N *Pol* **1** *Br (in department)* chef *m* de cabinet **2** *(politician)* sous-secrétaire *m*; **u. of state** sous-secrétaire d'État

undersell [ˌʌndəˈsel] *(pt & pp* **undersold** [-ˈsəʊld]) VT *(competitor)* vendre moins cher que; *(goods)* vendre au-dessous de la valeur de; *Fig* **to u. oneself** se sous-estimer; *Fig* **don't u. yourself at the interview** essaie de bien te vendre lors de l'entretien

VI *(goods)* se vendre mal

undersexed [ˌʌndəˈsekst] ADJ qui manque de libido

undersheet [ˈʌndəʃiːt] N alaise *f*

undershield [ˈʌndəʃiːld] N *Aut* bouclier *m* inférieur

undershirt [ˈʌndəʃɜːt] N *Am* maillot *m ou* tricot *m* de corps

undershoot [ˌʌndəˈʃuːt] *(pt & pp* **undershot** [-ˈʃɒt]) VT **the plane undershot the runway** l'avion s'est posé avant d'atteindre la piste d'atterrissage; **he undershot the target** son coup n'a pas atteint la cible

underside [ˈʌndəsaɪd] N **the u.** le dessous, la face inférieure

undersigned [ˈʌndəsaɪnd] *(pl* inv*) Formal* N **the u.** le (la) soussigné(e); **I, the u.** je soussigné
ADJ soussigné

undersize [ˌʌndəˈsaɪz], **undersized** [ˌʌndəˈsaɪzd] ADJ trop petit

underskirt [ˈʌndəskɜːt] N jupon *m*

underslung [ˌʌndəˈslʌŋ] ADJ très bas; *Aut* surbaissé

undersold [ˌʌndəˈsəʊld] *pt & pp of* **undersell**

understaffed [ˌʌndəˈstɑːft] ADJ qui manque de personnel

understaffing [ˌʌndəˈstɑːfɪŋ] N manque *m ou* pénurie *f* de personnel

understand [ˌʌndəˈstænd] *(pt & pp* **understood** [-ˈstʊd]) VT **1** *(meaning)* comprendre; **I u. what you mean** je comprends ce que vous voulez dire; **is that understood?** est-ce compris?; **to make oneself understood** se faire comprendre; **do I make myself understood?** *(as threat)* est-ce que je me suis bien fait comprendre?; **I can't u. it!** je ne comprends pas!, cela me dépasse!
2 *(subject, theory)* comprendre, entendre; **I don't u. a thing about economics** je ne comprends rien à l'économie
3 *(character, person)* comprendre; **I u. your need to be independent** je comprends bien que vous ayez besoin d'être indépendant; **we u. each other perfectly** nous nous comprenons parfaitement; **she didn't u. why no one was interested** elle ne comprenait pas pourquoi personne n'était intéressé
4 *(believe)* comprendre, croire; **I u. you need a loan** j'ai cru comprendre que *ou* si j'ai bien compris, vous avez besoin d'un prêt; **I understood that I was to be paid for my work** j'ai cru comprendre que je devais être payé pour mon travail; **am I to u. that they refused?** dois-je comprendre qu'ils ont refusé?; **they are understood to have fled the country** il paraît qu'ils ont fui le pays; **we were given to u. that he was very ill** on nous a fait comprendre *ou* donné à entendre qu'il était très malade; **so I u.** c'est ce que j'ai compris
5 *(interpret)* entendre; **what do you u. by "soon"?** qu'est-ce que vous entendez par "bientôt"?; **as I u. it, there's nothing to pay** d'après ce que j'ai compris, il n'y a rien à payer
6 *(leave implicit)* entendre, sous-entendre; **she let it be understood that she preferred to be alone** elle a laissé entendre *ou* donné à entendre qu'elle préférait être seule; *Gram* **the object of the sentence is understood** l'objet de la phrase est sous-entendu
VI comprendre; **of course, I u.** bien sûr, je comprends (bien); **if you do that once more you're out, u.?** faites ça encore une fois et vous êtes viré, compris?; **they u. about international finance** ils s'y connaissent en finance internationale

understandable [ˌʌndəˈstændəbəl] ADJ compréhensible; **that's perfectly u.** cela se comprend parfaitement

understandably [ˌʌndəˈstændəblɪ] ADV **1** *(naturally)* naturellement; **they were, u. (enough), deeply embarrassed** ils étaient profondément gênés, ce qui se comprend parfaitement **2** *(speak, write)* de manière compréhensible

understanding [ˌʌndəˈstændɪŋ] N **1** *(UNCOUNT) (comprehension)* compréhension *f*; *(intelligence)* intelligence *f*; *(knowledge)* connaissance *f*, connaissances *fpl*; **it is our u. that they have now left the country** d'après ce que nous avons compris, ils ont quitté le pays à présent; **they have little u. of what the decision involves** ils ne comprennent pas très bien ce que la décision entraînera; **it's beyond all u.!** cela dépasse l'entendement!, c'est à n'y rien comprendre!
2 *(agreement)* accord *m*, arrangement *m*; **to come to** *or* **reach an u. about sth (with sb)** s'entendre (avec qn) sur qch; **there's some kind of u. between them** il y a quelque arrangement entre eux
3 *(interpretation)* compréhension *f*, interprétation *f*; *(conception)* conception *f*; **my u. of the matter is that he's resigned** d'après ce que j'ai compris, il a démissionné; **my u. was that the venue would be paid for by the organizers** j'avais compris que les organisateurs paieraient pour la location des locaux
4 *(relationship ▸ between people)* bonne intelligence *f*, entente *f*; *(▸ between nations)* entente *f*
5 *(sympathy)* **he showed great u.** il a fait preuve de beaucoup de compréhension
6 *(condition)* condition *f*
ADJ compréhensif, bienveillant
• **on the understanding that** CONJ à condition que; **on the u. that the money is given to charity** à condition que l'argent soit donné à des bonnes œuvres

understandingly [ˌʌndəˈstændɪŋlɪ] ADV avec compréhension, avec bienveillance

understate [ˌʌndəˈsteɪt] VT **1** *(minimize)* minimiser (l'importance de); **the deliberately understated figures in the foreground** les silhouettes volontairement estompées au premier plan **2** *(state with restraint)* dire avec retenue, modérer l'expression de

understated [ˌʌndəˈsteɪtɪd] ADJ discret(ète); **the acting was very u.** le jeu des acteurs était très sobre

understatement [ˌʌndəˈsteɪtmənt] N euphémisme *m*; *Ling & Literature* litote *f*; **that's a bit of an u.!** c'est peu dire!; **to say it's expensive is an u.** dire que c'est cher est un euphémisme; **calling him lazy is something of an u.** le traiter de paresseux, c'est peu dire; **with typical British u.** avec un sens de l'euphémisme tout britannique

understeer [ˈʌndəˌstɪə(r)] VI *Aut* sous-virer

understeering [ˈʌndəˌstɪərɪŋ] N *Aut* sous-virage *m*, comportement *m* sous-vireur

understood [ˌʌndəˈstʊd] *pt & pp of* **understand**

understudy [ˈʌndəˌstʌdɪ] *(pl* **understudies**, *pt & pp* **understudied**) N *Theat* doublure *f*
VT *(role)* apprendre un rôle en tant que doublure; *(actor)* doubler

undersubscribed [ˌʌndəsʌbˈskraɪbd] ADJ *Fin & St Exch (issue, share)* non-souscrit

undertake [ˌʌndəˈteɪk] *(pt* **undertook** [-ˈtʊk], *pp* **undertaken** [-ˈteɪkən]) VT **1** *Formal (take up ▸ job, project, journey)* entreprendre; *(▸ experiment)* entreprendre, se lancer dans; *(▸ responsibility)* assumer, se charger de; *(▸ change)* entreprendre, mettre en œuvre **2** *Formal (agree, promise)* s'engager à; **he undertook to pay half the costs** il s'est engagé à payer la moitié des frais **3** *Fam (vehicle)* doubler par l'intérieur
VI *Fam (driver, vehicle)* doubler par l'intérieur

undertaker [ˈʌndəˌteɪkə(r)] N entrepreneur *m* des pompes funèbres; **we'd better call the undertakers** il faut appeler les pompes funèbres

undertaking [ˌʌndəˈteɪkɪŋ] N **1** *(promise)* engagement *m*; **to give a written u. to do sth** s'engager par écrit à faire qch; **she gave an u. that she wouldn't intervene** elle a promis de ne pas intervenir **2** *(enterprise)* entreprise *f*; **it's quite an u.** c'est toute une affaire **3** *Fam (of vehicle)* dépassement *m* par l'intérieur

undertax [ˌʌndəˈtæks] VT *(goods, product)* taxer insuffisamment; *(person)* ne pas faire payer assez d'impôts à

under-the-counter *Fam* ADJ *(agreement, offer, sale)* en douce, clandestin; **an u. payment** un dessous-de-table
ADV clandestinement, sous le manteau; **to sell sth u.** vendre qch sous le manteau

undertone [ˈʌndətəʊn] N **1** *(in speech)* voix *f* basse; **to speak in an u.** parler à voix basse *ou* à mi-voix **2** *(of feeling)* nuance *f*; **the situation had comic undertones** au fond, la situation avait quelque chose de comique; **all her poetry has a tragic u.** toute sa poésie a un fond de tragique **3** *(in colour)* nuance *f*; **grey with blue undertones** gris nuancé de bleu

undertook [ˌʌndəˈtʊk] *pt of* **undertake**

undertow [ˈʌndətəʊ] N courant *m* sous-marin *(causé par le reflux de la vague)*; *Fig* **I sensed an u. of resentment in her words** je sentais un vague ressentiment dans ses paroles

underuse N [ˌʌndəˈjuːs] *(gen)* sous-utilisation *(of resources, land)* sous-exploitation *f*
VT [ˌʌndəˈjuːz] *(gen)* sous-utiliser; *(resource land)* sous-exploiter

underutilization, -isation [ˈʌndəˌjuːtɪla zeɪʃən] N *(gen)* sous-utilisation *f*, *(of resource land)* sous-exploitation *f*

underutilize, -ise [ˌʌndəˈjuːtɪlaɪz] VT *(gen)* sou utiliser; *(resources, land)* sous-exploiter

undervalue [ˌʌndəˈvæljuː] VT *(object, good* sous-évaluer, sous-estimer; *(person, help)* sou estimer

undervest [ˈʌndəvest] N *Br* tricot *m ou* maillot de corps

underwater ADJ [ˈʌndəwɔːtə(r)] sous-marin
ADV [ˌʌndəˈwɔːtə(r)] sous l'eau

underwear [ˈʌndəweə(r)] N *(UNCOUNT)* sou vêtements *mpl*

underweight [ˈʌndəˈweɪt] ADJ **1** *(person)* qui pèse pas assez, trop maigre; **to be u.** être en de sous de son poids normal; **I'm half a stone u.** devrais peser trois kilos de plus **2** *(goods)* d' poids insuffisant; **all the packets are 20 grams** il manque 20 grammes à chaque paquet

underwent [ˌʌndəˈwent] *pt of* **undergo**

underwhelm [ˌʌndəˈwelm] VT *Hum* décevo **she felt rather underwhelmed by it all** elle a é plutôt déçue par tout ça; **he was obviously und whelmed by his present** le cadeau l'avait lais manifestement indifférent; **the critics we underwhelmed by his next film** son nouveau fil fut accueilli avec un enthousiasme très rela par la critique

underwired [ˈʌndəˌwaɪəd] ADJ *(bra)* avec arm ture

underworld [ˈʌndəˌwɜːld] N **1** *(of criminals)* p gre *f*, milieu *m* **2** *Myth* **the u.** les Enfers *mpl*
COMP *(activity)* du milieu; *(contact)* dans *ou* av le milieu

underwrite [ˈʌndəraɪt] *(pt* **underwrote** [-ˈrəʊt], **underwritten** [-ˈrɪtən]) VT **1** *Ins (policy)* garant *(risk)* garantir, assurer contre **2** *St Exch (ne issue)* garantir, souscrire **3** *(support ▸ financial* soutenir *ou* appuyer financièrement; *(▸ agreement)* soutenir, souscrire à

underwriter [ˈʌndəˌraɪtə(r)] N **1** *Ins (of poli risk)* assureur *m* **2** *St Exch (of new issue)* syndic taire *mf*; **the underwriters** le syndicat de garan

underwriting [ˈʌndəˌraɪtɪŋ] N *Ins (of policy, ris* garantie *f*; **marine u.** assurance *f* maritime
▸▸ *St Exch* ***underwriting agent*** agent *m* souscri teur; *Ins* ***underwriting commission*** commissio de garantie

underwritten [ˌʌndəˈrɪtən] *pp of* **underwrot**

underwrote [ˌʌndəˈrəʊt] *pt of* **underwrite**

undeserved [ˌʌndɪˈzɜːvd] ADJ immérité, injus

undeservedly [ˌʌndɪˈzɜːvɪdlɪ] ADV injustemer indûment

undeserving [ˌʌndɪˈzɜːvɪŋ] ADJ *(person)* p méritant; *(cause)* peu méritoire; **he is quite u. such praise** il est parfaitement indigne de *ou* il mérite pas du tout de telles louanges

undesirable [ˌʌndɪˈzaɪərəbəl] ADJ indésirab **highly u.** tout à fait inopportun; **to have an u. fluence on sb** avoir une mauvaise influence s qn
N indésirable *mf*
▸▸ ***undesirable alien*** étranger(ère) *m,f* indés rable

undetected [ˌʌndɪˈtektɪd] ADJ *(error)* non d tecté, non décelé; *(disease)* non détecté, non d pisté; **to go u.** passer inaperçu

undetermined [ˌʌndɪˈtɜːmɪnd] ADJ **1** *(unknow* inconnu, indéterminé; **an artefact of u. origin** objet fabriqué d'origine inconnue; **for an u. su of money** pour une somme d'argent non fixée *(hesitant)* irrésolu, indécis

undeterred [ˌʌndɪˈtɜːd] ADJ sans se laisser d courager; **she was u. by this setback** elle ne s'e pas laissé décourager par ce revers; **u. by t weather, he went out for a walk** en dépit du ma vais temps, il est sorti se promener

undeveloped [ˌʌndɪˈveləpt] ADJ **1** *(ideas, su gestions)* non développé; *(country)* en dévelo pement; *(muscles, organs)* non formé; *(lan* esources) non exploité **2** *(immature)* immature **3** *'hot (film)* non développé

ndeviating [ˌʌn'di:vieɪtɪŋ] **ADJ** *(course, path)* lroit, direct; *(faithfulness)* qui ne se dément pas

ndid [ˌʌn'dɪd] *pt of* **undo**

ndies ['ʌndɪz] **NPL** *Fam (abbr* **underwear***)* sous-êtements *mpl* féminins

ndifferentiated [ˌʌndɪfə'renʃieɪtɪd] **ADJ** indifférencié

ndigested [ˌʌndɪ'dʒestɪd] **ADJ** mal digéré, non ligéré

ndignified [ˌʌn'dɪgnɪfaɪd] **ADJ** *(behaviour, person)* qui manque de dignité; **to be u.** manquer de lignité; **their business venture came to an u. end** eur entreprise a échoué de façon lamentable

ndiluted [ˌʌndaɪ'lju:tɪd] **ADJ 1** *(liquid)* non dilué; *(acid)* concentré **2** *Fig (emotion)* sans mélange, parfait; **it's pure, u. malice** c'est de la néchanceté à l'état pur

ndiminished [ˌʌndɪ'mɪnɪʃt] **ADJ** intact, non diminué; **my respect for him remains u.** mon respect pour lui n'a pas diminué *ou* est resté ntact; **30 years later, the appeal of the film remains u.** 30 ans plus tard, le film n'a rien perdu le son intérêt

ndiplomatic [ˌʌndɪplə'mætɪk] **ADJ** *(action)* peu liplomatique; *(person)* peu diplomate, qui nanque de diplomatie

ndiplomatically [ˌʌndɪplə'mætɪkəlɪ] **ADV** de nanière peu diplomatique

ndipped [ˌʌn'dɪpt] **ADJ** *Br Aut* **to drive with u. eadlights** rouler en pleins phares

ndiscerning [ˌʌndɪ'sɜ:nɪŋ] **ADJ** *(eater, wine-rinker)* peu raffiné, peu connaisseur; *(mind)* eu pénétrant; **to be u.** *(person)* manquer de discernement

ndischarged [ˌʌndɪs'tʃɑ:dʒd] **ADJ** *Fin & Law bankrupt)* non réhabilité, non déchargé; *(debt)* on liquidé

ndisciplined [ˌʌn'dɪsɪplɪnd] **ADJ** indiscipliné

ndisclosed [ˌʌndɪs'kləʊzd] **ADJ** non divulgué; **or an u. sum** pour une somme dont le montant a pas été révélé

ndiscountable [ˌʌndɪs'kaʊntəbəl] **ADJ** *Fin* nescomptable

ndiscovered [ˌʌndɪ'skʌvəd] **ADJ** non découvert; **the manuscript lay u. for centuries** le manuscrit est resté inconnu des siècles durant; **an . land** une terre inconnue

ndiscriminating [ˌʌndɪs'krɪmɪˌneɪtɪŋ] **ADJ** qui nanque de discernement

ndiscriminatingly [ˌʌndɪs'krɪmɪˌneɪtɪŋlɪ] **ADV** ans discernement

ndisguised [ˌʌndɪs'gaɪzd] **ADJ** *(hatred, contempt, pleasure)* non dissimulé

ndisguisedly [ˌʌndɪs'gaɪzɪdlɪ] **ADV** ouvertement

ndismayed [ˌʌndɪs'meɪd] **ADJ** qui ne se laisse pas décourager; **he seemed quite u. by his defeat** a défaite ne semblait pas du tout l'avoir découragé

ndisputed [ˌʌndɪ'spju:tɪd] **ADJ** incontesté

ndistinguished [ˌʌndɪ'stɪŋgwɪʃt] **ADJ 1** *(person)* peu distingué, sans distinction **2** *(style, aste)* banal, quelconque

ndistributed [ˌʌndɪs'trɪbjətəd] **ADJ** *Fin (money, earnings)* non distribué

▸▸ ***undistributed profits*** bénéfices *mpl* non distribués

ndisturbed [ˌʌndɪ'stɜ:bd] **ADJ 1** *(in peace)* tranquille; **I want to be left u. for a while** je veux qu'on me laisse tranquille un moment **2** *(unchanged, untroubled)* inchangé, tranquille; **village life has gone on here u. for centuries** la vie du village se poursuit tranquillement depuis des siècles; **the population remained largely u. by the war** en général, la population n'a pas été affectée par la guerre **3** *(untouched* ▸ *body, ground, papers)* non dérangé, non déplacé

ndivided [ˌʌndɪ'vaɪdɪd] **ADJ 1** *(whole)* entier; **this job requires your u. attention** ce travail nécessite toute votre attention *ou* votre entière attention; **you have my u. love** vous avez tout mon amour **2** *(unanimous)* unanime

undo [ˌʌn'du:] *(pt* **undid** [-'dɪd], *pp* **undone** [-'dʌn]*)* **VT 1** *(bow, knot, button, knitting)* défaire; *(tie, lace)* défaire, dénouer; *(fastening)* défaire; *(screw)* desserrer; *(parcel)* défaire, déficeler; *(shoes)* délacer; *(garment, belt)* défaire

2 *(ruin* ▸ *work)* détruire; *(*▸ *effect)* annuler; *(*▸ *plan)* mettre en échec; **you can't u. the past** ce qui est fait est fait

3 *(repair* ▸ *wrong, mistake)* réparer

4 *Comput (command)* annuler, défaire; **can't u.** impossible d'annuler; **u. changes** annuler les révisions; **u. last** annuler dernière opération

5 *Literary or Hum (hope, plan)* ruiner, anéantir; *(person)* être la ruine de

VI *(tie, bra, belt, lace, knot)* se défaire; *(zip)* s'ouvrir; *(shirt)* se déboutonner

▸▸ *Comput* ***undo command*** commande *f* d'annulation

undocumented [ˌʌn'dɒkjʊmentɪd] **ADJ** non documenté

undoing [ˌʌn'du:ɪŋ] **N** perte *f*; **that man will be her u.** cet homme la conduira à sa perte; **his indecision proved to be his u.** son indécision a causé sa perte

undomesticated [ˌʌndə'mestɪˌkeɪtɪd] **ADJ** *(animal)* non domestiqué; *(person)* sans talent pour les travaux ménagers; **she's completely u.** elle ne sait rien faire dans la maison

undone [ˌʌn'dʌn] *pp of* **undo**

ADJ 1 *(button, hair)* défait; *(fastening)* défait; *(blouse)* déboutonné; *(flies)* ouvert; **to come u.** se défaire **2** *(task)* non accompli; **we had to leave it u.** nous n'avons pas pu le terminer; **we have left u. those things that we ought to have done** nous n'avons pas fait les choses que nous aurions dû faire **3** *Literary or Hum (hope, plan)* ruiné, anéanti; **we are u.!** nous sommes perdus!

undoubted [ˌʌn'daʊtɪd] **ADJ** indubitable

undoubtedly [ˌʌn'daʊtɪdlɪ] **ADV** indubitablement

undramatic [ˌʌndrə'mætɪk] **ADJ** *(lacking in interest)* pas très intéressant; **this seemingly u. incident...** cet incident apparemment anodin...

undrawn [ˌʌn'drɔ:n] **ADJ 1** *(cheque)* qu'on n'a pas tiré **2** *(curtains)* ouvert

undreamed-of [ˌʌn'dri:md-], **undreamt-of** [ˌʌn'dremt-] **ADJ** inconcevable, impensable, auquel on ne songe pas

undress [ˌʌn'dres] **VT** déshabiller

VI se déshabiller

N *Hum* **in a state of u.** en petite tenue

undressed [ˌʌn'drest] **ADJ 1** *(person)* déshabillé; **to get u.** se déshabiller

2 *(wound)* non pansé

3 *(lobster, crab)* nature; *(salad)* non assaisonné

4 *(cloth)* inapprêté; *(wood)* en grume; *(stone)* non taillé

undrinkable [ˌʌn'drɪŋkəbəl] **ADJ 1** *(bad-tasting)* imbuvable **2** *(unfit for drinking)* non potable

undubbed [ˌʌn'dʌbd] **ADJ** *Cin & TV* non doublé; **the u. version of the film** la version originale du film

undue [ˌʌn'dju:] **ADJ** excessif; **with u. haste** avec une hâte excessive

undulate ['ʌndjʊleɪt] **VI** onduler

undulating ['ʌndjʊleɪtɪŋ] **ADJ** *(curves, hills)* onduleux

undulation [ˌʌndjʊ'leɪʃən] **N** ondulation *f*

unduly [ˌʌn'dju:lɪ] **ADV** excessivement, trop; **not u. expensive/concerned** pas excessivement cher/inquiet; **he worries u.** *or* **he's u. worried about his health** sa santé le préoccupe trop

undying [ˌʌn'daɪɪŋ] **ADJ** *(faith)* éternel; **to swear one's u. love (for sb)** jurer un amour éternel (à qn)

unearned [ˌʌn'ɜ:nd] **ADJ 1** *(undeserved* ▸ *fame, privilege)* non mérité, immérité **2** *Econ* non gagné en travaillant *ou* par le travail

▸▸ ***unearned income*** *(UNCOUNT)* revenus *mpl* non professionnels, rentes *fpl*

unearth [ˌʌn'ɜ:θ] **VT 1** *(dig up)* déterrer **2** *Fig (find* ▸ *object, equipment, fact)* dénicher, trouver; *(*▸ *old ideas)* ressortir, ressusciter

unearthly [ˌʌn'ɜ:θlɪ] **ADJ 1** *(weird)* étrange; *(unnatural)* surnaturel; *(mysterious)* mystérieux; *(sinister)* sinistre **2** *Fig* **at an u. hour** à une heure indue; **u. din** vacarme *m* de tous les diables; **for some u. reason** pour une raison absurde

unease [ˌʌn'i:z] **N** *Literary* **1** *(of mind)* inquiétude *f*, malaise *m*; *(embarrassment)* malaise *m*, gêne *f*; **I tried to ignore my growing u.** j'essayais d'ignorer mon malaise grandissant **2** *Pol (unrest)* troubles *mpl*; *(tension)* tension *f*

uneasily [ˌʌn'i:zɪlɪ] **ADV 1** *(anxiously* ▸ *wait, watch)* anxieusement, avec inquiétude; *(*▸ *sleep)* d'un sommeil agité **2** *(with embarrassment)* avec gêne, mal à l'aise

uneasy [ˌʌn'i:zɪ] *(compar* **uneasier**, *superl* **uneasiest***)* **ADJ 1** *(troubled* ▸ *person)* inquiet(ète); *(*▸ *sleep)* agité; **I've just got an u. feeling that it won't work** j'ai la fâcheuse impression que ce ne marchera pas; **she was u. in her mind** elle se sentait inquiète; **to feel u. about sth/doing sth** se sentir inquiet à l'idée de qch/de faire qch; **I had an u. conscience** je n'avais pas la conscience tranquille **2** *(embarrassed* ▸ *person)* mal à l'aise, gêné; *(*▸ *silence)* gêné; **I feel u. in her presence** je me sens mal à l'aise en sa présence **3** *(uncertain* ▸ *peace, situation)* précaire

uneatable [ˌʌn'i:təbəl] **ADJ** immangeable

uneaten [ˌʌn'i:tn] **ADJ** qui n'a pas été mangé; **he left his meal u.** il n'a pas touché à son repas

uneconomic ['ʌnˌi:kə'nɒmɪk] **ADJ 1** *(expensive)* peu économique **2** *(wasteful)* peu rentable

uneconomical ['ʌnˌi:kə'nɒmɪkəl] **ADJ** *(wasteful)* peu rentable

unedifying [ˌʌn'edɪfaɪɪŋ] **ADJ** peu édifiant

unedited [ˌʌn'edɪtɪd] **ADJ** *Cin & TV* non monté; *(speech, text)* non édité, non révisé

uneducated [ˌʌn'edjʊkeɪtɪd] **ADJ 1** *(person)* sans instruction **2** *(behaviour, manners)* sans éducation, inculte; *(writing)* informe; *(speech, accent)* populaire

unelectable [ˌʌnɪ'lektəbəl] **ADJ** *(person)* inéligible; *(party)* incapable de remporter des élections

unemotional [ˌʌnɪ'məʊʃənəl] **ADJ** *(person)* impassible; *(behaviour, reaction)* qui ne trahit aucune émotion; *(voice)* neutre; *(account, style)* sans passion, neutre

unemotionally [ˌʌnɪ'məʊʃənəlɪ] **ADV** froidement

unemployable [ˌʌnɪm'plɔɪəbəl] **ADJ** *(person)* inapte au travail, que l'on ne peut pas embaucher

unemployed [ˌʌnɪm'plɔɪd] **NPL the u.** les chômeurs *mpl*, les demandeurs *mpl* d'emploi

ADJ 1 *(person)* en *ou* au chômage; **she was u. for months** elle est restée au chômage pendant des mois **2** *Fin (capital, funds)* inactif

unemployment [ˌʌnɪm'plɔɪmənt] **N** chômage *m*

▸▸ *Br Formerly* ***unemployment benefit*** allocation *f* (de) chômage; *Am* ***unemployment compensation*** allocation *f* (de) chômage; ***unemployment figures*** les chiffres *mpl* du chômage; ***unemployment fund*** caisse *f* de chômage; ***unemployment insurance*** assurance *f* chômage; ***unemployment level, unemployment rate*** taux *m* de chômage; ***unemployment trap*** cercle *m* vicieux du chômage

unencumbered [ˌʌnɪn'kʌmbəd] **ADJ** *(passage)* dégagé, non encombré; *(person)* non encombré; **u. by children or mortgage** sans enfants ni emprunt immobilier à rembourser

▸▸ *Law* ***unencumbered estate*** propriété *f* franche d'hypothèques

unending [ˌʌn'endɪŋ] **ADJ** sans fin, interminable

unendorsed [ˌʌnɪn'dɔ:st] **ADJ** *Fin (cheque)* non endossé

unendurable [ˌʌnɪn'djʊərəbəl] **ADJ** intolérable

unenforceable [ˌʌnɪn'fɔ:səbəl] **ADJ** inapplicable

un-English **ADJ** peu anglais; **he's very u.** ce n'est pas du tout l'Anglais type

unenlightened [ˌʌnɪn'laɪtənd] **ADJ** *(person)* ignorant, peu éclairé; *(practice)* arriéré; **an u. age** une époque où règne/régnait l'ignorance; **I remained completely u.** je suis resté dans l'ignorance la plus totale

unenlightening [ˌʌnɪnˈlaɪtənɪŋ] ADJ *(comment)* qui n'apporte pas grand-chose

unenterprising [ˌʌnˈentəpraɪzɪŋ] ADJ *(person)* peu entreprenant; *(measure)* timoré

unenthusiastic [ˌʌnɪnθjuːzɪˈæstɪk] ADJ peu enthousiaste; **she seemed rather u. about it** ça n'avait pas l'air de l'enthousiasmer

unenthusiastically [ˌʌnɪnθjuːzɪˈæstɪkəlɪ] ADV *(say)* sans enthousiasme; *(welcome)* tièdement

unenviable [ˌʌnˈenvɪəbəl] ADJ *(conditions, situation, task)* peu enviable

unequal [ˌʌnˈiːkwəl] ADJ **1** *(amount, number, result)* inégal **2** *(contest, struggle)* inégal, non équilibré **3** *Formal (incapable)* **to be u. to a job/to a task** ne pas être à la hauteur d'un travail/d'une tâche

unequalled, *Am* **unequaled** [ˌʌnˈiːkwəld] ADJ inégalé, sans pareil

unequally [ˌʌnˈiːkwəlɪ] ADV inégalement

unequivocal [ˌʌnɪˈkwɪvəkəl] ADJ sans équivoque

unequivocally [ˌʌnɪˈkwɪvəkəlɪ] ADV sans équivoque, clairement

unerring [ˌʌnˈɜːrɪŋ] ADJ infaillible, sûr; *(aim)* sûr

unerringly [ˌʌnˈɜːrɪŋlɪ] ADV infailliblement

UNESCO [juːˈneskəʊ] N *(abbr* **United Nations Educational, Scientific and Cultural Organization***)* Unesco *f*

unescorted [ˌʌnɪsˈkɔːtɪd] ADJ non accompagné

unessential [ˌʌnɪˈsenʃəl] ADJ non essentiel

unesthetic *Am* = **unaesthetic**

unethical [ˌʌnˈeθɪkəl] ADJ contraire à l'éthique

unethically [ˌʌnˈeθɪkəlɪ] ADV contrairement à l'éthique

uneven [ˌʌnˈiːvən] ADJ **1** *(line)* irrégulier, qui n'est pas droit; *(surface)* irrégulier, rugueux; *(ground)* raboteux, accidenté; *(edge)* inégal; **she has u. teeth** ses dents sont irrégulières; **the floorboards are u.** les lattes du plancher ne sont pas toutes au même niveau **2** *(unequal ▸ contest, quality, distribution)* inégal; *Fig* **his performance was very u.** il a joué de façon très inégale **3** *(number)* impair

unevenly [ˌʌnˈiːvənlɪ] ADV **1** *(divide, spread)* inégalement; **the contestants are u. matched** les adversaires ne sont pas de force égale **2** *(cut, draw)* irrégulièrement **3** *(breathe)* irrégulièrement

unevenness [ˌʌnˈiːvnɪs] N **1** *(of line, surface, ground, edge)* irrégularité *f* **2** *(of contest, quality, distribution)* inégalité *f*

uneventful [ˌʌnɪˈventfʊl] ADJ *(day)* sans événement marquant, sans histoires; *(career)* sans histoires; *(journey)* sans histoires, sans encombre; **to lead an u. life** mener une vie sans histoires *ou* paisible

uneventfully [ˌʌnɪˈventfʊlɪ] ADV sans incidents

unexceptionable [ˌʌnɪkˈsepʃnəbəl] ADJ *Formal* irréprochable

unexceptional [ˌʌnɪkˈsepʃənəl] ADJ qui n'a rien d'exceptionnel, banal

unexchangeable [ˌʌnɪksˈtʃeɪndʒəbəl] ADJ *Fin (securities)* impermutable, inéchangeable

unexciting [ˌʌnɪkˈsaɪtɪŋ] ADJ *(life)* peu passionnant; *(film)* sans grand intérêt; *(food)* quelconque; *(person, orator etc)* terne

unexpected [ˌʌnɪkˈspektɪd] ADJ *(gen)* inattendu, imprévu; *(pleasure, gift)* inattendu; *(success)* inattendu, inespéré; *(departure, death)* inopiné; **their marriage was totally u.** leur mariage était totalement inattendu; **it was completely u.** on ne s'attendait pas du tout

N **the u.** l'imprévu *m*

unexpectedly [ˌʌnɪkˈspektɪdlɪ] ADV **1** *(arrive)* à l'improviste, de manière imprévue; *(fail, succeed)* contre toute attente, de manière inattendue **2** *(surprisingly)* étonnamment

unexpired [ˌʌnɪkˈspaɪəd] ADJ *(lease)* non expiré; *(passport, ticket)* non périmé, encore valable

unexplained [ˌʌnɪkˈspleɪnd] ADJ inexpliqué

unexploded [ˌʌnɪkˈspləʊdɪd] ADJ non explosé

unexploited [ˌʌnɪkˈsplɔɪtɪd] ADJ inexploité

unexplored [ˌʌnɪkˈsplɔːd] ADJ inexploré, inconnu; *(solution, possibility)* inexploré

unexposed [ˌʌnɪkˈspəʊzd] ADJ **1** *Phot (film)* vierge **2** *(criminal)* non démasqué **3** *(not subject to)* **she has been u. to the influences of the outside world** elle n'a pas été en contact avec le monde extérieur; **u. to the influence of TV** qui n'est pas soumis à l'influence de la télévision

unexpressed [ˌʌnɪkˈsprest] ADJ inexprimé

unexpurgated [ˌʌnˈekspəgeɪtɪd] ADJ non expurgé, intégral

unfading [ˌʌnˈfeɪdɪŋ] ADJ *(colour, feeling, pleasure)* toujours vif *(malgré le temps)*; *(memory)* toujours vif, ineffaçable

unfailing [ˌʌnˈfeɪlɪŋ] ADJ *(courage, good mood, loyalty, support)* inébranlable, à toute épreuve; *(means, remedy, memory)* infaillible; *(zeal)* infatigable; *(energy, supply)* intarissable, inépuisable; *(interest)* constant; *(kindness)* inaltérable

unfailingly [ˌʌnˈfeɪlɪŋlɪ] ADV inlassablement, toujours

unfair [ˌʌnˈfeə(r)] ADJ *(advantage, decision, treatment)* injuste; *(system)* injuste, inique; *(judgment)* inique; *(competition, play)* déloyal; **to be u. to sb** se montrer injuste envers qn; **to have an u. advantage over everybody else** être injustement avantagé par rapport à tous les autres; **he has been put at an u. disadvantage** il a été désavantagé

▸▸ *Com* ***unfair competition*** concurrence *f* déloyale; *Ind* ***unfair dismissal*** licenciement *m* abusif; **he's claiming u. dismissal** il prétend avoir fait l'objet d'un licenciement abusif

unfairly [ˌʌnˈfeəlɪ] ADV *(treat)* inéquitablement, injustement; *(compete)* déloyalement; *Ind* **to be u. dismissed** être victime d'un licenciement abusif

unfairness [ˌʌnˈfeənɪs] N *(UNCOUNT)* injustice *f*

unfaithful [ˌʌnˈfeɪθfʊl] ADJ infidèle; **to be u. to sb** être infidèle à qn

unfaithfully [ˌʌnˈfeɪθfʊlɪ] ADV infidèlement

unfaithfulness [ˌʌnˈfeɪθfʊlnɪs] N infidélité *f*

unfaltering [ʌnˈfɔːltərɪŋ] ADJ *(speech, voice, steps)* ferme, assuré; **she was u. in her support of the reform** elle soutenait fermement la réforme

unfalteringly [ʌnˈfɔːltərɪŋlɪ] ADV *(speak)* d'une voix ferme *ou* assurée; *(walk)* d'un pas ferme *ou* assuré

unfamiliar [ˌʌnfəˈmɪljə(r)] ADJ **1** *(not known ▸ face, person, surroundings)* inconnu; *(▸ ideas)* peu familier, que l'on connaît mal **2** *(strange)* étrange; **the u. sounds of the language** les sonorités étranges de cette langue **3 to be u. with sth** *(of person)* ne pas connaître *ou* mal connaître qch, ne pas être au fait de qch; **I'm u. with his writings** je connais mal ses écrits

unfamiliarity [ˈʌnfəˌmɪlɪˈærətɪ] N **1** *(strangeness ▸ of faces, ideas, surroundings)* aspect *m* peu familier, étrangeté *f* **2** *(lack of knowledge)* ignorance *f* (**with** de); **my u. with the city put me at a disadvantage** mon inexpérience de la ville a été un handicap

unfashionable [ˌʌnˈfæʃənəbəl] ADJ **1** *(clothes, ideas)* démodé **2** *(area, restaurant)* pas très chic; *(term)* démodé; *(writer)* qui n'est plus à la mode

unfashionably [ˌʌnˈfæʃənəblɪ] ADV *(dress)* sans se préoccuper de la mode; **u. long skirts** des jupes trop longues pour être à la mode; **he has u. conservative views** il a des opinions conservatrices assez démodées; **u. romantic films** des films romantiques comme on n'en fait plus

unfasten [ˌʌnˈfɑːsən] VT *(garment, tie, lace, knot, belt, button, bracelet)* défaire; *(gate)* ouvrir

unfathomable [ˌʌnˈfæðəməbəl] ADJ insondable

unfathomed [ˌʌnˈfæðəmd] ADJ inexploré, insondé

unfavourable, *Am* **unfavorable** [ˌʌnˈfeɪvərəbəl] ADJ *(gen)* défavorable; *(terms)* désavantageux

unfavourably, *Am* **unfavorably** [ˌʌnˈfeɪvərəblɪ] ADV défavorablement; **to be u. disposed towards sb/sth** être mal disposé envers qn/qch; **his work compares u. with his brother's** son travail supporte mal la comparaison avec celui de son frère

unfazed [ˌʌnˈfeɪzd] ADJ *Fam* pas du tout impre sionné; **he was totally u. by the prospect of ha ing to speak in front of thousands of people** l'idé d'avoir à prendre la parole devant des millie de personnes ne l'inquiétait pas le moins d monde

UNFCCC [juːenˌefsiːsiːˈsiː] N *(abbr* **United Natio Framework Convention on Climate Chang**) CCNUCC *f*

unfeeling [ˌʌnˈfiːlɪŋ] ADJ insensible, dur

unfeelingly [ˌʌnˈfiːlɪŋlɪ] ADV avec dureté, san pitié

unfeigned [ˌʌnˈfeɪnd] ADJ non feint, réel

unfeminine [ˌʌnˈfemɪnɪn] ADJ qui manque d féminité, peu féminin

unfenced [ˌʌnˈfenst] ADJ *(land etc)* sans clôtur

unfermented [ˌʌnfəˈmentɪd] ADJ non ferment

unfertilized, -ised [ˌʌnˈfɜːtɪlaɪzd] ADJ *(egg)* no fécondé

unfettered [ˌʌnˈfetəd] ADJ *Formal (action)* sa contrainte, sans entrave; *(imagination, violenc* débridé; **u. by moral constraints** libre de tou contrainte morale

unfilial [ˌʌnˈfɪlɪəl] ADJ peu filial

unfinished [ˌʌnˈfɪnɪʃt] ADJ **1** *(incomplete)* i complet(ète), inachevé; **an u. piece of work** u travail inachevé **2** *(rough ▸ furniture)* brut, no fini; *(▸ material)* sans apprêt; *(▸ wood)* brut

▸▸ ***unfinished business*** affaires *fpl* à régler; *F* questions *fpl* à régler

unfit [ˌʌnˈfɪt] *(pt & pp* **unfitted,** *cont* **unfitting)** A **1** *(unsuited ▸ permanently)* inapte; *(▸ temporaril* qui n'est pas en état; **he is u. for life in the army** est inapte à la vie militaire; **u. for human co sumption** impropre à la consommation; **u. f publication** impubliable; **she is u. for social wo** *or* **to be a social worker** elle n'est pas faite pou être assistante sociale; **he's still u. for work** n'est toujours pas en état de reprendre le trava **this house is u. for habitation** cette maison est i habitable **2** *(unhealthy ▸ person)* qui n'est pas e forme, qui est en mauvaise forme; *(▸ conditio* mauvais; **three of our star players have been d clared u.** trois de nos joueurs vedettes ont été d clarés hors d'état de jouer

VT *Formal* rendre inapte; **his past record unfitte him for public office** sa conduite passée lui inte disait toute fonction officielle

unfitness [ˌʌnˈfɪtnɪs] N **1** *(unsuitability)* inapt tude *f*; **his u. for public office** son inaptitude toute fonction officielle **2** *(lack of health, physic fitness)* mauvaise forme *f*

unfitted [ˌʌnˈfɪtɪd] ADJ *Formal (unprepared)* m préparé; *(unsuitable)* inapte; **to be u. to do st** être inapte à faire qch; **u. for** inapte à

unfitting [ˌʌnˈfɪtɪŋ] ADJ *(remarks)* déplacé, i convenant; *(behaviour)* inconvenant

unfittingly [ʌnˈfɪtɪŋlɪ] ADV *(say, remark)* mal propos; *(behave)* de manière peu convenable

unfix [ˌʌnˈfɪks] VT *(bayonet)* remettre

unflagging [ˌʌnˈflægɪŋ] ADJ *(courage)* infat gable, inlassable; *(enthusiasm)* inépuisabl **with u. interest** avec un intérêt toujours soute

unflaggingly [ˌʌnˈflægɪŋlɪ] ADV infatigabl ment, inlassablement

unflappability [ˌʌnflæpəˈbɪlɪtɪ] N *Fam* impe turbabilité *f*

unflappable [ˌʌnˈflæpəbəl] ADJ *Fam* impertu bable, qui ne se laisse pas démonter

unflattering [ˌʌnˈflætərɪŋ] ADJ *(gen)* peu fla teur; *(clothes, hat)* qui n'arrange pas; **her hat wa most u.** son chapeau ne la mettait certes pas e valeur; **it shows him in an u. light** ça le montr sous un jour défavorable; **he was rather u. abou your playing** il ne s'est pas montré très flatteu quant à votre jeu

unflatteringly [ˌʌnˈflætərɪŋlɪ] ADV d'une m nière peu flatteuse; **her dress was u. tight** s robe, trop étroite, ne la flattait guère; **she spok rather u. about him** elle a parlé de lui en term assez peu flatteurs

unfledged [ˌʌnˈfledʒd] ADJ **1** *(bird)* sans plume **2** *Fig* inexpérimenté, novice

nflinching [ˌʌn'flɪntʃɪŋ] ADJ *(person)* intrépide, ui ne bronche pas; *(resolve, courage)* inébranable

nflinchingly [ˌʌn'flɪntʃɪŋlɪ] ADV stoïquement, ans broncher

nfold [ˌʌn'fəʊld] VT **1** *(spread out* ▸ *cloth, map)* éplier **2** *(reveal* ▸ *intentions, plans)* exposer, rééler; *(*▸ *story)* raconter, dévoiler; *(*▸ *secret)* déoiler; *(*▸ *reasons)* faire connaître **3 to u. one's rms** décroiser les bras

VI **1** *(cloth, map)* se déplier; *(wings)* se déployer **2** *truth)* être révélé; *(events, story)* se dérouler; *view)* se dérouler, s'étendre; **the drama unfolded efore our eyes** le drame se déroulait devant nos eux

nforced [ˌʌn'fɔːst] ADJ qui n'est pas forcé, pontané

▸▸ *Sport* **unforced error** faute *f* directe; **unforced augh** rire *m* franc

nforeseeable [ˌʌnfɔː'siːəbəl] ADJ imprévisible

nforeseen [ˌʌnfɔː'siːn] ADJ imprévu, inattendu

▸▸ ***unforeseen expenses*** dépenses *fpl* non préues au budget

nforgettable [ˌʌnfə'getəbəl] ADJ inoubliable

nforgivable [ˌʌnfə'gɪvəbəl] ADJ impardonable; **it's u. of me** je suis impardonnable

nforgivably [ˌʌnfə'gɪvəblɪ] ADV impardonnalement

nforgiven [ˌʌnfə'gɪvən] ADJ non pardonné

nforgiving [ˌʌnfə'gɪvɪŋ] ADJ *(person)* implacable, impitoyable, sans merci; *(garment)* qui évèle toutes les imperfections

nforgotten [ˌʌnfə'gɒtən] ADJ inoublié

nformatted [ˌʌn'fɔːmætɪd] ADJ *Comput (disk)* on formaté; *(text)* non mis en forme

▸▸ ***unformatted capacity*** *(of disk)* capacité *f* rute

nformed [ˌʌn'fɔːmd] ADJ **1** *(undeveloped)* non ormé; *(mind)* inculte; *(idea)* en gestation **2** *shapeless)* informe, sans forme

nformulated [ˌʌn'fɔːmjʊˌleɪtɪd] ADJ informulé

nforthcoming [ˌʌnfɔːθ'kʌmɪŋ] ADJ **he was ery u. about the date of the elections** il s'est monré très discret sur la date des élections

nfortified [ˌʌn'fɔːtɪfaɪd] ADJ *(place)* non fortiié, sans fortifications

nfortunate [ʌn'fɔːtʃnət] ADJ **1** *(unlucky)* maleureux, malchanceux; **hundreds of u. people re now homeless** des centaines de malheureux ont maintenant sans abri; **he's been most u.** il n'a raiment pas eu de chance **2** *(regrettable* ▸ *incilent, situation)* fâcheux, regrettable; *(*▸ *joke, renark)* malencontreux; **it's just u. things turned out this way** il est malheureux *ou* regrettable ue les choses se soient passées ainsi; **an u. hoice of words** un choix de mots peu heureux; **n u. state of affairs** une situation regrettable *ou* âcheuse; **in u. circumstances** dans des circonsances regrettables

N *Euph Formal* malheureux(euse) *m,f*

NPL **the u.** les infortunés *mpl*

nfortunately [ʌn'fɔːtʃnətlɪ] ADV malheureuement; **u. not** malheureusement pas; **u. for im** malheureusement pour lui

nfounded [ˌʌn'faʊndɪd] ADJ infondé, dénué de ondement

nframed [ˌʌn'freɪmd] ADJ sans cadre

nfreeze [ˌʌn'friːz] *(pt* **unfroze** [-'frəʊz], *pp* **unrozen** [-'frəʊzən]) VT **1** *(thaw)* dégeler **2** *Fin (credit, ent)* débloquer, dégeler

VI (se) dégeler

nfrequented [ˌʌnfrɪ'kwentɪd] ADJ peu fréuenté

nfriendliness [ˌʌn'frendlɪnɪs] N froideur *f*

nfriendly [ˌʌn'frendlɪ] *(compar* **unfriendlier,** *superl* **unfriendliest)** ADJ *(person)* froid, peu sympathique; *(welcome, tone)* froid; *(behaviour, gesure, remark)* inamical; **to be u. to** *or* **towards sb** raiter qn avec froideur

▸▸ *Mil* ***unfriendly action*** action *f* hostile

nfrock [ˌʌn'frɒk] VT défroquer

nfrozen [ˌʌn'frəʊzən] *pp of* **unfreeze**

unfruitful [ˌʌn'fruːtfʊl] ADJ **1** *(barren)* stérile, improductif **2** *Fig (efforts, search)* infructueux, vain

unfulfilled [ˌʌnfʊl'fɪld] ADJ *(person)* insatisfait, frustré; *(dream, hopes)* non réalisé; *(ambition)* inaccompli; *(promise)* non tenu; **to feel u.** éprouver un sentiment d'insatisfaction

unfunded [ˌʌn'fʌndɪd] ADJ sans subvention

▸▸ *Fin* ***unfunded debt*** dette *f* flottante *ou* non consolidée

unfunny [ˌʌn'fʌnɪ] ADJ *(experience, joke, situation)* qui n'a rien d'amusant; **I find that most u.** je ne trouve pas ça amusant du tout

unfurl [ˌʌn'fɜːl] VT *(flag, sail)* déferler, déployer

VI se déployer

unfurnished [ˌʌn'fɜːnɪʃt] ADJ *(flat, room)* non meublé

ungainliness [ˌʌn'geɪnlɪnɪs] N maladresse *f*, gaucherie *f*

ungainly [ˌʌn'geɪnlɪ] *(compar* **ungainlier,** *superl* **ungainliest)** ADJ *(in movement)* maladroit, gauche; *(in appearance)* dégingandé, disgracieux

ungallant [ˌʌn'gælənt] ADJ peu galant, discourtois

ungeared [ˌʌn'gɪəd] ADJ *Fin* sans endettement

▸▸ ***ungeared balance sheet*** bilan *m* sans emprunts *ou* à faible endettement

ungenerous [ˌʌn'dʒenərəs] ADJ **1** *(allowance, person)* peu généreux **2** *(criticism, remark)* mesquin

ungentlemanly [ˌʌn'dʒentəlmənlɪ] ADJ *(attitude, conduct, remark)* peu galant, discourtois

ungetatable [ˌʌnget'ætəbəl] ADJ *Fam* inaccessible□, hors de portée□

ungird [ˌʌn'gɜːd] *(pt & pp* **ungirded** *or* **ungirt** [ˌʌn'gɜːt]) VT *(sword)* détacher

unglazed [ʌn'gleɪzd] ADJ **1** *(window)* sans vitres **2** *(paper)* mat, non glacé **3** *Cer* non verni, non émaillé; *(brick)* non vitrifié

▸▸ ***unglazed porcelain*** biscuit *m*; *Phot* ***unglazed print*** épreuve *f* mate

ungodliness [ˌʌn'gɒdlɪnɪs] N impiété *f*

ungodly [ˌʌn'gɒdlɪ] ADJ **1** *Literary* irréligieux, impie **2** *Hum Fig (noise)* infernal; **at an u. hour** à une heure impossible *ou* indue

ungovernable [ˌʌn'gʌvənəbəl] ADJ **1** *(feelings, temper)* irrépressible **2** *(country)* ingouvernable

ungraceful [ˌʌn'greɪsfʊl] ADJ sans grâce, gauche

ungracefully [ˌʌn'greɪsfʊlɪ] ADV sans grâce, gauchement

ungracious [ˌʌn'greɪʃəs] ADJ désobligeant; **it would be u. of me to refuse** j'aurais mauvaise grâce à refuser

ungraciously [ˌʌn'greɪʃəslɪ] ADV de mauvaise grâce

ungraciousness [ˌʌn'greɪʃəsnɪs] N mauvaise grâce *f*

ungrammatical [ˌʌngrə'mætɪkəl] ADJ agrammatical, non grammatical

ungrammatically [ˌʌngrə'mætɪklɪ] ADV incorrectement

ungrateful [ʌn'greɪtfʊl] ADJ **1** *(person)* ingrat; **to be u. to sb** manquer de reconnaissance envers qn **2** *Formal or Literary (task)* ingrat

ungratefully [ʌn'greɪtfʊlɪ] ADV de manière ingrate, avec ingratitude

ungratefulness [ʌn'greɪtfʊlnɪs] N ingratitude *f*

ungratified [ˌʌn'grætɪfaɪd] ADJ *(desire)* inassouvi

ungrudging [ˌʌn'grʌdʒɪŋ] ADJ *(offer, help)* généreux

ungrudgingly [ˌʌn'grʌdʒɪŋlɪ] ADV généreusement, de bon cœur

unguarded [ˌʌn'gɑːdɪd] ADJ **1** *(house)* non surveillé, non gardé; *(suitcase)* non surveillé; *(town)* sans défense

2 *(fire)* sans pare-feu

3 *(machinery, mechanism)* sans dispositif de protection

4 *(remark)* irréfléchi; **in an u. moment** dans un moment d'inattention

unguent ['ʌŋgwənt] N *Literary* onguent *m*, pommade *f*

ungulate ['ʌŋgjʊleɪt] ADJ ongulé

N ongulé *m*

unhallowed [ˌʌn'hæləʊd] ADJ **1** *Rel (ground)* non consacré **2** *(ungodly* ▸ *act, behaviour)* impie

unhampered [ˌʌn'hæmpəd] ADJ non entravé, libre

unhand [ˌʌn'hænd] VT *Arch or Hum* lâcher; **u. me, sir!** monsieur, lâchez-moi!

unhappily [ʌn'hæpɪlɪ] ADV **1** *(sadly)* tristement; **she looked at me u.** elle me regarda d'un air triste *ou* malheureux; **they're u. married** ils ne sont pas heureux en ménage **2** *Formal (unfortunately)* malheureusement

unhappiness [ʌn'hæpɪnɪs] N **1** *(sadness)* chagrin *m*, peine *f*; **her departure caused me great u.** son départ m'a fait beaucoup de peine; **there's so much u. in the world** il y a tellement de misère dans le monde **2** *(disaffection)* mécontentement *m*; **their u. with the situation at work is growing** leur insatisfaction au travail est de plus en plus grande

unhappy [ʌn'hæpɪ] *(compar* **unhappier,** *superl* **unhappiest)** ADJ **1** *(sad)* triste, malheureux; **to make sb u.** rendre qn malheureux; **he had an u. time abroad** il a fait un mauvais séjour à l'étranger

2 *Formal (unfortunate* ▸ *coincidence)* malheureux, regrettable; *(*▸ *remark)* malheureux, malencontreux; **an u. turn of phrase** une tournure malheureuse; **it's a most u. state of affairs** c'est une situation tout à fait regrettable *ou* fâcheuse; *Br* **the u. fellow drowned** le pauvre malheureux s'est noyé

3 *(displeased)* mécontent; **to be u. about** *or* **with sth** être mécontent de qch; **she was u. about me spending so much money** elle n'aimait pas que je dépense tant d'argent

4 *(worried)* inquiet(ète); **I'm u. about leaving the house empty** je n'aime pas laisser *ou* ça m'inquiète de laisser la maison vide

unharmed [ˌʌn'hɑːmd] ADJ **1** *(person)* sain et sauf, indemne; **to escape u.** s'en sortir indemne; **they released two boys u.** ils ont relâché deux garçons sains et saufs **2** *(object)* intact; *(house, paintwork)* non endommagé

unharness [ˌʌn'hɑːnɪs] VT *(remove harness from)* déharnacher; *(unhitch)* dételer

UNHCR [ˌjuːenˌeɪtʃsiː'ɑː(r)] N *(abbr* **United Nations High Commission for Refugees)** HCR *m*

unhealthiness [ˌʌn'helθɪnɪs] N **1** *(of person)* mauvaise santé *f*; **the u. of her complexion** son teint maladif **2** *(of air, place)* insalubrité *f* **3** *Fig (of curiosity, interest)* caractère *m* malsain *ou* morbide; *(of influence, relationship)* caractère *m* malsain

unhealthy [ˌʌn'helθɪ] *(compar* **unhealthier,** *superl* **unhealthiest)** ADJ **1** *(person)* malade; *(complexion)* maladif; **he had an u. look about him** il avait un air maladif; *Fam* **the car's sounding rather u.** la voiture fait un drôle de bruit **2** *(air, place)* malsain, insalubre **3** *Fig (curiosity, interest)* malsain, morbide; *(influence, relationship)* malsain

unheard [ˌʌn'hɜːd] ADJ **1** *(voice, complaints)* non entendu; **his cries for help went u.** personne n'a entendu ses appels à l'aide; **the opinions of the immigrant population go u.** personne ne tient compte des opinions des immigrés **2** *Law (case)* non jugé; **to be judged u.** être jugé sans être entendu

unheard-of ADJ **1** *(extraordinary)* inouï, sans précédent; **u. cruelty** une cruauté inouïe **2** *(unprecedented)* inconnu, sans précédent; **such an occurrence is quite unheard of** pareil événement n'est jamais arrivé **3** *(unknown)* inconnu, ignoré; **several previously u. painters were included in the exhibition** plusieurs peintres inconnus jusqu'alors ont participé à l'exposition; **it was u. in my day** de mon temps ça n'existait pas

unheated [ˌʌn'hiːtɪd] ADJ sans chauffage

unheeded [ˌʌn'hiːdɪd] ADJ *(ignored* ▸ *message, warning)* ignoré, dont on ne tient pas compte; *(unnoticed)* inaperçu; **his instructions went** *or* **were u.** ses instructions n'ont pas été suivies;

the announcement went u. on n'a pas tenu compte de l'annonce

unheeding [ˌʌnˈhiːdɪŋ] ADJ **1** *(unconcerned)* insouciant, indifférent **2** *(inattentive)* inattentif

unhelpful [ˌʌnˈhelpfʊl] ADJ *(person)* peu secourable *ou* serviable; *(instructions, map)* qui n'est d'aucun secours; *(advice)* inutile; **you're being deliberately u.** vous faites exprès de ne pas nous aider

unhelpfully [ˌʌnˈhelpfʊlɪ] ADV **1** *(act)* sans aider, sans coopérer; **someone very u. left the disk on a radiator** quelqu'un de très négligent a laissé la disquette sur un radiateur **2** *(advise, say, suggest)* inutilement; **she u. suggested that I go and see a clairvoyant** elle n'a rien trouvé de mieux que de me conseiller d'aller voir un voyant

unheralded [ˌʌnˈherəldɪd] ADJ *(unannounced)* non annoncé; *(unexpected)* inattendu

unhesitating [ʌnˈhezɪteɪtɪŋ] ADJ *(reaction, reply)* immédiat, spontané; *(belief)* résolu, ferme; *(person)* résolu, qui n'hésite pas

unhesitatingly [ʌnˈhezɪteɪtɪŋlɪ] ADV sans hésitation

unhindered [ʌnˈhɪndəd] ADJ sans entrave *ou* obstacle; **we crossed the border u.** nous avons passé la frontière sans encombre; **u. by all that luggage** sans être encombré par tous ces bagages; **to be u. by petty regulations** ne pas être gêné par des règlements tatillons; **u. by any moral scruples** nullement encombré de scrupules

unhinge [ˌʌnˈhɪndʒ] VT **1** *(door, window)* démonter, enlever de ses gonds **2** *Fig (mind, person)* déséquilibrer, déranger

unhinged [ˌʌnˈhɪndʒd] ADJ déséquilibré

unhip [ˌʌnˈhɪp] ADJ *Fam* ringard

unhitch [ˌʌnˈhɪtʃ] VT **1** *(rope)* détacher, décrocher **2** *(horse, ox)* dételer

unholy [ˌʌnˈhəʊlɪ] *(compar* **unholier**, *superl* **unholiest**) ADJ **1** *Rel* profane, impie; *Fig* **an u. alliance** une alliance contre nature **2** *Fam (awful* ▸ *noise, mess)* impossible[□], invraisemblable[□]; **at an u. hour** à une heure impossible *ou* indue

unhook [ˌʌnˈhʊk] VT **1** *(remove, take down)* décrocher **2** *(garment)* dégrafer, défaire
VI *(garment)* se dégrafer

unhoped-for [ʌnˈhəʊpt-] ADJ inespéré

unhorse [ˌʌnˈhɔːs] VT *Horseriding* démonter, désarçonner

unhurried [ʌnˈhʌrɪd] ADJ *(person)* qui ne se presse pas; *(manner)* tranquille, serein; **we enjoyed an u. lunch** nous avons pris plaisir à déjeuner sans nous presser

unhurt [ˌʌnˈhɜːt] ADJ indemne, sans blessure; **to escape u.** sortir sain et sauf *ou* indemne

unhygienic [ˌʌnhaɪˈdʒiːnɪk] ADJ antihygiénique, non hygiénique

uni [ˈjuːnɪ] N *Fam* **1** *Br & Austr (abbr* **university**) fac *f*, *Suisse* Uni *f*; **he's doing law at u.** il fait une fac de droit **2** *Am (abbr* **uniform**) uniforme[□] *m*

unibrow [ˈjuːnɪbraʊ] N *Fam Hum* **to have a u.** avoir les sourcils qui se rejoignent au milieu[□]

UNICEF [ˈjuːnɪsef] *(abbr* **United Nations International Children's Emergency Fund**) N Unicef *m*

unicellular [ˌjuːnɪˈseljʊlə(r)] ADJ *Biol* unicellulaire

unicorn [ˈjuːnɪkɔːn] N *Myth & Her* licorne *f*

unicycle [ˈjuːnɪsaɪkəl] N monocycle *m*

unidentifiable [ˌʌnaɪˈdentɪfaɪəbəl] ADJ non identifiable

unidentified [ˌʌnaɪˈdentɪfaɪd] ADJ non identifié
▸▸ ***unidentified flying object*** objet *m* volant non identifié

unidirectional [ˌjuːnɪdɪˈrekʃənəl] ADJ unidirectionnel

UNIDO [juːˈniːdəʊ] N *(abbr* **United Nations Industrial Development Organization**) ONUDI *f*

unification [ˌjuːnɪfɪˈkeɪʃən] N unification *f*; **the U. Church** = nom officiel de la secte mooniste

uniform [ˈjuːnɪfɔːm] N uniforme *m*; **in u.** *(gen)* en uniforme; *Mil* sous les drapeaux; **in school u.** en uniforme d'école; **to wear u.** porter l'uniforme
ADJ *(identical)* identique, pareil; *(constant)* constant; *(unified)* uniforme; **these boxes are all of u. size** ces boîtes sont toutes de la même grandeur
▸▸ *Com* ***uniform business rate*** = taxe assise sur la valeur des locaux commerciaux, ≃ taxe *f* professionnelle; ***uniform rate*** taux *m* uniforme

uniformed [ˈjuːnɪfɔːmd] ADJ *(gen)* en uniforme; *(policeman, soldier)* en tenue

uniformity [ˌjuːnɪˈfɔːmətɪ] *(pl* **uniformities**) N uniformité *f*

uniformly [ˈjuːnɪfɔːmlɪ] ADV uniformément

unify [ˈjuːnɪfaɪ] *(pt & pp* **unified**) VT *(unite* ▸ *country)* unifier

unifying [ˈjuːnɪfaɪɪŋ] ADJ unificateur

unilateral [ˌjuːnɪˈlætərəl] ADJ **1** *(action, decision)* unilatéral; **u. declaration of independence** déclaration *f* unilatérale d'indépendance **2** *Med (paralysis)* hémiplégique
▸▸ ***unilateral disarmament*** désarmement *m* unilatéral

unilaterally [ˌjuːnɪˈlætərəlɪ] ADV *(act, decide)* unilatéralement

unilingual [ˌjuːnɪˈlɪŋgwəl] ADJ monolingue, unilingue

unimaginable [ˌʌnɪˈmædʒɪnəbəl] ADJ inimaginable, inconcevable

unimaginably [ˌʌnɪˈmædʒɪnəblɪ] ADV incroyablement, invraisemblablement

unimaginative [ˌʌnɪˈmædʒɪnətɪv] ADJ manquant d'imagination, peu imaginatif; **they're very u. about their holidays** ils ne font preuve d'aucune imagination pour ce qui est de partir en vacances; **you're so u.!** vous n'avez aucune imagination!

unimaginatively [ˌʌnɪˈmædʒɪnətɪvlɪ] ADV sans imagination

unimaginativeness [ˌʌnɪˈmædʒɪnətɪvnɪs] N manque *m* d'imagination

unimpaired [ˌʌnɪmˈpeəd] ADJ *(faculty, strength)* intact; *(health)* non altéré; **her political prestige remains u.** son prestige politique demeure intact

unimpeachable [ˌʌnɪmˈpiːtʃəbəl] ADJ **1** *Formal (source, evidence)* incontestable; *(reputation, honesty, character)* irréprochable **2** *Law (witness, judge)* irrécusable

unimpeded [ˌʌnɪmˈpiːdɪd] ADJ sans obstacle, libre
ADV **to do sth u.** faire qch sans rencontrer d'obstacles

unimportant [ˌʌnɪmˈpɔːtənt] ADJ **1** *(detail, matter, question)* sans importance, insignifiant **2** *(person)* sans importance

unimposing [ˌʌnɪmˈpəʊzɪŋ] ADJ **1** *(unimpressive)* peu imposant *ou* impressionnant **2** *(insignificant)* insignifiant

unimpressed [ˌʌnɪmˈprest] ADJ non impressionné; **I was u. by her** elle ne m'a pas fait une grosse impression; **they were u. by your threats** vos menaces ne les ont pas impressionnés

unimpressive [ˌʌnɪmˈpresɪv] ADJ guère impressionnant; **their record is u.** leur dossier n'est pas très impressionnant *ou* est très quelconque

uninflammable [ˌʌnɪnˈflæməbəl] ADJ ininflammable

uninfluential [ˌʌnɪnflʊˈenʃəl] ADJ sans influence

uninformed [ˌʌnɪnˈfɔːmd] ADJ *(person)* non informé; *(opinion)* mal informé; *(reader, critic)* non averti; **to make an u. guess** deviner au hasard

uninhabitable [ˌʌnɪnˈhæbɪtəbəl] ADJ inhabitable

uninhabited [ˌʌnɪnˈhæbɪtɪd] ADJ inhabité

uninhibited [ˌʌnɪnˈhɪbɪtɪd] ADJ *(person)* sans inhibition *ou* inhibitions; *(behaviour, reaction)* non réfréné, non réprimé; *(laughter)* franc et massif, sans retenue

uninitialized, -ised [ˌʌnɪˈnɪʃəlaɪzd] ADJ *Comput* non initialisé

uninitiated [ˌʌnɪˈnɪʃɪeɪtɪd] NPL **the u.** les profanes *mpl*, les non-initiés *mpl*; **to** *or* **for the u.** pour le profane
ADJ non initié

uninjured [ˌʌnˈɪndʒəd] ADJ *(person)* indemne

uninspired [ˌʌnɪnˈspaɪəd] ADJ qui manque d'inspiration; **the team gave an u. performance** l'équipe n'a pas été très performante

uninspiring [ˌʌnɪnˈspaɪrɪŋ] ADJ *(dull)* qui n'inspire pas; *(mediocre)* médiocre; *(unexciting)* qui n'est pas passionnant; *(uninteresting)* sans intérêt

uninstall, *Am* **uninstal** [ˌʌnɪnˈstɔːl] VT *Comput* désinstaller, supprimer

uninsured [ˌʌnɪnˈʃʊəd] ADJ non assuré (**against** contre)

unintelligent [ˌʌnɪnˈtelɪdʒənt] ADJ inintelligent, qui manque d'intelligence; **he's not an u. boy** c'est un garçon n'est pas bête

unintelligible [ˌʌnɪnˈtelɪdʒəbəl] ADJ inintelligible

unintelligibly [ˌʌnɪnˈtelɪdʒəblɪ] ADV inintelligiblement

unintended [ˌʌnɪnˈtendɪd] ADJ *(outcome, consequence)* non recherché, non voulu; *(pun, irony)* involontaire

unintentional [ˌʌnɪnˈtenʃənəl] ADJ involontaire, non intentionnel; **it was quite u.** ce n'était pas fait exprès

unintentionally [ˌʌnɪnˈtenʃnəlɪ] ADV sans le vouloir, involontairement; **he did it quite u.** il ne l'a pas fait exprès

uninterested [ˌʌnˈɪntrəstɪd] ADJ *(indifferent)* indifférent; **to be u. in sb/sth** être indifférent à qn/qch

> Attention: ne pas confondre avec l'adjectif **disinterested.**

uninteresting [ˌʌnˈɪntrəstɪŋ] ADJ *(subject)* inintéressant, sans intérêt; *(book)* inintéressant, ennuyeux; *(person)* ennuyeux

uninterrupted [ˈʌnˌɪntəˈrʌptɪd] ADJ continu, ininterrompu

uninterruptedly [ˈʌnˌɪntəˈrʌptɪdlɪ] ADV de façon ininterrompue, sans interruption

uninvited [ˌʌnɪnˈvaɪtɪd] ADJ **1** *(person)* qu'on n'a pas invité; **an u. guest** une personne non invitée; **he turned up u. at the party** il a débarqué à la soirée sans y avoir été invité **2** *(comment)* non sollicité

uninviting [ˌʌnɪnˈvaɪtɪŋ] ADJ *(place)* peu accueillant; *(prospect)* peu attrayant; *(smell)* peu attirant; *(food)* peu appétissant

union [ˈjuːnjən] N **1** *(act of linking, uniting)* union *f*, *Com* regroupement *m*, fusion *f*
2 *Ind* syndicat *m*; **to join a u.** se syndiquer; **to form a u.** créer un syndicat; **unions and management** les syndicats *mpl* et la direction, les partenaires *mpl* sociaux
3 *(association)* association *f*, union *f*; *Fig* **a u. of French and British skills** un mariage entre le savoir-faire français et britannique
4 *(marriage)* union *f*, mariage *m*
5 *Math* union *f*
6 *Univ (premises)* ≃ foyer *m* des étudiants; *(organization)* syndicat *m ou* union *f* des étudiants
COMP *(dues, meeting)* syndical
• **Union** N *Hist* **the U.** *Br (between Scotland and England)* l'Union *f* de l'Angleterre et de l'Écosse; *(between Great Britain and Northern Ireland)* l'Union *f* de la Grande Bretagne et de l'Irlande du Nord; *Am* les États *mpl* de l'Union
▸▸ ***union agreement*** convention *f* collective; ***union card*** carte *f* syndicale; ***union catalogue*** = catalogue des publications commun à plusieurs bibliothèques; ***the Union Jack*** l'Union Jack *m (drapeau officiel du Royaume-Uni)*; ***union leader*** dirigeant(e) *m,f* syndical(e); ***union member*** *(in general)* membre *m* d'un syndicat, syndiqué(e) *m,f*; *(of particular union)* membre *m* du syndicat, syndiqué(e) *m,f*; ***union official*** responsable *m* syndical(e); ***union regulations*** règles *fpl* syndicales; ***union representative*** délégué(e) *m,f ou* représentant(e) *m,f* syndical(e); ***union rights*** liberté syndicale; *Am* ***union shop*** atelier *m* d'ouvriers syndiqués, union shop *m*; *Formerly* ***the Union of Soviet Socialist Republics*** l'Union *f* des républiques socialistes soviétiques; *Am* ***union suit*** combinaison *f*

unionism [ˈjuːnjənɪzəm] N **1** *Ind* syndicalisme *m* **2** *Pol* unionisme *m*
• **Unionism** N *Pol (in Northern Ireland)* unionisme *m*

nionist ['ju:njənɪst] ADJ *Ind* syndicaliste
N **1** *Ind* syndicaliste *mf* **2** *Pol* unioniste *mf*; *(in American Civil War)* nordiste *mf*
▸ **Unionist** *Pol (in Northern Ireland)*
N unioniste *mf*
ADJ unioniste

nionize, -ise ['ju:njənaɪz] VI se syndicaliser, se yndiquer
VT syndicaliser, syndiquer

niparous [ju:'nɪpərəs] ADJ unipare

nique [ju:'ni:k] ADJ **1** *(sole, single)* unique; *(particular)* particulier, propre; **a problem u. to this region** un problème propre à cette région; **to be u. n doing sth** être le seul à faire qch; **you're not u.** on cas n'est pas unique, tu n'es pas le seul **2** *(exceptional)* exceptionnel, remarquable; **his work s quite u.** son travail est tout à fait exceptionnel
▸▸ *Mktg* ***unique selling point, unique selling proposition*** proposition *f* unique de vente

niquely [ju:'ni:klɪ] ADV *(particularly)* particulièrement; *(remarkably)* exceptionnellement, emarquablement; **he is u. placed to get this information** il est exceptionnellement bien placé pour obtenir ce renseignement

niqueness [ju:'ni:knɪs] N originalité *f*

nisex ['ju:nɪseks] ADJ unisexe

nison ['ju:nɪsən] N unisson *m*; **in u. (with)** à l'unisson (de)

nissued [ˌʌn'ɪʃu:d] ADJ *St Exch (shares, share capital)* non encore émis

nit ['ju:nɪt] N **1** *(constituent, component)* unité *f*; **the parish is the basic church u.** la paroisse est l'unité de base de l'Église
2 *(group)* unité *f*; *(team)* équipe *f*, unité *f*; **army u.** unité *f* de l'armée; **family u.** cellule *f* familiale; **production u.** unité *f* de production
3 *(department* ▸ *in hospital)* service *m*; (▸ *in school, university, company)* groupe *m*, section *f*; *(centre)* centre *m*; *(building)* locaux *mpl*; *(offices)* bureaux *mpl*; **child care u.** service *m* de protection de l'enfance; **operating u.** bloc *m* opératoire
4 *(in amounts, measurement)* unité *f*; **a glass of wine equals one u. of alcohol** un verre de vin compte pour une unité d'alcool; **u. of length/time** unité *f* de longueur/de temps
5 *(part* ▸ *of furniture)* élément *m*; (▸ *of mechanism, system)* bloc *m*, élément *m*; **the knives are in the u. there** les couteaux sont dans ce placard
6 *Austr (apartment)* appartement *m*
7 *Sch (lesson)* unité *f*; **u. 5** unité 5
▸ **units** NPL *Math* **the units** les unités *fpl*
▸▸ *Fin* ***unit of account*** unité *f* de compte; *Tel* ***unit charge*** taxe *f* unitaire; *Constr* ***unit construction*** préfabrication *f*; *Com & Ind* ***unit cost*** coût *m* unitaire; ***unit of currency*** unité *f* monétaire; ***unit furniture*** mobilier *m* par éléments; ***unit price*** prix *m* unitaire *ou* à l'unité; *Br St Exch* ***unit trust*** fonds *m* commun de placement, ≃ SICAV *f*

nitarian [ju:nɪ'teərɪən] N *Rel* unitaire *mf*, unitarien(enne) *m,f*
ADJ unitaire, unitarien

nitarianism [ju:nɪ'teərɪənɪzəm] N *Rel* unitarisme *m*

nitary ['ju:nɪtrɪ] ADJ **1** *(united, single)* unitaire **2** *(government)* centralisé

nite [ju:'naɪt] VT **1** *(join, link* ▸ *forces)* unir, rassembler
2 *(unify* ▸ *country, party)* unifier, unir; **more unites us than separates us** ce qui nous unit est plus fort que ce qui nous divise; **common interests that u. two countries** intérêts communs qui unissent deux pays
3 *(bring together* ▸ *people, relatives)* réunir
4 *Formal (marry)* unir (en mariage)
VI s'unir; **they united in their efforts to defeat the enemy** ils ont conjugué leurs efforts pour vaincre l'ennemi; **the two countries united in opposing or to oppose oppression** les deux pays se sont unis pour s'opposer à l'oppression; **to u. against** s'unir contre

nited [ju:'naɪtɪd] ADJ *(family)* uni; *(efforts)* conjugué; *(country, party)* uni, unifié; **to present a u. front** montrer un front uni; **to be u. against sb/sth** être uni contre qn/qch; **we are u. in our aims** nous sommes d'accord dans nos objectifs, nous partageons les mêmes objectifs; *Prov* **u. we stand, divided we fail** l'union fait la force
▸▸ ***the United Arab Emirates*** les Émirats *mpl* arabes unis; ***the United Kingdom*** le Royaume-Uni; ***the United Nations*** les Nations *fpl* unies; ***United Nations Organization*** Organisation *f* des Nations unies; ***the United Reformed Church*** = église fondée en 1972 par la réunion de l'Église presbytérienne et l'Église congrégationnaliste; ***the United States*** les États-Unis *mpl*; ***the United States of America*** les États-Unis *mpl* d'Amérique

unity ['ju:nətɪ] *(pl* **unities)** N **1** *(union)* unité *f*, union *f*; **national/political u.** unité *f* nationale/politique; **strength lies in u.** l'union fait la force
2 *(identity* ▸ *of purpose)* identité *f*; (▸ *of views)* unité *f*
3 *(harmony)* harmonie *f*; **to live in u.** vivre en harmonie
4 *Theat* unité *f*; **the dramatic unities** les unités *fpl* dramatiques
5 *Math* unité *f*

Univ. *(written abbr* **university)** Univ.

univalent [ˌju:nɪ'veɪlənt] ADJ *Biol & Chem* univalent, monovalent

universal [ju:nɪ'vɜ:səl] ADJ **1** *(concerning all people, things)* universel; **topics of u. interest** sujets *mpl* qui intéressent tout le monde **2** *(general)* unanime; **to meet with u. agreement** faire l'unanimité; **to meet with u. acclaim** être applaudi par tout le monde
N **1** *(truth)* vérité *f* universelle; *(proposition)* proposition *f* universelle **2** *Ling & Phil* **universals** universaux *mpl*
▸▸ ***universal blood donor*** donneur(euse) *m,f* universel(elle); ***the Universal Declaration of Human Rights*** la Déclaration universelle des droits de l'homme; ***universal grammar*** grammaire *f* universelle; *Chem* ***universal indicator*** indicateur *m* universel de pH; *Tech* ***universal joint*** (joint *m* de) cardan *m*; *Am* ***universal product code*** code *m* barres; ***universal remote control*** télécommande *f* universelle; *Comput* ***universal serial bus*** norme *f* USB, port *m* série universel; ***universal suffrage*** suffrage *m* universel

universality [ju:nɪvɜ:'sælətɪ] N universalité *f*

universalize, -ise [ju:nɪ'vɜ:səlaɪz] VT universaliser, généraliser

universally [ju:nɪ'vɜ:səlɪ] ADV universellement; **a u. held opinion** une opinion qui prévaut partout; **he is u. liked/admired** tout le monde l'aime bien/l'admire

universe ['ju:nɪvɜ:s] N **1** *(space)* univers *m*; **in the u.** dans l'univers **2** *Mktg (number of people in group or segment)* univers *m*

university [ju:nɪ'vɜ:sətɪ] *(pl* **universities)** N université *f*; **to go to u.** aller à l'université, faire des études universitaires; **to be at u.** être à l'université *ou* en faculté; **she studied at Cambridge u.** elle était à l'université de Cambridge; *Fig* **I studied at the u. of life** je me suis formé à l'école de la vie
COMP *(building, campus, team)* universitaire; *(professor, staff)* d'université; *(education, studies)* supérieur, universitaire
▸▸ ***university fees*** frais *mpl* d'inscription à l'université; ***university student*** étudiant(e) *m,f (à l'université)*; *Belg & Suisse* universitaire *mf*; ***university town*** ville *f* universitaire

UNIX® ['ju:nɪks] N *Comput (abbr* **Uniplexed Information and Computing System)** UNIX® *m*

UNIX®-based ADJ *Comput* basé sur UNIX®

unjust [ˌʌn'dʒʌst] ADJ injuste

unjustifiable [ˌʌndʒʌstɪ'faɪəbəl] ADJ *(behaviour)* injustifiable, inexcusable; *(claim)* que l'on ne peut justifier; *(error)* injustifié

unjustifiably [ˌʌndʒʌstɪ'faɪəblɪ] ADV sans justification

unjustified [ˌʌn'dʒʌstɪfaɪd] ADJ **1** *(unwarranted)* injustifié; **u. absences** absences *fpl* sans motif valable **2** *Typ* non justifié

unjustly [ˌʌn'dʒʌstlɪ] ADV injustement, à tort

unkempt [ˌʌn'kempt] ADJ *(hair)* mal peigné, en bataille; *(beard)* hirsute; *(appearance, person)* négligé, débraillé; *(garden)* mal entretenu, en friche

unkind [ʌn'kaɪnd] ADJ *(person)* peu aimable, qui n'est pas gentil; *(manner)* peu aimable; *(thought)* vilain, méchant; *(remark)* désobligeant, méchant; **he was rather u. to me** il n'a pas été très gentil à mon égard *ou* avec moi; **to say u. things to sb** dire des méchancetés à qn; **to be u. to animals** être cruel avec les animaux; *Literary* **the unkindest cut of all** la pire des trahisons

unkindly [ʌn'kaɪndlɪ] ADV *(cruelly)* méchamment, cruellement; *(roughly)* sans ménagement; **to take u. to sth** mal accepter qch; **she didn't mean it u.** elle n'a voulu blesser *ou* offenser personne

unkindness [ʌn'kaɪndnɪs] N *(of person)* manque *m* de gentillesse, méchanceté *f*; *(of behaviour, manner)* méchanceté *f*

unknot [ˌʌn'nɒt] *(pt & pp* **unknotted**, *cont* **unknotting)** VT dénouer

unknowing [ˌʌn'nəʊɪŋ] ADJ inconscient; **they went, all u., to their deaths** ils allaient, sans le savoir, au-devant de leur mort

unknowingly [ˌʌn'nəʊɪŋlɪ] ADV à mon/son/*etc* insu, sans m'en/s'en/*etc* apercevoir

unknown [ˌʌn'nəʊn] ADJ **1** *(not known)* inconnu; **for reasons u. to us** pour des raisons que nous ignorons *ou* qui nous sont inconnues; **these drugs are u. to most family doctors** ces médicaments sont inconnus de la plupart des généralistes; *Law* **verdict against person or persons u.** verdict *m* contre inconnu **2** *(obscure* ▸ *cause)* inconnu, mystérieux; (▸ *place)* inconnu; (▸ *actor, writer)* inconnu, méconnu
N **1** *(person)* inconnu(e) *m,f* **2** *(place, situation)* inconnu *m*; **the great u.** le grand inconnu, l'inconnu *m*; **the explorers set off into the u.** les explorateurs se lancèrent vers l'inconnu **3** *Math & (in logic)* inconnue *f*
ADV **u. to his son, he sold the house** à l'insu de son fils *ou* sans que son fils le sache, il a vendu la maison; **u. to us, the bus had already gone** nous ne le savions pas, mais le bus était déjà parti
▸▸ *Math & Fig* ***unknown quantity*** inconnue *f*; **the new minister is a bit of an u. quantity** le nouveau ministre est un personnage dont on ne sait pas grand-chose; **the new drug is an u. quantity** on ne sait pas grand-chose des effets de ce nouveau médicament; ***the Unknown Soldier, the Unknown Warrior*** le Soldat inconnu

unlace [ˌʌn'leɪs] VT *(bodice, shoe)* délacer

unladen [ˌʌn'leɪdən] ADJ **1** *(goods)* déchargé **2** *(lorry, ship)* à vide
▸▸ ***unladen weight*** poids *m* à vide

unladylike [ˌʌn'leɪdɪlaɪk] ADJ *(girl)* mal élevé; *(behaviour, posture)* peu distingué; **it's u. to whistle** une jeune fille bien élevée ne siffle pas

unlaid [ˌʌn'leɪd] *pt & pp of* **unlay**
ADJ **the table was still u.** la table n'était pas encore mise

unlamented [ˌʌnlə'mentɪd] ADJ regretté de personne; **his death was u., he died u.** personne n'a pleuré sa mort

unlatch [ˌʌn'lætʃ] VT *(door)* soulever le loquet de, ouvrir; **the door was left unlatched** la porte est restée entrouverte, on n'avait pas fermé le loquet de la porte
VI *(door)* s'ouvrir

unlawful [ˌʌn'lɔ:fʊl] ADJ illicite, illégal; **it is u. to use a television set without a licence** il est interdit d'utiliser une télévision sans payer de redevance; **their marriage was deemed u.** leur mariage fut jugé illégitime
▸▸ ***unlawful arrest*** arrestation *f* illégale; *Law* ***unlawful assembly*** réunion *f* illégale, attroupement *m* illégal; ***unlawful detention*** détention *f* abusive; ***unlawful means*** moyens *mpl* illicites

unlawfully [ˌʌn'lɔ:fʊlɪ] ADV illicitement, illégalement

unleaded [ˌʌn'ledɪd] ADJ *(petrol)* sans plomb

unlearn [ˌʌn'lɜ:n] *(pt & pp* **unlearned** *or* **unlearnt** [-'lɜ:nt]) VT désapprendre

unlearned ADJ **1** [ˌʌn'lɜ:nɪd] *(person)* non instruit, ignorant **2** [ˌʌn'lɜ:nd] *(lesson)* non appris; *(reflex)* inné, non acquis

unlearnt [ˌʌn'lɜ:nt] *pt & pp of* **unlearn**

unleash [ˌʌn'li:ʃ] VT **1** *(dog)* lâcher **2** *Fig (anger, violence)* déchaîner; *(wave of repression)* provoquer, déclencher; **she unleashed a stream of invective** elle lâcha une bordée d'injures

unleavened [ˌʌn'levənd] ADJ *Culin* sans levain; *Rel* azyme; *Literary* **the speech was u. by even a trace of humour** le discours n'était même pas égayé par une pointe d'humour

unless [ən'les] CONJ à moins que + *subjunctive*, à moins de + *infinitive*; **I'll go u. he phones first** j'irai, à moins qu'il (ne) téléphone d'abord; **u. I'm very much mistaken** à moins que je ne me trompe; **u. he pays me tomorrow, I'm leaving** s'il ne m'a pas payé demain, je m'en vais; **we won't get there on time u. we leave now** nous ne serons pas à l'heure à moins de partir maintenant; **I would always be back by 6.15, u. I was working late** je rentrais toujours à 6 heures 15 au plus tard, sauf quand je travaillais tard; **you won't win u. you practise** vous ne gagnerez pas si vous ne vous entraînez pas; **don't speak u. spoken to** ne parle que lorsqu'on t'adresse la parole; **u. I hear otherwise** *or* **to the contrary** sauf avis contraire, sauf contrordre; **u. otherwise stated** sauf indication contraire

unlettered [ˌʌn'letəd] ADJ *Literary (uneducated)* sans instruction; *(illiterate)* illettré, analphabète

unliberated [ˌʌn'lɪbəreɪtɪd] ADJ non libéré; **u. slaves** les esclaves non émancipés

unlicensed [ˌʌn'laɪsənst] ADJ *(parking, sale)* illicite, non autorisé; *(fishing, hunting)* sans permis, illicite; *(car)* sans vignette; *(premises)* qui n'a pas de licence de débit de boissons

unlikable [ˌʌn'laɪkəbəl] ADJ *(person)* peu sympathique; *(place, thing)* peu agréable

unlike [ˌʌn'laɪk] ADJ *(dissimilar)* dissemblable; *(different)* différent; *(showing no likeness)* peu ressemblant; *(unequal)* inégal; **the two sisters are quite u. each other** les deux sœurs ne se ressemblent pas du tout

PREP **1** *(different from)* différent de, qui ne ressemble pas à; **he's quite u. his brother** il ne ressemble pas à son frère; **she is not u. your sister in looks** elle n'est pas sans ressembler à votre sœur; **your situation is quite u. mine** votre situation est très différente de la mienne **2** *(uncharacteristic of)* **that's (very) u. him!** cela ne lui ressemble pas (du tout)! **3** *(in contrast to)* à la différence de, contrairement à; **u. you, I prefer a quiet life** contrairement à vous, je préfère une vie tranquille

unlikeable = **unlikable**

unlikelihood [ˌʌn'laɪklɪhʊd], **unlikeliness** [ˌʌn'laɪklɪnɪs] N improbabilité *f*

unlikely [ˌʌn'laɪklɪ] ADJ **1** *(improbable ▸ event, outcome)* improbable, peu probable; **it is very** *or* **most u. that it will rain** il est très peu probable qu'il pleuve, il y a peu de chances pour qu'il pleuve; **in the u. event of my winning** au cas improbable où je gagnerais

2 *(person)* peu susceptible, qui a peu de chances; **he is u. to come/to fail** il est peu probable qu'il vienne/échoue, il est peu susceptible de venir/d'échouer; **she is u. to choose him** il est peu probable qu'elle le choisisse, il y a peu de chances pour qu'elle le choisisse

3 *(implausible ▸ excuse, story)* invraisemblable

4 *(unexpected ▸ situation, undertaking, costume)* extravagant, invraisemblable; *(▸ person)* peu indiqué; **he turns up at the most u. times** il débarque à des heures invraisemblables; **the manager chose the most u. person to run the department** on ne s'attendait pas du tout à ce que le directeur choisisse cette personne pour diriger le service; **we found the ring in a most u. place** nous avons retrouvé la bague dans un endroit auquel nous n'aurions jamais pensé

unlimited [ˌʌn'lɪmɪtɪd] ADJ *(possibilities, space)* illimité, sans limites; *(power)* illimité, sans bornes; *(time)* infini, illimité; *Mktg (guarantee, warranty)* illimité; **there was u. coffee** il y avait du café à volonté; **he has an u. fund of stories** il a un stock d'histoires inépuisable; **u. travel** nombre *m* de voyages illimité

▸▸ *Br Fin* ***unlimited company*** société *f* à responsabilité illimitée *ou* infinie; ***unlimited liability*** responsabilité *f* illimitée;

unlined [ˌʌn'laɪnd] ADJ **1** *(paper)* non réglé, uni **2** *(curtain, clothes)* sans doublure **3** *(face)* sans rides

unlisted [ʌn'lɪstɪd] ADJ **1** *(not on list ▸ name)* qui ne paraît pas sur la liste; **she was u. in the standard reference works** son nom ne figurait pas dans les livres de référence classiques **2** *Am Tel* qui est sur la liste rouge **3** *St Exch* non coté (en Bourse), non inscrit à la cote

▸▸ *St Exch* ***unlisted market*** Bourse *f* coulisse

unlit [ˌʌn'lɪt] ADJ **1** *(candle, fire)* non allumé **2** *(room, street)* non éclairé

unload [ˌʌn'ləʊd] VT **1** *(remove load from ▸ gun, ship, truck)* décharger; **have you unloaded the washing machine?** avez-vous enlevé le linge de la machine?

2 *(remove ▸ cargo, furniture)* décharger; *(▸ film)* enlever; **to u. bricks from a cart** décharger des briques d'une charrette

3 *Fam (get rid of)* se débarrasser de[□], se défaire de[□]

4 *Fig (responsibility, worries)* décharger; **to u. one's problems onto sb** se décharger de ses problèmes sur qn

VI *(ship, truck)* décharger

unloaded [ˌʌn'ləʊdɪd] ADJ **1** *(lorry, ship ▸ with load removed)* déchargé; *(▸ without a load)* non chargé, sans chargement **2** *(gun, camera)* non chargé; **don't worry, the gun's u.** n'aie pas peur, le fusil n'est pas chargé

unloading [ˌʌn'ləʊdɪŋ] N déchargement *m*

COMP *(platform, permit)* de déchargement

▸▸ ***unloading dock*** quai *m* de déchargement

unlock [ˌʌn'lɒk] VT **1** *(door)* ouvrir

2 *Fig (mystery, puzzle)* résoudre, donner la clé de; *(secret)* dévoiler

3 *Comput (file, diskette, keyboard)* déverrouiller

4 *Tel (mobile phone)* débloquer

5 *Fin (assets)* débloquer

VI s'ouvrir

unlocked [ˌʌn'lɒkt] ADJ *(door)* qui n'est pas fermé à clef

unlooked-for [ˌʌn'lʊkt-] ADJ inattendu, imprévu

unloose [ˌʌn'luːs], **unloosen** [ˌʌn'luːsən] VT *(belt, grip)* relâcher, desserrer

unlovable, unloveable [ˌʌn'lʌvəbəl] ADJ peu attachant

unloved [ˌʌn'lʌvd] ADJ privé d'affection, aimé de personne; **to feel u.** ne pas se sentir aimé, se sentir mal aimé

unlovely [ˌʌn'lʌvlɪ] ADJ laid, déplaisant

unloving [ˌʌn'lʌvɪŋ] ADJ peu affectueux

unluckily [ˌʌn'lʌkɪlɪ] ADV malheureusement; **u. for us, it rained** malheureusement pour nous, il a plu

unlucky [ˌʌn'lʌkɪ] *(compar* **unluckier**, *superl* **unluckiest)** ADJ **1** *(person)* malchanceux; *(day)* de malchance; **we were u. enough to get caught in a jam** nous avons eu la malchance d'être pris dans un embouteillage; **it was u. for him that she arrived just at that moment** malheureusement pour lui, elle est arrivée à cet instant précis; **to be u. in love** être malheureux en amour **2** *(colour, number)* qui porte malheur; *(omen)* funeste, mauvais; **it's supposed to be u. to break a mirror** c'est censé porter malheur de casser un miroir

unmade [ˌʌn'meɪd] *pt & pp of* **unmake**

ADJ **1** *(bed)* défait **2** *Br (road)* non goudronné

unmade-up ADJ *(face)* non maquillé, sans maquillage

unmake [ˌʌn'meɪk] *(pt & pp* **unmade** [-'meɪd]) VT **1** *(bed)* défaire **2** *Formal or Literary (reputation)* démolir, ruiner; *(man)* briser, ruiner; *(ruler)* déposer

unman [ˌʌn'mæn] *(pt & pp* **unmanned**, *cont* **unmanning)** VT *Literary (person)* faire perdre courage à

unmanageable [ˌʌn'mænɪdʒəbəl] ADJ **1** *(vehicle, ship)* difficile à manœuvrer; *(object)* peu maniable, difficile à manier

2 *(animal)* difficile, indocile; *(children)* difficile, impossible

3 *(situation)* difficile à gérer; **the problem has become u.** le problème est devenu impossible à gérer *ou* à régler

4 *(hair)* difficile à coiffer, rebelle

unmanly [ˌʌn'mænlɪ] *(compar* **unmanlier**, *supe* **unmanliest)** ADJ **1** *(effeminate)* efféminé, peu viri **2** *(cowardly)* lâche

unmanned [ˌʌn'mænd] ADJ *(without crew ▸ plane, ship)* sans équipage; *(▸ spacecraft, fligh* inhabité; *Rail (▸ station)* sans personnel; *(▸ leve crossing)* non gardé, automatique; **the borde post/switchboard was u.** il n'y avait personne a poste frontière/au standard; **the control centr was left u.** le centre de contrôle est resté san surveillance

▸▸ ***unmanned space travel*** vols *mpl* spatiaux no habités

unmannerliness [ˌʌn'mænəlɪnɪs] N *Forma* manque *m* de courtoisie, impolitesse *f*

unmannerly [ˌʌn'mænəlɪ] ADJ *Formal* discour tois, impoli

unmapped [ˌʌn'mæpt] ADJ *(area)* pour lequel n'existe pas de carte, dont on n'a pas dressé l carte

unmarked [ˌʌn'mɑːkt] ADJ **1** *(face, furniture page)* sans marque, sans tache

2 *(without identifying features)* **the radioactiv waste was carried in u. drums** les déchets ra dioactifs étaient transportés dans des baril non identifiés; **an u. police car** une voiture d police banalisée; **to be buried in an u. grave** êtr enterré dans une tombe anonyme

3 *(without name tag, label)* sans nom, no marqué

4 *(essay)* non corrigé

5 *Ling* non marqué

6 *Sport (player)* démarqué

unmarketable [ˌʌn'mɑːkɪtəbəl] ADJ invendabl

unmarriageable [ˌʌn'mærɪdʒəbəl] ADJ imma riable

unmarried [ˌʌn'mærɪd] ADJ non marié, céliba taire

▸▸ ***unmarried mother*** mère *f* célibataire; ***unma ried state*** célibat *m*

unmask [ˌʌn'mɑːsk] VT *(person)* démasquer *(plot, conspiracy)* dévoiler

unmatched [ˌʌn'mætʃt] ADJ inégalé, sans éga *ou* pareil; **she is u. as a novelist** comme roman cière, elle n'a pas sa pareille

unmentionable [ˌʌn'menʃənəbəl] ADJ *(subjec* dont il ne faut pas parler, interdit; *(word)* qu'i ne faut pas prononcer, interdit

N **the u.** *(forbidden subject)* le sujet interdit o dont il ne faut pas parler; *(taboo)* le sujet tabou

• **unmentionables** NPL *Euph Hum (underwea* dessous *mpl*, sous-vêtements *mpl*

unmerciful [ʌn'mɜːsɪfʊl] ADJ impitoyable, san pitié; **to be u. to** *or* **towards sb** être sans pitié pou qn

unmercifully [ʌn'mɜːsɪfʊlɪ] ADV *(treat)* impi toyablement, sans pitié; *(tease)* sans répit

unmerited [ˌʌn'merɪtɪd] ADJ *(undeserved)* im mérité; *(unjust)* injuste

unmethodical [ˌʌnmɪ'θɒdɪkəl] ADJ peu métho dique

unmindful [ˌʌn'maɪndfʊl] ADJ *Formal (uncaring* peu soucieux; *(forgetful)* oublieux; *(inattentive* inattentif; **he is u. of other people's feelings** il es peu soucieux des sentiments des autres, il n tient pas compte des sentiments des autres

unmistakable [ˌʌnmɪ'steɪkəbəl] ADJ *(distinctive* aisément reconnaissable, caractéristique *(clear, obvious)* indubitable, manifeste, évident **the u. sound of bagpipes** le son caractéristiqu de la cornemuse; **these symptoms are u.** on n peut pas se tromper sur ces symptômes; **she be gan to show u. signs of fatigue** elle commença à montrer des signes évidents de fatigue

unmistakably [ˌʌnmɪ'steɪkəblɪ] ADV **1** *(undeni ably)* indéniablement, sans erreur possible; **th style is u. French** le style est français, il n'y a pas s'y tromper **2** *(visibly)* visiblement, manifeste ment

unmistakeable, unmistakeably = **un mistakable, unmistakably**

unmitigated [ˌʌn'mɪtɪgeɪtɪd] ADJ **1** *(total ▸ disas ter, chaos)* total; *(▸ horror)* absolu; *(▸ stupidity* pur, total; **the whole project was an u. disaste**

tout le projet a été un véritable désastre **2** *(undiminished)* non mitigé

nmixed [ˌʌnˈmɪkst] **ADJ** non mélangé, pur

nmolested [ˌʌnməˈlestɪd] **ADJ** sans encombre; **to leave sb u.** *(not bother)* laisser qn en paix

nmortgaged [ˌʌnˈmɔːgɪdʒd] **ADJ** *Fin* libre d'hypothèques

nmotivated [ˌʌnˈməʊtɪveɪtɪd] **ADJ** sans mobile; *(person)* non motivé; *(without ambition)* dépourvu d'ambition; **his actions were u. by any desire for personal glory** ses actes n'étaient pas motivés par un quelconque désir de gloire personnelle

nmounted [ˌʌnˈmaʊntɪd] **ADJ 1** *(rider)* sans monture **2** *(photograph)* non monté **3** *(jewel)* non serti

nmourned [ˌʌnˈmɔːnd] **ADJ he died u.** personne ne l'a pleuré

nmoved [ˌʌnˈmuːvd] **ADJ** indifférent, insensible; **to be u. by sth** rester insensible à qch; **the music left me u.** la musique ne m'a pas ému; **he remained u.** il est resté de marbre

nmusical [ˌʌnˈmjuːzɪkəl] **ADJ 1** *(sound)* peu mélodieux **2** *(person)* peu musicien

nnameable [ˌʌnˈneɪməbəl] **ADJ** innommable, sans nom

nnamed [ˌʌnˈneɪmd] **ADJ 1** *(anonymous)* anonyme; *(unspecified)* non précisé **2** *(having no name* ▸ *child)* sans nom, qui n'a pas reçu de nom; *(*▸ *desire, fear)* inavoué

nnatural [ˌʌnˈnætʃərəl] **ADJ 1** *(affected* ▸ *behaviour, laughter, walk)* peu naturel **2** *(odd, abnormal* ▸ *circumstances, state)* anormal; *(*▸ *phenomenon)* surnaturel; **it's u. for him (to)** cela ne lui ressemble pas (de) **3** *(perverse* ▸ *love, passion)* contre nature

nnaturally [ˌʌnˈnætʃərəlɪ] **ADV** *(behave, laugh, walk)* de façon peu naturelle; **it was u. hot** il faisait anormalement chaud; **he not u. decided to resign** naturellement, il a décidé de démissionner; **the text reads very u.** ce texte est très forcé

nnavigable [ˌʌnˈnævɪgəbəl] **ADJ** non navigable

nnecessarily [*Br* ʌnˈnesəsərɪlɪ, *Am* ˌʌnnesəˈserəlɪ] **ADV** *(worry)* sans raison; *(do, say)* inutilement; **the questions were u. complicated** les questions étaient inutilement compliquées; **you're being u. hard on yourself** tu te fais du mal pour rien; **she works u. hard** elle n'a pas besoin de travailler aussi dur

nnecessary [ˌʌnˈnesəsərɪ] **ADJ** superflu, inutile; **it's quite u. for you all to attend** il n'est vraiment pas nécessaire *ou* utile que vous y alliez tous; **it's a lot of u. fuss** c'est beaucoup d'agitation pour rien

nneeded [ˌʌnˈniːdɪd] **ADJ** inutile

nnegotiable [ˌʌnnɪˈgəʊʃəbəl] **ADJ** *Fin (cheque, bill)* non négociable

nneighbourly, *Am* **unneighborly** [ˌʌnˈneɪbəlɪ] **ADJ** *(unfriendly)* peu obligeant, qui n'agit pas en bon voisin; *(unhelpful)* peu serviable

nnerve [ˌʌnˈnɜːv] **VT** déconcerter, troubler

Note that the French verb **énerver** is a false friend. It means **to irritate** or **to make nervous**, depending on the context.

nnerving [ˌʌnˈnɜːvɪŋ] **ADJ** *(event, experience)* déconcertant, perturbant

nnervingly [ˌʌnˈnɜːvɪŋlɪ] **ADV he can be u. flippant** il est parfois d'une désinvolture déconcertante; **there was something u. peaceful about the village** le calme qui régnait dans le village avait quelque chose de troublant

nnoticed [ˌʌnˈnəʊtɪst] **ADJ** inaperçu; **to go** *or* **pass u.** passer inaperçu; **she left the party u.** elle a quitté la soirée sans que personne ne s'en rende compte *ou* ne s'en aperçoive

nnumbered [ˌʌnˈnʌmbəd] **ADJ 1** *(seats, tickets, copies)* non numéroté; *(house)* sans numéro **2** *Fig Formal (descendants, followers, stars)* innombrable, sans nombre

NO [ˈjuːnəʊ, juːenˈəʊ] **N** *(abbr* **United Nations Organization***)* ONU *f*

unoaked [ˌʌnˈəʊkt] **ADJ** *(wine)* qui n'a pas été vieilli en fûts de chêne

unobjectionable [ˌʌnəbˈdʒekʃnəbəl] **ADJ** *(idea, activity)* acceptable; *(behaviour, person)* qui ne peut être critiqué

unobservant [ˌʌnəbˈzɜːvənt] **ADJ** peu observateur; **you're so u.!** tu n'es vraiment pas observateur!

unobserved [ˌʌnəbˈzɜːvd] **ADJ** inaperçu; **she crept past u.** elle s'est faufilée sans se faire remarquer

unobstructed [ˌʌnəbˈstrʌktɪd] **ADJ 1** *(view, road, entry, passage)* dégagé; *(tube, pipe)* non bouché **2** *(activity, progress)* sans obstacle

unobtainable [ˌʌnəbˈteɪnəbəl] **ADJ 1** *(goods, item)* introuvable; *(tickets)* impossible à obtenir; *Tel (number)* qui n'est pas en service **2** *(person)* inaccessible

▸▸ *Br Tel* ***unobtainable tone*** = tonalité continue indiquant qu'un numéro n'est pas en service

unobtrusive [ˌʌnəbˈtruːsɪv] **ADJ** *(person)* discret (ète), effacé; *(object)* discret(ète), pas trop visible; *(smell)* discret(ète); **he always tried to remain u.** il cherchait toujours à s'effacer

unobtrusively [ˌʌnəbˈtruːsɪvlɪ] **ADV** discrètement; **she stood u. in a corner** elle se tenait dans un coin sans se faire remarquer

unoccupied [ˌʌnˈɒkjʊpaɪd] **ADJ 1** *(person)* qui ne fait rien, oisif **2** *(house)* inoccupé, inhabité; *(hotel room)* libre; *(seat)* libre **3** *Mil (territory)* non occupé; **the u. zone** *(in WW2 France)* la zone libre

unofficial [ˌʌnəˈfɪʃəl] **ADJ 1** *(unconfirmed* ▸ *report)* officieux, non officiel **2** *(informal* ▸ *meeting, visit)* non officiel, privé; **in an u. capacity** à titre privé; **from an u. source** de source officieuse

▸▸ *Ind* ***unofficial strike*** grève *f* sauvage

unofficially [ˌʌnəˈfɪʃəlɪ] **ADV** *(informally)* officieusement; *(in private)* en privé

unopened [ˌʌnˈəʊpənd] **ADJ** *(letter, bottle)* non ouvert, qui n'a pas été ouvert; **the letters lay u. on the table** les lettres étaient sur la table, non décachetées

unopposed [ˌʌnəˈpəʊzd] **ADJ** sans opposition; **to advance u.** avancer sans rencontrer d'opposition *ou* de résistance; **we cannot allow this sort of thing to go u.** on ne peut pas laisser faire ce genre de choses; **she was elected u.** elle était la seule candidate (et elle a été élue)

unorganized, -ised [ˌʌnˈɔːgənaɪzd] **ADJ** *(event, group, person)* non organisé; *(disorganized)* désorganisé

▸▸ *Ind* ***unorganized labour*** main-d'œuvre *f* non syndiquée

unoriginal [ˌʌnəˈrɪdʒənəl] **ADJ** sans originalité

unorthodox [ˌʌnˈɔːθədɒks] **ADJ** non orthodoxe, pas très orthodoxe; *Rel* hétérodoxe

unostentatious [ˌʌnɒstenˈteɪʃəs] **ADJ** *(person, behaviour, house, party)* simple; *(dress)* sobre, simple

unostentatiously [ˌʌnɒstenˈteɪʃəslɪ] **ADV** *(act)* simplement; *(dressed)* simplement, sobrement

unostentatiousness [ˌʌnɒstenˈteɪʃəsnɪs] **N** *(of person, lifestyle, house etc)* absence *f* d'ostentation, simplicité *f*

unpack [ˌʌnˈpæk] **VT 1** *(bag, suitcase)* défaire; *(books, clothes, shopping)* déballer; *(car)* décharger; **to get unpacked** défaire ses bagages **2** *Comput* décompresser, décompacter

VI *(after travelling)* défaire ses bagages; *(after moving)* déballer *ou* vider ses cartons

unpacking [ˌʌnˈpækɪŋ] **N** déballage *m*; **to do the u.** déballer ses affaires

unpaid [ˌʌnˈpeɪd] **ADJ 1** *(helper, job)* bénévole, non rémunéré **2** *(bill, salary)* impayé; *(employee)* non payé; **the money is still u.** l'argent n'a toujours pas été versé

▸▸ ***unpaid holiday, unpaid leave*** congé *m* sans solde

unpalatable [ˌʌnˈpælətəbəl] **ADJ** *(food)* immangeable; *Fig (idea)* dérangeant; *(truth)* désagréable à entendre

unparalleled [ˌʌnˈpærəleld] **ADJ** *(unequalled)* sans pareil; *(unprecedented)* sans précédent

unpardonable [ˌʌnˈpɑːdənəbəl] **ADJ** impardonnable, inexcusable

unpardonably [ˌʌnˈpɑːdənəblɪ] **ADV** de manière inexcusable; **he was u. rude** il a été d'une impolitesse inexcusable *ou* impardonnable

unparliamentary [ˈʌnˌpɑːləˈmentərɪ] **ADJ** *(language, action)* contraire aux règles du parlement

▸▸ *Br Pol* ***unparliamentary language*** langage *m* grossier

unpatented [*Br* ˌʌnˈpeɪtəntɪd, *Am* ˌʌnˈpætəntɪd] **ADJ** non breveté

unpatriotic [*Br* ˌʌnpætrɪˈɒtɪk, *Am* ˌʌnpeɪtrɪˈɒtɪk] **ADJ** *(person)* peu patriote; *(sentiment, song)* peu patriotique

unpatriotically [*Br* ˌʌnpætrɪˈɒtɪkəlɪ, *Am* ˌʌnpeɪtrɪˈɒtɪkəlɪ] **ADV** *(act)* de manière peu patriotique

unpaved [ˌʌnˈpeɪvd] **ADJ** *(street)* non pavé

unperceived [ˌʌnpəˈsiːvd] **ADJ** non perçu

unperforated [ˌʌnˈpɜːfəreɪtɪd] **ADJ** non perforé, non percé

unperson [ˈʌnpɜːsən] **N** *Pol* non-personne *f*

unperturbed [ˌʌnpəˈtɜːbd] **ADJ** imperturbable, impassible; **to be u. by sth** rester imperturbable face à qch; **he remained u.** il est resté impassible

unpick [ˌʌnˈpɪk] **VT** *(seam, hem)* défaire; *(garment)* découdre

unpin [ˌʌnˈpɪn] *(pt & pp* **unpinned,** *cont* **unpinning)** **VT** *(seam)* enlever les épingles de

unplaced [ˌʌnˈpleɪst] **ADJ** *(horse, competitor)* non placé

unplanned [ˌʌnˈplænd] **ADJ** *(visit, activity)* imprévu; *(child)* non prévu

unplayable [ˌʌnˈpleɪəbəl] **ADJ** *(pitch)* impraticable; *(ball, shot* ▸ *in tennis, squash etc)* impossible à rattraper; *(*▸ *in golf)* injouable; *(music)* injouable

unpleasant [ʌnˈplezənt] **ADJ** *(person, experience)* désagréable; *(smell, taste, weather)* désagréable, mauvais; *(remark)* désagréable, désobligeant; *(memory)* pénible; **the boss was most u. to her** le patron était très désagréable avec elle

unpleasantly [ʌnˈplezəntlɪ] **ADV** désagréablement, de façon déplaisante; **I found the wine u. sweet** le vin était trop sucré à mon goût; **it was u. cold** il faisait trop froid pour moi

unpleasantness [ʌnˈplezəntnɪs] **N 1** *(of person)* côté *m* désagréable; *(of food)* caractère *m* peu appétissant; **the u. of the experience** cette expérience désagréable; **the u. of the weather** le mauvais temps **2** *(discord)* friction *f*, dissension *f*; **the disputes caused a lot of u.** le conflit a provoqué beaucoup de frictions; **there was some u. between them** il y avait des frictions *ou* tensions entre eux

unpleasing [ˌʌnˈpliːzɪŋ] **ADJ** déplaisant, désagréable

unpledged revenue [ˌʌnˈpledʒd-] **N** *Fin* recettes *fpl* non gagées

unplug [ʌnˈplʌg] *(pt & pp* **unplugged,** *cont* **unplugging)** **VT 1** *Elec* débrancher **2** *(opening, pipe)* déboucher

unplumbed [ˌʌnˈplʌmd] **ADJ** *(depths, area of knowledge)* insondé

unpoetic [ˌʌnpəʊˈetɪk], **unpoetical** [ˌʌnpəʊˈetɪkəl] **ADJ** peu poétique

unpoetically [ˌʌnpəʊˈetɪkəlɪ] **ADV** de façon peu poétique

unpolished [ˌʌnˈpɒlɪʃt] **ADJ 1** *(furniture, brass)* non poli; *(floor, shoes)* non ciré **2** *Fig (person)* qui manque de savoir-vivre; *(manners, style)* peu raffiné, peu élégant

unpolluted [ˌʌnpəˈluːtɪd] **ADJ** non pollué

unpopular [ˌʌnˈpɒpjʊlə(r)] **ADJ** impopulaire, peu populaire; **this style is u. with the younger generation** ce style est peu populaire chez les jeunes, les jeunes n'aiment pas beaucoup ce style; **an u. make of car** une marque de voiture qui n'est pas très populaire; **at school she had been an u. child** quand elle était à l'école les autres enfants ne l'aimaient pas beaucoup; **I'm rather u. with the bosses** je ne suis pas très bien vu des patrons; **to make oneself u.** se rendre impopulaire

unpopularity ['ʌnˌpɒpjʊ'lærɪtɪ] N impopularité *f*

unpopulated [ˌʌn'pɒpjʊleɪtɪd] ADJ désert, non peuplé

unpractical [ˌʌn'præktɪkəl] ADJ **1** *(person)* peu pratique; **he's completely u.** il n'a aucun sens pratique **2** *(plan)* irréalisable

unpractised, *Am* **unpracticed** [ˌʌn'præktɪst] ADJ inexpérimenté; **to be u. in the art of public speaking** ne pas avoir l'habitude de parler en public; **to the u. ear/eye** pour les oreilles non exercées/l'œil non exercé

unprecedented [ʌn'presɪdəntɪd] ADJ sans précédent; **this was quite u. in the continent's history** c'était du jamais vu dans l'histoire du continent

unpredictability [ˌʌnprɪdɪktə'bɪlətɪ] N imprévisibilité *f*

unpredictable [ˌʌnprɪ'dɪktəbəl] ADJ *(person, behaviour, mood)* imprévisible; *(weather)* incertain

unprejudiced [ˌʌn'predʒʊdɪst] ADJ impartial, sans parti pris

unpremeditated [ˌʌnprɪ'medɪteɪtɪd] ADJ non prémédité

unprepared [ˌʌnprɪ'peəd] ADJ **1** *(food)* non préparé; *(speech)* improvisé, impromptu; **to find everything u.** ne rien trouver de prêt; **the hall was quite u. for the party** la salle n'était pas du tout prête pour la soirée **2** *(person)* **to be u. for sth** ne pas s'attendre à qch; **to embark on sth u.** faire qch sans être préparé; **I was quite u. for the exam** *(hadn't studied for it)* je n'étais pas du tout préparé à l'examen

unpreparedness [ˌʌnprɪ'peərɪdnɪs] N manque *m* de préparation

unprepossessing ['ʌnˌpri:pə'zesɪŋ] ADJ *(place)* peu attrayant; *(person, appearance, smile)* peu avenant *ou* engageant

unpresentable [ˌʌnprɪ'zentəbəl] ADJ *(person, room)* qui n'est pas présentable; *(clothes)* immettable

unpretentious [ˌʌnprɪ'tenʃəs] ADJ *(person)* sans prétention, simple; *(tastes, house)* simple

unpretentiously [ˌʌnprɪ'tenʃəslɪ] ADV simplement

unpriced [ˌʌn'praɪst] ADJ non étiqueté, qui n'a pas d'étiquette de prix

unprincipled [ʌn'prɪnsɪpəld] ADJ *(person)* dénué de principes, peu scrupuleux; *(behaviour)* sans scrupules

unprintable [ˌʌn'prɪntəbəl] ADJ **1** *(language)* grossier; **her reply was u.** la décence m'empêche de rapporter sa réponse **2** *(article)* impubliable

unprocessed [ʌn'prəʊsest] ADJ **1** *(food, wool)* non traité, naturel **2** *Phot (film)* non développé **3** *(data)* brut

unproductive [ˌʌnprə'dʌktɪv] ADJ *(land)* improductif, stérile; *(discussion, weekend, worker)* improductif

unprofessional [ˌʌnprə'feʃənəl] ADJ *(attitude, conduct)* peu professionnel; **it looks u. not to send a covering letter** ça ne fait pas très professionnel de ne pas envoyer une lettre de motivation

unprofessionally [ˌʌnprə'feʃənəlɪ] ADV *(do job, work, carry out contract, behave)* de manière peu professionnelle; **he dealt with the whole situation rather u.** la façon dont il s'est occupé de l'affaire n'était pas très professionnelle

unprofitable [ˌʌn'prɒfɪtəbəl] ADJ **1** *(business)* peu rentable **2** *(discussions)* peu profitable; *(action)* inutile

unprofitably [ˌʌn'prɒfɪtəblɪ] ADV sans profit

Unprofor ['ʌnprəʊfɔ:(r)] N *(abbr* **United Nations Protection Force***)* FORPRONU *f*

unpromising [ˌʌn'prɒmɪsɪŋ] ADJ peu prometteur; **the weather looks u.** on dirait qu'il ne va pas faire beau; **that's an u. start** c'est un mauvais départ *ou* un départ qui augure mal de la suite

unprompted [ˌʌn'prɒmptɪd] ADJ *(action, words)* spontané; **that was quite u. by any self-interest** ce n'était motivé par aucun intérêt personnel

unpronounceable [ˌʌnprə'naʊnsəbəl] ADJ imprononçable

unprotected [ˌʌnprə'tektɪd] ADJ **1** *(person)* sans protection, non défendu; **children over 15 are u. by the legislation** les enfants de plus de 15 ans ne sont pas protégés par la législation
2 *(machinery)* sans protection, non protégé
3 *(wood)* non traité
4 *(exposed)* exposé (aux intempéries); **the house is u. from the east wind** la maison est exposée aux vents d'est
▸▸ ***unprotected sex*** rapports *mpl* non protégés

unproved [ˌʌn'pru:vd], **unproven** [ˌʌn'pru:vən] ADJ non prouvé

unprovided-for [ˌʌnprə'vaɪdɪd-] ADJ *(family)* sans ressources; *(eventuality)* non prévu; **he left his family u. in his will** il n'a rien laissé à sa famille dans son testament

unprovoked [ˌʌnprə'vəʊkt] ADJ *(attack, insult)* injustifié

unpublicized, -ised [ˌʌn'pʌblɪsaɪzd] ADJ dont on n'a pas parlé

unpublishable [ˌʌn'pʌblɪʃəbəl] ADJ impubliable

unpublished [ˌʌn'pʌblɪʃt] ADJ *(manuscript, book)* inédit, non publié

unpunctual [ˌʌn'pʌŋktʃʊəl] ADJ peu ponctuel

unpunctuality ['ʌnˌpʌŋktʃʊ'ælɪtɪ] N manque *m* de ponctualité

unpunished [ˌʌn'pʌnɪʃt] ADJ impuni; **he can't be allowed to go u.** il ne peut pas rester impuni

unputdownable [ˌʌnpʊt'daʊnəbəl] ADJ *Br Fam (book, novel)* passionnant[□], auquel on a du mal à s'arracher[□]; **I found it absolutely u.** je ne pouvais pas m'arrêter de lire[□]

unqualified [ˌʌn'kwɒlɪfaɪd] ADJ **1** *(unskilled)* non qualifié; *(without diploma)* qui n'a pas les diplômes requis; *(unsuitable)* qui n'a pas les qualités requises; **he is u. for the job of chairman** il n'est pas qualifié pour le poste de président **2** *(not competent)* non qualifié *ou* compétent; **she is u. to decide** elle n'est pas qualifiée pour décider **3** *(unrestricted* ▸ *admiration, approval, support)* inconditionnel, sans réserve; (▸ *praise)* sans réserve; (▸ *success)* complet(ète)

unquenchable [ˌʌn'kwentʃəbəl] ADJ *Literary (curiosity, desire, passion)* insatiable, inassouvissable; *(thirst)* impossible à étancher

unquenched [ˌʌn'kwentʃt] ADJ *(fire)* non éteint; *Literary (curiosity, desire, passion)* inassouvi; **u. thirst** soif *f* non étanchée

unquestionable [ˌʌn'kwestʃənəbəl] ADJ **1** *(undeniable)* incontestable, indubitable **2** *(above suspicion)* qui ne peut être mis en question

unquestionably [ʌn'kwestʃənəblɪ] ADV indéniablement, incontestablement

unquestioned [ʌn'kwestʃənd] ADJ *(decision, leader, principle)* indiscuté, incontesté; **to let a statement pass** *or* **go u.** laisser passer une affirmation sans la relever

unquestioning [ʌn'kwestʃənɪŋ] ADJ *(faith, love, obedience, belief)* absolu, aveugle

unquestioningly [ʌn'kwestʃənɪŋlɪ] ADV aveuglément

unquiet [ˌʌn'kwaɪət] ADJ *Literary (person)* troublé, inquiet(ète), tourmenté; *(mind)* perturbé, tourmenté; *(period)* troublé, agité

unquote [ˌʌn'kwəʊt] ADV fin de citation; *(in dictation)* fermez les guillemets

unquoted [ˌʌn'kwəʊtɪd] ADJ *St Exch* non coté

unratified [ˌʌn'rætɪfaɪd] ADJ non ratifié

unravel [ˌʌn'rævəl] *(Br pt & pp* **unravelled,** *cont* **unravelling,** *Am pt & pp* **unraveled,** *cont* **unraveling***)* VT **1** *(knitting)* défaire; *(textile)* effiler, effilocher **2** *(untangle* ▸ *knots, string)* démêler; *Fig* (▸ *mystery)* débrouiller, éclaircir; (▸ *plot)* dénouer, démêler
VI **1** *(knitting)* se défaire; *(textile)* s'effilocher **2** *Fig (mystery)* s'éclaircir; *(plan)* s'effondrer

unread [ˌʌn'red] ADJ **1** *(person)* qui a peu lu **2** *(book, report)* qui n'a pas été lu; **he left the magazine on the table u.** il a laissé la revue sur la table sans l'avoir lue

unreadable [ˌʌn'ri:dəbəl] ADJ **1** *(handwriting, signature)* illisible **2** *(book, report)* illisible, ennuyeux **3** *Comput (file, data)* illisible

unreadiness [ˌʌn'redɪnɪs] N **1** *(unpreparednes*… manque *m* de préparation **2** *(unwillingnes*… manque *m* d'empressement; **their u. to co**… **tribute** la mauvaise volonté qu'ils ont mise… contribuer; *(refusal)* leur refus de contribuer

unready [ˌʌn'redɪ] ADJ **1** *(unprepared)* non pr… paré, qui n'est pas prêt **2** *(unwilling)* peu dispo…

unreal [ˌʌn'rɪəl] ADJ **1** *(appearance, feeling)* **it**… **seems so u.** tout paraît si irréel; **an u. situati**… une situation artificielle **2** *Fam (unbelievab*… pas possible, pas croyable, dingue; **his arr**… **gance is u.!** il est d'une arrogance pas possib… *ou* pas croyable *ou* dingue! **3** *Fam (excellent)* d… ment, super *(inv)*, génial

unrealistic [ˌʌnrɪə'lɪstɪk] ADJ irréaliste, peu ré… liste

unreality [ˌʌnrɪ'ælɪtɪ] N irréalité *f*

unrealizable, -isable [ˌʌnrɪə'laɪzəbəl] ADJ… *(hope, wish)* irréalisable **2** *Fin (capital, asse*… non réalisable

unrealized, -ised [ˌʌn'rɪəlaɪzd] ADJ **1** *(hop*… *wish)* irréalisé **2** *Fin (capital, assets)* non réalis…

unreasonable [ˌʌn'ri:zənəbəl] ADJ **1** *(absu*… *preposterous)* déraisonnable; *(unfair)* injust… **you're being u.** vous n'êtes pas raisonnable; **i**… **u. to stay up so late** ce n'est pas raisonnable… veiller si tard; **surely it's not u. to expect that** on peut tout de même raisonnablement s'atte… dre à ce que…; **at this u. hour** à cette heure i… due **2** *(excessive)* excessif, déraisonnable

unreasonably [ˌʌn'ri:zənəblɪ] ADV *(behave)*… manière *ou* façon déraisonnable; **they aske**… **and not altogether u., that in future they shou**… **be kept informed about such matters** ils ont d… mandé, ce qui est tout à fait raisonnable *ou* l… gitime, que dorénavant on les tienne… courant de ces choses

unreasoning [ʌn'ri:zənɪŋ] ADJ *(fear, hatred)*… rationnel

unrecognizable, -isable ['ʌnˌrekəg'naɪzəb… ADJ méconnaissable

unrecognized, -ised [ˌʌn'rekəgnaɪzd] ADJ… *(without being recognized)* **he slipped out u.** il s'e… glissé vers la sortie sans être reconnu **2** *(not a*… *knowledged* ▸ *talent, achievement)* méconnu; **h**… **is u. by the scientific community** il n'est pas reco… nu par la communauté scientifique; **her disco**… **eries went largely u.** ses découvertes so… restées méconnues pour la plupart

unrecorded [ˌʌnrɪ'kɔ:dɪd] ADJ **1** *(remark, fa*… qui n'a pas été enregistré; **to go u.** *(crime, in*… *dent)* ne pas être signalé; **the details of the ca**… **went u.** il n'y a pas eu de trace écrite sur les d… tails de l'affaire **2** *(music)* qui n'a pas encore é… enregistré

unrecoverable [ˌʌnrɪ'kʌvərəbəl] ADJ **1** *Comp*… irrécouvrable **2** *Fin (debt)* inexigible

unredeemed [ˌʌnrɪ'di:md] ADJ **1** *(from pau*… non dégagé *ou* racheté
2 *(promise)* non tenu; *(obligation)* non rempli
3 *(sinner)* impénitent; *(sin)* inexpié, non r… cheté; *Fig* **the town's ugliness is u. by any char**… **whatsoever** la ville n'a aucun charme qui puis… racheter sa laideur
4 *Fin (loan)* non amorti, non remboursé; *(dra*… non honoré; *(mortgage)* non purgé

unreel [ˌʌn'ri:l] VT dérouler
VI se dérouler

unrefined [ˌʌnrɪ'faɪnd] ADJ **1** *(petroleum)* bru… non raffiné; *(sugar)* non raffiné; *(flour)* non blu… **2** *(person, manners)* peu raffiné, fruste

unreformed [ˌʌnrɪ'fɔ:md] ADJ *(person)* qui r… s'est pas corrigé; *(law)* non amendé; **to rema**… **u.** *(person)* rester incorrigible

unrefreshed [ˌʌnrɪ'freʃt] ADJ encore fatigu… non reposé

unregistered [ˌʌn'redʒɪstəd] ADJ **1** *(luggag*… *complaint)* non enregistré
2 *(mail)* non recommandé
3 *(car)* non immatriculé
4 *(voter, student)* non inscrit; *(birth)* non décla…

unregretted [ˌʌnrɪ'gretɪd] ADJ que l'on ne r… grette pas; **she died u.** personne n'a regretté… mort

nrehearsed [ˌʌnrɪˈhɜːst] ADJ **1** *(improvised)* im-rovisé, spontané **2** *Mus & Theat* sans répéti-on, qui n'a pas été répété

nrelated [ˌʌnrɪˈleɪtɪd] ADJ **1** *(unconnected)* sans apport; **the two incidents are u.** les deux inci-ents sont sans rapport l'un avec l'autre; **his an-wer was completely u. to the question** sa réponse avait absolument aucun rapport *ou* absolu-ent rien à voir avec la question **2** *(people)* sans en de parenté

nrelenting [ˌʌnrɪˈlentɪŋ] ADJ **1** *(relentless ▸ ac-ivity, effort)* soutenu, continuel; *(▸ struggle, criti-sm)* acharné; *(▸ pressure, rain)* incessant **2** *erson ▸ tenacious)* tenace, obstiné; *(▸ merci-ss)* implacable; **he was u.** *(would not be per-uaded, influenced)* il restait inflexible; *erciless)* il était implacable

nreliability [ˈʌnrɪˌlaɪəˈbɪlɪtɪ] N **1** *(of person)* anque *m* de sérieux **2** *(of method, machine)* anque *m* de fiabilité

nreliable [ˌʌnrɪˈlaɪəbəl] ADJ **1** *(person)* peu able, sur qui on ne peut pas compter; **he's too** on ne peut vraiment pas compter sur lui *ou* lui aire confiance
2 *(car, machinery)* peu fiable
3 *(service)* peu fiable, peu sûr; *(business, com-any)* qui n'inspire pas confiance
4 *(information, memory)* peu fiable

nrelieved [ˌʌnrɪˈliːvd] ADJ **1** *(unvarying ▸ oom, misery)* constant, permanent; *(▸ bore-om)* mortel; *(▸ black)* uniforme; *(▸ landscape, outine)* monotone; **vast expanses of grey, u. by ny bright colour** de vastes étendues de gris u'aucune couleur vive ne vient égayer **2** *(pain)* ans rémission, sans répit

nremarkable [ˌʌnrɪˈmɑːkəbəl] ADJ peu remar-uable, quelconque

nremitting [ˌʌnrɪˈmɪtɪŋ] ADJ *(activity, rain)* in-essant, ininterrompu; *(demands, efforts)* inlas-able, infatigable; *(opposition)* implacable, piniâtre; **they were u. in their efforts to find a so-ution** ils se sont efforcés avec assiduité de trou-er une solution

nremittingly [ˌʌnrɪˈmɪtɪŋlɪ] ADV *(work)* sans esse, inlassablement; *(rain)* sans cesse, sans nterruption; *(hostile, opposed)* implacable-ent, opiniâtrement

nremunerative [ˌʌnrɪˈmjuːnərətɪv] ADJ peu émunérateur

nrepealed [ˌʌnrɪˈpiːld] ADJ *(law)* non abrogé

nrepeatable [ˌʌnrɪˈpiːtəbəl] ADJ **1** *(remark)* u'on n'ose pas répéter, trop grossier pour être épété; **what he said was quite u.** ce qu'il a dit 'est pas répétable **2** *(offer, performance)* excep-onnel, unique

nrepentant [ˌʌnrɪˈpentənt] ADJ impénitent; **to ie u.** mourir dans le péché; **she was u. about what she had done** *(gen)* elle ne regrettait pas du out ce qu'elle avait fait; *(about sin)* elle ne se re-entissait aucunement de ce qu'elle avait fait

nreported [ˌʌnrɪˈpɔːtɪd] ADJ non signalé *ou* entionné; **the accident went u.** l'accident n'a as été signalé

nrepresentative [ˌʌnreprɪˈzentətɪv] ADJ non eprésentatif; **it's completely u. of the style of he period** ce n'est pas du tout représentatif du tyle de l'époque; **his opinions are u. of the group** es opinions ne représentent pas celles du roupe

nrepresented [ˌʌnreprɪˈzentɪd] ADJ *Pol* qui 'est pas représenté

nrequited [ˌʌnrɪˈkwaɪtɪd] ADJ *Literary* non ré-iproque, non partagé
▸▸ ***unrequited love*** amour *m* non partagé

nreserved [ˌʌnrɪˈzɜːvd] ADJ **1** *(place)* non ré-ervé **2** *(unqualified)* sans réserve, entier; **to be . in one's praise of sth** ne pas tarir d'éloges à pro-os de qch

nreservedly [ˌʌnrɪˈzɜːvɪdlɪ] ADV **1** *(without ualification)* sans réserve, entièrement; **to trust b u.** avoir pleine confiance en qn **2** *(frankly)* ans réserve, franchement

nresisting [ˌʌnrɪˈzɪstɪŋ] ADJ soumis, docile

nresolved [ˌʌnrɪˈzɒlvd] ADJ *(issue, problem)* on résolu

unresponsive [ˌʌnrɪˈspɒnsɪv] ADJ **1** *(without re-action)* qui ne réagit pas; *Aut & Tech (steering)* qui ne répond pas bien; *(engine)* qui manque de nervosité; **management was u. to workers' de-mands** l'administration n'a pas répondu aux exi-gences des ouvriers; **the patient has been u. to medical treatment** le traitement n'a pas agi sur le malade, le malade n'a pas réagi au traitement **2** *(mentally ▸ gen)* insensible; *(▸ audience)* passif; *(sexually ▸ woman)* frigide; **she complains that her husband is u. in bed** elle se plaint du fait que son mari manque d'enthousiasme au lit

unrest [ʌnˈrest] N *(UNCOUNT)* agitation *f*, trou-bles *mpl*; **labour** *or* **industrial u.** agitation *f* ou-vrière; **social u.** *(discontent)* malaise *m* social; *(disorder)* troubles *mpl* sociaux

unrestrained [ˌʌnrɪˈstreɪnd] ADJ *(anger, growth, joy)* non contenu; **the u. use of force** l'usage sans limites de la force

unrestrainedly [ˌʌnrɪˈstreɪnɪdlɪ] ADV librement, sans contrainte

unrestricted [ˌʌnrɪˈstrɪktɪd] ADJ *(access, park-ing)* libre; *(number, time)* illimité; *(power)* absolu

unrevealed [ˌʌnrɪˈviːld] ADJ non révélé

unrewarded [ˌʌnrɪˈwɔːdɪd] ADJ *(person)* non ré-compensé; *(effort, search)* vain, infructueux; **our efforts went u.** nos efforts sont restés sans ré-compense

unrewarding [ˌʌnrɪˈwɔːdɪŋ] ADJ **1** *(financially)* pas très intéressant financièrement **2** *Fig (work, experience)* ingrat

unrhythmic [ˌʌnˈrɪðmɪk], **unrhythmical** [ˌʌn-ˈrɪðmɪkəl] ADJ *(person)* qui n'a pas le sens du rythme; *(music)* peu rythmé

unrig [ˌʌnˈrɪg] *(pt & pp* **unrigged**, *cont* **unrigging)** VT *Naut (ship)* dégréer

unrighteous [ˌʌnˈraɪtʃəs] NPL *Literary* **the u.** *(not pious)* les impies *mpl*; *(sinful)* les pécheurs *mpl*

unripe [ˌʌnˈraɪp] ADJ vert

unrivalled, *Am* **unrivaled** [ʌnˈraɪvəld] ADJ sans égal *ou* pareil, incomparable

unroadworthy [ˌʌnˈrəʊdˌwɜːðɪ] ADJ *(vehicle)* qui n'est pas en état de rouler

unroll [ˌʌnˈrəʊl] VT dérouler

unromantic [ˌʌnrəˈmæntɪk] ADJ *(person ▸ unsen-timental)* peu romantique; *(▸ down-to-earth)* prosaïque, terre à terre *(inv)*; *(ideas, place)* peu romantique

unrope [ˌʌnˈrəʊp] VI *(in mountaineering)* se déta-cher (de la cordée)

unruffled [ˌʌnˈrʌfəld] ADJ **1** *(person)* impertur-bable, qui ne perd pas son calme; **she remained completely u.** elle n'a pas sourcillé *ou* bronché **2** *(hair)* lisse; *(water)* calme, lisse

unruled [ˌʌnˈruːld] ADJ *(paper)* blanc (blanche), non réglé

unruliness [ˌʌnˈruːlɪnɪs] N *(of child)* indiscipline *f*, turbulence *f*; *(of mob)* agitation *f*; *(of horse)* ca-ractère *m* fougueux

unruly [ˌʌnˈruːlɪ] *(compar* **unrulier**, *superl* **un-ruliest)** ADJ **1** *(children)* indiscipliné, turbulent; *(mob)* incontrôlé; *(horse)* fougueux **2** *(hair)* in-discipliné

unsaddle [ˌʌnˈsædəl] VT *(horse)* desseller; *(rider)* désarçonner

unsafe [ˌʌnˈseɪf] ADJ **1** *(dangerous ▸ machine, neighbourhood)* peu sûr, dangereux; *(▸ building, bridge)* peu solide, dangereux; **the water is u. to drink** l'eau n'est pas potable; **it's u. to leave it near the fire** c'est dangereux de le laisser près du feu **2** *(endangered)* en danger; **I feel very u. here** je ne me sens pas du tout en sécurité ici
▸▸ ***unsafe sex*** rapports *mpl* non protégés

unsaid [ʌnˈsed] *pt & pp of* **unsay**
ADJ non dit, inexprimé; **a lot was left u.** beau-coup de choses ont été passées sous silence; **there was a lot that was left u. between them** il y a eu beaucoup de non-dits entre eux; **some things are better left u.** parfois il faut savoir se taire

unsalaried [ˌʌnˈsælərɪd] ADJ *(position)* non ré-munéré; *(person)* non salarié

unsaleable [ˌʌnˈseɪləbəl] ADJ *(goods)* inven-dable

unsalted [ˌʌnˈsɔːltɪd] ADJ non salé
▸▸ ***unsalted butter*** beurre *m* doux

unsatisfactorily [ˌʌnsætɪsˈfæktərɪlɪ] ADV d'une manière peu satisfaisante

unsatisfactory [ˌʌnsætɪsˈfæktərɪ] ADJ peu satis-faisant, qui laisse à désirer; **this situation is most u.** cette situation n'est pas du tout satisfaisante

unsatisfied [ˌʌnˈsætɪsfaɪd] ADJ **1** *(person ▸ un-happy)* insatisfait, mécontent; *(▸ unconvinced)* non convaincu; **they remain u. with her work** ils sont toujours mécontents de son travail **2** *(de-sire)* insatisfait, inassouvi; *(appetite)* non rassa-sié

unsatisfying [ˌʌnˈsætɪsfaɪɪŋ] ADJ **1** *(activity, task)* peu gratifiant, ingrat **2** *(unconvincing)* peu convaincant **3** *(meal ▸ insufficient)* insuffisant, peu nourrissant; *(▸ disappointing)* décevant

unsavoury, *Am* **unsavory** [ˌʌnˈseɪvərɪ] ADJ **1** *(behaviour, habits)* peu ragoûtant, très déplai-sant; *(person)* peu recommandable; *(place)* lou-che; *(reputation, film, novel)* douteux **2** *(smell)* fétide, nauséabond; *(food)* mauvais; **the food looked u.** la nourriture était peu ragoûtante

unsay [ˌʌnˈseɪ] *(pt & pp* **unsaid** [-ˈsed]) VT retirer, revenir sur; **what's said cannot be unsaid** ce qui est dit est dit

unscathed [ˌʌnˈskeɪðd] ADJ *(physically)* in-demne, sain et sauf; *(psychologically)* non af-fecté; **luckily he emerged u. from the experience** heureusement, il est sorti indemne de cette aventure; **the city survived the bombing relatively u.** la ville a survécu au bombardement sans trop de dégâts

unscented [ˌʌnˈsentɪd] ADJ *(soap etc)* sans par-fum, non parfumé

unscheduled [*Br* ˌʌnˈʃedjuːld, *Am* ˌʌnˈskedʒʊld] ADJ imprévu

unscholarly [ˌʌnˈskɒləlɪ] ADJ *(not appropriate for a scholar)* qui n'est pas digne d'un intellectuel; *(not written etc in a scholarly way)* peu acadé-mique

unschooled [ˌʌnˈskuːld] ADJ *Formal* **1** *(person)* qui n'a pas d'instruction; **he is u. in such matters** il est ignorant en la matière, il n'a jamais été ini-tié à ces choses **2** *(talent)* inné, naturel

unscientific [ˌʌnsaɪənˈtɪfɪk] ADJ *(method, ap-proach)* non *ou* peu scientifique

unscientifically [ˌʌnsaɪənˈtɪfɪkəlɪ] ADV peu scientifiquement

unscramble [ˌʌnˈskræmbəl] VT *(code, message)* déchiffrer; *Tel* désembrouiller; *Fig (problem)* ré-soudre

unscrambler [ˌʌnˈskræmblə(r)] N *TV* décodeur *m*

unscrambling [ˌʌnˈskræmblɪŋ] N *TV* décodage *m*

unscrew [ˌʌnˈskruː] VT dévisser
VI se dévisser

unscripted [ˌʌnˈskrɪptɪd] ADJ *(play, speech)* im-provisé; *(item, subject)* non programmé

unscrupulous [ˌʌnˈskruːpjʊləs] ADJ *(person)* sans scrupules, peu scrupuleux; *(behaviour, methods)* malhonnête, peu scrupuleux

unscrupulously [ˌʌnˈskruːpjʊləslɪ] ADV sans scrupules, peu scrupuleusement

unscrupulousness [ˌʌnˈskruːpjʊləsnɪs] N *(of person)* manque *m* de scrupules, malhonnêteté *f*; *(of behaviour, methods)* malhonnêteté *f*

unseal [ˌʌnˈsiːl] VT *(open ▸ letter)* ouvrir, déca-cheter; *(▸ deed, testament)* desceller; *Fig* **to u. one's lips** rompre le silence

unsealed [ˌʌnˈsiːld] ADJ *(letter)* ouvert, déca-cheté; *(deed, testament)* descellé

unseasonable [ˌʌnˈsiːzənəbəl] ADJ *(clothing, weather)* qui n'est pas de saison; **this weather's very u.** ce n'est pas un temps de saison

unseasonably [ˌʌnˈsiːzənəblɪ] ADV **an u. cold night** une nuit fraîche pour la saison

unseasoned [ˌʌnˈsiːzənd] ADJ **1** *(food)* non as-saisonné **2** *(wood)* vert

unseat [ˌʌnˈsiːt] VT *(rider)* désarçonner; *(govern-ment, king)* faire tomber; *Parl (MP)* faire perdre son siège à

unseaworthy [ˌʌn'siːwɜːðɪ] ADJ *(ship)* innavigable

unsecured [ˌʌnsɪ'kjʊəd] ADJ **1** *(door, window ▸ unlocked)* qui n'est pas fermé à clé; *(▸ open)* mal fermé **2** *Fin (loan, overdraft)* sans garantie, non garanti
▸▸ *Fin* ***unsecured advance*** avance *f* à découvert; *Fin* ***unsecured creditor*** créancier(ère) *m,f* ordinaire *ou* chirographaire; *Fin* ***unsecured debt*** créance *f* chirographaire *ou* sans garantie

unseeded [ˌʌn'siːdɪd] ADJ *Sport* non classé

unseeing [ˌʌn'siːɪŋ] ADJ *Literary* aveugle; **he looked at her with u. eyes** il l'a regardée sans (vraiment) la voir

unseemliness [ˌʌn'siːmlɪnɪs] N *Literary (of behaviour, dress)* inconvenance *f*

unseemly [ˌʌn'siːmlɪ] *(compar* **unseemlier,** *superl* **unseemliest)** ADJ *Literary (improper ▸ behaviour)* inconvenant, déplacé; *(▸ dress)* inconvenant, peu convenable; *(rude)* indécent, grossier

unseen [ˌʌn'siːn] ADJ **1** *(invisible)* invisible; *(unnoticed)* inaperçu; **she passed u. through the crowd** elle est passée inaperçue dans la foule **2** *(not seen previously)* **to buy sth sight u.** acheter qch sans l'avoir vu; *Br Sch & Univ* **an u. translation** une traduction sans préparation *ou* à vue
N *Br Sch & Univ* traduction *f* sans préparation *ou* à vue

unselfconscious [ˌʌnself'kɒnʃəs] ADJ *(charm)* naturel; *(laugh)* spontané; *(person ▸ spontaneous)* naturel; *(▸ uninhibited)* sans complexes; **he's got a big scar on his face but he's quite u. about it** il a une grande cicatrice sur le visage mais n'est pas complexé; **she's quite u. about speaking up** elle n'a vraiment pas peur de dire ce qu'elle pense, elle dit ce qu'elle pense sans aucun complexe

unselfconsciously [ˌʌnself'kɒnʃəslɪ] ADV *(spontaneously)* avec naturel; *(uninhibitedly)* sans complexes

unselfish [ˌʌn'selfɪʃ] ADJ *(person, act)* généreux, désintéressé

unselfishly [ˌʌn'selfɪʃlɪ] ADV généreusement, sans penser à soi

unselfishness [ˌʌn'selfɪʃnɪs] N *(of person, act)* générosité *f*, désintéressement *m*

unsellable [ˌʌn'seləbəl] ADJ invendable

unsentimental [ˌʌnsentɪ'mentəl] ADJ *(person)* qui ne fait pas de sentiment; *(book, description)* qui ne tombe pas dans le sentimental, sans sentimentalisme; **to be u. about animals** ne pas faire de sentiment au sujet des animaux

unserviceable [ˌʌn'sɜːvɪsəbəl] ADJ inutilisable

unsettle [ˌʌn'setəl] VT **1** *(person)* inquiéter, troubler **2** *(stomach)* déranger

unsettled [ˌʌn'setəld] ADJ **1** *(unstable ▸ conditions, situation)* instable, incertain; *(▸ person)* troublé, perturbé, inquiet(ète); *(▸ stomach)* dérangé; *(▸ weather)* incertain, changeant; **I feel u. in my job** je ne suis pas bien dans mon travail
2 *(unfinished ▸ issue, argument, dispute)* qui n'a pas été réglé
3 *(account, bill)* non réglé, impayé
4 *(area, region)* inhabité, sans habitants

unsettling [ˌʌn'setəlɪŋ] ADJ *(disturbing)* troublant, perturbateur

unsex [ˌʌn'seks] VT *Literary (woman)* faire perdre sa féminité à; *(man)* faire perdre sa virilité à

unshackle [ˌʌn'ʃækəl] VT désenchaîner, ôter ses fers à; *Fig* libérer, émanciper

unshackled [ˌʌn'ʃækəld] ADJ sans entraves, libre; **to be u. by convention** ne pas porter le poids des conventions

unshakeable [ˌʌn'ʃeɪkəbəl] ADJ *(conviction, faith)* inébranlable; *(decision)* ferme

unshaken [ˌʌn'ʃeɪkən] ADJ inébranlable

unshaven [ˌʌn'ʃeɪvən] ADJ non rasé

unsheathe [ˌʌn'ʃiːð] VT dégainer

unsheltered [ˌʌn'ʃeltəd] ADJ non abrité, non protégé (**from** contre)

unship [ˌʌn'ʃɪp] VT *(pt & pp* **unshipped,** *cont* **unshipping)** *Naut* décharger, débarquer

unshod [ˌʌn'ʃɒd] ADJ **1** *(horse)* qui n'est pas ferré **2** *(person)* sans chaussures; *(having removed shoes)* déchaussé

unsighted [ˌʌn'saɪtɪd] ADJ **1** *(with one's view blocked)* **I didn't see what happened, I was u.** je n'ai pas vu ce qui s'est passé, quelqu'un bloquait ma vue; **the goalkeeper was u.** quelqu'un empêchait le gardien de but de voir le ballon **2** *(sightless)* aveugle

unsightliness [ʌn'saɪtlɪnɪs] N laideur *f*, aspect *m* disgracieux

unsightly [ʌn'saɪtlɪ] *(compar* **unsightlier,** *superl* **unsightliest)** ADJ disgracieux, laid

unsigned [ˌʌn'saɪnd] ADJ non signé, sans signature

unsinkable [ˌʌn'sɪŋkəbəl] ADJ *(boat)* insubmersible; *Fig (person)* qui ne se démonte pas facilement

unskilful, *Am* **unskillful** [ˌʌn'skɪlfʊl] ADJ *(lacking skill)* malhabile; *(clumsy)* maladroit

unskilled [ˌʌn'skɪld] ADJ **1** *(worker)* sans formation professionnelle, non spécialisé, non qualifié **2** *(job, work)* qui ne nécessite pas de connaissances professionnelles **3** *(person)* inexpérimenté; **to be u. in** *or* **at doing sth** ne pas être doué pour faire qch
▸▸ *Br* ***unskilled labourer*** ouvrier *m* non spécialisé, ouvrière *f* non spécialisée

unskimmed [ʌn'skɪmd] ADJ *(milk)* entier

unslept-in [ˌʌn'slept-] ADJ *(bed)* non défait

unsling [ˌʌn'slɪŋ] *(pt & pp* **unslung** [-'slʌŋ]) VT dégréer; *(hammock)* décrocher; **to u. one's rifle** enlever son fusil de l'épaule

unsmiling [ˌʌn'smaɪlɪŋ] ADJ *(person, face)* austère, sérieux

unsmoked [ʌn'sməʊkt] ADJ non fumé

unsociable [ˌʌn'səʊʃəbəl] ADJ *(person)* sauvage, peu sociable; *(place)* peu accueillant; **to feel u.** ne pas avoir envie de voir du monde; **don't be so u.!** ne sois pas si sauvage!

unsocial [ˌʌn'səʊʃəl] ADJ **she works u. hours** elle travaille en dehors des heures normales

unsold [ˌʌn'səʊld] ADJ invendu

unsoldierly [ˌʌn'səʊldʒəlɪ] ADJ peu militaire

unsolicited [ˌʌnsə'lɪsɪtɪd] ADJ *(comment)* non sollicité; *(contribution)* volontaire; *(application)* spontané; **u. manuscript** manuscrit *m* non commandé; **to do sth u.** faire qch spontanément

unsolvable [ˌʌn'sɒlvəbəl] ADJ insoluble

unsolved [ˌʌn'sɒlvd] ADJ *(mystery)* non résolu, inexpliqué; *(problem)* non résolu

unsophisticated [ˌʌnsə'fɪstɪkeɪtɪd] ADJ **1** *(person ▸ in dress, tastes)* simple; *(▸ in attitude)* simple, naturel
2 *(dress, style)* simple, qui n'est pas sophistiqué
3 *(device, machine, technology)* simple; *(approach, method)* rudimentaire, *Pej* simpliste
4 *(inexperienced)* inexpérimenté; **guidelines for the financially u.** des conseils pour ceux qui ne sont pas très au fait *ou* manquent d'expérience en matière de finances

unsound [ˌʌn'saʊnd] ADJ **1** *(argument, conclusion, reasoning)* mal fondé, peu pertinent; *(advice, decision)* peu judicieux, peu sensé; *(enterprise, investment)* peu sûr, risqué; *(business)* peu sûr, précaire; **the project is economically u.** le projet n'est pas sain *ou* viable sur le plan économique; **ideologically/politically u.** *(theory, beliefs, system)* pas valable sur le plan idéologique/politique; **scientifically u.** qui ne repose *ou* s'appuie pas sur des bases scientifiques solides; **this method of waste disposal is environmentally u.** ce système de traitement des ordures est nuisible à l'environnement **2** *(building, bridge)* peu solide, dangereux; **the building is structurally u.** le bâtiment n'est pas solide **3** *(idiom)* **to be of u. mind** ne pas jouir de toutes ses facultés mentales

unsparing [ˌʌn'speərɪŋ] ADJ **1** *(generous)* généreux, prodigue; **to be u. of one's time/with one's advice** ne pas être avare de son temps/de conseils; **they were u. in their efforts to help us** ils n'ont pas ménagé leurs efforts pour nous aider **2** *(harsh)* sévère

unsparingly [ˌʌn'speərɪŋlɪ] ADV **1** *(lavishly)* généreusement, libéralement **2** *(criticize, moc*…*)* sévèrement, sans mâcher ses mots

unspeakable [ˌʌn'spiːkəbəl] ADJ **1** *(crime, pai*…*)* épouvantable, atroce **2** *(beauty, joy)* indicibl… ineffable

unspeakably [ˌʌn'spiːkəblɪ] ADV **1** *(cruel, rud*…*)* épouvantablement, atrocement **2** *(beautifu*…*)* indiciblement, ineffablement

unspecified [ˌʌn'spesɪfaɪd] ADJ non spécifi… **certain u. persons** certaines personnes, dont o… taira les noms

unspectacular [ˌʌnspek'tækjʊlə(r)] ADJ pe… spectaculaire

unspent [ˌʌn'spent] ADJ non dépensé, restant

unspoiled [ˌʌn'spɔɪld], **unspoilt** [ˌʌn'spɔɪlt] AD… **1** *(person)* (qui est resté) naturel; **they were u. b… fame** ils étaient simples *ou* naturels malgré leu… succès, le succès ne leur était pas monté à … tête **2** *(beauty, town)* intact **3** *(flavour)* naturel

unspoken [ˌʌn'spəʊkən] ADJ **1** *(agreement)* tacit… **2** *(thought, wish)* inexprimé; *(word)* non pr… noncé; **although his name remained u....** bie… que son nom n'ait pas été prononcé…

unsporting [ˌʌn'spɔːtɪŋ] ADJ *(person)* déloya… *(behaviour ▸ gen)* déloyal; *(▸ in sport)* peu spo… tif, peu fair-play *(inv)*; **it was u. of him not to he… us** ce n'était pas très chic de sa part de ne pa… nous aider; **he was suspended for u. behaviour** a été suspendu pour conduite indigne d'u… sportif

unstable [ˌʌn'steɪbəl] ADJ **1** *(chair, governmen*… *price, situation)* instable **2** *(marriage)* peu solid… **3** *(person)* déséquilibré, instable

unstained [ˌʌn'steɪnd] ADJ **1** *(reputation)* sans ta… che **2** *(wood)* non teinté

unstamped [ˌʌn'stæmpt] ADJ *(letter)* non affran… chi, non timbré; *(document)* non tamponné

unstated [ˌʌn'steɪtɪd] ADJ **1** *(agreement)* tacite *(desire)* inexprimé

unstatesmanlike [ˌʌn'steɪtsmənlaɪk] ADJ *(beha*… *viour)* peu digne d'un homme d'État

unsteadily [ˌʌn'stedɪlɪ] ADV *(walk)* d'un pa… chancelant *ou* incertain, en titubant; *(spea*…*)* d'une voix mal assurée; *(hold, write)* d'une mai… tremblante

unsteadiness [ˌʌn'stedɪnɪs] N *(of step, voic*… *writing)* manque *m* d'assurance; *(of table*…*)* manque *m* de stabilité

unsteady [ˌʌn'stedɪ] *(compar* **unsteadier,** *supe*… **unsteadiest)** ADJ **1** *(chair, ladder)* instable, bran… lant
2 *(step, voice)* mal assuré, chancelant; *(hand*…*)* tremblant; **to be u. on one's feet** *(from illnes*… *tiredness, drink)* ne pas tenir très bien sur se… jambes
3 *(rhythm, speed, temperature)* irrégulier; *(flam*…*)* vacillant
4 *Fin (prices)* variable; *(market)* agité

unsterilized, -ised [ˌʌn'sterɪlaɪzd] ADJ non sté… rilisé

unstick [ˌʌn'stɪk] *(pt & pp* **unstuck** [-'stʌk]) VT dé… coller

unstinted [ˌʌn'stɪntɪd] ADJ **1** *(supplies)* abondan… **2** *(praise, admiration)* sans réserve

unstinting [ˌʌn'stɪntɪŋ] ADJ *(care)* infini; *(help*… généreux; *(efforts)* incessant, illimité; *(suppor*…*)* sans réserve, inconditionnel; *(person)* géné… reux, prodigue; **the firm has been u. in its effor… to help us** l'entreprise n'a pas ménagé ses effort… pour nous aider; **to be u. in one's praise of sb/st…** ne pas tarir d'éloges au sujet de qn/qch; **to giv… u. praise** ne pas ménager ses louanges

unstintingly [ˌʌn'stɪntɪŋlɪ] ADV généreuse… ment; *(help, work)* sans se ménager; *(suppor*…*)* sans réserve, inconditionnellement; **to prais… sb u.** ne pas tarir d'éloges sur qn

unstitch [ˌʌn'stɪtʃ] VT découdre; **the hem cam… unstitched** l'ourlet s'est décousu

unstop [ˌʌn'stɒp] *(pt & pp* **unstopped,** *cont* **u…** **stopping)** VT *(drain, sink)* déboucher

unstoppable [ˌʌn'stɒpəbəl] ADJ qu'on ne peu… pas arrêter; *(force)* irrésistible; *Sport (shot)* im… parable; **the u. rise in property prices** la hauss…

ıexorable des prix de l'immobilier; **he's u. now** 'ésormais rien ne peut l'arrêter

nstressed [ˌʌn'strest] ADJ *Ling* inaccentué, ıtone

nstring [ˌʌn'strɪŋ] *(pt & pp* **unstrung** [-'strʌŋ]) VT *(bow)* débander; **to u. a violin** ôter les cordes l'un violon **2** *(beads etc)* ôter le fil de

nstructured [ˌʌn'strʌktʃəd] ADJ *(activity, essay)* non structuré; *(group)* non organisé; *Mktg interview)* non structuré, libre

nstuck [ˌʌn'stʌk] *pt & pp of* **unstick**

ADJ *(envelope, label)* décollé; **to come u.** se décoller; *Fig (plan, policy)* tomber à l'eau; *(person)* e casser la figure

nstudied [ˌʌn'stʌdɪd] ADJ *(natural)* naturel; *spontaneous)* spontané

nsubdued [ˌʌnsəb'djuːd] ADJ indompté

nsubscribe [ˌʌnsəb'skraɪb] VI *Comput (from SP)* résilier son abonnement; *(from mailing list)* ;e désinscrire

nsubscribed [ˌʌnsəb'skraɪbd] ADJ *Fin (capital)* ıon souscrit

nsubsidized, -ised [ˌʌn'sʌbsɪdaɪzd] ADJ non ;ubventionné

nsubstantiated [ˌʌnsəb'stænʃɪeɪtɪd] ADJ *(report, story)* non confirmé *ou* corroboré; *(accusation)* non fondé

nsubtle [ˌʌn'sʌtəl] ADJ *(person, remark)* peu ubtil, sans finesse; *(joke)* gros (grosse); **how ould anyone be so u.!** comment peut-on manuer de subtilité à ce point!

nsuccessful [ˌʌnsək'sesful] ADJ *(plan, project)* ıui est un échec, qui n'a pas réussi; *(attempt)* ain, infructueux; *(person)* qui n'a pas de sucès; *(demand)* refusé, rejeté; *(marriage, outome)* malheureux; **after several u. attempts** près plusieurs essais infructueux; **to be u.** échouer; **I was u. in my attempts to find her** je n'ai as réussi *ou* je ne suis pas arrivé à la trouver, je 'ai cherchée en vain *ou* sans succès; **to be u. in n exam** échouer *ou* ne pas être reçu à un exanen; **your application has been u.** votre candidaure n'a pas été retenue; **u. applications will not be acknowledged** nous ne répondrons pas aux personnes dont les candidatures n'ont pas été reteues; **u. candidate** *(at election)* candidat *m* non Elu

nsuccessfully [ˌʌnsək'sesfulɪ] ADV en vain, ;ans succès

nsuitability [ˌʌnsuːtə'bɪlɪtɪ] N *(of person)* inapitude *f* (**for sth** à qch); *(of behaviour, language)* caractère *m* inconvenant; **due to the u. of the climate...** *(for person)* le climat étant peu indiqué...; *(for plants)* le climat ne convenant as...; **this seems proof of his u. for the job** ceci emble indiquer qu'il n'est pas la personne qu'il 'aut pour ce poste; **he pointed out the u. of that date for the meeting** il a fait remarquer que cette late ne convenait pas pour la réunion; **the u. of the tools meant that the job took twice as long** le ravail a pris deux fois plus longtemps parce que les outils ne convenaient pas

nsuitable [ˌʌn'suːtəbəl] ADJ *(arrangement, candidate, qualities, tool)* qui ne convient pas; *(behaviour, language)* inconvenant; *(moment, time)* nopportun; *(clothing)* peu approprié, inadéquat; *(friend, people)* peu recommandable; *(climate ▸ for person)* peu indiqué; *(▸ for plants)* qui ne convient pas; **he chose an u. time to call** il a nal choisi le moment pour appeler; **this is an u. time to bring the matter up** ce n'est pas le moment de parler de cela; **u. for children** *(on packaging)* ne convient pas aux enfants; **the land is u. for farming** le sol n'est pas propice aux culures *ou* n'est pas cultivable; **he's quite u. for the job** ce n'est pas la personne qu'il faut pour ce poste; **u. for the occasion** qui ne convient pas à a circonstance

nsuitably [ˌʌn'suːtəblɪ] ADV *(behave)* de façon inconvenante; *(dress)* de façon inappropriée; **they're u. matched** *(couple)* ils sont mal assortis

nsuited [ˌʌn'suːtɪd] ADJ *(person)* inapte; *(machine, tool)* mal adapté, impropre; **he is u. to politics** il n'est pas fait pour la politique; **as a couple they seem totally u.** ils forment un couple mal assorti, ils ne vont pas du tout ensemble

unsulfured *Am* = **unsulphured**

unsullied [ˌʌn'sʌlɪd] ADJ *Literary* sans souillure, sans tache; **her reputation was u. by...** sa réputation n'a pas souffert de...

unsulphured, *Am* **unsulfured** [ˌʌn'sʌlfəd] ADJ *(dried fruit)* non traité au dioxyde de soufre

unsung [ˌʌn'sʌŋ] ADJ *Literary (deed, hero)* méconnu

unsupervised [ʌn'suːpəvaɪzd] ADJ *(child)* non surveillé; **u. minors not admitted** *(sign)* interdit aux enfants non accompagnés

unsupported [ˌʌnsə'pɔːtɪd] ADJ **1** *(argument, theory)* non vérifié; *(accusation, statement)* non fondé; **the theories were u. by any evidence** ces théories n'ont été étayées par aucune preuve **2** *(wall, aperture)* sans support; **to walk u.** *(invalid)* marcher sans se faire aider **3** *Fig (person ▸ financially, emotionally)* **to be u.** n'avoir aucun soutien

unsure [ˌʌn'ʃɔː(r)] ADJ *(lacking self-confidence)* qui manque d'assurance, qui n'est pas sûr de soi; *(hesitant)* incertain; **to be u. of oneself** manquer d'assurance, ne pas être sûr de soi; **I'm u. about going** je ne suis pas certain d'y aller; **they were u. of his reaction** ils ignoraient quelle serait sa réaction

unsurpassable [ˌʌnsə'pɑːsəbəl] ADJ insurpassable

unsurpassed [ˌʌnsə'pɑːst] ADJ sans égal *ou* pareil

unsurprised [ˌʌnsə'praɪzd] ADJ non surpris; **I was u. by his decision** je n'ai pas été surpris par sa décision

unsurprising [ˌʌnsə'praɪzɪŋ] ADJ peu surprenant

unsurprisingly [ˌʌnsə'praɪzɪŋlɪ] ADV bien entendu, évidemment; **u., this suggestion was rejected** évidemment *ou* comme on pouvait s'y attendre, cette suggestion fut rejetée

unsuspected [ˌʌnsə'spektɪd] ADJ insoupçonné

unsuspecting [ˌʌnsə'spektɪŋ] ADJ qui ne soupçonne rien, qui ne se doute de rien

unsuspicious [ˌʌnsəs'pɪʃəs] ADJ peu soupçonneux

unsustainable [ˌʌnsə'steɪnəbəl] ADJ non viable

unsweetened [ˌʌn'swiːtənd] ADJ sans sucre, non sucré

unswerving [ˌʌn'swɜːvɪŋ] ADJ *(devotion, loyalty)* indéfectible, à toute épreuve; *(determination)* inébranlable

unswervingly [ˌʌn'swɜːvɪŋlɪ] ADV **u. loyal** d'une loyauté à toute épreuve

unsympathetic [ˈʌnˌsɪmpəˈθetɪk] ADJ **1** *(unfeeling)* insensible, incompréhensif; **to be u. to a cause** être opposé *ou* hostile à une cause; **they were very u. about our problems** nos problèmes les laissaient complètement indifférents; **he was generally u. to modern art** *(didn't like)* de manière générale il appréciait peu l'art moderne; *(made critical statements about)* il n'était généralement pas tendre avec l'art moderne; **the idea met with an u. reception** l'idée a reçu un accueil plutôt froid **2** *(unlikeable)* antipathique; **I find the characters of this novel u.** les personnages de ce roman me sont peu sympathiques

unsympathetically [ˈʌnˌsɪmpəˈθetɪklɪ] ADV *(speak)* froidement, sans compassion; *(behave)* sans compassion; **"tough!" she said u.** "tant pis pour vous!", dit-elle froidement

unsystematic [ˌʌnsɪstə'mætɪk] ADJ non systématique, non méthodique

unsystematically [ˌʌnsɪstə'mætɪkəlɪ] ADV sans méthode

untainted [ˌʌn'teɪntɪd] ADJ *(water)* pur; *Fig (reputation)* sans tache; **his work is u. by commercialism** son œuvre n'est pas entachée par le mercantilisme

untalented [ˌʌn'tæləntɪd] ADJ peu doué

untamable, untameable [ˌʌn'teɪməbəl] ADJ indomptable, inapprivoisable

untamed [ˌʌn'teɪmd] ADJ **1** *(animal ▸ undomesticated)* sauvage, inapprivoisé; *(▸ untrained)* non dressé; *(lion, tiger)* indompté **2** *(land)* sauvage **3** *(person)* insoumis, indompté; *(spirit)* indompté, rebelle

untangle [ˌʌn'tæŋgəl] VT *(hair, necklace, rope)* démêler; *Fig (mystery)* débrouiller, éclaircir

untapped [ˌʌn'tæpt] ADJ inexploité

untarnished [ˌʌn'tɑːnɪʃt] ADJ *(silver)* non terni; *Fig (reputation)* non terni, sans tache

untasted [ˌʌn'teɪstɪd] ADJ auquel on n'a pas goûté; **he sent the wine back u.** il a renvoyé le vin sans y avoir goûté *ou* touché

untaught [ˌʌn'tɔːt] ADJ **1** *(person)* sans instruction, ignorant **2** *(skill)* inné, naturel

untaxable [ˌʌn'tæksəbəl] ADJ *Fin* non imposable

untaxed [ˌʌn'tækst] ADJ *Fin (items)* non imposé, exempt de taxes, non taxé; *(income)* non imposable, exempt d'impôt, exonéré d'impôt; *(car)* = sans vignette

unteachable [ˌʌn'tiːtʃəbəl] ADJ *(person)* à qui on ne peut rien apprendre; *(skill)* impossible à enseigner *ou* à inculquer

untenable [ˌʌn'tenəbəl] ADJ *(argument, theory)* indéfendable; *(position)* intenable

untenanted [ˌʌn'tenəntɪd] ADJ inoccupé, sans locataire

untended [ˌʌn'tendɪd] ADJ *(sick person)* non soigné, sans soins; *(garden)* non entretenu; *(sheep)* sans surveillance

untested [ˌʌn'testɪd] ADJ *(employee, method, theory)* qui n'a pas été mis à l'épreuve; *(invention, machine, product)* qui n'a pas été essayé; *(drug)* non encore expérimenté

unthinkable [ˌʌn'θɪŋkəbəl] ADJ impensable, inconcevable; **it's u. that...** il est inconcevable que... + *subjunctive*; **if the u. should happen** si l'inconcevable se produisait

unthinking [ˌʌn'θɪŋkɪŋ] ADJ *(action, remark)* irréfléchi, inconsidéré; *(person)* irréfléchi, étourdi

unthinkingly [ˌʌn'θɪŋkɪŋlɪ] ADV sans réfléchir, inconsidérément

unthread [ˌʌn'θred] VT *(beads)* ôter le fil de

untidily [ˌʌn'taɪdɪlɪ] ADV sans soin, d'une manière négligée; **the children's clothes were strewn u. across the floor** les vêtements des enfants jonchaient le plancher

untidiness [ˌʌn'taɪdɪnɪs] N *(of dress)* manque *m* de soin, débraillé *m*; *(of cupboard, desk, room)* désordre *m*; *(of person ▸ in appearance)* aspect *m* négligé; *(▸ characteristic)* manque *m* d'ordre

untidy [ˌʌn'taɪdɪ] *(compar* **untidier**, *superl* **untidiest**) ADJ *(cupboard, desk, room)* mal rangé, en désordre; *(appearance)* négligé, débraillé; *(person ▸ as characteristic)* désordonné; **u. appearance** tenue *f* débraillée; **his room/desk always gets u.** sa chambre/son bureau est toujours en désordre; **his playing is u.** *(of musician)* son jeu manque de netteté

untie [ˌʌn'taɪ] VT *(string)* dénouer; *(knot)* défaire; *(bonds)* défaire, détacher; *(package)* défaire, ouvrir; *(prisoner)* détacher, délier

until [ən'tɪl] PREP **1** *(up to)* jusqu'à; **u. midnight/Monday** jusqu'à minuit/lundi; **u. 1989** jusqu'en 1989; **stay on the motorway u. junction 13** restez sur l'autoroute jusqu'à la sortie 13; **u. such time as you are ready** jusqu'à ce que *ou* en attendant que vous soyez prêt; **she was here (up) u. February** elle était ici jusqu'en février; **(up) u. now** jusqu'ici, jusqu'à présent; **(up) u. then** jusque-là **2** *(with negative ▸ before)* **not u. tomorrow** pas avant demain; **they didn't arrive u. 8 o'clock** ils ne sont arrivés qu'à 8 h; **your car won't be ready u. next week** votre voiture ne sera pas prête avant la semaine prochaine; **I've never seen it u. now** c'est la première fois que je le vois

CONJ **1** *(up to the specified moment ▸ in present)* jusqu'à ce que + *subjunctive*; *(▸ in past)* avant que + *subjunctive*, jusqu'à ce que + *subjunctive*; **wait u. she says hello** attendez qu'elle dise bonjour; **they stayed u. everybody had gone** ils sont restés jusqu'à ce que tout le monde soit parti; **I laughed u. I cried** j'ai ri aux larmes **2** *(with negative main clause)* **u. she spoke I didn't realize she was Spanish** jusqu'à ce qu'elle commence à parler, je ne m'étais pas rendu compte qu'elle était espagnole; **she won't go to sleep u. her mother comes home** elle ne s'endormira pas avant que sa mère (ne) soit rentrée *ou* tant que sa mère n'est pas rentrée; **don't sign anything u. the boss gets there** ne signez rien avant que le patron n'arrive, attendez le patron pour signer quoi que ce soit; **the play didn't start u. everyone was seated** la pièce n'a commencé qu'une fois que tout le monde a été assis

untilled [ˌʌnˈtɪld] **ADJ** *(uncultivated)* non cultivé; *(not ploughed)* non labouré

untimely [ʌnˈtaɪmlɪ] **ADJ 1** *(premature)* prématuré, précoce; **an u. death** une mort prématurée; **to meet** *or* **to come to an u. end** *(person)* mourir avant l'âge; *(reign, project)* connaître une fin prématurée **2** *(inopportune ▸ remark)* inopportun, déplacé; *(▸ moment)* inopportun, mal choisi; *(▸ visit)* intempestif

untiring [ˌʌnˈtaɪərɪŋ] **ADJ** *(efforts)* inlassable, infatigable; **they were u. in their efforts** ils n'ont pas ménagé leurs efforts

untiringly [ˌʌnˈtaɪərɪŋlɪ] **ADV** inlassablement, infatigablement

unto [ˈʌntuː] **PREP** *Arch or Literary* **1** *(to)* à; *Bible* **u. us a child is born** un enfant nous est né; *Bible* **and I say u. you...** en vérité je vous le dis...; **do u. others as you would have them do u. you** ne faites pas à autrui ce que vous ne voudriez pas qu'il vous fît **2** *(until)* jusqu'à; **u. death** jusqu'à la mort

untold [ˌʌnˈtəʊld] **ADJ 1** *(tale)* jamais raconté; *(secret)* jamais dévoilé; **the story remains u.** cette histoire reste secrète *ou* n'a jamais été racontée **2** *(great ▸ joy, suffering)* indicible, indescriptible; *(▸ amount, number)* incalculable; **the war caused u. suffering** la guerre a causé des souffrances indicibles

untouchable [ˌʌnˈtʌtʃəbəl] **ADJ** intouchable
N *(in India)* intouchable *mf*; *Fig* paria *m*

untouched [ˌʌnˈtʌtʃt] **ADJ 1** *(not changed)* auquel on n'a pas touché, intact; **he'd left the meal u.** il n'avait pas touché à son repas
2 *(unaffected)* **to be u. by the influence of television** ne pas avoir subi l'influence de la télévision; **these artefacts have lain u. by human hand for thousands of years** ces objets sont restés inconnus de l'homme pendant des milliers d'années
3 *(unharmed ▸ person)* indemne, sain et sauf; *(▸ thing)* indemne, intact; **most of the city centre has remained u.** une grande partie du centre ville est resté intact
4 *(unmoved ▸ person)* indifférent, insensible (**by** à)

untoward [ˌʌntəˈwɔːd] **ADJ** *Formal (unfortunate ▸ circumstances)* fâcheux, malencontreux; *(▸ effect)* fâcheux, défavorable; **I hope nothing u. has happened** j'espère qu'il n'est rien arrivé de fâcheux

untraceable [ˌʌnˈtreɪsəbəl] **ADJ** introuvable

untradable, untradeable [ˌʌnˈtreɪdəbəl] **ADJ** *St Exch* incotable

untrained [ˌʌnˈtreɪnd] **ADJ** *(person)* sans formation; *(ear)* inexercé; *(mind)* non formé; *(voice)* non travaillé; *(dog, horse)* non dressé; **to the u. eye** pour un œil inexercé

untrammelled, *Am* **untrammeled** [ˌʌnˈtræməld] **ADJ** *Literary* sans contrainte, sans entraves; **u. by convention** libre de toute convention

untransferable [ˌʌntrænsˈfɜːrəbəl] **ADJ** non transmissible; *Law (right, property)* incessible

untranslatable [ˌʌntrænsˈleɪtəbəl] **ADJ** intraduisible

untravelled, *Am* **untraveled** [ˌʌnˈtrævəld] **ADJ** *(road)* peu utilisé *ou* fréquenté; *(person)* qui n'a pas beaucoup voyagé

untried [ˌʌnˈtraɪd] **ADJ 1** *(method, recruit, theory)* qui n'a pas été mis à l'épreuve; *(invention, product)* qui n'a pas été essayé **2** *Law (prisoner, case)* qui n'a pas encore été jugé

untrodden [ˌʌnˈtrɒdən] **ADJ** *(ground, wilderness)* inexploré, vierge; *(path)* non utilisé *ou* fréquenté
▸▸ ***untrodden snow*** neige *f* immaculée *ou* vierge

untroubled [ˌʌnˈtrʌbəld] **ADJ** tranquille, paisible; **they seemed u. by the situation** la situation ne paraissait pas les inquiéter

untrue [ˌʌnˈtruː] **ADJ 1** *(incorrect ▸ belief, statement)* faux (fausse), erroné; *(▸ measurement, reading)* erroné, inexact **2** *(disloyal)* **to be u. to sb** être déloyal envers *ou* infidèle à qn; **to be u. to oneself** trahir ses principes

untrustworthiness [ˌʌnˈtrʌstˌwɜːðɪnɪs] **N** *(of information, machine)* manque *m* de fiabilité; **he was noted for his u.** il avait la réputation de quelqu'un à qui on ne peut pas faire confiance

untrustworthy [ˌʌnˈtrʌstˌwɜːðɪ] **ADJ** *(person)* qui n'est pas digne de confiance; *(information, machine)* peu fiable

untruth [ˌʌnˈtruːθ] **N** *Euph Formal (lie)* mensonge *m*, invention *f*; **to tell an u.** mentir, dire un mensonge

untruthful [ˌʌnˈtruːθfʊl] **ADJ** *(statement)* mensonger; *(person)* menteur; **to say u. things** mentir, dire des mensonges

untruthfully [ˌʌnˈtruːθfʊlɪ] **ADV** d'une façon mensongère

untruthfulness [ˌʌnˈtruːθfʊlnɪs] **N** *(of evidence)* caractère *m* mensonger; **he was notorious for his u.** c'était un menteur notoire

untuned [ˌʌnˈtjuːnd] **ADJ** *(instrument)* non accordé; *(engine)* qui n'est pas réglé

untuneful [ˌʌnˈtjuːnfʊl] **ADJ** *(song, voice)* peu mélodieux

untutored [ˌʌnˈtjuːtəd] **ADJ** *(person)* sans instruction; *(eye, ear)* inexercé; *(voice)* non travaillé; *(mind)* non formé

untwine [ˌʌnˈtwaɪn] **VT** détordre, détortiller

untwist [ˌʌnˈtwɪst] **VT** détordre

untypical [ˌʌnˈtɪpɪkəl] **ADJ** peu typique; **it's very u. of her** ce n'est pas d'elle, ça ne lui ressemble pas du tout

untypically [ˌʌnˈtɪpɪklɪ] **ADJ** anormalement; **it was an u. sunny day** il faisait anormalement beau; **u. for him, he didn't complain** il ne s'est pas plaint, ce qui n'est pas dans ses habitudes *ou* ce qui ne lui ressemble guère

unusable [ˌʌnˈjuːzəbəl] **ADJ** inutilisable

unused ADJ 1 [ˌʌnˈjuːzd] *(not in use)* inutilisé; *(new ▸ machine, material)* neuf, qui n'a pas servi; *(▸ clothing, shoes)* neuf, qui n'a pas été porté **2** [ʌnˈjuːst] *(unaccustomed)* **to be u. to sth** ne pas avoir l'habitude de qch, ne pas être habitué à qch; **I'm u. to (eating) spicy food** je n'ai pas l'habitude de manger *ou* je ne suis pas habitué à manger épicé

unusual [ʌnˈjuːʒəl] **ADJ** *(uncommon)* peu commun, inhabituel; *(odd)* insolite, étrange, bizarre; **it's u. for her to be so brusque** il est rare qu'elle soit si brusque, ça ne lui ressemble pas *ou* ce n'est pas son genre d'être aussi brusque; **it's not u. to see flooding in these parts** il n'est pas rare *ou* il arrive assez fréquemment qu'il y ait des inondations par ici; **what do you think of my new haircut? – well, it's certainly u.!** que pensestu de ma nouvelle coupe de cheveux? – ah pour ça c'est original!; **nothing u.** rien d'anormal

unusually [ʌnˈjuːʒəlɪ] **ADV 1** *(exceptionally)* exceptionnellement, extraordinairement; **she is u. intelligent** elle est d'une intelligence exceptionnelle **2** *(abnormally)* exceptionnellement, anormalement; **he was u. silent that day** il était étrangement *ou* anormalement silencieux ce jour-là; **u., it wasn't raining** chose rare, il ne pleuvait pas

unutterable [ʌnˈʌtərəbəl] **ADJ** *Formal (misery, pain)* indicible, indescriptible; *(boredom)* mortel; *(joy)* inexprimable; **he's an u. fool!** c'est vraiment un imbécile fini!

unutterably [ʌnˈʌtərəblɪ] **ADV** *Formal (miserable, tired)* terriblement, horriblement; *(happy)* extrêmement, extraordinairement; **he's u. stupid** il est d'une stupidité invraisemblable *ou* inouïe

unvaried [ʌnˈveərɪd] **ADJ** qui manque de variété, monotone; **an u. diet** une alimentation peu variée

unvarnished [ʌnˈvɑːnɪʃt] **ADJ 1** *(furniture)* non verni; *(pottery)* non vernissé **2** *Fig (plain, simple)* simple, sans fard; **the plain u. truth** la vérité pure et simple *ou* toute nue

unvarying [ˌʌnˈveərɪŋ] **ADJ** invariable, ur forme

unveil [ˌʌnˈveɪl] **VT** *(painting, statue, plaque)* d voiler, inaugurer; *(new car ▸ at a show)* prése ter; *Fig (secret, details, plans)* révéler, dévoile *(profits)* annoncer

unveiling [ˌʌnˈveɪlɪŋ] **N** *(of painting, statu plaque, car)* inauguration *f*; *Fig (of secret, detai plans)* révélation *f*; *(of profits)* annonce *f*
▸▸ ***unveiling ceremony*** (cérémonie *f* d')inaug ration *f*

unverifiable [ˌʌnˌverɪˈfaɪəbəl] **ADJ** invérifiable

unverified [ˌʌnˈverɪfaɪd] **ADJ** non vérifié

unversed [ˌʌnˈvɜːst] **ADJ** *Formal* peu versé; **to b u. in sth** être peu versé dans qch

unvoiced [ˌʌnˈvɔɪst] **ADJ 1** *(desire, objectio* inexprimé **2** *Ling (sound)* non voisé, sourd

unwaged [ˌʌnˈweɪdʒd] **ADJ** *(unsalaried)* non s larié; *(unemployed)* sans emploi, au chômage
NPL the u. les sans-emploi *mpl*

unwanted [ˌʌnˈwɒntɪd] **ADJ** *(child, pregnanc* non désiré, non souhaité; *(books, clothing)* do on n'a plus besoin, dont on veut se séparer; **hair** poils *mpl* superflus; **to feel u.** *(in the way)* s sentir de trop; *(unloved)* se sentir mal-aimé

unwarlike [ˌʌnˈwɔːlaɪk] **ADJ** non belliqueux

unwarrantable [ˌʌnˈwɒrəntəbəl] **ADJ** injus fiable

unwarrantably [ˌʌnˈwɒrəntəblɪ] **ADV** d'une m nière injustifiable

unwarranted [ˌʌnˈwɒrəntɪd] **ADJ** *(concern, cri cism)* injustifié; *(remark, interference)* déplacé

unwary [ˌʌnˈweərɪ] **ADJ** *(person, animal)* qui n'e pas méfiant *ou* sur ses gardes; **an u. reader u** lecteur non averti; **u. consumers** les consomm teurs non avertis

unwashed [ˌʌnˈwɒʃt] **ADJ** *(dishes, feet, floor)* no lavé; *(person)* qui ne s'est pas lavé
NPL *Br Hum Pej* **the great u.** la populace

unwavering [ʌnˈweɪvərɪŋ] **ADJ** *(devotion, sup port)* indéfectible, à toute épreuve; *(look)* fixe *(person)* inébranlable, ferme; **they were u. their belief** ils étaient inébranlables dans le conviction

unwaveringly [ʌnˈweɪvərɪŋlɪ] **ADV** *(believ support)* sans réserve, fermement; *(look)* fixe ment

unweaned [ˌʌnˈwiːnd] **ADJ** *(child, kitten)* non se vré

unwearable [ˌʌnˈweərəbəl] **ADJ** pas mettable

unwearying [ˌʌnˈwɪərɪŋ] **ADJ** inlassable, infat gable

unwed [ˌʌnˈwed] **ADJ** célibataire

unweighted [ˌʌnˈweɪtɪd] **ADJ** *Econ (index)* no pondéré; **u. figures** chiffres *mpl* bruts

unwelcome [ʌnˈwelkəm] **ADJ** *(advances, atte tion)* importun; *(advice)* non sollicité; *(visi* inopportun; *(visitor)* importun, gênant; *(new situation)* fâcheux; **he made his mother feel u.** a donné l'impression à sa mère qu'elle gênai **the extra £50 was not u.** les 50 livres supplémer taires ne tombaient pas mal du tout

unwell [ʌnˈwel] **ADJ** *(indisposed)* souffrant, *Fo mal* indisposé; *(ill)* malade

unwholesome [ˌʌnˈhəʊlsəm] **ADJ** *(climate)* ma sain, insalubre; *(activity, habits, thoughts)* ma sain, pernicieux; *(fascination, interest)* malsair morbide; *(drink, food)* peu sain, nocif

unwieldy [ʌnˈwiːldɪ] **ADJ 1** *(piece of furniture package)* encombrant **2** *(argument, method)* ma ladroit; *(bureaucracy, system)* lourd

unwilling [ˌʌnˈwɪlɪŋ] **ADJ** *(helper, student)* rét cent, peu enthousiaste; **he was u. to cooperate** n'était pas vraiment disposé à coopérer; **I was u that my wife should know** *or* **for my wife to know** je ne voulais pas que ma femme le sache; **I wa their u. accomplice** j'étais leur complice malgr moi *ou* à mon corps défendant

unwillingly [ˌʌnˈwɪlɪŋlɪ] **ADV** à contrecœur contre mon/son/*etc* gré

unwillingness [ˌʌnˈwɪlɪŋnɪs] **N** manque *m* d'en thousiasme, réticence *f*; **she showed her usual u to compromise** comme d'habitude, elle s'es montrée réticente à accepter le compromis

unwind [ʌn'waɪnd] *(pt & pp* **unwound** [-'waʊnd]) **VT** dérouler
VI 1 *(ball of yarn, cord)* se dérouler **2** *Fig (relax)* se détendre, se relaxer

unwise [ˌʌn'waɪz] **ADJ** *(action, decision)* peu judicieux, imprudent; **it would be u. of you to go** vous auriez tort *ou* il serait imprudent de votre part d'y aller

unwisely [ˌʌn'waɪzlɪ] **ADV** imprudemment

unwitting [ˌʌn'wɪtɪŋ] **ADJ** *Formal (accomplice)* involontaire; *(insult)* non intentionnel, involontaire

unwittingly [ˌʌn'wɪtɪŋlɪ] **ADV** involontairement, sans (le) faire exprès

unwomanly [ˌʌn'wʊmənlɪ] **ADJ** peu féminin

unwonted [ˌʌn'wəʊntɪd] **ADJ** *Formal (event)* exceptionnel; *(generosity, kindness)* inaccoutumé, inhabituel

unworkable [ˌʌn'wɜːkəbəl] **ADJ** *(idea, plan)* impraticable, impossible à réaliser; **your project is u.** votre projet ne marchera pas *ou* est infaisable

unworldliness [ˌʌn'wɜːldlɪnɪs] **N 1** *(lack of materialism)* détachement *m* de ce monde **2** *(naivety)* simplicité *f*, candeur *f*

unworldly [ˌʌn'wɜːldlɪ] **ADJ 1** *(not materialistic* ▸ *person)* détaché de ce monde, indifférent aux biens de ce monde; *(*▸ *existence)* détaché de ce monde **2** *(naive)* naïf, ingénu **3** *(otherworldly* ▸ *beauty)* surnaturel, céleste, qui n'est pas de ce monde

unworn [ˌʌn'wɔːn] **ADJ** *(clothing)* qui n'a pas été porté, (comme) neuf; *(carpet)* qui n'est pas usé

unworthiness [ˌʌn'wɜːðɪnɪs] **N** *(of person)* indignité *f*, manque *m* de mérite; *(of action)* indignité *f*

unworthy [ˌʌn'wɜːðɪ] *(compar* **unworthier**, *superl* **unworthiest)** **ADJ** *(unbefitting)* indigne; *(undeserving)* indigne, peu méritant; **he felt u. of such praise** il se croyait indigne de *ou* il ne croyait pas mériter de telles louanges; **such behaviour is u. of you!** une telle conduite est indigne de vous!; **such details are u. of her attention** de tels détails ne méritent pas son attention

unwounded [ˌʌn'wuːndɪd] **ADJ** non blessé, indemne

unwrap [ˌʌn'ræp] *(pt & pp* **unwrapped**, *cont* **unwrapping)** **VT** *(parcel)* défaire; *(goods)* déballer

unwritten [ˌʌn'rɪtən] **ADJ** *(legend, story)* non écrit; *(agreement)* verbal, tacite; **an u. rule** une règle tacitement admise
▸▸ *Law* **unwritten law** droit *m* coutumier

unyielding [ˌʌn'jiːldɪŋ] **ADJ** *(ground, material)* très dur; *(person)* inflexible, intransigeant; *(determination, principles)* inébranlable

unyoke [ˌʌn'jəʊk] **VT** dételer

unzip [ˌʌn'zɪp] *(pt & pp* **unzipped**, *cont* **unzipping)** **VT 1** *(garment, bag etc)* défaire la fermeture Éclair® de **2** *Comput (file)* dézipper, décompresser
VI it unzips at the side il y a une fermeture Éclair® sur le côté

UP [juː'piː] **N** *(abbr* **unit price)** PU *m*

UP [ʌp] *(pt & pp* **upped**, *cont* **upping)** **ADV A. 1** *(towards a higher position or level)* en haut; **all the way up, the whole way up, right up (to the top)** *(of stairs, hill)* jusqu'en haut; **he's on his way up** il monte; **hang it higher up** accrochez-le plus haut; *Fam* **he doesn't have very much up top** c'est pas une lumière, il a pas inventé l'eau chaude *ou* le fil à couper le beurre; *Fam* **she's got plenty up top** elle en a dans le ciboulot
2 *(in a higher position, at a higher level)* **she wears her hair up** elle porte ses cheveux relevés; **hold your head up high!** redressez la tête!; **heads up!** attention!; **up above** au-dessus; **the glasses are up above the plates** les verres sont au-dessus des assiettes; **up in the air** en l'air; **look at the kite up in the sky** regardez le cerf-volant (là-haut) dans le ciel; **I live eight floors up** j'habite au huitième (étage); **she lives three floors up from us** elle habite trois étages au-dessus de chez nous; **she's up in her room** elle est en haut dans sa chambre; **we spend our holidays up in the mountains** nous passons nos vacances à la montagne; **from up on the mountain** du haut de la montagne; **do you see her up on that hill?** la voyez-vous en haut de *ou* sur cette colline?; **what are you doing up there?** qu'est-ce que vous faites là-haut?; **the captain is up on deck** le capitaine est en haut sur le pont; **have you ever been up in a plane?** avez-vous déjà pris l'avion?; **up the top** tout en haut; **it's up on top of the wardrobe** c'est sur le dessus de l'armoire; *Fig* **she's up there with the best (of them)** elle est parmi *ou* dans les meilleurs
3 *(in a raised position)* levé; **Charles has his hand up** Charles a la main levée; **put your hood up** relève *ou* mets ta capuche; **she turned her collar up** elle a relevé son col
4 *(into an upright position)* debout; **up you get!** debout!; **he helped me up** il m'a aidé à me lever *ou* à me mettre debout; *Fam* **up and at them!** grouillez-vous!
5 *(out of bed)* **get up!** debout!; **she got up late this morning** elle s'est levée tard ce matin; **she's always up and doing** elle n'arrête jamais
6 *(facing upwards)* **the body was lying face up** le corps était couché sur le dos; **I turned the poster right side up** j'ai mis l'affiche dans le bon sens *ou* à l'endroit; **put it the other way up** retournez-le; **he turned his hand palm up** il a tourné la main paume vers le haut; **fragile – this way up** *(on packaging)* fragile – haut
7 *(erected, installed)* **they're putting up a new hotel there** ils construisent un nouvel hôtel là-bas; **help me get the curtains/the pictures up** aide-moi à accrocher les rideaux/les tableaux
8 *(on wall)* **up on the blackboard** au tableau; **I saw an announcement up about it** je l'ai vu sur une affiche
9 *(removed)* **careful, we've got some of the floorboards up** attention au plancher, il manque des lattes; **when we've got the carpet up…** quand nous aurons enlevé la moquette…
B. 1 *(towards north)* **they came up for the weekend** ils sont venus pour le week-end; **it's cold up here** il fait froid ici; **up there** là-bas; **up north** dans le nord
2 *(in, to or from a larger place)* **up in Madrid** à Madrid; **she's up in Maine for the week** elle passe une semaine dans le Maine; **we're up from Munich** nous venons *ou* arrivons de Munich
3 *Br (at university)* **he's up at Oxford** il est à Oxford
4 *(further)* **there's a café up ahead** il y a un café plus loin; **the sign up ahead says 10 miles** la pancarte là-bas indique 10 miles
5 *(in phrasal verbs)* **the clerk came up to him** le vendeur s'est approché de lui *ou* est venu vers lui; **a car drew up at the petrol pump** une voiture s'est arrêtée à la pompe à essence; **up came a small, blonde child** un petit enfant blond s'est approché
6 *(close to)* **up close** de près; **I like to sit up front** j'aime bien m'asseoir devant; **when you get right up to her** quand vous la voyez de près; **they stood up close to one another** ils se tenaient l'un contre l'autre *ou* tout près l'un de l'autre
C. *(towards a higher level)* **the temperature soared up into the thirties** la température est montée au-dessus de trente degrés; **they can cost anything from £750 up** ils coûtent au moins 750 livres, on en trouve à partir de 750 livres; **suitable for children aged seven and up** convient aux enfants âgés de sept ans et plus; **all ranks from sergeant up** tous les rangs à partir de celui de sergent
D. *Fam (indicating support)* **up (with) the Revolution!** vive la Révolution!; *Sport* **up the Lakers!** allez les Lakers!
ADJ A. 1 *(at or moving towards higher level)* haut; **the river is up** le fleuve est en crue; **the tide is up** la marée est haute; **before the sun was up** avant le lever du soleil; **prices are up on last year** les prix ont augmenté par rapport à l'année dernière; **the temperature is up in the twenties** la température a dépassé les vingt degrés
2 *(in a raised position)* levé; **the blinds are up** les stores sont levés; **keep the windows up** *(in car)* n'ouvrez pas les fenêtres; **her hair was up (in a bun)** elle avait un chignon; **her hood was up so I couldn't see her face** sa capuche était relevée, si bien que je ne voyais pas sa figure; *Fig* **his defences were up** il était sur ses gardes
3 *(in an upwards direction)* **the up escalator** l'escalier roulant qui monte
4 *Br Rail (heading for a larger city)* **the up train** le train qui va en ville; **the up platform** le quai où l'on prend le train qui va en ville
5 *(out of bed)* **is she up yet?** est-elle déjà levée *ou* debout?; **we're normally up at 6** d'habitude nous nous levons à 6 heures; **she was up late last night** elle s'est couchée *ou* elle a veillé tard hier soir; **they were up all night** ils ne se sont pas couchés de la nuit, ils ont passé une nuit blanche
6 *(in tennis)* **was the ball up?** la balle était-elle bonne?
B. 1 *(road)* en travaux; **road up** *(sign)* travaux
2 *(erected, installed)* **these buildings haven't been up long** ça ne fait pas longtemps que ces immeubles ont été construits; **are the new curtains up yet?** les nouveaux rideaux ont-ils été posés?; **when the tent's up** quand la tente sera montée
3 *(on wall)* **are the results up yet?** les résultats sont-ils déjà affichés?
C. 1 *(finished, at an end)* terminé; **time is up!** *(on exam, visit)* c'est l'heure!; *(in game, on meter)* le temps est écoulé!; **when the month was up he left** à la fin du mois, il est parti
2 *(ahead) Sport* **Madrid was two goals up** Madrid menait de deux buts; *Sport* **Georgetown was 13 points up on Baltimore** Georgetown avait 13 points d'avance sur Baltimore; *Golf* **to be one hole up** avoir un trou d'avance; *Fam* **I'm $50 up on you** j'ai 50 dollars de plus que vous❑; *Fam* **to be one up on sb** avoir un avantage sur qn❑
3 *Fam (ready)* prêt❑; **dinner's up** le dîner est prêt
4 *(in operation)* **the computer's up again** l'ordinateur fonctionne à nouveau
D. 1 *Fam (cheerful)* gai❑; **he seemed very up when I saw him** il avait l'air en pleine forme quand je l'ai vu
2 *(well-informed)* **to be up on sth** être au fait de qch❑; **he's really up on history** il est fort *ou* calé en histoire❑; **she's always up with the latest trends** elle est toujours au courant de la dernière mode❑
E. 1 to be up *(before an authority)* comparaître; **to be up before a court/a judge** comparaître devant un tribunal/un juge; **she's up before the board tomorrow** elle comparaît devant le conseil demain
2 *Fam (idioms)* **something's up** *(happening)* il se passe quelque chose❑; *(wrong)* quelque chose ne va pas❑; **what's up?** *(happening)* qu'est-ce qui se passe?❑; *(wrong)* qu'est-ce qu'il y a?❑; *Am (as greeting)* quoi de neuf?; **what's up with you?** *(happening)* quoi de neuf?; *(wrong)* qu'est-ce que tu as?❑; **something's up with Mum** il y a quelque chose qui ne va pas chez maman❑, maman a quelque chose❑; **there's something up with the TV** la télé débloque
PREP 1 *(indicating motion to a higher place or level)* **we carried our suitcases up the stairs** nous avons monté nos valises; **he ran up the stairs** il a monté l'escalier en courant; **she was up and down the stairs all day** elle montait et descendait les escaliers toute la journée; **I climbed up the ladder** je suis monté à l'échelle; **the cat climbed up the tree** le chat a grimpé dans l'arbre; **the smoke went up my nose** la fumée m'est montée par le nez; **the gas goes up this pipe** le gaz monte par ce tuyau; **further up the wall** plus haut sur le mur; *Literary* **up hill and down dale** par monts et par vaux
2 *(at or to the top of)* **her flat is up those stairs** son appartement est en haut de cet escalier; **the cat is up a tree** le chat est (perché) sur un arbre; **we walked up the street** nous avons monté la rue; **she pointed up the street** elle a montré le haut de la rue; **she lives up this street** elle habite dans cette rue; **the café is just up the road** le café se trouve plus loin *ou* plus haut dans la rue
3 *(towards the source of)* **up the river** en amont; **a voyage up the Amazon** une remontée de l'Amazone
4 *Br Fam (at, to)* à❑; **he's up the pub** il est au pub; **I'm going up the shops** je vais faire les courses❑
5 *Br very Fam* **he's a good-looking guy but he's totally up himself** c'est un beau mec, mais il ne se prend pas pour de la merde
6 *(idiom) Br very Fam* **up yours!** va te faire voir!
VT 1 *(increase)* augmenter; **they have upped their**

prices by 25 percent ils ont augmenté leurs prix de 25 pour cent; *also Fig* **to up the stakes** monter la mise

2 *(promote)* lever, relever; **the boss upped him to district manager** le patron l'a bombardé directeur régional

3 *(idiom)* **to up sticks** plier bagages

VI *Fam* **she upped and left** elle a fichu le camp; **he just upped and hit him** tout à coup il (s'est levé et) l'a frappé; **he upped and married her** en moins de deux, il l'a épousée

N 1 *(high point)* haut *m*; **ups and downs** *(in land, road)* accidents *mpl*; *(of market)* fluctuations *fpl*; **I've had a lot of ups and downs in my life** j'ai connu des hauts et des bas; **we all have our ups and downs** nous avons tous des hauts et des bas

2 *(increase)* **the market is on the up** le marché est à la hausse; **prices are on the up** les prix sont en hausse

3 *Fam (drug)* amphet *f*, amphé *f*

• **up against** **PREP 1** *(touching)* contre; **lean the ladder up against the window** appuyez l'échelle contre la fenêtre

2 *(in competition or conflict with)* **you're up against some good candidates** vous êtes en compétition avec de bons candidats; **they don't know what they're up against!** ils ne se rendent pas compte de ce qui les attend!; *Fam* **to be up against it** être dans le pétrin

• **up and about, up and around** **ADJ** **I've been up and about since 7 o'clock** *(gen)* je suis levé depuis 7 heures; **so you're up and about again?** *(after illness)* alors tu n'es plus alité?

• **up and down** **ADV 1** *(upwards and downwards)* **he was jumping up and down** il sautait sur place; **she looked us up and down** elle nous a regardés de haut en bas; **the bottle bobbed up and down on the waves** la bouteille montait et descendait sur les vagues; **I was up and down all night** *(in and out of bed)* je n'ai pas arrêté de me lever la nuit dernière

2 *(to and fro)* de long en large; **I could hear him walking up and down** je l'entendais faire les cent pas *ou* marcher de long en large; **she walked up and down the platform** elle faisait les cent pas sur le quai

3 *(in all parts of)* **up and down the country** dans tout le pays

• **up for** **PREP 1** *(under consideration, about to undergo)* à; **the house is up for sale** la maison est à vendre; **the project is up for discussion** on va discuter du projet; **she's up for election** elle est candidate *ou* elle se présente aux élections

2 *(due to be tried for)* **he's up for murder/speeding** il va être jugé pour meurtre/excès de vitesse

3 *Fam (interested in, ready for)* **are you still up for supper tonight?** tu veux toujours qu'on dîne ensemble ce soir?; **he's up for anything** il est toujours partant

• **up front** **ADV** *(pay)* en avance

• **up to** **PREP 1** *(as far as)* jusqu'à; **he can count up to 100** il sait compter jusqu'à 100; **the river is up to 25 feet wide** le fleuve a jusqu'à 25 pieds de largeur; **the bus can take up to 50 passengers** le bus peut accueillir jusqu'à 50 passagers; **I'm up to page 120** j'en suis à la page 120; **up to and including Saturday** jusqu'à samedi inclus; **up to here** jusqu'ici; **up to** *or* **up until now** jusqu'à maintenant, jusqu'ici; **up to** *or* **up until then** jusqu'alors, jusque-là; **we were up to our knees in mud** nous avions de la boue jusqu'aux genoux

2 *(the decision of)* **should he attend the meeting? – that's up to him** est-ce qu'il doit assister à la réunion? – il fait ce qu'il veut *ou* c'est à lui de voir; **which film do you fancy? – it's up to you** quel film est-ce que tu veux voir? – c'est comme tu veux; **it's entirely up to you whether you go or not** il ne tient qu'à toi de rester ou de partir; **if it were up to me...** si c'était moi qui décidais *ou* à moi de décider...; **it's up to them to pay damages** *(their responsibility)* c'est à eux *ou* il leur appartient de payer les dégâts

3 *(capable of)* **to be up to doing sth** être capable de faire qch; **my German is not up to translating novels** mon niveau d'allemand ne me permet pas de traduire des romans; **he's not up to it** *(not good enough)* il n'est pas capable de le faire; **are you going out tonight? – no, I don't feel up to it** tu sors ce soir? – non, je ne me sens pas assez en forme; **he's not up to the journey** il n'est pas à même de faire le voyage; **are you up to working** *or* **to work?** êtes-vous capable de *ou* en état de travailler?; **I'm not up to going back to work** je ne suis pas encore en état de reprendre le travail; *Fam* **the football team isn't up to much** l'équipe de foot ne vaut pas grand-chose; *Fam* **I don't feel up to much** je ne me sens pas en super forme

4 *(as good as)* **his work is not up to his normal standard** son travail n'est pas aussi bon que d'habitude; **the levels are up to standard** les niveaux sont conformes aux normes; **I don't feel up to par** je ne me sens pas en forme

5 *(engaged in, busy with)* **let's see what she's up to** allons voir ce qu'elle fait *ou* fabrique; **what have you been up to lately?** qu'est-ce que tu deviens?; **what's he been up to now?** qu'est-ce qu'il a encore inventé?; **what's he up to with that ladder?** qu'est-ce qu'il fabrique avec cette échelle?; **what are you up to with my girlfriend?** qu'est-ce que tu lui veux à ma copine?; **they're up to something** ils manigancent quelque chose; **she's up to no good** elle prépare un mauvais coup; **the things we got up to in our youth!** qu'est-ce qu'on *ou* ce qu'on ne faisait pas quand on était jeunes!

►► *Comput* ***up arrow*** flèche *f* vers le haut; ***up arrow key*** touche *f* de déplacement vers le haut

---

up-and-coming **ADJ** *(athlete, star, politician)* qui monte; **the u. generation of politicians** la nouvelle génération d'hommes politiques

up-and-down **ADJ 1** *(movement)* qui monte et qui descend, ascendant et descendant **2** *(unstable)* **his career has been very u.** sa carrière a connu des hauts et des bas; *Br* **I've been very u. lately** j'ai eu des hauts et des bas ces derniers temps

up-and-over **ADJ**

►► ***up-and-over door*** porte *f* basculante *(d'un garage etc)*

up-and-under **N** *(in rugby)* chandelle *f*

upbeat ['ʌpbi:t] **ADJ** *(mood, person)* optimiste; *(music)* entraînant

N *Mus* levé *m*

upbraid [ˌʌp'breɪd] **VT** *Formal* réprimander

upbringing ['ʌpbrɪŋɪŋ] **N** éducation *f*; **he had a strict u.** il a eu une éducation très stricte

upchuck ['ʌpˌtʃʌk] **VI** *Fam Hum* dégobiller, dégueuler

upcoming ['ʌpˌkʌmɪŋ] **ADJ** *(event)* à venir, prochain; *(book)* à paraître, qui va paraître; *(film)* qui va sortir; **Ford's u. film** le prochain film de Ford; **the u. elections** les élections qui vont bientôt avoir lieu

►► ***upcoming attractions*** *(film, theatre advertisement)* prochainement

up-country **ADJ** *(inland)* de l'intérieur; *Pej (unsophisticated)* provincial

N intérieur *m*

ADV *(go, move)* vers l'intérieur; *(live)* dans l'intérieur

update **VT** [ˌʌp'deɪt] *(information, record)* mettre à jour; *Comput (computer software)* mettre à jour, actualiser; *(army, system)* moderniser; *(person)* mettre au courant; **could you u. me on what's been happening?** pourriez-vous me mettre au courant de ce qui s'est passé?; **it hasn't been updated since 1933** il n'a pas été remis à jour depuis 1933

N ['ʌpdeɪt] *(of information, record)* mise *f* à jour; *Comput (of software package)* mise *f* à jour, actualisation *f*; *(of army, system)* modernisation *f*; **an u. on the situation** une mise au point sur la situation; **to give sb an u. on sth** mettre qn au courant de qch

updating [ˌʌp'deɪtɪŋ] **N** mise *f* à jour

updo ['ʌpdu:] *(pl* **updos***)* **N** *Fam* coiffure *f* en hauteur

up-draught, *Am* **up-draft** **N** *Aviat* courant *m* d'air ascendant

upend [ˌʌp'end] **VT 1** *(object)* mettre debout; *(person)* mettre la tête en bas **2** *Fig (upset)* bouleverser

upfront [ˌʌp'frʌnt] **ADJ** *Fam* **1** *(frank* ► *person)* franc (franche), ouvert; *(*► *remark)* franc (franche), direct **2** *(payment)* d'avance

upgradability ['ʌpˌgreɪdə'bɪlɪtɪ] **N** *Comput* possibilités *fpl* d'extension

upgradable [ˌʌp'greɪdəbəl] **ADJ** *Comput (hardware, system)* évolutif; *(memory)* extensible

upgrade **VT** [ˌʌp'greɪd] **1** *(improve)* améliorer; *(increase)* augmenter; **I was upgraded to business class** *(on plane)* on m'a mis en classe affaires **2** *Comput (system)* optimiser; *(software)* améliorer, perfectionner; *(hardware)* mettre à niveau **3** *(job)* revaloriser; *(employee)* promouvoir; **I was upgraded** je suis monté en grade; **she was upgraded to sales manager** elle a été promue directrice des ventes

VI [ˌʌp'greɪd] **we've upgraded to a more powerful system** on est passés à un système plus puissant

N ['ʌpgreɪd] **1** *Am (slope)* pente *f* ascendante; *(on railway line)* montée *f*

2 *Comput (of software)* mise *f* à jour, actualisation *f*; *(of hardware, system)* mise *f* à niveau

3 *(on plane)* **I managed to get an u. to business class** j'ai réussi à obtenir une place en classe affaires

4 *(idiom)* **to be on the u.** *(price, salary)* augmenter, être en hausse; *(business, venture)* progresser, être en bonne voie; *(sick person)* être en voie de guérison; **his career is on the u.** sa carrière est en bonne voie

►► ***upgrade kit*** ensemble *m* de mise à niveau

upgradeability, upgradeable = **upgradability, upgradable**

upgrading [ˌʌp'greɪdɪŋ] **N 1** *(of system)* amélioration *f*; *(of person)* avancement *m* **2** *Comput (of software)* mise *f* à jour, actualisation *f*; *(of hardware, system)* mise *f* à niveau

upheaval [ˌʌp'hi:vəl] **N** *(emotional, political etc)* bouleversement *m*; *(social unrest)* agitation *f*, perturbations *fpl*; **the war brought a lot of u.** la guerre a entraîné de nombreux bouleversements

uphill [ˌʌp'hɪl] **ADJ 1** *(road, slope)* qui monte; **it's u. all the way** ça monte tout le long du chemin; *Fig* c'est une lutte permanente **2** *Fig (task)* ardu, pénible; *(battle)* rude, acharné; **it was an u. struggle convincing him** j'ai eu beaucoup de mal à le convaincre

ADV **to go u.** *(car, person)* monter (la côte); *(road)* monter; **to ski u.** skier en amont

►► ***uphill ski*** ski *m* amont

uphold [ˌʌp'həʊld] *(pt & pp* **upheld** [-'held]*)* **VT** *(right)* défendre, faire respecter; *(law, rule)* faire respecter *ou* observer **2** *Law (conviction, decision)* maintenir, confirmer

upholder [ˌʌp'həʊldə(r)] **N** défenseur *m*; **an u. of law and order** un défenseur de l'ordre public

upholster [ˌʌp'həʊlstə(r)] **VT** *(cover)* recouvrir, tapisser; *(pad)* capitonner, rembourrer; **upholstered in leather** garni de cuir; *Hum* **to be well upholstered** être bien rembourré

upholsterer [ˌʌp'həʊlstərə(r)] **N** tapissier(ère) *m,f (en ameublement)*

upholstery [ˌʌp'həʊlstərɪ] **N** *(UNCOUNT)* *(covering* ► *fabric)* tissu *m* d'ameublement; *(padding)* capitonnage *m*, rembourrage *m*; *(*► *leather)* cuir *m*; *(*► *in car)* garniture *f* **2** *(trade)* tapisserie *f*

►► ***upholstery tack*** clou *m* de tapissier

UPI [ju:pi:'aɪ] **N** *(abbr* **United Press International***)* UPI *f (agence de presse)*

upkeep ['ʌpki:p] **N** *(UNCOUNT)* *(maintenance)* entretien *m*; *(cost)* frais *mpl* d'entretien; **he pays nothing towards the u. of the children** il ne donne pas d'argent pour subvenir aux besoins matériels des enfants

upland ['ʌplənd] **N** **the u.** *or* **uplands** les hautes terres *fpl*

ADJ *(landscape, stream, farm)* de montagne; **u. areas** hautes terres *fpl*

uplift **VT** [ʌp'lɪft] *(person* ► *spiritually)* élever (l'âme de); *(*► *morally)* édifier; **to u. sb's spirits** remonter le moral à qn, redonner du cœur à qn; **he was uplifted by the news** la nouvelle lui a remonté le moral *ou* lui a redonné du cœur

N ['ʌplɪft] **1** *(in the economy)* nouvel essort *m* **2** *(person)* **spiritual u.** élévation *f* de l'esprit; **moral** édification *f* **3** *Geol* soulèvement *m*

►► ***uplift bra*** soutien-gorge *m* de maintien

uplifted [ʌp'lɪftɪd] ADJ **1** *(hand)* levé **2** *(person)* **she was spiritually u.** cela lui a élevé l'âme; **they left the cinema feeling u.** ils se sentaient plus gais en sortant du cinéma

uplifting [ʌp'lɪftɪŋ] ADJ *(experience, sermon)* édifiant; *(film, book)* qui remonte le moral

uplighter ['ʌplaɪtə(r)] N = applique ou lampadaire diffusant la lumière vers le haut

uplink ['ʌplɪŋk] N *TV* liaison *f* montante
▸▸ ***uplink receiver*** récepteur *m* de liaison terre/satellite

upload *Comput* N ['ʌpləʊd] téléchargement *m* *(vers le serveur)*
VT [ʌp'ləʊd] télécharger *(vers le serveur)*

upmarket ADJ ['ʌpmɑːkɪt] *(goods, service)* haut de gamme, de première qualité; *(restaurant)* haut de gamme; *(neighbourhood)* riche; *(newspaper, television programme)* qui vise un public cultivé; *(audience)* cultivé
ADV [ˌʌp'mɑːkɪt] **to move u.** *(company)* se repositionner à la hausse; **she's moved u.** elle fait dans le haut de gamme maintenant

upmost ['ʌpməʊst] = **uppermost**

upon [ə'pɒn] PREP **1** *Formal (indicating position or place)* **u. the grass/the table** sur la pelouse/la table; **she had a sad look u. her face** elle avait l'air triste; **the ring u. her finger** la bague à son doigt
2 *Formal (indicating person or thing affected)* **attacks u. old people are on the increase** les attaques contre les personnes âgées sont de plus en plus fréquentes; **you brought it u. yourself** ne t'en prends qu'à toi-même!
3 *Formal (immediately after)* à; **u. our arrival in Rome** à notre arrivée à Rome; **u. hearing the news, he rang home** lorsqu'il a appris la nouvelle, il a appelé chez lui; **u. request** sur simple demande
4 *(indicating large amount)* et; **mile u. mile of desert** des kilomètres et des kilomètres de désert; **we receive thousands u. thousands of offers each year** nous recevons plusieurs milliers de propositions chaque année
5 *(indicating imminence)* **the holidays are nearly u. us** les vacances approchent
6 *(idiom) Old-fashioned* **u. my word!** ma parole!

upper ['ʌpə(r)] ADJ **1** *(physically higher)* supérieur, plus haut *ou* élevé; *(top)* du dessus, du haut; **temperatures are in the u. 30s** la température atteint presque les 40 degrés; **the u. atmosphere** les couches supérieures de l'atmosphère; **companies operating at the u. end of the market** sociétés spécialisées dans le haut de gamme; **to have the u. hand** avoir le dessus; **to get** *or* **to gain the u. hand** prendre le dessus *ou* l'avantage; **to let sb get the u. hand** laisser qn prendre le dessus, laisser qn dominer
2 *(higher in order, rank)* supérieur; **the u. echelons of the civil service** les plus hauts échelons de l'administration
3 *Geog (inland)* haut; **the u. valley of the Nile** la haute vallée du Nil; **the u. Rhine** le haut Rhin
N **1** *(of shoe)* empeigne *f*; *Br Fam* **to be on one's uppers** manger de la vache enragée, être fauché
2 *Fam Drugs slang* amphé *f*
▸▸ ***Upper Canada*** le Haut-Canada; ***upper case*** *Typ* haut *m* de casse; *Comput* majuscule *f*; ***the upper class, the upper classes*** = l'aristocratie et la haute bourgeoisie; ***Upper Egypt*** la Haute-Égypte; *Parl* ***the Upper House*** *(gen)* la Chambre haute; *(the House of Lords)* la Chambre des lords; ***upper limit*** plafond *m*; ***upper lip*** lèvre *f* supérieure; ***upper middle class*** = classe sociale réunissant les professions libérales, les universitaires, les cadres de l'industrie et les hauts fonctionnaires; ***upper reaches*** *(of river)* amont *m*; *Br* ***the upper school*** les grandes classes *fpl*; *Br Sch* ***upper sixth*** terminale *f*

upper-case ADJ **an u. letter** une majuscule

upper-class ADJ **1** *(accent, family)* aristocratique **2** *Am Univ (student)* = de troisième ou quatrième année
▸▸ *Fam Pej* ***upper-class twit*** = aristocrate bête et prétentieux

upper-crust ADJ *Fam* aristo, de la haute

uppercut ['ʌpəkʌt] *(pt & pp* **uppercut,** *cont* **uppercutting)** N uppercut *m*
VT frapper d'un uppercut

uppermost ['ʌpəməʊst] ADJ **1** *(part, side)* le plus haut *ou* élevé; *(drawer, storey)* du haut, du dessus **2** *(most prominent)* le plus important; **it's not u. in my mind** ce n'est pas ma préoccupation essentielle en ce moment; **human rights are u. on his list of priorities** les droits de l'homme sont en tête de ses priorités

uppity ['ʌpɪtɪ], **uppish** ['ʌpɪʃ] ADJ *Fam* bêcheur, arrogant▫; **he's getting very u.** il se croit quelqu'un; **don't you get u. with me!** ne joue pas les arrogants avec moi!

upright ['ʌpraɪt] ADJ **1** *(erect)* droit **2** *(honest)* droit, honnête
ADV **1** *(sit, stand)* droit; **he sat bolt u.** il se redressa (sur son siège) **2** *(put)* droit, debout; **to put** *or* **to stand sth u.** mettre qch debout *ou* d'aplomb
N **1** *(of door, bookshelf)* montant *m*, portant *m*; *(of goal post)* montant *m* du but; *Archit* pied-droit *m* **2** *(piano)* piano *m* droit
▸▸ ***upright freezer*** congélateur *m* armoire; ***upright piano*** piano *m* droit; ***upright vacuum cleaner*** aspirateur-balai *m*

uprightly ['ʌpraɪtlɪ] ADV droitement, honnêtement

uprightness ['ʌpraɪtnɪs] N droiture *f*, honnêteté *f*

uprising ['ʌpˌraɪzɪŋ] N soulèvement *m*, révolte *f*

uproar ['ʌprɔː(r)] N *(noise)* tumulte *m*, vacarme *m*; *(protest)* protestations *fpl*, tollé *m*; **his speech caused quite an u.** *(protests)* son discours a déclenché un tollé; *(shouting)* son discours a déclenché le tumulte; **the town was in (an) u. over the new taxes** la ville entière s'est élevée contre le nouvel impôt

uproarious [ʌp'rɔːrɪəs] ADJ *(crowd, group)* hilare; *(film, joke)* hilarant, désopilant; *(laughter)* tonitruant

uproariously [ʌp'rɔːrɪəslɪ] ADV *(laugh)* aux éclats; **u. funny** désopilant, tordant

uproot [ˌʌp'ruːt] VT *also Fig* déraciner; **to feel uprooted** se sentir déraciné

UPS [juːpiː'es] N *Comput (abbr* **uninterruptible power supply)** onduleur *m*

upset *(pt & pp* **upset,** *cont* **upsetting)** VT [ʌp'set] **1** *(overturn ▸ chair, pan)* renverser; *(▸ milk, paint)* renverser, répandre; *(▸ boat)* faire chavirer
2 *(disturb ▸ plans, routine)* bouleverser, déranger; *(▸ procedure)* bouleverser; *(▸ calculations, results)* fausser; *(▸ balance)* rompre, fausser
3 *(person ▸ annoy)* contrarier, ennuyer; *(▸ offend)* fâcher, vexer; *(▸ worry)* inquiéter, tracasser; *(▸ distress)* faire de la peine à, blesser; **the least little thing upsets her** un rien la contrarie; **it's not worth upsetting yourself over** ce n'est pas la peine de te mettre dans tous tes états
4 *(make ill ▸ stomach)* déranger; *(▸ person)* rendre malade; **seafood always upsets me** *or* **my stomach** les fruits de mer me rendent toujours malade
ADJ [ʌp'set] **1** *(annoyed)* contrarié, ennuyé; *(offended)* vexé, fâché; *(worried)* inquiet(ète); *(grieved)* peiné; *(distressed)* bouleversé; **there's no reason to get so u.** il n'y a pas de quoi en faire un drame; **he's u. about losing the deal** il est contrarié d'avoir perdu l'affaire; **I was most u. that she left** j'ai été très peiné qu'elle parte; **what are you so u. about?** qu'est-ce qui te met dans cet état?; **she was clearly u. by the pictures** *(distraught, moved)* ces images l'avaient manifestement bouleversée
2 *(stomach)* dérangé; **to have an u. stomach** avoir une indigestion
N ['ʌpset] **1** *(in plans)* bouleversement *m*; *(of government)* renversement *m*; *(of team)* défaite *f*; **the result caused a major political u.** le résultat a entraîné de grands bouleversements politiques
2 *(emotional)* bouleversement *m*
3 *(of stomach)* indigestion *f*; **he often gets stomach upsets** il a souvent des indigestions
▸▸ *Am & Scot* ***upset price*** mise *f* à prix

upsetting [ʌp'setɪŋ] ADJ *(annoying)* ennuyeux, contrariant; *(offensive)* vexant; *(saddening)* attristant, triste; *(worrying)* inquiétant; *(disturbing)* perturbant, troublant; *(more seriously)* bouleversant; **viewers might find some of these scenes u.** certaines des scènes qui vont suivre peuvent être de nature à perturber les téléspectateurs; **I didn't find the experience in the least u.** l'expérience ne m'a pas du tout perturbé

upshift ['ʌpʃɪft] N *(of gears)* passage *m* à la vitesse supérieure

upshot ['ʌpʃɒt] N résultat *m*, conséquence *f*; **what will be the u. of it?** cela finira comment?; **the u. of it all was that he resigned** le résultat, c'est qu'il a donné sa démission

upside ['ʌpsaɪd] N **1** *(surface)* dessus *m* **2** *(of situation)* avantage *m*, bon côté *m*

upside down ADJ **1** *(cup, glass)* à l'envers, retourné; *(person, animal)* la tête en bas **2** *(room, house)* sens dessus dessous
ADV **1** *(in inverted fashion)* à l'envers; **she hung u. from the bar** elle s'est suspendue à la barre la tête en bas; **to read sth u.** lire qch à l'envers **2** *(in disorderly fashion)* sens dessus dessous; **we turned the house u. looking for the keys** nous avons mis la maison sens dessus dessous en cherchant les clés; **the news turned our world u.** la nouvelle a bouleversé notre univers
▸▸ ***upside down cake*** gâteau *m* renversé; *Fig* ***upside down logic*** raisonnement *m* tordu

upstage [ˌʌp'steɪdʒ] ADV *(move)* vers le fond de la scène; *(enter, exit)* par le fond de la scène; *(stand)* au fond de la scène
VT *Fig* éclipser, voler la vedette à

upstairs ADV [ˌʌp'steəz] **1** *(on or to higher level)* en haut, à l'étage; **there are three bedrooms u.** il y a trois chambres en haut *ou* à l'étage; **to go u.** monter (à l'étage); **she ran back u.** elle est remontée en courant; **he chased me u.** il m'a poursuivi dans l'escalier; **I'll take your bags u.** je monterai vos bagages; *Fam Fig* **he hasn't got much u.** il n'a pas grand-chose dans le crâne **2** *(in house with masters and servants)* chez les maîtres
ADJ ['ʌpsteəz] *(room, window)* du haut, (situé) à l'étage; *(flat, neighbour)* du dessus
N ['ʌpsteəz] étage *m*; **we rent out the u.** nous louons (les pièces de) l'étage

upstanding [ˌʌp'stændɪŋ] ADJ **1** *(in character)* intègre, droit; *(in build)* bien bâti; **a fine u. young man** un jeune homme bien comme il faut **2** *Formal (on one's feet)* **be u.** levez-vous

upstart ['ʌpstɑːt] N *Pej* parvenu(e) *m,f*; **that young u.!** ce petit morveux!

upstate [ˌʌp'steɪt] *Am* ADV *(live)* dans le nord (de l'État); *(move)* vers le nord (de l'État); **he moved u.** il est allé s'installer dans le nord (de l'État)
ADJ au nord (de l'État); **u. New York** = la partie nord de l'État de New York

upstream [ˌʌp'striːm] ADV **1** *(live)* en amont; *(move)* vers l'amont; *(row, swim)* contre le courant **2** *Econ* en amont
ADJ **1** *(gen)* d'amont, (situé) en amont **2** *Econ* en amont

upstroke ['ʌpstrəʊk] N *(of pen)* délié *m*; *(of piston)* mouvement *m* ascendant

upsurge ['ʌpsɜːdʒ] N *(gen)* mouvement *m* vif; *(of anger, enthusiasm)* vague *f*, montée *f*; *(of interest)* recrudescence *f*, regain *m*; *(in production, sales)* forte augmentation *f*

upswept ['ʌpswept] ADJ **1** *Aut & Aviat* profilé **2** *(hairstyle)* en hauteur

upswing ['ʌpswɪŋ] N **1** *(movement)* mouvement *m* ascendant, montée *f* **2** *(improvement)* amélioration *f*, **the stock market is on the u.** la Bourse est en hausse; **there's been an u. in sales** il y a eu une progression des ventes

uptake ['ʌpteɪk] N **1** *(of air)* admission *f*; *(of water)* prise *f*, adduction *f*; *Physiol (of oxygen, calcium etc)* assimilation *f* **2** *(of offer, allowance)* **a campaign to improve the u. of child benefit** une campagne pour inciter les gens à réclamer leurs allocations familiales **3** *(idioms)* **to be quick on the u.** avoir l'esprit vif *ou* rapide, comprendre vite; **to be slow on the u.** être lent à comprendre *ou* à saisir

uptight [ˌʌp'taɪt] ADJ *Fam* **1** *(tense)* tendu▫, crispé; *(irritable)* irritable▫, énervé▫; *(nervous)* nerveux▫, inquiet(ète)▫; **he gets so u. whenever I mention it** il se crispe chaque fois que j'en parle; *(annoyed)* il s'énerve chaque fois que j'en parle **2** *(repressed, prudish)* coincé, collet monté *(inv)*; **he's very u. about sex** il est très coincé quand il s'agit de sexe

up-to-date ADJ **1** *(information, report ▸ updated)* à jour; *(▸ most current)* le plus récent; **I try to keep u. on** *or* **with the news** j'essaie de me tenir au courant de l'actualité; **to bring sb u. on** *or* **with sth** mettre qn au courant de qch; **they brought the reports u.** ils ont mis les rapports à jour **2** *(modern ▸ machinery, methods)* moderne

up-to-the-minute ADJ le plus récent; **u. news reporting** bulletins *mpl* (d'information) de dernière minute

uptown *Am* ADJ [ˈʌptaʊn] des quartiers résidentiels

ADV [ˌʌpˈtaʊn] *(be, live)* dans les quartiers résidentiels; *(move)* vers les quartiers résidentiels

N [ˈʌptaʊn] les quartiers *mpl* résidentiels

upturn N [ˈʌptɜːn] *(in economy, situation)* amélioration *f*; *(in production, sales)* progression *f*, reprise *f*; **there's been an u. in the market** il y a eu une progression du marché

VT [ʌpˈtɜːn] *(turn over)* retourner; *(turn upside down)* mettre à l'envers; *(overturn)* renverser

upturned [ʌpˈtɜːnd] ADJ **1** *(nose)* retroussé; **he gazed down at her u. face** il contemplait son visage, qu'elle tenait levé vers lui **2** *(upside down)* retourné, renversé

upward [ˈʌpwəd] ADJ *(movement)* ascendant; *Fin (trend)* à la hausse

ADV *Am* = **upwards**

▸▸ ***upward mobility*** ascension *f* sociale

upward-compatible ADJ *Comput* compatible vers le haut

upwardly mobile [ˈʌpwədlɪ-] ADJ *(moving up)* qui s'élève rapidement sur l'échelle sociale; *(in a position to move)* qui peut s'élever rapidement sur l'échelle sociale

upwards [ˈʌpwədz] ADV **1** *(move, climb, look)* vers le haut; **to slope u.** monter; **if you look u. you can see…** si vous levez la tête *ou* les yeux, vous voyez…; **prices are moving u.** les prix sont à la hausse **2** *(facing up)* **she placed the photos (face) u. on the table** elle a posé les photos à l'endroit sur la table; **he lay on the floor face u.** il était allongé par terre sur le dos **3** *(onwards)* **from 15 years u.** à partir de 15 ans

• **upwards of** PREP **u. of 100 candidates applied** plus de 100 candidats se sont présentés; **they can cost u. of £150** ils peuvent coûter 150 livres et plus

upwind [ˌʌpˈwɪnd] ADV du côté du vent, contre le vent

ADJ dans le vent, au vent; **to be u. of sth** être dans le vent *ou* au vent par rapport à qch

Ural [ˈjʊərəl] ADJ

▸▸ ***the Ural Mountains*** les monts *mpl* Oural, l'Oural *m*

uranium [jʊˈreɪnjəm] N uranium *m*

Uranus [ˈjʊərənəs] N *Astron* Uranus *f*

PR N *Myth* Uranus

urban [ˈɜːbən] ADJ urbain

▸▸ ***urban area*** zone *f* urbaine, agglomération *f*; ***urban blight*** dégradation *f* urbaine; ***urban centre*** centre *m* urbain, agglomération *f* urbaine; ***urban decay*** dégradation *f* urbaine; ***urban guerrilla*** guérillero *m* urbain; ***the urban jungle*** la jungle de la ville; ***urban legend*** légende *f*, faux fait *m* divers; ***urban music*** musiques *fpl* urbaines; ***urban myth*** légende *f*, faux fait *m* divers; ***urban planner*** urbaniste *mf*; ***urban renewal*** rénovations *fpl* urbaines; ***urban sprawl*** étalement *m* urbain; ***urban studies*** études *fpl* d'urbanisme; ***urban unemployment*** chômage *m* en zones urbaines

> Attention: ne pas confondre avec **urbane**.

urbane [ɜːˈbeɪn] ADJ *(person)* courtois, d'une politesse raffinée; *(manner)* poli, raffiné

> Attention: ne pas confondre avec **urban**.

urbanely [ɜːˈbeɪnlɪ] ADV avec mondanité

urbanism [ˈɜːbənɪzəm] N urbanisme *m*

urbanite [ˈɜːbənaɪt] N citadin(e) *m,f*

urbanity [ɜːˈbænətɪ] N savoir-vivre *m inv*, *Formal* urbanité *f*

urbanization, -isation [ˌɜːbənaɪˈzeɪʃən] N urbanisation *f*

urbanize, -ise [ˈɜːbənaɪz] VT urbaniser

urchin [ˈɜːtʃɪn] N galopin *m*, polisson(onne) *m,f*

▸▸ ***urchin cut*** coupe *f ou* coiffure *f* à la garçonne

Urdu [ˈʊədu:] N ourdou *m*, urdu *m*

urea [ˈjʊərɪə] N *Biol & Chem* urée *f*

ureter [jʊˈriːtə(r)] N uretère *m*

urethra [jʊˈriːθrə] N urètre *m*

urge [ɜːdʒ] N forte envie *f*, désir *m*; *Psy* pulsion *f*; **I felt** *or* **I had a sudden u. to tell her** j'avais tout à coup très envie de lui dire; **I'll let you know if I ever get the u.** je te le dirai si j'en ai envie *ou* si ça me chante; **the sexual u.** les pulsions *fpl* sexuelles

VT **1** *(person ▸ incite)* exhorter, presser; **I u. you to reconsider** je vous conseille vivement de reconsidérer votre position; **she urged us not to sell the house** elle nous a vivement déconseillé de vendre la maison; **he urged them to revolt** il les a incités à la révolte *ou* à se révolter **2** *(course of action)* conseiller vivement, préconiser; *(need, point)* insister sur; **we urged caution** nous avons préconisé la prudence **3** *(goad, encourage etc)* **to u. a horse forward** pousser un cheval; **he urged his men into battle** il poussa ses hommes dans la bataille

▸ **urge on** VT SEP talonner, presser; *(person, troops)* faire avancer; **to u. sb on to do sth** inciter qn à faire qch

urgency [ˈɜːdʒənsɪ] N urgence *f*; **it's a matter of great u.** c'est une affaire très urgente; **there's no great u.** cela n'est pas urgent *ou* ne presse pas; **could you do this as a matter of the utmost u.?** pourriez-vous faire ceci de toute urgence?; **there was a note of u. in her voice** il y avait quelque chose de pressant dans sa voix

urgent [ˈɜːdʒənt] ADJ **1** *(matter, need)* urgent, pressant; *(message)* urgent; **it's not u.** ce n'est pas urgent, ça ne presse pas; **is it u.?** est-ce urgent?; **the roof is in u. need of repair** le toit a un besoin urgent d'être réparé; **I was in u. need of a drink** il me fallait absolument quelque chose à boire **2** *(manner, voice)* insistant

urgently [ˈɜːdʒəntlɪ] ADV d'urgence, de toute urgence; **they appealed u. for help** ils ont demandé du secours avec insistance; **the matter is u. in need of attention** l'affaire demande à être traitée immédiatement *ou* sans délais; **supplies are u. needed** un ravitaillement est absolument nécessaire

uric [ˈjʊərɪk] ADJ urique

▸▸ ***uric acid*** acide *m* urique

urinal [*Br* jʊəˈraɪnəl *Am* ˈjʊərɪnəl] N *(fitting)* urinal *m*; *(building)* urinoir *m*

urinary [ˈjʊərɪnərɪ] ADJ urinaire

▸▸ ***urinary tract*** appareil *m* urinaire

urinate [ˈjʊərɪˌneɪt] VI uriner

urine [ˈjʊərɪn] N urine *f*

URL [ˌjuːɑːˈrel] N *Comput* (*abbr* **uniform resource locator**) (adresse *f*) URL *m*

urn [ɜːn] N **1** *(container ▸ gen)* urne *f* **2** *(for ashes)* urne *f* (funéraire) **3** *(for coffee, tea)* fontaine *f*

urogenital [ˌjʊərəʊˈdʒenɪtəl] ADJ urogénital

urological [ˌjʊərəˈlɒdʒɪkəl] ADJ urologique

urologist [jʊəˈrɒlədʒɪst] N urologue *mf*

urology [jʊəˈrɒlədʒɪ] N urologie *f*

Ursa [ˈɜːsə] N *Astron* **U. Major/Minor** la Grande/Petite Ourse

urticaria [ˌɜːtɪˈkeərɪə] N *Med* urticaire *f*

Uruguay [ˈjʊərəgwaɪ] N Uruguay *m*

Uruguayan [ˌjʊərʊˈgwaɪən] N Uruguayen(enne) *m,f*

ADJ uruguayen

COMP *(embassy)* d'Uruguay; *(history)* de l'Uruguay

US [ˌjuːˈes] (*abbr* **United States**) N **the US** les USA *mpl*, les États-Unis *mpl*

COMP des États-Unis, américain

us [ʌs] PRON **1** *(object form of "we")* nous; **tell us the truth** dites-nous la vérité; **it's us!** c'est nous!; **it's us she's looking for** c'est nous qu'elle cherche; **most of us are students** nous sommes presque tous des étudiants; **all four of us went** nous y sommes allés tous les quatre; **there are three of us** nous nous sommes trois; **those of us who were left…** ceux d'entre nous qui restaient…; **they're with us** ils sont avec nous; **as for us Scotsmen** quant à nous autres Écossais **2** *Fam (me ▸ direct object)* me□; *(▸ indirect object)* me□, moi□; **give us a kiss!** embrasse-moi!; **give us a chance, I've only just got here!** je t'en prie, je viens d'arriver!□

USA [ˈjuːesˈeɪ] N **1** *Geog* (*abbr* **United States of America**) **the U.** les USA *mpl*, les États-Unis *mpl*; **in the U.** aux USA, aux États-Unis **2** *Mil* (*abbr* **United States Army**) = armée des États-Unis

usability [ˌjuːzəˈbɪlɪtɪ] N facilité *f* d'utilisation

usable [ˈjuːzəbəl] ADJ utilisable

USAF [ˌjuːesˌeɪˈef] N *Mil* (*abbr* **United States Air Force**) = armée de l'air des États-Unis

usage [ˈjuːzɪdʒ] N **1** *(custom, practice)* coutume *f*, usage *m*; **sanctified** *or* **hallowed by u.** consacré par l'usage **2** *(of term, word)* usage *m*; **accepted u.** le bon usage; **the term is in common u.** le terme est employé couramment; **that phrase has long since dropped out of u.** cette expression n'est plus usitée depuis longtemps **3** *(employment)* usage *m*, emploi *m*; *(treatment ▸ of material, tool)* manipulation *f*; *(▸ of person)* traitement *m*; **designed for rough u.** conçu pour résister aux chocs; **these books are not meant for rough u.** ces livres ne sont pas faits pour être malmenés

usance [ˈjuːzəns] N *Banking & Fin (time limit)* usance *f*; **at thirty days' u.** à usance de trente jours

USB [ˌjuːesˈbiː] *Comput* (*abbr* **universal serial bus**) N norme *f* USB

COMP USB

USE

N	
• utilisation **1, 2**	• emploi **1, 3**
• consommation **1**	• usage **1–4, 6, 7**
• besoin **4**	
VT	
• se servir de **1, 2**	• utiliser **1, 3**
• employer **1**	• prendre **1, 5**
• profiter de **2**	• consommer **3**
• finir **3**	• traiter **4**

N [juːs] **1** *(utilization ▸ of materials)* utilisation *f*, emploi *m*; *(consumption ▸ of water, resources etc)* consommation *f*; *(being used, worn etc)* usage *m*; **to stretch with u.** se détendre à l'usage; **to wear out with u.** s'user; **the dishes are for everyday u.** c'est la vaisselle de tous les jours; **ready for u.** prêt à l'emploi; **directions** *or* **instructions for u.** *(on packaging)* mode d'emploi; **for your personal u.** *(on packaging)* pour votre usage personnel; **for customer u. only** *(sign)* réservé à notre clientèle; *Med* **for external/internal u. only** *(on packaging)* à usage externe/interne; **for u. in case of emergency** *(sign)* à utiliser en cas d'urgence; **the film is for u. in teaching** le film est destiné à l'enseignement; **in u.** *(machine, system)* en usage, utilisé; *(lift, cashpoint)* en service; *(phrase, word)* usité; **in general u.** d'emploi courant, d'utilisation courante; **not in u., out of u.** *(machine, system)* hors d'usage; *(lift, cash point)* hors service; **the phrase is no longer in u.** l'expression est inusitée *ou* ne s'utilise plus; **to come into u.** entrer en service; **to go out of u.** *(machine)* être mis au rebut; **steam engines went out of u. in 1950** on a cessé d'utiliser *ou* d'employer les machines à vapeur en 1950; **to make u. of sth** se servir de *ou* utiliser qch; **to make good u. of, to put to good u.** *(machine, money)* faire bon usage de; *(opportunity, experience)* tirer profit de

2 *(ability or right to use)* usage *m*, utilisation *f*; **we gave them the u. of our car** nous leur avons laissé l'usage de notre voiture; **he only has the u. of one arm** il n'a l'usage que d'un bras; **she lost the u. of her legs** elle a perdu l'usage de ses jambes; **the old man still has the full u. of his faculties** le vieil homme jouit encore de toutes ses facultés

3 *(practical application)* usage *m*, emploi *m*; **this tool has many uses** cet outil a de nombreux usages *ou* emplois; **we found a u. for the old fridge** nous avons trouvé un emploi pour le vieux frigo; *Hum* **I have my uses** il m'arrive de servir à quelque chose

4 *(need)* besoin *m*, usage *m*; **do you have any u. for this book?** avez-vous besoin de ce livre?; **to have no u. for sth** ne pas avoir besoin de qch; *Fig* n'avoir que faire de qch; **I have no u. for idle**

gossip je n'ai que faire des cancans; **this department has no u. for slackers** il n'y a pas de place pour les fainéants dans ce service

5 *(usefulness)* **to be of u. (to sb)** être utile (à qn), servir (à qn); **were the instructions (of) any u.?** est-ce que le mode d'emploi a servi à quelque chose?; **I found his advice to be of little u., his advice was of little u. to me** je n'ai pas trouvé ses conseils très utiles; **the book would be of more u. if it had illustrations** le livre serait plus utile s'il contenait des illustrations; **it's not much u.** cela ne sert pas à grand-chose; **he's not much u. as a secretary** il n'est pas brillant comme secrétaire; **to be (of) no u.** *(thing)* ne servir à rien; *(person)* n'être bon à rien; **they were no u. at all during the move** ils n'ont rien fait pendant le déménagement; **it's** *or* **there's no u. complaining** inutile de *ou* ça ne sert à rien de se plaindre; **it's no u., we might as well give up** c'est inutile *ou* ça ne sert à rien, autant abandonner; **I tried to convince her but it was no u.** j'ai essayé de la convaincre mais il n'y avait rien à faire; **is it any u. calling her?** est-ce que ça servira à quelque chose de l'appeler?; **what's the u. of waiting?** à quoi bon attendre?, à quoi ça sert d'attendre?; **oh, what's the u.?** à quoi bon?; *Fam Ironic* **that's a fat lot of u.!** ça nous fait une belle jambe!

6 *Ling* usage *m*; **that's an old-fashioned u.** c'est un usage vieilli

7 *Rel* usage *m*

VT [ju:z] **1** *(put into action ▸ service, tool, skills)* se servir de, utiliser; *(▸ product, name)* utiliser; *(▸ method, phrase, word)* employer; *(▸ vehicle, form of transport)* prendre; **these are the notebooks he used** ce sont les cahiers dont il s'est servi *ou* qu'il a utilisés; **is anyone using this book?** est-ce que quelqu'un se sert de *ou* a besoin de ce livre?; **it's very easy to u.** c'est très facile à utiliser; **it's no longer used** *(machine, tool)* ça ne sert plus; *(word, expression)* ça n'est plus usité; **am I using the term correctly?** est-ce comme ça qu'on utilise le terme?; **I'd like to u. my language skills more** j'aimerais utiliser davantage mes connaissances en langues; **I always u. public transport** je prends toujours les transports en commun; **we u. this room as an office** nous nous servons de cette pièce comme bureau, cette pièce nous sert de bureau; **what is this used for** *or* **as?** à quoi cela sert-il?; **it's used for identifying the blood type** cela sert à identifier le groupe sanguin; **I u. it for opening** *or* **to open letters** je m'en sers *ou* je l'utilise pour ouvrir les lettres; **I used the money to rebuild my garage** j'ai utilisé *ou* employé l'argent pour reconstruire mon garage; **what battery does this radio u.?** quelle pile faut-il pour cette radio?; **my car uses unleaded petrol** ma voiture marche à l'essence sans plomb; **may I u. the phone?** puis-je téléphoner?; **he asked to u. the** *Br* **toilet** *or Am* **bathroom** il a demandé à aller aux toilettes; **to u. force/violence** avoir recours à la force/violence; **the police often u. tear gas** la police a souvent recours au gaz lacrymogène; **to u. one's intelligence/intuition** faire marcher son intelligence/intuition; **to u. diplomacy** user de diplomatie; **to u. discretion** agir avec discrétion; **to u. one's influence** user de son influence; **u. your imagination!** utilise ton imagination!; **u. your initiative!** fais preuve d'initiative!; **u. your head** *or* **your brains!** réfléchis un peu!; **u. your eyes!** ouvrez l'œil!; *Fam* **he could certainly u. some help** un peu d'aide ne lui ferait pas de mal; *Fam* **we could all u. a holiday!** nous aurions tous bien besoin de vacances!▫

2 *(exploit, take advantage of ▸ opportunity)* profiter de; *(▸ person)* se servir de; **u. it to your advantage!** profitez-en!; **I feel used** j'ai l'impression qu'on s'est servi de moi

3 *(consume)* consommer, utiliser; *(finish, use up)* finir, épuiser; **the car's using a lot of oil** la voiture consomme beaucoup d'huile; **have you used all the shampoo?** as-tu utilisé tout le shampooing?

4 *Formal (treat physically)* traiter; *(behave towards)* agir envers; **I consider I was ill used** je considère qu'on ne m'a pas traité comme il faut; **how's the world been using you?** comment ça va?

5 *(drug)* prendre

V AUX [ju:z] *(only in past tense)* **they used to live here** (avant) ils habitaient ici; **he used to drink a lot** il buvait beaucoup avant; **it used to be true** c'était vrai autrefois; **it used to be a pleasant town to live in** autrefois c'était une ville agréable; **things aren't what they used to be** les choses ne sont plus ce qu'elles étaient; **she can't get about the way she used to** elle ne peut plus se déplacer comme avant; **we used not** *or* **we didn't u. to eat meat** avant, nous ne mangions pas de viande; **did he u. to visit her?** venait-il la voir avant?; **do you travel much? – I used to** vous voyagez beaucoup? – autrefois, oui

VI [ju:z] *Fam (use drugs)* se camer

> Note that the French verb **user** is a false friend. Its most common meaning is **to wear out**.

▸ **use up VT SEP** *(consume)* consommer, prendre; *(exhaust ▸ paper, soap)* finir; *(▸ patience, energy, supplies)* épuiser; **she used up the leftovers to make soup** elle a utilisé les restes pour faire un potage; **did you u. up all your money?** as-tu dépensé tout ton argent?; **the paper was all used up** il ne restait plus de papier

---

use-by date **N** date *f* de péremption

used¹ [ju:zd] **ADJ** *(book, car)* d'occasion; *(clothing)* d'occasion, usagé; *(glass, linen)* sale, qui a déjà servi; *(stamp)* oblitéré, qui a déjà servi; **hardly u.** presque neuf

used² [ju:st] **ADJ** *(accustomed)* **to be u. to (doing) sth** avoir l'habitude de *ou* être habitué à (faire) qch; **I'm u. to working alone** j'ai l'habitude de *ou* je suis habitué à travailler tout seul; **they're not u. to it** ils n'y sont pas habitués, ils n'en ont pas l'habitude; **to be u. to sb** être habitué à qn; **to get u. to sth** s'habituer à qch; **he can't get u. to it** il n'arrive pas à s'y habituer; **I'm not u. to being spoken to like that!** je n'ai pas l'habitude qu'on me parle comme ça!; **you'll soon get u. to the idea** tu te feras à l'idée

useful ['ju:sfʊl] **ADJ 1** *(handy ▸ book, information, machine)* utile, pratique; *(▸ discussion, experience)* utile, profitable; *(▸ method)* utile, efficace; **does it serve any u. purpose?** est-ce utile?, est-ce que cela sert à quelque chose?; **it will come in very u.** cela rendra bien service; **you could be u. to the director** vous pourriez rendre service au directeur; **the information was u. to us in making a decision** les renseignements nous ont aidés à prendre une décision; **make yourself u. and help me tidy up** rends-toi utile et aide-moi à ranger; **it's u. to know** c'est bon à savoir; **she's a u. person to know** c'est une femme qu'il est bon de connaître; **he's very u. around the house** il est très utile *ou* il rend beaucoup de services dans la maison; **they're u. when it comes to financial affairs** ils sont très compétents dans le domaine financier; **this map could be very u.** cette carte pourrait être très utile *ou* d'une grande utilité

2 *Fam (satisfactory ▸ performance, score)* honorable▫; **he's a very u. player** c'est un joueur très compétent▫

3 *Fam (skilful)* **to be u. with one's fists** savoir se servir de ses poings; **to be u. with a gun** savoir manier un fusil▫

▸▸ ***useful life*** vie *f* utile; **this machine has a u. life of ten years** cette machine a une durée de vie de dix ans

usefully ['ju:sfʊlɪ] **ADV** utilement; **his free time was u. employed in improving his languages** il a employé utilement son temps libre à améliorer ses connaissances en langues; **you could u. devote a further year's study to the subject** tu pourrais consacrer avec profit une année d'étude supplémentaire au sujet; **his work might u. be compared to that of Joyce** il est intéressant de comparer son œuvre à celle de Joyce

usefulness ['ju:sfʊlnɪs] **N** utilité *f*; **it's outlived its u.** ça a fait son temps, ça ne sert plus à rien

useless ['ju:slɪs] **ADJ 1** *(bringing no help ▸ book, information, machine)* inutile; *(▸ discussion, experience)* vain, qui n'apporte rien; *(▸ advice, suggestion)* qui n'apporte rien, qui ne vaut rien; *(▸ attempt, effort)* inutile, vain; *(▸ remedy)* inefficace; *(unusable)* inutilisable; **the contract is u. to them** le contrat ne leur est d'aucune utilité; **it's u. trying to reason with him, it's u. to try and reason with him** ça ne sert à rien *ou* c'est inutile d'essayer de lui faire entendre raison; **the computer is u. without the instructions** l'ordinateur est inutilisable *ou* on ne peut pas se servir de l'ordinateur sans mode d'emploi **2** *Fam (incompetent)* nul; **I'm u. at history/maths** je suis nul en histoire/math; **she's u. as a navigator** elle est nulle *ou* elle ne vaut rien en tant que navigatrice; **her brother is absolutely u.** son frère est nul *ou* bon à rien

uselessly ['ju:slɪslɪ] **ADV** inutilement

uselessness ['ju:slɪsnɪs] **N** inutilité *f*; *(of remedy)* inefficacité *f*; *Fam (of person)* nullité *f*

Usenet® ['ju:znet] **N** *Comput* Usenet® *m*

user ['ju:zə(r)] **N** *(of computer, machine, product, dictionary)* utilisateur(trice) *m,f*; *(of telephone)* abonné(e) *m,f*; *(of airline, public service, road)* usager *m*; *(of electricity, gas, oil)* usager *m*, utilisateur(trice) *m,f*; *(of drugs)* consommateur (trice) *m,f*; **users of public transport** usagers *mpl* des transports en commun

▸▸ *Comput* ***user ID, user identification*** identification *f* de l'utilisateur; *Comput* ***user interface*** interface *f* utilisateur; *Comput* ***user language*** langage *m* utilisateur; *Comput* ***user manual*** manuel *m* d'utilisation; *Comput* ***user name*** nom *m* de l'utilisateur; *Comput* ***user network*** réseau *m* d'utilisateurs; *Comput* ***user software*** logiciel *m* utilisateur; *Comput* ***user support*** assistance *f* à l'utilisateur

user-definable **ADJ** *Comput (characters, keys)* définissable par l'utilisateur

user-defined [ju:zədɪ'faɪnd] **ADJ** *Comptr* défini par l'utilisateur

user-friendliness **N** *(gen) & Comput* convivialité *f*

user-friendly **ADJ** *(gen) & Comput* convivial, facile à utiliser

user-interface **N** *Comput & Fig* interface *f* utilisateur

user-programmable **ADJ** *Comput* programmable par l'utilisateur

user-specific **ADJ** spécifique à l'utilisateur

U-shaped **ADJ** en U

usher ['ʌʃə(r)] **VT** conduire, accompagner; **I ushered them to their seats** je les ai conduits à leur place; **he ushered us into/out of the living room** il nous a fait entrer au/sortir du salon

N 1 *(at concert, theatre, wedding)* placeur(euse) *m,f* **2** *(doorkeeper)* portier *m*; *Law* huissier *m*

▸ **usher in VT SEP** *Fig* inaugurer, marquer le début de; **the printing press ushered in a new era** l'imprimerie a marqué le début d'une ère nouvelle

usherette [ˌʌʃə'ret] **N** ouvreuse *f*

USM [ju:es'em] **N 1** *Am (abbr* **United States Mail***)* ≃ la Poste **2** *Br Formerly St Exch (abbr* **unlisted securities market***)* marché *m* hors cote, second marché *m*

USN [ˌju:es'en] **N** *Mil (abbr* **United States Navy***)* = marine de guerre des États-Unis

USP [ˌju:es'pi:] **N** *Mktg (abbr* **unique selling point or proposition***)* proposition *f* unique de vente

USS [ˌju:es'es] **N** *Naut (abbr* **United States Ship***)* = initiales précédant le nom des navires américains; **the U. Washington** le Washington

USSR [ˌju:esˌes'ɑ:(r)] **N** *Formerly (abbr* **Union of Soviet Socialist Republics***)* **the U.** l'URSS *f*

usual ['ju:ʒʊəl] **ADJ** *(customary ▸ activity, place)* habituel; *(▸ practice, price)* habituel, courant; *(▸ expression, word)* courant, usité; *(▸ doctor)* habituel, traitant; **they asked the u. questions** ils ont posé les questions habituelles; **I didn't get my u. bus this morning** je n'ai pas pris le bus que je prends d'habitude ce matin; **my u. diet consists of fish and vegetables** généralement *ou* d'habitude je mange du poisson et des légumes; **let's meet at the u. time** retrouvons-nous à l'heure habituelle *ou* à la même heure que d'habitude; **later than u.** plus tard que d'habitude; **he drank more than u.** il a bu plus que d'habitude; **she was her u. cheery self** elle était gaie comme d'habitude; **she's her u. self again** elle est redevenue elle-même; **with her u. optimism** avec son optimisme habituel, avec l'optimisme qui est le sien *ou* qui la caractérise; **it's not u. for him to be so bitter** il est rarement si amer, c'est rare qu'il soit si amer; **it's the u. story** c'est toujours la même histoire; **it's quite u. to see flooding in the spring** il y a souvent des inondations au printemps; **it's u. to pay in advance** il est d'usage de payer d'avance; **I believe it's the u. practice** je crois que c'est ce qui se fait d'habitude; **as is u. with young mothers** comme d'habitude avec les jeunes mamans

N *Fam (drink, meal)* **what will you have? – the u., please** que prends-tu? – comme d'habitude, s'il te plaît

• **as per usual ADV** comme d'habitude; **as per u., he was late** comme d'habitude, il était en retard

• **as usual ADV** comme d'habitude; **as u., the opposition objected** comme d'habitude *ou* comme toujours, l'opposition a élevé une objection; **life goes on as u.** la vie continue; **business as u.** *(during building work)* le magasin reste ouvert pendant la durée des travaux; **despite recent events it was business as u.** malgré les récents événements, la vie continuait comme si de rien n'était

usually ['juːʒəlɪ] **ADV** d'habitude, généralement, d'ordinaire; **I u. get to work early** généralement *ou* d'habitude j'arrive tôt au bureau; **she's not u. late** il est rare qu'elle soit en retard, elle est rarement en retard; **we don't u. eat dessert** d'habitude nous ne mangeons pas de dessert; **the roads were more than u. busy** il y avait encore plus de circulation que d'habitude *ou* d'ordinaire *ou* de coutume sur les routes

usufruct ['juːzjʊˌfrʌkt] **N** *Law* usufruit *m*

usufructuary [ˌjuːzjʊ'frʌktjərɪ] *Law* **N** usufruitier(ère) *m,f*

ADJ usufruitier

usurer ['juːʒərə(r)] **N** usurier(ère) *m,f*

usurious [juː'ʒʊrɪəs] **ADJ** *(interest etc)* usuraire

usurp [juː'zɜːp] **VT** usurper

usurpation [ˌjuːzɜː'peɪʃən] **N** usurpation *f*

usurper [juː'zɜːpə(r)] **N** usurpateur(trice) *m,f*

usury ['juːʒʊrɪ] **N** usure *f (intérêt)*

UT *(written abbr* **Utah**) Utah *m*

utensil [juː'tensəl] **N** ustensile *m*, outil *m*; **cooking utensils** ustensiles *mpl* de cuisine

uterine ['juːtəraɪn] **ADJ** utérin

uterus ['juːtərəs] *(pl* **uteri** [-raɪ] *or* **uteruses**) **N** utérus *m*

utilitarian [juːtɪlɪ'teərɪən] **ADJ 1** *(functional)* utilitaire, fonctionnel **2** *Phil* utilitariste

N utilitariste *mf*

utilitarianism [juːtɪlɪ'teərɪənɪzəm] **N** utilitarisme *m*

utility [juː'tɪlətɪ] *(pl* **utilities**) **N 1** *(usefulness)* utilité *f*

2 *(service)* service *m*; **they plan to improve (public) utilities** ils ont l'intention d'améliorer les services publics

3 *Comput* utilitaire *m*, programme *m* utilitaire

4 *Am (room)* ≃ buanderie *f*

ADJ *(fabric, furniture)* utilitaire, fonctionnel

►► *Am* ***utility man*** *(worker)* ouvrier *m* polyvalent; *(for gas, electricity)* = employé des services publics; *(actor)* = acteur qui joue les utilités; *Sport* ***utility player*** joueur(euse) *m,f* polyvalent; *Am* ***utility pole*** = poteau pour câbles électriques et téléphoniques; *Comput* ***utility program*** (logiciel *m*) utilitaire *m*; ***utility room*** ≃ buanderie *f*; *Austr & NZ* ***utility vehicle*** = grosse voiture tout-terrain

utilizable, -isable [juːtɪ'laɪzəbəl] **ADJ** utilisable

utilization, -isation [juːtɪlaɪ'zeɪʃən] **N** utilisation *f*

utilize, -ise ['juːtɪlaɪz] **VT** *(use)* utiliser, se servir de; *(make best use of)* exploiter; **you could have utilized your time better** vous auriez pu tirer meilleur parti de votre temps *ou* mieux profiter de votre temps

utmost ['ʌtməʊst] **ADJ 1** *(greatest)* le plus grand; **it's a matter of the u. seriousness** c'est une affaire extrêmement sérieuse; **in the u. secrecy** dans le plus grand secret; **it's of the u. importance that I see him** il est extrêmement important *ou* il est d'une importance capitale que je le voie; **with the u. respect, I cannot agree with your conclusions** avec tout le respect que je vous dois, je ne peux pas partager vos conclusions; **it was only with the u. difficulty that we were able to persuade them** nous avons eu toutes les peines du monde à les convaincre **2** *(farthest)* **to the u. ends of the earth** au bout du monde

N 1 *(maximum)* maximum *m*, plus haut degré *m*; **at the u.** au grand maximum; **to do sth to the u. of one's abilities** faire qch au maximum de ses capacités; **to live life to the u.** profiter pleinement de la vie; **the u. in comfort** ce qui se fait de mieux en matière de confort **2** *(best effort)* **we did our u. to fight the new taxes** nous avons fait tout notre possible *ou* tout ce que nous pouvions pour lutter contre les nouveaux impôts; **she tried her u.** elle a fait de son mieux

utopia, Utopia [juː'təʊpɪə] **N** utopie *f*

utopian, Utopian [juː'təʊpɪən] **ADJ** utopique

N utopiste *mf*

utter ['ʌtə(r)] **VT 1** *(pronounce* ► *word)* prononcer, proférer; *(*► *cry, groan)* pousser; **he didn't u. a sound** il n'a pas ouvert la bouche, il n'a pas soufflé mot; **never u. his name in her presence** il ne faut jamais prononcer son nom devant elle **2** *Law (libel)* publier; *(counterfeit money)* émettre, mettre en circulation

ADJ *(amazement, bliss)* absolu, total; **he shows an u. disregard for his family's welfare** il affiche une indifférence absolue pour le bien-être de sa famille; **he's talking u. rubbish** ce qu'il dit n'a aucun sens *ou* est absolument idiot; **it's u. madness** c'est de la folie totale *ou* pure; **an u. fool** un parfait crétin, un crétin fini; **to her u. amazement** à sa plus grande stupéfaction

utterance ['ʌtərəns] **N 1** *(statement)* déclaration *f*; *Ling* énoncé *m*; **they taped the child's first utterances** ils ont enregistré les premiers mots de l'enfant **2** *(expression)* expression *f*, énonciation *f*; **to give u. to sth** exprimer qch

utterly ['ʌtəlɪ] **ADV** complètement, tout à fait

uttermost ['ʌtəməʊst] = **utmost**

U-tube **N** tube *m* en U

U-turn **N 1** *Aut* demi-tour *m*; **to make a U.** faire (un) demi-tour **2** *Fig* volte-face *f inv*, revirement *m*; **the government were accused of making a U. on health policy** le gouvernement a été accusé de faire volte-face en matière de politique de santé

UV [juː'viː] **N** *(abbr* **ultra-violet**) UV *m*

uvula ['juːvjʊlə] *(pl* **uvulas** *or* **uvulae** [-liː]) **N** luette *f*, *Spec* uvule *f*, uvula *f*

uvular ['juːvjʊlə(r)] **ADJ** uvulaire

uxorious [ʌk'sɔːrɪəs] **ADJ** *Formal* **1** *(devoted to one's wife)* excessivement dévoué à sa femme; **an u. husband** un mari dévoué **2** *(submissive to one's wife)* soumis à sa femme; **an u. husband** un mari soumis

uxoriousness [ʌk'sɔːrɪəsnɪs] **N** *Formal (devotion to one's wife)* dévotion *f* excessive (à sa femme); *(submission to one's wife)* soumission *f* (à sa femme)

Uzbekistan [ʊzˌbekɪ'stɑːn] **N** Ouzbékistan *m*

V

/[1], v[1] [viː] **N** *(letter)* V, v *m inv*; **two v's** deux v; **V for Victor** V comme Victor; **V-1 (bomb)** V1 *m*; **V-2 (rocket)** V2 *m*; **V-8 (engine)** moteur *m* à huit cylindres en V

/[2] *Elec (written abbr* **volt***)* V

/[2] 1 *(written abbr* **velocity***)* v
2 *Gram (written abbr* **verb***)* v
3 *Bible & Rel (written abbr* **verse***)* v
4 *(written abbr* **versus***)* contre
5 *(written abbr* **vide***)* v

/A *(written abbr* **Virginia***)* Virginie *f*

ac [væk] **N** *Br Univ Fam (abbr* **vacation***)* vacances *fpl*

acancy ['veɪkənsɪ] *(pl* **vacancies***)* **N 1** *(job)* poste *m* vacant *ou* libre, vacance *f*; **do you have any vacancies?** avez-vous des postes à pourvoir?, est-ce qu'il y a de l'embauche?; **we have a v. for a sales clerk** nous cherchons un vendeur; **the v. has been filled** le poste a été pourvu; **no vacancies** *(sign)* pas d'embauche
2 *(in hotel)* chambre *f* libre; **no vacancies** *(sign)* complet
3 *(lack of intelligence)* ineptie *f*, esprit *m* vide; **he had a look of utter v. on his face** il avait l'air complètement idiot
4 *(emptiness)* vide *m*

> Note that the French word **vacances** is a false friend. It means **holiday**.

acant ['veɪkənt] **ADJ 1** *(house, room ▸ to rent)* libre, à louer; *(▸ empty)* inoccupé; *(seat)* libre, inoccupé; **is this seat v.?** est-ce que cette place est libre?
2 *(job, position)* vacant, libre; **there are several v. places to be filled** il y a plusieurs postes à pourvoir; **the situations v. column** la rubrique des offres d'emploi
3 *(empty ▸ mind, look)* vide; *(stupid ▸ person, expression)* niais, idiot; **I asked a question and she just looked v.** j'ai posé une question et elle a eu l'air de ne pas comprendre
4 *(time)* de loisir, perdu; *(hour)* creux, de loisir
▸▸ *Am* ***vacant lot*** terrain *m* vague; *Br* ***vacant possession*** libre possession *f*; **apartments sold with v. possession** appartements libres à la vente; *Pol* ***vacant seat*** siège *m* à pourvoir *ou* vacant

acantly ['veɪkəntlɪ] **ADV** *(expressionlessly)* d'un air absent *ou* vague; *(stupidly)* d'un air niais *ou* idiot; **he looked at us v.** *(expressionlessly)* il nous a regardés avec des yeux vides *ou* sans expression; *(stupidly)* il nous a regardés bêtement; **she stared v. into space** elle avait le regard perdu dans le vague

acate [və'keɪt] **VT** *(hotel room)* libérer, quitter; *(flat, house)* quitter, déménager de; *(job)* démissionner de

acation [və'keɪʃən] **N 1** *Br Univ (recess)* vacances *fpl*; *Law* vacations *fpl*, vacances *fpl* judiciaires; **over the v.** pendant les vacances **2** *Am (holiday)* vacances *fpl*; **to be on v.** être en vacances; **they went to Italy on v.** ils ont passé leurs vacances en Italie; **when are you going on** *or* **taking v.?** quand est-ce que vous prenez vos vacances?
COMP *Am (job)* de vacances
VI *Am* passer des vacances; **they're vacationing in the mountains** ils sont en vacances à la montagne
▸▸ *Am* ***vacation center*** club *m* de vacances; *Univ* ***vacation course*** cours *mpl* d'été; ***vacation home*** résidence *f* secondaire; *Admin* ***vacation leave*** congé *m* annuel; *Am* ***vacation resort*** camp *m* de vacances; ***vacation work*** travail *m* effectué pendant les vacances *(par un étudiant)*

vacationer [və'keɪʃənə(r)], **vacationist** [və'keɪʃənɪst] **N** *Am* vacancier(ère) *m,f*

vaccinate ['væksɪneɪt] **VT** vacciner; **to get vaccinated** se faire vacciner

vaccination [ˌvæksɪ'neɪʃən] **N** vaccination *f*; **polio v., v. against polio** vaccination *f* contre la polio

vaccine [*Br* 'væksiːn, *Am* væk'siːn] **N** vaccin *m*; **smallpox v.** vaccin *m* contre la variole
▸▸ ***vaccine point*** plume *f* à vaccin

vaccinee [ˌvæksɪ'niː] **N** *Am* personne *f* vaccinée

vacillate ['væsəleɪt] **VI** hésiter

vacillating ['væsəleɪtɪŋ] **ADJ** *(behaviour)* indécis, irrésolu
N indécision *f*

vacillation [ˌvæsə'leɪʃən] **N** hésitation *f*, indécision *f*

vacuity [væ'kjuːətɪ] *(pl* **vacuities***)* **N** *Formal* **1** *(of person, reasoning)* vacuité *f* **2** *(statement)* ânerie *f*, niaiserie *f*

vacuous ['vækjʊəs] **ADJ** *Formal (eyes, look)* vide, sans expression; *(remark)* sot (sotte), niais; *(film, novel)* idiot, dénué de tout intérêt; *(life)* vide de sens; **he's completely v.** il n'a rien dans la tête

vacuously ['vækjʊəslɪ] **ADV** *Formal (gaze)* sans expression; *(say)* niaisement

vacuousness ['vækjʊəsnɪs] **N** *Formal (of laugh)* bêtise *f*, niaiserie *f*; *(of remark, debate)* vacuité *f*

vacuum ['vækjʊəm] *(pl* **vacuums** *or* **vacua** [-jʊə]*)* **N 1** *(void)* vide *m*; **a cultural v.** un vide sur le plan culturel **2** *Phys* vacuum *m* **3** *(machine)* **v. (cleaner)** aspirateur *m*; **I gave the room a quick v.** j'ai passé l'aspirateur en vitesse dans la pièce
VT *(carpet)* passer l'aspirateur sur; *(flat, room)* passer l'aspirateur dans
▸▸ *Am* ***vacuum bottle*** (bouteille *f*) Thermos® *f*; ***vacuum brake*** frein *m* à vide; ***vacuum chamber*** chambre *f* à dépression; ***vacuum cleaner*** aspirateur *m*; *Br* ***vacuum flask*** (bouteille *f*) Thermos® *f*; ***vacuum pack*** emballage *m* sous vide; ***vacuum packing*** emballage *m* sous vide; ***vacuum pump*** pompe *f* à vide; *Am* ***vacuum tube*** tube *m* électronique *ou* à vide

vacuuming ['vækjʊəmɪŋ] **N to do the v.** passer l'aspirateur

vacuum-packed **ADJ** emballé sous vide

vade mecum [ˌvɑːdɪ'meɪkʊm] *(pl* **vade mecums***)* **N** vade-mecum *m inv*

vagabond ['vægəbɒnd] **N** *(wanderer)* vagabond (e) *m,f*; *(tramp)* clochard(e) *m,f*
ADJ vagabond, errant

vagary ['veɪgərɪ] *(pl* **vagaries***)* **N** caprice *m*; **the vagaries of fashion** les caprices de la mode

vagina [və'dʒaɪnə] *(pl* **vaginas** *or* **vaginae** [-niː]*)* **N** vagin *m*

vaginal [və'dʒaɪnəl] **ADJ** vaginal
▸▸ ***vaginal discharge*** pertes *fpl* blanches; ***vaginal smear*** frottis *m* vaginal

vagrancy ['veɪgrənsɪ] **N** *(gen) & Law* vagabondage *m*

vagrant ['veɪgrənt] **N** *(wanderer)* vagabond(e) *m,f*; *(tramp)* clochard(e) *m,f*; *(beggar)* mendiant(e) *m,f*
ADJ vagabond

vague [veɪg] **ADJ 1** *(imprecise ▸ promise, statement)* vague, imprécis; *(▸ person)* vague; **she had only a v. idea of what he meant** elle ne comprenait que vaguement ce qu'il voulait dire; **they were v. about their activities** *(imprecise)* ils n'ont pas précisé la nature de leurs activités; *(evasive)* ils sont restés vagues sur la nature de leurs activités; **I'm still v. about how to get there** *(unsure)* je ne comprends toujours pas comment y aller; **I haven't the vaguest idea** je n'en ai pas la moindre idée
2 *(dim ▸ memory, feeling)* vague, confus; **I have a v. recollection of summers spent in Greece** je me rappelle vaguement les étés passés en Grèce
3 *(indistinct ▸ shape)* flou, indistinct
4 *(absent-minded)* distrait; **she looked v.** elle avait un air distrait

vaguely ['veɪglɪ] **ADV 1** *(not clearly ▸ promise, say)* vaguement; *(▸ remember, understand)* vaguement, confusément; **I v. remember dining here before** j'ai le vague souvenir *ou* je me souviens vaguement d'avoir déjà mangé ici **2** *(a bit)* vaguement, peu; **it tastes v. like coffee** cela a vaguement un goût de café; **she resembles her sister only v.** elle ne ressemble pas beaucoup à sa sœur **3** *(absent-mindedly)* distraitement; **he looked v. around him** il regardait autour de lui d'un air vague *ou* distrait

vagueness ['veɪgnɪs] **N 1** *(imprecision ▸ of promise, statement)* imprécision *f*, manque *m* de clarté
2 *(of memory)* imprécision *f*, manque *m* de précision; *(of feeling)* vague *m*, caractère *m* vague *ou* indistinct
3 *(of shape)* flou *m*, caractère *m* indistinct
4 *(absent-mindedness)* distraction *f*

vain [veɪn] **ADJ 1** *(conceited)* vaniteux; **he's very v. about his looks** il s'occupe beaucoup de sa petite personne **2** *(unsuccessful ▸ attempt, effort)* vain, inutile; *(▸ hope, plea, search)* vain, futile **3** *(idle ▸ promise)* vide, en l'air; *(▸ word)* creux, en l'air
• **in vain** **ADV** *(unsuccessfully)* en vain; **they tried in v. to free the driver** ils ont essayé sans succès *ou* en vain de libérer le conducteur; **all their efforts were in v.** leurs efforts n'ont servi à rien *ou* ont été vains; **it was all in v.** c'était peine perdue; **to take sb's name in v.** *(show disrespect)* manquer de respect envers le nom de qn; *(mention name)* parler de qn en son absence; *Hum* **are you taking my name in v. again?** vous parlez encore de moi derrière mon dos?

vainglorious [ˌveɪn'glɔːrɪəs] **ADJ** *Literary (proud)* vaniteux, orgueilleux; *(boastful)* vantard

vaingloriously [ˌveɪn'glɔːrɪəslɪ] **ADV** *Literary (proudly)* vaniteusement, orgueilleusement; *(boastfully)* en se vantant

vainglory [ˌveɪn'glɔːrɪ] **N** *Literary (pride)* vanité *f*, orgueil *m*; *(boastfulness)* vantardise *f*

vainly ['veɪnlɪ] **ADV 1** *(conceitedly)* avec vanité, vaniteusement **2** *(unsuccessfully ▸ try)* en vain, inutilement; *(▸ hope)* en vain

valance ['væləns] **N** *(round bed frame)* frange *f* de lit; *(round shelf, window)* lambrequin *m*, frange *f*

valanced sheet ['vælənst-] **N** housse *f* cache-sommier

vale [veɪl] **N** *Literary* vallée *f*, val *m*; *Fig* **this v. of tears** cette vallée de larmes

valediction [ˌvælɪ'dɪkʃən] **N 1** *(act)* adieux *mpl*; **2** *Am Sch & Univ (at graduation)* discours *m* d'adieu

valedictorian [ˌvælɪdɪk'tɔːrɪən] **ADJ** d'adieu
N *Am Sch & Univ* = major de la promotion (qui prononce le discours d'adieu)

valedictory [ˌvælɪ'dɪktərɪ] *(pl* **valedictories**) *Formal* **ADJ** *(mass, service, ceremony, speech)* d'adieu; **the v. mood of the meeting** l'ambiance de la réunion, qui annonçait la fin
N *Am Sch & Univ (at graduation)* discours *m* d'adieu

valence ['veɪləns] **N 1** *Am Chem* valence *f* **2** *(bonding capacity)* atomicité *f*

valency ['veɪlənsɪ] *(pl* **valencies**) **N** *Chem* valence *f*

Valentine ['væləntaɪn] **PR N (Saint) V.'s Day** la Saint-Valentin

valentine ['væləntaɪn] **N 1** *(card)* carte *f* de la Saint-Valentin **2** *(recipient of card)* = celui/celle qui reçoit une carte envoyée le jour de la Saint-Valentin; **George is my v.** c'est George que j'aime
►► ***valentine card*** carte *f* de la Saint-Valentin

valerian [və'lɪərɪən] **N** *Bot* valériane *f*

valet N ['væleɪ] **1** *(manservant)* valet *m* de chambre **2** *(clothing rack)* valet *m*
VT ['vælɪt] **can I have my suit valeted?** puis-je faire nettoyer mon costume?; **to have one's car valeted** faire faire un lavage-route à sa voiture
►► ***valet parking*** *(sign)* service de voiturier; ***valet service*** *(in hotel)* pressing *m* de l'hôtel

valetudinarian [ˌvælɪtjuːdɪ'neərɪən] *Arch or Literary* **ADJ** valétudinaire
N valétudinaire *mf*

Valhalla [væl'hælə] **N** *Myth* Walhalla *m*

valiant ['væljənt] **ADJ** *(person)* vaillant, courageux; *(behaviour, deed)* courageux, brave; **she made a v. attempt to put out the fire** elle a tenté courageusement d'éteindre l'incendie; **he made a v. effort not to cry out** il a fait un gros effort pour ne pas crier

valiantly ['væljəntlɪ] **ADV** vaillamment, courageusement

valid ['vælɪd] **ADJ 1** *(argument, reasoning)* valable, bien fondé; *(excuse)* valable **2** *(contract, passport)* valide, valable; **a v. driving licence** un permis de conduire valable *ou* valide *ou* en règle; **my driver's licence is no longer v.** mon permis de conduire est périmé

> Note that the French word **valide** also means **able-bodied**.

validate ['vælɪdeɪt] **VT 1** *(argument, claim)* confirmer, prouver la justesse de; *Am* **to v. an election** valider une élection **2** *(document)* valider **3** *Comput* valider

validation [ˌvælɪ'deɪʃən] **N 1** *(of argument, claim)* confirmation *f*, preuve *f* **2** *(of document)* validation *f*

validity [və'lɪdətɪ] **N 1** *(of argument, reasoning)* justesse *f*, solidité *f* **2** *(of document)* validité *f*

validly ['vælɪdlɪ] **ADV** avec raison

valise [*Br* və'liːz, *Am* və'liːs] **N** *Old-fashioned or Am (case)* mallette *f*; *(bag)* sac *m* de voyage

Valium® ['vælɪəm] *(pl* **inv**) **N** Valium® *m*; **to be on V.** être sous Valium®

Valkyrie [væl'kɪərɪ] **N** Walkyrie *f*, Valkyrie *f*

valley ['vælɪ] **N** vallée *f*; *(small)* vallon *m*; **the Valleys** = le sud du pays de Galles; **the Loire v.** la vallée de la Loire
►► *Am Fam Pej* ***valley girl*** = jeune Californienne frivole venant d'un milieu aisé; ***Valley of the Kings*** la Vallée des Rois

valor *Am* = **valour**

valorization, -isation [ˌvælərаɪ'zeɪʃən] **N** valorisation *f*

valorize, -ise ['væləraɪz] **VT** valoriser

valorous ['vælərəs] **ADJ** *Literary* valeureux, vaillant

valour, *Am* **valor** ['vælə(r)] **N** *Literary* vaillance *f*, bravoure *f*

valuable ['væljʊəbəl] **ADJ 1** *(of monetary worth)* de (grande) valeur **2** *(advice, friendship, time)* précieux
N *(usu pl)* **valuables** objets *mpl* de valeur
►► *Law* ***valuable consideration*** contrepartie *f* de valeur

valuation [ˌvæljʊ'eɪʃən] **N** *(act)* évaluation *f*, estimation *f*, expertise *f*; *(price)* évaluation *f*; **to get a v. of sth** faire évaluer *ou* estimer *ou* expertiser qch; **to make a v. of sth** évaluer *ou* estimer *ou* expertiser qch; **the v. of** *or* **the v. (put) on the business is £50,000** l'affaire a été estimée *ou* évaluée à 50 000 livres
►► *Fin* ***valuation charge*** taxation *f* à la valeur

valuator ['væljʊeɪtə(r)] **N** expert *m (en expertise de biens)*

value ['væljuː] **N 1** *(monetary worth)* valeur *f*; **to be of v.** avoir de la valeur; **they own nothing of v.** ils ne possèdent rien de valeur; **this necklace is of great v.** ce collier vaut cher; **this necklace is of little v.** ce collier ne vaut pas grand-chose *ou* a peu de valeur; **it's of no v.** c'est sans valeur; **to be good/poor v. (for money)** être d'un bon/mauvais rapport qualité-prix; **it's excellent v. for money** le rapport qualité-prix est excellent; **it's good v. at £10** ce n'est pas cher à 10 livres; **we got good v. for our money** nous en avons eu pour notre argent; **he gives you v. for money** il vous en donne pour votre argent; **to go up/down in v.** prendre/perdre de la valeur; **to depreciate in v.** se déprécier; **the increase/loss in v.** la hausse/perte de valeur, l'appréciation *f*/la dépréciation; **to set** *or* **to put a v. on sth** estimer la valeur de qch; **they put a v. of £80,000 on the house** ils ont estimé *ou* expertisé la maison à 80 000 livres; **of no commercial v.** sans valeur commerciale; **goods to the v. of £50 or more are subject to duty** les marchandises d'une valeur égale ou supérieure à 50 livres sont soumises à une taxe; **what will this do to the v. of property?** quel effet est-ce que ça va avoir sur le prix de l'immobilier?
2 *(merit, importance* ► *of method, work)* valeur *f*; *(*► *of person)* valeur *f*, mérite *m*; **he had nothing of v. to add** il n'avait rien d'important à ajouter; **these books may be of v. to them** ces livres peuvent leur servir, ils peuvent avoir besoin de ces livres; **they place little/a high v. on punctuality** ils font peu de cas/grand cas de l'exactitude, ils attachent peu d'importance/beaucoup d'importance à l'exactitude; **your help was of great v.** votre aide a été très précieuse; **she has been of great v. to the company** elle a apporté une contribution précieuse à l'entreprise
3 *(usu pl) (principles)* **values** valeurs *fpl*; **sense of values** sens *m* des valeurs; **moral values** valeurs *fpl* morales; **he has old-fashioned values** il est très traditionaliste
4 *(feature)* particularité *f*
5 *(of colour)* valeur *f*
6 *Ling, Math & Mus* valeur *f*
VT 1 *(assess worth of)* expertiser, estimer, évaluer; **to have sth valued** faire évaluer *ou* estimer *ou* expertiser qch; **they valued the house at £50,000** ils ont estimé *ou* évalué la maison à 50 000 livres **2** *(have high regard for* ► *friendship)* apprécier, estimer; *(*► *honesty, punctuality)* faire grand cas de; **if you v. your life you'd better leave** si vous tenez à la vie, vous feriez mieux de partir; **we greatly v. your help** nous apprécions beaucoup *ou* nous vous sommes très reconnaissants de votre aide; **does he v. your opinion?** votre opinion lui importe-t-elle?
►► *Fin* ***value added*** valeur *f* ajoutée; *Fin* ***value analysis*** analyse *f* de valeur; *Mktg* ***value brand*** marque *f* de valeur; *Com* ***value chain*** chaîne *f* de valeur; *Fin* ***value for collection*** valeur *f* à l'encaissement; *Fin* ***value date*** date *f* de valeur; *Fin* ***value day*** jour *m* de valeur; *Fin* ***value engineering*** analyse *f* de valeur; *Fin* ***value in exchange*** valeur *f* d'échange, contre-valeur *f*; ***value judgment*** jugement *m* de valeur; *Fin* ***value at maturity*** valeur *f* à l'échéance; *Fin* ***value in use*** valeur *f* d'usage

value-added ADJ *(product, service)* à valeur ajoutée
►► *Br* ***value-added tax*** taxe *f* sur la valeur ajoutée, *Can* taxe *f* sur les ventes

valued ['væljuːd] **ADJ** *(opinion)* estimé; *(advice, friend)* précieux
►► *Ins* ***valued policy*** assurance *f* forfaitaire

valueless ['væljʊlɪs] **ADJ** sans valeur

> Attention: ne pas confondre avec **invaluable** qui signifie **inestimable**.

valuer ['væljʊə(r)] **N** expert *m (en expertise de biens)*; **official v.** commissaire-priseur *m*

valve [vælv] **N 1** *(in pipe, tube, air chamber)* valve *f*; *(in machine)* soupape *f*, valve *f*
2 *Anat* valve *f*; *(small)* valvule *f*
3 *Bot & Zool* valve *f*
4 *Mus (of brass instrument)* piston *m*
5 *Elec (of radio)* lampe *f*, valve *f*

valved [vælvd] **ADJ** *Tech (pipe, tube, air chamber)* à valve(s); *(machine)* à valve(s), à soupape(s); *Mus (instrument)* à pistons

valvular ['vælvjʊlə(r)] **ADJ 1** *(machine)* à soupapes *ou* valves **2** *Anat, Bot & Zool* valvulaire *Mus (instrument)* à pistons

vamoose [və'muːs] **VI** *Am Fam* décamper, filer; **v.!** fiche le camp!

vamp[1] [væmp] *Fam* **N** *(woman)* vamp *f*
VT *(seduce)* vamper
VI 1 *(woman)* jouer la vamp **2** *Am (leave)* se casser, se tirer

vamp[2] *Fam* **N 1** *(piecing together)* rafistolage *m*; *(of story)* enjolivement□ *m* **3** *Mus* improvisation *f*
VT 1 *(repair)* rafistoler; *(renovate)* retaper; *(story)* enjoliver□ **3** *Mus (piece, song)* improviser des accompagnements à□; *(accompaniment)* improviser□

► **vamp up VT SEP** *Fam* = **vamp**[2] **VT**

vampire ['væmpaɪə(r)] **N** *(bat, monster)* vampire *m*; *(person)* vampire *m*, sangsue *f*
►► *Zool* ***vampire bat*** vampire *m*

vampiric [væm'pɪrɪk] **ADJ** vampirique

vampirism ['væmpaɪərɪzəm] **N** vampirisme *m*

vampish ['væmpɪʃ] **ADJ** *Fam (looks, dress)* de vamp, de femme fatale

VAN [væn] **N** *Comput (abbr* **value-added network**) réseau *m* à valeur ajoutée

van[1] [væn] **N 1** *(small vehicle)* camionnette *f*, fourgonnette *f*; *(large vehicle)* camion *m*, fourgon *m* **2** *Br Rail* fourgon *m*, wagon *m* **3** *(caravan)* caravane *f*
►► *Am* ***van pool*** = covoiturage *m* en minibus *(souvent aux frais de l'entreprise)*

van[2] **N** *Mil (vanguard)* avant-garde *f*; **in the v.** en tête; *Fig* **in the v. of abstract art** à l'avant-garde de l'art abstrait

van[3] **N** *Br Fam (advantage* ► *in tennis)* avantage *m*; **v. in/out** avantage dedans/dehors

vanadium [və'neɪdɪəm] **N** *Chem* vanadium *m*

V and A [ˌviːən'eɪ] **N** *Br Art (abbr* **Victoria and Albert Museum**) = grand musée londonien des arts décoratifs

vandal ['vændəl] **N** *(hooligan)* vandale *mf*
• **Vandal N** *Hist* Vandale *mf*

vandalism ['vændəlɪzəm] **N** vandalisme *m*

vandalize, -ise ['vændəlaɪz] **VT** *(building, telephone box)* saccager; **several pictures have been vandalized** plusieurs tableaux ont été mutilés (par des vandales)

vane [veɪn] **N 1** *(blade* ► *of propeller)* pale *f*; *(*► *of windmill)* aile *f*; *(*► *of turbine)* aube *f*; *(*► *of bomb, torpedo)* ailette **2 (weather) v.** girouette *f* **3** *Orn (of feather)* barbe *f*

vanguard ['vængɑːd] **N** *Mil* avant-garde *f*; **in the v. of the division** en tête de la division; *Fig* **to be in the v. of a movement** être un des pionniers d'un mouvement; **in the v. of progress** à l'avant-garde *ou* à la pointe du progrès

vanilla [və'nɪlə] **N** *(plant)* vanillier *m*; *(flavour)* vanille *f*; **flavoured with v., v. flavoured** vanillé (parfumé) à la vanille
COMP v. ice cream/flavour glace *f*/parfum *m* à la vanille
►► ***vanilla bean*** gousse *f* de vanille; ***vanilla essence*** extrait *m* de vanille; ***vanilla pod*** gousse *f* de vanille; ***vanilla sugar*** sucre *m* vanillé

vanillin [ˈvænılın] N vanilline *f*

vanish [ˈvænıʃ] VI *(object, person, race)* disparaître; *(hopes, worries)* s'évanouir, disparaître; **the aeroplane vanished from sight** l'avion a disparu; **elephants are vanishing from the earth** les éléphants sont en voie de disparition

vanishing [ˈvænıʃıŋ] ADJ *Fig* **she did a v. act** elle s'est éclipsée

►► *Old-fashioned* ***vanishing cream*** crème *f* de jour; ***vanishing point*** point *m* de fuite; *Fig* **profits have dwindled to v. point** les bénéfices se sont trouvés réduits à néant; ***vanishing trick*** tour *m* de passe-passe; *Fig* **he did a v. trick** *(disappeared)* il a disparu

vanity [ˈvænətı] *(pl* **vanities)** N **1** *(conceit)* vanité *f*, orgueil *m*; **she refused to use a walking stick out of (sheer) v.** par (pure) vanité elle a refusé d'utiliser une canne; **I think I can without v. claim to be the most competent** sans vanité *ou* sans vouloir me vanter, je peux prétendre être le plus compétent **2** *Formal or Literary (futility)* futilité *f*, insignifiance *f*, *Literary* vanité *f*; **all is v.** tout n'est que vanité **3** *Am (dressing table)* coiffeuse *f*, table *f* de toilette

►► ***vanity bag*** trousse *f* de toilette *(pour femme)*; ***vanity case*** mallette *f* de toilette, vanity-case *m*; ***vanity mirror*** miroir *m* de courtoisie; *Am* ***vanity plate*** plaque *f* d'immatriculation personnalisée; ***vanity press*** maison *f* d'édition à compte d'auteur; ***vanity publishing*** publication *f* à compte d'auteur; ***vanity table*** coiffeuse *f*, table *f* de toilette; ***vanity unit*** = meuble de salle de bains avec lavabo encastré

vanquish [ˈvæŋkwıʃ] VT vaincre

vanquisher [ˈvæŋkwıʃə(r)] N vainqueur *m*

vantage [ˈvɑːntıdʒ] N **1** *(advantageous situation)* avantage *m*, supériorité *f*; **point of v.** point de vue *m* privilégié **2** *(in tennis)* avantage *m*

►► ***vantage ground*** *(gen)* point de vue *m* (privilégié); *Mil* position *f* stratégique; ***vantage point*** point de vue *m* (privilégié), position *f* (avantageuse); **from our v. point we could see…** de la position avantageuse où nous étions nous voyions…; *Fig* **from the v. point of contemporary society, it is easy to…** d'un point de vue contemporain, il est facile de…

Vanuatu [ˈvænuːˌætuː] N *Geog* Vanuatu

vapid [ˈvæpıd] ADJ *(conversation, remark)* fade, insipide; *(style)* fade, plat; *(person)* fade, terne

vapidity [væˈpıdətı] N *(of conversation)* insipidité *f*; *(of style)* platitude *f*, caractère *m* plat; *(of person)* fadeur *f*

vapor *Am* = **vapour**

vaporization, -isation [ˌveıpəraıˈzeıʃən] N vaporisation *f*

vaporize, -ise [ˈveıpəraız] VT vaporiser

VI se vaporiser

vaporizer, -iser [ˈveıpəraızə(r)] N **1** *(gen)* vaporisateur *m*; *(for perfume, spray)* atomiseur *m*, pulvérisateur *m* **2** *Med (inhaler)* inhalateur *m*; *(for throat)* pulvérisateur *m*

vaporous [ˈveıpərəs] ADJ vaporeux

vapour, *Am* vapor [ˈveıpə(r)] N vapeur *f*; *(on window)* buée *f*

VI **1** *Phys* s'évaporer **2** *Am Fam (brag)* se vanter[❑], fanfaronner

• **vapours** NPL *Arch* **to have (an attack of) the vapours** avoir des vapeurs

►► *Constr* ***vapour barrier*** coupe-vapeur *m inv*; ***vapour bath*** bain *m* de vapeur; ***vapour density*** densité *f* de vapeur; ***vapour pressure*** pression *f ou* tension *f* de vapeur; *Aviat* ***vapour trail*** traînée *f* de condensation

variability [ˌveərıəˈbılətı] N variabilité *f*

variable [ˈveərıəbəl] ADJ **1** *(weather)* variable, changeant; *(quality)* variable, inégal; *(performance, work)* de qualité inégale, inégal; **the combinations are infinitely v.** les combinaisons peuvent varier à l'infini **2** *Comput & Math* variable

N variable *f*

►► *Fin* ***variable capital*** capital *m* variable; ***variable cost*** coût *m* variable; *Fin* ***variable costs*** coûts *mpl* variables, frais *mpl* variables; ***variable interest rate*** taux *m* d'intérêt variable; *Banking* ***variable rate*** taux *m* variable; ***variable star*** étoile *f* variable

variable-income ADJ *Fin (bond, investment)* à revenu variable

variable-rate ADJ

►► ***variable-rate interest*** intérêt *m* variable; ***variable-rate security*** valeur *f* à revenu variable

variable-yield ADJ *Fin (investments, securities)* à revenu variable

variably [ˈveərıəblı] ADV variablement

variance [ˈveərıəns] N **1** *(in statistics)* variance *f*; *(in law)* divergence *f*, différence *f*

2 *Acct* variance *f*, écart *m*; **v. analysis** analyse *f* des écarts

3 *Chem & Math* variance *f*

4 *(idioms)* **to be at v. with sb** être en désaccord avec qn; **to be at v. with sth** ne pas cadrer avec *ou* ne pas concorder avec qch; **she is at v. with her colleagues on *or* over this issue** elle est en désaccord avec ses collègues à ce sujet; **this announcement is at v. with his previous statements** cette annonce est en contradiction avec ses déclarations antérieures

variant [ˈveərıənt] N *(gen) & Ling* variante *f*

ADJ **1** *(different)* autre, différent; **v. interpretation *or* reading** interprétation *f ou* lecture *f* différente; **a v. spelling** une variante orthographique **2** *(various)* varié, divers **3** *Ling* variant

variation [ˌveərıˈeıʃən] N **1** *(change, modification)* variation *f*, modification *f*; **variations in temperature** variations *fpl ou* changements *mpl* de température; **the level of demand is subject to considerable v.** le niveau de la demande peut varier considérablement; **v. between two readings** *(using scientific instrument)* écart *m* entre deux lectures

2 *Mus* variation *f*; **theme and variations** thème *m* et variations *fpl*

3 *(different version)* variation *f*; **another v. on the same theme** une autre variation sur le même thème

4 *Biol* variation *f*

varicoloured, *Am* varicolored [ˈveərıˌkʌləd] ADJ multicolore, aux couleurs variées; *Fig* divers

varicose [ˈværıkəʊs] ADJ *(ulcer)* variqueux; **to have *or* to suffer from v. veins** avoir des varices

varied [ˈveərıd] ADJ varié, divers

variegated [ˈveərıgeıtıd] ADJ **1** *(gen)* bigarré **2** *Bot* panaché

variegation [ˌveərıˈgeıʃən] N bigarrure *f*

varietal [vəˈraıətəl] ADJ variétal

variety [vəˈraıətı] *(pl* **varieties)** N **1** *(diversity)* variété *f*, diversité *f*; **there isn't much v. in the menu** le menu n'est pas très varié *ou* n'offre pas un grand choix; **the work lacks v.** le travail manque de variété *ou* n'est pas assez varié; **it adds v. to the job** ça rend le travail plus intéressant; *Prov* **v. is the spice of life** = la diversité est le sel de la vie

2 *(number, assortment)* nombre *m*, quantité *f*; **for a v. of reasons** *(various)* pour diverses raisons; *(many)* pour de nombreuses raisons; **in a v. of ways** de diverses manières; **there is a wide v. of colours/styles to choose from** il y a un grand choix de couleurs/styles

3 *(type)* espèce *f*, genre *m*; **different varieties of cheese** différentes sortes *fpl* de fromage, des fromages *mpl* variés

4 *Bot & Zool (strain)* variété *f*

5 *(UNCOUNT) Theat & TV* variétés *fpl*

COMP *(artiste, show, theatre)* de variétés, de music-hall

►► *Am* ***variety meat*** abats *mpl*; *Am* ***variety store*** grand magasin *m*

variola [vəˈraıələ] N *Med* variole *f*, petite vérole *f*

various [ˈveərıəs] ADJ **1** *(diverse)* divers, différent; *(several)* plusieurs; **she writes under v. names** elle écrit sous divers pseudonymes; **at v. times in his life** à plusieurs reprises dans sa vie; **at v. intervals** de temps à autre **2** *(varied, different)* varié; **his reasons were many and v.** ses raisons étaient nombreuses et variées

variously [ˈveərıəslı] ADV *(in different ways)* diversement, de différentes *ou* diverses façons; **v. estimated at…** estimé par diverses sources à…; **he is v. known as soldier, king and emperor** on le connaît à la fois comme soldat, roi et empereur

varlet [ˈvɑːlıt] N **1** *Arch (servant)* valet *m* **2** *Pej Literary* fripon *m*, gredin *m*

varmint [ˈvɑːmınt] N *Fam Old-fashioned* coquin(e) *m,f*, vaurien(enne) *m,f*

varnish [ˈvɑːnıʃ] N *also Fig* vernis *m*

VT *(nails, painting, wood)* vernir; *(pottery)* vernir, vernisser; **to v. one's nails** se mettre du vernis à ongles; *Fig* **to v. (over) the truth** maquiller la vérité

varnisher [ˈvɑːnıʃə(r)] N vernisseur *m*

varnishing [ˈvɑːnıʃıŋ] N vernissage *m*

►► *Art* ***varnishing day*** (jour *m* du) vernissage *m*

varsity [ˈvɑːsətı] *(pl* **varsities)** *Fam* N *Br Old-fashioned* université[❑] *f*, fac *f*

ADJ *Am Sport* = qui représente l'université au plus haut niveau

►► *Br* ***varsity match*** match *m* interuniversitaire *(entre Oxford et Cambridge)*

vary [ˈveərı] *(pt & pp* **varied)** VI **1** *(be different)* varier; **opinions on this question v.** les opinions varient sur ce sujet; **the students v. considerably in ability** les étudiants ont des niveaux très différents; **they v. in size from small to extra large** ils vont de la plus petite taille à la plus grande; **to v. from year to year** varier d'une année à l'autre *ou* selon les années **2** *(change, alter)* changer, se modifier; **his mood varies with the weather** il est très lunatique; **the colour of the wood varies with age** ce bois change de couleur en vieillissant

VT *(diet, menu)* varier; *(temperature)* faire varier

varying [ˈveərıŋ] ADJ variable, qui varie; **with v. degrees of success** avec plus ou moins de succès

vascular [ˈvæskjʊlə(r)] ADJ vasculaire

►► *Bot* ***vascular bundle*** faisceau *m* fibro-vasculaire; *Med* ***vascular disease*** maladie *f* vasculaire; *Anat* ***vascular tissue*** tissu *m* vasculaire

vascularization, -isation [ˌvæskjʊləraıˈzeıʃən] N *Med* vascularisation *f*

vas deferens [ˈvæsˈdefərenz] *(pl* **vasa deferentia** [ˈveısədefəˈrenʃıə]) N *Anat* canal *m* déférent

vase [*Br* vɑːz, *Am* veız] N vase *m*

vasectomy [væˈsektəmı] *(pl* **vasectomies)** N vasectomie *f*; **to have a v.** subir une vasectomie

Vaseline® [ˈvæsəliːn] N vaseline *f*

VT enduire de vaseline, vaseliner

►► ***Vaseline® jelly*** vaseline *f*

vasoconstriction [ˌveızəʊkənˈstrıkʃən] N *Physiol & Med* vasoconstriction *f*

vasoconstrictor [ˌveızəʊkənˈstrıktə(r)] N *Physiol & Med* vasoconstricteur *m*

vasodilation [ˌveızəʊdaıˈleıʃən] N *Physiol & Med* vasodilatation *f*

vasodilator [ˌveızəʊdaıˈleıtə(r)] N *Physiol & Med* vasodilatateur *m*

vasomotor [ˌveızəʊˈməʊtə(r)] ADJ *Physiol* vasomoteur

vassal [ˈvæsəl] ADJ vassal

N vassal *m*

►► ***vassal state*** pays *m* vassal

vassalage [ˈvæsəlıdʒ] N vassalité *f*, vasselage *m*

vast [vɑːst] ADJ vaste, immense, énorme; **v. sums of money** des sommes *fpl* énormes, énormément d'argent; **she has v. experience in this area** elle a beaucoup d'expérience dans ce domaine

vastly [ˈvɑːstlı] ADV *(wealthy)* extrêmement, immensément; *(grateful)* infiniment; *(different)* extrêmement; **the show was v. successful** le spectacle a eu un immense succès; **he is v. improved** *(in health)* il va infiniment mieux; *(in work, performance)* il est bien meilleur

vastness [ˈvɑːstnıs] N immensité *f*

VAT [væt, ˌviːeıˈtiː] N *Br* *(abbr* **value added tax)** TVA *f*; **exclusive of *or* excluding V.** hors TVA; **subject to V.** soumis à la TVA; **to be V. registered** être assujetti à la TVA

►► ***VAT credit*** crédit *m* de TVA; *Fam* ***VAT man*** = inspecteur *m* de la TVA[❑]; ***VAT rate*** taux *m* de TVA; ***VAT registration number*** code *m* assujetti TVA; ***VAT return*** déclaration *f* de TVA; ***VAT statement*** état *m* TVA

vat [væt] **N** cuve *f*, bac *m*
▸▸ ***vat dye*** matière *f* colorante insoluble

vatful ['vætfʊl] **N** *(quantity)* cuvée *f*

Vatican ['vætɪkən] **N** the V. le Vatican
COMP *(edict, bank, policy)* du Vatican; **the First/Second V. council** le premier/deuxième concile du Vatican
▸▸ ***Vatican City*** l'État *m* de la cité du Vatican, le Vatican; *Fam Hum* ***Vatican roulette*** = méthode de contraception basée sur l'abstinence périodique

vaudeville ['vɔːdəvɪl] **N** *Am* vaudeville *m*
COMP *(artiste, theatre)* de vaudeville, de music-hall

vault [vɔːlt] **N 1** *Archit* voûte *f*; *Fig* **the v. of heaven** la voûte céleste
2 *Anat* voûte *f*
3 *(cellar)* cave *f*, cellier *m*; *(burial chamber)* caveau *m*; **a family v.** un caveau de famille
4 *(in bank)* chambre *f* forte; **a bank v.** les coffres *mpl* d'une banque, la salle des coffres
5 *(jump)* (grand) saut *m*; *Sport* saut *m* (à la perche)
VI *(jump)* sauter; *Sport* sauter (à la perche); **he vaulted over the fence** il a sauté par-dessus la clôture
VT 1 *Archit* voûter, cintrer **2** *(jump)* sauter par-dessus

vaulted ['vɔːltɪd] **ADJ** *Archit* voûté, en voûte

vaulting ['vɔːltɪŋ] **N 1** *Archit* voûte *f*, voûtes *fpl* **2** *Sport* saut *m* à la perche
ADJ 1 *Sport (pole)* de saut **2** *Fig Literary (ambition, pride)* démesuré
▸▸ ***vaulting horse*** cheval-d'arçons *m inv*

vaunt [vɔːnt] *Literary* **VT** vanter, se vanter de; **her much vaunted charms** ses charmes tant vantés
VI se vanter, fanfaronner

VC [ˌviː'siː] **N 1** *Br Mil (abbr* **Victoria Cross***)* Victoria Cross *f*
2 *Br Univ (abbr* **vice-chancellor***)* ≃ président *m* d'université
3 *(abbr* **vice-chairman***)* VP *m*
4 *Am Hist (abbr* **Vietcong***)* Viêt-cong *mf*

V-chip **N** *Comput & TV* puce *f* anti-violence

vCJD [ˌviːsiːˌdʒeɪ'diː] **N** *Med (abbr* **new-variant Creutzfeldt-Jakob disease***)* vMCJ *m*

VCR [ˌviːsiː'ɑː(r)] **N** *esp Am (abbr* **video cassette recorder***)* magnétoscope *m*

VCT [ˌviːsiː'tiː] **N** *Fin (abbr* **venture capital trust***)* FCPR *m*

VD [ˌviː'diː] **N** *(UNCOUNT) (abbr* **venereal disease***)* MST *f*
▸▸ ***VD clinic*** centre *m* de traitement des maladies vénériennes

VDT [ˌviːdiː'tiː] **N** *Comput (abbr* **visual display terminal***)* moniteur *m*

VDU [ˌviːdiː'juː] **N** *Comput (abbr* **visual display unit***)* moniteur *m*
▸▸ *Comput* ***VDU operator*** = personne travaillant sur écran

veal [viːl] **N** veau *m (viande)*
COMP *(stew, chop)* de veau

vector ['vektə(r)] **N 1** *Math & Med* vecteur *m* **2** *Aviat* direction *f*
COMP *Math* vectoriel
VT *Aviat* radioguider
▸▸ *Comput* ***vector graphics*** image *f* vectorielle

vectorial [vek'tɔːrɪəl] **ADJ** vectoriel

VE day [ˌviː'iː-] **N** *(abbr* **Victory in Europe Day***)* = jour de l'armistice du 8 mai 1945

veep [viːp] **N** *Am Fam* vice-président(e)▫ *m,f*

veer [vɪə(r)] **VI 1** *(vehicle, road)* virer, tourner; *(ship)* virer de bord; *(wind)* tourner, changer de direction; **the car veered (over) to the left** la voiture a viré vers la *ou* à gauche; **the wind has veered (round) to the east** le vent a tourné à l'est; **to v. off course** *(car)* quitter sa route; *(boat, plane, wind-surfer)* quitter sa trajectoire **2** *Fig* **the conversation veered round to the elections** la conversation a dévié sur les élections; **the speaker kept veering off the subject** l'orateur s'éloignait sans cesse du sujet
VT 1 *(ship, car)* faire virer **2** *(cable)* filer

▸ **veer round VI** *(vehicle, person)* faire demi-tour; *(wind)* changer de direction; *Fig (person)* se ranger à l'opinion contraire

veg [vedʒ] *Fam* **NPL** *(vegetables)* légumes▫ *mpl*
VI traîner, glandouiller; **I just feel like vegging in front of the TV tonight** j'ai envie de comater *ou* larver devant la télé ce soir

▸ **veg out VI** = **veg VI**

vegan ['viːgən] **N** végétalien(enne) *m,f*
ADJ végétalien

veganism ['viːgənɪzəm] **N** végétalisme *m*

vegeburger ['vedʒɪˌbɜːgə(r)] **N** hamburger *m* végétarien

vegetable ['vedʒtəbəl] **N 1** *Culin & Hort* légume *m*; *Bot (plant)* végétal *m*; **early vegetables** primeurs *mpl*; **green vegetables** légumes *mpl* verts; **root vegetables** racines *fpl (comestibles)* **2** *Fam Fig (person)* légume *m*; **the accident has left her a v.** depuis son accident, c'est un légume
COMP *(matter)* végétal; *(soup)* de légumes
▸▸ ***vegetable butter*** beurre *m* végétal; ***vegetable dish*** plat *m* à légumes, légumier *m*; ***vegetable garden*** (jardin *m*) potager *m*; ***vegetable knife*** couteau *m* à légumes, éplucheur *m*; ***vegetable marrow*** courge *f*; ***vegetable oil*** huile *f* végétale; ***vegetable peeler*** couteau *m* à légumes, éplucheur *m*; ***vegetable slicer*** coupe-légumes *m inv*; ***vegetable wax*** cire *f* végétale

vegetal ['vedʒɪtəl] **ADJ** végétal

vegetarian [ˌvedʒɪ'teərɪən] **N** végétarien(enne) *m,f*
ADJ végétarien

vegetarianism [ˌvedʒɪ'teərɪənɪzəm] **N** végétarisme *m*

> **VEGETARIANISM**
>
> Que ce soit pour des raisons éthiques, religieuses ou diététiques, le végétarisme s'est considérablement répandu au cours des dernières années en Grande-Bretagne – sensiblement plus que dans les autres pays européens ou aux États-Unis. Aujourd'hui, la majorité des restaurants proposent un menu avec un ou plusieurs plats sans viande, et lorsque l'on invite des gens à dîner, il est d'usage de s'enquérir s'ils sont végétariens ou non.

vegetate ['vedʒɪteɪt] **VI** *also Fig* végéter

vegetation [ˌvedʒɪ'teɪʃən] **N** végétation *f*

vegetative ['vedʒɪtətɪv] **ADJ** *also Fig* végétatif
▸▸ *Bot* ***vegetative propagation*** multiplication *f* végétative

veggie ['vedʒɪ] *Fam* **ADJ** *(abbr* **vegetarian***)* végétarien▫
N végétarien(enne)▫ *m,f*
• **veggies NPL** *(abbr* **vegetables***)* légumes▫ *mpl*, verdure▫ *f*

veggieburger ['vedʒɪˌbɜːgə(r)] **N** hamburger *m* végétarien

vehemence ['viːɪməns] **N** *(of emotions)* ardeur *f*, véhémence *f*; *(of actions, gestures)* violence *f*, véhémence *f*; *(of language)* véhémence *f*, passion *f*

vehement ['viːɪmənt] **ADJ** *(emotions)* ardent, passionné, véhément; *(actions, gestures)* violent, véhément; *(language)* véhément, passionné; **she launched a v. attack on the government** elle a violemment attaqué le gouvernement

vehemently ['viːɪməntlɪ] **ADV** *(speak)* avec passion, avec véhémence; *(deny)* avec véhémence; *(attack)* avec violence; *(gesticulate)* frénétiquement

vehicle ['viːɪkəl] **N 1** *(gen) & Aut* véhicule *m*; **heavy vehicles turning** *(sign)* passage d'engins; **v. emissions** gaz *mpl* d'échappement **2** *Pharm* véhicule *m* **3** *Fig (of thought, for propaganda)* véhicule *m*; **the play is merely a v. for his talents** la pièce n'est qu'un moyen de mettre ses talents en valeur
▸▸ ***vehicle excise duty*** taxe *f*, impôt *m* direct; ***vehicle identification number*** numéro *m* d'immatriculation

vehicular [vɪ'hɪkjʊlə(r)] **ADJ** *(gen) & Aut* de véhicules, de voitures
▸▸ ***vehicular access*** accès *m* aux véhicules; ***vehicular traffic*** circulation *f* automobile

veil [veɪl] **N 1** *(over face)* voile *m*; *(on hat)* voilette *f*; **she was wearing a v.** elle était voilée **2** *Fig* voile *m*; **to draw a v. over sth** mettre un voile sur qch; **under the v. of secrecy** sous le voile du secret **3** *Rel* **to take the v.** prendre le voile
VT 1 *(face)* voiler, couvrir d'un voile; **to v. oneself** se voiler **2** *Fig (truth, feelings, intentions)* voiler, dissimuler, masquer

veiled [veɪld] **ADJ 1** *(wearing a veil)* voilé **2** *(hidden, disguised* ▸ *expression, meaning)* voilé, caché; *(*▸*allusion, insult)* voilé; *(*▸*hostility)* sourd

vein [veɪn] **N 1** *Anat* veine *f*; **she has Polish blood in her veins** elle a du sang polonais dans les veines
2 *(on insect wing)* veine *f*; *(on leaf)* nervure *f*
3 *(in cheese, wood, marble)* veine *f*; *(of ore, mineral)* filon *m*, veine *f*; **a rich v. of irony runs through the book** le livre est parcouru d'une ironie sous-jacente
4 *(mood)* esprit *m*; *(style)* veine *f*, style *m*; **in a more frivolous v.** dans un esprit plus frivole; **in the same v.** dans le même style *ou* la même veine; **written in an imaginative v.** écrit dans un style plein d'imagination

veined [veɪnd] **ADJ 1** *(hand, skin)* veiné **2** *(leaf)* nervuré **3** *(cheese, stone)* marbré, veiné

veining ['veɪnɪŋ] **N** *(UNCOUNT)* **1** *Anat* veines *fpl* **2** *Bot (on leaf)* nervures *fpl* **3** *(in wood, marble, cheese)* veines *fpl*

velar ['viːlə(r)] **ADJ** *Anat & Ling* vélaire

Velcro® ['velkrəʊ] **N** (bande *f*) Velcro® *m*

veld, veldt [velt] **N** veld *m*, veldt *m*

vellum ['veləm] **N** vélin *m*
ADJ de vélin
▸▸ ***vellum paper*** papier *m* vélin

velocipede [vɪ'lɒsɪpiːd] **N** vélocipède *m*

velocity [vɪ'lɒsətɪ] *(pl* **velocities***)* **N** vélocité *f*
▸▸ *Econ* ***velocity of circulation (of money), velocity of money*** vitesse *f* de circulation de la monnaie

velodrome ['velədrəʊm] **N** vélodrome *m*

velour, velours [və'lʊə(r)] *(pl* **velours** [-'lʊəz]*)* **N** velours *m*
COMP de *ou* en velours

velum ['viːləm] **N 1** *Anat* vélum *m*, voile *m* du palais **2** *Zool & Bot* vélum *m*

velvet ['velvɪt] **N 1** *(material)* velours *m*; **as smooth as v.** *(skin)* doux comme du *ou* le velours; *(drink)* velouté; *Fam Fig* **to be on v.** jouer sur le velours **2** *Am Fam (profit)* bénef *m*; *(easy money)* argent *m* facile▫
COMP *(curtains, dress)* de *ou* en velours; *Fig (skin, voice)* velouté, de velours; **to walk with a v. tread** marcher à pas feutrés *ou* de velours; *Fig* **an iron hand in a v. glove** une main de fer dans un gant de velours
▸▸ *Hist* ***the Velvet Revolution*** la Révolution de Velours

velveteen [ˌvelvɪ'tiːn] **N** veloutine *f*
ADJ en *ou* de veloutine

velvety ['velvɪtɪ] **ADJ** *(cloth, complexion, texture)* velouteux, velouté; *Fig (cream, voice)* velouté

venal ['viːnəl] **ADJ** vénal

venality [viː'nælətɪ] **N** vénalité *f*

vend [vend] **VT** *Law or Formal* vendre

vendee [ven'diː] **N** *Law* acquéreur *m*

vendetta [ven'detə] **N** vendetta *f*; **to wage a v. against sb** mener une vendetta contre qn

vending ['vendɪŋ] **N** *Law or Formal* vente *f*
▸▸ ***vending machine*** distributeur *m* automatique

vendor ['vendɔː(r)] **N 1** *Com* marchand(e) *m,f*; **ice cream v.** marchand *m* de glaces
2 *(machine)* distributeur *m* automatique
3 *Law & Fin* vendeur(euse) *m,f*
4 *Comput* fournisseur *m*
▸▸ *Law & Fin* ***vendor's lien*** privilège *m* du vendeur

veneer [və'nɪə(r)] **N 1** *(of wood)* placage *m* (de bois); **walnut v.** placage *m* noyer **2** *Fig* vernis *m*, masque *m*, apparence *f*; **a v. of respectability** un vernis de respectabilité
VT plaquer; **veneered in** *or* **with walnut** plaqué noyer

venerable ['venərəbəl] **ADJ** *(gen) & Rel* vénérabl

enerate ['venəreɪt] **VT** vénérer

eneration [ˌvenə'reɪʃən] **N** vénération *f*

enereal [vɪ'nɪərɪəl] **ADJ** vénérien

►► ***venereal disease*** maladie *f* vénérienne

enereology [vɪˌnɪərɪ'blədʒɪ] **N** vénérologie *f*, vénéréologie *f*

enetian [vɪ'niːʃən] **N** Vénitien(enne) *m,f*

ADJ vénitien, de Venise

►► ***Venetian blind*** store *m* vénitien; ***Venetian glass*** verre *m ou* cristal *m* de Venise; *Archit* ***Venetian window*** (fenêtre *f*) serlienne *f*

enezuela [ˌvenɪ'zweɪlə] **N** Venezuela *m*

enezuelan [ˌvenɪ'zweɪlən] **N** Vénézuélien (enne) *m,f*

ADJ vénézuélien

COMP *(embassy, history)* du Venezuela

engeance ['vendʒəns] **N 1** *(revenge)* vengeance *f*; **to take** *or* **to wreak v. on** *or* **upon sb (for sth)** se venger de qn (pour qch); **to seek v. for sth** vouloir tirer vengeance de qch, chercher à se venger de qch **2** *(idiom)* **with a v.** très fort; **by then it was raining with a v.** à ce moment-là, la pluie tombait à torrents; **to work with a v.** travailler d'arrache-pied; **she's back with a v.** elle fait un retour en force

engeful ['vendʒful] **ADJ** vindicatif

engefully ['vendʒfulɪ] **ADV** d'une manière vindicative

engefulness ['vendʒfulnɪs] **N** *(of action)* caractère *m* vindicatif; *(of person)* esprit *m* de vengeance

enial ['viːnɪəl] **ADJ** *(gen) & Rel* véniel

eniality [ˌviːnɪ'ælətɪ] **N** caractère *m* véniel

enice ['venɪs] **N** Venise

enison ['venɪsən] **N** venaison *f*; **haunch of v.** quartier *m* de chevreuil

enn diagram [ven-] **N** diagramme *m* de Venn

enom ['venəm] **N** *also Fig* venin *m*; *Fig* **with v.** d'une manière venimeuse

enomous ['venəməs] **ADJ** venimeux; *Fig (remark, insult)* venimeux, malveillant; *(look)* haineux, venimeux; **he has a v. tongue** il a une langue de vipère

enomously ['venəməslɪ] **ADV** d'une manière venimeuse

enous ['viːnəs] **ADJ** veineux

ent [vent] **N 1** *(outlet ► for air, gas, liquid)* orifice *m*, conduit *m*; *(► in chimney)* conduit *m*, tuyau *m*; *(► in volcano)* cheminée *f*; *(► in barrel)* trou *m*; *(► for ventilation)* conduit *m* d'aération; *Ich & Orn (of fish, bird)* orifice *m* anal **2** *(in jacket, skirt)* fente *f* **3** *(idiom)* **to give v. to sth** donner *ou* laisser libre cours à qch; **he gave full v. to his feelings** il a donné *ou* laissé libre cours à ses émotions; **she gave v. to her anger** elle a laissé échapper sa colère

VT 1 *(barrel)* pratiquer un trou dans, trouer; *(pipe, radiator)* purger **2** *(release ► smoke)* laisser échapper; *(► gas)* évacuer **3** *Fig (express ► anger)* décharger; **to v. one's anger/one's spleen on sb** décharger sa colère/sa bile sur qn

entilate ['ventɪleɪt] **VT 1** *(room)* ventiler, aérer; **a well/badly ventilated room** une pièce bien/mal aérée **2** *Fig (controversy, question)* agiter (au grand jour); *(grievance)* étaler (au grand jour) **3** *Med (blood)* oxygéner

entilation [ˌventɪ'leɪʃən] **N** aération *f*, ventilation *f*; **a v. shaft** un conduit d'aération *ou* de ventilation

entilator ['ventɪˌleɪtə(r)] **N 1** *(in room, building)* ventilateur *m*; *Aut* déflecteur *m* **2** *Med* respirateur *m* (artificiel); **to be on a v.** être sur respirateur

enting screw ['ventɪŋ-] **N** *Aut* vis *f* de mise à l'air libre *ou* de purge

entral ['ventrəl] **ADJ** ventral

►► *Ich* ***ventral fin*** nageoire *f* pelvienne *ou* abdominale

entricle ['ventrɪkəl] **N** *Anat* ventricule *m*

entriloquism [ven'trɪləkwɪzəm] **N** ventriloquie *f*

entriloquist [ven'trɪləkwɪst] **N** ventriloque *mf*; **v.'s dummy** marionnette *f* de ventriloque

venture ['ventʃə(r)] **N 1** *(undertaking)* entreprise *f* périlleuse *ou* risquée; *(adventure)* aventure *f*; *(project)* projet *m*, entreprise *f*; **his latest film v.** sa dernière entreprise cinématographique; **it's his first v. into politics** c'est la première fois qu'il s'aventure dans la politique; **this v. into advertising** cette incursion dans la publicité

2 *Com & Fin (firm)* entreprise *f*; **a business v.** une entreprise commerciale, un coup d'essai commercial

3 *(idiom)* **at a v.** au hasard

VT 1 *(risk ► fortune, life)* hasarder, risquer; **he ventured a glance at her** il risqua un coup d'œil dans sa direction; *Prov* **nothing ventured nothing gained** qui ne risque rien n'a rien

2 *(proffer ► opinion, suggestion)* hasarder, avancer, risquer; **she didn't dare v. an opinion on the subject** elle n'a pas osé exprimer sa pensée à ce sujet; **if I may v. a guess** si je peux me permettre d'avancer une hypothèse

3 *(dare)* oser; **to v. to do sth** s'aventurer *ou* se hasarder à faire qch; **he ventured to contradict her** il a osé la contredire

VI 1 *(embark)* se lancer; **to v. into politics** se lancer dans la politique

2 *(go)* **to v. in/out** prendre le risque d'entrer/de sortir, se risquer à entrer/à sortir; **I wouldn't v. out of doors in this weather** je ne me risquerais pas à sortir par ce temps; **don't v. too far from the beach** ne t'éloigne pas trop de la plage; **he ventured into the woods** il s'est hasardé dans les bois; *Literary* **the explorers ventured forth into the jungle** les explorateurs se sont lancés dans la jungle

►► *Fin* ***venture capital*** capital-risque *m*; ***venture capital company*** société *f* à capital-risque; *Fin* ***venture capitalist*** pourvoyeur(euse) *m,f* de capital-risque, spécialiste *mf* de la prise de risques *(dans la finance)*; ***venture capital trust*** fonds *m* commun de placement à risques; *Br* ***Venture Scout*** éclaireur *m (de grade supérieur)*

venturesome ['ventʃəsəm] **ADJ** *Literary* **1** *(daring ► nature, person)* aventureux, entreprenant **2** *(hazardous ► action, journey)* hasardeux, risqué

venue ['venjuː] **N 1** *(setting)* lieu *m* (de rendezvous *ou* de réunion); *(for football match)* terrain *m*; *(for tennis)* court *m*; **he hasn't decided on a v. for the concert** il n'a pas décidé où le concert aura lieu; **they've changed the v. for tonight's meeting** ils ont changé le lieu de réunion de ce soir; **the band have played at all of the biggest London venues** l'orchestre a joué dans toutes les grandes salles (de concert) de Londres **2** *Law* lieu *m* du procès; **to lay the v.** désigner la cour qui sera saisie de l'affaire

> Note that the French word **venue** is a false friend and is never a translation for the English word **venue**. It means **coming, arrival**.

venule ['venjuːl] **N** *Anat* veinule *f*

Venus ['viːnəs] **N** *Astron* Vénus *f*

PR N *Myth* Vénus

►► *Bot* ***Venus flytrap*** dionée *f*; *Zool* ***Venus shell*** vénus *f*

veracious [və'reɪʃəs] **ADJ** véridique

veracity [və'ræsɪtɪ], **veraciousness** [və'reɪʃəsnɪs] **N** véracité *f*

veranda, verandah [və'rændə] **N** véranda *f*

verb [vɜːb] **N** verbe *m*

►► ***verb phrase*** syntagme *m ou* groupe *m* verbal

verbal ['vɜːbəl] **ADJ 1** *(spoken ► account, agreement, promise)* verbal, oral; *(► confession)* oral; *Fam* **to have v. diarrhoea** être atteint de diarrhée verbale **2** *(literal ► copy, translation)* mot à mot, littéral, textuel **3** *Gram* verbal

N *Br Fam* **to give sb v.** *(shout at)* engueuler qn; **they were given some v.** ils se sont fait engueuler

• **verbals** **NPL** *Law* aveux *mpl* faits oralement *ou* de vive voix

►► ***verbal memory*** mémoire *f* auditive; *Gram* ***verbal noun*** nom *m* verbal; ***verbal skills*** aptitudes *fpl* à l'oral

verbalize, -ise ['vɜːbəlaɪz] **VT** *(feelings, ideas)* verbaliser, exprimer par des mots

verbally ['vɜːbəlɪ] **ADV 1** *(orally)* verbalement, oralement; **to be v. abused** se faire insulter; **to agree v. to do sth** se mettre d'accord verbalement pour faire qch; **v. deficient** illettré, analphabète **2** *(as a verb)* en tant que verbe

verbatim [vɜː'beɪtɪm] **ADJ** mot pour mot

ADV textuellement; **to report a speech v.** rendre compte mot à mot d'un discours

►► ***verbatim report*** procès-verbal *m (d'une réunion)*

verbena [vɜː'biːnə] **N** *(herb, plant)* verveine *f*; *(genus)* verbénacées *fpl*

verbiage ['vɜːbɪɪdʒ] **N** verbiage *m*

verbose [vɜː'bəʊs] **ADJ** verbeux, prolixe

verbosely [vɜː'bəʊslɪ] **ADV** avec verbosité, verbeusement; **v. worded** verbeux

verbosity [vɜː'bɒsətɪ] **N** verbosité *f*

verdant ['vɜːdənt] **ADJ** *Literary* verdoyant

verdict ['vɜːdɪkt] **N 1** *Law* verdict *m*; **to reach a v.** arriver à un verdict; **a v. of guilty/not guilty** un verdict de culpabilité/non-culpabilité; **the jury returned a v. of not guilty/guilty** le jury a déclaré l'accusé non coupable/coupable; **open v.** *(at inquest)* = jugement qui ne formule aucune conclusion sur les circonstances dans lesquelles la mort a eu lieu **2** *Fig (conclusion)* verdict *m*, jugement *m*; **to give one's v. on sth** se prononcer sur qch

verdigris ['vɜːdɪgrɪs] **N** vert-de-gris *m inv*

ADJ vert-de-grisé

verdure ['vɜːdʒə(r)] **N** *Literary* verdure *f*

verge [vɜːdʒ] **N 1** *(edge ► of lawn)* bord *m*; *(► of forest)* orée *f*; *Br (► by roadside)* accotement *m*, bas-côté *m*; **grass v.** *(round flowerbed)* bordure *f* en gazon; *(by roadside)* herbe *f* au bord de la route; *(in park, garden)* bande *f* d'herbe; *Br Aut* **soft verges** *(sign)* accotement instable; **the car skidded onto the v.** la voiture a dérapé et est montée sur l'accotement *ou* sur le bas-côté **2** *Fig (brink)* bord *m*; *(threshold)* seuil *m*; **to be on the v. of tears/of a nervous breakdown** être au bord des larmes/de la dépression nerveuse; **to be on the v. of adolescence** être au seuil de l'adolescence; **to be on the v. of doing sth** être sur le point de faire qch; **I was on the v. of telling him** j'étais sur le point de lui dire, j'étais à deux doigts de lui dire; **he's on the v. of sixty** il frise la soixantaine

VT *(road, lawn)* border

►**verge on, verge upon** **VT INSEP** *(be close to)* côtoyer, s'approcher de; **they are verging on bankruptcy** ils sont au bord de la faillite; **his feeling was one of panic verging on hysteria** il ressentait une sorte de panique qui frôlait l'hystérie; **she's verging on thirty** elle frise la trentaine; **green verging on blue** du vert qui tire sur le bleu

verger ['vɜːdʒə(r)] **N** *Rel* bedeau *m*, suisse *m*; *(at ceremony)* huissier *m* à verge, massier *m*

Vergil = **Virgil**

verifiable [ˌverɪ'faɪəbəl] **ADJ** vérifiable

verification [ˌverɪfɪ'keɪʃən] **N** vérification *f*

verify ['verɪfaɪ] *(pt & pp* **verified***)* **VT** *(prove ► information, rumour)* vérifier; *(confirm ► truth)* vérifier, confirmer; **I have witnesses who can v. what I have said** j'ai des témoins qui peuvent confirmer mes dires

verily ['verəlɪ] **ADV** *Arch* vraiment, véritablement

verisimilitude [ˌverɪsɪ'mɪlɪtjuːd] **N** *Formal* vraisemblance *f*

veritable ['verɪtəbəl] **ADJ** véritable; **he is a v. genius** c'est un véritable *ou* vrai génie

veritably ['verɪtəblɪ] **ADV** véritablement

verity ['verɪtɪ] *(pl* **verities***)* **N** *Formal* vérité *f*

vermicelli [ˌvɜːmɪ'selɪ] **N** *(UNCOUNT)* vermicelle *m*, vermicelles *mpl*

vermicide ['vɜːmɪsaɪd] **N** vermicide *m*

vermiculite [vɜː'mɪkjʊlaɪt] **N** *Miner* vermiculite *f*

vermiform ['vɜːmɪfɔːm] **ADJ** vermiforme

vermifugal [ˌvɜːmɪ'fjuːgəl] **ADJ** vermifuge

vermifuge ['vɜːmɪfjuːdʒ] **N** vermifuge *m*

vermilion, vermillion [və'mɪlɪən] **N** vermillon *m*

ADJ vermillon *(inv)*

vermin ['vɜːmɪn] NPL **1** *(rodents)* animaux *mpl* nuisibles; *(insects)* vermine *f* **2** *Pej (people)* vermine *f*, racaille *f*

verminous ['vɜːmɪnəs] ADJ **1** *(place)* infesté de vermine *ou* d'animaux nuisibles, pouilleux; *(clothes)* pouilleux, couvert de vermine; *Med (disease)* vermineux **2** *Pej (person)* infect, ignoble

vermouth [vɜː'muːθ] N vermouth *m*

vernacular [və'nækjʊlə(r)] N **1** *Ling* (langue *f*) vernaculaire *m*; **in the v.** en langue vernaculaire; *(everyday language)* en langage courant; *(not Latin)* en langue vulgaire
2 *(jargon)* jargon *m*; **the sporting v.** le jargon sportif
3 *Bot & Zool* nom *m* vernaculaire
4 *Archit* style *m* typique (du pays)
ADJ **1** *Bot, Ling & Zool* vernaculaire **2** *(architecture, style)* indigène

vernal ['vɜːnəl] ADJ *Literary (flowers, woods, breeze)* printanier
▸▸ ***vernal equinox*** équinoxe *m* de printemps

veronal ['verənəl] N *Pharm* véronal *m*

veronica [və'rɒnɪkə] N *Bot* véronique *f*

verruca [və'ruːkə] (*pl* **verrucas** *or* **verrucae** [-kaɪ]) N verrue *f* (plantaire)

versant ['vɜːsənt] N *(of mountain)* versant *m*

versatile ['vɜːsətaɪl] ADJ **1** *(person)* aux talents variés, doué dans tous les domaines; *(mind)* souple; *(tool)* polyvalent, à usages multiples; *(dress, jacket* ▸ *which can be worn anywhere)* passe-partout; **a politician has to be very v.** un politicien doit avoir des talents variés **2** *Bot* versatile **3** *Zool* mobile, pivotant

> Note that the French word **versatile** is a false friend and is almost never a translation for the English word **versatile**. It means **fickle, changeable**.

versatility [ˌvɜːsə'tɪlətɪ] N **1** *(of person)* faculté *f* d'adaptation, variété *f* de talents; *(of mind)* souplesse *f*; *(of tool)* polyvalence *f* **2** *Bot & Zool* versatilité *f*

verse [vɜːs] N **1** *(stanza* ▸ *of poem)* strophe *f*; *(▸ of song)* couplet *m*; *(▸ in bible)* verset *m* **2** *(UNCOUNT) (poetry)* vers *mpl*, poésie *f*; **in v.** en vers; **free v.** vers *mpl* libres
COMP *(line, epic)* en vers

versed [vɜːst] ADJ **v. in** *(knowledgeable)* versé dans; *(experienced)* rompu à; **he is well/not very well v. in current affairs** il est/n'est pas très au courant de l'actualité, *Formal* il est très/peu versé dans les questions d'actualité; **I am well v. in his ways** je le connais bien, je sais bien comment il est

versification [ˌvɜːsɪfɪ'keɪʃən] N versification *f*

versifier ['vɜːsɪˌfaɪə(r)] N *Pej* versificateur(trice) *m,f*

versify ['vɜːsɪfaɪ] (*pt & pp* **versified**) VT versifier, mettre en vers
VI rimer, faire des vers

version ['vɜːʃən] N **1** *(account of events)* version *f*; **her v. differs from mine** sa version des faits diffère de la mienne
2 *(form* ▸ *of book, song)* version *f*; **did you see the film in the original v.?** est-ce que vous avez vu le film en version originale?; **the screen** *or* **film v. of the book** l'adaptation cinématographique du livre; *Fig* **he looks like a younger v. of his father** c'est l'image de son père en plus jeune
3 *(model* ▸ *of car, plane)* modèle *m*, version *f*
4 *(translation)* version *f*

verso ['vɜːsəʊ] (*pl* **versos**) N *(of page)* verso *m*; *(of coin, medal)* revers *m*

versus ['vɜːsəs] PREP **1** *(against)* contre; **it's the government v. the trade unions** c'est le gouvernement contre les syndicats; *Sport* **Italy v. France** Italie-France; *Law* **Dickens v. Dickens** Dickens contre Dickens **2** *(compared with)* par rapport à, par opposition à; **the advantages of living in a house v. (living in) a flat** les avantages d'une maison par rapport à un appartement; **the advantage of a higher salary v. the loss of security** l'avantage d'un salaire plus élevé en contrepartie d'une sécurité moindre

vertebra ['vɜːtɪbrə] (*pl* **vertebras** *or* **vertebrae** [-briː]) N vertèbre *f*

vertebral ['vɜːtɪbrəl] ADJ vertébral
▸▸ ***vertebral column*** colonne *f* vertébrale

vertebrate ['vɜːtɪbreɪt] ADJ vertébré
N vertébré *m*

vertex ['vɜːteks] (*pl* **vertexes** *or* **vertices** [-tɪsiːz]) N *Math* sommet *m*; *Astron* apex *m*; *Anat & Zool* vertex *m*

vertical ['vɜːtɪkəl] ADJ **1** *(gen) & Geom* vertical; **a v. cliff** une falaise à pic *ou* qui s'élève à la verticale; **a v. line** une ligne verticale **2** *Fig (structure, organization)* vertical
N verticale *f*; **out of the v.** écarté de la verticale, hors d'aplomb
▸▸ *Geom* ***vertical angles*** angles *mpl* de pointe; *Astron* ***vertical circle*** vertical *m*; *Econ* ***vertical concentration*** concentration *f* verticale; *Fin* ***vertical equity*** équité *f* verticale; *Am* ***vertical file*** *(cabinet)* = casier des documents qui ne font pas partie de la collection permanente d'une bibliothèque; *(documents)* = documents qui ne font pas partie de la collection permanente d'une bibliothèque; *TV* ***vertical hold*** bouton *m* de commande de synchronisme vertical; *Com* ***vertical integration*** intégration *f* verticale; *Comput* ***vertical justification*** justification *f* verticale; ***vertical landing*** atterrissage *m* vertical; *Com* ***vertical merger*** fusion *f* verticale; *Fin* ***vertical spread*** écart *m* vertical; ***vertical takeoff*** décollage *m* vertical; *Am* ***vertical union*** confédération *f* syndicale

verticality [ˌvɜːtɪ'kælɪtɪ] N verticalité *f*

vertically ['vɜːtɪklɪ] ADV verticalement; *Aviat* **to take off v.** décoller à la verticale
▸▸ *Hum* ***vertically challenged*** de petite taille

vertiginous [vɜː'tɪdʒɪnəs] ADJ *Formal* vertigineux

vertigo ['vɜːtɪgəʊ] N *(UNCOUNT)* vertige *m*; **to suffer from** *or* **to have v.** avoir le vertige

verve [vɜːv] N verve *f*, brio *m*

Very ['vɪərɪ-] N
▸▸ ***Very light*** fusée *f* éclairante; ***Very pistol*** pistolet *m* lance-fusées

VERY ['verɪ] ADV **1** *(with adj or adv)* très, bien; **it was v. pleasant** c'était très *ou* bien agréable; **was the pizza good? – v./not v.** la pizza était-elle bonne? – très/pas très; **I'm not v. impressed with the results** je ne suis pas très *ou* tellement impressionné par les résultats; **be v. careful** faites très *ou* bien attention; **he was v. hungry/thirsty** il avait très faim/soif; **I v. nearly fell** j'ai bien failli tomber; **v. few/little** très peu; **so v. little** si peu; **there were v. few of them** *(people)* ils étaient très peu nombreux; *(objets)* il y en avait très peu; **he takes v. little interest in what goes on** il s'intéresse très peu à ce qui se passe; **there's v. little one can do to help** on ne peut pas faire grand-chose pour aider; **there weren't v. many people** il n'y avait pas grand monde; **it isn't so v. difficult** ce n'est pas si difficile que ça; **v. good!, v. well!** *(expressing agreement, consent)* très bien!; **you can't v. well ask outright** tu ne peux pas vraiment demander directement; **that's all v. well but...** tout ça, c'est très bien mais…
2 *(with superlative* ▸ *emphatic use)* **our v. best wine** notre meilleur vin; **the v. best of friends** les meilleurs amis du monde; **it's the v. worst thing that could have happened** c'est bien ce qui pouvait arriver de pire; **the v. latest designs** les créations les plus récentes; **at the v. latest** au plus tard; **at the v. least/most** tout au moins/plus; **the v. first/last person** la (toute) première/dernière personne; **the v. next day** le lendemain même, dès le lendemain; **the v. next person I met was his brother** la première personne que j'ai rencontrée était son frère; **we'll stop at the v. next town** nous nous arrêterons à la prochaine ville; **it's nice to have your v. own car** c'est bien d'avoir une voiture à soi; **it's my v. own** c'est à moi; **the v. same day** le jour même; **on the v. same date** exactement à la même date; *Rel* **the V. Reverend Alan Scott** le très révérend Alan Scott
ADJ **1** *(extreme, far)* **at the v. end** *(of street, row etc)* tout au bout; *(of story, month etc)* tout à la fin; **to the v. end** *(in space)* jusqu'au bout; *(in time)* jusqu'à la fin; **at the v. beginning** au tout début; **at the v. back** tout au fond; **at the v. top/bottom of the page** tout en haut/en bas de la page; **at th v. bottom of the sea** au plus profond de la mer
2 *(exact)* **at that v. moment** juste à ce moment-là; **the v. man I need** juste l'homme qu'il me fau; **those were his v. words** ce sont ses propos mê mes, c'est exactement ce qu'il a dit; **this is the v room where they were murdered** c'est dans cett pièce même qu'ils ont été tués; **it was a year ag to the v. day** c'était il y a un an jour pour jour
3 *(emphatic use)* **the v. idea!** quelle idée!; **the v thought of it makes me shiver** je frissonne rie que d'y penser; **it happened before my v. eyes** ce la s'est passé sous mes yeux; *Arch* **the veriest foo could do it** le premier imbécile venu pourrait l faire
• **very much** ADV **1** *(greatly)* beaucoup, bien; **like French cinema v. much** j'aime beaucoup l cinéma français; **I v. much hope to be able t come** j'espère bien que je pourrai venir; **v. muc better/bigger** beaucoup mieux/plus grand; **ur less I'm v. much mistaken** à moins que je ne m trompe; **were you impressed? – v. much so** ça vou a impressionné? – beaucoup
2 *(to a large extent)* **the situation remains v. muc the same** la situation n'a guère évolué; **it's v. muc a question of who to believe** la question est su tout de savoir qui on doit croire ADJ beaucou de; **there wasn't v. much wine** il n'y avait pa beaucoup de vin PRON beaucoup; **she doesn say v. much** elle parle peu, elle ne dit pas granc chose
▸▸ ***very high frequency*** très haute fréquence (gamme *f* des) ondes *fpl* métriques; ***very low fre quency*** très basse fréquence *f*

vesical ['vesɪkəl] ADJ *Anat & Med* vésical

vesicle ['vesɪkəl] N *(sac)* vésicule *f*; *(blister)* am poule *f*

vespers ['vespəz] NPL vêpres *fpl*

vessel ['vesəl] N **1** *Literary (container)* récipient *n*; **a drinking v.** une timbale, un gobelet **2** *Naut* vais seau *m* **3** *Anat & Bot* vaisseau *m*

vest[1] [vest] N **1** *Br (singlet* ▸ *for boy, man)* maillo *m* de corps, tricot *m* de peau; *(▸ for woman)* che mise *f* **2** *Am (waistcoat)* gilet *m* (de costume)

> Note that the French word **veste** is a false friend and is never a translation for the English word **vest**. It means **jacket**.

vest[2] VT *Formal* investir; **to v. sb with the powe to do sth** investir qn du pouvoir de faire qch; **to v sth in sb** assigner *ou* attribuer qch à qn; **th president is vested with the power to veto the gov ernment** le président a le pouvoir d'opposer so veto aux projets du gouvernement; **legislativ authority is vested in Parliament** le Parlement es investi du pouvoir législatif

vestal ['vestəl] *Antiq* ADJ *(relating to Vesta)* de Ves ta; *(relating to the vestal virgins)* de vestale, de vestales
N vestale *f*
▸▸ ***vestal virgin*** vestale *f*

vested interest ['vestɪd-] N intérêt *m* (direct o personnel); **she has a v. in keeping it secret/in th success of the venture** elle a tout intérêt à garde le secret/à ce que l'entreprise réussisse; *Fin* **t have a v. in a business** avoir des capitaux investi dans une entreprise, être intéressé dans un entreprise
• **vested interests** NPL *(rights)* droits *mpl* ac quis; *(investments)* capitaux *mpl* investis; *(ac vantages)* intérêts *mpl*; **there are vested interest in industry opposed to trade union reform** ceu qui ont des intérêts dans l'industrie s'opposen à la réforme des syndicats; **that case will neve come to trial, there are too many vested interest** cette affaire ne sera jamais jugée, cela dérang trop de gens

vestibule ['vestɪbjuːl] N **1** *(in house, church)* ves tibule *m*; *(in hotel)* vestibule *m*, hall *m* d'entrée *Med* vestibule *m* **3** *Am Rail* sas *m*

vestige ['vestɪdʒ] N **1** *(remnant)* vestige *m*; **there not a v. of truth in the story** il n'y a pas un grain o une once de vérité dans cette histoire **2** *Anat Zool* organe *m* rudimentaire; **the v. of a tail** un queue rudimentaire

vestigial [veˈstɪdʒɪəl] ADJ **1** *(remaining)* résiduel; **some v. sense of decency prevented him from doing it** le peu de décence qui lui restait l'a empêché de le faire **2** *Anat & Zool (organ, tail)* rudimentaire, atrophié

vestment [ˈvestmənt] N habit *m* de cérémonie; *Rel* vêtement *m* sacerdotal

vest-pocket *Am* N poche *f* de gilet
ADJ *(book, camera, pistol)* de poche; *Fig (farm, park)* grand comme un mouchoir de poche

vestry [ˈvestrɪ] *(pl* **vestries**) N **1** *(room)* sacristie *f* **2** *(committee)* conseil *m* paroissial

Vesuvius [vɪˈsuːvɪəs] N **(Mount) V.** le Vésuve

vet[1] [vet] N *(abbr* **veterinary surgeon, veterinarian**) vétérinaire *mf*

vet[2] *Am Fam (abbr* **veteran**) N ancien combattant□ *m*, vétéran□ *m*
ADJ *(association, rally)* d'anciens combattants□

vet[3] *(pt & pp* **vetted**, *cont* **vetting**) VT **1** *(check ▸ application)* examiner minutieusement, passer au crible; *(▸ claims, facts, figures)* vérifier soigneusement, passer au crible; *(▸ documents)* contrôler; *(▸ person)* enquêter sur; **she was thoroughly vetted for the job** ils ont soigneusement examiné sa candidature avant de l'embaucher; **the committee has to v. any expenditure exceeding £100** le comité doit approuver toute dépense au-delà de 100 livres; **all his girlfriends were vetted by his mother** toutes ses copines devaient recevoir l'approbation maternelle **2** *Vet (examine)* examiner; *(treat)* soigner

vetch [vetʃ] N *Bot* vesce *f*

veteran [ˈvetərən] N **1** *Mil* ancien combattant *m*, vétéran *m* **2** *(experienced person)* vétéran *m*, ancien(enne) *m,f* **3** *(car)* voiture *f* ancienne *ou* d'époque; *(machinery)* vieille machine *f*
ADJ *(experienced)* expérimenté, chevronné; **she's a v. campaigner for civil rights** c'est une ancienne de la campagne pour les droits civiques
▸▸ ***Veterans Association*** association *f* d'anciens combattants; *Br* ***veteran car*** voiture *f* de collection *(normalement antérieure à 1905)*; *Am* ***Veterans Day*** fête *f* de l'armistice *(le 11 novembre)*, *Can* le Jour du Souvenir; ***veteran soldier*** vieux soldat *m*

veterinarian [ˌvetərɪˈneərɪən] N *Am* vétérinaire *mf*

veterinary [ˈvetərɪnrɪ] ADJ *(medicine, science)* vétérinaire
▸▸ *Br* ***veterinary surgeon*** vétérinaire *mf*

veto [ˈviːtəʊ] *(pl* **vetoes**) N **1** *(power)* droit *m* de veto; **to use one's v.** exercer son droit de veto **2** *(refusal)* veto *m*; **to put a v. on sth** mettre *ou* opposer son veto à qch
VT *Pol & Fig* mettre *ou* opposer son veto à

vetting [ˈvetɪŋ] N *(UNCOUNT) (of things)* contrôle *m*; *(of people)* enquête *f* (**of** sur); **to undergo positive v.** être soumis à une enquête de sécurité; **security v.** enquêtes *fpl* de sécurité

vex [veks] VT contrarier, ennuyer

> Note that the French verb **vexer** is a false friend. It means **to hurt somebody's feelings**.

vexation [vekˈseɪʃən] N *Formal* **1** *(anger)* ennui *m*, agacement *m*; **she threw it down in v.** elle le jeta avec agacement **2** *(difficulty, annoyance)* ennui *m*, tracasserie *f*; **one of life's vexations** une de ces contrariétés que nous réserve la vie

vexatious [vekˈseɪʃəs] ADJ *Formal* contrariant, ennuyeux

vexed [vekst] ADJ *Formal* **1** *(annoyed)* fâché, ennuyé, contrarié; **to become v.** se fâcher; **to be v. with sb** être fâché contre qn, en vouloir à qn; **she was v. at his behaviour** son comportement l'avait contrariée **2** *(question, issue ▸ controversial)* controversé; *(▸ difficult)* épineux; **the v. question of crime and punishment** le problème constamment débattu du crime et du châtiment; **it remains a v. question** c'est un sujet qui continue à soulever les controverses; **it's a very v. period in our history** c'est une période délicate de notre histoire

vexing [ˈveksɪŋ] ADJ **1** *(annoying)* contrariant, ennuyeux, fâcheux **2** *(frustrating ▸ issue, riddle)* frustrant

VGA [ˌviːdʒiːˈeɪ] N *Comput (abbr* **Video Graphics Array**) VGA *m*
▸▸ ***VGA monitor*** moniteur *m* VGA

VHF [ˌviːeɪtʃˈef] N *TV & Rad (abbr* **very high frequency**) VHF *f*

VHS [ˌviːeɪtʃˈes] N *TV (abbr* **video home system**) VHS *m*

via [ˈvaɪə] PREP **1** *(by way of)* via, par; **they travelled from Paris to Rome v. Florence** ils ont voyagé de Paris à Rome via *ou* en passant par Florence; **the trip is shorter if you travel v. Calais** le trajet est plus court par Calais **2** *(by means of)* par, au moyen de; **contact me v. this number/v. my secretary** contactez-moi à ce numéro/par l'intermédiaire de ma secrétaire; **these pictures come v. satellite** ces images arrivent par satellite; **the best way to get into films is v. drama school** le meilleur moyen d'entrer dans le monde du cinéma est de passer par une école d'art dramatique

viability [ˌvaɪəˈbɪlɪtɪ] N *(UNCOUNT)* **1** *Econ (of company, state)* viabilité *f* **2** *(of plan, programme, scheme)* chances *fpl* de réussite, viabilité *f* **3** *Med & Bot* viabilité *f*

viable [ˈvaɪəbəl] ADJ **1** *Econ (company, economy, state)* viable **2** *(practicable ▸ plan, programme)* viable, qui a des chances de réussir; **there is no v. alternative** il n'y a pas d'autre solution viable **3** *Med & Bot* viable

viaduct [ˈvaɪədʌkt] N viaduc *m*

via ferrata [ˌviːəfəˈrɑːtə] N *Sport* via ferrata *f inv*

Viagra® [ˌvaɪˈægrə] N *Pharm* Viagra® *m*

vial [ˈvaɪəl] N *Literary* fiole *f*; *Pharm* ampoule *f*

viaticum [vaɪˈætɪkəm] *(pl* **viaticums** *or* **viatica** [-kə]) N viatique *m*

vibe [vaɪb] N *Fam (abbr* **vibration**) atmosphère□ *f*, ambiance□ *f*; **this bar's got a really nice relaxed v.** l'ambiance est très cool dans ce bar; **their new album's got a bit of an R&B v.** leur nouvel album a un petit côté R&B

vibes [vaɪbz] NPL *Fam* **1** *Mus (abbr* **vibraphone**) vibraphone□ *m* **2** *(abbr* **vibrations**) atmosphère□ *f*, ambiance□ *f*; **they give off really good/bad v.** avec eux le courant passe vraiment bien/ne passe vraiment pas; **I get really bad v. from her** je la sens vraiment mal; **I don't like the v. in this place** je n'aime pas l'ambiance ici

vibrancy [ˈvaɪbrənsɪ] N *(of person, painting, description)* vivacité *f*; *(of style)* vigueur *f*; *(of new company)* dynamisme *m*; *(of colour)* éclat *m*; *(of sound, voice)* caractère *m* vibrant

vibrant [ˈvaɪbrənt] ADJ **1** *(vigorous, lively ▸ person, painting, description)* plein de vie; *(▸ town, cultural scene, atmosphere)* très animé; *(▸ style)* plein de vigueur; *(▸ speech)* vibrant; *(▸ new company)* très dynamique; **to be v. with life** être plein de vie **2** *(resonant ▸ sound, voice)* vibrant **3** *(bright ▸ colour, light)* éclatant
N *Ling* vibrante *f*

vibraphone [ˈvaɪbrəfəʊn] N vibraphone *m*

vibrate [vaɪˈbreɪt] VI **1** *(shake, quiver)* vibrer **2** *(sound)* vibrer, retentir **3** *Phys (oscillate)* osciller, vibrer

vibrating [vaɪˈbreɪtɪŋ] ADJ vibrant

vibration [vaɪˈbreɪʃən] N vibration *f*
• **vibrations** NPL *Fam (feeling)* ambiance□ *f*; **good vibrations** une bonne ambiance

vibrato [vɪˈbrɑːtəʊ] *(pl* **vibratos**) *Mus* N vibrato *m*
ADV avec vibrato

vibrator [vaɪˈbreɪtə(r)] N **1** *Elec* vibrateur *m* **2** *(for massage, sexual)* vibromasseur *m*

vibratory [ˈvaɪbrətrɪ] ADJ vibratoire

viburnum [vaɪˈbɜːnəm] N viorne *f*

vicar [ˈvɪkə(r)] N pasteur *m (de l'Église anglicane)*; **the V. of Christ** le vicaire de Jésus-Christ
▸▸ ***vicar apostolic*** vicaire *m* apostolique; ***vicar general*** vicaire *m* général

vicarage [ˈvɪkərɪdʒ] N presbytère *m*

vicarious [vɪˈkeərɪəs] ADJ **1** *(indirect, secondhand ▸ feeling, pride, enjoyment)* indirect, par procuration *ou* contrecoup; **to lead a v. existence** vivre par procuration
2 *(punishment)* (fait) pour autrui; *(suffering, pain)* subi pour autrui
3 *(power, authority)* délégué
4 *Physiol* vicariant
▸▸ *Rel* ***vicarious sacrifice*** = le sacrifice du Christ mort pour racheter les hommes

vicariously [vɪˈkeərɪəslɪ] ADV **1** *(experience)* indirectement; **she lived v. through her reading** elle vivait par procuration à travers ses lectures **2** *(authorize)* par délégation, par procuration

vice N [vaɪs] **1** *(depravity)* vice *m*
2 *(moral failing)* vice *m*; *(less serious)* défaut *m*; *Hum* **it's my only v.** c'est mon seul vice
3 *Tech* étau *m*; **he had a grip like a v.** il avait une poigne de fer
4 *Am* brigade *f* des mœurs, brigade *f* mondaine
PREP [ˈvaɪsɪ] *Formal (instead of)* à la place de, en remplacement de
▸▸ ***vice ring*** organisation *f* criminelle *(impliquée dans la prostitution, le trafic de drogue, etc)*; ***vice squad*** brigade *f* mondaine *ou* des mœurs

vice-admiral N vice-amiral *m* d'escadre

vice-chairman N vice-président(e) *m,f*

vice-chairmanship N vice-présidence *f*

vice-chancellor N *Br Univ* ≃ président(e) *m,f* d'université

vice-chancellorship N *Br Univ* ≃ présidence *f* d'université

vice-consul N vice-consul *m*

vice-consulate N *(post or premises)* vice-consulat *m*

vicelike [ˈvaɪslaɪk] ADJ **held in a v. grip** serré dans une poigne de fer, serré comme dans un étau

vice-presidency N vice-présidence *f*

vice-president N vice-président(e) *m,f*

vice-presidential ADJ vice-présidentiel
▸▸ ***vice-presidential candidate*** candidat *m* à la vice-présidence; ***vice-presidential hopeful*** prétendant(e) *m,f* à la vice-présidence

viceroy [ˈvaɪsrɔɪ] N vice-roi *m*

vice versa [ˌvaɪsəˈvɜːsə] ADV vice versa, inversement

vicinity [vɪˈsɪnɪtɪ] *(pl* **vicinities**) N **1** *(surrounding area)* environs *mpl*, alentours *mpl*; *(neighbourhood)* voisinage *m*, environs *mpl*; *(proximity)* proximité *f*; **is there a good school in the v.?** est-ce qu'il y a une bonne école dans les environs?; **he's somewhere in the v.** il est quelque part dans le coin; **in the v. of the town centre** *(in the area)* dans les environs du centre-ville; *(close)* à proximité du centre-ville; **in the immediate v.** dans les environs immédiats; *Formal* **one good thing about the house is its v. to the station** un des bons côtés de la maison, c'est qu'elle est située tout près de la gare **2** *(approximate figures, amounts)* **his salary is in the v. of £18,000** son salaire se situe aux alentours de *ou* est de l'ordre de 18 000 livres; **its weight is in the v. of 500 lb** cela pèse dans les 500 livres

vicious [ˈvɪʃəs] ADJ **1** *(cruel, savage ▸ attack, blow)* brutal, violent; **a v. wind** un vent violent
2 *(malevolent ▸ criticism, gossip, remarks)* méchant, malveillant; **he has a v. tongue** il a une langue de vipère
3 *(dog)* méchant; *(horse)* vicieux, rétif
4 *(perverse ▸ behaviour, habits)* vicieux, pervers
▸▸ ***vicious circle*** cercle *m* vicieux

> Note that the French word **vicieux** usually means **depraved** or **underhand**, depending on the context.

viciously [ˈvɪʃəslɪ] ADV *(attack, beat)* brutalement, violemment; *(criticize, gossip)* avec malveillance, méchamment

viciousness [ˈvɪʃəsnɪs] N *(of attack, beating)* brutalité *f*, violence *f*; *(of criticism, gossip)* méchanceté *f*, malveillance *f*

vicissitude [vɪˈsɪsɪtjuːd] N *Formal* vicissitude *f*

victim [ˈvɪktɪm] N **1** *(physical sufferer)* victime *f*; *(of earthquake, floods, disaster)* sinistré(e) *m,f*; **to fall v. to sth** être victime de qch; **the fire claimed many victims** l'incendie a fait de nombreuses victimes; **road accident victims** les victimes *ou* les accidentés de la route; **a fund for victims of cancer** des fonds pour les cancéreux *ou* les malades du cancer **2** *Fig* victime *f*; **to fall v. to sb's charms** succomber aux charmes de qn;

the game fell v. to the weather le match a été annulé à cause du temps; **many people fall v. to these fraudulent schemes** beaucoup de gens se font avoir par ces combines frauduleuses; **he was a v. of his own success** il a été victime de son propre succès

victimization, -isation [ˌvɪktɪmaɪˈzeɪʃən] **N** *(for beliefs, race, differences)* persécution *f*; *(reprisals)* représailles *fpl*; **there must be no further v. of workers** il ne doit pas y avoir d'autres représailles contre les ouvriers

victimize, -ise [ˈvɪktɪmaɪz] **VT** *(make victim of)* persécuter; *(take reprisals against)* exercer des *ou* user de représailles sur; **she was victimized at school** elle a été victime de brimades à l'école; **immigrant workers are being victimized by some of the foremen** les travailleurs immigrés sont pris pour cibles par certains contremaîtres; **the strikers feel they are being victimized** les grévistes estiment qu'ils sont victimes de représailles; **it victimizes the lower paid** cela constitue un traitement discriminatoire à l'égard des petits salaires

victimless crime [ˈvɪktɪmlɪs-] **N** délit *m* sans victime

victor [ˈvɪktə(r)] **N** vainqueur *m*; **Labour were the victors in the election** le Parti travailliste a remporté la victoire aux élections

Victoria [vɪkˈtɔːrɪə] **PR N** *(person)* **Queen V.** la reine Victoria

N *Geog* **1** *(state)* le Victoria **2** *(lake)* **Lake V.** le lac Victoria

▸▸ *Mil* ***Victoria Cross*** Victoria Cross *f (en Grande-Bretagne, la plus haute décoration militaire)*; ***Victoria Day*** *(Canada)* = fête *f* de Victoria *(jour férié en mai)*; ***Victoria Falls*** les chutes *fpl* Victoria; ***Victoria Island*** l'île *f* Victoria; *Culin* ***Victoria sponge (cake)*** gâteau *m* de Savoie *(à la confiture, à la chantilly etc)*

victoria [vɪkˈtɔːrɪə] **N 1** *(carriage)* victoria *f* **2** *(plum)* = sorte de prune anglaise

▸▸ ***victoria plum*** = sorte de prune anglaise

Victorian [vɪkˈtɔːrɪən] **ADJ** victorien; **a return to V. values** un retour aux valeurs victoriennes *ou* de l'époque victorienne

N Victorien(enne) *m,f*

Victoriana [ˌvɪktɔːrɪˈɑːnə] **N** *(UNCOUNT)* antiquités *fpl* victoriennes, objets *mpl* de l'époque victorienne

victorious [vɪkˈtɔːrɪəs] **ADJ** *(army, campaign, party)* victorieux; *(army)* vainqueur; *(cry)* de victoire; **to be v. over sb** être victorieux de qn, remporter la victoire sur qn

victoriously [vɪkˈtɔːrɪəslɪ] **ADV** victorieusement

victory [ˈvɪktərɪ] *(pl* **victories***)* **N** victoire *f*; **to gain** *or* **to win a v. over sb** remporter la victoire sur qn

▸▸ ***Victory in Europe Day*** = jour de l'armistice du 8 mai 1945; ***victory parade*** défilé *m* de la victoire, défilé *m* pour célébrer une victoire; ***victory sign*** V *m* de la victoire

victual [ˈvɪtəl] *(pt & pp* **victualled**, *cont* **victualling***)* *Arch* **VT** ravitailler, approvisionner

VI se ravitailler, s'approvisionner

• **victuals NPL** victuailles *fpl*

victualler [ˈvɪtlə(r)] **N** *Arch* fournisseur *m* (de provisions)

vicuna [vɪˈkjuːnə] **N** *Zool* vigogne *f*

vid [vɪd] **N** *Fam (abbr* **video***)* vidéo◻ *f*, vidéocassette◻ *f*

video [ˈvɪdɪəʊ] *(pl* **videos***)* **N 1** *(medium)* vidéo *f*; **I use v. a lot in my teaching** j'utilise beaucoup la vidéo pendant mes cours

2 *Br (VCR)* magnétoscope *m*; **have you set the v.?** est-ce que tu as mis le magnétoscope en marche *ou* programmé le magnétoscope?

3 *(cassette)* vidéocassette *f*; *(recording)* vidéo *f*; *(for pop song)* clip *m*, vidéoclip *m*; **they rented a v. for the night** ils ont loué une vidéo *ou* vidéocassette pour la soirée; **we've got a v. of the film** on a le film en vidéocassette

4 *Am Fam (television)* télé *f*

COMP 1 *(film, version)* (en) vidéo; *(services, shop, equipment, signal)* vidéo *(inv)* **2** *Am (on TV)* télévisé

VT 1 *(film, programme)* enregistrer sur magnétoscope, magnétoscoper **2** *(using camcorder)* filmer (à la caméra vidéo); **they didn't know they were being videoed** ils ne savaient pas qu'ils étaient filmés

▸▸ ***video arcade*** salle *f* de jeux vidéo; ***video art*** art *m* vidéo; *Comput* ***video board*** carte *f* vidéo; ***video camera*** caméra *f* vidéo; *Comput* ***video card*** carte *f* vidéo; ***video cartridge*** cartouche *f* vidéo; ***video cassette*** vidéocassette *f*; ***video cassette recorder*** magnétoscope *m*; ***video clip*** vidéoclip *m*, clip *m* (vidéo); ***video club*** vidéoclub *m*; ***video compact disc*** disque *m* compact vidéo; ***video conference*** vidéoconférence *f*, visioconférence *f*; ***video conferencing*** vidéoconférences *fpl*; ***video diary*** journal *m* vidéo; ***video editing*** montage *m* vidéo; ***video effects*** effets *mpl* vidéo; ***video flux*** flux *m* vidéo; ***video frequency*** vidéofréquence *f*; ***video game*** jeu *m* vidéo; ***video installation*** installation *f* vidéo; *Fam* ***video jock*** présentateur(trice) *m,f* de vidéoclips◻; ***video jockey*** présentateur (trice) *m,f* de vidéoclips; ***video library*** vidéothèque *f*; ***video link*** liaison *f* vidéo; ***video machine*** magnétoscope *m*; ***video monitor*** moniteur *m* vidéo; *Br Fam* ***video nasty*** = film vidéo à caractère violent et souvent pornographique; ***video operator*** opérateur(trice) *m,f* magnétoscope *ou* vidéo; ***video piracy*** duplication *f* pirate de cassettes vidéo; ***video playback*** visualisation *f* de vidéo; ***video player*** magnétoscope *m*; ***video projection*** vidéoprojection *f*; ***video projector*** vidéoprojecteur *m*; ***video publisher*** éditeur *m* de vidéo; ***video recorder*** magnétoscope *m*; ***video recording*** enregistrement *m* sur magnétoscope; ***video streaming*** streaming *m* vidéo; ***video teleconferencing*** visiophonie *f*; ***video telephone*** vidéophone *m*; ***video transmission*** vidéotransmission *f*; ***video wall*** mur *m* d'écrans de télévision

videodisc [ˈvɪdɪəʊdɪsk] **N** vidéodisque *m*

videogram [ˈvɪdɪəʊgræm] **N** vidéogramme *m*

videographic [ˌvɪdɪəʊˈgræfɪk] **ADJ** vidéographique

videography [ˌvɪdɪˈɒgrəfɪ] **N** vidéographie *f*

video-maker N vidéaste *mf*

video-on-demand N vidéo *f* à la demande

videophone [ˈvɪdɪəʊfəʊn] **N** vidéophone *m*

▸▸ ***videophone conference*** visioconférence *f*

videotape [ˈvɪdɪəʊteɪp] **N** bande *f* vidéo

VT enregistrer sur magnétoscope, magnétoscoper

▸▸ ***videotape recorder*** magnétoscope *m*

Videotex® [ˈvɪdɪəʊteks] **N** vidéotex *m*, vidéographie *f* interactive

videotext [ˈvɪdɪəʊtekst] **N** vidéotex *m*, vidéographie *f* interactive

vie [vaɪ] *(pt & pp* **vied**, *cont* **vying***)* **VI** rivaliser, lutter; **to v. with sb for sth** disputer qch à qn; **the two children vied with each other for attention** les deux enfants rivalisaient pour attirer l'attention; **several companies were vying with each other to sponsor the event** plusieurs firmes se battaient pour parrainer l'évènement

Vienna [vɪˈenə] **N** Vienne

COMP viennois, de Vienne

▸▸ ***Vienna bread*** pain *m* viennois; ***Vienna roll*** ≃ pain *m* au lait

Viennese [ˌvɪəˈniːz] *(pl* **inv***)* **N** Viennois(e) *m,f*

ADJ viennois

Vietcong [ˌvjetˈkɒŋ] *(pl* **inv***)* **N** Viêt-cong *mf*

Vietnam [*Br* ˌvjetˈnæm, *Am* ˌvjetˈnɑːm] **N** Viêt-nam *m*

▸▸ ***the Vietnam War*** la guerre du Viêt-nam

Vietnamese [ˌvjetnəˈmiːz] *(pl* **inv***)* **N 1** *(person)* Vietnamien(enne) *m,f* **2** *(language)* vietnamien *m*

ADJ vietnamien

COMP *(embassy, history)* du Viêt-nam; *(teacher)* de vietnamien

Viet Vet [vietˈvet] **N** *Am Fam Mil* ancien *m* du Viêt-nam◻

view [vjuː] **N 1** *(sight)* vue *f*; **to come into v.** apparaître; **we came into v. of the shore** nous sommes arrivés en vue du rivage, nous avons aperçu le rivage; **he turned the corner and disappeared from v.** il a tourné au coin et on l'a perdu de vue *ou* il a disparu; **it happened in full v. of the television cameras/police** cela s'est passé juste devant les caméras de télévision/sous les yeux de la police; **to be on v.** *(house)* être ouvert aux visites; *(picture)* être exposé; **the woods are within v. of the house** de la maison on voit les bois; **to hide sth from v.** *(accidentally)* cacher qch; *(deliberately)* cacher qch aux regards; **to keep sth in v.** ne pas perdre qch de vue

2 *(prospect)* vue *f*; **the house has a good v. of the sea** la maison a une belle vue sur la mer; **a room with a v.** une chambre avec vue; **there's a nice v. from the window** de la fenêtre il y a une très belle vue; **from here we have a side v. of the cathedral** d'ici nous avons une vue de profil de la cathédrale; **you get a better v. from here** on voit mieux d'ici; **the man in front of me blocked my v. of the stage** l'homme devant moi m'empêchait de voir la scène; *Fig* **a comprehensive v. of English literature** une vue d'ensemble de la littérature anglaise

3 *(future perspective)* **in v.** en vue; **there appears to be no solution in v.** il semble n'y avoir aucune solution en vue; **what do you have in v. as regards work?** quelles sont vos intentions en ce qui concerne le travail?; **with this (end) in v.** avec *ou* dans cette intention; **she has in v. the publication of a new book** elle envisage de publier un nouveau livre; **to take the long v. of sth** voir qch à long terme

4 *(aim, purpose)* but *m*, intention *f*; **with a v. to doing sth** en vue de faire qch, dans l'intention de faire qch; **they bought the house with a v. to their retirement** ils ont acheté la maison en pensant à leur retraite

5 *(interpretation)* vue *f*; **an overall v.** une vue d'ensemble; **he has** *or* **takes a gloomy v. of life** il a une vue pessimiste de la vie, il envisage la vie d'une manière pessimiste

6 *(picture, photograph)* vue *f*; **an aerial v. of New York** une vue aérienne de New York

7 *(opinion)* avis *m*, opinion *f*; **in my v.** à mon avis; **in the v. of many of our colleagues** de l'avis de beaucoup de nos collègues; **I respect her political views** je respecte ses opinions politiques; **that seems to be the generally accepted v.** ceci semble être l'opinion générale *ou* courante; **that's the official v.** c'est le point de vue officiel; **he takes the v. that they are innocent** il pense *ou* estime qu'ils sont innocents; **I don't take that v.** je ne partage pas cet avis; **she took a poor** *or* **dim v. of his behaviour** elle n'appréciait guère son comportement; **what is your v. on the matter?** quelle est votre opinion sur la question?; **she holds** *or* **has strong views on the subject** elle a des opinions *ou* des idées bien nettes sur le sujet; **he's changed his views on disarmament** il a changé d'avis sur le désarmement

VT 1 *(look at)* voir, regarder; *(film, programme)* regarder; **viewed from above/from afar/from the outside** vu d'en haut/de loin/de l'extérieur

2 *(examine ▸ slides)* visionner; *(▸ through microscope)* regarder; *(▸ flat, showhouse)* visiter, inspecter; *(exhibition, paintings)* voir; **the house may be viewed at weekends only** on peut visiter la maison pendant les week-ends uniquement

3 *Fig (consider, judge)* considérer, envisager; **the committee viewed his application favourably** la commission a porté un regard favorable sur sa candidature; **he was viewed as a dangerous maniac** on le considérait comme un fou dangereux; **how do you v. this matter?** quel est votre avis sur cette affaire?; **the government views the latest international developments with alarm** le gouvernement porte un regard inquiet sur les derniers développements internationaux; **when viewed in this light** vu sous cet angle

4 *Hunt (fox)* apercevoir

5 *Comput (codes, document)* visualiser, afficher

VI *TV* regarder la télévision

• **in view of PREP** étant donné, vu; **in v. of his age** étant donné son âge, vu son âge; **in v. of what has happened** en raison de *ou* étant donné ce qui s'est passé; **in v. of this** ceci étant

viewable area [ˈvjuːəbəl-] **ADJ** *Comput (of monitor)* zone *f* d'affichage

Viewdata® [ˈvjuːˌdeɪtə] **N** vidéotex *m*, vidéographie *f* interactive

viewer [ˈvjuːə(r)] **N 1** *TV* téléspectateur(trice) *m,f*; **the programme has** *or* **attracts a lot of women viewers/young viewers** l'émission est très regardée par les femmes/les jeunes **2** *Phot (for slides)*

ʼisionneuse *f*; *(viewfinder)* viseur *m* **3** *Comput program)* visualiseur *m*

iewership ['vjuːəʃɪp] **N** *Am TV* public *m*

iewfinder ['vjuːˌfaɪndə(r)] **N** *Cin & Phot* viseur *n*

iewing ['vjuːɪŋ] **N** *(UNCOUNT)* **1** *TV* programme *m*, programmes *mpl*, émissions *fpl*; **ate-night v. on BBC2** émissions de fin de soirée ur BBC2; **his latest film makes exciting v.** son dernier film est un spectacle passionnant **2** *(of showhouse, exhibition)* visite *f*; **v. at weekends only** visites uniquement le week-end **3** *Astron* observation *f*

COMP 1 *TV (time, patterns)* d'écoute; **a young v. audience** de jeunes téléspectateurs **2** *Astron & Met (conditions)* d'observation

▸▸ *TV* ***viewing figures*** taux *m ou* indice *m* d'écoute; *TV* ***viewing hours*** heures *fpl* d'écoute; **at peak v. hours** aux heures de grande écoute

iewpoint ['vjuːpɔɪnt] **N 1** *(opinion)* point *m* de vue **2** *(viewing place)* point *m* de vue, panorama *n*

igil ['vɪdʒɪl] **N 1** *(watch)* veille *f*; *(in sickroom)* veillée *f*; *(for dead person)* veillée *f* funèbre; **to keep (an all-night) v. by sb's bedside** veiller (toute la nuit) au chevet de qn **2** *(demonstration)* manifestation *f* silencieuse (nocturne) **3** *Rel* vigile *f*

> Note that the French word **vigile** is a false friend. Its most common meaning is **security guard**.

igilance ['vɪdʒɪləns] **N** vigilance *f*

▸▸ *Am* ***vigilance committee*** groupe *m* d'autodéfense

igilant ['vɪdʒɪlənt] **ADJ** vigilant, éveillé

igilante [ˌvɪdʒɪ'læntɪ] **N** = membre d'un groupe d'autodéfense

▸▸ ***vigilante group*** groupe *m* d'autodéfense

igilantism [ˌvɪdʒɪ'læntɪzəm] **N** = attitude agressive typique des groupes d'autodéfense

igilantly ['vɪdʒɪləntlɪ] **ADV** avec vigilance, attentivement

ignette [vɪ'njet] **N** *(illustration)* vignette *f*; *Art & Phot* portrait *m* en buste dégradé; *Literature* esquisse *f* de caractère, portrait *m*; *Fig* **this ten-minute v. of city life** cet aperçu de dix minutes de la vie dans une grande ville

VT *(picture, photograph)* dégrader, estomper; *character)* esquisser; *(book, page)* orner de vignettes

igor *Am* = **vigour**

igorous ['vɪgərəs] **ADJ 1** *(robust ▸ person, plant)* vigoureux; *(enthusiastic ▸ person)* enthousiaste **2** *(forceful ▸ opposition, campaign, support)* vigoureux, énergique; *(▸ denial)* formel **3** *(energetic ▸ exercise)* énergique

igorously ['vɪgərəslɪ] **ADV** vigoureusement, énergiquement; **he nodded his head v.** il acquiesça vivement de la tête

igour, *Am* **vigor** ['vɪgə(r)] **N 1** *(physical vitality)* vigueur *f*, énergie *f*, vitalité *f*; *(mental vitality)* vigueur *f*, vivacité *f*; **he is no longer in the full v. of youth** il n'a plus toute la vigueur de la jeunesse **2** *(of attack, style)* vigueur *f*; *(of storm)* violence *f* **3** *Am Law* **in v.** en vigueur

iking ['vaɪkɪŋ] **ADJ** viking

N Viking *mf*

▸▸ ***Viking ship*** drakkar *m*

ile [vaɪl] **ADJ 1** *(morally wrong ▸ deed, intention, murder)* vil, ignoble, infâme; **to be v. to sb** être ignoble envers qn **2** *(disgusting ▸ person, habit, taste)* abominable, exécrable; *(▸ food)* infect, exécrable; *(▸ smell)* infect, nauséabond; **it smells v.!** ça pue!; **spitting is a v. habit** cracher est une sale habitude; **he used some v. language** il a employé des termes ignobles **3** *(very bad ▸ temper)* exécrable, massacrant; *(▸ weather)* exécrable; **to be in a v. temper** être d'une humeur massacrante; **what v. weather!** quel sale temps!

ilely ['vaɪllɪ] **ADV 1** *(basely, despicably)* vilement, bassement **2** *(decorated)* d'une manière abominable *ou* exécrable

ileness ['vaɪlnɪs] **N 1** *(of deed, intention)* vilenie *f*, bassesse *f* **2** *(of smell, taste, weather)* caractère *n* exécrable *ou* abominable

vilification [ˌvɪlɪfɪ'keɪʃən] **N** *Formal* diffamation *f*, calomnie *f*

vilify ['vɪlɪfaɪ] *(pt & pp* **vilified***)* **VT** *Formal* diffamer, calomnier

villa ['vɪlə] **N** *(in country)* maison *f* de campagne; *(by sea)* villa *f*; *Br (in town)* villa *f ou* pavillon *m* (de banlieue); *Hist* villa *f*

village ['vɪlɪdʒ] **N** village *m*; *Am* **the V.** = surnom de Greenwich Village, quartier de New York

COMP du village

▸▸ *Br* ***village green*** = pelouse se trouvant au centre du village; ***village hall*** salle *f* des fêtes; ***village idiot*** idiot *m* du village

villager ['vɪlɪdʒə(r)] **N** villageois(e) *m,f*

villain ['vɪlən] **N 1** *(ruffian, scoundrel)* scélérat(e) *m,f*, vaurien(enne) *m,f*; *(in film, story)* méchant (e) *m,f*, traître(esse) *m,f*; *Theat & Fig* **the v. of the piece** le méchant, le coupable

2 *Fam (rascal)* coquin(e) *m,f*, vilain(e) *m,f*; **you little v.!** petit coquin!, vilain!

3 *Fam Crime slang (criminal)* bandit *m*, malfaiteur *m*

4 *Hist (free)* vilain(e) *m,f*; *(unfree)* serf (serve) *m,f*

villainous ['vɪlənəs] **ADJ 1** *(evil ▸ act, person)* vil, ignoble, infâme; **a v. deed** une infamie, une bassesse **2** *(foul ▸ food, weather)* abominable, exécrable

villainously ['vɪlənəslɪ] **ADV** d'une manière infâme *ou* ignoble

villainy ['vɪlənɪ] *(pl* **villainies***)* **N** infamie *f*, bassesse *f*

> **-VILLE** SUFFIXE
>
> Ce suffixe, qui s'emploie surtout en anglais américain, est à la fois péjoratif, humoristique et quelque peu désuet. Il sert à former des noms de lieux fictifs décrivant un ÉTAT caractérisé par le mot auquel il est attaché, que ce soit un nom ou un adjectif. On rajoute souvent un 's' entre le terme de départ et **-ville**, et le nom ainsi formé est le plus souvent (mais pas systématiquement) utilisé comme adjectif :
>
> **his party was dullsville** (formé à partir de l'adjectif *dull*) sa fête était ennuyeuse à mourir; **it's dragsville** (formé à partir du nom *drag*) c'est galère; **she's from squaresville** (formé à partir du nom *square*) elle est vraiment ringarde; **it's sleazeville in politics** (formé à partir du nom *sleaze*) le monde de la politique est hyper corrompu.

villein ['vɪlɪn] **N** *Hist (free)* vilain(e) *m,f*; *(unfree)* serf (serve) *m,f*

villus ['vɪləs] *(pl* **villi** [-laɪ]*)* **N** *Bot* poil *m*; *Anat & Zool* villosité *f*

Vilnius ['vɪlnɪəs] **N** Vilnius

vim [vɪm] **N** *Fam* énergie*f*, entrain *m*; **full of v. (and vigour)** plein d'entrain

vinaigrette [ˌvɪnɪ'gret] **N** *Culin* vinaigrette *f*

vindaloo [ˌvɪndə'luː] **N** vindaloo *m (plat indien au curry très épicé)*

vindicate ['vɪndɪkeɪt] **VT 1** *(justify)* justifier; **this vindicates my faith in him** ceci prouve que j'avais raison d'avoir confiance en lui

2 *(show to be correct ▸ opinions, theory)* confirmer; *(▸ person)* donner raison à

3 *(uphold ▸ claim, right)* faire valoir, revendiquer

4 *Law (exonerate ▸ person)* innocenter

vindication [ˌvɪndɪ'keɪʃən] **N** justification *f*; **he spoke in v. of his behaviour** il s'expliqua pour justifier son comportement

vindicatory ['vɪndɪˌkeɪtərɪ] **ADJ 1** *(justifying)* justificatif; *Rel* apologétique **2** *(avenging)* vindicatif, vengeur(eresse)

▸▸ ***vindicatory justice*** justice *f* vindicative

vindictive [vɪn'dɪktɪv] **ADJ** vindicatif

▸▸ *Law* ***vindictive damages*** dommages-intérêts *mpl* à titre punitif

vindictively [vɪn'dɪktɪvlɪ] **ADV** *(say)* vindicativement; *(act)* par esprit de vengeance; **he had quite v. made sure she would not get the job** par esprit de vengeance, il avait tout fait pour qu'elle n'obtienne pas le poste

vindictiveness [vɪn'dɪktɪvnɪs] **N** caractère *m* vindicatif; **she did it out of sheer v.** elle l'a fait par esprit de vengeance

vine [vaɪn] **N 1** *(grapevine)* vigne *f* **2** *(plant ▸ climbing)* plante *f* grimpante; *(▸ creeping)* plante *f* rampante

COMP *(leaf)* de vigne; *(disease)* de la vigne

• **vines NPL** *Am Fam (clothes)* fringues *fpl*

▸▸ ***vine fruit*** raisin *m*; ***vine grower*** viticulteur (trice) *m,f*, vigneron(onne) *m,f*; ***vine growing*** viticulture *f*; ***vine harvest*** vendange *f*, vendanges *fpl*

vinegar ['vɪnɪgə(r)] **N** vinaigre *m*

▸▸ ***vinegar fly*** mouche *f* du vinaigre

vinegary ['vɪnɪgərɪ] **ADJ 1** *(smell, taste)* de vinaigre; *(wine)* qui a un goût de vinaigre **2** *Fig (tone, reply)* acide, acerbe; *(temper)* acide, acariâtre

vinery ['vaɪnərɪ] *(pl* **vineries***)* **N 1** *(hothouse)* = serre où l'on cultive la vigne **2** *(vineyard)* (champ *m* de) vigne *f*; *(commercial)* vignoble *m*

vineyard ['vɪnjəd] **N** (champ *m* de) vigne *f*; *(commercial)* vignoble *m*

viniculture ['vɪnɪkʌltʃə(r)] **N** viniculture *f*

vino ['viːnəʊ] *(pl* **vinos***)* **N** *Fam* pinard *m*

vinous ['vaɪnəs] **ADJ** vineux

vintage ['vɪntɪdʒ] **N 1** *(wine)* vin *m* de cru; *(year)* cru *m*, millésime *m*; **this claret is an excellent v.** ce bordeaux est un très grand cru; **1982 was a good v.** 1982 a été une bonne année pour le vin; **a 1983 v.** un vin de 1983; **what v. is this wine?** quel est le millésime *ou* quelle est l'année de ce vin?

2 *(crop)* récolte *f*; *(harvesting)* vendange *f*, vendanges *fpl*

3 *(period)* époque *f*; **an old radio of pre-war v.** une vieille radio d'avant-guerre; **our parents are of the same v.** nos parents sont de la même génération

4 *(fashion)* vintage *m*

ADJ 1 *(old)* antique, ancien

2 *(classic, superior)* classique; **a season of v. films** un cycle de films classiques; **it was v. Agatha Christie** c'était de l'Agatha Christie du meilleur style *ou* cru

3 *(champagne)* millésimé; *(port)* de grand cru

4 *(clothes, accessories)* vintage

VT vendanger

▸▸ *Br* ***vintage car*** voiture *f* de collection *(normalement construite entre 1919 et 1930)*; ***vintage model*** modèle *m ou* pièce *f* d'époque; ***vintage wine*** vin *m* millésimé; ***vintage year*** *(for wine)* grand millésime *m*, grande année *f*; *(for books, films)* très bonne année *f*; **it was a v. year for the British film industry** ce fut une excellente année pour l'industrie cinématographique britannique

vintner ['vɪntnə(r)] **N** négociant *m* en vins

vinyl ['vaɪnɪl] **N** vinyle *m*

ADJ *(wallpaper, tiles, coat)* de *ou* en vinyle; *(paint)* vinylique

viol ['vaɪəl] **N** viole *f*

▸▸ ***viol player*** violiste *mf*

viola [vɪ'əʊlə] **N 1** *Mus* alto *m* **2** *Bot (genus)* violacée *f*; *(flower)* pensée *f*, violette *f*

▸▸ ***viola player*** altiste *mf*

violate ['vaɪəleɪt] **VT 1** *(promise, secret, treaty)* violer; *(law)* violer, enfreindre; *(rights)* violer, bafouer

2 *(frontier, property)* violer; **to v. a country's territorial waters** violer les eaux territoriales d'un pays

3 *(peace, silence)* troubler, rompre; **to v. sb's privacy** violer l'intimité de qn

4 *(sanctuary, tomb)* violer, profaner

5 *Formal (rape)* violer, violenter

violation [ˌvaɪə'leɪʃən] **N 1** *(of promise, rights, secret)* violation *f* (**of** de); *(of law)* violation (**of** de), infraction *f* (**of** à); *Sport* faute *f*; **they acted in v. of the treaty** ils ont contrevenu au traité

2 *(of frontier, property)* violation *f*; **it's a v. of my privacy** c'est une atteinte à ma vie privée

3 *Admin* **v. of the peace** trouble *m* de l'ordre public

4 *(of sanctuary, tomb)* profanation *f*, violation *f*

5 *Am Law (offence)* infraction *f*

6 *Formal (rape)* viol *m*

violator ['vaɪəleɪtə(r)] **N 1** *(gen)* violateur *m* **2** *Am Law (offender)* contrevenant *m*

violence ['vaɪələns] **N** *(UNCOUNT)* **1** *(physical)* violence *f*; **acts/scenes of v.** actes *mpl*/scènes *fpl* de violence; **football/TV v.** la violence sur les terrains de football/à la télévision; **the men of v.** *(terrorists)* les terroristes *mpl*; **v. broke out in the streets** il y a eu de violents incidents *ou* des bagarres ont éclaté dans les rues

2 *Law* violences *fpl*; **crimes of v.** crimes *mpl* de violence; **robbery with v.** vol *m* avec coups et blessures

3 *(of language, passion, storm)* violence *f*

4 *(idiom)* **to do v. to** faire violence à

violent ['vaɪələnt] **ADJ 1** *(attack, crime, person, behaviour)* violent; **by v. means** par la violence; **to be v. with sb** se montrer *ou* être violent avec qn; **to die a v. death** mourir de mort violente

2 *(intense ▸ pain)* violent, aigu(ë); *(furious ▸ temper)* violent; *(strong, great ▸ contrast, change)* violent, brutal; *(▸ explosion, storm)* violent; **she took a v. dislike to him** elle s'est prise d'une vive aversion à son égard; **to be in a v. temper** être furieux; **I've got a v. toothache/headache** j'ai une rage de dents/un mal de tête atroce

3 *(forceful, impassioned ▸ argument, language, emotions)* violent

4 *(wind, weather)* violent

5 *(colour)* criard, voyant

violently ['vaɪələntlɪ] **ADV** *(attack, shake, struggle)* violemment; *(act, react)* violemment, avec violence; **to behave v.** avoir un comportement violent; **he was v. sick** il fut pris de vomissements violents

violet ['vaɪələt] **N 1** *Bot* violette *f* **2** *(colour)* violet *m*

ADJ violet

violin [ˌvaɪə'lɪn] **N** violon *m*

COMP *(concerto)* pour violon; *(lesson)* de violon

▸▸ ***violin case*** étui *m* à violon; ***violin maker*** luthier *m*

violinist [ˌvaɪə'lɪnɪst] **N** violoniste *mf*

violoncellist [ˌvaɪələn'tʃelɪst] **N** violoncelliste *mf*

violoncello [ˌvaɪələn'tʃeləʊ] *(pl* **violoncellos***)* **N** violoncelle *m*

VIP [ˌviːaɪ'piː] *(abbr* **very important person***)* **N** VIP *mf*, personnalité *f*, personnage *m* de marque

COMP *(guests, visitors)* de marque, éminent, très important; **to give sb the V. treatment** traiter qn comme un personnage de marque; **we got V. treatment** on nous a réservé un accueil princier, on nous a traités comme des rois

▸▸ ***VIP lounge*** *(in airport)* = salon d'accueil réservé aux personnages de marque

viper ['vaɪpə(r)] **N** *Zool & Fig* vipère *f*; *Fig* **a vipers' nest** un nœud de vipères

▸▸ *Bot* ***viper's bugloss*** vipérine *f*

viperine ['vaɪpəraɪn] **ADJ** *Zool* vipérin

viperish ['vaɪpərɪʃ], **viperous** ['vaɪpərəs] **ADJ** vipérin, de vipère; *(person)* qui a une langue de vipère; *Fig* **a v. tongue** une langue de vipère

virago [vɪ'rɑːgəʊ] *(pl* **viragoes** *or* **viragos***)* **N** mégère *f*, virago *f*

viral ['vaɪrəl] **ADJ** viral; **a v. infection** une infection virale

▸▸ *Med* ***viral load*** charge *f* virale; *Mktg* ***viral marketing*** marketing *m* viral

Virgil ['vɜːdʒɪl] **PR N** Virgile

virgin ['vɜːdʒɪn] **N** *(girl)* vierge *f*, pucelle *f*; *(boy)* puceau *m*

ADJ 1 *(sexually)* vierge **2** *(forest, soil, wool)* vierge; *(fresh)* virginal; **v. white sheets** draps d'un blanc immaculé

• **Virgin PR N** *Rel* **the V.** la Vierge

▸▸ *Rel* ***the Virgin birth*** l'Immaculée Conception *f*; ***virgin birth*** *(parthenogenesis)* parthénogenèse *f*; ***the Virgin Islands*** les îles *fpl* Vierges; *Bible* ***the Virgin Mary*** la Vierge Marie; ***the Virgin Queen*** la reine *f* vierge *(Élisabeth Ière)*; ***virgin snow*** neige *f* fraîche; ***virgin territory*** territoire *m* vierge; *Fig* **this market is v. territory for the company** ce marché constitue un territoire vierge pour la société

virginal ['vɜːdʒɪnəl] **ADJ** virginal

• **virginals NPL** *Mus* virginal *m*

Virginia [və'dʒɪnjə] **N** *Geog* la Virginie

▸▸ *Bot* ***Virginia creeper*** vigne *f* vierge; ***Virginia tobacco*** virginie *m*, tabac *m* de Virginie

virginity [və'dʒɪnɪtɪ] **N** virginité *f*; **to lose one's v.** perdre sa virginité

Virgo ['vɜːgəʊ] **N 1** *Astron* Vierge *f* **2** *Astrol* Vierge *f*; **he's a V.** il est (du signe de la) Vierge

ADJ *Astrol* de la Vierge; **he's V.** il est (du signe de la) Vierge

Virgoan ['vɜːgəʊən] *Astrol* **N to be a V.** être (du signe de la) Vierge

ADJ de la Vierge; **the V. male** l'homme Vierge

viricidal [ˌvaɪrɪ'saɪdəl] **ADJ** *Biol* virucide

viricide ['vaɪrɪsaɪd] **ADJ** *Biol* virucide

virile ['vɪraɪl] **ADJ** viril

virility [vɪ'rɪlɪtɪ] **N** virilité *f*

viroid ['vɪrɔɪd] **N** *Biol* viroïde *m*

virologist [ˌvaɪ'rɒlədʒɪst] **N** *Biol & Med* virologue *mf*, virologiste *mf*

virology [ˌvaɪ'rɒlədʒɪ] **N** *Biol & Med* virologie *f*

virtual ['vɜːtʃʊəl] **ADJ 1** *(near, as good as)* **the country is in a state of v. anarchy** c'est pratiquement l'anarchie dans le pays; **it's a v. impossibility/dictatorship** c'est une quasi-impossibilité/une quasi-dictature; **he's a v. prisoner** il est quasiment prisonnier; **the v. extinction of this species** la disparition quasi-totale de cette espèce **2** *(actual, effective)* **they are the v. rulers of the country** en fait, ce sont eux qui dirigent le pays, ce sont eux les dirigeants de fait du pays **3** *Comput & Phys* virtuel

▸▸ *Phys* ***virtual image*** image *f* virtuelle; *Comput* ***virtual memory*** mémoire *f* virtuelle; ***virtual reality*** réalité *f* virtuelle; ***virtual reality helmet*** casque *m* de réalité virtuelle; *Comput* ***virtual reality simulator*** simulateur *m* de réalité virtuelle; *Comput* ***virtual storage*** mémoire *f* virtuelle

virtually ['vɜːtʃʊəlɪ] **ADV 1** *(almost)* pratiquement, quasiment; **it's v. impossible** c'est pratiquement *ou* quasiment impossible; **it's v. finished** c'est presque *ou* quasiment fini; **she v. insulted me** elle m'a pratiquement insulté; **v. every country in Europe** chaque pays européen ou presque **2** *(actually, in effect)* en fait; **he is v. the manager** en fait *ou* en pratique, c'est lui le directeur

virtue ['vɜːtjuː] **N 1** *(goodness)* vertu *f*; **to make a v. of necessity** faire de nécessité vertu; **a woman of easy v.** une femme de petite vertu; *Prov* **v. is its own reward** = la vertu est sa propre récompense **2** *(merit)* mérite *m*, avantage *m*; **she at least has the v. of being discreet** elle a au moins le mérite d'être discrète; **the flat has the v. of being centrally heated** l'appartement a l'avantage d'avoir le chauffage central **3** *(power)* vertu *f*; **the healing virtues of certain plants** les vertus curatives de certaines plantes

• **by virtue of PREP** en vertu *ou* en raison de; **by v. of her age** en vertu *ou* en raison de son âge; **by v. of being the eldest, he…** en vertu *ou* en raison du fait qu'il est l'aîné, il…

virtuosity [ˌvɜːtjʊ'ɒsɪtɪ] **N** virtuosité *f*

virtuoso [ˌvɜːtjʊ'əʊzəʊ] *(pl* **virtuosos** *or* **virtuosi** [-ziː]*)* **N** *(gen) & Mus* virtuose *mf*

ADJ de virtuose; **it was a v. performance** *Mus* c'était une interprétation de virtuose; *Fig* c'était un tour de force

virtuous ['vɜːtʃʊəs] **ADJ** vertueux

▸▸ ***virtuous circle*** cercle *m* vertueux

virtuously ['vɜːtʃʊəslɪ] **ADV** vertueusement

virucidal [ˌvaɪrə'saɪdəl] **ADJ** *Biol* virucide

virucide ['vaɪrəsaɪd] **N** *Biol* virucide *m*

virulence ['vɪrjʊləns] **N** virulence *f*

virulent ['vɪrjʊlənt] **ADJ** *Med & Fig* virulent

virulently ['vɪrjʊləntlɪ] **ADV** avec virulence

virus ['vaɪrəs] **N 1** *Med* virus *m*; **the flu v.** le virus de la grippe; *Fam* **the v.** *(Aids)* le sida ▫ **2** *Comput* virus *m*; **to disable a v.** désactiver un virus

▸▸ *Comput* ***virus check*** détection *f* de virus; **to run a v. check** activer le détecteur de virus; *Comput* ***virus detection*** détection *f* de virus; *Comput* ***virus detector*** détecteur *m* de virus; *Med* ***virus infection*** infection *f* virale; *Comput* ***virus program*** programme *m* virus

virus-checked ADJ *Comput* qui a été passé a[u] détecteur de virus

virus-free ADJ *Comput* dépourvu de virus

virus-infected ADJ *Comput* contaminé pa[r] un/des virus

Visa® ['viːzə] **N** carte Visa® *f*; **to pay by V.** pay[er] par carte Visa®

▸▸ ***Visa® card*** carte *f* Visa®

visa ['viːzə] **N** visa *m*; **he has applied for an Ame[ri]can v.** il a demandé un visa pour l'Amérique

VT *Admin* viser

visage ['vɪzɪdʒ] **N** *Literary* visage *m*, figure *f*

vis-à-vis [ˌviːzɑː'viː] *(pl* **inv***)* **PREP 1** *(in relation t[o])* par rapport à **2** *(opposite)* vis-à-vis de

ADV vis-à-vis

N 1 *(person or thing opposite)* vis-à-vis *m inv* *(counterpart)* homologue *mf*

viscera ['vɪsərə] **NPL** viscères *mpl*

visceral ['vɪsərəl] **ADJ** viscéral

viscid ['vɪsɪd] **ADJ** visqueux

viscidity [vɪ'sɪdɪtɪ] **N** viscosité *f*

viscose ['vɪskəʊs] **N** viscose *f*

ADJ visqueux

viscosity [vɪ'skɒsɪtɪ] *(pl* **viscosities***)* **N** viscosité *f*

viscount ['vaɪkaʊnt] **N** vicomte *m*

viscountcy ['vaɪkaʊntsɪ] **N** vicomté *f*

viscountess ['vaɪkaʊntɪs] **N** vicomtesse *f*

viscounty ['vaɪkaʊntɪ] = **viscountcy**

viscous ['vɪskəs] **ADJ** visqueux, gluant

vise [vaɪs] *Am* = **vice N**

visibility [ˌvɪzɪ'bɪlɪtɪ] **N** visibilité *f*; **good/poor** bonne/mauvaise visibilité *f*; **v. is down to a fe[w] yards** la visibilité est réduite à quelques mètre[s]

visible ['vɪzəbəl] **ADJ 1** *(gen) & Opt* visible; **to be[-] come v.** devenir visible; **clearly v. to the naked ey[e]** clairement visible à l'œil nu; **the beach is not [visible] from the road** on ne peut pas voir la plage de [la] route **2** *(evident)* visible, apparent, manifest[e]; **his nervousness was clearly v.** sa nervosité éta[it] manifeste *ou* évidente; **it serves no v. purpos[e]** on n'en voit pas vraiment l'utilité, on ne vo[it] pas vraiment à quoi cela sert; *Admin* **with no means of support** sans ressources apparentes

▸▸ *Com* ***visible assets*** actif *m* corporel; *Com* ***vi[s]ible defect*** défaut *m* apparent; ***visible horizon*** ho[-] rizon *m*; *Phys* ***visible spectrum*** spectre *m* visibl[e]; *Com* ***visible trade*** commerce *m* de biens

visibly ['vɪzɪblɪ] **ADV** visiblement; **he was v. su[r]prised** il était visiblement surpris

Visigoth ['vɪzɪˌgɒθ] **N** Visigoth(e) *m,f*, Wisigo[th] (e) *m,f*

vision ['vɪʒən] **N 1** *(UNCOUNT) Opt (sight)* visio[n] *f*, vue *f*; **to suffer from defective v.** avoir mauvais[e] vue; **outside/within one's field of v.** hors de/e[n] vue

2 *(UNCOUNT) (insight)* vision *f*, clairvoyance; **a man of v.** un visionnaire; **we need people with and imagination** nous avons besoin de gens ins[-] pirés et imaginatifs

3 *(dream, fantasy)* vision *f*; *Rel* **to have a v.** avo[ir] une vision; *Med & Psy* **to have visions** avoir de[s] visions; **he has visions of being rich and famous** se voit riche et célèbre; **I had visions of you lyin[g] in a hospital bed** je vous voyais couché dans u[n] lit d'hôpital

4 *(conception)* vision *f*, conception *f*; **what your v. of the new town centre?** comment voye[z-] vous *ou* comment concevez-vous le nouvea[u] centre-ville?

5 *(apparition)* vision *f*, apparition *f*; *(lovely sigh[t])* magnifique spectacle *m*; **she was a v. in whi[te] lace** elle était ravissante en dentelle blanche; **v. of loveliness** une apparition de charme

6 *TV* image *f*

▸▸ *TV* ***vision mixer*** *(equipment)* mixeur *m*, mé[-] langeur *m* de signaux; *(person)* opérateur(trice) *m,f* de mixage; *TV* ***vision mixing*** mixage *m* d'ima[-] ges

visionary ['vɪʒənərɪ] *(pl* **visionaries***)* **ADJ** visio[n]naire

N visionnaire *mf*

visit ['vɪzɪt] **N 1** *(call)* visite *f*; **to pay sb a v.** rendr[e] visite à qn; **I haven't paid a v. to the cathedral yet** j['] n'ai pas encore visité *ou* je ne suis pas encor[e] allé voir la cathédrale; **I had a v. from your aunt last week** j'ai eu la visite de ta tante la semaine dernière; **you must pay them a return v.** il faut leur rendre leur visite; **she met him on a return v. to her home town** elle l'a rencontré quand elle est retournée en visite dans sa ville natale; *Br Fam Euph* **to pay a v.** aller au petit coin

2 *(stay)* visite *f*, séjour *m*; *(trip)* voyage *m*, séjour *m*; **she's on a v. to her aunt's** elle est en visite chez sa tante; **she's on a v. to Amsterdam** elle fait un séjour à Amsterdam; **did you enjoy your v. to California?** avez-vous fait un bon séjour en Californie?; **the President is on an official v. to Australia** le président est en visite officielle en Australie; **this is my first v. to your country** c'est la première fois que je viens dans votre pays

3 *Am (chat)* causette *f*, bavardage *m*

VT 1 *(person ▸ go to see)* rendre visite à, aller voir; *(▸ stay with)* rendre visite à, séjourner chez; **to v. the doctor** aller voir le médecin, aller chez le médecin; **not many people come to v. her** il n'y a pas beaucoup de gens qui viennent lui rendre visite; **to v. the sick** visiter les malades; **he's away visiting friends at the moment** il séjourne *ou* il est chez des amis en ce moment

2 *(museum, town)* visiter, aller voir; **in the afternoon they went to v. Pisa** l'après-midi, ils sont allés visiter *ou* voir Pise

3 *(inspect ▸ place, premises)* visiter, inspecter, faire une visite d'inspection à; *Law* **to v. the scene of the crime** se rendre sur les lieux du crime

4 *Literary (inflict)* **to v. a punishment on sb** punir qn; **the sins of the fathers are visited upon their sons** les fils sont punis pour les péchés de leurs pères; **the city was visited by the plague in the 17th century** la ville a été atteinte par la peste au XVIIème siècle

VI être de passage; **we're just visiting** nous sommes simplement de passage

visit with **VT INSEP** *Am (call on)* passer voir; *(talk with)* bavarder avec

visitation [ˌvɪzɪˈteɪʃən] **N 1** *(official visit, inspection)* visite *f ou* tour *m* d'inspection; *Rel (of bishop)* visite *f* épiscopale *ou* pastorale; *Hum* **we're having a v. from the managing director next week** le directeur général nous fait l'honneur de sa visite la semaine prochaine **2** *(social visit)* visite *f*; *Hum (prolonged)* visite *f* trop prolongée **3** *Formal (affliction)* punition *f* du ciel; *(reward)* récompense *f* divine

• **Visitation** **N** *Rel* **the V.** la Visitation

▸▸ *Am Law* **visitation rights** *(of divorced parent to child)* droits *mpl* de visite

visiting [ˈvɪzɪtɪŋ] **ADJ** *(circus, performers)* de passage; *(lecturer)* invité; *(birds)* de passage, migrateur; *Sport* **the v. team** les visiteurs *mpl*

▸▸ *Br* **visiting card** carte *f* de visite; *Am Fam* **visiting fireman** visiteur *m* de marque[□]; **visiting hours** heures *fpl* de visite; *Am* **visiting nurse** infirmier (ère) *m,f* à domicile; *Univ* **visiting professor** professeur *m* associé *ou* invité; *Law* **visiting rights** *(of divorced parent)* droit *m* de visite; **visiting time** heures *fpl* de visite

visitor [ˈvɪzɪtə(r)] **N 1** *(caller ▸ at hospital, house, prison)* visiteur(euse) *m,f*; **you have a v.** vous avez de la visite; **I rarely have visitors** c'est rare que j'aie de la visite; **they are not allowed any visitors after 10 p.m.** ils n'ont pas le droit de recevoir des visiteurs *ou* des visites après 22 heures

2 *(guest ▸ at private house)* visiteur(euse) *m,f*, invité(e) *m,f*; *(▸ at hotel)* client(e) *m,f*; **we have visitors** on a du monde *ou* des invités

3 *(tourist)* visiteur(euse) *m,f*, touriste *mf*; **we had 40,000 visitors last year** on a eu 40 000 visiteurs l'an dernier

4 *Orn* oiseau *m* passager; **this bird is a v. to these shores** cet oiseau est seulement de passage sur ces côtes; **this species is a winter v. to Britain** cette espèce vient passer l'hiver en Grande-Bretagne

▸▸ **visitors' book** *(in house, museum)* livre *m* d'or; *(in hotel)* registre *m*; **visitor centre** *(in park, at tourist attraction etc)* centre *m* d'accueil pour les visiteurs; **visitors' gallery** tribune *f* du public; **visitor's passport** passeport *m* temporaire

visor [ˈvaɪzə(r)] **N** *(on hat)* visière *f*; *(in car)* pare-soleil *m inv*

vista [ˈvɪstə] **N 1** *(view)* vue *f*, perspective *f*; **a mountain v.** une vue sur les montagnes, une perspective de montagnes **2** *Fig (perspective)* perspective *f*, horizon *m*; *(image ▸ of past)* vue *f*, vision *f*; *(▸ of future)* perspective *f*, vision *f*; **to open up new vistas** ouvrir de nouvelles perspectives *ou* de nouveaux horizons

▸▸ **vista point** point *m* de vue

vistadome [ˈvɪstədəʊm] **N** *Am Rail* vistadôme *m*

visual [ˈvɪʒjʊəl] **ADJ 1** *(gen) & Opt (image, impression, faculty)* visuel; **her comedy is very v.** son comique repose sur les effets visuels **2** *Aviat (landing, navigation)* à vue

• **visuals** **NPL** supports *mpl* visuels

▸▸ **visual aid** support *m* visuel; **visual arts** arts *mpl* plastiques; **visual display terminal, visual display unit** visuel *m*, écran *m* de visualisation; *Cin & TV* **visual effects** effets *mpl* spéciaux; **visual field** champ *m* visuel; **visual handicap** handicap *m* visuel; **visual identity** identité *f* visuelle; **visual memory** mémoire *f* visuelle; *Biol* **visual purple** pourpre *m* rétinien

visualization, -isation [ˌvɪʒjʊəlaɪˈzeɪʃən] **N 1** *(visual presentation)* visualisation *f* **2** *(imagination)* visualisation *f*, évocation *f*

visualize, -ise [ˈvɪʒjʊəlaɪz] **VT 1** *(call to mind ▸ scene)* se représenter, évoquer; *(imagine)* s'imaginer, visualiser, se représenter; **I remember the name but I can't v. his face** je me souviens de son nom mais je ne revois plus son visage; **she tried to v. herself travelling through the Amazon** elle essayait de s'imaginer en train de traverser l'Amazone **2** *(foresee)* envisager, prévoir; **I can't v. things getting any better** je n'envisage aucune amélioration **3** *Tech (make visible)* visualiser; *Med* rendre visible par radiographie

visually [ˈvɪʒjʊəlɪ] **ADV** visuellement; **v. handicapped, v. impaired** malvoyant, *Spec* amblyope; **the v. handicapped** les malvoyants *mpl*

vital [ˈvaɪtəl] **ADJ 1** *(essential ▸ information, services, supplies)* vital, essentiel, indispensable; **of v. importance** d'une importance capitale; **this drug is v. to the success of the operation** ce médicament est indispensable au succès de l'opération; **it's v. that I know the truth** il est indispensable que je sache la vérité; **to play a v. role** jouer un rôle capital *ou* primordial

2 *(very important ▸ decision, matter)* vital, fondamental; **tonight's match is v.** le match de ce soir est décisif

3 *Biol (function, organ)* vital

4 *(energetic)* plein d'entrain, dynamique

• **vitals** **NPL 1** *Anat or Hum* organes *mpl* vitaux **2** *(essential elements)* parties *fpl* essentielles

▸▸ *Physiol* **vital capacity** capacité *f* thoracique; **vital force** force *f* vitale; *Med* **vital signs** = température, rythme cardiaque et respiration; **vital statistics** *(demographic)* statistiques *fpl* démographiques; *Fam (of woman)* mensurations *fpl*

vitality [vaɪˈtælɪtɪ] **N** vitalité *f*

vitalize, -ise [ˈvaɪtəlaɪz] **VT** vivifier, dynamiser

vitally [ˈvaɪtəlɪ] **ADV** absolument; **it's v. important that you attend this meeting** il est extrêmement important que vous assistiez à cette réunion; **this question is v. important** cette question est d'une importance capitale; **supplies are v. needed** on a un besoin vital de vivres; **v. for the British, the European Commission has agreed** la Commission Européenne a accepté, ce qui est capital pour les Britanniques

vitamin [*Br* ˈvɪtəmɪn, *Am* ˈvaɪtəmɪn] **N** vitamine *f*; **v. C/E** vitamine C/E; **with added vitamins** vitaminé

▸▸ **vitamin deficiency** *(gen)* carence *f* vitaminique; *(disease)* avitaminose *f*; **vitamin pill** comprimé *m* de vitamines

vitiate [ˈvɪʃɪeɪt] **VT** *Formal* vicier

vitiation [ˌvɪʃɪˈeɪʃən] **N** *Formal* viciation *f*

viticulture [ˈvɪtɪˌkʌltʃə(r)] **N** viticulture *f*

vitreous [ˈvɪtrɪəs] **ADJ 1** *(china, rock)* vitreux; *(enamel)* vitrifié **2** *Anat* vitré

▸▸ **vitreous body** *(in eye)* corps *m* vitré; **vitreous humour** humeur *f* vitrée

vitrifaction [ˌvɪtrɪˈfækʃən], **vitrification** [ˌvɪtrɪfɪˈkeɪʃən] **N** vitrification *f*

vitrified [ˈvɪtrɪfaɪd] **ADJ** vitrifié

vitrify [ˈvɪtrɪfaɪ] *(pt & pp* **vitrified***)* **VT** vitrifier

VI se vitrifier

vitriol [ˈvɪtrɪəl] **N** *Chem & Fig* vitriol *m*

vitriolic [ˌvɪtrɪˈɒlɪk] **ADJ 1** *Chem* de vitriol **2** *(attack, description, portrait)* au vitriol; *(tone)* venimeux

▸▸ **vitriolic criticism** critique *f* mordante

vitriolize, -ise [ˈvɪtrɪəlaɪz] **VT** vitrioler

vituperate [vɪˈtjuːpəreɪt] *Literary* **VT** vitupérer (contre), vilipender

VI vitupérer; **to v. against sb/sth** vitupérer (contre) qn/qch

vituperation [vɪˌtjuːpəˈreɪʃən] **N** *(UNCOUNT)* vitupérations *fpl*

vituperative [vɪˈtjuːpərətɪv] **ADJ** injurieux

viva[1] [ˈviːvə] **EXCLAM** vive!

N vivat *m*

viva[2] [ˈvaɪvə] = **viva voce N**

vivacious [vɪˈveɪʃəs] **ADJ 1** *(manner, person)* enjoué, plein de vivacité **2** *Bot* vivace

vivaciously [vɪˈveɪʃəslɪ] **ADV** avec vivacité

vivacity [vɪˈvæsɪtɪ] **N** *(in action)* vivacité *f*; *(in speech)* verve *f*

vivarium [vaɪˈveərɪəm] *(pl* **vivariums** *or* **vivaria** [-rɪə]*)* **N** vivarium *m*

viva voce [ˌvaɪvəˈvəʊtʃɪ] **N** *Br Univ (gen)* épreuve *f* orale, oral *m*; *(for thesis)* soutenance *f* de thèse

ADJ oral

ADV de vive voix, oralement

vivid [ˈvɪvɪd] **ADJ 1** *(bright ▸ colour, light)* vif, éclatant; *(▸ clothes)* voyant; **v. green paint** peinture d'un vert éclatant

2 *(intense ▸ feeling)* vif

3 *(lively ▸ personality)* vif, vivant; *(▸ imagination)* vif; *(▸ language)* coloré; **it was a very v. performance** c'était une interprétation pleine de verve

4 *(graphic ▸ account, description)* vivant; *(▸ memory)* vif, net; *(▸ example)* frappant; *(▸ imagery)* saisissant

vividly [ˈvɪvɪdlɪ] **ADV 1** *(coloured)* de façon éclatante; *(painted, decorated)* avec éclat, de façon éclatante **2** *(describe)* de façon frappante *ou* vivante; **I can v. remember the day we first met** j'ai un vif souvenir du jour où nous nous sommes rencontrés

vividness [ˈvɪvɪdnɪs] **N 1** *(of colour, light)* éclat *m*, vivacité *f* **2** *(of description, language)* vivacité *f*; *(of memory)* clarté *f*; **she could remember him with great v.** elle se souvenait très nettement de lui; **the v. of the imagery in this poem** les images saisissantes dans ce poème

vivify [ˈvɪvɪfaɪ] *(pt & pp* **vivified***)* **VT** vivifier

viviparous [vɪˈvɪpərəs] **ADJ** *Biol* vivipare

vivisect [ˌvɪvɪˈsekt] **VT** pratiquer la vivisection sur

vivisection [ˌvɪvɪˈsekʃən] **N** vivisection *f*

vivisectionist [ˌvɪvɪˈsekʃənɪst] **N 1** *(practitioner)* vivisecteur(trice) *m,f* **2** *(advocate)* partisan(e) *m,f* de la vivisection

vixen [ˈvɪksən] **N 1** *Zool* renarde *f* **2** *Pej (woman)* mégère *f*

viz [vɪz] **ADV** *(abbr* **videlicet***)* c.-à-d.

vizier [vɪˈzɪə(r)] **N** vizir *m*

vizor = **visor**

VJ [ˌviːˈdʒeɪ] **N** *(abbr* **video jockey***)* présentateur (trice) *m,f* de (vidéo)clips

VJ Day **N** *(abbr* **Victory in Japan Day***)* = jour de la victoire des alliés sur le Japon, le 15 août 1945

VLE [ˌviːelˈiː] **N** *(abbr* **virtual learning environment***)* système *m* de formation en ligne

VLF [ˌviːelˈef] **N** *TV & Rad (abbr* **very low frequency***)* VLF *f*

vlog [ˈviːˌlɒg] **N** *Comput* vlog *m*, blog *m* vidéo

VLSI [ˌviːelˌesˈaɪ] **N** *Comput (abbr* **very large-scale integration***)* VLSI *f*

V-neck **N** encolure *f* en V

ADJ à encolure en V

V-necked **ADJ** à encolure en V

VO [ˌviːˈəʊ] **N** *Cin & TV (abbr* **voice-over***)* voix *f* off

vocab [ˈvəʊkæb] **N** *Fam* vocabulaire[□] *m*

vocabulary [və'kæbjʊlərɪ] (*pl* **vocabularies**) N vocabulaire *m*; *Ling* vocabulaire *m*, lexique *m*
COMP *(test, guide, book)* de vocabulaire

vocal ['vəʊkəl] ADJ **1** *Anat* vocal; **the v. organs** les organes *mpl* vocaux
2 *(oral ▸ communication)* oral, verbal
3 *(outspoken ▸ person, minority)* qui se fait entendre; **the most v. member of the delegation** le membre de la délégation qui s'est fait le plus entendre *ou* qui s'est exprimé le plus énergiquement; **one of the government's most v. critics** l'un de ceux qui critiquent le gouvernement avec le plus de véhémence; **he is very v. about…** il se fait entendre souvent au sujet de…
4 *(noisy ▸ assembly, meeting)* bruyant
5 *Mus* vocal
6 *Ling (sound)* vocalique; *(consonant)* voisé
N *Ling* son *m* vocalique
• **vocals** NPL *Mus* chant *m*, musique *f* vocale; **Lucy Johnston on vocals** au chant: Lucy Johnston
▸▸ ***vocal cords*** cordes *fpl* vocales; ***vocal frequency*** fréquence *f* vocale; ***vocal score*** partition *f* chorale

vocalic [və'kælɪk] ADJ vocalique

vocalist ['vəʊkəlɪst] N chanteur(euse) *m,f (de groupe pop)*; **backing v.** choriste *mf*

vocalization, -isation [ˌvəʊkəlaɪ'zeɪʃən] N vocalisation *f*

vocalize, -ise ['vəʊkəlaɪz] VT **1** *(gen ▸ articulate)* exprimer **2** *Ling (sound)* vocaliser **3** *(text)* vocaliser, marquer des points-voyelles sur
VI *Mus* vocaliser, faire des vocalises

vocally ['vəʊkəlɪ] ADV vocalement; *(protest)* à haute voix

vocation [vəʊ'keɪʃən] N *(gen) & Rel* vocation *f*; **he has no v. for teaching/acting** il n'a pas la vocation de l'enseignement/du théâtre; **to miss one's v.** manquer sa vocation

vocational [vəʊ'keɪʃənəl] ADJ professionnel
▸▸ ***vocational course*** *(short)* stage *m* de formation professionnelle; *(longer)* enseignement *m* professionnel; ***vocational guidance*** orientation *f* professionnelle; *Am & Ir* ***vocational school*** lycée *m* professionnel; ***vocational training*** formation *f* professionnelle

vocative ['vɒkətɪv] *Gram* N vocatif *m*; **in the v.** au vocatif
ADJ **the v. case** le vocatif

vociferate [və'sɪfəreɪt] VI vociférer, hurler

vociferation [vəˌsɪfə'reɪʃən] N *(shout)* cri *m*; *(shouting)* vociférations *fpl*, cris *mpl*

vociferous [və'sɪfərəs] ADJ bruyant, véhément; **to be v. in one's criticism of sth** critiquer qch avec véhémence

vociferously [və'sɪfərəslɪ] ADV *(argue, complain)* bruyamment; *(criticize, protest, condemn)* avec véhémence

VOD [ˌviːəʊ'diː] N *(abbr* **video on demand***)* vidéo *f* à la demande, VOD *f*

vodka ['vɒdkə] N vodka *f*; **v. and orange** vodka-orange *f*

vogue [vəʊg] N *(fashion)* vogue *f*, mode *f*; **to come into v.** devenir à la mode; **that hairstyle was much in v. in the 1930s** cette coiffure était très en vogue *ou* très à la mode dans les années trente; **the v. for long hair is on the way out** les cheveux longs passent de mode; **mini skirts are back in v.** les minijupes sont de nouveau à la mode
ADJ *(style, word)* en vogue, à la mode

voice [vɔɪs] N **1** *(of speaker)* voix *f*; **in a low v.** à voix basse; **in a loud v.** d'une voix forte; **to have a good speaking v.** avoir une bonne voix; **we heard the sound of voices** on entendait des gens parler; **he likes the sound of his own v.** *(is talkative)* il parle beaucoup; *(is conceited)* il s'écoute parler; **to shout at the top of one's v.** crier à tue-tête; **to give v. to sth** exprimer qch; **to hear voices** entendre des voix; **keep your voices down** ne parlez pas si fort; **to raise one's v.** *(speak louder)* parler plus fort; *(get angry)* hausser le ton; **don't you raise your v. at** *or* **to me!** ne prenez pas ce ton-là avec moi!; **several voices were raised in protest** plusieurs voix se sont élevées pour protester; **to make one's v. heard** se faire entendre; *Fig* **the v. of reason** la voix de la raison; **a little v. inside her told her it was wrong** *(her conscience told her)* une petite voix en elle lui dit que c'était mal; **the government must be seen to speak with one v.** le gouvernement doit donner l'impression qu'il parle d'une seule voix; *Am Rad* **V. of America** = station de radio américaine émettant dans le monde entier
2 *(of singer)* voix *f*; **to have a good (singing) v.** avoir une belle voix; **to be in good v.** être bien en voix
3 *(say)* voix *f*; **we have no v. in the matter** nous n'avons pas voix au chapitre; **did you have a v. in deciding who should be invited?** avez-vous participé à l'élaboration de la liste des invités?
4 *Gram* voix *f*; **in the active/passive v.** à la voix active/passive
VT **1** *(express ▸ feelings)* exprimer, formuler; *(▸ opposition, support)* exprimer; **to v. one's anxieties** exprimer ses angoisses **2** *Ling (consonant)* voiser, sonoriser **3** *Mus (organ)* harmoniser
▸▸ ***voice box*** larynx *m*; *Cin, Theat & TV* ***voice coach*** répétiteur(trice) *m,f* vocal(e); *Comput* ***voice input*** entrée *f* vocale; *Mus* ***voice part*** partie *f* vocale; *Comput* ***voice recognition*** reconnaissance *f* de la parole; *Comput* ***voice recognition software*** logiciel *m* de reconnaissance vocale; *Comput* ***voice response*** réponse *f* vocale; *Comput* ***voice synthesizer*** synthétiseur *m* de paroles; ***voice test*** audition *f*; ***voice training*** (UNCOUNT) *Mus* cours *mpl* de chant; *Theat* cours *mpl* de diction *ou* d'élocution; *Am Pol* ***voice vote*** vote *m* par acclamation

voice-activated ADJ à commande vocale

voiced [vɔɪst] ADJ *Ling (consonant)* sonore, voisé

-voiced [vɔɪst] SUFF **low-/soft-v.** à voix basse/douce

voiceless ['vɔɪslɪs] ADJ **1** *Med* aphone **2** *(with no say)* sans voix; **the v. masses** les masses sans voix *ou* qui ne peuvent pas s'exprimer **3** *Ling (consonant)* non-voisé, sourd

voicemail ['vɔɪsmeɪl] N *Tel (message service)* messagerie *f* vocale; *(message)* message *m* vocal

voice-over N *Cin & TV* voix *f* off

void [vɔɪd] N **1** *Phys & Astron* vide *m* **2** *(chasm)* vide *m* **3** *(emptiness)* vide *m*; **to fill a v.** combler un vide; **her husband's death left an aching v. in her life** la mort de son mari a laissé un grand vide dans sa vie
ADJ **1** *(empty)* vide; **v. of interest** dépourvu d'intérêt, sans aucun intérêt **2** *Law (deed, contract)* **(null and) v.** nul; **to make sth v.** annuler *ou* rendre nul qch **3** *(vacant ▸ position)* vacant
VT **1** *Formal (empty)* vider; *(discharge ▸ bowels)* évacuer **2** *Law* annuler, rendre nul

voidable ['vɔɪdəbəl] ADJ *Law (deed, contract)* annulable, résiliable

voile [vɔɪl, vwɑːl] N *Tex* voile *m*

vol. *(written abbr* **volume***)* vol

volatile [*Br* 'vɒlətaɪl, *Am* 'vɒlətəl] ADJ **1** *Chem* volatil
2 *(person ▸ changeable)* versatile, inconstant; *(▸ temperamental)* lunatique
3 *(unstable ▸ situation)* explosif, instable; *(▸ market)* instable; *(▸ Stock Exchange)* volatil
4 *Literary (transitory)* fugace
5 *Comput (memory)* volatil
N *Chem* substance *f* volatile

volatility [ˌvɒlə'tɪlɪtɪ] N **1** *Chem* volatilité *f* **2** *(of person ▸ changeability)* versatilité *f*, inconstance *f* **3** *(of situation, market)* caractère *m* explosif, instabilité *f*; *(of Stock Exchange)* volatilité *f*

volatilize, -ise [vɒ'lætɪlaɪz] VT volatiliser
VI se volatiliser, s'évaporer

vol-au-vent ['vɒləʊvɑ̃] N *Culin* vol-au-vent *m inv*

volcanic [vɒl'kænɪk] ADJ volcanique

volcano [vɒl'keɪnəʊ] (*pl* **volcanoes** *or* **volcanos**) N volcan *m*

vole [vəʊl] N *Zool* campagnol *m*

volition [və'lɪʃən] N *(gen) & Phil* volition *f*, volonté *f*; **of one's own v.** de son propre gré

volley ['vɒlɪ] N **1** *(of gunshots)* volée *f*, salve *f*; *(of arrows, missiles, stones)* volée *f*, grêle *f*; *(of blows)* volée *f* **2** *(of insults, curses)* bordée *f*, torrent *m*; *(of questions)* feu *m* roulant; *(of applause)* salve *f* **3** *Sport* volée *f*; **half v.** *(in tennis)* demi-volée *f*
VT **1** *Mil (missiles, shots)* tirer une volée *ou* une salve de **2** *(curses, insults)* lâcher une bordée o[u] un torrent de **3** *Sport* reprendre de volée
VI **1** *Mil* tirer par salves **2** *Sport (in tennis)* vol[]leyer, reprendre la balle de volée; *(in footbal[l])* reprendre le ballon de volée

volleyball ['vɒlɪbɔːl] N volley-ball *m*, volley *m*
▸▸ ***volleyball player*** volleyeur(euse) *m,f*

volt[1] [vəʊlt] N *Elec* volt *m*

volt[2] [vɒlt, vəʊlt] N *Fencing* volte *f*; **to make a v.** volter

voltage ['vəʊltɪdʒ] N voltage *m*, *Spec* tension *f*; **high/low v.** haute/basse tension *f*

voltaic [vɒl'teɪɪk] ADJ voltaïque
▸▸ ***voltaic pile*** pile *f* voltaïque

volte-face [ˌvɒlt'fɑːs] N volte-face *f inv*; **to make a v.** faire volte-face; **the speech represents a complete v.** ce discours marque un revirement complet

voltmeter ['vəʊltˌmiːtə(r)] N voltmètre *m*

volubility [ˌvɒljʊ'bɪlɪtɪ] N volubilité *f*

voluble ['vɒljʊbəl] ADJ volubile, loquace

volubly ['vɒljʊblɪ] ADV avec volubilité

volume ['vɒljuːm] N **1** *(gen) & Phys* volume *m* *(capacity)* volume *m*, capacité *f*; *(amount)* volume *m*, quantité *f*; **to increase in v.** augmenter de volume; **the v. of traffic/imports** le volume de la circulation/des importations; **a huge v. of work** une énorme quantité de travail
2 *(loudness)* volume *m*; **to turn the v. up/down** augmenter/baisser le volume; *Rad* **at full v.** à fond, à plein volume
3 *(book)* volume *m*, tome *m*; **v. one** volume *m* o[u] tome *m* premier, premier volume *m*; **an encyclopedia in 20 volumes** une encyclopédie en 20 volumes; *Fig* **to speak volumes (about)** *(of action, remark etc)* en dire long (sur), être révélateu[r] (de)
4 *(of hair)* volume *m*
▸▸ *Rad & TV* ***volume control*** bouton *m* de réglag[e] du volume; *Mktg* ***volume mailing*** multipostag[e] *m*, publipostage *m* groupé; *Typ* ***volume numbering*** tomaison *f*

volumetric [ˌvɒljʊ'metrɪk], **volumetrical** [ˌvɒljʊ'metrɪkəl] ADJ volumétrique

voluminous [və'luːmɪnəs] ADJ *(gen)* volumineux; *(garment)* ample; *(correspondence)* abondant

voluminously [və'luːmɪnəslɪ] ADV *(write)* abondamment

volumizing ['vɒljuːmaɪzɪŋ] ADJ *(shampoo, mascara)* volumateur

voluntarily [*Br* 'vɒləntrɪlɪ, *Am* ˌvɒlən'terəlɪ] ADV *(willingly)* volontairement, de son plein gré *(without payment)* bénévolement

voluntary ['vɒləntrɪ] (*pl* **voluntaries**) ADJ **1** *(freely given ▸ statement, donation)* volontaire
2 *(optional)* facultatif; **attendance on the course is purely v.** la participation au cours est facultative
3 *(unpaid ▸ help, service)* bénévole; **the shop is run on a v. basis** le magasin est tenu par des bénévoles
4 *Physiol* volontaire
N **1** *Rel & Mus* morceau *m* d'orgue **2** *(unpaid work)* travail *m* bénévole, bénévolat *m*
▸▸ ***voluntary agency*** organisme *m* bénévole; *B[r] Fin* ***voluntary arrangement*** = arrangement entre une entreprise et ses créanciers de façon à éviter la mise en liquidation; ***voluntary body*** organisme *m* bénévole; *Br Com* ***voluntary liquidation*** liquidation *f* volontaire; **to go into v. liquidation** déposer son bilan; *Law* ***voluntary manslaughter*** homicide *m* volontaire; *Anat* ***voluntary muscle*** muscle *m* strié *ou* squelettique; *Br* ***voluntary redundancy*** départ *m* volontaire; **he decided to take v. redundancy** il a accepté d'être licencié et échange d'indemnités; ***voluntary school*** = école privée qui reçoit une aide de l'État mais garde un certain pouvoir de décision, notamment sur le contenu des cours d'instruction religieuse et le choix des enseignants; ***voluntary service*** service *m* volontaire; ***Voluntary Service Overseas*** = coopération technique à l'étrange[r]

(non rémunérée); *voluntary work* travail *m* bénévole, bénévolat *m*; *voluntary worker* bénévole *mf*

'olunteer [ˌvɒlən'tɪə(r)] N 1 *(gen) & Mil* volontaire *mf*; **can I have a v. from the audience?** y a-t-il une personne dans la salle qui voudrait bien venir sur scène? 2 *(unpaid worker)* bénévole *mf*
COMP 1 *(army, group)* de volontaires 2 *(work, worker)* bénévole
VT 1 *(advice, information, statement)* donner *ou* fournir spontanément; *(help, services)* donner *ou* proposer volontairement; **he volunteered his services as a guide** il s'est proposé comme guide; **to v. to do sth** se proposer pour *ou* offrir de faire qch 2 *(say)* dire spontanément; **"I saw them yesterday," she volunteered** "je les ai vus hier", dit-elle spontanément; **she seemed unwilling to v. anything more than this** elle n'avait pas l'air de vouloir en dire plus
VI *(gen)* se porter volontaire; *Mil* s'engager comme volontaire; **to v. for guard duty** se porter volontaire pour être de garde

'oluptuary [və'lʌptʃʊərɪ] *(pl* **voluptuaries***)* *Literary* N voluptueux(euse) *m,f*, sybarite *mf*
ADJ voluptueux, sensuel

'oluptuous [və'lʌptʃʊəs] ADJ voluptueux, sensuel

'oluptuously [və'lʌptʃʊəslɪ] ADV voluptueusement

'oluptuousness [və'lʌptʃʊəsnɪs] N volupté *f*, sensualité *f*

'om [vɒm] *Fam* N dégueulis *m*
VI dégueuler, gerber

'omit ['vɒmɪt] N vomissement *m*, vomi *m*
VT *also Fig* vomir

'omiting ['vɒmɪtɪŋ] N *(UNCOUNT)* vomissements *mpl*

'oodoo ['vu:du:] *(pl* **voodoos***)* N vaudou *m*
ADJ vaudou *(inv)*
VT envoûter, ensorceler
►► *Am* ***voodoo economics*** = politique économique qui tient de l'illusionnisme

'oodooism ['vu:du:ɪzəm] N vaudou *m*

'oracious [və'reɪʃəs] ADJ *(appetite, energy, person)* vorace; *(reader)* avide

'oraciously [və'reɪʃəslɪ] ADV *(consume, eat)* voracement, avec voracité; *(read)* avec voracité, avidement

'oracity [vɒ'ræsɪtɪ] N voracité *f*

'ortex ['vɔ:teks] *(pl* **vortexes** *or* **vortices** [-tɪsi:z]*)* N *(of water, gas)* vortex *m*, tourbillon *m*; *Fig* tourbillon *m*, maelström *m*

'otary ['vəʊtərɪ] *(pl* **votaries***)* N *Rel & Fig* fervent(e) *m,f*

'ote [vəʊt] N 1 *(ballot)* vote *m*; **to have a v. on sth** voter sur qch, mettre qch aux voix; **to put a question to the v.** mettre une question aux voix; **let's put it to the v.** votons; **to take a v. on sth** *(gen)* voter sur qch; *Admin & Pol* procéder au vote de qch; **v. of thanks** discours *m* de remerciement; **I propose a v. of thanks to our charming hostesses** je propose que l'on remercie chaleureusement nos charmantes hôtesses
2 *(in parliament)* vote *m*, scrutin *m*; **the v. went in the government's favour/against the government** les députés se sont prononcés en faveur du/contre le gouvernement; **v. of confidence** vote *m* de confiance; **v. of no confidence** motion *f* de censure
3 *(individual choice)* vote *m*, voix *f*; **to give one's v. to sb** voter pour qn; **they've got my v.** je vote pour eux; **to count the votes** *(gen)* compter les votes *ou* les voix; *Pol* dépouiller le scrutin; **the candidate got 15,000 votes** le candidat a recueilli 15 000 voix; **to be elected by one v.** être élu à une voix de majorité; **one member, one v.** = système de scrutin "un homme, une voix"
4 *(ballot paper)* bulletin *m* de vote
5 *(suffrage)* droit *m* de vote; **to have the v.** avoir le droit de vote; **to give the v. to sb** accorder le droit de vote à qn; **they campaigned for votes for women** ils ont fait campagne pour qu'on accorde le droit de vote aux femmes
6 *(UNCOUNT) (collectively ▸ voters)* vote *m*, voix *fpl*; *(▸ votes cast)* voix *fpl* exprimées; **they hope to win the working-class v.** ils espèrent gagner les voix des ouvriers; **they won 40 percent of the v.** ils ont remporté 40 pour cent des voix *ou* des suffrages; **they increased their v. by 12 percent** ils ont amélioré leurs résultats de 12 pour cent
7 *Br Pol (grant)* vote *m* de crédits; **a v. of £100,000** un vote de crédits de 100 000 livres
VT 1 *(in election)* voter; **v. Malone!** votez Malone!; **to v. Labour/Republican** voter travailliste/républicain
2 *(in parliament, assembly ▸ motion, law, money)* voter; **they voted that the sitting (should) be suspended** ils ont voté la suspension de la séance
3 *(elect)* élire; *(appoint)* nommer; **she was voted president** elle a été élue présidente
4 *(declare)* proclamer; **the party was voted a great success** de l'avis de tous, la soirée a été un grand succès
5 *(suggest)* proposer; **I v. we all go to bed** je propose qu'on aille tous se coucher
VI voter; **France is voting this weekend** la France va aux urnes ce week-end; **to v. for/against sb** voter pour/contre qn; **I'm going to v. for Barron** je vais voter (pour) Barron *ou* donner ma voix à Barron; **to v. in favour of/against sth** voter pour/contre qch; **let's v. on it!** mettons cela aux voix!; **to v. by a show of hands** voter à main levée; *Fig* **to v. with one's feet** *(by leaving)* manifester *ou* signifier son mécontentement en partant; *(by not turning up)* manifester *ou* signifier son mécontentement par le boycott
▸ **vote down** VT SEP *(bill, proposal)* rejeter *(par le vote)*
▸ **vote in** VT SEP *(person, government)* élire; *(new law)* voter, adopter
▸ **vote out** VT SEP *(suggestion)* rejeter; *(minister)* relever de ses fonctions; **the bill was voted out** le projet de loi n'a pas été adopté *ou* a été rejeté
▸ **vote through** VT SEP *(bill, reform)* voter, ratifier

vote-buying N achat *m* de voix *ou* de votes; **the Japanese government was accused of v. to secure an agreement** on a accusé le gouvernement japonais d'avoir acheté des voix afin d'obtenir un accord

vote-catcher N politique *f* électoraliste

vote-loser N politique *f* qui risque de faire perdre des voix, politique *f* peu populaire

vote-losing ADJ = peu populaire, qui risque de faire perdre des voix

voter ['vəʊtə(r)] N électeur(trice) *m,f*; **the voters** l'électorat *m*; **French voters go to the polls tomorrow** les Français vont aux urnes demain
►► ***voter apathy*** apathie *f* électorale *ou* des électeurs; ***voter registration*** inscription *f* sur les listes électorales; *Am* ***voter registration card*** carte *f* d'électeur; ***voter turnout*** taux m de participation électorale

vote-rigging N manipulations *fpl* électorales

vote-selling N vente *f* de voix *ou* de votes

vote-trading N échange *m* de voix *ou* de votes

vote-winner N = politique populaire permettant de remporter une victoire électorale; **Labour believes its plans to cut taxes were a v. in last year's elections** le Parti travailliste pense que c'est son intention de réduire les impôts qui lui a valu la victoire aux élections de l'année dernière

vote-winning ADJ = qui permet de remporter une victoire électorale

voting ['vəʊtɪŋ] N vote *m*, scrutin *m*; **v. takes place on Sunday** le scrutin a lieu dimanche
COMP *(assembly)* électoral; *(member)* votant
►► ***voting behaviour*** comportement *m* électoral; ***voting booth*** isoloir *m*; ***voting card*** carte *f* d'électeur; *Am* ***voting machine*** machine *f* pour enregistrer les votes; ***voting method*** méthode *f* électorale; ***voting paper*** bulletin *m* de vote; ***voting pattern*** répartition *f* des votes; *Am* ***voting precinct*** circonscription *f* électorale; ***voting rights*** droits *mpl* de vote; *Fin* ***voting shares*** actions *fpl* donnant droit au vote

votive ['vəʊtɪv] ADJ votif
►► ***votive offering*** ex-voto *m inv*

vouch [vaʊtʃ] VI **to v. for sb/sth** se porter garant de qn/qch, répondre de qn/qch; **he needs somebody to v. for his honesty** il lui faut quelqu'un qui se porte garant de son honnêteté; **I can v. for the truth of her story** je peux attester *ou* témoigner de la véracité de sa déclaration

voucher ['vaʊtʃə(r)] N 1 *Br (for restaurant, purchase, petrol)* bon *m*; **(gift) v.** bon-cadeau *m*
2 *(receipt)* reçu *m*, récépissé *m*
3 *Law* pièce *f* justificative
4 *Acct* pièce *f* comptable

vouchsafe [vaʊtʃ'seɪf] VT *Formal* 1 *(grant ▸ help, support)* accorder, octroyer; *(▸ answer)* accorder; **he vouchsafed us no reply** il n'a pas daigné nous répondre 2 *(undertake)* **to v. to do sth** *(willingly)* accepter gracieusement de faire qch; *(reluctantly)* condescendre à *ou* daigner faire qch

vow [vaʊ] N 1 *(promise)* serment *m*, promesse *f*; **to make** *or* **to take a v. to do sth** faire serment *ou* jurer de faire qch; **I'm under a v. of silence** j'ai fait serment *ou* j'ai juré de ne rien dire; **she took a solemn v. to return once a year** elle a juré solennellement de revenir une fois par an 2 *Rel* vœu *m*; **to take one's vows** prononcer ses vœux; **to take a v. of poverty/chastity** faire vœu de pauvreté/chasteté; **to take a v. of silence** *(monk etc)* faire vœu de silence
VT *(swear ▸ gen)* jurer; *(▸ to oneself)* se jurer; **to v. to do sth** jurer de faire qch; **to v. obedience/secrecy** jurer obéissance/de garder le secret; **to v. revenge on sb** jurer de se venger de qn

vowel ['vaʊəl] N voyelle *f*
COMP *(harmony, pattern, sound)* vocalique
►► ***vowel point*** point-voyelle *m*; ***vowel shift*** mutation *f* vocalique

vox pop [ˌvɒks'pɒp] N *Br Fam* micro-trottoir *m*

voyage ['vɔɪɪdʒ] N voyage *m*; **a transatlantic v.** un voyage *ou* une traversée transatlantique; **to go on a v.** partir en voyage; **a round-the-world v.** un voyage autour du monde; **great voyages of discovery** grands voyages d'exploration
VT *Naut* traverser, parcourir
VI 1 *Naut* voyager par mer; **they voyaged across the Atlantic/the desert** ils ont traversé l'Atlantique/le désert; **to v. round the world** voyager autour du monde 2 *Am Aviat* voyager par avion

voyager ['vɔɪɪdʒə(r)] N 1 *(traveller)* voyageur(euse) *m,f* 2 *(explorer)* navigateur(trice) *m,f*

voyeur [vwɑ:'jɜ:(r)] N voyeur(euse) *m,f*

voyeurism [vwɑ:'jɜ:rɪzəm] N voyeurisme *m*

voyeuristic [ˌvɔɪə'rɪstɪk] ADJ voyeuriste

VP [ˌvi:'pi:] N *(abbr* **vice-president***)* VP *m*

VPL [ˌvi:pi:'el] N *Fam Hum (abbr* **visible panty line***)* = contours du slip visibles sous les vêtements

VR [ˌvi:'ɑ:(r)] *Br (abbr* **Victoria Regina***)* la Reine Victoria

VRAM ['vi:ræm] N *Comput (abbr* **video random access memory***)* VRAM *f*

VRML [ˌvi:ɑ:ˌrem'el] N *Comput (abbr* **virtual reality modelling language***)* VRML *m*

vs *(written abbr* **versus***)* contre

V-shaped ADJ en (forme de) V

V-sign N **to give the V.** *(for victory, approval)* faire le V de la victoire; *Br* **to give sb the V.** *(as insult)* ≃ faire un bras d'honneur à qn

VSO [ˌvi:es'əʊ] N *Br (abbr* **Voluntary Service Overseas***)* = coopération technique à l'étranger (non rémunérée)

VT[1] [ˌvi:'ti:] N *Cin & TV (abbr* **videotape***)* bande *f* vidéo
►► ***VT editing*** montage *m* vidéo; ***VT operator*** opérateur(trice) *m,f* magnétoscope *ou* vidéo

VT[2], **Vt** *(written abbr* **Vermont***)* Vermont *m*

VTOL ['vi:tɒl] N *Aviat (abbr* **vertical takeoff and landing***)* *(system)* décollage *m* et atterrissage *m* vertical; *(plane)* ADAV *m*

VTR [ˌvi:ti:'ɑ:(r)] N *TV (abbr* **video tape recorder***)* magnétoscope *m*

vulcanite ['vʌlkənaɪt] N ébonite *f*

vulcanization, -isation [ˌvʌlkənaɪ'zeɪʃən] N vulcanisation *f*

vulcanize, -ise ['vʌlkənaɪz] VT vulcaniser

vulgar ['vʌlgə(r)] ADJ 1 *(rude)* vulgaire, grossier 2 *(common ▸ person, taste, decor)* vulgaire, commun; **the v. tongue** la langue commune
►► ***vulgar fraction*** fraction *f* ordinaire; ***Vulgar Latin*** latin *m* vulgaire

vulgarian [vʌl'geərɪən] N personne *f* vulgaire

vulgarism ['vʌlgərɪzəm] **N 1** *(uneducated language)* vulgarisme *m*; *(rude word)* grossièreté *f* **2** *(vulgarity)* vulgarité *f*

vulgarity [vʌl'gærɪtɪ] **N** vulgarité *f*

vulgarization, -isation [ˌvʌlgəraɪ'zeɪʃən] **N** vulgarisation *f*

vulgarize, -ise ['vʌlgəraɪz] **VT 1** *(appearance, language)* rendre vulgaire **2** *(popularize)* vulgariser, populariser

vulgarly ['vʌlgəlɪ] **ADV 1** *(coarsely)* vulgairement, grossièrement **2** *(commonly)* vulgairement, communément

Vulgate ['vʌlgeɪt] **N** Vulgate *f*

vulnerability [ˌvʌlnərə'bɪlɪtɪ] **N** vulnérabilité *f*

vulnerable ['vʌlnərəbəl] **ADJ 1** *(gen)* vulnérable; **to be v. to sth** être vulnérable à qch; **that's her v. spot** c'est son point faible *ou* son talon d'Achille; **the v. spot in our defences** le point faible de nos défenses **2** *Cards (in bridge)* vulnérable

vulture ['vʌltʃə(r)] **N** *also Fig* vautour *m*

vulva ['vʌlvə] (*pl* **vulvas** *or* **vulvae** [-viː]) **N** *Ana*[t] vulve *f*

vulvitis [vʌl'vaɪtɪs] **N** *Med* vulvite *f*

VU meter [ˌviː'juː-] **N** vumètre *m*

vv 1 (*written abbr* **verses**) v. **2** (*written abbr* **versus**) contre

vying ['vaɪɪŋ] **N** rivalité *f*

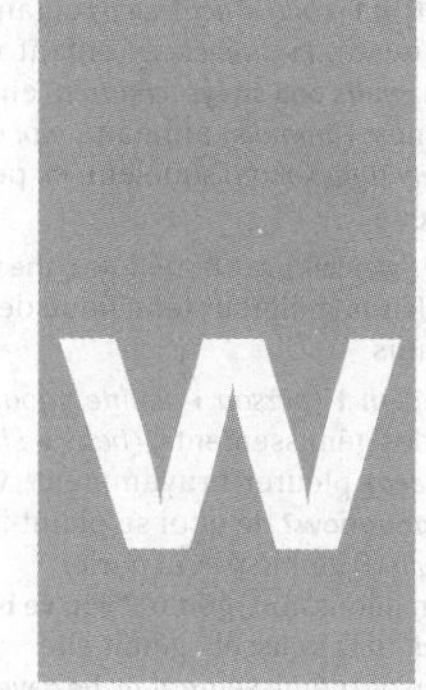

W¹, w ['dʌbəlju:] **N** *(letter)* W, w *m inv*; **two w's** deux w; **W for William** W comme William

W² **1** *(written abbr* **west)** O **2** *Elec (written abbr* **watt)** w

W3 [ˌdʌbəlju:'θri:] **N** *Comput (abbr* **World Wide Web)** W3 *m*, le Web *m*

WAAF [wæf] **N** *Br Hist & Mil (abbr* **Women's Auxiliary Air Force)** = pendant la Seconde Guerre mondiale, section féminine auxiliaire de l'armée de l'air britannique

wack ['wæk] **ADJ** *Am Fam* **1** *(worthless)* nul **2** *(mad)* cinglé, dingue **3** *(stupid)* débile

wack-job **N** *Am Fam* cinglé(e) *m,f*, dingue *mf*

wacko ['wækəʊ] *(pl* **wackos)** *Fam* **N** cinglé(e) *m,f*, dingue *mf*

ADJ cinglé, dingue

wacky ['wæki] *(compar* **wackier,** *superl* **wackiest)** **ADJ** *Fam* loufoque, farfelu

▸▸ *Hum* ***wacky baccy*** *(marijuana)* herbe *f*

wad [wɒd] *(pt & pp* **wadded,** *cont* **wadding)** **N 1** *(of cotton wool, paper)* tampon *m*, bouchon *m*; *(of tobacco)* chique *f*; *(of straw)* bouchon *m*; *(of gum)* boulette *f*; *Mil (for cannon, gun)* bourre *f* **2** *(of letters, documents)* liasse *f*, paquet *m*; **he pulled out a thick w. of banknotes** il a sorti une grosse liasse de billets; **to shoot one's w.** *Fam (spend all one's money)* claquer tout son fric; *esp Am Vulg (have orgasm)* décharger, envoyer la sauce

VT 1 *(cloth, paper)* faire un tampon de; *(tobacco, chewing gum)* faire une boulette de **2** *(hole, aperture)* boucher (avec un tampon); *Mil (barrel, cannon)* bourrer **3** *(quilt, garment)* ouater; **a wadded jacket** une veste ouatée *ou* doublée d'ouate

▸ **wad up** **VT SEP** = **wad** *vt* 2

wadding ['wɒdɪŋ] **N 1** *Mil (in gun, cartridge)* bourre *f* **2** *(stuffing* ▸ *for furniture, packing)* rembourrage *m*, capitonnage *m*; *(*▸ *for clothes)* ouate *f*, ouatine *f*

waddle ['wɒdəl] **VI** *(duck, person)* se dandiner; **to w. along/in** avancer/entrer en se dandinant

N dandinement *m*; **to walk with a w.** *(person)* marcher en se dandinant

wade [weɪd] **VI** avancer, marcher; **they waded across the stream** ils ont traversé le ruisseau à pied; **we waded into the water** nous sommes entrés dans l'eau; **she waded out to the boat** elle s'avança dans l'eau vers le bateau

VT *(river)* passer *ou* traverser à pied

▸ **wade in** **VI** *Br (in fight, quarrel)* s'en mêler

▸ **wade into** **VT INSEP** *Br (work, task)* attaquer, s'atteler à, se mettre à; *(meal)* attaquer, entamer; *(person* ▸ *verbally)* s'attaquer à, s'en prendre à; *(*▸ *physically)* attaquer, se jeter sur; **critics have waded into his latest film** la critique a démoli son dernier film

▸ **wade through** **VT INSEP** avancer *ou* marcher dans; **to w. through piles of dirty clothing** *(walk through them)* se tailler un chemin à travers des piles de linge sale; *Fig* **I'm still wading through 'War and Peace'** je suis toujours aux prises avec 'Guerre et paix'; **it took me a month to w. through that book** il m'a fallu un mois pour venir à bout de ce livre; **she's got a 100-page report to w. through** elle a un rapport de 100 pages à lire

wader ['weɪdə(r)] **N** *Orn* échassier *m*

waders ['weɪdəz] **NPL** cuissardes *fpl (de pêcheur)*

wadi ['wɒdɪ] **N** *Geog* oued *m*

wading ['weɪdɪŋ] **N** *(in water)* marche *f* dans l'eau

▸▸ ***wading bird*** échassier *m*; *Am* ***wading pool*** *(in swimming pool)* petit bassin *m*; *(inflatable)* piscine *f* gonflable

wafer ['weɪfə(r)] **N 1** *Culin* gaufrette *f*, *Belg* galette *f*

2 *Rel* hostie *f*

3 *(seal)* cachet *m* (de papier rouge)

4 *Comput & Tech* tranche *f*

VT 1 *(seal)* cacheter (avec du papier rouge) **2** *Comput & Tech* diviser en tranches

wafer-thin **ADJ** mince comme une feuille de papier à cigarette *ou* comme une pelure d'oignon; **a w. majority** une majorité infime

waffle ['wɒfəl] **N 1** *Culin* gaufre *f* **2** *Br Fam (spoken)* baratin *m*, bla-bla *m inv*; *(written)* remplissage *m*, baratin *m*; **it's just a load of w.** ce n'est que du baratin

VI *Fam (in speaking)* baratiner, parler pour ne rien dire; *(in writing)* faire du remplissage; **he's been waffling away for over an hour** cela fait plus d'une heure qu'il raconte son baratin; *Br* **to w. on** bavarder, faire des laïus; **she's always waffling on about her children** elle n'arrête pas de parler de ses enfants

▸▸ *Culin* ***waffle iron*** gaufrier *m*

waft [wɑ:ft, wɒft] **VT** *(scent, sound)* porter, transporter; **the breeze wafted the curtains gently to and fro** le vent léger faisait ondoyer les rideaux

VI *(scent, sound)* flotter; **a delicious smell wafted into the room** une délicieuse odeur envahit la pièce; **the papers wafted off the table** un souffle d'air emporta les papiers qui étaient sur la table; **her voice wafted gently down the stairs** sa voix douce parvenait jusqu'en bas de l'escalier; *Fig* **Vanessa wafted into/out of the room** Vanessa entra dans/sortit de la pièce d'un pas léger

N *(of smoke, air)* bouffée *f*

WAG [wæg] **N** *Fam (abbr* **wives and girlfriends)** = femme ou petite amie d'une star du monde du sport, le plus souvent un footballeur

wag [wæg] *(pt & pp* **wagged,** *cont* **wagging)** **VT** *(tail, finger)* agiter, remuer; **she wagged her finger at him** elle le menaça du doigt

VI *(tail)* remuer, frétiller; **tongues were wagging about her behaviour** son comportement faisait jaser *ou* parler les gens; **if you carry on like this tongues will begin to w.** si tu continues comme ça, les gens vont jaser

N 1 *(of tail)* remuement *m*, frétillement *m*; **with a w. of its tail** en agitant *ou* en remuant la queue **2** *Br (person)* plaisantin *m*, farceur(euse) *m,f*

wage [weɪdʒ] **N 1** *(pay* ▸ *of worker)* salaire *m*, paye *f*, paie *f*; *(*▸ *of servant)* gages *mpl*; **her w. is** *or* **her wages are only £100 a week** elle ne gagne que 100 livres par semaine; *Br* **a w.-price spiral** une spirale des prix et des salaires; *Hum* **I'm fed up with being a w. slave** j'en ai assez d'être obligé de gagner ma vie **2** *(reward)* salaire *m*, récompense *f*; *Bible* **the wages of sin is death** la mort est le prix du péché

COMP *(demand, settlement)* salarial; *(increase, incentive)* de salaire

VT **to w. war on** *or* **against** faire la guerre contre; **the government have decided to w. war on drug trafficking** le gouvernement a résolu de partir en guerre contre les trafiquants de drogue; **to w. a campaign for/against sth** faire campagne pour/contre qch

▸▸ ***wage adjustment*** ajustement *m* des salaires; ***wage bargaining*** *(UNCOUNT)* négociations *fpl* salariales; ***wage bill*** masse *f* salariale, charges *fpl* salariales; ***wage bracket*** fourchette *f* de salaire; ***wage ceiling*** salaire *m* plafonné; ***wage claim*** revendication *f* salariale; ***wage cut*** réduction *f* de salaire, réduction *f* salariale; *Br* ***wage differential*** écart *m* salarial; ***wage dispute*** conflit *m* salarial; ***wage drift*** dérive *f* salariale; ***wage earner*** salarié(e) *m,f*; **they are both w. earners** ils sont salariés tous les deux, ils ont tous les deux un salaire; ***wage economy*** économie *f* salariale; ***wage freeze*** gel *m ou* blocage *m* des salaires; ***wage inflation*** inflation *f* des salaires; *Br* ***wage packet*** *(envelope)* enveloppe *f* contenant la paie; *(money)* paie *f*, salaire *f*; ***wage policy*** politique *f* salariale *ou* des salaires; ***wage and price index*** indice *m* des prix et des salaires; ***wage pyramid*** pyramide *f* des salaires; ***wage rate*** taux *m* des salaires; ***wage restraint*** restriction *f* salariale; ***wage rise*** augmentation *f* de salaire; ***wage round*** série *f* de négociations salariales; ***wage scale*** échelle *f* des salaires; ***wage slip*** fiche *f* de paie, bulletin *m* de salaire; ***wage structure*** structure *f* des salaires

wager ['weɪdʒə(r)] **VT** parier

VI parier, faire un pari

N pari *m*; **to make** *or* **to lay a w.** faire un pari

waggish ['wægɪʃ] **ADJ** facétieux

waggle ['wægəl] **VT** *(tail)* agiter, remuer; *(pencil)* agiter; *(loose tooth, screw)* faire jouer; *(ears, nose)* remuer

VI *(tail)* bouger, frétiller; *(loose tooth, screw)* bouger

N **to give sth a w.** agiter *ou* remuer qch

waggon, waggonette *etc Br* = **wagon, wagonette** *etc*

Wagnerian [vɑ:g'nɪərɪən] **ADJ** wagnérien

N wagnérien(enne) *m,f*

Wagon ['wægən] **N** *Astron* **the W.** la Grande Ourse

wagon ['wægən] **N 1** *(horse-drawn)* chariot *m*

2 *(truck)* camionnette *f*, fourgon *m*; *Am* **(patrol) w.** fourgon *m* cellulaire; *Am* **(station) w.** break *m*

3 *Br Rail* wagon *m* (de marchandises)

4 *Am (drinks trolley)* chariot *m*

5 *Fam (idiom)* **to be on the w.** être au régime sec; **to be off** *or* **have fallen off the w.** s'être remis à boire

▸▸ ***wagon train*** convoi *m* de chariots *(en particulier de colons américains)*

wagoner ['wægənə(r)] **N** charretier *m*

wagonette [ˌwægə'net] **N** break *m* (attelé)

wagonload ['wægənləʊd] **N** *Agr* charretée *f*, *Rail* wagon *m*

wagtail ['wægteɪl] **N** *Orn* hochequeue *m*, bergeronnette *f*

wah-wah ['wɑ:ˌwɑ:] **N** *Mus* effet *m* wah-wah *ou* wa-wa

▸▸ ***wah-wah pedal*** pédale *f* wah-wah

waif [weɪf] **N 1** *(child ▸ neglected)* enfant *mf* malheureux(euse); *(▸ homeless)* enfant *mf* abandonné(e); **waifs and strays** *(children)* enfants *mpl* abandonnés; *(animals)* animaux *mpl* errants **2** *(excessively thin person)* squelette *m*, personne *f* famélique

waiflike ['weɪflaɪk] **ADJ** famélique; **the w. look of some models** la maigreur famélique de certains mannequins

wail [weɪl] **VI 1** *(person ▸ whine, moan)* gémir, pousser des gémissements; *(baby ▸ shout)* hurler; *(▸ weep)* pleurer bruyamment; **what's he wailing about now?** de quoi se plaint-il maintenant? **2** *(wind)* gémir; *(siren)* hurler

VT dire en gémissant, gémir; **"you've broken it!" she wailed** "tu l'as cassé!", gémit-elle

N 1 *(of person)* gémissement *m*; **he gave a loud w.** il poussa un profond gémissement; **"he's gone!" she said with a w.** "il est parti!" dit-elle en gémissant **2** *(of wind)* gémissement *m*; *(of siren)* hurlement *m*

wailing ['weɪlɪŋ] **N** *(UNCOUNT) (of person)* gémissements *mpl*, plaintes *fpl*; *(of wind)* gémissements *mpl*, plainte *f*; *(of siren)* hurlement *m*, hurlements *mpl*

ADJ *(person)* gémissant; *(sound)* plaintif

▸▸ ***the Wailing Wall*** le mur des Lamentations

wain [weɪn] **N** *Literary* chariot *m (de ferme)*

• **Wain N** *Astron* **the W.** le Grand Chariot, la Grande Ourse

wainscot ['weɪnskət] **N** lambris *m (en bois)*

wainscoting, wainscotting ['weɪnskətɪŋ] **N** *Br* lambrissage *m (en bois)*

WAIS [weɪz] **N** *Comput (abbr* **wide area information service** *or* **system)** WAIS *m*

waist [weɪst] **N 1** *(of person, garment)* taille *f*; **he measures 80 cm around the w.** il fait 80 cm de tour de taille; **he put his arm around her w.** il l'a prise par la taille; **it's too tight at** *or* **round the w.** ça serre à la taille; **he was up to the** *or* **his w. in water** l'eau lui arrivait à la ceinture *ou* à la taille **2** *(of ship, plane)* partie *f* centrale; *(of violin)* partie *f* resserrée de la table; *(of pipe)* rétrécissement *m*

▸▸ ***waist lock*** *(in wrestling)* ceinture *f*; ***waist measurement, waist size*** tour *m* de taille

waistband ['weɪstbænd] **N** ceinture *f (d'un vêtement)*

waistcoat ['weɪskəʊt] **N** *Br* gilet *m (de costume)*

waist-deep ADJ he was w. in water l'eau lui arrivait à la ceinture *ou* à la taille; **the water was w.** l'eau arrivait à la ceinture

waisted ['weɪstɪd] **ADJ** *(coat, jacket)* cintré

waist-high ADJ *(grass)* à hauteur de la taille

waistline ['weɪstlaɪn] **N** taille *f*; **to watch one's w.** surveiller sa ligne

wait [weɪt] **VI 1** *(person, bus, work)* attendre; **I've been waiting for half an hour/since Easter** j'attends depuis une demi-heure/depuis Pâques; **just you w.!** *(as threat)* attends un peu, tu vas voir!, tu ne perds rien pour attendre!; *(you'll see)* vous verrez!; **we'll just have to w. and see** on verra bien; **w. and see!** attends voir!; **he didn't w. to be told twice** il ne se l'est pas fait dire deux fois; **letters waiting to be delivered** lettres qui attendent d'être distribuées, *Admin* lettres en souffrance; **we're waiting to be served** nous attendons qu'on s'occupe de nous; **to keep sb waiting** faire attendre qn; **they do it while you w.** ils le font devant vous; **repairs while you w.** *(sign)* réparations minute; *Prov* **everything comes to him** *or* **to he who waits** tout vient à point à qui sait attendre

2 *(with "can")* **it can w.** cela peut attendre; **he can w.** laisse-le attendre; *also Ironic* **I can't w.!** je brûle d'impatience!; **it can't w.** cela ne peut pas attendre, c'est très urgent; **I can hardly w. to see them again** j'ai hâte de les revoir; **I can't w. for the weekend (to arrive)** j'attends le week-end avec impatience!, vivement le week-end!

3 *(with "until" or "till")* **w. until I've finished** attendez que j'aie fini; **w. until the film is over** attendez la fin du film; **can't that w. until tomorrow?** cela ne peut pas attendre jusqu'à demain?; **just w. till your parents hear about it** attends un peu que tes parents apprennent cela

4 *(serve)* servir, faire le service; **to w.** *Br* **at** *or Am* **on table** servir à table, faire le service

VT 1 *(period of time)* attendre; **I waited half an hour** j'ai attendu (pendant) une demi-heure; **I waited all day for the repairman to come** j'ai passé toute la journée à attendre le réparateur; **w. a minute!** (attendez) une minute *ou* un instant!; **w. your turn!** attendez votre tour! **2** *Am (delay)* **don't w. dinner for me** ne m'attendez pas pour vous mettre à table **3** *Am (serve at)* **to w. tables** servir à table, faire le service

N attente *f*; **we had a long w.** nous avons dû attendre (pendant) longtemps; **she had a half-hour** *or* **half-hour's w. at Gatwick** il a fallu qu'elle attende une demi-heure *ou* elle a eu une demi-heure d'attente à Gatwick; **there was an hour's w. between trains** il y avait une heure de battement *ou* d'attente entre les trains; **it was worth the w.** ça valait la peine d'attendre; **to lie in w. for** être à l'affût de, guetter; **the gunmen were lying in w. for the convoy** les bandits guettaient l'arrivée du convoi

• **waits NPL** *Br Mus* chanteurs *mpl* de Noël

▸▸ *Comput* ***wait loop*** boucle *f* d'attente; *Comput* ***wait state*** état *m* d'attente

▸ **wait about VI** *Br* traîner, faire le pied de grue; **to w. about for sb** attendre qn, faire le pied de grue en attendant qn; **don't keep me waiting about** ne me fais pas attendre

▸ **wait behind VI** rester; **to w. behind for sb** rester pour attendre qn

▸ **wait in VI** rester à la maison; **I waited in all evening for her** je suis resté chez moi à l'attendre toute la soirée

▸ **wait on VT INSEP 1** *(serve)* **I'm not here to w. on you!** *(male)* je ne suis pas ton serviteur!; *(female)* je ne suis pas ta servante *ou* ta bonne! **to w. on sb hand and foot** être aux petits soins pour qn; **he expects to be waited on hand and foot** il veut que tout le monde soit à son service *ou* à ses petits soins **2** *Am (in restaurant)* **to w. on tables** faire le service, servir à table

▸ **wait out VT SEP** *(war, storm)* attendre la fin de; *(concert, film)* rester jusqu'à la fin *ou* jusqu'au bout de, attendre la fin de

▸ **wait up VI 1** *(at night)* rester debout, veiller; **I'll be late so don't w. up (for me)** je rentrerai tard, ne m'attendez pas; **her parents always w. up for her** ses parents ne se couchent jamais avant qu'elle soit rentrée; **the children were allowed to w. up until midnight** on a permis aux enfants de veiller jusqu'à minuit **2** *Fam (wait)* **hey, w. up!** attendez-moi!ᵒ

waiter ['weɪtə(r)] **N 1** *(in restaurant)* serveur *m*, garçon *m*; **w.!** s'il vous plaît!, monsieur! **2** *St Exch* coursier *m*

▸▸ ***waiter service*** service *m* à table

waiting ['weɪtɪŋ] **N** attente *f*; **after two hours of w.** après deux heures d'attente, après avoir attendu deux heures; **I can't stand all this waiting about** cela m'énerve d'être obligé d'attendre comme ça; **no w.** *(sign)* stationnement interdit; **to be in w. on sb** être au service de qn

ADJ *(person, taxi)* qui attend; **to play a w. game** *Mil & Pol* mener une politique d'attentisme; *Fig* jouer la montre, attendre son heure

▸▸ ***waiting list*** liste *f* d'attente; **to be on the w. list** être sur la liste d'attente; **there's a two-month w. list for an operation** il faut attendre deux mois pour une opération; ***waiting period*** période *f* d'attente; ***waiting room*** *(in office, surgery, station)* salle *f* d'attente

waitlist ['weɪtlɪst] **VT** *Am* mettre sur la liste d'attente; **I'm waitlisted for the next flight** je suis sur la liste d'attente pour le prochain vol

waitperson ['weɪtpɜːsən] **N** *Am* serveur(euse) *m,f*

waitress ['weɪtrɪs] **N** serveuse *f*; **w.!** s'il vous plaît!, mademoiselle!

▸▸ ***waitress service*** service *m* à table

waitstaff ['weɪt,stɑːf] **N** *Am* serveurs *mpl*

waive [weɪv] **VT** *(condition, requirement)* ne pas insister sur, abandonner; *(law, rule)* déroger à; *(claim, right)* renoncer à, abandonner

> Attention: ne pas confondre avec **wave**.

waiver ['weɪvə(r)] **N** *(of condition, requirement)* abandon *m*; *(of law, rule)* dérogation *f*; *(of claim, right)* renonciation *f*, abandon *m*

wake [weɪk] *(pt* **woke** [wəʊk] *or* **waked,** *pp* **woken** ['wəʊkən] *or* **waked) VI** *(stop sleeping)* se réveiller, s'éveiller; **the baby woke at six** le bébé s'est réveillé à six heures; **he woke to the news that war had broken out** à son réveil, il a appris que la guerre avait éclaté

VT 1 *(rouse from sleep)* réveiller, tirer *ou* sortir du sommeil; **the noise was enough to w. the dead** il y avait un bruit à réveiller les morts

2 *(arouse ▸ curiosity, jealousy)* réveiller, éveiller, exciter; *(▸ memories)* réveiller, éveiller, ranimer **3** *(alert)* éveiller l'attention de

N 1 *(vigil)* veillée *f* (mortuaire); **to have a w. for sb** organiser une veillée de commémoration en souvenir de qn; *Fig* **it is too soon to hold a w. for the ideal of European unity** il est encore trop tôt pour enterrer l'idéal de l'unité européenne

2 *(of ship)* sillage *m*, eaux *fpl*; *Fig* sillage *m*; **famine followed in the w. of the drought** la famine a suivi la sécheresse; **he always brings trouble in his w.** il amène toujours des ennuis (dans son sillage); **to follow in sb's w.** marcher sur les traces *ou* dans le sillage de qn; **since then many other countries have followed in our w.** depuis lors bon nombre d'autres pays nous ont suivis; **he left the other athletes trailing in his w.** il a laissé les autres athlètes à la traîne *ou* loin derrière lui; **in the w. of the storm** après l'orage

3 = wakes

• **wakes NPL** *(in Northern England)* = congé annuel (dans le Nord de l'Angleterre)

▸▸ *Aviat* ***wake effect*** effet *m* de sillage; ***wakes week*** *(in Northern England)* = la semaine de congé annuel (dans le Nord de l'Angleterre)

▸ **wake up VI 1** *(stop sleeping)* se réveiller, s'éveiller; **w. up!** réveille-toi!; **they woke up to find themselves famous** du jour au lendemain, ils se sont retrouvés célèbres **2** *(become alert)* se réveiller, prendre conscience; **w. up and do some work!** réveille-toi *ou* secoue-toi et mets-toi au travail! **3** *(become aware of truth, reality)* ouvrir les yeux; **it's time you woke up to the truth** il est temps que tu regardes la vérité en face; **it took him a while to w. up to what was going on** il lui fallut un certain temps pour réaliser ce qui se passait; **oh, w. up (and smell the roses** *or* **the coffee)!** ouvre les yeux!

VT SEP 1 *(rouse from sleep)* réveiller, tirer *ou* sortir du sommeil; **w. me up at seven** réveillez-moi à sept heures **2** *(make alert)* réveiller, secouer; **a little exercise will w. you up!** un peu d'exercice va vous réveiller!; **the accident woke us up to the dangers of nuclear power** l'accident a attiré notre attention sur les dangers de l'énergie nucléaire **3** *(make aware of truth, reality)* ouvrir les yeux à qn; **that woke her up to what was going on** ça lui a ouvert les yeux sur ce qui se passait

wakeboard ['weɪkbɔːd] **N** *Sport* monoski *m* nautique

wakeboarding ['weɪkbɔːdɪŋ] **N** *Sport* monoski *m* nautique

wakeful ['weɪkfʊl] **ADJ 1** *(person ▸ unable to sleep)* qui ne dort pas, éveillé; *(▸ alert)* vigilant **2** *(night, week)* sans sommeil; **I had** *or* **I spent a w. night** j'ai passé une nuit blanche

wakefulness ['weɪkfʊlnɪs] **N** *(sleeplessness)* insomnie *f*; *(alertness)* vigilance *f*

waken ['weɪkən] *Literary* **VI** se réveiller, s'éveiller; **to w. from sleep** se réveiller, s'éveiller, sortir du sommeil

VT réveiller, tirer *ou* sortir du sommeil

wake-up call N *(in hotel)* réveil *m* téléphonique; *Fig* **the bomb scare was a w. to the government to tighten security** avec cette alerte à la bombe, le gouvernement a compris qu'il devait renforcer les mesures de sécurité

wakey wakey [,weɪkɪ'weɪkɪ] **EXCLAM** *Br Fam* réveille-toi!ᵒ, debout!ᵒ

waking ['weɪkɪŋ] **ADJ** *(hours)* de veille; **she spends all her w. hours reading** elle passe tout son temps à lire; **a w. dream** une rêverie, une rêvasserie

N *(state)* (état *m* de) veille *f*

Waldorf salad [ˈwɔːldɔːf-] N = salade composée de pommes, de céleri et de noix, assaisonnée avec de la mayonnaise

wale [weɪl] N **1** *(on skin)* zébrure *f*, marque *f* de coup **2** *(on cloth)* côte *f* **3** *Naut* plat-bord *m*

Wales [weɪlz] N pays *m* de Galles

WALK [wɔːk]

VI
- marcher **1**
- se promener **1**
- aller à pied **2**
- aller au pas **3**
- être relâché **4**
- disparaître **5**

VT
- faire à pied **1**
- accompagner **2**
- faire marcher **3**
- promener **3**

N
- promenade **2, 4**
- randonnée **2**
- démarche **3**
- allée **4**
- sentier **4**
- trottoir **6**

VI **1** *(gen)* marcher; *(go for a walk)* se promener; **w., don't run!** ne cours pas!; *Am* **w.!/don't w.!** *(traffic sign)* (piétons) passez!/attendez!; **he walked along the beach** il marchait *ou* se promenait le long de la plage; **we walked down/up the street** nous avons descendu/monté la rue à pied; **to w. across the street** traverser la rue; **they walked through the park** ils ont traversé le parc à pied; **he walked slowly towards the door** il s'est dirigé lentement vers la porte; **she walked back and forth** elle faisait les cent pas; **w. with me to the shop** accompagnez-moi au magasin; **he walks in his sleep** il est somnambule; **he walked downstairs in his sleep** il a descendu l'escalier en dormant; **to w. on one's hands** marcher sur les mains; *Fig* **you have to w. before you can run** il faut apprendre petit à petit; **I'm walking on air!** je suis aux anges!; **to w. on water** marcher sur l'eau; **as far as the party faithful are concerned, he can w. on water** aux yeux des fidèles du parti, il est capable de miracles; *Am* **he's walking tall** il marche la tête haute

2 *(as opposed to drive, ride)* aller à pied; **to w. home** rentrer à pied; **I w. to work** je vais au travail à pied; **did you w. all the way?** avez-vous fait tout le chemin à pied?; **is it too far to w.?** est-ce trop loin pour y aller à pied?

3 *(horse, rider)* aller au pas

4 *(go free)* être relâché

5 *Fam (disappear, be stolen ▸ money, object)* disparaître[□]; **the money seems to have walked** l'argent semble s'être envolé

VT **1** *(cover on foot)* faire à pied; **we w. 3 km a day** nous faisons 3 km (de marche) à pied par jour; **you can w. it in ten minutes** il faut dix minutes (pour y aller) à pied; **I can't w. another step** je ne peux pas faire un pas de plus; **she walks this road every day** elle passe à pied par cette rue tous les jours; **to w. the streets** *(wander)* se promener dans les rues; *(looking for something)* arpenter les rues, battre le pavé; *(as prostitute)* faire le trottoir; **to w. a beat** *(policeman)* faire sa ronde

2 *(escort)* accompagner, marcher avec; **I'll w. you to the station** je vais vous accompagner (à pied) à la gare; **may I w. you home?** puis-je vous raccompagner?

3 *(take for walk ▸ person)* faire marcher; *(▸ dog)* promener; *(▸ horse)* conduire à pied; **she walked her mother round the garden** elle a fait faire un tour de jardin à sa mère; **they walked him forcibly to the door** ils l'ont dirigé de force vers la porte; **she walked the bike up the hill** elle a poussé le vélo dans la côte; *Br Fam* **she has walked me off my feet** elle m'a fait tellement marcher que je ne tiens plus debout[□]

4 *Fam (idiom)* **to w. it** *(succeed easily)* gagner les doigts dans le nez

N **1** *(movement)* **she slowed to a w.** elle a ralenti et s'est mise à marcher; **they moved along at a brisk w.** ils marchaient d'un pas rapide

2 *(stroll)* promenade *f*; *(long)* randonnée *f*; **to go for** *or* **to take a w.** aller se promener, faire une promenade *ou* un tour; **we had a nice/long w. through the woods** nous avons fait une belle/grande promenade *ou* balade en forêt; **it's a long w. to the office** ça fait loin pour aller à pied au bureau; **the station is a five-minute w. from here** la gare est à cinq minutes à pied d'ici; **I took my mother for a w.** j'ai emmené ma mère en promenade *ou* faire un tour; **did you take the dog for a w.?** as-tu sorti le chien?; *Fam* **it was a w. in the park** c'était un jeu d'enfant; *Am Fam* **take a w.!** dégage!

3 *(gait)* démarche *f*, façon *f* de marcher; **you'll recognize her from her w.** tu la reconnaîtras à sa démarche *ou* à sa façon de marcher

4 *(path)* promenade *f*; *(in garden)* allée *f*; *(in forest)* sentier *m*, chemin *m*; **a coastal w.** un chemin côtier; *Am* **the front w.** l'allée *f (de devant la maison)*

5 *(occupation)* **I meet people from all walks** *or* **from every w. of life** je rencontre des gens de tous milieux

6 *Am (sidewalk)* trottoir *m*

▸ **walk away** VI partir, s'en aller; **she walked away from the group** elle s'est éloignée du groupe, elle a quitté le groupe; *Fig* **he walked away from the accident** il est sorti de l'accident indemne; *Fig* **to w. away from trouble** éviter les problèmes; **you can't just w. away from the situation** tu ne peux pas te désintéresser comme ça de la situation

▸ **walk away with** VT INSEP **to w. away sth** emporter qch; *Fig (win easily)* remporter *ou* gagner qch haut la main; **I walked away with an antique dressing table for just 30 pounds** j'ai réussi à avoir une coiffeuse ancienne pour seulement 30 livres; **he walked away with a small fine** il s'en est tiré avec une petite amende; **she walked away with all the credit** c'est elle qui a reçu tous les honneurs

▸ **walk back** VI *(return)* revenir *ou* retourner (à pied)

VT SEP raccompagner (à pied)

▸ **walk in** VI entrer; **she walked in and started complaining** elle est entrée et a commencé à se plaindre; **we walked in on her as she was getting dressed** nous sommes entrés sans prévenir alors qu'elle s'habillait

VT SEP faire entrer

▸ **walk into** VT INSEP **1** *(enter ▸ house, room)* entrer dans; *(▸ job)* obtenir (sans problème); *(▸ situation)* se retrouver dans; *(▸ trap)* tomber dans; *Fam* **you walked right into that one!** tu t'es bien fait piéger! **2** *(bump into ▸ chair, wall)* se cogner à, rentrer dans; *(▸ person)* rentrer dans; **he walked right into me/it** il m'est rentré en plein dedans/il est rentré en plein dedans

▸ **walk off** VI partir, s'en aller

VT SEP *(get rid of ▸ headache)* faire passer en marchant; *(▸ weight)* perdre en faisant de la marche; **to w. off one's lunch** faire une promenade pour digérer

▸ **walk off with** VT INSEP **to w. off with sth** *(take)* emporter qch; *(steal)* voler qch; **he walked off with all the prizes** il a remporté tous les prix (haut la main)

▸ **walk out** VI **1** *(go out)* sortir; *(leave)* partir, s'en aller; **we walked out of the meeting** nous sommes partis de la réunion en signe de protestation **2** *(worker)* se mettre en grève **3** *Br Old-fashioned (court)* **to w. out with sb** faire la cour à qn, courtiser qn

▸ **walk over** VT INSEP *(bridge)* traverser; *Sport* **to w. over the course** inspecter le terrain (avant l'épreuve); *Fig* **don't let them w. all over you** ne vous laissez pas marcher sur les pieds

VI aller, faire un saut; **I'll w. over to her place tomorrow** je ferai un saut *ou* je passerai chez elle demain; **the boss walked over to congratulate him** le patron s'est approché de lui pour le féliciter

▸ **walk round** VT INSEP *(museum, shops etc)* faire le tour de

▸ **walk through** VT INSEP *(one's exams etc)* réussir sans effort

VT SEP **to w. sb through sth** expliquer qch à qn étape par étape

walkabout [ˈwɔːkəˌbaʊt] N **1** *Br* **to go on a w.** *(celebrity, politician, member of royal family)* prendre un bain de foule **2** *Austr (of Aborigine)* = excursion périodique dans la brousse; **to go w.** partir dans la brousse **3** *Fam* **to go w.** *(become mislaid)* disparaître[□]

walkaway [ˈwɔːkəˌweɪ] N *Am Fam* victoire *f* facile[□]; **the race was a w. for him** il a gagné la course haut la main

walker [ˈwɔːkə(r)] N **1** *(person ▸ stroller)* promeneur(euse) *m,f*, marcheur(euse) *m,f*; *(▸ in mountains)* randonneur(euse) *m,f*, *Sport* marcheur (euse) *m,f*; **are you a keen w.?** aimez-vous la marche?; **she's a fast/slow w.** elle marche vite/lentement **2** *(apparatus ▸ for babies)* trotte-bébé *m*; *(▸ for invalids)* déambulateur *m*

walkie-talkie [ˌwɔːkɪˈtɔːkɪ] *(pl* **walkie-talkies***)* N (poste *m*) émetteur-récepteur *m* portatif, talkie-walkie *m*

walk-in N *(customer in hotel)* client(e) *m,f* sans réservation; *esp Am (patient)* patient(e) *m,f* sans rendez-vous

ADJ **1** *(safe, wardrobe)* de plain-pied; **the flat is in w. condition** l'appartement est libre d'occupation **2** *Am Fam (victory)* facile[□]

▸▸ ***walk-in closet*** *or* ***cupboard*** *(gen)* débarras *m*; *(for clothes)* dressing *m*; ***walk-in fridge*** armoire *f* réfrigérante

walking [ˈwɔːkɪŋ] N **1** *(activity ▸ gen)* marche *f* (à pied), promenade *f*, promenades *fpl*; *(▸ hiking)* randonnée *f*, *Sport* marche *f* (athlétique); **w. is the best form of exercise** la marche est le meilleur des exercices **2** *(in basketball)* marcher *m*

ADJ *(clothing, shoes)* de marche; **at w. pace** au pas; **is it within w. distance?** est-ce qu'on peut y aller à pied?; **a w. holiday in the Vosges** un séjour randonnée dans les Vosges; **we went on a w. tour of the Alps** nous avons fait de la randonnée dans les Alpes; **the w. wounded** les blessés qui peuvent encore marcher; *Fam* **she's a w. dictionary** c'est un dictionnaire ambulant; **that man's a w. disaster area!** ce type est une catastrophe ambulante!; *Am Fam* **to hand** *or* **to give sb their w. papers** *(employee)* renvoyer qn[□], flanquer qn à la porte; *(lover)* plaquer qn; **to get one's w. papers** *(employee)* se faire mettre à la porte; *(lover)* se faire plaquer

▸▸ ***walking frame*** déambulateur *m*; ***walking race*** épreuve *f* de marche; ***walking shoes*** chaussures *fpl* de marche; ***walking stick*** **1** *(cane)* canne *f* **2** *Am (stick insect)* phasme *m*

walking-out dress N *Mil* tenue *f* de ville

Walkman® [ˈwɔːkmən] *(pl* **Walkmans***)* N Walkman® *m*, *Offic* baladeur *m*

walk-on N rôle *m* de figurant

▸▸ *Cin & TV* ***walk-on actor*** figurant(e) *m,f*; ***walk-on part, walk-on role*** bout *m* de rôle, rôle *m* muet

walkout [ˈwɔːkaʊt] N *(of members, spectators)* départ *m* (en signe de protestation); *(of workers)* grève *f*; **to stage a w.** *(negotiators, students)* partir (en signe de protestation); *(workers)* se mettre en grève

walkover [ˈwɔːkˌəʊvə(r)] N **1** *Br Fam (victory)* victoire *f* facile[□]; **the race was a w. for the German team** l'équipe allemande a gagné la course haut la main **2** *(in horseracing)* walk-over *m inv*

walk-through N **1** *Theat* répétition *f* **2** *Comput* guide *m* détaillé **3** *(explanation)* explication *f* donnée étape par étape

walk-up *Am* ADJ *(apartment)* situé dans un immeuble sans ascenseur; *(building)* sans ascenseur

N *(apartment, office)* = appartement ou bureau situé dans un immeuble sans ascenseur; *(building)* = immeuble sans ascenseur; **they live in a fifth-floor w.** ils habitent un quatrième étage sans ascenseur

walkway [ˈwɔːkweɪ] N *(path)* sentier *m*, chemin *m*; *(passage)* passage *m ou* passerelle *f (pour piétons, entre deux bâtiments)*

wall [wɔːl] N **1** *(of building, room)* mur *m*; *(round field, garden)* mur *m* de clôture; *(round castle, city)* murs *mpl*, murailles *fpl*, remparts *mpl*; **the city walls of Langres** les remparts *ou* murs de Langres; **within the city walls** dans les murs, dans la ville, intra-muros; **the prisoners went over the w.** les prisonniers ont fait le mur; **people like him should be put up against a w. and shot** les gens comme lui méritent la peine de mort; *Fam* **to drive** *or* **to send sb up the w.** rendre qn fou (folle) *ou* dingue; *Fam* **I'll go up the w. if I have to work with her** je vais devenir fou si je dois travailler avec elle; **this is between you, me and these four walls** garde ça pour toi, que ça reste entre nous; *Br* **to go to the w.** *(business)* faire faillite; *(employee)* perdre la partie; **walls have ears** les murs ont des oreilles

2 *(side ▸ of box, cell, artery, cave, tunnel)* paroi *f*; *(▸ of tyre)* flanc *m*

3 *(of mountain)* paroi *f*, face *f*

4 *Fig* **a w. of fire** une muraille de feu; **a w. of silence** un mur de silence

VT *(garden, land)* clôturer, entourer d'un mur; *(city)* fortifier

▸▸ ***wall bars*** espalier *m (pour exercices)*; ***wall bracket*** support *m* mural; ***wall clock*** pendule *f* murale; ***wall covering*** tapisserie *f*, revêtement *m* mural; ***wall cupboard*** placard *m* mural; ***wall hanging*** tenture *f* murale; ***wall lamp, wall light*** applique *f (lampe)*; ***wall lighting*** éclairage *m* par appliques; ***wall painting*** peinture *f* murale; ***wall socket*** prise *f* murale; ***Wall Street*** Wall Street *(quartier de la Bourse de New York)*; **according to W. Street...** selon la Bourse de New York..., selon Wall Street...; ***wall unit*** élément *m* mural

▸ **wall in** VT SEP *(garden)* clôturer, entourer d'un mur; **the park was walled in on all four sides by giant buildings** le parc était bordé sur les quatre côtés par des immeubles gigantesques

▸ **wall off** VT SEP séparer par un mur *ou* par une cloison; **part of the garden was walled off from the rest** une partie du jardin était isolée du reste par un mur

▸ **wall up** VT SEP *(door, window)* murer, condamner; *(body, treasure)* emmurer

wallaby ['wɒləbɪ] *(pl* **wallabies**) N *Zool* wallaby *m*

wallah ['wɒlə] N *Fam Old-fashioned* préposé▫ *m*; **the tea w.** le préposé au thé

wallchart ['wɔːltʃɑːt] N panneau *m* mural

walled [wɔːld] ADJ *(city)* fortifié; *(garden)* clos

wallet ['wɒlɪt] N portefeuille *m*

walleyed ['wɔːlˌaɪd] ADJ *(person, eyes)* qui louche

wallflower ['wɔːlˌflaʊə(r)] N **1** *Bot* giroflée *f* **2** *Fam (person)* **I'm tired of being a w.** j'en ai assez de faire tapisserie

wall-mounted ADJ *(clock, telephone)* mural

Walloon [wɒ'luːn] N **1** *(person)* Wallon(onne) *m,f* **2** *Ling* wallon *m*

ADJ wallon

wallop ['wɒləp] *Fam* VT **1** *(hit ▸ person)* flanquer un coup à, cogner sur; *(▸ ball)* donner un grand coup dans▫; **she walloped him on the jaw** elle lui a flanqué son poing sur la figure; **w. him one!** fiche-lui une beigne! **2** *(defeat)* mettre une raclée à

N **1** *(blow)* beigne *f*; **she gave him a w. across the face** elle lui a flanqué *ou* filé une beigne; **he packs a real w.** il a du punch; **give it a w. with the hammer** mets-y un coup de marteau **2** *(impact)* **she fell down with a w.** et vlan! elle est tombée par terre **3** *Br Fam (beer)* bière▫ *f*

ADV *Br* **to run w. into sth** rentrer en plein dans qch

walloping ['wɒləpɪŋ] *Fam* ADJ énorme▫, phénoménal; **a w. great lie** un énorme mensonge▫

ADV vachement

N **1** *(beating)* raclée *f*; **his mother gave him a good w.** sa mère lui a flanqué une raclée **2** *(defeat)* raclée *f*; **they gave our team a w.** ils ont flanqué une raclée à notre équipe

wallow ['wɒləʊ] VI **1** *(roll about)* se vautrer, se rouler **2** *(indulge)* se vautrer, se complaire; **to w. in a bath** se prélasser dans un bain; **to w. in misery/self-pity** se complaire dans la tristesse/s'apitoyer sur soi-même **3** *Naut* être ballotté

N **1** *(mud)* boue *f*, bourbe *f*; *(place)* mare *f* bourbeuse **2** *Fam (act of wallowing)* **there's nothing like a w. in a warm bath to unwind** rien de tel qu'un bon bain pour se détendre; **to have a w. in the mud** se vautrer dans la boue; **we all enjoy a good w. in nostalgia** tout le monde aime se laisser aller à la nostalgie de temps en temps

wallpaper ['wɔːlˌpeɪpə(r)] N *(gen) & Comput* papier *m* peint

VT tapisser (de papier peint)

▸▸ ***wallpaper paste*** colle *f* badigeon

wallpapering ['wɔːlˌpeɪpərɪŋ] N **w. is easy** poser du papier peint est facile

▸▸ ***wallpapering brush*** *(for applying paste)* pinceau *m* à encoller le papier peint; *(for smoothing paper)* balai *m* de colleur

wall-to-wall ADJ *(widespread, complete)* **w. sound** son enveloppant; **the room was w. with people** la pièce était bondée; *Fig* **the hostage crisis was given w. coverage** la prise d'otages était à la une de tous les médias

▸▸ ***wall-to-wall carpet, wall-to-wall carpeting*** moquette *f*

wally ['wɒlɪ] *(pl* **wallies**) N *Br Fam* imbécile▫ *mf*, andouille *mf*; **I felt a bit of a w.** je me suis senti un peu idiot▫; **he looked a real** *or* **a right w.** il avait vraiment l'air d'un imbécile▫

walnut ['wɔːlnʌt] N *(tree, wood)* noyer *m*; *(nut)* noix *f*

COMP *(furniture)* de *ou* en noyer; *(oil)* de noix; *(cake)* aux noix

walrus ['wɔːlrəs] *(pl* **inv** *or* **walruses**) N *Zool* morse *m*

▸▸ ***walrus moustache*** moustache *f* à la gauloise

Walter Mitty [ˌwɔːltə'mɪtɪ] ADJ **to lead a W. existence** vivre dans un monde imaginaire; **a W. character** un rêveur

waltz [wɔːls] N valse *f*

VI **1** *(dancer)* valser, danser une valse **2** *(move)* danser; **she waltzed in/out of his office** *(jauntily)* elle est entrée dans/sortie de son bureau d'un pas joyeux; *(brazenly)* elle est entrée dans/sortie de son bureau avec effronterie; **he waltzed right up to the boss** il s'est approché du patron sans hésitation; **to w. off** partir, s'en aller; **he waltzed off with her bag** il lui a volé son sac à main; **they waltzed off with first prize** ils ont remporté le premier prix haut la main

VT **1** *(dance)* valser avec, faire valser **2** *(propel)* pousser, propulser

waltzer ['wɔːlsə(r)] N **1** *(dancer)* valseur(euse) *m,f* **2** *(at fairground)* Mont-Blanc *m*

wampum ['wɒmpəm] N *(UNCOUNT)* **1** *(beads)* wampum *m* **2** *Am Fam (money)* pognon *m*

WAN [wæn] N *Comput (abbr* **wide area network**) réseau *m* longue distance

wan [wɒn] *(compar* **wanner**, *superl* **wannest**) ADJ *Literary (person ▸ pale)* pâle, blême, blafard; *(▸ sad)* triste; *(smile)* pâle, faible; *(light, star)* pâle

wand [wɒnd] N *(of fairy, magician)* baguette *f* (magique)

wander ['wɒndə(r)] VI **1** *(meander ▸ person)* errer, flâner; *(▸ stream)* serpenter, faire des méandres; **she wandered into a café** elle est entrée dans un café d'un pas nonchalant; **we wandered round the town** nous avons flâné en ville; **I'll just w. down to the beach later** j'irai faire un tour *ou* je descendrai à la plage plus tard; **her eyes wandered over the crowd** elle a promené son regard sur la foule

2 *(stray ▸ person)* s'égarer; **he's wandered off somewhere** il est parti mais il n'est pas loin; **don't w. too far** ne vous éloignez pas trop; **don't w. off the path** ne vous écartez pas du chemin

3 *(mind, thoughts)* vagabonder, errer; **he wandered off the topic** il s'est écarté du sujet; **her attention began to w.** elle commença à être de moins en moins attentive; **I can't concentrate, my mind keeps wandering** je ne peux pas me concentrer, je suis trop distrait; **my mind wandered back to when we first met** j'ai repensé au moment où nous nous sommes rencontrés

4 *(become confused)* divaguer, déraisonner; **her mother's mind** *or* **her mother has begun to w.** sa mère commence à divaguer

VT errer dans, parcourir (au hasard); **their children w. the streets at night** leurs enfants errent dans les rues *ou* courent les rues le soir; **the nomads w. the desert** les nomades parcourent le désert; **he spent his life wandering the world** il a passé sa vie à parcourir le monde

N promenade *f*, tour *m*; **we went for a w. round the town** nous sommes allés faire un tour dans la ville

wanderer ['wɒndərə(r)] N vagabond(e) *m,f*; *Fig* **she's a bit of a w.** elle n'aime pas trop se fixer; *Hum* **the w. returns** voilà un revenant!

wandering ['wɒndərɪŋ] ADJ **1** *(roaming ▸ person)* errant, vagabond; *(▸ tribe)* nomade; *(▸ stream)* qui serpente, qui fait des méandres **2** *(distracted ▸ mind, thoughts, attention)* distrait, vagabond *(confused ▸ mind, person)* qui divague, qui délire *(▸ thoughts)* incohérent

N **1** *(roaming)* vagabondage *m*, voyages *mpl* **2** *(c… mind)* délire *m*

• **wanderings** NPL *(roaming)* vagabondage *m*, voyages *mpl*; **during his wanderings** pendant ses voyages

▸▸ *Fam* ***wandering hands*** mains *fpl* baladeuses; ***wandering minstrels*** ménestrels *mpl*

wanderlust ['wɒndəlʌst] N envie *f* de voyager

wane [weɪn] VI *(moon)* décroître, décliner; *(interest, power, popularity, influence)* diminuer; *(civilization, empire)* décliner, être en déclin; *(beauty)* se faner

N **to be on the w.** *(moon)* décroître, décliner; *(interest, power, popularity, influence)* diminuer; *(civilization, empire)* décliner, être en déclin; *(beauty)* se faner

wangle ['wæŋgəl] *Fam* N combine *f*, embrouille *f*, truc *m*

VT *(obtain ▸ through cleverness)* se débrouiller pour avoir; *(▸ through devious means)* resquiller, carotter; **can you w. me an invitation?** est-ce que tu peux me dégotter une invitation?; **can you w. it?** est-ce que tu peux arranger ça▫?; **he wangled his way into the job** c'est par combine qu'il a décroché le poste; **I wangled myself a trip to Rome** je me suis débrouillé pour resquiller un voyage à Rome; **they wangled their way out of paying the fine** ils se sont débrouillés pour ne pas payer l'amende

wangler ['wæŋglə(r)] N *Fam* resquilleur(euse) *m*

wangling ['wæŋglɪŋ] N *Fam* resquillage *m*, carottage *m*; **with a bit of w. I managed to get myself a ticket** j'ai eu mon ticket en faisant marcher le système D; **it just needs a bit of w.** il suffit de resquiller un peu

waning ['weɪnɪŋ] N *(of moon)* décroissement *m*; *(of interest, power, popularity, influence)* diminution *f*; *(of civilization, empire)* déclin *m*

ADJ *(moon)* décroissant, à son déclin; *(interest, power, popularity, influence)* qui diminue; *(civilization, empire)* sur son déclin, en déclin

wank [wæŋk] *Br Vulg* VI se branler

N **1** *(masturbation)* branlette *f*; **to have a w.** se faire une branlette **2** *Fig (nonsense)* connerie*s fpl*; **he was talking a load of w.** il disait que des conneries

▸ **wank off** *Br Vulg* VI se branler

VT SEP **to w. oneself off** se branler; **to w. sb off** branler qn

wanker ['wæŋkə(r)] N *Br Vulg* connard *m*

wankered ['wæŋkəd] ADJ *Br Vulg (drunk)* rond comme une queue de pelle, plein comme une barrique

wanky ['wæŋkɪ] *(compar* **wankier**, *superl* **wankiest**) ADJ *Br Vulg* débile, con

wanly ['wɒnlɪ] ADV **1** *(answer, smile)* faiblement, tristement **2** *(shine)* faiblement, avec une pâle *ou* une faible clarté

wanna ['wɒnə] *Fam* **1** = **want to 2** = **want a**

wannabe ['wɒnəˌbiː] N *Fam* = se dit de quelqu'un qui veut être ce qu'il ne peut pas être; **Brad Pitt w.** un clone de Brad Pitt

wanness ['wɒnnɪs] N *(of person ▸ paleness)* pâleur *f*; *(▸ sadness)* tristesse *f*; *(of light)* pâleur, manque *m* de clarté

WANT [wɒnt]

VT
- vouloir **1**
- avoir envie de **1, 2**
- vouloir voir **3**
- avoir besoin de **5**
- désirer **1, 2**
- demander **3**
- (re)chercher **4**

N
- désir **1**
- besoin **2, 4**
- misère **4**
- envie **1**
- manque **3**

VT **1** *(expressing a wish or desire)* vouloir, désirer; **to w. sth badly** avoir très envie de qch; **what do you w.?** qu'est-ce que vous voulez?; **what do you**

/. now? qu'est-ce que tu veux encore?; **what** **ıore do you w.?** que voulez-vous de plus?; **I w. a** **up of coffee** je veux *ou* voudrais une tasse de afé; **all he wants is to go to bed** tout ce qu'il veut, 'est aller se coucher; **to w. to do sth** avoir envie le *ou* vouloir faire qch; **she doesn't w. to go** elle 'a pas envie d'y aller, elle ne veut pas y aller; **she** **oesn't w. to** elle n'en a pas envie; **he doesn't w. to** **now** il ne veut rien savoir; **I w. you to wait here** je eux que tu attendes ici; **I don't w. it known** je ne eux pas que cela se sache; **what do you w.** **one?** que désirez-vous qu'on fasse?; **I don't w.** **ou turning everything upside down** je ne veux as que vous mettiez tout sens dessus dessous; **don't w. any trouble** je ne veux pas d'ennuis; **vhat do you w. with her?** qu'est-ce que tu lui eux?; **what do you w. from her?** que voulez-vous 'elle?; *Ironic* **she doesn't w. much!** elle n'est pas ifficile, elle au moins; *Fig* **now I've got you** **vhere I w. you!** je te tiens!

2 *(desire sexually)* désirer, avoir envie de

3 *(require to be present)* demander, vouloir voir; **ou're wanted** on vous demande; **the boss wants** **ou** le patron vous demande *ou* veut vous voir *u* demande à vous voir; **someone wants you** *or* **ou're wanted on the phone** quelqu'un vous de- ıande au téléphone; **where do you w. this ward-** **obe?** où voulez-vous qu'on mette cette rmoire?; **you won't be wanted this afternoon** on 'aura pas besoin de vous cet après-midi; **go** **way, you're not wanted here** va-t-en, tu n'es pas e bienvenu ici; **I know when I'm not wanted** je ais quand je suis de trop

4 *(hunt, look for)* chercher, rechercher; **to be** **vanted by the police** être recherché par la police

5 *(need ▸ of person)* avoir besoin de; *(▸ of task, hing)* avoir besoin de, nécessiter; **do you have** **verything you w.?** avez-vous tout ce qu'il vous aut?; **I have more than I w.** j'en ai plus qu'il n'en aut; **I've had all I w.** j'en ai eu assez; **that's the** **ery thing I w., that's just what I w.** c'est juste ce ıu'il me faut, cela fera parfaitement mon af- aire; **this room wants a fresh coat of paint** cette ièce a besoin d'une nouvelle couche de pein- ure; **that child wants a good hiding** cet enfant a esoin d'une bonne correction; **your hair wants** **utting** tu as besoin de te faire couper les che- eux, tu devrais te faire couper les cheveux; **here are still a couple of things that w. doing** il y encore quelques petites choses à faire; **what** **o you w. with a car that size?** qu'allez-vous faire l'une voiture de cette taille?

6 *Fam (ought)* **you w. to see a doctor about that** **eg** vous devez montrer *ou* il faut que vous mon- riez cette jambe à un médecin; **she wants to** **vatch out, the boss is looking for her** elle devrait aire attention, le patron la cherche

7 *Literary (lack ▸ food, shelter)* manquer de

VI *Fam* **the cat wants in/out** le chat veut entrer/ ortir; *Fig* **he wants in (on the deal)** il veut une part lu gâteau; **I w. out!** je ne suis plus de la partie!

N 1 *(desire, wish)* désir *m*, envie *f*; **to satisfy sb's** **vants** satisfaire les envies *ou* les désirs de qn

2 *(requirement)* besoin *m*; **I have few wants, my** **vants are few** j'ai besoin de peu; **she attends to** **ll his wants** elle pourvoit à tous ses besoins

3 *(lack)* manque *m*; **a w. of generosity** un nanque de générosité; **there's certainly no w. of** **oodwill** ce ne sont certainement pas les bon- ıes volontés qui manquent; **to be in w. of sth** voir besoin de qch

4 *(poverty)* misère *f*, besoin *m*; **to be in w.** être lans le besoin *ou* dans la misère

▸ **for want of** PREP faute de; **I'll take this novel** **or w. of anything better** faute de mieux, je vais rendre ce roman; **for w. of anything better to** **lo, she went for a walk** n'ayant rien de mieux à aire, elle est allée se promener; **if we failed, it** **vasn't for w. of trying** nous avons échoué mais e n'est pas faute d'avoir essayé

▸▸ *Am* ***want ad*** petite annonce *f*

vanted ['wɒntɪd] ADJ **1** *(in advertisements)* **car-** **enter/cook w.** on recherche (un) charpentier/ un) cuisinier; **accommodation w.** cherche ap- artement **2** *(murderer, thief)* recherché; **w. for** **rmed robbery** *(sign)* recherché pour vol à main rmée

▸▸ ***wanted notice*** avis *m* de recherche

wanting ['wɒntɪŋ] ADJ **1** *(inadequate)* **to be found** **w.** *(person)* ne pas convenir, ne pas faire l'affaire; *(machine)* ne pas convenir, ne pas être au point **2** *(lacking)* manquant; **to be w. in sth** manquer de qch; **there is something w.** le compte n'y est pas **3** *Euph (weak-minded)* simple d'esprit

wanton ['wɒntən] ADJ **1** *(malicious ▸ action, cruelty)* gratuit, injustifié; *(▸ destroyer)* vicieux

2 *Formal (immoral ▸ behaviour, thoughts)* licencieux; *(▸ person)* dévergondé

3 *Arch or Literary (playful ▸ breeze)* capricieux

4 *Arch or Literary (uncontrolled ▸ vegetation)* abondant, exubérant

N *Literary (man)* dévergondé *m*; *(woman)* dévergondée *f*, femme *f* légère

wantonly ['wɒntənlɪ] ADV **1** *(maliciously)* gratuitement, sans justification

2 *Formal (immorally)* licencieusement

3 *Arch or Literary (playfully)* capricieusement

4 *Arch or Literary (grow ▸ vegetation)* surabondamment, profusément

wantonness ['wɒntənnɪs] N **1** *(of action, cruelty)* gratuité *f* **2** *Formal (immorality)* libertinage *m*

WAP [wæp] N *Comput & Tel (abbr* **wireless application protocol)** WAP *m*

▸▸ ***WAP phone*** téléphone *f* WAP

wapiti ['wɒpɪtɪ] N *Zool* wapiti *m*

War. = **Warks**

war [wɔː(r)] *(pt & pp* **warred**, *cont* **warring)** N **1** *(armed conflict)* guerre *f*; **to be at w./to go to w.** **with sb** être en guerre/entrer en guerre avec qn; **Israel went to w. with Syria over border disagreements** Israël est entré en guerre avec *ou* contre la Syrie pour des problèmes territoriaux; **the Allies waged w. against** *or* **on the Axis** les Alliés ont fait la guerre aux puissances de l'Axe; **he fought in the w.** il a fait la guerre; **the troops went off to w.** les troupes sont parties pour la guerre; *Fam Hum* **you've been through the wars!** on dirait que tu reviens de la guerre!, tu t'es bien arrangé!; *Fam Hum* **that carpet (looks like it) has been through the wars!** cette moquette est dans un état lamentable!; **to have a good w.** *(soldier)* être vaillant au combat; **the w. to end all wars** la der des der; *Literary* **to let loose the dogs of w.** déchaîner les fureurs de la guerre; **w. of attrition/nerves** guerre *f* d'usure/des nerfs; **the American W. of Independence** la guerre d'Indépendance américaine; **the W. between the States, the W. of Secession** la guerre de Sécession; **the Wars of the Roses** la guerre des Deux-Roses **2** *(conflict, struggle)* guerre *f*, lutte *f*; **to declare** *or* **to wage w. on sth** partir en guerre contre *ou* déclarer la guerre à qch; **a w. of words** une guerre des mots; **the w. against crime/drugs** la lutte contre le crime/la drogue

COMP *(diary, hero, pension)* de guerre; **during the w. years** pendant la guerre

VI faire la guerre; **to w. with sb** faire la guerre à qn

▸▸ ***war baby*** = enfant né pendant la guerre; ***war bond*** titre *m* d'emprunt de guerre *(émis pendant la Seconde Guerre mondiale)*; ***war bride*** mariée *f* de la guerre; ***war cabinet*** cabinet *m* de guerre; ***war cemetery*** cimetière *m* militaire; *also Fig* ***war chest*** trésor *m* de guerre; ***war clouds*** nuages *mpl ou* signes *mpl* précurseurs de guerre; **the w. clouds are gathering** la guerre menace; ***war correspondent*** correspondant(e) *m,f* de guerre; ***war crime*** crime *m* de guerre; ***war criminal*** criminel(elle) *m,f* de guerre; *also Fig* ***war cry*** cri *m* de guerre; ***war dance*** danse *f* de guerre *ou* guerrière; ***the war effort*** l'effort *m* de guerre; ***war film*** film *m* de guerre; ***war game*** *Mil (simulated battle with maps)* kriegspiel *m*, wargame *m*; *(manoeuvres)* manœuvres *fpl* militaires; *(game)* wargame *m*; ***war grave*** = tombeau d'un soldat tombé au champ d'honneur; ***war machine*** machine *f* de guerre; ***war memorial*** monument *m* aux morts; ***war movie*** film *m* de guerre; ***war museum*** musée *m* de la guerre; ***the War Office*** = ancien nom du ministère de la Défense britannique; ***war record*** passé *m* militaire; **he has a good w. record** il s'est conduit honorablement pendant la guerre; **what's his w. record?** qu'est-ce qu'il a fait pendant la guerre?; ***war victims*** victimes *fpl* de guerre; ***war widow*** veuve *f* de guerre; ***war wound*** blessure *f* de guerre; ***war zone*** zone *f* de guerre

warble[1] ['wɔːbəl] VI *(bird)* gazouiller; *(person)* chanter (avec des trilles)

VT *(of bird)* gazouiller; *(of person)* chanter (avec des trilles)

N gazouillis *m*, gazouillement *m*

warble[2] N *Vet* **1** *(on horse)* cors *m* **2** *(of cattle)* varron *m*

warbler ['wɔːblə(r)] N *Orn* fauvette *f*, pouillot *m*

warbling ['wɔːblɪŋ] N gazouillis *m*, gazouillement *m*

ADJ *(bird)* gazouillant; *(sound)* mélodieux

> **SUFFIXE**
>
> **-WARD, -WARDS**
>
> Ces suffixes servent à indiquer l'idée de DIRECTION :
>
> • Le suffixe **-ward** sert à former des adjectifs :
>
> **the homeward trip** le (voyage de) retour; **an upward movement** un mouvement ascendant; **in a downward direction** vers le bas; **they sailed a southward course** ils naviguaient vers le sud.
>
> • Les suffixes **-wards** (surtout employé en anglais britannique) and **-ward** (surtout employé en anglais américain) servent à former des adverbes :
>
> **eastward(s)** vers l'est, en direction de l'est; **he fell backwards** il est tombé en arrière; **the plane plunged earthwards** l'avion piqua vers le sol; **prices are moving upward** les prix sont à la hausse.

ward [wɔːd] N **1** *(of hospital ▸ room)* salle *f*; *(▸ section)* pavillon *m*; *(of prison)* quartier *m* **2** *Pol (district)* circonscription *f* électorale **3** *Law (person)* pupille *mf*; *(guardianship)* tutelle *f*; **to be in w.** être sous tutelle judiciaire

▸▸ *Law* ***ward of court*** pupille *mf* sous tutelle judiciaire; *Am Pol* ***ward heeler*** agent *m* électoral *(qui sollicite des voix)*

▸ **ward off** VT SEP *(danger, disease)* éviter; *(blow)* parer, éviter

warden ['wɔːdn] N **1** *(director ▸ of building, institution)* directeur(trice) *m,f*; *Am (▸ of prison)* directeur(trice) *m,f* **2** *(public official ▸ of fortress, town)* gouverneur *m*; *(▸ of park, reserve)* gardien(enne) *m,f*; *Br* **W. of the Cinque Ports** gouverneur des Cinq Ports **3** *Br Univ* portier *m*

warder ['wɔːdə(r)] N *Br (prison guard)* gardien (enne) *m,f*, surveillant(e) *m,f*

wardress ['wɔːdrɪs] N *Br (prison guard)* gardienne *f*, surveillante *f*

wardrobe ['wɔːdrəʊb] N **1** *(cupboard)* armoire *f*, penderie *f* **2** *(clothing)* garde-robe *f*; *Theat* costumes *mpl*; *Cin & Theat* **Nicole Kidman's w. by…** Nicole Kidman est habillée par…, les costumes de Nicole Kidman sont de chez…; **to have a large w.** avoir une garde-robe importante; *Theat* **to work in w.** être costumier/costumière, s'occuper des costumes

▸▸ ***wardrobe department*** service *m* costumes; *Fam Hum* ***wardrobe malfunction*** incident *m* vestimentaire, = incident au cours duquel une personne révèle accidentellement une partie de son anatomie; ***wardrobe mistress*** costumière *f*; ***wardrobe supervisor*** chef costumier *m*; ***wardrobe trunk*** malle *f (penderie)*

wardroom ['wɔːdrʊm] N *Naut (quarters)* quartiers *mpl* des officiers *(excepté le capitaine)*; *(officers)* officiers *mpl (excepté le capitaine)*

wardship ['wɔːdʃɪp] N tutelle *f*

warehouse N ['weəhaʊs, *pl* -haʊzɪz] entrepôt *m*, dépôt *m* de marchandises; *(for furniture)* garde-meuble *m*

VT ['weəhaʊz] entreposer, mettre en entrepôt

▸▸ *Com* ***warehouse charges*** frais *mpl* d'entreposage; *Com* ***warehouse club*** club *m* de gros; ***warehouse manager*** responsable *mf* d'entrepôt; ***warehouse party*** = soirée house dans un local désaffecté; *Com* ***warehouse sale*** vente *f* au déballage; *Com* ***warehouse warrant*** certificat *m* d'entreposage

warehouseman ['weəhaʊsmən] *(pl* **warehousemen** [-mən]**)** N magasinier *m*

warehousing ['weəˌhaʊzɪŋ] **N**(*UNCOUNT*) **1** (*of goods*) entreposage *m* **2** (*of shares*) parcage *m*
►► ***warehousing company*** société *f* d'entrepôts; ***warehousing costs*** frais *mpl* d'entreposage

wares [weəz] **NPL** marchandises *fpl*

warfare ['wɔːfeə(r)] **N** (*UNCOUNT*) *Mil* guerre *f*; *Fig* lutte *f*, guerre *f*; **class w.** lutte *f* des classes; **economic w.** guerre *f* économique; *Mil & Fig* **open w.** guerre *f* ouverte

warhead ['wɔːhed] **N** ogive *f*

warhorse ['wɔːhɔːs, *pl* -hɔːsɪz] **N 1** *Hist* (*horse*) cheval *m* de bataille **2** *Fam Fig* (*person*) dur(e) *m,f* à cuire; **he's an old w. of the party** c'est un vétéran du parti **3** *Mktg* cheval *m* de bataille

warily ['weərɪlɪ] **ADV** (*carefully*) prudemment, avec prudence *ou* circonspection; (*distrustfully*) avec méfiance

wariness ['weərɪnɪs] **N**(*caution*) prudence *f*, circonspection *f*; (*distrust*) méfiance *f*

Warks (*written abbr* **Warwickshire**) Warwickshire *m*

warlike ['wɔːlaɪk] **ADJ** guerrier, belliqueux

warlock ['wɔːlɒk] **N** sorcier *m*

warlord ['wɔːlɔːd] **N** seigneur *m* de la guerre

warm [wɔːm] **ADJ 1** (*moderately hot*) chaud; **to be w.** (*water*) être chaud; (*person*) avoir chaud; *Met* **a w. front** un front chaud; **a w. oven** un four moyen; **I can't wait for the w. weather** j'ai hâte qu'il fasse chaud; **it's getting warmer** (*weather*) il commence à faire plus chaud; **this soup is barely w.** cette soupe est à peine chaude *ou* est tiède; **will you keep dinner w. for me?** peux-tu me garder le dîner au chaud?; **does that coat keep you w.?** est-ce que ce manteau te tient chaud?; **it's a difficult house to keep w.** c'est une maison difficile à chauffer; **are you w. enough?** avez-vous assez chaud?; **I can't seem to get w.** je n'arrive pas à me réchauffer; **the room is too w.** il fait trop chaud *ou* on étouffe dans cette pièce; **the bedroom was nice and w.** il faisait bon dans la chambre; **am I right? – you're getting warmer!** est-ce que j'y suis? – tu chauffes!
2 (*clothing*) chaud, qui tient chaud
3 (*work*) qui donne chaud
4 (*affectionate* ► *feelings*) chaud, chaleureux; (► *personality*) chaleureux; **he's a very w. person, he has a w. heart** il est très chaleureux; **she has a w. relationship with her mother** elle a une relation très affectueuse avec sa mère; **give my warmest wishes to your wife** toutes mes amitiés à votre femme
5 (*hearty* ► *greeting, welcome*) chaleureux, cordial; (► *thanks*) vif; (► *admirer, support*) ardent, enthousiaste; (► *applause*) chaleureux, enthousiaste; (► *smile*) accueillant
6 (*colour, sound*) chaud; (*voice*) chaud, chaleureux
7 (*scent, trail*) récent
VT 1 (*heat* ► *person, room*) réchauffer; (► *food*) (faire) chauffer; **she warmed her hands by the fire** elle s'est réchauffé les mains près du feu; **come and w. yourself at the fire** viens te réchauffer près du feu; **the sight was enough to w. the cockles of your heart!** c'était un spectacle à vous réchauffer le cœur!
2 (*reheat*) (faire) réchauffer
VI 1 (*food*) chauffer
2 *Fig* **to w. to** *or* **towards** (*person*) se prendre de sympathie pour; (*idea, topic*) s'enthousiasmer pour; **you'll soon w. to the idea** tu verras, cette idée finira par te plaire; **"then...," he continued, warming to his theme** "puis...", poursuivit-il, entraîné par son sujet
N *Fam* **come into the w.** viens au chaud *ou* où il fait chaud□; **to give sth a w.** réchauffer qch□; **give your hands a w. at the fire** réchauffe-toi les mains devant le feu
►► *Comput* ***warm boot, warm start*** redémarrage *m* à chaud

► **warm over VT SEP** *Am* **1** (*food*) (faire) réchauffer **2** *Pej* (*idea*) ressasser

► **warm up VT SEP 1** (*heat* ► *person, room*) réchauffer; (► *food*) (faire) chauffer; (► *engine, machine*) faire chauffer **2** (*reheat*) (faire) réchauffer **3** (*animate* ► *audience*) mettre en train, chauffer
VI 1 (*become hotter* ► *person*) se chauffer, se réchauffer; (► *room, engine, food*) se réchauffer; (► *weather*) devenir plus chaud, se réchauffer **2** (*get ready* ► *athlete, comedian*) s'échauffer, se mettre en train; (► *audience*) commencer à s'animer **3** (*debate, discussion, party*) s'animer

warm-blooded [-'blʌdɪd] **ADJ** *Zool* à sang chaud; *Fig* (*ardent*) ardent, qui a le sang chaud

warm-hearted [-'hɑːtɪd] **ADJ** (*kindly*) chaleureux, bon; (*generous*) généreux

warm-heartedly [-'hɑːtɪdlɪ] **ADV** (*kindly*) chaleureusement, avec chaleur; (*generously*) généreusement

warming ['wɔːmɪŋ] **ADJ** (*drink*) qui réchauffe; (*thought*) réconfortant
N réchauffage *m*
►► ***warming pan*** bassinoire *f*; *Sport* ***warming up*** échauffement *m*; **w.-up exercises** exercices *mpl* d'échauffement

warmly ['wɔːmlɪ] **ADV 1** (*dress*) chaudement; **the sun shone w.** le soleil chauffait **2** (*greet, smile, welcome*) chaleureusement, chaudement; (*recommend, thank*) vivement, chaudement; (*support*) avec enthousiasme, ardemment; (*applaud*) avec enthousiasme, chaleureusement; **his suggestion was not w. received** sa proposition n'a pas été chaudement accueillie; **the film was w. received by the critics** le film a été accueilli par la critique avec enthousiasme

warmonger ['wɔːˌmʌŋgə(r)] **N** belliciste *mf*

warmongering ['wɔːˌmʌŋgərɪŋ] **N** (*UNCOUNT*) (*activities*) activités *fpl* bellicistes; (*attitude*) bellicisme *m*; (*propaganda*) propagande *f* belliciste
ADJ belliciste

warmth [wɔːmθ] **N 1** (*of temperature*) chaleur *f*; **we huddled together for w.** nous nous sommes blottis les uns contre les autres pour nous tenir chaud
2 (*of greeting, welcome*) chaleur *f*, cordialité *f*; (*of recommendation, thanks*) chaleur *f*, vivacité *f*; (*of applause, support*) enthousiasme *m*
3 (*of colour*) chaleur *f*
4 (*anger*) emportement *m*, vivacité *f*; **...she said with some w.** ...dit-elle d'un ton vif

warm-up **N** (*gen*) préparation *f*, préparations *fpl*; (*of athlete, singer*) échauffement *m*; (*of audience*) mise *f* en train; **they get a ten-minute w.** ils ont dix minutes d'échauffement
►► ***warm-up exercises*** exercices *mpl* d'échauffement; ***warm-up man*** chauffeur *m* de salle; ***warm-up match*** match *m* préparatoire *ou* d'entraînement; *esp Am* ***warm-up suit*** survêtement *m*

warn [wɔːn] **VT 1** (*inform*) avertir, prévenir; **I warned them of the danger** je les ai avertis *ou* prévenus du danger; **w. them that the bridge is unsafe** prévenez-les *ou* avertissez-les que le pont n'est pas sûr; **she warned them that she would be late** elle les a prévenus qu'elle serait en retard; **you've been warned!** te voilà averti *ou* prévenu!; **w. the police!** alertez la police!; **don't say I didn't w. you!** je t'aurai prévenu!; **I'm warning you for the last time** je te préviens pour la dernière fois **2** (*advise*) conseiller, recommander; **he warned her about** *or* **against travelling at night** il lui a déconseillé de voyager la nuit; **he warned me not to do it** il m'a déconseillé de le faire

► **warn off VT SEP 1** (*tell to leave*) **to w. sb off** demander à qn de quitter les lieux; **he warned them off his land** il leur demanda instamment de quitter ses terres; **the signs are meant to w. people off** les panneaux sont là pour interdire aux gens d'entrer **2** (*advise against*) **to w. sb off sth** déconseiller qch à qn; **to w. sb off doing sth** déconseiller à qn de faire qch

warning ['wɔːnɪŋ] **N 1** (*caution*) avertissement *m*; **let that be a w. to you** que cela vous serve d'avertissement; **thanks for the w.** merci de m'avoir prévenu *ou* m'avoir averti; **this is your last w.** (*to child*) c'est la dernière fois que je te le dis; (*to worker*) c'est votre dernier avertissement; **there was a note of w. in her voice** il y avait comme un avertissement dans sa voix; **the police gave him a w. (about speeding)** la police lui a donné un avertissement (pour excès de vitesse); **to issue a w. against sth** émettre une mise en garde à propos de qch
2 (*advance notice*) avis *m*, préavis *m*; **we only received a few days' w.** nous n'avons été prévenus que quelques jours à l'avance; **the boss visite[d] the office without (any) w.** le patron est venu vi[siter] le bureau inopinément *ou* à l'improviste; **he left without any w.** il est parti sans préveni[r]; **they gave us advance w. of the meeting** ils nou[s] ont prévenus de la réunion
3 (*alarm, signal*) alerte *f*, alarme *f*
4 (*advice*) conseil *m*; **he gave them a stern w[arning] about the dangers of smoking** il les a sévèremen[t] mis en garde contre les dangers du tabac
ADJ d'avertissement; **they fired a w. shot** (*gen*) [...] *Mil* ils ont tiré une fois en guise d'avertissement; *Naut* ils ont tiré un coup de semonce
►► ***warning beep*** signal *m* sonore; ***warning be[ll]*** sonnette *f ou* sonnerie *f* d'alarme; ***warning buzz[er]*** avertisseur *m* sonore; ***warning device*** avertis[]seur *m*; ***warning light*** voyant *m* (avertisseur), avertisseur *m* lumineux; *Comput* ***warning mes[sage]*** message *m* d'avertissement; ***warning notic[e]*** avis *m*, avertissement *m*; ***warning sign*** pannea[u] *m* avertisseur; *Fig* **he's going to go crazy, I've see[n] all the w. signs** il va perdre la tête, ça se voit; **dia[]betes is often a w. sign of heart disease** le diabèt[e] est souvent un signe avant-coureur des mala[]dies cardio-vasculaires; ***warning signal*** (*gen*) si[]gnal *m* d'alarme *ou* d'alerte; *Aut* signal *m* d[e] détresse; *Ind* ***warning strike*** grève *f* d'avertisse[]ment; ***warning system*** système *m ou* disposit[if] *m* d'alarme; *Br Aut* ***warning triangle*** triangle *m* d[e] signalisation

warp [wɔːp] **VT 1** (*wood*) gauchir, voiler; (*meta[l], plastic*) voiler **2** *Fig* (*person, character, mind*) pe[r]vertir; (*thinking*) fausser, pervertir
VI (*wood*) gauchir, se voiler; (*metal, plastic*) s[e] voiler
N 1 (*fault* ► *in wood*) gauchissement *m*, voilure (► *in metal, plastic*) voilure *f* **2** *Tex* (*of yarn*) chaîn[e] *f*; (*for tapestry*) lisse *f*, lice *f*

warpath ['wɔːpɑːθ] **N to be on the w.** être sur l[e] sentier de la guerre; *Fig* **be careful, the boss is o[n] the w.** fais attention, le patron est d'une humeu[r] massacrante

warped [wɔːpt] **ADJ 1** (*wood*) gauchi, voil[é]; (*metal, plastic*) voilé **2** *Fig* (*person, characte[r], mind*) perverti; (*thinking, view*) faux (fausse[]), perverti; **you've got a w. mind!, your mind is w[arped]** tu as l'esprit tordu!; **what a w. sense of humou[r]** quel humour tordu!; **you must be a bit w. if yo[u] think that's funny!** tu dois être un peu tordu pou[r] trouver ça drôle!

warplane ['wɔːpleɪn] **N** avion *m* de guerre

warrant ['wɒrənt] **N 1** *Law* (*written order*) manda[t] *m*; **there's a w. (out) for his arrest** il y a un manda[t] d'arrêt contre lui **2** *Com & Fin* (*for payment*) bo[n] *m*; (*guarantee*) garantie *f*; (*for shares*) bon *m* d[e] souscription d'actions; (*for goods*) certificat [] d'entrepôt **3** *Mil* brevet *m*
VT 1 (*justify*) justifier; **costs are too high to w[arrant] further investment** les frais sont trop élevés pou[r] permettre *ou* justifier d'autres investissement[s] **2** *Old-fashioned* (*declare with certainty*) assure[r], certifier; **I'll w. (you) that's the last we see of h[im]** c'est la dernière fois qu'on la voit, je vous le g[a]rantie **3** *Com* (*goods*) warranter
►► ***warrant officer*** adjudant *m* (*auxiliaire d'un o[f]ficier*)

warrantable ['wɒrəntəbəl] **ADJ** (*justifiable*) ju[s]tifiable

warrantee [ˌwɒrən'tiː] **N** *Law* titulaire *mf* d'un[e] garantie

warrantor, warranter ['wɒrəntɔː(r)] **N** *Law* g[a]rant(e) *m,f*, débiteur(trice) *m,f*

warranty ['wɒrəntɪ] (*pl* **warranties**) **N 1** (*guaran[tee]*) garantie *f*; **a one-year w.** une garantie d'u[n] an; **this computer has a five-year w.** cet ordinate[ur] est garanti cinq ans; **under w.** sous garantie [] *Law* garantie *f*
►► ***warranty certificate*** certificat *m* de garantie

warren ['wɒrən] **N 1** (*of rabbit*) terriers *mpl*, g[a]renne *f* **2** *Fig* (*maze of passageways*) labyrinth[e] *m*, dédale *m*

warring ['wɔːrɪŋ] **ADJ** (*nations, tribes*) en guerr[e]; *Fig* (*beliefs*) en conflit; (*interests*) contradictoir[e], contraire; **w. factions within the Labour Party** d[es] factions adverses au sein du Labour Party

warrior ['wɒrɪə(r)] **N** guerrier(ère) *m,f*

Warsaw ['wɔːsɔː] N Varsovie
▸▸ *Hist* **the Warsaw Pact** le pacte de Varsovie; ***Warsaw Pact countries*** pays *mpl* (membres) du pacte de Varsovie

war-scarred ADJ *(city, country)* dévasté par la guerre

warship ['wɔːʃɪp] N navire *m ou* bâtiment *m* de guerre

wart [wɔːt] N **1** *Med* verrue *f*; *Fig* **a biography of Charles de Gaulle, warts and all** une biographie de Charles de Gaulle écrite sans complaisance *ou* qui ne fait pas de cadeaux; *Fig* **she'll have to accept him as he is, warts and all** il faudra qu'elle l'accepte comme il est, avec tous ses défauts **2** *Bot* excroissance *f*

warthog ['wɔːthɒg] N *Zool* phacochère *m*

wartime ['wɔːtaɪm] N période *f* de guerre; **in w.** en temps de guerre
COMP de guerre; **w. London** le Londres des années de guerre

warty ['wɔːtɪ] *(compar* **wartier**, *superl* **wartiest)** ADJ couvert de verrues, *Spec* verruqueux

wary ['weərɪ] *(compar* **warier**, *superl* **wariest)** ADJ *(prudent ▸ person)* prudent, sur ses gardes; *(▸ look)* prudent; *(▸ smile)* hésitant; *(distrustful)* méfiant; **I'm w. about promoting these ideas** j'hésite à promouvoir ces idées; **the people were w. of the new regime** les gens se méfiaient du nouveau régime; **he kept a w. eye on the dog** il surveillait le chien attentivement

> Attention: ne pas confondre avec **weary**.

was [wɒz, *unstressed* wəz] *pt of* **be**

Wash *(written abbr* **Washington)** Washington *f*

WASH [wɒʃ]

VT
- laver **1, 4**
- emporter **2**
- baigner **2**
- badigeonner **3**

VI
- se laver **1, 2**
- être lavable **2**
- faire sa toilette **1**
- laver **3**

N
- nettoyage **1**
- linge sale **2**
- badigeon **4**
- lessive **2**
- remous **3**
- lotion **5**

VT **1** *(clean)* laver; **to w. oneself** *(person)* se laver, faire sa toilette; *(cat, dog)* faire sa toilette; **go and w. your hands** va te laver les mains; **she washed her hair** elle s'est lavé la tête *ou* les cheveux; **he washed the walls clean** il a bien lavé *ou* nettoyé les murs; **to w. the dishes** faire *ou* laver la vaisselle; **to w. clothes** faire la lessive; **w. in cold/hot water** *(on clothing label)* laver à l'eau froide/chaude; **I w. my hands of the whole affair** je me lave les mains de toute cette histoire; **she washed her hands of him** elle s'est désintéressée de lui
2 *(of current, river, waves ▸ move over)* baigner; *(▸ carry away)* emporter, entraîner; **the waves washed the shore** les vagues baignaient la côte; **the body was washed ashore** le cadavre s'est échoué *ou* a été rejeté sur la côte; **the crew was washed overboard** l'équipage a été emporté par une vague; **he was washed out to sea** il a été emporté par la mer
3 *(coat, cover)* badigeonner
4 *Mining (gold, ore)* laver
VI **1** *(clean oneself ▸ person)* se laver, faire sa toilette; **have you washed properly?** est-ce que tu as bien fait ta toilette?
2 *(be washable)* se laver, être lavable; **this dress doesn't w. very well** cette robe ne supporte pas bien le lavage; *Br Fam* **his story just doesn't w. with me** son histoire ne marche pas avec moi, il ne me fera pas avaler cette histoire
3 *(do dishes)* **you w. and I'll dry** tu laves et j'essuie
4 *(waves, sea)* **the waves washed against the cliff** les vagues baignaient la falaise
N **1** *(act of cleaning)* nettoyage *m*; **this floor needs a good w.** ce plancher a bien besoin d'être lavé *ou* nettoyé; **your hair needs a w.** il faut que tu te laves la tête; **I gave the car a w.** j'ai lavé la voiture; **he's having a w.** il se lave, il fait sa toilette; **I could do with a quick w. and brush-up** j'aimerais faire un brin de toilette
2 *(clothes to be washed)* lessive *f*, linge *m* sale; **your shirt is in the w.** *(laundry basket)* ta chemise est au (linge) sale; *(machine)* ta chemise est à la lessive; **the stain came out in the w.** la tache est partie au lavage; *Br* **it'll all come out in the w.** *(become known)* ça finira par se savoir; *(turn out for the best)* tout cela finira par s'arranger
3 *(movement of water ▸ caused by current)* remous *m*; *(▸ caused by ship)* sillage *m*, remous *m*; *(sound of water)* clapotis *m*
4 *(of paint)* badigeon *m*
5 *Med (lotion)* solution *f*, lotion *f*
6 *Art (of watercolour)* lavis *m*
ADJ *Am* lavable
▸▸ *Art* ***wash drawing*** dessin *m* au lavis; *Am St Exch* ***wash sale*** vente *f* fictive

▸ **wash away** VT SEP *(carry off ▸ boat, bridge, house)* emporter; *(▸ river bank, soil)* éroder; **the rain washed away the road** la route s'est effondrée sous l'action de la pluie; *Fig* **to w. one's sins away** laver ses péchés

▸ **wash down** VT SEP **1** *(clean)* laver (à grande eau) **2** *(food)* arroser; *(tablet)* faire descendre; **roast beef washed down with Burgundy wine** rosbif arrosé d'un bourgogne

▸ **wash off** VT SEP *(remove ▸ with soap)* enlever *ou* faire partir au lavage; *(▸ with water)* enlever *ou* faire partir à l'eau
VI *(disappear ▸ with soap)* s'en aller *ou* partir au lavage; *(▸ with water)* s'en aller *ou* partir à l'eau; **the paint won't w. off** la peinture ne s'en va pas *ou* ne part pas

▸ **wash out** VT SEP **1** *(remove ▸ with soap)* enlever *ou* faire partir au lavage; *(▸ with water)* enlever *ou* faire partir à l'eau
2 *(clean)* laver
3 *(carry away ▸ bridge)* emporter; *(▸ road)* dégrader
4 *(cancel, prevent)* **the game was washed out** le match a été annulé à cause de la pluie
VI = **wash off**

▸ **wash over** VT INSEP *(of waves)* balayer; *Fig (have no effect on)* ne faire aucun effet à; **anything I say just washes over her** rien de ce que je lui dis ne lui fait le moindre effet

▸ **wash up** VI **1** *Br (wash dishes)* faire *ou* laver la vaisselle **2** *Am (wash oneself)* se laver, faire sa toilette
VT SEP **1** *Br (glass, dish)* laver; **whose turn is it to w. up the dishes?** c'est à qui de faire la vaisselle? **2** *(of sea)* rejeter; **several dolphins were washed up on shore** plusieurs dauphins se sont échoués sur la côte

washable ['wɒʃəbəl] ADJ lavable, lessivable

wash-and-wear ADJ qui ne nécessite aucun repassage

washbasin ['wɒʃ,beɪsən] N *(basin)* cuvette *f*, bassine *f*; *(sink)* lavabo *m*

washboard ['wɒʃbɔːd] N planche *f* à laver
▸▸ *Fam* ***washboard stomach*** ventre *m* plat[❑]

washbowl ['wɒʃbəʊl] N *Am (basin)* cuvette *f*, bassine *f*; *(sink)* lavabo *m*

washcloth ['wɒʃklɒθ] N *(for dishes)* lavette *f*; *Am (face flannel)* ≃ gant *m* de toilette

washday ['wɒʃdeɪ] N jour *m* de lessive

washed-out ['wɒʃt-] ADJ **1** *(faded ▸ colour)* délavé; *(▸ curtain, jeans)* décoloré, délavé **2** *Fam (exhausted)* épuisé[❑], lessivé; *(pale)* pâle de fatigue[❑]

washed-up ['wɒʃt-] ADJ *Fam* fichu; **he's w. as a singer** sa carrière de chanteur est fichue *ou* est finie[❑]

washer ['wɒʃə(r)] N **1** *Constr* joint *m*, rondelle *f*; *(in tap)* joint *m* **2** *(washing machine)* machine *f* à laver, lave-linge *m inv*

washer-dryer, washer-drier N machine *f* à laver séchante

washer-up *(pl* **washers-up)**, **washer-upper** *(pl* **washer-uppers)** N *Br Fam (gen)* laveur(euse) *m,f* de vaisselle[❑]; *(in restaurant)* plongeur (euse)[❑] *m,f*

washerwoman ['wɒʃə,wʊmən] *(pl* **washerwomen** [-wɪmɪn]) N blanchisseuse *f*

wash-hand basin *Br* = **washbasin**

washing ['wɒʃɪŋ] N **1** *(UNCOUNT) (act ▸ of car, floors)* lavage *m*; *(▸ of laundry)* lessive *f*; *Rel (of feet, hands)* lavement *m* **2** *(laundry)* linge *m*, lessive *f*; **a pile of dirty w.** une pile de linge sale; **to do the w.** faire la lessive, laver le linge; **where can I hang the w.?** où puis-je étendre le linge?
▸▸ ***washing day*** jour *m* de lessive; ***washing line*** corde *f* à linge; ***washing liquid*** lessive *f* liquide; ***washing machine*** machine *f* à laver, lave-linge *m inv*; ***washing powder*** lessive *f ou* détergent *m (en poudre)*; ***washing soda*** cristaux *mpl* de soude

Washington ['wɒʃɪŋtən] N *Geog* **1** *(state)* **W. (State)** l'État *m* de Washington **2** *(town)* **W. (DC)** Washington *f*

washing-up N *Br* vaisselle *f (à laver)*; **to do the w.** faire la vaisselle
▸▸ ***washing-up bowl*** cuvette *f*, bassine *f*; ***washing-up liquid*** liquide *m* vaisselle

wash-leather N *Br* peau *f* de chamois

washout ['wɒʃaʊt] N *Fam (party, plan)* fiasco *m*; *(person)* raté(e) *m,f*; **the whole thing's a w.** c'est une perte sèche

washrag ['wɒʃræg] N *Am* lavette *f*

washroom ['wɒʃrʊm] N **1** *(for laundry)* buanderie *f* **2** *Am Euph (lavatory)* toilettes *fpl*

washstand ['wɒʃstænd] N table *f* de toilette

washtub ['wɒʃtʌb] N *(for laundry)* bassine *f*, cuvette *f*

wash-wipe N *Aut* lavage-balayage *m*

wasn't [wɒzənt] = **was not**

Wasp, WASP [wɒsp] N *Am (abbr* **White Anglo-Saxon Protestant)** = Blanc d'origine anglo-saxonne et protestante, appartenant aux classes aisées et influentes

wasp [wɒsp] N guêpe *f*; **a w.'s nest** un guêpier; *Fig* **to have a w. waist** avoir une taille de guêpe

waspish ['wɒspɪʃ] ADJ *(person ▸ by nature)* méchant; *(▸ in bad mood)* qui est de mauvaise humeur; *(reply, remark)* acerbe, mordant, méchant

waspishly ['wɒspɪʃlɪ] ADV *(say)* d'un ton acerbe *ou* mordant, méchamment

wassail ['wɒseɪl] *Arch & Literary* N **1** *(drink ▸ beer)* bière *f* épicée; *(▸ wine)* vin *m* chaud **2** *(festivity)* beuverie *f* **3** *(toast)* toast *m*
VI chanter (des chants de Noël); **to go wassailing** aller chanter des noëls de maison en maison

wastage ['weɪstɪdʒ] N *(UNCOUNT)* **1** *(loss ▸ of materials, money)* gaspillage *m*, gâchis *m*; *(▸ of heat)* déperdition *f*, perte *f*; *(▸ of time)* perte *f*; *(▸ through leakage)* fuites *fpl*, pertes *fpl* **2** *(what is wasted)* déchets *mpl*, rebuts *mpl* **3** *(in numbers, workforce)* réduction *f*; **many students are lost by w.** beaucoup d'étudiants abandonnent en cours de route

waste [weɪst] VT **1** *(misuse ▸ materials, money)* gaspiller; *(▸ time)* perdre; *(▸ life)* gâcher; **very little is wasted in this family** on ne gaspille pas dans cette famille; **I hate wasting food** j'ai horreur de gâcher la nourriture; **I wasted an hour at the post office** j'ai perdu une heure à la poste; **you're wasting your time trying to convince her** tu perds ton temps à essayer de la convaincre; **she wasted no time in telling us about it** elle s'est empressée de nous le raconter; *Fam* **you didn't w. any time, did you!** tu n'as pas perdu de temps, hein?; **expensive wine is wasted on me** je suis incapable d'apprécier le bon vin; **the joke was wasted on him** il n'a pas compris la plaisanterie; **you're wasting your energy** vous vous dépensez inutilement; **you're wasting your breath!** tu uses ta salive pour rien!; **don't w. your breath trying to convince them** ne te fatigue pas à essayer de les convaincre; *Prov* **w. not, want not** = l'économie protège du besoin
2 *(wear away ▸ limb, muscle)* atrophier; *(▸ body, person)* décharner; **her body was completely wasted by cancer** son corps était complètement miné par le cancer
3 *Fam (attack)* casser la gueule à, démonter le portrait à; *(kill)* buter, refroidir, zigouiller; **to w. sb's face** casser la gueule à qn, faire une tête au carré à qn
N **1** *(misuse ▸ of materials, money)* gaspillage *m*, gâchis *m*; *(▸ of time)* perte *f*; **what a w.!** quel gâchis *ou* gaspillage!; **it's a w. of breath arguing about it** ce n'est pas la peine d'en discuter; **it's a complete w. of money** c'est de l'argent jeté par les fenêtres *ou* gaspillé; **it's a w. of time talking to her**

tu perds ton temps à discuter avec elle; **what a w. of time!** que de temps perdu!; **our trip was a w. of time and energy** notre voyage a été une perte de temps et d'énergie; **it's an enormous w. of talent** c'est énormément de talent gâché; **to go to w.** *(gen)* se perdre, être gaspillé; *(land)* tomber en friche; **don't let all this food go to w.!** ne laissez pas *ou* n'allez pas laisser tout ça se perdre!; **I'm not going to let the opportunity go to w.** je ne vais pas laisser passer l'occasion; *Fam* **he's a w. of space** il est nul
2 *(UNCOUNT) (refuse ▸ gen)* déchets *mpl*; *(▸ household)* ordures *fpl* (ménagères); *(▸ water)* eaux *fpl* usées; **industrial w.** déchets *mpl* industriels
3 *(land)* terrain *m* vague
4 *(idiom)* **to lay w. to sth, to lay sth w.** ravager *ou* dévaster qch
ADJ **1** *(paper)* de rebut; *(energy)* perdu; *(water)* sale, usé; *(food)* qui reste **2** *(ground)* en friche; *(region)* désert, désolé; **the children were playing on w. ground** les enfants jouaient sur un terrain vague
• **wastes** NPL terres *fpl* désolées, désert *m*; **the polar wastes** le désert polaire
▸▸ *Br* ***waste bin*** *(in kitchen)* poubelle *f*, boîte *f* à ordures; *(for paper)* corbeille *f* (à papier); ***waste collection*** ramassage *m* des ordures; ***waste disposal*** élimination *f ou* destruction *f* des déchets *ou* des ordures; ***waste disposal site*** dépôt *m* d'ordures; ***waste disposal unit*** broyeur *m* d'ordures; ***waste heat*** chaleur *f* perdue; ***waste heat recovery*** récupération *f* de la chaleur perdue; ***waste material*** déchets *mpl*; ***waste matter*** déchets *mpl*; ***waste paper*** *(UNCOUNT)* papier *m ou* papiers *mpl* de rebut; ***waste pipe*** (tuyau *m* de) vidange *f*; ***waste product*** *Ind* déchet *m* de production *ou* de fabrication; *Physiol* déchet *m (de l'organisme)*; ***waste segregation*** tri *m* sélectif (des ordures ménagères); *Typ* ***waste sheet*** maculature *f*, macule *f*

▸ **waste away** VI dépérir

wastebasket [ˈweɪstbæskɪt] N *esp Am* corbeille *f* (à papier); *Comput* poubelle *f*

wasted [ˈweɪstɪd] ADJ **1** *(material, money)* gaspillé; *(energy, opportunity, time)* perdu; *(attempt, effort)* inutile, vain; *(food)* inutilisé; **a w. journey** un voyage pour rien; **she's w. in that job** cet emploi est bien au-dessous de ses capacités **2** *(figure, person)* décharné; *(limb ▸ emaciated)* décharné; *(▸ enfeebled)* atrophié **3** *Fam (drunk)* pété, bourré, fait; *(on drugs)* défoncé

wasteful [ˈweɪstfʊl] ADJ *(habits)* de gaspillage; *(person)* gaspilleur; *(procedure)* inefficace, peu rentable; **a w. use of natural resources** un gaspillage des ressources naturelles

wastefully [ˈweɪstfʊlɪ] ADV en gaspillant; **we spend our time so w.** on gaspille un temps fou

wastefulness [ˈweɪstfʊlnɪs] N *(of person)* gaspillage *m*, manque *m* d'économie; *(of procedure)* inefficacité *f*

wasteland [ˈweɪstlænd] N *(land ▸ disused)* terrain *m* vague; *(▸ uncultivated)* terres *fpl* en friche *ou* abandonnées; *(of desert, snow)* désert *m*; *Fig* **a cultural w.** un désert culturel

waster [ˈweɪstə(r)] N **1** *(wasteful person)* gaspilleur(euse) *m,f*; *(who wastes money)* dépensier(ère) *m,f* **2** *Br (good-for-nothing)* bon (bonne) *m,f* à rien

wastewater [ˌweɪstˈwɔːtə(r)] N *Ecol* eaux *fpl* usées

wasting [ˈweɪstɪŋ] N **1** *(of resources, time)* gaspillage *m* **2** *(of body)* dépérissement *m*, amaigrissement *m*; *(of limb)* atrophie *f*
▸▸ *Acct* ***wasting asset*** actif *m* qui se déprécie; ***wasting disease*** maladie *f* qui ronge

wastrel [ˈweɪstrəl] = **waster**

WATCH [wɒtʃ]

VT
• regarder **1** • observer **1, 2**
• surveiller **2, 3** • faire attention à **4**
• suivre de près **4**
VI
• regarder **1** • observer **1**
• veiller **2**
N
• montre **1** • surveillance **2**
• garde **3, 4**

VT **1** *(look at, observe ▸ event, film)* regarder; *(▸ animal, person)* regarder, observer; **they w. a lot of television** ils regardent beaucoup la télévision; **I watched her working** je la regardais travailler; **the crowds were watching the lions being fed** la foule regardait les lions qu'on était en train de nourrir; **we sat outside watching the world go by** nous étions assis dehors à regarder les gens passer; **w. how I do it, w. me** regardez *ou* observez comment je fais; **I bet he ignores us, just you w.!** je parie qu'il va nous ignorer, tu vas voir!; *Prov* **a watched pot never boils** = inutile de s'inquiéter, ça ne fera pas avancer les choses
2 *(spy on ▸ person)* surveiller, observer; *(▸ activities, suspect)* surveiller; **you'd better w. him** vous feriez bien de le surveiller *ou* de l'avoir à l'œil; **I think we're being watched** *(gen)* j'ai l'impression qu'on nous observe; *(by police, thieves)* j'ai l'impression qu'on nous surveille
3 *(guard, tend ▸ children, pet)* surveiller, s'occuper de; *(▸ belongings, house)* surveiller, garder; *Mil* monter la garde devant, garder
4 *(pay attention to ▸ health, weight)* faire attention à; *(▸ development, situation)* suivre de près; **w. where you're going!** regardez devant vous!; **w. what you're doing!** faites attention (à ce que vous faites)!; **w. you don't spill the coffee** fais attention à ne pas renverser le café; **can you w. the milk?** peux-tu surveiller le lait?; **I'm watching the classifieds for any job opportunities** je regarde les petites annonces pour les offres d'emploi; **we'd better w. the time** il faut que nous surveillions l'heure; **w. this space** = annonce d'une publicité ou d'informations à paraître; *Fig* affaire à suivre; **w. your head!** attention *ou* gare à votre tête!; **w. your language!** surveille ton langage!; **w. it!** *(warning)* (fais) attention!; *(threat)* attention!, gare à vous!; *also Fig* **w. your step** faites attention *ou* regardez où vous mettez les pieds; **you should w. your step** *or* **w. yourself with the boss** vous feriez bien de vous surveiller quand vous êtes avec le patron
VI **1** *(observe)* regarder, observer; **I watched to see how she would react** j'ai attendu pour voir quelle serait sa réaction; **he watched closely as I removed the bandage** il a regardé *ou* observé attentivement quand j'ai enlevé le bandage; **I just came to w.** je suis simplement venu regarder, je suis venu en simple spectateur
2 *(keep vigil)* veiller; **his mother watched by his bedside** sa mère a veillé à son chevet
N **1** *(timepiece)* montre *f*; **it's six o'clock by my w.** il est six heures à ma montre
2 *(lookout)* surveillance *f*; *Br* **be on the w. for pickpockets** faites attention *ou* prenez garde aux voleurs à la tire; *Br* **tax inspectors are always on the w. for fraud** les inspecteurs des impôts sont toujours à l'affût des fraudeurs; **a sentry was on w.** *or* **kept w.** une sentinelle montait la garde; **to keep w. by sb's bed** veiller au chevet de qn; **the police kept a close w. on the suspect** la police a surveillé le suspect de près; **we'll keep w. on your house during your absence** nous surveillerons votre maison pendant votre absence
3 *(person on guard ▸ gen) & Mil* sentinelle *f*; *Naut* homme *m* de quart; *(group of guards ▸ gen) & Mil* garde *f*; *Naut* quart *m*
4 *(period of duty ▸ gen) & Mil* garde *f*; *Naut* quart *m*; **who's on w.?** *(gen) & Mil* qui monte la garde?; *Naut* qui est de quart?; *Fig* **it won't happen on my w.** ça n'arrivera pas tant que ce sera moi le responsable
5 *Literary (period of the night)* **in the slow watches of the night** pendant les longues nuits sans sommeil
▸▸ ***watch chain*** chaîne *f* de montre; ***watch crystal*** verre *m* de montre; ***watch night*** nuit *f* de la Saint-Sylvestre; ***watch night service*** messe *f* (de minuit) de la Saint-Sylvestre; ***watch pocket*** gousset *m*

▸ **watch back** VT SEP *Fam* **when I watched the tape back I noticed some mistakes** quand j'ai regardé la cassette j'ai remarqué qu'il y avait quelques erreurs

▸ **watch for** VT INSEP guetter, surveiller; **he watched for a chance to approach the President** il attendait une occasion d'approcher le Président; **something to w. for this month is the London marathon** la chose à ne pas rater ce mois-ci, c'est le marathon de Londres

▸ **watch out** VI faire attention, prendre garde; **w[…] out!** *(warning)* (faites) attention!; **you'd better w[…] out, the boss knows** tu devrais te méfier, le pa[…]tron est au courant; **to w. out for sth** *(be on look[…] out for)* guetter qch; *(be careful of)* faire attentio[…] *ou* prendre garde à qch; **w. out for the bus** gue[…]tez le bus; **w. out for Ronnie!** gare à Ronnie!

▸ **watch over** VT INSEP garder, surveiller; **sh[…] watched over the children while we were gone** ell[…] a surveillé les enfants *ou* elle s'est occupée de[…] enfants pendant notre absence; **God will w. ove[…] you** Dieu vous protégera

watchband [ˈwɒtʃbænd] N *Am* bracelet *m* d[…] montre

watchdog [ˈwɒtʃdɒg] N *(dog)* chien(enne) *m[…]* de garde; *Fig (person)* gardien(enne) *m,f*; *(o[…]ganization)* organisme *m* de surveillance *ou* d[…] contrôle; **the committee acts as w. on environmen[…]tal issues** le comité veille aux problèmes d'env[…]ronnement
COMP *(body, committee)* de surveillance
▸▸ *Comput* ***watchdog program*** programme *r[…]* sentinelle

watcher [ˈwɒtʃə(r)] N observateur(trice) *m,[…]* *(spectator)* spectateur(trice) *m,f*; *(idle onlooke[…])* curieux(euse) *m,f*; **Downing Street watchers** le[…] observateurs de Downing Street

watchful [ˈwɒtʃfʊl] ADJ vigilant, attentif; **he wa[…] w. for any unusual behaviour** il était attentif à tou[…] comportement inhabituel; **under the w. eye o[…] her mother** sous l'œil vigilant de sa mère; **to kee[…] a w. eye on sb/sth** avoir qn/qch à l'œil; **she kept […] w. eye on the situation** elle a suivi la situation d[…] près

watchfully [ˈwɒtʃfʊlɪ] ADV avec vigilance, d'u[…] œil attentif

watching brief [ˈwɒtʃɪŋ-] N **to have a w.** avo[…] un mandat de contrôle

watchmaker [ˈwɒtʃˌmeɪkə(r)] N horloger(ère[…]) *m,f*

watchmaking [ˈwɒtʃˌmeɪkɪŋ] N *(UNCOUNT[…])* horlogerie *f*

watchman [ˈwɒtʃmən] *(pl* **watchmen** [-mən]*)* […] gardien *m*

watchstrap [ˈwɒtʃstræp] N bracelet *m* de mon[…]tre

watchtower [ˈwɒtʃˌtaʊə(r)] N tour *f* de guet

watchword [ˈwɒtʃwɜːd] N *(password)* mot *m* d[…] passe; *(slogan)* mot *m* d'ordre

water [ˈwɔːtə(r)] N **1** *(gen)* eau *f*; **I took a drink of w[…]** j'ai bu de l'eau; **is the w. safe to drink?** est-ce qu[…] l'eau est potable?; **hot and cold running w.** eau courante chaude et froide; **turn on the w.** *(a[…] main)* ouvre l'eau; *(at tap)* ouvre le robinet; **pris[…]oners were put on bread and w.** on mit les prison[…]niers au pain (sec) et à l'eau; **they held his hea[…] under w.** ils lui ont tenu la tête sous l'eau; **m[…] shoes let in w.** mes chaussures prennent l'ea[…] **the w.** *or* **waters of the Seine** l'eau *ou* les eaux d[…] la Seine; **the ship was making w.** le bateau pre[…]nait l'eau *ou* faisait eau; *Fig* **they're in rough fi[…]nancial waters** ils sont dans une situatio[…] financière difficile; **that idea won't hold w.** cett[…] idée ne tient pas debout; *Fam* **you're in hot w[…] now** tu vas avoir de gros ennuis[□], tu es dans d[…] beaux draps; *Fam* **her statement got us into hot w[…]** sa déclaration nous a mis dans le pétrin *ou* dan[…] de beaux draps; *Fam* **I'm trying to keep my hea[…] above w.** *or* **to stay above w.** j'essaye de me main[…]tenir à flot *ou* de faire face; **the wine flowed lik[…] w.** le vin coulait à flots; **to spend money like w[…]** jeter l'argent par les fenêtres; **they poured c[…] threw cold w. on our suggestion** ils n'ont pas ét[…] enthousiasmés par notre suggestion; **it's like w[…] off a duck's back** ça n'a aucun effet; **it's w. unde[…] the bridge** c'est du passé; **a lot of w. has passe[…] under the bridge since then** il a coulé beaucou[…] d'eau sous les ponts depuis; *Br Formal* **he's an ar[…]ist of the first w.** c'est un artiste de premier ordr[…]
2 *(body of water)* eau *f*; **the children played at th[…] w.'s edge** les enfants ont joué au bord de l'eau[…] **she fell in the w.** elle est tombée à l'eau; **they sen[…] the goods by w.** ils ont envoyé la marchandis[…] par bateau
3 *(tide)* marée *f*; **at high/low w.** à marée haute[…] basse

4 *Euph (urine)* urine *f*; **to make** *or* **to pass w.** uriner
5 *Med* **w. on the brain** hydrocéphalie *f*; **the baby has w. on the brain** le bébé est hydrocéphale; **to have w. on the knee** avoir un épanchement de synovie
6 *Tex (of cloth)* moiré *m*

VT 1 *(land, plants)* arroser; **the land here is watered by the Seine** ici, la terre est arrosée *ou* irriguée par la Seine
2 *(animal)* donner à boire à, faire boire
3 *(dilute ▸ alcohol)* couper (d'eau)
4 *Tex (cloth)* moirer

VI 1 *(eyes)* larmoyer **2** *(mouth)* **the smell made my mouth w.** l'odeur m'a donné *ou* m'a mis l'eau à la bouche

• **waters NPL 1** *(territorial)* eaux *fpl*; **in Japanese waters** dans les eaux (territoriales) japonaises
2 *(spa water)* **to take the waters** prendre les eaux, faire une cure thermale
3 *(of pregnant woman)* poche *f* des eaux; **her waters broke** elle a perdu les eaux, la poche des eaux s'est rompue
4 *Prov* **to cast one's bread upon the waters** = se comporter de façon altruiste

▸▸ ***water bag*** outre *f* à eau; *Br* ***water bailiff*** garde-pêche *m (personne)*; ***water bed*** lit *m* à matelas d'eau; ***water bird*** oiseau *m* aquatique; ***water birth*** accouchement *m* sous l'eau; *Br* ***water biscuit*** = biscuit salé croquant; ***water blister*** ampoule *f*, *Spec* phlyctène *f*; *Br Admin* ***water board*** service *m* des eaux; *Entom* ***water boatman*** notonecte *f*; ***water bomb*** bombe *f* à eau; ***water bottle*** *(gen)* bouteille *f* d'eau; *(soldier's, worker's)* bidon *m* à eau; *(in leather)* gourde *f*; ***water buffalo*** *(in India)* buffle *m* d'Inde; *(in Malaysia)* karbau *m*, kérabau *m*; *(in Asia)* buffle *m* d'Asie; ***water bus*** navette *f (sur eau)*; ***water butt*** citerne *f* (à eau de pluie); ***water cannon*** canon *m* à eau; ***water carrier*** *(container)* bidon *m* à eau; *(person)* porteur(euse) *m,f* d'eau; *Astrol & Astron* **the Water Carrier** le Verseau; ***water cart*** *(to sprinkle water)* arroseuse *f*; *(to sell water)* voiture *f* de marchand d'eau; ***water chestnut*** châtaigne *f* d'eau; ***water chute*** *(in swimming-pool)* toboggan *m*; ***water clock*** horloge *f* à eau, clepsydre *f*; *Old-fashioned* ***water closet*** W-C *mpl*, toilettes *fpl*, cabinets *mpl*; ***water cooler*** distributeur *m* d'eau fraîche; *Fam TV* ***water cooler show*** = émission dont tout le monde parle; ***water cooling*** refroidissement *m* par eau; *Am* ***water cracker*** = biscuit salé craquant; *Biol & Meteo* ***water cycle*** cycle *m* de l'eau *ou* d'évaporation; ***water damage*** dégâts *mpl* des eaux; *Entom* ***water flea*** daphnie *f*, puce *f* d'eau; ***water fountain*** *(for decoration)* jet *m* d'eau; *(for drinking)* distributeur *m* d'eau fraîche; ***water gas*** gaz *m* à l'eau; ***water gauge*** jauge *f* d'eau; ***water glass*** *(for drinking out of)* verre *m* à eau; *(water gauge)* jauge *f* d'eau; *Chem* silicate *m* de potasse; ***water gun*** pistolet *m* à eau; ***water hammer*** *(in pipes)* cognements *mpl* dans la canalisation; ***water heater*** chauffe-eau *m inv*; ***water hen*** poule *f* d'eau; *Br* ***water ice*** sorbet *m*; ***water jacket*** chemise *f* d'eau; *Aut* ***water jet*** gicleur *m* d'eau; ***water jump*** brook *m*; ***water level*** *(of river, sea)* niveau *m* de l'eau; *(in tank)* niveau *m* d'eau; *Bot* ***water lily*** nénuphar *m*; ***water main*** conduite *f* d'eau; ***water mattress*** matelas *m* à eau; ***water meadow*** prairie *f (souvent inondée)*; ***water meter*** compteur *m* d'eau; ***water nymph*** naïade *f*; ***water park*** parc *m* aquatique; ***water pipe*** *Constr* conduite *f ou* canalisation *f* d'eau; *(hookah)* narguilé *m*; ***water pistol*** pistolet *m* à eau; ***water plant*** plante *f* aquatique; *Ecol* ***water pollution*** pollution *f* des eaux; ***water polo*** water-polo *m*; ***water power*** énergie *f* hydraulique, houille *f* blanche; ***water pump*** pompe *f* à eau; ***water purification*** dépollution *f ou* épuration *f* de l'eau; *Orn* ***water rail*** râle *m* d'eau; *Zool* ***water rat*** rat *m* d'eau; *Br* ***water rate*** taxe *f* sur l'eau; *Astrol* ***water sign*** signe *m* d'eau; ***water ski*** ski *m* nautique; ***water skier*** skieur(euse) *m,f* nautique; ***water skiing*** ski *m* nautique; *Zool* ***water snake*** serpent *m* d'eau; ***water softener*** adoucisseur *m* d'eau; *Zool* ***water spaniel*** épagneul *m (qui chasse du gibier d'eau)*; *Entom* ***water spider*** araignée *f* d'eau, *Spéc* argyronète *m*; ***water sports*** *(water skiing, windsurfing etc)* sports *mpl* nautiques; *Myth* ***water sprite*** ondin(e) *m,f*; ***water supply*** *(for campers, troops)* provision *f* d'eau; *(to house)* alimentation *f* en eau; *(to area, town)* distribution *f* des eaux, approvisionnement *m* en eau; **the w. supply has been cut off** l'eau a été coupée; ***water table*** niveau *m* de la nappe phréatique; ***water tank*** réservoir *m* d'eau, citerne *f*; ***water torture*** supplice *m* de l'eau; ***water tower*** château *m* d'eau; ***water transport*** transport *m* par voie d'eau; ***water vapour*** vapeur *f* d'eau; *Zool* ***water vole*** rat *m* d'eau

▸ **water down VT SEP 1** *(alcohol)* couper (d'eau) **2** *Fig (speech)* édulcorer; *(complaint, criticism)* atténuer

water-based ADJ à l'eau

waterborne ['wɔːtəbɔːn] **ADJ** *(vehicle)* flottant; *(commerce, trade)* effectué par voie d'eau; *(disease)* d'origine hydrique

watercolour, *Am* **watercolor** ['wɔːtəˌkʌlə(r)] **N** *(paint)* couleur *f* pour aquarelle; *(painting)* aquarelle *f*; **painted in w.** peint à l'aquarelle
ADJ *(paint)* pour aquarelle, à l'eau; *(landscape, portrait)* à l'aquarelle
▸▸ ***watercolour artist*** aquarelliste *mf*

water-cooled [-kuːld] **ADJ** à refroidissement par eau

watercourse ['wɔːtəkɔːs] **N** *(river, stream)* cours *m* d'eau; *(bed)* lit *m (d'un cours d'eau)*

watercress ['wɔːtəkres] **N** cresson *m* (de fontaine)

watered ['wɔːtəd] **ADJ**
▸▸ *Tex* ***watered silk*** soie *f* moirée; *Fin* ***watered stock*** titres *mpl* dilués

waterfall ['wɔːtəfɔːl] **N** cascade *f*, chute *f* d'eau

waterfowl ['wɔːtəfaʊl] *(pl* **inv** *or* **waterfowls) N** *(bird)* oiseau *m* aquatique; *(collectively)* gibier *m* d'eau

waterfront ['wɔːtəfrʌnt] **N** *(in harbour)* quais *mpl*; *(seafront)* front *m* de mer; **on the w.** *(in harbour)* sur les quais; *(on seafront)* face à la mer

wateriness ['wɔːtərɪnɪs] **N** *(of ground, soil)* excès *m* d'eau; *(of coffee, tea)* manque *m* de goût; *(of soup)* insipidité *f*, fadeur *f*; *(of beer)* insipidité *f*; *(of light)* faiblesse *f*; *(of colour)* ton *m* délavé

watering ['wɔːtərɪŋ] **N 1** *(of garden, plants)* arrosage *m*; *(of crops, fields)* irrigation *f*; **azaleas need daily w.** il faut arroser les azalées chaque jour **2** *(of animals)* abreuvage *m* **3** *Tex (of silk)* moirage *m*
▸▸ ***watering can*** arrosoir *m*; ***watering hole*** *(for animals)* point *m* d'eau; *Fam Hum (pub)* troquet *m*; ***watering place*** *(waterhole)* point *m* d'eau; *Br (spa)* station *f* thermale; *Br (seaside resort)* station *f* balnéaire; ***watering pot*** arrosoir *m*

waterlogged ['wɔːtəlɒgd] **ADJ** *(land, soil)* détrempé; *(boat)* plein d'eau; *(clothing, shoes, carpet)* saturé d'eau, trempé

Waterloo [ˌwɔːtə'luː] **N 1** *Geog* Waterloo; *Hist* **the Battle of W.** la bataille de Waterloo **2** *Fig* **to meet one's W.** essuyer un revers

watermark ['wɔːtəmɑːk] **N 1** *(left by river)* ligne *f* des hautes eaux; *(left by tide)* laisse *f* de haute mer **2** *(on paper)* filigrane *m*
VT filigraner

watermelon ['wɔːtəˌmelən] **N** pastèque *f*

waterproof ['wɔːtəpruːf] **ADJ** *(clothing, material)* imperméable; *(container, wall, watch)* étanche; **w. mascara** mascara *m* waterproof *ou* résistant à l'eau
N imperméable *m*
VT *(clothing, material)* imperméabiliser; *(barrel, wall)* rendre étanche
• **waterproofs NPL** vêtements *mpl* imperméables

waterproofing ['wɔːtəpruːfɪŋ] **N** *(process ▸ for clothing, material)* imperméabilisation *f*; *(▸ for barrel, wall)* action *f* de rendre étanche; *(coating)* imperméabilisation *f*

water-repellent ADJ imperméable, hydrofuge

water-resistant ADJ *(material)* semi-imperméable; *(lotion)* qui résiste à l'eau; *(ink)* indélébile, qui résiste à l'eau

watershed ['wɔːtəʃed] **N 1** *Geog (line)* ligne *f* de partage des eaux; *Am (area)* bassin *m* hydrographique **2** *Fig (event)* grand tournant *m*; **the concert was a w. in her career as a singer** ce concert marqua un grand tournant dans sa carrière de chanteuse; **at this w. in her life** à ce moment critique de sa vie **3** *Br TV* **the w.** = l'heure après laquelle l'émission de programmes destinés aux adultes est autorisée

waterside ['wɔːtəsaɪd] **N** bord *m* de l'eau
ADJ *(house, path)* au bord de l'eau; *(flower)* du bord de l'eau; **w. residents** riverains *mpl*
▸▸ *Am* ***waterside workers*** dockers *mpl*

water-ski VI faire du ski nautique

water-skiing N ski *m* nautique

water-soluble ADJ soluble dans l'eau

waterspout ['wɔːtəspaʊt] **N 1** *(pipe)* (tuyau *m* de) descente *f* **2** *Met* trombe *f*

watertight ['wɔːtətaɪt] **ADJ 1** *(box, door)* étanche **2** *Fig (argument, reasoning)* inattaquable, indiscutable; *(alibi)* en béton
▸▸ *Naut* ***watertight bulkhead*** cloison *f* étanche

waterway ['wɔːtəweɪ] **N** cours *m* d'eau, voie *f* navigable

waterworks ['wɔːtəwɜːks] *(pl* **inv) N** *(establishment)* station *f* hydraulique; *(system)* système *m* hydraulique
NPL 1 *(fountain)* jet *m* d'eau **2** *Br Fam Euph (urinary system)* voies *fpl* urinaires[□]; **he has problems with his w.** il a des problèmes de vessie[□] **3** *Fam Hum (tears)* **she turned on the w.** elle s'est mise à pleurer comme une Madeleine

watery ['wɔːtərɪ] **ADJ 1** *(surroundings, world)* aquatique; *(ground, soil)* détrempé, saturé d'eau; **the sailors found a w. grave** les marins ont été ensevelis par les eaux
2 *(eyes)* larmoyant, humide
3 *(coffee, tea)* trop léger; *(soup)* trop liquide; *(milk)* qui a trop d'eau; *(vegetables, beer)* insipide; *(taste)* fade, insipide
4 *(light, sun, smile)* faible; *(colour)* délavé, pâle; *(sky)* chargé de pluie

watt [wɒt] **N** watt *m*

wattage ['wɒtɪdʒ] **N** puissance *f ou* consommation *f* (en watts)

watt-hour N wattheure *m*

wattle ['wɒtəl] **N 1** *(of bird, lizard)* caroncule *f* **2** *(sticks)* clayonnage *m*
▸▸ ***wattle and daub*** clayonnage *m* enduit de torchis

wave [weɪv] **N 1** *(in sea)* vague *f*, lame *f*; *(on lake)* vague *f*; **the waves** les flots *mpl*; *Fig* **don't make waves** ne faites pas de vagues, ne créez pas de remous
2 *(of earthquake, explosion)* onde *f*; *Fig (of crime, panic, pain, disgust)* vague *f*; *(of anger)* bouffée *f*; **the refugees arrived in waves** les réfugiés sont arrivés par vagues; *Mil* **there were several waves of attack** il y eut plusieurs vagues d'assaut
3 *(in hair)* cran *m*, ondulation *f*; **her hair has a natural w. to it** ses cheveux ondulent naturellement
4 *(gesture)* geste *m ou* signe *m* de la main; **our neighbour gave us a friendly w.** notre voisin nous a fait un signe amical; **with a w. of the hand** d'un geste *ou* d'un signe de la main; **with a w. of her magic wand** d'un coup de baguette magique
5 *Phys & Rad (electric, magnetic)* onde *f*

VI 1 *(gesture)* faire un signe *ou* un geste de la main; **his sister waved at** *or* **to him** *(greeted)* sa sœur l'a salué d'un signe de la main; *(signalled)* sa sœur lui a fait signe de la main; **he waved to us as he left** il nous fit au revoir de la main en partant; **she waved at** *or* **to them to come in** elle leur a fait signe d'entrer; **he waved vaguely towards the door** il a montré vaguement la porte d'un geste de la main
2 *(move ▸ flag)* flotter; *(▸ wheat)* onduler, ondoyer; *(▸ branch)* être agité

VT 1 *(brandish ▸ flag)* agiter, brandir; *(▸ pistol, sword)* brandir; **to w. a magic wand** donner un coup de baguette magique; *Fig* **I can't just w. a magic wand!** je ne peux pas faire de miracle!, je n'ai pas de baguette magique!
2 *(gesture)* **his mother waved him away** sa mère l'a écarté d'un geste de la main; **the guard waved us back/on** le garde nous a fait signe de reculer/d'avancer; **the policeman waved us through the crossroads** le policier nous a fait signe de traverser le carrefour; **we waved goodbye** nous avons fait au revoir de la main; *Fam Fig* **you can w.**

goodbye to your promotion! tu peux dire adieu à ta promotion!
3 *(hair)* onduler
►► ***wave band*** bande *f* de fréquences; ***wave energy*** énergie *f* des vagues; ***wave function*** fonction *f* d'onde; ***wave machine*** machine *f* à vagues; ***wave mechanics*** *(UNCOUNT)* mécanique *f* ondulatoire; ***wave power*** énergie *f* des vagues

> Attention: ne pas confondre avec **to waive**.

►**wave aside** VT SEP *(person)* écarter *ou* éloigner d'un geste; *(protest)* écarter; *(help, suggestion)* refuser, rejeter

►**wave down** VT SEP **to w. sb/a car down** faire signe à qn/à une voiture de s'arrêter

wavelength ['weɪvleŋθ] N *Phys & Rad* longueur *f* d'onde; *Fig* **we're just not on the same w.** nous ne sommes pas sur la même longueur d'onde
►► ***wavelength range*** plage *f* des longueurs d'onde

waver ['weɪvə(r)] VI **1** *(person)* vaciller, hésiter; *(confidence, courage)* vaciller, faiblir; **they didn't w. in their loyalty to the cause** leur attachement à la cause n'a pas faibli **2** *(flame, light)* vaciller, osciller; *(temperature)* osciller; **the price wavered around the £46 per kilo mark** le prix tournait autour des 46 livres le kilo **3** *(voice)* trembloter, trembler

waverer ['weɪvərə(r)] N irrésolu(e) *m,f*, indécis (e) *m,f*

wavering ['weɪvərɪŋ] ADJ **1** *(person)* irrésolu, indécis; *(confidence, courage)* vacillant, défaillant **2** *(flame, light)* vacillant, oscillant; *(steps)* vacillant, chancelant; *(temperature)* oscillant **3** *(voice)* tremblotant, tremblant
N **1** *(of person)* irrésolution *f*, indécision *f*; *(of confidence, courage)* défaillance *f* **2** *(of flame, light)* vacillement *m*, oscillation *f*; *(of temperature)* oscillation *f* **3** *(of voice)* tremblement *m*

waviness ['weɪvɪnɪs] N *(of line, surface)* ondulation *f*; *(of hair)* ondulations *fpl* naturelles

waving ['weɪvɪŋ] ADJ *(fields, corn)* ondulant, ondoyant

wavy ['weɪvɪ] *(compar* **wavier**, *superl* **waviest)** ADJ *(line, surface, hair)* ondulé

wax [wæks] N **1** *(for car, floor, furniture)* cire *f*; *(in ear)* cérumen *m*; *(for skis)* fart *m* **2** *Br Fam Old-fashioned* **to be in a w.** être en rogne *ou* en colère
COMP *(candle, figure)* de *ou* en cire
VT **1** *(floor, table)* cirer, encaustiquer; *(skis)* farter; *(car)* enduire de cire **2** *(legs)* épiler (à la cire); **to w. one's legs** s'épiler les jambes (à la cire)
VI **1** *(moon)* croître; *Fig (influence, power)* croître, augmenter; **to w. and wane** *(moon)* croître et décroître; *Fig (influence, power)* croître et décliner **2** *Arch (become)* devenir; **he waxed poetic/sentimental** il se fit poète/sentimental; *Hum* **she waxed eloquent** *or* **lyrical on the subject of country life** elle s'est montrée éloquente sur le thème de la vie à la campagne
►► *Am* ***wax beans*** haricots *mpl* beurre; ***wax crayons*** crayons *mpl* gras; ***wax jacket*** veste *f* en toile huilée; ***wax museum*** musée *m* de cire; ***wax paper*** papier *m* paraffiné *ou* sulfurisé; *Bot* ***wax tree*** *(Chinese)* troène *m* de Chine; *(Japanese)* arbre *m* à cire, sumac *m* cirier

waxed [wækst] ADJ *(floor, tablecloth)* ciré; *(thread)* poissé; *(moustache)* gominé; *(lemon)* traité à la cire alimentaire
►► ***waxed cotton*** coton *m* ciré; ***waxed jacket*** veste *f* en toile huilée; ***waxed paper*** papier *m* paraffiné *ou* sulfurisé

waxen ['wæksən] ADJ **1** *(made of wax* ► *candle, figure)* de *ou* en cire **2** *(resembling wax* ► *complexion, face)* cireux

waxing ['wæksɪŋ] N **1** *(of floor, furniture)* cirage *m*, encaustiquage *m*; *(of skis)* fartage *m* **2** *(of moon)* croissance *f* **3** *(of legs)* épilation *f*

waxwing ['wækswɪŋ] N *Orn* jaseur *m*

waxwork ['wækswɜːk] N *(object)* objet *m* de *ou* en cire; *(statue of person)* statue *f* de cire

waxworks ['wækswɜːks] *(pl* **inv)** N musée *m* de cire

waxy ['wæksɪ] *(compar* **waxier**, *superl* **waxiest)** ADJ *(complexion, texture)* cireux; *(colour)* cireux, jaunâtre; *(potato)* ferme, pas farineux

WAY [weɪ]

N	
• chemin **A1–3**	• voie **A1**
• route **A1, 3**	• direction **A4**
• sens **A4, 5**	• parages **A6**
• moyen **B1**	• méthode **B1**
• façon **B2**	• manière **B2, 3**
• coutume **B3**	• habitude **B3**
• égard **B6**	• rapport **B6**
ADV	
• très loin **1**	• vachement **3**

N **A. 1** *(thoroughfare, path)* chemin *m*, voie *f*; *(for cars)* rue *f*, route *f*; **we took the w. through the woods** nous avons pris le chemin qui traverse le bois; **they live across** *or* **over the w. from the school** ils habitent en face de l'école; **the people over** *or* **across the w.** les gens d'en face; **pedestrian w.** voie *f ou* rue *f* piétonne; **private/public w.** voie *f* privée/publique; *Rel* **the W. of the Cross** le chemin de Croix
2 *(route leading to a specified place)* chemin *m*; **this is the w. to the library** la bibliothèque est par là; **could you tell me the w. to the library?** pouvez-vous me dire comment aller à la bibliothèque?; **what's the shortest** *or* **quickest w. to town?** quel est le chemin le plus court pour aller en ville?; **that's the w. to ruin** c'est le chemin de la ruine; **we took the long w. (round)** nous avons pris le chemin le plus long; **which w. does this bus go?** par où passe ce bus?; **I had to ask the** *or* **my w.** il a fallu que je demande mon chemin; **she knows the w. to school** elle connaît le chemin de l'école; **to know one's w. about a place** connaître un endroit; **you'll soon find your w. about** tu trouveras bientôt ton chemin tout seul; **they went the wrong w.** ils se sont trompés de chemin; **to lose one's w.** s'égarer, perdre son chemin; *Fig* s'égarer, se fourvoyer; **to know one's w. around** savoir s'orienter; *Fig* savoir se débrouiller; **the w. to a man's heart is through his stomach** = pour conquérir le cœur d'un homme, il faut lui faire de bons petits plats
3 *(route leading in a specified direction)* chemin *m*, route *f*; **the w. back** le chemin *ou* la route du retour; **I got lost on the w. back home** je me suis perdu sur le chemin du retour; **he couldn't find the w. back home** il n'a pas trouvé le chemin pour rentrer (à la maison); **on our w. back we stopped for dinner** au retour *ou* sur le chemin du retour, nous nous sommes arrêtés pour dîner; **she showed us the easiest w. down/up** elle nous a montré le chemin le plus facile pour descendre/monter; **the w. up is difficult but the w. down will be easier** la montée est difficile mais la descente sera plus facile; **do you know the w. down/up?** savez-vous par où on descend/on monte?; **we looked for a w. in/out** nous cherchions un moyen d'entrer/de sortir; **I took the back w. out** je suis sorti par derrière; **can you find your w. out?** vous connaissez le chemin pour sortir?; **I can find my own w. out** je trouverai mon chemin; **w. in** *(sign)* entrée; **w. out** *(sign)* sortie; **miniskirts are on the w. back in** la minijupe est de retour; **miniskirts are on the w. out** la minijupe n'est plus tellement à la mode; **the director is on the w. out** le directeur ne sera plus là très longtemps; **they found a w. out of the deadlock** ils ont trouvé une solution pour sortir de l'impasse; **is there no w. out of this nightmare?** n'y a-t-il pas moyen de mettre fin à ce cauchemar?; **their decision left her no w. out** leur décision l'a mise dans une impasse; **he left himself a w. out** il s'est ménagé une porte de sortie
4 *(direction)* direction *f*, sens *m*; **come this w.** venez par ici; **he went that w.** il est allé par là; **is this the w.?** c'est par ici?; **this w. to the chapel** *(sign)* vers la chapelle; **this w. and that** de-ci de-là, par-ci par-là; **look this w.** regarde par ici; **I never looked their w.** je n'ai jamais regardé dans leur direction; **to look the other w.** détourner les yeux; *Fig* fermer les yeux; **he didn't know which w. to look** *(embarrassed)* il ne savait plus où se mettre; **which w. is the library from here?** par où faut-il passer pour aller à la bibliothèque?; **which w. did you come?** par où êtes-vous venu?; **which w. did she go?** par où est-elle passée?; **which w. is the wind blowing?** d'où vient le vent?; *Fig* **I could tell which w. the wind was blowing** je voyais très bien ce qui allait se passer; **which w. does the tap turn?** dans quel sens faut-il tourner le robinet?; **which w. do I go from here?** où est-ce que je vais maintenant?; *Fig* qu'est-ce que je fais maintenant?; **get in, I'm going your w.** montez, je vais dans la même direction que vous; **they set off, each going his own w.** ils sont partis chacun de leur côté; **to go one's own w.** *(follow own wishes)* faire à sa guise; *(differ from others)* faire bande à part, suivre son chemin; **we each went our separate ways** *(on road)* nous sommes partis chacun de notre côté; *(in life)* chacun de nous a suivi son propre chemin; **he went the wrong w.** il a pris la mauvaise direction; *(down one-way street)* il a pris la rue en sens interdit; **to come one's w.** se présenter; **any job that comes my w.** n'importe quel travail qui se présente; **if ever the opportunity comes your w.** si jamais l'occasion se présente; *Fam* **everything's going my w.** tout marche comme je veux en ce moment; **the vote went our w.** le vote nous a été favorable; **the vote couldn't have gone any other w.** les résultats du vote étaient donnés d'avance; **to go the w. of all flesh** *or* **of all things** mourir
5 *(side)* sens *m*; **stand the box the other w. up** posez le carton dans l'autre sens; **this w. up** *(on packaging)* haut; **hold the picture the right w. up** tenez le tableau dans le bon sens; **is it the right w. round?** est-ce qu'il est à l'endroit?; **it's the wrong w. up** c'est dans le mauvais sens; **the curtains are the wrong w. round** les rideaux sont à l'envers *ou* dans le mauvais sens; **your sweater is the right/wrong w. out** votre pull est à l'endroit/à l'envers; **try it the other w. round** essayez dans l'autre sens; **cats hate having their fur brushed the wrong w.** les chats détestent qu'on les caresse à rebrousse-poil; **SHE insulted HIM?** **you've got it the wrong w. round** elle, elle l'a insulté? mais c'est le contraire; **he invited her tonight, last time it was the other w. round** ce soir c'est lui qui l'a invitée, la dernière fois c'était l'inverse
6 *(area, vicinity)* parages *mpl*; **call in when you're up our w.** passez nous voir quand vous êtes dans le coin *ou* dans les parages; **I was out** *or* **over your w. yesterday** j'étais près de *ou* du côté de chez vous hier; **the next time you're that w.** la prochaine fois que vous passerez par là; **the village is rather out of the w.** le village est un peu isolé
7 *(distance)* **we came part of the w. by foot** nous avons fait une partie de la route à pied; **to go part of the w. with sb** faire un bout de chemin avec qn; **they were one-third of the w. through their trip** ils avaient fait un tiers de leur voyage; **we've come most of the w.** nous avons fait la plus grande partie du chemin; **he talked the entire** *or* **whole w.** il a parlé pendant tout le trajet; **he can swim quite a w.** il peut nager assez longtemps; **a long w. off** *or* **away** loin; **a little** *or* **short w. off** pas très loin, à courte distance; **Susan sat a little w. off** Susan était assise un peu plus loin; **I saw him from a long w. off** je l'ai aperçu de loin; **it's a long w. to Berlin** Berlin est loin; **we're a long w. from home** nous sommes loin de chez nous; **we've come a long w.** *(from far away)* nous venons de loin; *(made progress)* nous avons fait du chemin; **we've a long w. to go** *(far to travel)* il nous reste beaucoup de route à faire; *(a lot to do)* nous avons encore beaucoup à faire; *(a lot to collect, pay)* nous sommes encore loin du compte; **he has a long w. to go to be ready for the exam** il est loin d'être prêt pour l'examen
8 *(in time)* **it's a long w. to Christmas** Noël est encore loin; **you have to go back a long w.** il faut remonter loin; *Fig* **I'm a long w. from trusting him** je suis loin de lui faire confiance; **you're a long w. off** *or* **out** *(in guessing)* vous n'y êtes pas du tout; **that's a long w. from what we thought** ce n'est pas du tout ce qu'on croyait; **she'll go a long w.** elle ira loin; **the scholarship will go a long w. towards helping with expenses** la bourse va beaucoup aider à faire face aux dépenses; **a little goodwill goes a long w.** un peu de bonne volonté facilite

oien les choses; **she makes her money go a long w.** elle sait ménager son argent; **a little bit goes a long w.** il en faut très peu; *Hum* **a little of him goes a long w.** il est sympa, mais à petites doses

9 *(space in front of person, object)* **you're in the w.** u gênes le passage; *Fig* tu gênes, tu me/nous/ *etc* déranges; **a tree was in the w.** un arbre bloquait *ou* barrait le passage; **a car was in his w.** une voiture lui barrait le passage *ou* l'empêchait de passer; **is the lamp in your w.?** la lampe vous gêne-t-elle?; **put the suitcases under the bed out of the w.** rangez les valises sous le lit pour qu'elles ne gênent pas; **to get out of the w.** s'écarter (du chemin); **we got out of his w.** nous l'avons laissé passer; **out of my w.!** pousse-toi!, laisse-moi passer!; **the cars got out of the ambulance's w.** les voitures ont laissé passer l'ambulance; **to get sb out of the w.** se débarrasser de qn, écarter *ou* éloigner qn; **to get sth out of the w.** enlever *ou* pousser qch; *Fig* **let's get the subject of holidays out of the w. first** réglons d'abord la question des vacances; **keep out of the w.!** ne reste pas là!; **make w.!** écartez-vous!; **make w. for the parade!** laissez passer le défilé!; **make w. for the President!** faites place au Président!; **to get in one another's w.** se gêner (les uns les autres); *Fig* **her social life got in the w. of her studies** ses sorties l'empêchaient d'étudier; **I don't want to get in the w. of your happiness** je ne veux pas entraver votre bonheur; **I kept out of the boss's w.** j'ai évité le patron; *Fam* **he wants his boss out of the w.** il veut se débarrasser de son patron□; *Fam* **once the meeting is out of the w.** dès que nous serons débarrassés de la réunion; **he is retiring to make w. for a younger man** il prend sa retraite pour céder la place à un plus jeune; **they tore down the slums to make w. for blocks of flats** ils ont démoli les taudis pour pouvoir construire des immeubles; **to clear** *or* **prepare the w. for sth** préparer la voie à qch; **to put difficulties in sb's w.** créer des difficultés à qn; **couldn't you see your w. (clear) to doing it?** ne trouveriez-vous pas moyen de le faire?

10 *(indicating a progressive action)* **the acid ate its w. through the metal** l'acide est passé à travers le métal; **I fought** *or* **pushed my w. through the crowd** je me suis frayé un chemin à travers la foule; **we made our w. towards the train** nous nous sommes dirigés vers le train; **to make one's w. home** rentrer; **I made my w. back to my seat** je suis retourné à ma place; **they made their w. across the desert** ils ont traversé le désert; **they made their w. down/up the hill** ils ont descendu/ monté la colline; **she made her w. up through the hierarchy** elle a gravi les échelons de la hiérarchie un par un; **she had to make her own w. in the world** elle a dû faire son chemin toute seule; **she talked her w. out of it** elle s'en est sortie avec de belles paroles; **he worked** *or* **made his w. through the pile of newspapers** il a lu les journaux un par un; **I worked my w. through college** j'ai travaillé pour payer mes études

B. 1 *(means, method)* moyen *m*, méthode *f*; **in what w. can I help you?** comment *ou* en quoi puis-je vous être utile?; **there are several ways to go** *or* **of going about it** il y a plusieurs façons *ou* plusieurs moyens de s'y prendre; **I do it this w.** voilà comment je fais; **in one w. or another** d'une façon ou d'une autre; **they thought they would win that w.** ils pensaient pouvoir gagner comme ça; **he's going to handle it his w.** il va faire ça à sa façon; **she has her own w. of cooking fish** elle a sa façon à elle de cuisiner le poisson; **the right/ wrong w. to do it** la bonne/mauvaise façon de le faire; **you're doing it the right/wrong w.** c'est comme ça/ce n'est pas comme ça qu'il faut (le) faire; **do it the usual w.** faites comme d'habitude; **there's no w.** *or* **I can't see any w. we'll finish on time** nous ne finirons jamais *ou* nous n'avons aucune chance de finir à temps; *Pol* **ways and means** financement *m*; **there are ways and means** il y a des moyens; **to find a w. of doing sth** trouver (le) moyen de faire qch; *Hum* **love will find a w.** l'amour finit toujours par triompher; **that's the w. to do it!** c'est comme ça qu'il faut faire!; *Am Fam* **w. to go!** *(congratulations)* bravo! c'est bien!□; **what a w. to go!** *(manner of dying)* quelle belle mort!

2 *(particular manner, fashion)* façon *f*, manière *f*; **in this w.** de cette façon; **in a friendly w.** gentiment; **he spoke in a general w. about the economy** il a parlé de l'économie d'une façon générale; **she doesn't like the w. he is dressed** elle n'aime pas la façon dont il est habillé; **he doesn't speak the w. his family does** il ne parle pas comme sa famille; **they see things in the same w.** ils voient les choses de la même façon; **in their own (small) w. they fight racism** à leur façon *ou* dans la limite de leurs moyens, ils luttent contre le racisme; **in the same w., we note that...** de même, on notera que...; **that's one w. to look at it** *or* **of looking at it** c'est une façon de voir les choses; **my w. of looking at it** mon point de vue sur la question; **that's not my w. (of doing things)** ce n'est pas mon genre; **try to see it my w.** mettez-vous à ma place; **w. of speaking/writing** façon de parler/ d'écrire; **to her w. of thinking** à son avis; **the w. she feels about him** les sentiments qu'elle éprouve à son égard; **I didn't think you would take it this w.** je ne pensais pas que vous le prendriez comme ça; **if that's the w. you feel about it!** si c'est comme ça que vous le prenez!; **the American w. of life** la manière de vivre des Américains, le mode de vie américain; **dieting has become a w. of life with some people** certaines personnes passent leur vie à faire des régimes; **yearly strikes have become a w. of life** les grèves annuelles sont devenues une habitude

3 *(custom)* coutume *f*, usage *m*; *(habitual manner of acting)* manière *f*, habitude *f*; **we soon got used to her ways** nous nous sommes vite habitués à ses manières; **I know his little ways** je connais ses petites manies; **the ways of God and men** les voies de Dieu et de l'homme; **he knows nothing of their ways** il les connaît très mal; **they're happy in their own w.** ils sont heureux à leur manière; **he's a genius in his w.** c'est un génie dans son genre; **it's not my w. to criticize** ce n'est pas mon genre *ou* ce n'est pas dans mes habitudes de critiquer; **he's not in a bad mood, it's just his w.** il n'est pas de mauvaise humeur, c'est sa façon d'être habituelle; **she got into/out of the w. of rising early** elle a pris/perdu l'habitude de se lever tôt; **you'll get into the w. of it** vous vous y ferez

4 *(facility, knack)* **he has a w. with children** il sait (comment) s'y prendre *ou* il a le chic avec les enfants; **she has a w. with words** elle a le chic pour s'exprimer; **trouble has a w. of showing up when least expected** les ennuis ont le chic pour se manifester quand on ne s'y attend pas

5 *(indicating a condition, state of affairs)* **let me tell you the w. it was** laisse-moi te raconter comment ça s'est passé; **we can't invite him given the w. things are** on ne peut pas l'inviter étant donné la situation; **we left the flat the w. it was** nous avons laissé l'appartement tel qu'il était *ou* comme il était; **is he going to be staying here? – it looks that w.** est-ce qu'il va loger ici? – on dirait (bien); **it's not the w. it looks!** ce n'est pas ce que vous pensez!; **it's not the w. it used to be** ce n'est pas comme avant; **that's the w. things are** c'est comme ça; **that's the w. of the world** ainsi va le monde; **business is good and we're trying to keep it that w.** les affaires vont bien et nous faisons en sorte que ça dure; **that's always the w. with him** c'est toujours comme ça avec lui; **life goes on (in) the same old w.** la vie va son train *ou* suit son cours; **I don't like the w. things are going** je n'aime pas la tournure que prennent les choses; **we'll never finish the w. things are going** au train où vont les choses, on n'aura jamais fini; **to be in a bad w.** être en mauvais état; **he's in a bad w.** il est dans un triste état; **their business is in a bad/ good w.** leurs affaires marchent mal/bien; **she's in a fair w. to succeed/to becoming president** elle est bien partie pour réussir/pour devenir président

6 *(respect, detail)* égard *m*, rapport *m*; **in what w.?** à quel égard?, sous quel rapport?; **in this w.** à cet égard, sous ce rapport; **it's important in many ways** c'est important à bien des égards; **in some ways** à certains égards, par certains côtés; **the job suits her in every w.** le poste lui convient à tous égards *ou* à tous points de vue; **I'll help you in every possible w.** je ferai tout ce que je peux pour vous aider; **she studied the problem in every w. possible** elle a examiné le problème sous tous les angles possibles; **useful in more ways than one** utile à plus d'un égard; **these two books, each interesting in its (own) w.** ces deux livres, qui sont intéressants chacun dans son genre; **he's clever that w.** sur ce plan-là, il est malin; **in one w.** d'un certain point de vue; **in a w. you're right** en un sens vous avez raison; **I see what you mean in a w.** d'une certaine manière, je vois ce que tu veux dire; **I am in no w. responsible** je ne suis absolument pas responsable; **this in no w. changes your situation** ceci ne change en rien votre situation; **without wanting in any w. to criticize** sans vouloir le moins du monde critiquer; **I was not involved with this in any w., shape or form** je n'ai absolument rien à voir avec ça

7 *(scale)* **to do things in a big w.** faire les choses en grand; **she went into politics in a big w.** elle s'est lancée à fond dans la politique; **they helped out in a big w.** ils ont beaucoup aidé; **a grocer in a big/small w.** un gros/petit épicier; **we live in a small w.** nous vivons modestement; **the restaurant is doing quite well in a small w.** le restaurant marche bien à son échelle; **it does change the situation in a small w.** ça change quand même un peu la situation

8 *(usu pl) (part, share)* **we divided the money four ways** nous avons partagé l'argent en quatre; **the committee was split three ways** le comité était divisé en trois groupes

9 *Naut* **we're gathering/losing w.** nous prenons/ perdons de la vitesse; **the ship has w. on** le navire a de l'erre

10 *(idioms)* **she always gets** *or* **has her (own) w.** elle arrive toujours à ses fins; **he only wants it his w.** il n'en fait qu'à sa tête; **I'm not going to let you have it all your (own) w.** je refuse de te céder en tout; **if I had my w., he'd be in prison** si cela ne tenait qu'à moi, il serait en prison; **I refuse to go – have it your (own) w.** je refuse d'y aller – fais ce que *ou* comme tu veux; **no, it was 1789 – have it your (own) w.** non, c'était en 1789 – soit; **you can't have it both ways** il faut choisir; **I can stop too, it works both ways** je peux m'arrêter aussi, ça marche dans les deux sens; **there are no two ways about it** il n'y a pas le choix; **no two ways about it, he was rude** il n'y a pas à dire, il a été grossier; *Hum* **to have one's (wicked) w. with sb** séduire qn

ADV **1** *(far ▸ in space, time)* très loin□; **they live w. over yonder** ils habitent très loin par là-bas; **w. up the mountain** très haut dans la montagne; **w. down south** là-bas dans le sud; **w. back in the distance** au loin derrière; **w. back in the 1930s** déjà dans les années 30

2 *Fam Fig* **we know each other from w. back, we go w. back** nous sommes amis depuis très longtemps□; **you're w. below the standard** tu es bien en-dessous du niveau voulu□; **he's w. over forty** il a largement dépassé la quarantaine□; **she's w. ahead of her class** elle est très en avance sur sa classe□; **he's w. off** *or* **out in his guess** il est loin d'avoir deviné□

3 *Fam (very)* vachement; **he is w. crazy** il est vachement atteint

• **ways** NPL *Naut (in shipbuilding)* cale *f*

• **all the way** ADV **the baby cried all the w.** le bébé a pleuré tout le long du chemin; **don't close the curtains all the w.** ne fermez pas complètement les rideaux; **prices go all the w. from 200 to 1,000 dollars** les prix vont de 200 à 1000 dollars; *Fig* **I'm with you all the w.** je vous suis *ou* je vous soutiens jusqu'au bout; *Fam* **to go all the w. (with sb)** aller jusqu'au bout (avec qn)

• **along the way** ADV en route; *Fig* **their project had some problems along the w.** leur projet a connu quelques problèmes en cours de route

• **by a long way** ADV **I prefer chess by a long w.** je préfère de loin les échecs; **this is bigger by a long w.** c'est nettement *ou* beaucoup plus grand; **he's not as capable as you are by a long w.** il est loin d'être aussi compétent que toi; **is your project ready? – not by a long w.!** ton projet est-il prêt? – loin de là!

• **by the way** ADV *(incidentally)* à propos; **by the w., where did he go?** à propos, où est-il allé?; **I bring up this point by the w.** je signale ce point au passage *ou* en passant ADJ *(incidental)* secondaire; **that point is quite by the w.** ce détail est tout à fait secondaire

• **by way of** PREP **1** *(via)* par, via; **to go by w. of Brussels** passer par Bruxelles

2 *(as a means of)* **by w. of illustration** à titre d'exemple; **she outlined the situation by w. of**

introduction elle a présenté un aperçu de la situation en guise d'introduction; **they receive money by w. of grants** ils reçoivent de l'argent sous forme de bourses

• **either way** ADV **1** *(in either case)* dans les deux cas; **either w. I lose** dans les deux cas, je suis perdant; **there's nothing in it either w.** c'est pareil; **shall we take the car or the bus? – I don't mind either w.** tu préfères prendre la voiture ou le bus? – n'importe, ça m'est égal

2 *(more or less)* en plus ou en moins; **a few days either w. could make all the difference** quelques jours en plus ou en moins pourraient tout changer

3 *(in either direction)* **the match could have gone either w.** le match était serré

• **in such a way as to** CONJ de façon à ce que + *subjunctive*; **she answered in such a w. as to make me understand** elle a répondu de façon à ce que je comprenne

• **in such a way that** CONJ de telle façon *ou* manière que

• **in the way of** PREP **1** *(in the form of)* **she receives little in the w. of salary** son salaire n'est pas bien gros; **what is there in the w. of food?** qu'est-ce qu'il y a à manger?; **he doesn't have much in the w. of brains** il n'a rien dans la tête

2 *(within the context of)* **we met in the w. of business** nous nous sommes rencontrés dans le cadre du travail; **they put me in the w. of making some money** ils m'ont indiqué un moyen de gagner de l'argent

• **no way** ADV *Fam* pas question; **will you do it for me? – no w.!** tu feras ça pour moi? – pas question!; **no w. am I going to tell him!** (il n'est) pas question que je le lui dise!; **there's no w. that's Jeanne Moreau!** tu rigoles?, ce n'est pas Jeanne Moreau!

• **on one's way, on the way** ADJ & ADV **1** *(along the route)* **it's on my w.** c'est sur mon chemin; **to stop on the w.** s'arrêter en chemin; **I'm on my w.!** j'y vais!; **she's on her w. home** elle rentre chez elle; **he's on his w. to Paris** il est en route pour Paris; **on his w. to town/to work he met his father** en allant en ville/au travail, il a rencontré son père; **we must be on our w.** il faut que nous y allions; **to go one's w.** repartir, reprendre son chemin

2 *Fig* **she has a baby on the w.** elle attend un bébé; **her second book is on the w.** *(being written)* elle a presque fini d'écrire son deuxième livre; *(being published)* son deuxième livre est sur le point de paraître; **she's on the w. to success** elle est sur le chemin de la réussite; **the patient is on the w. to recovery** le malade est en voie de guérison; **she's (well) on the w. to becoming president** elle est en bonne voie de devenir président; **the new school is well on the w. to being finished** la nouvelle école est presque terminée

• **one way and another** ADV en fin de compte

• **one way or the other, one way or another** ADV **1** *(by whatever means)* d'une façon ou d'une autre; **one w. or the other I'm going to get that job!** d'une façon ou d'une autre, j'aurai ce boulot!

2 *(expressing impartiality or indifference)* **I've nothing to say one w. or the other** je n'ai rien à dire, ni pour ni contre; **it doesn't matter to them one w. or the other** ça leur est égal

3 *(more or less)* **a month one w. or the other** un mois de plus ou de moins

• **out of one's way** ADV **to go out of one's w.** faire un détour; **I don't want to take you out of your w.** je ne veux pas vous faire faire un détour; *Fig* **don't go out of your w. for me!** ne vous dérangez pas pour moi!; *Fig* **she went out of her w. to find me a job** elle s'est donné du mal pour me trouver du travail

• **under way** ADJ **to be under w.** *(person, vehicle)* être en route; *Fig (meeting, talks, project)* être en cours **the meeting was already under w.** la réunion avait déjà commencé ADV **to get under w.** *(person, train)* se mettre en route, partir; *(car)* se mettre en route, démarrer; *Fig (meeting, plans, talks)* démarrer; **they got the plans under w.** ils ont mis le projet en route; **the captain got (the ship) under w.** le capitaine a appareillé; **the ship got under w.** le navire a appareillé *ou* a levé l'ancre

▸▸ *Am* ***way station*** *Rail* petite gare *f*; *Fig* étape *f*; **a w. station on the road to success** une étape sur la route du succès

waybill [ˈweɪbɪl] N feuille *f* de route, lettre *f* de voiture

wayfarer [ˈweɪfeərə(r)] N voyageur(euse) *m,f*

wayfaring [ˈweɪfeərɪŋ] N *(UNCOUNT)* voyages *mpl*

ADJ voyageur; **a w. life** une vie de voyages; **w. man** voyageur *m* (à pied)

waylay [ˌweɪˈleɪ] *(pt & pp* **waylaid** [-ˈleɪd]*)* VT *(attack)* attaquer, assaillir; *(stop)* intercepter, arrêter (au passage); **sorry I'm late, I got waylaid** excuse mon retard, quelqu'un m'a arrêté au passage *ou* je me suis fait harponner

way-out ADJ *Fam* **1** *(unusual ▸ film, style)* bizarre▫, curieux▫; *(▸ person)* excentrique▫, bizarre▫ **2** *Old-fashioned (excellent)* géant

wayside [ˈweɪsaɪd] N bord *m ou* côté *m* de la route

ADJ au bord de la route; **a w. inn** une auberge au bord de la route; **w. flowers** les fleurs qui bordent la route

wayward [ˈweɪwəd] ADJ **1** *(person ▸ wilful)* entêté, têtu; *(▸ unpredictable)* qui n'en fait qu'à sa tête, imprévisible; *(behaviour)* imprévisible; *(horse)* rétif **2** *(fate)* fâcheux, malencontreux **3** *(shot, pass)* manqué

waywardness [ˈweɪwədnɪs] N *(wilfulness)* entêtement *m*; *(unpredictability)* caractère *m* imprévisible; **a certain w. became apparent in his character** il est apparu comme quelqu'un qui n'en faisait qu'à sa tête

wazz [wæz] *Br Fam* N **to have/go for a w.** faire/aller faire la petite commission

VI faire la petite commission

wazzock [ˈwæzək] N *Br Fam* andouille *f*, cloche *f*

WC [ˌdʌbəljuːˈsiː] N *(abbr* **water closet***)* W-C *mpl*

w/e *(written abbr* **week ending***)* semaine se terminant

we [wiː] PRON **1** *(oneself and others)* nous; **we went for a walk** nous sommes allés nous promener; **we all stood up** nous nous sommes tous levés; **we both thank you** nous vous remercions tous (les) deux; **we, the people** nous, le peuple; **we Democrats believe that…** nous, les démocrates, croyons que…; **as we say back home** comme on dit chez nous; **as we will see in chapter two** comme nous le verrons *ou* comme on le verra dans le chapitre deux; **you don't think that WE did it!** vous ne pensez pas que c'est nous qui l'avons fait?; **we all make mistakes** tout le monde peut se tromper **2** *Formal (royal)* nous; **the royal we** le nous *ou* le pluriel de majesté **3** *Fam (you)* **and how are we today, John?** alors, comment ça va aujourd'hui, John?▫

weak [wiːk] ADJ **1** *(physically ▸ animal, person)* faible; *(▸ health)* fragile, délicat; *(▸ eyes, hearing)* faible, mauvais; **to become** *or* **to get** *or* **to grow w.** *or* **weaker** s'affaiblir; **we were w. with** *or* **from hunger** nous étions affaiblis par la faim; **he felt w. with fear** il avait les jambes molles de peur; **I went w. at the knees** mes jambes se sont dérobées sous moi, j'avais les jambes en coton; *Br* **it's always the weakest who go to the wall** ce sont toujours les plus faibles qui trinquent; *Pej* **the weaker sex** le sexe faible

2 *(morally, mentally)* mou (molle), faible; **he's far too w. to be a leader** il est beaucoup trop mou pour être dirigeant; **in a w. moment** dans un moment de faiblesse; **to be w. in the head** être faible d'esprit

3 *(feeble ▸ argument, excuse)* faible, peu convaincant; *(▸ army, government, institution)* faible, impuissant; *(▸ structure)* fragile, peu solide; *(▸ light, signal, currency, economy)* faible; *(market)* en baisse, baissier; **she managed a w. smile** elle a réussi à sourire faiblement; **she answered in a w. voice** elle répondit d'une voix faible; **to have a w. hand** *(in cards)* avoir des cartes faibles; **he's the w.** *or* **weakest link (in the chain)** c'est lui le maillon faible de la chaîne

4 *(deficient, poor ▸ pupil)* faible; **geography is my w. subject** mon point faible, c'est la géographie; **she's rather w. on discipline** elle est plutôt laxiste

5 *(chin)* fuyant; *(mouth)* tombant

6 *(acid, solution)* faible; *(drink, tea)* léger; *Aut & Tech (mixture)* pauvre

7 *Gram & Ling (verb)* faible, régulier; *(syllable)* faible, inaccentué

NPL **the w.** les faibles *mpl*

weaken [ˈwiːkən] VT **1** *(person)* affaiblir; *(heart)* fatiguer; *(health)* miner

2 *(government, institution, team)* affaiblir

3 *(argument)* enlever du poids *ou* de la force à *(position)* affaiblir; *(determination)* affaiblir, faire fléchir

4 *(structure)* affaiblir, rendre moins solide *(foundations, cliff)* miner, saper

5 *Fin (currency)* affaiblir, faire baisser; *(market prices)* faire fléchir

VI **1** *(person ▸ physically)* s'affaiblir, faiblir; *(▸ morally)* faiblir; *(voice, health, determination)* faiblir; **he finally weakened and gave in** il s'est finalement laissé fléchir et a cédé

2 *(influence, power)* diminuer, baisser

3 *(structure)* faiblir, devenir moins solide

4 *Fin (currency)* s'affaiblir, baisser; *(market prices)* fléchir; **the pound has weakened against the dollar** la livre est en baisse par rapport au dollar

weakening [ˈwiːkənɪŋ] ADJ **1** *(debilitating)* affaiblissant **2** *(losing strength)* faiblissant

N **1** *(of person, resolve)* affaiblissement *m* **2** *(of structure)* fléchissement *m*, affaiblissement *m* *Fin (of currency)* fléchissement *m*, affaiblissement *m*

weakhearted [wiːkˈhɑːtɪd] ADJ sans courage

weak-kneed [-niːd] ADJ *Fam* mou (molle)▫, lâche▫

weakling [ˈwiːklɪŋ] N **1** *(physically)* gringalet *m* petite nature *f* **2** *(morally)* faible *mf*, mauviette *f*

weakly [ˈwiːklɪ] *(compar* **weaklier**, *superl* **weakliest***)* ADJ *(person)* débile, chétif

ADV *(get up, walk)* faiblement; *(speak, protest)* faiblement, mollement

weak-minded ADJ **1** *(not intelligent)* faible ou simple d'esprit **2** *(lacking willpower)* faible, irrésolu

weakness [ˈwiːknɪs] N **1** *(of person ▸ physical)* faiblesse *f*; *(▸ moral)* point *m* faible; **in a moment of w.** dans un moment de faiblesse; **he has a w. for sports cars** il a un faible pour les voitures de sport

2 *(of government, institution)* faiblesse *f*, fragilité *f*

3 *(of structure)* fragilité *f*

4 *Fin (of currency)* faiblesse *f*

weak-willed ADJ faible, velléitaire

weal [wiːl] N **1** *(mark)* marque *f* de coup, zébrure *f*; **his back was covered in weals** il avait le dos couvert de traces de coups **2** *Arch or Literary (well being)* bien *m*, bonheur *m*; **the common** *or* **public w.** le bien public

wealth [welθ] N *(UNCOUNT)* **1** *(richness ▸ of family, person)* richesse *f*, richesses *fpl*, fortune *f*; *(▸ of nation)* richesse *f*, prospérité *f*; **a young woman of great w.** une jeune femme très fortunée *(large amount ▸ of details, ideas)* abondance *f*, profusion *f*; **a w. of knowledge about Egyptian art** une profonde connaissance de l'art égyptien; **she has had a w. of opportunities to prove** elle a eu plein d'occasions de le prouver

▸▸ ***wealth creation*** création *f* de richesses; ***wealth distribution*** répartition *f* des richesses; *Fin* ***wealth tax*** impôt *m* de solidarité sur la fortune

wealth-creating [-kriːˈeɪtɪŋ] ADJ générateur de richesses

wealthy [ˈwelθɪ] *(compar* **wealthier**, *superl* **wealthiest***)* ADJ *(person)* riche, fortuné; *(country)* riche; **a w. heiress** une riche héritière

NPL **the w.** les riches *mpl*

wean [wiːn] VT *(baby)* sevrer; **youngsters today are being weaned on computers** les jeunes d'aujourd'hui sont nourris d'informatique; **she has been weaned on Mozart** elle a grandi sur les airs de Mozart

weaner [ˈwiːnə(r)] N *(pig)* = porcelet venant d'être sevré et pesant moins de 40 kg

weaning [ˈwiːnɪŋ] N sevrage *m*

ADJ *(animal)* en sevrage

weapon ['wepən] N also Fig arme f; weapons of mass destruction armes fpl de destruction massive; carrying a w. is illegal le port d'armes est illégal; Fig patience is your best w. in this situation la patience est votre meilleure arme dans cette situation

▸▸ *weapons inspector* inspecteur m du désarmement; *weapon system* dispositif m ou système m militaire

weaponry ['wepənrɪ] N (UNCOUNT) armes fpl; Mil matériel m de guerre, armements mpl

WEAR [weə(r)]

VT
- porter 1
- avoir 2
- afficher 2
- user 3

VI
- durer 1
- s'user 2
- passer 3

N
- vêtements 1
- usage 2
- usure 3

(pt wore [wɔː(r)], pp worn [wɔːn])

VT 1 (beard, glasses, clothing etc) porter; what shall I w.? qu'est-ce que je vais mettre?; I haven't a thing to w. je n'ai rien à me mettre; she wore a dress elle portait une robe, elle était en robe; Aut to w. a seat belt mettre la ceinture (de sécurité); to w. black porter du noir; the miniskirt is being worn again this year la minijupe se porte de nouveau cette année; he always wears good clothes il est toujours bien habillé; he was wearing slippers/a dressing gown il était en chaussons/en robe de chambre; he wears a beard il porte la barbe; she wears her hair in a bun elle a un chignon; he wears his hair long il a les cheveux longs; do you always w. make-up? tu te maquilles tous les jours?; she wore lipstick elle s'était mis du rouge à lèvres; I often w. perfume/aftershave je mets souvent du parfum/de la lotion après-rasage

2 (expression) avoir, afficher; (smile) arborer; he wore an anxious look il avait l'air inquiet; he wore a frown il fronçait les sourcils

3 (make by rubbing) user; to w. holes in sth trouer ou percer peu à peu qch; her shoes were worn thin ses chaussures étaient complètement usées; he wore his coat threadbare il a usé son manteau jusqu'à la corde; the wheel had worn a groove in the wood la roue avait creusé le bois

4 Br Fam (accept ▸ argument, behaviour) supporter□, tolérer□; I won't w. it! je ne marcherai pas!

5 (idioms) to w. oneself to a frazzle or a shadow s'éreinter

VI 1 (endure, last) durer; wool wears better than cotton la laine résiste mieux à l'usure que le coton; this coat has worn well ce manteau a bien servi; this rug should w. for years ce tapis devrait faire des années; it will w. forever c'est inusable; Fig their friendship has worn well leur amitié est restée intacte malgré le temps; the film has not worn well le film n'a pas bien vieilli; Br Fam she's worn well elle est bien conservée

2 (be damaged through use) s'user; this rug has worn badly in the middle ce tapis est très usé au milieu; the carpet had worn thin le tapis était usé ou élimé; the stone had worn smooth la pierre était polie par le temps; Fig her patience was wearing thin elle était presque à bout de patience; his excuses/jokes are wearing a bit thin ses excuses ne prennent plus/ses plaisanteries ne sont plus drôles

3 Literary (time) passer; as morning wore into afternoon comme la matinée passait ou l'après-midi approchait; as the year wore to its close comme l'année tirait à sa fin

N (UNCOUNT) 1 (of clothes) for everyday w. pour porter tous les jours; clothes suitable for evening w. tenue f de soirée; a suit for business w. un costume pour le bureau; women's w. vêtements mpl pour femmes; winter w. vêtements mpl d'hiver

2 (use) usage m; these shoes will stand hard w. ces chaussures feront un bon usage ou résisteront bien à l'usure; there's still plenty of w. in that dress cette robe peut tout à fait encore être portée; to get a lot of w. from or out of sth faire durer qch; is there any w. left in them? feront-ils encore de l'usage?

3 (deterioration) w. (and tear) usure f; Acct w. and tear dépréciation f fonctionnelle; fair or normal w. and tear usure f normale; living in the big city puts a lot of w. and tear on people les grandes villes sont une source de stress pour leurs habitants; the sheets are beginning to show signs of w. les draps commencent à être un peu usés

▸ **wear away** VT SEP (soles) user; (cliff, land) ronger, éroder; (stone) éroder; (paint, design) effacer

VI (metal) s'user; (land) être rongé, s'éroder; (grass, topsoil) disparaître (par usure); (stone) s'éroder; (design) s'effacer

▸ **wear down** VT SEP (steps) user; Fig (patience, strength) épuiser petit à petit; (courage, resistance) saper, miner; in the end she wore me down (I gave in to her) elle a fini par me faire céder; the busy schedule finally wore her down son emploi du temps chargé a fini par l'épuiser

VI (pencil, steps, tyres) s'user; (courage) s'épuiser; the heels have worn down les talons sont usés

▸ **wear off** VI 1 (marks, design) s'effacer, disparaître 2 (excitement) s'apaiser, passer; (anaesthetic, effects) se dissiper; (pain) se calmer, passer; the novelty soon wore off l'attrait de la nouveauté a vite passé

VT SEP effacer par l'usure, user

▸ **wear on** VI (day, season) avancer lentement; (battle, discussion) se poursuivre lentement; as time wore on au fur et à mesure que le temps passait

▸ **wear out** VT SEP 1 (clothing, machinery) user 2 (patience, strength, reserves) épuiser; to w. out one's welcome abuser de l'hospitalité de ses hôtes 3 (tire) épuiser; you're wearing yourself out working so hard tu t'épuises ou tu t'exténues à tant travailler; to be worn out être exténué ou éreinté; worn out from arguing, he finally accepted their offer de guerre lasse, il a fini par accepter leur offre

VI (clothing, shoes) s'user; this material will never w. out ce tissu est inusable

wearable ['weərəbəl] ADJ portable

wearer ['weərə(r)] N good news for wearers of glasses bonnes nouvelles pour les personnes qui portent des lunettes; designed with the w.'s comfort in mind conçu pour le confort de celui qui le portera

wearily ['wɪərɪlɪ] ADV avec lassitude; "all right, if I must," she said w. "bien, s'il le faut", dit-elle d'un ton las; he smiled w. il sourit d'un air fatigué

weariness ['wɪərɪnɪs] N 1 (tiredness) lassitude f, fatigue f 2 (discontent) lassitude f, ennui m

wearing ['weərɪŋ] ADJ fatigant, épuisant; their company is rather w. je trouve leur présence assez pénible

wearisome ['wɪərɪsəm] ADJ 1 (tiring) fatigant, épuisant 2 (annoying) ennuyeux, lassant

weary ['wɪərɪ] (compar wearier, superl weariest, pt & pp wearied) ADJ 1 (tired ▸ physically, morally) las (lasse), fatigué; she grew w. of reading elle s'est lassée de lire; I'm w. of his silly jokes j'en ai assez de ses plaisanteries stupides; he gave a w. sigh il a soupiré d'un air las; he spoke in a w. voice il parlait d'une voix lasse; I'm w. of life j'en ai assez ou je suis las de la vie 2 (tiring ▸ day, journey) fatigant, lassant

VT (tire) fatiguer, lasser; (annoy) lasser, agacer

VI se lasser

Attention: ne pas confondre avec wary.

wearying ['wɪərɪɪŋ] ADJ fatigant, ennuyeux; I find her quite w. je la trouve très pénible; I find it very w. cela me fatigue beaucoup

weasel ['wiːzəl] N 1 Zool belette f 2 Pej (person) fouine f

VI Am ruser; (in speaking) parler d'une façon ambiguë

VT he weaseled his way into the conversation il s'est insinué dans la conversation

▸▸ *weasel words* paroles fpl ambiguës ou équivoques, discours m ambigu ou équivoque

▸ **weasel out** VI Am Fam he weaseled out of the contract il s'est débrouillé pour se dégager du contrat; she always weasels out of doing the dishes elle se débrouille toujours pour échapper à la vaisselle

weather ['weðə(r)] N 1 Met temps m; (forecast) météo f; what's the w. like? quel temps fait-il?; it's beautiful/terrible w. il fait beau/mauvais; the w. is awful or foul il fait un temps de chien; w. permitting si le temps le permet; surely you're not going out in this w.? vous n'allez tout de même pas sortir par un temps pareil?; we had good w. for the time of year nous avons eu du beau temps pour la saison; in hot w. par temps chaud, en période de chaleur; in all weathers par tous les temps 2 (idioms) Fam to feel under the w. ne pas être dans son assiette; Fam keep your w. eye open! veillez au grain!; Fam I'll keep a w. eye on the kids je vais surveiller les enfants□

VT 1 (survive ▸ storm) réchapper à; (▸ crisis) survivre à, réchapper à; the ship weathered the storm le navire a traversé la tempête; Fig will he w. the storm? va-t-il se tirer d'affaire ou tenir le coup? 2 (wood) exposer aux intempéries; (rock) éroder

VI (bronze, wood) se patiner; (rock) s'éroder; this paint weathers well cette peinture résiste bien aux intempéries

▸▸ *weather balloon* ballon-sonde m; *weather bulletin* bulletin m météorologique; Am *weather bureau* ≃ office m national de la météorologie; Br *weather centre* ≃ centre m météorologique régional; the London w. centre la station de météorologie de Londres; *weather chart* carte f météorologique; *weather conditions* conditions fpl météo; *weather deck* (on ship) pont m découvert; (on bus) impériale f découverte; *weather forecast* prévisions fpl météorologiques, météo f; what's the w. forecast for tomorrow? quelle est la météo pour demain?; *weather map* carte f météorologique; *weather report* bulletin m météorologique; *weather satellite* satellite m météorologique; *weather ship* navire m météorologique; *weather side* (of house etc) côté m exposé au vent; Naut bord m du vent; *weather station* station f ou observatoire m météorologique; *weather strip* (for door, window) bourrelet m isolant, calfeutrage m; *weather vane* girouette f; *weather warning* alerte f météorologique; to issue a w. warning lancer une alerte météorologique

weather-beaten ADJ (face, person) buriné; (building, stone) dégradé par les intempéries

weatherboarding ['weðəbɔːdɪŋ] N (UNCOUNT) planches fpl à recouvrement

weather-bound ADJ (aircraft, ship) immobilisé par le mauvais temps; (event) reporté pour cause de mauvais temps

weathercock ['weðəkɒk] N also Fig girouette f

weathergirl ['weðəgɜːl] N présentatrice f de la météo

weathering ['weðərɪŋ] N désagrégation f, érosion f

weatherman ['weðəmæn] (pl weathermen [-men]) N the w. le météorologue, le météorologiste; Rad & TV le journaliste météo

weatherproof ['weðəpruːf] ADJ (paint, coating) résistant à l'eau; (clothing) imperméable; (building, windows) étanche; (equipment, machinery) qui résiste aux intempéries

VT (paint, coating, clothing) imperméabiliser; (building, windows) rendre étanche; (equipment, machinery) traiter à l'antirouille

weave [wiːv] (vt senses 1, 2, 3 & vi senses 1 & 2 pt wove [wəʊv], pp woven ['wəʊvən], vt sense 4 & vi sense 3 pt & pp weaved) VT 1 (cloth, web) tisser; (basket, garland) tresser; she wove the strands together into a necklace elle a tressé ou entrelacé les fils pour en faire un collier

2 (story) tramer, bâtir; (plot) tisser, tramer; also Fig to w. a spell over sb ensorceler qn, jeter un sort à qn; a tightly woven plot une intrigue bien ficelée

3 (introduce) introduire, incorporer; he managed to w. all the facts together to make a fascinating report il a réussi à incorporer tous les faits dans un rapport passionnant

4 (as verb of movement) he weaved his way across the crowd/towards the bar il s'est frayé un chemin à travers la foule/vers le bar; the cyclist

weaved his way through the traffic le cycliste se faufilait entre les voitures

VI 1 *Tex* tisser **2** *(road, river)* serpenter **3** *(as verb of movement)* se faufiler, se glisser; **to w. in and out of the crowd** se faufiler dans la foule; **the boxer ducked and weaved** le boxeur a esquivé tous les coups; *Fam* **come on, get weaving!** allons, grouillez-vous!

N tissage *m*

weaver ['wi:və(r)] **N 1** *Tex* tisserand(e) *m,f* **2** *Orn* tisserin *m*

weaving ['wi:vɪŋ] **N 1** *(of cloth)* tissage *m*; *(of baskets, garlands)* tressage *m* **2** *(of story)* récit *m*; *(of plot)* trame *f*

COMP *(industry, mill)* de tissage

Web [web] **N** *Comput* **the W.** le Web, *Offic* la Toile

▸▸ ***Web authoring*** création *f* de pages Web; ***Web authoring tool*** outil *m* de création de pages Web; ***Web browser*** navigateur *m*, logiciel *m* de navigation; ***Web consultancy*** société *f* conseil pour la création et l'administration de sites Web; ***Web designer*** concepteur(trice) *m,f* de sites Web; ***Web hosting*** hébergement *m* de sites Web; ***Web master*** Webmaster *m*, Webmestre *m*, responsable *mf* de site Web; ***Web page*** page *f* Web; ***Web server*** serveur *m* Web; ***Web site*** site *m* Web; ***Web space*** espace *m* Web

web [web] **N 1** *(of fabric, metal)* tissu *m*; *(of spider)* toile *f*; *Fig (of lies)* tissu *m*; *(of intrigue)* réseau *m* **2** *(on feet ▸ of duck, frog)* palmure *f*; *(▸ of humans)* palmature *f*

▸▸ *Typ* ***web press*** rotative *f*

webbed [webd] **ADJ** palmé; **to have w. feet** *(duck, frog)* avoir les pattes palmées; *(human)* avoir une palmature

webbing ['webɪŋ] **N** *(UNCOUNT)* **1** *Tex (material)* toile *f* à sangles; *(on chair)* sangles *fpl* **2** *Anat (animal)* palmure *f*; *(human)* palmature *f*

webcam [webkæm] **N** *Comput* webcam *f*, caméra *f* Internet

webcast ['webkɑ:st] *Comput* **N** webcast *m*

VT diffuser sur Internet

webcasting ['webkɑ:stɪŋ] **N** *Comput* diffusion *f* sur Internet

web-footed [-'fʊtɪd] **ADJ** *(duck, frog)* palmipède, qui a les pattes palmées; *(human)* qui a une palmature

weblog ['weblɒg] **N** *Comput* weblog *m*

webmail ['webmeɪl] **N** *Comput* webmail *m*

webmaster ['web,mɑ:stə(r)] **N** *Comput* Webmaster *m*, Webmestre *m*, responsable *mf* de site Web

web-offset printing **N** impression *f* (offset) continue

website ['websaɪt] **N** site *m* Web

webzine ['webzi:n] **N** *Comput* webzine *m*

Wed. *(written abbr* **Wednesday***)* mer

we'd [wi:d] **1** = **we would 2** = **we had**

wed [wed] *(pt & pp* **wed** *or* **wedded**, *cont* **wedding***)* **VT** *Literary* **1** *(marry)* épouser, se marier avec; **to get w.** se marier **2** *(of clergyman)* marier **3** *(usu passive) (unite, combine)* allier; **intelligence wedded to beauty** l'intelligence alliée à la beauté; **he's wedded to the cause** il est véritablement marié à cette cause; **the fate of the project was wedded to that of the Chairman** la destinée du projet était liée à celle du Président

VI *(in headline)* se marier; **PM's son to w.** le fils du Premier ministre se marie

wedded ['wedɪd] **ADJ** *(person)* marié; *(bliss, life)* conjugal; **her lawful w. husband** son époux légitime; **the newly w. couple** les jeunes mariés *mpl*

wedding ['wedɪŋ] **N 1** *(marriage)* mariage *m*, noces *fpl*; **to have a church w.** se marier à l'église; **we had a quiet w.** nous nous sommes mariés dans l'intimité **2** *(uniting)* union *f*

COMP *(night)* de noces; *(ceremony, photograph, present)* de mariage

▸▸ ***wedding anniversary*** anniversaire *m* de mariage; ***wedding band*** alliance *f*, anneau *m* de mariage; ***wedding breakfast*** repas *m* de noces; ***wedding cake*** gâteau *m* de noces, ≃ pièce *f* montée; ***wedding day*** jour *m* du mariage; **on their w. day** le jour de leur mariage; ***wedding dress*** robe *f* de mariée; ***wedding guest*** invité(e) *m,f (au mariage)*; ***wedding invitation*** invitation *f* de mariage; ***wedding list*** liste *f* de mariage; ***wedding march*** marche *f* nuptiale; ***wedding planner*** organisateur(trice) *m,f* de mariages; ***wedding reception*** réception *f* de mariage; ***wedding ring*** alliance *f*, anneau *m* de mariage; ***wedding singer*** = chanteur qui anime les mariages; *Fam Hum* ***wedding tackle*** *(man's genitals)* bijoux *mpl* de famille

wedge [wedʒ] **N 1** *(under door, wheel)* cale *f*; **put a w. under the door** calez la porte, mettez une cale sous la porte; *Fig* **their political differences drove a w. between the two friends** les deux amis se sont brouillés à cause de leurs divergences politiques

2 *(for splitting wood)* coin *m*

3 *(of cheese, cake, pie)* morceau *m*, part *f*

4 *(golf club)* cale *f*

5 *(for climber)* coin *m*

6 *(shoe heel)* semelle *f* compensée; *(shoe)* chaussure *f* à semelle compensée

7 *Br Fam (money)* fric *m*, flouze *m*, pognon *m*

VT 1 *(make fixed or steady)* caler; **the window was wedged open** la fenêtre était maintenue ouverte à l'aide d'une cale; **I wedged the door open/shut** j'ai maintenu la porte ouverte/fermée par une cale; **w. the table with something, it's wobbling** mets une cale sous la table, elle est branlante **2** *(squeeze, push)* enfoncer; **to w. sth apart** fendre *ou* forcer qch; **he wedged his foot in the door** il a bloqué la porte avec son pied; **she sat wedged between her two aunts** elle était assise coincée entre ses deux tantes; **I found the ring wedged down behind the cushion** j'ai trouvé la bague enfoncée derrière le coussin

▸▸ ***wedge heel*** semelle *f* compensée

wedge-shaped **ADJ** en forme de coin

wedgie ['wedʒi:] **N** *Fam* **1** *(shoe)* chaussure *f* à semelle compensée◻ **2** *Hum* **to give sb a w.** = tirer le slip de qn pour le lui faire rentrer dans les fesses; **I've got a w.** j'ai mon slip coincé entre les fesses◻

wedlock ['wedlɒk] **N** *Formal* mariage *m*; **to be born out of w.** être un enfant naturel, être né hors du mariage

Wednesday ['wenzdɪ] **N** mercredi *m*; *see also* **Friday**

wee [wi:] **ADJ** *esp Scot* petit; **a w. bit** un peu; **a w. drop of whisky** une larme de whisky; **in the w. (small) hours of the morning** au petit matin; **a w. boy** un petit garçon

VI *Fam* faire pipi

N *Fam* pipi *m*; **to have a w.** faire pipi

weed [wi:d] **N 1** *(plant)* mauvaise herbe *f*; **that plant grows like a w.** cette plante pousse comme du chiendent

2 *Pej (person ▸ physically)* gringalet *m*; *(▸ in character)* mauviette *f*

3 *Fam (tobacco)* **the w.** le tabac◻; **I've given up the w.** j'ai arrêté de fumer◻

4 *Fam Drugs slang (marijuana)* herbe *f*

VT désherber, arracher les mauvaises herbes de; *(with hoe)* sarcler

VI désherber, arracher les mauvaises herbes; *(with hoe)* sarcler

• **weeds** **NPL** vêtements *mpl* de deuil; **in widow's weeds** en deuil

▸**weed out** **VT SEP** éliminer; *(troublemakers)* expulser; **to w. out the bad from the good** faire le tri

weeding ['wi:dɪŋ] **N** désherbage *m*; *(with hoe)* sarclage *m*; **he does a little w. every day** il désherbe un peu tous les jours

weedkiller ['wi:d,kɪlə(r)] **N** herbicide *m*, désherbant *m*

weedy ['wi:dɪ] *(compar* **weedier**, *superl* **weediest***)* **ADJ 1** *(ground)* couvert de *ou* envahi par les mauvaises herbes **2** *Fam Pej (person ▸ physically)* gringalet, malingre◻; *(▸ in character)* faible◻, mou

weegie [wi:dʒɪ] **N** *Scot Fam Pej (inhabitant of Glasgow)* habitant(e) *m,f* de Glasgow◻; *(native of Glasgow)* originaire *mf* de Glasgow◻

week [wi:k] **N** semaine *f*; **next/last w.** la semaine prochaine/dernière; **see you next w.** à la semaine prochaine; **in one w., in one w.'s time** dans huit jours, d'ici une semaine; **two weeks ago** il y a deux semaines *ou* quinze jours; **a w. ago today** il y a (aujourd'hui) huit jours; **within a w.** *(gen)* dans la semaine, d'ici une semaine; *Admin Com* sous huitaine; **w. ending 25 March** la se maine du 25 mars; **a w. (from) today** d'ici hu jours; **a w. (from) tomorrow** demain en huit; **ye terday w., a w. yesterday** il y a eu une semain hier; **Monday w., a w. on Monday** lundi en hui **twice a w.** deux fois par semaine; **w. in w. ou w. after w.** semaine après semaine; **from w. t w.** de semaine en semaine; **it rained for week on end** il a plu pendant des semaines; **I haven seen you in** *or* **for weeks** ça fait des semaine que je ne t'ai pas vu; **we're taking a w.'s holida** nous prenons huit jours de congé; **the workir w.** la semaine de travail; **a forty-hour/five-da w.** une semaine de quarante heures/de cin jours; **she's paid by the w.** elle est payée à la se maine; **I lost a w.'s pay** j'ai perdu une semaine c salaire

weekday ['wi:k,deɪ] **N** jour *m* de la semain *Admin & Com* jour *m* ouvrable; **on weekdays** e semaine; **weekdays only** sauf samedi et dima che

COMP *(activities)* de la semaine; **on w. morning** le matin en semaine

weekend [,wi:k'end] **N** week-end *m*, fin *f* de se maine; *Br* **at** *or Am* **on the w.** le week-end; **have good w.!** bon week-end!, bonne fin de semaine **I'll do it at the w.** je le ferai pendant le week-en **what do you do at weekends?** que fais-tu (pe dant) le week-end *ou* les week-ends?; **what a you doing at the w.?** qu'est-ce que tu fais c week-end?; **he's staying with them for the w.** passe le week-end chez eux; **I'm going away fo the w.** je pars en week-end; **a long w.** un wee end prolongé

COMP *(schedule, visit)* de *ou* du week-end; *(gol er, rugby player)* qui ne joue que le week-end

VI passer le week-end

▸▸ ***weekend bag*** sac *m* de voyage; ***weeken break*** = séjour d'un week-end; ***weekend cottag*** maison *f* secondaire *ou* de campagne *(où c passe le week-end)*

weekender [,wi:k'endə(r)] **N** = personne e voyage pour le week-end; **he's one of the weel enders who come here to ski** il fait partie des gen qui viennent skier ici le week-end; **most of th cottages belong to weekenders** la plupart de maisons sont des résidences secondaires

weekly ['wi:klɪ] *(pl* **weeklies***)* **ADJ** *(visit, meeting* de la semaine, hebdomadaire; *(publicatio payment, wage)* hebdomadaire; *(tenant)* à la se maine; **these incidents were an almost w. occu rence** ces incidents avaient lieu presqu chaque semaine

N hebdomadaire *m*; **the weeklies** la presse heb domadaire

ADV *(once a week)* chaque semaine, une fois pa semaine; *(each week)* chaque semaine, tous le huit jours; **twice w.** deux fois par semaine; **he paid w.** il est payé à la semaine

weeknight ['wi:knaɪt] **N** soir *m* de la semaine; **can't go out on weeknights** je ne peux pas sort le soir en semaine

weenie ['wi:nɪ] **N** *Am Fam* **1** *(frankfurter)* sau cisse *f* (de Francfort)◻ **2** *(penis)* zizi *m*; **to pla hide the w.** *(have sex)* s'envoyer en l'air **3** *(person* imbécile *mf*

weeny ['wi:nɪ] *(compar* **weenier**, *superl* **weenies** **ADJ** *Fam* tout petit◻, minuscule◻

weenybopper ['wi:nɪ,bɒpə(r)] **N** *Fam* = gamin férue de musique pop

weep [wi:p] *(pt & pp* **wept** [wept]*)* **VI 1** *(person* pleurer, verser des larmes; **to w. for joy/wit vexation** pleurer de joie/de dépit; **she wept fo her lost youth** elle pleurait sa jeunesse perdue **to w. for sb** pleurer qn; **he wept to see her so ill** a pleuré de la voir si malade; **that's nothing to w about** *or* **over** il n'y a pas de quoi pleurer; *Hum* **it enough to make you w.!** c'est à faire pleurer!; **could have wept!** j'en aurais pleuré! **2** *(walls wound)* suinter

VT *(tears)* verser

N **to have a w.** pleurer, verser quelques larmes

weepie = **weepy N**

weeping ['wi:pɪŋ] **ADJ** *(person)* qui pleure *(walls, wound)* suintant

N *(UNCOUNT)* larmes *fpl*, pleurs *mpl*; **a fit of w**

w. fit une crise de larmes; **we could hear w. rom the next room** on pouvait entendre quelu'un qui pleurait dans la pièce d'à côté
►► *weeping willow* saule *m* pleureur

veepy ['wi:pɪ] (*compar* **weepier**, *superl* **weepiest**, *l* **weepies**) ADJ **1** (*tone, voice*) larmoyant; (*peron*) qui pleure; **she is** *or* **feels w.** elle a envie de leurer, elle est au bord des larmes **2** (*film, story*) entimental, larmoyant
N *Br Fam* (*film*) mélo *m*, film *m* sentimental; *book*) mélo *m*, roman *m* à l'eau de rose

veevil ['wi:vəl] N *Entom* charançon *m*

vee-wee *Br Fam* N pipi *m*; **to go (for a) w.** faire ipi
VI faire pipi

VEF [ˌdʌbəlju:i:'ef] N (*abbr* **World Economic Forum**) orum *m* économique mondial *m*

veft [weft] N *Tex* trame *f*

veigh [weɪ] VT **1** (*person, thing*) peser; **to w. oneelf** se peser; **to w. sth in one's hand** soupeser qch **2** (*consider*) considérer, peser; **let's w. the evidence** considérons les faits; **to w. the consequences** calculer les conséquences; **she weighed her words carefully** elle a bien pesé ses mots; **you have to w. the pros and cons** il faut peser le pour et le contre; **to w. one thing against another** mettre deux choses en balance **3** *Naut* **to w. anchor** lever l'ancre
VI **1** (*person, object*) peser; **how much do you w.?** combien est-ce que tu pèses?, quel poids faisu?; **the fish weighs one kilo** le poisson pèse un kilo; **he doesn't w. much** il ne pèse pas lourd **2** (*influence*) **his silence began to w. (heavy)** son silence commençait à devenir pesant; **his past record weighed against him** son passé a joué en sa défaveur; **her qualifications weighed in her favour** ses qualifications ont fait pencher la balance en sa faveur *ou* ont joué en sa faveur
• **under weigh** ADJ *Naut* appareillé, en marche

weigh down VT SEP **1** faire plier, courber; **the branches were weighed down with snow** les branches ployaient sous le poids de la neige **2** *Fig* **weighed down with debts/with sorrow** accablé de dettes/de tristesse

weigh in VI **1** *Boxing & Horseracing* se faire peser (*avant une épreuve*); **the boxer weighed in at 85 kilos** le boxeur faisait 85 kilos avant le match; **the jockey weighed in at 45 kilos** le jockey pesait 45 kilos avant la course **2** (*join in*) intervenir; **he always has to w. in with his opinions** il faut toujours qu'il intervienne pour imposer ses opinions

weigh into VT INSEP *Br Fam* rentrer dans le lard à

weigh out VT SEP peser; **w. out 200 grams of flour for me** pèse-moi 200 grammes de farine

weigh up VT SEP **1** (*consider*) examiner, calculer; (*compare*) mettre en balance; **to w. up the situation** peser la situation; **I'm weighing up whether to take the job or not** je me demande si je dois prendre le poste; **to w. up one's chances of doing sth** calculer ses chances de faire qch; **to w. up the pros and cons** peser le pour et le contre **2 to w. sb up** (*their character*) estimer la valeur de qn; (*their intentions*) estimer les intentions de qn

veighbridge ['weɪbrɪdʒ] N pont-bascule *m*

veigh-in N *Boxing & Horseracing* pesage *m*, pesée *f*

veighing machine ['weɪɪŋ-] N (*for people*) balance *f*; (*for loads*) bascule *f*

weight [weɪt] N **1** (*of person, package, goods*) poids *m*; **she tested** *or* **felt the w. of the package** elle a soupesé le paquet; **what's your normal w.?** combien pesez-vous *ou* quel poids faites-vous normalement?; **my w. is 50 kg, I'm 50 kilos in w.** je pèse *ou* je fais 50 kilos; **we're the same w.** nous faisons le même poids; **he's twice your w.** il pèse deux fois plus lourd que toi; **to gain** *or* **to put on w.** grossir, prendre du poids; **to lose w.** maigrir, perdre du poids; **she's watching her w.** elle fait attention à sa ligne; **what a w.!** (*person*) qu'il est lourd!; (*stone, parcel*) que c'est lourd!; **that case must be quite a w.** cette valise doit être drôlement lourde; **don't lift any heavy weights** ne soulève pas trop de poids; **to sell sth by w.** vendre qch au poids; **she's worth her w. in gold** elle vaut son pesant d'or; *Hum* **take the w. off your feet** assieds-toi un peu; *Horseracing* **to carry w.** être handicapé
2 (*force*) poids *m*; **he put his full w. behind the blow** il a frappé de toutes ses forces; *Fig* **to pull one's w.** faire sa part du travail; *Fig* **to throw one's w. about** *or* **around** bousculer les gens
3 (*burden*) poids *m*; **the w. of years** le poids des années; **he quailed under the w. of responsibility** le poids de la responsabilité l'a effrayé; **that's a w. off my mind** je suis vraiment soulagé
4 (*importance, influence*) poids *m*, influence *f*; **the facts lend considerable w. to her argument** les faits donnent un poids considérable à son raisonnement; **their opinion carries quite a lot of w.** leur opinion a un poids *ou* une autorité considérable; **she put** *or* **threw all her w. behind the candidate** elle a apporté tout son soutien au candidat
5 (*for scales*) poids *m*; **weights and measures** poids *mpl* et mesures *fpl*; **a set of weights** une série de poids; **a one-kilogramme w.** un poids d'un kilogramme
6 *Sport* poids *m*; **to lift weights** soulever des poids *ou* des haltères
7 (*of clock*) poids *m*; (*for fishing net*) lest *m*
8 *Phys* pesanteur *f*, poids *m*
COMP **to have a w. problem** avoir un problème de poids
VT **1** (*put weights on*) lester **2** (*hold down*) retenir *ou* maintenir avec un poids **3** *Econ* (*index, average*) pondérer; *Fig* **the circumstances are weighted in his favour** les circonstances jouent en sa faveur *ou* lui sont favorables; **the electoral system was weighted against him** le système électoral lui était défavorable *ou* jouait contre lui
►► *weight allowance* (*in aeroplane*) poids *m* de bagages autorisé; *weight charge* taxation *f* au poids; *weight loss* perte *f* de poids; *weight training* entraînement *m* aux haltères

►**weight down** VT SEP **1** (*body, net*) lester **2** (*papers, tarpaulin*) maintenir avec un poids

weighted ['weɪtɪd] ADJ **1** (*body, net*) lesté **2** (*index, average*) pondéré
►► *Fin weighted average* moyenne *f* pondérée; *Acct weighted average cost* coût *m* moyen pondéré

weightily ['weɪtɪlɪ] ADV (*reason*) puissamment, avec force

weighting ['weɪtɪŋ] N **1** (*extra salary*) indemnité *f*, allocation *f* **2** (*of statistics*) pondération *f*; *Sch* coefficient *m*

weightless ['weɪtlɪs] ADJ très léger; *Astron* en état d'apesanteur

weightlessness ['weɪtlɪsnɪs] N extrême légèreté *f*; *Astron & Phys* apesanteur *f*

weightlifter ['weɪtˌlɪftə(r)] N haltérophile *mf*

weightlifting ['weɪtˌlɪftɪŋ] N haltérophilie *f*

weighty ['weɪtɪ] (*compar* **weightier**, *superl* **weightiest**) ADJ **1** (*heavy*) lourd, pesant **2** (*important* ► *responsibility*) lourd; (► *problem*) important, grave; (► *argument, reasoning*) probant, de poids

weir [wɪə(r)] N barrage *m* (*sur un cours d'eau*)

weird [wɪəd] ADJ **1** (*mysterious*) mystérieux, surnaturel **2** *Fam* (*odd*) bizarre, étrange; **he has some w. ideas** il a de drôles d'idées

►**weird out** VT SEP *Am Fam* **to w. sb out** faire flipper qn

weirdie ['wɪədɪ] N *Fam* tordu(e) *m,f*

weirdly ['wɪədlɪ] ADV **1** (*mysteriously*) mystérieusement **2** (*oddly*) bizarrement, singulièrement

weirdness ['wɪədnɪs] N étrangeté *f*, singularité *f*

weirdo ['wɪədəʊ] (*pl* **weirdos**) *Fam* N tordu(e) *m,f*
COMP (*hairdo, clothes*) extravagant; (*habits, ideas*) zarbi

WELCOME ['welkəm]

VT	
• accueillir **1**	• être heureux d'avoir **2**
N	
• accueil	
ADJ	
• bienvenu **1, 2**	• opportun **2**
EXCLAM	
• bienvenue!	

VT **1** (*greet, receive* ► *people*) accueillir; **I welcomed her warmly** je lui ai fait bon accueil *ou* un accueil chaleureux; **they welcomed me in** ils m'ont chaleureusement invité à entrer; **we welcomed him with open arms** nous l'avons accueilli à bras ouverts; **a dinner to w. the new members** un dîner pour accueillir les nouveaux membres; **the dog welcomes them home every evening** le chien leur fait la fête chaque soir lorsqu'ils rentrent; **would you please w. Melissa Harte!** (*to audience*) voulez-vous applaudir Melissa Harte!
2 (*accept gladly*) être heureux d'avoir, recevoir avec plaisir; **I welcomed the opportunity to speak to her** j'étais content d'avoir l'occasion de lui parler; **he welcomed the news** il s'est réjoui de la nouvelle, il a accueilli la nouvelle avec joie; **she welcomed any comments** elle accueillait volontiers les remarques que l'on pouvait lui faire; **his efforts weren't welcomed** ses efforts ont reçu peu d'encouragement; **we'd w. a cup of coffee** nous prendrions volontiers une tasse de café
N accueil *m*; **she said a few words of w.** elle a prononcé quelques mots de bienvenue; **we bid them w.** nous leur souhaitons la bienvenue; **they gave him a warm w.** ils lui ont fait bon accueil *ou* réservé un accueil chaleureux; **we gave her a big w. home** nous lui avons fait fête à son retour à la maison; **let's give a warm w. to Norah Jones!** (*to audience*) applaudissons très fort Norah Jones!; **to overstay** *or* **to outstay one's w.** abuser de l'hospitalité de ses hôtes; **I don't want to outstay my w.** je ne veux pas abuser de sa/votre/*etc* hospitalité
ADJ **1** (*person*) bienvenu; **to be w.** être le bienvenu; **she's always w. here** elle est toujours la bienvenue ici; **they made us very w.** ils nous ont fait un très bon accueil; **she didn't feel very w.** elle s'est sentie de trop; **the card is w. in over 1,000 outlets** la carte est acceptée dans plus de 1000 points de vente
2 (*pleasant, desirable* ► *arrival*) bienvenu; (► *change, interruption, remark*) opportun; **a w. cup of coffee** une bonne tasse de café; **that's w. news** nous sommes heureux de l'apprendre; **that would be most w.** (*food, drink*) ça me ferait le plus grand bien; **their offer was most w.** leur suggestion m'a fait grand plaisir; **this cheque is most w.** ce chèque arrive opportunément *ou* tombe bien; **that's a w. sight!** c'est un spectacle à réjouir le cœur!; **a helping hand is always w.** un coup de main est toujours le bienvenu *ou* ne fait jamais de mal; **the holiday came as a w. break** les vacances ont été une coupure bienvenue *ou* appréciable
3 (*permitted*) **you're w. to join us** n'hésitez pas à vous joindre à nous; **he's w. to borrow my book** qu'il n'hésite pas à emprunter mon livre; **I don't need it, she's w. to it** je n'en ai pas besoin, elle peut bien le prendre *ou* je le lui donne volontiers; **you're w. to anything you need** servez-vous si vous avez besoin de quelque chose; **they're w. to stay with us** ils peuvent venir chez nous; **you're w. to try** je vous en prie, essayez; **he's w. to try!** (*grudgingly*) libre à lui d'essayer!, qu'il essaie donc!; **take it and w.!** je te le donne bien volontiers!
4 (*acknowledgment of thanks*) **you're w.!** je vous en prie!, il n'y a pas de quoi!, **tell her she's w.** dislui que ce n'est rien
EXCLAM bienvenue!, soyez le bienvenu!; **w. back** *or* **home!** content de vous revoir!; **w. to my home!** bienvenue chez moi *ou* à la maison!; **w. to Wales** (*sign*) bienvenue au pays de Galles
►► *welcome committee* comité *m* d'accueil; *welcome mat* paillasson *m*; *Fig* **they put out the w. mat for him** ils l'ont accueilli à bras ouverts; *welcome pack* (*at conference, in hotel*) documentation *f* (*remise à l'accueil*); *welcome reception* réception *f* de bienvenue

welcoming ['welkəmɪŋ] ADJ (*person, greeting, smile, atmosphere*) accueillant; (*ceremony, committee*) d'accueil; **the w. party took them to their hotel** la délégation venue les accueillir les a conduits à leur hôtel

weld [weld] VT **1** *Tech* souder; **to w. parts together** souder des pièces ensemble; **he welded the bracket onto the shelf** il a soudé le support à l'étagère **2** (*unite*) amalgamer, réunir; **a set of policies that will w. the party into a united political force**

un ensemble de mesures qui cimentera le parti et en force politique unie

VI souder

N 1 *Tech* soudure *f* 2 *Bot* réséda *m* des teinturiers

▸▸ ***weld spot*** point *m* de soudure

welder [weldə(r)] N *(person)* soudeur(euse) *m,f*; *(machine)* soudeuse *f*, machine *f* à souder

welding ['weldɪŋ] N *Tech* soudage *m*; *(of groups)* union *f*

▸▸ ***welding helmet*** casque *m* de soudeur; ***welding machine*** soudeuse *f*, machine *f* à souder; ***welding mask*** masque *m* de soudeur; ***welding rod*** baguette *f* de soudure; ***welding torch*** chalumeau *m*

welfare ['welfeə(r)] N 1 *(wellbeing)* bien-être *m*; **the w. of the nation** le bien public; **the physical and spiritual w. of the people** le bien-être physique et moral du peuple; **I am concerned about** *or* **for her w.** je m'inquiète pour elle; **she's looking after his w.** elle s'occupe de lui 2 *Am (state aid)* aide *f* sociale; **his family is on w.** sa famille touche l'aide sociale; **to live on w.** vivre de l'aide sociale; **people on w.** les personnes *ou* ceux qui touchent l'aide sociale

COMP *(meals, milk)* gratuit; *Am* **to stand in the w. line** recevoir les allocations chômage

▸▸ *Am* ***welfare benefits*** avantages *mpl* sociaux; ***welfare centre*** ≃ centre *m* d'assistance sociale; *Am* ***welfare check*** (chèque *m* d')allocations *fpl*; ***welfare hotel*** foyer *m* d'accueil; ***welfare officer*** = travailleur social ayant la charge d'une personne mise en liberté surveillée; ***welfare payments*** prestations *fpl* sociales; ***welfare service*** ≃ service *m* d'assistance sociale; ***the Welfare State*** *(concept)* l'État *m* providence; **the government wants to cut back on the W. State** le gouvernement veut réduire les dépenses d'aide sociale; ***welfare work*** travail *m* social; ***welfare worker*** assistant(e) *m,f* social(e)

we'll [wi:l] 1 = **we shall** 2 = **we will**

well¹ [wel] N 1 *(for water, oil)* puits *m*

2 *(for lift, staircase)* cage *f*; *(between buildings)* puits *m*, cheminée *f*

3 *Br Law* barreau *m (au tribunal)*

4 *Literary* source *f*, fontaine *f*

VI = **well up**

▸▸ ***well head*** tête *f* de puits

▸ **well out** VI *(water)* jaillir

▸ **well up** VI *(blood, spring, tears)* monter, jaillir; **tears welled up in her eyes** les larmes lui montèrent aux yeux; **joy welled up within her** la joie monta en elle

WELL² *(compar* **better** ['betə(r)], *superl* **best** [best]*)*

ADV 1 *(satisfactorily, successfully)* bien; **she speaks French very w.** elle parle très bien (le) français; **he plays the piano w.** il joue bien du piano; **she came out of it rather w.** elle s'en est plutôt bien sortie; **it's extremely w. done** c'est vraiment très bien fait; **everything is going w.** tout se passe bien; **the meeting went w.** la réunion s'est bien passée; **those colours go really w. together** ces couleurs vont vraiment bien ensemble; **the machine/system works w.** la machine/le système marche bien; **things have worked out w.** les choses se sont bien passées; **does she work as w. as I do?** fait-elle son travail aussi bien que moi?; **to do w.** s'en sortir; **she's doing very w.** elle s'en sort très bien; **he did very w. for a beginner** il s'est très bien débrouillé pour un débutant; **to do w. for oneself** bien réussir; **to do w. out of sb/sth** bien s'en sortir avec qn/qch; **that boy will do w.!** ce garçon ira loin!; **the patient is doing w.** le malade se rétablit bien *ou* est en bonne voie de guérison; **we would do w. to keep quiet** nous ferions bien de nous taire; **w. done!** bravo!; **w. said!** bien dit!; **it was money w. spent** ce n'était pas de l'argent gaspillé; *Arch* **w. met!** heureuse rencontre!, vous arrivez bien à propos!

2 *(favourably, kindly)* bien; **she treats her staff very w.** elle traite très bien son personnel; **everyone speaks w. of you** tout le monde dit du bien de vous; **his action speaks w. of his courage** son geste montre bien son courage; **she won't take it w.** elle ne va pas apprécier; **she thinks w. of you** elle a de l'estime pour vous; **he wished her w.** il lui souhaita bonne chance; **to do w. by sb** traiter qn comme il se doit

3 *(easily, readily)* bien; **he could w. decide to leave** il se pourrait tout à fait qu'il décide de partir; **I couldn't very w. accept** je ne pouvais guère accepter; **you may w. be right** il se peut bien que tu aies raison; **I can w. believe it** je le crois facilement *ou* sans peine; **she was angry, and w. she might be** elle était furieuse, et à juste titre

4 *(to a considerable extent or degree)* bien; **she's w. over** *or* **past 40** elle a bien plus de 40 ans; **he's w. into his seventies** il a largement dépassé les soixante-dix ans; **there were w. over 5,000 demonstrators** il y avait bien plus de 5000 manifestants; **he's w. on in years** il n'est plus tout jeune; **w. on into the morning** jusque tard dans la matinée; **it's w. above/within the limit** c'est bien au-dessus de/inférieur à la limite; **it's w. after midday** il est bien plus de midi; **the play went on until w. after midnight** la pièce s'est terminée bien après minuit; **I woke w. before dawn** je me suis réveillé bien avant l'aube; **let me know w. in advance** prévenez-moi longtemps à l'avance

5 *(thoroughly)* bien; **shake/stir w.** bien secouer/remuer; **be sure to cook it w.** veillez à ce que ce soit bien cuit; **w. cooked** *or* **done** bien cuit; **let it dry w. first** attendez d'abord que ce soit bien sec; **I know her w.** je la connais bien; **I know only too w. how hard it is** je ne sais que trop bien à quel point c'est difficile; **how w. I understand her feelings!** comme je comprends ce qu'elle ressent!; **I'm w. aware of the problem** je suis bien conscient *ou* j'ai bien conscience du problème; *Ironic* **I bet he was w. pleased!** il devait être content!; **I like him w. enough** il ne me déplaît pas; **we got w. and truly soaked** nous nous sommes fait tremper jusqu'aux os; **it's w. and truly over** c'est bel et bien fini; **it's w. worth the money** ça vaut largement la dépense; **it's w. worth trying** ça vaut vraiment la peine d'essayer; *Fam* **he was w. annoyed** il était super-énervé

6 *(idioms)* **to be w. away** *(making good progress)* être sur la bonne voie; *(drunk)* être complètement parti; **to be w. in with sb** être bien avec qn; **she's w. in with all the right people** elle est très bien avec tous les gens qui peuvent servir; **to be w. out of it** s'en sortir à bon compte; **you're w. out of it** tu as bien fait de partir; **she's w. rid of him/it!** quel bon débarras pour elle!; **to be w. up on sth** s'y connaître en qch; **she's w. up on European law** elle s'y connaît en droit européen; **to leave** *or* **let w. alone** *(equipment)* ne pas toucher; *(situation)* ne pas s'occuper de; *(person)* laisser tranquille

ADJ 1 *(good)* bien, bon; **all is not w. with them** il y a quelque chose qui ne va pas chez eux; **owning a home is all very w. but...** c'est bien beau d'être propriétaire mais...; **it's all very w. pretending you don't care but...** c'est bien beau de dire que ça t'est égal mais...; **it's all very w. for you to say that** tu peux bien dire ça, toi; *Mil* **all's w.!** rien à signaler!

2 *(advisable)* bien; **it would be w. to start soon** nous ferions bien de commencer bientôt; *Br* **you'd be just as w. to tell him** tu ferais mieux de (le) lui dire

3 *(in health)* **to be w.** aller *ou* se porter bien; **how are you? – w., thank you** comment allez-vous? – bien, merci; **he's been ill but he's better now** il a été malade mais il va mieux (maintenant); **I don't feel w.** je ne me sens pas bien; **she's not very w.** elle ne va pas très bien; **to get w.** se remettre, aller mieux; **get w. soon** *(on card)* bon rétablissement; **I hope you're w.** j'espère que vous allez bien; **you're looking** *or* **you look w.** vous avez l'air en forme; **are you okay?, you don't sound very w.** ça va?, tu n'as pas l'air bien; **he's not a w. man** il ne se porte pas bien

EXCLAM 1 *(indicating start or continuation of speech)* bon, bien; **w., I would just say one thing** bon, je voudrais simplement dire une chose; **w., let me just add that...** alors, laissez-moi simplement ajouter que...

2 *(indicating change of topic or end of conversation)* **w., as I was saying...** donc, je disais que..., je disais donc que...; **right, w., let's move on to the next subject** bon, alors passons à la question suivante; **w. thank you Mr Alderson, I'll be in touch** eh bien merci M. Alderson, je vous contacterai

3 *(softening a statement)* **w., obviously I'd like to come but...** disons que, bien sûr, j'aimerais venir mais...; **he was, w., rather unpleasant really** il a été, disons, assez désagréable, c'est le mot

4 *(expanding on or explaining a statement)* **he was rather fat, w. stout might be a better word** il était plutôt gros, enfin disons corpulent; **I've known her for ages, w. at least three years** ça fait des années que je la connais, enfin au moins trois ans; **you know John? – w. I saw him yesterday** tu connais John? – eh bien je l'ai vu hier

5 *(expressing hesitation or doubt)* ben, eh bien; **did you ask? – w.... I didn't dare actually** as-tu demandé? – eh bien *ou* ben, je n'ai pas osé; **are you coming? – w., I should really stay in and work** tu viens? – eh bien, il vaudrait mieux que je reste à la maison pour travailler

6 *(asking a question)* eh bien, alors; **w., who was it?** alors *ou* eh bien, qui était-ce?; **w., what of it?** et alors?; **w. then, why worry about it?** eh bien alors, pourquoi se faire du mauvais sang?

7 *(expressing surprise or anger)* **w., look who's here!** ça alors, regardez qui est là!; **w., w., w.,** tiens, tiens; **w., really!** ça alors!; *Fam* **w. I never!** ça par exemple!; **(w.,) w., what do you know!** eh bien *ou* ça alors, qui l'aurait cru!

8 *(in relief)* eh bien; **w., at least that's over!** eh bien, en tout cas, c'est terminé!

9 *(in resignation)* bon; **(oh) w., it can't be helped** bon tant pis, on n'y peut rien; **(oh) w., that's life** bon enfin, c'est la vie; **(oh) w., all right** bon alors, d'accord; **can I come too? – oh, very w., if you must** je peux venir aussi? – bon d'accord, si tu y tiens

NPL **the w.** ceux *mpl* qui sont en bonne santé

• **all well and good** ADV tout ça, c'est très bien; **so you want to go to drama school, all very well and good, but...** alors comme ça, tu veux faire une école de théâtre? tout ça, c'est très bien mais...

---

well-adjusted ADJ *(person* ▸ *psychologically)* équilibré; *(*▸ *to society, work)* bien adapté

well-advised ADJ sage, prudent; **he would be w. to leave** il aurait intérêt à partir

well-appointed [-ə'pɔɪntɪd] ADJ *Br Formal (house)* bien équipé; *(hotel)* de catégorie supérieure

well-argued [-'ɑ:gju:d] ADJ bien argumenté; **w. case** un point de vue bien argumenté

well-attended [-ə'tendɪd] ADJ **the meeting was w.** il y avait beaucoup de monde à la réunion; **the classes were not w.** les cours étaient peu suivis

well-balanced ADJ *(person)* équilibré, posé; *(diet)* bien équilibré; *(sentence)* bien construite

well-behaved [-bɪ'heɪvd] ADJ *(person)* bien élevé; *(animal)* bien dressé

wellbeing [,wel'bi:ɪŋ] N bien-être *m inv*; **the general w. of the population** le bien-être général de la population; **he felt a sense of w.** il éprouva une impression de bien-être; **for your own w.** pour votre bien

well-born ADJ de bonne famille; **she was not sufficiently w. to marry him** elle n'était pas assez bien née pour l'épouser

well-bred ADJ 1 *(well-behaved)* bien élevé 2 *(from good family)* de bonne famille 3 *(animal)* de (bonne) race; *(horse)* pur-sang *(inv)*

well-built ADJ 1 *(person)* bien bâti 2 *(building)* bien construit

well-chilled ADJ *(wine)* frais (fraîche)

well-chosen ADJ *(present, words)* bien choisi

well-connected ADJ *(of good family)* de bonne famille; *(having influential friends)* qui a des relations

well-defined [-dɪ'faɪnd] ADJ 1 *(distinct* ▸ *colours, contrasts, shape)* bien défini, net 2 *(precise* ▸ *problem)* bien défini, précis; **within w. limits** dans des limites bien définies

well-developed ADJ 1 *(person)* bien fait; *(body, muscles)* bien développé 2 *(scheme)* bien développé; *(idea)* bien exposé

well-disposed [-dɪs'pəʊzd] ADJ bien disposé; **to be w. to** *or* **towards sb** être bien disposé envers qn; **to be w. to** *or* **towards sth** voir qch d'un bon œil

well-documented [-ˈdɒkjʊmentɪd] ADJ bien documenté

well-done ADJ *(work)* bien fait; *(meat)* bien cuit

well-dressed ADJ bien habillé

well-earned [-ɜːnd] ADJ bien mérité

well-educated ADJ cultivé, instruit

well-endowed [-ɪnˈdaʊd] ADJ *Euph Fig* **a w. young man/woman** un jeune homme bien doté/une jeune femme bien dotée par la nature; **she's w.!** elle a une belle poitrine!, il y a du monde au balcon!

well-equipped [-ɪˈkwɪpt] ADJ *(garage, kitchen, person)* bien équipé; *(with tools)* bien outillé; **the vans are w. to deal with any emergency** les camionnettes sont équipées pour faire face à toute urgence

well-established ADJ bien établi

well-fed ADJ *(animal, person)* bien nourri

well-fixed ADJ *Am Fam* à l'aise❑

well-founded [-ˈfaʊndɪd] ADJ *(doubt, suspicion)* fondé, légitime

well-groomed ADJ *(person)* soigné; *(hair)* bien coiffé; *(horse)* bien pansé; *(garden, lawn)* bien entretenu

well-grounded ADJ fondé

wellhead [ˈwelhed] N *also Fig* source *f*

well-heeled [-hiːld] ADJ *Fam* à l'aise financièrement❑

well-hung ADJ **1** *(game)* bien faisandé **2** *very Fam (man)* bien monté

well-in ADJ *Fam* **1** *Br* **to be w. with sb** être bien avec qn❑ **2** *Austr (rich)* à l'aise financièrement❑

well-informed ADJ *(having information)* bien informé *ou* renseigné; *(knowledgeable)* instruit; **in w. circles** dans les milieux bien informés; **he's very w. about current affairs** il est très au courant de l'actualité

wellington [ˈwelɪŋtən] N *Br (boot)* botte *f* (en caoutchouc)

►► ***wellington boot*** botte *f* en caoutchouc

well-intentioned [-ɪnˈtenʃənd] ADJ bien intentionné

well-judged [-ˈdʒʌdʒd] ADJ *(remark)* bien vu, judicieux; *(shot, throw)* bien jugé; *(estimate)* juste; *(moment)* opportun

well-kept ADJ **1** *(hands, nails)* soigné; *(hair)* bien coiffé; *(house)* bien tenu; *(garden)* bien entretenu **2** *(secret)* bien gardé

well-known ADJ *(person)* connu, célèbre; *(fact)* bien connu; **it is w.** *or* **it is a w. fact that she disagrees with the policy** tout le monde sait qu'elle n'est pas d'accord avec cette politique; **what is less w. is that she's an accomplished actress** ce qu'on sait moins, c'est que c'est une très bonne actrice

well-liked [-laɪkt] ADJ apprécié

well-loved ADJ très aimé

well-made ADJ *(furniture)* bien fait, de fabrication soignée; *(garment)* de coupe soignée; *(play)* bien construit

►► *Theat* ***well-made play*** pièce *f* bien faite

well-mannered ADJ qui a de bonnes manières, bien élevé

well-matched ADJ *(couple)* faits l'un pour l'autre; *(teams)* de force égale

well-meaning ADJ bien intentionné

well-nigh ADV presque; **it's w. impossible** c'est presque *ou* quasi impossible

well-off ADJ **1** *(financially)* aisé **2** *(in a good position)* **they were still w. for supplies** ils avaient encore largement assez de provisions; *Fig* **you don't know when you're w.** vous ne connaissez pas votre bonheur

NPL **the w.** les riches *mpl*; **the less w.** ceux qui ont des moyens modestes

well-oiled ADJ **1** *(machinery)* bien graissé; **the operation ran like a w. machine** l'opération s'est parfaitement déroulée **2** *Fam (drunk)* pompette

well-paid ADJ bien payé

well-preserved [-prɪˈzɜːvd] ADJ *(person, building)* bien conservé

well-proportioned [-prəˈpɔːʃənd] ADJ bien proportionné

well-read [-red] ADJ cultivé, érudit; **she's very w.** elle est très cultivée

well-respected ADJ respecté

well-rounded ADJ **1** *(complete* ► *education)* complet(ète); *(*► *life)* bien rempli **2** *(figure)* rondelet **3** *(style)* harmonieux; *(sentence)* bien tourné

well-spent ADJ *(time)* bien utilisé, qui n'est pas perdu; *(money)* utilement dépensé, que l'on n'a pas gaspillé; **it's money w.** c'est un bon investissement

well-spoken ADJ *(person)* qui s'exprime avec élégance

well-stacked ADJ *Br very Fam (woman)* qui a de gros nichons; **she's w.** il y a du monde au balcon

well-stocked [-stɒkt] ADJ *(shop)* bien approvisionné

well-thought-of ADJ bien considéré

well-thought-out ADJ bien conçu

well-thumbed [-θʌmd] ADJ *(magazine)* qui a été beaucoup feuilleté; *(book)* lu et relu

well-timed [-taɪmd] ADJ *(arrival, remark)* opportun, qui tombe à point; *(blow)* bien calculé

well-to-do ADJ aisé, riche

NPL **the w.** les nantis *mpl*

well-tried ADJ éprouvé, qui a fait ses preuves

well-trodden ADJ **a w. path** un chemin très fréquenté; *Fig* **a w. path to fame** le parcours classique vers la célébrité

well-turned ADJ *(ankle)* fin; *(leg)* bien galbé; *Br (sentence)* bien tourné

well-versed ADJ **to be w. in sth** bien connaître qch

well-wisher [-ˈwɪʃə(r)] N *(gen)* = personne qui offre son soutien; *(of cause, group)* sympathisant (e) *m,f*, partisan *m*

well-woman clinic N centre *m* de santé pour femmes

well-worn ADJ **1** *(carpet, clothes)* usé, usagé **2** *(path)* battu **3** *(expression, joke)* rebattu; **a w. phrase** une banalité, un lieu commun

well-written ADJ bien écrit

welly [ˈwelɪ] *(pl* **wellies***)* N *Br Fam* **1** *(boot)* botte *f* (en caoutchouc)❑ **2** *(idiom)* **give it some w.!** du nerf!

Welsh [welʃ] NPL **the W.** les Gallois *mpl*

N *Ling* gallois *m*

ADJ gallois

►► ***the Welsh Assembly*** l'Assemblée *f* galloise *ou* du pays de Galles; ***Welsh dresser*** vaisselier *m*; ***the Welsh Office*** = secrétariat d'État aux affaires galloises; *Br* ***Welsh rabbit, Welsh rarebit*** ≃ toast *m* au fromage

THE WELSH ASSEMBLY

L'assemblée nationale du pays de Galles fut établie dans le cadre de la décentralisation (voir aussi l'encadré à **devolution**) engagée par le gouvernement travailliste et fut inaugurée à Cardiff en mai 1999. Les soixante membres de l'assemblée forment le "Welsh Cabinet" et siègent sous la houlette du "First Secretary" qui représente les intérêts gallois au parlement de Westminster. L'assemblée nationale du pays de Galles, la première depuis six siècles, a toutefois moins de pouvoirs que le parlement écossais mis en place en même temps.

welsh [welʃ] VI *Br Fam* décamper sans payer; **to w. on a debt** décamper sans payer une dette; **to w. on a promise** ne pas tenir une promesse❑

Welshman [ˈwelʃmən] *(pl* **Welshmen** [-mən]) N Gallois *m*

Welshwoman [ˈwelʃˌwʊmən] *(pl* **Welshwomen** [-ˈwɪmɪn]) N Galloise *f*

welt [welt] N **1** *(on skin)* zébrure *f* **2** *(on garment)* bordure *f*; *(on shoe)* trépointe *f*

welter [ˈweltə(r)] VI *Literary* se vautrer, se rouler

N confusion *f*; **a w. of detail** une profusion de détails; **a w. of conflicting information** une avalanche d'informations contradictoires

welterweight [ˈweltəweɪt] *Boxing* N poids *m* welter

COMP *(champion)* des poids welter; *(fight, title)* de poids welter

wen [wen] N **1** *Med* loupe *f*, *Spec* kyste *m* sébacé **2** *(city)* **the great w.** Londres *f*

wench [wentʃ] N **1** *Arch or Hum (young woman)* jeune fille *f*, jeune femme *f* **2** *Arch* **(serving) w.** *(in inn)* serveuse *f* **3** *Arch (prostitute)* fille *f* de joie

VI *Arch* **to go wenching** aller courir le jupon

wencher [ˈwentʃə(r)] N *Arch or Hum* coureur *m* de jupons

wend [wend] VT *Literary* **to w. one's way home** s'acheminer vers chez soi; **he wended his way through the forest** il s'achemina à travers la forêt

Wendy house [ˈwendɪ-] N *Br* = maison en miniature dans laquelle les jeunes enfants peuvent jouer

Wensleydale [ˈwenzlɪdeɪl] N = fromage anglais à pâte dure originaire de Wensleydale

went [went] *pt of* **go**

wept [wept] *pt & pp of* **weep**

we're [wɪə(r)] = **we are**

were [wɜː(r)] *pt of* **be**

weren't [wɜːnt] = **were not**

werewolf [ˈwɪəwʊlf] *(pl* **werewolves** [-wʊlvz]) N loup-garou *m*

Wesleyan [ˈwezlɪən] *Rel* ADJ de Wesley, wesleyen

N disciple *m* de Wesley

►► ***Wesleyan Methodists*** méthodistes *mpl* wesleyens

west [west] N **1** *Geog* ouest *m*; **in the w.** à l'ouest, dans l'ouest; **the house lies to the w. (of the town)** la maison se trouve à l'ouest (de la ville); **two miles to the w.** trois kilomètres à l'ouest; **look towards the w.** regardez vers l'ouest; **I was born in the w.** je suis né dans l'Ouest; **in the w. of Austria** dans l'ouest de l'Autriche; **on the w. of the island** à l'ouest de l'île; **the wind is in the w.** le vent est à l'ouest; **the wind is coming from the w.** le vent vient *ou* souffle de l'ouest; **the W.** *(the Occident)* l'Occident *m*, les pays *mpl* occidentaux; *(in US)* l'Ouest *m (États situés à l'ouest du Mississippi)* **2** *Cards* ouest *m*

ADJ **1** *Geog* ouest *(inv)*, de l'ouest; *(country)* de l'Ouest; *(wall)* exposé à l'ouest; **the w. coast** la côte ouest; **in w. London** dans l'ouest de Londres; **on the w. side** du côté ouest **2** *(wind)* d'ouest

ADV à l'ouest; *(travel)* vers l'ouest, en direction de l'ouest; **the village lies w. of Manchester** le village est situé à l'ouest de Manchester; **the living room faces w.** la salle de séjour est exposée à l'ouest; **the path heads (due) w.** le chemin va *ou* mène (droit) vers l'ouest; **drive w. until you come to a main road** roulez vers l'ouest jusqu'à ce que vous arriviez à une route principale; **I travelled w.** je suis allé vers l'ouest; **he travelled w. for three days** pendant trois jours, il a voyagé en direction de l'ouest; **to sail w.** naviguer cap sur l'ouest; **it's 20 miles w. of Edinburgh** ≃ c'est à 32 kilomètres à l'ouest d'Édimbourg; **w. by north/by south** ouest-quart-nord-ouest/ouest-quart-sud-ouest; **the school lies further w. of the town hall** l'école se trouve plus à l'ouest de la mairie; **to go w.** aller à *ou* vers l'ouest; *Fam Hum (person)* passer l'arme à gauche; *(thing)* tomber à l'eau; *Fam* **there's another job gone w.!** encore un emploi de perdu!

►► ***West Africa*** Afrique *f* occidentale; ***West African*** N habitant(e) *m,f* de l'Afrique occidentale ADJ *(languages, states)* de l'Afrique occidentale, ouest-africain; ***the West Bank*** la Cisjordanie; *Formerly* ***West Berlin*** Berlin *m* Ouest; *Formerly* ***West Berliner*** habitant(e) *m,f* de Berlin Ouest; ***the West Coast*** la côte ouest *(des États-Unis)*; ***the West Country*** = le sud-ouest de l'Angleterre (Cornouailles, Devon et Somerset); ***the West End*** N *(in general)* les quartiers *mpl* ouest; *(of London)* le West End *(centre touristique et commercial de la ville de Londres connu pour ses théâtres)*; *Formerly* ***West German*** N Allemand(e) *m,f* de l'Ouest ADJ ouest-allemand; *Formerly* ***West Germany*** Allemagne *f* de l'Ouest; ***West Indian*** N Antillais(e) *m,f* ADJ antillais; ***the West Indies*** les Antilles *fpl*; *Med* ***West Nile virus*** virus *m* du Nil occidental

West Point = importante école militaire américaine; ***West Virginia*** la Virginie-Occidentale

westbound ['westbaʊnd] ADJ *(traffic)* en direction de l'ouest; *(lane, carriageway)* de l'ouest; *(road)* qui va vers l'ouest; **w. traffic is subject to delays** la circulation est ralentie dans le sens ouest; *Br* **the w. carriageway of the motorway is closed** l'axe ouest de l'autoroute est fermé (à la circulation); **there's a jam on the w. carriageway** il y a un bouchon en direction de l'ouest

westerly ['westəlɪ] *(pl* **westerlies***)* ADJ **1** *Geog* ouest *(inv)*, de l'ouest; **to travel in a w. direction** aller vers l'ouest; **w. point** point *m* situé à l'ouest *ou* vers l'ouest; **the most w. point on the island** le point le plus à l'ouest de l'île; **a room with a w. aspect** une pièce exposée à l'ouest; *Naut* **to steer a w. course** faire route vers l'ouest; *(when setting out)* mettre le cap à l'ouest **2** *(wind)* d'ouest

ADV vers l'ouest, en direction de l'ouest

N vent *m* d'ouest

western ['westən] ADJ **1** *Geog* ouest *(inv)*, de l'ouest; *(of West)* occidental; **the w. wing of the castle** l'aile ouest du château; **in w. Spain** dans l'ouest de l'Espagne; **the w. side of the country** la partie ouest du pays **2** *(wind)* d'ouest **3** *Pol (powers, technology, world)* occidental

N *(film)* western *m*; *(book)* roman-western *m*

▸▸ *Pol* ***Western Australia*** l'Australie-Occidentale *f*; ***the Western Church*** l'Église *f* d'Occident *ou* latine; ***Western Europe*** Europe *f* occidentale; ***Western Isles*** les Hébrides *fpl*; *Sport* ***western roll*** rouleau *m* costal; ***Western Sahara*** le Sahara occidental; ***Western Samoa*** Samoa *fpl* occidentales

Westerner ['westənə(r)] N habitant(e) *m,f* de l'ouest; *Pol* Occidental(e) *m,f*

westernization, -isation [ˌwestənaɪ'zeɪʃən] N occidentalisation *f*

westernize, -ise ['westənaɪz] VT occidentaliser; **Japan is becoming increasingly westernized** le Japon s'occidentalise de plus en plus

Westminster ['westmɪnstə(r)] N = quartier du centre de Londres où se trouvent le Parlement et le palais de Buckingham

▸▸ ***Westminster Abbey*** l'abbaye *f* de Westminster

> **WESTMINSTER**
>
> C'est dans ce quartier que se trouvent le Parlement et le palais de Buckingham. Le nom de "Westminster" est également employé pour désigner le Parlement lui-même.

westward ['westwəd] ADJ vers l'ouest, en direction de l'ouest

ADV vers l'ouest, en direction de l'ouest; **to sail w.** naviguer cap sur l'ouest

N ouest *m*

westwards ['westwədz] ADV en direction de *ou* vers l'ouest; **to sail w.** naviguer cap sur l'ouest

wet [wet] *(compar* **wetter**, *superl* **wettest**, *pt & pp* **wet** *or* **wetted**, *cont* **wetting***)* ADJ **1** *(ground, person, umbrella ▸ gen)* mouillé; *(▸ damp)* humide; *(▸ soaked)* trempé; **to get w.** se mouiller; **I got my jacket w.** j'ai mouillé ma veste; **I got my feet w.** je me suis mouillé les pieds; **try not to get your shoes w.** essaie de ne pas mouiller tes chaussures; **to be w. through** *(person)* être trempé jusqu'aux os *ou* complètement trempé; *(clothes, towel)* être complètement trempé; **her eyes were w. with tears** elle avait les yeux baignés de larmes; **the roads can be slippery when w.** les routes mouillées peuvent être glissantes; *Fig* **to be (still) w. behind the ears** manquer d'expérience

2 *(ink, paint, concrete)* frais (fraîche); **w. paint!** *(sign)* peinture fraîche!

3 *(climate, weather ▸ damp)* humide; *(▸ rainy)* pluvieux; *(day)* pluvieux, de pluie; **it's going to be very w. all weekend** il va beaucoup pleuvoir tout ce week-end; **the wettest summer on record** l'été le plus humide dont on se souvienne; **in w. weather** par temps de pluie, quand il pleut; **the w. season** la saison des pluies

4 *Br Fam (feeble)* faible▫, mou (molle); **don't be so w.!** tu es une vraie lavette!; **he thinks it's w. to discuss emotions** il trouve ça mièvre de parler des sentiments▫

5 *Br Pol* modéré, mou (molle) *(du parti conservateur)*

6 *Am Fam (wrong)* **to be all w.** avoir tort▫

7 *Am (state, town)* = où l'on peut acheter librement des boissons alcoolisées

VT *(hair, sponge, towel)* mouiller; **to w. oneself** *or* **one's pants** mouiller sa culotte; **to w. the bed** faire pipi au lit; **to w. one's lips** s'humecter les lèvres; **to w. oneself** *(from worry)* se faire de la bile; *(from laughter)* rire aux larmes; *Fam* **to w. one's whistle** boire un coup; *Fam Fig* **we'll have to w. the baby's head** il faudra qu'on arrose la naissance du bébé▫

N **1** *Br (rain)* pluie *f*; *(damp)* humidité *f*; **to go out in the w.** sortir sous la pluie; **let's get in out of the w.** entrons, ne restons pas sous la pluie; **he left his bike out in the w.** il a laissé son vélo dehors sous la pluie

2 *Austr* **the w.** la saison des pluies

3 *Br Pol* modéré(e) *m,f*, mou (molle) *m,f (du parti conservateur)*

4 *Br Fam Pej (feeble person)* lavette *f*

▸▸ *Am* ***wet bar*** = minibar avec un petit évier; *Fam* ***wet blanket*** rabat-joie *m inv*; ***wet dock*** bassin *m* à flot; ***wet dream*** éjaculation *f ou* pollution *f* nocturne; ***wet fish*** poisson *m* frais; ***wet nurse*** nourrice *f*; ***wet room*** salle *f* de douche; ***wet rot*** *(UNCOUNT)* moisissure *f* humide; ***wet signature*** signature *f* manuscrite; ***wet suit*** combinaison *f ou* ensemble *m* de plongée

wetback ['wetbæk] N *Am* = terme injurieux désignant un ouvrier mexicain entré illégalement aux États-Unis

wether ['weðə(r)] N bélier *m* châtré, mouton *m*

wetland ['wetlənd] N marécage *m*, marais *m*

wetness ['wetnɪs] N humidité *f*; **the area is renowned for the w. of its climate** la région est connue pour son climat pluvieux

wetting ['wetɪŋ] N

▸▸ *Chem* ***wetting agent*** (agent *m*) mouillant *m*; *Typ* ***wetting board*** ais *m*; ***wetting solution*** *(for contact lenses)* solution *f* de rinçage

wet-weather tyre, *Am* **wet-weather tire** N pneu *m* pluie

WEU [ˌdʌbəljuːiː'juː] N *Pol (abbr* **Western European Union***)* UEO *f*

we've [wiːv] = **we have**

WFP [ˌdʌbəljuːef'piː] N *(abbr* **World Food Programme***)* PAM *m*

whack [wæk] *Fam* N **1** *(thump)* claque *f*, grand coup▫ *m*; *(sound)* claquement▫ *m*, coup *m* sec▫; **to give sb/sth a w.** donner un grand coup à qn/qch

2 *(try)* essai▫ *m*; **to have a w. at sth** essayer qch▫

3 *Br (share)* part▫ *f*; **he paid more than his w.** il a payé plus que sa part; **she didn't do her fair w.** elle n'a pas fait sa part du travail

4 *(amount, rate)* **you're already earning the top w. for this job** tu gagnes déjà le maximum pour ce travail▫; **I'll pay 50 pounds, top w.** je paierai 50 livres, et pas un sou de plus; **we can offer you £50,000, top w.** nous pouvons vous offrir 50 000 livres, dernier prix *ou* grand maximum

5 *(idioms)* **the price is out of w. with the marketplace** le prix ne correspond pas au cours du marché; **to be out of w. with reality** ne pas être en phase avec la réalité; *Am* **out of the w.** déglingué

VT **1** *(person ▸ hit)* donner un coup *ou* des coups à▫; *(▸ spank)* donner une claque sur les fesses à; *(ball ▸ hit)* donner un grand coup dans▫; *(▸ kick)* donner un grand coup de pied dans▫; **to w. sb over the head** frapper qn sur la tête▫; **to w. sb with a stick/a ruler** donner un coup de bâton/de règle à qn▫ **2** *Br (defeat)* flanquer une dérouillée *ou* raclée à

VI **to w. at sth with a stick** donner un coup de bâton à qch

EXCLAM vlan!

▸**whack off** VI *Vulg* se branler

whacked [wækt] ADJ *Br Fam* vanné, crevé

whacking ['wækɪŋ] *Fam* ADJ *Br* énorme▫, colossal▫

ADV vachement; **a w. great dog/house** un chien/une maison absolument énorme▫

N **1** *(beating)* rossée *f*, raclée *f*; **his father gave him a w.** son père lui a donné une raclée; **to get a w.** prendre une raclée **2** *(defeat)* **we gave them a w.** on leur a mis la pâtée; **to get a w.** prendre une raclée *ou* une déculottée

whacko [ˌwæk'əʊ] EXCLAM *Fam Old-fashioned* épatant!, bath!

whacky *(compar* **whackier**, *superl* **whackiest***)* = **wacky**

whale [weɪl] N **1** *(mammal)* baleine *f* **2** *Fam (idioms)* **we had a w. of a time** on s'est drôlement bien amusés; **a w. of a difference** une différence énorme▫

VI **1** *(hunt whales)* pêcher la baleine **2** *Am Fam* **to w. away at sth** s'en prendre à qch▫

VT *Am Fam* **1** *(thump)* mettre une raclée à, rosser; **I'll w. the living daylights out of you!** je vais te mettre une de ces raclées! **2** *(defeat)* mettre une raclée à

▸▸ ***whale calf*** baleineau *m*; ***whale hunter*** baleinier *m*; ***whale oil*** huile *f* de baleine; ***whale shark*** requin-baleine *m*

whaleboat ['weɪlbəʊt] N baleinière *f*

whalebone ['weɪlbəʊn] N fanon *m* de baleine; *(in corset, dress)* baleine *f*

whaler ['weɪlə(r)] N **1** *(person)* pêcheur *m* de baleine **2** *(ship)* baleinier *m*

whaling ['weɪlɪŋ] N **1** *(industry)* pêche *f* à la baleine **2** *Am Fam (thrashing)* rossée *f*, raclée *f*

COMP *(industry, port)* baleinier

▸▸ ***whaling ship*** baleinier *m*

wham [wæm] *(pt & pp* **whammed**, *cont* **whamming***)* *Fam* N **we hit the wall with a w.** et vlan! on est rentrés dans le mur

EXCLAM vlan!; **it was w., bam, thank you ma'am** il a tiré son coup et il s'est cassé

VT **1** *(hit ▸ person)* donner une raclée à; *(▸ ball)* donner un grand coup dans; **she whammed the ball over the net** d'un grand coup, elle a envoyé la balle par-dessus le filet **2** *(crash ▸ heavy object, vehicle)* rentrer dans▫

VI **to w. into sth** rentrer dans qch▫; **the ball whammed into the back of the net** le ballon a filé dans les buts; **she whammed into the wall** elle s'est écrasée contre le mur; **the car whammed into the lamppost** la voiture est rentrée dans le réverbère

wharf [wɔːf] *(pl* **wharves** [wɔːvz] *or* **wharfs***)* N quai *m*

VT **1** *(goods ▸ store)* entreposer sur le quai; *(▸ unload)* débarquer **2** *(ship)* amarrer à quai

VI *(ship)* venir à quai, amarrer à quai

wharfage ['wɔːfɪdʒ] N droits *mpl* de quai

WHAT [wɒt]

PRON	
• qu'est-ce qui **1**	• que **1**
• qu'est-ce que **1**	• quoi **1, 2, 4, 6, 9**
• ce qui **2, 6**	• ce que **2, 6, 7**
• comment **3**	• combien **5**
ADJ	
• quel **1**	
PREDET	
• quel	

PRON **1** *(in direct questions ▸ as subject)* qu'est-ce qui, que; *(▸ as object)* (qu'est-ce) que, quoi; *(▸ after preposition)* quoi; **w. do you want?** qu'est-ce que tu veux?, que veux-tu?; **w.'s happening?** qu'est-ce qui se passe?, que se passe-t-il?; **w.'s new?** quoi de neuf?; *Fam* **w.'s up?** qu'est-ce qu'il y a?▫; *Am (as greeting)* quoi de neuf?; **w.'s that for?** à quoi cela sert-il?, à quoi ça sert?; **w.'s the matter?, w. is it?** qu'est-ce qu'il y a?; *Fam* **w.'s it to you?** qu'est-ce que ça peut te faire?; **w.'s that?** qu'est-ce que c'est que ça?; *(what did you say)* quoi?; **w.'s that building?** qu'est-ce que c'est que ce bâtiment?; **w.'s your phone number?** quel est votre numéro de téléphone?; **w.'s her name?** comment s'appelle-t-elle?; **w.'s the Spanish for "light"?** comment dit-on "light" en espagnol?; **w.'s the boss like?** comment est le patron?; **w. is life without friends?** que vaut la vie sans amis?; *Fam* **w.'s up with him?** qu'est-ce qu'il a?▫; **w. did I tell you?** *(gen)* qu'est-ce que je vous ai dit?; *(I told you so)* je vous l'avais bien dit!; **she must be, w., 50?** elle doit avoir, quoi, 50 ans?; **Mum? – w.? – can I go out?** Maman? – quoi? – est-ce que je peux sortir?; **w. are you thinking about?** à quoi pensez-vous?; **w. did he die of?** de quoi est-il mort?; **w. do you take me for?** pour qui me prenez-vous?; **w. could be more beautiful?** quoi de plus beau?; *Formal or Hum* **to w. do I owe this honour?** qu'est-ce qui me vaut cet honneur?

2 *(in indirect questions ▸ as subject)* ce qui; (▸ *as object)* ce que, quoi; **tell us w. happened** dites-nous ce qui s'est passé; **I wonder w. she was thinking about!** je me demande ce qui lui est passé par la tête!; **I asked w. it was all about** j'ai demandé de quoi il était question; **he didn't understand w. I said** il n'a pas compris ce que j'ai dit; **I don't know w. to do** je ne sais pas quoi faire; **I don't know w. to do to help him** je ne sais pas quoi faire pour l'aider

3 *(asking someone to repeat something)* comment; **w.'s that?** qu'est-ce que tu dis?; **they bought w.?** quoi, qu'est-ce qu'ils ont acheté?

4 *(expressing surprise)* quoi; **w., another new dress?** quoi, encore une nouvelle robe?; **w., no coffee!** comment *ou* quoi? pas de café?; **he's going into the circus – w.!** il va travailler dans un cirque – quoi?; **I found $350 – you w.!** j'ai trouvé 350 dollars – quoi?; **I told her to leave – you did w.!** je lui ai dit de partir – tu lui as dit quoi?

5 *(how much)* **w.'s 17 minus 4?** combien *ou* que fait 17 moins 4?; **w. does it cost?** combien est-ce que ça coûte?; **w. do I owe you?** combien vous dois-je?

6 *(that which ▸ as subject)* ce qui; (▸ *as object)* ce que, quoi; **w. you need is a hot bath** ce qu'il vous faut, c'est un bon bain chaud; **they spent w. amounted to a week's salary** ils ont dépensé l'équivalent d'une semaine de salaire; **she has w. it takes to succeed** elle a ce qu'il faut pour réussir; **that's w. life is all about!** c'est ça la vie!; **education is not w. it used to be** l'enseignement n'est plus ce qu'il était; **w. is most remarkable is that…** ce qu'il y a de plus remarquable c'est que…; **w.'s done cannot be undone** ce qui est fait est fait; **and w. is worse…** et ce qui est pire…

7 *(whatever, everything that)* **they rescued w. they could** ils ont sauvé ce qu'ils ont pu; **say w. you will** vous pouvez dire *ou* vous direz tout ce que vous voudrez; **say w. you will, I don't believe you** racontez tout ce que vous voulez, je ne vous crois pas; **come w. may** *(regardless of the consequences)* advienne que pourra; *(no matter what)* quoi qu'il arrive

8 *Br Fam Old-fashioned (inviting agreement)* n'est-ce pas□; **an interesting book, w.?** un livre intéressant, n'est-ce pas *ou* pas vrai?

9 *(idioms)* **I'll tell you w.…** écoute!; **you know w.…?** tu sais quoi…?; **I know w.** j'ai une idée; **you'll never guess w.** tu ne devineras jamais (quoi); *Fam* **documents, reports and w. have you** *or* **and w. not** des documents, des rapports et je ne sais quoi encore□; *Fam* **and I don't know w.** et que sais-je encore□; *Fam* **and God knows w.** et Dieu sait quoi; **look, do you want to come or w.?** alors, tu veux venir ou quoi?; **a trip to Turkey? – w. next!** un voyage en Turquie? – et puis quoi encore!; **w. have we here?** mais que vois-je?; **w. then?** et après?; *Old-fashioned* **w. ho!** eh! ho!; *(as greeting)* salut!; *Fam* **we need to find out w.'s w.** il faut qu'on sache où en sont les choses; *Fam* **she told me w. was w.** elle m'a mis au courant; *Fam* **they know w.'s w. in art** ils s'y connaissent en art□; *Fam* **I'll show him w.'s w.!** je vais lui montrer de quel bois je me chauffe!

ADJ 1 *(in questions ▸ singular)* quel (quelle); (▸ *plural)* quels (quelles); **w. books did you buy?** quels livres avez-vous achetés?; **w. colour/size is it?** de quelle couleur/taille c'est?; **(at) w. time will you be arriving?** à quelle heure arriverez-vous?; **w. day is it?** quel jour sommes-nous?; **w. good** *or* **use is this?** à quoi ça sert?

2 *(as many as, as much as)* **I gave her w. money I had** je lui ai donné le peu d'argent que j'avais; **I gave her w. comfort I could** je l'ai consolée autant que j'ai pu

PREDET *(expressing an opinion or a reaction)* **w. a suggestion!** quelle idée!; **w. a strange thing!** comme c'est bizarre!; **w. a pity!** comme c'est *ou* quel dommage!; **w. an idiot he is!** comme il est bête!, qu'il est bête!; **w. lovely children you have!** quels charmants enfants vous avez!; **w. a lot of people!** que de gens!, que de monde!; **you can't imagine w. a time we had getting here** vous ne pouvez pas vous imaginer le mal qu'on a eu à venir jusqu'ici

ADV *(in rhetorical questions)* **w. do I care?** qu'est-ce que ça peut me faire?; **w. does it matter?** qu'est-ce que ça peut faire?; **well, w. of it?** et bien?, et après?

• **what about ADV w. about lunch?** et si on déjeunait?; **when shall we go? – w. about Monday?** quand est-ce qu'on y va? – (et si on disait) lundi?; **w. about your promise? – w. about my promise?** et ta promesse? – ben quoi, ma promesse?; *Fam* **w. about it?** et alors?; **do you remember Lauryn? – w. about her?** tu te souviens de Lauryn? – oui, et alors?; **and w. about you?** et vous donc?

• **what for ADV** *(why)* pourquoi?; **w. did you say that for?** pourquoi as-tu dit cela?; **I'm leaving town – w. for?** je quitte la ville – pourquoi?

• **what if CONJ w. if we went to the beach?** et si on allait à la plage?; **he won't come – and w. if he doesn't?** *(supposing)* il ne va pas venir – et alors?

• **what with CONJ w. with work and the children I don't get much sleep** entre le travail et les enfants, je ne dors pas beaucoup; **w. with paying for dinner and the cab he was left with no cash** après avoir payé le dîner et le taxi, il n'avait plus d'argent; **w. with one thing and another I never got there** pour un tas de raisons je n'y suis jamais allé

what-d'ye-call-her ['wɒtjəkɔːlə(r)] **N** *Fam (person)* Machine *f*

what-d'ye-call-him ['wɒtjəkɔːlɪm] **N** *Fam (person)* Machin *m*

what-d'ye-call-it ['wɒtjəkɔːlɪt] **N** *Fam (thing)* machin *m*, truc *m*

whate'er [wɒt'eə(r)] *Literary* = **whatever**

whatever [wɒt'evə(r)] **PRON 1** *(anything, everything)* tout ce que; **do w. he asks you** faites tout ce qu'il vous demande; **take w. you need** prenez tout ce dont vous avez besoin; **I'll do w. is necessary** je ferai le nécessaire; **w. you like** ce que tu veux

2 *(no matter what)* quoi que + *subjunctive*; **w. I say, he always disagrees** quoi que je dise, il n'est jamais d'accord; **w. happens, stay calm** quoi qu'il arrive, restez calme; **w. you do, don't tell her what I said** surtout, ne lui répète pas ce que je t'ai dit; **w. it may be** quoi que ce soit; **w. the reason** quelle que soit la raison; **the doctors must operate w. the risk** les médecins doivent opérer quel que soit le risque; **w. it costs, I want that house** je veux cette maison à tout prix; **I won't do it, w. you say** vous aurez beau dire *ou* vous pouvez dire tout ce que vous voulez, je ne le ferai pas; **w. you say, w. you think best** comme tu voudras; **w. you may think, I am telling the truth** vous pouvez penser ce que vous voulez, mais je dis la vérité

3 *(indicating surprise)* **w. can that mean?** qu'est-ce que ça peut bien vouloir dire?; **w. do you want to do that for?** et pourquoi donc voulez-vous faire ça?; **he wants to join the circus – w. next!** il veut travailler dans un cirque – qu'est-ce qu'il ne va pas chercher!

4 *(indicating uncertainty)* **it's an urban regeneration area, w. that means** c'est une zone de rénovation urbaine, si tu sais ce qu'ils entendent par là

5 *Fam (some similar thing or things)* **they sell newspapers, magazines and w.** ils vendent des journaux, des revues et ainsi de suite *ou* et que sais-je encore

6 *Fam (indicating lack of interest)* **shall I take the red or the green? – w.** je prends le rouge ou le vert? – n'importe; **I'll call you next week – w.** je t'appellerai la semaine prochaine – comme tu veux

ADJ 1 *(any, all)* tout, n'importe quel; **she read w. books she could find** elle lisait tous les livres qui lui tombaient sous la main; **I'll take w. fruit you have** je prendrai ce que vous avez comme fruits **2** *(no matter what)* **for w. reason, he changed his mind** pour une raison quelconque, il a changé d'avis; **she likes all films, w. subject they have** elle aime tous les films quel qu'en soit le sujet

ADV choose any topic w. choisissez n'importe quel sujet; **I have no doubt w.** je n'ai pas le moindre doute; **we have no intention w. of giving up** nous n'avons pas la moindre intention d'abandonner; **he knew nothing w. about it** il n'en savait absolument rien *ou* rien du tout; **she has no money w.** elle n'a pas un sou

what-ho EXCLAM *Br Old-fashioned* **1** *(in surprise)* eh bien!, tiens! **2** *(greeting)* bonjour!, salut!

whatnot ['wɒtnɒt] **N 1** *(furniture)* étagère *f* **2** *Fam (idiom)* **and w.** et ainsi de suite; **there was champagne, caviar and w.** il y avait du champagne, du caviar et tout le tralala

what's [wɒts] **1** = **what is 2** = **what has**

whatshername ['wɒtsəneɪm] **N** *Fam* Machine *f*; **Mrs w.** Madame Machin

whatshisname ['wɒtsɪzneɪm] **N** *Fam* Machin *m*, Machin Chouette *m*; **Mr w.** Monsieur Machin

whatsit ['wɒtsɪt] **N** *Fam* machin *m*, truc *m*

whatsoever [ˌwɒtsəʊ'evə(r)] **ADV none w.** aucun; **he gave us no encouragement w.** il ne nous a pas prodigué le moindre encouragement

wheat [wiːt] **N** blé *m*; **to separate the w. from the chaff** séparer le bon grain de l'ivraie

COMP *(flour)* de blé, de froment; *(field)* de blé

▸▸ ***wheat beer*** bière *f* blanche; ***wheat germ*** germe *m* de blé; ***wheat rust*** rouille *f* du blé

wheatear ['wiːtˌɪə(r)] **N** *Orn* traquet *m* (motteux)

wheaten ['wiːtən] **ADJ 1** *(bread)* de blé, de froment **2** *(colour)* blond comme les blés

wheatgrass ['wiːtgrɑːs] **N** herbe *f* de blé; **w. juice** jus *m* d'herbe de blé

wheatmeal ['wiːtmiːl] **N** *(flour)* farine *f* complète

▸▸ ***wheatmeal flour*** farine *f* complète

wheatsheaf ['wiːtʃiːf] **N** gerbe *f* de blé

wheedle ['wiːdəl] **VT** enjôler; **to w. sb into doing sth** convaincre qn de faire qch à force de cajoleries; **to w. sth out of sb** obtenir qch de qn par des cajoleries; **he wheedled his way into the old lady's confidence** il s'est assuré la confiance de la vieille dame à force de cajoleries

wheedling ['wiːdlɪŋ] **N** *(UNCOUNT)* cajolerie *f*, cajoleries *fpl*

ADJ cajoleur, enjôleur; **a w. voice** une voix pateline

wheel [wiːl] **N 1** *(of bicycle, car, train)* roue *f*; *(smaller)* roulette *f*; *(for potter)* tour *m*; **on wheels** sur roues/roulettes; *Fig* **the w. has come full circle** la boucle est bouclée; **the w. of fortune** la roue de la fortune; *Fig* **the wheels have come off** les choses ont commencé à mal tourner

2 *Aut* **(steering) w.** volant *m*; **to be at the w.** être au volant; *Fig* être aux commandes; **to get behind** *or* **to take the w.** se mettre au *ou* prendre le volant

3 *Naut* barre *f*, gouvernail *m*; **at the w.** à la barre

4 *Hist (of torture)* roue *f*; **to break sb on the w.** rouer qn

VI 1 *(birds)* tournoyer; *(procession)* faire demi-tour; *Mil (column)* effectuer une conversion; **to w. to the left** tourner sur la gauche; *Mil* **left w.!** à gauche! **2** *(idiom) Fam* **to w. and deal** *(do business)* brasser des affaires; *Pej* magouiller

VT *(bicycle, trolley, barrow)* pousser; *(suitcase)* tirer; **she wheeled the baby around the park** elle a promené le bébé dans le parc; **she wheeled in a trolley full of cakes** elle entra en poussant un chariot plein de gâteaux; *Fig* **they wheeled on** *or* **out the usual celebrities** ils ont ressorti les mêmes célébrités

• **wheels NPL 1** *(workings)* rouages *mpl*; **the wheels of government** les rouages du gouvernement; **there are wheels within wheels** c'est plus compliqué que ça n'en a l'air **2** *Fam (car)* bagnole *f*; **he's got a new set of wheels** il a une nouvelle bagnole

▸▸ *Aut* ***wheel alignment*** parallélisme *m* des roues; ***wheel brace*** clef *f* en croix; *Aut* ***wheel chain*** chaîne *f* (de pneu); *Aut* ***wheel cover*** enjoliveur *m*

▸ **wheel about, wheel around VI 1** *(turn)* faire demi-tour *ou* se retourner (brusquement); *(procession)* faire demi-tour; *(horse)* pirouetter; *(birds)* tournoyer; **she wheeled around to face him** elle s'est retournée brusquement pour lui faire face **2** *(circle)* tourner en rond *ou* en cercle, tournoyer; **vultures wheeling about in the sky** des vautours qui tournoient dans le ciel

VT SEP *(turn)* tourner; *(dancing partner)* faire tourner

wheelbarrow ['wiːlˌbærəʊ] **N** brouette *f*

wheelbase ['wi:lbeɪs] **N** *Aut* empattement *m*

wheelchair ['wi:l͵tʃeə(r)] **N** fauteuil *m* roulant; **she'll be in a w. for the rest of her life** elle sera dans un fauteuil roulant pour le reste de ses jours

▸▸ ***wheelchair access*** accès *m* aux handicapés; ***the Wheelchair Olympics*** les jeux *mpl* Olympiques handisport *ou* pour handicapés; ***wheelchair ramp*** rampe *f* d'accès pour les handicapés; ***wheelchair user*** handicapé(e) *m,f*

wheelclamp ['wi:lklæmp] **N** sabot *m* de Denver

VT my car was wheelclamped on a mis un sabot à ma voiture

-wheeled [wi:ld] **SUFF** à roues; **four-w.** à quatre roues

wheeled [wi:ld] **ADJ** à roues, muni de roues

-wheeler [wi:lə(r)] **SUFF** à roues; **three-w.** véhicule *m* à trois roues

wheeler-dealer N *Fam Pej* magouilleur(euse) *m,f*

wheelhouse ['wi:lhaʊs, *pl* -haʊzɪz] **N** *Naut* timonerie *f*

wheelie ['wi:lɪ] **N** *Fam* **to do a w.** faire une roue arrière, cabrer

▸▸ ***wheelie bin*** poubelle *f* (*avec des roues*)

wheeling and dealing ['wi:lɪŋ-] **N** (*UNCOUNT*) *Fam* combines *fpl*, manigances *fpl*

wheelwright ['wi:lraɪt] **N** charron *m*

wheeze [wi:z] **VI** (*person*) respirer bruyamment, avoir une respiration sifflante; (*animal*) souffler

VT dire d'une voix rauque; **the old accordion can still w. out a note or two** on peut encore tirer quelques notes du vieil accordéon

N 1 (*sound of breathing*) respiration *f* bruyante *ou* sifflante

2 *Br Fam* (*trick*) combine *f*; **the government's latest w. for cutting unemployment** la dernière trouvaille du gouvernement pour réduire le chômage▫

3 *Br Fam* (*joke*) blague▫ *f*

4 *Am* (*saying*) dicton *m*

wheezing ['wi:zɪŋ] **N** (*of person*) respiration *f* bruyante *ou* sifflante, *Med* sibilance *f* respiratoire

wheezy ['wi:zɪ] (*compar* **wheezier**, *superl* **wheeziest**) **ADJ** (*person*) asthmatique; (*voice, chest*) d'asthmatique; (*musical instrument, horse*) poussif; **she's still a little bit w. after her cold** elle a encore un peu de mal à respirer après son rhume; *Fig* **a w. old barrel organ** un vieil orgue de Barbarie asthmatique

whelk [welk] **N** *Zool* (*mollusc*) bulot *m*, buccin *m*

whelp [welp] **N 1** (*animal*) petit(e) *m,f* **2** *Pej* (*youth*) petit(e) morveux(euse) *m,f*

VI (*animals*) mettre bas

WHEN [wen]

> **ADV**
> - quand
>
> **CONJ**
> - quand **1–7**
> - lorsque **3**
> - dès que **4**
> - après que **4**
> - chaque fois que **6**
> - étant donné que **7**
> - alors que **8**
>
> **REL PRON**
> - où **1, 3**

ADV quand; **w. are we leaving?** quand partons-nous?; **w. is the next bus?** à quelle heure est *ou* quand passe le prochain bus?; **w. did the war end?** quand la guerre s'est-elle terminée?; **w. did the accident happen?** quand l'accident a-t-il eu lieu?; **w. do you start your new job?** quand commencez-vous votre nouveau travail?; **you're open until w.?** vous êtes ouvert jusqu'à quand?; **w. did you last see her?** quand l'avez-vous vue pour la dernière fois?; **w. do the Easter holidays begin?** quand commencent les vacances de Pâques?; **w. is the best time to call?** quel est le meilleur moment pour appeler?; **the homework is due w.?** quand doit-on rendre les devoirs?

CONJ 1 (*how soon*) quand; **I don't know w. we'll see you again** je ne sais pas quand nous vous reverrons; **do you remember w. we met?** te souviens-tu du jour où nous nous sommes connus?; **do you know w. he was born?** savez-vous quand il est né?, connaissez-vous sa date de naissance?; **I wonder w. the shop opens** je me demande à quelle heure ouvre le magasin; **your contract states w. you will be paid** votre contrat spécifie quand vous serez payé; **we don't agree on w. it should be done** nous ne sommes pas d'accord sur le moment où il faudrait le faire

2 (*at which time*) quand; **come back next week w. we'll have more time** revenez la semaine prochaine quand nous aurons plus de temps; **he returned in the autumn, w. the leaves were beginning to turn** il est revenu à l'automne, alors que les feuilles commençaient à jaunir; **the prince will arrive on the 10th, w. he will open the new university** le prince arrivera le dix et inaugurera la nouvelle université

3 (*indicating a specific point in time*) quand, lorsque; **he turned round w. she called his name** il s'est retourné quand *ou* lorsqu'elle l'a appelé; **w. I was a student** lorsque j'étais *ou* à l'époque où j'étais étudiant; **will you still love me w. I'm old?** m'aimeras-tu encore quand je serai vieux?; **they were talking w. he came in** ils étaient en train de discuter quand il est entré; **she's thinner than w. I last saw her** elle a maigri depuis la dernière fois que je l'ai vue; **w. she was a child** quand *ou* lorsqu'elle était enfant; **on Sunday, w. I go to the market** (*this week*) dimanche, quand j'irai au marché; (*every week*) le dimanche, quand je vais au marché; **I had just walked in the door/he was about to go to bed w. the phone rang** je venais juste d'arriver/il était sur le point de se coucher quand le téléphone a sonné; **we hadn't been gone five minutes w. Susan wanted to go home** ça ne faisait pas cinq minutes que nous étions partis et Susan voulait déjà rentrer

4 (*as soon as*) quand, dès que; (*after*) quand, après que; **put your pencils down w. you have finished** posez votre crayon quand vous avez terminé; **w. completed, the factory will employ 100 workers** une fois terminée, l'usine emploiera 100 personnes; **w. he starts drinking, he can't stop** une fois qu'il a commencé à boire, il ne peut plus s'arrêter; **I'll answer any questions w. the meeting is over** quand la réunion sera terminée, je répondrai à toutes vos questions; *Culin* **w. cool, turn out onto a dish** une fois refroidi, démouler sur un plat; **w. they had finished dinner, he offered to take her home** quand *ou* après qu'ils eurent dîné, il lui proposa de la ramener; **w. you see her you'll understand** quand vous la verrez vous comprendrez

5 (*the time that*) **remember w. a coffee cost 10 cents?** vous souvenez-vous de l'époque où un café coûtait 10 cents?; **he talked about w. he was a soldier** il parlait de l'époque où il était soldat; **that's w. it snowed so hard** c'est quand il a tant neigé; **that's w. he got up and left** c'est à ce moment-là *ou* c'est alors qu'il s'est levé et qu'il est parti; **that's w. the shops close** c'est l'heure où les magasins ferment; *Fig* **now is w. we should stand up and be counted** c'est le moment d'avoir le courage de nos opinions

6 (*whenever*) quand, chaque fois que; **w. I hear that song, I think of her** chaque fois que *ou* quand j'entends cette chanson, je pense à elle; **w. I think of what she must have suffered!** quand je pense à ce qu'elle a dû souffrir!; **I get very irritated w. talking to her** je m'énerve chaque fois que je lui parle

7 (*since, given that*) quand, étant donné que; **what good is it applying w. I don't qualify for the job?** à quoi bon me porter candidat quand *ou* si je n'ai pas les capacités requises pour faire ce travail?; **how can you treat her so badly w. you know she loves you?** comment pouvez-vous la traiter si mal quand *ou* alors que vous savez qu'elle vous aime?; **why change jobs w. you like what you do?** pourquoi changer de travail quand *ou* puisque vous aimez ce que vous faites?

8 (*whereas*) alors que; **she described him as being lax w. in fact he's quite strict** elle l'a décrit comme étant négligent alors qu'en réalité il est assez strict

RELATIVE PRON 1 (*at which time*) **in a period w. business was bad** à une période où les affaires allaient mal; **she was president until 1980, w. she left the company** elle fut présidente jusqu'en 1980, année où elle a quitté l'entreprise

2 (*which time*) **she started her job in May, since w. she has had no free time** elle a commencé à travailler en mai et elle n'a pas eu de temps libre depuis; **the new office will be ready in January until w. we will use the old one** le nouveau bureau sera prêt en janvier, jusque là *ou* en attendant nous utiliserons l'ancien

3 (*that*) où; **do you remember the year w. we went to Alaska?** tu te rappelles l'année où on est allé en Alaska?; **what about the time w. she didn't show up?** et la fois où elle n'est pas venue?; **one day w. he was out** un jour où il était sorti *ou* qu'il était sorti; **on Monday, the day w. I was supposed to start work** lundi, le jour où je devais commencer à travailler; **it's one of those days w. everything goes wrong** c'est un de ces jours où tout va de travers; **there were times w. she didn't know what to do** il y avait des moments où elle ne savait plus quoi faire

N the w. and the how of it quand et comment cela s'est-il passé/se passera-t-il/*etc*

whence [wens] *Formal* **ADV** d'où

PRON d'où

whenever [wen'evə(r)] **CONJ 1** (*every time that*) quand, chaque fois que; **w. we go on a picnic, it rains** chaque fois qu'on part en pique-nique, il pleut; **w. it snows there's chaos on the roads** chaque fois qu'il neige, c'est la panique sur les routes; **he can come w. he likes** il peut venir quand il veut; **I go to visit her w. I can** je vais la voir dès que je peux **2** (*at whatever time*) quand; **call me w. you need me** appelez-moi si vous avez besoin de moi; **you can leave w. you're ready** vous pouvez partir dès que vous serez prêt; **they try to help w. possible** ils essaient de se rendre utiles quand c'est possible

ADV 1 (*expressing surprise*) quand; **w. did you find the time?** mais quand donc avez-vous trouvé le temps? **2** (*referring to an unknown or unspecified time*) **I'll pick you up at six o'clock or w. is convenient** je te prendrai à six heures ou quand ça te convient; *Fam* **let's assume he started work in April or w.** supposons qu'il ait commencé à travailler en avril ou quelque chose comme ça; *Fam* **we could have lunch on Thursday or Friday or w.** on pourrait déjeuner ensemble jeudi, vendredi ou un autre jour

WHERE [weə(r)]

> **ADV**
> - où **1, 2**
>
> **CONJ**
> - où **1**
> - là où **1–4**
> - là que **2**
> - quand **3**
> - alors que **4**
>
> **REL PRON**
> - où **1, 2**

ADV 1 (*at, in, to what place*) où; **w. is the restaurant?** où est le restaurant?; **w. are we going?** où allons-nous?; **w. are you from?** d'où est-ce que vous venez?, d'où êtes-vous?; **w. did you put them?** où les avez-vous mis?; **w. is the entrance?** où est l'entrée?; **the school is near w.?** l'école est près d'où?; **w. does this road lead?** où va cette route?

2 (*at what stage, position*) **w. are you in your work/in the book?** où en êtes-vous dans votre travail/dans votre lecture?; **w. were we?** où en étions-nous?; **w. do you stand on this issue?** quelle est votre position *ou* opinion sur cette question?; **w. do you stand with the boss?** quels sont vos rapports avec le patron?; **w. do I come into it?** qu'est-ce que j'ai à faire là-dedans, moi?; **w. would I be without you?** que serais-je devenu sans toi?

CONJ 1 (*the place at or in which*) (là) où; **it rains a lot w. we live** il pleut beaucoup là où nous habitons; **she told me w. to go** (*gave me directions*) elle m'a dit où (il fallait) aller; (*was rude*) elle m'a envoyé promener; **there is a factory w. I used to go to school** il y a une usine là où *ou* à l'endroit où j'allais autrefois à l'école; **how did you know w. to find me?** comment avez-vous su où me trouver?; **I wonder w. my keys are** je me demande où sont mes clés; **you'll find your key w. you left it** tu trouveras ta clé (là) où tu l'as laissée; **sit w. you like** asseyez-vous où vous voulez *ou* voudrez; *Fig* ıst don't know w. to begin je ne sais vraiment ·as par où commencer

2 *(the place that)* là que, là où; **this is w. I work** 'est là que je travaille; **he showed me w. the students live** il m'a montré l'endroit où habitent les tudiants; **this is w. we get off the bus** c'est là que ous descendons; **the child ran up to w. her** ıother **was sitting** l'enfant a couru jusqu'à l'enroit où sa mère était assise; **we can't see well** ·om **w. we're sitting** nous ne voyons pas bien 'où *ou* de là où nous sommes assis; *Fig* **I see w. went wrong** je vois où je me suis trompé; **that's** ⁄. **she's mistaken** c'est là qu'elle se trompe, voilà on erreur; **this is w. you have to make up your** ıind là, il faut que tu te décides

3 *(whenever, wherever)* quand, là où; **the situation is hopeless w. defence is concerned** pour la éfense, la situation est sans espoir; **he can't be** ·**bjective w. she's concerned** il ne peut pas être ·bjectif lorsqu'il s'agit d'elle; *Math* **w. x equals y** ù x égale y; **w. possible** là où *ou* quand c'est posible; **delete w. inapplicable** *(on form)* rayer les ıentions inutiles; *Prov* **w. there's life, there's** ·**ope** tant qu'il y a de la vie, il y a de l'espoir

4 *(whereas, while)* là où, alors que; **w. others see** **horrid brat, I see a shy little boy** là où les autres oient un affreux moutard, je vois un petit garon timide

RELATIVE PRON 1 *(in which, at which)* où; **the place** ⁄. **we went on holiday** l'endroit où nous sommes llés en vacances; **the room w. he was working** la ièce où *ou* dans laquelle il travaillait; **the table** ⁄. **they were sitting** la table où *ou* à laquelle ils taient assis; **it was the kind of restaurant w. tourists go** c'était le genre de restaurant que fréuentent les touristes; *Fig* **I'm at the part w. they** **liscover the murder** j'en suis au moment où ils écouvrent le meurtre; **it's reached a stage w.** **m finding it difficult to work** ça en est au point ·ù travailler me devient pénible

2 *(in or at which place)* **Boston, w. I was born** Boson, où je suis né, Boston, ma ville natale; **they** **vent to Paris, w. they stayed a week** ils sont allés à 'aris et y sont restés huit jours; **sign at the botom, w. I've put a cross** signez en bas, là où j'ai ıis une croix

N they discussed the w. and how of his accident ils ·nt parlé en détail des circonstances de son acident; **the w. and the when** le lieu et la date/ heure; **you can find that any old w.** vous pouvez rouver cela n'importe où

'hereabouts ADV [ˌweərə'baʊts] où; **w. are you** **rom?** d'où êtes-vous?; **I used to live in Cumbria –** ·**h, really, w.?** j'habitais dans le Cumbria – vraiıent? où ça *ou* dans quel coin?; **do you know w.** **he town hall is?** savez-vous de quel côté se rouve l'hôtel de ville?; **w. in France do you live?** ·ù est-ce que tu habites en France?

NPL ['weərəbaʊts] **to know the w. of sb/sth** savoir ·ù se trouve qn/qch; **her exact w. are unknown** ·ersonne ne sait exactement où elle se trouve

'hereafter [weər'ɑːftə(r)] **CONJ** *Arch or Formal* ·près quoi

'hereas [weər'æz] **CONJ 1** *(gen)* alors que, tanlis que **2** *Law or Formal* attendu que, considéant que

'hereat [weər'æt] *Arch or Formal* **CONJ** sur *ou* ·près quoi, sur ce

ADV où

'hereby [weə'baɪ] **RELATIVE PRON** *Formal* par leuel, au moyen duquel; **there's a new system w.** **veryone gets one day off a month** il y a un noueau système qui permet à tout le monde 'avoir un jour de congé par mois

'herefore ['weəfɔː(r)] **ADV** *Arch or Formal* pouruoi, pour quelle raison

CONJ *Arch or Formal* pour cette raison, donc

N *see* **why**

'herein [weər'ɪn] *Arch or Formal* **RELATIVE PRON** ·ù, dans lequel (laquelle)

ADV en quoi, dans quoi

CONJ en quoi, dans quoi

'hereof [weər'ɒv] *Arch or Formal* **RELATIVE PRON** *oerson)* dont, de qui; *(thing)* dont, duquel (de aquelle)

ADV de quoi

whereon [weər'ɒn] *Arch or Formal* **RELATIVE PRON** sur quoi, sur lequel (laquelle)

ADV sur quoi

wheresoever [ˌweəsəʊ'evə(r)] *Formal or Literary* = **wherever**

whereupon [ˌweərə'pɒn] **CONJ** sur *ou* après quoi, sur ce; **w. he left us** sur quoi il nous a quittés

ADV *Arch* sur quoi

wherever [weər'evə(r)] **CONJ 1** *(every place)* partout où; *(no matter what place)* où que; **w. you go in Europe, you meet other tourists** où que vous alliez en Europe, vous rencontrez d'autres touristes; **w. you go it's the same thing** c'est la même chose où que vous alliez, c'est partout pareil; **w. we went, he complained about the food** partout où nous sommes allés, il s'est plaint de la nourriture

2 *(anywhere, in whatever place)* (là) où; **he can sleep w. he likes** il peut dormir (là) où il veut; **we'll have to sit w. there's room** il faudra s'asseoir là où il y aura de la place; **she works w. she's needed** elle travaille là où on a besoin d'elle; **he takes on work w. he can find it** il accepte du travail où il en trouve; **we can go w. we please** nous pouvons aller où bon nous semble; **w. there is poverty there are social problems** là où il y a de la misère, il y a des problèmes sociaux; **they're from Little Pucklington, w. that is** ils viennent d'un endroit qui s'appelle Little Pucklington

3 *(in any situation)* quand; **I wish, w. possible, to avoid job losses** je souhaite éviter toute perte d'emploi quand c'est possible; **grants are given w. needed** des bourses sont accordées à chaque fois que c'est nécessaire

ADV *Fam* **1** *(indicating surprise)* mais où donc; **w. did you get that idea?** mais d'où sors-tu cette idée?; **w. have you been?** où étais-tu donc passé?

2 *(indicating unknown or unspecified place)* **they're holidaying in Marbella or Malaga or w.** ils passent leurs vacances à Marbella ou à Malaga ou Dieu sait où

wherewithal ['weəwɪðɔːl] **N** *Br* **the w.** les moyens *mpl*; **I don't have the w. to buy a new coat** je n'ai pas les moyens de me payer un manteau neuf

whet [wet] *(pt & pp* **whetted**, *cont* **whetting)** **VT** *(cutting tool)* affûter, aiguiser; *(appetite)* aiguiser, ouvrir; **to w. sb's appetite** ouvrir l'appétit à qn; *Fig* **her few days in Spain only whetted her appetite for more** ces quelques jours passés en Espagne n'ont fait que lui donner envie d'y revenir

whether ['weðə(r)] **CONJ 1** *(if)* si; **I asked w. I could come** j'ai demandé si je pouvais venir; **I don't know w. she's ready or not** je ne sais pas si elle est prête ou non; **I don't know now w. it's such a good idea** je ne suis plus sûr que ce soit vraiment une bonne idée; **I doubt w. he'll come** je doute qu'il vienne; **the question now is w. you want the job or not** la question est maintenant de savoir si tu veux cet emploi ou pas **2** *(no matter if)* **w. it rains or not** qu'il pleuve ou non; **w. you want to or not** que tu le veuilles ou non; **w. by accident or design** que ce soit par hasard ou fait exprès; **everyone, w. rich or poor, needs it** chacun, qu'il soit riche ou pauvre, en a besoin

whetstone ['wetstəʊn] **N** pierre *f* à aiguiser

whew [hwjuː] **EXCLAM** *(in relief)* ouf!; *(admiration)* oh là là!; **w.! I'm glad that's over!** ouf! je suis bien content que ça soit fini!

whey [weɪ] **N** petit-lait *m*

WHICH [wɪtʃ]

ADJ	
• quel **1**	
PRON	
• lequel **1**	• celui qui **2**
• celui que **2**	
REL PRON	
• qui **1**	• que **1**
• ce qui **2**	• ce que **2**

ADJ 1 *(in questions ▸ singular)* quel (quelle); *(▸ plural)* quels (quelles); **w. book did you buy?** quel livre as-tu acheté?; **w. candidate are you voting for?** pour quel candidat allez-vous voter?; **w. one?** lequel?/laquelle?; **w. ones?** lesquels?/lesquelles?; **w. one of you spoke?** lequel de vous a parlé?; **w. one of the twins got married?** lequel des jumeaux s'est marié?; **I saw several films – w. ones?** j'ai vu plusieurs films – lesquels?; **I wonder w. route would be best** je me demande quel serait le meilleur chemin; **w. way should we go?** par où devrions-nous aller?; **keep track of w. employees come in late** notez le nom des employés qui arrivent en retard

2 *(referring back to preceding noun or statement)* **he may miss his plane, in w. case he'll have to wait** il est possible qu'il rate son avion, auquel cas il devra attendre; **she arrives at 5 p.m. at w. time I'll still be at the office** elle arrive à 17 heures, heure à laquelle je serai encore au bureau; **they lived in Madrid for one year, during w. time their daughter was born** ils ont habité Madrid pendant un an, et c'est à cette époque que leur fille est née

PRON 1 *(in questions ▸ singular)* lequel (laquelle) *m,f*; *(▸ plural)* lesquels (lesquelles) *mpl, fpl*; **w. of the houses do you live in?** dans quelle maison habitez-vous?; **w. of these books is yours?** lequel de ces livres est le tien?; **w. is the freshest?** quel est le plus frais?; **w. is the more interesting of the two films?** lequel de ces deux films est-il le plus intéressant?; **w. of you saw the accident?** qui de vous a vu l'accident?; **w. of you three is the oldest?** lequel de vous trois est le plus âgé?, qui est le plus âgé de vous trois?; **we can play bridge or poker, I don't care w.** on peut jouer au bridge ou au poker, peu m'importe; **I can't tell w. is w.** je n'arrive pas à les distinguer (l'un de l'autre)

2 *(the one or ones that ▸ as subject) (singular)* celui qui (celle qui) *m,f*; *(plural)* ceux qui (celles qui) *mpl,fpl*; *(▸ as object) (singular)* celui que (celle que) *m,f*; *(plural)* ceux que (celles que) *mpl,fpl*; **show me w. you prefer** montrez-moi celui que vous préférez; **tell her w. is yours** dites-lui lequel est le vôtre

RELATIVE PRON 1 *(adding further information ▸ as subject)* qui; *(▸ as object)* que; **the house, w. is very old, needs urgent repairs** la maison, qui est très vieille, a besoin d'être réparée sans plus attendre; **the vases, each of w. held white roses, were made of crystal** les vases, qui contenaient chacun des roses blanches, étaient en cristal; **the hand with w. I write** la main avec laquelle j'écris; **the office in w. she works** le bureau dans lequel *ou* où elle travaille; **the hotels at w. they stayed** les hôtels où ils sont allés *ou* descendus; **the house of w. I am speaking** la maison dont je parle; **the countries to w. we are going** *or* **w. we're going to** les pays où nous allons

2 *(commenting on previous statement ▸ as subject)* ce qui; *(▸ as object)* ce que; **it took her an hour, w. isn't bad really** elle a mis une heure, ce qui n'est pas mal en fait; **he looked like a military man, w. in fact he was** il avait l'air d'un militaire, et en fait c'en était un; **he says it was an accident, w. I don't believe for an instant** il dit que c'était un accident, ce que je ne crois absolument pas *ou* mais je ne le crois pas un seul instant; **then they arrived, after w. things got better** puis ils sont arrivés, après quoi tout est allé mieux; **she lied about the letter, from w. I guessed she was up to something** elle a menti au sujet de la lettre, d'où j'ai deviné qu'elle combinait quelque chose; **he insists that actors should have talent, in w. he is right** il exige que les acteurs aient du talent, (ce) en quoi il a raison; **he started shouting, upon w. I left the room** il s'est mis à crier, sur quoi *ou* et sur ce j'ai quitté la pièce

whichever [wɪtʃ'evə(r)] **PRON 1** *(the one or ones that ▸ as subject) (singular)* celui (celle) qui *m,f*; *(plural)* ceux (celles) qui *mpl,fpl*; *(▸ as object) (singular)* celui (celle) que *m,f*; *(plural)* ceux (celles) que *mpl,fpl*; **choose w. most appeals to you** choisissez celui/celle qui vous plaît le plus; **choose w. most appeal to you** choisissez ceux/ celles qui vous plaisent le plus; **will w. of you arrives first turn on the heating?** celui d'entre vous qui arrivera le premier pourra-t-il allumer le chauffage?; **take w. is (the) cheapest** prenez (celui qui est) le moins cher; **shall we go to the cinema or the theatre? – w. you prefer** on va au cinéma ou au théâtre? – choisis ce que tu préfères; **let's meet at 3 or 4, w. is best for you** donnons-nous rendez-vous à trois heures ou quatre heures, comme cela vous arrange le mieux

2 *(no matter which one)* **w. of the routes you choose, allow about two hours** quel que soit le chemin que vous choisissiez, comptez environ deux heures; **w. of the houses you buy it will be a good investment** quelle que soit la maison que vous achetiez, ce sera un bon investissement; **w. of the computers you buy will be installed free of charge** quel que soit l'ordinateur que vous achetiez, l'installation sera gratuite; **I'd like to speak either to Mr Brown or Mr Jones, w. is available** j'aimerais parler à M. Brown ou à M. Jones, celui des deux qui est disponible

ADJ 1 *(indicating the specified choice or preference)* **I'll buy w. car does the best mileage** je prendrai la voiture qui consomme le moins(, peu importe laquelle); **take w. seat you like** asseyez-vous (là) où vous voulez; **we'll travel by w. train is fastest** nous prendrons le train le plus rapide(, peu importe lequel); **keep w. one appeals to you most** gardez celui/celle qui vous plaît le plus

2 *(no matter what* ▸ *as subject)* quel que soit… qui; *(*▸ *as object)* quel que soit… que; **w. job you take, it will mean a lot of travelling** quel que soit le poste que vous preniez, vous serez obligé de beaucoup voyager; **w. party is in power** quel que soit le parti au pouvoir; **we'll still be late w. way we go** nous serons en retard de toute façon quel que soit le chemin que nous prenions; **w. way you look at it, it's not fair** peu importe la façon dont on considère la question, c'est vraiment injuste

whiff [wɪf] **N 1** *(inhalation)* bouffée *f*; *Fam* **one w. of this gas and you'd be out cold** une seule bouffée de ce gaz et vous tombez dans les pommes **2** *(smell)* odeur *f*; **he got a sudden w. of her perfume/of rotten eggs** il sentit soudain l'odeur de son parfum/une odeur d'œufs pourris; *Fam* **get a w. of this!** sens-moi un peu ça!; *Fig* **a w. of scandal** une odeur de scandale; **he had caught a w. of something suspicious** il avait senti que quelque chose de louche était dans l'air

VI *Fam* schlinguer

whiffy ['wɪfɪ] *(compar* **whiffier**, *superl* **whiffiest)** **ADJ** *Fam* qui schlingue; **the dog's a bit w.** le chien schlingue un peu; **it's a bit w. in here, don't you think?** ça schlingue ici, tu ne trouves pas?

Whig [wɪg] *Pol* **ADJ** whig

N whig *m*

while [waɪl] **CONJ 1** *(during the time that)* pendant que; **he read the paper w. he waited** il lisait le journal en attendant; **w. (you're) in London you should visit the British Museum** pendant que vous serez à Londres *ou* pendant votre séjour à Londres, il faut visiter le British Museum; **he cut himself w. (he was) shaving** il s'est coupé en se rasant; **w. this was going on** pendant ce temps-là; **heels repaired/keys cut w. you wait** *(sign)* talons/clés minute; **w. you're up could you fetch me some water?** puisque tu es debout, peux-tu aller me chercher de l'eau?; **w. you're at** *or* **about it, could you photocopy this too?** pendant que tu y es, peux-tu aussi me photocopier cela?

2 *(although)* bien que, quoique; **w. I admit it's difficult, it's not impossible** j'admets que c'est difficile, mais ce n'est pas impossible; **w. comprehensive, the report lacked clarity** bien que détaillé le rapport manquait de clarté

3 *(whereas)* alors que, tandis que; **w. he loves opera, I prefer jazz** il adore l'opéra alors que moi je préfère le jazz; **she's left-wing, w. he's rather conservative** elle est de gauche tandis que lui est plutôt conservateur

N to wait a w. attendre (un peu); **after a w.** au bout de quelque temps; **for a w./a long w. I believed her** pendant un certain temps/pendant assez longtemps je l'ai crue; **it took me a w. to realize what she meant** j'ai mis un certain temps à comprendre ce qu'elle voulait dire; **a long w. ago** il y a longtemps; **she was in the garden a short w. ago** elle était dans le jardin il y a un instant; **it's been a good w. since I've seen her** ça fait pas mal de temps que je ne l'ai pas vue; **it will be a good w. before you see him again** vous ne le reverrez pas de si tôt; **it takes quite a w. to get there** il faut un certain temps pour y aller; **all the w.** (pendant) tout ce temps; **once in a w.** de temps en temps, de temps à autre

▸ **while away VT SEP** faire passer; **to w. away the time** passer le temps; **she whiled away the hours reading until he returned** elle passa le temps à lire jusqu'à son retour

whilst [waɪlst] *Br* = **while CONJ**

whim [wɪm] **N** caprice *m*, fantaisie *f*; **it's just one of his little whims** ce n'est qu'une de ses petites lubies; **she indulges his every w.** elle lui passe tous ses caprices; **whenever the w. takes him** chaque fois que l'idée lui prend; **on a sudden w. I telephoned her mother** tout à coup, l'idée m'a pris de téléphoner à sa mère

whimper ['wɪmpə(r)] **VI** *(person)* gémir, geindre; *Pej* pleurnicher; *(dog)* gémir, pousser des cris plaintifs

VT gémir

N gémissement *m*, geignement *m*; **"don't," he said with a w.** "non", dit-il d'un ton larmoyant *ou* gémit-il; **I don't want to hear a w. out of you** je ne veux pas t'entendre; **she did it without a w.** elle l'a fait sans se plaindre

whimpering ['wɪmpərɪŋ] **N** *(UNCOUNT)* gémissements *mpl*, plaintes *fpl*; **stop your w.!** arrête de pleurnicher!

ADJ *(voice)* larmoyant; *(person)* qui pleurniche; *(dog)* qui gémit

whimsical ['wɪmzɪkəl] **ADJ** *(person* ▸ *capricious)* capricieux, fantasque; *(*▸ *playful)* malicieux; *(behaviour, sense of humour, story, remark)* farfelu; *(smile)* malicieux

whimsicality [wɪmzɪ'kælɪtɪ] **N** *(of person* ▸ *capriciousness)* caractère *m* capricieux *ou* fantasque; *(*▸ *playfulness)* malice *f*; *(of behaviour, sense of humour, story, remark)* caractère *m* farfelu

whimsically ['wɪmzɪkəlɪ] **ADV** *(capriciously)* capricieusement; *(playfully)* malicieusement; *(directed, written)* de façon farfelue; *(smile)* malicieusement

whimsy ['wɪmzɪ] *(pl* **whimsies)** **N 1** *(whimsicality)* caractère *m* fantasque *ou* fantaisiste; **a piece of pure w.** de la pure fantaisie; **full of w.** plein de fantaisie *ou* de malice **2** *(idea)* caprice *m*, fantaisie *f*

whin [wɪn] **N** ajonc *m*

whine [waɪn] **VI 1** *(in pain, discomfort* ▸ *person)* gémir, geindre; *(*▸ *dog)* gémir, pousser des gémissements **2** *(complain)* se lamenter, se plaindre; **to w. about sth** se plaindre de qch; **don't come whining to me about it** ne viens pas t'en plaindre à moi

VT dire en gémissant; **"I'm hungry," she whined** "j'ai faim", dit-elle d'une voix plaintive

N 1 *(from pain, discomfort)* gémissement *m* **2** *(complaint)* plainte *f* **3** *(of machinery, engine)* bruit *m* strident

whinge [wɪndʒ] *(cont* **whingeing)** *Br & Austr Fam Pej* **VI** geindre❑, pleurnicher❑; **he's always whingeing about something** il est toujours en train de geindre à propos de quelque chose; **don't come whingeing to me about your problems** ne venez pas vous plaindre à moi de vos problèmes

N plainte❑ *f*, pleurnicherie❑ *f*; **to have a w. about sth** se plaindre (à propos) de qch❑

whinger [wɪndʒə(r)] **N** *Br & Austr Fam* râleur (euse) *m,f*

whining ['waɪnɪŋ] **N** *(UNCOUNT)* **1** *(of person)* gémissements *mpl*, pleurnicheries *fpl*; *(of dog)* gémissements *mpl*; **I've had enough of your w.!** j'en ai assez de tes pleurnicheries *ou* de tes jérémiades! **2** *(of machinery, engine)* gémissement *m*

ADJ *(person)* geignard, pleurnicheur; *(voice)* geignard; *(dog)* qui gémit

whinny ['wɪnɪ] *(pt & pp* **whinnied**, *pl* **whinnies)** **VI** hennir

N hennissement *m*

whinnying ['wɪnɪɪŋ] **N** hennissement *m*

ADJ a w. laugh un rire qui ressemble à un hennissement

whiny ['waɪnɪ] *(compar* **whinier**, *superl* **whiniest)** **ADJ** pleurnichard

whip [wɪp] *(pt & pp* **whipped**, *cont* **whipping)** **VT 1** *(person, animal)* fouetter; **the cold wind whipped her face** le vent glacial lui fouettait le visage; **th… wind whipped her hair about** le vent agitait s… chevelure

2 *Fam (defeat)* vaincre❑, battre❑; **I know whe… I'm whipped** je sais quand déclarer forfait❑

3 *Culin* fouetter, battre au fouet

4 *(move quickly)* **she whipped it out of sight** el… l'a caché d'un mouvement rapide; **she wa… whipped into hospital** elle a été transportée … l'hôpital de toute urgence

5 *Fig* **his speech whipped them all into a frenz…** son discours les a tous rendus frénétiques; **I… soon w. the team into shape** j'aurai bientôt fa… de mettre l'équipe en forme; **I need time to w… the project into shape** il me faut du temps pou… donner forme au projet; **to w. sb into line** mett… qn au pas

6 *Br Fam (steal)* faucher, piquer; **someone whipped my wallet** on m'a piqué mon porte… feuille

7 *Sewing* surfiler

8 *(cable, rope)* surlier

VI 1 *(lash)* fouetter; **the rain whipped against th… windows** la pluie fouettait *ou* cinglait les vitre… **the flags whipped about in the wind** les drapeau… claquaient au vent

2 *(move quickly)* aller vite, filer; **the car whippe… along the road** la voiture filait sur la route; **sh… whipped around the corner** elle a pris le virag… sur les chapeaux de roue; **the sound of bulle… whipping through the air** le bruit des balles q… sifflaient; **I'll just w. down to the shop** je vais just… faire un saut au magasin; **can you w. round to th… library for me?** est-ce que tu peux faire un saut … la bibliothèque pour moi?

N 1 *(lash)* fouet *m*; *(for riding)* cravache *f*; *Fig* **t… have the w. hand** être le maître; **to have the w… hand over sb** avoir le dessus sur qn

2 *Pol (MP)* = parlementaire chargé de la disc… pline de son parti et qui veille à ce que ses d… putés participent aux votes

3 *Br Pol (summons)* convocation *f*

4 *Br Pol (paper)* = calendrier des travaux parle… mentaires envoyé par le "whip" aux députés d… son parti

5 *(dessert* ▸ *with cream)* crème *f*; *(*▸ *with eg… whites)* mousse *f*; **pineapple w.** *(with crea…)* crème *f* à l'ananas; *(with egg whites)* mousse *f* … l'ananas

▸ **whip away VT SEP** *(of wind)* emporter brus… quement; **a sudden gust whipped my hat awa…** une rafale de vent a emporté mon chapeau

▸ **whip in VT SEP 1** *Hunt* ramener, rassembler **2** *… Pol (in parliament)* battre le rappel de *(pour vote…* **3** *(supporters)* rallier

VI 1 *(rush in)* entrer précipitamment **2** *Hunt* êt… piqueur

▸ **whip off VT SEP** *(take off* ▸ *jacket, shoes)* se d… barrasser de; *(write quickly* ▸ *letter, memo)* écri… en vitesse

▸ **whip out VT SEP 1** *(take out)* sortir vivement; **h… whipped a notebook out of his pocket** il a vite sor… un carnet de sa poche; **she whipped out a gu…** elle a soudain sorti un pistolet; **they had to w… out his appendix** on a dû l'opérer d'urgence d… l'appendicite **2** *(grab)* **someone whipped my ba… out of my hand** quelqu'un m'a arraché mon sa… des mains

VI sortir précipitamment; **I'm just whipping ou… to the library** je file à la bibliothèque

▸ **whip round VI** *(person)* se retourner viv… ment, faire volte-face

▸ **whip up VT SEP 1** *(curiosity, emotion)* attise… *(support)* obtenir; **to w. up an audience** galvanis… *ou* exalter un public **2** *(typhoon)* susciter, provo… quer; *(dust)* soulever (des nuages de) **3** *Cul…* battre au fouet, fouetter; *(egg whites)* battre à … neige; *Fam* **I'll w. up some lunch** je vais prépar… de quoi déjeuner en vitesse

whipcord ['wɪpkɔːd] **N 1** *(cord)* mèche *f* de fou… **2** *Tex (fabric)* whipcord *m*

COMP en whipcord

whiplash ['wɪplæʃ] **N** *(stroke of whip)* coup *m* d… fouet

▸▸ *Med* ***whiplash effect*** effet *m* du coup du lapi… ***whiplash injury*** coup *m* du lapin, *Spec* syndrom… *m* cervical traumatique

whipper-in ['wɪpər-] (*pl* **whippers-in**) N *Hunt* piqueur *m*

whippersnapper ['wɪpəˌsnæpə(r)] N *Old-fashioned* freluquet *m*

whippet ['wɪpɪt] N *Zool (dog)* whippet *m*

whipping ['wɪpɪŋ] N **1** *(as punishment ▸ of child)* correction *f*; *(▸ of prisoner)* coups *mpl* de fouet; **his father gave him a good w.** son père lui a donné une bonne correction **2** *Fam (defeat)* raclée *f*; **the team got a w.** l'équipe a pris une raclée
▸▸ ***whipping boy*** bouc *m* émissaire; ***whipping cream*** ≃ crème *f* fraîche (à fouetter); ***whipping post*** poteau *m (auquel étaient attachés les condamnés au fouet)*; ***whipping top*** toupie *f*

whippoorwill ['wɪpˌpuəwɪl] N *Orn* engoulevent *m* d'Amérique du Nord

whip-round N *Br Fam* collecte☐ *f*; **they had a w. for her** ils ont fait une collecte pour elle

whir = **whirr**

whirl [wɜːl] VI **1** *(person, skater)* tourner, tournoyer; **she whirled round the ice rink** elle a fait le tour de la piste en tourbillonnant
2 *(leaves, smoke)* tourbillonner, tournoyer; *(dust, water)* tourbillonner; *(spindle, top)* tournoyer; *(propeller)* tourner; **snowflakes whirled past the window** des flocons de neige passaient devant la fenêtre en tourbillonnant; **the water whirled away down the sink** l'eau s'est écoulée en tourbillonnant dans l'évier
3 *(head, ideas)* tourner; **my head is whirling** (j'ai) la tête (qui) me tourne
4 *(move quickly)* aller à toute vitesse; **the horses whirled past us** les chevaux sont passés devant nous à toute allure
VT **1** *(dancer, skater)* faire tourner; **he whirled his partner around the floor** il faisait tournoyer sa partenaire autour de la piste
2 *(leaves, smoke)* faire tourbillonner *ou* tournoyer; *(dust, sand)* faire tourbillonner; **the wind whirled the leaves about** le vent faisait tourbillonner les feuilles
3 *(take rapidly)* **she whirled us off on a trip round Europe** elle nous a embarqués pour un tour d'Europe
N **1** *(of dancers, leaves, events)* tourbillon *m*; *Fig* **my head's in a w.** la tête me tourne; **her thoughts were in a w.** tout tourbillonnait dans sa tête; *Hum* **the mad social w.** la folle vie mondaine; **the kitchen was a w. of activity** la cuisine bourdonnait d'activité
2 *Fam (try)* **to give sth a w.** s'essayer à qch☐; **why don't you give it a w.?** pourquoi n'essayez-vous pas?
3 *Fam (trip)* promenade☐ *f*, tour☐ *m*

whirl round VI **1** *(person)* se retourner brusquement; *(dancer, skater)* pirouetter; **she whirled round and round in the middle of the dance floor** elle tournait et tournait au milieu de la piste de danse **2** *(leaves)* tourbillonner, tournoyer
VT SEP **to w. sb round** faire tournoyer qn

whirligig ['wɜːlɪgɪg] N *Br* **1** *(top)* toupie *f*; *(toy windmill)* moulin *m* à vent *(jouet)* **2** *(merry-go-round)* manège *m* **3** *(of activity, events)* tourbillon *m*
▸▸ *Entom* ***whirligig beetle*** tourniquet *m*, gyrin *m*

whirlpool ['wɜːlpuːl] N *also Fig* tourbillon *m*
▸▸ ***whirlpool bath*** bain *m* à remous, Jacuzzi® *m*

whirlwind ['wɜːlwɪnd] N tornade *f*, trombe *f*; *Fig* **he went through the office accounts like a w.** il a passé les comptes de la société en revue en un rien de temps
▸▸ ***whirlwind romance*** aventure *f* enivrante; ***whirlwind tour*** visite *f* éclair

whirlybird ['wɜːlɪbɜːd] N *Fam Old-fashioned* hélico *m*

whirr [wɜː(r)] N *(of wings)* bruissement *m*; *(of camera, machinery)* bruit *m*, ronronnement *m*; *(of helicopter, propeller)* bruit *m*, vrombissement *m*; **we could hear the w. of the cameras** on entendait le ronronnement des caméras
VI *(wings)* bruire; *(camera, machinery)* ronronner; *(propeller)* vrombir

whisk [wɪsk] VT **1** *(put or take quickly)* **we whisked the money into the tin/off the counter** nous avons vite fait disparaître l'argent dans la boîte/du comptoir; **she whisked the gun back into her bag** elle remit vivement le pistolet dans son sac; **the car whisked us to the embassy** la voiture nous emmena à l'ambassade à toute allure; **she whisked the children out of the room** elle emmena rapidement les enfants hors de la pièce **2** *Culin (cream, eggs)* battre; *(egg whites)* battre en neige; **w. in the cream** incorporer la crème avec un fouet **3** *(flick)* **the horse/the cow whisked its tail** le cheval/la vache agitait la queue
VI *(move quickly)* aller vite; **she just whisked in and out** elle n'a fait qu'entrer et sortir; **the train whisked through the countryside** le train filait *ou* roulait à vive allure à travers la campagne
N **1** *(of tail, stick, duster)* coup *m*; **the horse gave a w. of its tail** le cheval agita la queue *ou* donna un coup de queue; **give the bedroom a quick w. with a duster** passez un coup de chiffon dans la chambre **2** *(for sweeping)* époussette *f*; *(for flies)* chasse-mouches *m inv* **3** *Culin* fouet *m*; *(electric)* batteur *m*; **give the batter a good w.** bien travailler la pâte au fouet

▸ **whisk away** VT SEP **1** *(dust)* enlever, chasser; *(dishes, tablecloth)* faire disparaître; *(flies ▸ with fly swatter)* chasser à coups de chasse-mouches; *(▸ with tail)* chasser d'un coup de queue **2** *(take off)* **the president was whisked away in a helicopter** le président a été emmené à toute vitesse en hélicoptère; **he was whisked away to hospital in an ambulance** il a été transporté de toute urgence en ambulance à l'hôpital

▸ **whisk off** VT SEP *(quickly)* emporter *ou* emmener à vive allure; *(suddenly, immediately)* conduire sur-le-champ; **the bus whisked us off to the airport** le bus nous emmena rapidement jusqu'à l'aéroport; **we were whisked off to the police station** on nous emmena sur-le-champ au poste de police

whisker ['wɪskə(r)] N poil *m*; *Fam* **she won the contest by a w.** elle a gagné le concours de justesse☐; *Fam* **he came within a w. of discovering the truth** il s'en est fallu d'un cheveu *ou* d'un poil qu'il n'apprenne la vérité
• **whiskers** NPL *(beard)* barbe *f*, *(moustache)* moustache *f*, *(on animal)* moustaches *fpl*

whiskered ['wɪskəd] ADJ *(bearded)* qui a une barbe; *(with moustache)* qui a une moustache; *(animal)* qui a des moustaches

whisky ['wɪskɪ] (*pl* **whiskies**) N whisky *m*; **a w. and soda** un whisky soda; **a w. on the rocks** un whisky avec des glaçons
▸▸ ***whisky distillery*** distillerie *f* de whisky; ***whisky glass*** verre *m* à whisky; ***whisky sour*** = cocktail à base de whisky et de jus de citron

whisper ['wɪspə(r)] VI **1** *(person)* chuchoter, parler à voix basse; **to w. to sb** parler *ou* chuchoter à l'oreille de qn; **stop whispering!** arrêtez de chuchoter!; **what are you whispering about?** qu'est-ce que vous avez à chuchoter? **2** *(leaves)* bruire; *(water, wind)* murmurer
VT **1** *(person)* chuchoter, dire à voix basse; **to w. sth to sb** chuchoter qch à qn; **I whispered the answer to her** je lui ai soufflé la réponse; **to w. sweet nothings to sb** susurrer des mots doux à l'oreille de qn **2** *Br (rumour)* **it's whispered that her husband's left her** le bruit court *ou* on dit que son mari l'a quittée; **I've heard it whispered that he's lost his fortune** j'ai entendu dire qu'il avait perdu toute sa fortune
N **1** *(of voice)* chuchotement *m*; **to speak in a w.** parler tout bas *ou* à voix basse; **we never raised our voices above a w.** nous n'avons fait que murmurer; **...she said in a loud w.** ...chuchota-t-elle assez fort; *Fig* **not a w. of this to anyone!** n'en soufflez mot à personne! **2** *(of leaves)* bruissement *m*; *(of water, wind)* murmure *m* **3** *Br (rumour)* rumeur *f*, bruit *m*; **there are whispers of his leaving** le bruit court *ou* on dit qu'il va partir; **I've heard whispers that they're getting married** j'ai entendu dire qu'ils allaient se marier

whispering ['wɪspərɪŋ] N **1** *(of voices)* chuchotement *m*, chuchotements *mpl* **2** *(of leaves)* bruissement *m*; *(of water, wind)* murmure *m* **3** *(usu pl) Br (rumour)* rumeur
ADJ **1** *(voice)* qui chuchote **2** *(leaves, tree)* qui frémit *ou* murmure; *(water, wind)* qui murmure
▸▸ ***whispering campaign*** campagne *f* de diffamation; *Archit* ***whispering gallery*** galerie *f* à écho

whist [wɪst] N whist *m*; **to have a game of w.** faire une partie de whist; **to play w.** jouer au whist
▸▸ ***whist drive*** tournoi *m* de whist

whistle ['wɪsəl] VI **1** *(person ▸ using lips)* siffler; *(▸ using whistle)* donner un coup de sifflet, siffler; **he walked in whistling happily** il est entré en sifflant joyeusement; **to w. to sb** siffler qn; **I whistled to my dog** j'ai sifflé mon chien; **the porter whistled for a taxi** le portier a sifflé un taxi; **he whistles at all the girls** il siffle toutes les filles; **the audience booed and whistled** le public a hué et sifflé; *Br Fam* **you can w. for it!** tu peux toujours courir *ou* te brosser!; *Br* **let him w. for his lunch!** il peut toujours l'attendre, son repas!; *Fig* **to w. in the dark** essayer de se donner du courage
2 *(bird, kettle, train)* siffler; **bullets whistled past him** des balles passaient près de lui en sifflant; **the wind whistled through the trees** le vent gémissait dans les arbres
VT *(tune)* siffler, siffloter; **the coach whistled them off the field** l'entraîneur a sifflé pour qu'ils quittent le terrain; **the players were whistled off the field by the crowd** les joueurs ont quitté le terrain sous les sifflements de la foule
N **1** *(whistling ▸ through lips)* sifflement *m*; *(▸ from whistle)* coup *m* de sifflet; **the cheers and whistles of the crowd** les acclamations et les sifflements de la foule; **if you need me, just give a w.** tu n'as qu'à siffler si tu as besoin de moi
2 *(of bird, kettle, train)* sifflement *m*
3 *(instrument ▸ of person, on train)* sifflet *m*; **to blow a w.** donner un coup de sifflet; **the w. blew for the end of the shift** le sifflet a signalé la fin du service; **the referee blew his w. for half-time** l'arbitre a sifflé la mi-temps; **to be as clean as a w.** briller comme un sou neuf; *Fig* **it's got all the bells and whistles** il a tous les accessoires possibles et imaginables
4 *Mus* **(penny** *or* **tin) w.** flûtiau *m*, pipeau *m*
5 *SEng Fam (rhyming slang* **whistle and flute** = **suit)** costard *m*

▸ **whistle up** VT SEP *Br* **1** *(by whistling)* siffler; **I'll w. up a cab** je vais siffler un taxi **2** *(find)* dénicher, dégoter; **I managed to w. up a van for the move** j'ai réussi à dégoter un camion pour le déménagement; **I can't w. up a sofa just like that!** je ne peux pas faire apparaître un canapé comme par enchantement!

whistle-blower N *Fam* = personne qui vend la mèche; **we need a few more whistle-blowers like her** il faudrait d'autres personnes comme elle pour tirer sur la sonnette d'alarme

whistler ['wɪslə(r)] N **1** *(person)* siffleur(euse) *m,f* **2** *(bird)* oiseau *m* siffleur **3** *(animal)* siffleur *m*, marmotte *f* canadienne, *Can* siffleux *m*

whistle-stop N *Am Rail* arrêt *m* facultatif; *(town)* village *m* perdu
VI *Am Pol* = faire une tournée électorale en passant par des petites villes
ADJ **he made a w. tour of the West** il a fait une tournée rapide dans l'ouest
▸▸ ***whistle-stop town*** village *m* perdu

whistling ['wɪslɪŋ] N sifflement *m*

Whit [wɪt] N Pentecôte *f*
COMP *(holidays, week)* de Pentecôte
▸▸ ***Whit Monday*** lundi *m* de Pentecôte; ***Whit Sunday*** dimanche *m* de Pentecôte

whit [wɪt] N *Literary* **he hasn't changed a w.** il n'a absolument pas changé; **I don't care a w. what people think** je me moque éperdument de ce que les gens pensent; **it won't make a w. of difference** ça ne changera rien à rien; **it doesn't matter a w.** ça n'a aucune espèce d'importance

white [waɪt] ADJ **1** *(in colour)* blanc (blanche); **he painted his house w.** il a peint sa maison en blanc; **his hair has turned w.** ses cheveux ont blanchi; **he went w. overnight** ses cheveux sont devenus blancs du jour au lendemain
2 *(pale)* **she was w. with fear/with rage** elle était verte de peur/blanche de colère; **his face suddenly went w.** il a blêmi tout d'un coup; **whiter than w.** plus blanc que blanc; *Fig* sans tache; **you're as w. as a ghost/as a sheet** vous êtes pâle comme la mort/comme un linge; **as w. as snow** blanc comme neige
3 *(flour, rice, sugar)* blanc (blanche); **(a loaf of) w. bread** du pain blanc

4 *(race)* blanc (blanche); **a w. man** un Blanc; **a w. woman** une Blanche; **an all-w. neighbourhood** un quartier blanc; **w. schools** écoles *fpl* pour les Blancs

5 *(coffee)* au lait; **do you take your coffee w.?** tu prends du lait dans ton café?

N 1 *(colour)* blanc *m*; **the bride wore w.** la mariée était en blanc; **he was dressed all in w.** il était tout en blanc; **dazzling w.** blanc éclatant

2 *Anat (of eye)* blanc *m*; *Fig* **don't shoot until you see the whites of their eyes** ne tirez qu'au dernier moment

3 *Culin (of egg)* blanc *m*

4 *(Caucasian)* Blanc (Blanche) *m,f*; **whites only** *(sign)* réservé aux Blancs; **they're trying to set w. against black** ils essaient de monter les Blancs contre les Noirs

5 *Chess* **W.** les blancs *mpl*

6 *(in snooker, pool)* **the w.** la blanche

VT *Arch* blanchir

VI *Arch* blanchir

• **whites** **NPL** *(sportswear)* tenue *f* de sport blanche; *(linen)* blanc *m*

▸▸ *Am* ***White Anglo-Saxon Protestant*** = Blanc d'origine anglo-saxonne et protestante, appartenant aux classes aisées et influentes; ***white ball*** *(in snooker, pool)* blanche *f*; *Biol* ***white blood cell*** globule *m* blanc; ***white coat*** blouse *f* blanche; ***white chocolate*** chocolat *m* blanc; ***white Christmas*** Noël *m* sous la neige; ***white coffee*** café *m* au lait; *Bot* ***white dead-nettle*** ortie *f* blanche; *Astron* ***white dwarf*** naine *f* blanche; ***white elephant*** *(useless construction)* = réalisation de prestige dont l'utilité ne justifie pas le coût; *Br* ***white elephant stall*** *(at fair, jumble sale)* stand *m* de bibelots; ***White Ensign*** = pavillon de la marine royale britannique; *Br Hist* ***white feather*** = symbole de lâcheté; **to show the w. feather** battre en retraite; *Br* ***white fish*** = poisson à chair blanche; ***white flag*** drapeau *m* blanc; *Am* ***white folks*** les Blancs *mpl*; ***white gold*** or *m* blanc; ***white goods*** *(household equipment)* produits *mpl* blancs, appareils *mpl* ménagers; *(linen)* linge *m* de maison, blanc *m*; *Phys & Fig* ***white heat*** chaleur *f* incandescente; **in the w. heat of passion** au plus fort de la passion; ***white hope*** espoir *m*; **he's the (great) w. hope of British athletics** c'est le grand espoir de l'athlétisme britannique; ***white horses*** *(waves)* moutons *mpl*; ***the White House*** la Maison-Blanche; *Fig* ***white knight*** sauveur *m*, chevalier *m* blanc; ***white lead*** blanc *m* de céruse *ou* de plomb; ***white lie*** pieux mensonge *m*; ***white light*** lumière *f* blanche; *Fam* ***white lightning*** tord-boyaux *m inv (distillé illégalement)*; ***white line*** *(on road)* ligne *f* blanche; ***white magic*** magie *f* blanche; ***white man's burden*** = obligation pour les Blancs d'assurer l'instruction des habitants noirs de leurs colonies; ***white meat*** viande *f* blanche; *(of poultry)* blanc *m*; *Br* ***white meter*** = système économique de chauffage qui utilise l'électricité pendant les heures où elle coûte moins cher; ***the White Nile*** le Nil Blanc; ***white noise*** bruit *m* de fond; *Bot* ***white oak*** *(tree, wood)* chêne *m* blanc; *Am* ***White Out®*** correcteur *m* liquide; ***white owl*** harfang *m*, chouette *f* blanche; *Am* ***the White Pages*** l'annuaire *m* (du téléphone); *Br* ***white paper*** *(government report)* livre *m* blanc; ***white pepper*** poivre *m* blanc; *Culin* ***white pudding*** boudin *m* blanc; *Zool* ***white rhinoceros*** rhinocéros *m* blanc; ***White Russia*** Russie *f* Blanche; ***White Russian*** **ADJ 1** *Ling & Geog* biélorusse **2** *Hist (soldier)* russe blanc (blanche); **the W. Russian Army** les armées *fpl* blanches **N 1** *Hist (person)* Russe *m* blanc, Russe *f* blanche **2** *Ling & Geog* biélorusse *m* **3** *(cocktail)* = cocktail à base de Kahlua, de vodka et de crème fraîche; *Am* ***white sale*** promotion *f* sur le blanc; ***white sauce*** sauce *f* blanche; ***the White Sea*** la mer Blanche; ***white shark*** requin *m* blanc; ***white slave*** victime *f* de la traite des Blanches; ***white slavery, white slave trade*** traite *f* des Blanches; ***white space*** *(on page)* espace *m* blanc; ***white spirit*** white-spirit *m*; ***white stick*** *(of blind person)* canne *f* blanche; ***white supremacist*** partisan(e) *m,f* de la suprématie blanche; ***white supremacy*** suprématie *f* blanche; ***white tea*** thé *m* blanc; ***white tie*** *(formal clothes)* habit *m*; *(on invitation)* ≃ tenue de soirée exigée; *Zool* ***white tiger*** tigre *m* blanc; *Pej* ***white trash*** Blancs *mpl* pauvres; *Med* ***white tumour*** tumeur *f* blanche; *Br Fam* ***white van man*** = jeune ouvrier en camionnette à la conduite agressive; ***white water*** eau *f* vive; ***white wedding*** mariage *m* en blanc; **she's having a w. wedding** elle se marie en blanc; *Zool* ***white whale*** bélouga *m*, béluga *m*; ***white wine*** vin *m* blanc; ***white witch*** = sorcière qui a recours à la magie blanche

▸ **white out** **VT SEP** effacer (au correcteur liquide); **can you w. out this word?** peux-tu effacer ce mot?

whitebait ['waɪtbeɪt] **N** *(for fishermen)* blanchaille *f*; *Culin* petite friture *f*

whiteboard ['waɪtbɔːd] **N** tableau *m* blanc

whitebread ['waɪtbred] **ADJ** *Am Fam Pej* conventionnel[□]

whitecaps ['waɪtkæps] **NPL** *(waves)* moutons *mpl*

whitecoat seal ['waɪtkəʊt-] **N** *Zool* bébé *m* phoque

white-collar **ADJ**

▸▸ ***white-collar crime*** délinquance *f* économique et financière; ***white-collar job*** poste *m* d'employé de bureau; ***white-collar union*** syndicat *m* d'employés de bureau; ***white-collar workers*** les employés *mpl* de bureau, les cols *mpl* blancs

white-faced **ADJ** au visage pâle

whitefish ['waɪtfɪʃ] *(pl* **inv** *or* **whitefishes)** **N** *Ich* corégone *m*

white-haired **ADJ** *(person)* aux cheveux blancs; *(animal)* aux poils blancs; **his w. old mother** sa vieille mère aux cheveux blancs

▸▸ *Am Fig* ***white-haired boy*** chouchou *m*

Whitehall ['waɪthɔːl] **N** = rue du centre de Londres

> **WHITEHALL**
>
> De nombreux services gouvernementaux ont leurs bureaux dans cette rue londonienne dont le nom est souvent employé pour désigner le gouvernement lui-même.

white-headed **ADJ** *(person)* aux cheveux blancs; *(animal, bird)* à la tête blanche

▸▸ *Am Fig* ***white-headed boy*** chouchou *m*

white-hot **ADJ** *Phys & Fig* chauffé à blanc

white-knuckle **ADJ**

▸▸ ***white-knuckle ride*** tour *m* de manège terrifiant; *Fig* **the film was a bit of a w. ride** le film était palpitant

whitelist ['waɪtlɪst] **N** liste *f* blanche, whitelist *f*

white-livered [-lɪvəd] **ADJ** *Fig (person)* poltron

whiten ['waɪtən] **VT 1** *(hair, linen, shoes)* blanchir **2** *(with whitewash)* blanchir à la chaux, badigeonner de chaux

VI blanchir; *(with fear, rage)* pâlir, blêmir

whiteness ['waɪtnɪs] **N 1** *(gen)* blancheur *f*; *(of skin)* blancheur *f*, pâleur *f* **2** *Literary* innocence *f*, pureté *f*

whiteout ['waɪtaʊt] **N** voile *m* blanc; **in w. conditions** dans des conditions de visibilité nulle

white-slaver **N** = personne qui se livre à la traite des Blanches

whitethorn ['waɪtθɔːn] **N** *Bot* aubépine *f*

whitethroat ['waɪtθrəʊt] **N** *Orn* fauvette *f* grisette

whitewall ['waɪtwɔːl] **N** pneu *m* à flanc blanc

whitewash ['waɪtwɒʃ] **N 1** *(substance)* lait *m* de chaux **2** *Fig (cover-up)* **the police report was simply a w.** le rapport de police visait seulement à étouffer l'affaire **3** *Sport (crushing defeat)* défaite *f* cuisante

VT 1 *(building, wall)* blanchir à la chaux **2** *Fig (cover up)* blanchir, étouffer; **the minister tried to w. the affair** le ministre essaya d'étouffer l'affaire **3** *Sport (defeat)* écraser

whitewashing ['waɪt,wɒʃɪŋ] **N 1** *(painting)* peinture *f* à la chaux, badigeonnage *m* **2** *Fig (of reputation)* blanchiment *m*

whitewood ['waɪtwʊd] **N** bois *m* blanc

whitey ['waɪtɪ] **N** *Am very Fam Pej* = terme injurieux désignant un Blanc

whither ['wɪðə(r)] *Arch or Literary* **ADV** (vers) où; **w. Christianity?** *(in headlines, titles)* où va le christianisme?

CONJ (vers) où; **I shall go w. fate leads me** j'irai là où me mènera le destin

whiting ['waɪtɪŋ] **N 1** *Ich* merlan *m* **2** *(colouring agent)* blanc *m* d'Espagne

whitish ['waɪtɪʃ] **ADJ** blanchâtre; **her hair was w. blond** ses cheveux étaient d'un blond presque blanc

whitlow ['wɪtləʊ] **N** panaris *m*

Whitsun ['wɪtsən], **Whitsuntide** ['wɪtsəntaɪd] **N** Pentecôte *f*; **at W.** à la Pentecôte

whittle ['wɪtəl] **VT** tailler (au couteau); **he whittled an arrow from an old stick, he whittled an old stick into an arrow** il a taillé une flèche dans un vieux bâton

VI tailler (au couteau)

▸ **whittle away** **VT SEP** *Fig* amoindrir, diminuer; **they whittled away his resistance** ils ont amoindri sa résistance

VI *(with knife)* tailler; **he sat there whittling away at a piece of wood** il était assis à tailler un morceau de bois avec un couteau; *Fig* **their constant teasing whittled away at his patience** leurs moqueries constantes ont mis sa patience à bout

▸ **whittle down** **VT SEP** *(with knife)* tailler (au couteau); *Fig* amenuiser, amoindrir; **rising fuel costs have whittled down our profits** l'augmentation du prix du pétrole a fait baisser nos bénéfices; **we've whittled down the number of candidates** nous avons réduit le nombre de candidats

whizz [wɪz] *(pt & pp* **whizzed**, *cont* **whizzing)** **VI 1** *(rush)* filer; **a car whizzed past** une voiture est passée à toute allure; **the holiday has just whizzed by** les vacances ont passé à toute vitesse **2** *(hiss)* **bullets whizzed around** *or* **past him** des balles sifflaient tout autour *ou* passaient près de lui en sifflant

N 1 *(hissing sound)* sifflement *m*

2 *Fam (swift movement)* **I'll just have a (quick) w. round with the Hoover®/the duster** je vais juste passer un petit coup d'aspirateur/de chiffon

3 *Fam (bright person)* as *m*; **she's a w. at chemistry** c'est un as en chimie; **she's a real computer w.** c'est vraiment un as de l'informatique; **he's a real w. in the kitchen** il cuisine comme un chef

4 *Br Fam Drugs slang (amphetamines)* amphés *fpl*, amphets *fpl*

5 *Am Fam* **to take a w.** *(urinate)* faire pipi

▸▸ *Fam* ***whizz kid*** jeune prodige[□] *m*; **she's a computer w. kid** c'est un vrai génie de l'informatique

▸ **whizz through** **VT INSEP** *Fam (work)* faire à toute vitesse[□]; *(meal)* avaler[□]; *(book)* lire à toute vitesse[□]

WHO [,dʌbəljuːeɪtʃ'əʊ] **N** *(abbr* **World Health Organization)** OMS *f*

who [huː] **PRON** *(what person or persons* ▸ *as subject)* (qui est-ce) qui; (▸ *as object)* qui est-ce que, qui; **w. are you?** qui êtes-vous?; **w. is it?** *(at door)* qui est-ce?, qui est là?; **w.'s speaking?** *(on telephone)* qui est à l'appareil?; *(asking for third person)* c'est de la part de qui?; **w.'s going with you?** qui est-ce qui *ou* qui t'accompagne?; **it's Michael – w.?** c'est Michael – qui ça?; **I told him w. I was** je lui ai dit qui j'étais; **find out w. they are** voyez qui c'est *ou* qui sont ces gens; **bring w. you want** amenez qui vous voulez; **w. do you think you are?** vous vous prenez pour qui?; **w. do you think you are, giving me orders?** de quel droit est-ce que vous me donnez des ordres?; **w. did you say was coming to the party?** qui avez-vous dit qui viendrait à la soirée?; **w. did they invite?** qui est-ce qu'ils ont invité?, qui ont-ils invité?; **you'll have to tell me w.'s w.** il faudra que tu me dises qui est qui; **w. is the film by?** de qui est le film?; **w. is the letter from?** la lettre est de qui?, de qui est la lettre?; **w. did he go with?** avec qui y est-il allé?; **w. were you talking to?** à qui parliez-vous?

RELATIVE PRON *(subject)* qui; *(object)* que; **the family w. lived here moved away** la famille qui habitait ici a déménagé; **those of you w. were late** ceux d'entre vous qui sont arrivés en retard; **anyone w. so wishes may leave** ceux qui le souhaitent peuvent partir; **Charles, w. is a policeman, lives upstairs** Charles, qui est policier, vit en haut; **my mother, w. I believe you've met...** ma mère, que vous avez déjà rencontrée je crois...

whoa [wəʊ] EXCLAM ho!, holà!; *Fam (to person)* doucement!, attendez!

who'd [hu:d] **1** = **who had 2** = **who would**

whodunit, whodunnit [ˌhu:ˈdʌnɪt] N *Fam* polar *m*

whoever [hu:ˈevə(r)] PRON **1** *(any person who)* qui; **w. wants it can have it** celui qui le veut peut le prendre; **I'll give it to w. needs it** je le donnerai à qui en a besoin; **invite w. you like** invitez qui vous voulez
2 *(the person who)* celui qui (celle qui) *m,f*; *(the people who)* ceux qui (celles qui) *mpl,fpl*; **w. answered the phone had a nice voice** la personne qui a répondu au téléphone avait une voix agréable
3 *(no matter who)* **come out, w. you are!** montrez-vous, qui que vous soyez!; **w. gets the job will find it a real challenge** celui qui obtiendra cet emploi n'aura pas la tâche facile; **it's from Sandy Campbell, w. he is** c'est de la part d'un certain Sandy Campbell, si ça te dit quelque chose; **ask Mark or Paul or w.** demande à Mark ou à Paul ou à n'importe qui
4 *(emphatic use)* qui donc; **w. can that be?** qui cela peut-il bien être?

whole [həʊl] ADJ **1** *(entire, complete) (with singular nouns)* entier, tout; *(with plural nouns)* entier; **it took me a w. day to paint the kitchen** j'ai mis une journée entière *ou* toute une journée pour peindre la cuisine; **I didn't read the w. book** je n'ai pas lu tout le livre *ou* le livre en entier; **I've never seen anything like it in my w. life** je n'ai jamais vu une chose pareille de toute ma vie; **that was the w. point** c'était précisément pour cette raison; **she said nothing the w. time we were there** elle n'a rien dit tout le temps que nous étions là; **I never saw her the w. evening** je ne l'ai pas vue de (toute) la soirée; **the w. truth** toute la vérité; **the w. world was watching** le monde entier regardait; **do you have to tell the w. world?** est-ce que tu tiens à ce que tout le monde le sache?; **w. cities were devastated** des villes entières furent dévastées; **there are two w. months still to go** il reste deux mois entiers; **the w. thing** *or* **the w. business was a farce** ce fut un véritable fiasco; **I had to start the w. thing over again** j'ai dû tout recommencer; **forget the w. thing** n'en parlons plus
2 *(as intensifier)* tout; *Fam* **a w. pile of records** tout un tas de disques; **he's got a w. collection of old photographs** il a toute une collection de vieilles photographies; **a w. new way of living** une façon de vivre tout à fait nouvelle
3 *(unbroken ▸ china, egg yolk)* intact; *(unhurt ▸ person)* indemne, sain et sauf; **the cups were still w.** les tasses étaient toujours intactes; *Arch or Bible* **to make w.** sauver; **thy faith hath made thee w.** ta foi t'a sauvé
4 *Culin (milk)* entier; *(grain)* complet(ète)
5 *(brother, sister)* **w. brothers** des frères qui ont les mêmes parents
N **1** *(complete thing, unit)* ensemble *m*; **the w. of which this is just a part** l'ensemble dont ceci n'est qu'une partie; **the w. is greater than the sum of its parts** le tout est plus grand que la somme des parties **2** *(as quantifier)* **the w. of** tout; **it will be cold over the w. of England** il fera froid sur toute l'Angleterre; **we spent the w. of August at the seaside** nous avons passé tout le mois d'août au bord de la mer; **can you pay the w. of the amount?** pouvez-vous payer toute la somme *ou* l'intégralité de la somme?
ADV **cook the fish w.** faites cuire le poisson entier; **to swallow sth w.** avaler qch en entier; *Fam Fig* **he swallowed her story w.** il a gobé tout ce qu'elle lui a dit
• **as a whole** ADV **1** *(as a unit)* entièrement; **as a w. or in part** entièrement ou en partie **2** *(overall)* dans son ensemble; **is it true of America as a w.?** est-ce vrai pour toute l'Amérique *ou* l'Amérique en général?; **considered as a w., the festival was a remarkable success** dans son ensemble, le festival a été un vrai succès
• **a whole lot** ADV *Fam* beaucoup□; **he's a w. lot younger than his wife** il est beaucoup plus jeune que sa femme; **I don't think it will make a w. lot of difference** je ne pense pas que ça fasse une énorme différence; **for a w. lot of reasons** pour tout un tas de raisons
• **on the whole** ADV dans l'ensemble; **on the w. he made a good impression** dans l'ensemble, il a fait bonne impression; **I agree with that on the w.** je suis d'accord dans l'ensemble
▸▸ *Am Mus* ***whole note*** *(semibreve)* ronde *f*; *Math* ***whole number*** *(integer)* nombre *m* entier; *Am Mus* ***whole rest*** pause *f*

wholefood [ˈhəʊlfu:d] N aliment *m* complet; **the w. section of the supermarket** le rayon diététique du supermarché; **w. shop** magasin *m* diététique

wholehearted [ˌhəʊlˈhɑ:tɪd] ADJ *(unreserved)* sans réserve; **she gave them her w. support** elle leur a donné un soutien sans réserve *ou* sans faille; **he is a w. supporter of our cause** il est dévoué corps et âme à notre cause

wholeheartedly [ˌhəʊlˈhɑ:tɪdlɪ] ADV *(unreservedly)* de tout cœur; **I agree w.** j'accepte de tout (mon) cœur; **he flung himself w. into his new job** il s'est jeté corps et âme dans son nouveau travail

wholemeal [ˈhəʊlmi:l] ADJ *Br (bread, flour)* complet(ète)

wholeness [ˈhəʊlnɪs] N *(indivisibility)* intégrité *f*, intégralité *f*

wholesale [ˈhəʊlseɪl] N (vente *f* en) gros *m*; **w. and retail** le gros et le détail
ADJ **1** *(business, price, shop)* de gros **2** *Fig (indiscriminate)* en masse; **there was a w. massacre of civilians** il y a eu un énorme massacre de civils
ADV **1** *(buy, sell)* en gros; **they only sell w.** ils vendent uniquement en gros; **I can get it for you w.** je peux vous le procurer au prix de gros **2** *Fig (in entirety)* **to reject sth w.** rejeter qch en bloc; **communities have been destroyed w.** des communautés entières ont été détruites
▸▸ *Fin* ***wholesale dealer*** grossiste *mf*; ***wholesale distribution*** distribution *f* en gros; ***wholesale goods*** marchandises *fpl* de gros; ***wholesale price*** prix *m* de gros; ***wholesale trade*** commerce *m* de gros; ***wholesale trader*** grossiste *mf*

wholesaler [ˈhəʊlˌseɪlə(r)] N grossiste *mf*, commerçant(e) *m,f* en gros

wholesaling [ˈhəʊlˌseɪlɪŋ] N vente *f* en gros

wholesome [ˈhəʊlsəm] ADJ *(healthy ▸ food, attitude, image, life)* sain; *(▸ air, climate, environment)* salubre, salutaire; *(advice)* salutaire; **a w.-looking boy** un garçon sain d'aspect

wholesomeness [ˈhəʊlsəmnɪs] N *(of food, attitude, image, life)* nature *f* saine; *(of air, climate, environment)* salubrité *f*; **the w. of her appearance** son côté rangé *ou* (bien) comme il faut

wholewheat [ˈhəʊlwi:t] ADJ *(bread, flour)* complet(ète)

who'll [hu:l] **1** = **who will 2** = **who shall**

wholly [ˈhəʊlɪ] ADV entièrement; **you will be w. compensated for the damage** les dommages vous seront intégralement remboursés

wholly-owned subsidiary N *Com* filiale *f* à cent pour cent; **the firm has two wholly-owned subsidiaries** la société a deux filiales à cent pour cent

whom [hu:m] *Formal* PRON *(in questions)* qui; **w. did you contact?** qui avez-vous contacté?; **w. did she see?** qui a-t-elle vu?; **for w. was the book written?** pour qui le livre a-t-il été écrit?
RELATIVE PRON **1** *(as object of verb)* que; **she is the person w. I most admire** c'est la personne que j'admire le plus; **she saw two men, neither of w. she recognized** elle a vu deux hommes mais elle n'a reconnu ni l'un ni l'autre **2** *(after preposition)* **the person to w. I am writing** la personne à qui *ou* à laquelle j'écris; **a composer about w. little is known** un compositeur sur qui *ou* sur lequel on sait peu de choses

whoop [wu:p] N **1** *(yell)* cri *m*; **whoops of delight came from the nursery** il y avait des cris de joie venant de la garderie **2** *Med* quinte *f* de toux
VI **1** *(yell)* **she whooped with joy** elle poussa un cri de joie **2** *Med* avoir un accès de toux coquelucheuse

whoopee *Fam* EXCLAM [wʊˈpi:] youpi!
N [ˈwʊpi:] **to make w.** *(celebrate)* faire la noce; *(have sex)* faire l'amour□
▸▸ ***whoopee cushion*** coussin-péteur *m*

whooping cough [ˈhu:pɪŋ-] N *Med* coqueluche *f*

whoops [wʊps], **whoops-a-daisy** EXCLAM *Fam* houp-là!

whop [wɒp] *(pt & pp* **whopped**, *cont* **whopping**) *Fam* VT *(beat)* rosser; *(defeat)* écraser
N *(blow)* coup□ *m*

whopper [ˈwɒpə(r)] N *Fam* **1** *(large object)* **he caught a real w.** *(fish)* il a attrapé un poisson super gros; **he's got a w. of a nose** il a un nez énorme□; **that sandwich is a real w.** c'est un énorme sandwich□ *ou* un sandwich gigantesque; **what a w.!** il est gigantesque! **2** *(lie)* gros mensonge□ *m*, mensonge *m* énorme□; **to tell a w.** dire un mensonge gros comme une maison

whopping [ˈwɒpɪŋ] *Fam* ADJ énorme□, géant; **inflation increased to a w. 360 percent** l'inflation a atteint le taux colossal de 360 pour cent□
ADV **a w. great lie** un mensonge énorme□; **a w. great fish** un poisson super gros
N *(beating, defeat)* raclée *f*

who're [ˈhu:ə(r)] = **who are**

whore [hɔ:(r)] *Pej* N putain *f*; *Bible (sinner)* pécheresse *f*
VI **1 to go whoring** *(prostitute oneself)* se prostituer; *(frequent prostitutes)* fréquenter les prostituées, courir la gueuse **2** *Fig* **to w. after sth** se prostituer pour obtenir qch

whorehouse [ˈhɔ:haʊs, *pl* -haʊzɪz] N *Fam* maison *f* close□

whoremonger [ˈhɔ:ˌmʌŋgə(r)] N *Arch or Bible* vicieux *m*, fornicateur *m*

whoring [ˈhɔ:rɪŋ] N *Old-fashioned & Literary* **1** *(by woman)* prostitution *f* **2** *(by man)* **because of all his w.** parce qu'il n'arrêtait pas de fréquenter les prostituées

whorl [wɜ:l] N **1** *(on shell)* spire *f*; *(on finger)* sillon *m*; **whorls of smoke rose from the chimney** la fumée montait en spirale de la cheminée, des volutes de fumée s'échappaient de la cheminée **2** *Bot* verticille *m*

whorled [wɜ:ld] ADJ *(flower)* verticillé; *(shell)* convoluté

whortleberry [ˈwɜ:təlˌberɪ] *(pl* **whortleberries**) N myrtille *f*

who's [hu:z] **1** = **who is 2** = **who has**

whose [hu:z] POSSESSIVE PRON à qui; **w. is it?** à qui est-ce?; **w. could it be?** à qui pourrait-il bien être?; **w. was the winning number?** à qui était le numéro gagnant?
POSSESSIVE ADJ **1** *(in a question)* à qui, de qui; **w. car was he driving?** à qui était la voiture qu'il conduisait?; **w. child is she?** de qui est-elle l'enfant?; **w. side are you on?** de quel côté êtes-vous?; **w. fault is it?** à qui la faute? **2** *(in a relative clause)* dont; **isn't that the man w. photograph was in the newspaper?** n'est-ce pas l'homme qui était en photo dans le journal?; **the girl, both of w. parents had died, lived with her aunt** la fille, dont les parents étaient morts, vivait avec sa tante; **they had twins neither of w. names I can remember** ils avaient des jumeaux mais je ne me souviens pas de leurs prénoms

whosoever [ˌhu:səʊˈevə(r)] PRON *Formal or Literary* celui (celle) qui, quiconque

Who's Who N ≃ le Bottin® mondain

who've [hu:v] = **who have**

why [waɪ] ADV pourquoi; **w. is it that he never phones?** pourquoi est-ce qu'il ne téléphone jamais?; **w. continue the war at all?** pourquoi *ou* à quoi bon continuer la guerre?; **w. pay more?** pourquoi payer davantage?; **w. the sudden panic?** pourquoi toute cette agitation?; **w. not?** pourquoi pas?; **w. not join us?** vous pourriez vous joindre à nous, joignez-vous donc à nous; **w. me?** pourquoi moi?
CONJ pourquoi; **I wonder w. he left** je me demande pourquoi il est parti; **that's w. he dislikes you** c'est pour ça qu'il *ou* voilà pourquoi il ne vous aime pas; **is that w. she hasn't written?** est-ce pour ça qu'elle n'a pas écrit?; **they've gone, I can't think w.** ils sont partis, je ne sais pas pourquoi
RELATIVE PRON *(after "reason")* **the reason w. I lied was that I was scared** j'ai menti parce que j'avais peur; **he didn't tell me the reason w.** il ne m'a pas dit pourquoi; **this is the reason w. I lied** voilà pourquoi j'ai menti; **there is no (good) reason w. she shouldn't come** il n'y a pas de raison qu'elle ne vienne pas
EXCLAM *(expressing surprise, indignation etc)* **w., it's your sister!** tiens, c'est ta sœur!; **w., Mr Ricks,**

how kind of you to call! M. Ricks! comme c'est gentil à vous de téléphoner!; **w., there's nothing to it!** oh, il n'y a rien de plus simple!; **w., he's an impostor!** mais enfin, c'est un imposteur!

N the whys and wherefores le pourquoi et le comment

WI[1] [ˌdʌbəljuːˈaɪ] **N** (*abbr* **Women's Institute**) = association britannique de femmes particulièrement active en milieu rural, à qui l'on prête une image démodée

NPL (*abbr* **West Indies**) Antilles *fpl*

WI[2] (*written abbr* **Wisconsin**) Wisconsin *m*

wick [wɪk] **N 1** (*for candle, lamp*) mèche *f* **2** *very Fam* **to dip one's w.** (*have sex*) tremper son biscuit **3** *Br Fam (idiom)* **to get on sb's w.** taper sur les nerfs à qn

wicked [ˈwɪkɪd] **ADJ 1** (*evil* ▸ *person, action, thought*) mauvais, méchant; (*immoral, indecent*) vicieux; **he's a w. man** c'est un méchant *ou* un mauvais homme; **what a w. thing to say!** c'est vraiment méchant de dire ça!; **she felt as if she had done something very w.** elle avait le sentiment d'avoir fait quelque chose de très mal; *Fig* **it's a w. waste of natural resources** c'est un gâchis scandaleux de ressources naturelles; **w. witch** méchante sorcière *f*; *Hum* **to have one's w. way with sb** séduire qn

2 (*very bad* ▸ *weather*) épouvantable; (▸ *temper*) mauvais, épouvantable; **he's got a w. temper** il a très mauvais caractère; **there are some w. bends on those mountain roads** il y a quelques méchants virages sur ces routes de montagne; **they're asking a w. price for their house** ils ont mis leur maison en vente à un prix exorbitant; *Fam* **prices have gone up something w.** les prix ont augmenté quelque chose d'incroyable

3 (*mischievous* ▸ *person*) malicieux; (▸ *smile, look, sense of humour*) malicieux, coquin; **you're a w. little boy** tu es un petit coquin; **a w. remark** une réflexion malicieuse *ou* espiègle

4 *Fam* (*skilful* ▸ *goal, shot*) super; **she has a w. forehand** elle a un sacré coup droit; **that was a w. goal** c'était un sacré *ou* super but

5 *Fam* (*very good*) génial; **she makes a w. curry** elle fait un curry d'enfer

ADV *Am Fam* vachement; **this bed is w. comfortable** il est vachement confortable, ce lit

EXCLAM *Fam* génial!

NPL the w. les méchants *mpl*; *Hum* **(there's) no rest for the w.** pas de repos pour les braves

wickedly [ˈwɪkɪdlɪ] **ADV 1** (*with evil intent*) méchamment, avec méchanceté **2** (*mischievously*) malicieusement

wickedness [ˈwɪkɪdnɪs] **N 1** *Rel* (*sin, evil*) iniquité *f*, vilenie *f*; (*cruelty* ▸ *of action, crime*) méchanceté *f*; (▸ *of thought*) méchanceté *f*, vilenie *f*; **he spoke of the w. in the world** il parla du mal qui règne dans le monde **2** (*mischievousness* ▸ *of look, sense of humour, smile*) caractère *m* malicieux *ou* espiègle, malice *f*

wicker [ˈwɪkə(r)] **N** osier *m*; **made of w.** en osier

ADJ (*furniture*) en osier

▸▸ ***wicker basket*** panier *m* en osier

wickerwork [ˈwɪkəwɜːk] **N** (*material*) osier *m*; (*objects*) vannerie *f*; **is the chair made of w.?** est-ce que la chaise est en osier?; **they sell w.** ils vendent de la vannerie

COMP (*furniture*) en osier; (*shop*) de vannerie

wicket [ˈwɪkɪt] **N 1** *Am* (*window*) guichet *m* **2** (*gate*) (petite) porte *f*, portillon *m* **3** (*in cricket* ▸ *stumps*) guichet *m*; (▸ *area of grass*) terrain *m* (entre les guichets); **to keep w.** garder les guichets; **to take a w.** éliminer un batteur

wicketkeeper [ˈwɪkɪtkiːpə(r)] **N** gardien *m* de guichet (*au cricket*)

widdle [ˈwɪdəl] *Br Fam* **N to have a w.** (*urinate*) faire pipi

VI faire pipi

-WIDE — SUFFIXE

Le suffixe **-wide** sert à créer des adjectifs et des adverbes. Ajouté à des noms de lieux ou d'organisations, il indique le fait que ces derniers sont concernés par ce dont on parle DANS LEUR INTÉGRALITÉ :

nationwide (*employé comme adjectif*) national; (*employé comme adverbe*) à l'échelle nationale, dans tout le pays; **the product is sold worldwide** ce produit se vend dans le monde entier; **she enjoys countrywide support** tout le pays la soutient; **the regulation applies citywide** cette règle est valable dans toute la ville; **companywide changes** des changements qui concernent l'ensemble de l'entreprise.

wide [waɪd] **ADJ 1** (*broad*) large; **how w. is it?** cela fait combien (de mètres) de large?, quelle largeur ça fait?; **do you know how w. it is?** savez-vous combien ça fait de large?; **the road is 30 metres w.** la route fait 30 mètres de large; **they're making the street wider** ils élargissent la route; **he gave a w. grin** il a fait un large sourire; **we need to see the problem in a wider context** il faut que nous envisagions le problème dans un contexte plus général; **I'm using the word in its widest sense** j'emploie ce mot au sens le plus large; **to disappear into the w. blue yonder** disparaître, s'évanouir dans la nature

2 (*fully open* ▸ *eyes*) grand ouvert; **she watched with w. eyes** elle regardait les yeux grands ouverts; **his eyes were w. with terror** ses yeux étaient écarquillés par l'épouvante

3 (*extensive, vast*) étendu, vaste; **a w. plain** une vaste plaine; **to travel the w. world** parcourir le vaste monde; **she has w. experience in this area** elle a une longue *ou* une grande expérience dans ce domaine; **he has very w. interests** il a des centres d'intérêt très larges; **he has a w. knowledge of music** il a de vastes connaissances *ou* des connaissances approfondies en musique; **there are w. gaps in her knowledge** il y a des lacunes importantes dans ses connaissances; **the incident received w. publicity** l'événement a été largement couvert par les médias; *Com* **a w. range of products** une gamme importante de produits; **a w. range of views was expressed** des points de vue très différents furent exprimés; **a w. variety of colours** un grand choix de couleurs

4 (*large* ▸ *difference*) **the gap between rich and poor remains w.** l'écart (existant) entre les riches et les pauvres demeure considérable

5 *Sport* **the ball was w.** la balle est passée à côté; **the shot was w.** le coup est passé à côté; *Br* **to be w. of the mark** rater *ou* être passé loin de la cible; *Fig* être loin de la vérité *ou* du compte

ADV 1 (*to full extent*) **open (your mouth) w.** ouvrez grand votre bouche; **she opened the windows w.** elle ouvrit les fenêtres en grand; **he flung his arms w.** il a ouvert grand les bras; **place your feet w. apart** écartez bien les pieds **2** (*away from target*) à côté; **the missile went w.** le missile est tombé à côté

N (*in cricket*) balle *f* écartée *ou* qui passe hors de la portée du batteur

▸▸ *Comput* ***wide area network*** réseau *m* longue distance; *Br Fam Pej* ***wide boy*** escroc[□] *m*, fricoteur *m*; *Cin* ***wide screen*** grand écran *m*, écran *m* panoramique; *Cin & TV* ***wide shot*** plan *m* d'ensemble

wide-angle ADJ

▸▸ ***wide-angle lens*** grand-angle *m*, grand-angulaire *m*; *Cin & TV* ***wide-angle shot*** panoramique *m*

wide-body ADJ a w. aircraft avion *m* à fuselage élargi, gros-porteur *m*

wide-eyed ADJ 1 (*with fear, surprise*) les yeux agrandis *ou* écarquillés; **he looked at me in w. astonishment** il me regarda, les yeux écarquillés d'étonnement; **she watched w.** elle regardait, les yeux écarquillés **2** (*naive*) candide, ingénu; **he listened with w. innocence** il écoutait, l'air tout innocent

widely [ˈwaɪdlɪ] **ADV 1** (*broadly*) **to smile w.** faire un grand sourire; **to yawn w.** bâiller profondément; **the houses were w. scattered/spaced** les maisons étaient très dispersées/espacées **2** (*extensively*) **she has travelled w.** elle a beaucoup voyagé; **the talk ranged w. over a variety of topics** la discussion embrassa des sujets très variés; **the drug is now w. available/used** le médicament est maintenant largement répandu/utilisé; **it was w. believed that war was inevitable** il était largement *ou* communément admis que la guerre était inévitable; **w. held beliefs/opinions** des croyances/des opinions très répandues; **to be w. read** (*writer, book*) être très lu, avoir un grand public; (*person*) avoir beaucoup lu, être très cultivé; **she is w. read in history** elle est très érudite en histoire **3** *Fig* (*significantly*) **prices vary w.** les prix varient très sensiblement; **the two versions differed w.** les deux versions étaient sensiblement différentes; **the students came from w. differing backgrounds** les étudiants venaient d'horizons très différents

widen [ˈwaɪdən] **VT** élargir, agrandir; *Fig* (*experience, influence, knowledge*) accroître, étendre; **the tax reform will w. the gap between rich and poor** la réforme fiscale va accentuer *ou* agrandir l'écart entre les riches et les pauvres; **I've widened my study to include recent events** j'ai développé mon étude afin d'y inclure les derniers événements

VI s'élargir; (*eyes*) s'agrandir; (*smile*) s'accentuer; **the gulf between skilled and unskilled workers is widening** l'écart entre les travailleurs qualifiés et non qualifiés va en s'accentuant; **turn left where the road widens out** tournez à gauche à l'endroit où la route s'élargit

wideness [ˈwaɪdnɪs] **N** largeur *f*

widening [ˈwaɪdənɪŋ] **N 1** (*of road, channel*) élargissement *m* **2** (*of influence*) extension *f*

widescreen [ˈwaɪdskriːn] **N** grand écran *m*; **in w.** en grand écran

ADJ grand écran (*inv*); **a w. epic** un film à grand spectacle

▸▸ ***widescreen television*** téléviseur *m* grand écran

widespread [ˈwaɪdspred] **ADJ 1** (*arms*) en croix; (*wings*) déployé; **she stood there arms w.** elle se tenait là, les bras en croix **2** (*extensive*) (très) répandu; **there has been w. public concern** l'opinion publique se montre extrêmement préoccupée

widgeon = **wigeon**

widget [ˈwɪdʒɪt] **N 1** *Fam* (*thing, gadget*) truc *m*, machin *m* **2** (*in beer can*) = dispositif fixé au fond des canettes de bière afin de produire de la mousse lorsque le contenu est versé dans le verre

widow [ˈwɪdəʊ] **N 1** (*woman*) veuve *f*; **she's a w.** elle est veuve; *Br Fam Hum* **a golf w.** = une femme que son mari délaisse pour jouer au golf; *Bible* **the w.'s mite** le denier de la veuve **2** *Typ & Comput* (ligne *f*) veuve *f*

VT (*usu passive*) **he/she was widowed last year** il a perdu sa femme/elle a perdu son mari l'année dernière; **she is recently widowed** elle est veuve depuis peu, elle a perdu son mari il n'y a pas longtemps; **he is twice widowed** il est deux fois veuf

▸▸ ***widow's peak*** = ligne de cheveux sur le front en forme de v; ***widow's pension*** allocation *f* veuvage; ***widow's weeds*** deuil *m* de veuve

widowed [ˈwɪdəʊd] **ADJ** (*man*) veuf; (*woman*) veuve; **his w. mother** sa mère qui est/était veuve

widower [ˈwɪdəʊə(r)] **N** veuf *m*

widowhood [ˈwɪdəʊhʊd] **N** veuvage *m*

width [wɪdθ] **N 1** (*breadth*) largeur *f*; **the room was ten metres in w.** la pièce faisait dix mètres de largeur; **she swam the entire w. of the river** elle a traversé le fleuve à la nage **2** (*of swimming pool*) largeur *f*; **she swam two widths** elle a fait deux largeurs de piscine **3** *Tex* laize *f*, lé *m*; **half a w. of cloth** une demi-laize *ou* un demi-lé de tissu

widthways [ˈwɪdθweɪz], **widthwise** [ˈwɪdθwaɪz] **ADV** dans le sens de la largeur

wield [wiːld] **VT 1** (*weapon*) brandir; (*pen, tool*) manier **2** (*influence, power*) exercer, user de

wiener [ˈwiːnə(r)] **N** *Am* **1** (*frankfurter*) saucisse *f* de Francfort **2** *very Fam* (*penis*) zizi *m*

Wiener schnitzel [ˈviːnəˈʃnɪtsəl] **N** *Culin* escalope *f* viennoise

wife [waɪf] (*pl* **wives** [waɪvz]) **N 1** (*spouse*) femme *f*, épouse *f*; *Admin* conjointe *f*; *Arch* **to take a w.** prendre femme; *Formal* **do you take this woman to be your lawful, wedded w.?** prenez-vous cette femme pour épouse légitime?; *Arch* **to take sb to w.** prendre qn pour femme; **she's his second w.** elle est sa deuxième femme, il l'a épousée en secondes noces; **she's been a good w. to him** elle a été une bonne épouse pour lui; **the farmer's w.**

la fermière; *Br Fam* **the w.** la bourgeoise **2** *Arch or Fam (woman)* femme *f*

wife-beater N **1** *(man)* = homme qui bat sa femme **2** *Am Fam (vest)* marcel *m*

wifely ['waɪflɪ] *(compar* **wifelier**, *superl* **wifeliest)** ADJ de bonne épouse

wife-swapping N échangisme *m*

▸▸ ***wife-swapping party*** soirée *f* échangiste

WiFi ['waɪˌfaɪ] *Comput (abbr* **wireless fidelity)** N WiFi *m*

ADJ WiFi

wig [wɪg] *(pt & pp* **wigged**, *cont* **wigging)** N perruque *f*; *(hairpiece)* postiche *m*; *Br (for lawyers)* perruque *f*

▸▸ *Bot* ***wig tree*** arbre *m* à perruque, fustet *m*

▸**wig out** VI *esp Am Fam (get angry)* piquer une crise, péter les plombs; *(go mad)* devenir cinglé, perdre la boule; *(get excited)* devenir dingue

wigeon ['wɪdʒən] N *Orn* canard *m* siffleur

wigged [wɪgd] ADJ à perruque

wigging ['wɪgɪŋ] N *Br Fam Old-fashioned (scolding)* savon *m*; **to get a (good) w.** se faire disputer, se faire passer un savon; **to give sb a (good) w.** passer un savon à qn

wiggle ['wɪgəl] VT remuer; *(hips)* remuer, tortiller; **to w. one's toes** remuer les orteils; **to w. one's hips** tortiller des hanches

VI *(person)* (se) remuer, frétiller; *(loose object)* branler

N **1** *(movement)* tortillement *m*; **he gave his toes a w.** il remua ses orteils **2** *(wavy line)* trait *m* ondulé

▸▸ *Fam* ***wiggle room*** marge*f*; **that doesn't leave much w. room** ça ne laisse pas beaucoup de marge

wiggly ['wɪglɪ] *(compar* **wigglier**, *superl* **wiggliest)** ADJ frétillant, qui remue; **a w. line** un trait ondulé

wiggy ['wɪgɪ] *(compar* **wiggier**, *superl* **wiggiest)** ADJ *Am Fam (mad)* cinglé, tapé; *(eccentric)* loufoque, allumé

wigmaker ['wɪgˌmeɪkə(r)] N perruquier(ère) *m,f*

wigwam ['wɪgwæm] N wigwam *m*

wiki ['wɪkɪ] *Comput* N wiki *m*

ADJ wiki

wilco ['wɪlkəʊ] EXCLAM *Tel* j'exécute

wild [waɪld] ADJ **1** *(undomesticated)* sauvage; *(untamed)* farouche; **a w. beast** une bête sauvage; *Fig* une bête féroce; **a pack of w. dogs** une meute de chiens féroces *ou* sauvages; **a w. rabbit** un lapin de garenne

2 *(uncultivated* ▸ *fruit)* sauvage; (▸ *flower, plant)* sauvage, des champs; **w. strawberries** fraises *fpl* des bois; **many parts of the country are still w.** beaucoup de régions du pays sont encore à l'état sauvage

3 *(violent)* **w. weather** du gros temps; **a w. wind** un vent violent *ou* de tempête; **a w. sea** une mer très agitée; **it was a w. night** ce fut une nuit de tempête

4 *(mad)* fou (folle), furieux; **to be w. with grief/happiness/jealousy** être fou de douleur/de joie/de jalousie; **that noise is driving me w.** ce bruit me rend fou; **he had w. eyes** *or* **a w. look in his eyes** il avait une lueur de folie dans le regard

5 *(dishevelled* ▸ *appearance)* débraillé; (▸ *hair)* en bataille, ébouriffé; **a w.-looking young man** un jeune homme à l'air farouche

6 *(enthusiastic)* **the speaker received w. applause** l'orateur reçut des applaudissements frénétiques; *Fam* **to be w. about sb** être dingue de qn; *Fam* **to be w. about sth** être dingue de qch, être emballé par qch; **I'm not really w. about modern art** l'art moderne ne m'emballe pas vraiment

7 *(outrageous* ▸ *idea, imagination)* insensé, fantaisiste; (▸ *promise)* insensé; (▸ *rumour)* délirant; (▸ *plan)* extravagant; **he has some w. scheme for getting rich quick** il a un projet farfelu *ou* abracadabrant pour devenir riche en peu de temps; **the book's success was beyond his wildest dreams** le succès de son livre dépassait ses rêves les plus fous

8 *(reckless)* fou (folle); **they're always having w. parties** ils organisent toujours des soirées démentes; **that was in my w. youth** c'était au temps de ma folle jeunesse; **we had some w. times together** nous en avons fait des folies ensemble; **there was a lot of w. talk about revolution/going to court** on a parlé à tort et à travers de révolution/de porter l'affaire devant les tribunaux

9 *(random)* **to take a w. swing at sth** lancer le poing au hasard pour atteindre qch; **to make a w. guess (at the answer)** répondre à tout hasard *ou* à l'aveuglette; **at a w. guess** à vue de nez; *Cards* **aces are w.** les as sont libres; *Fig* **to play a w. card** prendre un risque

10 *Fam Euph* **to sow one's w. oats** jeter sa gourme

11 *Fam (idiom)* **w. and woolly** *(idea, plan)* peu réfléchi; *(place)* sauvage, primitif

N **in the w.** en liberté; **the call of the w.** l'appel *m* de la nature; **he spent a year living in the w.** *or* **the wilds** il a passé un an en pleine cambrousse; **the wilds of northern Canada** les étendues sauvages du nord du Canada

ADV **1** *(grow, live)* en liberté; **strawberries grow w. in the forest** des fraises poussent à l'état sauvage dans la forêt; **the deer live w. in the hills** les cerfs vivent en liberté dans les collines

2 *(emotionally)* **to go w. with joy/rage** devenir fou de joie/de colère; **when he came on stage the audience went w.** les spectateurs hurlèrent d'enthousiasme quand il arriva sur le plateau

3 *(unconstrained)* **to run w.** *(animals)* courir en liberté; *(children)* être déchaîné; **they let their children run w.** ils laissent leurs enfants traîner dans la rue; *Fig* ils ne disciplinent pas du tout leurs enfants; **they've left the garden to run w.** ils ont laissé le jardin à l'abandon *ou* revenir à l'état sauvage

▸▸ *Zool* ***wild ass*** âne *m* sauvage; *Zool* ***wild boar*** sanglier *m*; ***wild card*** *(in card games)* joker *m*; *Comput* joker *m*; *Sport (player)* = sportif invité à participer à une compétition sans s'être qualifié; *(in American football)* = équipe qualifiée pour la finale sans pour autant avoir remporté sa poule; *Comput* ***wild card character*** caractère *m* joker; ***wild cherry*** *(fruit)* merise *f*; *(tree)* merisier *m*; *Bot* ***wild chicory*** chicorée *f* sauvage, mignonnette *f*; *Bot* ***wild garlic*** ail *m* des ours; *Zool* ***wild goat*** chèvre *f* sauvage; *(ibex)* bouquetin *m*; ***wild horse*** cheval *m* sauvage; *Fig* **w. horses couldn't drag it out of me** je serai muet comme une tombe; *Bot* ***wild hyacinth*** jacinthe *f* des bois; ***wild man*** *(savage)* sauvage *m*; *Culin* ***wild rice*** zizania *m*, riz *m* sauvage; ***wild rose*** *(dog rose)* églantine *f*; *(sweetbrier)* églantier *m* odorant; *Bot* ***wild thyme*** serpolet *m*; *Cin* ***wild track*** piste *f* non synchrone; ***Wild West*** Far West *m*; **a W. West show** = un spectacle sur le thème du Far West

wildcat ['waɪldkæt] *(pl sense* **1** *inv or* **wildcats**, *sense* **2** **wildcats)** N **1** *Zool* chat *m* sauvage; *Fig* **she's a real w.** c'est une vraie tigresse **2** *Am (product, company)* dilemme *m*

ADJ *(imprudent, ill-considered)* aléatoire, hasardeux

VI *Petr* creuser un puits d'exploration

▸▸ ***wildcat strike*** grève *f* sauvage

wildebeest ['wɪldɪbiːst] *(pl* **inv** *or* **wildebeests)** N *Zool* gnou *m*

wilderness ['wɪldənɪs] N **1** *(uninhabited area)* pays *m* désert, région *f* sauvage; *Bible* désert *m*; **a w. of snow and ice** une région *ou* une étendue de neige et de glace; **his warnings came like a voice in the w.** ses avertissements étaient comme une voix dans le désert; *Fig* **she's been relegated to the political w.** elle en est réduite à une traversée du désert sur le plan politique; **a concrete w.** un désert de béton; *Fig* **a cultural w.** un désert culturel **2** *(overgrown piece of land)* jungle *f*; **the garden's like a w.** le jardin est une véritable jungle

ADJ *(region)* reculé; *Fig* **the w. years** la traversée du désert; **the party believes that the w. years may be about to end** le parti pense que sa traversée du désert touche à sa fin

▸▸ ***wilderness area*** *(gen)* région *f* déserte; *Am (protected area)* parc *m* naturel

wildfire ['waɪldˌfaɪə(r)] N **to spread like w.** se répandre comme une traînée de poudre; **news of the attack spread like w.** la nouvelle de l'attaque s'est répandue comme une traînée de poudre

wildfowl ['waɪldfaʊl] NPL oiseaux *mpl* sauvages; *Hunt (collectively)* sauvagine *f*, gibier *m* à plume

wild-goose chase N **to go on a w.** faire fausse route; **you're on a w.** tu es sur une fausse piste, tu perds ton temps; **I was sent on a w.** on m'a envoyé courir au diable pour rien

wilding ['waɪldɪŋ] N **1** *(crab apple)* pomme *f* sauvage

2 *(wild plant)* plante *f* sauvage

3 *(wild animal)* animal *m* sauvage

4 *Am Fam* = actes de violence extrême effectués par une bande de voyous contre des personnes

wildlife ['waɪldlaɪf] N *(UNCOUNT) (wild animals)* faune *f*; *(wild animals and plants)* la faune et la flore

COMP de la vie sauvage; *(photographer)* de la nature; *(programme)* sur la nature *ou* la vie sauvage; *(expert, enthusiast)* de la faune et de la flore

▸▸ ***wildlife park*** réserve *f* naturelle; ***wildlife sanctuary*** réserve *f* animale

wildly ['waɪldlɪ] ADV **1** *(violently)* violemment, furieusement; **waves beat w. against the rocks** les vagues venaient se heurter furieusement contre les rochers; **she struggled w. to free herself** elle se débattait furieusement pour tenter de se libérer

2 *(enthusiastically)* frénétiquement; **the crowd applauded w.** la foule applaudissait frénétiquement

3 *(randomly)* au hasard; **"you're a Scorpio, aren't you," I said, guessing w.** "tu es Scorpion, non?", ai-je demandé au hasard; **to swing w. at sb/sth** lancer le poing au hasard en direction de qn/qch; **he dashed about w.** il courait dans tous les sens

4 *(extremely)* excessivement; **exchange rates fluctuated w.** les taux de change fluctuaient énormément; **the reports are w. inaccurate** les comptes rendus sont complètement faux; **to be w. excited** être surexcité; **w. expensive** follement cher; **he is w. funny!** il est d'un drôle!; **his stories are w. funny** ses histoires sont à mourir de rire; **to be w. jealous/happy** être fou de jalousie/de bonheur; **I'm not w. happy about the decision** cette décision ne m'enchante pas spécialement; **it's not w. encouraging** ça n'est pas franchement encourageant; **I'm not w. enthusiastic about it** je ne suis pas franchement emballé

wildness ['waɪldnɪs] N **1** *(of country, animal)* état *m* sauvage; *(of region, landscape)* aspect *m* sauvage

2 *(violence, intensity* ▸ *of storm)* violence *f*; *(of wind, waves)* fureur *f*, violence *f*; (▸ *of applause)* frénésie *f*; (▸ *of imagination)* caractère *m* insensé *ou* fantaisiste

3 *(disorderliness* ▸ *of party)* ambiance *f* démente; **the w. of the atmosphere** l'ambiance démente; **the w. of her appearance** son apparence débraillée

4 *(madness)* **the w. of his eyes** la lueur de folie qui brillait dans son regard

5 *(outrageousness* ▸ *of ideas, words)* extravagance *f*

wiles [waɪlz] NPL ruses *fpl*; **he fell victim to her feminine w.** il se laissa prendre à ses ruses de femme

wilful, Am willful ['wɪlfʊl] ADJ **1** *(deliberate)* délibéré; *(damage)* volontaire, délibéré; **he rebuked her for w. disobedience** il l'a réprimandée pour avoir désobéi délibérément *ou* à dessein **2** *(obstinate)* entêté, obstiné

wilfully, Am willfully ['wɪlfʊlɪ] ADV **1** *(deliberately)* délibérément; **he w. disregarded my advice** il n'a délibérément *ou* sciemment tenu aucun compte de mes conseils **2** *(obstinately)* obstinément, avec entêtement; **she has behaved quite w. over this issue** elle n'en a fait qu'à sa tête à ce sujet

wilfulness, Am willfulness ['wɪlfʊlnɪs] N **1** *(deliberateness)* caractère *m* délibéré; *(of damage)* caractère *m* intentionnel **2** *(obstinacy)* obstination *f*, entêtement *m*

wiliness ['waɪlɪnɪs] N *(of person)* ruse *f*, caractère *m* rusé; *(of scheme, trick)* habileté *f*

WILL[1] [wɪl]

On trouve généralement **I/you/he/***etc* **will** sous leurs formes contractées **I'll/you'll/he'll/***etc.* La forme négative correspondante est **won't** que l'on écrira **will not** dans des contextes formels.

MODAL AUX V1 *(indicating the future)* **what time w. you be home tonight?** à quelle heure rentrez-vous ce soir?; **the next meeting w. be held in July** la prochaine réunion aura lieu en juillet; **I w. be there before ten o'clock** j'y serai avant dix heures; **I don't think he w.** *or* **he'll come today** je ne pense pas qu'il vienne *ou* je ne crois pas qu'il viendra aujourd'hui; **do you think she'll marry him? – I'm sure she w./she won't** est-ce que tu crois qu'elle va se marier avec lui? – je suis sûr que oui/non; **he doesn't think he'll be able to fix it** il ne pense pas pouvoir *ou* il ne croit pas qu'il pourra le réparer; **she's sure she'll have to work next weekend** elle est sûre qu'elle devra *ou* elle est sûre de devoir travailler le week-end prochain; **while he's on holiday his wife w. be working** pendant qu'il sera en vacances, sa femme travaillera; **when they come home the children w. be sleeping** quand ils rentreront, les enfants dormiront *ou* seront endormis

2 *(indicating probability)* **that'll be the postman** ça doit être *ou* c'est sans doute le facteur; **they'll be wanting their dinner** ils doivent attendre *ou* ils attendent sans doute leur dîner; **she'll be grown up by now** elle doit être grande maintenant; **it won't be ready yet** ce n'est sûrement pas prêt

3 *(indicating resolution, determination)* **I'll steal the money if I have to** je volerai l'argent s'il le faut; **I won't go!** je n'irai pas!; **I won't have it!** je ne supporterai *ou* je n'admettrai pas ça!; **you must come! – I won't!** il faut que vous veniez! – non, je ne viendrai pas!; **I won't go – oh yes you w.!** je n'irai pas – oh (que) si!; **he can't possibly win – he w.!** il ne peut pas gagner – mais si!

4 *(indicating willingness)* **I'll carry your suitcase** je vais porter votre valise; **who'll volunteer? – I w.!** qui se porte volontaire? – moi!; **w. you marry me? – yes, I w./no, I won't** veux-tu m'épouser? – oui/non; **my secretary w. answer your questions** ma secrétaire répondra à vos questions; *Fam* **w. do!** d'accord!▫

5 *(in requests, invitations)* **w. you please stop smoking?** pouvez-vous éteindre votre cigarette, s'il vous plaît?; **you won't forget, w. you?** tu n'oublieras pas, n'est-ce pas?; **you WILL remember to lock the door, won't you?** tu n'oublieras pas de fermer à clef, hein?; **won't you join us for lunch?** vous déjeunerez bien avec nous?; **if you w. come with me** si vous voulez bien venir avec moi

6 *(in orders)* **stop complaining, w. you!** arrête de te plaindre, tu veux!; **he'll do as he's told** il fera ce qu'on lui dira; **you'll stop arguing this minute!** vous allez arrêter de vous disputer tout de suite!; **you'll be here at three** soyez ici à trois heures; **w. you be quiet!** vous allez vous taire!

7 *(indicating basic ability, capacity)* **the machine w. wash up to five kilos of laundry** la machine peut laver jusqu'à cinq kilos de linge; **this car won't do more than 75 miles per hour** ≃ cette voiture ne peut pas faire plus de 120 kilomètres à l'heure; **this hen w. lay up to six eggs a week** cette poule pond jusqu'à six œufs par semaine

8 *(indicating temporary state or capacity)* **the car won't start** la voiture ne veut pas démarrer; **it w. start, but it dies after a couple of seconds** elle démarre, mais elle s'arrête tout de suite; **the television won't switch on** la télévision ne veut pas s'allumer

9 *(indicating habitual action)* **she'll play in her sandpit for hours** elle peut jouer des heures dans son bac à sable

10 *(indicating obstinacy)* **she WILL insist on calling me Uncle Roger** elle insiste pour *ou* elle tient à m'appeler Oncle Roger; **it WILL keep on doing that** ça n'arrête pas de faire ça; **she WILL have the last word** il faut toujours qu'elle ait le dernier mot; **accidents WILL happen** on ne peut pas éviter les accidents

11 *(used with "have")* **another ten years w. have gone by** dix autres années auront passé

will² **N1** *(desire, determination)* volonté *f*; **he has a weak/a strong w.** il a peu/beaucoup de volonté; **she succeeded by force of w.** elle a réussi à force de volonté; **a battle of wills** une lutte d'influences; **she no longer has the w. to live** elle n'a plus envie de vivre; **you must have the w. to win/to succeed** il faut avoir envie de gagner/de réussir; **it is the w. of the people that...** le peuple veut que...; *Bible* **thy w. be done** que ta volonté soit faite; **to have a w. of iron** *or* **an iron w.** avoir une volonté de fer; **to have a w. of one's own** n'en faire qu'à sa tête, être très indépendant; **this shopping trolley has a w. of its own** ce chariot est impossible à guider; **with the best w. in the world** avec la meilleure volonté du monde; *Prov* **where there's a w. there's a way** quand on veut on peut

2 *Law* testament *m*; **last w. and testament** dernières volontés *fpl*; **to make a w.** faire un testament; **did he leave me anything in his w.?** m'a-t-il laissé quelque chose dans son testament?

VT1 *(using willpower)* **I was willing her to say yes** j'espérais qu'elle allait dire oui; **she willed herself to keep walking** elle s'est forcée à continuer à marcher; **I could feel the crowd willing me on** je sentais que la foule me soutenait; **you can't just w. these things to happen** on ne peut pas faire arriver ces choses par un simple acte de volonté **2** *(bequeath)* léguer; **she willed her entire fortune to charity** elle a légué toute sa fortune à des œuvres de charité **3** *Literary (wish, intend)* vouloir; **the Lord so willed it** le Seigneur a voulu qu'il en soit ainsi; **say what you w., you won't be believed** quoi que vous disiez, on ne vous croira pas

VI *Arch or Literary (wish)* vouloir; **as you w.** comme vous voulez

• **against one's will** **ADV** contre sa volonté; **he left home against his father's w.** il est parti de chez lui contre la volonté de son père

• **at will** **ADV** à sa guise; **they can come and go at w. here** ils peuvent aller et venir à leur guise ici; **fire at w.!** feu à volonté!

• **with a will** **ADV** avec ardeur, avec acharnement; **we set to with a w.** nous nous attelâmes à la tâche avec ardeur

willful, willfully *etc Am* = **wilful, wilfully** *etc*

William ['wɪlɪəm] **PR N W. Tell** Guillaume Tell; **W. the Conqueror** Guillaume le Conquérant

willie = **willy**

willies ['wɪlɪz] **NPL** *Fam* **he/it gives me the w.** il/ça me fiche la trouille

willing ['wɪlɪŋ] **ADJ1** *(ready, prepared)* **are you w. to cooperate with us?** êtes-vous prêt à collaborer avec nous?; **he isn't even w. to try** il ne veut même pas essayer; **to be w. and able (to do sth)** avoir l'envie et les moyens (de faire qch); **he's more than w. to change jobs** il ne demande pas mieux que de changer d'emploi; **w. or not, they must lend a hand** qu'ils le veuillent ou non, ils devront nous aider

2 *(compliant)* **he's a w. victim** c'est une victime complaisante

3 *(eager, enthusiastic* ▸ *helper)* bien disposé, plein de bonne volonté; **she's a w. pupil** c'est une élève pleine de bonne volonté

4 *(idiom)* **to show w.** faire preuve de bonne volonté

willingly ['wɪlɪŋlɪ] **ADV1** *(eagerly, gladly)* de bon cœur, volontiers; **they w. gave up their time** ils n'ont pas été avares de leur temps; **I'll do it w., I'll w. do it** je le ferai volontiers **2** *(voluntarily)* volontairement, de plein gré; **I bet he didn't do it w.** je parie qu'il ne l'a pas fait de bon cœur; **he came along quite w.** il est venu de son plein gré

willingness ['wɪlɪŋnɪs] **N1** *(enthusiasm)* **he set to with great w.** il s'est attelé à la tâche avec un grand enthousiasme **2** *(readiness)* **the soldiers were surprised at the enemy's w. to fight** les soldats furent surpris par la combativité de l'ennemi; **he admired her w. to sacrifice her own happiness** il admirait le fait qu'elle soit prête à sacrifier son propre bonheur

will-o'-the-wisp **N** *also Fig* feu *m* follet

willow ['wɪləʊ] **N1** *Bot* saule *m* **2** *Fam Old-fashioned (in cricket)* **the w.** la batte▫

COMP de saule

▸▸ ***willow pattern*** = motif de céramique; **w. pattern plates** des assiettes à motifs chinois; ***willow tree*** saule *m*; *Orn* ***willow warbler*** pouillot *m* fitis

willowy ['wɪləʊɪ] **ADJ** *(figure, person)* élancé, svelte; *(object)* souple, flexible

willpower ['wɪl,paʊə(r)] **N** volonté *f*; **he lacks the w. to diet** il n'a pas suffisamment de volonté pour se mettre au régime; **he gave up smoking through sheer w.** il a arrêté de fumer à force de volonté

willy ['wɪlɪ] *(pl* **willies)** **N** *Br Fam (penis)* zizi *m*

willy-nilly [-'nɪlɪ] **ADV 1** *(without order, randomly)* au hasard; **the editor just altered a few words w.** le rédacteur a simplement changé quelques mots au hasard **2** *(willingly or not)* bon gré mal gré

wilt¹ [wɪlt] **N** *Eng or Arch or Literary 2nd pers sing of* **will¹**

wilt² **VI1** *(flower, plant)* se faner, se flétrir **2** *(person* ▸ *with heat, fatigue)* languir, s'alanguir; *(*▸ *lose courage)* se dégonfler; **I'm beginning to w.** je commence à fatiguer; **to w. under pressure** fléchir sous la pression; **he wilted under her fierce gaze** il perdit contenance sous son regard furieux

VT *(flower, plant)* faner, flétrir

Wilts *(written abbr* **Wiltshire)** Wiltshire *m*

wily ['waɪlɪ] *(compar* **wilier**, *superl* **wiliest)** **ADJ** *(person)* rusé, malin(igne); *(scheme, trick)* habile, astucieux; **a w. old devil** *or* **fox** un vieux malin *ou* rusé

wimp [wɪmp] **N** *Fam Pej (person* ▸ *physically weak)* mauviette *f*; *(*▸ *morally weak, irresolute)* mou (molle), pâte *f* molle; **don't be such a w.!** quel mollasson tu fais!

▸ **wimp out** **VI** *Fam* se dégonfler; **he wimped out of the fight** il s'est dégonflé au dernier moment et a refusé de se battre; **he wimped out of telling her the truth** finalement, il a eu la trouille de lui dire la vérité

wimpish ['wɪmpɪʃ] **ADJ** *Fam Pej* mollasson; **stop being so w.!** quel mollasson tu fais!

wimple ['wɪmpəl] **N** guimpe *f*

win [wɪn] *(pt & pp* **won** [wʌn], *cont* **winning)** **VI** *(in competition)* gagner; **she always wins at tennis** elle gagne toujours au tennis; **they're winning three nil** ils gagnent trois à zéro; **he won by only one point** il a gagné d'un point seulement; **did you w. at cards?** avez-vous gagné aux cartes?; **to let sb w.** laisser gagner qn; **OK, you w.!** bon, d'accord!; **I (just) can't w.!** j'ai toujours tort!; **to w. hands down** gagner haut la main

VT 1 *(award, prize, race, competition)* gagner; *(scholarship)* obtenir; *(contract)* gagner, remporter; **he won first prize** il a gagné *ou* il a eu le premier prix; **he won £100 at poker** il a gagné 100 livres au poker; **w. yourself a dream holiday!** gagnez des vacances de rêve!; **she won a gold medal in the Olympics** elle a obtenu une médaille d'or aux jeux Olympiques; **his superior finishing speed won him the race** il a gagné la course grâce à sa vitesse supérieure dans la dernière ligne *ou* au finish; *Br* **to w. a place at university** obtenir une place à l'université; **we have won a great victory** nous avons remporté une grande victoire; **this offensive could w. them the war** cette offensive pourrait leur faire gagner la guerre; **you w. some, you lose some** on ne peut pas toujours avoir ce qu'on veut dans la vie; **you can't w. them all** on ne peut pas réussir à tous les coups

2 *(acquire, secure* ▸ *friendship, love)* gagner; *(*▸ *sympathy)* s'attirer; *(*▸ *popularity)* acquérir; **to w. sb's heart** gagner *ou* conquérir le cœur de qn; **to w. the right to do sth** obtenir le droit de faire qch; *Arch* **to w. sb's hand** obtenir la main de qn; **she was desperate to w. his favour** elle cherchait désespérément à attirer ses bonnes grâces; **intransigence has won him many enemies** son intransigeance lui a valu de nombreux ennemis; **his impartiality has won him the respect of his colleagues** son impartialité lui a valu *ou* fait gagner le respect de ses collègues; **you've just won yourself a friend** tu viens juste de te faire un ami

3 *Mining* extraire

4 *Formal or Literary (reach)* **we finally won the shore after three days at sea** nous avons fini par gagner le rivage après trois jours de mer

5 *Arch or Literary (earn)* **to w. one's living** *or* **one's daily bread** gagner sa vie *ou* son pain quotidien

N1 *Sport* victoire *f*; **they've had an unprecedented run of wins** ils ont eu une série de victoires sans précédent; **we haven't had one w. all season** nous n'avons pas remporté une seule victoire de toute la saison

▸ **win back** VT SEP *(money, trophy)* reprendre, recouvrer; *(land)* reprendre, reconquérir; *(loved one)* reconquérir; *(esteem, respect, support)* retrouver, recouvrer; *Pol (votes, voters, seats)* récupérer, recouvrer; **they were determined to w. back the Cup from the Australians** ils étaient décidés à reprendre la Coupe aux Australiens; **I won every penny back from him** je lui ai repris jusqu'au dernier centime; **you won't w. back your wife with threats** tu ne vas pas reconquérir *ou* retrouver l'amour de ta femme avec des menaces

▸ **win out** VI triompher; **the need for peace won out over the desire for revenge** le besoin de paix triompha du désir de revanche

▸ **win over** VT SEP *(convert, convince)* rallier; **he has won several of his former opponents over to his ideas** il a rallié plusieurs de ses anciens adversaires à ses idées; **we won him over in the end** nous avons fini par le convaincre; **I won him over to my point of view** j'ai réussi à le rallier à mon point de vue

▸ **win through** VI remporter; **the striking rail workers won through in the end** les cheminots en grève ont fini par obtenir gain de cause

wince [wɪns] VI *(from pain)* crisper le visage, grimacer; **she didn't even w.** elle n'a pas fait la moindre grimace; **to w. with pain** grimacer de douleur; *Fig* grimacer (de dégoût); **she winced at the thought** cette pensée l'a fait grimacer de dégoût

N grimace *f*

winceyette [ˌwɪnsɪ'et] *Br* N flanelle *f* de coton

COMP *(nightdress, pyjamas, sheets)* en flanelle de coton

winch [wɪntʃ] N treuil *m*

VT **to w. sb/sth up/down** monter/descendre qn/qch au treuil; **the survivors were winched to safety** à l'aide d'un treuil, on a hissé les rescapés hors de danger

wind[1] [wɪnd] N **1** *Met* vent *m*; **there's quite a w.** il y a beaucoup de vent; **the w. has risen/dropped** le vent s'est levé/est tombé; **the w. is changing** le vent tourne; *Naut* **into the w.** contre le vent; *Naut* **off the w.** dans le sens du vent; *Naut* **before the w.** le vent en poupe; *Fig* **the winds of change are blowing** il y a du changement dans l'air; *Fig* **with a fair w.** si tout va bien; **to get w. of sth** avoir vent de qch; **to run like the w.** courir comme le vent; **to be scattered to the four winds** être éparpillés aux quatre vents; **there's something in the w.** il se prépare quelque chose; **to take the w. out of sb's sails** couper l'herbe sous le pied à qn; **let's wait and see which way the w. blows** attendons de voir quelle tournure les événements vont prendre

2 *(breath)* souffle *m*; **to get one's w. back** reprendre haleine *ou* son souffle; **to get one's second w.** reprendre haleine *ou* son souffle; **the fall knocked the w. out of her** la chute lui a coupé le souffle; *Fam* **to put the w. up sb** flanquer la frousse à qn; *Fam* **to have the w. up** avoir la frousse

3 *Fam (empty talk)* vent *m*; **his speech was just a lot of w.** son discours n'était que du vent

4 *(UNCOUNT) (air in stomach)* vents *mpl*, gaz *mpl*; **beans give me w.** les haricots me donnent des vents *ou* des gaz; **I've got terrible w.** j'ai des gaz, quelque chose de terrible; **to break w.** lâcher des vents; **to get a baby's w. up** faire faire son renvoi à un bébé

5 *Mus* **the w. (section)** les instruments *mpl* à vent, les vents *mpl*; **the w. is** *or* **are too loud** les instruments à vent sont trop forts

VT **1** *(make breathless)* **to w. sb** couper le souffle à qn; **the blow winded him** le coup l'a mis hors d'haleine *ou* lui a coupé le souffle; **she was quite winded by the walk uphill** la montée de la côte l'a essoufflée *ou* lui a coupé le souffle; **don't worry, I'm only winded** ne t'inquiète pas, j'ai la respiration coupée, c'est tout

2 *(horse)* laisser souffler

3 *(baby)* faire faire son renvoi à

4 *Hunt (prey)* avoir vent de

▸▸ ***wind chimes*** carillon *m* éolien; ***wind cone*** manche *f* à air; ***wind energy*** énergie *f* éolienne; ***wind farm*** champ *m* d'éoliennes, parc *m* éolien; ***wind gauge*** anémomètre *m*; *Mus* ***wind harp*** harpe *f* éolienne; *Mus* ***wind instrument*** instrument *m* à vent; *Theat* ***wind machine*** machine *f* à souffler le vent; ***wind power*** énergie *f* du vent *ou* éolienne; ***wind rose*** rose *f* des vents; *Aviat* ***wind sleeve*** manche *f* à air; ***wind tunnel*** tunnel *m* aérodynamique; ***wind turbine*** éolienne *f*

wind[2] [waɪnd] *(pt & pp* **wound** [waʊnd]*)* VI *(bend ▸ procession, road)* serpenter; *(coil ▸ thread)* s'enrouler; **the river winds through the valley** le fleuve décrit des méandres dans la vallée *ou* traverse la vallée en serpentant

VT **1** *(wrap ▸ bandage, rope)* enrouler; **I wound a scarf round my neck** j'ai enroulé une écharpe autour de mon cou; **w. the string into a ball** enroulez la ficelle pour en faire une pelote; **the snake had wound itself around the man's arm** le serpent s'était enroulé autour du bras de l'homme; *Literary* **to w. sb in one's arms** enlacer qn; **to w. sb round** *or* **around one's little finger** mener qn par le bout du nez **2** *(clock, watch, toy)* remonter; *(handle)* tourner, donner un tour de; **have you wound your watch?** avez-vous remonté votre montre? **3** *Arch or Hum (travel)* **to w. one's way home** prendre le chemin du retour

N **1** *Tech* **give the clock/the watch a w.** remontez l'horloge/la montre; **she gave the handle another w.** elle tourna la manivelle encore une fois, elle donna un tour de manivelle de plus **2** *(bend ▸ of road)* tournant *m*, courbe *f*; *(▸ of river)* coude *m*

▸ **wind down** VI **1** *(person)* se détendre, décompresser **2** *(party, meeting)* tirer à sa fin; **the party didn't begin to w. down until nearly 4 a.m.** la fête a continué à battre son plein jusqu'à environ 4 heures du matin **3** *Tech (clock, watch)* ralentir

VT SEP **1** *Tech (lower)* faire descendre; *(car window)* baisser **2** *(bring to an end ▸ business)* mener (doucement) vers sa fin

▸ **wind up** VT SEP **1** *(conclude ▸ meeting)* terminer; *(▸ account, business)* liquider; **the chairman wound up the debate** le président a clos le *ou* mis fin au débat; **the business will be wound up by the end of the year** l'entreprise sera liquidée avant la fin de l'année

2 *(raise)* monter, faire monter; *(car window)* monter, fermer

3 *(string, thread)* enrouler; *(on a spool)* dévider

4 *Tech (clock, watch, toy)* remonter; *Fam Fig* **to be wound up (about sth)** être à cran (à cause de qch)

5 *Br Fam (annoy)* asticoter; *(tease)* faire marcher; *(fool)* mettre en boîte; **they're only winding you up** ils te font marcher, ils essaient seulement de te mettre en boîte; **don't you know when you're being wound up?** tu ne te rends même pas compte quand on te fait marcher *ou* quand on essaie de te mettre en boîte?

VI *Fam (end up)* finir[□]; **he wound up in jail** il a fini *ou* s'est retrouvé en prison; **she'll w. up begging in the streets** elle finira par mendier dans la rue; **he wound up with a broken nose** il a fini avec le nez cassé; **we usually w. up back at my place** généralement, nous finissons chez moi; **we wound up working for the same company** nous nous sommes retrouvés à travailler pour la même société **2** *(end speech, meeting)* conclure; **I'd like to w. up by saying…** je voudrais conclure en disant…

windbag ['wɪndbæg] N *Fam Pej* moulin *m* à paroles, jaseur(euse) *m,f*

windblown ['wɪndbləʊn] ADJ *(hair)* ébouriffé par le vent; *(trees)* fouetté *ou* cinglé par le vent

windborne ['wɪndbɔːn] ADJ transporté par le vent

windbreak ['wɪndbreɪk] N abri-vent *m*, coupe-vent *m inv*

windcheater ['wɪndˌtʃiːtə(r)] N *Br* anorak *m*, coupe-vent *m inv*

windchill factor ['wɪndtʃɪl-] N facteur *m* de refroidissement au vent

winder ['waɪndə(r)] N *(for clock)* remontoir *m*; *(for car window)* lève-vitre *m*, lève-glace *m*; *(for thread, yarn)* dévidoir *m*

windfall ['wɪndfɔːl] N **1** *(fruit)* fruit *m* tombé **2** *Fig (unexpected gain)* (bonne) aubaine *f*; **I've had a bit of a w. from my aunt** j'ai eu la chance d'hériter d'un peu d'argent de ma tante

ADJ *(fruit)* tombé *ou* abattu par le vent

▸▸ ***windfall dividends*** dividendes *mpl* exceptionnels; ***windfall payment*** paiement *m* exceptionnel; ***windfall profits*** bénéfices *mpl* exceptionnels; ***windfall tax*** impôt *m* sur les bénéfices exceptionnels

winding ['waɪndɪŋ] ADJ *(road, street)* tortueux, sinueux; *(river)* sinueux; *(staircase)* en hélice, en colimaçon

N **1** *(process)* enroulement *m*; *Elec (of wire)* bobinage *m*, enroulement *m* **2** *(in a river)* méandres *mpl*, coudes *mpl*; *(in a road)* zigzags *mpl*

▸▸ ***winding gear*** *(of lift)* treuil *m*; *Mining* appareils *mpl ou* machine *f* d'extraction; ***winding sheet*** linceul *m*

winding-up N *(of account, meeting)* clôture *f*; *(of business)* liquidation *f*

▸▸ ***winding-up arrangement*** *(in bankruptcy)* concordat *m*

windjammer ['wɪndˌdʒæmə(r)] N **1** *Naut* grand voilier *m* marchand **2** *Br (light jacket)* anorak *m*, coupe-vent *m inv*

windlass ['wɪndləs] N treuil *m*; *Naut* guindeau *m*

VT *(raise)* monter au treuil; *(haul)* tirer au treuil

windmill ['wɪndmɪl] N **1** *(building)* moulin *m* à vent; *(toy)* moulinet *m* **2** *(wind turbine)* aéromoteur *m*, éolienne *f*

window ['wɪndəʊ] N **1** *(in room)* fenêtre *f*; *(in car)* vitre *f*, glace *f*; *(in front of shop)* vitrine *f*, devanture *f*; *(in church)* vitrail *m*; *(at ticket office)* guichet *m*; *(on envelope)* fenêtre *f*; **she looked out of** *or* **through the w.** elle regarda par la fenêtre; **he jumped out of the w.** il a sauté par la fenêtre; **to break a w.** casser une vitre *ou* un carreau; **can I try on that dress in the w.?** puis-je essayer la robe qui est dans la *ou* en vitrine?; *Fam* **all our plans have gone out the w.** tous nos projets sont partis en fumée; *Fam* **that's my chances of promotion out the w.** je peux faire une croix sur mon avancement

2 *Comput* fenêtre *f*

3 *(in diary)* créneau *m*, moment *m* libre; **a w. of opportunity** une chance; **to create a w. of opportunity for sth** créer une conjoncture favorable à qch; **they saw this as a w. of opportunity to advance the cause of human rights** ils ont vu là l'occasion de faire progresser la cause des droits de l'homme

4 *(insight)* **a w. on the world of finance** un aperçu des milieux financiers

5 *(opportune time) Astron* **launch w.** fenêtre *f ou* créneau *m* de lancement; **weather w.** accalmie *f (permettant de mener à bien des travaux)*

▸▸ ***window box*** jardinière *f*; ***window cleaner*** *(person)* laveur(euse) *m,f* de vitres *ou* de carreaux; *(substance)* nettoyant *m* pour vitres; ***window display*** étalage *m*; ***window envelope*** enveloppe *f* à fenêtre; ***window frame*** châssis *m* de fenêtre; ***window ledge*** *(inside)* appui *m* de fenêtre; *(outside)* rebord *m* de fenêtre; ***window seat*** *(in room)* banquette *f* sous la fenêtre; *(in train, plane)* place *f* côté fenêtre; *Am* ***window shade*** store *m*; *Am* ***window washer*** laveur(euse) *m,f* de vitres *ou* de carreaux; *Aut* ***window winder*** lève-vitre *m*

window-dress VT *Acct (accounts, balance sheet)* camoufler, habiller

window-dresser étalagiste *mf*

window-dressing **1** *(merchandise on display)* présentation *f* de l'étalage; *(activity)* art *m* de l'étalage; **they need someone to do the w.** ils ont besoin de quelqu'un pour composer *ou* pour faire l'étalage **2** *Fig (facade)* façade *f*; **that's just w.** ce n'est qu'une façade; **no amount of w. can hide the fact that the party is in crisis** rien ne pourra camoufler l'état de crise dans lequel se trouve le parti **3** *Acct* habillage *m* de bilan

windowing ['wɪndəʊɪŋ] N *Comput* fenêtrage *m*

windowless ['wɪndəʊlɪs] ADJ sans fenêtres

windowpane ['wɪndəʊpeɪn] N carreau *m*, vitre *f*

window-shop VI faire du lèche-vitrines

window-shopper N = personne qui fait du lèche-vitrines; **the streets were full of window-shoppers** les rues étaient pleines de gens en train de faire du lèche-vitrines

window-shopping N lèche-vitrines *m inv*; **to go w.** faire du lèche-vitrines

windowsill ['wɪndəʊsɪl] N rebord *m* de fenêtre

windpipe ['wɪndpaɪp] N trachée *f*

wind-pollinated ['wɪnd'pɒləneɪtɪd] ADJ pollinisé par le vent

wind-pollination [wɪnd-] N pollinisation *f* par le vent

windscreen ['wɪndskriːn] N *Br* pare-brise *m inv*
►► ***windscreen washer*** lave-glace *m*; ***windscreen wiper*** essuie-glace *m*

windshield ['wɪndʃiːld] N *Am* pare-brise *m inv*
►► ***windshield wiper*** essuie-glace *m*

windsock ['wɪndsɒk] N *Aviat* manche *f* à air

windstorm ['wɪndstɔːm] N (vent *m* de) tempête *f*

windsurf ['wɪndsɜːf] VI faire de la planche à voile

windsurfer ['wɪnd,sɜːfə(r)] N *(board)* planche *f* à voile; *(person)* véliplanchiste *mf*, planchiste *mf*

windsurfing ['wɪnd,sɜːfɪŋ] N planche *f* à voile; **to go w.** faire de la planche à voile

windswept ['wɪndswept] ADJ *(place)* balayé par le vent; *(hair)* ébouriffé par le vent; **you're looking very w.** tu as l'air tout ébouriffé par le vent

wind-up [waɪnd-] ADJ *(mechanism)* **a w. toy/watch** un jouet/une montre à remontoir
N **1** *Br Fam (joke)* **is this a w.?** est-ce qu'on veut me faire marcher? **2** *(conclusion)* conclusion *f*

windward ['wɪndwəd] *Naut* ADJ **on the w. side** du côté du vent
N côté *m* du vent; **to w.** au vent, contre le vent
ADV contre le vent; **to sail w.** avoir le vent debout

windy ['wɪndɪ] (*compar* **windier**, *superl* **windiest**)
ADJ **1** *Met* **it's w. today** il y a du vent aujourd'hui; **it was terribly w. up on deck** il y avait un vent terrible *ou* le vent soufflait terriblement sur le pont; **a cold, w. morning** un matin froid et de grand vent; **it's a very wet and w. place** c'est un endroit très pluvieux et très venteux **2** *Fam (pompous, verbose)* ronflant, pompeux[□] **3** *Fam Old-fashioned (nervous)* **to be** *or* **to get w. about sth** paniquer à propos de qch
►► ***the Windy City*** = surnom de Chicago

wine [waɪn] N **1** *(drink)* vin *m*; **a bottle/a glass of w.** une bouteille/un verre de vin; **red/white w.** vin *m* rouge/blanc; **the wines of Spain** les vins espagnols; **w. and cheese evening** = petite fête où l'on déguste du vin et du fromage; **wines and spirits** *(shop sign)* vins et spiritueux **2** *(colour)* lie-de-vin *f inv*
COMP *(bottle, glass)* à vin
VT **to w. and dine sb** inviter qn dans les bons restaurants
VI **to go out wining and dining** faire la fête au restaurant
ADJ *(colour)* lie-de-vin *(inv)*
►► ***wine bar*** *(drinking establishment)* bistrot *m*; ***wine box*** Cubitainer® *m*; ***wine cellar*** cave *f* (à vin), cellier *m*; ***wine cooler*** *(container)* seau *m* à rafraîchir (le vin); *Am (drink)* = mélange de vin, de jus de fruit et d'eau gazeuse; *Br* ***wine gum*** = bonbon gélifié aux fruits; ***wine list*** carte *f* des vins; ***wine merchant*** *(shopkeeper)* marchand(e) *m,f* de vin(s); *(wholesaler)* négociant(e) *m,f* en vin(s); ***wine rack*** casier *m* à vin; ***wine shop*** magasin *m* de vin(s); ***wine taster*** *(person)* dégustateur (trice) *m,f*; *(cup)* tâte-vin *m inv*, taste-vin *m inv*; ***wine tasting*** dégustation *f* (de vins); ***wine vinegar*** vinaigre *m* de vin; ***wine waiter*** sommelier *m*

wine-coloured, *Am* **wine-colored** ADJ lie-de-vin *(inv)*; **a w. dress** une robe lie-de-vin

wineglass ['waɪnglɑːs] N verre *m* à vin

winepress ['waɪnpres] N pressoir *m* à vin

wing [wɪŋ] N **1** *(of bird, insect)* aile *f*; *Literary* **to take w.** prendre son envol *ou* son essor; **my heart took w.** mon cœur s'emplit de joie; *Literary* **to be on the w.** être en (plein) vol; **he shot the bird on the w.** il tira l'oiseau en vol; *Literary* **desire gave** *or* **lent him wings** le désir lui donnait des ailes; **to take sb under one's w.** prendre qn sous son aile
2 *Aviat* aile *f*; *Fig* **on a w. and a prayer** en s'en remettant à la Providence
3 *Br (of car)* aile *f*
4 *Pol* aile *f*; **the radical w. of the party** l'aile *f ou* la fraction radicale du parti; **the left/right w.** l'aile *f* gauche/droite
5 *(of building)* aile *f*; *(of hospital)* pavillon *m*; *(of door)* battant *m*; **the west w.** l'aile *f* ouest
6 *Sport (of field)* aile *f*; *(player)* ailier *m*; **she plays on the w.** elle est ailier
7 *(of nut)* oreille *f*, ailette *f*
8 *Mil & Aviat (unit)* escadre *f* aérienne
9 *(of windmill)* aile *f*
10 *(of armchair)* oreille *f*
VT **1** *(wound ► bird)* blesser, toucher à l'aile; *(► person)* blesser *ou* toucher légèrement
2 *(fly) also Fig* **to w. one's way** voler; **while the letters were winging their way over the ocean** pendant que les lettres survolaient l'océan; **my report should be winging its way towards you now** mon rapport devrait te parvenir incessamment sous peu
3 *Literary (cause to fly ► arrow)* darder, décocher
4 *Fam* **to w. it** *(improvise)* improviser[□]
VI *Literary (fly)* **the plane winged over the mountains** l'avion survola les montagnes
● **wings** NPL **1** *Theat* coulisse *f*, coulisses *fpl*; *also Fig* **to wait in the wings** se tenir dans la coulisse *ou* dans les coulisses; *Fig* **younger politicians are waiting in the wings to seize power** les jeunes politiciens se tiennent dans la coulisse *ou* dans les coulisses en attendant de prendre le pouvoir **2** *Am (for non-swimmer)* brassards *mpl*, flotteurs *mpl* **3** *Aviat (badge)* **to win one's wings** faire ses preuves, prendre du galon
►► ***wing back*** *(in football)* arrière *m* d'aile; *Zool* ***wing case*** élytre *m*; ***wing chair*** bergère *f* à oreilles; ***wing collar*** col *m* cassé; ***wing commander*** ≃ lieutenant-colonel *m*; ***wing flap*** *(of plane)* volet *m*; ***wing forward*** *(in rugby)* ailier *m*; ***wing mirror*** rétroviseur *m* extérieur; ***wing nut*** papillon *m*, écrou *m* à ailettes; ***wing three-quarter*** *(in rugby)* trois-quarts aile *m*; ***wing tip*** *(of plane, bird)* bout *m* de l'aile

wingding ['wɪŋdɪŋ] N *Am Fam (party)* fête[□] *f*, bringue *f*; **we had a real w.** on a vraiment fait la bringue

-winged [wɪŋd] SUFF **white-w.** aux ailes blanches

winged [wɪŋd] ADJ **1** *(possessing wings)* ailé **2** *(wounded ► bird, animal)* blessé à l'aile; *(► person)* blessé légèrement

winger ['wɪŋə(r)] N *Sport* ailier *m*

wingless ['wɪŋlɪs] ADJ sans ailes; *(insect)* aptère

wingspan ['wɪŋspæn] N envergure *f*

wink [wɪŋk] VI **1** *(person)* faire un clin d'œil; **to w. at sb** faire un clin d'œil à qn; *Fig* **to w. at sth** fermer les yeux sur qch; **it's as easy as winking** c'est simple comme bonjour **2** *Literary (light, star)* clignoter
VT **to w. an eye at sb** faire un clin d'œil à qn
N clin *m* d'œil; **she gave them a knowing w.** elle leur a fait un clin d'œil entendu; **"hello darling," he said with a big w.** "bonjour chérie", dit-il en faisant un grand clin d'œil; **I didn't get a w. of sleep** *or* **I didn't sleep a w. last night** je n'ai pas fermé l'œil de la nuit; **(as) quick as a w.** en un clin d'œil; **it was all over in the w. of an eye** c'était fini en un clin d'œil

winker ['wɪŋkə(r)] N *Br Aut Fam* clignotant[□] *m*

winking ['wɪŋkɪŋ] ADJ *(lights)* clignotant
N **1** *(of an eye)* clins *mpl* d'œil; **it was all over in the w. of an eye** c'était fini en un clin d'œil **2** *(of lights, stars)* clignotement *m*

winkle ['wɪŋkəl] N *Br* **1** *(shellfish)* bigorneau *m*, vigneau *m* **2** *Fam (penis)* zizi *m*

► **winkle out** VT SEP *Fam (information)* arracher; *(person)* déloger; **to w. information out of sb** arracher des informations à qn; **we finally managed to w. him out of his room** nous avons finalement réussi à l'extirper de sa chambre

Winnebago® [,wɪnɪ'beɪgəʊ] N camping-car *m*

winner ['wɪnə(r)] N **1** *(of prize, competition, race)* gagnant(e) *m,f*; *(of battle, war)* vainqueur *m*; *(of match)* vainqueur *m*, gagnant(e) *m,f*; **there will be neither winners nor losers in this war** il n'y aura ni vainqueurs ni vaincus dans cette guerre; **to back a w.** *Horseracing* jouer un cheval gagnant; *Fig* jouer gagnant, bien miser **2** *Sport (winning point)* **he scored the w.** c'est lui qui a marqué le but décisif; **he played a w.** *(successful shot)* il a joué un coup gagnant **3** *(successful person)* gagneur(euse) *m,f*; *(successful thing)* succès *m*; **she's one of life's winners** c'est une gagneuse, elle est de celles qui gagnent; **her latest book is a sure w.** son dernier livre va faire un vrai tabac; **to be onto a w.** avoir tiré le bon numéro, être parti pour gagner

Winnie the Pooh [,wɪnɪðə'puː] PR N Winnie l'ourson

winning ['wɪnɪŋ] ADJ **1** *(successful)* gagnant; *Sport (goal, stroke)* décisif; **to be on a w. streak** remporter victoire sur victoire; **w. number** *(in lottery)* numéro *m* gagnant *ou* sortant **2** *(charming)* engageant, charmant; **that child has a w. way with her** cette enfant est très gracieuse
● **winnings** NPL gains *mpl*
►► ***winning post*** poteau *m* d'arrivée

winnow ['wɪnəʊ] VT *Agr* vanner; *Fig (separate)* démêler, trier; **to w. the chaff from the grain** *or* **the wheat** vanner; *Fig* séparer le bon grain de l'ivraie; **to w. out fact from fiction** démêler le réel d'avec l'imaginaire
N *(machine)* tarare *m*, vanneuse *f*

winnowing ['wɪnəʊɪŋ] N *Agr* vannage *m*; *Fig* examen *m* minutieux; **winnowings** *(of grain)* vannure *f*
►► ***winnowing basket*** van *m*

wino ['waɪnəʊ] (*pl* **winos**) N *Fam* poivrot(e) *m,f*

winsome ['wɪnsəm] ADJ *(person)* charmant, gracieux; *(smile)* engageant, charmeur

winsomely ['wɪnsəmlɪ] ADV de façon charmante

winsomeness ['wɪnsəmnɪs] N charme *m*

winter ['wɪntə(r)] N hiver *m*; **it never snows here in (the) w.** il ne neige jamais ici en hiver; **she was born in the w. of 1913** elle est née pendant l'hiver 1913; **we spent the w. in Nice** nous avons passé l'hiver à Nice; **a cold w.'s day** une froide journée d'hiver; *Literary* **a man of 75 winters** un homme qui a vu passer 75 hivers
COMP *(clothing, holiday)* d'hiver
VI *Formal (spend winter)* passer l'hiver, hiverner
VT *(farm animals)* hiverner
►► ***winter garden*** *(conservatory)* jardin *m* d'hiver; ***the Winter Olympics*** les jeux *mpl* Olympiques d'hiver; ***winter resort*** station *f* de sports d'hiver; ***winter season*** saison *f* d'hiver; ***winter solstice*** solstice *m* d'hiver; ***winter sports*** sports *mpl* d'hiver

winter-flowering ADJ hibernal

wintergreen ['wɪntəgriːn] N *Bot* gaulthérie *f*

winterize, -ise ['wɪntəraɪz] VT *Am* aménager pour l'hiver

wintertime ['wɪntətaɪm] N hiver *m*; **in (the) w.** en hiver

winterval ['wɪntəvəl] N festivités *fpl* de fin d'année

winterweight ['wɪntəweɪt] ADJ *(clothes)* d'hiver

wintery, wintry ['wɪntrɪ] ADJ hivernal; *Fig (look, smile)* glacial; **it's quite w., this morning** c'est presque un jour d'hiver, ce matin; **because of the w. conditions** parce qu'il fait/faisait un temps d'hiver

win-win situation N situation *f* gagnant-gagnant

WIP [,dʌbəljuːaɪ'piː] N *Acct (abbr* **work in progress***)* travail *m* en cours, encours *m* de production de biens

wipe [waɪp] VT **1** *(with cloth)* essuyer; **he wiped the plate dry** il a bien essuyé l'assiette; **to w. one's hands** s'essuyer les mains; **to w. one's feet** s'essuyer les pieds; **to w. one's nose** se moucher; **to w. one's bottom** s'essuyer; **she wiped the sweat from his brow** elle essuya la sueur de son front; **she wiped her knife clean** elle nettoya son couteau (d'un coup de torchon); *Fam* **to w. the floor with sb** réduire qn en miettes; **he wiped the floor with me** il m'a complètement démoli; **to w. the slate clean** passer l'éponge, tout effacer; *Br Vulg* **it's not fit to w. your arse with** tu peux te torcher avec **2** *(delete ► from written record, magnetic tape)* effacer; **the remark was wiped from the minutes** l'observation fut retirée du compte-rendu; **the tape has been wiped** la bande a été effacée
VI essuyer; **she wiped round the sink with a wet cloth** elle a essuyé l'évier avec un chiffon humide
N **1** *(action of wiping)* **he gave the plate a quick w.**

il essuya rapidement l'assiette d'un coup de torchon **2** *(moist tissue)* lingette *f* **3** *TV & Cin* volet *m*

▸ **wipe away** VT SEP *(blood, tears)* essuyer; *(dirt, dust)* enlever; **he wiped the mud away with a cloth** il enleva *ou* il ôta la boue avec un chiffon

▸ **wipe off** VT SEP **1** *(remove)* enlever; *Fam* **w. that smile** *or* **that grin off your face!** enlève-moi ce sourire idiot!; *Fam* **that'll w. the smile off his face** ça va lui enlever le sourire **2** *(erase)* effacer; *Rad & TV* **he wiped off half the programme by accident** il a effacé la moitié de l'émission par mégarde **3** *Fin (debt)* annuler; **several millions of pounds were wiped off the value of shares** la valeur des actions a baissé de plusieurs millions de livres

VI *(stain)* s'enlever

▸ **wipe out** VT SEP **1** *(clean)* nettoyer

2 *(erase)* effacer; *Fig (insult, disgrace)* effacer, laver

3 *(debt)* liquider, amortir; **his gambling debts wiped out his entire fortune** ses dettes de jeu ont eu raison de toute sa fortune; **many small traders were wiped out in the recession** de nombreux petits commerçants ont été balayés par la récession

4 *(destroy)* anéantir, décimer; **whole families were wiped out by the disease** des familles entières ont été exterminées par la maladie; **the fire wiped out the whole district** l'incendie a détruit tout le quartier

5 *Fam (exhaust)* crever; **that match really wiped me out** le match m'a complètement crevé

▸ **wipe up** VT SEP éponger, essuyer

VI *Br* essuyer (la vaisselle)

wiper ['waɪpə(r)] N *Aut* essuie-glace *m*

wire ['waɪə(r)] N **1** *(of metal)* fil *m* (métallique *ou* de fer); **a w. fence** un grillage; **telephone wires** fils *mpl* téléphoniques; *Fam* **we got our wires crossed** nous ne nous sommes pas compris❑, il y a eu un malentendu❑

2 *Old-fashioned (telegram)* télégramme *m*

3 *esp Am Horseracing (finishing line)* ligne *f* d'arrivée; *Fig* **down to the w.** jusqu'à la dernière minute; *Fig* **to just get in under the w.** *(application etc)* arriver de justesse; *Fig* **the peace talks went right down to the w.** les pourparlers de paix se sont poursuivis jusqu'à la toute dernière minute

4 *Am Fam (hidden microphone)* micro *m* caché

VT **1** *(attach with wire)* relier avec du fil de fer; *(jaw)* mettre en place avec du fil de fer; *(flowers etc)* monter sur fil de fer; *(opening, fence)* grillager

2 *Elec (building, house)* mettre l'électricité dans, faire l'installation électrique de; *(connect electrically)* brancher; **the lamp is wired to the switch on the wall** la lampe est branchée sur *ou* reliée à l'interrupteur placé sur le mur; **the room had been wired (up) for sound** la pièce avait été sonorisée

3 *(send telegram to* ▸ *person)* envoyer un télégramme à, télégraphier à; *(send by telegram* ▸ *money, information)* envoyer par télégramme, télégraphier

4 *Am Fam (police officer, detective)* munir d'un micro

▸▸ ***wire brush*** brosse *f* métallique; ***wire gauze*** toile *f* métallique; ***wire mesh, wire netting*** grillage *m*, treillis *m* métallique; ***wire rope*** câble *m* métallique; *Am* ***wire service*** agence *f* de presse *(envoyant des dépêches télégraphiques)*; ***wire wool*** éponge *f* métallique

▸ **wire into** VT INSEP *Fam* **to w. into sb** *(scold)* engueuler qn; **to w. into sth** attaquer qch; **he wired into his colleagues about their failure to keep him informed** il a engueulé ses collègues parce qu'ils ne l'avaient pas tenu au courant; **they wired into the food as if they hadn't eaten for days** ils ont attaqué la nourriture comme s'ils n'avaient pas mangé depuis des jours

▸ **wire up** VT SEP **1** *(attach with wire)* relier avec du fil de fer; *(jaw)* mettre en place avec du fil de fer; *(opening, fence)* grillager **2** *Am Fam (make nervous)* énerver❑; **he gets all wired up before exams** il est à cran avant les examens

wirecutter ['waɪə,kʌtə(r)], **wirecutters** ['waɪə,kʌtəz] N coupe-fil *m inv*, pince *f* coupante

wired ['waɪəd] ADJ **1** *Elec (to an alarm)* relié à un système d'alarme

2 *(wiretapped)* mis sur écoute

3 *(bra)* à tiges métalliques

4 *Fam (highly strung)* sur les nerfs, à cran; *(after taking drugs)* défoncé *(après avoir pris de la cocaïne ou des amphétamines)*

wire-haired ADJ *(dog)* à poils durs

wireless ['waɪəlɪs] N *Br Old-fashioned* TSF *f*; **on the w.** à la TSF; **he sent us a message by w.** il nous envoya un message par sans-fil

ADJ sans fil

COMP *(broadcast, waves)* de TSF

▸▸ ***wireless headset*** oreillette-micro *f*; *Comput* ***wireless mouse*** souris *f* sans fil; *Old-fashioned* ***wireless set*** poste *m* de TSF, TSF *f*

wirepuller ['waɪə,pʊlə(r)] N *Am Fam* personne *f* qui a du piston

wirepulling ['waɪə,pʊlɪŋ] N *Am Fam* piston *m*; **he did some w. for me** il m'a pistonné

wiretap ['waɪətæp] *(pt & pp* **wiretapped**, *cont* **wiretapping)** VT mettre sur écoute

N **they put a w. on his phone** ils ont mis son téléphone sur écoute

wiretapping ['waɪə,tæpɪŋ] N mise *f* sur écoute des lignes téléphoniques

wireworm ['waɪəwɜːm] N larve *f* de taupin

wiring ['waɪərɪŋ] N installation *f* électrique; **the house needs new w.** il faut refaire l'installation électrique de *ou* l'électricité dans la maison

▸▸ ***wiring diagram*** schéma *m* de branchement *ou* de câblage

wiry ['waɪərɪ] *(compar* **wirier**, *superl* **wiriest)** ADJ **1** *(person)* sec (sèche) et musclé; *(animal)* nerveux, vigoureux **2** *(hair)* rêche

Wis *(written abbr* **Wisconsin**) Wisconsin *m*

Wisconsin [wɪs'kɒnsɪn] N *Geog* le Wisconsin

wisdom ['wɪzdəm] N **1** *(advisability, judgement)* sagesse *f*; **I have my doubts about the w. of moving house this year** j'ai des doutes sur l'opportunité de déménager cette année **2** *(store of knowledge)* sagesse *f* **3** *(opinion)* avis *m* (général), jugement *m*; **(the) received** *or* **conventional w.** les idées *fpl* reçues

▸▸ ***wisdom tooth*** dent *f* de sagesse

> **-WISE** SUFFIXE
>
> • Le suffixe **-wise** s'emploie avec des noms pour former des adjectifs. Il signifie POUR CE QUI EST DE. Il s'agit d'un suffixe très générateur qui peut se combiner avec de très nombreux noms. En français ce sens est souvent rendu en plaçant les mots **côté** ou **question** en apposition devant ce dont on parle :
>
> **work-wise things are OK** côté travail, ça va; **money-wise, I'm struggling a bit** question argent, j'ai du mal; **order-wise, the company is doing well** pour ce qui est des commandes, l'entreprise marche bien; **the film is very dull plot-wise** côté intrigue, le film est très ennuyeux; **relaxation-wise, it could have been better** côté repos, ça aurait pu être mieux.
>
> • Lorsqu'on l'emploie avec des noms pour former des adverbes, **-wise** signifie COMME, À LA MANIÈRE DE :
>
> **she walked crab-wise through the crowd** elle marchait en crabe à travers la foule; **the ivy is growing serpent-wise up the column** le lierre grimpe comme un serpent vers le haut de la colonne; **he was sitting Buddha-wise on the floor** il était assis par terre comme un Bouddha.
>
> • Dans certain cas, utilisé avec des adverbes et des adjectifs, **-wise** peut aussi véhiculer la notion de DIRECTION :
>
> **lengthwise/widthwise** dans le sens de la longueur/de la largeur; **in a clockwise direction** dans le sens des aiguilles d'une montre.

wise [waɪz] ADJ **1** *(learned, judicious)* sage; **a w. man** un sage; **you'd be w. to take my advice** vous seriez sage de suivre mes conseils; **do you think it's w. to invite his wife?** crois-tu que ce soit prudent d'inviter sa femme?

2 *(clever, shrewd)* habile, astucieux; **a w. move** *(in board games)* un coup habile *ou* astucieux; **the president made a w. move in dismissing the attorney general** le président a été bien avisé de renvoyer le ministre de la Justice; **it's always easy to be w. after the event** c'est toujours facile d'avoir raison après coup; **the Three W. Men** les Rois Mages *mpl*; **to be none the wiser** ne pas être plus avancé; **do it while he's out, he'll be none the wiser** fais-le pendant qu'il est sorti et il n'en saura rien; *Fam* **to be w. to sth** être au courant de qch; **I'm w. to you** *or* **to your schemes** je sais ce que tu manigances; *Fam* **to get w. to sb** percer qn à jour; *Fam* **you'd better get w. to what's going on** vous feriez bien d'ouvrir les yeux sur ce qui se passe; *Fam* **to put sb w. to sth** avertir qn de qch❑; *Fam* **to put sb w. to sb** prévenir qn contre qn❑

N *Literary (way)* manière *f*, façon *f*; **he is in no w.** *or* **not in any w. satisfied with his new position** il n'est point *ou* aucunement satisfait de son nouveau poste

▸▸ *Fam* ***wise guy*** malin(igne) *m,f*; **don't be a w. guy!** ne fais pas le malin!; **OK, w. guy, what would you do?** OK, gros malin, qu'est-ce que tu ferais?

-wise [waɪz] SUFF **1** *(in the direction of)* dans le sens de; **length-w.** dans le sens de la longueur **2** *(in the manner of)* à la manière de, comme; **he edged crab-w. up to the bar** il s'approcha du bar en marchant de côté comme un crabe **3** *Fam (as regards)* côté; **money-w. the job leaves a lot to be desired** le poste laisse beaucoup à désirer côté argent

▸ **wise up** *Fam* VI **he'd better w. up!** il ferait bien de se mettre dans le coup!; **to w. up to sb** voir qn sous son vrai jour❑; **to w. up to sth** se rendre compte de qch❑; **she finally wised up to the fact that she'd never be a great musician** elle a enfin compris qu'elle ne serait jamais une grande musicienne❑

VT SEP *Am* mettre dans le coup

wiseacre ['waɪz,eɪkə(r)] N *Pej* bel esprit *m*

wiseass ['waɪzæs] N *Am Fam* je-sais-tout *mf inv*

wisecrack ['waɪzkræk] N *Fam* sarcasme❑ *m*

wisecracking ['waɪz,krækɪŋ] ADJ *Fam* blagueur

wisely ['waɪzlɪ] ADV sagement, avec sagesse

WISH [wɪʃ]

> **VT**
> - souhaiter **1, 3, 4**
> - vouloir **3**
>
> **VI**
> - souhaiter **1**
> - vouloir **1**
> - faire un vœu **2**
>
> **N**
> - souhait **1**
> - vœu **1, 3**
> - désir **2**
> - amitiés **3**

VT **1** *(expressing something impossible or unlikely)* souhaiter; **to w. sb dead** souhaiter la mort de qn; **I w. I were a bird!** je voudrais être un oiseau!; **she wished herself far away** elle aurait souhaité être loin; *Fam* **I w. I were** *or Br* **was somewhere else** j'aimerais bien être ailleurs; **w. you were here** *(on postcard)* j'aimerais bien que tu sois là; **I w. you didn't have to leave** j'aimerais que tu ne sois pas *ou* ce serait bien si tu n'étais pas obligé de partir; **I w. you hadn't said that** tu n'aurais pas dû dire ça; **I w. I'd never come!** je n'aurais jamais dû venir; **I w. I'd thought of that before** je regrette de n'y avoir pas pensé plus tôt; **why don't you come with us? – I w. I could** pourquoi ne venez-vous pas avec nous? – j'aimerais bien

2 *(expressing criticism, reproach)* **I w. you'd be more careful** j'aimerais que vous fassiez plus attention; **I w. you wouldn't talk so much!** tu ne peux pas te taire un peu?

3 *Formal (want)* souhaiter, vouloir; **I don't w. to appear rude, but...** je ne voudrais pas paraître impoli mais...; **he no longer wishes to discuss it** il ne veut *ou* il ne souhaite plus en parler; **how do you w. to pay?** comment désirez-vous payer?

4 *(in greeting, expressions of goodwill)* souhaiter; **I wished her a pleasant journey** je lui ai souhaité (un) bon voyage; **he wished them success in their future careers** il leur a souhaité de réussir dans leur carrière; **he wished us good day** il nous a souhaité le bonjour; **I w. you no harm** je ne vous veux pas de mal; **I w. you well** j'espère que tout ira bien pour vous; **I w. you (good) luck** je vous souhaite bonne chance

VI **1** *Formal (want, like)* vouloir, souhaiter; **may I**

see you again? – if you w. puis-je vous revoir? – si vous le voulez *ou* le souhaitez; **do as you w.** faites comme vous voulez; *Ironic* **did you get a pay rise/go on holiday this year? – I w.!** tu as eu une augmentation/tu es allé en vacances cette année? – tu parles!

2 *(make a wish)* faire un vœu; **close your eyes and w. hard** ferme les yeux et fais un vœu; *Literary* **to w. upon a star** faire un vœu en regardant une étoile

N 1 *(act of wishing, thing wished for)* souhait *m*, vœu *m*; **make a w.!** fais un souhait *ou* un vœu!; **to grant a w.** exaucer un vœu; **he got his w., his w. came true** son vœu s'est réalisé

2 *(desire)* désir *m*; **to express a w. for sth** exprimer le désir de qch; *Formal* **it is my (dearest) w. that...** c'est mon vœu le plus cher que...; **it was his last w.** c'était sa dernière volonté; *Literary or Hum* **your w. is my command** vos désirs sont des ordres; *Formal* **I have no w. to appear melodramatic, but...** je ne voudrais pas avoir l'air de dramatiser mais...; **she had no great w. to travel** elle n'avait pas très envie de voyager; **to respect sb's wishes** respecter les vœux de qn; **she went against my wishes** elle a agi contre ma volonté; **he joined the navy against** *or* **contrary to my wishes** il s'est engagé dans la marine contre mon gré *ou* ma volonté

3 *(regards)* **give your wife my best wishes** transmettez toutes mes amitiés à votre épouse; **my parents send their best wishes** mes parents vous font toutes leurs amitiés; **best wishes for the coming year** meilleurs vœux pour la nouvelle année; **best wishes on your graduation (day)** toutes mes/nos félicitations à l'occasion de l'obtention de votre diplôme; **(with) best wishes** *(in letter)* bien amicalement, toutes mes amitiés

►► *Psy* ***wish fulfilment*** accomplissement *m* d'un désir; ***wish list*** liste *f* de vœux; **the unions presented a w. list of their conditions** les syndicats ont présenté une liste de conditions

► **wish away** VT SEP **you can't simply w. away the things you don't like** on ne peut pas faire comme si les choses qui nous déplaisent n'existaient pas

► **wish on** VT SEP **1** *(fate, problem)* souhaiter à; **I wouldn't w. this headache on anyone** je ne souhaite à personne d'avoir un mal de tête pareil **2** *(foist on)* **it's a terribly complicated system wished on us by head office** c'est un système très compliqué dont nous a fait cadeau la direction

wishbone ['wɪʃbəʊn] **N 1** *(bone)* bréchet *m*, fourchette *f*; **to pull a w. with sb** = tirer à deux sur le bréchet en faisant un vœu (le vœu de celui qui casse le plus long morceau sera exaucé) **2** *(in windsurfing)* wishbone *m*

►► *Aut* ***wishbone suspension*** suspension *f* triangulée

wishful thinking [wɪʃful-] **N I suppose it was just w.** je prenais mes rêves pour la réalité; **he thinks a peace deal can be achieved but that's just w.** il pense qu'un accord de paix peut être conclu mais ce n'est pas réaliste; **they dismissed her predictions as mere w.** ils ont qualifié ses prédictions d'irréalistes

wishy-washy ['wɪʃɪ,wɒʃɪ] **ADJ** *Fam (behaviour)* mou (molle); *(person)* sans personnalité[□]; *(colour)* délavé[□]; *(taste)* fadasse

wisp [wɪsp] **N 1** *(of grass, straw)* brin *m*; *(of hair)* petite mèche *f*; *(of smoke, steam)* ruban *m*; *Fig* **a w. of a girl** un petit bout de fillette **2** *Literary (hint, trace)* soupçon *m*, pointe *f*; **there wasn't a w. of a cloud** il n'y avait pas le moindre nuage

wispy ['wɪspɪ] *(compar* **wispier**, *superl* **wispiest**) **ADJ** *(beard)* effilé; *(hair)* épars; *(person)* (tout) menu

wisteria [wɪ'stɪərɪə] **N** glycine *f*

wistful ['wɪstful] **ADJ** mélancolique, nostalgique; **he sounded w. when he spoke of her** il parlait d'elle avec une nuance de regret dans la voix

wistfully ['wɪstfulɪ] **ADV** d'un air triste et rêveur

wit [wɪt] **N 1** *(humour)* esprit *m*; **to have a quick/a ready w.** avoir de la vivacité d'esprit/beaucoup d'esprit **2** *(humorous person)* bel esprit *m*, homme *m*/femme *f* d'esprit; **he was a great w.** c'était un homme plein d'esprit **3** *(intelligence)* esprit *m*, intelligence *f*; *Fam* **he didn't have the w. to keep his mouth shut** il n'a pas eu l'intelligence de *ou* il n'a pas été assez futé pour fermer son bec; **she has quick wits** elle a l'esprit fin, elle est très fine; **you need your wits about you in this job** il faut avoir de la présence d'esprit dans ce métier; **keep your wits about you while you're travelling** sois prudent *ou* attentif pendant que tu voyages; **to live by one's wits** vivre d'expédients; **to collect** *or* **to gather one's wits** se ressaisir, reprendre ses esprits; **I was at my wits' end** je ne savais plus quoi faire; **you frightened me out of my wits** *or* **the wits out of me!** tu m'as fait une de ces peurs!

• **to wit** ADV *Formal* à savoir

witch [wɪtʃ] **N** *(sorceress)* sorcière *f*, *Fig* **it's that old w. of a landlady** c'est cette vieille sorcière de propriétaire; *Fam* **you little w.!** petite garce!

witchcraft ['wɪtʃkrɑːft] **N** *(UNCOUNT)* sorcellerie *f*; **he claimed to have been a victim of w.** il a prétendu qu'on lui avait jeté un sort

witchdoctor ['wɪtʃ'dɒktə(r)] **N** sorcier *m* (de tribu), shaman *m*

witchery ['wɪtʃərɪ] **N** *Literary* **1** *(witchcraft)* sorcellerie *f* **2** *(charm, enchantment)* ensorcellement *m*

witch-hazel **N** *Bot* hamamélis *m*

witch-hunt **N** chasse *f* aux sorcières; *Fig* chasse *f* aux sorcières, persécution *f* (politique)

witching hour ['wɪtʃɪŋ-] **N the w.** l'heure *f* fatale

WITH [wɪð]

• avec **1, 3, 7, 10, 11**	• à **2, 5, 9**
• chez **4, 5, 11**	• contre **8**
• de **8, 10, 12**	

PREP 1 *(by means of)* avec; **she broke it w. her hands** elle l'a cassé avec ses *ou* les mains; **what did you fix it w.?** avec quoi l'as-tu réparé?; **I need something to open this can w.** j'ai besoin de quelque chose pour ouvrir cette boîte; **she painted the wall w. a roller** elle a peint le mur avec un *ou* au rouleau; **they fought w. swords** ils se sont battus à l'épée; **she filled the vase w. water** elle a rempli le vase d'eau; **his eyes filled w. tears** ses yeux se remplirent de larmes; **covered/lined w.** couvert/doublé de

2 *(describing a feature or attribute)* à; **a woman w. green eyes/long hair** une femme aux yeux verts/aux cheveux longs; **which boy? – the one w. the torn jacket** quel garçon? – celui qui a la veste déchirée; **a man w. one eye/a limp** un homme borgne/boiteux; **w. his/her hat on** le chapeau sur la tête; **the house w. the red roof** la maison au toit rouge; **a table w. three legs** une table à trois pieds; **an old woman w. no teeth** une vieille femme édentée; **a child w. no home** un enfant sans foyer *ou* sans famille; **she was left w. nothing to eat or drink** on l'a laissée sans rien à manger ni à boire

3 *(accompanied by, in the company of)* avec; **she went out w. her brother** elle est sortie avec son frère; **she came in w. a suitcase** elle est entrée avec une valise; **I'm sorry I don't have a handkerchief w. me** je suis désolé, je n'ai pas de mouchoir; **can I go w. you?** puis-je aller avec vous *ou* vous accompagner?; **I have no one to go w.** je n'ai personne avec qui aller; **she stayed w. him all night** *(gen)* elle est restée avec lui toute la nuit; *(sick person)* elle est restée auprès de lui toute la nuit; **are you w. him?** *(accompanying)* êtes-vous avec lui?; **to leave a child w. sb** laisser un enfant à la garde de qn; **I'll be w. you in a minute** je suis à vous dans une minute; **are you w. me?** *(supporting)* vous êtes avec moi?; *(understanding)* vous me suivez?; **I'm w. you there** là, je suis d'accord avec toi; **I'm w. you one hundred per cent** *or* **all the way** je suis complètement d'accord avec vous; **I'm not w. you** *(don't understand)* je ne vous suis pas; **this is a problem that will always be w. us** ce problème sera toujours d'actualité

4 *(in the home of)* chez; **he stayed w. a family** il a logé dans une famille; **she lives w. her mother** elle vit chez sa mère; **I live w. a friend** je vis avec un ami

5 *(an employee of)* **isn't he w. Ford any more?** ne travaille-t-il plus chez Ford?

6 *(a client of)* **we're w. the Galena Building Society** nous sommes à la Galena Building Society

7 *(indicating joint action)* avec; **who did you dance w.?** avec qui as-tu dansé?; **stop fighting w. your brother** arrête de te battre avec ton frère

8 *(indicating feelings towards someone else)* **angry/at war w.** fâché/en guerre contre; **in love w.** amoureux de; **pleased w.** content de

9 *(including)* **does the meal come w. wine?** est-ce que le vin est compris dans le menu?; **the bill came to £85 w. the tip** l'addition était de 85 livres avec le pourboire; **the radio didn't come w. batteries** la radio était livrée sans piles; **coffee w. milk** café *m* au lait; **duck w. orange sauce** canard *m* à l'orange; **some cheese to eat w. it** du fromage pour manger avec

10 *(indicating manner)* de, avec; **he knocked the guard out w. one blow** il assomma le gardien d'un (seul) coup; **he spoke w. ease** il s'exprima avec aisance; **w. a cry** en poussant un cri; **she hit him w. all her might** elle le frappa de toutes ses forces; **"you'll be late again," she said w. a smile** "tu vas encore être en retard", dit-elle avec un sourire *ou* en souriant; **w. these words** *or* **w. that he left** sur ces mots, il partit

11 *(as regards, concerning)* **you never know w. him** avec lui, on ne sait jamais; **all is well w. her** elle va bien; **it's an obsession w. her** c'est une manie chez elle; *Fam* **what's w. you?, what's wrong w. you?** qu'est-ce qui te prend?; **he isn't very good w. animals** il ne sait pas vraiment s'y prendre avec les bêtes

12 *(because of, on account of)* de; **white w. fear** vert de peur; **sick** *or* **ill w. malaria** atteint du paludisme; *Fig* **I was sick w. worry** j'étais malade d'inquiétude; **w. crime on the increase, elderly people are afraid to go out** avec l'augmentation du taux de criminalité, les personnes âgées ont peur de sortir; **what will happen to her w. both her parents dead?** *(now that they are dead)* que va-t-elle devenir maintenant que son père et sa mère sont morts?; **I can't draw w. you watching** je ne peux pas dessiner si tu me regardes; **w. your intelligence you'll easily guess what followed** intelligent comme vous l'êtes, vous devinerez facilement la suite; **he'll never stop smoking w. his friends offering him cigarettes all the time** il n'arrêtera jamais de fumer si ses amis continuent à lui proposer des cigarettes

13 *(in spite of)* **w. all his bragging he's just a coward** il a beau se vanter, ce n'est qu'un lâche; **w. all his faults** malgré tous ses défauts

• **with it** ADJ *Fam* **1** *(alert)* réveillé[□]; **she's not really w. it this morning** elle n'est pas très bien réveillée ce matin; **get w. it!** réveille-toi![□], secoue-toi!

2 *Old-fashioned (fashionable)* dans le vent

withal [wɪ'ðɔːl] **ADV** *Literary (as well, besides)* de plus, en outre; *(nevertheless)* néanmoins

withdraw [wɪð'drɔː] *(pt* **withdrew**, *pp* **withdrawn**) **VT 1** *(remove)* retirer; **they have withdrawn their support/their offer** ils ont retiré leur soutien/leur offre; **the car has been withdrawn (from sale)** la voiture a été retirée de la vente; **he withdrew his hand from his pocket** il a retiré la main de sa poche

2 *(money)* retirer; **I withdrew £500 from my account** j'ai retiré 500 livres de mon compte

3 *(bring out ► diplomat)* rappeler; *(► troops)* retirer, désengager

4 *(statement, remark)* retirer, rétracter; *Law (charge)* retirer

VI 1 *(retire)* se retirer; **the waiter withdrew discreetly** le serveur s'est discrètement retiré; **she has decided to w. from politics** elle a décidé de se retirer de la politique

2 *(retreat)* se retirer; *(move back)* reculer; *Mil* désengager; **he withdrew ten paces** il a reculé de dix pas; **they are being urged to w. from Iraq** on les presse de se retirer d'Irak; **he tends to w. into himself** il a tendance à se replier sur lui-même; **she often withdrew into a fantasy world** elle se réfugiait souvent dans un monde imaginaire

3 *(back out ► candidate, competitor)* se retirer, se désister; *(► partner)* se rétracter, se dédire

4 *(after sex)* se retirer

withdrawal [wɪð'drɔːəl] **N 1** *(removal ► of funding, support, troops)* retrait *m*; *(► of envoy)* rappel *m*; *(► of candidate)* retrait *m*, désistement *m*; *(► o*

love) privation *f*; **I support w. from NATO** je soutiens notre retrait de l'OTAN
2 *(of statement, remark)* rétraction *f*; *Law (of charge)* retrait *m*, annulation *f*
3 *Psy* repli *m* sur soi-même, introversion *f*
4 *Med (from drugs)* état *m* de manque; **to experience w.** être en (état de) manque
5 *(of money)* retrait *m*; **to make a w.** faire un retrait
►► *Banking* **withdrawal limit** plafond *m* (d'autorisation) de retrait; ***withdrawal method*** *(of contraception)* coït *m* interrompu; *Banking* ***withdrawal notice*** avis *m* de retrait; *Banking* ***withdrawal slip*** bordereau *m* de retrait; ***withdrawal symptoms*** symptômes *mpl* de manque; **to have** *or* **to suffer from w. symptoms** être en (état de) manque

withdrawn [wɪð'drɔːn] *pp of* **withdraw**
ADJ *(shy)* renfermé, réservé

wither ['wɪðə(r)] **VI 1** *(flower, plant)* se flétrir, se faner; *(body ► from age)* se ratatiner; *(► from sickness)* s'atrophier; *Fig* **to w. on the vine** *(project)* ne rien donner, ne pas aboutir **2** *Fig (beauty)* se faner; *(hope, optimism)* s'évanouir; *(memory)* s'étioler; **without the steel industry the region will simply w. and die** sans l'industrie sidérurgique, la région va mourir lentement; **the party gradually withered and died** le parti s'est peu à peu éteint
VT *(plant)* flétrir, faner; *(body ► of age)* ratatiner; *(► of sickness)* atrophier; *Fig* **to w. sb with a look** foudroyer qn du regard

► **wither away VI** *(flower, plant)* se dessécher, se faner; *(beauty)* se faner, s'évanouir; *(hope, optimism)* s'évanouir; *(memory)* disparaître, s'atrophier

withered ['wɪðəd] **ADJ 1** *(flower, plant)* flétri, fané; *(face, cheek)* fané, flétri; **he was old and w.** il était vieux et complètement desséché **2** *(arm)* atrophié

withering ['wɪðərɪŋ] **ADJ** *(heat, sun)* desséchant; *(criticism, remark)* cinglant, blessant; **she gave me a w. look** elle m'a lancé un regard méprisant, elle m'a foudroyé du regard; **she spoke of him with w. scorn** elle parlait de lui avec un mépris cinglant
N *(of plant)* flétrissure *f*; *(of arm)* atrophie *f*; *(of beauty)* déclin *m*; *(of hope, optimism)* évanouissement *m*

witheringly ['wɪðərɪŋlɪ] **ADV** avec un profond mépris

withers ['wɪðəz] **NPL** garrot *m* (du cheval)

withhold [wɪð'həʊld] *(pt & pp* **withheld** [-'held]) **VT 1** *(refuse ► love, permission, consent, support, loan)* refuser; *(refuse to pay ► rent, tax)* refuser de payer; **to w. payment** refuser de payer **2** *(keep back ► criticism, news)* taire, cacher; *(► information, facts)* ne pas divulguer; **to w. the truth from sb** cacher la vérité à qn; **I managed to w. my indignation/my laughter** j'ai réussi à contenir mon indignation/mon rire; **they w. 2 percent of the profits** ils retiennent 2 pour cent des bénéfices

withholding [wɪð'həʊldɪŋ] **N 1** *(refusal)* **the w. of taxes** le refus de payer les impôts; **the government's w. of aid to developing countries** le refus du gouvernement d'aider les pays en voie de développement **2** *(of information, facts)* rétention *f*

within [wɪ'ðɪn] **PREP 1** *(inside ► place)* à l'intérieur de, dans; *Fig (► group, system)* à l'intérieur de, au sein de; *(► person)* en; **he lived and worked w. these four walls** il a vécu et travaillé entre ces quatre murs; **a play w. a play** une pièce dans une pièce; **new forces are at work w. our society** des forces nouvelles sont à l'œuvre dans notre société; **the man's role w. the family is changing** le rôle de l'homme au sein de la famille est en train de changer; **a small voice w. her** une petite voix intérieure *ou* au fond d'elle-même
2 *(inside the limits of)* dans les limites de; **you must remain w. the circle** tu dois rester dans le *ou* à l'intérieur du cercle; **to be w. the law** être dans les limites de la loi; **w. the framework of the agreement** dans le cadre de l'accord; **to live w. one's means** vivre selon ses moyens; **the car is well w. his price range** la voiture est tout à fait dans ses prix *ou* dans ses moyens; **w. reason** dans des limites raisonnables
3 *(before the end of a specified period of time)* en moins de; **w. the hour** *or* **an hour she had finished** en moins d'une heure, elle avait fini; **I'll let you know w. a week** je vous dirai ce qu'il en est dans le courant de la semaine; **w. the required time** dans le délai prescrit; **w. 24 hours/two days** dans les 24 heures/les deux jours; **w. a week of taking the job, she knew it was a mistake** moins d'une semaine après avoir accepté cet emploi, elle sut qu'elle avait fait une erreur; **w. the next five years, w. five years from now** d'ici cinq ans
4 *(indicating distance, measurement)* **they were w. 10 km of Delhi** ils étaient à moins de 10 km de Delhi; **we are w. walking distance of the shops** nous pouvons aller faire nos courses à pied; **accurate to w. 0.1 of a millimetre** précis au dixième de millimètre près; **w. a radius of ten kilometres** dans un rayon de dix kilomètres; **she came w. seconds of beating the record** elle a failli battre le record à quelques secondes près; **we were w. sight of the shore** nous avions la côte en vue
5 *(during)* **enormous changes have taken place w. a single generation** de grands changements ont eu lieu en l'espace d'une seule génération; **did the accident take place w. the period covered by the insurance?** l'accident a-t-il eu lieu pendant la période couverte par l'assurance?
ADV dedans, à l'intérieur; **enquire w.** *(sign)* renseignements à l'intérieur; **from w.** de l'intérieur

without [wɪ'ðaʊt] **PREP** sans; **three nights w. sleep** trois nuits sans dormir; **we couldn't have done it w. you** on n'aurait pas pu le faire sans vous; **w. milk or sugar** sans lait ni sucre; **with or w. chocolate sauce?** avec ou sans sauce au chocolat?; **to be w. fear/shame** ne pas avoir peur/honte; **not w. irony** non sans ironie; **he took it w. so much as a thank you** il l'a pris sans même dire merci; **w. any difficulty** sans aucune difficulté; **the rumour is w. foundation** la rumeur est dénuée de fondement *ou* n'est pas fondée; **she did it w. asking/being asked** elle l'a fait sans demander/sans qu'on le lui demande; **w. looking up** sans lever les yeux; **I knocked w. getting a reply** j'ai frappé sans obtenir de réponse; **leave the house w. anybody knowing** quittez la maison sans que personne le sache
ADV *Literary* au dehors, à l'extérieur; **a voice from w.** une voix de l'extérieur

with-pack premium N *Mktg* prime *f* directe

with-profits ADJ *Fin (pension fund)* avec participation aux bénéfices

withstand [wɪð'stænd] *(pt & pp* **withstood** [-'stʊd]) **VT** *(heat, punishment)* résister à; **to w. the test of time** résister à l'épreuve du temps

withy ['wɪðɪ] *(pl* **withies) N** brin *m ou* lien *m* d'osier

witless ['wɪtlɪs] **ADJ** sot (sotte), stupide; *Fam* **to scare sb w.** faire une peur bleue à qn

witness ['wɪtnɪs] **N 1** *(onlooker) (► at accident, event)* témoin *m*
2 *Law (in court, to signature, will, document)* témoin *m*; **to call sb as (a) w.** citer qn comme témoin; **w. for the prosecution/defence** témoin *m* à charge/à décharge; **two people must be witnesses to my signature/will** deux personnes doivent signer comme témoins de ma signature/de mon testament; **will you act as a w. at our wedding?** est-ce que vous voulez bien être témoin à notre mariage?
3 *(testimony)* **in w. of sth** en témoignage de qch; **to be** *or* **to bear w. to sth** témoigner de qch; **to give w. on behalf of sb** témoigner en faveur de qn
4 *Rel* témoignage *m*; **to bear false w.** porter un faux témoignage
VT 1 *(see)* être témoin de, témoigner de; **did she w. the accident?** a-t-elle été témoin de l'accident?; **millions witnessed the first moon landing** des millions de gens ont vu le premier atterrissage sur la lune; **we are witnessing a historic event** nous assistons à un événement historique; **he had witnessed the entire scene from his window** il avait vu *ou* il avait assisté à toute la scène depuis sa fenêtre; **never in my entire life have I witnessed such stupidity** je n'ai jamais, de ma vie entière, vu une telle stupidité **2** *(signature)* être témoin de; *(will, document)* signer comme témoin **3** *(experience ► change)* voir, connaître; **the 19th century witnessed many revolutions** le XIXème siècle a connu beaucoup de révolutions
VI *(gen) & Law* témoigner, être témoin; **to w. to sth** témoigner de qch; **to w. against sb** témoigner contre qn; **she witnessed to finding the body** elle a témoigné avoir découvert le cadavre
►► *Br* ***witness box*** barre *f* des témoins; **in the w. box** à la barre; ***witness protection programme, witness protection scheme*** programme *f* de protection des témoins; *Am* ***witness stand*** barre *f* des témoins; **to take the w. stand** venir à la barre

-witted ['wɪtɪd] **SUFF quick-w.** à l'esprit vif; **dim-w.** à l'esprit lent

witter ['wɪtə(r)] **VI** *Br Fam Pej* **they were wittering (on) about diets** ils parlaient interminablement de régimes□; **do stop wittering on** arrête de parler pour ne rien dire, arrête tes jacasseries

wittering ['wɪtərɪŋ] **N** *Br Fam Pej* jacasseries *fpl*

witticism ['wɪtɪsɪzəm] **N** bon mot *m*, trait *m* d'esprit

wittily ['wɪtɪlɪ] **ADV** spirituellement, avec beaucoup d'esprit

wittiness ['wɪtɪnɪs] **N** esprit *m*, humour *m*

wittingly ['wɪtɪŋlɪ] **ADV** *Formal* en connaissance de cause, sciemment

witty ['wɪtɪ] *(compar* **wittier**, *superl* **wittiest) ADJ** spirituel, plein d'esprit

wizard ['wɪzəd] **N 1** *(magician)* enchanteur *m*, sorcier *m* **2** *Fig (expert)* génie *m*; **she's a real w. at drawing** elle est vraiment douée en dessin; **she's a w. with computers** c'est un champion de l'ordinateur; **a financial w.** un génie de la finance **3** *Comput* assistant *m*
ADJ *Br Fam Old-fashioned* épatant

wizardry ['wɪzədrɪ] **N 1** *(magic)* magie *f*, sorcellerie *f* **2** *Fig (genius)* génie *m*; **financial w.** le génie de la finance; **they've installed a new piece of technical w. in the office** ils ont installé une nouvelle merveille de la technique dans le bureau; **that was sheer w. with the ball** c'était un jeu purement et simplement génial

wizened ['wɪzənd] **ADJ** *(skin, hands)* desséché; *(old person)* desséché, ratatiné; *(face, fruit, vegetables)* ratatiné

wk *(written abbr* **week)** sem

WMD [ˌdʌbəljuːem'diː] **NPL** *(abbr* **weapons of mass destruction)** ADM *fpl*

WO [ˌdʌbəljuː'əʊ] **N** *Br Mil (abbr* **warrant officer)** adjt

wo = whoa

woad [wəʊd] **N** guède *f*

wobble ['wɒbəl] **VI** *(hand, jelly, voice)* trembler; *(chair, table)* branler, être branlant *ou* bancal; *(drunkard)* tituber, chanceler; *(building, tooth)* bouger; *(cyclist)* aller de travers, aller en zigzag; **the stone wobbled as I stood on it** la pierre a oscillé quand je suis monté dessus; **the pile of books wobbled dangerously** la pile de livres oscilla dangereusement; **the child wobbled across the room** l'enfant traversa la pièce en chancelant; **she wobbled off/past on her bike** elle partit/passa sur son vélo, en équilibre instable
VT faire bouger; **don't w. the table when I'm writing** ne fais pas bouger la table quand j'écris
N the chair has got a bit of a w. la chaise est légèrement bancale *ou* branlante; **after a few wobbles, he finally got going** après avoir cherché son équilibre, il se mit enfin en route

wobbly ['wɒblɪ] *(compar* **wobblier**, *superl* **wobbliest**, *pl* **wobblies) ADJ 1** *(table, chair)* branlant, bancal; *(pile)* chancelant, instable; *(jelly)* qui tremble **2** *(hand, voice)* tremblant; **I feel a bit w.** je me sens un peu faible; **she's rather w. on her feet** elle flageole un peu *ou* elle ne tient pas très bien sur ses jambes **3** *(line)* qui n'est pas droit; *(handwriting)* tremblé
N *Br Fam (idiom)* **to throw a w.** piquer une crise

wodge [wɒdʒ] **N** *Br Fam* gros bloc *m*, gros morceau *m*

woe [wəʊ] *Literary or Hum* **N** malheur *m*, infortune *f*; **a tale of w.** une histoire pathétique; **tell me your woes** raconte-moi tes malheurs, dis-moi ce qui ne va pas; **w. betide anyone who lies to me** malheur à celui qui me raconte des mensonges
EXCLAM hélas; **w. is me!** pauvre de moi!

woebegone ['wəʊbɪˌgɒn] **ADJ** *Literary or Hum* désolé, abattu

woeful ['wəʊfʊl] ADJ **1** *(sad ▸ person, look, news, situation)* malheureux, très triste; *(▸ scene, tale)* affligeant, très triste **2** *(very poor)* lamentable, épouvantable, consternant

woefully ['wəʊfʊlɪ] ADV **1** *(sadly ▸ look, smile)* très tristement **2** *(badly ▸ perform, behave)* lamentablement; **he is w. lacking in common sense** le bon sens lui fait cruellement défaut; **the garden was w. neglected for several years** le jardin avait été très négligé pendant plusieurs années

wog [wɒg] N *Br very Fam* nègre (négresse) *m,f*, = terme raciste désignant un Noir

wok [wɒk] N wok *m (poêle chinoise)*

wold [wəʊld] N haute plaine *f*, plateau *m*

wolf [wʊlf] *(pl* **wolves** [wʊlvz]) N loup *m*; *also Fig* **the big bad w.** le grand méchant loup; **he's a w. in sheep's clothing** c'est un loup déguisé en brebis; **it helps keep the w. from the door** ça me/le/*etc* met à l'abri du besoin; **to throw sb to the wolves** sacrifier qn

▸▸ ***wolf cub*** *(animal)* louveteau *m*; ***wolf pack*** meute *f* de loups; ***wolf whistle*** sifflement *m (au passage d'une femme)*

▸ **wolf down** VT SEP *Fam (food)* engloutir▫, dévorer▫

wolfhound ['wʊlfhaʊnd] N chien-loup *m*

wolfish ['wʊlfɪʃ] ADJ *(appearance)* de loup; *(appetite)* vorace

wolfram ['wʊlfrəm] N tungstène *m*, wolfram *m*

wolfsbane ['wʊlfsbeɪn] N aconit *m* jaune

wolf-whistle VT siffler *(une femme)*

wolverine ['wʊlvəri:n] *(pl* **inv** *or* **wolverines**) N *Zool* glouton *m*

woman ['wʊmən] *(pl* **women** ['wɪmɪn]) N **1** *(gen)* femme *f*; **a young/an old w.** une jeune/vieille femme; *Fam Pej* **he's an old w.** il fait des histoires pour rien; **she's quite the young w. now** elle fait très jeune fille maintenant; **women and children first** les femmes et les enfants d'abord; **man's perception of w.** la façon dont les hommes voient les femmes, la vision de la femme qu'a l'homme; **women live longer than men** les femmes vivent plus longtemps que les hommes; **I don't even know the w.!** je ne sais même pas qui elle est *ou* qui c'est!; **a w. of letters** une femme de lettres; **a w. of the world** *(cultivated)* une femme du monde; *(worldly-wise)* une femme d'expérience; **she's a working/career w.** elle travaille/elle a une carrière; **a w.'s** *or* **women's magazine** un magazine féminin

2 *(employee)* femme *f*; **a w. minds the children for me** j'ai une femme qui me garde les enfants; **the factory women left for work** les ouvrières sont parties travailler; **(cleaning) w.** femme *f* de ménage

3 *Fam (wife)* femme▫ *f*; *(girlfriend, mistress)* nana *f*; **he's bringing his new w. with him** il amène sa nouvelle copine; **the other w.** *(mistress)* l'autre femme

4 *Fam (patronizing term of address)* **that's enough, w.!** assez, femme!

▸▸ ***woman doctor*** (femme *f*) médecin *m*; ***woman driver*** conductrice *f*; ***woman friend*** amie *f*; *Euph* ***women's problems*** problèmes *mpl* de femmes

woman-hater N misogyne *mf*

womanhood ['wʊmənhʊd] N *(UNCOUNT)* **1** *(female nature)* féminité *f*; **to reach w.** devenir une femme **2** *(women collectively)* les femmes *fpl*

womanish ['wʊmənɪʃ] ADJ *Pej (man)* efféminé; *(characteristic)* de femme, féminin

womanize, -ise ['wʊmənaɪz] VI courir les femmes

womanizer, -iser ['wʊmənaɪzə(r)] N coureur *m* de jupons

womanizing, -ising ['wʊmənaɪzɪŋ] N **she was fed up with his w.** elle en avait assez qu'il coure le jupon

ADJ **her w. husband** son coureur de jupon de mari

womankind [ˌwʊmən'kaɪnd] N les femmes *fpl*

womanliness ['wʊmənlɪnɪs] N féminité *f*

womanly ['wʊmənlɪ] ADJ *(virtue, figure)* féminin, de femme; *(act)* digne d'une femme, féminin

womb [wu:m] N *Anat* utérus *m*; **in his mother's w.** dans le ventre de sa mère

wombat ['wɒmbæt] N *Zool* wombat *m*

women ['wɪmɪn] *pl of* **woman**

▸▸ ***Women's Lib*** MLF *m*, mouvement *m* de libération de la femme; ***Women's Libber*** féministe *f*; ***Women's Liberation*** mouvement *m* de libération de la femme, MLF *m*; ***Women's Movement*** mouvement *m* féministe; ***women's refuge*** centre *m* d'accueil pour les femmes; ***women's rights*** droits *mpl* de la femme; ***women's shelter*** centre *m* d'accueil pour les femmes; ***women's studies*** = discipline universitaire ayant pour objet la sociologie et l'histoire des femmes, la création littéraire féminine etc

womenfolk ['wɪmɪnfəʊk] NPL **the w.** les femmes *fpl*

won [wʌn] *pt & pp of* **win**

wonder ['wʌndə(r)] N **1** *(marvel)* merveille *f*; **the seven wonders of the world** les sept merveilles du monde; **the wonders of science** les miracles de la science; **to work** *or* **to do wonders** *(person)* faire des merveilles; *(action, event)* faire merveille; **a hot bath worked wonders for her aching body** un bain chaud la soulagea à merveille de ses douleurs

2 *(amazing event or circumstances)* **the w. (of it) is that he manages to get any work done at all** le plus étonnant dans tout cela, c'est qu'il arrive à travailler; **it's a w. (that) she didn't resign on the spot** c'est étonnant qu'elle n'ait pas démissionné sur-le-champ; **no w. they refused** ce n'est pas étonnant qu'ils aient refusé; **no w.!** ce n'est pas étonnant!, cela vous étonne?; **is it any w. that he got lost?** cela vous étonne qu'il se soit perdu?; **it's little** *or* **small w. no one came** ce n'est guère étonnant que personne ne soit venu; *Hum* **wonders will never cease!** on n'a pas fini d'être étonné!

3 *(awe)* émerveillement *m*; **the children were filled with w.** les enfants étaient émerveillés; **there was a look of w. in his eyes** il avait les yeux pleins d'étonnement

4 *(prodigy)* prodige *m*, génie *m*; **a boy w.** un petit prodige *ou* génie

COMP *(drug, detergent)* miracle; *(child)* prodige

VT **1** *(ask oneself)* se demander; **I w. where she's gone** je me demande où elle est allée; **I w. how he managed it** je me demande comment il s'y est pris; **I w. why** je me demande bien pourquoi; **I w. who invented that** je suis curieux de savoir qui a inventé cela; **it makes you w. how safe these power stations are** on en vient à se demander si ces centrales électriques sont vraiment sûres; **I often w. that myself** je me pose souvent la question; **I w. whether** *or* **if she'll come** je me demande si elle viendra

2 *(in polite requests)* **I was wondering if you were free tomorrow** est-ce que par hasard vous êtes libre demain?; **I w. if you could help me** pourriez-vous m'aider, s'il vous plaît?

3 *(be surprised)* s'étonner; **I w. that he wasn't hurt** je m'étonne *ou* cela m'étonne qu'il n'ait pas été blessé; **I shouldn't w. if he were already married** cela ne m'étonnerait pas *ou* cela ne me surprendrait pas qu'il soit déjà marié

VI **1** *(think, reflect)* penser, réfléchir; **it makes you w.** cela donne à penser *ou* à réfléchir; **I'm wondering about going tomorrow** je me demande si je ne vais pas y aller demain; **I was wondering about it too** je me posais la même question; **the war will be over in a few days – I w.** la guerre sera finie dans quelques jours – je n'en suis pas si sûr; **why? – oh, I just wondered** pourquoi? – oh, pour rien, comme ça

2 *(marvel, be surprised)* s'étonner, s'émerveiller; **to w. at sth** s'émerveiller de qch; **the people wondered at the magnificent sight** les gens s'émerveillaient de ce magnifique spectacle; **I don't w. (that) you're annoyed** cela ne m'étonne pas que vous soyez contrarié; **I don't w.** cela ne m'étonne pas

Wonderbra® ['wʌndəbrɑ:] N Wonderbra® *m*

wonderful ['wʌndəfʊl] ADJ *(enjoyable)* merveilleux, formidable; *(beautiful)* superbe, magnifique; *(delicious)* excellent; *(astonishing)* étonnant, surprenant; **we had a w. time/holiday** nous avons passé des moments/des vacances formidables; **the weather was w.** il a fait un temps superbe; **what w. news!** quelle nouvelle formidable!; **that's w.!** c'est merveilleux!; **you look w.** tu es superbe

wonderfully ['wʌndəfʊlɪ] ADV **1** *(with adj or adv)* merveilleusement, admirablement; **you look w. well** vous avez une mine superbe; **she was w. kind** elle était d'une gentillesse merveilleuse **2** *(with verb)* merveilleusement, à merveille; **they got on w.** ils s'entendirent à merveille; **I slept w.** j'ai dormi à merveille, j'ai merveilleusement bien dormi

wondering ['wʌndərɪŋ] ADJ *(pensive)* songeur, pensif; *(surprised)* étonné; **she looked at him with w. eyes** elle le regarda d'un air perplexe

wonderingly ['wʌndərɪŋlɪ] ADV *(look ▸ pensively)* d'un air songeur; *(▸ in surprise)* d'un air étonné; *(speak)* avec étonnement

wonderland ['wʌndəlænd] N pays *m* des merveilles; **a winter w.** un paysage hivernal féerique

wonderment ['wʌndəmənt] N *(wonder)* émerveillement *m*; *(surprise)* étonnement *m*

wondrous ['wʌndrəs] *Literary* ADJ merveilleux

ADV merveilleusement

wondrously ['wʌndrəslɪ] ADV *Literary* merveilleusement

wonga ['wɒŋgə] N *Br Fam (money)* fric *m*, flouze *m*, pognon *m*

wonk [wɒŋk] N *Am Fam* **1** *(student)* bûcheur (euse) *m,f* **2** *(intellectual, expert)* intello *mf (qui ne s'intéresse qu'à sa discipline)*

wonky ['wɒŋkɪ] *(compar* **wonkier**, *superl* **wonkiest**) ADJ *Br Fam (table, chair, floorboards)* bancal▫, branlant▫; *(bicycle)* détraqué; *(gadget, zip, switch)* qui débloque; *(radio, TV)* déréglé▫, détraqué; *(line)* qui n'est pas bien droit▫; *(collar, picture)* de travers▫; **your tie is a bit w.** ta cravate est un peu de travers; **this sentence is a bit w.** il y a quelque chose qui cloche dans cette phrase

won't [wəʊnt] = **will not**

wont [wəʊnt] *Literary* N coutume *f*, habitude *f*; **as was his/her w.** comme de coutume

ADJ **to be w. to do sth** avoir l'habitude *ou* coutume de faire qch; **he is w. to panic** il a tendance à paniquer, il panique facilement

woo [wu:] *(pt & pp* **wooed**) VT **1** *Old-fashioned (court)* courtiser, faire la cour à **2** *(attract ▸ customers, voters)* chercher à plaire à, rechercher les faveurs de; **they tried to w. the voters with promises of lower taxes** ils cherchaient à s'attirer les faveurs de l'électorat en promettant de baisser les impôts; **they wooed him away from their rivals by promising him more money** ils lui ont fait quitter leurs concurrents en lui promettant plus d'argent

wood [wʊd] N **1** *(timber)* bois *m*; **a piece of w.** un bout de bois; *Br* **touch w.!**, *Am* **knock on w.!** touchons du bois!

2 *(group of trees)* bois *m*; **we went for a walk in the woods** nous sommes allés nous promener dans les bois; *Fig* **he can't see the w. for the trees** les arbres lui cachent la forêt; *Fig* **we're not out of the woods yet** on n'est pas encore sortis de l'auberge, on n'est pas encore tirés d'affaire

3 *(casks, barrels)* tonneau *m*; **matured in the w.** vieilli au tonneau

4 *(in bowls)* boule *f*

5 *Golf* bois *m*; **a (number) 3 w.** un bois 3

6 *Am Fam* **to put the w. to sb** *(beat up)* tabasser qn; *(defeat)* battre qn à plates coutures

7 *Vulg* **to get w.** *(erection)* bander

COMP **1** *(wooden ▸ floor, table, house)* en bois, de bois **2** *(for burning wood ▸ stove)* à bois; *(▸ fire)* de bois

▸▸ ***wood alcohol*** esprit-de-bois *m*, alcool *m* méthylique; ***wood ash*** cendre *f* de bois; ***wood carver*** sculpteur *m* sur bois; ***wood nymph*** nymphe *f* des bois, dryade *f*; *Orn* ***wood pigeon*** ramier *m*; ***wood pulp*** pâte *f* à papier; ***wood stain*** teinture *f* pour bois

woodbine ['wʊdbaɪn] N *Bot (honeysuckle)* chèvrefeuille *m*; *Am (Virginia creeper)* vigne *f* vierge

woodchuck ['wʊdtʃʌk] N marmotte *f* d'Amérique *ou* du Canada

woodcock ['wʊdkɒk] *(pl* **inv** *or* **woodcocks**) N *Orn* bécasse *f*

woodcraft ['wʊdkrɑːft] **N** *Am* **1** *(in woodland)* connaissance *f* des bois et des forêts **2** *(artistry)* art *m* de travailler le bois

woodcut ['wʊdkʌt] **N** gravure *f* sur bois

woodcutter ['wʊd,kʌtə(r)] **N** bûcheron(onne) *m,f*

woodcutting ['wʊd,kʌtɪŋ] **N 1** *(in forest)* abattage *m* des arbres **2** *(engraving)* gravure *f* sur bois

wooded ['wʊdɪd] **ADJ** boisé; **densely w.** très boisé

wooden ['wʊdən] **ADJ 1** *(made of wood)* en bois, de bois; **a w. leg** une jambe de bois; **the W. Horse of Troy** le cheval de Troie **2** *Fig (stiff ▸ gesture, manner)* crispé, raide; *(▸ performance, actor)* raide, qui manque de naturel
▸▸ *Fam Hum* ***wooden overcoat*** *(coffin)* costume *m* de sapin; ***wooden spoon*** cuillère *f* en bois; *Br Sport* **to win the w. spoon** gagner la cuillère de bois

woodenhead ['wʊdən,hed] **N** *Fam* idiot(e) *m,f*, imbécile[□] *mf*

woodenheaded ['wʊdən,hedɪd] **ADJ** *Fam (stupid)* stupide[□], bouché

woodenness ['wʊdənnɪs] **N** *Fig (of gesture, manner)* raideur *f*; *(of performance, actor)* manque *m* de naturel

woodfree ['wʊdfriː] **ADJ** *(paper)* sans bois

woodie ['wʊdɪ] **N** *Am very Fam (erection)* érection[□] *f*, bandaison *f*; **to have a w.** bander

woodland ['wʊdlənd] **N** région *f* boisée
ADJ *(fauna)* des bois; **w. walks** promenades *fpl* à travers bois

woodlark ['wʊdlɑːk] **N** *Orn* alouette *f* des bois, lulu *m*

woodlouse ['wʊdlaʊs] *(pl* **woodlice** [-laɪs]*)* **N** *Entom* cloporte *m*

woodman ['wʊdmən] *(pl* **woodmen** [-mən]*)* **N** forestier *m*

woodpecker ['wʊd,pekə(r)] **N** *Orn* pic *m*, pivert *m*

woodpile ['wʊdpaɪl] **N** tas *m* de bois

woodshed ['wʊdʃed] **N** bûcher *m (abri)*

woodsman ['wʊdzmən] *(pl* **woodsmen** [-mən]*)* **N** *Am* forestier *m*

woodstack ['wʊdstæk] **N** tas *m* de bois

woodwind ['wʊdwɪnd] **ADJ** *(music)* pour les bois
N 1 *(single instrument)* bois *m* **2** *(UNCOUNT) (family of instruments)* bois *mpl*
▸▸ ***woodwind instruments, woodwind section*** bois *mpl*

woodwork ['wʊdwɜːk] **N** *(UNCOUNT)* **1** *(craft ▸ carpentry)* menuiserie *f*; *(▸ cabinet-making)* ébénisterie *f*; *(school subject)* menuiserie *f* **2** *(in building ▸ doors, window frames)* boiseries *fpl*; *(▸ beams)* charpente *f*; *Fam* **to come** *or* **to crawl out of the w.** sortir d'un peu partout

woodworm ['wʊdwɜːm] **N 1** *(insect)* ver *m* de bois **2** *(infestation)* **a chair affected** *or* **damaged by w.** une chaise vermoulue *ou* mangée aux vers; **the sideboard has got w.** le buffet est vermoulu

woody ['wʊdɪ] *(compar* **woodier,** *superl* **woodiest)** **ADJ 1** *(plant, vegetation)* ligneux **2** *(countryside)* boisé **3** *(taste, texture)* de bois; *(smell)* boisé

wooer ['wuːə(r)] **N** *Old-fashioned* prétendant *m*

woof¹ [wuːf] **N** *Tex* trame *f*

woof² [wʊf] **N** *(bark)* aboiement *m*
VI *(animal)* aboyer
ONOMAT ouah! ouah!

woofer ['wʊfə(r)] **N** haut-parleur *m* de graves, woofer *m*

woofter ['wʊftə(r)] **N** *Br Fam* pédé *m*, = terme injurieux désignant un homosexuel

wool [wʊl] **N** laine *f*; **pure new w.** pure laine vierge; **a ball of w.** une pelote de laine; **to pull the w. over sb's eyes** berner *ou* duper qn
ADJ 1 *(made of wool ▸ cloth)* de laine; *(▸ socks, dress)* en laine **2** *(relating to wool)* **the w. industry** l'industrie *f* lainière; **w. shop** magasin *m* de laines

woolen *Am* = **woollen**

woolgathering ['wʊl,gæðərɪŋ] **N to be** *or* **to go w.** rêvasser

woollen, *Am* **woolen** ['wʊlən] **ADJ 1** *(fabric)* de laine; *(jacket, gloves, blanket)* en laine **2** *(industry)* lainière; *(manufacture)* de lainages
• **woollens,** *Am*
• **woolens NPL** lainages *mpl*, vêtements *mpl* de laine
▸▸ ***woollen mill*** lainerie *f*

woolliness, *Am* **wooliness** ['wʊlɪnɪs] **N 1** *(of reasoning, ideas, style)* flou *m*, caractère *m* confus; *(of outline)* manque *m* de netteté, flou *m* **2** *(resemblance to wool)* nature *f* laineuse (**of** de)

woolly, *Am* **wooly** ['wʊlɪ] *(Br compar* **woollier,** *superl* **woolliest,** *Am compar* **woolier,** *superl* **wooliest,** *Br pl* **woollies,** *Am pl* **woolies)** **ADJ 1** *(socks, hat)* en laine
2 *(sheep)* laineux
3 *(clouds)* cotonneux; *(hair)* frisé
4 *(vague ▸ reasoning, ideas, style)* confus, flou; *(▸ outline)* flou, peu net
N *Br Fam (jumper)* tricot *m*, lainage *m*; **winter woollies** lainages *mpl* d'hiver

woolly-headed, *Am* **wooly-headed ADJ** *(person)* écervelé; *(ideas)* vague, confus

woolly-minded, *Am* **wooly-minded ADJ** à l'esprit confus

woolsack ['wʊlsæk] **N** *Br Parl* **the w., the W.** *(seat)* = coussin rouge sur lequel s'assoit le Lord Chancellor (à la Chambre des lords); *(office)* = le siège du Lord Chancellor (à la Chambre des lords)

woozy ['wuːzɪ] *(compar* **woozier,** *superl* **wooziest)** **ADJ** *Fam (dazed)* hébété[□], dans les vapes; *(from drink)* éméché, pompette; *(sick)* **to feel w.** avoir mal au cœur[□]

wop [wɒp] **N** *very Fam* macaroni *mf*, = terme injurieux désignant un Italien

Worcester sauce ['wʊstə-] **N** sauce *f* Worcestershire, = sauce épicée au soja et au vinaigre

Worcs *(written abbr* **Worcestershire)** Worcestershire *m*

WORD [wɜːd]

N	
• mot **1–3**	• parole **1, 2, 4**
• nouvelle(s) **3**	• message **3**
• promesse **4**	• conseil **5**
• bruit **6**	• ordre **7**
VT	
• rédiger **1**	• formuler **1**

N 1 *(gen ▸ written)* mot *m*; *(▸ spoken)* mot *m*, parole *f*; **the words of a song** les paroles d'une chanson; *Ironic* **(what) fine words!** quelles belles paroles!; **what is the Russian w. for "head"?, what is the w. for "head" in Russian?** comment dit-on "head" en russe?; **the Japanese don't have a w. for it** les Japonais n'ont pas de mot pour dire cela; **she can't put her ideas/her feelings into words** elle ne trouve pas les mots pour exprimer ses idées/ce qu'elle ressent; **there are no words to describe** *or* **words cannot describe how I feel** aucun mot ne peut décrire ce que je ressens; **they left without (saying) a w.** ils sont partis sans (dire) un mot; **lazy isn't the w. for it!** paresseux, c'est peu dire!; **idle would be a better w.** oisif serait plus juste; *Fig* **he doesn't know the meaning of the w. "generosity"** il ne sait pas ce que veut dire le mot "générosité"; **he's mad, there's no other w. for it** il est fou, il n'y a pas d'autre mot; **there's a w. for people like you, it's "thief"** les gens dans ton genre, on les appelle des voleurs; **I didn't understand a w. of the lecture** je n'ai pas compris un mot de la conférence; **he doesn't know a w. of German** il ne sait pas un mot d'allemand; **I don't believe a w. of it!** je n'en crois pas un mot!; **that's my last** *or* **my final w. on the matter** c'est mon dernier mot (sur la question); **those were his dying words** ce sont les dernières paroles qu'il a prononcées avant de mourir; **she said a few words of welcome** elle a dit quelques mots de bienvenue; **I gave him a few words of advice** je lui ai donné quelques conseils; **can I give you a w. of warning/of advice?** puis-je vous mettre en garde/vous conseiller?; **he didn't say a w.** il n'a rien dit, il n'a pas dit un mot; **I can't get a w. out of her** je ne peux pas en tirer un mot; **and now a w. from our sponsors** et maintenant, voici un message publicitaire de nos sponsors; **he's a man of few words** c'est un homme peu loquace, c'est quelqu'un qui n'aime pas beaucoup parler; **in the words of Shelley** comme l'a dit Shelley; **in the words of his boss, he's a layabout** à en croire son patron *ou* d'après (ce que dit) son patron, c'est un fainéant; **tell me in your own words** dites-le moi à votre façon *ou* avec vos propres mots; **he told me in so many words that I was a liar** il m'a dit carrément *ou* sans mâcher ses mots que j'étais un menteur; **she didn't say it in so many words but her meaning was quite clear** elle n'a pas dit exactement cela, mais c'était sous-entendu; **a 600-w. article** un article de 600 mots; **by** *or* **through w. of mouth** oralement; **the news spread by w. of mouth** la nouvelle se répandit de bouche à oreille; **too stupid for words** vraiment trop bête; **w. for w.** *(translate)* littéralement, mot à mot; *(repeat)* mot pour mot; **from the w. go** dès le départ; **(upon) my w.!** ma parole!, oh la la!; **not a w.!** pas un mot!, bouche cousue!; **don't put words into my mouth** ne me faites pas dire ce que je n'ai pas dit; **he took the words right out of my mouth** il a dit exactement ce que j'allais dire; **words fail me!** j'en perds la parole!, je suis stupéfait!; **he never has a good w. to say about anyone** personne ne trouve jamais grâce à ses yeux; **to put in a (good) w. for sb** glisser un mot en faveur de qn; **to have the last w.** avoir le dernier mot; *Br* **it's the last w. in luxury** c'est ce qu'on fait de plus luxueux
2 *(talk)* mot(s) *m(pl)*, parole(s) *f(pl)*; **to have a w. with sb about sth** toucher un mot *ou* deux mots à qn au sujet de qch; **can I have a w. with you about the meeting?** est-ce que je peux vous dire deux mots à propos de la réunion?; **can I have a w.?** je voudrais vous parler un instant
3 *(UNCOUNT) (news)* nouvelle(s) *f(pl)*; *(message)* message *m*, mot *m*; **the w. got out that there had been a coup** la nouvelle d'un coup d'État a circulé; **w. came from Tokyo that the strike was over** la nouvelle arriva de Tokyo que la grève était terminée; **she brought them w. of Tom** elle leur a apporté des nouvelles de Tom; **have you had any w. from him?** avez-vous eu de ses nouvelles?; **she left w. for us to follow** elle nous a laissé un message pour dire que nous devions la suivre; **to spread the w.** *(proselytize)* annoncer la bonne parole; **spread the w. that Mick's back in town** faites passer la nouvelle *ou* faites dire que Mick est de retour en ville; **he sent w. to say he had arrived safely** il a envoyé un mot pour dire qu'il était bien arrivé
4 *(promise)* parole *f*, promesse *f*; **he gave his w. that we wouldn't be harmed** il a donné sa parole qu'il ne nous ferait aucun mal; **I give you my w. on it** je vous en donne ma parole; **to break one's w.** manquer à sa parole; **to go back on one's w.** revenir sur sa parole; **we held** *or* **we kept her to her w.** nous l'avons obligée à tenir sa parole; **to keep one's w.** tenir parole, tenir (sa) promesse; **he was as good as his w.** il a tenu parole; **I'm a man of my w.** je suis un homme de parole; **w. of honour!** parole d'honneur!; **you can take my w. for it** vous pouvez me croire sur parole; **we'll have to take your w. for it** nous sommes bien obligés de vous croire; **take my w. (for it), it's a bargain!** croyez-moi, c'est une affaire!; **I took her at her w.** je l'ai prise au mot; **it's your w. against mine** c'est votre parole contre la mienne; **my w. is my bond** je n'ai qu'une parole, je tiens toujours parole
5 *(advice)* conseil *m*; **a w. to travellers, watch your luggage!** un petit conseil aux voyageurs, surveillez vos bagages!; **a quick w. in your ear** je vous glisse un mot à l'oreille
6 *(rumour)* bruit *m*; **(the) w. went round that he was dying** le bruit a couru qu'il était sur le point de mourir
7 *(order)* ordre *m*; **he gave the w. to march** il a donné l'ordre *ou* le signal de se mettre en marche; **his w. is law** c'est lui qui fait la loi; **just give** *or* **say the w. and we'll be off** vous n'avez qu'à donner le signal et nous partons
8 *(watchword)* mot *m* d'ordre; *(password)* mot *m* de passe; **the w. now is "democracy"** le mot d'ordre maintenant, c'est "démocratie"
VT *(letter, document)* rédiger, formuler; *(con-*

tract) rédiger; **they worded the petition carefully** ils ont choisi les termes de la pétition avec le plus grand soin; **we sent a strongly worded protest** nous avons envoyé une lettre de protestation bien sentie

• **Word** N *Rel* **the W.** le Verbe; **the W. of God** la parole de Dieu

• **words** NPL *Br Fam (argument)* dispute f; **to have words** se disputer, avoir des mots; **they had words about her drinking** ils se sont disputés sur le fait qu'elle boit

• **in a word** ADV en un mot

• **in other words** ADV autrement dit, en d'autres termes

▸▸ ***word association*** association *f* d'idées par les mots; *Comput & Typ* ***word break*** césure *f*; *Comput* ***word count*** nombre *m* des mots; **to do a w. count** compter les mots; ***word count facility*** fonction *f* de comptage de mots; ***word game*** = jeu de lettres; ***word group*** groupe *m* de mots, membre *m* de phrase; ***word order*** ordre *m* des mots; ***word processing*** traitement *m* de texte; ***word processor*** logiciel *m* de traitement de texte; *Typ* ***word split*** coupure *f* de mot; *Comput* ***word wrap*** retour *m* à la ligne automatique

wordbook ['wɜːdbʊk] N lexique *m*, vocabulaire *m*

word-for-word ADJ *(repetition, imitation)* mot pour mot; *(translation)* littéral

wordiness ['wɜːdɪnɪs] N verbosité *f*

wording ['wɜːdɪŋ] N *(UNCOUNT)* **1** *(of letter, speech)* termes *mpl*, formulation *f*; *(of contract)* termes *mpl*; **I think you should change the w. of the last sentence** je crois que vous devriez reformuler la dernière phrase; **the w. is rather strange** c'est bizarrement formulé **2** *Admin & Law* rédaction *f*; **I don't really understand the w. of the contract** je ne comprends pas vraiment les termes du contrat

wordless ['wɜːdlɪs] ADJ **1** *Literary (silent ▸ admiration)* muet **2** *(without words ▸ music)* sans paroles

wordlessly ['wɜːdlɪslɪ] ADV sans dire un mot

word-process VI travailler sur traitement de texte

VT *(text)* réaliser par traitement de texte

wordsmith ['wɜːdsmɪθ] N manieur *m* de mots

wordy ['wɜːdɪ] *(compar* **wordier**, *superl* **wordiest)** ADJ verbeux

wore [wɔː(r)] *pt of* **wear**

WORK [wɜːk]

N	
• travail **1–5, 7, 10**	• œuvre **1, 6, 8**
• besogne **2**	• emploi **3**
• ouvrage **6**	• recherches **7**
• acte **8**	• effet **9**
VI	
• travailler **A1–5**	• fonctionner **B1**
• marcher **B1, 2**	• réussir **B2**
• agir **B3, 4**	
VT	
• faire travailler **A1**	• travailler **A2, 3, 5, C1**
• faire marcher **B1**	• façonner **C1**
NPL	
• mécanisme **1**	• travaux **2**

N **1** *(effort, activity)* travail *m*, œuvre *f*; **computers take some of the w. out of filing** les ordinateurs facilitent le classement; **this report needs more w.** il y a encore du travail à faire sur ce rapport, ce rapport demande plus de travail; **she's done a lot of w. for charity** elle a beaucoup travaillé pour des associations caritatives; **it will take a lot of w. to make a team out of them** ça va être un drôle de travail de faire d'eux une équipe; **keep up the good w.!** continuez comme ça!; **nice** *or* **good w.!** c'est du bon travail!, bravo!; **that's fine w.** *or* **a fine piece of w.** c'est du beau travail; **w. on the tunnel is to start in March** *(existing tunnel)* les travaux sur le tunnel doivent commencer en mars; *(new tunnel)* la construction du tunnel doit commencer en mars; **w. in progress** *Admin* travail *m* en cours; *Acct* travaux *mpl* en cours, inventaire *m* de production; *(sign)* travaux en cours; **she put a lot of w. into that book** elle a beaucoup travaillé sur ce livre; **to make w. for sb** compliquer la vie à qn; **to start w., to set to w.** se mettre au travail; **she set** *or* **went to w. on the contract** elle a commencé à travailler sur le contrat; **I set him to w. (on) painting the kitchen** je lui ai donné la cuisine à peindre; **they put him to w. in the kitchen** ils l'ont mis au travail dans la cuisine; **let's get (down) to w.!** (mettons-nous) au travail!

2 *(duty, task)* travail *m*, besogne *f*; **I've got loads of w. to do** j'ai énormément de travail à faire; **she gave us too much w.** elle nous a donné trop de travail; **he's trying to get some w. done** il essaie de travailler un peu; **it's hard w.** c'est du travail, ce n'est pas facile; **it's thirsty w.** ça donne soif; **to make short** *or* **light w. of sth** expédier qch; *Fig* **to make short w. of sb** ne faire qu'une bouchée de qn; *Fam* **(it's) nice w. if you can get it!** c'est une bonne planque, encore faut-il la trouver!

3 *(paid employment)* travail *m*, emploi *m*; **what (kind of) w. do you do?** qu'est-ce que vous faites dans la vie?, quel travail faites-vous?; **I do translation w.** je suis traducteur, je fais des traductions; **to find w.** trouver du travail; **to look for w.** chercher du travail *ou* un emploi; **to be in w.** travailler, avoir un emploi; **to be out of w.** être au chômage *ou* sans travail *ou* sans emploi; **he had a week off w.** *(holiday)* il a pris une semaine de vacances; *(illness)* il n'est pas allé au travail pendant une semaine; **to take time off w.** prendre des congés; **she's off w. today** elle ne travaille pas aujourd'hui; **to do a full day's w.** faire une journée entière de travail; **people out of w.** *(gen)* les chômeurs *mpl*; *Admin & Econ* les inactifs *mpl*

4 *(place of employment)* travail *m*; *Admin* lieu *m* de travail; **I go to w. by bus** je vais au travail en bus; **I'm late for w.** je suis en retard pour le travail; **he's a friend from w.** c'est un ami qui travaille avec moi

5 *(papers, material etc being worked on)* travail *m*; **to take w. home** prendre du travail à la maison; **her w. was all over the table** son travail était étalé sur la table

6 *(creation, artefact etc)* œuvre *f*; *(on smaller scale)* ouvrage *m*; *Sewing* ouvrage *m*; **it's all my own w.** j'ai tout fait moi-même; **it's an interesting piece of w.** *(gen)* c'est un travail intéressant; *Art, Literature & Mus* c'est une œuvre intéressante; **very detailed/delicate w.** *(embroidery, carving etc)* ouvrage très détaillé/délicat; **the silversmith sells much of his w. to hotels** l'orfèvre vend une grande partie de ce qu'il fait *ou* de son travail à des hôtels; **the complete works of Shakespeare** les œuvres complètes *ou* l'œuvre de Shakespeare; **a w. of art** une œuvre d'art; **works of fiction** des ouvrages de fiction

7 *(research)* travail *m*, recherches *fpl*; **there hasn't been a lot of w. done on the subject** peu de travail a été fait *ou* peu de recherches ont été faites sur le sujet

8 *(deed)* œuvre *f*, acte *m*; **good works** bonnes œuvres *fpl*; **charitable works** actes *mpl* de charité, actes *mpl* charitables; **the murder is the w. of a madman** le meurtre est l'œuvre d'un fou; **these formations are the w. of the wind** ces formations sont l'œuvre du vent

9 *(effect)* effet *m*; **wait until the medicine has done its w.** attendez que le médicament ait agi *ou* ait produit son effet

VI **A. 1** *(exert effort on a specific task, activity etc)* travailler; **we worked for hours cleaning the house** nous avons passé des heures à faire le ménage; **they worked in the garden** ils ont fait du jardinage; **we w. hard** nous travaillons dur; **she's working on a novel just now** elle travaille à un roman en ce moment; **a detective is working on this case** un détective est sur cette affaire; **he works at** *or* **on keeping himself fit** il fait de l'exercice pour garder la forme; **we have to w. to a deadline** nous devons respecter des délais dans notre travail; **we have to w. to a budget** nous devons travailler avec un certain budget; **I've worked with the handicapped before** j'ai déjà travaillé avec les handicapés

2 *(be employed)* travailler; **he works as a teacher** il a un poste d'enseignant; **I w. in advertising** je travaille dans la publicité; **who do you w. for?** chez qui est-ce que vous travaillez?; **she works in** *or* **for a bank** elle travaille dans *ou* pour une banque; **I w. a 40-hour week** je travaille 40 heures par semaine, je fais une semaine de 40 heures; **to w. for a living** travailler pour gagner sa vie; *Ind* **to w. to rule** faire la grève du zèle

3 *(strive for a specific goal or aim)* **to w. for a good cause** travailler pour une bonne cause; **they're working for better international relations** ils s'efforcent d'améliorer les relations internationales

4 *(study)* travailler, étudier; **you're going to have to w. if you want to pass the exam** il va falloir que tu travailles *ou* que tu étudies si tu veux avoir ton examen

5 *(use a specified substance)* travailler; **this sculptor works in** *or* **with copper** ce sculpteur travaille avec le cuivre; **she has always worked in** *or* **with watercolours** elle a toujours travaillé avec de la peinture à l'eau

B. 1 *(function, operate ▸ machine, brain, system)* fonctionner, marcher; **the lift doesn't w. at night** l'ascenseur ne marche pas la nuit; **the lift never works** l'ascenseur est toujours en panne; **the radio works off batteries** la radio fonctionne avec des piles; **a pump worked by hand** une pompe actionnée à la main *ou* manuellement; **they soon got** *or* **had it working** ils sont vite parvenus à le faire fonctionner; **she sat still, her brain** *or* **her mind working furiously** elle était assise immobile, le cerveau en ébullition; **that argument works both ways** ce raisonnement est à double tranchant; **how does the law w. exactly?** comment la loi fonctionne-t-elle exactement?

2 *(produce results, succeed)* marcher, réussir; **your idea won't w.** ton idée ne peut pas marcher; **it worked brilliantly** ça a très bien marché; **their scheme didn't w.** leur complot a échoué; **that/flattery won't w. with me** ça/la flatterie ne prend pas avec moi; **this relationship isn't working** cette relation ne marche pas

3 *(drug, medicine)* agir, produire *ou* faire son effet

4 *(act)* agir; **the acid works as a catalyst** l'acide agit comme *ou* sert de catalyseur; **events have worked against us/in our favour** les événements ont agi contre nous/en notre faveur; **I'm working on the assumption that they'll sign the contract** je pars du principe qu'ils signeront le contrat

C. 1 *(reach a condition or state gradually)* **to w. loose** se desserrer; **to w. free** se libérer; **the nail worked through the sole of my shoe** le clou est passé à travers la semelle de ma chaussure

2 *(face, mouth)* se contracter, se crisper

VT **A. 1** *(worker, employee, horse)* faire travailler; **the boss works his staff hard** le patron exige beaucoup de travail de ses employés; **you w. yourself too hard** tu te surmènes; **to w. oneself to death** se tuer à la tâche; **to w. one's fingers to the bone** s'user au travail

2 *(pay for with labour or service)* **they worked their passage to India** ils ont payé leur passage en Inde en travaillant; **I worked my way through college** j'ai travaillé pour payer mes études à l'université

3 *(carry on activity in)* **he works the southern sales area** il travaille pour le service commercial de la région sud; **the pollster worked both sides of the street** le sondeur a enquêté des deux côtés de la rue; *Fig* **the candidate worked the crowd** le candidat s'efforçait de soulever l'enthousiasme de la foule; **she works the bars** *(prostitute)* elle travaille dans les bars

4 *(achieve, accomplish)* **the new policy will w. major changes** la nouvelle politique opérera *ou* entraînera des changements importants; **the story worked its magic** *or* **its charm on the public** l'histoire a enchanté le public; **to w. miracles** faire *ou* accomplir des miracles; **to w. wonders** faire merveille; **she has worked wonders with the children** elle a fait des merveilles avec les enfants

5 *(make use of, exploit ▸ land)* travailler, cultiver; *(▸ mine, quarry)* exploiter, faire valoir

B. 1 *(operate)* faire marcher, faire fonctionner; **this switch works the furnace** ce bouton actionne *ou* commande la chaudière; **he knows how to w. the drill** il sait se servir de la perceuse

2 *(manoeuvre)* **I worked the handle up and down** j'ai remué la poignée de haut en bas; **to w. one's hands free** parvenir à dégager ses mains

3 *(by slow progression)* **he worked his way down/up the cliff** il a descendu/monté la falaise lentement; **they worked their way through the list** ils ont traité chaque élément de la liste tour à tour; **he's worked his way through the whole grant** il a épuisé toute la subvention; **a band of rain working its way across the country** un front de pluie qui traverse le pays; **they have worked themselves into a corner** ils se sont mis dans une impasse

4 *Fam (contrive)* s'arranger; **I worked it** *or* **worked things so that she's never alone** j'ai fait en sorte qu'elle *ou* je me suis arrangé pour qu'elle ne soit jamais seule

C. 1 *(shape ▸ leather, metal, stone)* travailler, façonner; *(▸ clay, dough)* travailler, pétrir; *(▸ object, sculpture)* façonner; *Sewing (design, initials)* broder; **she worked the silver into earrings** elle a travaillé l'argent pour en faire des boucles d'oreilles; **she worked a figure out of the wood** elle a sculpté une silhouette dans le bois; **the flowers are worked in silk** les fleurs sont brodées en soie; **w. the putty into the right consistency** travaillez le mastic pour lui donner la consistance voulue

2 *(excite, provoke)* **the orator worked the audience into a frenzy** l'orateur a enflammé *ou* a galvanisé le public; **she worked herself into a rage** elle s'est mise dans une colère noire

• **works** NPL 1 *(mechanism)* mécanisme *m*, rouages *mpl*; *(of clock)* mouvement *m*; *Fam* **to foul up** *or* **to gum up the works** tout foutre en l'air

2 *Constr* travaux *mpl*; *(installation)* installations *fpl*; **road works** travaux *mpl*; *(sign)* travaux; **Minister/Ministry of Works** ministre *m*/ministère *m* des Travaux publics N1 *Ind (factory)* usine *f*; **a printing works** une imprimerie; **a gas works** une usine à gaz

2 *Fam (everything)* **the (whole) works** tout le bataclan *ou* le tralala; **they had eggs, bacon, toast, the works** ils mangeaient des œufs, du bacon, du pain grillé, tout, quoi!; **to give sb the works** *(special treatment)* dérouler le tapis rouge pour qn; *(beating)* passer qn à tabac

• **at work** ADJ 1 *(person)* **to be at w. on sth/(on) doing sth** travailler (à) qch/à faire qch; **he's at w. on a new book** il travaille à un nouveau livre; **they're hard at w. painting the house** ils sont en plein travail, ils repeignent la maison

2 *(having an effect)* **there are several factors at w. here** il y a plusieurs facteurs qui entrent en jeu *ou* qui jouent ici; **there are evil forces at w.** des forces mauvaises sont en action ADV *(at place of work)* **she's at w.** *(gen)* elle est au travail; *(office)* elle est au bureau; *(factory)* elle est à l'usine; **we met at w.** on s'est connus au travail

▸▸ ***work area*** *(in school, home)* coin *m* de travail; *Comput* zone *f* de travail; ***works committee, works council*** comité *m* d'entreprise; ***work ethic*** = exaltation des valeurs liées au travail; ***work experience*** stage *m* (en entreprise); **two months' w. experience** un stage en entreprise de deux mois; *Comput* ***work file*** fichier *m* de travail; ***work flow*** déroulement *m* des opérations; ***work group*** *(committee ▸ for study)* groupe *m* de travail; *(▸ for enquiry)* commission *f* d'enquête; ***work permit*** permis *m* de travail; ***work rate*** cadence *f* *ou* rhythme *m* de travail; *Comput* ***work sheet*** feuille *f* de travail; ***work space*** *(at home)* coin-travail *m*; *(in office) & Comput* espace *m* de travail; **I need more w. space** j'ai besoin de plus d'espace pour travailler; ***work surface*** plan *m* de travail; *Am* ***work week*** semaine *f* de travail

▸ **work in** VT SEP 1 *(incorporate)* incorporer; **w. the ointment in thoroughly** faites bien pénétrer la pommade; *Culin* **w. the butter into the flour** incorporez le beurre à la farine 2 *(insert)* faire entrer *ou* introduire petit à petit; **he worked in a few sly remarks about the boss** il a réussi à glisser quelques réflexions sournoises sur le patron

▸ **work off** VT SEP 1 *(dispose of ▸ fat, weight)* se débarrasser de, éliminer; *(▸ anxiety, frustration)* passer, assouvir; **I worked off my excess energy chopping wood** j'ai dépensé mon trop-plein d'énergie en cassant du bois; **he worked off his tensions by running** il s'est défoulé en faisant du jogging 2 *(debt, obligation)* **it took him three months to w. off his debt** il a dû travailler trois mois pour rembourser son emprunt

▸ **work on** VT INSEP 1 *(person)* essayer de convaincre; **we've been working on him but he still won't go** nous avons essayé de le persuader mais il ne veut toujours pas y aller 2 *(task, problem)* **the police are working on who stole the jewels** la police s'efforce de retrouver celui qui a volé les bijoux; **he's been working on his breaststroke/emotional problems** il a travaillé sa brasse/essayé de résoudre ses problèmes sentimentaux; **have you got any ideas? – I'm working on it** as-tu des idées? – je cherche 3 *(use as basis)* **have you any data to w. on?** avez-vous des données sur lesquelles vous fonder?

VI *(continue to work)* continuer à travailler

▸ **work out** VT SEP 1 *(discharge fully)* acquitter en travaillant; **to w. out one's notice** faire son préavis

2 *(calculate ▸ cost, distance, sum)* calculer; *(▸ answer, total)* trouver; **I w. it out at £22** d'après mes calculs, ça fait 22 livres

3 *(solve ▸ calculation, problem)* résoudre; *(▸ puzzle)* faire, résoudre; *(▸ code)* déchiffrer; **have they worked out their differences?** est-ce qu'ils ont réglé *ou* résolu leurs différends?; **I'm sure we can w. this thing out** *(your problem)* je suis sûr que nous pouvons arranger ça; *(our argument)* je suis sûr que nous finirons par nous mettre d'accord; **things will w. themselves out** les choses s'arrangeront toutes seules *ou* d'elles-mêmes

4 *(formulate ▸ idea, plan)* élaborer, combiner; *(▸ agreement, details)* mettre au point; **to w. out a solution** trouver une solution; **have you worked out yet when it's due to start?** est-ce que tu sais quand ça doit commencer?; **she had it all worked out** elle avait tout planifié

5 *(figure out)* arriver à comprendre; **I finally worked out why he was acting so strangely** j'ai enfin découvert *ou* compris pourquoi il se comportait si bizarrement; **the dog had worked out how to open the door** le chien avait compris comment ouvrir la porte; **I can't w. her out** je n'arrive pas à la comprendre

VI 1 *(happen)* se passer; **it depends on how things w. out** ça dépend de la façon dont les choses se passent; **the trip worked out as planned** le voyage s'est déroulé comme prévu; **it all worked out for the best** tout a fini par s'arranger pour le mieux; **but it didn't w. out that way** mais il en a été tout autrement; **it worked out badly for them** les choses ont mal tourné pour eux

2 *(have a good result ▸ job, plan)* réussir; *(▸ problem, puzzle)* se résoudre; **she worked out fine as personnel director** elle s'est bien débrouillée comme directeur du personnel; **are things working out for you OK?** est-ce que ça se passe bien pour toi?; **did the new job w. out?** ça a marché pour le nouveau boulot?; **it didn't w. out between them** les choses ont plutôt mal tourné entre eux; **their project didn't w. out** leur projet est tombé à l'eau

3 *(amount to)* **how much does it all w. out at?** ça fait combien en tout?; **the average price for an apartment works out to** *or* **at $5,000 per square metre** le prix moyen d'un appartement s'élève *ou* revient à 5000 dollars le mètre carré; **that works out at three hours a week** ça fait trois heures par semaine; **electric heating works out expensive** le chauffage électrique revient cher

4 *(exercise)* faire de l'exercice; *(professional athlete)* s'entraîner

▸ **work up** VT SEP 1 *(stir up, rouse)* exciter, provoquer; **he worked up the crowd** il a excité la foule; **he worked the crowd up into a frenzy** il a rendu la foule frénétique; **he works himself up** *or* **he gets himself worked up over nothing** il s'énerve pour rien; **she had worked herself up into a rage** elle s'était mise dans une rage 2 *(develop)* développer; **I want to w. these ideas up into an article** je veux développer ces idées pour en faire un article; **to w. up an appetite** se mettre en appétit; **we worked up a sweat/a thirst playing tennis** jouer au tennis nous a donné chaud/soif; **he tried to w. up an interest in the cause** il a essayé de s'intéresser à la cause 3 *(idiom)* **to w. one's way up** faire son chemin; **she worked her way up from secretary to managing director** elle a commencé comme secrétaire et elle a fait son chemin jusqu'au poste de P-DG; **I worked my way up from nothing** je suis parti de rien

VI 1 *(clothing)* remonter 2 *(build up)* **things were working up to a crisis** une crise se préparait, on était au bord d'une crise; **she's working up to what she wanted to ask** elle en vient à ce qu'elle voulait demander; **what are you working up to?** où veux-tu en venir?

workability [ˌwɜːkəˈbɪlɪtɪ] N 1 *(of plan, proposal)* caractère *m* réalisable 2 *(of mine, field)* caractère *m* exploitable

workable [ˈwɜːkəbəl] ADJ 1 *(plan, proposal)* réalisable, faisable 2 *(mine, field)* exploitable

workaday [ˈwɜːkədeɪ] ADJ *(clothes, routine)* de tous les jours; *(man)* ordinaire, banal; *(incident)* courant, banal; **the w. world of the office** la routine du bureau

workaholic [ˌwɜːkəˈhɒlɪk] N *Fam* bourreau *m* de travail

workbag [ˈwɜːkbæg] N sac *m* à ouvrage

workbasket [ˈwɜːkˌbɑːskɪt] N corbeille *f* à ouvrage

workbench [ˈwɜːkbentʃ] N établi *m*

workbook [ˈwɜːkbʊk] N 1 *Sch (exercise book)* cahier *m* d'exercices; *(record book)* cahier *m* de classe 2 *(manual)* manuel *m*

workbox [ˈwɜːkbɒks] N boîte *f* à ouvrage

workday [ˈwɜːkdeɪ] N 1 *(day's work)* journée *f* de travail 2 *(working day)* jour *m* ouvré *ou* où l'on travaille

ADJ = **workaday**

worker [ˈwɜːkə(r)] N 1 *Ind (gen)* travailleur(euse) *m,f*, employé(e) *m,f*; *(manual)* ouvrier(ère) *m,f*, travailleur(euse) *m,f*; **relations between workers and management** les relations entre les travailleurs *ou* les employés et la direction; **he's a fast w.!** il travaille vite!; **she's a good/hard w.** elle travaille bien/dur 2 *Entom* ouvrière *f*

▸▸ ***worker ant*** (fourmi *f*) ouvrière *f*; ***worker bee*** (abeille *f*) ouvrière *f*; ***worker director*** = ouvrier qui fait partie du conseil d'administration; ***workers' organization*** organisation *f* de travailleurs; ***worker participation*** participation *f* ouvrière; ***worker representation*** représentation *f* du personnel

worker-priest N prêtre-ouvrier *m*

workfare [ˈwɜːkfeə(r)] N *Pol* = principe selon lequel les bénéficiaires de l'allocation de chômage doivent fournir un travail en échange

workflow [ˈwɜːkfləʊ] N rythme *m* de travail

▸▸ ***workflow schedule*** plan *m* de travail

workforce [ˈwɜːkfɔːs] N main-d'œuvre *f*, effectifs *mpl*

workhorse [ˈwɜːkhɔːs, *pl* -hɔːsɪz] N 1 *(horse)* cheval *m* de labour 2 *Fig (worker)* bourreau *m* de travail

workhouse [ˈwɜːkhaʊs, *pl* -haʊzɪz] N 1 *Hist (in UK)* asile *m* des pauvres 2 *(in US ▸ prison)* maison *f* de correction

workie [ˈwɜːkɪ] N *Br Fam* ouvrier[□] *m*

working [ˈwɜːkɪŋ] ADJ 1 *(mother)* qui travaille; *(population)* actif; **ordinary w. people** les travailleurs ordinaires; **the party of the w. man** le parti des travailleurs

2 *(day, hours)* de travail; **w. day** *(gen)* journée *f* de travail; *Admin* jour *m* ouvrable; **during a normal w. day** pendant la journée de travail; **Sunday is not a w. day** le dimanche est chômé, on ne travaille pas le dimanche; **a w. week of 40 hours** une semaine de 40 heures; **he spent his entire w. life with the firm** il a travaillé toute sa vie dans l'entreprise; **to be of w. age** être en âge de travailler

3 *(clothes, conditions)* de travail; **a relaxed w. environment** un milieu professionnel détendu; **we have a close w. relationship** nous travaillons bien ensemble

4 *(functioning ▸ farm, factory)* qui marche; **in (good) w. order** en (bon) état de marche;

5 *(theory, definition)* de travail; *(majority)* suffisant; *(knowledge)* adéquat, suffisant; **w. agreement** modus vivendi *m*; **to have a w. knowledge of French/the law** posséder une connaissance suffisante du français/du droit

N 1 *(work)* travail *m* 2 *(operation ▸ of machine)* fonctionnement *m* 3 *(of mine)* exploitation *f*

• **workings** NPL 1 *(mechanism)* mécanisme *m*; *Fig (of government, system)* rouages *mpl*; **it's diffi-**

cult to understand the workings of his mind il est difficile de savoir ce qu'il a dans la tête *ou* ce qui se passe dans sa tête **2** *Mining* chantier *m* d'exploitation; **old mine workings** anciennes mines *fpl*

▸▸ *Fin* ***working account*** compte *m* d'exploitation; *Fin* ***working capital*** *(UNCOUNT)* fonds *mpl* de roulement, capital *m* de roulement; *Fin* ***working capital cycle*** cycle *m* du besoin en fonds de roulement; *Fin* ***working capital fund*** compte *m* d'avances; ***the working class, the working classes*** la classe ouvrière, le prolétariat; ***working copy*** *(of document, text)* copie *f* de travail; *Comput* ***working file*** fichier *m* de travail; ***working girl*** *(prostitute)* professionnelle *f*; ***working group*** *(committee ▸ for study)* groupe *m* de travail; *(▸ for enquiry)* commission *f* d'enquête; ***working lunch*** déjeuner *m* d'affaires *ou* de travail; ***working majority*** majorité *f* suffisante; *Br* ***working man*** ouvrier *m*; ***working men's club*** = club d'ouvriers, comportant un bar et une scène où sont présentés des spectacles; ***working model*** modèle *m* qui fonctionne; *Math* ***working out*** *(of problem)* résolution *f*; **show all w. out** *(in exam paper)* montrez les étapes de votre raisonnement; ***working party*** *(committee ▸ for study)* groupe *m* de travail; *(▸ for enquiry)* commission *f* d'enquête; *(group ▸ of prisoners, soldiers)* groupe *m* de travail; ***working speed*** vitesse *f* de régime; *Br Law* ***working time directive*** loi *f* sur le temps de travail; ***working title*** titre *m* provisoire; ***working woman*** *(worker)* ouvrière *f*, employée *f*; *(woman with job)* femme *f* qui travaille

working-class ADJ *(district, origins)* ouvrier; *(accent)* des classes populaires; **she's w.** elle appartient à la classe ouvrière; **a w. hero** un héros de la classe ouvrière *ou* du prolétariat

workload ['wɜːkləʊd] N travail *m* à effectuer, charge *f* de travail; **I have a heavy w.** je suis surchargé de travail

workman ['wɜːkmən] *(pl* **workmen** [-mən]) N **1** *(manual worker)* ouvrier *m*; **the workmen came to fix the drainpipe** les ouvriers sont venus réparer la gouttière; *Prov* **a bad w. always blames his tools** les mauvais ouvriers ont toujours de mauvais outils **2** *(craftsman)* artisan *m*; **he is a good w.** il travaille bien, il fait du bon travail

workmanlike ['wɜːkmənlaɪk] ADJ **1** *(efficient ▸ approach, person)* professionnel; **she did the job in a w. way** elle a fait du très bon travail **2** *(well made ▸ artefact)* bien fait, soigné; **he wrote a w. report** il a fait un compte rendu très sérieux **3** *(serious ▸ attempt, effort)* sérieux

workmanship ['wɜːkmənʃɪp] N *(UNCOUNT)* **1** *(skill)* métier *m*, maîtrise *f*; **he was famous for his w.** il était connu pour la finesse de son travail **2** *(quality)* exécution *f*, fabrication *f*; *(of clothes)* façon *f*; **she admired the fine w. of the carving** elle admira le ciselage délicat; **it was a shoddy piece of w.** c'était du travail mal fait *ou* bâclé

workmate ['wɜːkmeɪt] N camarade *mf* de travail

workout ['wɜːkaʊt] N **to have a w.** faire de l'exercice; *(professional athlete)* s'entraîner, faire une séance d'entraînement

workpeople ['wɜːkˌpiːpəl] NPL travailleurs *mpl*

workplace ['wɜːkpleɪs] N lieu *m* de travail

workroom ['wɜːkrʊm] N salle *f* de travail

workshare ['wɜːkʃeə(r)] N travail *m* en temps partagé; *(person)* travailleur(euse) *m,f* en temps partagé; **workshares are becoming more common** le partage du travail devient de plus en plus courant

worksharing ['wɜːkˌʃeərɪŋ] N partage *m* du travail; **w. arrangement** système *m* de partage du travail; **w. is becoming popular** le partage du travail est de plus en plus courant

workshop ['wɜːkʃɒp] N **1** *Ind (gen)* atelier *m* **2** *(study group)* atelier *m*, groupe *m* de travail

workshy ['wɜːkʃaɪ] ADJ fainéant, tire-au-flanc *(inv)*

workstation ['wɜːkˌsteɪʃən] N *Comput* poste *m ou* station *f* de travail

worktable ['wɜːkˌteɪbəl] N table *f* de travail

worktop ['wɜːktɒp] N *(in kitchen)* plan *m* de travail, *Can* comptoir *m* de cuisine

work-to-rule N *Br* grève *f* du zèle

WORLD [wɜːld] N **A. 1** *(earth)* monde *m*; **to travel round the w.** faire le tour du monde, voyager autour du monde; **to see the w.** voir du pays, courir le monde; **throughout the w.** dans le monde entier; **in this part of the w.** dans cette région; **the best in the w.** le meilleur du monde; **I'm the w.'s worst photographer** il n'y a pas pire photographe que moi; **there isn't a nicer spot in the whole w.** il n'y a pas d'endroit plus agréable au monde; **the w. over, all over the w.** dans le monde entier, partout dans le monde; **love is the same the w. over** l'amour, c'est la même chose partout dans le monde; **(it's a) small w.!** (que) le monde est petit!

2 *(planet)* monde *m*; **there may be other worlds out there** il existe peut-être d'autres mondes quelque part

3 *(universe)* monde *m*, univers *m*; **since the w. began** depuis que le monde existe

B. 1 *(part of the world) & Hist & Pol* monde *m*; **the Arab W.** le monde arabe; **the developing w.** les pays *mpl* en voie de développement; **the Gaelic-speaking w.** les régions où l'on parle le gaélique

2 *(society)* monde *m*; **she wants to change the w.** elle veut changer le monde; **the modern w.** le monde moderne; **she's gone up in the w.** elle a fait du chemin; **he's gone down in the w.** il a connu de meilleurs jours; **to come into the w.** venir au monde; **to bring a child into the w.** mettre un enfant au monde; **to be alone in the w.** être seul au monde; **to make one's way in the w.** faire son chemin; **what's the w. coming to?** où allons-nous?, où va le monde?

3 *(general public)* monde *m*; **the news shook the w.** la nouvelle a ébranlé le monde entier; **the singer had the w. at her feet** la chanteuse avait tout le monde à ses pieds

4 *(people in general)* **we don't want the whole w. to know** nous ne voulons pas que tout le monde le sache; *Fam Fig* **(all) the w. and his wife** le monde entier[□]

C. 1 *(existence, particular way of life)* monde *m*, vie *f*; **a whole new w. opened up to me** un monde nouveau s'ouvrit à moi; **we live in different worlds** nous ne vivons pas sur la même planète; **it's a different w. up north** c'est complètement différent au nord; **to be worlds apart** *(in lifestyle)* avoir des styles de vie complètement différents; *(in opinions)* avoir des opinions complètement différentes

2 *(realm)* monde *m*; **he lives in a w. of his own** il vit dans un monde à lui; **a fantasy w.** un monde de rêve; **the child's w.** l'univers *m* des enfants; **they knew nothing of the w. outside** ils ignoraient tout du monde extérieur; **the underwater w.** le monde sous-marin

3 *(field, domain)* monde *m*, milieu *m*, milieux *mpl*; **in the theatre w.** dans le milieu du théâtre; **the publishing w.** le monde de l'édition

4 *(group of living things)* monde *m*; **the animal/the plant w.** le règne animal/végétal

5 *Rel* monde *m*; **in this w. and the next** dans ce monde(-ci) et dans l'autre; **he isn't long for this w.** il n'en a pas pour longtemps

6 *(idioms)* **a holiday will do you a** *or* **the w. of good** des vacances vous feront le plus grand bien; **it made a w. of difference** ça a tout changé; **there's a w. of difference between them** il y a un monde entre eux; **he thinks the w. of his daughter** il tient à sa fille comme à la prunelle de ses yeux; **it means the w. to me** c'est quelque chose qui me tient beaucoup à cœur

COMP *(champion, championship, record)* mondial, du monde; *(language, history, religion)* universel; *(population)* mondial; **on a w. scale** à l'échelle mondiale

• **for all the world** ADV exactement; **she behaved for all the w. as if she owned the place** elle faisait exactement comme si elle était chez elle

• **for (anything in) the world** ADV **I wouldn't hurt her for (anything in) the w.** je ne lui ferais de mal pour rien au monde

• **in the world** ADV **1** *(for emphasis)* **nothing in the w. would change my mind** rien au monde ne me ferait changer d'avis; **I felt as if I hadn't a care in the w.** je me sentais libre de tout souci; **we've got all the time in the w.** nous avons tout le *ou* tout notre temps; **I wouldn't do it for all the money in the w.!** je ne le ferais pas pour tout l'or du monde!

2 *(expressing surprise, irritation, frustration)* **who in the w. will believe you?** qui donc va vous croire?; **where in the w. have you put it?** où l'avez-vous donc mis?; **what in the w. made you do it?** pourquoi donc avez-vous fait ça?; **why in the w. didn't you tell me?** pourquoi donc ne me l'as-tu pas dit?

• **out of this world** ADJ *Fam* extraordinaire[□], sensationnel

▸▸ ***the World Bank*** la Banque mondiale; ***the World Council of Churches*** le Conseil œcuménique des Églises; ***the World Cup*** la Coupe du monde; ***world domination*** domination *f* du monde; ***World Economic Forum*** Forum *m* économique mondial; ***world economy*** conjoncture *f* économique mondiale; ***World Fair*** exposition *f* universelle; ***World Food Programme*** programme *m* alimentaire mondial; ***the World Health Organization*** l'Organisation *f* mondiale de la santé; ***world map*** carte *f* du monde; *(in two hemispheres)* mappemonde *f*; *Com* ***world market*** marché *m* mondial *ou* international; ***world music*** world music *f*; ***world opinion*** l'opinion internationale; ***world peace*** la paix mondiale; ***world power*** puissance *f* mondiale; *Fin* ***world reserves*** réserves *fpl* mondiales; ***world rights*** droits *mpl* d'exploitation pour le monde entier; ***World Series*** = le championnat américain de base-ball; *Rad* ***the World Service*** = service étranger de la BBC; ***world television*** mondovision *f*; ***world tour*** voyage *m* autour du monde; ***world trade*** commerce *m* international; ***the World Trade Center*** le World Trade Center; ***the World Trade Organization*** l'Organisation *f* mondiale du commerce; ***world view*** = vue métaphysique du monde; ***world war*** guerre *f* mondiale; ***World War I, the First World War*** la Première Guerre mondiale; ***World War II, the Second World War*** la Seconde Guerre mondiale; *Fam* ***world war three*** la troisième guerre mondiale; *Comput* ***the World Wide Web*** le World Wide Web

world-beater N *Fam (person)* champion (onne) *m,f*; *Fig* **this new car is going to be a w.** cette nouvelle voiture va faire un tabac

world-beating ADJ *Fam (performance, achievement)* inégalé[□], qui supasse tous les autres[□]; **of w. quality** d'une qualité inégalée; **the new w. X52** le X52, nouveau leader mondial

world-famous ADJ de renommée mondiale, célèbre dans le monde entier

worldliness ['wɜːldlɪnɪs] N **1** *(materialism)* matérialisme *m* **2** *(experience of the world)* mondanité *f*; **there was an air of w. about her** elle avait l'air de quelqu'un qui a l'expérience du monde

worldly ['wɜːldlɪ] *(compar* **worldlier,** *superl* **worldliest)** ADJ **1** *(material ▸ possessions, pleasures, matters)* matériel, de ce monde, terrestre; *Rel* temporel, de ce monde; **he is not interested in w. things** les choses de ce monde ne l'intéressent pas; **all my w. goods** tout ce que je possède au monde; **w. wisdom** la sagesse du monde *ou* du siècle **2** *(materialistic ▸ person, outlook)* matérialiste **3** *(sophisticated ▸ person)* qui a l'expérience du monde; *(▸ attitude, manner)* qui démontre une expérience du monde; **she was very w. for one so young** elle avait une bien grande expérience du monde pour quelqu'un d'aussi jeune

worldly-wise ADJ qui a l'expérience du monde

world-weary *(compar* **world-wearier,** *superl* **world-weariest)** ADJ *(person)* las (lasse) du monde

worldwide ['wɜːldwaɪd] ADJ *(depression, famine, reputation)* mondial, global

ADV partout dans le monde, dans le monde entier; **this product is sold w.** ce produit se vend dans le monde entier

▸▸ ***worldwide rights*** droits *mpl* d'exploitation pour le monde entier

WORM [wɜːm] *Comput (abbr* **write once read many times)** WORM

worm [wɜːm] N **1** *(in earth, garden)* ver *m* (de terre); *(in fruit)* ver *m*; *(for fishing)* ver *m*, asticot *m*; *Br Fig* **the w. has turned** j'en ai eu/il en a eu/*etc* assez de se faire marcher dessus; *Fig* **the w. in the bud** le ver dans le fruit

2 *(parasite ▸ in body)* ver *m*; **to have worms** avoir des vers
3 *Fam Fig (person)* minable *mf*
4 *Literary (troublesome thing)* tourment *m*, tourments *mpl*; **the w. of jealousy** les affres *fpl* de la jalousie
5 *Tech (of screw)* filet *m*; **w. and roller steering** direction *f* à vis et galet
VT 1 *(move)* **to w. one's way under sth** passer sous qch à plat ventre *ou* en rampant; **she wormed her way through a gap in the fence** en se tortillant, elle s'est faufilée par une ouverture dans la palissade; **he managed to w. his way to the front** il a réussi à se faufiler jusqu'à l'avant **2** *Pej (sneak)* **they have wormed their way into our party** ils se sont infiltrés *ou* immiscés dans notre parti; **he wormed his way into her affections** il a trouvé le chemin de son cœur *(par sournoiserie)* **3** *(dog, sheep)* débarrasser de ses vers
▸▸ ***worm cast*** déjections *fpl* de ver; *Tech* ***worm drive*** transmission *f* par vis sans fin; *Tech* ***worm gear*** engrenage *m* de vis sans fin

worm-eaten ADJ *(apple)* véreux; *(furniture)* vermoulu, mangé aux vers; *Fig (ancient)* désuet (ète), antédiluvien

wormhole [ˈwɜːmhəʊl] N trou *m* de ver

wormwood [ˈwɜːmwʊd] N **1** *(plant)* armoise *f* **2** *Literary (bitterness)* fiel *m*, amertume *f*; **life to him was gall and w.** la vie pour lui n'était qu'amertume et dégoût

wormy [ˈwɜːmɪ] *(compar* **wormier**, *superl* **wormiest)** ADJ **1** *(apple)* véreux; *(furniture)* vermoulu, piqué aux vers **2** *(soil)* plein de vers **3** *(in shape)* vermiculaire

worn [wɔːn] *pp of* **wear**
ADJ **1** *(shoes, rug, tyre)* usé **2** *(weary ▸ person)* las (lasse)

worried [ˈwʌrɪd] ADJ *(person, look)* inquiet(ète) *m,f*; **I'm w. that they may get lost** *or* **in case they get lost** j'ai peur qu'ils ne se perdent; **to be w. about sb/sth** être inquiet pour qn/qch; **she's w. about the future** elle est inquiète pour l'avenir; **I'm w. about him** je suis inquiet *ou* je m'inquiète pour lui; **to be w. sick** *or* **to death (about sb)** être fou *ou* malade d'inquiétude (pour qn); **you had me w. for a minute** vous m'avez fait peur pendant une minute; **I'm not w. either way** ça m'est égal; **I was w. it would be the wrong size** j'avais peur que ce ne soit pas la bonne taille

worriedly [ˈwʌrɪdlɪ] ADV *(say)* avec un air inquiet

worrier [ˈwʌrɪə(r)] N anxieux(euse) *m,f*, inquiet (ète) *m,f*; **don't be such a w.** arrête de t'inquiéter comme ça

worrisome [ˈwʌrɪsəm] ADJ *Old-fashioned* inquiétant

worry [ˈwʌrɪ] *(pt & pp* **worried**, *pl* **worries)** VT **1** *(make anxious)* inquiéter, tracasser; **you really worried me** je me suis vraiment inquiété à cause de toi; **he was worried by her sudden disappearance** il était inquiet de sa disparition subite; **I sometimes w. that they'll never be found** parfois, je crains qu'on ne les retrouve jamais; **that boiler worries me, suppose it blows up?** la chaudière m'inquiète, si elle explosait?; **she is worrying herself sick** *or* **to death about it** elle en est malade d'inquiétude; **something is worrying her** il y a quelque chose qui la préoccupe *ou* qui la travaille; **nothing seems to w. her** rien ne semble l'inquiéter *ou* la tracasser; **what's worrying you?** qu'est-ce qui vous tracasse?; **it doesn't w. me if you want to waste your life** cela m'est égal *ou* ne me gêne pas si vous voulez gâcher votre vie; *Fam* **don't w. your head** *or* **yourself about the details** ne vous inquiétez pas pour les détails▫
2 *(disturb, bother)* inquiéter, ennuyer; **why w. him with your problems?** pourquoi l'ennuyer avec vos problèmes?; **it doesn't seem to w. you if other people get hurt** que d'autres souffrent ne semble pas te préoccuper
3 *(of dog ▸ bone, ball)* secouer dans la gueule; *(▸ sheep)* harceler
VI s'inquiéter, se faire du souci, se tracasser; **don't tell them, they'll only w.** ne le leur dis pas, ça ne fera que les inquiéter; **to w. about** *or* **over sth** s'inquiéter pour *ou* au sujet de qch; **she has enough to w. about** elle a assez de soucis comme ça; **there's nothing to w. about** il n'y a pas lieu de s'inquiéter; **it's only a scratch, nothing to w. about** ce n'est qu'une égratignure, pas de quoi s'inquiéter; **don't w.** ne vous inquiétez *ou* ne vous tracassez pas; **they'll be found, don't (you) w.** on va les trouver, ne t'en fais pas; **stop worrying!** ne t'en fais donc pas!; **not to w.!** ce n'est pas grave!; **what's the use of worrying?** à quoi bon se tourmenter?; *Ironic* **YOU should w.** ce n'est pas votre problème, il n'y a pas de raisons de vous en faire
N **1** *(anxiety)* inquiétude *f*, souci *m*; **money is a constant source of w.** l'argent est un perpétuel souci *ou* une perpétuelle source d'inquiétude; **her sons are a constant w. to her** ses fils lui causent constamment des soucis *ou* du souci; **he was sick with w. about her** il se rongeait les sangs pour elle *ou* à son sujet
2 *(concern)* sujet *m* d'inquiétude, souci *m*; *(problem)* problème *m*; **my greatest w. is my health** mon plus grand souci, c'est ma santé; **he doesn't seem to have any worries** il n'a pas l'air d'avoir de soucis; **it's a real w. for her** cela la tracasse vraiment; **that's my w.** c'est mon problème; **that's the least of my worries** c'est le moindre *ou* le cadet *ou* le dernier de mes soucis; *Austr Fam* **no worries!** pas de problème!
▸▸ ***worry beads*** ≃ komboloï *m*

worryguts [ˈwʌrɪgʌts] N *Br Fam* anxieux (euse)▫ *m,f*, éternel(elle) inquiet(ète) *m,f*

worrying [ˈwʌrɪɪŋ] ADJ inquiétant
N inquiétude *f*; **w. won't solve anything** cela ne résoudra rien de se faire du souci

worrywart [ˈwʌrɪwɔːt] *Am Fam* = **worryguts**

WORSE [wɜːs]

> **ADJ**
> • pire **1** • plus mauvais **1**
> • plus mal **2**
> **ADV**
> • plus mal **1** • moins bien **1**
> • plus fort **2**
> **N**
> • pire

ADJ *(compar of* **bad)** **1** *(not as good, pleasant)* pire, plus mauvais; **I'm a w. player than he is** je joue plus mal que lui; **you're bad at French but he's w.** tu es mauvais en français mais il est plus mauvais que toi; **the news is even w. than we expected** les nouvelles sont encore plus mauvaises que nous ne pensions; **your writing is w. than mine** votre écriture est pire que la mienne; **my writing is bad, but yours is w.** j'écris mal, mais vous, c'est pire; **things are w. than you imagine** les choses vont plus mal que vous l'imaginez; **it could have been w.!** ça aurait pu être pire!; **I lost my money, and w. still** *or* **and what's w., my passport** j'ai perdu mon argent, et ce qui est plus grave, mon passeport; **w. than before/than ever** pire qu'avant/que jamais; **how are things? – no w. than before** comment ça va? – pas plus mal qu'avant; **the rain is w. than ever** il pleut de plus en plus; **w. than useless** complètement inutile; **to get** *or* **to grow w.** empirer, s'aggraver; **to get w. and w.** aller de mal en pis; **conditions got w.** les conditions se sont aggravées *ou* détériorées; **things will get w. before they get better** les choses ne sont pas près de s'améliorer; **his memory is getting w.** sa mémoire est de moins en moins bonne; **you're only making things** *or* **matters w.** vous ne faites qu'aggraver les choses; **she's only making things** *or* **matters w. for herself** elle ne fait qu'aggraver son cas; **and, to make matters w., he swore at the policeman** et pour tout arranger, il a insulté le policier; **there's nothing w. than arriving too early** il n'y a rien de pire que d'arriver trop tôt; **w. things happen at sea!** on a vu pire!, ce n'est pas la fin du monde!; *Fam* **w. luck!** quelle poisse!
2 *(in health)* plus mal; **I feel w.** je me sens encore plus mal *ou* encore moins bien; **her headache got w.** son mal de tête s'est aggravé; **you'll only get w. if you go out in this awful weather** ton état ne peut que s'aggraver si tu sors par ce temps
3 *(idioms)* **this carpet is looking rather the w. for wear** cette moquette est plutôt défraîchie; **he's looking/feeling rather the w. for wear** *(tired, old)* il n'a pas l'air/il ne se sent pas très frais; *(drunk)* il a l'air/il se sent plutôt éméché; *(ill)* il n'a pas l'air/il ne se sent pas très bien; **he was rather the w. for drink** il était plutôt éméché
ADV *(compar of* **badly)** **1** *(less well)* plus mal, moins bien; **he behaved w. than ever** il ne s'est jamais aussi mal conduit; **he is w. off than before** *(in worse situation)* sa situation a empiré; *(even poorer)* il est encore plus pauvre qu'avant; **you could** *or* **you might do w. than (to) marry him** l'épouser, ce n'est pas ce que vous pourriez faire de pire; **she doesn't think any the w. of her for it** elle ne l'en estime pas moins pour ça
2 *(more severely ▸ snow, rain)* plus fort; **the noise went on w. than ever** le vacarme a repris de plus belle
N pire *m*; **there's w. to come, w. is to come** *(in situation)* le pire est à venir; *(in story)* il y a pire encore; **w. was to follow** le pire était encore à venir; **I have seen w.** j'en ai vu bien d'autres, j'ai vu pire; **there's been a change for the w.** les choses se sont aggravées; **to take a turn for the w.** *(health, situation)* se détériorer, se dégrader; **the economy has taken a turn for the w.** la situation économique s'est aggravée; **the patient has taken a turn for the w.** l'état du patient s'est aggravé; *Am* **if w. comes to w.** au pire, dans le pire des cas
• **none the worse** ADJ pas plus mal; **the little girl is none the w. for the experience** la petite fille ne se ressent pas de son expérience

worsen [ˈwɜːsən] VI *(depression, crisis, pain, illness)* empirer, s'aggraver; *(weather, situation)* se gâter, se détériorer
VT *(situation)* empirer, rendre pire; *(crisis, infection, bad mood)* aggraver; *(relations, driving conditions)* rendre plus difficile

worsening [ˈwɜːsənɪŋ] ADJ *(situation)* qui empire; *(health)* qui se détériore; *(weather)* qui se gâte, qui se détériore
N aggravation *f*, détérioration *f*

worship [ˈwɜːʃɪp] *(Br pt & pp* **worshipped**, *cont* **worshipping**, *Am pt & pp* **worshiped**, *cont* **worshiping)** N **1** *Rel (service)* culte *m*, office *m*; *(liturgy)* liturgie *f*; *(adoration)* adoration *f*; **church w.** office *m* religieux; **an act of w.** *(veneration)* un acte de dévotion; *(service)* un culte, un office; **freedom of w.** la liberté de culte; **place of w.** lieu *m* de culte **2** *Fig (veneration)* adoration *f*, culte *m*; **the rock star has become an object of w.** la rock star est devenue un véritable objet de culte; **the w. of wealth and power** le culte de l'argent et du pouvoir
VT **1** *Rel* adorer, vénérer; **they worshipped Venus** ils rendaient un culte à Vénus, ils adoraient Vénus **2** *(person)* adorer, vénérer; *(money, possessions)* vouer un culte à, avoir le culte de; **he worships his mother** il adore sa mère; **they worshipped the ground she walked on** ils vénéraient jusqu'au sol sur lequel elle marchait
VI faire ses dévotions; **the church where she worshipped for ten years** l'église où elle a fait ses dévotions pendant dix ans; *Fig* **to w. at the altar of success** vouer un culte au succès
• **Worship** N *Br Formal* **Your W.** *(to judge)* monsieur le Juge; *(to mayor)* monsieur le Maire

worshipful [ˈwɜːʃɪpful] ADJ **1** *(respectful)* respectueux **2** *Br Formal (in titles)* **the W. Mayor of Portsmouth** monsieur le Maire de Portsmouth; **the W. Company of Mercers** l'honorable compagnie des marchands de tissus

worshipper, *Am* **worshiper** [ˈwɜːʃɪpə(r)] N **1** *Rel* adorateur(trice) *m,f*, fidèle *mf* **2** *Fig (of possessions, person)* adorateur(trice) *m,f*

WORST [wɜːst]

> **ADJ**
> • le pire **1** • le plus mauvais **1**
> • le plus grave **2**
> **ADV**
> • le plus mal
> **N**
> • le pire **1, 2**

ADJ *(superl of* **bad)** **1** *(least good, pleasant etc)* le pire, le plus mauvais; **the w. book I've ever read** le plus mauvais livre que j'aie jamais lu; **this is the w. thing that could have happened** c'est la pire chose qui pouvait arriver; **the w. thing about it**

was the heat le pire, c'était la chaleur; **it has happened at the w. possible time** c'est arrivé au plus mauvais moment; **and, w. of all, I lost my keys** et le pire de tout, c'est que j'ai perdu mes clés; **we came off w.** *(in deal)* c'est nous qui étions perdants; *(in fight)* c'est nous qui avons reçu le plus de coups; **I felt w. of all just after the operation** c'est juste après l'opération que je me suis senti le plus mal

2 *(most severe, serious ▸ disaster, error)* le plus grave; *(▸ winter)* le plus rude; **the fighting was w. near the border** les combats les plus violents se sont déroulés près de la frontière

ADV *(superl of* **badly***)* **out of all of us I played w.** j'ai joué le plus mal de nous tous; **that frightened me w. of all** c'est ce qui m'a fait le plus peur; **they are the w. paid** ce sont les plus mal payés

N **1** *(thing)* **the w.** le pire; **the w. that can happen** le pire qui puisse arriver; **the w. of it is she knew all along** le pire, c'est qu'elle le savait depuis le début; **that's the w. of cheap shoes** c'est l'inconvénient des chaussures bon marché; **money brings out the w. in people** l'argent réveille les pires instincts (chez les gens); **to expect/to be prepared for the w.** s'attendre/être préparé au pire; **I fear the w.** je crains le pire; **the w. is still to come** le pire est encore à venir; **the w. was yet to come** le pire restait à venir; **the w. is over** le plus mauvais moment est passé; **if the w. comes to the w., if it comes to the w.** au pire, dans le pire des cas; **he got the w. of it** c'est lui qui s'en est le moins bien sorti; **and that's not the w. of it!** et ce n'est pas le pire!, et il y a pire encore!; *Hum* **do your w.!** allez-y, je suis prêt; **when the storm was at its w.** au plus fort de l'orage; **when the situation was at its w.** alors que la situation était désespérée; **things** *or* **matters were at their w.** les affaires étaient au plus mal, les choses ne pouvaient pas aller plus mal; **I'm at my w. in the morning** le matin est mon plus mauvais moment de la journée; **even at her w. she is still a brilliant player** même quand elle joue mal, elle reste une joueuse fantastique

2 *(person)* **the w.** le (la) pire de tous; **to be the w. in the class** être le (la) dernier(ère) de la classe; **when it comes to dancing, he's the world's w.** pour ce qui est de danser, il n'y a pas pire que lui

VT *Literary (opponent, rival)* battre, avoir le dessus sur

• **at (the) worst** CONJ au pire, dans le pire des cas

worst-case ADJ **the w. scenario** le scénario catastrophe; **the w. scenario is that we lose all the money** dans le pire des cas *ou* au pire, nous perdrions tout l'argent

worsted ['wʊstɪd] N worsted *m*, laine *f* peignée
ADJ *(suit)* en worsted, en laine peignée

WORTH [wɜːθ] ADJ **1** *(financially, in value)* **to be w. £40,000** valoir 40 000 livres; **how much is the picture w.?** combien vaut le tableau?; **it isn't w. much** cela ne vaut pas grand-chose; **to be w. a lot of money** *(thing)* valoir cher, avoir beaucoup de valeur; *(person)* être riche; **his uncle is w. several million pounds** la fortune de son oncle s'élève à plusieurs millions de livres; **it was w. every penny** ça en valait vraiment la peine; **what's it w. to you?** vous êtes prêt à y mettre combien?; *Fig* **it isn't w. the paper it's written on** ça ne vaut pas le papier sur lequel c'est écrit; **to be w. one's weight in gold** valoir son pesant d'or; *Br* **any proofreader w. his salt would have spotted the mistake** n'importe quel correcteur digne de ce nom aurait relevé l'erreur

2 *(emotionally)* **the bracelet is w. a lot to me** j'attache beaucoup de prix au bracelet; **their friendship is w. a lot to her** leur amitié a beaucoup de prix pour elle; **she's w. ten of you** elle en vaut dix comme toi; **it's more than my job's w. to cause a fuss** je ne veux pas risquer ma place en faisant des histoires; **I can't do it, it's more than my life is w.** je ne peux absolument pas prendre le risque de faire cela

3 *(valid, deserving)* **the church is (well) w. a visit** l'église vaut la peine d'être visitée *ou* vaut le détour; **it's w. a try** *or* **trying** cela vaut la peine d'essayer; **it wasn't w. the effort** *or* **the trouble** cela ne valait pas la peine de faire un tel effort, ça n'en valait pas la peine; **it's not w. waiting for him** cela ne vaut pas la peine de l'attendre; **is the film w. seeing?** est-ce que le film vaut la peine d'être vu?; **without you, life wouldn't be w. living** sans toi, la vie ne vaudrait pas la peine d'être vécue; **it's w. thinking about** cela mérite réflexion; **it's w. knowing** c'est bon à savoir; **don't bother to phone, it isn't w. it** inutile de téléphoner, cela n'en vaut pas la peine; **don't get upset, he isn't w. it** ne te rends pas malade, il n'en vaut pas la peine; *Prov* **if something's w. doing, it's w. doing well** = si une chose vaut la peine d'être faite, elle vaut la peine d'être bien faite; *Br Fam* **the game isn't w. the candle** le jeu n'en vaut pas la chandelle

4 *(idioms)* **it would be w. your while to check** *or* **checking** vous auriez intérêt à vérifier; **it's not w. (my) while waiting** cela ne vaut pas la peine d'attendre *ou* que j'attende; **I'll make it w. your while** je vous récompenserai de votre peine; **she was running for all she was w.** elle courait de toutes ses forces *ou* aussi vite qu'elle pouvait; **for what it's w.** pour ce que cela vaut

N **1** *(in money, value)* valeur *f*; **of great/little/no w.** de grande/de peu de/d'aucune valeur; **£2,000 w. of damage** pour 2000 livres de dégâts, des dégâts qui se montent à 2000 livres

2 *(of person)* valeur *f*; **she knows her own w.** elle sait ce qu'elle vaut, elle connaît sa propre valeur

3 *(equivalent value)* équivalent *m*; **he got a day's w. of work out of me for nothing** j'ai travaillé pour lui l'équivalent d'une journée, pour rien; **a week's w. of supplies** suffisamment de provisions pour une semaine

worthily ['wɜːðɪlɪ] ADV *(live, behave)* dignement; *(donate, sacrifice)* honorablement

worthiness ['wɜːðɪnɪs] N *(dignity)* caractère *m* digne; *(praiseworthiness)* caractère *m* louable

worthless ['wɜːθlɪs] ADJ **1** *(goods, land etc)* sans valeur, qui ne vaut rien **2** *(useless ▸ attempt)* inutile; *(▸ advice, suggestion)* inutile, sans valeur **3** *(person)* incapable, qui ne vaut rien

> Attention: ne pas confondre avec l'adjectif **priceless**, qui signifie **inestimable**.

worthlessness ['wɜːθlɪsnɪs] N **1** *(of goods, land etc)* absence *f* totale de valeur **2** *(of attempt, advice, suggestion)* inutilité *f* **3** *(of person)* nullité *f*

worthwhile [,wɜːθ'waɪl] ADJ **1** *(useful ▸ action, visit)* qui vaut la peine; *(▸ job)* utile, qui a un sens; **they didn't think it was w. buying** *or* **to buy a new car** ils ne pensaient pas que ça valait la peine d'acheter une nouvelle voiture **2** *(deserving ▸ cause, project, organization)* louable, méritoire **3** *(interesting ▸ book)* qui vaut la peine d'être lu; *(▸ film)* qui vaut la peine d'être vu

worthy ['wɜːðɪ] *(compar* **worthier***, superl* **worthiest***, pl* **worthies***)* ADJ **1** *(deserving ▸ person)* digne, méritant; *(▸ cause)* louable, digne; **to be w. of sth** être digne de *ou* mériter qch; **to be w. to do sth** être digne *ou* mériter de faire qch; **they are w. of praise/of contempt** ils sont dignes d'éloges/de mépris; **surely my letter was at least w. of an answer?** ma lettre méritait quand même une réponse, non?; **she was a w. winner** elle méritait bien de gagner; **it is w. of note that...** il est intéressant de remarquer *ou* de noter que...; **the town has no museum w. of the name** la ville n'a aucun musée digne de ce nom **2** *Hum* excellent, brave; **the w. captain** l'excellent *ou* le brave capitaine

N *(important person)* notable *mf*; *Hum* brave citoyen(enne) *m,f*

wot [wɒt] *Br Fam* = **what**

wotcha, wotcher ['wɒtʃə] EXCLAM *Br Fam* salut!

WOULD [wʊd] *pt of* **will**

> On trouve généralement **I/you/he/***etc* **would** sous leurs formes contractées **I'd/you'd/he'd/***etc*. La forme négative correspondante est **wouldn't** que l'on écrira **would not** dans des contextes formels.

MODAL AUX V **A. 1** *(speculating, hypothesizing)* **I'm sure they w. come if you invited them** je suis sûr qu'ils viendraient si vous les invitiez; **he w. if he could** il le ferait s'il le pouvait; **he w. be 30 now if he had lived** il aurait 30 ans maintenant s'il avait vécu; **I wouldn't do that if I were you** je ne ferais pas ça si j'étais vous *ou* à votre place; **you w. think they had better things to do** on pourrait penser qu'ils ont mieux à faire; **I thought he w. understand** je pensais qu'il comprendrait; **they wouldn't have come if they'd known** ils ne seraient pas venus s'ils avaient su; **he wouldn't have finished without your help** il n'aurait pas terminé sans votre aide; **she w. have been 16 by now** elle aurait 16 ans maintenant

2 *(making polite offers, requests)* **w. you please be quiet!** voulez-vous vous taire, s'il vous plaît!; **w. you pass the mustard please?** voudriez-vous bien me passer la moutarde?; **w. you mind driving me home?** est-ce que cela vous dérangerait de me reconduire chez moi?; **w. you like to see her?** aimeriez-vous *ou* voudriez-vous la voir?; **w. you like another cup?** en voulez-vous encore une tasse?; **I'll do it for you – w. you?** je vais m'en occuper – vraiment?

3 *(expressing preferences, desires)* **I w. prefer to go** *or* **I w. rather go alone** j'aimerais mieux *ou* je préférerais y aller seul; **I w. have preferred to go** *or* **I w. rather have gone alone** j'aurais mieux aimé *ou* j'aurais préféré y aller seul; **I w. love to go** je serais ravi d'y aller

B. 1 *(indicating willingness, responsiveness ▸ of person, mechanism)* **they w. give their lives for the cause** ils donneraient leur vie pour la cause; **she wouldn't touch alcohol** elle refusait de toucher à l'alcool; **I couldn't find anyone who w. lend me a torch** je n'ai trouvé personne pour me prêter une lampe électrique; **the car wouldn't start** la voiture ne voulait pas démarrer

2 *(indicating habitual or characteristic behaviour)* **she w. often complain about the neighbours** elle se plaignait souvent des voisins; **they w. go and break something!** il fallait qu'ils aillent casser quelque chose!; **I didn't really enjoy the fish – you wouldn't, w. you?** je n'ai pas tellement aimé le poisson – ça m'aurait étonné!; **he w.!** c'est bien de lui!; **he w. say that, wouldn't he** il fallait qu'il dise ça

3 *(expressing opinions)* **I w. imagine it's warmer than here** j'imagine qu'il fait plus chaud qu'ici; **I w. think he'd be pleased** j'aurais cru que ça lui ferait plaisir; **I wouldn't know** *(I don't know)* je ne saurais dire

4 *(giving advice)* **I w. have a word with her about it (, if I were you)** moi, je lui en parlerais (à votre place)

5 *(expressing surprise, incredulity)* **you wouldn't think she was only 15, w. you?** on ne dirait pas qu'elle n'a que 15 ans, n'est-ce pas?; **who w. have thought it?** qui l'aurait cru?; **I wouldn't have thought it possible** je ne l'aurais pas cru possible; **w. you credit it!** tu te rends compte!

6 *(indicating likelihood, probability)* **there was a woman there – that w. be his wife** il y avait une femme – ça devait être sa femme; **w. that be your cousin you have in mind?** c'est à votre cousin que vous pensez?

C. 1 *(in reported speech)* **it was to be the last time I w. see him before he left** c'était la dernière fois que je le voyais avant son départ

2 *(used with "have")* **they w. have been happy if it hadn't been for the war** ils auraient vécu heureux si la guerre n'était pas survenue; *Am* **if you w. have told the truth, this w. never have happened** si tu m'avais dit la vérité, ça ne serait jamais arrivé

3 *(subjunctive use) Formal or Literary (expressing wishes)* **w. that it were true!** si seulement c'était vrai!; **what w. you have me do?** que voulez-vous que je fasse?

would-be ADJ **1** *(hopeful)* **a w. writer/MP** une personne qui veut être écrivain/député; **troops seized the w. assassin** les militaires ont attrapé l'assassin avant qu'il ne commette le crime **2** *Pej (so-called)* prétendu, soi-disant *(inv)*

wouldn't ['wʊdənt] = **would not**

would've ['wʊdəv] = **would have**

wound[1] [wuːnd] N **1** *(physical injury)* blessure *f*, plaie *f*; **a bullet w.** une blessure par balle; **she had three bullet wounds** elle avait été blessée par trois balles; **she had three knife wounds** elle avait reçu trois coups de couteau; **they had serious**

head wounds ils avaient été gravement blessés à la tête; **to dress a w.** panser une blessure *ou* une plaie **2** *Fig (emotional or moral)* blessure *f*; **he was still suffering from deep psychological wounds** il souffrait encore de graves blessures psychologiques; **to reopen an old w.** rouvrir une plaie

VT 1 *(physically)* blesser; **they were wounded by flying glass** ils ont été blessés par des éclats de verre; **she was wounded in the shoulder** elle a été blessée à l'épaule **2** *Fig (emotionally)* blesser; **he was deeply wounded by their criticism** il a été profondément blessé par leurs critiques; **to w. sb's pride** heurter l'amour-propre de qn, blesser qn dans son amour-propre

VI causer une blessure

wound[2] [waʊnd] *pt & pp of* **wind**[2]

wounded ['wu:ndɪd] **ADJ 1** *(soldier, victim)* blessé; **a w. woman** une blessée **2** *Fig (feelings, pride)* blessé

NPL the w. les blessés *mpl*

wounding ['wu:ndɪŋ] **ADJ** *Fig (hurtful)* blessant

wove [wəʊv] *pt of* **weave**

woven ['wəʊvən] *pp of* **weave**

wow [waʊ] *Fam* **EXCLAM** oh là là!, la vache!

N it's a real w.! c'est vraiment super!; **he's a w. at hockey** c'est un super joueur de hockey

VT *(impress)* impressionner[□], emballer

WP [ˌdʌbəlju:'pi:] **N 1** *(abbr* **word processing***)* TTX *m*, traitement *m* de texte **2** *(abbr* **word processor***)* machine *f* à traitement de texte

WPC [ˌdʌbəlju:pi:'si:] **N** *Br (abbr* **woman police constable***)* = femme agent de police; **W. Roberts** l'agent Roberts

wpm *(written abbr* **words per minute***)* mots/min

WRAC [ræk] **N** *Br Mil (abbr* **Women's Royal Army Corps***)* = section féminine de l'armée de terre britannique

wrack [ræk] **N 1** *(seaweed)* varech *m* **2** = **shindig rack**

WRAF [ræf] **N** *Br Mil (abbr* **Women's Royal Air Force***)* = section féminine de l'armée de l'air britannique

wraith [reɪθ] **N** *Literary* apparition *f*, spectre *m*

wraithlike ['reɪθlaɪk] **ADJ** *Literary* spectral

wrangle ['ræŋgəl] **VI** se disputer, se chamailler; **to w. about** *or* **over sth** se disputer à propos de qch; **they were wrangling over who should pay** ils se disputaient pour savoir qui devait payer; **to w. with sb** se disputer *ou* se chamailler avec qn

VT *Am (cattle, horses)* garder

N dispute *f*; **a long legal w. over the amount of damages** une longue dispute juridique sur le montant des dommages-intérêts

wrangler ['ræŋglə(r)] **N 1** *Am (cowboy)* cowboy *m* **2** *Cin* animalier *m*

wrangling ['ræŋglɪŋ] **N** *(UNCOUNT)* disputes *fpl*, querelles *fpl*; **there has been a lot of w. over who to give the job to** il y a eu beaucoup de querelles pour décider à qui donner le poste

wrap [ræp] *(pt & pp* **wrapped***)* **VT 1** *(goods, parcel, gift, food)* emballer, envelopper; **the fish was wrapped in foil** le poisson était enveloppé dans du papier d'aluminium; **would you like it wrapped?** *(gift)* c'est pour offrir?

2 *(cocoon, envelop)* envelopper, emmailloter; **the baby was wrapped in a blanket** le bébé était enveloppé dans une couverture; *Fig* **her visit was wrapped in mystery** sa visite était entourée de mystère

3 *(twist, wind)* **to w. round** *or* **around** enrouler; **she had a towel wrapped round her head** sa tête était enveloppée dans une serviette; **she had a towel wrapped round her body** elle s'était enveloppée dans une serviette; **w. this blanket round you/your shoulders** enroule cette couverture autour de toi/de tes épaules; **he wrapped the bandage round her hand** il lui a enroulé la main dans une bande; **he wrapped his arms round her** il l'a prise dans ses bras; *Fam Fig* **he wrapped the car round a tree** il s'est payé un arbre

VI *Comput (lines)* se boucler

N 1 *(housecoat)* peignoir *m*; *(shawl)* châle *m*; *(over ballgown)* sortie-de-bal *f*; *(blanket, rug)* couverture *f*

2 *Cin* **it's a w.!** c'est dans la boîte!

3 *Culin (sandwich)* = tortilla fourrée

4 *Fam Drugs Slang (for powdered drugs)* sachet *m* de drogue[□]

• **wraps NPL** *Fig* **to keep a plan/one's feelings under wraps** garder un plan secret/ses sentiments secrets; **the wraps were taken off the new car today** la voiture a été montrée au public pour la première fois aujourd'hui

▸ **wrap up VT SEP 1** *(goods, parcel, gift, food)* envelopper, emballer, empaqueter; **he wrapped the sandwiches up in foil** il a enveloppé les sandwiches dans du papier d'aluminium

2 *(person ▸ in clothes, blanket)* envelopper; **w. him up in a blanket** enveloppez-le dans une couverture; **she was well wrapped up in a thick coat** elle était bien emmitouflée dans un épais manteau; **w. yourself up warmly** couvrez-vous bien

3 *Fig* **politicians are skilled at wrapping up bad news in an acceptable form** les politiciens s'y connaissent pour présenter les mauvaises nouvelles sous un jour acceptable; **his meaning was wrapped up in diplomatic jargon** il enrobait ce qu'il disait de jargon diplomatique

4 *Fam (conclude ▸ job)* terminer[□], conclure[□]; *(▸ deal, contract)* conclure[□], régler[□]; **let's get this matter wrapped up** finissons-en avec cette question[□]

5 *(engross)* **to be wrapped up in sth** être absorbé par qch; **he's very wrapped up in his work** il est très absorbé par son travail; **she's very wrapped up in herself** elle est très repliée sur elle-même; **she is too wrapped up in her own problems** elle est trop préoccupée par ses propres problèmes

6 *(implicate)* **he was wrapped up in some shady dealings** il a été impliqué dans des transactions louches

7 *Am (summarize)* résumer; **she wrapped up her talk with three points** elle a résumé son discours en trois points

VI 1 *(dress)* s'habiller, se couvrir; **w. up warmly** *or* **well!** couvrez-vous bien! **2** *Br Fam (be quiet)* la fermer; **w. up!** la ferme!

wraparound ['ræpəˌraʊnd] **ADJ** *(dress, skirt)* portefeuille *(inv)*

N 1 *(dress)* robe *f* portefeuille; *(skirt)* jupe *f* portefeuille **2** *Comput* mise *f* à la ligne automatique des mots

• **wraparounds NPL** *(sunglasses)* lunettes *fpl* de soleil panoramiques

▸▸ *Aut* ***wraparound bumper*** pare-chocs *m* enveloppant; ***wraparound sunglasses*** lunettes *fpl* de soleil panoramiques

wrapover ['ræpˌəʊvə(r)] **N** *(dress)* robe *f* portefeuille; *(skirt)* jupe *f* portefeuille

ADJ *(dress, skirt)* portefeuille *(inv)*

wrapped [ræpt] **ADJ** *(bread, cheese)* préemballé

wrapper ['ræpə(r)] **N 1** *(for sweet)* papier *m*; *(for parcel)* papier *m* d'emballage; *(of cigar)* emballage *m* **2** *(cover ▸ on book)* jaquette *f*; *(▸ on magazine, newspaper)* bande *f*

wrapping ['ræpɪŋ] **N** *(packaging)* emballage *m*; *(on parcel)* papier *m* d'emballage; *(on sweet)* papier *m*

▸▸ ***wrapping paper*** *(for gift)* papier *m* cadeau; *(for parcel)* papier *m* d'emballage

wrapround ['ræpraʊnd] **N** *(in word processing)* bouclage *m*, renouement *m* (des mots)

▸▸ *Aut* ***wrapround rear window*** lunette *f* arrière panoramique; ***wrapround windscreen*** pare-brise *m* panoramique

wrath [rɒθ] **N** *Literary* colère *f*, courroux *m*

wrathful ['rɒθful] **ADJ** *Literary* en colère, courroucé

wreak [ri:k] *(pt & pp sense* **1 wreaked** *or* **wrought** [rɔ:t]) **VT 1** *(cause ▸ damage, chaos)* causer, provoquer; **the damage wreaked by the explosion** les dommages provoqués par l'explosion; **to w. havoc** faire des ravages, tout mettre sens dessus dessous; **the storm wreaked havoc with telephone communications** la tempête a sérieusement perturbé les communications téléphoniques; *Fig* **it wreaked havoc with my holiday plans** cela a bouleversé mes projets de vacances **2** *(inflict ▸ revenge, anger)* assouvir; **to w. vengeance on sb** assouvir sa vengeance sur qn

wreath [ri:θ] *(pl* **wreaths** [ri:ðz]) **N 1** *(for funeral)* couronne *f* **2** *(garland)* guirlande *f*; **a holly w.** une guirlande de houx; **a laurel w.** une couronne de laurier **3** *Fig (of mist)* nappe *f*; *(of smoke)* volute *f*

wreathe [ri:ð] **VT 1** *(shroud)* envelopper; **the mountain top was wreathed in mist** le sommet de la montagne était enveloppé *ou* disparaissait dans la brume; *Fig* **to be wreathed in smiles** être rayonnant **2** *(with flowers ▸ person)* couronner; *(▸ grave, window)* orner

VI *(smoke)* monter en volutes

wreck [rek] **N 1** *(wrecked remains ▸ of ship)* épave *f*; *(▸ of plane)* avion *m* accidenté, épave *f*; *(▸ of train)* train *m* accidenté; *(▸ of car, lorry, bus)* véhicule *m* accidenté, épave *f*; **the car was a w.** la voiture était une épave; **the burnt-out w. of a bus** les restes calcinés d'un bus

2 *(wrecking ▸ of ship)* naufrage *m*; *(▸ of plane, car)* accident *m*; *(▸ of train)* déraillement *m*

3 *Fam (dilapidated car)* guimbarde *f*; *(old bike)* clou *m*

4 *Fam (person)* épave *f*, loque *f*; **he's a w.** *(physically)* c'est une épave; *(mentally)* il est à bout; **I must look a w.** je dois avoir une mine de déterré; **I'm a nervous w.** je suis à bout; **the man's an emotional w.** le type est une loque, au niveau émotionnel

5 *Fig (of hopes, plans)* effondrement *m*, anéantissement *m*

VT 1 *(in accident, explosion ▸ ship)* provoquer le naufrage de; *(▸ car, plane)* détruire totalement; *(▸ building)* démolir; **the tanker was wrecked off the African coast** le pétrolier a fait naufrage au large des côtes africaines; **the car was completely wrecked in the accident** la voiture a été totalement détruite dans l'accident; **the store was wrecked by a bomb blast** une bombe a fait sauter le magasin, le magasin a été détruit par l'explosion d'une bombe

2 *(damage ▸ furniture)* casser, démolir; *(▸ mechanism)* détruire, détraquer

3 *(upset ▸ marriage, relationship)* briser; *(▸ hopes, chances)* anéantir; *(▸ health)* briser, ruiner; *(▸ negotiations)* faire échouer, saboter; **she's wrecked my plans** elle a ruiné mes plans; **this defeat has wrecked the team's chances** cette défaite a anéanti les chances de l'équipe; **the accident wrecked her hopes** l'accident a anéanti ses espoirs; **you've wrecked my life!** tu as brisé ma vie!

wreckage ['rekɪdʒ] **N 1** *(UNCOUNT) (debris ▸ from ship, car)* débris *mpl*; *(▸ from building)* décombres *mpl*; **pieces of w. from the building lay in the street** les décombres du bâtiment jonchaient la rue; **a body was found in the w. of the plane** un corps a été trouvé dans les débris de l'avion; **to pull sb from the w.** tirer qn des décombres **2** *(wrecked ship)* épave *f*, navire *m* naufragé **3** *Fig (of hopes, relationship)* anéantissement *m*

wrecked [rekt] **ADJ 1** *(ship)* naufragé; *(car, plane)* complètement détruit; *(house)* complètement démoli; **w. cars** épaves *fpl* d'automobiles, voitures *fpl* accidentées

2 *Fig (relationship, hopes)* anéanti

3 *Fam (drunk)* bourré, pété; *(on drugs)* défoncé, raide

4 *Fam (exhausted)* crevé, naze

wrecker ['rekə(r)] **N 1** *(destroyer)* destructeur (trice) *m,f*, démolisseur(euse) *m,f*; **marriage-w.** briseur(euse) *m,f* de ménages **2** *Am (demolition man ▸ for buildings)* démolisseur *m*; *(▸ for cars)* ferrailleur *m*, casseur *m* **3** *Am (breakdown van)* dépanneuse *f*

Wren [ren] **N** *Br* = membre du "Women's Royal Naval Service"; **the Wrens** = section féminine de la marine britannique

wren [ren] **N** *Orn* roitelet *m*

wrench [rentʃ] **VT 1** *(pull)* tirer violemment sur; **she wrenched the door open** elle a ouvert la porte d'un geste violent; **we'll have to w. the lid off** nous allons être obligés de forcer le couvercle pour l'ouvrir; **someone wrenched the bag out of my hands** *or* **from my grasp** quelqu'un m'a arraché le sac des mains; **to w. oneself free** se dégager d'un mouvement violent **2** *(eyes, mind)* arracher, détacher; **I couldn't w. my gaze (away) from the horrible sight** je ne pouvais pas détacher mon regard de cet horrible spectacle; **nothing could w. her away from her book** rien ne pouvait l'arracher à son livre **3** *(ankle, arm)* se faire une entorse à; **I've wrenched my shoulder**

je me suis foulé l'épaule; **to w. one's back** se donner *ou* se faire un tour de reins

VI he wrenched free of his bonds il s'est dégagé de ses liens d'un mouvement violent; *Fig* il s'est libéré de ses liens

N 1 *(tug, twist)* mouvement *m* violent *(de torsion)*; **with a sudden w. she pulled herself free** elle se dégagea d'un mouvement brusque; **he gave the handle a w.** il a tiré brusquement *ou* violemment sur la poignée

2 *(to ankle, knee)* entorse *f*; **I gave my ankle a w.** je me suis fait une entorse à *ou* je me suis foulé la cheville; **I gave my back a w.** je me suis donné *ou* fait un tour de reins

3 *Fig (emotional)* déchirement *m*; **it was a terrible w. for me to leave home** ce fut un déchirement terrible pour moi de quitter la maison

4 *Tech (spanner)* clé *f*, clef *f*; *(adjustable)* clé *f* anglaise; *(for wheels)* clé *f* en croix; *Am* **he threw a w. into the works** il nous a mis des bâtons dans les roues

wrest [rest] **VT** *Literary* **1** *(grab ▸ object)* arracher violemment; **he wrested the gun from me** *or* **from my grasp** il m'a arraché violemment le fusil des mains **2** *(extract ▸ truth, secret)* arracher; **he wrested the truth from her** il lui a arraché la vérité; **they just manage to w. a living from the land** ils réussissent tout juste à vivre de la terre; **we could w. no meaning from the coded message** nous n'avons rien pu tirer du message codé **3** *(control, power)* ravir, arracher; **to w. power from sb** ravir le pouvoir à qn; **we wrested victory from the jaws of defeat** nous avons arraché la victoire des mains de l'ennemi

wrestle ['resəl] **VI 1** *(fight)* lutter, pratiquer la lutte; *Sport (in freestyle wrestling)* catcher, pratiquer le catch; **to w. with sb** lutter (corps à corps) avec qn, se battre avec qn; **the two men wrestled briefly** les deux hommes ont brièvement lutté **2** *Fig (struggle)* se débattre, lutter; **she wrestled with her conscience** elle se débattait avec sa conscience; **I wrestled with the problem all evening** je me suis débattu avec ce problème toute la soirée **3** *(try to control)* **to w. with sth** se débattre avec qch; **the woman wrestled to keep control of the car** la femme luttait pour garder le contrôle de la voiture

VT *(fight ▸ intruder, enemy)* lutter contre; *Sport (in Greek or Sumo wrestling)* rencontrer à la lutte; *(in freestyle wrestling)* rencontrer au catch; **he wrestled his attacker to the ground** luttant avec son agresseur, il réussit à le clouer au sol

N lutte *f*; **to have a w. with sb** lutter avec *ou* contre qn; **after a w. with the knot, she was free** après s'être débattue avec le nœud, elle était libre; *Fig* **after a w. with his conscience, he agreed** après une lutte avec sa conscience, il a accepté

wrestler ['reslə(r)] **N** *Sport* lutteur(euse) *m,f*; *(in freestyle wrestling)* catcheur(euse) *m,f*

wrestling ['reslɪŋ] *Sport* **N** lutte *f*; *(freestyle)* catch *m*

COMP *(hold, match)* de lutte; *(in freestyle wrestling)* de catch

wretch [retʃ] **N 1** *(unfortunate person)* pauvre diable *m*, malheureux(euse) *m,f*; **the poor w.** le pauvre malheureux **2** *Literary or Hum (scoundrel)* scélérat(e) *m,f*, misérable *mf*; **the w. who stole my bag** le scélérat qui m'a volé mon sac **3** *(child)* vilain(e) *m,f*, coquin(e) *m,f*; **you little w.!** petit coquin!

wretched ['retʃɪd] **ADJ 1** *(poor ▸ dwelling, clothes)* misérable; **she had a w. existence** elle a eu une existence misérable; **their living conditions are w.** leurs conditions de vie sont misérables *ou* sont épouvantables

2 *(unhappy)* malheureux; *(depressed)* déprimé, démoralisé; **he was** *or* **felt w. about what he had said** il se sentait coupable à cause de ce qu'il avait dit; **I felt cold and w.** j'avais froid et je me sentais malheureux

3 *(ill)* malade; **the flu made me feel really w.** je me sentais vraiment très mal avec cette grippe

4 *Fam (as expletive)* fichu, maudit; **keep your w. money!** garde-le, ton fichu argent!

5 *(abominable ▸ behaviour, performance, weather)* lamentable; **I'm a w. singer/writer** je suis un piètre chanteur/écrivain; **it's a w. business** c'est une affaire *ou* une histoire lamentable

wretchedly ['retʃɪdlɪ] **ADV 1** *(poorly ▸ live, dress)* misérablement, pauvrement **2** *(unhappily ▸ cry, look)* pitoyablement, misérablement; **he apologized w.** il a fait des excuses pitoyables **3** *(abominably ▸ behave)* abominablement; *(▸ play, perform)* très mal, lamentablement; **a w. small amount** une somme absolument dérisoire

wretchedness ['retʃɪdnɪs] **N 1** *(poverty ▸ of living conditions)* extrême pauvreté *f*, misère *f*

2 *(unhappiness)* tristesse *f*, malheur *m*

3 *(meanness ▸ of behaviour)* mesquinerie *f*; *(▸ of sum, wage)* caractère *m* dérisoire

4 *(in quality ▸ of performance, of weather, of meal)* médiocrité *f*

wriggle ['rɪgəl] **VT** *(toes, fingers)* tortiller; **he wriggled his way under the fence** il est passé sous la clôture en se tortillant *ou* à plat ventre; *Fig* **I'd like to see him w. his way out of that!** j'aimerais bien voir comment il va se sortir de cette situation!

VI *(person)* remuer, gigoter; *(snake, worm)* se tortiller; *(fish)* frétiller; **stop wriggling!** arrête de t'agiter!; **the children were wriggling in their seats** les enfants gigotaient sur leur siège; **to w. along** *(person)* avancer en rampant *ou* à plat ventre; *(snake)* avancer en se tortillant; **the fish/the little boy wriggled from her grasp** le poisson/le petit garçon réussit à s'échapper de ses mains en se tortillant; **she wriggled under the fence** elle est passée sous la clôture à plat ventre *ou* en se tortillant; **she wriggled under the blankets** elle s'est enfoncée sous les couvertures en se tortillant; **to w. free** se libérer en se tortillant; *Fig* s'en sortir

N to give a w. *(snake)* se tortiller; *(fish)* frétiller; *(person)* se tortiller; **with a w. the rabbit shook itself free from the trap** en se tortillant, le lapin parvint à se dégager du piège

wriggler ['rɪgələ(r)] **N** *(person)* **he's a terrible w.** il n'arrête pas de gigoter, il ne se tient jamais tranquille

wriggling ['rɪgəlɪŋ] **ADJ** = **wriggly**

N tortillement *m*; **a w. movement** un tortillement

wriggly ['rɪgəlɪ] *(compar* **wrigglier**, *superl* **wriggliest) ADJ** *(eel, snake, worm)* qui se tortille; *(fish)* frétillant; *(person)* remuant, qui gigote

wring [rɪŋ] *(pt & pp* **wrung** [rʌŋ]) **VT 1** *(wet cloth, clothes)* essorer, tordre; **he wrung the towel dry** il a essoré la serviette en la tordant; **she wrung the water from the sponge** elle a exprimé l'eau de l'éponge

2 *(neck)* tordre; **she wrung the chicken's neck** elle a tordu le cou au poulet; *Fig* **I'll w. his neck!** je vais lui tordre le cou!

3 *(hand ▸ in handshake)* serrer; **he wrung her hand** il lui a serré la main vigoureusement; **to w. one's hands (in despair)** se tordre les mains (de désespoir); *Fig* **it's no use sitting there wringing your hands** cela ne sert à rien de rester assis à vous désespérer

4 *(extract ▸ confession)* arracher; *(▸ money)* extorquer; **she wrung every last detail from him** elle a réussi à lui extorquer tous les renseignements; **I'll w. the truth out of them** je vais leur arracher la vérité; **the blackmailer wrung £5,000 from her** le maître chanteur lui a extorqué 5000 livres; **he's wringing the maximum publicity from the situation** il profite de la situation pour en tirer le maximum de publicité

5 *Fig (heart)* fendre; **her efforts to cope with four children on her own wrung my heart** ses efforts pour se débrouiller toute seule avec quatre enfants me fendaient le cœur

VI essorer

N give the cloth a w. essorez la serpillière

▸ wring out VT SEP *(wet cloth, clothes)* essorer, tordre

wringer ['rɪŋə(r)] **N** essoreuse *f* (à rouleaux); **to put clothes through the w.** essorer des vêtements (à la machine); *Fig* **he's really been through the w.** on lui en a fait voir de toutes les couleurs

wringing ['rɪŋɪŋ] **N 1** *(of washing)* tordage *m*; *(by machine)* essorage *m* **2** *(of hands)* **she told us the news, with much w. of hands** elle nous a annoncé la nouvelle, en se tordant les mains

ADJ w. (wet) *(clothes)* complètement trempé; *(person)* complètement trempé, trempé jusqu'aux os; **the shirt was w. with sweat** la chemise était trempée de sueur

wrinkle ['rɪŋkəl] **VT 1** *(nose)* froncer; *(brow)* plisser **2** *(paper, rug, cloth)* froisser

VI 1 *(skin, hands)* se rider; *(brow)* se contracter, se plisser; *(nose)* se froncer, se plisser; *(fruit)* se ratatiner, se rider **2** *(skirt, stocking)* faire des plis

N 1 *(on skin, fruit)* ride *f* **2** *(in paper, carpet)* pli *m*; *(in cloth)* faux pli *m*; *Fig* **there are still some wrinkles in the plan which need ironing out** il reste encore quelques difficultés à aplanir

wrinkled ['rɪŋkəld] **ADJ 1** *(skin, hands)* ridé; *(brow, nose)* plissé, froncé; *(fruit)* ridé, ratatiné; **a w. old man** un vieillard ratatiné **2** *(rug, skirt)* qui fait des plis; *(stockings, tights)* en accordéon

wrinkly ['rɪŋklɪ] *(compar* **wrinklier**, *superl* **wrinkliest**, *pl* **wrinklies) ADJ 1** *(skin, hands)* ridé; *(after bath)* fripé; *(fruit)* ridé, ratatiné **2** *(stockings, tights)* en accordéon

N *Br Fam Pej* croulant(e) *m,f*

wrist [rɪst] **N** poignet *m*

▸▸ *Comput* **wrist rest** repose-poignets *m inv*

wristband ['rɪstbænd] **N** *(on shirt, blouse)* poignet *m*; *(sweatband)* poignet *m*; *(of watch)* bracelet *m*

wristbone ['rɪstbəʊn] **N** *Anat* os *m* du carpe

wristlet ['rɪstlɪt] **N** bracelet *m*

wristlock ['rɪstlɒk] **N** *(in wrestling)* clef *f* de poignet; **to put a w. on sb** faire une clef de poignet à qn

wristwatch ['rɪstwɒtʃ] **N** montre-bracelet *f*

writ [rɪt] *pt & pp Arch see* **write**

N 1 *Law* ordonnance *f*; **to issue a w. against sb** *(for arrest)* lancer un mandat d'arrêt contre qn; *(for libel)* assigner qn en justice; **to serve a w. on sb, to serve sb with a w.** assigner qn (en justice) **2** *Pol (for elections)* ordonnance *f (émanant du président de la Chambre des communes et convoquant les députés pour un vote)*

ADJ astonishment was w. large on everybody's face l'étonnement se lisait sur tous les visages

write [raɪt] *(pt* **wrote** [rəʊt], *pp* **written** ['rɪtən], *pt & pp Arch* **writ** [rɪt]) **VT 1** *(letter)* écrire; *(address, name)* écrire, inscrire; *(initials)* écrire, tracer; *(prescription, cheque)* écrire, faire; *(will)* faire; *(application form)* compléter, rédiger; **to w. a letter to sb** écrire *ou* envoyer une lettre à qn; **w. her a letter** envoyez-lui une lettre, écrivez-lui; **I have some letters to w.** j'ai du courrier à faire; **they wrote me a letter of thanks** ils m'ont écrit pour me remercier; **he wrote her a postcard** il lui a envoyé une carte postale; **can I w. you a cheque (for it)?** est-ce que je peux vous faire un chèque?; *Am* **to w. sb** écrire à qn; *Am* **she wrote me about her father's illness** elle m'a écrit au sujet de la maladie de son père; **he can't speak Italian very well, but he can w. it** il ne parle pas très bien l'italien mais il peut l'écrire; **it is written in the Bible "thou shalt love thy neighbour as thyself"** il est écrit dans la bible "tu aimeras ton prochain comme toi-même"; *Fig* **perplexity was written all over his face** la perplexité se lisait sur son visage; *Fig* **he had success written all over him** on voyait bien qu'il avait réussi; **he's got journalist written all over him** on voit tout de suite que c'est un journaliste

2 *(book)* écrire; *(article, report)* écrire, faire; *(essay)* faire; *(music)* écrire, composer; **well written** bien écrit

3 *(send letter about)* écrire; **he wrote that he was getting married** il a écrit (pour annoncer) qu'il se mariait

4 *(spell)* écrire; **I never know how to w. her name** je ne sais jamais comment s'écrit son nom

5 *Comput (program)* écrire; *(CD-ROM)* graver, enregistrer; *(data ▸ store)* stocker, sauvegarder; *(▸ transfer)* transférer; **to w. sth to disk** écrire qch sur disque

VI 1 *(gen)* écrire; **to w. in pencil/in ink** écrire au crayon/à l'encre; **to learn to read and w.** apprendre à lire et à écrire; **I don't w. very well** je n'ai pas une belle écriture

2 *(send letter)* écrire; **to w. to sb** écrire à qn; **we still w.** *(to each other)* nous nous écrivons toujours; **to w. to thank/to invite sb** écrire pour remercier/pour inviter qn; **she wrote and told me about it** elle m'a écrit pour me le raconter; **please w. (again) soon** écris-moi vite (à nouveau), s'il te plaît; **they wrote (to him) asking** *or* **to ask for permission** ils (lui) ont écrit pour demander l'autorisation; **I've written for a catalogue** j'ai écrit pour demander *ou* pour qu'on m'envoie un catalogue

3 *(professionally ▸ as author)* écrire, être écrivain; *(▸ as journalist)* écrire, être journaliste; **he writes on home affairs for 'The Economist'** il fait des articles de politique intérieure dans 'The Economist'; **she writes for children's television** elle fait des émissions pour les enfants à la télévision; **she writes under a pseudonym** elle écrit sous un pseudonyme; **he writes on** *or* **about archeology** il écrit sur l'archéologie, il traite de questions d'archéologie

4 *(pen, typewriter)* écrire; **this pen doesn't w. very well** ce stylo n'écrit pas *ou* ne marche pas très bien

▸▸ *Comput* ***write access*** accès *m* en écriture; *Comput* ***write area*** zone *f* d'écriture; *Comput* ***write density*** densité *f* d'écriture; *Tech* ***write head*** tête *f* d'enregistrement; *Comput* ***write protection*** protection *f* contre l'écriture *ou* en écriture; *Comput* ***write speed*** vitesse *f* d'écriture

▸ **write back** VI *(answer)* répondre (à une lettre); **w. back soon** réponds-moi vite; **he wrote back to say he couldn't come** il a répondu qu'il ne pouvait pas venir; **he wrote back rejecting their offer** il a renvoyé une lettre refusant leur offre

▸ **write down** VT SEP **1** *(note)* écrire, noter; *(put in writing)* mettre par écrit; *Fig* **I had them written down as layabouts** je les considérais comme des bons à rien **2** *Fin & Com (in price)* réduire le prix de; *(in value)* réduire la valeur de; *(undervalue)* sous-évaluer; *(asset)* déprécier

▸ **write in** VI écrire; **to w. in for a refund** écrire pour demander un remboursement; **hundreds wrote in to complain** des centaines de personnes ont écrit pour se plaindre

VT SEP **1** *(on list, document ▸ word, name)* ajouter, insérer **2** *Am Pol (add ▸ name)* ajouter, inscrire *(sur un bulletin de vote)*; *(vote for ▸ person)* voter pour *(en ajoutant le nom sur le bulletin de vote)*

▸ **write off** VT SEP **1** *Fin (capital, stock)* amortir; *(bad debt, asset)* passer aux profits et pertes

2 *(consider lost, useless)* faire une croix sur, considérer comme perdu; *(cancel)* renoncer à, annuler; **the plan had to be written off** le projet a dû être abandonné; **three months' hard work was simply written off** on a perdu trois mois de travail acharné; **he was written off as a failure** on a considéré qu'il n'y avait rien de bon à en tirer

3 *(in accident ▸ of insurance company)* considérer comme irréparable, mettre à la casse; *(▸ of driver)* rendre inutilisable; *Br* **she wrote off her new car** elle a complètement démoli sa voiture neuve

4 *(letter, poem)* écrire en vitesse

▸ **write out** VT SEP **1** *(report)* écrire, rédiger; *(list, cheque)* faire, établir; *(prescription)* rédiger **2** *(copy up ▸ notes)* recopier, mettre au propre **3** *Rad & TV (character)* faire disparaître

▸ **write up** VT SEP **1** *(diary, impressions)* écrire, rédiger; *Press (event)* faire un compte rendu de, rendre compte de; **the demonstration was written up in the local newspaper** le journal local a fait un compte rendu de la manifestation; **he wrote up his ideas in a report** il a consigné ses idées dans un rapport **2** *(copy up ▸ notes, data)* recopier, mettre au propre **3** *Fin & Com (in price)* augmenter le prix de; *(in value)* augmenter la valeur de; *(overvalue)* surévaluer; *(asset)* revaloriser

write-back N *Acct* **w. of provisions** reprises *fpl* sur provisions

write-down N *Fin* dépréciation *f*

write-off N **1** *Fin* annulation *f* par écrit, passation *f* par pertes et profits **2** *Br* **to be a w.** *(motor vehicle)* être irréparable *ou* bon pour la casse; *(garment)* être bon à jeter; *(business venture)* être une perte de temps et d'argent

write-protect VT *Comput* protéger contre l'écriture *ou* en écriture

write-protected ADJ *Comput (disk)* protégé contre l'écriture *ou* en écriture

writer ['raɪtə(r)] N **1** *(of novel, play)* écrivain *m*, auteur *m*; *(of letter)* auteur *m*; **a w. of novels/of poetry** un romancier/poète; **she's a fine w.** c'est un excellent écrivain; **I'm a bad letter-w.** je suis un mauvais correspondant **2** *(in handwriting)* **to be a good w.** avoir une belle écriture; **to be a bad w.** écrire mal **3** *Scot Law* notaire *m*; **W. to the Signet** ≃ avoué *m*

▸▸ ***writer's block*** angoisse *f* de la page blanche; ***writer's cramp*** crampe *f* de l'écrivain

writer-director N *Cin & TV* auteur-réalisateur (trice) *m,f*

write-up N **1** *(review)* compte rendu *m*, critique *f*; **the play got a good w.** la pièce a eu une bonne critique *ou* a été bien accueillie par la critique **2** *Acct* augmentation *f*

writhe [raɪð] VI **1** *(person ▸ in pain)* se tordre, se contorsionner; *(snakes, worms)* se tortiller; **to w. in** *or* **with agony** se tordre de douleur, être en proie à d'atroces souffrances **2** *Fig* **her remarks made him w.** *(in disgust)* ses remarques l'ont fait frémir; *(in embarrassment)* ses remarques l'ont atrocement gêné; **the memory still makes me w. with embarrassment** ce souvenir me fait encore rougir

writing ['raɪtɪŋ] N **1** *(of books, letters)* écriture *f*; **to take up w.** *(author)* commencer à écrire; **to devote one's time to w.** se consacrer à l'écriture; **it's a good piece of w.** c'est bien écrit; **this is clear, concise w.** c'est un style clair et concis, c'est écrit avec clarté et concision; **the report was four years in the w.** il a fallu quatre ans pour rédiger le rapport; **at the time of w.** au moment où j'écris/il écrit/*etc*; *Press* à l'heure où nous mettons sous presse

2 *(handwriting)* écriture *f*; **I can't read your w.** je ne peux pas déchiffrer votre écriture *ou* ce que vous avez écrit

3 *(written text)* **there was w. all over the board** il n'y avait plus de place pour écrire quoi que ce soit sur le tableau noir; *Fig* **the w.'s on the wall** l'issue est inéluctable; **the w. was on the wall for the Roman Empire** la fin de l'empire romain était imminente; **I could see the w. on the wall** je savais ce qui allait arriver

4 *Sch (spelling)* orthographe *f*; *(written language)* écriture *f*; **to learn reading and w.** apprendre à lire et à écrire, apprendre la lecture et l'écriture

• **writings** NPL *(written works)* œuvre *f*, écrits *mpl*; **the writings of Karl Marx** les écrits *mpl ou* l'œuvre *m* de Karl Marx; **selected writings** morceaux *mpl* choisis

• **in writing** ADV par écrit; **to put sth in w.** mettre qch par écrit; **can we have that in w.?** pouvons-nous avoir cela par écrit?; **you need her agreement in w.** il vous faut son accord écrit; **I won't be satisfied until I see it in w.** je ne serai pas satisfait tant que ce ne sera pas écrit noir sur blanc

▸▸ ***writing case*** nécessaire *m* de correspondance; ***writing desk*** secrétaire *m (meuble)*; ***writing materials*** matériel *m* nécessaire pour écrire; ***writing pad*** bloc-notes *m*; ***writing paper*** papier *m* à lettres; ***writing table*** secrétaire *m (meuble)*

written ['rɪtən] *pp of* **write**

ADJ *(form, text, examination)* écrit; *(confirmation, consent)* par écrit; **to make a w. request** faire une demande par écrit; **w. law** droit *m* écrit; **the w. word** l'écrit *m*; **her w. French is not as good as her oral French** elle parle le français mieux qu'elle ne l'écrit

written-down cost, written-down value N *Fin* valeur *f* amortie

WRNS [renz] N *Br Mil* (*abbr* **Women's Royal Naval Service**) = section féminine de la marine de guerre britannique

WRONG [rɒŋ]

ADJ	
• mauvais **1, 3**	• faux **1**
• erroné **1**	• tort **2**
• mal **4**	• injuste **4**
ADV	
• mal	
N	
• mal **1**	• tort **2–4**
• injustice **2**	
VT	
• faire du tort à	

ADJ **1** *(incorrect ▸ address, answer, information)* mauvais, faux (fausse), erroné; *(▸ decision)* mauvais; *Mus (note)* faux (fausse); *Tel (number)* faux (fausse); **to get things in the w. order** mettre les choses dans le mauvais ordre; **these cups are in the w. place** ces tasses ne sont pas à leur place; **they came on the w. day** ils se sont trompés de jour pour leur venue; **to take the w. road/train** se tromper de route/de train; **this is the w. road for Munich** ce n'est pas la bonne route pour aller à Munich; **to drive on the w. side of the road** conduire du mauvais côté de la route; **you've put your shoes on the w. feet** vous vous êtes trompé (de pied) en mettant vos chaussures; **to be (the) w. side up** être à l'envers; **to be (the) w. side out** *(clothing)* être à l'envers; **the biscuit went down the w. way** j'ai avalé le gâteau de travers; **it was a w. number** c'était une erreur; **to dial the w. number** se tromper de numéro; **I'm sorry, you've got the w. number** désolé, vous vous êtes trompé de numéro *ou* vous faites erreur; **you've got the w. man, Jack Taylor isn't a murderer** vous faites erreur, Jack Taylor n'est pas un meurtrier; **the clock/my watch is w.** le réveil/ma montre n'est pas à l'heure

2 *(mistaken ▸ person)* **to be w. (about sth)** avoir tort *ou* se tromper (à propos de qch); **you were w. to lose your temper** vous avez eu tort de vous emporter; **to be w. about sb** se tromper sur (le compte de) qn; **how w. can you be!** comme quoi on peut se tromper!; **that's just where you are w.** c'est justement ce qui vous trompe, c'est justement là que vous vous trompez; **I hope he won't get the w. idea about me** j'espère qu'il ne se fera pas de fausses idées sur mon compte; **I hope you won't take this the w. way, but…** ne le prends pas mal mais…

3 *(unsuitable)* mauvais, mal choisi; **you've got the w. attitude** vous n'avez pas l'attitude qu'il faut *ou* la bonne attitude; **it was the w. thing to do/to say** ce n'était pas la chose à faire/à dire; **I said all the w. things** j'ai dit tout ce qu'il ne fallait pas dire; **his ideas are all w.** il a des idées tout de travers; **you're going about it in the w. way** vous vous y prenez mal; **it's the w. way to deal with the situation** ce n'est pas comme cela qu'il faut régler la situation; **to come at the w. time** venir à un mauvais moment *ou* mal à propos; **I'm the w. person to ask** il ne faut pas me demander ça à moi; **I think you're in the w. job** je pense que ce n'est pas le travail qu'il vous faut; *Hum* vous vous êtes trompé de métier!; **this village is the w. place for a nightclub** ce village n'est pas l'endroit qui convient *ou* n'est pas le bon endroit pour une boîte de nuit

4 *(immoral, bad)* mal; *(unjust)* injuste; **cheating is w.** c'est mal de tricher; **slavery is w.** l'esclavage est inacceptable; **it was w. of him to take the money** ce n'était pas bien de sa part de prendre l'argent; **what's w. with reading comics?** qu'est-ce qu'il y a de mal à lire des bandes dessinées?; **what's w. with that?** qu'est-ce qu'il y a de mal à ça?; **there's nothing w. with it** il n'y a rien à redire à cela, il n'y a pas de mal à cela; **it's w. that anyone should have to live in poverty** il est injuste que des gens soient obligés de vivre dans la misère

5 *(amiss)* **something is w.** *or* **there's something w. with the lamp** la lampe ne marche pas bien *ou* a un défaut; **something is w.** *or* **there's something w. with my elbow** j'ai quelque chose au coude; **there's something w. with me** *(ill)* j'ai quelque chose qui ne va pas; **there must be something w. with me** *(that people don't like me)* il doit y avoir quelque chose qui ne va pas chez moi; **there must be something seriously w.** il doit y avoir un gros problème; **there's something w. somewhere** il y a quelque chose qui ne va pas quelque part; **I hope there's nothing w.** j'espère qu'il n'est rien arrivé; **there's nothing at all w. with the clock** la pendule marche parfaitement bien; **there's nothing w. with your work** votre travail est très bon; **there's nothing w. with her decision/her reasoning** sa décision/son raisonnement est parfaitement valable; **there's nothing w. about wanting a holiday without the kids** il n'y a pas de mal à vouloir des vacances sans les enfants; **there's nothing w. with you** vous êtes en parfaite santé; **there's nothing w., thank you** tout va bien, merci; **there's nothing w. with your eyes/your hearing!** vous avez de bons yeux/de bonnes oreilles!; **what's w.?** qu'est-ce qui ne va pas?; **what's w. with the car?** qu'est-ce qu'elle a, la voi-

ture?; **what's w. with your elbow?** qu'est-ce qu'il a, votre coude?; **what's w. with you?** qu'est-ce que vous avez?; **what's w. with these people?** *(that they don't understand)* qu'est-ce qu'ils ont qui ne va pas, ces gens?; **what's w. with going to France?** quel mal y a-t-il à aller en France?; **there's very little w. with you** dans l'ensemble, vous êtes en très bonne santé; **there wasn't much w. with the car** la voiture n'avait pas grand-chose; *Br Fam* **to be w. in the head** avoir la tête fêlée *ou* le cerveau fêlé, être fêlé *ou* timbré
6 *(idioms)* **he got hold of the w. end of the stick** il a tout compris de travers; *Br* **to be caught on the w. foot** être pris au dépourvu; **they got off on the w. foot** ils se sont mal entendus au départ; *Br* **I'm (on) the w. side of 50** j'ai 50 ans bien sonnés; **to get out of bed on the w. side** se lever du pied gauche; **to get on the w. side of sb** se faire mal voir de qn
ADV mal; **you did w.** vous avez mal agi; **I guessed w.** je suis tombé à côté, je me suis trompé; **you've spelt the word w.** vous avez mal écrit *ou* mal orthographié ce mot; **she got the time/address/name w.** *(was mistaken about)* elle s'est trompée d'heure/d'adresse/de nom; *(misunderstood)* elle a mal compris l'heure/l'adresse/le nom; **I got the answer w.** je n'ai pas donné la bonne réponse; **to get one's sums w.** *Math* faire des erreurs dans ses opérations; *Fig* se tromper dans ses calculs; **she's got her facts w.** elle se trompe, ce qu'elle avance est faux; **you've got it w., I never said that** vous vous trompez *ou* vous n'avez pas compris, je n'ai jamais dit cela; **don't get me w.** comprenez-moi bien; **you've got her all w.** vous vous trompez complètement sur son compte; **to go w.** *(person)* se tromper; *(plan)* mal marcher, mal tourner; *(deal)* tomber à l'eau; *(machine)* tomber en panne; **something has gone w. with the TV** la télé est tombée en panne; **something went w. with her eyesight** elle a eu des ennuis avec sa vue; **the space flight went disastrously w.** le vol spatial a tourné à la catastrophe; **we must have gone w. somewhere** nous avons dû nous tromper quelque part; **you can't go w.** vous ne pouvez pas vous tromper, c'est très simple; **you won't go far w. if you follow her advice** vous ne risquez guère de vous tromper si vous suivez ses conseils; **you can't go w. with a pair of jeans** vous êtes tranquille avec un jean; **you can't go w. with a good book** *(for reading)* vous ne risquez pas de vous ennuyer avec un bon livre; *(as present)* un bon livre, cela plaît toujours; **where I went w. was in being too kind to him** là où j'ai commis une erreur, c'est en me montrant trop gentil avec lui; **when did things start going w.?** quand est-ce que les choses ont commencé à se gâter?; **she used to be a normal, happy little girl, but something went w.** c'était une petite fille normale et heureuse mais quelque chose a mal tourné; **everything that could go w. went w.** tout ce qui pouvait aller de travers est allé de travers; **to turn out w.** *(event)* mal (se) terminer; *(calculation)* se révéler faux; *(person)* mal tourner
N 1 *(immorality, immoral act)* mal *m*; **to know the difference between right and w.** savoir distinguer le bien du mal; **I did no w.** je n'ai rien fait de mal; *Prov* **two wrongs don't make a right** = on ne répare pas une injustice par une autre
2 *(harm)* tort *m*, injustice *f*; **to do sb w.** faire du tort à *ou* se montrer injuste envers qn; **he did them a great w.** il leur a fait subir une grave injustice, il leur a fait (un) grand tort
3 *(error)* tort *m*, erreur *f*; **he can do no w. in her eyes** tout ce qu'il fait trouve grâce à ses yeux
VT faire du tort à, traiter injustement; **he wronged his wife by accusing her of being unfaithful** il a traité injustement sa femme en l'accusant d'infidélité; **she felt deeply wronged** elle se sentait gravement lésée; **she has been badly wronged** *(by words)* on a dit à tort beaucoup de mal d'elle; *(by actions)* on a agi de manière injuste envers elle
• **in the wrong ADJ** dans son tort; **to be in the w.** être dans son tort, avoir tort **ADV to put sb in the w.** mettre qn dans son tort

wrongdoer [ˌrɒŋˈduːə(r)] **N 1** *(delinquent)* malfaiteur *m*, délinquant(e) *m,f* **2** *(sinner)* pécheur (eresse) *m,f*

wrongdoing [ˌrɒŋˈduːɪŋ] **N** mal *m*, méfait *m*; **his many wrongdoings** ses nombreux méfaits

wrong-foot VT *Sport* prendre à contre-pied; *Fig* prendre au dépourvu

wrongful [ˈrɒŋfʊl] **ADJ** *(unjust)* injuste; *(unjustified)* injustifié; *(illegal)* illégal, illicite
►► *Law* ***wrongful arrest*** arrestation *f* arbitraire; *Ind* ***wrongful dismissal*** renvoi *m* injustifié; ***wrongful imprisonment*** emprisonnement *m* injustifié

wrongfully [ˈrɒŋfʊlɪ] **ADV** injustement; *Ind* **I was w. dismissed** j'ai été renvoyé à tort

wrongheaded [ˌrɒŋˈhedɪd] **ADJ** *(person)* buté; *(idea)* insensé

wrongheadedly [ˌrɒŋˈhedɪdlɪ] **ADV** *(wrongly, mistakenly)* à tort; *(obstinately)* avec une obstination que rien ne justifie

wrongheadedness [ˌrɒŋˈhedɪdnɪs] **N** *(of person)* persistance *f* dans l'erreur; *(of idea)* absurdité *f*

wrongly [ˈrɒŋlɪ] **ADV 1** *(unjustly)* à tort, injustement; **to be w. accused** être accusé à tort *ou* injustement accusé **2** *(incorrectly)* à tort, mal; **to be w. informed** être mal renseigné; **this word is spelt w.** ce mot est mal écrit *ou* mal orthographié; **I guessed w.** je suis tombé à côté, je me suis trompé; **the cat was w. described as a Siamese** le chat a été décrit à tort comme un siamois **3** *(by mistake)* par erreur, à tort; **he was w. assigned to the night shift** il a été affecté par erreur *ou* à tort à l'équipe de nuit

wrongness [ˈrɒŋnɪs] **N 1** *(error)* erreur *f* **2** *(injustice)* injustice *f* **3** *(immorality)* immoralité *f*, mal *m*

wrote [rəʊt] *pt of* **write**

wrought [rɔːt] *Arch pt & pp of* **work the havoc w. by the hurricane** les ravages causés par l'ouragan; **the changes w. by industrialization** les (profonds) changements occasionnés par la révolution industrielle
ADJ *(silver, gold)* travaillé, ouvragé, façonné; *(metal)* ouvré, forgé; *(copper)* martelé; *Literary* **carefully w. prose** prose *f* finement ciselée
►► ***wrought iron*** fer *m* forgé

wrought-iron ADJ en fer forgé

wrought-up ADJ énervé

WRVS [ˌdʌbəljuːɑːˌviːˈes] **N** *Br (abbr* **Women's Royal Voluntary Service**) = association de femmes au service des déshérités

wry [raɪ] *(compar* **wrier** *or* **wryer**, *superl* **wriest** *or* **wryest**) **ADJ 1** *(ironic* ▸ *comment, smile)* ironique, désabusé; **w. humour** ironie *f*; **the film is a w. comedy** le film est plein d'ironie **2** *(expression, glance* ▸ *of distaste)* désabusé; **she made a w. face** elle a fait la grimace

wryly [ˈraɪlɪ] **ADV** de manière désabusée, ironiquement; **he smiled back at me w.** il m'a répondu par un sourire ironique *ou* désabusé; **her w. observed portrait** son portrait ironique

wt *(written abbr* **weight**) poids

wtf *(written abbr* **what the fuck?**) hein ?, quoi ?, = abréviation employée sur Internet ou dans les SMS pour exprimer la surprise, l'agacement ou l'incrédulité

WTO [ˌdʌbəljuːtiːˈəʊ] **N** *(abbr* **World Trade Organization**) OMC *f*

wulfenite [ˈwʊlfənaɪt] **N** *Miner* wulfénite *f*

wunderkind [ˈwʌndəkɪnd] **N** enfant *mf* prodige

wuss [wʊs] **N** *Fam* mauviette *f*, lavette *f*

wussy [ˈwʊsɪ] *Fam* **N** mauviette *f*, lavette *f*
ADJ mou (molle), mollasson

WV, WVa *(written abbr* **West Virginia**) Virginie-Occidentale *f*

WW *(written abbr* **World War**) guerre *f* mondiale

WWW [ˌdʌbəljuːdʌbəljuːˈdʌbəljuː] **N** *Comput (abbr* **world wide web**) WWW, W3

WY *(written abbr* **Wyoming**) Wyoming *m*

wych elm [wɪtʃ-] **N** *Bot* orme *m* blanc

wynd [waɪnd] **N** *Scot* allée *f*

Wyo *(written abbr* **Wyoming**) Wyoming *m*

Wyoming [waɪˈəʊmɪŋ] **N** *Geog* le Wyoming

WYSIWYG [ˈwɪzɪwɪg] **N & ADJ** *Comput (abbr* **what you see is what you get**) tel écran-tel écrit *m*, tel-tel *m*, Wysiwyg *m*
►► ***WYSIWYG display*** affichage *m* tel écran-tel écrit *ou* tel-tel *ou* Wysiwyg

X¹, x¹ [eks] **N** *(letter)* X, x *m inv*; **two x's** deux x; **X for xylophone** ≃ X comme Xavier

X² *(pt & pp* **X-ed** *or* **X'd)** **N** *(unknown factor)* X *m*; **X marks the spot** l'endroit est marqué d'une croix; **Mr X** monsieur X; **for X number of years** pendant x années

VT marquer d'une croix

►► *X chromosome* chromosome *m* X

X³ 1 *(written abbr* **kiss)** = formule affectueuse placée après la signature à la fin d'une lettre **2** *(written abbr* **Christ)** Christ *m*

x-axis **N** *Math* axe *m* des X, abscisse *f*

X-Dax **N** *St Exch* **the X. (index)** le X-Dax, l'indice *m* X-Dax

xenon ['zi:nɒn] **N** *Chem* xénon *m*

xenophobe ['zenəfəʊb] **N** xénophobe *mf*

xenophobia [ˌzenə'fəʊbɪə] **N** xénophobie *f*

xenophobic [ˌzenə'fəʊbɪk] **ADJ** xénophobe

xerography [ˌzɪə'rɒgrəfɪ] **N** *(UNCOUNT)* photocopie *f*, *Spec* électrocopie *f*

Xerox® ['zɪərɒks] **N 1** *(machine)* copieur *m*, photocopieuse *f* **2** *(process, copy)* photocopie *f*

Xetra-Dax ['ekstrədæks] **N** *St Exch* **the X. index** l'indice *m* Xetra-Dax

XL [ˌeks'el] **N** *(abbr* **extra-large)** XL *m*

Xmas *(written abbr* **Christmas)** Noël *m*

XMCL [ˌeksemsi:'el] **N** *Comput (abbr* **Extensible Media Commerce Language)** XMCL *m*

XML [ˌeksem'el] **N** *Comput (abbr* **Extensible Markup Language)** XML *m*

X-rated [-reɪtɪd] **ADJ** *Formerly Cin (film)* interdit aux mineurs *ou* aux moins de dix-huit ans; *Fam* **some of the stuff she told me was pretty X.** elle m'a dit des choses assez corsées

x-ray, X-ray **VT 1** *Med (examine* ► *chest, ankle)* radiographier, faire une radio de; *(*► *patient)* faire une radio à; *(treat)* traiter aux rayons X **2** *(inspect* ► *luggage)* passer aux rayons X

N 1 *Med* radio *f*; **to have an x.** passer une radio; **to take an x. of sth** radiographier qch, faire une radiographie de qch **2** *Phys* rayon *m* X

COMP 1 *Med (examination)* radioscopique; *(treatment)* radiologique, par rayons X **2** *Phys (astronomy, tube)* à rayons X

►► *Med* ***x-ray photograph*** radiographie *f*, radio *f*; *Med* ***x-ray therapy*** radiothérapie *f*; *Med* ***x-ray unit*** service *m* de radiologie

xylograph ['zaɪləˌgrɑ:f] **N** xylographie *f*

xylographic [ˌzaɪlə'græfɪk] **ADJ** xylographique

xylography [zaɪ'lɒgrəfɪ] **N** *(UNCOUNT)* xylographie *f*

xylophone ['zaɪləfəʊn] **N** xylophone *m*

xylophonist [zaɪ'lɒfənɪst] **N** joueur(euse) *m,f* de xylophone

-Y SUFFIXE

Il s'agit d'un suffixe très courant et extrêmement générateur, qui sert à former des adjectifs.

• On peut employer **-y** avec des verbes pour former des adjectifs :

shiny luisant; **curly hair** cheveux frisés; **leaky bucket** seau qui fuit; **runny sauce** sauce liquide; **smelly socks** chaussettes qui sentent mauvais; **I feel sleepy** j'ai envie de dormir.

• Employé avec certains noms, **-y** signifie COUVERT DE la chose qui précède :

dirty clothes vêtements sales; **inky hands** mains tachées d'encre; **hairy arms** bras poilus; **spotty face** visage couvert de boutons *ou* boutonneux; **cloudy/starry sky** ciel nuageux/étoilé; **grassy plain** plaine verdoyante.

• Employé avec d'autres noms, le préfixe **-y** suggère que ce dont on parle POSSÈDE LES QUALITÉS du référent du nom auquel il est accolé :

rubbery caoutchouteux; **wint(e)ry** hivernal; **icy wind** vent glacial; **leathery skin** peau parcheminée; **sandy soil** sol sablonneux; **smoky taste** goût de fumé; **lemony taste** goût citronné; **rubbishy film** film nul.

On notera que dans certains cas l'on ajoute un **e** devant le **y**, bien que cela ne soit pas strictement nécessaire : **the cake isn't chocolat(e)y enough** le gâteau n'a pas assez le goût de chocolat; **a hors(e)y face** un visage chevalin.

On remarquera par ailleurs que le suffixe **-y** peut servir à créer à volonté des néologismes à partir de noms. Ainsi on pourra dire :

the film was a bit too science-fictiony for me le film faisait un peu trop science-fiction à mon goût; **she's doing something businessy at college** elle fait des études de commerce ou quelque chose dans le genre; **she'd tied some weird scarfy thing round her waist** elle s'était attaché une sorte d'écharpe autour de la taille.

Y[1], **y**[1] [waɪ] **N** *(letter)* Y, y *m inv*; **two y's** deux y; **Y for yellow** ≃ Y comme Yvonne

►► ***Y chromosome*** chromosome *m* Y

Y[2] **1** *(written abbr* **yen***)* y **2** *(written abbr* **yuan***)* yuan

Y2K [ˌwaɪtuːˈkeɪ] *(abbr* **year 2000***)* **N** l'an *m* 2000

ADJ *Comput* **Y. compatible, Y. compliant** conforme à l'an 2000

yacht [jɒt] **N** *(sailing boat)* voilier *m*; *(pleasure boat)* yacht *m*

VI faire du yachting

►► ***yacht club*** yacht-club *m*; ***yacht race*** régate *f*

yachting [ˈjɒtɪŋ] **N** yachting *m*; **to go y.** faire du yachting

yachtsman [ˈjɒtsmən] *(pl* **yachtsmen** [-mən]*)* **N** yachtman *m*, yachtsman *m*

yachtswoman [ˈjɒtsˌwʊmən] *(pl* **yachtswomen** [-ˈwɪmɪn]*)* **N** yachtwoman *f*

yack [jæk] = **yak N & VI**

yackety-yak [ˌjækətɪˈjæk] **ADV** *Fam* **to go y.** jacasser

yada [ˈjædə] *Am Fam (to avoid repetition)* **y. y. (y.)** et patati et patata

yah [jɑː] **N** *Br Fam Pej* **(OK) y.** bourge *mf*

yahoo [jɑːˈhuː] *(pl* **yahoos***)* **N** rustre *m*, butor *m*

yak [jæk] *(pt & pp* **yakked**, *cont* **yakking***)* **N 1** *Zool* yak *m*, yack *m* **2** *(UNCOUNT) Fam* papotage *m*; **to have a y.** papoter; **it's ages since we've had a really good y.** ça fait longtemps qu'on ne s'est pas taillé une bonne bavette

VI *Fam* **1** *(chat)* jacasser; **it's y., y., y. all day long with that woman!** cette femme n'arrête pas de jacasser toute la journée! **2** *Am (vomit)* gerber, dégueuler

y'all [jɑːl] = **you-all**

yam [jæm] **N 1** *(plant, vegetable)* igname *f* **2** *Am Culin* patate *f* douce

yammer [ˈjæmə(r)] **VI** *Fam (person* ► *whine)* pleurnicher, geindre; *(*► *chatter)* jacasser; **what are you yammering (on) about?** qu'est-ce que tu as à jacasser comme ça?

yang [jæŋ] **N** yang *m*

Yank [jæŋk] *Fam* **N 1** *Am (inhabitant of New England)* habitant(e) *m,f* de la Nouvelle Angleterre ; *(native of New England)* originaire *mf* de Nouvelle Angleterre; *(inhabitant of Northern US)* habitant(e) *m,f* du Nord (des États-Unis); *(native of Northern US)* originaire *mf* du Nord (des États-Unis) **2** *Br Pej* Yankee *mf*, Amerloque *mf*

ADJ 1 *Am* yankee **2** *Br Pej* yankee, amerloque

yank [jæŋk] **VT** *(hair, sleeve)* tirer brusquement (sur), tirer d'un coup sec; **he was yanked to his feet** on l'a tiré brutalement pour l'obliger à se lever; **I yanked the lever back** j'ai tiré le levier en arrière d'un coup sec

N coup *m* sec; **I gave the wire/her hair a y.** j'ai tiré d'un coup sec sur le fil/sur ses cheveux

Yankee [ˈjæŋkɪ] = **Yank**

yap [jæp] *(pt & pp* **yapped**, *cont* **yapping***)* **VI 1** *(dog)* japper **2** *Fam Fig (person)* jacasser; **she's always yapping away** elle n'arrête pas de jacasser

N 1 *(yelp)* jappement *m* **2** *Fam (mouth)* clapet *m*, gueule *f*; **shut your y.!** ferme ton clapet!, la ferme! **3** *Am Fam (idiot)* andouille *f*, truffe *f*

yapping [ˈjæpɪŋ] **ADJ** *(dog)* jappeur

N *(UNCOUNT)* **1** *(of dog)* jappement *m*; **I wish that dog would stop its y.!** si ce chien pouvait arrêter ses jappements! **2** *Fam Fig (of person)* jacasseries *fpl*

yappy [ˈjæpɪ] *(compar* **yappier**, *superl* **yappiest***)* **ADJ 1** *(dog)* jappeur **2** *Fam (person)* jacasseur

yard [jɑːd] **N 1** *(of factory, farm, house, school)* cour *f*

2 *(work site)* chantier *m*; **builder's y.** chantier *m* de construction; *Naut* **repair y.** chantier *m* de radoub

3 *(for storage)* dépôt *m*

4 *(for animals* ► *enclosure)* enclos *m*; *(*► *pasture)* pâturage *m*

5 *Br Fam* **the Y.** Scotland Yard

6 *Am (garden)* jardin *m*

7 *(unit of measurement)* = 0,914m, yard *m*; *(in Canada)* verge *f*; **square y.** = 0,836m^2, yard *m* carré; **it was about ten yards away** c'était à environ dix mètres; **it was ten yards wide** il avait dix mètres de large; **to buy cloth by the y.** acheter le tissu au mètre; *Fig* **we still have yards of green velvet** nous avons toujours des quantités de velours vert; *Fig* **his calculations were yards out** il s'était complètement trompé dans ses calculs; **his face was a y. long** il en faisait une tête, il faisait une tête d'enterrement

8 *Old-fashioned Sport* **the 100 yards, the 100 yards' dash** le cent mètres

►► ***yard of ale*** *(container)* = long récipient à bière d'une contenance d'environ un litre et demi; *Am* ***yard sale*** vide-grenier *m*; ***yard work*** jardinage *m*

yardage [ˈjɑːdɪdʒ] **N** *Tex* ≃ métrage *m*

yardarm [ˈjɑːdɑːm] **N** extrémité *f* d'une vergue carrée; *Fam Hum* **the sun's over the y.** c'est l'heure de l'apéro

Yardie [ˈjɑːdɪ] **N** truand *m* d'origine jamaïcaine

yardman [ˈjɑːdmæn] *(pl* **yardmen** [-mən]*)* **N** *Am* jardinier *m*

yardstick [ˈjɑːdstɪk] **N 1** *(instrument)* mètre *m (en bois ou en métal)* **2** *Fig* critère *m*, point *m* de référence; *Fig* **salary seems to be a y. for success** il semble que le salaire soit un critère de réussite

yarmulka, yarmulke [ˈjɑːməlkə] **N** *Rel* kippa *f*

yarn [jɑːn] **N 1** *(UNCOUNT) Tex* fil *m (à tricoter ou à tisser)* **2** *(tall story)* histoire *f* à dormir debout; *(long story)* longue histoire *f*

VI *(tell tall stories)* raconter des histoires; *(tell long stories)* raconter de longues histoires

yarrow [ˈjærəʊ] **N** *Bot* mille-feuille *f*, achillée *f*

yashmak [ˈjæʃmæk] **N** litham *m*, litsam *m*

yaw [jɔː] **VI 1** *(ship)* être déporté, faire une embardée **2** *(plane, missile)* faire un mouvement de lacet

N 1 *(of ship)* écart *m*, embardée *f* **2** *(of plane, missile)* mouvement *m* de lacet

yawl [jɔːl] **N 1** *(sailing boat)* yawl *m*; *(fishing boat)* yole *f* **2** *(carried on ship)* chaloupe *f*

yawn [jɔːn] **VI 1** *(person)* bâiller **2** *(chasm, opening)* être béant, s'ouvrir; **the gulf yawned at his feet** le gouffre s'ouvrait *ou* béait à ses pieds

VT *(utter with yawn)* dire en bâillant; *Fam* **she was yawning her head off** elle bâillait à se décrocher la mâchoire

N 1 *(of person)* bâillement *m*; **to give a big y.** bâiller (bruyamment) la bouche grande ouverte **2** *Fam Fig* **to be a y.** *(meeting)* être ennuyeux à mourir; *(film, book)* être rasoir; **what a y.!** qu'est-ce que c'est rasoir!

yawning [ˈjɔːnɪŋ] **ADJ 1** *(person)* qui bâille **2** *(gap, chasm)* béant

N *(UNCOUNT)* bâillement *m*, bâillements *mpl*

yaws [jɔːz] **N** *(UNCOUNT) Med* pian *m*

y-axis **N** *Math* axe *m* des Y *ou* des ordonnées

yd *(written abbr* **yard***)* yd

ye [jiː] **PRON** *Arch or Bible* vous; **ye who weep** vous qui versez des larmes

DEF ART *Arch* **ye olde inne** la vieille hostellerie

yea [jeɪ] **ADV 1** *(yes)* oui; **you know you can say y. or nay to the plan** vous savez bien que vous avez la faculté d'accepter ou de refuser ce projet **2** *Arch or Literary (indeed)* voire, vraiment

N *(in vote)* oui *m*; **the yeas and nays** les oui et les non, les voix pour et contre

yeah [jeə] *Fam* ADV *(yes)* ouais; *Ironic* **y., right!** oui, c'est ça!

year [jɪə(r)] N **1** *(period of time)* an *m*, année *f*; **this y.** cette année; **last y.** l'an dernier, l'année dernière; **next y.** l'année prochaine; **the y. after next** dans deux ans; **y. by y.** d'année en année; **y. after y.** année après année; **all (the) y. round** (pendant) toute l'année; **y. in y. out** année après année; **it was five years last Christmas** ça a fait cinq ans à Noël; **we'll have been here five years next Christmas** cela fera cinq ans à Noël que nous sommes là; **after ten years in politics** après dix ans passés dans la politique; **he spent many years working for the same company** il a passé de nombreuses années dans la même société; **in a few years, in a few years' time** dans quelques années; **in ten years, in ten years' time** dans dix ans; **in years to come** dans les années à venir; **in all my years as a social worker** au cours de toutes mes années d'assistante sociale; **I haven't seen her for years** je ne l'ai pas vue depuis des années; **for a few years** pendant quelques années; **I haven't been home for two long years** cela fait deux longues années que je ne suis pas rentré chez moi; **for years and years** pendant des années; **she'll be busy writing her memoirs for years** elle en a pour des années de travail à écrire ses mémoires; **two years ago** il y a deux ans; **that was many years ago** cela remonte à bien des années; **the batteries last (for) years** les piles durent des années; **it took me years to build up the collection** cela m'a demandé des années pour *ou* j'ai mis des années à rassembler cette collection; **he earns over £40,000 a y.** il gagne plus de 40 000 livres par an; **it cost me a y.'s salary** cela m'a coûté un an de salaire

2 *(in calendar)* an *m*, année *f*; **in the y. 1607** en (l'an) 1607; *Br* **since the y. dot**, *Am* **since y. one** depuis une éternité, de tout temps; *Fin* **the y. under review** l'exercice écoulé; *Fin* **y. ended 31 December 2005** exercice clos le 31 décembre 2005

3 *(in age)* **he is 15 years old** *or* **of age** il a 15 ans; **the foundations are 4,000 years old** les fondations sont vieilles de 4000 ans; **a man of 80 years** un homme (âgé) de 80 ans; **a man of your years** un homme de votre âge; **she died in her fiftieth y.** elle est morte dans sa cinquantième année; **she's young for her years** elle fait jeune pour son âge, elle ne fait pas son âge; **to be old for one's years** *(of child)* être précoce; *(of adult)* faire plus vieux que son âge; **I'm getting on in years** je prends de l'âge; **the experience put years on/took years off her** l'expérience l'a beaucoup vieillie/rajeunie; **that dress takes years off her** cette robe la fait paraître des années plus jeune *ou* la rajeunit beaucoup; **smoking can take years off your life** fumer peut raccourcir la durée de votre vie

4 *Br (as student)* année *f*; **he's in the first y.** *(at school)* ≃ il est en sixième; *(at university)* il est en première année; **first-y. students** les étudiants de première année; **all the third y.** *(at school)* tous les élèves de quatrième; *(at university)* tous les étudiants de troisième année; **he was in my y.** *(at school)* il était dans ma classe; *(at university)* il est de ma promotion; **she was in the y. above/below me** elle était dans la classe au-dessus/en dessous de la mienne

5 *(for wine, coin)* année *f*; **1965 was a good y.** 1965 fut une bonne année *ou* un bon millésime

►► *Fin* ***year of assessment*** année *f* d'imposition; *Fin* ***year end*** fin *f* d'exercice

> When translating the word **year**, note that the French words **an** and **année** are not interchangeable. **Année** is used when the emphasis is on duration, while in cases where it is preceded by a number, **year** is usually translated by **an**.

yearbook [ˈjɪəbʊk] N annuaire *m*, recueil *m* annuel

year-end ADJ *Acct* de fin d'année, de fin d'exercice

N **at the y.** à la fin de l'année, en fin d'année

►► ***year-end accounts*** compte *m* de résultats; ***year-end audit*** vérification *f* comptable de fin d'exercice; ***year-end closing of accounts*** clôture *f* annuelle des livres; ***year-end loss*** perte *f* de fin d'exercice; ***year-end profits*** bénéfices *mpl* de fin d'exercice; ***year-end report*** rapport *m* annuel

yearling [ˈjɪəlɪŋ] N *Zool* petit *m* d'un an; *Horse-riding* yearling *m*

ADJ *Zool* (âgé) d'un an

yearlong [jɪəˈlɒŋ] ADJ de toute une année; **a y. drought** une sécheresse qui a duré toute une année

yearly [ˈjɪəlɪ] *(pl* **yearlies***)* ADJ annuel

ADV annuellement

N *Press* publication *f* annuelle

yearn [jɜːn] VI **to y. for** *(freedom, peace)* aspirer à; *(child, somebody's company)* désirer ardemment; **she yearned for love** *or* **to be loved** elle aspirait à l'amour, elle avait très envie d'être aimée; **she yearned for home** elle avait la nostalgie du pays; **to y. to do sth** brûler de faire qch; **he was yearning to see her again** il brûlait de la revoir

yearning [ˈjɜːnɪŋ] N *(longing)* désir *m* ardent; *(pining)* nostalgie *f*; **he feels a constant y. to see his old friends** *or* **for his old friends** il n'aspire qu'à une chose, revoir ses vieux amis; **I felt a sudden y. for company** j'ai eu un soudain désir *ou* besoin de compagnie

yearningly [ˈjɜːnɪŋlɪ] ADV *(longingly)* avec désir, avec envie; *(piningly)* avec nostalgie

year-on-year, year-over-year ADJ *(growth, decline)* sur un an

ADV *(grow, decline)* sur un an

year-round ADJ *(activity)* qui dure toute l'année, sur toute l'année; *(facility)* qui fonctionne toute l'année

yeast [jiːst] N levure *f*

VI mousser

►► *Culin* ***yeast extract*** extrait *m* de levure; *Med* ***yeast infection*** *(vaginal thrush)* mycose *f* vaginale

yeasty [ˈjiːstɪ] *(compar* **yeastier**, *superl* **yeastiest***)* ADJ **1** *(in taste)* qui a un goût de levure; *(in smell)* à l'odeur de levure **2** *(frothy)* écumeux, qui mousse

yell [jel] VI hurler; **to y. at sb** hurler après qn; **to y. about sth** brailler au sujet de qch; **to y. with pain/with laughter** hurler de douleur/de rire; **to y. at the top of one's voice** crier à tue-tête; **if you need me, just y.** si vous avez besoin de moi, vous n'avez qu'à crier

VT *(shout out)* hurler; *(proclaim)* clamer, crier; *Fam* **he was yelling his head off** il beuglait comme un veau

N **1** *(shout)* hurlement *m* **2** *Am (from students, supporters)* cri *m* de ralliement

yelling [ˈjelɪŋ] N *(UNCOUNT)* hurlements *mpl*; **stop that y.!** cesse de hurler comme ça!

yellow [ˈjeləʊ] ADJ **1** *(in colour)* jaune; **the papers had gone** *or* **turned y. with age** les papiers avaient jauni avec le temps **2** *Fam (cowardly)* lâche[□], trouillard; **you're y.!** tu n'es qu'un trouillard *ou* qu'un lâche!; **we all have a y. streak** on est tous un peu lâches; **to turn** *or* **to go y.** se dégonfler

N **1** *(colour)* jaune *m* **2** *(yolk)* jaune *m* (d'œuf)

VI jaunir; **to y. with age** jaunir avec le temps

VT jaunir; **newspapers yellowed with age** des journaux jaunis par le temps

►► ***yellow card*** *(in football, rugby)* carton *m* jaune, *Belg* carte *f* jaune; ***yellow fever*** fièvre *f* jaune; *Am* ***yellow jacket*** guêpe *f*; *Cycling* ***yellow jersey*** *(in Tour de France)* maillot *m* jaune; *Am* ***yellow light*** feu *m* orange; ***yellow line*** bande *f* jaune; **to park on a y. line** ≃ se mettre en stationnement irrégulier; **double y. line** *or* **y. lines** double ligne *f* jaune; ***yellow metal*** *(brass)* cuivre *m* jaune, laiton *m*; *(gold)* métal *m* jaune, or *m*; ***yellow ochre*** ocre *f* jaune; ***Yellow Pages®*** les Pages *fpl* Jaunes®

> **YELLOW LINES**
>
> En Grande-Bretagne, une ligne jaune parallèle au trottoir signifie "arrêt autorisé réglementé"; une double ligne jaune signifie "stationnement interdit".

yellow-bellied [-ˈbelɪd] ADJ *Fam* trouillard

yellow-belly *(pl* **yellow-bellies***)* N *Fam* trouillard(e) *m,f*

yellowhammer [ˈjeləʊˌhæmə(r)] N *Orn* **1** *(European bunting)* bruant *m* jaune **2** *Am (American woodpecker)* colapte *m* doré

yellowish [ˈjeləʊɪʃ] ADJ jaunâtre, qui tire sur le jaune

yellowness [ˈjeləʊnɪs] N **1** *(colour)* couleur *f* jaune; *(of person, complexion)* teint *m* jaune **2** *Fam (cowardice)* lâcheté[□] *f*, poltronnerie *f*

yelp [jelp] VI *(dog)* japper, glapir; *(person)* crier, glapir; **to y. in** *or* **with pain** *(dog)* glapir de douleur; *(person)* crier de douleur

N *(of dog)* jappement *m*, glapissement *m*; *(of person)* cri *m*, glapissement *m*

yelping [ˈjelpɪŋ] N *(of dog)* jappements *mpl*, glapissements *mpl*; *(of person)* cris *mpl*, glapissements *mpl*

Yemen [ˈjemən] N Yémen *m*

Yemeni [ˈjemənɪ], **Yemenite** [ˈjemənaɪt] N Yéménite *mf*

ADJ yéménite

COMP *(embassy, history)* du Yemen

yen [jen] *(pl sense* **1** inv*)* N **1** *(currency)* yen *m* **2** *Fam (desire)* envie *f*; **to have a y. for sth/to do sth** avoir très envie de *ou* mourir d'envie de qch/faire qch

yeoman [ˈjəʊmən] *(pl* **yeomen** [-mən]*)* N **1** *Hist (small freeholder)* franc-tenancier *m*; *Fig* **to do y. service** rendre des services inestimables **2** *Br Mil & Hist* soldat *m* du "yeomanry"; **Y. of the Guard** yeoman *m* de la garde

yeomanry [ˈjəʊmənrɪ] N *(UNCOUNT)* **1** *Hist (small freeholders)* francs-tenanciers *mpl* **2** *Br Mil & Hist* = corps de cavalerie composé de volontaires

yep [jep] EXCLAM *Fam* ouais!

yer [jə(r)] *Fam* = **your**

yes [jes] ADV **1** *(gen)* oui; *(in answer to negatives)* si; *(answering phone)* allô, oui; *(encouraging a speaker to continue)* oui, et puis?, oui, et alors?; **to say/to vote y.** dire/voter oui; **is it raining? – y. (it is)** est-ce qu'il pleut? – oui; **will you tell her? – y. (I will)** le lui direz-vous? – oui (je vais le faire); **are you hungry? – y. (I am)** avez-vous faim?– oui; **y.? what do you want?** oui? que voulez-vous?; **did they enjoy the cruise? – oh, y.!** ont-ils aimé leur croisière? – oh, oui!; **oh y.?** *(doubtful)* c'est vrai?; **you don't like me, do you? – y. I do!** vous ne m'aimez pas, n'est-ce pas? – mais si (voyons)!; **y. please** oui, s'il vous plaît; **y. of course, y. certainly** oui, bien sûr

2 *(introducing a contrary opinion)* **y. but…** oui *ou* d'accord mais…

3 *(in response to command or call)* oui; **y., sir** oui *ou* bien, monsieur; **James! – y.?** James! – oui?

4 *(indeed)* en effet, vraiment; **she was rash, y., terribly rash** elle a été imprudente, vraiment très imprudente

N *(person, vote)* **there are ten yeses and sixteen noes** il y a dix oui et seize non

• **yes and no** ADV oui et non; **do you like him? – well, y. and no** vous l'aimez bien?– ben, oui et non

►► ***yes vote*** vote *m* pour; **to give a y. vote** voter pour

yes-man N *Fam* béni-oui-oui *m inv*

yesterday [ˈjestədeɪ] ADV **1** *(the day before today)* hier; **he came y.** il est venu hier; **y. morning/afternoon** hier matin/après-midi; **a week y., a week ago y.**, *Br* **y. week** il y a huit jours; **I wasn't born y.** je ne suis pas né de la dernière pluie **2** *(in the past)* hier, naguère

N **1** *(day before)* hier *m*; **y. was Monday** hier c'était lundi; **y.'s programme** l'émission d'hier; **the day before y.** avant-hier; **it seems like (only) y.** c'est comme si c'était hier **2** *(former times)* temps *mpl* passés *ou* anciens; **y.'s fashions** la mode d'hier *ou* d'autrefois; *Pej* **y.'s men** les hommes qui appartiennent au passé; **all our yesterdays** tout notre passé

yesteryear [ˈjestəjɪə(r)] N *Formal or Literary* temps *m* jadis; **the heroes of y.** les héros d'antan

yet [jet] ADV **1** *(up to now)* déjà; **is he here y.?** est-il déjà là?; **have you been to London y.?** êtes-vous déjà allés à Londres?; *Am* **did you go to the zoo y.?** êtes-vous déjà allés au zoo?; **not as y.** pas encore; **as y. unexplored jungle** jungle pas encore explorée

2 *(at the present time)* **not y.** pas encore; **not just y.** pas tout de suite; **she isn't here y.** elle n'est pas encore là; **I haven't finished y.** je n'ai pas encore fini; **it isn't time for a break y.** il n'est pas encore l'heure de faire une pause

3 *(in affirmative statements) (still)* encore, toujours; **I have y. to meet her** je ne l'ai pas encore rencontrée; **the best is y. to come** le meilleur est encore à venir *ou* reste à venir; **there are another ten miles to go y.** il reste encore une quinzaine de kilomètres; **I won't be ready for another hour y.** j'en ai encore pour une heure; **they won't be here for another hour y.** ils ne seront pas là avant une heure; **they may y. be found** on peut encore les retrouver, il se peut encore qu'on les retrouve

4 *(with comparatives and superlatives) (even)* encore, même; **y. more expensive** encore plus cher; **y. more snow was expected** on prévoyait encore de la neige; **y. higher interest rates** des taux d'intérêt encore plus élevés; **a life of parties and y. more parties** une existence qui consiste à aller de fête en fête; *Literary* **he is not handsome, nor y. well-dressed** il n'est pas beau, ni même bien habillé

5 *(emphasizing amount, frequency etc)* **y. another bomb** encore une bombe; **y. again** encore une fois

6 *(so far ▸ in present)* jusqu'ici, jusque-là; *(▸ in past)* jusque-là; **it's her best play y.** c'est sa meilleure pièce

7 *(despite everything)* après tout, quand même; **she may y. surprise you all** elle va peut-être vous surprendre tous après tout; **I shall catch him y.!** je finirai bien par l'attraper!

CONJ *(nevertheless)* néanmoins, toutefois; *(however)* cependant, pourtant; *(but)* mais; **they had no income y. they still had to pay taxes** ils n'avaient pas de revenus et pourtant ils devaient payer des impôts; **he was firm y. kind** il était sévère mais juste

yeti ['jetɪ] **N** yéti *m*

yew [juː] **N 1** *(tree)* if *m* **2** *(wood)* (bois d')if *m*

▸▸ ***yew tree*** if *m*

Y-fronts® **NPL** slip *m* kangourou

YHA [ˌwaɪeɪtʃ'eɪ] **N** *Br* (*abbr* **Youth Hostels Association**) = fédération unie des auberges de jeunesse

yid, Yid [jɪd] **N** *very Fam* youpin(e) *m,f*, = terme antisémite désignant un juif

Yiddish ['jɪdɪʃ] **N** yiddish *m*

ADJ yiddish

yield [jiːld] **VI 1** *(person ▸ give in)* céder; *(▸ surrender)* se rendre; **he refused to y.** il a refusé de céder *ou* de se laisser fléchir; **to y. to** *(argument)* céder *ou* s'incliner devant; *(criticism, force)* céder devant; *(blackmail, demand)* céder à; *(pressure, threat)* céder sous; *(desire, temptation)* succomber à, céder à; **to y. to reason** se rendre à la raison; **I had to y. to them on that point** j'ai dû leur céder sur ce point; **the city yielded after a month-long siege** la ville a capitulé après un mois de siège; **the countryside has had to y. to suburbia** la campagne a dû reculer au profit de la banlieue

2 *(break, bend ▸ under weight, force)* céder, fléchir; **the ice yielded under his weight** la glace céda sous son poids; **the window catch eventually yielded** le loqueteau de la fenêtre a fini par céder

3 *Am Aut* céder le passage *ou* la priorité; **y.** *(sign)* cédez le passage; **y. to pedestrians** *(sign)* priorité aux piétons

4 *Agr (field)* rapporter, rendre; *(crop)* rapporter

VT 1 *(produce, bring in ▸ gen)* produire, rapporter; *(▸ crops)* produire, rapporter, donner; *(▸ results)* donner; *Fin (▸ dividend, interest)* rapporter; *(▸ income)* créer; **the orchard yielded plentiful amounts of fruit** le verger a produit *ou* a donné des fruits à profusion; **to y. a profit** rapporter *ou* dégager un bénéfice; **the investment bond will y. 11 percent** le bon d'épargne rapportera 11 pour cent; **their research has yielded some interesting results** leur recherche a fourni *ou* a donné quelques résultats intéressants

2 *(relinquish, give up)* céder, abandonner; *Mil & Fig* **to y. ground** céder du terrain; **he was forced to y. control of the party** il a dû céder le contrôle du parti; **to y. a point to sb** céder à qn sur un point, concéder un point à qn

3 *Am Aut* **to y. right of way** céder la priorité

N 1 *Agr & Ind (output)* rendement *m*, rapport *m*; *(of wheat, fruit)* récolte *f*; *(of crops)* rendement *m*; **high-y. crops** récoltes *fpl* à rendement élevé; **y. per acre** ≃ rendement *m* à l'hectare **2** *Fin (from investments)* rapport *m*, rendement *m*; *(profit)* bénéfice *m*, bénéfices *mpl*; *(from tax)* recette *f*, rapport *m*; **an 8 percent y. on investments** des investissements qui rapportent 8 pour cent

▸▸ *Fin* ***yield capacity*** productivité *f*; *Fin* ***yield gap*** prime *f* de risque; *Am* ***yield sign*** panneau *m* de priorité

yielding ['jiːldɪŋ] **ADJ 1** *(soft ▸ ground)* mou (molle); *(material, metal)* flexible, extensible **2** *(person)* complaisant, accommodant; *(character)* docile

N *(of town)* reddition *f*; *(of rights, control)* cession *f*

yikes [jaɪks] **EXCLAM** *Fam* mince!

yin [jɪn] **N y. and yang** le yin et le yang

yippee [*Br* jɪ'piː, *Am* 'jɪpɪ] **EXCLAM** *Fam* hourra!

Y-junction **N** fourche *f*

YMCA [ˌwaɪemˌsiː'eɪ] **N** (*abbr* **Young Men's Christian Association**) = association chrétienne de jeunes gens (surtout connue pour ses centres d'hébergement)

yo [jəʊ] **EXCLAM** *esp Am Fam* salut!

yob [jɒb] **N** *Br Fam Pej* voyou m, loubard *m*; **the y. culture that prevails in this country today** l'agressivité et l'anti-intellectualisme qui règnent aujourd'hui dans notre pays

yobbish ['jɒbɪʃ] **ADJ** *Br Fam* de voyou, de loubard; **it makes you look y.** ça te donne l'air d'un voyou *ou* d'un loubard; **don't be so y.** arrête de jouer les voyous *ou* les loubards

yobbo ['jɒbəʊ] (*pl* **yobbos**) = **yob**

yodel ['jəʊdəl] (*Br pt & pp* **yodelled**, *cont* **yodelling**, *Am pt & pp* **yodeled**, *cont* **yodeling**) **VI** jodler, iodler

yodeller, yodler, *Am* **yodeler** ['jəʊdələ(r)] **N** jodleur(euse) *m,f*, iodleur(euse) *m,f*

yoga ['jəʊgə] **N** yoga *m*; **to do y.** faire du yoga

COMP *(class, teacher)* de yoga

▸▸ ***yoga mat*** tapis *m* de yoga

yoghourt, yoghurt [*Br* 'jɒgət, *Am* 'jəʊgərt] **N** yaourt *m*, yogourt *m*, yoghourt *m*

yogi ['jəʊgɪ] **N** yogi *m*

yogurt = **yoghourt**

yoke [jəʊk] **N 1** *(frame ▸ for hitching oxen)* joug *m*; *(▸ for carrying buckets)* joug *m*, palanche *f*

2 *Fig (burden, domination)* joug *m*; **a country struggling to cast off the y. of foreign domination** un pays qui lutte pour briser le joug de la domination étrangère

3 *(pair of animals)* attelage *m*, paire *f*

4 *(of dress, skirt, blouse)* empiècement *m*

5 *Literary* **the y. of marriage** les liens *mpl* du mariage

VT 1 *(oxen)* atteler; **to y. (up) oxen/bullocks to a plough** atteler des bouvillons/des bœufs à une charrue **2** *(ideas, qualities)* lier, joindre

yokel ['jəʊkəl] **N** *Pej* péquenot *m*

yolk [jəʊk] **N 1 (egg)** y. jaune *m* (d'œuf) **2** *Biol* vitellus *m*

▸▸ ***yolk bag, yolk sac*** sac *m* vitellin, vésicule *f* vitelline

Yom Kippur [jɒm'kɪpʊə(r)] **N** *Rel* Yom Kippour *m inv*

yomp [jɒmp] **VI** *Br Fam Mil slang* crapahuter

yon [jɒn] **ADJ** *Scot & NEng or Arch* ce …-là; **y. tree** cet arbre-là, l'arbre là-bas

yonder ['jɒndə(r)] *Literary* **ADJ y. tree** l'arbre là-bas

ADV là-bas; **way over y.** loin là-bas

yonks [jɒŋks] **N** *Br Fam* **I haven't been there for y.** il y a une paie *ou* ça fait un bail que je n'y suis pas allé

yore [jɔː(r)] **N** *Arch or Literary* **in days of y.** au temps jadis

Yorks. *(written abbr* **Yorkshire)** Yorkshire *m*

Yorkshire ['jɔːkʃə(r)] **N** le Yorkshire

▸▸ ***the Yorkshire Moors*** les Landes *fpl* du Yorkshire; ***Yorkshire pudding*** = crêpe épaisse salée traditionnellement servie avec du rôti de bœuf; ***Yorkshire terrier*** yorkshire-terrier *m*, yorkshire *m*

Yoruba ['jɒrʊbə] **N 1** *(person)* Yoruba *mf*, Yorouba *mf* **2** *Ling* yoruba *m*, yorouba *m*

ADJ yoruba, yorouba

you [juː] **PRON 1** *(as plural subject)* vous; *(as singular subject ▸ polite use)* vous; *(▸ familiar use)* tu; *(as plural object)* vous; *(as singular object ▸ polite use)* vous; *(▸ familiar use)* te; **y. didn't ask** vous n'avez pas/tu n'as pas demandé; **don't y. dare!** je te le déconseille!; **y. and I will go together** vous et moi/toi et moi irons ensemble; **would y. like a drink?** voulez-vous boire/veux-tu boire quelque chose?; **y. and yours** vous et les vôtres/toi et les tiens; **y. there!** vous là-bas/toi là-bas!; **did he see y.?** est-ce qu'il vous a vu/t'a vu?; **I'll get y. some dinner** je vais vous/te préparer à manger; **she gave y. the keys** elle vous a donné/elle t'a donné les clés

2 *(after preposition)* vous; *(familiar use)* toi; **all of y.** vous tous; **with y.** avec vous/toi; **for y.** pour vous/toi; **that's men for y.** ah! les hommes!; **she gave the keys to y.** elle vous a donné/elle t'a donné les clés; **between y. and me** entre nous; **now there's a typical politician for y.** voilà un politicien type; **now there's manners for y.!** ça au moins, c'est quelqu'un de bien élevé/ce sont des gens bien élevés!; *Ironic* en voilà des manières!

3 *(before noun or adjective) very Fam* **y. idiot!** espèce d'idiot!; **y. sweetie!** oh, le mignon/la mignonne!; **y. Americans are all the same** vous les Américains *ou* vous autres Américains, vous êtes tous pareils

4 *(emphatic use)* vous; *(familiar form)* toi; **y. mean they chose y.** tu veux dire qu'ils t'ont choisi toi; **y. wouldn't do that, would y.?** vous ne feriez pas cela/tu ne ferais pas cela, n'est-ce pas?; **silly/lucky (old) y.!** quel gros bêta/veinard tu fais!; *Fam* **that jacket/job wasn't y.** cette veste/ce travail n'était pas ton style; **just y. try!** essaye un peu pour voir!

5 *(impersonal use)* **y. never know** on ne sait jamais; **a hot bath does y. a world of good** un bon bain chaud vous fait un bien immense

you-all [jɔːl] **PRON** *Am Fam (in southern states)* vous (tous)

you'd [juːd] **1** = **you had 2** = **you would**

you-know-who **N** *Fam Euph* qui tu sais/qui vous savez

you'll [juːl] = **you will**

young [jʌŋ] *(compar* **younger** ['jʌŋgə(r)], *superl* **youngest** ['jʌŋgɪst]) **ADJ 1** *(in age, style, ideas ▸ person, clothes)* jeune; **the y. men and women of today** les jeunes gens et les jeunes femmes d'aujourd'hui; **a y. woman** une jeune femme; **y. people** les jeunes *mpl*, la jeunesse *f*; **families with y. children** les familles qui ont des enfants en bas âge; **the younger generation** la jeune génération; **my younger brother** mon frère cadet, mon petit frère; **I'm ten years younger than she is** j'ai dix ans de moins qu'elle; **I'm not as y. as I was!** je n'ai plus (mes) vingt ans!; **he is y. for such responsibility** il est bien jeune pour de telles responsabilités; **you're only y. once!** la jeunesse ne dure qu'un temps!; **in my younger days** dans ma jeunesse, quand j'étais jeune; *Br* **how is y. Christopher?** comment va le jeune Christopher?; **the y. Mr Ford, Mr Ford the younger** le jeune M. Ford, M. Ford fils; **now listen here y. man!** écoutez-moi bien, jeune homme!; *Old-fashioned* **her y. man** son petit ami, son amoureux; *Old-fashioned* **his y. lady** sa petite amie, son amoureuse; **she's quite a y. lady now** c'est une vraie jeune fille maintenant; **what do you have to say for yourself, y. lady?** qu'avez-vous à dire, mademoiselle?

2 *(youthful)* jeune; **he is y. for 45** il fait jeune pour 45 ans; **she is a y. 45** elle a 45 ans, mais elle ne les fait pas; **he's y. for his age** il est jeune pour son âge, il ne fait pas son âge; **to be y. at heart** avoir la jeunesse du cœur

3 *(recent ▸ grass, plant)* nouveau(elle); *(▸ wine)* jeune, vert; **a y. country/company** un pays/une société de création récente

NPL 1 *(people)* **the y.** les jeunes (gens) *mpl*, la jeunesse; **suitable for y. and old alike** pour les jeunes et les moins jeunes

2 *(of animal)* petits *mpl*; **a lioness and her y.** une lionne et ses petits; **to be with y.** *(animal)* être pleine *ou* grosse

▸▸ ***young blood*** *(new attitudes, ideas, people)* sang *m* nouveau *ou* neuf; *Br Pol* ***Young Conservatives*** jeunes conservateurs *mpl*; *Br* ***young offender*** jeune délinquant(e) *m,f*; *Br* ***Young Offenders' Institution*** = centre de détention pour mineurs

youngish [ˈjʌŋɪʃ] **ADJ** plutôt jeune

youngster [ˈjʌŋstə(r)] **N** *(young person)* jeune *mf*

your [jɔː(r)] **ADJ 1** *(with singular possession* ▸ *familiar use)* ton (ta); *(*▸ *plural and polite use)* votre; *(with plural possession* ▸ *familiar use)* tes; *(*▸ *plural and polite use)* vos; **y. book** votre/ton livre; **y. car** votre/ta voiture; **y. books** vos/tes livres; **y. father and mother** votre père et votre mère/ton père et ta mère; **I object to y. visiting the children** je m'oppose à ce que tu rendes visite aux enfants

2 *(with parts of body, clothes)* **don't put y. hands in y. pockets** ne mets pas tes mains dans les poches; **why are you scratching y. head?** pourquoi est-ce que tu te grattes la tête?; **hold on to y. hat!** tenez-bien votre chapeau!; **I think you've broken y. finger** je crois que vous vous êtes cassé le doigt; **does y. wrist hurt?** est-ce que tu as mal au poignet?

3 *(emphatic form)* **is this y. book or his?** est-ce que c'est votre livre ou le sien?; **oh it's YOUR book, is it?** ah, c'est à toi ce livre!; **that's YOUR problem** c'est TON problème

4 *(impersonal use)* **if you don't stand up for y. rights, no one else will** si vous ne défendez pas vos droits vous-même, personne ne le fera à votre place; **swimming is good for y. heart and lungs** la natation est un bon exercice pour le cœur et les poumons; **where are y. Churchills and y. De Gaulles when you need them?** où sont vos Churchill et vos De Gaulle quand vous avez besoin d'eux?; **it's not a film for y. average cinema goer** ce n'est pas un film pour n'importe quel public; **I like y. London buses** j'aime bien les bus que vous avez à Londres

5 *(in titles)* **Y. Highness** Votre Majesté *(à un roi, une reine, un prince ou une princesse)*; **Y. Holiness** Très Saint Père; **Y. Honour** Votre Honneur; **Y. Majesty** Votre Majesté *(à un roi ou une reine uniquement)*

you're [jɔː(r)] = **you are**

yours [jɔːz] **PRON 1** *(replacing singular possession* ▸ *familiar use)* le tien (la tienne) *m,f*; *(*▸ *plural and polite use)* le vôtre (la vôtre) *m,f*; *(replacing plural possession* ▸ *familiar use)* les tiens (les tiennes) *mpl, fpl*; *(*▸ *plural and polite use)* les vôtres *mfpl*; **is this book y.?** est-ce que ce livre est à vous/toi?; **is this car y.?** c'est votre/ta voiture?; **are these books y.?** ces livres sont-ils à vous/toi?; **is he a friend of y.?** est-ce un de vos/tes amis?; **y. is an unenviable task** votre tâche est peu enviable; **can't you control that wretched dog of y.?** vous ne pouvez pas retenir votre satané chien?; **the bathroom's all y.** la salle de bains est libre maintenant; **can I use your telephone? – it's all y.** est-ce que je peux utiliser ton téléphone? – vas-y

2 *(up to you)* **it is not y. to decide** ce n'est pas à vous *ou* il ne vous appartient pas de décider

3 *Fam (your house, flat)* chez vous/chez toi, votre/ta maison; **let's go to y.** allons chez vous/chez toi

4 *(in letter)* **y., Peter** ≃ bien à vous *ou* à bientôt, Peter; **y. sincerely, y. faithfully** *(in letters)* ≃ je vous prie d'agréer, Madame/Monsieur, l'expression de mes sentiments distingués

yourself [jɔːˈself] *(pl* **yourselves** [-ˈselvz]*)* **PRON 1** *(personally* ▸ *polite use)* vous-même; *(*▸ *familiar use)* toi-même; **do it y.** faites-le vous-même/fais-le toi-même; **do it yourselves** faites-le vous-mêmes; **you've kept the best seats for yourselves** vous avez gardé les meilleures places pour vous; **sort it out among yourselves** débrouillez-vous entre vous; **see for y.** tu n'as qu'à voir par toi-même; **tell us something about y.** parle-nous de toi/parlez-nous de vous; **did you come by y.?** vous êtes venu tout seul?/tu es venu tout seul?; **did you mend the fuse (by) y.?** vous avez remplacé le fusible tout seul?/tu as remplacé le fusible tout seul?; **did you make it y.?** l'avez-vous fait vous-même?/l'as-tu fait toi-même?; **you don't look** *or* **seem quite y.** vous n'avez pas l'air dans votre assiette/tu n'as pas l'air dans ton assiette; **just be y.** sois naturel/soyez naturel

2 *(reflexive use)* **did you hurt y.?** est-ce que vous vous êtes/tu t'es fait mal?; **did you enjoy y.?** est-ce que c'était bien?; **you were talking to y.** tu parlais tout seul/vous parliez tout seul; **speak for y.!** parle pour toi!; **just look at y.!** regarde-toi donc!

3 *(emphatic use)* **you told me y., you y. told me** vous me l'avez dit vous-même, c'est vous-même qui me l'avez dit/tu me l'as dit toi-même, c'est toi-même qui me l'as dit; **you must have known y. that they wouldn't accept** vous-même, vous auriez dû savoir qu'ils n'accepteraient pas/toi-même, tu aurais dû savoir qu'ils n'accepteraient pas

4 *(impersonal use)* **you have to know how to look after y. in the jungle** dans la jungle, il faut savoir se défendre tout seul *ou* se débrouiller soi-même; **you're supposed to help y.** on est censé se servir soi-même

youth [juːθ] *(pl* **youths** [juːðz]*)* **N 1** *(young age)* jeunesse *f*; **in my y.** dans ma jeunesse, quand j'étais jeune; **in his early y.** dans sa première jeunesse; **he is no longer in his first y.** il n'est plus de la première jeunessse **2** *(young man)* adolescent *m*, jeune *m*

NPL *(young people)* **the y. of today** les jeunes *mpl ou* la jeunesse d'aujourd'hui

COMP to go y. hostelling passer ses vacances en auberges de jeunesse

▸▸ *Br* ***youth club*** ≃ maison *f* des jeunes; ***youth culture*** culture *f* des jeunes; ***youth hostel*** auberge *f* de jeunesse; ***youth hosteller*** habitué(e) *m,f* des auberges de jeunesse; ***Youth Hostels Association*** association *f* des auberges de jeunesse; *Mktg* ***youth market*** marché *m* de la jeunesse; *Mktg* ***youth marketing*** marketing *m* de la classe des jeunes, marketing *m* des juniors; ***youth orchestra*** orchestre *m* de jeunes; ***youth worker*** éducateur(trice) *m,f*

youthful [ˈjuːθfʊl] **ADJ 1** *(young* ▸ *person)* jeune; *(*▸ *appearance)* d'allure jeune; **to look y.** avoir l'air jeune; **y. good looks** *(of men)* air *m* de jeune homme; **he is a y. 52** il est jeune pour ses 52 ans **2** *(typical of youth* ▸ *idea, error)* de jeunesse; *(*▸ *enthusiasm, humour, expectations, attitude)* juvénile

youthfulness [ˈjuːθfʊlnɪs] **N** *(of person)* jeunesse *f*; *(of appearance)* allure *f* jeune; *(of mind, ideas)* jeunesse *f*, fraîcheur *f*

you've [juːv] = **you have**

yowl [jaʊl] **VI** *(cat)* miauler (fort); *(dog, person)* hurler; **to y. in pain** *(cat)* miauler de douleur; *(dog, person)* hurler de douleur

N *(of cat)* miaulement *m* (déchirant); *(of dog, person)* hurlement *m*

yo-yo [ˈjəʊjəʊ] *(pl* **yo-yos***)* **N** *(toy)* Yo-Yo® *m inv*; *Fam* **he was jumping up and down like a y.** il sautait sur place comme s'il était monté sur un ressort; *Fam* **I've been up and down the stairs like a y. all day** je n'ai pas arrêté de monter et de descendre l'escalier toute la journée; **to y. diet** faire le régime yo-yo *ou* yoyo

VI *Fam* fluctuer

▸▸ ***yo-yo dieting*** régime *m* yo-yo *ou* yoyo

yr *(written abbr* **year***)* année *f*

YTS [ˌwaɪtiːˈes] **N** *Br (abbr* **Youth Training Scheme***)* *(programme)* = programme gouvernemental britannique d'insertion des jeunes dans la vie professionnelle; *(person)* = personne participant au programme "YTS"

yuan [juːˈɑːn] *(pl* **inv***)* **N** yuan *m*

yucca [ˈjʌkə] **N** yucca *m*

yuck [jʌk] **EXCLAM** *Fam* berk!, beurk!

yucky [ˈjʌkɪ] *(compar* **yuckier**, *superl* **yuckiest***)* **ADJ** *Fam* dégueulasse

Yugoslav [ˈjuːgəʊˌslɑːv] **N** Yougoslave *mf*

ADJ yougoslave

Yugoslavia [ˌjuːgəʊˈslɑːvɪə] **N** *Formerly* Yougoslavie *f*

Yugoslavian [ˌjuːgəʊˈslɑːvɪən] **N** Yougoslave *mf*

ADJ yougoslave

yuk = **yuck**

yule, Yule [juːl] **N** *Arch or Literary* Noël *m*

▸▸ ***yule log*** bûche *f* de Noël

yuletide, Yuletide [ˈjuːltaɪd] *Literary* **N** (époque *f* de) Noël *m*; **at y.** à Noël

COMP *(greetings, festivities)* de Noël

yum, [jʌm], **yummy** [ˈjʌmɪ] *(compar* **yummier**, *superl* **yummiest***)* *Fam* **ADJ** *(food)* succulent[□], délicieux[□]

EXCLAM miam-miam!

▸▸ *Br Fam* ***yummy mummy*** = femme, souvent très en vue, qui, tout en ayant des enfants, reste séduisante et branchée

yum-yum **EXCLAM** *Fam* miam-miam!

N *Br (cake)* chichi *m*

yup [jʌp] **ADV** *Am Fam* ouais

yuppie [ˈjʌpɪ] *(abbr* **young upwardly mobile professional***)* **N** yuppie *mf*, ≃ jeune cadre *m* dynamique

ADJ *(club)* pour jeunes cadres dynamiques; *(lifestyle, neighbourhood)* de yuppies

▸▸ ***yuppie flu*** encéphalomyélite *f* myalgique

yuppify [ˈjʌpɪfaɪ] *(pt & pp* **yuppified***)* **VT to become yuppified** s'embourgeoiser

YWCA [ˌwaɪdʌbəljuːˌsiːˈeɪ] **N** *(abbr* **Young Women's Christian Association***)* = association chrétienne de jeunes filles (surtout connue pour ses centres d'hébergement)

Z

Z, z [*Br* zed, *Am* ziː] **N** *(letter)* Z, z *m inv*; **two z's** deux z; **Z for zebra** ≃ Z comme Zoé; *Am Fam* **to get** *or* **score some z's** faire une petite somme

Zaïre [zɑːˈɪə(r)] **N** Zaïre *m*

Zaïrean [zɑːˈɪərɪən], **Zaïrese** [ˌzɑːɪəˈriːz] **N** Zaïrois(e) *m,f*
ADJ zaïrois

Zambesi, Zambezi [zæmˈbiːzɪ] **N** **the Z.** le Zambèze

Zambia [ˈzæmbɪə] **N** Zambie *f*

Zambian [ˈzæmbɪən] **N** Zambien(enne) *m,f*
ADJ zambien
COMP *(embassy)* de Zambie; *(history)* de la Zambie

zaniness [ˈzeɪnɪnɪs] **N** *Fam* loufoquerie *f*

zany [ˈzeɪnɪ] *(compar* **zanier**, *superl* **zaniest**, *pl* **zanies**) *Fam* **ADJ** farfelu, loufoque
N *Theat* bouffon *m*, zani *m*, zanni *m*

Zanzibar [ˌzænzɪˈbɑː(r)] **N** Zanzibar *m*

zap [zæp] *(pt & pp* **zapped**, *cont* **zapping**) *Fam* **VI 1** *(go quickly)* courir; **I'll z. over to see her** je file la voir, je vais faire un saut chez elle **2** *TV* zapper
VT 1 *(destroy by bombing ▸ town)* ravager, bombarder; *(▸ target)* atteindre
2 *(kill ▸ victim)* tuer, descendre; *(▸ in video game)* éliminer
3 *Comput (display, data)* effacer, supprimer; *(file)* écraser
4 *(send quickly)* **z. it in the microwave** passe-le vite fait au micro-ondes; **we'll z. it across to you by courier** on vous l'enverra *ou* expédiera vite fait par coursier
N *(energy)* pêche *f*, punch *m*
EXCLAM vlan!
▸ **zap up VT SEP** *Fam (make more exciting)* **to z. up one's style** rendre son style plus coloré *ou* plus vivant; **to z. up the colour scheme** *(in house etc)* rehausser les couleurs

zapped [zæpt] **ADJ** *Fam (exhausted)* crevé, claqué

zapper [ˈzæpə(r)] **N** *Fam (for TV)* télécommande *f*

zapping [ˈzæpɪŋ] **N** *(changing TV channels)* zapping *m*

zappy [ˈzæpɪ] *(compar* **zappier**, *superl* **zappiest**) **ADJ** *Br Fam* qui a la pêche, plein de punch; **a z. little car** une petite voiture nerveuse

ZBB [*Br* ˌzedbiːˈbiː, *Am* ˌziːbiːˈbiː] **N** *Fin (abbr* **zero-base budgeting**) BBZ *m*

Z-bed **N** *Br* lit *m* pliant

zeal [ziːl] **N** zèle *m*, ferveur *f*, ardeur *f*; **she undertook the work with great z.** elle a entrepris le travail avec beaucoup de zèle; **political/religious z.** ferveur *f* politique/religieuse

zealot [ˈzelət] **N** *(fanatic)* fanatique *mf*, zélateur (trice) *m,f*; **religious zealots** fanatiques *mpl* religieux

zealotry [ˈzelətrɪ] **N** fanatisme *m*

zealous [ˈzeləs] **ADJ** *(worker, partisan)* zélé, actif; *(opponent)* zélé, acharné; **she is z. in carrying out her duties** elle fait ce qu'elle a à faire avec beaucoup de zèle *ou* d'ardeur

zealously [ˈzeləslɪ] **ADV** avec zèle *ou* ardeur

zebra [*Br* ˈzebrə, *Am* ˈziːbrə] *(pl* **inv** *or* **zebras**) **N** zèbre *m*
▸▸ *Br* ***zebra crossing*** passage *m* clouté *ou* pour piétons

zebu [ˈziːbuː] **N** *Zool* zébu *m*

zed [zed] **N** *Br* (lettre *f*) z *m inv*; *Fam* **to catch some zeds** piquer un roupillon

zee [ziː] *Am* = **zed**

Zen [zen] **N** zen *m*
ADJ zen *(inv)*
▸▸ ***Zen Buddhism*** les préceptes *mpl* du zen, le bouddhisme zen; ***Zen Buddhist*** bouddhiste *mf* zen

zenith [*Br* ˈzenɪθ, *Am* ˈziːnəθ] **N 1** *Astron* zénith *m*; **the sun at its z.** le soleil en son zénith **2** *(peak)* zénith *m*; **at the z. of his fame** à l'apogée *ou* au sommet de sa gloire; **when the British Empire was at its z.** lorsque l'empire britannique était à son apogée, à l'apogée de l'empire britannique

zephyr [ˈzefə(r)] **N** *Literary (wind)* zéphyr *m*

zeppelin [ˈzepəlɪn] **N** zeppelin *m*

zero [ˈzɪərəʊ] *(pl* **zeros** *or* **zeroes**) **N 1** *Math* zéro *m*
2 *(in temperature)* zéro *m*; **40 below z.** 40 degrés au-dessous de zéro, moins 40
3 *Sport* **to win three z.** gagner trois (à) zéro
4 *(nothing, nought)* **our chances have been put at z.** on considère que nos chances sont nulles
5 *Fam (person)* nul (nulle) *m,f*
COMP *(altitude)* zéro *(inv)*; *(visibility)* nul; **he's got z. intelligence/charm** il n'a aucune intelligence/aucun charme
VT *(instrument)* régler sur zéro
▸▸ ***zero gravity*** apesanteur *f*; ***zero growth*** croissance *f* zéro; ***zero hour*** heure *f* H; *Pol* ***the zero option*** l'option *f* zéro; ***zero tolerance*** tolérance *f* zéro *(politique d'intransigeance à l'égard de toute infraction à la loi ou au règlement)*; **to have a z. tolerance approach to crime/to vagrancy** ne rien tolérer *ou* ne rien laisser passer en matière de délinquance/de vagabondage
▸ **zero in on VT INSEP 1** *Mil (aim for)* se diriger *ou* piquer droit sur; *(aim weapon at)* régler le tir sur; *Fam* **the police zeroed in on the terrorists' hideout** la police a investi la cachette des terroristes **2** *Fam (concentrate on)* se concentrer sur **3** *Fam (pinpoint)* mettre le doigt sur

zero-base budgeting **N** *Fin* budget *m* base zéro, budgétisation *f* base zéro

zeroed [ˈzɪərəʊd] **ADJ** *(milometer)* à zéro

zeroing [ˈzɪərəʊɪŋ] **N** *Comput* initialisation *f* du compteur

zero-rated **ADJ z. (for VAT)** exempt de TVA, exonéré de TVA; **in Britain, books are z.** en Grande-Bretagne, les livres sont exempts *ou* exonérés de TVA

zero-rating **N** *Fin* taux *m* zéro

zest [zest] **N 1** *(piquancy)* piquant *m*, saveur *f*; **to add z. to a situation** ajouter du sel *ou* du piquant à une situation **2** *(enthusiasm)* enthousiasme *m*, entrain *m*; **with z.** *(fight)* avec élan, avec entrain; *(eat)* avec appétit, de bon appétit; **z. for life** joie *f* de vivre **3** *Culin (of orange, lemon)* zeste *m*
VT *(orange, lemon)* zester

zestful [ˈzestfʊl] **ADJ** *(person)* enthousiaste; *(performance)* plein de vie

zeugma [ˈzjuːgmə] **N** *Ling* zeugma *m*, zeugme *m*

zigzag [ˈzɪgzæg] *(pt & pp* **zigzagged**, *cont* **zigzagging**) **VI** *(walker, vehicle)* avancer en zigzags, zigzaguer; *(road)* zigzaguer; *(river)* serpenter; **to z. across/up the road** traverser/monter la rue en zigzaguant; **the road zigzags through the valley** la route traverse la vallée en zigzaguant *ou* serpente à travers la vallée
N *(in design)* zigzag *m*; *(on road)* lacet *m*; *(in river)* boucle *f*
ADJ *(path, line)* en zigzag; *(pattern)* à zigzag, à zigzags; **the path follows a z. course across the fields** le chemin traverse les champs en zigzaguant
ADV en zigzag

zilch [zɪltʃ] **N** *Fam* que dalle

zillion [ˈzɪlɪən] *(pl* **inv** *or* **zillions**) *Fam* **N** foultitude *f*; **they earn/cost zillions** ils gagnent/coûtent des milliards; **we got zillions of replies** nous avons eu des tas *ou* des tonnes de réponses

Zimbabwe [zɪmˈbɑːbwɪ] **N** Zimbabwe *m*

Zimbabwean [zɪmˈbɑːbwɪən] **N** Zimbabwéen (enne) *m,f*
ADJ zimbabwéen
COMP *(embassy, history)* du Zimbabwe

Zimmer (frame)® [ˈzɪmə-] **N** déambulateur *m*

zinc [zɪŋk] **N** zinc *m*
COMP *(chloride, sulphate, sulphide)* de zinc; *(ointment)* à l'oxyde de zinc
▸▸ ***zinc ointment*** pommade *f* à l'oxyde de zinc; ***zinc oxide*** oxyde *m* de zinc; ***zinc white*** blanc *m* de zinc, oxyde *m* de zinc

zing [zɪŋ] *Fam* **ONOMAT** zim!
N 1 *(of bullet)* sifflement *m* **2** *(of person)* punch *m*; **this drink's got real z.!** cette boisson est vraiment costaud!
VI 1 *(projectile)* siffler, passer dans un sifflement; **the bullet zinged past me** la balle est passée à côté de moi dans un sifflement **2** *Am Fam (tease)* vanner, chambrer

zinnia [ˈzɪnɪə] **N** *Bot* zinnia *m*

Zion [ˈzaɪən] **N** Sion

Zionism [ˈzaɪənɪzəm] **N** sionisme *m*

Zionist [ˈzaɪənɪst] **N** sioniste *mf*
ADJ sioniste

Zip® **N** *Comput*
▸▸ ***Zip® disk*** cartouche *f* Zip®; ***Zip® drive*** lecteur *m* Zip®

zip [zɪp] *(pt & pp* **zipped**, *cont* **zipping**) **N 1** *Br (fastener)* fermeture *f* Éclair® *ou* à glissière
2 *(sound of bullet)* sifflement *m*
3 *Fam (liveliness)* vivacité *f*, entrain *m*; **put some z. into it!** mets-y du nerf!; **your style needs more z.** ton style a besoin d'un peu plus de punch
4 *Am (zip code)* code *m* postal
5 *Am Fam (nothing)* rien *m*
VI 1 *(with zip fastener)* **to z. open/shut** s'ouvrir/se fermer à l'aide d'une fermeture Éclair® *ou* à glissière
2 *Fam (verb of movement)* **to z. past** passer comme une flèche; **to z. upstairs** monter l'escalier quatre à quatre; **she zipped out to get a paper** elle a filé chercher un journal; **I zipped through the book/my work** j'ai lu ce livre/j'ai fait mon travail en quatrième vitesse
3 *(arrow, bullet)* siffler; **bullets zipped past us** des balles sifflaient à nos oreilles
VT 1 *(with zip fastener)* **to z. sth open/shut** fermer/

ouvrir la fermeture Éclair® *ou* à glissière de qch; **I zipped myself into my sleeping bag** je me suis mis dans mon sac de couchage et j'ai tiré la fermeture
2 *Fam (do quickly)* **I'll just z. this cake into the oven** je glisse en vitesse ce gâteau dans le four
3 *Fam* **to z. it** *(be quiet)* la fermer, la boucler; **z. it!** la ferme!
4 *Comput (file)* zipper, compresser
►► *Am* ***zip code, ZIP code*** code *m* postal; *Br* ***zip fastener*** fermeture *f* Éclair® *ou* à glissière

►**zip on** VT SEP attacher (avec une fermeture à glissière)
VI s'attacher avec une fermeture Éclair® *ou* à glissière

►**zip up** VT SEP **1** *(clothing, sleeping bag)* fermer avec la fermeture Éclair® *ou* à glissière **2** *(of person)* fermer la fermeture Éclair® *ou* à glissière de; **z. me up** remonte ma fermeture
VI *(dress)* se fermer avec une fermeture Éclair® *ou* à glissière

zip-on ADJ *(flap, hood)* qui s'attache avec une fermeture Éclair® *ou* à glissière

zipper ['zɪpə(r)] *Am* = **zip** *n* 1

zipperhead ['zɪpəhed] N *Fam* bridé *m*, = terme injurieux pour désigner un Asiatique

zippy ['zɪpɪ] *(compar* **zippier**, *superl* **zippiest**) ADJ *Fam (person)* vif; *(car)* nerveux

zip-up ADJ *(bag, coat)* à fermeture Éclair®, zippé

zircon ['zɜ:kɒn] N *Miner* zircon *m*

zit [zɪt] N *Fam* bouton ▫ *m (sur la peau)*

zither ['zɪðə(r)] N cithare *f*

zizz [zɪz] N *Br Fam* **to have a z.** faire un somme

Z-list ['zedlɪst, *Am* 'zi:lɪst] ADJ *Pej* **a Z. celebrity** une petite célébrité ▫

Z-lister ['zedlɪstə(r), *Am* 'zi:lɪstə(r)] N *Pej (celebrity)* petite célébrité ▫ *f*

zodiac ['zəʊdɪæk] N zodiaque *m*

zodiacal [zəʊ'daɪəkəl] ADJ zodiacal

zombie ['zɒmbɪ] N *Rel & Fig* zombi(e) *m*; **he walks about like a z.** il a tout le temps l'air abruti *ou* l'air d'un zombi

zonal ['zəʊnəl] ADJ zonal

zone [zəʊn] N **1** *(area)* zone *f*, secteur *m*; *Mil* **battle/war z.** zone *f* des combats/de guerre
2 *(sphere)* zone *f*, domaine *m*
3 *Geog & Met* zone *f*
4 *Fam Sport* **to be in the z.** être au top de sa forme
5 *Am Fam* **to be in a z.** *(dazed)* être dans le coaltar; *(after taking drugs)* être raide, planer
VT **1** *(partition)* diviser en zones **2** *(classify)* désigner; **to z. an area as industrial/residential** classer un secteur zone industrielle/résidentielle

►**zone out** VI *Fam* planer, rêvasser

zoning ['zəʊnɪŋ] N zonage *m*

zonked [zɒŋkt] ADJ *Fam* **1** *(exhausted)* vanné, claqué **2** *(drunk)* bourré; *(on drugs)* défoncé

zoo [zu:] *(pl* **zoos**) N zoo *m*, jardin *m* zoologique

zookeeper ['zu:ˌki:pə(r)] N gardien(enne) *m,f* de zoo

zoological [ˌzəʊə'lɒdʒɪkəl] ADJ zoologique
►► ***zoological gardens*** jardin *m ou* parc *m* zoologique

zoologist [zəʊ'ɒlədʒɪst] N zoologiste *mf*

zoology [zəʊ'ɒlədʒɪ] N zoologie *f*

zoom [zu:m] VI **1** *(verb of movement)* **the car zoomed up/down the hill** la voiture a monté/descendu la côte à toute allure *ou* en trombe; **the rocket zoomed up into the clouds** la fusée est montée en chandelle dans les nuages; **I'm just going to z. into town to get some food** je vais faire un saut en ville pour acheter de quoi manger
2 *(prices, costs, sales)* monter en flèche; **inflation zoomed up** *or* **upwards** l'inflation est montée en flèche
3 *(engine)* vrombir
4 *Aviat (climb steeply)* monter en chandelle
N **1** *(of engine)* vrombissement *m* **2** *Phot (lens, effect)* zoom *m*
ONOMAT vroum!
►► *Comput* ***zoom box*** case *f* zoom; ***zoom lens*** zoom *m*

►**zoom in** VI *Phot* faire un zoom; **the camera zoomed in on the laughing children** la caméra a fait un zoom sur les enfants en train de rire

►**zoom off** VI filer; **they're zooming off on holiday tomorrow** ils filent en vacances demain

►**zoom out** VI *Phot* faire un zoom arrière

zoophyte ['zəʊəfaɪt] N zoophyte *m*

zooted ['zu:tɪd] ADJ *Am Fam* **1** *(drunk)* bourré, pété **2** *(on drugs)* raide, défoncé

zoot suit [zu:t-] N costume *m* zazou *(des années quarante)*

zounds [zaʊndz] EXCLAM *Arch* morbleu!, sacrebleu!

zowie ['zaʊɪ] EXCLAM *Am Fam* oh là là!, la vache!

zucchini [zu:'ki:nɪ] *(pl* **inv** *or* **zucchinis**) N *Am* courgette *f*

Zulu ['zu:lu:] *(pl* **inv** *or* **Zulus**) N **1** *(person)* Zoulou (e) *m,f* **2** *Ling* zoulou *m*
ADJ zoulou

Zululand ['zu:lu:lænd] N Zoulouland *m*

Zürich ['zjʊərɪk] N Zurich *m*

zwieback® ['zwi:bæk] N *Am* biscotte *f*, *Suisse* zwieback *m*

zygote ['zaɪgəʊt] N *Biol* zygote *m*

Supplément
Supplement

La Langue en action

a langue en action a été conçu spécialement pour permettre aux étudiants d'anglais de s'exprimer e façon naturelle et avec aisance. Ce guide, indispensable pour tout apprenant, se compose de trois arties principales: LES OPINIONS: EXPRIMER CE QUE L'ON PENSE; LES EMOTIONS: EXPRIMER CE UE L'ON RESSENT et enfin COMMUNICATION: PARLER, ECRIRE, ECHANGER. Chaque partie est ubdivisée en sous-sections comprenant de nombreux exemples en anglais accompagnés de leur aduction française. Ces phrases peuvent s'employer pour décrire un large éventail d'opinions et 'émotions et pour communiquer dans toutes sortes de situations, à l'oral comme à l'écrit. Essentiel our l'apprentissage de la langue et la préparation aux examens écrits et oraux, ce supplément onstitue également l'outil idéal pour quiconque souhaite communiquer en anglais de façon plus fficace, que ce soit par e-mail, au téléphone ou encore dans la conversation.

.ES OPINIONS: EXPRIMER CE QUE L'ON PENSE

la certitude

I'm certain *or* sure (that) he'll come
Je suis certain qu'il viendra

I don't know for sure *or* for certain
Je n'en suis pas sûr

They're not convinced (that) it's necessary
Ils ne sont pas convaincus que c'est nécessaire

She is definitely innocent
Elle est innocente, c'est sûr

Of course he loves you
Bien sûr qu'il t'aime

I know for a fact (that) he is dead
Je sais avec certitude qu'il est mort

She made certain *or* sure (that) all the doors were locked
Elle s'est assurée que toutes les portes étaient fermées

Our success is guaranteed
Notre succès est garanti

There's no question about it
Il n'y a pas de doute là-dessus

It's anybody's guess
Dieu seul le sait

The wisdom of this decision is open to question
Le bien-fondé de la décision est discutable

There are no two ways about it
Il n'y a pas à discuter

On second *Br* thoughts *or Am* thought I'd better go myself
Réflexion faite, il vaut mieux que j'y aille moi-même

Fam He's a dead cert for the job
À tous les coups, il a le poste

• la comparaison

You are as tall as he is *or* as him
Vous êtes aussi grand que lui

The cedars are older than the oaks (are)
Les cèdres sont plus vieux que les chênes

He plays tennis better/worse than I do *or* than me
Il joue au tennis mieux/plus mal que moi

I have as much money/as many books as you (do *or* have)
J'ai autant d'argent/autant de livres que vous

Fewer/more than ten
Moins/plus de dix

As much/soon as possible
Autant/aussitôt que possible

The film was better than I expected (it to be)
Le film était meilleur que je ne m'y attendais

Compared with *or* to the others she's brilliant
Elle est brillante par rapport aux autres

His paintings have been compared to Manet's
On a comparé ses tableaux à ceux de Manet

The book makes *or* draws a comparison between London and New York
Le livre établit une comparaison entre Londres et New York

He can't compare with you
On ne peut pas le comparer à vous

There's no comparison
Il n'y a pas de comparaison

This music is melodic by *or* in comparison
En comparaison, cette musique est mélodieuse

In comparison with his brother, he was shy
Comparé à son frère, il était timide

• la compréhension

I don't understand the question
Je ne comprends pas la question

He claims his wife doesn't understand him
Il prétend que sa femme ne le comprend pas

I can't make myself understood in English
Je ne peux pas me faire comprendre en anglais

Are you clear about what you have to do?
Es-tu sûr de ce que tu as à faire?

Would you mind repeating that?
Auriez-vous l'obligeance de répéter?

I see what you're getting at
Je vois où vous voulez en venir

I didn't quite grasp what she meant
Je n'ai pas bien saisi ce qu'elle a voulu dire

I just can't fathom it
Je n'y comprends rien

I heard what you said, but it didn't sink in at the time
Je vous ai entendu, mais je n'ai pas vraiment saisi sur le moment

I don't think (that) the bad news has registered with her yet
On lui a annoncé la mauvaise nouvelle mais je ne crois pas qu'elle ait bien réalisé

He took in the situation at a glance
Il a compris la situation en un clin d'œil

Why he wants to go there is beyond me
Je ne comprends pas pourquoi il veut y aller

Her lecture was completely over my head
Sa conférence m'a complètement dépassé

She's a bit out of her depth in her new job
Elle est un peu dépassée dans son nouveau travail

I intend to get to the bottom of this affair
J'entends aller au fond de cette affaire

I'll get back to you once I've got a handle on the situation
Je vous recontacterai quand j'aurai la situation en main

Fam I don't get it
Je ne pige pas

Fam It's all Greek to me
Tout ça, c'est de l'hébreu pour moi

Fam It's as clear as mud
C'est clair comme du jus de boudin

Fam I can't make head nor tail of this
Pour moi ça n'a ni queue ni tête

Br Fam Suddenly the penny dropped
Tout à coup ça a fait tilt

• convenir

Blue/This hat suits you
Le bleu/Ce chapeau te va bien

This climate/This food doesn't suit me
Ce climat/Cette nourriture ne me convient pas

The house is not suitable for a large family
La maison ne conviendrait pas à une famille nombreuse

You are not appropriately dressed for such an occasion
Tu n'es pas convenablement habillé pour ce genre d'occasion

That tie doesn't go with your shirt
Cette cravate ne va pas avec ta chemise

It fits (me) like a glove
Ça me va comme un gant

It's the perfect *or* ideal gift
C'est le cadeau idéal

Now is not the right time to mention it
Ce n'est pas le moment d'en parler

I'm the wrong person to ask
Il ne faut pas me demander ça à moi

When would be the best time for you?
Quelle heure vous conviendrait le mieux?

That's all right with *or* by me
Moi, ça me va

He's not cut out to be a politician
Il n'a pas l'étoffe d'un homme politique

That's right up my street
C'est tout à fait mon rayon

Rachel was in her element, telling everybody what to do
Rachel était dans son élément, disant à chacun ce qu'il devait faire

• croire

I believe (that) it's true
Je crois que c'est vrai

I can't believe it
Je n'arrive pas à le croire

He believes in God/in ghosts
Il croit en Dieu/aux revenants

I believe in free enterprise
Je crois à la libre entreprise

He couldn't believe his eyes/his ears
Il n'en croyait pas ses yeux/ses oreilles

Don't you believe it!
N'en croyez rien!

She is a great believer in taking exercise
Elle est convaincue qu'il faut faire de l'exercice

It's my belief (that) he's lying
Je suis convaincu qu'il ment

Contrary to popular belief …
Contrairement à ce que l'on croit …

It's beyond belief *or* unbelievable
C'est incroyable

Believe it or not, he fell for her
Tu le croiras si tu veux, il s'est épris d'elle

She's a smart one, believe (you) me!
C'est une maligne, crois-moi!

The government has lost credibility with the public
Le gouvernement a perdu sa crédibilité aux yeux du public

Your story is a bit far-fetched
Ton histoire est un peu tirée par les cheveux

They took her at her word
Ils l'ont prise au mot

She took it as gospel
Elle l'a pris pour parole d'évangile

Fam I told her a lie and she bought *or* swallowed it
Je lui ai raconté un mensonge et elle l'a gobé

Formal Do you give (any) credence to the rumours?
Ajoutez-vous foi aux rumeurs?

• la curiosité

I wonder whether he'll come
Je me demande s'il viendra

I wonder who invented that
Je suis curieux de savoir qui a inventé cela

They weren't at all curious as to how it had happened
Ils n'étaient pas du tout curieux de savoir comment cela s'était produit

He went there out of curiosity
Il y est allé par curiosité

She has an inquisitive mind
C'est un esprit curieux

He's an awful busybody
Il se mêle des affaires de tout le monde

They were agog to hear the latest news
Ils brûlaient d'impatience d'apprendre les dernières nouvelles

Fam Don't be so nosy!
Occupe-toi donc de tes oignons!

Fam I didn't mean to be nosy
Je ne voulais pas être indiscret

• la déception

He was disappointed at *or* about not being invited
Il a été déçu de ne pas être invité

Are you disappointed with the results?
Les résultats vous ont-ils déçu?

I'm very disappointed in him
Il m'a beaucoup déçu

I found the film very disappointing
J'ai trouvé le film vraiment décevant

She has suffered many disappointments
Elle a essuyé bien des déboires

I've become disillusioned *or* disenchanted with politics
J'ai perdu mes illusions sur la politique

It was worse than I expected
C'était pire que je pensais

His performance didn't come up *or* live up to their expectations
Il n'a pas répondu à leurs attentes

His winnings fell far short of what he had expected
Ses gains ont été bien inférieurs à ce qu'il attendait

She has been badly let down
Elle a été profondément déçue

The party was a bit of an anticlimax *or Fam* a bit of a letdown
La fête a été plutôt décevante

• la différence

This book is very different from *or* to her first
Ce livre est très différent de son premier

He put on a different shirt
Il a mis une autre chemise

I can't tell the difference between the two
Je ne vois pas la différence entre les deux

They differ in size/colour
Ils sont de tailles/couleurs différentes

They are as different as chalk and cheese
C'est le jour et la nuit

He is quite unlike his brother
Il ne ressemble pas du tout à son frère

Unlike you, I prefer a quiet life
Contrairement à vous, je préfère une vie tranquille

No two are alike
Il n'y en a pas deux de pareils

These facts are totally unrelated
Il n'y a aucun rapport entre ces faits

This version diverges from the truth
Cette version s'écarte de la vérité

By *or* in contrast, the president was almost optimistic
Par contraste, le président était presque optimiste

They have nothing in common
Ils n'ont rien de commun

Their positions on disarmament are poles apart *or* diametrically opposed
Leurs positions sur le désarmement sont diamétralement opposées

Formal This announcement is at variance with his previous statements
Cette annonce est en contradiction avec ses déclarations antérieures

• la difficulté

I find it difficult *or* hard to believe (that) she has gone
Il m'est difficile de croire qu'elle est partie

Don't be so difficult!
Ne fais pas le/la difficile!

He had difficulty *or* trouble (in) climbing the stairs
Il a eu du mal à monter l'escalier

They are in financial difficulties
Ils rencontrent des difficultés financières

What seems to be the problem?
Où est le problème?

I can't come – I've got problems with the car
Je ne peux pas venir; j'ai des problèmes avec la voiture

La Langue en action

There's been a hitch *or* snag
Il y a eu un problème

We had the devil of a job finding the house
On a eu un mal fou à trouver la maison

I've really got my work cut out
J'ai du pain sur la planche

It's easier said than done
C'est plus facile à dire qu'à faire

That's a tall order
Voilà qui va être difficile

You'll be hard pressed or pushed or put to find a shop open at this time
Tu vas avoir du mal à trouver une boutique ouverte à cette heure-ci

They were in dire straits
Ils étaient dans une très mauvaise passe

We had our backs to the wall
Nous étions au pied du mur

Fam She's in a fix *or* in a mess *or* up against it
Elle est dans le pétrin

Fam It's a hard *or* tough nut to crack
C'est difficile à résoudre

Fam It can be a headache finding somewhere to park
Parfois c'est la croix et la bannière pour trouver à se garer

LA DISSERTATION

Mots et expressions pour relier les arguments dans une dissertation

Ajouter: also, furthermore, in addition, moreover, what is more
It must also be emphasized that …
Il faut souligner de plus que ...

The experiment failed. Moreover *or* What is more, many scientists lost their jobs.
L'expérience a échoué. En outre, de nombreux chercheurs ont perdu leur emploi.

Comparer: by the same token, likewise, similarly
The pursuit of weapons of mass destruction only invites isolation. By the same token, leaders who abandon the pursuit of those weapons will find an open path to better relations.
La course aux armes de destruction massive n'apporte que l'isolement. De la même manière, les dirigeants qui l'abandonnent ouvriront la voie à de meilleures relations internationales.

La conséquence: accordingly, as a result, consequently, hence, therefore, thus
Prices went higher and higher. As a result *or* Consequently, the government was obliged to put a curb on public-sector wage increases.
Les prix augmentaient de plus en plus. En conséquence, le gouvernement fut obligé de mettre un frein aux augmentations de salaire dans le secteur public.

We all have a duty to help others. Accordingly *or* Therefore, we should contribute to the disaster fund.
Nous avons tous le devoir d'aider les autres. Par conséquent, nous devons contribuer au fonds de solidarité pour les catastrophes naturelles.

L'enchaînement des arguments: at the same time, earlier, first of all, in the first place, in the meantime, meanwhile, next, simultaneously, then, to begin with, while
He admits he's lied and at the same time he wants us to trust him!
Il admet avoir menti et en même temps il veut qu'on le croie!

In the first place *or* To begin with, the statistics are wrong; and then they have been misinterpreted.
En premier lieu, ces statistiques sont fausses; et puis elles ont été mal interprétées.

Illustrer: for example, for instance

Mettre en contraste: but, conversely, however, in contrast, instead, nevertheless, nonetheless, on the contrary, on the other hand, rather, yet
Nearly every young person has a mobile phone. Conversely *or* In contrast, very few senior citizens carry one.
Chaque jeune ou presque possède un téléphone portable. Par contraste, très peu de personnes âgées en possèdent un.

Such measures are frequently criticized; on the contrary, they should be welcomed.
De telles mesures sont fréquemment critiquées; elles devraient au contraire être bien accueillies.

Récapituler: in brief, in essence, in other words, in short, namely, that is
There are some differences, but in essence this is a classic case of plagiarism.
Il existe des différences, mais dans le fond il s'agit là d'un exemple classique de plagiat.

There is one important objection to this plan: namely *or* that is, the high cost.
Le projet soulève une objection de taille, à savoir son coût élevé.

Résumer: all in all, all things considered, by and large, in any case, in conclusion, in the final analysis, on balance, on the whole, to sum up, to summarize
By and large *or* On the whole, the new system is working well. However, there are some areas where improvements could be made.
Dans l'ensemble, le nouveau système fonctionne bien. Cependant, certains aspects pourraient bénéficier d'une amélioration.

All things considered *or* On balance, capital punishment cannot be said to reduce the number of murders committed.
Tout bien considéré, on ne peut pas dire que la peine capitale diminue le nombre de meurtres.

• le doute

I doubt if *or* whether he'll come
Je doute qu'il vienne

I doubt it
J'en doute

It's doubtful whether they're really serious
Il est douteux qu'ils soient vraiment sérieux

I have (my) doubts about him
J'ai des doutes sur lui

We are in no doubt as to *or* have no doubts about her competence
Nous n'avons aucun doute sur ses compétences

Without (a *or* any) doubt, she is the best in the world
C'est, sans aucun doute, la meilleure au monde

The facts have been established beyond (all) doubt
Ces faits ont été avérés sans le moindre doute

I'm very sceptical of *or* about their claims
Je suis très sceptique quant à ce qu'ils affirment

She had misgivings about allowing them to go
Elle hésitait à les laisser y aller

He is hesitating about buying the house
Il hésite à acheter la maison

It is debatable whether he is to blame or she is
Il est difficile de dire si c'est lui ou elle qui est à blâmer

I'm in two minds about going
Je ne sais pas si je vais y aller

Make up your mind!
Décidez-vous!

She is in a bit of a dilemma *or* quandary over whether to tell him or not
Elle ne sait pas trop si elle doit le lui dire ou non

His employer called his honesty into question
Son employeur a mis son honnêteté en question

You must take what he says with a pinch of salt
Il ne faut pas prendre ce qu'il dit pour argent comptant

• l'erreur

I took the wrong road/train
Je me suis trompé de route/train

This is the wrong road for Paris
Ce n'est pas la bonne route pour aller à Paris

I was mixing you up with your brother
Je vous confondais avec votre frère

I'm getting all mixed up
Je ne sais plus où j'en suis

You're confusing me and *or* with my sister
Vous me confondez avec ma sœur

My things are all in a jumble *or* muddle
Mes affaires sont tout en désordre

The pages got all jumbled
Les pages se sont complètement mélangées

Paul was in a real muddle over his holiday plans
Paul ne savait plus où il en était dans ses projets de vacances

I mistook him for someone else
Je l'ai pris pour quelqu'un d'autre

There is some confusion as to who won
Il y a incertitude sur le vainqueur

It is a hotchpotch *or* ragbag of ideas
C'est un fatras d'idées

• l'espoir

We're hoping for good weather
Nous espérons avoir beau temps

I hope (that) your brother is better
J'espère que votre frère va mieux

She has hopes of succeeding
Elle a bon espoir de réussir

La Langue en action

Don't raise his hopes too much
Ne lui donne pas trop d'espoir

Hopefully, they'll leave tomorrow
On espère qu'ils partiront demain

It's everybody's dream to win the lottery
Tout le monde rêve de gagner à la loterie

There is little prospect of their winning the match
Il y a peu d'espoir qu'ils remportent le match

The outlook for the New Year is promising
Cette nouvelle année s'annonce prometteuse

Things are looking quite optimistic
Les choses se présentent plutôt bien

We must look on the bright side – at least we're still alive
Nous devons voir les choses du bon côté: au moins nous sommes toujours vivants

That's a bit of wishful thinking
C'est prendre ses désirs pour des réalités

Every cloud has a silver lining
À quelque chose malheur est bon

She sees the world through rose-coloured glasses
Elle voit la vie en rose

He's always building castles in the air
Il ne cesse de bâtir des châteaux en Espagne

Formal They were sanguine about the company's prospects
Ils voyaient l'avenir de l'entreprise avec optimisme

• l'évidence

It's obvious *or* clear *or* plain (that) she's lying
Il est évident qu'elle ment

He is obviously *or* clearly *or* plainly wrong
Il est clair qu'il a tort

Of course I believe you
Bien sûr que je te crois

There is no denying (that) we have a problem
Il est indéniable que nous avons un problème

It goes without saying that we'll travel together
Il va sans dire que nous voyagerons ensemble

It was a blatant attempt to win him over
C'était une tentative flagrante de s'attacher son soutien

The experiment was a conspicuous failure
L'expérience s'est soldée par un échec retentissant

It really stands out that he's not a local
Ça se voit vraiment qu'il n'est pas d'ici

The mistake jumped out at me
L'erreur m'a sauté aux yeux

It's as plain as the nose on your face
C'est clair comme de l'eau de roche

The answer's staring you in the face!
La réponse saute aux yeux!

It was right under my nose all the time
C'était en plein sous mon nez

Fam It stands out a mile!
Ça se voit comme le nez au milieu de la figure!

• la facilité

The exam was very easy
L'examen était très facile

She is easy to get on with
Elle est facile à vivre

This will make your job easier
Cela vous facilitera la tâche

You can easily imagine my disappointment
Vous concevez sans peine ma déception

It's easier said than done
C'est plus facile à dire qu'à faire

It's as easy as pie or as ABC or as falling off a log
C'est simple comme bonjour

It's child's play
C'est un jeu d'enfant

It should be a simple matter to change your ticket
Tu ne devrais avoir aucun mal à changer ton billet

It's a rather undemanding book
C'est un livre plutôt facile à lire

You made short work of that!
Tu n'y es pas allé par quatre chemins!

They've always taken exams *Br* in their stride *or Am* in stride
Ils ont toujours réussi leurs examens facilement

He won hands down
Il a gagné haut la main

Fam I haven't got a car – no problem *or* no sweat, I'll take you
Je n'ai pas de voiture – pas de problème, je t'emmènerai

Fam He's found a cushy job
Il a trouvé une bonne planque

Fam It was a piece of cake!
C'était du gâteau!

Fam That's the kind of thing he could do standing on his head
C'est le genre de choses qu'il peut faire les yeux fermés

• faire semblant

They pretended not to see us
Ils ont fait semblant de ne pas nous voir

She made no pretence of being interested
Elle n'a pas feint d'être intéressée

Make believe (that) you're a bird
Imagine que tu es un oiseau

Stop putting on an act!
Arrête de jouer la comédie!

It's all show *or* a facade *or* a pose
Ce n'est qu'une façade

He posed as *or* passed himself off as a hero
Il s'est fait passer pour un héros

It's just an excuse
Ce n'est qu'un prétexte

She came on the pretext of consulting her brother
Elle est venue sous prétexte de consulter son frère

You've got me here under false pretences
Tu m'as fait venir ici sous un faux prétexte

I feigned illness so (that) I wouldn't have to go
J'ai feint d'être malade afin de ne pas y aller

He's malingering *or Fam* swinging the lead
Il tire au flanc

Deep down he's very kind
Au fond, il est très gentil

Don't play *or* come the innocent with me!
Ne fais pas l'innocent avec moi!

He gave a forced laugh
Il a ri du bout des lèvres

She's just going through the motions
Elle fait juste semblant

She said it tongue in cheek
Elle l'a dit sur un ton pince-sans-rire

Fam Don't worry, he's just putting it on
Ne t'inquiète pas, il fait du chiqué

Formal When she heard of it, she affected surprise
Lorsqu'elle en a entendu parler, elle a affecté la surprise

• ignorer

We don't know her
Nous ne la connaissons pas

I don't know if she's ready or not
Je ne sais pas si elle est prête ou non

I don't know anything at all *or* the first thing about cars
Je n'y connais absolument rien en voitures

I've never heard of him
Je n'ai jamais entendu parler de lui

I haven't the faintest idea *or Fam* the foggiest (idea) what you're talking about
Je n'ai pas la moindre idée de ce dont vous parlez

He was unaware *or* didn't realize (that) he was being watched
Il ne se rendait pas compte qu'on l'observait

We were completely in the dark about their plans
Nous ignorions tout de leurs projets

She was ignorant of the facts
Elle ignorait les faits

I'm unfamiliar with his writings
Je connais mal ses écrits

There has been no news of them so far
Il n'y a aucune nouvelle d'eux pour l'instant

The police have nothing to go on
La police n'a rien sur quoi se fonder

Your guess is as good as mine
Je n'en sais pas plus que toi

Economics is a closed book to me
Je ne comprends rien à l'économie

The new minister is a bit of an unknown quantity
Le nouveau ministre est un personnage dont on ne sait pas grand-chose

I'm stumped for something to say
Je ne sais pas quoi dire

Fam It's all Greek to me
Tout ça, c'est de l'hébreu pour moi

• l'importance

It's important to know (that) …
Il est important de savoir que …

It is of no importance *or* consequence
Cela n'a pas d'importance

It is an event of great significance
C'est un événement de la plus haute importance

Don't attach too much importance to this survey
N'accordez pas trop d'importance à cette enquête

What he says carries weight
Sa parole a du poids

It doesn't matter how much it costs
Peu importe le prix

I don't count around here
Je ne compte pas ici

A knowledge of economics is essential *or* fundamental to a proper understanding of this problem
Il est essentiel d'avoir des connaissances en économie pour bien comprendre ce problème

She was appointed to a key post
Elle a été nommée à un poste clé

I don't set much store by his advice
Je ne fais pas grand cas de ses conseils

It's a matter of life and death
C'est une question de vie ou de mort

It's a trifling matter
Ce n'est qu'une bagatelle

Br It was a storm in a teacup
Ce fut une tempête dans un verre d'eau

The press played up her divorce
La presse a monté son divorce en épingle

The government is trying to play down its role
Le gouvernement tente de minimiser l'importance de son rôle

She thinks (that) she's somebody
Elle se croit quelqu'un

He's a bit of a nonentity
Il est plutôt insignifiant

Never mind!
Ça ne fait rien!

So what?
Et alors?

Fam It's *Br* small beer *or Am* small potatoes
C'est de la petite bière

• l'intention

How do you intend to do it?
Comment avez-vous l'intention de vous y prendre?

We arrived later than (we had) intended
Nous sommes arrivés plus tard que prévu

I have every intention of calling her
J'ai bien l'intention de l'appeler

I have no intention of accepting
Je n'ai aucune intention d'accepter

She's thinking of starting a business
Elle pense monter une affaire

His aim is to get rich quickly
Son but est de s'enrichir rapidement

She has set her sights on the presidency
Elle vise la présidence

He's going for her job
Il va essayer d'obtenir son poste

What kind of party did you have in mind?
À quelle sorte de soirée est-ce que tu pensais?

They bought the house with a view to letting it
Ils ont acheté la maison en vue de la louer

She didn't mean (to do) it
Elle ne l'a pas fait exprès

I avoided the subject on purpose *or* purposely *or* deliberately *or* intentionally
J'ai fait exprès d'éviter la question

In order to simplify things, I have …
Afin de simplifier les choses, j'ai …

By doing that, he unwittingly broke the law
Ce faisant, il a involontairement enfreint la loi

• l'intérêt

She is interested in fashion
Elle s'intéresse à la mode

Would you be interested in meeting him?
Ça t'intéressait de le rencontrer?

He takes an active interest in politics
Il s'intéresse activement à la politique

This may be of interest to you
Ceci peut vous intéresser

He paid attention to everything she said
Il a prêté attention à tout ce qu'elle disait

May I have your attention for a moment?
Pourriez-vous m'accorder votre attention un instant?

The government should concentrate *or* focus on improving the economy
Le gouvernement devrait s'attacher à améliorer la situation économique

Concentrate on *or* Apply yourself to your work!
Appliquez-vous à votre travail!

Take no notice of him!
Ne faites pas attention à lui!

I need to study the proposal before I decide
J'ai besoin d'étudier cette proposition avant de me décider

She was poring over the details of the contract
Elle passait au crible les détails du contrat

He is wrapped up *or* engrossed in his work
Il est entièrement absorbé par son travail

She pricked up her ears at the sound of her name
Elle a dressé l'oreille en entendant son nom

Have you had any news of her?
Avez-vous eu de ses nouvelles?

What's new?
Quoi de neuf?

• les opinions

What is your opinion *or* do you think of him?
Que pensez-vous de lui?

I'm of the opinion *or* My opinion is that we should wait
Je suis d'avis que l'on attende

It's a good film in my opinion *or* view
C'est un bon film à mon avis

She has strong views on the subject
Elle a des opinions marquées sur le sujet

It's a matter of opinion
C'est une question d'opinion

Personally, I think (that) it's a silly idea
Pour ma part, je trouve que c'est une idée stupide

To be honest, I don't think (that) it will work
À vrai dire, je ne crois pas que ça marchera

I feel *or* I have the feeling (that) things have changed between us
J'ai l'impression que les choses ont changé entre nous

I regard her as *or* look on her as *or* consider her a good friend
Je la considère comme une bonne amie

What is your attitude to abortion?
Que pensez-vous de l'avortement?

What is the American position *or* stance on this issue?
Quelle est la position des Américains sur ce problème?

What's your outlook on life?
Quelle est votre conception de la vie?

To my way of thinking, this would be a good solution
Selon moi, cela serait une bonne solution

She got it into her head (that) she was being persecuted
Elle s'est mis en tête qu'on la persécutait

I've changed my mind about him
J'ai changé d'avis à son égard

I'll stick to my guns come what may
Rien ne m'en fera démordre

• la pertinence

What relevance do his remarks have to the situation?
Quel est le rapport entre ses remarques et la situation?

Such considerations are not relevant
De telles considérations sont hors de propos

It has to do with *or* concerns your mother, I'm afraid
J'ai bien peur que ça concerne ta mère

It has nothing to do with the colour of your skin
Cela n'a rien à voir avec la couleur de la peau

I had nothing to do with it
Je n'y suis pour rien

I don't see the point of redoing it
Je ne vois pas l'intérêt de le refaire

That's beside the point!
Ce n'est pas le problème!

I have a few things to say in connection with this
J'ai quelques remarques à faire à ce propos

It is very apt *or* appropriate that it should end in this way
Il est tout à fait approprié que cela se termine de cette manière

This law applies *or* is applicable to all citizens
Cette loi s'applique à tous les citoyens

Your confidence in her was totally misplaced
Ta confiance en elle était bien mal placée

This ties in with what I said before
Cela rejoint ce que j'ai dit avant

His comments have some bearing on the present situation
Ses remarques ont un certain rapport avec la situation actuelle

It's just a red herring
Ce n'est qu'une fausse piste

Her conversation was full of non sequiturs
Il n'y avait pas de suite dans sa conversation

Formal The evidence pertaining to the case is not strong
Les preuves se rapportant au dossier sont plutôt minces

• la possession

Paul has (got) a lot of money
Paul a beaucoup d'argent

That letter is mine
Cette lettre est à moi

Whose are these gloves? *or* Whose gloves are these?
À qui sont ces gants?

Who does this book belong to?
À qui appartient ce livre?

The shop is owned by her father
Le magasin appartient à son père

She is the proud owner of a Rolls Royce
Elle est l'heureuse propriétaire d'une Rolls Royce

He's one of the Murphy gang
Il fait partie de la bande à Murphy

My job includes sorting the mail
Trier le courrier fait partie de mon travail

Their son has a house of his own
Leur fils a sa propre maison

She made the song her own
Elle s'est approprié la chanson

Fam Stop hogging the computer!
Arrête de squatter l'ordinateur!

Formal Do they possess/Are they in possession of the necessary documents?
Possèdent-ils les documents nécessaires?

Formal When do you take possession of your new yacht?
Quand prenez-vous possession de votre nouveau yacht?

Formal She has a million pounds at her disposal
Elle dispose d'un million de livres

Formal I lay claim to no specialist knowledge
Je ne prétends pas posséder des connaissances approfondies

• la possibilité

It isn't possible *or* It's impossible for her to come
Il ne lui est pas possible de venir

Is there any possibility of you coming up for the weekend?
Vous serait-il possible de venir ce week-end?

He is possibly the greatest musician of his time
C'est peut-être le plus grand musicien de son temps

Avoid touching the sides as far as possible
Évitez autant que possible de toucher les côtés

She comes to see me whenever possible
Elle vient me voir quand elle le peut

He may *or* might *or* could return at any moment
Il pourrait revenir d'un moment à l'autre

La Langue en action

Perhaps *or* Maybe she won't accept
Peut-être qu'elle n'acceptera pas

That boy is a potential genius
Ce garçon est un génie en puissance

The idea has potential
L'idée a de l'avenir

I would go if I were you, it's the opportunity *or* chance of a lifetime
À ta place j'irais, c'est la chance de ta vie

I phoned on the off-chance of catching him at home
J'ai appelé en espérant qu'il serait chez lui

The plans stand little chance of being approved
Les projets ont peu de chances d'être approuvés

It is not financially feasible to keep the shop open
Ce n'est pas faisable financièrement de maintenir le magasin ouvert

You might win, you never know!
Tu pourrais gagner, on ne sait jamais!

In the event of fire, evacuate the building
En cas d'incendie, évacuez le bâtiment

• pouvoir

Can you come to the party?
Peux-tu venir à la fête?

I'm sorry, I can't
Je suis désolé, je ne peux pas

He could still walk
Il pouvait encore marcher

She can play the violin
Elle sait jouer du violon

I'll be able to visit you more often now
Je pourrai te rendre visite plus souvent désormais

They are capable of looking after themselves
Ils sont capables de se débrouiller tout seuls

We managed to persuade her
Nous avons réussi à la persuader

Would it be possible for you to lend me £5?
Vous serait-il possible de me prêter 5 livres?

That made it impossible for me to do my work
Cela m'a mis dans l'impossibilité de faire mon travail

They are in a position to offer it you
Ils sont en mesure de vous l'offrir

She couldn't very well refuse
Il lui aurait été difficile de refuser

He has the power to decide
Il a le pouvoir de décider

Who gave him (the) authority to enter?
Qui lui a donné l'autorisation d'entrer?

Are you up to doing it?
Êtes-vous capable de le faire?

I didn't think she had it in her
Je ne l'en croyais pas capable

• la probabilité

It's the most probable *or* likely hypothesis
C'est l'hypothèse la plus vraisemblable

I think it highly improbable *or* unlikely (that) he ever came here
Il me paraît fort peu probable qu'il soit jamais venu ici

Will you be able to come? – Probably (not)
Pourrez-vous venir? – Probablement (pas)

The probability *or* likelihood is that it will get even hotter
Il est probable qu'il fasse encore plus chaud

There's little/a good chance of that happening
Il y a peu de chances/de bonnes chances que cela se produise

It's a pretty safe bet (that) he'll be late
Il y a fort à parier qu'il arrivera en retard

She's liable to make mistakes
Elle est susceptible de faire des erreurs

As likely as not he's already home
Il est sûrement déjà rentré

You will doubtless be surprised at my decision
Vous serez sans doute surpris de ma décision

The affair has all the makings of a national scandal
Il y a dans cette affaire largement de quoi déclencher un scandale national

It was *Br* on *or Am* in the cards that the project would fail
Il était prévisible que le projet échouerait

That's a bit of a tall *Br* story *or Am* tale
C'est un peu dur à avaler

It's a long shot, but we may be successful
C'est un pari risqué mais nous réussirons peut-être

• les progrès

He was making slow progress with learning the language
Il progressait lentement dans son apprentissage de la langue

Negotiations are making good progress
Les négociations sont en bonne voie

The patient is progressing satisfactorily
Le malade fait des progrès satisfaisants

There have been significant advances in genetics in recent years
Il y a eu des avancées significatives en génétique ces dernières années

How are you getting on with the painting?
Alors, ça avance la peinture?

The rehearsal went well/badly
La répétition a bien/mal marché

I'm not getting anywhere with this essay
Je tourne en rond avec cette dissertation

Your maths has improved by leaps and bounds
Vous avez fait des progrès phénoménaux en maths

The building work is coming on *or* along fine
La construction avance bien

He is making great strides with his research
Sa recherche avance à grand pas

The company has taken a great leap forward
La société a fait un grand bond en avant

I've made a good start on my Christmas shopping
J'ai déjà fait une bonne partie de mes achats de Noël

We've broken the back of the job
Nous avons fait le plus gros du travail

The two sides have made some headway in their negotiations
Les deux parties ont avancé dans leurs négociations

We are gaining ground on/losing ground to our competitors
Nous gagnons/perdons du terrain sur nos concurrents

They've fallen behind with their reading
Ils ont pris du retard dans leurs lectures

The economy is treading water
L'économie fait du surplace

• les projets

We're planning to go to the States
Nous projetons d'aller aux États-Unis

The plan is to meet up at Rachel's
L'idée, c'est de se retrouver chez Rachel

We don't have anything planned tomorrow afternoon
Nous n'avons rien de prévu demain après-midi

They had made plans to stay at a hotel
Ils avaient prévu de descendre à l'hôtel

There has been a change of plan
Il y a eu un changement de programme

Everything went according to plan
Tout a marché comme prévu

It's still at the planning stage
C'est encore à l'état de projet

They arrived later than expected
Ils sont arrivés plus tard que prévu

The proposal to build a new prison was rejected
La proposition de construction d'une nouvelle prison a été rejetée

I've organized a visit to a dairy for them
J'ai organisé la visite d'une laiterie à leur intention

I've arranged with the boss to leave early tomorrow
Je me suis arrangé avec le patron pour partir de bonne heure demain

He is already making preparations for next year's trip to Russia
Il prépare déjà le voyage en Russie de l'année prochaine

We worked out an easier route
Nous avons trouvé un itinéraire plus facile

• résumer

In short *or* In brief *or* To cut a long story short, it's not possible
Bref, ce n'est pas possible

To sum up, I will say (that) …
En résumé, je dirai que …

In conclusion *or* To conclude, I would just like to say (that) …
En conclusion, je voudrais simplement dire que …

In a word, no
En un mot, non

That's the whole thing in a nutshell
Voilà toute l'affaire en deux mots

All in all *or* On the whole he made a good impression
Dans l'ensemble, il a fait bonne impression

So, not to beat *Br* about *or Am* around the bush, I've lost my job
Enfin bref, j'ai perdu mon emploi

I'll come straight to the point
Je serai bref

• souligner

She emphasized *or* stressed *or* underlined the need for caution
Elle a mis l'accent sur la nécessité d'être prudent

The report highlights the desperate plight of the refugees
Le rapport souligne la situation désespérée des réfugiés

The thin dress only accentuated her frailness
La robe légère ne faisait qu'accentuer son air fragile

I must insist on this point
Je dois insister sur ce point

I repeat, I have never heard of him
Je le répète, je n'ai jamais entendu parler de lui

Don't dwell on your problems
Ne vous attardez pas sur vos problèmes

The revolt brought these issues to the fore
La révolte a mis ces problèmes en évidence

The defence made much of the witness's criminal record
La défense a beaucoup insisté sur le casier judiciaire du témoin

My uncle impressed on me the importance of hard work
Mon oncle a instillé en moi l'importance du travail

Good manners were dinned into us at school
Les bonnes manières nous ont été inculquées à l'école

I've told you hundreds of times!
Je vous l'ai dit cent fois!

She would not wear a hat
Elle refusait absolument de porter un chapeau

He will get in my way
Il va me gêner

I won't have it!
Je ne le permettrai pas!

It wasn't me, I swear (it)!
Ce n'était pas moi, je le jure!

• le succès

The film was a great success *or* was hugely successful in Italy
Le film a eu énormément de succès en Italie

We all want to succeed in life
Nous voulons tous réussir dans la vie

She succeeded only in confusing things further
Elle n'a réussi qu'à compliquer davantage les choses

He was successfully operated on for a stomach ulcer
Il a été opéré avec succès d'un ulcère à l'estomac

The experiment was a failure
L'expérience a été un échec

This agreement will be seen as a personal triumph for the President
Cet accord sera considéré comme un triomphe personnel pour le président

The discussions have failed to bring any progress
Les discussions n'ont produit aucune avancée

We managed to persuade her
Nous avons réussi à la persuader

The plan didn't achieve its objectives
Le plan n'a pas atteint ses objectifs

She had a hit with her song 'Bye, Bye'
Sa chanson 'Bye, Bye' a été un tube

That's a feather in her cap
Elle peut en être fière

The team rose to the occasion and won by a large margin
L'équipe s'est montrée à la hauteur des circonstances et s'est imposée facilement

He has reached the top of his profession
Il est arrivé en haut de l'échelle dans sa profession

She passed the exam with flying colours
Elle a réussi l'examen haut la main

Fam Will she (manage to) pull it off?
Est-ce qu'elle va y arriver?

Fam He's made a go of the business
Il a réussi à faire marcher l'affaire

• le sujet

What are they talking about?
De quoi parlent-ils?

It's a book about the life of Mozart
C'est un livre sur la vie de Mozart

What do you want to see me about?
Vous voulez me voir à quel sujet?

Talking of Switzerland *or* While we're on the subject of Switzerland, have you ever been skiing?
À propos de la Suisse, vous avez déjà fait du ski?

Don't try to change the subject!
N'essaie pas de changer de sujet!

She's taking exams in four subjects
Elle passe des examens dans quatre matières

That's not my field
Ce n'est pas mon domaine

Tonight's topic for debate is unemployment
Le débat de ce soir porte sur le chômage

In my lecture, I shall deal with …
Dans mon cours, je traiterai de …

Let's get back to the matter in hand
Revenons à nos moutons

The problem of the homeless doesn't come very high on the government's agenda
Le problème des sans-abri ne figure pas parmi les priorités du gouvernement

The matter is still under consideration
La question est encore à l'étude

The rising cost of living must also be taken into account *or* into consideration
Il faut aussi prendre en compte l'augmentation du coût de la vie

• la supposition

What makes you suppose *or* assume *or* presume (that) I trust you?
Qu'est-ce qui vous fait croire que j'ai confiance en vous?

I don't suppose (that) you remember me
Vous ne vous souvenez sans doute pas de moi

I suppose so/not
Je suppose que oui/que non

Supposing *or* (let's) suppose (that) you're right
Supposons que vous ayez raison

In the absence of proof, he must be assumed *or* presumed to be innocent
En l'absence de preuves, il doit être présumé innocent

I'm working on the assumption *or* the premise (that) …
Je me fonde sur l'hypothèse que …

She must have been talking about someone else
Elle devait parler de quelqu'un d'autre

At a guess, there'll be about 40 people at the party
Je pense qu'il y aura environ 40 personnes à la soirée

I dare say *or* I expect you're hungry after your journey
Je suppose que vous êtes affamés après ce voyage

We can only speculate
Nous ne pouvons que faire des suppositions

It was pure speculation *or* pure conjecture on his part
C'était pure conjecture de sa part

This confirms my hypothesis that …
Cela confirme mon hypothèse selon laquelle …

You take too much for granted
Vous présumez trop

Formal I can only surmise what the circumstances were
Je ne puis que conjecturer quelles étaient les circonstances

- **vouloir**

I want a cup of coffee
Je veux une tasse de café

They want to go to Spain on holiday
Ils veulent aller en vacances en Espagne

I want you to wait here
Je veux que tu attendes ici

I have no wish to offend you, but …
Je n'ai aucune envie de te blesser, mais …

I wish I were in your place
Je voudrais bien être à votre place

She had no desire to go back
Elle n'avait aucune envie d'y retourner

I was longing *or Fam* dying to tell her the truth
Je mourais d'envie de lui dire la vérité

He was yearning to see her again
Il brûlait de la revoir

She aspires to political power
Elle aspire au pouvoir politique

His ambition was to become a doctor
Il avait l'ambition de devenir médecin

I had an *or* the urge to hit him
J'ai eu envie de le frapper

I got a sudden craving for chocolate
J'ai eu une soudaine fringale de chocolat

He was driven by a hunger *or* a thirst for knowledge
Il était poussé par une soif de savoir

LES ÉMOTIONS: EXPRIMER CE QUE L'ON RESSENT

- **l'admiration**

They admire him for sticking to his principles
Ils l'admirent de s'en tenir à ses principes

I have great admiration for doctors
J'ai beaucoup d'admiration pour les médecins

She is held in high esteem *or* high regard by her colleagues
Elle est tenue en haute estime par ses collègues

I don't think very highly of my boss
Je n'ai pas une très haute opinion de mon patron

Children need someone to look up to
Les enfants ont besoin de prendre exemple sur quelqu'un

He looked at her in wonder
Il l'a regardée avec émerveillement

She worships her mother
Elle adore sa mère

She went into raptures over my geraniums
Elle s'est extasiée devant mes géraniums

I take my hat off to you!
Chapeau!

He stared at her in awe
Il la regardait, plein d'admiration

She has some wonderful ideas
Elle a des idées formidables

She looked stunning in her black velvet dress
Elle était superbe dans sa robe de velours noir

Fam What a fantastic goal!
Quel but fantastique!

Fam Wow!
Ouah!

- **l'amour**

They love one another
Ils s'aiment

My brother is/has fallen in love with her
Mon frère est/est tombé amoureux d'elle

It was love at first sight
C'était le coup de foudre

I have a lot of affection for you
J'ai beaucoup d'affection pour toi

We're just good friends
Nous sommes bons amis, c'est tout

He wanted to keep things platonic
Il voulait que leur relation reste platonique

Karen became infatuated with her teacher
Karen s'est entichée de son professeur

She had an affair *or Fam* a fling with my brother
Elle a eu une aventure avec mon frère

He's just a flirt
Il fait du charme à tout le monde

I don't have a steady boyfriend
Je n'ai pas vraiment de petit ami

They've been going out together for a month
Ils sortent ensemble depuis un mois

He's totally smitten
Il est sous le charme

I'm fond of you but I don't love you
Je t'aime bien mais c'est tout

She had a soft spot for Dan
Elle avait un faible pour Dan

Fam How's your love life?
Comment vont tes amours?

Fam She swears it's the real thing this time
Elle jure que cette fois-ci c'est le grand amour

Br Fam He fancies her something rotten
Elle lui plaît vachement

• l'aversion

I don't like *or* I dislike him
Je ne l'aime pas

She doesn't like dancing *or* to dance
Elle n'aime pas danser

If he doesn't like it he can go elsewhere
Si ça ne lui plaît pas il peut aller ailleurs

I detest *or* hate *or* loathe modern art/doing housework
Je déteste l'art moderne/faire le ménage

I can't stand smokers/hypocrisy
Je ne peux pas supporter les fumeurs/l'hypocrisie

Paul can't stand (the sight of) *or Br Fam* can't stick her
Paul ne peut pas la voir en peinture

The boss took an instant dislike to him
Le patron l'a tout de suite pris en grippe

I'm not keen on *or Fam* mad about *or Fam* crazy about Indian food
Je ne raffole pas de la cuisine indienne

He had a horror of being seen naked
Il avait horreur qu'on le voie nu

Rachel is allergic to hard work
Rachel est allergique au travail

Why are you so averse to the idea of helping?
Pourquoi l'idée d'apporter ton aide te répugne-t-elle tant?

The film wasn't at all to my taste
Le film n'était pas du tout à mon goût

I didn't care for his last book
Son dernier livre ne m'a pas plu

I've no time for that sort of attitude
Je ne supporte pas ce genre de mentalité

Fam Computers aren't my thing
L'informatique, ce n'est pas mon truc

Fam I'm not really into wearing ties
Les cravates, ce n'est pas vraiment mon truc

Formal There has always been some antipathy between the two actors
Il y a toujours eu une certaine inimitié entre les deux acteurs

• la beauté

What a beautiful woman/song!
Quelle belle femme/chanson!

She was a beauty in her day
C'était une beauté dans son temps

Beauty is in the eye of the beholder
Il n'y a pas de laides amours

Do you find him attractive?
Il te plaît?

Their daughter is as pretty as a picture
Leur fille est mignonne comme tout

He's very good-looking *or* handsome
Il est beau garçon

She's quite good-looking
Elle n'est pas mal

He's lost his looks
Il n'est plus aussi beau qu'avant

The new building is not very aesthetically pleasing
Le nouveau bâtiment n'est pas des plus agréables à l'œil

The landscape took my breath away
Le paysage m'a coupé le souffle

Fam Your baby is really cute
Ton bébé est vraiment mignon

Fam She's a real looker *or* stunner
Elle est vraiment canon

Fam He's a real hunk
C'est vraiment un beau mec

• la colère

She's angry at not having been invited
Elle est en colère parce qu'elle n'a pas été invitée

He got angry with her
Il s'est fâché contre elle

Her remarks made me angry
Ses observations m'ont mis en colère

In a moment of anger, he …
Dans un accès de colère, il …

My father was in a rage *or* was furious *or* was fuming
Mon père était furieux

It's infuriating the way she's always right
Ça me met hors de moi qu'elle ait toujours raison

Promise me (that) you won't get annoyed
Promets-moi que tu ne vas pas t'énerver

You're really getting on my nerves with your stupid comments
Tu commences vraiment à me taper sur les nerfs avec tes commentaires stupides

I resent your remarks
Je n'aime pas du tout vos remarques

He lost his temper with *or* flared up at me
Il s'est emporté contre moi

All of a sudden, she blew her top *or* flew off the handle *or* hit the roof and insulted me
D'un coup, elle est sortie de ses gonds et m'a insulté

He gets (himself) worked up over nothing
Il s'énerve pour rien

The boss is on the warpath
Le patron est d'une humeur massacrante

Behaviour like that really gets my back up
Ce genre de comportement m'horripile

How dare you speak to me in that tone of voice!
Comment oses-tu me parler sur ce ton!

Just wait till I get hold of him!
Attends un peu que je l'attrape!

That's the (absolute) limit!
Ça c'est le comble!

• la confiance

Are you feeling confident?
Tu te sens sûr de toi?

We are confident (that) it will work
Nous sommes confiants que ça marchera

I'm not confident of success
Je ne suis pas sûr de réussir

He is a very (self-)confident *or* (self-)assured person
C'est quelqu'un de très sûr de lui

She is full of/lacks (self-)confidence *or* (self-)assurance
Elle a une grande/manque de confiance en elle

He's very sure of himself for one so young
Il est très sûr de lui pour quelqu'un de si jeune

She was very poised during the interview
Elle était très sûre d'elle pendant l'entretien

You're not assertive enough
Vous n'avez pas assez d'autorité

You can tell (that) she's insecure
On sent qu'elle est mal dans sa peau

You're being overconfident about the exam
Tu présumes un peu trop de ta réussite à l'examen

Fam Don't be cocky!
Ne fais pas le malin!

• le courage

You'll have to be brave *or* courageous and tell him
Tu vas devoir être courageux et le lui dire

I don't have the courage to jump from a plane
Je n'ai pas le courage de sauter d'un avion

He's a soldier and an intrepid explorer
C'est un soldat et un explorateur intrépide

She's trying to pluck up courage *or* summon up her courage to invite him to the party
Elle essaie de rassembler son courage pour l'inviter à la fête

(Keep your) chin up!
Courage!

It takes pluck to do that
Il faut du courage pour faire ça

She was fearless in her pursuit of criminals
Elle était intrépide dans sa poursuite des criminels

Paul put a brave face on it, doing his best to appear unconcerned
Paul a fait bonne contenance, s'efforçant de paraître indifférent

Don't be such a coward
Ne sois pas aussi lâche

It was very cowardly of him
C'était lâche de sa part

You have no backbone
Vous n'avez rien dans le ventre

Fam She was too chicken to ask him out
Elle avait trop la frousse de lui demander de sortir avec elle

Fam I didn't have the guts to tell them
Je n'ai pas eu le cran de leur dire

Formal She bore her final illness with quiet fortitude
Elle a enduré la maladie qui devait l'emporter avec stoïcisme

• le dégoût

I'm disgusted with him/his behaviour
Il/Son comportement m'écœure

I resigned in disgust
Dégoûté, j'ai démissionné

How disgusting!
C'est dégoûtant!

They're disgustingly rich
Ils sont scandaleusement riches

It made him (feel) sick to think of all that waste
Ça l'écœurait de penser à tout ce gâchis

You make me sick!
Tu me dégoûtes!

It's sickening the way the refugees are treated
C'est écœurant, la façon dont on traite les réfugiés

The sight was enough to turn your stomach
Le spectacle avait de quoi vous soulever le cœur

He finds her/the idea repellent *or* repugnant *or* repulsive
Elle/l'idée lui répugne

Their attitude is abhorrent to me
Je trouve leur attitude détestable

It smells/tastes revolting
Ça a une odeur infecte/un goût infâme

La Langue en action

The soup was vile *or* foul
La soupe était infecte

I found his hypocrisy nauseating
J'ai trouvé son hypocrisie écœurante

That was a loathsome thing to do/say!
C'était vraiment dégoûtant de faire/dire ça!

That's disgusting! Ugh *or Fam* Yuck!
C'est dégoûtant, ça! Berk!

• les divertissements

Did you enjoy it?
Cela t'a plu?

She enjoys going to the cinema
Elle aime aller au cinéma

Enjoy yourself!
Amusez-vous bien!

I don't get much enjoyment out of teaching
Je ne tire guère de plaisir à enseigner

He amused himself building sandcastles
Il s'est amusé à faire des châteaux de sable

I love *or* adore walking in the rain
J'adore marcher sous la pluie

Skiing is great fun
C'est très amusant de faire du ski

We had fun *or Fam* a great time at the party
Nous nous sommes bien amusés à la soirée

We painted the town red at the weekend
On a fait la tournée des grands-ducs ce week-end

It was bliss to plunge into the water
C'était un bonheur de se plonger dans l'eau

He revelled in *or* took great delight in criticizing his employees
Il prenait grand plaisir à critiquer ses employés

She gets a thrill *or Fam* a kick out of driving fast
Elle s'éclate en conduisant vite

When I'm on holiday I really let myself go
Lorsque je suis en vacances, je me laisse vraiment aller

It was absolutely wonderful!
C'était absolument merveilleux!

Fam I'm having a ball!
Je me marre comme un fou!

Fam Come on, John, let your hair down a bit!
Vas-y John, laisse-toi un peu aller

Fam She's been living it up in London
Elle a mené la grande vie à Londres

• la douleur

Are you in pain?
Avez-vous mal?

I've a pain in my side
J'ai une douleur au côté

I have a shooting pain in my thigh
J'ai des élancements dans la cuisse

My foot hurts
Mon pied me fait mal

He has a bad back
Il a des problèmes de dos

I've got stomach ache/toothache/a headache
J'ai mal au ventre/aux dents/à la tête

Where is it sore?
Où as-tu mal?

He's bruised his arm
Il s'est fait un bleu au bras

My eyes are stinging *or* smarting
Les yeux me brûlent

He injured his knee skiing
Il s'est blessé au genou en faisant du ski

She has sprained her ankle/broken her arm
Elle s'est foulé la cheville/s'est cassé le bras

I've been bitten by mosquitoes
J'ai été piqué par des moustiques

This remedy will relieve the pain
Ce remède soulagera la douleur

Ow!
Aïe!

• l'embarras

It would be embarrassing *or* awkward if we met
Une rencontre serait embarrassante

Much to my embarrassment, I had to admit that…
À mon grand embarras, j'ai dû avouer que…

He blushed *or* went red at the thought
Il rougit à cette pensée

She was red in the face with embarrassment
Elle était rouge de gêne

Have you no shame?
Tu n'as pas honte?

The shame of it!
Quelle honte!

They tried to shame her into donating more
Ils ont essayé de lui faire honte pour qu'elle donne davantage

There's nothing to be ashamed of
Il n'y a pas de quoi avoir honte

He admitted, rather shamefacedly, that it was his fault
Il a reconnu, d'un air plutôt penaud, que c'était de sa faute

She just sat there with a sheepish grin on her face
Elle restait assise là, un sourire penaud sur son visage

I was mortified to discover that I had been deceived
J'étais mortifié de découvrir que l'on m'avait trompé

Don't be shy *or* bashful, tell me what you want
Ne soyez pas timide, dites-moi ce que vous voulez

When he said that I didn't know where to put my face!
Lorsqu'il a dit ça, je ne savais plus où me mettre!

Hearing myself say that, I just wanted the ground to open and swallow me up
J'aurais voulu rentrer sous terre quand je me suis rendu compte de ce que j'avais dit

He went off with his tail between his legs
Il s'en est allé la queue entre les jambes

• l'ennui

His speech was really boring *or* tedious *or* dull
Son discours était vraiment ennuyeux

It's a tedious *or* boring business collecting signatures
Recueillir des signatures est un travail fastidieux

He eats to keep boredom at bay
Il mange pour tromper l'ennui

She's a real bore on the subject of gardening
Elle est vraiment barbante quand elle se met à parler de jardinage

I'm bored with him/this conversation
Il/Cette conversation m'ennuie

I'm beginning to get bored
Je commence à m'ennuyer

I got tired of *or Fam* fed up with playing cards
J'en ai eu assez de jouer aux cartes

We had a dreary time (of it)
Ce n'était pas très gai

Her visits broke *or* relieved the monotony of his life
Les visites qu'elle lui rendait rompaient la monotonie de son existence

She went on about her holiday ad nauseam
Elle nous a raconté ses vacances à n'en plus finir

Fam Housework bores me stiff *or* silly *or* to tears *or* to death
Faire le ménage m'ennuie à mourir

Fam His latest film is deadly (dull)
Son dernier film est rasant

Fam This book is as dull as ditchwater
Ce livre est ennuyeux comme la pluie

Fam The exams are a real drag!
Quelle barbe ces examens!

• l'envie

I envy him his success
Je lui envie son succès

I don't envy her having to catch such an early train
Je ne l'envie pas d'avoir à prendre le train de si bonne heure

Your dress is wonderful; I'm green with envy
Ta robe est merveilleuse; je suis verte d'envie

She was the envy of all her friends
Elle faisait l'envie de tous ses amis

He is envious of their new house
Il est envieux de leur nouvelle maison

My daughter is jealous of me
Ma fille est jalouse de moi

He became jealous of her sudden success
Sa réussite soudaine l'a rendu jaloux

There's a lot of rivalry between the two brothers
Il y a une forte rivalité entre les deux frères

Vous n'avez rien à lui envier
You have no reason to be envious of him

She looked longingly at my delicious sandwiches
Elle regardait avec convoitise mes délicieux sandwichs

I'd really love to have your musical talents
J'aimerais vraiment avoir tes talents musicaux

Formal The Booker Prize is a highly coveted award
Le Booker Prize est un prix très convoité

• l'exécration

I hate *or* detest *or* loathe my boss/modern art/doing housework
Je déteste mon patron/l'art moderne/faire le ménage

She had an intense hatred of the police
Elle avait une haine profonde de la police

He's such a horrible *or* horrid little man!
C'est un affreux petit bonhomme!

I sensed the animosity between them
Je sentais une certaine animosité entre eux

My father-in-law is very hostile towards me
Mon beau-père fait preuve de beaucoup d'hostilité à mon égard

She only succeeded in antagonizing him further
Elle n'a réussi qu'à le rendre encore plus hostile

He has strong aversion to *or Formal* abhors travelling
Il déteste voyager

This building is an abomination
L'immeuble est une abomination

There is bad blood *or* ill feeling between the two families
Il y a de la rancune entre les deux familles

There's no love lost between them
Ils se détestent cordialement

Formal It's/He's anathema to me
C'est ma bête noire

• la faiblesse

I got weaker the farther we walked
Plus nous marchions, plus je devenais faible

She has a weak heart
Elle a le cœur faible

He's far too weak to be a leader
Il est beaucoup trop mou pour être un meneur

In a moment of weakness I gave in to temptation
Dans un moment de faiblesse j'ai cédé à la tentation

Punctuality is my weak point
La ponctualité est mon point faible

I haven't the strength to lift these boxes/to start again
Je n'ai pas la force de soulever ces cartons/ de recommencer

John was a sickly child
John était un enfant maladif

She fell to the floor in a faint
Elle est tombée en syncope

He's feeling emotionally fragile after his divorce
Il se sent fragile sur le plan émotionnel après son divorce

They were powerless to prevent the scandal
Ils n'ont rien pu faire pour éviter le scandale

That's a pretty feeble excuse
C'est une bien piètre excuse

The pound has weakened against the dollar
La livre est en baisse par rapport au dollar

There was a rickety bridge over the river
Un pont branlant enjambait la rivière

He was condemned on the flimsiest evidence
On l'a condamné en s'appuyant sur des preuves très peu convaincantes

Fam Don't be such a wimp!
Ne sois pas si dégonflé!

• la faim

Can I get you something to eat?
Est-ce que je peux vous offrir quelque chose à manger?

I'm getting hungry
Je commence à avoir faim

That night he went hungry
Cette nuit-là il est resté sur sa faim

I'm ravenous! *or* I could eat a horse!
J'ai une faim de loup!

We stopped for a snack *or Fam* a bite to eat
Nous nous sommes arrêtés pour manger un morceau

I've got no appetite
Je n'ai pas d'appétit

The walk gave him an appetite
La marche lui a ouvert l'appétit

The smell made my mouth water
L'odeur m'a mis l'eau à la bouche

I can't work on an empty stomach
Je ne peux pas travailler l'estomac vide

He's a big eater
C'est un gros mangeur

She's a fussy eater
Elle est difficile sur la nourriture

My uncle eats like a horse
Mon oncle mange comme quatre

Don't be so greedy *or* such a glutton!
Ne sois pas si goulu!

Drink some water to stave off your hunger
Buvez de l'eau pour tromper la faim

Fam I'm starving *or* famished!
Je meurs de faim

Fam I eat some fruit if I'm feeling peckish
Je mange un fruit si j'ai un petit creux

Fam I didn't have enough for breakfast and I've got the munchies
Je n'ai pas suffisamment déjeuné et j'ai la fringale

• la fatigue

He gets tired *or* tires easily
Il se fatigue facilement

The walk made me tired
La marche m'a fatigué

You'll tire yourself out moving all those boxes
Vous allez vous épuiser à déplacer toutes ces caisses

I'm tired out *or* worn out *or* exhausted
Je n'en peux plus

I always start to flag about mid-afternoon
Je commence toujours à faiblir vers le milieu de l'après-midi

He always feels sleepy after a meal
Il a toujours sommeil après un repas

She has rings under her eyes
Elle a les yeux cernés

You look weary
Vous avez l'air fatigué

I'm ready to drop
Je tombe de fatigue

Don't kill yourself working
Ne te tue pas au travail

Fam I'm dead beat *or Br Fam* I'm whacked
Je suis crevé

Br Fam I was absolutely done in *or* shattered *or* knackered!
J'étais complètement crevé!

• les goûts

I like my teacher/my new job
J'aime bien mon professeur/mon nouveau travail

She likes dancing *or* to dance
Elle aime danser

I've taken a liking to him
Il m'est devenu sympathique

He has a passion for music
Il a la passion de la musique

I'm very keen on *or Fam* mad about *or Fam* crazy about golf
Je suis fou de golf

She's not averse to a glass of wine
Elle boit volontiers un verre de vin

I'm a big fan of hers
Je suis un de ses fans les plus fervents

Did you like it at your grandmother's?
Tu t'es bien amusé chez ta grand-mère?

It's nice *or* good to be back again
Cela fait plaisir d'être de retour

It's a lovely idea
C'est une très bonne idée

Her parents are lovely people
Ses parents sont des gens charmants

Fam He's really into jogging
Il est fou de jogging

Formal Is it to your liking?
Cela vous convient-il?

• l'horreur

It was an awful *or* a dreadful *or* a terrible crime
C'était un crime horrible

To my horror, I noticed (that) …
À ma grande horreur, je me suis aperçu que …

I was horrified by the murder
J'ai été horrifié par le meurtre

He suffered horrific injuries to the head
Il a subi des blessures horribles à la tête

I'm appalled!
C'est un scandale!

It appals me to think (that) …
Je suis horrifié à la pensée que …

Her behaviour shocked them
Son comportement les a choqués

How shocking!
Quelle horreur!

Horror films give me nightmares
Les films d'horreur me donnent des cauchemars

The army was guilty of many atrocities during the war
L'armée s'est rendue coupable de nombreuses atrocités pendant la guerre

She goes *or* lives in terror of her father
Elle vit dans la terreur de son père

I stared at him aghast
Je l'ai regardé, atterré

Her blood ran cold *or* froze at the thought
À cette pensée, son sang s'est figé dans ses veines

It was enough to make your hair stand on end
C'était à faire dresser les cheveux sur la tête

It sent cold shivers down my spine
Cela m'a fait froid dans le dos

• l'impatience

The children were eager *or* keen to learn
Les enfants étaient avides d'apprendre

He's eager *or* keen for me to see his work
Il a très envie que je voie son travail

They aren't so keen on going out tonight
Ça ne leur dit pas grand-chose de sortir ce soir

I can't wait to go
J'ai hâte d'y aller

I'm looking forward to seeing her again
Il me tarde de la revoir

He was anxious for them to go
Il attendait impatiemment qu'ils partent

She's very enthusiastic about the project
Elle est très enthousiaste à l'idée de ce projet

I can't get excited about it
Ça ne me dit vraiment rien

I was longing *or Fam* dying to tell her the truth
Je mourais d'envie de lui dire la vérité

He is a fervent believer in reincarnation
Il croit ardemment à la réincarnation

There were 10,000 troops in the region raring to go *or* champing at the bit *or* straining at the leash
Il y avait 10 000 soldats dans la région qui brûlaient d'en découdre

• l'indignation

He was indignant at her attitude
Il était indigné par son attitude

To my indignation, I discovered I hadn't been invited
À mon indignation, j'ai découvert que je n'avais pas été invité

It really annoys *or* irritates me when people throw litter in my garden
Cela m'agace vraiment lorsque les gens jettent des détritus dans mon jardin

The annoying thing about it is (that) …
L'ennuyeux là-dedans c'est que …

I did it out of sheer exasperation
J'ai fait cela parce que j'étais exaspéré

It's/He's outrageous!
Cela/Il dépasse les bornes!

You must be joking! *or* You're joking!
Vous voulez rire!

Who does he think he is?
Pour qui se prend-il?

He had the cheek to ask her age!
Il a eu le culot de lui demander son âge!

How dare you!
Comment oses-tu!

Fam He went off in a huff
Il a pris la mouche et s'en est allé

Formal She was vexed at his behaviour
Elle était contrariée par son comportement

La Langue en action

• l'indifférence

It's a matter of complete indifference to me
Cela m'est parfaitement indifférent

She was indifferent to the beauty of the landscape
Elle était indifférente à la beauté du paysage

He wasn't interested in what I was saying
Il n'était pas intéressé par ce que je disais

I worked hard but my heart wasn't in it
J'ai beaucoup travaillé mais le cœur n'y était pas

I don't care what people think
Je me moque de ce que pensent les gens

I couldn't care less if he comes or not
Ça m'est complètement égal qu'il vienne ou non

It's all the same to me *or* It makes no difference to me
Cela m'est égal

He's not particularly bothered *or Br Fam* fussed whether we go or not
Ça lui est égal qu'on y aille ou pas

Do you like opera? – I can take it or leave it
Vous aimez l'opéra?– Pas plus que ça

I don't mind if people laugh at me
Cela m'est égal si les gens se moquent de moi

It all comes (down) to the same thing
Tout cela revient au même

Who cares?
Qu'est-ce que ça peut faire?

Never mind!
Ça ne fait rien!

So what?
Et alors?

Fam I don't give a damn about the money
Je me fiche pas mal de l'argent

Fam It's six of one and half a dozen of the other
C'est blanc bonnet et bonnet blanc

• l'intolérance

He is very intolerant of noisy children
Il ne supporte absolument pas les enfants bruyants

She is narrow-minded about sex
Elle est étroite d'esprit en ce qui concerne le sexe

It is not good to have an inflexible attitude to change
Il n'est pas bon d'adopter une attitude intransigeante face au changement

I don't share their fanatical devotion to the cause.
Je ne partage pas leur dévotion fanatique à la cause

He's full of prejudice
Il est plein de préjugés

Let's not be prejudiced about this
Essayons de ne pas avoir d'idées préconçues là-dessus

You're biased in her favour
Tu as un parti pris pour elle

My aunt has a closed mind
Ma tante est hermétique aux idées nouvelles

You shouldn't be dogmatic about grammar
Il ne faut pas être dogmatique au sujet de la grammaire

Don't be such a pedant!
Ne sois pas aussi pédant!

I won't put up with this noise any longer!
Je ne supporterai pas ce bruit une minute de plus!

Br Fam He couldn't be doing with living in London
Il ne pouvait pas supporter de vivre à Londres

• la patience

You'll have to be patient
Il vous faudra être patient

I've no patience with him
Je n'ai aucune patience avec lui

I'm getting impatient
Je commence à m'impatienter

To do that you need the patience of Job *or* of a saint
Pour faire cela il faut avoir une patience d'ange

Take your time over it
Prenez le temps qu'il faudra

What's the rush *or* hurry?
Qu'est-ce qui presse tant?

There's no (great) urgency
Ce n'est pas urgent

Can't it wait until the weekend?
Cela ne peut-il pas attendre ce week-end?

I can't wait to go
J'ai hâte d'y aller

I was longing *or Fam* dying to tell her the truth
Je mourais d'envie de lui dire la vérité

I'm determined not to give in
Je suis résolu à ne pas céder

We'll just have to grin and bear it
Il faudra le prendre avec le sourire

More haste less speed
Plus on se hâte moins on avance

Fam Go and wash your hands and make it snappy *or* jump to it!
Va te laver les mains et que ça saute!

• la peur

We feared for our lives
Nous craignions pour nos vies

We spoke quietly for fear of being discovered
Nous parlions tout bas de peur d'être découverts

She's afraid *or* frightened *or* scared of the dark
Elle a peur du noir

I'm not afraid *or* frightened *or* scared of you
Tu ne me fais pas peur

They frightened *or* scared him into leaving
Ils lui ont fait peur jusqu'à ce qu'il parte

There's nothing to be afraid of
Il n'y a rien à craindre

I have a phobia of spiders
J'ai la phobie des araignées

He got into a panic about his debts
Il était complètement paniqué à cause de ses dettes

Don't be alarmed, it's not serious
Ne vous alarmez pas, ce n'est pas grave

I'm nervous about flying
Je suis mal à l'aise à l'idée de prendre l'avion

I dread having them both here
J'appréhende de les avoir tous les deux en même temps

I was petrified (that) he would shoot me
J'étais mort de peur à l'idée qu'il me tire dessus

You gave me a terrible fright!
Vous m'avez fait une de ces peurs!

Her heart was in her mouth as she watched
Elle regardait en retenant son souffle

Just thinking about it brings me out in a cold sweat
Rien que d'y penser, j'en ai des sueurs froides

He has a voice that makes your flesh creep
Il a une voix qui donne la chair de poule

Fam The film scared me stiff!
Le film m'a flanqué une de ces frousses!

Fam This ghost story frightened the living daylights out of me
Cette histoire de fantômes m'a flanqué une peur bleue

Fam He's got the jitters about his exam
Il a la trouille à cause de son examen

Fam Her threats really put the wind up me
Ses menaces m'ont vraiment fichu la frousse

• le plaisir

I'm delighted *or* very pleased (that) you could come
Je suis ravi que tu aies pu venir

(I'm) pleased to meet you!
Enchanté de faire votre connaissance!

I'd accept your invitation with pleasure, but …
J'accepterais votre invitation avec plaisir, seulement …

He plays cards for pleasure, not for money
Il joue aux cartes pour le plaisir, non pas pour l'argent

It gives me great pleasure to join the team
Ça me fait énormément plaisir de me joindre à l'équipe

Thank you for a very pleasant evening
Merci pour cette merveilleuse soirée

She was very pleasant to us as a rule
Elle était en général très aimable à notre égard

I'm very happy *or* satisfied *or* content with his work
Je suis très satisfait de son travail

They were delighted at the news
La nouvelle leur a fait très plaisir

I'm glad you like him
Je suis content que vous l'aimiez bien

We had a lovely day at the beach
Nous avons passé une très agréable journée à la plage

Have a nice day!
Bonne journée!

The laid-back atmosphere of the village made a welcome change from London
L'atmosphère détendue du village nous changeait en bien de Londres

Fam She's over the moon about it
Elle en est ravie

• les préférences

Which would you prefer, wine or beer?
Tu préfères du vin ou de la bière?

I have no preference
Je n'ai pas de préférence

Come tomorrow, preferably in the evening
Venez demain, de préférence dans la soirée

I'd rather go by car
J'aimerais mieux y aller en voiture

Would you like to make the presentations? – I'd rather not
Voudriez-vous faire les présentations? – Je n'y tiens pas

Tuesday suits me best
C'est mardi qui me convient le mieux

It would be better if you called me tomorrow
Il vaudrait mieux que tu m'appelles demain

There's nothing to choose between them
L'un vaut l'autre

Spain would be my choice
Je choisirais l'Espagne

You have no choice (in the matter)
Vous n'avez pas le choix

We have no option but to agree
Nous n'avons pas d'autre option que d'accepter

Which do you want? – Either (one) will do
Lequel veux-tu? – N'importe

You're biased in her favour
Tu as un parti pris pour elle

La Langue en action

He took Tom's side against me
Il a pris le parti de Tom contre moi

She has right-wing leanings
Ses sympathies vont à la droite

I'm inclined to favour the suicide theory
Je pencherais plutôt pour l'hypothèse du suicide

He could do (a lot) worse than accept their offer
Il pouvait faire pire que d'accepter leur proposition

Fam Which course have you plumped for?
Quels cours as-tu choisi?

• les regrets

Sorry to have bothered you
Excusez-moi de vous avoir dérangé

I'm sorry (that) we won't be able to fetch you
Je regrette que nous ne puissions venir vous chercher

I regret ever mentioning it
Je regrette d'en avoir jamais parlé

I have no regrets
Je ne regrette rien

It's a shame *or* a pity (that) you can't come
C'est dommage que vous ne puissiez pas venir

I'm afraid I can't help you
Je suis désolé, mais je ne peux pas vous aider

Unfortunately, I don't know if I'm going to be able to take part
Malheureusement je ne sais pas si je vais pouvoir y participer

If only I had known!
Si seulement j'avais su!

They ought not to have *or* should not have been allowed in
On n'aurait pas dû les laisser entrer

I wish (that) I hadn't left so early
Je regrette d'être parti si tôt

He was filled with remorse at what he had done
Il était pris de remords en songeant à ce qu'il avait fait

She has no qualms *or* scruples about lying to them
Elle n'a aucun scrupule à leur mentir

If he dies, I'll never forgive myself
S'il meurt, je ne me le pardonnerais jamais

I could have kicked myself!
Je me serais donné des gifles!

It's no use crying over spilt milk
Ce qui est fait est fait

• la résignation

I was resigned to *or* had resigned myself to going alone
Je m'étais résigné à y aller seul

We have to accept the fact that war is imminent
Nous devons accepter le fait que la guerre est imminente

He's finding it hard to come to terms with his wife's death
Il a du mal à accepter la mort de sa femme

We'll have to make the best of the situation
Il faudra nous accommoder de la situation

You give in too easily
Tu abandonnes trop facilement

That's life!
C'est la vie!

That's the way things are
C'est comme ça

There's nothing I can do about it
Je ne peux rien y faire

We'll have to put up with it
Il faut nous y résigner

I won't take this lying down!
Je ne vais pas me laisser faire comme ça!

She shrugged her shoulders *or* gave a shrug and carried on regardless
Elle a haussé les épaules et continué comme si de rien n'était

Fam He shouldn't let people push him around *or* walk all over him
Il ne devrait pas se laisser piétiner ainsi

Formal She submitted to her fate
Elle acceptait son destin

• la soif

Can I get you something to drink?
Est-ce que je peux vous offrir quelque chose à boire?

I'm getting thirsty
Je commence à avoir soif

Tea is good for quenching your thirst
Le thé est très désaltérant

I could do with *or* I wouldn't mind a cup of coffee
Je prendrais bien une tasse de café

A cold drink just now would be very refreshing
Une bonne boisson froide nous rafraîchirait maintenant

She drained her glass
Elle a vidé son verre

My uncle is a heavy drinker
Mon oncle boit beaucoup

Fam I'm parched
Je crève de soif

• les soucis

Tell me what's worrying you
Dites-moi ce qui vous préoccupe

There's nothing to worry about
Il n'y a pas lieu de s'inquiéter

That's the least of my worries
C'est le cadet de mes soucis

She's worried *or* concerned about her nephew
Elle est inquiète pour son neveu

He's worried sick about it
Il en est malade d'inquiétude

I'm anxious about losing my job
J'ai peur de perdre mon travail

Her husband's health is causing her great anxiety
La santé de son mari est source d'angoisse pour elle

Nothing seems to trouble him
Il ne s'en fait jamais

She's fretting because her pony is missing
Elle est dans tous ses états parce que son poney a disparu

The thought continued to prey on my mind
L'idée continuait à me ronger l'esprit

That's a weight off my mind
Je suis vraiment soulagé

She doesn't have a care in the world
Elle n'a aucun souci

You shouldn't agonize so much about these decisions
Tu ne devrais pas te ronger les sangs comme ça à propos de ces décisions

• la surprise

I'm surprised to see you *or* at seeing you here
Je m'étonne de vous voir ici

What a lovely *or* pleasant surprise!
Quelle bonne surprise!

Their arrival took me by surprise *or* caught me unawares
Leur arrivée m'a pris au dépourvu

Well, it's not surprising, is it?
Ça n'a vraiment rien de surprenant

I'm surprised *or* astonished (that) the question has never been asked
Cela m'étonne que la question n'ait jamais été posée

To our astonishment, the shop was closed
À notre grand étonnement, le magasin était fermé

I was amazed *or* astounded when she left like that
J'étais stupéfait qu'elle parte comme ça

We were dumbfounded at the news
La nouvelle nous a frappés de stupeur

I was staggered to learn of his decision
J'ai été stupéfait d'apprendre sa décision

The noise startled her *or* made her jump
Le bruit l'a fait sursauter

I can't get over how much he's grown!
Qu'est-ce qu'il a grandi, je n'en reviens pas!

When he said that, her jaw dropped
Lorsqu'il le lui a dit, elle en est restée bouche bée

I'm speechless! *or* I don't know what to say!
Je ne sais pas quoi dire!

Fam I was flabbergasted by how much progress he had made
J'ai été sidéré par ses progrès

Br Fam Never!
Pas possible!

• la tristesse

I shall be sad to see you leave
Je serai désolé de vous voir partir

It makes me sad or saddens me to see what's become of them
Ça me rend triste de voir ce qu'ils sont devenus

I am writing to express my sadness *or* my sorrow at your loss
Je vous écris pour vous faire part de la tristesse que j'ai éprouvée en apprenant votre deuil

He had an unhappy time abroad
Il a passé des moments difficiles à l'étranger

What are you so upset about?
Qu'est-ce qui te met dans cet état?

I'm upset about losing it/her
Ça me fait mal au cœur de le/la perdre

Don't upset yourself
Arrête, tu te fais du mal

She was crying her heart *or* eyes out
Elle pleurait toutes les larmes de son corps

We are grieving for *or* mourning our father
Nous pleurons notre père

In despair, she took her own life
De désespoir elle a mis fin à ses jours

We found him alone and in a very distressed state
Nous l'avons trouvé seul, complètement bouleversé

Visiting her grandparents made her feel depressed *or* got her down
Le fait de rendre visite à ses grands-parents la déprimait

I tried to comfort him but he was inconsolable
J'ai essayé de le réconforter mais il était inconsolable

They made her life a misery
Ils lui ont rendu la vie insupportable

La Langue en action

COMMUNICATION: PARLER, ÉCRIRE, ÉCHANGER

• accepter

Please accept my apologies
Je vous prie de bien vouloir accepter mes excuses

Will you accept *or* take a cheque?
Vous acceptez les chèques?

His wife accepted the prize on his behalf
Sa femme a accepté le prix en son nom

I refuse to accept that he's guilty
Je refuse de croire qu'il soit coupable

He took the news better than I thought he would
Il a pris la nouvelle mieux que je ne l'aurais cru

We must take things as they come
Il faut prendre les choses comme elles viennent

Did she say yes to your offer?
A-t-elle dit oui à votre offre?

I wouldn't say no to a cold drink
Je prendrais volontiers une boisson fraîche

The plans met with little opposition
Les projets n'ont rencontré que peu d'opposition

The government will not take in any refugees
Le gouvernement n'accueillera aucun réfugié

He was granted asylum
On lui a accordé l'asile

My boss gave in to *or Formal* deferred to my wishes
Mon patron a exaucé mes souhaits

That's what they decided and I went along with it
C'est la décision qu'ils ont prise et je l'ai acceptée

I admit (that) I was wrong
J'ai eu tort, je le reconnais

• l'âge

How old are you?
Quel âge avez-vous?

She's 25 (years old *or* years of age)
Elle a 25 ans

Paul is as old as *or* is the same age as David
Paul a le même âge que David

She is older than me *or* than I am
Elle est plus âgée que moi

I'm two years younger than her *or* two years her junior
J'ai deux ans de moins qu'elle

He's old enough to be my father!
Il pourrait être mon père!

When I was your age, I …
Quand j'avais votre âge, je …

She doesn't look her age
Elle ne fait pas son âge

He's tall for his age
Il est grand pour son âge

The president is getting on for sixty
Le président approche de la soixantaine

She's getting on a bit
Elle commence à se faire vieille

My uncle lived to a ripe old age
Mon oncle a vécu jusqu'à un âge avancé

When will I be able to retire?
Quand pourrai-je prendre ma retraite?

Pneumonia cut him down in the prime of life *or* in his prime
Une pneumonie l'a emporté à la fleur de l'âge

My oldest daughter has just turned 20
Ma fille aînée vient d'avoir 20 ans

This is my youngest, Stephen
Voici mon cadet, Stephen

They have a ten-year-old boy
Ils ont un garçon de dix ans

We go back a long way, Brad and me
Ça remonte à loin, Brad et moi

Fam She's a bit long in the tooth
Elle n'est plus toute jeune

Fam He's no spring chicken
Ce n'est pas un perdreau de l'année

• annoncer

We are pleased to announce the birth/ marriage of our son
Nous sommes heureux de vous faire part de la naissance/du mariage de notre fils

Management have announced a cut in pay
La direction a annoncé une réduction des salaires

She was declared the winner
Elle a été déclarée vainqueur

He refused to reveal *or Formal* disclose *or Formal* divulge the identity of his attacker
Il a refusé de révéler l'identité de son agresseur

He let it be known that he was available
Il a fait savoir qu'il était disponible

She went public with the story
Elle a révélé toute l'histoire

There are rumours of a takeover
Il y a des rumeurs de rachat

It's being put about by her rivals that …
Ses rivaux font circuler le bruit que …

He made a statement in the press to the effect that …
Il a fait une déclaration à la presse selon laquelle …

I'm so happy I want to shout it from the rooftops!
Je suis si heureux que j'ai envie de le crier sur tous les toits!

His mother didn't know he was gay until he came out
Sa mère ne savait pas qu'il était gay avant qu'il fasse son outing

Formal He proclaimed himself emperor
Il s'est proclamé empereur

• approuver

Do you approve of the proposal?
Êtes-vous d'accord avec la proposition?

She doesn't approve of *or* She disapproves of them smoking
Ça ne lui plaît pas qu'ils fument

I'm in favour of this line of action
Je suis favorable à ce plan d'action

I'm opposed to the idea
Je m'oppose à cette idée

I welcomed the opportunity to speak to her
J'étais content d'avoir l'occasion de lui parler

I disagree with everything they've done
Je désapprouve tout ce qu'ils ont fait

He gave the plan his seal *or* stamp of approval
Il a donné son approbation au projet

Has the boss given his blessing to the project?
Est-ce que le patron a donné sa bénédiction au projet?

She takes a dim view of him going out with other women
Elle n'apprécie guère qu'il sorte avec d'autres femmes

I take exception to that remark
Je n'apprécie pas du tout ce commentaire

They got the green light or the go-ahead to buy the company
Ils ont obtenu le feu vert pour acheter la société

I've nothing against it
Je n'ai rien contre

His mother doesn't hold with private schools
Sa mère est contre les écoles privées

Fam Her plan has been okayed
Son projet a reçu le feu vert

• au revoir!

Goodbye, Mike!
Au revoir, Mike!

She said goodbye to me
Elle m'a dit au revoir

We said our goodbyes and left
On a fait nos adieux et on est partis

He gave her a goodbye kiss
Il l'a embrassée en partant

Thank you for calling, goodbye
Merci d'avoir appelé, au revoir

Good night, sleep tight!
Bonne nuit, dors bien!

They left the cinema and said good night
Ils sont sortis du cinéma et se sont dit bonsoir

She came to see me off at the station
Elle est venue à la gare me dire au revoir

We waved goodbye
Nous avons fait au revoir de la main

They held a farewell party for him
Ils ont fait une fête pour son départ

Have a nice day!
Bonne journée!

See you! *or* (I'll) be seeing you! *or* *Fam* So long!
À bientôt!

Well, I must be going *or* I have to go
Bon, je dois y aller

It's been really nice meeting you – And you
C'est un plaisir de vous avoir rencontré – Pareillement

Have a good trip home!
Je vous souhaite un bon retour!

Fam Bye! *or* Take care! *or* *Br* Cheerio!
Salut!

• bonjour!

Hello, Jim, how are you?
Bonjour, Jim, comment ça va?

Say hello to him for me
Dis-lui bonjour de ma part

She asked me to say hello to you
Elle m'a demandé de vous donner le bonjour

Hello, Anne Johnson speaking
Allô, Anne Johnson à l'appareil

Good morning/afternoon!
Bonjour!

Good evening!
Bonsoir!

Welcome to my home/to England!
Bienvenue chez moi/en Angleterre!

How do you do? My name is Robert Green
Bonjour! Je m'appelle Robert Green

Charles greeted *or* welcomed them warmly
Charles les a chaleureusement accueillis

He isn't well enough to receive visitors
Il n'est pas en état de recevoir des visites

They shook hands
Ils se sont serré la main

Fam Hi, how's things?
Salut, ça roule?

• la compassion

I was sorry to hear about your father's death
J'ai été désolé d'apprendre la mort de votre père

It's the children I feel sorry for
Ce sont les enfants que je plains

La Langue en action

La Langue en action

That poor woman, I feel for her
La pauvre, ça me fait de la peine pour elle

I sympathize because I used to have similar problems
Je compatis car j'ai connu des problèmes du même genre

Her heart went out to them
Elle a ressenti de la compassion pour eux

He consoled me in my grief
Il m'a consolé de ma peine

If it's any consolation, the same thing happened to me
Si cela peut te consoler, il m'est arrivé la même chose

I tried to comfort him but he was inconsolable
J'ai essayé de le réconforter mais il était inconsolable

If there's anything I can do for you, please let me know
Si je peux vous aider en quoi que ce soit, n'hésitez pas à me le faire savoir

How awful for you!
Ça a dû être vraiment terrible pour vous!

You poor thing, Alice!
Ma pauvre Alice!

Formal You have my deepest sympathy *or* Please accept my condolences
Je vous présente toutes mes condoléances

Formal We commiserated with him on his misfortune
Nous avons compati à ses malheurs

• la concession

He admitted *or* acknowledged *or* conceded (that) he was wrong
Il a admis qu'il avait tort

She has a point
Elle n'a pas tort

To be fair (to them) *or* In all justice to them, they did contribute their time
Rendons-leur cette justice, ils ont donné de leur temps

You're honest, I'll say that for you
Je dirais en votre faveur que vous êtes honnête

That's fair enough, but don't you think that …?
Très bien, mais ne pensez-vous pas que …?

Owning a home is all very well, but …
C'est bien beau d'être propriétaire, mais …

To be honest (with you), I don't think it'll work
À vrai dire, je ne crois pas que ça marchera

Granted, he's not very intelligent, but …
D'accord, il n'est pas très intelligent, mais …

I had to yield to them on that point
J'ai dû leur céder sur ce point

Please can I stay up late? – Oh, I suppose so
S'il te plaît, est-ce que je peux veiller tard? – Bon, si tu veux

Formal I defer to your knowledge in these matters
Je m'en remets à vos connaissances en la matière

• la confiance

You can trust me
Vous pouvez me faire confiance

I can't rely on *or* trust her to do the job properly
Je ne peux pas compter sur elle pour faire le travail correctement

I certainly wouldn't trust him with any of my secrets
Je ne lui confierais certainement pas un de mes secrets

It's a car you can rely on *or* trust *or* It's a reliable car
C'est une voiture fiable

We must put our trust in science
Nous devons placer notre confiance en la science

He has a deep distrust *or* mistrust of doctors
Il éprouve une profonde méfiance à l'égard des médecins

They have good reason to distrust *or* mistrust her
Ils ont de bonnes raisons de se méfier d'elle

I don't have much faith in him
Je ne lui fais pas beaucoup confiance

I'm relying on you to find a solution
Je compte sur vous pour trouver une solution

She swears by those vitamin tablets
Elle ne jure que par ces vitamines

Be on your guard: he's devious
Prenez garde: il est sournois

Children should be wary of strangers
Les enfants devraient se méfier des étrangers

We are reliably informed that …
Nous avons appris de bonne source que …

He's a loyal *or* faithful friend
C'est un ami fidèle

• confirmer

Could you confirm your name and address, please?
Pourriez-vous, s'il vous plaît, confirmer vos nom et adresse?

We confirm receipt of your letter
Nous accusons réception de votre lettre

His diagnosis confirmed my fears
Son diagnostic a confirmé mes craintes

Could you tell me if the meeting is taking place?
Pourriez-vous me dire si la réunion aura bien lieu?

Are you quite sure he hasn't left yet?
Êtes-vous bien sûr qu'il n'est pas encore parti?

I owe you £20, (is that) right?
Je te dois 20 livres, c'est ça?

Am I right in thinking you're German?
Je me trompe ou vous êtes allemand?

That's right!
C'est ça!

I told you so! *or* What did I tell you!
Je vous l'avais bien dit!

There was no evidence of his stay in the house
Rien ne montrait qu'il avait séjourné dans la maison

I feel, and I'm sure Peter will bear me out *or* back me up on this …
J'estime, et je suis sûr que Peter confirmera ce point …

I can verify that Gillian Brown was present
Je peux confirmer que Gillian Brown était bien là

Formal What you say corroborates her story
Ce que vous dites corrobore sa version des faits

• les conseils

Let me give you some advice
Permettez que je vous donne un conseil

Take my advice and say nothing to her
Suis mon conseil, ne lui dis rien

What do you advise (me to do)?
Que me conseillez-vous?

He advised them against taking legal action
Il leur a déconseillé d'intenter une action en justice

I recommend going *or* that you go via Leeds
Je vous recommande de passer par Leeds

If you want my advice, you'll wait a bit longer before selling
Si vous voulez un bon conseil, attendez encore un peu avant de vendre

She needs guidance concerning her education
Elle a besoin de conseils pour son éducation

He cautioned them against deciding before they knew all the facts
Il leur a bien dit de se garder de prendre une décision avant de connaître les tenants et aboutissants

They warned me about you
On m'avait mis en garde contre toi

You ought to get a second opinion
Vous devriez consulter quelqu'un d'autre

What would you do (if you were) in my place *or* if you were me?
Que feriez-vous à ma place?

Do you want to know what I think?
Vous voulez savoir ce que j'en pense?

It's expensive, don't you think?
C'est cher, tu ne trouves pas?

The best thing (to do) is to keep quiet
Le mieux, c'est de ne rien dire

• convaincre

They persuaded him to come/dissuaded him from coming
Ils l'ont persuadé/dissuadé de venir

I urged him to accept
Je lui ai vivement conseillé d'accepter

His arguments don't convince me
Ses arguments ne me convainquent pas

I'm convinced (that) we will succeed
Je suis convaincu que nous réussirons

I managed to convince *or* persuade myself that everything would be all right
J'ai réussi à me persuader que tout irait bien

She wasn't very convincing as Juliet
Elle n'était pas très convaincante dans le rôle de Juliette

You'll never get him to admit it
Tu ne le lui feras jamais admettre

Do you think you could use your influence with the boss and get me a pay rise?
Tu crois que tu pourrais utiliser ton influence auprès du patron pour m'obtenir une augmentation?

I talked *or* brought them round to my way of thinking
Je les ai amenés à partager mon avis

She allowed herself to be talked into going
Elle s'est laissé convaincre d'y aller

I won him over to my point of view
J'ai réussi à le rallier à mon point de vue

I tried to reason with them
J'ai essayé de leur faire entendre raison

He'd have me believe (that) it's an antique
Il voudrait me faire croire que c'est un objet d'époque

Yes, but I'm sure you'd agree (that) he does have a point
Oui, mais vous conviendrez certainement qu'il n'a pas tort

LA CONVERSATION

We had a long conversation *or* talk about fishing. *Nous avons eu une longue conversation sur la pêche.*
I got into conversation with him. *Nous avons engagé la conversation.*
I'm not much of a conversationalist. *Je ne suis pas brillant causeur.*
She was just making conversation. *Elle faisait juste la conversation.*

They sat talking *or* chatting about this and that. *Ils étaient assis là à bavarder de choses et d'autres.*
He was chatting to the man next to him. *Il bavardait avec l'homme qui était à côté de lui.*
I often pass the time of day with my neighbours. *Je fais souvent un brin de causette avec mes voisins.*
Have you heard the latest bit of gossip? *Tu ne connais pas la dernière?*
Fam Two old men were standing on the corner chewing the fat. *Deux hommes âgés taillaient une bavette au coin de la rue*

Engager la conversation

It's lovely/terrible weather, isn't it? *Il fait un temps magnifique/horrible, n'est-ce pas?*
That's a nice jacket/car/camera. *C'est une jolie veste/une jolie voiture/un bel appareil photo.*
Is this your first time here? *C'est la première fois que vous venez ici?*
Have you been waiting long? *Vous attendez depuis longtemps?*
So, how long have you known Peter? *Et depuis combien de temps connaissez-vous Peter?*

Alimenter la conversation et manifester son intérêt

Sons: Oh / Uh-huh / Mm
Répétition: Ten years? *Dix ans?* / The oldest in Europe? *Le plus vieux d'Europe?* / Right next door? *Juste à côté?*
Mots et expressions: Really? *Vraiment?* / OK *OK* / I see. *Je vois.* / Amazing! *Incroyable!* / I know. *Je sais.* / You're joking! *Vous plaisantez!* / That's terrible! *Mais c'est terrible!* / I didn't know that. *Je ne le savais pas.* / I can't believe it. *Je n'arrive pas à le croire.*
Questions (pour encourager la personne à continuer): And what did you do? *Et qu'avez-vous fait?* / And then what? *Et que s'est-il passé ensuite?* / And what will happen? *Et que va-t-il se passer?* / Did you? *or* Can he? *or* Are they? *Ah oui, vraiment?*

Demander à la personne de répéter

Br Sorry? *or* Pardon? *or Am* Excuse me? *or* Pardon me? *Excusez-moi?*
I didn't catch what you said. Could you repeat that, please? *Je n'ai pas bien compris ce que vous avez dit. Pourriez-vous répéter s'il vous plaît?*
Sorry, what did you say? *Pardon, qu'avez-vous dit?*

Demander à la personne d'être plus claire

What do you mean exactly? *Que voulez-vous dire exactement?*
What do you mean by ...? I'm not sure I follow. *Qu'entendez-vous par ...? Je ne vous suis pas bien.*
I don't understand. Could you explain that again? *Je ne comprends pas bien. Pourriez-vous me réexpliquer?*
I'm sorry, could you repeat that? I didn't quite understand. *Je suis désolé, pourriez-vous répéter? Je n'ai pas vraiment compris.*
Could you say that again a little more slowly, please? *Pourriez-vous répéter un peu plus lentement, s'il vous plaît?*

Quitter la conversation lorsque les autres personnes sont encore en train de parler

I'm afraid I've got to go now. I'll talk to you later. *Si vous le voulez bien, je vais vous laisser pour le moment. Je reviendrai vous voir plus tard.*
I must go and get another drink. *Je vais aller chercher un autre verre.*
Excuse me a moment. I have to check something/see someone. *Veuillez m'excuser un instant. Je dois aller vérifier quelque chose/voir quelqu'un.*
Sorry, I'll be back in a minute. *Excusez-moi, je reviens dans une minute.*
Fam I'll catch you later. *À plus tard.*

- **corriger**

He had the nerve to correct my French
Il a eu le culot de corriger mon français

Correct me if I'm wrong, but ...
Reprenez-moi si je me trompe, mais ...

I stand corrected
Au temps pour moi

She made a few corrections to the text
Elle a apporté quelques corrections au texte

I got the date wrong *or* I was mistaken *or* wrong about the date
Je me suis trompé de date

There must be some mistake
Il doit y avoir erreur

It was done by mistake *or* in error
Cela a été fait par erreur

That can't be right
Ça ne peut pas être juste

You're not doing it the right way
Ce n'est pas comme ça qu'il faut faire

He made a mess of it and I had to put things right
Il a bâclé le travail et j'ai dû réparer les dégâts

You misunderstood the message
Vous avez mal compris le message

I think (that) you have been misinformed
Je pense qu'on vous a mal renseigné

It appears (that) I misjudged you
Il semblerait que je vous aie mal jugé

Your guess is *or* You're wide of the mark
Vous êtes loin du compte

It was a slip of the tongue; I meant to say …
Ma langue a fourché; je voulais dire …

- **demander**

I asked them to be quiet
Je leur ai demandé de se taire

He asked for some water
Il a demandé de l'eau

Mr and Mrs Booth request the pleasure of your company
M. et Mme Booth vous prient de leur faire l'honneur de votre présence

As requested, I enclose a cheque for £50
Conformément à votre demande, je joins un chèque de 50 livres

She applied for the job but didn't get it
Elle a posé sa candidature mais n'a pas obtenu le poste

The mayor demanded an apology
Le maire a exigé des excuses

You make too many demands on her
Vous exigez trop d'elle

He made an appeal *or* a plea on behalf of the victims
Il a lancé un appel au nom des victimes

She appealed to me for help
Elle a imploré mon aide

They were pleading with him *or* begging him *or Formal* imploring him *or Formal* entreating him to stop
Ils le suppliaient de s'arrêter

The police are calling for tougher penalties
La police réclame des sanctions plus fermes

Could you pass the salt, please?
Pouvez-vous me passer le sel, s'il vous plaît?

Would you mind if I opened the window?
Vous permettez que j'ouvre la fenêtre?

They got up a petition against the council's plans
Ils ont lancé une pétition pour protester contre les projets de la municipalité

ÉCRIRE UNE LETTRE

Formule d'appel	**Formule de politesse**
Lorsqu'on ne connaît pas le nom de la personne à qui l'on s'adresse:	
Dear Sir **Dear Madam**	***Br* Yours faithfully** ***Am* Faithfully yours**

[Lorsqu'on ne sait pas s'il agit d'un homme ou d'une femme:]
Dear Sir or Madam *or* Dear Sir/Madam

[Lorsqu'on s'adresse à une société ou à un organisme sans préciser le nom du destinataire:]
***Br* Dear Sirs**
***Am* Gentlemen**

Lorsqu'on connaît le nom de la personne à qui l'on s'adresse:	
Dear Mr Jameson **Dear Mrs Lucas** **Dear Miss Crookshaw** **Dear Ms Greening**	***Br* Yours sincerely** ***Am* Sincerely yours** ***Am* Sincerely**

[L'abréviation Ms est employée car elle permet de ne pas préciser s'il agit d'une femme mariée (Mrs) ou non (Miss).]

La Langue en action

Dear Dr Johnston	**[Style moins soutenu:]**
	With best wishes
	Kind regards

[Aux États-Unis, l'abréviation est généralement suivie d'un point: Mr., Mrs., Ms., Dr.]

Lorsqu'on s'adresse à de la famille ou à des amis:

Dear Paul	**With love**
Dear Erin	**Love**
Dear David and Joanne	**Love from**
Dear All	**Love and best wishes**
Dear Mum and Dad	
Dear Uncle Mark/Auntie Laura	**[Plus affectueux:]**
Dearest/My dearest Jill	**With all my/our love**
	Much love
[Très familier:]	**[Plus familier:]**
Hi John!	**Lots of love**
Hello Alice	
	[Plus soutenu:]
	Yours
	Br **All the best**
	Best wishes
	Regards
	[Familier:]
	See you soon
	Bye for now
	Br **Cheers**

E-MAILS & TEXTOS

Can I email you? *Est-ce que je peux vous contacter par e-mail?*
Email the details to us. *Envoyez-nous les coordonnées par e-mail.*
I check my email twice a day. *Je vérifie mes e-mails deux fois par jour.*
He sent it as an attachment. *Il l'a envoyé en fichier joint.*
Can you forward her email to me? *Pouvez-vous me transférer son message?*
I'll print their email out for you. *Je vais vous imprimer leur message.*
Can you text them *or* send them a text? *Pouvez-vous leur envoyer un texto?*

Abréviations communes utilisées dans les e-mails, les forums et les textos

2	**to/too**	**KIT**	**keep in touch**
2DAY	**today**	**L8**	**late**
2MORO	**tomorrow**	**L8R**	**later**
2NITE	**tonight**	**LOL**	**laughing out loud/lots of love**
4	**for**	**M8**	**mate (pote)**
4EVER	**forever**	**MSG**	**message**
AAMOF	**as a matter of fact**	**MYOB**	**mind your own business**
AFAICT	**as far as I can tell**	**NE**	**any**
AFAIK	**as far as I know**	**NE1**	**anyone**
AFK	**away from keyboard**	**NETHING**	**anything**
AIUI	**as far as I understand**	**NO1**	**no one**
ASAP	**as soon as possible**	**NP**	**no problem**
ATB	**all the best**	**NRN**	**no reply necessary**
B	**be**	**NW**	**no way!**
B4	**before**	**OIC**	**oh, I see**
BAK	**back at keyboard**	**OTOH**	**on the other hand**
BBL	**be back later**	**OTT**	**over the top**

BCNU	be seeing you	**PCM**	please call me
BRB	be right back	**PLS**	please
BTDT	been there, done that	**POV**	point of view
BTW	by the way	**R**	are
C	see	**RTFM**	read the f***ing manual
CID	consider it done	**RUOK**	are you OK?
CLD	could	**SB**	somebody
COS	because	**SHLD**	should
CU	see you	**SMTG**	something
CUL8R	see you later	**SRY**	sorry
D8	date	**THNQ**	thank you
EZ	easy	**THX**	thanks
F2F	face to face	**TIA**	thanks in advance
FAQ	frequently asked questions	**TMB**	text me back
FOC	free of charge	**TTFN**	ta-ta for now
FWIW	for what it's worth	**TTYL**	talk to you later
FYI	for your information	**TXT**	text
GAL	get a life	**TYVM**	thank you very much
GBTM	get back to me	**U**	you
GR8	great	**UR**	your/you're
GTG	got to go	**W8**	wait
HTH	hope this helps	**WAN2**	want to
IAC	in any case	**WBS**	write back soon
IDK	I don't know	**WLD**	would
IIRC	if I recall correctly	**W/O**	without
ILU	I love you	**WRK**	work
IM(H)O	in my (humble) opinion	**WRT**	with regard to
IOW	in other words	**X**	kiss
ISTM	it seems to me	**XLNT**	excellent
ITRO	in the region of	**Y**	why
IYKWIM	if you know what I mean	**YR**	your
IYSS	if you say so		

• encourager

Her mother encouraged her to play the piano
Sa mère l'a encouragée à jouer du piano

His success was a great encouragement to us
Sa réussite nous a beaucoup encouragés

It is encouraging to see the progress that has been made
C'est encourageant de constater les progrès accomplis

No amount of coaxing *or* cajoling would get him to agree
Rien n'a pu l'amener à accepter malgré tous les efforts pour l'amadouer

He was egged on by the other boys to steal it.
Les autres garçons l'ont poussé à le voler

The programme inspired her to study biology
L'émission l'a incitée à étudier la biologie

His parents supported *or* backed him in his attempt to become an actor
Ses parents l'ont soutenu lorsqu'il a essayé de devenir acteur

The government has introduced a number of measures to stimulate investment
Le gouvernement a introduit un certain nombre de mesures afin de stimuler l'investissement

Their shouts spurred us on
Leurs cris nous aiguillonnaient

Keep up the good work!
Continuez à bien travailler!

Come on, the Reds!
Allez, les Rouges!

Go on, you can do it!
Allez, tu peux y arriver!

• être d'accord

I quite agree (with you)
Je suis tout à fait d'accord (avec vous)

They agreed to share the cost
Ils se sont mis d'accord pour partager les frais

That was the price we agreed on
C'était le prix dont nous avions convenu

They disagree *or* They are in disagreement about what action to take
Ils ne sont pas d'accord sur les mesures à prendre

She is for/against free trade
Elle est pour/contre le libre-échange

He accused the oil companies of colluding to raise prices
Il a accusé les compagnies pétrolières de s'entendre pour augmenter les prix

By mutual agreement *or* consent they went their separate ways
Ils se sont séparés d'un commun accord

Opinion is divided on the matter
Les avis sont partagés sur ce problème

There is a discrepancy between the two stories
Les deux récits ne cadrent pas

Don't contradict me!
Ne me contredisez pas!

You were right/wrong (about him)
Vous aviez raison/tort (à son sujet)

I'm with you there
Là, je suis d'accord avec toi

I'm opposed to the idea
Je m'oppose à cette idée

I think I can go along with that
Je pense que je peux être d'accord là-dessus

The government is hopeless! – Hear, hear!
Ce gouvernement est nul! – Bravo!

Her father and I don't see eye to eye
Son père et moi ne partageons pas les mêmes points de vue

Fam Are you sure he'll be okay about letting us use the car?
Tu es sûr qu'il ne fera pas d'histoires pour nous laisser la voiture?

Formal He proposed a different approach and she concurred
Il a proposé une approche différente et elle a approuvé

• s'excuser

I owe you an apology
Je vous dois des excuses

Please accept my apologies
Je vous prie d'accepter mes excuses

There's no need to apologize
Vous n'avez pas à vous excuser

(I'm) sorry to have kept you waiting
Désolé de vous avoir fait attendre

Sorry, I can't help – It doesn't matter *or* Don't worry about it
Désolé, je ne peux pas vous aider – Ça ne fait rien

I've said I'm sorry; what more can I do?
J'ai déjà dit que j'étais désolé, qu'est-ce que je peux faire d'autre?

Sorry!
Pardon!

There's no excuse for that kind of behaviour
Ce genre de comportement est inexcusable

I don't want any excuses!
Je ne veux pas d'excuse!

If you will excuse me, I have to finish my work
Si vous voulez bien m'excuser, il faut que je finisse mon travail

Excuse me, can I get past?
Excusez-moi, je peux passer?

She was very apologetic for being late
Elle s'est excusée plusieurs fois d'être arrivée en retard

When the story turned out to be false, the editor had to eat humble pie
Lorsqu'il s'est avéré que l'histoire était fausse, l'éditeur a dû manger son chapeau

I'm afraid (that) it's my fault *or* I'm to blame
Je crains que ce ne soit de ma faute

• expliquer

Sorry, I don't quite follow you
Pardon, mais je ne vous suis pas vraiment

Could you be a bit more specific?
Pourriez-vous être un peu plus précis?

I'm sorry, but could you explain in a little more detail?
Pardonnez-moi mais pourriez-vous me donner des explications un peu plus détaillées?

Could you explain *or* clarify what you mean by that?
Pourriez-vous expliquer ce que vous entendez par là?

What are you getting at?
Où voulez-vous en venir?

Perhaps I didn't explain myself very well
Je ne me suis peut-être pas très bien expliqué

The teacher gave an explanation of the term
Le professeur a donné une explication de ce terme

What I meant was …
Ce que je voulais dire, c'est que …

Now let's get this clear: I want no nonsense
Comprenons-nous bien: je ne supporterai pas de sottises

How do you account for your behaviour?
Comment justifiez-vous votre comportement?

The reason I did it was to make him happy
C'est pour le contenter que j'ai fais ça

Do I have to spell it out for you?
Faut-il que je te fasse un dessin?

Formal She expounded her theory at great length
Elle a exposé fort longuement sa théorie

• féliciter

Congratulations (on your new job)!
Félicitations (pour ton nouveau poste)!

I congratulate you
Je vous félicite

Her parents congratulated her on passing her exams
Ses parents l'ont félicitée d'avoir été reçue à ses examens

I congratulated myself *or* gave myself a pat on the back for having kept my temper
Je me suis félicité d'avoir gardé mon sang-froid

She complimented him on his English
Elle lui a fait des compliments sur son anglais

Give him my compliments
Faites-lui mes compliments

They raised their glasses *or* drank a toast to the newly married couple
Ils ont levé leurs verres à la santé des jeunes mariés

The actors received a standing ovation
Tout le monde s'est levé pour applaudir les acteurs

Three cheers for Sarah!
Un ban pour Sarah!

Well done!
Bravo!

You've done a really good job
Tu as vraiment fait du bon travail

Happy birthday! *or* Many happy returns!
Bon anniversaire!

• fêter

Let's open a bottle of wine to celebrate!
Ouvrons une bouteille de vin pour fêter ça!

This calls for a celebration!
Il faut fêter ça!

The festivities ended with a firework display
Les festivités se sont terminées par un feu d'artifice

They had a party *or Fam* a do to celebrate their wedding anniversary
Ils ont fait une fête pour leur anniversaire de mariage

We painted the town red at the weekend
On a fait la tournée des grands-ducs ce week-end

The association marked the occasion with a special ceremony
L'association a organisé une cérémonie spéciale pour célébrer l'événement

The streets of the capital were full of revellers
Les rues de la capitale étaient pleines de joyeux fêtards

They toasted the birth of their baby with champagne
Ils ont fêté au champagne la naissance de leur bébé

They cheered loudly when he came into the room
Ils l'ont acclamé bruyamment lorsqu'il est entré dans la pièce

Three cheers for Mary!
Un ban pour Mary!

Fam We partied all night
Nous avons fait la fête toute la nuit

• former des vœux

He wished them success in their future careers
Il leur a souhaité de réussir dans leur carrière

I wish you all the best in your new job
Tous mes vœux de réussite dans votre nouvelle vie professionnelle

Give her my best wishes for a speedy recovery
Transmettez-lui mes meilleurs vœux de prompt rétablissement

Give them my regards
Transmettez-leur mon bon souvenir

Good luck (with the exams)!
Bonne chance (pour les examens)!

Have a good weekend!
Bon week-end!

Enjoy yourselves!
Amusez-vous bien!

I hope you have a pleasant journey
Je vous souhaite un agréable voyage

Merry Christmas (and happy New Year)!
Joyeux Noël (et Bonne année)!

All the best for 2009!
Meilleurs vœux pour 2009!

• l'interdiction

Drinking alcohol at work is prohibited *or* forbidden
Il est interdit de boire de l'alcool sur le lieu de travail

He was forbidden to see *or* from seeing her again
On lui a interdit de la revoir

She was banned from driving for a year
Elle a eu une suspension de permis de conduire d'un an

He vetoed it
Il y a mis son veto

They put an embargo on further spending
Ils ont gelé toute nouvelle dépense

Speed limits *or* restrictions have been introduced on that section of road
Des limitations de vitesse ont été mises en place sur cette portion de route

These subjects are taboo
Ces sujets sont tabous

La Langue en action

The theatre in Britain is not subject to censorship
Le théâtre en Grande-Bretagne n'est pas soumis à la censure

It's against the law *or* It's illegal to do that
C'est illégal de faire ça

The police are clamping down *or* cracking down on illegal parking
La police prend des mesures énergiques contre le stationnement interdit

You've (got) no right to talk to me like that!
Tu n'as pas le droit de me parler ainsi!

I won't have it!
Ça ne va pas se passer comme ça!

• inviter

My boss has invited me for lunch
Mon chef m'a invité à déjeuner

I asked her up for a coffee
Je l'ai invitée à monter prendre un café

We must have them round *or* over for dinner
Il faudra qu'on les invite à dîner

Do come in and make yourself at home
Entrez donc, faites comme chez vous

Would you like to go out for dinner tomorrow night? – Sorry, I can't make it
Aimerais-tu sortir dîner avec moi demain soir? – Désolée, je ne peux pas

Would you like to come to my house for dinner? – I'd be delighted
Voudriez-vous venir dîner chez moi? – Avec grand plaisir

We're going out for a drink later; would you like to join us? – Yes, I'd love to
Nous allons prendre un verre tout à l'heure; voulez-vous vous joindre à nous? – Oui, avec grand plaisir

Are you free to come to the theatre with me tomorrow? – Thanks, but I've got something else on
Tu es libre demain pour aller au théâtre avec moi? – Merci mais je suis déjà pris

I'm afraid I can't make it tonight, but thank you
Je regrette, mais ce soir je ne vais pas pouvoir. Merci quand même

Are you expecting company?
Vous attendez de la visite?

They entertain a great deal
Ils reçoivent beaucoup

Fam How about meeting for a drink after work? – That'd be nice
Ça te dirait de prendre un pot après le travail? – Oui, ça serait sympa

Formal I'm sorry but I have another engagement
Je regrette mais je suis déjà pris

• les menaces

We were threatened with the sack
On nous a menacés de licenciement

She's threatening to cancel the concert if her demands aren't met
Elle menace d'annuler le concert si ses exigences ne sont pas satisfaites

You shouldn't use threatening language
Vous ne devriez pas utiliser un langage menaçant

The new weapon is a threat *or* menace to world peace
Cette nouvelle arme constitue une menace pour la paix mondiale

He stared at her menacingly
Il la dévisageait d'un air menaçant

Don't let yourself be intimidated by him
Ne te laisse pas intimider par lui

Don't be such a bully!
Ne te comporte pas comme une brute!

They bullied me into going with them
Ils m'ont forcé la main pour que je les accompagne

You've been warned! *or* I'm warning you!
Te voilà averti!

Watch it or you'll be in trouble!
Attention ou tu vas avoir des ennuis!

Do what I tell you, or else!
Fais ce que je te dis, sinon!

You'll be sorry if you do that again!
Si tu recommences, tu vas le regretter!

Woe betide anyone who lies to me
Malheur à celui qui me raconte des mensonges

Formal Her confession was obtained under duress
Ses aveux ont été obtenus sous la contrainte

• l'obligation

You are under no obligation to reply
Rien ne vous oblige à répondre

I feel obliged to tell him
Je me vois contraint de lui dire

Attendance is obligatory *or* compulsory
La présence est obligatoire

I have (got) to go to the meeting
Je dois aller à la réunion

I don't have to *or* need to work
Je n'ai pas besoin de travailler

You mustn't touch it!
Il ne faut pas y toucher!

There's no need to wait *or* You needn't wait
Inutile d'attendre

Is this visit really necessary?
Est-ce que cette visite est vraiment indispensable?

No one's forcing you!
Personne ne t'y force!

They made me wait
Ils m'ont fait attendre

Ill health compelled *or* forced her to retire
Elle a été obligée de prendre sa retraite pour raisons de santé

The law requires you to wear a seatbelt
La loi exige que vous mettiez la ceinture de sécurité

A qualification in Greek is no longer a requirement
Un diplôme de grec n'est plus nécessaire

I had no choice *or* option but to leave
Je n'avais pas d'autre choix que partir

• offrir

She offered me £800 for my car
Elle m'a offert 800 livres pour ma voiture

Can I offer you a drink?
Je vous offre un verre?

I had several offers of help
Plusieurs personnes ont proposé de m'aider

We gave her a pony as a present
Nous lui avons fait cadeau d'un poney

This is just a small gift to say thank you
Ce n'est qu'un petit cadeau pour vous remercier

I've brought you some flowers – Thank you, they're lovely
Je vous ai apporté des fleurs – Merci, elles sont ravissantes

Please take a seat
Veuillez vous asseoir

Would you like something to eat?
Voulez-vous manger quelque chose?

Is there anything you need?
Avez-vous besoin de quelque chose?

If I can help in any way, please let me know
Si je peux faire quoi que ce soit, n'hésitez pas à me le demander

Can I give you a lift to the station? – Yes, please, if it's no trouble
Je peux vous déposer à la gare?– Si ça ne vous dérange pas, oui, merci

This is on me
C'est moi qui offre

• les ordres

He gave the order to open fire
Il a donné l'ordre d'ouvrir le feu

Our orders are to wait here
Nous avons l'ordre d'attendre ici

I'm just following orders
Je ne fais qu'exécuter les ordres

We were ordered out of the room
On nous a ordonné de quitter la pièce

The doctor ordered him to rest for three weeks
Le médecin lui a prescrit trois semaines de repos

The troops were withdrawn at his command
Les troupes ont été retirées sur ses ordres

She likes ordering people about
Elle aime commander les autres

You can't tell me what to do!
Tu n'as pas à me dire ce que je dois faire!

Who's (the person) in charge here?
Qui est le responsable ici?

She's at her mother's beck and call
Elle obéit à sa mère au doigt et à l'œil

I could hear him laying down the law to his employees
Je l'entendais dicter sa loi à ses employés

I am instructed by the board to inform you that ...
La direction me charge de vous faire savoir que ...

Quiet please!
Silence, s'il vous plaît!

Formal They were summoned to the headmaster's office
Ils ont été convoqués au bureau du directeur

• la permission

You are not permitted *or* allowed to enter the building
Vous n'avez pas le droit de pénétrer dans l'immeuble

Who gave them permission to smoke?
Qui leur a permis de fumer?

You have my permission
Je te donne la permission

She let them watch *or* allowed them to watch the programme
Elle les a laissés regarder l'émission

He is authorized *or* has authorization to act for his father
Il est autorisé à représenter son père

I'll need to clear it with the boss
Il faut que j'obtienne la permission du patron

Could *or* Can *or Formal* May I join you? – Yes, of course
Est-ce que je pourrais me joindre à vous? – Mais oui, bien sûr

Do you mind if I borrow your pen? – I'd rather you didn't
Je peux vous emprunter votre stylo? – J'aimerais mieux pas, non

Allow me!
Permettez(-moi)!

Formal The government has granted their request
Le gouvernement a accédé à leur demande

Formal He asked leave to address the meeting
Il a demandé la permission de prendre la parole devant l'assemblée

LES PETITES ANNONCES

1. Abréviations utilisées dans les petites annonces

AC	air conditioning
adj.	adjoining
all mod cons	all modern conveniences
appt.	appointment
apt.	apartment
avail.	available
bed, b/room	bedroom(s)
bsmt.	basement
bldg.	building
bus.	business
c/h	central heating
CT, C/T *Br*	council tax
del.	deliver, delivery
det.	detached
din.	dining
dr.	door
dbl.	double
ea.	each
elec.	electric
exc.	excellent
exch.	exchange
fl.	floor
ft.	foot, feet
furn.	furniture, furnishes
g.	good
gar.	garage
GCH	gas central heating
H/CW	hot/cold water
K	thousand
kit.	kitchen
lg.	large
m.	month
msg.	message
nr.	near
NS, N/S	non-smoking
obo *Am*	or best offer
ono *Br*	or nearest offer
orig.	originally
pkg.	parking
pls.	please
prof.	professional
ref.	reference
reqd.	required
rm.	room
sgl.	single
terr.	terrace
unfurn.	unfurnished
vac.	vacancy
vg.	very good
w.	with
wk.	week
yr.	year

►DRYER: Kenmore elec. Exc. cond. $95 obo. Call 364-9999 between 6-8pm

►Plasma TV 42-inch screen. As new. Orig. £800, asking £380 ono. 0113 794958, leave msg.

☎ Hello. I'm calling about the dryer you want to sell. *Bonjour, je vous appelle à propos du sèche-linge à vendre.*

☎ Hello. I saw your advertisement in yesterday's paper. Do you still have the TV for sale? … What model is it? … Would you accept £350 for it? *Bonjour, j'ai vu votre annonce dans le journal d'hier. Votre télé est-elle toujours à vendre? … De quel modèle s'agit-il? … En accepteriez-vous 350 livres?*

►2-rm. apt. to rent in city centre. All mod cons., TV, fitted kit., bathroom w. shower. £600 per month. Tel: 0786 554321

►Lg. rm. to rent in shared house, SE London. £80 per wk, + CT + bills. Deposit reqd. Suit NS young prof. Tel: 0206 555655

►For sale: 5 bed det. house, big garden, dbl. gar. South facing. £250K ono. Tel: 09987 66589

☎ Hello. I'm calling about the room advertised in this evening's paper … Already? Oh well, thank you. *Bonjour, j'appelle au sujet de l'annonce pour une chambre à louer dans le journal d'aujourd'hui … Déjà? Bon, tant pis. Je vous remercie.*

☎ Hello. Is your house still for sale? … When would be a suitable time for me to come and view it? *Bonjour, votre maison est-elle toujours en vente? … Quand pourrais-je venir la visiter?*

2. Abréviations utilisées dans les petites annonces pour rencontres

A	Asian
B	Black
NA	Native American
NBM	Never Been Married

Bi	**Bisexual**	**ND**	**Non Drinker**
C	**Christian**	**NS, N/S**	**Non Smoker**
D	**Divorced**	**S**	**Single**
F	**Female**	**SD**	**Social Drinker**
G	**Gay**	**SI**	**Similar Interests**
GSOH	**Good Sense of Humour**	**SOH**	**Sense of Humour**
H	**Hispanic**	**W**	**White**
ISO	**In Search Of**	**Wi**	**Widowed**
LTR	**Long-Term Relationship**	**WLTM**	**Would Like To Meet**
M	**Male**	**YO**	**Years Old**

►SWM, 37YO, Aquarius. Caring, strong, romantic. Likes art, travel, photography. WLTM lady 30-50 for outings, meals and maybe more. London area.

►Attractive prof. F, mid 40s, seeks caring, solvent, N/S M w. GSOH for LTR. Interests opera, fine wine and dogs.

• se plaindre

He complained of a headache/that she was always late
Il s'est plaint d'un mal de tête/qu'elle était toujours en retard

Do you have any complaints about the company?
Est-ce que vous avez à vous plaindre de l'entreprise?

I would like to make a complaint
J'aimerais faire une réclamation

I want to see the manager!
Je veux voir le responsable!

You should ask for your money back
Vous devriez demander un remboursement

I'm not at all happy with the work you've done on the patio
Je ne suis pas du tout satisfait du travail que vous avez fait sur le patio

It's not good enough!
Ça ne va pas!

She's always whining *or Fam* moaning *or Fam* bellyaching about something
Elle est toujours en train de se lamenter à propos d'une chose ou d'une autre

He often finds fault with my style of writing
Il trouve souvent à redire à ma manière d'écrire

They have been criticized for not trying
On leur a reproché de ne pas avoir essayé

Her letter contained the usual grumbles
Sa lettre contenait les récriminations habituelles

Really, I protest, that's too much!
Non, vraiment, je proteste, c'est trop!

The unions are up in arms over the new legislation
Les syndicats s'élèvent contre la nouvelle législation

• les présentations

I don't think we've been introduced
Je ne crois pas que nous ayons été présentés

I don't think you know Ken, do you?
Je ne pense pas que vous connaissiez Ken, n'est-ce pas?

She introduced me to her sister
Elle m'a présenté à sa sœur

Let me introduce myself: I'm John
Je me présente, je m'appelle John

Would you make the introductions?
Peux-tu faire les présentations?

This is Sonya – Hello, I'm Samantha
Voici Sonya – Bonjour, je m'appelle Samantha

I'd like you to meet *or* I'd like to introduce my mother
Je vous présente ma mère

(I'm) pleased to meet you! *or* How do you do?
Enchanté!

(It's) good to see you again
Ça fait plaisir de vous revoir

I got to know her *or Formal* made her acquaintance at Mike's party
J'ai fait sa connaissance à la fête de Mike

• refuser

I refuse to accept that all is lost
Je refuse de croire que tout est perdu

They were refused a loan
On leur a refusé un prêt

We don't understand your refusal to compromise
Nous ne comprenons pas pourquoi vous refusez de transiger

He declined my invitation
Il a décliné mon invitation

She turned me down flat
Elle m'a envoyé balader

They won't take no for an answer
Ils n'accepteront aucun refus

I draw the line at lying
Je refuse de mentir

He was denied access to his children
On lui a refusé le droit de visite de ses enfants

La Langue en action

You can't go, it's out of the question!
Tu ne peux pas y aller, c'est hors de question!

He shook his head
Il a hoché la tête en signe de refus

I won't do it!
Je refuse de le faire!

I'm not moving, and that's final!
Je ne bouge pas, un point c'est tout!

Fam Will you do it for me? – No way!
Tu feras ça pour moi? – Pas question!

• rejeter

My application was rejected *or* turned down
Ma candidature a été rejetée

They offered him a job but he turned them down
Ils lui ont proposé un emploi mais il a rejeté leur offre

You can't go on dismissing the evidence
Vous ne pouvez pas continuer à ignorer ces preuves

She rejected *or* repudiated the accusation
Elle a réfuté cette accusation

He spurned all offers of help
Il a décliné toute offre d'aide

Send the chocolates back to the shop
Renvoyez les chocolats au magasin

He's quite unsuitable for the job
Ce n'est pas la personne qu'il faut pour ce poste

She turned her nose up at the food on her plate
Elle a pris l'air dégoûté devant la nourriture dans son assiette

It was a real slap in the face for the Prime Minister
Cela a été un vrai camouflet pour le Premier ministre

We gave them the cold shoulder
Nous les avons snobés

Take it away, I don't want it!
Enlevez-moi ça, je n'en veux pas!

Fam My proposal was given the thumbs-down
Ma proposition a été rejetée

Fam I got the brush-off
On m'a envoyé sur les roses

Br Fam She gave her boyfriend the elbow
Elle a largué son petit ami

• remercier

Thank you *or Fam* Thanks for the flowers/for coming – My pleasure
Merci pour les fleurs/d'être venu – Je t'en prie

Will you have some tea? – No, thank you *or Fam* thanks
Veux-tu du thé? – Non merci

Thank you very much *or Fam* Thanks a lot – Don't mention it *or* Not at all *or* It's nothing
Merci beaucoup – De rien

I can't thank you enough for what you've done
Je ne sais comment vous remercier pour ce que vous avez fait

Say thank you to your grandma
Dis merci à ta grand-mère

You should write a thank-you letter to him
Tu devrais lui écrire une lettre de remerciement

I'm grateful for *or* I appreciate your help
Je vous suis reconnaissant de votre aide

I'd really appreciate that
Ça me rendrait vraiment service

Br Fam Here's your book – Ta!
Voici ton livre – Merci!

Formal Please accept this gift as a token of my gratitude
Acceptez ce présent en témoignage de ma gratitude

• se rencontrer

I arranged to meet him at three o'clock
J'ai pris rendez-vous avec lui à trois heures

I get to meet a lot of people in my job
Mon travail m'amène à rencontrer beaucoup de gens

Have you met my wife?
Vous connaissez ma femme?

I have a meeting with the boss this morning
J'ai rendez-vous avec le patron ce matin

We'll have to meet up the next time I'm in Paris
Il faudra qu'on se voie la prochaine fois que je passerai à Paris

When shall I see you again?
Quand vais-je vous revoir?

I bumped into *or* ran into an old school friend this morning
Je suis tombé sur un ancien camarade d'école ce matin

They joined us for lunch
Ils nous ont retrouvés pour déjeuner

My date didn't show up *or Fam* I was stood up
On m'a posé un lapin

I'll see you on Monday then at four o'clock
Je vous verrai donc lundi, à quatre heures

Are you free for lunch today?
Êtes-vous libre à déjeuner aujourd'hui?

I'll pick you up *or* collect you at *or* from the station
Je viendrai vous chercher à la gare

• le soupçon

Does your husband suspect anything?
Est-ce que ton mari se doute de quelque chose?

She is suspected of corruption
Elle est soupçonnée de corruption

I had my suspicions about it
J'avais mes soupçons là-dessus

I'm suspicious of his motives
Je me méfie de ses intentions

He's a dubious character
C'est un type douteux

The detective smelt a rat
Le détective a flairé quelque chose de louche

I don't like the look of him
Sa tête ne me revient pas

There's something about her (that) I don't like
Il y a en elle quelque chose qui me déplaît

I don't know why I distrust them; it's just a feeling (that) I have
Je ne sais pas pourquoi je me méfie d'eux; c'est juste une impression que j'ai

Fam There's something shifty about her
Il y a quelque chose de pas net chez elle

Fam They were involved in a couple of shady *or Br* dodgy business deals
Ils ont été impliqués dans des transactions plutôt louches

Fam There's something fishy about her alibi
Il y a quelque chose qui ne colle pas dans son alibi

• suggérer

She suggested going for a walk
Elle a proposé de faire une promenade

I suggest (that) we adjourn the meeting until next Monday
Je suggère que nous ajournions la réunion jusqu'à lundi prochain

We're open to suggestions
Toute suggestion est la bienvenue

I propose (that) we vote on it
Je propose que nous votions sur ce point

She accepted his proposal (of marriage)
Elle a accepté sa demande en mariage

Are you implying *or* insinuating (that) I'm lying?
Est-ce que vous insinuez que je mens?

Your silence implies (that) you are guilty
Votre silence laisse penser que vous êtes coupable

I recommend (that) we make them an offer
Je recommande que nous leur fassions une offre

I have come on the recommendation of one of your customers
Je viens sur la recommandation d'un de vos clients

The play is full of innuendo
La pièce est pleine de sous-entendus

Management has nothing new to put on the table
La direction n'a rien de nouveau à proposer

Couldn't we at least talk about it?
Ne pourrions-nous pas au moins en discuter?

We could always increase our prices
Nous pourrions toujours augmenter nos prix

Why don't we take a break?
Et si nous faisions une pause?

It might be a good idea to have a word with him
Ce serait peut-être une bonne idée de lui en toucher un mot

Perhaps *or* Maybe we could go to an Italian restaurant later
Nous pourrions peut-être aller manger italien plus tard

How about *or* What about going for a quick drink?
Que diriez-vous d'aller prendre un petit verre?

Shall we meet up at six o'clock?
18h, ça vous va?

TÉLÉPHONER

I'll call *or* phone *or Br* ring you tonight. *Je t'appellerai ce soir.*
Give me a call *or Br* a ring when you arrive at the station. *Passe-moi un coup de fil quand tu arriveras à la gare.*
I need to phone home. *Il faut que j'appelle chez moi.*
The phone's ringing. *Le téléphone sonne.*
Can someone answer the phone? *Quelqu'un peut répondre au téléphone?*
She's been on the phone for two hours! *Cela fait deux heures qu'elle est au téléphone!*
Are you having a phone put in? – No, I'm going to use my mobile. *Tu vas faire mettre le téléphone? – Non, je me servirai de mon portable.*
You can find his number either in the phone book or online. *Vous trouverez son numéro dans l'annuaire ou bien sur Internet*
I let the phone ring ten times before I hung up. *J'ai laissé le téléphone sonner dix fois avant de raccrocher.*

La Langue en action

Passer un coup de téléphone

Hello, is that Sarah? *Allô, c'est bien Sarah?*
Hello, is Dave there, please? *Allô, est-ce que Dave est là, s'il vous plaît?*
Hi, it's Alex. Can I speak to Tom, please? *Salut, c'est Alex. Est-ce que je peux parler à Tom, s'il te plaît?*
Hello, can I speak to John Clark, please? *Bonjour, pourrais-je parler à John Clark, s'il vous plaît?*
Hello, this is Jessica Roberts. I'd like to speak to Alan Parks, please. *Bonjour, ici Jessica Roberts. Je voudrais parler à Alan Parks, s'il vous plaît.*
This is Michelle Brown calling from Global Communications. Can you put me through to David Walker, please? *Ici Michelle Brown, de Global Communications. Pourriez-vous me passer David Walker, s'il vous plaît?*

Recevoir un appel

Hello? *Allô?*
(Hello,) Simon Johnson. *(Allô,) Simon Johnson.*
3160123 (= three one six *Br* oh *or Am* zero one two three) *Ici le trois cent seize, zéro un, vingt- trois*
Good morning, Management Solutions? *Management Solutions, bonjour?*
Hello, City Leisure Centre, Jane speaking. How can I help you? *City Leisure Centre, bonjour, Jane à l'appareil. Que puis-je faire pour vous?*
I've got Susan Wallace on the line for you. – OK, you can put her through. *Vous avez Susan Wallace en ligne. – D'accord, passez-la moi.*
There's a call for you from the London office. – I'm a bit busy right now. Could you take a message? *Vous avez un appel du bureau de Londres. – Je suis un peu occupé pour l'instant. Pourriez-vous prendre un message?*

Obtenir la communication

Hi, can I speak to Paul, please? – Yes, hang on a minute, I'll just get him for you. *Bonjour, pourrais-je parler à Paul, s'il vous plaît? – Oui, un instant, je vais le chercher.*
Can I speak to Peter Davis, please? – Speaking! – Oh, hi, Peter! *Pourrais-je parler à Peter Davis, s'il vous plaît? – Lui-même! – Oh, salut Peter!*
Hello, can I speak to Jason Wright, please? – Can I ask who's calling, please? – It's Sarah Green from World Travel. – OK, hold on a moment and I'll transfer you. *Allo, pourrais-je parler à Jason Wright, s'il vous plaît? – De la part de qui, s'il vous plaît? – De la part de Sarah Green de World Travel – Entendu, ne quittez pas, je vous passe son poste.*
Hi, could I have extension 535, please? – Certainly. May I ask who's calling? – This is Tom's wife. – Oh, right! Just a minute, I'll put you through. *Bonjour, pourrais-je avoir le poste 535 s'il vous plaît? – Certainement, de la part de qui, s'il vous plaît? – Je suis la femme de Tom – Ah d'accord, je vous le passe tout de suite.*
How do I get an outside line? – Press 0 to dial out. *Comment fait-on pour avoir la ligne? – Composez le 0 pour téléphoner à l'extérieur.*
There's no answer. *Ça ne répond pas.*
The line's *Br* engaged *or Am* busy. *La ligne est occupée.*
He's on the other line. *Il est sur l'autre ligne.*
She's out *or* not in at the moment. *Elle est absente pour l'instant.*
He's busy just now. *Il est occupé en ce moment.*
She's in a meeting. *Elle est en réunion.*
She's on holiday all week. *Elle est en vacances cette semaine.*
He's not in the office today. *Il n'est pas au bureau aujourd'hui.*

Les messages

I'm afraid John's not back from work yet. Can I take a message *or* give him a message? – Yes, can you tell him Phil called, and ask him to give me a ring when he gets in? *Je regrette mais John n'est pas encore rentré du travail. Vous voulez laisser un message? – Oui, pouvez-vous lui dire que Phil a appelé et lui demander de me rappeler lorsqu'il rentrera?*
He's in a meeting at the moment. Would you like to leave a message? – Yes, could you ask him to call me back as soon as possible? *Il est en réunion. Voulez-vous laisser un message? – Oui, pouvez-vous lui dire de me rappeler dès que possible?*
Hi, Rachel, it's Alan Brown here. I'm just returning your call. – Oh yes, I tried to ring you this morning but you weren't in the office. *Bonjour Rachel, ici Alan Brown. Je te rappelle comme tu me l'as demandé. – Ah oui, j'ai essayé de te joindre ce matin mais tu n'étais pas au bureau.*

Hello, you've reached the Jones family. We're not available right now, but please leave a message after the tone and we'll get back to you as soon as we can. *Bonjour, vous êtes bien chez la famille Jones. Nous ne sommes pas là pour le moment mais laissez-nous un message après le bip et nous vous rappellerons dès que possible.*
Hi, this is Sarah. Leave a message after the beep. *Bonjour, ici Sarah. Laissez votre message après le bip.*

Terminer une conversation

Nice talking to you. Speak to you soon, bye! *Ça m'a fait plaisir de te parler. À bientôt, salut!*
Listen, I've got to go. Can I call you back later? *Écoute, il faut que je te laisse. Est-ce que je peux te rappeler plus tard?*
Thank you for calling, goodbye. *Merci d'avoir appelé, au revoir.*
Thanks for your help, bye. *Merci pour votre aide, au revoir.*
How rude, he hung up on me! *Quel malpoli, il m'a raccroché au nez!*

Les numéros

2546731 = two five four six seven three one
0130 = *Br* oh one three oh *or Am* zero one three zero
3112944 = three one one *or* double one two nine four four *or* double four
Can I take your phone number? – Yes, it's oh double one three, two five four six seven three one. – Thanks. So is oh double one three the dialling code for the UK? – No, it's the code for Leeds. The code for the UK is oh oh four four. – OK. So from France I'll have to dial oh oh four four, one one three, etc. – That's right. *Pouvez-vous me donner votre numéro de téléphone? – Oui, c'est le zéro cent treize, vingt-cinq, quarante-six, sept cent trente et un. – Merci. Donc zéro cent treize est l'indicatif de la Grande-Bretagne, c'est ça? – Non, c'est l'indicatif de Leeds. L'indicatif de la Grande-Bretagne est zéro zéro quarante-quatre – D'accord. Donc depuis la France il faut que je compose zéro zéro quarante-quatre, cent treize etc. – C'est cela, oui.*

Les problèmes

Pardon? *or* Sorry? *Pardon?*
I'm sorry, I didn't quite catch that. *Pardon, je n'ai pas bien compris.*
Could you repeat that, please? *Pourriez-vous répéter, s'il vous plaît?*
Could you say that again more slowly, please? *Pourriez-vous répéter plus lentement, s'il vous plaît?*
Can you spell that for me, please? *Pourriez-vous me l'épeler, s'il vous plaît?*
Sorry, I can't hear you very well. It's a really bad line. *Pardon, je ne vous entends pas très bien. La ligne est très mauvaise.*
The reception isn't very good where I am. *La réception est plutôt mauvaise là où je me trouve.*
Hello? Are you still there? *Allo? Tu es encore là?*
Can you hear me? *Vous m'entendez?*
I was in the middle of a conversation and I got cut off! *J'étais en pleine conversation et j'ai été coupé!*
There's no *Br* dialling *or Am* dial tone. *Il n'y a pas de tonalité.*
Oh, I'm sorry. I think I've dialled the wrong number. *Oh, pardon. Je crois que je me suis trompé de numéro.*
I'm sorry, I think you've got the wrong number. *Désolé, je crois que vous avez fait un faux numéro.*
The number you have dialled has not been recognized. *Il n'y a pas d'abonné au numéro que vous avez demandé.*
The line's dead. *Il n'y a pas de tonalité.*

En cas d'urgence

There's been an accident. Quick, call *Br* 999 *or Am* 911! *Il y a eu un accident. Appelez vite le 999/911!*
Which service do you require? *Quel service demandez-vous?*

Les téléphones portables

There's no reception *or* signal in this bar. *Il n'y a pas de réseau dans ce bar.*
My mother called but my phone was on silent and I didn't hear it, so she left me a voicemail. *Ma mère m'a appelé mais mon portable était sur silencieux et je ne l'ai pas entendu, alors elle m'a laissé un message.*

My battery's flat. I need to recharge it. *Ma batterie est à plat. Il faut que je la recharge.*
Can I plug my phone charger in here? *Est-ce que je peux brancher le chargeur de mon portable ici?*
Br Could I have a £10 Eurofone top-up card, please? *Est-ce que je pourrais avoir une recharge Eurofone à 10 livres, s'il vous plaît?*
Am Where can I buy a refill card for my cellphone? *Où est-ce que je peux acheter une recharge pour mon portable?*
I'm nearly out/I've run out of *Br* credit *or Am* minutes. *Je n'ai presque plus/Je n'ai plus de crédit.*
Listen to this cool new ringtone I've downloaded! *Écoute un peu cette nouvelle sonnerie géniale que j'ai téléchargée!*

LE TEMPS ET L'HEURE

I don't have (the) time to do the shopping. *Je n'ai pas le temps de faire les courses.*
It's time I was going. *Il est temps que je parte.*
I start in three weeks' time. *Je commence dans trois semaines.*
He waited for a long time. *Il a attendu longtemps.*
How long will it take? *Combien de temps cela va prendre?*
You took a long time! *Tu en a mis du temps!*
They haven't been married (for) long. *Ça ne fait pas longtemps qu'ils sont mariés.*
I'm keeping my options open for the time being. *Je préfère ne pas m'engager pour le moment.*
On what date are you flying to France? *À quelle date est ton vol pour la France?*
They moved here ten years ago. *Ils ont emménagé ici il y a dix ans.*
She arrived right on time. *Elle est arrivée juste à l'heure.*
I'll be back in time for the film. *Je serai de retour à temps pour le film.*
What are you up to these days? *Qu'est-ce que tu fais de beau ces temps-ci?*
I'll be with you in a minute *or* second. *Je serai à vous dans un instant.*
Do you know how to tell the time? *Est-ce que tu sais lire l'heure?*
What's the time? *or* What time is it? *Quelle heure est-il?*
Do you have the time? *Vous avez l'heure?*
It's four o'clock/midnight. *Il est quatre heures/minuit.*
They are coming at five o'clock/at 3am/at 6pm. *Ils viennent à cinq heures/à trois heures du matin/à dix-huit heures.*
It'll soon be half *Br* past *or Am* after ten. *Il sera bientôt dix heures et demie.*
It's nearly a quarter to *or Am* of eight. *Il est presque huit heures moins le quart.*
We're leaving at a quarter *Br* past *or Am* after eleven. *Nous partons à onze heure et quart.*
It's five (minutes) *Br* past *or Am* after four. *Il est quatre heures cinq.*
What time do trains for London leave? – Every hour on the hour/on the half-hour/at ten minutes to. *À quelle heure partent les trains pour Londres? – Toutes les heures à l'heure pile/à la demie/à moins dix.*

LE TEMPS QU'IL FAIT

It's lovely weather, isn't it? *Il fait un temps magnifique, non?*
Nice today, isn't it? – Yes, it is. *Il fait beau aujourd'hui, n'est-ce pas? – Oui.*
Saturday is supposed to be sunny. *Il devrait faire beau samedi.*
I can't wait for the warm weather. *J'ai hâte qu'il fasse chaud.*
There was a pleasant breeze blowing. *Il y avait une agréable petite brise.*
It was a cold night, wasn't it? – It certainly was. *La nuit a été froide, non? – Oui, en effet.*
It feels chilly this morning. *Il fait frais ce matin.*
March is usually a windy month. *En général il y a du vent au mois de mars.*
It's pouring with rain. *Il pleut à verse.*
There was a light drizzle all day. *Il a pleuvoté toute la journée.*
Heavy snow is forecast. *La météo prévoit d'abondantes chutes de neige.*
We got caught in a snowstorm. *Nous avons été pris dans une tempête de neige.*
There's a storm coming *or* brewing. *Le temps est à l'orage.*

It's sleeting. *Il tombe de la neige fondue.*
It's hailing. *Il grêle.*
It wouldn't stop raining. Hundreds of people have been flooded out. *La pluie ne cessait pas. Des centaines de personnes ont vu leurs maisons inondées.*
What's the weather like in Nantes at this time of year? – Much the same as here. *Quel temps fait-il à Nantes en cette saison? – A peu près le même temps qu'ici.*
How are you finding the weather here? – Well, it's very wet! *Comment trouvez-vous le temps ici? – Eh bien, c'est très humide!*
I blame it all on global warming. *Pour moi, tout est la faute du réchauffement climatique.*

Living Language

This supplement has been specially conceived and compiled to enable learners of French to express themselves naturally and fluently. Divided into three main sections: OPINIONS: EXPRESSING WHAT YOU THINK; EMOTIONS: EXPRESSING WHAT YOU FEEL; and COMMUNICATION: ENGAGING WITH OTHERS, each section is further subdivided into topic headings containing many example sentences with their English translations. These sentences may be used to describe a wide range of opinions and emotions and to communicate in many types of situation, be it orally or using the written word. An essential language-learning tool for essay-writing and oral tests, this supplement will also equip the user with the linguistic tools necessary for natural communication in a wide variety of contexts, be it in conversation with French native speakers, sending an email or making a phone call.

OPINIONS: EXPRESSING WHAT YOU THINK

• ability

Peux-tu venir à la fête?
Can you come to the party?

Je suis désolé, je ne peux pas
I'm sorry, I can't

Il pouvait encore marcher
He could still walk

Elle sait jouer du violon
She can play the violin

Je pourrai te rendre visite plus souvent désormais
I'll be able to visit you more often now

Ils sont capables de se débrouiller tout seuls
They are capable of looking after themselves

Nous avons réussi à la persuader
We managed to persuade her

Vous serait-il possible de me prêter 5 livres?
Would it be possible for you to lend me £5?

Cela m'a mis dans l'impossibilité de faire mon travail
That made it impossible for me to do my work

Ils sont en mesure de vous l'offrir
They are in a position to offer it you

Il lui aurait été difficile de refuser
He/She couldn't very well refuse

Il a le pouvoir de décider
He has the power to decide

Qui lui a donné l'autorisation d'entrer?
Who gave him/her the authority to enter?

• belief

Je crois que c'est vrai
I believe it's true

Je n'arrive pas à le croire
I can't believe it

Il croit en Dieu/aux revenants
He believes in God/in ghosts

Je crois à la libre entreprise
I believe in free enterprise

Il n'en croyait pas ses yeux/ses oreilles
He couldn't believe his eyes/his ears

N'en croyez rien!
Don't you believe it!

Je suis convaincu qu'il ment
It's my belief he's lying

Contrairement à ce que l'on croit …
Contrary to popular belief …

C'est incroyable!
It's unbelievable!

Je n'en crois pas un mot
I don't believe a word of it

Je ne suis pas celle que vous croyez
I'm not that kind of person

C'est une maligne, crois-moi!
She's a smart one, believe (you) me!

Le gouvernement a perdu sa crédibilité aux yeux du public
The government has lost credibility with the public

Ton histoire est un peu tirée par les cheveux
Your story is a bit far-fetched

Ils l'ont prise au mot
They took her at her word

Elle a pris ça pour parole d'évangile
She took it as gospel

Fam Je lui ai raconté un mensonge et elle l'a gobé
I told her a lie and she swallowed it

Formal Ajoutez-vous foi aux rumeurs?
Do you give any credence to the rumours?

• belonging

Paul a beaucoup d'argent
Paul has a lot of money

Cette lettre est à moi
That letter is mine

À qui sont ces gants?
Whose gloves are these?

À qui appartient ce livre?
Who does this book belong to?

Elle est l'heureuse propriétaire d'une Rolls Royce
She is the proud owner of a Rolls Royce

Il fait partie de la bande à Dupont
He's one of the Dupont gang

Trier le courrier fait partie de mon travail
My job includes sorting the mail

Leur fils a sa propre maison
Their son has a house of his own

Cette région possède de grandes réserves d'eau
This region has large water reserves

Possèdent-ils les documents nécessaires?
Are they in possession of the necessary documents?

Quand prenez-vous possession de votre nouveau yacht?
When do you take possession of your new yacht?

Elle dispose d'un million de livres
She has a million pounds at her disposal

Ils détiennent 30 pour cent des parts de la société
They have a 30 percent shareholding in the company

Fam Arrête de squatter l'ordinateur!
Stop hogging the computer!

• certainty

Je suis certain qu'il viendra
I'm certain he'll come

Je n'en suis pas sûr
I don't know for sure

Ils ne sont pas convaincus que c'est nécessaire
They're not convinced it's necessary

Elle est innocente, c'est sûr
She is definitely innocent

Mais bien sûr qu'il t'aime
Of course he loves you

Êtes-vous sûr que c'était lui? – J'en suis certain!
Are you sure it was him? – I'm positive!

Elle s'est assurée que toutes les portes étaient fermées
She made sure that all the doors were locked

Ce n'est pas une hypothèse, c'est une certitude
It's not a possibility, it's a certainty

Il n'y a pas de doute là-dessus
There's no question about it

C'est sûr et certain
It's a hundred percent sure

Le bien-fondé de la décision est discutable
The wisdom of this decision is open to question

Il n'y a pas à discuter
There are no two ways about it

Réflexion faite, il vaut mieux que j'y aille moi-même
On second thoughts I'd better go myself

Fam À tous les coups, il a le poste
He's a dead cert for the job

• comparison

Vous êtes aussi grand que lui
You are as tall as he is

Les cèdres sont plus vieux que les chênes
The cedars are older than the oaks

Il joue au tennis mieux/plus mal que moi
He plays tennis better/worse than me

J'ai autant d'argent/autant de livres que vous
I have as much money/as many books as you

J'ai travaillé autant que lui
I worked as much as he did

Le film était meilleur que je ne m'y attendais
The film was better than I expected

Elle est brillante par rapport *ou* comparée aux autres
Compared with the others she's brilliant

On a comparé ses tableaux à ceux de Manet
His paintings have been compared to Manet's

Le livre établit une comparaison entre Londres et New York
The book makes a comparison between London and New York

Autant que je me souvienne, il n'était pas là
As far as I can remember he wasn't there

Il n'y a pas de comparaison
There's no comparison

En comparaison, cette musique est mélodieuse
This music is melodic by comparison

Comparé à son frère, il était timide
In comparison with his brother, he was shy

Il me le faut aussitôt que possible *ou* dès que possible
I need it as soon as possible

• confusion

Je me suis trompé de route/train
I took the wrong road/train

Ce n'est pas la bonne route pour aller à Paris
This is not the right road for Paris

Je vous confondais avec votre frère
I was mixing you up with your brother

Je ne sais plus où j'en suis
I'm getting all mixed up

Mes affaires sont tout en désordre
My things are all in a jumble

Les pages se sont complètement mélangées
The pages got all jumbled

La confusion entre les deux notions est fréquente
The two notions are often confused

Je l'ai pris pour quelqu'un d'autre
I mistook him for someone else

Ne mélange pas tout
Don't get everything mixed up

C'est un fatras d'idées
It is a hotchpotch of ideas

• curiosity

Je me demande s'il viendra
I wonder whether he'll come

Je suis curieux de savoir qui a inventé cela
I'd like to know who invented that

Ils n'étaient pas du tout curieux de savoir comment cela s'était produit
They weren't at all curious as to how it had happened

Il y est allé par curiosité
He went there out of curiosity

C'est un esprit curieux
He/She has an inquisitive mind

Il se mêle des affaires de tout le monde
He pokes his nose into everybody's business

Ils brûlaient d'impatience d'apprendre les dernières nouvelles
They were dying to hear the latest news

Fam Mêle-toi *ou* occupe-toi de tes oignons!
Mind your own business!

La curiosité est un vilain défaut
Curiosity killed the cat

• difference

Ce livre est très différent de son premier
This book is very different from his/her first

Leur version contredit la tienne
Their version is at variance with yours

Je ne vois pas la différence entre les deux
I can't tell the difference between the two

Ils sont de tailles/couleurs différentes
They're different sizes/colours

C'est ce qui fait toute la différence!
That's what makes all the difference!

Il ne ressemble pas du tout à son frère
He's not at all like his brother

Contrairement à vous, je préfère une vie tranquille
Unlike you, I prefer a quiet life

Il n'y en a pas deux de pareils
No two are alike

Il n'y a aucun rapport entre ces faits
These facts are totally unrelated

Comment distinguer le diamant du zircon?
How can you tell the difference between diamond and zircon?

Par contraste, le président était presque optimiste
By contrast, the president was almost optimistic

Ils n'ont rien de commun
They have nothing in common

Leurs positions sur le désarmement sont diamétralement opposées
Their positions on disarmament are poles apart

Il y a deux ans de différence d'âge entre eux
There are two years between them

• difficulty

Ne fais pas le difficile!
Don't be so difficult!

Il a eu du mal à monter l'escalier
He had trouble climbing the stairs

Ils rencontrent des difficultés financières
They are in financial difficulties

Où est le problème?
What's the problem?

Je ne peux pas venir, j'ai des problèmes avec la voiture
I can't come – I've got problems with the car

La crise a mis plusieurs banques en difficulté
The crisis put several banks in a difficult position

On a eu un mal fou à trouver la maison
We had the devil of a job finding the house

Elle traverse une période difficile
She's going through a bad time

C'est plus facile à dire qu'à faire
It's easier said than done

Il s'endort difficilement
He finds it hard to get to sleep

Tu vas avoir du mal à trouver une boutique ouverte à cette heure-ci
You'll be hard pressed to find a shop open at this time

Ils étaient dans une très mauvaise passe
They were in dire straits

Nous étions au pied du mur
We had our backs to the wall

Fam Elle est dans le pétrin
She's in a fix

Fam Elle est tombée sur un os
She hit a snag

Fam Parfois c'est la croix et la bannière pour trouver à se garer
It can be a headache finding somewhere to park

• disappointment

Il a été déçu de ne pas être invité
He was disappointed at not being invited

Les résultats vous ont-ils déçu?
Are you disappointed with the results?

Tu me déçois
I'm disappointed in you

Cela a été la grande déception de sa vie
It was the great disappointment of his/her life

J'ai trouvé le film vraiment décevant
I found the film very disappointing

Quelle ne fut pas ma déconvenue lorsque …
I was so disappointed when …

C'était pire que je pensais
It was worse than I expected

Il n'a pas répondu à leurs attentes
He didn't live up to their expectations

Leurs gains ont été bien inférieurs à ce qu'ils attendaient
Their winnings fell far short of what they had expected

Elle a essuyé bien des déboires
She has suffered many disappointments

• doubt

Je doute qu'il vienne
I doubt whether he'll come

J'en doute
I doubt it

J'ai des doutes sur lui
I have my doubts about him

Nous n'avons aucun doute sur ses compétences
We are in no doubt as to his/her competence

C'est, sans aucun doute, la meilleure au monde
Without any doubt, she is the best in the world

Ces faits ont été avérés sans le moindre doute
The facts have been established beyond doubt

Je suis très sceptique quant à ce qu'ils affirment
I'm very sceptical of their claims

Il a toujours été indécis
He's always been indecisive

Il hésite à acheter la maison
He's hesitating about buying the house

Je n'ai jamais douté de ton talent
I've never doubted your talent

Je suis très partagé sur ce point
I have very mixed feelings on the subject

Décidez-vous!
Make up your mind!

Elle ne sait pas trop si elle doit le leur dire ou non
She's in a bit of a dilemma over whether to tell them or not

Son employeur a mis son honnêteté en question
His/Her employer called his/her honesty into question

Il ne faut pas prendre ce qu'il dit pour argent comptant
You must take what he says with a pinch of salt

• easiness

L'examen était très facile
The exam was very easy

Elle est facile à vivre
She's easy to get on with

Cela vous facilitera la tâche
This will make your job easier

Vous concevez sans peine ma déception
You can easily imagine my disappointment

Tu ne devrais avoir aucun mal à changer ton billet
You shouldn't have any trouble changing your ticket

C'est plus facile à dire qu'à faire
It's easier said than done

C'est simple comme bonjour
It's as easy as pie

C'est un jeu d'enfant
It's child's play

Essaie, c'est facile comme tout!
Have a go, it's as easy as anything!

Il a gagné haut la main
He won hands down

C'est le genre de choses qu'il peut faire les yeux fermés
That's the kind of thing he could do standing on his head

Fam Il a trouvé une bonne planque
He's found a cushy job

Fam C'était du gâteau!
It was a piece of cake!

Fam C'était hyper fastoche
It was a walk in the park

• emphasizing

Elle a mis l'accent sur la nécessité d'être prudent
She emphasized the need for caution

On ne saurait trop insister sur cette différence
This difference cannot be overemphasized

Je dois insister sur ce point
I must insist on this point

Je le répète, je n'ai jamais entendu parler de lui
I repeat, I have never heard of him

Ne vous attardez pas sur vos problèmes
Don't dwell on your problems

Je ne vous dirai rien, inutile d'insister
I'm not telling you anything, so there's no point pressing me any further

La révolte a mis ces problèmes en évidence
The revolt brought these issues to the fore

La défense a beaucoup insisté sur le casier judiciaire du témoin
The defence made much of the witness's criminal record

Mon oncle a instillé en moi l'importance du travail
My uncle impressed on me the importance of hard work

Les bonnes manières nous ont été inculquées à l'école
Good manners were dinned into us at school

Il a tellement insisté que j'ai fini par accepter
He was so insistent about it that I ended up accepting

Je vous l'ai dit cent fois!
I've told you hundreds of times!

Ce n'était pas moi, je le jure!
It wasn't me, I swear!

Fam Je ne reviendrai pas, enfonce-toi bien ça dans la tête!
I won't be back, just get that into your thick head!

ESSAY WRITING

Words and phrases for linking points in an essay

Adding: aussi, également, de plus, en outre, en plus de cela, outre cela, de même
Il convient aussi *ou* également *ou* de plus de souligner que ...
It must also be emphasized that ...

L'expérience s'est soldée par un échec. De plus *ou* En outre, de nombreux chercheurs ont perdu leur emploi.
The experiment failed. Moreover, many scientists lost their jobs.

Comparing: de la même manière, de la même façon, de même, ainsi, pareillement
La course aux armes de destruction massive n'apporte que l'isolation. De la même manière *ou* De la même façon *ou* De même, les dirigeants qui l'abandonnent ouvriront la voie à de meilleures relations internationales.
The pursuit of weapons of mass destruction only invites isolation. By the same token, leaders who abandon the pursuit of those weapons will find an open path to better relations.

Consequence: par conséquent, en conséquence, donc, il en résulte que, dès lors
En l'absence de législation, le droit à l'éducation est impossible à mettre en œuvre. Il convient dès lors *ou* par conséquent de moderniser la constitution des pays concernés.
Without legislation it is impossible to implement the right to education. Consequently, it is advisable to modernize the constitutions of the countries concerned.

Nous avons tous le devoir d'aider les autres. Par conséquent *ou* En conséquence, nous devons contribuer au fonds de solidarité pour les catastrophes naturelles.
We all have a duty to help others. Therefore, we should contribute to the disaster fund.

Contrasting: mais, cependant, toutefois, néanmoins, par contraste, d'un autre côté, au contraire, contrairement à, au lieu de cela
Chaque jeune ou presque possède un téléphone portable. Par contraste, très peu de personnes âgées en possèdent un.
Nearly every young person has a mobile phone. By contrast, very few senior citizens have one.

De telles mesures sont fréquemment critiquées; elles devraient au contraire être bien accueillies.
Such measures are frequently criticized; on the contrary, they should be welcomed.

Illustrating: par exemple

Restating: en résumé, en un mot, dans le fond, au fond, à savoir, c'est-à-dire
Il existe des différences, mais dans le fond *ou* au fond, il s'agit là d'un exemple classique de plagiat.
There are some differences, but in essence this is a classic case of plagiarism.

Le projet soulève une objection de taille, à savoir son coût élevé.
There is one important objection to this plan: namely, the high cost.

Sequence: en même temps, parallèlement, tout d'abord, en premier lieu, premièrement, pour commencer, et puis, puis, tandis que, alors que
Il admet avoir menti et en même temps il veut qu'on le croie!
He admits he's lied and at the same time he wants us to trust him!

En premier lieu *ou* Tout d'abord, ces statistiques sont fausses; et puis elles ont été mal interprétées.
To begin with, the statistics are wrong; and then they have been misinterpreted.

Summarizing: tout bien considéré, tout compte fait, dans l'ensemble, globalement, en gros, en conclusion, pour conclure, en dernier ressort, en fin de compte, finalement, en résumé

Dans l'ensemble *ou* Globalement, le nouveau système fonctionne bien. Cependant, certains aspects pourraient bénéficier d'une amélioration.
By and large, the new system is working well. However, there are some areas where improvements could be made.

Tout bien considéré *ou* Tout compte fait, on ne peut pas dire que la peine capitale diminue le nombre de meurtres.
All things considered, capital punishment cannot be said to reduce the number of murders committed.

• hope

Nous espérons avoir beau temps
We're hoping for good weather

J'espère que votre frère va mieux
I hope your brother is better

Elle a bon espoir de réussir
She has hopes of succeeding

Ne lui donne pas trop d'espoir
Don't raise his/her hopes too much

On espère qu'ils partiront demain
Hopefully, they'll leave tomorrow

Tout le monde rêve de gagner à la loterie
Everyone dreams of winning the lottery

Il y a peu d'espoir qu'ils remportent le match
There is little prospect of their winning the match

Cette nouvelle année s'annonce prometteuse
The outlook for the New Year is promising

Les choses se présentent plutôt bien
Things are looking quite optimistic

Nous devons voir les choses du bon côté: au moins nous sommes toujours vivants
We must look on the bright side – at least we're still alive

C'est prendre ses désirs pour des réalités
That's a bit of wishful thinking

À quelque chose malheur est bon
Every cloud has a silver lining

Elle voit la vie en rose
She sees the world through rose-coloured glasses

Il ne cesse de bâtir des châteaux en Espagne
He's always building castles in the air

Ils voyaient l'avenir de l'entreprise avec optimisme
They were optimistic about the company's prospects

• ignorance

Nous ne la connaissons pas
We don't know her

Je ne sais pas si elle est prête ou non
I don't know if she's ready or not

Je n'y connais absolument rien en voitures
I don't know anything at all about cars

Je n'ai jamais entendu parler de lui
I've never heard of him

Je n'ai pas la moindre idée de ce dont vous parlez
I haven't the faintest idea what you're talking about

Il ne se rendait pas compte qu'on l'observait
He was unaware he was being watched

Nous ignorions tout de leurs projets
We were completely in the dark about their plans

Elle ignorait les faits
She was ignorant of the facts

Je connais mal ses écrits
I'm unfamiliar with his/her writing

Il n'y a aucune nouvelle d'eux pour l'instant
There has been no news of them so far

La police n'a rien sur quoi se fonder
The police have nothing to go on

Je n'en sais pas plus que toi
I don't know any more than you do

Je ne comprends rien à l'économie
I haven't a clue about economics

Le nouveau ministre est un personnage dont on ne sait pas grand-chose
The new minister is a bit of an unknown quantity

Fam Là, vous me posez une colle!
You've got me there!

Fam Tout ça, c'est de l'hébreu pour moi
It's all Greek to me

• importance

Il est important de savoir que …
It's important to know that …

Vous êtes en bonne santé, c'est l'essentiel
You're healthy, that's the main thing

C'est un événement de la plus haute importance
It is an event of great significance

N'accordez pas trop d'importance à cette enquête
Don't attach too much importance to this survey

Sa parole a du poids
What he/she says carries weight

Peu importe le prix
It doesn't matter how much it costs

Je ne compte pas ici
I don't count around here

Il est vital que …
It's vital that …

Elle a été nommée à un poste clé
She was appointed to a key post

Je ne fais pas grand cas de leurs conseils
I don't set much store by their advice

C'est une question de vie ou de mort
It's a matter of life and death

C'est d'une importance capitale
It's of the utmost importance

C'était une tempête dans un verre d'eau
It was a storm in a teacup

La presse a monté son divorce en épingle
The press played up his/her divorce

Le gouvernement tente de minimiser l'importance de son rôle
The government is trying to play down its role

Elle se croit quelqu'un
She thinks she's somebody

Il est plutôt insignifiant
He's a bit of a nonentity

Ça ne fait rien!
Never mind!

Et alors?
So what?

Fam C'est de la petite bière
It's small beer

• intention

Comment avez-vous l'intention de vous y prendre?
How do you intend to do it?

Nous sommes arrivés plus tard que prévu
We arrived later than intended

J'ai bien l'intention de les appeler
I have every intention of calling them

Je n'ai aucune intention d'accepter
I have no intention of accepting

Elle pense monter une affaire
She's thinking of starting a business

Son but est de s'enrichir rapidement
His/Her aim is to get rich quickly

Elle vise la présidence
She has set her sights on the presidency

Il ambitionne de monter sur les planches
His ambition is to go on the stage

Je ne voulais pas te vexer
I didn't mean to offend you

Ils ont acheté la maison en vue de la louer
They bought the house with a view to letting it

Elle ne l'a pas fait exprès
She didn't do it on purpose

C'est l'intention qui compte
It's the thought that counts

Afin de simplifier les choses, j'ai …
In order to simplify things, I have …

Ce faisant, il a involontairement enfreint la loi
By doing that, he unwittingly broke the law

• interest

Elle s'intéresse à la mode
She is interested in fashion

Ça t'intéressait de le rencontrer?
Would you be interested in meeting him?

Il s'intéresse activement à la politique
He takes an active interest in politics

Cela peut vous intéresser
This may be of interest to you

Il a prêté attention à tout ce qu'elle disait
He paid attention to everything she said

Pourriez-vous m'accorder votre attention un instant?
May I have your attention for a moment?

Le gouvernement devrait s'attacher à améliorer la situation économique
The government should focus on improving the economy

J'ai suivi votre émission avec un grand intérêt
I watched your programme with great interest

Ne faites pas attention à lui!
Take no notice of him!

J'ai besoin d'étudier cette proposition avant de me décider
I need to study the proposal before I decide

Elle passait au crible les détails du contrat
She was poring over the details of the contract

Il est entièrement absorbé par son travail
He is wrapped up in his work

Elle a dressé l'oreille en entendant ton nom
She pricked up her ears at the sound of your name

Avez-vous eu de leurs nouvelles?
Have you had any news of them?

Quoi de neuf?
What's new?

• obviousness

Il est évident qu'elle ment
It's obvious she's lying

Il est clair qu'il a tort
He is clearly wrong

Bien sûr que je te crois
Of course I believe you

Il est indéniable que nous avons un problème
There is no denying that we have a problem

Il va sans dire que nous voyagerons ensemble
It goes without saying that we'll travel together

C'était une tentative flagrante de s'attacher son soutien
It was a blatant attempt to win him/her over

L'expérience s'est soldée par un échec retentissant
The experiment was a conspicuous failure

Ça se voit vraiment qu'il n'est pas d'ici
It really stands out that he's not a local

L'erreur m'a sauté aux yeux
The mistake jumped out at me

La réponse saute aux yeux!
The answer's staring you in the face!

C'est clair comme de l'eau de roche
It's as plain as the nose on your face

C'était en plein sous mon nez
It was right under my nose all the time

Fam Ça se voit comme le nez au milieu de la figure!
It stands out a mile!

• opinions

Que pensez-vous de lui?
What do you think of him?

Je suis d'avis que l'on attende
My opinion is that we should wait

C'est un bon film à mon avis
It's a good film in my opinion

Elle a des opinions marquées sur le sujet
She has strong views on the subject

C'est une question d'opinion
It's a matter of opinion

Pour ma part, je trouve que c'est une idée stupide
Personally, I think it's a silly idea

À vrai dire, je ne crois pas que ça marchera
To be honest, I don't think it will work

J'ai l'impression que les choses ont changé entre nous
I have the feeling things have changed between us

Je la considère comme une bonne amie
I regard her as a good friend

J'estime avoir mon mot à dire
I think I've got the right to offer an opinion

Quelle est la position des Américains sur ce problème?
What is the American position on this issue?

Il n'a pas estimé nécessaire de me prévenir
He didn't consider it necessary to warn me

Selon moi, cela serait une bonne solution
To my way of thinking, this would be a good solution

Elle s'est mis en tête qu'on la persécutait
She got it into her head she was being persecuted

J'ai changé d'avis à leur égard
I've changed my mind about them

Rien ne m'en fera démordre
I'll stick to my guns come what may

• planning

Nous projetons d'aller aux États-Unis
We're planning to go to the States

L'idée, c'est de se retrouver chez Amélie
The plan is to meet up at Amélie's

Nous n'avons rien de prévu demain après-midi
We don't have anything planned tomorrow afternoon

Ils avaient prévu de descendre à l'hôtel
They had made plans to stay at a hotel

Il y a eu un changement de programme
There's been a change of plan

Tout a marché comme prévu
Everything went according to plan

C'est encore à l'état de projet
It's still at the planning stage

Ils sont arrivés plus tard que prévu
They arrived later than expected

La proposition de construction d'une nouvelle prison a été rejetée
The proposal to build a new prison was rejected

J'ai organisé la visite d'une laiterie à leur intention
I've organized a visit to a dairy for them

Je me suis arrangé avec le patron pour partir de bonne heure demain
I've arranged with the boss to leave early tomorrow

Il prépare déjà le voyage en Russie de l'année prochaine
He's already making preparations for next year's trip to Russia

Nous avons trouvé un itinéraire plus facile
We worked out an easier route

• possibility

Il ne lui est pas possible de venir
It isn't possible for him/her to come

C'est peut-être le plus grand musicien de son temps
He is possibly the greatest musician of his time

Évitez autant que possible de toucher les côtés
Avoid touching the sides as far as possible

Elle vient me voir à chaque fois que c'est possible *ou* quand elle le peut
She comes to see me whenever possible

Il pourrait revenir d'un moment à l'autre
He could return at any moment

Peut-être qu'elle n'acceptera pas
Perhaps she won't accept

Ce garçon est un génie en puissance
That boy is a potential genius

L'idée a de l'avenir
The idea has potential

À ta place j'irais, c'est la chance de ta vie
I would go if I were you, it's the opportunity of a lifetime

Prends un parapluie au cas où
Take an umbrella just in case

Les projets ont peu de chances d'être approuvés
The plans stand little chance of being approved

Ce n'est pas faisable financièrement de maintenir le magasin ouvert
It is not financially feasible to keep the shop open

Tu pourrais gagner, on ne sait jamais!
You might win, you never know!

En cas d'incendie, évacuez le bâtiment
In the event of fire, evacuate the building

• pretending

Ils ont fait semblant de ne pas nous voir
They pretended not to see us

Elle n'a pas feint d'être intéressée
She made no pretence of being interested

Imagine que tu es un oiseau
Make believe you're a bird

Arrête de jouer la comédie!
Stop putting on an act!

Ce n'est qu'une façade
It's all show

Il s'est fait passer pour un héros
He passed himself off as a hero

Ce n'est qu'un prétexte
It's just an excuse

Elle est venue sous prétexte de consulter son frère
She came on the pretext of consulting her brother

Tu m'as fait venir ici sous un faux prétexte
You've got me here under false pretences

J'ai feint d'être malade afin de ne pas y aller
I feigned illness so I wouldn't have to go

Lorsqu'elle en a entendu parler, elle a affecté la surprise
When she heard of it, she affected surprise

Au fond, il est très gentil
Deep down he's very kind

Ne fais pas l'innocent avec moi!
Don't play the innocent with me!

Il a ri du bout des lèvres
He gave a forced laugh

Je ne pense pas qu'elle simule
I don't think she's pretending

Elle l'a dit sur un ton pince-sans-rire
She said it tongue in cheek

Fam Ne t'inquiète pas, il fait du chiqué
Don't worry, he's just putting it on

Fam Il tire au flanc
He's swinging the lead

• probability

C'est l'hypothèse la plus vraisemblable
It's the most likely hypothesis

Il me paraît fort peu probable qu'il soit jamais venu ici
I think it highly unlikely that he ever came here

Pourrez-vous venir? – Probablement (pas)
Will you be able to come? – Probably (not)

Il est probable qu'il fasse encore plus chaud
The likelihood is that it will get even hotter

Il y a peu de chances/de bonnes chances que cela se produise
There's little/a good chance of that happening

Il y a fort à parier qu'il arrivera en retard
It's a pretty safe bet that he'll be late

Elle est susceptible de faire des erreurs
She's liable to make mistakes

Il est sûrement déjà rentré
As likely as not he's already home

Vous serez sans doute surpris de ma décision
You will doubtless be surprised at my decision

Il y a dans cette affaire largement de quoi déclencher un scandale national
The affair has all the makings of a national scandal

Il était prévisible que le projet échouerait
It was on the cards that the project would fail

C'est un peu dur à avaler
That's a bit hard to swallow

C'est un pari risqué mais nous réussirons peut-être
It's a long shot, but we may be successful

• progress

Il progressait lentement dans son apprentissage de la langue
He was making slow progress with learning the language

Les négociations sont en bonne voie
Negotiations are making good progress

Living Language

Le malade fait des progrès satisfaisants
The patient is progressing satisfactorily

Il y a eu des avancées significatives en génétique ces dernières années
There have been significant advances in genetics in recent years

Alors, ça avance la peinture?
How are you getting on with the painting?

La répétition a bien/mal marché
The rehearsal went well/badly

Je tourne en rond avec cette dissertation
I'm not getting anywhere with this essay

Vous avez fait des progrès phénoménaux en maths
Your maths has improved by leaps and bounds

La construction avance bien
The building work is coming along fine

Sa recherche avance à grand pas
He/She is making great strides with his/her research

Notre chiffre d'affaires est en constante progression
Our turnover is constantly improving

J'ai déjà fait une bonne partie de mes achats de Noël
I've already done quite a bit of my Christmas shopping

Nous avons fait le plus gros du travail
We've done the bulk of the work

Les deux parties ont avancé dans leurs négociations
The two sides have made some headway in their negotiations

Nous gagnons/perdons du terrain sur nos concurrents
We are gaining ground on/losing ground to our competitors

Ils ont pris du retard dans leurs lectures
They've fallen behind with their reading

L'économie fait du surplace
The economy is treading water

• relevance

Quel est le rapport entre ses remarques et la situation?
What relevance do his/her remarks have to the situation?

De telles considérations sont hors de propos
Such considerations are not relevant

J'ai bien peur que ça concerne ta mère
It has to do with your mother, I'm afraid

Cela n'a rien à voir avec la couleur de la peau
It has nothing to do with skin colour

Je n'y suis pour rien
I had nothing to do with it

Je ne vois pas l'intérêt de le refaire
I don't see the point of redoing it

Ce n'est pas le problème!
That's not the problem!

J'ai quelques remarques à faire à ce propos
I have a few things to say in connection with this

Il est tout à fait approprié que cela se termine de cette manière
It is very apt that it should end in this way

Cette loi s'applique à tous les citoyens
This law applies to all citizens

Ta confiance en elle était bien mal placée
Your confidence in her was totally misplaced

Cela rejoint ce que j'ai dit avant
That ties in with what I said before

Ses remarques ont un certain rapport avec la situation actuelle
His/Her comments have some bearing on the present situation

Vos critiques ne sont pas pertinentes
Your criticisms are irrelevant

Il n'y avait pas de suite dans sa conversation
His/Her conversation was full of non sequiturs

Les preuves se rapportant au dossier sont plutôt minces
The evidence relating to the case is not strong

• subject

De quoi parlent-ils?
What are they talking about?

C'est un livre sur la vie de Mozart
It's a book about the life of Mozart

Vous voulez me voir à quel sujet?
What do you want to see me about?

À propos de la Suisse, vous avez déjà fait du ski?
Talking of Switzerland, have you ever been skiing?

N'essaie pas de changer de sujet!
Don't try to change the subject!

Elle passe des examens dans quatre matières
She's taking exams in four subjects

Ce n'est pas mon domaine
That's not my field

Le débat de ce soir porte sur le chômage
Tonight's topic for debate is unemployment

Là n'est pas la question
That's not the point

Revenons à nos moutons
Let's get back to the matter in hand

Le problème des sans-abri ne figure pas parmi les priorités du gouvernement
The problem of the homeless doesn't come very high on the government's agenda

La question est encore à l'étude
The matter is still under consideration

Il faut aussi prendre en compte l'augmentation du coût de la vie
The rising cost of living must also be taken into account

• success

Le film a eu énormément de succès en Italie
The film was a great success in Italy

L'opération est un succès total
The operation is a complete success

Nous voulons tous réussir dans la vie
We all want to succeed in life

Le programme de vaccination a été couronné de succès
The vaccination programme was a great success

Il a été opéré avec succès d'un ulcère à l'estomac
He was successfully operated on for a stomach ulcer

L'expérience a été un échec
The experiment was a failure

Cet accord sera considéré comme un triomphe personnel pour le président
This agreement will be seen as a personal triumph for the President

Les discussions n'ont produit aucune avancée
The discussions have failed to bring any progress

Nous avons réussi à la persuader
We managed to persuade her

Le plan n'a pas atteint ses objectifs
The plan didn't achieve its objectives

Leur chanson 'Bye, Bye' a été un tube
They had a hit with their song 'Bye, Bye'

L'équipe s'est montrée à la hauteur des circonstances et s'est imposée facilement
The team rose to the occasion and won by a large margin

Il est arrivé en haut de l'échelle dans sa profession
He has reached the top of his profession

Elle a réussi l'examen haut la main
She passed the exam with flying colours

C'est une réussite!
It's a real success!

La société a le vent en poupe
The company is riding high

Sa nouvelle pièce fait un malheur
His/Her latest play is a big hit

• suitability

Le bleu/Ce chapeau te va bien
Blue/This hat suits you

Ce climat/Cette nourriture ne me convient pas
This climate/This food doesn't suit me

La maison ne conviendrait pas à une famille nombreuse
The house is not suitable for a large family

Tu n'es pas convenablement habillé pour ce genre d'occasion
You are not appropriately dressed for such an occasion

Cette cravate ne va pas avec ta chemise
That tie doesn't go with your shirt

Ça me va comme un gant
It fits me like a glove

C'est le cadeau idéal
It's the perfect gift

Ce n'est pas le moment d'en parler
Now is not the right time to mention it

Il ne faut pas me demander ça à moi
I'm the wrong person to ask

Quelle heure vous conviendrait le mieux?
When would be the best time for you?

Moi, ça me va
That's all right by me

Il n'a pas l'étoffe d'un homme politique
He's not cut out to be a politician

C'est tout à fait mon rayon
That's right up my street

Isabelle était dans son élément, disant à chacun ce qu'il devait faire
Isabelle was in her element, telling everybody what to do

• summarizing

Bref, ce n'est pas possible
In short, it's not possible

En résumé, je dirai que …
To sum up, I will say that …

En conclusion, je voudrais simplement dire que …
To conclude, I would just like to say that …

En un mot, non
In a word, no

Voilà toute l'affaire en deux mots
That's the whole thing in a nutshell

Dans l'ensemble, il a fait bonne impression
On the whole he made a good impression

Enfin bref, j'ai perdu mon emploi
So, not to beat about the bush, I've lost my job

Je serai bref
I'll come straight to the point

• supposition

Qu'est-ce qui vous fait croire que j'ai confiance en vous?
What makes you suppose I trust you?

Vous ne vous souvenez sans doute pas de moi
I don't suppose you remember me

Je suppose que oui/que non
I suppose so/not

Supposons que vous ayez raison
Let's suppose you're right

En l'absence de preuves, il doit être présumé innocent
In the absence of proof, he must be assumed innocent

Je me fonde sur l'hypothèse que …
I'm working on the assumption that …

Elle devait parler de quelqu'un d'autre
She must have been talking about someone else

Je pense qu'il y aura environ 40 personnes à la soirée
I reckon there'll be about 40 people at the party

Tu veux de l'argent, j'imagine
You want some money, I suppose

Je présume que vous êtes sa sœur
I take it you're his/her sister

Nous ne pouvons que faire des suppositions
We can only speculate

C'était pure conjecture de sa part
It was pure speculation on his/her part

Cela confirme mon hypothèse selon laquelle …
This confirms my hypothesis that …

De fortes présomptions pèsent sur lui
He is under great suspicion

• understanding

Je ne comprends pas la question
I don't understand the question

Il prétend que sa femme ne le comprend pas
He claims his wife doesn't understand him

Je ne peux pas me faire comprendre en anglais
I can't make myself understood in English

J'ai compris à demi-mot
I took the hint

Auriez-vous l'obligeance de répéter?
Would you mind repeating that?

Je vois où vous voulez en venir
I see what you're getting at

Je n'ai pas bien saisi ce qu'elle a voulu dire
I didn't quite grasp what she meant

Je n'y comprends rien
It makes no sense to me

Est-ce que je me fais bien comprendre?
Do I make myself clear?

Je vous ai entendu, mais je n'ai pas vraiment saisi sur le moment
I heard what you said, but it didn't sink in at the time

Il a compris la situation en un clin d'œil
He took in the situation at a glance

Elle est un peu dépassée dans son nouveau travail
She's a bit out of her depth in her new job

J'entends aller au fond de cette affaire
I intend to get to the bottom of this affair

Ce que je n'arrive pas à comprendre c'est …
What I can't work out is …

Pour moi ça n'a ni queue ni tête
I can't make head nor tail of this

Fam Je ne pige pas
I don't get it

Fam Tout ça, c'est de l'hébreu pour moi
It's all Greek to me

Fam C'est clair comme du jus de boudin
It's as clear as mud

Fam Il a la comprenette difficile
He's a bit slow on the uptake

Fam Tout à coup ça a fait tilt
Suddenly the penny dropped

• wanting

Je veux une tasse de café
I want a cup of coffee

Ils veulent aller en vacances en Espagne
They want to go to Spain on holiday

Je veux que tu attendes ici
I want you to wait here

Tes désirs sont des ordres!
Your wish is my command!

Je voudrais bien être à votre place
I wish I were in your place

Elle n'avait aucune envie d'y retourner
She had no desire to go back

Je mourais d'envie de lui dire la vérité
I was longing to tell him/her the truth

Il brûlait de la revoir
He was dying to see her again

Elle aspire au pouvoir politique
She aspires to political power

Il avait l'ambition de devenir médecin
His ambition was to become a doctor

J'ai eu envie de le frapper
I had the urge to hit him

J'ai eu une soudaine fringale de chocolat
I got a sudden craving for chocolate

Il était poussé par une soif de savoir
He was driven by a thirst for knowledge

EMOTIONS: EXPRESSING WHAT YOU FEEL

• admiration

Chapeau!
I take my hat off to you!

J'ai beaucoup d'admiration pour les médecins
I have great admiration for doctors

Elle est tenue en haute estime par ses collègues
She is held in high esteem by her colleagues

Je n'ai pas une très haute opinion de mon patron
I don't think very highly of my boss

Les enfants ont besoin de prendre exemple sur quelqu'un
Children need someone to look up to

Il l'a regardée avec émerveillement
He looked at her in wonder

Elle adore sa mère
She worships her mother

Je l'admire beaucoup, ça n'a pas dû être facile pour lui
I admire him enormously, it can't have been easy for him

Elle s'est extasiée devant mes géraniums
She went into raptures over my geraniums

Il est tombé en admiration devant ses photos
He was speechless with admiration for his/her photos

Elle a des idées formidables
She has some wonderful ideas

Elle était superbe dans sa robe de velours noir
She looked stunning in her black velvet dress

Quel but fantastique!
What a fantastic goal!

Fam Ouah!
Wow!

• anger

Je vais me mettre en colère!
I'm going to get angry!

Elle est en colère parce qu'elle n'a pas été invitée
She's angry at not having been invited

Il s'est fâché contre elle
He got angry with her

Dans un accès de colère, il …
In a moment of anger, he …

Il est très coléreux
He's got quite a temper

Mon père était furieux
My father was furious

Elle ne décolérait pas
She was still fuming

Promets-moi que tu ne vas pas t'énerver
Promise me you won't get annoyed

Tu commences vraiment à me taper sur les nerfs avec tes commentaires stupides
You're really getting on my nerves with your stupid comments

Je n'aime pas du tout vos remarques
I resent your remarks

Il s'est emporté contre moi
He lost his temper with me

Elle s'énerve pour rien
She gets worked up over nothing

Le patron est d'une humeur massacrante
The boss is on the warpath

Ce genre de comportement m'horripile
Behaviour like that really gets my back up

Comment oses-tu me parler sur ce ton!
How dare you speak to me in that tone of voice!

Attends un peu que je l'attrape!
Just wait till I get hold of him/her!

Ça c'est le comble!
That's the limit!

• beauty

Quelle belle femme/chanson!
What a beautiful woman/song!

C'était une beauté dans son temps
She was a beauty in her day

Il te plaît?
Do you find him/it attractive?

Leur fille est mignonne comme tout
Their daughter is as pretty as a picture

Il est très beau garçon
He's very good-looking

Elle n'est pas mal
She's quite good-looking

Il n'est plus aussi beau qu'avant
He's lost his looks

Elle n'est pas belle mais elle a du charme
She's not beautiful but she's attractive

Le nouveau bâtiment n'est pas des plus agréables à l'œil
The new building is not very aesthetically pleasing

Le paysage m'a coupé le souffle
The landscape took my breath away

Ton bébé est vraiment mignon
Your baby is really cute

Fam Elle est vraiment canon
She's a real looker

Fam C'est vraiment un beau mec
He's a real hunk

• boredom

Son discours était vraiment ennuyeux
His/Her speech was really boring

Recueillir des signatures est un travail fastidieux
It's a tedious business collecting signatures

Il mange pour tromper l'ennui
He eats to keep boredom at bay

Elle est vraiment barbante quand elle se met à parler de jardinage
She's a real bore on the subject of gardening

Je commence à m'ennuyer
I'm beginning to get bored

J'en ai eu assez de jouer aux cartes
I got tired of playing cards

Les visites qu'elle leur rendait rompaient la monotonie de leur existence
Her visits broke the monotony of their lives

Living Language

Faire le ménage m'ennuie à mourir
Housework bores me stiff

Ce livre est ennuyeux comme la pluie
This book is as dull as ditchwater

Repasser, quelle corvée!
Ironing's such a chore!

Fam Son dernier film est rasant
His/Her latest film is deadly

Fam Quelle barbe ces examens!
The exams are a real drag!

Fam Je la trouve assommante
She's a real pain

• confidence

Tu te sens sûr de toi?
Are you feeling confident?

Nous sommes confiants que ça marchera
We are confident it will work

Je ne suis pas sûr de réussir
I'm not confident of success

C'est quelqu'un de très sûr de lui
He is a very self-confident person

Elle a une grande/manque de confiance en elle
She is full of/lacks self-confidence

Vous n'avez pas assez d'autorité
You're not assertive enough

On sent qu'elle est mal dans sa peau
You can tell she's insecure

Tu présumes un peu trop de ta réussite à l'examen
You're being overconfident about the exam

Fam Ne fais pas le malin!
Don't be cocky!

• courage

Tu vas devoir être courageux et le lui dire
You'll have to be brave and tell him/her

Je ne me sens pas le courage d'aller travailler/de le leur dire
I don't feel up to going to work/to telling them

C'est un soldat et un explorateur intrépide
He's a soldier and an intrepid explorer

Elle essaie de rassembler son courage pour l'inviter à la fête
She's trying to pluck up courage to invite him/her to the party

Courage!
Chin up!

Il faut du courage pour faire ça
It takes courage to do that

Tu ne manques pas d'audace!
You've got some cheek!

Ne te décourage pas
Don't give up

Ne sois pas aussi lâche
Don't be such a coward

C'était lâche de sa part
It was very cowardly of him/her

Vous n'avez rien dans le ventre
You have no backbone

Il est courageux mais pas téméraire
He's brave but not reckless

Elle a enduré avec stoïcisme la maladie qui devait l'emporter
She bore her final illness with fortitude

Fam Je n'ai pas eu le cran de le leur dire
I didn't have the guts to tell them

• disgust

C'est dégoûtant, ça! Berk!
That's disgusting! Ugh!

Il/Son comportement m'écœure
I'm disgusted with him/his behaviour

Ça l'écœurait de penser à tout ce gâchis
It made him/her sick to think of all that waste

Tu me dégoûtes!
You make me sick!

C'est écœurant, la façon dont on traite les réfugiés
It's sickening the way the refugees are treated

Le spectacle avait de quoi vous soulever le cœur
The sight was enough to turn your stomach

Elle/l'idée me répugne
I find her/the idea repellent

Il est d'une laideur repoussante
He's repulsively ugly

Cela m'a dégoûté de la viande
That put me off meat

Ça a une odeur infecte/un goût infâme
It smells/tastes revolting

La soupe était infecte
The soup was vile

J'ai trouvé son hypocrisie écœurante
I found his/her hypocrisy nauseating

C'était vraiment dégoûtant de faire/dire ça!
That was a disgusting thing to do/say!

La chambre était d'une saleté répugnante
The room was revoltingly filthy

Elle m'a regardé d'un air dégoûté
She gave me a look of disgust

• dislike

Je ne les aime pas
I don't like them

Elle n'aime pas danser
She doesn't like dancing

Si ça ne lui plaît pas il peut aller ailleurs
If he doesn't like it he can go elsewhere

Je déteste l'art moderne/faire le ménage
I hate modern art/doing housework

Je ne peux pas supporter les fumeurs/l'hypocrisie
I can't stand smokers/hypocrisy

Paul ne peut pas la voir en peinture
Paul can't stand the sight of her

Le patron l'a tout de suite pris en grippe
The boss took an instant dislike to him

Je ne raffole pas de la cuisine indienne
I'm not keen on Indian food

Il avait horreur qu'on le voie nu
He had a horror of being seen naked

Rachel est allergique au travail
Rachel is allergic to hard work

Jamais tu ne me feras aimer la voile!
You'll never persuade me to like sailing!

Le film n'était pas du tout à mon goût
The film wasn't at all to my taste

Son dernier livre ne m'a pas plu
I didn't like his last book

Il y a toujours eu une certaine inimitié entre les deux acteurs
There has always been some antipathy between the two actors

Fam L'informatique/Les cravates, ce n'est pas vraiment mon truc
Computers/Ties aren't really my thing

• eagerness

Il est impatient de commencer
He's impatient to start

Les enfants étaient avides d'apprendre
The children were keen to learn

Il a très envie que je voie son travail
He's eager for me to see his work

Ça ne leur dit pas grand-chose de sortir ce soir
They aren't so keen on going out tonight

J'ai hâte d'y aller
I can't wait to go

Il me tarde de la revoir
I'm looking forward to seeing her again

Il attendait impatiemment qu'ils partent
He was anxious for them to go

Elle est très enthousiaste à l'idée de ce projet
She's very enthusiastic about the project

Ça ne me dit vraiment rien
I can't get excited about it

Je mourais d'envie de lui dire la vérité
I was longing to tell him/her the truth

Il y avait 10 000 soldats dans la région qui brûlaient d'en découdre
There were 10,000 troops in the region raring to go

• embarrassment

À mon grand embarras, j'ai dû avouer que …
Much to my embarrassment, I had to admit that …

Il éprouve une certaine gêne à parler en public
He feels rather ill at ease when speaking in public

Il rougit à cette pensée
He blushed at the thought

Tu n'as pas honte?
Have you no shame?

Quelle honte!
The shame of it!

Cela m'embarrasse de lui demander son âge
I'm embarrassed to ask him/her how old he/she is

Il n'y a pas de quoi avoir honte
There's nothing to be ashamed of

Il a reconnu, d'un air plutôt penaud, que c'était de sa faute
He admitted, rather shamefacedly, that it was his fault

Elle restait assise là, un sourire penaud sur son visage
She just sat there with a sheepish grin on her face

J'étais mortifié de découvrir que l'on m'avait trompé
I was mortified to discover that I had been deceived

Ne soyez pas timide, dites-moi ce que vous voulez
Don't be shy, tell me what you want

Lorsqu'il a dit ça, je ne savais plus où me mettre!
When he said that I didn't know where to put my face!

J'aurais voulu rentrer sous terre quand je me suis rendu compte de ce que j'avais dit
Hearing myself say that, I just wanted the ground to open up and swallow me

Ses remarques m'avaient troublé
His/Her remarks had unsettled me

Il s'en est allé la queue entre les jambes
He went off with his tail between his legs

• enjoyment

Cela t'a plu?
Did you enjoy it?

Elle aime aller au cinéma
She enjoys going to the cinema

Amusez-vous bien!
Enjoy yourself/yourselves!

Je ne tire guère de plaisir à enseigner
I don't get much enjoyment out of teaching

Il s'est amusé à faire des châteaux de sable
He amused himself building sandcastles

J'adore marcher sous la pluie
I love walking in the rain

C'est très amusant de faire du ski
Skiing is great fun

Living Language

Nous nous sommes bien amusés à la soirée
We had fun at the party

On a fait la tournée des grands-ducs ce week-end
We painted the town red at the weekend

C'était un bonheur de se plonger dans l'eau
It was bliss to plunge into the water

Il prenait grand plaisir à critiquer ses employés
He took great delight in criticizing his employees

Je vais t'apprendre un petit jeu amusant
I'm going to teach you an entertaining little game

Lorsque je suis en vacances, je me laisse vraiment aller
When I'm on holiday I really let myself go

C'était absolument merveilleux!
It was absolutely wonderful!

Vas-y Étienne, laisse-toi un peu aller!
Come on, Étienne, let your hair down a bit!

Elle a mené la grande vie à Londres
She's been living it up in London

Fam Je me marre comme un fou!
I'm having a ball!

• envy

Je leur envie leur succès
I envy them their success

Je ne l'envie pas d'avoir à prendre le train de si bonne heure
I don't envy him/her having to catch such an early train

Ta robe est merveilleuse; je suis verte d'envie
Your dress is wonderful; I'm green with envy

Elle faisait l'envie de tous ses amis
She was the envy of all her friends

Cela va faire des envieux
That will make people envious

Ma fille est jalouse de moi
My daughter is jealous of me

Leur réussite soudaine l'a rendu jaloux
He became jealous of their sudden success

Il y a une forte rivalité entre les deux frères
There's a lot of rivalry between the two brothers

Vous n'avez rien à lui envier
You have no reason to be envious of him

Elle regardait avec convoitise mes délicieux sandwichs
She looked longingly at my delicious sandwiches

J'aimerais tant avoir tes talents musicaux
I'd really love to have your musical talents

Le Goncourt est un prix très convoité
The Goncourt Prize is a highly coveted award

• fear

Nous craignions pour nos vies
We feared for our lives

Nous parlions tout bas de peur d'être découverts
We spoke quietly for fear of being discovered

Elle a peur du noir
She's afraid of the dark

Tu ne me fais pas peur
I'm not frightened of you

Il n'y a rien à craindre
There's nothing to be afraid of

J'ai la phobie des araignées
I have a phobia of spiders

Il était complètement paniqué à cause de ses dettes
He got into a panic about his debts

Ne vous alarmez pas, ce n'est pas grave
Don't be alarmed, it's not serious

Je suis mal à l'aise à l'idée de prendre l'avion
I'm nervous about flying

J'appréhende de les avoir tous les deux en même temps
I dread having them both here

J'étais mort de peur à l'idée qu'il me tire dessus
I was petrified he would shoot me

Vous m'avez fait une de ces peurs!
You gave me a terrible fright!

Elle regardait en retenant son souffle
She held her breath as she watched

Il a vécu trois jours très angoissants
He lived through three harrowing days

Rien que d'y penser, j'en ai des sueurs froides
Just thinking about it brings me out in a cold sweat

Il a une voix qui donne la chair de poule
He has a voice that makes your flesh creep

Fam Le film m'a flanqué une de ces frousses!
The film scared me stiff!

Fam Cette histoire de fantômes m'a flanqué une peur bleue
This ghost story frightened the living daylights out of me

Fam Il a la trouille à cause de son examen
He's got the jitters about his exam

Fam Ses menaces m'ont vraiment fichu la frousse
His/Her threats really put the wind up me

• grief

Je serai désolé de vous voir partir
I shall be sad to see you leave

Ça me rend triste de voir ce qu'ils sont devenus
It makes me sad to see what's become of them

Je vous écris pour vous faire part de la tristesse que j'ai éprouvée en apprenant votre deuil
I am writing to express my sorrow at your loss

Il a passé des moments difficiles à l'étranger
He had an unhappy time abroad

Qu'est-ce qui te met dans cet état?
What are you so upset about?

Ça me fait mal au cœur de le perdre
I'm upset about losing it/him

Arrête, tu te fais du mal
Don't upset yourself

Elle pleurait toutes les larmes de son corps
She was crying her heart out

Nous pleurons notre père
We are grieving for our father

De désespoir elle a mis fin à ses jours
In despair, she took her own life

Nous l'avons trouvé seul, complètement bouleversé
We found him alone and in a very distressed state

Rendre visite à ses grands-parents la déprimait
Visiting her grandparents made her feel depressed

J'ai essayé de le réconforter mais il était inconsolable
I tried to comfort him but he was inconsolable

Ils lui ont rendu la vie insupportable
They made his/her life a misery

• hate

Je déteste mon patron/l'art moderne/faire le ménage
I hate my boss/modern art/doing housework

Sans rancune?
No hard feelings?

Je sentais une certaine animosité entre eux
I sensed a certain animosity between them

Mon beau-père fait preuve de beaucoup d'hostilité à mon égard
My father-in-law is very hostile towards me

Elle n'a réussi qu'à le rendre encore plus hostile
She only succeeded in antagonizing him further

Elle me lança un regard haineux
She gave me a look full of hate

Cet immeuble est une abomination
This building is an abomination

Il y a de la rancune entre les deux familles
There is bad blood between the two families

Ils se détestent cordialement
There's no love lost between them

C'est un homme aigri, plein de ressentiment
He's embittered and full of resentment

Il a été condamné pour incitation à la haine raciale
He was convicted of incitement to racial hatred

• horror

C'était un crime horrible
It was an awful crime

À ma grande horreur, je me suis aperçu que …
To my horror, I noticed that …

Je suis horrifié à la pensée que …
It appals me to think that …

Elle a reculé, horrifiée
She shrank back in horror

Son comportement les a choqués
His/Her behaviour shocked them

Quelle horreur!
How shocking!

Les films d'horreur me donnent des cauchemars
Horror films give me nightmares

L'armée s'est rendue coupable de nombreuses atrocités pendant la guerre
The army was guilty of many atrocities during the war

Il décrit la guerre des tranchées dans toute son horreur
He describes trench warfare in all its horror

Elle vit dans la terreur de son père
She lives in terror of her father

Je l'ai regardé, atterré
I stared at him aghast

À cette pensée, son sang s'est figé dans ses veines
His/Her blood ran cold or froze at the thought

C'était à faire dresser les cheveux sur la tête
It was enough to make your hair stand on end

Cela m'a fait froid dans le dos
It sent cold shivers down my spine

• hunger

Est-ce que je peux vous offrir quelque chose à manger?
Can I get you something to eat?

Je commence à avoir faim
I'm getting hungry

J'ai une faim de loup!
I'm ravenous!

Nous nous sommes arrêtés pour manger un morceau
We stopped for a bite to eat

Je n'ai pas d'appétit
I've got no appetite

La marche lui a ouvert l'appétit
The walk gave him/her an appetite

L'odeur m'a mis l'eau à la bouche
The smell made my mouth water

Je ne peux pas travailler l'estomac vide
I can't work on an empty stomach

C'est un gros mangeur
He's a big eater

Elle est difficile sur la nourriture
She's a fussy eater

Mon oncle mange comme quatre
My uncle eats like a horse

Ne sois pas si goulu!
Don't be so greedy!

Buvez de l'eau pour tromper la faim
Drink some water to stave off your hunger

Je meurs de faim!
I'm starving!

Ça va te couper l'appétit
It'll spoil your appetite

Elle a un appétit d'oiseau
She has a poor appetite

• indifference

Cela m'est parfaitement indifférent
It's a matter of complete indifference to me

Elle était indifférente à la beauté du paysage
She was indifferent to the beauty of the landscape

Il n'était pas intéressé par ce que je disais
He wasn't interested in what I was saying

J'ai beaucoup travaillé mais le cœur n'y était pas
I worked hard but my heart wasn't in it

Je me moque de ce que pensent les gens
I don't care what people think

Ça m'est complètement égal qu'il vienne ou non
I couldn't care less if he comes or not

Cela m'est égal
It's all the same to me

Ça lui est égal qu'on y aille ou pas
He's/She's not particularly bothered whether we go or not

Cela m'est égal si les gens se moquent de moi
I don't mind if people laugh at me

Vous aimez l'opéra?– Pas plus que ça
Do you like opera? – I can take it or leave it

Tout cela revient au même
It all comes down to the same thing

Qu'est-ce que ça peut faire?
Who cares?

Ça ne fait rien!
Never mind!

Et alors?
So what?

Fam Je me fiche pas mal de l'argent
I don't give a damn about the money

Fam C'est blanc bonnet et bonnet blanc
It's six of one and half a dozen of the other

• indignation

Il était indigné par leur attitude
He was indignant at their attitude

Cela m'agace vraiment lorsque les gens jettent des détritus dans mon jardin
It really annoys me when people throw litter in my garden

Ils sont scandaleusement riches
They're outrageously rich

Son cynisme a scandalisé la classe politique
His/Her cynicism scandalized the politicians

C'est un scandale!
It's an outrage!

Cela a soulevé un tollé général
It provoked a general outcry

Ça ne révolte pas toi?
Don't you think that's revolting?

Cela/Il dépasse les bornes!
It's/He's outrageous!

Vous voulez rire!
You must be joking!

Pour qui se prend-il?
Who does he think he is?

Il a eu le culot de me demander mon âge!
He had the cheek to ask my age!

Comment oses-tu!
How dare you!

• intolerance

Il ne supporte absolument pas les enfants bruyants
He is very intolerant of noisy children

Elle est étroite d'esprit en ce qui concerne le sexe
She is narrow-minded about sex

Il n'est pas bon d'adopter une attitude intransigeante face au changement
It is not good to have an inflexible attitude to change

Je ne partage pas leur dévotion fanatique à la cause
I don't share their fanatical devotion to the cause

Il est plein de préjugés
He's full of prejudice

Essayons de ne pas avoir d'idées préconçues là-dessus
Let's not be prejudiced about this

Tu as un parti pris pour elle
You're biased in her favour

Ma tante est hermétique aux idées nouvelles
My aunt has a closed mind

Il est intransigeant sur la discipline
He's a stickler for discipline

Je ne supporterai pas ce bruit une minute de plus!
I won't put up with this noise any longer!

Il est très compréhensif
He is very understanding

Comment lutter contre l'intolérance et le fanatisme religieux?
How do we fight against intolerance and religious fanaticism?

• liking

J'aime bien mon professeur/mon nouveau travail
I like my teacher/my new job

Elle aime danser
She likes dancing

Il m'est devenu sympathique
I've taken a liking to him

Il a la passion de la musique
He has a passion for music

Je suis fou de golf
I'm mad about golf

C'est affaire de goût
It's a matter of taste

Il manifeste un goût marqué pour le dessin
He has a great liking for drawing

Avec le temps, elle y a pris goût
She developed a liking for it

Cela fait plaisir d'être de retour
It's good to be back again

C'est une très bonne idée
It's a very good idea

Ses parents sont des gens charmants
His/Her parents are lovely people

Cela vous convient-il?
Is it to your liking?

J'ai beaucoup apprécié cette soirée
I enjoyed the evening very much

• love

Ils s'aiment
They love one another

Mon frère est/est tombé amoureux d'elle
My brother is/has fallen in love with her

C'était le coup de foudre
It was love at first sight

J'ai beaucoup d'affection pour toi
I have a lot of affection for you

Nous sommes bons amis, c'est tout
We're just good friends

Elle voulait que leur relation reste platonique
She wanted to keep things platonic

Simone s'est entichée de son professeur
Simone became infatuated with her teacher

Elle a eu une aventure avec mon frère
She had an affair with my brother

Il fait du charme à tout le monde
He's just a flirt

Je n'ai pas vraiment de petit ami
I don't have a steady boyfriend

Ils sortent ensemble depuis un mois
They've been going out together for a month

Il la regardait amoureusement
He watched her lovingly

Je t'aime bien mais c'est tout
I'm fond of you but I don't love you

Elle avait un faible pour Georges
She had a soft spot for Georges

Comment vont tes amours?
How's your love life?

Elle jure que cette fois-ci c'est le grand amour
She swears it's the real thing this time

Fam Elle lui plaît vachement
He fancies her something rotten

• pain

Avez-vous mal?
Are you in pain?

Où as-tu mal?
Where does it hurt?

Mon pied me fait mal
My foot hurts

Il a des problèmes de dos
He has a bad back

J'ai mal au ventre/aux dents/à la tête
I've got stomach ache/toothache/a headache

J'ai une douleur au côté
I've a pain in my side

J'ai des élancements dans la cuisse
I have a shooting pain in my thigh

Il s'est fait un bleu au bras
He's bruised his arm

Les yeux me brûlent
My eyes are stinging

Il s'est blessé au genou en faisant du ski
He injured his knee skiing

Elle s'est foulé la cheville/s'est cassé le bras
She has sprained her ankle/broken her arm

J'ai été piqué par des moustiques
I've been bitten by mosquitoes

Ce remède soulagera la douleur
This remedy will relieve the pain

Aïe!
Ow!

• patience

Il vous faudra être patient
You'll have to be patient

Je n'ai aucune patience avec lui
I've no patience with him

Je commence à m'impatienter
I'm getting impatient

Pour faire cela il faut avoir une patience d'ange
To do that you need the patience of Job

Prenez le temps qu'il faudra
Take your time over it

Living Language

Qu'est-ce qui presse tant?
What's the rush?

Ce n'est pas urgent
It's not urgent

Cela ne peut-il pas attendre ce week-end?
Can't it wait until the weekend?

J'ai hâte d'y aller
I can't wait to go

Je mourais d'envie de lui dire la vérité
I was longing to tell him/her the truth

Je suis résolu à ne pas céder
I'm determined not to give in

Il faudra le prendre avec le sourire
We'll just have to grin and bear it

Plus on se hâte moins on avance
More haste less speed

Fam Va te laver les mains et que ça saute!
Go and wash your hands and make it snappy!

• pleasure

Je suis ravi que tu aies pu venir
I'm delighted you could come

Enchanté de faire votre connaissance!
Pleased to meet you!

J'accepterais votre invitation avec plaisir, seulement …
I'd accept your invitation with pleasure, but …

Il joue aux cartes pour le plaisir, non pas pour l'argent
He plays cards for pleasure, not for money

La nouvelle leur a fait très plaisir
They were delighted at the news

Ça me fait énormément plaisir de me joindre à l'équipe
I'm delighted to join the team

Merci pour cette merveilleuse soirée
Thank you for a wonderful evening

Elle était en général très aimable à notre égard
She was very pleasant to us as a rule

Je suis très satisfait de son travail
I'm very happy with his/her work

Je suis content que vous les aimiez
I'm glad you like them

Nous avons passé une très agréable journée à la plage
We had a lovely day at the beach

Bonne journée!
Have a nice day!

Tout le plaisir est pour moi
The pleasure is all mine

Elle en est ravie
She's delighted about it

• preference

Tu préfères du vin ou de la bière?
Do you prefer wine or beer?

Je n'ai pas de préférence
I have no preference

Venez demain, de préférence dans la soirée
Come tomorrow, preferably in the evening

J'aimerais mieux y aller en voiture
I'd rather go by car

Voudriez-vous faire les présentations? – Je n'y tiens pas
Would you like to make the presentations? – I'd rather not

C'est mardi qui me convient le mieux
Tuesday suits me best

Il vaudrait mieux que tu m'appelles demain
It would be better if you called me tomorrow

L'un vaut l'autre
There's nothing to choose between them

Je choisirais l'Espagne
Spain would be my choice

Vous n'avez pas le choix
You have no choice in the matter

Nous n'avons pas d'autre option que d'accepter
We have no option but to agree

Lequel veux-tu? – N'importe
Which do you want? – Either will do

Tu as un parti pris pour elle
You're biased in her favour

Il a pris le parti de Tom contre moi
He took Tom's side against me

Ses sympathies vont à la droite
He/She has right-wing leanings

Je pencherais plutôt pour l'hypothèse du suicide
I'm inclined to favour the suicide theory

Il pouvait faire pire que d'accepter leur proposition
He could do a lot worse than accept their offer

Des goûts et des couleurs, on ne discute pas
There's no accounting for taste

• regret

Excusez-moi de vous avoir dérangé
Sorry to have bothered you

Je regrette que nous ne puissions venir vous chercher
I'm sorry we won't be able to fetch you

Je regrette d'en avoir jamais parlé
I regret ever mentioning it

Je ne regrette rien
I have no regrets

C'est dommage que vous ne puissiez pas venir
It's a shame you can't come

Je suis désolé, mais je ne peux pas vous aider
I'm sorry, but I can't help you

Malheureusement je ne sais pas si je vais pouvoir y participer
Unfortunately, I don't know if I'm going to be able to take part

Si seulement j'avais su!
If only I had known!

On n'aurait pas dû les laisser entrer
They should not have been allowed in

Il était pris de remords en songeant à ce qu'il avait fait
He was filled with remorse at what he had done

Elle n'a aucun scrupule à leur mentir
She has no qualms about lying to them

S'il meurt, je ne me le pardonnerais jamais
If he dies, I'll never forgive myself

Je me serais donné des gifles!
I could have kicked myself!

Ce qui est fait est fait
What's done is done

• resignation

Je m'étais résigné à y aller seul
I was resigned to going alone

Nous devons accepter le fait que la guerre est imminente
We have to accept the fact that war is imminent

Il a du mal à accepter la mort de sa femme
He's finding it hard to come to terms with his wife's death

Il faudra nous accommoder de la situation
We'll have to make the best of the situation

Tu abandonnes trop facilement
You give in too easily

C'est la vie!
That's life!

C'est comme ça
That's the way things are

Je n'y peux rien
There's nothing I can do about it

Il faut nous y résigner
We'll have to put up with it

Je ne vais pas me laisser faire comme ça!
I won't take this lying down!

Elle a haussé les épaules et continué comme si de rien n'était
She gave a shrug and carried on regardless

Il ne devrait pas se laisser piétiner ainsi
He shouldn't let people push him around

Elle acceptait son destin
She submitted to her fate

• surprise

Je m'étonne de vous voir ici
I'm surprised to see you here

Quelle bonne surprise!
What a lovely surprise!

Leur arrivée m'a pris au dépourvu
Their arrival took me by surprise

Ça n'a vraiment rien de surprenant
Well, it's not surprising, is it?

Cela m'étonne que la question n'ait jamais été posée
I'm surprised the question has never been asked

J'étais stupéfait qu'elle parte comme ça
I was astounded when she left like that

La nouvelle nous a frappés de stupeur
We were dumbfounded at the news

J'ai été stupéfait d'apprendre sa décision
I was staggered to learn of his/her decision

Le bruit les a fait sursauter
The noise made them jump

Qu'est-ce qu'il a grandi, je n'en reviens pas!
I can't get over how much he's grown!

Lorsqu'il le lui a dit, elle en est restée bouche bée
When he said that, her jaw dropped

Ça a l'air de vous surprendre
You seem surprised

Je ne sais pas quoi dire!
I don't know what to say!

Fam J'ai été sidéré par ses progrès
I was flabbergasted by how much progress he/she had made

Ne lui dis pas, je veux lui faire la surprise
Don't tell him/her, I want it to be a surprise

• thirst

Est-ce que je peux vous offrir quelque chose à boire?
Can I get you something to drink?

Je commence à avoir soif
I'm getting thirsty

Le thé est très désaltérant
Tea is good for quenching your thirst

Je prendrais bien une tasse de café
I wouldn't mind a cup of coffee

Elle a vidé son verre
She drained her glass

Mon oncle boit beaucoup
My uncle is a heavy drinker

Ça donne soif de bêcher au soleil
Digging in the sun makes you thirsty

Fam Je crève de soif
I'm parched

• tiredness

Il se fatigue facilement
He tires easily

La marche m'a fatigué
The walk made me tired

Vous allez vous épuiser à déplacer toutes ces caisses
You'll tire yourself out moving all those boxes

Je n'en peux plus
I'm worn out

Je commence toujours à faiblir vers le milieu de l'après-midi
I always start to flag about mid-afternoon

Il a toujours sommeil après un repas
He always feels sleepy after a meal

Elle a les yeux cernés
She has rings under her eyes

Vous avez l'air fatigué
You look tired

Essaie de ne pas trop te fatiguer
Try not to overtire yourself

Je tombe de fatigue
I'm ready to drop

Ne te tue pas au travail
Don't kill yourself working

Fam Je suis crevé
I'm dead beat

- **weakness**

Plus nous marchions, plus je devenais faible
I got weaker the farther we walked

Elle a le cœur faible
She has a weak heart

Il est faible avec ses enfants
He's lax with his children

Dans un moment de faiblesse j'ai cédé à la tentation
In a moment of weakness I gave in to temptation

La ponctualité est mon point faible
Punctuality is my weak point

Je n'ai pas la force de soulever ces cartons/ de recommencer
I haven't the strength to lift these boxes/to start again

Marcel était un enfant maladif
Marcel was a sickly child

Elle est tombée en syncope
She fell to the floor in a faint

Il se sent fragile sur le plan émotionnel après son divorce
He's feeling emotionally fragile after his divorce

Sa maladie l'a beaucoup affaibli
His illness has weakened him a lot

C'est une bien piètre excuse
That's a pretty feeble excuse

On est impuissant devant un tel malheur
One is powerless in the face of such a misfortune

Un pont branlant enjambait la rivière
There was a rickety bridge over the river

C'est un faible
He's weak-willed

Fam Ne sois pas si dégonflé!
Don't be such a wimp!

- **worry**

Dites-moi ce qui vous préoccupe
Tell me what's worrying you

Il n'y a pas lieu de s'inquiéter
There's nothing to worry about

C'est le cadet de mes soucis
That's the least of my worries

Elle est inquiète pour son neveu
She's worried about her nephew

Il en est malade d'inquiétude
He's worried sick about it

J'ai peur de perdre mon travail
I'm anxious about losing my job

La santé de son mari est source d'angoisse pour elle
Her husband's health is causing her great anxiety

Il ne s'en fait jamais
Nothing seems to trouble him

Elle est dans tous ses états parce que son poney a disparu
She's fretting because her pony is missing

L'idée continuait à me ronger l'esprit
The thought continued to prey on my mind

Je suis vraiment soulagé
That's a weight off my mind

Mon fils me donne bien du souci
My son is a great worry to me

Tu ne devrais pas te ronger les sangs comme ça à propos de ces décisions
You shouldn't agonize so much about these decisions

COMMUNICATION: ENGAGING WITH OTHERS

- **accepting**

Je vous prie de bien vouloir accepter mes excuses
Please accept my apologies

Vous acceptez les chèques?
Will you take a cheque?

Sa femme a accepté le prix en son nom
His wife accepted the prize on his behalf

Je refuse de croire qu'il soit coupable
I refuse to believe that he's guilty

C'est la décision qu'ils ont prise et je l'ai acceptée
That's what they decided and I accepted it

Il a pris la nouvelle mieux que je ne l'aurais cru
He took the news better than I thought he would

Il faut prendre les choses comme elles viennent
We must take things as they come

A-t-elle dit oui à votre offre? *ou* A-t-elle accepté votre offre?
Did she say yes to your offer?

Je prendrais volontiers une boisson fraîche
I wouldn't say no to a cold drink

Les projets n'ont rencontré que peu d'opposition
The plans met with little opposition

Le gouvernement n'accueillera aucun réfugié
The government will not take in any refugees

On lui a accordé l'asile
He/She was granted asylum

Mon patron a exaucé mes souhaits
My boss deferred to my wishes

J'ai eu tort, je le reconnais *ou* je l'admets
I admit I was wrong

ADVERTISEMENTS

1. Abbreviations used in classified advertisements

à deb.	à débattre	**kitch.**	kitchenette
apt., appt.	appartement	**jard.**	jardin
arr.	arrondissement	**mezz.**	mezzanine
asc.	ascenseur	**nf, nve**	neuf, neuve
balc.	balcon	**pkg**	parking
be	bon état	**pkgss**	parking au sous sol
buand.	buanderie	**plac.**	placard
carl	carrelage	**poss.**	possibilité de
cc	charges comprises	**pqt**	parquet
chauf., chauff.	chauffage	**PP, pces**	pièces
chauf. ind.	chauffage individuel	**prox.**	proximité
chbre	chambre	**px**	prix
compr.	comprenant	**rdc**	rez-de-chaussée
cuis.	cuisine	**rdv**	rendez-vous
cuis. éqp	cuisine équipée	**rés.**	résidence
cuis. US	cuisine américaine	**rnv**	rénové
dble séj.	double séjour	**sdb**	salle de bain [1]
disp./dispo	disponible	**sde**	salle d'eau [2]
disp. im.	disponible immédiatement	**séc.**	sécurisé
ds	dans	**séj.**	séjour
et.	étage	**ss, s/sol**	sous sol
FA	frais d'agence	**tbe**	très bon état
gar., Gge, Gg	garage	**terr., terras.**	terrasse
gd, gde	grand, grande	**ttc**	toutes taxes comprises
gren.	grenier	**tt cft, tt conf.**	tout confort
hc	hors charges	**ugt**	urgent
hon.	honoraires	**vds**	vends

[1] with bathtub [2] without bathtub

► Vds cause dém.[1] canapé cuir 3 pl.[2] tbe. 500€ à déb. Tél: 03 20 34 28 75

► Vds cause dble empl.[3] TV LCD 81 cm, TNT intégrée, nve. 600€ px ferme. Tél : 05 40 32 18 16

[1] pour cause de déménagement [2] places [3] pour cause de double emploi

☎ Bonjour, je vous appelle à propos du canapé cuir à vendre. *Hello. I'm calling about the leather sofa you want to sell.*

☎ Bonjour, j'ai vu votre annonce dans le journal d'hier. Votre télé est-elle toujours à vendre?... De quel modèle s'agit-il?... Et le prix n'est vraiment pas négociable? *Hello. I saw your advertisement in yesterday's paper. Do you still have the TV for sale? ... And the price really is non-negotiable?*

▶Ds rés. nve loue gd studio 35 m² tt cft: entrée, plac., cuis. équip.[1], sde. Prox. ts[2] commerces. 400€ cc. Tél 02 20 55 12 12

▶Paris 1er arr. Ugt, partage appt. 3 pces tt cft. (2 chbres, cuis. US, WIFI) avec pers. sér.[3] et ordonnée. Loyer 650€ cc. Tél : 01 40 62 18 24

▶Vds maison 100 m² habit.[4] + gren. sur gd terrain arboré 500 m². 4 chbres, 2 sdb, dble séj. Prox. plage. 500 000 € à déb.
Tél 05 55 40 12 13 après 18 h.

[1] cuisine équipée [2] tous [3] personne sérieuse [4] habitation

☎ Oui, bonjour, je vous appelle au sujet du trois pièces à partager … Ah, vous avez déjà trouvé quelqu'un? Bon, tant pis. *Au revoir. Yes, hello. I'm calling about the flat that's to share … Oh, you've already found someone? Oh well, goodbye.*

☎ Bonjour, je vous appelle au sujet de la maison. Est-elle toujours en vente? … Quand pourrais-je venir la visiter? *Hello. I'm calling about the house. Is it still for sale? … When could I come and view it?*

2. Abbreviations used in personal advertisements

bcp	beaucoup
b. éduc	bonne éducation
bi	bisexuel, bisexuelle
bien phys.	bien physiquement
bon niv soc	bon niveau social
bon. sit	bonne situation
cél.	célibataire
ch	cherche
cple	couple
dyn.	dynamique
div.	divorcé, divorcée
et + si aff.	et plus si affinités
F	femme
gd, gde	grand, grande
H	homme
JF, JH	jeune femme, jeune homme
nat.	nature
pr	pour
rech.	recherche
rel. dur.	relation durable
s'abst.	s'abstenir
souh. renc.	souhaite rencontrer
ss enf.	sans enfant
vf, vve	veuf, veuve

▶H 44 ans, div., gd, brun, yeux noisette, bien phys., sportif, bon. sit., ch JF tendre et mince pr sorties, ciné, danse, et + si aff.

▶F 57 ans, phys. agréable, aimant nat. et balades, souh. renc. H sérieux pour rompre solitude. Aventuriers s'abst.

• advice

Permettez que je vous donne un conseil
Let me give you some advice

Suis mon conseil, ne lui dis rien
Take my advice and say nothing to him/her

Que me conseillez-vous?
What do you advise me to do?

Il leur a déconseillé d'intenter une action en justice
He advised them against taking legal action

Je vous recommande de passer par Leeds
I recommend that you go via Leeds

Si vous voulez un bon conseil, attendez encore un peu avant de vendre
If you want my advice, you'll wait a bit longer before selling

On m'a bien/mal conseillé
I was given good/bad advice

Je ne vous le conseille pas
I wouldn't recommend it

On m'avait mis en garde contre toi
They warned me about you

Vous devriez consulter quelqu'un d'autre
You ought to get a second opinion

Que feriez-vous à ma place?
What would you do in my place?

Vous voulez savoir ce que j'en pense?
Do you want to know what I think?

C'est cher, tu ne trouves pas?
It's expensive, don't you think?

Le mieux, c'est de ne rien dire
The best thing is to keep quiet

• age

Quel âge avez-vous?
How old are you?

Elle a 25 ans
She's 25

Paul a le même âge que David
Paul is as old as David

Elle est plus âgée que moi
She is older than me

J'ai deux ans de moins qu'elle
I'm two years younger than her

Il pourrait être mon père!
He's old enough to be my father!

Quand j'avais ton âge, je …
When I was your age, I …

Elle ne fait pas son âge
She doesn't look her age

Il est grand pour son âge
He's tall for his age

Le président approche de la soixantaine
The president is getting on for sixty

Elle commence à se faire vieille
She's getting on a bit

Mon oncle a vécu jusqu'à un âge avancé
My uncle lived to a ripe old age

Quand pourrai-je prendre ma retraite?
When will I be able to retire?

Une pneumonie l'a emporté à la fleur de l'âge
Pneumonia cut him down in his prime

Ma fille aînée vient d'avoir 20 ans
My oldest daughter has just turned 20

Voici mon cadet, Stephen
This is my youngest, Stephen

Ils ont un garçon de dix ans
They have a ten-year-old boy

Ça remonte à loin, Fabrice et moi
We go back a long way, Fabrice and me

Elle n'est plus toute jeune *ou* de la première jeunesse
She's not as young as she was

Fam Ce n'est pas un perdreau de l'année
He's no spring chicken

• agreement

Je suis tout à fait d'accord (avec vous)
I quite agree (with you)

Ils sont un peu jeunes, je vous l'accorde, mais …
Granted, they're a bit young, but …

C'était le prix dont nous avions convenu
That was the price we agreed on

Ils ne sont pas d'accord sur les mesures à prendre
They disagree about what action to take

Elle est pour/contre le libre-échange
She is for/against free trade

Il a accusé les compagnies pétrolières de s'entendre pour augmenter les prix
He accused the oil companies of colluding to raise prices

Ils se sont séparés d'un commun accord
By mutual agreement they went their separate ways

Les avis sont partagés sur ce problème
Opinion is divided on the matter

Les deux récits ne cadrent pas
There is a discrepancy between the two stories

Ne me contredisez pas!
Don't contradict me!

Vous aviez raison/tort (à son sujet)
You were right/wrong (about him/her)

Ils s'entendent comme larrons en foire
They're as thick as thieves

Je m'oppose à cette idée
I'm opposed to the idea

Ce gouvernement est nul! – Bravo!
This government is hopeless! – Hear, hear!

Son père et moi ne partageons pas les mêmes points de vue
Her father and I don't see eye to eye

Ils n'arrivent pas à se mettre d'accord
They can't manage to agree

Il a proposé une approche différente et elle a approuvé
He proposed a different approach and she agreed to it

Fam Ils étaient de mèche
They were in it together

• announcing

Nous sommes heureux de vous faire part de la naissance/du mariage de notre fils
We are pleased to announce the birth/marriage of our son

Je n'ose pas le lui annoncer
I daren't break it to him/her

Elle a été déclarée vainqueur
She was declared the winner

Il a refusé de révéler l'identité de son agresseur
He refused to reveal the identity of his attacker

Il a fait savoir qu'il était disponible
He let it be known that he was available

On annonce des réductions d'impôts
Tax reductions have been announced

Il y a des rumeurs de rachat *ou* On parle d'un rachat
There are rumours of a takeover

Ses rivaux font circuler le bruit que …
It's being put about by his/her rivals that …

Il a fait une déclaration à la presse selon laquelle …
He made a statement in the press to the effect that …

Je suis si heureux que j'ai envie de le crier sur tous les toits!
I'm so happy I want to shout it from the rooftops!

On vient de lui notifier son renvoi
He's/She's just received notice of his/her dismissal

Il s'est proclamé empereur
He proclaimed himself emperor

• apologizing

Je vous dois des excuses
I owe you an apology

Je vous prie de bien vouloir accepter mes excuses
Please accept my apologies

Vous n'avez pas à vous excuser
There's no need to apologize

Désolé de vous avoir fait attendre
Sorry to have kept you waiting

Désolé, je ne peux pas vous aider – Ça ne fait rien
Sorry, I can't help – It doesn't matter

J'ai déjà dit que j'étais désolé, qu'est-ce que je peux faire d'autre?
I've said I'm sorry; what more can I do?

Pardon!
Sorry!

Ce genre de comportement est inexcusable
There's no excuse for that kind of behaviour

Je ne veux pas d'excuse!
I don't want any excuses!

Si vous voulez bien m'excuser, il faut que je finisse mon travail
If you will excuse me, I have to finish my work

Excusez-moi, je peux passer?
Excuse me, can I get past?

Elle s'est excusée plusieurs fois d'être arrivée en retard
She apologized several times for being late

Lorsqu'il s'est avéré que l'histoire était fausse, l'éditeur a dû manger son chapeau
When the story turned out to be false, the editor had to eat humble pie

Je crains que ce ne soit de ma faute
I'm afraid it's my fault

• approval

Êtes-vous d'accord avec cette proposition?
Do you approve of the proposal?

Ça ne lui plaît pas qu'ils fument
He/She doesn't approve of them smoking

Je suis favorable à ce plan d'action
I'm in favour of this line of action

Je m'oppose à cette idée
I'm opposed to the idea

J'étais content d'avoir l'occasion de lui parler
I welcomed the opportunity to speak to him/her

Je désapprouve tout ce qu'ils ont fait
I disagree with everything they've done

Il a donné son approbation au projet
He gave his approval to the plan

Elle n'apprécie guère qu'il sorte avec d'autres femmes
She takes a dim view of him going out with other women

Je n'apprécie pas du tout ce commentaire
I take exception to that remark

Ils ont obtenu le feu vert pour acheter la société
They got the green light to buy the company

Je n'ai rien contre
I've nothing against it

Est-ce que le patron a donné sa bénédiction au projet?
Has the boss given his blessing to the project?

Je ne vous reproche rien
I'm not blaming you for anything

Le bruit court qu'elle s'adonne à des pratiques que la morale réprouve
Rumour has it that she is involved in morally unacceptable practices

• celebration

Il faut fêter ça!
This calls for a celebration!

Ouvrons une bouteille de vin pour fêter ça!
Let's open a bottle of wine to celebrate!

Les festivités se sont terminées par un feu d'artifice
The festivities ended with a firework display

Ils ont fait *ou* donné une fête pour leur anniversaire de mariage
They had a party to celebrate their wedding anniversary

On a fait la tournée des grands-ducs ce week-end
We painted the town red at the weekend

L'association a organisé une cérémonie spéciale pour célébrer l'événement
The association organized a special ceremony to mark the event

Les rues de la capitale étaient pleines de joyeux fêtards
The streets of the capital were full of revellers

Ils ont fêté au champagne la naissance de leur bébé
They toasted the birth of their baby with champagne

Ils l'ont acclamé bruyamment lorsqu'il est entré dans la pièce
They cheered loudly when he came into the room

Un ban pour Louis! *ou* Pour Louis, hip hip hip! hourra!
Three cheers for Louis!

Nous avons fait la fête toute la nuit
We partied all night

• complaining

Il s'est plaint d'un mal de tête/qu'elle était toujours en retard
He complained of a headache/that she was always late

Est-ce que vous avez à vous plaindre de l'entreprise?
Do you have any complaints about the company?

Arrête de te plaindre tout le temps!
Stop complaining all the time!

J'aimerais faire une réclamation
I would like to make a complaint

Je veux voir le responsable!
I want to see the manager!

Vous devriez demander un remboursement
You should ask for your money back

Je ne suis pas du tout satisfait du travail que vous avez fait sur le patio
I'm not at all happy with the work you've done on the patio

Elle est toujours en train de se lamenter à propos d'une chose ou d'une autre
She's always whining about something

Il trouve souvent à redire à ma manière d'écrire
He often finds fault with my style of writing

On leur a reproché de ne pas avoir essayé
They have been criticized for not trying

Sa lettre contenait les récriminations habituelles
His/Her letter contained the usual grumbles

Mais qu'est-ce qu'elle a encore à râler?
What is she moaning about now?

Les syndicats s'élèvent contre la nouvelle législation
The unions are up in arms over the new legislation

• conceding

Il a admis qu'il avait tort
He admitted he was wrong

Elle n'a pas tort
She has a point

Rendons-leur cette justice, ils ont donné de leur temps
To be fair, they did contribute their time

Elle parle bien, ça je te le concède *ou* je te l'accorde
She's a good speaker, I grant you

Très bien, mais ne pensez-vous pas que …?
That's fair enough, but don't you think that …?

C'est bien beau d'être propriétaire, mais …
Owning a home is all very well, but …

Pour être honnête *ou* À vrai dire, je ne crois pas que ça marchera
To be honest, I don't think it'll work

D'accord *ou* Je vous l'accorde, il n'est pas très intelligent, mais …
Granted, he's not very intelligent, but …

J'ai dû leur céder sur ce point
I had to yield to them on that point

Il faut admettre que c'est un résultat inattendu
You have to admit the result is unexpected

Je m'en remets à vos connaissances en la matière
I defer to your knowledge in these matters

• confirmation

Nous accusons réception de votre lettre
We confirm receipt of your letter

Son diagnostic a confirmé mes craintes
His/Her diagnosis confirmed my fears

Pourriez-vous me dire si la réunion aura bien lieu?
Could you tell me if the meeting is taking place?

Êtes-vous bien sûr qu'il n'est pas encore parti?
Are you quite sure he hasn't left yet?

Je te dois 20 euros, c'est ça?
I owe you 20 euros, right?

Je me trompe ou vous êtes allemand?
Am I right in thinking you're German?

C'est ça!
That's right!

Je vous l'avais bien dit!
I told you so!

Les derniers chiffres confirment cette tendance
The latest figures confirm this trend

J'estime, et je suis sûr que Peter confirmera ce point …
I feel, and I'm sure Peter will bear me out on this …

Je te le garantis
I can vouch for it

Il m'a assuré qu'il viendrait
He assured me he'd come

Ce que vous dites corrobore sa version des faits
What you say corroborates his/her story

• congratulations

Félicitations (pour ton nouveau poste)!
Congratulations (on your new job)!

Je vous félicite
I congratulate you

Ses parents l'ont félicitée d'avoir été reçue à ses examens
Her parents congratulated her on passing her exams

Je me suis félicité d'avoir gardé mon sang-froid
I congratulated myself for having kept my temper

Elle lui a fait des compliments sur son anglais
She complimented him/her on his/her English

Tous mes compliments!
Congratulations!

Ils ont levé leurs verres à la santé des jeunes mariés
They raised their glasses to the newly married couple

Tout le monde s'est levé pour applaudir les acteurs
The actors received a standing ovation

Un ban pour Sarah! *ou* Pour Sarah, hip hip hip! hourra!
Three cheers for Sarah!

Bravo!
Well done!

Tu as vraiment fait du bon travail
You've done a really good job

Bon anniversaire!
Happy birthday!

Living Language

CONVERSATION

Nous avons eu une longue conversation sur la pêche. *We had a long conversation about fishing.*
Nous avons engagé la conversation. *We got into conversation.*
Je ne suis pas (un) brillant causeur. *I'm not much of a conversationalist.*
Elle faisait juste la conversation. *She was just making conversation.*
Ils étaient assis là, à parler de choses et d'autres. *They sat talking about this and that.*
Il bavardait avec l'homme qui était à côté de lui. *He was chatting to the man next to him.*
Je fais souvent un brin de causette avec mes voisins. *I often pass the time of day with my neighbours.*
Tu connais la dernière? *Have you heard the latest bit of gossip?*
Fam Deux hommes âgés taillaient une bavette *ou* discutaient le bout de gras au coin de la rue. *Two old men were standing on the corner chewing the fat.*

Starting a conversation

Il fait un temps magnifique/horrible, n'est-ce pas? *It's lovely/terrible weather, isn't it?*
C'est une jolie veste/une jolie voiture/un bel appareil photo. *That's a nice jacket/car/camera.*
C'est la première fois que vous venez ici? *Is this your first time here?*
Vous attendez depuis longtemps? *Have you been waiting long?*
Et depuis combien de temps connaissez-vous Peter? *So, how long have you known Peter?*

Keeping the conversation going and showing interest

Sounds: Oh / Ah / Hum
Repetition: Dix ans? *Ten years?* / Le plus vieux d'Europe? *The oldest in Europe?* / Juste à côté? *Right next door?*
Words and expressions: Vraiment? *Really?* / OK *OK* / Je vois. *I see.* / Incroyable! *Amazing!* / Je sais. *I know.* / Vous plaisantez! *You're joking!* / Mais c'est terrible! *That's terrible!* / Je ne (le) savais pas. *I didn't know that.* / Je n'arrive pas à le croire. *I can't believe it.*
Questions (to encourage somebody to continue): Et qu'avez-vous fait? *And what did you do?* / Et que s'est-il passé ensuite? *And then what?* / Et que va-t-il se passer maintenant? *And what will happen?* / Ah oui, vraiment? *Did you?* or *Can he?* or *Are they?* etc

Asking somebody to repeat something

Excusez-moi? *ou* Pardon? *Sorry?*
Je n'ai pas bien compris ce que vous avez dit. Pourriez-vous répéter s'il vous plaît? *I didn't catch what you said. Could you repeat that, please?*
Pardon, qu'avez-vous dit? *Sorry, what did you say?*

Asking somebody to clarify something

Que voulez-vous dire exactement? *What do you mean exactly?*
Qu'entendez-vous par …? Je ne vous suis pas bien *ou* Je ne suis pas sûr de comprendre. *What do you mean by …? I'm not sure I follow.*
Je ne comprends pas. Pourriez-vous me réexpliquer? *I don't understand. Could you explain that again?*
Je suis désolé, pourriez-vous répéter? Je n'ai pas vraiment compris. *I'm sorry, could you repeat that? I didn't quite understand.*
Pourriez-vous répéter un peu plus lentement, s'il vous plaît? *Could you say that again a little more slowly, please?*

Dropping out of the conversation while the others are still talking

Si vous le voulez bien, je vais vous laisser pour le moment. Je reviendrai vous voir plus tard. *I'm afraid I've got to go now. I'll talk to you later.*
Je vais aller chercher un autre verre. *I'm going to get another drink.*
Veuillez m'excuser un instant. Je dois aller vérifier quelque chose/voir quelqu'un. *Excuse me a moment. I have to check something/see someone.*
Excusez-moi, je reviens dans une minute. *Sorry, I'll be back in a minute.*
Fam À plus (tard). *I'll catch you later.*

• correcting

Il a eu le culot de corriger mon français
He had the nerve to correct my French

Reprenez-moi *ou* Corrigez-moi si je me trompe, mais ...
Correct me if I'm wrong, but ...

Au temps pour moi
I stand corrected

Elle a apporté quelques corrections au texte
She made a few corrections to the text

Je me suis trompé de date
I got the date wrong

Il doit y avoir erreur
There must be some mistake

Cela a été fait par erreur
It was done by mistake

Ça ne peut pas être juste
That can't be right

Tu t'y prends mal *ou* Ce n'est pas comme ça qu'il faut faire
You're not doing it the right way

Il a bâclé le travail et j'ai dû réparer les dégâts
He made a mess of it and I had to put things right

Vous avez mal compris le message
You misunderstood the message

Je pense qu'on vous a mal renseigné
I think you have been misinformed

Il semblerait que je vous aie mal jugé
It appears that I misjudged you

Vous êtes loin du compte
You're wide of the mark

Ma langue a fourché; je voulais dire ...
It was a slip of the tongue; I meant to say ...

EMAIL & TEXTING

Est-ce que je peux vous contacter par e-mail *ou* par courrier électronique? *Can I email you?*
Envoyez-nous les coordonnées par e-mail. *Email the details to us.*
Je vérifie mes e-mails *ou* mes courriels deux fois par jour. *I check my email twice a day.*
Il l'a envoyé en fichier joint. *He sent it as an attachment.*
Pouvez-vous me transférer son message *ou* mail *ou* courriel? *Can you forward his/her email to me?*
Je vais vous imprimer leur message *ou* mail *ou* courriel. *I'll print their email out for you.*
Pouvez-vous leur envoyer un texto *ou* un SMS? *Can you text them?*

Common abbreviations used in email, newsgroups and texting

1	un, une, in...
10kuT, 10kut	discuter, discute
1stant	instant
1viT, 1vit	inviter, invite
2	de, de...
2m1	demain
2mand, 2manD	demande, demander
2pui	depuis
2van	devant
2vine	devine
5pa	sympa
6né	ciné, cinéma
7	cet, cette
id, ID	idée
IR	hier
jenémar	j'en ai marre
jt'M	je t'aime
Kdo	cadeau
ke	que
kekina	qu'est-ce qu'il y a
keske C	qu'est-ce que c'est
kestufé	qu'est-ce que tu fais
ki	qui
kL	quel, quelle
kLq1	quelqu'un
koa, koi	quoi

@2m1, a2m1	à demain
@+	à plus, à plus tard
A12C4	à un des ces quatre
a l1di, al'1di	à lundi
ASV	âge sexe ville
ayé	ça y est
b1, b1sur	bien, bien sûr
bap	bon après-midi
bi1to	bientôt
bjr	bonjour
bsr	bonsoir
c, C	c'est
cad	c'est-à-dire
C cho	c'est chaud
chanG	changer
chuis	je suis
C mal1	c'est malin
C pa grave	ce n'est pas grave
ct, CT	c'était
d1gue	dingue
d6d, D6D	décider
dak	d'accord
DanC	danser
DpenC	dépenser
ds	dans
Dzolé	désolé
empr1T	emprunter
en +	en plus
épaT	épater, épaté
fo	il faut
fR	faire
g, G	j'ai
G la N	j'ai la haine
Gnial	génial
grat8	gratuit
HT	acheter
koi29	quoi de neuf
l, L	elle
l8, L8	lui
l'StomB	laisse tomber
manG	manger
mdr, MDR	mort de rire
mé, mè	mais
mn	minute
msg	message
nrv	énervé
oqp, OQP	occupé
pb	problème
pr	pour
PTDR	pété de rire
Q	cul
qd	quand
ras	rien à signaler
raT	rater
rdv	rendez vous
ri1	rien
rstp	réponds s'il te plaît
savapa	ça ne va pas
semN	semaine
slt	salut
stp	s'il te plaît
strC	stressé
tabitou	tu habites où
tjrs	toujours
tps	temps
vi1	viens
Vlo	vélo
vR	vers
vs	vous
WE	week-end
xqzé, xqze	excuser, excuse

• encouragement

Sa mère l'a encouragée à jouer du piano
Her mother encouraged her to play the piano

Leur réussite nous a beaucoup encouragés
Their success was a great encouragement to us

C'est encourageant de constater les progrès accomplis
It is encouraging to see the progress that has been made

Rien n'a pu l'amener à accepter malgré tous les efforts pour l'amadouer
No amount of coaxing would get him/her to agree

Les autres garçons l'ont poussé à le voler
He was egged on by the other boys to steal it

L'émission l'a incitée *ou* l'a poussée à étudier la biologie
The programme inspired her to study biology

Ses parents l'ont soutenu lorsqu'il a essayé de devenir acteur
His parents supported him in his attempt to become an actor

Le gouvernement a introduit un certain nombre de mesures afin de stimuler l'investissement
The government has introduced a number of measures to stimulate investment

Leurs cris nous aiguillonnaient
Their shouts spurred us on

Continuez à bien travailler!
Keep up the good work!

Allez, les Rouges!
Come on, the Reds!

Allez, tu peux y arriver!
Go on, you can do it!

explaining

Pardon, mais je ne vous suis pas vraiment
Sorry, I don't quite follow you

Pourriez-vous être un peu plus précis?
Could you be a bit more specific?

Pardonnez-moi mais pourriez-vous me donner des explications un peu plus détaillées?
I'm sorry, but could you explain in a little more detail?

Pourriez-vous expliquer ce que vous entendez par là?
Could you explain what you mean by that?

Où voulez-vous en venir?
What are you getting at?

Je ne me suis peut-être pas très bien expliqué
Perhaps I didn't explain myself very well

J'exige des explications!
I demand an explanation!

Ce que je voulais dire, c'est que …
What I meant was …

Comprenons-nous bien: je ne supporterai pas d'âneries
Now let's get this clear: I want no nonsense

Comment justifiez-vous votre comportement?
How do you account for your behaviour?

Ce n'est pas une raison!
That's no excuse!

Faut-il que je te fasse un dessin?
Do I have to spell it out for you?

Elle a exposé fort longuement sa théorie
She expounded her theory at great length

goodbye

Au revoir, Sophie!
Goodbye, Sophie!

Elle m'a dit au revoir
She said goodbye to me

On a fait nos adieux et on est partis
We said our goodbyes and left

Il l'a embrassée en partant
He gave her a goodbye kiss

Merci d'avoir appelé, au revoir
Thank you for calling, goodbye

Bonne nuit, dors bien!
Good night, sleep tight!

Ils sont sortis du cinéma et se sont dit bonsoir
They left the cinema and said good night

Elle est venue à la gare me dire au revoir
She came to see me off at the station

Il a fait au revoir de la main
He waved goodbye

Ils ont fait une fête pour son départ
They held a farewell party for him/her

Bonne journée!
Have a nice day!

À bientôt! *ou Fam* À la prochaine!
See you!

Bon, je dois y aller *ou* il faut que j'y aille
Well, I must be going

C'est un plaisir de vous avoir rencontré – Pareillement
It's been really nice meeting you – And you

Je vous souhaite un bon retour!
Have a good trip home!

Fam Salut!
Bye!

• good wishes

Souhaite-moi bonne chance!
Wish me luck!

Tous mes vœux de réussite dans votre nouvelle vie professionnelle
I wish you all the best in your new job

Transmettez-lui mes meilleurs vœux de prompt rétablissement
Give him/her my best wishes for a speedy recovery

Transmettez-leur mon bon souvenir
Give them my regards

Bonne chance (pour les examens)!
Good luck (with the exams)!

Bon week-end!
Have a good weekend!

Amusez-vous bien!
Enjoy yourselves!

Je vous souhaite un agréable voyage
I hope you have a pleasant journey

Joyeux Noël (et bonne année)!
Merry Christmas (and happy new year)!

Meilleurs vœux pour 2009!
All the best for 2009!

• hello

Bonjour, Jim, comment ça va?
Hello, Jim, how are you?

Dis-lui bonjour de ma part
Say hello to him/her for me

Elle m'a demandé de vous donner le bonjour
She asked me to say hello to you

Allô, Stéphane Lenoir à l'appareil
Hello, Stéphane Lenoir speaking

Bonjour!
Good morning/afternoon!

Bonsoir!
Good evening!

Bienvenue chez moi/en France!
Welcome to my home/to France!

Living Language

Bonjour! Je m'appelle Éric Maréchal
How do you do? My name is Éric Maréchal

Charles les a chaleureusement accueillis
Charles greeted them warmly

Il n'est pas en état de recevoir des visites *ou* des visiteurs
He isn't well enough to receive visitors

Ils se sont serré la main
They shook hands

Fam Salut, ça roule? *ou* ça biche? *ou* ça boume?
Hi, how's things?

• introducing

Je ne crois pas que nous ayons été présentés
I don't think we've been introduced

I don't think you know Jean-Pierre, do you?
Je ne pense pas que vous connaissiez Jean-Pierre, n'est-ce pas?

Elle m'a présenté à sa sœur
She introduced me to her sister

Je me présente, je m'appelle Véronique
Let me introduce myself: I'm Véronique

Peux-tu faire les présentations?
Would you make the introductions?

Voici Manon – Bonjour, je m'appelle Béatrice
This is Manon – Hello, I'm Béatrice

Je vous présente ma mère
I'd like you to meet my mother

Enchanté!
Pleased to meet you!

Ça fait plaisir de vous revoir
It's good to see you again

J'ai fait sa connaissance à la fête de Mike
I got to know him/her at Mike's party

• inviting

Mon chef m'a invité à déjeuner
My boss has invited me for lunch

Je l'ai invitée à monter prendre un café
I asked her up for a coffee

Il faudra qu'on les invite à dîner
We must have them round for dinner

Entrez donc, faites comme chez vous
Do come in and make yourself at home

Aimerais-tu sortir dîner avec moi demain soir? – Désolée, je ne peux pas
Would you like to go out for dinner tomorrow night? – Sorry, I can't make it

Voudriez-vous venir dîner chez moi? – Avec grand plaisir
Would you like to come to my house for dinner? – I'd be delighted

Nous allons prendre un verre tout à l'heure; voulez-vous vous joindre à nous? – Oui, avec grand plaisir
We're going out for a drink later; would you like to join us? – Yes, I'd love to.

Tu es libre demain pour aller au théâtre avec moi? – Merci mais je suis déjà pris
Are you free to come to the theatre with me tomorrow? – Thanks, but I've got something else on

Je regrette, mais ce soir je ne vais pas pouvoir. Merci quand même
I'm afraid I can't make it tonight, but thank you

Vous attendez de la visite?
Are you expecting company?

Ils reçoivent beaucoup
They entertain a great deal

Fam Ça te dirait de prendre un pot après le travail? – Oui, ça serait sympa
How about meeting for a drink after work? – That'd be nice

• meeting

J'ai pris rendez-vous avec lui à trois heures
I arranged to meet him at three o'clock

Mon travail m'amène à rencontrer beaucoup de gens
I get to meet a lot of people in my job

Vous connaissez ma femme?
Have you met my wife?

J'ai rendez-vous avec le patron ce matin
I have a meeting with the boss this morning

Il faudra qu'on se voie la prochaine fois que je passerai à Paris
We'll have to meet up the next time I'm in Paris

Quand vais-je vous revoir?
When shall I see you again?

Je suis tombé sur un ancien camarade d'école ce matin
I bumped into an old school friend this morning

Ils nous ont retrouvés *ou* Ils se sont joints à nous pour déjeuner
They joined us for lunch

Je vous verrai donc lundi, à quatre heures
I'll see you on Monday then at four o'clock

Êtes-vous libre à déjeuner aujourd'hui?
Are you free for lunch today?

Je viendrai vous chercher à la gare
I'll pick you up at the station

Fam On m'a posé un lapin
I was stood up

• obligation

Rien ne vous oblige à répondre
You are under no obligation to reply

Je me vois contraint de lui dire
I feel obliged to tell him/her

La présence est obligatoire
Attendance is compulsory

Je dois aller à la réunion
I have to go to the meeting

Je n'ai pas besoin de travailler
I don't have to work

Il ne faut pas y toucher! *ou* Tu ne dois pas y toucher!
You mustn't touch it!

Inutile d'attendre
There's no need to wait

Est-ce que cette visite est vraiment indispensable?
Is this visit really necessary?

Personne ne t'y force!
No one's forcing you!

Ils m'ont fait attendre
They made me wait

Elle a été obligée de prendre sa retraite pour raisons de santé
Ill health forced her to retire

La loi exige que vous mettiez *ou* La loi vous impose de mettre la ceinture de sécurité
The law requires you to wear a seatbelt

Un diplôme de grec n'est plus nécessaire
A qualification in Greek is no longer a requirement

Je n'avais (pas) d'autre choix que partir
I had no choice but to leave

• offering

Elle m'a offert *ou* m'a proposé 800 euros pour ma voiture
She offered me 800 euros for my car

Puis-je vous offrir un verre?
Can I offer you a drink?

Plusieurs personnes ont proposé *ou* offert de m'aider
Several people offered to help me

Nous lui avons fait cadeau d'un poney
We gave him/her a pony as a present

Ce n'est qu'un petit cadeau pour vous remercier
This is just a small gift to say thank you

Je vous ai apporté des fleurs – Merci, elles sont ravissantes
I've brought you some flowers – Thank you, they're lovely

Veuillez vous asseoir
Please take a seat

Voulez-vous manger quelque chose?
Would you like something to eat?

Avez-vous besoin de quelque chose?
Do you need anything?

Si je peux faire quoi que ce soit, n'hésitez pas à me le demander
If I can help in any way, please let me know

Je peux vous déposer à la gare?– Si ça ne vous dérange pas, oui, merci
Can I give you a lift to the station? – Yes, please, if it's no trouble

C'est moi qui offre *ou Fam* C'est moi qui régale
This is on me

• orders

Il a donné l'ordre d'ouvrir le feu
He gave the order to open fire

Nous avons (l')ordre d'attendre ici
Our orders are to wait here

Je ne fais qu'exécuter les ordres
I'm just following orders

On nous a ordonné de quitter la pièce
We were ordered to leave the room

Le médecin lui a prescrit trois semaines de repos
The doctor ordered him/her to rest for three weeks

Les troupes ont été retirées sur ses ordres
The troops were withdrawn at his/her command

Elle aime commander les autres
She likes ordering people about

Tu n'as pas à me dire ce que je dois faire!
You can't tell me what to do!

Qui est le responsable ici?
Who's in charge here?

Elle obéit à sa mère au doigt et à l'œil
She's at her mother's beck and call

Je l'entendais dicter sa loi à ses employés
I could hear him/her laying down the law to his/her employees

La direction me charge de vous faire savoir que ...
I am instructed by the board to inform you that ...

Silence, s'il vous plaît!
Quiet please!

Ils ont été convoqués au bureau du directeur
They were summoned to the headmaster's office

• permission

Vous n'avez pas le droit de *ou* Vous n'êtes pas autorisé à pénétrer dans l'immeuble
You are not allowed to enter the building

Qui leur a permis de fumer? *ou* Qui les a autorisés à fumer? *ou* Qui leur a donné la permission de fumer?
Who gave them permission to smoke?

Je te donne la permission
You have my permission

Elle les a laissés regarder l'émission
She let them watch the programme

Il est autorisé à représenter son père
He is authorized to act for his father

Il faut que j'obtienne la permission du patron
I'll need to clear it with the boss

Est-ce que je pourrais *ou* Puis-je me joindre à vous? – Mais oui, bien sûr
Can I join you? – Yes, of course

Je peux vous emprunter votre voiture? – J'aimerais mieux pas, non
Do you mind if I borrow your car? – I'd rather you didn't

Permettez(-moi)!
Allow me!

Le gouvernement a accédé à leur demande
The government has granted their request

- **persuasion**

Ils l'ont persuadé/dissuadé de venir
They persuaded him to come/dissuaded him from coming

Je lui ai vivement conseillé d'accepter
I urged him/her to accept

Leurs arguments ne me convainquent pas
Their arguments don't convince me

Je suis convaincu que nous réussirons
I'm convinced we will succeed

J'ai réussi à me persuader que tout irait bien
I managed to convince myself that everything would be all right

Elle n'était pas très convaincante dans le rôle de Juliette
She wasn't very convincing as Juliet

Tu ne le lui feras jamais admettre
You'll never get him/her to admit it

Tu crois que tu pourrais utiliser ton influence auprès du patron pour m'obtenir une augmentation?
Do you think you could use your influence with the boss and get me a pay rise?

Je les ai amenés à partager mon avis
I talked them round to my way of thinking

Elle s'est laissé convaincre d'y aller
She allowed herself to be talked into going

J'ai réussi à le rallier à mon point de vue
I won him over to my point of view

J'ai essayé de leur faire entendre raison
I tried to reason with them

Il voudrait me faire croire que c'est un objet d'époque
He'd have me believe it's an antique

Oui, mais vous conviendrez certainement qu'il n'a pas tort
Yes, but I'm sure you'd agree that he does have a point

- **prohibition**

Il est interdit de boire de l'alcool sur le lieu de travail
Drinking alcohol at work is forbidden

On lui a interdit de la revoir
He/She was forbidden to see her again

Elle a eu une suspension de permis de conduire d'un an
She was banned from driving for a year

Il y a mis son veto
He vetoed it

Ils ont gelé toute nouvelle dépense
They put an embargo on further spending

Des limitations de vitesse ont été mises en place sur cette portion de route
Speed limits have been introduced on that section of road

Ces sujets sont tabous
These subjects are taboo

Le théâtre en Grande-Bretagne n'est pas soumis à la censure
The theatre in Britain is not subject to censorship

C'est illégal de faire ça
It's illegal to do that

La police prend des mesures énergiques contre le stationnement interdit
The police are clamping down on illegal parking

Tu n'as pas le droit de me parler ainsi!
You've got no right to talk to me like that!

Ça ne va pas se passer comme ça!
I won't have it!

- **refusing**

Je refuse de croire que tout est perdu
I refuse to accept that all is lost

On leur a refusé un prêt
They were refused a loan

Il a décliné mon invitation
He declined my invitation

Elle m'a envoyé promener
She turned me down flat

Une offre pareille, ça ne se refuse pas
Such an offer can't be turned down

On lui a refusé le droit de visite de ses enfants
He/She was denied access to his/her children

Tu ne peux pas y aller, c'est hors de question!
You can't go, it's out of the question!

Il a hoché la tête en signe de refus
He shook his head

Je refuse de le faire! *ou* Je ne le ferai pas!
I won't do it!

Je ne bouge pas, un point c'est tout!
I'm not moving, and that's final!

Tu feras ça pour moi? – Pas question!
Will you do it for me? – No way!

Fam Ce n'est pas de refus!
I don't mind if I do!

- **rejecting**

Ma candidature a été rejetée
My application was rejected

Ils lui ont proposé un emploi mais il a rejeté *ou* décliné leur offre
They offered him a job but he turned them down

Il a décliné toute offre d'aide
He turned down all offers of help

Vous ne pouvez pas continuer à ignorer ces preuves
You cannot go on dismissing the evidence
Elle a réfuté cette accusation
She rejected the accusation

Ce n'est pas la personne qu'il faut pour ce poste
He's/She's quite unsuitable for the job

Elle a pris l'air dégoûté devant la nourriture dans son assiette
She turned her nose up at the food on her plate
Cela a été un vrai camouflet pour le Premier ministre
It was a real slap in the face for the Prime Minister

Nous les avons snobés
We snubbed them

Enlevez-moi ça, je n'en veux pas!
Take it away, I don't want it!

Il nie l'avoir tuée
He denies killing her

Fam Elle s'est fait éjecter
She got thrown out

Fam On m'a envoyé sur les roses
I got the brush-off

Fam Elle a largué son petit ami
She gave her boyfriend the elbow

- **requesting**

Je leur ai demandé de se taire
I asked them to be quiet

Il a demandé de l'eau
He asked for some water

M. et Mme Chevalier vous prient de leur faire l'honneur de votre présence
Mr and Mrs Chevalier request the pleasure of your company

Conformément à votre demande, je joins un chèque de 50 euros
As requested, I enclose a cheque for 50 euros

Elle a posé sa candidature mais n'a pas obtenu le poste
She applied for the job but didn't get it

Le maire a exigé des excuses
The mayor demanded an apology
Vous exigez trop d'elle
You make too many demands on her

Il a lancé un appel au nom des victimes
He made an appeal on behalf of the victims

Elle a imploré mon aide
She appealed to me for help

Ils le suppliaient de s'arrêter
They were begging him to stop
La police réclame des sanctions plus fermes
The police are calling for tougher penalties

Pouvez-vous me passer le sel, s'il vous plaît?
Could you pass me the salt, please?

Vous permettez que j'ouvre la fenêtre?
Would you mind if I opened the window?

Ils ont lancé une pétition pour protester contre les projets de la municipalité
They got up a petition against the council's plans

- **suggesting**

Elle a proposé *ou* suggéré de faire une promenade
She suggested going for a walk

Je suggère que nous ajournions la réunion jusqu'à lundi prochain
I suggest we adjourn the meeting until next Monday

Nous sommes ouverts aux suggestions *ou* Toute suggestion est la bienvenue
We're open to suggestions

Je propose que nous votions sur ce point
I propose that we vote on it

Elle a accepté sa demande en mariage
She accepted his proposal of marriage

Est-ce que vous insinuez que je mens?
Are you insinuating that I'm lying?

Votre silence laisse penser que vous êtes coupable
Your silence implies you are guilty
Je recommande que nous leur fassions une offre
I recommend that we make them an offer

Je viens sur la recommandation d'un de vos clients
I have come on the recommendation of one of your customers

La pièce est pleine de sous-entendus
The play is full of innuendo

Qu'est-ce que tu proposes?
What do you suggest?

Ne pourrions-nous pas au moins en discuter?
Couldn't we at least talk about it?

Nous pourrions toujours augmenter nos prix
We could always increase our prices

Et si nous faisions une pause? *ou* Pourquoi ne pas faire une pause?
Why don't we take a break?

Ce serait peut-être une bonne idée de lui en toucher un mot
It might be a good idea to have a word with him/her about it

Nous pourrions peut-être aller manger italien plus tard
Perhaps we could go for an Italian meal later

Que diriez-vous d'aller prendre un petit verre?
How about going for a quick drink?
18h, ça vous va?
Is six o'clock okay?

- **suspicion**

Est-ce que ton mari se doute de quelque chose *ou* soupçonne quelque chose?
Does your husband suspect anything?

Elle est soupçonnée de corruption
She is suspected of corruption

J'avais mes soupçons là-dessus
I had my suspicions about it

Je me méfie de ses intentions
I'm suspicious of his motives

C'est un type louche *ou* douteux
He's a dubious character

Le détective a flairé quelque chose de louche
The detective smelt a rat

Sa tête ne me revient pas
I don't like the look of him/her

Il y a en elle quelque chose qui me déplaît
There's something about her I don't like

Je ne sais pas pourquoi je me méfie d'eux; c'est juste une impression que j'ai
I don't know why I distrust them; it's just a feeling I have

Il l'a regardé d'un air soupçonneux
He looked at her suspiciously

Fam Il y a quelque chose de pas net chez elle
There's something shifty about her

Fam Il y a quelque chose qui ne colle pas dans son alibi
There's something fishy about her alibi

- **sympathy**

J'ai été désolé *ou* navré d'apprendre la mort de votre père
I was sorry to hear about your father's death

Ce sont les enfants que je plains
It's the children I feel sorry for

La pauvre, ça me fait de la peine pour elle
That poor woman, I feel for her

Je compatis car j'ai connu des problèmes du même genre
I sympathize because I used to have similar problems

Elle a ressenti de la compassion pour eux
Her heart went out to them

Je compatis à votre douleur
I sympathize with you in your grief

Si cela peut te consoler, il m'est arrivé la même chose
If it's any consolation, the same thing happened to me

J'ai essayé de le réconforter mais il était inconsolable
I tried to comfort him but he was inconsolable

Si je peux vous aider en quoi que ce soit, n'hésitez pas à me le faire savoir
If there's anything I can do for you, please let me know

Ça a dû être vraiment terrible pour vous!
That must have been awful for you!

Ma pauvre Alice!
You poor thing, Alice!

Je vous présente toutes mes condoléances
Please accept my condolences

Nous avons compati à ses malheurs
We commiserated with him/her on his/her misfortune

TELEPHONING

Je t'appellerai *ou* te téléphonerai ce soir. *I'll call you tonight.*
Passe-moi un coup de téléphone *ou* de fil quand tu arriveras à la gare. *Give me a call when you arrive at the station.*
Il faut que j'appelle chez moi. *I need to phone home.*
Le téléphone sonne. *The phone's ringing.*
Quelqu'un peut répondre au téléphone? *Can someone answer the phone?*
Cela fait deux heures qu'elle est au téléphone! *She's been on the phone for two hours!*
Tu vas faire mettre le téléphone? – Non, je me servirai de mon portable. *Are you having a phone put in? – No, I'm going to use my mobile.*
Vous trouverez son numéro dans l'annuaire ou bien sur Internet *ou* dans un annuaire papier ou (un annuaire) en ligne. *You can find his/her number either in the phone book or online.*
J'ai laissé le téléphone sonner dix fois avant de raccrocher. *I let the phone ring ten times before I hung up.*

Making a call

Allô, c'est bien Pascale? *Hello, is that Pascale?*
Allô, est-ce que Pierre est là, s'il te plaît? *Hello, is Pierre there, please?*
Salut, c'est Robert. Est-ce que je peux parler à Henri, s'il te plaît? *Hi, it's Robert. Can I speak to Henri, please?*
Bonjour, pourrais-je parler à John Clark, s'il vous plaît? *Hello, can I speak to John Clark, please?*

Bonjour, ici Claude Laurent. Je voudrais parler à Nicole Bernard, s'il vous plaît. *Hello, this is Claude Laurent. I'd like to speak to Nicole Bernard, please.*
Ici Michelle Colin, de Global Communications. Pourriez-vous me passer André Rey, s'il vous plaît? *This is Michelle Colin calling from Global Communications. Can you put me through to André Rey, please?*

Taking a call

Allô? *Hello?*
(Allô,) Simone Marchand. *(Hello,) Simone Marchand.*
(Ici le) trois cent seize, zéro un, vingt-trois *3160123 (= three one six oh one two three)*
Management Solutions, bonjour? *Good morning, Management Solutions?*
City Leisure Centre, bonjour, Isabelle à l'appareil. Que puis-je faire pour vous? *Hello, City Leisure Centre, Isabelle speaking. How can I help you?*
Vous avez Françoise Pilard en ligne. – D'accord, passez-la moi. *I've got Françoise Pilard on the line for you. – OK, you can put her through.*
Vous avez un appel du bureau de Londres. – Je suis un peu occupé pour l'instant. Pourriez-vous prendre un message? *There's a call for you from the London office. – I'm a bit busy right now. Could you take a message?*

Getting through

Bonjour, pourrais-je parler à Paul s'il vous plaît? – Oui, un instant, je vais le chercher. *Hi, can I speak to Paul, please? – Yes, hang on a minute, I'll just get him for you.*
Pourrais-je parler à Pierre Thibault, s'il vous plaît? – Lui-même! – Oh, salut Pierre! *Can I speak to Pierre Thibault, please? – Speaking! – Oh, hi, Pierre!*
Allô, pourrais-je parler à Jean Vienne, s'il vous plaît? – De la part de qui s'il vous plaît? – De la part de Sophie Beau de World Travel – Entendu, ne quittez pas je vous passe son poste. *Hello, can I speak to Jean Vienne, please? – Can I ask who's calling, please? – It's Sophie Beau from World Travel. – OK, hold on a moment and I'll transfer you.*
Bonjour, pourrais-je avoir le poste 535 s'il vous plaît? – Certainement, de la part de qui s'il vous plaît? – Je suis la femme de Maurice. – Ah d'accord, je vous le passe tout de suite. *Hi, could I have extension 535, please? – Certainly. May I ask who's calling? – This is Maurice's wife. – Oh, right! Just a minute, I'll put you through.*
Comment fait-on pour avoir la ligne? – Composez le 0 pour téléphoner à l'extérieur. *How do I get an outside line? – Press 0 to dial out.*
Ça ne répond pas. *There's no answer.*
La ligne est occupée. *The line's engaged.*
Il est sur l'autre ligne. *He's on the other line.*
Elle est absente pour l'instant. *She's not in at the moment.*
Il est occupé en ce moment. *He's busy just now.*
Elle est en réunion. *She's in a meeting.*
Elle est en vacances cette semaine. *She's on holiday all week.*
Il n'est pas au bureau aujourd'hui. *He's not in the office today.*

Messages

Je regrette mais Jean n'est pas encore rentré du travail. Vous voulez laisser un message? – Oui, pouvez-vous lui dire que Paul a appelé et lui demander de me rappeler lorsqu'il rentrera? *I'm afraid Jean's not back from work yet. Can I take a message? – Yes, can you tell him Paul called, and ask him to give me a ring when he gets in?*
Il est en réunion. Voulez-vous laisser un message? – Oui, pouvez-vous lui dire de me rappeler dès que possible? *He's in a meeting at the moment. Would you like to leave a message? – Yes, could you ask him to call me back as soon as possible?*
Bonjour Rachel, ici Alain Raynaud. Je te rappelle comme tu me l'as demandé. – Ah oui, j'ai essayé de te joindre ce matin mais tu n'étais pas au bureau. *Hi, Rachel, it's Alain Raynaud here. I'm just returning your call. – Oh yes, I tried to ring you this morning but you weren't in the office.*
Bonjour, vous êtes bien chez la famille Larroche. Nous ne sommes pas là pour le moment mais laissez-nous un message après le bip et nous vous rappellerons dès que possible. *Hello, you've reached the Larroche family. We're not available right now, but please leave a message after the tone and we'll get back to you as soon as we can.*
Bonjour, ici Véronique. Laissez votre message après le bip. *Hi, this is Véronique. Leave a message after the beep.*

Ending a call

Écoute, il faut que je te laisse. Est-ce que je peux te rappeler plus tard? *Listen, I've got to go. Can I call you back later?*
Ça m'a fait plaisir de te parler. À bientôt, salut! *Nice talking to you. Speak to you soon, bye!*
Merci d'avoir appelé, au revoir. *Thank you for calling, goodbye.*
Merci pour votre aide, au revoir. *Thanks for your help, bye.*
Quel malpoli, il m'a raccroché au nez! *How rude, he hung up on me!*

Numbers

01 55 42 64 13 = zéro un, cinquante-cinq, quarante-deux, soixante-quatre, treize
00 33 = zéro zéro trente-trois
Pouvez-vous me donner votre numéro de téléphone? – Oui, c'est le zéro un, cinquante-cinq, quarante-deux, soixante-quatre, treize. – Merci. Mais, depuis la Grande-Bretagne, quel indicatif dois-je composer? – Il vous faut composer le zéro zéro trente-trois pour la France. – Donc, je fais le zéro zéro trente-trois, zéro un, cinquante-cinq etc? – Non, depuis l'étranger, il ne faut pas composer le premier zéro du numéro français. – D'accord, donc zéro zéro trente-trois, un, cinquante-cinq, quarante-deux, soixante-quatre, treize. C'est bien ça? – Oui, c'est ça. *Can you give me your phone number? – Yes, it's oh one double five four two six four one three. – Thanks. But what code do I have to dial from Great Britain? – You have to dial oh oh three three for France. – So I dial oh oh three three, oh one double five, etc? – No, if you're ringing from abroad you don't have to dial the first oh of the French number. – OK. So oh oh three three, oh one double five four two six four one three. Is that it? – That's right.*

Problems

Pardon? *Sorry?*
Pardon, je n'ai pas bien compris. *I'm sorry, I didn't quite catch that.*
Pourriez-vous répéter, s'il vous plaît? *Could you repeat that, please?*
Pourriez-vous répéter plus lentement, s'il vous plaît? *Could you say that again more slowly, please?*
Pourriez-vous me l'épeler, s'il vous plaît? *Can you spell that for me, please?*
Pardon, je ne vous entends pas très bien. La ligne est très mauvaise. *Sorry, I can't hear you very well. It's a really bad line.*
La réception est plutôt mauvaise là où je me trouve. *The reception isn't very good where I am.*
Allô? Tu es encore là? *Hello? Are you still there?*
Vous m'entendez? *Can you hear me?*
J'étais en pleine conversation et j'ai été coupé! *I was in the middle of a conversation and I got cut off!*
Il n'y a pas de tonalité. *There's no dialling tone.*
Oh, pardon. Je crois que je me suis trompé de numéro. *Oh, I'm sorry. I think I've dialled the wrong number.*
Désolé, je crois que vous avez fait un faux numéro. *I'm sorry, I think you've got the wrong number.*
Il n'y a pas d'abonné au numéro que vous avez demandé. *The number you have dialled has not been recognized.*
Il n'y a pas de tonalité. *The line's dead.*

Emergency calls

Il y a eu un accident. Appelez vite le 15 (*France) ou* le 144 (*Switzerland) ou* le 100 (*Belgium*) *ou* le 112 *(EU) ou* le 911 *(Canada). There's been an accident. Quick, call 15/144/100/112/911!*
Quel service demandez-vous? *Which service do you require?*

Mobile phones

Il n'y a pas de réseau *ou* de réception dans ce bar. *There's no reception in this bar.*
Ma mère m'a appelé mais mon portable était sur silencieux et je ne l'ai pas entendu, alors elle m'a laissé un message. *My mother called but my phone was on silent and I didn't hear it, so she left me a voicemail.*
Ma batterie est à plat. Il faut que je la recharge. *My battery's flat. I need to recharge it.*
Est-ce que je peux brancher le chargeur de mon portable ici? *Can I plug my phone charger in here?*
Est-ce que je pourrais avoir une recharge Eurofone à 20 euros, s'il vous plaît? *Could I have a €20 Eurofone top-up card please?*

Où est-ce que je peux acheter une recharge pour mon portable? *Where can I get a top-up for my mobile?*
Je n'ai presque plus/Je n'ai plus de crédit. *I'm nearly out/I've run out of credit.*
Écoute un peu cette nouvelle sonnerie géniale que j'ai téléchargée! *Listen to this cool new ringtone I've downloaded!*

thanking

Merci pour les fleurs/d'être venu – Je t'en prie
Thank you for the flowers/for coming – My pleasure

Veux-tu du thé? – Non merci
Do you want some tea? – No, thank you

Merci beaucoup – De rien *ou* Il n'y a pas de quoi
Thank you very much – Don't mention it

Je ne sais comment vous remercier pour ce que vous avez fait
I can't thank you enough for what you've done

Dis merci à ta grand-mère
Say thank you to your grandma

Tu devrais lui écrire une lettre de remerciement
You should write a thank-you letter to him/her

Je vous suis reconnaissant de votre aide
I'm grateful for your help

Ça me rendrait vraiment service
I'd really appreciate that

Merci mille fois!
Thank you so much!

Sout Acceptez ce présent en témoignage de ma gratitude
Please accept this gift as a token of my gratitude

threats

On nous a menacés de licenciement
We were threatened with the sack

Elle menace d'annuler le concert si ses exigences ne sont pas satisfaites
She's threatening to cancel the concert if her demands aren't met

Il est menacé de mort
He's being threatened with death

Cette nouvelle arme constitue une menace pour la paix mondiale
The new weapon is a threat to world peace

Il la dévisageait d'un air menaçant
He stared at her menacingly

Ne te laisse pas intimider par lui
Don't let yourself be intimidated by him

Ne te comporte pas comme une brute!
Don't be such a bully!

Ils m'ont forcé la main pour que je les accompagne
They bullied me into going with them

Te voilà averti!
You've been warned!

Attention ou tu vas avoir des ennuis!
Watch it or you'll be in trouble!

Fais ce que je te dis, sinon!
Do what I tell you, or else!

Si tu recommences, tu vas le regretter!
You'll be sorry if you do that again!

Malheur à celui qui me raconte des mensonges
Woe betide anyone who lies to me

Ses aveux ont été obtenus sous la contrainte
His/Her confession was obtained under duress

TIME

Je n'ai pas le temps de faire les courses. *I don't have time to do the shopping.*
Il est temps que je parte. *It's time I was going.*
Je commence dans trois semaines. *I start in three weeks' time.*
Il a attendu longtemps. *He waited for a long time.*
Combien de temps cela va prendre? *How long will it take?*
Tu en a mis du temps! *You took a long time!*
Ça ne fait pas longtemps qu'ils sont mariés. *They haven't been married for long.*
Je préfère ne pas m'engager pour le moment. *I'm keeping my options open for the time being.*
À quelle date est ton vol pour la France? *On what date are you flying to France?*
Ils ont emménagé ici il y a dix ans. *They moved here ten years ago.*
Elle est arrivée juste à l'heure. *She arrived right on time.*
Je serai de retour à temps pour le film. *I'll be back in time for the film.*

Qu'est-ce que tu fais de beau ces temps-ci? *What are you up to these days?*
Je serai à vous dans un instant. *I'll be with you in a minute.*

Est-ce que tu sais lire l'heure? *Do you know how to tell the time?*
Quelle heure est-il? *What's the time?*
Vous avez l'heure? *Do you have the time?*
Il est quatre heures/minuit. *It's four o'clock/midnight.*
Ils viennent à cinq heures/à trois heures du matin/à dix-huit heures. *They are coming at five o'clock/at 3am/at 6pm.*
Il sera bientôt dix heures et demie. *It'll soon be half past ten.*
Il est presque huit heures moins le quart. *It's nearly a quarter to eight.*
Nous partons à onze heure et quart. *We're leaving at a quarter past eleven.*
Il est quatre heures cinq. *It's five past four.*
À quelle heure partent les trains pour Londres? – Toutes les heures à l'heure pile/à la demie/à moins dix. *What time do trains for London leave? – Every hour on the hour/on the half-hour/ at ten minutes to.*

- **trust**

Vous pouvez me faire confiance
You can trust me

Je ne peux pas compter sur elle pour faire le travail correctement
I can't rely on her to do the job properly

Peut-on lui faire confiance?
Can he/she be trusted?

C'est une voiture fiable
It's a reliable car

Nous devons placer notre confiance en la science
We must put our trust in science

Il éprouve une profonde méfiance à l'égard des médecins
He has a deep mistrust of doctors

Ils ont de bonnes raisons de se méfier d'elle
They have good reason to distrust her

Je suis confiant dans la réussite de notre programme
I have confidence in the success of our programme

Je compte sur vous pour trouver une solution
I'm relying on you to find a solution

Elle ne jure que par ces vitamines
She swears by those vitamin tablets

Prenez garde: il est sournois
Be on your guard: he's devious

Les enfants devraient se méfier des étrangers
Children should be wary of strangers

Nous avons appris de bonne source que …
We are reliably informed that …

C'est un ami fidèle
He's a faithful friend

WEATHER

Il fait un temps magnifique, non? *It's lovely weather, isn't it?*
Il fait beau aujourd'hui, n'est-ce pas? – Oui. *Nice today, isn't it? – Yes, it is.*
Il devrait faire beau samedi. *Saturday is supposed to be sunny.*
J'ai hâte qu'il fasse chaud. *I can't wait for the warm weather.*
Il y avait une agréable petite brise. *There was a pleasant breeze.*
La nuit a été froide, non? – Oui, en effet. *It was a cold night, wasn't it? – It certainly was.*
Il fait frais ce matin. *It feels chilly this morning.*
En général il y a du vent au mois de mars. *March is usually a windy month.*
Il pleut à verse. *It's pouring with rain.*
Il a pleuvoté toute la journée. *There was a light drizzle all day.*
La météo prévoit d'abondantes chutes de neige. *Heavy snow is forecast.*
Nous avons été pris dans une tempête de neige. *We got caught in a snowstorm.*
Le temps est à l'orage. *There's a storm brewing.*
Il tombe de la neige fondue. *It's sleeting.*
Il grêle. *It's hailing.*
La pluie ne cessait pas. Des centaines de personnes ont vu leurs maisons inondées. *It wouldn't stop raining. Hundreds of people have been flooded out.*
Quel temps fait-il à Londres en cette saison? – À peu près le même temps qu'ici. *What's the weather like in London at this time of year? – Much the same as here.*

Comment trouvez-vous le temps ici? – Eh bien, c'est très humide! *How are you finding the weather here? – Well, it's very wet!*
Pour moi, tout est la faute du réchauffement climatique. *I blame it all on global warming.*

WRITING LETTERS

Letter beginning	**Letter ending**
If you do not know the person you are writing to:	
Monsieur, Madame,	Veuillez agréer, Monsieur/Madame, l'expression de mes sentiments distingués.
[When you are unsure whether the recipient of the letter is male or female:]	
Madame, Monsieur, *or* Monsieur ou Madame,	Veuillez agréer, Monsieur ou Madame, l'expression de mes sentiments distingués.
[When the letter is addressed to a company rather than an individual:]	
Messieurs,	Veuillez agréer, Messieurs, mes salutations distinguées.
When you know the person you are writing to and/or want to sound less formal:	
Cher Monsieur, Chère Madame, Chère Mademoiselle*, [*for an unmarried young woman; if in doubt, use 'Madame']	Veuillez agréer, Cher Monsieur/Chère Madame/Chère Mademoisellel'expression de mes sentiments les pluscordiaux.
[Simplified and more informal endings are becoming more common. The following endings are found more and more in everyday business letters, emails and faxes:]	
	Salutations distinguées Cordialement [more friendly] Bien à vous [even more friendly]
When you are writing to a relative or friend, or to a colleague with whom you are on first name terms:	
Cher Nicolas, Chère Pascale,	[Polite endings] Amitiés Amicalement Bien amicalement Bien affectueusement Bien à toi
[When writing to a relative or close friend, especially if they are younger than you, you can also use:] Mon cher Nicolas, Ma chère Pascale,	[Friendly endings] Je t'embrasse À bientôt Embrasse Olivier de ma part [Informal endings] Grosses bises Bisous

Le Monde du travail

Introduction

De nombreux apprenants choisissent de pratiquer leur anglais dans le cadre d'un petit boulot d'été ou d'un stage en pays anglophone. Au niveau universitaire, il est fréquent que les étudiants soient amenés à passer une année à l'étranger dans le cadre de leur formation et nombreux sont ceux qui souhaitent également exercer un emploi à temps partiel pendant cette période. Les étudiants d'un niveau plus avancé choisiront peut-être de mettre à profit leurs compétences linguistiques en allant travailler à plein-temps dans un pays anglophone. Que vous cherchiez un emploi temporaire ou à long terme, ce guide vous fournira toutes les informations nécessaires à une recherche d'emploi efficace, du déchiffrage des petites annonces d'emploi aux questions à poser lors de vos entretiens d'embauche.

La correspondance commerciale et administrative

Dans une lettre, la présentation est aussi importante que l'expression. La correspondance commerciale et administrative doit respecter certains codes si l'on veut être pris au sérieux par son interlocuteur.

Dans ce type de courrier, les paragraphes sont alignés à gauche, sans retrait, et séparés par une ligne de blanc. Chaque paragraphe doit comporter un maximum de trois ou quatre phrases et traiter d'un seul sujet.

Un style direct et concis est nécessaire. On évitera les abréviations ou les contractions telles que **don't**, **I've** et **she'd** pour **do not**, **I have**, et **she had/would** qui sont réservées au courrier privé ou à la communication orale.

Lorsque l'on répond à une lettre ou à une annonce, il peut être utile de s'y reporter pour y relever les points essentiels développés par l'expéditeur, ainsi que les formules à reprendre.

Les coordonnées de l'expéditeur se placent en haut à droite, le nom et la fonction du destinataire se trouvent en-dessous mais sur le côté gauche. On écrit la date soit à gauche, soit à droite, sous les coordonnées de l'expéditeur.

La formule de politesse varie en fonction de la formule d'appel utilisée et, comme en français, elle est suivie d'une virgule. La signature se situe à gauche, en retrait, sous la formule de politesse.

Formules d'appel et formules de politesse

■ formule d'appel	■ formule de politesse

Lorsque l'on ne connaît pas le nom de la personne à qui l'on s'adresse :

Dear Sir **Dear Madam**	**Yours faithfully** (Br) En anglais américain, la formule de politesse est toujours inversée : **Faithfully yours** (Am)

Lorsque l'on ne sait pas s'il s'agit d'un homme ou d'une femme :
Dear Sir or Madam
Dear Sir/Madam

Lorsque l'on s'adresse à une société ou à un organisme sans préciser le nom du destinataire :
Dear Sirs (Br)
Dear Gentlemen (Am)

Lorsque l'on connaît le nom de la personne à qui l'on s'adresse :

Dear Mr Jameson **Dear Mrs Lucas** **Dear Miss Crookshaw** **Dear Ms Greening**	**Yours sincerely** (Br) **Sincerely yours** (Am) **Sincerely** (Am)
(L'abréviation Ms est employée lorsque l'on s'adresse à une femme car elle permet de ne pas préciser s'il agit d'une femme mariée (Mrs) ou non (Miss).)	Style moins soutenu : **Best wishes** **Kind regards** **Regards** **Best** (Am)

Dear Dr Johnston
Aux États-Unis, l'abréviation est généralement uivie d'un point : Mr., Mrs., Ms., Dr.

à un professeur titulaire de chaire :
Dear Professor Smith

à un avocat :
Dear Mr Franks

à un député :
Dear Mr Brown
Dear Mrs Alexander

à un représentant ou membre du Congrès :
Sir/Madam
Dear Congressman/Congresswoman Fox
Dear Senator Mitcham

Le Monde du travail

Adresses et enveloppes

L'adresse doit être aussi précis que possible. Les sites Web des services postaux des différent pays peuvent être utiles pour trouver l'adresse complète d'un particulier, d'un organisme ou d'une entreprise, y compris le code postal précis.

Royaume-Uni : www.royalmail.com
Canada : www.canadapost.ca
Irlande : www.anpost.ie
États-Unis : www.usps.gov
Australie : www.auspost.com.au
Nouvelle-Zélande : www.nzpost.co.nz

Il est recommandé de n'inclure aucun signe de ponctuation et, surtout aux États-Unis et au Canada de rédiger l'adresse en majuscules (voir les modèles ci-dessous).

- **Adresse au Royaume-Uni :** Mr (Mrs, Ms, Dr, etc.), prénom (ou initiale), nom de famille
  Fonction
  Société
  (Dénomination du lieu et/ou) Numéro, nom de la rue
  Localité (ville, village)
  COMTÉ ou GRANDE VILLE
  CODE POSTAL

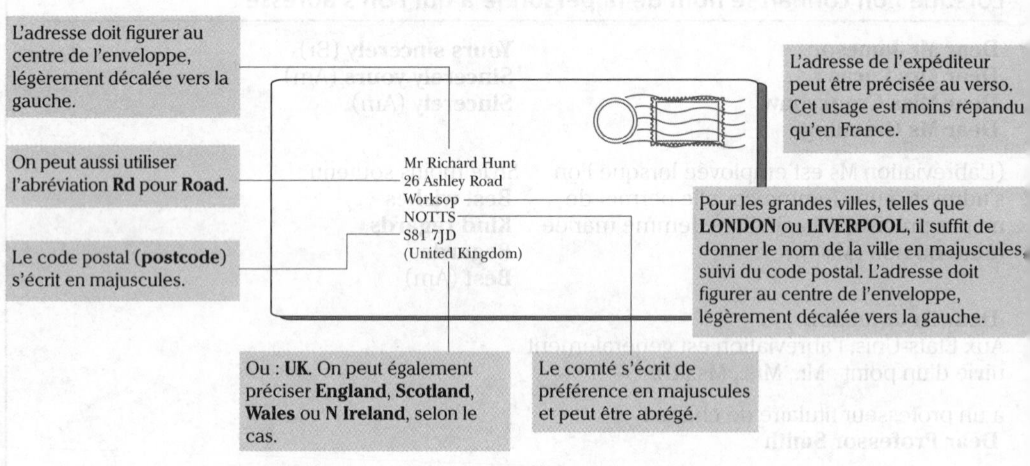

L'adresse doit figurer au centre de l'enveloppe, légèrement décalée vers la gauche.
On peut aussi utiliser l'abréviation **Rd** pour **Road**.
Le code postal (**postcode**) s'écrit en majuscules.
Mr Richard Hunt
26 Ashley Road
Worksop
NOTTS
S81 7JD
(United Kingdom)
L'adresse de l'expéditeur peut être précisée au verso. Cet usage est moins répandu qu'en France.
Pour les grandes villes, telles que **LONDON** ou **LIVERPOOL**, il suffit de donner le nom de la ville en majuscules, suivi du code postal. L'adresse doit figurer au centre de l'enveloppe, légèrement décalée vers la gauche.
Ou : **UK**. On peut également préciser **England**, **Scotland**, **Wales** ou **N Ireland**, selon le cas.
Le comté s'écrit de préférence en majuscules et peut être abrégé.

- **Adresse aux États-Unis :** Mr (Mrs, Ms, Dr, etc.), PRÉNOM (ou INITIALE), NOM DE FAMILLE
  Fonction
  Société
  (DÉNOMINATION DU LIEU et/ou) NUMÉRO, NOM DE LA RUE
  LOCALITÉ (ville, village), ÉTAT et CODE POSTAL

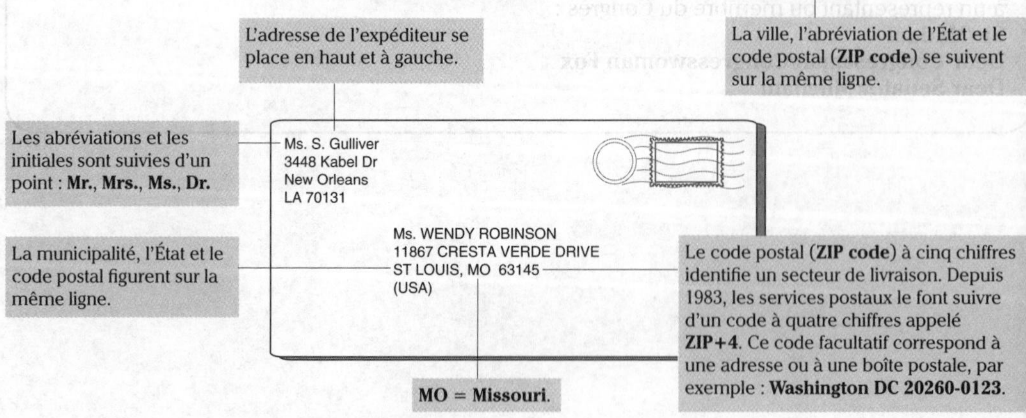

L'adresse de l'expéditeur se place en haut et à gauche.
La ville, l'abréviation de l'État et le code postal (**ZIP code**) se suivent sur la même ligne.
Les abréviations et les initiales sont suivies d'un point : **Mr.**, **Mrs.**, **Ms.**, **Dr.**
Ms. S. Gulliver
3448 Kabel Dr
New Orleans
LA 70131
La municipalité, l'État et le code postal figurent sur la même ligne.
Ms. WENDY ROBINSON
11867 CRESTA VERDE DRIVE
ST LOUIS, MO 63145
(USA)
Le code postal (**ZIP code**) à cinq chiffres identifie un secteur de livraison. Depuis 1983, les services postaux le font suivre d'un code à quatre chiffres appelé **ZIP+4**. Ce code facultatif correspond à une adresse ou à une boîte postale, par exemple : **Washington DC 20260-0123**.
MO = Missouri.

- **Adresse en Irlande :**

Jonathan O'Donnell
Creative Director
Tiger Advertising Agency
48A The Glen
Roden Park
Rathfarnham
Dublin 14
(Ireland)

a mention A ou B après le numéro est équivalent de 'bis' ou 'ter' dans une dresse française.

)u : Republic of Ireland.

Il n'y a pas de code postal en Irlande, sauf à Dublin où l'on utilise un nombre entre 1 et 24 pour désigner les différents secteurs de la ville. Pour les adresses rurales, on emploie l'abréviation **Co.** pour désigner le comté où le destinataire est domicilié : par example, **Co. Clare** pour le comté de Clare.

- **Adresse au Canada :**

Mr. S. Fitzgerald
Head of Finance
Studio One
28 Alpine Boulevard
St Albert AB T8N 2M7
(Canada)

AB = Alberta. Les deux premières lettres du code postal canadien représente la province ou le territoire.

la place du numéro et de la rue, certaines sociétés utilisent une boîte postale, notée **PO Box**. Cette ıention est suivie du numéro de la boîte postale.

.es annonces et la lettre de motivation

a lettre de motivation (**covering letter** pour les Britanniques et **cover letter** pour les Américains) doit ›ujours être dactylographiée, sauf si l'annonce spécifie qu'il faut envoyer une lettre manuscrite.

omme pour toute lettre commerciale ou administrative, le style doit être clair, concis et courtois. dressez votre lettre à la personne responsable, en précisant son nom et sa fonction si vous les onnaissez.

ous devez montrer dans votre lettre que vous connaissez l'entreprise et qu'elle vous intéresse. Si otre lettre est accompagnée d'un CV, il est inutile de répéter les informations qui s'y trouvent déjà.

e CV et la lettre de motivation peuvent être envoyés par e-mail si l'annonce le précise. L'envoi d'une andidature spontanée par e-mail est possible mais il est préférable d'opter pour un pli traditionnel, ui aura davantage d'impact.

'ans le premier paragraphe :

- Précisez à quel poste vous êtes candidat et comment vous avez été informé du recrutement en cours, en précisant la date et le lieu de parution de l'annonce.
- S'il s'agit d'une candidature spontanée (**speculative letter**), décrivez le type de poste que vous recherchez et la manière dont vous avez entendu parler de l'entreprise.
- Confirmez que votre CV est joint.

es paragraphes intermédiaires s'articulent autour de trois thèmes principaux :

- La présentation de votre situation professionnelle actuelle.
- L'explication détaillée de votre intérêt pour l'entreprise et la raison pour laquelle vous souhaitez l'intégrer.
- Vos principaux points forts et les raisons pour lesquelles votre profil correspond au poste.

.e dernier paragraphe :

- Contient des informations pratiques (disponibilité pour un entretien, autres renseignements).
- Se termine par une formule de politesse.

Réponse à une annonce

Assistant Hotel Receptionist

This busy city-centre 5* hotel is looking for an assistant receptionist to join the front-of-house team. Duties will include: taking reservations, both telephone and online, running the reception desk, meeting and greeting guests, checking guests in and out, answering the telephone and redirecting calls, and dealing with guests' enquiries. Candidates must have some experience as a hotel receptionist in a 4* or 5* hotel, and excellent communication and telephone skills. Working knowledge of at least one foreign language is highly desirable.

To apply, please send a CV with current salary details to: Colin Manning, Human Resources Manager, New Town Hotel, 30 Gordon Street, Edinburgh, EH1 1LP. Closing date 31 August 2009

30 Union Street
Edinburgh
EH1 1JK

Tel: 0131 449 7274
Email: Ebonnici@free.fr

Colin Manning
Human Resources Manager
New Town Hotel
30 Gordon Street
Edinburgh
EH1 1LP

19 August 2009

Dear Mr Manning

Assistant Hotel Receptionist

I would like to apply for the above post as advertised in The Scotsman of 14 August, and enclose my CV for your attention.

After graduating from Toulouse University earlier this year with a degree in hotel management, I spent three months working in a small, family-run 4* hotel in the busy tourist resort of Antibes in France. I have now come to the UK with the aim of using my university degree in a role which will also enable me to put my language skills to further use.

My degree and my recent experience as a receptionist have gven me a good grounding in the many duties involved in hotel reception work. I am accustomed to dealing with the public on a daily basis and have excellent communication skills. A French native speaker, I also speak fluent English and have a good working knowledge of Spanish and Italian; I am therefore confident that my educational background coupled with my linguistic expertise would be of benefit in the demanding position of assistant receptionist with your hotel. Above all I am excited at the prospect of working for a renowned establishment such as yours.

I would be available for interview at your convenience and can supply references on request.

Yours sincerely

Emeline Bonnici

Emeline Bonnici

Tournures utiles :

In response to your advertisement in … I would like to be considered for the post of ...
I have several years' experience in a sales/marketing environment.
As you can see from my CV, I am computer literate and have extensive experience of customer service/of working with children.
I enjoy working as part of a team and am self-motivated/a skilled multitasker
Thank you for considering my application. I would be happy to attend an interview at any time and look forward to hearing from you.

Candidature spontanée

143 rue des Pins
75015 Paris
France

Tel: 00 33 1 42 28 38 74
Email: valerieroch@voila.fr

Rebecca McIntyre
Managing Director
Outloud PR Agency
30 Baillie Square
Brighton
BN7 8YH

1 September 2009

Dear Ms McIntyre

I am writing to enquire about any vacancies you may have within your agency as I shall shortly be moving to the UK and am seeking full-time employment within the field of marketing and/or PR.

As you can see from the enclosed CV, I have a degree in marketing from the university of Nantes and since graduating eight years ago have worked for a large PR agency in Paris, first as PR assistant and for the last three years as PR executive, a role in which I manage a team of three. My written and spoken English is fluent and I believe that this together with my experience and skills in the field would make me an asset to your company.

Having recently got married, I shall be moving to the UK permanently next month as my husband is English and is based in the south-east. I shall therefore be free to start any job from mid-October onwards and would be very grateful if you could let me know if you have any suitable vacancies.

I am happy to attend an interview at any time and can supply references on request.

Yours sincerely

Valérie Roch

Valérie Roch

Demande de stage

Les entreprises reçoivent de nombreuses demandes de stages (**work placement** ou **work experience** en anglais britannique et **internship** en anglais américain), aussi, essayez de faire ressortir votre candidature. Renseignez-vous au préalable sur l'entreprise. Mettez l'accent sur votre motivation ainsi que sur votre flexibilité en ce qui concerne les tâches qui vous seront confiées et précisez si vous n'exigez pas de rémunération.

50 rue de Bach
92800 Puteaux
France

Ms Sarah Hamilton
Personnel Manager
Hill's Press
18 Douglas Avenue
Worsley
MANCHESTER
M28 2SG

Tel: 00 33 1 49 74 44 44
E-mail: franlesc@allo.fr

20 March 2009

Dear Ms Hamilton

I am writing to enquire about the possibility of obtaining a work placement in your company. I have been advised that you offer work placements and the profile of your company matches my training and background.

I will be graduating from university in June with a Master of Arts degree. My studies included courses in English and French language and literature, desktop publishing and applied linguistics.

I am a good communicator and a capable linguist. I enjoy working as part of a team and have good organizational skills. I am very interested in publishing and would appreciate an opportunity to work for a dynamic and internationally recognized firm like Hill's Press.

I enclose my CV for your consideration. Should you need any further information, you may contact me at the above address and telephone number. I would be available for interview at your convenience.

Yours sincerely

François Lescourant

François Lescourant

Réponse à une petite annonce

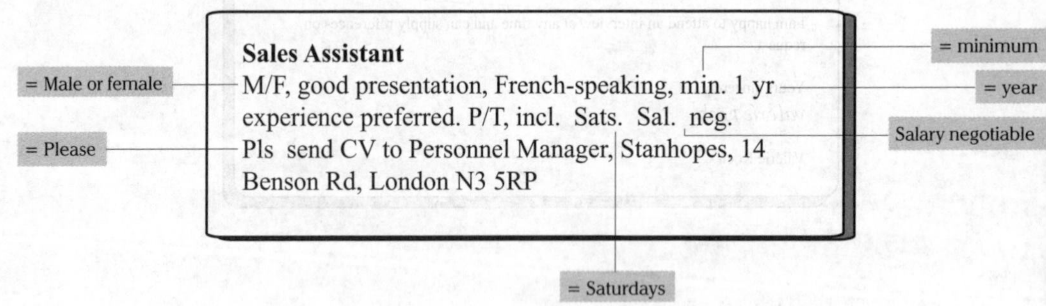
Sales Assistant
M/F, good presentation, French-speaking, min. 1 yr experience preferred. P/T, incl. Sats. Sal. neg.
Pls send CV to Personnel Manager, Stanhopes, 14 Benson Rd, London N3 5RP

2 James Street
London
N3 6PQ
Mobile: 07777 143231

Email: jp_rousseau@mail.fr

Personnel Manager
Stanhopes
14 Benson Road
London
N3 5RP

20 July 2009

Dear Sir/Madam

Sales Assistant

I am writing in response to your small ad featured in the Daily News on 15 July and enclose my CV for your consideration.

I am currently studying for a degree in English at City University and am looking for part time work. I have two years' experience as a sales assistant at Roberts Department Store, where it was essential to be well presented and have excellent customer service skills. In addition I can operate an electronic cash register and am bilingual in English and French.

I would be available to work four days per week, including Saturdays, and could start immediately.

Should you require any further details, please do not hesitate to contact me. I look forward to hearing from you.

Yours sincerely

Jean-Pierre Rousseau
Jean-Pierre Rousseau

Enc.

Le dossier de candidature

Certaines entreprises demandent aux candidats de compléter un formulaire ou un dossier de candidature (**application form**) spécialement conçu pour les besoins de l'entreprise. Si cette information est precisée dans l'annonce qui vous intéresse, il vous faudra demander le formulaire le plus tôt possible, par e-mail ou par téléphone.

D'autres entreprises utilisent des formulaires à compléter en ligne. Remplissez ses questionnaires avec le même soin que pour une candidature traditionnelle car ils peuvent remplacer votre CV et/ou votre lettre de motivation. Il est important d'y mentionner toutes les données figurant sur votre CV et de les personnaliser autant que possible. Cependant, vous pouvez également joindre votre CV, ainsi qu'une lettre de motivation ou un e-mail.

Si un espace consacré aux informations supplémentaires existe, utilisez-le pour enrichir votre candidature, par exemple avec un résumé de vos compétences et de votre expérience.

Attention à ne jamais laisser de case vide. Le cas échéant, écrire **N/A** (**not applicable**).

Demande de dossier de candidature

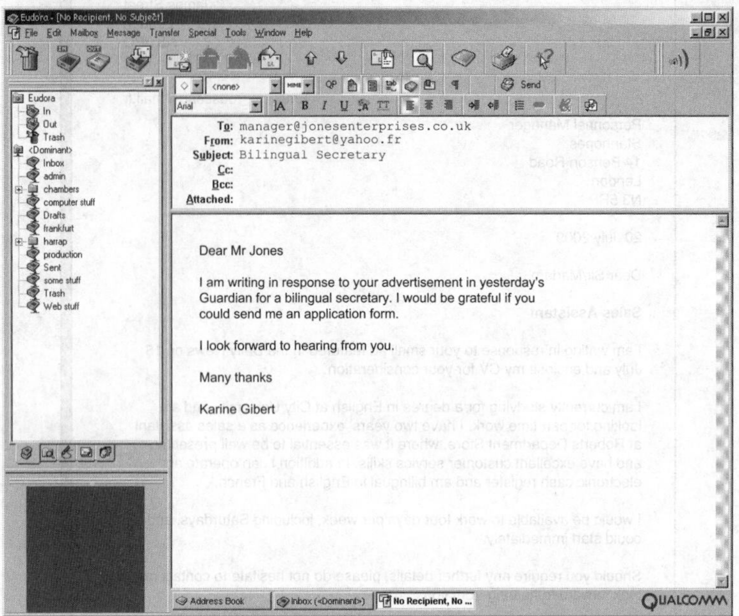
To: manager@jonesenterprises.co.uk
From: karinegibert@yahoo.fr
Subject: Bilingual Secretary
Cc:
Bcc:
Attached:

Dear Mr Jones

I am writing in response to your advertisement in yesterday's Guardian for a bilingual secretary. I would be grateful if you could send me an application form.

I look forward to hearing from you.

Many thanks

Karine Gibert

Les candidatures en ligne

Aujourd'hui, de plus en plus de recrutements s'effectuent grâce à Internet et il est courant de devoir envoyer son CV et sa lettre de motivation par e-mail. De nombreuses entreprises utilisent les services de sites de recrutement en ligne. Ne négligez donc pas cet outil indispensable.

- Exemple de candidature par e-mail

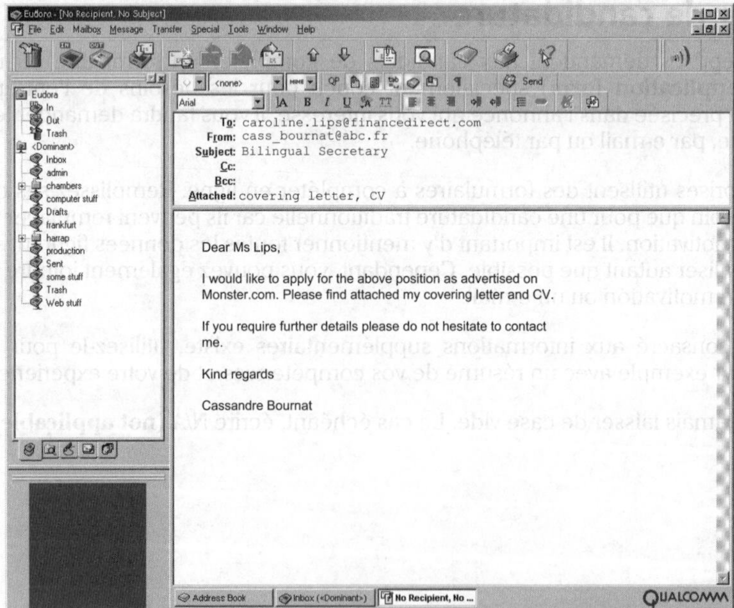
To: caroline.lips@financedirect.com
From: cass_bournat@abc.fr
Subject: Bilingual Secretary
Cc:
Bcc:
Attached: covering letter, CV

Dear Ms Lips,

I would like to apply for the above position as advertised on Monster.com. Please find attached my covering letter and CV.

If you require further details please do not hesitate to contact me.

Kind regards

Cassandre Bournat

Le curriculum vitae

Un bon CV (les Américains emploient le mot **résumé**) doit être clair, concis et facile à lire. Si vous répondez à une annonce, vérifiez bien les documents requis (voir **Dossier de candidature**), et adaptez votre CV en fonction du profil recherché en mettant en valeur certaines expériences ou compétences.

En haut de la page, précisez vos coordonnées (**Name**, **Address**, **Telephone Number**, **Email**). Les informations personnelles telles que **Nationality**, **Date of Birth** et **Marital Status** (situation de amille) ne sont pas obligatoires. Notez qu'en Grande-Bretagne et aux États-Unis, les candidats ne ɔignent généralement pas de photo à leur CV.

ous pouvez commencer votre CV en résumant vos points forts dans une section **Profile** ou **Career rofile**. Une partie **Objective** ou **Target** peut également être utilisée pour préciser vos objectifs rofessionnels (très populaire aux États-Unis). Ces sections ne sont pas obligatoires et doivent être xtrêmement brèves (deux ou trois lignes).

es deux parties les plus importantes d'un CV sont intitulées **Education** et **Professional/ Vork Experience**. Elles récapitulent les diplômes obtenus, la formation suivie et l'expérience rofessionnelle, présentés dans chaque rubrique par ordre chronologique inversé, du plus récent u plus ancien.

ans la partie **Education**, énumérez vos diplômes et votre formation. Si vous avez peu d'expérience rofessionnelle, mettez en valeur cette rubrique. Vous pouvez par exemple la placer avant **rofessional Experience** et détailler les matières principales étudiées pour l'obtention du Bac ou u cours de vos études supérieures.

our présenter votre carrière professionnelle, vous préciserez le nom des sociétés pour lesquelles ous avez travaillé, l'intitulé de votre poste et les tâches que vous effectuiez. N'oubliez pas de nentionner vos stages. Si vous venez de finir vos études, vous pouvez ajouter vos emplois saisonniers, s peuvent témoigner de compétences utiles dans différentes situations.

Contrairement à l'usage français, un CV rédigé en anglais comporte presque toujours des références **referees**). Les personnes citées en référence sont généralement des employeurs (**professional eferee**) ou des enseignants (**academic referee**). Vous pouvez soit mentionner leurs noms et oordonnées à la fin de votre CV sous la rubrique **References**, soit indiquer que vous communiquerez es informations sur demande (**References upon request** ou **References available on request**).

l est bon de contacter les personnes concernées afin de leur demander la permission de ommuniquer leurs coordonnées et de leur préciser la nature de l'emploi auquel vous postulez.

l n'y a pas de règles absolues pour rédiger un CV. Vous pouvez ajouter d'autres catégories en onction de vos aptitudes et du poste recherché, par exemple : **Languages**, **Courses Attended**, **pecial Skills**, **Publications**, **Awards**, **Military Service**, **Interests**, etc.

Diplomés français ayant une première expérience

Isabelle Murat
40, impasse de la Colline
75003 Paris
Tel: 00 33 (0)1 40 30 40 40
E-mail: imurat@ubet.fr

Date of Birth 13/2/1988
Nationality French

Professional Experience

April/May 2009	Three-month placement at Cabinet Desmoulin, Paris Customer Services
Summer 2008	Organiser in school summer camp, Port-de-Bouc

Education

2006-2009	Ecole Technique Supérieure, Bordeaux Three-year diploma course in Civil Engineering
2005-2006	Baccalauréat S (equivalent A Levels) in: Maths, Physics, Chemistry, Biology, French, English, Geography, History

Languages	French, English (fluent) German, Greek (basic)
Interests	Horse-riding, mountaineering Opera singing

References available on request

On commence par les études et les diplômes les plus récents.

Cette formule n'est pas obligatoire. Vous pouvez inclure sur une deuxième page les coordonnées des personnes pouvant fournir des références.

La date de naissance est facultative mais souvent précisée. Le lieu de naissance est moins courant.

MARC DUFOUR
42 rue Alsace-Lorraine
69000 Lyon
France
00 33 (0)4 78 55 32 14
madufo@voila.fr
Born: 26/2/86 in Nice, France

OBJECTIVE
A post using my IT knowledge and communication skills to train others

WORK EXPERIENCE
2007 – present Helpdesk Operator (French/English)
QCX Systems, Lyon
Provide telephone assistance with computer problems to international clients
Troubleshoot computer problems within the company
Train company staff in using new software

2004 – 2005 Student Computer Assistant
Université de Lyon 1
Assisted students with computer problems
Carried out minor installations/repairs

Summer 2006 Work placement at Softworld, Leeds
Tested new software and provided feedback

EDUCATION
2003 – 2007 Bachelor's Degree in Computer Science with English,
Université de Lyon 1
(2005 – 2006 Exchange year at University of Leeds)
2003: French "Baccalauréat"

LANGUAGES
French, English
JAVA, HTML, SQL, BASIC

ACTIVITIES
Running (Paris Marathon 2005), tae kwondo, online gaming

Cadre français

Name: Laurent Marie
Address: 25, rue des Arquebusiers
76000 Rouen
Tel: 00 33 (0)2 24 24 45 73
E-mail: mariel@battisto.com

Human Resources Consultant

Work Experience
2006 – present Personnel Manager, Conseil général, Le Havre
Recruiting, planning of training programmes, staff follow-up
2004 – 2005 Assistant to Personnel Manager, Société Pierre et Fils, Le Havre

Education
2003 Master of Business Administration, Boston University
2001 – 2002 DEA "Langage et Médias" - Paris X
2000 Master's Degree in History - Paris IV
1996 Baccalauréat (equivalent A Levels), specialising in Maths, Académie de Paris.

Other Experience
Year spent in Africa (2003/4) as part of a mission with the voluntary medical aid organisation, "Médecins sans frontières"
Member of a voluntary association promoting adult literacy

Languages Fluent English and Spanish

Computer Skills Mac OS, Word, Excel

Précisez pour chaque emploi les tâches principales que vous deviez effectuer.

Les entretiens

Lors d'un entretien d'embauche, tout candidat doit faire preuve d'un vif intérêt pour le poste à pourvoir. Il est important de rester naturel, mais une bonne présentation et de l'enthousiasme sont indispensables.

uelques conseils :

1. Renseignez-vous sur l'entreprise (le site Web est un outil idéal). Ne prétendez pas non plus tout savoir, quelques connaissances de base suffisent à montrer votre intérêt.
2. La présentation est très importante. Que ce soit dans votre correspondance, dans le choix de vos vêtements ou dans votre attitude, veillez à donner une image positive à votre employeur potentiel.
3. Préparez-vous aux questions qu'on est susceptible de vous poser, et répondez-y sincèrement. N'essayez pas d'éluder les questions concernant d'éventuels points faibles : réfléchissez à la façon dont vous avez appris de vos erreurs passées et à celle dont vous envisagez de combler vos lacunes.
4. Posez vous-même quelques questions. Non seulement vous montrerez toute l'attention que vous portez à l'entreprise, mais vous pourrez aussi vérifier que le poste vous convient. En général, on vous donne la possibilité de poser des questions à la fin de l'entretien.
5. Soyez confiant par rapport à vos compétences linguistiques. Pour la plupart des postes, vous ne serez pas tenu d'avoir un accent parfait. Écoutez attentivement les questions et prenez votre temps pour y répondre clairement.

:xemples de questions posées lors de l'entretien

/hat university did you attend and why did you choose it?
uelle université avez-vous fréquentée, et pourquoi l'avez-vous choisie ?

It offered the course that best suited my chosen career.
Elle proposait le cursus qui convenait le mieux à mes projets professionnels.
Its business faculty had an excellent reputation.
Son école de commerce avait une excellente réputation.

/hy do you want this job?
ourquoi souhaitez-vous obtenir cet emploi ?

I'm looking for a new challenge.
J'ai envie de relever un nouveau défi.
It's an opportunity for me to further my career.
C'est l'occasion pour moi de faire évoluer ma carrière.
I feel that this post would give me the new responsibilites I have been seeking.
Je pense que ce poste m'apportera les nouvelles responsabilités que je recherche.

Iow do you feel about managing a small team?
ous sentez-vous capable de diriger une équipe ?

I have no problem about that.
Cela ne me pose aucun problème.
I had to supervise small project teams in my last job.
J'ai déjà eu à superviser des équipes sur de petits projets dans mon emploi précédent.
I think that I have the right skills to deal with potential problems.
Je pense avoir les qualités requises pour gérer d'éventuels problèmes.
I'm quite confident that I have good interpersonal skills.
Je pense sincèrement avoir de bonnes capacités relationnelles.

/hat do you dislike about your current job?
ourquoi est-ce que votre emploi actuel ne vous satisfait pas ?

I don't have enough freedom to use my own initiative.
Je ne dispose pas d'une liberté suffisante pour faire preuve d'initiative.
It's a very small company.
C'est une toute petite entreprise.
I feel that I don't have enough opportunity to develop my interest in...
J'estime ne pas avoir la possibilité de développer mon intérêt pour...
I'm not learning enough.
Je n'apprends pas assez.

What are your future career plans?
Quels sont vos projets de carrière pour l'avenir ?

I hope to be... by the time I'm 40.
J'espère être... à l'âge de 40 ans.
Ultimately, I would like to...
Par la suite, j'aimerais...
I'm interested in the possibility of working in the US.
L'éventualité de travailler aux États-Unis m'intéresse.
Eventually, I'd like to be managing my own team.
Par la suite, j'aimerais diriger ma propre équipe.

What are your strengths and weaknesses?
Quels sont vos points forts et vos points faibles ?

On the positive side, I'm a good communicator/listener/organizer.
Mes qualités : je sais communiquer/écouter/organiser.
I'm able to manage my time well.
Je sais bien gérer mon temps.
On the negative side, I can be very demanding.
Parmi mes défauts : je peux être très exigeant.
I do have a tendency to get frustrated if a project is not advancing quickly enough.
J'ai tendance à être contrarié si un projet n'avance pas assez vite.

Les questions à poser lors de l'entretien

Can you describe a typical day?
Pouvez-vous me décrire une journée de travail typique ?

What training do you offer?
Quelle formation proposez-vous ?

What kind of opportunities are there for growth in this company?
Quelles sont les possibilités d'évolution dans cette entreprise ?

I read about your new product/recent takeover of/new plans to... Can you tell me more about that?
J'ai lu un article au sujet de votre nouveau produit/votre récente prise de contrôle de/vos nouveaux projets pour... Pouvez-vous m'en dire plus ?

What are the best things about working here?
Quels sont les principaux avantages à travailler ici ?

Could you tell me about the salary and benefits?
Pourriez-vous me parler du salaire et des avantages ?

Attention :
Toutes les questions relatives à la paie doivent être posées avec le plus de tact possible. Ne posez jamais de questions sur : les vacances, les augmentations, les décisions de gestion ou les décisions commerciales avec lesquelles vous n'êtes pas d'accord.

L'entretien téléphonique

C'est un deuxième contact après votre candidature écrite. Un employeur ou son représentant vous appellera à un moment prédéterminé afin de procéder à un entretien par téléphone. N'oubliez pas que même si un appel téléphonique peut sembler informel, il fait partie intégrante du processus de recrutement et doit être pris très au sérieux. Veillez à être au calme, tenez-vous droit pour parler clairement, réfléchissez aux questions qui vous seront posées et prenez le temps d'y répondre de manière exhaustive.

L'entretien classique

L'entretien face à face (**face-to-face interview**) est généralement mené par une ou deux personnes ou bien par un jury (**panel**). Vous pourrez être amené à faire une courte présentation (**presentation**) ou encore à passer une série d'entretiens en tête à tête avec différentes personnes.

L'entretien en situation

Ce type d'entretien se pratique de plus en plus. Il permet à l'employeur de comparer aisément les réponses de chaque candidat, en utilisant un formulaire préétabli. Au cours de cet entretien, en plus de détailler vos expériences précédentes, vous aurez à décrire vos réactions face à une situation réelle. Les questions ont tendance à être plus spécifiques au poste à pourvoir que dans un entretien classique.

Accepter un poste

Lorsque l'on vous offre un poste, l'usage est de refuser ou d'accepter dans les 24 heures qui suivent. Il est conseillé d'annoncer votre décision par téléphone à la personne qui vous a offert le poste et de confirmer cette décision par écrit. Pour cela, vous enverrez soit une lettre soit un e-mail selon le type de communication qui convient à votre employeur.

Si vous acceptez le poste, veillez à remercier votre nouvel employeur pour son offre et à confirmer certaines informations importantes comme la date à laquelle vous prendrez vos fonctions.

Confirmer par lettre que vous acceptez le poste offert

35 Field Crescent
Birmingham
B6 1PE

Mr S. Simpson
Human Resources Manager
Wilson & Wilson Ltd.
12 Bedford Road
Birmingham
B7 6ST

29 July 2009

Dear Mr Simpson

Thank you for your phone call offering me the position of marketing assistant within your company. Please consider this letter as formal notification that I accept your offer.

I am dedicated to a career in this sector and very much look forward to contributing to the future success of your organisation.

As agreed, I will be able to start work on 1 September. In the meantime please do not hesitate to contact me if you require any further documentation.

Yours sincerely

Amélie Lebrun

Amélie Lebrun

La communication au bureau

Le téléphone

- Pour répondre à un appel

  Robert McQueen speaking, how can I help you?
  Yes, ... speaking (pour confirmer que l'on est bien la personne demandée).

- Pour demander un interlocuteur

  Could I speak to... ?
  (Could I have) extension 539, please?
  Could you put me through to the manager, please?

- Comprendre les phrases utilisées par le réceptionniste

  Pour vous demander votre nom :
  Who should I say is calling?
  Who's speaking, please?

Pour vous passer quelqu'un :
Please hold, I'll put you through.

Quand la ligne est occupée :
He/she is on another line, would you like to hold?

Pour vous demander si vous désirez un message :
Would you like to leave a message?

Pour conclure un appel
Thank you, I look forward to seeing you on Wednesday. Goodbye.

- Message de répondeur téléphonique
  We are unable to take your call at the moment/I am not here at the moment. Please leave a message after the tone (and we/I will get back to you as soon as possible).

Les e-mails

Vous aurez probablement à utiliser l'e-mail pour correspondre avec un employeur potentiel (voir Le dossier de candidature p 97 et Les candidatures en ligne p 98). L'e-mail permet une communication rapide et peut donc s'avérer plus pratique que le courrier traditionnel dans certains cas, comme pour confirmer un entretien d'embauche par exemple.

Le ton employé dans un e-mail peut être celui d'un courrier classique ou alors plus proche du discours parlé, en restant concis. Les formules d'appel et de politesse sont généralement plus informelles que dans une lettre. Mais si l'e-mail est considéré comme un support de communication relativement informel, il faut néanmoins respecter certaines normes de rédaction.

Faites attention à l'emploi des majuscules qui peuvent laisser penser à votre interlocuteur que vous haussez le ton. Par ailleurs, il faut éviter de souligner à cause du risque de confusion avec un lien hypertexte renvoyant à un site Web.

Veillez à envoyer vos e-mails depuis votre boîte personnelle et non celle de votre employeur actuel. Votre adresse électronique doit être neutre et ne pas contenir de surnom ou de termes déplacés. Il peut être judicieux de créer une adresse à usage exclusivement professionnel qui soit différente de votre adresse habituelle.

Confirmer un entretien par e-mail

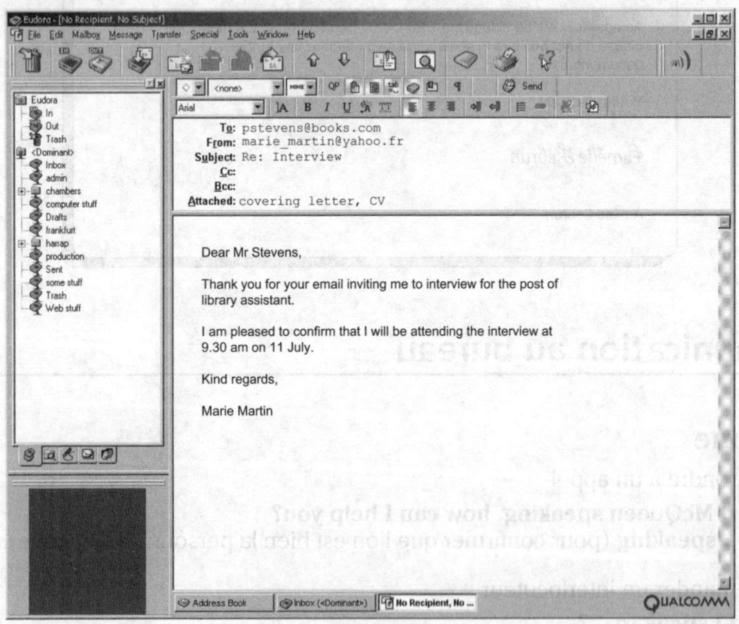
To: pstevens@books.com
From: marie_martin@yahoo.fr
Subject: Re: Interview
Cc:
Bcc:
Attached: covering letter, CV

Dear Mr Stevens,

Thank you for your email inviting me to interview for the post of library assistant.

I am pleased to confirm that I will be attending the interview at 9.30 am on 11 July.

Kind regards,

Marie Martin

World of Work

Introduction

Many learners of French choose to practise their language skills by finding a summer job or work placement in a French-speaking country. Indeed, for most students at university level an academic year spent abroad is a requirement of the course and many will choose to spend at least part of the year in some sort of employment. More advanced learners may go on to use their language skills directly by working full-time for a company based in a French-speaking country. Whether you are seeking a summer job or a more permanent position, this guide will provide you with all the information you need to cope with every step of the job-seeking process, from deciphering job ads to asking the right questions at an interview.

Letter-writing: general principles

When sending letters or other written communication particular attention should be paid to the grammar and spelling as errors in a letter are considered very bad form, especially as part of a job application. Note that in French the symbols **?** **!** **;** and **:** are all preceded by a space.

The style should be simple and clear. The introductory paragraph should summarize the intent of the letter and each subsequent paragraph should give further detail, but focus on one idea only.

- In formal letters, the sender's name and address should appear in the top left-hand corner. On company headed paper, the name of the company and its address are centred at the top of the letter.
- Below this on the right is the name and address of the recipient.
- Underneath this is the date, written in full and usually preceded by the name of the town from which you are writing. The only punctuation is a comma between the name of the town and the date. Days and months are written without capitals.
- The main body should start with a greeting, then an opening paragraph. Once the letter has been written it is finished with a standard complimentary ending.
- Unlike in English the signature below the letter is on the right, with the printed name immediately below it.

Opening greetings

The opening greetings and endings used in letters written in French follow certain well-established rules:

- If you do not know the person you are writing to, whether you know their name or not, or if you know them only slightly:

  Monsieur
  Madame

  The greetings **Monsieur** and **Madame** are equivalent to "Dear Sir" and "Dear Madam" in English. They are not followed by the person's name.

- When you are unsure whether the recipient of the letter is male or female:

  Madame, Monsieur

- When the letter is addressed to a company rather than to an individual:

  Messieurs

- When writing to the head of a company or institution:

  Monsieur le Directeur
  Madame la Directrice
  Monsieur le Président
  Madame la Présidente

- When writing to a minister:

  Monsieur le Ministre
  Madame le Ministre

  The form **Madame la Ministre** is equally acceptable now.

- When writing to a lawyer or solicitor:

  Cher Maître

  This form is used irrespective of whether one is addressing a man or a woman in this context.

- When you know the person you are writing to and want to sound less formal:

  Cher Monsieur
  Chère Madame
  Chère Mademoiselle (for an unmarried young woman)

These greetings are never followed by the name of the person. The equivalent of "Dear Mr Allen" is **Monsieur** if you don't know him very well, or **Cher Monsieur** if you know him better and want to sound less formal. Always write the title in full and avoid abbreviations like **M.**, **Mme** and **Mlle**.

If you are writing to more than one person, you need to repeat **Cher** before each title:
Cher Monsieur,
Chère Madame,

Endings

Although the formal endings of French business or administrative letters may appear slightly florid or pompous, it must be remembered that this is all part of a code of politeness integral to French correspondence etiquette. The complimentary ending should correspond in form and tone to the opening greeting. The title used at the beginning (**Monsieur**, **Cher Monsieur** etc) is always repeated in the ending of the letter.

- The most appropriate endings for a job application letter are:

  Veuillez agréer, Monsieur (Madame), mes salutations distinguées.
  Veuillez recevoir, Monsieur (Madame), mes salutations distinguées.
  Veuillez agréer, Monsieur (Madame), l'expression de mes sentiments distingués.
  Je vous prie d'agréer, Monsieur le Directeur (Madame la Directrice), mes salutations distinguées.
  Je vous prie d'agréer, cher Maître, mes salutations distinguées.
  Je vous remercie d'avance et vous prie d'agréer, Monsieur (Madame), mes salutations distinguées.
  Dans l'attente d'une réponse de votre part, veuillez agréer, Messieurs, mes salutations distinguées.
  Veuillez agréer, Monsieur (Madame), l'expression de ma considération distinguée.

This form is used when addressing a lawyer or solicitor specifically.

Addresses and postcodes

- The first two numbers of a French postcode correspond to the administrative code number of the relevant "département". All postcodes for Paris begin with 75. For example:

  Société Dupont
  20, boulevard Arago
  75013 Paris

In the example above, the first two numbers indicate the city of Paris while the last two figures indicate that the address is located in the thirteenth "arrondissement" [district] of the city. Note that in French addresses the postcode is usually written before the town, on the same line.The structure of a French business address is otherwise very similar to an English one. For example:

Monsieur Georges Trenay
Directeur des exportations
Société Delacour
77170 Fontainebleau Cedex

The abbreviation "Cedex" is often found in French business addresses. This is a special postcode ensuring rapid delivery of mail to businesses and certain institutions. The first two figures, as in other postcodes, denote geographical location, but the following three figures denote an individual code assigned to the company in question.

- In Belgium addresses are often written with the building number coming after the street name. For a building where there are more than three letterboxes it is usual to add the letterbox number. For example:

  Monsieur Luc Dujardin
  Directeur adjoint
  Agence Mercure
  rue du Clocher 143, bte 4
  1040 Bruxelles

- Swiss addresses are also usually written with the street number appearing after the street name, and the postcode before the town. When writing from outside Switzerland the abbreviation CH (for "Confederatio Helvetica") is often added. For example:

Monsieur André Roux
Service du Marketing
Société Cochet
Avenue du Peyrou 4
CH-2000 Neuchâtel

- In Canada, it is usual to write the name of the town or municipality, followed by the province in which it is located, followed by the postcode, all on the same line. For example:

Madame Chantal Lemoine
Directrice du Personnel
Hôtel Lenoir
3567 rue Drummond
Montréal (Québec) H3G 1M8

The name of the province is usually given in brackets after the name of the town or municipality. Alternatively an abbreviation can be used to designate the province: for example **QC** for **Québec**. If the abbreviated form is used then there is no need for brackets.

The websites of the various postal services in French-speaking countries are a useful source of information regarding addresses and postcodes in particular:

France: www.laposte.fr (www.laposte.com is in English)
Belgium: www.post.be
Luxembourg: www.pt.lu
Switzerland: www.poste.ch
Canada: www.canadapost.ca

Envelopes

In administrative letters the surname usually precedes the forename: **Madame Guimard Annie**.

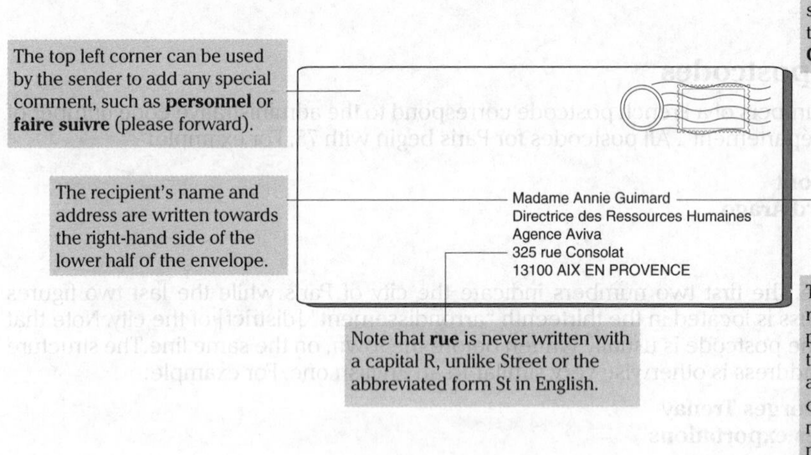

Madame Annie Guimard
Directrice des Ressources Humaines
Agence Aviva
325 rue Consolat
13100 AIX EN PROVENCE

The top left corner can be used by the sender to add any special comment, such as **personnel** or **faire suivre** (please forward).

The recipient's name and address are written towards the right-hand side of the lower half of the envelope.

Note that **rue** is never written with a capital R, unlike Street or the abbreviated form St in English.

The French postal services recommend that no punctuation be used on the envelope (no commas at the ends of lines, no comma after the street number etc) and that the name of the town should be written in capital letters, without any accents or hyphens.

It is standard practice to write a return address on the back of the envelope at the top, in case the letter gets lost.

Job advertisements and covering letters

When applying for a job in France, it is customary to write the covering letter ("lettre de motivation") by hand.

letter of application is quite formal in its presentation. It should be concise, properly structured n paragraphs and have the standard opening and closing formulas. You should cover the following oints:

- Emphasize what you consider important in your CV
- Add information about your objectives
- Explain why you are interested in the company
- Convince the reader that you are the right person for the job

eplying to an advertisement

Le centre culturel « La Vague » recherche secrétaire à plein temps dans le cadre d'un contrat à durée indéterminée.
Vous serez chargé(e) de gérer les activités culturelles du centre en collaboration étroite avec le directeur.
Vous assurerez également le suivi des différents fichiers et de la communication avec les partenaires.
Une bonne connaissance des métiers de la culture est souhaitable.
Anglais courant et bonne maîtrise de l'outil informatique (en particulier Excel et Powerpoint) exigés.
Salaire à définir en fonction de l'expérience.

Envoyer candidatures à l'adresse suivante avant le 10 octobre 2009 :
Centre culturel La Vague
3, place de la Mairie
37000 Tours

Marielle Gondrand
Villa La Tourelle
37000 Tours

Centre culturel La Vague
3, place de la Mairie
37000 Tours

Tours, le 1er octobre 2009

Madame, Monsieur,

Votre annonce parue dans Les Nouvelles de Tours du 28 septembre 2009 pour un poste de secrétaire a retenu toute mon attention.

Introductory paragraph mentioning where you saw the vacancy advertised.

Je viens de terminer mon BTS de secrétariat et je suis à la recherche d'un emploi. Au cours de mes études, j'ai eu l'occasion de faire deux stages : l'un à la Banque Moreau et l'autre à la Maison des Jeunes de Tours. Par ailleurs, je m'occupe bénévolement du secrétariat d'une association à but non lucratif de mon quartier.

Outline of your current employment situation, qualifications and previous experience.

Je suis très attirée par les métiers de la culture, et ceci, ainsi que le rayonnement de votre société au niveau régional, m'incite à vouloir rejoindre votre équipe.

Why you are interested in the company.

Je me tiens à votre disposition pour un entretien éventuel.

Indicate that you are available for interview.

Je vous prie d'agréer, Madame, Monsieur, mes salutations distinguées.

Standard complimentary ending.

Marielle Gondrand

Marielle Gondrand

World of Work

Useful phrases

En réponse à votre annonce parue dans Les Nouvelles de Tours du…, je me permets de vous adresser mon curriculum vitae pour le poste de secrétaire.
Je dispose de plusieurs années d'expérience dans différentes entreprises.
Au cours de mes cinq années d'expérience auprès de la société X, j'ai acquis une bonne maîtrise de…
Je souhaite élargir mon expérience professionnelle tout en acquérant de nouvelles responsabilités et serais donc ravi d'intégrer une entreprise aussi dynamique et réputée que la vôtre.
En espérant que ma candidature retiendra votre attention, je vous prie d'agréer, Madame, Monsieur, l'expression de mes sentiments distinguées.

Making an unsolicited application

Wilfrid Garnier
10, impasse des Petites Écuries
37000 Tours
Tél : 02 47 30 60 30
E-mail : wilf.garnier@free.fr

Tours, le 17 février 2009

M. le Directeur des Ressources Humaines
Supermarchés Guévara
Z. I. de la Gravière
37042 TOURS CEDEX

Monsieur,

Show what you have to offer.

Titulaire d'un BTS de gestion et après une expérience réussie en tant qu'assistant du responsable de la gestion des stocks de la société des Engrais Santic (voir CV ci-joint), je vous écris pour vous proposer mes services. Je souhaiterais désormais élargir mon expérience en utilisant mes compétences dans le domaine de la grande distribution. Ce secteur m'a toujours intéressé et je crois disposer des aptitudes nécessaires pour donner entière satisfaction dans toute mission que vous voudriez bien me confier.

Votre société m'intéresse particulièrement car elle jouit d'une réputation d'excellence sans pareil, et j'admire les efforts qu'elle a fournis pour le développement du commerce éthique.

Explain your interest in this particular company.

Je me tiens à votre entière disposition pour vous fournir tout renseignement complémentaire.

Dans l'attente de vous lire, je vous prie d'agréer, Monsieur, l'expression de mes sentiments les meilleurs.

W Garnier

W Garnier

PJ : un CV avec photo

Asking for a work placement

Work placements are very popular in France and are a compulsory part of many courses. It is therefore advisable to send your request well in advance.

This type of letter is always handwritten in French (see Covering letter p. 109).

Katherine Dixon
28 Fallowfield Road
COLCHESTER
Essex CM16 3JF

Cabinet d'urbanisme Alphacité
22 boulevard des Dames
33000 Bordeaux

Colchester, le 17 octobre 2009

Monsieur,

Mention your course.

Étudiante en licence d'urbanisme à l'Université de Colchester, je dois effectuer dans le cadre de mes études un stage en entreprise d'une durée de six semaines minimum, entre le mois de janvier et le mois d'avril 2008. Ce stage est destiné à enrichir l'enseignement reçu à l'université, d'une part en permettant à l'étudiant de se perfectionner dans une langue étrangère, d'autre part en le mettant en situation réelle.

Specify the length of the placement and the dates.

Explain what is expected from the placement.

Très intéressée par la signalétique urbaine, et attirée par la réputation de votre cabinet, je souhaite mettre mes compétences et mon savoir-faire au bénéfice de votre entreprise.

Explain your reasons for choosing the company.

Dans l'espoir que ma candidature retiendra votre attention, je vous prie d'agréer, Monsieur, mes salutations distinguées.

Katherine Dixon

Katherine Dixon

Replying to a small ad

If you are not familiar with the abbreviations and style used, small ads can seem very cryptic.

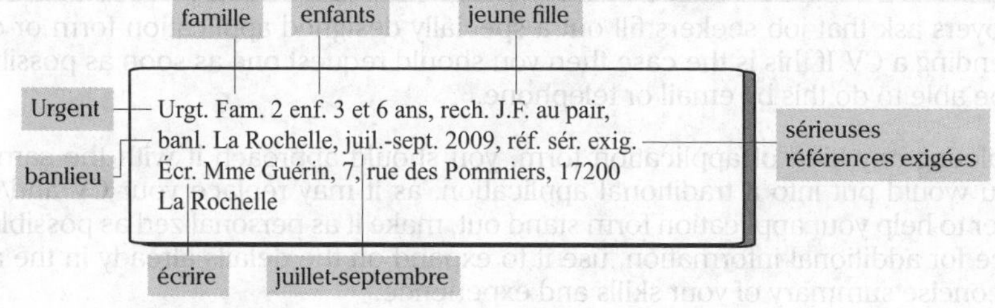

famille
enfants
jeune fille
Urgent
Urgt. Fam. 2 enf. 3 et 6 ans, rech. J.F. au pair,
banl. La Rochelle, juil.-sept. 2009, réf. sér. exig.
Écr. Mme Guérin, 7, rue des Pommiers, 17200
La Rochelle
sérieuses
références exigées
banlieu
écrire
juillet-septembre

Gemma Lewis
16 The Avenue
Luton
LU6 2BY
Grande-Bretagne

Mme Guérin
7, rue des Pommiers
17200 La Rochelle

Luton, le 10 juin 2009

Madame,

Je me permets de vous écrire concernant votre petite annonce parue dans Le Quotidien.
Jeune femme de 22 ans, je viens de finir mes études et je souhaiterais maintenant passer quelques mois en France afin de perfectionner mon français.
L'emploi que vous proposez m'intéresse car j'adore travailler avec les enfants. J'ai beaucoup d'expérience en tant que baby-sitter dans mon quartier et je peux donc vous fournir des références. En outre, je possède une bonne connaissance des premiers soins et je sais faire la cuisine et le ménage.
Je serai disponible de juillet à septembre et demeure à votre disposition pour toute information complémentaire.
Dans l'attente d'une réponse de votre part, veuillez agréer, Madame, mes salutations distinguées.

Gemma Lewis

Gemma Lewis

PJ : deux lettres de recommandation.

Useful phrases

Vous trouverez ci-joint mon curriculum vitae.
Je vous remercie de l'attention que vous porterez à ma demande et reste à votre disposition pour un entretien.
Je reste à votre disposition pour vous rencontrer et vous fournir tout autre renseignement.
En vous remerciant à l'avance de bien vouloir examiner ma demande, je vous prie d'agréer …

Application forms

Some employers ask that job seekers fill out a specially designed application form or online form instead of sending a CV. If this is the case then you should request one as soon as possible. You will most likely be able to do this by email or telephone.

When completing any kind of application form, you should approach it with the same care and attention you would put into a traditional application, as it may replace your CV and/or covering letter. In order to help your application form stand out, make it as personalized as possible: if you are offered space for additional information, use it to expand on the details already in the application, including a concise summary of your skills and experience.

Application forms tend to be less common in France, where they are mostly used in the Civil Service.

Requesting an application form

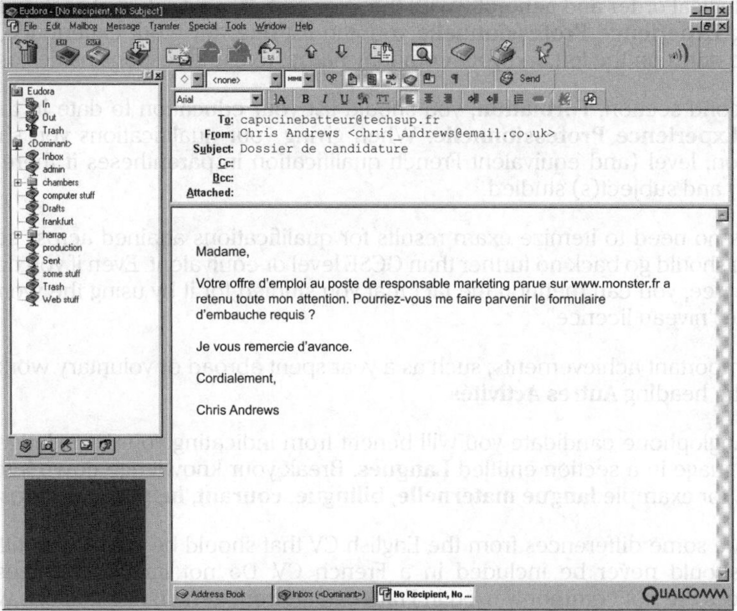
To: capucinebatteur@techsup.fr
From: Chris Andrews <chris_andrews@email.co.uk>
Subject: Dossier de candidature
Cc:
Bcc:
Attached:

Madame,

Votre offre d'emploi au poste de responsable marketing parue sur www.monster.fr a retenu toute mon attention. Pourriez-vous me faire parvenir le formulaire d'embauche requis ?

Je vous remercie d'avance.

Cordialement,

Chris Andrews

Online applications

Companies are increasingly turning to the Internet as a means to recruit new employees and many now require you to send in your CV and covering letter via email. The use of specialist recruitment websites is also becoming more widespread, so do not overlook this useful tool when searching for employment.

Making an online application

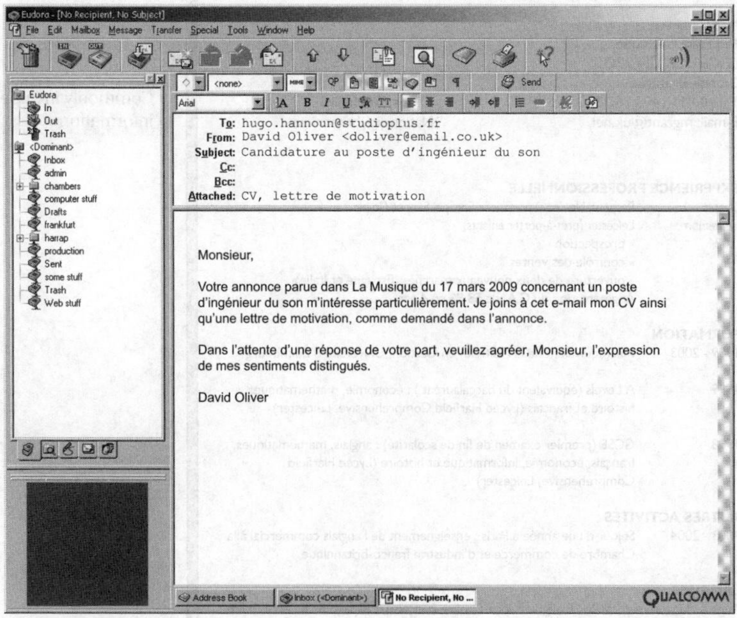
To: hugo.hannoun@studioplus.fr
From: David Oliver <doliver@email.co.uk>
Subject: Candidature au poste d'ingénieur du son
Cc:
Bcc:
Attached: CV, lettre de motivation

Monsieur,

Votre annonce parue dans La Musique du 17 mars 2009 concernant un poste d'ingénieur du son m'intéresse particulièrement. Je joins à cet e-mail mon CV ainsi qu'une lettre de motivation, comme demandé dans l'annonce.

Dans l'attente d'une réponse de votre part, veuillez agréer, Monsieur, l'expression de mes sentiments distingués.

David Oliver

Curriculum vitae

The presentation of a CV in French is in many ways similar to an English or American CV.

- Your personal details should be in the upper left-hand corner, and include **nom**, **adresse**, **numéro de téléphone** and **e-mail**. Other commonly included details are **âge**, **date de naissance**, **situation familiale**, **nationalité** and often a passport photo too.

- The main sections of your CV will summarize your education and experience, listed in reverse chronological order and generally with the strongest or most relevant section first. Under the heading **Expérience Professionnelle** you can list relevant work experience, with the start and end dates on the left and your company name, role and responsibilities on the right.
- In a second section, **Formation**, you should list your education to date in the same layout as the **Expérience Professionnelle**. When giving your qualifications you should state the institution, level (and equivalent French qualification in parentheses if there is no obvious parallel) and subject(s) studied.
- There is no need to itemize exam results for qualifications attained across several subjects and you should go back no further than GCSE level or equivalent. Even if you do not complete your degree, you can mention the fact that you studied for it by using the word "niveau", for example "niveau licence".
- Other important achievements, such as a year spent abroad or voluntary work, can be listed under the heading **Autres Activités**.
- As an Anglophone candidate you will benefit from indicating your knowledge of more than one language in a section entitled **Langues**. Break your knowledge down into categories of fluency, for example **langue maternelle**, **bilingue**, **courant**, **lu**, **parlé**, **notions**.
- There are some differences from the English CV that should be noted. The title "Curriculum Vitae" should never be included in a French CV. Do not include referees on your CV: references are not commonly used in France apart from certain occupations where personal recommendation would be expected such as catering, cleaning, child care etc. Similarly, only mention hobbies if they add something personal to your profile or if they are particularly relevant to the job. It is assumed that everybody likes reading, going to the cinema, listening to music and travelling.
- You should add any additional information you feel would be helpful in brief in a section entitled **Divers**. This might include, for example, non-work related expertise in an area that would be helpful to your application, with a short list of capabilities.

Experienced (British)

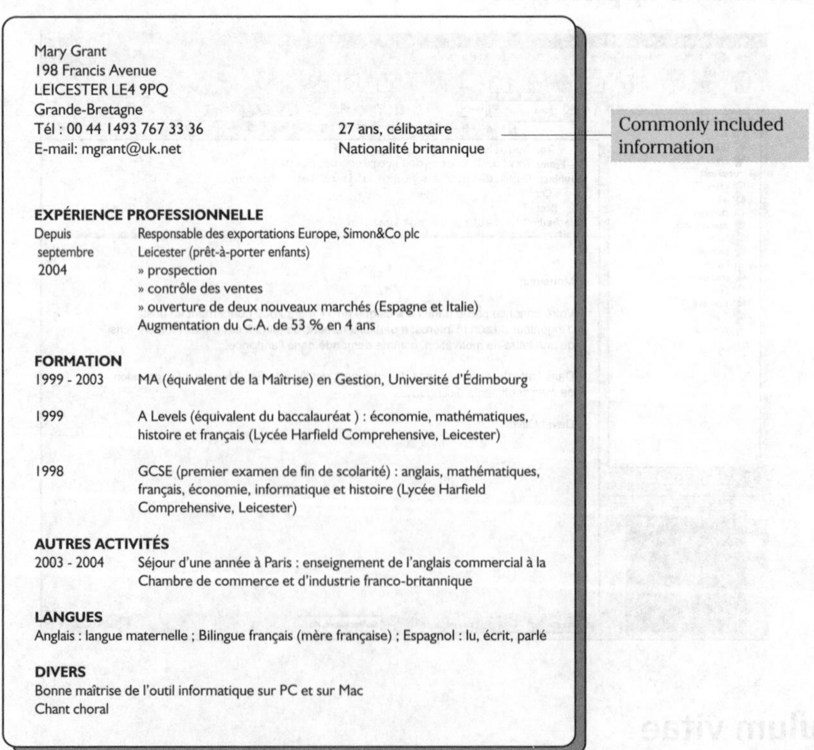

Mary Grant
198 Francis Avenue
LEICESTER LE4 9PQ
Grande-Bretagne
Tél : 00 44 1493 767 33 36 — 27 ans, célibataire
E-mail: mgrant@uk.net — Nationalité britannique

Commonly included information

EXPÉRIENCE PROFESSIONNELLE

Depuis septembre 2004	Responsable des exportations Europe, Simon&Co plc Leicester (prêt-à-porter enfants) » prospection » contrôle des ventes » ouverture de deux nouveaux marchés (Espagne et Italie) Augmentation du C.A. de 53 % en 4 ans

FORMATION

1999 - 2003	MA (équivalent de la Maîtrise) en Gestion, Université d'Édimbourg
1999	A Levels (équivalent du baccalauréat) : économie, mathématiques, histoire et français (Lycée Harfield Comprehensive, Leicester)
1998	GCSE (premier examen de fin de scolarité) : anglais, mathématiques, français, économie, informatique et histoire (Lycée Harfield Comprehensive, Leicester)

AUTRES ACTIVITÉS

2003 - 2004	Séjour d'une année à Paris : enseignement de l'anglais commercial à la Chambre de commerce et d'industrie franco-britannique

LANGUES

Anglais : langue maternelle ; Bilingue français (mère française) ; Espagnol : lu, écrit, parlé

DIVERS

Bonne maîtrise de l'outil informatique sur PC et sur Mac
Chant choral

Experienced (American)

John Farmer
18 rue de Turenne
75004 Paris
Tél: 01 42 22 37 89
E-mail: jfarmer@nxl.fr

Né le 17 juin 1978
Marié, 2 enfants (1 et 3 ans)
Nationalité américaine

9 ans d'expérience dans la fonction commerciale

Connaissance approfondie du marché informatique

Depuis 2004 — ICN Europe, Amsterdam
Directeur commercial
· Responsable de la politique commerciale et du marketing opérationnel
· Recrutement et encadrement d'une équipe de 7 commerciaux
· Définition des objectifs commerciaux
· Augmentation du chiffre d'affaires (+53 %)

2000 - 2003 — Société ADB, Paris
Ingénieur commercial grands comptes
· Responsable du développement des ventes pour le secteur de la grande distribution sur la région parisienne
· Ouverture de nouveaux comptes
· Atteinte des objectifs fixés

Formation

2004	MBA, Harvard Business School
2000	MS (équivalent de la maîtrise) en Économie et Gestion, Université de Harvard
1996	High school diploma (équivalent du baccalauréat)

Langues
Anglais : langue maternelle
Français : bilingue
Espagnol : notions

Recent graduate (British)

Stephen Forbes
81 Lincoln Walk
STEVENAGE
Herts SE19 2DN
Tél: 00 44 1283 671621
E-mail: sforbes@teaser.org.uk

22 ans, célibataire
Nationalité britannique

Formation

2005 - 2008	BSc (équivalent de la licence) en Biologie, Université de Swansea, Grande-Bretagne.
2005	A Levels (équivalent du baccalauréat) : Mathématiques, Chimie, Biologie et Français, Lycée Whitton Comprehensive, Bristol, Grande-Bretagne.
2003	GCSE (premier examen de fin de scolarité) : Anglais, Mathématiques, Chimie, Biologie, Français, Histoire et Informatique, Lycée Whitton Comprehensive, Bristol, Grande-Bretagne.

Expérience professionnelle

juillet - septembre 2008	Stage de 3 mois auprès du service d'hématologie de l'hôpital Frenchay de Bristol : analyse de prélèvements sanguins.
octobre 2008 - novembre 2009	Enseignement de l'anglais langue étrangère, École de langues Babel, Osaka, Japon.

Langues
Anglais : langue maternelle
Français : courant
Japonais : notions

Divers
Bonnes connaissances informatiques : animateur du club d'informatique d'une maison des jeunes et de la culture (Bristol)

Titulaire du brevet de secourisme

Recent graduate (American)

Martha Jacobs
493 Huntington Avenue
Boston
MA 02575
États-Unis
Tél : (617) 267-1680
E-mail: mjacobs@totem.com

25 ans, célibataire
Nationalité américaine

Traductrice anglais/français/espagnol

Début de spécialisation en informatique

FORMATION

2007 - 2009 Diplôme de traducteur technique
Université McGill, Montréal

2004 - 2007 BA (équivalent de la licence) en français et espagnol, mention très bien
Université de Boston

2002 High school diploma (équivalent du baccalauréat)

EXPÉRIENCE PROFESSIONNELLE

2007 - 2008 **Éditions Dulis**, Montréal
Travaux de traduction en free-lance

juillet 2006 - septembre 2007 **Société AX Networks**, Boston
Stage de 3 mois dans le service de traduction : adaptation de logiciels pour le marché européen

2005 - 2006 **Lycée Dupuis**, Grenoble
Assistante de français

LANGUES

Anglais : langue maternelle
Français : bilingue (2 ans à Montréal, 1 an à Grenoble)
Espagnol : courant

CONNAISSANCES INFORMATIQUES

Word, Excel et Access (sur PC et Mac)

LOISIRS

Escrime, violoncelle

Interviews

As a prospective employee you will be expected to show a strong interest in the position at an interview. You should be enthusiastic and well presented. There are several ways that presentation and preparation can help you in an interview situation:

1. Learn a little about the company background. The company website is an ideal tool for this. Do not pretend to know more than you do – a healthy interest and proof of some background knowledge is enough.
2. Presentation is very important. Whether it is a written form, your choice of clothes or your manner you should take care of your image throughout the application process. Dress smartly, smile, make eye contact and sit up straight.
3. Anticipate and be prepared for questions that an employer is likely to ask you, and answe openly and honestly. Do not try to avoid questions about your possible weaknesses: thinl about how you have learned from your past mistakes and how you plan to develop you shortcomings.
4. Ask a few questions of your own: this will not only reinforce your image as someone wh cares about the job and the company, but is also the perfect occasion to see whether th position would be suitable for you. The interviewer will generally give you a chance to d this at the end. Do not ask about salary and benefits.
5. Be positive about your language skills and do not worry too much about sounding like native speaker. For most positions you will not be expected to have a perfect accent, as lon as you can communicate confidently and effectively. Listen carefully to the questions an take your time to answer clearly.

Examples of questions asked in an interview

Quelle université/école avez-vous fréquentée, et pourquoi l'avez-vous choisie ?
What university did you attend and why did you choose it?

Elle proposait le cursus qui convenait le mieux à mes projets professionnels.
It offered the course that best suited my chosen career.
Cette école de commerce avait une excellente réputation.
This business school had an excellent reputation.

Pourquoi souhaitez-vous obtenir cet emploi ?
Why do you want this job?

J'ai envie de relever un nouveau défi.
I'm looking for a new challenge.
C'est l'occasion pour moi de faire évoluer ma carrière.
It's an opportunity for me to further my career.
Je pense que ce poste m'apportera les nouvelles responsabilités que je recherche.
I feel that this post would give me the new responsibilities I have been seeking.

Vous sentez-vous capable de diriger une équipe ?
How do you feel about managing a small team?

Cela ne me pose aucun problème.
I have no problem with that.
J'ai déjà eu à superviser des équipes sur de petits projets dans mon emploi précédent.
I had to supervise small project teams in my last job.
Je pense avoir les qualités requises pour gérer d'éventuels problèmes.
I think that I have the right skills to deal with potential problems.
Je pense sincèrement avoir de bonnes capacités relationnelles.
I'm quite confident that I have good interpersonal skills.

Pourquoi est-ce que votre emploi actuel ne vous satisfait pas ?
What do you dislike about your current job?

Je ne dispose pas d'une liberté suffisante pour faire preuve d'initiative.
I don't have enough freedom to use my own initiative.
C'est une toute petite entreprise.
It's a very small company.
J'estime ne pas avoir la possibilité de développer mon intérêt pour…
I feel that I don't have enough opportunity to develop my interest in…
Je n'apprends pas assez.
I'm not learning enough.

Quels sont vos projets de carrière pour l'avenir ?
What are your future career plans?

J'espère être… à l'âge de 40 ans.
I hope to be… by the time I'm 40.
Par la suite, j'aimerais…
Ultimately, I would like to…
L'éventualité de travailler aux États-Unis m'intéresse.
I'm interested in the possibility of working in the US.
Par la suite, j'aimerais diriger ma propre équipe.
Eventually, I'd like to be managing my own team.

Quels sont vos points forts et vos points faibles ?
What are your strengths and weaknesses?

Mes qualités : je sais communiquer/écouter/organiser.
On the positive side, I'm a good communicator/listener/organizer.
Je sais bien gérer mon temps.
I'm able to manage my time well.
Parmi mes défauts : je peux être très exigeant.
On the negative side, I can be very demanding.
J'ai tendance à être contrarié si un projet n'avance pas assez vite.
I do have a tendency to get frustrated if a project is not advancing quickly enough.

Questions to ask during an interview

Beware of asking questions about salary and benefits. If you feel that it is appropriate or the topic is raised by the employer, be tactful and try not to appear driven solely by the salary. Note that you should never ask questions about holidays, pay rises or business decisions you disagree with.

Pourriez-vous me décrire une journée de travail typique ?
Can you describe a typical day?

Quelle formation proposez-vous ?
What training do you offer?

Quelles sont les possibilités d'évolution dans cette entreprise ?
What kind of opportunities are there for growth in this company?

J'ai lu un article au sujet de votre nouveau produit/votre récente prise de contrôle de/vos nouveaux projets pour... Pourriez-vous m'en dire plus ?
I read an article about your new product/recent takeover of/new plans to... Can you tell me more about that?

Quels sont les principaux avantages à travailler ici ?
What are the best things about working here?

Pourriez-vous me parler du salaire et des avantages ?
Can you tell me about the salary and benefits?

Telephone interview

This is a common second point of contact after an application in writing. Here an employer or their representative will call you at a prearranged time to conduct an interview based on the details of your application. Remember that although a phone call can seem informal, it is still part of the application process and should be taken seriously: make sure you have peace and quiet, sit up straight to ensure you speak clearly, think about the questions you may be asked and take your time answering them fully.

Standard interview

This will be a face-to-face talk with one or more members of the company you are looking to work for.

Competency-based interview

This increasingly common type of interview is designed to ensure all candidates answer the same questions and can be compared on an equal footing. It will usually follow a very rigid format. The interviewer will have a set list of questions that require you to talk in detail about specific experiences, or describe how you would deal with hypothetical situations. The questions tend to be highly specific to the position and organization, and the interviewer will take notes throughout.

Accepting an offer

Once you have been offered a position, it is courteous to accept or decline within 24 hours. You should telephone the company to inform your contact of your decision and follow up the call with written confirmation. This could take the form of a letter or email, according to the employer's preference.

It is important to thank your new employer for the opportunity and confirm any important details, such as your start date.

Writing a letter of acceptance

Joanne Bennett
3 South Lane
York
YO5 6TH

Samuel Fossard
Directeur adjoint
Hôtel Mercure
56260 Vannes

York, le 14 juillet 2009

Monsieur,

Je vous écris pour vous remercier de m'avoir téléphoné pour me proposer le poste de réceptionniste bilingue. Je confirme officiellement par cette lettre que j'accepte votre offre.

Je suis très heureuse d'avoir été choisie pour ce poste et je suis impatiente de mettre mes compétences et mon savoir-faire au service de votre entreprise.

Comme convenu, je serai disponible pour commencer à travailler le 1er septembre. N'hésitez pas à me contacter avant cette date si nécessaire.

Je vous prie d'agréer, Monsieur, mes salutations distinguées.

Joanne Bennett

Joanne Bennett

Office communication

Telephone calls

- Pronunciation of telephone numbers

  When giving their phone numbers, French people say them two by two: 01 45 67 44 32: zéro un, quarante-cinq, soixante-sept, quarante-quatre, trente-deux. This can be a little disconcerting for the English speaker and you may have to ask them to say it again one number at a time.

- Answering the telephone

  Allô, Ruth Jarvis à l'appareil(, je vous écoute).
  Hôtel de la Paix, bonjour.

- Asking to speak to someone

  Je voudrais parler à Monsieur Dupont.

- Phrases used by a receptionist or secretary taking a call

  When asking for the caller's name:

  Qui dois-je annoncer ?
  C'est de la part de qui ?

  When putting a caller through:

  Je vous le/la passe.
  Ne quittez pas, je vous le/la passe.

When the caller cannot be connected immediately:

C'est occupé.
Il/Elle est en communcation, voulez-vous patienter ?

Asking the caller if he or she wishes to leave a message:

Voulez-vous lui laisser un message ?

To which the caller may reply:

Pouvez-vous lui demander de me rappeler ?

- Recorded messages

  If you are put on hold, the standard recorded message while waiting is:

  Nous vous demandons de bien vouloir patienter quelques instants. Nous allons donner suite à votre appel.

Emails

It may be essential to email a potential employer as part of the job application process (see Application forms p00 and Online applications p00). Email may also be more convenient for shorter correspondence or when you need to respond quickly, for example when confirming an interview.

Emails in French are often written in a slightly less telegraphic style than tends to be the case in English, mainly due to the fact that French contains fewer of the abbreviated forms that characterize so much of this type of communication in English.

Opening greetings and endings are usually rather informal for emails, and nowhere near as stylized as the ones typically found in letters. Although the style of the email will also be more informal than for a letter, the register should still remain fairly high – affectionate endings like **Bisous** would not be appropriate, nor should you add kisses or emoticons!

Make sure you send your email from a personal address and not from your current employer. Be careful about the address you use; it should not contain nicknames or other inappropriate references – it might be a good idea to create a separate account for professional use.

Confirming an interview

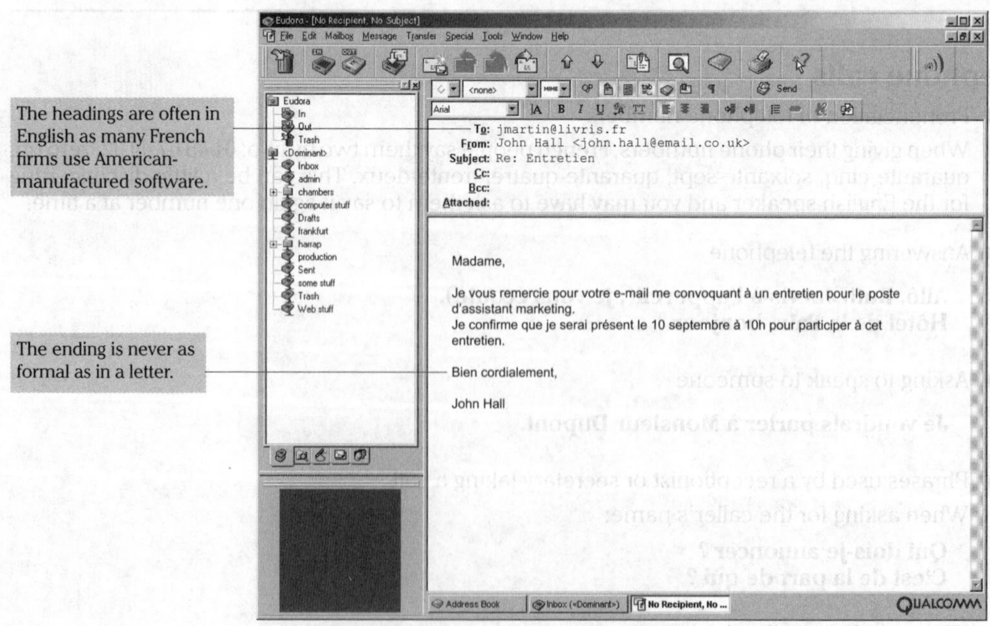

250 Expressions anglaises à connaître

250 Expressions anglaises à connaître

L'amour et l'affection

he is the apple of his eye
tient à elle comme à la prunelle de ses yeux

ⓘ L'expression anglaise est toujours au singulier (the apple of his/her eye) et s'applique toujours à une personne, jamais à une chose.

o sweep someone off their feet
ire perdre la tête à quelqu'un

o carry a torch for someone
voir un faible pour quelqu'un

o fall head over heels for someone
mber follement amoureux de quelqu'un

Aimer/ne pas aimer

o be in someone's good books
re dans les petits papiers de quelqu'un

o have been bitten by the bug
voir la folie de quelque chose

o get on like a house on fire
entendre à merveille

o turn one's nose up at something
édaigner quelque chose

to give someone the cold shoulder
snober quelqu'un

to make someone's toes curl
donner des frissons de plaisir à quelqu'un

to ruffle someone's feathers
froisser quelqu'un

to get up someone's nose
taper sur les nerfs à quelqu'un

to look daggers at someone
foudroyer quelqu'un du regard

to cut someone dead
faire semblant de ne pas voir quelqu'un

S'amuser

to let one's hair down
se détendre, se laisser aller

ⓘ Cette expression fait référence au fait qu'autrefois les femmes ne laissaient retomber leurs cheveux que dans l'intimité.

to have a blast
s'éclater

to paint the town red
faire la noce

to be out on the tiles
sortir faire la bringue

ⓘ L'expression compare ceux qui sortent s'amuser aux chats qui se promènent sur les toits la nuit.

Le bonheur

to be on top of the world
être en pleine forme

to be walking on air
to be on cloud nine
to be over the moon
être ravi, être aux anges

La tristesse

with one's heart in one's boots
complètement abattu

to hit rock bottom
toucher le fond

to be down in the mouth
être déprimé

to be in the doldrums
avoir le moral à zéro

ⓘ Le terme "doldrums" désigne la zone des calmes équatoriaux, où les vents sont faibles et où les bateaux à voiles ont donc du mal à avancer.

La colère

to hit the ceiling
péter les plombs

to go off at the deep end
piquer une crise

to blow one's top
sortir de ses gonds

to go ballistic
piquer une crise

to be like a red rag to a bull to someone
avoir le don de mettre quelqu'un hors de soi

to get hot under the collar
se mettre en rogne

to be at the end of one's tether
être à bout

ⓘ Littéralement : avoir atteint le bout de sa longe. Quand l'herbe à portée de l'animal attaché est épuisée, il tire sur sa longe pour tenter de brouter plus loin.

Attention: cette expression n'est pas l'équivalent du français "être au bout du rouleau".

La mauvaise humeur

to be like a bear with a sore head
être d'humeur massacrante

to get out of bed on the wrong side
se lever du pied gauche

Les critiques

to drive a coach and horses through something
tailler quelque chose en pièces

to haul someone over the coals
démolir quelqu'un (en le critiquant)

the pot calling the kettle black
l'hôpital qui se moque de la charité

to give someone the rough side of one's tongue
parler brutalement à quelqu'un

to cut someone down to size
remettre quelqu'un à sa place

to pick holes in something
relever des erreurs dans quelque chose

to take a pot shot at someone
lancer une critique à quelqu'un

Les réprimandes

to throw the book at someone
passer un savon à quelqu'un

ⓘ L'expression fait référence au code pénal.

to send someone away with a flea in their ear
envoyer quelqu'un promener

to bite someone's head off
rembarrer quelqu'un

to jump down someone's throat
rabrouer quelqu'un

to have someone's guts for garters
massacrer quelqu'un

ⓘ Cette expression s'emploie toujours sous forme de menace.

to get it in the neck
en prendre pour son grade

La peur

to brick it
avoir les jetons

to get cold feet
avoir la frousse

to scare the pants off someone
faire une peur bleue à quelqu'un

o have one's heart in one's mouth
voir le cœur qui bat la chamade

o get the wind up
voir une peur bleue

.es opinions

o nail one's colours to the mast
fficher ses opinions

ⓘ Au cours d'une bataille navale, un navire voulant abandonner le combat descendait jadis son pavillon en signe de défaite. Impossible de déclarer forfait lorsque le pavillon est cloué au mât.

o get on one's soapbox
aranguer les foules

ⓘ Littéralement : monter sur sa caisse à savon (soapbox), c'est-à-dire sur une tribune improvisée, pour faire un discours.

o be in bed with someone
tre allié avec quelqu'un de façon officieuse

o see eye to eye (with someone)
oir les choses du même œil (que quelqu'un)

o vote with one's feet
ıdiquer sa désapprobation en quittant les lieux

o change horses in midstream
: raviser en cours de route

o stick to one's guns
ester sur ses positions, tenir bon

ⓘ L'expression fait référence au soldat qui continue à tirer au lieu de s'enfuir devant l'ennemi.

o stick one's oar in
ıettre son grain de sel

o put one's pennyworth in/two cents in
ıettre son grain de sel

ıot to pull any punches
e pas y aller de main morte

o give something one's seal of approval
onner son approbation à quelque chose

ıot to mince one's words
e pas mâcher ses mots

o have a change of heart
hanger d'avis

o be out of tune with someone
e pas être d'accord avec quelqu'un

Contrôle et manipulation

o have someone eating out of one's hand
ıire faire ce qu'on veut à quelqu'un

to wrap someone round one's little finger
faire ce qu'on veut de quelqu'un

to be in the saddle
tenir les rênes

to run a tight ship
mener tout le monde à la baguette

to twist someone's arm
exercer une pression sur quelqu'un

La tromperie

a wolf in sheep's clothing
un loup déguisé en agneau

to lead someone up the garden path
duper quelqu'un, faire marcher quelqu'un

to sell someone down the river
trahir quelqu'un, vendre quelqu'un

ⓘ Cette expression idiomatique fait allusion aux esclaves que l'on transportait sur le Mississippi jusqu'aux marchés aux esclaves de la Nouvelle-Orléans.

to pull the wool over someone's eyes
faire croire n'importe quoi à quelqu'un

ⓘ "The wool" était une perruque portée autrefois par les riches. Un voleur ou un plaisantin pouvait les désorienter en tirant la perruque sur leur visage.

L'âge

to be long in the tooth
ne plus être tout jeune

ⓘ On peut estimer l'âge d'un cheval à la longueur de ses dents. En général, plus les dents sont longues, plus le cheval est âgé.

to have been around the block a few times
ne plus être de la première jeunesse

to be over the hill
commencer à se faire vieux

to be as old as the hills
dater de Mathusalem

L'entraide

to bend over backwards
se mettre en quatre

to give someone a hand
donner un coup de main à quelqu'un

to get someone off the hook
tirer quelqu'un d'affaire

to give someone a leg up
donner un coup de pouce à quelqu'un

L'apparence

to look like death warmed up
avoir une mine de déterré

to be knee-high to a grasshopper
être haut comme trois pommes

to look like something the cat brought in
être en piteux état

to look like a million dollars
être superbe

L'argent

to be made of money
être plein aux as, rouler sur l'or

to bring home the bacon
faire bouillir la marmite

to laugh all the way to the bank
s'en mettre plein les poches

to cost an arm and a leg
coûter les yeux de la tête

to pay through the nose for something
payer quelque chose les yeux de la tête

it's daylight robbery
c'est du vol organisé

to cut corners
faire des économies exagérées

to push the boat out
ne pas regarder à la dépense

to throw money around
jeter l'argent par les fenêtres

to go Dutch
payer chacun sa part

to take someone to the cleaners
nettoyer quelqu'un, plumer quelqu'un

La boisson et l'ivresse

to drink like a fish
boire comme un trou

to be on the wagon
être au régime sec

ⓘ À l'origine, cette expression d'origine américaine était "on the water wagon", terme qui désignait le chariot qui transportait la citerne d'eau.

to wet one's whistle
se rincer le gosier

to be three sheets to the wind
avoir du vent dans les voiles

La prise de risques

a leap in the dark
un saut dans l'inconnu

to sail close to the wind
jouer un jeu dangereux

ⓘ Si on navigue au plus près, c'est-à-dire presque contre le vent, le bateau risque de chavirer.

better the devil you know
mieux vaut se contenter de ce que l'on a plutôt que de risquer de trouver pire

ⓘ L'expression anglaise est la forme tronquée du proverbe "better the devil you know than the devil you don't know" : mieux vaut un danger que l'on connaît qu'un danger que l'on ne connaît pas.

on a wing and a prayer
Dieu sait comment

ⓘ Il s'agit d'une référence à une chanson des années 40 à propos d'un pilote d'avion.

to dice with death
risquer sa vie

to go out on a limb
prendre des risques

ⓘ Dans cette expression, l'image est celle d'une personne s'aventurant sur une branche d'arbre.

to skate on thin ice
toucher à un sujet délicat

to stick one's neck out
prendre des risques

Le changement et la continuité

to break the mould
rompre avec la tradition

to turn the tables
retourner la situation

the worm has turned
j'en ai/il en a/etc. assez de me/se/etc. laisser mener par le bout du nez

to be in a rut
être enlisé dans la routine

to turn the clock back
revenir en arrière

you can't teach an old dog new tricks
on ne peut pas apprendre un nouveau métier à quelqu'un une fois passé un certain âge

to turn over a new leaf
s'acheter une conduite

ⓘ Contrairement aux apparences, cette expression ne signifie pas "tourner la page".

Les ressemblances et les différences

to be cut from the same cloth
être coulé dans le même moule

to be as alike as two peas in a pod
se ressembler comme deux gouttes d'eau

it's a different kettle of fish
c'est une autre affaire

to be poles apart
être diamétralement opposés

to be like chalk and cheese
c'est le jour et la nuit

La supériorité

to be head and shoulders above someone
surpasser quelqu'un

to have someone for breakfast
ne faire qu'une bouchée de quelqu'un

to knock spots off someone
être bien supérieur à quelqu'un

to put someone/something in the shade
éclipser quelqu'un/quelque chose

to make mincemeat of someone
démolir quelqu'un, écraser quelqu'un

to wipe the floor with someone
ne faire qu'une bouchée de quelqu'un

La compréhension et l'incompréhension

to get one's head around something
piger quelque chose

the penny dropped
j'ai/il a/etc. fini par comprendre

to put two and two together
faire le rapprochement

to get the wrong end of the stick
mal comprendre

to get one's wires crossed
mal se comprendre

S'informer

to pick someone's brains
avoir recours aux lumières de quelqu'un

to have one's ear to the ground
se tenir aux écoutes

ⓘ Les Indiens d'Amérique sont souvent représentés l'oreille au sol en train d'estimer la position de personnes ou d'animaux.

to put out feelers
tâter le terrain

ⓘ Les "feelers" sont les antennes d'un insecte.

to keep abreast of something
se tenir au courant de quelque chose

to see how the land lies
tâter le terrain

to get wind of something
avoir vent de quelque chose

Savoir

to know one's onions
connaître son affaire

ⓘ Cette expression n'a rien à voir avec "s'occuper de ses oignons".

to know something like the back of one's hand
connaître quelque chose comme sa poche

to hear something on the grapevine
apprendre quelque chose par le téléphone arabe

ⓘ Les premières lignes télégraphiques aux États-Unis étaient si mal installées que parfois les fils s'entremêlaient et l'ensemble ressemblait à des pieds de vigne. D'où le terme "grapevine telegraph" qui est à l'origine de l'expression.

to read someone like a book
savoir toujours ce que pense quelqu'un

to hear something from the horse's mouth
apprendre quelque chose de source sûre

ⓘ Pour se faire une idée de l'âge d'un cheval, la meilleure façon est de lui examiner les dents.

to be in the picture
être au courant

La détermination

to grasp the nettle
prendre le taureau par les cornes

to leave no stone unturned
remuer ciel et terre

to bite the bullet
serrer les dents

ⓘ Littéralement : mordre la balle. Lorsque les produits anesthésiques n'existaient pas, les médecins des armées demandaient à leurs patients de mordre une balle de fusil de façon à mieux supporter la douleur.

to put one's foot down
faire preuve de fermeté

come hell or high water
quoi qu'il arrive

La parole

to shoot the breeze
bavarder

to bend someone's ear
casser les oreilles à quelqu'un, pomper l'air à quelqu'un

to talk through one's hat
parler à tort et à travers

to talk the hind legs off a donkey
être bavard comme une pie

to shoot one's mouth off
ouvrir sa grande gueule, l'ouvrir

to spin a yarn
raconter une histoire à dormir debout

to put a sock in it
la fermer

to spill the beans
révéler un secret

ⓘ Il faut noter que l'expression anglaise ne signifie pas nécessairement "trahir un secret".

to be all mouth and no trousers
être une grande gueule

:o talk nineteen to the dozen
'tre un vrai moulin à paroles

:o chew the fat
ailler une bavette

:o take the floor
rendre la parole

:o pass the time of day
avarder

L'effort

:o bust a gut
e décarcasser, se donner un mal de chien

:o sing for one's supper
lonner quelque chose en échange

:o put one's shoulder to the wheel
e mettre à l'œuvre avec énergie

La réussite et l'échec

:o be cooking with gas
narcher très fort

ⓘ Selon une vieille réclame américaine, rien ne valait la cuisine au gaz.

.o bring the house down
asser la baraque, faire un tabac

ⓘ Il s'agit d'une allusion aux applaudissements qui font trembler les murs d'une salle de spectacle.

o set the world alight
aire sensation

o go belly up
aire faillite

o bite the dust
nordre la poussière, être battu

o go by the board
tre abandonné, tomber à l'eau

o go great guns
archer très fort

ⓘ Le terme "great guns" désignait l'artillerie lourde par opposition aux armes légères.

to come up roses
marcher parfaitement

to make the grade
se montrer à la hauteur

ⓘ Le terme "grade" désigne un tronçon de voie ferrée en pente raide. Aux États-Unis, "to make the grade" se disait d'un train qui pouvait monter cette côte.

La folie

to be out to lunch
débloquer

to have a screw loose
avoir une case de vide

to be barking mad
être complètement cinglé

to lose one's marbles
perdre la boule

Les difficultés et les problèmes

out of the frying pan into the fire
tomber de Charybde en Scylla

ⓘ L'expression anglaise s'utilise beaucoup plus fréquemment que sa traduction habituelle "tomber de Charybde en Scylla".

to go through the mill
en baver

ⓘ L'image est celle du grain écrasé par la meule du moulin.

to go to hell and back
connaître des moments très difficiles (mais s'en sortir)

to paint oneself into a corner
se mettre dans une impasse

to tie oneself in knots
s'embrouiller

to shoot oneself in the foot
faire une gaffe

to score an own goal
se faire du tort à soi-même

to leave someone holding the baby
refiler le bébé à quelqu'un

to cook someone's goose
couler quelqu'un

to pull the rug from under someone's feet
faire capoter les projets de quelqu'un

a hard nut to crack
un problème difficile à résoudre

a hot potato
un sujet délicat

to be an albatross around someone's neck
être un boulet pour quelqu'un

ⓘ Dans le poème de Coleridge *The Rime of the Ancient Mariner* (La Chanson du vieux marin), le mauvais sort s'abat sur un navire après qu'un marin a abattu un albatros. L'équipage force alors le coupable à porter l'oiseau mort autour du cou.

to cut off one's nose to spite one's face
se punir soi-même

La vanité

to be too big for one's boots
avoir les chevilles qui enflent

to blow one's own trumpet
chanter ses propres louanges

to throw one's weight around
faire l'important

to think one is the bee's knees
ne pas se prendre pour n'importe qui

Les relations

to play the field
papillonner, avoir de nombreuses aventures amoureuses

to have been left on the shelf
être en passe de devenir vieille fille

to tie the knot
se marier

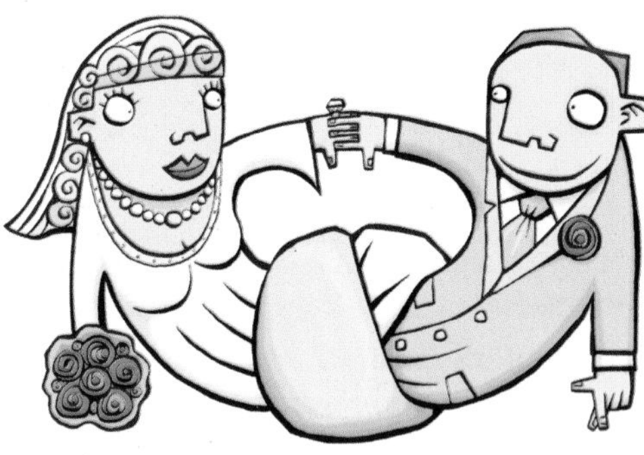

to take the plunge
se marier

to sow one's wild oats
jeter sa gourme

to make a pass at someone
draguer quelqu'un

to get one's oats
prendre son pied

Les gaffes

to have egg on one's face
s'être couvert de ridicule

to blot one's copybook
se faire mal voir

to put one's foot in one's mouth
faire une gaffe

Le passé

to rake over the ashes
remuer le passé

it's a blast from the past
ça nous ramène des années en arrière

to put the clock back
revenir en arrière

to go down memory lane
se plonger dans ses souvenirs

it's all water under the bridge
c'est du passé

La revanche et la vengeance

to pay someone back in their own coin
rendre à quelqu'un la monnaie de sa pièce

to get one's own back
prendre sa revanche

to give someone a taste of their own medicine
rendre à quelqu'un la monnaie de sa pièce

La surprise

to blow someone away
en boucher un coin à quelqu'un

o come out of left field
tre complètement inattendu

ⓘ Il s'agit d'une expression issue du monde du base-ball : les joueurs renvoient moins de balles dans la partie du terrain appelée "left field", d'où l'effet de surprise quand cela se produit.

o raise eyebrows
aire tiquer, provoquer des froncements de sourcils

o knock someone for six
basourdir quelqu'un

ⓘ Il s'agit d'une expression issue du monde du cricket.

ut of the blue
e manière complètement inattendue

ⓘ Dans cette expression, "the blue" fait référence au ciel bleu. L'image est celle d'un éclair qui frappe un jour de beau temps.

.es secrets et les confidences

etween you, me and the gatepost
ntre nous soit dit

o keep something under one's hat
arder quelque chose pour soi

o be in on something
tre au courant de quelque chose

num's the word
otus et bouche cousue

o keep something under wraps
arder quelque chose secret

.e travail

o be up to one's eyeballs
re débordé de travail

to do the donkey work
faire le sale boulot

to work one's finger to the bone
se tuer à la tâche

to keep one's nose to the grindstone
travailler d'arrache-pied

to pull one's weight
faire sa part de travail

to burn the midnight oil
travailler tard dans la nuit

L'idéalisme et les chimères

to live in a fool's paradise
se bercer d'illusions

to be pie in the sky
relever de l'utopie

ⓘ Il s'agit d'une formule extraite d'une chanson américaine datant de 1906. La chanson disait "you'll get pie in the sky when you die" (tu auras le droit à de la tarte quand tu seras au ciel).

to build castles in the air
bâtir des châteaux en Espagne

to tilt at windmills
se battre contre des moulins à vent

to live in cloud-cuckoo-land
ne pas avoir les pieds sur terre

ⓘ Dans la comédie d'Aristophane Les Oiseaux (414 av. J.-C.), "Cloud-Cuckoo-Land" est l'adaptation anglaise de la ville Néphélococcygie (en français, "Coucouville-les-Nuées"), une ville aérienne fondée entre ciel et terre par les oiseaux pour faire obstacle aux relations entre les hommes et les dieux de l'Olympe.

to set the world to rights
refaire le monde

La violence et les menaces

to put the boot in
donner des coups de pied

ⓘ Au sens figuré cette expression signifie "remuer le couteau dans la plaie".

to beat the living daylights out of someone
tabasser quelqu'un

I'll have his guts for garters!
je vais en faire de la chair à pâté!

to make mincemeat out of someone
ne faire qu'une bouchée de quelqu'un

to settle someone's hash
régler son compte à quelqu'un

to tan someone's hide
tanner le cuir à quelqu'un

Les décisions et l'indécision

to be caught between a rock and a hard place
se trouver face à un dilemme

to sleep on it
remettre sa décision au lendemain

to be in a cleft stick
se trouver dans une impasse

to think on one's feet
réfléchir vite et bien

to um and aah
hésiter, se tâter

ⓘ Les "um" et les "aah" sont censés être les sons émis par ceux qui réfléchissent et essaient de parvenir à une décision.

La mort

to pop one's clogs
casser sa pipe

to be pushing up the daisies
manger les pissenlits par la racine

to be as dead as a doornail
être mort et bien mort

to kick the bucket
casser sa pipe

250 Essential French Idioms

250 Essential French Idioms

Anger

éter les plombs
blow one's top

> ⓘ Here, the word "plombs" refers to the fuses that melt in order to avoid a short-circuit.

ortir de ses gonds
fly off the handle

> ⓘ The image is that of a door that has come off its hinges.

e fâcher tout rouge
go up the wall

'ai la moutarde qui me monte au nez
'm beginning to lose my temper

nonter sur ses grands chevaux
get on one's high horse

rendre la mouche
fly off the handle

> ⓘ This expression is close to "quelle mouche vous a piqué?" (what's with you?). The idea is that a person's sudden outburst is the result of having being stung by an insect.

tre hors de soi
be beside oneself (with rage)

tre vert de rage
be livid with rage

voir les nerfs en pelote
be on edge, to be nervy

> ⓘ Although this expression is reminiscent of the English "to be a bundle of nerves", it is used to describe someone's exasperation, and not a permanent state.

e mettre en boule
fly off the handle

e mettre en pétard
blow one's top

e lever du pied gauche
get out of bed on the wrong side

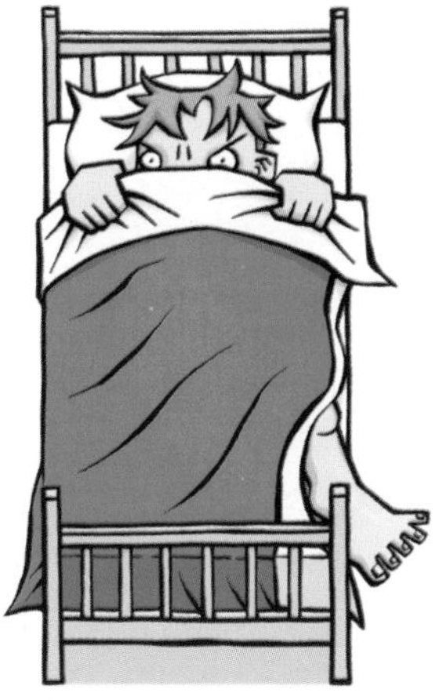

être soupe au lait
to flare up very easily

> ⓘ This expression comes from the fact that soup with added milk boils over quickly.

ne pas être à prendre avec des pincettes
to be like a bear with a sore head

> ⓘ Originally the expression "être à prendre avec des pincettes" ("to have to be handled with tongs") was used about people who were unspeakably dirty or immoral.

avoir la tête près du bonnet
to have a short fuse

être de mauvais poil
to be in a bad mood

Telling someone off

faire passer un mauvais quart d'heure à quelqu'un
to give someone a bad time

remonter les bretelles à quelqu'un
to bawl someone out

> ⓘ The image is that of someone shaking someone else violently by their braces.

passer un savon à quelqu'un
to give someone a telling-off

souffler dans les bronches à quelqu'un
to bawl someone out

fusiller quelqu'un du regard
to look daggers at someone

Criticizing

casser du sucre sur le dos de quelqu'un
to bad-mouth someone

tailler un costard à quelqu'un
to slag someone off

> ⓘ The idea here is that once you have a bad reputation, it is difficult to lose it, in the same way that a suit cannot be altered once it has been cut to a certain shape.

descendre quelqu'un en flammes
to shoot someone down in flames

être une langue de vipère
to be a malicious gossip

il ne faut pas cracher dans la soupe
don't bite the hand that feeds you

il se plaint que la mariée est trop belle
he doesn't know how lucky he is

Annoyance

casser les pieds à quelqu'un
to do someone's head in

courir sur le haricot à quelqu'un
to get up someone's nose

rendre quelqu'un chèvre
to drive someone up the wall

faire tourner quelqu'un en bourrique
to drive someone round the bend

Getting along (and not)

s'entendre comme larrons en foire
to be as thick as thieves

être comme cul et chemise
to be inseparable

être comme les doigts de la main
to be very close

être dans les petits papiers de quelqu'un
to be in someone's good books

ⓘ Here "petits papiers" refers to fictitious notes that people would keep about who they liked and disliked.

je ne peux pas le voir en peinture
I can't stand the sight of him

se regarder en chiens de faïence
to glare at one another

ⓘ This is a reference to china dogs which were sometimes used to decorate mantelpieces, one being placed at either end.

je l'ai dans le nez
he gets up my nose

il me sort par les trous de nez
I can't stand the sight of him

il y a de l'eau dans le gaz
there's trouble brewing

entre eux le torchon brûle
they're at loggerheads

ⓘ Even though most French speakers think that the literal translation of this expression is "the dishcloth is on fire", in this context the word "torchon" originally referred to a small torch and not to a dishcloth.

Love

avoir le coup de foudre
to fall in love at first sight

être un bourreau des cœurs
to be a ladykiller

avoir un cœur d'artichaut
to be fickle (in love)

ⓘ The full form of this expression used to be "cœur d'artichaut, une feuille pour tout le monde" (in an artichoke heart, there's a leaf for everyone), suggesting fickleness in love.

avoir quelqu'un dans la peau
to be crazy about someone

être mordu
to be madly in love

en pincer pour quelqu'un
to be crazy about someone

ⓘ It is believed that this expression might come from the image of someone serenading their loved one while playing a stringed instrument.

avoir un faible pour quelqu'un
to have a soft spot for someone

Truth and lies

mentir comme un arracheur de dents
to be a compulsive liar

ⓘ In the days before anaesthetic, patients were wise enough not to believe the dentist when he said "relax, you won't feel a thing".

raconter des salades
to tell fibs

mener quelqu'un en bateau
to take someone for a ride

faire avaler des couleuvres à quelqu'un
to take someone in

ne pas savoir si c'est du lard ou du cochon
o wonder what to make of it

> ⓘ This expression – the literal meaning of which is "not to know if this is bacon or pork"– is used in situations where the significance of an event is open to a few different interpretations.

mener quelqu'un par le bout du nez
o have someone wrapped around one's little finger

une histoire à dormir debout
cock-and-bull story

Appearance

être une grande perche
o be a beanpole

avoir un œil qui dit merde à l'autre
o have a squint

être haut comme trois pommes
o be knee-high to a grasshopper

avoir les dents du bonheur
o have a gap between one's teeth

se mettre sur son trente-et-un
o get all dressed up

être tiré à quatre épingles
o be dressed up to the nines

> ⓘ This is a reference to the fact that four pins are needed to stretch a piece of fabric and eliminate creases.

avoir les cheveux en bataille
o have dishevelled hair

être fagoté comme l'as de pique
o be dressed any old how

c'est une armoire à glace
he's built like a tank

> ⓘ A variant of this expression is "être bâti comme une armoire normande" – to be built like a Normandy wardrobe – such items of furniture being particularly large and sturdy.

être laid comme un pou
to be as ugly as sin

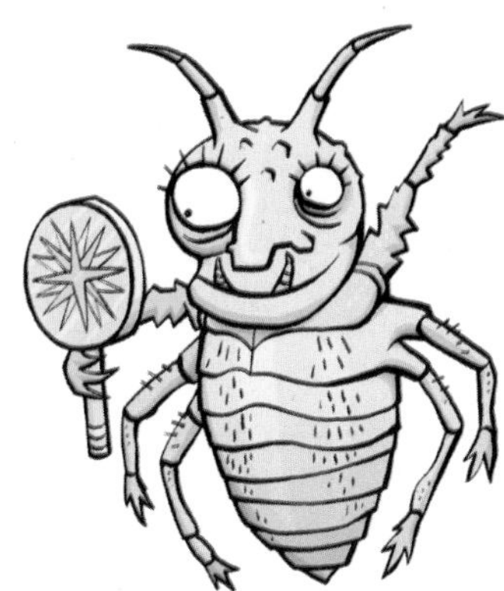

être joli comme un cœur
to be as pretty as a picture

avoir une mine de déterré
to look like death warmed up

Embarrassment

être dans ses petits souliers
to feel awkward

> ⓘ In this expression embarrassment is likened to the sort of discomfort one experiences when wearing shoes that are too small.

il ne savait plus où se mettre
he didn't know where to put himself

être rouge comme une tomate
to be as red as a beetroot

Fear and worry

ne pas en mener large
to have one's heart in one's boots

serrer les fesses
to have the wind up

avoir les jetons
to have the jitters

avoir une peur bleue
to be scared to death

avoir les foies
to be scared out of one's wits

donner la chair de poule à quelqu'un
to make someone's flesh creep

avoir les fesses qui font bravo
to have the jitters

> ⓘ In this colloquial expression, the imaginary clapping motion of someone's buttocks conveys the notion of fear in a very colourful way.

se faire des cheveux (blancs)
to worry oneself (sick)

se faire un sang d'encre
to worry oneself (sick)

ⓘ This expression – which means literally "to worry so much that one's blood turns the colour of ink" – is similar to "se faire du mauvais sang" (in both cases worry is believed to alter the quality of one's blood) and to "se faire de la bile" (to produce bile).

Directness

ne pas y aller par quatre chemins
to go straight to the point

ne pas tourner autour du pot
not to beat around the bush

ⓘ The expression evokes the directness of someone going straight to the cooking pot to check its contents instead of wondering what's for dinner.

ne pas y aller de main morte
not to pull one's punches

ne pas mâcher ses mots
not to mince one's words

être franc du collier
to be very frank and open

ne pas y aller avec le dos de la cuillère
not to go in for half-measures

ⓘ Literally, "not to dish things out using the back of a spoon".

Speaking and keeping silent

tenir la jambe à quelqu'un
to bore someone with one's talk

être un moulin à paroles
to be a chatterbox

soûler quelqu'un
to bore someone silly

avoir la langue bien pendue
to have the gift of the gab

ne pas avoir sa langue dans sa poche
never to be at a loss for words

discuter le bout de gras
to chew the fat

tailler une bavette
to have a chat

se mettre à table
to come clean

cracher le morceau
to spill the beans

ⓘ The origin of the expressions "se mettre à table" and "manger le morceau", which both mean "to confess", dates back to the time when suspects were deliberately starved by the police in order to force them to confess. They were only given food once they had agreed to confess, hence the expression.

vendre la mèche
to give the game away

ne pas desserrer les dents
not to open one's mouth

avoir perdu sa langue
to have lost one's tongue

tenir sa langue
to keep a secret

Surprise

couper le sifflet à quelqu'un
to shut someone up

en boucher un coin à quelqu'un
to take the wind out of someone's sails

en rester comme deux ronds de flan
to be flabbergasted

tomber de haut
to be dumbfounded

tomber des nues
to be flabbergasted

je n'en reviens pas
I can't get over it

y a de quoi tomber à la renverse
's staggering

Iappiness

tre au septième ciel
be in seventh heaven

tre aux anges
be walking on air

tre comme un coq en pâte
be in clover

tre heureux comme un poisson dans l'eau
be in one's element

tre bien dans ses baskets
be sorted

Sadness

tre malheureux comme les pierres
be utterly miserable

royer du noir
be down in the dumps

tre au trente-sixième dessous
be extremely depressed

leurer comme une madeleine
cry one's heart out

ⓘ This expression has nothing to do with the fairy cakes called "madeleines" but is a biblical allusion to Mary Magdalene, who cried over the body of Christ after his crucifixion.

ller comme une âme en peine
wander around like a lost soul

voir le cafard
feel down

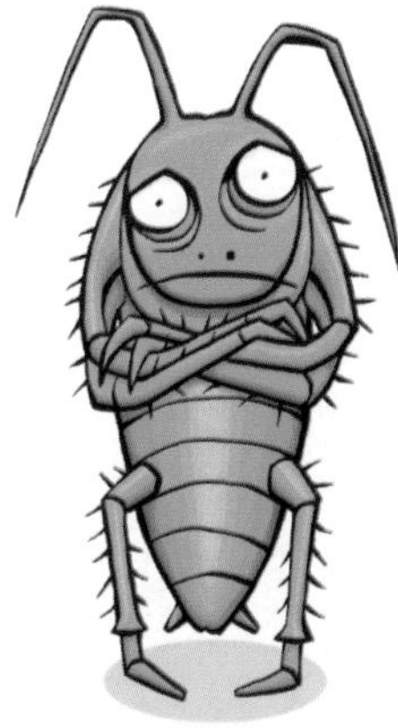

voir une tête d'enterrement
look sombre

voir le moral à zéro
be feeling down in the dumps

Laughter

e fendre la pipe
split one's sides (laughing)

tre plié en deux
be doubled up with laughter

rire comme un bossu/comme une baleine
to laugh one's head off

ⓘ It is believed that "rire comme une baleine" (to laugh like a whale) might have derived from "se tordre comme une baleine de parapluie retourné", playing on the words "se tordre", which means both "to bend" and "to laugh" (in colloquial language), and "baleine", which of course means "whale", but which also means the rib of an umbrella.

rire à s'en décrocher la mâchoire
to split one's sides (laughing)

Madness

il ne tourne pas rond
he's not all there

travailler du chapeau
to have a screw loose

avoir un petit vélo dans la tête
to be off one's rocker

perdre la boule
to go round the bend

être marteau
to be nuts

être tombé sur la tête
to have a screw loose

avoir une araignée au plafond

to have bats in the belfry

être timbré
to be cracked

Stupidity

il n'a pas inventé l'eau chaude/la poudre
he'll never set the Thames on fire

être bête à manger du foin
to be as thick as two short planks

ⓘ This expression plays on the two meanings of the word "bête"; as a noun it means "animal" but as an adjective it means "stupid".

être bête comme ses pieds
to be unbelievably stupid

raisonner comme un tambour
to talk through one's hat

ⓘ This expression plays on the verbs "raisonner" (to think) and "résonner" (to echo). The hollowness of the drum (tambour) also suggests a person of little intelligence.

avoir une case de vide
to have a screw loose

avoir une cervelle de moineau
to be feather-brained

être dur à la détente
to be slow on the uptake

ⓘ The image is that of a weapon that is difficult to fire because of a stiff trigger.

il comprend vite mais il faut lui expliquer longtemps
he's a bit slow on the uptake

il est un peu bas de plafond
he's not the sharpest knife in the drawer

en tenir une couche
to be thick as two short planks

ce n'est pas une flèche
he'll never set the Thames on fire

Hunger and eating

avoir l'estomac dans les talons
to be ravenous

avoir les crocs
to be famished

avoir la dalle
to be hungry

avoir une faim de loup
to be ravenous

avoir les dents du fond qui baignent
to have stuffed oneself

tu as les yeux plus grands que le ventre
your eyes are bigger than your belly

manger sur le pouce
to have a quick snack

manger avec un lance-pierres
to gulp one's meal down

dîner avec les chevaux de bois
to go without food

ⓘ This humorous expression means literally "to have dinner with the wooden horses". The wooden horses in question are those of a merry-go-round which, of course do not need to be fed.

Drinking

boire comme un trou
to drink like a fish

avoir la gueule de bois
to be hungover

avoir du vent dans les voiles
to be three sheets to the wind

ⓘ This expression likens the teetering drunkard to a ship that is buffeted by the wind.

lever le coude
to booze

ne pas sucer que de la glace
to drink like a fish

s'en jeter un derrière la cravate
to knock back a drink

se rincer la dalle
to have a drink

ⓘ In traditional French slang the word "dalle" means "throat".

avoir une casquette en plomb
to be badly hungover

avoir mis ses chaussures à bascule
to be swaying

Doing things easily

ce n'est pas la mer à boire
it's no big deal

c'est du gâteau
it's a piece of cake

faire quelque chose les doigts dans le nez
to do something very easily

e n'est pas le bout du monde
's no big deal

ⓘ Do not confuse with the expression "ce n'est pas la fin du monde", which means "it isn't the end of the world".

'est simple comme bonjour
's as easy as pie

.eaving

rendre ses jambes à son cou
take to one's heels

nettre les bouts/les voiles
skedaddle

rendre le large
clear off

rendre la poudre d'escampette
make off

ⓘ The word "escampette" only occurs in this expression and derives from "escamper", an old French verb which means "to flee".

e faire la malle
clear off

iler à l'anglaise
sneak off, to take French leave

ⓘ Interestingly, but unsurprisingly, the French and the English credit each other with this type of rude behaviour.

rendre ses cliques et ses claques
pack one's bags and go

Work and effort

mettre la main à la pâte
to lend a hand

ⓘ In this expression the word "pâte" refers to the dough prepared and kneaded by bakers.

retrousser ses manches
to roll up one's sleeves

en mettre un coup
to pull out all the stops

mettre les bouchées doubles
to really get a move on

être un bourreau de travail
to be a workaholic

un travail de Romain
a Herculean task

se mettre en quatre pour faire quelque chose
to do one's utmost to do something

faire des pieds et des mains pour faire quelque chose
to move heaven and earth to do something

donner un coup de main à quelqu'un
to give someone a hand

rendre son tablier
to hand in one's resignation

ⓘ This expression means literally "to return one's apron" and was originally used about unhappy domestic staff quitting their job on the spur of the moment.

ne pas avoir les deux pieds dans le même sabot
to have a lot of initiative

Laziness

avoir les côtes en long
to be bone-idle

ⓘ Literally, this expression means "to have vertical ribs", a condition that would make it impossible to bend over and do any kind of physical work.

se tourner les pouces
to twiddle one's thumbs

peigner la girafe
to do damn all

ne pas se fouler la rate
not to strain oneself

les avoir palmées
to be a complete layabout

ⓘ This expression means "to have webbed hands", a condition that would, obviously, make work somewhat difficult.

avoir un poil dans la main
to be workshy

Success

marcher comme sur des roulettes
to be going very smoothly

casser la baraque
to bring the house down

faire un malheur
to be a sensation

avoir le vent en poupe
to have the wind in one's sails

Failure

battre de l'aile
to be in a bad way

faire chou blanc
to draw a blank

tomber à l'eau
to fall through

s'en aller en eau de boudin
to go down the drain

rester le bec dans l'eau
to be left high and dry

c'est la fin des haricots
we've had it now

ⓘ It is believed that this expression came to describe a hopeless situation because beans used to be the main staple of a soldier's diet and running out of beans was therefore considered a disaster.

Money

ne pas attacher son chien avec des saucisses
to be tight with one's money

ⓘ Obviously, using link sausage as a lead for one's dog would be a sign that one doesn't care too much about money.

être près de ses sous
to be a penny-pincher

avoir des oursins dans le porte-monnaie
to be tight-fisted

ⓘ Literally, "to have sea urchins in one's purse". The idea is that someone does not want to put his hand into his purse because the spikes of the sea urchins might hurt him.

coûter les yeux de la tête/la peau des fesses
to cost an arm and a leg

jeter l'argent par les fenêtres
to throw money down the drain

l'argent lui fond entre les doigts
money runs through his fingers

être un panier percé
to be a spendthrift

plaie d'argent n'est pas mortelle
money isn't everything

être plein aux as
to be rolling in it

rouler sur l'or
to be rolling in money

tirer le diable par la queue
to be hard up

mener la vie de château
to lead a life of luxury

s'en mettre plein les poches
to make a packet

un chèque en bois
a rubber cheque

être sans un radis
to be stony broke

être raide (comme un passe-lacets)
to be stony broke

être sur la paille
to be on one's uppers

plumer quelqu'un
to fleece someone

être payé au lance-pierres
to be paid peanuts

faire bouillir la marmite
to bring home the bacon

obtenir quelque chose à l'œil
to get something for free

obtenir quelque chose pour une bouchée de pain
to get something for next to nothing

Enjoying oneself

s'en payer une tranche
to have a whale of a time

s'éclater comme une bête
to have a wild time

faire la noce
to live it up

Vanity

avoir la grosse tête
to be big-headed

il se croit le premier moutardier du pape
he thinks he's the bee's knees

se hausser du col
to blow one's own trumpet

elle a les chevilles qui enflent
she's getting too big for her boots

il ne se mouche pas du pied
he thinks he's the cat's whiskers

il pète plus haut que son cul
he thinks he's the business

se croire sorti de la cuisse de Jupiter
to think one is God's gift (to mankind)

ⓘ This expression is an allusion to the fact that in Graeco-Roman mythology, the god Dionysus/Bacchus was born from Zeus/Jupiter's thigh.

Authority and obedience

mener quelqu'un à la baguette
to rule someone with a rod of iron

obéir au doigt et à l'œil (à quelqu'un)
to do exactly as one is told (by someone)

avoir le petit doigt sur la couture du pantalon
to toe the line

ⓘ This expression means literally "to have one's little finger on the seams of one's trouser leg". It is an allusion to the position of a soldier standing to attention and taking orders from his superiors.

faire les quatre volontés de quelqu'un
to pander to someone's every whim

tenir la dragée haute à quelqu'un
to make someone dance to one's tune

manger dans la main de quelqu'un
to be eating out of someone's hand

Inferiority

ses rivaux ne lui arrivent pas à la cheville
none of his rivals can touch him

ça ne vaut pas un clou
it's not worth a bean

c'est du pipi de chat
it's a load of bilge

ne faire qu'une bouchée de quelqu'un
to make short work of someone

Similarities and differences

être le jour et la nuit
to be like chalk and cheese

c'est du pareil au même
it's the same difference

c'est bonnet blanc et blanc bonnet
it's six of one and half a dozen of the other

c'est une autre paire de manches
that's a different kettle of fish

c'est kif-kif
it's all the same

ⓘ This expression comes from the Arabic "kif", which means "like", and entered the French language via the colonial soldiers stationed in North Africa.

Death

casser sa pipe
to kick the bucket

passer l'arme à gauche
to snuff it

ⓘ The expression "passer l'arme à gauche", meaning "to die", comes from military terminology, referring to the position in which soldiers hold their weapons when they stand at ease; this is because in French the expression for "to stand at ease" is "être au repos" which can also mean "to be at rest", ie dead.

manger les pissenlits par la racine
to be pushing up the daisies

lâcher la rampe
to kick the bucket

partir les pieds devant
to leave feet first

avaler son bulletin de naissance
to cash in one's chips

Verbes anglais irréguliers

Liste des verbes irréguliers

Les américanismes sont indiqués par *. Les formes peu courantes, archaïques ou littéraires sont données entre parenthèses. Les traductions ci-dessous ne sont pas restrictives et ne donnent qu'un des sens de base.

Infinitif		Prétérit	Participe passé
arise	*surgir*	arose	arisen
awake	*s'éveiller*	awoke, awaked	awoken, (awaked)
bear	*porter*	bore	borne
beat	*battre*	beat	beaten
become	*devenir*	became	become
befall	*arriver*	befell	befallen
beget	*engendrer*	begot	begotten
begin	*commencer*	began	begun
behold	*apercevoir*	beheld	beheld
bend	*courber*	bent	bent
bereave	*priver*	bereaved	bereft
beseech	*implorer*	besought	besought
bet	*parier*	bet, betted	bet, betted
bid	*offrir*	bid	bid
bid	*commander*	bade	bidden
bind	*attacher*	bound	bound
bite	*mordre*	bit	bitten
bleed	*saigner*	bled	bled
blow	*souffler*	blew	blown
break	*casser*	broke	broken
breed	*élever*	bred	bred
bring	*apporter*	brought	brought
broad-cast	*diffuser*	broadcast	broadcast
build	*construire*	built	built
burn	*brûler*	burnt, burned	burnt, burned
burst	*éclater*	burst	burst
buy	*acheter*	bought	bought
cast	*jeter*	cast	cast
catch	*attraper*	caught	caught
chide	*gronder*	chid, chided	chid, (chidden), chided
choose	*choisir*	chose	chosen
cleave	*fendre*	clove, cleft	cloven, cleft
cleave	*adhérer*	cleaved, (clave)	cleaved
cling	*s'accrocher à*	clung	clung
clothe	*habiller*	clothed, (clad)	clothed, (clad)
come	*venir*	came	come
cost	*coûter*	cost	cost
creep	*ramper*	crept	crept
crow	*chanter*	crowed, (crew)	crowed
cut	*couper*	cut	cut
dare	*oser*	dared, (durst)	dared, (durst)
deal	*traiter*	dealt	dealt
dig	*fouiller*	dug	dug
dive	*plonger*	dived, dove*	dived
draw	*dessiner, tirer*	drew	drawn
dream	*rêver*	dreamt, dreamed	dreamt, dreamed
drink	*boire*	drank	drunk
drive	*conduire*	drove	driven
dwell	*demeurer*	dwelt, dwelled	dwelt, dwelled
eat	*manger*	ate	eaten
fall	*tomber*	fell	fallen
feed	*nourrir*	fed	fed
feel	*sentir*	felt	felt
fight	*battre*	fought	fought
find	*trouver*	found	found
fit	*aller à*	fit*, fitted	fit*, fitted
flee	*s'envoler*	fled	fled
fling	*lancer*	flung	flung
fly	*voler*	flew	flown
forbid	*interdire*	forbad(e)	forbidden
forget	*oublier*	forgot	forgotten
forgive	*pardonner*	forgave	forgiven
forsake	*abandonner*	forsook	forsaken
freeze	*geler*	froze	frozen
get	*obtenir*	got	got, gotten*
gild	*dorer*	gilt, gilded	gilt, gilded
gird	*ceindre*	girt, girded	girt, girded
give	*donner*	gave	given
go	*aller*	went	gone
grind	*grincer*	ground	ground
grow	*pousser*	grew	grown
hang	*accrocher, suspendre*	hung, hanged	hung, hanged
hear	*entendre*	heard	heard
hew	*tailler*	hewed	hewn, hewed
hide	*cacher*	hid	hidden
hit	*frapper*	hit	hit
hold	*tenir*	held	held
hurt	*blesser*	hurt	hurt
keep	*garder*	kept	kept
kneel	*s'agenouiller*	knelt, kneeled	knelt, kneeled
knit	*tricoter*	knit, knitted	knit, knitted
know	*savoir, connaître*	knew	known
lay	*coucher*	laid	laid
lead	*mener*	led	led
lean	*s'appuyer*	leant, leaned	leant, leaned
leap	*sauter*	leapt, leaped	leapt, leaped
learn	*apprendre*	learnt, learned	learnt, learned
leave	*laisser*	left	left
lend	*prêter*	lent	lent
let	*laisser*	let	let
lie	*coucher*	lay	lain
light	*allumer*	lit	lit
lose	*perdre*	lost	lost

Infinitif		Prétérit	Participe passé
make	*faire*	made	made
mean	*signifier*	meant	meant
meet	*rencontrer*	met	met
melt	*fondre*	melted	melted,
mow	*faucher*	mowed	mown, mowed
pay	*payer*	paid	paid
plead	*plaider*	pled*, pleaded	pled*, pleaded
put	*poser*	put	put
quit	*quitter*	quit, (quitted)	quit, (quitted)
read	*lire*	read	read
rend	*déchirer*	rent	rent
rid	*débarrasser*	rid, (ridded)	rid
ride	*monter à*	rode	ridden
ring	*sonner*	rang	rung
rise	*se lever*	rose	risen
run	*courir*	ran	run
saw	*scier*	sawed	sawn, sawed
say	*dire*	said	said
see	*voir*	saw	seen
seek	*chercher*	sought	sought
sell	*vendre*	sold	sold
send	*envoyer*	sent	sent
set	*mettre*	set	set
sew	*coudre*	sewed	sewn, sewed
shake	*secouer*	shook	shaken
shear	*tondre*	sheared	shorn, sheared
shed	*perdre*	shed	shed
shine	*briller*	shone	shone
shoe	*chausser*	shod	shod
shoot	*abattre, tirer*	shot	shot
show	*montrer*	showed	shown, showed
shrink	*rétrécir*	shrank	shrunk
shut	*fermer*	shut	shut
sing	*chanter*	sang	sung
sink	*couler*	sank	sunk
sit	*s'asseoir*	sat	sat
slay	*tuer*	slew	slain
sleep	*dormir*	slept	slept
slide	*glisser*	slid	slid
sling	*lancer*	slung	slung
slink	*se glisser furtuvement*	slunk	slunk
slit	*fendre*	slit	slit
smell	*sentir*	smelt, smelled	smelt, smelled
smite	*frapper*	smote	smitten
sneak	*se faufiler,*	snuck*, sneaked	snuck*, sneaked
sow	*semer*	sowed	sown, sowed
speak	*parler*	spoke	spoken
speed	*aller vite*	sped, speeded	sped, speeded
spell	*écrire*	spelt, spelled	spelt, spelled
spend	*dépenser*	spent	spent
spill	*renverser*	spilt, spilled	spilt, spilled
spin	*filer*	spun	spun
spit	*cracher*	spat, spit*	spat, spit*
split	*se briser*	split	split
spoil	*abîmer*	spoilt, spoiled	spoilt, spoiled
spread	*étendre*	spread	spread
spring	*bondir*	sprang	sprung
stand	*se tenir*	stood	stood
steal	*voler*	stole	stolen
stick	*enfoncer, coller*	stuck	stuck
sting	*piquer*	stung	stung
stink	*puer*	stank	stunk
strew	*répandre*	strewed	strewn, strewed
stride	*marcher à grands pas*	strode	stridden
strike	*frapper*	struck	struck
string	*enfiler*	strung	strung
strive	*s'efforcer*	strove	striven
swear	*jurer*	swore	sworn
sweat	*suer*	sweat*, sweated	sweat*, sweated
sweep	*balayer*	swept	swept
swell	*gonfler*	swelled	swollen, swelled
swim	*nager*	swam	swum
swing	*se balancer*	swung	swung
take	*prendre*	took	taken
teach	*enseigner*	taught	taught
tear	*déchirer*	tore	torn
tell	*dire*	told	told
think	*penser*	thought	thought
thrive	*fleurir*	thrived, (throve)	thrived, (thriven)
throw	*jeter*	threw	thrown
thrust	*pousser*	thrust	thrust
tread	*marcher*	trod	trodden
under-stand	*comprendre*	understood	understood
under-take	*s'engager*	undertook	undertaken
wake	*se réveiller*	woke, waked	woken, waked
wear	*porter*	wore	worn
weave	*tisser*	wove	woven
weep	*pleurer*	wept	wept
wet	*mouiller*	wet*, wetted	wet, wetted
win	*gagner*	won	won
wind	*remonter*	wound	wound
wring	*tordre*	wrung	wrung
write	*écrire*	wrote	written

French Conjugation Tables

The following section is a comprehensive list of the conjugation patterns of French verbs in simple tenses; these are the present, imperfect, future, conditional, past historic, present subjunctive and imperfect subjunctive.

Compound tenses can be derived by using avoir or être as auxiliaries in the appropriate simple tense, combined with the past participle of the verb.

This section starts with être and avoir, followed by -er, -ir and -re verbs.

Each verb that features as an entry in the French-English part of this dictionary is followed by a number from 1 to 116 in brackets. This number tells the user which conjugated verb pattern to look up in this section.

	1 avoir	2 être	3 chanter	4 baisser	5 pleurer
Present	j'ai	je suis	je chante	je baisse	je pleure
	tu as	tu es	tu chantes	tu baisses	tu pleures
	il, elle a	il, elle est	il, elle chante	il, elle baisse	il, elle pleure
	nous avons	nous sommes	nous chantons	nous baissons	nous pleurons
	vous avez	vous êtes	vous chantez	vous baissez	vous pleurez
	ils, elles ont	ils, elles sont	ils, elles chantent	ils, elles baissent	ils, elles pleurent
Imperfect	il, elle avait	il, elle était	il, elle chantait	il, elle baissait	il, elle pleurait
Past Historic	il, elle eut	il, elle fut	il, elle chanta	il, elle baissa	il, elle pleura
	ils, elles eurent	ils, elles furent	ils, elles chantèrent	ils, elles baissèrent	ils, elles pleurèrent
Future	j'aurai	je serai	je chanterai	je baisserai	je pleurerai
	il, elle aura	il, elle sera	il, elle chantera	il, elle baissera	il, elle pleurera
Conditional	j'aurais	je serais	je chanterais	je baisserais	je pleurerais
	il, elle aurait	il, elle serait	il, elle chanterait	il, elle baisserait	il, elle pleurerait
Present Subjunctive	que j'aie	que je sois	que je chante	que je baisse	que je pleure
	qu'il, elle ait	qu'il, elle soit	qu'il, elle chante	qu'il, elle baisse	qu'il, elle pleure
	que nous ayons	que nous soyons	que nous chantions	que nous baissions	que nous pleurions
	qu'ils, elles aient	qu'ils, elles soient	qu'ils, elles chantent	qu'ils, elles baissent	qu'ils, elles pleurent
Imperfect Subjunctive	qu'il, elle eût	qu'il, elle fût	qu'il, elle chantât	qu'il, elle baissât	qu'il, elle pleurât
	qu'ils, elles eussent	qu'ils, elles fussent	qu'ils, elles chantassent	qu'ils, elles baissassent	qu'ils, elles pleurassent
Imperative	aie	sois	chante	baisse	pleure
	ayons	soyons	chantons	baissons	pleurons
	ayez	soyez	chantez	baissez	pleurez
Present Participle	ayant	étant	chantant	baissant	pleurant
Past Participle	eu, eue	été	chanté, -e	baissé, -e	pleuré, -e

	6 jouer	7 saluer	8 arguer	9 copier	10 prier
Present	je joue	je salue	j'argue, arguë	je copie	je prie
	tu joues	tu salues	tu argues, arguës	tu copies	tu pries
	il, elle joue	il, elle salue	il, elle argue, arguë	il, elle copie	il, elle prie
	nous jouons	nous saluons	nous arguons	nous copions	nous prions
	vous jouez	vous saluez	vous arguez	vous copiez	vous priez
	ils, elles jouent	ils, elles saluent	ils, elles arguent, arguënt	ils, elles copient	ils, elles prient
Imperfect	il, elle jouait	il, elle saluait	il, elle arguait	il, elle copiait	il, elle priait
Past Historic	il, elle joua	il, elle salua	il, elle argua	il, elle copia	il, elle pria
	ils, elles jouèrent	ils, elles saluèrent	ils, elles arguèrent	ils, elles copièrent	ils, elles prièrent
Future	je jouerai	je saluerai	j'arguerai, arguërai	je copierai	je prierai
	il, elle jouera	il, elle saluera	il, elle arguera, arguëra	il, elle copiera	il, elle priera
Conditional	je jouerais	je saluerais	j'arguerais, arguërais	je copierais	je prierais
	il, elle jouerait	il, elle saluerait	il, elle arguerait, arguërait	il, elle copierait	il, elle prierait
Present Subjunctive	que je joue	que je salue	que j'argue, arguë	que je copie	que je prie
	qu'il, elle joue	qu'il, elle salue	qu'il, elle argue, arguë	qu'il, elle copie	qu'il, elle prie
	que nous jouions	que nous saluions	que nous arguions	que nous copiions	que nous priions
	qu'ils, elles jouent	qu'ils, elles saluent	qu'ils, elles arguent, arguënt	qu'ils, elles copient	qu'ils, elles prient
Imperfect Subjunctive	qu'il, elle jouât	qu'il, elle saluât	qu'il, elle arguât	qu'il, elle copiât	qu'il, elle priât
	qu'ils, elles jouassent	qu'ils, elles saluassent	qu'ils, elles arguassent	qu'ils, elles copiassent	qu'ils, elles priassent
Imperative	joue	salue	argue, arguë	copie	prie
	jouons	saluons	arguons	copions	prions
	jouez	saluez	arguez	copiez	priez
Present Participle	jouant	saluant	arguant	copiant	priant
Past Participle	joué, -e	salué, -e	argué, -e	copié, -e	prié, -e

	11 payer[1]		12 grasseyer	13 ployer	14 essuyer
Present	je paie	je paye	je grasseye	je ploie	j'essuie
	tu paies	tu payes	tu grasseyes	tu ploies	tu essuies
	il, elle paie	il, elle paye	il, elle grasseye	il, elle ploie	il, elle essuie
	nous payons	nous payons	nous grasseyons	nous ployons	nous essuyons
	vous payez	vous payez	vous grasseyez	vous ployez	vous essuyez
	ils, elles paient	ils, elles payent	ils, elles grasseyent	ils, elles ploient	ils, elles essuient
Imperfect	il, elle payait	il, elle payait	il, elle grasseyait	il, elle ployait	il, elle essuyait
Past Historic	il, elle paya	il, elle paya	il, elle grasseya	il, elle ploya	il, elle essuya
	ils, elles payèrent	ils, elles payèrent	ils, elles grasseyèrent	ils, elles ployèrent	ils, elles essuyèrent
Future	je paierai	je payerai	je grasseyerai	je ploierai	j'essuierai
	il, elle paiera	il, elle payera	il, elle grasseyera	il, elle ploiera	il, elle essuiera
Conditional	je paierais	je payerais	je grasseyerais	je ploierais	j'essuierais
	il, elle paierait	il, elle payerait	il, elle grasseyerait	il, elle ploierait	il, elle essuierait
Present Subjunctive	que je paie	que je paye	que je grasseye	que je ploie	que j'essuie
	qu'il, elle paie	qu'il, elle paye	qu'il, elle grasseye	qu'il, elle ploie	qu'il, elle essuie
	que nous payions	que nous payions	que nous grasseyions	que nous ployions	que nous essuyions
	qu'ils, elles paient	qu'ils, elles payent	qu'ils, elles grasseyent	qu'ils, elles ploient	qu'ils, elles essuient
Imperfect Subjunctive	qu'il, elle payât	qu'il, elle payât	qu'il, elle grasseyât	qu'il, elle ployât	qu'il, elle essuyât
	qu'ils, elles payassent	qu'ils, elles payassent	qu'ils, elles grasseyassent	qu'ils, elles ployassent	qu'ils, elles essuyassent
Imperative	paie	paye	grasseye	ploie	essuie
	payons	payons	grasseyons	ployons	essuyons
	payez	payez	grasseyez	ployez	essuyez
Present Participle	payant	payant	grasseyant	ployant	essuyant
Past Participle	payé, -e	payé, -e	grasseyé, -e	ployé, -e	essuyé, -e

[1] According to some grammarians, the verb **rayer** should keep the **-y-** in all its conjugated forms.

	15 créer	16 avancer	17 manger	18 céder[1]	19 semer
Present	je crée	j'avance	je mange	je cède	je sème
	tu crées	tu avances	tu manges	tu cèdes	tu sèmes
	il, elle crée	il, elle avance	il, elle mange	il, elle cède	il, elle sème
	nous créons	nous avançons	nous mangeons	nous cédons	nous semons
	vous créez	vous avancez	vous mangez	vous cédez	vous semez
	ils, elles créent	ils, elles avancent	ils, elles mangent	ils, elles cèdent	ils, elles sèment
Imperfect	il, elle créait	il, elle avançait	il, elle mangeait	il, elle cédait	il, elle semait
Past Historic	il, elle créa	il, elle avança	il, elle mangea	il, elle céda	il, elle sema
	ils, elles créèrent	ils, elles avancèrent	ils, elles mangèrent	ils, elles cédèrent	ils, elles semèrent
Future	je créerai	j'avancerai	je mangerai	je céderai	je sèmerai
	il, elle créera	il, elle avancera	il, elle mangera	il, elle cédera	il, elle sèmera
Conditional	je créerais	j'avancerais	je mangerais	je céderais	je sèmerais
	il, elle créerait	il, elle avancerait	il, elle mangerait	il, elle céderait	il, elle sèmerait
Present Subjunctive	que je crée	que j'avance	que je mange	que je cède	que je sème
	qu'il, elle crée	qu'il, elle avance	qu'il, elle mange	qu'il, elle cède	qu'il, elle sème
	que nous créions	que nous avancions	que nous mangions	que nous cédions	que nous semions
	qu'ils, elles créent	qu'ils, elles avancent	qu'ils, elles mangent	qu'ils, elles cèdent	qu'ils, elles sèment
Imperfect Subjunctive	qu'il, elle créât	qu'il, elle avançât	qu'il, elle mangeât	qu'il, elle cédât	qu'il, elle semât
	qu'ils, elles créassent	qu'ils, elles avançassent	qu'ils, elles mangeassent	qu'ils, elles cédassent	qu'ils, elles semassent
Imperative	crée	avance	mange	cède	sème
	créons	avançons	mangeons	cédons	semons
	créez	avancez	mangez	cédez	semez
Present Participle	créant	avançant	mangeant	cédant	semant
Past Participle	créé, -e	avancé, -e	mangé, -e	cédé, -e	semé, -e

[1] The Académie française recommends **je cèderai** and **je cèderais** in the future and conditional tenses respectively.

	20 rapiécer[1]	21 acquiescer	22 siéger[1,2]	23 déneiger	24 appeler
Present	je rapièce tu rapièces il, elle rapièce nous rapiéçons vous rapiécez ils, elles rapiècent	j'acquiesce tu acquiesces il, elle acquiesce nous acquiesçons vous acquiescez ils, elles acquiescent	je siège tu sièges il, elle siège nous siégeons vous siégez ils, elles siègent	je déneige tu déneiges il, elle déneige nous déneigeons vous déneigez ils, elles déneigent	j'appelle tu appelles il, elle appelle nous appelons vous appelez ils, elles appellent
Imperfect	il, elle rapiéçait	il, elle acquiesçait	il, elle siégeait	il, elle déneigeait	il, elle appelait
Past Historic	il, elle rapiéça ils, elles rapiécèrent	il, elle acquiesça ils, elles acquiescèrent	il, elle siégea ils, elles siégèrent	il, elle déneigea ils, elles déneigèrent	il, elle appela ils, elles appelèrent
Future	je rapiécerai il, elle rapiécera	j'acquiescerai il, elle acquiescera	je siégerai il, elle siégera	je déneigerai il, elle déneigera	j'appellerai il, elle appellera
Conditional	je rapiécerais il, elle rapiécerait	j'acquiescerais il, elle acquiescerait	je siégerais il, elle siégerait	je déneigerais il, elle déneigerait	j'appellerais il, elle appellerait
Present Subjunctive	que je rapièce qu'il, elle rapièce que nous rapiécions qu'ils, elles rapiècent	que j'acquiesce qu'il, elle acquiesce que nous acquiescions qu'ils, elles acquiescent	que je siège qu'il, elle siège que nous siégions qu'ils, elles siègent	que je déneige qu'il, elle déneige que nous déneigions qu'ils, elles déneigent	que j'appelle qu'il, elle appelle que nous appelions qu'ils, elles appellent
Imperfect Subjunctive	qu'il, elle rapiéçât qu'ils, elles rapiéçassent	qu'il, elle acquiesçât qu'ils, elles acquiesçassent	qu'il, elle siégeât qu'ils, elles siégeassent	qu'il, elle déneigeât qu'ils, elles déneigeassent	qu'il, elle appelât qu'ils, elles appelassent
Imperative	rapièce rapiéçons rapiécez	acquiesce acquiesçons acquiescez	siège siégeons siégez	déneige déneigeons déneigez	appelle appelons appelez
Present Participle	rapiéçant	acquiesçant	siégeant	déneigeant	appelant
Past Participle	rapiécé, -e	acquiescé	siégé	déneigé, -e	appelé, -e

[1] The Académie française recommends **je rapiècerai**; **je siègerai** and **je rapiècerais**; **je siègerais** in the future and conditional tenses respectively.

[2] **Assiéger** conjugates like **siéger**, except that its past participle is variable.

	25 peler	26 interpeller	27 jeter	28 acheter	29 dépecer
Present	je pèle tu pèles il, elle pèle nous pelons vous pelez ils, elles pèlent	j'interpelle tu interpelles il, elle interpelle nous interpellons vous interpellez ils, elles interpellent	je jette tu jettes il, elle jette nous jetons vous jetez ils, elles jettent	j'achète tu achètes il, elle achète nous achetons vous achetez ils, elles achètent	je dépèce tu dépèces il, elle dépèce nous dépeçons vous dépecez ils, elles dépècent
Imperfect	il, elle pelait	il, elle interpellait	il, elle jetait	il, elle achetait	il, elle dépeçait
Past Historic	il, elle pela ils, elles pelèrent	il, elle interpella ils, elles interpellèrent	il, elle jeta ils, elles jetèrent	il, elle acheta ils, elles achetèrent	il, elle dépeça ils, elles dépecèrent
Future	je pèlerai il, elle pèlera	j'interpellerai il, elle interpellera	je jetterai il, elle jettera	j'achèterai il, elle achètera	je dépècerai il, elle dépècera
Conditional	je pèlerais il, elle pèlerait	j'interpellerais il, elle interpellerait	je jetterais il, elle jetterait	j'achèterais il, elle achèterait	je dépècerais il, elle dépècerait
Present Subjunctive	que je pèle qu'il, elle pèle que nous pelions qu'ils, elles pèlent	que j'interpelle qu'il, elle interpelle que nous interpellions qu'ils, elles interpellent	que je jette qu'il, elle jette que nous jetions qu'ils, elles jettent	que j'achète qu'il, elle achète que nous achetions qu'ils, elles achètent	que je dépèce qu'il, elle dépèce que nous dépecions qu'ils, elles dépècent
Imperfect Subjunctive	qu'il, elle pelât qu'ils, elles pelassent	qu'il, elle interpellât qu'ils, elles interpellassent	qu'il, elle jetât qu'ils, elles jetassent	qu'il, elle achetât qu'ils, elles achetassent	qu'il, elle dépeçât qu'ils, elles dépeçassent
Imperative	pèle pelons pelez	interpelle interpellons interpellez	jette jetons jetez	achète achetons achetez	dépèce dépeçons dépecez
Present Participle	pelant	interpellant	jetant	achetant	dépeçant
Past Participle	pelé, -e	interpellé, -e	jeté, -e	acheté, -e	dépecé, -e

	30 envoyer	31 aller[1]	32 finir	33 haïr	34 ouvrir
Present	j'envoie tu envoies il, elle envoie nous envoyons vous envoyez ils, elles envoient	je vais tu vas il, elle va nous allons vous allez ils, elles vont	je finis tu finis il, elle finit nous finissons vous finissez ils, elles finissent	je hais tu hais il, elle hait nous haïssons vous haïssez ils, elles haïssent	j'ouvre tu ouvres il, elle ouvre nous ouvrons vous ouvrez ils, elles ouvrent
Imperfect	il, elle envoyait	il, elle allait	il, elle finissait	il, elle haïssait	il, elle ouvrait
Past Historic	il, elle envoya ils, elles envoyèrent	il, elle alla ils, elles allèrent	il, elle finit ils, elles finirent	il, elle haït ils, elles haïrent	il, elle ouvrit ils, elles ouvrirent
Future	j'enverrai il, elle enverra	j'irai il, elle ira	je finirai il, elle finira	je haïrai il, elle haïra	j'ouvrirai il, elle ouvrira
Conditional	j'enverrais il, elle enverrait	j'irais il, elle irait	je finirais il, elle finirait	je haïrais il, elle haïrait	j'ouvrirais il, elle ouvrirait
Present Subjunctive	que j'envoie qu'il, elle envoie que nous envoyions qu'ils, elles envoient	que j'aille qu'il, elle aille que nous allions qu'ils, elles aillent	que je finisse qu'il, elle finisse que nous finissions qu'ils, elles finissent	que je haïsse qu'il, elle haïsse que nous haïssions qu'ils, elles haïssent	que j'ouvre qu'il, elle ouvre que nous ouvrions qu'ils, elles ouvrent
Imperfect Subjunctive	qu'il, elle envoyât qu'ils, elles envoyassent	qu'il, elle allât qu'ils, elles allassent	qu'il, elle finît qu'ils, elles finissent	qu'il, elle haït qu'ils, elles haïssent	qu'il, elle ouvrît qu'ils, elles ouvrissent
Imperative	envoie envoyons envoyez	va allons allez	finis finissons finissez	hais haïssons haïssez	ouvre ouvrons ouvrez
Present Participle	envoyant	allant	finissant	haïssant	ouvrant
Past Participle	envoyé, -e	allé, -e	fini, -e	haï, -e	ouvert, -e

[1] The imperative form of **aller** is **vas** in the construction **vas-y**. The imperative forms of **s'en aller** are **va-t'en**, **allons-nous-en** and **allez-vous-en**. In compound tenses, the verb **être** may be used instead of **aller**, for example **avoir été**, **j'ai été** etc. In compound tenses of the reflexive verb **s'en aller**, **en** is usually placed before the auxiliary verb, eg **je m'en suis allé(e)**, but in everyday language **je me suis en allé(e)** is becoming increasingly common.

	35 fuir	36 dormir[1]	37 mentir[2]	38 servir	39 acquérir
Present	je fuis tu fuis il, elle fuit nous fuyons vous fuyez ils, elles fuient	je dors tu dors il, elle dort nous dormons vous dormez ils, elles dorment	je mens tu mens il, elle ment nous mentons vous mentez ils, elles mentent	je sers tu sers il, elle sert nous servons vous servez ils, elles servent	j'acquiers tu acquiers il, elle acquiert nous acquérons vous acquérez ils, elles acquièrent
Imperfect	il, elle fuyait	il, elle dormait	il, elle mentait	il, elle servait	il, elle acquérait
Past Historic	il, elle fuit ils, elles fuirent	il, elle dormit ils, elles dormirent	il, elle mentit ils, elles mentirent	il, elle servit ils, elles servirent	il, elle acquit ils, elles acquirent
Future	je fuirai il, elle fuira	je dormirai il, elle dormira	je mentirai il, elle mentira	je servirai il, elle servira	j'acquerrai il, elle acquerra
Conditional	je fuirais il, elle fuirait	je dormirais il, elle dormirait	je mentirais il, elle mentirait	je servirais il, elle servirait	j'acquerrais il, elle acquerrait
Present Subjunctive	que je fuie qu'il, elle fuie que nous fuyions qu'ils, elles fuient	que je dorme qu'il, elle dorme que nous dormions qu'ils, elles dorment	que je mente qu'il, elle mente que nous mentions qu'ils, elles mentent	que je serve qu'il, elle serve que nous servions qu'ils, elles servent	que j'acquière qu'il, elle acquière que nous acquérions qu'ils, elles acquièrent
Imperfect Subjunctive	qu'il, elle fuît qu'ils, elles fuissent	qu'il, elle dormît qu'ils, elles dormissent	qu'il, elle mentît qu'ils, elles mentissent	qu'il, elle servît qu'ils, elles servissent	qu'il, elle acquît qu'ils, elles acquissent
Imperative	fuis fuyons fuyez	dors dormons dormez	mens mentons mentez	sers servons servez	acquiers acquérons acquérez
Present Participle	fuyant	dormant	mentant	servant	acquérant
Past Participle	fui, -e	dormi	menti	servi, -e	acquis, -e

[1] **Endormir** conjugates like **dormir**, except that its past participle is variable.

[2] **Démentir** conjugates like **mentir**, except that its past participle is variable.

	40 venir	41 cueillir	42 mourir	43 partir	44 revêtir
Present	je viens tu viens il, elle vient nous venons vous venez ils, elles viennent	je cueille tu cueilles il, elle cueille nous cueillons vous cueillez ils, elles cueillent	je meurs tu meurs il, elle meurt nous mourons vous mourez ils, elles meurent	je pars tu pars il, elle part nous partons vous partez ils, elles partent	je revêts tu revêts il, elle revêt nous revêtons vous revêtez ils, elles revêtent
Imperfect	il, elle venait	il, elle cueillait	il, elle mourait	il, elle partait	il, elle revêtait
Past Historic	il, elle vint ils, elles vinrent	il, elle cueillit ils, elles cueillirent	il, elle mourut ils, elles moururent	il, elle partit ils, elles partirent	il, elle revêtit ils, elles revêtirent
Future	je viendrai il, elle viendra	je cueillerai il, elle cueillera	je mourrai il, elle mourra	je partirai il, elle partira	je revêtirai il, elle revêtira
Conditional	je viendrais il, elle viendrait	je cueillerais il, elle cueillerait	je mourrais il, elle mourrait	je partirais il, elle partirait	je revêtirais il, elle revêtirait
Present Subjunctive	que je vienne qu'il, elle vienne que nous venions qu'ils, elles viennent	que je cueille qu'il, elle cueille que nous cueillions qu'ils, elles cueillent	que je meure qu'il, elle meure que nous mourions qu'ils, elles meurent	que je parte qu'il, elle parte que nous partions qu'ils, elles partent	que je revête qu'il, elle revête que nous revêtions qu'ils, elles revêtent
Imperfect Subjunctive	qu'il, elle vînt qu'ils, elles vinssent	qu'il, elle cueillît qu'ils, elles cueillissent	qu'il, elle mourût qu'ils, elles mourussent	qu'il, elle partît qu'ils, elles partissent	qu'il, elle revêtît qu'ils, elles revêtissent
Imperative	viens venons venez	cueille cueillons cueillez	meurs mourons mourez	pars partons partez	revêts revêtons revêtez
Present Participle	venant	cueillant	mourant	partant	revêtant
Past Participle	venu, -e	cueilli, -e	mort, -e	parti, -e	revêtu, -e

	45 courir	46 faillir[1]	47 défaillir[2]	48 bouillir	49 gésir[3]
Present	je cours tu cours il, elle court nous courons vous courez ils, elles courent	je faillis, faux tu faillis, faux il, elle faillit, faut nous faillissons, faillons vous faillissez, faillez ils, elles faillissent, faillent	je défaille tu défailles il, elle défaille nous défaillons vous défaillez ils, elles défaillent	je bous tu bous il, elle bout nous bouillons vous bouillez ils, elles bouillent	je gis tu gis il, elle gît nous gisons vous gisez ils, elles gisent
Imperfect	il, elle courait	il, elle faillissait, faillait	il, elle défaillait	il, elle bouillait	il, elle gisait
Past Historic	il, elle courut ils, elles coururent	il, elle faillit ils, elles faillirent	il, elle défaillit ils, elles défaillirent	il, elle bouillit ils, elles bouillirent	
Future	je courrai il, elle courra	je faillirai, faudrai il, elle faillira, faudra	je défaillirai il, elle défaillira	je bouillirai il, elle bouillira	
Conditional	je courrais il, elle courrait	je faillirais, faudrais il, elle faillirait, faudrait	je défaillirais il, elle défaillirait	je bouillirais il, elle bouillirait	
Present Subjunctive	que je coure qu'il, elle coure que nous courions qu'ils, elles courent	que je faillisse, faille qu'il, elle faillisse, faille que nous faillissions, faillions qu'ils, elles faillissent, faillent	que je défaille qu'il, elle défaille que nous défaillions qu'ils, elles défaillent	que je bouille qu'il, elle bouille que nous bouillions qu'ils, elles bouillent	
Imperfect Subjunctive	qu'il, elle courût qu'ils, elles courussent	qu'il, elle faillît qu'ils, elles faillissent	qu'il, elle défaillît qu'ils, elles défaillissent	qu'il, elle bouillît qu'ils, elles bouillissent	
Imperative	cours courons courez	faillis, faux faillissons, faillons faillissez, faillez	défaille défaillons défaillez	bous bouillons bouillez	
Present Participle	courant	faillissant, faillant	défaillant	bouillant	gisant
Past Participle	couru, -e	failli	défailli	bouilli, -e	

[1] The more common conjugation of the verb **faillir** is the one modelled on the verb **finir**. This verb is rarely found in its conjugated form.

[2] **Je défaillerai, tu défailleras** etc and **je défaillerais**, **tu défaillerais** etc are also used in the future and conditional tenses respectively. The same forms are also used for **tressaillir** and **assaillir**.

[3] **Gésir** is not used in other tenses and moods.

	50 saillir[1]	51 ouïr[2]	52 recevoir	53 devoir	54 mouvoir
Present		j'ouïs, ois	je reçois	je dois	je meus
		tu ouïs, ois	tu reçois	tu dois	tu meus
	il, elle saille	il, elle ouït, oit	il, elle reçoit	il, elle doit	il, elle meut
		nous ouïssons, oyons	nous recevons	nous devons	nous mouvons
		vous ouïssez, oyez	vous recevez	vous devez	vous mouvez
	ils, elles saillent	ils, elles ouïssent, oient	ils, elles reçoivent	ils, elles doivent	ils, elles meuvent
Imperfect	il, elle saillait	il, elle ouïssait, oyait	il, elle recevait	il, elle devait	il, elle mouvait
Past Historic	il, elle saillit	il, elle ouït	il, elle reçut	il, elle dut	il, elle mut
	ils, elles saillirent	ils, elles ouïrent	ils, elles reçurent	ils, elles durent	ils, elles murent
Future		j'ouïrai, orrai	je recevrai	je devrai	je mouvrai
	il, elle saillera	il, elle ouïra, orra	il, elle recevra	il, elle devra	il, elle mouvra
Conditional		j'ouïrais, orrais	je recevrais	je devrais	je mouvrais
	il, elle saillerait	il, elle ouïrait, orrait	il, elle recevrait	il, elle devrait	il, elle mouvrait
Present Subjunctive		que j'ouïsse, oie	que je reçoive	que je doive	que je meuve
	qu'il, elle saille	qu'il, elle ouïsse, oie	qu'il, elle reçoive	qu'il, elle doive	qu'il, elle meuve
		que nous ouïssions, oyions	que nous recevions	que nous devions	que nous mouvions
	qu'ils, elles saillent	qu'ils, elles ouïssent, oient	qu'ils, elles reçoivent	qu'ils, elles doivent	qu'ils, elles meuvent
Imperfect Subjunctive	qu'il, elle saillît	qu'il, elle ouït	qu'il, elle reçût	qu'il, elle dût	qu'il, elle mût
	qu'ils, elles saillissent	qu'ils, elles ouïssent	qu'ils, elles reçussent	qu'ils, elles dussent	qu'ils, elles mussent
Imperative	*not used*	ouïs, ois	reçois	dois	meus
		ouïssons, oyons	recevons	devons	mouvons
		ouïssez, oyez	recevez	devez	mouvez
Present Participle	saillant	oyant	recevant	devant	mouvant
Past Participle	sailli, -e	ouï, -e	reçu, -e	dû, due, dus, dues	mû, mue, mus, mues

[1] This conjugation table refers to **saillir**[2] in the dictionary.

[2] In modern French, the verb **ouïr** is used only in the infinitive, in compound tenses and in the expressions **par ouï-dire** and **oyez, braves gens**.

	55 émouvoir	56 promouvoir[1]	57 vouloir	58 pouvoir[2]	59 savoir
Present	j'émeus	je promeus	je veux	je peux, puis	je sais
	tu émeus	tu promeus	tu veux	tu peux	tu sais
	il, elle émeut	il, elle promeut	il, elle veut	il, elle peut	il, elle sait
	nous émouvons	nous promouvons	nous voulons	nous pouvons	nous savons
	vous émouvez	vous promouvez	vous voulez	vous pouvez	vous savez
	ils, elles émeuvent	ils, elles promeuvent	ils, elles veulent	ils, elles peuvent	ils, elles savent
Imperfect	il, elle émouvait	il, elle promouvait	il, elle voulait	il, elle pouvait	il, elle savait
Past Historic	il, elle émut	il, elle promut	il, elle voulut	il, elle put	il, elle sut
	ils, elles émurent	ils, elles promurent	ils, elles voulurent	ils, elles purent	ils, elles surent
Future	j'émouvrai	je promouvrai	je voudrai	je pourrai	je saurai
	il, elle émouvra	il, elle promouvra	il, elle voudra	il, elle pourra	il, elle saura
Conditional	j'émouvrais	je promouvrais	je voudrais	je pourrais	je saurais
	il, elle émouvrait	il, elle promouvrait	il, elle voudrait	il, elle pourrait	il, elle saurait
Present Subjunctive	que j'émeuve	que je promeuve	que je veuille	que je puisse	que je sache
	qu'il, elle émeuve	qu'il, elle promeuve	qu'il, elle veuille	qu'il, elle puisse	qu'il, elle sache
	que nous émouvions	que nous promouvions	que nous voulions	que nous puissions	que nous sachions
	qu'ils, elles émeuvent	qu'ils, elles promeuvent	qu'ils, elles veuillent	qu'ils, elles puissent	qu'ils, elles sachent
Imperfect Subjunctive	qu'il, elle émût	qu'il, elle promût	qu'il, elle voulût	qu'il, elle pût	qu'il, elle sût
	qu'ils, elles émussent	qu'ils, elles promussent	qu'ils, elles voulussent	qu'ils, elles pussent	qu'ils, elles sussent
Imperative	émeus	promeus	veux, veuille	*not used*	sache
	émouvons	promouvons	voulons, veuillons		sachons
	émouvez	promouvez	voulez, veuillez		sachez
Present Participle	émouvant	promouvant	voulant	pouvant	sachant
Past Participle	ému, -e	promu, -e	voulu, -e	pu	su, -e

[1] This verb is rarely found in its conjugated forms.

[2] When the subject and verb are inverted in the interrogative, **puis-je** is the only possible conjugated form.

	60 valoir	61 prévaloir	62 voir	63 prévoir	64 pourvoir
Present	je vaux tu vaux il, elle vaut nous valons vous valez ils, elles valent	je prévaux tu prévaux il, elle prévaut nous prévalons vous prévalez ils, elles prévalent	je vois tu vois il, elle voit nous voyons vous voyez ils, elles voient	je prévois tu prévois il, elle prévoit nous prévoyons vous prévoyez ils, elles prévoient	je pourvois tu pourvois il, elle pourvoit nous pourvoyons vous pourvoyez ils, elles pourvoient
Imperfect	il, elle valait	il, elle prévalait	il, elle voyait	il, elle prévoyait	il, elle pourvoyait
Past Historic	il, elle valut ils, elles valurent	il, elle prévalut ils, elles prévalurent	il, elle vit ils, elles virent	il, elle prévit ils, elles prévirent	il, elle pourvut ils, elles pourvurent
Future	je vaudrai il, elle vaudra	je prévaudrai il, elle prévaudra	je verrai il, elle verra	je prévoirai il, elle prévoira	je pourvoirai il, elle pourvoira
Conditional	je vaudrais il, elle vaudrait	je prévaudrais il, elle prévaudrait	je verrais il, elle verrait	je prévoirais il, elle prévoirait	je pourvoirais il, elle pourvoirait
Present Subjunctive	que je vaille qu'il, elle vaille que nous valions qu'ils, elles vaillent	que je prévale qu'il, elle prévale que nous prévalions qu'ils, elles prévalent	que je voie qu'il, elle voie que nous voyions qu'ils, elles voient	que je prévoie qu'il, elle prévoie que nous prévoyions qu'ils, elles prévoient	que je pourvoie qu'il, elle pourvoie que nous pourvoyions qu'ils, elles pourvoient
Imperfect Subjunctive	qu'il, elle valût qu'ils, elles valussent	qu'il, elle prévalût qu'ils, elles prévalussent	qu'il, elle vît qu'ils, elles vissent	qu'il, elle prévît qu'ils, elles prévissent	qu'il, elle pourvût qu'ils, elles pourvussent
Imperative	vaux valons valez	prévaux prévalons prévalez	vois voyons voyez	prévois prévoyons prévoyez	pourvois pourvoyons pourvoyez
Present Participle	valant	prévalant	voyant	prévoyant	pourvoyant
Past Participle	valu, -e	prévalu, -e	vu, -e	prévu, -e	pourvu, -e

	65 asseoir[1]		66 surseoir	67 seoir[2]	68 pleuvoir[3]
Present	j'assieds tu assieds il, elle assied nous asseyons vous asseyez ils, elles asseyent	j'assois tu assois il, elle assoit nous assoyons vous assoyez ils, elles assoient	je sursois tu sursois il, elle sursoit nous sursoyons vous sursoyez ils, elles sursoient	il, elle sied ils, elles siéent	il pleut
Imperfect	il, elle asseyait	il, elle assoyait	il, elle sursoyait	il, elle seyait	il pleuvait
Past Historic	il, elle assit ils, elles assirent	il, elle assit ils, elles assirent	il, elle sursit ils, elles sursirent	*not used*	il plut
Future	j'assiérai il, elle assiéra	j'assoirai il, elle assoira	je surseoirai il, elle surseoira	il, elle siéra	il pleuvra
Conditional	j'assiérais il, elle assiérait	j'assoirais il, elle assoirait	je surseoirais il, elle surseoirait	il, elle siérait	il pleuvrait
Present Subjunctive	que j'asseye qu'il, elle asseye que nous asseyions qu'ils, elles asseyent	que j'assoie qu'il, elle assoie que nous assoyions qu'ils, elles assoient	que je sursoie qu'il, elle sursoie que nous sursoyions qu'ils, elles sursoient	qu'il, elle siée qu'ils, elles siéent	qu'il pleuve
Imperfect Subjunctive	qu'il, elle assît qu'ils, elles assissent	qu'il, elle assît qu'ils, elles assissent	qu'il, elle sursît qu'ils, elles sursissent	*not used*	qu'il plût
Imperative	assieds asseyons asseyez	assois assoyons assoyez	sursois sursoyons sursoyez	*not used*	*not used*
Present Participle	asseyant	assoyant	sursoyant	seyant	pleuvant
Past Participle	assis, -e	assis, -e	sursis	*not used*	plu

[1] In written French, the preferred spelling of the **-oi-** forms is **-eoi-**, eg **j'asseois**, **il, elle asseoira**, **que tu asseoies**, **ils, elles asseoiraient**.

[2] In this case, **seoir** has the sense of "to suit". When it means "to be located" it exists only in the past participle (**sis**, **-e**).

[3] The figurative use of the verb **pleuvoir** allows a conjugation in the third-person plural, eg **les insultes pleuvent**, **pleuvaient**, **pleuvront**, **plurent**, **pleuvraient**.

	69 falloir	70 échoir	71 déchoir	72 choir	73 vendre
Present	il faut	il, elle échoit ils, elles échoient	je déchois tu déchois il, elle déchoit nous déchoyons vous déchoyez ils, elles déchoient	je chois tu chois il, elle choit *not used* *not used* ils, elles choient	je vends tu vends il, elle vend nous vendons vous vendez ils, elles vendent
Imperfect	il fallait	il, elle échoyait	*not used*	*not used*	il, elle vendait
Past Historic	il fallut	il, elle échut ils, elles échurent	il, elle déchut ils, elles déchurent	il, elle chut ils, elles churent	il, elle vendit ils, elles vendirent
Future	il faudra	il, elle échoira, écherra	je déchoirai il, elle déchoira	je choirai, cherrai il, elle choira, cherra	je vendrai il, elle vendra
Conditional	il faudrait	il, elle échoirait, écherrait	je déchoirais il, elle déchoirait	je choirais, cherrais il, elle choirait, cherrait	je vendrais il, elle vendrait
Present Subjunctive	qu'il faille	qu'il, elle échoie qu'ils, elles échoient	que je déchoie qu'il, elle déchoie que nous déchoyions qu'ils, elles déchoient	*not used*	que je vende qu'il, elle vende que nous vendions qu'ils, elles vendent
Imperfect Subjunctive	qu'il fallût	qu'il, elle échût qu'ils, elles échussent	qu'il, elle déchût qu'ils, elles déchussent	qu'il, elle chût *not used*	qu'il, elle vendît qu'ils, elles vendissent
Imperative	*not used*	*not used*	*not used*	*not used*	vends vendons vendez
Present Participle	*not used*	échéant	*not used*	*not used*	vendant
Past Participle	fallu	échu, -e	déchu, -e	chu, -e	vendu, -e

	74 répandre	75 répondre	76 mordre	77 perdre	78 rompre
Present	je répands tu répands il, elle répand nous répandons vous répandez ils, elles répandent	je réponds tu réponds il, elle répond nous répondons vous répondez ils, elles répondent	je mords tu mords il, elle mord nous mordons vous mordez ils, elles mordent	je perds tu perds il, elle perd nous perdons vous perdez ils, elles perdent	je romps tu romps il, elle rompt nous rompons vous rompez ils, elles rompent
Imperfect	il, elle répandait	il, elle répondait	il, elle mordait	il, elle perdait	il, elle rompait
Past Historic	il, elle répandit ils, elles répandirent	il, elle répondit ils, elles répondirent	il, elle mordit ils, elles mordirent	il, elle perdit ils, elles perdirent	il, elle rompit ils, elles rompirent
Future	je répandrai il, elle répandra	je répondrai il, elle répondra	je mordrai il, elle mordra	je perdrai il, elle perdra	je romprai il, elle rompra
Conditional	je répandrais il, elle répandrait	je répondrais il, elle répondrait	je mordrais il, elle mordrait	je perdrais il, elle perdrait	je romprais il, elle romprait
Present Subjunctive	que je répande qu'il, elle répande que nous répandions qu'ils, elles répandent	que je réponde qu'il, elle réponde que nous répondions qu'ils, elles répondent	que je morde qu'il, elle morde que nous mordions qu'ils, elles mordent	que je perde qu'il, elle perde que nous perdions qu'ils, elles perdent	que je rompe qu'il, elle rompe que nous rompions qu'ils, elles rompent
Imperfect Subjunctive	qu'il, elle répandît qu'ils, elles répandissent	qu'il, elle répondît qu'ils, elles répondissent	qu'il, elle mordît qu'ils, elles mordissent	qu'il, elle perdît qu'ils, elles perdissent	qu'il, elle rompît qu'ils, elles rompissent
Imperative	répands répandons répandez	réponds répondons répondez	mords mordons mordez	perds perdons perdez	romps rompons rompez
Present Participle	répandant	répondant	mordant	perdant	rompant
Past Participle	répandu, -e	répondu, -e	mordu, -e	perdu, -e	rompu, -e

	79 prendre	80 craindre	81 peindre	82 joindre	83 battre
Present	je prends	je crains	je peins	je joins	je bats
	tu prends	tu crains	tu peins	tu joins	tu bats
	il, elle prend	il, elle craint	il, elle peint	il, elle joint	il, elle bat
	nous prenons	nous craignons	nous peignons	nous joignons	nous battons
	vous prenez	vous craignez	vous peignez	vous joignez	vous battez
	ils, elles prennent	ils, elles craignent	ils, elles peignent	ils, elles joignent	ils, elles battent
Imperfect	il, elle prenait	il, elle craignait	il, elle peignait	il, elle joignait	il, elle battait
Past Historic	il, elle prit	il, elle craignit	il, elle peignit	il, elle joignit	il, elle battit
	ils, elles prirent	ils, elles craignirent	ils, elles peignirent	ils, elles joignirent	ils, elles battirent
Future	je prendrai	je craindrai	je peindrai	je joindrai	je battrai
	il, elle prendra	il, elle craindra	il, elle peindra	il, elle joindra	il, elle battra
Conditional	je prendrais	je craindrais	je peindrais	je joindrais	je battrais
	il, elle prendrait	il, elle craindrait	il, elle peindrait	il, elle joindrait	il, elle battrait
Present Subjunctive	que je prenne	que je craigne	que je peigne	que je joigne	que je batte
	qu'il, elle prenne	qu'il, elle craigne	qu'il, elle peigne	qu'il, elle joigne	qu'il, elle batte
	que nous prenions	que nous craignions	que nous peignions	que nous joignions	que nous battions
	qu'ils, elles prennent	qu'ils, elles craignent	qu'ils, elles peignent	qu'ils, elles joignent	qu'ils, elles battent
Imperfect Subjunctive	qu'il, elle prît	qu'il, elle craignît	qu'il, elle peignît	qu'il, elle joignît	qu'il, elle battît
	qu'ils, elles prissent	qu'ils, elles craignissent	qu'ils, elles peignissent	qu'ils, elles joignissent	qu'ils, elles battissent
Imperative	prends	crains	peins	joins	bats
	prenons	craignons	peignons	joignons	battons
	prenez	craignez	peignez	joignez	battez
Present Participle	prenant	craignant	peignant	joignant	battant
Past Participle	pris, -e	craint, -e	peint, -e	joint, -e	battu, -e

	84 mettre	85 moudre	86 coudre	87 absoudre[1]	88 résoudre[2]
Present	je mets	je mouds	je couds	j'absous	je résous
	tu mets	tu mouds	tu couds	tu absous	tu résous
	il, elle met	il, elle moud	il, elle coud	il, elle absout	il, elle résout
	nous mettons	nous moulons	nous cousons	nous absolvons	nous résolvons
	vous mettez	vous moulez	vous cousez	vous absolvez	vous résolvez
	ils, elles mettent	ils, elles moulent	ils, elles cousent	ils, elles absolvent	ils, elles résolvent
Imperfect	il, elle mettait	il, elle moulait	il, elle cousait	il, elle absolvait	il, elle résolvait
Past Historic	il, elle mit	il, elle moulut	il, elle cousit	il, elle absolut	il, elle résolut
	ils, elles mirent	ils, elles moulurent	ils, elles cousirent	ils, elles absolurent	ils, elles résolurent
Future	je mettrai	je moudrai	je coudrai	j'absoudrai	je résoudrai
	il, elle mettra	il, elle moudra	il, elle coudra	il, elle absoudra	il, elle résoudra
Conditional	je mettrais	je moudrais	je coudrais	j'absoudrais	je résoudrais
	il, elle mettrait	il, elle moudrait	il, elle coudrait	il, elle absoudrait	il, elle résoudrait
Present Subjunctive	que je mette	que je moule	que je couse	que j'absolve	que je résolve
	qu'il, elle mette	qu'il, elle moule	qu'il, elle couse	qu'il, elle absolve	qu'il, elle résolve
	que nous mettions	que nous moulions	que nous cousions	que nous absolvions	que nous résolvions
	qu'ils, elles mettent	qu'ils, elles moulent	qu'ils, elles cousent	qu'ils, elles absolvent	qu'ils, elles résolvent
Imperfect Subjunctive	qu'il, elle mît	qu'il, elle moulût	qu'il, elle cousît	qu'il, elle absolût	qu'il, elle résolût
	qu'ils, elles missent	qu'ils, elles moulussent	qu'ils, elles cousissent	qu'ils, elles absolussent	qu'ils, elles résolussent
Imperative	mets	mouds	couds	absous	résous
	mettons	moulons	cousons	absolvons	résolvons
	mettez	moulez	cousez	absolvez	résolvez
Present Participle	mettant	moulant	cousant	absolvant	résolvant
Past Participle	mis, -e	moulu, -e	cousu, -e	absous, -oute	résolu, -e

[1] The past historic and imperfect subjunctive forms are rarely used.

[2] The past participle **résous, -oute** may also be used when the verb means "to transform, to become", eg **un brouillard résous en pluie**, although this form is rare.

	89 suivre	90 vivre[1]	91 paraître	92 naître	93 croître[2]
Present	je suis tu suis il, elle suit nous suivons vous suivez ils, elles suivent	je vis tu vis il, elle vit nous vivons vous vivez ils, elles vivent	je parais tu parais il, elle paraît nous paraissons vous paraissez ils, elles paraissent	je nais tu nais il, elle naît nous naissons vous naissez ils, elles naissent	je croîs tu croîs il, elle croît nous croissons vous croissez ils, elles croissent
Imperfect	il, elle suivait	il, elle vivait	il, elle paraissait	il, elle naissait	il, elle croissait
Past Historic	il, elle suivit ils, elles suivirent	il, elle vécut ils, elles vécurent	il, elle parut ils, elles parurent	il, elle naquit ils, elles naquirent	il, elle crût ils, elles crûrent
Future	je suivrai il, elle suivra	je vivrai il, elle vivra	je paraîtrai il, elle paraîtra	je naîtrai il, elle naîtra	je croîtrai il, elle croîtra
Conditional	je suivrais il, elle suivrait	je vivrais il, elle vivrait	je paraîtrais il, elle paraîtrait	je naîtrais il, elle naîtrait	je croîtrais il, elle croîtrait
Present Subjunctive	que je suive qu'il, elle suive que nous suivions qu'ils, elles suivent	que je vive qu'il, elle vive que nous vivions qu'ils, elles vivent	que je paraisse qu'il, elle paraisse que nous paraissions qu'ils, elles paraissent	que je naisse qu'il, elle naisse que nous naissions qu'ils, elles naissent	que je croisse qu'il, elle croisse que nous croissions qu'ils, elles croissent
Imperfect Subjunctive	qu'il, elle suivît qu'ils, elles suivissent	qu'il, elle vécût qu'ils, elles vécussent	qu'il, elle parût qu'ils, elles parussent	qu'il, elle naquît qu'ils, elles naquissent	qu'il, elle crût qu'ils, elles crûssent
Imperative	suis suivons suivez	vis vivons vivez	parais paraissons paraissez	nais naissons naissez	croîs croissons croissez
Present Participle	suivant	vivant	paraissant	naissant	croissant
Past Participle	suivi, -e	vécu, -e	paru, -e	né, -e	crû, crue, crus, crues

[1] **Survivre** conjugates like **vivre**, except that its past participle is always invariable.

[2] The Académie française recommends that **crusse**, **crusses**, **crussions**, **crussiez** and **crussent** be used in the imperfect subjunctive.

	94 accroître[1]	95 rire	96 conclure[2]	97 nuire[3]	98 conduire
Present	j'accrois tu accrois il, elle accroît nous accroissons vous accroissez ils, elles accroissent	je ris tu ris il, elle rit nous rions vous riez ils, elles rient	je conclus tu conclus il, elle conclut nous concluons vous concluez ils, elles concluent	je nuis tu nuis il, elle nuit nous nuisons vous nuisez ils, elles nuisent	je conduis tu conduis il, elle conduit nous conduisons vous conduisez ils, elles conduisent
Imperfect	il, elle accroissait	il, elle riait	il, elle concluait	il, elle nuisait	il, elle conduisait
Past Historic	il, elle accrut ils, elles accrurent	il, elle rit ils, elles rirent	il, elle conclut ils, elles conclurent	il, elle nuisit ils, elles nuisirent	il, elle conduisit ils, elles conduisirent
Future	j'accroîtrai il, elle accroîtra	je rirai il, elle rira	je conclurai il, elle conclura	je nuirai il, elle nuira	je conduirai il, elle conduira
Conditional	j'accroîtrais il, elle accroîtrait	je rirais il, elle rirait	je conclurais il, elle conclurait	je nuirais il, elle nuirait	je conduirais il, elle conduirait
Present Subjunctive	que j'accroisse qu'il, elle accroisse que nous accroissions qu'ils, elles accroissent	que je rie qu'il, elle rie que nous riions qu'ils, elles rient	que je conclue qu'il, elle conclue que nous concluions qu'ils, elles concluent	que je nuise qu'il, elle nuise que nous nuisions qu'ils, elles nuisent	que je conduise qu'il, elle conduise que nous conduisions qu'ils, elles conduisent
Imperfect Subjunctive	qu'il, elle accrût qu'ils, elles accrussent	qu'il, elle rît qu'ils, elles rissent	qu'il, elle conclût qu'ils, elles conclussent	qu'il, elle nuisît qu'ils, elles nuisissent	qu'il, elle conduisît qu'ils, elles conduisissent
Imperative	accrois accroissons accroissez	ris rions riez	conclus concluons concluez	nuis nuisons nuisez	conduis conduisons conduisez
Present Participle	accroissant	riant	conluant	nuisant	conduisant
Past Participle	accru, -e	ri	conclu, -e	nui	conduit, -e

[1] **Recroître** conjugates like **accroître**, except that its past participle is **recrû**, **recrue**, **recrus**, **recrues.**

[2] **Inclure** and **occlure** conjugate like **conclure**, except that their past participles are **inclus, -e** and **occlus, -e** respectively.

[3] **Luire** and **reluire** conjugate like **nuire** but also have the alternative forms **je luis** etc in the past historic.

	99 écrire	100 suffire	101 confire[1]	102 dire	103 contredire
Present	j'écris	je suffis	je confis	je dis	je contredis
	tu écris	tu suffis	tu confis	tu dis	tu contredis
	il, elle écrit	il, elle suffit	il, elle confit	il, elle dit	il, elle contredit
	nous écrivons	nous suffisons	nous confisons	nous disons	nous contredisons
	vous écrivez	vous suffisez	vous confisez	vous dites	vous contredisez
	ils, elles écrivent	ils, elles suffisent	ils, elles confisent	ils, elles disent	ils, elles contredisent
Imperfect	il, elle écrivait	il, elle suffisait	il, elle confisait	il, elle disait	il, elle contredisait
Past Historic	il, elle écrivit	il, elle suffit	il, elle confit	il, elle dit	il, elle contredit
	ils, elles écrivirent	ils, elles suffirent	ils, elles confirent	ils, elles dirent	ils, elles contredirent
Future	j'écrirai	je suffirai	je confirai	je dirai	je contredirai
	il, elle écrira	il, elle suffira	il, elle confira	il, elle dira	il, elle contredira
Conditional	j'écrirais	je suffirais	je confirais	je dirais	je contredirais
	il, elle écrirait	il, elle suffirait	il, elle confirait	il, elle dirait	il, elle contredirait
Present Subjunctive	que j'écrive	que je suffise	que je confise	que je dise	que je contredise
	qu'il, elle écrive	qu'il, elle suffise	qu'il, elle confise	qu'il, elle dise	qu'il, elle contredise
	que nous écrivions	que nous suffisions	que nous confisions	que nous disions	que nous contredisions
	qu'ils, elles écrivent	qu'ils, elles suffisent	qu'ils, elles confisent	qu'ils, elles disent	qu'ils, elles contredisent
Imperfect Subjunctive	qu'il, elle écrivît	qu'il, elle suffît	qu'il, elle confît	qu'il, elle dît	qu'il, elle contredît
	qu'ils, elles écrivissent	qu'ils, elles suffissent	qu'ils, elles confissent	qu'ils, elles dissent	qu'ils, elles contredissent
Imperative	écris	suffis	confis	dis	contredis
	écrivons	suffisons	confisons	disons	contredisons
	écrivez	suffisez	confisez	dites	contredisez
Present Participle	écrivant	suffisant	confisant	disant	contredisant
Past Participle	écrit, -e	suffi	confit, -e	dit, -e	contredit, -e

[1] **Circoncire** conjugates like **confire**, except that its past participle is **circoncis, -e**.

	104 maudire	105 bruire[1]	106 lire	107 croire	108 boire
Present	je maudis	je bruis	je lis	je crois	je bois
	tu maudis	tu bruis	tu lis	tu crois	tu bois
	il, elle maudit	il, elle bruit	il, elle lit	il, elle croit	il, elle boit
	nous maudissons	*not used*	nous lisons	nous croyons	nous buvons
	vous maudissez		vous lisez	vous croyez	vous buvez
	ils, elles maudissent		ils, elles lisent	ils, elles croient	ils, elles boivent
Imperfect	il, elle maudissait	il, elle bruyait	il, elle lisait	il, elle croyait	il, elle buvait
Past Historic	il, elle maudit	*not used*	il, elle lut	il, elle crut	il, elle but
	ils, elles maudirent		ils, elles lurent	ils, elles crurent	ils, elles burent
Future	je maudirai	je bruirai	je lirai	je croirai	je boirai
	il, elle maudira	il, elle bruira	il, elle lira	il, elle croira	il, elle boira
Conditional	je maudirais	je bruirais	je lirais	je croirais	je boirais
	il, elle maudirait	il, elle bruirait	il, elle lirait	il, elle croirait	il, elle boirait
Present Subjunctive	que je maudisse	*not used*	que je lise	que je croie	que je boive
	qu'il, elle maudisse		qu'il, elle lise	qu'il, elle croie	qu'il, elle boive
	que nous maudissions		que nous lisions	que nous croyions	que nous buvions
	qu'ils, elles maudissent		qu'ils, elles lisent	qu'ils, elles croient	qu'ils, elles boivent
Imperfect Subjunctive	qu'il, elle maudît	*not used*	qu'il, elle lût	qu'il, elle crût	qu'il, elle bût
	qu'ils, elles maudissent		qu'ils, elles lussent	qu'ils, elles crussent	qu'ils, elles bussent
Imperative	maudis	*not used*	lis	crois	bois
	maudissons		lisons	croyons	buvons
	maudissez		lisez	croyez	buvez
Present Participle	maudissant	*not used*	lisant	croyant	buvant
Past Participle	maudit, -e	bruit	lu, -e	cru, -e	bu, -e

[1] **Bruire** is normally used only in the present indicative, imperfect (**je bruyais**, **tu bruyais** etc), future and conditional forms. **Bruisser** (see table 3) is often used instead of **bruire**, particularly for the forms in which the latter is defective.

	109 faire	110 plaire	111 taire	112 extraire	113 clore[1]
Present	je fais	je plais	je tais	j'extrais	je clos
	tu fais	tu plais	tu tais	tu extrais	tu clos
	il, elle fait	il, elle plaît	il, elle tait	il, elle extrait	il, elle clôt
	nous faisons	nous plaisons	nous taisons	nous extrayons	*not used*
	vous faites	vous plaisez	vous taisez	vous extrayez	*not used*
	ils, elles font	ils, elles plaisent	ils, elles taisent	ils, elles extraient	ils, elles closent
Imperfect	il, elle faisait	il, elle plaisait	il, elle taisait	il, elle extrayait	*not used*
Past Historic	il, elle fit	il, elle plut	il, elle tut	*not used*	*not used*
	ils, elles firent	ils, elles plurent	ils, elles turent		
Future	je ferai	je plairai	je tairai	j'extrairai	je clorai
	il, elle fera	il, elle plaira	il, elle taira	il, elle extraira	il, elle clora
Conditional	je ferais	je plairais	je tairais	j'extrairais	je clorais
	il, elle ferait	il, elle plairait	il, elle tairait	il, elle extrairait	il, elle clorait
Present Subjunctive	que je fasse	que je plaise	que je taise	que j'extraie	que je close
	qu'il, elle fasse	qu'il, elle plaise	qu'il, elle taise	qu'il, elle extraie	qu'il, elle close
	que nous fassions	que nous plaisions	que nous taisions	que nous extrayions	que nous closions
	qu'ils, elles fassent	qu'ils, elles plaisent	qu'ils, elles taisent	qu'ils, elles extraient	qu'ils, elles closent
Imperfect Subjunctive	qu'il, elle fît	qu'il, elle plût	qu'il, elle tût	*not used*	*not used*
	qu'ils, elles fissent	qu'ils, elles plussent	qu'ils, elles tussent		
Imperative	fais	plais	tais	extrais	clos
	faisons	plaisons	taisons	extrayons	*not used*
	faites	plaisez	taisez	extrayez	*not used*
Present Participle	faisant	plaisant	taisant	extrayant	closant
Past Participle	fait, -e	plu	tu, -e	extrait, -e	clos, -e

[1] **Déclore**, **éclore** and **enclore** conjugate like **clore**, although the Académie française recommends **il, elle éclot** and **il, elle enclot** in the present tense. The verb **enclore** also has the forms **nous enclosons**, **vous enclosez** in the present tense and **enclosons**, **enclosez** in the imperative.

	114 vaincre	115 frire	116 foutre
Present	je vaincs	je fris	je fous
	tu vaincs	tu fris	tu fous
	il, elle vainc	il, elle frit	il, elle fout
	nous vainquons	*not used*	nous foutons
	vous vainquez		vous foutez
	ils, elles vainquent		ils, elles foutent
Imperfect	il, elle vainquait	*not used*	il, elle foutait
Past Historic	il, elle vainquit	*not used*	*not used*
	ils, elles vainquirent		
Future	je vaincrai	je frirai	je foutrai
	il, elle vaincra	il, elle frira	il, elle foutra
Conditional	je vaincrais	je frirais	je foutrais
	il, elle vaincrait	il, elle frirait	il, elle foutrait
Present Subjunctive	que je vainque	*not used*	que je foute
	qu'il, elle vainque		qu'il, elle foute
	que nous vainquions		que nous foutions
	qu'ils, elles vainquent		qu'ils, elles foutent
Imperfect Subjunctive	qu'il, elle vainquît	*not used*	*not used*
	qu'ils, elles vainquissent		
Imperative	vaincs	fris	fous
	vainquons	*not used*	foutons
	vainquez		foutez
Present Participle	vainquant	*not used*	foutant
Past Participle	vaincu, -e	frit, -e	foutu, -e

Français – Anglais

French – English

A¹, a¹ [a] **NM INV 1** *(lettre)* A, a; **de A (jusqu')à Z** from A to Z; **A comme Anatole** ≃ A for Andrew **2** *Mus (note)* A

A² **1** *Élec (abrév écrite* **ampère***)* A, Amp

2 *Météo (abrév écrite* **anticyclone***)* anticyclone

3 *(abrév* **autoroute***) Br* ≃ M, motorway, *Am* ≃ I, interstate

4 *(abrév écrite* **apprenti conducteur***) (sur une voiture)* = indicates that the driver has recently obtained his or her licence, *Br* ≃ L

a² [a] *voir* **avoir²**

À [a]

- to **A2, E, J3**
- in **A1, B1**
- from **A3**
- of **D**
- at **A1, B1**
- on **A1, B1**
- with **C1, I**
- by **F2, G3**

à + le contracts to form **au**, **à + les** contracts to form **aux** [o].

PRÉP A. *DANS L'ESPACE* **1** *(indiquant la position)* at; *(à l'intérieur de)* in; *(sur)* on; **il habite à la campagne** he lives in the country; **elle habite au Canada** she lives in Canada; **j'habite au Havre** I live in Le Havre; **je suis aux Bermudes** I'm in Bermuda; **j'aimerais vivre à la Martinique** I'd like to live in Martinique; **il est à l'hôpital** he's in *Br* hospital *or Am* the hospital; **elle travaille à l'hôpital** she works at the hospital; **au jardin** in the garden; **à l'orée du bois** at the edge of the wood; **au marché** at the market; **il fait 45°C au soleil** it's 45°C in the sun; **quand on est à 2000 mètres d'altitude** when you're 2,000 metres up; **au niveau de la mer** at sea level; **elle attendait à la porte** she was waiting at *or* by the door; **tenez-vous correctement à table** behave (properly) at the table; **au mur/plafond** on the wall/ceiling; **à terre** on the ground; **c'est au rez-de-chaussée** it's on the *Br* ground floor *or Am* first floor; **j'ai mal à la tête** I've got a headache; **j'ai une ampoule au pied** I've got a blister on my foot; **à ma droite** on *or* to my right; **vous tournez à gauche après le feu** you turn left after the traffic lights; **la gare est à 500 mètres d'ici** the station is 500 metres from here

2 *(indiquant la direction)* to; **aller à Paris/aux États-Unis/à la Jamaïque** to go to Paris/to the United States/to Jamaica; **aller au cinéma** to go to the movies *or Br* cinema; **aller à la piscine** to go swimming, to go to the swimming pool; **est-ce qu'elle est allée à l'université?** has she been to university?; **il a lancé le javelot à 74 mètres** he threw the javelin 74 metres; **lever les bras au ciel** to throw up one's arms

3 *(indiquant la provenance, l'origine)* **puiser de l'eau à la fontaine** to get water from the fountain; **retenir l'impôt à la source** to deduct tax at source; **remonter à l'origine d'une affaire** to get to the root of a matter; **je l'ai entendu à la radio** I heard it on the radio; **je l'ai vu à la télé** I saw it on TV; **on en a parlé aux informations** they mentioned it *or* it was mentioned on the news

B. *DANS LE TEMPS* **1** *(indiquant un moment précis)* at; *(devant une date, un jour)* on; *(indiquant une époque, une période)* in; **à 6 heures** at 6 o'clock; **il ne rentrera qu'à 8 heures** he won't be back before 8; **à Pâques** at Easter; **à Noël** at Christmas; **à l'aube/l'aurore/midi** at dawn/daybreak/midday; **au crépuscule** at dusk; **le 12 au soir** on the evening of the 12th; **à dater de ce jour** from that day on *or* onwards; **à mon arrivée** on my arrival; **à ma naissance** when I was born; **à l'automne** in *Br* (the) autumn *or Am* the fall; **à la Renaissance** in the Renaissance; **au XVIIème siècle** in the 17th century; **à chaque fois** every time; **à chaque instant** every minute; **vous allez quelque part à Noël?** are you going somewhere for Christmas?; **je te le donnerai à ton anniversaire** I'll give it to you on your birthday; **à trois, tu pars!** when I count three, go!

2 *(indiquant un délai)* **nous sommes à deux semaines de Noël** there are only two weeks to go before Christmas, Christmas is only two weeks away; **il me tarde d'être à dimanche** I can't wait till Sunday; **à demain/la semaine prochaine/mardi** see you tomorrow/next week/(on) Tuesday

C. *MARQUANT LE MOYEN, LA MANIÈRE* **1** *(indiquant le moyen, l'instrument, l'accompagnement)* **peindre à l'eau/à l'huile** to paint in watercolours/oils; **marcher au fuel** to run off *or* on oil; **couper qch au couteau** to cut sth with a knife; **cousu à la main** hand-sewn; **cousu à la machine** machine-sewn; **des mots écrits à la craie** words written in chalk; **jouer qch à la guitare** to play sth on the guitar; **cuisiner au beurre** to cook with butter; **aller à pied/à bicyclette/à cheval** to go on foot/by bicycle/on horseback

2 *(indiquant la manière)* **à voix haute** out loud; **on a ri aux larmes** we laughed till we cried; **agir à son gré** to do as one pleases *or* likes; **tout fonctionne à merveille** everything works perfectly; **je l'aime à la folie** I love him/her to distraction; **nous pourrions multiplier les exemples à l'infini** we could cite an infinite number of examples; **il s'assit à califourchon sur la chaise** he sat astride the chair; **à toute vitesse** at full speed; **à petits pas** at a slow pace; **au ralenti** in slow motion; **au rythme de deux par semaine** at the rate of two a week; **à jeun** on *or* with an empty stomach; **faire qch à la russe/turque** to do sth the Russian/Turkish way; **la vie à l'américaine** the American way of life; **un film policier à la Hitchcock** a thriller in the style of *or* à la Hitchcock; *Fam* **encore une blague à la Marie** another one of Marie's little jokes

D. *MARQUANT L'APPARTENANCE* **je veux une chambre à moi** I want my own room *or* a room of my own; **à qui est ce livre? – à moi** whose book is it? – (it's) mine; **c'est un ami à moi qui m'a parlé de vous** it was a friend of mine who told me about you; *Fam* **encore une idée à Papa!** another of Dad's ideas!

E. *INDIQUANT L'ATTRIBUTION, LA DESTINATION* **je suis à vous dans une minute** I'll be with you in a minute; **c'est à moi de jouer/parler** it's my turn to play/to speak; **ce n'est pas à moi de le faire** it's not up to me to do it; **à l'attention de M. le directeur** *(dans la correspondance)* for the attention of the manager; **à Jacques** to *or* for Jacques; **à notre fille bien-aimée** *(sur une tombe)* in memory of our beloved daughter; **à toi pour toujours** yours for ever

F. *INTRODUISANT UNE ÉVALUATION, UN RAPPORT DISTRIBUTIF* **1** *(introduisant un prix)* **un livre à 30 euros** a book which costs 30 euros, a book worth 30 euros; **un tableau à 100 000 euros** a painting worth 100,000 euros; **ne fais pas la difficile pour une robe à 50 euros** don't make so much fuss about a 50-euro dress

2 *(indiquant un rapport, une mesure)* **vendus à la douzaine/au poids/au détail** sold by the dozen/by weight/individually; **payé à la page** paid by the page; **les promotions s'obtiennent au nombre d'années d'ancienneté** promotion is in accordance with length of service; **faites-les aligner deux à deux** line them up two by two

3 *(introduisant un nombre de personnes)* **ils ont soulevé le piano à quatre** it took four of them to lift the piano; **à deux, on aura vite fait de repeindre la cuisine** between the two of us, it won't take long to repaint the kitchen; **nous travaillons à sept dans la même pièce** there are seven of us working in the same room; **on peut dormir à six dans le chalet** the chalet can sleep six; **ils sont venus à plusieurs** several of them came

4 *(indiquant une approximation)* **je m'entraîne trois à cinq heures par jour** I practise three to five hours a day; **j'en ai vu 15 à 20** I saw 15 or 20 of them

G. *MARQUANT DES RAPPORTS DE CAUSE OU DE CONSÉQUENCE* **1** *(indiquant la cause)* **à ces mots, il s'est tu** on hearing these words, he fell silent; **à ces cris, je me suis retourné** when I heard the cries, I turned round; **on l'a distribué à sa demande** it was given out at his request

2 *(indiquant la conséquence)* **il lui a tout dit, à ma grande surprise** he told him/her everything, much to my surprise; **à la satisfaction générale** to the satisfaction of all concerned

3 *(d'après)* **je t'ai reconnu à ta voix/démarche** I recognized (you by) your voice/walk; **au tremblement de ses mains, je voyais bien qu'il avait peur** I could tell he was scared from *or* by the way his hands were shaking; **à sa mine, on voit qu'il est en mauvaise santé** you can tell from the way he looks that he's ill; **à ce que je vois/comprends** from what I see/understand; **à ce qu'elle dit, la lettre n'est jamais arrivée** according to her *or* to what she says, the letter never arrived

H. *SUIVI DE L'INFINITIF* **1** *(indiquant l'hypothèse, la cause)* **il s'est fait des ennemis à se conduire ainsi** he's made enemies by behaving that way; **tu vas te fatiguer à rester debout** you'll get tired standing up; **à t'entendre, on dirait que tu t'en moques** listening to you, I get the feeling you don't care; **une histoire à vous faire rougir** an embarrassing story; **à bien considérer les choses...** all things considered...

2 *(exprimant l'obligation)* **la somme est à régler avant le 10** the full amount has to *or* must be paid by the 10th; **le mur est à repeindre** the wall needs to be repainted; **à consommer avec modération** drink in moderation; **c'est une pièce à voir absolument** this play is really worth seeing; **un livre à lire et à relire** a book which can be read over and over again; **les vêtements à laver/repasser** the clothes to be washed/ironed; **la phrase à retenir** the sentence to be *or* which should be remembered

3 *(exprimant la possibilité)* **il n'y a rien à voir/à manger** there's nothing to see/to eat

4 *(en train de)* **il était assis là à bâiller** he was sitting there yawning; **j'étais sur la terrasse à lire** I was reading on the patio; **ne restez pas là à rêvasser** don't just sit there daydreaming

5 *(au point de)* **il en est à regretter ce qu'il a fait** he's come to regret what he did; **ils en sont à se demander si ça en vaut la peine** they've got to the stage of wondering whether it's worth the effort **I.** *MARQUANT LA CARACTÉRISATION* **une fille aux cheveux longs** a girl with long hair; **l'homme au pardessus** the man in *or* with the overcoat; **une bête à cornes** a horned animal, an animal with horns; **une chemise à manches courtes** a short-sleeved shirt, a shirt with short sleeves; **un pyjama à fleurs/rayures** flowery/stripy pyjamas; **une voiture à cinq vitesses** a five-gear car, a car with five gears; **une fugue à trois voix** a fugue in three parts; **des sardines à l'huile** sardines in oil; **concombre à la vinaigrette** cucumber in vinaigrette; **poulet aux épices** spicy chicken; **glace à la framboise** raspberry ice cream; **arme à feu** firearm; **avion à réaction** jet plane; **chauffage au charbon/gaz** coal/gas heating; **calculette à piles** battery-operated calculator; **tasse à thé** tea cup; **mousse à raser** shaving cream; **machine à coudre** sewing machine; **papier à lettres** writing paper; **bureau à louer** *(dans petite annonce, sur panneau)* office for rent

J. *SERVANT DE LIEN SYNTAXIQUE* **1** *(introduisant le complément du verbe)* **parler à qn** to talk to sb; **téléphoner à qn** to phone sb; **croire à qch** to believe in sth; **penser à qn** to think of *or* about sb; **convenir à qn** to suit sb; *Littéraire* **aimer à faire qch** to like to do sth, to like doing sth; **il consent à ce que nous y allions** he agrees to our going; **dire à qn de faire qch** to tell sb to do sth; **rendre qch à qn** to give sth back to sb, to give sth sb back; **dérober qch à qn** to steal sth from sb; **autoriser qn à faire qch** to authorize sb to do sth

2 *(introduisant le complément d'un nom)* **l'aspiration à la liberté** hopes for freedom; **l'appartenance à un parti** membership of a party; **son dévouement à notre cause** his/her devotion to our cause

3 *(introduisant le complément de l'adjectif)* **c'est difficile à dessiner** it's difficult to draw; **perpendiculaire à la droite B** perpendicular to line B; **dévoué à la cause** devoted to the cause; **agréable aux yeux** pleasant to look at; **doux au toucher** soft to the touch

---

A3 [ɑtrwa] **NM** A3

A4 [ɑkatr] **NM** A4

AA [ɑɑ] **NF** *Banque & Bourse* **(notation) AA** AA (rating), double-A rating

AAA [ɑɑɑ] **NF** *Banque & Bourse* **(notation) A.** AAA (rating), triple-A rating

abaissant, -e [abesɑ̃, -ɑ̃t] **ADJ** degrading, humiliating

abaisse [abɛs] **NF** *Culin (en pâtisserie)* piece of rolled-out pastry; **faites une a. de 3mm** roll the pastry to a thickness of 3mm

abaisse-langue [abɛslɑ̃g] **NM INV** *Méd Br* tongue spatula, *Am* tongue depressor

abaissement [abɛsmɑ̃] **NM 1** *(d'une vitre)* lowering; *(d'un store)* pulling down; *(d'une manette ▸ en tirant)* pulling down; *(▸ en poussant)* pushing down

2 *(du niveau d'un fleuve etc)* lowering; *(de la température)* fall, drop

3 *Écon (des prix, des taux, d'un impôt)* lowering, reduction; *(d'une monnaie)* weakening

4 *Fig Vieilli & Littéraire* abasement, humbling

abaisser **[4]** [abese] **VT 1** *(faire descendre ▸ vitre)* to lower; *(▸ store)* to pull down; *(▸ voilette)* to let down; *(▸ pont-levis)* to lower, to let down; **a. la manette** *(en tirant)* to pull the lever down; *(en poussant)* to push the lever down

2 *(réduire ▸ température)* to lower; *(▸ prix, taux, impôt)* to lower, to reduce; *(monnaie)* to weaken

3 *Fig Littéraire (individu, pays)* to abase, to humble

4 *Math (perpendiculaire)* to drop; *(chiffre)* to bring down, to carry

5 *Culin* to roll out

6 *Cartes* to lay down

VPR s'abaisser 1 *(vitre, pont-levis)* to be lowered; *(voile, rideau)* to fall; *(paupière)* to droop **2** *(être en pente ▸ champ)* to slope down **3 s'a. à qch** to stoop to sth; **s'a. à des compromissions** to stoop to compromise; **je ne m'abaisserais jamais à un tel niveau** I'd never stoop so low as that; **s'a. à faire qch** to stoop so low as to do sth

abaisseur [abesœr] **ADJ 1** *Élec (transformateur)* step-down **2** *Anat* **muscle a.** depressor

NM *Anat* depressor; **a. de tension** depressor

abandon [abɑ̃dɔ̃] **NM 1** *(fait de rejeter)* abandonment, rejection; *Jur (de biens, de droit)* surrender; **son a. de toute ambition politique** the fact that he/she gave up all political ambition; **faire a. de qch à qn** to donate sth (freely) to sb; *Jur* **a. du domicile conjugal** desertion of the marital home; *Mil & Jur* **a. de poste** dereliction of duty

2 *(fait d'être rejeté)* **éprouver un sentiment d'a.** to feel abandoned

3 *(état négligé)* neglected state; **les lieux étaient dans un (état de) grand a.** the place was shamefully neglected

4 *(absence de contraintes)* abandon, freedom; **avec a.** *(parler)* freely; *(danser, rire)* with gay abandon

5 *Sport* withdrawal; **il y a eu a. par Roger juste avant l'arrivée** Roger dropped out just before the finish

6 *Ordinat* abort

7 *Bourse* **a. de l'option** *ou* **de prime** relinquishment *or* abandonment of the option

• à l'abandon ADJ un potager à l'a. a neglected vegetable garden **ADV laisser son affaire/ses enfants à l'a.** to neglect one's business/one's children

abandonné, -e [abɑ̃dɔne] **ADJ 1** *(parc)* neglected; *(mine, exploitation)* disused; *(village)* deserted; *(maison, voiture)* abandoned; *(vêtement, chaussure)* discarded **2** *(enfant, animal)* abandoned

abandonner **[3]** [abɑ̃dɔne] **VT 1** *(quitter ▸ enfant, chien, voiture, lieu)* to abandon; *(▸ épouse)* to leave, to desert; *Mil (▸ poste)* to desert, to abandon; **ils ont abandonné la ville pour la campagne** they left city life behind and settled in the country; **les troupes abandonnèrent le village** the troops withdrew from the village

2 *(faire défaut à)* to fail, to desert, to forsake; *Littéraire* **mes forces m'abandonnent** my strength is failing me

3 *(renoncer à ▸ projet, principe, hypothèse)* to abandon; *(▸ espoir)* to give up, to abandon; *(▸ cours)* to drop out of; *(▸ études, carrière)* to give up; *Jur (▸ droit, privilège)* to relinquish, to renounce; **a. le pouvoir** to leave *or* to retire from *or* to give up office; **elle abandonne la géographie** she's dropping geography; **elle a abandonné l'enseignement** she's given up *or* left teaching; **a. la partie** to give up; *Fig* to throw in the sponge *or* towel; **il a abandonné sa part d'héritage à sa sœur** he gave up his share of the inheritance in favour of his sister

4 *(livrer)* **a. qn à** to leave *or* to abandon sb to; **ils abandonnent le pays à la famine** they are condemning the country to starvation

5 *Naut (navire)* to abandon; *(homme)* to maroon

6 *Ordinat* to abort

7 *Bourse* **a. l'option** *ou* **la prime** to relinquish *or* abandon *or* surrender the option

USAGE ABSOLU *(dans une lutte, une discussion)* to give up; **il ne comprendra jamais, j'abandonne** he'll never understand, I give up

VPR s'abandonner 1 *(se laisser aller)* to let (oneself) go **2** *(s'épancher)* to open one's heart, to pour out one's feelings **3 s'a. à** *(désespoir)* to give way to; *(rêverie)* to drift off into

abaque [abak] **NM 1** *(pour compter)* abacus **2** *Math* chart, graph **3** *Archit* abacus

abasourdir **[32]** [abazurdir] **VT 1** *(stupéfier)* to stun; **la nouvelle nous a abasourdis** we were stunned by the news **2** *(sujet: bruit, clameur)* to stun, to deafen

abasourdissant, -e [abazurdisɑ̃, -ɑ̃t] **ADJ** *(nouvelle)* stunning; *(bruit)* shattering, deafening

abasourdissement [abazurdismɑ̃] **NM** amazement

abat *etc voir* **abattre**

abatage [abataʒ] = **abattage**

abâtardir **[32]** [abɑtardir] **VT** *(race, individu)* to cause to degenerate; *(valeur)* to debase

VPR s'abâtardir *(race, individu)* to degenerate; *(valeur)* to become debased

abâtardissement [abɑtardismɑ̃] **NM** *(d'une race)* degeneration; *(d'une valeur)* debasement

abat-jour [abaʒur] **NM INV** lampshade; *Fig* **elle a mis sa main en a.** she shaded her eyes with her hand

abats [aba] **NMPL** *Culin Br* offal *(UNCOUNT)*, *Am* variety meat; **a. de volaille** giblets

abattage [abataʒ] **NM 1** *(d'arbres)* felling

2 *(d'animaux)* slaughter, slaughtering; **45 kilos à l'a.** 45 kilos at the time of slaughter

3 *Mines* cutting, working; **face d'a.** working face, coalface

4 *Naut* **a. en carène** careening

5 *Com* **vente à l'a.** sale at knock-down prices

6 *Fam (locution)* **avoir de l'a.** *Vieilli* to be full of energy□; *Fig (d'un acteur, d'un politicien etc)* to have charisma

abattant [abatɑ̃] **NM** flap, drop-leaf

abattement [abatmɑ̃] **NM 1** *(épuisement ▸ physique)* exhaustion; *(▸ mental)* despondency, dejection **2** *Fin (rabais)* reduction; *(d'impôts)* allowance; **donnant droit à a.** eligible for tax relief; **a. à la base** basic personal allowance; **a. fiscal** tax allowance; **a. forfaitaire** fixed-rate rebate

> Il faut noter que le nom anglais **abatement** est un faux ami. Il signifie **apaisement**.

abatteur [abatœr] **NM 1** *(d'arbres)* feller **2** *(d'animaux)* slaughterer, slaughterman **3** *Fam (de travail)* slogger, hard worker□

abattis [abati] **NM 1** *Mil* abatis, abattis **2** *(dans une forêt)* felled trees

NMPL 1 *(de volaille)* giblets **2** *Fam (bras et jambes)* limbs□, arms and legs□; **t'as intérêt à numéroter tes a.!** start saying your prayers!

abattoir [abatwar] **NM** slaughterhouse, abattoir; *Fig* **envoyer des hommes à l'a.** to send men to the slaughter *or* to be slaughtered *or* butchered

abattre **[83]** [abatr] **VT 1** *(faire tomber ▸ arbre)* to cut down, to fell; *(▸ mur, quille)* to knock down; *(▸ adversaire)* to bring down; *Fam Fig* **a. de la besogne** *ou* **du travail** to get through a lot of work□

2 *(sujet: vent, tempête etc)* to knock down; **l'arbre fut abattu par le vent** the tree was blown down

3 *(mettre à plat ▸ main, battant)* to bring down; **elle a abattu son poing sur le buffet** she slammed her fist down on the sideboard; **a. ses cartes** *ou* **son jeu** to lay down one's cards; *Fig* to lay one's cards on the table

4 *(faire retomber ▸ blé, poussière)* to settle; *(▸ vent)* to bring down

5 *(tuer ▸ personne, avion)* to shoot down; *(▸ animal domestique)* to put down; *(▸ animal de boucherie)* to slaughter; **c'est un homme à a.** this man is on the hit-list

6 *Fig (démoraliser)* to dishearten, to depress; *(épuiser)* to drain, to wear out; **la défaite l'a complètement abattu** *(moralement)* the defeat completely crushed him; **ne pas se laisser a.** to keep one's spirits up;

VI *Naut (bateau à moteur)* to pay off; *(voilier)* to bear away

VPR s'abattre 1 *(s'écrouler ▸ maison)* to fall down; *(▸ personne)* to fall (down), to collapse; **l'arbre s'est abattu** the tree came crashing down **2 s'a. sur** *(pluie)* to come pouring down on; *(grêle)* to come pelting *or* beating down on; *(coups)* to rain down on; *(se jeter sur ▸ oiseau, personne)* to swoop down on; **le malheur/la maladie venait de s'a. sur nous** suddenly we'd been struck by disaster/disease; *aussi Fig* **s'a. sur sa proie** to swoop down on one's prey

abattu, -e [abaty] **ADJ 1** *(démoralisé)* despondent, dejected, downcast; **d'un air a.** dejectedly, dispiritedly; **a. par la chaleur** limp with the heat **2** *(épuisé)* exhausted, worn-out

NM fusil à l'a. uncocked rifle

abbatial, -e, -aux, -ales [abasjal, -o] **ADJ** abbey *(avant n)*

• abbatiale NF abbey

abbaye [abei] **NF** abbey

abbé [abe] **NM 1** *(d'une abbaye)* abbot **2** *(ecclésiastique)* = title formerly used in France for members of the secular clergy; *Vieilli* **monsieur l'a.** *(en s'adressant à lui)* Father; *(en parlant de lui)* the Reverend Father

abbesse [abɛs] **NF** abbess

abc [abese] NM INV **1** *(base)* basics, fundamentals; **elle ignore même l'a. du métier** she doesn't even know the basics of the job **2** *(livre pour apprendre à lire)* ABC, alphabet (book); *(livre scolaire)* primer

abcès [apsɛ] NM *Méd* abscess; **a. à la gencive** gumboil; *Fig* **crever** *ou* **vider l'a.** to clear the air

abdication [abdikasjɔ̃] NF abdication

abdiquer [3] [abdike] VT *(pouvoir)* to abdicate, to surrender; *(responsabilité, opinion)* to abdicate, to renounce
VI to abdicate, to give in

abdomen [abdɔmɛn] NM *Anat* abdomen

abdominal, -e, -aux, -ales [abdɔminal, -o] ADJ *Anat* abdominal
• **abdominaux** NMPL *Anat* **1** *(muscles)* stomach *or* abdominal muscles **2** *(exercices)* **faire des abdominaux** to do stomach exercises *or* sit-ups

abdominoplastie [abdɔminoplasti] NF *Méd* abdominoplasty

abdos [abdo] NMPL *Fam* *(abrév* **abdominaux***)* **1** *(muscles)* abs, stomach *or* abdominal muscles[□] **2** *(exercices)* **faire des a.** to do stomach exercises *or* sit-ups[□], to work one's abs

abducteur [abdyktœr] ADJ M **1** *Anat* abductor **2** *Chim (tube)* delivery *(avant n)*
NM *Anat* abductor muscle

abécédaire [abesedɛr] NM primer, alphabet book

abeille [abɛj] NF *Entom* bee; *Fam* **avoir les abeilles** to be hacked off *or Br* cheesed off; **a. ouvrière** worker (bee)

aber [abɛr] NM (deep) estuary *(in Brittany)*

aberrant, -e [aberɑ̃, -ɑ̃t] ADJ **1** *(comportement)* aberrant, illogical; *(prix)* ridiculous; *(idée)* preposterous, absurd; **c'est a.!** it's absurd!, it's ridiculous! **2** *Biol* aberrant

aberration [aberasjɔ̃] NF **1** *(absurdité)* aberration; **dans un moment d'a.** in a moment of aberration; **c'est une a.!** it's absurd!, it's ridiculous! **2** *Astron, Biol & Opt* aberration; *Biol* **a. chromosomique** chromosome abnormality

abêtir [32] [abetir] VT to dull the mind of; **abêti de fatigue** numb *or* dazed with fatigue
VPR **s'abêtir** to become mindless *or* half-witted

abêtissant, -e [abetisɑ̃, -ɑ̃t] ADJ *(activité, tâche)* mind-numbing; *(émission)* mindless

abhorrer [3] [abɔre] VT *Littéraire* to loathe, to abhor

abîme [abim] NM **1** *Géog (gouffre)* abyss, chasm, gulf **2** *Fig (moral)* despair; *(financier)* ruin; **il est au bord de l'a.** *(moral)* he is on the brink *or* verge of despair; *(financier)* he is on the brink *or* verge of ruin; **être au fond de l'a.** to have reached rock bottom, to be at one's lowest ebb **3** *Fig (distance mentale)* gulf, chasm, abyss; **il y avait comme un a. entre nous** a great abyss seemed to open up between us
• **abîmes** NMPL *Littéraire (infini)* depths; **les abîmes de son cœur** the depths of his/her heart

abîmer [3] [abime] VT **1** *(gâter* ► *aliment, vêtement, livre)* to spoil; *(*► *meuble)* to damage; *(*► *yeux)* to ruin; **tu vas a. ta poupée!** you'll break your doll! **2** *Fam (meurtrir)* to injure[□]; **ils l'ont bien abîmé** they've made a right mess of him; **a. le portrait à qn** to smash sb's face in; **se faire a. le portrait** to get one's face smashed in **3** *Littéraire* **abîmé dans ses pensées** deep in thought; **abîmé dans le désespoir** in the depths of despair
VPR **s'abîmer 1** *(endommager)* to ruin; **tu t'abîmes les yeux** you're ruining your eyes *or* eyesight; **s'a. la santé** to ruin one's health
2 *(aliment)* to go bad *or Br* off; *(livre, meuble)* to get damaged; *(vêtement, chaussures)* to wear out
3 *Littéraire (navire)* to sink, to founder
4 *Littéraire* **s'a. dans qch** *(se plonger dans)* to be deeply absorbed in sth; **s'a. dans ses pensées** to be lost *or* deep in thought; **s'a. dans le désespoir** to be plunged into despair

abject, -e [abʒɛkt] ADJ despicable, contemptible; **il a été a. avec elle** he behaved despicably towards her

abjectement [abʒɛktəmɑ̃] ADV *Littéraire* abjectly

abjection [abʒɛksjɔ̃] NF **1** *(état)* utter humiliation **2** *(caractère vil)* abjectness, vileness; **l'a. de son comportement** his/her vile behaviour **3** *(chose vile)* **ce film est une a.** this film is a complete outrage *or* a disgrace

abjuration [abʒyrasjɔ̃] NF *(d'un serment)* renunciation; *(d'une menace, d'une hérésie)* recantation

abjurer [3] [abʒyre] VT to abjure; *(serment)* to renounce; *(menace, hérésie)* to recant

ablatif, -ive [ablatif, -iv] ADJ *Astron* ablative
NM *Gram* ablative (case); **à l'a.** in the ablative; **a. absolu** ablative absolute

ablation [ablasjɔ̃] NF *Méd* removal, *Spéc* ablation

ablative [ablativ] *voir* **ablatif**

> **-ABLE** SUFFIX
>
> • This very productive suffix expresses the idea of POSSIBILITY and is used to create adjectives, mainly from transitive verbs but also sometimes from intransitive verbs or nouns. Its equivalent in English is, in a lot of cases, *-able* or *-ible*. When there is no equivalent form in *-able*, the translation often includes an expression like "which can be…" or "easy to…":
>
> **payable** payable; **mangeable** edible; **abordable** affordable; **maniable** easy to handle; **négligeable** negligible; **simplifiable** which can be made simpler; **variable** variable; **valable** valid; **effroyable** horrifying
>
> • **-able** is often found in conjunction with a base and the prefix **in-** (or **im-**), with the idea of IMPOSSIBILITY, even if there is no equivalent positive form:
>
> **intolérable** intolerable, unbearable; **inusable** which will never wear out; **immuable** unchanging; **impitoyable** merciless
>
> • One recent trend is to use **-able** to create adjectives applied to people, meaning, in contexts of election or award-giving, "who can be elected…" or "who can be awarded…":
>
> **un nobélisable** a potential Nobel prizewinner; **les oscarisables** potential Oscar winners, Oscar hopefuls; **les cardinaux papables** the cardinals who are likely candidates for the papacy; **les présidentiables** would-be presidential candidates; **il est considéré comme premier ministrable** he's considered Prime Minister material; **un académisable** a potential future member of the Académie française

ablette [ablɛt] NF *Ich* bleak

ablution [ablysjɔ̃] NF **1** *Rel (du corps, du calice)* ablution **2** *Fam (toilette)* **faire ses ablutions** to perform one's ablutions

abnégation [abnegasjɔ̃] NF abnegation, self-denial

aboi [abwa] NM *Chasse* bay
• **aux abois** ADJ **être aux abois** *Chasse* to stand at bay; *Fig* to have one's back against *or* to the wall ADV *Chasse* at bay; *Fig* **mettre qn aux abois** to have sb with his/her back against the wall

aboie *etc voir* **aboyer**

aboiement [abwamɑ̃] NM *(d'un chien)* bark; **des aboiements** barking *(UNCOUNT)*; *Fig* **l'officier répondit par un a.** the officer barked (out) an answer
• **aboiements** NMPL *Fig Péj* ranting, raving; **les aboiements de la presse** the rantings of the press

abolir [32] [abɔlir] VT **1** *(une loi, la peine de mort)* to abolish **2** *Fig* **le téléphone abolit les distances** the telephone makes distance irrelevant

abolitionnisme [abɔlisjɔnism] NM abolitionism

abolitionniste [abɔlisjɔnist] ADJ abolitionist
NMF abolitionist

abominable [abɔminabl] ADJ **1** *(désagréable* ► *temps, odeur)* abominable, foul **2** *(abject* ► *crime)* heinous, abominable, vile; **l'a. homme des neiges** the abominable snowman

abominablement [abɔminabləmɑ̃] ADV *(laid, cher)* horribly; *(habillé)* hideously; **a. (mal) organisé** appallingly *or* abominably badly organized

abomination [abɔminasjɔ̃] NF **1** *(acte, propos)* abomination; **cette soupe, c'est une a.** that soup is revolting; **il dit des abominations** he says appalling things **2** *(sentiment)* loathing, detestation, abomination; **avoir qch en a.** to abhor *or* to loathe sth

abominer [3] [abɔmine] VT *Littéraire* to loathe, to abhor, to abominate

abondamment [abɔ̃damɑ̃] ADV *(servir, saler)* copiously; *(manger, boire)* in copious amounts; *(rincer)* thoroughly; *(pleuvoir)* heavily; **elle a a. traité la question** she has amply *or* fully dealt with the question; **je vous l'ai a. répété** I have told you again and again; **a. illustré** lavishly illustrated

abondance [abɔ̃dɑ̃s] NF **1** *(prospérité)* affluence; **vivre dans l'a.** to live in affluence **2** *(grande quantité)* **une a. de qch** an abundance *or* a wealth of sth; **parler avec a.** to be eloquent; **parler d'a.** to speak off-the-cuff, to extemporize
• **en abondance** ADV in abundance

abondant, -e [abɔ̃dɑ̃, -ɑ̃t] ADJ *(en quantité* ► *nourriture)* abundant, copious; *(*► *récolte)* bountiful; *(*► *vivres)* plentiful; *(*► *végétation)* luxuriant, lush; *(*► *larmes)* copious; *(*► *chevelure)* luxuriant, thick; **peu a.** *(vivres)* scarce; *(récolte)* poor; *(végétation)* sparse; *(chevelure)* sparse, thin; **d'abondantes illustrations/recommandations** a wealth of illustrations/recommendations

abondement [abɔ̃dmɑ̃] NM *Fin* = employer's contribution to company savings scheme

abonder [3] [abɔ̃de] VI **1** *(foisonner)* to be plentiful; **le raisin abonde cet automne** the grapes are plentiful this autumn; **a. en** to abound in, to be full of; **la rivière abonde en poissons** the river is teeming with fish; **son livre abonde en anecdotes** his/her book is rich in anecdotes **2** *Fig* **a. dans le sens de** to be in complete agreement with

abonné, -e [abɔne] NM,F **1** *(à un journal, à une revue, au téléphone etc)* subscriber; **abonnés au gaz/à l'électricité** gas/electricity consumers; **il n'y a pas d'a. au numéro que vous avez demandé** ≃ the number you have dialled has not been recognized; **a. numérique** digital subscriber **2** *(pour un trajet, au théâtre, au stade)* season-ticket holder

abonnement [abɔnmɑ̃] NM **1** *(à un journal, à une revue, au téléphone etc)* subscription; **prendre un a. à** to take out a subscription to **2** *(pour un trajet, au théâtre, au concert, au stade)* season ticket; **prendre un a.** to take out a season ticket **3** *(tarif* ► *pour gaz, électricité)* standing charge; *Tél* line rental; **a. à un service en ligne** on-line subscription

abonner [3] [abɔne] VT **1 a. qn à qch** *(journal)* to take out a subscription for sb to sth; *(théâtre, stade)* to buy sb a season ticket for sth; **être abonné à un journal** to subscribe to a paper **2** *(pour un service)* **être abonné au gaz** to have gas; **être abonné au téléphone** to have a phone, *Br* to be on the phone
VPR **s'abonner le trajet revient moins cher si l'on s'abonne** the journey works out cheaper with a season ticket; **s'a. à** *(journal)* to take out a subscription to; *(théâtre, stade)* to buy a season ticket for

abord [abɔr] NM **1** *(contact)* **elle est d'un a. déconcertant/chaleureux** she has an offputting/a warm manner; **être d'un a. facile/difficile** to be approachable/unapproachable **2** *(accès* ► *à une côte)* approach; *(*► *à une maison)* access; **d'un a. facile** *(demeure)* easy to get to; *(texte)* easy to understand *or* to get to grips with
• **abords** NMPL *(alentours)* surroundings; *(d'une ville)* outskirts; **les abords de la tour** the area around the tower
• **aux abords** ADV all around; **dans le château et aux abords** in and around the castle
• **aux abords de** PRÉP **aux abords de la ville** on the outskirts of the town; **aux abords du château/de la maison** (in the area) around the castle/house
• **d'abord** ADV **1** *(en premier lieu)* first; **il vaut mieux en parler d'a.** it's better to talk about it first;

il faudrait (tout) d'a. avoir l'argent et le temps first you'd need the money and the time
2 *(au début)* at first, initially, to begin with; **d'a., elle a été gentille** at first *or* initially she was nice
3 *(introduisant une restriction)* to start with, for a start; **d'a., tu n'es même pas prêt!** to start with *or* for a start, you're not even ready!; **d'a., il ne dit jamais bonjour** for a start, he never says hello
4 *(de toute façon)* anyway; **je n'ai jamais aimé ça, d'a.** I've never liked it anyway; **et puis d'a., qu'est-ce que tu veux?** and anyway, what do you want?
• **dès l'abord** ADV at the outset, from the (very) beginning
• **de prime abord, au premier abord** ADV at first sight *or* glance

abordabilité [abɔrdabilite] ADJ *Can* affordability

abordable [abɔrdabl] ADJ **1** *(peu cher ▸ prix)* reasonable; *(▸ produit)* reasonably priced, affordable
2 *(ouvert ▸ patron, célébrité)* approachable
3 *(facile ▸ texte)* accessible
4 *Naut (côte)* accessible; **le rivage n'était pas a.** the shore was not easy to approach

abordage [abɔrdaʒ] NM *Naut* **1** *(manœuvre ▸ d'assaut)* boarding **2** *(collision)* collision; **l'a. s'est produit à la sortie du chenal** the two boats collided as they came out of the fairway **3** *(approche ▸ du rivage)* coming alongside; *(▸ d'un quai)* berthing

aborder [3] [abɔrde] VT **1** *(accoster ▸ passant)* to accost, to approach; **on n'aborde pas les gens dans la rue!** you don't just walk up to people in the street!; **quand le policier l'a abordé** when the detective came *or* walked up to him; **quand vas-tu l'a. pour cette augmentation?** when are you going to approach him/her about your pay rise?
2 *(arriver à l'entrée de)* to enter; **je suis tombé de vélo au moment où j'abordais le virage** I fell off my bike as I was coming up to the bend
3 *(faire face à ▸ nouvelle vie)* to embark on; *(▸ tâche)* to tackle, to get to grips with; *(▸ retraite)* to approach
4 *(se mettre à examiner ▸ texte, problème)* to approach; **on n'aborde Pascal qu'en dernière année** we only start studying Pascal in the final year; **il n'a pas eu le temps d'a. le sujet** he didn't have time to get onto *or* to broach the subject
5 *Naut (attaquer)* to board; *(percuter)* to collide with, to ram into
VI to touch *or* to reach land; **nous abordons à Gênes demain** we reach Genoa tomorrow

aborigène [abɔriʒɛn] ADJ **1** *(autochtone)* aboriginal; *(d'Australie)* Aboriginal, native Australian **2** *Bot* indigenous
NMF *(autochtone)* aborigine; *(autochtone d'Australie)* Aborigine, Aboriginal; **les aborigènes d'Australie** the (Australian) Aborigines, native Australians

abortif, -ive [abɔrtif, -iv] ADJ abortive
NM *Méd* abortifacient

aboucher [3] [abuʃe] VT **1** *(tuyaux)* to butt, to join up, to join end to end **2** *(gens)* to put in touch *or* contact; **a. qn avec qn** to put sb in touch *or* contact with sb
VPR **s'aboucher s'a. avec qn** *(se mettre en rapport avec qn)* to get in touch *or* contact with sb; *(se lier avec qn)* to team up with sb

abouler [3] [abule] *Fam* VT to hand over[□], to give[□]; **la clé, là, aboule!** sling us that key, will you!
VPR **s'abouler** to turn up, to show up, to roll up

about [abu] NM *Tech* butt *(of a beam)*

abouter [3] [abute] VT *Tech* to join end-to-end, to butt

aboutir [32] [abutir] VI **1** *(réussir ▸ projet, personne)* to succeed; **l'entreprise n'a pas abouti** the venture fell through *or* never came to anything; **faire a. des négociations** to bring talks to a satisfactory conclusion **2** *(finir)* **le chemin aboutit sur la berge du fleuve** the path leads to the river bank; **a. en prison** to end up in prison
• **aboutir à** VT IND **1** *(voie, rue)* to end at *or* in, to lead to; *(fleuve)* to end in; **cette route aboutit à la prison** this road ends at the prison; **où aboutit cette allée?** where does this lane go to *or* end up? **2** *(avoir pour résultat)* to lead to, to result in; **cela aboutira à une guerre** that will lead to a war; **tu aboutiras au même résultat** you'll arrive at *or* get the same result; **j'ai abouti à la conclusion que…** I finally came to the conclusion that…

aboutissant [abutisɑ̃] NM *Littéraire (conclusion)* (final) outcome, result; *(résultat positif)* success
• **aboutissants** NMPL abuttals; *Fig* **les tenants et les aboutissants** the ins and outs

aboutissement [abutismɑ̃] NM *(conclusion)* (final) outcome, result; *(résultat positif)* success

aboyer [13] [abwaje] VI **1** *(chien)* to bark; *(chien de meute)* to bay **2** *Fig (personne)* to bark; **a. après** *ou* **contre qn** to yell at sb **3** *(locution)* **a. à la lune** to howl at the moon; *Fig* to complain to no avail

aboyeur, -euse [abwajœr, -øz] ADJ barking

abracadabra [abrakadabra] NM abracadabra

abracadabrant, -e [abrakadabrɑ̃, -ɑ̃t] ADJ *Fam* bewildering[□]

abraser [3] [abraze] VT to wear off, *Sout* to abrade

abrasif, -ive [abrazif, -iv] ADJ abrasive
NM abrasive

abrasion [abrazjɔ̃] NF **1** *(action de frotter, résultat)* abrasion **2** *Géol* abrasion

abrasive [abraziv] *voir* **abrasif**

abrégé [abreʒe] NM **1** *(d'un texte)* summary; **faire un a. de qch** to make a summary of sth, to summarize sth **2** *(livre)* abstract; **un a. d'histoire de France** a short history of France; **un a. de philosophie** a short guide to philosophy
• **en abrégé** ADJ *(mot, phrase)* in abbreviated form ADV *(écrire)* in brief, in abbreviated form

abrègement [abrɛʒmɑ̃] NM **1** *(d'un texte)* summary; *(d'un mot)* abbreviation; *(d'une syllabe)* shortening **2** *(d'un délai)* shortening; *(d'un congé)* cutting short, curtailing

abréger [22] [abreʒe] VT **1** *(interrompre ▸ vacances)* to cut short, to shorten; *(▸ vie)* to cut short, to put an (early) end to; **pour a. votre attente** so as not to keep you waiting **2** *(tronquer ▸ discours)* to cut; *(▸ texte)* to cut, to abridge; *(▸ conversation)* to cut short; *(▸ mot)* to abbreviate
USAGE ABSOLU *Fam* **abrège!** get to the point!, cut to the chase!
• **pour abréger** ADV **Catherine, ou Cath pour a.** Catherine, or Cath for short; **pour a., nous avons échoué** to cut a long story short, we failed
VPR **s'abréger** to be abbreviated *or* shortened (à to)

abreuvement [abrœvmɑ̃] NM watering

abreuver [5] [abrœve] VT **1** *(faire boire ▸ animaux)* to water **2** *Fig* **a. qn de critiques/d'éloges** to heap criticism/praise on sb; **a. qn d'insultes** to shower sb with abuse; **nous sommes abreuvés d'images de violence** we get swamped with violent images
VPR **s'abreuver 1** *(animal)* to drink **2** *Fam (personne)* to drink[□]

abreuvoir [abrœvwar] NM *(bac)* (drinking) trough; *(plan d'eau)* watering place; **mener les chevaux à l'a.** to lead the horses to water, to water the horses

abréviation [abrevjasjɔ̃] NF abbreviation

abri [abri] NM **1** *(cabane, toit, refuge)* shelter; **a. antiatomique** *ou* **antinucléaire** (nuclear) fallout shelter; **a. anti-aérien** air-raid shelter; **a. à vélos** bike shed **2** *Fig* refuge; **un a. contre la solitude** a refuge from *or* a guard against loneliness
• **à l'abri** ADV **1** *(des intempéries)* **être à l'a.** to be sheltered; **mets ton vélo à l'a., il va se mouiller** put your bike away, it'll get wet; **mettre qn à l'a.** to find shelter for sb; **se mettre à l'a.** to take cover, to shelter **2** *(en lieu sûr)* in a safe place; **j'ai mis ma collection de verres à l'a.** I've put my collection of glasses away in a safe place; **mettre sa fortune à l'a. dans le pétrole** to invest one's money safely in oil
• **à l'abri de** PRÉP **1 être à l'a. de** *(pluie, chaleur)* to be sheltered from; *(obus)* to be sheltered *or* shielded from; *(regards)* to be hidden from; **se mettre à l'a. de** *(pluie, chaleur)* to (take) shelter from; *(obus)* to take cover from **2** *Fig* **nos économies nous mettront à l'a. du besoin** our savings will shield us against poverty *or* will protect us from hardship; **à l'a. du danger** safe from danger; **à l'a. de tout soupçon** free from (all) suspicion; **personne n'est à l'a. d'une erreur/d'un maître-chanteur** anyone can make a mistake/fall victim to a blackmailer; **il l'a mis dans un tiroir à l'a. des regards indiscrets** he locked it in a drawer safe from prying eyes

Abribus® [abribys] NM bus shelter

abricot [abriko] NM **1** *Bot (fruit)* apricot **2** *(couleur)* apricot
ADJ INV apricot, apricot-coloured

abricoté, -e [abrikɔte] ADJ apricot-flavoured

abricotier [abrikɔtje] NM *Bot* apricot tree

abricotine [abrikɔtin] NF *Suisse* apricot brandy

abrier [10] [abrije] *Can* VT to cover up *(to protect from the cold)*
VPR **s'abrier** to wrap up (well)

abri-garage *(pl* **abris-garages)** NM carport

abri-sous-roche [abrisurɔʃ] *(pl* **abris-sous-roche)** NM *Géol* rock-shelter

abriter [3] [abrite] VT **1** *(protéger ▸ de la pluie, des intempéries)* to shelter; *(▸ du soleil)* to shade, to shelter; **abritant ses yeux avec un journal** shading his/her eyes with a newspaper; **cet auvent nous abrite des regards indiscrets** *(des passants)* the awning gives us some privacy; *(des intrus)* the awning shields us from prying eyes **2** *(loger ▸ personnes)* to house, to accommodate; *(▸ société, machine)* to house
VPR **s'abriter s'a. des tirs** to take cover; **s'a. de la pluie/du vent** to (take) shelter from the rain/from the wind; **s'a. du soleil** to go into the shade; *Fig* **s'a. derrière la loi/ses parents** to hide behind the law/one's parents

abrivent [abrivɑ̃] NM windbreak

abrogation [abrɔgasjɔ̃] NF *Jur* repeal, rescinding, abrogation

abrogeable [abrɔʒabl] ADJ *Jur* repealable

abroger [17] [abrɔʒe] VT *Jur* to repeal, to rescind, to abrogate

abrupt, -e [abrypt] ADJ **1** *(raide ▸ côte)* steep; *(▸ versant)* sheer **2** *(brusque ▸ manières, personne, réponse)* abrupt, brusque; *(▸ changement)* abrupt, sudden
NM steep slope

abruptement [abryptəmɑ̃] ADV *(répondre)* abruptly, brusquely; *(changer)* abruptly, suddenly

abruti, -e [abryti] NM,F *Fam* fool, idiot; **arrête de rire comme un a.** stop laughing like an idiot

abrutir [32] [abrytir] VT **1** *(abêtir)* to turn into an idiot **2** *(étourdir)* to stupefy; **abruti de soleil** dazed by sunshine; **abruti de fatigue** numb *or* dazed with tiredness; **abruti par l'alcool** stupefied with drink **3** *(accabler)* **a. qn de travail** to overwork sb; **a. qn de conseils** to pester sb with endless advice
VPR **s'abrutir 1** *(s'accabler)* **s'a. de travail** to overwork oneself, to work oneself into the ground **2** *(s'abêtir)* to turn into an idiot; **on s'abrutit à trop regarder la télévision** too much television rots the brain

abrutissant, -e [abrytisɑ̃, -ɑ̃t] ADJ **1** *(qui rend bête)* mind-numbing **2** *(qui étourdit)* stupefying **3** *(qui fatigue)* wearing, exhausting

abrutissement [abrytismɑ̃] NM mindless state; **l'a. des enfants par la télévision** the mind-numbing effects of television on children

ABS [abeɛs] NM INV *Aut (abrév* **Antiblockiersystem)** ABS

abscisse [apsis] NF *Math* abscissa

abscons, -e [apskɔ̃, -ɔ̃s] ADJ *Littéraire* abstruse

absence [apsɑ̃s] NF **1** *(fait de n'être pas là)* absence; **cette décision a été prise pendant mon a.** this decision was taken in my absence *or* while I was away; **sa troisième a.** *(à l'école)* the third time he's/she's been away from *or* missed school; *(au travail)* the third time he's/she's been off work; *(à une réunion)* the third time he's/she's stayed away from *or* not attended the meeting; **nous avons regretté votre a.** we were sorry that you weren't with us; **on a remarqué ses absences répétées** his/her persistent absenteeism didn't go unnoticed
2 *(de goût, d'imagination etc)* lack, absence; **a. d'idéaux** lack of ideals; **une rassurante a. de préjugés** a reassuring lack of prejudice
3 *(défaillance)* **j'ai eu une a.** *ou* **un moment d'a.** my mind went blank; **elle a des absences** *ou* **des mo-**

ments d'a. her mind wanders at times, at times she can be absent-minded

4 *Jur* absence

• **en l'absence de** PRÉP in the absence of; **en mon a.** during *or* in my absence; **en l'a. de mon fils** in my son's absence, while my son is/was away

absent, -e [apsɑ̃, -ɑ̃t] ADJ 1 *(personne ▸ de l'école)* absent; *(▸ du travail)* off work, absent; *(▸ de son domicile)* away; **il était a. de la réunion** he was not present at the meeting; **il est a. de Paris en ce moment** he isn't in Paris at the moment 2 *(inattentif)* absent; **regard a.** vacant look; **d'un air a.** absent-mindedly 3 *(chose)* missing; *(sentiment)* lacking; **un regard d'où toute tendresse est absente** a look entirely devoid of tenderness

NM,F *(du travail, de l'école)* absentee; *(dans une famille)* absent person; **on ne fait pas cours, il y a trop d'absents** we're not having a lesson today, there are too many pupils missing *or* away; **les Russes ont été les grands absents lors de la Coupe du Monde** the Russians were the most notable absentees from the World Cup

absentéisme [apsɑ̃teism] NM absenteeism; **a. scolaire** truancy

absentéiste [apsɑ̃teist] ADJ absentee

NMF absentee; **les absentéistes** *(au travail)* persistent absentees

absenter [3] [apsɑ̃te] **s'absenter** VPR to be absent; **s'a. de son travail** to be off work; **s'a. du lycée** to be off *or* away from *or* to miss school; **je ne m'étais absentée que quelques minutes** I'd only gone out for a few minutes

absidal, -e, -aux, -ales [apsidal, -o] ADJ *Archit* apsidal

abside [apsid] NF *Archit* apse

absidial, -e, -aux, -ales [apsidjal, -o] = **absidal**

absidiole [apsidjɔl] NF *Archit* apsidiole

absinthe [apsɛ̃t] NF 1 *(alcool)* absinthe 2 *Bot* wormwood, absinthe

absolu, -e [apsɔly] ADJ 1 *(total ▸ liberté, silence)* absolute, complete; *(▸ repos)* complete; **en cas d'absolue nécessité** when absolutely necessary; **nous sommes dans l'impossibilité absolue de vous aider** we are quite unable to help you; **vous avez notre soutien a.** you have our unconditional support

2 *Pol (pouvoir, monarque, majorité)* absolute

3 *(sans nuances)* absolute; **elle voit les choses de manière absolue** she sees things in absolute terms *or* in black and white

4 *(intransigeant)* uncompromising, rigid

5 *Chim, Math & Phys* absolute

6 *Ling (ablatif, construction)* absolute

NM 1 *Phil* **l'a.** the Absolute 2 *Ling* absolute construction

• **dans l'absolu** ADV in absolute terms

absolument [apsɔlymɑ̃] ADV 1 *(entièrement ▸ croire, avoir raison)* absolutely, entirely; *(▸ ravi, faux)* absolutely, completely; *(▸ défendu)* strictly; **a. pas** absolutely not, not at all; **a. rien** absolutely nothing, nothing whatsoever

2 *(à tout prix)* absolutely; **il faut a. leur parler** we (absolutely) must speak to them, it's imperative that we speak to them; **elle veut a. venir avec moi** she insists on coming with me

3 *(oui)* absolutely; **il a raison! – a.!** he's right! – absolutely!

4 *Ling* absolutely; **employé a.** used absolutely *or* in an absolute construction

absolution [apsɔlysjɔ̃] NF 1 *Rel* absolution; **donner l'a. à qn** to give sb absolution 2 *Jur* acquittal

absolutisme [apsɔlytism] NM *Pol* absolutism

absolvait *etc voir* **absoudre**

absorbant, -e [apsɔrbɑ̃, -ɑ̃t] ADJ 1 *(tissu)* absorbent

2 *(lecture)* absorbing, gripping

3 *Phys* absorbative

4 *Bot* **poils absorbants** root hairs

absorber [3] [apsɔrbe] VT 1 *(éponger ▸ gén)* to absorb, to soak up; *(▸ avec un buvard)* to blot

2 *(lumière)* to absorb; *(bruit)* to absorb, to deaden

3 *(consommer ▸ aliment)* to take, to consume; *(▸ boisson)* to drink; *(▸ bénéfices, capitaux)* to absorb; *Écon (▸ entreprise)* to take over, to absorb

4 *(préoccuper ▸ sujet: travail)* to absorb, to engross, to occupy; *(▸ sujet: pensée)* to absorb, to grip; **être absorbé dans ses pensées** to be lost *or* deep in thought

VPR **s'absorber s'a. dans** to become absorbed in; **s'a. dans un livre** to be engrossed in a book; **s'a. dans ses pensées** to be lost *or* deep in thought

absorption [apsɔrpsjɔ̃] NF 1 *(ingestion)* swallowing, taking 2 *(pénétration)* absorption; **masser jusqu'à a. complète par la peau** massage well into the skin 3 *(intégration)* assimilation; *Écon (d'une entreprise)* takeover

absorption-fusion [absɔrpsjɔ̃fyzjɔ̃] *(pl* **absorptions-fusions)** NF *Écon* merger

absoudre [87] [apsudr] VT 1 *Rel* to absolve; **a. qn de ses péchés** to absolve sb from his/her sins, to forgive sb his/her sins 2 *Littéraire (pardonner)* to absolve 3 *Jur* to dismiss

abstenir [40] [apstənir] **s'abstenir** VPR 1 *Pol* to abstain 2 **s'a. de** *(éviter de)* to refrain *or* to abstain from; **s'a. de fumer** to refrain from smoking; **abstiens-toi de la critiquer** don't criticize her; **s'a. de tout commentaire** to refrain from comment

USAGE ABSOLU *(ne pas agir)* **dans ce cas, mieux vaut s'a.** in that case, it's better not to do anything; **pas sérieux s'a.** *(dans une offre d'emploi)* serious applicants only; *(dans une petite annonce)* no timewasters please; **dans le doute, abstiens-toi** when in doubt, don't

abstention [apstɑ̃sjɔ̃] NF 1 *Pol* abstention; **a. électorale** abstention 2 *(renoncement)* abstention 3 *Jur* **a. délictueuse** failure to act

abstentionnisme [apstɑ̃sjɔnism] NM *Pol* abstention

abstentionniste [apstɑ̃sjɔnist] *Pol* ADJ abstentionist

NMF abstainer

abstenu, -e [apstəny] *pp voir* **abstenir**

abstient *etc voir* **abstenir**

abstinence [apstinɑ̃s] NF 1 *Rel* abstinence; **faire a.** to refrain from eating meat 2 *(chasteté)* abstinence 3 *(tempérance)* abstemiousness

abstinent, -e [apstinɑ̃, -ɑ̃t] ADJ 1 *Rel* abstinent 2 *(chaste)* abstinent, chaste 3 *(tempérant)* abstemious

NM,F 1 *Rel* abstinent person 2 *(chaste)* abstinent *or* chaste person 3 *(tempérant)* abstemious person

abstint *etc voir* **abstenir**

abstraction [apstraksjɔ̃] NF 1 *(notion)* abstraction, abstract idea; **se perdre dans des abstractions** to lose oneself in abstractions; **un esprit capable d'a.** a mind capable of abstract thought 2 *(fait d'isoler)* abstraction; **faire a. de** *(ignorer)* to take no account of, to ignore, to disregard; **a. faite de** apart from, leaving aside; **a. faite de la forme** style apart

abstractionnisme [apstraksjɔnism] NM *Phil* abstractionism

abstractionniste [apstraksjɔnist] *Phil* ADJ abstractionist

NMF abstractionist

abstraire [112] [apstrer] VT 1 *(séparer)* to abstract 2 *Phil* to abstract

VPR **s'abstraire** to cut oneself off

abstrait, -e [apstrɛ, -ɛt] PP *voir* **abstraire**

ADJ 1 *(conçu par l'esprit)* abstract 2 *(non appliqué ▸ science, pensée)* theoretical, abstract, pure

NM 1 *Phil* **l'a.** the abstract; *(notions)* abstract ideas, the theoretical plane 2 *Beaux-Arts (art)* abstract *or* non-representational art; *(artiste)* abstract *or* non-representational artist

• **dans l'abstrait** ADV in the abstract; **dans l'a., il est facile de critiquer** it's easy to be critical if you just look at things in the abstract

abstraitement [apstretmɑ̃] ADV in the abstract, abstractly

abstrayait *etc voir* **abstraire**

abstrus, -e [apstry, -yz] ADJ abstruse

absurde [apsyrd] ADJ 1 *(remarque, idée)* absurd, preposterous; *(personne)* ridiculous, absurd; **ne soyez pas a.!** don't be absurd!, don't talk nonsense! 2 *(oubli, contretemps)* absurd 3 *Phil* absurd

NM 1 *(absurdité)* absurd 2 *Littérature, Théât & Phil* **l'a.** the absurd

absurdement [apsyrdəmɑ̃] ADV absurdly, ludicrously

absurdité [apsyrdite] NF 1 *(irrationalité)* absurdity 2 *(parole, action)* absurdity; **ne dis pas d'absurdités!** don't be absurd!, don't talk nonsense!; **cette réaction est une a.** this reaction is completely absurd

abus [aby] NM 1 *(excès ▸ de café)* excess consumption; *(▸ de stupéfiants, d'alcool)* abuse; **a. d'alcool** alcohol abuse; **l'a. de somnifères** taking too many sleeping pills; **faire des a.** to overindulge *(in food or drink)*; **il y a de l'a.** that's a bit much *or* over the top

2 *(injustice)* injustice; **une pratique qui a donné lieu à des a.** a practice which has given rise to abuse; **les a.** excesses

3 *Jur* misuse; **a. d'autorité** misuse *or* abuse of authority; **a. de biens sociaux** misappropriation of funds; **a. de confiance** breach of trust; **a. de droit** abuse of power; **a. de pouvoir** abuse of power

4 *Ling* **a. de langage** misuse of language

abuser [3] [abyze] VT *Littéraire* to deceive, to mislead

• **abuser de** VT IND 1 *(consommer excessivement)* to overuse; **a. de la boisson** to drink too much; **il ne faut pas a. des bonnes choses** good things should be enjoyed in moderation, enough is as good as a feast; **a. de ses forces** to overtax oneself

2 *(mal utiliser ▸ pouvoir, privilège)* to abuse, to misuse; **le directeur abuse de son autorité** the manager is abusing his position

3 *(exploiter ▸ ami, bonté, patience)* to take advantage of, to exploit; *(▸ confiance)* to abuse; **tu abuses de lui** you take advantage of him; **je ne voudrais pas a. de votre gentillesse** I don't want to impose; **je ne veux pas a. de votre temps** I don't want to take up your time

4 *Euph (violer)* to abuse sexually

USAGE ABSOLU *(exagérer)* **je crains d'a.** I wouldn't like to impose; **vraiment, il abuse!** he's going a bit far *or* pushing it a bit!

VPR **s'abuser** to be mistaken; **si je ne m'abuse** if I'm not mistaken, correct me if I'm wrong

> Il faut noter que le verbe anglais **to abuse** ne s'emploie jamais dans le sens d'**exagérer**.

abuseur, -euse [abyzœr, -øz] ADJ abusive

NM,F abuser

abusif, -ive [abyzif, -iv] ADJ 1 *(immodéré)* excessive; **l'emploi a. de la force** excessive *or* unwarranted use of force; **l'usage a. des médicaments** the excessive use of prescription drugs; **100 euros, c'est a.!** 100 euros, that's a bit much! 2 *(outrepassant ses droits ▸ père, mère)* domineering 3 *(incorrect ▸ emploi)* incorrect

abusive [abyziv] *voir* **abusif**

abusivement [abyzivmɑ̃] ADV 1 *(de façon injuste)* wrongly, unfairly 2 *(de façon incorrecte)* wrongly, improperly 3 *(de façon excessive)* excessively

abuter [abyte] VT **a. un camion à un quai** to back a lorry against a platform

abyme [abim] NM **tableau/film/pièce avec mise en a.** painting within a painting/film within a film/play within a play

abyssal, -e, -aux, -ales [abisal, -o] ADJ *Géog (faune, relief)* abyssal; **les fosses abyssales** deep-sea trenches

abysse [abis] NM **l'a.** the abyssal zone

Abyssinie [abisini] NF **l'A.** Abyssinia

abyssinien, -enne [abisinjɛ̃, -ɛn] ADJ *Hist* Abyssinian

• **Abyssinien, -enne** NM,F Abyssinian

acabit [akabi] NM *Péj* **de cet a.** of that type; **son amie est du même a.** he/she and his/her friend are two of a kind; **ils sont tous du même a.** they are all (pretty much) the same

acacia [akasja] NM *Bot* acacia; **faux a.** false acacia, robinia

académicien, -enne [akademisjɛ̃, -ɛn] NM,F *(membre ▸ d'une académie)* academician; *(▸ de* *l'Académie française)* member of the French Academy *or* the Académie française

académie [akademi] **NF 1** *(société savante)* learned society, academy; **l'A. française** the French Academy, the Académie Française *(learned society of leading men and women of letters)*; **l'A. (des) Goncourt** = literary society whose members choose the winner of the "Prix Goncourt"
2 *(école)* academy; **a. de danse/musique** school of dance/music
3 *(salle)* **a. de billard** billiard hall
4 *Admin & Scol Br* ≃ education authority area, *Am* ≃ school district
5 *Beaux-Arts* nude
6 *Fam (corps)* body[□], figure[□]

ACADÉMIE FRANÇAISE

This was originally a group of men of letters who were encouraged by Cardinal Richelieu in 1635 to become an official body. Consisting of 40 distinguished writers ("les Quarante" or "les Immortels"), the Académie's chief task was, and is, to produce a definitive dictionary and to be the ultimate authority in matters concerning the French language.

académique [akademik] **ADJ 1** *(d'une société savante)* academic; *(de l'Académie française)* of the French Academy *or* Académie française; **elle occupe un fauteuil a.** *(à l'Académie française)* she is a member of the French Academy *or* Académie française
2 *Péj (conventionnel)* academic; **danse a.** ballet dancing; **style a.** academic *or* pedantic style
3 *Belg, Suisse & Can Scol* **l'année a.** the academic year
4 *Phil* **philosophe a.** Platonic philosopher

académisme [akademism] **NM** academicism

Acadie [akadi] **NF l'A.** Acadia

acadien, -enne [akadjɛ̃, -ɛn] **ADJ** Acadian
NM *(dialecte)* Acadian
• **Acadien, -enne NM,F** Acadian

acajou [akaʒu] **NM 1** *(arbre)* mahogany (tree) **2** *(bois)* mahogany
ADJ INV *(couleur)* mahogany

acanthe [akɑ̃t] **NF 1** *Bot* acanthus **2** *Archit* **(feuille d')a.** acanthus (leaf)

a cappella, a capella [akapela] *Mus* **ADV** a cappella
ADJ INV a cappella

Acapulco [akapylko] **N** Acapulco

acardiaque [akardjak] **ADJ** *Méd* acardiac

acariâtre [akarjɑtr] **ADJ** *(caractère)* sour; *(personne)* bad-tempered, cantankerous; **être d'humeur a.** to be bad-tempered

acarien [akarjɛ̃] **NM** *Entom* mite, house dust mite, *Spéc* acarid

accablant, -e [akablɑ̃, -ɑ̃t] **ADJ** *(chaleur)* oppressive; *(preuve, témoignage, vérité)* damning; *(travail)* exhausting; *(douleur)* excruciating; *(chagrin)* overwhelming; **il est d'une stupidité accablante** he's too stupid for words

accablement [akabləmɑ̃] **NM 1** *(désespoir)* dejection, despondency; **saisi d'un grand a.** utterly dejected **2** *(dû à la chaleur)* (heat) exhaustion

accabler **[3]** [akable] **VT 1** *(abattre ▸ sujet: fatigue, chaleur)* to overcome, to overwhelm; *(▸ sujet: soucis)* to overcome; *(▸ sujet: chagrin, deuil, travail)* to overwhelm; **accablé de chagrin** grief-stricken; **accablé de fatigue/par la chaleur** overwhelmed *or* overcome with fatigue/with the heat; **accablé de soucis** careworn; **accablé de dettes** burdened with debts **2** *(accuser ▸ sujet: témoignage)* to condemn **3** *(couvrir)* **a. qn d'injures** to heap abuse upon *or* to hurl insults at sb; **a. qn de mépris** to show utter contempt for sb; **a. qn de critiques** to be highly critical of sb; **a. qn de questions** to bombard sb with questions; **a. qn de conseils** to pester sb with advice

accalmie [akalmi] **NF** *(du bruit, du vent, de la pluie, d'un combat, d'une crise politique)* lull; *(d'une maladie)* temporary improvement; *(de souffrances)* temporary relief *or* respite; *(du commerce)* slack period; *(dans le travail, l'agitation)* break; **un instant d'a.** a moment's respite

accaparant, -e [akaparɑ̃, -ɑ̃t] **ADJ** *(travail, études, enfant)* demanding

accaparement [akaparmɑ̃] **NM 1** *Écon (des stocks)* buying up; *(du marché)* cornering **2** *(d'une conversation, d'une personne)* monopolization

accaparer **[3]** [akapare] **VT 1** *Écon (stocks)* to buy up; *(marché)* to corner; **a. des marchandises** *(pour contrôler le marché)* to withhold goods from the market **2** *(monopoliser ▸ conversation, personne)* to monopolize; *(▸ victoires, récompenses)* to carry off; *(▸ places)* to grab; **n'accapare pas le téléphone** don't monopolize the phone; **ne laisse pas les enfants t'a.** don't let the children monopolize you **3** *(absorber ▸ sujet: travail, soucis)* to absorb; **il est complètement accaparé par ses études** he's wrapped up *or* completely absorbed in his studies; **son travail l'accapare** his/her work takes up all his/her time

accapareur, -euse [akaparœr, -øz] **NM,F** *Péj* hoarder

accastillage [akastijaʒ] **NM** *Naut* **1** *(ensemble des structures)* superstructure **2** *(quincaillerie marine)* deck fittings

accastiller **[3]** [akastije] **VT** *Naut* **1** *(doter d'une structure)* to provide with a superstructure **2** *(équiper en quincaillerie)* to fit out

accédant, -e [aksedɑ̃, -ɑ̃t] **NM,F un a. à la propriété** a new home-owner, a first-time buyer

accéder **[18]** [aksede] **accéder à VT IND 1** *(atteindre ▸ trône)* to accede to; *(▸ poste, rang)* to rise to; *(▸ indépendance, gloire)* to gain, to attain; *(▸ lieu)* to reach; **on accède à la maison par un petit chemin** you get to the house via a narrow path, access to the house is by a narrow path; **a. à la propriété** to become a home-owner; **a. à de hautes responsabilités** to acquire important responsibilities; **faire a. qn au pouvoir** to bring sb to power
2 *(accepter ▸ demande, requête)* to grant; *(▸ désir)* to meet, to give in to
3 *(connaître ▸ culture)* to attain a degree of; *(▸ secrets, documents)* to gain access to
4 *Ordinat (programme)* to access

accélérateur, -trice [akseleratœr, -tris] **ADJ** accelerating
NM accelerator; *Chim* accelerant; **a. de bronzage** tanning accelerator; *Ordinat* **a. graphique** graphic *or* graphics accelerator; **a. de particules** particle accelerator

accélération [akselerasjɔ̃] **NF 1** *Aut, Tech & Phys* acceleration; **avoir de l'a.** to have good acceleration; **a. de la pesanteur** gravitational acceleration **2** *(accroissement du rythme ▸ du cœur, du pouls)* acceleration; *(▸ d'un processus, de travaux)* speeding up

accélératrice [akseleratris] *voir* **accélérateur**

accéléré, -e [akselere] **ADJ** accelerated; **ils reprirent le travail à un rythme a.** they started working at a faster pace; **un stage a.** a crash course
NM fast motion
• **en accéléré ADJ** speeded-up, accelerated
ADV speeded-up

accélérer **[18]** [akselere] **VT** *(allure)* to accelerate; *(rythme cardiaque)* to raise, to increase; *(pouls)* to quicken; *(démarches, travaux)* to speed up; **a. le pas** to quicken one's pace; *Fam* **a. le mouvement** to get things moving
VI 1 *Aut* to accelerate; **allez, accélère!** come on, step on it! **2** *Fam (se dépêcher)* **accélère un peu!** come on, get going *or* move!
VPR s'accélérer *(pouls, cœur)* to beat faster; *(rythme, mouvement)* to accelerate, to speed up

accent [aksɑ̃] **NM 1** *(prononciation)* accent; **avoir un a.** to speak with *or* to have an accent; **il n'a pas d'a.** he doesn't have an accent; **elle a un bon a. (en anglais/chinois)** her (English/Chinese) accent is very good; **elle avait l'a. italien** she spoke with an Italian accent; **l'a. du Midi** a southern (French) accent
2 *(de la voix)* stress; **a. de hauteur** pitch; **a. d'intensité** tonic *or* main stress; **a. secondaire** secondary stress; **a. tonique** tonic accent; *(signe)* stress mark; **mettre l'a. sur** to stress; *Fig* to stress, to emphasize
3 *(signe graphique)* accent; **a. grave/circonflexe/aigu** grave/circumflex/acute (accent); **e a. grave/aigu** e grave/acute
4 *Fig (inflexion)* note, accent; **un a. de sincérité/d'émotion** a note of sincerity/of emotion; **avec un a. plaintif** in plaintive tones; **avoir l'a. de la vérité** to ring true

accentuation [aksɑ̃tɥasjɔ̃] **NF 1** *(phonétique)* stressing, accentuation; **l'a., en anglais, se définit ainsi** the stress pattern of English is defined as follows; **les règles de l'a. espagnole** the stress rules in Spanish **2** *(système graphique)* use of accents; **faire des fautes d'a.** to put accents in the wrong place **3** *(intensification ▸ d'une ressemblance, d'une différence, des traits)* emphasizing; *(▸ du chômage, d'une crise)* increase, rise

accentué, -e [aksɑ̃tɥe] **ADJ 1** *(son, syllabe)* stressed, accented; **une voyelle non accentuée** an unstressed vowel **2** *(dans l'écriture)* accented; **un e a.** an e with an accent, an accented e **3** *(exagéré ▸ traits, défaut)* marked, pronounced; *(▸ tendance)* increased, stronger

accentuer **[7]** [aksɑ̃tɥe] **VT 1** *(son, syllabe)* to stress, to accent
2 *(dans l'écriture)* to put an accent on
3 *(rendre plus visible ▸ ressemblance, différence)* to accentuate, to bring out, to emphasize; *(▸ forme, traits)* to emphasize, to accentuate, to highlight; **le maquillage accentue la forme de l'œil** make-up accentuates the outline of the eye
4 *(augmenter ▸ efforts)* to increase, to intensify; *(▸ chômage, crise)* to increase
VPR s'accentuer *(contraste, ressemblance)* to become more marked *or* apparent *or* pronounced; *(tendance)* to become more noticeable; *(chômage)* to rise, to increase; *(crise)* to increase in intensity

acceptabilité [akseptabilite] **NF 1** *Ling* acceptability **2** *Mktg* **a. de la marque** brand acceptability, brand acceptance

acceptable [akseptabl] **ADJ** *(offre, condition)* acceptable; *(attitude)* decent, acceptable; *(travail)* fair, acceptable; *(prix)* fair, reasonable

acceptablement [akseptabləmɑ̃] **ADV** acceptably, in an acceptable manner

acceptant, -e [akseptɑ̃, -ɑ̃t] **ADJ** acceptant
NM,F acceptant

acceptation [akseptasjɔ̃] **NF 1** *(accord)* acceptance; **a. sous condition** conditional acceptance; **sous réserve d'a. du dossier** subject to a favourable report **2** *Fin & Jur* acceptance; **a. bancaire** banker's acceptance

accepter **[4]** [aksepte] **VT 1** *(recevoir volontiers ▸ cadeau, invitation)* to accept; *(s'engager volontiers dans ▸ défi, lutte)* to take up
2 *(admettre ▸ hypothèse, situation, excuse)* to accept; *(▸ condition)* to agree to, to accept; *(▸ mort, échec, sort)* to accept, to come to terms with; *(▸ requête)* to grant; **j'accepte que cela soit difficile** I agree that it is *or* might be difficult; **j'accepte qu'il vienne** I agree to him coming; **a. de faire qch** to agree to do sth; **je n'ai pu leur faire a. votre proposition** I was unable to persuade them to accept your offer
3 *(tolérer ▸ critique, hypocrisie)* to take, to stand for, to put up with; **il accepte tout de sa femme** he'd put up with anything from his wife; **il n'a pas accepté qu'elle le quitte** he just couldn't take *or* accept her leaving him; **j'accepte de ne rien dire** I'm prepared to say nothing
4 *(accueillir)* to accept; **acceptez-vous Jean-Guy Pierre pour époux?** do you take this man, Jean-Guy Pierre, to be your lawfully wedded husband?; **les animaux ne sont pas acceptés** *(sur vitrine)* no animals allowed, no pets; **acceptez-vous les cartes de crédit?** do you take credit cards?
5 *Fin (chèque, effet)* to accept, to sign, to honour
USAGE ABSOLU ne fais pas tant d'histoires, accepte! don't make such a fuss, say yes!
VPR s'accepter to accept oneself

accepteur, -euse [akseptœr, -øz] **NM,F** *(gén)* accepter; *Fin (d'une facture, d'un effet)* acceptor, drawee
NM *Chim & Phys* acceptor

acception [aksepsjɔ̃] **NF** *Ling* meaning, sense; **dans toutes les acceptions du mot** *ou* **du terme** in every sense of the word

• **sans acception de** PRÉP without taking into account; **sans a. de race/de sexe** *(dans une offre d'emploi)* open to candidates of all races/of both sexes, irrespective of race/sex

accès [aksɛ] NM **1** *(entrée)* access; **un a. direct à** *ou* **sur la route** direct access to the road; **l'a. de la chambre t'est interdit** you're forbidden to enter the bedroom; **a. gratuit** *(sur panneau)* free admission; **a. interdit** *(sur panneau ou porte)* no entry, no admittance; **a. réservé aux voyageurs munis de billets** *(sur panneau)* ticket-holders only; **d'a. facile** *(lieu)* easy to get to; *(personne)* approachable; *(œuvre)* accessible; **d'a. difficile** *(lieu)* hard to get to; *(personne)* unapproachable; *(œuvre)* difficult; **facile/difficile d'a.** *(lieu)* easy/hard to get to; **avoir a. à** *(lieu, personne, études, profession)* to have access to; **donner a. à** *(lieu)* to lead to; *(musée, exposition)* to allow entry to; *(études, profession)* to lead to, to open the way to; **l'a. au statut de membre de l'Union européenne** entry into the European Union

2 *(chemin, voie)* way in, access, entrance; **les a. de la ville** the approaches to the town; **les a. de la maison** the ways in to *or* entrances to the house; **a. aux trains** *ou* **quais** *(sur panneau)* to the trains

3 *(crise ▸ de rhumatisme, de goutte)* attack; *(▸ de folie, de jalousie)* fit; **a. de colère** fit of anger, angry outburst; **un a. de fièvre** a sudden high temperature; *Fig* a burst of intense activity; **un a. de toux** a fit of coughing, a coughing fit; **un a. de joie** a burst of happiness; **un a. de tristesse** a wave of sadness

4 *Ordinat* access; *(à une page Web)* hit; **avoir a. à** to be able to access; **a. aléatoire** random access; **a. commuté** dial-up access; **a. direct** direct access; **a. à distance** remote access; **a. par ligne commutée** dial-up access; **a. mémoire simultané** interleaving; **à a. multiple** multi-access; **a. sécurisé par mot de passe** password-protected access; **a. séquentiel** sequential access

• **par accès** ADV in spurts, in fits and starts; **ça le prenait par a.** it came over him in waves

accessibilité [aksesibilite] NF accessibility

accessible [aksesibl] ADJ *(livre, œuvre)* accessible; *(personne)* approachable; *(lieu)* accessible; *(prix)* affordable; **a. au public** *(sur panneau)* open to the public; **un luxe qui n'est pas a. à tous** a luxury that not everyone can afford; **être a. à la pitié** to be capable of pity; **être a. à la flatterie** to be susceptible to flattery

accession [aksesjɔ̃] NF **1** *(arrivée)* **a. au trône** accession *or* acceding to the throne; **depuis son a. au poste/rang de...** since he/she rose to the post/rank of...; **le pays fête son a. à l'indépendance** the country's celebrating becoming independent *or* achieving independence; **a. à la propriété** home ownership; **faciliter l'a. à la propriété** to make it easier for people to become home-owners; **a. au statut de membre de l'Union européenne** entry into the European Union **2** *Jur* accession

accessit [aksesit] NM *Br* ≃ certificate of merit, *Am* ≃ Honorable Mention

accessoire [akseswar] ADJ *(détail, considération)* of secondary importance, less important; *(rôle)* subordinate; **des frais accessoires** incidentals, incidental expenses; **des avantages accessoires** fringe benefits

NM **1** *(considérations secondaires)* minor details; **laissons l'a. de côté** let's forget about the (minor) details for now **2** *(dispositif, objet)* accessory; **a. automobile/informatique/vestimentaire** car/computer/fashion accessory **3** *Cin, Théât & TV* prop; **a. cassable** breakaway

accessoirement [akseswarmɑ̃] ADV **1** *(secondairement)* secondarily **2** *(éventuellement)* if necessary, if need be

accessoiriser [3] [akseswarize] VT *(voiture, tenue)* to accessorize

accessoiriste [akseswarist] NMF **1** *Cin, Théât & TV* props person, propman, *f* props girl; *(au générique)* props **2** *Aut* car accessories dealer

accident [aksidɑ̃] NM **1** *(chute, coup)* accident; *(entre véhicules)* crash, accident; **la police est sur le lieu de l'a.** the police are at the scene of the accident; **a. d'avion** plane crash; **a. de chemin de fer** rail accident; **a. de la circulation** road accident; *Jur* **a. avec délit de fuite** hit-and-run; **a. mortel** fatal accident; **a. de la route** road accident; **a. du travail** industrial accident; **a. de voiture** car crash

2 *(fait imprévu)* mishap, accident; **a. (de parcours)** hitch; **Anne a eu un petit a. avec la confiture** Anne had a little accident *or* mishap with the jam

3 *Méd* **a. cardiaque** heart attack; **a. cérébrovasculaire, a. vasculaire cérébral** stroke, *Spéc* cerebral vascular accident

4 *Euph (incontinence)* accident; **à six ans, il a encore des accidents la nuit** although he's six, he still has accidents *or* wets the bed at night

5 *Géol* **un a. de terrain** an uneven piece of ground; **les accidents du relief** the unevenness *or* irregularity of the contours

6 *Mus* accidental

• **par accident** ADV accidentally, by accident *or* chance

accidenté, -e [aksidɑ̃te] ADJ **1** *(endommagé ▸ voiture, avion)* damaged **2** *(inégal ▸ terrain)* uneven, broken, irregular **3** *(mouvementé ▸ destin, vie)* eventful, chequered

NM,F injured person, casualty; **a. du travail** victim of an industrial injury; **a. de la route** person in a road accident

accidentel, -elle [aksidɑ̃tɛl] ADJ **1** *(dû à un accident)* accidental; *(dû au hasard)* incidental, accidental, *Sout* fortuitous; **je l'ai rencontré de façon totalement accidentelle** I met him quite by accident **2** *Mus* **signes accidentels** accidentals

accidentellement [aksidɑ̃tɛlmɑ̃] ADV *(dans un accident)* in an accident; *(par hasard)* incidentally, accidentally, by accident

accidenter [3] [aksidɑ̃te] VT *(personne)* to injure, to wound; *(véhicule)* to damage

accidentogène [aksidɑ̃tɔʒɛn] ADJ unsafe, dangerous; **c'est un carrefour très a.** that crossroads is a real accident blackspot; **une mesure a.** a measure that increases the risk of accidents; **le snowboard est le sport d'hiver le plus a.** snowboarding results in more accidents than any other winter sport

accidentologie [aksidɑ̃tolɔʒi] NF road accident research

accidentologue [aksidɑ̃tɔlɔg] NMF accident researcher, person who specializes in the study of road accidents

acclamation [aklamasjɔ̃] NF cheering *(UNCOUNT)*, *Littéraire* acclamation; **être accueilli par les acclamations de la foule** to be greeted with cheers from the crowd; **son discours fut salué par des acclamations** his/her speech was greeted with cheers

• **par acclamation** ADV by popular acclaim, by acclamation; **motion adoptée par a.** motion carried by acclamation

acclamer [3] [aklame] VT to cheer, *Littéraire* to acclaim

acclimatable [aklimatabl] ADJ acclimatizable, *Am* acclimatable

acclimatation [aklimatasjɔ̃] NF acclimatization, *Am* acclimation

acclimatement [aklimatmɑ̃] NM acclimatization, *Am* acclimation

acclimater [3] [aklimate] VT **1** *Bot & Zool* to acclimatize, *Am* to acclimate **2** *(adopter)* **a. un usage étranger** to adopt a foreign practice

VPR **s'acclimater 1** *Bot & Zool* to acclimatize, to become acclimatized *or Am* acclimated **2** *(personne)* to adapt; **il s'est bien acclimaté à la vie parisienne** he's adapted *or* taken to the Parisian way of life very well

accointances [akwɛ̃tɑ̃s] NFPL *Péj* contacts, links; **avoir des a. avec le milieu** to have contacts with *or* to be connected to the criminal underworld; **il a des a. en haut lieu** he has friends in high places

accointer [3] [akwɛ̃te] **s'accointer** VPR *Péj Vieilli* **s'a. avec** to take up with, to team up with

accolade [akɔlad] NF **1** *(embrassade)* embrace; **donner l'a. à qn** to embrace sb; **recevoir l'a.** to be embraced **2** *Hist* accolade; **recevoir l'a.** to be knighted **3** *(signe typographique)* brace, bracket

accolement [akɔlmɑ̃] NM *Littéraire* association, bracketing (together)

accoler [3] [akɔle] VT **1** *(disposer ensemble)* to place *or* to put side by side; **a. deux photographies, a. une photographie à une autre** to put two photographs side by side; **le nom de l'épouse est accolé à celui du mari** the wife's surname is joined *or* added to that of the husband **2** *(joindre par une accolade)* to bracket together **3** *Hort (vigne, arbres)* to tie up

accommodant, -e [akɔmɔdɑ̃, -ɑ̃t] ADJ accommodating, obliging

accommodation [akɔmɔdasjɔ̃] NF **1** *(acclimatement)* acclimatization, *Am* acclimation; *(adaptation)* adaptation **2** *Opt* focusing

accommodement [akɔmɔdmɑ̃] NM **1** *(accord)* arrangement **2** *Pol* compromise; **propositions d'a. en vue d'une trêve** compromise proposals for a truce

accommoder [3] [akɔmɔde] VT **1** *(adapter)* to adapt, to adjust, to fit; **a. un produit aux désirs des clients** to adapt *or* to tailor a product to the clients' wishes **2** *Culin* to prepare; **a. les restes** to use up the leftovers

VI *Opt* to focus

VPR **s'accommoder 1 s'a. à qch** to adapt to sth; **il s'est accommodé à la vie à la campagne** he has adapted to country life **2 s'a. avec qn** to come to an agreement with sb **3 s'a. de qch** to put up with sth, to make the best of sth; **il s'accommode d'une modeste retraite** he's content *or* satisfied with a small pension

> Il faut noter que le verbe anglais **to accommodate** est un faux ami. Il ne signifie jamais **accommoder**.

accompagnant, -e [akɔ̃paɲɑ̃, -ɑ̃t] NM,F = person who accompanies another; **les accompagnants des excursionnistes bénéficient de réductions** those accompanying the day trippers receive a discount; **un a. adulte** an accompanying adult

accompagnateur, -trice [akɔ̃paɲatœr, -tris] NM,F **1** *(de touristes)* guide, courier; *(d'enfants)* group leader, accompanying adult; *(de malades)* nurse **2** *Mus* accompanist **3** *Belg Rail* **a. de train** ticket inspector

accompagnement [akɔ̃paɲmɑ̃] NM **1** *Culin (d'un rôti) Br* trimmings, *Am* fixings; *(d'un mets)* garnish; **servi avec un a. de petits légumes** served with mixed vegetables **2** *Mus* accompaniment; **chanter sans a.** to sing unaccompanied

• **d'accompagnement** ADJ *Mil voir* **tir**

accompagner [3] [akɔ̃paɲe] VT **1** *(aller avec)* to go with; *(venir avec)* to come with; **tu vas chez Paul? je t'accompagne** you're going to see Paul? I'll come along *or* I'll go with you; **a. qn à l'aéroport** to go to the airport with sb; *(en voiture)* to take sb to the airport; **a. qn en ville** *(à pied)* to walk into town with sb; *(en voiture)* to drive sb into town; **être accompagné de gardes du corps** to be accompanied by bodyguards; **elle vient toujours accompagnée** she never comes alone, she always brings somebody with her; **les enfants doivent être accompagnés** children must be accompanied by an adult; **je serai accompagné de ma cousine** I'll come with my cousin; *Prov* **il vaut mieux être seul que mal accompagné** you're better off alone than in bad company; *Fig* **a. qn du regard** to follow sb with one's eyes; **nos vœux/pensées vous accompagnent** our wishes/thoughts are with you

2 *(compléter)* to go with; **un échantillon de parfum accompagne tout achat** a sample of perfume comes with every purchase; **le dictionnaire est accompagné d'un CD de prononciation** the dictionary comes with a pronunciation CD; **ce gratin accompagne agréablement toutes les viandes** this gratin goes well with any meat dish; **il a accompagné ses mots d'un sourire** he said it with a smile; **un sourire accompagné d'un regard complice** a smile and a knowing glance

3 *Mus* to accompany, to provide an accompaniment for; **a. qn au piano** to accompany sb on the piano

VPR **s'accompagner 1** *Mus* **il chante et s'accompagne à l'accordéon** he sings and accompanies himself on the accordion **2 s'a. de qch** to come with sth; **ses remarques s'accompagnaient d'une menace** his remarks contained a threat

accompli, -e [akɔ̃pli] **ADJ 1** *(parfait)* accomplished **2** *(révolu)* **elle a 20 ans accomplis** she's turned *or* over 20

accomplir [32] [akɔ̃plir] **VT 1** *(achever ▸ mandat, obligation)* to fulfil; *(▸ mission, travail)* to accomplish, to carry out; *(▸ formalités)* to go through; **a. son devoir** to perform one's duty; **il n'a rien accompli à ce jour** up to now he hasn't achieved *or* accomplished anything **2** *(réaliser ▸ miracle)* to perform; *(▸ souhait, promesse)* to fulfil; **a. les dernières volontés de qn** to carry out sb's last wishes

VPR s'accomplir *(être exécuté ▸ vœu)* to come true, to be fulfilled; *(▸ prophétie)* to come true; **ce qui s'accomplit autour de nous** the things happening all around us; **la volonté de Dieu s'accomplira** God's will shall be done

accomplissement [akɔ̃plismɑ̃] **NM 1** *(exécution)* **cinq ans pour l'a. de ce travail** five years to carry out *or* to complete this work; **après l'a. de votre mission** after carrying out your mission **2** *(concrétisation)* **l'a. d'une prophétie** the realization of a prophecy; **l'a. d'un exploit sportif/d'un miracle** the performance of an athletic feat/of a miracle

accord [akɔr] **NM 1** *(entente)* agreement; *(harmonie)* harmony; **il faut un bon a. entre les participants** the participants must all get on well with each other; **d'un commun a.** by common consent, by mutual agreement; **vivre en parfait a.** to live in perfect harmony; **vivre en a. avec ses principes** to live by one's principles; **être en a. avec soi-même** to be true to oneself; **la décision doit être prise en a. avec les différents intéressés** the decision must be made with the agreement *or* the consent of the different parties involved

2 *(convention)* & *Com* agreement; *(non formel)* understanding; *(pour résoudre un conflit)* settlement; **signer un a.** to sign an agreement; **conclure un a. avec** to come to an agreement with; **arriver** *ou* **parvenir à un a.** to come to an agreement, to reach (an) agreement; **a. d'achat et de vente** buy-sell agreement; **a. atypique** atypical contract; *Banque* **a. de clearing** clearing agreement; **a. collectif** collective agreement; **a. commercial** trade agreement; **a. de commercialisation** marketing agreement; *Écon* **a. de compensation** offset agreement; *Banque* **a. de crédit** credit agreement; **a. dérogatoire** derogatory agreement; **a. de distribution exclusive** exclusive distribution agreement; *Fin* **a. d'entreprise** *ou* **d'établissement** collective agreement; **a. d'exclusivité** exclusivity agreement; **a. en forme simplifié** executive agreement; **a. de franchise** franchise agreement; **a. de licence** licensing agreement; **a. de paiement** payment agreement; **a. de partenariat** partnership agreement; **a. de principe** agreement in principle; **a. procédural** choice of law agreement; **a. régional** regional agreement; **a. de représentation** agency agreement; **a. de reprise** buyback agreement; **a. salarial** pay *or* wage agreement; **a. de siège** headquarters agreement; *Bourse* **a. de taux futur** Future Rate Agreement; *Bourse* **a. de taux à terme** Forward Rate Agreement; **les accords d'Évian** = the agreement signed on 18 March 1962, establishing a ceasefire in Algeria and recognizing the country's independence; **A. Général sur les Tarifs Douaniers et le Commerce** General Agreement on Tariffs and Trade; **les accords de Grenelle** = an agreement between the government and trade unions (27 May 1968) improving wages and working conditions and aimed at ending workers' support for student disturbances; **accords d'Helsinki** Helsinki Agreement; **A. de libre-échange nord-américain** North American Free Trade Agreement; *UE* **A. monétaire européen** European monetary agreement; **A. multilatéral sur l'investissement** multilateral investment agreement; **A. sur la réduction du temps de travail** = French agreement to reduce the working week to 35 hours

3 *(approbation)* consent, agreement; **demander l'a. de qn** to ask for sb's agreement *or* consent; **donner son a. à** to consent to; **donner son a. oralement** to give one's verbal consent

4 *Ling* agreement, concord; **a. en genre/nombre** gender/number agreement; **a. en genre et en nombre** agreement in number and in gender; **y a-t-il a. entre le sujet et le verbe?** does the verb agree with the subject?

5 *Mus (de sons)* chord, concord; *(d'un instrument)* tuning; **a. arpégé** broken chord; **a. parfait** triad *or* common chord

6 *Tech* tuning

• **d'accord ADV** OK; **tu viens? – d'a.** are you coming? – OK; **dix euros chacun, d'a.?** ten euros each, OK?; **(c'est) d'a. pour ce soir** it's OK for tonight; **d'a., puisque c'est comme ça, je n'irai pas!** OK *or* all right *or* I see, if that's the way it is I won't go!; **être d'a. (avec qn)** to agree (with sb); **ils ne sont pas d'a.** they don't agree, they disagree; **je suis d'a. pour qu'on lui dise** I agree to him/her being told *or* that he/she should be told; **(je ne suis) pas d'a.!** *(je refuse)* no (way)!; *(c'est faux)* I disagree!; **alors là, je ne suis plus d'a.!** now there I disagree!; *Sout* **nous en sommes** *ou* **demeurons d'a.** we are in agreement; **j'ai enfin réussi à les mettre d'a.** I've finally managed to get them to agree; **se mettre d'a. (sur qch)** to agree (on sth); **ils n'arrivent pas à se mettre d'a.** they can't manage to agree *or* to reach an agreement; **mettez-vous d'a., je ne comprends rien à ce que vous dites** get your story straight, I can't understand a word of what you're saying; **mettons-nous bien d'a., c'est vous le responsable** let's get one thing straight, you're in charge; **tomber d'a.** to come to an agreement; **tomber d'a. sur qch** to agree on sth

• **en accord avec PRÉP 1** *(personne)* **en a. avec lui** in agreement with him **2** *(suivant)* **en a. avec les directives** according to the guidelines; **en a. avec notre politique commerciale** in line with *or* in keeping with our business policy

accordage [akɔrdaʒ] **NM** *Mus* tuning

accord-cadre [akɔrkadr] *(pl* **accords-cadres)** **NM** framework *or* outline agreement

accordéon [akɔrdeɔ̃] **NM** *Mus* accordion; **a. diatonique/chromatique** diatonic/chromatic accordion; *Fig* **coup d'a.** sudden reversal

• **en accordéon ADJ** *(chaussettes)* wrinkled; *(voiture)* crumpled

accordéoniste [akɔrdeonist] **NMF** *Mus* accordionist

accorder [3] [akɔrde] **VT 1** *(octroyer ▸ congé, permission)* to give, to grant; *(▸ faveur, pardon)* to grant; *(▸ subvention)* to grant, to award; *(▸ dommages-intérêts)* to award; *(▸ découvert bancaire, remise)* to allow, to give; *(▸ prêt)* to authorize, to extend; *(▸ interview)* to give; **a. le droit de vote à qn** to give sb the right to vote, to enfranchise sb; **a. toute sa confiance à qn** to give sb one's complete trust; **a. de l'importance à qch** to attach importance to sth; **a. de la valeur aux objets** to set a value on things; **je vous accorde une heure, pas plus** I'll allow you one hour, no more; **voulez-vous m'a. cette danse?** may I have this dance?

2 *(concéder)* **a. à qn que** to admit to *or* to grant sb that; **vous m'accorderez que, là, j'avais raison** you must admit that on this point I was right; **ils sont un peu jeunes, je vous l'accorde, mais...** granted, they're a bit young, but..., they're a bit young, I grant you, but...

3 *(harmoniser)* **a. les couleurs d'une pièce** to coordinate the colours in a room

4 *Gram* to make agree; **a. le verbe avec le sujet** to make the verb agree with the subject

5 *Mus* to tune; **les musiciens accordent leurs instruments** *(avant un concert)* the players are tuning up; *Fig* **a. ses violons** to agree; **il faudrait a. vos violons!** make your minds up!, get your stories straight!

VPR s'accorder 1 *(être du même avis)* **tous s'accordent à dire que...** they all agree *or* concur that...; **ils se sont accordés pour baisser leurs prix** they agreed among themselves that they would drop their prices

2 *(se mettre d'accord)* to agree, to come to an agreement (**avec qn** with sb; **sur qch** on sth); **s'a. sur le prix** to agree on the price

3 *(s'entendre)* **on ne s'est jamais accordés (tous les deux)** we two never saw eye to eye *or* got along

4 *(être en harmonie ▸ caractères)* to blend; *(▸ opinions)* to match, to tally, to converge; **le moderne et l'ancien s'accordent parfaitement** old and new blend perfectly together; **ce qu'il dit ne s'accorde pas avec sa personnalité** he's saying things which are out of character

5 *Gram* to agree; **s'a. en genre avec** to agree in gender with

6 *Mus* to tune up

7 *(s'autoriser)* to allow oneself; **s'a. dix minutes de repos** to allow *or* to give oneself ten minutes' rest

accordeur [akɔrdœr] **NM** *Mus* (piano) tuner

accordoir [akɔrdwar] **NM** *Mus* (piano) tuning key

accort, -e [akɔr, -ɔrt] **ADJ** *Littéraire* pleasant, comely

accostable [akɔstabl] **ADJ** *Naut* **le rivage n'est pas a.** you can't get near the shore

accostage [akɔstaʒ] **NM 1** *Naut* drawing *or* coming alongside **2** *(d'une personne)* accosting

accoster [3] [akɔste] **VT 1** *(personne)* to go up to, to accost; **je me suis fait a. dans la rue** I got accosted in the street **2** *Naut* to come *or* to draw alongside

VI *Naut* to berth

accotement [akɔtmɑ̃] **NM 1** *(d'une route)* shoulder, *Br* verge; **accotements stabilisés** *(sur panneau)* hard shoulders; **accotements non stabilisés** *(sur panneau)* soft shoulders, *Br* soft verges **2** *Rail (rail)* shoulder

accoter [3] [akɔte] **VT** to lean; **a. une échelle contre un mur** to lean a ladder against a wall

VPR s'accoter s'a. à *ou* **contre** to lean against

accotoir [akɔtwar] **NM** armrest

accouchée [akuʃe] **NF** = woman who has recently given birth

accouchement [akuʃmɑ̃] **NM** *Obst (travail)* childbirth, labour; *(expulsion)* delivery; **première/deuxième phase de l'a.** first/second stage of labour; **pendant mon a.** while I was giving birth *or* in labour; **procéder à un a.** to deliver a woman; **elle a eu un a. difficile** she had a difficult delivery; **on a dû provoquer l'a.** she had to be induced; **a. avant terme** premature delivery; **a. dirigé** induced delivery; **a. sans douleur** painless delivery *or* childbirth; **a. au forceps** forceps delivery; **a. naturel** natural childbirth; **a. prématuré** premature delivery; **a. par le siège** breech birth; **a. à terme** full-term delivery

accoucher [3] [akuʃe] **VI 1** *Obst (avoir un bébé)* to have a baby, to give birth; **pendant qu'elle accouchait** while she was giving birth *or* in labour; **elle a accouché chez elle** she had a home birth; **Diane a accouché l'été dernier/avant terme** Diane had her baby last summer/prematurely; **j'accouche en juin** my baby's due in June; **ils ont été obligés de la faire a. avant terme** they had to induce her **2** *Fam (parler)* **accouche!** spit it out!, let's have it!

VT c'est lui qui l'a accouchée he delivered her baby

• **accoucher de VT IND 1** *Obst (enfant)* to give birth to, to have; **a. d'une fille** to give birth to a girl **2** *Fam (produire)* to come up with, to produce▫; **six mois de travail pour a. d'une pièce aussi nulle!** six months of work to produce such a useless play!

accoucheur, -euse [akuʃœr, -øz] **NM,F** *Obst* obstetrician

accouder [3] [akude] **s'accouder VPR s'a. à** *ou* **sur qch** to lean (one's elbows) on sth; **s'a. à la fenêtre** to lean out of the window; **être accoudé à qch** to lean on sth; **il était accoudé au bar** he was leaning on the bar

accoudoir [akudwar] **NM** armrest

accouple [akupl] **NF** *Chasse* leash

accouplement [akupləmɑ̃] **NM 1** *(raccordement)* linking, joining; *Tech* coupling, connecting; *Élec* connecting; *Aut* **a. direct** direct drive; **a. à glissement** slip clutch; *Aviat* **a. à griffe** *ou* **à griffes** dog clutch, jaw clutch **2** *Agr* yoking, coupling **3** *Zool* mating

accoupler [3] [akuple] **VT 1** *(raccorder ▸ mots)* to link *or* to join (together); *Tech* to couple, to connect; *Élec* to connect **2** *Agr (pour le trait)* to yoke *or* to couple together **3** *Zool* to mate

VPR s'accoupler *(animaux)* to mate

accourir [45] [akurir] **VI** to run, to rush; **ils sont accourus (pour) m'annoncer la nouvelle** they came running to tell me the news; **ses hurlements ont fait a. tout le voisinage** his/her screams brought all the neighbours rushing to the scene

accoutrement [akutrəmɑ̃] **NM** *Péj* outfit

accoutrer [3] [akutre] *Péj* **VT** to dress up; **comme te voilà accoutré!** you do look ridiculous in that outfit!; **accoutré d'une vieille capote** rigged out in an old army greatcoat

VPR s'accoutrer to get dressed up

accoutumance [akutymɑ̃s] **NF 1** *(adaptation)* habituation (**à** to) **2** *(d'un toxicomane)* addiction, dependency; **l'effet d'a. des drogues dures** the habit-forming effect of hard drugs

accoutumé, -e [akutyme] **ADJ** usual, customary

• **comme à l'accoutumée ADV** as usual, as always

accoutumer [3] [akutyme] **VT a. qn à qch/à faire qch** to accustom sb to sth/to doing sth, to get sb used to sth/to doing sth; **être accoutumé à qch/à faire qch** to be accustomed *or* used to sth/to doing sth

VPR s'accoutumer s'a. à to get used to; **il faudra vous a. à vous lever tôt** you'll have to get used to getting up early

accouvage [akuvaʒ] **NM** artificial incubation

accréditation [akreditasjɔ̃] **NF** *Fin* accreditation

accrédité, -e [akredite] **ADJ** *Fin* accredited; **notre représentant dûment a.** our duly authorized agent

NM,F 1 *Fin (détenteur d'une lettre de crédit)* holder of a letter of credit **2** *Compta* beneficiary, payee

accréditer [3] [akredite] **VT** *(rumeur, nouvelle)* to substantiate, to give credence to; *(personne, représentant)* to accredit; *Banque (client)* to open an account for, to open credit facilities for; *Banque* **être accrédité auprès d'une banque** to have credit facilities at a bank

VPR s'accréditer *(rumeur)* to gain ground

accréditif, -ive [akreditif, -iv] *Banque* **ADJ lettre accréditive** letter of credit

NM 1 *(lettre de crédit)* letter of credit; *Compta* credential **2** *(crédit)* credit; **loger un a. sur une banque** to open credit facilities with a bank; **a. permanent** permanent credit

accro [akro] *Fam* **ADJ** hooked; **être a. à qch** *(drogue)* to be hooked on sth; *Fig* to be hooked on *or* really into sth; **il va à tous les matchs de foot, il est vraiment a.** he goes to all the football matches, he's a real football junkie

NMF *(toxicomane)* addict[□]; *(passionné)* fanatic[□]; **les accros de la hi-fi** hi-fi fanatics

accrobranche® [akrobrɑ̃ʃ] **NM** aerial assault course

accroc [akro] **NM 1** *(déchirure)* tear, rip; **faire un a. à sa chemise** to tear *or* to rip one's shirt **2** *Fam (entorse)* breach, violation; **faire un a. au règlement** to bend the rules; **faire un a. un contrat** to breach *or* to violate a contract **3** *(incident)* snag, hitch; **un voyage sans a.** *ou* **accrocs** an uneventful trip

accrochage [akrɔʃaʒ] **NM 1** *(suspension ▸ d'un tableau)* hanging; *Beaux-Arts* small exhibition

2 *(fixation ▸ d'un wagon)* hitching (up), coupling; *(▸ d'une remorque)* hitching (up)

3 *Aut (collision ▸ entre véhicules)* collision

4 *(querelle)* quarrel, squabble; **avoir un a. avec qn** to quarrel *or* squabble with sb

5 *Mil* skirmish, engagement

6 *Sport (en boxe)* clinch; *(entre deux coureurs)* tangle

accroche [akrɔʃ] **NF** gimmick; *(slogan)* slogan

accroche-casseroles [akrɔʃkasrɔl] **NM INV** saucepan rack

accroche-cœur [akrɔʃkœr] *(pl inv ou* **accroche-cœurs**) **NM** *Br* kiss-curl, *Am* spit curl; **se faire des accroche-cœurs** to put one's hair into *Br* kiss curls *or Am* spit curls

accrocher [3] [akrɔʃe] **VT 1** *(suspendre ▸ tableau)* to hang; *(▸ manteau, rideau)* to hang up; **un petit miroir accroché au moyen d'un clou** a small mirror hanging on *or* from a nail

2 *(saisir)* to hook; *Fam Fig* **il a accroché une bonne commande** he landed a big order

3 *(relier)* **a. qch à** to tie sth (on) to; **a. un wagon à un train** to couple *or* to hitch a wagon to a train; **a. un pendentif à une chaîne** to attach a pendant to a chain

4 *Fam (aborder)* to corner, to buttonhole, to collar; **le curé m'a accroché à la sortie de l'église** the priest cornered me outside the church

5 *Fig (retenir l'intérêt de)* to grab the attention of; *(attirer ▸ regard)* to catch; **il faut a. le lecteur dès les premières pages** we must make the reader sit up and take notice from the very beginning of the book; **qui accroche le regard** eye-catching; **ses bijoux accrochaient la lumière** her jewellery was catching the light

6 *(déchirer ▸ collant, vêtement)* to snag, to catch; **a. sa robe à des ronces** to catch one's dress on brambles

7 *(heurter ▸ piéton)* to hit; **il a accroché l'aile de ma voiture** he caught *or* scraped my wing

8 *Rad* **a. une station** to tune in to a station

USAGE ABSOLU *Fig (attirer l'attention)* **un slogan qui accroche** a catchy slogan

VI 1 *(coincer ▸ fermeture, tiroir)* to jam, to stick; *Fig (buter)* to be stuck; *Fig* **la discussion accroche sur la composition du comité** the discussion has got bogged down over the composition of the committee; *Fig* **j'accroche sur la traduction de ce mot** I just can't come up with a good translation for this word **2** *Fam (bien marcher)* **ça n'a pas accroché entre eux** they didn't hit it off; **je n'ai jamais accroché en physique** I never really got into physics

VPR s'accrocher 1 *(emploi passif)* to hang, to hook on; **la médaille s'accroche au bracelet avec un fermoir** the medallion fixes *or* fastens on to the bracelet with a clasp; **la remorque s'accroche à la voiture** the trailer hooks *or* hitches on to the (back of the) car

2 *(emploi réciproque) (entrer en collision ▸ voitures)* to crash (into each other), to collide; *(▸ boxeurs)* to clinch; *(se disputer ▸ personnes)* to quarrel, to squabble; *Fam* **ils ne peuvent pas se supporter, ils vont s'a. tout de suite** they can't stand each other so they're bound to start arguing straight away;

3 *Fam (persévérer ▸ athlète, concurrent)* to apply oneself; **avec lui, il faut s'a.!** he's hard work!; **accroche-toi, tu n'as pas tout entendu!** brace yourself, you haven't heard everything yet!

4 s'a. à to cling on to; **accroche-toi à la poignée!** hang on (tight) to the handle!; *Fig* **s'a. au pouvoir/à la vie/à qn** to cling to power/to life/to sb

5 *Fam* **s'a. avec** to clash with

6 *très Fam (locution)* **tu peux te l'a.!** *(tu ne l'auras jamais)* you can whistle for it!; *(tu ne l'auras plus)* you can kiss it goodbye!

accrocheur, -euse [akrɔʃœr, -øz] **ADJ 1** *(attirant ▸ titre, slogan, chanson)* catchy; *(▸ sourire)* beguiling **2** *(tenace ▸ vendeur)* pushy

NM,F fighter

accroire [akrwar] **VT** *(à l'infinitif seulement) Littéraire* **faire** *ou* **laisser a. qch à qn** to mislead sb into believing sth; **en faire a. à qn** to try to deceive sb

accrois *voir* **accroître**

accroissait *etc voir* **accroître**

accroissement [akrwasmɑ̃] **NM 1** *(augmentation)* increase (**de** in); *(▸ du capital)* accumulation; **l'a. de la population** population growth; **les nouveaux équipements ont permis un a. de la productivité** the new equipment has led to an increase in productivity; *Fin* **a. global net** aggregate net increment **2** *Math* increment

accroître [94] [akrwatr] **VT** *(fortune, sentiment)* to increase; *(domaine)* to add (on) to; *(popularité)* to enhance

VPR s'accroître *(fortune)* to increase; *(tension)* to rise; *(sentiment, population)* to grow, to increase

accroupir [32] [akrupir] **s'accroupir VPR** to squat *or* to crouch (down); **il était accroupi** he was squatting *or* crouching

accroupissement [akrupismɑ̃] **NM 1** *(action)* squatting, crouching **2** *(position)* squatting *or* crouching position

accru, -e [akry] **PP** *voir* **accroître**

ADJ *(fortune)* increased, larger; *(sentiment)* deeper; *(popularité)* enhanced

NM *Bot* sucker

accu [aky] **NM** *Fam* battery[□]; **les accus sont morts** the battery's dead

accueil [akœj] **NM 1** *(manière d'accueillir)* welcome, greeting; **nous avons reçu le plus chaleureux des accueils** we were given the heartiest of welcomes; **faire bon a. à qn** to give sb a warm welcome; **faire mauvais a. à qn** to give sb a cool reception; *Fig* **faire bon/mauvais a. à une proposition** to receive a proposal warmly/coldly; *Fin* **faire (bon) a. à une traite** to meet *or* to honour a bill **2** *(bureau, comptoir)* desk, reception; **passez à l'a.** go to the reception desk, go to reception; **tenir l'a.** to be on reception

• **d'accueil ADJ** *(discours, cérémonie)* welcoming; *(hôtesse, hall)* reception *(avant n)*; *(pays)* host *(avant n)*

accueillant, -e [akœjɑ̃, -ɑ̃t] **ADJ** *(peuple, personne, sourire)* welcoming, friendly; *(maison, endroit)* hospitable; **peu a.** *(maison, endroit)* inhospitable; *(peuple, personne, sourire)* unwelcoming, cold

accueillir [41] [akœjir] **VT 1** *(aller chercher)* to meet; **a. qn à l'aéroport** to meet sb at the airport **2** *(recevoir)* **a. qn froidement** to give sb a cool reception; **être très bien/mal accueilli** to get a very pleasant/poor welcome; **il a été accueilli par des bravos** he was greeted with cheers; **le projet a été très mal accueilli par la direction** the project got a frosty reception *or* response from the management; *Fin* **a. une traite** to meet *or* to honour a bill **3** *(héberger)* to house, to accommodate; **l'hôpital peut a. 1000 malades** the hospital can accommodate 1,000 patients; **j'ai un ami qui pourrait vous a. pendant un certain temps** I have a friend who could put you up for a while

acculer [3] [akyle] **VT 1** *(bloquer)* **a. qn contre qch** to drive sb back against sth; *Chasse* **a. un animal** to bring an animal to bay; **tel un animal acculé** like an animal at bay **2** *(contraindre)* **a. qn à la faillite** to push sb into bankruptcy; **a. qn au désespoir** to drive sb to despair

acculturation [akyltyrasjɔ̃] **NF** acculturation

accumulateur [akymylatœr] **NM** accumulator

accumulation [akymylasjɔ̃] **NF 1** *(action)* accumulation, amassing, building up; *(collection)* mass; *(de marchandises ▸ action)* stockpiling; *(▸ résultat)* stockpile; *(de dettes)* accumulation; *(de stocks)* accumulation, build-up; *(d'erreurs)* series; **devant cette a. de preuves/démentis** faced with this mass of proof/with repeated denials; **a. de capital** capital accumulation; *Fin* **a. des intérêts** accrual of interest **2** *Élec* storage; **chauffage par a.** storage heating

accumuler [3] [akymyle] **VT 1** *(conserver ▸ boîtes, boutons)* to keep *or* to hoard (in large quantities), to accumulate; *(▸ denrées)* to stockpile, to hoard; *(▸ papiers)* to keep; *(marchandises)* to stockpile; *(stocks)* to accumulate, to build up; *(dettes)* to accumulate; *Fin* **intérêts accumulés** accrued interest **2** *(réunir ▸ preuves)* to pile on, to accumulate; *(▸ fortune, argent)* to amass; **a. les gaffes/erreurs** to make a series of blunders/mistakes; *Fam* **mais tu les accumules!** *(les bêtises)* you never stop, do you?

VPR s'accumuler *(dettes, travail)* to accumulate, to mount (up), to pile up; *(nuages)* to gather, to build up; *Fin (intérêts)* to accrue; **le linge sale s'accumule** the dirty laundry is piling up; **les toxines s'accumulent dans l'organisme** there is a build-up of toxins in the body

accusateur, -trice [akyzatœr, -tris] **ADJ** *(silence, regard)* accusing; *(document)* incriminating; **il a pointé vers elle un index a.** he pointed an accusing finger at her

NM,F *(dénonciateur)* accuser

NM *Hist* **a. public** public prosecutor *(during the French Revolution)*

accusatif [akyzatif] **NM** *Ling* accusative; **à l'a.** in the accusative

accusation [akyzasjɔ̃] **NF 1** *Jur* charge, indictment; **mettre qn en a.** to indict *or* to charge sb; **a. fondée** substantiated charge **2** *(reproche)* accusation, charge; **lancer** *ou* **porter une a. contre** to make an accusation against

accusatrice [akyzatris] *voir* **accusateur**

accusé, -e [akyze] **ADJ** *(traits)* sharp, pronounced; *(rides)* deep; *Écon & Fin (baisse, hausse)* sharp

NM,F *Jur* defendant; **l'a.** the accused; **a., levez-vous!** the accused will stand!

• **accusé (de) réception NM** *(d'une lettre)* acknowledgement (of receipt); *(d'un colis)* receipt; *Ordinat* acknowledge, acknowledgement; **envoyer qch en recommandé avec a. de réception** to send sth by *Br* recorded delivery *or Am* certified mail

accuser [3] [akyze] **VT 1** *(désigner comme coupable)* to accuse; **je ne t'accuse pas!** I'm not accusing you!; **a. qn de qch** to accuse sb of sth; **on m'accuse d'avoir menti** I'm being accused of lying; *Jur* **a. qn de meurtre/viol** to charge sb with murder/rape

2 *(rejeter la responsabilité sur)* to blame, to put the blame on; **je ne t'accuse pas!** I'm not blaming you!

3 *(accentuer)* to highlight, to emphasize, to accentuate; **la lumière accuse les reliefs** sunlight emphasizes the outlines

4 *(indiquer)* **la Bourse accuse une forte baisse** the stock market is registering heavy losses; **son visage accuse une grande fatigue** you can see on his/her face how tired he/she is; **il accuse ses 50 ans** he's 50 and looks it

5 *(locutions)* **a. réception de** to acknowledge receipt of; **a. le coup** *Boxe* to reel with the punch; *Fig (de fatigue)* to show the strain; *(moralement)* to take it badly

VPR s'accuser to confess; **il s'est accusé d'avoir volé** he confessed to having committed a theft

acerbe [asɛrb] **ADJ** *(parole, critique)* cutting, acerbic; **d'un ton a.** crisply

acéré, -e [asere] **ADJ 1** *(lame, pointe)* sharp **2** *Fig (critique, propos)* biting, caustic

acérer [18] [asere] **VT** to sharpen

acériculteur, -trice [aserikyltœr, -tris] **NM,F** *Can* maple producer

acériculture [aserikyltyr] **NF** *Can* maple production, maple sugaring

acétate [asetat] **NM** *Chim* acetate; **a. d'aluminium** aluminium acetate; **a. de cellulose** cellulose acetate

acétique [asetik] **ADJ** *Chim* acetic; **une odeur a.** a vinegary smell

acétocellulose [asetɔselyloz] **NF** *Chim* cellulose acetate

acétone [asetɔn] **NF** *Chim* acetone

acétylène [asetilɛn] **NM** *Chim* acetylene

acétylsalicylique [asetilsalisilik] **ADJ** *Pharm* acetylsalicylic

ACF [aseɛf] **NM** *Aut (abrév* **Automobile Club de France)** = French automobile association, *Br* ≃ AA, ≃ RAC, *Am* ≃ AAA

achalandage [aʃalɑ̃daʒ] **NM** *(clientèle)* custom, clientele

achalandé, -e [aʃalɑ̃de] **ADJ bien a.** *(bien approvisionné)* well-stocked; *(qui compte de nombreux clients)* with a large clientele; **mal a.** *(mal approvisionné)* poorly-stocked; *(qui compte peu de clients)* with a small clientele

achalander [3] [aʃalɑ̃de] **VT** *(magasin)* to stock

achaler [3] [aʃale] **VT** *Can Fam* to bug

achards [aʃar] **NMPL** *Culin* achar, relish

acharné, -e [aʃarne] **ADJ** *(combat, lutte, concurrence)* fierce; *(travail)* relentless; *(travailleur)* hard; *(joueur)* hardened; **il est a. à votre perte** *ou* **à vous perdre** he is set *or* bent *or* intent on ruining you

NM,F un a. du travail a workaholic

acharnement [aʃarnəmɑ̃] **NM** *(dans un combat)* fury; *(dans le travail)* relentlessness, perseverance; **son a. à réussir** his/her determination to succeed; **a. au travail** dedication to work; *Méd* **a. thérapeutique** use of intensive treatment *(to keep a patient alive)*

• **avec acharnement ADV** *(combattre)* tooth and nail, furiously; *(travailler)* relentlessly; *(résister)* fiercely

acharner [3] [aʃarne] **VT** *Vieilli (chien)* to flesh, to blood

VPR s'acharner 1 s'a. sur *ou* **contre** *ou* **après qn** *(le tourmenter)* to persecute *or* to hound sb; **les médias s'acharnent sur** *ou* **contre moi** I'm being hounded by the press; **le meurtrier s'est acharné sur sa victime** the murderer savaged his victim; **les examinateurs se sont acharnés sur le candidat** the examiners had a real go at the candidate; **le sort s'acharne sur lui** he's dogged by bad luck **2 s'a. sur qch** *(persévérer)* to work (away) at sth; **s'a. à faire qch** *(persévérer)* to strive to do sth; *(vouloir à tout prix)* to be determined to do sth; **il s'acharne à vous nuire** he is determined to do you harm, he is set on harming you

USAGE ABSOLU inutile de t'a., tu ne la convaincras pas you might as well give up, you won't convince her

achat [aʃa] **NM 1** *(fait d'acheter)* purchasing, buying; **l'a. d'une voiture neuve** the purchasing of a new car; **faire un a.** to make a purchase; **faire un a. à crédit** to buy *or* to purchase something on credit; **faire l'a. de qch** to buy *or* to purchase sth; **aller faire ses achats** to go shopping; **a. sur catalogue** mail-order purchasing; **achats centralisés** centralized purchasing; **achats comparatifs** comparison shopping; **a. au comptant** cash purchase; **a. à crédit** credit purchase, purchase for the account; *(location-achat)* buying on hire purchase *or Am* on the installment plan; **achats directs** direct purchasing; **achats à domicile** teleshopping; *Mktg* **a. d'émotion** emotional purchase; *Ordinat* **a. en ligne** on-line purchase; **a. d'espace** media buying; **a. en espèces** cash purchase; **achats hors taxes** tax-free shopping; *Mktg* **a. impulsif, a. d'impulsion** impulse buy; *Fin* **achats institutionnels** institutional buying; *Mktg* **a. juste à temps** just-in-time purchasing; **a. à petit prix** low-cost purchase; *Mktg* **a. prévu** destination purchase; **achats regroupés** one-stop buying; *Mktg* **a. renouvelé** repeat purchase; **achats spéculatifs** speculative buying; *Mktg* **a. spontané** impulse buy; *Com* **a. de système** systems buying; *Bourse* **a. à terme** forward buying; *Pol* **a. de voix** vote-buying

2 *(article acheté)* purchase, buy; **réglez vos achats à la caisse** pay at the cash desk; **un sac rempli d'achats** a bag full of shopping; **montre-nous tes achats** show us what you've bought; **c'est un bon/mauvais a.** it's a good/bad buy

• **à l'achat ADV la livre vaut 1,50 euros à l'a.** the buying rate for sterling is 1.50 euros; **cette machine est chère à l'a. mais vous l'amortirez en quelques années** this machine involves a high initial outlay but it will pay for itself in a few years

acheminement [aʃminmɑ̃] **NM 1** *(de marchandises)* conveying, forwarding, shipment; *(de troupes)* moving; *(de trains)* routing; **l'a. des marchandises se fait par Calais** the goods are routed through Calais; **a. du courrier** mail handling **2** *(progression)* progress

acheminer [3] [aʃmine] **VT 1** *(marchandises)* to ship, to dispatch, to forward; *(courrier)* to handle; **a. des produits par avion** to ship products by plane; **a. un colis vers** to ship a parcel to

VPR s'acheminer s'a. vers *(endroit, succès)* to head for; *(accord, solution)* to move towards; **nous nous acheminons vers la résolution du conflit** we're moving towards a solution to the conflict

acheter [28] [aʃte] **VT 1** *(cadeau, objet d'art, denrée)* to buy, *Sout* to purchase; **j'ai acheté ce livre cinq euros** I bought this book for five euros; **a. qch au kilo** to buy sth by the kilo; **a. qch comptant/en gros/d'occasion/à crédit** to buy sth cash/wholesale/second-hand/on credit; **a. qch à tempérament** to buy sth on hire purchase *or Am* on the installment plan; **a. qch au détail** to buy sth retail; *(à l'unité)* to buy sth individually; **a. qch par correspondance** to buy sth by mail order; **a. qch à qn** *(pour soi)* to buy sth from sb; *(pour le lui offrir)* to buy sb sth, to buy sth for sb; *Bourse* **a. à terme** to buy forward **2** *(échanger ▸ liberté, paix)* to buy **3** *(soudoyer ▸ témoin, juge)* to bribe, to buy (off); *(▸ électeurs)* to buy; **ils ont été achetés** they were bribed

USAGE ABSOLU *(gén)* to buy; **achetez français!** buy French (products)!

VPR s'acheter 1 *(emploi passif)* to be on sale; **où est-ce que ça s'achète?** where can you buy it?; **ces choses-là ne s'achètent pas** such things cannot be bought *or* are not for sale **2 s'a. qch** to buy oneself sth; **s'a. une conduite** to turn over a new leaf

acheteur, -euse [aʃtœr, -øz] **NM,F 1** *(client)* buyer, purchaser; **on n'a pas pu trouver a. pour ce produit** there are no buyers for *or* there is no market for this product; **je suis a.!** I'm interested!; *Mktg* **a. anonyme** anonymous buyer; *Mktg* **a. cible** target buyer; **a. éventuel** potential buyer; *Mktg* **a. impulsif** impulse buyer; *Com* **a. industriel** business buyer; *Mktg* **a. non-identifié** anonymous buyer; **a. potentiel** potential buyer **2** *(professionnel)* buyer; **a. principal** head buyer **3** *Jur* vendee

achevé, -e [aʃve] **ADJ** *(sportif, artiste)* accomplished; *(œuvre)* perfect; *(idiot)* downright, absolute; **c'est d'un ridicule a.** it's utterly preposterous

achèvement [aʃɛvmɑ̃] **NM** completion

> Il faut noter que le nom anglais **achievement** est un faux ami. Il signifie **réussite**.

achever [19] [aʃve] **VT 1** *(finir ▸ discours, lettre, repas)* to finish, to end; *(▸ journal, livre)* to reach the end of, to finish; **a. sa vie à l'hôpital** to end one's days in hospital; **laisse-le a. sa phrase** let him finish what he's saying; **a. de faire qch** to finish doing sth; **cette remarque acheva de le décourager** this remark discouraged him completely

2 *(tuer ▸ animal)* to destroy; *(▸ personne)* to finish off

3 *Fam (accabler)* to finish off; **la mort de sa femme l'a achevé** his wife's death really finished him off; **toutes ces courses m'ont achevé** all this shopping has finished me off *or Br* done me in

4 *Fam (ruiner)* to finish off, to clean out; **les frais d'avocat l'ont achevé** the lawyer's fees cleaned him out

USAGE ABSOLU *(finir de parler)* to finish (talking); **à peine avais-je achevé que...** I'd hardly finished (talking) *or* stopped talking when...

VPR s'achever *(vie, journée, vacances)* to come to an end, to draw to a close *or* an end; *(dîner, film)* to end, to finish; **le livre s'achève sur une note d'espoir/un chapitre consacré à la peinture** the book ends on a hopeful note/with a chapter on painting

> Il faut noter que le verbe anglais **to achieve** est un faux ami. Il ne signifie jamais **achever**.

achigan [aʃigɑ̃] **NM** *Can Ich* black-bass

Achille [aʃil] **NPR** *Myth* Achilles

achoppement [aʃɔpmɑ̃] *voir* **pierre**

achopper [3] [aʃɔpe] **VI** *Vieilli* **a. au problème de...** to come up against the problem of...; *Vieilli* **a. sur** to stumble on *or* over *Fig* to come up against

achromatique [akrɔmatik] **ADJ** *Opt* achromatic

achrome [akrom] **ADJ 1** *Phot* achromous, achromatous **2** *Méd* achromic

acide [asid] **ADJ 1** *(goût, fruit)* sour, acidic; *(propos)* acid, cutting, caustic **2** *Chim & Écol* acid

NM 1 *Biol & Chim* acid; **a. aminé** amino acid; **a. ascorbique** ascorbic acid; **a. désoxyribonucléique** deoxyribonucleic acid; **a. folique** folic acid, folacin; **a. gras** fatty acid; **a. sulfhydrique** hydrogen sulphide; **a. sulfurique** sulphuric acid **2** *Fam (LSD)* acid

acidificateur [asidifikatœr] **NM** *Chim* acidifier, acidifying agent

acidification [asidifikasjɔ̃] **NF** *Chim* acidification

acidifier [9] [asidifje] *Chim* **VT** to acidify

VPR s'acidifier to acidify

acidité [asidite] **NF 1** *(d'un goût, d'un fruit)* acidity, sourness; *(d'un propos)* tartness, sharpness **2** *Chim, Géol & Méd* acidity; *Physiol* **a. gastrique** acid stomach

acidose [asidoz] **NF** *Méd* acidosis

acidulé, -e [asidyle] **ADJ** *(goût)* acidulous; *Fig (coloris)* vivid, (very) bright

acier [asje] **NM** *Métal* steel; **a. haute tension** high-tensile steel; **a. inoxydable/trempé** stainless/tempered steel

• **d'acier ADJ** steel *(avant n)*; *Fig (regard)* steely; **muscles/cœur d'a.** muscles/heart of steel

aciérie [asjeri] **NF** *Métal* steelworks *(singulier)*, steel plant

aciériste [asjerist] **NMF** *Métal* steel manufacturer

acmé [akme] **NM OU NF 1** *Littéraire (apogée)* acme, summit, height **2** *Méd* climax

acné [akne] NF *Méd* acne; **avoir de l'a.** to suffer from *or* to have acne; **a. juvénile** teenage acne

acolyte [akɔlit] NM **1** *Rel* acolyte **2** *(complice)* sidekick

acompte [akɔ̃t] NM **1** *(versement régulier)* instalment; *(avance sur ▸ une commande, des travaux)* down payment; *(▸ un salaire)* advance; *(▸ un loyer)* deposit; **payer par** *ou* **en plusieurs acomptes** to pay by *or* in instalments; **donner** *ou* **verser un a. de 500 euros (sur), payer** *ou* **verser 500 euros en a. (sur)** *(achat)* to make a down payment of 500 euros (on), to pay a deposit of 500 euros (on); **recevoir un a. sur son salaire** to receive an advance on one's salary; **a. de** *ou* **sur dividende** interim dividend; *Admin* **a. provisionnel** interim *or* advance payment **2** *(avant-goût)* taster, preview; **j'ai pris un petit a.** I had a little taster (of how things would be)

aconit [akɔnit] NM *Bot* aconite, monkshood

a contrario [akɔ̃trarjo] ADJ INV converse
ADV conversely

acoquiner [3] [akɔkine] **s'acoquiner** VPR *Péj* **s'a. à** *ou* **avec qn** to fall in with sb; *Fig* to cosy up to sb

Açores [asɔr] NFPL **les A.** the Azores

à-côté [akote] *(pl* **à-côtés***)* NM **1** *(aspect ▸ d'une question)* side issue; *(▸ d'une histoire, d'un événement)* side *or* secondary aspect **2** *Fam (gain)* bit of extra money□; *(frais)* incidental expense□; **se faire des à-côtés** to make a bit on the side; **les frais d'hôtel plus les à-côtés** hotel expenses plus incidentals

à-coup [aku] *(pl* **à-coups***)* NM **1** *(secousse ▸ d'un moteur, d'un véhicule)* cough, judder; *(▸ d'une machine)* jerk, jolt; **le moteur a des à-coups** the engine judders; **sans à-coups** smoothly **2** *(de l'économie)* upheaval

• **par à-coups** ADV *(travailler)* in spurts; *(avancer)* in fits and starts

acousticien, -enne [akustisjɛ̃, -ɛn] NM,F acoustician

acoustique [akustik] ADJ acoustic; **appareil a.** hearing aid
NF *(science)* acoustics *(singulier)*; *(qualité sonore)* acoustics

acquéreur, -euse [akerœr, -øz] NM,F purchaser, buyer; *Jur* vendee; **se porter a. de qch** to offer to buy sth; **elle a trouvé un a. pour sa voiture** she found a buyer for her car
ADJ **les pays acquéreurs de cette technologie** countries which buy *or* acquire this technology; *Com* **société acquéreuse** takeover company

acquérir [39] [akerir] VT **1** *(biens)* to buy, to purchase, to acquire; *(fortune)* to acquire; **a. qch par héritage** to come into sth; *Prov* **bien mal acquis ne profite jamais** ill-gotten gains seldom prosper **2** *Fig (habitude)* to develop; *(célébrité)* to attain, to achieve; *(droit)* to obtain; *(expérience)* to gain; *(savoir-faire)* to acquire; *(information, preuve)* to obtain, to acquire, to get hold of; **a. de la valeur** to increase in value; **a. la conviction/la certitude que...** to become convinced/certain that...; **ce stage est destiné à leur faire a. une expérience pratique** this placement is designed to give them practical experience **3** *(au passif)* **il vous est entièrement acquis** he backs you fully; **mon soutien vous est acquis** you can be certain of my support
VPR **s'acquérir 1** *(emploi passif)* **cette habitude s'acquiert facilement** it's easy to get into the habit; **la souplesse s'acquiert par des exercices** you become supple by exercising **2** *(gagner)* **s'a. la confiance de qn** to gain *or* to win sb's trust

acquêt [akɛ] NM *Jur* marital property; **communauté réduite aux acquêts** = marriage settlement whereby only goods acquired since the marriage are deemed to be held in common

acquiert *etc voir* **acquérir**

acquiescement [akjesmɑ̃] NM *(accord)* agreement; *(consentement)* assent, agreement; **hocher la tête en signe d'a.** to nod one's agreement

• **d'acquiescement** ADJ *(geste, signe)* approving

acquiescer [21] [akjese] VI to agree, to approve; **a. d'un signe de tête** to nod (one's) approval; **a. à qch** to assent *or* to agree to sth

acquis, -e [aki, -iz] PP *voir* **acquérir**
ADJ **1** *(avantage, droit, fait)* established; *(fortune, titre)* acquired; **je tiens votre soutien pour a.** I take it for granted that you'll support me **2** *(tournure impersonnelle)* **il est a. que vous ne participerez pas aux frais** it's understood that you won't contribute financially; **il est a. que la couche d'ozone est en danger** it is an established fact that the ozone layer is at risk
NM **1** *(savoir)* knowledge **2** *(expérience)* experience; **avoir de l'a.** to be experienced **3** *(avantages, droits)* established privileges, rights to which one is entitled; *UE* **a. communautaire** acquis communautaire *(entire body of legislation ratified by the EU since its inception, to which all new member states must adhere)*; **les a. sociaux** social benefits

acquisitif, -ive [akizitif, -iv] ADJ *Jur* acquisitive

acquisition [akizisjɔ̃] NF **1** *(apprentissage)* acquisition **2** *(achat ▸ gén)* purchase; *(d'entreprise)* acquisition; **faire l'a. de qch** to buy *or* to purchase sth; **regarde ma dernière a.** look at my latest buy; *UE* **a. intracommunautaire** intra-Community acquisition **3** *Ordinat* **a. de données** data acquisition

acquisitive [akizitiv] *voir* **acquisitif**

acquit [aki] NM *Com* receipt; **donner a. de qch** to give a receipt for sth; **pour a.** *(sur facture, quittance)* received (with thanks), paid; **a. de paiement** receipt

• **par acquit de conscience** ADV in order to set my/his/*etc* mind at rest

acquit-à-caution [akiakosjɔ̃] *(pl* **acquits-à-caution** [akiakosjɔ̃]*)* NM *Com* bond note

acquittement [akitmɑ̃] NM **1** *(règlement ▸ d'une facture, d'un droit, d'une dette)* payment; *(▸ d'une obligation)* discharge; *(▸ d'une promesse, d'un engagement)* fulfilment; *(▸ d'une fonction, d'un travail)* performance **2** *Jur* acquittal

acquitter [3] [akite] VT **1** *(payer ▸ facture, note)* to pay, to settle; *(▸ dette)* to pay off, to discharge; *(▸ droits)* to pay; *(▸ chèque)* to endorse **2** *(libérer)* **a. qn d'une dette/d'une obligation** to release sb from a debt/from an obligation **3** *Jur* to acquit
VPR **s'acquitter s'a. de** *(obligation)* to discharge; *(promesse)* to carry out; *(dette)* to pay off, to discharge; *(facture, droits)* to pay; *(fonction, travail)* to perform; *(engagement)* to fulfil; **s'a. envers qn** to repay sb

acre [akr] NF **1** *Anciennement (en France)* ≃ 5200m^2 **2** *Can* acre (= 4047m^2)

âcre [akr] ADJ **1** *(saveur, odeur)* acrid **2** *Littéraire (propos, ton)* bitter

âcreté [ɑkrəte] NF **1** *(d'une saveur, d'une odeur)* acridness, acridity **2** *Littéraire (d'un propos, d'un ton)* bitterness

acrimonie [akrimɔni] NF acrimony, acrimoniousness

acrimonieux, -euse [akrimɔnjø, -øz] ADJ acrimonious

acrobate [akrɔbat] NMF *(gén)* acrobat; *(au trapèze)* trapeze artist
NM *Zool (mammifère)* flying squirrel

acrobatie [akrɔbasi] NF **1** *Sport* acrobatics **2** *Fig* **faire des acrobaties pour obtenir un crédit** to turn cartwheels to get credit **3** *Aviat* **a. aérienne** aerobatics

acrobatique [akrɔbatik] ADJ acrobatic

acrobranche = **accrobranche**

acromégalie [akrɔmegali] NF *Méd* acromegaly

acromégalique [akrɔmegalik] ADJ *Méd* acromegalic

acronyme [akrɔnim] NM *Ling* acronym

acropole [akrɔpɔl] NF acropolis, citadel

acrostiche [akrɔstiʃ] NM *Littérature* acrostic

acrylique [akrilik] *Chim & Tex* ADJ acrylic; **en a.** acrylic *(avant n)*
NM acrylic

ACT [ɑsete] NMF *Belg Rail (abrév* **accompagnateur de train***)* ticket inspector

ACTE [akt] NM **A.** *SÉQUENCE* **1** *Mus & Théât* act; **a. III, scène 2** Act III, scene 2; **un opéra en trois/cinq actes** an opera in three/five acts **2** *Fig* period, episode; **sa mort annonçait le dernier a. de la campagne d'Italie/de la Révolution** his death ushered in the last episode of the Italian campaign/the Revolution

B. *ACTION* **1** *(gén)* action, act; **nous ne voulons pas des promesses mais des actes** we don't want promises but action; **son premier a. a été d'ouvrir la fenêtre** the first thing he/she did was to open the window; **juger qn sur ses actes** to judge sb by his/her actions; **passer aux actes** to take action, to act; **le dossier est prêt, nous passerons aux actes vendredi** the plans are ready, we'll set things in motion on Friday; **faire a. d'héritier** to come forward as a beneficiary; **faire a. de témoin** to act as a witness, to testify; **faire a. de candidature** *(chercheur d'emploi)* to submit one's application, to apply; *(maire) Br* to stand, *Am* to run; **faire a. d'autorité** to show one's authority; **faire a. de bonne volonté** to show willing *or* one's good will; **elle a fait a. de courage** she proved *or* showed her courage; **faire a. de présence** to put in a token appearance; **a. de bravoure** act of bravery, brave deed, courageous act; **a. de charité** act of charity; **a. criminel** criminal offence, crime; **un a. de Dieu** an act of God; **a. de folie** act of madness; **a. de guerre** act of war; **a. d'hostilité** hostile act; **a. manifeste** overt act; **un a. contre nature** an unnatural act; **a. simulé** bogus deed; **a. de terrorisme** terrorist action, act of terrorism; **a. de vandalisme** act of vandalism; **a. de vengeance** act of revenge
2 *Méd* **a. chirurgical** *ou* **opératoire** operation; **a. de laboratoire** laboratory test; **a. (médical)** *(consultation)* (medical) consultation; *(traitement)* (medical) treatment
3 *Physiol (mouvement)* **a. instinctif/réflexe** instinctive/reflex action; **a. volontaire/involontaire** voluntary/involuntary action
4 passer à l'a. *(gén)* to act; *Psy* to act out; *(sexuellement)* to do the deed
5 *Psy* **a. manqué** acte manqué; **c'était peut-être un a. manqué** maybe subconsciously I/he/*etc* did it deliberately
6 *Rel* **a. d'amour** act of love; **a. de foi** act of faith; *Hist (pendant l'Inquisition)* auto-da-fé
7 *Phil* **a. gratuit** motiveless act, *Spéc* acte gratuit

C. *ACTION LÉGALE, POLITIQUE* **1** *Jur* act, action; **a. administratif** administrative act; **a. d'administration** administrative act; **a. bilatéral** bilateral act; **a. de commerce** commercial transaction; **a. judiciaire** judicial act; **a. juridictionnel** legal ruling; **a. juridique** legal transaction; **a. du Palais** ≃ act between *Br* two counsels *or Am* attorneys at law; **a. de procédure** procedure; **a. à titre gratuit** act without consideration; **a. à titre onéreux** act for valuable consideration; **a. translatif** deed of transfer; **a. unilatéral** act of benevolence **2** *Pol* **a. de gouvernement** *(en France)* act of State; **A. du Parlement** *(en Grande-Bretagne)* Act of Parliament; **c'est maintenant un A. du Parlement** it has now become law; *UE* **a. unique européen** Single European Act

D. *DOCUMENT ADMINISTRATIF, LÉGAL* **1** *Admin* certificate; *Jur* deed; **demander a. de qch** to ask for formal acknowledgement of sth; **je demande a. de cette remarque** I want this remark to be minuted; **je demande a. du fait que...** I want it on record that...; **donner a. de qch** *(constater légalement)* to acknowledge sth formally; *Fig* **donner a. à qn de qch** to acknowledge the truth of what sb said; **dont a.** duly noted *or* acknowledged; **prendre a. de qch** *(faire constater légalement)* to record sth; *(noter)* to take a note of *or* to note sth; **je prends a. de votre refus** I have taken note of *or* noted your refusal; **le comité prendra a.** the committee will note; **a. de cession** conveyance; **a. de décès** death certificate; **a. de l'état civil** ≃ certificate delivered by the Registrar of births, deaths and marriages; **a. hypothécaire** mortgage deed; **a. de mariage** marriage certificate; **a. de naissance** birth certificate; **a. de propriété** title deed; **a. de renonciation** quitclaim deed; **a. de transfert** deed of assignment
2 *(en droit pénal)* **a. d'accusation** (bill of) indictment, charge; **lire l'a. d'accusation** to read out the bill of indictment *or* the charge; **quel est l'a. d'accusation?** what is the defendant being charged with?, what is the charge?; **a. d'instruction** measure of enquiry; **a. de poursuite** initiation of legal proceedings; **actes préparatoires** preparation *(of a crime)*
3 *(en droit civil)* **a. apparent** act apparent; **a. d'appel** notice of appeal; **a. authentique** *ou* **notarié** notarial act; **a. d'avocat à avocat** ≃ act between

two *Br* counsels *or Am* attorneys at law; **a. d'avoué à avoué** ≃ act between two *Br* counsels *or Am* attorneys at law; **a. en brevet** = contract delivered by a notary in the original; **a. à cause de mort** = instrument not taking effect until death; **a. consensuel** consensual contract, contract of mutual assent; **a. conservatoire** conservation measure; **a. constitutif** incorporation of legal status, recognition of right; **a. déclaratif** declaration of legal status, recognition of right; **a. de disposition** act of disposal; **a. de donation** deed of covenant, gift; **a. fictif** ficitious action; **a. extrajudiciaire** = document served by a "huissier" without legal proceedings; **a. d'huissier** writ; **a. de notoriété** sworn affidavit; **a. récognitif** deed of recognition; **a. de simple tolérance** = tolerated access to another's property which does not result in its acquisition; **a. sous seing privé** private agreement; **a. de succession** attestation of inheritance *or* will; **a. de suscription** (testamentary) superscription

4 *(en droit commercial)* **a. d'association** partnership agreement *or* deed, articles of partnership; **a. de commerce** act of merchant; **a. mixte** = bilateral action which is commercial for one party but private for the other; **a. de vente** bill of sale

5 *(dans la diplomatie)* **a. diplomatique** diplomatic instrument

• **actes** NMPL **1** *(procès-verbaux)* proceedings; *(annales)* annals; **les actes de l'Académie des sciences** the annals of the Academy of Science **2** *Rel* **les Actes des apôtres** the Acts of the Apostles; **les Actes des martyrs** the acts of the martyrs

• **en acte** ADV *Phil* in action

acter [3] [akte] VT **1** *(noter)* to take a note of, to note; *Jur* to record **2** *Can Fam (jouer ▸ rôle)* to play (the part of)□, to act□; *(▸ pièce de théâtre)* to perform□; *(faire semblant)* to pretend□

VI *Can Fam* to act□; **a. dans un film/une pièce** to be in a film/a play□

acteur, -trice [aktœr, -tris] NM,F *Cin, Théât & TV* actor, *f* actress; **a. de cinéma/de théâtre** screen actor, movie *or Br* film/stage actor; **a. comique** comic actor; **a. de composition** versatile actor; **a. enfant** child actor; **a. de genre** character actor; **a. virtuel** *ou* **de synthèse** virtual-reality actor, synthespian

NM *Fig* protagonist; **les différents acteurs de la négociation** the different participants in *or* parties involved in the negotiations; **a. économique** economic agent *or* player; **a. du marché, a. sur le marché** market participant, market player; **les acteurs sociaux** = employer, workers and trade unions

actif, -ive [aktif, -iv] ADJ **1** *(qui participe ▸ membre, militaire, supporter)* active; **être a. dans une organisation** to be active within an organization; **participer de façon** *ou* **prendre une part active à** to take part fully *or* an active part in; **a. sur le plan politique** politically active

2 *(dynamique ▸ vie)* busy, active; *(▸ personne)* active, lively, energetic; **les années les plus actives de ma vie** the busiest years of my life

3 *(qui travaille ▸ population)* working, active

4 *Écon (marché)* active; **balance commerciale active** favourable trade balance; **la Bourse a été très active aujourd'hui** trading on the stock market was brisk today

5 *(efficace ▸ remède, substance)* active, potent; *(▸ shampooing)* active; **le principe a. de ce détachant** the active ingredient in this stain remover

6 *Élec & Opt* active

7 *Gram* active; **à la voix active** in the active voice

8 *Chim* active, activated

9 *Ordinat (fichier, fenêtre)* active

NM **1** *Gram* active voice; **à l'a.** in the active voice **2** *(travailleur)* member of the active *or* working population; **les actifs** the active *or* working population **3** *Com, Compta & Fin (patrimoine)* assets; *Jur (d'une succession)* estate; **mettre** *ou* **porter une somme à l'a. de qn** to add a sum to sb's assets; **excédent de l'a. sur le passif** excess of assets over liabilities; **a. brut** gross assets; **a. brut de succession** gross estate; **a. circulant** floating *or* current assets; **a. circulant net** net current assets; **a. corporel** tangible assets; **a. corporel net** net tangible assets; **a. différé** deferred asset; **a. disponible liquide** available assets; **a. d'exploitation** operating assets; **a. fictif** fictitious assets; **a. immobilisé** fixed *or* capital assets; **a. incorporel** intangible assets; **a. liquide** liquid assets; **a. net** net assets *or* worth; **a. net comptable** net accounting *or* book assets; **a. net réévalué** net revalued assets; **a. non-disponible immobilisé** illiquid assets; **a. principal** core assets; **a. réalisable** realizable assets; **a. réel** real assets; **a. de roulement** current assets; **a. sous-jacent** underlying asset

• **active** NF *Mil* **l'active** the regular army

• **à l'actif de** PRÉP **mettre qch à l'a. de qn** to credit sb with sth; **avoir qch à son a.** to have sth to one's credit; **elle a de nombreuses victoires à son a.** she has many achievements to her credit; **à son a., on peut mettre la conception du nouveau musée** to his/her credit, it should be said that he/she was the creator of the new museum

action [aksjõ] NF **1** *(acte)* act, action; **l'a. de marcher** the act of walking; **responsable de ses actions** responsible for his/her actions; **bonne/mauvaise a.** good/evil deed; **faire une bonne a.** to do a good deed; **faire une mauvaise a.** to commit an evil deed; **une a. de grâces** an offering of thanks

2 *(actes)* action; **passer à l'a.** *(gén)* to take action; *Mil* to go into action; **assez parlé, il est temps de passer à l'a.** enough talking, let's get down to it *or* take some action; **dans le feu de l'a., en pleine a.** right in the middle *or* at the heart of the action; **l'a.** *(l'intrigue)* the action *or* plot; **l'a. se passe en Europe/l'an 2000** the action is set in Europe/the year 2000

3 *(intervention)* action; **un conflit qui nécessite une a. immédiate de notre part** a conflict necessitating immediate action on our part; **une a. syndicale est à prévoir** some industrial action is expected; **a. revendicative** *(des travailleurs)* industrial action; *(des étudiants)* protests; **a. directe** direct action; **A. directe** = right-wing terrorist organization; **l'A. française** = French nationalist and royalist group founded in the late 19th century

4 *(activités)* work, activities; *(mesures)* measures; *(campagne)* campaign; **l'a. gouvernementale en faveur des sans-abri** the government's measures to help the homeless; **l'a. du gouvernement a été de laisser les forces s'équilibrer** the government's policy *or* course of action was to let the various forces balance each other out; **l'a. de l'institut dépasse le cadre strict de la médecine** the institute's sphere of activities goes beyond the purely medical field; **il est chargé de l'a. culturelle dans l'association** he has responsibility for cultural affairs in the organization

5 *(effet)* action, effect; **cette campagne aura une a. psychologique sur les consommateurs** this campaign will have a psychological effect *or* influence on the consumer; **l'a. de l'acide sur le métal** the action of acid on metal; **l'a. de la morphine** the effect of morphine

6 *Bourse (titre, valeur)* share; *(document)* share certificate; **actions** shares, equity, *Am* stock; **avoir des actions dans une société, détenir des actions d'une société** to have shares *or* a shareholding in a company; **émettre des actions sur un marché** to issue shares on a market; **les actions Comtel sont en hausse/à la baisse** Comtel shares are up/down; *Fig Hum* **ses actions ont baissé/monté** his stock has fallen/risen; **capital en actions** equity capital; **dividende en actions** *Br* bonus issue, *Am* stock dividend; **a. d'apport** *(délivrée au fondateur d'une société)* founder's share; *(émise par une société en échange d'un apport en nature)* vendor's share; **a. d'attribution** bonus share; **a. de capital** ≃ ordinary share; **a. de capitalisation** capital share; **a. cotée (en Bourse)** quoted share; **actions cotées en Bourse** common stock; **a. différée** deferred stock; **a. de distribution** income share; **a. à dividende cumulatif** cumulative share; **a. gratuite** bonus share; **a. de jouissance** dividend share; **a. libérée** paid-up share; **a. nominative** registered stock; **a. nouvelle** new share; **a. ordinaire** *Br* ordinary share, *Am* common stock; **a. au porteur** bearer share; **a. de premier rang** *ou* **de priorité** *ou* **privilégiée** *Br* preference share, *Am* preferred stock; **a. privilégiée cumulative** cumulative *Br* preference share *or Am* preferred stock; **a. reflet** tracker share; **a. syndiquée** syndicated share

7 *Mktg* campaign; **a. commerciale** marketing campaign; **a. promotionnelle** promotional campaign; **a. de vente** sales campaign, sales drive

8 *Jur* action, lawsuit; **intenter une a. contre** *ou* **à qn** to bring an action against sb, to take legal action against sb, to take sb to court *or* to bring a lawsuit against sb; **a. civile** civil action; **a. collective** class action; **a. confessoire** action in recognition of easement; **a. contractuelle** action for breach of contract; **a. en contrefaçon** action for infringement of patent; **a. déclaratoire** action in definition of right; **a. en diffamation** libel action; **a. disciplinaire** disciplinary action; **a. en dommages-intérêts** action *or* claim for damages; **a. à fins de subsides** action for child maintenance; **a. immobilière** action concerning real property; **a. judiciaire** action; **a. en justice** legal action, lawsuit; **a. mixte** mixed real and personal action; **a. mobilière** action concerning movable property; **a. négatoire** negatory action; **a. en nullité** action for (a) voidance of contract; **a. oblique** derivative action; **a. personnelle** personal action, action in personam; **a. en pétition d'hérédité** = claim to succeed to an estate held by a third party; **a. pétitoire** claim of ownership; **a. possessoire** possessory action; **a. publique** = public prosecution initiated by the public prosecutor; **déclencher l'a. publique** to bring about a public prosecution; **a. en recherche de maternité naturelle** maternity suit; **a. en recherche de paternité naturelle** paternity suit; **a. réelle** real action, action in rem; **a. récursoire** claim for contribution; **a. rédhibitoire** remedy for latent defect; **a. rescisoire** rescissory action

9 *Mil, Mus & Phys* action; **à double/simple a.** *(arme à feu, détente)* double-/single-action

10 *Gram* action; **l'a. du verbe** the action of the verb

11 *Suisse (vente promotionnelle)* sale, special offer

12 *Sport* **une magnifique a.** a great bit of play; **il y a eu quelques belles actions lors de cette rencontre** there were some fine passages of play *or* there was some good play during the match; **l'équipe a gagné grâce à l'a. de Marchand** some neat play from Marchand won the game for the team; **on va revoir l'a. de Thierry Henry** let's see that bit of play from Thierry Henry again

13 *Admin* **a. sanitaire et sociale** health and social services

• **d'action** ADJ **1** *(mouvementé ▸ roman)* action-packed, full of action; **film d'a.** action movie **2** *(entreprenant)* **homme/femme d'a.** man/woman of action **3** *Pol & Ind* **journée/semaine d'a.** day/week of action

• **en action** ADJ in action; **être en a.** to be in action; **ils sont déjà en a. sur les lieux** they're already busy at the scene ADV **entrer en a.** *(pompiers, police)* to go into action; *(loi, règlement)* to become effective, to take effect; **mettre qch en a.** to set sth in motion; **la sirène s'est/a été mise en a.** the alarm went off/was set off

• **sous l'action de** PRÉP due to, because of; **sous l'a. de la pluie** due to the effect *or* because of the rain

actionnaire [aksjɔnɛr] NMF *Bourse Br* shareholder, *Am* stockholder; **les petits actionnaires** small *Br* shareholders *or Am* stockholders; **a. majoritaire** majority *Br* shareholder *or Am* stockholder; **a. minoritaire** minority *Br* shareholder *or Am* stockholder; **a. de référence** major *Br* shareholder *or Am* stockholder

actionnariat [aksjɔnarja] NM *Bourse* **1** *(système) Br* shareholding, *Am* stockholding; **a. intermédiaire** nominee *Br* shareholding *or Am* stockholding; **a. ouvrier** worker *Br* shareholding *or Am* stockholding; **a. des salariés** employee *Br* shareholding *or Am* stockholding, employee share ownership **2** *(actionnaires)* **l'a.** *Br* the shareholders, *Am* the stockholders

actionnement [aksjɔnmɑ̃] NM activation; **a. à distance** remote-control operation

actionner [3] [aksjɔne] VT **1** *(mettre en marche ▸ appareil)* to start up; *(▸ sirène)* to set off; *(▸ sonnette)* to ring; **le moteur est actionné par la vapeur** the engine is steam-powered *or* steam-driven; **actionné à la main** hand-operated **2** *Jur* **a. qn** to bring an action against *or* to sue sb

actionneur [aksjɔnœr] NM *Tech* actuator

activation [aktivasjɔ̃] NF **1** *(d'un processus, de travaux)* speeding up *or* along, hastening **2** *Chim & Phys* activation

active [aktiv] *voir* **actif**

activé, -e [aktive] ADJ **1** *Chim & Phys* activated **2** *Ordinat (fichier, fenêtre)* active; *(option)* enabled

activement [aktivmɑ̃] ADV actively; **participer a. à qch** to take an active part *or* to be actively engaged in sth

activer [3] [aktive] VT **1** *(feu)* to stoke (up); *(travaux, processus)* to speed up
2 *Fam (presser)* **active le pas!** get a move on!
3 *Chim & Phys* to activate
4 *Ordinat* to activate; **a. une option** to select an option
USAGE ABSOLU *Fam (se dépêcher)* **active un peu!** get a move on!
VPR **s'activer 1** *(s'affairer)* to bustle about **2** *Fam (se dépêcher)* **il est tard, dis-leur de s'a.!** it's late, tell them to get a move on!

activisme [aktivism] NM activism

activiste [aktivist] ADJ activist, militant
NMF activist, militant

activité [aktivite] NF **1** *(animation)* activity *(UNCOUNT)*; **déborder d'a.** *(sujet: personne)* to be extraordinarily active; **le restaurant/l'aéroport débordait d'a.** the restaurant/airport was very busy; **elle déploie une grande a. au travail** she invests a lot of energy in her work; *Bourse* **sans a.** *(marché)* slack, dull
2 *Admin & Écon* **avoir une a. professionnelle** to be actively employed; **mes activités professionnelles** my professional activities; **être sans a.** to be unemployed; **avoir une a. non rémunérée** to be in unpaid work; **a. bancaire** banking; **a. commerciale** business activity; **a. économique** economic activity; **a. industrielle** industrial activity; **a. lucrative** gainful employment; **a. politique** political activity; **a. primaire/secondaire/tertiaire** primary/secondary/tertiary-sector employment
3 *(occupation ▸ d'une personne, d'un marché, d'une entreprise)* activity; **une a. différente leur est proposée tous les soirs** they can do a different activity every evening; **pensez-vous conserver une a. après la retraite?** do you intend to carry on some form of activity *or* occupation after retirement?; **activités dirigées** guided activities; **activités d'éveil** discovery classes
4 *Astron & Physiol* activity; **a. cérébrale** brain activity; **l'a. solaire** solar activity
• **en activité** ADJ *(fonctionnaire, militaire)* (currently) in post; *(médecin)* practising; *(volcan)* active, live; *Admin* **rester en a.** to remain in gainful employment
• **en pleine activité** ADJ *(industrie, usine)* fully operational; *(bureau, restaurant)* bustling; *(marché boursier, secteur)* active, brisk; **être en pleine a.** *(très affairé)* to be very busy; *(non retraité)* to be in the middle of one's working life

actrice [aktris] *voir* **acteur**

actuaire [aktɥɛr] NMF *Fin & Assur* actuary

actualisation [aktɥalizasjɔ̃] NF **1** *(mise à jour ▸ d'un texte, d'un ouvrage)* updating; **faire l'a. d'un ouvrage** to update a work
2 *Phil* actualization
3 *Écon & Fin* discounting
4 *Ordinat (d'écran)* refresh; *(d'un logiciel)* update

actualiser [3] [aktɥalize] VT **1** *(texte, ouvrage)* to update, to bring up to date
2 *Phil* to actualize
3 *Écon* to discount
4 *Ordinat (écran)* to refresh; *(logiciel)* to update

actualité [aktɥalite] NF **1** *(caractère actuel)* topicality **2** *(événements récents)* current developments; **l'a. médicale/scientifique** medical/scientific developments; **se tenir au courant de l'a. politique/théâtrale** to keep abreast of political/theatrical events; **il s'intéresse à l'a.** he's interested in current affairs; **une question d'une a. brûlante** a highly topical issue **3** *Phil* actuality, reality
• **actualités** NFPL **les actualités** *(les informations)* the news *(singulier)*; **les actualités télévisées** the television news; **il est passé aux actualités** he was on the news
• **d'actualité** ADJ *(film, roman, débat)* topical; **cette question est toujours d'a.** this is still a topical question

actuariat [aktɥarja] NM *Fin & Assur* **1** *(fonction)* **l'a.** the actuarial profession **2** *(corporation)* body of actuaries

actuariel, -elle [aktɥarjɛl] ADJ *Fin & Assur* actuarial

actuel, -elle [aktɥɛl] ADJ **1** *(présent)* present, current; **sous le gouvernement a.** under the present government; **le monde a.** today's world; **à l'époque actuelle** nowadays, in this day and age; **le cours a. du dollar** the current (exchange) rate for the dollar **2** *(d'actualité)* topical **3** *Phil & Rel* actual

> Il faut noter que l'adjectif anglais **actual** est un faux ami. Il ne signifie jamais **actuel**.

actuellement [aktɥɛlmɑ̃] ADV *(à présent)* at present, at the moment; *(de nos jours)* nowadays, currently

> Il faut noter que l'adverbe anglais **actually** est un faux ami. Il signifie **en fait**.

acuité [akɥite] NF **1** *(du son)* shrillness **2** *(intensité ▸ de l'intelligence)* sharpness; *(▸ d'une crise)* severity; *(▸ du regard)* penetration; *(▸ d'un chagrin)* keenness; *(▸ d'une douleur)* intensity, acuteness **3** *Méd* acuity, acuteness; **a. visuelle** acuteness of vision

acuponcteur, -trice [akypɔ̃ktœr, -tris] NM,F *Méd* acupuncturist

acuponcture [akupɔ̃ktyr] NF *Méd* acupuncture

acupressing [akuprɛsiŋ] NM *Méd* acupressure

acupuncteur, -trice [akypɔ̃ktœr, -tris] = **acuponcteur, -trice**

acupuncture [akupɔ̃ktyr] = **acuponcture**

acutangle [akytɑ̃gl] ADJ *Géom* acute-angled

ADAC [adak] NM *Aviat (abrév* **avion à décollage et atterrissage courts***)* STOL

adage [adaʒ] NM *(maxime)* adage, saying; **selon l'a.** as the saying goes

adagio [adadʒjo] *Mus* NM adagio
ADV adagio

Adam [adɑ̃] NPR *Bible* Adam

adaptabilité [adaptabilite] NF adaptability

adaptable [adaptabl] ADJ adaptable

adaptateur, -trice [adaptatœr, -tris] NM,F *(personne)* adapter, adaptor
NM *Élec (objet)* adapter, adaptor; *Phot* **a. graphique couleur** colour graphics adapter

adaptation [adaptasjɔ̃] NF **1** *(flexibilité)* adaptation; **faculté d'a.** adaptability; **ils n'ont fait aucun effort d'a.** they didn't try to adapt **2** *Biol* adaptation **3** *Cin, Théât & TV* adaptation, adapted version; **a. scénique** *ou* **théâtrale/cinématographique** stage/screen adaptation

adaptatrice [adaptatris] *voir* **adaptateur**

adapter [3] [adapte] VT **1** *(fixer)* **a. un embout à un tuyau/un filtre sur un objectif** to fit a nozzle on to a pipe/a filter on to a lens **2** *(ajuster)* **a. son discours à son public** to fit one's language to one's audience; **la méthode n'est pas vraiment adaptée à la situation** the method isn't very appropriate for this situation; **adapté aux besoins du client** adapted *or* tailored to the needs of the customer **3** *Cin, Théât & TV* to adapt; **a. un roman au théâtre** *ou* **à la scène/au cinéma** to adapt a novel for the stage/for the cinema; **a. une pièce pour la télévision** to adapt a play for TV
VPR **s'adapter 1** *(s'ajuster)* **la clé s'adapte à la serrure** the key fits the lock; **le couvercle s'adapte sur le bocal par un crochet/par un pas de vis** the lid clips/screws onto the jar **2** *(s'habituer)* to adapt (oneself); **tu t'adapteras!** you'll get used to it!; **elle n'a pas pu s'a. à ce milieu** she couldn't adjust to this social circle

adaptif, -ive [adaptif, -iv] ADJ *Biol* adaptive

ADAV [adav] NM *Aviat (abrév* **avion à décollage et atterrissage verticaux***)* VTOL

addenda [adɛ̃da] NMPL addenda

addict [adikt] ADJ **être a. de qch** to be addicted to *ou* hooked on sth
NMF **mon frère est un vrai a. de jeux vidéo** my brother's hooked on video games

addictologie [adiktɔlɔʒi] NF study of addiction, addictology

addictologue [adiktɔlɔg] NMF addiction specialist, addictologist

additif, -ive [aditif, -iv] ADJ *Math & Phot* additive
NM **1** *(à un texte)* additional clause **2** *(ingrédient)* additive; **sans additifs** additive-free

addition [adisjɔ̃] NF **1** *(ajout)* addition; **l'a. d'une aile au bâtiment** the addition of a new wing to the building; **faire des additions à un texte** to add to a text **2** *Math* sum; **faire une a.** to add (figures) up, to do a sum **3** *(facture) Br* bill, *Am* check

additionnel, -elle [adisjɔnɛl] ADJ additional; *Ordinat* add-on

additionner [3] [adisjɔne] VT **1** *Math (nombres)* to add (up); **a. 15 et 57** to add 15 and 57, to add 15 to 57, to add together 15 and 57 **2** *(altérer)* **a. un alcool d'un peu d'eau** to add a little water to a drink; **du vin/lait additionné d'eau** watered-down wine/milk
VPR **s'additionner** to build up; **aux longues heures de travail s'additionnent celles passées dans le métro** along with the long working hours, there are those spent on the underground

additionneur [adisjɔnœr] NM *Électron* adder

additive [aditiv] *voir* **additif**

adducteur [adyktœr] ADJ M *Anat (muscle)* adductor *(avant n)*; *(canal)* feeder *(avant n)*
NM *Anat (muscle)* adductor; *(canal)* feeder (canal)

adduction [adyksjɔ̃] NF **1** *Physiol* adduction **2** *(en travaux publics)* **a. d'eau** water conveyance

> **-ADE** SUFFIX
>
> This suffix is used to form feminine nouns.
>
> • In the majority of cases, the basis is a verb. The idea is that of an ACTION or the RESULT of an action, and the register is often colloquial:
>
> **une bousculade** a scramble, a stampede; **une engueulade** a bawling out, a quarrel; **la rigolade** fun; **des embrassades** hugging and kissing; **une embuscade** an ambush
>
> Occasionally, the basis for derivation is a noun:
>
> **des fanfaronnades** (from *fanfaron*) boasting; **une œillade** (from *œil*) a wink
>
> • Adding the suffix **-ade** to a noun can result in a COLLECTIVE noun:
>
> **une fusillade** a volley of shots; **une arcade** arches; **une colonnade** a colonnade
>
> • When added to a noun, **-ade** can also convey the idea of something MADE OF the ingredient that the noun refers to:
>
> **une orangeade** an orange drink; **une persillade** chopped parsley; **une grillade** grilled meat

adénoïde [adenɔid] ADJ *Anat* adenoidal

adénopathie [adenɔpati] NF *Méd* adenopathy

adent [adɑ̃] NM *Menuis* dovetail

adepte [adɛpt] NMF **1** *Rel & Pol* follower; **un a. de la non-violence** a supporter of non-violence **2** *Fig* **faire des adeptes** to become popular, to attract a following; **les adeptes du tennis** tennis enthusiasts

adéquat, -e [adekwa, -at] ADJ suitable, appropriate

adéquation [adekwasjɔ̃] NF appropriateness; **l'a. entre l'offre et la demande favorise la stabilité des prix** the balance between supply and demand encourages stable prices; *Fin* **a. des fonds propres** capital adequacy

adhérence [aderɑ̃s] NF **1** *(par la colle, le ciment)* adhesion **2** *(au sol)* adhesion, grip; **le manque d'a. d'une voiture** a car's lack of *or* poor road-holding **3** *Anat* adhesion

adhérent, -e [aderɑ̃, -ɑ̃t] ADJ **1** *(gén)* adherent; **a. à la route** with good road-holding **2** *Bot* adherent, adnate
NM,F member

adhérer [18] [adere] **adhérer à** VT IND **1** *(coller sur)* to adhere to; **a. à la route** to hold the road **2** *(se rallier à ▸ opinion)* to adhere to, to support; *(▸*

cause) to support; (► *idéal)* to adhere to; (► *association)* to join, to become a member of
USAGE ABSOLU une colle qui adhère rapidement a quick-setting glue; **pour une France moderne, adhérez!** join us in building a new France!

adhésif, -ive [adezif, -iv] **ADJ** adhesive, sticky
NM 1 *(substance)* adhesive **2** *(ruban)* sticky tape, *Br* Sellotape®, *Am* Scotch® tape

adhésion [adezjɔ̃] **NF 1** *(accord)* support, adherence; **donner son a. à un projet** to give one's support to *or* to support a project **2** *(inscription)* membership; **de plus en plus d'adhésions** more and more members; **après leur a. à l'Union européenne** after joining the European Union

adhésive [adeziv] *voir* **adhésif**

ad hoc [adɔk] **ADJ INV 1** *(approprié)* appropriate, suitable **2** *(destiné à tel usage* ► *règle, raisonnement, commission)* ad hoc

adieu, -x [adjø] **NM** goodbye, *Littéraire* farewell; **faire ses adieux à qn** to say goodbye *or* one's farewells to sb; **faire ses adieux à la scène** to make one's final appearance on stage; **dire a. à qn** to say goodbye *or* farewell to sb; **tu peux dire a. à ta voiture** you can say goodbye to your car *or* kiss your car goodbye
• **adieu EXCLAM** *(pour toujours)* goodbye, *Littéraire* farewell
• **d'adieu ADJ INV** *(baiser)* farewell *(avant n)*; *(regard, cadeau)* parting *(avant n)*

adipeux, -euse [adipø, -øz] **ADJ** *(tissu, cellule)* adipose; *(visage)* puffed up, puffy

adiposité [adipozite] **NF** *Physiol* adiposity

adjacent, -e [adʒasɑ̃, -ɑ̃t] **ADJ** adjoining, adjacent; *Math (angles)* adjacent; **a. à qch** adjoining sth, adjacent to sth

adjectif, -ive [adʒɛktif, -iv] **ADJ** adjectival
NM *Gram* adjective; **a. attribut** predicative adjective; **a. épithète** attributive adjective

adjectival, -e, -aux, -ales [adʒɛktival, -o] **ADJ** *Gram* adjectival

adjective [adʒɛktiv] *voir* **adjectif**

adjectiver [3] [adʒɛktive], **adjectiviser [3]** [adʒɛktivize] **VT** *Gram* to use as an adjective

adjoindre [82] [adjwɛ̃dr] **VT 1** *(ajouter)* **a. à** to add to; **a. une véranda à une pièce** to add a conservatory onto a room; **a. une pièce à une lettre** to enclose a document with a letter **2** *(associer)* **on m'a adjoint un secrétaire/une assistante** I was given a secretary/an assistant
VPR s'adjoindre s'a. qn to take sb on; **ils se sont adjoint des collaborateurs** they've taken on some helpers

adjoint, -e [adʒwɛ̃, -ɛ̃t] **ADJ** assistant, deputy *(avant n)*; *(directeur)* assistant, associate
NM,F *(assistant)* assistant, deputy; **a. au maire** deputy mayor

adjonction [adʒɔ̃ksjɔ̃] **NF 1** *(fait d'ajouter)* adding; **sans a. de sucre/sel** with no added sugar/salt; *(sur emballage)* no added sugar/salt **2** *(chose ajoutée)* addition; **faire une a. à un texte** to make an addition to a text

adjudant [adʒydɑ̃] **NM** *Mil (dans l'armée de terre) Br* ≃ staff sergeant, *Am* ≃ sergeant major; *(dans l'armée de l'air) Br* ≃ warrant officer, *Am* ≃ master sergeant

adjudant-chef [adʒydɑ̃ʃɛf] *(pl* **adjudants-chefs)** **NM** *Mil (dans l'armée de terre) Br* ≃ warrant officer 2nd class, *Am* ≃ warrant officer; *(dans l'armée de l'air) Br* ≃ warrant officer, *Am* ≃ senior master sergeant

adjudant-major [adʒydɑ̃maʒɔr] *(pl* **adjudants-majors)** **NM** *Mil (dans l'armée de terre) Br* ≃ warrant officer 1st class, *Am* ≃ warrant officer; *(dans l'armée de l'air) Br* ≃ warrant officer, *Am* ≃ chief master sergeant

adjudicataire [adʒydikatɛr] **NMF 1** *Jur (aux enchères)* successful bidder **2** *Com (d'un appel d'offres)* successful *Br* tenderer *or Am* bidder

adjudicateur, -trice [adʒydikatœr, -tris] **NM,F 1** *Jur (dans des enchères)* seller **2** *Com (dans un appel d'offres)* awarder *(of a contract)*

adjudication [adʒydikasjɔ̃] **NF 1** *Jur (enchères)* auction sale; *(attribution)* auctioning (off); **a. forcée** compulsory sale **2** *Com (appel d'offres)* invitation to *Br* tender *or Am* bid; *(attribution)* awarding, allocation
• **en adjudication ADV mettre une propriété en a.** to put a property up for (sale by) auction; **mettre un marché en a.** to put a contract out to tender
• **par adjudication, par voie d'adjudication ADV 1** *Jur (aux enchères)* by auction **2** *Com* by *Br* tender *or Am* bid

adjudicatrice [adʒydikatris] *voir* **adjudicateur**

adjuger [17] [adʒyʒe] **VT 1** *Jur (aux enchères)* **a. qch à qn** to knock sth down to sb; **la statuette a été adjugée pour 1000 euros** the statuette was knocked down for 1,000 euros; **une fois, deux fois, trois fois, adjugé, vendu!** going, going, gone! **2** *(attribuer)* **a. un contrat à qn** to award a contract to sb; **a. une note à qn** to give sb a *Br* mark *or Am* grade; **a. une place à qn** to give sb a seat
VPR s'adjuger to take; **elle s'est adjugé la plus jolie chambre** she took *or* commandeered the nicest room

adjuration [adʒyrasjɔ̃] **NF** plea, entreaty

adjurer [3] [adʒyre] **VT** to entreat, to implore; **a. qn de faire qch** to implore *or* to entreat sb to do sth

adjuvant, -e [adʒyvɑ̃, -ɑ̃t] **ADJ** adjuvant, auxiliary
NM 1 *Méd & Pharm (médicament)* adjuvant **2** *(produit)* additive **3** *Littérature & Théât* companion, partner

ADM [adeɛm] **NFPL** *(abrév* **armes de destruction massive)** WMD

admettre [84] [admɛtr] **VT 1** *(laisser entrer* ► *client, spectateur)* to allow *or* to let in; **le public sera admis après 8 heures** the public will be allowed in after 8; **les enfants de moins de dix ans ne sont pas admis** children under the age of ten are not admitted
2 *Tech* to let in; **la soupape admet les liquides** the valve lets the fluid in
3 *(recevoir)* **a. qn chez soi** to allow sb into one's house; **a. qn dans un club** to admit sb to (membership of) a club; **elle a été admise à l'Académie/à l'hôpital** she was elected to the Académie/admitted to hospital; **a. les femmes à** *ou* **dans la prêtrise** to admit women to the priesthood; *Bourse* **a. une société à la cote** to list a company
4 *Scol & Univ* to pass; **être admis** to pass; **il ne sera pas admis dans la classe supérieure** he won't be admitted to *or* allowed into the next *Br* year *or Am* class
5 *(autoriser)* **il a été admis à passer les épreuves à la session de septembre** he was allowed *or* permitted to take the tests in September
6 *(reconnaître)* to admit to; **a. un vol** to admit to a theft *or* to having stolen something; **j'admets m'être trompé** I admit *or* accept that I made a mistake; **il faut a. que c'est un résultat inattendu** you've got to admit the result is unexpected
7 *(accepter)* **il n'a pas reçu ta lettre, admettons** OK, so he didn't get your letter; **j'admets que les choses se sont/se soient passées ainsi** I accept that things did happen/may have happened that way
8 *(permettre* ► *sujet: personne)* to tolerate, to stand for; (► *sujet: chose)* to allow, to admit, *Sout* to be susceptible of; **tout texte admet de multiples interprétations** any text can lend itself to many different readings; **l'usage admis** the accepted custom; **ces insolences ne seront pas admises** this kind of rudeness won't be tolerated
9 *(supposer)* to assume; **si on admet qu'il gagne 1000 euros par mois** if one assumes he earns 1,000 euros a month
• **admettons que CONJ** let's suppose *or* assume, supposing, assuming; **admettons qu'il soit venu, pourquoi n'a-t-il pas laissé un message sur mon bureau?** assuming he did come, why didn't he leave a message on my desk?
• **en admettant que CONJ** supposing *or* assuming (that); **en admettant que je parte à 3 heures, je peux être à Nice dans la soirée** supposing I leave at 3, I could be in Nice by the evening

administrateur, -trice [administratœr, -tris] **NM,F 1** *Admin (dans une société)* (non-executive) director; *Jur* **a. de biens** *Br* estate agent, *Am* real estate agent; **a. judiciaire** (official) receiver
2 *Admin (dans les affaires publiques)* administrator; **a. civil** senior civil servant; **a. délégué** associate administrator
3 *Admin (dans une institution, une fondation)* trustee; *Jur* **a. légal** *(de biens)* trustee; *(d'un enfant)* legal guardian
4 *Ordinat* **a. de réseau** network manager; **a. de serveur** server administrator

administratif, -ive [administratif, -iv] **ADJ** *Admin* administrative

administration [administrasjɔ̃] **NF 1** *(fait de donner)* **l'a. d'un remède/sédatif** administering a remedy/sedative; **l'a. de la justice** applying the law
2 *Admin (gestion* ► *d'une entreprise)* management; (► *d'une institution)* administration; (► *de biens)* management, administration; (► *d'un pays)* government, running; **la mauvaise a. d'une société** the mismanagement of a company; **les frais d'a.** spending on administration, administration costs; **a. économique** e-government; **a. fiscale** tax authorities; **a. légale** guardianship; **a. des ventes** sales management
3 *Admin (fonction publique)* **l'A.** ≃ the Civil Service; **entrer dans l'A.** ≃ to become a civil servant, to enter the Civil Service
4 *Admin (service public)* **a. communale** local government; **l'a. des Douanes** *Br* ≃ the Customs and Excise, *Am* ≃ the Customs Service; **l'a. des Eaux et Forêts** *Br* ≃ the Forestry Commission, *Am* ≃ the Forest Service; **l'a. de l'Enregistrement** the Registration Department; **l'a. des Impôts** *Br* ≃ the Inland Revenue, *Am* ≃ the Internal Revenue Service; **a. locale** local authority; **a. municipale** local government; **a. portuaire** port authorities; **a. privée** private administration; **a. publique** public administration; *(fonction)* ≃ Civil Service
5 *(équipe présidentielle)* **l'A. Bush** the Bush administration
6 *Ordinat* **a. de réseau** network management

administrative [administrativ] *voir* **administratif**

administrativement [administrativmɑ̃] **ADV** *Admin* administratively

administratrice [administratris] *voir* **administrateur**

administré, -e [administre] **NM,F** ≃ constituent; **le maire informera ses administrés** the mayor will inform those people who come under his/her jurisdiction

administrer [3] [administre] **VT 1** *Admin (diriger* ► *entreprise)* to manage; (► *institution, fondation, département)* to administer, to run; (► *biens)* to manage; (► *succession)* to be a trustee of; (► *pays)* to govern, to run; (► *commune)* to run **2** *(donner* ► *remède, sacrement)* to administer; (► *gifle, fessée)* to give; **on lui a administré les derniers sacrements** he/she was given the last rites; **a. un malade** to administer *or* to give the last rites to a sick person **3** *Jur (preuve)* to produce, to adduce; **a. la justice** to administer justice

admirable [admirabl] **ADJ** admirable; **elle a été a. de courage/volonté** she showed admirable courage/willpower

admirablement [admirabləmɑ̃] **ADV** wonderfully; **ils s'entendent a. bien** they get along wonderfully

admirateur, -trice [admiratœr, -tris] **NM,F** admirer

admiratif, -ive [admiratif, -iv] **ADJ** admiring

admiration [admirasjɔ̃] **NF** admiration, wonder; **avoir** *ou* **éprouver de l'a. pour qn/qch** to admire sb/sth; **être en a. devant qn/qch** to be filled with admiration for sb/sth; **susciter** *ou* **soulever l'a. de qn** to fill sb with admiration; **tomber en a. devant qch** to be stopped in one's tracks by the beauty of sth

admirative [admirativ] *voir* **admiratif**

admiratrice [admiratris] *voir* **admirateur**

admirer [3] [admire] **VT** to admire; **il m'a fait a. sa voiture** he showed off his car to me; **elle nous a fait a. la vue de la terrasse** she took us on to the terrace so that we could admire the view

admis, -e [admi, -iz] **PP** *voir* **admettre**
NM,F *Scol & Univ (à un examen)* successful candidate

admissibilité [admisibilite] **NF 1** *(d'une proposition, d'un procédé)* acceptability **2** *Univ (après la première partie)* = eligibility to take the second part of an exam; *(après l'écrit)* = eligibility to take the oral exam **3** *(à un emploi)* eligibility

admissible [admisibl] **ADJ 1** *(procédé, excuse)* acceptable **2** *Univ (après la première partie)* = eligible to take the second part of an exam; *(après l'écrit)* = eligible to take the oral exam **3** *(à un emploi)* eligible; **il faut remplir certaines conditions pour être a. à ce poste** you must meet certain requirements in order to be eligible for this job
NMF *Univ (après la première partie)* = student who is allowed to take the second part of an exam; *(après l'écrit)* = student who is allowed to take the oral exam

admission [admisjɔ̃] **NF 1** *(accueil)* admission, admittance, entry; **l'a. des pays de l'Est dans l'Union européenne** the entry *or* admission of Eastern European countries into the European Union; **demande d'a.** *(à l'hôpital)* admission form; *(dans un club)* membership application
2 *Univ* **a. à un examen** passing an exam; **son a. à l'université** his admission to *or* his being admitted to the university; **a. sur concours** entry by competitive examination; **a. sur dossier** entry by written application
3 *Tech* intake; *Aut* induction
4 *Bourse* **a. à la cote** admission to quotation, listing; **faire une demande d'a. à la cote** to seek admission to quotation
5 *Com (en douane)* **a. temporaire** temporary entry
6 *Jur* **a. des créances** recognizance of debts

admixtion [admiksjɔ̃] **NF** *Pharm* admixture

admonestation [admɔnestasjɔ̃] **NF** *Littéraire* admonition, rebuke

admonester [3] [admɔneste] **VT** *Littéraire* to admonish

admonition [admɔnisjɔ̃] **NF 1** *Littéraire (reproche)* admonition, rebuke **2** *Rel* admonition

ADN [adeen] **NM** *Biol (abrév* **acide désoxyribonucléique**) DNA

ado [ado] **NMF** *Fam* teenager[□], teen

adobe [adɔb] **NM** *Constr* adobe

adolescence [adɔlesɑ̃s] **NF** adolescence; **je me souviens de mon a.** I remember when I was a teenager

adolescent, -e [adɔlesɑ̃, -ɑ̃t] **ADJ** adolescent, teenage
NM,F adolescent, teenager

adon [adɔ̃] **NM** *Can* coincidence

Adonis [adɔnis] **NPR** *Myth* Adonis

adonis [adɔnis] **NM 1** *(bel homme)* Adonis; **ce n'est pas un a.!** he's no oil painting! **2** *(papillon)* adonis

adonner [3] [adɔne] **V IMPERSONNEL** *Can* to suit, to be convenient; **viens me voir quand ça t'adonnera** come and see me whenever it suits you
VI *Can* **a. avec qch** *(vêtements etc)* to go with sth
VPR s'adonner 1 s'a. à *(lecture, sport, loisirs)* to go in for; *(travail, études)* to devote oneself to; **s'a. à la boisson/au jeu** to take to drink/to gambling; **être adonné à qch** to be addicted to sth **2** *Can* **s'a. avec qn** to get on *or* along with sb

adoptant, -e [adɔptɑ̃, -ɑ̃t] **ADJ** adopting
NM,F adopter, adoptive parent

adopté, -e [adɔpte] **ADJ** adopted; **enfants adoptés** adopted children
NM,F adoptee

adopter [3] [adɔpte] **VT 1** *(enfant)* to adopt; *Fig* **ses beaux-parents l'ont tout de suite adoptée** her in-laws took an instant liking to her
2 *(choisir ▸ cause)* to take up; *(▸ point de vue)* to adopt, to approve; *(▸ politique)* to adopt, to take up; *(▸ loi)* to adopt, to pass; *(▸ mode)* to follow, to adopt; *(▸ produit)* to adopt; **le projet de loi a été adopté** the bill went through
3 *(se mettre dans ▸ position, posture)* to adopt, to assume; **a. la démarche de Charlot** to walk like Charlie Chaplin
4 *(emprunter ▸ nom)* to assume; *(▸ accent)* to put on; **a. un profil bas** to keep a low profile

adopteur [adɔptœr] **NM** *Mktg (d'un produit)* adopter; **a. précoce** early adopter

adoptif, -ive [adɔptif, -iv] **ADJ** *(enfant)* adopted; *(parent)* adoptive; *(patrie)* adopted

adoption [adɔpsjɔ̃] **NF 1** *(d'un enfant)* adoption; **a. plénière** full adoption; **a. simple** simple adoption **2** *(d'une loi, d'un projet)* adoption, passing **3** *Mktg (d'un produit)* adoption
• **d'adoption ADJ** *(pays)* adopted; **c'est un Parisien d'a.** he's Parisian by adoption, he's adopted Paris as his home town

adoptive [adɔptiv] *voir* **adoptif**

adorable [adɔrabl] **ADJ** *(charmant ▸ personne)* adorable; *(▸ endroit)* beautiful; *(▸ vêtement)* lovely; *(▸ sourire)* charming; **une a. petite maison** an adorable little house

adorablement [adɔrabləmɑ̃] **ADV** adorably

adorateur, -trice [adɔratœr, -tris] **NM,F 1** *Rel* worshipper **2** *(admirateur ▸ d'un chanteur)* fan, admirer; *(▸ d'une femme)* admirer

adoration [adɔrasjɔ̃] **NF 1** *Rel* worship, adoration **2** *(admiration)* adoration; **être en a. devant qn** to dote on *or* to worship sb

adoratrice [adɔratris] *voir* **adorateur**

adorer [3] [adɔre] **VT 1** *(aimer)* to adore, to love; **elle adore qu'on lui écrive** she loves to get letters **2** *Rel* to adore, to worship
VPR s'adorer to adore each other

adossé, -e [adose] **ADJ elle était adossée au mur** she was leaning against the wall; **une maison adossée à la colline** a house built right up against the hillside; **la cabane adossée au garage** the shed backing on to the garage

adosser [3] [adose] **VT a. qch à** *ou* **contre qch** to put sth (up) against sth; **a. une armoire à** *ou* **contre un mur** to put a wardrobe against a wall; **a. une échelle contre un mur** to put *or* to lean a ladder against a wall
VPR s'adosser s'a. à *ou* **contre qch** to lean against sth

adouber [3] [adube] **VT 1** *Hist (chevalier)* to dub **2** *Échecs* to adjust

adoucir [32] [adusir] **VT 1** *(rendre plus doux ▸ peau, regard, voix, eau)* to soften; *(▸ boisson, goût)* to sweeten; *(▸ amertume, caractère, acidité)* to take the edge off; **l'âge l'a beaucoup adouci** he's mellowed a lot with age
2 *(atténuer ▸ couleur, propos, dureté)* to tone down; *(▸ difficulté, antagonisme)* to ease
3 *(rendre supportable ▸ peine, punition)* to reduce, to lessen the severity of; *(▸ chagrin)* to ease; **le tribunal a adouci la sentence** the court reduced the sentence; **ils s'efforcent d'a. les conditions de vie des prisonniers** they try to make the prisoners' living conditions less harsh
4 *Métal* to temper down, to soften
VPR s'adoucir 1 *(devenir plus doux ▸ peau, regard, voix, lumière)* to soften; *(▸ personne, caractère)* to mellow
2 *Météo (temps, température)* to become milder
3 *(s'atténuer ▸ pente)* to become less steep; *(▸ accent)* to become less broad
4 *Agr (▸ vin)* to mellow

adoucissage [adusisaʒ] **NM 1** *(des couleurs)* toning down **2** *Métal* tempering down, softening

adoucissant, -e [adusisɑ̃, -ɑ̃t] **ADJ** emollient; **crème adoucissante pour les mains** hand cream; **produit a. pour le linge** fabric softener
NM 1 *Méd* emollient **2** *(pour le linge)* fabric conditioner

adoucissement [adusismɑ̃] **NM 1** *(de la peau, de l'eau, de la voix)* softening; *(d'un caractère)* softening, mellowing
2 *(estompage ▸ d'une couleur, d'un contraste)* softening, toning down
3 *(atténuation ▸ d'une peine)* reduction
4 *Métal* tempering, softening

adoucisseur [adusisœr] **NM a. (d'eau)** water softener

ADP [adepe] **NF** *Chim (abrév* **adénosine diphosphate**) ADP

ad patres [adpatres] **ADV** *Fam* **aller a.** to go to meet one's Maker; **envoyer qn a.** to send sb to (meet) his/her Maker

adrénaline [adrenalin] **NF** *Physiol* adrenalin, adrenaline

adressable [adresabl] **ADJ** *Ordinat* addressable

adressage [adresaʒ] **NM** *Ordinat* addressing; **a. direct** direct addressing; **mode d'a.** address mode

adresse [adres] **NF 1** *(domicile)* address; **a. bibliographique** imprint; **a. de facturation** invoicing address, address for invoicing; **a. du lieu de travail** business address; **a. de livraison** delivery address; *(d'objets volumineux)* shipping address
2 *(discours)* formal speech, address
3 *Ordinat* address; *Can* **a. de courriel** e-mail address; **a. électronique** e-mail address; **a. Internet** Internet address; **a. IP** IP address; **a. URL** URL; **a. virtuelle** virtual address
4 *(dextérité)* skill, dexterity, deftness; **jongler avec a.** to juggle skilfully *or* with dexterity; **jeu d'a.** game of skill
5 *(subtilité)* cleverness, adroitness; **répondre avec a.** to give a tactful answer
• **à l'adresse de PRÉP** intended for, aimed at; **une observation à votre a.** a remark aimed at *or* intended for you; **je l'ai dit à l'a. de ceux qui…** I said it for the benefit of those who…

adresser [4] [adrese] **VT 1** *(envoyer)* **a. qch à qn** *(gén)* to address *or* to direct sth to sb; *(par courrier)* to send *or* to forward sth to sb; **adressez toute requête au Bureau 402** direct *or* address all requests to Department 402; **a. CV détaillé à Monique Bottin** send detailed CV to Monique Bottin
2 *(destiner)* **a. qch à qn** *(▸ remarque)* to address sth to *or* to direct sth at sb; *(▸ geste, regard)* to aim sth at sb; *(▸ paquet, enveloppe)* to address sth to sb; **le colis était mal adressé** the address on the parcel was wrong; **cette lettre vous est adressée** this letter is addressed to you; **il faudra a. vos remarques au président** please address your remarks to the chair; **a. des questions à qn** to ask sb questions, to direct questions at sb; **a. la parole à qn** to speak to sb; **a. un compliment à qn** to pay sb a compliment; **il leur adressa des regards furieux** he looked at them with fury in his eyes, he shot furious glances at them; **a. un signe à qn** to wave at sb; **a. un signe de tête à qn** *(positif)* to nod at sb; *(négatif)* to shake one's head at sb
3 *(diriger ▸ personne)* **a. un malade à un spécialiste** to refer a patient to a specialist; **on m'a adressé à vous** I've been referred to you
4 *Ordinat* to address
VPR s'adresser 1 *(emploi réciproque)* **ils ne s'adressent plus la parole** they don't talk to each other any more; **s'a. à** *(parler à)* to speak to, to address; **c'est à vous que je m'adresse** I'm talking to you; **comment s'adresse-t-on à un archevêque?** how do you address an archbishop?; *Fig* **s'a. à la générosité de qn** to appeal to sb's generosity
2 s'a. à *(être destiné à)* to be meant for *or* aimed at; **à qui s'adresse cette remarque?** who's this remark aimed at?; **une émission qui s'adresse aux adolescents** a show aimed at a teenage audience
3 s'a. à *(pour se renseigner ▸ personne)* to go and see; *(▸ guichet, bureau)* to go to; **adressez-vous à la concierge** go and ask *or* see the porter

Adriatique [adrijatik] **ADJ** Adriatic; **la mer A.** the Adriatic Sea
NF l'A. the Adriatic (Sea)

adroit, -e [adrwa, -at] **ADJ 1** *(habile ▸ gén)* deft, dexterous; *(▸ apprenti, artisan, sportif)* skilful; **être a. de ses mains** to be clever with one's hands **2** *(astucieux ▸ manœuvre)* clever; *(▸ diplomate)* skilful; *(▸ politique)* clever; *(▸ phrase)* neatly turned; **la remarque n'était pas bien adroite** it was a rather clumsy thing to say

adroitement [adrwatmɑ̃] **ADV 1** *(avec des gestes habiles)* skilfully **2** *(astucieusement)* cleverly

ADSL [adeesel] **NM** *Ordinat & Tél (abrév* **Asymmetric Digital Subscriber Line**) ADSL; **est-ce que tu as l'A. chez toi?** have you got broadband at home?

adsorber [3] [atsɔrbe] **VT** *Phys & Biol* to adsorb

adsorption [atsɔrpsjɔ̃] **NF** *Phys & Biol* adsorption

adulateur, -trice [adylatœr, -tris] *Littéraire* **ADJ** adulatory
NM,F adulator

adulation [adylasjɔ̃] **NF** *Littéraire* adulation

adulatrice [adylatris] *voir* **adulateur**

aduler [3] [adyle] **VT** *Littéraire* to adulate, to fawn upon

adulte [adylt] **ADJ 1** *(individu)* adult; *(attitude)* mature; **devenir a.** to become an adult, to grow up **2** *Zool* full-grown, adult; *Bot* full-grown
NMF adult; **livres/films pour adultes** adult books/films

adultère [adyltɛr] **ADJ** *(relation)* adulterous; **femme a.** adulteress; **homme a.** adulterer
NMF *Littéraire* adulterer, *f* adulteress
NM *(infidélité)* adultery; **commettre l'a. avec qn** to have an adulterous relationship with sb, to commit adultery with sb

adultérin, -e [adylterɛ̃, -in] **ADJ** adulterine

ad valorem [advalɔrem] **ADJ INV** *Jur (droit, taxe)* ad valorem

advenir [40] [advənir] **V IMPERSONNEL** to happen; **qu'est-il advenu de lui?** what's become of him?; **il advient que...** it (so) happens that...; **quoi qu'il advienne, quoi qu'il puisse a.** come what may, whatever may happen; **advienne que pourra** come what may

adventice [advɑ̃tis] **ADJ 1** *Phil* adventitious **2** *Bot* adventitious
NF *Bot* adventitious plant

adventif, -ive [advɑ̃tif, -iv] **ADJ 1** *Bot (racine)* adventitive **2** *Géol (cône, cratère)* adventive, parasitic

advenu, -e [advəny] *pp voir* **advenir**

adverbe [advɛrb] **NM** *Gram* adverb; **a. de lieu/temps/quantité** adverb of place/time/degree

adverbial, -e, -aux, -ales [advɛrbjal, -o] **ADJ** *Gram* adverbial

adversaire [advɛrsɛr] **NMF** adversary, opponent; *(dans un conflit, une guerre)* enemy, adversary

adverse [advɛrs] **ADJ 1** *(camp, opinion)* opposing **2** *Littéraire (circonstances)* adverse **3** *Jur* opposing

adversité [advɛrsite] **NF** adversity; **dans l'a.** in the face of adversity

advertorial [advɛrtɔrjal] **NM** *Presse* advertorial

advient *etc voir* **advenir**

advint *etc voir* **advenir**

AELE [aəɛlə] **NF** *UE (abrév* **Association européenne de libre-échange**) EFTA

aérage [aeraʒ] **NM** ventilation, air supply

aérateur [aeratœr] **NM** ventilator

aération [aerasjɔ̃] **NF** *Tech* ventilation; *Chim* aeration; *(d'une pièce)* airing, ventilation; **il faudrait un peu d'a. dans cette chambre** this room needs airing

aéré, -e [aere] **ADJ** *(chambre)* well-ventilated, airy; *Chim* aerated; **bien a.** well-ventilated, airy; **mal a.** poorly-ventilated, stuffy

aérer [18] [aere] **VT 1** *(ventiler ▸ chambre, maison)* to air, to ventilate; *Chim* to aerate **2** *(rendre moins dense ▸ texte)* to space out
VPR s'aérer to get some fresh air; **s'a. l'esprit/les idées** to clear one's mind/one's thoughts

aérien, -enne [aerjɛ̃, -ɛn] **ADJ 1** *Aviat (tarif, base, raid, catastrophe)* air *(avant n)*; *(combat, photographie)* aerial *(avant n)* ; **nos forces aériennes** our air forces **2** *(à l'air libre ▸ câble)* overhead **3** *(léger ▸ mouvement, démarche)* light, floating

aérium [aerjɔm] **NM** *Méd Br* sanatorium, *Am* sanatarium

aérobic [aerobik] **NM** *Sport* aerobics *(singulier)*; **faire de l'a.** to do aerobics

aérobie [aerobi] **ADJ** *Biol & Aviat* aerobic

aérocâble [aerokabl] **NM** cableway

aéro-club [aeroklœb] *(pl* **aéro-clubs**) **NM** *Aviat* flying club

aérodrome [aerodrom] **NM** *Aviat* airfield

aérodynamique [aerodinamik] **ADJ** *(étude, soufflerie)* aerodynamic; *(ligne, profil, voiture)* streamlined
NF aerodynamics *(singulier)*

aérodynamisme [aerodinamism] **NM** aerodynamics *(singulier)*

aérodyne [aerodin] **NM** *Aviat* aerodyne

aérofrein [aerofrɛ̃] **NM** air brake

aérogare [aerogar] **NF** *Aviat (pour les marchandises)* airport building; *(pour les voyageurs)* air terminal

aérogastrie [aerogastri] **NF** *Méd* aerogastria

aérogel [aeroʒel] **NM** *Tech* aerogel

aéroglisseur [aeroglisœr] **NM** *Transp* hovercraft

aérogramme [aerogram] **NM** *(lettre)* aerogramme, air letter

aérographe [aerograf] **NM** airbrush; **retoucher qch à l'a.** to airbrush sth

aérologie [aerolɔʒi] **NF** *Météo* aerology

aéromodélisme [aeromɔdelism] **NM** aeromodelling

aéromoteur [aeromotœr] **NM** wind power engine

aéronaute [aeronot] **NMF** *Aviat* aeronaut

aéronautique [aeronotik] *Aviat* **ADJ** aeronautic, aeronautical
NF aeronautics *(singulier)*

aéronaval, -e, -als, -ales [aeronaval] **ADJ** *(bataille)* air and sea *(avant n)*
• **aéronavale NF l'aéronavale** *Br* ≃ the Fleet Air Arm, *Am* ≃ Naval Aviation

aéronef [aeronef] **NM** *Aviat* aircraft

aérophagie [aerofaʒi] **NF** *Méd* wind, *Spéc* aerophagia; **avoir** *ou* **faire de l'a.** to have wind

aérophobe [aerɔfɔb] **NMF** aerophobe

aérophotographie [aerofotografi] **NF** aerial photography

aéroplane [aeroplan] **NM** *Vieilli Br* aeroplane, *Am* airplane

aéroport [aeropɔr] **NM** *Aviat* airport

aéroporté, -e [aeropɔrte] **ADJ** *Mil* airborne

aéroportuaire [aeropɔrtɥɛr] **ADJ** *Aviat* airport *(avant n)*

aéropostal, -e, -aux, -ales [aeropɔstal, -o] **ADJ** *Aviat* airmail *(avant n)*
• **Aéropostale NF** *Hist* **l'Aéropostale** = first French airmail service between Europe and South America; *(filiale d'Air France)* = subsidiary of Air France

aérosol [aerosɔl] **NM** aerosol
ADJ INV bombe a. aerosol (can)
• **en aérosol ADJ** spray *(avant n)*; **nous l'avons aussi en a.** we also have it in spray form

aérospatial, -e, -aux, -ales [aerospasjal, -o] *Aviat & Astron* **ADJ** aerospace *(avant n)*
• **aérospatiale NF 1** *(science)* aerospace science **2** *(industrie)* aerospace industries

aérostat [aerosta] **NM** *Aviat* aerostat

aérostatique [aerostatik] **ADJ** *Aviat* aerostatic, aerostatical
NF *Phys* aerostatics *(singulier)*

aérostier [aerostje] **NM** *Aviat* balloonist

Aérotrain® [aerotrɛ̃] **NM** *Transp* hovertrain

aérotransporté, -e [aerotrɑ̃spɔrte] **ADJ** *Mil* airborne

AF[1] **1** *(abrév écrite* **allocations familiales**) family allowance *(UNCOUNT)*, child benefit *(UNCOUNT)* **2** *Suisse (abrév écrite* **Assemblée fédérale**) (Swiss) federal assembly

AF[2] *(abrév écrite* **Air France**) Air France

AFB [aɛfbe] **NF** *Banque (abrév* **Association française des banques**) = French Bankers' Association

affabilité [afabilite] **NF** affability, friendliness; **être d'une grande a.** to be very affable *or* friendly

affable [afabl] **ADJ** affable, friendly

affablement [afabləmɑ̃] **ADV** affably

affabulateur, -trice [afabylatœr, -tris] **NM,F** compulsive liar, storyteller

affabulation [afabylasjɔ̃] **NF 1** *Littérature* plot construction **2** *Psy* mythomania

affabulatrice [afabylatris] *voir* **affabulateur**

affabuler [3] [afabyle] **VI** to invent things, to make things up

affacturage [afaktyraʒ] **NM** *Com* factoring

affactureur [afaktyrœr] **NM** *Com* factor

affadir [32] [afadir] **VT 1** *(aliments)* to make bland *or* tasteless **2** *(ternir ▸ couleurs)* to make dull, to cause to fade; *(▸ style, personnalité)* to make dull *or* uninteresting
VPR s'affadir 1 *(aliments)* to become tasteless **2** *(couleur)* to fade; *(style, personnalité)* to become dull *or* uninteresting

affaiblir [32] [afeblir] **VT 1** *(personne)* to weaken; **sa maladie l'a beaucoup affaibli** his illness has weakened him a lot *or* sapped all his energy **2** *(atténuer)* to weaken; **le brouillard affaiblit tous les sons** the fog muffles all sounds; **l'usage a affaibli le sens original du mot** the original meaning of the word has become weakened through use **3** *(armée, institution)* to weaken, to undermine; **un pays affaibli par la guerre** a country weakened by war
VPR s'affaiblir 1 *(dépérir)* to weaken, to become weaker; **elle s'est beaucoup affaiblie depuis le mois dernier** she has grown a lot weaker since last month **2** *(s'atténuer ▸ signification, impact)* to weaken, to grow weaker; *(▸ lumière)* to fade; *(▸ son)* to grow fainter, to fade away; **la lumière du jour s'affaiblissait peu à peu** the daylight was fading gradually

affaiblissement [afeblismɑ̃] **NM** *(d'une personne, d'un sentiment, du sens d'un mot)* weakening; *(d'une lumière, d'un bruit)* fading

affaiblisseur [afeblisœr] **NM** *Phot* reducer

affaire [afɛr] **NF 1** *(entreprise)* business, firm, company; **monter une a.** to set up a business; **remonter une a.** to put a business back on its feet; **administrer** *ou* **gérer** *ou* **diriger une a.** to run a business; **elle a une grosse a. de meubles** she's got a big furniture business; **faire entrer qn dans une a.** to bring sb into a firm; **l'a. familiale** the family business

2 *(transaction)* deal, transaction; **faire a. avec qn** to do a deal with sb; **conclure une a. (avec qn)** to clinch a deal (with sb); **faire beaucoup d'affaires** to do a lot of business; **(c'est une) a. conclue!, c'est une a. faite!** (it's a) deal!; **a. blanche** profitless *or* break-even deal; **l'a. ne s'est jamais faite** the deal was never clinched; **l'a. ne se fera pas** the deal's off; **c'est une a. entendue!** we agree on that!

3 *Fam (achat à bon marché)* **une a. (en or)** an unbeatable bargain; **faire une (bonne) a.** to get a (good) bargain; **à mon avis, ce n'est pas une a.!** I wouldn't exactly call it a bargain!; **lui, c'est vraiment pas une a.!** he's no bright spark!

4 *(problème, situation délicate)* business; **une mauvaise** *ou* **sale a.** a nasty business; *Ironique* **quelle** *ou* **la belle a.!** so what (does it matter)?; **c'est une autre a.** that's another story *or* a different proposition; **pour lui faire manger des légumes, c'est toute une a.!** we have a terrible time getting him to eat vegetables!; **je n'en fais pas toute une a.** I'm not making an issue of it; **c'est une a. de gros sous** it's a huge scam; **sortir** *ou* **tirer qn d'a.** *(par amitié)* to get sb out of trouble; *(médicalement)* to pull sb through; **être sorti** *ou* **tiré d'a.** *(après une aventure, une faillite)* to be out of trouble *or* in the clear; *(après une maladie)* to be off the danger list; **se sortir** *ou* **se tirer d'a.** *(après une aventure, une faillite)* to get oneself out of trouble; *(après une maladie)* to make a full recovery; **on n'est pas encore tirés d'a.** we're not out of the woods yet

5 *(scandale)* scandal *or* affair; *(crime)* murder; *(escroquerie)* business, job; **l'a. des pots-de-vin** the bribery scandal; **l'a. Dreyfus** the Dreyfus affair; *Pol* **a. d'État** affair of state; *Fig* **n'en fais pas une a. d'État!** don't blow it up out of all proportion!, *Am* don't make a federal case out of it!; **être sur une a.** to be in on a job

6 *(procès)* trial, lawsuit, case; **l'a. est jugée demain** the trial concludes tomorrow; **plaider/juger une a.** to act for one of the parties/to be a judge in a lawsuit; **saisir un tribunal d'une a.** to bring a case before a judge; **a. en cause** case before the court; **a. civile** civil action; **a. correctionnelle** criminal action; **a. en état** = case which is ready for trial; **a. politique** political scandal *or* affair

7 *Fam (ce qui convient)* **j'ai votre a.** I've got just the thing for you; **la mécanique, c'est pas/c'est son a.** car engines aren't exactly/are just his/her thing; **la vieille casserole fera l'a.** the old saucepan'll do; **leur maison ferait bien mon a.** I'd be quite happy with their house; **je vais lui faire son a.** I'll sort *or* straighten him/her out!

8 *(responsabilité)* **c'est mon/leur a.** it's my/their business; **l'a. d'autrui** other people's business; **en faire son a.** to take the matter in hand, to make it one's business; **l'architecte? j'en fais mon a.** I'll deal with *or* handle the architect

9 *(question)* **dis-moi l'a. en deux mots** tell me

briefly what the problem is; **l'âge/l'argent/le temps ne fait rien à l'a.** age/money/time doesn't make any difference; *Fam* **c'est l'a. d'un coup de fil** all it takes is a phone call; **c'est une a. de vie ou de mort** it's a matter of life and death; **pour moi, c'est une a. d'honnêteté intellectuelle** for me, it's a matter of *or* it's a question of intellectual honesty; **a. de principe** matter of principle; **je ne le lui dirai jamais, a. de principe!** I'll never tell him, as *or* it's a matter of principle; **a. de goût** question of taste; **c'est (une) a. de goût** to each his own, it's a question of taste; **pour une a. de souveraineté territoriale** over some business to do with territorial sovereignty; **faut-il les emprisonner? – a. d'opinion** should they be sent to prison? – it's a matter of opinion

10 *(locutions)* **avoir a. à** to (have to) deal with; **avoir a. à forte partie** to have a strong *or* tough opponent; **avoir a. à plus fort/plus malin que soi** to be dealing with someone stronger/more cunning than oneself; **il vaut mieux ne pas avoir a. à lui** it's better to avoid having anything to do with him; **je n'ai eu a. qu'à sa femme** I only ever dealt with *or* had to do with his wife; **à la cuisine, il est à son a.** when he's cooking, he's in his element; **tout à son a., il ne m'a pas vu entrer** he was so absorbed in what he was doing, he didn't see me come in; *Belg* **être tout en a.** *ou* **affaires** to be all of a flutter

• **affaires** NFPL **1** *Com & Écon (activités commerciales)* business *(UNCOUNT)*; **comment vont les affaires?** how's business?; **parler affaires** to talk business; **les affaires vont bien/mal** business is good/bad; **être dans les affaires** to be in business; **les affaires sont les affaires!** business is business!; **pour affaires** *(voyager, rencontrer)* for business purposes, on business; **voyage/repas d'affaires** business trip/lunch

2 *Admin & Pol* affairs; **être aux affaires** to run the country, to be the head of state; **depuis qu'il est revenu aux affaires** since he's been back in power; **les affaires courantes** everyday matters; **les affaires de l'État** the affairs of state; **affaires étrangères** foreign affairs; **affaires intérieures** internal *or* domestic affairs; **affaires internationales** international affairs; **affaires publiques** public affairs; **les Affaires sociales** the Social Services (department); **les Affaires** *(scandale)* = financial scandals involving members of government

3 *(situation matérielle)* **ses affaires** his business affairs, his financial situation; **il connaît bien les affaires de son père** he's well acquainted with his father's business affairs; **mettre de l'ordre dans ses affaires (avant de mourir)** to put one's affairs in order (before dying)

4 *(situation personnelle)* **s'il revient, elle voudra le revoir et ça n'arrangera pas tes affaires** if he comes back, she'll want to see him and that won't help the situation; **mêle-toi de tes affaires!** mind your own business!, keep your nose out of this!; *Fam* **c'est mes affaires, ça te regarde pas!** that's MY business!; *ou* **affaires de cœur** love life

5 *(objets personnels)* things, belongings, (personal) possessions; **tes affaires de classe** your school things; **mes affaires de plage** my beach *or* swimming things; **range tes affaires** tidy up your things; *Hum* **ses petites affaires** his/her little things; *Péj* his/her precious belongings

• **en affaires** ADV when (you're) doing business, in business; **être dur en affaires** to drive a hard bargain, to be a tough businessman, *f* businesswoman

• **toutes affaires cessantes** ADV forthwith; **toutes affaires cessantes, ils sont allés chez le maire** they dropped everything and went to see the mayor

affairé, -e [afere] ADJ busy; **ils entraient et sortaient d'un air a.** they were bustling in and out; **être a. à faire qch** to be busy doing sth

affairement [afɛrmɑ̃] NM *Littéraire* bustle

affairer [4] [afere] **s'affairer** VPR to bustle; **il est toujours à s'a. dans la maison** he's always bustling about the house; **s'a. auprès de qn** to fuss around sb; **s'a. à faire qch** to be busy doing sth

affairisme [aferism] NM *Péj* wheeling and dealing

affairiste [aferist] NMF *Péj* wheeler-dealer

affaissement [afesmɑ̃] NM **1** *(effondrement ▸ gén)* subsidence; *(▸ du plancher, d'une poutre, d'un canapé)* sagging; **a. de sol** *ou* **de terrain** subsidence **2** *(relâchement ▸ d'un muscle, des traits)* sagging **3** *(dépression)* collapse, breakdown

affaisser [4] [afese] VT *Géol (terrain, sol)* to cause to sink *or* to subside

VPR **s'affaisser 1** *(se tasser ▸ gén)* to subside, to collapse, to sink; *(▸ bâtiment)* to collapse; *(▸ plancher, poutre, canapé)* to sag; **la route s'est affaissée en plusieurs endroits** the road has subsided in several places **2** *(s'affaler)* to collapse, to slump; **s'a. sur un canapé** to collapse *or* to slump onto a couch

affaler [3] [afale] VT *Naut (voile)* to haul down

VPR **s'affaler s'a. dans un fauteuil** to flop into an armchair; **s'a. sur le sol** to collapse on the ground; **s'a. sur un divan** to flop down onto a couch

affamé, -e [afame] ADJ famished, starving; *Littéraire* **a. de** hungry for

NM,F starving person; **les affamés** the starving

affamer [3] [afame] VT to starve

affectation [afektasjɔ̃] NF **1** *(manière)* affectation; **il n'y a aucune a. dans son langage** his/her language is not at all affected; **avec a.** affectedly

2 *(attribution ▸ gén)* allocation; *Fin (▸ d'une somme, de crédits)* assignment, allocation; **l'a. de crédits à la recherche** the allocation of funds to research; *Écon & Compta* **affectations budgétaires** budget appropriations; **a. aux dividendes** sum available for dividend; **a. de fonds** appropriation of funds; **a. hypothécaire** mortgage charge

3 *(nomination ▸ à une fonction)* appointment, nomination; *(▸ à une ville, un pays)* posting

4 *Mil* posting; **il a reçu son a. en Allemagne** he was posted to Germany

5 *Ordinat (de touche)* assignment; **a. de mémoire** memory allocation

affecté, -e [afekte] ADJ *(personne)* affected, mannered; **parler d'une manière affectée** to speak affectedly

affecter [4] [afekte] VT **1** *(feindre)* to affect, to put on a show of; **a. une grande joie** to pretend to be overjoyed; **a. de faire qch** to pretend to do sth

2 *(présenter ▸ une forme)* to assume; **a. l'apparence de** to take on *or* to assume the appearance of

3 *(assigner)* to allocate, to assign; **a. des crédits à la recherche** to allocate funds to research

4 *(nommer ▸ à une fonction)* to appoint, to nominate; *(▸ à une ville, un pays)* to post; **être affecté à un poste** to be appointed to a post; **son père l'a fait a. à Paris** his father got him a post in Paris

5 *Mil* to post

6 *(atteindre)* to affect; **la grève a affecté plusieurs usines** the strike has affected *or* hit several factories; **le virus a affecté les deux reins** both kidneys were affected by the virus

7 *(émouvoir)* to affect, to move; **il est très affecté par cette lettre** he's greatly moved by this letter

VPR **s'affecter** *Littéraire* **s'a. de** to be affected *or* moved *or* stirred by

affectif, -ive [afektif, -iv] ADJ *(problème, réaction)* emotional

affection [afeksjɔ̃] NF **1** *(attachement)* affection, fondness, liking; **avoir de l'a. pour** to be fond of, to feel affection for; **prendre qn en a.** to become fond of sb; **une marque** *ou* **un signe d'a.** a token of love *or* affection; **en manque d'a.** in need of affection **2** *Méd* disease, disorder

affectionné, -e [afeksjɔne] ADJ *(dans une lettre)* loving, devoted; **votre petite-fille affectionnée** your loving *or* devoted granddaughter

affectionner [3] [afeksjɔne] VT **1** *(objet, situation)* to be fond of **2** *(personne)* to like, to feel affection for

affective [afektiv] *voir* **affectif**

affectivité [afektivite] NF *(caractère)* sensitivity

affectueuse [afektɥøz] *voir* **affectueux**

affectueusement [afektɥøzmɑ̃] ADV **1** *(tendrement)* affectionately, fondly **2** *(dans une lettre)* **bien a.** with love

affectueux, -euse [afektɥø, -øz] ADJ loving, affectionate; **elle le regardait d'un air a.** she was looking at him fondly *or* affectionately

afférent, -e [aferɑ̃, -ɑ̃t] ADJ **1** *Jur* **a. à** accruing to, relating to; **la part** *ou* **portion afférente à qn** the portion accruing to sb **2 a. à** *(qui se rapporte à)* relating *or* relevant to; **voici les renseignements afférents à l'affaire** here is information relating *or* relevant to the matter **3** *Physiol (nerf, vaisseau)* afferent

affermage [afermaʒ] NM **1** *Jur (d'un bien rural)* tenant farming **2** *(d'un emplacement publicitaire)* contracting

affermer [3] [aferme] VT **1** *Jur (bien rural)* to lease (out), to rent (out) **2** *(emplacement publicitaire)* to contract for

affermir [32] [afermir] VT **1** *Constr (consolider ▸ mur)* to reinforce, to strengthen **2** *(rendre plus ferme)* to strengthen, to tone up, to firm up; **a. ses muscles par la natation** to strengthen one's muscles by swimming **3** *(assurer)* to strengthen; **a. sa position** to strengthen one's position; **a. sa voix** to steady one's voice

VPR **s'affermir 1** *(puissance, influence)* to be strengthened; *(investissements, monnaie)* to strengthen **2** *(muscle, chair)* to firm up, to tone up, to get firmer

affermissement [afermismɑ̃] NM *(d'un pont)* strengthening, consolidating; *(de la peau)* toning; *(des muscles)* strengthening, toning *or* firming up; *(d'une monnaie, du pouvoir)* strengthening

affichage [afiʃaʒ] NM **1** *(sur une surface)* posting; **a. interdit** *(sur panneau)* stick no bills, post no bills **2** *Mktg (activité)* bill-sticking, bill-posting; *(ensemble d'affiches)* posters; *(publicité)* poster advertising, display advertising; **a. transport** transport advertising **3** *Ordinat* display; **a. couleur** colour display; **a. à cristaux liquides** liquid crystal display, LCD; **a. digital** digital display; **a. graphique** graphics display; **a. numérique** digital display; **a. plasma** plasma display; **a. tel écran-tel écrit, a. tel-tel, a. Wysiwyg** WYSIWYG display

affiche [afiʃ] NF **1** *(annonce officielle)* public notice; *(image publicitaire)* advertisement, poster; *(d'un film, d'une pièce, d'un concert)* poster; **a. publicitaire** poster, advertisement; **a. électorale** election poster **2** *Cin & Théât* **en tête d'a., en haut de l'a.** at the top of the bill; **tenir l'a.** to run; **la pièce a tenu l'a. pendant plusieurs années** the play ran for several years; **quitter l'a.** to close

• **à l'affiche** ADV *Cin & Théât* **être à l'a.** to be on; **qu'est-ce qui est à l'a. en ce moment?** what's on at the moment?; **mettre une pièce à l'a.** to put a play on, to stage a play; **rester à l'a.** to run; **la pièce est restée à l'a. pendant deux ans** the play ran for two years

afficher [3] [afiʃe] VT **1** *(placarder ▸ annonce, poster)* to post (up), to stick up; *(mettre en évidence ▸ prix, produit)* to display, to put up

2 *Cin & Théât (annoncer)* to bill, to have on the bill; **une des salles affichait du Mozart** one of the concert halls had Mozart on the bill; **a. une vente** to advertise a sale, *Am* to post a sale

3 *Péj (exhiber)* to show off, to display, to flaunt; **a. son désespoir** to make one's despair obvious; **a. sa fortune/une liaison** to flaunt one's wealth/an affair

4 *Com (présenter)* to show; **a. un déficit/un excédent** to show a deficit/a surplus

5 *Ordinat (message)* to display; *(fichiers, articles)* to show; **l'écran affiche...** the on-screen message reads..., the screen displays the message...

VPR **s'afficher 1** *Péj (s'exhiber)* **elle s'affiche avec lui** she makes a point of being seen with him **2** *Ordinat (sur un écran)* to be displayed

affichette [afiʃet] NF small poster

afficheur [afiʃœr] NM **1** *(personne)* billposter, billsticker; *(entreprise d'affichage)* poster advertising company **2** *Ordinat* visual display unit, VDU; **a. LCD** LCD display

affichiste [afiʃist] NMF poster designer

affidavit [afidavit] NM *Jur* affidavit

affidé, -e [afide] *Péj Littéraire* ADJ accomplice

NM,F accomplice

affilage [afilaʒ] NM *Tech (d'un couteau, d'une lame)* sharpening

affilé, -e [afile] ADJ *(aiguisé)* sharp

• **d'affilée** ADV **il a pris plusieurs semaines de**

congé d'affilée he took several weeks' leave in a row; pendant deux/trois heures d'affilée for two/three hours at a stretch

affiler [3] [afile] VT *(couteau, lame)* & *Can (crayon)* to sharpen

affiliation [afiljasjɔ̃] NF affiliation; **demander son a. à une organisation** to apply for membership of an organization

affilié, -e [afilje] ADJ affiliated

NM,F affiliate, affiliated member

affilier [9] [afilje] **s'affilier** VPR **s'a. à** to affiliate oneself to, to become affiliated to

affinage [afinaʒ] NM *(d'un fromage)* maturing; *(du coton)* fining; *(d'un métal, du sucre)* fining, refining

affinement [afinmɑ̃] NM refinement

affiner [3] [afine] VT 1 *(purifier ▸ verre, métal)* to refine

2 *(adoucir ▸ traits)* to soften

3 *(raffiner ▸ goût, sens)* to refine; *(▸ esprit, jugement)* to sharpen, to make more acute

4 *(mûrir)* **a. du fromage** to allow cheese to mature

VPR **s'affiner** 1 *(se raffiner ▸ traits, goûts)* to become more refined; *(▸ esprit, jugement)* to become sharper *or* more acute 2 *(mincir)* to become thinner

affinité [afinite] NF 1 *(sympathie)* affinity; **avoir des affinités avec qn** to have an affinity with sb; **ils ont de fortes affinités l'un avec l'autre** there's a strong rapport between them 2 *Chim* affinity

affirmatif, -ive [afirmatif, -iv] ADJ 1 *(catégorique)* affirmative; **il a été très a. à ce sujet** he was quite positive about it; **faire un signe de tête a.** to nod in agreement 2 *Ling* affirmative

ADV *Mil & Tél* **a.!** affirmative!

• **affirmative** NF **répondre par l'affirmative** to answer yes *or* in the affirmative

affirmation [afirmasjɔ̃] NF 1 *(gén)* affirmation; *(de la personnalité)* assertion 2 *Jur* solemn affirmation

affirmative [afirmativ] *voir* **affirmatif**

affirmativement [afirmativmɑ̃] ADV affirmatively

affirmer [3] [afirme] VT 1 *(assurer)* to assert, *Sout* to affirm; **rien ne permet encore d'a. qu'il s'agit d'un acte terroriste** there is no firm evidence as yet that terrorists were involved; **je ne pourrais pas l'a.** I couldn't swear to it, I can't be (absolutely) positive about it; **elle affirme ne pas l'avoir vu de la soirée** she maintains she didn't see him all evening; **le Premier ministre a affirmé son désir d'en finir avec le terrorisme** the Prime Minister stated his desire to put an end to terrorism 2 *(exprimer ▸ volonté, indépendance)* to assert

VPR **s'affirmer** *(personne)* to assert oneself; *(qualité, désir, volonté)* to assert *or* to express itself

affleurement [aflœrmɑ̃] NM 1 *Géol* outcrop 2 *Menuis* levelling

affleurer [5] [aflœre] VT *Menuis (étagère, planches)* to level

VI *(écueil)* to show on the surface; *Géol (filon)* to outcrop; *Fig* to show through; **l'espace d'une seconde, il laissa a. ses sentiments** for a second he let his feelings show through

affliction [afliksjɔ̃] NF *Littéraire* affliction; **plongé dans l'a.** deeply distressed

affligé, -e [afliʒe] ADJ *(air, ton)* upset

affligeant, -e [afliʒɑ̃, -ɑ̃t] ADJ 1 *Littéraire (attristant)* distressing 2 *(lamentable)* appalling, pathetic; **d'une ignorance affligeante** appallingly ignorant

affliger [17] [afliʒe] VT 1 *(atteindre)* to afflict, to affect; **être affligé d'un handicap** to be afflicted with a handicap; *Fig Hum* **elle est affligée d'un prénom ridicule** she's cursed with a ridiculous first name 2 *Littéraire (attrister)* to aggrieve, to affect; **sa mort m'a beaucoup affligé** his/her death affected me greatly

VPR **s'affliger** *Littéraire* to be distressed, to feel grief; **s'a. de** to be distressed about, to grieve over

affluence [aflyɑ̃s] NF 1 *(foule)* crowd; **il y a a.** it's crowded 2 *Littéraire (abondance)* abundance

affluent, -e [aflyɑ̃, -ɑ̃t] ADJ *(fleuve, rivière)* tributary

NM tributary, affluent

affluer [7] [aflye] VI 1 *(couler)* to rush; **le sang afflua à son visage** blood rushed to his/her face 2 *(arriver)* to surge; **les manifestants affluaient vers la cathédrale** the demonstrators were flocking to the cathedral

afflux [afly] NM 1 *(de sang)* rush, *Sout* afflux 2 *(de voyageurs)* influx, flood; *(de capitaux)* inflow, influx; **a. de capitaux** *ou* **de fonds** capital inflow 3 *Élec* surge

affolant, -e [afɔlɑ̃, -ɑ̃t] ADJ 1 *(inquiétant)* frightening, terrifying 2 *Fam (en intensif)* appalling; **c'est a. ce qu'il y a comme circulation** the traffic's appalling; **c'est a. ce qu'elle a grandi** it's frightening *or* scary how much she's grown

affolé, -e [afɔle] ADJ 1 *(bouleversé)* panic-stricken; **il avait l'air complètement a. au téléphone** he sounded totally panic-stricken *or* in a complete panic over the phone 2 *(boussole)* spinning

affolement [afɔlmɑ̃] NM 1 *(panique)* panic; **l'a. était si grand que nous avons oublié de fermer la porte** there was such a panic that we forgot to lock the door; **pas d'a.!** don't panic! 2 *(d'une boussole)* spinning 3 *Métal & Phys* perturbation

affoler [3] [afɔle] VT 1 *(terrifier)* to throw into a panic; *(bouleverser)* to throw into turmoil; **les poulains étaient affolés** the foals were running around panic-stricken 2 *Littéraire (sexuellement)* to drive wild with desire

VPR **s'affoler** 1 *(s'effrayer)* to panic; **ne t'affole pas, tout va bien!** don't panic, everything's OK! 2 *(boussole)* to spin

affouiller [3] [afuje] VT *Géol (rive, fondation etc)* to undermine, to erode, to wash away

affranchi, -e [afrɑ̃ʃi] ADJ 1 *(esclave)* freed 2 *(émancipé)* emancipated, liberated

NM,F 1 *(esclave libéré)* freed slave 2 *Fam Arg crime* shady character

affranchir [32] [afrɑ̃ʃir] VT 1 *(libérer ▸ esclave)* to (set) free; **a. qn de qch** to free *or* to release sb from sth

2 *(colis, lettre)* to stamp, to put a stamp *or* stamps on; **paquet insuffisamment affranchi** parcel with insufficient postage on it

3 *Fam Arg crime (renseigner)* **a. qn** to give sb the lowdown, to tip sb off

4 *Cartes* to clear

VPR **s'affranchir** *(colonie)* to gain one's freedom; *(adolescent)* to gain one's independence; *(opprimé)* to become emancipated *or* liberated

affranchissement [afrɑ̃ʃismɑ̃] NM 1 *(libération)* freeing; **après leur a.** after they were set free 2 *(d'une lettre ▸ action)* stamping; *(▸ coût)* postage; **tarifs d'a. pour l'Afrique** postage *or* postal rates to Africa; **a. insuffisant** insufficient postage; **dispensé d'a.** post-free, postage paid

affranchisseuse [afrɑ̃ʃisøz] NF franking machine

affres [afr] NFPL *Littéraire* pangs; **les a. de la jalousie** the pangs of jealousy; **les a. de la mort** the pangs *or* throes of death; **les a. de la création** the throes of creativity

affrètement [afrɛtmɑ̃] NM chartering

affréter [18] [afrete] VT *(avion, navire)* to charter

affréteur [afretœr] NM charterer, charter company

affreuse [afrøz] *voir* **affreux**

affreusement [afrøzmɑ̃] ADV 1 *(en intensif)* dreadfully, horribly, terribly; **ce tableau est a. laid** this painting is terribly ugly; **il parle a. mal l'anglais** his English is awful 2 *(laidement)* **a. habillé/décoré** hideously dressed/decorated

affreux, -euse [afrø, -øz] ADJ 1 *(répugnant)* horrible, ghastly; **quelle ville affreuse!** what a horrible city! 2 *(très désagréable)* dreadful, awful; **nous avons connu quelques années affreuses** we have been through a few dreadful years; **il a fait un temps a. pendant toute la semaine** the weather was awful all week long; **qu'est-ce que ça a augmenté, c'est a.!** it's dreadful *or* shocking how the price has gone up!

NM *Fam* 1 *(mercenaire)* (white) mercenary *(in Africa)* 2 *(en appellatif)* **tu viens, l'a.?** coming, you little terror *or* monster?

affriander [3] [afrijɑ̃de] VT *Littéraire* to allure, to entice

affriolant, -e [afrijɔlɑ̃, -ɑ̃t] ADJ alluring, appealing; **des dessous affriolants** sexy underwear; *Fig* **ce travail n'a rien d'a.** it's not the world's most exciting job

affrioler [3] [afrijɔle] VT to excite, to allure

affriquée [afrike] *Ling* ADJ F *(consonne)* affricative

NF affricate

affront [afrɔ̃] NM affront; **essuyer** *ou* **subir un a.** to be affronted *or* offended; **faire un a. à qn** to affront sb

affrontement [afrɔ̃tmɑ̃] NM 1 *(heurt)* confrontation; **les derniers affrontements ont fait plusieurs morts** the last confrontation claimed several lives 2 *(mise de niveau) Menuis* joining edge to edge; *Méd* closing up

affronter [3] [afrɔ̃te] VT 1 *(ennemi, mort)* to face, to confront; *(problème)* to face (up to); *(équipe, adversaire)* to meet, to clash with; **il n'a pas hésité à a. le danger/l'incendie** he didn't hesitate to face danger/the fire; **a. la colère de qn** to brave sb's wrath 2 *Menuis (planche)* to butt-joint 3 *Méd* **a. les lèvres d'une plaie** to close up a wound

VPR **s'affronter** *(gén)* to confront one another; *(équipes, joueurs)* to meet, to clash; **deux thèses s'affrontent dans le débat sur la peine de mort** there are two opposing theories in the debate on the death penalty

affubler [3] [afyble] VT *Péj (habiller)* to attire; **affublé d'une veste rouge** attired in a red jacket; **qui l'a affublé ainsi?** who on earth dressed him like that?

VPR **s'affubler** *Péj* **s'a. de** to don; **elle s'était affublée d'une robe à froufrous** she had donned a flouncy dress

affût [afy] NM 1 *Mil (d'un canon)* carriage, mount 2 *Opt (d'un télescope)* frame 3 *Chasse* hide, *Am* blind

• **à l'affût** ADV *Chasse* **se mettre à l'a.** to hide out; **être à l'a.** to be lying in wait

• **à l'affût de** PRÉP 1 *Chasse* **être à l'a. de** to be lying in wait for 2 *(à la recherche de)* **il est toujours à l'a. des ragots** he's always on the look-out for juicy bits of gossip

affûtage [afytaʒ] NM *Tech* 1 *(aiguisage)* grinding, sharpening 2 *(outils)* set of bench tools

affûter [3] [afyte] VT 1 *Tech (outils)* to grind, to sharpen 2 *Équitation* **a. un cheval** to bring a horse to the top of its form

affûteur [afytœr] NM *Tech* grinder

affûteuse [afytøz] NF *Tech* grinding machine

afghan, -e [afgɑ̃, -an] ADJ Afghan

NM *(langue)* Afghan

• **Afghan, -e** NM,F Afghan, Afghani

Afghanistan [afganistɑ̃] NM **l'A.** Afghanistan

aficionado [afisjɔnado] NM aficionado; **les aficionados du football** football enthusiasts

afin [afɛ̃] **afin de** PRÉP in order to, so as to; **il s'est levé tôt a. d'éviter les embouteillages** he got up early (in order) to avoid traffic jams

• **afin que** CONJ *(suivi du subjonctif)* in order *or* so that; **préviens-moi si tu viens a. que je puisse préparer ta chambre** tell me if you're coming so that I can prepare your bedroom

AFNOR, Afnor [afnɔr] NF *Ind (abrév* **Association française de normalisation***)* = French industrial standards authority, *Br* ≃ BSI, *Am* ≃ ASA

à-fond [afɔ̃] *(pl* **à-fonds***)* NM *Belg* **faire un à.** to down one's drink in one

• **à-fonds** NMPL *Suisse* spring-cleaning *(UNCOUNT)*; **faire les à-fonds** to spring-clean, to do the spring-cleaning

a fortiori [afɔrsjɔri] ADV a fortiori, even more so, with all the more reason

AF-P [ɑɛfpe] NF *Presse (abrév* **Agence France-Presse***)* Agence France-Presse *(French national news agency)*

AFPA [ɑɛfpeɑ] NF *(abrév* **Association pour la formation professionnelle des adultes***)* = government body promoting adult vocational training

AFR [ɑɛfɛr] NF *(abrév* **allocation de formation reclassement***)* = allowance paid to employees requiring further training or new qualifications

africain, -e [afrikɛ̃, -ɛn] ADJ African
• **Africain, -e** NM,F African

africanisation [afrikanizasjɔ̃] NF Africanization, Africanizing

africaniser [3] [afrikanize] VT to Africanize
VPR **s'africaniser** to become Africanized

africaniste [afrikanist] NMF Africanist, specialist on Africa

afrikaans [afrikans] NM *(langue)* Afrikaans

Afrikander [afrikɑ̃dɛr] NMF Afrikaner

Afrique [afrik] NF **l'A.** Africa; **l'A. du Nord** North Africa; **l'A. du Sud** South Africa

afro [afro] ADJ INV afro; **coiffure a.** afro hairstyle
NM afro

afro-américain, -e [afroamerikɛ̃, -ɛn] *(mpl* **afro-américains,** *fpl* **afro-américaines)** ADJ Afro-American
• **Afro-Américain, -e** NM,F Afro-American

afro-asiatique [afroazjatik] *(pl* **afro-asiatiques)** ADJ **1** *Géog* Afro-Asian **2** *Ling* Afro-Asiatic
• **Afro-Asiatique** NMF Afro-Asian

afro-cubain, -e [afrokybɛ̃, -ɛn] *(mpl* **afro-cubains,** *fpl* **afro-cubaines)** ADJ Afro-Cuban
• **Afro-Cubain, -e** NM,F Afro-Cuban

after [aftœr] NM OU NF *Fam (soirée)* after-party; **on a décidé d'aller faire l'a. chez Alex** we finished the night off at Alex's place; **je fais un** *ou* **une a. après la soirée en boîte, d'accord?** everybody back to mine after the clubs shut, yeah?

after-shave [aftœrʃɛv] ADJ INV aftershave; **une lotion a.** aftershave (lotion)
NM INV aftershave (lotion)

AG [aʒe] NF *(abrév* **assemblée générale)** general meeting

agaçant, -e [agasɑ̃, -ɑ̃t] ADJ *(irritant)* irritating, annoying; **ce qu'il peut être a.!** he can be so annoying!

agacement [agasmɑ̃] NM irritation, annoyance; **montrer de l'a.** to show irritation

agacer [16] [agase] VT **1** *(irriter)* to irritate, to annoy; **ses plaisanteries m'agacent** his/her jokes get on my nerves; **il m'agace avec ses questions** he's getting on my nerves, asking all those questions **2** *(dents)* **le jus de citron agace les dents** lemon juice sets one's teeth on edge

agaceries [agasri] NFPL charms, wiles; **faire des a.** to use one's charm(s) *or* wiles

agaceur, -euse [agasœr, -øz], **agaceux, -euse** [agasø, -øz] ADJ *Can* irritating, annoying; **ce qu'il peut être a.!** he can be so annoying!

agapanthe [agapɑ̃t] NF *Bot* agapanthus

agape [agap] NF *Arch Rel* agape
• **agapes** NFPL *Hum* feast; **faire des agapes** to have a feast

agar-agar [agaragar] *(pl* **agars-agars)** NM *Biol & Pharm* agar, agar-agar

agaric [agarik] NM *Bot* agaric

agate [agat] NF **1** *Minér* agate **2** *(bille)* glass marble

agave [agav], **agavé** [agave] NM *Bot* agave; **a. americana** century plant

AGC [aʒese] NM *Phot (abrév* **adaptateur graphique couleur)** CGA

AGE [aʒeœ] NF *(abrév* **assemblée générale extraordinaire)** EGM

âge [ɑʒ] NM **1** *(nombre d'années)* age; **quel â. as-tu?** how old are you?; **quand j'avais ton â.** when I was your age; **être du même â. que** to be the same age *or* as old as; **à ton â., je lisais beaucoup** when I was your age, I used to read a lot; **à ton â., on ne pleure plus** you're old enough not to cry now; **un garçon/une fille de ton â. ne doit pas parler comme ça** a boy/a girl (of) your age shouldn't talk like that; **d'un â. avancé** getting on *or* advanced in years; *Hum* **d'un â. canonique** ancient; *Euph* **d'un certain â.** *(dame, monsieur)* middle-aged; *Hum* **un canapé d'un certain â.** a couch which is past its best *or* prime; **d'â. mûr** middle-aged; **à cause de son jeune/grand â.** because he's so young/old; **avancer en â.** to be getting on in years; **il veut se marier, c'est normal, il a l'â.** he wants to get married, it's normal at his age; **je n'ai plus l'â.** *ou* **je ne suis plus en â. de grimper à la corde** I'm too old for climbing ropes; **quand tu auras l'â.!** when you're old enough!; **j'ai passé l'â.!** I'm too old (for this kind of thing)!; **les boums, c'est de son â.** they all want to have parties at that age; **ce n'est pas de ton â.!** *(tu es trop jeune)* you're not old enough!; *(tu es trop vieux)* you're too old (for it)!; **ce sont des choses qui ne sont plus de mon â.** I'm too old for that sort of thing now; **tu es en â. de comprendre** you're old enough to understand; **ils ne sont pas en â. de se marier** they're not old enough to get married; **je n'ai plus l'â.** *ou* **je ne suis plus en â. de faire du camping** I'm too old to go camping; **sans â.** ageless; **elle n'a pas d'â.** she seems ageless; **on ne lui donne vraiment pas son â.** he/she doesn't look his/her age at all; **quel â. me donnez-vous?** how old do you think I am?; **faire** *ou* **paraître son â.** to look one's age; **elle ne fait** *ou* **ne paraît pas son â.** she doesn't look her age, she looks younger than she actually is; **elle est bien pour son â.** she looks good for her age; **on a l'â. de ses artères** you're as old as you feel; **l'â. d'un arbre/vin** the age of a tree/wine; **un whisky 20 ans d'â.** a 20-year-old whisky
2 *(période)* age, time (of life); **la quarantaine, c'est l'â. des grandes décisions** forty is the time (of life) for making momentous decisions; **une fois passé l'â. des poupées** when one's too old for dolls; **c'est le bel â.!** these are the best years of one's life!; **l'â. adulte** *(gén)* adulthood; *(d'un homme)* manhood; *(d'une femme)* womanhood; **l'â. ingrat** *ou Fam* **bête** the awkward *or* difficult age; **l'â. critique** the change of life; **l'â. mûr** maturity; **l'â. pubertaire** *ou* **de la puberté** the age of puberty; **l'â. de raison** the age of reason; **avoir l'â. de raison** to have reached the age of reason; **l'â. tendre** the tender years; **l'â. viril** manhood; **le premier â.** infancy; **le troisième â.** *(période)* old age; *(groupe social)* senior citizens; **le quatrième â.** *(période)* advanced old age; *(groupe social)* very old people
3 *(vieillissement)* ageing; **avec l'â., il s'est calmé** he became more serene with age *or* as he grew older; **les effets de l'â.** the effects of ageing; **prendre de l'â.** to age, to get older; **j'ai mal aux genoux – c'est l'â.!** my knees hurt – it's your age!
4 *Admin* age; **quel est l'â. de la retraite en France?** what's the retirement age in France?; **avoir l'â. légal (pour voter)** to be old enough to vote, to be of age; **l'â. scolaire** compulsory school age; **un enfant d'â. scolaire** a school-age child, a child of school age
5 *Archéol* age; **l'â. de bronze** the Bronze Age; **l'â. de fer** the Iron Age; *Fig & Myth* **l'â. d'or** the golden age; **l'â. néolithique** *ou* **de la pierre polie** the Neolithic Age; **l'â. paléolithique** *ou* **de la pierre taillée** the Palaeolithic Age; **c'est une tradition venue du fond des âges** it's a tradition which has come down through the ages
6 *Psy* **â. mental** mental age; **il a un â. mental de cinq ans** he has a mental age of five
• **à l'âge de** PRÉP **je l'ai connu à l'â. de 17 ans** *(j'avais 17 ans)* I met him when I was 17; *(il avait 17 ans)* I met him when he was 17; **on est majeur à l'â. de 18 ans** 18 is the age of majority
• **en bas âge** ADJ *(enfant)* very young *or* small
• **entre deux âges** ADJ *(personne)* middle-aged

âgé, -e [ɑʒe] ADJ **1** *(vieux)* old; **c'est un monsieur très â. maintenant** he's a very old man now; **elle est plus/moins âgée que moi** she's older/younger than I am **2 â. de** *(de tel âge)* aged; **être â. de 20 ans** to be 20 years old; **une jeune fille âgée de 15 ans** a 15-year-old girl, a girl of 15

Aged [aʒɛd] NF *(abrév* **allocation de garde d'enfant à domicile)** = allowance paid to working parents who employ a childminder at home

agence [aʒɑ̃s] NF **1** *(bureau)* agency, bureau; **a. commerciale** sales office; *Fin* mercantile agency; **a. conseil en communication** public relations agency, PR agency; **a. de coupures de presse** press cuttings agency; **a. de design** design agency; **a. de distribution** distribution agency; **a. immobilière** *Br* estate agent's, *Am* real-estate office; **a. d'intérim** temping agency; **a. maritime** shipping *or* forwarding agency; **a. matrimoniale** marriage bureau; **a. de notation** *Br* credit (rating) agency, *Am* credit bureau; **a. photographique** photographic agency; **a. de placement** employment agency *or* bureau; **a. de presse** press *or* news agency; **a. de promotion** promotions agency; **a. de promotion des ventes** sales promotion agency; **a. de publicité** advertising agency; **a. de recouvrements** debt collection agency; **a. de renseignements** information bureau; **a. de tourisme** tourist agency; **a. de voyages** travel agency *or* agent's; **A. pour l'énergie nucléaire** = French atomic energy agency, ≃ AEA; **A. de l'environnement et de la maîtrise de l'énergie** = French public body responsible for environmental and energy management; **A. française de lutte contre le sida** = French Aids research and care agency; **A. France-Presse** = French national news agency; **A. internationale de l'énergie atomique** International Atomic Energy Agency; **A. nationale pour l'emploi** = national employment agency; **A. nationale de recherches sur le sida** = Aids research institute; **A. spatiale européenne** European Space Agency **2** *(succursale)* branch (office); **quand vous passerez à l'a.** when you next visit the branch; **a. bancaire** bank branch

agencé, -e [aʒɑ̃se] ADJ *Suisse (cuisine)* fitted

agencement [aʒɑ̃smɑ̃] NM *(d'un lieu)* layout, design; *(d'un texte)* layout; *(d'éléments)* order, ordering

agencer [16] [aʒɑ̃se] VT **1** *(aménager)* to lay out; **a. une pièce** to arrange the furniture in a room **2** *(organiser)* to put together, to construct; **des phrases mal agencées** badly constructed sentences
VPR **s'agencer les parties du discours s'agencent bien/mal** the different parts of the speech go/don't hang well together

agencier [aʒɑ̃sje] NM *Journ* freelance journalist *(working for a press agency)*

agenda [aʒɛ̃da] NM **1** *(livre)* diary; **a. de bureau** desk diary; **a. électronique** personal organizer; **a. de poche** pocket diary; *Fig* **avoir un a. très chargé** to have a very full diary **2** *Ordinat* notebook

> Il faut noter que le nom anglais **agenda** est un faux ami. Il signifie **ordre du jour**.

agender [3] [aʒɑ̃de] VT *Suisse (rendez-vous, date)* to note down (in a *Br* diary *or Am* notebook)

agenouiller [3] [aʒnuje] **s'agenouiller** VPR to kneel (down); **s'a. devant une statue** to kneel (down) before a statue; *Fig* **il refuse de s'a. devant le pouvoir** he refuses to bow to authority

agenouilloir [aʒnujwar] NM *(prie-dieu)* hassock, kneeling stool; *(planche)* kneeling plank

agent [aʒɑ̃] NM **1** *(employé)* **a. d'affaires** business agent; **a. artistique** agent; **a. d'assurances** insurance agent; **a. attitré** appointed agent; *Bourse* **a. de change** stockbroker, exchange dealer *or* broker; **a. commercial** sales representative; **a. commercial exclusif** sole agent, sole representative; **a. commissionnaire** commission agent; **a. comptable** accountant; **a. contractuel** *Admin* contract public servant; *(agent de police) Br* traffic warden, *Am* traffic policeman; *Com* **a. direct** commission agent; **a. de distribution** distribution agent; **a. double** double agent; **a. électoral** canvasser; **a. exclusif** sole agent; **a. exportateur** export agent; **a. du fisc** tax official; **a. de fret** freight forwarder, forwarding agent; **un a. du gouvernement** a government official; **a. immobilier** *Br* estate agent, *Am* real estate agent, realtor; **a. importateur** import agent; **a. indépendant** free agent; **a. intermédiaire** middleman; *Jur* **a. de justice** = officer of the court; *Mil* **a. de liaison** liaison officer; **a. lié** tied agent; **a. de ligne** forwarding agent; **a. littéraire** literary agent; **agents de maîtrise** lower management; **a. mandataire** authorized agent; **a. maritime** shipping agent; **a. provocateur** agent provocateur; **a. publicitaire, a. de publicité** advertising agent, publicity agent; *Belg* **a. de quartier** community policeman, policeman on the beat; **a. de recouvrement** *ou* **de recouvrements** debt collector; **a. secret** secret agent; **a. de sécurité** security officer; **a. souscripteur** underwriting *or* underwriter agent; **a. technico-commercial** sales technician, sales engineer; *Mil* **a. de transmission** dispatch rider; **a. du trésor** government broker
2 *(policier)* **a. (de police)** *(homme)* policeman, police officer *Br* constable, *Am* patrolman;

(femme) policewoman, *Br* woman police constable, *Am* woman police officer; **a. de la circulation, a. contractuel** *Br* (male) traffic warden *or Am* traffic policeman; **s'il vous plaît, monsieur l'a.** excuse me, officer

3 *(émissaire)* agent, official; *Péj* **des agents de l'étranger** foreign agents

4 *(cause ▸ humaine)* agent; *(▸ non humaine)* factor; **elle a été l'un des principaux agents de la révolution** she was a prime mover in the revolution; **a. atmosphérique/économique** atmospheric/economic factor

5 *Méd* **a. asphyxiant** asphyxiant; *Méd* **a. carcinogène** *ou* **cancérogène** carcinogen; *Chim* **a. chimique** chemical agent; **a. conservateur** *ou* **de conservation** preservative; *Chim* **a. mouillant** wetting agent

6 *Gram & Phil* agent

7 *Ordinat* **a. intelligent** intelligent agent

AGETAC [aʒetak] **NM** *(abrév* **Accord général sur les tarifs et le commerce)** GATT

aggiornamento [adʒɔrnamento] **NM** *Rel & Fig* aggiornamento; **le parti doit faire son a.** the party has to move with the times

agglomérant [aglɔmerɑ̃] **NM** *Constr* binder

agglomérat [aglɔmera] **NM 1** *Géol* agglomerate **2** *Ling* cluster

agglomération [aglɔmerasjɔ̃] **NF 1** *(ville et sa banlieue)* town; **l'a. parisienne** Paris and its suburbs, greater Paris **2** *Transp* built-up area; **en a.** in a built-up area **3** *Mines (de sable)* aggregation

aggloméré, -e [aglɔmere] **ADJ** agglomerate

NM 1 *Mines* briquet, briquette **2** *Constr* chipboard, particle board; **a. de liège** agglomerated cork **3** *Géol* conglomerate

agglomérer [18] [aglɔmere] **VT** *(pierre, sable)* to aggregate; *(charbon)* to briquet; *(métal)* to agglomerate

VPR s'agglomérer *(sable, particules)* to agglomerate; **les populations pauvres s'agglomèrent dans les favelas** the poor are packed together in the shanty towns

agglutinant, -e [aglytinɑ̃, -ɑ̃t] **ADJ** *Ling & Méd* agglutinative

NM bond

agglutination [aglytinasjɔ̃] **NF 1** *Ling & Méd* agglutination **2** *Péj (masse)* mass

agglutiner [3] [aglytine] **VT** to mass *or* to pack together

VPR s'agglutiner to congregate; **ils s'agglutinaient à la fenêtre** they were all pressing up against the window

aggravant, -e [agravɑ̃, -ɑ̃t] **ADJ** aggravating

aggravation [agravasjɔ̃] **NF 1** *(d'une maladie, d'un problème)* aggravation, worsening; *(de l'inflation)* increase; **son état de santé a connu une a.** his/her health has worsened **2** *(d'une peine)* increase

aggraver [3] [agrave] **VT** *(mal, problème)* to aggravate, to make worse, to exacerbate; *(mécontentement, colère)* to increase; **ces mesures ne feront qu'a. l'inflation** these measures will only serve to worsen inflation; **pour a. les choses** to make matters worse

VPR s'aggraver to get worse, to worsen; **son état s'est aggravé** his/her condition has worsened; **la situation s'aggrave** the situation is getting worse

agile [aʒil] **ADJ** nimble, agile; **un esprit a.** an agile mind

agilement [aʒilmɑ̃] **ADV** *(grimper, se mouvoir)* nimbly, agilely

agilité [aʒilite] **NF** agility

agios [aʒjo] **NMPL** *Fin* premium; *(dans un échange de devises)* agio; *(quand on est à découvert)* bank charges; *(d'un emprunt)* interest payments

agiotage [aʒjɔtaʒ] **NM** *Bourse* speculating, speculation

agioter [3] [aʒjɔte] **VI** *Bourse* to speculate, to gamble

agioteur, -euse [aʒjɔtœr, -øz] **NM,F** *Bourse* speculator, gambler

agir [32] [aʒir] **VI A.** *AVOIR UNE ACTIVITÉ* **1** *(intervenir)* to act, to take action; **il faut a. rapidement pour enrayer l'épidémie** we have to act quickly *or* to take swift action to prevent the epidemic from developing; **en cas d'incendie, il faut a. vite** in the event of a fire, it is important to act quickly; **sur les ordres de qui avez-vous agi?** on whose orders did you act?; **c'est l'ambition qui le fait a.** he is motivated by ambition; **a. auprès de qn** *(essayer de l'influencer)* to try to influence sb; **a. auprès de qn pour obtenir qch** to approach sb for sth; **a. au nom de** *ou* **pour qn** to act on behalf of *or* for sb

2 *(passer à l'action)* to do something; **parler et a. sont deux choses différentes** there's quite a difference between talking and actually doing something; **elle parle, mais elle n'agit pas** she talks, but she doesn't do anything; **assez parlé, maintenant il faut a.!** enough talk, let's have some action!

3 *(se comporter)* to act, to behave; **elle agit bizarrement ces temps-ci** she's been acting *or* behaving strangely of late; **bien/mal a. envers qn** to behave well/badly towards sb; **tu n'as pas agi loyalement** you didn't play fair; **il a agi en bon citoyen** he did what any honest citizen would have done; **a. à la légère** to act rashly; **a. selon sa conscience** to act according to one's conscience, to let one's conscience be one's guide

B. *AVOIR UN EFFET* **1** *(fonctionner ▸ poison, remède)* to act, to take effect, to work; *(▸ élément nutritif)* to act, to have an effect; *(▸ détergent)* to work; **laisser a. un décapant** to allow a paint stripper to work; **laisser a. la justice** to let justice take its course

2 *(avoir une influence)* **a. sur** to work *or* to have an effect on; **tes larmes n'agissent plus sur moi** your tears don't have any effect on me *or* don't move me any more; *Bourse* **a. sur le marché** to manipulate the market

C. *DANS LE DOMAINE JURIDIQUE* to act in a court of law; **a. contre qn** *(en droit pénal)* to prosecute sb; *(en droit civil)* to sue sb; **a. en diffamation** to sue for libel; **a. en recherche de paternité** to bring a paternity suit

• **s'agir de V IMPERSONNEL 1** *(être question de)* **je voudrais te parler – de quoi s'agit-il?** I'd like to talk to you – what about?; **de qui s'agit-il?** who is it?; **je voudrais vous parler d'une affaire importante, voici ce dont il s'agit** I'd like to talk to you about an important matter, namely this; **le criminel dont il s'agit** the criminal in question; **l'affaire dont il s'agit** the matter at issue; **ne la mêle pas à cette affaire, il s'agit de toi et de moi** don't bring her into this, it's between you and me; **il ne s'est agi que de littérature toute la soirée** the only thing talked about all evening was literature; **mais enfin, il s'agit de sa santé!** but his/her health is at stake (here)!; **je peux te prêter de l'argent – il ne s'agit pas de ça** *ou* **ce n'est pas de ça qu'il s'agit** I can lend you some money – that's not the point *or* the question; **s'il ne s'agissait que de moi, la maison serait déjà vendue** if it were just up to me, the house would already be sold; **s'il ne s'agissait que d'argent, la solution serait simple!** if it were only a question of money, the answer would be simple!; *Ironique* **une augmentation? il s'agit bien de cela à l'heure où l'on parle de licenciements** a rise? that's very likely now there's talk of redundancies; **quand il s'agit de râler, tu es toujours là!** you can always be relied upon to moan!; **une voiture a explosé, il s'agirait d'un accident** a car has exploded, apparently by accident; **il s'agirait d'une grande première scientifique** it is said to be an important first for science

2 *(falloir)* **maintenant, il s'agit de lui parler** now we must talk to him/her; **c'est qu'il s'agit de gagner ce match!** we must win this match!; **il s'agissait pour moi d'être convaincant** I had to be convincing; **il s'agit de savoir si...** the question is whether...; **il s'agirait d'obéir!** *(menace)* you'd better do as you're told!; **dis donc, il ne s'agit pas de se perdre!** come on, we mustn't get lost now!; **il s'agit bien de pleurer maintenant que tu l'as cassé!** you may well cry, now that you've broken it!; **il ne s'agit pas que tu ailles tout lui raconter!** you'd better not go and repeat everything to him/her!

• **s'agissant de PRÉP 1** *(en ce qui concerne)* as regards, with regard to; **s'agissant de lui, vous pouvez avoir toute confiance** as far as he's concerned, you've got nothing to worry about **2** *(puisque cela concerne)* **un service d'ordre ne s'imposait pas, s'agissant d'une manifestation pacifique** there was no need for a police presence, given that this was a peaceful demonstration

âgisme [aʒism] **NM** ageism, age discrimination

agissant, -e [aʒisɑ̃, -ɑ̃t] **ADJ 1** *(entreprenant)* active **2** *(efficace)* efficient, effective; **un remède a.** an effective remedy

agissements [aʒismɑ̃] **NMPL** machinations, schemes

agitateur, -trice [aʒitatœr, -tris] **NM,F** *Pol* agitator

NM *Chim* beater, agitator

agitation [aʒitasjɔ̃] **NF 1** *(mouvement ▸ de l'air)* turbulence; *(▸ de l'eau)* roughness; *(▸ de la rue)* bustle

2 *(fébrilité)* agitation, restlessness; **être dans un état d'a. extrême** to be extremely agitated; **l'a. régnait dans la salle** *(excitation)* the room was buzzing with excitement; *(inquiétude)* there was an uneasy atmosphere in the room

3 *Méd & Psy* agitated depression

4 *Pol* unrest; **a. parmi la population** civil unrest; **a. syndicale** industrial unrest

5 *(sur le marché de la Bourse)* activity

agitatrice [aʒitatris] *voir* **agitateur**

agité, -e [aʒite] **ADJ 1** *(mer)* rough, stormy **2** *(personne ▸ remuante)* restless; *(▸ angoissée)* agitated, worried; **c'était un enfant très a.** he was a very restless child **3** *(troublé ▸ vie)* hectic; *(▸ nuit, sommeil)* restless; *(▸ esprit)* perturbed, troubled; *(▸ époque)* unsettled

NM,F 1 *Méd & Psy* disturbed (mental) patient **2** *(excité)* **c'est un a.** he can't sit still for a minute; *Fam Hum* **a. du bocal** headcase, *Br* nutter

agiter [3] [aʒite] **VT 1** *(remuer ▸ liquide)* to shake; *Chim* to agitate; *(▸ mouchoir, journal, drapeau)* to wave about; *(sujet: vent ▸ arbre, branches)* to sway; **a. les bras** to flap *or* to wave one's arms; **a. la queue** *(chien)* to wag its tail; *(cheval)* to flick its tail; **une petite brise agite la surface du lac** a soft breeze is ruffling the surface of the lake; **a. avant usage** *ou* **de s'en servir** *(sur mode d'emploi)* shake well before use

2 *(brandir)* to brandish

3 *(troubler)* to trouble, to upset; **cette nouvelle risque de l'a. encore plus** this news could upset him/her even more; **une violente colère l'agitait** he/she was in the grip of a terrible rage; **a. le peuple contre le gouvernement** to incite the people to rise up against the government

4 *(débattre)* to debate, to discuss

VPR s'agiter 1 *(bouger)* to move about; **s'a. dans son sommeil** to toss and turn in one's sleep

2 *(s'énerver)* to become agitated *or* excited, to get upset *or* worked up; **il ne faut pas que le malade s'agite** care should be taken not to upset *or* excite the patient

3 *Fam (se dépêcher)* to get a move on; *(s'affairer)* to rush about; **il faut t'a. un peu si tu veux être à l'heure/avoir ton examen** you'd better get a move on if you want to be on time/to pass your exam

4 *(se révolter)* to be in a state of unrest

5 *(mer)* to become rough

agit-prop [aʒitprɔp] **NF INV** *Pol* agit-prop

agneau, -x [aɲo] **NM 1** *Zool (animal)* lamb; *Fig* **il est doux comme un a.!** he's as meek *or* gentle as a lamb! **a. de lait** suckling lamb

2 *Culin* lamb *(UNCOUNT)*; **l'a. est gras, la viande d'a. est grasse** lamb is fatty; **côtelettes d'a.** lamb chops

3 *(en appellatif)* **viens mon a. (joli)!** come on, my lamb!; **mes agneaux, vous allez me dire la vérité maintenant!** now, my little friends, you're going to tell me the truth!

4 *(fourrure)* lamb, lambskin; *(peau)* lambskin; **une veste en a.** a lambskin jacket

5 *Rel* **l'A. (de Dieu)** the Lamb (of God)

agnelage [aɲəlaʒ] **NM** *Zool (naissance)* lambing; *(période)* lambing season *or* time

agneler [24] [aɲəle] **VI** *Zool* to lamb

agnelet [aɲəlɛ] **NM** *Vieilli Zool* small lamb, lambkin

agneline [aɲlin] *Tex* **ADJ** lambswool

NF lambswool

agnelle [aɲɛl] **NF** *Zool* ewe lamb, young ewe

agnosticisme [agnɔstisism] **NM** *Phil* agnosticism

agnostique [agnɔstik] *Phil* **ADJ** agnostic
NMF agnostic

agonie [agɔni] **NF 1** death throes, pangs of death, death agony; **il a eu une longue a.** he died a slow and painful death; *Fig* **l'a. de l'empire** the death throes of the empire; **être à l'a.** to be at the point of death; *Fig* to suffer agonies; *Fig* **ne prolongez pas son a.** please put him/her out of his/her misery **2** *Vieilli Littéraire* anguish

> Il faut noter que le nom anglais **agony** est un faux ami. Il signifie **douleur atroce** ou **angoisse**, selon le contexte.

agonir [32] [agɔnir] **VT a. qn d'injures** *ou* **d'insultes** to hurl abuse at sb; **elle s'est fait a.** she was reviled

agonisant, -e [agɔnizɑ̃, -ɑ̃t] **ADJ** dying
NM,F dying person

agoniser [3] [agɔnize] **VI** to be dying

> Il faut noter que le verbe anglais **to agonize** est un faux ami. Il signifie **se tourmenter**.

agoraphobe [agɔrafɔb] *Psy* **ADJ** agoraphobic
NMF agoraphobic

agoraphobie [agɔrafɔbi] **NF** *Psy* agoraphobia; **souffrir d'a.** to be agoraphobic

Agra [agra] **N** *Géog* Agra

agrafage [agrafaʒ] **NM 1** *(de papiers, de tentures)* stapling; *(de vêtements)* hooking, fastening **2** *(de bois ou de métal)* clamping, cramping **3** *Méd* clamping

agrafe [agraf] **NF 1** *(pour papier)* staple; *(pour vêtement)* hook, fastener; *(bijou)* clasp; *Com* **a. antivol** anti-theft *or* security tag **2** *(pour bois ou métal)* clamp **3** *Méd* clamp

agrafer [3] [agrafe] **VT 1** *(papiers)* to staple (together); *(vêtement)* to fasten (up) **2** *Méd* to clamp **3** *Fam Arg crime (arrêter) Br* to nick, *Am* to bust; **il s'est fait a.** he got *Br* nicked *or Am* busted

agrafeuse [agraføz] **NF** stapler

agraire [agrɛr] **ADJ** *Agr (société)* agrarian; *(réforme, lois)* land *(avant n)*

agrammatical, -e, -aux, -ales [agramatikal, -o] **ADJ** *Gram* ungrammatical

agrandir [32] [agrɑ̃dir] **VT 1** *(élargir ▸ trou)* to enlarge, to make bigger; *(▸ maison, jardin)* to extend; *(▸ couloir, passage)* to widen; **a. le cercle de ses activités** to enlarge the scope of one's activities
2 *Littéraire (exalter ▸ âme, pensée)* to elevate, to uplift
3 *(faire paraître grand)* **ce papier peint agrandit la pièce** this wallpaper makes the room look larger
4 *Typ & Phot (cliché, copie)* to enlarge, to blow up; *(sur écran)* to magnify; *Ordinat (fenêtre)* to maximize
VPR s'agrandir 1 *(s'élargir)* to grow, to get bigger; **le cercle de famille s'agrandit** the family circle is getting bigger; **quand elle le vit, ses yeux s'agrandirent** when she saw him, her eyes widened **2** *Écon* to expand; **le marché des logiciels s'agrandit** the software market is expanding **3** *(avoir plus de place)* **nous voudrions nous a.** we want more space for ourselves

agrandissement [agrɑ̃dismɑ̃] **NM 1** *Phot* enlargement; **je voudrais faire un a. de cette photo** I'd like to get this photo blown up *or* enlarged **2** *(d'un appartement, d'une affaire)* extension

agrandisseur [agrɑ̃disœr] **NM** *Phot* enlarger

agrarien, -enne [agrarjɛ̃, -ɛn] *Hist* **ADJ** agrarian
NM,F agrarian

agréable [agreabl] **ADJ** pleasant, nice, agreeable; **une corvée pas très a.** a rather unpleasant chore; **il me serait bien a. de le revoir** I would love to see him again; **une couleur a. à l'œil** a colour (which is) pleasing to the eye; **être a. au toucher** to feel nice; **voilà quelqu'un qui est a. à vivre** he's/she's really easy to get on with
NM l'a., ici, c'est la grande terrasse the nice thing *or* what's nice about this place is the big terrace

agréablement [agreabləmɑ̃] **ADV** pleasantly, agreeably

agréé, -e [agree] **ADJ 1** *(organisme, agent)* recognized, authorized; *Jur* registered **2** *(produit)* approved

agréer [15] [agree] **VT** to approve, to authorize; *(dans la correspondance)* **veuillez a., Madame/Monsieur, mes salutations distinguées** *(à une personne dont on connaît le nom) Br* yours sincerely, *Am* sincerely (yours); *(à une personne dont on ne connaît pas le nom) Br* yours faithfully, *Am* sincerely (yours)
• **agréer à VT IND** *Littéraire* to please, to suit; **si cela vous agrée, nous nous verrons la semaine prochaine** if it suits you, we shall meet next week

agrég [agrɛg] **NF** *Fam Univ (abrév* **agrégation***)* = high-level competitive examination for teachers

agrégat [agrega] **NM 1** *(de roches, de substances)* aggregate; *Fig Péj* conglomeration, mish-mash **2** *Fin* **a. monétaire** monetary aggregate

agrégatif, -ive [agregatif, -iv] *Univ* **ADJ** *(candidat, étudiant)* = who is studying to take the "agrégation"
NM,F "agrégation" candidate

agrégation [agregasjɔ̃] **NF 1** *Univ* = high-level competitive examination for teachers **2** *(assemblage)* agglomeration

> **AGRÉGATION**
>
> This is a prestigious professional qualification for teachers in France. Those who pass the challenging competitive exam for the "agrég" become teachers in secondary education or universities and are entitled to higher pay and a less onerous timetable than those who have passed the **CAPES** (see box at this entry).

agrégative [agregativ] *voir* **agrégatif**

agrégé, -e [agreʒe] **ADJ 1** *Univ* = who has passed the "agrégation" **2** *(assemblé)* agglomerated
NM,F *Univ* = person who has passed the "agrégation"

agréger [22] [agreʒe] **VT 1** *(assembler)* to agglomerate (together) **2** *(intégrer)* **a. qn à** to incorporate sb into
VPR s'agréger 1 *(s'assembler)* to form a mass **2 s'a. à** to incorporate oneself into

agrément [agremɑ̃] **NM 1** *(attrait)* charm, appeal, attractiveness; *(plaisir)* pleasure; **sa maison est pleine d'a.** his house is delightful *or* very attractive; **un visage sans a.** an unattractive face
2 *(accord)* approval, consent; *Mktg (du consommateur, du client)* approval; **agir avec l'a. de ses supérieurs** to act with one's superiors' approval *or* consent
3 *Fin (garantie financière)* bonding scheme
4 *Mus* ornament
• **d'agrément ADJ** *(jardin, voyage)* pleasure *(avant n)*

> Il faut noter que le nom anglais **agreement** est un faux ami. Il signifie **accord**.

agrémenter [3] [agremɑ̃te] **VT a. qch avec** *ou* **de** to decorate sth with; **vous pouvez a. votre plat avec quelques feuilles de menthe** decorate *or* garnish the dish with a few sprigs of mint

agrès [agrɛ] **NMPL 1** *Sport* apparatus; **elle a eu 20 aux (exercices aux) a.** she got 20 for apparatus work **2** *Naut* lifting gear; *(sur un ballon)* tackle **3** *Can* **a. de pêche** fishing tackle

agresser [4] [agrese] **VT 1** *(physiquement)* to attack, to assault; *(pour voler)* to mug; **se faire a.** to be assaulted; *(pour son argent)* to be mugged **2** *(verbalement)* to attack; **je me suis sentie agressée** I felt I was being got at **3** *(psychologiquement)* to stress

agresseur [agresœr] **ADJ M** *(État, pays)* attacking
NM *(d'une personne)* attacker, assailant, aggressor; *(d'un pays)* aggressor

agressif, -ive [agresif, -iv] **ADJ 1** *(hostile ▸ personne)* aggressive, hostile **2** *(oppressant ▸ musique, image)* aggressive; **la laideur agressive des monuments** the sheer ugliness of the buildings **3** *(dynamique)* dynamic, aggressive; **une concurrence agressive** aggressive competitors

agression [agresjɔ̃] **NF** *(attaque ▸ contre une personne)* attack, assault; *(▸ pour voler)* mugging; *(▸ contre un pays)* aggression; **être victime d'une** *ou* **subir une a.** to be assaulted; *(pour son argent)* to be mugged; **a. sexuelle** sexual assault; *Fig* **les agressions de la vie moderne** the stresses and strains of modern life; **les agressions du soleil contre votre peau** the harm the sun does to your skin

agressive [agresiv] *voir* **agressif**

agressivement [agresivmɑ̃] **ADV** aggressively

agressivité [agresivite] **NF** aggressivity, aggressiveness

agreste [agrest] **ADJ** *Littéraire* rustic

agricole [agrikɔl] **ADJ** *(économie, pays)* agricultural; *(population)* farming *(avant n)*; *(produit)* farm *(avant n)*

agriculteur, -trice [agrikyltœr, -tris] **NM,F** farmer

agriculture [agrikyltyr] **NF** agriculture, farming

agripper [3] [agripe] **VT 1** *(prendre)* to grab, to snatch **2** *(tenir)* to grip, to grasp, to clutch
VPR s'agripper to hold on; **s'a. à qch** to cling to *or* to hold on (tight) to sth; **elle s'agrippait à mon bras** she was gripping my arm

agritourisme [agriturism] **NM** agritourism

agroalimentaire [agroalimɑ̃tɛr] *Agr* **ADJ** food-processing *(avant n)*
NM l'a. the food-processing industry, agribusiness

agrochimie [agroʃimi] **NF** *Agr* agrochemistry

agrochimiste [agroʃimist] **NMF** *Agr* agrochemist

agronome [agronɔm] **NMF** *Agr* agronomist, agriculturalist

agronomie [agronɔmi] **NF** *Agr* agronomy

agronomique [agronɔmik] **ADJ** *Agr* agronomic, agronomical

agroterrorisme [agroterɔrism] **NM** agroterrorism

agrotourisme [agroturism] **NM** agrotourism

agrume [agrym] **NM** *Bot* citrus fruit

agrumicole [agrymikɔl] **ADJ** *Agr* citrus fruit-producing

aguerrir [32] [agerir] **VT** to harden, to toughen (up); *(troupes)* to train (for battle)
VPR s'aguerrir to become hardened *or* tougher; **s'a. à** *ou* **contre qch** to become hardened to sth

aguets [agɛ] **aux aguets ADV être aux a.** to be on watch *or* the lookout

aguichage [agiʃaʒ] **NM** *(technique publicitaire)* teaser advertising

aguichant, -e [agiʃɑ̃, -ɑ̃t] **ADJ** seductive, enticing, alluring

aguiche [agiʃ] **NF** *(publicité)* teaser

aguicher [3] [agiʃe] **VT** to seduce, to entice, to allure

aguicheur, -euse [agiʃœr, -øz] **ADJ** seductive, enticing, alluring
NM,F tease

Ah *Élec (abrév écrite* **ampère-heure***)* ah

ah [a] **EXCLAM 1** *(renforce l'expression d'un sentiment)* ah, oh; **ah, ne va pas croire cela!** oh please, you mustn't believe that!; **ah, ça y est, je l'ai trouvé!** ah *or* aha, here we are, I've found it!; **ah, c'est un secret** aha, that's a secret; **ah là là, qu'est-ce qu'il m'énerve!** oh, he's a real pain in the neck! **2** *(dans une réponse)* **il est venu – ah bon?** he came – did he (really)?; **ils n'en ont plus en magasin – ah bon!** *(ton résigné)* they haven't got any more in stock – oh well!; **ah non alors!** certainly not!; **ah oui?** really?
NM INV ah; **pousser des oh et des ah** to ooh and ah

ahaner [3] [aane] **VI** *Littéraire* to puff and pant

ahuri, -e [ayri] **ADJ 1** *(surpris)* dumbfounded, amazed, stunned; **il a eu l'air a.** he looked dumbfounded **2** *(hébété)* stupefied, dazed; **il avait l'air complètement a.** he looked as if he was in a daze
NM,F idiot

ahurir [32] [ayrir] **VT** to stun, to daze

ahurissant, -e [ayrisɑ̃, -ɑ̃t] **ADJ** stunning, staggering

ahurissement [ayrismɑ̃] **NM** daze; **son a. était tel qu'il ne m'entendait pas** he was so stunned that he didn't even hear me

ai *voir* **avoir**[2]

aï [ai] NM *Zool* ai, three-toed sloth

AIDA [aidea] NM *Mktg* (*abrév* **attention-intérêt-désir-action**) AIDA

aide¹ [ɛd] NM **1** *(assistant ▸ payé)* assistant; *(▸ bénévole)* helper; **les aides du président** the presidential aides; **a. familial (étranger)** (male) au pair **2** *(comme adj; avec ou sans trait d'union)* assistant *(avant n)* **3** *Mil* **a. de camp** aide-de-camp

NF **a. à domicile, a. familiale, a. ménagère** home help

aide² [ɛd] NF **1** *(appui)* help, assistance, aid; **avoir besoin d'a.** to need help; **elle y est arrivée sans l'a. de personne** she succeeded unaided *or* without anyone's help; **à l'a.!** help!; **j'ai eu de l'a.** I had help; **appeler à l'a.** to call for help; **quand elle s'est retrouvée au chômage, elle a appelé ses parents à l'a.** when she found herself unemployed, she asked *or* turned to her parents for help; **offrir son a. à qn** to give sb help, to go to sb's assistance; **venir en a. à qn** to come to sb's aid **2** *(don d'argent)* aid; **recevoir l'a. de l'État** to receive government aid; **a. financière** financial aid *or* assistance; **a. fiscale** tax credit; **a. humanitaire** humanitarian aid; **a. juridictionelle** ≃ legal aid; **a. personnalisée au logement** ≃ housing benefit *(UNCOUNT)*; **A. publique au développement** Official Development Assistance; **a. au retour** = policy aimed at discouraging immigration by giving support to foreign nationals returning to their country of origin; **a. sociale** *Br* social security, *Am* welfare **3** *Ordinat* **a. à la césure** hyphenation help; **a. contextuelle** context-sensitive help; **a. en ligne** on-line help

• **à l'aide de** PRÉP **1** *(avec)* with the help of; **marcher à l'a. de béquilles** to walk with crutches **2** *(au secours de)* **aller/venir à l'a. de qn** to go/to come to sb's aid

aide-comptable [ɛdkɔ̃tabl] *(pl* **aides-comptables***)* NMF *Compta* junior accountant

aide-cuisinier [ɛdkɥizinje] *(pl* **aides-cuisiniers***)* NMF kitchen assistant

aide-éducateur, -trice [ɛdedykatœr, -tris] *(mpl* **aides-éducateurs**, *fpl* **aides-éducatrices***)* NM,F *Br* ≃ classroom assistant, *Am* ≃ teacher's assistant

aide-électricien [ɛdelɛktrisjɛ̃] *(pl* **aides-électriciens***)* NM *Cin & TV* best boy

aide-gouvernante [ɛdguvɛrnɑ̃t] *(pl* **aides-gouvernantes***)* NF assistant housekeeper

aide-infirmière [ɛdɛ̃firmjɛr] *(pl* **aides-infirmières***)* NF *Br* healthcare assistant, auxiliary nurse, *Am* nurse's aid

aide-mécanicien [ɛdmekanisjɛ̃] *(pl* **aides-mécaniciens***)* NM garage hand

aide-mémoire [ɛdmemwar] NM INV notes

aide-monteur, -euse [ɛdmɔ̃tœr, -øz] *(mpl* **aides-monteurs**, *fpl* **aides-monteuses***)* NM,F *Cin & TV* assistant film editor

aide-opérateur, -trice [ɛdɔperatœr, -tris] *(mpl* **aides-opérateurs**, *fpl* **aides-opératrices***)* NM,F assistant cameraman, *f* assistant camerawoman

aider [4] [ede] VT **1** *(apporter son concours à)* to help; **que puis-je faire pour vous a.?** how may I help you?; **je me suis fait a. par mon frère** I got my brother to help me; **a. qn à faire qch** to help sb (to) do sth; **il a aidé la vieille dame à monter/descendre** he helped the old lady up/down; **aide-moi à rentrer/sortir la table** help me move the table in/out **2** *(financièrement)* to help out, to aid, to assist; **il a fallu l'a. pour monter son affaire** he/she needed help to set up his/her business

USAGE ABSOLU to help (out); *(favoriser, être utile)* to help; *Fam* **ça aide** it helps, it's a help; **avoir un père richissime, ça aide** it helps if your dad's loaded; **la fatigue aidant, je me suis endormi tout de suite** helped by exhaustion, I fell asleep right away; *Fam* **il n'est pas aidé!** he hasn't got much going for him!; **Dieu aidant** with the help of God, God willing

• **aider à** VT IND to aid, to help; **a. à la digestion** to aid digestion; **ça aide à passer le temps** it helps to pass the time

VPR **s'aider 1** *(emploi réfléchi) Prov* **aide-toi, le ciel t'aidera** God helps those who help themselves **2** *(emploi réciproque)* to help each other; **entre femmes, il faut s'a.** we women should help each other **3 s'a. de** to use; **elle s'est aidée de plusieurs ouvrages** she made use of *or* used several books; **marcher en s'aidant d'une canne** to walk with a stick

aide-serveur [ɛdsɛrvœr] *(pl* **aides-serveurs***)* NM waiter's assistant, *Am* busboy

aide-soignant, -e [ɛdswaɲɑ̃, -ɑ̃t] *(mpl* **aides-soignants**, *fpl* **aides-soignantes***)* NM,F *Méd Br* healthcare assistant, auxiliary nurse, *Am* nurse's aid

aie *etc voir* **avoir²**

aïe [aj] EXCLAM *(cri ▸ de douleur)* ouch!; *(▸ de surprise)* **a., la voilà!** oh dear *or* oh no, here she comes!; **a., a., a., il était dur, l'examen!** boy, was that exam tough!

AIEA [aiəa] NF *Nucl* (*abrév* **Agence internationale de l'énergie atomique**) IAEA

aïeul, -e [ajœl] NM,F grandparent; *(grand-père)* grandfather; *(grand-mère)* grandmother

aigle [ɛgl] NM **1** *Orn* eagle; **a. ravisseur** tawny eagle; **a. royal** golden eagle; **avoir des yeux** *ou* **un regard d'a.** to be eagle-eyed; *Hum* **ce n'est pas un a.** he's no rocket scientist **2** *Ich* **a. de mer** eagle ray **3** *(lutrin)* lectern

NF **1** *Orn* (female) eagle **2** *Mil* eagle **3** *Hér* eagle

aiglefin [ɛgləfɛ̃] = **églefin**

aiglette [ɛglɛt] NF *Hér* eaglet

aiglon, -onne [ɛglɔ̃, -ɔn] NM,F *Orn* eaglet

aigre [ɛgr] ADJ **1** *(acide ▸ vin)* acid, sharp; *(▸ goût, lait)* sour; **le vin a un goût a.** the wine tastes sour

2 *(perçant ▸ voix, son)* shrill, sharp

3 *(vif ▸ bise, froid)* bitter

4 *(méchant)* cutting, harsh, acid

NM **ton vin sent l'a.** your wine smells sour; **tourner à l'a.** *(lait)* to turn sour; *Fig (discussion)* to turn sour *or* nasty

aigre-doux, -douce [ɛgrədu, -dus] *(mpl* **aigres-doux**, *fpl* **aigres-douces***)* ADJ *Culin* sweet-and-sour; *Fig* **ses lettres étaient aigres-douces** his/her letters were tinged with bitterness

aigrefin [ɛgrəfɛ̃] NM swindler

aigrelet, -ette [ɛgrəlɛ, -ɛt] ADJ *(odeur, saveur)* sourish; *(son, voix)* shrillish; *(propos)* tart, sour, acid

aigrement [ɛgrəmɑ̃] ADV sourly, tartly, acidly

aigrette [ɛgrɛt] NF **1** *Orn (oiseau)* egret, tufted heron; **a. garzette, petite a.** little egret

2 *(décoration ▸ d'un héron)* aigrette; *(▸ d'un perroquet)* crest; *(▸ d'une chouette)* horn

3 *(panache)* aigrette, plume

4 *Bot* egret; *(du maïs)* tassel

aigreur [ɛgrœr] NF **1** *(acidité)* sourness, acidity **2** *(animosité)* sharpness, bitterness; **ses propos étaient pleins d'a.** his remarks were very bitter

• **aigreurs** NFPL **avoir des aigreurs (d'estomac)** to have heartburn *or* acid indigestion

aigri, -e [egri] ADJ bitter, embittered

NM,F embittered person; **ce n'est qu'un a.** he's just bitter

aigrir [32] [egrir] VT *(lait, vin)* to make sour; *(personne)* to embitter, to make bitter

VI *(lait)* to turn (sour), to go off; *(vin)* to turn sour

VPR **s'aigrir** *(lait)* to turn (sour), to go off; *(vin)* to turn sour; *(caractère)* to sour; *(personne)* to become embittered

aigu, -ë [egy] ADJ **1** *(perçant ▸ voix)* high-pitched; *(▸ glapissement, hurlement)* piercing, shrill; *Mus* high-pitched

2 *(effilé)* sharp; **ses petites dents aiguës** his/her sharp little teeth

3 *(pénétrant ▸ esprit, intelligence)* sharp, keen; **avoir un sens a. de l'observation** *ou* **un regard a.** to be an acute observer

4 *(grave ▸ crise, douleur)* sharp, acute; *Méd (▸ phase, appendicite)* acute

5 *Math (angle)* acute

NM high pitch; **l'a., les aigus** treble range; **dans les aigus** in treble

aigue-marine [ɛgmarin] *(pl* **aigues-marines***)* NF *Minér* aquamarine

aiguillage [egɥijaʒ] NM **1** *Rail (manœuvre)* shunting, switching; *(dispositif)* shunt, switch **2** *Ordinat* switching **3** *Fig* orientation; **erreur d'a.** wrong turning

aiguille [egɥij] NF **1** *(pour coudre, pour tricoter)* needle; **a. à coudre/tricoter/repriser** sewing/knitting/darning needle

2 *Méd* needle; **a. hypodermique** hypodermic needle

3 *(d'une montre, d'une pendule)* hand; *(d'une balance)* pointer; *(d'une boussole)* needle; **l'a. des secondes** the second hand; **la grande a., l'a. des minutes** the minute hand; **la petite a., l'a. des heures** the hour hand

4 *Géog* needle, high peak

5 *Bot* needle; **a. de pin/de sapin** pine/fir tree needle

6 *Rail* switch, shunt, points

7 *Ich* **a. de mer** *(syngnathe)* pipefish; *(orphie)* needlefish

8 *(tour, clocher)* spire

aiguillée [egɥije] NF length of thread *(on a needle)*

aiguiller [3] [egɥije] VT **1** *Rail* to shunt, to switch **2** *(orienter ▸ recherche)* to steer; **a. la police sur une fausse piste** to put the police on a false scent; **on l'a aiguillé vers une section scientifique** he was steered *or* guided towards the sciences; **il a été mal aiguillé dans ses études** he was badly advised about his studies

aiguilleur [egɥijœr] NM **1** *Rail Br* pointsman, *Am* switchman **2** *Aviat* **a. (du ciel)** air traffic controller

aiguillon [egɥijɔ̃] NM **1** *Entom* sting

2 *Bot* prickle

3 *(bâton)* goad

4 *Littéraire (motivation)* incentive, stimulus, motivating force; **l'a. du remords** the pricks of remorse

aiguillonner [3] [egɥijɔne] VT **1** *(piquer ▸ bœuf)* to goad **2** *(stimuler ▸ curiosité)* to arouse; *(▸ personne)* to spur on, to goad on; **aiguillonné par son ambition** goaded on by his ambition

aiguise-crayon [egizkrɛjɔ̃] *(pl* **inv** *ou* **aiguise-crayons***)* NM *Can Fam* pencil sharpener

aiguiser [3] [egize] VT **1** *(rendre coupant ▸ couteau, lame)* to sharpen; *(▸ faux)* to whet; **bien aiguisé** sharp **2** *(stimuler ▸ curiosité)* to stimulate, to rouse; *(▸ faculté, sens)* to sharpen; *(▸ appétit)* to whet, to stimulate

aiguiseur, -euse [egizœr, -øz] NM,F *Tech* sharpener, grinder

aiguisoir [egizwar] NM **1** *Tech* sharpener **2** *Can* pencil sharpener

aïkido [ajkido] NM *Sport* aikido; **faire de l'a.** to do aikido

ail [aj] *(pl* **ails** *ou* **aulx** [o]*)* NM *Bot* garlic

• **à l'ail** ADJ garlic *(avant n)*

aile [ɛl] NF **1** *Orn (d'un oiseau)* wing; **avoir des ailes** to run like the wind; *Fam* **avoir un petit coup dans l'a.** to be tipsy; **couper** *ou* **rogner les ailes à qn** to clip sb's wings; **c'est la peur qui lui donne des ailes** fear lends him/her wings; **prendre qn sous son a.** to take sb under one's wing

2 *(d'un moulin)* sail; *(d'un avion)* wing; **a. (delta), a. libre, a. volante** hang glider; *Aviat* **a. (en) delta** delta wing

3 *Aut Br* wing, *Am* fender

4 *Anat* **les ailes du nez** the sides of the nostrils

5 *Archit* wing

6 *Sport* wing

7 *Mil* wing, flank

8 *(d'un parti)* wing

ailé, -e [ele] ADJ winged, *Spéc* alate

aileron [ɛlrɔ̃] NM **1** *Ich (d'un poisson, d'un requin)* fin; *Orn (d'un oiseau)* pinion

2 *Aviat* aileron

3 *(d'une voiture de course)* aerofoil

4 *(de roue à eau)* paddle board

5 *(d'un sous-marin)* fin keel; *(d'une planche à voile)* skeg

ailette [ɛlɛt] NF **1** *(d'un radiateur)* fin **2** *(d'une turbine)* blade **3** *Tech* fin

ailier [elje] NM *Sport* wing; *(au football)* winger

aille *etc voir* **aller²**

SUFFIX

-AILLE

This suffix is used to form feminine nouns.

• When added to a noun or a verb, it generates a COLLECTIVE noun. This noun can be of a neutral register:

des broussailles undergrowth, scrub; **de la pierraille** loose stones, scree; **de la rocaille** loose stones; **une rocaille** a rockery

Very often, however, there are derogatory connotations, especially when the noun used as a basis is itself colloquial:

ferraille scrap iron; **marmaille** kids; **flicaille** cops; **tripaille** guts; **boustifaille** (an alteration of *boufaille*, itself derived from *bouffer*) grub

• The resulting noun, when derived from a verb, can refer to an ACTION, often, but not exclusively, to do with a ritual or a celebration:

fiançailles engagement, engagement party; **semailles** sowing, sowing season; **retrouvailles** reunion; **bataille** battle

• Again in conjunction with a verb, **-aille** refers to tools or instruments:

des tenailles pincers; **une cisaille** shears

ailler [3] [aje] **VT** *Culin (gigot, rôti)* to put garlic in; *(croûton)* to rub garlic on

ailleurs [ajœr] **ADV** somewhere else, elsewhere; **allons voir a.** let's go and look somewhere else *or* elsewhere; **tu sais, ce n'est pas mieux a. qu'ici** you know, it's no better anywhere else than it is here; **on ne trouve ça nulle part a.** you won't find that anywhere else; **il fera beau partout a.** the weather will be fine everywhere else; **il a toujours l'air a.** he always looks as if he's miles away; **l'erreur doit provenir d'a.** the mistake must come from somewhere else

NM *Littéraire* **il rêvait d'un a. impossible** he was dreaming of a distant world he would never see

• **d'ailleurs ADV 1** *(de toute façon)* besides, anyway; **je n'ai pas envie de sortir, d'a. il fait trop froid** I don't want to go out and anyway *or* besides, it's too cold **2** *(de plus)* what's more; **je n'en sais rien et d'a. je ne tiens pas à le savoir** I don't know anything about it and what's more I don't want to know **3** *(du reste)* for that matter; **je ne les aime pas, elle non plus d'a.** I don't like them, nor does she for that matter **4** *(à propos)* incidentally; **nous avons dîné dans un restaurant, très bien d'a.** we had dinner in a restaurant which, incidentally, was very good **5** *(bien que)* although, while; **votre inquiétude – d'a. légitime – n'en est pas moins exagérée** your concern – although justified *or* justified as it is – is nonetheless exaggerated

• **par ailleurs ADV 1** *(d'un autre côté)* otherwise; **il est charmant, mais pas très efficace par a.** he's charming but otherwise not very efficient **2** *(de plus)* besides, moreover; **la pièce est trop longue et par a. pas très intéressante** the play's too long and not very interesting (either) for that matter

ailloli [ajɔli] = **aïoli**

aimable [ɛmabl] **ADJ 1** *(gentil)* kind, pleasant, amiable; **il a dit quelques mots aimables avant de partir** he said a few kind words before leaving; **soyez assez a. de nous prévenir si vous ne venez pas** please be kind enough to let us know if you aren't coming; **vous êtes trop a., merci beaucoup** you're most kind, thank you very much; **c'est très a. à vous** it's very kind of you **2** *(poli)* nice **3** *Littéraire (digne d'amour)* lovable; *(séduisant)* attractive

aimablement [ɛmabləmɑ̃] **ADV** kindly, pleasantly, amiably

aimant[1] [ɛmɑ̃] **NM** *(instrument)* magnet

aimant[2], **-e** [ɛmɑ̃, -ɑ̃t] **ADJ** loving, caring

aimantation [ɛmɑ̃tasjɔ̃] **NF** *Tech* magnetization

aimante [ɛmɑ̃t] *voir* **aimant**[2]

aimanter [3] [ɛmɑ̃te] **VT** *Tech* to magnetize

aimer [4] [eme] **VT 1** *(d'amour)* to love **2** *(apprécier)* to like, to be fond of; **je l'aime beaucoup** I'm very fond of him/her; **je l'aime bien** I like him/her; **les chats aiment le canapé** the cats like the sofa; **jamais tu ne me feras a. la voile!** you'll never persuade me to like sailing!; **il a réussi à se faire a. de tous** he got everybody to like him; **nous aimions à nous promener au bord du lac** we used to enjoy walking by the lake; **j'aime à croire** *ou* **à penser que tu m'as dit la vérité cette fois** I'd like to think that you told me the truth this time; **il aime que ses enfants l'embrassent avant d'aller au lit** he loves his children to kiss him good night; **je n'aime pas qu'on me mente/que tu rentres si tard** I don't like being lied to/your coming home so late; *Prov* **qui aime bien châtie bien** spare the rod and spoil the child **3 a. autant** *ou* **mieux** *(préférer)* to prefer; **j'aime mieux la rouge** I prefer the red one; **pas de dessert, merci, j'aime autant** *ou* **mieux le fromage** no dessert, thanks, I'd rather have *or* I'd prefer cheese; **j'aime autant** *ou* **mieux ça** (it's) just as well; **il aimerait autant** *ou* **mieux prendre son bain tout de suite** he'd rather have *or* he'd prefer to have his bath now; **elle aime autant** *ou* **mieux que tu y ailles** she'd rather you *or* she'd prefer it if you went **4** *(au conditionnel) (souhaiter)* **j'aimerais un café, s'il vous plaît** I'd like a coffee, please; **j'aimerais bien te voir** I'd really like to see you; **j'aurais aimé le voir** I would like to have seen him

VPR s'aimer 1 *(emploi réfléchi)* to like oneself; **je ne m'aime pas** I don't like myself; **je m'aime bien habillé en bleu/avec les cheveux courts** I think I look good in blue/with short hair **2** *(emploi réciproque) (d'amour)* to love each other; *(s'apprécier)* to like each other; **un couple qui s'aime** a loving *or* devoted couple; **les trois frères ne s'aimaient pas** the three brothers didn't care for *or* like each other

-AIN, -AINE SUFFIX

• This suffix conveys the idea of ORIGIN or BELONGING.

(i) It appears in nouns and adjectives of nationality, or refers to inhabitants of regions, cities etc:

africain(e), Africain(e) African; **américain(e), Américaine(e)** American; **lorrain(e)** of or from Lorraine; **toulousain(e)** of or from Toulouse; **napolitain(e), Napolitain(e)** Neapolitan

(ii) The idea can also be more general, ie that of "relating to..." It is translated in most cases by using the suffix *-an*:

républicain(e) republican; **humain(e)** human; **élisabéthain(e)** Elizabethan

(iii) Following the idea of belonging or origin, nouns ending in **-ain(e)** can refer to social status, trade or membership of a particular group:

châtelain(e) (person who comes from a *château*) lord or lady of the manor; **sacristain** (who looks after the *sacristie*) sacristan; **forain(e)** (who works on a *foire*) stallholder; **dominicain(e)** (member of a religious order founded by saint *Dominique*) Dominican

• When coupled with a number, **-ain** and **-aine** are used to form nouns referring to a group of X units, or a quantity close to X units. The latter is conveyed only by the feminine suffix **-aine**:

une douzaine d'œufs a dozen eggs; **une douzaine de pages** roughly twelve pages; **un quatrain** a quatrain = (a stanza of four lines); **une centaine d'invités** a hundred or so guests; **sous huitaine** within a week; **il doit avoir la cinquantaine** he must be about fifty

aine [ɛn] **NF** *Anat* groin

aîné, -e [ene] **ADJ l'enfant a.** *(de deux)* the elder *or* older child; *(de plusieurs)* the eldest *or* oldest child; **la branche aînée de la famille** the senior branch of the family

NM,F 1 *(entre frères et sœurs)* **l'a.** *(de deux)* the elder *or* older boy; *(de plusieurs)* the eldest *or* oldest boy; **l'aînée** *(de deux)* the elder *or* older girl; *(de plusieurs)* the eldest *or* oldest girl; **notre aînée est étudiante** *(de deux)* our elder daughter's a student; *(de plusieurs)* our eldest (daughter) is a student **2** *(le plus âgé)* **l'a.** *(de deux)* the older man; *(de plusieurs)* the oldest man; **l'aînée** *(de deux)* the older woman; *(de plusieurs)* the oldest woman; **il est mon a.** he is older than me; **il est mon a. de deux ans** he is two years older than me

• **aînés NMPL** *(d'une famille, d'une tribu)* **les aînés** the elders

aînesse [enɛs] *voir* **droit**[3]

ainsi [ɛ̃si] **ADV 1** *(de cette manière)* this *or* that way; **je suis a. faite** that's the way I am; **puisqu'il en est a.** since that is the case, since that is the way things are; **s'il en était vraiment a.** if this were really so *or* the case; **c'est toujours a.** it's always like that; **c'est a. que cela s'est passé** this is how it happened; **on voit a. que...** in this way *or* thus we can see that...; *Rel* **a. soit-il** amen; *Hum* so be it **2** *(par conséquent)* so, thus; **nous n'avons rien dérangé, a. vous retrouverez tout plus facilement** we didn't move anything, so you'll find everything again easily; **a. tu n'as pas réussi à le voir?** so you didn't manage to see him?; **a. (donc) tout est fini entre nous** so it's all over between us **3** *(par exemple)* for instance, for example; **je n'arrête pas de faire des bêtises: a., l'autre jour...** I keep doing silly things: for example, the other day...

• **ainsi que CONJ 1** *(comme)* as; **tout s'est passé a. que je l'ai dit** everything happened as I said (it would); **a. que je l'ai fait remarquer...** as I pointed out... **2** *(et)* as well as; **mes parents a. que mes frères seront là** my parents will be there as well as my brothers

• **et ainsi de suite ADV** and so on, and so forth

• **pour ainsi dire ADV 1** *(presque)* virtually; **nous ne nous sommes pour a. dire pas vus** we virtually didn't see each other **2** *(si l'on peut dire)* so to speak, as it were; **elle est pour a. dire sa raison de vivre** she's his/her reason for living, so to speak *or* as it were

AIO [aio] **NM** *Mktg (abrév* **activités, intérêts et opinions)** AIO

aïoli [ajɔli] **NM** *Culin* **1** *(sauce)* aïoli, garlic mayonnaise **2** *(plat provençal)* = dish of cod and poached vegetables served with aïoli sauce

AIR [ɛr]

- air **1, 4, 6**
- likeness **2**
- atmosphere **7**
- look **1**
- tune **3**

NM 1 *(apparence)* air, look; **"bien sûr", dit-il d'un a. guilleret/inquiet** "of course," he said, jauntily/looking worried; **elle l'écoute de l'a. de quelqu'un qui s'ennuie** when she listens to him/her, she looks bored; **il avait un a. angoissé/mauvais** he looked anxious/very nasty; **avoir bel** *ou* **bon a.** to look impressive; **avoir mauvais a.** to look shifty; **ne te laisse pas prendre à son faux a. de gentillesse** don't be taken in by his/her apparent kindness; **son témoignage a un a. de vérité qui ne trompe pas** his/her testimony sounds unmistakably genuine; **Maria, tu as l'a. heureux** *ou* **heureuse** Maria, you look happy; **cette poire a l'a. mauvaise, jette-la** this pear looks (as though it's) rotten, throw it away; **l'armoire avait l'a. ancienne** the wardrobe looked like an antique *or* looked old; *Fam* **j'avais l'a. fin!** I looked a real fool!; **il a l'a. de t'aimer beaucoup** he seems to be very fond of you; **je ne voudrais pas avoir l'a. de lui donner des ordres** I wouldn't like (it) to look as though I were ordering him/her about; **ça a l'a. d'un** *ou* **d'être un scarabée** it looks like a beetle; *Fam* **ça m'a tout l'a. (d'être) traduit de l'anglais** it looks to me as though it's been translated from English; **il a peut-être la rougeole – il en a tout l'a.** he may have measles – it certainly looks like it; *aussi Ironique* **avoir un petit a. penché** *ou* **des petits airs penchés** to look pensive; **avec son a. de ne pas y toucher** *ou* **sans avoir l'a. d'y toucher, il arrive toujours à ses fins** though you wouldn't think it to look at him, he always manages to get his way; *Fam* **je me suis approchée, l'a. de rien** *ou* **de ne pas en avoir, et je lui ai flanqué ma main sur la figure** I walked up, all innocent, and gave him/her a slap in the face; **ça n'a l'a. de rien comme ça, mais c'est une lourde tâche** it doesn't look much but it's quite a big job; *Fam* **elle n'a pas l'a. comme ça, mais elle sait ce qu'elle veut!** you wouldn't think it to look at her, but she knows what she wants!; **sans en avoir l'a., elle a tout rangé en une heure** she tidied up everything in an hour without even looking busy; **je suis arrivée au bout de mon tricot, sans en avoir l'a.!** I managed to finish my knitting, though it didn't seem that I was making any progress!; **prendre** *ou* **se donner des airs** to give oneself airs; **prendre de grands airs** to put on airs (*Br* and graces)

2 *(ressemblance)* likeness, resemblance; **un a. de famille** *ou* **parenté** a family resemblance *or* likeness; **il a un faux a. de James Dean** he looks a bit like James Dean; *Can* **avoir l'a. de qn** to look like sb

3 *Mus (mélodie)* tune; *(à l'opéra)* aria; **siffloter un petit a. joyeux** to whistle a happy little tune; **le grand a. de la Tosca** Tosca's great aria; *Fig Péj* **avec lui c'est toujours le même a.!** he should change his tune! **c'est l'a. qui fait la chanson** it's not what you say, it's the way you say it

4 *(qu'on respire)* air; **la pollution/température de l'a.** air pollution/temperature; **l'a. de la mer/des montagnes** (the) sea/mountain air; **l'a. était chargé d'une odeur de jasmin** a smell of jasmine filled the air; **ça manque d'a. ici** it's stuffy in here; **donne un peu d'a., on étouffe ici** let's have some air, it's stifling in here; **j'ouvre la porte pour faire de l'a.** I'll open the door to let some air in; **a. conditionné** *(système)* air-conditioning; **ils ont l'a. conditionné dans leur immeuble** their building is air-conditioned; **a. comprimé** compressed air; **outil à a. comprimé** pneumatic tool; **a. liquide** liquid air; **prendre l'a.** to get some fresh air; *Péj* **déplacer** *ou* **remuer beaucoup d'a.** to make a lot of noise; *Fam* **(allez,) de l'a.!** come on, beat it!; *Fam* **vous, les gosses, de l'a.!** come on you lot, scram!

5 *Fam (vent)* **il y a** *ou* **il fait de l'a. aujourd'hui** *(un peu)* it's breezy today; *(beaucoup)* it's windy today

6 *(ciel)* air; **dans l'a.** *ou* **les airs** (up) in the air *or* sky; **prendre l'a.** *(avion)* to take off, to become airborne, to take to the air; **transport par a.** air transport

7 *(ambiance)* atmosphere; **de temps en temps, il me faut l'a. du pays natal** I need to go back to my roots from time to time; **c'est dans l'a. du temps** it's the in thing; **vivre de l'a. du temps** to live on (thin) air; **c'est bien joli d'être amoureux, mais on ne vit pas de l'a. du temps** love is all very well but you can't exist on love alone

• **à l'air** ADV **laisser qch à l'a.** to leave sth uncovered; **mets les draps à l'a. sur le balcon** put the sheets on the balcony to air; **j'ai mis tous les vêtements d'hiver à l'a.** I put all the winter clothes out for an airing; **mettre son derrière à l'a.** to bare one's bottom

• **à l'air libre** ADV out in the open

• **au grand air** ADV *(dehors)* (out) in the fresh air

• **dans l'air** ADV in the air; **il y a du printemps dans l'a.** spring is in the air; **il y a de la bouderie dans l'a.** somebody's sulking around here; *aussi Fig* **il y a de l'orage dans l'a.** there's a storm brewing; **influencé par les idées qui sont dans l'a.** influenced by current ideas; **la maladie est dans l'a.** the illness is going around; **il y a quelque chose dans l'a.!** there's something going on!

• **en l'air** ADJ **1** *(levé)* in the air, up; **les pattes en l'a.** with its feet in the air; **les mains en l'a.!** hands up! **2** *(non fondé ▸ promesse)* empty; **encore des paroles en l'a.!** more empty words!; **je ne fais pas de projets en l'a.** when I make a plan, I stick to it

ADV **1** *(vers le haut)* (up) in the air; **jeter** *ou* **lancer qch en l'a.** to throw sth (up) in the air; **tirer en l'a.** to fire in the air; **regarde en l'a.** look up **2** *Fig (sans réfléchir)* **parler en l'a.** to say things without meaning them; **vous dites que vous montez votre affaire? – oh, nous parlions en l'a.** did you say you're setting up your own business? – oh, we were just tossing *or* kicking ideas around **3** *Fig (sens dessus dessous)* **mettre qch en l'a.** to make an awful mess of sth; *Fam* **flanquer** *ou très Fam* **foutre qch en l'a.** *(jeter)* to chuck sth out, to bin sth; *(gâcher)* to screw sth up

airain [ɛrɛ̃] NM *Littéraire* bronze; *Fig* **avoir un cœur d'a.** to have a heart of stone

air-air [ɛrɛr] ADJ INV *Mil* air-to-air

Airbag® [ɛrbag] NM **1** *(dispositif)* Airbag **2** *Fam* **airbags** *(seins)* boobs

Airbus® [ɛrbys] NM Airbus®

aire [ɛr] NF **1** *(terrain)* area; **a. de jeu(x)** playground; **a. de pique-nique** picnic site *or* area; **a. de repos** rest area *(along a road)*, *Br* ≃ lay-bys; **a. de stationnement** parking area

2 *(région ▸ linguistique)* area; *(▸ économique)* sphere

3 *Aviat & Astron* **a. d'atterrissage** landing area; **a. de lancement** launching site

4 *Géol* **a. continentale** continental shield

5 *Math* area

6 *Agr* floor; **a. de battage** threshing floor

7 *(nid d'aigle)* eyrie

airedale [ɛrdɛl], **airedale-terrier** [ɛrdɛltɛrje] *(pl* **airedale-terriers)** NM *(chien)* Airedale (terrier)

airelle [ɛrɛl] NF *Bot (myrtille)* blueberry, bilberry; *(rouge)* cranberry; **a. canneberge** cranberry

air-sol [ɛrsɔl] ADJ INV *Mil* air-to-ground

ais [ɛ] NM **1** *Arch* board, plank **2** *Typ* wetting board; *(en reliure)* press-board

> SUFFIX
>
> **-AIS, -AISE**
>
> • Placed at the end of a place name, **-ais** and **-aise** denote the ORIGIN of a person, be it a country, a region or a city:
>
> **anglais(e)** English; **un(e) Anglais(e)** an Englishman, an Englishwoman; **japonais(e), Japonais(e)** Japanese; **charentais(e)** of or from the Charente; **Bordelais(e)** inhabitant of or person from Bordeaux.
>
> • Additionally, the masculine form ending in **-ais** can be used, without a capital, to refer to a language:
>
> **ils parlent anglais** they speak English; **en français** in French

aisance [ɛzɑ̃s] NF **1** *(naturel)* ease; **aller et venir avec a.** to walk back and forth with ease; **danser/jongler/s'exprimer avec a.** to dance/to juggle/to express oneself with great ease **2** *(prospérité)* affluence; **vivre dans l'a.** to live a life of ease **3** *Jur* **aisances de voirie** public easement

aise [ɛz] ADJ *Littéraire* delighted; **je suis bien a. de vous revoir** I'm delighted to see you again

NF **1** *(plaisir)* pleasure, joy; **il ne se sentait plus d'a.** he was utterly contented **2** *(locutions)* **je suis plus à l'a. avec mes vieilles pantoufles** I feel more comfortable with my old slippers on; **on est mal à l'a. dans ce fauteuil** this armchair isn't very comfortable; **nous sommes bien plus à l'a. depuis que ma femme travaille** we're much better off now my wife's working; **il se sent à l'a.** *ou* **à son a.** he feels at ease; *Fig* **il s'est senti mal à l'a. pendant toute la réunion** he felt ill-at-ease during the entire meeting; **il nous a mis tout de suite à l'a.** *ou* **à notre a.** he put us at (our) ease right away; **mettez-vous donc à l'a.** *ou* **à votre a.** make yourself comfortable; **à ton a.!** please yourself!; **à votre a.** as you please; **tu en parles à ton a.** it's easy for you to talk; **il en prend à son a. avec ses collègues** he takes his colleagues for granted; *Fam* **être à l'a. dans ses baskets** to be together; *Fam* **on y sera ce soir, à l'a.!** we'll be there tonight, no hassle *or* sweat!; *Fam* **tu crois qu'on va y arriver? – à l'a.!** do you think we'll manage? – easily!; *Fam Ironique* **tu ne te gênes pas toi au moins, à l'a., Blaise!** you go right ahead, don't mind me!

• **aises** NFPL creature comforts

aisé, -e [eze] ADJ **1** *(facile)* easy; **ce n'est pas chose aisée que de le faire** it's no easy thing *or* not easy to do **2** *(prospère)* well-to-do, well-off **3** *(naturel ▸ manières)* easy, free; *(▸ style)* flowing

aisément [ezemɑ̃] ADV easily

aisselle [ɛsɛl] NF **1** *Anat* armpit **2** *Bot* axil

AITA [aitea] NF *(abrév* **Association internationale des transports aériens)** IATA

Aix-la-Chapelle [ɛkslaʃapɛl] NF *Géog* Aachen

ajiste [aʒist] ADJ = who is a member of the "Fédération des auberges de jeunesse"

NMF = member of the "Fédération des auberges de jeunesse", ≃ youth-hosteller

ajointer [3] [aʒwɛ̃te] VT to join up; *(planches, tuyaux etc)* to fit end to end

ajonc [aʒɔ̃] NM *Bot* gorse *(UNCOUNT)*, furze *(UNCOUNT)*

ajour [aʒur] NM **1** *(laissant passer la lumière)* opening, hole, orifice; *(en sculpture etc)* (ornamental) perforation, openwork **2** *Couture* **ajours** hemstitching *(UNCOUNT)*; *(dans une dentelle)* openwork *(UNCOUNT)*

ajouré, -e [aʒure] ADJ **1** *Couture (nappe, napperon)* openwork *(avant n)*, hemstitched **2** *Archit* with an openwork design

ajourer [3] [aʒure] VT **1** *Couture (nappe)* to hemstitch **2** *Archit* to decorate with openwork

ajournement [aʒurnəmɑ̃] NM **1** *(d'une réunion, d'une décision, d'un voyage)* postponement; *(après le début de la séance)* adjournment **2** *Jur* **a. du prononcé de la peine** deferment (of sentence) **3** *(d'un étudiant)* referral; *(d'un soldat)* deferment

ajourner [3] [aʒurne] VT **1** *(réunion, décision, voyage etc)* to postpone, to put off; *(après le début de la séance)* to adjourn; **l'avocat a fait a. le procès** the lawyer requested a postponement of the trial *or* asked for the trial to be postponed **2** *Jur* to summon, to subpoena **3** *(étudiant)* to refer; *(soldat)* to defer

ajout [aʒu] NM *(à un texte)* addition; *(à un bâtiment)* extension; **quelques ajouts dans la marge** a few additions *or* addenda in the margin; *Mktg* **a. à la gamme** range addition; *Mktg* **a. à la ligne** line addition; *Ordinat* **a. de mémoire** memory upgrade

ajoute [aʒut] NF *Belg* addition

ajouté [aʒute] NM addition, addendum

ajouter [3] [aʒute] VT **1** *(mettre)* to add; **ajoute donc une assiette pour ton frère** lay an extra place *or* add a plate for your brother

2 *Math* to add; **ils ont ajouté 15 pour cent de service** they added on 15 percent for the service; **a. 10 à 15** to add 10 and 15 (together), to add 10 to 15

3 *(dire)* to add; **il est parti sans rien a.** he left without saying another word; **je n'ai plus rien à a.** I have nothing further to say *or* to add; **"venez aussi", ajouta-t-il** "you come too," he added

4 a. foi à *(croire)* to believe

5 *Ordinat (à une base de données)* to append

• **ajouter à** VT IND to add to; **ça ne fait qu'a. à mon embarras** it only adds to my confusion

VPR **s'ajouter** to be added; **vient s'a. là-dessus le loyer** on top of this you have to add the rent

ajustable [aʒystabl] ADJ adjustable

ajustage [aʒystaʒ] NM **1** *Ind* fitting **2** *(des pièces de monnaie)* gauging

ajustement [aʒystəmɑ̃] NM **1** *(modification ▸ d'un projet)* adjustment, adaptation; *(▸ des prix, des salaires, d'une monnaie, des statistiques)* adjusting, adjustment; **a. saisonnier** seasonal adjustment; **a. structurel** structural adjustment **2** *Ind* fitting

ajuster [3] [aʒyste] VT **1** *(adapter)* to fit; *Couture* **a. un vêtement** to alter a garment; **a. qch à** *ou* **sur** to fit sth to *or* on; **a. l'offre à la demande** to adjust *or* adapt supply to demand, to match supply and demand

2 *(mécanisme, réglage)* to adjust

3 *Fin (salaires, prix, monnaie)* to adjust

4 *Chasse* **a. son coup** *ou* **tir** to aim one's shot

5 *(arranger ▸ robe, coiffure)* to rearrange; *(▸ cravate)* to straighten

VPR **s'ajuster 1** *(s'adapter)* to fit; **l'embout s'ajuste sur le** *ou* **au tuyau** the nozzle fits onto the pipe **2** *(emploi réfléchi)* to straighten one's clothes, to tidy oneself up

ajusteur [aʒystœr] NM fitter

alacrité [alakrite] NF *Littéraire* alacrity, eagerness

Aladin [aladɛ̃] NPR *Littérature* Aladdin

alaire [alɛr] ADJ *Aviat* wing *(avant n)*

alaise [alɛz] NF drawsheet; **a. en caoutchouc** rubber sheet *or* undersheet

alambic [alɑ̃bik] NM still *(for making alcohol)*

alambiqué, -e [alɑ̃bike] ADJ *Littéraire (style)* convoluted; *(explication)* involved, tortuous; *(esprit)* oversubtle

alangui, -e [alɑ̃gi] ADJ languid

alanguir [32] [alɑ̃gir] VT *(sujet: chaleur, fatigue)* to make listless *or* languid *or* languorous; *(sujet: oisiveté, paresse)* to make indolent *or* languid; *(sujet: fièvre)* to make feeble, to enfeeble

VPR **s'alanguir** to grow languid; **elle s'alanguissait peu à peu** *(devenait triste)* her spirits gradually fell; *(n'offrait plus de résistance)* she was weakening gradually

alanguissement [alɑ̃gismɑ̃] NM languor

alarmant, -e [alarmɑ̃, -ɑ̃t] ADJ alarming; **son état est a.** his/her condition is giving serious cause for concern

alarme [alarm] NF **1** *(dispositif)* **a. antivol** burglar alarm; *(d'une voiture)* car alarm; **a. incendie** fire alarm **2** *(alerte)* alarm; **donner l'a.** to give *or* to raise the alarm; *Fig* to raise the alarm; **sonner l'a.** to sound the alarm **3** *(inquiétude)* alarm, anxiety; **à la première a.** at the first sign of danger • **d'alarme** ADJ *(dispositif, signal, sonnette)* alarm *(avant n)*

alarmer [3] [alarme] VT **1** *(inquiéter ▸ sujet: personne, remarque)* to alarm; *(▸ sujet: bruit)* to startle **2** *(alerter ▸ opinion, presse)* to alert
VPR **s'alarmer** to become alarmed; **il n'y a pas de quoi s'a.** there's no cause for alarm

alarmisme [alarmism] NM alarmism

alarmiste [alarmist] ADJ alarmist
NMF alarmist

Alaska [alaska] NM **l'A.** Alaska; **en A.** in Alaska; **la route de l'A.** the Alaska Highway

albanais, -e [albane, -ez] ADJ Albanian
NM *(langue)* Albanian
• **Albanais, -e** NM,F Albanian

Albanie [albani] NF **l'A.** Albania

albanophone [albanɔfɔn] ADJ Albanian-speaking
NMF Albanian speaker

albâtre [albɑtr] NM **1** *Minér* alabaster **2** *(objet)* alabaster (object)
• **d'albâtre** ADJ *Littéraire (blanc)* **des épaules d'a.** alabaster shoulders, shoulders of alabaster

albatros [albatros] NM **1** *Orn (oiseau)* albatross; **a. hurleur** wandering albatross **2** *Golf* albatross

albigeois, -e [albiʒwa, -az] ADJ of/from Albi
• **Albigeois, -e** NM,F = inhabitant of or person from Albi
• **albigeois** NMPL *Hist* Albigensians

albinisme [albinism] NM *Méd & Vét* albinism

albinos [albinos] ADJ & NMF *Méd & Vét* albino

Albion [albjɔ̃] NF *Géog* Albion; *Littéraire* **la perfide A.** perfidious Albion

album [albɔm] NM **1** *(livre)* album; **a. à colorier** *ou* **de coloriage** colouring *or* painting book; **a. (de) photos** photograph album; **a. de bandes dessinées** comic book **2** *(disque)* album, LP **3** *Ordinat (sur Macintosh)* scrapbook

albumen [albymen] NM *Biol & Bot* albumen

albumine [albymin] NF *Biol* albumin

alcali [alkali] NM *Chim* alkali; **a. volatil** ammonia

alcalin, -e [alkalɛ̃, -in] ADJ **1** *Chim* alkaline **2** *Méd* **médicament a.** antacid
NM *Chim* alkali

alcaloïde [alkalɔid] NM *Chim* alkaloid

alchimie [alʃimi] NF alchemy; *Fig* chemistry

alchimiste [alʃimist] NM alchemist

alcolo [alkɔlo] = **alcoolo**

alcool [alkɔl] NM **1** *(boissons alcoolisées)* **l'a.** alcohol; **je ne touche pas à l'a.** I never touch alcohol, I don't drink; **l'a. au volant accroît considérablement les risques d'accidents** *Br* drink-driving *or Am* drunk-driving greatly increases the risk of accidents; **boisson sans a.** non-alcoholic drink; **bière sans a.** alcohol-free beer **2** *(spiritueux)* **voulez-vous un petit a.?** would you like a digestif?; **a. de prune** plum brandy; **a. de fruit, a. blanc** = clear spirit made of distilled fruit wine **3** *Chim & Pharm* alcohol, spirit; **a. à 90°** *Br* surgical spirit, *Am* rubbing alcohol; **a. absolu** pure *or* absolute alcohol; **a. à brûler** methylated spirits; *Ind* **a. dénaturé** methylated spirits; **a. éthylique** ethyl alcohol, ethanol; **a. pur** raw spirits
• **à alcool** ADJ *(réchaud, lampe)* spirit *(avant n)*

alcoolémie [alkɔlemi] NF presence of alcohol in the blood; **taux d'a.** blood alcohol concentration

alcoolique [alkɔlik] ADJ alcoholic
NMF alcoholic; **Alcooliques anonymes** Alcoholics Anonymous

alcoolisation [alkɔlizasjɔ̃] NF **1** *Chim* alcoholization **2** *Méd* alcoholism

alcoolisé, -e [alkɔlize] ADJ **1** *(qui contient de l'alcool)* **boissons alcoolisées** alcoholic drinks *or* beverages, *Sout* intoxicating liquors; **non a.** non-alcoholic; **bière peu alcoolisée** low-alcohol beer **2** *Fam (personne)* drunk

alcooliser [3] [alkɔlize] VT **1** *(convertir en alcool)* to alcoholize, to convert to alcohol **2** *(additionner d'alcool)* to add alcohol to
VPR **s'alcooliser** *Fam (s'enivrer)* to get drunk[□]; *(être alcoolique)* to drink

alcoolisme [alkɔlism] NM *Méd* alcoholism

alcoolo [alkɔlo] NMF *Fam* alkie

alcoolodépendance [alkɔlodepɑ̃dɑ̃s] NF alcohol dependency

alcoolodépendant, -e [alkɔlodepɑ̃dɑ̃, -ɑ̃t] ADJ alcohol-dependent
NM,F = person with an alcohol dependency

alcoologie [alkɔlɔʒi] NF medical study of alcoholism

alcoologue [alkɔlɔg] NMF = specialist in the treatment of alcoholism

alcoomètre [alkɔmɛtr] NM alcoholometer

alcopop [alkopɔp] NM alcopop

Alcotest®, Alcootest® [alkɔtest] NM **1** *(appareil)* breathalyser **2** *(vérification)* breath test; **subir un A.** to take a breath test; **soumettre qn à un A.** to give sb a breath test, to breath-test *or* to breathalyse sb

alcôve [alkov] NF *Archit* alcove, recess
• **d'alcôve** ADJ *(secret, histoire)* intimate

aldéhyde [aldeid] NM *Chim* aldehyde; **a. formique** formaldehyde

al dente [aldente] *Culin* ADJ INV al dente
ADV al dente

aldin, -e [aldɛ̃, -in] ADJ *Typ (édition, caractère)* Aldine

ALE [ɑelø] NF *Com (abrév* **Association de libre-échange***)* FTA

ale [ɛl] NF *(alcool)* ale

aléa [alea] NM unforeseen turn of events; **les aléas de l'existence** the ups and downs of life; **ça fait partie des aléas du métier** *(risque)* it's one of the risks you have to take in this job; *(désagrément)* it's one of the disadvantages of the job

aléatoire [aleatwar] ADJ **1** *(entreprise, démarche)* risky, hazardous, chancy; **c'est a.** it's uncertain, there's nothing definite about it
2 *Jur (contrat)* aleatory
3 *Fin* **gain a.** chance *or* contingent gain; **marché/spéculation a.** risky market/speculation
4 *Mktg (sondage, échantillonnage)* random
5 *Math* random

alémanique [alemanik] ADJ & NMF *Géog & Ling* Alemannic

ALENA [alena] NM *Com (abrév* **Accord de libre-échange nord-américain***)* NAFTA

alêne [alɛn] NF *Tech* awl

alentour [alɑ̃tur] ADV **dans la campagne a.** in the surrounding countryside; **les églises a.** the churches in the neighbourhood; **tout a.** all around
• **alentours** NMPL neighbourhood, vicinity, (surrounding) area; **les alentours de la ville** the area around the city; **il doit être dans les alentours** *(tout près)* he's somewhere around (here); **il n'y avait personne aux alentours** there was no one around *or* in the vicinity; **aux alentours de** *(dans l'espace, le temps)* around; **aux alentours de Paris** near Paris; **aux alentours de minuit** round (about) *or* some time around midnight; **aux alentours de 50 m/500 euros** around 50 m/500 euros

aléoute [aleut], **aléoutien, -enne** [aleusjɛ̃, -ɛn] ADJ Aleutian; **les îles aléoutiennes** the Aleutian Islands
• **Aléoutien, -enne** NM,F Aleut, Aleutian

alerte[1] [alɛrt] ADJ *(démarche)* quick, alert; *(esprit)* lively, alert; *(style)* lively, brisk; *(personne)* spry

alerte[2] [alɛrt] NF **1** *(signal)* alert; **donner l'a.** to give the alert; **a.!** *(aux armes)* to arms!; *(attention)* watch out! **fausse a.** false alarm; **a. aérienne** air raid *or* air strike warning; **a. à la bombe** bomb scare; **a. rouge** red alert; **fin d'a.** all clear **2** *(signe avant-coureur)* alarm, warning sign; **à la première a.** at the first warning; **je ne suis pas surpris de son hospitalisation, elle avait déjà eu une a. le mois dernier** I'm not surprised she's in hospital, she had a warning sign last month; **l'a. a été chaude** that was a close call
• **d'alerte** ADJ warning *(avant n)*, alarm *(avant n)*
• **en alerte, en état d'alerte** ADV on the alert; **être en état d'a.** to be in a state of alert; **toutes les casernes de pompiers étaient en état d'a.** the entire fire service was on standby *or* the alert

alerter [3] [alɛrte] VT **1** *(alarmer)* to alert; **un bruit insolite l'avait alerté** he'd been alerted by an unusual sound **2** *(informer ▸ autorités)* to notify, to inform; *(▸ presse)* to alert; **nous avons été alertés par les résidents eux-mêmes** the local residents themselves drew our attention to the problem; **a. qn de** to alert sb to; **a. qn des dangers de l'alcool** to alert *or* to awaken sb to the dangers of alcohol

alésage [alezaʒ] NM *Tech* **1** *(technique)* reaming, boring (out) **2** *(diamètre d'un cylindre, du canon d'un fusil)* bore

alèse [alɛz] = **alaise**

aléser [18] [aleze] VT *Tech* to ream, to bore

aléseuse [alezøz] NF boring *or* reaming machine

alevin [alvɛ̃] NM *Ich* alevin, young fish

alevinage [alvinaʒ] NM *Pêche (repeuplement)* stocking with young fish

aleviner [3] [alvine] VT *Pêche* to stock (with young fish)

alevinier [alvinje] NM *Pêche* breeding-pond

Alexandre [alɛksɑ̃dr] NPR **A. le Grand** Alexander the Great

Alexandrie [alɛksɑ̃dri] NF *Géog* Alexandria

alexandrin, -e [alɛksɑ̃drɛ̃, -in] ADJ **1** *Hist* Alexandrian **2** *Littérature* Alexandrine
NM *Littérature* Alexandrine
• **Alexandrin, -e** NM,F Alexandrian

> **ALEXANDRIN**
>
> First favoured as the "vers héroïque" by sixteenth-century poets like Ronsard, the Alexandrine became the pre-eminent verse form of seventeenth-century classical French literature: it reached its highest development in the writings of Boileau, and in the classical tragedies of Corneille and Racine, who regarded it as being the form best suited to express the idea of "grandeur". The Alexandrine (based on a syllable count like all other French verse) consists of a line of twelve syllables with a medial caesura after the sixth syllable.

alexie [alɛksi] NF *Méd* acquired dyslexia, alexia

alezan, -e [alzɑ̃, -an] ADJ *(cheval)* chestnut
NM,F *(cheval)* chestnut

alfa [alfa] NM **1** *Bot* esparto (grass) **2** *(papier)* esparto paper

algarade [algarad] NF quarrel

algèbre [alʒɛbr] NF *Math* algebra; *Fam* **pour moi, c'est de l'a.** it's all Greek to me, I can't make head nor tail of it

algébrique [alʒebrik] ADJ *Math* algebraic, algebraical

Alger [alʒe] NF *Géog* Algiers

Algérie [alʒeri] NF **l'A.** Algeria; *Hist* **la guerre d'A.** the Algerian War

> **LA GUERRE D'ALGÉRIE**
>
> This was the most bitter of France's post-colonial struggles, and lasted from 1954 to 1962. In a country dominated by a million white settlers, the **pieds noirs** (see box at this entry), the French government's attempts to crush the revolt of the "Front de libération nationale" (**FLN**) (see entry), and to put an end to their struggle for independence with massive military intervention, came to nothing. The return to power of General de Gaulle in 1958, and the Accords d'Évian in 1962, led to Algerian independence and the resettlement of the "pieds noirs" in France.

algérien, -enne [alʒerjɛ̃, -ɛn] ADJ Algerian
• **Algérien, -enne** NM,F Algerian

algérois, -e [alʒerwa, -az] ADJ of/from Algiers
• **Algérois, -e** NM,F = inhabitant of or person from Algiers

algie [alʒi] NF *Méd* ache, pain

algol [algɔl] NM *Ordinat* ALGOL

algonkien, -enne [algɔ̃kjɛ̃, -ɛn] *Géol* ADJ Algonkian
• **Algonkien, -enne** NM,F Algonkian

algonkin, -e [algɔ̃kɛ̃, -in] ADJ Algonquin, Algonkian
NM *Ling* Algonquin, Algonkian
• **Algonkin, -e** NM,F Algonquin, Algonkian; **les Algonkins** the Algonquin

algonquin, -e [algɔ̃kɛ̃, -in] = **algonkin**

algorithme [algɔritm] NM *Math* algorithm

algorithmique [algɔritmik] ADJ *Math* algorithmic

algothérapie [algɔterapi] NF *Méd* algotherapy

algue [alg] NF *Bot* (piece of) seaweed
• **algues** NFPL seaweed *(UNCOUNT)*, *Spéc* algae

alias [aljas] NM *Ordinat (de courrier électronique, de bureau)* alias
ADV alias, aka; **Frédo, a. le Tueur** Frédo, aka the Killer

aliassage [aljasaʒ] NM *Ordinat* aliasing

alibi [alibi] NM **1** *Jur* alibi **2** *(prétexte)* alibi, excuse

alicament [alikamɑ̃] NM nutraceutical, dietary supplement

alien [aljɛn] NM **1** *(extra-terrestre)* alien **2** *Fig* **il fait figure d'a. dans le milieu de la politique** he's not at all what you'd expect from a politician; **ce portable est un alien sur le marché** this mobile is completely unlike anything else on the market

aliénable [aljenabl] ADJ *Jur* alienable

aliénant, -e [aljenɑ̃, -ɑ̃t] ADJ *Jur* alienating

aliénation [aljenasjɔ̃] NF **1** *Phil & Pol* alienation
2 *Psy* **a. (mentale)** insanity, mental illness
3 *(perte ▸ d'un droit, d'un bien)* loss, removal
4 *Jur* alienation, transfer of property

aliéné, -e [aljene] ADJ **1** *Phil & Pol* alienated **2** *Psy* insane, mentally disturbed
NM,F *Psy* insane person, mentally disturbed person

aliéner [18] [aljene] VT **1** *(abandonner ▸ indépendance, liberté, droit)* to give up; *Jur* to alienate
2 *(supprimer ▸ droit, liberté, indépendance)* to remove, to confiscate
3 *(faire perdre)* **ce commentaire vous a aliéné la sympathie de l'auditoire** that comment lost you the audience's sympathy
4 *Phil & Pol* to alienate; **les dirigeants ont aliéné la base** the leadership has alienated the rank and file
VPR **s'aliéner s'a. qn** to alienate sb; **elle s'est aliéné la presse** she has alienated the press; **je me suis aliéné leur amitié** I caused them to turn away *or* to become estranged from me

alignement [aliɲmɑ̃] NM **1** *(rangée)* line, row; **d'interminables alignements d'arbres** line upon line of trees; **être à** *ou* **dans l'a.** to be *or* to stand in line; **ne pas être à** *ou* **dans l'a.** to be out of line; **mettre qch à** *ou* **dans l'a. de** to bring sth into line *or* alignment with; **se mettre à** *ou* **dans l'a.** to fall into line; **perdre l'a.** to get out of line *or* alignment
2 *Fig (gén)* aligning, bringing into alignment; *Com (des prix)* alignment (**sur** with); *(d'une monnaie, d'une économie)* alignment; **l'a. des salaires sur le coût de la vie** bringing salaries into line with the cost of living; **leur a. sur la politique des socialistes** their coming into line with the socialists' policy; **a. monétaire** monetary alignment *or* adjustment
3 *Compta (d'un compte)* making up, balancing
4 *Ordinat* alignment

aligner [3] [aliɲe] VT **1** *(mettre en rang)* to line up, to align; **a. des dominos** to line up dominoes (end to end)
2 *Mil (soldats, tanks)* to line up, to form into lines; *(divisions)* to line up
3 *(présenter ▸ preuves)* to produce one by one; *(▸ en écrivant)* to string together; *(▸ en récitant)* to string together, to reel off; **je passe ma journée à a. des chiffres** I spend my day producing lists of figures
4 *(mettre en conformité)* **a. qch sur** to line sth up with, to bring sth into line with; **chaque membre doit a. sa politique sur celle de la Communauté** each member state must bring its policies into line with those of the Community
5 *Ordinat* to align
6 *Compta (compte)* to make up, to balance
7 *Écon (prix, monnaie)* to align, to bring into line (**sur** with)
8 *Fam (réprimander)* **a. qn** to tell sb off; **il s'est fait a. par un flic en moto** a motorcycle cop slapped a fine on him
9 *très Fam (locution)* **les a.** *(payer)* to cough up, to fork out
VPR **s'aligner 1** *(foule, élèves)* to line up, to form a line; *(soldats)* to fall into line **2** *très Fam (locutions)* **il peut toujours s'a.!** he's got no chance (of getting anywhere)!; **elle s'entraîne tous les jours, alors tu peux toujours t'a.!** she trains every day, so you don't stand a chance! **3 s'a. sur** *(imiter ▸ nation, gouvernement)* to fall into line *or* to align oneself with; **la Corée du Sud sera obligée de s'a. sur les prises de position nipponnes** South Korea will be forced to fall into line with the Japanese position

aliment [alimɑ̃] NM *(nourriture)* (type *or* kind of) food; *(portion)* (piece of) food; **des aliments** food *(UNCOUNT)*, foodstuffs; **aliments pour bébé/chien** baby/dog food; **aliments congelés/diététiques** frozen/health food; **aliments préparés** processed food
• **aliments** NMPL *Jur Br* maintenance *(UNCOUNT)*, *Am* alimony *(UNCOUNT)*

alimentaire [alimɑ̃tɛr] ADJ **1** *Com & Méd* food *(avant n)*; **sac/papier a.** bag/paper for wrapping food; **mauvaises habitudes alimentaires** bad eating habits **2** *(de la digestion)* alimentary **3** *Jur (obligation)* maintenance *(avant n)*

alimentation [alimɑ̃tasjɔ̃] NF **1** *(fait de manger)* (consumption of) food; *(fait de faire manger)* feeding; **combien dépensez-vous pour l'a.?** how much do you spend on food?; *Méd* **a. par perfusion** drip-feeding
2 *(régime)* diet; **une a. saine** a healthy diet
3 *Com (magasin) Br* grocer's (shop), *Am* grocery store; *(rayon)* groceries; **au fond à droite, après l'a.** on the right at the bottom, past the grocery shelves *or* groceries
4 *Ordinat* **a. papier** paper feed; **a. feuille à feuille, a. page par page** cut sheet feed, single sheet feed
5 *(approvisionnement)* feed, supply; **assurer l'a. d'une pompe en électricité** to supply electricity to a pump; **l'a. d'une ville en eau** the water supply to a town

alimenter [3] [alimɑ̃te] VT **1** *(nourrir ▸ malade, bébé)* to feed
2 *(rivière, lac)* to flow into; *Tech (moteur, pompe)* to feed, to supply; *(ville)* to supply; **a. qn en eau** to supply sb with water; **a. un ordinateur en données** to feed data into a computer; *(dans l'imprimerie)* **alimenté par bobine** web-fed
3 *(approvisionner ▸ compte)* to pay money into; **a. les caisses de l'État** to be a source of revenue *or* cash for the Government
4 *(entretenir ▸ conversation)* to sustain; *(▸ curiosité, intérêt)* to feed, to sustain; *(▸ doute, désaccord)* to fuel
VPR **s'alimenter 1** *(emploi réfléchi) (gén)* to eat; *(▸ bébé)* to feed oneself; **s'a. bien/mal** to have a good/poor diet; **il a l'âge de s'a. tout seul** he's old enough to feed himself **2 s'a. en** *(se procurer)* to be supplied with; **comment le village s'alimente-t-il en eau?** how does the village get its water?

alinéa [alinea] NM *(espace)* indent; *(paragraphe)* paragraph; **faire un a.** to indent

alitement [alitmɑ̃] NM confinement *(to one's bed)*

aliter [3] [alite] VT to confine to bed
VPR **s'aliter** to take to one's bed; **rester alité** to be confined to one's bed, to be bedridden

alizé [alize] ADJ M *(vent)* trade *(avant n)*
NM trade wind

Allah [ala] NPR Allah

allaitant, -e [aletɑ̃, -ɑ̃t] ADJ **1** *(femme)* breast-feeding; **mère allaitante** nursing mother **2** *Agr* **troupeau a.** weaning herd

allaitement [alɛtmɑ̃] NM *(processus)* feeding, *Br* suckling, *Am* nursing; *(période)* breast-feeding period; **a. au biberon** *ou* **artificiel** bottle-feeding; **a. maternel** *ou* **au sein** breast-feeding; **a. mixte** mixed feeding

allaiter [4] [alete] VT *(enfant)* to breast-feed; *(sujet: animal)* to suckle

allant, -e [alɑ̃, -ɑ̃t] ADJ *Littéraire* lively, active
NM energy, drive; **être plein d'a.** to have plenty of drive

alléchant, -e [aleʃɑ̃, -ɑ̃t] ADJ **1** *(plat, odeur)* mouthwatering, appetizing **2** *(proposition, projet, offre)* enticing, tempting

allécher [18] [aleʃe] VT **1** *(sujet: odeur, plat)* **a. qn** to give sb an appetite **2** *(sujet: offre, proposition, projet ▸ gén)* to tempt, to seduce, to entice; *(▸ dans le but de tromper)* to lure

allée [ale] NF *(à la campagne)* footpath, lane; *(dans un jardin)* alley; *(dans un parc)* walk, path; *(en ville)* avenue; *(devant une maison, une villa)* drive, driveway; *(dans un cinéma, un train, un magasin)* aisle; **les allées du pouvoir** the corridors of power
• **allées et venues** NFPL comings and goings; **toutes ces allées et venues pour rien** all this running around *or* about for nothing; **nous faisons des allées et venues entre Québec et Toronto** we go *or* we shuttle back and forth between Quebec and Toronto

allégation [alegasjɔ̃] NF allegation, (unsubstantiated) claim

allège [alɛʒ] NF **1** *Constr (d'une fenêtre)* basement; *(mur)* dwarf wall **2** *Naut* barge, lighter

allégé, -e [aleʒe] ADJ *Culin (yaourt, chips)* low-fat; *(confiture)* low-sugar

allégeance [aleʒɑ̃s] NF **1** *Hist* allegiance; **a. politique** political allegiance **2** *Naut* handicap

allégement, allègement [alɛʒmɑ̃] NM **1** *(diminution ▸ d'un fardeau)* lightening; *(▸ d'une douleur)* relief, alleviation, soothing **2** *Écon (d'impôts, de charges, de dépenses)* reduction; **ils sont en faveur de l'a. des charges sociales pour les entreprises** they are in favour of reducing employers' national insurance contributions; **a. fiscal** tax relief

alléger [22] [aleʒe] VT **1** *(rendre moins lourd ▸ malle, meuble)* to make lighter, to lighten; **il va falloir a. le paquet de 10 grammes** we'll have to take 10 grams off the parcel; **pour a. votre silhouette** to make your body look trimmer **2** *Écon (impôts, charges, dépenses)* to reduce; **a. les impôts de 10 pour cent** to reduce tax by 10 percent, to take 10 percent off tax **3** *(soulager ▸ douleur)* to relieve, to soothe; **je me suis senti allégé d'un grand poids** *ou* **fardeau** I felt (that) a great weight had been taken off my shoulders

allégorie [alegɔri] NF *Littérature* allegory

allégorique [alegɔrik] ADJ *Littérature* allegorical

allégoriquement [alegɔrikmɑ̃] ADV *Littérature* allegorically

allègre [alɛgr] ADJ cheerful, light-hearted; **d'un ton a.** cheerfully, light-heartedly; **marcher d'un pas a.** to walk with a light step

allègrement, allégrement [alɛgrəmɑ̃] ADV **1** *(joyeusement)* cheerfully, light-heartedly **2** *Hum (carrément)* heedlessly, blithely; **il s'est a. moqué de nous** he has been blithely making fools of us

allégresse [alegrɛs] NF cheerfulness, liveliness; **des cris d'a.** cries of joy; **accueillir qn avec a.** to give sb a cheerful welcome; **a. générale** general rejoicing

allegretto [alegreto] ADV *Mus (tempo)* allegretto

allegro [alegro] ADV *Mus (tempo)* allegro

alléguer [18] [alege] VT **1** *(prétexter)* to argue; **a. comme excuse/prétexte que** to put forward as an excuse/a pretext that; **il allégua que personne ne l'avait informé de ce projet** he alleged that no one had informed him of the plan; **alléguant du fait que** arguing that; **a. l'ignorance** to plead ignorance, to argue that one didn't know **2** *(citer)* to cite, to quote; **a. un texte de loi** to quote a legal text

alléluia [aleluja] NM *Rel* alleluia, hallelujah

Allemagne [almaɲ] NF **l'A.** Germany; *Anciennement* **l'A. de l'Est/de l'Ouest** East/West Germany

allemand, -e [almɑ̃, -ɑ̃d] ADJ German
NM *(langue)* German

• **Allemand, -e** NM,F German; **A. de l'Est/de l'Ouest** East/West German
• **allemande** NF *(danse, musique)* allemande

aller¹ [ale] **NM 1** *(voyage)* outward journey; **je suis passé les voir à l'a.** I dropped in to see them on the way (there); **à l'a., nous sommes passés par Anchorage** on the flight out, we went via Anchorage; **l'avion était en retard à l'a. et au retour** the flight was delayed both ways; **un a. (et) retour** a round trip; **l'a. est plus long que le retour** *(gén)* the outward journey is longer than the return journey; *(en avion)* flying out takes longer than flying back; **faire des allers et retours** *(personne, document)* to go back and forth, to shuttle back and forth; **je fais plusieurs allers et retours par jour entre l'hôpital et la maison** I go back and forth between the hospital and home several times a day; **je vais à la banque, mais je ne fais qu'un a. et retour** I'm going to the bank, but I'll be right back
2 *(billet)* **a. (simple)** *Br* single (ticket), *Am* one-way ticket; **viens donc nous voir, je t'offre l'a.** come and see us, I'll pay half the price of the trip; **a. (et) retour** *Br* return *or Am* round-trip (ticket); **deux allers et retours pour Paris** *Br* two returns *or Am* round-trip tickets to Paris; **c'est combien l'a. retour?** how much is the *Br* return *or Am* round-trip (ticket)?
3 *Fam* **a. et retour** *(gifle)* slap□
4 *Bourse* **a. et retour** bed and breakfasting

ALLER² [31] [ale]

V AUX
- to be going to **1**
- to go **2**

VI
- to go **A, B, C**
- to run **A5**
- to be **D**
- to fit **A6, E1**
- to be right **E3**

VPR
- to go (away) **1**
- to come undone **2**
- to die **3**
- to come off **4**
- to fade **4**

V AUX 1 *(suivi de l'infinitif) (exprime le futur proche)* to be going *or* about to; **tu vas tomber!** you're going to fall!, you'll fall!; **attendez-le, il va arriver** wait for him, he'll be here any minute now; **attends, tu vas comprendre!** wait, all will become clear *or* will be revealed!; **j'allais justement te téléphoner** I was just going to phone you, I was on the point of phoning you; **fais vite, la pièce va commencer** be quick, the play is about *or* is going to start; **il va être cinq heures** it's going on five; **il va pleuvoir, on dirait** it looks like rain *or* as if it's going to rain; **est-ce que ça va durer longtemps?** is it going to be long?; **tu vas faire ce que je te dis, oui ou non?** will you do as I say or won't you?
2 *(suivi de l'infinitif) (en intensif)* to go; **pourquoi es-tu allé tout lui raconter?** why did you go and tell him/her everything?; *Ironique* **je voudrais apprendre à skier – c'est ça, va te casser une jambe!** I'd like to learn how to ski – that's right, go and break your leg!; **pour a. me faire tuer?** why should I go and get killed?; **ne va pas croire/penser que...** don't go and believe/think that...; **tu ne vas pas me faire croire que tu ne savais rien!** you can't fool me into thinking that you didn't know anything!; **pourvu qu'elle n'aille pas se trouver mal!** let's hope she doesn't go and faint!; **qu'est-ce que tu vas t'imaginer!** you know me/him/her/*etc* better than that!; **que n'iront-ils pas s'imaginer!** God knows what they'll think!; **où est-elle? – allez savoir!** where is she? – God knows!; **allez expliquer ça à un enfant de cinq ans!** try and explain *or* try explaining that to a five-year-old!
3 *(exprime la continuité)* **a. en s'améliorant** to get better and better, to improve; **a. en empirant** to get worse and worse, to worsen; **a. en augmentant** to keep increasing; **le bruit allait en diminuant** the noise was getting fainter and fainter; **a. croissant** *(tension)* to be rising; *(nombre)* to be rising *or* increasing

VI A. *EXPRIME LE MOUVEMENT* **1** *(se déplacer)* to go; **qui va là?** who goes there?; *Vieilli* **tu sais a. à cheval?** can you ride a horse?; **va vite!** hurry up!; *(à un enfant)* run along (now)!; **a. à grands pas** to stride along; **vous alliez à plus de 90 km/h** *(en voiture)* you were driving at *or* doing more than 90 km/h; **va moins vite!** drive more slowly!, slow down!; **a. çà et là** to flit about; **a. (et) venir** *(de long en large)* to pace up and down; *(entre deux destinations)* to come and go, to go to and fro; **je vais et viens entre la France et la Suisse** I go *or* I shuttle back and forth between France and Switzerland; **je n'ai fait qu'a. et venir toute la matinée** I was in and out all morning; **il allait et venait dans la pièce** he was pacing up and down the room
2 *(se rendre ▸ personne)* **a. à** to go to; **en allant à Limoges** on the way to Limoges; **a. à la mer/à la montagne** to go to the seaside/mountains; **il n'ira pas aux jeux Olympiques** he won't go to the Olympic Games; **son film ira au festival de Cannes** his/her film will go to *or* be shown at the Cannes festival; **a. à l'université** *(bâtiment)* to go to the university; *(institution)* to go to university *or* college; **a. à l'école** *(bâtiment)* to go to the school; *(institution)* to go to school; **a. à l'église** *(bâtiment)* to go to the church; *(institution)* to go to church, to be a churchgoer; **les gens qui vont à l'église/au concert** *(gén)* the people who go to church/to the concert; *(habitués)* churchgoers/concertgoers; **a. à la messe** to go to *or* to attend mass; *(être pratiquant)* to be a churchgoer; **a. à la chasse/pêche** to go hunting/fishing; **a. aux champignons** to go mushroom-picking; **a. aux escargots** to go snail-collecting; **où vas-tu?** where are you going?; **comment y va-t-on?** how do you get there?; **il y est allé en courant** he ran there; **on y va!** let's go!; **je n'irai pas** I won't go; **j'irai en avion/voiture** I'll fly/drive, I'll go by plane/car; **j'irai à** *ou* **en vélo** I'll go (there) by bike, I'll cycle (there); **a. chez un ami** to go to see a friend, to go to a friend's; **a. chez le dentiste** to go to the dentist's; **tu n'iras plus chez eux, tu m'entends?** you will not visit them again, do you hear me?; **je vais toujours chez Burthot pour mes chocolats** I always go to Burthot for my chocolates *or* buy my chocolates from Burthot; **il a peur d'a. dans l'eau** he's afraid to go into the water; **je vais dans les Pyrénées** I'm going to the Pyrenees; **a. en Autriche** to go *or* to travel to Austria; **a. en Avignon/Arles** to go to Avignon/to Arles; **a. en haut/bas** to go up/down; **j'allais vers le nord** I was heading *or* going north
3 *(suivi de l'infinitif) (pour se livrer à une activité)* **a. faire qch** to go and do sth, *Am* to go do sth; **je vais faire mes courses tous les matins** I go shopping every morning; **va ramasser les poires dans le jardin** go and pick the pears in the garden; *très Fam* **va voir là-bas si j'y suis!** push off!, clear off!; *très Fam* **va te faire voir!**, *Vulg* **va te faire foutre!** go to hell!, get lost *or Br* stuffed!
4 *(mener ▸ véhicule, chemin)* to go; **ce train ne va pas à Pau** this train doesn't go to Pau; **cette route ne va pas à Bruges** this road doesn't go to Bruges; **cette rue va vers le centre** this street leads towards the city centre; **a. droit au cœur de qn** to go straight to sb's heart; **il choisit des mots qui vont droit au cœur** he uses words which speak to the heart
5 *(fonctionner ▸ machine)* to go, to run; *(▸ moteur)* to run; *(▸ voiture, train)* to go; **le manège allait de plus en plus vite** the roundabout was going faster and faster; **son pouls va trop vite** his/her pulse (rate) is too fast
6 *(se ranger ▸ dans un contenant)* to go, to belong; *(▸ dans un ensemble)* to fit; **où vont les tasses?** where do the cups go?; **les poupées russes vont l'une dans l'autre** Russian dolls fit one inside the other
7 *(être remis)* **a. à** to go to; **l'argent collecté ira à une œuvre** the collection will go *or* be given to (a) charity; **le prix d'interprétation masculine est allé à Jean Dufour** Jean Dufour was awarded the prize for best actor, the prize for best actor went to Jean Dufour

B. *S'ÉTENDRE* **1** *(dans l'espace)* **leur propriété va de la rivière à la côte** their land stretches from the river to the coast; **le passage qui va de la page 35 à la page 43** the passage which goes from page 35 to page 43; **a. jusqu'à** *(vers le haut)* to go *or* to reach up to; *(vers le bas)* to go *or* to reach down to; *(en largeur, en longueur)* to go to, to stretch as far as; **la tapisserie va jusqu'au plafond** the tapestry goes up to the ceiling
2 *(dans le temps)* **a. de... à...** to go from... to...; **sa période productive va de 1867 à 1892** his/her most productive period was from 1867 to 1892; **a. jusqu'à** *(bail, contrat)* to run till; **mon congé maladie va jusqu'au 15 janvier** my sick leave runs till 15 January; **jusqu'à quand vont les congés de février?** when does the February break finish?
3 *(dans une série)* **a. de... à...** to go *or* to range from... to...; **vos notes vont de 11 à 18** your *Br* marks *or Am* grades go *or* range from 11 to 18; **avec des températures allant de 10°C à 15°C** with temperatures (of) between 10°C and 15°C *or* ranging from 10°C to 15°C; **les prix vont jusqu'à 5000 euros** prices go as high as 5,000 euros; **sa voix va jusqu'au do** his/her voice reaches *or* goes up to C

C. *PROGRESSER* **1** *(se dérouler)* **a. vite/lentement** to go fast/slow; **arrêtez-moi si je vais trop vite** *(en parlant)* stop me if I'm going too fast; **à partir de ce moment-là, le divorce est allé très vite** from that moment onwards, the divorce proceedings went very fast; **plus ça va, moins je comprends la politique** the more I see of politics, the less I understand it; **plus ça va, plus je l'aime** I love him/her more each day
2 *(personne)* **j'irai jusqu'à 300 euros pour le fauteuil** I'll pay *or* go up to 300 euros for the armchair; **a. jusqu'à faire** to go as far as doing, to go so far as to do; **il est allé jusqu'à publier le tract** he went as far as publishing the pamphlet; **j'irais même jusqu'à dire que...** I would even go so far as to say that...; **sans a. jusque-là** without going that far; **il va sur** *ou* **vers la cinquantaine** he's getting on for *or* going on fifty; **elle va sur ses cinq ans** she's nearly *or* almost five, she'll be five soon; **a. à la faillite/l'échec** to be heading for bankruptcy/failure; **a. à sa ruine** to be on the road to ruin; **où va-t-on** *ou* **allons-nous s'il faut se barricader chez soi?** what's the world coming to if people have to lock themselves in nowadays?; **allons (droit) au fait** let's get (straight) to the point; **a. au plus pressé** to do the most urgent thing first

D. *ÊTRE DANS TELLE OU TELLE SITUATION* **1** *(en parlant de l'état de santé)* **bonjour, comment ça va? – ça va** hello, how are you? – all right; **comment vas-tu? – ça va** how are you? – fine; **comment va ta mère?** how's your mother?; *Fam* **comment va la santé?, comment va?** how are you keeping?; **ça va?** *(après un choc)* are you all right?; **ça ne va pas du tout** I'm not at all well; **je vais bien** I'm fine *or* well; **ça va bien?** are you OK?; **mon cœur ne va plus trop bien** my heart's not as good as it used to be; **elle va beaucoup mieux** she's (feeling) much better; **ton genou va mieux?** is your knee better?, does your knee feel (any) better?; **bois ça, ça ira mieux** drink this, you'll feel better; **il va mal** he's not at all well, he's very poorly; *Fam* **ça va pas (bien)** *ou* **la tête!, ça va pas, non?** you're off your head!, you must be mad!□; *Fam* **ça va? – on fait a.** how are you? – mustn't grumble *or* muddling along
2 *(se passer)* **comment vont les affaires? – elles vont bien** how's business? – (it's doing) OK *or* fine; **ça va de moins en moins bien entre eux** things have gone from bad to worse between them; **ça a l'air d'a. beaucoup mieux avec son mari** things seem to be much better between her and her husband; **les choses vont** *ou* **ça va mal** things aren't too good *or* aren't going too well; **ça va mal dans le sud du pays** there's trouble in the south of the country; **obéis-moi ou ça va mal a. (pour toi)!** do as I say or you'll be in trouble!; **comment ça va dans ton nouveau service?** how are you getting on *or* how are things in the new department?; **ça a l'air d'a.** you seem to be coping; **et le lycée, ça va?** and how's school?; **quelque chose ne va pas?** is there anything wrong *or* the matter?; **il y a quelque chose qui ne va pas dans l'imprimante** there's something wrong with the printer; **ça ne va pas tout seul** *ou* **sans problème** it's not an *or* it's no easy job; *Fam* **et le travail, ça va comme tu veux?** is work going all right?; *Fam* **faire a.** *(commerce)* to run, to manage□

E. *EXPRIME L'ADÉQUATION* **1** *(être seyant)* **a. (bien) à qn** *(taille d'un vêtement)* to fit sb; *(style d'un vêtement)* to suit sb; **le bleu lui va** blue suits him/her, he/she looks good in blue; **rien ne me va** I don't look good in anything, nothing suits me; **mon manteau te va mieux qu'à moi** my coat looks much better on you (than on me), my coat suits you better than (it does) me; **ça ne te va pas de parler vulgairement** coarse language doesn't suit *or* become you; *Ironique* **ça te va bien de donner des conseils!** you're a fine one to give advice!; **cela te va à ravir** *ou* **à merveille** that looks wonderful on you, you look wonderful in that

2 *(être en harmonie)* **a. avec qch** to go with sth, to match sth; **j'ai acheté un chapeau pour a. avec ma veste** I bought a hat to go with *or* to match my jacket; **a. ensemble** *(couleurs, styles)* to go well together, to match; *(éléments d'une paire)* to belong together; **ils vont bien ensemble, ces deux-là!** those two make quite a pair!; **je trouve qu'ils vont très mal ensemble** I think (that) they're an ill-matched couple *or* they make a very odd pair

3 *(convenir)* **le ton de ta voix ne va pas, reprends à la ligne 56** your tone isn't right, do it again from line 56; **la clé de 12 devrait a.** spanner number 12 should do (the job); **nos plats vont au four** our dishes are oven-proof; **tu veux de l'aide? – non, ça ira** do you want a hand? – no, I'll manage *or* it's OK; **tu ne rajoutes pas de crème? – ça ira comme ça** don't you want to add some cream? – that'll do (as it is) *or* it's fine like this; **ça ira pour aujourd'hui** that'll be all for today, let's call it a day; **pour un studio, ça peut a.** as far as studio apartments go, it's not too bad; **la robe ne va pas à la taille** the dress isn't right at the waist; **on dînera après le spectacle – ça me va** we'll go for dinner after the show – that's all right *or* fine by me *or* that suits me (fine); **je vous fais un rabais de 10 pour cent, ça vous va?** I'll give you a 10 percent discount, is that all right?; **je vous ai mis un peu plus de la livre, ça (vous) va?** it's a bit over a pound, is that all right?

F. *LOCUTIONS* **allez, un petit effort** come on, put some effort into it; **allez, ne pleure plus** come on (now), stop crying; **allez, je m'en vais!** right, I'm going now!; **zut! j'ai cassé un verre! – et allez (donc), le troisième en un mois!** damn! I've broken a glass! – well done, that's the third in a month!; **allez** *ou* **allons donc!** *(tu exagères)* go on *or* get away (with you)!, come off it!; **allez-y!** go on!, off you go!; **vas-y, lance-toi!** go on then, do it!; **allons-y!** let's go!; *Fam Hum* **allons-y Alonzo!** let's go!, *Am* let's go Cisco!; **allons-y, après la troisième mesure!** let's take it from the third bar!; *Ironique* **allons-y, ne nous gênons pas!** don't mind me!; **allons bon, j'ai perdu ma clef maintenant!** oh no, now I've lost my key!; **allons bon, voilà qu'il recommence à pleurer!** here we go, he's crying again!; **il n'est pas encore rentré – allons bon!** he's not home yet – oh no *or* dear!; **c'est mieux comme ça, va!** it's better that way, you know!; **tu ne seras pas en retard, va, tu as une heure devant toi!** you won't be late, you know, you've got an hour to go yet!; *Fam* **(espèce de) frimeur, va!** you show-off!; *Fam* **va donc, eh, chauffard!** roadhog!; *Fam* **va donc, eh, minable!** get lost, you little creep!; *Fam* **ça va, ça va bien, ça va comme ça** OK; **je t'aurai prévenu! – ça va, ça va!** don't say I didn't warn you! – OK, OK!; **c'est toujours moi qui fais la vaisselle – oh, eh, ça va!** it's always me who does the dishes – give it a rest!; **ça va comme ça, hein! j'en ai assez de tes jérémiades!** just shut up, will you! I'm fed up with your moaning!; *Fam* **une fois que tu es sur le plongeoir, il faut y a.!** once you're on the diving board, you've got to jump!; *Fam* **quand faut y a., faut y a.** when you've got to go, you've got to go; *Fam* **vas-y doucement, c'est fragile** gently *or* easy does it, it's fragile; *Fam* **vas-y mollo avec le vin!** go easy on the wine!; **ils n'y sont pas allés doucement avec les meubles** they were a bit rough with the furniture; *Fam* **j'en veux 500 euros – comme tu y vas!** I want 500 euros for it – isn't that a bit steep?; **c'est un fasciste – comme vous y allez!** he's a fascist – that's going a bit far!; *Fam* **où tu vas?** are you mad?□, have you got a screw loose?, *Br* are you off your head?; *Fam* **ça y va, les billets de 50 euros!** 50-euro notes are going as if there was no tomorrow!; **ça y allait, les bouteilles de champagne!** champagne flowed like water!; **aux réunions de famille, il y va toujours d'une** *ou* **de sa chansonnette** every time there's a family gathering, he sings a little song; *Hum* **elle y est allée de sa petite larme** she had a little cry; **il** *ou* **cela** *ou* **ça va de soi (que)** it goes without saying (that); **il va de soi que je vous paierai** it goes without saying that I'll pay you; **il** *ou* **cela** *ou* **ça va sans dire (que)** it goes without saying (that); **il y va de ta vie/carrière/réputation** your life/career/reputation is at stake; **il n'y va pas seulement de sa dignité** his/her dignity isn't the only thing at stake here; **il en va de la littérature comme de la peinture** it's the same with literature as with painting; **il n'en va pas de même pour toi** the same doesn't apply to you; **il en irait autrement si ta mère était encore là** things would be very different if your mother was still here; *Fam* **va pour le saint-émilion!** all right *or* OK then, we'll have the Saint-Émilion!; **je vous en donne 50 euros – va pour 50 euros!** I'll give you 50 euros for it – very well *or* all right, 50 euros (it is)!; **si tu vas par là, si vous allez par là** on those grounds, on that account; **tout le monde est égoïste, si tu vas par là!** everybody's selfish, if you look at it like that!

VPR s'en aller 1 *(partir ▸ personne)* to go; **il faut que je m'en aille** I must be off, I must go; **je lui donnerai la clé en m'en allant** I'll give him/her the key on my way out; **ne t'en va pas** don't go; **va-t'en!** go away!; **s'en a. discrètement** to slip away (quietly); **les employés qui ont 58 ans sont encouragés à s'en a.** employees who are 58 are encouraged to leave; **tous les jeunes s'en vont du village** all the young people are leaving the village; **va-t'en de là!** get away from there!; **il regarda le bateau s'en a.** he watched the boat leaving *or* leave

2 *(se défaire, se détacher)* to come undone; **attention! ta barrette s'en va!** careful, your hair slide is coming out!

3 *(mourir ▸ personne)* to die, to pass away; **si je m'en vais avant toi** if I die before you; *Hum* **il s'en va de la poitrine** his cough will carry him off

4 *(disparaître ▸ tache)* to come off, to go (away); *(▸ son)* to fade away; *(▸ forces)* to fail; *(▸ jeunesse)* to pass; *(▸ lumière, soleil, couleur)* to fade (away); *(▸ peinture, vernis)* to come off; **ça s'en ira au lavage/avec du savon** it'll come out in the wash/wash out with soap; **leur dernière lueur d'espoir s'en est allée** their last glimmer of hope has gone *or* vanished; **la morale, la politesse, tout s'en va!** morals and good manners just don't exist any more!

5 *(suivi de l'infinitif) (en intensif)* **il s'en alla trouver le magicien** off he went to find the wizard; *Fam* **je m'en vais lui dire ses quatre vérités!** I'm going to tell him/her a few home truths!

---

allergène [alɛrʒɛn] **NM** *Méd* allergen

allergénique [alɛrʒenik] **ADJ** *Méd* allergenic

allergie [alɛrʒi] **NF 1** *Méd* allergy; **avoir** *ou* **faire une a. à** to be allergic to **2** *Fam Fig* allergy; **avoir une a. à** to be allergic to

allergique [alɛrʒik] **ADJ 1** *Méd (réaction)* allergic; **être a. à qch** to be allergic to sth **2** *Fam Fig* allergic; **je suis a. au sport** I'm allergic to sport

allergologiste [alɛrgɔlɔʒist], **allergologue** [alɛrgɔlɔg] **NMF** *Méd* allergist

alliage [aljaʒ] **NM** *Métal & Tech* alloy; **structure en a. léger** alloy structure

alliance [aljɑ̃s] **NF 1** *(pacte)* alliance, pact, union; **conclure une a. avec un pays** to enter into *or* to forge an alliance with a country; **conclure une a. avec qn** to ally oneself with sb; **faire a. avec/contre qn** to ally *or* to team up with/against sb; *Mktg* **a. de marque** co-branding; **l'A. française** = organization promoting French language and culture abroad; **a. stratégique** strategic alliance

2 *(mariage)* union, marriage

3 *(combinaison)* union, blending, combination; *Ling* **a. de mots** oxymoron

4 *(bague)* wedding ring

> **L'ALLIANCE FRANÇAISE**
>
> In many respects, the activities of the Alliance française are similar to those of the British Council, although it is a private body. It organizes classes in French language and civilization and has branches all over the world.

allié, -e [alje] **ADJ 1** *(nation, pays)* allied **2** *(dans une famille)* related by marriage

NM,F 1 *(pays, gouvernement)* ally; *Hist* **les Alliés** the Allies **2** *(ami)* ally, supporter

allier [9] [alje] **VT 1** *(unir ▸ pays, gouvernements, chefs)* to unite, to ally (together); *(▸ familles)* to relate *or* to unite by marriage **2** *(combiner ▸ efforts, moyens, qualités)* to combine; *(▸ sons, couleurs, parfums)* to match, to blend (together); **elle allie l'intelligence à l'humour** she combines intelligence and humour **3** *Tech* to (mix into an) alloy

VPR s'allier 1 *(pays)* to become allied; **s'a. avec un pays** to ally oneself to a country, to form an alliance with a country; **s'a. contre** to unite against

2 *(par le mariage ▸ personnes)* to marry; *(▸ familles)* to become allied *or* related by marriage; **s'a. à une famille** to marry into a family

3 *(se combiner ▸ couleurs, sons, parfums)* to match, to blend (together); *(▸ qualités, talents, arts)* to combine, to unite

4 *Tech* to (become mixed into an) alloy

alligator [aligatɔr] **NM** *Zool* alligator

allitération [aliterasjɔ̃] **NF** *Ling* alliteration; **a. en s** alliteration of the letter s

allô [alo] **EXCLAM** hello, hullo; **a., qui est à l'appareil?** hello, who's speaking?; **a., je voudrais parler à Damien** hello, I'd like to speak to Damien

alloc [alɔk] **NF** *Fam (abrév* **allocation)** benefit□; **les allocs** *(allocations familiales)* child benefit□ *(UNCOUNT)*

allocataire [alɔkatɛr] **NMF** beneficiary

allocation [alɔkasjɔ̃] **NF 1** *(attribution ▸ d'argent)* allocation; *(▸ de dommages-intérêts, d'une indemnité)* awarding; *Fin & Bourse (▸ de titres)* allocation, allotment **2** *Admin (prestation financière)* allowance, *Br* benefit, *Am* welfare; **avoir** *ou* **toucher des allocations** to be on *Br* benefit *or Am* welfare; **a. (de) chômage** *Br* unemployment benefit, *Am* welfare; **allocations familiales** family allowance *(UNCOUNT)*, child benefit *(UNCOUNT)*; **a. de formation reclassement** = allowance paid to employees requiring further training or new qualifications; **a. de garde d'enfant à domicile** = allowance paid to working parents who employ a childminder at home; **a. (de) logement, a.-logement** *Br* housing benefit, *Am* rent subsidy *or* allowance; **a. (de) maternité** maternity allowance; **a. de parent isolé** = allowance paid to single parents; **a. de rentrée scolaire** = allowance paid to parents to help cover costs incurred at the start of the school year; **a. de solidarité spécifique** = allowance paid to long-term unemployed people who are no longer entitled to unemployment benefit; **a. unique dégressive** = unemployment allowance that gradually decreases over time, the sum depending on age, previous salary and amount of national insurance paid; **a. vieillesse** old-age pension

• **allocations NFPL** *Fam* **les allocations** *(service) Br* social security□, *Am* welfare□; *(bureau)* the *Br* social security *or Am* welfare office□

allocution [alɔkysjɔ̃] **NF** *(discours)* (formal) speech

allogène [alɔʒɛn] **ADJ** *(gén)* foreign; *(population)* non-native

NMF alien

allogreffe [alɔgrɛf] **NF** *Méd* allograft, homograft

allonge [alɔ̃ʒ] **NF 1** *(rallonge ▸ gén)* extension; *(▸ d'une table)* leaf **2** *(crochet)* (butcher's) hook **3** *Sport* reach; **avoir une bonne a.** to have a long reach

allongé, -e [alɔ̃ʒe] **ADJ 1** *(forme, silhouette)* elongated **2** *(couché)* **il était a. sur le canapé** he was lying on the sofa; **il est resté a. pendant trois mois** he was bedridden for three months

allongement [alɔ̃ʒmɑ̃] **NM** *(extension ▸ d'une route, d'un canal)* extension; *(▸ d'une distance)* increasing, lengthening; *(▸ d'une durée, de la vie)* lengthening, extension; *(▸ des jours)* lengthening; **l'a. du temps de loisir** the increased time available for leisure pursuits; **a. de l'espérance de vie des femmes** increase in women's life expectancy

allonger [17] [alɔ̃ʒe] **VT 1** *(rendre plus long ▸ robe, route, texte)* to lengthen, to make longer; *(▸ espérance de vie, délai)* to prolong; **le dernier chapitre allonge inutilement le récit** the last chapter just drags the story out pointlessly; **la coupe vous allonge la silhouette** the cut of the garment makes you look thinner; **a. le pas** to take longer strides **2** *(étirer ▸ bras, jambe)* to stretch out; **a. le cou** to stretch one's neck; **a. le bras pour prendre qch** *(devant soi)* to stretch out one's hand to get sth; *(en* *l'air)* to stretch up to reach sth; *(par terre)* to bend down to pick up sth

3 *(coucher ▸ blessé, malade)* to lay down; *très Fam (assommer)* to knock down❑, to floor; **vite, allongez-la par terre** quick, lay her down on the floor

4 *très Fam (donner ▸ argent)* to produce❑, to come up with; **a. un pourboire au coiffeur** to slip the hairdresser a tip; **cette fois-ci, il a fallu qu'il les allonge** this time, he had to cough up *or* to fork out; **a. une taloche à qn** to give sb a slap❑

5 a. la sauce *Culin* to make the sauce thinner; *Fig* to spin things out

VI les jours allongent the days are drawing out *or* getting longer

VPR s'allonger 1 *(se coucher)* to stretch out; **allongez-vous!** lie down!; **il/le chien s'allongea sur le tapis** he/the dog stretched out on the rug; **allonge-toi un peu** have a little lie-down

2 *(se prolonger ▸ visite, récit)* to drag on; *(▸ vie, période)* to become longer

3 *(grandir ▸ enfant)* to get taller, to grow

4 *(se renfrogner)* **son visage s'allongea** his/her face fell, he/she *Br* pulled *or Am* made a long face

allopathe [alɔpat] *Méd* **ADJ** allopathic

NMF allopathist, allopath

allopathie [alɔpati] **NF** *Méd* allopathy

allouer [6] [alwe] **VT 1** *(attribuer ▸ argent)* to allocate; *(▸ dommages-intérêts, indemnité)* to award, to grant; *(▸ dépense, budget)* to allow, to pass; *Fin & Bourse (▸ actions)* to allocate, to allot; *Admin (▸ salaire, pension)* to grant, to award **2** *(temps)* to allot, to allow; **au terme du temps alloué** at the end of the allotted time

allouf [aluf] **NF** *Fam* match❑ *(for lighting fire)*

allumage [alymaʒ] **NM 1** *(d'un feu, d'une chaudière)* lighting; *(du gaz)* lighting, turning on **2** *(d'une ampoule, d'un appareil électrique)* turning *or* switching on **3** *Aut & Tech* ignition; **avance/retard à l'a.** advanced/retarded ignition; **a. électronique/à induction** electronic/coil ignition

allumé, -e [alyme] **ADJ 1** *(feu, chaudière)* alight, burning; *(haut-fourneau)* in blast **2** *Fam (ivre)* trashed, wasted **3** *Fam (dingue)* crazy, off one's head *or* rocker

NM,F *Fam* **1** *(fou)* crackpot, crank **2** *(fanatique)* fanatic❑; **c'est un a. de l'informatique/du cinéma** he's mad *or* crazy about computers/the cinema

allume-cigare, allume-cigares [alymsigar] *(pl* **allume-cigares)** **NM** cigarette lighter

allume-gaz [alymgaz] **NM INV** gas lighter

allumer [3] [alyme] **VT 1** *(enflammer ▸ bougie, réchaud, cigarette, torche, gaz)* to light; *(▸ bois, brindille)* to light, to kindle; *(▸ feu, incendie)* to light, to start

2 *(mettre en marche ▸ lampe, appareil, lumière)* to turn on, to switch on, to put on; *(▸ phare)* to put on, to turn on; *Ordinat* to power up; **laisse la pièce allumée** leave the lights on in the room; **j'ai laissé la radio allumée!** I forgot to turn off the radio!

3 *Littéraire (commencer ▸ guerre)* to start; *(▸ passion, haine)* to stir up

4 *Fam (sexuellement)* to turn on, to make horny

5 *Fam (battre)* to beat up, *Br* to do over; **se faire a.** to get beaten up *or Br* done over

6 *Fam (tuer)* to kill❑, *Br* to do in

USAGE ABSOLU allume! turn the light on!; **comment est-ce qu'on allume?** how do you turn *or Br* switch it on?; **où est-ce qu'on allume?** where's the switch?

VPR s'allumer 1 *(s'éclairer)* **leur fenêtre vient de s'a.** a light has just come on at their window

2 *Fig (visage, œil, regard)* to light up

3 *(se mettre en marche ▸ appareil, radio)* to switch on, to turn on; *(▸ lumière)* to come on; *Ordinat* to power up; **ça ne s'allume pas** the light's not working; **où est-ce que ça s'allume?** where's the light switch?

4 *(prendre feu ▸ bois, brindille)* to catch (fire); *(▸ incendie)* to start, to flare up

5 *Littéraire (commencer ▸ haine, passion)* to be aroused; *(▸ guerre)* to break out

allumette [alymet] **NF 1** *(pour allumer)* match, matchstick; **a. suédoise** *ou* **de sûreté** safety match; **être gros** *ou* **épais comme une a.** to be as thin as a rake; **avoir des jambes comme des allumettes** to have legs like matchsticks **2** *Culin (gâteau)* allumette

allumeur [alymœr] **NM 1** *Tech* igniter **2** *Aut* (ignition) distributor

allumeuse [alymøz] **NF** *Fam Péj* tease

allure [alyr] **NF 1** *(vitesse d'un véhicule)* speed; **à grande/faible a.** at (a) high/low speed; **rouler à petite a.** *ou* **à une a. réduite** to drive at a slow pace *or* slowly; **aller** *ou* **rouler à toute a.** to go at (top *or* full) speed **2** *(vitesse d'un marcheur)* pace; **marcher à vive a.** to walk at a brisk pace; **courir à toute a.** to run as fast as one can; *Fig* **à cette a., tu n'auras pas fini avant demain** at that speed *or* rate, you won't have finished before tomorrow **3** *(apparence ▸ d'une personne)* look, appearance; **avoir de l'a., avoir grande a.** to have style; **une femme d'a. élégante entra** an elegant-looking woman came in; **il a une drôle d'a.** he looks odd *or* weird; **je n'aime pas l'a. qu'elle a** I don't like the look of her; **le projet prend une mauvaise a.** the project is taking a turn for the worse; **prendre des allures de** to take on an air of

> Il faut noter que le nom anglais **allure** est un faux ami. Il signifie **attrait**.

allusif, -ive [alyzif, -iv] **ADJ** allusive; **il est resté très a.** he wasn't very specific

allusion [alyzjɔ̃] **NF 1** *(référence)* allusion, reference; **faire a. à qch** to allude to sth, to refer to sth; **il n'y a fait a. qu'en passant** he only made passing reference to it; **par a. à** alluding to **2** *(sous-entendu)* hint; **c'est une a.?** are you hinting at something?; **l'a. m'échappe** I don't get it; **s'exprimer par allusions** to express oneself obliquely *or* allusively

allusive [alyziv] *voir* **allusif**

allusivement [alyzivmɑ̃] **ADV** allusively

alluvial, -e, -aux, -ales [alyvjal, -o] **ADJ** *Géol* alluvial

alluvions [alyvjɔ̃] **NFPL** *Géol* alluvium

alma mater [almamater] **NM OU NF** *Belg, Can & Suisse* alma mater

almanach [almana] **NM** almanac

aloès [alɔɛs] **NM** *Bot* aloe; *Pharm* bitter aloes

aloe vera [alɔevera] **NM INV** *Bot & Pharm* aloe vera

aloi [alwa] **NM de bon a.** *(marchandise, individu)* of sterling *or* genuine worth; *(plaisanterie)* in good taste; *(succès)* well-deserved, worthy; **de mauvais a.** *(marchandise)* worthless; *(individu)* worthless, no-good *(avant n)*; *(plaisanterie)* in bad taste; *(succès)* cheap

alopécie [alɔpesi] **NF** *Méd* alopecia

alors [alɔr] **ADV 1** *(à ce moment-là)* then; **j'étais jeune a.** I was young then; **Rome était a. à la tête d'un grand empire** at that time Rome was at the head of a great empire, Rome was then at the head of a great empire; **le Premier ministre d'a. refusa de signer les accords** the then Prime Minister refused to sign the agreement; **jusqu'a.** until then; **a. seulement, il se rendit compte de la situation** it was only then that he understood the situation; **venez la semaine prochaine, j'aurai plus de temps a.** come next week, I'll have more time then

2 *(en conséquence)* so; **il s'est mis à pleuvoir, a. nous sommes rentrés** it started to rain, so we came back in; **a., il n'y a pas d'autre solution?** so there's no other solution then?

3 *(dans ce cas)* then, so, in that case; **s'il mourait, a. elle devrait reprendre son travail** if he died, then she would have to go back to work; **je préfère renoncer tout de suite, a.!** in that case, I'd just as soon give up straight away!; **mais a., ça change tout!** but that changes everything!

4 *(emploi expressif)* **et a.?** so?, so what?; **il va se mettre en colère, et a.?** if he gets angry, so what?; **et a., qu'est-ce qui s'est passé?** so what happened then?; **a., qu'est-ce qu'on fait?** so what are we going to do?, what are we going to do, then?; **a. là, il exagère!** he's going a bit far there!; **a. quoi, t'as un problème?** what do you mean you've got a problem?; **ça a., je ne l'aurais jamais cru!** my goodness, I would never have believed it!; **non mais a., pour qui vous vous prenez?** well really, who do you think you are?

• **alors que CONJ 1** *(au moment où)* while, when; **l'orage éclata a. que nous étions encore loin de la maison** the storm broke while *or* when we were still a long way from the house **2** *(bien que, même si)* even though; **il a parlé tout le temps, a. qu'on ne lui avait rien demandé** he talked non-stop, even though no one had asked him anything; **a. même qu'il ne nous resterait que ce moyen, je refuserais de l'utiliser** even if this were the only means left to us, I wouldn't use it **3** *(tandis que)* while; **il part en vacances, a. que je reste ici tout l'été** he's going on holiday, while I stay here all summer

alouette [alwɛt] **NF 1** *Orn* lark; **a. des bois** woodlark; **a. des champs** skylark; **a. de mer** sealark; *Fam* **il attend que les alouettes lui tombent toutes cuites dans le bec** he's waiting for things to just fall into his lap **2** *Culin* **a. sans tête** ≃ veal olive

alourdir [32] [alurdir] **VT 1** *(ajouter du poids à)* to weigh down, to make heavy *or* heavier; **l'emballage alourdit le paquet de 200 g** the wrapping makes the parcel heavier by 200 g; **alourdi par la fatigue** heavy with exhaustion **2** *(style, allure, traits)* to make heavier *or* coarser; *(impôts)* to increase; **la grossesse commençait à a. sa démarche** her pregnancy was beginning to make her walk more heavily; **cette répétition alourdit la phrase** the repetition makes the sentence unwieldy

VPR s'alourdir 1 *(grossir ▸ personne)* to put on weight; *(▸ taille)* to thicken, to get thicker

2 *(devenir lourd)* to become heavy *or* heavier; **ses paupières s'alourdissaient** his/her eyelids were beginning to droop *or* were getting heavy; **sa démarche s'est alourdie** he/she walks more heavily

3 *(devenir plus grossier)* to get coarser; **ses traits s'alourdissent** his/her features are getting coarser

4 *(augmenter ▸ charges, impôts)* to increase

alourdissement [alurdismɑ̃] **NM 1** *(d'un paquet, d'un véhicule)* increased weight **2** *(d'un style)* heaviness; *(des impôts)* increase

aloyau [alwajo] **NM** *Culin* sirloin

alpaga [alpaga] **NM** *Zool* alpaca

alpage [alpaʒ] **NM 1** *(pâturage)* high (mountain) pasture **2** *(saison)* grazing season *(spent by livestock in high pastures)*

alpaguer [3] [alpage] **VT** *très Fam* **1** *(arrêter)* to nab, *Am* to bust; **se faire a.** to get nabbed *or Am* busted **2** *(accaparer)* to nab

alpe [alp] **NF** (high) alpine pasture

Alpes [alp] **NFPL les A.** the Alps; **les A. suisses** the Swiss Alps

alpestre [alpɛstr] **ADJ** alpine; **plante a.** alpine plant

alpha [alfa] **NM INV** alpha; *Fig* **l'a. et l'oméga de** the beginning and the end of

alphabet [alfabɛ] **NM 1** *(d'une langue)* alphabet; **a. arabe/cyrillique/grec/romain** Arab/Cyrillic/Greek/Roman alphabet **2** *(abécédaire)* spelling *or* ABC book, alphabet **3** *(code)* **a. Morse** Morse code; **a. phonétique** phonetic alphabet; **a. phonétique international** International Phonetic Alphabet

alphabétique [alfabetik] **ADJ** alphabetic, alphabetical

alphabétiquement [alfabetikmɑ̃] **ADV** alphabetically

alphabétisation [alfabetizasjɔ̃] **NF** elimination of illiteracy; **campagne/taux d'a.** literacy campaign/rate; **l'a. de la population** teaching the population to read and write

alphabétiser [3] [alfabetize] **VT** to teach to read and write

alpha-hydroxy-acide [alfaidrɔksiasid] **NM** *Chim* alpha hydroxy acid

alphanumérique [alfanymerik] **ADJ** alphanumeric

Alphapage® [alfapaʒ] **NM** = radiopaging system run by France Télécom

alpha-test [alfatɛst] **NM** *Ordinat* alphatest; **alpha-tests** *(procédure)* alpha testing

alpin, -e [alpɛ̃, -in] **ADJ 1** *Biol, Bot & Géol* alpine **2** *Sport (club)* mountaineering *(avant n)*, mountain-climbing *(avant n)*; *(ski)* downhill

alpinisme [alpinism] NM *Sport* mountaineering, mountain-climbing; **faire de l'a.** to climb, to go mountain-climbing

alpiniste [alpinist] NMF *Sport* mountaineer, climber

Alsace [alzas] NF **l'A.** Alsace
NM Alsace (wine)

Alsace-Lorraine [alzaslɔrɛn] NF **l'A.** Alsace-Lorraine

ALSACE-LORRAINE

The chief subjects of the longstanding conflict between Germany and France, these two provinces were seized by the Germans at the end of the Franco-Prussian War in 1871, becoming part of the German Reich. They reverted to France after the First World War, were seized by Germany again in 1940, and were finally restored to France at the end of the Second World War.

alsacien, -enne [alzasjɛ̃, -ɛn] ADJ Alsatian
NM *(dialecte)* Alsatian
• **Alsacien, -enne** NM,F Alsatian; **les Alsaciens** the people of Alsace

alter [altɛr] NMF *Fam (abrév* **altermondialiste**) alterglobalist

ALTER- PREFIX

• This prefix, from the Latin *alter* meaning *other*, has emerged in recent years to refer to the antiglobalization movement or **altermondialisme**. The idea in French, unlike the English, is not strictly that of opposition but rather of a possible alternative to globalization. The prefix has also given rise to **altermondialiste** (adjective and noun), as in:
le mouvement altermondialiste the antiglobalization movement; **les idées altermondialistes** antiglobalization ideas; **les altermondialistes** those in favour of antiglobalization, supporters of antiglobalization
• **Alter-** has become a very productive prefix, which can be seen and heard in neologisms such as **alterconsommation, alterconsommateurs, alteréconomie, altereuropéen,** etc. In order to translate these, a periphrasis would probably have to be used: *an alternative to mass consumption/the liberal economy* or *a new form of consumption/economy, people looking for an alternative to mass consumption* or *new consumers, which offers a new vision of Europe*, etc.
• Due to its relatively recent coinage (the late 1990s), the prefix **alter-** does not yet have a fixed grammatical status, as evidenced by the occurrence of, variously, **alter** or **alters** as a plural adjective.
• As is often the case with prefixes and suffixes, there is some uncertainty as to the use of the hyphen, even if the unhyphenated forms seem to be outweighing their hyphenated equivalents (**altermondialisme** rather than **alter-mondialisme**, but **alter-européen** rather than **altereuropéen**, maybe for greater ease of reading).

altérable [alterabl] ADJ *(aliment, matériel)* liable to deteriorate *or* be damaged; *(couleur ▸ à l'usage)* liable to fade; *(▸ au lavage)* liable to run

altéragène [alteraʒɛn] ADJ *Biol (substance)* harmful to the environment, noxious

altérant, -e [alterɑ̃, -ɑ̃t] ADJ **1** *(qui modifie)* altering **2** *(qui donne soif)* thirst-inducing

altération [alterasjɔ̃] NF **1** *(dégradation ▸ d'aliments, de matériel, de la santé)* deterioration; *(▸ de couleurs ▸ à l'usage)* fading; *(▸ au lavage)* running
2 *(falsification ▸ de monnaie, de document)* falsification; *(▸ de texte)* garbling; *(dilution ▸ du vin)* adulteration
3 *Mus (dièse)* sharp (sign); *(bémol)* flat (sign)
4 *Ordinat (d'un fichier)* corruption

altercation [alterkasjɔ̃] NF quarrel, altercation; **j'ai eu une violente a. avec elle** I had a violent quarrel *or* a huge row with her

alterconsommateur [alterkɔ̃sɔmatœr] NM ethical consumer

alterconsommation [alterkɔ̃sɔmasjɔ̃] NF ethical consumption, ethical purchasing

altéré, -e [altere] ADJ **1** *(aliments)* spoiled, damaged; *(couleurs)* faded; *(santé, amitié)* impaired, affected; *(traits)* drawn, distorted
2 *(falsifié ▸ faits)* altered, falsified; *(dilué ▸ vin)* adulterated
3 *(assoiffé)* thirsty
4 *Ordinat* corrupted

alter ego [alterego] NM INV **1** *Hum (ami)* alter ego **2** *(homologue)* counterpart, alter ego

altérer [18] [altere] VT **1** *(dégrader ▸ couleur)* to fade; *(▸ denrée)* to affect *or* to impair the quality of; *(▸ amitié)* to affect
2 *(falsifier ▸ fait, histoire)* to distort; *(▸ vérité)* to distort, to twist; *(▸ monnaie)* to falsify; *(▸ document)* to tamper with, to falsify; *(diluer ▸ vin)* to adulterate
3 *(changer ▸ composition, équilibre)* to change, to alter, to modify; **les traits altérés par le chagrin/la fatigue/la maladie** his/her face pinched with grief/drawn with tiredness/drawn with illness; **la voix altérée par l'angoisse** his/her voice strained with anxiety
4 *Ordinat* to corrupt
5 *Littéraire (assoiffer)* to make thirsty; **altéré de** thirsty *or* thirsting for; **altéré de sang** bloodthirsty
6 *Mus (accord)* to alter; *(note)* to inflect
VPR **s'altérer 1** *(se dégrader ▸ denrée)* to spoil; *(▸ sentiment, amitié)* to deteriorate; *(▸ couleurs)* to fade; *(▸ voix)* to be distorted; **leurs rapports se sont altérés** their relationship has deteriorated; **sa santé s'est altérée** his/her health has got worse **2** *Ordinat* to corrupt **3** *(se transformer ▸ substance, minéral)* to alter, to (undergo a) change

altérité [alterite] NF otherness

altermondialisation [altɛrmɔ̃djalizasjɔ̃] NF alterglobalization, ethical globalization

altermondialisme [altɛrmɔ̃djalism] NM alterglobalism, ethical globalization movement

altermondialiste [altɛrmɔ̃djalist] ADJ alterglobalist
NMF alterglobalist

alternance [altɛrnɑ̃s] NF **1** *(succession)* alternation; **l'a. des saisons** the alternating *or* changing seasons; **a. des cultures** crop rotation **2** *Pol* **a. (du pouvoir)** changeover of political power; **pratiquer l'a.** to take turns running a country; **l'A.** = transfer of power **3** *Élec* alternation
• **en alternance** ADV **ils donnent** *ou* **programment 'Manon' et 'la Traviata' en a.** they're putting on 'Manon' and 'la Traviata' alternately; **faire qch en a. avec qn** to take turns with sb to do sth

alternateur [alternatœr] NM *Élec* alternator

alternatif, -ive [alternatif, -iv] ADJ **1** *(périodique)* alternate, alternating **2** *(à option)* alternative; **modèle a. de croissance** alternative model of growth; **rock a.** alternative rock
• **alternative** NF **1** *(choix)* alternative, option; **se trouver devant une pénible alternative** to be faced with a difficult choice, to be in a difficult dilemma **2** *(solution de remplacement)* alternative; **l'alternative écologiste** the green alternative; **alternatives économiques** economic alternatives

alternativement [alternativmɑ̃] ADV (each) in turn, alternately

alterne [altɛrn] ADJ *Bot & Géom* alternate

alterner [3] [alterne] VT **1** *(faire succéder)* to alternate **2** *Agr (cultures)* to rotate
VI *(se succéder ▸ phases)* to alternate; *(▸ personnes)* to alternate, to take turns; **faire a.** to alternate

altesse [altɛs] NF Highness; **Son A. Royale** *(prince)* His Royal Highness; *(princesse)* Her Royal Highness

altier, -ère [altje, -ɛr] ADJ haughty, arrogant; **avoir un port a.** to carry oneself proudly; **avoir une démarche altière** to walk proudly

altimètre [altimɛtr] NM altimeter

altiport [altipɔr] NM *Aviat* (ski-resort) airfield

altiste [altist] NMF *Mus* viola player, violist

altitude [altityd] NF altitude; **a. au-dessus du niveau de la mer** height above sea level; **à une a. de 4500 m, à 4500 m d'a.** at an altitude of 4,500 m; **à haute/basse a.** at high/low altitude; **prendre/perdre de l'a.** to gain/lose altitude
• **d'altitude** ADJ *(restaurant, station)* mountain-top
• **en altitude** ADV high up, at high altitude

alto [alto] NM *Mus* **1** *(instrument à cordes)* viola; *(saxophone)* alto **2** *(voix)* contralto *or* alto (voice); *(chanteuse)* contralto, alto; **je suis a.** I sing alto *or* contralto

altocumulus [altokymylys] NM *Météo* altocumulus

altostratus [altostratys] NM *Météo* altostratus

altruisme [altrɥism] NM altruism

altruiste [altrɥist] ADJ altruistic
NMF altruist

Altuglas® [altyglas] NM *Br* ≃ Perspex®, *Am* ≃ Plexiglas®

alumine [alymin] NF *Chim* alumina, *Br* aluminium *or Am* aluminum oxide

aluminé, -e [alymine] ADJ *Chim* aluminized

aluminium [alyminjɔm] NM *Br* aluminium, *Am* aluminum

alun [alœ̃] NM *Chim* alum

alunir [32] [alynir] VI *Astron* to land (on the moon)

alunissage [alynisaʒ] NM *Astron* (moon *or* lunar) landing

alvéolaire [alveɔlɛr] ADJ *Anat & Ling* alveolar

alvéole [alveɔl] NF **1** *(d'une ruche)* cell, *Spéc* alveolus **2** *Anat* **a. dentaire** tooth socket, *Spéc* alveolus; **a. pulmonaire** air cell, *Spéc* alveolus **3** *Géol* cavity, pit

alvéolé, -e [alveɔle] ADJ honeycombed

AM *(abrév écrite* **Assurance maladie**) health insurance

amabilité [amabilite] NF *(qualité)* kindness, friendliness, amiability; **un homme plein d'a.** a very kind man; **ils ont eu l'a. de...** they were kind enough to...; **d'un ton sans a.** rather curtly; **veuillez avoir l'a. de...** please be so kind as to...
• **amabilités** NFPL *(politesses)* polite remarks; **faire des amabilités à qn** to be polite to sb; **trêve d'amabilités, passons aux choses sérieuses** enough of the pleasantries, let's get down to business

amadou [amadu] NM *Bot* touchwood, tinder

amadouement [amadumɑ̃] NM *(fait d'enjôler)* wheedling, coaxing; *(apaisement)* softening

amadouer [6] [amadwe] VT **1** *(enjôler)* to cajole; **elle essaie de l'a. pour qu'il accepte** she's trying to cajole *or* to coax him into agreeing **2** *(apaiser)* to mollify, to soften (up); **c'est pour m'a. que tu me dis ça?** are you saying this to soften me up?

amaigrir [32] [amegrir] VT **1** *(sujet: maladie, régime)* to make thin *or* thinner; **son séjour en prison l'a beaucoup amaigri** he's lost a lot of weight while he's been in prison; **le visage amaigri par la maladie** his/her face emaciated from illness **2** *Tech (épaisseur)* to reduce; *(pâte)* to thin down **3** *Agr (sol)* to impoverish
VPR **s'amaigrir** to lose weight

amaigrissant, -e [amegrisɑ̃, -ɑ̃t] ADJ slimming, *Am* reducing

amaigrissement [amegrismɑ̃] NM **1** *(perte de poids ▸ du corps)* weight loss; *(▸ des cuisses, de la silhouette)* weight reduction; **un a. de 10 kg** a weight reduction of 10 kg **2** *Tech (de l'épaisseur)* reducing; *(d'une pâte)* thinning down

amalgamation [amalgamasjɔ̃] NF *Chim* amalgamation

amalgame [amalgam] NM **1** *Métal* amalgam **2** *(mélange)* mixture, amalgam; **il ne faut pas faire l'a. entre ces deux questions** the two issues must not be confused

amalgamer [3] [amalgame] VT **1** *Métal* to amalgamate **2** *(mélanger ▸ ingrédients)* to combine, to mix up **3** *(réunir ▸ services, sociétés)* to amalgamate; **les deux unités ont été amalgamées** the two units have been amalgamated
VPR **s'amalgamer 1** *Métal* to amalgamate **2** *(s'unir)* to combine, to amalgamate **3** *(se mélanger)* to get mixed up

amanché, -e [amɑ̃ʃe] ADJ *Can Fam* **1** *(habillé)* **bien/mal a.** well/badly dressed; **être a. comme la chienne de Jacques** to be dressed like a dog's dinner **2 être a.** *(dans une mauvaise passe)* to be up the creek; **je la plains d'être amanchée avec cette ivrogne** I feel really sorry for her being stuck with that drunk

amande [amɑ̃d] NF *Bot* **1** *(fruit)* almond; **chocolat aux amandes** almond chocolate; **a. douce/amère** sweet/bitter almond **2** *(noyau)* kernel
• **d'amande(s)** ADJ almond *(avant n)*
• **en amande** ADJ *(yeux)* almond-shaped

amandier [amɑ̃dje] NM *Bot* almond tree

amanite [amanit] NF *Bot* amanita; **a. phalloïde** death-cap; **a. tue-mouches** fly agaric; **a. vineuse** blushing amanita, blushing mushroom

amant [amɑ̃] NM (male) lover; **prendre un a.** to take a lover
• **amants** NMPL lovers; **devenir amants** to become lovers; **les amants de Vérone** Romeo and Juliet

amarante [amarɑ̃t] ADJ INV *(couleur)* amaranthine
NF *Bot* amaranth, love-lies-bleeding

amariner [3] [amarine] VT *Naut* **1** *(habituer à la mer)* to accustom to life at sea **2** *(navire)* to take over
VPR **s'amariner** to find one's sea legs

amarrage [amaraʒ] *Naut* NM **1** *(dans un port)* mooring **2** *(à un objet fixe)* lashing
• **à l'amarrage** ADJ moored

amarre [amar] NF *Naut* mooring line *or* rope; **larguer les amarres** to cast off, to slip the moorings; *Fig* to set off; **rompre les amarres** to break its moorings; *Fig* to break off all links

amarrer [3] [amare] VT **1** *Naut (cordages)* to fasten, to make fast; *(navire)* to hitch, to moor **2** *(bagages)* to tie down; **nous avons amarré les valises sur le toit de la voiture** we tied the luggage to the car roof
USAGE ABSOLU *Naut* **a. à quai** to wharf
VPR **s'amarrer** *Naut (à une berge)* to moor; *(dans un port)* to dock, to berth

amaryllis [amarilis] NF *Bot* amaryllis

amas [amɑ] NM **1** *(tas)* heap, mass, jumble **2** *Astron* cluster; **a. globulaire/ouvert** globular/open cluster

amasser [3] [amase] VT **1** *(entasser ▸ vivres, richesses)* to amass, to hoard; **a. une fortune** to amass a fortune; **après avoir amassé un petit pécule** having got together a bit of money **2** *(rassembler ▸ preuves, information)* to amass
VPR **s'amasser** *(foule, troupeau)* to gather *or* to mass (in large numbers); *(preuves)* to accumulate, to pile up

amateur [amatœr] ADJ **1** *(avec ou sans trait d'union) (non professionnel)* amateur *(avant n)*; *Sport* amateur, non-professional; **théâtre a.** amateur theatre; **photographe/peintre a.** amateur photographer/painter; *Sport* **rencontre a.** amateur event **2** *(friand, adepte)* **être a. de qch** to be very interested in sth; **elle est a. de concerts** she's a keen concertgoer
NM **1** *(non professionnel ▸ gén) & Sport* amateur
2 *Péj (dilettante)* dilettante, mere amateur
3 *(connaisseur)* **a. de** connoisseur of; **a. d'art** art lover *or* enthusiast
4 *Fam (preneur)* taker; **il y a des amateurs?** any takers?; **je ne suis pas a.** I'm not interested, I don't go in for that sort of thing
• **d'amateur** ADJ *Péj* amateurish; **c'est du travail d'a.** it's a shoddy piece of work
• **en amateur** ADV non-professionally; **je fais de la compétition en a.** I compete non-professionally *or* as an amateur; **s'intéresser à qch en a.** to have an amateur interest in sth

amateurisme [amatœrism] NM **1** *(gén) & Sport* amateurism, amateur sport **2** *Péj (dilettantisme)* amateurism, amateurishness

amazone [amazon] NF **1** *(cavalière)* horsewoman **2** *(tenue)* (woman's) riding habit; *(jupe)* riding skirt
• **en amazone** ADV **monter en a.** to ride side-saddle

Amazonie [amazoni] NF **l'A.** the Amazon (Basin)

ambages [ɑ̃baʒ] **sans ambages** ADV without beating about the bush

ambassade [ɑ̃basad] NF **1** *(bâtiment)* embassy; **l'a. du Canada** the Canadian Embassy
2 *(fonction)* ambassadorship
3 *(personnel)* embassy (staff)
4 *(mission)* mission; **être envoyé en a. auprès de qn** to be sent on a mission to sb

ambassadeur, -drice [ɑ̃basadœr, -dris] NM,F **1** *(diplomate)* ambassador; **c'est l'a. du Canada** he's the Canadian Ambassador; **a. auprès de** ambassador to; **a. extraordinaire** ambassador extraordinary **2** *Fig (représentant)* representative, ambassador; **vous êtes les ambassadeurs de votre pays** you are ambassadors for your country
• **ambassadrice** NF *(femme d'ambassadeur)* ambassador's wife; *(diplomate)* ambassador, ambassadress

ambassadorial, -ale, -aux, -ales [ɑ̃basadɔrjal, -o] ADJ ambassadorial

ambiance [ɑ̃bjɑ̃s] NF **1** *(atmosphère)* mood, atmosphere; **l'a. qui règne à Paris** the general atmosphere *or* mood in Paris; **l'a. générale du marché** the prevailing mood of the market; **comment créer une a. intime** how to create an intimate atmosphere **2** *(cadre)* surroundings, ambiance **3** *Fam (animation)* **il y a de l'a. ici!** it's pretty lively in here!; **mettre de l'a.** to liven things up; **il va y avoir de l'a. quand elle saura ça!** there'll be hell to pay when she hears this!
• **d'ambiance** ADJ *(éclairage)* soft, subdued; *(musique)* mood *(avant n)*

ambiant, -e [ɑ̃bjɑ̃, -ɑ̃t] ADJ **température ambiante** room temperature; *Tech* ambient temperature; **les préjugés ambiants** the reigning *or* prevailing prejudices

ambidextre [ɑ̃bidɛkstr] ADJ ambidextrous
NMF ambidexter

ambient [ambjɛnt] NM *Mus* ambient, ambient music

ambigu, -ë [ɑ̃bigy] ADJ **1** *(à deux sens)* ambiguous, equivocal; **l'expression est ambiguë** the phrase has two possible meanings *or* is ambiguous; **de façon ambiguë** ambiguously, equivocally **2** *(difficile à cerner)* ambiguous; **c'est un personnage a.** he/she is an ambiguous character

ambiguïté [ɑ̃bigɥite] NF *(équivoque)* ambiguity; **réponse sans a.** unequivocal *or* unambiguous answer; **répondre sans a.** to answer unequivocally *or* unambiguously

ambigument [ɑ̃bigymɑ̃] ADV ambiguously

ambitieuse [ɑ̃bisjøz] *voir* **ambitieux**

ambitieusement [ɑ̃bisjøzmɑ̃] ADV ambitiously

ambitieux, -euse [ɑ̃bisjø, -øz] ADJ ambitious; **trop a.** overambitious
NM,F ambitious man, *f* ambitious woman

ambition [ɑ̃bisjɔ̃] NF **1** *(désir)* ambition, aspiration; **j'ai l'a.** *ou* **mon a. est de...** it's my ambition to... **2** *(désir de réussite)* ambition; **avoir de l'a.** to be ambitious; **je n'ai pas beaucoup d'a.** I'm not particularly ambitious; **être plein d'a.** to be very ambitious; **manquer d'a.** to lack ambition; **un homme sans a.** an unambitious man

ambitionner [3] [ɑ̃bisjɔne] VT *(poste)* to have one's heart set on; **elle ambitionne de monter sur les planches** her ambition is to go on the stage
VPR **s'ambitionner** *Can* to drive oneself hard

ambivalence [ɑ̃bivalɑ̃s] NF ambivalence

ambivalent, -e [ɑ̃bivalɑ̃, -ɑ̃t] ADJ ambivalent

amble [ɑ̃bl] NM *(chameau, cheval)* amble; **aller l'a.** to amble

ambler [3] [ɑ̃ble] VI *Arch* to amble

ambre [ɑ̃br] ADJ INV amber
NM **a. (gris)** ambergris; *Bot* **a. (jaune)** amber

ambré, -e [ɑ̃bre] ADJ *(couleur)* amber; *(parfum)* amber-scented; **un vin a.** an amber-coloured wine

ambroisie [ɑ̃brwazi] NF **1** *Myth* ambrosia **2** *Bot* ragweed, ambrosia

ambulance [ɑ̃bylɑ̃s] NF ambulance; **en a.** in an ambulance; *Fig* **on ne tire pas sur une a.** you shouldn't kick a man when he's down

ambulancier, -ère [ɑ̃bylɑ̃sje, -ɛr] NM,F **1** *(chauffeur)* ambulance driver **2** *(infirmier)* ambulance man, *f* ambulance woman

ambulant, -e [ɑ̃bylɑ̃, -ɑ̃t] ADJ itinerant, travelling; *Fam* **c'est un dictionnaire a.** he's/she's a walking dictionary

ambulatoire [ɑ̃bylatwar] ADJ *Méd & Jur* ambulatory

AME [aœmø] NM *Écon (abrév* **Accord monétaire européen)** EMA

âme [ɑm] NF **1** *(vie)* soul; **avoir l'â. chevillée au corps** to hang on grimly to life; **rendre l'â.** to pass away
2 *(personnalité)* soul, spirit; **avoir** *ou* **être une â. généreuse** to have great generosity of spirit; **avoir une â. de chef** to be a born leader
3 *(principe moral)* **en mon â. et conscience** in all conscience
4 *(cœur)* soul, heart; **faire qch avec/sans â.** to do sth with/without feeling; **sans â.** *(personne)* unfeeling; *(tableau, ville)* soulless, that has no soul; **touché jusqu'au fond de l'â.** deeply moved; **de toute mon â.** with all my heart *or* soul; **c'est un artiste dans l'â.** he's a born artist
5 *(personne)* soul; **un village de cinq cents âmes** a village of five hundred souls; **mon â., ma chère â.** *(en appellatif)* (my) dearest; **â. charitable, bonne â.** kind soul; *Ironique* **il y a toujours de bonnes âmes pour conseiller quand c'est trop tard!** there are always plenty of people ready with helpful advice when it's too late!; **son â. damnée** the person who does his/her evil deeds *or* dirty work for him/her; **aller** *ou* **errer comme une â. en peine** to wander around like a lost soul; **â. sensible** sensitive person; **âmes sensibles, s'abstenir** not for the squeamish; **â. sœur** kindred spirit, soul mate; **il n'y a pas â. qui vive** there isn't a (living) soul around
6 *Littéraire (inspirateur)* soul; *Fig* **c'était elle, l'â. du groupe** she was the inspiration of the group; **celui qui était l'â. du dadaïsme** he who was the moving spirit behind Dadaism
7 *(d'une arme)* bore; **â. rayée** rifled bore
8 *(centre ▸ d'un aimant, d'une statue)* core; *(▸ d'un câble)* heart, core; *(d'une poutre)* web
9 *(d'un violon)* soundpost

améliorable [ameljɔrabl] ADJ improvable, that can be improved

améliorant, -e [ameljɔrɑ̃, -ɑ̃t] ADJ soil-improving

amélioration [ameljɔrasjɔ̃] NF **1** *(action)* improving, bettering; **assurer l'a. des conditions de travail** to ensure that working conditions are improved **2** *(résultat)* improvement; *Ordinat (d'image, de qualité)* enhancement; **apporter des améliorations à qch** to improve on sth, to carry out improvements to sth; **on observe une nette a. de son état de santé** his/her condition has improved considerably; **a. (du temps)** better weather; **pas d'a. prévue cet après-midi** no improvement expected in the weather this afternoon; *Mktg* **a. du produit** product augmentation, product improvement
• **améliorations** NFPL *Jur* improvements; **apporter des améliorations à qch** to carry out improvements to sth

amélioré, -e [ameljɔre] ADJ improved; *(modèle, version)* enhanced; **un petit mousseux a.** a very good quality sparkling wine

améliorer [3] [ameljɔre] VT **1** *(changer en mieux ▸ sol)* to improve; *(▸ relations)* to improve, to make better; *(▸ productivité)* to increase, to improve **2** *(perfectionner ▸ technique)* to improve, to better; **a. son anglais** to improve one's (knowledge of) English **3** *Ordinat (logiciel)* to upgrade; *(image, qualité)* to enhance
VPR **s'améliorer** to improve; **le vin s'améliore en vieillissant** wine improves with age; **le temps s'améliore** the weather's getting better, the weather's improving; **ça ne s'améliore pas** it's not getting any better

amen [amɛn] NM INV *Rel* amen; **tu dis a. à tout ce qu'elle fait** you agree with everything she does

aménagement [amenaʒmɑ̃] NM **1** *(d'une pièce, d'un local)* fitting (out); *(d'un parc)* laying out, designing; *(d'un terrain)* landscaping; **on prévoit l'a. d'un des bureaux en salle de réunion** we're planning to convert one of the offices into a meeting room

2 *Admin* **a. rural** rural development *or* planning; **a. du territoire** town and country planning, regional development; **a. urbain** urban planning; **a. urbain et rural** town and country planning

3 *(refonte ▸ d'un texte)* redrafting, adjusting

4 *(assouplissement)* **a. du temps de travail** flexibility of working hours; **a. fiscal** tax adjustment

• **aménagements** NMPL **aménagements intérieurs** (fixtures and) fittings

aménager [17] [amenaʒe] VT **1** *(parc)* to design, to lay out; *(terrain)* to landscape; *(région)* to develop; **a. une sortie sur une autoroute** to build an exit onto a motorway

2 *(équiper)* to fit out, to equip; **camping aménagé** fully equipped camping site; **plage aménagée** beach with full amenities

3 *(transformer)* **a. une pièce en atelier** to convert a room into a workshop; **grenier aménagé** loft conversion

4 *(installer)* to install, to fit; **a. un placard sous un escalier** to fit *or* to install a cupboard under a staircase

5 *(assouplir ▸ horaire)* to plan, to work out

6 *(refaire ▸ texte)* to adapt, to redraft

amende [amɑ̃d] NF fine; **une a. de 30 euros, 30 euros d'a.** a 30-euro fine; **avoir une a. de 30 euros** to be fined 30 euros; **être condamné à une grosse a.** to be heavily fined; **défense d'entrer sous peine d'a.** *(sur panneau)* trespassers will be fined *or* prosecuted; **a. forfaitaire** on-the-spot fine; **mettre qn à l'a.** to fine sb; *Fig* to penalize sb; **faire a. honorable** to make amends

amendement [amɑ̃dmɑ̃] NM **1** *Jur & Pol* amendment; **a. constitutionnel** constitutional amendment; **a. européen** European amendment **2** *Agr (incorporation)* fertilizing, enrichment; *(substance)* fertilizer

amender [3] [amɑ̃de] VT **1** *Jur & Pol* to amend

2 *Agr* to fertilize

3 *Littéraire (corriger)* to amend

4 *Suisse (infliger d'une amende)* to fine

VPR **s'amender** to mend one's ways, to turn over a new leaf

amène [amɛn] ADJ *Littéraire* affable, amiable; **d'une façon peu a.** in a very unpleasant manner

amenée [amne] **d'amenée** ADJ supply *(avant n)*

amener [19] [amne] VT **1** *(faire venir ▸ personne)* to bring (along); **amenez vos amis!** (do) bring your friends!; **qu'est-ce qui vous amène?** what brings you here?; **a. l'eau à ébullition** to bring the water to the boil; **a. la conversation sur un sujet** to bring the conversation round to a subject; *Fig* **qu'est-ce qui vous a amené à la musique/à Dieu?** what got you involved with music/made you turn to God?

2 *Fam (apporter)* to bring (along)ᵔ; **amène les couteaux** bring *or* get the knives; **j'amènerai mon travail** I'll bring some work along

3 *(acheminer)* to bring, to convey; *(conduire ▸ sujet: véhicule, chemin)* to take; **le pipeline amène le pétrole au terminal** the pipeline brings the oil to the terminal; **les journaux sont amenés par avion** the papers are brought (over) by air; **la petite route vous amène à la plage** the path will take you to the beach

4 *(provoquer ▸ perte, ruine)* to bring about, to cause; *(▸ guerre, maladie, crise)* to bring (on) *or* about, to cause; *(▸ paix)* to bring about

5 *(entraîner)* **mon métier m'amène à voyager** my job involves a lot of travelling; **son travail l'amène à rencontrer beaucoup de monde** he/she meets a lot of people through his/her work; **et ceci nous amène à parler de la ponctualité** which brings us to the question of punctuality

6 *(inciter)* **a. qn à faire qch** to lead sb to do sth; *(en lui parlant)* to talk sb into doing sth

7 *(introduire ▸ sujet)* to introduce; **un bon auteur sait a. le dénouement de son récit** a good author knows how to bring his/her story to a conclusion

8 *Naut (drapeau)* to strike

9 *(tirer ▸ filets)* to draw in

VPR **s'amener** *Fam* to come alongᵔ, to turn up, to show up; **alors, tu t'amènes?** are you coming or aren't you?; **elle s'est amenée avec deux types** she showed up with two guys

> Do not confuse **amener** and **apporter**. The former should be used with animate objects and the latter with inanimate objects.

aménité [amenite] NF *(caractère)* amiability, affability; **sans a.** ungraciously, somewhat curtly

• **aménités** NFPL *Ironique* insults, cutting remarks

aménorrhée [amenɔre] NF *Méd* amenorrhoea

amenuisement [amənɥizmɑ̃] NM *(de rations, de l'espoir)* dwindling; *(des chances)* lessening

amenuiser [3] [amənɥize] VT **1** *(amincir ▸ planche, bande)* to thin down **2** *(diminuer ▸ économies, espoir)* to diminish, to reduce

VPR **s'amenuiser** *(rations, espoir)* to dwindle, to run low; *(chances)* to grow *or* to get slimmer; *(distance)* to grow smaller

amer, -ère [amɛr] ADJ **1** *(fruit)* bitter **2** *Fig (déception)* bitter

NM *(alcool)* bitters

amèrement [amɛrmɑ̃] ADV bitterly

américain, -e [amerikɛ̃, -ɛn] ADJ American

NM **1** *Ling* American English **2** *Belg Fam Culin (steak tartare)* steak tartareᵔ

• **Américain, -e** NM,F American

• **américaine** NF **1** *(voiture)* American car **2** *(course cycliste)* track relay (race)

• **à l'américaine** ADJ **1** *Archit* American-style **2** *Culin* à l'américaine *(cooked with tomatoes)*

américanisation [amerikanizasjɔ̃] NF Americanization

américaniser [3] [amerikanize] VT to Americanize

VPR **s'américaniser** to become Americanized

américanisme [amerikanism] NM **1** *(science)* American studies **2** *(tournure)* Americanism

américaniste [amerikanist] ADJ *(étudiant)* specializing in American studies

NMF Americanist

amérindien, -enne [amerɛ̃djɛ̃, -ɛn] ADJ Amerindian, American Indian

• **Amérindien, -enne** NM,F Amerindian, American Indian

Amérique [amerik] NF **l'A.** America; **l'A. centrale/latine/du Nord/du Sud** Central/Latin/North/South America

amerlo [amɛrlo] NMF *Fam Vieilli* Yank, Yankee

amerloque [amɛrlɔk] NMF *Fam* Yank, Yankee

amerlot [amɛrlo] = **amerlo**

amerrir [32] [amerir] VI *Aviat* to land (on the sea), to make a sea landing; *Astron* to splash down

amerrissage [amerisaʒ] NM *Aviat* sea landing; *Astron* splashdown; *Aviat* **faire un a. forcé** to make an emergency landing at sea

amertume [amɛrtym] NF bitterness; **être plein d'a.** to be very bitter; **avec a.** bitterly

améthyste [ametist] NF *Minér* amethyst

ameublement [amœbləmɑ̃] NM **1** *(meubles)* furniture; **articles d'a.** furnishings **2** *(installation)* furnishing; *(décoration)* (interior) decoration

ameublir [32] [amœblir] VT **1** *Agr (sol)* to loosen, to break down **2** *Jur & Fin (biens immobiliers)* to convert into personalty

ameublissement [amœblismɑ̃] NM **1** *Agr (du sol)* loosening, breaking up **2** *Jur & Fin (biens immobiliers)* conversion into personalty, inclusion in the communal estate

ameuter [4] [amœte] VT **1** *(attirer l'attention de)* **le bruit a ameuté les passants** the noise drew a crowd of passers-by; **a. l'opinion publique sur qch** to awaken public opinion to sth; **il faut a. la presse** we must get the press onto this **2** *(chiens)* to form into a pack

VPR **s'ameuter** to gather, to band together

AMF [aemɛf] NF *Bourse (abrév* **Autorité des marchés financiers)** = French Stock Exchange authority

AMI [aemi] NM *Fin (abrév* **Accord multilatéral sur l'investissement)** MAI

ami, -e [ami] ADJ *(voix, peuple, rivage)* friendly; **un pays a.** a friendly country, an ally; **dans une maison amie** in the house of friends

NM,F **1** *(camarade)* friend; **c'est un de mes amis/une de mes amies** he's/she's a friend of mine; *Fam* **des amis à nous** friends of ours; **Tom et moi sommes restés amis** I stayed friends with Tom; **un médecin de mes amis** a doctor friend of mine; **un a. de la famille** *ou* **maison** a friend of the family; **se faire un a. de qn** to make friends with sb; **je m'en suis fait une amie** she became my friend *or* a friend (of mine); **devenir l'a. de qn** to become friends *or* friendly with sb; **ne pas avoir d'amis** to have no friends; **être entre amis** to be among friends; **amis d'enfance** childhood friends; **les amis de mes amis sont mes amis** any friend of yours is a friend of mine

2 *(amoureux)* boyfriend; *(amoureuse)* girlfriend; **petit a.** boyfriend; **petite amie** girlfriend

3 *(bienfaiteur)* **l'a. des pauvres/du peuple** the friend of the poor/of the people; **un a. des arts** a patron of the arts; **les amis de la nature/des bêtes** nature/animal lovers

4 *(comme interjection)* **mon pauvre a.!** you poor fool!; **écoutez, mon jeune a.!** now look here, young man!; **mon a.!** *(entre amis)* my friend!; *(entre époux)* (my) dear!

5 *Fam (locution)* **il a essayé de faire a.-a. avec moi** he came on all buddy-buddy with me

• **en ami** ADV *(par amitié)* as a friend; *(en non-professionnel)* as a friend, on a friendly basis; **je te le dis en a.** I'm telling you as a friend *or* because I'm your friend; **vous êtes là professionnellement ou en a.?** are you here in your professional capacity or as a friend?

amiable [amjabl] ADJ *(accord, compromis)* amicable, friendly; *Jur* **a. compositeur** = arbitrator who makes a decision in accordance with what is fair rather than in accordance with the law

• **à l'amiable** ADV privately, amicably; **régler qch à l'a.** *(gén)* to reach an amicable agreement about sth; *(sans procès)* to settle sth out of court

ADJ **divorce à l'a.** no-fault divorce

amiante [amjɑ̃t] NM *Minér* asbestos

amibe [amib] NF *Biol* amoeba

amibiase [amibjaz] NF *Méd* amoebiasis

amibien, -enne [amibjɛ̃, -ɛn] ADJ *Méd* amoebic

amical, -e, -aux, -ales [amikal, -o] ADJ friendly; **peu a.** unfriendly; **un match a.** a friendly (match)

• **amicale** NF association, club

amicalement [amikalmɑ̃] ADV in a friendly manner; **discuter a.** to have a friendly chat; **bien a.** *(en fin de lettre)* yours

amide [amid] NM *Chim* amide

amidon [amidɔ̃] NM *Chim* starch

amidonnage [amidɔnaʒ] NM *Tex* starching

amidonner [3] [amidɔne] VT *Tex* to starch

amigne [amiɲ] NF *Suisse* = grape variety from the Valais canton, or white wine produced from these grapes

amincir [32] [amɛ̃sir] VT **1** *(amaigrir)* to make thin *or* thinner; *(rendre svelte)* to slim down; **cette veste t'amincit** this jacket makes you look slimmer; **je cherche une coiffure qui amincisse le visage** I'm looking for a hairstyle that'll make my face look thinner **2** *(planche)* to fine down, to thin down

VPR **s'amincir** to get thin *or* thinner

amincissant, -e [amɛ̃sisɑ̃, -ɑ̃t] ADJ slimming, *Am* reducing

amincissement [amɛ̃sismɑ̃] NM *(d'une épaisseur)* thinning down; *(d'une personne, de la taille, des hanches)* slimming; **après deux mois de régime, elle a constaté un a. de la taille de 2 cm** after dieting for two months, she found that she had lost 2 cm from around the waist

amine [amin] NF *Chim* amine

aminé, -e [amine] *voir* **acide**

aminoacide [aminoasid] NM *Chim* amino acid

amiral, -e, -aux, -ales [amiral, -o] ADJ **vaisseau** *ou* **navire a.** flagship

NM admiral; **a. de la flotte** Admiral of the Fleet

• **amirale** NF admiral's wife

amirauté [amirote] NF *Naut & Mil (corps des amiraux)* admiralty; *(grade)* admiralship, admiralty; **accéder à l'a.** to become an admiral

amitié [amitje] NF **1** *(sentiment)* friendship; **faire qch par a.** to do sth out of friendship; **se lier d'a. avec qn** to make friends *or* to strike up a friendship with sb; **prendre qn en a., se prendre d'a. pour qn** to befriend sb, to make friends with sb; **avoir de l'a. pour qn** to be fond of sb; **l'a. qui lie nos deux pays** the friendship between our two countries **2** *(relation)* friendship; **lier** *ou* **nouer une a. avec qn** to strike up a friendship with sb; *Euph* **a. particulière** homosexual relationship, special relationship **3** *(faveur)* kindness, favour; **faites-moi l'a. de rester** please do me the kindness *or* favour of staying

• **amitiés** NFPL *(salutations, compliments)* **faites-lui** *ou* **présentez-lui mes amitiés** give him/her my best regards *or* wishes; **mes amitiés à vos parents** best regards to your parents; **(toutes) mes amitiés** *(en fin de lettre)* best regards *or* wishes; **amitiés, Marie** *(en fin de lettre)* love *or* yours, Marie

amitieux, -euse [amitjø, -øz] ADJ *Belg* friendly, affectionate

ammoniac, -aque [amɔnjak] ADJ *Chim* ammoniac; **gaz a.** ammonia; **sel a.** salt ammoniac
NM *Chim* ammonia

ammoniacal, -e, -aux, -ales [amɔnjakal, -o] ADJ *Chim* ammoniacal

ammoniaque [amɔnjak] *voir* **ammoniac**

ammoniaqué, -e [amɔnjake] ADJ *Chim* ammoniated

ammonite [amɔnit] NF *Zool & Géol* ammonite

amnésie [amnezi] NF *Méd* amnesia; **souffrir d'a.** to have amnesia

amnésique [amnezik] *Méd* ADJ *(patient)* amnesic; **être a.** to have amnesia
NMF amnesic, amnesiac

amniocentèse [amnjɔsɛ̃tɛz] NF *Méd* amniocentesis

amnioscopie [amnjɔskɔpi] NF *Méd* amnioscopy

amniotique [amnjɔtik] ADJ *Anat & Obst* amniotic

amnistie [amnisti] NF *Jur* amnesty; **accorder une a. à qn** to grant sb amnesty; **l'a. des contraventions** = traditional waiving of parking fines by the French president after a presidential election

> **AMNISTIE**
>
> Parking fines as well as some prison sentences are traditionally waived by the French president immediately after a presidential election. The latter is known as "la grâce présidentielle".

amnistier [9] [amnistje] VT *Jur (personne)* to grant an amnesty to, to amnesty; *(délit)* to grant amnesty for

amocher [3] [amɔʃe] *Fam* VT *(meubles, vêtements)* to ruin[□], to mess up; *(voiture)* to bash up; *(adversaire, boxeur)* to smash up; *(visage, jambe)* to mess up; **se faire a.** to get smashed up; *très Fam* **il s'est fait a. le portrait** he got his face smashed in
VPR **s'amocher** to get badly bashed; **il s'est salement amoché le genou en tombant de vélo** he fell off his bike and really messed up his knee

amoindrir [32] [amwɛ̃drir] VT **1** *(faire diminuer ▸ valeur, importance)* to diminish, to reduce; *(▸ forces)* to weaken; *(▸ autorité, faculté)* to weaken, to lessen, to diminish; *(▸ réserves)* to diminish **2** *(rendre moins capable)* to weaken, to diminish; **il est sorti de son accident très amoindri** *(physiquement)* his accident left him physically much weaker; *(moralement)* his accident left him psychologically impaired; **se sentir amoindri** to feel weakened
VPR **s'amoindrir** *(autorité, forces)* to weaken, to grow weaker; *(réserves)* to diminish, to dwindle

amoindrissement [amwɛ̃drismɑ̃] NM *(d'une autorité, de facultés)* weakening; *(de forces)* diminishing, weakening; *(de réserves)* reduction, diminishing

amollir [32] [amɔlir] VT *(beurre, pâte)* to soften, to make soft; *(volonté, forces)* to weaken, to diminish; **a. qn** *(l'adoucir)* to soften sb; *(l'affaiblir)* to weaken sb
VPR **s'amollir 1** *(beurre, pâte, plastique)* to soften, to become soft **2** *(s'affaiblir ▸ énergie, courage)* to weaken

amollissement [amɔlismɑ̃] NM debilitation

amonceler [24] [amɔ̃sle] VT **1** *(entasser ▸ boîtes, livres, chaussures)* to heap up, to pile up; *(▸ neige, sable, feuilles)* to bank up; *(▸ vivres, richesses)* to amass, to hoard **2** *(rassembler ▸ documents, preuves, informations)* to amass
VPR **s'amonceler** *(papiers, boîtes, feuilles)* to heap up, to pile up; *(preuves)* to accumulate, to pile up; *(dettes)* to mount, to pile up; *(neige, sable, nuages)* to bank up

amoncellement [amɔ̃sɛlmɑ̃] NM *(d'objets divers, d'ordures)* heap, pile; *(de neige, de sable, de feuilles, de nuages)* heap; *(de richesses)* hoard; **devant cet a. de preuves** faced with this wealth of evidence

amoncellerai *etc voir* **amonceler**

amont [amɔ̃] NM *(d'une rivière)* upstream water; *(d'une montagne)* uphill slope; **vent d'a.** land breeze; **vers l'a.** *(d'une rivière)* upstream
ADJ INV *(ski, skieur)* uphill *(avant n)*

• **en amont** ADV *aussi Fig* upstream

• **en amont de** PRÉP *(rivière)* upstream from; *(montagne)* uphill from, above; **la Tamise en a. de Londres** the Thames upstream from London; *Fig* **les étapes en a. de la production** the stages upstream of production, the pre-production stages

amoral, -e, -aux, -ales [amɔral, -o] ADJ amoral

amoralité [amɔralite] NF amorality

amorçage [amɔrsaʒ] NM **1** *Tech (d'une pompe, d'une cartouche)* priming; *(d'un arc électrique)* striking **2** *Pêche* baiting **3** *Ordinat* booting

amorce [amɔrs] NF **1** *Tech (détonateur)* primer, detonator; *(d'une balle)* cap, primer; *(pétard)* cap; **pistolet à amorces** cap gun
2 *Pêche* bait
3 *(début)* beginning; **l'a. d'une réforme** the beginnings of a reform
4 *Cin* leader

amorcer [16] [amɔrse] VT **1** *(commencer ▸ travaux)* to start, to begin; *(▸ réforme)* to initiate, to begin; *(▸ discussion, réconciliation)* to start, to begin, to initiate; *(▸ virage)* to go into; *(▸ descente)* to start, to begin; **les travaux sont bien amorcés** the work is well under way; **elle amorça un pas vers la porte** she made as if to go to the door
2 *Tech (pompe, cartouche)* to prime; *(arc)* to strike
3 *Pêche* to bait
4 *Ordinat* to boot (up); **a. de nouveau** to reboot
VPR **s'amorcer 1** *(commencer)* to begin; **le processus ne fait que s'a.** the process has only just begun *or* got under way **2** *Ordinat* to boot (up)

amorçoir [amɔrswar] NM **1** *Pêche* bait box **2** *Tech (arme)* gunpowder container

amorphe [amɔrf] ADJ **1** *Fam (indolent)* lifeless[□], passive[□]; **cette chaleur me rend totalement a.** this heat is making me lethargic *or* listless[□] **2** *Biol & Chim* amorphous

amorti [amɔrti] NM **1** *Ftbl* **faire un a.** to trap the ball **2** *Tennis* drop shot

amortir [32] [amɔrtir] VT **1** *(absorber ▸ choc)* to cushion, to absorb; *(▸ son)* to deaden, to muffle; *(▸ douleur)* to deaden; **l'herbe a amorti sa chute** the grass broke his/her fall; **a. le coup** to cushion *or* to soften the blow; *Fig* to soften the blow
2 *(rentabiliser)* **il a amorti sa nouvelle voiture en six mois** he recouped the cost of his new car in six months; **le matériel a été amorti dès la première année** the equipment paid for itself by the end of the first year, the cost of the equipment was written off by the end of the first year
3 *Fin (dette)* to pay off, to amortize; *(prêt)* to repay; *(équipement)* to depreciate, to write off, to amortize; *(investissement)* to amortize; *Bourse (titre)* to redeem
4 *Ftbl (ballon)* to trap; *Tennis (balle)* to kill
VPR **s'amortir 1** *(dépenses, investissement)* to pay for itself; **un achat qui s'amortit en deux ans** *Écon* a purchase that can be paid off in two years; *Bourse* a purchase that can be redeemed in two years **2** *(s'affaiblir ▸ bruit)* to fade (away)

amortissable [amɔrtisabl] ADJ *(dette)* redeemable

amortissant [amɔrtisɑ̃] ADJ shock-absorbent

amortissement [amɔrtismɑ̃] NM **1** *(adoucissement ▸ d'un choc)* absorption, cushioning; *(▸ d'un coup)* cushioning; *(▸ d'un son)* deadening, muffling **2** *Fin (d'une dette)* paying *or* writing off; *(d'un titre)* redemption; *(d'un emprunt)* paying off, amortization **3** *Compta (perte de valeur)* depreciation; **l'a. d'un équipement est plus rapide si on emprunte à court terme** equipment pays for itself faster if it's paid for with a short-term loan; **a. accéléré** accelerated depreciation; **a. annuel** annual depreciation; **a. anticipé** redemption before due date; **a. du capital** depreciation of capital; **a. dégressif** declining balance depreciation, sliding scale depreciation; **a. linéaire** straight-line depreciation, diminishing balance (method)

amortisseur [amɔrtisœr] NM shock absorber; **a. de vibrations** vibration damper; **a. à gaz** gas strut; **a. hydraulique** hydraulic shock absorber, hydraulic damper; **a. pneumatique** air cushion

amour [amur] NM **1** *(sentiment)* love; **une vie sans a.** a loveless life; **son a. des** *ou* **pour les enfants** his/her love of *or* for children; **l'a. de ma mère** *(qu'elle a pour moi)* my mother's love; *(que j'ai pour elle)* my love for my mother; **le grand a.** true love; **éprouver de l'a. pour qn** to feel love for sb; **aimer qn d'a.** to be in love with sb; **être fou d'a. pour qn** to be madly in love with sb; *Can* **être/tomber en a. (avec qn)** to be/fall in love (with sb); **l'a. filial** *(d'un fils)* a son's love; *(d'une fille)* a daughter's love; **l'a. libre** free love; **l'a. maternel/paternel** motherly/fatherly love, a mother's/father's love; **l'a. du prochain** love of one's neighbour
2 *(amant)* lover, love; **un a. de jeunesse** an old flame
3 *(liaison)* (love) affair, romance; **ils ont vécu un grand a.** they had a passionate affair
4 *(acte sexuel)* love-making; **faire l'a. à** *ou* **avec qn** to make love to *or* with sb; **pendant/après l'a.** while/after making love
5 *(vif intérêt)* love; **l'a. de la nature** love of nature; **l'a. de la justice** passion for justice; **faire qch avec a.** to do sth with loving care *or* with love
6 *(terme affectueux)* **mon a.** my love *or* darling; **un a. de petite fille** a delightful little girl; **apporte les glaçons, tu seras un a.** be a darling and bring the ice
7 *Beaux-Arts* cupid

• **amours** NFPL *Hum (relations amoureuses)* love life; **comment vont tes amours?** how's your love life (these days)?; **à vos amours!** *(pour trinquer)* cheers!, here's to you!; *(après un éternuement)* bless you!
NMPL *Suisse (vin)* **les amours** = the last drops of wine in a bottle

• **d'amour** ADJ *(chagrin, chanson)* love *(avant n)*

• **par amour** ADV out of *or* for love; **par a. pour qn** for the love of sb

• **pour l'amour de** PRÉP for the love *or* sake of; **pour l'a. de Dieu!** *(ton suppliant)* for the love of God!; *(ton irrité)* for God's sake!; **pour l'a. du ciel!** for heaven's sake!; **faire qch pour l'a. de l'art** to do sth for the sake of it

amouracher [3] [amuraʃe] **s'amouracher** VPR **s'a. de qn** to become infatuated with sb

amourette [amurɛt] NF *(liaison)* casual love affair

• **amourettes** NFPL *Culin* marrowbone jelly *(UNCOUNT)*

amoureuse [amurøz] *voir* **amoureux**

amoureusement [amurøzmɑ̃] ADV lovingly; **il la regardait a.** he watched her lovingly *or* with love in his eyes

amoureux, -euse [amurø, -øz] ADJ **1** *(tendre ▸ regard, geste)* loving, tender; *(vie, exploit)* love *(avant n)* **2** *(épris)* **un homme a.** a man in love; **être a. de qn** to be in love with sb; **ils sont a. (l'un de l'autre)** they're in love (with each other); **tomber a. de qn** to fall in love with sb; **être éperdument** *ou* **follement a. de qn** to be head over heels *or* madly in love with sb; **être fou a.** *ou* **a. fou** to be madly in love **3** *(amateur)* **elle est amoureuse de la montagne** she has a passion for mountains

NM,F 1 *(amant)* lover; **un couple d'a.** a pair of lovers **2** *(adepte)* lover; **a. des beaux-arts** a lover of fine arts; **les a. de la nature** nature-lovers

• **en amoureux ADV si nous sortions en a. ce soir?** how about going out tonight, just the two of us?

amour-propre [amurprɔpr] *(pl* **amours-propres)** **NM** pride; **elle est blessée dans son a.** her pride is hurt

amovible [amɔvibl] **ADJ** *(housse, doublure, couvercle, manche)* removable, detachable; *(col)* detachable; *Ordinat (disque dur)* removable

AMP [aɛmpe] **NF** *Méd (abrév* **assistance médicale à la procréation)** (medically) assisted conception

ampérage [ɑ̃peraʒ] **NM** *Élec* amperage

ampère [ɑ̃pɛr] **NM** *Élec* ampere

ampère-heure [ɑ̃pɛrœr] *(pl* **ampères-heures)** **NM** *Élec* ampere hour

ampèremètre [ɑ̃pɛrmɛtr] **NM** *Élec* ammeter, amperometer

amphé [ɑ̃fe] **NF** *Fam Pharm (amphétamine)* speed

amphétamine [ɑ̃fetamin] **NF** *Pharm* amphetamine

amphi [ɑ̃fi] **NM** *Fam (abrév* **amphithéâtre)** lecture hall□ *or Br* theatre□

amphibie [ɑ̃fibi] **ADJ** *Aviat & Mil* amphibious

NM *Écol* amphibian

amphibien [ɑ̃fibjɛ̃] *Zool* **NM** amphibian

• **amphibiens NMPL** Amphibia

amphithéâtre [ɑ̃fiteɑtr] **NM** *Antiq* amphitheatre; *Univ* lecture hall *or* theatre; *(d'un théâtre)* amphitheatre, (upper) gallery; *(salle de dissection)* dissection room

amphore [ɑ̃fɔr] **NF** *Antiq* amphora

ample [ɑ̃pl] **ADJ 1** *(large ▸ pull)* loose, baggy; *(▸ cape, jupe)* flowing, full **2** *(mouvement, geste)* wide, sweeping; *(style)* rich; *(voix)* sonorous **3** *(abondant ▸ stock, provisions)* extensive, ample; **de plus amples renseignements** further details *or* information

amplement [ɑ̃pləmɑ̃] **ADV** fully, amply; **gagner a. sa vie** to make a very comfortable living; **ça suffit a., c'est a. suffisant** that's more than enough; **nous avons a. le temps** we have plenty of time

ampleur [ɑ̃plœr] **NF 1** *(largeur ▸ d'un pull)* looseness; *(▸ d'une cape, d'une jupe)* fullness; **coupez en biais pour donner plus d'a.** cut on the bias to give more fullness **2** *(rondeur ▸ d'un mouvement, d'un geste)* fullness **3** *(importance ▸ d'un projet)* scope; *(▸ d'un stock, de ressources)* abundance; **l'a. de la crise** the scale *or* extent of the crisis; **des événements d'une telle a.** events of such magnitude; **prendre de l'a.** to gain in importance

ampli [ɑ̃pli] **NM** *Fam (abrév* **amplificateur)** amp

amplificateur, -trice [ɑ̃plifikatœr, -tris] **ADJ** *Élec & Phys* amplifying; *Opt* magnifying; *Phot* enlarging

NM 1 *Élec & Rad* amplifier; **a. de puissance** power amplifier **2** *Phot* enlarger

• **amplificatrice NF** *Phot* enlarger

amplification [ɑ̃plifikasjɔ̃] **NF 1** *Élec & Phys* amplification, amplifying; *Phot (action)* enlarging, enlargement; *Opt* magnifying **2** *(développement ▸ d'une tendance, de tensions)* development, increase; *(▸ d'un conflit)* deepening; *(▸ d'une différence)* widening; *(▸ d'échanges, de relations)* development, expansion **3** *Péj (exagération)* exaggeration, magnification

amplificatrice [ɑ̃plifikatris] *voir* **amplificateur**

amplifier [9] [ɑ̃plifje] **VT 1** *Élec & Phys* to amplify; *Opt* to magnify; *Phot* to enlarge **2** *(développer ▸ tendance, tensions)* to develop, to increase; *(▸ conflit)* to deepen; *(▸ différence)* to widen; *(▸ échanges, relations)* to develop, to expand **3** *Péj (exagérer)* to exaggerate, to magnify; **les médias ont amplifié le scandale** the scandal has been blown up out of all proportion by the media

VPR s'amplifier *(augmenter ▸ courant, tendance)* to develop, to increase; *(▸ conflit)* to deepen; *(▸ tensions, revendications, hausse)* to increase; *(▸ différence)* to widen; *(▸ échanges, relations)* to develop, to expand

ampliforme [ɑ̃plifɔrm] **ADJ soutien-gorge a.** padded bra

NM *(soutien-gorge)* padded bra

amplitude [ɑ̃plityd] **NF 1** *Astron, Math & Phys* amplitude

2 *Météo* range; **a. thermique** temperature range **3** *Écon* **a. des fluctuations** amplitude of fluctuations

4 *Littéraire (étendue)* magnitude, extent

ampoule [ɑ̃pul] **NF 1** *Élec* bulb; **a. à baïonnette/vis** bayonet/screw-in bulb; *Phot* **a. de flash** flashbulb, flashlight **2** *(récipient)* phial, vial; **a. autocassable** break-open phial *or* vial **3** *(cloque)* blister; *Fam Hum* **toi, tu ne vas pas attraper** *ou* **te faire des ampoules!** don't strain yourself, will you!

ampoulé, -e [ɑ̃pule] **ADJ** *Péj* pompous, bombastic

amputation [ɑ̃pytasjɔ̃] **NF 1** *Méd* amputation **2** *Fig (suppression)* removal, cutting out; **ce texte a subi de nombreuses amputations** this text has been heavily cut

amputé, -e [ɑ̃pyte] **NM,F** *Méd* amputee

amputer [3] [ɑ̃pyte] **VT 1** *Méd (membre)* to amputate, to remove; **a. un bras à qn** to amputate sb's arm; **elle a été amputée d'un pied** she had a foot amputated **2** *(ôter une partie de ▸ texte)* to cut (down), to reduce; *(▸ budget)* to cut back; **l'article a été amputé d'un tiers** the article was cut by a third; **le pays a été amputé de deux provinces** the country lost two provinces; **le palais a été amputé de son aile sud** the south wing of the palace was demolished

amulette [amylɛt] **NF** amulet

amusant, -e [amyzɑ̃, -ɑ̃t] **ADJ 1** *(drôle)* funny, amusing; **les gags ne sont même pas amusants** the jokes aren't even funny; **le plus a., c'est que...** the funniest *or* most amusing thing is that... **2** *(divertissant)* entertaining; **je vais t'apprendre un petit jeu a.** I'm going to teach you an entertaining little game **3** *(curieux)* funny; **tiens, c'est a., je n'avais pas remarqué...** that's funny, I hadn't noticed...

amuse-gueule [amyzgœl] *(pl* **inv** *ou* **amuse-gueules)** **NM** *Culin* appetizer; **des a.** *ou* **amuse-gueules** appetizers, *Br* nibbles

amusement [amyzmɑ̃] **NM 1** *(sentiment)* amusement; **à son grand a.** much to his/her amusement **2** *(chose divertissante)* entertainment; *(jeu)* recreational activity, pastime; *Ironique* **tu parles d'un a.!** this isn't exactly my idea of fun!

amuser [3] [amyze] **VT 1** *(faire rire)* to make laugh, to amuse; **elle m'amuse** she makes me laugh; **cela ne m'amuse pas du tout** I don't find that in the least bit funny; **ah, ça t'amuse, toi!** you think that's funny, do you?; **il nous a regardés d'un air amusé** he looked at us in amusement; *Fam* **a. la galerie** to play to the gallery

2 *(plaire à)* to appeal to; **ça ne l'amuse pas de travailler chez eux** he/she doesn't enjoy *or* like working there; **tu crois que ça m'amuse d'être pris pour un imbécile?** do you think I enjoy being taken for a fool?; **si ça t'amuse, fais-le** do it if that's what you want, if it makes you happy, do it

3 *(divertir)* to entertain

VPR s'amuser 1 *(jouer ▸ enfant)* to play; **elle s'amuse dehors avec son cousin** she's outside playing with her cousin; **à cet âge-là, on s'amuse avec presque rien** at that age, they amuse themselves very easily; **s'a. avec** *(manipuler)* to fiddle *or* to play with

2 *(se divertir)* to have fun; **je ne me suis jamais autant amusé** I've never had so much fun; **ils se sont bien amusés** they really had a good time; **amusez-vous bien!** enjoy yourselves!, have a good time!; **qu'est-ce qu'on s'est amusés!** we had so much fun!; **mais, papa, c'était pour s'a.!** but, dad, we were only having fun!; **ils ne vont pas s'a. avec le nouveau colonel** they won't have much fun with the new colonel; **s'a. aux dépens de qn** to make fun of sb

3 s'a. à faire qch *(jouer à)* to have fun doing sth; *(s'occuper à)* to be busy doing sth; **ils s'amusaient à imiter le professeur** they were having fun imitating the teacher; **ils s'amusent à dessiner** they're busy drawing; **il s'amuse à faire des avions en papier en cours** he spends his time making paper aeroplanes in class; **si tu crois que je vais m'a. à ça!** if you think I have nothing better to do!; *Fam* **si je dois m'a. à tout lui expliquer, j'ai pas fini!** if I've got to go and explain everything to him/her, I'll still be there next week!; **ne t'amuse pas à toucher ce fil!** don't you (go and) touch *or* go touching that wire!

> Il faut noter que le verbe anglais **to amuse oneself** est un faux ami. Il signifie **s'occuper, passer le temps.**

amusette [amyzɛt] **NF 1** *(distraction)* idle amusement **2** *Belg (personne frivole)* frivolous person

amuseur, -euse [amyzœr, -øz] **NM,F 1** *(artiste)* entertainer **2** *Péj (personne peu sérieuse)* smooth talker

amygdale [amidal] **NF** *Anat* tonsil; **se faire opérer des amygdales** to have one's tonsils removed *or* out

amygdalectomie [amidalɛktɔmi] **NF** *Méd* tonsillectomy

amygdalite [amidalit] **NF** *Méd* tonsillitis

an [ɑ̃] **NM 1** *(durée de douze mois)* year; **dans un an** one year from now; **encore deux ans et je m'arrête** two more years and then I'll stop; **une amitié de 20 ans** a friendship of 20 years' standing; **un prêt sur 20 ans** a loan over 20 years; **un an plus tard** *ou* **après** one year *or* twelve months later; **voilà deux ans qu'elle est partie** she's been gone for two years now; **par an** a year; **deux fois par an** twice a year; **je gagne tant par an** I earn so much a year *or* per year; **tous les ans** *(gén)* every *or* each year; *(publier, réviser)* yearly, on a yearly basis; **bon an mal an, je dois gagner dans les 20000 euros** in an average year, I earn 20,000 euros, on average, I earn 20,000 euros a year **2** *(avec l'art déf) (division du calendrier)* (calendar) year; **l'an dernier** *ou* **passé** last year; **l'an prochain** next year; **en l'an 10 apr. J.-C.** in (the year) 10 AD; **en l'an 200 avant notre ère** in (the year) 200 BC; **en l'an 2000** in the year 2000; **le jour** *ou* **le premier de l'an** New Year's Day; *Fam* **je m'en fiche** *ou* **moque comme de l'an quarante!** I don't give two hoots! **3** *(pour exprimer l'âge)* **à trois ans** at three (years of age); **elle a cinq ans** she's five (years old); **on fête ses vingt ans** we're celebrating his/her twentieth birthday; **un enfant de cinq ans** a five-year-old (child)

anabaptisme [anabatism] **NM** *Rel* Anabaptism

anabaptiste [anabatist] **ADJ & NMF** *Rel* Anabaptist

anabolisant, -e [anabɔlizɑ̃, -ɑ̃t] *Biol* **ADJ** anabolic

NM anabolic steroid

anabolisme [anabɔlism] **NM** *Physiol* anabolism

anacarde [anakard] **NM** *Bot* cashew (nut)

anacardier [anakardje] **NM** *Bot* cashew (tree)

anachorète [anakɔrɛt] **NM** recluse; *Rel* anchorite; *Fig* **il mène une vie d'a.** he lives the life of a recluse

anachronique [anakrɔnik] **ADJ** anachronistic, anachronic

anachronisme [anakrɔnism] **NM** anachronism

anaconda [anakɔ̃da] **NM** *Zool* anaconda, eunectes

anaérobie [anaerɔbi] *Biol* **ADJ** anaerobic

NM anaerobe

anagrammatique [anagramatik] **ADJ** anagrammatic(al)

anagramme [anagram] **NF** *Ling* anagram

ANAH [ana, ɑenɑaʃ] **NF** *(abrév* **Agence nationale pour l'amélioration de l'habitat)** = national agency responsible for housing projects and restoration grants

anal, -e, -aux, -ales [anal, -o] **ADJ** *Anat & Psy* anal

analeptique [analɛptik] *Méd* **ADJ** analeptic

NM analeptic

analgésie [analʒezi] **NF** *Méd* analgesia

analgésique [analʒezik] Pharm ADJ analgesic
NM analgesic

anallergique [analɛrʒik] ADJ Méd hypoallergenic

analogie [analɔʒi] NF analogy; il y a une a. entre ces deux histoires there's an analogy between the two stories; trouver une a. entre deux choses to draw an analogy between two things
• **par analogie** ADV by analogy; par a. avec by analogy with

analogique [analɔʒik] ADJ 1 (présentant un rapport) analogical; dictionnaire a. thesaurus 2 Ordinat analog; calculateur a. analog computer; convertisseur a. numérique analog-to-digital converter

analogue [analɔg] ADJ analogous, similar; a. par la forme analogous in shape; une histoire a. à une autre a story similar to another one
NM analogue; ce mot anglais n'a pas d'a. en français this English word has no equivalent in French

analphabète [analfabɛt] ADJ & NMF illiterate

analphabétisme [analfabetism] NM illiteracy

analysable [analizabl] ADJ 1 (que l'on peut examiner) analysable 2 Ordinat scannable

analyse [analiz] NF 1 (étude) analysis; cet argument ne résiste pas à l'a. this argument doesn't stand up to analysis; l'a. des faits montre que... an examination of the facts shows that...; en dernière a. in the last or final analysis, when all is said and done, all things considered; Com a. des besoins needs analysis; Com & Mktg a. conjointe conjoint analysis, trade-off analysis; Compta & Fin a. des coûts cost analysis; Compta & Fin a. coûts-bénéfices cost-benefit analysis; Compta & Fin a. de coût et d'efficacité cost-effectiveness analysis; Compta & Fin a. coût-profit cost-benefit analysis; Compta & Fin a. des coûts et rendements cost-benefit analysis; a. démographique demographic analysis; a. des écarts variance analysis; a. économique economic analysis; a. de faisabilité feasibility study; Mktg a. des forces et faiblesses strengths and weaknesses analysis; Mktg a. des forces, faiblesses, opportunités et menaces SWOT analysis; a. de marché market survey or research; a. du marché market analysis; a. des marchés market research; a. des médias media analysis; Mktg a. des opportunités et des menaces opportunity and threat analysis; Compta & Fin a. du point mort break-even analysis; a. de portefeuille portfolio analysis; a. des postes de travail job analysis; Compta & Fin a. du prix de revient cost analysis; a. de produit product analysis; Compta & Fin a. du rendement rate of return analysis; a. des résultats processing of results; a. des risques risk analysis; a. par secteur d'activité segment reporting; Mktg a. par segment cluster analysis; a. du style de vie lifestyle analysis; a. des tendances trend analysis; a. de valeur value analysis or engineering; a. des ventes sales analysis
2 Scol analysis; faire l'a. d'un texte to analyse a text; a. de texte textual analysis; Gram a. logique/grammaticale sentence/grammatical analysis; faire une a. grammaticale to parse; faites l'a. grammaticale de cette phrase parse this sentence
3 Biol analysis; a. de sang blood analysis or test; faire une a. de sang to have a blood test
4 Psy analysis, psychoanalysis; être en a. to be in analysis; faire une a. to undergo analysis
5 Ordinat analysis; Électron scan, scanning; a. de données data analysis; a. factorielle factor analysis; a. fonctionnelle functional or systems analysis; a. lexicale lexical scan; a. numérique numerical analysis; a. organique systems design; a. des performances du système system evaluation; Ordinat a. de système, a. systémique systems analysis
6 Chim & Math analysis

analyser [3] [analize] VT 1 (étudier) to analyse
2 Gram to parse; a. une phrase en constituants to parse a sentence into its constituents
3 Biol & Chim to analyse, to test
4 Psy to analyse; se faire a. to undergo analysis
VPR s'analyser elle s'analyse trop she goes in for too much self-analysis

analyseur [analizœr] NM 1 Ordinat analyser; a. logique/différentiel logic/differential analyser; a. syntaxique parser 2 Électron scanner, analyser 3 Chim analyst

analyste [analist] NMF 1 (gén) analyst; a. financier financial analyst; a. du marché market analyst; a. des médias media analyst; a. en placements investment analyst 2 Psy analyst, psychoanalyst

analyste-programmeur, -euse [analistprɔgramœr, -øz] (mpl analystes-programmeurs, fpl analystes-programmeuses) NM,F Ordinat systems analyst

analytique [analitik] ADJ analytic, analytical; géométrie/philosophie a. analytical geometry/philosophy
NM abstract
NF analytics (singulier)

analytiquement [analitikmɑ̃] ADV analytically

anamnèse [anamnɛz], **anamnésie** [anamnezi] NF Psy & Rel anamnesis

anamorphique [anamɔrfik] ADJ Cin & TV anamorphic

anamorphose [anamɔrfoz] NF Zool & Opt anamorphosis

ananas [anana(s)] NM Bot pineapple

anaphore [anafɔr] NF Littérature & Ling anaphora

anaphorique [anafɔrik] ADJ Ling anaphoric, anaphorical

anaphylactique [anafilaktik] ADJ Méd anaphylactic

anar [anar] NMF Fam (abrév anarchiste) anarchist

anarchie [anarʃi] NF 1 Pol anarchy 2 (désordre) anarchy, lawlessness

anarchique [anarʃik] ADJ anarchic, anarchical

anarchiquement [anarʃikmɑ̃] ADV anarchically

anarchisant, -e [anarʃizɑ̃, -ɑ̃t] ADJ Pol & Hist anarchistic

anarchiser [3] [anarʃize] VT Pol to anarchize

anarchisme [anarʃism] NM Pol & Hist anarchism

anarchiste [anarʃist] ADJ anarchist, anarchistic
NMF anarchist

anarcho-syndicaliste [anarkosɛ̃dikalist] (pl anarcho-syndicalistes) ADJ & NMF Ind anarcho-syndicalist

anathématiser [3] [anatematize] VT 1 Littéraire (condamner) to censure 2 Rel to anathematize

anathème [anatɛm] NM 1 (condamnation) anathema; jeter l'a. sur to pronounce an anathema upon, to anathematize 2 Rel anathema

anatife [anatif] NM Zool (crustacé) barnacle

anatomie [anatɔmi] NF Anat 1 (étude, structure) anatomy; a. pathologique pathological anatomy 2 Fam (corps) body; une belle a. a gorgeous figure; Euph son pantalon révélait tous les détails de son a. his/her trousers didn't leave much to the imagination

anatomique [anatɔmik] ADJ Anat anatomical; faire l'étude a. d'un corps to anatomize or to dissect a body

anatomiquement [anatɔmikmɑ̃] ADV Anat anatomically

anatomiste [anatɔmist] NMF Anat anatomist

ancestral, -e, -aux, -ales [ɑ̃sɛstral, -o] ADJ 1 (venant des ancêtres) ancestral 2 (ancien ▸ tradition, coutume) ancient, age-old, time-honoured

ancêtre [ɑ̃sɛtr] NMF 1 (ascendant) ancestor, forefather; c'était mon a. he/she was an ancestor of mine; la maison de ses ancêtres his/her family home 2 Fam (vieille personne) Br old boy, f old girl, Am old-timer

anche [ɑ̃ʃ] Mus NF reed
• **anches** NFPL les anches reed instruments, the reeds

anchois [ɑ̃ʃwa] NM anchovy

anchorman [ɑ̃kɔrman] NM TV anchorman, anchor

ancien, -enne [ɑ̃sjɛ̃, -ɛn] ADJ 1 (vieux ▸ coutume, tradition, famille) old, ancient, time-honoured; (▸ amitié, relation) old, long-standing; (▸ bague, châle) old, antique; un meuble a. an antique; livres anciens antiquarian books; une de nos règles déjà ancienne stipule que... one of our long-standing rules stipulates or states that...
2 Antiq (langue, histoire, civilisation) ancient; la Grèce ancienne ancient or classical Greece
3 (avant le nom) (ex ▸ président, époux, employé) former, ex-; (▸ stade, église) former; mon a. patron my former boss or ex-boss; ses anciens camarades his/her old or former comrades; c'est une ancienne infirmière she used to work as a nurse; mon ancienne école my old school; une ancienne colonie française a former French colony; l'ancienne rue de la Gare what used to be rue de la Gare; un a. combattant a (war) veteran, an ex-serviceman; un a. élève a former pupil, Br an old boy, Am an alumnus; une ancienne élève a former pupil, Br an old girl, Am an alumna
4 (passé) former; dans les temps anciens, dans l'a. temps in former times, in olden or bygone days
5 (qui a de l'ancienneté) senior; vous n'êtes pas assez a. dans la profession you've not been in the job long enough; ils sont plus anciens que moi dans la fonction they're senior to me (in the job)
NM,F 1 (qui a de l'expérience) old hand 2 (qui est plus vieux) elder; respectez les anciens have some respect for your elders 3 (qui a participé) un a. du parti communiste an ex-member of the Communist Party; un a. de la guerre de Corée a Korean War veteran, a veteran of the Korean War
NM 1 (objets) l'a. antiques; meublé entièrement en a. entirely furnished with antiques 2 (construction) l'a. old or older buildings; les murs sont plus épais dans l'a. walls are thicker in old or older buildings
• **Anciens** NMPL Antiq & Littérature Ancients
• **à l'ancienne** ADJ old-fashioned; des fiançailles à l'ancienne an old-fashioned or old-style engagement; bœuf à l'ancienne beef in the traditional style
• **Ancien Testament** NM l'A. Testament the Old Testament

> Il faut noter que le mot anglais **ancient** est un faux ami. Il correspond au français **antique**.

> **ANCIEN RÉGIME**
> This refers to the government and social structure of France before the Revolution of 1789, an absolutist monarchy consisting of three "estates": the nobility, the clergy (both enjoying institutional privileges) and the "Third Estate", or commoners. The privileges which characterized the Ancien Régime were abolished on 4 August 1789.

anciennement [ɑ̃sjɛnmɑ̃] ADV previously, formerly

ancienneté [ɑ̃sjɛnte] NF 1 (d'une chose) oldness 2 (d'une personne) length of service; (avantages acquis) seniority; elle a beaucoup d'a. chez nous she's been with us for a long time; avoir 15 ans d'a. dans une entreprise to have 15 years' service with a firm; avancer ou être promu à l'a. to be promoted by seniority
• **de toute ancienneté** ADV from time immemorial

ancillaire [ɑ̃silɛr] ADJ (avec une servante) les amours ancillaires love affairs with servants

ancolie [ɑ̃kɔli] NF Bot columbine, aquilegia

ancrage [ɑ̃kraʒ] NM 1 Tech (fixation) anchorage; a. des câbles d'un pont suspendu cable anchorage of a suspension bridge
2 Naut (arrêt) moorage, anchorage; (droits) anchorage or moorage or berthing (dues)
3 (enracinement) l'a. d'un parti dans l'électorat a party's electoral base; l'action de la pièce n'a aucun a. dans la réalité the plot of the play has no basis in reality
4 Ordinat & Typ justification; a. à droite/gauche right/left justification

ancre [ɑ̃kr] NF 1 Naut a. (de marine) anchor; Fig a. de salut last resort; elle est mon a. de salut she's my last hope; être à l'a. to ride or to lie at anchor; jeter l'a. to cast or to drop anchor; Fig to put down roots; lever l'a. to weigh anchor; Fig allez, on lève l'a.! come on, let's go! 2 Constr a. de mur cramp (iron); **a. de tête/voûte** wall/tie anchor **3** *Ordinat* anchor

ancrer [3] [ɑ̃kre] **VT 1** *Naut* to anchor **2** *(attacher)* to anchor; **a. un câble** to anchor a cable **3** *Fig* to root; **la propagande a ancré le parti dans la région** propaganda has established the party firmly in this area; **c'est une idée bien ancrée** it's a firmly rooted idea

VPR s'ancrer 1 *Naut* to drop *or* to cast anchor **2** *(se fixer)* to settle; **sa famille s'est ancrée dans la région** his/her family has settled in the area

andain [ɑ̃dɛ̃] **NM** *Agr* swath *(of cut grass, hay etc)*

andalou, -se [ɑ̃dalu, -uz] **ADJ** Andalusian

NM *(dialecte)* Andalusian

• **Andalou, -se NM,F** Andalusian

Andalousie [ɑ̃daluzi] **NF l'A.** Andalusia

andante [ɑ̃dɑ̃t(e)] *Mus* **ADV** *(tempo)* andante

NM *(morceau de musique)* andante

andantino [ɑ̃dɑ̃tino] *Mus* **ADV** *(tempo)* andantino

NM *(morceau de musique)* andantino

Andes [ɑ̃d] **NFPL les A.** the Andes; **la cordillère des A.** the Andes Mountain Ranges; **le climat des A.** the climate of the Andes, the Andean climate

andin, -e [ɑ̃dɛ̃, -in] **ADJ** Andean

• **Andin, -e NM,F** Andean

andorran, -e [ɑ̃dɔrɑ̃, -an] **ADJ** Andorran

• **Andorran, -e NM,F** Andorran

Andorre [ɑ̃dɔr] **NF (la principauté d')A.** (the principality of) Andorra

andouille [ɑ̃duj] **NF 1** *Culin* chitterlings sausage *(eaten cold)* **2** *Fam (imbécile)* dummy; **faire l'a.** to fool around; **espèce d'a.!** you great dummy!; **fais pas l'a., tu sais bien qu'elle t'aime!** don't do anything stupid, you know she loves you!

andouiller [ɑ̃duje] **NM** *Zool (d'un cerf)* antler

andouillette [ɑ̃dujɛt] **NF** *Culin* chitterlings sausage *(for grilling)*

androgène [ɑ̃drɔʒɛn] *Biol* **ADJ** androgenic

NM androgen

androgyne [ɑ̃drɔʒin] *Biol & Bot* **ADJ** androgynous

NM androgyne

androïde [ɑ̃drɔid] **NMF** android

andrologie [ɑ̃drɔlɔʒi] **NF** *Méd* andrology

andrologue [ɑ̃drɔlɔg] **NMF** *Méd* andrologist

Andromaque [ɑ̃drɔmak] **NPR** *Myth* Andromache

Andromède [ɑ̃drɔmɛd] **NPR** *Myth* Andromeda

andropause [ɑ̃drɔpoz] **NF** *Méd* male menopause

âne [ɑn] **NM 1** *(animal)* donkey, ass; **il est comme l'â. de Buridan** he can't make up his mind; **être mauvais** *ou* **méchant comme un â. rouge** to be vicious *or* nasty; **â. sauvage** wild ass **2** *(imbécile)* idiot, fool; **faire l'â.** to play the fool; **c'est un â. bâté** he's a complete idiot

anéantir [32] [aneɑ̃tir] **VT 1** *(détruire* ► *armée, ville)* to annihilate, to destroy; *(*► *rébellion, révolte)* to quell, to crush; *(*► *espoir)* to dash, to destroy; *(*► *succès, effort)* to ruin, to wreck; *(*► *amour, confiance)* to destroy; **leur équipe a été anéantie** their team was annihilated **2** *(accabler* ► *sujet: nouvelle, événement)* to overwhelm, to crush; **ça l'a anéanti** it was a tremendous blow to him; **être anéanti par le chagrin** to be overcome by grief; **elle est anéantie** she's devastated **3** *(épuiser)* to exhaust; **elle est anéantie par la chaleur/fatigue** she's overwhelmed by the heat/utterly exhausted

VPR s'anéantir to disappear, to vanish; **s'a. dans l'oubli** to sink into oblivion; **tous nos espoirs se sont anéantis** all our hopes were dashed

anéantissement [aneɑ̃tismɑ̃] **NM 1** *(destruction)* ruin, annihilation, destruction; **c'est l'a. d'un mois de travail** it's a whole month's work lost; **cette nouvelle fut l'a. de tous mes espoirs** this news dashed all my hopes **2** *(accablement)* prostration; **être dans l'a. le plus total** to be completely devastated

anecdote [anɛkdɔt] **NF** anecdote; *Péj* **tout cela, c'est de l'a.** this is all trivial detail, this is just so much trivia

anecdotique [anɛkdɔtik] **ADJ 1** *(qui contient des anecdotes)* anecdotal **2** *(sans intérêt)* trivial

anémie [anemi] **NF 1** *Méd* anaemia; **faire de l'a.** to have anaemia; **a. falciforme, a. à hématies falciformes** sickle cell anaemia; **a. pernicieuse** pernicious anaemia **2** *Fig* **nous constatons une a. de la production** we can see that output has slowed to a trickle

anémier [9] [anemje] **VT 1** *Méd* to make anaemic **2** *(affaiblir)* to weaken

anémique [anemik] **ADJ 1** *Méd* anaemic **2** *(faible* ► *personne)* feeble, ineffectual; *(*► *économie, industrie)* weak, slow, sluggish; **un texte plutôt a.** a rather colourless piece of writing

anémomètre [anemɔmɛtr] **NM** *Météo* anemometer

anémone [anemɔn] **NF 1** *Bot* anemone; **a. des bois** wood anemone **2** *Zool* **a. de mer** sea anemone

ânerie [ɑnri] **NF 1** *(caractère stupide)* stupidity; **tu es d'une â.!** you are so stupid!, you're such an idiot! **2** *(parole)* stupid *or* silly remark; **dire des âneries** to make stupid *or* silly remarks, to talk rubbish **3** *(acte)* stupid blunder *or* mistake; **faire des âneries** to make stupid mistakes

anéroïde [anerɔid] **ADJ** *Météo* aneroid

ânesse [ɑnɛs] **NF** *Zool* she-ass, jenny; **lait d'â.** ass's milk

anesthésiant, -e [anestezjɑ̃, -ɑ̃t] = **anesthésique**

anesthésie [anestezi] **NF** *Méd* anaesthesia; **faire une a. à qn** to anaesthetize sb, to give sb an anaesthetic; **être sous a.** to be anaesthetized *or* under an anaesthetic; **a. épidurale** epidural (anaesthesia); **a. locale/générale** local/general anaesthesia; **a. péridurale** epidural (anaesthesia)

anesthésier [9] [anestezje] **VT 1** *Méd* to anaesthetize; **docteur, allez-vous m'a.?** doctor, are you going to give me an anaesthetic? **2** *(insensibiliser* ► *bras, jambe)* to numb, to deaden; **le glaçon m'a anesthésié la gencive** the ice cube numbed *or* took all the feeling out of my gum **3** *Fig (opinion publique)* to anaesthetize; *Hum* **on ressort de ses cours complètement anesthésié** your brain is numb with boredom when you come out of his/her lectures

anesthésiologie [anestezjɔlɔʒi] **NF** *Méd Br* anaesthetics *(singulier)*, *Am* anesthesiology

anesthésique [anestezik] *Méd* **ADJ** anaesthetic

NM anaesthetic; **un a. local** a local anaesthetic

anesthésiste [anestezist] **NMF** *Méd (médecin) Br* anaesthetist, *Am* anesthesiologist; *(infirmière) Br* anaesthetic nurse, *Am* anesthetist

aneth [anɛt] **NM** *Bot* dill

anévrisme, anévrysme [anevrism] **NM** *Méd* aneurism, aneurysm

anfractuosité [ɑ̃fraktɥozite] **NF** *Géol (cavité)* crevice, crack

ange [ɑ̃ʒ] **NM 1** *Rel* angel; **c'est mon bon a.** he's/she's my guardian angel; **c'est mon mauvais a.** he's/she's a bad influence on me; **a. déchu/gardien** fallen/guardian angel; **un a. passa** there was a sudden silence, there was a lull in the conversation; **ah, un a. passe!** hasn't anybody got anything to say?, don't all talk at once!; **discuter du sexe des anges** to engage in pointless intellectual arguments, to argue about how many angels can fit on the end of a pin; **être aux anges** to be beside oneself with joy; **elle était aux anges quand je le lui ai dit** when I told her, she was ecstatic; **il riait** *ou* **souriait aux anges dans son sommeil** he was smiling happily in his sleep **2** *(personne parfaite)* angel; **passe-moi le pain, tu seras un a.** be an angel and pass me the bread; **c'est un a. de douceur** he's/she's sweetness itself; **mon a.** my darling *or* angel **3** *Ich* **a. (de mer)** monkfish, angel shark

angéiographie [ɑ̃ʒeiɔgrafi] = **angiographie**

angélique [ɑ̃ʒelik] **ADJ** *Rel & Fig* angelic; **un sourire a.** an angelic smile

NF *Bot & Culin* angelica

angélisme [ɑ̃ʒelism] **NM** otherworldliness

angelot [ɑ̃ʒlo] **NM** *Beaux-Arts* cherub

angélus [ɑ̃ʒelys] **NM** *Rel* Angelus

angevin, -e [ɑ̃ʒvɛ̃, -in] **ADJ 1** *(d'Angers)* of/from Angers **2** *(de l'Anjou)* of/from Anjou

• **Angevin, -e NM,F 1** *(d'Angers)* = inhabitant of or person from Angers **2** *(de l'Anjou)* = inhabitant of or person from Anjou

angine [ɑ̃ʒin] **NF** *Méd* **1** *(infection* ► *des amygdales)* tonsillitis; *(*► *du pharynx)* pharyngitis; **avoir une a.** to have a sore throat **2** *(douleur cardiaque)* angina; **a. de poitrine** angina (pectoris)

angiogenèse [ɑ̃ʒjɔʒenɛz] **NF** *Méd* angiogenesis

angiographie [ɑ̃ʒjɔgrafi] **NF** *Méd* angiography

angiome [ɑ̃ʒjom] **NM** *Méd* angioma

angioplastie [ɑ̃ʒjoplasti] **NF** *Méd* angioplasty

anglais, -e [ɑ̃glɛ, -ɛz] **ADJ** *(d'Angleterre)* English; *(de Grande-Bretagne)* British; **l'équipe anglaise** the England team

NM *(langue)* English; **a. américain/britannique** American/British English

• **Anglais, -e NM,F** *(d'Angleterre)* Englishman, *f* Englishwoman; *(de Grande-Bretagne)* Briton; **les A.** *(d'Angleterre)* English people, the English; *(de Grande-Bretagne)* British people, the British; *Fam* **les A. ont débarqué** I have my period ▫

• **anglaises NFPL** ringlets; **elle était coiffée avec des anglaises** her hair was in ringlets

• **à l'anglaise ADJ 1** *Culin* boiled **2** *Hort* **jardin/parc à l'anglaise** landscaped garden/park **ADV se sauver** *ou* **filer à l'anglaise** to slip away

angle [ɑ̃gl] **NM 1** *(coin* ► *d'un meuble, d'un mur, d'une pièce)* corner, angle; *(*► *d'une rue, d'une table)* corner; **faire un a.** *(chemin)* to bend, to turn; *(maison)* to be L-shaped, to form an angle; **la maison qui est à** *ou* **qui fait l'a.** the house on the corner; **la statue est à l'a. de deux rues** the statue stands at a crossroads; **le buffet a des angles arrondis/pointus** the dresser has rounded/sharp corners

2 *Géom* angle; **a. aigu/droit/obtus** acute/right/obtuse angle; **la rue fait un a. droit avec l'avenue** the street is at right angles to the avenue; **les rues se coupent à a. droit** the roads cross at right angles; **a. mort** *(en voiture)* blind spot; **a. ouvert** wide angle; **a. plat** straight angle; **a. plein** 360-degree angle

3 *(aspect)* angle, point of view; **je ne vois pas cela sous cet a.** I don't see it quite in that light *or* from that angle; **présenter les choses sous un certain a.** to present things from a certain point of view; **sous quel a. avez-vous abordé le sujet?** how did you approach the subject?; **vu sous l'a. économique/du rendement, cette décision se comprend** from an economic/a productivity point of view, the decision makes sense

4 *Opt* angle; **a. d'incidence/de réflexion/de réfraction** angle of incidence/of reflection/of refraction

5 *Cin* **a. de prise de vue** camera angle; **a. du regard** point of view

angledozer [ɑ̃glədɔzɛr] **NM** angledozer

Angleterre [ɑ̃glətɛr] **NF l'A.** England; *(Grande-Bretagne)* (Great) Britain; *Hist* **la bataille d'A.** the Battle of Britain

anglican, -e [ɑ̃glikɑ̃, -an] **ADJ** *Rel* Anglican

NM,F Anglican

anglicanisme [ɑ̃glikanism] **NM** *Rel* Anglicanism

anglicisant, -e [ɑ̃glisizɑ̃, -ɑ̃t] **ADJ** *(étudiant)* specializing in English

angliciser [3] [ɑ̃glisize] **VT** to anglicize

VPR s'angliciser to become anglicized

anglicisme [ɑ̃glisism] **NM** *Ling* anglicism

angliciste [ɑ̃glisist] **NMF 1** *(étudiant)* student of English **2** *(enseignant)* teacher of English **3** *(spécialiste)* Anglicist, expert in English language and culture

anglo- [ɑ̃glo] **PRÉF** Anglo-

anglo-américain, -e [ɑ̃glɔamerikɛ̃, -ɛn] *(mpl* **anglo-américains,** *fpl* **anglo-américaines)** **ADJ** Anglo-American

NM *(langue)* American English

• **Anglo-Américain, -e NM,F** Anglo-American

anglo-irlandais, -e [ɑ̃glɔirlɑ̃dɛ, -ɛz] *(mpl* **inv,** *fpl* **anglo-irlandaises)** **ADJ** Anglo-Irish

• **Anglo-Irlandais, -e NM,F** Anglo-Irishman, *f* Anglo-Irishwoman; **les A.** the Anglo-Irish

anglomane [ɑ̃glɔman] **NMF** Anglomaniac
anglomanie [ɑ̃glɔmani] **NF** Anglomania
anglo-normand, -e [ɑ̃glɔnɔrmɑ̃, -ɑ̃d] *(mpl* **anglo-normands,** *fpl* **anglo-normandes) ADJ 1** *Hist* Anglo-Norman **2** *Géog* of/from the Channel Islands; **les îles anglo-normandes** the Channel Islands
NM *(langue)* Anglo-Norman
anglophile [ɑ̃glɔfil] **ADJ** Anglophilic, Anglophiliac
NMF Anglophile
anglophilie [ɑ̃glɔfili] **NF** Anglophilia
anglophobe [ɑ̃glɔfɔb] **ADJ** Anglophobic
NMF Anglophobe
anglophobie [ɑ̃glɔfɔbi] **NF** Anglophobia
anglophone [ɑ̃glɔfɔn] **ADJ** English-speaking, Anglophone
NMF English speaker, Anglophone
anglo-saxon, -onne [ɑ̃glɔsaksɔ̃, -ɔn] *(mpl* **anglo-saxons,** *fpl* **anglo-saxonnes) ADJ 1** *(culture, civilisation, littérature)* Anglo-American, British and American, Anglo-Saxon; **les coutumes anglo-saxonnes** customs in English-speaking countries **2** *Hist* Anglo-Saxon
NM *(langue)* Old English, Anglo-Saxon
• **Anglo-Saxon, -onne NM,F** Anglo-Saxon; **les Anglo-Saxons** *(peuples)* British and American people; *Hist* the Anglo-Saxons

ANGLO-SAXON

Note that the adjective "anglo-saxon" and the noun "Anglo-Saxon" are often used in French to refer to British and American people, culture, customs etc: "la musique anglo-saxonne", "la littérature anglo-saxonne".

angoissant, -e [ɑ̃gwasɑ̃, -ɑ̃t] **ADJ 1** *(expérience)* distressing, harrowing, agonizing; *(nouvelle, livre, film)* distressing, harrowing; **il a vécu trois jours très angoissants** he lived through three harrowing days **2** *(sens affaibli)* **j'ai trouvé l'attente très angoissante** the wait was a strain on my nerves; **une période angoissante** an anxious time
angoisse [ɑ̃gwas] **NF** *(inquiétude)* anxiety; *(tourment)* anguish; **l'a. de la mort** the fear of death; **être** *ou* **vivre dans l'a.** to live in (a constant state of) anxiety; **vivre dans l'a. de qch** to live in dread of *or* to dread sth; **l'a. de devoir faire un choix** the anguish of having to make a choice; **a. existentielle** (existential) angst; *Fam* **c'est l'a.!, bonjour l'a.!** what a pain *or* drag *or* bummer!
• **angoisses NFPL avoir des angoisses** to suffer from anxiety attacks
angoissé, -e [ɑ̃gwase] **ADJ** *(personne)* anxious; *(regard)* haunted, anguished, agonized; *(voix, cri)* agonized, anguished; **être a. avant un examen** to feel anxious before an exam
NM,F anxious person
angoisser [3] [ɑ̃gwase] **VT a. qn** *(inquiéter)* to cause sb anxiety, to cause anxiety to sb; *(tourmenter)* to cause sb anguish; **ça m'angoisse de devoir parler en public** I get very nervous if I have to speak in public, I find speaking in public a real ordeal
VI *Fam* to worry; **j'angoisse à mort pour l'examen de demain** I'm worried sick about tomorrow's exam
VPR s'angoisser *Fam* to get worked up; **elle s'angoisse pour un rien** she gets worked up over nothing
Angola [ɑ̃gɔla] **NM l'A.** Angola
angolais, -e [ɑ̃gɔlɛ, -ɛz] **ADJ** Angolan
• **Angolais, -e NM,F** Angolan
angora [ɑ̃gɔra] **ADJ** angora; **chat/chèvre/lapin a.** Angora cat/goat/rabbit; **de la laine a.** angora wool
NM 1 *(chat, lapin)* Angora **2** *(laine)* angora
• **en angora ADJ** angora *(avant n)*
angstrœm, angström [ɑ̃gstrœm] **NM** *Phys* angstrom
anguille [ɑ̃gij] **NF** *Ich* eel; **a. de mer/électrique** conger/electric eel; **mince/souple comme une a.** thin/supple as a reed; *Fig* **il y a a. sous roche** there's something fishy going on
angulaire [ɑ̃gylɛr] **ADJ** angular

anguleux, -euse [ɑ̃gylø, -øz] **ADJ** *(objet)* angular; *(visage)* bony, sharp-featured, angular; *(personne)* skinny, bony; *(esprit, caractère)* stiff
anicroche [anikrɔʃ] **NF** hitch, snag; **il pourrait bien y avoir des anicroches** there might well be a few snags *or* hitches; **sans a.** smoothly, without a hitch
aniline [anilin] **NF** *Chim* aniline
animal, -e, -aux, -ales [animal, -o] **ADJ** *Zool* animal *(avant n)*; **l'instinct a.** the animal instinct
NM 1 *(gén)* animal; **les animaux de la ferme** *(dans les livres d'enfants)* farm animals; **a. familier** *ou* **domestique** pet; **a. de boucherie** animal bred for meat; **animaux de laboratoire** laboratory animals; **grands animaux** larger animals **2** *Fam (personne)* dope, oaf; **qu'est-ce qu'il a encore fait, ce grand a.(-là)?** what's that great oaf been up to this time?; **quel a.!** what a brute!, what a beast!
animalerie [animalri] **NF 1** *(de laboratoire)* breeding farm *(for laboratory animals)* **2** *(magasin)* pet shop
animalier, -ère [animalje, -ɛr] **ADJ** *(peintre, sculpteur)* animal *(avant n)*
NM 1 *Beaux-Arts* animalier **2** *(employé)* animal keeper *(in a laboratory)*
animalité [animalite] **NF** animality, animal nature
animateur, -trice [animatœr, -tris] **NM,F 1** *(responsable ▸ de maison de jeunes, de centre sportif)* (youth) leader; *(▸ de groupe)* leader; *(▸ d'entreprise, de service)* coordinator
2 *Rad & TV (gén)* presenter; *(de jeux, de variétés)* host; *(d'un débat)* moderator
3 *Cin* animator
4 *Mktg (d'une réunion de groupe)* leader, moderator; **a. des ventes** marketing executive
animation [animasjɔ̃] **NF 1** *(entrain)* life, liveliness, excitement; **mettre un peu d'a. dans une réunion** to liven up a meeting; **son arrivée a créé beaucoup d'a.** his/her arrival caused a great deal of excitement
2 *(vivacité)* liveliness, vivacity, animation; **elles discutaient de politique avec a.** they were having a lively discussion about politics
3 *(d'un quartier, d'une ville)* life; **il y a de l'a. dans les rues le soir** the streets are very lively *or* full of life at night
4 *(coordination ▸ d'un groupe)* running; *(▸ d'un débat)* chairing; **chargé de l'a. culturelle** in charge of cultural activities; **responsable de l'a. de l'équipe** responsible for coordinating the team; **faire de l'a., travailler dans l'a.** *(dans une maison des jeunes, dans une colonie de vacances)* to be a youth leader, to run activities; **organiser des animations de rue** to organize street shows
5 *(promotion ▸ d'un produit)* promotion; **a. commerciale** marketing campaign; **a. des ventes** sales drive, sales promotion
6 *Cin* animation; **a. par ordinateur** computer animation
7 *Météo* **a. satellite** satellite picture
animatique [animatik] **NF** *Ordinat* board test
animatrice [animatris] *voir* **animateur**
animé, -e [anime] **ADJ 1** *(doué de vie)* animate
2 *(doté de mouvement)* moving, animated; **les vitrines animées de Noël** moving *or* animated window displays at Christmas
3 *(plein de vivacité ▸ personne, discussion)* lively, animated; *(▸ marché, ville, rue)* busy, bustling; *(▸ quartier)* lively, busy
4 *Fin & Bourse (marché)* brisk, buoyant
animer [3] [anime] **VT 1** *(doter de mouvement ▸ mécanisme, robot)* to move, to actuate
2 *(inspirer)* to prompt, to motivate; **c'est la générosité qui l'anime** he's/she's prompted *or* motivated by generous feelings; **être animé de qch** to be motivated *or* prompted by sth; **être animé des meilleures intentions** to have the best of intentions
3 *(égayer ▸ soirée, repas, quartier)* to liven up; *(▸ pièce)* to brighten up; *(▸ regard)* to light up; **le plaisir animait son visage** his/her face was lit up with joy; **a. un personnage** to make a character come to life
4 *Rad & TV (présenter ▸ débat)* to chair; *(▸ émission d'actualité)* to present; *(▸ émission de variétés)* to host

VPR s'animer *(personne, conversation)* to become animated; *(quartier, rue, visage, yeux)* to come alive; *(pantin, poupée)* to come to life
animisme [animism] **NM** *Phil & Rel* animism
animiste [animist] *Phil & Rel* **ADJ** animistic
NMF animist
animosité [animosite] **NF** animosity, hostility, resentment; **avoir de l'a. contre qn** to feel resentment *or* hostility towards sb; **un regard plein d'a.** a hostile look
anion [anjɔ̃] **NM** *Phys* anion
anis [ani(s)] **NM 1** *Bot* anise **2** *Culin* aniseed; **à l'a.** aniseed *(avant n)*, aniseed-flavoured
aniser [3] [anize] **VT** *Culin* to flavour with aniseed
anisette [anizet] **NF** *(alcool)* anisette
ankylose [ɑ̃kiloz] **NF 1** *Méd* ankylosis **2** *(engourdissement)* stiffness, numbness
ankyloser [3] [ɑ̃kiloze] **VT** to ankylose
VPR s'ankyloser 1 *Méd* to ankylose **2** *(devenir engourdi ▸ bras, jambe)* to become numb; *(▸ personne)* to go stiff **3** *Fig (dans un métier)* to get into a rut
annal, -e, -aux, -ales [anal, -o] **ADJ** valid for one year, yearly
annales [anal] **NFPL 1** *(chronique)* annals; **rester dans les a.** to go down in history **2** *(d'examen)* past examination papers *(with annotations)* **3** *(revue)* review
annamite [anamit] **ADJ** Annamese
• **Annamite NMF** Annamese
anneau, -x [ano] **NM 1** *(gén)* ring; **un simple a. d'or** a plain band of gold; **en forme d'a.** ring-shaped; **a. épiscopal/nuptial** bishop's/wedding ring
2 *(pour rideaux)* ring; *(maillon)* link; *(boucle ▸ de ficelle)* loop
3 *Math* ring
4 *Zool (d'un serpent)* coil
5 *Astron* ring; **les anneaux de Saturne** the rings of Saturn
6 *Sport* **a. de vitesse** *(pour patinage)* rink; *(pour bicyclette)* racetrack
• **anneaux NMPL** *Sport* rings; **exercices aux anneaux** ring exercises
• **en anneau ADJ** ring-shaped
année [ane] **NF 1** *(division du calendrier)* year; **a. bissextile** leap year; *Fin* **a. budgétaire** *Br* financial year, *Am* fiscal year; **a. civile** calendar *or* civil year; **a. comptable** accounting year; **a. en cours** current year; **a. d'exercice** *Br* financial year, *Am* fiscal year; **a. fiscale** tax year, *Am* fiscal year
2 *(date)* year; **quelle est son a. de naissance?** what year was he/she born?; **l'a. 1789** the year 1789; **l'a. prochaine/dernière** next/last year
3 *(durée)* year; **il y a des années que je ne l'ai pas vue** I haven't seen her for years; **ce projet durera toute l'a.** this project will last the whole year; **d'a. en a.** from year to year; **d'une a. à l'autre** from one year to the next; **tout au long de l'a., toute l'a.** all year long *or* round; **j'ai encore deux années à faire** I have two more years to do; **entrer dans sa trentième a.** to enter one's thirtieth year; **elle entre dans sa trentième a.** she'll be thirty (on her) next birthday; **années d'abondance** prosperous years; **les plus belles années de ma vie** the best years of my life; *Univ* **première a.** *Br* first year, *Am* freshman year; *Univ* **dernière a.** *Br* final year, *Am* senior year; **c'est une étudiante de troisième a.** *Br* she's a third-year student, *Am* she's in her junior year; **elle est en troisième a. de médecine** she's in her third year at medical school; **l'a. scolaire/universitaire/judiciaire** the school/academic/legal year; **une a. sabbatique** a sabbatical (year); *Fam* **années de vaches maigres/grasses** lean/prosperous years; **années de plomb** dark years
4 *(célébration)* **l'a. de** the Year of; **l'a. du Dragon** the Year of the Dragon; **l'a. de la Femme** International Women's Year
5 *(nouvel an)* **bonne a.!** happy New Year!; **souhaiter la bonne a. à qn** to wish sb a happy New Year
• **années NFPL les années soixante/soixante-dix** the sixties/seventies
• **à l'année ADV** *(louer, payer)* annually, on a yearly basis

année-lumière [anelymjɛr] (*pl* **années-lumière**) **NF** *Astron* light year; *Fig* **à des années-lumière de** light years away from; **mon cousin et moi, nous sommes à des années-lumière l'un de l'autre** my cousin and I are poles apart

annelé, -e [anle] **ADJ** *(colonne, ver etc)* ringed

annexe [anɛks] **ADJ 1** *(accessoire ▸ tâche, détail, fait)* subsidiary, related; *(sans importance)* minor; **des considérations annexes** side issues; **ne parlons pas de cela, c'est tout à fait a.** let's forget about this, it's not relevant to the matter in hand **2** *(dossier)* additional; **les documents** *ou* **pièces annexes** the attached documents

3 bâtiment a. annexe

4 *(revenus, frais)* supplementary

NF 1 *(bâtiment)* annexe; *(d'une ferme, d'un château)* outbuilding **2** *(supplément ▸ d'un document)* annexe; *(▸ d'un dossier)* appendix; *(▸ d'un contrat)* rider; *(▸ d'un bilan)* schedule; *Jur (▸ d'une loi)* rider, annexe; **mettre qch en a. à** to append sth to; **les détails du sondage sont en a.** the details of the survey are in the appendix; **en a. à ma lettre** enclosed with my letter; **en a. veuillez trouver...** *(dans une lettre)* please find enclosed...; *(dans un e-mail)* please find attached... **3** *(d'un bateau)* dinghy

• **annexes NFPL** *Compta* notes to the accounts

annexer [4] [anɛkse] **VT 1** *(joindre)* to annex, to append, to attach; **pièces annexées** *(à une lettre)* enclosures; *(à un dossier)* appended documents, appendices; **a. un témoignage à un dossier** to append a testimony to a file **2** *Hist & Pol* to annex

VPR s'annexer *Fam* **s'a. qch** *(le monopoliser)* to hog sth; *Euph (le voler)* to filch sth

annexion [anɛksjɔ̃] **NF** annexation

annihilation [aniilasjɔ̃] **NF** *Sout (destruction)* annihilation, destruction

annihiler [3] [aniile] **VT** *Sout (efforts, révolte)* to annihilate, to destroy; *(personne)* to crush, to destroy

anniversaire [anivɛrsɛr] **ADJ** anniversary *(avant n)*; **le jour** *ou* **la date a. de leur rencontre** the anniversary of the day they first met

NM 1 *(d'une naissance)* birthday; **une fête d'a.** a birthday party; **bon** *ou* **joyeux a.!** happy birthday! **2** *(d'un mariage, d'une mort, d'un événement)* anniversary; **le cinquantième a. de leur mariage** their fiftieth wedding anniversary **3** *(fête)* birthday party

> Attention: ne pas confondre **anniversary** et **birthday** lorsqu'on traduit **anniversaire**. **Birthday** s'utilise pour l'anniversaire d'une personne et **anniversary** pour celui d'un événement.

annonce [anɔ̃s] **NF 1** *(nouvelle)* notice, notification; *(fait de dire)* announcement; **tu as lu l'a. de sa nomination?** did you read the notification of his/her appointment?; **faire une a.** *(gén)* to make an announcement; **faire l'a. de la sortie d'un disque** to announce the release of a new record **2** *(texte ▸ d'information)* notice; *(▸ pour une transaction)* advert, ad; **mettre** *ou* **passer une (petite) a. dans un journal** to put an advertisement *or* an ad in a paper; **annonces classées, petites annonces** *(de location, de vente)* classified advertisements *or* ads, *Br* small ads, *Am* want ads; *(courrier du cœur)* personal ads *or* column

3 *Rad & TV* **a. de continuité** continuity announcement

4 *Can (publicité)* advert, ad

annoncer [16] [anɔ̃se] **VT 1** *(communiquer ▸ renseignement)* to announce; *(▸ mauvaise nouvelle)* to announce, to break; *(▸ météo)* to predict, to forecast; **je n'ose pas le lui a.** I daren't break it to him/her; **a. la naissance d'un enfant** to announce the birth of a child; **ils annoncent du soleil pour demain** sunshine is forecast for tomorrow, the forecast for tomorrow is sunny; **a. qch à qn** to inform sb of sth, to tell sb sth; **on m'a annoncé sa mort hier** I was told *or* informed of his/her death yesterday; **a. à qn que** to inform sb that; **je vous annonce que je me marie** I'd like to inform you that I'm getting married

2 *Com (proposer)* to quote; **a. un prix** to quote a price

3 *(présenter ▸ visiteur)* to announce; *(▸ projet, changement)* to introduce, to usher in; **qui dois-je a.?** what name shall I say?; **se faire a.** to give one's name; **elle est arrivée sans se faire a.** she came unannounced

4 *(présager)* to announce, to foreshadow, *(être signe de)* to be a sign *or* an indication of; **ça n'annonce rien de bon** it doesn't bode well, it isn't a very good sign

VPR s'annoncer 1 *(prévenir de sa visite)* to notify *or* to warn (that one will visit); **viens quand tu veux, ce n'est pas la peine de t'a.** come whenever you like, there's no need to let me know beforehand **2** *(se profiler)* to be looming *or* on the horizon; **une grave crise s'annonce** a serious crisis is looming **3** *(dans des constructions attributives)* **la journée s'annonce très belle** it looks like it's going to be a beautiful day; **cela s'annonce très bien** things are looking very promising *or* good; **cela s'annonce plutôt mal** it doesn't look very promising, the picture doesn't look *or* isn't too good

annonceur, -euse [anɔ̃sœr, -øz] **NM,F** *(présentateur)* announcer

NM a. (publicitaire) advertiser

annonciateur, -trice [anɔ̃sjatœr, -tris] **ADJ** announcing, foreshadowing; **bourgeons annonciateurs du printemps** buds heralding spring; **les secousses annonciatrices d'un tremblement de terre** the tremors that are the warning signs of an earthquake

annonciation [anɔ̃sjasjɔ̃] **NF** *Rel* annunciation; **fête de l'A.** Feast of the Annunciation, Lady Day

annonciatrice [anɔ̃sjatris] *voir* **annonciateur**

annotateur, -trice [anɔtatœr, -tris] **NM,F** annotator

annotation [anɔtasjɔ̃] **NF 1** *(note explicative)* annotation **2** *(note personnelle)* note; **faire des annotations dans un texte** *(gén)* to write notes in the margins of a text; *(éditeur, correcteur)* to annotate a text

annotatrice [anɔtatris] *voir* **annotateur**

annoter [3] [anɔte] **VT 1** *(commenter)* to annotate **2** *(de remarques personnelles)* to write notes on; **entièrement annoté** *(livre)* covered with notes; *(édition)* fully annotated

annuaire [anɥɛr] **NM** *(recueil ▸ d'une association, d'une société)* yearbook, annual; *(liste d'adresses)* directory; **a. (téléphonique)** telephone directory *or* book; **je suis dans l'a.** I'm in the (phone) book; **a. électronique** electronic directory

annualisation [anɥalizasjɔ̃] **NF** annualization; **l'a. du temps de travail permettra de répondre à une demande saisonnière** calculating working hours across the year will enable us to meet seasonal demand

annualiser [3] [anɥalize] **VT** to annualize

annuel, -elle [anɥɛl] **ADJ 1** *(qui revient chaque année)* yearly, annual; **budget a.** annual budget; **congé a.** annual leave; **chiffre d'affaires a.** annual *or* yearly turnover; **consommation annuelle** yearly *or* annual consumption **2** *(qui dure un an)* annual; **une plante annuelle** an annual

annuellement [anɥɛlmɑ̃] **ADV** annually, yearly, on a yearly basis

annuitaire [anɥitɛr] **ADJ** *Compta & Fin (dette)* redeemable by yearly payments

annuité [anɥite] **NF 1** *Fin (dans le remboursement d'un emprunt)* annual instalment *or* repayment; **remboursement par annuités** repayment by annual payments *or* yearly instalments; *Compta* **a. d'amortissement** annual depreciation *or* write-down; *Compta* **a. constante** *(de remboursement)* fixed annual payment **2** *Can & Suisse (rente)* annuity

annulaire [anylɛr] **ADJ** *(circulaire)* annular, ring-shaped

NM *Anat (doigt)* third *or* ring finger

annulation [anylasjɔ̃] **NF 1** *(d'un ordre, d'un rendez-vous, d'un projet)* cancellation, calling off; *(d'une réservation)* cancellation; *(d'une commande)* cancellation, withdrawal; *(d'une proposition)* withdrawal; *(d'une dette)* cancellation, writing off; *Banque (d'un chèque)* cancellation **2** *Jur (d'un décret, d'un acte judiciaire)* revocation, annulment; *(d'un jugement, d'un verdict)* quashing; *(d'une loi)* revocation, rescindment; *(d'un contrat)* annulment, invalidation; *(d'un mariage)* annulment; *(d'un testament)* setting aside; *(d'un droit)* abolition, defeasance **3** *Ordinat* deletion; **a. d'entrée** *(commande)* cancel entry; **a. des révisions** *(commande)* undo changes

annuler [3] [anyle] **VT 1** *(ordre, rendez-vous, projet)* to cancel, to call off; *(réservation)* to cancel; *(commande)* to cancel, to withdraw; *(dette)* to cancel, to write off; *Banque (chèque)* to cancel **2** *Jur (décret, acte judiciaire)* to revoke, to annul; *(jugement, verdict)* to quash; *(loi)* to rescind, to revoke; *(contrat)* to annul, to render null and void, to invalidate; *(mariage)* to annul; *(testament)* to set aside, to nullify; *(droit)* to abolish

3 *(remplacer)* to supersede, to cancel; **ce catalogue annule les précédents** this catalogue supersedes all previous issues

4 *Ordinat* to cancel; *(opération)* to undo; **a. les révisions** *(commande)* undo changes

5 *Sport (but)* to disallow

VPR s'annuler to cancel each other out

anoblir [32] [anɔblir] **VT** to ennoble, to confer a title on

> Do not confuse with **ennoblir**, which means **to elevate morally**.

anoblissement [anɔblismɑ̃] **NM** ennoblement

anode [anɔd] **NF** *Chim & Électron* anode

anodin, -e [anɔdɛ̃, -in] **ADJ 1** *(inoffensif ▸ remarque, plaisanterie)* harmless; *(▸ blessure)* slight, minor **2** *(insignifiant ▸ personne, propos)* ordinary, commonplace; *(▸ détail)* trifling, insignificant; *(▸ événement)* meaningless, insignificant

anodique [anɔdik] **ADJ** *Chim & Électron* anodic, anodal, anode *(avant n)*

anomalie [anɔmali] **NF 1** *(bizarrerie ▸ d'une expérience, d'une attitude)* anomaly; *(▸ d'une procédure, d'une nomination)* irregularity **2** *Astron & Ling* anomaly **3** *Biol* abnormality

ânon [ɑnɔ̃] **NM** *Zool* young donkey *or* ass

ânonnement [ɑnɔnmɑ̃] **NM** *(balbutiement)* **les ânonnements des enfants qui apprennent à lire** the faltering tones of children learning to read

ânonner [3] [ɑnɔne] **VT** to stumble through; **â. son rôle** to stumble through one's lines

VI to stammer out one's words; **il lisait en ânonnant** he read haltingly

anonymat [anɔnima] **NM** anonymity; **conserver** *ou* **garder l'a.** to remain anonymous; **l'a. le plus total est garanti** confidentiality is guaranteed; **sous le couvert de** *ou* **en gardant l'a.** anonymously; **sortir de l'a.** *(devenir célèbre)* to come to public attention, to emerge from obscurity

anonyme [anɔnim] **ADJ 1** *(sans nom ▸ manuscrit, geste, appel)* anonymous; **rester a.** to remain unnamed *or* anonymous **2** *(inconnu ▸ auteur, attaquant)* anonymous, unknown **3** *(sans personnalité ▸ vêtement, meuble)* drab, nondescript; *(▸ maison, appartement)* anonymous, soulless

NMF anonym; **c'était signé "a."** it was signed "anon"

anonymement [anɔnimmɑ̃] **ADV** anonymously

anonymisation [anɔnimizasjɔ̃] **NF** anonymization

anonymiser [anɔnimize] **VT** to anonymize

anophèle [anɔfɛl] **NM** *Entom* anopheles

anorak [anɔrak] **NM** anorak

anorexie [anɔrɛksi] **NF** *Méd* anorexia; **faire de l'a.** to suffer from anorexia; *Psy* **a. mentale** anorexia nervosa

anorexique [anɔrɛksik] **ADJ** anorexic

NMF *Méd* anorexic

anormal, -e, -aux, -ales [anɔrmal, -o] **ADJ 1** *(inhabituel ▸ événement)* abnormal, unusual; *(▸ comportement)* abnormal, *Sout* aberrant; **il fait une chaleur anormale** it's abnormally hot

2 *(non réglementaire)* irregular; **la procédure que vous avez utilisée est tout à fait anormale** it was most irregular for you to proceed in that way

3 *(injuste)* unfair, unjustified; **il est parfaitement a. qu'ils ne vous aient pas payé** it's intolerable that they didn't pay you

4 *(handicapé)* mentally handicapped
NM,F mentally handicapped person

anormalement [anɔrmalmɑ̃] **ADV** *(inhabituellement)* unusually, abnormally

anormalité [anɔrmalite] **NF** abnormality

ANP [ɑenpe] **NM** *(abrév* **assistant numérique personnel***)* PDA

ANPE [ɑenpeə] **NF** *(abrév* **Agence nationale pour l'emploi***)* = national employment agency; **s'inscrire à l'A.** to sign on

ANRS [ɑenɛrɛs] **NF** *(abrév* **Agence nationale de recherches sur le sida***)* = Aids research institute

anse [ɑ̃s] **NF 1** *(poignée)* handle; *Fig* **faire danser** *ou* **valser l'a. du panier** to fiddle the books **2** *Géog* cove **3** *Archit* **a. (de panier)** basket-handle arch

antagonique [ɑ̃tagɔnik] **ADJ** *(forces, personnes)* antagonistic; *(intérêts, influences)* conflicting

antagonisme [ɑ̃tagɔnism] **NM** antagonism

antagoniste [ɑ̃tagɔnist] **ADJ** *(attitude, relation, forces, personnes)* antagonistic; **avoir des positions antagonistes** to have opposing *or* conflicting opinions; **les partis antagonistes** the opposing parties; **les muscles antagonistes** antagonistic muscles
NMF antagonist

antalgique [ɑ̃talʒik] *Méd* **ADJ** analgesic
NM analgesic

antan [ɑ̃tɑ̃] **d'antan ADJ** of yesteryear; **le Paris d'a.** the Paris of yesteryear; **mes amis d'a.** my friends from the old days

antarctique [ɑ̃tarktik] **ADJ** Antarctic; **le cercle polaire a.** the Antarctic Circle
• **Antarctique NM** *Géog* **l'A.** Antarctica

anté- [ɑ̃te] **PRÉF** ante-, pre-

antécédence [ɑ̃tesedɑ̃s] **NF** *Géol* antecedence

antécédent, -e [ɑ̃tesedɑ̃, -ɑ̃t] **ADJ 1** *(précédent* ▸ *élément)* antecedent; *(*▸ *événement)* prior, previous; **a. à** prior to **2** *Géol* antecedent
NM *Gram, Ling & Math* antecedent
• **antécédents NMPL 1** *(faits passés)* antecedents, past *or* previous history; **avoir de bons/mauvais antécédents** to have a good/bad record **2** *Méd* **antécédents (médicaux)** past *or* previous (medical) history, case history; **il y a des antécédents cancéreux dans ma famille** my family has a history of cancer

Antéchrist [ɑ̃tekrist] **NM** *Bible* Antichrist

antédiluvien, -enne [ɑ̃tedilyvjɛ̃, -ɛn] **ADJ 1** *Bible* antediluvian **2** *Fam (vieux)* antiquated, ancient

antémémoire [ɑ̃tememwar] **NF** *Ordinat* cache (memory); **mettre en a.** to cache

anténatal, -e, -aux, -ales [ɑ̃tenatal, -o] **ADJ** *Méd Br* antenatal, *Am* prenatal

antenne [ɑ̃tɛn] **NF 1** *Zool & Entom* antenna, feeler; *Fam* **avoir des antennes** *(avoir de l'intuition)* to be very intuitive□; *(avoir des contacts)* to know all the right people
2 *Électron Br* aerial, *Am* antenna; **a. cadre** loop *Br* aerial *or Am* antenna; **a. collective** shared aerial; **a. directive** beam *Br* aerial *or Am* antenna; **a. parabolique** satellite dish, dish *Br* aerial *or Am* antenna; **mini a. parabolique** minidish; **a. télescopique** telescopic mast
3 *Rad & TV* **à vous l'a.** over to you; **être à l'a.** to be on (the air); **passer à/garder l'a.** to go/stay on the air; **je passe l'a. à notre prochain invité** I'll hand you over to our next guest; **prendre l'a.** to come on the air; **rendre l'a.** to hand back to the studio; **sur notre a.** *Rad* on this frequency *or* station; *TV* on this channel
4 *(agence, service)* office; **notre a. à Genève** our agent in Geneva, our Geneva office; **a. chirurgicale** surgical unit

antépénultième [ɑ̃tepenyltjɛm] **ADJ** antepenultimate

antérieur, -e [ɑ̃terjœr] **ADJ 1** *(précédent)* anterior, prior; **la situation antérieure** the previous *or* former situation; **une vie antérieure** a former life; **a. à** prior to, before; **c'était bien a. à cette époque** it was long before that time; **la période antérieure à la révolution** the period before the revolution **2** *Anat (de devant)* anterior

antérieurement [ɑ̃terjœrmɑ̃] **ADV** previously
• **antérieurement à PRÉP** prior to, previous to, before

antériorité [ɑ̃terjɔrite] **NF 1** *(d'un événement)* anteriority, antecedence, precedence **2** *Gram* anteriority

anthère [ɑ̃tɛr] **NF** *Bot* anther

anthologie [ɑ̃tɔlɔʒi] **NF** *Littérature* anthology

anthracite [ɑ̃trasit] **ADJ INV** charcoal grey
NM *Minér* anthracite, hard coal

anthrax [ɑ̃traks] **NM** *Méd* carbuncle, anthrax *(sore)*

anthropique [ɑ̃trɔpik] **ADJ** anthropogenic

anthropocentrique [ɑ̃trɔposɑ̃trik] **ADJ** *Phil* anthropocentric

anthropocentrisme [ɑ̃trɔposɑ̃trism] **NM** *Phil* anthropocentrism

anthropoïde [ɑ̃trɔpɔid] *Zool* **ADJ** anthropoid
NM anthropoid ape

anthropologie [ɑ̃trɔpɔlɔʒi] **NF** anthropology

anthropologique [ɑ̃trɔpɔlɔʒik] **ADJ** anthropological

anthropologue [ɑ̃trɔpɔlɔg], **anthropologiste** [ɑ̃trɔpɔlɔʒist] **NMF** anthropologist

anthropométrie [ɑ̃trɔpɔmetri] **NF** anthropometry

anthropométrique [ɑ̃trɔpɔmetrik] **ADJ** anthropometric, anthropometrical; **service a.** criminal anthropometry department, *Br* ≃ Criminal Records Office; **fiche a.** = record containing fingerprints and details of height, weight etc

anthropomorphe [ɑ̃trɔpɔmɔrf] **ADJ** anthropomorphous, anthropomorphic

anthropomorphisme [ɑ̃trɔpɔmɔrfism] **NM** anthropomorphism

anthropophage [ɑ̃trɔpɔfaʒ] **ADJ** cannibal *(avant n)*, cannibalistic
NMF cannibal

anthropophagie [ɑ̃trɔpɔfaʒi] **NF** cannibalism

anti-[1] [ɑ̃ti] **PRÉF** *(contre, qui s'oppose à)* anti-; **être anti-télévision** to be anti-television, to be against television; **être antisport** not to like sport

anti-[2] [ɑ̃ti] **PRÉF** *(qui précède)* ante-

antiacnéique [ɑ̃tiakneik] **ADJ** anti-acne
NM acne treatment

antiadhésif, -ive [ɑ̃tiadezif, -iv] **ADJ** antiadhesive *(avant n)*; *(poêle)* nonstick
NM antiadhesive

antiaérien, -enne [ɑ̃tiaerjɛ̃, -ɛn] **ADJ** *Mil* anti-aircraft

anti-âge [ɑ̃tiɑʒ] **ADJ INV crème a.** anti-ageing cream

antialcoolique [ɑ̃tialkɔlik] **ADJ** anti-alcohol *(avant n)*

antialcoolisme [ɑ̃tialkɔlism] **NM** anti-alcoholism

anti-aliassage [ɑ̃tialjasaʒ] *(pl* **anti-aliassages***)* **NM** *Ordinat* anti-aliasing

antiallergique [ɑ̃tialɛrʒik] *Méd* **ADJ** antiallergenic
NM antiallergen

antiatomique [ɑ̃tiatɔmik] **ADJ** *Mil* antiatomic

antiavortement [ɑ̃tiavɔrtəmɑ̃] **ADJ INV** pro-life, anti-abortion

antibactérien, -enne [ɑ̃tibakterjɛ̃, -ɛn] **ADJ** *Biol* antibacterial

antibalistique [ɑ̃tibalistik] **ADJ** *Astron* antiballistic

antibiogramme [ɑ̃tibjɔgram] **NM** *Biol* antibiogram

antibiotique [ɑ̃tibjɔtik] **ADJ** antibiotic
NM antibiotic; **prendre des antibiotiques** to take antibiotics; **être sous antibiotiques** to be on antibiotics

antiblocage [ɑ̃tiblɔkaʒ] **ADJ** *Aut* antilock *(avant n)*

antibrouillage [ɑ̃tibrujaʒ] **NM** *Électron* antijamming

antibrouillard [ɑ̃tibrujar] **ADJ INV** *Aut* fog *(avant n)*; **phare** *ou* **dispositif a.** fog *Br* lamp *or Am* light

antibruit [ɑ̃tibrɥi] **ADJ INV** *(matériau)* soundproof; **mur a.** antinoise barrier

antibuée [ɑ̃tibɥe] *Aut* **ADJ INV** demisting, antimisting
NM 1 *(dispositif)* demister **2** *(produit)* antimist agent, clear vision agent

anticalcaire [ɑ̃tikalkɛr] **ADJ** antiscale *(avant n)*

anticancéreux, -euse [ɑ̃tikɑ̃serø, -øz] **ADJ** *Méd* **1** *(centre, laboratoire)* cancer *(avant n)* **2** *(médicament)* anticancer *(avant n)*

anticapitalisme [ɑ̃tikapitalism] **NM** *Pol* anticapitalism

anticathode [ɑ̃tikatɔd] **NF** *Électron* anticathode

antichambre [ɑ̃tiʃɑ̃br] **NF** anteroom, antechamber; **dans les antichambres du pouvoir** on the fringes of power; **faire a.** to wait quietly (to be received)

antichar [ɑ̃tiʃar] **ADJ** *Mil* antitank

antichoc [ɑ̃tiʃɔk] **ADJ** shockproof

anti-chute [ɑ̃tiʃyt] **ADJ INV traitement a.** treatment to stop hair loss

anticipatif, -ive [ɑ̃tisipatif, -iv] **ADJ paiement a.** prepayment

anticipation [ɑ̃tisipasjɔ̃] **NF 1** *(prévision)* anticipation; **a. des résultats** anticipation *or* forecasting of the results **2** *Com* **a. de paiement** *(somme)* advance payment; *(action)* paying in advance **3** *(science-fiction)* science-fiction
• **d'anticipation ADJ** *(roman, film)* science-fiction *(avant n)*, futuristic; **littérature d'a.** science fiction
• **par anticipation ADJ** *Fin* advance *(avant n)*; **paiement par a.** advance payment, prepayment
ADV *(payer, régler)* in advance

anticipative [ɑ̃tisipativ] *voir* **anticipatif**

anticipé, -e [ɑ̃tisipe] **ADJ 1** *(avant la date prévue* ▸ *retraite, départ)* early; *(*▸ *remboursement)* before due date; *(*▸ *dividende, paiement)* advance; *(*▸ *ventes)* expected **2** *(fait à l'avance)* **avec nos remerciements anticipés** thanking you in advance *or* anticipation

anticiper [3] [ɑ̃tisipe] **VT 1** *Com & Fin* **a. un paiement** to pay *or* to settle a bill in advance **2** *(prévoir)* to anticipate; **il a bien anticipé la réaction de son adversaire** he anticipated *or* foresaw his opponent's reaction
USAGE ABSOLU il a bien anticipé he anticipated his opponent's moves; **n'anticipons pas!** let's just wait and see!, all in good time!
• **anticiper sur VT IND a. sur ce qui va se passer** *(deviner)* to guess what's going to happen; *(raconter)* to explain what's going to happen

anticlérical, -e, -aux, -ales [ɑ̃tiklerikal, -o] *Rel* **ADJ** anticlerical
NM,F anticlerical

anticléricalisme [ɑ̃tiklerikalism] **NM** *Rel* anticlericalism

anticlinal, -e, -aux, -ales [ɑ̃tiklinal, -o] **ADJ** *Géol & Biol* anticlinal
NM *Géol* anticline

anticoagulant, -e [ɑ̃tikoagylɑ̃, -ɑ̃t] *Méd* **ADJ** anticoagulating
NM anticoagulant

anticolonialisme [ɑ̃tikɔlɔnjalism] **NM** anticolonialism

anticolonialiste [ɑ̃tikɔlɔnjalist] **ADJ** anticolonialist
NMF anticolonialist

anticommercial, -e, -aux, -ales [ɑ̃tikɔmɛrsjal, -o] **ADJ** *Com (attitude)* unbusinesslike

anticommunisme [ɑ̃tikɔmynism] **NM** *Pol* anticommunism; **faire de l'a. primaire** to be fiercely anticommunist

anticommuniste [ɑ̃tikɔmynist] **ADJ** anticommunist
NMF *Pol* anticommunist

anticonceptionnel, -elle [ɑ̃tikɔ̃sɛpsjɔnɛl] **ADJ** *(pilule, méthode, mesures)* contraceptive, birth-control *(avant n)*

anticonformisme [ɑ̃tikɔ̃fɔrmism] **NM** nonconformism

anticonformiste [ɑ̃tikɔ̃fɔrmist] **ADJ** nonconformist
NMF nonconformist

anticonstitutionnel, -elle [ɑ̃tikɔ̃stitysjɔnɛl] ADJ *Jur* unconstitutional

anticonstitutionnellement [ɑ̃tikɔ̃stitysjɔnɛlmɑ̃] ADV *Jur* unconstitutionally

anticopie [ɑ̃tikɔpi] ADJ INV *Ordinat* copy-protected

anticorps [ɑ̃tikɔr] NM *Physiol* antibody

anticorrosion [ɑ̃tikɔrozjɔ̃] ADJ INV anticorrosive, rust-resistant

anti-crevaison [ɑ̃ticrœvezɔ̃] ADJ INV *(pneu)* puncture-proof, anti-puncture

anticyclique [ɑ̃tisiklik] ADJ *Écon* anticyclic

anticyclonal, -e, -aux, -ales [ɑ̃tisiklɔnal, -o] ADJ *Météo* anticyclonic

anticyclone [ɑ̃tisiklon] NM *Météo* anticyclone

anticyclonique [ɑ̃tisiklɔnik] ADJ *Météo* anticyclonic

antidate [ɑ̃tidat] NF antedate

antidater [3] [ɑ̃tidate] VT to antedate, to predate

antidéflagrant, -e [ɑ̃tideflagrɑ̃, -ɑ̃t] ADJ *Mines* explosion-proof

antidémarrage [ɑ̃tidemaraʒ] NM *Aut* engine immobilizer; **a. codé** security-coded immobilizer

antidémocratique [ɑ̃tidemɔkratik] ADJ *Pol* antidemocratic

antidépresseur [ɑ̃tidepresœr] *Pharm*
ADJ M antidepressant
NM antidepressant

antidérapant, -e [ɑ̃tiderapɑ̃, -ɑ̃t] ADJ **1** *(surface, tapis)* nonslip **2** *Aut* nonskid, antiskid
NM non-slip coating

antidétonant, -e [ɑ̃tidetɔnɑ̃, -ɑ̃t] ADJ antiknock *(avant n)*
NM antiknock (compound)

antidiphtérique [ɑ̃tidifterik] ADJ *Méd* diphtheria *(avant n)*; **sérum a.** diphtheria serum

anti-discriminatoire [ɑ̃tidiskriminatwar] ADJ *(mesures, politique)* anti-discriminatory

antidopage [ɑ̃tidɔpaʒ], **antidoping** [ɑ̃tidɔpiŋ] ADJ INV **contrôle/mesure a.** drug detection test/measure

antidote [ɑ̃tidɔt] NM antidote; **l'a. de l'arsenic** the antidote to arsenic; **un a. contre la tristesse** a remedy for sadness

antidumping [ɑ̃tidœmpiŋ] ADJ INV *Jur (loi, législation)* anti-dumping

anti-éblouissant, -e [ɑ̃tiebluisɑ̃, -ɑ̃t] *(mpl* **anti-éblouissants,** *fpl* **anti-éblouissantes)** ADJ anti-dazzle; **écran a.** anti-glare screen; **rétroviseur a.** anti-dazzle rear-view mirror

antiéconomique [ɑ̃tiekɔnɔmik] ADJ *Com* contrary to economic principles, uneconomic

antiémétique [ɑ̃tiemetik], **antiémétisant, -e** [ɑ̃tiemetizɑ̃, -ɑ̃t] *Pharm* ADJ antiemetic
NM antiemetic

antiémeute [ɑ̃tiemøt] ADJ antiriot

antienne [ɑ̃tjɛn] NF **1** *Mus & Rel* antiphon **2** *Fig* refrain; **chanter toujours la même a.** to be always harping on about the same thing

antiesclavagisme [ɑ̃tiɛsklavaʒism] NM *Pol* opposition to slavery; *Hist (aux États-Unis)* abolitionism

antiesclavagiste [ɑ̃tiɛsklavaʒist] ADJ antislavery *(avant n)*; *Hist (aux États-Unis)* abolitionist
NMF *Pol* opponent of slavery; *Hist (aux États-Unis)* abolitionist

antifading [ɑ̃tifediŋ] NM *Élec & Rad* automatic volume control

antifascisme [ɑ̃tifaʃism] NM *Pol* antifascism

antifasciste [ɑ̃tifaʃist] *Pol* ADJ antifascist
NMF antifascist

antifongique [ɑ̃tifɔ̃ʒik] *Méd* ADJ antifungal, fungicidal
NM fungicide, antifungal

antifriction [ɑ̃tifriksjɔ̃] ADJ INV *Métal* antifriction; **alliage a.** antifriction metal, white metal

antigang [ɑ̃tigɑ̃g] *voir* **brigade**

antigaz [ɑ̃tigaz] ADJ anti-gas

antigel [ɑ̃tiʒɛl] NM **1** *Aut* antifreeze **2** *Chim* antigel

antigène [ɑ̃tiʒɛn] NM *Biol* antigen

antigivrant, -e [ɑ̃tiʒivrɑ̃, -ɑ̃t] ADJ *Aviat* anti-ice *(avant n)*
NM anti-icer

antigivreur [ɑ̃tiʒivrœr] NM anti-icer

antiglisse [ɑ̃tiglis] ADJ INV *Ski* antislip, nonslip

antigrippal, -e, -aux, -ales [ɑ̃tigripal, -o] ADJ *Méd & Pharm (médicament, traitement)* flu *(avant n)*

antiguerre [ɑ̃tigɛr] NMF INV person opposed to the war; **les a.** the people opposed to the war

antihalo [ɑ̃tialo] *Phot* ADJ INV antihalation
NM antihalation

antihéros [ɑ̃tiero] NM *Littérature* antihero

antihistaminique [ɑ̃tiistaminik] *Chim* ADJ antihistamine
NM antihistamine

antihygiénique [ɑ̃tiiʒjenik] ADJ unhygienic

anti-inflammatoire [ɑ̃tiɛ̃flamatwar] *(pl* **anti-inflammatoires)** *Méd* ADJ anti-inflammatory
NM anti-inflammatory agent

anti-inflationniste [ɑ̃tiɛ̃flasjɔnist] *(pl* **anti-inflationnistes)** ADJ *Écon* anti-inflationary

antillais, -e [ɑ̃tijɛ, -ɛz] ADJ West Indian
• **Antillais, -e** NM,F West Indian

Antilles [ɑ̃tij] NFPL **les A.** the Antilles, the West Indies; **les A. françaises/néerlandaises** the French/Dutch West Indies; **la mer des A.** the Caribbean Sea

> **ANTILLES**
>
> The French West Indies include the overseas "départements" of Martinique and Guadeloupe, the latter including the islands of La Désirade, Marie-Galante, Saint-Barthélemy (Saint Bart), Les Saintes and part of Saint-Martin.

antilogarithme [ɑ̃tilɔgaritm] NM *Math* antilogarithm

antilope [ɑ̃tilɔp] NF *Zool* antelope

antimatière [ɑ̃timatjɛr] NF *Phys* antimatter

antimilitarisme [ɑ̃timilitarism] NM *Mil* antimilitarism

antimilitariste [ɑ̃timilitarist] *Mil* ADJ antimilitarist
NMF antimilitarist

antimissile [ɑ̃timisil] ADJ INV *Mil* antimissile

antimite [ɑ̃timit] ADJ INV **boules a.** mothballs; **produit a.** moth repellent
NM moth repellent

antimoine [ɑ̃timwan] NM *Chim* antimony

antimonarchique [ɑ̃timɔnarʃik] ADJ *Pol* antimonarchical

antimonarchiste [ɑ̃timɔnarʃist] *Pol* ADJ antimonarchist
NMF antimonarchist

antimondialisation [ɑ̃timɔ̃djalizasjɔ̃] NF *Pol* antiglobalization

antimondialiste [ɑ̃timɔ̃djalist] ADJ antiglobalist
NMF antiglobalist

antimycosique [ɑ̃timikozik] *Méd* ADJ antimycotic
NM antimycotic

antinationalisme [ɑ̃tinasjɔnalism] NM *Pol* antinationalism

antinazi, -e [ɑ̃tinazi] *Pol* ADJ anti-Nazi
NM,F anti-Nazi

antinévralgique [ɑ̃tinevralʒik] ADJ *Pharm* antineuralgic

antinomie [ɑ̃tinɔmi] NF *Ling* antinomy

antinomique [ɑ̃tinɔmik] ADJ *Ling* antinomic

antinucléaire [ɑ̃tinykleɛr] *Nucl* ADJ antinuclear
NMF supporter of antinuclear policies

Antiope [ɑ̃tjɔp] NPR *Myth* Antiope

antioxydant [ɑ̃tiɔksidɑ̃] NM *Biol & Chim* antioxidant, oxidation inhibitor

antipaludéen, -enne [ɑ̃tipalydeɛ̃, -ɛn], **antipaludique** [ɑ̃tipalydik] *Méd* ADJ antimalarial, antipaludal
NM antimalarial, antipaludal

antipape [ɑ̃tipap] NM *Rel* antipope

antiparasitage [ɑ̃tiparazitaʒ] NM *Élec* interference suppression

antiparasite [ɑ̃tiparazit] *Élec* ADJ INV anti-interference *(avant n)*
NM interference suppressor, interference eliminator, *Br* noise blanker

antiparlementaire [ɑ̃tiparləmɑ̃tɛr] ADJ *Pol* antiparliamentary

antiparlementarisme [ɑ̃tiparləmɑ̃tarism] NM *Pol* antiparliamentarism

antipathie [ɑ̃tipati] NF antipathy; **avoir** *ou* **éprouver de l'a. pour qn** to dislike sb

antipathique [ɑ̃tipatik] ADJ unpleasant; **je le trouve assez a.** I don't like him much

antipatinage [ɑ̃tipatinaʒ] ADJ *Tech (système, dispositif)* antiskid *(avant n)*

antipelliculaire [ɑ̃tipelikylɛr] ADJ *(shampooing, traitement)* dandruff *(avant n)*, antidandruff *(avant n)*

antipersonnel [ɑ̃tipersɔnɛl] ADJ INV *Mil* antipersonnel; **mine a.** anti-personnel mine

antiphrase [ɑ̃tifraz] NF *Ling* antiphrasis
• **par antiphrase** ADV ironically; **il a dit ça par a.** he was being ironic

antipiratage [ɑ̃tipirataʒ] ADJ INV anti-piracy

antipode [ɑ̃tipɔd] NM antipode; **les antipodes** the antipodes; **la Nouvelle-Zélande est aux antipodes de la France** New Zealand is at the opposite point of the globe from France; *Fig* **c'est aux antipodes de ce que je pensais** it's light years away from what I imagined

antipoétique [ɑ̃tipoetik] ADJ *Littérature* unpoetic

antipoison [ɑ̃tipwazɔ̃] ADJ INV **centre a.** emergency poisons unit

antipoliomyélitique [ɑ̃tipɔljomjelitik] ADJ *Méd* antipolio, polio *(avant n)*

antipollution [ɑ̃tipɔlysjɔ̃] ADJ INV antipollution *(avant n)*; **contrôle/mesure a.** pollution control/measure

antiprotectionniste [ɑ̃tiprɔteksjɔnist] *Écon* ADJ antiprotectionist, free trade *(avant n)*
NMF antiprotectionist, free-trader

antipsychiatrie [ɑ̃tipsikjatri] NF *Psy* antipsychiatry

antipub [ɑ̃tipyb] ADJ anti-advertising
NMF anti-advertising campaigner

antipyrétique [ɑ̃tipiretik] *Méd* ADJ antipyretic, antifebrile
NM antipyretic, antifebrile

antipyrine [ɑ̃tipirin] NF *Pharm* antipyrine

antiquaille [ɑ̃tikaj] NF *Péj* (worthless) antique, piece of bric-a-brac

antiquaire [ɑ̃tikɛr] NMF antique dealer

antique [ɑ̃tik] ADJ **1** *(d'époque ▸ meuble, bijou, châle)* antique, old **2** *(démodé)* antiquated, ancient
NM **l'a.** *(œuvres)* antiquities; *(art)* classical art

antiquité [ɑ̃tikite] NF **1** *(objet)* antique; **des antiquités** antiques; **magasin d'antiquités** antique shop; *Fig Hum* **sa voiture, c'est une a.!** his/her car is ancient *or* an old wreck! **2** *Antiq (période)* **l'a.** ancient times, antiquity; **l'A. (grecque et romaine)** Ancient Greece and Rome **3** *(ancienneté)* great age; **ça remonte à la plus haute a.** that goes back *or* dates back to time immemorial
• **antiquités** NFPL *Beaux-Arts* antique art
• **de toute antiquité** ADV from time immemorial

antirabique [ɑ̃tirabik] ADJ *Méd* anti-rabies *(avant n)*

antirachitique [ɑ̃tiraʃitik] ADJ *Méd* antirachitic

antiracisme [ɑ̃tirasism] NM *Pol* antiracism

antiraciste [ɑ̃tirasist] ADJ antiracist
NMF antiracist

antiradar [ɑ̃tiradar] *Mil* ADJ INV antiradar
NM anti-radar device

antireflet [ɑ̃tirəflɛ] ADJ INV coated, *Spéc* bloomed; *Ordinat* non-reflecting, antiglare; **verre a.** non-reflecting glass

antiréglementaire [ɑ̃tireglәmɑ̃tɛr] ADJ against regulations

antireligieux, -euse [ɑ̃tirəliʒjø, -øz] **ADJ** *Rel* antireligious

antirépublicain, -e [ɑ̃tirepyblikɛ̃, -ɛn] *Pol* **ADJ** antirepublican
NM,F antirepublican

antirétroviral, -e, -aux, -ales [ɑ̃tiretrɔviral, -o] **ADJ** *(molécule, traitement)* antiretroviral

antirévolutionnaire [ɑ̃tirevɔlysjɔnɛr] *Pol* **ADJ** antirevolutionary
NMF antirevolutionary

antirides [ɑ̃tirid] **ADJ** anti-wrinkle *(avant n)*

antiroman [ɑ̃tirɔmɑ̃] **NM** *Littérature* anti-novel

antirouille [ɑ̃tiruj] **ADJ INV** antirust *(avant n)*, rust-resistant
NM *(pour protéger de la rouille)* rust inhibitor; *(pour enlever la rouille)* rust remover

antiroulis [ɑ̃tiruli] **ADJ** *Aut & Naut* anti-roll *(avant n)*

antiscorbutique [ɑ̃tiskɔrbytik] **ADJ** *Méd* antiscorbutic

antisèche [ɑ̃tisɛʃ] **NF** *Fam Arg scol Br* crib, *Am* cheat sheet

antiségrégationniste [ɑ̃tisegregasjɔnist] **ADJ & NMF** *Pol* antisegregationist

antisémite [ɑ̃tisemit] *Rel* **ADJ** anti-Semitic
NMF anti-Semite

antisémitisme [ɑ̃tisemitism] **NM** *Rel* anti-Semitism

antisepsie [ɑ̃tisɛpsi] **NF** *Méd* antisepsis

antiseptique [ɑ̃tisɛptik] *Méd & Pharm* **ADJ** antiseptic
NM antiseptic

antisérum [ɑ̃tiserɔm] **NM** *Physiol* antiserum

antisocial, -e, -aux, -ales [ɑ̃tisɔsjal, -o] **ADJ** antisocial

anti-sous-marin, -e [ɑ̃tisumarɛ̃, -in] *(mpl* **anti-sous-marins,** *fpl* **anti-sous-marines)** **ADJ** *Mil* antisubmarine

antisoviétique [ɑ̃tisɔvjetik] **ADJ** *Pol* anti-Soviet

antispasmodique [ɑ̃tispasmɔdik] *Pharm* **ADJ** antispasmodic
NM antispasmodic

antisportif, -ive [ɑ̃tispɔrtif, -iv] **ADJ** *Sport* **1** *(hostile au sport)* anti-sport **2** *(contraire à l'esprit sportif)* unsporting, unsportsmanlike

antistrophe [ɑ̃tistrɔf] **NF** *Littérature* antistrophe

antisudoral, -e, -aux, -ales [ɑ̃tisydɔral, -o] **ADJ** *Physiol* antiperspirant

antisyndicalisme [ɑ̃tisɛ̃dikalism] **NM** union-bashing

antitabac [ɑ̃titaba] **ADJ INV** *(campagne, lutte)* anti-smoking

antiterreur [ɑ̃titɛrœr] **ADJ** anti-terror

antiterrorisme [ɑ̃titerɔrism] **NM** anti-terrorism

antiterroriste [ɑ̃titɛrɔrist] **ADJ** anti-terrorist

antitétanique [ɑ̃titetanik] **ADJ** *Méd* antitetanic

antithèse [ɑ̃titɛz] **NF** *Ling* antithesis; *Fig* **je suis l'a. de ma sœur** I'm the complete opposite of my sister

antithétique [ɑ̃titetik] **ADJ** *Ling* antithetical, antithetic

antitoxine [ɑ̃titɔksin] **NF** *Biol & Pharm* antitoxin

antitoxique [ɑ̃titɔksik] **ADJ** *Biol & Pharm* antitoxic

antitrust [ɑ̃titrœst] **ADJ INV** *Br* anti-monopoly, *Am* antitrust

antituberculeux, -euse [ɑ̃tityberkylø, -øz] **ADJ** *Méd* antitubercular, antituberculous; **centre a.** tuberculosis centre

antitussif, -ive [ɑ̃titysif, -iv] **ADJ** *Pharm* **sirop a.** cough syrup

antivariolique [ɑ̃tivarjɔlik] **ADJ** **vaccin a.** smallpox vaccine

antivénérien, -enne [ɑ̃tivenerjɛ̃, -ɛn] **ADJ** *Méd* antivenereal

antivenimeux, -euse [ɑ̃tivənimø, -øz] **ADJ** *Méd* antivenin

antivieillissement [ɑ̃tivjɛjismɑ̃] **NM** *(produit qui ralentit le vieillissement)* anti-ageing product; **traitement a.** anti-ageing treatment

antiviral, -e, -aux, -ales [ɑ̃tiviral, -o] *Méd & Pharm* **ADJ** antiviral, antivirus *(avant n)*
NM antiviral

antivirus [ɑ̃tivirys] **NM** *Ordinat* antivirus

antivivisection(n)iste [ɑ̃tiviviseksjɔnist] **NMF** antivivisectionist
ADJ antivivisectionist, antivivisection *(avant n)*; **société a.** antivivisection society

antivol [ɑ̃tivɔl] **ADJ INV** antitheft *(avant n)*
NM 1 *Aut* theft protection; *(sur la direction)* steering (wheel) lock **2** *(de vélo)* (bicycle) lock

antonomase [ɑ̃tɔnɔmaz] **NF** *Ling* antonomasia

antonyme [ɑ̃tɔnim] **NM** *Ling* antonym

antre [ɑ̃tr] **NM 1** *(abri)* cavern, cave **2** *(repaire ▸ d'un fauve, d'un ogre) & Fig* lair, den; *(▸ d'un brigand)* hideout **3** *Anat* antrum

anurie [anyri] **NF** *Méd* anuria

anus [anys] **NM** *Anat* anus; **a. artificiel** colostomy

Anvers [ɑ̃vɛr(s)] **NF** *Géog* Antwerp

anversois, -e [ɑ̃vɛrswa, -az] **ADJ** of/from Antwerp
• **Anversois, -e NM,F** = inhabitant of or person from Antwerp

anxiété [ɑ̃ksjete] **NF** anxiety, worry; **attendre qch avec a.** to wait anxiously for sth; *Psy* **a. névrotique** anxiety neurosis

anxieuse [ɑ̃ksjøz] *voir* **anxieux**

anxieusement [ɑ̃ksjøzmɑ̃] **ADV** anxiously, worriedly

anxieux, -euse [ɑ̃ksjø, -øz] **ADJ** *(inquiet ▸ attente)* anxious; *(▸ regard, voix, personne)* anxious, worried; **être a. de qch** to be anxious *or* impatient about sth; **être a. de réussir** to be impatient to succeed *or* for success
NM,F worrier; **c'est un grand a.** he's the anxious type

anxiogène [ɑ̃ksjɔʒɛn] **ADJ** *Psy* anxiety-provoking

anxiolytique [ɑ̃ksjɔlitik] **ADJ** anxiolytic
NM tranquillizer

AOC [aose] **NF** *(abrév* **appellation d'origine contrôlée)** appellation (d'origine) contrôlée *(official certification guaranteeing the quality of French produce, especially wines and cheeses)*

aorte [aɔrt] **NF** *Anat* aorta

aortique [aɔrtik] **ADJ** *Anat* aortic, aortal

août [u(t)] **NM** August; **le 15 a.** = national holiday in France, well-known as a time of heavy traffic congestion; *voir aussi* **mars**

aoûtien, -enne [ausjɛ̃, -ɛn] **NM,F** August *Br* holidaymaker *or Am* vacationer

apache [apaʃ] **ADJ** Apache
• **Apache NMF** Apache

apaisant, -e [apɛzɑ̃, -ɑ̃t] **ADJ 1** *(qui calme la douleur)* soothing **2** *(qui calme la colère ▸ paroles, voix)* soothing; *(▸ influence)* calming

apaisement [apɛzmɑ̃] **NM 1** *(fait de calmer ▸ soif)* quenching; *(▸ faim, désir)* assuaging; *(▸ chagrin)* easing, alleviation; *(▸ douleur)* soothing, alleviation; **attendre l'a. d'une tempête** to wait for a storm to die down; **j'attendais l'a. de ses colères** I would wait for him/her to calm down after his/her angry outbursts **2** *(fait de se calmer)* quietening down
• **apaisements NMPL** *(paroles)* assurances; **donner des apaisements à qn** to give sb assurances

apaiser [4] [apeze] **VT** *(calmer ▸ opposants, mécontents)* to calm down, to pacify, to appease; *(▸ soif)* to quench; *(▸ faim, désir)* to assuage; *(▸ chagrin)* to ease, to alleviate; *(▸ douleur)* to soothe, to alleviate; **je ne savais pas quoi dire pour a. sa colère** I didn't know what to say to calm him/her down; **a. les esprits** to calm things down
VPR s'apaiser *(se calmer ▸ personne)* to calm down; *(▸ bruit, dispute, tempête, vent)* to die down, to subside; *(▸ colère, chagrin, douleur)* to subside; *(▸ faim, désir)* to be assuaged; *(▸ soif)* to be quenched

apanage [apanaʒ] **NM** prerogative, privilege; **avoir l'a. de qch** to have a monopoly on sth; **être l'a. de qn** to be sb's privilege

aparté [aparte] **NM 1** *(discussion)* private conversation **2** *Théât* aside
• **en aparté ADV** as an aside; **il me l'a dit en a.** he took me aside to tell me

apartheid [apartɛd] **NM** *Hist & Pol* apartheid

apathie [apati] **NF** apathy, listlessness

apathique [apatik] **ADJ** apathetic, listless

apatride [apatrid] *Jur* **ADJ** stateless
NMF stateless person

apatridie [apatridi] **NF** *Jur* statelessness

APD [apede] **NF** *(abrév* **Aide publique au développement)** ODA

APE [apeə] **NF** *UE (abrév* **Assemblée parlementaire européenne)** EP

APEC [apɛk] **NF** *(abrév* **Association pour l'emploi des cadres)** = agency providing information and employment and training opportunities for professionals

Apennin [apenɛ̃] **NM l'A., les Apennins** the Apennines

aperception [apersɛpsjɔ̃] **NF** *Phil* apperception

apercevoir [52] [apersəvwar] **VT 1** *(voir brièvement)* to glimpse, to catch sight of; **il était pressé, je n'ai fait que l'a.** he was in a hurry, so I just caught a glimpse of him **2** *(distinguer)* to make out; **on apercevait le phare au loin** you could (just) make out the lighthouse in the distance **3** *(remarquer)* to see, to notice; **elle cherche à ne pas laisser a. sa fatigue** she's trying not to let her tiredness show; **si on y pense bien, on aperçoit des difficultés** if you think about it, you start to see difficulties
VPR s'apercevoir 1 *(emploi réfléchi)* to catch sight of oneself **2** *(emploi réciproque)* to catch a glimpse of one another **3 s'a. de** *(voir)* to notice, to see; *(réaliser)* to become aware of, to realize; **il ne s'est aperçu de rien** he didn't notice *or* see anything; **on s'en aperçoit à peine** it's hardly noticeable; **sans s'en a.** inadvertently, without realizing it; **s'a. que** to realize *or* to understand that; **je m'aperçois que c'est plus difficile que je ne croyais** I now realize it's more difficult than I thought; **il s'en est aperçu peu à peu** it gradually dawned on him

aperçu [apɛrsy] **NM 1** *(idée générale)* outline, idea; **avoir un a. de la situation** to have a general idea of the situation; *Ordinat* **a. avant impression** print preview **2** *(observation)* insight

aperçut *etc voir* **apercevoir**

apériodique [aperjɔdik] **ADJ** aperiodic

apéritif, -ive [aperitif, -iv] **ADJ faire une promenade apéritive** to take a walk to work up an appetite; **prendre une boisson apéritive** to have an aperitif
NM drink, aperitif; **prendre l'a.** to have a drink *(before lunch or dinner)*, to have an aperitif

L'APÉRITIF

In France, the "apéritif", or "apéro", is an informal social ritual. It is quite usual to invite people for before-dinner drinks without actually providing dinner, or to arrange to meet someone in a café "pour l'apéritif" before going out for a meal.

apéro [apero] **NM** *Fam* aperitif^□, drink^□ *(before lunch or dinner)*

aperture [apɛrtyr] **NF** *Ling* aperture

apesanteur [apəzɑ̃tœr] **NF** *Astron & Phys* weightlessness; **en état d'a., en a.** in weightless conditions

à-peu-près [apøprɛ] **NM INV** *(approximation)* approximation; **il y a trop d'à. dans votre rapport** your report is too vague

apeuré, -e [apœre] **ADJ** scared, frightened

apeurer [5] [apœre] **VT** to scare, to frighten

APEX [apɛks] **NM** *(ticket)* APEX

apex [apɛks] **NM** *Anat & Astron* apex

aphasie [afazi] **NF** *Méd* aphasia

aphasique [afazik] *Méd* **ADJ** aphasic
NMF aphasic

aphone [afɔn] **ADJ** *(sans voix)* hoarse; **j'étais complètement a.** I'd lost my voice; **il est devenu a., tellement il a crié** he's shouted himself hoarse

aphonie [afɔni] **NF** *Méd* aphonia

aphorisme [afɔrism] NM *Ling* aphorism; *Péj* **s'exprimer par aphorismes** to speak in platitudes

aphrodisiaque [afrɔdizjak] ADJ aphrodisiac
NM aphrodisiac

aphte [aft] NM mouth ulcer

aphteux, -euse [aftø, -øz] ADJ aphthous; *Méd & Vét* **fièvre aphteuse** foot-and-mouth disease

API [ɑpei] NM *Ling (abrév* **alphabet phonétique international***)* IPA
NF *(abrév* **allocation de parent isolé***)* = allowance paid to single parents

à-pic [apik] NM INV sheer cliff

apicole [apikɔl] ADJ beekeeping *(avant n)*, *Spéc* apiarian; **exploitation a.** honey farm

apiculteur, -trice [apikyltœr, -tris] NM,F beekeeper

apiculture [apikyltyr] NF beekeeping

apitoie *etc voir* **apitoyer**

apitoiement [apitwamɑ̃] NM pity, compassion; **pas d'a.!** *(ne sois pas indulgent)* don't feel sorry for him/her/*etc*!; *(sois sans pitié)* show no mercy!

apitoyer [13] [apitwaje] VT to arouse the pity of; **il veut m'a.** he's trying to make me feel sorry for him
VPR **s'apitoyer s'a. sur qn** to feel sorry for *or* to pity sb; **s'a. sur soi-même** *ou* **sur son sort** to feel sorry for oneself

ap. J.-C. *(abrév écrite* **après Jésus-Christ***)* AD

APL [apeɛl] NF *(abrév* **aide personnalisée au logement***)* ≃ housing benefit

aplanir [32] [aplanir] VT **1** *(niveler ▸ terrain)* to level (off), to grade; *(▸ surface)* to smooth, to level off **2** *Fig (difficulté)* to smooth out *or* over, to iron out; *(obstacle)* to remove
VPR **s'aplanir 1** *(surface)* to level out *or* off **2** *(difficulté, obstacle)* **les difficultés se sont peu à peu aplanies** the difficulties gradually smoothed themselves out

aplanissement [aplanismɑ̃] NM *(d'un jardin, d'une surface)* levelling (off); *Fig* **nous lui devons l'a. de toutes nos difficultés** we have him/her to thank for ironing out all our problems

aplat, à-plat [apla] *(pl* **à-plats***)* NM *(couleur)* flat tint, solid colour

aplati, -e [aplati] ADJ *(gén)* flattened; *(nez)* flat; **la Terre est aplatie aux pôles** the Earth is flat at the poles

aplatir [32] [aplatir] VT **1** *(rendre plat ▸ tôle, verre, surface)* to flatten (out); *(▸ couture, pli)* to press (flat), to smooth (out); *(▸ cheveux)* to smooth *or* to plaster down; **aplatissez le morceau de pâte avec votre main** flatten out the piece of dough with your hand; **a. qch à coups de marteau** to hammer sth flat
2 *(écraser)* to flatten, to squash, to crush; **a. son nez contre la vitre** to flatten *or* to squash one's nose against the window
3 *Fam (vaincre)* to crush, to flatten; **encore un mot et je t'aplatis!** one more word and I'll flatten you!
4 *Sport* **a. le ballon** *(au rugby)* to score a try, to ground the ball; **a. un essai** to score a try, to ground the ball
USAGE ABSOLU *Sport (en rugby)* to score a try
VPR **s'aplatir 1** *(être plat)* to be flat; *(devenir plat ▸ terrain)* to flatten (out), to become flat; *(▸ cheveux)* to go flat; *(▸ chapeau)* to get flattened; **après la rivière, le relief commence à s'a.** the contours flatten out *or* get flatter beyond the river
2 *(se coller)* **s'a. par terre** to lie flat on the ground; **s'a. contre le mur** to flatten oneself against the wall; **sa voiture s'est aplatie contre un arbre** his/her car smashed into a tree
3 *Fam (s'humilier)* to crawl; **s'a. devant qn** to go crawling to sb
4 *Fam (tomber)* to fall flat on one's face

aplatissage [aplatisaʒ] NM *(de la tôle, du verre, d'une surface)* flattening; *(d'une couture, d'un pli)* pressing (flat), smoothing (out)

aplatissement [aplatismɑ̃] NM **1** *Astron & Géom* **l'a. de la Terre** the flattening of the Earth **2** *(fait de rendre plat)* flattening **3** *Fam (servilité)* crawling

aplomb [aplɔ̃] NM **1** *(verticalité)* perpendicularity; **à l'a. de** *(au-dessus de)* directly above; *(au-dessous de)* directly below **2** *(confiance en soi)* self-assurance, self-possession; **avoir de l'a.** to be self-possessed *or* self-assured; **répondre avec a.** to answer with self-assurance *or* self-possession **3** *Péj (insolence)* nerve; **avoir l'a. de faire qch** to have the nerve to do sth; **il ne manque pas d'a.** he really has a nerve
• **d'aplomb** ADJ **1** *(vertical)* perpendicular; **être d'a.** to be vertical; *Constr* **ne pas être d'a.** to be out of plumb *or* off plumb; *(en déséquilibre)* to be askew; **être bien d'a. sur ses jambes** to be steady on one's feet **2** *(en bonne santé)* well; **être d'a.** to be well *or* in good health; **ne pas être d'a.** to feel unwell *or* out of sorts ADV **1** *(à la verticale) Constr* **mettre qch d'a.** to plumb sth (up); *(redresser)* to straighten sth up **2** *(en bonne santé)* **remettre qn d'a.** to put sb back on his/her feet, to make sb better

aplomber [3] [aplɔ̃be] *Can* VT *(verticalement)* to make straight; *(horizontalement)* to make level
VPR **s'aplomber** to straighten up

apnée [apne] NF apnoea; **descendre** *ou* **plonger en a.** to dive without breathing apparatus

apnéiste [apneist] NMF apnoea diver, breath-holding diver

apocalypse [apɔkalips] NF *(catastrophe)* apocalypse; **une a. nucléaire** a nuclear holocaust
• **Apocalypse** NF *Rel* **l'A.** the Apocalypse, the (Book of) Revelation
• **d'apocalypse** ADJ *(vision)* apocalyptic; *(récit)* doom-laden; **un paysage d'a.** a scene of total devastation

apocalyptique [apɔkaliptik] ADJ apocalyptic, cataclysmic; *Fig* **un paysage a.** a scene of total devastation; **un silence a.** a doom-laden silence

apocope [apɔkɔp] NF *Ling* apocope

apocryphe [apɔkrif] ADJ apocryphal
NM *Littérature* apocryphal text; **les apocryphes (de la Bible)** the Apocrypha

apogée [apɔʒe] NM **1** *Astron* apogee **2** *(sommet)* peak, summit, apogee; **à l'a. de sa carrière** at the height *or* at the peak of his/her career; **atteindre son a.** to reach one's peak

apolitique [apɔlitik] *Pol* ADJ *(sans convictions politiques)* apolitical; *(non affilié)* nonpolitical
NMF apolitical person

apolitisme [apɔlitism] NM *Pol (refus de s'engager)* apolitical stance; *(engagement sans affiliation)* nonpolitical stance

Apollon [apɔlɔ̃] NPR *Myth* Apollo; **l'A. du Belvédère** the Apollo Belvedere
• **apollon** NM *(bel homme)* Adonis; **un jeune a.** a young Adonis; **ce n'est pas un a.** he's no oil painting

apologétique [apɔlɔʒetik] ADJ apologetic
NF *Rel* apologetics *(singulier)*

apologie [apɔlɔʒi] NF *(défense)* apologia (**de** for); *(éloge)* encomium, eulogy (**de** of); **faire l'a. de qn/qch** *(défendre)* to (seek to) justify sb/sth; *(louer)* to eulogize sb/sth

> Il faut noter que le nom anglais **apology** est un faux ami. Il signifie **excuses**.

apologiste [apɔlɔʒist] NMF apologist

apologue [apɔlɔg] NM *Littérature* apologue

apophyse [apɔfiz] NF *Anat* apophysis

apoplectique [apɔplɛktik] *Méd* ADJ apoplectic
NMF apoplectic

apoplexie [apɔplɛksi] NF *Méd* apoplexy; **attaque d'a.** stroke; *Fig* **il était au bord de l'a.** he nearly had a fit

apostasie [apɔstazi] NF *Rel* apostasy

apostasier [9] [apɔstazje] *Rel* VT to apostatize
VI to apostatize

apostat, -e [apɔsta, -at] *Rel & Littéraire* ADJ apostate, renegade *(avant n)*
NM,F apostate, renegade

a posteriori [apɔsterjɔri] ADJ INV a posteriori
ADV afterwards; **il est facile de juger a.** it's easy to be wise after the event; **je m'en suis aperçu a.** I realized later *or* afterwards

apostolat [apɔstɔla] NM **1** *Rel* apostolate, discipleship **2** *(prosélytisme)* evangelism, proselytism **3** *(vocation)* dedication, vocation; **pour lui, l'enseignement est un a.** he is wholeheartedly devoted to teaching, teaching is his mission in life

apostolique [apɔstɔlik] ADJ *Rel* apostolic

apostrophe [apɔstrɔf] NF **1** *(interpellation)* invective **2** *Gram* apostrophe; **mis en a.** used in apostrophe; **le vocatif est le cas de l'a.** the vocative is the case of direct address **3** *(signe)* apostrophe; **s a. s** apostrophe

apostropher [3] [apɔstrɔfe] VT to shout at
VPR **s'apostropher** to shout at each other

apothéose [apɔteoz] NF **1** *(apogée)* summit; **l'a. du courage** the height of bravery; **ce concert a été l'a. du festival** the concert was the highlight of the festival **2** *Théât* (grand) finale; **cela s'est terminé en a.** it ended in grand style

apothicaire [apɔtikɛr] NM *Arch* apothecary

apôtre [apotr] NM **1** *Rel* apostle, disciple **2** *(avocat)* advocate; **se faire l'a. d'une idée** to champion *or* to speak for an idea; **un a. de la tolérance** an advocate *or* a champion of tolerance; *Péj* **faire le bon a.** to be holier-than-thou

Appalaches [apalaʃ] NMPL **les A.** the Appalachian Mountains, the Appalachians

appalachien, -enne [apalaʃjɛ̃, -ɛn] ADJ Appalachian

apparaître [91] [aparɛtr] VI **1** *(à la vue)* to appear; **des nuages menaçants apparaissaient dans le ciel** menacing clouds were appearing in the sky; **après le bosquet, on voit a. le village** after you pass the copse, the village comes into view; **a. à qn en songe** *ou* **rêve** to appear *or* to come to sb in a dream
2 *(à l'esprit)* to appear, to transpire, to emerge; **ce qui apparaît, c'est surtout sa méchanceté** what emerges above all is his/her wickedness; **la vérité m'est apparue un beau jour** the truth came to *or* dawned on me one day; **faire a. la vérité** to bring the truth to light
3 *(surgir)* to appear, to materialize; **il est apparu tout d'un coup au coin de la rue** he appeared suddenly at the street corner; **le chat est apparu au milieu des couvertures** the cat emerged from the blankets
4 *(figurer)* to appear, to feature; **la liste des ingrédients doit a. sur le paquet** the list of ingredients must appear *or* feature on the packet
5 *(se manifester ▸ symptôme, bouton)* to appear; *(▸ maladie)* to develop; *(▸ préjugé, habitude)* to develop, to surface; **faire a.** to reveal
6 *(sembler)* to seem, to appear; **il m'apparaît comme le seul capable d'y parvenir** he seems to me to be the only person capable of doing it
7 *(tournure impersonnelle)* **il apparaît impossible de faire...** it appears to be *or* it seems impossible to do...; **il apparaît que...** it appears *or* emerges that...

apparat [apara] NM *(cérémonie)* pomp; **en grand a.** with great pomp (and ceremony); **tenue/discours d'a.** ceremonial dress/speech

apparatchik [aparatʃik] NM *Pol* apparatchik

apparaux [aparo] NMPL **1** *Naut* handling gear, tackle **2** *Gym* apparatus

appareil [aparej] NM **1** *(dispositif)* apparatus, device; **a. acoustique** hearing aid; **a. dentaire** *(prothèse)* dentures, (dental) plate; *(pour corriger)* brace, plate; *Tél* **a. mains libres** hands-free device; **a. ménager** household appliance; **a. de mesure** measuring device *or* apparatus; **a. orthopédique** orthopedic device; **a. photo** camera; **a. photo APS** APS camera; **a. photo compact** compact camera; **a. photo jetable** disposable camera; **a. photo numérique** digital camera; **a. plâtré** plaster cast; **a. de projection** film projector; **a. de prothèse** surgical appliance; **a. reflex** reflex camera; **a. (téléphonique)** telephone; **qui est à l'a.?** who's speaking?
2 *Aviat* craft, aircraft
3 *Anat* apparatus, system; **a. digestif** digestive apparatus *or* system; **a. respiratoire** respiratory apparatus
4 *Gym (agrès)* apparatus
5 *Constr* bond
6 *(système)* apparatus; **l'a. du parti** the party apparatus *or* machinery; **l'a. législatif** the machinery of the law; **a. de production** production facilities
7 *Littéraire (cérémonial)* trappings; **l'a. somptueux du couronnement** the pomp and circum-

stance *or* sumptuous trappings of the coronation

appareillage [apareja3] **NM 1** *Naut* casting off, weighing anchor **2** *Tech* equipment **3** *Constr* bonding

appareillement [aparejmɑ̃] **NM** *(d'animaux)* matching, pairing

appareiller [4] [apareje] **VT 1** *Constr* to bond **2** *Naut (bateau)* to rig out; *(filet)* to spread **3** *(assortir)* to match, to pair **4** *Zool (animaux)* to mate

VI *Naut* to cast off, to get under way

apparemment [aparamɑ̃] **ADV** apparently; **a., tout va bien** everything seems to be *or* apparently everything's all right

apparence [aparɑ̃s] **NF 1** *(aspect ▸ d'une personne)* appearance; *(▸d'un objet, d'une situation)* appearance, look; **ça a l'a. du bois** it looks like wood; **avoir belle a.** to look impressive; **avoir une a. maladive** to look sickly, to be sickly-looking; **à l'a. soignée** *(personne)* well-groomed; **à l'a. négligée** *(personne)* untidy-looking, unkempt(-looking); **il a l'air gentil, mais ce n'est qu'une (fausse) a.** he seems nice, but it's only a façade; **les apparences** appearances; **il va très bien, malgré les apparences** he's perfectly well, contrary to all appearances; **juger sur** *ou* **d'après les apparences** to judge *or* to go by appearances; **les apparences sont trompeuses, il ne faut pas se fier aux apparences** *(en jugeant une personne)* looks are deceptive; *(en jugeant une situation)* there's more to it than meets the eye, appearances can be deceptive; **faire qch pour sauver les apparences** to do sth for appearances' sake; **heureusement pour nous, les apparences sont sauvées** fortunately, we've been able to save face **2** *(trace)* semblance, vestige; **elle n'a plus la moindre a. de respect pour lui** she no longer has the slightest semblance of respect for him

• **en apparence ADV** apparently, by *or* to all appearances; **en a. il travaille, mais comment le savoir vraiment?** it may look as though he's working, but how can one be sure?

apparent, -e [aparɑ̃, -ɑ̃t] **ADJ 1** *(visible)* visible; **devenir a.** to become apparent, to surface, to emerge; **il n'y a aucun danger a.** there's no apparent *or* visible danger **2** *(évident)* obvious, apparent, evident; **sans raison apparente** for no obvious *or* apparent reason **3** *(superficiel)* apparent; **une tranquillité apparente** outward *or* surface calm; **sous cette apparente bonté se cache un grand égoïsme** beneath that kind exterior there lies great selfishness

apparenté, -e [aparɑ̃te] **ADJ 1** *(parent)* related **2** *(allié)* allied; **des listes apparentées** grouped electoral lists *(in proportional elections)*; **les socialistes et apparentés** the socialists and their allies **3** *(ressemblant)* similar; **deux styles apparentés** two similar *or* closely related styles

apparentement [aparɑ̃tmɑ̃] **NM 1** *(lien)* link; **son a. à la bourgeoisie** his/her links to the bourgeoisie **2** *Pol (alliance)* alliance; **a. à un groupe parlementaire** alliance with a parliamentary group; **a. de listes électorales** grouping of electoral lists *(in proportional elections)*

apparenter [3] [aparɑ̃te] **s'apparenter VPR 1** *Pol* to enter into an alliance **2 s'a. à** *(ressembler à)* to be like; *(s'allier à ▸ un parti)* to enter into an alliance with; *(▸une famille)* to marry into; **cette histoire s'apparente à une aventure que j'ai vécue** this story is similar to *or* is like an experience I once had

apparier [10] [aparje] **VT 1** *(chaussures, gants)* to match, to pair **2** *Zool* to mate

VPR s'apparier to mate

appariteur [aparitœr] **NM 1** *Jur (huissier)* usher **2** *Univ Br* porter, *Am* campus policeman

apparition [aparisjɔ̃] **NF 1** *(arrivée ▸ d'une personne, d'une saison)* arrival, appearance; **avec l'a. du printemps** with the coming *or* arrival of spring; **faire une a.** to put in *or* to make an appearance; **faire son a.** *(maladie)* to develop; *(soleil)* to come out; **la star a finalement fait son a. vers 18 heures** the star finally appeared *or* made his/her appearance around 6 o'clock **2** *(première manifestation)* (first) appearance; **dès l'a. des premiers symptômes** as soon as the first symptoms appear **3** *(vision)* apparition, vision; **avoir une a.** to be visited by an apparition; **avoir des apparitions** to have visions

appart [apart] **NM** *Fam Br* flat, *Am* apartment

appartement [apartəmɑ̃] **NM** *(logement) Br* flat, *Am* apartment; **a. de fonction** company *Br* flat *or Am* apartment; **a. témoin** *ou* **modèle** *Br* show flat, *Am* model apartment; **a. thérapeutique** sheltered accommodation *(UNCOUNT)*

• **appartements NMPL** *(d'un château)* apartments; *Hum* **se retirer dans ses appartements** to withdraw *or* to retire to one's quarters

appartenance [apartənɑ̃s] **NF 1** *(statut de membre)* **son a. à la tendance symboliste** his/her links *or* his/her association with the Symbolist group; **a. à un club/une communauté** membership of a club/a community; **a. à un parti** affiliation to *or* membership of a party **2** *Math* membership

appartenir [40] [apartənir] **appartenir à VT IND 1** *(être la propriété de)* to belong to; **à qui appartient la voiture verte?** whose is the green car?; **cet argent m'appartient en propre** this money is my own

2 *(faire partie de ▸ groupe)* to belong to, to be part of; *(▸ professorat, syndicat)* to belong to; **il appartient à la même section que toi** he's a member of *or* he belongs to the same group as you; **elle appartient à une famille très riche** she comes from a very wealthy family

3 *(dépendre de)* **pour des raisons qui m'appartiennent** for my own reasons; **l'éducation des enfants appartient aux deux parents** bringing up children is the responsibility of both parents

4 *(tournure impersonnelle)* **il appartient à chacun de faire attention** it's everyone's responsibility to be careful; **il ne vous appartient pas d'en décider** it's not for you to decide, the decision is not yours (to make)

5 *Math* to be a member of

VPR s'appartenir *(être libre)* **avec tout ce travail, je ne m'appartiens plus** I have so much work, my time isn't my own any more

apparu, -e [apary] *pp voir* **apparaître**

appas [apɑ] **NMPL** *Littéraire* charms

appât [apɑ] **NM 1** *Chasse & Pêche* bait *(UNCOUNT)*; **mordre à l'a.** to take the bait; *Fig* to rise to the bait **2** *(attrait)* **l'a. de** the lure of; **l'a. du gain** the lure *or* attraction of money

appâter [3] [apɑte] **VT 1** *(attirer ▸ poisson, animal)* to lure; *(▸ personne)* to lure, to entice; **a. qn par des promesses** to entice sb with promises **2** *(engraisser ▸ volaille)* to forcefeed

appauvrir [32] [apovrir] **VT** *(rendre pauvre ▸ personne, pays)* to impoverish; *(▸ terre)* to impoverish, to drain, to exhaust; *(▸ sang)* to make thin, to weaken; *(▸ langue)* to impoverish

VPR s'appauvrir *(personne, famille, pays)* to get *or* to grow poorer; *(sol)* to become exhausted; *(sang)* to become thin; *(langue)* to become impoverished, to lose its vitality

appauvrissement [apovrismɑ̃] **NM** *(gén)* impoverishment; *(du sang)* thinning

appeau, -x [apo] **NM** *Chasse* **1** *(sifflet)* birdcall **2** *(oiseau)* decoy (duck); *Fig* **servir d'a. à qn** to act as a decoy for sb

appel [apel] **NM 1** *(cri)* call; **un a. au secours** a shout *or* cry for help; **tu n'as pas entendu mes appels?** didn't you hear me calling (out)?; **le mâle répond à l'a. de la femelle** the male answers the call of the female; **l'a. des sens/du large** the call of the senses/of the sea; **l'a. de la nature** the call of the wild; **a. à l'insurrection** call to insurrection; **a. aux armes** call to arms; **un a. à la grève** a call for strike action; **a. au peuple** appeal to the people; **a. au rassemblement** call for unity; **a. de détresse** *Naut* distress signal, call for help; *(d'une personne)* call for help; **faire un a. de phares (à qn)** to flash one's lights (at sb); **a. radio** radio message

2 *(coup de téléphone)* **a. (téléphonique)** (telephone) *or* phone call; *Mktg* **a. à froid** cold call; **a. gratuit** *Br* Freefone®, *Am* toll-free call; **a. interurbain** long-distance call; **a. en PCV** *Br* reverse charge call, *Am* collect call; **a. avec préavis** person-to-person call; **a. de réveil** wake-up *or* alarm call

3 *(demande)* request; **lancer un a. pour l'aide aux sinistrés** to launch an appeal for the disaster victims; **il est resté sourd aux appels (à l'aide) de sa famille** he ignored his family's calls *or* appeals *or* pleas (for help); **faire a. à** *(clémence, générosité)* to appeal to; *(courage, intelligence, qualité)* to summon (up); *(souvenirs)* to summon (up); **faire a. à la générosité publique** to appeal to public generosity; **faire a. à tout son courage** to summon (up) all one's courage, to take one's courage in both hands; **faire a. à la force** to resort to force; **faire a. à un spécialiste** to call in a specialist; **il a fait a. à elle pour son déménagement** he asked her to help him when he moved house

4 *Écon* call; **a. de fonds** call for funds; **faire un a. de fonds** to call up capital; **a. d'offres** invitation to tender; **répondre à un a. d'offres** to make a bid; *Bourse* **a. de couverture** *ou* **de garantie** *ou* **de marge** margin call

5 *Jur* appeal; **en a.** on appeal; **faire a.** to appeal; **faire a. d'un jugement** to appeal against a decision; **aller en a.** to appeal, to go to appeal; **a. à témoins** appeal for witnesses (to come forward)

6 *(liste de présence)* roll call; *Mil (mobilisation)* call-up; **faire l'a.** *Scol Br* to call the register, *Am* to call (the) roll; *Mil* to call the roll; **répondre à l'a.** to be present

7 *Typ* **a. de note** reference mark

8 *Ordinat* call; **a. par référence/valeur** call by reference/value; **programme/séquence d'a.** call routine/sequence

9 *Sport* take-off; **prendre son a.** to take off

• **sans appel ADJ 1** *Jur* without (the possibility of an) appeal **2** *(irrévocable)* irrevocable; **une décision sans a.** an irrevocable *or* a final decision; **répondre d'un ton sans a.** to reply dismissively

appelant, -e [aplɑ̃, -ɑ̃t] **NM,F** *Jur* appellant

appelé, -e [aple] **NM,F il y a beaucoup d'appelés et peu d'élus** many are called but few are chosen

NM *Mil* conscript

appeler [24] [aple] **VT 1** *(interpeller)* to call (out) to, to shout to; **attendez que je vous appelle** wait till I call you; **a. qn par la fenêtre** to call out to sb from the window; **a. le nom de qn** to call out sb's name; **a. au secours** to shout "help", to call for help; *Fig* to call for help

2 *(au téléphone)* to call (up); **appelle-moi demain** call me tomorrow; **appelez ce numéro en cas d'urgence** dial this number in an emergency; **elle appelle Londres** she's on the phone to London

3 *(faire venir ▸ médecin)* to call, to send for; *(▸ police)* to call; *(▸ renforts)* to call up *or* out; *(▸ ascenseur)* to call; **a. du secours** to go for help; **a. qn à l'aide** to call to sb for help; **a. un taxi** *(dans la rue)* to hail a taxi; *(par téléphone)* to phone for *or* to call a taxi; **le patron m'a appelé pour me faire signer le contrat** the boss called me in to get me to sign the contract; **a. qn à qch** to call sb to sth; **a. qn à une fonction importante** to call *or* to appoint sb to a high office; **être appelé sous les drapeaux** to be called up *or* conscripted; **faire a. qn** to send for sb, to summon sb; *Hum* **le devoir m'appelle!** duty calls!; **une affaire m'appelle en ville** I have to go to town on business

4 *Jur* to summon; **être appelé à comparaître** to be summoned *or* issued with a summons; **être appelé à la barre** to be called *or* summoned to the witness stand; **être appelé devant le juge** to be called up before the magistrate

5 *(nécessiter)* to require, to call for; **la situation appelle des mesures immédiates** the situation calls for *or* requires immediate action; **un acte qui appelle une condamnation immédiate** an act which calls for immediate censure

6 *(entraîner)* to lead to; **un coup en appelle un autre** one blow leads to another

7 *(inviter)* **a. qn à qch** to call sb to sth; **a. (des travailleurs) à la grève** to call a strike, to put out a strike call; **a. les gens à la révolte** to incite people to rebel; **a. aux armes** to call to arms

8 *(destiner)* **être appelé à faire qch** to be bound to do sth; **ce quartier est appelé à disparaître** this part of town is due to be demolished (eventually); **j'étais appelée à devenir religieuse** I had a vocation to become a nun

9 *(nommer)* to call; **comment on appelle ça en chinois?** what's (the word for) this in Chinese?; **ici, on appelle tout le monde par un surnom** here we give everybody a nickname; **appelez-moi Jo** call me Jo; **nous appellerons le bébé Marie** we'll call *or*

name the baby Marie; **elle se fait a. Jaspe** she wants to be called Jaspe

10 *Ordinat (programme, fichier)* to call (up); *(réseau)* to dial

USAGE ABSOLU la pauvre, elle a appelé toute la nuit the poor thing called out all night

• **en appeler à VT IND** to appeal to; **j'en appelle à votre bon cœur** I'm appealing to your generosity; **j'en appelle à vous en dernier recours** I'm appealing to you as a last resort

VPR s'appeler 1 *(emploi passif)* to be called; **comment s'appelle-t-il?** what's his name?, what's he called?; **voilà ce qui s'appelle une gaffe!** that's what's called *or* that's what I call putting your foot in it! **2** *(emploi réciproque)* to call one another; **vous vous appelez par vos prénoms?** are you on first-name terms?

> Il faut noter que le verbe anglais **to appeal** est un faux ami. Il ne signifie jamais **appeler**.

appellation [apelasjɔ̃] **NF** appellation, designation; **une a. injurieuse** an insulting name **a. d'origine contrôlée** appellation (d'origine) contrôlée *(official certification guaranteeing the quality of French produce, especially wines and cheeses)*; **a. d'origine** label of quality; **un vin sans a.** a non-vintage wine

appelle *etc voir* **appeler**

appendice [apɛ̃dis] **NM 1** *(supplément)* appendix

2 *(prolongement)* appendage

3 *Hum (nez)* snout

4 *Anat* appendix

appendicectomie [apɛ̃disɛktɔmi] **NF** *Méd* appendicectomy, appendectomy; **j'ai eu une a.** I had my appendix out

appendicite [apɛ̃disit] **NF** appendicitis; **crise d'a.** appendicitis; **se faire opérer de l'a.** to have one's appendix removed

appentis [apɑ̃ti] **NM 1** *(bâtiment)* lean-to **2** *(toit)* lean-to, sloping roof

appesantir [32] [apəzɑ̃tir] **VT** *(rendre pesant ▸ démarche)* to slow down; *(▸ tête, corps)* to weigh down; *(▸ facultés)* to dull; **les paupières appesanties par le sommeil** eyes heavy with sleep; *Fig* **a. son bras** *ou* **autorité sur un pays** to strengthen one's authority over a country

VPR s'appesantir 1 *(devenir lourd ▸ tête)* to become heavier; *(▸ gestes, démarche)* to become slower; *(▸ esprit)* to grow duller; *Fig* **la main de fer de l'Inquisition s'appesantit sur eux** the iron fist of the Inquisition weighed down on them **2** *(insister)* **s'a. sur un sujet** to concentrate on *or* to dwell at length on a subject

appesantissement [apəzɑ̃tismɑ̃] **NM** *(de l'esprit)* (growing) dullness; *(des gestes, de la démarche)* increased heaviness

appétence [apetɑ̃s] **NF** *Littéraire* appetence, appetency; **une a. d'aventure** an appetence for adventure

appétissant, -e [apetisɑ̃, -ɑ̃t] **ADJ 1** *(odeur, mets)* appetizing, mouthwatering; **peu a.** unappetizing **2** *Fam (attirant)* attractive

appétit [apeti] **NM 1** *(envie de manger)* appetite; **avoir de l'a.** *ou* **bon a.** to have a good *or* hearty appetite; **je n'ai plus d'a.** I've lost my appetite, I'm off my food; **manger avec a.** *ou* **de bon a.** to eat heartily; **manger sans a.** to pick at one's food; **la promenade m'a donné de l'a.** *ou* **m'a ouvert l'a.** *ou* **m'a mis en a.** the walk has given me an appetite; **quelques diapositives d'abord, pour vous ouvrir l'a.** first, a few slides, to whet your appetite; **ça va te couper l'a.** it'll spoil your appetite; **perdre l'a.** to lose one's appetite; **bon a.!** enjoy your meal!; **avoir un a. d'oiseau** to eat like a bird; **avoir un a. de loup** *ou* **d'ogre** to eat like a horse; *Prov* **l'a. vient en mangeant** = the more you have, the more you want **2** *(désir)* **a. de** appetite for; **un insatiable a. de vivre/de connaissances** an insatiable thirst for life/for knowledge; **a. sexuel** sexual appetite

applaudimètre [aplodimɛtr] **NM** *Br* clapometer, *Am* applause meter

applaudir [32] [aplodir] **VT 1** *(acteur, orateur)* to applaud, to clap; *(discours, pièce)* to applaud; **et on l'applaudit encore une fois!** let's give him/her another big hand!, let's hear it for him/her one more time!; **il a longuement fait a. le pianiste** he led a long round of applause for the pianist **2** *Fig Littéraire (approuver)* to applaud, to praise; **la décision du gouvernement a été vivement applaudie** the government's decision has been much praised

VI to clap, to applaud; **les gens applaudissaient à tout rompre** there was thunderous applause; *Fig* **a. à une initiative** to praise *or* to applaud an initiative

VPR s'applaudir s'a. de qch/d'avoir fait qch to congratulate oneself on sth/on having done sth

applaudissement [aplodismɑ̃] **NM** *(approbation)* approval

• **applaudissements NMPL** applause *(UNCOUNT)*, clapping *(UNCOUNT)*; **un tonnerre** *ou* **une tempête d'applaudissements** thunderous applause; **soulever des applaudissements** to be applauded

applicable [aplikabl] **ADJ** applicable; **cette règle est a. à tous les cas** this rule applies to all cases; **loi a. à partir du 1er mars** law to be applied *or* to come into force as of 1 March

applicateur [aplikatœr] **ADJ M** applicator *(avant n)*

NM applicator; **tampon avec a.** applicator tampon

application [aplikasjɔ̃] **NF 1** *(pose)* application; **laisser sécher après a. de la première couche** allow to dry after applying the first coat of paint

2 *(mise en pratique ▸ d'une loi)* application, enforcement; *(▸ d'une sentence)* enforcement; **mesures prises en a. de la loi** measures taken to enforce the law, law-enforcement measures; **mettre qch en a.** *(théorie)* to put sth into practice; *(loi, règlement)* to enforce sth, to implement sth; **entrer en a.** to come into force

3 *Tech* application; **les applications pratiques des voyages dans l'espace** the practical applications of space travel

4 *(soin)* application; **travailler avec a.** to work diligently, to apply oneself (to one's work); **il y mettait une a. inhabituelle** he was doing it with unusual application *or* zeal

5 *Couture* **a. de dentelle** (piece of) appliqué lace

6 *Ordinat* application, *Fam* app; **a. bureautique** business application; **a. graphique** graphics application; **a. phare** killer app; **a. en service** current application

applique [aplik] **NF 1** *(lampe)* wall lamp **2** *Couture* piece of appliqué work; **l'a.** appliqué work

appliqué, -e [aplike] **ADJ 1** *(personne)* assiduous, hard-working; *(écriture)* careful **2** *Univ* applied; **informatique appliquée à la gestion** computer technology applied to management

appliquer [3] [aplike] **VT 1** *(poser ▸ masque, crème, ventouse)* to apply; *(▸ enduit)* to apply, to lay on; **a. sur le cou et le visage** *(sur mode d'emploi)* apply to neck and face; **a. son oreille contre la porte** to put one's ear to the door

2 *(mettre en pratique ▸ décret, règlement, mesures)* to enforce, to apply; *(▸ peine)* to enforce; *(▸ idée, réforme)* to put into practice, to implement; *(▸ recette, méthode)* to use; *(▸ théorie, invention)* to apply, to put into practice; **la règle n'est pas toujours appliquée** the rule is not always applied; **a. une loi à un cas particulier** to apply a law to a particular case; **ces juges sont chargés de faire a. les peines** these judges are responsible for ensuring that sentences are carried out

3 *(donner ▸ sobriquet, gifle)* to give; *(▸ baiser)* to plant; **un coup de pied bien appliqué** a powerful kick; **elle lui fit une bise bien appliquée** she planted a kiss on his/her cheek

4 *(consacrer)* **a. qch à** to devote sth to; **a. toute son énergie à son travail** to devote all one's energy to one's work; **a. son esprit à ses études** to apply one's mind to one's studies

VPR s'appliquer 1 *(se poser)* **s'a. sur** *(sujet: objet)* to be laid *or* to fit over; *(sujet: enduit)* to go over, to be applied on; **le pansement s'applique directement sur la lésion** the dressing is applied directly to the wound

2 *(être utilisé)* to apply; **à qui s'applique cette remarque?** who is that remark intended for?; **cela ne s'applique pas dans notre cas** it doesn't apply in *or* it's not applicable to our case

3 *(être attentif ▸ élève, apprenti)* to take care (over one's work), to apply oneself (to one's work); **tu ne t'appliques pas assez!** you don't take enough care over your work!, you don't apply yourself sufficiently!; **s'a. à ses devoirs** to apply oneself to one's homework

4 *(s'acharner)* **s'a. à faire qch** to try to do sth; **je me suis appliqué à faire ce qu'on attendait de moi** I took the trouble to do what was expected of me; **elle s'applique à me contredire** she is making a point of contradicting me

appoint [apwɛ̃] **NM 1** *(argent)* **faire l'a.** to give the exact money *or* change **2** *(revenu supplémentaire)* extra *or* additional income; **ce travail à mi-temps lui fait un petit a.** this part-time job brings him/her a little extra income **3** *Littéraire (aide)* assistance, contribution; **apporter son a. à qch** to contribute to sth

• **d'appoint ADJ** extra; **salaire d'a.** extra income

appointements [apwɛ̃tmɑ̃] **NMPL** salary; **toucher ses a.** to draw one's salary

> Il faut noter que le nom anglais **appointment** est un faux ami. Il signifie **rendez-vous** ou **nomination**, selon le contexte.

appointer [3] [apwɛ̃te] **VT 1** *(rémunérer)* to pay a salary to; **être appointé à la semaine** to be paid weekly *or* by the week **2** *Tech* to sharpen

appondre [75] [apɔ̃dr] **VT** *Suisse* to join (together)

appontage [apɔ̃taʒ] **NM** *Aviat* landing *(on an aircraft carrier)*

appontement [apɔ̃tmɑ̃] **NM** *Naut* wharf, landing stage

apponter [3] [apɔ̃te] **VI** *Aviat* to land *(on an aircraft carrier)*

apport [apɔr] **NM 1** *(fait d'apporter)* contribution; **l'a. culturel des immigrés** the cultural contribution of immigrants; **a. journalier recommandé** recommended daily intake; **l'a. journalier en fer et en calcium** *(fourni)* the daily supply of iron and calcium; *(reçu)* the daily intake of iron and calcium **2** *Fin (fait d'apporter)* contribution; *Écon* inflow, influx; *(dans une entreprise)* initial share; **cette région bénéficie de l'a. (en devises) du tourisme** this area benefits from the financial contribution made *or* the money brought in by tourism; **un a. d'argent frais** an injection of new money; **a. en capital** capital contribution; **a. en espèces** cash contribution; **a. de gestion** management buy-in

apporter [3] [apɔrte] **VT 1** *(objet)* to bring; **apporte-le ici** bring it over here; **apporte-le à papa dans la cuisine** take it to Dad in the kitchen; **apportez vos livres avec vous** bring your books along, bring your books with you; **on lui apporte ses repas au lit** he/she has his/her meals brought to him/her in bed; **Marie, apportez une chaise** Marie, bring *or* fetch a chair; **faut-il a. à boire?** should we bring a bottle?; **les marins qui ont apporté le virus en Europe** the sailors who brought *or* carried the virus (with them) to Europe **2** *(fournir ▸ message, nouvelle)* to give; *(▸ preuve)* to give, to provide, to supply; *(▸ résultat)* to produce; *(▸ capitaux)* to bring in, to contribute; *(▸ soulagement, satisfaction)* to bring; *(▸ modification)* to introduce; **a. de l'attention** *ou* **du soin à qch/à faire qch** to exercise care in sth/in doing sth; **elle apporte à ce projet l'enthousiasme de la jeunesse** she brings the enthusiasm of youth to the project; **vous avez des qualités à a. à notre société** you have skills to bring to our company; **a. de l'aide à qn** to help sb; **cette expérience lui a beaucoup apporté** the experience has been very beneficial for him/her; **ce travail ne m'apporte pas grand-chose** I don't get very much out of this work; **qu'est-ce que ça peut t'a.?** what good can that do you?

> Do not confuse **apporter** and **amener**. The former should be used with inanimate objects and the latter with animate objects.

apposer [3] [apoze] **VT 1** *(ajouter ▸ cachet, signature)* to affix, to append; *Jur (insérer ▸ clause)* to insert **2** *(poser ▸ affiche, plaque)* to put up; *Jur* **a. les scellés sur une porte** to affix the seals on a door

apposition [apozisjɔ̃] **NF 1** *(ajout)* affixing, appending **2** *(pose)* putting up; *Jur (des scellés)* affixing 3 *Gram* apposition; **un substantif en a.** a noun in apposition

appréciable [apresjabl] **ADJ 1** *(perceptible ▸ changement)* appreciable, noticeable; **de manière a.** appreciably **2** *(considérable ▸ somme, effort)* appreciable **3** *(précieux)* **il a des qualités appréciables** he has some good qualities; **c'est a. de pouvoir se lever une heure plus tard** it's nice to be able to get up an hour later

appréciateur, -trice [apresjatœr, -tris] **NM,F** appreciator (**de** of); *Com* appraiser, valuer; **un a. du talent** a good judge of talent

appréciatif, -ive [apresjatif, -iv] **ADJ 1** *(estimatif)* evaluative; **état a. du mobilier** evaluation *or* estimate of the value of the furniture **2** *(admiratif)* appreciative

appréciation [apresjasjɔ̃] **NF 1** *(estimation ▸ d'un poids, d'une valeur)* estimation, assessment; *(▸ d'une situation)* assessment, appreciation, grasp; **je laisse cela à votre a.** I leave it to your judgement; **le pourboire est laissé à votre a.** *(sur carte)* gratuities to be given at your discretion; **son a. du problème laisse à désirer** his/her grasp of the problem isn't all it should be; **a. des risques** risk assessment **2** *(observation)* remark, comment; *Scol* **il a obtenu d'excellentes appréciations** he got a very good report from his teachers **3** *(augmentation ▸ d'une devise)* appreciation; **a. monétaire** currency appreciation

appréciative [apresjativ] *voir* **appréciatif**

appréciatrice [apresjatris] *voir* **appréciateur**

apprécier [9] [apresje] **VT 1** *(évaluer ▸ poids, valeur)* to estimate, to assess; *(▸ distance)* to estimate, to judge; **je ne crois pas que tu apprécies mon travail à sa juste valeur** I don't think you appreciate just how good my work is; **il est impossible d'a. l'étendue des dégâts** it's impossible to estimate *or* assess the extent of the damage

2 *(discerner ▸ ironie, subtilités)* to appreciate; **a. l'importance de qch** to appreciate the significance of sth

3 *(aimer)* to appreciate; **a. qn pour qch** to appreciate sb for sth, to like sb because of sth; **on l'apprécie pour son humour** he's/she's appreciated for his/her sense of humour; **j'ai beaucoup apprécié cette soirée** I liked *or* enjoyed the evening very much; **un vin très apprécié des connaisseurs** a wine much appreciated by connoisseurs; **je n'apprécie pas du tout ce genre de blagues** I don't care for *or* like that sort of joke at all; *Fam* **le sel dans son café, il n'a pas apprécié!** he was not amused when he found his coffee had salt in it!; *Fam* **les premières chaleurs à la sortie de l'hiver, on apprécie!** the first spell of mild weather after the winter is really welcome!

VPR s'apprécier 1 *Fin (monnaie)* to appreciate (in value), to rise; **l'euro s'est apprécié par rapport au dollar** the euro has risen against the dollar **2** *(emploi réciproque)* to like each other

appréhender [3] [apreɑ̃de] **VT 1** *(craindre ▸ examen, réaction)* to feel apprehensive about; **j'appréhende mon opération** I am apprehensive *or* worried about my operation; **elle appréhendait de partir** she was apprehensive about leaving **2** *(comprendre)* to comprehend, to grasp **3** *Jur (arrêter)* to arrest, to apprehend

appréhensif, -ive [apreɑ̃sif, -iv] **ADJ** apprehensive

appréhension [apreɑ̃sjɔ̃] **NF 1** *(crainte)* fear, apprehension; **avoir** *ou* **éprouver de l'a.** to feel apprehensive, to have misgivings; **avec a.** apprehensively; **je n'y pense pas sans une certaine a.** I'm a little apprehensive about it **2** *Phil (compréhension)* apprehension

appréhensive [apreɑ̃siv] *voir* **appréhensif**

apprenant, -e [aprənɑ̃, -ɑ̃t] **NM,F** learner

apprendre [79] [aprɑ̃dr] **VT 1** *(s'initier à)* to learn; **j'apprends le russe** I'm learning Russian; **a. qch de qn** to learn sth from sb, to be taught sth by sb; **a. qch par cœur** to learn sth (off) by heart; **a. à faire qch** to learn (how) to do sth; **a. à être patient** to learn patience, to learn to be patient; **a. à connaître qn** to get to know sb

2 *(enseigner)* **a. qch à qn** to teach sb sth *or* sth to sb; **a. à qn à faire qch** to teach sb (how) to do sth; **elle m'a appris le français/à nager** she taught me French/(how) to swim; *Fig* **ça t'apprendra à faire l'imbécile** that'll teach you (not) to fool around; **il/ça va lui a. à vivre!** he'll/it'll teach him/her a thing or two!

3 *(donner connaissance de)* to tell; **a. qch à qn** to tell sb sth; **qui te l'a appris?** who told you?; **vous ne m'apprenez rien!** tell me something new!

4 *(être informé de ▸ départ, mariage)* to learn *or* to hear of; *(▸ nouvelle)* to hear; **j'ai appris sa mort à la radio** I heard of his/her death on the radio; **qu'est-ce que j'apprends, vous démissionnez?** what's this I hear about you resigning?; **apprenez** *ou* **vous apprendrez qu'ici on ne fait pas ce genre de choses** you'll have to learn that we don't do things like that here; *Fam* **tiens, tiens, on en apprend des choses!** well, well, who'd have thought such a thing?; *Hum* **on en apprend tous les jours!** you learn something new every day!

USAGE ABSOLU il apprend facilement/avec difficulté learning comes/doesn't come easily to him; **a. lentement/vite** to be a slow/fast learner; **on apprend à tout âge** it's never too late to learn; **ça lui apprendra!** that'll teach him/her!; *Prov* **on n'apprend pas à un vieux singe à faire la grimace** don't teach your grandmother to suck eggs

VPR s'apprendre to be learnt; **le style, ça ne s'apprend pas** style isn't something you can learn; **ça s'apprend vite** it's easy to learn, it can be learned quickly; **le chinois ne s'apprend pas facilement** it isn't easy to learn Chinese

apprenti, -e [aprɑ̃ti] **NM,F** apprentice; **a. maçon** builder's apprentice; **être placée comme apprentie chez une couturière** to be apprenticed to a seamstress; *Fig* **jouer les apprentis sorciers** *ou* **à l'a. sorcier** to play at being God

apprentissage [aprɑ̃tisaʒ] **NM 1** *(fait d'apprendre)* **l'a. des langues** language learning, learning languages; *Fig* **faire l'a. de qch** to learn one's first lessons in sth; **faire l'a. de la vie** to gain some experience of life **2** *(durée)* (period of) apprenticeship

• d'apprentissage ADJ *(centre, école)* training; *(contrat)* of apprenticeship

• en apprentissage ADV être en a. chez qn to be apprenticed to *or* to be serving one's apprenticeship with sb; **mettre qn en a. chez un artisan** to apprentice sb to a craftsman

apprêt [aprɛ] **NM 1** *(affectation)* affectation, affectedness; **un style sans a.** an unaffected style; **parler sans a.** to speak unaffectedly *or* without affectation **2** *Tech (préparation ▸ du cuir, d'un tissu)* dressing; *(▸ du papier)* finishing; *(▸ d'un plafond, d'un mur)* sizing; *(produit ▸ pour cuir, tissu)* dressing; *(▸ pour papier)* finish; *(▸ pour plafond, mur)* size

apprêtage [aprɛtaʒ] **NM** *Tech (d'un cuir, d'un tissu)* dressing, finishing; *(d'un papier)* finishing; *(d'un plafond, d'un mur)* sizing

apprêté, -e [aprete] **ADJ** affected, fussy

apprêter [4] [aprete] **VT 1** *Tech (cuir, tissu)* to dress, to finish; *(papier)* to finish; *(plafond, mur)* to size **2** *Littéraire (préparer ▸ repas)* to get ready, to prepare; *(habiller)* to get ready, to dress

VPR s'apprêter 1 *Littéraire (emploi réfléchi)* to prepare *or* to dress oneself **2 s'a. à faire qch** to be getting ready to do sth

appris, -e [apri, -iz] *pp voir* **apprendre**

apprivoisable [aprivwazabl] **ADJ** tameable, which can be tamed

apprivoisé, -e [aprivwaze] **ADJ** tame

apprivoisement [aprivwazmɑ̃] **NM** taming

apprivoiser [3] [aprivwaze] **VT** *(animal)* to tame, to domesticate; *(enfant, peur)* to tame; **apprivoisez votre corps** get to know your body

VPR s'apprivoiser 1 *(animal)* to become tame; *(personne)* to become more sociable **2** *Littéraire* **s'a. à** *(se familiariser avec)* to get used *or* accustomed to

approbateur, -trice [aprɔbatœr, -tris] **ADJ** *(regard, sourire)* approving; *(commentaire)* supportive; **faire un signe de tête a.** to give an approving nod, to nod (one's head) in approval

approbation [aprɔbasjɔ̃] **NF 1** *(assentiment)* approval, approbation; **il sourit en signe d'a.** he gave a smile of approval, he smiled approvingly; **recevoir/gagner l'a. de qn** to meet with/to win sb's approval; **donner son a. à un projet** to approve a plan **2** *(autorisation)* approval; **soumettre qch à l'a. de qn** to submit sth to sb for approval

approbatrice [aprɔbatris] *voir* **approbateur**

approchable [aprɔʃabl] **ADJ** approachable, accessible; **une vedette difficilement a.** an inaccessible *or* unapproachable star

approchant, -e [aprɔʃɑ̃, -ɑ̃t] **ADJ** similar; **voici quelque chose d'a.** here's something quite similar; **rien d'a.** nothing like that; **il a dû le traiter d'escroc ou quelque chose d'a.** he must have called him a crook or something like that *or* something of the sort

ADV *Suisse* about, around; **gagner a. 500 euros, gagner 500 euros a.** to earn about 500 euros

approche [aprɔʃ] **NF 1** *(venue)* approach; **l'a. des examens** the approaching exams; **il sentait l'a. de la mort** he felt that death was approaching *or* upon him

2 *(accès)* approachability; **il est d'a. facile/difficile** he is approachable/unapproachable; **sa fiction est plus facile d'a. que son théâtre** his/her novels are more accessible than his/her plays

3 *(manière d'aborder)* approach; **une a. écologique du problème** an ecological approach to the problem; **cette étude a nécessité un long travail d'a.** the study required a great deal of preliminary work; *Mktg* **a. directe** cold calling

4 *Typ (espacement)* spacing; *(erreur)* spacing error; *(signe)* close-up mark

5 *Aviat* approach; **être en a. (finale)** to be on one's final approach

• approches NFPL les approches de l'aéroport the area surrounding the airport, the vicinity of the airport

• à l'approche de PRÉP 1 *(dans le temps)* **à l'a. de l'épreuve, j'ai commencé à m'inquiéter** as the contest drew near, I started to worry; **à l'a. de la trentaine** as one nears *or* approaches (the age of) thirty **2** *(dans l'espace)* **à l'a. de son père, il s'est enfui** he ran away as his father approached

• aux approches de PRÉP 1 *(dans le temps)* **aux approches de l'épreuve, j'ai pris peur** as the test drew near, I panicked; **aux approches de la trentaine elle a voulu avoir des enfants** as she approached thirty she wanted to have children **2** *(dans l'espace)* **aux approches de la frontière, il y avait davantage de soldats** there were more soldiers as we approached *or* neared the border; **il y a plusieurs centres commerciaux aux approches de la ville** there are several shopping centres on the outskirts of the town

approché, -e [aprɔʃe] **ADJ** *(idée, calcul)* approximate

approcher [3] [aprɔʃe] **VT 1** *(mettre plus près ▸ lampe, chaise)* to move *or* to draw nearer, to move *or* to draw closer; **approche un peu ton tabouret** draw *or* bring your stool a bit nearer *or* closer; **approche la table du mur** move *or* draw the table closer to the wall

2 *(aller près de)* to go near, to approach; *(venir près de)* to come near, to approach; **ne l'approchez/m'approchez surtout pas!** please don't go near him/her/come near me!

3 *(côtoyer ▸ personnalité)* to approach; **il n'est pas facile de l'a.** he's/she's not very approachable; **il approche les grands de ce monde** he rubs shoulders with the people at the top

4 *(faire des démarches auprès de) (personne)* to approach; **il a été approché par diverses sociétés** he was approached by various companies

VI 1 *(dans l'espace)* to come *or* to get nearer, to approach; **toi, approche!** you, come over here!; **faire a. qn** *(d'un signe)* to beckon to sb; **on approche de Paris** we're getting near to *or* we're nearing Paris; **a. de la perfection** to be *or* to come close to perfection; **tu approches de la vérité** you're getting close to the truth; **nous approchions alors des 200 km/heure** we were going at almost 200 km an hour **2** *(dans le temps ▸ nuit, aube)* to draw near; *(▸ événement, saison)* to approach, to draw near; **l'heure** *ou* **le moment approche** it will soon be time; **on approchait de l'hiver** winter was drawing near; **quand on approche de la cinquantaine** when you're *Br* getting on for fifty *or Am* going on fifty

VPR s'approcher 1 *(venir)* to come near, to approach; *(aller)* to go near, to approach; **approche-toi** come here *or* closer; **je me suis approché**

pour voir I went closer to have a look **2 s'a. de qn** *(venir)* to come up to sb, to approach sb; *(aller)* to go up to sb, to approach sb; **s'a. de qch** *(venir)* to go near sth, to approach sth; *(aller)* to go up to sth, to approach sth; *(correspondre à)* to be *or* to come close to sth; **qu'elle ne s'approche pas trop du bord** see that she doesn't go too near the edge; **on s'approche de la côte** we're nearing *or* approaching the coast; **leurs thèses s'approchent beaucoup des nôtres** their ideas are very close to ours; **s'a. de la perfection** to be *or* to come close to perfection

approfondi, -e [aprɔfɔ̃di] **ADJ** thorough, detailed, extensive; **une connaissance approfondie de la langue** a thorough command *or* knowledge of the language; **traiter qch de façon approfondie** to go into sth thoroughly

approfondir **[32]** [aprɔfɔ̃dir] **VT 1** *(creuser ▸ puits)* to deepen, to dig deeper **2** *(détailler davantage ▸ sujet, étude)* to go deeper *or* more thoroughly into; **il faut a. la question** the question needs to be examined in more detail; **tu n'approfondis jamais (les choses)** you only ever skim the surface of things; **sans a.** superficially **3** *(parfaire ▸ connaissances)* to improve, to deepen; **a. sa connaissance de qch** to improve one's knowledge of sth, to acquire a deeper knowledge of sth

approfondissement [aprɔfɔ̃dismɑ̃] **NM 1** *(d'un puits)* increasing the depth of, deepening **2** *(des connaissances)* extending; **l'a. de la question est réservé au deuxième volume** there will be a more thorough examination of the issue in volume two

appropriation [aprɔprijasjɔ̃] **NF** *Jur (saisie)* appropriation; **a. de fonds** misappropriation of funds, embezzlement; **a. par violence** forcible seizure

approprié, -e [aprɔprije] **ADJ** *(solution, technique)* appropriate, suitable; *(tenue)* proper, right; **peu a.** inappropriate; **de manière peu appropriée** inappropriately; **un discours a. aux circonstances** a speech appropriate *or* suited to the circumstances; **on ne peut pas entrer si on n'a pas la tenue appropriée** they won't let you in if you're not wearing the proper *or* right clothes

approprier **[10]** [aprɔprije] **VT** *(adapter)* to adapt, to suit; **il a su a. son style à un public d'adolescents** he's managed to adapt his style to a teenage audience

VPR s'approprier 1 *(biens, invention)* to appropriate; *(pouvoir)* to seize **2 s'a. à** *(s'adapter à)* to be suitable *or* appropriate for, to be in keeping with

approuver **[3]** [apruve] **VT 1** *(être d'accord avec ▸ méthode, conduite)* to approve of; **je n'approuve pas la manière dont tu les traites** I don't approve *or* I disapprove of the way you treat them; **elle m'a approuvé de ne pas avoir cédé** she approved of my not giving in; **nous vous approuvons dans votre choix** we approve of your choice; **je vous approuve entièrement** I think you're entirely right; **elle approuve tout ce qu'il dit/fait** she agrees with everything he says/does; **la proposition a été approuvée par tout le monde** the proposition met with *or* received general approval **2** *(autoriser ▸ alliance, fusion)* to approve, to agree to; *(▸ médicament, traitement)* to approve; *(▸ facture)* to pass; *(▸ contrat)* to ratify; *(▸ projet de loi)* to approve, to pass

approvisionné, -e [aprɔvizjɔne] **ADJ bien a.** *(magasin, rayon)* well-stocked

approvisionnement [aprɔvizjɔnmɑ̃] **NM 1** *(action)* supplying (**en** with); *(d'un magasin)* stocking (**en** with); **faire un a. de qch** to stock up with sth; **l'approvisionnement du pays en pétrole/en matières premières** the supply of oil/raw materials to the country **2** *(provisions)* supply, provision, stock; **a. en eau/gaz** water/gas supply; **approvisionnements de réserve** reserve stocks

approvisionner **[3]** [aprɔvizjɔne] **VT 1** *(village, armée)* to supply; *(magasin)* to supply; **être approvisionné en électricité** to be supplied with electricity; **a. qn en qch** to supply sb with sth **2** *Banque (compte)* to pay money *or* funds into; **son compte n'a pas été approvisionné depuis six mois** no funds have been paid into his/her account for six months

VPR s'approvisionner *(personne)* to shop; *(commerce, entreprise)* to stock up; **où est-ce que vous vous approvisionnez?** *(individu)* where do you do your shopping?; *(commerce, entreprise)* where do you get your supplies from?; **s'a. en qch** *(stocker)* to stock up on sth, to get in supplies of sth

approximatif, -ive [aprɔksimatif, -iv] **ADJ** *(coût, évaluation)* approximate, rough; *(traduction)* rough; *(réponse)* vague; **nous nous sommes exprimés dans un anglais a.** we expressed ourselves in broken English; **ce chiffre est très a.** this figure is only a rough estimate

approximation [aprɔksimasjɔ̃] **NF 1** *(estimation)* approximation; **ce chiffre n'est qu'une a.** this is only an approximate figure *or* a rough estimate **2** *Péj (à-peu-près)* generality, (vague) approximation

approximative [aproksimativ] *voir* **approximatif**

approximativement [aprɔksimativmɑ̃] **ADV** *(environ)* approximately, roughly; *(vaguement)* vaguely

appt *(abrév écrite* **appartement***)* apt.

appui [apɥi] **NM 1** *Constr (d'un balcon, d'un garde-fou)* support; **a. de fenêtre** windowsill, window ledge **2** *(dans les positions du corps)* **prendre a. sur qch** to lean (heavily) on sth; **prenant a. sur les épaules de son partenaire** leaning *or* resting on his/her partner's shoulders; **prendre a. sur le pied gauche** *(pour sauter)* to take off from the left foot; **trouver un a.** *(pied)* to gain *or* to get a hold **3** *(soutien)* support, backing; *Mil* support; **a. moral** moral support; **apporter son a. à une initiative** to back *or* to support an initiative; **avoir l'a. de qn** to have sb's support *or* backing; **avoir des appuis en haut lieu** to have friends in high places; **a. aérien/naval** air/naval support; **a. financier** (financial) backing

• à l'appui ADV il a lu, à l'a., une lettre datée du 24 mai in support of this *or* to back this up, he read out a letter dated 24 May; **preuves à l'a.** supporting evidence

• à l'appui de PRÉP in support of, supporting; **à l'a. de ses dires** in support of *or* to support what he/she was saying

appui-bras [apɥibra] *(pl* **appuis-bras***)* **NM** armrest

appuie *etc voir* **appuyer**

appuie-bras [apɥibra] **NM INV** = **appui-bras**

appui-tête, appuie-tête [apɥitɛt] *(pl* **appuis-tête** *ou* **appuie-tête***)* **NM** headrest

appuyé, -e [apɥije] **ADJ** *(allusion)* heavy, laboured; *(regard)* insistent

appuyer **[14]** [apɥije] **VT 1** *(faire reposer)* to lean, to rest; **a. son bras/sa main sur le dos d'une chaise** to rest one's arm/hand on the back of a chair; **le vélo était appuyé contre la grille** the bicycle was resting *or* leaning against the railings

2 *(faire peser)* to press; **appuie ta main sur le couvercle** press down on the lid

3 *(étayer)* to support; **mur appuyé sur des contreforts** wall supported by buttresses

4 *(donner son soutien à ▸ candidat, réforme)* to back, to support; *(▸ proposition)* to second; **la police, appuyée par l'armée** the police, backed up *or* supported by the army

5 *Fin (apporter un soutien financier)* to back, to support; **a. qn financièrement** to back sb (financially), to give sb financial backing

6 *(fonder)* to ground, to base; **a. son raisonnement sur des faits** to base one's argument on *or* to ground one's argument in facts

VI 1 *(exercer une pression)* to press, to push down; **il faut a. de toutes ses forces** you have to press as hard as you can; **a. sur qch** *(avec le doigt)* to press sth, to push sth; *(avec le pied)* to press down on sth; **a. sur la gâchette** to pull the trigger; *Fam* **appuie sur le 3ème étage** *(dans un ascenseur)* press *or* push the button for the third floor **2** *(insister)* **a. sur** *(mot, urgence, argument, aspect)* to stress, to emphasize; *(note)* to sustain; **il a beaucoup appuyé sur les qualités nécessaires pour ce poste** he put great emphasis on the qualities necessary for the job; **inutile d'a. là-dessus, on a compris** you don't need to keep going on about it, we understand **3** *Aut* **a. sur la** *ou* **à droite/gauche** to bear right/left; **a. sur la pédale de frein** to brake; **a. sur l'accélérateur** *(aller vite)* *Br* to put one's foot down, *Am* to step on the gas

VPR s'appuyer 1 *Fam* to have to put up with; **s'a. qn** to get stuck *or Br* landed *or* lumbered with sb; **je me suis appuyé cinq heures de voiture pour te voir** I had to drive for five hours just to see you❑; **qui c'est qui va encore s'a. le ménage?** guess who's going to get stuck with the housework again?

2 s'a. à *(physiquement)* to lean *or* to rest on; **il entra, s'appuyant à son bras** he came in leaning on his/her arm

3 s'a. contre qch to lean against sth

4 s'a. sur *(se soutenir sur)* to lean on; *(s'en remettre à ▸ ami)* to lean *or* to depend *or* to rely on; *(▸ amitié, aide)* to count *or* to rely on; *(▸ témoignage)* to rely on; *(se fonder sur)* to be based on; **le voilà, appuyé sur sa canne** there he is, leaning on his stick; **ce récit s'appuie sur une expérience vécue** this story is based on a real-life experience

apr. *(abrév écrite* **après***)* after; **a. J.-C.** AD

âpre [apr] **ADJ 1** *(âcre ▸ goût)* sour; *(▸ vin)* rough **2** *(rude ▸ voix, ton)* harsh, rough; *(▸ hiver)* harsh; *(▸ froid)* bitter, biting; *(▸ reproche)* bitter, harsh; *(féroce ▸ concurrence, lutte)* bitter, fierce; *Péj* **â. au gain** greedy, money-grabbing

âprement [aprəmɑ̃] **ADV** *(sévèrement)* bitterly, harshly; **on me l'a â. reproché** I was harshly *or* bitterly criticized for it; **se battre â.** to fight bitterly

après- [aprɛ] **PRÉF** post-...; **la période de l'a.-soixante-huit** the period after 1968, the post-1968 period; **le Moscou de l'a.-Gorbatchev** Moscow in the post-Gorbachev era

après [aprɛ] **PRÉP 1** *(dans le temps)* after; **a. le départ de Paul** after Paul left; **a. (le) dîner** after dinner; **le but a été marqué a. deux minutes de jeu** the goal was scored two minutes into the game *or* after kick-off; **530 a. Jésus-Christ** 530 AD; **c'était peu a. 3 heures** it was shortly *or* soon after 3 o'clock; **a. toutes ses promesses, voilà qu'elle change d'avis!** after all her promises, now she's changed her mind!; *Fam* **qu'est-ce qu'il fait froid aujourd'hui, a. le beau temps qu'on a eu hier!** it's so cold today, after the nice weather we had yesterday!; **a. cela, que prendrez-vous?** what would you like after that?; **tu le contredis en public, et a. ça tu t'étonnes qu'il s'énerve!** you contradict him in public (and) then you're surprised that he's annoyed!; **a. ça, il ne te reste plus qu'à aller t'excuser** the only thing you can do now is apologize; **a. quoi, nous verrons** then we'll see; **a. avoir dîné, ils bavardèrent** after dining *or* after dinner they chatted; **jour a. jour** day after day

2 *(dans l'espace)* after; **la gare est a. le parc** the station is past *or* after the park; **a. la fontaine, tournez à gauche** turn left after the fountain; *Fam* **son foulard est resté accroché a. les ronces** his/her scarf got caught on the brambles❑

3 *(dans un rang, un ordre, une hiérarchie)* after; **a. les livres, il aime la musique** after books, music is his second love; **a. vous, je vous en prie** after you; **vous êtes a. moi** *(dans une file d'attente)* you're after me; **le travail passe a. la santé** your health is more important than your work

4 *(indiquant un mouvement de poursuite, l'attachement, l'hostilité)* **courir a. qn** to run after sb; **le chien aboie a. les passants** the dog barks at the passers-by; **crier a. qn** to shout at sb; **il est furieux a. toi** he's furious with you; **s'énerver a. qch** to get angry with sth; **il est constamment a. moi** *(me surveille)* he's always breathing down my neck; *(me harcèle)* he's always nagging *or* going on at me; **ils sont a. une invitation, c'est évident** it's obvious they're angling for *or* they're after an invitation; **être a. une bonne affaire** to be onto a bargain; **demander a. qn** to ask after sb

ADV 1 *(dans le temps)* **un mois a.** a month later; **aussitôt a.** straight *or* immediately after *or* afterwards; **bien a.** a long *or* good while after, much later; **longtemps a.** a long time after *or* afterwards; **peu a.** shortly after *or* afterwards; **garde tes forces pour a.** conserve your strength for afterwards *or* later; **nous sommes allés au cinéma et a. au restaurant** we went to the movies *or Br* cinema and then to a restaurant; **a. on ira dire que je suis avare!** and then people will say I'm mean!; **a., tu ne viendras pas te plaindre!** don't come

moaning to me afterwards!; **et a.?** *(pour demander la suite)* and then what?; *(marquant l'indifférence)* so what?; **et a.? qu'a-t-il fait?** and then what did he do?; *Fam* **et a.? qu'est-ce que ça peut faire?** so what? who cares? **2** *(dans l'espace)* after; **vous tournez au feu, c'est tout de suite a.** you turn at the lights, and it's just after that **3** *(dans un rang, un ordre, une hiérarchie)* next; **qui est a.?** *(dans une file d'attente)* who's next?; **et qu'est-ce qui vient a.?** and what's next?
• **après coup** ADV afterwards, later; **c'est a. coup que j'ai compris** it was only later *or* afterwards that I understood; **laissez les journalistes parler, nous démentirons a. coup** let the press talk, we'll deny it all afterwards *or* later; **n'essaie pas d'inventer une explication a. coup** don't try to invent an explanation after the event
• **après que** CONJ after; **a. qu'il eut terminé...** after he had finished...; **je te dirai ce que j'en pense a. que tu auras décidé** I'll tell you what I think after you've made a decision; **je me suis couché a. que tu aies téléphoné** I went to bed after you phoned
• **après tout** ADV **1** *(introduisant une justification)* after all; **a. tout, ça n'a pas beaucoup d'importance** after all, it's not particularly important **2** *(emploi expressif)* then; **il peut bien venir, a. tout, s'il veut** he can come, then, if he wants *or* likes; **débrouille-toi tout seul, a. tout!** sort it out yourself then!
• **d'après** PRÉP **1** *(introduisant un jugement)* according to; **d'a. moi/eux** in my/their opinion; **alors, d'a. vous, qui va gagner?** so who do you think is going to win?; **d'a. les informations qui nous parviennent** from *or* according to the news we're getting; **d'a. mon expérience** in my experience **2** *(introduisant un modèle, une citation)* **d'a. Tolstoï** *(adaptation)* adapted from Tolstoy; **d'a. une idée originale de...** based on *or* from an original idea by... ADJ **1** *(dans le temps)* following, next; **le jour d'a., il était là** the following *or* next day, he was there; **l'instant d'a.** the next moment **2** *(dans l'espace)* next; **je descends à la station d'a.** I'm getting off at the next station; **la maison d'a. est la nôtre** the next house is ours

après-coup [aprɛku] *(pl* **après-coups***)* NM *Psy* aftereffect

après-demain [aprɛdmɛ̃] ADV the day after tomorrow; **a. matin/soir** the day after tomorrow in the morning/evening

après-dîner [apredine] *(pl* **après-dîners***)* NM evening; **discours d'a.** after-dinner speech

après-guerre [apreger] *(pl* **après-guerres***)* NM OU NF post-war era *or* period; **le théâtre d'a.** post-war drama; **l'a. froide** the post-Cold War period

après-midi [apremidi] NM INV OU NF INV afternoon; **en début/fin d'a.** early/late in the afternoon; **à 2 heures de l'a.** at 2 (o'clock) in the afternoon, at 2 p.m.; **je le ferai dans l'a.** I'll do it this afternoon

après-rasage [apreraza3] *(pl* **après-rasages***)* ADJ INV aftershave *(avant n)*
NM aftershave (lotion)

après-shampoing, après-shampooing [aprɛʃɑ̃pwɛ̃] NM conditioner

après-ski [apreski] *(pl* **après-skis***)* NM *(botte)* snow boot

> Il faut noter que le nom anglais **après-ski** est un faux ami. Il désigne les activités récréatives auxquelles on se livre après une séance de ski.

après-vente [aprɛvɑ̃t] ADJ INV *Com* after-sales

âpreté [aprəte] NF **1** *(âcreté ▸ d'un goût)* sourness; *(▸ d'un vin)* roughness **2** *(dureté ▸ d'une voix, d'un ton)* harshness, roughness; *(▸ de l'hiver)* harshness; *(▸ du froid)* bitterness; *(▸ d'un reproche)* bitterness, harshness; **combattre avec â.** to struggle bitterly *or* grimly

a priori [aprijɔri] ADJ INV *Phil* a priori
ADV in principle, on the face of it; **a., c'est une bonne idée** on the face of it *or* in principle it's a good idea
NM INV *(préjugé)* preconception, preconceived idea; **avoir un a. favorable envers qn** to be biased *or* prejudiced in favour of sb; **avoir des a.** to be biased *or* prejudiced; **être sans a.** to be impartial

à-propos [apropo] NM INV aptness, relevance; **votre remarque manque d'à.** your remark is not relevant *or* to the point; **répondre avec à.** to give a suitable *or* an appropriate reply; **quelle que soit la situation, il réagit avec à.** whatever the situation, he always does *or* says the right thing; **faire preuve d'à.** to show presence of mind

apte [apt] ADJ **a. à qch** *(par sa nature)* fit for *or* suited to sth; *(par ses qualifications)* qualified for sth; **a. (au service militaire)** fit (for military service); **a. à faire qch** *(par sa nature)* suited to doing sth; *(par ses qualifications)* qualified to do sth

aptère [aptɛr] ADJ *Zool* wingless

aptéryx [apteriks] NM *Orn* kiwi

aptitude [aptityd] NF *(capacité)* ability, aptitude; **il n'a aucune a. dans ce domaine** he has *or* shows no aptitude in that direction; **avoir une a. au bonheur/à la patience** to have a capacity for happiness/for patience
• **aptitudes** NFPL **aptitudes (intellectuelles)** abilities; **avoir/montrer des aptitudes en langues** to have/to show a gift for languages; **aptitudes relationnelles** people skills

apurement [apyrmɑ̃] NM *Compta* **1** *(des comptes)* auditing **2** *(d'une dette, du passif)* discharge

apurer [3] [apyre] VT *Compta* **1** *(comptes)* to audit **2** *(dette, passif)* to discharge

aquaculteur, -trice [akwacyltœr, -tris] NM,F aquaculturalist, aquiculturalist

aquaculture [akwakyltyr] NF aquaculture, aquiculture

aquaplanage [akwaplanaʒ] NM *Aut* aquaplaning

aquaplane [akwaplan] NM *Sport* **1** *(activité)* aquaplaning **2** *(planche)* aquaplane

aquaplaning [akwaplaniŋ] = **aquaplanage**

aquarelle [akwarɛl] NF *Beaux-Arts* *(tableau)* watercolour; **peindre à l'a.** to paint in watercolours

aquarelliste [akwarelist] NMF *Beaux-Arts* watercolourist

aquarium [akwarjɔm] NM **1** *(décoratif)* fish tank, aquarium **2** *(au zoo)* aquarium; **a. d'eau de mer** oceanarium

aquatinte [akwatɛ̃t] NF *Beaux-Arts* aquatint

aquatique [akwatik] ADJ aquatic, water *(avant n)*

aqueduc [akdyk] NM **1** *(conduit)* aqueduct **2** *Anat* duct

aqueux, -euse [akø, -øz] ADJ **1** *Anat & Chim* aqueous **2** *(plein d'eau)* watery

à quia [akɥija] ADV *Littéraire Vieilli* **être à.** to be dumbfounded *or* nonplussed; **réduire qn à.** to leave sb dumbfounded *or* nonplussed

aquiculteur, -trice [akɥikyltœr, -tris] = **aquaculteur**

aquiculture [akɥikyltyr] = **aquaculture**

aquifère [akɥifer] *Géol* ADJ water-bearing, *Spéc* aquiferous
NM aquifer

aquilin [akilɛ̃] ADJ M *(nez)* aquiline

aquilon [akilɔ̃] NM *Littéraire* north wind

aquitain, -e [akitɛ̃, -ɛn] ADJ of/from Aquitaine, Aquitaine *(avant n)*
• **Aquitain, -e** NM,F = inhabitant of or person from Aquitaine
• **Aquitaine** NF **l'Aquitaine** Aquitaine

ara [ara] NM *Orn* macaw

arabe [arab] ADJ *(cheval)* Arab, Arabian; *(pays)* Arab, Arabic; *(langue, littérature)* Arabic; *(civilisation)* Arab; **chiffres arabes** Arabic numerals, Arabics
NM *(langue)* Arabic; **a. dialectal/littéral** vernacular/written Arabic
• **Arabe** NMF Arab

> **ARABE**
>
> Note that in a French context this word usually refers to people from the former colonies of North Africa, who make up the largest ethnic minority in France.

arabesque [arabesk] NF arabesque

arabica [arabika] NM *Bot* arabica

Arabie [arabi] NF **l'A.** Arabia; **l'A. Saoudite** Saudi Arabia

arabique [arabik] ADJ Arabic

arabisant, -e [arabizɑ̃, -ɑ̃t] ADJ Arabic
NM,F Arabist, Arabic scholar

arabisation [arabizasjɔ̃] NF Arabization

arabiser [3] [arabize] VT to Arabize, to Arabicize

arable [arabl] ADJ *Agr* arable

arabophone [arabɔfɔn] ADJ Arabic-speaking
NMF Arabic speaker

arachide [araʃid] NF *Bot* peanut, *Spéc* groundnut

arachnéen, -enne [arakneɛ̃, -ɛn] ADJ **1** *Littéraire (dentelle)* gossamer *(avant n)*, gossamery **2** *Zool* arachnidan

arachnide [araknid] *Zool* NM arachnid
• **arachnides** NMPL Arachnida

arachnoïde [araknɔid] NF *Anat* arachnoid

araignée [areɲe] NF **1** *Zool* spider; **a. d'eau** water spider; **a. de mer** spider crab, sea spider; **a. rouge** red spider; *Fam Hum* **avoir une a. au plafond** to have bats in the belfry; *Prov* **a. du matin, chagrin, a. du soir, espoir** = seeing a spider in the morning brings bad luck, seeing one in the evening brings good luck **2** *Pêche* gill net **3** *Ordinat* crawler

araire [arɛr] NM *Agr* swing-plough

araméen, -enne [arameɛ̃, -ɛn] ADJ Aramaic, Aramean, Aramaean
NM *(langue)* Aramaic
• **Araméen, -enne** NM,F Aramean, Aramaean

araser [3] [araze] VT **1** *Constr (égaliser ▸ mur)* to level, to make level *or* flush; *(▸ planche)* to plane down **2** *Géol* to erode

aratoire [aratwar] ADJ *Agr* ploughing

araucaria [arokarja] NM *Bot* araucaria

arbalète [arbalɛt] NF crossbow

arbalétrier [arbaletrije] NM **1** *(soldat)* crossbowman **2** *Constr* rafter

arbitrage [arbitraʒ] NM **1** *Jur* arbitration; **a. international** international arbitration; **recourir à l'a.** to go to arbitration; **soumettre un différend à un a.** to refer a dispute to arbitration **2** *Sport (gén)* refereeing; *(au volley-ball, au tennis, au cricket)* umpiring **3** *Bourse* arbitrage; **a. de change** arbitration of exchange; **a. comptant-terme** cash and carry arbitrage; **a. risque** risk arbitrage

arbitragiste [arbitraʒist] NM *Bourse* arbitrageur, arbitrager

arbitraire [arbitrɛr] ADJ **1** *(choix, décision)* arbitrary **2** *(gouvernement, pouvoir, action)* arbitrary, despotic
NM arbitrariness, arbitrary nature

arbitrairement [arbitrɛrmɑ̃] ADV arbitrarily

arbitral, -e, -aux, -ales [arbitral, -o] ADJ **1** *Jur* arbitral; **tribunal a.** tribunal, court of arbitration **2** *Sport* **décision arbitrale** *(gén)* referee's decision; *(au volley-ball, au tennis, au cricket)* umpire's decision

arbitre [arbitr] NM **1** *Jur* arbiter, arbitrator; **exercer un rôle d'a.** to act as arbitrator, to arbitrate; *Fig* **elle va devenir l'a. de la situation** she will hold the key to the situation; **a. rapporteur** referee *(in commercial suit)*; *Fig* **l'a. de l'élégance** the arbiter of style **2** *Sport (gén)* referee; *(au volley-ball, au tennis, au cricket)* umpire **3** *Phil* **libre a.** free will

arbitrer [3] [arbitre] VT **1** *(différend)* to arbitrate, to settle by arbitration **2** *Sport (gén)* to referee; *(au volley-ball, au tennis, au cricket)* to umpire **3** *Bourse (valeurs)* to carry out an arbitrage operation on

arboré, -e [arbɔre] ADJ *Écol* planted with trees, wooded, *Spéc* arboreous

arborer [3] [arbɔre] VT **1** *(porter ▸ veste, insigne)* to sport, to wear; *(▸ drapeau)* to bear, to display **2** *(afficher ▸ sourire, air)* to wear; *(▸ idées)* to parade; *(▸ manchette, titre)* to carry

arborescence [arbɔresɑ̃s] NF **1** *Bot* arborescence **2** *Ordinat (structure)* tree diagram, directory structure; *(chemin)* directory path

arborescent, -e [arbɔresɑ̃, -ɑ̃t] ADJ **1** *Bot* arborescent **2** *Ordinat* **structure arborescente** tree diagram, directory structure

arboretum [arbɔretɔm] NM *École* arboretum

arboricole [arbɔrikɔl] ADJ **1** *Hort* arboricultural **2** *Zool* tree-dwelling, *Spéc* arboreal

arboriculteur, -trice [arbɔrikyltœr, -tris] NM,F *Hort* tree grower, *Spéc* arboriculturist

arboriculture [arbɔrikyltyr] NF *Hort* arboriculture; **a. fruitière** cultivation of fruit trees

arborisation [arbɔrizasjɔ̃] NF arborization

arborisé, -e [arbɔrize] ADJ **1** *(qui présente des arborisations)* dendritic **2** *Suisse (boisé)* planted with trees

arbouse [arbuz] NF *Bot* arbutus berry

arbousier [arbuzje] NM *Bot* strawberry tree, *Spéc* arbutus

arbre [arbr] NM **1** *Bot* tree; **jeune a.** sapling; *Prov* **entre l'a. et l'écorce il ne faut pas mettre le doigt** = one shouldn't get involved in other people's family quarrels; **a. d'agrément** *ou* **d'ornement** ornamental tree; **a. d'amour** Judas tree, (Eastern) redbud; **a. à caoutchouc** rubber tree; *Bible* **l'a. de la Croix** the Rood; **a. à feuille(s) caduque(s)** deciduous tree; **a. feuillu** hardwood (tree); **a. fruitier** fruit tree; *Rel & Beaux-Arts* **a. de Jessé** tree of Jesse; **a. de Judée** Judas tree, (Eastern) redbud; *Hist* **a. de la liberté** tree of liberty; **a. de Moïse** pyracantha; **a. nain** dwarf tree; **a. de Noël** Christmas tree; **a. à pain** breadfruit tree; **a. à perruque** wig tree, Venetian sumach; **a. résineux** softwood (tree); *Bible* **l'a. de la science du bien et du mal** the tree of knowledge; **a. vert** evergreen (tree); **a. de vie** *Bot* thuya; *Anat* arbor vitae; *Bible* tree of life; **a. du voyageur** traveller's tree, ravenala

2 *Fig* **faire l'a. fourchu** to do a headstand *(with one's legs apart)*; **a. généalogique** family tree; **faire son a. généalogique** to draw up one's family tree

3 *Tech* shaft; **a. d'accouplement** coupling shaft; *Aut* **a. arrière** back axle shaft; **a. à cames** camshaft; **a. à cames en tête** overhead camshaft; *Aut* **a. à cardan** cardan shaft; *Aut* **a. de commande** driveshaft; *Naut* **a. de couche** engine shaft; **a. coudé** crankshaft; **a. creux** hollow shaft; *Aut* **a. de distribution** distributor shaft, camshaft; **a. d'entraînement** driveshaft; **a. d'entrée** input *or* primary shaft; *Aut* **a. d'essieu** axle shaft; **a. à excentrique** *ou* **d'excentrique** eccentric shaft; *Naut* **a. d'hélice, a. porte-hélice** propeller shaft; *Élec* **a. d'induit** armature shaft; **a. intermédiaire** intermediate shaft, layshaft, countershaft; **a. manivelle** crankshaft; **a. mené** driven shaft; **a. moteur** driving shaft; **a. de pompe** pump shaft; **a. primaire** primary *or* input shaft; **a. principal** main shaft; **a. de renvoi** jackshaft; *Aut* **a. de roue** axle shaft; **a. secondaire** secondary shaft, layshaft, countershaft; **a. de sortie** output shaft; **a. de transmission** driveshaft

4 *Anat* **a. respiratoire** respiratory system

5 *(diagramme)* tree; *Mktg* **a. de décision** decision tree

6 *(locutions)* **abattre** *ou* **couper l'a. pour avoir le fruit** to kill the goose that lays the golden eggs; **les arbres cachent la forêt** you can't see the *Br* wood *or Am* forest for the trees

arbrisseau, -x [arbriso] NM *Bot* shrub; **plantation** *ou* **parterre d'arbrisseaux** shrubbery

arbuste [arbyst] NM *Bot* shrub, bush; **plantation d'arbustes** shrubbery

arc [ark] NM **1** *(arme)* bow

2 *Géom* arc; **a. de cercle** arc of a circle; **être assis en a. de cercle** to be seated in a semicircle

3 *Anat* arch; **a. aortique** arch of the aorta

4 *Électron* **a. électrique** electric arc

5 *Archit* arch; **a. brisé** pointed arch; **a. en fer à cheval/en plein cintre** horseshoe/semicircular arch; **a. en ogive** ogee arch; **a. surbaissé/surhaussé** depressed/raised arch; **a. de triomphe** triumphal arch; **l'a. de triomphe (de l'Étoile)** the Arc de Triomphe

• **à arc** ADJ *(lampe, soudure)* arc *(avant n)*

arcade [arkad] NF **1** *Archit* archway; **des arcades** arches, an arcade **2** *Anat* arch; **a. dentaire** dental arch; **a. sourcilière** arch of the eyebrows; **il s'est ouvert l'a. sourcilière** he was cut above the eye **3** *Suisse (dans le canton de Genève) (boutique) Br* shop, *Am* store

arcane [arkan] NM *(secret)* mystery, *Littéraire* arcanum; **les arcanes de la politique/de la science** the mysteries of politics/of science

• **arcanes** NMPL *(cartes de tarot)* arcana

arcature [arkatyr] NF *Archit* arcature, blind arcade

arc-boutant [arkbutɑ̃] *(pl* **arcs-boutants***)* NM *Archit* flying buttress

arc-bouter [3] [arkbute] VT *Archit (mur)* to buttress

VPR **s'arc-bouter** to brace oneself; **s'a. contre un mur** to brace one's back against a wall

arc-doubleau [arkdublo] *(pl* **arcs-doubleaux***)* NM *Archit* transverse rib

arceau, -x [arso] NM **1** *Archit* arch (of vault) **2** *(de croquet)* hoop; *(d'une voiture)* roll bar **3** *Méd* cradle

arc-en-ciel [arkɑ̃sjel] *(pl* **arcs-en-ciel***)* NM rainbow

> **ARCH-, ARCHI-** — PREFIX
>
> • The prefixes **arch-** and **archi-**, like *arch-* in English, have a non-colloquial use that denotes the HIGHEST RANK in a given hierarchy. Thus an **archevêque** (archbishop) has several *évêques* under his command, whereas an **archiduc** (archduke) was in fact a prince in the Austrian imperial dynasty.
>
> • The colloquial use of **archi-** is a common and productive one, whereby virtually any adjective can be prefixed to indicate the HIGHEST DEGREE of a quality or a fault. This idea is often conveyed in the English translation by the use of an adverb like *very, totally, completely* etc:
>
> **archiconnu** very well known; **archidrôle** hilarious; **archifaux** totally wrong; **archinul** completely useless

archaïque [arkaik] ADJ **1** *(vieux)* archaic, outmoded, antiquated **2** *Beaux-Arts & Ling* archaic

archaïsant, -e [arkaizɑ̃, -ɑ̃t] ADJ archaistic

archaïsme [arkaism] NM *(mot)* archaism, archaic term; *(tournure)* archaism, archaic turn of phrase

archange [arkɑ̃ʒ] NM archangel

arche [arʃ] NF **1** *Archit* arch; **la Grande A. (de la Défense)** = large office block at La Défense near Paris, shaped like a square archway **2** *Rel* ark; **l'a. d'alliance** the Ark of the Covenant; **l'a. de Noé** Noah's Ark; **l'a. sainte** the Holy Ark

archéologie [arkeɔlɔʒi] NF archaeology

archéologique [arkeɔlɔʒik] ADJ archaeological

archéologue [arkeɔlɔg] NMF archaeologist

archer [arʃe] NM archer, bowman

archet [arʃe] NM **1** *Mus* bow; **avoir un excellent coup d'a.** to be an outstanding violonist **2** *Tech* bow-saw

archétypal, -e, -aux, -ales [arketipal, -o] ADJ archetypal

archétype [arketip] NM **1** *(symbole)* archetype; **c'est l'a. du père de famille** he is the archetypal family man **2** *Biol* prototype

archevêché [arʃəveʃe] NM *Rel* **1** *(fonction, territoire)* archbishopric **2** *(palais)* archbishop's palace

archevêque [arʃəvɛk] NM *Rel* archbishop

archiconnu, -e [arʃikɔny] ADJ *Fam* very well known[□]; **c'est a.!** everybody knows that!, that's common knowledge!

archidiacre [arʃidjakr] NM *Rel* archdeacon

archidiocèse [arʃidjɔsɛz] NM *Rel* archdiocese

archiduc [arʃidyk] NM archduke

archiduchesse [arʃidyʃɛs] NF archduchess

Archie [arʃi] NM *Ordinat* Archie

archiépiscopal, -e, -aux, -ales [arʃiepiskɔpal, -o] ADJ *Rel* archiepiscopal

archiépiscopat [arʃiepiskɔpa] NM *Rel* archiepiscopate

archifaux, -fausse [arʃifo, -fos] ADJ *Fam* totally wrong; **c'est faux et a.** it couldn't be more wrong

Archimède [arʃimɛd] NPR Archimedes

archipel [arʃipɛl] NM *Géol* archipelago; **l'a. frison** the Frisian Islands; **l'a. de la Sonde** the Sunda Islands

archisec, -sèche [arʃisɛk, -sɛʃ] ADJ *Fam* bone-dry

architecte [arʃitɛkt] NMF **1** *(gén)* architect; **avoir un diplôme d'a.** to have a degree in architecture; **a. d'intérieur** interior designer; **a. naval** naval architect; **a. paysagiste** landscape architect; **a. urbaniste** *Br* town planner, *Am* city planner **2** *Fig (d'une réforme, d'une politique)* architect **3** *Ordinat* **a. de réseaux** network architect

architectonique [arʃitɛktɔnik] ADJ architectonic

NF architectonics *(singulier)*

architectural, -e, -aux, -ales [arʃitɛktyral, -o] ADJ architectural

architecture [arʃitɛktyr] NF **1** *Archit (art, style)* architecture; **a. d'intérieur** interior design; **a. navale** naval architecture **2** *(structure ▸ d'une œuvre d'art)* structure, architecture **3** *Ordinat* architecture

architecturer [3] [arʃitɛktyre] VT to structure; **un exposé bien architecturé** a well-structured talk; *Ordinat* **architecturé autour de...** with its architecture built around...

architrave [arʃitrav] NF *Archit* architrave

archivage [arʃivaʒ] NM filing *or* storing (away)

archive [arʃiv] NF archive

archiver [3] [arʃive] VT **1** *(document, revue)* to file *or* to store (away) **2** *Ordinat* to archive

archives [arʃiv] NFPL **1** *(documents)* archives, records; *Ordinat* archive; **a. audiovisuelles/sonores** audiovisual/sound archives; **a. cinématographiques** movie *or Br* film archives; **a. familiales** family records **2** *(lieu)* record office; **les A. nationales** the French Historical Archives, *Br* ≃ the Public Record Office, *Am* ≃ the National Archives

• **d'archives** ADJ library *(avant n)*; *TV* **document/images d'a.** library document/pictures; *Ordinat* **copie d'a.** archive file

archiviste [arʃivist] NMF archivist; *(dans une entreprise)* filing clerk; *(dans la fonction publique)* keeper of public records

arçon [arsɔ̃] NM **1** *(de selle)* saddletree; **être ferme sur ses arçons** to be steady in the saddle; *Fig Vieilli* to have fixed opinions **2** *Tex* bow

arçonner [3] [arsɔne] VT *Tex* to card *or* to clean with a bow

arctique [arktik] ADJ Arctic; **le cercle polaire a.** the Arctic Circle

• **Arctique** NM **l'A.** the Arctic

> **-ARD, -ARDE** — SUFFIX
>
> • These two suffixes are applied to adjectives, nouns and verbs, and serve mostly to describe people in a DEROGATORY way. The register is often colloquial as the basic word to which they are attached is itself colloquial:
>
> **trouillard(e)** (from *trouille*) lily-livered, chicken; **connard** (from *con*) stupid bastard [note that the feminine is *connasse*; see **-ASSE**]; **nullard(e)** (from *nul*) thick, stupid; **braillard(e)** (from *brailler*) bawler
>
> • **-ard** and **-arde** can also simply refer to the idea of BELONGING, without any pejorative connotations. This is the case for adjectives and nouns relating to places or to political or social concepts:
>
> **banlieusard(e)** suburban, suburbanite; **soixante-huitard(e)** veteran of the 1968 students' revolt; **smicard(e)** minimum-wage earner

ardemment [ardamɑ̃] ADV ardently, fervently, passionately; **désirer qch a.** to yearn for *or* to crave sth; **désirer a. faire qch** to yearn to do sth

Ardennes [ardɛn] NFPL **les A.** the Ardennes; **la bataille des A.** the Battle of the Bulge

ardent, -e [ardɑ̃, -ɑ̃t] ADJ **1** *(brûlant ▸ chaleur)* burning, scorching; *(▸ soleil)* blazing, scorching; *(▸ fièvre)* burning, raging; *(▸ soif)* raging;

un rouge a. a fiery red **2** *(vif ▸ tempérament)* fiery, passionate; *(▸ désir)* ardent, eager, fervent; *(▸ imagination)* vivid, fiery; *(▸ conviction)* deep-seated; *(▸ lutte)* fierce **3** *(passionné ▸ amant)* ardent, eager, hot-blooded; *(▸ révolutionnaire, admirateur)* ardent, fervent

ardeur [ardœr] **NF 1** *(fougue)* passion, ardour, fervour; **soutenir une cause avec a.** to support a cause passionately *or* ardently *or* fervently; **il n'a jamais montré une grande a. au travail** he's never shown much enthusiasm for work; *Hum* **modérez vos ardeurs!** control yourself! **2** *Littéraire (chaleur)* (burning) heat

ardoise [ardwaz] **NF 1** *Géol (matière, tuile)* slate; **crayon d'a.** slate pencil
2 *(objet)* slate; **a. magique** magic slate
3 *Fam (compte)* bill, slate; **mets-le sur mon a.** put it on my bill *or* on the slate; **on a une a. de 50 euros chez le boucher** we've run up a bill of 50 euros at the butcher's; **il a des ardoises dans tous les bars de la ville** he owes money in all the bars in town
4 *Ordinat* **a. électronique** notepad computer
• **d'ardoise, en ardoise ADJ** slate *(avant n)*

ardoisé, -e [ardwaze] **ADJ** slate-grey

ardoisier, -ère [ardwazje, -ɛr] **ADJ 1** *(contenant de l'ardoise)* slaty **2** *(ressemblant à l'ardoise)* slate-like **3** *(industrie, production)* slate *(avant n)*
NM 1 *(exploitant)* slate-quarry owner **2** *(ouvrier)* slate-quarry worker **3** *Belg (couvreur)* roofer
• **ardoisière NF** slate quarry

ardt *Admin (abrév écrite* **arrondissement***)* **1** *(dans une ville)* = administrative subdivision of major French cities such as Paris, Lyons or Marseilles **2** *(au niveau départemental)* = administrative subdivision of a "département", governed by a "sous-préfet"

ardu, -e [ardy] **ADJ** *(difficile ▸ problème, question)* tough, difficult; *(▸ tâche)* arduous, hard

are [ar] **NM** are, $=100m^2$

arec [arɛk] **NM** *Bot* areca

areligieux, -euse [arəliʒjø, -øz] **ADJ** *Rel* not religious

aréna [arena] **NM OU NF** *Can* = sports centre with skating rink, *Am* arena

arène [arɛn] **NF 1** *(d'amphithéâtre)* arena; *(pour la corrida)* bullring; *Fig* **l'a. politique** the political arena; *Fig* **descendre** *ou* **entrer dans l'a.** to enter the fray *or* the arena **2** *Géol (sable)* arenite, sand; **a. granitique** granitic sand
• **arènes NFPL** *(amphithéâtre)* amphitheatre; *(pour la corrida)* bullring

arénicole [arenikɔl] *Zool* **ADJ** sand-dwelling, *Spéc* arenicolous
NF sandworm; **a. des pêcheurs** lobworm, lugworm

aréole [areɔl] **NF** *Anat, Bot & Méd* areola

aréomètre [areɔmɛtr] **NM** *Phys* hydrometer

aréométrie [areɔmetri] **NF** *Phys* hydrometry

aréopage [areɔpaʒ] **NM** learned assembly *or* gathering
• **Aréopage NM** *Antiq* **l'A.** the Areopagus

arête [arɛt] **NF 1** *Ich (de poisson)* bone; **cabillaud sans arêtes** boneless cod fillet; **enlever les arêtes d'un poisson** to bone a fish; **poisson plein d'arêtes** fish full of bones, bony fish
2 *Archit (angle ▸ d'un toit)* arris; *(▸ d'un cube)* edge; *(▸ d'une voûte)* groin; *(▸ d'un comble)* hip
3 *Anat* **l'a. du nez** the bridge of the nose
4 *Géog* crest, ridge
5 *Bot* beard

argent [arʒɑ̃] **NM 1** *Minér (métal)* silver **2** *(richesse)* money; **avoir de l'a.** to have money, to be wealthy; **une famille qui a de l'a.** a well-to-do family; *Fin* **placer son a.** to invest one's money; *Fin* **trouver de l'a.** to raise money; **(se) faire de l'a.** to make money; **pour de l'a.** for money; **l'a. lui fond dans les mains** money just runs through his/her fingers; **tu en auras pour ton a.** you'll get your money's worth, you'll get value for money; **je n'en ai pas vraiment eu pour mon a.** I didn't get my money's worth, I felt rather short-changed; **en être pour son a.** to end up out of pocket; **jeter l'a. par les fenêtres** to throw money down the drain, to squander money; *Prov* **l'a. n'a pas** *ou* **point d'odeur** = it's all money!; *Prov* **l'a. ne fait pas le bonheur** money can't buy happiness; *Prov* **l'a. (trouvé) n'a pas de maître** money knows no master; *Prov* **le temps, c'est de l'a.** time is money; *Fin* **a. à bon marché** cheap money; *Compta* **a. en caisse** cash in hand; *(recettes)* takings; **a. comptant** cash; **payer** *ou* **régler en a. comptant** to pay cash; **accepter** *ou* **prendre qch pour a. comptant** to take sth at face value; *Ordinat* **a. électronique** e-cash, electronic money; **a. frais** new money; *Fin* **a. au jour le jour** call money, day-to-day money; **a. liquide** ready cash *or* money; *Fin* **a. mal acquis** dirty money; *Fin* **a. mort** dead money; **a. de poche** pocket money; **se faire de l'a. de poche** to make a bit of extra money; **l'a. sale** dirty money; *Ordinat* **a. virtuel** e-cash, electronic money; *Fin* **a. à vue** call money **3** *(couleur)* silver (colour)
ADJ INV silver, silver-coloured; **robe en lamé a.** silver lamé dress
• **d'argent ADJ 1** *(en métal)* silver *(avant n)*
2 *(couleur)* silver, silvery, silver-coloured; **des reflets d'a.** silvery reflections
3 *(pécuniaire)* money *(avant n)*
4 *(intéressé)* **homme/femme d'a.** man/woman for whom money matters
• **en argent ADJ** silver *(avant n)*

argenté, -e [arʒɑ̃te] **ADJ 1** *(renard)* silver *(avant n)*; *(tempes)* silver, silvery; *(reflet)* silvery **2** *(plaqué)* silver-plated, silver *(avant n)*; **métal a.** silver plate **3** *Fam (fortuné)* well-heeled; **on n'était pas très argentés à l'époque** we weren't very well-off *or* we were rather hard up at the time

argenter [3] [arʒɑ̃te] **VT 1** *(miroir)* to silver; *(cuillère)* to plate, to silver-plate **2** *Littéraire (faire briller)* **la lune argentait la mer** the moon turned the sea silver

argenterie [arʒɑ̃tri] **NF** silver, silverware

argenteur [arʒɑ̃tœr] **NM** silverer

argentier [arʒɑ̃tje] **NM 1** *(meuble)* silver cabinet **2** *Hist* **le Grand a.** = the superintendent of the Royal Household; *Fam (ministre)* the Finance Minister

argentin[1], -e[1] [arʒɑ̃tɛ̃, -in] **ADJ** *(son)* silvery
• **argentine NF** *Bot* silverweed

argentin[2], -e[2] [arʒɑ̃tɛ̃, -in] **ADJ** Argentinian, Argentine
• **Argentin, -e NM,F** Argentinian, Argentine

argile [arʒil] **NF** *Minér* clay; **a. grasse** fat clay; **a. réfractaire** fire clay

argileux, -euse [arʒilø, -øz] **ADJ** *Minér* clayey, clayish

argon [argɔ̃] **NM** *Chim* argon

argonaute [argɔnot] **NM** *Zool (mollusque)* argonaut, paper nautilus

Argonautes [argɔnot] **NMPL** *Myth* **les A.** the Argonauts

argot [argo] **NM** *Ling* slang; **parler a.** to talk (in) slang; **un mot d'a.** a slang word; **l'a. scolaire** school slang; **a. de métier** jargon

> **ARGOT**
>
> This term can refer to both **la langue verte** (the slang of the underworld) and the jargon of particular social or professional groups (such as butchers, soldiers, students etc). Some "argot" has evolved from being part of the secret language of a select group to becoming part of everyday speech, while other terms have become obsolete, supplanted by **verlan** (see box at this entry), the slang used by young people in the suburbs of big cities.

argotique [argɔtik] **ADJ 1** *(propre à l'argot)* slang *(avant n)* **2** *(familier)* slangy

argotisme [argɔtism] **NM** *Ling (mot)* slang word; *(tournure)* slang expression

arguer [8] [argɥe] **VT 1** *(conclure)* to deduce; **que peut-on a. de ces écrits?** what can we deduce from *or* what conclusion can be drawn from these writings? **2** *(prétexter)* **a. que...** to put forward the fact that...; **arguant qu'il avait une mauvaise vue** pleading his poor eyesight **3** *Jur* **a. une pièce de faux** to assert a deed to be forged
• **arguer de VT IND** to use as an excuse, to plead; **elle argua d'une migraine pour se retirer** she pleaded a headache in order to retire

argument [argymɑ̃] **NM 1** *Ling (raison)* argument; **ses arguments** his/her reasoning; **les arguments pour/contre la réforme** the arguments supporting/opposing *or* for/against the reform; **présenter ses arguments** to state one's case; **avoir de bons/solides arguments** to have a good/strong case; **tirer a. de qch** to use sth as an argument
2 *Com* **a. de vente** selling point
3 *Littérature (sommaire)* general description, outline
4 *Math* argument

argumentaire [argymɑ̃tɛr] **NM 1** *Com* promotion leaflet; **l'a. est très convaincant** the sales pitch is very convincing **2** *Ling (arguments)* arguments

argumentateur, -trice [argymɑ̃tatœr, -tris] *Péj*
ADJ argumentative
NM,F arguer

argumentation [argymɑ̃tasjɔ̃] **NF** *Ling* **1** *(raisonnement)* argumentation, rationale **2** *(fait d'argumenter)* reasoning

argumentatrice [argymɑ̃tatris] *voir* **argumentateur**

argumenter [3] [argymɑ̃te] *Ling* **VI 1** *(débattre)* to argue; **a. en faveur de/contre qch** to argue for/against sth; **a. de qch** *(en tirer des conséquences)* to base an argument on sth; **a. de qch avec qn** to argue with sb about sth **2** *(ergoter)* to be argumentative, to quibble
VT *(texte, démonstration)* to support with (relevant) arguments; **motion bien/mal argumentée** impressively/poorly argued motion

argus [argys] **NM 1** *(publication)* **l'a. de l'automobile** the price guide for used cars; **ta voiture vaut à peine 1000 euros à l'a.** the book price for your car would only be 1,000 euros; **acheter/vendre qch à l'a.** to buy/sell sth for the book price **2** *Orn* argus pheasant **3** *Littéraire (gardien)* guardian

argutie [argysi] **NF** *Ling* quibble; **arguties** quibbling, hairsplitting

aria [arja] **NF** *Mus* aria

aride [arid] **ADJ 1** *(sec ▸ terre, région)* arid, barren; *(▸ climat)* arid; *(▸ vent)* dry; *(▸ cœur)* unfeeling **2** *(difficile ▸ sujet)* arid, dull, uninteresting

aridité [aridite] **NF 1** *(de la terre, d'une région)* aridity, barrenness; *(du climat)* aridity **2** *(d'un sujet)* dullness, *Sout* aridity

arien, -enne [arjɛ̃, -ɛn] **ADJ** Aryan
• **Arien, -enne NM,F** Aryan

ariette [arjɛt] **NF** *Mus* arietta, ariette

aristo [aristo] *Fam* **ADJ** *(abrév* **aristocratique***)* aristocratic[□]
NMF *(abrév* **aristocrate***)* aristocrat[□], *Br* toff; **les aristos** the upper crust, *Br* the toffs

aristocrate [aristɔkrat] **ADJ** aristocratic
NMF aristocrat; **une famille d'aristocrates** an aristocratic family

aristocratie [aristɔkrasi] **NF** aristocracy

aristocratique [aristɔkratik] **ADJ** aristocratic; **avoir du sang a. (dans les veines)** to have aristocratic blood (in one's veins), to be blue-blooded

Aristote [aristɔt] **NPR** Aristotle

aristotélicien, -enne [aristɔtelisjɛ̃, -ɛn] *Phil*
ADJ Aristotelian
NM,F Aristotelian

arithméticien, -enne [aritmetisjɛ̃, -ɛn] **NM,F** *Math* arithmetician

arithmétique [aritmetik] **ADJ 1** *Math (moyenne, progression)* arithmetical **2** *Tech* **machine a.** adding machine
NF 1 *(matière)* arithmetic; **faire de l'a.** to do arithmetic **2** *(livre)* arithmetic book

Arlequin [arləkɛ̃] **NPR** Harlequin
• **arlequin NM** Harlequin

arlequinade [arləkinad] **NF 1** *Théât* harlequinade **2** *Fig Péj* (piece of) buffoonery

arlésien, -enne [arlezjɛ̃, -ɛn] **ADJ** of/from Arles
• **Arlésien, -enne NM,F** = inhabitant of or person from Arles; *Fig* **sa copine, c'est l'Arlésienne!** does this much talked-about girlfriend really exist?

armada [armada] **NF 1** *(quantité)* **une a. de touristes** an army of tourists; **toute une a. de motos est arrivée tout à coup** a whole fleet of motorbikes suddenly appeared **2** *Hist* **l'(Invincible) A.** the Spanish Armada

armagnac [armaɲak] **NM** *(alcool)* Armagnac (brandy)

armailli [armaji] **NM** *Suisse* shepherd *(in Fribourg)*

armateur [armatœr] **NM** *Naut (propriétaire ▸ d'un navire)* ship owner; *(▸ d'une flotte)* fleet owner; *(locataire)* shipper

armature [armatyr] **NF 1** *(cadre ▸ d'une fenêtre, d'une tente, d'un abat-jour)* frame; *(structure ▸ d'un exposé, d'une théorie)* structure, framework
2 *Constr (de charpente)* framework; *(dans le béton)* reinforcement; *(d'un câble)* armouring
3 *Couture* underwiring; **soutien-gorge à a.** underwired bra
4 *Phys (d'un condensateur)* plate; *(d'un aimant)* armature
5 *Mus* key signature

arme [arm] **NF 1** *(objet)* arm, weapon; *(arsenal)* weapons; **l'a. du crime** the murder weapon; **porter une a. sur soi** to carry a weapon; **il chargea son a.** he loaded his gun; **l'a. biologique** biological weapons, bioweapons; **a. blanche** knife; **l'a. chimique** chemical weapons; **a. à feu** firearm; **l'a. nucléaire** nuclear weapons; **rester l'a. au pied** to be ready for action; *Fam* **passer l'a. à gauche** *(mourir)* to kick the bucket
2 *(armée)* force, service; **dans quelle a. est-il?** which service *or* which branch of the army is he in?; **l'a. de l'artillerie** the artillery
3 *(instrument)* weapon; **contre ses accusations, j'ai l'a. absolue** I have the perfect response to his/her accusations; **une bonne a. psychologique** a good psychological weapon; **son sourire est une a. fatale** his/her smile is a deadly weapon; *Fig* **une a. à double tranchant** a double-edged sword; **tu lui as donné une a. contre toi** you've given him/her a stick to beat you with
• **armes NFPL 1** *(matériel de guerre)* arms, weapons, weaponry; **le métier des armes** the military profession, soldiering; **prendre les armes** to take up arms; **porter les armes** to be a soldier; **portez/présentez/reposez armes!** shoulder/present/order arms!; **aux armes!** to arms!; **une nation en armes** a nation in arms; **régler** *ou* **résoudre qch par les armes** to settle sth by force; *Fig* **tourner ses armes contre qn** to turn (one's weapons) against sb; **passer qn par les armes** to send sb to the firing squad; **mettre bas** *ou* **déposer** *ou* **rendre les armes** to lay down one's arms; **partir avec armes et bagages** to leave with bag and baggage; **armes conventionnelles** conventional weapons; **armes de destruction massive** weapons of mass destruction; **armes de dissuasion** deterrent; **armes de guerre** weapons of war, weaponry; **armes de jet** projectiles, missiles **2** *Escrime* fencing **3** *Hér* coat of arms
• **à armes égales ADV** on equal terms
• **d'armes ADJ frère d'armes** brother-in-arms; *Hist* **homme d'armes** man-at-arms

armé, -e[1] [arme] **ADJ 1** *(personne)* armed (**de** with); **attention, il est a.!** watch out, he's armed *or* he's carrying a weapon!; **il sort toujours a.** he always carries a weapon when he goes out; **a. jusqu'aux dents** armed to the teeth; *Fig* **a. de ses lunettes/d'une loupe, il explorait la paroi rocheuse** armed with his glasses/a magnifying glass, he examined the rock face; **a. de pied en cap** *Hist* in full armour; *Fig* (well) prepared, fully armed; **bien/mal a. contre le froid** well-protected/defenceless against the cold; **je suis a. contre ce genre de sarcasme** I have become inured to this kind of sarcasm; **mal a. (pour lutter) contre la concurrence** defenceless in the face of the competition **2** *Constr (béton)* reinforced; *(poutre)* trussed; *(verre)* wired
NM *(position)* cock

armée[2] [arme] **NF 1** *(forces militaires) Mil* army; **être dans l'a.** to be in the army; **être à l'a.** to be doing one's military service; **a. active** *ou* **régulière** regular army; **l'a. de l'air** the Air Force; **l'a. de mer** the Navy; **a. de métier** professional army; **a. nationale** conscript army; **a. d'occupation** army of occupation; **a. de réserve** reserves; **l'A. rouge** the Red Army; **l'A. du Salut** the Salvation Army; **l'a. de terre** the Army **2** *Fig* army, host; **une a. de figurants/sauterelles** an army of extras/grasshoppers

armement [arməmɑ̃] **NM 1** *Mil (militarisation ▸ d'un pays, d'un groupe)* arming
2 *Naut* commissioning, fitting-out
3 *(d'un appareil photo)* winding (on); *(d'un pistolet)* cocking
4 *(armes)* arms, weapons, weaponry; **limitation** *ou* **réduction des armements stratégiques** strategic arms limitation

Arménie [armeni] **NF l'A.** Armenia; **vivre en A.** to live in Armenia

arménien, -enne [armenjɛ̃, -ɛn] **ADJ** Armenian
NM *(langue)* Armenian
• **Arménien, -enne NM,F** Armenian

armer [3] [arme] **VT 1** *Mil (guérilla, nation)* to arm, to supply with weapons *or* arms; **a. qn chevalier** to knight sb, to dub sb a knight
2 *Fig (préparer)* to equip, to arm; **a. qn contre les difficultés de la vie** to equip sb to deal with the difficulties of life
3 *(arme)* to cock
4 *Phot* to wind (on)
5 *Naut* to commission, to fit out
6 *Constr (béton, ciment)* to reinforce; *(poutre)* to truss
7 *Tech (câble)* to sheathe
VPR s'armer 1 *(prendre une arme ▸ policier, détective)* to arm oneself; *(▸ nation)* to arm **2 s'a. de qch** *(s'équiper de ▸ arme)* to arm oneself with sth; *(▸ instrument)* to equip oneself with sth; *Fig (prendre)* **s'a. de courage/patience** to muster *or* to summon up one's courage/patience

armistice [armistis] **NM** armistice; **(l'anniversaire de) l'A.** Armistice Day, *Br* Remembrance Day, *Am* Veterans Day

armoire [armwar] **NF** *(placard) Br* cupboard, *Am* closet; *(pour vêtements) Br* wardrobe, *Am* closet; **a. frigorifique** cold room *or* store; **a. à glace** mirrored wardrobe; *Fig Hum* **c'est une véritable a. à glace** he's/she's built like the side of a house; **a. à linge** linen cupboard; **a. normande** large wardrobe; **a. à pharmacie** medicine cabinet *or* chest; **a. de toilette** bathroom cabinet

armoiries [armwari] **NFPL** *Hér* coat of arms, armorial bearings
• **aux armoiries de PRÉP** bearing the arms of

armorial, -e, -aux, -ales [armɔrjal, -o] *Hér* **ADJ** armorial
NM armorial

armoricain, -e [armɔrikɛ̃, -ɛn] **ADJ** Armorican; *Littérature* **le cycle a.** the Breton cycle
• **Armoricain, -e NM,F** Armorican

Armorique [armɔrik] **NF l'A.** Armorica

armoriste [armɔrist] **NM** heraldic artist

armure [armyr] **NF 1** *Hist* armour; **vêtu de son a.** armour-clad
2 *(protection)* defence; **cette insolence est une a.** he/she/*etc* uses insolence as a defence mechanism
3 *Tex* weave, pattern, design; **a. toile** plain weave
4 *(d'un câble)* sheathing
5 *Mus* key signature

armurier [armyrje] **NM 1** *(fabricant)* gunsmith, armourer; *(vendeur)* gun dealer **2** *Mil* armourer

ARN [aɛrɛn] **NM** *Biol (abrév* **acide ribonucléique***)* RNA

arnaque [arnak] **NF** *Fam* swindle, rip-off; **c'est de l'a.!** what a rip-off!

arnaquer [3] [arnake] **VT 1** *Fam (duper)* to rip off; **a. qn de 100 euros** to do sb out of 100 euros; **il nous a joliment arnaqués** he really ripped us off; **je me suis fait a. en achetant cette voiture** I was conned *or* I got ripped off when I bought this car **2** *Fam Arg crime (arrêter)* to nab; **se faire a. par les flics** to get nabbed by the cops

arnaqueur [arnakœr] **NM** *Fam* swindler, rip-off merchant

arnica [arnika] **NM OU NF** *Bot* arnica

arobas [arobas], **arobase** [arobaz] **NF** *Ordinat (dans une adresse électronique)* at (sign)

aromate [arɔmat] **NM** *(herbe)* herb; *(condiment)* spice; **aromates** seasoning

aromathérapeute [arɔmaterapøt] **NMF** aromatherapist

aromathérapie [arɔmaterapi] **NF** aromatherapy

aromatique [arɔmatik] **ADJ** aromatic, fragrant
NM *Chim* aromatic compound

aromatisation [arɔmatizasjɔ̃] **NF** flavouring

aromatiser [3] [arɔmatize] **VT** to flavour; **chocolat aromatisé au rhum** chocolate flavoured with rum, rum-flavoured chocolate

arôme [arom] **NM** *(parfum)* aroma, fragrance; *(goût)* flavour; **crème glacée a. vanille** vanilla-flavoured ice-cream; **a. artificiel** artificial flavouring

arpège [arpɛʒ] **NM** *Mus* arpeggio

arpéger [22] [arpeʒe] **VT** *Mus (accord)* to play as an arpeggio, to spread, to arpeggiate

arpent [arpɑ̃] **NM** *Arch* ≃ acre; **un petit a. de terre** a few acres of *or* a patch of land

arpentage [arpɑ̃taʒ] **NM** land-surveying, land-measuring

arpenter [3] [arpɑ̃te] **VT 1** *(parcourir ▸ couloir)* to pace up and down; **a. un quai** to pace up and down a platform **2** *(mesurer)* to survey, to measure

arpenteur [arpɑ̃tœr] **NM** surveyor, land-surveyor

arpion [arpjɔ̃] **NM** *Fam (pied)* foot, *Br* plate, *Am* dog; *(orteil)* toe

arqué, -e [arke] **ADJ** *(sourcils)* arched; *(nez)* hooked; *(jambes)* bandy, bow *(avant n)*; **aux jambes arquées** bandy-legged, bow-legged

arquebuse [arkəbyz] **NF** *Mil* arquebus, harquebus

arquebusier [arkəbyzje] **NM** *Mil* arquebusier, harquebusier

arquer [3] [arke] **VT** *(courber ▸ planche)* to bend, to curve; **a. le dos** to arch one's back
VI 1 *(fléchir ▸ poutre)* to sag **2** *Fam (marcher)* to walk; **il peut plus a.** he can't walk any more
VPR s'arquer to bend, to curve

arr *Admin (abrév écrite* **arrondissement***)* **1** *(dans une ville)* = administrative subdivision of major French cities such as Paris, Lyons or Marseilles **2** *(au niveau départemental)* = administrative subdivision of a "département", governed by a "sous-préfet"

arrachage [araʃaʒ] **NM** *(d'une plante)* pulling up, uprooting; *(de pommes de terre)* lifting; *(d'une dent, d'un clou)* pulling out, extraction; **l'a. des mauvaises herbes** weeding

arraché [araʃe] **NM** *Sport* snatch; *Fig* **gagner à l'a.** to snatch a victory; **une victoire à l'a.** a hard-won victory; **ils ont obtenu le contrat à l'a.** it was a struggle for them to get the contract

arrache-agrafes [araʃagraf] **NM INV** staple remover

arrache-clou [araʃklu] *(pl* **arrache-clous***)* **NM** nail claw

arrachement [araʃmɑ̃] **NM 1** *(fait d'enlever ▸ plante)* uprooting, pulling up; *(▸ feuille)* ripping *or* tearing out; *(▸ papier peint)* ripping *or* tearing off **2** *Fig (déchirement)* wrench; **l'a. des adieux** the wrench of saying goodbye

arrache-pied [araʃpje] **d'arrache-pied ADV** *(travailler)* flat out, relentlessly

arracher [3] [araʃe] **VT 1** *(extraire ▸ clou, cheville)* to pull out, to draw out; *(▸ arbuste)* to pull up, to root up; *(▸ pommes de terre, betteraves)* to lift; *(▸ mauvaises herbes, liseron)* to pull out, to root out; *(▸ poil, cheveu)* to pull out; *(▸ dent)* to pull out, to draw, to extract; **se faire a. une dent** to have a tooth out; **il a eu un bras arraché dans l'explosion** he had an arm blown off in the explosion; *Fam Fig* **ça arrache la gorge!** *(alcool fort, piment)* it blows your head off!; **elle t'arracherait les yeux s'il savait** she'd scratch your eyes out if he knew; **des images à vous a. le cœur** a heart-rending spectacle; **a. son masque à qn** to unmask sb; *très Fam* **ça t'arracherait la gueule de dire merci/de t'excuser?** it wouldn't kill you to say thanks/to apologize

2 *(déchirer ▸ papier peint, affiche)* to tear off, to rip off; *(▸page)* to tear out, to pull out; **la dernière page de mon agenda a été arrachée** the last page was torn out of my diary

3 *(prendre ▸ sac, billet)* to snatch, to grab; **j'ai réussi à lui a. le pistolet des mains** *(très vite)* I managed to snatch the gun away *or* to grab the gun from him/her; *(après une lutte)* I managed to wrest the gun from his/her grip

4 *(obtenir ▸ victoire)* to snatch; **a. des aveux/une signature à qn** to wring a confession/a signature out of sb; **a. des larmes à qn** to bring tears to sb's eyes; **a. un sourire à qn** to force a smile out of sb; **a. une parole à qn** to get *or* to squeeze a word out of sb; **pas moyen de lui a. le moindre commentaire** it's impossible to get him/her to say anything

5 *(enlever ▸ personne)* **a. qn à son lit** to drag sb out of *or* from his/her bed; **comment l'a. à son ordinateur?** how can we get *or* drag him/her away from his/her computer?; **arraché très jeune à sa famille** torn from the bosom of his/her family at an early age; **a. un bébé à sa mère** to take a child from its mother; **a. qn au sommeil** to force sb to wake up; **l'arrivée de sa sœur l'arracha à ses rêveries** he/she was awoken from his/her daydreams by the arrival of his/her sister; **a. qn à la mort** to snatch sb from (the jaws of) death; **a. qn à l'enfer du jeu** to rescue sb from the hell of gambling

USAGE ABSOLU *Fam* **ça arrache!** *(alcool fort, piment)* it blows your head off!

VI *Can* **en a.** to have a hard time (of it)

VPR s'arracher 1 *(s'écorcher)* **je me suis arraché la peau du genou en tombant** I fell (over) and scraped my knee; *Fam* **c'est à s'a. les cheveux** it's enough to drive you crazy; **s'a. les yeux** to scratch each other's eyes out

2 *(se disputer ▸ personne, héritage)* to fight over; **on s'arrache les droits d'adaptation du roman** people are fighting over the film rights to the novel

3 *très Fam (partir)* **allez, on s'arrache!** come on, let's be off!ᵒ

4 s'a. à, s'a. de to tear oneself away from; **s'a. au sommeil** to tear oneself from sleep; **s'a. à ses rêveries** to snap out of one's daydreams; **s'a. à son travail/à son ordinateur/de son fauteuil** to tear oneself away from one's work/one's computer/out of one's armchair

arracheur, -euse [araʃœr, -øz] *Agr* **NM,F** *(de pommes de terre, de betteraves)* lifter; *Arch* **a. de dents** tooth-puller

• **arracheuse NF** lifter, grubber

arrachoir [araʃwar] **NM** *Agr (de pommes de terre)* (potato) lifter; *(de betteraves)* (beet) puller

arraisonnement [arezɔnmɑ̃] **NM** *Naut* boarding (for inspection)

arraisonner [3] [arezɔne] **VT** *Naut (navire)* to board (for inspection)

arrangeant, -e [arɑ̃ʒɑ̃, -ɑ̃t] **ADJ** accommodating, obliging

arrangement [arɑ̃ʒmɑ̃] **NM 1** *(fait de disposer)* arrangement, laying out; *(résultat)* arrangement, layout; **modifier l'a. d'une pièce** to change the layout of a room; **l'a. des vers dans un sonnet** the order of lines in a sonnet **2** *(accord)* arrangement, settlement; **parvenir à un a.** to reach an agreement, to come to an arrangement; **a. à l'amiable** amicable settlement; **nous avons un a.** we have an understanding; **c'était un a. entre nous** we'd agreed it between ourselves; **sauf a. contraire** unless otherwise agreed **3** *Mus* arrangement, setting; **a. pour piano** arrangement for (the) piano

arranger [17] [arɑ̃ʒe] **VT 1** *(mettre en ordre ▸ chignon)* to tidy up; *(▸ tenue)* to straighten; *(▸ bouquet)* to arrange; *(▸pièce)* to lay out, to arrange; **c'est bien arrangé, chez toi** your place is nicely decorated

2 *(organiser ▸ rencontre, entrevue)* to arrange, to fix; *(▸emploi du temps)* to organize; **c'est Paul qui a arrangé la cérémonie/l'exposition** Paul organized the ceremony/put the exhibition together; **a. qch à l'avance** to prearrange sth; **ils ont arrangé ça entre eux** they've fixed it up between them

3 *(résoudre ▸ dispute, conflit)* to settle, to sort out; **je vais a. ça avec ton professeur** I'll sort this out with your teacher; **c'est arrangé, tu peux partir** it's all settled, you're free to leave now; **et mes rhumatismes n'arrangent pas les choses** *ou* **n'arrangent rien à l'affaire** my rheumatism doesn't help matters either; **voilà qui n'arrange pas mes affaires!** that's all I needed!

4 *Mus* to arrange; **a. un morceau pour la guitare** to arrange a piece for (the) guitar

5 *(convenir à)* to suit; **ce soir ou demain, comme ça t'arrange** tonight or tomorrow, whichever is convenient for you; **mardi? non, ça ne m'arrange pas** Tuesday? no, that's no good for me; **ça m'arrange (à merveille)** it suits me (down to the ground); **on ne peut pas a. tout le monde** you can't please *or* satisfy everybody

6 *Fam (réparer ▸ radio, réveil)* to fixᵒ; *(▸chaussures)* to repairᵒ, to mendᵒ; *(▸ robe)* to alterᵒ; **je vais t'a. ça en moins de deux** I'll fix this for you in no time

7 *(modifier ▸ traduction, présentation)* to alter, to modify; **je ne t'ai jamais rien promis, tu arranges l'histoire (à ta façon)** I never promised you anything, you're just twisting things

8 *Fam (maltraiter) Br* to sort out, *Am* to work over; **eh bien, on t'a joliment arrangé!** well, they certainly gave you a good going over!

VPR s'arranger 1 *(emploi réfléchi)* **va donc t'a.!** go and tidy yourself up!; **elle sait s'a.** she knows how to make the best of herself; *Fam Ironique* **tu t'es encore bien arrangé/bien arrangé la figure!** you've made a fine mess of yourself/of your face again!

2 *(emploi réciproque) (se mettre d'accord)* to come to an agreement; **on trouvera bien un moyen de s'a.** we'll come to some sort of an arrangement; **on s'était arrangé pour que ce soit une surprise** we'd arranged it so that it would be a surprise

3 *(se débrouiller)* to manage; **je m'arrangerai, ne t'en fais pas** I'll find a way *or* work something out, don't worry; **arrangez-vous pour avoir l'argent, sinon...** make sure *or* see that you have the money, or else...; **je me suis arrangé pour vous faire tous inviter** I've managed to get an invitation for all of you

4 *(s'améliorer)* to improve, to get better; **les choses s'arrangeront d'elles-mêmes** things'll sort themselves out *or* take care of themselves; **ça ne risque pas de s'a. tout seul** things are hardly likely to work themselves out on their own; **tout a fini par s'a.** everything worked out fine in the end; *Fam* **comment ça s'est arrangé, tes histoires de bagnole?** how did things turn out in the end after all that trouble you had with your car?; *Hum* **tu ne t'arranges pas avec les années!** you're not getting any better in your old age!; **et Louis? – ça ne s'arrange pas!** what about Louis? – he's no better!; *Fam* **et maintenant il veut faire construire, ça s'arrange pas!** now he wants to build a house, he's completely off his head!

5 s'a. avec to come to an agreement with; **on s'est arrangé avec les voisins** we sorted something out with the neighbours; **je m'arrangerai avec lui pour qu'il garde les enfants** I'll arrange for him to look after the children; **il s'est arrangé à l'amiable avec ses créanciers** he came to an amicable agreement with his creditors; **arrange-toi avec ma mère pour les meubles** see my mother about the furniture; **je m'arrangerai avec ce que j'ai** I'll make do with what I've got

6 s'a. de to put up with, to make do with; **ce n'est pas confortable, mais on s'en arrange** it's not comfortable, but we make do with it; **il s'arrange de tout** he's very easy-going

arrangeur, -euse [arɑ̃ʒœr, -øz] **NM,F** *Mus* arranger

arrérages [areraʒ] **NMPL** *Jur* arrears

arrestation [arestasjɔ̃] **NF** arrest; **procéder à une a.** to make an arrest; **procéder à l'a. de qn** to arrest sb; **être en état d'a.** to be under arrest; **mettre qn en état d'a.** to place sb under arrest

arrêt [arɛ] **NM 1** *(interruption)* stopping; **il a décidé l'a. du match** he decided to put a stop to *or* to call a halt to *or* to stop the match; **a. momentané des programmes** temporary blackout; **annoncer l'a. des poursuites** to announce that there will be no more prosecutions; **l'a. se fait automatiquement** it stops automatically; **appuyer sur le bouton "a."** press the "stop" button; **temps d'a.** pause; **marquer un temps d'a.** to stop *or* to pause for a moment; *Ordinat* **a. de fin de session** shutdown; **a. des hostilités** cessation of hostilities; **a. de paiement** stoppage of pay; **a. de travail** *(grève)* stoppage; *(congé)* sick leave; *(certificat)* doctor's *or* medical certificate; **être en a. de travail** to be on sick leave

2 *Transp (pause)* stop, halt; **avant l'a. complet de l'appareil** before the aircraft has come to a complete stop *or* standstill; **ce train est sans a. jusqu'à Arcueil** this train is non-stop *or* goes straight through to Arcueil; **en cas d'a. entre deux gares** if the train stops between stations; **Brive, Brive, deux minutes d'a.** this is Brive, there will be a two-minute stop

3 *(lieu)* **a. (d'autobus)** bus stop; **je descends au prochain a.** I'm getting off at the next stop

4 *Ftbl* **faire un a. du pied gauche** to make a save with one's left foot; **a. de jeu** stoppage; **jouer les arrêts de jeu** to play injury time; **faire un a. de volée** to make a mark

5 *Cin & TV* **a. sur image** freeze frame; **faire un a. sur image** to freeze a frame

6 *Méd* **a. cardiaque** *ou* **du cœur** cardiac arrest, cardiac failure; **a. cardiocirculatoire** asystole

7 *Jur (décision)* judgment, ruling; **a. de mise en accusation** committal for trial on indictment; **a. de mort** death sentence; *Fig* **signer son a. de mort** to sign one's own death warrant; **a. de non-lieu** dismissal of the charges; **rendre un a. de non-lieu** to dismiss a case for lack of evidence; **a. de renvoi** committal for trial at the Criminal Court; **rendre un a.** to deliver *or* to pronounce a judgment; *Littéraire* **les arrêts de la Providence** the decrees of Fate

8 *(arrestation)* arrest; **faire a. sur des marchandises** to seize *or* to impound goods

• **arrêts NMPL** *Mil* arrest; **mettre qn aux arrêts** to place sb under arrest; **être aux arrêts** to be under arrest; **arrêts forcés** *ou* **de rigueur** close arrest

• **à l'arrêt ADJ** *(véhicule)* stationary; **l'appareil est à l'a. sur la piste** the aircraft is at a standstill on the runway

• **d'arrêt ADJ 1** *Tech (dispositif)* stopping, stop *(avant n)* **2** *Couture* **point d'a.** finishing-off stitch

• **en arrêt ADV rester en a. devant qch** to stop dead *or* short before sth; **tomber en a.** *(chien)* to point; **je suis tombé en a. devant un magnifique vaisselier** I stopped to admire a beautiful dresser

• **sans arrêt ADV** *(sans interruption)* non-stop; *(à maintes reprises)* constantly

arrêté¹ [arete] **NM 1** *Jur (décret)* order, decree; **a. ministériel** ministerial order; **a. municipal** *Br* ≃ bylaw, *Am* ≃ ordinance; **a. préfectoral** *Br* ≃ bylaw, *Am* ≃ ordinance *(issued by a prefecture)*; **par a. royal** by royal decree **2** *Banque* **a. de compte** *(bilan)* statement of account; *(fermeture)* settlement of account

arrêté², -e [arete] **ADJ** *(opinion)* fixed, set; *(intention)* firm

arrêter [4] [arete] **VT 1** *(empêcher d'avancer ▸ passant, taxi)* to stop; **arrêtez-le! il a volé mon portefeuille!** stop that man, he's stolen my wallet!; **la circulation est arrêtée sur la N7** traffic is held up *or* has come to a standstill on the N7 (road); *Fam* **arrête-moi à la gare** drop me off at the station; *Sport* **a. un ballon** to make a save, to save a goal; *Fam Hum* **arrête ton char!** *(je ne te crois pas)* come off it!; *(arrête de te vanter)* stop showing off!

2 *(retenir ▸ personne)* to stop; *(▸regard)* to catch, to fix; **qu'est-ce qui t'arrête?** what's stopping you?; **rien ne peut plus l'a.** nothing can stop him/her now

3 *(interrompre)* to interrupt; **arrêtez-moi si je parle trop vite** stop me if I'm speaking too fast

4 *(éteindre ▸ radio, télévision)* to turn off; *(▸moteur)* to stop, to switch off; *Ordinat (système)* to shut down

5 *(mettre fin à ▸ élan)* to stop, to check; *(▸écoulement, saignement)* to stem, to stop; *(▸ croissance, chute)* to stop, to arrest, to bring to a halt; *Fam Hum* **on n'arrête pas le progrès!** what will they think of next!; **a. les frais** to stop messing about

6 *(abandonner ▸ construction, publication, traitement)* to stop; *(▸ sport, chant)* to give up; *(cesser de fabriquer)* to discontinue (the manufacture of); **j'ai arrêté le piano/ma carrière d'acteur** I've given up the piano/my acting career

7 *(sujet: police)* to arrest; **se faire a.** to get *or* to be arrested

8 *(déterminer ▸ date, lieu)* to appoint, to decide on, to fix; *(▸plan, procédure)* to decide on, to settle on, to settle upon; **a. sa décision** to make up one's mind; **a. son choix** to make one's choice

9 *(sujet: médecin)* **a. qn** to put sb on sick leave; **ça fait un mois que je suis arrêté** I've been on sick leave for a month

10 *Banque (compte)* to close, to settle; *Compta (comptes de l'exercice)* to close

11 *Couture (point)* to fasten off; **a. les mailles** to cast off

12 *(gibier)* to point

VI arrête, tu me fais mal! stop it, you're hurting me!; **vous allez a. un peu, tous les deux!** stop it, the pair of you!; **quatre albums en un an! mais vous n'arrêtez pas!** four albums in a year! you never stop *or* you don't ever take a break, do you?; **a. de faire qch** to stop doing sth; **arrête de pleurer** stop crying; **il a arrêté de travailler l'an dernier** he retired last year; **j'ai arrêté de fumer** I've given up *or* stopped smoking; **a. de se droguer** to give up *or* to come off drugs; *(tournure impersonnelle)* **il n'a pas arrêté de neiger** it hasn't stopped snowing, it's been snowing non-stop

VPR s'arrêter 1 *(cesser ▸ bruit, pluie, saignement)* to stop; **notre histoire ne s'arrête pas là** this isn't the end of our story; **les émissions s'arrêtent à 4 heures** broadcasting stops *or* ends at 4 a.m.; **s'a. de faire qch** *(cesser de)* to stop doing sth; *(renoncer à)* to give up doing sth, to stop doing sth; **elle s'est arrêtée de jouer en me voyant** she stopped playing when she saw me; **s'a. de composer/fumer** to stop writing music/smoking; **le monde ne va pas s'a. de tourner pour autant** that won't stop the world from turning

2 *(s'immobiliser ▸ montre)* to stop; *(▸ascenseur, véhicule)* to stop, to come to a stop *or* halt; *(▸système)* to shut down; **dites au chauffeur de s'a.** tell the driver to stop; **une voiture vint s'a. à ma hauteur** a car pulled up alongside me; **s'a. net** to stop dead *or* short

3 *(faire une halte, une pause)* to stop; **passer sans s'a. devant qn** to pass by sb without stopping; **on va s'a. à un Restoroute** we'll stop at a *Br* motorway *or Am* highway café; **on s'est arrêtés plusieurs fois en route** we made several stops on the way; **s'a. chez qn** to call at sb's; **tu peux t'a. chez l'épicier en venant?** could you stop off at the *Br* grocer's *or Am* grocery store on your way here?; **on va s'a. un quart d'heure** we'll stop for fifteen minutes, we'll take a fifteen-minute break; **nous nous étions arrêtés à la page 56** we'd left off at page 56

4 *(se fixer)* **son regard s'arrêta sur leur ami** his/her gaze fell on their friend; **notre choix s'est arrêté sur le canapé en cuir** we decided *or* settled on the leather couch

5 s'a. à *(faire attention à)* to pay attention to; **il ne faut pas s'a. aux apparences** one mustn't go by appearances

arrêt-maladie [arɛmaladi] *(pl* **arrêts-maladies)** **NM** *(congé)* sick leave; *(certificat)* medical certificate; **être en a.** to be on sick leave

arrhes [ar] **NFPL** *Fin* deposit; **verser des a.** to pay a deposit; **verser 300 euros d'a.** to leave 300 euros as a deposit *or* a deposit of 300 euros

arriération [arjerasjɔ̃] **NF** *Vieilli Psy* backwardness, retardation

arrière [arjɛr] **ADJ INV 1** *Aut (roue, feu)* rear; *(siège)* back **2** *Sport* backward; **roulade a.** backward roll

NM 1 *(d'une maison)* back, rear; *(d'un véhicule)* rear (end), back (end); **à l'a. du véhicule** at the rear of the vehicle; **asseyez-vous à l'a.** sit in the back

2 *Sport (au basket-ball)* guard; *(au football, au rugby)* back; *(au volley-ball)* rearline player; *Ftbl* **jouer a. droit/gauche** to play right/left back; **a. central** centre-back; **a. latéral** side back; **a. volant** sweeper; **la ligne des arrières, les arrières** the back line, the backs

3 *Naut* stern; **à l'a.** astern; **à l'a. de** at the stern of

4 *Mil* **les blessés ont été transportés à l'a.** the wounded were carried behind the lines

EXCLAM (stand) back!

• **arrières NMPL** *Mil* rear; **assurer** *ou* **protéger ses arrières** to protect one's rear; *Fig* to leave oneself a way out *or* an escape route

• **en arrière ADV 1** *(regarder)* back; *(se pencher, tomber)* backward, backwards; **revenir en a.** *(sur une route)* to retrace one's steps; *(avec un magnétophone)* to rewind (the tape); **reviens en a., je n'ai pas vu le début du film** rewind (the tape), I didn't see the beginning of the film; **se balancer d'avant en a.** to rock to and fro; **ramener ses cheveux en a.** to sweep one's hair back; **rester en a.** *(d'un convoi, d'un défilé)* to stay at the back *or* rear; **ne restez pas en a., rapprochez-vous** don't stay at the back, come closer; *Naut* **en a. toute!** full astern!

2 *(dans le temps)* back; **revenir en a.** to go back in time; **cela nous ramène plusieurs mois en a.** this takes us back several months; *Suisse* **il y a un siècle en a.** a century ago; *Suisse* **il date de cent ans en a.** it dates back a hundred years

• **en arrière de PRÉP** behind; *Mil* **rester en a. de la colonne** to fall behind (in the line); **il reste en a. des autres élèves** he's fallen behind the other pupils; **se tenir en a. de qn** to stand behind sb

arriéré, -e [arjere] **ADJ 1** *Fin (impayé ▸ loyer, intérêt)* overdue, in arrears; *(▸dette)* outstanding **2** *(mentalement retardé)* backward, (mentally) retarded **3** *(archaïque ▸ idée, technologie)* outdated; *(▸pays, région)* backward; **ils sont un peu arriérés dans sa famille** they're a bit old-fashioned *or* behind the times in his/her family; **le pays est économiquement a.** the country is economically backward

NM,F *(retardé mental)* backward *or* mentally retarded person

NM 1 *Fin (dette)* arrears; **avoir des arriérés** to be in arrears; **a. d'impôts** tax arrears, back taxes; **avoir 400 euros d'a. de loyer/d'impôts** to be 400 euros in arrears with one's rent/taxes; **solder un a.** to pay off arrears **2** *(retard)* backlog; **j'ai beaucoup d'a. dans mon travail** I have a big backlog of work *or* a lot of work to catch up on

arrière-ban [arjɛrbɑ̃] *(pl* **arrière-bans)** **NM** *Hist (levée)* arrière-ban *(summons to the king's vassals to do military service)*; *(vassaux)* vassals

arrière-bouche [arjɛrbuʃ] *(pl* **arrière-bouches)** **NF** *Anat* back of the mouth

arrière-boutique [arjɛrbutik] *(pl* **arrière-boutiques)** **NF** *Br* back-shop, *Am* back-store; **dans mon a.** at the back of my *Br* shop *or Am* store

arrière-cour [arjɛrkur] *(pl* **arrière-cours)** **NF** *Br* backyard

arrière-cuisine [arjɛrkɥizin] *(pl* **arrière-cuisines)** **NF** scullery

arrière-fond [arjɛrfɔ̃] *(pl* **arrière-fonds)** **NM** innermost depths

arrière-garde [arjɛrgard] *(pl* **arrière-gardes)** **NF** *Mil* rearguard; *Fig* **d'a.** *(idées)* old-fashioned

arrière-gorge [arjɛrgɔrʒ] *(pl* **arrière-gorges)** **NF** *Anat* back of the throat

arrière-goût [arjɛrgu] *(pl* **arrière-goûts)** **NM** aftertaste; **ça vous laisse un a. d'amertume** one is left with a bitter aftertaste; **le vin a un petit a. de cassis** there's an aftertaste of blackcurrant to the wine

arrière-grand-mère [arjɛrgrɑ̃mɛr] *(pl* **arrière-grands-mères)** **NF** great-grandmother

arrière-grand-oncle [arjɛrgrɑ̃tɔ̃kl] *(pl* **arrière-grands-oncles)** **NM** great-great-uncle, great-granduncle

arrière-grand-père [arjɛrgrɑ̃pɛr] *(pl* **arrière-grands-pères)** **NM** great-grandfather

arrière-grands-parents [arjɛrgrɑ̃parɑ̃] **NMPL** great-grandparents

arrière-grand-tante [arjɛrgrɑ̃tɑ̃t] *(pl* **arrière-grands-tantes)** **NF** great-great-aunt, great-grand-aunt

arrière-main [arjɛrmɛ̃] *(pl* **arrière-mains)** **NM 1** *Tennis* **(coup d')a.** backhand (stroke) **2** *(d'un cheval)* (hind)quarters

arrière-neveu [arjɛrnəvø] *(pl* **arrière-neveux)** **NM** great-nephew, grandnephew

arrière-nièce [arjɛrnjɛs] *(pl* **arrière-nièces)** **NF** great-niece, grandniece

arrière-pays [arjɛrpei] **NM INV** hinterland; **dans l'a.** in the hinterland; **aller dans l'a.** to go inland

arrière-pensée [arjɛrpɑ̃se] *(pl* **arrière-pensées)** **NF** ulterior motive; **son acceptation cachait une a. de revanche** behind his/her acceptance lay a lurking idea of revenge; **sans arrière-pensées** without any ulterior motives

arrière-petite-fille [arjɛrpətitfij] *(pl* **arrière-petites-filles)** **NF** great-granddaughter

arrière-petite-nièce [arjɛrpətitnjɛs] *(pl* **arrière-petites-nièces)** **NF** great-great-niece

arrière-petit-fils [arjɛrpətifis] *(pl* **arrière-petits-fils)** **NM** great-grandson

arrière-petit-neveu [arjɛrpətinəvø] *(pl* **arrière-petits-neveux)** **NM** great-great-nephew

arrière-petits-enfants [arjɛrpətizɑ̃fɑ̃] **NMPL** great-grandchildren

arrière-plan [arjɛrplɑ̃] *(pl* **arrière-plans)** **NM** *(gén) & Ordinat* background; **on la voit à l'a. sur la photo** she's in the background of the picture; *Fig* **être à l'a.** to remain in the background; *Fig* **ce projet est passé à l'a.** this project has been put on the back burner; *Fig* **se trouver relégué à l'a.** to be upstaged

arrière-port [arjɛrpɔr] *(pl* **arrière-ports)** **NM** *Naut* inner harbour

arriérer [18] [arjere] **VT** *Fin (paiement)* to postpone, to delay, to defer

arrière-saison [arjɛrsɛzɔ̃] *(pl* **arrière-saisons)** **NF 1** *(fin de l'automne)* end of the *Br* autumn *or Am* fall **2** *Agr* end of the season

arrière-salle [arjɛrsal] *(pl* **arrière-salles)** **NF** inner room, back room

arrière-train [arjɛrtrɛ̃] *(pl* **arrière-trains)** **NM 1** *Zool* hindquarters **2** *Hum (fesses)* hindquarters, behind

arrimage [arimaʒ] **NM 1** *Naut* stowage **2** *Astron (d'une navette spatiale)* docking

arrimer [3] [arime] **VT 1** *Naut* to stow **2** *(attacher)* to secure, to fasten; **a. un chargement sur le toit d'une voiture** to secure *or* to fasten a load to the roof of a car **3** *Astron* to dock

arrimeur [arimœr] **NM** *Naut* stevedore

arrivage [arivaʒ] **NM 1** *(de produits)* delivery, consignment; **nous venons d'avoir un a.** we've just had a (fresh) consignment in; **prix selon a.** *(dans une poissonnerie)* price according to availability **2** *Fin (de fonds)* accession **3** *Hum (de personnes)* influx; **il y a encore eu un a. de touristes ce matin** another horde of tourists arrived this morning, there was another influx of tourists this morning

arrivant, -e [arivɑ̃, -ɑ̃t] **NM,F** newcomer, new arrival; **il y a dix nouveaux arrivants** there are ten newcomers *or* new arrivals

arrivé, -e [arive] **ADJ 1** *(qui a réussi)* **être a.** to have made it, to have arrived **2 le dernier/premier a.** the last/first (person) to arrive

• **arrivée NF 1** *(venue ▸ d'une saison, du froid)* arrival, coming; *(▸d'un avion, d'un ami)* arrival; **l'arrivée de nouveaux produits sur le marché** the arrival of new products onto the market; **on attend son arrivée pour le mois prochain** we're expecting him/her to arrive *or* he's/she's expected to arrive next month; **à mon arrivée à la gare** on *or* upon my arrival at the station, when I arrived at the station; **quelques mois après son arrivée au pouvoir** a few months after he/she came to power; **on viendra t'attendre à l'arrivée du train** we'll be waiting for you at the station; **heure d'arrivée** *(d'un train)* time of arrival; *(du courrier)* time of delivery **2** *Sport* finish **3** *Tech* **arrivée d'air/de gaz** *(robinet)* air/gas inlet; *(passage)* inflow of air/gas

ARRIVER [3] [arive] **VI** *(aux être)* **A.** *DANS L'ESPACE* **1** *(parvenir à destination ▸ voyageur, véhicule, courrier)* to arrive; **a. à l'école** to arrive at school, to get to school; **a. chez qn** to arrive at sb's house; **a. chez soi** to get *or* to arrive home; **a. au sommet** to reach the summit; **elle doit a. à Paris vers midi** she should arrive *or* be in Paris at around twelve; **Colomb croyait être arrivé aux Indes** Columbus thought he'd reached the Indies; **le bateau arrive à quai** the ship's coming alongside the quay; **j'étais à peine arrivé que le téléphone sonna** no sooner had I arrived than the phone rang; **on arrive à quelle heure?** what time do we get there?; **nous sommes bientôt** *ou* **presque arrivés** we're almost there; **les invités vont bientôt a.** the guests will be arriving soon; **qui est arrivé après l'appel?** *(en classe)* who came in after I *Br* called the register *or Am* called roll?; **je serai chez toi dans un quart d'heure, qui est déjà**

arrivé? I'll be at your place in fifteen minutes, who's already there?; **le courrier est-il arrivé?** has the mail *or Br* post arrived *or* come yet?; **être bien arrivé** *(personne, colis)* to have arrived safely; **vous voilà enfin arrivés, je m'inquiétais** *(ici)* here you are *or* you've arrived at last, I was getting worried; *(là-bas)* you got there at last, I was getting worried; **si tu n'arrives pas à l'heure, je pars sans toi** *(ici)* if you aren't here on time, I'll go without you; *(là-bas)* if you don't get there on time, I'll go without you; **par où es-tu arrivé?** *(ici)* which way did you come?; *(là-bas)* which way did you take to get there?; **a. de** to have (just) come from; **ils arrivent de Tokyo** they've just arrived *or* come from Tokyo; **d'où arrives-tu pour être si bronzé?** where did you get that tan?; **j'arrive tout juste de vacances** I'm just back from my holidays; **y aller sans réserver? t'arrives d'où, toi?** go there without booking? you must be joking!; **même en roulant vite ça nous fait a. après minuit** even if we drive fast we won't get there before midnight

2 *(finir ▸ dans un classement)* to come (in); **a. le premier** *(coureur)* to come in first, to take first place; *(invité)* to arrive first, to be the first to arrive; **a. le dernier** *(coureur)* to come in last, to take last place; *(invité)* to be the last to arrive; **il est arrivé cinquième au marathon** he took (the) fifth place *or* came in fifth in the marathon; **ils sont arrivés dans un mouchoir** it was a close finish

3 *(venir)* to come, to approach; **je l'ai vu a.** I saw him approaching *or* coming; **les voilà qui arrivent** here they come; **tu es prêt? – j'arrive tout de suite/dans une minute** are you ready? – I'm coming/I'll be with you in a minute; **j'arrive, j'arrive!** I'm coming!; **je n'ai pas vu la voiture a.** I didn't see the car (coming); **ils sont arrivés en voiture** they came by car; **l'express arrivait en gare** the express train was pulling in; **une odeur de chocolat arrivait de la cuisine** a smell of chocolate wafted in *or* came from the kitchen; **le courant/l'eau n'arrive plus** there's no more power/no more water coming through

B. *DANS LE TEMPS* **1** *(événement, jour, moment)* to come; **Noël arrive bientôt** it'll soon be Christmas; **le jour arrivera où...** the day will come when...; **la soixantaine/retraite est vite arrivée** sixty/retirement is soon upon us; **le printemps est arrivé** spring is here *or* has come; **le grand jour est arrivé!** the big day's here at last!

2 *(se produire)* to happen; **comment est-ce arrivé?** how did it happen?; **un accident est si vite arrivé!** accidents will happen!; **ce sont des choses qui arrivent** these things happen; **ça n'arrive pas dans la vie** it doesn't happen in real life; **a. à qn** to happen to sb; **il s'est fait renvoyer – ça devait lui a.** he got fired – it was bound to happen; **ce genre d'histoires n'arrive qu'à moi!** these things only happen to me!; **ça peut a. à tout le monde** it could happen to anyone; **ça peut a. à tout le monde de se tromper!** everybody makes mistakes!; **un malheur lui est arrivé** something bad's happened to him/her; **ça n'arrive pas qu'aux autres** it's easy to think it'll never happen to you; **ça ne t'arrive jamais d'être de mauvaise humeur?** aren't you ever in a bad mood?; **tu ne te décourages jamais? – si, ça m'arrive** don't you ever get discouraged? – yes, from time to time; **tu es encore en retard? que cela ne t'arrive plus!** late? don't let it happen again!

V IMPERSONNEL 1 *(venir)* **il est arrivé des dizaines de photographes** dozens of photographers arrived; **il arrive un train toutes les heures** there's a train every hour

2 *(aventure, événement)* **il est arrivé un accident** there's been an accident; **il est arrivé tant de choses depuis deux semaines** so many things have happened during the last two weeks; **comme il arrive souvent en pareilles circonstances** as is often the case in such circumstances; **il m'est arrivé une histoire incroyable!** something incredible happened to me!; **s'il m'arrivait quelque chose, prévenez mon père** if anything happens *or* should anything happen to me, let my father know; **pourvu qu'il ne lui soit rien arrivé!** let's hope nothing's happened to him/her!

3 *(se produire parfois)* **ne peut-il pas a. que l'ordinateur se trompe?** couldn't the computer ever make a mistake?; **il arrive bien qu'ils se disputent mais...** they do quarrel sometimes *or* from time to time but...; **il m'arrive rarement de me mettre en colère** I don't get angry very often; **il lui arrivait de s'enfermer des heures dans sa bibliothèque** sometimes he'd/she'd spend hours shut away in his/her library; **s'il arrivait que je sois** *ou* **fusse absent** if I happened to be away

• **arriver à VT IND 1** *(niveau, taille, lieu)* **le bas du rideau arrive à 20 cm du sol** the bottom of the curtain is 20 cm above the ground; **on arrive au carrefour, tu vas tourner à droite** we're coming up to *or* approaching the crossroads, you want to turn right; **le fil du téléphone n'arrive pas jusqu'à ma chambre** the phone cord doesn't reach *or* isn't long enough to reach my room; **des bruits de conversation arrivaient jusqu'à nous** the sound of people chatting reached us; **ses cheveux lui arrivent à la taille** his/her hair comes down to his/her waist; **ma nièce m'arrive à l'épaule** my niece comes up to my shoulder; **la boue m'arrivait jusqu'aux genoux** the mud came up to my knees, I was knee-deep in mud; **la neige nous arrivait à mi-corps** the snow came up to our waists

2 *(étape, moment, conclusion)* to come to, to reach; **nous arrivons à une phase cruciale du projet** we're reaching a crucial stage in our project; **où (en) étions-nous arrivés la semaine dernière?** *(dans une leçon)* where did we get up to *or* had we got to last week?; **arrivée à la fin de son discours** when she reached the end of her speech; **maintenant qu'il est arrivé au terme de son mandat** now that he's come to *or* reached the end of his term of office; **arrivée à la fin de sa carrière/vie** having reached the end of her career/life; **j'arrive à un âge où...** I've reached an age when...; **arrivez-en au fait** get to the point; **et ses tableaux? – j'y arrive/arrivais** what about his/her paintings? – I'm/I was coming to that

3 *(rang, résultat)* to get; *(succès)* to achieve; **pour a. à une meilleure rentabilité** to get better results; **tu as refait l'addition? – oui, j'arrive au même total que toi** did you redo the calculations? – yes, I get the same result as you; **alors, tu es arrivé à ce que tu voulais?** so, did you manage to get *or* to achieve what you wanted?; **si tu veux a.** if you want to get on *or* to succeed in life

4 *(pouvoir, réussir à)* **a. à faire qch** to manage to do sth, to succeed in doing sth; **tu arrives à nager le crawl?** can you do the crawl?; **tu n'arriveras jamais à la convaincre** you'll never succeed in convincing her, you'll never manage to convince her; **je n'arrive pas à m'y habituer** I just can't get used to it; **je n'arrive pas à comprendre son refus** I can't understand why he/she said no; **il n'arrive pas à prononcer ce mot** he can't pronounce this word; **je ne suis pas encore arrivé à lui écrire ce mois-ci** I still haven't got round to writing to him/her this month; **je parie que tu n'y arriveras pas!** I bet you won't be able to do it!; **tu m'aides? je n'y arrive pas!** can you help me? I can't do *or* manage it!; **tu n'arriveras jamais à rien** you'll never get anywhere; **je n'arriverai jamais à rien avec lui!** I'll never be able to do anything with him!

5 *(locutions)* **(en) a. à qch** *(en venir à)* **comment peut-on en a. au suicide?** how can anybody get to the point of contemplating suicide?; **j'en arrive à penser que...** I'm beginning to think that...; **j'en arrive parfois à me demander si...** sometimes I (even) wonder if...; **elle en arrive même à ne plus le souhaiter** she's even starting to hope it won't happen; **je ne veux pas me faire opérer – il faudra pourtant bien en a. là** I don't want to have an operation – you have no choice; **depuis, je ne lui parle plus – c'est malheureux d'en a. là** since then, I haven't spoken to him/her – it's a shame when it comes to that

USAGE ABSOLU *(réussir socialement)* to succeed, to arrive

---

arrivisme [arivism] **NM** pushiness, ambitiousness; **elle n'est entrée au comité que par a.** for her, joining the committee was just a way of furthering her career *or* ambitions

arriviste [arivist] **ADJ** self-seeking, careerist

NMF careerist

arrobase [arɔbaz] = **arobas**

arrogance [arɔgɑ̃s] **NF** arrogance; **parler avec a.** to speak arrogantly

arrogant, -e [arɔgɑ̃, -ɑ̃t] **ADJ** arrogant; **prendre un air a.** to take on an arrogant *or* haughty air

NM,F arrogant person

arroger [17] [arɔʒe] **s'arroger VPR** to assume, to arrogate (to oneself); **s'a. le droit de faire qch** to assume the right to do sth

arrondi, -e [arɔ̃di] **ADJ 1** *(objet, forme)* rounded, round; *(visage)* round **2** *(voyelle)* rounded

NM 1 *Couture* hemline

2 *(forme ▸ d'une sculpture)* rounded form *or* shape; *(▸ du visage)* round shape, roundness; *(▸ d'un parterre)* circular line *or* design

3 *Aviat* flaring out, flattening out

4 *Ordinat & Math* rounding

arrondir [32] [arɔ̃dir] **VT 1** *(rendre rond)* to make into a round shape, to round (off); *(incurver)* to round off; **le potier arrondit son bloc d'argile** the potter rounds off his lump of clay; **cette coiffure lui arrondit le visage** that haircut makes his/her face look round; **a. les lignes d'un dessin** to make the lines of a drawing rounder; **a. un angle de table** to round off a table corner; *Fig* **a. les angles** to smooth things over

2 *(augmenter ▸ capital, pécule)* to increase; *(▸ patrimoine, domaine)* to extend; *Fam* **a. ses fins de mois** to make a little extra on the side; *Fam* **cela m'aide à a. mes fins de mois** it keeps the wolf from the door

3 *Math* to round off; *(vers le haut)* to round up; *(vers le bas)* to round down; **a. un total à l'euro supérieur/inférieur** to round a sum up/down to the nearest euro

4 *Couture* to level (off)

5 *(dégrossir ▸ style, phrase)* to refine, to polish; *(▸ parfum, goût, personnalité)* to make smoother, to round out

VPR s'arrondir 1 *(grossir ▸ femme enceinte, ventre)* to get bigger *or* rounder; *(▸ visage)* to become rounder, to fill out; *(▸ somme)* to mount up; **mes économies se sont arrondies!** my nest-egg is a nice size now! **2** *(devenir rond ▸ voyelle)* to become rounded

arrondissement [arɔ̃dismɑ̃] **NM** *Admin* **1** *(dans une ville)* = administrative subdivision of major French cities such as Paris, Lyons or Marseilles **2** *(au niveau départemental)* = administrative subdivision of a "département", governed by a "sous-préfet"

> **ARRONDISSEMENT**
>
> In Paris, Lyons and Marseilles, the number of the "arrondissement" corresponds to the last two figures in a postcode: thus, you can tell from the postcode 75012 that it refers to the 12th arrondissement of Paris.

arrosage [arozaʒ] **NM 1** *(d'un jardin, de plantes)* watering; *(de la chaussée)* spraying

2 *Fam (corruption)* bribing

3 *(par les médias)* bombardment

4 *Mil (avec des bombes)* heavy bombing; *(avec des obus)* heavy shelling; *(avec des balles)* spraying

arroser [3] [aroze] **VT 1** *(asperger ▸ plante, jardin, pelouse)* to water; **arrosez légèrement le dessus des feuilles** sprinkle some water on the surface of the leaves; **a. une voiture au jet** to hose down *or* to spray a car; **arrête, tu m'arroses!** stop it, you're spraying water (all) over me *or* I'm getting wet!; *Fam* **se faire a.** *(par la pluie)* to get drenched *or* soaked

2 *(inonder)* to soak; **attention les enfants, vous allez a. mon parquet!** careful, children, you'll get my floor all wet!; **a. qn de qch** to pour sth over sb, to drench sb in sth

3 *Culin (gigot, rôti)* to baste

4 *(repas)* **une mousse de saumon arrosée d'un bon sauvignon** a salmon mousse washed down with a fine Sauvignon; *Fam* **(bien) a. son déjeuner** to drink (heavily) with one's lunch

5 *Fam (fêter)* to drink to; **tu as été reçu premier, on va a. ça!** you came first, this calls for a celebration!; **a. une naissance** to drink to a new baby, *Br* to wet a baby's head

6 *Géog (couler à travers)* to water, to irrigate; **la Seine arrose Paris** the river Seine flows through Paris

7 *Mil (avec des bombes, des obus)* to bombard; *(avec des balles)* to spray

8 *Fam (soudoyer)* to grease the palm of
9 *(sujet: médias)* to bombard
VPR s'arroser *Fam* **une nouvelle comme ça, ça s'arrose!** a piece of news like that calls for a celebration!

arroseur [arozœr] **NM 1** *(personne)* waterer; *Fig* **c'est (le gag de) l'a. arrosé** the boot's on the other foot **2** *(dispositif)* sprinkler

arroseuse [arozøz] **NF** water cart

arrosoir [arozwar] **NM** watering *Br* can *or Am* pot

arrt = **arr**

ARS [aεrεs] **NF** *(abrév* **allocation de rentrée scolaire)** = allowance paid to parents to help cover costs incurred at the start of the school year

arsenal, -aux [arsənal, -o] **NM 1** *Mil & Naut* arsenal; **ils ont découvert un véritable a.** *(armes)* they've stumbled on a major arms cache; *(bombes)* they've stumbled on a bomb factory; **a. maritime** naval dockyard **2** *Fam (panoplie)* equipment, gear; **l'a. législatif** *ou* **des lois** the might of the law

arsenic [arsənik] **NM** *Chim* arsenic

art [ar] **NM 1** *Beaux-Arts* art; **l'a. de Cézanne** Cézanne's art; **l'a. pour l'a.** art for art's sake; **a. abstrait** abstract art; *Ordinat* **a. ASCII** ASCII art; **a. brut** art brut; **a. cinétique** kinetic art; **a. contemporain** contemporary art; **a. déco** art deco; **a. figuratif** figurative art; **l'a. grec** Greek art; **a. minimal** minimalist art; **l'a. moderne** modern art; **a. multimédia** multimedia art; **a. naïf** naive art; **A. nouveau** Art nouveau; **a. numérique** digital art; **a. pauvre** process art; **a. primitif** primitive art; **a. religieux** *ou* **sacré** religious art; **a. vidéo** video art; **cinéma** *ou* **salle d'a. et d'essai** art house; **regardez cette pyramide de fruits, c'est du grand a.!** look at this pyramid of fruit, it's a work of art!; **vos graffiti dans le couloir, ce n'est pas du grand a.!** your graffiti in the corridor is hardly a work of art!
2 *(goût)* art, taste, artistry; **une maison décorée avec/sans a.** a house decorated with/without taste
3 *(technique)* art; *Fig* **découper un poulet, c'est tout un a.!** carving a chicken is quite an art!; **l'a. culinaire** the art of cooking; **l'a. dramatique** dramatic art, dramatics; **cours d'a. dramatique** *(classe)* drama class; *(école)* drama school; **a. floral** flower arranging, floral art; **l'a. de la guerre** the art of warfare; **l'a. oratoire** the art of public speaking; **l'a. poétique** poetics; **l'a. sacré, le grand a.** (the art of) alchemy
4 *(don)* art, talent; **avoir l'a. du compromis** to have mastered the art of compromise; **il a l'a. de m'énerver** he has a knack of getting on my nerves; **l'a. d'aimer/de vivre** the art of loving/living; **l'Orient nous apprend un nouvel a. de vivre** from the East, we are learning a new way of living; **je voulais juste le prévenir! – oui, mais il y a l'a. et la manière** I didn't want to offend him, just to warn him! – yes, but there are ways of going about it
• **arts NMPL** arts; **être un ami des arts** to be a friend of the arts; **arts appliqués** ≃ art and design; **arts décoratifs** decorative arts; **arts graphiques** graphic arts; **arts martiaux** martial arts; *Scol* **arts ménagers** home economics; *Univ* **les arts et métiers** = college for the advanced education of those working in commerce, manufacturing, construction and design; **les arts plastiques** the visual arts; **les arts premiers** ethnic art; **les arts du spectacle** the performing arts; **arts et traditions populaires** arts and crafts

Arte [arte] **NF** *TV* = Franco-German cultural television channel created in 1992

artefact [artefakt] **NM** artefact, artifact

artère [artεr] **NF 1** *Anat* artery **2** *(route)* (main) road; *(rue)* (main) street *or* thoroughfare; **les grandes artères** the main roads

artériel, -elle [arterjεl] **ADJ** *Anat* arterial

artériole [arterjɔl] **NF** *Anat* arteriole

artériosclérose [arterjɔskleroz] **NF** *Méd* arteriosclerosis

artésien, -enne [artezjε̃, -εn] **ADJ** *(langue, patois)* of/from Artois
• **Artésien, -enne NM,F** = inhabitant of or person from Artois

arthrite [artrit] **NF** *Méd* arthritis; **a. déformante** rheumatoid arthritis

arthritique [artritik] *Méd* **ADJ** arthritic
NMF arthritis sufferer

arthropode [artrɔpɔd] *Zool & Entom* **NM** arthropod
• **arthropodes NMPL** the Arthropoda

arthrose [artroz] **NF** *Méd* arthrosis

Arthur [artyr] **NPR** *Myth* Arthur; **la légende du roi A.** Arthurian legend; *Fam* **se faire appeler A.** to get one's head bitten off, to get bawled out

artichaut [artiʃo] **NM** artichoke

artiche [artiʃ] **NM** *Fam (argent)* dough, *Br* dosh, *Am* bucks

article [artikl] **NM 1** *Com* article, item; **nous ne suivons** *ou* **faisons plus cet a.** we don't stock that item any more; **articles d'alimentation** foodstuffs; **a. d'appel** loss leader, traffic builder; **a. bas de gamme** bottom-of-the-range item; **a. de base** staple; **articles de bureau** office equipment and stationery; **articles de consommation courante** consumer goods; **a. démarqué** mark-down; **articles d'exportation** export goods, exports; **a. en fin de série** discontinued item; **a. à forte rotation** fast mover; **articles de grande consommation** consumables, consumer goods; **a. haut de gamme** top-of-the-range item; **articles d'importation** import goods, imports; **articles de luxe** luxury goods; **a. de marque** branded article; **articles de mercerie** *Br* haberdasher's goods, *Am* notions; **articles de mode** fashion accessories; **a. de première nécessité** basic commodity; **articles en promotion** *(sur vitrine)* special offers; **a. de rebut** reject; **a. en réclame** special offer; **articles sans suite** discontinued line; **articles de toilette** toiletries; **articles de voyage** travel goods; **faire l'a. pour** to do a sales pitch for; *Fig* to praise; *Fam* **elle a fait l'a. pour son bouquin toute la soirée** she went on about her book all evening
2 *Compta & Fin (d'une facture)* item; *(d'un compte)* entry; **facture détaillée par articles** itemized bill; **a. de contre-passation** transfer entry; **articles de dépense** items of expenditure; **articles divers** sundries
3 *Journ* article; *(d'un dictionnaire, d'un guide)* entry; **a. de fond** leading article, *Br* leader
4 *(sujet)* point; **elle dit qu'on lui doit trois millions, et sur cet a., tu peux lui faire confiance!** she says she's owed three million, and you can believe her on that score *or* point
5 *Rel* **articles de foi** articles of faith; *Fig* **le socialisme, pour moi, c'est un a. de foi** socialism is an article of faith for me
6 *(paragraphe)* article, clause; **les articles de la Constitution** the articles *or* clauses of the Constitution; **l'a. 10 du contrat** point *or* paragraph *or* clause 10 of the contract; **a. de loi** article of law
7 *Gram* article; **a. défini/indéfini** definite/indefinite article; **a. élidé** elided article
8 *Ordinat (d'un menu)* command; *(dans des groupes de discussion)* article; *(dans une base de données)* record
9 *(locution)* **à l'a. de la mort** at death's door, on the point of death

articulaire [artikylεr] **ADJ** articular; **douleurs articulaires** sore joints, joint pain

articulation [artikylasjɔ̃] **NF 1** *Anat* joint; **a. du coude/du genou/de la hanche** elbow/knee/hip joint; **a. immobile/mobile** fixed/hinge joint; **j'ai mal aux articulations** my joints ache
2 *(prononciation)* articulation; **lieu** *ou* **point d'a.** point of articulation
3 *(liaison)* link, link-up; *(structure)* structure; **l'a. des deux parties** the link between the two parts; **l'a. des idées dans le texte** the structuring of ideas in the text
4 *Jur* enumeration, setting forth *or* out
5 *Tech* connection, joint

articulé, -e [artikyle] **ADJ 1** *(mobile)* articulated
2 *Anat* articulated, jointed
3 *Tech* hinged, jointed; **jouet a.** jointed toy; **poupée articulée** jointed doll
4 *Ling* articulated

articuler [3] [artikyle] **VT 1** *(prononcer)* to articulate
2 *(dire)* to utter; **j'étais si ému que je ne pouvais plus a. un seul mot** I was so moved that I couldn't utter *or* say a single word
3 *(enchaîner* ▸ *démonstration, thèse)* to link up *or* together; *(*▸ *faits)* to connect
4 *Tech* to joint
5 *Jur (accusations)* to enumerate, to set forth *or* out
USAGE ABSOLU *(parler clairement)* **articule, je ne comprends rien** speak more clearly, I don't understand; **il articule mal** he doesn't speak clearly; **bien a.** to pronounce clearly
VPR s'articuler 1 *(former une articulation)* to be joined together; **la façon dont les os s'articulent** the way the bones are joined together; **ces deux parties s'articulent assez bien** the two parts of the text hang together well **2 s'a. autour de** to hinge *or* to turn on; **son article s'articule autour d'une idée originale** his/her article hinges on an original idea **3** *Anat, Tech & Zool* **s'a. sur** to be articulated *or* jointed with

artifice [artifis] **NM 1** *(stratagème)* (clever) device *or* trick; **ils ont réussi à dissimuler la situation financière par des artifices de calcul** they managed to hide the financial situation by tweaking the figures; **ils ont usé de tous les artifices pour faire passer la proposition** they used every trick in the book to get the motion through; **beauté sans artifices** artless beauty **2** *(explosif)* firework

artificialité [artifisjalite] **NF** artificiality

artificiel, -elle [artifisjεl] **ADJ 1** *(colorant, fleur, lumière, intelligence, insémination)* artificial; *(lac, soie)* artificial, man-made; *(perle)* artificial, imitation *(avant n)*; *(dent)* false; *(bras, hanche)* replacement *(avant n)*
2 *(factice* ▸ *besoin, plaisir)* artificial
3 *(affecté* ▸ *manières)* artificial; *(*▸ *sourire)* false, artificial; *(*▸ *rire)* forced; **je le trouve totalement a.** I find him totally artificial; **le style est très a.** the style is very contrived *or* artificial
4 *(arbitraire)* artificial; **la comparaison est totalement artificielle** it's a very artificial comparison

artificiellement [artifisjεlmɑ̃] **ADV 1** *(fabriqué, créé)* artificially **2** *(arbitrairement)* arbitrarily

artificier [artifisje] **NM 1** *(en pyrotechnie)* fireworks expert **2** *Mil (soldat)* blaster; *(spécialiste)* bomb disposal expert

artificieuse [artifisjøz] *voir* **artificieux**

artificieusement [artifisjøzmɑ̃] **ADV** *Littéraire* deceitfully

artificieux, -euse [artifisjø, -øz] **ADJ** *Littéraire* deceitful

artillerie [artijri] **NF** *Mil* artillery; **a. anti-aérienne** anti-aircraft artillery; **a. anti-chars** anti-tank artillery; **a. d'assaut** assault artillery *or* guns; **a. de campagne** field artillery; **a. légère/lourde** light/heavy artillery; *Fig* **ils ont envoyé la grosse a.** *ou* **l'a. lourde** they used drastic measures; **pièce/tir d'a.** artillery cannon/fire

artilleur [artijœr] **NM** *Mil* artilleryman

artimon [artimɔ̃] **NM** *Naut (mât)* mizzen, mizzenmast; *(voile)* mizzen; **mât d'a.** mizzenmast

artisan, -e [artizɑ̃, -an] **NM,F 1** *(travailleur)* craftsman, *f* craftswoman, artisan; **a. ébéniste** cabinet-maker; **a. verrier** (skilled) glassmaker **2** *(responsable)* architect, author; **Churchill fut l'a. de la défense nationale** Churchill was the architect of national defence; **l'a. de la paix** the peacemaker; **être l'a. de sa propre chute/ruine** to bring about one's own downfall/ruin

artisanal, -e, -aux, -ales [artizanal, -o] **ADJ 1** *(des artisans* ▸ *classe, tradition)* artisan *(avant n)*; **métier a.** craft **2** *(traditionnel* ▸ *méthode, travail)* traditional; **ils font toujours leur pain de façon artisanale** they still make their bread in the traditional way; **un fauteuil fabriqué de façon artisanale** a hand-made armchair; **une bombe de fabrication artisanale** a home-made bomb **3** *(rudimentaire)* basic, crude; **leur production est restée à un niveau a.** their production has remained small-scale

artisanalement [artizanalmɑ̃] **ADV ils savent encore travailler a. dans cette région** they still use traditional work methods in this area; **produire des fromages a.** to make cheese on a small scale

artisanat [artizana] **NM 1** *(profession)* **l'a.** the craft industry, the crafts **2** *(ensemble des artisans)* artisans **3** *(produits)* arts and crafts; **a. d'art** *(sur panneau)* arts and crafts; **le travail du cuir fait partie de l'a. local** leatherwork is part of local industry

artiste [artist] **ADJ 1** *(personne)* artistic **2** *(bohème ▸ genre, vie)* bohemian
NMF 1 *Beaux-Arts (créateur)* artist; **mener une vie d'a.** to lead an artist's life; **a. peintre** painter; **représentation** *ou* **vue d'a.** artist's impression **2** *Cin & Théât (interprète)* performer; *(comédien)* actor; *(chanteur)* singer; *(de music-hall)* artiste, entertainer; **a. de cabaret** cabaret entertainer; **a. comique** comedian; **a. dramatique** actor, *f* actress **3** *(personne habile)* artist; **notre boulanger est un véritable a.** our baker is a true artist; **voilà ce que j'appelle un travail d'a.!** now that's what I call the work of an artist!

Il faut noter que le terme anglais **artist** désigne généralement un peintre, un dessinateur ou un sculpteur.

artistement [artistəmɑ̃] **ADV** *Littéraire* artistically
artistique [artistik] **ADJ** *(enseignement, richesses)* artistic; **elle a un certain sens a.** she has a certain feeling for art; **genre a.** art form
artistiquement [artistikmɑ̃] **ADV** artistically
arum [arɔm] **NM** *Bot* arum
arvine [arvin] **NF** *Suisse* = grape variety from the Valais canton, and white wine produced from these grapes
aryen, -enne [arjɛ̃, -ɛn] **ADJ** Aryan
• **Aryen, -enne NM,F** Aryan
AS [aɛs] **NF 1** *Sport (abrév* **association sportive***)* sports club **2** *(abrév* **assistante (de service) sociale***)* social worker
a/s *(abrév écrite* **aux soins de***)* c/o
as[1] [a] *voir* **avoir**[2]
as[2] [as] **NM 1** *(carte, dé, domino)* ace; *(aux courses)* number one; **l'as de cœur/pique** the ace of hearts/spades; *Fam* **t'es fagoté** *ou* **ficelé** *ou* **fichu comme l'as de pique** you look as if you've been dragged through a hedge backwards; *Fam* **et mon sandwich, alors, il passe à l'as?** what about my sandwich, then?; **mon augmentation est passée à l'as** I might as well forget the idea of getting a pay rise **2** *Fam (champion)* ace, champ, wizard; **Delphine, t'es un as!** Delphine, you're a marvel!; **un as du traitement de texte** a word-processing wizard; **un as de la route** *ou* **du volant** a crack driver; **un as de la gâchette** a crack shot **3** *Antiq (poids, monnaie)* as
asbeste [asbɛst] **NF** *Minér* asbestos
asbestose [asbɛstoz] **NF** *Méd* asbestosis
ASBL [aɛsbeɛl] **NF** *(abrév* **association sans but lucratif***)* *Br* non-profit-making *or Am* not-for-profit organization
ascendance [asɑ̃dɑ̃s] **NF 1** *(ancêtres)* ancestry
2 *(extraction)* **être d'a. allemande** to be of German descent; **être d'a. paysanne** to be of peasant origin
3 *Astron* ascent, rising
4 *Aviat & Météo* ascending current
ascendant, -e [asɑ̃dɑ̃, -ɑ̃t] **ADJ 1** *(mouvement)* rising, ascending; *(courbe)* rising; *(série)* ascending **2** *Anat (aorte, côlon)* ascending
NM 1 *(emprise)* influence, ascendancy; **avoir de l'a. sur qn** to have influence over sb; **je n'ai aucun a. sur eux** I have no influence over them; **subir l'a. de qn** to be under the influence of sb **2** *Astrol* ascendant; **Verseau a. Cancer** Aquarius with Cancer as the rising sign *or* with Cancer in the ascendant
• **ascendants NMPL** *Jur (parents)* ascendants, ancestors
ascenseur [asɑ̃sœr] **NM 1** *(dans un bâtiment)* *Br* lift, *Am* elevator; **il habite au quatrième sans a.** *Br* he lives on the fourth floor of a building with no lift, *Am* he lives in a fifth-floor walk-up **2** *Ordinat* scroll box
ascension [asɑ̃sjɔ̃] **NF 1** *(montée ▸ d'un ballon)* ascent; *(▸ d'un avion)* climb, ascent
2 *(escalade ▸ d'un alpiniste)* ascent, climb; **faire l'a. d'un pic** to climb a peak; **il a fait plusieurs ascensions dans les Alpes** he did several climbs in the Alps
3 *(progression)* ascent, rise; **ses affaires connaissent une a. rapide** his/her business is booming; **l'a. des Dumot dans le monde de la finance** the rising fortunes of the Dumot family in the world of finance; **a. professionnelle** climb up the professional ladder; **a. sociale** social climbing
4 *Rel* **l'A.** *(élévation du Christ)* the Ascension; **l'A., le jeudi de l'A.** Ascension Day
5 *Astron* ascension

L'ASCENSION

Ascension Day is on the fortieth day after Easter and is a public holiday in France. Many people take an extended weekend break during this period.

ascensionnel, -elle [asɑ̃sjɔnɛl] **ADJ** *(mouvement)* upward
ascensionner [3] [asɑ̃sjɔne] *Vieilli* **VT** to climb
VI to climb
ascensionniste [asɑ̃sjɔnist] **NMF** *Vieilli (en montagne ou en ballon)* ascensionist
ascèse [asɛz] **NF** *Rel* asceticism, ascetic lifestyle
ascète [asɛt] **NMF** *Rel* ascetic; **vivre en a.** to live an ascetic life
ascétique [asetik] **ADJ** *Rel* ascetic
ascétisme [asetism] **NM** *Rel* asceticism
ASCII [aski] **NM** *Ordinat (abrév* **American Standard Code for Information Interchange***)* ASCII
ascorbique [askɔrbik] **ADJ** *Méd* ascorbic
asdic [asdik] **NM** *Naut* asdic
ASE [ɑesə] **NF** *Astron (abrév* **Agence spatiale européenne***)* ESA
asepsie [asɛpsi] **NF** *Méd* asepsis
aseptique [asɛptik] **ADJ** *Méd* aseptic
aseptisation [asɛptizasjɔ̃] **NF** *(d'une blessure, d'un pansement)* sterilization, asepsis; *(d'une pièce)* disinfection
aseptiser [3] [asɛptize] **VT** *(blessure)* to sterilize; *(pièce)* to disinfect
asexué, -e [asɛksɥe] **ADJ** *(plante, reproduction)* asexual; *(individu)* asexual, sexless
asiatique [azjatik] **ADJ 1** *(d'Extrême-Orient)* Oriental; **un restaurant a.** = a restaurant serving Oriental cuisine **2** *(de l'Asie en général)* Asian
• **Asiatique NMF 1** *(d'Extrême-Orient)* Oriental **2** *(de l'Asie en général)* Asian

Il faut noter qu'en anglais britannique le nom **Asian** désigne le plus souvent une personne originaire du sous-continent indien.

ASIATIQUE

This word tends to refer to Oriental people (ie from countries such as China, Japan, Laos etc), rather than Asia as a whole. Note that it does not refer to the British English sense of "Asian" meaning someone from the Indian subcontinent.

Asie [azi] **NF** *Géog* Asia; **l'A. centrale** Central Asia; *Hist* **l'A. Mineure** Asia Minor; **l'A. du Sud-Est** South-east Asia
asile [azil] **NM 1** *(abri)* refuge; **offrir à qn un a. pour la nuit** to give sb shelter for the night; **chercher/trouver a.** to seek/to find refuge; **votre jardin est un a. de paix et de verdure** your garden is a haven of peace and greenery; *Littéraire* **le dernier a.** the final resting place, the grave
2 *Hist & Pol* asylum; **demander l'a. diplomatique/politique** to seek diplomatic protection/political asylum
3 *(établissement ▸ gén)* home; **a. d'aliénés** *ou* **de fous** mental home, *Vieilli* (lunatic) asylum; **a. de nuit** night shelter; *Fam* **il est bon pour l'a.!** he ought to be locked up!
4 *Mktg (document publicitaire)* stuffer, insert
asinien, -enne [azinjɛ̃, -ɛn] **ADJ** *Zool* asinine
asocial, -e, -aux, -ales [asɔsjal, -o] **ADJ** antisocial, *Sout* asocial
NM,F dropout, social outcast
asparagus [asparagys] **NM** *Bot* asparagus fern
aspartam, aspartame [aspartam] **NM** *Chim* aspartame; **yaourt à l'a.** yoghurt sweetened with aspartame
aspect [aspɛ] **NM 1** *(apparence)* appearance, look; **un bâtiment d'a. imposant** an imposing-looking building; **des fromages d'un bel a.** fine-looking cheeses; **tu ne trouves pas que la viande a un a. bizarre?** don't you think the meat looks odd?; **donner l'a. de qch à qn** to give sb the appearance of sth, to make sb look like sth; **ces couleurs sombres donnent à la pièce un a. bien terne** all those dark colours make the room look very dull; **prendre l'a. de qch** *(ressembler à quelque chose)* to take on the appearance of sth; *(se métamorphoser en quelque chose)* to turn into sth; **offrir** *ou* **présenter l'a. de qch** to look like *or* to resemble sth **2** *(point de vue)* aspect, facet; **envisager** *ou* **examiner une question sous tous ses aspects** to consider a question from all angles; **vu sous cet a.** seen from this angle *or* point of view; **sous un a. nouveau** in a new light **3** *Astrol & Ling* aspect
• **à l'aspect de PRÉP** at the sight of, upon seeing; **elle s'est évanouie à l'a. du sang** she fainted at the sight of the blood
asperge [aspɛrʒ] **NF 1** *(plante)* asparagus; **des asperges** asparagus **2** *Fam (personne)* **une (grande) a.** a beanpole
asperger [17] [aspɛrʒe] **VT 1** *(légèrement)* to sprinkle; **a. qn d'eau** to spray sb with water **2** *(tremper)* to splash, to splatter; **se faire a.** to get splashed; **on s'est fait copieusement a.** we got drenched *or* soaked; **a. qn/qch de qch** to splash sb/sth with sth, to splash sth on sb/sth
VPR s'asperger 1 *(emploi réfléchi)* **s'a. de qch** to splash oneself with sth, to splash sth on oneself **2** *(emploi réciproque)* to splash *or* to spray one another
aspergès [aspɛrʒɛs] **NM** *Rel* **1** *(goupillon)* aspergillum, holy-water sprinkler **2** *(rite)* Asperges
aspérité [asperite] **NF 1** *(proéminence)* rough bit; **les aspérités de la roche** the rough edges of the rock; **les aspérités d'une surface** the roughness of a surface **2** *Littéraire (rudesse)* asperity, harshness
asperme [aspɛrm] **ADJ** *Bot* seedless
aspersion [aspɛrsjɔ̃] **NF 1** *(d'eau)* sprinkling, spraying **2** *Rel* sprinkling, aspersion
aspersoir [aspɛrswar] **NM 1** *Rel (goupillon)* aspersorium **2** *(pomme d'arrosoir)* rose
asphaltage [asfaltaʒ] **NM** asphalting
asphalte [asfalt] **NM 1** *(bitume)* asphalt **2** *Fam (chaussée)* street[□]
asphalter [3] [asfalte] **VT** to asphalt
asphodèle [asfɔdɛl] **NM** *Bot* asphodel; **a. blanc** king's spear
asphyxiant, -e [asfiksjɑ̃, -ɑ̃t] **ADJ 1** *(obus, vapeur)* asphyxiating, suffocating **2** *(oppressant ▸ ambiance)* stifling, suffocating
asphyxie [asfiksi] **NF 1** *Méd* asphyxia; **mourir par a.** to die of asphyxiation; **a. par submersion** drowning **2** *Fig* paralysis; **la guerre conduit le pays à l'a.** war is paralysing the country; **a. économique** economic paralysis *or* strangulation
asphyxié, -e [asfiksje] **ADJ 1** *(personne ▸ par manque d'air)* suffocated; *(▸ au gaz)* asphyxiated **2** *Fig (personne)* oppressed; *(pays, économie)* paralysed
NM,F *(personne ▸ par manque d'air)* suffocated person; *(▸ au gaz)* asphyxiated person
asphyxier [9] [asfiksje] **VT 1** *(priver d'air)* to suffocate; *(faire respirer du gaz à)* to asphyxiate; **mourir asphyxié** to die of asphyxiation **2** *Fig (personne)* to oppress; *(pays, économie)* to paralyse
VPR s'asphyxier 1 *(volontairement, au gaz)* to gas oneself **2** *(accidentellement)* to suffocate; **un enfant peut s'a. avec un sac en plastique** a child could suffocate (itself) with a plastic bag **3** *Fig (pays, économie)* to become paralysed
aspic [aspik] **NM 1** *Zool* asp **2** *Bot & Culin* aspic
aspidistra [aspidistra] **NM** *Bot* aspidistra
aspirant, -e [aspirɑ̃, -ɑ̃t] **ADJ** sucking, pumping
NM,F candidate; **un a. à un poste** a job candidate, a candidate for a post
NM *Mil (dans l'armée de terre, de l'air)* officer cadet; *(dans la marine)* midshipman
aspirateur [aspiratœr] **NM 1** *(domestique)* vacuum cleaner, *Br* Hoover®; **passer l'a.** to do the vacuuming *or Br* hoovering; **j'ai passé l'a. dans la chambre** I vacuumed *or Br* hoovered the bedroom **2** *Méd & Tech* aspirator

aspiration [aspirasjɔ̃] **NF 1** *(ambition)* aspiration, ambition
2 *(souhait)* yearning, longing, craving
3 *(absorption ▸ d'air)* inhaling; *(▸ d'un gaz, d'un fluide)* sucking up
4 *Tech* induction
5 *Ling (d'une voyelle)* aspiration
6 *Méd* **IVG par a.** abortion by vacuum extraction

aspiré, -e [aspire] **ADJ** *(voyelle)* aspirate
• **aspirée NF** aspirate

aspirer [3] [aspire] **VT 1** *(inspirer)* to inhale, to breathe in; **il aspira goulûment l'air frais** he took long deep breaths of *or* he gulped in the fresh air
2 *(pomper)* to suck up; **a. une boisson avec une paille** to suck a drink through a straw; **a. de l'air/des gaz d'une conduite** to pump air/gas out of a main
3 *(avec un aspirateur)* to vacuum, *Br* to hoover; **a. la poussière d'un tapis** to vacuum *or Br* to hoover a carpet
4 *Ling (voyelle)* to aspirate
• **aspirer à VT IND** *(paix, repos)* to crave, to long for, to yearn for; *(rang, dignité)* to aspire to; **a. à faire qch** to long to do sth

aspirine [aspirin] **NF** *Pharm* aspirin; **un comprimé** *ou* **cachet d'a.** an aspirin; **prenez deux aspirines** take two aspirin(s)

aspiro-batteur [aspirobatœr] *(pl* **aspiro-batteurs)** **NM** beating vacuum cleaner *or Br* Hoover®

ASS [aɛsɛs] **NF** *(abrév* **allocation de solidarité spécifique)** = allowance paid to long-term unemployed people who are no longer entitled to unemployment benefit

assagir [32] [asaʒir] **VT** *Littéraire* **1** *(apaiser ▸ personne)* to quieten down; *(▸ passion, violence)* to soothe, to allay; **l'âge assagit les passions** passions wane *or* become less intense with age; **un visage aux traits assagis** a face with composed features; **l'expérience l'a assagie** experience has made her a wiser person **2** *(faire se ranger)* to cause to settle down; **c'est un homme assagi maintenant** he's calmed down a lot
VPR s'assagir *(se calmer ▸ enfant)* to calm down, to *Br* quieten *or Am* quiet down; *(se ranger ▸ adulte)* to settle down

assagissement [asaʒismɑ̃] **NM** settling *or* quietening down

assaillant, -e [asajɑ̃, -ɑ̃t] **ADJ** *Mil (armée, troupe)* assailing, assaulting, attacking
NM assailant, attacker

assaillir [47] [asajir] **VT** *Mil* to attack; *(esprit, imagination)* to beset; **le doute m'assaillit** I was beset with doubt; **le bureau est assailli de demandes** the office is swamped *or* besieged with inquiries; **à mon retour j'ai été assailli de questions** when I came back I was bombarded with questions

assainir [32] [asenir] **VT 1** *(nettoyer ▸ quartier, ville)* to clean up, to improve; *(▸ logement)* to clean up; *(▸ air)* to purify **2** *(assécher ▸ plaine, région)* to improve the drainage of; *(▸ marécage)* to drain **3** *(stabiliser ▸ situation)* to clear up; *(▸ bilan)* to balance; *(▸ budget, monnaie, économie)* to stabilize; **a. ses finances** to put one's finances in order; **a. le climat social** to put an end to social strife
VPR s'assainir to improve, to become healthier; **la situation s'est assainie** the situation has improved

assainissant, -e [asenisɑ̃, -ɑ̃t] **ADJ** cleansing, purifying

assainissement [asenismɑ̃] **NM 1** *(nettoyage ▸ d'un quartier, d'une ville)* cleaning-up, improvement; *(▸ d'un logement, d'un appartement)* cleaning up; *(▸ de l'air)* purification; **un nouveau projet d'a. pour notre quartier** a new project for improving our area **2** *(assèchement)* draining **3** *(d'un budget, d'une monnaie, de l'économie)* stabilization; *(d'un bilan)* balancing; *(des finances)* putting in order; **a. monétaire** stabilization of the currency

assaisonnement [asezɔnmɑ̃] **NM** *Culin* **1** *(processus)* dressing, seasoning **2** *(condiments)* seasoning; *(sauce)* dressing

assaisonner [3] [asezɔne] **VT 1** *Culin (plat, sauce)* to season; *(salade)* to dress; **ta salade est trop assaisonnée** there's too much dressing on your salad; **a. des poireaux avec de la** *ou* **à la vinaigrette** to give leeks a vinaigrette dressing
2 *Fig (agrémenter)* **a. qch de** to spice *or* to lace sth with
3 *Fam (malmener)* **a. qn** to tell sb off; **on va l'a., celui-là!** we'll certainly take care of HIM!
4 *Fam (escroquer)* to sting, to rip off; **un restaurant où on se fait a.** a restaurant where you get ripped off

assassin, -e [asasɛ̃, -in] **ADJ** *Littéraire Hum* **1** *(méchant ▸ regard)* murderous; *(▸ remarque)* crushing **2** *(provocant ▸ sourire)* provocative; **jeter une œillade assassine à qn** to give someone a smouldering look
NM *(gén)* murderer, killer; *(d'une personnalité connue)* assassin; **à l'aide, à l'a.!** help, murder!

assassinat [asasina] **NM** *(gén)* murder; *(d'une personnalité connue)* assassination

assassine [asasin] *voir* **assassin**

assassiner [3] [asasine] **VT 1** *(tuer ▸ gén)* to murder; *(▸ personnalité connue)* to assassinate; **se faire a.** to be murdered
2 *Fam Péj (malmener ▸ musique, symphonie)* to murder, to slaughter
3 *Fam (ruiner)* to bleed; **on assassine le contribuable!** the taxpayer is being bled dry!
4 *Fam (critiquer ▸ livre, film)* to slate, to pan; **si je dis ce que je pense vraiment, je vais me faire a.** if I say what I really think I'll get crucified

assaut [aso] **NM 1** *Mil* assault, attack, onslaught; **un a. contre** an assault on *or* against; *aussi Fig* **aller** *ou* **monter à l'a.** to attack; **à l'a.!** charge!; **donner l'a.** to launch *or* to mount an attack; **donner l'a. à** to launch *or* mount an attack on, to storm; **se lancer à l'a. d'une ville** to launch an attack *or* to mount an onslaught on a town; **ils se sont lancés à l'a. de la face nord** they launched *or* mounted an assault on the north face; *Fig* **ils se sont lancés à l'a. du marché japonais** they set out to capture the Japanese market; **résister aux assauts de l'ennemi** to withstand enemy attacks; **prendre d'a. un palais** to storm a palace; *Fig* **le bar était pris d'a.** the bar was mobbed; **les otages libérés ont subi les assauts de la presse** the released hostages had to put up with press harassment; **les assauts répétés de la maladie** the repeated attacks *or* onslaughts of the disease; *Littéraire* **elles font a. de politesse/gentillesse** they're falling over each other to be polite/nice; **troupes d'a.** storm troops
2 *Escrime* bout

> **-ASSE** — SUFFIX
>
> • The main connotation of this suffix is a DEROGATORY one, when coupled with a noun, an adjective or a verb:
>
> **vinasse** cheap wine, plonk; **paperasse** paperwork, forms; **blondasse** yellowish, blondish; **connasse** stupid bitch; **la chiasse** the runs
>
> • Note that the resulting nouns are always feminine (**la vinasse, la paperasse**), whereas the adjectives are masculine or feminine (**des cheveux blondasses, un style fadasse**).

assèchement [asɛʃmɑ̃] **NM** draining, drying-up

assécher [18] [aseʃe] **VT** *(drainer ▸ terre, sol)* to drain (the water off); *(vider ▸ étang, réservoir)* to empty
VI *(à marée basse)* to become dry, to dry up
VPR s'assécher to become dry, to dry up

ASSEDIC, Assedic [asedik] **NFPL** *(abrév* **Association pour l'emploi dans l'industrie et le commerce)** = French unemployment insurance scheme, *Br* ≃ Unemployment Benefit Office, *Am* ≃ Unemployment Office; **toucher les A.** to get unemployment benefit

assemblage [asɑ̃blaʒ] **NM 1** *(fait de mettre ensemble)* assembling, constructing, fitting together; *Couture* sewing together; *(d'un tricot)* making up; *Menuis* joining; **procéder à l'a. de pièces** to assemble parts; **a. par soudage** soldering together; **a. par tenons et mortaises** tenon and mortise joining
2 *Aut & Ind* assembly
3 *(ensemble)* assembly; *Constr* framework, structure; *Menuis* joint; **a. à tenon et mortaise** mortise-and-tenon joint
4 *Beaux-Arts* assemblage
5 *Péj (amalgame)* collection, concoction; **son livre n'est qu'un a. d'idées bizarres** his/her book is just a collection of weird ideas thrown together
6 *Ordinat* assembly; **langage d'a.** assembly language

assemblée [asɑ̃ble] **NF 1** *(groupe)* gathering; *(auditoire)* audience; **en présence d'une nombreuse a.** in front of a large audience; *Rel* **l'a. des fidèles** the congregation
2 *(réunion)* meeting; **a. des actionnaires** shareholders' meeting; **a. générale** general meeting; **a. générale d'actionnaires** general meeting of shareholders; **a. générale annuelle** annual general meeting; **a. (générale) ordinaire/extraordinaire** ordinary/extraordinary (general) meeting
3 *Pol (élus)* **la Haute A.** the (French) Senate; **a. constituante** constituent assembly; **a. fédérale** *(en Suisse)* (Swiss) federal assembly; *Hist* **l'A. législative** the Legislative Assembly; **l'A. (nationale)** the (French) National Assembly; **A. parlementaire européenne** European Parliament
4 *(bâtiment)* **l'A.** ≃ the House

> **ASSEMBLÉE NATIONALE**
>
> The French parliament has two chambers: the National Assembly and the Senate. The members of the National Assembly (the "députés") are elected in the "élections législatives" held every five years.

assembler [3] [asɑ̃ble] **VT 1** *(monter)* to assemble, to put *or* to fit together; *Menuis* to joint; **elle a tout assemblé elle-même à partir d'un kit** she put it together herself from a kit; **a. des poutres bout à bout** to butt beams; **a. deux pièces par collage/soudure** to glue/to solder two parts together
2 *(combiner ▸ pensées)* to gather (together); *(▸ documents)* to collate
3 *Vieilli (personnes)* to call together, to assemble
4 *Ordinat* to assemble
VPR s'assembler *(foule, badauds)* to gather; *(députés, actionnaires)* to gather, to assemble

assembleur, -euse [asɑ̃blœr, -øz] **NM,F** *(ouvrier)* fitter
NM *Ordinat* assembler (language)
• **assembleuse NF** *Typ* gathering machine

assener [19], asséner [18] [asene] **VT** *(coup)* to deliver, to strike; *Fig* **je lui ai asséné quelques vérités bien senties** I hurled a few home truths at him/her; **on nous assène des publicités toute la journée** we're bombarded with adverts all day long; **c'est là qu'il lui a asséné l'argument final** that's when he produced the argument that clinched matters

assentiment [asɑ̃timɑ̃] **NM** assent, agreement; **donner/refuser son a. (à qch)** to give/withhold one's assent (to sth); **hocher la tête en signe d'a.** to nod one's head (in agreement)

asseoir [65] [aswar] **VT 1** *(mettre en position assise)* **a. qn** *(le mettre sur un siège)* to sit sb down; *(le redresser dans son lit)* to sit sb up; **il assit les enfants sur un banc** he placed *or* sat the children on a bench; **huit personnes seront là pour dîner, où vais-je les a.?** there will be eight people at dinner, where am I going to put them all?; **assois-le bien, il va tomber** sit him up properly, he's going to fall over; **a. qn sur le trône** *(le couronner)* to put sb on the throne
2 *(consolider)* to establish; **a. son autorité** to establish *or* to strengthen one's authority; **a. sa réputation sur qch** to base one's reputation on sth
3 *(faire reposer ▸ statue)* to sit, to rest; **veillez à bien a. l'appareil sur son pied** make sure the camera is resting securely on its stand
4 *Fam (étonner)* to stun, to astound[□]; **son insolence nous a tous assis** we were stunned by his/her insolence; **j'en suis resté assis** I was flabbergasted
5 *Fin (impôt, taxe)* to base, to calculate the basis for; **a. l'impôt sur le revenu** to base taxation on income
VI faire a. qn to ask sb to sit down; **je n'ai pas pu le faire a.** I couldn't get him to sit down
VPR s'asseoir 1 *(s'installer)* to sit down; **elle s'est**

assise she sat down; **asseyez-vous donc** please, do sit down; **asseyons-nous par terre** let's sit on the floor; **venez vous a. à table avec nous** come and sit at the table with us; **tu devrais t'a. un peu dans ton lit, tu serais mieux** you should sit up a bit in bed, you'd be more comfortable; **s'a. en tailleur** to sit cross-legged; **il s'assit sur ses talons** he sat down on his heels **2** *très Fam (locution)* **ton opinion, je m'assois dessus** I couldn't give a damn about your opinion; **votre dossier, vous pouvez vous a. dessus** you know what you can do with your file

assermentation [asermɑ̃tasjɔ̃] **NF** *Can & Suisse* swearing in, taking of an oath

assermenté, -e [asermɑ̃te] **ADJ** *(fonctionnaire, médecin)* sworn (in); *(expert, témoin)* on *or* under oath

NM,F person on *or* under oath

assermenter [3] [asermɑ̃te] **VT** *Jur (fonctionnaire, médecin)* to swear in; *(expert, témoin)* to put on *or* under oath

assertion [asersjɔ̃] **NF** assertion

asservir [32] [aservir] **VT 1** *(assujettir ▸ gén)* to enslave; *(▸ nation)* to reduce to slavery, to enslave; **être asservi à une cause** to be in thrall to a cause; *Vieilli* **a. ses instincts** to control one's instincts, to keep one's instincts under control **2** *Tech* to put under servo *or* remote control; **moteur asservi** servomotor

VPR s'asservir à to submit *or* to bow to

asservissant [aservisɑ̃] **ADJ** enslaving; **avoir un emploi a.** to be a slave to one's job

asservissement [aservismɑ̃] **NM 1** *(assujettissement)* enslavement (**de** of); **on note un a. de plus en plus grand à la mode** people are following fashion more and more slavishly **2** *Tech* servomechanism

assesseur [asesœr] **NM** assessor

asseyait *etc voir* **asseoir**

assez [ase] **ADV 1** *(suffisamment)* enough; **je suis a. fatigué comme ça** I'm tired enough as it is; **la maison est a. grande pour nous tous** the house is big enough for all of us; **tu n'as pas crié a. fort** you didn't shout loud enough; **j'ai a. travaillé pour aujourd'hui** I've done enough work for today; **il n'a pas a. fait attention** he didn't pay (careful) enough attention; **est-ce que c'est a.?** is that enough?; **c'est bien a.** that's plenty; **c'est plus qu'a.** that's more than enough; **ça a a. duré!** it's gone on long enough!; **a. parlé, agissons!** that's enough talk *or* talking, let's DO something!; **en voilà** *ou* **c'(en) est a.!** that's enough!, enough's enough!; **elle est a. grande pour s'habiller toute seule** she's old enough to dress herself

2 *(plutôt, passablement)* quite, rather; **disons qu'elle est a. jolie, sans plus** let's say she's quite pretty, no more than that; **c'est un a. bon exemple de ce qu'il ne faut pas faire** it's a pretty good example of what not to do; **je suis a. contente de moi** I'm quite pleased with myself; **la situation est a. grave** the situation is quite serious; **ils sont arrivés a. tard** they arrived rather late; **ils se connaissent depuis a. longtemps** they've known each other for quite a long time; **j'ai a. peu mangé aujourd'hui** I haven't eaten much today; **il y a a. peu de monde** there aren't many people, it isn't very busy

• **assez de ADJ** enough; **il y a a. de monde** there are enough people; **nous n'aurons pas a. de temps** we won't have enough time; **il y en a a.** there is/are enough; **il en reste juste a.** there is/are just enough left; **il n'a pas besoin de venir, nous sommes (bien) a. de deux** he doesn't need to come, two of us will be (quite) enough; **j'aurai bien a. d'une couverture** one blanket will be quite enough *or* sufficient; **j'ai juste a. d'essence pour finir le trajet** I've got just enough petrol to last the journey; *Fam* **j'en ai a. de vous écouter râler** I've had enough of (listening to) your moaning; **j'en ai (plus qu')a. de toutes ces histoires!** I've had (more than) enough of all this fuss!

assidu, -e [asidy] **ADJ 1** *(zélé)* assiduous, diligent, hard-working; **élève a.** hard-working pupil; **il n'est pas très brillant mais au moins il est a.** he's not very bright but at least he's conscientious; **un amoureux a.** a persistent lover; **il lui faisait une cour assidue** he courted her assiduously **2** *(constant)* unflagging, unremitting, untiring; **grâce à un travail a.** by dint of hard work; **elle a fourni des efforts assidus** she made unremitting efforts **3** *(fréquent)* regular, constant; **un visiteur a. des expositions** a frequent *or* dedicated exhibition-goer

assiduité [asidɥite] **NF 1** *(zèle)* assiduity; **travailler avec a. (à qch)** to work assiduously *or* zealously (at sth) **2** *(régularité)* regular attendance; **je fréquente les musées avec a.** I visit museums regularly

• **assiduités NFPL** attentions; **importuner** *ou* **poursuivre qn de ses assiduités** to force one's attentions upon sb

assidûment [asidymɑ̃] **ADV 1** *(avec zèle)* assiduously; **il y travaille a.** he is hard at work on it **2** *(régulièrement)* assiduously, unremittingly, untiringly

assied *etc voir* **asseoir**

assiégé, -e [asjeʒe] **NM,F** besieged person; **les assiégés** the besieged

assiégeant, -e [asjeʒɑ̃, -ɑ̃t] **ADJ** besieging

NM besieger

assiégée [asjeʒe] *voir* **assiégé**

assiéger [22] [asjeʒe] **VT 1** *Mil (ville, forteresse)* to lay siege to, to besiege **2** *(se présenter en foule à)* to besiege, to mob; **la maison fut assiégée par les journalistes** the house was besieged by journalists; **les guichets ont été assiégés** the ticket office was stormed by the public; **la ville est assiégée par les touristes** the town is overrun with *or* by tourists **3** *Littéraire (importuner ▸ sujet: personne)* to harass, to plague, to pester; *(▸ sujet: pensées)* to beset

assiéra *etc voir* **asseoir**

assiette [asjet] **NF 1** *(récipient)* plate; **grande a.** dinner plate; **petite a.** dessert *or* side plate; *Belg* **a. profonde** soup dish; **a. en carton** paper plate; **a. creuse** *ou* **à soupe** soup dish; **a. à dessert** dessert plate; **a. plate** (dinner) plate; *Fam* **c'est l'a. au beurre** it's a cushy number

2 *(contenu)* plate, plateful; **une (pleine) a. de soupe** a (large) plateful of soup; **finis d'abord ton a.** eat up what's on your plate first; **faire une a. de légumes** to prepare a dish of (mixed) vegetables; **a. anglaise** assorted cold meats

3 *(assise)* foundation, basis; *(d'une voie ferrée, d'une route)* bed

4 *Fin (d'un impôt, d'un taux)* base; *(d'une hypothèque)* = property or funds on which a mortgage is secured; **a. de l'amortissement** depreciation, depreciable base; **a. fiscale** *ou* **de l'impôt** taxable income

5 *Equitation* seat

6 *Naut* trim

7 *(locution)* **je ne suis pas** *ou* **je ne me sens pas dans mon a.** I don't feel too well, I'm feeling (a bit) out of sorts

assiettée [asjete] **NF 1** *(mesure)* **une a. de** a plate *or* plateful of **2** *(contenu)* **il a jeté toute l'a. par terre** he threw all the contents of the plate on the floor

assignable [asiɲabl] **ADJ 1** *(attribuable)* ascribable, attributable **2** *Jur* liable to be subpoenaed

assignataire [asiɲater] **NMF** *Jur* beneficiary of an allocation

assignation [asiɲasjɔ̃] **NF 1** *(attribution ▸ d'une tâche, d'un poste)* allocation, assignment

2 *Jur* **a. (à comparaître)** *(d'un témoin)* subpoena; *(d'un accusé)* summons; **a. à résidence** house arrest

3 *Fin (de parts, de fonds)* allotment, allocation (**de** to)

4 *Bourse* exercise notice

assigner [3] [asiɲe] **VT 1** *(attribuer ▸ tâche, poste)* to allocate, to assign; *(▸ valeur)* to attach, to ascribe; *(▸ délai)* to set; **a. un même objectif à deux projets** to set the same goal for two projects **2** *Jur* **a. un témoin (à comparaître)** to subpoena a witness; **a. le prévenu** to summon the defendant; **a. qn à résidence** to put sb under house arrest; **être assigné à résidence** to be under house arrest; **a. qn (en justice) pour diffamation** to issue a writ for libel against sb **3** *Fin (part, fonds, crédits)* to allocate; **a. des crédits à la recherche** to allocate funds for *or* to research

assimilable [asimilabl] **ADJ 1** *Physiol* assimilable, easily absorbed *or* assimilated

2 *(abordable)* easily acquired *or* assimilated; **l'informatique est a. à tout âge** computer skills are easy to acquire at any age

3 *(population)* easily assimilated *or* integrated; **des populations difficilement assimilables** groups of people difficult to integrate

4 *(similaire)* comparable (**à** to); **son travail est souvent a. à celui d'un médecin** his/her work can often be compared to that of a doctor

assimilation [asimilasjɔ̃] **NF 1** *Physiol* assimilation

2 *Bot* **a. chlorophyllienne** photosynthesis

3 *(fait de comprendre)* **avoir un grand pouvoir d'a.** to acquire knowledge very easily; **l'a. des connaissances se fait à un rythme différent selon les élèves** pupils assimilate knowledge at different rates

4 *(intégration)* assimilation, integration; **politique d'a.** policy of assimilation

5 *(identification)* comparison; **l'a. de ses théories au marxisme** the way his/her theories have been likened to Marxism

6 *(d'une voyelle)* assimilation

assimilé, -e [asimile] **ADJ** comparable, similar; **talc pour bébé et produits assimilés** baby powder and similar products

NM cadres et assimilés executives and their equivalent

assimiler [3] [asimile] **VT 1** *Physiol* to assimilate, to absorb, to metabolize; *(digérer)* to digest

2 *(comprendre)* to assimilate, to take in; **il n'assimile rien** he doesn't take anything in; **j'ai du mal à a. les logarithmes** I have trouble mastering logarithms

3 *(intégrer)* to assimilate, to integrate

4 *(une voyelle)* to assimilate

• **assimiler à VT IND** to compare to, to put in the same category as; **être assimilé à un cadre supérieur** to be given equivalent status to an executive

VPR s'assimiler 1 *Physiol* to become absorbed *or* metabolized; *(être digéré)* to be assimilated *or* digested; **les aliments riches en fibres s'assimilent plus facilement** high-fibre food is easier to digest **2** *(s'intégrer)* to become assimilated **3** *(se comparer)* to compare oneself (**à** to *or* with); *(être comparable)* to be comparable (**à** with)

assis, -e [asi, -iz] **PP** *voir* **asseoir**

ADJ 1 *(établi)* stable; **position bien assise** well-established position **2** *(non debout)* sitting (down); **il est plus à l'aise dans la position assise que dans la position couchée** he feels more comfortable sitting than lying down; **j'étais assise sur un tabouret** I was sitting on a stool; **nous étions a. au premier rang** we were seated in the first row; **êtes-vous bien a.?** are you sitting comfortably?; **être a. en tailleur** to be sitting cross-legged; **je vous en prie, restez a.** please don't get up; **tout le monde est resté a.** everyone remained seated; **se tenir a.** to be sitting up; **a.!** *(à un chien)* sit!

• **assise NF 1** *(fondement)* foundation, basis **2** *Constr* course; *(d'une route)* bed **3** *Anat, Bot & Géol* stratum

• **assises NFPL 1** *Jur* Assize Court, *Br* ≃ crown court; **être envoyé aux assises** to be committed for trial **2** *(réunion ▸ gén)* meeting; *(▸ d'un parti, d'un syndicat)* conference

Assise [asiz] **NF** *Géog* Assisi

assistanat [asistana] **NM 1** *Scol* (foreign) assistant exchange scheme **2** *Univ* assistantship **3** *(secours ▸ privé)* aid; *(▸ public)* state aid

assistance [asistɑ̃s] **NF 1** *(aide)* assistance; **prêter a. à qn** to lend *or* to give assistance to sb, to assist sb; **trouver a. auprès de qn** to get help from sb; **a. éducative** = measure ordered by a judge to protect a child's physical, psychological or educational wellbeing; **a. judiciaire** legal aid; **a. médicale pour les pays du tiers-monde** medical aid for Third World countries; **l'A. (publique)** *(à Paris et Marseille)* = authority which manages the social services and state-owned hospitals; *Vieilli* **c'est un enfant de l'A.** he was brought up in an institution; **a. sociale** *(aux pauvres)* welfare; *(métier)* social work; *Ordinat* **a. technique** technical support; *Ordinat* **a. technique téléphonique** support line; *Ordinat* **a. à l'utilisateur** user support

2 *Méd* **a. médicale à la procréation** assisted conception; **a. respiratoire** artificial respiration

3 *(spectateurs ▸ d'une pièce, d'un cours)* audience; *(▸ d'une messe)* congregation; **la remarque a ému toute l'a.** the entire audience was moved by the remark; **y a-t-il quelqu'un dans l'a. qui souhaiterait intervenir?** does anyone in the audience wish to speak?

4 *(présence)* attendance (**à** at); **l'a. aux conférences n'est pas obligatoire** attendance at lectures is not compulsory

assistant, -e [asistɑ̃, -ɑ̃t] **NM,F 1** *(second)* assistant; **l'a. du directeur** the director's assistant; **a. de direction** personal assistant, PA; *Cin & TV* **a. de réalisation** assistant director; *Cin & TV* **a. du producteur** assistant producer; *Cin & TV* **a. du régisseur de plateau** assistant floor manager; *Cin & TV* **a. de production** production assistant; *Cin & TV* **a. de plateau** floor assistant

2 *Scol* (foreign language) assistant; **a. scolaire** classroom assistant, *Br* teaching assistant

3 *Univ Br* lecturer, *Am* assistant teacher

4 *(aide)* **a. maternel** *(à son domicile)* childminder; *(en collectivité) Br* crèche *or Am* daycare center worker; **a. social** social worker

NM *Ordinat (programme)* assistant; **a. numérique** personal digital assistant, PDA; **a. personnel** personal assistant

• **assistante NF assistante de police** policewoman, *Br* WPC *(in charge of minors)*

assistant-réalisateur, assistante-réalisatrice [asistɑ̃realizatœr, asistɑ̃trealizatris] *(mpl* **assistants-réalisateurs,** *fpl* **assistantes-réalisatrices) NM,F** *Cin & TV* assistant director

assisté, -e [asiste] **ADJ 1** *Admin (aidé)* **enfants assistés** children in *Br* care *or Am* custody; **chômeurs assistés** unemployed people receiving state aid; **être a.** to receive state aid; **je ne veux pas être a.!** I don't want charity! **2** *Ordinat* **a. par ordinateur** computer-aided, computer-assisted

NM,F *Admin* **les assistés** recipients of state aid; **ils ont une mentalité d'assistés** they expect everything to be done for them

assister [3] [asiste] **VT** *(aider)* to assist, to aid; *(soutenir financièrement)* to help (financially); **je l'ai assisté pendant l'opération/dans son travail** I assisted him during the operation/in his work; **le prêtre est assisté d'un enfant de chœur** the priest is attended by a choirboy; **nous vous ferons a. par un avocat** we will make sure you get a lawyer to assist you; **se faire a. par qn** to be assisted by sb; **a. qn dans ses derniers moments** *ou* **dernières heures** to comfort sb in his/her last hours; **que Dieu vous assiste!** (may) God be with you *or* help you!; *Jur* **a. (qn) d'office** to be appointed by the court (to defend sb)

• **assister à VT IND 1** *(être présent à ▸ messe, gala)* to attend; *(▸ concert de rock, enregistrement de télévision)* to be at **2** *(être témoin de)* to witness, to be a witness to; **il a assisté à l'accident** he was a witness to *or* he witnessed the accident **3** *(remarquer)* to note, to witness; **on assiste à une recrudescence de la criminalité/du chômage** we are witnessing a new increase in crime/unemployment

> Il faut noter que le verbe anglais **to assist** n'a jamais le sens de **être présent** (à un événement).

associatif, -ive [asɔsjatif, -iv] **ADJ** *(règle, activité)* of an association *or* organization; *(militant, regroupement)* organized; **la vie associative est très développée dans ce pays** a lot of people in this country belong to clubs and associations; **le mouvement syndical et le mouvement a.** trade unions and organizations

association [asɔsjasjɔ̃] **NF 1** *(groupement)* society, association; *(organisation)* organization; **protéger la liberté d'a.** to protect freedom of association; **a. des anciens élèves** association of *Br* former pupils *or Am* alumni; **a. d'avocats** ≃ chambers; **a. de bienfaisance** charity, charitable organization; **a. à but non lucratif** *ou* **sans but lucratif** *Br* non-profit-making *or Am* not-for-profit organization; **a. de consommateurs** consumer association; **a. de défense des consommateurs** consumer protection association; **A. pour l'emploi des cadres** = agency providing information and employment and training opportunities for professionals; **A. européenne de libre-échange** European Free Trade Association; **A. pour la formation professionnelle des adultes** = government body promoting adult vocational training; **A. française des banques** French Bankers' Association; **A. française de normalisation** = French industrial standards authority, *Br* ≃ British Standards Institution, *Am* ≃ American Standards Association; **a. humanitaire** charity organization; **A. de libre-échange** Free Trade Association; **a. loi 1901** = type of non-profit-making organization; **a. de malfaiteurs** criminal conspiracy; **a. de parents d'élèves** *Br* ≃ Parent-Teacher Association, *Am* ≃ Parent-Teacher Organization; **A. de recherche sur le cancer** = French national cancer research charity; **a. sportive** sports club

2 *(collaboration)* partnership, association; **notre a. n'a pas duré longtemps** we weren't partners for long; **travailler en a. avec l'État** to work in association with the state; **un opéra produit en a. avec une chaîne italienne** an opera produced in association with an Italian TV channel; *Fin* **a. capital-travail** profit-sharing scheme

3 *(d'images)* association; *(de couleurs)* combination; **l'a. de nos intérêts devrait nous être profitable à tous les deux** combining our interests should be profitable to us both; **a. d'idées** association of ideas; *Psy* **a. libre** free association; *Psy* **associations verbales** free associations

associative [asɔsjativ] *voir* **associatif**

associé, -e [asɔsje] **ADJ** associate; **directeur/membre a.** associate director/member

NM,F *Com & Fin* associate, partner; **je l'ai pris comme a.** I took him into partnership; **a. commanditaire** *Br* sleeping partner, *Am* silent partner; **a. commandité** active partner; **a. fictif** nominal partner; **a. fondateur** founding partner; **a. gérant** active partner; **a. majoritaire** senior partner; **a. minoritaire** junior partner; **associés à part égale** equal partners; **a. passif** *Br* sleeping partner, *Am* silent partner; **a. principal** senior partner; **a. en second** junior partner

associer [9] [asɔsje] **VT 1** *(idées, images, mots)* to associate; **a. qn/qch à** to associate *or* to connect *or* to link sb/sth with; **on associe souvent rhumatismes et humidité** rheumatism and damp conditions are frequently associated

2 *(faire participer)* **il m'a associé à son projet** he included me in his project; **son entreprise est associée au projet** his/her company is taking part in the project; **a. les travailleurs aux profits de leur entreprise** to allow workers to share in their company's profits; **j'aurais voulu l'a. à mon bonheur** I would have liked to share my happiness with him/her

3 *(saveurs, couleurs)* to combine (**qch à** sth with)

VPR s'associer 1 *(s'allier)* to join forces (**à** with); *Com* to enter *or* to go into partnership, to become partners (**à** *ou* **avec** with); *(prendre part à)* to share (**à** in); **associons-nous pour réussir** let us join forces in order to succeed; **la France et l'Allemagne se sont associées pour le projet Hermès** France and Germany are partners in the Hermes project; **il s'est associé à** *ou* **avec son frère pour monter une petite société d'ingénierie** he went into partnership with his brother and set up a small engineering company; **je m'associe pleinement à votre malheur** I share your grief; **s'a. à une entreprise criminelle** to be an accomplice to *or* to take part in a crime

2 *(s'harmoniser)* to be combined

3 s'a. qn to take sb on as a partner

assoiffé, -e [aswafe] **ADJ** thirsty; **a. de sang** bloodthirsty; **a. de savoir/de vengeance** thirsty *or* hungry for knowledge/for revenge

assoiffer [3] [aswafe] **VT** to make thirsty; **a. une ville** to cut off the water supply to a town

assoit *etc voir* **asseoir**

assolement [asɔlmɑ̃] **NM** *Agr* crop rotation; **a. triennal** three-course system

assoler [3] [asɔle] **VT** *Agr (terres)* to rotate crops on

assombrir [32] [asɔ̃brir] **VT 1** *(rendre sombre)* to darken, to make dark *or* darker; **l'orage assombrit le ciel** the sky's getting dark with the impending storm; **sous un ciel assombri** under darkened skies; **le mur brun assombrit la pièce** the brown wall makes the room look darker **2** *(rendre triste)* to cast a shadow *or* a cloud over, to mar; **la mort de son père a bien assombri notre séjour** his/her father's death cast a shadow over our stay; **aucun incident n'a assombri la cérémonie** no incident marred the ceremony

VPR s'assombrir 1 *(s'obscurcir)* to darken, to grow dark; **à l'approche du cyclone, le ciel s'est assombri** with the approaching hurricane, the sky grew very dark **2** *(s'attrister ▸ visage)* to cloud over; *(▸ personne, humeur)* to become gloomy

assombrissement [asɔ̃brismɑ̃] **NM** darkening

assommant, -e [asɔmɑ̃, -ɑ̃t] **ADJ** *Fam* **1** *(ennuyeux)* boring, tedious; **j'ai passé une demi-heure assommante** I spent an excruciatingly boring half-hour **2** *(fatigant)* annoying; **tu es a., à la fin, avec tes questions!** all these questions are getting really annoying!

assommer [3] [asɔme] **VT 1** *(frapper)* to knock out; **se faire a.** to be knocked out

2 *(tuer)* **a. un bœuf** to fell an ox; *Fam* **à a.** *ou* **qui assommerait un bœuf** powerful[□]; *Fam* **l'eau-de-vie de sa grand-mère, elle assommerait un bœuf** his/her grandmother's brandy could kill a horse

3 *Fam (ennuyer)* **a. qn** to bore sb stiff *or* to tears; **ils m'assomment avec leurs statistiques** they bore me to tears with their statistics

4 *Fam (importuner)* to harass[□], to wear down[□]

assommeur, -euse [asɔmœr, -øz] **NM,F** slaughterer

assommoir [asɔmwar] **NM** *Arch* **1** *(matraque)* club **2** *Fam (bar)* gin palace

assomption [asɔ̃psjɔ̃] **NF 1** *Rel* **l'A.** the Assumption **2** *(hypothèse)* assumption

> **L'ASSOMPTION**
>
> The Feast of the Assumption, on the 15th of August, is a Catholic feast day and an important holiday in France.

assonance [asɔnɑ̃s] **NF** *Littérature* assonance

assorti, -e [asɔrti] **ADJ 1** *(en harmonie)* **un couple bien a.** a well-matched couple; **un couple mal a.** an ill-matched *or* ill-assorted couple; **les deux couleurs sont très bien assorties** the two colours match (up) *or* blend (in) perfectly; **pantalon avec veste assortie** *Br* trousers *or Am* pants with matching jacket **2** *(chocolats)* assorted; **fromages assortis** choice of cheeses **3** *(approvisionné)* **un magasin bien/mal a.** a well-stocked/poorly-stocked shop

assortiment [asɔrtimɑ̃] **NM 1** *(ensemble)* assortment, selection; **a. de charcuterie** selection of *or* assorted cold meats; **a. d'outils** set of tools, tool kit **2** *Com (choix)* selection, range, stock; **nous avons un vaste a. de jupes** we stock a large selection of skirts; **nous avons un vaste a. de desserts** we offer a large selection *or* a wide range of desserts; *Mktg* **a. de produits** product mix

assortir [32] [asɔrtir] **VT 1** *(teintes, vêtements)* to match; *(personnes)* to match, to mix **j'ai acheté le couvre-lit assorti au papier peint** I bought a bedspread to match the wallpaper; **a. ses chaussures à sa ceinture** to match one's shoes with *or* to one's belt **2** *Com (approvisionner)* to supply, to stock **3** *(accompagner)* **il a assorti son discours d'un paragraphe sur le racisme** he included a paragraph on racism in his speech; **une peine de prison assortie d'une amende de 1000 euros** a prison sentence accompanied by a fine of 1,000 euros

VPR s'assortir 1 *(s'harmoniser)* to match, to go together well; **sa manière de s'habiller s'assortit à sa personnalité** the way he/she dresses matches *or* reflects his/her personality **2** *(être complété)* **son étude s'assortit de quelques remarques sur la situation actuelle** his/her study includes a few comments on the present situation **3** *Com* to buy one's stock; **il s'assortit dans les magasins de gros** he buys his stock wholesale

assoupi, -e [asupi] **ADJ 1** *(endormi ▸ personne)* asleep, sleeping, dozing **2** *Littéraire (calme ▸ ville)* sleepy; *(▸ passion)* dormant

assoupir [32] [asupir] **VT 1** *(endormir)* to make drowsy *or* sleepy **2** *Littéraire (atténuer ▸ soupçon, douleur)* to dull

VPR s'assoupir 1 *(s'endormir)* to doze off, to fall asleep **2** *Littéraire (s'affaiblir ▸ crainte, douleur)* to be dulled

assoupissant, -e [asupisɑ̃, -ɑ̃t] **ADJ** soporific

assoupissement [asupismɑ̃] **NM 1** *(sommeil léger)* doze; *(état somnolent)* drowsiness; **tomber dans un léger a.** to doze off **2** *Littéraire (atténuation ▸ des soupçons, de la douleur)* dulling, numbing

assouplir [32] [asuplir] **VT 1** *(rendre moins dur ▸ corps)* to make supple, to loosen up; *(▸ linge, cuir)* to soften; **ajoutez du lait pour a. la pâte** add milk until the dough is pliable **2** *(rendre moins strict ▸ règlement)* to relax; **a. ses positions** to take a softer line; **l'âge n'a pas assoupli son caractère** he/she hasn't mellowed with age; **le règlement de l'école a été considérablement assoupli** the school rules have been considerably relaxed

VPR s'assouplir 1 *(devenir moins strict)* to become looser *or* more supple, to loosen up **2** *(devenir moins strict)* to become more flexible

assouplissant [asuplisɑ̃] **NM** (fabric) softener

assouplissement [asuplismɑ̃] **NM 1** *Sport* warming-up; **des exercices** *ou* **une séance d'a.** warming-up exercises **2** *(d'un linge, d'un cuir)* softening **3** *Écon (de la réglementation, du contrôle)* relaxing; *(du crédit)* easing; **demander l'a. d'un règlement** to ask for regulations to be relaxed

assouplisseur [asuplisœr] = **assouplissant**

assourdir [32] [asurdir] **VT 1** *(personne)* to deafen; *(bruit, son)* to dull, to deaden, to muffle **2** *Ling* to make voiceless *or* unvoiced

VPR s'assourdir *Ling* to become voiceless *or* unvoiced

assourdissant, -e [asurdisɑ̃, -ɑ̃t] **ADJ** deafening, ear-splitting

assourdissement [asurdismɑ̃] **NM 1** *(d'un bruit)* deadening, dulling, muffling **2** *(d'une personne ▸ processus)* deafening; *(▸ résultat)* temporary deafness **3** *Ling* devoicing

assouvir [32] [asuvir] **VT** *(désir, faim)* to appease, *Sout* to assuage; *(soif)* to quench; *(curiosité)* to satisfy; **a. sa vengeance** to satisfy one's desire for revenge

assouvissement [asuvismɑ̃] **NM** *(d'une passion, de la faim)* appeasing, *Sout* assuaging; *(de la soif)* quenching; *(de la curiosité)* satisfying

assoyait *etc voir* **asseoir**

assuétude [asɥetyd] **NF** *Méd* addiction

assujetti, -e [asyʒeti] **ADJ 1** *Littéraire (peuple)* subjugated **2** *Jur* **être a. à l'impôt** to be liable for tax

NM,F *Jur* person liable for tax; **les assujettis** those who are liable for tax

assujettir [32] [asyʒetir] **VT 1** *(astreindre)* **a. qn à qch** to subject sb to sth; *Jur* **être assujetti à l'impôt** to be liable for tax **2** *(arrimer)* to fasten, to secure; **a. une porte avec une chaîne** to secure a door with a chain **3** *Littéraire (asservir ▸ nation, peuple)* to subjugate, to hold under a yoke

VPR s'assujettir à to submit (oneself) to

assujettissant, -e [asyʒetisɑ̃, -ɑ̃t] **ADJ** demanding

assujettissement [asyʒetismɑ̃] **NM 1** *Littéraire (asservissement)* subjection **2** *Littéraire (contrainte)* tie **3** *Jur* **a. à l'impôt** liability to taxation

assumer [3] [asyme] **VT 1** *(endosser)* to take on, to take upon oneself, to assume; **j'en assume l'entière responsabilité** I take *or* I accept full responsibility for it; **il assume la charge de directeur depuis la mort de son père** he's been director since his father died; **nous assumerons toutes les dépenses** we'll meet all the expenses; **elle assume à la fois les fonctions de présidente et de trésorière** she acts both as chairperson and treasurer; **j'ai assumé ces responsabilités pendant trop longtemps** I held that job for too long **2** *(accepter)* to accept; **il assume mal ses origines** he's never been able to come to terms with his background

USAGE ABSOLU *Fam* **ils font des gosses et après ils n'assument pas!** they have kids and then they don't face up to their responsibilities as parents!; **j'assume!** I don't care what other people think!

VPR s'assumer il a du mal à s'a. en tant que père he's finding it hard to come to terms with his role as father; *Fam* **il serait temps que tu t'assumes!** it's time you accepted yourself as you are!

> Il faut noter que le verbe anglais **to assume** est un faux ami. Il signifie le plus souvent **supposer**.

assurable [asyrabl] **ADJ** *Assur* insurable

assurance [asyrɑ̃s] **NF 1** *(contrat)* insurance (policy); **placer des assurances** to sell insurance (policies); **les assurances** insurance companies; *Fam* **il est dans les assurances** he's in insurance[▫]; *Fam* **je vais écrire à mon a.** I'll write to my insurance company[▫]; **a. contre les accidents** *Br* insurance against (personal) accidents, accident insurance; **a. auto** *ou* **automobile** car *or Am* automobile insurance; **a. bagage** baggage insurance; *Suisse* **a. casco** comprehensive insurance, all-risks insurance; **a. chômage** *(payée par le patron et le salarié)* ≃ unemployment insurance; *(reçue par le chômeur)* ≃ unemployment benefit(s); **a. crédit** loan repayment insurance; **a. contre l'incendie** insurance against fire, fire insurance; **a. décès** life insurance, *Br* life assurance; **a. invalidité** *Br* critical illness cover, *Am* disability insurance; **a. maladie** health insurance; **a. maritime** marine insurance; **a. maternité** maternity benefit; **a. mixte** endowment policy; **a. multirisque** comprehensive insurance; **a. personnelle** private health insurance *or* cover; **a. de portefeuille** portfolio insurance; **a. responsabilité civile** *ou* **au tiers** third party insurance; *Com* **a. de responsabilité du produit** product liability insurance; **a. tous risques** comprehensive insurance; **les assurances sociales** *Br* ≃ National Insurance, *Am* ≃ Welfare; **a. vieillesse** retirement pension; *Suisse* **a. vieillesse et survivants** = Swiss pension scheme; **a. contre le vol** insurance against theft; **a. volontaire** private health insurance *or* cover

2 *(garantie)* guarantee (**de** of); **je vous donne l'a. que tout sera fait d'ici demain** I assure you *or* I guarantee (you) that everything will be done by tomorrow; **j'ai reçu l'a. formelle que l'on m'aiderait financièrement** I was assured I would receive financial help; **demander/recevoir des assurances** to ask for/to receive assurance; **le retour à la démocratie constitue une a. de paix pour le pays** the return of democracy will guarantee peace for the country

3 *(aisance)* self-confidence, assurance; **manque d'a.** insecurity; **manquer d'a.** to be insecure; **s'exprimer avec a.** to speak with assurance; **elle a perdu toute sa belle a.** she's lost all her cockiness; **je chantonnais pour me donner un peu d'a.** I was singing to give myself some confidence; **elle a de l'a. dans la voix** she sounds confident

4 *(certitude)* **avoir l'a. que...** to feel certain *or* assured that...; **j'ai l'a. qu'il viendra** I'm sure he'll come

5 *(dans la correspondance)* **veuillez croire à l'a. de ma considération distinguée** *(à quelqu'un dont on connaît le nom) Br* yours sincerely, *Am* sincerely (yours); *(à quelqu'un dont on ne connaît pas le nom) Br* yours faithfully, *Am* sincerely (yours)

6 *Sport (en alpinisme)* **(point d')a.** belay

assuré, -e [asyre] **ADJ 1** *(incontestable)* certain, sure; **succès a. pour son nouvel album!** his/her new album is sure to be a hit!; **discrétion assurée** confidentiality guaranteed **2** *(résolu)* assured, self-confident; **marcher d'un pas a.** to walk confidently; **d'une voix mal assurée** quaveringly, in an unsteady voice; **avoir un air a.** to look self-confident

NM,F insured person, policyholder; **les assurés** the insured; *Admin* **a. social** *Br* ≃ contributor to the National Insurance scheme, *Am* ≃ contributor to Social Security

assurément [asyremɑ̃] **ADV** assuredly, undoubtedly, most certainly; **a. non!** certainly *or* indeed not!; **a. (oui)!** yes, indeed!, (most) definitely!

assurer [3] [asyre] **VT 1** *(certifier)* to assure; **il m'a assuré qu'il viendrait** he assured me he'd come; **je t'assure qu'elle est sincère** I assure you she's sincere; **mais si, je t'assure!** yes, I swear!; **il faut de la patience avec elle, je t'assure!** you need a lot of patience when dealing with her, I'm telling you!

2 *(rendre sûr)* to assure; **je l'assurai qu'il pouvait signer** I assured him he could sign; **laissez-moi vous a. de ma reconnaissance** let me assure you of my gratitude

3 *(procurer)* to maintain, to provide; **a. le ravitaillement des populations sinistrées** to provide disaster victims with supplies; **une permanence est assurée le samedi après-midi** there is someone on duty on Saturday afternoons; **a. la surveillance de qch** to guard sth; **pour mieux a. la sécurité de tous** to ensure greater safety for all; **a. une liaison aérienne/ferroviaire** to operate an air/a rail link; **a. le ramassage scolaire** to operate a school bus service; **a. à qn un bon salaire** to secure a good salary for sb

4 *(mettre à l'abri)* to ensure, to secure; **a. l'avenir** to make provision *or* provide for the future; **a. ses arrières** *Mil* to protect one's rear; *Fig* to leave oneself a way out *or* something to fall back on

5 *(arrimer)* to secure, to steady; **a. le chargement d'une voiture avec des cordes** to secure the load on a car with ropes

6 *Com* to insure; **a. ses bagages/sa voiture** to insure one's luggage/one's car; **j'ai fait a. mes bijoux** I had my jewellery insured; **être mal assuré contre le vol** to be under-insured in case of theft; **a. qch pour 10 000 euros** to insure sth for 10,000 euros

7 *Sport (en alpinisme)* to belay

8 *Naut (bout)* to belay, to make fast

VI *Fam* **il assure en physique/anglais** he's good at physics/English[▫]; **elle a beau être nouvelle au bureau, elle assure bien** she may be new to the job but she's certainly doing OK; **les femmes d'aujourd'hui, elles assurent!** modern women can do anything![▫]; **il va falloir a.!** we'll have to show that we're up to it!; **tu as encore oublié ton rendez-vous! t'assures pas** you missed your appointment again! you're useless!; **il assure pas une cacahuète** *ou* **un clou quand il s'agit de draguer** he hasn't got a clue when it comes to *Br* chatting up *or Am* hitting on women

VPR s'assurer 1 *(par contrat d'assurance)* to insure oneself; **s'a. contre le vol/l'incendie** to insure oneself against theft/fire; **il est obligatoire pour un automobiliste de s'a.** by law, a driver must be insured

2 *(s'affermir)* to steady oneself

3 *(se fournir ▸ revenu)* to secure, to ensure

4 s'a. de qch *(contrôler)* to make sure of sth; **assurez-vous de la validité de votre passeport** make sure your passport is valid; **je vais m'en a. immédiatement** I'll check right away; **s'a. que** to make sure (that), to check (that); **assure-toi que tout va bien** make sure everything's OK; **pouvez-vous vous a. qu'elle est bien rentrée?** could you check she got back all right?

assureur [asyrœr] **NM** *Assur* underwriter; *(agent)* insurance agent; *(compagnie)* insurance company; *(courtier)* insurance broker

assureur-conseil [asyrœrkɔ̃sɛj] *(pl* **assureurs-conseils) NM** *Assur* insurance adviser

Assyrie [asiri] **NF l'A.** Assyria

assyrien, -enne [asirjɛ̃, -ɛn] **ADJ** Assyrian

NM *(langue)* Assyrian

• **Assyrien, -enne NM,F** Assyrian

aster [astɛr] **NM 1** *Bot* aster; **a. (d'automne)** Michaelmas daisy; **a. maritime** sea aster **2** *Biol* aster

astérisque [asterisk] **NM** asterisk

astéroïde [asterɔid] **NM** *Astron* asteroid

asthénie [asteni] **NF** *Méd* asthenia

asthmatique [asmatik] *Méd* **ADJ** asthmatic

NMF asthmatic

asthme [asm] **NM** *Méd* asthma; **avoir de l'a.** to suffer from asthma; **crise d'a.** attack of asthma, asthma attack

asticot [astiko] **NM 1** *Entom (ver)* maggot; *Pêche* gentle **2** *Fam (individu) Br* bloke, *Am* guy

asticoter [3] [astikɔte] **VT** *Fam* to bug

astigmate [astigmat] *Opt* **ADJ** astigmatic

NMF astigmatic

astigmatisme [astigmatism] **NM** *Opt* astigmatism

astiquage [astikaʒ] **NM** polishing, shining

astiquer [3] [astike] **VT** to polish, to shine

astragale [astragal] **NM 1** *Anat* astragalus, talus **2** *Archit* astragal **3** *Bot* astragalus

astrakan [astrakɑ̃] **NM** astrakhan (fur); **un manteau en a.** an astrakhan coat

astral, -e, -aux, -ales [astral, -o] **ADJ** *Astrol & Astron* astral

astre [astr] **NM** *Astrol & Astron* star; *Littéraire* **l'a. du jour/de la nuit** the sun/moon; **beau comme un a.** radiantly handsome *or* beautiful; **né sous un a. favorable** born under a lucky star

astreignait *etc voir* **astreindre**

astreignant, -e [astrɛɲɑ̃, -ɑ̃t] **ADJ** demanding, exacting; **un programme a.** a punishing schedule

astreindre [81] [astrɛ̃dr] **VT a. qn à qch** to tie sb down to sth; **il est astreint à un régime sévère** he's on a very strict diet; **a. qn à faire qch** to compel *or* to force *or* to oblige sb to do sth

VPR s'astreindre s'a. à faire qch to compel *or* to force oneself to do sth; **il s'astreint à un régime sévère** he sticks to a strict diet

astreinte [astrɛ̃t] **NF 1** *Jur* = daily penalty for delay in payment of debt **2** *(contrainte)* obligation, constraint

astringence [astrɛ̃ʒɑ̃s] **NF** *Méd* astringency, astringence

astringent, -e [astrɛ̃ʒɑ̃, -ɑ̃t] **ADJ** astringent; *(vin)* sharp

NM astringent

astrolabe [astrɔlab] **NM** *Astron* astrolabe

astrologie [astrɔlɔʒi] **NF** *Astrol* astrology

astrologique [astrɔlɔʒik] **ADJ** *Astrol* astrological

astrologue [astrɔlɔg] **NMF** *Astrol* astrologer

astronaute [astronot] **NMF** *Astron* astronaut

astronautique [astronotik] **NF** *Astron* astronautics *(singulier)*

astronef [astronɛf] **NM** spaceship

astronome [astrɔnɔm] **NMF** *Astron* astronomer

astronomie [astrɔnɔmi] **NF** *Astron* astronomy

astronomique [astrɔnɔmik] **ADJ 1** *Astron* astronomic, astronomical **2** *Fam (somme)* astronomic, astronomical; **ça a atteint des prix astronomiques!** it's become ridiculously expensive!

astronomiquement [astrɔnɔmikmɑ̃] **ADV** astronomically

astrophysicien, -enne [astrofizisjɛ̃, -ɛn] **NM,F** *Astron* astrophysicist

astrophysique [astrofizik] *Astron* **ADJ** astrophysical

NF astrophysics *(singulier)*

astuce [astys] **NF 1** *(ingéniosité)* astuteness, shrewdness; **il est plein d'a.** he's a shrewd individual **2** *Fam (plaisanterie)* joke▫, gag▫; *(jeu de mots)* pun▫; **je n'ai pas compris l'a.!** I didn't get it!; **encore une de tes astuces vaseuses!** another one of your awful puns! **3** *Fam (procédé ingénieux)* trick▫; *(conseil)* tip▫; **en page 23, notre rubrique "astuces"** our tips are on page 23; **je n'arrive pas à l'ouvrir – attends, il doit y avoir une a.** I can't open it – wait, there must be some knack *or* trick (to it); **comment fais-tu tenir le loquet? – ah, ah, c'est l'a.!** how do you get the latch to stay on? – aha, wouldn't you like to know!; **j'ai trouvé une a. formidable pour ne pas avoir à attendre** I've hit upon a great trick to avoid waiting; **les astuces du métier** the tricks of the trade

astucieuse [astysjøz] *voir* **astucieux**

astucieusement [astysjøzmɑ̃] **ADV** shrewdly, cleverly

astucieux, -euse [astysjø, -øz] **ADJ** *(personne)* shrewd, clever; *(solution, méthode)* clever

asymétrie [asimetri] **NF** asymmetry, lack of symmetry

asymétrique [asimetrik] **ADJ** asymmetric, asymmetrical

asymptomatique [asɛ̃ptɔmatik] **ADJ** *Méd (maladie)* asymptomatic; *(porteur)* without symptoms

asymptote [asɛ̃ptɔt] *Géom* **ADJ** *(courbe, plan)* asymptotic, asymptotical

NF asymptote

asynchrone [asɛ̃kron] **ADJ** *Phys & Ordinat* asynchronous

asyntaxique [asɛ̃taksik] **ADJ** *Ling* asyntactic

ataca [ataka] = **atoca**

atavique [atavik] **ADJ** *Biol* atavistic, atavic

atavisme [atavism] **NM** *Biol* atavism; **ils sont prudents, c'est un vieil a. paysan** they're very cautious, it's an old peasant instinct; **faire qch par a.** to do sth because it's in one's genes

atchoum [atʃum] **EXCLAM** atishoo!

atelier [atəlje] **NM 1** *(d'un bricoleur, d'un artisan)* workshop; *(d'un peintre, d'un photographe)* studio; *(d'un couturier)* workroom; **a. d'artiste** artist's studio; **a. de stylisme** designer's studio

2 *(d'une usine)* shop; **l'a. s'est mis en grève** the shopfloor has gone on strike; **il est devenu contremaître après cinq ans d'a.** he became a foreman after five years on the factory *or* shop floor; **a. d'assemblage** assembly shop; *Aut* **a. de carrosserie** bodyshop; **a. de montage** assembly room; **a. naval** shipyard; **a. protégé** sheltered workshop; **a. de réparations** repair shop

3 *(cours)* workshop; *Beaux-Arts* class; **a. chorégraphique** dance workshop; **un a. de peinture sur soie** a silk painting workshop, a workshop on silk painting

4 *(groupe de travail)* group, workgroup; **les enfants travaillent en ateliers** the children work in groups

5 *(de francs-maçons)* lodge

atemporel, -elle [atɑ̃pɔrɛl] **ADJ** timeless

atermoie *etc voir* **atermoyer**

atermoiement [atɛrmwamɑ̃] **NM** *Com & Jur* = arrangement with creditors for extension of time for payment

• **atermoiements NMPL** *(hésitations)* procrastination, delaying

atermoyer [13] [atɛrmwaje] **VI** to procrastinate, to delay

> **-ATEUR, -ATRICE** — SUFFIX
>
> These suffixes are usually attached to the radical of a noun in **-ation** minus its ending or to the radical of a verb. The idea conveyed is that of an AGENT, whether it is a person or a thing (such as a machine or a tool). The equivalent suffix in English is often *-er* or *-or*: **aviateur, aviatrice** pilot, aviator; **admirateur, admiratrice** admirer; **décorateur, décoratrice** interior designer; **commentateur, commentatrice** commentator; **aspirateur** vacuum cleaner; **calculatrice** calculator

ATF [ateɛf] **NM** *Bourse (abrév* **accord de taux futur***)* forward rate agreement, future rate agreement

athée [ate] *Rel* **ADJ** atheistic, atheist *(avant n)*

NMF atheist

athéisme [ateism] **NM** *Rel* atheism

athénée [atene] **NM 1** *Antiq* Atheneum **2** *Belg Br* secondary school, *Am* high school

Athènes [atɛn] **NM** *Géog* Athens

athénien, -enne [atenjɛ̃, -ɛn] **ADJ** Athenian

• **Athénien, -enne NM,F** Athenian

athlète [atlɛt] **NMF** athlete; **un corps/une carrure d'a.** an athletic body/build

athlétique [atletik] **ADJ** athletic

athlétisme [atletism] **NM** *Sport* athletics *(singulier)*; **épreuves d'a.** athletic events, track and field events

Atlantide [atlɑ̃tid] **NF** *Myth* **l'A.** Atlantis

atlantique [atlɑ̃tik] **ADJ** Atlantic; **l'Arc a.** the Atlantic arc; **la côte/l'océan a.** the Atlantic coast/ocean; **le Pacte a.** the Atlantic Charter

• **Atlantique NM l'A.** the Atlantic (Ocean)

Atlas [atlas] **NPR** *Myth* Atlas

NM *Géog* **l'A.** the Atlas Mountains

atlas [atlas] **NM 1** *(livre)* atlas **2** *Anat* atlas

atmosphère [atmɔsfɛr] **NF 1** *Géog* atmosphere **2** *(ambiance)* atmosphere, ambiance; **avoir besoin de changer d'a.** to need a change of scene **3** *(air que l'on respire)* air; **l'a. humide du littoral** the dampness of the air on the coast **4** *Phys (unité)* atmosphere

atmosphérique [atmɔsferik] **ADJ** *(condition, couche, pression)* atmospheric

atoca [atɔka] **NM** *Can Bot* cranberry

atoll [atɔl] **NM** *Géog* atoll

atome [atom] **NM** *Phys* atom; **l'ère de l'a.** the atomic age; *Fig* **pas un a. de** not an ounce of; *Fam* **avoir des atomes crochus avec qn** to have things in common with sb; **je n'ai pas d'atomes crochus avec elle** I don't have much in common with her

atome-gramme [atomgram] *(pl* **atomes-grammes)** **NM** *Phys* gram-atom

atomicité [atɔmisite] **NF** *Phys* atomicity

atomique [atɔmik] **ADJ** *(masse, bombe)* atomic; *(énergie)* atomic, nuclear; *(explosion)* nuclear

atomisation [atɔmizasjɔ̃] **NF** *Phys* atomization, atomizing; *Fig (du pouvoir, de forces politiques)* dispersal

atomisé, -e [atɔmize] **ADJ** *Phys* atomized

NM,F person suffering from the effects of radiation

atomiser [3] [atɔmize] **VT 1** *Phys* to atomize **2** *Nucl* to destroy with an atom bomb, to blast with a nuclear device **3** *Fig* to pulverize

atomiseur [atɔmizœr] **NM** spray; **parfum en a.** spray perfume

atomisme [atɔmism] **NM** *Phys & Phil* atomism

atomiste [atɔmist] **ADJ 1** *Phys* atomic **2** *Phil* atomistic, atomistical, atomist

NMF 1 *Phys* atomic scientist **2** *Phil* atomist

atomistique [atɔmistik] **ADJ** *Phil* atomistic, atomistical, atomist

NF *Phys* atomic science

atonal, -e, -aux, -ales [atɔnal, -o] **ADJ** *Mus* atonal

atonalité [atɔnalite] **NF** *Mus* atonality

atone [atɔn] **ADJ 1** *(expression, œil, regard)* lifeless, expressionless **2** *Ling* atonic, unaccented, unstressed **3** *Méd* atonic

atonie [atɔni] **NF 1** *(inertie)* lifelessness **2** *Méd* atony

atours [atur] **NMPL** *Arch* attire, array; *Hum* **elle avait revêtu ses plus beaux a.** she was dressed in all her finery

atout [atu] **NM 1** *Cartes* trump; **jouer a.** to play a trump; *(en ouvrant le jeu)* to lead trump *or* trumps; **il a joué a. carreau** diamonds were trumps; **l'a. est à pique** spades are trumps; **quel est l'a.?** what's trump *or* trumps?; **prendre avec de l'a.** to trump; **jouer trois sans a.** to play three no trumps; **a. maître** master trump; *Fig* trump card **2** *(avantage)* asset, *Fig* trump; **la connaissance d'une langue étrangère est un a.** knowledge of a foreign language is an asset *or* an advantage; **il a tous les atouts dans son jeu** *ou* **en main** he has all the trumps *or* all the winning cards; **mettre tous les atouts dans son jeu** to maximize one's chances of success

atoxique [atɔksik] **ADJ** *Méd* non-poisonous, non-toxic

âtre [atr] **NM** *Littéraire* hearth; **au coin de l'â.** by *or* round the fireplace

atriqué, -e [atrike] **ADJ** *Can Fam* **bien/mal a.** well/badly dressed▫

atroce [atrɔs] **ADJ 1** *(cruel)* atrocious, foul; **des scènes atroces** horrifying *or* gruesome scenes; **leur vengeance fut a.** their revenge was awesome **2** *(insupportable)* excruciating, dreadful, atrocious; **il est mort dans d'atroces souffrances** he died in dreadful pain **3** *(en intensif)* **d'une laideur a.** hideously ugly; *Fam* **il est a. avec son père** he's really awful to his father; *Fam* **il fait un temps a.** the weather's dreadful;

atrocement [atrɔsmɑ̃] **ADV 1** *(cruellement)* atrociously, horribly; **a. mutilé** horribly *or* hideously mutilated **2** *(en intensif)* atrociously, dreadfully, horribly; **elle a a. mal** she's in dreadful *or* terrible pain; **a. ennuyeux** excruciatingly boring; **j'ai a. froid** I'm frozen to death; **j'ai a. faim** I'm starving

atrocité [atrɔsite] **NF 1** *(cruauté)* atrociousness **2** *(crime)* atrocity; **les atrocités de la guerre** wartime atrocities **3** *(chose horrible)* **on m'a raconté des atrocités sur votre compte** I have been hearing dreadful things about you; **ce tableau est une a.** this picture is a real horror *or* an atrocity

atrophie [atrɔfi] **NF** *Méd* atrophy

atrophié, -e [atrɔfje] **ADJ** *Méd* atrophied

atrophier [9] [atrɔfje] *Méd & Fig* **VT** to atrophy
VPR s'atrophier to atrophy

atropine [atrɔpin] **NF** *Méd* atropin, atropine

attabler [3] [atable] **s'attabler VPR** to sit down (at the table); **tous les convives sont déjà attablés** all the guests are already seated at the table; **venez donc vous a. avec nous** do come and sit at our table

attachant, -e [ataʃɑ̃, -ɑ̃t] **ADJ** *(personnalité)* engaging, lovable; *(livre, spectacle)* captivating; **c'est un enfant très a.** he's such a lovable child

attache [ataʃ] **NF 1** *(lien ▸ gén)* tie; *(▸ en cuir, en toile)* strap; *(▸ en ficelle)* string; *(▸ d'un vêtement)* clip, fastener
2 *(ami)* tie, friend; *(parent)* relative, family tie; **il n'a plus aucune a. en France** he doesn't have any ties left in France; **elle a des attaches en Normandie** she has relatives in Normandy; **un homme sans attaches** *(sans partenaire)* an unattached man; *(sans relations)* a man without family or friends
3 *Anat* **a. de la main/du pied** wrist/ankle joint
4 *Bot* tendril
5 *Rail* **a. de rail** rail fastening
• attaches NFPL *Anat* joints; **avoir des attaches fines** to be small-boned
• à l'attache ADJ *(chien, cheval)* tied up

attaché, -e [ataʃe] **ADJ** *(affectivement)* **être a. à** to be attached to *or* fond of
NM,F attaché; **a. d'administration** administrative assistant; **a. d'ambassade** embassy attaché; **a. commercial** *(d'une ambassade)* commercial attaché; *(d'une entreprise)* sales representative; **a. culturel** cultural attaché; **a. militaire** military attaché; **a. de presse** press officer; *(dans le corps diplomatique)* press attaché

attaché-case [ataʃekez] *(pl* **attachés-cases***)* **NM** attaché case

attachement [ataʃmɑ̃] **NM 1** *(affection)* affection, attachment; **son a. pour sa mère** his/her affection for *or* attachment to his/her mother **2** *Constr* daily statement *(to record progress and costs)*

attacher [3] [ataʃe] **VT 1** *(accrocher)* to tie, to tie up; **a. son chien** to tie up one's dog; **a. les mains d'un prisonnier** to tie a prisoner's hands together; **a. qn/qch à** to tie sb/sth to; **a. un chien à une corde/à sa niche** to tie a dog to a rope/to his kennel; **pauvre bête, il l'a attachée à une chaîne** he's chained the poor thing up; **la barque est attachée à une chaîne** the boat's moored on the end of a chain *or* chained up; **a. qn à une chaise** to tie sb to a chair; **une photo était attachée à la lettre** *(avec un trombone)* a picture was clipped to the letter; *(avec une agrafe)* a picture was stapled to the letter
2 *(pour fermer)* to tie; **a. un colis avec une ficelle** to tie up a parcel; **une simple ficelle attachait la valise** the suitcase was held shut with a piece of string
3 *(vêtement)* to fasten; **peux-tu m'aider à a. ma robe?** can you help me do up my dress?; **a. ses lacets** to tie one's shoelaces; **attachez votre ceinture** fasten your seatbelt
4 *(accorder)* to attach; **j'attache beaucoup de prix** *ou* **de valeur à notre amitié** I attach great value to *or* set great store by our friendship; **elle attache trop d'importance à son physique** she attaches too much importance to the way she looks
5 *(fixer)* **a. ses yeux** *ou* **son regard sur qn** to fix one's eyes upon sb
6 *(associer)* to link, to connect; **le scandale auquel son nom est/reste attaché** the scandal with which his/her name is/remains linked; **plus rien ne l'attache à Paris** he/she has no ties in Paris now; **qu'est-ce qui m'attache à la vie maintenant?** what is there for me to live for now?
7 *(comme domestique, adjoint)* **a. un apprenti à un maître** to apprentice a young boy to a master; **elle est attachée à mon service depuis dix ans** she has been working for me for ten years
VI *Culin* to stick; **le riz a attaché** the rice has stuck; **poêle/casserole qui n'attache pas** nonstick pan/saucepan
VPR s'attacher 1 *(emploi réfléchi)* to tie oneself (up); **il s'est attaché avec une corde** he tied himself (up) with a rope
2 *(emploi passif)* to fasten, to do up; **la robe s'attache sur le côté** the dress does up *or* fastens at the side; **s'a. avec une fermeture Éclair®/des boutons** to zip/to button up
3 s'a. (les services de) qn to take sb on; **il s'est attaché les services d'un garde du corps** he's hired a bodyguard
4 s'a. à *(se lier avec)* to become fond of *or* attached to; *(s'efforcer de)* to devote oneself to; **s'a. aux pas de qn** to follow sb closely; **je m'attache à le rendre heureux** I try (my best) to make him happy; **elle s'est attachée à reproduire les fresques fidèlement** she took great pains to reproduce the frescoes faithfully

attaquable [atakabl] **ADJ 1** *Mil* open to attack **2** *(discutable)* contestable; **son système/testament n'est pas a.** his/her system/will cannot be contested; **ses déclarations seront difficilement attaquables** his/her statements will be difficult to contest

attaquant, -e [atakɑ̃, -ɑ̃t] **ADJ** attacking, assaulting, assailing
NM,F 1 *(assaillant)* attacker, assailant **2** *Sport* striker

attaque [atak] **NF 1** *(agression)* attack, assault; *(d'une voiture, d'un train)* hold-up; **à l'a.!** attack!; **passer à l'a.** to attack; *Fig* to attack, to go on the offensive; **a. aérienne** air attack *or* raid; **a. à main armée** *(contre une banque)* armed robbery; **a. préventive** pre-emptive strike
2 *(diatribe)* attack, onslaught; **il a été victime d'odieuses attaques dans les journaux** he was subjected to scurrilous attacks in the newspapers; **pas d'attaques personnelles, s'il vous plaît** let's not get personal, please
3 *Méd (d'apoplexie)* stroke; *(cardiaque)* heart attack; *(crise)* fit, seizure; **a. d'épilepsie** epileptic fit
4 *Sport* attack; *(en alpinisme)* start
5 *Mus* attack; **ton a. n'est pas assez nette** your attack is too weak
• d'attaque ADJ *Fam* **être** *ou* **se sentir d'a.** to be on top form; **je ne me sens pas d'a. pour aller à la piscine** I don't feel up to going to the swimming pool; **je ne me sens pas tellement d'a. ce matin** I don't really feel up to much this morning

attaquer [3] [atake] **VT 1** *(assaillir ▸ ennemi, pays, forteresse, marché)* to attack, to launch an attack on; *(▸ passant, touriste)* to attack; **il s'est fait a. par deux hommes** he was attacked *or* assaulted by two men; **madame, c'est lui qui m'a attaqué!** please Miss, he started it!; **nous avons été attaqués par les moustiques** we were attacked by mosquitoes; **a. une place par surprise** to make a surprise attack on a fort; **a. le mal à la racine** to tackle the root of the problem
2 *(abîmer ▸ sujet: rouille)* to damage, to corrode, to eat into; **l'humidité a même attaqué l'abat-jour** the damp even damaged the lampshade
3 *(critiquer)* to attack, to condemn; **il a été attaqué par tous les journaux** he was attacked by all the newspapers; **j'ai été personnellement attaqué** I suffered personal attacks; **le projet a été violemment attaqué** the project came in for some fierce criticism; *Jur* **a. qn en justice** to bring an action against sb, to take sb to court; **a. qn en diffamation** to bring a libel action against sb; **a. un testament** to contest a will
4 *(entreprendre ▸ tâche)* to tackle, to attack, to get started on; **j'ai attaqué ma pile de dossiers vers minuit** I got started on my pile of files around midnight; **prêt à a. le travail?** ready to get *or* to settle down to work?
5 *Fam (commencer ▸ repas, bouteille)* **a. le petit déjeuner** to dig into breakfast; **on attaque le beaujolais?** shall we have a go at that Beaujolais?
6 *Méd* to affect; **le poumon droit est attaqué** the right lung is affected
7 *Mus* to attack
8 *Cartes* **a. à carreau/à l'atout** to lead diamonds/trumps
USAGE ABSOLU *(commencer)* **bon, on attaque?** right, shall we get going?; **quand l'orchestre attaque** when the orchestra strikes up
VPR s'attaquer à 1 *(combattre)* to take on, to attack; **il ne faut pas s'a. à plus faible que soi** pick on somebody your own size!; **elle s'est attaquée aux institutions** she took on the establishment; **s'a. aux préjugés** to attack *or* to fight *or* to tackle prejudice; **il s'est tout de suite attaqué au problème** he tackled the problem right away **2** *(agir sur)* to attack; **cette maladie ne s'attaque qu'aux jeunes enfants** only young children are affected by this disease; **les bactéries s'attaquent à vos gencives** bacteria attack your gums

attardé, -e [atarde] **ADJ 1** *(qui traîne)* **il ne restait plus que quelques passants attardés** there were only a few people still about **2** *Vieilli (anormal)* backward, (mentally) retarded **3** *(démodé)* old-fashioned
NM,F *Vieilli (malade)* (mentally) retarded person

attarder [3] [atarde] **s'attarder VPR 1** *(rester tard ▸ dans la rue)* to linger; *(▸ chez quelqu'un, au bureau)* to stay late; **ne nous attardons pas, la nuit va tomber** let's not stay any longer, it's almost nightfall; **je me suis attardée près de la rivière** I lingered by the river; **rentre vite, ne t'attarde pas** be home early, don't stay out too late; **ils se sont attardés ici bien après minuit** they stayed around here long after midnight; **elles s'attardaient à boire leur café** they were lingering over their coffee **2 s'a. sur** *(s'intéresser à)* to linger over, to dwell on; **s'a. sur des détails** to get bogged down in detail; **attardons-nous quelques minutes sur le cas de cette malade** let's consider the case of this patient for a minute; **vous vous êtes trop attardé sur l'aspect technique** you spent too much time discussing the technical side; **l'image contenue dans la strophe vaut que l'on s'y attarde** the image in the stanza merits further consideration; **encore un mélodrame qui ne vaut pas que l'on s'y attarde** another forgettable melodrama

atteindre [81] [atɛ̃dr] **VT 1** *(lieu)* to reach, to get to; *Rad & TV* to reach; **aucun son ne nous atteignait** no sound reached us; **des émissions qui atteignent un large public** programmes reaching a wide audience
2 *(situation, objectif)* to reach, *Sout* to attain; **a. la gloire** to attain glory; **il a atteint son but** he's reached his goal *or* achieved his aim; **leur propagande n'atteint pas son but** their propaganda misses its target; **avez-vous atteint vos objectifs de vente?** have you reached *or* fulfilled your sales targets?; **les taux d'intérêt ont atteint un nouveau record** interest rates have reached a record high
3 *(âge, valeur, prix)* to reach; **a. 70 ans** to reach the age of 70; **le sommet atteint plus de 4000 mètres** the summit is over 4,000 metres high; **les dégâts atteignent 200 000 euros** 200,000 euros' worth of damage has been done
4 *(communiquer avec)* to contact, to reach; **il est impossible d'a. ceux qui sont à l'intérieur de l'ambassade** the people inside the embassy are incommunicado
5 *(toucher)* to reach, to get at, to stretch up to; **je n'arrive pas à a. le dictionnaire qui est là-haut** I can't reach the dictionary up there
6 *(frapper)* to hit; **a. la cible** to hit the target; **a. la cible en plein centre** to hit the bull's eye; **la balle/le policier l'a atteint en pleine tête** the bullet hit/the policeman shot him in the head; **atteint à l'épaule** wounded in the shoulder
7 *(blesser moralement)* to affect, to move, to stir; **il peut dire ce qu'il veut à mon sujet, ça ne m'atteint pas** he can say what he likes about me, it doesn't bother me at all; **rien ne l'atteint** nothing affects *or* can reach him/her
8 *(affecter ▸ sujet: maladie, fléau)* to affect; **les tumeurs secondaires ont déjà atteint le poumon** the secondary tumours have already spread to the lung; **être atteint d'un mal incurable** to be suffering from an incurable disease; **les pays atteints par la folie de la guerre** countries in the grip of war mania
• atteindre à VT IND *Littéraire* to achieve, to attain

atteint, -e [atɛ̃, -ɛ̃t] **ADJ 1** *(d'une maladie, d'un fléau)* affected; **quand le moral est a.** when depression sets in **2** *Fam (fou)* touched; **il est plutôt a.** he's not quite right in the head
• atteinte NF *(attaque)* attack; **je considère que c'est une atteinte à mon honneur** I consider it an attack on my honour; **atteinte aux bonnes mœurs**

offence against public decency; **atteinte à la liberté individuelle** infringement of personal freedom; **atteinte aux droits de l'homme** violation of human rights; **atteinte à la sûreté de l'État** high treason; **atteinte à la vie privée** violation of privacy; **porter atteinte au pouvoir de qn** to undermine sb's power; **porter atteinte à la réputation de qn** to damage sb's reputation; **porter atteinte à l'ordre public** to commit a breach of the peace, to disturb the peace; **hors d'atteinte** out of reach

• **atteintes** NFPL *(effets nocifs)* effects; **les premières atteintes du mal se sont manifestées quand il a eu 20 ans** *(épilepsie, diabète)* he first displayed the symptoms of the disease at the age of 20; *(alcoolisme, dépression)* the first signs of the problem came to light when he was 20

attelage [atlaʒ] **NM 1** *(fait d'attacher ▸ un cheval)* harnessing; *(▸un bœuf)* yoking; *(▸une charrette, une remorque)* hitching up

2 *(plusieurs animaux)* team; *(paire d'animaux)* yoke

3 *(véhicule)* carriage

4 *Rail (processus, dispositif)* coupling

atteler **[24]** [atle] **VT 1** *(cheval)* to harness; *(bœuf)* to yoke; *(charrette, remorque)* to hitch up; **a. une voiture** to attach horses to a carriage **2** *Rail* to couple

VPR s'atteler s'a. à to get down to, to tackle; **il va falloir que tu t'attelles à ces révisions!** you'll have to get down to that revision!

attelle [atɛl] **NF 1** *Méd* splint **2** *(pour un cheval)* hame

attellera *etc voir* **atteler**

attenant, -e [atnɑ̃, -ɑ̃t] **ADJ** adjoining, adjacent; **cour attenante à la maison** back yard adjoining the house

ATTENDRE **[73]** [atɑ̃dr] **VT A. 1** *(rester jusqu'à la venue de ▸ retardataire, voyageur)* to wait for; **je l'attends pour partir** I'm waiting till he/she gets here before I leave, I'll leave as soon as he/she gets here; **il va falloir t'a. encore longtemps?** are you going to be much longer?; **attendez-moi après le travail** wait for me after work; **a. qn à la sortie** to wait for sb outside; **(aller) a. qn à l'aéroport/la gare** to (go and) meet sb at the airport/the station; **le train ne va pas vous a.** the train won't wait (for you); **l'avion l'a attendu** they delayed the plane for him; *Fig* **a. qn au passage** *ou* **au tournant** to wait for a chance to pounce on sb; **elle se trompera, et je l'attends au tournant** she'll make a mistake and that's when I'll get her

2 *(escompter l'arrivée de ▸ facteur, invité)* to wait for, to expect; *(▸ colis, livraison)* to expect, to await; *(▸ réponse, événement)* to wait for, to await; **je ne t'attendais plus!** I'd given up waiting for you!; **a. qn d'une minute à l'autre** to expect sb any minute; **a. qn à** *ou* **pour dîner** to expect sb for dinner; **vous êtes attendu, le docteur va vous recevoir immédiatement** the doctor's expecting you, he'll see you straightaway; **j'attends un coup de téléphone** I'm expecting a telephone call; **qu'est-ce que tu attends?** *(ton interrogatif ou de reproche)* what are you waiting for?; **qu'est-ce qu'il attend pour les renvoyer?** why doesn't he just fire them?; **qu'attendez-vous pour déjeuner?** why don't you go ahead and have lunch?; **ils n'attendent que ça, c'est tout ce qu'ils attendent** that's exactly *or* just what they're waiting for; **il attend le grand jour avec impatience** he's eagerly looking forward to the big day; **a. fiévreusement des résultats** to be anxiously waiting for results; **nous attendons des précisions** we're awaiting further details; **a. son tour** to wait one's turn; **a. son heure** to bide one's time; **a. le bon moment** to wait for the right moment (to come along); **a. demain pour faire qch** to delay *or* to put off doing sth till *or* until tomorrow; **cela peut a. demain** that can wait till *or* until tomorrow; **je lui ai prêté 100 euros et je les attends toujours** I lent him/her 100 euros and I still haven't got it back *or* I'm still waiting for it; **se faire a.** to keep others waiting; **désolé de m'être fait a.** sorry to have kept you waiting; **les hors-d'œuvre se font a.** the starters are taking a long time to come; **la réforme se fait a.** the reform is taking a long time to materialize; **les résultats ne se sont pas fait a.** *(après une élection)* the results didn't take long to come in; *(conséquences d'une action)* there were immediate consequences; *Fam* **alors, tu attends le dégel?** are you going to hang around here all day?; **a. qn comme le Messie** to wait eagerly for sb

3 *(sujet: femme enceinte)* **a. un bébé** *ou* **un enfant,** *Belg* **a. famille** to be expecting (a child), to be pregnant; **a. des jumeaux** to be pregnant with *or* expecting twins; **j'attends une fille** I'm expecting a girl; **elle attend son bébé pour le 15 avril** her baby's due on 15 April; *Euph* **a. un heureux événement** to be expecting

4 *(être prêt pour)* to await, to be ready for; **ta chambre t'attend** your room's ready (for you); **la voiture vous attend** the car's ready, the car's waiting for you; **venez, le dîner nous attend** come along, dinner's ready *or* dinner is served

5 *(sujet: destin, sort, aventure)* to await, to be *or* to lie in store for; **une mauvaise surprise l'attendait** there was an unpleasant surprise in store for him/her; **c'est là que la mort l'attendait** that's where he/she was to meet his/her death; **une nouvelle vie vous attend là-bas** a whole new life awaits you there; **il ne sait pas quel sort l'attend** he doesn't know what fate has in store for him; **si tu savais** *ou* **tu ne sais pas ce qui t'attend!** you haven't a clue what you're in for, have you?; **avant de me porter volontaire, je voudrais savoir ce qui m'attend** before I volunteer, I'd like to know what I'm letting myself in for

6 *(espérer)* **a. qch de qn/qch** to expect sth from sb/sth; **qu'attendez-vous de moi?** what do you expect of me?; **j'attendais mieux d'elle** I expected better of her, I was expecting better things from her; **j'attends de lui une réponse** I expect him to answer *or* an answer from him; **nous attendons beaucoup de la réunion** we expect a lot (to come out) of the meeting; **sa réponse, je n'en attends pas grand-chose** I'm not expecting too much (to come) out of his/her response

7 *(avoir besoin de)* to need; **le document attend encore trois signatures** the document needs another three signatures

B. *AVEC COMPLÉMENT INTRODUIT PAR "QUE"* **nous attendrons qu'elle soit ici** we'll wait till she gets here *or* for her to get here; **j'attends qu'il réponde** I'm waiting till he answers, I'm waiting for his answer *or* for him to answer; **elle attendait toujours qu'il rentre avant d'aller se coucher** she would always wait up for him; **attends (un peu) que je le dise à ton père!** just you wait until I tell your father!

C. *AVEC COMPLÉMENT INTRODUIT PAR "DE"* **attends d'être grand** wait until you're older; **nous attendions de sortir** we were waiting to go out; **j'attends avec impatience de la revoir** I can't wait to see her again; **nous attendons de voir la suite des événements** we're waiting to see what happens next

VI 1 *(patienter)* to wait; **les gens n'aiment pas a.** people don't like to be kept waiting *or* to have to wait; **je passe mon temps à a.** I spend all my time waiting around; **il est en ligne, vous attendez?** he's on the other line, will you hold?; **faites-les a.** ask them to wait; **si tu crois qu'il va t'aider, tu peux toujours a.!** if you think he's going to help you, don't hold your breath!; **il peut toujours a.!** he'll have a long wait!; **attends, je vérifie** hold on, I'll check!; **mais enfin attends, je ne suis pas prêt!** wait a minute, will you, I'm not ready!; **elle s'appelle, attends, comment déjà?** her name is, hold on, what is it again?; **c'était en, attendez un peu, 1986** it was in, just a minute, 1986; **et attends, tu ne sais pas le plus beau!** wait (for it) *or* hold on, the best part's yet to come!; **attendez voir, je crois me souvenir...** let's see *or* let's think *or* let me see, I seem to remember...; **et alors là, attendez, il s'est mis à tout avouer** and at that point, wait for it *or* would you believe it, he started to come clean; *Fam* **attends voir, je vais demander** hold *or* hang on, I'll ask; *Fam* **attends voir, toi!** *(menace)* just you wait!; *Prov* **tout vient à point à qui sait a.** all things come to he who waits

2 *(sujet: plat chaud, soufflé)* to wait; *(sujet: vin, denrée)* to keep; **les spaghetti ne doivent pas a.** spaghetti must be served as soon as it's ready; **il fait trop a. ses vins** *(les sert trop vieux)* he keeps his wines too long

3 *(être reporté)* to wait; **votre projet attendra** your plan'll have to wait

• **attendre après** **VT IND** *Fam* **1** *(avoir besoin de)* **a. après qch** to be in desperate need of sth; **garde le livre, je n'attends pas après** keep the book, I'm not desperate *or* in a hurry for it **2** *(compter sur)* **a. après qn** to rely *or* to count on sb; **je n'ai pas attendu après toi pour me l'expliquer** I didn't exactly rely on you to explain it to me; **si tu attends après lui, tu n'auras jamais tes renseignements** if you're counting on him *or* if you leave it up to him, you'll never get the information you want; **elle est assez grande, elle n'attend plus après toi!** she's old enough to get along (perfectly well) without you!

VPR s'attendre 1 *(emploi réciproque)* **les enfants, attendez-vous pour traverser la rue** children, wait for each other before you cross the road **2 s'a. à** to expect; **on ne s'attendait pas à sa mort** his/her death was unexpected; **il faut s'a. à des embouteillages** traffic jams are expected; **il faut s'a. à tout** we should be prepared for anything; **s'a. au pire** to expect the worst; **savoir à quoi s'a.** to know what to expect; **je ne m'attendais pas à cela de votre part** I didn't expect this from you; **nous ne nous attendions pas à ce que la grève réussisse** we weren't expecting the strike to succeed; **il fallait s'y a.** that was to be expected; **comme il fallait s'y a.** as was to be expected, predictably enough; **tu aurais dû t'y a.** you should have known; **je m'y attendais** I expected as much

• **en attendant** **ADV 1** *(pendant ce temps)* **finis ton dessert, en attendant je vais faire le café** finish your dessert, and in the meantime I'll make the coffee; **le train aura un retard de 20 minutes – en attendant, allons boire un café** the train's going to be 20 minutes late – let's go and have a coffee while we wait **2** *Fam (malgré cela)* **oui mais, en attendant, je n'ai toujours pas mon argent** that's as may be but I'm still missing my money; **ris si tu veux mais, en attendant, j'ai réussi à mon examen** you can laugh if you like, but I still passed my exam

• **en attendant que** **CONJ** until (such time as); **en attendant qu'il s'explique, on ne sait rien** until (such time as) he's explained himself *or* as long as he hasn't provided any explanations, we don't know anything

> Il faut noter que le verbe anglais **to attend** est un faux ami. Il signifie le plus souvent **être présent, assister à**.

attendri, -e [atɑ̃dri] **ADJ 1** *(ému ▸ regard)* fond, tender **2** *(amolli ▸ viande)* tenderized

attendrir **[32]** [atɑ̃drir] **VT 1** *(émouvoir)* to move to tears *or* pity **2** *(apitoyer)* to move to pity; **s'il espère m'a. avec ses cadeaux, il se trompe** if he's hoping to soften me up with his presents, he's mistaken; **se laisser a.** to give in to pity **3** *(viande)* to tenderize

VPR s'attendrir 1 *(être ému)* to be moved *or* touched (**sur** by); **ne nous attendrissons pas!** let's not get emotional!; **il s'attendrit facilement** he gets emotional easily, he is easily moved; **s'a. sur un bébé** to gush over a baby **2** *(être apitoyé)* to feel compassion; **s'a. sur le sort de qn** to feel pity *or* sorry for sb; **s'a. sur soi-même** to indulge in self-pity, to feel sorry for oneself

attendrissant, -e [atɑ̃drisɑ̃, -ɑ̃t] **ADJ** moving, touching; **regarde-le essayer de s'habiller, c'est a.!** look at him trying to dress himself, how sweet!; **de façon attendrissante** touchingly

attendrissement [atɑ̃drismɑ̃] **NM 1** *(tendresse)* emotion *(UNCOUNT)*; **pas d'a.!** let's not get emotional! **2** *(pitié)* pity, compassion; **a. sur soi-même** self-pity

attendrisseur [atɑ̃drisœr] **NM** *(pour viande)* tenderizer; **passer de la viande à l'a.** to tenderize meat

attendu[1] [atɑ̃dy] **PRÉP** considering, given

• **attendu que** **CONJ** since, considering *or* given that; *Jur* whereas

attendu[2] [atɑ̃dy] **NM** *Jur* **les attendus d'un jugement** the reasons adduced for a verdict

attendu[3]**, -e** [atɑ̃dy] **PP** *voir* **attendre**

ADJ le train est a. pour cinq heures the train is expected at five o'clock; **un mariage très a.** an eagerly-awaited wedding

attentat [atɑ̃ta] **NM 1** *(assassinat)* assassination attempt; **commettre un a. contre qn** to make an attempt on sb's life **2** *(explosion)* attack; **a. à la bombe** bomb attack, bombing; **a. à la voiture piégée** car bomb attack *or* explosion; **l'ambassade a été hier la cible d'un a.** the Embassy was bombed yesterday **3** *(atteinte)* **a. aux libertés constitutionnelles** violation of constitutional liberties; **a. contre la sécurité de l'État** acts harmful to State security; *Jur* **a. aux mœurs** indecent behaviour; **a. à la pudeur** indecent assault

attentatoire [atɑ̃tatwar] **ADJ** *Jur* **a. à la dignité de l'homme** detrimental *or* prejudicial to human dignity

attentat-suicide [atɑ̃tasɥisid] *(pl* **attentats-suicides)** **NM** suicide (bomb) attack

attente [atɑ̃t] **NF 1** *(fait d'attendre)* waiting; *(période)* wait; **l'a. est longue** it's a long time to wait; **vous devez compter une a. de quatre heures** you should expect a four-hour wait; **le plus dur, c'est l'a.** the toughest part is the waiting; **j'étais là depuis 40 minutes et l'a. se prolongeait** I'd been there for 40 minutes and I was still waiting; **pendant l'a. du verdict/des résultats** while awaiting the verdict/the results; **deux heures d'a.** a two-hour wait **2** *(espérance)* expectation; **répondre à l'a. de qn** to come up to sb's expectations; **si la marchandise ne répond pas à votre a.** should the goods not meet your requirements

• **dans l'attente de PRÉP 1** *(dans le temps)* **être dans l'a. de qch** to be waiting for *or* awaiting sth; **il vit dans l'a. de ton retour** he lives for the moment when you return **2** *(dans la correspondance)* **dans l'a. de vous lire/de votre réponse/de vous rencontrer** looking forward to hearing from you/to your reply/to meeting you

• **en attente ADV laisser qch en a.** to leave sth pending **ADJ** *(dossier, affaire)* pending; **le projet est en a.** the project is on hold; *Ordinat* **liste de fichiers à imprimer en a.** print queue

attenter [3] [atɑ̃te] **attenter à VT IND 1** *(commettre un attentat contre)* **a. à la vie de qn** to make an attempt on sb's life; **a. à ses jours** *ou* **à sa vie** to attempt suicide **2** *(porter atteinte à)* **a. à l'honneur/à la réputation de qn** to undermine sb's honour/reputation; **a. à la liberté de qn** to infringe upon sb's liberty

attentif, -ive [atɑ̃tif, -iv] **ADJ 1** *(concentré ▸ spectateur, public, élève)* attentive; **soyez attentifs!** pay attention!; **écouter qn d'une oreille attentive** to listen to sb attentively, to listen to every word sb says

2 *(prévenant ▸ présence)* watchful; *(▸ gestes, parole)* solicitous, thoughtful; **avoir besoin de soins attentifs** to be in need of tender loving care

3 *(scrupuleux)* **un examen a.** a close *or* careful examination

4 il était a. au moindre bruit/mouvement he was alert to the slightest sound/movement; **être a. à ce qui se dit** to pay attention to *or* to listen carefully to what is being said; **être a. aux autres/aux besoins de qn** to be attentive to others/to sb's needs; **être a. à sa santé** to be mindful of one's health; **être a. à son travail** to be careful *or* painstaking in one's work; **a. à ne pas être impliqué** anxious not to be involved

attention [atɑ̃sjɔ̃] **NF 1** *(concentration)* attention; **appeler** *ou* **attirer l'a. de qn sur qch** to call sb's attention to sth, to point sth out to sb; **mon a. a été attirée sur le fait que...** it has come to my attention *or* notice that...; **avoir l'a. de qn** to have sb's attention; **vous avez toute mon a.** you have my undivided attention; **consacrer toute son a. à un problème** to devote one's attention to *or* to concentrate on a problem; **écouter qn avec a.** to listen to sb attentively, to listen hard to what sb's saying; **lire qch avec a.** to read sth carefully *or* attentively; **manque d'a.** carelessness; **porter son a. sur qch** to turn one's attention to sth; **faire a.** to pay attention; **faites bien a.** *(écoutez)* listen carefully, pay attention; *(regardez)* look carefully; **faire a. à** to pay attention to, to heed; **fais particulièrement a. au dernier paragraphe** pay special attention to the last paragraph; **faites a. à ces menaces** bear these threats in mind; **fais a. (à ce) qu'ils soient tous à l'heure** make sure (that) they're all on time

2 *(égard)* attention *(UNCOUNT)*, attentiveness *(UNCOUNT)*, thoughtfulness *(UNCOUNT)*; **elle avait eu l'a. délicate de mettre des géraniums dans ma chambre** she'd kindly put geraniums in my bedroom; **je n'ai jamais droit à la moindre petite a.** nobody ever does nice things for me; **les mille et une attentions de la vraie tendresse** the thousand and one ways in which people express their love for each other; **entourer qn d'attentions, être plein d'attentions pour qn** to lavish attention on sb

3 *(capacité à remarquer)* attention; **attirer l'a.** to attract attention; **arrête, tu vas attirer l'a.!** stop, people will start looking!; **attirer l'a. de qn** to catch *or* to attract sb's attention; **tu as fait a. au numéro de téléphone?** did you get the phone number?; **quand il est entré, je n'ai d'abord pas fait a. à lui** when he came in I didn't notice him at first; **ne fais pas a. à lui, il dit n'importe quoi** don't mind him *or* pay no attention to him, he's talking nonsense

4 faire a. à qn/qch *(surveiller, s'occuper de)* to pay attention to sb/sth; **faire a. à sa santé** to take care of *or* to look after one's health; **faire a. à soi** to look after *or* to take care of oneself; **faire a. à sa ligne** to watch one's weight; **il ne fait pas assez a. à sa femme** he doesn't pay enough attention to his wife; **elle fait trop a. aux autres hommes** she's too interested in other men

5 faire a. *(être prudent)* to be careful *or* cautious; **fais bien a. en descendant de l'escabeau** do be careful when you come off the stepladder; **fais a. aux voitures** watch out for the cars; **fais a. à ce que tu dis!** watch what you're saying!; **fais a. à toi** take care; **a. à la marche/porte** mind the step/door; **a. à tes bottes sales sur le tapis!** watch your muddy boots on that carpet!; **a. à la voiture!** mind the car!; **a. au départ!** stand clear of the doors!

EXCLAM 1 *(pour signaler un danger)* watch *or* look out!; **a., il est armé!** watch *or* look out, he's got a gun!; **a., a., tu vas le casser!** gently *or* easy (now), you'll break it!; **a. chien méchant** *(sur panneau)* beware of the dog; **a. fragile** *(sur emballage)* handle with care; **a. peinture fraîche** *(sur panneau)* wet paint; **a. travaux** *(sur panneau)* men at work **2** *(pour introduire une nuance)* **a., ce n'est pas ce que j'ai dit** now look, that's not what I said

• **à l'attention de PRÉP** *(sur une enveloppe)* **à l'a. de Madame Chaux** for the attention of Madame Chaux

attentionné, -e [atɑ̃sjɔne] **ADJ** considerate, thoughtful; **être a. envers qn** to be considerate *or* attentive towards sb; **comme mari, il était très a.** he was a very attentive *or* caring husband

attentisme [atɑ̃tism] **NM** wait-and-see policy

attentiste [atɑ̃tist] **ADJ** *(attitude, politique)* wait-and-see; **pratiquer une politique d'a.** to play a waiting game

NMF les attentistes those who play a waiting game

attentive [atɑ̃tiv] *voir* **attentif**

attentivement [atɑ̃tivmɑ̃] **ADV** *(en se concentrant ▸ écouter)* carefully, attentively; *(▸ lire, regarder)* closely

atténuant, -e [atenɥɑ̃, -ɑ̃t] **ADJ** *(excuse, circonstance)* mitigating

atténuateur [atenɥatœr] **NM** *Élec* attenuator

atténuation [atenɥasjɔ̃] **NF 1** *(d'une douleur)* easing; *(du chagrin)* relief; *(d'une couleur)* toning down, softening; *(d'un bruit)* muffling; *(de la lumière)* dimming, subduing; *(d'un choc)* cushioning; softening; *(d'un contraste)* softening **2** *(d'une responsabilité)* reduction, lightening; *(de propos, d'une accusation)* toning down; *(d'une faute)* mitigation

atténué, -e [atenɥe] **ADJ** *Méd (virus)* attenuated

atténuer [7] [atenɥe] **VT 1** *(rendre moins perceptible ▸ douleur)* to relieve, to soothe; *(▸ chagrin)* to ease; *(▸ couleur)* to tone down, to soften; *(▸ bruit)* to muffle; *(▸ lumière)* to dim, to subdue; *(▸ choc)* to cushion, to soften; *(▸ contraste)* to soften; **le temps a atténué les souvenirs** the memories have faded over time **2** *(rendre moins important, moins grave ▸ responsabilité)* to reduce, to lighten, to lessen; *(▸ propos, accusation)* to tone down; **le remords n'atténue pas la faute** remorse does not lessen the blame

VPR s'atténuer *(chagrin, cris, douleur)* to subside, to die down; *(effet)* to subside, to fade, to wane; *(lumière)* to fade, to dim; *(bruit)* to diminish, to tone down; *(couleur)* to dim

atterrant, -e [aterɑ̃, -ɑ̃t] **ADJ** appalling, shocking

atterrer [4] [atere] **VT** to dismay, to appal; **sa réponse m'a atterré** I was appalled at his/her answer; **il les regarda d'un air atterré** he looked at them aghast *or* in total dismay

atterrir [32] [aterir] **VI 1** *Aviat* to land, to touch down; **l'avion allait a.** the plane was coming in to land; **a. en catastrophe** to make an emergency landing; **a. sur le ventre** to make a belly landing; **a. trop court** to undershoot; **a. trop long** to overshoot; **faire a. un avion** to land an aircraft

2 *Fam (se retrouver)* to end up, to wind up, to land up; **a. en prison** to end up *or* to land up in jail; **le dossier finit par a. sur son bureau** the file eventually landed up *or* wound up on his/her desk; **la voiture a atterri dans un champ** the car ended up *or* landed in a field; **tous ses vêtements ont atterri dans la cour** all his/her clothes ended up in the yard

3 *Naut (voir la terre)* to make *or* sight land, to make a landfall; *(toucher terre)* to reach *or* to hit land

4 *Fam* **atterris, mon vieux!** what planet have you been on?

atterrissage [aterisaʒ] **NM 1** *Aviat* landing; **prêt à l'a.** ready to touch down *or* to land; **après l'a.** after touchdown *or* landing; **a. en catastrophe** emergency landing; **a. en douceur** soft landing; **a. forcé** emergency landing; **a. aux instruments** instrument landing; **a. raté** bad landing; **a. sur le ventre** belly landing; **a. sans visibilité** blind landing; **a. à vue** visual landing **2** *Naut (en voyant la terre)* making land, landfall; *(en touchant terre)* reaching *or* hitting land

• **d'atterrissage ADJ** landing *(avant n)*

attestation [atestasjɔ̃] **NF 1** *(document)* certificate; **a. d'assurance** insurance certificate; **a. de conformité** certificate of conformity; **a. médicale** doctor's *or* medical certificate

2 *Scol (diplôme)* certificate (of accreditation)

3 *Jur* attestation

4 *(preuve)* proof; **son échec est une nouvelle a. de son incompétence** his/her failure further demonstrates his/her incompetence

attester [3] [ateste] **VT 1** *(certifier)* to attest; **il atteste que sa femme était bien chez elle** he attests that his wife was at home; **ce document atteste que...** this is to certify that... **2** *(témoigner)* to attest *or* to testify to, to vouch for; **cette version des faits est attestée par la presse** this version of the facts is borne out by the press; **ce mot n'est attesté dans aucun dictionnaire** this word isn't attested *or* doesn't feature in any dictionary

• **attester de VT IND** to prove, to testify to, to show evidence of; **sa réponse atteste de sa sincérité** his/her answer shows evidence of *or* testifies to *or* demonstrates his/her sincerity; **ainsi qu'en attesteront ceux qui me connaissent** as those who know me will testify

attiédir [32] [atjedir] *Littéraire* **VT 1** *(refroidir ▸ air)* to cool; *(▸ liquide)* to make lukewarm **2** *(réchauffer)* to warm (up) **3** *Fig (sentiment)* to cool

VPR s'attiédir 1 *(se refroidir)* to cool (down), to become cooler **2** *(se réchauffer)* to warm up, to become warmer **3** *Fig (sentiment)* to cool, to wane

attifer [3] [atife] *Fam* **VT** *Péj* to get up, to rig out; **elle attife ses enfants n'importe comment** she dresses her children any old how; **être attifé de qch** to be got up *or* rigged out in sth

VPR s'attifer to get oneself up, to rig oneself out; **comment tu t'es attifé!** what DO you look like!

attique[1] [atik] **ADJ** Attic

• **Attique NF** Attica

attique[2] [atik] **NM 1** *Archit* attic **2** *Suisse (appartement luxueux)* penthouse

NF *Belg Menuis (d'une porte, d'une fenêtre) Br* fanlight, *Am* transom

attirail [atiraj] **NM** equipment *(UNCOUNT)*; **a. de pêche** fishing tackle; **il a tout un a. pour la pêche** he's got a full set of fishing tackle; **a. de plombier** plumber's tool kit; *Fam* **on emporte l'ordinateur et tout son a.** let's take the computer and all the bits that go with it; *Péj* **qu'est-ce que c'est que (tout) cet a.?** what's all this paraphernalia for?

attirance [atirɑ̃s] **NF** attraction; **l'a. entre nous deux a été immédiate** we were attracted to each other straight away; **éprouver de l'a. pour qn/qch** to feel attracted to sb/sth; **l'a. du vice** the lure of vice

attirant, -e [atirɑ̃, -ɑ̃t] **ADJ** attractive

attirer [3] [atire] **VT 1** *(tirer vers soi)* to draw; **elle a attiré l'enfant contre elle/sur son cœur** she drew the child to her/to her bosom; **il m'a attiré vers le balcon pour me montrer le paysage** he drew me towards the balcony to show me the view; **l'aimant attire le fer/les épingles** iron is/pins are attracted to a magnet

2 *(inciter à venir ▸ badaud)* to attract; *(▸ proie)* to lure; **couvre ce melon, il attire les guêpes** cover that melon up, it's attracting wasps; **a. les foules** to attract *or* to draw (in) the crowds; **les requins, attirés par l'odeur du sang** sharks attracted *or* drawn by the smell of blood; **le coup de feu les a attirés sur les lieux** the shot drew them to the scene; **a. qn dans un coin/un piège** to lure sb into a corner/a trap; **après l'avoir attirée derrière un paravent, il l'a embrassée** he kissed her after luring her behind a screen; **a. qn avec** *ou* **par des promesses** to lure *or* to entice sb with promises

3 *(capter ▸ attention, regard)* to attract, to catch; **a. l'attention de qn** to catch *or* to attract sb's attention; **a. l'attention de qn sur qch** to call sb's attention to sth, to point sth out to sb; **a. l'intérêt de qn** to attract sb's interest; **essayant d'a. l'œil du serveur** trying to catch the waiter's eye; **une affiche qui attire les regards** an eye-catching poster

4 *(plaire à)* to attract, to seduce; **les femmes mariées l'attirent, il est attiré par les femmes mariées** he's attracted to married women; **se sentir attiré par qn** to feel attracted to sb; **il a une façon de sourire qui attire les femmes** women find the way he smiles attractive; **ce qui m'attire dans ce projet** what attracts me *or* what I find attractive about this project; **la musique classique ne m'attire pas beaucoup** classical music doesn't appeal to me much

5 *(avoir comme conséquence)* to bring, to cause; **a. des ennuis à qn** to cause trouble for sb, to get sb into trouble; **sa démission lui a attiré des sympathies** his/her resignation won *or* earned him/her some sympathy; **a. sur soi la colère de qn** to incur sb's anger

6 *Astron & Phys* to attract

VPR s'attirer 1 *(emploi réciproque)* to attract one another; **les contraires s'attirent** opposites attract (each other) **2 s'a. des ennuis** to get oneself into trouble, to bring trouble upon oneself; **s'a. la colère de qn** to incur sb's anger; **s'a. les bonnes grâces de qn** to win *or* to gain sb's favour; **s'a. des ennemis** to make enemies

attiser [3] [atize] **VT 1** *(flammes, feu)* to poke; *(incendie)* to fuel **2** *Littéraire (colère, haine, désir)* to stir up, to rouse

attitré, -e [atitre] **ADJ 1** *(accrédité)* accredited, appointed **2** *(habituel ▸ fournisseur, marchand)* usual, regular **3** *(favori ▸ fauteuil, place)* favourite

attitude [atityd] **NF 1** *(comportement)* attitude; *Péj (affectation)* attitude; **son a. envers moi/les femmes** his/her attitude towards me/women; **elle a eu une a. irréprochable** her attitude was beyond reproach; **prendre une a.** to strike an attitude; **prendre des attitudes** to put on airs; **il prend des attitudes de martyr** he puts on a martyred look; **il a l'air indigné, mais ce n'est qu'une a.** he looks indignant but he's only putting it on **2** *(point de vue)* standpoint; **adopter une a. ambiguë** to adopt an ambiguous standpoint *or* attitude **3** *(maintien)* bearing, demeanour; *(position)* position, posture; **avoir une a. gauche** to move clumsily; **surpris dans une a. coupable** caught in a compromising position

attouchement [atuʃmɑ̃] **NM 1** *(sexuel)* **se livrer à des attouchements sur qn** to fondle sb, to interfere with sb **2** *(pour guérir)* laying on of hands

attractif, -ive [atraktif, -iv] **ADJ 1** *Phys* attractive **2** *(plaisant)* attractive, appealing

attraction [atraksjɔ̃] **NF 1** *Astron & Phys* attraction; **a. terrestre** earth's gravity; **a. universelle** gravity

2 *(attirance)* attraction, appeal; **l'a. qu'il éprouve pour elle/la mort** his attraction to her/death; **exercer une a. sur qn/qch** to attract sb/sth; **la religion exerce-t-elle encore une a. sur les jeunes?** does the younger generation still feel drawn towards religion?; **les automobiles allemandes suscitent une a. très marquée chez les Britanniques** German cars are very popular with the British

3 *(centre d'intérêt)* attraction; **la grande a. de la soirée** the chief attraction of the evening; **les attractions touristiques de la région** the area's tourist attractions

4 *(distraction)* attraction; **a. numéro un** *ou* **principale** star attraction; **il y aura des attractions pour les enfants** entertainment will be provided for children; **les attractions** *(dans un gala etc)* the show; **les attractions passent à 21 heures** the show starts at 9 o'clock

attractive [atraktiv] *voir* **attractif**

attrait [atrɛ] **NM 1** *(beauté ▸ d'un visage, d'une ville, d'une idéologie)* attraction, attractiveness; *(intérêt ▸ d'un produit)* attraction, appeal; **elle trouve beaucoup d'a. à ses romans** she finds his/her novels very appealing; **un des attraits du célibat** one of the attractions of celibacy; **un village sans (grand) a.** a rather charmless village; **ce produit présente un a. commercial certain** this product has definite market appeal **2** *(fascination)* attraction, appeal; **éprouver un a. pour qch** to feel an attraction towards sth

• **attraits NMPL** *Euph Littéraire* charms

attrapade [atrapad], **attrapage** [atrapaʒ] **NF** *Fam* telling-off

attrape [atrap] **NF** catch, trick; **il doit y avoir une a. là-dessous** there must be a catch in it somewhere

attrape-couillon [atrapkujɔ̃] *(pl* **attrape-couillons)** **NM** *très Fam* con trick

attrape-mouche [atrapmuʃ] *(pl* **attrape-mouches)** **NM 1** *Bot* flytrap **2** *(papier collant)* flypaper

attrape-nigaud [atrapnigo] *(pl* **attrape-nigauds)** **NM** confidence trick

attraper [3] [atrape] **VT 1** *(prendre)* to pick up; **a. un timbre délicatement avec des pinces** to pick a stamp up carefully with tweezers; **la chatte attrape ses chatons par la peau du cou** the cat picks up her kittens by the scruff of the neck; **elle attrapa sa guitare sur le sol** she picked up her guitar from the floor; **attrape la casserole par le manche** hold *or* grasp the pan by the handle

2 *(saisir au passage ▸ bras, main, ballon)* to grab; **a. qn par le bras** to grab sb by the arm; **a. qn par la taille** to grab sb round the waist; **il m'a attrapé par les épaules et m'a secoué** he took me by the shoulders and shook me; **il a attrapé un stylo et a couru répondre au téléphone** he grabbed a pen and ran to answer the phone; **attrape Rex, attrape!** come on Rex, get it!

3 *(saisir par force, par ruse)* to capture, to catch

4 *(surprendre ▸ voleur, tricheur)* to catch; *(▸ bribe de conversation, mot)* to catch; **a. qn à faire qch** to catch sb doing sth; **attends que je t'attrape!** just you wait till I get hold of you!; **si tu veux le voir, il faut l'a. au saut du lit** if you want to see him, you have to catch him as soon as he gets up; **que je ne t'attrape plus à écouter aux portes!** don't let me catch you listening at doors again!

5 *(réprimander)* to tell off; **papa m'a attrapé!** Daddy told me off!; **je vais l'a. quand il va rentrer** he'll catch it from me when he gets home; **se faire a.** to get a telling-off

6 *(prendre de justesse ▸ train)* to catch

7 *Fam (avoir)* to get; **a. une contravention** to get a ticket; **a. un coup de soleil** to get sunburnt; *Vieilli* **a. froid** *ou* **un rhume** *ou* **du mal** to catch *or* to get a cold; **elle a attrapé la rubéole de son frère** she got *or* caught German measles off *or* from her brother; **ferme la fenêtre, tu vas nous faire a. un rhume!** close the window or we'll all catch cold!; **tiens, attrape!** *(à quelqu'un qui vient d'être critiqué)* that's one in the eye for you!, take that!

8 *(tromper ▸ naïf, gogo)* to catch (out), to fool

VPR s'attraper 1 *(emploi passif) (être contracté ▸ maladie, mauvaise habitude)* to be catching; **le cancer ne s'attrape pas** you can't catch cancer; **la rougeole s'attrape facilement** measles is very contagious **2** *(emploi réciproque) (se disputer)* to fight, to squabble; **tu les as entendus s'a.?** did you hear them squabbling?

attrape-touristes [atrapturist] **NM INV** tourist trap

attrayant, -e [atrɛjɑ̃, -ɑ̃t] **ADJ** *(homme, femme)* good-looking, attractive; *(suggestion)* attractive, appealing; **peu a.** unattractive, unappealing

attribuable [atribɥabl] **ADJ a. à** attributable to

attribuer [7] [atribɥe] **VT 1** *(distribuer ▸ somme, bien)* to allocate; *(▸ titre, privilège)* to grant; *(▸ fonction, place, salaire, prime)* to allocate, to assign; *(▸ prix, récompense)* to award; *Fin & Bourse (▸ actions, dividendes)* to allocate, to allot; *Ordinat (mémoire)* to allocate; **nous ne sommes pas ici pour a. des blâmes** it is not up to us to lay the blame; **a. un rôle à qn** *Théât* to cast sb for a part; *Fig* to cast sb in a role

2 *(imputer)* **a. qch à qn** to ascribe *or* to attribute sth to sb; **ses contemporains ne lui attribuaient aucune originalité** his/her contemporaries did not credit him/her with any originality; **a. la paternité d'un enfant/d'une œuvre à qn** to consider sb to be the father of a child/author of a work; **un sonnet longtemps attribué à Shakespeare** a sonnet long thought to have been written by Shakespeare; **ces mots ont été attribués à Marat** these words were attributed to Marat, Marat is supposed to have said these words; **j'attribue sa réussite à son environnement** I put his/her success down *or* I attribute his/her success to his/her background; **un divorce qu'il faut a. à l'alcoolisme** a divorce which alcoholism must take the blame for; **à quoi a. cette succession de catastrophes?** what could account for this series of disasters?

3 *(accorder)* **a. de l'importance à qch** to attach importance to sth; **a. de la valeur à qch** to find value in sth

VPR s'attribuer s'a. qch to claim sth for oneself; **il s'est attribué la plus grande chambre** he claimed the largest room for himself; **s'a. un titre** to give oneself a title; **s'a. une fonction** to appoint oneself to a post; **s'a. tout le mérite de qch** to claim all the credit for sth

attribut [atriby] **NM 1** *(caractéristique)* attribute, (characteristic) trait; *Euph* **attributs (virils** *ou* **masculins)** (male) privates **2** *Gram* predicate; **adjectif a.** predicative adjective

attribution [atribysjɔ̃] **NF 1** *(distribution ▸ d'une somme, d'un bien)* allocation; *(▸ d'un titre, d'un privilège)* granting; *(▸ d'une place, d'une fonction, d'une part)* allocation, assignment; *(▸ d'un prix, d'une récompense)* awarding; *(▸ d'un salaire, d'une prime)* assigning, allocation; *Fin & Bourse (▸ d'actions, de dividendes)* allocation, allotment; *Ordinat (▸ de mémoire)* allocation; *Cin & TV* **attribution des rôles** casting **2** *(reconnaissance ▸ d'une œuvre, d'une responsabilité, d'une découverte)* attribution; **toiles d'a. douteuse** paintings of doubtful origin; **l'a. de la figurine à Rodin a été contestée** doubts have been cast on whether Rodin actually sculpted the figurine; *Jur* **a. de paternité** affiliation

• **attributions NFPL** responsibilities; **cela n'est pas** *ou* **n'entre pas dans mes attributions** that doesn't come within my remit, that's not part of my responsibilities

attriqué, -e [atrike] = **atriqué**

attristant, -e [atristɑ̃, -ɑ̃t] **ADJ** saddening, depressing; **il est a. de voir que...** it's such a pity to see that...; **comme c'est a.!** it's so depressing!

attristé, -e [atriste] **ADJ** *(visage, regard)* sad

attrister [3] [atriste] **VT** to sadden, to depress; **sa mort nous a tous profondément attristés** we were all greatly saddened by his/her death; **cela m'attriste de voir que...** it makes me sad *or* I find it such a pity to see that...

VPR s'attrister s'a. de qch to be saddened by sth, to be sad about sth; **je m'attriste d'apprendre qu'il est parti** I'm sad to hear that he's gone

attroupement [atrupmɑ̃] **NM** crowd; **un a. s'est formé** a crowd gathered; **provoquer un a.** to draw a crowd; *Jur* **a. illégal** unlawful assembly, rout

attrouper [3] [atrupe] **VT** *(foule)* to draw, to attract; **arrêtez de crier, vous allez a. les passants** stop shouting, you'll draw a crowd

VPR s'attrouper *(gén)* to gather

atypique [atipik] ADJ atypical

au [o] *voir* **à**

aubade [obad] NF *Mus* dawn serenade, aubade; **donner une a.** *ou* **l'a. à qn** to serenade sb (at dawn)

aubaine [obɛn] NF *(argent)* windfall; *(affaire)* bargain; *(occasion)* godsend, golden opportunity; **quelle a.!** what a godsend!; **c'est une véritable a. pour notre usine** it comes as *or* it is a godsend to our factory; **profiter de l'a.** to take advantage *or* to make the most of a golden opportunity; *Can* **à prix d'a.** at a reduced price

aube [ob] NF **1** *(aurore)* dawn; **à l'a.** at dawn, at daybreak; **il se leva à l'a.** he rose at dawn; **l'a. pointait quand il se leva** dawn was about to break when he got up; *Fig* **l'a. d'une ère nouvelle** the dawn *or* dawning of a new era

2 *Rel* alb

3 *Naut (en bois)* paddle; *(en métal)* blade

4 *(d'un moulin à vent)* vane, blade; *(pale)* blade

aubépine [obepin] NF *Bot* hawthorn; **fleur d'a.** may blossom

aubère [obɛr] ADJ *(cheval)* red roan

NM red roan (horse)

auberge [obɛrʒ] NF inn; *Fam* **tu prends la maison pour une a.?** you treat this house like a hotel!; **c'est un peu l'a. espagnole** you get out of it what you put in it in the first place; **a. de jeunesse** youth hostel; *Fam* **il n'est pas sorti/on n'est pas sortis de l'a.** he's/we're not out of the woods yet

aubergine [obɛrʒin] NF **1** *Bot (légume) Br* aubergine, *Am* eggplant **2** *Fam (contractuelle) Br* (female) traffic warden, *Am* meter maid

ADJ INV *(couleur)* aubergine

aubergiste [obɛrʒist] NMF inn-keeper

aubette [obɛt] NF *Belg* **1** *(kiosque à journaux)* news stand **2** *(abri)* bus shelter

auburn [obœrn] ADJ INV auburn

aucun, -e [okœ̃, -yn] ADJ INDÉFINI **1** *(avec une valeur négative)* no, not any; **il ne fait a. effort** he doesn't make any effort; **aucune décision n'a encore été prise** no decision has been reached yet; **a. article n'est encore prêt** none of the articles is ready yet; **a. mot ne sortit de sa bouche** he/she didn't utter a single word; **il n'y a aucune raison de croire que...** there's no reason *or* there isn't any reason to think that...; **il n'y a a. souci à se faire** there is nothing to worry about; **ils n'eurent a. mal à découvrir la vérité** they had no trouble (at all) finding out the truth; **elle n'en prend a. soin** she doesn't look after it at all; **je ne vois a. inconvénient à ce que vous restiez** I don't mind your staying at all; **en aucune façon** in no way; **sans aucune exception** without any exception; **sans a. doute** undoubtedly, without any doubt; **sans a. remords** quite remorselessly; **aucune idée!** no idea!

2 *(avec une valeur positive)* any; **il est plus rapide qu'a. autre coureur** he's faster than any other runner; **avez-vous aucune intention de le faire?** have you any intention of doing it?

PRON INDÉFINI **1** *(avec une valeur négative)* none; **a. d'entre eux n'a pu répondre** none of them could answer; **je sais qu'a. n'a menti** I know that none *or* not one of them lied; **je n'ai lu a. de ses livres** I haven't read any of his/her books; **a. (des deux)** neither (of them)

2 *(servant de réponse négative)* none; **combien d'entre eux étaient présents? – a.!** how many of them were present? – none!

3 *(avec une valeur positive)* any; **j'ai apprécié son dernier livre plus qu'a. de ses films** I enjoyed his/her last book more than any of his/her films; **il est plus fort qu'a. de vos hommes** he's stronger than any of your men; **d'aucuns** some; **d'aucuns pensent que la guerre est inévitable** some (people) think *or* there are those who think that war is unavoidable

aucunement [okynmɑ̃] ADV **1** *(dans des énoncés négatifs avec "ne" ou "sans")* in no way, not in the least *or* slightest; **il n'avait a. envie d'y aller** he didn't want to go there in the slightest; **je n'ai a. l'intention de me laisser insulter** I certainly have no *or* I haven't the slightest intention of letting myself be insulted **2** *(servant de réponse négative)* not at all; **a-t-il été question de cela? – a.** was it a question of that? – not at all

> **SUFFIX**
>
> **-AUD, -AUDE**
>
> This suffix is added to adjectives or nouns to form new adjectives or nouns with a DEROGATORY emphasis, always applied to people and referring to physical appearance or character traits. It has no direct equivalent in English and so in order to translate it accurately, a similarly negative word has to be used:
>
> **rougeaud(e)** ruddy; **courtaud(e)** short-legged, squat; **lourdaud(e)** oafish/oaf; **rustaud(e)** uncouth/yokel; **salaud** bastard

audace [odas] NF **1** *(courage)* daring, boldness, audaciousness; **il faut beaucoup d'a. pour réussir** you need to be very daring to succeed; **avec a.** audaciously; **ils ont eu l'a. de nous attaquer par le flanc droit** they were bold enough to attack our right flank; **elle a toutes les audaces** she's daring **2** *(impudence)* audacity; **il a eu l'a. de dire non** he dared (to) *or* he had the audacity to say no; **tu ne manques pas d'a.!** you've got some cheek!

audacieuse [odasjøz] *voir* **audacieux**

audacieusement [odasjøzmɑ̃] ADV audaciously

audacieux, -euse [odasjø, -øz] ADJ **1** *(courageux)* daring, bold, audacious **2** *(impudent)* bold, audacious, impudent

NM,F bold man, *f* bold woman; **c'était un a.** he was very daring

au-deçà [odəsa] ADV on this side

• **au-deçà de** PRÉP on this side of

au-dedans [odədɑ̃] ADV **1** *(à l'intérieur)* inside; **vert a., rouge au-dehors** green (on the) inside, red (on the) outside **2** *(mentalement)* inwardly; **elle a l'air confiante mais a. elle a des doutes** she looks confident but deep within herself *or* but inwardly she has doubts

• **au-dedans de** PRÉP inside, within; *Fig* **a. d'elle-même, elle regrette son geste** deep down *or* inwardly, she regrets what she did

au-dehors [odəɔr] ADV **1** *(à l'extérieur)* outside; **il fait bon ici, mais a. il fait froid** it's warm in here, but outside *or* outdoors it's cold **2** *(en apparence)* outwardly; **elle est généreuse même si a. elle paraît dure** she's generous even if she looks cold *or* if she's outwardly cold

• **au-dehors de** PRÉP outside, *Littéraire* without; **a. de ces murs, personne ne sait rien** nobody knows anything outside these walls

au-delà [odəla] NM **l'a.** the hereafter, the next world

ADV beyond; **a. il y a la mer** beyond *or* further on there is the sea; **tu vois le monument? l'école est un peu a.** can you see the monument? the school is a little further (on) *or* just beyond (that); **le désir d'aller a.** the desire to go further; **500 euros, et je n'irai pas a.** 500 euros and that's my final offer; **surtout ne va pas a.** *(d'une somme)* whatever you do, don't spend any more; **il a obtenu tout ce qu'il voulait et bien a.** he got everything he wanted and more

• **au-delà de** PRÉP *(dans l'espace)* beyond; *(dans le temps)* after; **a. de la frontière** on the other side of *or* beyond the border; **a. de 300 euros, vous êtes imposable** above 300 euros you must pay taxes; **ne va pas a. de 100 euros** don't spend more than 100 euros; **a. des limites du raisonnable** beyond the limits of what is reasonable, beyond what's reasonable; **réussir a. de ses espérances** to succeed beyond one's expectations; **c'est a. de sa juridiction** it is beyond *or* outside his/her jurisdiction; **a. de ses forces/moyens** beyond one's strength/means

au-dessous [odsu] ADV **1** *(dans l'espace)* below, under, underneath; **il habite à l'étage a.** he lives one floor below; **il n'y a personne (à l'étage) a.** there's no one on the floor below **2** *(dans une hiérarchie)* under, below; **les enfants âgés de dix ans et a.** children aged ten and below; **la taille a.** the next size down; *Mus* **un ton a.** one tone lower

• **au-dessous de** PRÉP **1** *(dans l'espace)* below, under, underneath; **elle habite a. de chez moi** she lives downstairs from me; **a. du genou** below the knee **2** *(dans une hiérarchie)* below; **a. du niveau de la mer** below sea level; **a. de zéro** below zero; **température a. de zéro** sub-zero temperature; **a. de la moyenne** below average; **a. de 65 ans** under 65; **les paquets a. de 10 kg** parcels of less than 10 kg; **le commandant est a. du colonel** a major is ranked lower than a colonel; **c'est a. de lui de supplier** it's beneath him to beg; **je suis a. de la tâche** I'm not up to the job; **il est vraiment a. de tout!** he's really useless!; **le service est a. de tout** the service is an absolute disgrace

au-dessus [odsy] ADV **1** *(dans l'espace)* above; **il habite a.** he lives upstairs; **il n'y a rien a.** *(dans une maison)* there is nothing upstairs *or* (up) above; **il y a une croix a.** there's a cross above it; **là-haut, il y a le hameau des Chevrolles, et il n'y a rien a.** up there is Chevrolles village, and there's nothing beyond it **2** *(dans une hiérarchie)* above; **les enfants de dix ans et a.** children aged ten and over; **la taille a.** the next size up; *Mus* **un ton a.** one tone higher

• **au-dessus de** PRÉP **1** *(dans l'espace)* above; **le placard est a. de l'évier** the cupboard is above the sink; **a. du genou** above the knee; **il habite a. de chez moi** he lives upstairs from me; **un avion passa a. de nos têtes** a plane flew overhead **2** *(dans une hiérarchie)* above; **a. du niveau de la mer** above sea level; **a. de 5000 pieds** above 5,000 feet; **10 degrés a. de zéro** 10 degrees above zero; **les paquets a. de 10 kg** parcels weighing more than 10 kg; **a. de la moyenne** above average; **a. de 15 ans** over 15 years old; **le colonel est a. du commandant** a colonel is ranked higher than a major; **vivre a. de ses moyens** to live beyond one's means; **a. de tout soupçon** above all *or* beyond suspicion; **elle est a. de ça** she's above all that; **c'était a. de mes forces** it was too much for *or* beyond me; **se situer a. des partis** to be politically neutral

au-devant [odvɑ̃] **au-devant de** PRÉP **aller** *ou* **se porter a. de qn** to go and meet sb; **courir** *ou* **se précipiter a. de qn** to run to meet sb; **aller a. des désirs de qn** to anticipate sb's wishes; **aller a. de ses obligations** to do more than what's expected of one; **il va a. de graves ennuis/d'une défaite** he's heading for serious trouble/for failure; **aller a. du danger** to court danger

audibilité [odibilite] NF audibility

audible [odibl] ADJ audible

audience [odjɑ̃s] NF **1** *(entretien)* audience; **donner a.** *ou* **accorder une a. à qn** to grant sb an audience

2 *Jur* hearing; **l'a. est suspendue** the case is adjourned

3 *(public touché ▸ par un livre)* readership; *(▸ par un film, une pièce, un concert)* public; *(▸ pour des idées, un parti)* following; **une émission à large a.** a very popular programme; **cette proposition a trouvé a. auprès de la population française** this proposal met with a favourable reception from the French population

4 *(public ▸ à la radio)* listeners; *(▸ à la télévision)* viewers; *(▸ chiffres)* ratings

5 *Mktg* audience; **a. captive** captive audience; **a. cible** target audience; **a. cumulée** cumulative audience; **a. globale** global audience; **a. instantanée** instantaneous audience; **a. télévisuelle** television audience; **a. utile** addressable audience

> Do not confuse with **auditoire**.

Audimat® [odimat] NM *TV (appareil)* = device used for calculating viewing figures for French television, installed for a period of time in selected households; *(résultats)* audience ratings, audience viewing figures; **la dictature de l'A.** the pressure to get good ratings

audimètre [odimɛtr] NM *TV* audience rating device

audimétrie [odimetri] NF *TV* = calculation of audience ratings

audio [odjo] ADJ INV audio; **cassette a.** audio cassette

audiocassette [odjɔkasɛt] NF (audio) cassette

audioconférence [odjɔkɔ̃ferɑ̃s] NF *Tél* audio conference

audiofréquence [odjɔfrekɑ̃s] **NF** *Tech* audio frequency

audioguide [odjɔgid] **NF** audioguide, headset

audiomètre [odjɔmɛtr] **NM** *Tech* audiometer

audionumérique [odjɔnymerik] **ADJ disque a.** compact disc

audio-oral, -e [odjɔɔral] (*mpl* **audio-oraux** [-o], *fpl* **audio-orales**) **ADJ** *Scol* audio-oral

audiophone [odjɔfɔn] **NM 1** *(de malentendant)* hearing aid **2** *(lors d'une visite de musée)* audioguide, headset

audioprothésiste [odjɔprɔtezist] **NMF** *Méd* hearing aid specialist

audiotypie [odjotipi] **NF** audio-typing

audiotypiste [odjotipist] **NMF** audio-typist

audiovisuel, -elle [odjɔvizɥɛl] **ADJ** *(dans l'enseignement)* audiovisual; *(des médias)* broadcasting

NM 1 *(matériel)* **l'a.** *(des médias)* radio and television equipment *(UNCOUNT)*; *(dans l'enseignement)* audiovisual aids **2** *(médias)* **l'a.** broadcasting **3** *(techniques)* **l'a.** media techniques

audiphone [odifɔn] **NM** *Tél* pre-recorded telephone message service

audit [odit] **NM** *Admin & Compta* **1** *(service)* audit; **être chargé de** *ou* **faire l'a. d'une société** to audit a company; **a. consommateur** consumer audit; **a. des détaillants** retail audit; **a. environnemental** environmental audit; **a. externe/interne** external/internal audit; **a. marketing** marketing audit; **a. opérationnel** operational audit; **a. de vente** sales audit **2** *(personne, entreprise)* auditor; **a. des détaillants** retail auditor; **a. externe/interne** external/internal auditor; **a. marketing** marketing auditor

auditer [3] [odite] **VT** to audit

auditeur, -trice [oditœr, -tris] **NM,F 1** *(d'une radio, d'un disque)* listener; **les auditeurs** the audience

2 *Ling* hearer

3 *(chargé de l'audit)* auditor; **a. à la Cour des comptes** junior official at the "Cour des comptes"; **a. des détaillants** retail auditor; **a. externe/interne** external/internal auditor; **a. marketing** marketing auditor

4 *Scol & Univ* **a. libre** unregistered student, *Am* auditor; **j'y vais en a. libre** *Br* I go to the lectures but I'm not officially on the course, *Am* I audit the lectures

5 *Jur* **A. à la Cour de cassation** = assistant judge at the "Cour de cassation"; **a. de justice** = student at the "École nationale de la magistrature"

auditif, -ive [oditif, -iv] **ADJ** hearing, *Spéc* auditory; **troubles auditifs** hearing disorder

audition [odisjɔ̃] **NF 1** *Cin, Mus & Théât* audition; **passer une a.** to audition; **faire passer une a. à qn** to audition sb

2 *Jur* **pendant l'a. des témoins** while the witnesses were being heard

3 *Physiol* hearing

4 *(fait d'écouter)* listening

auditionner [3] [odisjɔne] **VT a. qn** to audition sb, to give sb an audition

VI to audition

auditive [oditiv] *voir* **auditif**

auditoire [oditwar] **NM 1** *(public)* audience **2** *Belg & Suisse (salle de conférences)* conference hall; *(salle de cours)* lecture hall, lecture theatre

> Do not confuse with the French noun **audience**.

auditorium [oditɔrjɔm] **NM** auditorium; *Rad & TV* recording studio

auditrice [oditris] *voir* **auditeur**

auge [oʒ] **NF 1** *Constr* trough

2 *Géog & Géol* **a. glaciaire, vallée en a.** U-shaped valley

3 *Tech (d'un moulin)* channel

4 *(mangeoire)* trough; *Fam Hum* **amène ton a.** pass your plate[□]

5 *(d'un concasseur)* hopper

auget [oʒɛ] **NM** bucket *(of waterwheel)*

augmentation [ɔgmɑ̃tasjɔ̃] **NF 1** *(fait d'augmenter)* increase (**de** in); **une a. de 3 pour cent** a 3 percent increase; **l'a. des cas d'hépatite** the increase in the number of hepatitis cases; **constater l'a. des salaires/impôts** to note the increase in salaries/taxes; **en a.** rising, increasing; **a. des bénéfices** earnings growth; **a. de capital** increase in capital; **a. de prix** price increase; **a. du prix de vente** mark-up

2 *(action d'augmenter)* raising; **l'a. des prix par les producteurs** the raising of prices by producers

3 *(majoration de salaire)* *Br* (pay) rise, *Am* raise; **demander une a.** to ask for a *Br* rise *or Am* raise; **quand vas-tu toucher ton a.?** when will your rise come through?

4 *Ordinat* **a. de puissance** upgrade, upgrading

5 *(en tricot)* **faire une a.** to make a stitch, to make one

augmenter [3] [ɔgmɑ̃te] **VT 1** *(porter à un niveau plus élevé ▸ impôt, prix, nombre, taux d'intérêt)* to put up, to increase, to raise; *(▸ durée, dépenses)* to increase; *(▸ tarif)* to step up; *(▸ salaire)* to increase, to raise; **a. le pain** *ou* **le prix du pain** to put up bread prices; **la crise a fait a. le prix du pétrole** the crisis has pushed up the price of oil; *Fam* **elle a été augmentée** she got a *Br* (pay) rise *or Am* raise; **a. le temps passé au bureau** to increase the time spent in the office; **a. les impôts de 5 pour cent** to put up *or* to raise *or* to increase taxes by 5 percent; **nous voulons a. les ventes de 10 pour cent** we want to boost sales by 10 percent; *Fam* **ils ont augmenté les employés de 20 euros** they put up the employees' pay by 20 euros

2 *(intensifier ▸ tension, difficulté)* to increase, to step up, to make worse; **ces déclarations n'ont fait qu'a. la peur du peuple** these remarks only added to *or* fuelled the people's fear

3 *Mus* to augment; **en augmentant** crescendo

VI 1 *(dette, population)* to grow, to increase, to get bigger; *(quantité, poids, dépenses)* to increase; *(prix, impôt, taux d'intérêt, salaire)* to increase, to go up, to rise; **tout** *ou* **la vie augmente!** everything's going up!; **achetez maintenant, ça va a.!** buy now, prices are going up!; **le chiffre d'affaires a augmenté de 10 pour cent (par rapport à l'année dernière)** the turnover has increased by 10 percent *or* is 10 percent up (on last year); **a. de valeur** to increase in value; **les salaires n'ont pas augmenté depuis 2003** salaries have been pegged at the same level since 2003; *Fam* **la viande a augmenté, le prix de la viande a augmenté** meat's gone up, meat has increased in price; **ça va faire a. la viande** it'll put the price of meat up

2 *(difficulté, tension)* to increase, to grow; **la violence augmente dans les villes** urban violence is on the increase

VPR s'augmenter s'a. de to increase by; **la famille s'est augmentée de deux jumeaux** a set of twins has joined the family; **notre société s'est augmentée de trois nouveaux cadres** our company has acquired three new managers

augure [ogyr] **NM 1** *Antiq* augur; *(voyant)* prophet, soothsayer; **consulter les augures** to consult the oracle **2** *(présage)* omen; *Antiq* augury

• **de bon augure ADJ** auspicious; **c'est de bon a.** it's auspicious, it augurs well, it bodes well

• **de mauvais augure ADJ** ominous, inauspicious; **c'est de mauvais a.** it's ominous, it doesn't augur *or* bode well

augurer [3] [ogyre] **VT** to foresee; **sa visite ne laisse pas a. de progrès significatif** no significant progress can be expected as a result of his/her visit; **sa réponse augure mal/bien de notre prochaine réunion** his/her answer doesn't augur well/augurs well for our next meeting; **je n'augure rien de bon de tout cela** I don't see any good coming of all this; **que peut-on a. de cette rencontre prochaine?** what does this next meeting hold in store?

Auguste [ogyst] **NPR** *(empereur)* Augustus; **le siècle d'A.** the Augustan Age

auguste [ogyst] **ADJ 1** *(personnage)* august **2** *(majestueux ▸ geste, pas, attitude)* majestic, noble

NM clown

augustin, -e [ogystɛ̃, -in] **NM,F** *Rel* Augustinian

augustinien, -enne [ogystinjɛ̃, -ɛn] *Rel* **ADJ** Augustinian

NM,F Augustinian

aujourd'hui [oʒurdɥi] **ADV 1** *(ce jour)* today; **je l'ai vu a.** I've seen him today; **le journal d'a.** today's paper; **nous sommes le trois a.** today's the third; **il y a huit jours a.** a week ago today; **dès a.** today; *Fam* **qu'est-ce qu'il est paresseux! – c'est pas d'a.!** he's so lazy! – tell me something new!; *Fam* **alors! c'est pour a. ou pour demain?** come on, we haven't got all day! **2** *(à notre époque)* today, nowadays; **la France d'a.** modern *or* present-day France, the France of today **3** *Belg (locutions)* **a. matin** this morning; **a. soir** this evening, tonight

aula [ola] **NF** *Suisse* hall

aulne [on] **NM** *Bot* alder

aulx [o] *pl de* **ail**

aumône [omon] **NF** charity, alms; **faire l'a. à qn** to give alms to sb; **demander l'a.** to ask for charity; **je ne demande pas l'a., uniquement ce qui m'est dû** I'm not asking for any handouts, only for what's rightly mine; **vivre d'aumônes** to live on charity; *Littéraire* **il lui fit l'a. d'un regard** he spared him/her a glance

aumônier [omonje] **NM** *Rel* chaplain

aune[1] [on] **NF** ell; **un visage long** *ou* **une tête longue d'une a.** a face as long as a fiddle; *Littéraire* **savoir ce qu'en vaut l'a.** to know the value of things (through experience); **tout est mesuré à l'a. de la rentabilité** everything is assessed using profitability as the only criterion

aune[2] [on] = **aulne**

auparavant [oparavɑ̃] **ADV 1** *(avant)* before, previously; **dix ans a.** ten years before *or* previously; **il avait a. vécu à l'étranger** he had previously lived abroad **2** *(tout d'abord)* beforehand, first

auprès [opre] **ADV** *Littéraire* nearby

• **auprès de PRÉP 1** *(à côté de)* close to, near, by; **assis a. du feu** sitting by the fire; **rester a. de qn** to stay with *or* close to sb

2 *(dans l'opinion de)* **avoir de l'influence a. de qn** to have some influence with sb; **il passe pour un fin connaisseur a. de ses amis** he's considered a connoisseur by his friends

3 *(en s'adressant à)* **chercher du réconfort a. d'un ami** to seek comfort from a friend; **se renseigner a. de qn** to ask sb; **faire une demande a. d'un organisme** to make an application *or* to apply to an organization; **demander une autorisation a. de qn** to ask permission of sb; **agir a. de qn** to use one's influence with sb

4 *(comparé à)* compared with *or* to; **ce n'est rien a. de ce qu'il a gagné** it's nothing compared to *or* with what he made

5 *(dans un titre)* **ambassadeur a. du roi du Danemark** ambassador to the King of Denmark

auquel [okɛl] *voir* **lequel**

aura [ora] **NF** aura

auréole [oreɔl] **NF 1** *Beaux-Arts* halo; *Fig* **ils aiment à se parer de l'a. du sacrifice** they like to wear the crown of sacrifice; **il a toujours nimbé sa mère d'une a.** he's always worshipped his mother **2** *(tache)* ring; **produit détachant qui ne laisse pas d'a.** product that removes stains without leaving a mark **3** *Astron* halo

auréoler [3] [oreɔle] **VT 1** *(parer)* **a. qn de toutes les vertus** to turn sb into a saint **2** *Beaux-Arts* to paint a halo around the head of; *Fig* **tête auréolée de cheveux roux** head with a halo of red hair

VPR s'auréoler to be crowned with (**de** with); **elle aime à s'a. de mystère** she likes to wreathe *or* shroud herself in mystery

auréomycine [oreomisin] **NF** *Pharm* aureomycin

auriculaire [orikylɛr] **ADJ** auricular

NM *Anat* little finger

auricule [orikyl] **NF** *Anat* auricle

auriculothérapie [ɔrikyloterapi] **NF** *Méd* auriculotherapy

aurifère [orifɛr] **ADJ** gold-bearing, *Spéc* auriferous

aurifier [9] [orifje] **VT** to fill with gold

Aurigny [ɔriɲi] **NF** *Géog* Alderney

aurique[1] [orik] **ADJ** *Naut* **voile a.** gaffsail

aurique[2] [orik] **NF** *Chim* auric

aurochs [orɔk] **NM** *Zool* aurochs

aurore [ɔrɔr] NF **1** *(matin)* daybreak, dawn; **avant l'a.** before daybreak; *Fig* **nous voici à l'a. d'une ère nouvelle** we are witnessing the dawn *or* dawning of a new era **2** *Astron* aurora; **a. australe** aurora australis; **a. boréale** aurora borealis; **a. polaire** northern lights, aurora polaris
ADJ INV golden (yellow)
• **aux aurores** ADV *Hum* at the crack of dawn

auscultation [oskyltasjɔ̃] NF *Méd* listening with a stethoscope, *Spéc* auscultation

ausculter [3] [oskylte] VT *Méd* to listen to *or* to sound the chest of, *Spéc* to auscultate

auspices [ospis] NMPL **1** *(parrainage)* **faire qch sous les a. de qn** to do sth under the patronage *or* auspices of sb **2** *(présage)* **sous de bons/mauvais a.** under favourable/unfavourable auspices **3** *Antiq* auspices

aussi [osi] ADV **1** *(également)* too, also; **tu y vas? j'y vais a.** are you going? I'm going too *or* as well; **j'y étais moi a.** I was there too *or* as well; **elle a. travaille à Rome** she too works in Rome, she works in Rome as well; **il a faim, moi a.** he's hungry, and so am I *or* me too; **elle parle russe, moi a.** she speaks Russian and so do I; **c'est a. leur avis** they think so too; **joyeux Noël! – vous a.!** merry Christmas! – the same to you!
2 *(en plus)* too, also; **il parle anglais et a. espagnol** he speaks English and also Spanish; **le talent ne suffit pas, il faut a. travailler** it's not enough to be talented, you also have to work *or* you have to work too; **j'ai a. une maison à Paris** I also have a house in Paris
3 *(terme de comparaison) (devant adj)* **il est a. grand que son père** he's as tall as his father; **il est loin d'être a. riche qu'elle** he's far from being as rich as she is *or* as her; **elle est a. belle qu'intelligente** *ou* **qu'elle est intelligente** she is as beautiful as she is intelligent; **ils sont a. bons l'un que l'autre** they're (both) equally good
4 *(terme de comparaison)* **il ne s'attendait pas à être payé a. rapidement que cela** he didn't expect to be paid as quickly as that *or* that quickly; **il se conduit a. mal qu'autrefois** he behaves just as badly as before; **a. souvent/tard/cher que...** as often/late/expensive as...; **a. doucement que possible** as quietly as possible; **il ne s'est jamais senti a. bien que depuis qu'il a arrêté de fumer** he's never felt so well since he stopped smoking; **je ferais a. bien de partir** I might as well leave; *Fam* **a. sec** right away
5 *(tellement)* so; *(avec un adjectif épithète)* such; **je n'ai jamais rien vu d'a. beau** I've never seen anything so beautiful; **as-tu déjà mangé quelque chose d'a. bon?** have you ever eaten anything so delicious?; **je ne le savais pas a. têtu** I didn't know he was so stubborn; **d'a. beaux cheveux** such lovely hair; **une a. bonne occasion ne se représentera plus** such a good opportunity won't come up again; **a. léger qu'il soit** *ou* **a. léger soit-il, je ne pourrai pas le porter** light as it is, I won't be able to carry it; **a. curieux que cela puisse paraître** strange as *or* though it may seem
CONJ **1** *(indiquant la conséquence)* therefore, and so; **il était très timide, a. n'osa-t-il rien répondre** he was very shy, and so he didn't dare reply; **j'avais confiance en elle, a. n'avais-je pas fait de copie du contrat** I trusted her, and so I hadn't made a copy of the contract **2** *(d'ailleurs)* **on ne lui a rien dit, a. pourquoi n'a-t-il pas demandé?** we didn't tell him anything, but in any case, why didn't he ask?; *Littéraire* **a. bien est-ce ma faute, je ne l'avais pas prévenu** but it's my fault, I didn't warn him

aussitôt [osito] ADV immediately; **il vint a.** he came right away *or* immediately; **a. après son départ** immediately *or* right after he/she left; **je suis tombé malade a. après avoir acheté la maison** right after buying *or* as soon as I'd bought the house I was taken ill; **il est arrivé a. après** he arrived immediately after *or* afterwards; **a. rentré chez lui, il se coucha** as soon as he got home, he went to bed; **a. dit, a. fait** no sooner said than done
• **aussitôt que** CONJ as soon as; **a. que possible** as soon as possible; **il l'appela a. qu'il l'aperçut** he called out the moment *or* as soon as he saw her

austère [ostɛr] ADJ *(architecture, mode de vie)* austere, stark; *(paysage)* bleak, austere; *(style)* dry; *(personnalité)* stern, austere; *(expression)* stern; *(vêtement)* plain, severe

austèrement [ostɛrmɑ̃] ADV austerely

austérité [osterite] NF **1** *(dépouillement* ▸ *d'une architecture, d'un mode de vie)* austerity, starkness; *(*▸ *d'un style)* dryness; *(*▸ *d'une personnalité)* sternness, austerity; *(*▸ *d'une expression)* sternness **2** *Écon* austerity; **mesures d'a.** austerity measures
• **austérités** NFPL *Rel* **les austérités** the austerities

austral, -e, -als *ou* **-aux, -ales** [ostral, -o] ADJ *(hémisphère)* southern; *(pôle)* south *(avant n)*; *(constellation)* austral

Australasie [ostralazi] NF **l'A.** Australasia

australasien, -enne [ostralazjɛ̃, -ɛn] ADJ Australasian
• **Australasien, -enne** NM,F Australasian

australe [ostral] *voir* **austral**

Australie [ostrali] NF **l'A.** Australia

australien, -enne [ostraljɛ̃, -ɛn] ADJ Australian
• **Australien, -enne** NM,F Australian

austro-hongrois, -e [ostroɔ̃grwa, -az] ADJ Austro-Hungarian
• **Austro-Hongrois, -e** NM,F Austro-Hungarian

AUTANT [otɑ̃] ADV **1** *(marquant l'intensité)* **je ne le hais plus a.** I don't hate him as much as I did; **j'ignorais que tu l'aimais a.** I didn't know that you loved him/her so much; **s'entraîne-t-il toujours a.?** does he still train as much (as he used to)?; **pourquoi attendre a.?** why wait that *or* so long?
2 *(en corrélation avec "que")* as much as; **les chaussures valent a. que la robe** the shoes are worth as much as the dress; **rien ne me déplaît a. que d'être en retard** there's nothing I dislike so much as being late; **tu peux le nier a. que tu voudras** you can deny it as much as you like; **la patiente doit prendre du repos a. que faire se peut** the patient must have as much rest as (is) possible; **je l'aime a. que toi** *(que tu l'aimes)* I like him/her as much as you do; *(que je t'aime)* I like him/her as much as (I like) you; **j'ai travaillé a. que lui** I worked as much *or* as hard as he did; **cela me concerne a. que vous** it's of as much concern to me as it is to you
3 *(indiquant la quantité)* **je ne pensais pas qu'ils seraient a.** I didn't think there would be so many of them; **elle boit toujours a.** she still drinks just as much (as she used to); **on lui en remboursera a.** he'll/she'll get the same amount back; **ils sont a. que nous** there are as many of them as (there are of) us; **a. pour moi!** my mistake!
4 *(avec "en") (la même chose)* **tu devrais en faire a.** you should do the same; **pourriez-vous en faire a.?** could you do as much *or* the same?; **j'en aurais fait a. pour toi** I'd have done the same *or* as much for you; **tâchez d'en faire a.** try to do the same; **elle est honnête, tout le monde ne peut pas en dire a.** she's honest, and not everyone can say that *or* as much; **ce n'est pas toi qui pourrais en dire a.** you certainly couldn't say that *or* as much, could you?; *Fam* **j'en ai a. à votre service!** same to you!, likewise!
5 *(avec l'infinitif) (mieux vaut)* **a. revenir demain** I/you/*etc* might as well come back tomorrow; **a. dire la vérité** I/you/*etc* might as well tell the truth; **a. y aller tant qu'il ne pleut pas** I/you/*etc* might as well go while it's not raining
6 *(mieux)* **j'aurais a. fait de rester chez moi** I might as well have stayed at home, I'd have done as well to stay at home; **tu aurais a. fait de passer par Le Mans** you'd have done as well to go via Le Mans; **a. aurait valu demander à sa sœur** it'd have been as well to ask his/her sister
7 *Belg (tant)* **il gagne a. par mois** he earns so much a month
• **autant..., autant** ADV **a. il est cultivé, a. il est nul en mathématiques** he's highly educated, but he's no good at mathematics; **a. il est gentil avec moi, a. il est désagréable avec elle** he's very nice to me, but he's horrible to her; **a. j'aime le vin, a. je déteste la bière** I hate beer as much as I love wine
• **autant de** ADJ *(avec un nom non comptable)* as much; *(avec un nom comptable)* as many; **il y a a. d'eau ici** there's as much water here; **il y a a. de sièges ici** there are as many seats here; **je ne pensais pas qu'il aurait a. de patience** I didn't think he'd have so much patience; **je n'avais jamais vu a. d'eau/d'oliviers** I'd never seen so much water/so many olive trees; **ces livres sont a. de chefs-d'œuvre** every last one of these books is a masterpiece; **a. d'hommes, a. d'avis** as many opinions as there are men; **il y a a. de femmes que d'hommes** there are as many women as (there are) men; **(c'est) a. de gagné** *ou* **de pris** at least that's something, we've got that much out of it anyway; **c'est a. de perdu** that's that (gone); **c'est a. de fait** that's that done at least
• **autant dire** ADV in other words; **j'ai été payé 300 euros, a. dire rien** I was paid 300 euros, in other words a pittance
• **autant dire que** CONJ **trois heures dans le four, a. dire que le poulet était carbonisé!** after three hours in the oven, needless to say the chicken was burnt to a cinder!; **l'ambassade ne répond plus, a. dire que tout est perdu** the embassy's phones are dead, a sure sign that all is lost
• **autant que** CONJ **1** *(dans la mesure où)* as far as; **a. que possible** as far as (is) possible; **a. que je me souvienne** as far as I can remember; **a. que je (le) sache** as far as I know **2** *(il est préférable que)* **a. que je vous le dise tout de suite...** I may as well tell you straightaway...
• **d'autant** ADV **si le coût de la vie augmente de 2 pour cent, les salaires seront augmentés d'a.** if the cost of living goes up by 2 percent, salaries will be raised accordingly; **cela augmente d'a. mon intérêt pour cette question** it makes me all the more interested in this question; **si l'on raccourcit la première étagère de 5 centimètres, il faudra raccourcir la deuxième d'a.** if we shorten the first shelf by 5 centimetres, we'll have to shorten the second one by the same amount
• **d'autant mieux** ADV all the better, much better; **pars à la campagne, tu te reposeras d'a. mieux** you'll have a much better rest if you go to the country; **c'est d'a. mieux ainsi** it's much better like that
• **d'autant mieux que** CONJ **il a travaillé d'a. mieux qu'il se sentait encouragé** he worked all the better for feeling encouraged
• **d'autant moins que** CONJ **je le vois d'a. moins qu'il est très occupé en ce moment** I see even less of him now that he's very busy
• **d'autant moins... que** CONJ **elle est d'a. moins excusable qu'on l'avait prévenue** what she did is all the less forgivable as she'd been warned; **la promenade a été d'a. moins agréable que j'étais un peu souffrant** the walk wasn't very pleasant, particularly as *or* since I wasn't feeling well
• **d'autant plus** ADV all the more reason; **mais je ne l'ai jamais fait! – eh bien d'a. plus!** but I've never done it before! – so *or* well, all the more reason!
• **d'autant plus que** CONJ especially as; **il vous écoutera d'a. plus qu'il vous connaît** he'll listen to you, especially as *or* particularly as he knows you
• **d'autant plus... que** CONJ **c'est d'a. plus stupide qu'il ne sait pas nager** it's particularly *or* all the more stupid given (the fact) that he can't swim
• **d'autant que** CONJ *(vu que, attendu que)* especially as, particularly as; **il faut rentrer – oui, d'a. que je n'ai pas encore préparé le dîner** it's time to go home – yes particularly *or* especially as I haven't got dinner ready yet; **c'est une bonne affaire, d'a. que le crédit est très avantageux** it's a good deal, especially as the terms of credit are very advantageous
• **pour autant** ADV **la situation n'est pas perdue pour a.** the situation isn't hopeless for all that, it doesn't necessarily mean all is lost; **n'en perds pas l'appétit pour a.** don't let it put you off your food; **il t'aime bien, mais il ne t'aidera pas pour a.** just because he's fond of you (it) doesn't mean that he'll help you; **fais-le-lui remarquer sans pour a. le culpabiliser** point it out to him, but don't make him feel guilty about it
• **pour autant que** CONJ as far as; **pour a. que je (le) sache** as far as I know; **tu n'es pas inscrit, pour a. que je sache?** you're not on the register, as far as I know?; **pour a. qu'on puisse prévoir** as far as we can foresee *or* predict; **pour a. qu'on puisse faire la comparaison** inasmuch as a comparison

can be made; **pour a. qu'il ait pu être coupable** guilty though he might have been

autarcie [otarsi] **NF** *Écon* self-sufficiency, *Spéc* autarky; **vivre en a.** to be self-sufficient

autarcique [otarsik] **ADJ** *Écon* self-sufficient, *Spéc* autarkic

autel [otɛl] **NM** *Rel* altar; **conduire** *ou* **mener qn à l'a.** to take sb to the altar *or* down the aisle; *Fig* **être immolé sur l'a. de** to be sacrificed on the altar of

auteur [otœr] **NM 1** *(créateur ▸ d'un livre, d'un article, d'une chanson)* writer, author; *(▸ d'une toile)* painter; *(▸ d'un décor, d'un meuble, d'un vêtement)* designer; *(▸ d'un morceau de musique)* composer; *(▸ d'une statue)* sculptor; *(▸ d'un film, d'un clip)* director; **une marine d'un a. inconnu** a seascape by an unknown artist; **quelle jolie chanson, qui en est l'a.?** what a lovely song, who wrote it?; **Léonard de Vinci a été l'a. de nombreuses inventions** Leonardo da Vinci invented many things; **un a. dramatique** a playwright; **a. à sensation** sensationalist writer; **un a. à succès** a popular writer **2** *(responsable)* **l'a. d'un accident** the person who caused an accident; **l'a. du meurtre** the murderer; **les auteurs de ce crime** those who committed that crime; **les auteurs présumés de l'attentat** those suspected of having planted the bomb; **qui est l'a. de cette farce?** who's behind *or* who thought up this prank?; *Littéraire & Hum* **l'a. de mes jours** my progenitor

auteur-compositeur [otœrkɔ̃pozitœr] *(pl* **auteurs-compositeurs)** **NM** *Mus* composer and lyricist; **a. interprète** singer-songwriter; **je suis a. interprète** I write and sing my own material

auteur-réalisateur [otœrrealizatœr] *(pl* **auteurs-réalisateurs)** **NM** writer-director

authenticité [otɑ̃tisite] **NF 1** *(d'un document, d'un tableau, d'un tapis)* authenticity; *(d'un sentiment)* genuineness **2** *Jur* authenticity

authentification [otɑ̃tifikasjɔ̃] **NF** *(gén) & Ordinat* authentication

authentifier [9] [otɑ̃tifje] **VT** *(gén) & Ordinat* to authenticate

authentique [otɑ̃tik] **ADJ 1** *(document, tableau, tapis, objet d'art)* genuine, authentic; *(sentiment)* genuine, heartfelt **2** *Jur* authentic; *(copie)* certified

authentiquement [otɑ̃tikmɑ̃] **ADV** authentically, genuinely

autisme [otism] **NM** *Méd* autism

autiste [otist] *Méd* **ADJ** autistic
NMF autistic person

autistique [otistik] **ADJ** *Méd* autistic

auto [oto] **NF** car, *Am* automobile; **petite a.** toy car

auto- [oto] **PRÉF** *(de soi-même)* self-

auto-accusation [otoakyzasjɔ̃] *(pl* **auto-accusations)** **NF** self-accusation

auto-adhésif, -ive [otoadezif, -iv] **ADJ** self-adhesive

auto-allumage [otoalymaʒ] *(pl* **auto-allumages)** **NM** *Aut* spontaneous combustion

auto-amorçage [otoamɔrsaʒ] *(pl* **auto-amorçages)** **NM** *Tech* automatic priming

autoberge [otobɛrʒ] **NF (voie) a.** *Br* embankment road, *Am* expressway *(along riverbank)*

autobiographie [otobjɔgrafi] **NF** autobiography

autobiographique [otobjɔgrafik] **ADJ** autobiographical

autobronzant, -e [otobrɔ̃zɑ̃, -ɑ̃t] **ADJ** self-tanning
NM *(crème)* self-tanning cream, fake tan

autobus [otobys] **NM** *Transp* bus; **a. à impériale** double-decker (bus); *Can* **a. scolaire** school bus

autocar [otokar] **NM** *Transp* bus, *Br* coach; **a. pullman** luxury coach

autocariste [otokarist] **NMF** *(propriétaire)* coach operator; *(conducteur)* coach driver

autocélébrer [18] [otoselebre] **s'autocélébrer** **VPR** to sing one's own praises

autocensure [otosɑ̃syr] **NF** self-censorship, self-regulation; **pratiquer l'a.** to censor oneself

autocensurer [3] [otosɑ̃syre] **s'autocensurer** **VPR** to censor oneself

autochenille [otoʃnij] **NF** *Aut* half-track

autochrome [otokrom] *Phot* **ADJ** autochrome
NF autochrome

autochtone [ɔtɔktɔn, otokton] **ADJ** native
NMF native; *Hum* **les autochtones sont arrivés en masse** the locals turned up in droves

autocinétique [otosinetik] **ADJ** *Psy* autokinetic

autoclave [otoklav] **ADJ** pressure-sealed, autoclave *(avant n)*
NM *Tech* autoclave; *Culin & Vieilli* pressure cooker

autocollant, -e [otokɔlɑ̃, -ɑ̃t] **ADJ** self-adhesive; *(enveloppe)* self-sealing
NM sticker

autocommutateur [otokɔmytatœr] **NM** *Ordinat* autoswitch; **a. privé** private branch exchange, PBX

autoconduction [otokɔ̃dyksjɔ̃] **NF** *Électron* mutual induction

autoconsommation [otokɔ̃sɔmasjɔ̃] **NF les légumes qu'ils cultivent sont destinés à l'a.** the vegetables they grow are meant for their own consumption; **économie d'a.** subsistence economy

autocopiant, -e [otokɔpjɑ̃, -ɑ̃t] **ADJ** carbonless, self-copying

autocopie [otokɔpi] **NF 1** *(procédé)* duplication **2** *(document)* duplicate copy

autocorrecteur, -trice [otokɔrɛktœr, -tris] **ADJ** *Ordinat* self-correcting

autocorrection [otokɔrɛksjɔ̃] **NF** self-correcting

autocorrectrice [otokɔrɛktris] *voir* **autocorrecteur**

autocouchette [otokuʃɛt] = **autos-couchettes**

autocrate [otokrat] **NM** *Pol* autocrat

autocratie [otokrasi] **NF** *Pol* autocracy

autocratique [otokratik] **ADJ** *Pol* autocratic

autocratiquement [otokratikmɑ̃] **ADV** *Pol* autocratically

autocritique [otokritik] **NF** self-criticism; **faire son a.** to make a thorough criticism of oneself

autocuiseur [otokɥizœr] **NM** pressure cooker

autodafé [otodafe] **NM** *Hist* auto-da-fé; **faire un a. de livres** to burn books

autodécompactable [otodekɔ̃paktabl] **ADJ** *Ordinat* self-extracting

autodéfense [otodefɑ̃s] **NF** self-defence
• **d'autodéfense** **ADJ** *(arme)* defensive; **groupe d'a.** vigilante group

autodestructeur, -trice [otodestryktœr, -tris] **ADJ** self-destructive

autodestruction [otodɛstryksjɔ̃] **NF** self-destruction

autodestructrice [otodestryktris] *voir* **autodestructeur**

autodétermination [otodeterminasjɔ̃] **NF** self-determination

autodiagnostic [otodjagnɔstik] **NM** self-diagnosis

autodidacte [otodidakt] **ADJ** self-taught, self-educated
NMF autodidact

autodrome [otodrom] **NM** *Aut* motor-racing track; *(pour les essais)* car-testing track

auto-école [otoekɔl] *(pl* **auto-écoles)** **NF** driving-school; **voiture a.** driving-school car

autoédition [otoedisjɔ̃] **NF** self-publishing

auto-érotique [otoerɔtik] *(pl* **auto-érotiques)** **ADJ** autoerotic, onanistic

auto-érotisme [otoerɔtism] **NM** autoeroticism, onanism

autofécondation [otofekɔ̃dasjɔ̃] **NF** *Biol* self-fertilization, self-fertilizing

autofiction [otofiksjɔ̃] **NF** *Littérature* autofiction

autofinancé, -e [otofinɑ̃se] **ADJ** self-financed; **3 milliards d'euros autofinancés à un tiers seulement** 3 billion euros, only a third of which was self-financed

autofinancement [otofinɑ̃smɑ̃] **NM** self-financing; **capacité d'a.** cash flow

autofinancer [16] [otofinɑ̃se] **s'autofinancer** **VPR 1** *(entreprise)* to be self-financing **2** *(personne)* to be self-supporting

autoflagellation [otoflaʒelasjɔ̃] **NF** self-flagellation, autoflagellation

autoflageller [4] [otoflaʒele] **s'autoflageller** **VPR** to self-flagellate; *Fig* to be too self-critical, to beat oneself up; **inutile de t'a. pour ça** don't beat yourself up about it

autofocus [otofɔkys] *Phot* **ADJ** autofocus
NM 1 *(système)* autofocus system **2** *(appareil)* autofocus camera

autogène [otoʒɛn] **ADJ** *Méd & Tech* autogenous

autogenèse [otoʒənez] **NF** *Biol* autogenesis

autogéré, -e [otoʒere] **ADJ** self-managed, self-run

autogestion [otoʒɛstjɔ̃] **NF** (workers') self-management; **entreprise/université en a.** self-managed company/university

autogestionnaire [otoʒɛstjɔnɛr] **ADJ** based on workers' self-management
NMF advocate of workers' self-management

autogire [otoʒir] **NM** *Astron* autogiro

autographe [otograf] **ADJ** handwritten, autograph *(avant n)*
NM autograph

autogreffe [otogrɛf] **NF** *Méd* autograft; **faire une a.** to carry out an autograft

autoguidage [otogidaʒ] **NM** homing guidance

autoguidé, -e [otogide] **ADJ** *(avion)* remotely piloted; *(missile)* guided

auto-immun, -e [otoimœ̃, -yn] *(mpl* **auto-immuns,** *fpl* **auto-immunes)** **ADJ** *Méd* autoimmune

auto-immunisation [otoimynizasjɔ̃] *(pl* **auto-immunisations)** **NF** *Méd* autoimmunity

auto-induction [otoɛ̃dyksjɔ̃] *(pl* **auto-inductions)** **NF** *Élec* self-induction

auto-intoxication [otoɛ̃tɔksikasjɔ̃] *(pl* **auto-intoxications)** **NF** *Méd* self-poisoning, autointoxication

autolimitation [otolimitasjɔ̃] **NF** setting of voluntary limits

autolimiter [3] [otolimite] **VT** to set voluntary limits to; **les Japonais autolimitent leurs exportations de voitures** the Japanese set voluntary limits to their car exports

autolubrifiant, -e [otolybrifjɑ̃, -ɑ̃t] **ADJ** self-lubricating

autolubrification [otolybrifikasjɔ̃] **NF** self-lubrication

autolyse [otoliz] **NF** *Biol* autolysis

automate [ɔtɔmat] **NM 1** *(robot)* automaton, robot; **comme un a.** like a robot **2** *Suisse (machine)* vending machine; *(à billets) Br* cashpoint, *Am* ATM

automation [ɔtɔmasjɔ̃] **NF** automation

automatique [ɔtɔmatik] **ADJ** automatic; **de façon a.** automatically; **il est absent tous les lundis, c'est a.** he's off every Monday without fail
NM 1 *(téléphone)* **l'a.** direct dialling **2** *(arme)* automatic
NF 1 *Aut* automatic (car) **2** *(science)* automation, cybernetics *(singulier)*

automatiquement [ɔtɔmatikmɑ̃] **ADV** automatically

automatisable [ɔtɔmatizabl] **ADJ** automatable

automatisation [ɔtɔmatizasjɔ̃] **NF** automation

automatiser [3] [ɔtɔmatize] **VT** to automate
VPR s'automatiser to become automated

automatisme [ɔtɔmatism] **NM 1** *(habitude)* automatism; **fermer la porte à double tour est devenu un a.** double-locking the door has become automatic **2** *(dispositif)* automatic device

automédication [otomedikasjɔ̃] **NF** *Méd* self-medication

automitrailleuse [otomitrajøz] **NF** *Mil* armoured car

automnal, -e, -aux, -ales [otɔnal, -o] ADJ *Br* autumnal, autumn *(avant n)*, *Am* fall *(avant n)*; **des teintes automnales** autumnal hues

automne [otɔn] NM *Br* autumn, *Am* fall; *Littéraire* **l'a. de sa vie** the autumn of his/her life

automobile [otomɔbil] NF **1** *Aut (véhicule) Br* motor car, *Am* automobile **2** *Sport* driving, *Br* motoring **3** *(industrie)* car industry

ADJ **1** *(des voitures ▸ accessoire, industrie)* car *(avant n)*; *(▸ club)* automobile *(avant n)*; *(bateau, engin)* automotive, self-propelled **2** *Admin (vignette)* car *(avant n)*; *(assurance)* car, automobile *(avant n)*

automobilisme [otomɔbilism] NM *Aut* driving, *Br* motoring

automobiliste [otomɔbilist] NMF *Aut* driver, *Br* motorist

automoteur, -trice [otomɔtœr, -tris] ADJ automotive, motorized, self-propelled

NM **1** *Mil* self-propelled gun **2** *Naut* self-propelled barge

• **automotrice** NF electric railcar

automutilation [otomytilasjɔ̃] NF self-harm, self-mutilation

automutiler [3] [otomytile] **s'automutiler** VPR to self-mutilate; *Psy* to self-harm; **de nombreux soldats s'automutilaient pour ne pas être envoyés au front** many soldiers would deliberately injure themselves so as not to be sent to the front

autoneige [otonɛʒ] NF *Can* snowmobile *(used to carry several passengers)*

autonettoyant, -e [otonɛtwajɑ̃, -ɑ̃t] ADJ self-cleaning

autonome [otɔnɔm, otonom] ADJ **1** *(autogéré ▸ territoire, organisme)* autonomous, self-governing; *(▸ gouvernement)* autonomous; **gestion a.** managerial autonomy

2 *(non affilié ▸ syndicat)* independent

3 *(libre ▸ personne, caractère, personnalité)* self-sufficient, independent

4 *(appareil)* self-contained; *Ordinat* stand-alone

autonomie [otɔnɔmi, otonomi] NF **1** *(d'une personne)* autonomy, independence; *(d'un État, d'un pays)* autonomy, self-government **2** *(d'un véhicule, d'un avion)* range; *(d'une batterie)* life; **ce rasoir a une a. de 30 minutes** the razor will run for 30 minutes before it needs recharging; **a. de vol** flight range

autonomiste [otɔnɔmist, otonomist] *Pol* ADJ separatist

NMF separatist

autopalpation [otopalpasjɔ̃] NF *Méd* self-examination *(of breasts)*

auto-patrouille [otopatruj] *(pl* **autos-patrouilles)** NF *Can* patrol car

autopont [otopɔ̃] NM *Br* flyover, *Am* overpass

autoportant, -e [otopɔrtɑ̃, -ɑ̃t] ADJ *Constr* self-supporting

autoportrait [otopɔrtrɛ] NM self-portrait; **faire son a.** to paint a self-portrait

autoproduction [otoprɔdyksjɔ̃] NF *Écon* self-supply

autopropulsé, -e [otoprɔpylse] ADJ self-propelled

autopropulsion [otoprɔpylsjɔ̃] NF self-propulsion

autopsie [otɔpsi, otɔpsi] NF **1** *Méd* autopsy, *Br* post mortem (examination); **pratiquer une a.** to perform an autopsy *or Br* a post mortem (examination) **2** *(analyse)* critical analysis, autopsy, *Br* post mortem; **faire l'a. d'un conflit** to go into the causes of a conflict

autopsier [9] [otɔpsje, otɔpsje] VT *Méd* to perform an autopsy *or* a post mortem (examination) on

autopunition [otopynisjɔ̃] NF *Psy* self-punishment

autoradio [otoradjo] NM car radio

auto-rafraîchissement [otorafrɛʃismɑ̃] NM *Ordinat* auto-refresh

autorail [otoraj] NM *Rail* railcar

autoréglage [otoreglaʒ] NM *Tech* automatic control

autorégulateur, -trice [otoregylatœr, -tris] ADJ *Tech* self-regulating

autorégulation [otoregylasjɔ̃] NF **1** *Biol & Physiol* self-regulation **2** *Tech* automatic regulation

autorégulatrice [otoregylatris] *voir* **autorégulateur**

autorisation [otɔrizasjɔ̃] NF **1** *(consentement ▸ d'un parent)* permission, consent; *(▸ d'un supérieur)* permission, authorization; *(▸ d'un groupe)* authorization; **demander l'a. de faire qch** to ask permission to do sth; **donner son a. à qch** to consent to sth; **donner à qn l'a. de faire qch** to give sb permission to do sth; **qui t'a donné l'a. de prendre ces pommes?** who said you could have these apples?; **je n'ai pas eu l'a. de sortir ce soir** I didn't get permission to go out tonight; **faire qch sans a.** to do sth without permission; **a. maritale** husband's authorization; **a. de vol** flight clearance

2 *Admin (acte officiel)* authorization, licence, permit; **avoir l'a. de vendre qch** to be licensed to sell sth; **a. d'exporter** export permit; *Pharm* **a. de mise sur le marché** = official authorization for marketing a pharmaceutical product; **a. de sortie** *(d'un lycée)* (special) pass; **a. de sortie du territoire** parental authorization *(permitting a minor to leave a country)*

3 *Banque* **une a. de 1000 euros** a temporary overdraft of up to 1,000 euros; **a. de crédit** credit line, line of credit; **a. de découvert** overdraft facility; **a. de prélèvement** direct debit mandate

4 *Ordinat* **a. d'accès** access authorization

autorisé, -e [otɔrize] ADJ **1** *Journ* official; **de source autorisée, le président aurait déjà signé l'accord** sources close to the President say that he's already signed the agreement; **les milieux autorisés** official circles **2** *(agréé ▸ aliment, colorant)* permitted **3** *(qui a la permission)* **personnes autorisées** authorized persons

autoriser [3] [otɔrize] VT **1** *(permettre ▸ manifestation, réunion, publication)* to authorize, to allow; *(▸ emprunt)* to authorize, to approve; **le défilé n'avait pas été autorisé** no permission *or* authorization had been given for the march (to be held); **une pétition pour faire a. la sortie d'un film** a petition to have a film passed for release **2** *(donner l'autorisation à)* **a. qn à** to allow sb *or* to give sb permission to; **je ne t'ai pas autorisé à utiliser ma voiture** I never said you could use my car; **je ne t'autorise pas à me parler sur ce ton** I won't have you talk to me like that; **a. qn à faire** *(lui en donner le droit)* to entitle sb *or* to give sb the right to do; **sa réponse nous autorise à penser que...** from his/her reply we may deduce that..., his/her reply leads us to conclude that... **3** *(justifier)* to justify, *Sout* to permit of; **la jeunesse n'autorise pas tous les débordements** being young isn't an excuse for uncontrolled behaviour; **cette dépêche n'autorise plus le moindre espoir** this news spells the end of any last remaining hopes

VPR **s'autoriser 1** *(s'offrir)* **je m'autorise un petit verre de vin le soir** I allow myself a small glass of wine in the evening **2 s'a. de** *(se servir de)* to use as a pretext, to take advantage of; **elle s'autorise de sa confiance** she exploits his/her confidence in her

autoritaire [otɔritɛr] ADJ authoritarian

NMF authoritarian

autoritairement [otɔritɛrmɑ̃] ADV in an authoritarian way, with (excessive) authority

autoritarisme [otɔritarism] NM authoritarianism

autorité [otɔrite] NF **1** *(pouvoir)* authority, power; **l'a. de la loi** the authority *or* power of the law; **un territoire soumis à l'a. de...** an area within the jurisdiction of...; **par a. de justice** by order of the court; **avoir de l'a. sur qn** to be in *or* to have authority over sb; **il n'a aucune a. sur ses élèves** he can't keep order over *or* he has no control over his pupils; **être sous l'a. de qn** to be *or* to come under sb's authority; **se mettre sous l'a. de qn** to place oneself under sb's authority; **exercer son a. sur qn** to exercise authority over sb; **faire qch de sa propre a.** to do sth on one's own authority; **avoir a. pour faire qch** to have authority to do sth; **l'a. parentale** *(droits)* parental rights; *(devoirs)* parental responsibilities

2 *(fermeté)* authority; **ses parents n'ont aucune a.** his/her parents don't have any control over him/her; **faire preuve d'a. envers un enfant** to show some authority towards a child; **il a besoin d'un peu d'a.** he needs to be taken in hand

3 *(compétence)* authority; *(expert)* authority, expert; **dire qch en invoquant l'a. de qn** to say sth on sb's authority; **parler de qch avec a.** to talk authoritatively about sth; **édition/version qui fait a.** authoritative *or* definitive edition/version; **essai qui fait a.** seminal essay; **c'est une a. en matière de...** he's/she's an authority *or* expert on...

4 *Admin (pouvoir établi)* authority; **l'a., les autorités** *(personnel)* the authorities; **les autorités françaises** the French authorities; **a. judiciaire** judicial power, judiciary; **les autorités militaires/religieuses** the military/religious authorities; **s'adresser à l'a. compétente** to apply to the appropriate authority; **a. de régulation** regulating body; **un agent** *ou* **représentant de l'a.** an official; **les autorités ont dû intervenir** the authorities had to intervene

• **d'autorité** ADV without consultation; **si tu ne me le donnes pas, je le prendrai d'a.** if you won't give it to me I'll take it without asking you; **d'a., j'ai décidé de fermer la bibliothèque le mercredi** I decided on my own authority to close the library on Wednesdays; **ils ont gelé les crédits d'a.** they unilaterally stopped the funding

autoroute [otorut] NF **1** *Aut Br* motorway, *Am* freeway; **conduite sur a.** *Br* motorway *or Am* freeway driving; **a. à péage** *Br* toll motorway, *Am* turnpike **2** *Ordinat* **l'a. de l'information** the information superhighway

autoroutier, -ère [otorutje, -ɛr] *Aut* ADJ *Br* motorway *(avant n)*, *Am* freeway *(avant n)*

• **autoroutière** NF = car particularly suited to *Br* motorway *or Am* freeway driving conditions

autosatisfaction [otosatisfaksjɔ̃] NF self-satisfaction

autos-couchettes [otokuʃɛt] ADJ INV **train a.** car-sleeper train

auto-stop [otostɔp] NM hitch-hiking, hitching; **faire de l'a.** to hitch-hike, to hitch; **elle a fait de l'a. jusqu'à Chicago** she hitch-hiked to *or* she hitched (a ride) to Chicago; **nous allons faire le tour de l'Europe en a.** we're going to hitch-hike around Europe; **prendre qn en a.** to give sb a lift *or* a ride

auto-stoppeur, -euse [otostɔpœr, -øz] *(mpl* **auto-stoppeurs**, *fpl* **auto-stoppeuses)** NM,F hitch-hiker; **prendre un a.** to pick up a hitch-hiker

autosuffisance [otosyfizɑ̃s] NF *Écon* self-sufficiency

autosuggestion [otosygʒɛstjɔ̃] NF *Psy* autosuggestion

autotest [ototɛst] NM *Ordinat* self-test

autotester [3] [ototɛste] **s'autotester** VPR *Ordinat* to self-test

autour[1] [otur] NM *Orn* goshawk

autour[2] [otur] ADV around, round; **mets du papier de soie a.** wrap it up in tissue paper; **tout a.** all around; **il y avait un arbre et les enfants couraient (tout) a.** there was a tree and the children were running round it; **une nappe avec des broderies tout a.** a tablecloth with embroidery all around it *or* round the edges

• **autour de** PRÉP **1** *(dans l'espace)* around; **a. du village** around the village; **il observait les gens a. de lui** he looked at the people around him; **discuter qch a. d'un verre** to discuss sth over a drink **2** *(indiquant une approximation)* around; **il gagne a. de 12 000 euros** he earns around 12,000 euros; **elle a a. de 20 ans** she's about 20; **il a fait beaucoup de films a. des années 30** he made a lot of films around the 1930s; **ils sont arrivés a. de 20 heures** they arrived (at) around 8 p.m.

autovaccin [otovaksɛ̃] NM *Méd* autogenous vaccine

AUTRE [otr]

ADJ
- another **1, 2**
- different **1, 3**
- other **5, 7**

PRON
- other **1–3**
- else **1, 2**
- another **3**

NM
- other

ADJ INDÉFINI 1 *(distinct, différent)* **un a. homme** another *or* a different man; **il a rencontré une a. femme** he's met another woman; **vous avez cette jupe dans une a. taille?** do you have this skirt in another *or* in a different size?; **donnez-moi une a. tasse, celle-ci est ébréchée** give me another *or* a new cup, this one's chipped; **j'ai une a. idée** I've got another idea; **en d'autres lieux** elsewhere; **dans d'autres circonstances...** in other circumstances..., had the circumstances been different...; **tu veux a. chose?** do you want anything else?; **il n'y a que du fromage, je n'ai pas a. chose** there's only cheese, I haven't got anything else; **toute a. réaction m'aurait surpris** any other reaction would've surprised me; **la vérité est tout a.** the truth is quite *or* very *or* altogether different; **je me faisais une tout a. idée de la question** I had quite a different concept of the matter; *Fam* **ça c'est une a. histoire** *ou* **affaire** *ou* **paire de manches** that's something else altogether, that's another story *or* a different kettle of fish; **autres temps, autres mœurs** other days, other ways

2 *(supplémentaire)* **voulez-vous un a. café?** would you like another coffee?; **il n'y a pas d'autres verres?** aren't there any other glasses?; **une a. bière, s'il vous plaît** another beer please; **un a. mot sur le sujet** another *or* one more word on the subject; **elle est partie sans autres explications** she left without further explanation; **il nous faut une a. chaise** we need one more *or* an extra *or* another chair; **essaie une a. fois** try again *or* one more time

3 *(devenu différent)* different; **c'est un a. appartement maintenant!** it's quite a different *Br* flat *or Am* apartment now!, the *Br* flat *or Am* apartment is completely transformed now!; **je me sens un a. homme** I feel a different *or* new man; **je me sens, comment dire, a.** I feel, how can I put it, different; **un tout a. homme** a completely different man; **avec des fines herbes, ça a un tout a. goût!** it tastes completely different with some mixed herbs added!; **elle est tout a. désormais** she's completely different now

4 *(marquant la supériorité)* **leur ancien appartement avait un a. cachet!** their old *Br* flat *or Am* apartment had far more character!; **leurs émissions sont d'une a. qualité!** their programmes are far better!; **le Japon, ah c'est a. chose!** Japan, now that's really something else!; **Marc est bon en maths, mais Jean c'est a. chose!** Marc is good at maths, but Jean is in a different class altogether!

5 *(restant)* other, remaining; **les autres passagers ont été rapatriés en autobus** the other passengers were taken home by bus

6 *(avec les pronoms "nous" et "vous")* **nous autres consommateurs...** we consumers...; **vous autres Français...** you French people...; *Fam* **écoutez-le, vous autres!** listen to him, you lot!

7 *(dans le temps)* other; **on y est allés l'a. jour** we went there the other day; **on ira une a. année** we'll go another year; **l'a. fois** the other time; **d'autres fois** other times; **en d'autres temps** in other times; *(dans le passé)* in days gone by; **l'a. matin** the other morning; **je l'ai vu l'a. dimanche** I saw him the other Sunday; **un a. jour** some other day; **je reviendrai à un a. moment** I'll come back some other time; **dans l'a. vie** in the next world; **dans une a. vie** in another life

8 *(en corrélation avec "l'un")* **l'une et l'a. hypothèses sont valables** both hypotheses are valid; **l'un ou l'a. projet devra être accepté** one of the two projects will have to be accepted; **ni l'une ni l'a. explication n'est plausible** neither explanation is plausible

PRON 1 *(désignant des personnes)* **un a.** someone else, somebody else; **d'autres** other people, others; **on n'attend pas les autres?** aren't we going to wait for the others?; **d'autres que moi vous donneront les explications nécessaires** others will give you the necessary explanations; **plus que tout a., tu aurais dû prévoir que...** you of all people should have foreseen that...; **tout** *ou* **un a. que lui aurait refusé** anyone else but him would have refused; **quelqu'un d'a.** someone else; **aucun a., nul a.** no one else, nobody else, none other; **personne d'a.** no one else, nobody else; **bien d'autres ont essayé** a lot of other people have tried; **elle est plus futée que les autres** she's cleverer than (any of) the others; **comme dit** *ou* **dirait l'a.** as they say; *Fam* **à d'autres!** go on with you!, come off it!; *Fam* **et l'a. qui n'arrête pas de pleurer!** now the other one won't stop crying!; *Fam* **eh l'a., il est fou!** listen to that one *or* him, he's mad!

2 *(désignant des choses)* **un a.** another one; **d'autres** other ones, others; **une maison semblable à une a.** a house like any other; **le restaurant ne me disait rien, nous en avons cherché un a.** the restaurant didn't appeal to me, (so) we looked for another one; **ce livre ou l'a.** this book or the other one; **mes chaussures sont sales, il faut que je mette les autres** my shoes are dirty, I'll have to wear the other ones; **je n'en ai pas besoin d'autres** I don't need any more; **quelque chose d'a.** something else; **rien d'a.** nothing else; *Suisse* **sans a.** *(sans plus)* without further ado; *(facilement)* easily

3 *(en corrélation avec "l'un")* **l'une chante, l'a. danse** one sings, the other dances; **l'un et l'a.** both of them; **l'un ou l'a.** (either) one or the other, either one; **je l'ai su par l'une ou l'a. de ses collègues** I heard it through one or other of his colleagues; **l'un après l'a.** one after another *or* the other; **ils marchaient l'un derrière l'a./l'un à côté de l'a.** they were walking one behind the other/side by side; **ni l'un ni l'a. n'est venu** neither (of them) came; **je n'ai pu les joindre ni l'un ni l'a.** I couldn't get hold of either (one) of them; **on ne peut pas les distinguer l'un de l'a.** you can't tell one from the other, you can't tell them apart; **on les prend souvent l'un pour l'a.** people often mistake one for the other; **les uns le détestent, les autres l'adorent** he's loathed by some, loved by others; **aimez-vous les uns les autres** love one another; **aidez-vous les uns les autres** help each other *or* one another; **n'écoute pas ce que disent les uns et les autres** don't listen to what people say; **l'un ne va pas sans l'a.** you can't have one without the other; **présente-les l'un à l'a.** introduce them to each other; **ils sont tout l'un pour l'a.** they mean everything to each other; **l'un dans l'a.** all in all, at the end of the day

NM *Phil* **l'a.** the other

---

autrefois [otrəfwa] **ADV** in the past, in former times *or* days; **je l'ai bien connu a.** I knew him well once; **a. s'élevait ici un château médiéval** there used to be a medieval castle here; **d'a.** of old, of former times; **les maisons d'a. n'avaient aucun confort** in the past *or* in the old days, houses were very basic; **sa vie d'a.** his/her past life; **des chants d'a.** old-time songs

autrement [otrəmɑ̃] **ADV 1** *(différemment)* another *or* some other way; **la banque est fermée, je vais me débrouiller a.** the bank's closed, I'll find some other way (of getting money); **il est habillé a. que d'habitude** he hasn't got his usual clothes on; **comment pourrait-il en être a.** how could things be different?; **il n'en a jamais été a.** things have always been this way *or* have never been any other way *or* have never been any different; **nous ne les laisserons pas construire la route ici, il faudra qu'ils fassent a.** we won't let them build the road here, they'll have to find another *or* some other way; **il n'y a pas moyen de faire a.** there's no other way *or* no alternative; **j'ai accepté, je n'ai pas pu faire a.** I had no alternative but to say yes; **je n'ai pu faire a. que de les entendre** I couldn't help but overhear them; **on ne peut faire a. que d'admirer son audace** one can't but admire his/her daring

2 *(sinon)* otherwise, or else; **payez car a. vous aurez des ennuis** pay up or else you'll get into trouble; **les gens sont désagréables, a. le travail est intéressant** the people are unpleasant, but otherwise *or* apart from that the work's interesting

3 *(beaucoup)* far; *(beaucoup plus)* far more; **c'est a. plus grave cette fois-ci** it's far more serious this time; **il est a. moins intelligent que son premier mari** he's much less bright than her first husband

• **autrement dit ADV** in other words

• **pas autrement ADV** not particularly; **cela ne me surprend pas a.** that does not particularly surprise me

Autriche [otriʃ] **NF l'A.** Austria

autrichien, -enne [otriʃjɛ̃, -ɛn] **ADJ** Austrian

• **Autrichien, -enne NM,F** Austrian; *Hist* **l'Autrichienne** (Queen) Marie-Antoinette

autruche [otryʃ] **NF** *Orn* ostrich; **des chaussures en a.** ostrich-skin shoes; *Fig* **faire l'a.** to bury one's head in the sand

autrui [otrɥi] **PRON INDÉFINI** others, other people; **la liberté d'a.** other people's freedom, the freedom of others; *Prov* **ne fais pas à a. ce que tu ne voudrais pas qu'on te fît** do as you would be done by

auvent [ovɑ̃] **NM 1** *(en dur)* porch roof; **un toit en a.** a sloping roof **2** *(en toile)* awning, canopy

auvergnat, -e [ovɛrɲa, -at] **ADJ** of/from the Auvergne

NM *Ling* = dialect spoken in the Auvergne

• **Auvergnat, -e NM,F** = inhabitant of or person from the Auvergne

aux [o] *voir* **à**

auxiliaire [oksiljɛr] **ADJ 1** *Ling* auxiliary **2** *(personnel)* auxiliary, extra; **services auxiliaires de l'armée** non-combatant services **3** *Tech* auxiliary, standby

NMF 1 *(employé temporaire)* temporary worker; **ce n'est qu'un a.** he's only temporary

2 *Jur* **a. de justice** representative of the law

3 *Méd* **a. médical** paramedic; **les auxiliaires médicaux** the paramedical profession

4 *(travailleur social)* **a. de vie sociale** ≃ social worker

5 *(aide)* helper, assistant; **elle m'a été une a. infatigable** she was a constant help to me

6 *Mil* **a. féminin de l'armée de terre** = female member of the French army

NM 1 *Ling* auxiliary **2** *(outil, moyen)* aid

• **auxiliaires NMPL 1** *Antiq* = foreign troops of the Roman Army **2** *Naut (moteurs)* auxiliary engines; *(équipement)* auxiliary equipment *(UNCOUNT)*

auxquels, auxquelles *voir* **lequel**

AV 1 *Banque (abrév écrite* **avis de virement***)* (bank) transfer advice **2** *(abrév écrite* **avant***)* front

Av., av. *(abrév écrite* **avenue***)* Ave.

avachi, -e [avaʃi] **ADJ 1** *(sans tenue ▸ vêtement)* crumpled, rumpled, shapeless; *(▸ sommier, canapé)* sagging; *(▸ chaussures, chapeau)* shapeless; *(▸ cuir)* limp; *(▸ gâteau, soufflé)* collapsed **mon vieux pantalon a.** my baggy old trousers **2** *(indolent)* flabby, spineless; **être a. dans un fauteuil** to be slumped in an armchair

avachir [32] [avaʃir] **VT** *(personne, muscles)* to make flabby; **la chaleur m'avachit** the heat makes me feel quite limp *or* floppy

VPR s'avachir 1 *(s'affaisser ▸ vêtement, chaussures)* to become shapeless; *(▸ sommier, canapé)* to start sagging; *(▸ cuir)* to go limp; *(▸ gâteau, soufflé)* to collapse **2** *(s'affaler)* **s'a. dans un fauteuil/sur une table** to slump into an armchair/over a table **3** *(se laisser aller)* to let oneself go

avachissement [avaʃismɑ̃] **NM 1** *(perte de tenue ▸ d'un vêtement)* becoming limp, losing (its) shape; *(▸ de chaussures)* wearing out; *(▸ d'un sommier, d'un canapé)* starting to sag; **lutter contre l'a. des tissus musculaires** to prevent the slackening of muscles

2 *(état déformé)* limp *or* worn-down appearance

3 *(perte de courage ▸ physique)* going limp; *(▸ moral)* loss of moral fibre

4 *(état physique ▸ temporaire)* limpness; *(▸ permanent)* flabbiness; *(découragement)* loss of moral fibre; *(veulerie)* spinelessness

aval, -als [aval] **NM 1** *Fin & Jur (d'un effet de commerce)* endorsement, guarantee; **donner son a. à une traite/un billet** to guarantee *or* to endorse a draft/a bill; **a. bancaire** bank guarantee

2 *(soutien)* support; **donner son a. à qn** to back sb (up)

3 *(autorisation)* authorization; **avoir l'a. des autorités** to have (an) official authorization; **donner son a. à qn/qch** to give sb/sth one's approval; **pour a.** *(sur document)* for approval

4 *(d'une rivière)* downstream water

5 *(d'une pente)* downhill side *(of a slope)*; **faites face à l'a.** face the valley; **regardez vers l'a.** look down the slope

ADJ ski/skieur a. downhill ski/skier

• **en aval de PRÉP 1** *(en suivant une rivière)* downstream *or* downriver from **2** *(en montagne)* downhill from **3** *(après)* following on from; **les**

étapes qui se situent en a. de la production the post-production stages

avalanche [avalɑ̃ʃ] **NF 1** *Géol* avalanche **2** *Fig (quantité ▸ de courrier, de protestations, de compliments, de lumière)* flood; *(▸ de coups, d'insultes)* shower; **il y eut une a. de réponses** the answers came pouring in

avalancheux, -euse [avalɑ̃ʃø, -øz] **ADJ** *Géol* avalanche-prone

avaler [3] [avale] **VT 1** *(consommer ▸ nourriture)* to swallow; *(▸ boisson)* to swallow, to drink; **a. qch d'un (seul) coup** *ou* **d'un trait** to swallow sth in one gulp; **j'ai dû a. quelque chose de travers** something went down the wrong way; **je n'ai rien avalé depuis deux jours** I haven't had a thing to eat for two days; **a. du lait à petites gorgées** to sip milk; **a. sa salive** to swallow; **à midi, elle prend à peine le temps d'a. son déjeuner** at lunchtime, she bolts her meal

2 *Fig* **le distributeur a avalé ma carte!** the *Br* cash machine *or Am* ATM has eaten *or* swallowed my card!; **tu as avalé ta langue?** have you lost your tongue?, has the cat got your tongue?; **a. les obstacles/les kilomètres** to make light work of any obstacle/of distances; **a. ses mots** to swallow one's words; **vouloir tout a.** to be hungry *or* thirsty for experience; **a. qn tout cru** to eat sb alive; *Fam* **a. son bulletin** *ou* **son acte de naissance** *ou* **sa chique** to kick the bucket, to go and meet one's maker; **comme quelqu'un qui aurait avalé son** *ou* **un parapluie** *(raide)* stiffly, with his/her back like a rod; *(manquant d'adaptabilité)* stiffly, starchily

3 *(inhaler ▸ fumée, vapeurs)* to inhale, to breathe in; **a. la fumée** to inhale

4 *(lire ▸ roman, article)* to devour; **une petite anthologie que vous avalerez en un après-midi** a short anthology which you will read *or* get through in one afternoon

5 *Fam (croire ▸ mensonge)* to swallow, to buy; **vous croyez que je vais a. ça?** do you think I'll buy that?; **il a avalé mon histoire (toute crue)** he swallowed my story hook, line and sinker; **je lui ai fait a. que j'étais malade** I got him/her to believe that I was sick; **on ne nous le fera pas a.** it won't wash (with us); **elle lui ferait a. n'importe quoi** he/she believes anything she says

6 *Fam (accepter ▸ insulte)* to swallow; *Fig* **pilule difficile à a.** hard *or* bitter pill to swallow; *Fig* **a. la pilule** to swallow the bitter pill; **a. des couleuvres** *(insultes)* to swallow insults; *(mensonges)* to be taken in; **faire a. des couleuvres à qn** *(insultes)* to humiliate sb; *(mensonges)* to take sb in

USAGE ABSOLU *(manger, boire)* to swallow

avaleur [avalœr] **NM a. de sabres** sword swallower

avaliser [3] [avalize] **VT 1** *Jur (effet de commerce)* to endorse, to guarantee; *(signature)* to guarantee **2** *(donner son accord à)* to back, to condone, to support

avaliseur [avalizœr], **avaliste** [avalist] **NM** *Jur* endorser, guarantor, backer

avaloir [avalwar] **NM 1** *(de conduit)* head; *(de cheminée)* hood **2** *Pêche* fish trap **3** *Fam* throat, gullet

à-valoir [avalwar] **NM INV** advance (payment)

AVANCE [avɑ̃s]

• ahead **1**	• early **1**
• lead **3**	• advance **4–6**

NF 1 *(par rapport au temps prévu)* **prendre de l'a. dans ses études** to get ahead in one's studies; **j'ai pris de l'a. sur le** *ou* **par rapport au planning** I'm ahead of schedule; **avoir de l'a. sur** *ou* **par rapport à ses concurrents** to be ahead of the competition *or* of one's competitors; **arriver avec dix minutes/jours d'a.** to arrive ten minutes/days early; **le livreur a une heure d'a.** the delivery man is an hour early; **le maillot jaune a pris 37 secondes d'a.** the yellow jersey's 37 seconds ahead of time

2 *(d'une montre, d'un réveil)* **ma montre a une minute d'a.** my watch is one minute fast; **ma montre prend une seconde d'a. toutes les heures** my watch gains a second every hour

3 *(avantage ▸ d'une entreprise)* lead; *(▸ d'une armée)* progress, advance; **l'a. prise par notre pays en matière de génétique** our country's lead in genetics; **perdre son a. sur un marché/dans une discipline scolaire** to lose one's lead in a market/ school subject; **conserver son a. sur ses concurrents** to retain one's lead over one's competitors; **ralentir l'a. de qn** to slow sb's progress; **avoir dix points d'a. sur qn** to have a ten-point lead over sb; **elle a une a. de dix mètres sur la Britannique** she leads the British girl by ten metres, she has a ten-metre lead over the British girl; **avoir une demi-longueur d'a.** to lead by half a length

4 *(dans un approvisionnement)* **prends ce beurre, j'en ai plusieurs paquets d'a.** have this butter, I keep several packs in reserve; **de la sauce tomate? j'en fais toujours d'a.** tomato sauce? I always make some in advance

5 *Fin (acompte)* advance; **donner à qn une a. sur son salaire** to give sb an advance on his/her salary; **faire une a. de 100 euros à qn** to advance 100 euros to sb; **avances** sums advanced; **a. bancaire** bank advance; **a. à découvert** unsecured *or* uncovered advance; **avances en devises** foreign currency loan; **a. de fonds** advance, loan; **a. sur honoraires** retainer; **a. en numéraire** cash advance; **a. sur recette** loan to a producer *(to be recouped against box-office takings)*; **a. sur titre** collateral loan; **a. de trésorerie** cash advance

6 *Aut* **a. à l'allumage** ignition advance

7 *Tech* **a. rapide** fast forward

8 *Ordinat* **a. automatique** automatic feed

• **avances NFPL** *(propositions ▸ d'amitié, d'association)* overtures, advances; *(▸ sexuelles)* advances; **faire des avances à qn** *(sujet: séducteur)* to make advances to sb; *(sujet: entreprise)* to make overtures to sb; **ils nous ont fait quelques avances mais rien n'a été signé** they made a few overtures but there was no actual deal

• **à l'avance ADV** *(payer, informer)* in advance, beforehand; **vous le saurez à l'a.** you'll know beforehand; **dites-le-moi bien à l'a.** tell me well in advance, give me plenty of notice; **je n'ai été averti que deux minutes à l'a.** I was only warned two minutes beforehand, I only got two minutes' notice; **acheter un billet deux mois à l'a.** to buy a ticket two months in advance; **réservez longtemps à l'a.** book early; **je savais à l'a. qu'il allait mentir** I knew in advance *or* I could tell beforehand that he would lie

• **d'avance, par avance ADV** *(payer, remercier)* in advance; **d'a. merci** thanking you in advance; **savourant d'a. sa revanche** already savouring his/ her planned revenge; **c'est joué d'a.** it's a foregone conclusion; *Fam* **c'est tout combiné d'a.** it's a put-up job; **d'a. je peux te dire qu'il n'est pas fiable** I can tell you right away *or* now that he's not reliable

• **en avance ADJ elle est en a. sur le reste de la classe** she's ahead of the rest of the class; **être en a. sur son temps** *ou* **époque** to be ahead of one's time; **être en a. sur la concurrence** to be ahead of the competition **ADV** *(avant l'heure prévue)* early; **arriver en a.** to arrive early; **elle arrive** *ou* **elle est toujours en a.** she's always early; **être en a.** to be early; **être en a. de dix minutes/jours** to be ten minutes/days early; **je me dépêche, je ne suis pas en a.!** I must rush, I'm (rather) late!

avancé, -e [avɑ̃se] **ADJ 1** *(dans le temps ▸ heure)* late; **à une heure avancée** late at night; **à une date avancée de la colonisation romaine** at a late stage in the colonization by Rome; **la saison est avancée** it's late in the season; **les pommiers sont bien avancés cette année** the apple trees are early this year; **à un âge a.** late (on) in life; **arriver à un âge a.** to be getting on in years

2 *(développé ▸ intelligence, économie)* advanced; **un garçon a. pour son âge** a boy who's mature for *or* ahead of his years; **pays parvenus à un stade/ état a. de la technologie** countries that have reached an advanced stage/state of technological development; **à un stade peu a.** at an early stage; **je ne suis pas assez a. dans mon travail pour pouvoir sortir ce soir** I'm not far enough ahead with my work to be able to go out tonight; *Ironique* **te voilà bien a.!** a (fat) lot of good that's done you!

3 *Mil (division, élément)* advance *(avant n)*; **ouvrage a.** outwork

4 *(pourri ▸ poisson, viande)* bad, *Br* off; *(▸ fruit)* overripe; **des pêches un peu avancées** peaches that are past their best

• **avancée NF 1** *(marche)* advance; *Fig (progression)* progress **2** *(d'un toit)* overhang **3** *Pêche* trace, cast, leader

avancement [avɑ̃smɑ̃] **NM 1** *(promotion)* promotion, advancement; **avoir** *ou* **obtenir de l'a.** to get (a) promotion, to get promoted

2 *(progression)* progress; **y a-t-il de l'a. dans les travaux?** is the work progressing?

3 *Jur* **a. d'hoirie** = gift of part of an inheritance given in advance

4 *Ordinat* **a. par friction** friction feed; **a. du papier** sheet feed

AVANCER [16] [avɑ̃se]

VT	
• to move forward **1**	• to bring forward **1, 3**
• to stick out **2**	• to put forward **3, 4**
• to advance **6**	
VI	
• to move forward **1**	• to advance **1**
• to progress **1–3**	• to be getting on **2**
• to stick out **5**	
VPR	
• to move forward **1**	• to make progress **2**
• to commit oneself **3**	• to stick out **4**

VT 1 *(pousser vers l'avant)* to push *or* to move forward; *(amener vers l'avant)* to bring forward; **tu es trop loin, avance ta chaise** you're too far away, move *or* bring your chair forward; **il m'avança un siège et me demanda de m'asseoir** he pulled up a chair for me and asked me to sit down; **a. son assiette** *(vers le plat de service)* to push one's plate forward; **a. les aiguilles d'une horloge** to put the hands of a clock forward; *Hum* **la voiture de Madame/Monsieur est avancée** Madam/Sir, your carriage awaits

2 *(allonger)* **a. la tête** to stick one's head out; **a. le cou** to crane one's neck; **a. sa** *ou* **la main vers qch** *(pour l'attraper)* to reach towards sth; *(pour qu'on vous le donne)* to hold out one's hand for sth

3 *(dans le temps)* to bring *or* to put forward, *Am* to move up; **ils ont dû a. la date de leur mariage** they had to bring the date of their wedding forward; **l'heure du départ a été avancée de dix minutes** the starting time was put forward ten minutes; **la réunion a été avancée à demain/lundi** the meeting was brought forward to tomorrow/ Monday; **a. sa montre (d'une heure)** to put one's watch forward (by an hour)

4 *(proposer ▸ explication, raison, opinion)* to put forward, to suggest, to advance; *(▸ argument, théorie, plan)* to put forward; **être sûr de ce que l'on avance** to be certain of what one is saying; **si ce qu'il avance est vrai** if his allegations are true

5 *(faire progresser)* **a. qn** to help sb along; **je vais rédiger les étiquettes pour vous a.** I'll write out the labels to make it quicker for you *or* to help you along; **voilà qui n'avance pas mes affaires** this isn't much good *or* help (to me), that doesn't get me very far; *Fam* **ça t'avance à quoi de mentir?** what do you gain by lying?; **voilà à quoi ça t'avance de tricher** this is where cheating gets you; **les insultes ne t'avanceront à rien** being abusive will get you nowhere

6 *(prêter ▸ argent, somme, loyer)* to lend, to advance

7 *Hort (plante)* to push, to force

VI 1 *(se déplacer dans l'espace)* to move forward, to proceed, to progress; *Mil* to advance, to progress; **a. d'un pas** to take one step forward; **a. à grands pas** to stride forward *or* along; **a. avec difficulté** to plod along; **a. vers** *ou* **sur qn d'un air menaçant** to advance on *or* towards sb threateningly; **avoir du mal à a.** to make slow progress, to be slowed down in one's progress; **le bus avançait lentement** the bus was moving slowly; **ne restez pas là, avancez!** don't just stand there, move on!; **avance!** *(en voiture)* move!; **faire a. qn/une mule** to move sb/a mule along; **a. vers un objectif** *(armée)* to advance toward *or* on a target; *(entreprise)* to make good progress in trying to fulfil an objective

2 *(progresser ▸ temps, action)* to be getting on, to progress; **l'heure avance** time's getting on, it's getting late; **l'été/l'hiver avance** we're well into the summer/winter; **au fur et à mesure que la nuit avançait** as the night wore on; **ça avance?** how's it going?; **alors, ce tricot, ça avance?** how's this knitting of yours coming along?; **ça avance bien** it's coming along nicely; **les réparations n'avançaient pas/avançaient** the repair work was getting nowhere/was making swift progress; **le projet n'avance plus** the project's come to a halt *or* standstill; **faire a.** *(cause)* to promote; *(connaissances)* to further, to advance; **faire a. les choses** *(accélérer une action)* to speed things up; *(améliorer la situation)* to improve matters

3 *(personne)* to (make) progress, to get further forward; **tu n'avanceras pas en remâchant tes idées noires** you won't get very far by going over the same depressing thoughts again and again; **j'ai l'impression de ne pas a.** I don't feel I'm getting anywhere *or* I'm making any headway; **a. dans une enquête/son travail** to (make) progress in an investigation/one's work; **les peintres avancent vite/lentement** the decorators are making good/slow progress; **a. en âge** *(enfant)* to grow up, to get older; *(personne mûre)* to be getting on in years; **a. en grade** to go up the promotion ladder

4 *(montre, réveil)* **votre montre avance** *ou* **vous avancez de dix minutes** your watch is *or* you are ten minutes fast; **pendule qui avance d'une seconde toutes les heures** clock that gains a second every hour

5 *(faire saillie ▸ nez, menton)* to jut out, to stick out, to protrude; *(▸piton, promontoire)* to jut out, to stick out

VPR s'avancer 1 *(approcher)* to move forward *or* closer; **avancez-vous, les enfants** move forward *or* come closer, children; **elle s'avançait discrètement vers les gâteaux** she was discreetly making her way toward the cakes; **il s'avança vers moi** he came towards me

2 *(prendre de l'avance)* **s'a. dans son travail** to make progress *or* some headway in one's work

3 *(prendre position)* to commit oneself; **je ne voudrais pas m'a., mais il est possible que...** I can't be positive, but it might be that...; **il s'est avancé à la légère** he committed himself rather rashly; **je me suis trop avancé pour me dédire** I've gone too far *or* I'm in too deep to pull out now; **je m'avance peut-être un peu trop en affirmant cela** it might be rash of me to say this

4 *(faire saillie)* to jut out, to stick out, to protrude; **la jetée s'avance dans la mer** the jetty sticks out into the sea

---

avanie [avani] **NF** *Littéraire* snub; **faire (subir) des avanies à qn** to snub sb; **subir des avanies** to be snubbed

---

AVANT [avɑ̃]

PRÉP	
• before **1–3**	• until **1**
ADV	
• before **1**	• far **2**
• first **3**	
ADJ INV	
• forward, front	
NM	
• front **1, 3**	• forward **2**

PRÉP 1 *(dans le temps)* before; **a. le lever du soleil** before sunrise; **il est arrivé a. la nuit/le dîner** he arrived before nightfall/dinner; **je voudrais te voir a. mon départ** I'd like to see you before I leave; **a. son élection** prior to his/her election, before being elected; **a. la guerre** in the pre-war period, before the war; **200 ans a. Jésus-Christ** 200 (years) BC; **je ne serai pas prêt a. une demi-heure** I won't be ready for another half hour; **ne me réveille pas a. onze heures** don't wake me up before eleven; **quand mon manteau sera-t-il prêt? – pas a. mardi** when will my coat be ready? – not before Tuesday; **nous n'ouvrons pas a. dix heures** we don't open until ten; **le contrat sera signé a. deux mois** the contract will be signed within two months; **vous recevrez votre livraison a. la fin du mois** you'll get your delivery before the end *or* by the end of the month; **il faut que je termine a. ce soir** I've got to finish by this evening; **il faut que tu y sois bien a./un peu a. onze heures** you have to be there well before/a bit before eleven; **peu a. les élections** a short while *or* time before the elections

2 *(dans l'espace)* before; **vous tournez à droite juste a. le feu** you turn right just before the lights; **il est tombé a. la ligne d'arrivée** he fell before the finishing line

3 *(dans un rang, un ordre, une hiérarchie)* before; **vous êtes a. moi** *(dans une file d'attente)* you're before me; **il était juste a. moi dans la file** he was just in front of me in the *Br* queue *or Am* line; **leur équipe est maintenant a. la nôtre dans le classement général** their team is now ahead of us in the league; **je place le travail a. tout le reste** I put work above *or* before everything else; **ta santé passe a. ta carrière** your health is more important than *or* comes before your career

ADV 1 *(dans le temps)* before; **quelques jours a.** some days before; **il fallait (y) réfléchir a.** you should have thought (about it) before; **a./après** *(légende de photo)* before/after; **a., j'avais plus de patience avec les enfants** I used to be more patient with children; **a., il n'y avait pas de machines à laver** before *or* in the old days, there weren't any washing machines; **la maison est comme a.** the house has remained the same *or* is the same as it was (before); **peu de temps a.** shortly before *or* beforehand; **quand j'ai un rendez-vous, j'aime arriver un peu a.** when I'm due to meet someone, I like to get there a little ahead of time; **bien** *ou* **longtemps a.** well *or* long before; **on n'a aucune chance de le rattraper, il est parti bien a.** there's no chance of catching up with him, he left well ahead of us; **il est parti quelques minutes a.** he left a few minutes before *or* earlier; **un jour/mois/an a.** a day/month/year earlier; **très a. dans la saison** very late in the season; **discuter/lire bien a. dans la nuit** to talk/to read late into the night

2 *(dans l'espace)* **vous voyez le parc? il y a un restaurant juste a.** see the park? there's a restaurant just before it *or* this side of it; **allons plus a.** let's go further; **il s'était aventuré trop a. dans la forêt** he'd ventured too far into the forest; *Fig* **sans entrer** *ou* **aller plus a. dans les détails** without going into any further *or* more detail; **il est allé trop a. dans les réformes** he went too far with the reforms

3 *(dans un rang, un ordre, une hiérarchie)* **est-ce que je peux passer a.?** can I go first?; **lequel met-on a.?** which one do you put first?; **il y a quelqu'un a.?** *(dans une file d'attente)* is someone else before me?; **tu sortiras cet été, mais tes examens, ça passe a.!** you can go out this summer, but your exams come first!

ADJ INV *(saut périlleux, roulade)* forward; *(roue, siège, partie)* front; **la partie a. du véhicule** the front part of the vehicle

NM 1 *(d'un véhicule)* front; *Naut* bow, bows; **tout l'a. de la voiture a été enfoncé** the front of the car was all smashed in; **il s'est porté vers l'a. du peloton** he moved to the front of the bunch; *Naut* **de l'a. à l'arrière** fore and aft; **à l'a.** in the front; **montez à l'a.** sit in the front; *aussi Fig* **aller de l'a.** to forge ahead; *Can* **mettre qch de l'a.** to put sth forward

2 *Sport* forward; *(au volley)* front-line player; **il est a. dans son équipe de foot** he's a forward in his football team; **jouer a. droit/gauche** to play right/left forward; **la ligne des avants, les avants** the forward line, the forwards

3 *Mil* **l'a.** the front

• **avant de PRÉP** before; **a. de partir, il faudra...** before leaving, it'll be necessary to...; **écoute-moi a. de crier** listen to me before you start shouting; **je ne signerai rien a. d'avoir vu les locaux** I won't sign anything until *or* before I see the premises; **a. d'arriver au pont, il y a un feu rouge** there is a set of traffic lights before you come to the bridge

• **avant que CONJ ne dites rien a. qu'il n'arrive** don't say anything until he arrives; **je viendrai la voir a. qu'elle (ne) parte** I'll come and see her before she leaves; **a. qu'il comprenne, celui-là!** by the time he's understood!

• **avant que de PRÉP** *Littéraire* before; **a. que de mourir...** before dying...; **a. que de donner mon avis, j'entendrai chacun d'entre vous** before I state my opinion, I'll hear what each of you has to say

• **avant tout ADV 1** *(surtout)* **c'est une question de dignité a. tout** it's a question of dignity above all (else) **2** *(tout d'abord)* first; **a. tout, je voudrais vous dire ceci** first (and foremost), I'd like to tell you this

• **avant toute chose ADV** first of all; **a. toute chose, je voudrais que vous sachiez ceci** first of all, I'd like you to know this; **a. toute chose, je vais prendre une douche** I'll have a shower before I do anything else

• **d'avant ADJ le jour/le mois d'a.** the previous day/month, the day/month before; **je vais essayer de prendre le train d'a.** I'll try to catch the earlier train; **les locataires d'a. étaient plus sympathiques** the previous tenants were much nicer

• **en avant ADV** *(marcher)* in front; *(partir)* ahead; *(se pencher, tomber, bondir)* forward; **envoyer qn en a.** to send sb on ahead *or* in front; **je pars en a., je t'attendrai là-bas** I'm going on ahead, I'll wait for you there; **il s'élança en a.** he rushed forward; **en a.!** forward!; *Mil* **en a., marche!** forward march!; *Naut* **en a., toute!** full steam ahead!; *Fig* **mettre qn en a.** *(pour se protéger)* to use sb as a shield; *(pour le faire valoir)* to push sb forward *or* to the front; **mettre qch en a.** to put sth forward; **se mettre en a.** to push oneself forward *or* to the fore

• **en avant de PRÉP il marche toujours en a. des autres** he always walks ahead of the others; **être en a. d'un convoi** *(dans les premiers)* to be at the front of a procession; *(en premier)* to be leading a procession; **le barrage routier a été installé en a. de Dijon** the roadblock was set up just before Dijon

---

avantage [avɑ̃taʒ] **NM 1** *(supériorité)* advantage; **sa connaissance du danois est un a. par rapport aux autres candidats** his/her knowledge of Danish gives him/her an advantage *or* the edge over the other candidates; **avoir un a. sur qn/qch** to have an advantage over sb/sth; **le nouveau système a des avantages sur l'ancien** the new system has advantages over the old one; **cela vous donne un a. sur eux** this gives you an advantage over them; **garder/perdre l'a.** to keep/to lose the upper hand; **prendre l'a.** *ou* **un a. sur qn** to gain the upper hand over sb; **avoir l'a. sur qn** to have the advantage over sb; **avoir l'a. de** to have the advantage of; **ils nous ont battus, mais ils avaient l'a. du nombre** they defeated us, but they had the advantage of numbers; **j'ai sur toi l'a. de l'âge** I have age on my side; **elle a l'a. d'avoir 20 ans/d'être médecin** she's 20/a doctor, which is an advantage; *Mktg* **a. absolu** absolute advantage; *Mktg* **a. comparatif** *ou* **comparé** comparative advantage; *Mktg* **a. concurrentiel** competitive advantage

2 *(intérêt)* advantage; **les avantages et les inconvénients d'une solution** the advantages and disadvantages *or* pros and cons of a solution; **cette idée présente l'a. d'être simple** the idea has the advantage of being simple; **à mon/son a.** in my/his/her interest; **c'est (tout) à ton a.** it's in your (best) interest; **exploiter une idée à son a.** to exploit an idea to one's own advantage; **avoir a. à faire qch** to be better off doing sth; **vous auriez a. à apprendre la comptabilité** it would be to your advantage *or* you'd do well to learn accounting; **tu as tout a. à l'acheter ici** you'd be much better off buying it here; **elle aurait a. à se taire** she'd be well-advised to keep quiet; **quel a. as-tu à déménager?** what do you gain from moving house?; **tirer a. de** to derive an advantage from, to take advantage of; **ne tirez pas a. de sa naïveté** don't take advantage of his/her naivety; **tirer a. de la situation** to turn the situation to (one's) advantage; **notre lien de parenté a tourné à mon a.** our family relationship worked to my advantage

3 *Fin (bénéfice)* benefit; **elle ne tire de sa participation aucun a. matériel** she derives no material benefit *or* gain from her contribution; **avantages accessoires** financial benefits; **avantages acquis** long-service benefits; **avantages collectifs** social welfare; **avantages complémentaires** perks; **avantages en espèces** cash benefits; **avantages financiers** financial benefits; **a. fiscal** tax benefit, tax incentive; **avantages en nature** benefits *or* payments in kind; **avantages sociaux** *(dans une entreprise)* fringe benefits; *(au sein de l'État)* welfare benefits

4 *(plaisir)* **je n'ai pas l'a. de vous avoir été présenté** I haven't had the privilege *or* pleasure of being introduced to you; **j'ai (l'honneur et) l'a. de vous annoncer que...** I am pleased *or* delighted to inform you that...

5 *Sport* advantage; **a. (à) Rops!** advantage Rops!
6 *(locutions)* **être à son a.** *(avoir belle allure)* to

look one's best; *(dans une situation)* to be at one's best; changer à son a. to change for the better

avantager [17] [avɑ̃taʒe] VT 1 *(favoriser)* to advantage, to give an advantage to; ils ont été avantagés par rapport aux étudiants étrangers they were given an advantage over the foreign students; être avantagé dès le départ par rapport à qn to have a head start on *or* over sb; être avantagé par la nature to be favoured by nature; il n'a pas été avantagé par la nature! nature hasn't been particularly kind to him! 2 *(mettre en valeur)* to show off, to show to advantage; son uniforme l'avantage he looks his best in (his) uniform; cette coupe ne t'avantage pas that hairstyle doesn't flatter you

avantageuse [avɑ̃taʒøz] *voir* avantageux

avantageusement [avɑ̃taʒøzmɑ̃] ADV 1 *(peu cher)* at *or* for a good price 2 *(favorablement)* il s'en est tiré a. he got away lightly; parler de qn a. to speak favourably of sb

avantageux, -euse [avɑ̃taʒø, -øz] ADJ 1 *(contrat, affaire)* profitable; *(prix)* attractive; *(conditions, situation)* favourable; c'est une offre très avantageuse it's an excellent bargain; les cerises sont avantageuses en ce moment cherries are a good buy at the moment 2 *(flatteur ▸ pose, décolleté, uniforme)* flattering; parler de qn en termes a. to speak favourably of sb; il a une idée un peu trop avantageuse de lui-même he's got too high an opinion of himself; prendre des airs a. to look self-satisfied

avant-après [avɑ̃aprɛ] NM INV *(d'une personne, d'une maison)* makeover

avant-bassin [avɑ̃basɛ̃] *(pl* avant-bassins) NM *Naut* outer basin, dock

avant-bras [avɑ̃bra] NM INV *Anat* forearm

avant-cale [avɑ̃kal] *(pl* avant-cales) NF *Naut* fore hold

avant-centre [avɑ̃sɑ̃tr] *(pl* avants-centres) NM *Sport* centre-forward

avant-corps [avɑ̃kɔr] NM INV *Archit (d'un bâtiment)* projecting part

avant-cour [avɑ̃kur] *(pl* avant-cours) NF forecourt

avant-coureur [avɑ̃kurœr] *(pl* avant-coureurs) *voir* signe

avant-dernier, -ère [avɑ̃dɛrnje, -ɛr] *(mpl* avant-derniers, *fpl* avant-dernières) ADJ second last, last but one; l'avant-dernière fois the time before last

NM,F second last, last but one; arriver a. to be second last *or* last but one

avant-garde [avɑ̃gard] *(pl* avant-gardes) NF 1 *Mil* vanguard 2 *(élite)* avant-garde; peinture/architecture d'a. avant-garde painting/architecture; être à l'a. de la mode/du progrès to be in the vanguard *or* at the forefront of fashion/progress

avant-gardisme [avɑ̃gardism] *(pl* avant-gardismes) NM avant-gardism

avant-gardiste [avɑ̃gardist] *(pl* avant-gardistes) ADJ avant-garde

NMF avant-gardist

avant-goût [avɑ̃gu] *(pl* avant-goûts) NM foretaste

avant-guerre [avɑ̃gɛr] *(pl* avant-guerres) NM OU NF *Hist* pre-war years *or* period; les voitures d'a. pre-war cars

avant-hier [avɑ̃tjɛr] ADV the day before yesterday; a. au soir the evening before last; a. matin two mornings ago

avant-main [avɑ̃mɛ̃] *(pl* avant-mains) NM 1 *(de cheval)* forequarters, forehand 2 *Sport (au tennis)* coup d'a. forehand (stroke)

avant-midi [avɑ̃midi] NM INV OU NF INV *Belg & Can* morning

avant-plan [avɑ̃plɑ̃] *(pl* avant-plans) NM *Belg* foreground

avant-port [avɑ̃pɔr] *(pl* avant-ports) NM *Naut* outer harbour

avant-poste [avɑ̃pɔst] *(pl* avant-postes) NM 1 *Mil* outpost 2 *(lieu de l'action)* il est toujours aux avant-postes he's always where the action is

avant-première [avɑ̃prəmjɛr] *(pl* avant-premières) NF 1 *Théât* dress rehearsal 2 *Cin* preview; présenter qch en a. to preview sth

avant-programme [avɑ̃prɔgram] *(pl* avant-programmes) NM *(d'un événement)* synopsis of events

avant-projet [avɑ̃prɔʒɛ] *(pl* avant-projets) NM pilot study; *Jur* a. de loi draft bill

avant-propos [avɑ̃prɔpo] NM INV foreword

avant-scène [avɑ̃sɛn] *(pl* avant-scènes) NF *Théât* 1 *(partie de la scène)* apron, proscenium 2 *(loge)* box

avant-spectacle [avɑ̃spɛktakl] *(pl* avant-spectacles) NM *Belg & Can* pre-show performance; en a. as a curtain-raiser

avant-titre [avɑ̃titr] *(pl* avant-titres) NM *(d'un livre)* half-title

avant-toit [avɑ̃twa] *(pl* avant-toits) NM *Archit* l'a. the eaves

avant-train [avɑ̃trɛ̃] *(pl* avant-trains) NM 1 *Zool* forequarters 2 *Aut* front-axle unit 3 *Mil* limber

avant-veille [avɑ̃vɛj] *(pl* avant-veilles) NF two days before *or* earlier; l'a. de son mariage two days before he/she got married; *Fig* à l'a. de la révolution on the eve of the revolution

avare [avar] ADJ 1 *(pingre)* mean, miserly, tightfisted 2 *Fig* être a. de to be sparing of; elle est plutôt a. de sourires she doesn't smile much; il n'a pas été a. de compliments/de conseils he was generous with his compliments/advice; il n'est pas a. de son temps he gives freely of his time

NMF miser; un vieil a. an old miser *or* skinflint

avarice [avaris] NF miserliness, avarice

avaricieux, -euse [avarisjø, -øz] *Arch* ADJ miserly, stingy

NM,F miser, skinflint

avarie [avari] NF damage *(sustained by vehicle, ship, cargo)*; subir des avaries to sustain damage; avaries communes/particulières/simples general/particular/ordinary damage; avaries de route damage in transit

avarié, -e [avarje] ADJ 1 *(aliment, marchandise)* spoilt, damaged; cette viande est avariée this meat has gone off 2 *Naut* navire a. damaged ship

avarier [10] [avarje] VT to damage; la chaleur a avarié les aliments the food has gone off in the heat

VPR s'avarier *(denrée alimentaire)* to rot, to go bad *or Br* off

avatar [avatar] NM 1 *Rel* avatar

2 *(changement)* change, metamorphosis

3 *(mésaventure)* misadventure, mishap; les avatars de la vie politique the vicissitudes of political life

4 *Ordinat* avatar

Ave [ave] NM INV *Rel* Ave Maria, Hail Mary

AVEC [avɛk]

- with 1–9
- despite 7
- to, towards 2

PRÉP 1 *(indiquant la complémentarité, l'accompagnement, l'accord)* with; et a. la viande, quels légumes voulez-vous? what vegetables would you like with your meat?; et a. ceci? anything else?; je ne prends jamais de sucre a. mon café I never take sugar in my coffee; une maison a. jardin a house with a garden; une chambre a. vue sur le lac a room with a view over the lake; un homme a. une blouse blanche a man in a white coat *or* with a white coat on; je viendrai a. ma femme I'll come with my wife, I'll bring my wife along; a. les encouragements de... encouraged by..., with the encouragement of...; a. la collaboration de... with contributions from *or* by...; tous les résidents sont a. moi all the residents support me *or* are behind me *or* are on my side; là-dessus, je suis a. vous I'm with you on that point; a., dans le rôle principal/dans son premier rôle, X starring/introducing X; un film a. Gabin a film featuring Gabin

2 *(envers)* être patient/honnête a. qn to be patient/honest with sb; être gentil a. qn to be kind *or* nice to sb; se comporter bien/mal a. qn to behave well/badly towards sb

3 *(en ce qui concerne)* a. lui, c'est toujours la même chose it's always the same with him; ce qu'il y a a. eux, c'est qu'ils ne comprennent rien the problem with them is that they don't understand anything; a. lui, tout est toujours simple everything is always simple according to him; a. ça, il faut compter les frais d'assurance the cost of insurance should also be added on top of that; il est compétent, et a. ça il ne prend pas cher he's very competent and he's cheap as well; et a. ça, il n'est pas content! *(en plus)* and on top of that *or* and what's more, he's not happy!; *(malgré tout)* with all that, he's still not happy!; a. tout ça, j'ai oublié de lui téléphoner with all that, I forgot to call him/her; et a. ça que je me gênerais! I should worry!

4 *(indiquant la simultanéité)* se lever a. le jour to get up at the crack of dawn; se coucher a. les poules to go to bed early; le paysage change a. les saisons the countryside changes with the seasons

5 *(indiquant une relation d'opposition)* with; se battre a. qn to fight with sb; être en guerre a. un pays to be at war with a country; se disputer a. qn to quarrel with sb; rivaliser a. qn to compete with sb

6 *(indiquant une relation de cause)* with; a. le temps qu'il fait, je préfère ne pas sortir I prefer not to go out in this weather; a. tout le chocolat que tu as mangé, tu vas être malade you're going to be ill with all that chocolate you've eaten; a. ce nouveau scandale, le ministre va tomber this new scandal will mean the end of the minister's career; au lit a. la grippe in bed with (the) flu; ils ont compris a. le temps in time, they understood; s'améliorer a. l'âge to improve with age; ne m'embête pas a. toutes ces histoires don't bother me with all that

7 *(malgré)* a. tous ses diplômes, Pierre ne trouve pas de travail even with all his qualifications, Pierre can't find work; a. ses airs aimables, c'est une vraie peste despite his/her pleasant manner, he's/she's a real pest

8 *(indiquant la manière)* with; elle est habillée a. goût she is tastefully dressed; faire qch a. plaisir to do sth with pleasure, to take pleasure in doing sth; faire qch a. beaucoup de soin to do sth with great care, to take great care in doing sth; regarder qn a. passion/mépris to look at sb passionately/contemptuously; ce n'est pas a. colère que je le fais I'm not doing it in anger

9 *(indiquant le moyen, l'instrument)* with; marcher a. une canne to walk with a stick, to use a walking-stick; couper qch a. un couteau to cut sth with a knife; fonctionner a. des piles to run on batteries, to be battery-operated; c'est fait a. de la laine it's made of wool; a. un peu de chance with a bit of luck; elle est partie a. un bateau de pêche she left on a fishing boat; nous avons continué a. cinq litres de carburant we carried on with five litres of fuel; tu peux conduire un poids lourd a. ton permis? can you drive a heavy goods vehicle with *or* on your licence?; voyager a. un faux passeport to travel with *or* on a forged passport

ADV 1 *Fam* il a pris la clef et il est parti a. he took the key and went off with it❑; ôtez vos chaussures, vous ne pouvez pas entrer a. take off your shoes, you can't come in with them on❑; je vous mets le poisson a.? shall I put the fish in with the rest?❑

2 *Belg* je vais faire des courses, tu viens a.? I'm going shopping, are you coming (with me)?

• **d'avec** PRÉP distinguer qch d'a. qch to distinguish sth from sth; divorcer d'a. qn to divorce sb; se séparer d'a. qn to separate from sb

aveline [avlin] NF *Bot* filbert, cobnut

avelinier [avlinje] NM *Bot* filbert, cob

aven [avɛn] NM *Géol* sinkhole, *Br* swallow hole

avenant[1] [avnɑ̃] NM *Jur* 1 *(gén)* amendment; a. à un contrat amendment to a contract 2 *(dans les assurances)* endorsement, additional clause; a. d'augmentation de la garantie endorsement for an increase in cover

• **à l'avenant** ADV un exposé sans intérêt et des questions à l'a. a boring lecture with equally boring questions; toutes les unes de journaux sont à l'a. all the front pages carry the same story

• **à l'avenant de** PRÉP in accordance with; ils se

sont conduits à l'a. de leurs principes they behaved according to their principles

avenant², -e [avnɑ̃, -ɑ̃t] **ADJ** pleasant; **le personnel est compétent mais peu a.** the staff are competent but not very pleasant; **une hôtesse avenante accueille les visiteurs** a gracious hostess greets the visitors

avènement [avɛnmɑ̃] **NM 1** *(d'un souverain)* accession; *Rel (du Messie)* advent, coming **2** *(d'une époque, d'une mode)* advent; **l'a. d'une ère nouvelle** the advent of a new era

avenir [avnir] **NM 1** *(période future)* future; **dans un a. indéterminé** sometime in the future; **dans un a. proche/lointain** in the near/distant future; **pas dans un a. proche** not in the foreseeable future; **ce que nous réserve l'a.** what the future holds (for us); **l'a. dira si j'ai raison** time will tell if I'm right; **espérer dans/croire en un a. meilleur** to hope for/to believe in a better future; **l'a. est à nous** the future is ours; **les moyens de transport de l'a.** the transport systems of the future

2 *(générations futures)* future generations

3 *(situation future)* future; **nous devons nous préoccuper de l'a. de notre fils** we should start thinking about our son's future; **tu as devant toi un brillant a.** you have a promising future ahead (of you); **assurer l'a. de qn** to make provision for sb

4 *(chances de succès)* future, (future) prospects; **une invention sans a.** an invention with no future; **avoir de l'a.** to have a future; **les nouveaux procédés techniques ont de l'a.** the new technical processes are promising *or* have a good future; **découverte d'un matériau d'a.** discovery of a promising new material; **les professions d'a.** up-and-coming professions

5 *Jur* writ of summons *(to opposing counsel)*

• **à l'avenir ADV** in future; **à l'a., vous êtes priés d'arriver à l'heure** in future, you are requested to be on time

Avent [avɑ̃] **NM** *Rel* advent; **l'A.** Advent; **calendrier de l'A.** Advent calendar

aventure [avɑ̃tyr] **NF 1** *(incident ▸ gén)* experience, incident; *(▸ extraordinaire)* adventure; **il m'est arrivé une drôle d'a. ce matin** a strange thing happened to me this morning; **le récit d'une a. en mer** the tale of an adventure at sea; **pour trouver un taxi le samedi soir, c'est tout une a.** finding a taxi on a Saturday night is quite a performance **2** *(risque)* adventure, venture; **l'a. est au coin de la rue** the unexpected is always round the corner; **adopter un tel projet, c'est se lancer dans l'a.** accepting such a project is a bit risky; **la grande a.** great adventure; **se lancer dans une grande a.** to set off on a big adventure; **dire la bonne a. à qn** to tell sb's fortune **3** *(liaison)* (love) affair

• **à l'aventure ADV** at random, haphazardly; **marcher/rouler à l'a.** to walk/to drive aimlessly; **partir à l'a.** to go off in search of adventure

• **d'aventure(s) ADJ** *(roman, film)* adventure *(avant n)*

• **d'aventure, par aventure ADV** by chance; **si d'a. tu le vois, transmets-lui mon message** if by any chance you see him, give him my message

aventuré, -e [avɑ̃tyre] **ADJ** *(hypothèse, théorie)* risky; *(démarche)* chancy, risky

aventurer [3] [avɑ̃tyre] **VT 1** *(suggérer ▸ hypothèse, analyse)* to venture **2** *(risquer ▸ fortune, réputation, bonheur)* to risk, to chance

VPR s'aventurer 1 *(aller)* to venture; **il n'avait pas peur de s'a. le soir dans des ruelles obscures** he wasn't afraid of venturing out into dark alleys at night **2 s'a. à faire** to venture to do; **téléphone-lui si tu veux, moi je ne m'y aventurerais pas** call him/her if you like, I wouldn't chance it myself

aventureuse [avɑ̃tyrøz] *voir* **aventureux**

aventureusement [avɑ̃tyrøzmɑ̃] **ADV 1** *(hardiment)* adventurously **2** *(dangereusement)* riskily

aventureux, -euse [avɑ̃tyrø, -øz] **ADJ 1** *(hardi ▸ héros)* adventurous **2** *(dangereux ▸ projet)* risky, chancy

aventurier [avɑ̃tyrje] **NM** *(explorateur)* adventurer; *(aimant le risque)* risk-taker

aventurisme [avɑ̃tyrism] **NM** *Pol* adventurism

avenue [avny] **NF** *(de ville)* avenue; *(menant à une maison)* drive(way); *Fig* **les avenues du pouvoir** the paths to power

avéré, -e [avere] **ADJ** *(fait, information)* known, established; **c'est un fait a. que…, il est a. que…** it is a known fact that…

avérer [18] [avere] **VT** *(affirmer)* **a. un fait** to vouch for the accuracy of a fact

VPR s'avérer 1 *(être prouvé)* to be proved (correct); **cette hypothèse ne s'est jamais avérée** this hypothesis was never proved correct **2** *(se révéler)* to prove (to be); **la solution s'est avérée inefficace** the solution turned out *or* proved (to be) inefficient **3** *(tournure impersonnelle)* **il s'avère difficile d'améliorer les résultats** it's proving difficult to improve on the results; **il s'avère que mon cas n'est pas prévu par le règlement** it turns out *or* it so happens that my situation isn't covered by the regulations

avers [avɛr] **NM** obverse

averse [avɛrs] **NF** showers *(rain)*; **sous l'a.** in the rain; *Fig* **laisser passer l'a.** to wait until the storm blows over; **une a. d'injures s'abattit sur moi** I was assailed by a string *or* stream of insults

aversion [avɛrsjɔ̃] **NF** aversion, dislike; **sa laideur m'inspirait de l'a.** his/her ugliness filled me with loathing; **avoir de l'a. pour** to have an aversion to *or* for, to have a dislike for; **il les a pris en a.** he took a violent dislike to them

averti, -e [averti] **ADJ** (well-)informed; **un critique a. en matière de musique** a critic well-informed about music; **pour lecteurs avertis seulement** for adult readers only; *Prov* **un homme a. en vaut deux** forewarned is forearmed

avertir [32] [avertir] **VT 1** *(informer)* to inform; **avertis-moi dès que tu (le) sauras** let me know as soon as you know; **l'avez-vous averti de votre départ?** have you informed him that *or* did you let him know that you are leaving?; **il faut l'a. que le spectacle est annulé** he/she must be informed *or* told that the show's off; **nous n'avons pas été avertis du danger** we were not warned about the danger **2** *(par menace, par défi)* to warn; **je t'avertis que la prochaine fois la punition sera sévère** I'm warning you that the next time the punishment will be severe; **tiens-toi pour averti!** be warned!; **vous voilà avertis!** I give you fair warning!, don't say I haven't warned you!

> Il faut noter que le verbe anglais **to advertise** est un faux ami. Il ne signifie jamais **avertir**.

avertissement [avertismɑ̃] **NM 1** *(signe)* warning, warning sign; **il est parti sans le moindre a.** he left without any warning

2 *(appel à l'attention)* notice, warning; **il n'a pas tenu compte de mon a.** he didn't take any notice of my warning

3 *(blâme)* warning, reprimand; *Sport (de l'arbitre)* warning, caution; *Admin (lettre)* warning letter; **donner un a. à qn** to give sb a warning, to warn sb; **premier et dernier a.!** I'm telling you now and I won't tell you again!

4 *(en début de livre)* **a. (au lecteur)** foreword

5 *Rail* warning signal

6 *Ordinat* **a. de réception** *(de message)* acknowledgement; **a. à réception d'un courrier** mail received message

> Il faut noter que le nom anglais **advertisement** est un faux ami. Il signifie **publicité** ou **annonce**, selon le contexte.

avertisseur, -euse [avertisœr, -øz] **ADJ** warning

NM alarm, warning signal; **a. lumineux** warning light; **a. sonore** *(gén)* alarm; *Aut* horn; **a. d'incendie** fire alarm

aveu, -x [avø] **NM 1** *(confession)* confession; **faire un a.** to acknowledge *or* to confess *or* to admit something; **je vais vous faire un a., j'ai peur en voiture** I must confess that I'm scared travelling in cars; **recueillir les aveux d'un criminel** to take down a criminal's confession; **faire des aveux complets** *(à la police)* to make a full confession; *Fig Hum* to confess all; *aussi Fig* **passer aux aveux** to confess; **faire l'a. de qch** to own up to sth; **faire l'a. de son inexpérience/amour** to confess to being inexperienced/in love; **(faire) l'a. de son ignorance lui a été pénible** he/she found it difficult to admit *or* to acknowledge his/her ignorance **2** *(autorisation)* permission, consent; **nous ne pouvons rien faire sans l'a. de l'intéressé** we can do nothing without the consent of the party concerned

• **de l'aveu de PRÉP** according to; **de l'a. des participants, il ressort que…** according to the participants, it seems that…; **la tour ne tiendra pas, de l'a. même de l'architecte** the tower will collapse, even the architect says so; **de son propre a.** by his/her own reckoning

aveuglant, -e [avœglɑ̃, -ɑ̃t] **ADJ** *(éclat, lueur)* blinding, dazzling; *(évidence, preuve)* overwhelming; *(vérité)* self-evident, glaring; **soudain, une vérité aveuglante lui est apparue** the truth came to his/her in a blinding flash

aveugle [avœgl] **ADJ 1** *(privé de la vue)* blind; **un enfant a. de naissance** a child born blind *or* blind from birth; **a. d'un œil** blind in one eye; **devenir a.** to go blind; **l'accident qui l'a rendu a.** the accident which blinded him *or* deprived him of his sight; **je ne suis pas a., je vois bien tes manigances** I'm not blind, I can see what you're up to; **la passion la rend a.** she's blinded by passion

2 *(extrême ▸ fureur, passion)* blind, reckless

3 *(absolu ▸ attachement, foi, soumission)* blind, unquestioning; **avoir une confiance a. en qn** to trust sb implicitly *or* unreservedly

4 *Constr (mur, fenêtre)* blind

NMF blind man, *f* blind woman; **les aveugles** the blind; **parler de/juger qch comme un a. des couleurs** to speak of/to judge sth blindly

• **en aveugle ADV faire qch en a.** to do sth blindly; **faire un test en a.** to do a blind test; **se lancer en a. dans une entreprise** to take a leap in the dark

aveuglement [avœgləmɑ̃] **NM** blindness, blinkered state; **dans son a., il est capable de tout** in his blindness, he's capable of anything

aveuglément [avœglemɑ̃] **ADV** *(inconsidérément)* blindly; **elle lui faisait a. confiance** she trusted him/her implicitly

aveugle-né, -e [avœglane] *(mpl* **aveugles-nés**, *fpl* **aveugles-nées) NM,F** *Méd* = person blind from birth; **c'est un a.** he was born blind, he's been blind from birth

aveugler [5] [avœgle] **VT 1** *(priver de la vue, éblouir)* to blind; **l'accident qui l'a aveuglée** the accident which blinded her *or* deprived her of her sight; **la lueur des phares m'aveuglait** the glare of the headlights blinded *or* dazzled me; *Fig* **la haine/l'amour l'aveugle** he's/she's blinded by hatred/love **3** *(fenêtre)* to wall up, to block

VPR s'aveugler to delude oneself; **il ne faut pas t'a., ça ne sera pas facile** don't delude yourself, it won't be easy; **s'a. sur** to close one's eyes to; **ne vous aveuglez pas sur vos chances de réussite** don't overestimate your chances of success

aveuglette [avœglɛt] **à l'aveuglette ADV 1** *(sans voir)* blindly; **il m'a fallu marcher à l'a. le long d'un tunnel** I had to grope my way through a tunnel; **elle conduisait à l'a. dans un brouillard épais** she drove blindly through thick fog **2** *Fig* **choisir qch à l'a.** to choose sth at random *or* in the dark *or* blindly; **lancer des coups à l'a.** to hit out blindly; **je ne veux pas agir à l'a.** I don't want to act without first weighing up the consequences

aveulir [32] [avølir] *Littéraire* **VT** to enervate

VPR s'aveulir to become enervated

aveulissement [avølismɑ̃] **NM** *Littéraire* enervation

aviaire [avjɛr] **ADJ** *Orn* avian; **grippe a.** bird flu; **peste a.** fowl pest

aviateur, -trice [avjatœr, -tris] **NM,F** pilot, *Vieilli* aviator

aviation [avjasjɔ̃] **NF 1** *(transport)* aviation; **a. civile** *ou* **de tourisme** civil aviation; **a. marchande** *ou* **commerciale** commercial aviation

2 *(activité)* flying; **faire de l'a.** to go flying; **elle était destinée à l'a.** she was meant to fly

3 *(fabrication)* aircraft industry

4 *Mil (armée de l'air)* air force; *(avions)* aircraft, air force; **l'a. ennemie a attaqué nos bases** enemy aircraft attacked our bases

aviatrice [avjatris] *voir* **aviateur**

avicole [avikɔl] **ADJ 1** *(parasite)* avicolous **2** *(de volailles ▸ ferme, producteur, élevage)* poultry *(avant n)*; *(d'oiseaux ▸ élevage)* bird *(avant n)*

aviculteur, -trice [avikyltœr, -tris] **NM,F** *(éleveur ▸ d'oiseaux)* bird breeder *or* farmer, *Spéc* aviculturist; *(▸ de volailles)* poultry breeder *or* farmer

aviculture [avikyltyr] **NF** *(élevage ▸ d'oiseaux)* bird breeding, *Spéc* aviculture; *(▸ de volailles)* poultry farming *or* breeding

avide [avid] **ADJ 1** *(cupide)* greedy, grasping; **un homme a.** a greedy man; **des mains avides se tendaient vers l'or** greedy *or* grasping hands reached towards the gold **2** *(enthousiaste)* eager, avid; **écouter d'une oreille a.** to listen eagerly *or* avidly; **a. de** greedy *or* avid for; **a. de louanges/succès** hungry for praise/success; **a. de savoir** eager to learn, thirsty for knowledge; **a. de connaître le monde** eager *or* anxious *or* impatient to discover the world

avidement [avidmɑ̃] **ADV 1** *(voracement)* greedily **2** *(avec enthousiasme)* eagerly, avidly, keenly; **écouter qn a.** to listen to sb eagerly **3** *(par cupidité)* greedily, covetously

avidité [avidite] **NF 1** *(voracité)* voracity, greed, *Péj* gluttony; **manger avec a.** to eat greedily *or* ravenously **2** *(enthousiasme)* eagerness, enthusiasm; **écouter avec a.** to listen eagerly **3** *(cupidité)* greed, cupidity, covetousness

Avignon [aviɲɔ̃] **NM** *Géog* Avignon; **à** *ou* **en A.** in Avignon; *Théât* **le festival d'A.** the Avignon festival

> **LE FESTIVAL D'AVIGNON**
>
> Founded by Jean Vilar in 1947 and held every summer in Avignon in the South of France, this arts festival is a showcase for new theatre and dance performances. Along with the programme of official shows ("le in") performed in prestigious venues such as the Court of Honour of the "Palais des Papes", a programme comprising numerous fringe shows, referred to as "le off", has also been performed since the 1970s.

avilir [32] [avilir] **VT 1** *(personne)* to debase, to shame; **vos mensonges vous avilissent** your lies are unworthy of you **2** *(monnaie)* to cause to depreciate, to devalue; *(marchandise)* to cause to depreciate; **l'inflation a avili l'euro** inflation has devalued the euro

VPR s'avilir 1 *(emploi réfléchi)* to demean *or* to debase *or* to disgrace oneself; **il s'avilit dans l'alcoolisme** he's sunk into alcoholism **2** *(monnaie, marchandise)* to depreciate

avilissant, -e [avilisɑ̃, -ɑ̃t] **ADJ** degrading, demeaning; **mon métier n'a rien d'a.** there is nothing shameful about my job

avilissement [avilismɑ̃] **NM 1** *(d'une personne)* degradation, debasement **2** *(d'une monnaie)* depreciation, devaluation

aviné, -e [avine] **ADJ** *(qui a trop bu)* drunken, intoxicated; *(qui sent le vin ▸ souffle)* wine-laden; *(altéré par la boisson ▸ voix)* drunken

aviner [3] [avine] **VT** *(fût, futaille)* to season

avion [avjɔ̃] **NM 1** *(véhicule)* plane, *esp Br* aeroplane, *Am* airplane; **a. bimoteur/quadrimoteur** twin-engined/four-engined plane; **a. charter** charter plane; **a. civil** civil aircraft; **a. commercial** commercial aircraft; **a. à décollage et atterrissage courts** short take-off and landing aircraft; **a. à décollage vertical** jump-jet; **a. furtif** stealth aircraft; **a. de guerre** warplane; **a. à hélices** propeller plane; **a. hôpital** hospital plane; **a. de ligne** airliner; **a. militaire/de chasse** military/fighter plane; **a. sans pilote** pilotless aircraft; **a. de ravitaillement (en vol)** refuelling aircraft; **a. à réaction** jet(plane); **a. de reconnaissance** reconnaissance aircraft; **a. de tourisme** private aircraft; **a. de transport** transport aircraft **2** *(mode de transport)* **l'a.** flying; **irez-vous en a. ou en train?** are you flying or going by train?; **j'ai fait une partie du trajet en a.** I flew part of the way; **je déteste (prendre) l'a.** I hate flying; **elle n'a jamais pris l'a.** she's never been on a plane, she's never flown; **courrier par a.** air mail

avion-cargo [avjɔ̃kargo] *(pl* **avions-cargos)** **NM** freight plane

avion-citerne [avjɔ̃sitɛrn] *(pl* **avions-citernes)** **NM** (air) tanker, supply plane

avion-école [avjɔ̃ekɔl] *(pl* **avions-écoles)** **NM** training plane *or* aircraft

avion-espion [avjɔ̃ɛspjɔ̃] *(pl* **avions-espions)** **NM** spy plane

avionique [avjɔnik] **NF** *Aviat & Électron* avionics *(singulier)*

avionneur [avjɔnœr] **NM** aircraft constructor

avion-suicide [avjɔ̃sɥisid] *(pl* **avions-suicide)** **NM** suicide plane

avion-taxi [avjɔ̃taksi] *(pl* **avions-taxis)** **NM** charter aircraft

aviron [avirɔ̃] **NM 1** *(rame)* oar; *Can* paddle; **tirer sur les avirons** to row; **coup d'a.** stroke; **en trois coups d'a. vous serez de l'autre côté** you'll row to the other side in no time at all **2** *Sport (activité)* rowing; **faire de l'a.** to row

avironner [3] [avirɔne] **VI** *Can* to paddle

avis [avi] **NM 1** *(point de vue)* opinion, viewpoint; **les a. sont partagés au sein du parti** opinions within the party are divided; **avoir son** *ou* **un a. sur qch** to have views on sth; **je n'ai pas d'a. sur la question** I have nothing to say *or* no opinion on the matter; **ne décide pas pour elle, elle a son a.!** don't decide for her, she knows her own mind!; **j'aimerais avoir votre a.** I'd like to hear your views *or* to know what you think (about it); **demande** *ou* **prends l'a. d'un second médecin** ask the opinion of another doctor; **toi, je ne te demande pas ton a.!** I didn't ask for your opinion!; **donner son a.** to give *or* to contribute one's opinion; **si vous voulez (que je vous donne) mon a.** if you ask me *or* want my opinion; **donner** *ou* **émettre un a. favorable** *(à une demande)* to give the go-ahead; *(à une proposition)* to give a positive response, to come out in favour; **après a. favorable, vous procéderez à l'expulsion** having obtained permission (from the authorities), you will start the eviction procedure; **émettre un a. défavorable** to give a negative response; **prendre l'a. de qn** to seek sb's advice; **je vais prendre des a. et je vous contacterai** I'll seek further advice before contacting you; **à mon a.** in my opinion; *Hum* **à mon humble a.** in my humble opinion; **être d'a. que...** to be of the opinion that...; **elle est d'a. qu'il est trop tard** she's of the opinion that it's too late; **je ne suis pas d'a. qu'on l'envoie en pension** I don't agree with his/her being sent away to boarding school; **de l'a. de** *(selon)* according to; **de l'a. général, ce film est un chef-d'œuvre** the general view is that the film is a masterpiece; **je suis de votre a.** I agree with you; **il n'est pas de ton a.** he doesn't agree with you; **lui et moi ne sommes jamais du même a.** he and I don't see eye to eye *or* never agree on anything; **je suis du même a. que toi** I agree with you; **il n'est pas du même a. que son père** he disagrees with his father; *Hum* **m'est a. que...** it seems to me that..., methinks...; **sur l'a. de** on the advice *or* at the suggestion of; **c'est sur leur a. que j'ai fait refaire la toiture** I had the roof redone on their advice

2 *(information)* announcement; *(sommation ▸ légale)* notice; *(▸ fiscale)* notice, demand; **j'ai reçu un a. du percepteur** I had a tax demand; **jusqu'à nouvel a.** until further notice; **nous irons sauf a. contraire** *(de votre part)* unless we hear otherwise *or* to the contrary, we'll go; *(de notre part)* unless you hear otherwise *or* to the contrary, we'll go; **il reste encore quelques parts de gâteau, a. aux amateurs** there's still some cake left if anyone's interested; **a. au lecteur** foreword; **a. au public** *(sur panneau)* public notice; *Fin* **a. d'appel de fonds** call letter; *Bourse* **a. d'attribution** allotment letter; **a. de la banque** bank notification *or* advice; *Jur* **a. contraire** dissent; *Banque* **a. de crédit** credit advice; *Banque* **a. de débit** debit advice; **a. de décès** death notice; *Jur* **a. défavorable** unfavourable verdict; **en cas d'a. défavorable du jury** should the jury return an unfavourable verdict; *Banque* **a. de domiciliation** notice of payment by banker's order; *Bourse* **a. d'exécution** contract note; *Fin* **a. d'imposition** tax assessment; **a. de licenciement** redundancy notice; *Fin* **a. de non-imposition** tax exemption document; *Bourse* **a. d'opération sur titres, a. d'opéré** trade ticket, contract note; **a. de paiement** payment advice; *Banque* **a. de prélèvement** direct debit advice; **a. de rappel** reminder; **a. de réception** acknowledgement of receipt; **a. de recherche** *(d'un criminel)* wanted (person) poster; *(d'un disparu)* missing person poster; *Banque* **a. de rejet** notice of returned cheque; *Banque* **a. de remise** remittance advice; *Banque* **a. de retrait (de fonds)** notice of withdrawal; *Banque* **a. de virement** (bank) transfer advice

avisé, -e [avize] **ADJ** shrewd, prudent; **un conseiller très a.** a shrewd counsellor; **bien a.** well-advised; **mal a.** ill-advised

aviser [3] [avize] **VT 1** *(informer)* to inform, to notify; **a. qn de qch** to inform *or* to notify sb of sth; **vous serez avisé par lettre** you will be notified *or* informed by letter; **il m'a avisé que ma candidature était retenue** he informed me that my application had been accepted **2** *Littéraire (voir)* to notice, to catch a glimpse of

VI to decide, to see (what one can do); **maintenant nous allons devoir a.** we'll have to see what we can do now; **s'il n'est pas là dans une heure, j'aviserai** I'll have another think if he isn't here in an hour; **avisons au plus pressé** let's attend *or* see to the most urgent matters

VPR s'aviser de 1 *(remarquer)* to notice, to become aware of; **je me suis avisé de sa présence quand elle a ri** I suddenly noticed her presence when she laughed; **il s'est avisé trop tard (de ce) qu'il n'avait pas sa clé** he realized too late that he didn't have his key **2** *(oser)* to dare to; **ne t'avise pas de l'interrompre quand elle parle** don't think of interrupting her while she's speaking; **et ne t'avise pas de recommencer!** and don't you dare do that again!; **le premier qui s'avise de tricher sera puni** the first one who takes it into his head to cheat will be punished

aviso [avizo] **NM** *Mil* sloop

avitaminose [avitaminoz] **NF** *Méd* vitamin deficiency, *Spéc* avitaminosis

aviver [3] [avive] **VT 1** *(intensifier ▸ flammes)* to fan, to stir up; *(▸ feu)* to revive, to rekindle; *(▸ couleur)* to brighten, to revive; *(▸ sentiment)* to stir up; *(▸ désir)* to excite, to arouse; *(▸ blessure)* to irritate; *(▸ querelle)* to stir up, to exacerbate; *(▸ crainte)* to heighten

2 *Menuis* to square off

3 *(métal)* to burnish; *(marbre)* to polish

4 *Méd* to open up

av. J.-C. *(abrév écrite* **avant Jésus-Christ)** BC

avocat[1] [avɔka] **NM** *(fruit)* avocado

avocat[2]**, -e** [avɔka, -at] **NM,F 1** *Jur* lawyer, *Am* attorney(-at-law); *(à la barre) Br* barrister, *Am* trial lawyer *or* attorney, *Scot* advocate; **mon a.** my lawyer *or* counsel; **mes avocats** my counsel; *Fam* **je lui mettrai mes avocats sur le dos!** I'll take him/her to court!; **a. d'affaires** business lawyer; **a. consultant** *Br* ≃ counsel in chamber, consulting barrister, *Am* ≃ attorney; **a. de la défense** counsel for the defence, *Br* ≃ defending counsel, *Am* ≃ defense counsel; **a. général** *Br* ≃ counsel for the prosecution, *Am* ≃ prosecuting attorney **2** *(porte-parole)* advocate, champion; **se faire l'a. d'une mauvaise cause** to advocate *or* to champion a lost cause; **je serai votre a. auprès de lui** I'll plead with him on your behalf; **se faire l'a. du diable** to be devil's advocate

avocat-conseil, avocate-conseil [avɔkakɔ̃sɛj, avɔkatkɔ̃sɛj] *(mpl* **avocats-conseils,** *fpl* **avocates-conseils)** **NM,F** *Jur* legal adviser

avocatier [avɔkatje] **NM** *Bot* avocado (tree)

avocette [avɔsɛt] **NF** *Orn* avocet

avoine [avwan] **NF** *Bot (plante)* oat; *(grains)* oats; **a. commune** common oats

avoir[1] [avwar] **NM 1** *Com (attestation de crédit)* credit note; *(en comptabilité)* credit side; **la fleuriste m'a fait un a.** the florist gave me a credit note; **j'ai un a. de 20 euros à la boucherie** I've got 20 euros' credit at the butcher's **2** *Écon & Fin (capital)* capital; **avoirs** assets, holdings; **a. en banque** bank credit; **a. en devises** foreign currency holding; **avoirs disponibles** liquid assets; **a. fiscal** tax credit; **avoirs numéraires** *ou* **en caisse** cash holdings **3** *Littéraire (possessions)* assets, worldly goods; **vivre d'un petit a. personnel** to live off a small personal income

AVOIR² [1] [avwar]

V AUX	
• to have **A1, 2**	• to have to **B2, 3**
VT	
• to have **A1–4, 6, 9, B1, 2, C1, D2, E**	• to have on **B3**
	• to own **A1**
• to be **B5, 6**	• to make **C2**
• to get **A5, 8, 10, D1**	• to feel **C3**
• to give **C2**	• to catch **A11**
• to take in **D3**	

V AUX A. 1 *(avec des verbes transitifs)* **as-tu lu sa lettre?** did you read *or* have you read his/her letter?; **les deux buts qu'il avait marqués** the two goals he had scored; **j'aurais voulu vous aider** I'd have liked to help you; **non content de les a. humiliés, il les a jetés dehors** not content with humiliating them, he threw them out

2 *(avec des verbes intransitifs)* **j'ai maigri** I've lost weight; **as-tu bien dormi?** did you sleep well?; **tu as dû rêver** you must have been dreaming

3 *(avec le verbe "être")* **j'ai été surpris** I was surprised; **il aurait été enchanté** he would've *or* would have been delighted

B. 1 *(exprime la possibilité)* **tu as à manger dans le réfrigérateur** there's something to eat in the fridge for you; **je n'ai rien à boire** I haven't got anything *or* I have nothing *or* I've got nothing to drink; **ils n'ont qu'à écrire au directeur** *(conseil)* all they have to do *or* all they've got to do is write to the manager; *(menace)* just let them (try and) write to the manager; **s'il vous manque quelque chose, vous n'avez qu'à me le faire savoir** if you're missing anything, just let me know; **tu n'as qu'à le recoller** all you've got to do is glue it back together; *Fam* **t'as qu'à la mettre à la porte!** just throw her out!; *Fam* **t'as qu'à me frapper, pendant que tu y es!** why don't you hit me while you're at it?

2 *(exprime l'obligation)* **a. à** to have to; **partez, j'ai à travailler** go away, I've got to work; **j'ai à ajouter une petite précision** I must add one point, I must just say one thing; **je n'ai pas à me justifier auprès de vous** I don't have to justify myself to you; **un jour, tu auras à t'expliquer** one day, you'll have to account for yourself; **et voilà, je n'ai plus qu'à recommencer!** so now I've got to start all over again!

3 *(exprime le besoin)* **a. à** to have to; **il a à te parler** he's got something to *or* there's something he wants to tell you; **j'ai à réfléchir** I need to think (it over); **tu n'as pas à t'inquiéter** you shouldn't worry, you have nothing to worry about

4 *(locutions)* **je n'ai que faire de tes états d'âme** I couldn't care less about your moods; **la démocratie, ils n'en ont que faire** they couldn't care less about democracy

VT A. 1 *(être propriétaire de ▸ action, bien, domaine etc)* to have, to own, to possess; *(▸ chien, hôtel, voiture)* to have, to own; **a. de l'argent** to have money; **tu n'aurais pas un stylo en plus?** have you got *or* do you happen to have a spare pen?; **je n'ai plus de sucre** I've run out of sugar

2 *Com* to have; **a. un article en magasin** to have an item in stock; **a. un article en vitrine** to display an item in the window; **nous avons plus grand si vous préférez** we have it in a larger size if you prefer; **j'ai encore quelques places à 25 euros/un vol à 17 heures 30** I still have some 25 euro seats/a flight at five thirty p.m. (available)

3 *(ami, collègue, famille etc)* to have; **il a encore sa grand-mère** his grandmother's still alive; **je n'ai plus ma mère** my mother's dead; **voilà sept ans qu'il n'a plus sa femme** he lost his wife *or* his wife died seven years ago; **elle a trois enfants** she has three children; **elle a eu des jumeaux** she had twins; **il n'a jamais eu d'enfants** he never had any children; **elle a un mari qui fait la cuisine** she's got the sort *or* kind of husband who does the cooking; *Fam* **j'ai la chaîne de mon vélo qui est cassée** the chain on my bike is broken[□]; *Fam* **il a sa tante qui est malade** his aunt's ill[□]

4 *(permis de conduire, titre)* to have, to hold; *(droits, privilège)* to have, to enjoy; *(emploi, expérience, devoirs, obligations)* to have; *(documents, preuves)* to have, to possess; *Sport* to have; **quand nous aurons le pouvoir** when we're in power; **a. l'arme nucléaire est devenu une de leurs priorités** possession of nuclear weapons has become one of their priorities; **a. l'heure** to have the time; **quelle heure avez-vous?** what time do you make it?; **a. le ballon** to be in possession of *or* to have the ball

5 *(obtenir ▸ amende, article)* to get; *(▸ information, rabais, récompense)* to get, to obtain; *(▸ au téléphone)* to get through to; **où as-tu eu tes chaussettes?** where did you get *or* buy your socks?; **elle a ses renseignements par Mirna** she gets her information from Mirna; **je pourrais vous a. des places gratuites** I could get you free tickets; **tu auras la réponse/le devis demain** you'll get the answer/estimate tomorrow; *Fam* **il a toutes les filles qu'il veut** he gets all the girls he wants; **j'ai essayé de t'a. toute la journée** I tried to get through to you *or* to contact you all day; **je l'ai eu au téléphone** I got him on the phone; **je n'arrive même pas à a. leur standard** I can't even get through to their switchboard; **pour a. Besançon, composez le 8513** for Besançon *or* to get through to Besançon, dial 8513

6 *(jouir de ▸ beau temps, bonne santé, liberté, bonne réputation)* to have, to enjoy; *(▸ choix, temps, mauvaise réputation)* to have; **a. la confiance de qn** to be trusted by sb; **a. l'estime de qn** to be held in high regard by sb; **vous avez toute ma sympathie** you have all my sympathy; **j'ai une heure pour me décider** I have an hour (in which) to make up my mind; **il a tout pour lui et il n'est pas heureux!** he's got everything you could wish for and he's still not happy!; **tu veux tout a.!** you want (to have) everything!

7 *(recevoir chez soi)* **il a son fils tous les dimanches** his son stays with him every Sunday; **a. de la famille/des amis à dîner** to have relatives/friends over for dinner; **j'aurai ma belle-famille au mois d'août** my in-laws will be staying with me in August

8 *Rad & TV (chaîne, station)* to receive, to get; **bientôt, nous aurons les chaînes européennes** soon, we'll be able to get the European channels

9 *(attraper ▸ otage, prisonnier)* to have; *Fam* **les flics ne l'auront jamais** the cops'll never catch him/her

10 *(atteindre ▸ cible)* to get, to hit; **vise la pomme – je l'ai eue!** aim at the apple – (I) got it!; **tu peux m'a. le pot de confiture?** can you reach the pot of jam for me?

11 *(monter à bord de ▸ avion, bus, train)* to catch; **je n'ai pas pu a. le train de cinq heures** I couldn't catch *or* get the five o'clock train

B. 1 *(présenter ▸ tel aspect)* to have (got); **elle a un joli sourire** she's got *or* she has a nice smile; **tu as de petits pieds** you've got *or* you have small feet; **il a les yeux verts** he's got *or* he has green eyes; **elle a le nez de sa mère** she's got *or* she has her mother's nose; **un monstre qui a sept têtes** a seven-headed monster, a monster with seven heads; **je cherche un acteur qui ait un grand nez** I'm looking for an actor with a big nose; **elle a une jolie couleur de cheveux** her hair's a nice colour; **elle a beaucoup de sa mère** she really takes after her mother; **il a tout de l'aristocrate** he's the aristocratic type; **tu as tout d'un fou avec cette coiffure** you look like a madman with that hairstyle; **les ordinateurs qui ont un disque dur** computers with a hard disk; **la méthode a l'avantage d'être bon marché** this method has the advantage of being cheap; **ton père a le défaut de ne pas écouter ce qu'on lui dit** your father's weakness is not listening to what people tell him; **l'appareil a la particularité de s'éteindre automatiquement** the machine's special feature is that it switches itself off automatically

2 *(avec pour complément une partie du corps)* to have; **a. l'estomac vide** to have an empty stomach; **j'ai la tête lourde** my head aches; **j'ai le bras ankylosé** my arm's stiff; **il a les yeux qui se ferment** he can't keep his eyes open; *très Fam* **en a.** to have a lot of balls; *très Fam* **ne pas en a.** to have no balls

3 *(porter sur soi ▸ accessoire, vêtement, parfum)* to have on, to wear; **tu vois la dame qui a le foulard?** do you see the lady with the scarf?; **faites attention, il a une arme** careful, he's got a weapon *or* he's armed

4 *(faire preuve de)* **a. de l'audace** to be bold; *Fam* **a. du culot** to be cheeky[□], to have a nerve; *Fam* **il a eu le culot de me le dire** he had the cheek[□] *or* the nerve to tell me; **a. du talent** to have talent, to be talented; **ayez la gentillesse de...** would you *or* please be kind enough to...; **aie la politesse de laisser parler les autres** please be polite enough to let the others talk; **il a eu la cruauté de lui dire** he was cruel enough to tell him/her

5 *(exprime la mesure)* to be; **le voilier a 4 m de large** *ou* **largeur** the yacht is 4 m wide; **j'ai 70 cm de tour de taille** I'm 70 cm round the waist, I have a 70 cm waist; **le puits a 2 m de profondeur** the well's 2 m deep; **la porte a 1,50 m de haut** *ou* **hauteur** the door is 1 m 50 cm high; **j'en ai pour 200 euros** it's costing me 200 euros; **tu en as pour 12 jours/deux heures** it'll take you 12 days/two hours; **j'ai pour 300 euros de frais!** I have 300 euros worth of expenses!; **j'en ai eu pour 27 euros** I had to pay *or* it cost me 27 euros; **on en a bien pour trois heures pour aller jusqu'à Lille** it's going to take us *or* we'll need at least three hours to get to Lille; *Fam* **si la police l'attrape, il en aura pour 20 ans!** if the police catch him, he'll get *or* cop 20 years!

6 *(exprime l'âge)* to be; **quel âge as-tu?** how old are you?; **j'ai 35 ans** I'm 35 (years old); **nous avons le même âge** we're the same age; **il a deux ans de plus que moi** he's two years older than me; **il vient d'a. 74 ans** he's just turned 74

C. 1 *(subir ▸ symptôme)* to have, to show, to display; *(▸ maladie, hoquet, mal de tête etc)* to have; *(▸ accident, souci, ennuis)* to have; *(▸ difficultés)* to have, to experience; *(▸ opération)* to undergo, to have; *(▸ crise)* to have, to go through; **a. de la fièvre** to have *or* to be running a temperature; **a. un cancer** to have cancer; **a. des migraines** to suffer from *or* to have migraines; **a. des contractions** to have contractions; **j'ai une rougeur au coude** I have a red blotch on my elbow; **je ne sais pas ce que j'ai aujourd'hui** I don't know what's the matter *or* what's wrong with me today; **qu'as-tu? tu es affreusement pâle** what's wrong? you're deathly pale; **sa sœur n'a rien eu** his/her sister escaped unscathed; *Fam* **le car n'a rien eu du tout, mais la moto est fichue** there wasn't a scratch on the bus, but the motorbike's a write-off; *Fam* **qu'est-ce qu'elle a encore, cette voiture?** NOW what's wrong with this car?[□]; **il a des souris chez lui** he's got mice; **un enfant/chaton qui a des vers** a child/kitten with worms

2 *(émettre, produire ▸ mouvement)* to make; *(▸ ricanement, regard, soupir)* to give; **a. un sursaut** to (give a) start; **elle eut un pauvre sourire** she smiled faintly *or* gave a faint smile; **elle eut cette phrase devenue célèbre** she said *or* uttered those now famous words; **il eut une moue de dédain** he pouted disdainfully

3 *(ressentir)* **a. faim** to be *or* to feel hungry; **a. peur** to be *or* to feel afraid; **a. des scrupules** to have qualms; **a. des remords** to feel remorse; **a. du chagrin** to feel *or* to be sad; **a. un pressentiment** to have a premonition; **a. de l'amitié pour qn** to regard *or* to consider sb as a friend; **a. de l'admiration pour qn** to admire sb; **je n'ai que mépris pour lui** I feel only contempt for him; **a. du respect pour qn** to have respect for *or* to respect sb; *Fam* **en a. après** *ou* **contre qn** to be angry with sb[□]; **après** *ou* **contre qui en as-tu?** who are you angry with?; **ce chien/cette guêpe en a après toi!** this dog/wasp has got it in for you!; **en a. après** *ou* **contre qch** to be angry about sth; **moi, j'en ai après** *ou* **contre la pollution!** pollution really makes me angry!

D. *Fam* **1** *(battre, surpasser)* to get, to beat[□]; **ne t'inquiète pas, on les aura dans la descente!** don't worry, we'll get them going downhill!; **tu essaies d'accaparer le marché, mais je t'aurai!** you're trying to corner the market, but I'll get the better of you!; **il m'a eu au cinquième set** he got *or* beat me in the fifth set; **il va se faire a. dans la dernière ligne droite** he's going to get beaten in the final straight

2 *(escroquer)* to have, to do, to con; **500 euros pour ce buffet? tu t'es fait a.!** 500 euros for that dresser? you were conned *or* had *or* done!; **les touristes, on les a facilement** tourists are easily conned

3 *(duper)* to take in, to take for a ride, to have; **je**

t'ai bien eu! I took you in *or* I had you there, didn't I?; **il m'a eu** he led me up the garden path, I was taken in by him; **tu t'es fait a.!** you've been had *or* taken in *or* taken for a ride!; **tu essaies de m'a.!** you're having *or* putting me on!; **n'essaie pas de m'a.** don't try it on with me

E. *(devoir participer à ▸ débat, élection, réunion)* to have, to hold; *(▸ rendez-vous)* to have; **j'ai (un) cours de chimie ce matin** I've got a chemistry lesson this morning; **avons-nous une réunion aujourd'hui?** is there *or* do we have a meeting today?

• **il y a** V IMPERSONNEL **1** *(dans une description, une énumération ▸ suivi d'un singulier)* there is; *(▸ suivi d'un pluriel)* there are; **il y avait trois chanteurs** there were three singers; **il n'y a pas de lit** there is no bed; **il y a du soleil** the sun is shining; **qu'est-ce qu'il y a dans la malle?** what's in the trunk?; **il n'y a qu'ici qu'on en trouve** this is the only place (where) you can find it/them; **il n'y a pas que moi qui le dis** I'm not the only one to say so; **il y a juste de quoi faire une jupe** there is just enough to make a skirt; **avoue qu'il y a de quoi être énervé!** you must admit it's pretty irritating!; **merci – il n'y a pas de quoi!** thank you – don't mention it *or* you're welcome!; **il n'y a rien à faire, la voiture ne démarre pas** it's no good, the car won't start; **il n'y a pas à dire, il sait ce qu'il veut** there's no denying he knows what he wants; **il n'y a que lui pour dire une chose pareille!** trust him to say something like that!; **circulez, il n'y a rien à voir,** *Fam* **y a rien à voir** move along, there's nothing to see; *Fam* **qu'est-ce qu'il y a? – il y a que j'en ai marre!** what's the matter? – I'm fed up, that's what!; **il y a voiture et voiture** there are cars and cars; *Fam* **il n'y en a que pour lui!** he's the one who gets all the attention!❑; *Fam* **il y en a** *ou* **il y a des gens, je vous jure!** some people, honestly *or* really!; *Fam* **quand il n'y en a plus, il y en a encore!** there's plenty more where that came from!

2 *(exprimant la possibilité, l'obligation etc)* **il n'y a plus qu'à payer les dégâts** we'll just have to pay for the damage; **il n'y a qu'à lui dire** you/we/*etc* just have to tell him; **il n'y a qu'à commander pour être servi** you only have to order to get served

3 *(indiquant la durée)* **il y a 20 ans de ça** 20 years ago; **il y a une heure que j'attends** I've been waiting for an hour

4 *(indiquant la distance)* **il y a bien 3 km d'ici au village** it's at least 3 km to the village

5 *(à l'infinitif)* **il va y a. de la pluie** there's going to be some rain; **il pourrait y a. un changement** there could be a change; **il doit y a. une raison** there must be a *or* some reason

---

avoir-client [avwarklijɑ̃] NM *Compta* customer credit

avoirdupoids, avoirdupois [avwardypwa] NM avoirdupois (weight)

avoir-fournisseur [avwarfurnisœr] NM *Compta* supplier credit

avoisinant, -e [avwazinɑ̃, -ɑ̃t] ADJ neighbouring, nearby; **les quartiers avoisinants ont été évacués** the surrounding streets were evacuated

avoisiner [3] [avwazine] VT **1** *(dans l'espace)* to be near *or* close to, to border on; **la propriété avoisine la rivière** the land borders on the river; *Fig* **son attitude avoisine l'insolence** his/her attitude verges on insolence **2** *(en valeur)* to be close on, to come close to; **les dégâts avoisinent le million** damages come close to one million; **une somme avoisinant les 80 euros** a sum in the region of 80 euros

avortement [avɔrtəmɑ̃] NM *Obst* abortion; **être contre l'a.** to be against abortion; *Fig* **l'a. d'une tentative** the failure of an attempt; **a. spontané** miscarriage; **a. thérapeutique** termination *(for medical reasons)*

avorter [3] [avɔrte] VI **1** *Obst (faire une fausse couche)* to miscarry; *(subir une IVG)* to abort, to have an abortion; *Zool* to abort; **faire a. qn** *(médicament, piqûre)* to induce a miscarriage in sb **2** *(plan, réforme, révolution)* to miscarry, to fall through

VT to abort, to carry out an abortion on; **se faire a.** to have an abortion

avorteur, -euse [avɔrtœr, -øz] NM,F *Obst* abortionist

avorton [avɔrtɔ̃] NM **1** *(personne ▸ chétive)* runt; *(▸ monstrueuse)* freak, monster; **espèce d'a.!** you little runt! **2** *(plante)* stunted plant

avouable [avwabl] ADJ worthy, respectable; **un motif a.** a worthy motive; **des mobiles peu avouables** disreputable motives

avoué[1] [avwe] NM *Jur Br* ≃ solicitor, *Am* ≃ attorney

avoué[2]**, -e** [avwe] ADJ *(partisan, auteur)* confessed; **il est allé là-bas dans le but a. de se venger** he went there with the declared aim of taking revenge

avouer [6] [avwe] VT **1** *(erreur, forfait)* to admit, to confess (to), to own up to; **elle a avoué voyager sans billet/tricher aux cartes** she owned up to travelling without a ticket/to cheating at cards **2** *(doute, sentiment)* to admit *or* to confess to; **elle refuse d'a. ses angoisses/qu'elle a des ennuis** she refuses to acknowledge her anxiety/to admit that she has problems; **je t'avoue que j'en ai assez** I must admit that I've had all I can take; **il faut a. qu'elle a de la patience** you have to admit (that) she's patient

USAGE ABSOLU **il a avoué** *(à la police)* he owned up, he made a full confession; **si personne n'avoue, tout le monde sera puni** if no one owns up, then everyone will be punished; **allez, avoue, elle te plaît** go on, admit it, you like her

VPR **s'avouer elle ne s'avoue pas encore battue** *ou* **vaincue** she won't admit defeat yet; **je m'avoue complètement découragé** I confess *or* admit to feeling utterly discouraged; **s'a. coupable** to admit one's guilt

avril [avril] NM April; *Prov* **en a., ne te découvre pas d'un fil** ≃ ne'er cast a clout till May is out; *voir aussi* **mars**

AVS [aveɛs] NF **1** *(abrév* **auxiliaire de vie sociale***)* ≃ social worker **2** *Suisse Assur (abrév* **assurance vieillesse et survivants***)* = Swiss pension scheme

avunculaire [avɔ̃kylɛr] ADJ avuncular

axe [aks] NM **1** *Géom* axis; **a. des abscisses** x-axis; **a. optique** principal axis; **a. des ordonnées** y-axis; **a. de rotation** axis of rotation; **a. de symétrie** axis of symmetry; **a. des X** x-axis; **a. des Y** y-axis; **a. des Z** z-axis

2 *(direction)* direction, line; **deux grands axes de développement** two major directions of development; **développer de nouveaux axes de recherche** to open up new areas of research; **sa politique s'articule autour de deux axes principaux** his/her policy revolves around two main themes *or* issues; **il est dans l'a. du parti** *(membre)* he's in the mainstream of the party; *Ftbl* **dans l'a. (du terrain)** down the middle

3 *(voie)* **ils vont ouvrir un nouvel a. Paris–Bordeaux** they're going to open up a new road link between Paris and Bordeaux; *Rail* **l'a. Lyon–Genève** the Lyons–Geneva line; **(grand) a.** *Br* major road, *Am* main highway; **tous les (grands) axes routiers sont bloqués par la neige** all major roads are snowed up

4 *Tech* axle

5 *Hist* **l'A.** the Axis

• **dans l'axe de** PRÉP *(dans le prolongement de)* in line with; **la perspective s'ouvre dans l'a. du palais** the view opens out from the palace

axer [3] [akse] VT **il est très axé sur le spiritisme** he is very keen on spiritualism; **toute sa vie est axée là-dessus** his whole life revolves around it; **a. une campagne publicitaire sur les enfants** to build an advertising campaign around children; **le premier trimestre sera axé autour de Proust** the first term will be devoted to Proust; **une modernisation axée sur l'importation des meilleures techniques étrangères** modernization based on importing the best foreign techniques; **une visite touristique axée sur...** a guided tour focusing on...

axial, -e, -aux, -ales [aksjal, -o] ADJ **1** *(d'un axe)* axial **2** *(central)* central; **éclairage a.** central overhead lighting *(in a street)*

axillaire [aksilɛr] ADJ *Anat* axillary

axiomatique [aksjɔmatik] ADJ *Ling* axiomatic
NF *Math* axiomatics *(singulier)*

axiome [aksjom] NM *Ling & Math* axiom

axis [aksis] NM *Anat & Zool* axis

ayant *voir* **avoir**[2]

ayant cause [ɛjɑ̃koz] *(pl* **ayants cause***)* NM *Jur* beneficiary, legal successor

ayant-compte [ɛjɑ̃kɔ̃t] *(pl* **ayants-comptes***)* NM *Banque* account holder

ayant droit [ɛjɑ̃drwa] *(pl* **ayants droit***)* NM *Jur (gén)* beneficiary; *(à une propriété)* rightful owner; *(à un droit)* eligible party

ayatollah [ajatɔla] NM *Rel* ayatollah; *Fam Fig* **les ayatollahs du libéralisme** fanatical advocates of the free market, those who preach the gospel of the free market

ayons *etc voir* **avoir**[2]

ayurvéda [ajurveda] NM *Méd* ayurveda

ayurvédique [ajurvedik] ADJ *Méd* ayurvedic

azalée [azale] NF *Bot* azalea

Azerbaïdjan [azɛrbajdʒɑ̃] NM **l'A.** Azerbaijan

azerbaïdjanais, -e [azɛrbaidʒanɛ, -ɛz] ADJ Azerbaijani
NM *(langue)* Azerbaijani

• **Azerbaïdjanais, -e** NM,F Azerbaijani; **les A.** the Azerbaijanis *or* Azerbaijani

azéri, -e [azeri] ADJ Azeri

• **Azéri, -e** NM,F Azeri

azimut [azimyt] NM azimuth; *Fam* **partir dans tous les azimuts** to be all over the place; **la discussion partait dans tous les azimuts** the discussion was all over the place

• **tous azimuts** *Fam* ADJ all-out, full-scale❑; **une attaque tous azimuts** an all-out attack ADV all over (the place); **prospecter tous azimuts** to canvass all over

azimutal, -e, -aux, -ales [azimytal, -o] ADJ azimuthal

azimuté, -e [azimyte] ADJ *Fam* crazy❑, *Br* round the bend

azotate [azɔtat] NM *Chim* nitrate; **a. de potasse** nitre, saltpetre

azote [azɔt] NM *Chim* nitrogen

azoté, -e [azɔte] ADJ *Chim* nitrogenous, azotic

azoter [3] [azɔte] VT *Chim* to nitrogenize

azotique [azɔtik] ADJ *Chim* nitric

azotite [azɔtit] NM *Chim* nitrite

AZT® [azedte] NM *Méd (abrév* **azidothymidine***)* AZT

aztèque [astɛk] ADJ Aztec

• **Aztèque** NMF Aztec

azur [azyr] NM **1** *(couleur)* azure, sky-blue; **la Côte d'A.** the French Riviera, the Côte d'Azur **2** *Littéraire (ciel)* skies
ADJ INV azure, sky-blue

azuré, -e [azyre] ADJ *Littéraire* azure, sky-blue

azurer [3] [azyre] VT to blue, to tinge with blue

azyme [azim] *voir* **pain**

B[1], b [be] **NM INV 1** *(lettre)* B, b; **B comme Berthe** ≃ B for Bob **2** *Mus (note)* B

B[2] *Scol (abrév écrite* **bien***)* = good grade (as assessment of schoolwork), ≃ B

B2B [bitubi] **ADJ** *(abrév* **business to business***)* B2B

B2C [bitusi] **ADJ** *(abrév* **business to consumer***)* B2C

BA [bea] **NF** *Fam (abrév* **bonne action***)* = good deed; **faire une BA** to do a good deed; **j'ai fait ma BA pour aujourd'hui** I've done my good deed for the day

baba [baba] **ADJ** *Fam* **en être** *ou* **rester b.** to be flabbergasted
NM 1 *Culin* **b. (au rhum)** (rum) baba **2** *Fam (locution)* **l'avoir dans le b.** to be let down; **après ils partiront en congé et c'est toi qui l'auras dans le b.!** then they'll go off on holiday and you'll be left holding the baby!
NMF *(hippie)* hippyish person; *(personne relax)* laid-back person

b.a.-ba [beaba] **NM** ABCs, rudiments; **apprendre le b. du métier** to learn the ABCs *or* basics of the trade

baba cool [babakul] *(pl* **babas cool***)* *Fam* **ADJ** *(hippie)* hippyish; *(relax)* laid-back; **elle est très b.** she's a bit of a hippy
NMF *(hippie)* hippyish person; *(décontractée)* laid-back person

Babel [babɛl] *voir* **tour**[1]

babeleer [babəlɛr] **NM** *Belg Fam* chatterbox

babeurre [babœr] **NM** buttermilk

babil [babil] **NM** *(des enfants, du ruisseau)* babbling; *(des oiseaux)* twittering

babillage [babijaʒ] **NM** *(des enfants)* babble, babbling; *(d'un bavard)* chatter

babillard, -e [babijar, -ard] **ADJ** *Littéraire (personne)* chattering; *(ruisseau)* babbling
NM,F *Littéraire (personne)* chatterbox
NM *Offic Ordinat* bulletin board, BBS
• **babillarde NF** *Fam* letter□

babillement [babijmɑ̃] = **babil**

babiller [3] [babije] **VI** *(oiseau)* to twitter; *(ruisseau)* to murmur, to babble; *(enfant)* to babble, to chatter; *(bavard)* to prattle (on), to chatter (away)

babines [babin] **NFPL 1** *Zool* chops **2** *Fam (lèvres)* lips□; **se lécher** *ou* **pourlécher les b.** to lick one's chops; **d'avance, je m'en lèche les b.** my mouth's watering in anticipation

babiole [babjɔl] **NF 1** *(objet)* knick-knack, trinket **2** *(incident)* trifle

bâbord [babɔr] **NM** *Naut* port; **à b.** on the port side

babouche [babuʃ] **NF** (oriental) slipper

babouin [babwɛ̃] **NM** *Zool* baboon

baboune [babun] *Fam* **NF** *Can (moue)* **faire la b.** to sulk□
• **babounes NFPL** *(lèvres)* big *or* full lips□

baby [bebi] **ADJ INV taille b.** baby-size(d); **whisky b.** small whisky
NM small whisky

baby-blues [bebibluz] **NM** baby blues

baby-boom [bebibum, babibum] *(pl* **baby-booms***)* **NM** baby boom; **les enfants du b.** the baby boomers

baby-foot [babifut] **NM INV** *(jeu)* table football; *(table)* football table

Babylone [babilɔn] **NF** *Géog* Babylon

Babylonie [babilɔni] **NF** *Antiq* Babylonia

babylonien, -enne [babilɔnjɛ̃, -ɛn] **ADJ** Babylonian
• **Babylonien, -enne NM,F** Babylonian

babyphone [babifɔn] **NM** baby monitor

baby-sitter [bebisitœr] *(pl* **baby-sitters***)* **NMF** baby-sitter

baby-sitting [bebisitiŋ] *(pl* **baby-sittings***)* **NM** baby-sitting; **faire du b.** to baby-sit

bac [bak] **NM 1** *Naut* (small) ferry *or* ferryboat
2 *(dans un réfrigérateur)* compartment, tray; **b. à glace** ice-cube tray; **b. à légumes** vegetable compartment
3 *Ordinat* **b. d'alimentation (papier)** *(d'une imprimante)* sheet feed; **b. de** *ou* **à papier, b. de** *ou* **à feuilles** *(d'imprimante)* paper tray
4 *(pour plantes)* **b. (à fleurs)** plant holder
5 *Com (présentoir)* dumpbin
6 *(fosse, réserve ▸ pour liquides)* tank, vat; *(▸ pour stockage de pièces)* container; **b. à douche** shower tray; **b. à sable** *(d'enfant) Br* sandpit, *Am* sandbox; *(pour routes)* grit bin
7 *Phot (cuvette ▸ vide)* tray; *(▸ pleine)* bath
8 *Fam Scol (diplôme)* = final secondary school examination, qualifying for university entrance, *Br* ≃ A-levels, *Am* ≃ high school diploma; **b. + 3** *(dans une annonce)* = three years of higher education required

bacante [bakɑ̃t] = **bacchante**

baccalauréat [bakalɔrea] **NM** *Scol* = final secondary school examination, qualifying for university entrance, *Br* ≃ A-levels, *Am* ≃ high school diploma; **b. international** international baccalaureate; **b. L** *ou* **littéraire** = arts-based baccalauréat; **b. S** *ou* **scientifique** = science-based baccalauréat

> **BACCALAURÉAT**
>
> The "baccalauréat", or "bac", is taken by pupils who have completed their final year at the "lycée"; successful candidates may go to university. Depending on which subjects pupils choose to study at "lycée", they prepare for a "baccalauréat général", "technologique" (vocational) or "professionnel" (vocational and including professional training). Since the last major reform, in 1995, there have been three main types of "baccalauréat général", each corresponding to a specific field: "bac L" (arts subjects), "bac ES" (economics and social studies) and "bac S" (sciences). Pupils study all major subjects for the "bac", each subject being given a particular **coefficient** (see box at this entry) depending on the "baccalauréat" chosen.

baccara, baccarat[1] [bakara] **NM** *Cartes* baccara, baccarat

baccarat[2] [bakara] **NM** Baccarat (crystal); **un vase en b.** a Baccarat crystal vase

bacchanale [bakanal] **NF** *Littéraire (débauche)* drunken revel, bacchanal; *(danse)* bacchanalian dance
• **bacchanales NFPL** *Antiq & Myth* bacchanalia

bacchante [bakɑ̃t] **NF** *Antiq & Myth* bacchante, bacchanal
• **bacchantes NFPL** *Fam Hum* moustache□, whiskers

bâche [baʃ] **NF 1** *(toile)* transport cover, canvas sheet, tarpaulin; **bâches imperméables** waterproof tarpaulin **2** *Tech (réservoir)* tank, cistern

bachelier, -ère [baʃəlje, -ɛr] **NM,F** *Scol* = student who has passed the baccalauréat

bâcher [3] [baʃe] **VT** to cover (with a tarpaulin)
VPR se bâcher *Fam* to hit the sack *or* the hay

bachi-bouzouk [baʃibuzuk] *(pl* **bachi-bouzouks***)* **NM** *Fam Hist* Bashi-Bazouk

bachique [baʃik] **ADJ** Bacchic; **chanson b.** drinking song

bachot [baʃo] **NM 1** *(barque)* wherry, skiff **2** *Fam Vieilli Scol* = **baccalauréat**

bachotage [baʃɔtaʒ] **NM** *Fam Scol & Univ* cramming; **faire du b.** to cram, *Br* to swot up, *Am* to bone up

bachoter [3] [baʃɔte] **VI** *Fam Scol & Univ* to cram, *Br* to swot up, *Am* to bone up; **il a été obligé de b. dans toutes les matières** he had to cram all the subjects

bachoteur, -euse [baʃɔtœr, -øz] **NM,F** *Fam Scol & Univ* crammer

bacillaire [basilɛr] *Biol & Méd* **ADJ** bacillar, bacillary; **malade b.** tubercular patient
NMF tubercular patient

bacille [basil] **NM 1** *Biol & Méd (bactérie)* bacillus **2** *Entom* stick insect

bacillose [basiloz] **NF** *Méd* pulmonary tuberculosis

backbone [bakbon] **NM** *Ordinat* backbone

background [bakgrawnd] **NM** background

back-office [bakofis] *(pl* **back-offices***)* **NM** *Banque* back office

bâclage [baklaʒ] **NM** *Fam (action)* botching; **cette toiture, c'est du b.!** they/you/*etc* made a really shoddy job of that roof!

bâcle [bakl] **NF** bar *(across a door or window)*

bâcler [3] [bakle] **VT** *Fam* to botch; **nous avons bâclé les formalités en deux jours** we pushed through the red tape in a couple of days; **b. sa toilette** to give oneself a quick wash□; **je vais b. les comptes vite fait** I'll throw the accounts together in no time; **c'est du travail bâclé** *(réparation)* it's a botched job; *(devoir)* it's slapdash work

bacon [bekɔn] **NM** *(lard)* bacon; *(porc fumé)* smoked loin of pork, Canadian bacon

bactéricide [bakterisid] *Biol* **ADJ** bactericidal
NM bactericide

bactérie [bakteri] **NF** *Biol* bacterium; **bactéries** bacteria

bactérien, -enne [bakterjɛ̃, -ɛn] **ADJ** *Biol* bacterial

bactériologie [bakterjɔlɔʒi] NF *Biol* bacteriology

bactériologique [bakterjɔlɔʒik] ADJ *Biol* bacteriological

bactériologiste [bakterjɔlɔʒist] NMF *Biol* bacteriologist

bactériophage [bakterjɔfaʒ] *Biol* ADJ bacteriophage
NM bacteriophage

badaboum [badabum] EXCLAM *(bruit de chute)* crash!, bang!

badaud, -e [bado, -od] NM,F **1** *(curieux)* curious onlooker; *(promeneur)* stroller; **un attroupement de badauds** a crowd of gaping onlookers; **attirer les badauds** to draw a crowd **2** *Ordinat (sur Internet)* lurker

badauder [3] [badode] VI *Littéraire* to stroll about full of idle curiosity

baderne [badɛrn] NF *très Fam* **une vieille b.** an old fogy, an old stick-in-the-mud

badge [badʒ] NM **1** *(insigne)* badge; **passer son b. de secouriste** to get one's first-aid badge **2** *(carte magnétique)* swipe card

badigeon [badiʒɔ̃] NM *Constr (pour l'extérieur)* whitewash; *(pour l'intérieur)* distemper; *(pigmenté)* coloured distemper, *Br* colourwash; **passer qch au b.** *(pour l'extérieur)* to whitewash sth; *(pour l'intérieur)* to distemper sth

badigeonnage [badiʒɔnaʒ] NM **1** *Constr (de l'extérieur)* whitewashing; *(de l'intérieur)* distempering; *(avec un badigeon pigmenté)* painting with coloured distemper, *Br* colourwashing **2** *Méd* painting; **le b. d'une plaie avec de l'alcool** painting a wound with surgical spirit

badigeonner [3] [badiʒɔne] VT **1** *Constr (intérieur)* to distemper; *(extérieur)* to whitewash; *(en couleur)* to paint with coloured distemper, *Br* to colourwash **2** *Méd* to paint; **b. la plaie d'alcool** paint *or* dab surgical spirit liberally onto the wound **3** *Culin* to brush; **b. la pâte de jaune d'œuf** brush the pastry with egg yolk

badin[1] [badɛ̃] NM *Aviat* airspeed indicator

badin[2], **-e**[1] [badɛ̃, -in] ADJ *(gai)* light-hearted; *(plaisant)* playful; **tenir des propos badins** to (indulge in light-hearted) banter; **répondre d'un ton b.** to answer playfully *or* jokingly

badinage [badinaʒ] NM banter, jesting, badinage

badine[2] [badin] NF switch, stick

badiner [3] [badine] VI to jest, to banter, to tease; **ne badine pas avec ta santé** don't trifle with your health; **elle ne badine pas sur le chapitre de l'exactitude** she's very strict about *or* she's a stickler for punctuality

badinerie [badinri] NF *Littéraire* jest, badinage

bad-lands [badlɑ̃ds] NFPL *Géol* badlands

badminton [badmintɔn] NM *Sport* badminton

bâdrant, -e [bɑdrɑ̃, -ɑ̃t] *Can Joual* ADJ annoying□
NM,F annoying person□, pain (in the neck)

bâdrer [3] [bɑdre] VT *Can* **b. qn** to bug sb

BAFA, Bafa [bafa] NM *(abrév* **brevet d'aptitude aux fonctions d'animation***)* = diploma for youth leaders and workers

baffe [baf] NF *Fam* slap□, clout, smack; **coller une b. à qn** to give sb a smack in the face; **recevoir/donner une paire de baffes** to get/to give a couple of slaps

baffer [3] [bafe] VT *Fam* to clout, to cuff

Baffin [bafɛ̃] *voir* **terre**

baffle [bafl] NM *(enceinte)* speaker; *Tech* baffle

bafouer [6] [bafwe] VT *(personne)* to ridicule, to jeer at; *(autorité, loi)* to flout, to defy; *(sentiment)* to ridicule, to scoff at

bafouillage [bafujaʒ] NM **1** *(bredouillage)* sputtering, stammering **2** *(propos ▸ incohérents)* gibberish; *(▸ inaudibles)* mumblings

bafouille [bafuj] NF *très Fam* letter□

bafouiller [3] [bafuje] VI *(bégayer)* to stutter, to stammer; **tellement embarrassé qu'il en bafouillait** stammering with embarrassment
VT to stammer; **"euh… oui, euh… non", bafouilla-t-elle** "well… yes, well… no," she stammered; **b. des propos incohérents** to talk (a lot of) gibberish

bâfrer [3] [bɑfre] *très Fam* VT to gobble, to wolf (down); **il a bâfré trois douzaines d'huîtres** he wolfed down three dozen oysters
VI to stuff one's face, to pig out

bâfreur, -euse [bɑfrœr, -øz] NM,F *très Fam* glutton, greedy guts, *Am* chowhound

bagage [bagaʒ] NM **1** *(pour voyager)* baggage *(UNCOUNT)*, luggage *(UNCOUNT)*; **mes bagages** my luggage; **chacun de mes bagages** *(sacs)* each (one) of my bags; *(valises)* each (one) of my suitcases; **il avait pour tout b. un sac et un manteau** he was carrying only a bag and a coat; **faire ses bagages** to pack one's bags; *Fig* **il a fait ses bagages sans demander son reste** he left without further ado; **en b. accompagné** *(expédier, voyager)* as registered baggage; **un b. à main** a piece of hand-baggage *or* hand-luggage; **bagages de soute** registered baggage *(in an aeroplane)* **2** *(formation)* background (knowledge); **son b. scientifique était insuffisant pour faire des études de médecine** his scientific knowledge was insufficient for studying medicine; **en musique, elle a déjà un bon b.** she already has a good grounding in music

bagagerie [bagaʒri] NF luggage room

bagagiste [bagaʒist] NM **1** *(dans un hôtel)* porter; *(dans un aéroport)* baggage handler **2** *(fabricant)* travel goods manufacturer

bagarre [bagar] NF **1** *(échange de coups)* fight, brawl; **une b. entre ivrognes** a drunken brawl; **il va y avoir de la b.** there's going to be a fight; **aimer la b.** to like a fight **2** *Fig* battle, fight; **se lancer dans la b. politique** to join the political fray; *Sport* **la b. a été très dure pendant la deuxième mi-temps/le deuxième set** it was a close fight during the second half/set

bagarrer [3] [bagare] VI *(physiquement)* to fight; *(verbalement)* to argue; **elle a bagarré dur pour arriver là où elle est** she fought hard to get where she is
VPR **se bagarrer 1** *(se combattre)* to fight, to scrap; **ils n'arrêtent pas de se b.** they're always fighting
2 *(se quereller)* to quarrel, to have a scene; **mes parents se bagarraient** my parents used to quarrel
3 *(combattre)* to fight; **il adore se b.** he loves a good fight
4 *Fig* to fight, to struggle; **se b. pour que justice soit faite** to fight *or* to struggle in order to see justice done

bagarreur, -euse [bagarœr, -øz] ADJ *Joual* aggressive; **elle a des enfants bagarreurs** her kids are always ready for a scrap
NM,F brawler

bagatelle [bagatɛl] NF **1** *(chose ▸ sans valeur)* trinket, bauble; *(▸ sans importance)* trifle, bagatelle; **se fâcher pour une b.** to take offence over nothing; *Ironique* **ça m'a coûté la b. de 5000 euros** it cost me a mere 5,000 euros **2** *Mus* bagatelle **3** *Fam (sexe)* **il est porté/elle est portée sur la b.** he/she likes to play around

baggy [bagi] ADJ baggy
NM **un b.** baggy *Br* trousers *or Am* pants, baggies

bagnard [baɲar] NM *Hist* convict

bagne [baɲ] NM *(prison)* prison; *Hist* penal colony; **condamné à cinq ans de b.** sentenced to five years' penal servitude; *Fig* **c'est le b., ici!** they work you to death in this place!; **son travail, c'est pas le b.!** he's not exactly overworked!

bagnole [baɲɔl] NF *Fam* car□; **une vieille b.** an old car *or Br* banger

bagou, bagout [bagu] NM *Fam* glibness (of tongue); **avoir du b.** to have the gift of the gab

baguage [bagaʒ] NM **1** *Hort* girdling **2** *Orn* ringing

bague [bag] NF **1** *(bijou)* ring; **passer la b. au doigt à qn** to marry sb; **b. de fiançailles** engagement ring **2** *(d'un champignon)* ring; *(d'un cigare)* band; *(d'une boîte de conserve)* ring-pull **3** *Tech* collar, ring; *Élec* **b. collectrice** collector ring; **b. de roulement** ball race, bearing race; **b. de serrage** jubilee clip

baguenauder [3] [bagnode] *Fam* VI to amble *or* to stroll *or* to drift along
VPR **se baguenauder** to amble *or* to stroll *or* to drift along

baguer [3] [bage] VT **1** *(oiseau)* to ring; *(doigt)* to put a ring on **2 un cigare bagué d'or** a cigar with a gold band **3** *Couture* to baste, to tack

baguette [bagɛt] NF **1** *(petit bâton)* switch, stick; **b. divinatoire** *ou* **de sourcier** divining rod; **b. magique** magic wand; *Fig* **d'un coup de b. magique** as if by magic; **elle a les cheveux raides comme des baguettes (de tambour)** her hair is poker straight
2 *Culin (pain)* baguette, French loaf *or Br* stick; *(pour manger)* chopstick; **manger avec des baguettes** to eat with chopsticks
3 *Mus (pour diriger)* baton; **sous la b. du jeune chef** under the baton of the young conductor; **b. de tambour** drumstick; **mener** *ou* **faire marcher qn à la b.** to rule sb with an iron hand *or* a rod of iron
4 *Aut* **b. de protection latérale** side trim
5 *Menuis* length of beading; **cacher les câbles avec des baguettes** to bead in the wires

baguier [bagje] NM ring case

bah [ba] EXCLAM *(marque l'indifférence)* who cares!; **b., on verra bien!** oh well, we'll have to see!

Bahamas [baamas] NFPL **les B.** the Bahamas; **vivre aux B.** to live in the Bahamas; **aller aux B.** to go to the Bahamas

Bahreïn [barɛjn], **Bahrayn** [barajn] NM *Géog* Bahrain, Bahrein; **vivre à B.** to live in Bahrain; **aller à B.** to go to Bahrain

bahut [bay] NM **1** *(buffet ▸ gén)* sideboard, buffet; *(▸ ancien)* trunk **2** *Fam (collège, lycée)* school□ **3** *Fam (taxi)* taxi□, cab□; *(camion)* lorry□, truck□; **avance ton b.!** get that heap of junk out of my way!

bai, -e[1] [bɛ] ADJ *(cheval)* bay

baie[2] [bɛ] NF **1** *Bot* berry; **b. d'acai** *ou* **açaï** acai berry; **b. de goji** goji berry
2 *Archit* opening; **b. vitrée** picture *or* bay window
3 *Géog* bay; **la b. de Baffin** Baffin Bay; **la b. de Cardigan** Cardigan Bay; *Hist* **la b. des Cochons** the Bay of Pigs; **la b. d'Hudson** Hudson Bay; **la b. de San Francisco** San Francisco Bay
4 *Ordinat* bay

baignade [bɛɲad] NF **1** *(activité)* swimming, *Br* bathing; **b. interdite** *(sur panneau)* no swimming
2 *(lieu)* swimming *or Br* bathing place

baigner [4] [beɲe] VT **1** *(pour laver) Br* to bath, *Am* to bathe; **c'est l'heure de b. les enfants** it's time *Br* to bath *or Am* to bathe the children; *(pour soigner)* to bathe; **baigne ton doigt malade dans de l'eau chaude** bathe your sore finger in hot water
2 *Littéraire (sujet: fleuve, mer)* to wash, to bathe; **la Seine baigne Paris** the Seine bathes *or* washes Paris; **un rayon de lumière baignait la pièce** light suffused the room, the room was bathed in light
3 *(mouiller)* to soak, to wet; **un visage baigné de larmes** a face bathed in tears; **il était baigné de sueur après sa course** he was soaked with sweat after the race
VI **1** *(être immergé ▸ dans l'eau, dans le lait)* to soak; *(▸ dans l'alcool, dans le vinaigre)* to steep; **des cerises baignant dans l'alcool** cherries steeping *or* soaking in alcohol; **les pommes de terre baignaient dans la sauce** the potatoes were swimming in sauce; **il baignait dans son sang** he was lying in a pool of his own blood
2 *Littéraire (être environné ▸ de brouillard, de brume)* to be shrouded *or* swathed; **le paysage baignait dans la brume** the countryside was shrouded in mist
3 *Fig* **nous baignons dans le mystère** we're deep in mystery; **elle baigne dans la musique depuis sa jeunesse** she's been immersed in music since she was young
4 *Fam (locution)* **ça** *ou* **tout baigne (dans l'huile)!** everything's great *or* fine!
VPR **se baigner 1** *(emploi réfléchi)* **se b. les yeux/le visage** to bathe one's eyes/face **2** *(dans une baignoire)* to have *or Am* to take a bath; *(dans un lac, la mer, une piscine)* to have a swim, to go swim-

ming; **à quelle heure on va se b.?** when are we going swimming?, when are we having a swim?

baigneur, -euse [beɲœr, -øz] **NM,F** swimmer, *Br* bather

NM baby doll

baignoire [beɲwar] **NF 1** *(dans une salle de bains)* bathtub, *Br* bath; **b. encastrée** sunken bath; **b. sabot** hip bath **2** *Théât* ground floor box **3** *Mil & Naut* conning tower

bail [baj] *(pl* **baux** [bo]) **NM 1** *Jur (de location)* lease; **donner qch à b.** to lease (out) sth; **prendre qch à b.** to take out a lease on sth; **faire/passer un b.** to draw up/to enter into a lease; **renouveler un b.** to renew a lease; **résilier un b.** to cancel a lease; **b. commercial/professionnel/rural** commercial/professional/rural lease; **b. à construction** construction lease; **b. emphytéotique** long lease; **b. à ferme** farm lease; **b. d'habitation** *Br* house-letting lease, *Am* rental lease; **b. à long terme** long-term lease *(18–25 years)*; **b. à loyer** rental agreement, lease **2** *Fam (locution)* **il y a** *ou* **ça fait un b. que...** it's been ages since...; **ça fait un b. qu'il ne m'a pas téléphoné** it's been ages since he last phoned me, he hasn't phoned me for ages

baille [baj] **NF 1** *Naut (baquet, mauvais bateau)* tub **2** *très Fam (eau)* water❑; **tomber** *ou* **se retrouver à la b.** to fall into the drink

bâillement [bajmɑ̃] **NM 1** *(action)* yawn; **étouffer un b.** to stifle a yawn; **des bâillements** yawning *(UNCOUNT)* **2** *(ouverture)* gap

bâiller [3] [baje] **VI 1** *(ouvrir la bouche)* to yawn; **b. de sommeil/d'ennui/de fatigue** to yawn drowsily/with boredom/with tiredness; **b. à s'en décrocher la mâchoire** *ou* **comme une carpe** to yawn one's head off; **ses discours me font b.** his speeches send me to sleep **2** *(être entrouvert ▸ porte, volet)* to be ajar *or* half-open; *(▸ col)* to gape; **son chemisier bâille aux emmanchures** her blouse gapes at the armholes

bailleresse [bajrɛs] *voir* **bailleur**

bâilles [bɑj] **NFPL** *Belg* **faire des b.** to yawn

bailleur, -eresse [bajœr, bajrɛs] **NM,F** *Jur* lessor; **b. de fonds** *(investisseur)* (financial) backer, sponsor; *(associé passif) Br* sleeping partner, *Am* silent partner; **b. de licence** licenser

bailli [baji] **NM** *Hist* bailiff

bailliage [bajaʒ] **NM** *Hist (circonscription)* bailiwick; *(tribunal)* bailiff's court

bâillon [bajɔ̃] **NM** *(sur une personne)* gag; **mettre un b. à qn** to gag sb; *Fig* **mettre un b. à l'opposition** to gag *or* to muzzle the opposition

bâillonner [3] [bajɔne] **VT** *(otage, victime)* to gag; *Fig (adversaire, opposant)* to gag, to muzzle

bain [bɛ̃] **NM 1** *(pour la toilette)* bath, bathing; **donner un b. à qn** to bath sb, to give sb a bath; **prendre un b.** to have *or Am* to take a bath; **vider/faire couler un b.** to empty/to run a bath; **mon b. refroidit** my bath's *or* bathwater's getting cold; **b. de bouche** mouthwash; **b. de boue** mudbath; **b. moussant/parfumé** bubble/scented bath; **b. de pieds** footbath; **prendre un b. de pieds** to soak *or* to bathe one's feet (in warm soapy water); **b. de siège** sitz-bath, hip bath; *Can* **b. tourbillon** whirlpool bath; **b. turc** Turkish bath; **b. de vapeur** steam bath; *Fig* **être dans le b.** *(s'y connaître)* to be in the swing of things; *(être compromis)* to be in it up to one's neck; *Fig* **quand on n'est plus dans le b.** when you've got out of the habit of things; **être dans le même b. (que)** to be in the same boat (as); **mettre deux choses dans le même b.** to lump two things together; **mettre qn dans le b.** *(l'initier)* to put sb in the picture; *(le compromettre)* to drag sb into it

2 *Can (baignoire)* bathtub, *Br* bath

3 b. à remous Jacuzzi®

4 *(activité)* bathing, swimming; **prendre un b.** *(nager)* to have a swim; *(patauger)* to have a paddle

5 *(à la piscine)* **grand b.** *(bassin)* big pool; *(côté)* deep end; **petit b.** *(bassin)* children's pool; *(côté)* shallow end

6 *Fig (immersion)* **b. de culture** feast of culture; **ce séjour à Paris était un véritable b. de culture** this stay in Paris was a complete cultural experience; **b. de foule** walkabout; **prendre un b. de foule** to go on a walkabout; **b. de jouvence** rejuvenating *or* regenerating experience; **cela a été pour moi un b. de jouvence** it's taken years off me; **b. linguistique** *ou* **de langue** immersion in a language; **la manifestation s'est terminée dans un b. de sang** the demonstration ended in a bloodbath; **b. de soleil** sunbathing; **prendre un b. de soleil** to sunbathe

7 *(substance pour trempage)* bath; *Phot* **b. d'arrêt** stop bath; *Phot* **b. de fixage** fixing bath; *Culin* **b. de friture** deep fat; *Phot* **b. révélateur** *ou* **de développement** developing bath, developer; *Chim* **b. de sable** sandbath; **b. de sels** salt bath; **b. de trempe** quenching bath; *(cuve)* vat

• **bains NMPL** *(établissement)* baths; **bains douches** public baths (with showers); **bains turcs** Turkish baths

• **de bain ADJ** *(sels, serviette)* bath *(avant n)*

bain-marie [bɛ̃mari] *(pl* **bains-marie)** *Culin* **NM 1** *(processus)* bain-marie cooking **2** *(casserole)* bain-marie

• **au bain-marie ADV** in a bain-marie

baïonnette [bajɔnɛt] **NF** bayonet; **ampoule à b.** bulb with a bayonet fitting

baïram [bairam] **NM** *Rel* Bairam

baisable [bɛzabl] **ADJ** *Vulg* fuckable, *Br* shaggable

baise [bɛz] **NF 1** *Belg (baiser)* kiss **2** *Vulg* **la b.** *(sexe)* sex❑, *Br* shagging

baise-en-ville [bɛzɑ̃vil] **NM INV** *Fam Hum Vieilli* overnight bag❑

baisemain [bɛzmɛ̃] **NM faire le b. à qn** to kiss sb's hand

baiser¹ [beze] **NM** kiss; **donner** *ou* **faire/envoyer un b. à qn** to give/to blow sb a kiss; **gros baisers** *(dans une lettre)* love and kisses; **b. d'adieu** parting *or* goodbye *or* farewell kiss; **b. de Judas** kiss of Judas; **b. de paix** kiss of peace

baiser² [4] [beze] **VT 1** *Littéraire (embrasser)* to kiss; **b. le front/la main de qn** to kiss sb's forehead/hand; **b. la terre** to kiss the ground

2 *Vulg (coucher avec)* to screw, to fuck; **il est mal baisé** he needs to get laid; **c'est une mal baisée** she's a frustrated old cow

3 *Vulg (tromper)* to shaft, to con; *(vaincre)* to outdo❑; **se faire b.** to get conned

4 *(prendre)* to nab; **ils se sont fait b. par le contrôleur** they got nabbed by the ticket inspector

VI *Vulg* to fuck; **il baise bien** he's a good fuck; **on a bien baisé** we had a good fuck; **b. avec qn** to screw sb

baiseur, -euse [bezœr, -øz] **NM,F** *Vulg* **c'est un sacré b./une sacrée baiseuse** he/she screws around; **c'est un bon b./une bonne baiseuse** he/she's good in bed

baisse [bɛs] **NF 1** *(des prix, du chômage, du taux de l'inflation)* fall, drop, decline (**de** in); **la b. du dollar** the fall in the value of the dollar; **b. des prix** *(résultat)* fall in prices; *(action)* price cutting **2** *Bourse (des cours, des valeurs)* fall; **le marché des obligations a connu une b. sensible** the bond market has dropped considerably **3** *(de la température, de la tension)* fall, drop (**de** in)

• **à la baisse ADJ spéculations à la b.** bear speculations; **le marché est à la b.** the market is falling *or* is bearish **ADV** on the downswing *or* downturn *or* decline; **jouer** *ou* **spéculer à la b.** to bear, to go a bear, to speculate for a fall; **revoir** *ou* **réviser à la b.** to revise downwards

• **en baisse ADJ être en b.** *(crédits, fonds)* to be sinking *or* decreasing; *(actions)* to be falling; *(température, nombre d'adhésions)* to be falling *or* dropping; *(popularité)* to be on the decline *or* the wane; **acheter en b.** to buy on a falling market

BAISSER [4] [bese] **VT 1** *(vitre de voiture)* to lower, to wind *or* to let down; *(store)* to lower, to take *or* to let down; *(tableau)* to lower; **il faudra b. l'étagère de deux crans** the shelf will have to be taken down two pegs; **le rideau est baissé** *Théât* the curtain's down; *(boutique)* the iron curtain's down; **b. son pantalon** to pull down one's trousers; *aussi Fig* **b.** *Fam* **son pantalon** *ou très Fam* **sa culotte (devant qn)** to climb *or* to back down

2 *(main, bras)* to lower; **b. les yeux** *ou* **paupières** to lower one's eyes, to look down, to cast one's eyes down; **b. les yeux (sur qn/qch)** to look down (at sb/sth); **faire b. les yeux à qn** to stare sb out *or* down; **marcher les yeux baissés** *(de tristesse)* to walk with downcast eyes; *(en cherchant)* to walk with one's eyes to the ground; **b. le nez dans/sur son journal** to bury one's head in/to look down at one's newspaper; **b. son chapeau sur ses yeux** to pull *or* to tip one's hat over one's eyes; **attention, baisse la tête!** look out, duck!; **les fleurs baissent la tête** the flowers are drooping; **en baissant la tête** *(posture)* with one's head down *or* bent; *(de tristesse)* head bowed (with sorrow); *Fig* **b. la tête** *ou* **le nez (de honte)** to hang one's head (in shame); *Fig* **b. les bras** to throw in the towel

3 *(en intensité, en valeur)* to lower, to turn down; **b. la radio/lumière** to turn the radio/light down; **b. la voix** to lower one's voice; **b. un prix/le loyer** to bring down *or* to lower *or* to reduce a price/the rent; **la concurrence fait b. les prix** competition brings prices down; **b. le ton** to calm down; *Fam* **baisse le ton!** cool it!, pipe down!

VI *(espoir, lumière)* to fade; *(marée)* to go out; *(soleil)* to go down, to sink; *(température)* to go down, to drop, to fall; *(prix, action boursière)* to drop, to fall; *(stocks)* to be running low; *(santé, faculté)* to decline; *(pouvoir)* to wane, to dwindle, to decline; **la crue baisse** the waters are subsiding; **le jour baisse** the daylight's fading; **la qualité baisse** the quality's deteriorating; **nos réserves de sucre ont baissé** our sugar reserves have run low, we're low on sugar; **le dollar a baissé** the dollar has weakened; **ces mesures visent à faire b. les prix du mètre carré** these measures are intended to bring down the price per square metre; **sa vue baisse** his eyesight's fading *or* getting weaker *or* failing; **son travail baisse** his work's deteriorating; **il a beaucoup baissé depuis sa maladie** he's deteriorated *or* declined considerably since his illness; **sa voix baissa, et il s'arrêta au milieu de la phrase** his voice trailed off in mid-sentence; **b. dans l'estime de qn** to go down in sb's estimation; **on l'a fait b. à 50 euros** we beat him/her down to 50 euros

VPR se baisser 1 *(personne)* to bend down; **il faut se b. pour passer** you have to bend down *or* to stoop to go through; **il n'y a qu'à se b. pour les prendre** *ou* **les ramasser** they're *Br* two a penny *or Am* a dime a dozen

2 *(store, vitre)* to go down; **la poignée ne se baisse plus** the handle won't go down now

baissier, -ère [besje, -ɛr] *Bourse* **ADJ** bear *(avant n)*, bearish

NM,F bear

bajoue [baʒu] **NF** *Zool* chop, chap

• **bajoues NFPL** *Hum* jowls; **il avait des bajoues** he had great big jowls

bakchich [bakʃiʃ] **NM** *Fam (pourboire)* tip❑; *(pot-de-vin)* bribe❑, *Br* backhander

Bakélite® [bakelit] **NF** Bakelite®; **téléphone en B.** Bakelite® telephone

baklava [baklava] **NM** *Culin* baklava

bal, -als [bal] **NM 1** *(réunion ▸ populaire)* dance; *(▸ solennelle)* ball, dance; **la tradition des bals de rue** the tradition of dancing in the streets; **aller au b.** to go dancing *or* to a dance; **donner un b.** to give a ball; **b. costumé** fancy-dress ball; **b. masqué** masked ball; **b. musette** dance (with accordion music); **b. populaire** = (local) dance open to the public; **b. travesti** costume ball; **mener le b.** to lead off (at a dance); *Fig* to have the upper hand; **ouvrir le b.** *(être le premier à danser)* to open the ball; *Fig (être le premier à faire quelque chose)* to start the ball rolling **2** *(lieu)* dance hall

balade [balad] **NF** *Fam* **1** *(promenade ▸ à pied)* walk❑, stroll, ramble; *(▸ en voiture)* drive❑, spin; *(▸ à vélo, à moto, à cheval)* ride❑; **faire une b.** *(à pied)* to go for a walk; *(en voiture)* to go for a drive; *(à vélo, à moto, à cheval)* to go for a ride; **être/partir en b.** *(à pied)* to be out for/go (out) for a walk; *(en voiture)* to be out for/go (out) for a drive; *(à vélo, à moto, à cheval)* to be out for/go (out) for a ride **2** *(voyage)* jaunt, trip; **une jolie b. à travers l'Italie** a delightful jaunt across Italy

balader [3] [balade] *Fam* **VT 1** *(promener ▸ enfant, chien)* to take (out) for a walk❑; *(▸ touriste, visiteur)* to take *or* to show around❑; **je les ai baladés en voiture** I took them (out) for a drive❑ **2** *(emporter)* to carry❑ *or Péj* to cart about; **b. le télé-**

phone d'une pièce à l'autre to carry the telephone from room to room❑

VPR se balader 1 *(se promener ▸ à pied)* to stroll *or* to amble along; **se b. sans but** to drift (aimlessly) along; **se b., aller se b.** *(à pied)* to go for a walk❑; *(en voiture)* to go for a drive❑; *(à vélo, à moto, à cheval)* to go for a ride❑ **2** *(voyager)* to go for a trip *or* jaunt; **aller se b. en Espagne** to go for a trip around Spain **3** *(traîner)* to lie around❑; **ses vêtements se baladent partout** his/her clothes are lying around all over the place; **je n'aime pas les fils électriques qui se baladent** I hate trailing wires

baladeur, -euse [baladœr, -øz] **ADJ** *Fam* **être de tempérament b.** to have wanderlust; **il est d'humeur baladeuse ce matin** he just can't stay in one place today; **avoir la main baladeuse** *ou* **les mains baladeuses** to have wandering hands

NM 1 *(Walkman®)* Walkman®, personal stereo; **b. numérique** portable digital music player **2** *Aut* sliding shaft **3** *Tech* sliding gear wheel

• **baladeuse NF 1** *(lampe)* inspection *or* portable lamp **2** *Aut* trailer

baladin [baladɛ̃] **NM** *Arch* wandering player, travelling artist

baladisque [baladisk] **NM** portable compact disc player, Discman®

balafre [balafr] **NF 1** *(entaille)* slash, gash, cut **2** *(cicatrice)* scar

balafré, -e [balafre] **ADJ** scarred; **un visage b.** a scarred face

NM,F scarface

balafrer [3] [balafre] **VT** to slash, to gash, to cut

balai [balɛ] **NM 1** *(de ménage)* broom; **b. éponge** mop; **b. mécanique** carpet sweeper; *Fam* **du b.!** scram!

2 *Élec* brush

3 *Aut* **b. d'essuie-glace** *Br* windscreen *or Am* windshield wiper blade

4 *Fam (autobus)* last bus❑; *(métro)* last underground *or Am* subway train❑

5 *très Fam (année)* year❑; **il a 50 balais** he's 50❑

balai-brosse [balɛbrɔs] *(pl* **balais-brosses) NM** (long-handled) *Br* scrubbing *or Am* scrub brush

balaie *etc voir* **balayer**

balaise [balɛz] = **balèze**

balalaïka [balalaika] **NF** *Mus* balalaika

balan [balɑ̃] **NM** *Suisse* **être sur le b.** *(être sur le point de tomber)* to be tottering; *(hésiter)* to be indecisive; *(être inquiet quant à son sort)* to wait nervously

Balance [balɑ̃s] **NF 1** *Astron* Libra **2** *Astrol* Libra; **être B.** to be Libra *or* a Libran

balance [balɑ̃s] **NF 1** *(instrument de mesure ▸ gén)* (pair of) scales; *(▸ pour pesées délicates)* balance; **monter sur la b.** to stand on the scales; **b. à bascule** weighing machine; **b. électronique** electronic scales; **b. à fléau** beam balance; **b. de ménage** kitchen scales; **b. de précision** precision balance; **b. romaine** steelyard; *Fig* **jeter qch dans la b.** to take sth into account, to take account of sth; *Fig* **mettre tout son poids** *ou* **tout mettre dans la b.** to use (all of) one's influence to tip the scales; *Fig* **tenir la b. égale entre deux personnes/opinions** to strike a balance between two people/opinions

2 *(équilibre)* balance; *Pol* **b. électorale** electoral balance; **b. des forces** *ou* **des pouvoirs** balance of power

3 *Écon & Compta* balance; **la b. est en excédent** there is a surplus; **faire la b.** to make up the balance sheet; **b. de l'actif et du passif** credit and debit balance, balance of assets and liabilities; **b. de caisse** cash balance; **b. commerciale** *ou* **du commerce** balance of trade; **b. commerciale déficitaire** trade deficit; **b. commerciale excédentaire** trade surplus; **b. courante** current balance; **b. (générale) des comptes, b. des paiements** balance of payments

4 *Pêche* crayfish net

5 *Fam Arg crime (dénonciateur)* squealer, *Br* grass, *Am* rat

• **en balance ADV mettre deux arguments en b.** to balance two arguments; **mettre en b. les avantages et les inconvénients** to weigh (up) the pros and cons

• **balances NFPL** balances; **balances dollars** dollar balances *or* holdings

> Il faut noter que le nom anglais **balance** est un faux ami. Il signifie le plus souvent **équilibre** et s'emploie rarement pour désigner un instrument de mesure.

balancé, -e [balɑ̃se] **ADJ** *Fam* **être bien b.** to have a stunning figure; **tout bien b.** all things considered❑, taking one thing with another❑

balancelle [balɑ̃sɛl] **NF** *(siège)* swing chair

balancement [balɑ̃smɑ̃] **NM 1** *(mouvement ▸ d'un train)* sway, swaying; *(▸ d'un navire)* pitching, roll, rolling; *(▸ de la tête)* swinging; *(▸ des hanches)* swaying; *(▸ d'une jupe)* swinging **2** *(équilibre)* balance, equilibrium, symmetry **3** *Littéraire (hésitation)* wavering, hesitation

balancer [16] [balɑ̃se] **VT 1** *(bras, hanches)* to swing; *(bébé)* to rock; *(personne ▸ dans un hamac)* to push

2 *(compenser)* to counterbalance, to counteract, to cancel out

3 *Fam (se débarrasser de ▸ objet)* to throw away❑, to chuck out; **je ne trouve plus sa lettre, j'ai dû la b.** I can't find his/her letter, I must have chucked it out; **b. qch par la fenêtre** to throw *or* to chuck *or* to pitch sth out of the window; **tout b.** to chuck it all in

4 *Fam (se débarrasser de ▸ personne)* **b. qn** to get rid of sb; **ils ont balancé le corps dans la rivière** they dumped the body in the river; **elle a balancé son mec** she's dumped *or* ditched her boyfriend

5 *Fam (donner ▸ coup)* to give❑; **b. une gifle à qn** to give sb a slap❑, to smack sb in the face

6 *(lancer ▸ livre, clefs)* to chuck *or* to toss (over); **balance le journal** can you chuck *or* sling me the paper?

7 *Fam (dire ▸ insulte)* to hurl; **elle n'arrête pas de me b. des trucs vraiment durs** she's always making digs at me; **elle m'a balancé ça en pleine figure** she came out with it just like that

8 *Fam Arg crime (dénoncer ▸ bandit)* to squeal on, *Br* to shop; *(▸ complice)* to rat on

9 *Fin (budget, compte)* to balance; **b. les comptes** to balance *or* to make up the books

VI *Littéraire (hésiter)* to waver, to dither; **sans b.** unhesitatingly, unreservedly; *Hum* **entre les deux, mon cœur balance** I can't choose between them

VPR se balancer 1 *(osciller ▸ personne)* to rock, to sway; *(▸ train)* to roll, to sway; *(▸ navire)* to roll, to pitch; *(▸ branche)* to sway; **se b. d'un pied sur l'autre** to shift from one foot to the other; **se b. sur sa chaise** to tip back one's chair

2 *(sur une balançoire)* to swing; *(sur une bascule)* to seesaw; *(au bout d'une corde)* to swing, to dangle; **quand on l'a retrouvé, il se balançait au bout d'une corde** *(pendu)* when they found him, he was swinging from the end of a rope

3 *(se compenser)* to balance; **profits et pertes se balancent** profits and losses cancel each other out, the account balances

4 *Fam (locution)* **je m'en balance** *(je m'en fous)* I don't give a damn; **tes opinions, tout le monde s'en balance!** who gives a damn about what you think?

balancier [balɑ̃sje] **NM 1** *(de moteur)* beam, rocker arm; *(d'horloge)* pendulum; *(de montre)* balance wheel; *(autour d'un axe)* walking beam; **retour de b.** backlash **2** *(de funambule)* pole

balançoire [balɑ̃swar] **NF 1** *(suspendue)* swing; **faire de la b.** to have a (go on the) swing, to play on the swing **2** *(bascule)* seesaw

balayage [balɛjaʒ] **NM 1** *(d'un sol, d'une pièce)* sweeping; *(d'épluchures, de copeaux)* sweeping up

2 *(avec un projecteur, un radar)* scanning, sweeping; **b. d'une zone/du ciel avec un faisceau lumineux** scanning an area/the sky with a light beam

3 *(de la chevelure)* highlighting; **se faire faire un b.** to get one's hair highlighted, to get highlights in one's hair

4 *Électron* scanning, sweep, sweeping; **circuit/fréquence/vitesse de b.** sweep current/frequency/speed

5 *Ordinat* scanning; **b. de ligne** row scanning; **b. télévision** *ou* **de trame** raster scan

balayer [11] [baleje] **VT 1** *(nettoyer ▸ sol, pièce)* to sweep *(▸ tapis)* to brush, to sweep; **le sol a besoin d'être balayé** the floor could do with a sweep; *Fig* **b. devant chez soi** *ou* **sa porte** to set one's own house in order

2 *(pousser ▸ feuilles, nuages)* to sweep (along *or* away *or* up); *(▸ poussière, épluchures, copeaux)* to sweep up *or* away; **le vent balayait les feuilles** the wind swept the leaves along *or* away; **balayé par le vent** windswept; **balayant les jetons de la main** *(pour les ramasser)* sweeping up the tokens with his/her hand; *(pour les éloigner)* sweeping the tokens away with his/her hand

3 *(parcourir ▸ sujet: vent, tir)* to sweep (across *or* over); *(▸ sujet: faisceau, regard)* to sweep, to scan; *(▸ sujet: caméra)* to pan across; **les vagues balayaient la jetée** the waves were sweeping (over) the jetty; **ses grandes ailes balayaient le sol** its large wings swept the ground; **ses yeux balayèrent l'assemblée** he scanned the audience

4 *(détruire ▸ obstacles, préjugés)* to sweep away *or* aside; *(repousser ▸ objections, critiques)* to brush aside; **la monarchie a été balayée par la révolution** the monarchy was swept aside by the revolution; **b. l'ennemi hors de ses positions** to sweep the enemy out of its positions

5 *Fam (renvoyer)* to push out, to get rid of; **il va falloir me b. ces incapables!** these incompetents have got to go!

6 *Électron* to scan

VI to sweep up; **il faudra b. ici** this place needs a good sweep

balayette [balɛjɛt] **NF** brush

balayeur, -euse [balɛjœr, -øz] **NM,F** street *or* road sweeper

• **balayeuse NF 1** *(machine)* road-sweeping machine **2** *Can (aspirateur)* vacuum cleaner, *Br* Hoover®

balayures [balɛjyr] **NFPL** sweepings

balbutiant, -e [balbysjɑ̃, -ɑ̃t] **ADJ 1** *(hésitant)* stuttering, stammering; **il répondit, tout b.** he stammered an answer **2** *(récent)* **c'est une technique encore balbutiante** it's a technique that's still in its infancy

balbutiement [balbysimɑ̃] **NM** stammer, stutter; **balbutiements** *(d'un bègue)* stammering, stuttering; *(d'un ivrogne)* slurred speech; *(d'un bébé)* babbling

• **balbutiements NMPL** *(d'une technique, d'un art)* early stages, beginnings, infancy; **l'informatique n'en était alors qu'à ses premiers balbutiements** data processing was then only in its infancy *or* in its early stages

balbutier [9] [balbysje] **VI 1** *(bègue)* to stammer, to stutter; *(ivrogne)* to slur (one's speech); *(bébé)* to babble; **la timidité le fait b.** he's so shy he stammers; **j'en balbutiais d'ahurissement** I was so astonished (that) I was stuck for words **2** *(débuter)* to be just starting *or* in its early stages *or* in its infancy

VT to stammer (out); **b. des remerciements** to stammer out one's thanks; **b. une prière** to mumble a prayer

balcon [balkɔ̃] **NM 1** *(plate-forme)* balcony **2** *(balustrade)* railings, railing **3** *Théât* balcony; **premier b.** dress circle; **deuxième b.** upper circle; **dernier b.** gallery

balconnet [balkɔnɛ] **NM 1** *(balustrade)* overhanging railing **2 (soutien-gorge à) b.** balcony *or* half-cup bra

baldaquin [baldakɛ̃] **NM 1** *(sur un lit)* canopy, tester **2** *(sur un autel, un trône)* canopy, baldachin

Bâle [bal] **NM** *Géog* Basel, Basle

Baléares [balear] **NFPL** *Géog* Baleares; **les (îles) B.** the Balearic Islands; **aux B.** in the Balearic Islands

baleine [balɛn] **NF 1** *Zool* whale; **b. blanche** beluga (whale); **b. bleue** blue whale; **b. à bosse** humpback whale; *Fam* **rire** *ou* **rigoler** *ou* **se tordre comme une b.** to split one's sides laughing

2 *(de parapluie)* rib

3 *(de corset ▸ en plastique)* bone, stay; *(▸ en métal)* steel; *(▸ en fanon)* (whalebone) stay

4 *(pour un col)* collar stiffener

baleiné, -e [balene] **ADJ 1** *(corset, gaine)* boned **2** *(col)* stiffened

baleineau, -x [baleno] **NM** *Zool* whale calf

baleinier, -ère [balenje, -ɛr] **ADJ** whaling; **industrie baleinière** whaling (industry); **port b.** whaling station

NM 1 *(navire)* whaling ship, whaler **2** *(chasseur)* whaler

• **baleinière NF 1** *Naut* lifeboat **2** *Pêche* whaleboat, whaler, whale catcher

balèze [balez] *Fam* **ADJ 1** *(grand)* hefty, huge❑; **un type b.** a great hulk (of a man) **2** *(doué)* great❑, brilliant❑; **b. en physique** ace *or Br* dead good at physics **3** *(difficile)* tough, tricky

NMF *(homme)* big guy; *(femme)* big woman❑; **un gros** *ou* **grand b.** a great hulk (of a man)

balier [9] [balje] *Can Fam* **VT** *(nettoyer ▸ sol, pièce)* to sweep (up *or* out)❑; *(▸ tapis)* to brush❑, to sweep❑

VI to sweep up❑

balisage [balizaʒ] **NM 1** *(signaux ▸ en mer)* markers, beacons, buoyage; *(▸ aériens)* lights, markers; *(▸ sur route)* markers, road markers; *Aviat* **b. des bords de piste** runway lights; *Aviat* **b. d'entrée de piste** airway markers; **b. maritime** navigational markers **2** *(pose ▸ de signaux, de signes)* marking out; *Ordinat (d'un texte)* tagging; **b. par radars** beacon signalling

balise [baliz] **NF 1** *Naut* beacon, (marker) buoy; *Aviat* marker, beacon; **b. de guidage** radar beacon; *(sur route)* road marker cone, police cone; *(sur sentier)* waymark; **b. maritime** navigational marker; **b. radio** (radio) beacon **2** *Ordinat (d'un texte)* tag; **b. de début** opening tag; **b. de fin** closing tag

baliser [3] [balize] **VT 1** *Naut* to mark out, to buoy **2** *Aviat* **b. une piste** to mark out a runway with lights

3 *(trajet)* to mark out *or* off; **b. une voie (pour l'interdire à la circulation)** to cone off a lane (from traffic); **balisé de drapeaux/piquets** marked out with flags/poles; **sentier balisé** waymarked path

4 *Ordinat (texte)* to tag

VI *très Fam* to be scared stiff; **ça me fait b. rien que d'y penser** the very thought of it scares me stiff

baliseur [balizœr] **NM** *Naut* **1** *(navire)* buoy *or* lighthouse tender **2** *(personne)* buoy keeper

balistique [balistik] **ADJ** ballistic

NF ballistics *(singulier)*

balivernes [balivɛrn] **NFPL 1** *(propos)* nonsense *(UNCOUNT)*; **ce sont des b.** it's all nonsense; **raconter des b.** to talk nonsense **2** *(bagatelles)* trivia *(pl)*, trifles; **s'inquiéter pour des b.** to worry over trivial details

balkanique [balkanik] **ADJ** Balkan

balkanisation [balkanizasjɔ̃] **NF 1** *Pol* Balkanization **2** *(fragmentation)* parcelling off into tiny units

Balkans [balkɑ̃] **NMPL les B.** the Balkans

ballade [balad] **NF** *Littérature & Mus* **1** *(poème narratif, chanson)* ballad **2** *(poème court à forme fixe, pièce musicale)* ballade

ballant, -e [balɑ̃, -ɑ̃t] **ADJ** *(jambes)* dangling; *(poitrine)* wobbling; **il était debout, les bras ballants** he stood with his arms dangling at his sides

NM 1 *(mouvement) (d'un véhicule)* sway, roll **2** *Naut (d'un cordage)* slack; **donner du b. à un câble** to give a cable some slack, to slacken off a cable

ballast [balast] **NM 1** *Naut* ballast tank *or* container **2** *Constr & Rail* ballast

ballaster [3] [balaste] **VT** *Naut & Rail* to ballast

balle [bal] **NF 1** *(d'arme)* bullet; **tirer à balles** to shoot with real bullets; **se tirer une b. dans la bouche/tête** to shoot oneself in the mouth/head; **tué par balles** shot dead; **b. à blanc** blank; **b. en caoutchouc** rubber bullet; **b. dum-dum/perdue/traçante** dum-dum/stray/tracer bullet

2 *(pour jouer)* ball; **jouer à la b.** to play with a ball; **la b., la b.!** *(dans les jeux d'équipe)* over here, over here!; *Fig* **la b. est dans son camp** the ball's in his/her court; **b. de caoutchouc** rubber ball; **b. de golf** golf ball; *Can* **b. molle** *(sport)* softball; **b. au mur** handball; *Can* **b. de neige** snowball; **b. de tennis** tennis ball

3 *(point, coup)* stroke, shot; **une belle b.** a fine stroke *or* shot; *Tennis* **faire des balles** to practise, *Br* to knock up; *Tennis* **b. de jeu/match** game/match point; **b. nulle** no-ball

4 *Bot & Agr* **la b.** the chaff, the husks

5 *Fam (visage)* face❑; **avoir une bonne b.** to have a friendly face

6 *Fam (locutions)* **c'est de la b.!** *Br* it's absolutely wicked!, *Am* it's totally awesome!; **trop de la b., ce film** *Br* that film's wicked!, *Am* that movie's awesome!

• **balles NFPL 1** *Anciennement Fam* francs; **t'as pas cent balles?** can you spare some change?❑; **j'ai dépensé cent balles aujourd'hui** I've spent a tenner today; **200 balles** 200 francs❑ **2** *Fam* **à deux balles** *(médiocre)* pathetic, lame; **une excuse à deux balles** a lame excuse; **de la philosophie/psychologie à deux balles** pop philosophy/psychology

baller [3] [bale] **VI** *Littéraire (bras, jambe)* to dangle

ballerine [balrin] **NF 1** *(danseuse)* ballerina, ballet dancer **2** *(chaussure ▸ de danse)* ballet *or* dancing shoe; *(▸ de ville)* pump

ballet [balɛ] **NM** *Mus & Théât* **1** *(genre)* ballet (dancing)

2 *(œuvre)* ballet (music); *(spectacle)* ballet; **le b. blanc** classical ballet *(in white tutus)*; *Fig* **l'incident a donné lieu à tout un b. diplomatique** the incident has given rise to intense diplomatic activity; **les Ballets russes** the Ballets Russes

3 *(troupe)* ballet company

4 *Sport* **b. aquatique** aquashow, *Am* aquacade

ballon [balɔ̃] **NM 1** *Sport* ball; **jouer au b.** to play with a ball; **b. de basket** basketball; **b. de foot** *ou* **football** football; **le b. ovale** *(le rugby)* rugby; **le b. rond** *(le foot)* soccer, *Br* football; **b. de rugby** rugby ball; **mon premier b.** the first time I touched the ball

2 *(sphère)* **b. (de baudruche)** (party) balloon; **b. d'hélium** helium balloon; **b. d'oxygène** *Méd* oxygen tank; *Fig* life-saver

3 *Aviat* (hot-air) balloon; **monter en b.** *(ascension)* to go up in a balloon; **b. de barrage** barrage balloon; **b. captif/libre** captive/free balloon; **b. dirigeable** airship, dirigible; **b. d'essai** pilot balloon; *Fig* test; **lancer un b. d'essai** *(se renseigner)* to put out feelers; *(faire un essai)* to do a trial run, to run a test

4 *Chim* round-bottomed flask, balloon; *(pour l'Alcotest®)* (breathalyser) bag; *Fam* **on m'a fait souffler dans le b.** I was breathalysed❑, I was made to blow into the bag

5 *(verre)* (round) wine glass, balloon glass; *(contenu)* glassful; **b. de rouge** glass of red wine; **il boit son b. de blanc tous les matins** he has a little glass of white wine every morning

6 *(réservoir)* **b. (d'eau chaude)** hot water tank

7 *Géog* **les ballons** the (rounded tops of the) Vosges mountains; **le b. d'Alsace/de Guebwiller** the Ballon d'Alsace/de Guebwiller

8 *Suisse (petit pain)* (bread) roll

9 *Suisse (de vin)* = decilitre of wine

10 *très Fam (locution)* **avoir le b.** to have a bun in the oven

ballonné, -e [balɔne] **ADJ** bloated; **être b.** to feel bloated

ballonnement [balɔnmɑ̃] **NM 1** *Méd* distension *(UNCOUNT)*, flatulence *(UNCOUNT)*; **j'ai des ballonnements** I feel bloated **2** *Vét* bloat

ballonner [3] [balɔne] **VT** to swell

ballon-panier [balɔ̃panje] **NM INV** *Can Sport* basketball

ballon-sonde [balɔ̃sɔ̃d] *(pl* **ballons-sondes***)* **NM** *Météo* sounding balloon

ballot [balo] **NM 1** *(paquet)* bundle, package **2** *Fam (sot)* nitwit, wally; **cette espèce de b. n'avait rien compris** the poor fool hadn't got the idea at all

ballotin [balɔtɛ̃] **NM** *Br* sweet *or Am* candy box; **un b. de chocolats** a small box of chocolates

ballottage [balɔtaʒ] **NM** *Pol* **il y a b. à Tours** there will be a second ballot in Tours; **être en b.** to have to *Br* stand *or Am* to run again in a second round

ballottement [balɔtmɑ̃] **NM** *(d'un véhicule)* rocking, swaying, shaking; *(d'un navire)* tossing (about); *(d'un passager, d'un sac)* shaking about, tossing about; *(d'un radeau)* tossing, bobbing about

ballotter [3] [balɔte] **VT** *(véhicule)* to rock, to sway, to shake; *(navire)* to toss (about); *(passager, sac)* to shake about, to toss about; *(radeau)* to toss, to bob about; **les détritus ballottés par les vagues** refuse bobbing up and down in the waves; *Fig* **être ballotté entre deux endroits** to be shifted *or* shunted around constantly from one place to the other; **être ballotté entre deux personnes** to waver between two people; **être ballotté par les événements** to be carried along by events

VI *(tête)* to loll, to sway; *(valise)* to bang *or* to shake about, to rattle around; *(poitrine)* to bounce (up and down)

ballottine [balɔtin] **NF** *Culin* stuffed and boned meat roll, ballottine

balloune [balun] **NF** *Can Joual* balloon❑; *(de savon)* bubble❑; **souffler dans la b.** to be breathalysed❑, to blow into the bag; *Fig* **prendre** *ou* **virer une b., partir en b.** to get trashed; **être en b.** *(enceinte)* to be in the club

ball-trap [baltrap] *(pl* **ball-traps***)* **NM 1** *(tir ▸ à une cible)* trapshooting, clay-pigeon shooting; *(▸ à deux cibles)* skeet, skeet shooting **2** *(appareil)* trap

balluchon [balyʃɔ̃] **NM** bundle; *aussi Fig* **faire son b.** to pack one's bags

balnéaire [balneɛr] **ADJ** seaside *(avant n)*

balnéothérapie [balneoterapi] **NF** *Méd* balneotherapy

baloche [balɔʃ] **NM** *Fam* local dance❑

balourd, -e [balur, -urd] **ADJ** *(physiquement)* clumsy; *(dans ses paroles, son comportement)* awkward

NM,F *(physiquement)* clumsy person; *(dans ses paroles, son comportement)* awkward person

NM *Tech* unbalance

balourdise [balurdiz] **NF 1** *(caractère ▸ physiquement)* clumsiness; *(▸ dans ses paroles, son comportement)* awkwardness **2** *(parole, acte)* blunder, gaffe; **dire des balourdises** to say the wrong thing

balsa [balza] **NM** *Bot* balsa, balsawood

balsamier [balzamje] **NM** *Bot* balsam tree

balsamine [balzamin] **NF** *Bot* balsam, busy Lizzie

balte [balt] **ADJ** Baltic; **les pays/républiques Baltes** the Baltic states/ republics

NM *Ling* Baltic

• **Balte NMF** Balt

balthazar [baltazar] **NM** *(bouteille)* Balthazar

Baltique [baltik] **NF la (mer) B.** the Baltic (Sea)

baluchon [balyʃɔ̃] = **balluchon**

balustrade [balystrad] **NF** *(d'un balcon)* balustrade; *(d'un pont)* railing

balustre [balystr] **NM 1** *(pilier ▸ de balustrade, de siège)* baluster **2** *(compas)* pair of compasses *(with spring bow dividers)*

balzacien, -enne [balzasjɛ̃, -ɛn] **ADJ un héros b.** *Littérature* a hero in a Balzac novel; *Fig* a hero reminiscent of Balzac; **une description balzacienne** *Littérature* a description from a Balzac novel; *Fig* a description reminiscent of Balzac

balzan, -e [balzɑ̃, -an] **ADJ** white-stockinged

• **balzane NF** *(d'un cheval)* white stocking (of a horse)

bambin [bɑ̃bɛ̃] **NM** *Fam* toddler❑

bambochard, -e [bɑ̃bɔʃar, -ard] = **bambocheur**

bamboche [bɑ̃bɔʃ] **NF** *Fam Vieilli* partying; **c'est la b. ce soir!** it's party-time tonight!; **faire b.** to party

bambocher [3] [bɑ̃bɔʃe] **VI** *Fam Vieilli* to party; **à l'époque où je bambochais** in the days when I was always partying

bambocheur, -euse [bɑ̃bɔʃœr, -øz] *Fam Vieilli* **ADJ être b.** to enjoy partying; **c'est un type très b.** he really enjoys partying

NM,F partygoer, reveller❑

bambou [bɑ̃bu] **NM** *Bot* bamboo; *Fam* **attraper un coup de b.** to get sunstroke❑; *Fam* **avoir le coup de b.** *(devenir fou)* to crack up, to go nuts; *(être fatigué)* to be wiped *or Br* shattered *or Am* pooped; *Fam* **c'est le coup de b. dans ce restaurant!** *(très cher)* this restaurant costs an arm and a leg *or Br* a packet

• **en bambou** **ADJ** *(meuble, cloison)* bamboo *(avant n)*

bamboula [bɑ̃bula] **NF** *très Fam (fête)* wild party; **faire la b.** to party

ban [bɑ̃] **NM 1** *(applaudissements)* **un b. pour...!** three cheers *or* a big hand for...!

2 *(roulement de tambour)* drum roll; *Fig* **fermer le b.** to bring the proceedings to a close; *Fig* **ouvrir le b.** to open the proceedings; *(sonnerie de clairon)* bugle call

3 *Hist (condamnation)* banishment, banning; *(convocation)* ban; *(vassaux)* vassals; *Fig* **le b. et l'arrière-b.** the world and his wife; **convoquer le b. et l'arrière-b.** to summon the (entire) family

4 *Arch (proclamation)* (public) proclamation

• **bans** **NMPL** *(de mariage)* banns; **les bans sont affichés** *ou* **publiés** the banns have been posted *or* published

• **au ban** **ADV** **mettre qn au b.** to banish sb

• **au ban de** **PRÉP** **être au b. de la société** to be an outcast *or* a pariah; **mettre un pays au b. des nations** to boycott a country; **mettre qn au b. d'un club** to blackball sb

banal, -e, -als, -ales [banal] **ADJ 1** *(courant)* commonplace, ordinary, everyday *(avant n)*; **ce n'est vraiment pas b.** it's most unusual, it's really strange **2** *(sans originalité ▸ idée, histoire, situation)* trite, banal; *(▸ objet, événement)* everyday *(avant n)*; *(▸ argument)* standard, well-worn; *(▸ vie)* humdrum, mundane; *(▸ tenue)* ordinary; **ce que je vais vous dire là est très b.** there's nothing original *or* unusual about what I'm going to say **3** *Ordinat* general-purpose

banalement [banalmɑ̃] **ADV** in an ordinary way; **nous nous sommes rencontrés fort b.** we met in very ordinary *or* unremarkable circumstances

banalisation [banalizasjɔ̃] **NF 1** *(généralisation)* spread; *Péj (perte d'originalité)* trivialization; **la b. des transports aériens** the fact that air travel has become commonplace *or* has become an everyday phenomenon; **son exposé est une b. des idées de Lacan** his account trivializes Lacan's ideas **2** *(d'un véhicule)* **la b. des voitures de police** the use of unmarked police cars **3** *Rail (d'une voie)* signalling for two-way working; *(d'une locomotive)* use of engine by several crews

banaliser [3] [banalize] **VT 1** *(rendre courant ▸ pratique)* to trivialize, to make commonplace; **maintenant que la téléphonie sans fil est banalisée** now that cordless phones have become commonplace

2 *Péj (œuvre)* to deprive *or* to rob of originality; *(idée)* to turn into a commonplace

3 *(véhicule)* to remove the markings from; *(marque déposée)* to turn into a household name

4 *Rail (voie)* to signal for two-way working; *(locomotive)* to man with several crews

VPR se banaliser to become commonplace *or* a part of (everyday) life

banalité [banalite] **NF 1** *(d'une idée, d'une histoire, d'une situation)* triteness, banality; *(d'un objet, d'un événement)* everydayness; *(d'un argument)* triteness, banality, triviality; *(de la vie)* mundanity; *(d'une tenue)* ordinariness **2** *(propos, écrit)* platitude, commonplace, cliché

banane [banan] **NF 1** *Bot (fruit)* banana; **b. plantain** *ou* **jaune** plantain; **b. verte** green banana

2 *Fam (pare-chocs)* overrider▫

3 *Fam (coiffure) Br* quiff

4 *Fam (hélicoptère)* chopper

5 *Fam (décoration)* medal▫, *Br* gong

6 *(sac) Br* bum bag, *Am* fanny pack

7 *très Fam (idiot)* nitwit, *Br* twit, *Am* dumbbell

ADJ INV banana-shaped

bananier, -ère [bananje, -ɛr] **ADJ** banana *(avant n)*

NM 1 *Bot* banana, banana tree **2** *Naut* banana boat

banc [bɑ̃] **NM 1** *(siège)* bench, seat; **sur le b. des ministres** on the government bench; **b. des accusés** dock; **au b. des accusés** in the dock; *Jur* **le b. des avocats** the lawyers' bench; **b. d'église** pew; *Sport* **b. des joueurs** player's bench; *Jur* **b. des pénalités** *ou* **des punitions** penalty box; **b. public** park bench; *Jur* **(au) b. des témoins** *Br* (in the) witness box, *Am* (on the) witness stand; **sur les bancs de l'école** in one's schooldays; **ils se sont connus sur les bancs de l'école** they got to know each other at school

2 *Menuis & Tech (établi)* bench, workbench; *(bâti)* frame, bed

3 *Cin & TV* **b. de montage** editing desk

4 *Ordinat* bank; **b. de mémoire** memory bank

5 *Naut* (oarsman's) bench, thwart

6 *(de poissons)* shoal, school; **b. de homards** lobster ground; **b. d'huîtres** oyster bed; **b. de pêche** fishing bank *or* ground **b. de sardines** school *or* shoal of sardines

7 *(amas)* bank; **b. de boue** mudbank, mudflats; **b. de brume** fog patch; **b. de glace** ice floe; **b. de gravier** gravel bank; **b. de sable** sandbank, sandbar

8 *Géol (couche)* bed, layer; *(au fond de la mer)* bank, shoal

• **banc d'essai** **NM** *Ind* test rig, test bed; *Mktg* benchtest; *Ordinat* benchmark; *Fig* test; *Aut* **faire un b. d'essai** to test (an engine); *Fig* to have a trial run; **mettre qn au b. d'essai** to give sb a test; **mettre une idée au b. d'essai** to test out an idea

bancable [bɑ̃kabl] **ADJ** *Com (effet)* bankable; **non b.** unbankable

bancaire [bɑ̃kɛr] **ADJ** *Banque (commission, crédit, dépôt, frais, prêt)* bank *(avant n)*; *(opération)* banking

bancal, -e, -als, -ales [bɑ̃kal] **ADJ 1** *(meuble)* rickety, wobbly; *(personne)* lame **2** *(peu cohérent ▸ idée, projet)* unsound; *(▸ raisonnement)* weak, unsound; **la proposition est un peu bancale** the proposal doesn't really stand up to examination

bancarisation [bɑ̃karizasjɔ̃] **NF** *Banque* **le taux de b.** the number of bank account holders; **la b. de l'économie** the growing role of banks in the economy; **la b. de la population française** the growing number of bank account holders in France

bancarisé, -e [bɑ̃karize] **ADJ** *Banque* **être b.** to have a bank account, to use the banking system

bancassurance [bɑ̃kasyrɑ̃s] **NF** *Banque* bancassurance

bancassureur [bɑ̃kasyrœr] **NM** *Banque* insurance banker, bancassurer

bancatique [bɑ̃katik] **NF** *Banque* electronic *or* computerized banking *(UNCOUNT)*

banco [bɑ̃ko] **NM** banco; **faire b.** to go banco

bancomat [bɑ̃koma] **NM** *Suisse Br* cashpoint, *Am* ATM

banc-titre [bɑ̃titr] *(pl* **bancs-titres***)* **NM** *Cin & TV* rostrum camera

bandage [bɑ̃daʒ] **NM 1** *Méd (pansement)* bandage, dressing; **b. herniaire** truss

2 *(fait de panser)* bandaging, binding (up)

3 *(fait de tendre ▸ un ressort)* stretching, tensing; *(▸ un arc)* bending, drawing

4 *Aut & Rail (en caoutchouc)* tyre; *(en métal)* hoop, band

bandagiste [bɑ̃daʒist] **NMF** bandage manufacturer

bandana [bɑ̃dana] **NM** *Tex* bandana, bandanna

bandant, -e [bɑ̃dɑ̃, -ɑ̃t] **ADJ** *Vulg* exciting▫; **elle est bandante** she's a real turn-on; *Hum (sens affaibli)* **pas très b. comme boulot!** this job's hardly the most exciting thing going!

BANDE [bɑ̃d]

- gang, group **A1**
- bunch **A2**
- reel **B4**
- cushion **B10**
- band **A1, B1, 3, 5, 8**
- strip **B1, 2**
- bandage **B7**
- list, heel **C**

NF A. 1 *(groupe ▸ de malfaiteurs)* gang; *(▸ d'amis)* group; *(▸ d'enfants)* troop, band; *(▸ d'animaux)* herd; *(▸ de chiens, de loups)* pack; **faire partie de la b.** to be one of the group; **b. armée** armed gang *or* band; **b. organisée** organized (criminal) gang; **la B. des Quatre** the Gang of Four; *Péj* **une b. de** a pack *or* bunch of; *Fam* **une b. de menteurs/voleurs** a bunch of liars/crooks; *très Fam* **vous y comprenez rien, b. de cons!** you just don't get it, do you, you *Br* bloody *or Am* goddamn idiots!

2 *(locutions)* **il fait toujours b. à part** he keeps (himself) to himself; **ceux de Bel-Air font b. à part** those who come from Bel-Air stick together

B. 1 *(d'étoffe, de papier etc)* strip, band; **b. gommée** gummed binding strip; **b. de journal** newspaper wrapper; **b. molletière** puttee, putty; **b. publicitaire** *(autour d'un livre)* belly band; *Aut* **b. de roulement** tyre tread

2 *(de territoire)* strip; **b. de terrain** strip of land; *Transp* **b. d'arrêt d'urgence** emergency lane, hard shoulder

3 *(sur une route)* band, stripe; **b. blanche** white line

4 *Cin* reel; *Cin & Phot* **b. amorce** start *or* head leader; **b. audionumérique** digital audio tape, DAT; **b. démo** demo tape; **b. (magnétique)** (magnetic) tape; **b. mère** master tape; **b. originale** soundtrack; **b. son magnétique** magnetic soundtrack; **b. sonore** soundtrack; **b. vidéo** videotape

5 *Électron & Rad* band; **b. de fréquence** frequency band; **sur la b. FM** on FM; **b. passante** pass-band

6 *Ordinat* **b. de défilement** scroll bar; **b. perforée** perforated tape, *Br* punched paper tape

7 *Méd* bandage; **b. Velpeau®** crêpe bandage, *Am* Ace bandage®

8 *Archit* band

9 *Littérature* **b. dessinée** *(dans un magazine)* comic strip, *Br* strip cartoon; *(livre)* comic book; **la b. dessinée** *(genre)* comic strips; **l'auteur d'une b. dessinée célèbre** the author of a well-known comic book; **magazine** *ou* **revue de bandes dessinées** comic

10 *(au billard)* cushion; **jouer la b.** to play off the cushion

11 *Phys* **b. de fréquences** frequency band

C. *Naut* list, heel; **donner de la b.** to heel over, to list

• **en bande** **ADV** as *or* in a group, all together; **ils ne se déplacent qu'en b.** they always go around in a gang

• **par la bande** **ADV** in a roundabout way; **apprendre qch par la b.** to learn sth through the grapevine; **faire qch par la b.** to do sth underhandedly

bandé, -e [bɑ̃de] **ADJ 1** *(recouvert)* bandaged; **avoir les yeux bandés** to be blindfolded; **pieds bandés** bound *or* bound-up feet **2** *(tendu)* stretched, tensed

bande-annonce [bɑ̃danɔ̃s] *(pl* **bandes-annonces***)* **NF** *Cin* trailer; **la b. de son dernier film** the trailer for his/her last film

bandeau, -x [bɑ̃do] **NM 1** *(serre-tête)* headband

2 *(coiffure)* coiled hair; **avoir les cheveux en b., porter des bandeaux** = to wear one's hair parted in the middle and swept back round the sides

3 *(sur les yeux)* blindfold; *(sur un œil)* eye patch; **avoir un b. sur les yeux** to be blindfolded; *Fig* to be blind to reality

4 *Archit* string *or* belt course

5 *Journ (titre)* streamer

6 *Mktg (espace publicitaire)* advertising space *(in the shape of a band around a vehicle)*; *Ordinat (dans un site Web)* banner; **b. publicitaire** banner advertisement

bandelette [bɑ̃dlɛt] **NF** *(bande)* strip; **les bandelettes d'une momie** the wrappings of a mummy

bander [3] [bɑ̃de] **VT 1** *(panser ▸ main, cheville)* to bandage (up); **b. les yeux à qn** *(pour qu'il ne voie pas)* to blindfold sb; **avoir les yeux bandés** *Méd* to have one's eyes bandaged; *(avec un bandeau)* to be blindfolded **2** *(tendre ▸ arc)* to draw, to bend; *(▸ ressort, câble)* to stretch, to tense; *Littéraire (muscle)* to tense, to tauten; **b. ses forces** to gather up *or* to muster one's strength; **bandant toutes ses forces vers ce seul but** his/her whole being directed towards that goal **3** *Archit* to arch, to vault

VI *Vulg* to have a hard-on; **ça me fait b.** it gives me a hard-on; **il bande pour elle** he's got the hots for her, he thinks she's really horny; *(sens affaibli)* **ça me fait pas b.** it doesn't turn me on

banderille [bɑ̃drij] **NF** banderilla

banderole [bɑ̃drɔl] **NF 1** *(bannière ▸ sur un mât, une lance)* banderole; *(▸ en décoration)* streamer; *(▸ dans une manifestation)* banner **2** *Archit* banderole

bandit [bɑ̃di] **NM 1** *(brigand)* bandit; *(gangster)* gangster; **b. de grand(s) chemin(s)** highwayman **2** *(escroc)* crook, conman; **b., va!** *(dit avec affection)* you rogue *or* rascal!

banditisme [bɑ̃ditism] **NM** crime; *Fig* **c'est du b.!** it's daylight robbery!; **grand b.** organized crime

bandonéon [bɑ̃dɔneɔ̃] **NM** *Mus* bandoneon

bandouiller [3] [bɑ̃duje] **VI** *Vulg* to have a semi

bandoulière [bɑ̃duljɛr] **NF 1** *(d'une arme)* sling; *(à cartouches)* bandolier **2** *(d'un sac)* shoulder strap

• **en bandoulière ADV porter un sac en b.** to carry a bag across one shoulder; **on peut aussi le mettre en b.** you can also wear it over your shoulder

bang[1] [bɑ̃g] **NM** *(franchissement du mur du son)* sonic boom

EXCLAM bang!, crash!; **b., b., t'es mort!** bang, bang, you're dead!; **et b., tout est tombé par terre!** and then crash, everything was on the floor!

bang[2] [bɑ̃g] **NM** *Fam Arg drogue (pipe à eau)* bong

Bangladesh [bɑ̃gladɛʃ] **NM le B.** Bangladesh

banian [banjɑ̃] **NM** *Bot* banyan

banjo [bɑ̃(d)ʒo] **NM** *Mus* banjo

banlieue [bɑ̃ljø] **NF** suburb; **la b.** the suburbs; **la maison est en b.** the house is on the outskirts of the town *or* in the suburbs; **vivre en b.** to live in the suburbs; **une b. de Londres** a suburb of London; **la b. rouge** = towns in the Paris suburbs with Communist mayors; **b. verte** garden suburb; **grande b.** = outer suburbs; **proche b.** inner suburbs

NM *Belg Transp* commuter train

BANLIEUE

In France the word "banlieue" often refers not to the upmarket areas of a city – as the word "suburbia" suggests in English-speaking countries – but to the impoverished suburban areas on the outskirts of some cities. These neighbourhoods are culturally and ethnically diverse and are frequently associated with social problems such as delinquency, unemployment and unrest.

banlieusard, -e [bɑ̃ljøzar, -ard] **ADJ** *Péj* suburban

NM,F *(gén)* suburbanite; *Transp* commuter; **les banlieusards** suburbanites, people who live in the suburbs

banne [ban] **NF 1** *(auvent)* awning, tilt **2** *(charrette)* cart **3** *(panier)* (wicker) basket

banneret [banrɛ] **NM** *Hist* banneret

banneton [bantɔ̃] **NM 1** *(de boulanger)* (baker's) bread-basket **2** *Pêche* corf

banni, -e [bani] **ADJ** banished, exiled

NM,F exile

bannière [banjɛr] **NF 1** *(étendard)* banner; **la b. étoilée** the Star-spangled Banner; **combattre** *ou* **lutter sous la b. de qn** to fight on sb's side; **se ranger sous la b. de** to join the ranks of **2** *Vieilli (de chemise)* shirt-tail; **se balader en b.** to go about in one's shirt-tails **3** *Ordinat (dans un site Web)* banner; **b. publicitaire** banner advertisement

bannir [32] [banir] **VT 1** *(expulser)* to banish, to exile **2** *Littéraire (éloigner)* to reject, to cast out; **b. qn de sa présence** to cast sb from one's presence; **banni à jamais de mes relations** forever banished from my circle of friends **3** *(supprimer ▸ idée, pensée)* to banish; *(▸ aliment)* to cut out; **j'ai banni cette idée** I banished *or* dismissed the idea from my mind; **bannissez la violence de vos comportements** banish all violence from your behaviour; **il a complètement banni la cigarette** he has completely given up smoking

bannissement [banismɑ̃] **NM** banishment

banquable [bɑ̃kabl] = **bancable**

banque [bɑ̃k] **NF 1** *(établissement)* bank; **avoir une somme à la** *ou* **en b.** to have some money in the bank; **mettre une somme à la b.** to bank a sum of money; **passer à la b.** to go to the bank; **b. d'acceptation** *Br* accepting *or Am* acceptance house; **b. d'affaires** investment bank, *Br* merchant bank; **b. centrale** central bank; **b. de clearing** clearing bank; **b. commerciale** commercial bank; **b. de compensation** clearing bank; **b. confirmatrice** confirming bank; **b. de crédit** credit bank; **b. de dépôt** deposit bank; **b. de détail** retail bank; **b. émettrice** *ou* **d'émission** issuing bank *or* house; **b. d'épargne** savings bank; **b. d'escompte** discount house *or* bank; **b. de gestion de patrimoine** trust bank; **b. de gros** wholesale bank; **b. hypothécaire** mortgage bank; **b. industrielle** industrial bank; **b. d'investissement** investment bank, *Br* merchant bank; **b. notificatrice** advising bank; **b. de placement** issuing bank *or* house; **b. privée** private bank; **b. de recouvrement** collecting agency *or* bank; **la B. d'Angleterre** the Bank of England; **B. centrale européenne** European Central Bank; **B. européenne d'investissement** European Investment Bank; **B. européenne pour la reconstruction et le développement** European Bank for Reconstruction and Development; **la B. de France** the Banque de France *(French issuing bank)*; **la B. mondiale** the World Bank

2 *(activité, secteur)* banking; **travailler dans la b.** to be *or* work in banking; **b. à distance** remote banking; **b. à domicile** telebanking, home banking; **b. électronique** *ou* **en ligne** e-banking, online banking; **b. d'entreprise** corporate banking; **b. universelle** global banking

3 *(centre de collecte)* bank; **b. alimentaire** food bank; **b. d'organes** organ bank; **b. du sang/du sperme** blood/sperm bank; **b. des yeux** eye bank

4 *Ordinat, Rad & TV* **b. de données** data bank; **b. d'images** picture data bank; **b. de programmes** programme library, programme archives

5 *(à un jeu ▸ réserve)* bank; **tenir la b.** to be the banker, to keep the bank; **faire sauter la b.** to break the bank

banquer [3] [bɑ̃ke] **VI** *très Fam* to fork out; **qui va b.?** who's going to foot the bill?; **à toi de b.** your turn to cough up

banqueroute [bɑ̃krut] **NF 1** *Fin (faillite)* bankruptcy; **faire b.** to go bankrupt; **b. frauduleuse** fraudulent bankruptcy; **b. simple** bankruptcy *(with irregularities amounting to a breach of the law)* **2** *(échec)* failure; **la b. d'une politique** the utter failure of a policy; **critiquant la b. de notre société** criticizing our bankrupt society

banqueroutier, -ère [bɑ̃krutje, -ɛr] **NM,F** *Fin* bankrupt; *(frauduleux)* fraudulent bankrupt

banquet [bɑ̃kɛ] **NM** banquet; **donner un b.** to give a banquet; **faire un b.** to have *or* to hold a banquet

banquette [bɑ̃kɛt] **NF 1** *(siège ▸ de salon)* seat, *Am* banquette; *(▸ de piano)* (duet) stool; *(▸ de restaurant)* wall seat; *(▸ de voiture, de métro)* seat; **b. avant/arrière** front/back seat; *Fig* **jouer devant les banquettes** to play to an empty house **2** *Archit* window seat **3** *(sur une route)* = kerb separating a bus lane from the rest of the roadway

banquier, -ère [bɑ̃kje, -ɛr] **NM,F** banker; **b. d'affaires** investment banker, *Br* merchant banker; **b. prêteur** lending banker

banquise [bɑ̃kiz] **NF** *Géol (côtière)* ice, ice shelf; *(dérivante)* pack ice, ice field *or* floe

bantou, -e [bɑ̃tu] **ADJ** Bantu

NM *(langue)* Bantu

• **Bantou, -e NM,F** Bantu; **les Bantous** the Bantu *or* Bantus

bantoustan [bɑ̃tustɑ̃] **NM** *Hist* Bantustan, Bantu Homeland

baobab [baɔbab] **NM** *Bot* baobab

baptême [batɛm] **NM 1** *Rel* baptism; *(cérémonie)* christening, baptism; **donner le b. à qn** to baptize *or* to christen sb; **recevoir le b.** to be baptized *or* christened; **b. civil** civil baptism, ≃ naming ceremony **2** *(d'un bateau)* christening, naming; *(d'une cloche)* blessing, dedication **3** *(première expérience)* **b. de l'air** first *or* maiden flight; *Mil & Fig* **b. du feu** baptism of fire; **b. de la ligne** (first) crossing of the line

EXCLAM *Can Fam* goddammit!

baptiser [3] [batize] **VT 1** *Rel* to christen, to baptize

2 *(personne, animal ▸ nommer)* to name, to call; *(▸ surnommer)* to nickname, to christen, to dub; **elle a baptisé son chien Victor** she named her dog Victor

3 *(bateau)* to christen, to name; *(cloche)* to bless, to dedicate

4 *Fam (diluer ▸ vin, eau)* to water down

baptismal, -e, -aux, -ales [batismal, -o] **ADJ** baptismal

baptisme [batism] **NM** *Rel* Baptist doctrine

baptistaire [batistɛr] **ADJ** *Rel* **registre b.** register of baptisms; **extrait b.** certificate of baptism

baptiste [batist] **ADJ** *Rel* baptist

NMF 1 *Rel* Baptist; **les baptistes** the Baptists **2** *Can Fam (Canadien français)* = nickname given to French Canadians (from their patron saint, John the Baptist)

baptistère [batistɛr] **NM** *Rel* baptistery

baquer [3] [bake] **VT** *Can Joual (aider)* to back[□]

VPR se baquer *Fam* to go for a dip

baquet [bakɛ] **NM 1** *(récipient)* tub **2** *(siège)* bucket seat

bar [bar] **NM 1** *(café)* bar; *Suisse* **b. à café** café; **b. à thème** theme bar; **b. à vin** wine bar

2 *(comptoir)* bar; **le prix au b. n'est pas le même que le prix en salle** the price for eating or drinking at the bar is not the same as the price in the rest of the establishment

3 *Ich* (European) sea bass

4 *Phys* bar

barachois [baraʃwa] **NM** *Can* sandbar *(at river mouth)*

baragouin [baragwɛ̃] **NM** *Fam* **1** *(langage incompréhensible)* jargon, gobbledegook, *Br* double-Dutch **2** *Péj (langue étrangère)* lingo

baragouinage [baragwinaʒ] **NM** *Fam* **1** *(manière de parler)* jabbering, gibbering **2** *(jargon)* jargon, gobbledegook

baragouiner [3] [baragwine] *Fam* **VT** *(langue)* to speak badly[□]; *(discours)* to gabble; **je baragouine l'espagnol** I can barely put two words of Spanish together; **qu'est-ce qu'elle baragouine?** *(langue étrangère)* what's that language she's jabbering in?; *(propos incompréhensibles)* what's she jabbering on about?

VI *(de façon incompréhensible)* to jabber, to gibber, to talk gibberish; *(dans une langue étrangère)* to jabber away

baragouineur, -euse [baragwinœr, -øz] **NM,F** *Fam* jabberer, gabbler

baraka [baraka] **NF 1** *Rel (dans l'Islam)* baraka **2** *Fam (chance)* luck[□]; **avoir la b.** to be lucky[□]

baraque [barak] **NF** *Archit* **1** *(cabane ▸ à outils)* shed; *(▸ d'ouvriers, de pêcheurs)* shelter, hut; *(▸ de forains)* stall; *(▸ de vente)* stall, stand, booth **2** *Fam (maison)* shack, shanty; **une vieille b.** an old shack; **t'en as une belle b.!** you've got a great place!; **qui commande dans cette b.?** who the hell's in charge around here?

Il faut noter que le nom anglais **barracks** est un faux ami. Il signifie **caserne**.

baraqué, -e [barake] **ADJ** *Fam* muscular[□], hefty, *Péj* beefy; **un type b.** a great hulk of a man

baraquement [barakmɑ̃] **NM 1** *(baraques)* shacks **2** *Mil* camp

baraquer [3] [barake] **VI** *(chameau)* to kneel down

baratin [baratɛ̃] **NM** *Fam (pour vendre)* sales talk, patter, spiel; **b. publicitaire** sales pitch; *(pour convaincre)* flannel; *(pour draguer)* sweet *or* smooth talk, *Br* patter; **avoir du b.** to be a smooth talker; **faire du b. à qn** *(pour convaincre)* to flannel sb; *(pour draguer) Br* to chat sb up, *Am* to hit on sb

baratiner [3] [baratine] *Fam* **VI** *(parler beaucoup)* to chatter; *(mentir)* to flannel

VT b. qn *(pour vendre)* to give sb the sales pitch *or* patter *or* spiel; *(pour convaincre) Br* to flannel sb; *(pour séduire) Br* to chat sb up, *Am* to hit on sb

baratineur, -euse [baratinœr, -øz] *Fam* **ADJ** *(menteur, séducteur)* smooth-talking; **il est très b.** he's a real smooth talker

NM,F 1 *(séducteur)* smooth talker **2** *(menteur)* fibber

baratte [barat] **NF** churn

baratter [3] [barate] **VT** to churn

barbacane [barbakan] NF **1** *Constr* weep hole, weeper **2** *Hist (construction)* barbican; *(meurtrière)* loophole

Barbade [barbad] NF **la B.** Barbados

barbant, -e [barbɑ̃, -ɑ̃t] ADJ *Fam* boring[□]; **il est b.** he's a drag *or* bore; **l'émission était barbante** the programme was boring[□] *or* a drag

barbaque [barbak] NF *très Fam (viande)* meat[□]; *Péj* tough meat[□]

barbare [barbar] ADJ **1** *Hist (primitif)* barbarian, barbaric **2** *(terme, emploi)* incorrect **3** *(cruel)* barbaric

NMF barbarian

barbaresque [barbarɛsk] *Hist* ADJ Barbary *(avant n)*; **les États barbaresques** the Barbary states

• **Barbaresque** NMF = inhabitant of or person from Barbary

Barbarie [barbari] NF *Hist* **la B.** Barbary

barbarie [barbari] NF **1** *(cruauté)* barbarity, barbarousness; **acte de b.** barbarous act **2** *Hist (état primitif)* barbarism

barbarisme [barbarism] NM barbarism

barbe[1] [barb] NM *(cheval)* barb

barbe[2] [barb] NF **1** *(d'homme ▸ drue)* (full) beard; *(▸ clairsemée)* stubble; *(▸ en pointe)* goatee; **avoir de la b.** *(homme)* to need a shave; *(adolescent)* to have some hairs on one's chin; **porter la b.** to have a beard; **se faire la b.** to (have a) shave; **se raser/se tailler la b.** to shave off/to trim one's beard; **un homme à la b. rousse** a red-bearded man, a man with a red beard; **sans b.** *(rasé)* beardless, clean-shaven; *(imberbe)* beardless, smooth-chinned; **b. de deux jours** two days' stubble *or* growth; **b. à papa** *Br* candy floss, *Am* cotton candy; **fausse b.** false beard; **femme à b.** bearded woman; *Fam* **vieille b.** (old) stick-in-the-mud, old fogy; **rien que des vieilles barbes** a bunch of *Br* wrinklies *or Am* greybeards; *Fam* **il n'a pas encore de la b.** he's still wet behind the ears; *Fam* **c'est la b.!, quelle b.!** what a drag *or* bore!; *Fam* **la b.!** *(pour faire taire)* shut up!, shut your mouth!, shut your trap!; *(pour protester)* damn!, hell!, blast!; **parler dans sa b.** to mutter under one's breath; **il a marmonné quelque chose dans sa b.** he muttered something under his breath; **rire dans sa b.** to laugh up one's sleeve; **faire qch à la b. de qn** to do sth under sb's very nose

2 *(d'animal)* tuft of hairs, beard

3 *Bot* beard, awn

4 *(filament ▸ de plume)* barb; *(▸ de coton)* tuft; *(▸ de métal, de plastique)* burr

5 *Tech* beard, bolt toe

• **barbes** NFPL *(de papier)* ragged edge; *(d'encre)* smudge

barbeau, -x [barbo] NM **1** *Ich* barbel **2** *très Fam (souteneur)* pimp **3** *Bot* cornflower, bluebottle

Barbe-Bleue [barbəblø] NPR Bluebeard

barbecue [barbəkju] NM **1** *(appareil)* barbecue (set); **faire cuire de la viande au b.** to barbecue meat **2** *(repas)* barbecue; **faire un b.** to have a barbecue

barbelé, -e [barbəle] ADJ barbed

NM *Br* barbed wire, *Am* barbwire; **derrière les barbelés** behind the *Br* barbed wire *or Am* barbwire

barber [3] [barbe] *Fam* VT **1** *(lasser)* to bore[□]; **je vais lui écrire, mais ça me barbe!** I'll write to him/her, but what a drag! **2** *(importuner)* to hassle; **ne me barbe pas avec ces histoires!** don't hassle me with this stuff!

VPR **se barber** to be bored stiff *or* to tears *or* to death; **qu'est-ce qu'on se barbe ici!** this place is so boring![□]

barbeuc, barbeuk [barbœk] NM *Fam (barbecue)* BBQ, *Br & Austr* barbie

barbeux, -euse [barbø, -øz] *Can Fam* ADJ **être b.** to be a pain (in the neck)

NM pain (in the neck)

barbiche [barbiʃ] NF goatee

barbichette [barbiʃɛt] NF (small) goatee

barbichu, -e [barbiʃy] *Fam* ADJ bearded[□], with a goatee[□]

NM man with a goatee[□]

barbier [barbje] NM *Can & Vieilli* barber

barbillon [barbijɔ̃] NM **1** *Zool & Ich (poisson)* barbel; **barbillons** *(replis ▸ de poisson)* barbels; *(▸ de cheval, de bœuf)* barbs **2** *très Fam (souteneur)* (young) pimp

barbital, -als [barbital] NM *Pharm* barbitone, *Am* barbital

barbiturique [barbityrik] *Pharm* ADJ barbituric

NM barbiturate

barbiturisme [barbityrism] NM *Méd* barbiturate poisoning; *(dépendance)* barbiturate addiction, barbiturism

barbon [barbɔ̃] NM *Littéraire* **(vieux) b.** *(homme ▸ âgé)* old man, greybeard; *(▸ aux idées dépassées)* (old) stick-in-the-mud

barbotage [barbɔtaʒ] NM **1** *Fam (baignade)* paddling[□], splashing about **2** *Chim* bubbling (through a liquid)

barboter [3] [barbɔte] VI **1** *(s'ébattre)* to paddle, to splash around *or* about; **b. dans son bain** to splash around in one's bath **2** *(patauger)* to wade **3** *Chim* **faire b. un gaz** to bubble a gas (through a liquid)

VT *Fam (dérober)* to pinch, to swipe; **quelqu'un m'a barboté mon stylo** someone's pinched my pen

• **barboter dans** VT IND *Fam* **1** *(être impliqué dans)* to have a hand in; **b. dans des affaires louches** to be mixed up in some shady business; **un scandale où barbotent quelques ministres** a scandal several ministers are mixed up in **2** *(être empêtré dans)* to be embroiled *or* to stew in; **je barbote dans ces histoires de divorce** I'm embroiled in this divorce business

barboteur, -euse [barbɔtœr, -øz] ADJ *Fam* light-fingered

NM,F *Fam (voleur)* pilferer

NM *Chim* bubbler, wash bottle

• **barboteuse** NF **1** *(vêtement)* (pair of) rompers *or* crawlers, playsuit **2** *Can (gonflable) Br* paddling pool, *Am* wading pool; *(dans une piscine)* children's pool, wading pool

barbotin [barbɔtɛ̃] NM *Tech* sprocket-wheel; *Naut* cable wheel

barbouillage [barbujaʒ] NM **1** *(application de couleur, de boue)* daubing **2** *(fait d'écrire)* scribbling, scrawling; *(écrit)* scribble, scrawl **3** *(tableau ▸ de mauvais artiste) Péj* daub; *(▸ d'enfant)* scribbled picture; **à l'âge des premiers barbouillages** when a child first learns to draw

barbouiller [3] [barbuje] VT **1** *(salir)* **tu as barbouillé ton tablier!** you've dirtied your apron!; **b. qch de qch** to smear sth with sth; **son menton était barbouillé de confiture** his chin was smeared with jam; **il avait le visage barbouillé de larmes** his face was tear-stained

2 *(peindre)* to daub; **b. des toiles** to mess about *or* around with paint; **b. qch de peinture** to slap paint on sth, to daub sth with paint

3 *(gribouiller)* to scrawl, to scribble; **il barbouille du papier** he's scribbling away; *Fig Péj* he's just a scribbler

4 *Fam (donner la nausée à)* to nauseate[□]; **ça me barbouille (l'estomac** *ou* **le cœur)** it turns my stomach; **avoir l'air barbouillé** to look green around the gills; **avoir l'estomac** *ou* **se sentir barbouillé** to feel queasy *or* nauseated

USAGE ABSOLU *(peinturlurer)* **je ne peins pas, je barbouille** I'm not really a painter, I just mess about with colours

barbouilleur, -euse [barbujœr, -øz] NM,F *Péj (écrivain)* scribbler; *(peintre)* dauber

barbouillis [barbuji] = **barbouillage**

barbouze [barbuz] NF *très Fam* **1** *(espion)* secret agent[□] **2** *(garde du corps)* heavy, minder[□]; *(intermédiaire)* minder[□] **3** *(barbe)* beard[□]

barbu, -e[1] [barby] ADJ bearded

NM **1** *(homme)* bearded man, man with a beard; *Fam* Islamic fundamentalist[□] **2** *très Fam (poils pubiens de la femme)* bush

barbue[2] [barby] NF *Ich* brill

barcarolle [barkarɔl] NF *Mus* barcarolle

barcasse [barkas] NF *Péj Naut* boat[□], tub

Barcelone [barsəlɔn] NF *Géog* Barcelona

barco® [barko] NM data projector

barda [barda, *Can* bardɑ] NM *Fam* **1** *Mil* gear, *Br* kit **2** *(chargement)* stuff, gear, paraphernalia

3 *Can (pagaille)* shambles *(singulier)*; **petit b.** household chores; **grand b.** big clean-up

4 *Can (bruit)* **faire du b.** to make a racket

bardage [bardaʒ] NM **1** *Constr (revêtement de maison) Br* weatherboarding, *Am* siding **2** *(autour d'un tableau)* (protective) boarding **3** *(transport de matériaux lourds)* hand transport

bardane [bardan] NF *Bot* burdock

bardas [bardas] NM *Can (pagaille)* shambles; **être de b.** *(déranger)* to be a nuisance

bardasser [3] [bardase] *Can* VI **1** *(faire des besognes)* to do chores **2** *(perdre son temps)* to waste one's time **3** *(montrer sa mauvaise humeur en faisant du bruit)* to bang about in a temper

VT **1** *(cogner)* to bang **2** *(secouer)* to shake up **3** *(traiter sans ménagement)* to be rough with

barde [bard] NM *Littérature (poète)* bard

NF *Culin* bard

bardeau, -x [bardo] NM **1** *Constr (pour toiture)* shingle; **un toit de bardeaux** a shingle roof **2** *Zool* hinny **3** *Can Fam* **manquer un b.** to be not quite right in the head, to have a slate loose

barder [3] [barde] VT **1** *Culin* to bard **2** *Fig* **être bardé de** *(être couvert de)* to be covered in *or* with; **coffre bardé de ferrures** chest bound with iron bands; **être bardé de diplômes** to have a string of academic titles

V IMPERSONNEL *Fam* **ça barde!** all hell's broken loose!; **quand il a dit ça, ça a bardé!** things really turned nasty when he said that!

bardot [bardo] NM *Zool* hinny

barème [barɛm] NM **1** *(tableau)* ready reckoner **2** *Fin (tarification)* scale; **b. fiscal** *ou* **d'imposition** tax rate schedule *or* structure, tax scale; **b. des prix** price list, schedule of prices; **b. des salaires** wage scale, variable sliding scale

Barents [barɛ̃s] *voir* **mer**

barge[1] [barʒ] NF *Naut* barge, lighter

barge[2] [barʒ] ADJ *Fam (fou)* nuts, bananas, *Br* off one's head

barguiner [3] [bargine] VI *Can Fam* **1** *(hésiter)* to dither **2** *(marchander)* to bargain[□], to haggle

baril [baril] NM *(de vin)* barrel, cask; *(de pétrole)* barrel; *(de lessive)* drum; **b. de poudre** powder keg

barillet [barijɛ] NM **1** *(baril)* small barrel *or* cask **2** *Tech (d'un revolver, d'une serrure)* cylinder; *(d'une horloge)* spring box, spring drum

bariolage [barjɔlaʒ] NM **1** *(action)* daubing with bright colours **2** *(motif)* gaudy colour scheme

bariolé, -e [barjɔle] ADJ *(tissu)* multicoloured; *(foule)* colourful

barioler [3] [barjɔle] VT to cover with gaudy colours, to splash bright colours on

bariolure [barjɔlyr] NF garish *or* gaudy colours

barjo(t) [barʒo] *Fam* ADJ nuts, bananas

NMF nut, *Br* nutter

barmaid [barmɛd] NF barmaid

barman [barman] NM *(pl* **barmans** *ou* **barmen** [-mɛn]) barman, *Am* bartender

barn [barn] NM *Phys* barn

barnache [barnaʃ] = **bernache**

barographe [barɔgraf] NM *Phys* barograph

baromètre [barɔmɛtr] NM *Phys* barometer, glass; **le b. est au beau fixe** the barometer is set *or* reads fair; **le b. est à la pluie** the barometer is set on rain; *Fig* **b. de l'opinion publique** barometer *or* indicator of public opinion; **b. anéroïde** aneroid barometer; *Mktg* **b. de clientèle** customer barometer; **b. enregistreur** recording barometer; *Mktg* **b. de marque** brand barometer

barométrique [barɔmetrik] ADJ *Phys* barometric, barometer *(avant n)*

baron, -onne [barɔ̃, -ɔn] NM,F **1** *(noble)* baron, *f* baroness

2 *(magnat)* **b. de la finance** tycoon

3 *Culin* **b. d'agneau** baron of lamb

4 *Fam Arg crime (compère)* plant

baronet [barɔnɛ] NM *Hist* baronet

baronnage [barɔnaʒ] NM *Hist* baronage

baronne [barɔn] *voir* **baron**

baronnet = **baronet**
baronnie [barɔni] NF *Hist* barony
baroque [barɔk] ADJ **1** *(gén)* baroque **2** *(étrange ▸ idée)* strange, peculiar **3** *(perle)* tear-shaped
NM Baroque
baroud [barud] NM *Fam* battle; **b. d'honneur** last stand
barouder [barude] VI *Fam (voyager)* to knock about
baroudeur [barudœr] NM *Fam (qui aime le combat)* fighter; **c'est un b.** *(voyageur)* he's knocked about a bit
barouf [baruf], **baroufle** [barufl] NM *Fam* din, row, racket; **faire du b.** to make a din *or* row *or* racket
barque [bark] NF *Naut* small boat; **b. de pêcheur** small fishing boat; *Fig* **mener sa b.** to look after oneself; **il est assez grand pour mener sa b.** he's old enough to look after himself; **il a bien/mal mené sa b.** he managed/didn't manage his affairs well; **c'est elle qui mène la b.** she's the boss, she's in charge; **charger la b.** to overdo it
barquette [barkɛt] NF **1** *Culin* = boat-shaped tartlet **2** *(récipient ▸ pour plat à emporter)* container; *(▸ de fraises, de framboises)* punnet
barracuda [barakuda] NM *Ich* barracuda
barrage [baraʒ] NM **1** *Archit (réservoir)* dam; *(régulateur)* weir, barrage; **b. (de retenue)** dam; *Fig* **faire b. à** to stand in the way of, to obstruct, to hinder; **b. flottant** floating dam; **b. mobile** movable dam; **le b. Hoover** the Hoover dam; **le b. de Kariba** the Kariba dam
2 *(dispositif policier)* **b. (de police)** police cordon; **b. routier** roadblock
3 *Mil* **b. roulant** creeping *or* rolling barrage
4 *Sport* **(match de) b.** play-off

BARRE [bar]

- bar **1, 2, 6–8**
- line **4**
- helm, tiller **3**
- level **5**

NF **1** *(tige ▸ de bois)* bar; *(▸ de métal)* bar, rod; **b. de fer** iron bar; **j'ai une b. sur l'estomac/au-dessus des yeux** *(douleur)* I have a pain across my stomach/above my eyes; *Aut* **b. d'accouplement** tie-rod; *Naut* **b. antiroulis** anti-roll bar; **b. d'appui** handrail; **b. de céréales** *Br* cereal *or Am* granola bar; **une b. de chocolat** a bar of chocolate; **b. chocolatée** *Br* chocolate *or Am* candy bar; **b. de remorquage** tow bar; *Aut* **b. de torsion** torsion bar
2 *Sport* **barres asymétriques/parallèles** asymmetric/parallel bars; **b. à disques** barbell; **b. fixe** high *or* horizontal bar; *(en danse)* barre; **exercices à la b.** barre work *or* exercises; *Fig* **avoir b. sur qn** to have an advantage over sb
3 *Naut* **b. (de gouvernail)** *(gén)* helm; *(sur un voilier)* tiller; *(sur un navire)* wheel; **prendre la b.** to take the helm; *Fig* to take charge; **être à la b.** to be at the helm, to steer; *Fig* to be at the helm *or* in charge
4 *(trait)* line; **faire des barres** to draw lines; **mets la b. sur ton T** cross your T; **b. de soustraction/fraction** subtraction/fraction line; **b. oblique** slash; **b. oblique inversée** backslash; **double b.** double bar
5 *(niveau)* level; **le dollar est descendu au-dessous de la b. des 0,50 euros** the dollar fell below the 0.50 euro level; **pour l'examen de physique, la b. a été fixée à 12** the *Br* pass mark *or Am* passing grade for the physics exam was set at 12; **mettre** *ou* **placer la b. trop haut** to set too high a standard; **à chaque fois, ils mettent la b. plus haut** they keep making it harder to meet the target
6 *Mus* **b. (de mesure)** bar line; **double b.** double bar
7 *Jur* **b. (du tribunal)** bar; **b. des témoins** *Br* witness box, *Am* witness stand; **appeler qn à la b.** to call sb to the *Br* witness box *or Am* witness stand; **comparaître à la b.** to appear as a witness
8 *Ordinat* **b. de défilement** scroll bar; **b. d'espacement** space bar; **b. d'état** status bar; **b. d'icônes** icon bar; **b. de lancement rapide** quick launch bar; **b. de menu** menu bar; **b. de navigation** navigation bar; **b. d'outils** tool bar; **b. de sélection** menu bar; **b. des tâches** taskbar; **b. de titre** title bar
9 b. HLM *Br* ≃ large block of council flats, *Am* ≃ large public housing unit
10 *Can Joual* **b. de savon** bar of soap
11 *Géog (crête)* ridge; *(banc de sable)* sandbar; *(houle)* race

barré, -e [bare] ADJ **1** *Banque (chèque)* crossed; **chèque non b.** open cheque **2** *(dent)* impacted **3** *Fam (locutions)* **on est mal barrés pour y être à huit heures** we haven't got a hope in hell *or* we don't stand a chance of being there at eight; *Ironique* **on est bien barrés!, on est mal barrés!** (that's) great!, (that's) marvellous!; **c'est mal b.** it's got off to a bad start; **entre eux deux, c'est mal b.** they started off on the wrong foot with each other; **il est bien b., ce mec-là** that guy's completely nuts; **c'est un film bien b.** *(loufoque)* it's a really wacky film; *(étrange)* it's a really weird *or* freaky film; *Can* **ne pas être b.** to be a live wire
NM *Mus* barré
barreau, -x [baro] NM **1** *(de fenêtre, de cage)* bar; *(d'échelle)* rung; *(de chaise)* rung, crosspiece; *Fam Hum* **b. de chaise** fat cigar; **être derrière les barreaux** to be behind bars **2** *Jur* **le b.** the Bar; **être admis** *ou* **reçu au b.** to be called to the Bar; **être radié du b.** to be disbarred
barrement [barmɑ̃] NM *Banque (sur un chèque)* crossing
barrer [3] [bare, *Can* bɑre] VT **1** *(bloquer ▸ porte, issue)* to bar; *(▸ voie, route)* to block, to obstruct; **les grévistes barrent la voie de chemin de fer** strikers are blocking the railway track; **la rue est temporairement barrée** the street has been temporarily closed; **b. le passage à qn** to block sb's way; *aussi Fig* **b. la route à qn** to stand in sb's way
2 *Can & (régional en France) (fermer à clef)* to lock
3 *(rayer ▸ chèque)* to cross; *(▸ erreur, phrase)* to cross out, to score out; **b. ses T** to cross one's Ts; **un pli lui barrait le front** he/she had a deep line running right across his/her forehead; **l'écharpe tricolore qui lui barrait la poitrine** the tricolour sash he/she wore across his/her chest
4 *Naut* to steer
VI *Naut* to steer, to be at the helm; *Sport (à l'aviron)* to cox
VPR **se barrer** *Fam* **1** *(partir)* to beat it, to clear off; **on se barre d'ici!** let's get out of here! **2** *(se détacher)* to come off
barrette [barɛt] NF **1** *(pince)* **b. (à cheveux)** *Br* (hair) slide, *Am* barrette; **b. de médaille** medal bar
2 *Couture* collar pin
3 *Élec* **b. de connexion** connecting strip
4 *Rel* biretta; **recevoir la b.** to be made a cardinal
5 *Fam (de haschisch)* thin strip
6 *Ordinat* **b. de mémoire vive** RAM module
barreur, -euse [barœr, -øz] NM,F **1** *Naut (gén)* helmsman, *f* helmswoman **2** *Sport (en aviron)* coxswain; **avec b.** coxed; **sans b.** coxless
barricade [barikad] NF barricade; *Fig* **être du même côté de la b.** to be on the same side of the fence
barricader [3] [barikade] VT *(porte, rue)* to barricade
VPR **se barricader 1** *(se retrancher)* to barricade oneself **2** *(s'enfermer)* to lock *or* to shut oneself away; **il s'est barricadé dans sa chambre** he's locked *or* shut himself in his room
barrière [barjɛr] NF **1** *(clôture)* fence; *(porte)* gate; **b. de dégel** = closure of road to heavy traffic during thaw; **b. Nadar** crowd barrier; **b. de passage à niveau** *Br* level *or Am* grade crossing gate; **b. de sécurité** guardrail; *Belg* **b. Vauban** security barrier
2 *(obstacle)* barrier; **la b. de la langue** the language barrier; **dresser** *ou* **mettre une b. entre...** to raise a barrier between...; **faire tomber une b./les barrières** to break down a barrier/the barriers
3 *Géog* **b. de corail** barrier reef; **b. écologique** ecological barrier; **b. naturelle** natural barrier; **la Grande B.** the Great Barrier Reef
4 *Écon* **b. commerciale** trade barrier; **barrières douanières** trade *or* tariff barrier; **b. à l'entrée** entry barrier; **b. non tarifaire** non-tariff barrier; **b. tarifaire** tariff barrier
barrique [barik] NF barrel, cask
barrir [32] [barir] VI *(éléphant)* to trumpet

barrissement [barismɑ̃] NM *(de l'éléphant)* trumpeting
bar-tabac [bartaba] *(pl* **bars-tabacs***)* NM = bar where tobacco, stamps and lottery tickets are also sold over the counter
bartavelle [bartavɛl] NF *Orn* rock partridge
barter [bartœr], **bartering** [bartœriŋ] NM *Rad & TV* bartering
barycentre [barisɑ̃tr] NM *Astron & Phys* barycentre
baryte [barit] NF *Chim* baryta, barium hydroxide
baryté, -e [barite] ADJ *Méd* **bouillie barytée** barium meal
baryton [baritɔ̃] NM *Mus (voix)* baritone (voice); *(chanteur)* baritone
baryum [barjɔm] NM *Chim* barium; **sulfate de b.** barium meal
barzoï [barzɔj] NM *Zool* borzoi, Russian wolfhound
BAS [beas] NM *Admin (abrév* **Bureau d'aide sociale***)* welfare office
bas[1] [ba] NM **1** *(de femme)* stocking; **le visage dissimulé sous un b.** wearing a stocking mask; **des b. avec/sans couture** seamed/seamless stockings; **b. fins** sheer stockings; **b. de laine** woollen stockings; *Fig* savings, nest egg; **b. (de) Nylon®** nylon stockings; **b. résille** fishnet stockings; **b. de soie** silk stockings; **b. à varices** support stockings **2** *Can (chaussette)* sock; **marcher en pied de b.** to walk around in stockinged feet

BAS[2]**, BASSE** [ba, bas]

ADJ
- low **A1, 2, B1–6**
- lower **A4, 5**
- mean **B6**
- bass **B4**
- short **A1**
- quiet **B5**
- crude **B7**

ADV
- low **1, 3**

NM
- bottom, lower part **1**

ADJ **A.** *DANS L'ESPACE* **1** *(de peu de hauteur ▸ bâtiment, mur)* low; *(▸ herbes)* low, short; *(▸ nuages)* low; **une petite maison basse** a squat little house; **une chaise basse** a low chair; **avoir le front b.** to be low-browed; **attrape les branches basses** grasp the lower *or* bottom branches; **le soleil était b. sur l'horizon** the sun was low on the horizon; **à basse altitude** at (a) low altitude
2 *(peu profond)* low; **les eaux sont basses** the water level's low *or* down; **la Seine est basse** the (level of the) Seine is low; **aux basses eaux** *(de la mer)* at low tide; *(d'une rivière)* when the water level is low; *Fig* at a time of stagnation; **c'est la basse mer** *ou* **marée basse** it's low tide, the tide is low
3 *(incliné vers le sol)* **être assis la tête basse** to sit with one's head down; **le chien s'enfuit, la queue basse** the dog ran away with its tail between its legs
4 *Naut* **basses voiles, voiles basses** lower sails *or* courses; **basses vergues** lower yards
5 *Géog* **les basses terres** the lowlands; **la basse Bretagne** the western part of Brittany; **les basses Alpes** the foothills of the Alps; **la basse Loire/Seine** the lower Loire/Seine (valley)
B. *DANS UNE HIÉRARCHIE* **1** *(en grandeur ▸ prix, fréquence, pression etc)* low; **à b. prix** cheap, for a low price; **acheter/vendre qch à b. prix** to buy/sell sth cheap; **à basse température** *(laver)* at low temperatures; **le thermomètre est b.** temperatures are low; **la note la plus basse est 8** the lowest mark is 8; **les enchères sont restées très basses** the bidding didn't get off the ground; **le moral de l'équipe est b.** the team's in low spirits, morale in the team is low
2 *(médiocre ▸ intérêt, rendement)* low, poor; *(▸ dans les arts)* inferior, minor, crude; **le niveau de la classe est très b.** the (achievement) level of the class is very low; **c'est du b. comique** it's low comedy; *Cartes* **les basses cartes** the small *or* low cards
3 *(inférieur dans la société)* low, humble, *Littéraire* lowly; **de basse origine** of humble origin; **de basse condition** from a poor family; **le b. peuple** the lower classes *or Péj* orders

4 *Mus (grave ▸ note)* low, bottom *(avant n)*; *(▸ guitare, flûte)* bass *(avant n)*; **sa voix tremble dans les notes basses** her voice quavers in the bottom of the range; **une voix basse** a deep voice

5 *(peu fort)* low, quiet; **parler à voix basse** to speak in a low *or* quiet voice; **sur un ton b.** in hushed tones

6 *Péj (abject, vil ▸ âme)* low, mean, villainous; *(▸ acte)* low, base, mean; *(▸ sentiment)* low, base, abject; **de basses compromissions** shabby compromises; **à moi toutes les basses besognes** I get stuck with all the dirty work

7 *Péj (vulgaire ▸ terme, expression)* crude, vulgar

8 *Ling* **b. allemand** Low German; **b. breton** Breton *(as spoken in southern Brittany)*

9 *(le plus récent)* **le B.-Empire** the late Empire; **le b. Moyen Âge** the late Middle Ages

ADV 1 *(à faible hauteur, à faible niveau)* low; **les oiseaux sont passés très b.** the birds flew very low; **la dernière étagère est placée trop b.** the last shelf is too low; **le thermomètre est descendu** *ou* **tombé très b. cette nuit** temperatures dropped very low last night; **leurs actions sont au plus b.** their shares have reached an all-time low; **elle est bien b.** *(physiquement)* she's very poorly; *(moralement)* she's very low *or* down; **vous êtes tombé bien b.** *(financièrement)* you've certainly gone down in the world; *(moralement)* you've sunk really low; **il est tombé bien b. dans mon estime** he's gone down a lot in my estimation; **plus b., vous trouverez la boulangerie** *(plus loin)* you'll find the baker's a little further on; **j'habite deux maisons plus b. que lui** I live two houses down from his place; **plus b.** *(dans un document)* below, further down *or* on; **voir plus b.** see below; **je sais tout maintenant, alors b. les masques** I know everything now, so you can stop pretending; *Fam* **b. les pattes!** hands off!

2 *(d'une voix douce)* in a low voice; *(d'une voix grave)* in a deep voice; **mets le son plus b.** turn the sound down; **il dit tout haut ce que les autres pensent tout b.** he voices the thoughts which others keep to themselves

3 *Mus* low; **tu prends la deuxième mesure un peu trop b.** *(à un chanteur, à un musicien)* you're taking the second bar a bit flat

4 *Vét* **mettre b.** to give birth; **elle a mis b. quatre chiots** she gave birth to four puppies

5 *Naut* **mettre pavillon b.** to lower *or* to strike the colours; **haler b.** to haul in *or* down; **mettre b. les feux** to draw the fires

NM 1 *(partie inférieure ▸ d'un pantalon, d'un escalier, d'une hiérarchie etc)* bottom; *(▸ d'un visage)* lower part; **le b. d'une robe** *(partie inférieure)* the bottom of a dress; **elle a le b. du visage de son père** the bottom *or* lower part of her face is like her father's; **le b. du dos** the small of the back; *Typ & Ordinat* **b. de page** footer; **b. de pyjama** pyjama bottoms

2 *Culin* **b. de carré** prime chops (of veal)

3 *Naut* **le b. de l'eau** low tide

4 *Mktg (du marché)* low end

5 *Can (appartement ▸ au rez-de-chaussée) Br* ground-floor flat, *Am* first-floor apartment; *(▸ en sous-sol) Br* basement flat, *Am* basement apartment

6 *Littéraire (ignominie)* baseness, vileness

• **basse NF 1** *Mus (partie)* bass (part *or* score); **basse chiffrée** figured bass; **basse continue** basso continuo; **basse contrainte** basso ostinato; **basse noble** basso profundo; **basse obstinée** basso ostinato; **basse profonde** basso profundo

2 *(voix d'homme)* bass (voice); **basse chantante** basso cantante; **basse profonde** basso profundo; *(chanteur)* bass

3 *(instrument ▸ gén)* bass (instrument); *(▸ violoncelle)* (double) bass

4 *Géog* shoal, flat, sandbank

• **à bas ADV mettre qch à b.** to pull sth down; **ils ont mis à b. tout le quartier** they razed the whole district to the ground; **à b. la dictature!** down with dictatorship!

• **à bas de PRÉP se jeter/sauter à b. de son cheval** to throw oneself/to jump off one's horse

• **au bas de PRÉP au b. des escaliers** at the foot *or* bottom of the stairs; **au b. de la page** at the foot *or* bottom of the page; **au b. de la hiérarchie/liste** at the bottom of the hierarchy/list; **au b. du jardin** at the bottom (end) *or* far end of the garden

• **de bas en haut ADV** from bottom to top, from the bottom up; **regarder qn de b. en haut** to look sb up and down

• **d'en bas ADJ les voisins d'en b.** the people downstairs; **la porte d'en b. est fermée** the downstairs door is shut; *Fig* **la France d'en b.** the French underclass **ADV** *(dans une maison)* from downstairs; *(d'une hauteur)* from the bottom; *Fig* **elle est partie d'en b.** she worked her way up, she started from nowhere

• **du bas ADJ 1** *(de l'étage inférieur)* **l'appartement du b.** the flat underneath *or* below *or* downstairs **2** *(du rez-de-chaussée)* downstairs *(avant n)*; **les chambres du b.** the downstairs rooms **3** *(de l'endroit le moins élevé)* lower; **le carreau du b. est cassé** the lower pane is broken

• **en bas ADV 1** *(à un niveau inférieur ▸ dans un bâtiment)* downstairs, down; *Fam* **je vais** *ou* **descends en b.** I'm going down *or* downstairs; **la maison a deux pièces en b. et deux en haut** the house has two rooms downstairs and two upstairs **2** *(dans la partie inférieure)* **prends le carton par en b.** take hold of the bottom of the box **3** *(vers le sol)* **je ne peux pas regarder en b., j'ai le vertige!** I can't look down, I feel dizzy; **le village semblait si petit tout en b.** the village looked so small down there *or* below; **suspendre qch la tête en b.** to hang sth upside down

• **en bas de PRÉP en b. de la côte/des marches** at the bottom *or* foot of the hill/the stairs; **signez en b. du contrat** sign at the bottom of the contract; **j'ai rangé les draps en b. de l'armoire** I've put the sheets at the bottom of the wardrobe; **ils se retrouvent en b. du classement général** they're now (at the) bottom of the league

---

basalte [bazalt] **NM** *Géol* basalt

basaltique [bazaltik] **ADJ** *Géol* basaltic

basané, -e [bazane] **ADJ 1** *(bronzé ▸ touriste)* suntanned; *(▸ navigateur)* tanned, weather-beaten **2** *très Fam (connotation raciste)* swarthy□, dark-skinned□ **3** *Can (en acadien)* freckled

basaner [3] [bazane] **VT** to tan

bas-bleu [bablø] *(pl* **bas-bleus***)* **NM** *Péj* bluestocking

bas-côté [bakote] *(pl* **bas-côtés***)* **NM** *(de route)* side, verge; *(d'église)* aisle

basculant, -e [baskylɑ̃, -ɑ̃t] *voir* **benne, pont**

bascule [baskyl] **NF 1** *(balance)* weighing machine; *(pèse-personne)* scales

2 *(balançoire)* seesaw; **mouvement de b.** seesaw motion; **pratiquer une politique de b.** to change allies frequently

3 *Tech* bascule; *Électron* **b. bistable** flip-flop

4 *Ordinat* toggle

5 *Can* **donner la b. à qn** *Br* to give sb the bumps

basculement [baskylmɑ̃] **NM** *(d'une pile)* toppling over; *(d'un récipient)* tipping out *or* over; **le b. de l'électorat vers les verts** the swing to the green party

basculer [3] [baskyle] **VI 1** *(personne)* to topple, to fall over; *(vase)* to tip over; *(benne)* to tip up; **un peu plus et il faisait b. la voiture dans le vide** it would only have taken a little push to send the car over the edge **2** *Fig* **son univers a basculé** his/her world collapsed; **nous étions heureux, et puis tout a basculé** we were happy, then everything turned upside down; **b. dans l'opposition** to go over to the opposition **3** *Ordinat* to toggle

VT 1 *(renverser ▸ chariot)* to tip up; *(▸ chargement)* to tip out; **b. son vote sur** to switch one's vote to **2** *Tél (appel)* to transfer

basculeur [baskylœr] **NM 1** *Tech* rocker switch **2** *Ordinat (touche)* toggle key

bas-de-casse [badəkas] **NM INV** *Typ* lower case; **en b.** lower-case, in lower case; **mettre en b.** to put in lower case

base [baz] **NF 1** *(support)* base; **à la b. du cou** at the base of the neck; **b. de maquillage** make-up base

2 *(fondement)* basis, groundwork *(UNCOUNT)*, foundations; **établir qch/reposer sur une b. solide** to set sth up/to rest on a sound basis; **quelle est votre b. de départ?** what's *or* where's your starting point?; *Jur* **b. légale** legal basis

3 *(centre)* **b. de plein air (et de loisirs)** outdoor recreation centre

4 *Mil* **b. (aérienne/militaire/navale)** (air/army/naval) base; **b. arrière** rear base; **b. de lancement** launch *or* launching site; **b. d'opérations/de ravitaillement** operations/supply base; **rentrer à la b.** to go back to base

5 *Astron* **b. de lancement** launching site

6 *Pol* **la b.** the grass roots, the rank and file

7 *Fin & Compta* **sur une b. nette** on a net basis; **b. amortissable** basis for depreciation; **b. de calcul** basis of calculations; **b. hors taxe** amount exclusive of *Br* VAT *or Am* sales tax; **b. d'imposition** taxable base; **b. monétaire** monetary base

8 *Géom, Ordinat & Math* base; **système de b. cinq/huit** base five/eight system; **b. de données** database; **mettre qch dans une b. de données** to enter sth into a database; **b. de données client-serveur** client-server database; *Mktg* **b. de données de consommateurs** customer database; **b. de données relationnelles** relational database

9 *Mktg* **b. de clientèle** customer base; **b. de consommateurs** customer base; *Écon* **b. de sondage** sample base

10 *Ling (en diachronie)* root; *(en synchronie)* base, stem; *(en grammaire générative)* base component

11 *Culin (d'un cocktail, d'une sauce)* basic ingredient

12 *Chim* base

• **bases NFPL 1** *(fondations)* foundations, basis; **les bases de la sémiotique** the basis of semiotics; **établir** *ou* **jeter les bases d'une alliance** to lay the foundations of *or* for an alliance **2** *(acquis)* basic knowledge; **votre enfant n'a pas les bases** your child lacks basic knowledge; **avoir de bonnes bases en arabe/musique** to have a good grounding in Arabic/ music

• **à base de PRÉP à b. de café** coffee-based; **une boisson à b. de gin** a gin-based drink

• **à la base ADV 1** *(en son fondement)* **le raisonnement est faux à la b.** the basis of the argument is false **2** *(au début)* at the beginning, to begin *or* to start off with; **à la b., nous étions un groupe de rock** to begin with *or* originally, we were a rock band

• **à la base de PRÉP être à la b. de qch** *(à la source de)* to be at the root *or* heart of sth

• **de base ADJ 1** *(fondamental ▸ vocabulaire, industrie)* basic; *(▸ principe)* basic, fundamental; **militant de b.** grass-roots militant **2** *(de référence ▸ prix, salaire, traitement)* basic; *(▸ documents, données)* source *(avant n)*

• **sur la base de PRÉP** on the basis of; **je suis payée sur la b. de 13 euros de l'heure** I am paid at a basic rate of 13 euros an hour

base-ball [bɛzbol] *(pl* **base-balls***)* **NM** *Sport* baseball

baser [3] [baze] **VT 1** *(fonder)* **b. qch sur qch** to base sth on sth; **tes soupçons ne sont basés sur rien** there are no grounds for your suspicions, your suspicions are groundless; **b. une doctrine sur le libéralisme** to base a doctrine on liberalism **2** *Mil & Com (installer)* to base; **être basé à** to be based at/in; **les soldats basés à Berlin** the soldiers based in Berlin, the Berlin-based soldiers; **l'entreprise est basée à Lyon** the firm's based in Lyons

VPR se baser se b. sur to base one's judgement on, to go by *or* on; **sur quoi te bases-tu?** what's your basis for that?, what are you going on?; **je me base sur les chiffres de l'année dernière** I'm going by last year's figures, I've taken last year's figures as the basis for my calculations

bas-fond [bafɔ̃] *(pl* **bas-fonds***)* **NM** *Géog* **1** *(dans la mer, la rivière)* shallow, shoal **2** *(dans le terrain)* low ground, hollow

• **bas-fonds NMPL** *Littéraire* **les bas-fonds de New York** the seedy parts of New York; **les bas-fonds de la société** the dregs of society

Basic [bazik] **NM** *Ordinat* BASIC

basilic [bazilik] **NM 1** *Bot* basil **2** *Myth & Zool* basilisk

basilical, -e, -aux, -ales [bazilikal, -o] **ADJ** *Archit* basilical

basilique¹ [bazilik] **NF** *Archit* basilica; **la b. Saint-Pierre** Saint Peter's Basilica

basilique² [bazilik] *Anat* **ADJ** basilic

NF basilic vein

basin [bazɛ̃] **NM** *Tex* dimity

basique [bazik] **ADJ** basic

basket [basket] **NF** *(chaussure) Br* trainer, *Am* sneaker; *Fam* **être bien dans ses baskets** to be very together *or Br* sorted

NM *Sport* basketball

basket-ball [basketbol] *(pl* **basket-balls**) **NM** *Sport* basketball

basketteur, -euse [basketœr, -øz] **NM,F** *Sport* basketball player

bas-mât [bama] *(pl* **bas-mâts**) **NM** *Naut* lower mast

basquaise [baskez] **ADJ F** Basque

NF Basque

• **(à la) basquaise** **ADJ** *Culin* basquaise, with a tomato and ham sauce

basque¹ [bask] **NF** *Couture* basque; **s'accrocher** *ou* **se pendre aux basques de qn** to dog sb's footsteps, to stick to sb like glue; **cet enfant est toujours pendu à mes basques** that child just won't let go of me

basque² [bask] **ADJ** Basque; **le Pays b.** the Basque Country

NM *(langue)* Basque

• **Basque NMF** Basque

> **BASQUE**
>
> The area covered by the Basque Country includes the far south-western corner of France. The French portion shares with its Spanish counterpart a common language and a strong sense of separate identity. Nevertheless, nationalist sentiment is much less radical there and Basque is not as widely spoken as it is on the other side of the Pyrenees. Basque, or "Euskera", stands out as one of the very few non-Indo-European languages surviving in Europe.

bas-relief [barəljɛf] *(pl* **bas-reliefs**) **NM** *Beaux-Arts* bas-relief, low relief

Bas-Rhin [barɛ̃] **NM le B.** Bas-Rhin

basse [bas] *voir* **bas**

basse-contre [baskɔ̃tr] *(pl* **basses-contres**) **NF** *Mus* basso profundo

basse-cour [baskur] *(pl* **basses-cours**) **NF 1** *(lieu)* farmyard **2** *(volaille)* **(animaux de) b.** poultry; **toute la b. était en émoi** the hens and chickens were extremely agitated

basse-fosse [basfos] *(pl* **basses-fosses**) **NF** *Archit* dungeon

bassement [basmɑ̃] **ADV** *(agir)* basely, meanly; **sa visite était b. intéressée** his/her visit was motivated by mere self-interest; **parlons de choses b. matérielles** let's talk money

Basse-Normandie [basnɔrmɑ̃di] **NF la B.** Basse-Normandie

bassesse [basɛs] **NF 1** *(caractère vil)* baseness; *(servilité)* servility; **il ne poussera pas la b. jusque-là** he won't stoop that low **2** *(action ▸ mesquine)* base *or* despicable act; *(▸ servile)* servile act; **il ne reculera devant aucune b.** he will stoop to anything; **faire des bassesses** to behave despicably

basset [basɛ] **NM** *Zool (chien)* basset (hound)

basse-taille [bastaj] *(pl* **basses-tailles**) **NF 1** *Mus* basso cantante, singing bass **2** *(en orfèvrerie)* **émaux de** *ou* **sur b.** basse-taille enamelling

bassin [basɛ̃] **NM 1** *Anat* pelvis

2 *(piscine)* pool; *(plan d'eau)* ornamental lake; *(plus petit)* pond; **petit b.** *(de la piscine)* small *or* children's pool; **grand b.** *(de la piscine)* main pool

3 *(récipient)* basin, bowl; *(d'une balance)* pan; **b. hygiénique** *ou* **de lit** bedpan

4 *École* **b. de décantation** settling tank

5 *Géog* basin; **b. houiller** coal basin; **b. hydrographique** drainage area; **b. minier** mining area; **b. sédimentaire** sedimentary basin; **b. versant** watershed; **le B. d'Aquitaine** the Aquitaine Basin; **le B. du Congo** the Congo Basin; **le B. parisien** the Paris Basin

6 *Naut* dock; **b. de radoub** dry dock

7 *Rad & TV* **b. d'audience** audience pool

bassinant, -e [basinɑ̃, -ɑ̃t] **ADJ** *Fam* boring□; **elle est vraiment bassinante** she's a real pain in the neck

bassine [basin] **NF** basin, bowl; **b. à confiture** preserving pan; **une b. de confiture** a panful of jam

bassiner [3] [basine] **VT 1** *(chauffer)* to warm *(with a warming pan)* **2** *(humecter)* to moisten **3** *Fam (ennuyer)* to bore□; **il nous bassine avec ses histoires de cœur** we're bored stiff hearing about his love affairs; **tu nous bassines avec ça!** stop going on and on about it!

bassinet [basinɛ] **NM 1** *Anat* renal pelvis **2** *Hist* bascinet, basinet

bassinette [basinɛt] **NF** *Can Br* carrycot, *Am* bassinet

bassinoire [basinwar] **NF 1** *Arch (à lit)* warming pan **2** *Fam (importun)* pain in the neck, crashing bore

bassiste [basist] **NMF** *Mus* **1** *(guitariste)* bass guitarist **2** *(contrebassiste)* double-bass player

basson [basɔ̃] **NM** *Mus* **1** *(instrument)* bassoon **2** *(musicien)* bassoonist

bassoniste [basɔnist] **NMF** *Mus* bassoonist

basta [basta] **EXCLAM** *Fam* (that's) enough!; **je la rembourse et puis b.!** I'll give her her money back and then that's it!

bastide [bastid] **NF 1** *Archit (maison)* Provençal cottage; *(ferme)* Provençal farmhouse **2** *Hist* walled town *(in south-west France)*

bastille [bastij] **NF 1** *Archit (fort)* fortress **2** *(à Paris)* **la B.** *(forteresse)* the Bastille; *(quartier)* Bastille, the Bastille area; **la prise de la B.** the storming of the Bastille; **l'Opéra B.** the Bastille opera house

bastingage [bastɛ̃gaʒ] **NM 1** *Naut* rail; **par-dessus le b.** overboard **2** *Hist* bulwark

bastion [bastjɔ̃] **NM 1** *Archit* bastion **2** *(d'une doctrine, d'un mouvement)* bastion; **b. du socialisme** socialist stronghold, bastion of socialism; **les derniers bastions de la chrétienté** the last outposts *or* bastions of Christianity

baston [bastɔ̃] **NF** *Fam* **il y a eu de la b.** there was a bit of a scuffle *or Br* punch-up *or Am* fist fight

bastonnade [bastɔnad] **NF** beating

bastonner [3] [bastɔne] *Fam* **V IMPERSONNEL ça a bastonné** there was a scuffle *or Br* a punch-up *or Am* a fist fight

VPR se bastonner to fight□

bastos [bastɔs] **NF** *Fam Arg crime* bullet□, slug

bastringue [bastrɛ̃g] **NM** *Fam* **1** *(attirail)* stuff, gear, *Br* clobber; **et tout le b.** and the whole caboodle *or* shebang

2 *(bal)* (sleazy) dance hall

3 *(orchestre)* dance band□

4 *(bruit)* din, racket

5 *Can (danse)* = type of folk dance

bas-ventre [bavɑ̃tr] *(pl* **bas-ventres**) **NM** *Anat* (lower) abdomen, pelvic area

BAT [beate] **NM** *(abrév* **bon à tirer**) press proof, final corrected proof; **donner le B.** to pass for press

bat *etc voir* **battre**

bât [ba] **NM** packsaddle; **cheval de b.** packhorse; *Fig* **c'est là que** *ou* **où le b. blesse** that's where the shoe pinches

bataclan [bataklɑ̃] **NM** *Fam (attirail)* stuff, junk, *Br* clobber; **et tout le b.** and the whole caboodle *or* shebang

bataille [bataj] **NF 1** *(combat)* battle, fight; **une b. d'idées** a battle of ideas; **une b. politique/électorale** a political/an electoral contest; **b. aérienne** *(à grande échelle)* air battle; *(isolée)* dogfight; **b. aéronavale** sea-air battle; **b. de boules de neige** snowball fight; **b. de polochons** pillow fight; **b. rangée** pitched battle; **b. de rue** street fight *or* brawl; *Fig* **arriver après la b.** to arrive when it's all over bar the shouting **2** *Cartes* ≃ beggar-my-neighbour; **b. navale** *(jeu)* battleships

• **en bataille** **ADJ 1** *Mil* in battle order **2** *(en désordre)* **avoir les cheveux en b.** to have tousled hair; **avoir les sourcils en b.** to have bushy eyebrows, to be beetle-browed

batailler [3] [bataje] **VI 1** *(physiquement)* to fight, to battle; **il est toujours prêt à b.** he's always spoiling *or* ready for a fight **2** *Fig* to struggle, to fight; **on a bataillé dur pour avoir ce contrat** we fought *or* struggled hard to win this contract; **j'ai dû b. pendant une heure pour ouvrir la porte** I had to struggle for an hour to get the door open

batailleur, -euse [batajœr, -øz] **ADJ** *(agressif)* quarrelsome, rowdy

NM,F fighter; **c'est un b.** *(agressif)* he's always spoiling *or* ready for a fight

bataillon [batajɔ̃] **NM 1** *Mil* battalion; **le b. d'Afrique** = disciplinary battalion originally stationed in Africa **2** *(foule)* **un b. de** scores of, an army of

bâtard, -e [batar, -ard] **ADJ 1** *(enfant)* illegitimate; *(animal)* crossbred; **chien b.** mongrel **2** *(genre, œuvre)* hybrid; *(solution)* half-baked, ill-thought-out

NM,F *(chien)* mongrel; *(enfant)* illegitimate child; *Péj* bastard

NM *(pain)* = short French loaf *or Br* stick

EXCLAM *Can Fam* goddammit!

• **bâtarde** **NF** slanting round-hand writing

bâtardise [batardiz] **NF** illegitimacy, *Péj Littéraire* bastardy

batavia [batavja] **NF** batavia lettuce

Bat d'Af [batdaf] **NM** *Hist* = the "bataillon d'Afrique", a disciplinary battalion originally stationed in North Africa (or, by extension, someone serving in it)

bateau, -x [bato] **NM 1** *Naut (navire, embarcation)* boat; *(grand)* ship; **je prends le b. à Anvers/à dix heures** I'm sailing from Antwerp/at ten; **faire du b.** *(en barque, en vedette)* to go boating; *(en voilier)* to go sailing; **b. à aubes** *ou* **roues** paddle steamer; **b. de guerre** warship, battleship; **b. hôtel** boatel; **b. à moteur** motor boat **b. de pêche** fishing boat; **b. de plaisance** pleasure boat *or* craft; **b. pneumatique** rubber boat, dinghy; **b. à rames** *Br* rowing boat, *Am* rowboat; **b. à vapeur** steamboat, steamer; **b. à voiles** yacht *or* sailing boat; *Fam* **mener** *ou* **conduire qn en b.** to lead sb up the garden path, to take sb for a ride; *Fam* **monter un b. à qn** to set sb up; *Can Fig* **manquer le b.** to miss the boat **2** *(charge)* **un b. de charbon** a boatload of coal **3** *(sur le trottoir)* dip (in the pavement)

ADJ INV 1 *Couture* **col** *ou* **encolure b.** boat neck **2** *Fam (banal)* hackneyed□; **un sujet b.** an old chestnut

bateau-mouche [batomuʃ] *(pl* **bateaux-mouches**) **NM** *Naut* river boat *(on the Seine)*

batelage [batlaʒ] **NM** *Naut* **1** *(transport)* ferry transport **2** *(salaire)* lighterage

bateleur, -euse [batlœr, -øz] **NM,F** tumbler, street entertainer

batelier, -ère [batəlje, -ɛr] *Naut* **ADJ** inland waterways *(avant n)*

NM,F *(marinier)* boatman, *f* boatwoman; *(sur un bac)* ferryman, *f* ferrywoman

batellerie [batɛlri] **NF** *Naut* **1** *(activité)* inland waterways transport **2** *(flotte)* inland *or* river fleet

bat-flanc [baflɑ̃] **NM INV** *Constr (cloison ▸ de dortoir)* wooden partition; *(▸ d'écurie)* bail

bath [bat] **ADJ INV** *Fam Vieilli* super, super-duper

bathymètre [batimɛtr] **NM** *Phys* bathometer, bathymeter

bathymétrie [batimetri] **NF** *Phys* bathymetry

bathyscaphe [batiskaf] **NM** *Phys* bathyscaph, bathyscaphe

bathysphère [batisfɛr] **NF** *Phys* bathysphere

bâti, -e [bati] **ADJ 1** *(personne)* **être bien b.** to be well-built; **être b. en force** to have a powerful build, to be powerfully built **2** *(terrain)* built-up, developed

NM 1 *Couture (technique)* basting, tacking; *(fil)* tacking; **défais le b.** take out the tacking **2** *(cadre)* frame; **b. d'assemblage** assembly jig

batifolage [batifɔlaʒ] **NM** *Fam* **1** *(amusement ▸ de personnes)* romping about, *Br* larking about; *(▸ d'animaux)* frolics, *Br* larking about **2** *(flirt)* flirting

batifoler [3] [batifɔle] **VI** *Fam* **1** *(s'amuser ▸ personnes)* to romp about, *Br* to lark about; *(▸ animaux)* to frolic, *Br* to lark about **2** *(flirter)* to flirt□

batik [batik] **NM** *Tex* batik; **en b.** batik *(avant n)*

bâtiment [batimɑ̃] NM **1** *Archit (édifice)* building; **bâtiments de ferme/d'usine** farm/factory buildings; **les bâtiments d'exploitation** the sheds and outhouses *(of a farm)* **2** *Constr (profession)* **le b., l'industrie du b.** the building trade, the construction industry; **bâtiments et travaux publics** building and civil engineering; **être dans le b.** to be a builder *or* in the building trade; *Fig* **il est du b.** *(il est du métier)* he's in the same line of business; *(il s'y connaît)* he knows what he's doing; **quand le b. va, tout va** a busy building trade is the sign of a healthy economy **3** *Naut* ship, (sea-going) vessel; **b. de charge** freighter; **b. de guerre** warship; **b. léger** light craft; **b. de soutien** support vessel

bâtir [32] [batir] VT **1** *Constr* to build; **se faire b. une maison** to have a house built; **b. (qch) sur le sable** to build (sth) on sand; *Fig* **b. des châteaux en Espagne** to build castles in the air **2** *(créer ▸ fortune)* to build up; *(▸ foyer)* to build; *(▸ théorie, hypothèse)* to build up, to develop; **bâtissons l'avenir ensemble** let's work together to build our future **3** *Couture* to baste, to tack

• **à bâtir** ADJ **1** *Constr (pierre, terrain)* building *(avant n)* **2** *Couture* basting *(avant n)*, tacking *(avant n)*

VPR **se bâtir 1** *(ville, maisons)* to be built **2 se b. une réputation (de)** to build up a reputation (as)

bâtisse [batis] NF **1** *aussi Péj Archit (bâtiment)* building; **une grande b.** a big barn of a place **2** *Constr (partie en maçonnerie)* masonry

bâtisseur, -euse [batisœr, -øz] NM,F *Constr* builder; *Fig* **b. d'empires** empire-builder

batiste [batist] NF *Tex* batiste, cambric

bâton [batɔ̃] NM **1** *(baguette ▸ gén)* stick; *(▸ d'agent de police) Br* truncheon, *Am* nightstick; *(▸ de berger)* staff, crook; *(▸ de skieur)* stick, pole; **donner des coups de b. à qn** to beat sb with a stick; **b. de maréchal** marshal's baton; *Fig* **cette nomination, c'est son b. de maréchal** this appointment is the high point of his/her career; **b. de pèlerin** pilgrim's staff; *Fig* **prendre son b. de pèlerin** to go on a crusade; **être le b. de vieillesse de qn** to be the staff of sb's old age; *Vulg* **b. merdeux** *(personne)* shit; *(situation)* shitty situation; **mettre des bâtons dans les roues à qn** *(continuellement)* to impede sb's progress; *(une fois)* to throw a *Br* spanner *or Am* wrench in the works for sb

2 *(barreau)* **b. de chaise** chair rung

3 *(de craie, de dynamite, de réglisse)* stick; **b. de rouge à lèvres** lipstick

4 *Scol (trait)* (vertical) line; **faire des bâtons** to draw vertical lines; **à l'âge où les enfants font des bâtons** at the age when children are in the earliest stages of learning to write

5 *Can & Suisse* **b. (de hockey)** *Br* ice hockey stick, *Am* hockey stick

6 *Anciennement Fam (10000 francs)* 10000 francs[□]

• **à bâtons rompus** ADJ **1** *Menuis* **parquet à bâtons rompus** herringbone flooring **2** *(conversation)* idle ADV **parler à bâtons rompus** to make casual conversation

bâtonner [3] [batɔne] VT to beat with a stick

bâtonnet [batɔnɛ] NM **1** *(petit bâton)* stick; **b. de manucure** orange stick **2** *Anat* **b. de la rétine** retinal rod **3** *Ordinat* **b. magnétique** magnetic strip

bâtonnier [batɔnje] NM *Jur* ≃ President of the Bar

battage [bataʒ] NM **1** *(du blé)* threshing; *(de l'or, d'un tapis)* beating; *(du beurre)* churning **2** *Fam* **b. médiatique** media hype; **b. (publicitaire)** hype, *Am* ballyhoo; **faire du b. autour de qch** to hype sth (up), *Am* to ballyhoo sth; **ils font tout un b. pour sa pièce** his/her play is getting a lot of hype

battant, -e [batɑ̃, -ɑ̃t] ADJ **porte battante** *(bruyante)* banging door; *(laissée ouverte)* swinging door; *(à battant libre)* swing door; **le cœur b.** with beating heart; **sous une pluie battante** in the driving *or* pelting rain; **à onze heures battantes** on the stroke of eleven

NM,F *Fig* fighter; **c'est une battante!** she's a real fighter!

NM **1** *(d'une cloche)* clapper, tongue

2 *(d'une table)* leaf; **le b. droit de la porte était ouvert** the right half of the double door was open; **porte à deux battants** double door

3 *Naut (d'un drapeau)* fly

4 *Fam (cœur)* ticker

batte [bat] NF **1** *Sport* bat; **b. de base-ball/cricket** baseball/cricket bat **2** *Culin* **b. à beurre** dasher **3** *(outil ▸ maillet)* mallet; *(▸ tapette)* beater

battement [batmɑ̃] NM **1** *(mouvement ▸ des ailes)* flapping *(UNCOUNT)*; *(▸ des paupières)* fluttter; **battements de mains** clapping *(UNCOUNT)*, applause *(UNCOUNT)*

2 *(en danse)* battement; **b. de jambes** *(d'un nageur)* leg movement

3 *(d'une porte)* banging *(UNCOUNT)*, beating *(UNCOUNT)*; **des battements de tambour** drumbeats

4 *(rythme du cœur, du pouls)* beating *(UNCOUNT)*, throbbing *(UNCOUNT)*, beat; **je sens les battements de son cœur** I can feel his/her heart beating; **chaque b. de cœur** every heartbeat; **j'ai des battements de cœur** *(palpitations)* I suffer from palpitations; *(émotion)* my heart's beating *or* pounding

5 *(pause)* break; **un b. de dix minutes** a ten-minute break

6 *(attente)* wait; **il y a un b. de cinq minutes entre les deux trains** there's a five-minute wait between the two trains

7 *(sur une fenêtre)* shutter catch

batterie [batri] NF **1** *Mil* battery; **mettre une arme en b.** to put a gun in battery; **b. antichars** antitank battery; **b. de canons** battery of artillery *or* guns

2 *Aut, Élec & Phys* battery; **ça fonctionne sur b.** it's battery-operated *or* battery-powered; **b. de cellules solaires** solar-powered battery; *Fig* **recharger** *ou* **regonfler ses batteries** to recharge one's batteries

3 *Mus (en jazz, rock, pop)* drums, drum kit; *(en musique classique)* percussion instruments; *(roulement)* drum roll; **tenir la b.** to play the *or* to be on drums; **Harvey Barton à la b.** Harvey Barton on drums

4 *(série)* battery; **b. de piles** batteries; **b. de tests/mesures** battery of tests/of measures; **b. de cuisine** set of kitchen utensils; *Hum* **les officiers avec leur b. de cuisine** the officers with all their decorations *or Br* gongs

5 *Agr* **poulet de b.** battery hen; **élevage en b.** battery farming

6 *(en danse)* batterie

batteur [batœr] NM **1** *Mus* drummer

2 *(ustensile de cuisine)* mixer

3 *(ouvrier)* beater; *Agr* thresher

4 *(au cricket)* batsman; *(au base-ball)* batter

5 *Agr (rouleau d'une batteuse)* beater drum

batteuse [batøz] NF **1** *Agr* thresher, threshing machine **2** *Métal* beater

battoir [batwar] NM *Arch (pour laver)* beetle, battledore

• **battoirs** NMPL *Fam* (great) paws, mitts

BATTRE [83] [batr]

VT	
• to beat **1–5, 8**	• to defeat **2**
• to churn **5**	• to whisk, to whip **5**
• to shuffle **7**	
VI	
• to bang **1**	• to beat **1**
VPR	
• to fight **1, 2**	• to struggle **2**

VT **1** *(brutaliser ▸ animal)* to beat; *(▸ personne)* to batter; **b. qn à mort** to batter sb to death; **il m'énerve tellement que je le battrais!** he annoys me so much that I could hit him!; **b. en brèche** *(mur)* to breach; *(gouvernement)* to topple; *(politique)* to demolish, *Br* to drive a coach and horses through; **b. qn comme plâtre** to beat sb severely

2 *(vaincre ▸ adversaire)* to beat, to defeat; **Bordeaux s'est fait b. 2 à 0** Bordeaux were beaten *or* defeated 2 nil; **b. qn aux échecs** to defeat *or* to beat sb at chess; **se tenir pour** *ou* **s'avouer battu** to admit defeat; **b. qn à plate couture** *ou* **à plates coutures** to beat sb hollow

3 *(surpasser ▸ record)* to beat; *aussi Fig* **b. tous les records** to set a new record; **j'ai battu tous les records de vitesse pour venir ici** I must have broken the record getting here; **cet hiver, nous battrons tous les records de froid** this winter will be the coldest on record

4 *(frapper ▸ tapis, or)* to beat (out); *(▸ blé, grain)* to thresh; **b. qch à froid** to cold-hammer sth; **b. froid à qn** to cold-shoulder sb; **b. la semelle** to stamp one's feet *(to keep warm)*; **b. monnaie** to mint (coins); *Prov* **il faut b. le fer quand il est chaud** strike while the iron is hot

5 *Culin (remuer ▸ beurre)* to churn; *(▸ blanc d'œuf)* to beat, to whip (up), to whisk; **œufs battus en neige ferme** stiffly beaten egg whites; **battez le sucre avec le beurre** cream together the sugar and the butter; *Fig* **b. l'air de ses bras** to beat the air with one's arms

6 *(sillonner)* **b. le secteur** to scour *or* to comb the area; **ils ont battu les bois pour retrouver l'enfant** they combed (every inch of) the woods to find the missing child; **b. le pavé parisien** to roam the streets of Paris; *Chasse* **b. les buissons** to beat the bushes; **b. la campagne** *ou* **le pays** to comb the countryside; *Fig* to be in one's own little world

7 *Cartes* **b. les cartes** to shuffle the cards *or* pack

8 *Mus (mesure)* to beat (out); *Mil & Mus (tambour)* to beat (on); *Mil* **b. la générale** to sound the call to arms; *Mil* **b. le rappel** to drum up troops; *Fig* **b. le rappel de la famille/du parti** to gather the family/party round; *Fam* **b. (le) tambour** *ou* **la grosse caisse** to make a lot of noise; **mon cœur bat la chamade** my heart's racing

9 *Naut* **b. pavillon** to sail under *or* to fly a flag; **un navire battant pavillon britannique** a ship flying the British flag

10 *(locution)* **b. son plein** *(fête)* to be in full swing

VI **1** *(cœur, pouls)* to beat, to throb; *(pluie)* to lash, to beat down; *(porte)* to rattle, to bang; *(store)* to flap; **l'émotion faisait b. mon cœur** my heart was beating *or* racing with emotion; **le vent faisait b. les volets** the shutters were banging in the wind

2 *(locutions)* **b. en retraite** to retreat; *Fig* to beat a retreat; *très Fam* **j'en ai rien à b.** I don't give a shit *or Br* a toss *or Am* a rat's ass

• **battre de** VT IND **b. des mains** to clap (one's hands); **b. des paupières** *(d'éblouissement)* to blink; **b. des cils** *(pour séduire)* to flutter one's eyelashes; **l'oiseau bat des ailes** *(lentement)* the bird flaps its wings; *(rapidement)* the bird flutters its wings; *Fig* **b. de l'aile** to be in a bad way

VPR **se battre 1** *(emploi réciproque)* to fight, to fight (with) one another; **se b. à mains nues** to fight with one's bare hands; **se b. à l'épée/au couteau** to fight with swords/knives; **se b. en duel** to fight (each other in) a duel; *Fig* **ne vous battez pas, il y en a pour tout le monde** don't get excited, there's enough for everyone; **on se bat pour assister à ses cours** people are falling over each other to get into his/her classes; *Ironique* **surtout ne vous battez pas pour m'aider!** don't all rush to help me!

2 *(lutter)* to fight; *Fig* to fight, to struggle; **se b. avec/contre qn** to fight with/against sb; **se b. contre des moulins à vent** to tilt at windmills; **j'ai dû me b. pour pouvoir entrer/sortir** I had to fight my way in/out; **il faut se b. pour le faire coucher à huit heures!** it's a real struggle to get him to bed at eight!; **nous nous battons pour la paix/contre l'injustice** we're fighting for peace/against injustice; *Hum* **je suis obligé de me b. avec la serrure chaque fois que je rentre** I have to struggle *or* to do battle with the lock every time I come home

3 *(frapper)* **se b. les flancs** to struggle pointlessly; *très Fam* **je m'en bats l'œil** I don't give a tinker's cuss

---

battu, -e[1] [baty] ADJ **1** *(maltraité)* battered

2 *(vaincu)* beaten, defeated; **on est battus d'avance** we've got no chance

3 avoir les yeux battus to have rings *or* circles round one's eyes

4 *(or, fer)* beaten

battue[2] [baty] NF **1** *Chasse* battue, beat **2** *(recherche)* search *(through an area)*

batture [batyr] NF *Can* **1** *(estran)* sandbank **2** *(glaces)* batture ice, = ice which builds up along the sides of a river

bau, -x [bo] NM *Naut* beam

baud [bo] NM *Ordinat & Tél* baud; **à (une vitesse de) 28 800 bauds** at 28,800 baud

baudet [bodɛ] NM **1** *Zool (âne)* donkey, ass **2** *Menuis* sawhorse, trestle

baudrier [bodrije] NM **1** *(bandoulière)* baldric **2** *Sport* harness

baudroie [bodrwa] NF *Ich* monkfish, anglerfish

baudruche [bodryʃ] NF **1** *(peau)* bladder **2** *Fam (personne)* wimp

bauge [boʒ] NF **1** *(du cochon, du sanglier)* wallow **2** *(lieu sale)* pigsty **3** *Constr* clay and straw mortar

baume [bom] NM *Bot & Pharm* balsam, balm; **b. de benjoin** friar's balsam; **b. du Canada** Canada balsam; **b. démêlant** hair conditioner; **b. du tigre** tiger balm; *Fig* **mettre un peu de b. au cœur de qn** to soothe sb's aching heart; *Fig* **si ça peut te mettre du b. au cœur** if it's any consolation (to you)

baumier [bomje] NM *Bot* balsam tree

baux [bo] **1** *pl de* **bail** **2** *pl de* **bau**

bauxite [boksit] NF *Géol* bauxite

bavard, -e [bavar, -ard] ADJ *(personne ▸ qui parle beaucoup)* talkative; *(▸ indiscrète)* indiscreet; *(roman, émission)* wordy, long-winded; **elle n'était pas bien bavarde ce soir** she hardly said a word *or* opened her mouth tonight; **il est b. comme une pie** he's a real chatterbox

NM,F **quelle bavarde, celle-là!** she's a real chatterbox!; **attention, c'est une bavarde!** watch out, she can't keep quiet!

NM *Fam Arg crime (avocat)* lawyer[◻], brief

• **bavarde** NF *Fam (langue)* tongue[◻]; **tenir sa bavarde** to hold one's tongue, to keep one's mouth shut

bavardage [bavardaʒ] NM **1** *(action de parler)* chatting, chattering **2** *Ordinat (sur Internet)* chat

• **bavardages** NMPL *(conversation)* chatter *(UNCOUNT)*; *Péj (racontars)* gossip *(UNCOUNT)*

bavarder [3] [bavarde] VI **1** *(parler)* to chat, to talk; **b. avec qn** to (have a) chat with sb; **on bavardait des heures au téléphone** we used to talk for hours on the phone

2 *(médire)* to gossip

3 *(être indiscret)* to talk

4 *Ordinat (sur Internet)* to chat

bavarois, -e [bavarwa, -az] ADJ Bavarian

NM *(dialecte)* Bavarian

• **Bavarois, -e** NM,F Bavarian

• **bavaroise** NF *Culin* Bavarian cream

bavasser [3] [bavase] VI *Fam Péj (parler)* to natter, to yack; *(médire)* to gossip[◻]

bave [bav] NF *(d'un bébé)* dribble; *(d'un chien)* slobber, slaver; *(d'un malade, d'un chien enragé)* foam, froth; *(d'un escargot)* slime; *(d'un crapaud)* spittle; *Prov* **la b. du crapaud n'atteint pas la blanche colombe** sticks and stones may break my bones, but names will never hurt me

baver [3] [bave] VI **1** *(bébé)* to dribble, to drool, to slobber; *(chien)* to slaver, to slobber; *(malade, chien enragé)* to foam *or* to froth at the mouth; **b. d'envie à la vue de qch** to drool over sth; **b. d'admiration devant qn** to worship the ground sb walks on **2** *(encre, stylo)* to leak **3** *Fam (locutions)* **en b.** *(souffrir)* to have a rough *or* hard time of it; **on va t'en faire b. à l'armée** they'll make you sweat blood *or* they'll put you through it in the army; **tu n'as pas fini d'en b.!** you've got a hard road *or Br* slog ahead of you!; **en b. des ronds de chapeau** *(être étonné)* to have eyes like saucers; *(souffrir)* to go through the mill, to have a rough time of it

VT **1** *Fam (dire)* **qu'est-ce que tu baves?** what are you rambling *or* jabbering *or Br* wittering on about? **2** *Can très Fam (contrarier)* to mess around, *Br* to wind up; **se faire b.** to be messed around, *Br* to be wound up

• **baver sur** VT IND *Fam (médire de)* to badmouth, to slag off

bavette [bavɛt] NF **1** *(bavoir)* bib **2** *(viande)* **b. (d'aloyau)** top of sirloin **3** *Aut* mudguard

baveux, -euse [bavø, -øz] ADJ *(bouche, enfant)* dribbling; *(baiser)* wet; *(omelette)* runny

NM,F *Can très Fam* jerk; **petit b.** *(enfant)* little devil

NM *Fam* **1** *(savon)* soap[◻] **2** *(journal)* newspaper[◻], rag **3** *(baiser)* sloppy kiss[◻]

Bavière [bavjɛr] NF **la B.** Bavaria

bavocher [bavɔʃe] VI *Typ* to smear

bavocheux, -euse [bavɔʃø, -øz] ADJ *Typ* mackled

bavochure [bavɔʃyr] NF *Typ* smear

bavoir [bavwar] NM bib

bavure [bavyr] NF **1** *Typ* smudge, ink stain **2** *Ind* burr **3** *(erreur)* mistake; **un spectacle sans b.** a faultless *or* flawless show; **b. (policière)** police error

bayer [3] [baje] VI **b. aux corneilles** to stand gaping; *(être inactif)* to stargaze

bazar [bazar] NM **1** *(souk)* bazaar, bazar; *(magasin)* general store, *Am* dime store

2 *Fam (désordre)* clutter, shambles *(singulier)*; **quel b., cette chambre!** what a shambles *or* mess this room is!; **il a mis un sacré b. dans mes papiers** he made a hell of a mess of my papers

3 *Fam (attirail)* stuff, junk, *Br* clobber; **et tout le b.** and the whole caboodle

4 *Belg Fam (chose)* thing[◻], thingy

• **de bazar** ADJ *Péj (psychologie, politique)* half-baked, *Am* two-bit *(avant n)*

bazarder [3] [bazarde] VT *Fam (jeter)* to dump, to chuck (out); *(vendre)* to sell off[◻], *Br* to flog

bazooka [bazuka] NM *Mil* bazooka

BBS [bebeɛs] NM *Ordinat (abrév* **bulletin board system***)* BBS

BBZ [bebezed] NM *Compta (abrév* **budget base zéro***)* ZBB

BCBG [besebeʒe, bɛsbɛʒ] ADJ INV *(abrév* **bon chic bon genre***)* = term used to describe an upper-middle-class lifestyle reflected especially in expensive but conservative clothes; **elle est très B.** *Br* ≃ she's really Sloaney, *Am* ≃ she's a real preppie type; **ils ont une clientèle plutôt B.** they have a largely upper-middle-class clientele

BCE [beseə] NF *(abrév* **Banque centrale européenne***)* European Central Bank

BCG® [beseʒe] NM *Méd (abrév* **bacille Calmette-Guérin***)* BCG®

BD [bede] NF **1** *Littérature (abrév* **bande dessinée***)* *(dans un magazine)* comic strip, *Br* strip cartoon; *(livre)* comic book **2** *Ordinat (abrév* **base de données***)* dbase

> **BD**
>
> This is a common abbreviation for "bande dessinée", or comic book. Considered a serious and important art form in France, the comic book has become popular among teenagers and intellectuals alike. An annual festival of comic book art is held in Angoulême.

bd *(abrév écrite* **boulevard***)* Blvd.

bdc *Typ (abrév écrite* **bas de casse***)* lc

B. de F. *(abrév écrite* **Banque de France***)* = the Banque de France *(French issuing bank)*

beach-volley [bitʃvɔlɛ] NM *Sport* beach volleyball

beagle [bigœl] NM *Zool (chien)* beagle

béant, -e [beɑ̃, -ɑ̃t] ADJ *(gouffre)* gaping, yawning; *(plaie)* gaping, open; **b. d'étonnement** gaping in surprise; **être b. d'admiration** to be open-mouthed *or Littéraire* agape with admiration

béarnais, -e [bearnɛ, -ɛz] ADJ of/from the Béarn

• **Béarnais, -e** NM,F = inhabitant of or person from the Béarn

• **béarnaise** NF *Culin* **(sauce à la) béarnaise** béarnaise sauce

béat, -e [bea, -at] ADJ *(heureux)* blissfully happy; *Péj (niais ▸ air, sourire)* vacant, vacuous; *(▸ optimisme)* smug; *(▸ admiration)* blind; **être b. d'admiration** to be open-mouthed *or Littéraire* agape with admiration; **elle nous observait d'un air b.** she watched us open-mouthed

béatement [beatmɑ̃] ADV *Péj (idiotement)* **il la regardait b.** he looked at her with a blissfully stupid expression

béatification [beatifikasjɔ̃] NF *Rel* beatification

béatifier [9] [beatifje] VT *Rel* to beatify

béatifique [beatifik] ADJ *Rel* beatific

béatitude [beatityd] NF **1** *Rel* beatitude; **les béatitudes** the Beatitudes **2** *(bonheur)* bliss, *Littéraire* beatitude

beatnik [bitnik] NMF *Littérature* beatnik; **les beatniks** the Beat Generation

BEAU, BELLE [bo, bɛl]

> **ADJ**
> - beautiful **A1–4**
> - good-looking **A1**
> - fine **A3, 4, B1, 3, C6**
> - smart **B4**
> - nice **C1**
> - good **A3, C3, 4**
> - Ironic use **D**
> - Emphatic use **C2**
>
> **ADV**
> - fine, warm, nice **1**

> **bel** is used before masculine singular nouns beginning with a vowel or h mute.

ADJ **A. 1** *(bien fait, joli ▸ femme)* beautiful, good-looking; *(▸ homme)* good-looking, handsome; *(▸ enfant, physique, objet, décor)* beautiful, lovely; **c'est très b.** it's gorgeous *or* exquisite *or* beautiful; **un b. chat** a beautiful *or* handsome cat; **de la tour, on a une belle vue** *ou* **la vue est belle** there's a lovely *or* beautiful view from the tower; **elle est belle fille** she's a good-looking *or* beautiful girl; *Fam* **il est b. garçon** *ou Fam* **gosse** he's good-looking, *Fam* he's a good-looking guy; **se faire b./belle** to get dressed up, to do oneself up; **ça, c'est une belle moto!** that's a terrific-looking bike!; **la robe a une très belle coupe** the dress is beautifully cut; *Fam* **ce n'était pas b. à voir** it wasn't a pretty sight; **il est b. comme l'amour** *ou* **un ange** *ou* **un astre** *ou* **le jour** *(homme)* he's a very handsome *or* good-looking man; *(petit garçon)* he's a very handsome *or* good-looking boy; **il est b. comme un dieu** he looks like a Greek god; **elle est belle comme un ange** *ou* **le jour** she's a real beauty

2 *(attrayant pour l'oreille ▸ chant, mélodie, voix)* beautiful, lovely; **quelques beaux accords** some fine chords; **le russe est une belle langue** Russian is a beautiful language

3 *(remarquable, réussi ▸ poème, texte)* fine, beautiful; *(▸ chanson, film)* beautiful, lovely; **de beaux vêtements** fine clothes; **de belles paroles de Brel** some fine lyrics by Brel; **le plus b. moment du match** the finest moment in the match; **il y a eu quelques beaux échanges** there were a few good *or* fine rallies; **quel b. coup!** what a magnificent shot!; **nous avons fait un b. voyage** we had a wonderful trip

4 *Météo* fine, beautiful; **il y aura un b. soleil sur tout le pays** the whole country will enjoy bright sunshine; **la mer sera belle** the sea will be calm; **du b. temps** nice *or* good weather; **on a eu du très b. temps** we had beautiful weather, the weather was beautiful; **une belle après-midi** a beautiful afternoon; **les derniers beaux jours** the last days of summer

B. 1 *(digne)* noble, fine; **une belle âme** a noble nature; **elle a eu un b. geste** she made a noble gesture; **je suis chirurgien – vous faites un b. métier** I'm a surgeon – yours is a fine profession

2 *(convenable)* nice; **ce n'est pas b. de tirer la langue!** it's not nice to stick your tongue out (at people)!; **ce n'est pas b. de mentir!** it's very naughty *or* it's not nice to lie!

3 *(brillant intellectuellement)* wonderful, fine; **c'est un b. sujet de thèse** it's a fine topic for a thesis; **en une belle expression, il résume le dilemme** he encapsulates the dilemma in one apt phrase

4 *(d'un haut niveau social)* smart; **faire un b. mariage** *(financièrement)* to marry into money *or* a fortune; *(socialement)* to marry into a very good family; *Fam* **le b. monde** *ou* **linge** the upper crust, the smart set

C. 1 *(gros, important ▸ gains, prime, somme)* nice, handsome, tidy; **donnez-moi un b. melon/poulet** give me a nice big melon/chicken; **il a un bel appétit** he has a good *or* hearty appetite; **manger avec un bel appétit** to eat heartily; **c'est un b. cadeau qu'il t'a fait là!** that's a nice *or* that's quite a present he gave you!

2 *(en intensif)* **je me suis fait une belle bosse** I got a great big bump; *Fam* **elle lui a mis une belle raclée** she gave him/her a good hiding; *Fam* **il y a un b. bazar dans ta chambre!** your room's in a fine *or*

real mess!; **il y a eu un b. scandale** there was a huge scandal; **tu m'as fait une belle peur** you gave me a real scare; **quel b. vacarme!** what a terrible noise!; **un bel hypocrite** a real hypocrite; *très Fam* **t'es un b. salaud!** you're a real bastard!; *Fam* **il y a b. temps de ce que je te dis là** what I'm telling you now happened ages ago

3 *(agréable)* good; **présenter qch sous un b. jour** to show sth in a good light; **ce serait trop b.!** that'd be too good to be true!; **c'est trop b. pour être vrai** it's too good to be true; **c'est b., l'amour!** love's a wonderful thing!

4 *(prospère)* good; **tu as encore de belles années devant toi** you still have quite a few good years ahead of you; **avoir une belle situation** *(financière)* to have a very well-paid job; *(prestigieuse)* to have a high-flying job; **il a fait une très belle carrière dans les textiles** he carved out a brilliant career for himself in textiles

5 *(dans des appellations)* **venez, ma belle amie** do come along, darling; **mais oui, mon bel ami, je vous accorde que...** yes, my friend, I'll grant you that...; *Fam* **alors, (ma) belle enfant, qu'en dis-tu?** what do you think about that, my dear?

6 *(certain)* **un b. jour/matin** one fine day/morning

7 *Can Fam (locution)* **c'est beau!** *(c'est d'accord)* OK!; **si vous n'êtes pas d'accord avec lui, vous pouvez lui écrire – c'est beau, je le ferai** if you don't agree with him, you can write to him – alright, I will!

D. *Ironique* **belle demande!** *(saugrenue)* what a question!; **que voilà un b. langage!** language, please!; **c'est du b. travail!** a fine mess this is!; **en voilà, une belle excuse!** that's a good excuse!, what an excuse!; **je vais le lui faire comprendre, et de la belle manière!** I'll make him/her understand, and in no uncertain terms!; **ils ont oublié tous leurs beaux discours** they've forgotten all their fine *or* fine-sounding words; **belles paroles** fine words; *Hum* **sur ces belles paroles, il faut que je m'en aille** on that note, I must go now; **il lui en a dit de belles!** the things he told her (you wouldn't believe)!; **j'en ai appris** *ou* **entendu de belles sur toi!** I heard some fine *or* right things about you!; **il est sorti de voiture et il m'en a dit de belles!** he got out of his car and gave me a right earful!; **il en a fait de belles quand il était petit!** he didn't half get up to some mischief when he was little!; **nous voilà beaux!** we're in a fine mess now!; **c'est bien b., tout ça, mais...** that's all very fine *or* well, but...; **c'est bien b. de critiquer les autres, mais toi, que fais-tu?** it's all very well to criticize, but what do YOU ever do?; *Fam* **le plus b., c'est que sa femme n'en savait rien!** the best part (of it) is that his wife knew nothing about it!; *Fam* **ça, c'est le plus b.!** that crowns it all!, that (really) takes the biscuit!

ADV 1 *Météo* **il fait b.** the weather's *or* it's fine; **il fera b. et chaud** it'll be warm and sunny

2 *(locutions)* **il ferait b. voir (cela)!** that'll be the day!; **il ferait b. voir qu'elle me donne des ordres!** her, boss me around? that'll be the day!; **j'avais b. tirer, la porte ne s'ouvrait pas** however hard I pulled, the door wouldn't open; **j'ai eu b. le lui répéter plusieurs fois, il n'a toujours pas compris** I have told him and told him but he still hasn't understood; **on a b. dire...** whatever you say..., say what you like...; *Fam* **on a b. dire, on a b. faire, les jeunes s'en vont un jour de la maison** whatever you do or say, young people eventually leave home; **tu auras b. faire, la pelouse ne repoussera plus ici** whatever you do, the lawn won't grow here again; **vous avez b. dire, elle a quand même tout financé elle-même** say what you like *or* you may criticize, but she's paid for it all herself; *Prov* **a b. mentir qui vient de loin** = it's easy to lie when there's nobody around to contradict you; **voir tout en b.** to see the world through rose-coloured spectacles; **alors, vous signez? – hé, tout b. (tout b.)!** you will sign then? – hey, steady on *or* not so fast!

NM 1 *(esthétique)* **elle aime le b.** she likes beautiful things

2 *(objets de qualité)* **pour les meubles du salon, je veux du b.** I want really good *or* nice furniture for the living room

3 *(homme)* beau, dandy; *Can* **faire le b.** to strut about

4 *(locutions)* **le temps est au b.** the weather looks fine; **le temps/baromètre est au b. fixe** the weather/barometer is set fair; *Fam* **nos relations sont au b. fixe** things between us are looking rosy; *Fam* **il a le moral au b. fixe** he's in high spirits; *Fam* **elle a dit un gros mot – c'est du b.!** she said a rude word! – how naughty!; **faire le b.** *(chien)* to sit up and beg

• **belle NF 1** *(jolie femme)* beauty; *(dame)* lady; **il se plaisait en compagnie de ces belles** he liked the company of these fair ladies

2 *Fam (en appellatif)* **bonjour ma belle!** good morning, beautiful!; **tu te trompes, ma belle!** you're quite wrong, my dear!

3 *Hum ou Littéraire (amie, amante)* lady friend, beloved; **sa belle l'a quitté** his lady (friend) has left him; **il chantait sous les fenêtres de sa belle** he was singing beneath the windows of his beloved

4 *Sport* decider, deciding match; *(jeux)* decider, deciding game; **on fait** *ou* **joue la belle?** shall we play the decider?

5 *(locutions) Fam* **(se) faire la belle** *Br* to do a runner, *Am* to cut and run; *Can (chien)* to stand up on its back legs; *Can Fig* **faire la belle devant qn** to suck up to sb

6 *Belg Fam (locutions)* **avoir belle à faire qch** to have no trouble doing sth▫, to find it easy to do sth▫; **en avoir une belle avec qn** to go through some hard times with sb; **en faire une (bien) belle** to do something really silly *or* stupid; **ne pas en faire une belle** to be a total disaster

• **au plus beau de PRÉP au plus b. de la fête** when the party is/was in full swing; **au plus b. du discours** right in the middle of the speech

• **bel et bien ADV** well and truly; **il m'aurait bel et bien frappé si tu n'avais pas été là** he really would have hit me if you hadn't been there; **elle s'est bel et bien échappée** she got away and no mistake; *Fam* **ils nous ont bel et bien eus** they well and truly conned us

• **bel et bon, bel et bonne ADJ** fine; *Ironique* **tout ceci est bel et bon, mais...** this is all very fine, but...

• **de plus belle ADV** *(aboyer, crier)* louder than ever, even louder; *(frapper)* harder than ever, even harder; *(taquiner, manger)* more than ever, even more; **la pluie a recommencé de plus belle** it started to rain again harder than ever; **il s'est mis à travailler de plus belle** he went back to work with renewed energy

• **belle page NF** *Typ* right-hand page, odd-number page; **chaque chapitre commence en belle page** each chapter starts on the right-hand page

> **LA BELLE ÉPOQUE**
>
> This refers to the period of apparent stability and prosperity from the closing years of the 19th century to the beginning of the First World War, which found its expression in café and theatre society, fashion, art and architecture. Its chief surviving monument is the area on the south side of the Champs-Élysées containing the "Petit Palais" and the "Grand Palais", erected at the time of the Universal Exhibition of 1900.

BEAUCOUP [boku]

> • a lot **1–3** • a great deal **1**
> • much **1, 2** • many **3**

ADV 1 *(modifiant un verbe)* a lot, a great deal; *(dans des phrases interrogatives ou négatives)* much, a lot, a great deal; **il boit b.** he drinks a lot *or* a great deal; **il ne mange pas b.** he doesn't eat much *or* a great deal *or* a lot; **je ne l'ai pas b. vu** I didn't see much of him; **je vous remercie b.** thank you very much (indeed); **on s'aimait b.** we liked each other a lot *or* a great deal; **il compte b. pour moi** he means a lot *or* a great deal to me; **ils ne s'apprécient pas b.** they don't like each other much; **dix bouteilles, ça ne fait pas b.?** ten bottles, isn't that a bit much?

2 *(modifiant un adverbe)* much, a lot; **c'est b. mieux comme ça** it's much *or* a lot better like that; **b. moins intéressant** much *or* a lot less interesting; **b. plus bête** much *or* a lot more stupid; **b. plus grand** much *or* a lot bigger; **b. trop fort** much *or* far too loud; **il parle b. trop** he talks far too much

3 *(de nombreuses personnes)* many, a lot; *(de nombreuses choses)* a lot; **b. pensent que...** a lot of people *or* many people think that...; **nous sommes b. à penser cela** there are a lot *or* many of us who think that; **il n'y en a pas b. qui réussissent** not a lot of people *or* not many succeed; **elle a b. à faire/à dire** she has a lot to do/to say; **c'est b.** that's a lot; **c'est déjà b. qu'il y soit allé!** at least he went!; **ça compte pour b.** that counts for a lot; **il est pour b. dans son succès** he played a large part in *or* he had a great deal to do with his/her success; **c'est b. dire** that's a bit of an overstatement

4 *(modifiant un adjectif)* **imprudent, il l'est même b.** he's really quite careless

• **beaucoup de ADJ** *(suivi d'un nom comptable)* many, a lot of; *(suivi d'un nom non comptable)* much, a lot of, a great deal of; **b. de monde** a lot of people; **b. de gens pensent que...** a lot of people *or* many people think that...; **j'ai b. de choses à dire** I've got many *or* a lot of things to say; **il n'a pas b. d'amis** he doesn't have many *or* a lot of friends, he has few friends; **b. d'entre nous** many *or* a lot of us; **il faut b. de courage** it takes a lot of *or* a great deal of courage; **il ne nous reste plus b. de temps** we've not got much time left; **il n'y a plus b. de lait** there isn't much milk left; **il y en a b.** there is/are a lot

• **de beaucoup ADV 1** *(avec un comparatif ou un superlatif)* by far; **il est de b. le plus jeune** he is the youngest by far, he is by far the youngest **2** *(avec un verbe)* **il a gagné de b.** he won easily; **il te dépasse de b.** he's far *or* much taller than you; **je préférerais de b. rester** I'd much rather stay; **as-tu raté ton train de b.?** did you miss your train by much?

beauf [bof] *très Fam* **NM 1** *(beau-frère)* brother-in-law▫ **2** *Fig Péj* = archetypal lower-middle-class Frenchman

ADJ *Fig Péj* = typical of the archetypal lower-middle-class Frenchman

beau-fils [bofis] *(pl* **beaux-fils)** **NM 1** *(gendre)* son-in-law **2** *(fils du conjoint)* stepson

Beaufort [bofɔr] *voir* **échelle**

beau-frère [bofrɛr] *(pl* **beaux-frères)** **NM** brother-in-law

beaujolais [boʒɔlɛ] **NM** *(vin)* Beaujolais (wine)

beaujolpif [boʒɔlpif] **NM** *Fam* Beaujolais▫

beau-père [bopɛr] *(pl* **beaux-pères)** **NM 1** *(père du conjoint)* father-in-law **2** *(conjoint de la mère)* stepfather

beaupré [bopre] **NM** *Naut* bowsprit

beauté [bote] **NF 1** *(d'une femme, d'une statue)* beauty, loveliness; *(d'un homme)* handsomeness; **avoir la b. du diable** to have a youthful glow **2** *(femme)* beauty, beautiful woman; **je vous offre un verre, b.?** can I get you a drink, darling? **3** *(élévation* ▸ *de l'âme)* beauty; *(*▸ *d'un raisonnement)* beauty, elegance; **pour la b. du geste** *ou* **de la chose** for the beauty of it; **je lui ai cédé mon tour, pour la b. du geste** I let him/her have my turn, just because it was a nice thing to do

• **beautés NFPL** *(d'un paysage)* beauties, beauty spots; *(d'une œuvre)* beauties

• **de beauté ADJ** *(concours, reine)* beauty *(avant n)*

• **de toute beauté ADJ** magnificent, stunningly beautiful

• **en beauté ADV être en b.** to look stunning; **gagner une course en b.** to win a race handsomely; **finir en b.** to end with a flourish *or* on a high note

beaux-arts [bozar] **NMPL 1** *(genre)* fine arts; **musée des B.** museum of fine art **2** *(école)* **les B.** art school; **être aux B., faire les B.** to be at art school

beaux-parents [boparɑ̃] **NMPL** father-in-law and mother-in-law, in-laws

bébé [bebe] **NM 1** *(nourrisson)* baby; **avoir un b.** to have a baby; **attendre un b.** to be expecting a baby; *Péj* **faire le b.** to act like *or* to be being a baby; *Can Joual Fig* **c'est mon b.** *(projet)* it's my baby; **b. à la carte** designer baby **2** *Zool* baby; **la lionne s'occupe de ses bébés** the lioness looks after her babies *or* young *or* cubs; **b. phoque/lapin** baby seal/rabbit **3** *Can Joual (jolie fille)* **un beau b.** a babe

ADJ INV *Péj* babyish, baby-like; **elle est restée b.** she's still very much a baby

bébé-éprouvette [bebeepruvet] (*pl* **bébés-éprouvette**) **NM** test-tube baby

bébelle [bebel] **NF** *Can* toy; *Péj (babiole)* trinket

bébé-médicament [bebemedikamɑ̃] (*pl* **bébés-médicaments**) **NM** designer baby *(selected to help a sick sibling)*

bébert [bebεr] **NM** *Fam* = stereotypical reactionary Frenchman

bébête [bebεt] **ADJ** silly

NF *(en langage enfantin)* little insect, *Br* creepy-crawly

bec [bεk] **NM 1** *(d'oiseau)* beak, bill; *(de tortue)* beak; **au b. long/court** long/short-billed; **donner des coups de b. à** to peck (at); **nez en b. d'aigle** hook nose; **avoir b. et ongles** to be well-equipped and ready to fight; **se défendre b. et ongles** to fight tooth and nail

2 *Fam (bouche)* mouth□; **ferme ton b.!** shut up!, pipe down!; **ouvre le b.!** *(en nourrissant un enfant)* open wide!; **il n'a pas ouvert le b. de la journée** he hasn't opened his mouth all day; **ça lui a bouclé** *ou* **cloué** *ou* **clos le b.** it shut him/her up; **avoir toujours la cigarette/pipe au b.** to have a cigarette/pipe always stuck in one's mouth; **se retrouver le b. dans l'eau** to be left high and dry; **être un b. sucré** to have a sweet tooth□

3 *(d'une plume)* nib

4 *(de casserole)* lip; *(de bouilloire, de théière)* spout

5 *Mus (de saxophone, de clarinette)* mouthpiece

6 *Géog* bill, headland

7 *Belg, Suisse & Can Fam (baiser)* kiss□, peck; **donner un b. à qn** to give sb a kiss *or* peck; *Can* **b. pincé** snob

8 *(d'un vêtement)* **faire un b.** to pucker

9 *Fam (locution)* **tomber sur un b.** to run into *or* to hit a snag

• **bec à gaz NM** gas burner

• **bec de gaz NM** lamppost, gaslight

• **bec fin NM** gourmet; *Can* **avoir le b. fin** to be picky

bécane [bekan] **NF** *Fam* **1** *(moto, vélo)* bike **2** *Hum (ordinateur)* computer□, puter; *(machine à écrire)* typewriter□

bécarre [bekar] *Mus* **ADJ la b.** A natural

NM natural

bécasse [bekas] **NF 1** *Orn* woodcock; **b. américaine** American woodcock **2** *Fam (sotte)* silly goose, *Br* twit

bécasseau, -x [bekaso] **NM** *Orn* **1** *(échassier)* sandpiper **2** *(petit de la bécasse)* young woodcock

bécassine [bekasin] **NF 1** *Orn* snipe **2** *Fam (sotte)* silly goose, nincompoop

bec-croisé [bεkkrwaze] (*pl* **becs-croisés**) **NM** *Orn* crossbill

bec-de-cane [bεkdəkan] (*pl* **becs-de-cane**) **NM 1** *(poignée)* door handle **2** *(serrure)* spring lock

bec-de-lièvre [bεkdəljevr] (*pl* **becs-de-lièvre**) **NM** *Méd* harelip

becfigue [bεkfig] **NM** *Orn (dans le Midi) (oiseau)* (garden) warbler; *(fauvette)* blackcap; *(jaseur)* waxwing; *(pipi)* pipit

bêchage [beʃaʒ] **NM** *Agr* digging (up)

béchamel [beʃamel] **NF** *Culin* **(sauce) b.** white sauce, béchamel (sauce)

bêche [bεʃ] **NF** spade

bêcher [4] [beʃe] **VT 1** *Agr (sol)* to dig (over); *(pommes de terre)* to dig (up *or* out) **2** *Fam (critiquer)* to run down, to pull apart *or* to pieces

VI *Fam (faire le snob)* to put on airs

bêcheur, -euse [bεʃœr, -øz] **NM,F** *Fam* **1** *(critiqueur)* knocker **2** *Péj (prétentieux)* stuck-up person, snooty person; **quelle bêcheuse, celle-là!** she's so stuck-up *or* snooty!

bécot [beko] **NM** *Fam (bise)* kiss□, peck; **gros b.** smacker

bécoter [3] [bekɔte] *Fam* **VT** *Br* to snog, *Am* to neck

VPR se bécoter *Br* to snog, *Am* to neck

becquée [beke] **NF** *Orn* beakful; **donner la b.** *(oiseau)* to feed; *Hum* **sa maman lui donne la b.** his/her mummy's feeding him/her little bits of food

becquerel [bεkrel] **NM** *Nucl* becquerel

becquet [bεke] **NM 1** *Aut* spoiler **2** *Typ (papier)* = slip of paper, showing the position of a query or addition in copy prepared for print

becquetance [bεktɑ̃s] **NF** *très Fam* grub, nosh, *Am* chow

becqueter [27] [bekte] **VT 1** *(picoter)* to peck (at) **2** *très Fam (manger)* to eat□; **il n'y avait rien à b.** there was no grub

bectance [bεktɑ̃s] **NF** *très Fam* grub, nosh, *Am* chow

becter [4] [bεkte] **VT** *très Fam (manger)* to eat□; **il n'y avait rien à b.** there was no grub

bedaine [bədεn] **NF** paunch, pot belly; **prendre de la b.** to develop a paunch *or* a pot belly; **un homme qui a de la b.** a man of ample girth

bédane [bedan] **NM** *(outil)* mortise chisel

bédé [bede] **NF** *Fam* **la b.** strip cartoons□; **une b.** a strip cartoon

bedeau, -x [bədo] **NM** *Rel* beadle, verger

bédéphile [bedefil] **NMF** comics fan

bédo [bedo] **NM** *Fam (cigarette de cannabis)* spliff, joint

bedon [bədɔ̃] **NM** *Vieilli (d'enfant)* tummy; *(gros ventre)* paunch

bedonnant, -e [bədɔnɑ̃, -ɑ̃t] **ADJ** paunchy

bedonner [3] [bədɔne] **VI** to get paunchy

bédouin, -e [bedwɛ̃, -in] **ADJ** Bedouin, Beduin

• **Bédouin, -e NM,F** Bedouin, Beduin

bée [be] **ADJ F être bouche b. devant** to gape at; **j'en suis restée bouche b.** I was flabbergasted

beefsteak [biftεk] = **bifteck**

béer [15] [bee] **VI** *Littéraire* to be wide open; **la valise béait à ses pieds** the case lay wide open at his/her feet; **b. d'admiration** to gape with *or* to be lost in admiration

beffroi [befrwa] **NM** *Archit* belfry

bégaie *etc voir* **bégayer**

bégaiement [begemɑ̃] **NM** *(trouble de la parole)* stammer, stutter; **bégaiements** *(d'un bègue)* stammering *(UNCOUNT)*, stuttering *(UNCOUNT)*; *(d'embarras, d'émotion)* faltering *(UNCOUNT)*; *Fig* **les premiers bégaiements d'une industrie nouvelle** the first hesitant steps of a new industry

bégayant, -e [begejɑ̃, -ɑ̃t] **ADJ** *(discours)* stammering, stuttering

bégayer [11] [begeje] **VI** *(hésiter ▸ bègue)* to stammer, to stutter; *(▸ ivrogne)* to slur (one's speech); **la colère le faisait b.** she was so angry she was stammering

VT to stammer (out); **b. des excuses** to stammer out an apology

bégayeur, -euse [begejœr, -øz] **ADJ** stuttering, stammering

bégonia [begɔnja] **NM** *Bot* begonia

bègue [bεg] **ADJ** stammering, stuttering; **être b.** to (have a) stammer

NMF stammerer, stutterer

bégueule [begœl] *Fam* **ADJ** prudish; **elle n'est pas b.** she's no prude

NF prude

béguin [begɛ̃] **NM 1** *Fam (attirance)* **avoir le b. pour qn** to have a crush on sb **2** *Fam (amoureux)* crush **3** *(coiffe)* bonnet

béguinage [beginaʒ] **NM** *Rel* beguine convent

béguine [begin] **NF** *Rel* beguine (nun)

bégum [begɔm] **NF** begum

béhaviorisme [beavjɔrism] **NM** *Psy* behaviourism

béhavioriste [beavjɔrist] *Psy* **ADJ** behaviourist

NMF behaviourist

Behring [beriŋ] = **Béring**

BEI [beəi] **NF** *(abrév* **Banque européenne d'investissement)** EIB

beige [bεʒ] **ADJ** beige

NM beige

beigne [bεɲ] **NF** *très Fam (gifle)* slap□, clout; **filer une b. à qn** to slap sb□, to give sb a smack; **tu veux une b.?** do you want a thick ear?

NM *Can Culin (beignet)* doughnut; *Fig* **se faire passer les beignes** to get a spanking

beignet [beɲε] **NM** *Culin (gén)* fritter; *(au sucre, à la confiture)* doughnut; **b. aux pommes** apple doughnut; **b. de crevettes** *(chips)* prawn cracker; *(avec de la pâte)* prawn fritter

beïram [beiram] = **baïram**

béké [beke] **NMF** Caribbean creole *(with white ancestry)*

bel [bεl] **ADJ** *voir* **beau**

NM *(unité d'intensité du son)* bel

bêlant, -e [belɑ̃, -ɑ̃t] **ADJ 1** *(mouton)* bleating **2** *(chevrotant ▸ voix)* bleating, shaky

bel canto [bεlkɑ̃to] **NM INV** *Mus* bel canto

bêlement [bεlmɑ̃] **NM** bleat; **les bêlements des moutons** the bleating of the sheep

bélemnite [belεmnit] **NF** *Zool & Géol* belemnite

bêler [4] [bele] **VI** to bleat

VT *(chanson)* to bleat out

bel-étage, bel étage [bεletaʒ] (*pl* **beaux(-)étages** [bozetaʒ]) **NM** *Belg* **1** *(rez-de-chaussée surélevé)* mezzanine *Br* ground *or Am* first floor **2** *(maison)* = house with mezzanine ground/first floor

belette [bəlεt] **NF 1** *Zool* weasel **2** *Fam (jeune femme) Br* bird, *Am* chick

Belga [belga] **NF** *Journ* = Belgian press agency

belge [bεlʒ] **ADJ** Belgian

• **Belge NMF** Belgian

belgicain, -e [bεlʒikɛ̃, -εn] *Belg Péj* **ADJ être b.** *(partisan de l'unité belge)* to be in favour of a united Belgium; *(attaché aux traditions nationales)* to be attached to conservative (Belgian) tradition

NM,F *(partisan de l'unité belge)* Belgian nationalist *(in favour of national unity)*; *(personne attachée aux traditions nationales)* conservative (Belgian)

belgicisme [bεlʒisism] **NM** *Ling (mot)* Belgian-French word; *(tournure)* Belgian-French expression

Belgique [bεlʒik] **NF la B.** Belgium

Belgrade [bεlgrad] **NM** *Géog* Belgrade

Bélier [belje] **NM 1** *Astron* Aries **2** *Astrol* Aries; **être B.** to be Aries *or* an Arian

bélier [belje] **NM 1** *Zool* ram

2 *Tech* **b. (hydraulique)** hydraulic ram

3 *Hist* battering ram

4 *Constr* pile driver, ram(mer)

bélière [beljεr] **NF 1** *(d'une cloche)* clapper ring; *(d'une montre)* ring **2** *(du bélier qui conduit le troupeau)* (sheep) bell

Belize [beliz] **NM le B.** Belize

belladone [beladɔn] **NF** *Bot* belladonna, deadly nightshade

bellâtre [bεlatr] **NM** *Péj* fop

belle [bεl] *voir* **beau**

belle-dame [bεldam] (*pl* **belles-dames**) **NF 1** *Bot* belladonna **2** *Entom* painted lady

belle-de-jour [bεldəʒur] (*pl* **belles-de-jour**) **NF** *Bot* convolvulus, morning-glory

belle-de-nuit [bεldənɥi] (*pl* **belles-de-nuit**) **NF 1** *Bot* marvel of Peru, four-o'clock **2** *(prostituée)* lady of the night

belle-doche [bεldɔʃ] (*pl* **belles-doches**) **NF** *Fam* mother-in-law□

belle-famille [bεlfamij] (*pl* **belles-familles**) **NF sa b.** *(de l'épouse)* her husband's family, her in-laws; *(de l'époux)* his wife's family, his in-laws

belle-fille [bεlfij] (*pl* **belles-filles**) **NF 1** *(bru)* daughter-in-law **2** *(fille du conjoint)* stepdaughter

bellement [bεlmɑ̃] **ADV 1** *(joliment)* nicely, finely **2** *(vraiment)* well and truly, in no uncertain manner; **il l'a b. remis à sa place** he really took him down a peg or two

belle-mère [bεlmεr] (*pl* **belles-mères**) **NF 1** *(mère du conjoint)* mother-in-law **2** *(conjointe du père)* stepmother

belles-lettres [bεllεtr] **NFPL** literature, *Sout* belles-lettres

belle-sœur [bεlsœr] (*pl* **belles-sœurs**) **NF** sister-in-law

bellicisme [belisism] **NM** warmongering, *Sout* bellicosity

belligérance [beliʒerɑ̃s] **NF** belligerence, belligerency

belligérant, -e [beliʒerɑ̃, -ɑ̃t] **ADJ** belligerent, warring

NM,F belligerent

• **belligérants NMPL les belligérants** the belligerents, the warring nations

belliqueux, -euse [belikø, -øz] **ADJ** *(peuple)* warlike; *(ton, discours)* aggressive, belligerent; *(enfant, humeur)* quarrelsome, *Sout* bellicose

belote [bəlɔt] **NF** *Cartes* belote *(card game)*; **faire une b.** to play a game of belote

bélouga, béluga [beluga] **NM 1** *Zool (mammifère)* beluga, white whale **2** *Culin (caviar)* beluga (caviar)

belvédère [belvedɛr] **NM** *Archit (pavillon)* belvedere, gazebo; *(terrasse)* panoramic viewpoint

Belzébuth [belzebyt] **NPR** Beelzebub

bémol [bemɔl] *Mus* **ADJ INV mi b.** E flat

NM flat; **double b.** double flat; **mettre un b.** *(parler moins fort)* to pipe down; *(modérer ses propos)* to climb down

bémoliser [3] [bemɔlize] **VT** *Mus* to flatten, *Am* to flat; *Fig* to tone down

ben [bɛ̃] **ADV** *Fam* **1** *(pour renforcer)* **b. quoi?** so what?; **b. non** well, no; **b. voilà, euh...** yeah, well, er...; **b. voyons (donc)!** what next! **2** *(bien)* **pt'êt b. qu'oui, pt'êt b. qu'non** maybe yes, maybe no

bénarde [benard] **NF** pin key lock, double-sided lock

bène [ben] **NM** *Fam Br* trousers[□], keks, *Am* pants[□]

bénédicité [benedisite] **NM** *Rel* grace; **dire le b.** to say grace

bénédictin, -e [benediktɛ̃, -in] *Rel* **ADJ** Benedictine

• **Bénédictin, -e NM,F** Benedictine

Bénédictine® [benediktin] **NF** *(liqueur)* Benedictine®

bénédiction [benediksjɔ̃] **NF 1** *Rel* benediction, blessing; *(d'une église)* consecration; **recevoir la b. papale** to be given *or* to receive the Pope's blessing; **donner la b. à qn** to pronounce the blessing on *or* to bless sb; **la b. nuptiale leur sera donnée à...** the marriage ceremony will take place *or Sout* the marriage will be solemnized at... **2** *(accord)* blessing; **donner sa b. à qch** to give sth one's blessing; **vous avez ma b.** you have my blessing; *Fam* **il peut déguerpir dès demain, et avec ma b.!** he can get lost tomorrow, with my blessing! **3** *(aubaine)* blessing, godsend; **c'est une b. qu'il soit vivant/qu'elle se porte volontaire** it's a blessing that he's alive/a godsend that she's volunteering to do it

bénef [benɛf] **NM** *Fam* profit[□]; **c'est tout b. pour elle** she gets quite a deal out of this

bénéfice [benefis] **NM 1** *Écon, Com & Fin* profit; **faire du b.** to make a profit; **faire** *ou* **enregistrer un b. brut/net de 200 euros** to gross/to net 200 euros; **donner un b.** to show a profit; **réaliser** *ou* **dégager un b.** to make a profit; **b. de** *ou* **pour l'exercice 2006** profits for the year 2006; **rapporter des bénéfices** to yield a profit; **vendre qch à b.** to sell sth at a profit; *Fam* **c'est tout b. à ce prix-là** at that price, you make a 100 percent profit on it; *Fig* **il leur apprend l'anglais en les amusant, c'est tout b.!** he teaches them English while entertaining them, what better way is there?; **b. par action** earnings per share; **b. brut/net** gross/net profit; **b. brut avant impôts** pre-tax profit; **b. consommateur** *(d'un produit)* consumer benefit; **b. cumulé** cumulative profit; **b. à distribuer, bénéfices distribuables** distributable profits; **b. escompté** desired profit; **bénéfices exceptionnels** excess *or* windfall profits; **bénéfices de l'exercice** current earnings; **b. d'exploitation** operating *or* trading profit; **bénéfices financiers** interest received; **b. fiscal** taxable profit; **b. imposable** taxable profit; **b. avant/après impôt** pre-tax/after-tax profit; **b. marginal** marginal profit; **b. net dilué par action** fully diluted earnings per share; **bénéfices non distribués** undistributed profits, retained profit; **b. transféré** profit transferred

2 *(avantage)* benefit, advantage; **il n'y a pas de b. à mentir** there's nothing to gain by lying; **tirer (un) b. de qch** to derive some benefit *or* an advantage from sth; **c'est le b. que l'on peut tirer de cette conduite** that's the reward for such behaviour; **laisser à qn le b. du doute** to give sb the benefit of the doubt

3 *Jur* **b. d'inventaire** = an heir's lack of liability for debts beyond inherited assets; **sous b. d'inventaire** = without liability to debts beyond inherited assets; *Fig* **j'accepte, sous b. d'inventaire** everything else being equal, I accept

4 *Rel* living, benefice

5 *Psy* **b. primaire/secondaire** primary/secondary gain

6 *Can* **concert/repas-b.** fundraising concert/dinner

• **à bénéfice ADV** *(exploiter, vendre)* at a profit

• **au bénéfice de PRÉP** *(en faveur de)* for (the benefit of); **match au b. de l'enfance handicapée** benefit match for handicapped children

bénéficiaire [benefisjɛr] **ADJ** *(opération)* profitable; *(entreprise)* profit-making; *(marge)* profit *(avant n)*; *(compte)* in credit; *(bilan)* showing a profit

NMF *(d'une mesure)* beneficiary; *(d'un mandat, d'un chèque)* payee, recipient; **qui en seront les principaux bénéficiaires?** who will benefit by it most?; **b. conjoint(e)** joint beneficiary

bénéficier [9] [benefisje] **bénéficier de VT IND 1** *(avoir)* to have, to enjoy; **b. de conditions idéales/d'avantages sociaux** to enjoy ideal conditions/welfare benefits; **cette carte d'abonnement vous fait b. d'une remise de 20 pour cent** this season ticket entitles you to a 20 percent reduction; *Jur* **b. de circonstances atténuantes** to have the benefit of *or* to be granted extenuating circumstances; *Jur* **il a bénéficié d'une ordonnance de non-lieu** he was discharged **2** *(profiter de)* to benefit by *or* from; **b. d'une forte remise** to get a big reduction; **b. d'une mesure** to benefit by *or* to profit from a measure; **faire b. qn de ses connaissances** to allow sb to benefit by *or* to give sb the benefit of one's knowledge

• **bénéficier à VT IND** to benefit; **à qui vont b. ces mesures?** who are these measures going to benefit?, who is going to benefit from these measures?

bénéfique [benefik] **ADJ 1** *(avantageux)* beneficial, advantageous; **ce séjour à la montagne vous sera b.** this stay in the mountains will do you good *or* will be beneficial to you **2** *Astrol* favourable

Benelux [benelyks] **NM le B.** Benelux; **les pays du B.** the Benelux countries

benêt [bənɛ] *Péj* **ADJ M** simple-minded, idiotic, silly

NM simpleton; **son grand b. de fils** his great fool of a son

bénévolat [benevɔla] **NM** *(travail)* voluntary work; *(système)* system of voluntary work

bénévole [benevɔl] **ADJ** *(aide, conseil)* voluntary, free; *(association)* voluntary; *(médecin)* volunteer *(avant n)*; **être employé à titre b.** to do voluntary work

NMF volunteer, voluntary worker

bénévolement [benevɔlmɑ̃] **ADV** voluntarily; **travailler b. pour qn** to do voluntary work for sb

Bengale [bɛ̃gal] **NM le B.** Bengal

bengali [bɛ̃gali] **ADJ** Bengali

NM *(langue)* Bengali

• **Bengali NMF** Bengali

bénigne [beniɲ] *voir* **bénin**

bénignité [beniɲite] **NF 1** *Méd (d'une maladie)* mildness; *(d'une tumeur)* non-malignancy **2** *Littéraire (mansuétude)* benignancy, kindness

Bénin [benɛ̃] **NM le B.** Benin

bénin, -igne [benɛ̃, -iɲ] **ADJ 1** *Méd (maladie)* minor; *(tumeur)* non-malignant, benign; **une forme bénigne de rougeole** a mild form of measles **2** *(accident)* slight, minor; *(sanction)* mild **3** *Littéraire (gentil)* benign, kindly

béninois, -e [beninwa, -az] **ADJ** Beninese

• **Béninois, -e NM,F** Beninese; **les B.** the Beninese

béni-oui-oui [beniwiwi] **NMF INV** *Péj* yes-man, *f* yes-woman

bénir [32] [benir] **VT 1** *Rel (fidèles)* to bless, to give one's blessing to; *(eau, pain, église)* to consecrate; *(union)* to solemnize **2** *(remercier)* **je bénis le passant qui m'a sauvé la vie** I'll be eternally thankful to the passer-by who saved my life; **béni soit le jour où je t'ai rencontré** blessed be the day I met you; **elle bénit le ciel de lui avoir donné un fils** she thanked God for giving her a son; *Ironique* **toi, je te bénis d'avoir perdu mes clés!** thanks a lot for losing my keys!

bénit, -e [beni, -it] **ADJ** consecrated, blessed

bénitier [benitje] **NM 1** *Rel (dans une église)* stoup, font **2** *Zool (mollusque)* giant clam

benjamin, -e [bɛ̃ʒamɛ̃, -in] **NM,F 1** *(d'une famille)* youngest child; **mon b.** my youngest (child) **2** *Sport* junior *(10 to 12 years old)*

benjoin [bɛ̃ʒwɛ̃] **NM** *Chim & Pharm* benzoin, benjamin

benne [bɛn] **NF** *Mines* tub, truck; *(de camion)* tipping *or* dump body; *(de grue)* scoop; *(de téléphérique)* (cable) car; **b. basculante** tipper; **b. à ordures** *(partie du camion) Br* skip, *Am* dumpster

benoît, -e [bənwa, -at] **ADJ 1** *Vieilli* kind, gentle; **b. lecteur** gentle reader **2** *Péj (doucereux)* bland, ingratiating

benthique [bɛ̃tik] **ADJ** *Géol* benthic

benthos [bɛ̃tɔs] **NM** *Écol* benthos

benzène [bɛ̃zen] **NM** *Chim* benzene

benzine [bɛ̃zin] **NF 1** *Chim* benzin, benzine **2** *Suisse (essence) Br* petrol, *Am* gas

benzol [bɛ̃zɔl] **NM** *Chim* benzol, benzole

benzolisme [bɛ̃zɔlism] **NM** *Méd* benzol poisoning

béotien, -enne [beɔsjɛ̃, -ɛn] **ADJ 1** *Antiq* Boeotian **2** *Péj (inculte)* uncultured, philistine

NM,F *Péj (rustre)* philistine

• **Béotien, -enne NM,F** *Antiq* Boeotian

BEP [beəpe] **NM** *Scol (abrév* **brevet d'études professionnelles)** = vocational diploma (taken after two years of study at a "lycée professionnel")

BEPC [beəpese] **NM** *Anciennement Scol (abrév* **brevet d'études du premier cycle)** = former school certificate taken after four years of secondary education

béquée [beke] = **becquée**

béquet [bekɛ] = **becquet**

béqueter [27] [bekte] = **becqueter**

béquille [bekij] **NF 1** *(canne)* crutch; **marcher avec des béquilles** to walk on *or* with crutches

2 *(de moto)* stand

3 *Fig (soutien)* prop

4 *Naut* shore, prop

5 *Aviat* tail skid

6 *(d'une serrure)* handle

7 *(d'une arme)* stand

8 *Fam (coup de genou dans la cuisse)* **faire une b. à qn** to give sb a dead leg

béquiller [3] [bekije] **VI** to hobble (along) on crutches

VT *Naut* to shore up, to prop up

berbère [bɛrbɛr] **ADJ** Berber

NM *(langue)* Berber

• **Berbère NMF** Berber

bercail [bɛrkaj] **NM** sheepfold; **ramener au b. la brebis égarée** to bring the lost sheep back to the fold; **rentrer** *ou* **revenir au b.** *(à la maison)* to get back home; *Rel* to return to the fold

berçante [bɛrsɑ̃t] **NF** *Can* **(chaise) b.** rocking chair

berce [bɛrs] **NF 1** *Bot* hogweed **2** *Belg (berceau)* cradle

berceau, -x [bɛrso] **NM 1** *(lit)* cradle; **du b. à la tombe** from the cradle to the grave; **on se connaît depuis le b.** we've known each other since we were babies; *Fam* **il/elle les prend au b.** *(séducteur)* he's/she's a cradle-snatcher; **prendre qn au b. pour lui apprendre qch** to teach sb sth right from the earliest age

2 *(lieu d'origine)* cradle, birthplace; **le b. de la civilisation** the cradle of civilization

3 *Archit* **(voûte en) b.** barrel vault

4 *(tonnelle)* arbour, bower

5 *(d'un moteur, d'un canon)* cradle

bercelonnette [bɛrsəlɔnɛt] **NF** rocking cradle

bercement [bɛrsəmɑ̃] **NM** rocking *or* swaying movement

bercer [16] [bɛrse] **VT 1** *(bébé)* to rock, to cradle; **b. un bébé dans ses bras** to cradle *or* to rock a baby in one's arms; **il faut la b. pour qu'elle s'endorme** you have to rock her to sleep; **un bateau bercé par la houle** a boat rocked by the waves **2** *(calmer ▸ douleur)* to lull, to soothe **3** *(tromper)* **b. qn de (belles) paroles/(vaines) promesses** to fob sb off with fine words/empty promises

VPR se bercer 1 se b. de qch to delude oneself with sth; **se b. d'illusions** to delude oneself, to entertain illusions **2** *Can (se balancer)* to rock (back and forth) *(in a rocking chair)*

berceur, -euse[1] [bɛrsœr, -øz] **ADJ** lulling, soothing

berceuse[2] [bɛrsøz] **NF 1** *(chanson d'enfant)* lullaby; *Mus* berceuse **2** *Can* rocking chair

BERD, Berd [bɛrd] **NF** *(abrév* **Banque européenne pour la reconstruction et le développement**) EBRD

béret [berɛ] **NM b. (basque)** (French) beret

bergamasque [bɛrgamask] **NF** *(danse)* bergamask

bergamote [bɛrgamɔt] **NF** *Bot* bergamot orange

• **à la bergamote ADJ** *(savon)* bergamot-scented; *(thé)* with bergamot, bergamot-flavoured

berge [bɛrʒ] **NF 1** *Géog (rive)* bank; **route** *ou* **voie sur b.** *(dans une grande ville)* embankment road **2** *très Fam (an)* year❑; **à 25 berges, elle a monté sa boîte** when she was 25, she set up her own business❑

berger, -ère [bɛrʒe, -ɛr] **NM,F 1** *(pâtre)* shepherd, *f* shepherdess; **des histoires de bergers et de bergères** pastoral stories **2** *(guide)* shepherd

NM *Zool (chien)* sheepdog; **b. allemand, b. d'Alsace** Alsatian, German shepherd; **b. d'Écosse** collie (dog); **b. des Pyrénées** Pyrenean mountain dog, Pyrenean shepherd

• **bergère NF** *(fauteuil)* bergère

bergerie [bɛrʒəri] **NF 1** *Agr* sheepfold **2** *Beaux-Arts (peinture)* pastoral (painting); *Littérature (poème)* pastoral **3** *Com* counter

bergeronnette [bɛrʒərɔnɛt] **NF** *Orn* wagtail

béribéri [beriberi] **NM** *Méd* beriberi

Béring [beriŋ] *voir* **mer**

berk [bɛrk] **EXCLAM** *Fam* ugh!, yuk!

berkélium [bɛrkeljɔm] **NM** *Chim* berkelium

berlander [3] [bɛrlɑ̃de] **VI** *Can (hésiter)* to dither; *(fainéanter)* to waste one's time

Berlin [bɛrlɛ̃] **NM** *Géog* Berlin; *Anciennement* **B.-Est** East Berlin; *Anciennement* **B.-Ouest** West Berlin; *Hist* **le mur de B.** the Berlin Wall

berline [bɛrlin] **NF 1** *Aut Br* saloon car, *Am* sedan; **grosse b.** *Br* big saloon (car), *Am* full-size sedan; **moyenne b.** compact car **2** *Hist* berlin, berline **3** *Mines* truck, tub

berlinette [bɛrlinɛt] **NF** *Aut* Berlinette

berlingot [bɛrlɛ̃go] **NM 1** *(bonbon) Br* ≃ boiled sweet, *Am* ≃ hard candy **2** *(emballage ▸ de lait)* carton; *(▸ de produit d'entretien)* pack

berlinois, -e [bɛrlinwa, -az] **ADJ** of/from Berlin

• **Berlinois, -e NM,F** Berliner; *Anciennement* **B. de l'Est/l'Ouest** East/West Berliner

berlue [bɛrly] **NF avoir la b.** to be seeing things; **si je n'ai pas la b., c'est bien Paul là-bas** if my eyes don't deceive me, that's Paul over there

berme [bɛrm] **NF 1** *(autour d'un château fort)* berm; *(le long d'un canal, d'un fossé etc)* (foot-) path, verge **2** *Belg & Suisse* **b. centrale** *(terre-plein) Br* central reservation, *Am* median (strip)

bermuda [bɛrmyda] **NM un b.** (a pair of) Bermuda shorts, Bermudas

Bermudes [bɛrmyd] **NFPL les B.** Bermuda; **vivre aux B.** to live in Bermuda; **aller aux B.** to go to Bermuda; **le triangle des B.** the Bermuda Triangle

bernache [bɛrnaʃ], **bernacle** [bɛrnakl] **NF 1** *Orn* barnacle goose **2** *Zool (crustacé)* (goose) barnacle

bernardin, -e [bɛrnardɛ̃, -in] **NM,F** *Rel* Bernardine

bernard-l'ermite, bernard-l'hermite [bɛrnarlɛrmit] **NM INV** *Zool (crustacé)* hermit crab

Berne [bɛrn] **NM** *Géog* Bern

berne [bɛrn] **en berne ADV** *(gén) & Mil & Naut* at half-mast; **mettre les drapeaux en b.** to half-mast the flags, to lower the flags to half-mast

berner [3] [bɛrne] **VT** *(tromper)* to fool, to dupe, to take in; **on s'est fait b.** we were taken in *or* duped; **je ne vais pas me laisser b. cette fois** I won't be made a fool of this time; **n'essaie pas de me b.** don't try to fool me

bernicle [bɛrnikl] **NF** *Zool (mollusque)* limpet

bernique [bɛrnik] **NF** *Zool (mollusque)* limpet

EXCLAM *Arch* nothing doing!

bernois, -e [bɛrnwa, -az] **ADJ** Bernese

• **Bernois, -e NM,F** Bernese

berrichon, -onne [bɛriʃɔ̃, -ɔn] **ADJ** of/from Berry

NM *(dialecte)* Berry dialect

• **Berrichon, -onne NM,F** = inhabitant of or person from Berry

Berry [beri] **NM le B.** Berry *(region in central France)*

bertillonnage [bɛrtijɔnaʒ] **NM** *(en anthropométrie)* Bertillon system

béryl [beril] **NM** *Géol* beryl

béryllium [beriljɔm] **NM** *Chim* beryllium, glucinium

berzingue [bɛrzɛ̃g] **à tout(e) berzingue ADV** *Fam* at full speed❑, double-quick

besace [bəzas] **NF** *(de mendiant)* bag; *(de pèlerin)* scrip; **sac b.** = large, soft handbag

bésef [bezɛf] **ADV** *très Fam* **pas b.** *(non comptable)* not much❑, not a lot❑; *(comptable)* not many❑, not a lot❑; **de la patience, j'en ai pas b.** I don't have tons of patience; **il n'y en avait pas b., des clients** there weren't tons of customers

bésicles [bezikl], **besicles** [bəzikl] **NFPL** *Arch* spectacles; *Hum* specs

bésigue [bezig] **NM** *Cartes* bezique

besogne [bəzɔɲ] **NF** *(travail)* task, job, work; **se mettre à la b.** to get down to work; **c'est de la belle** *ou* **bonne b.** it's a fine piece of work, it's a neat job; **une rude b.** a hard task

besogner [3] [bəzɔɲe] **VI** *Péj (travailler)* to drudge, to slave away, to toil away

VT *Vulg* to hump, to screw

besogneux, -euse [bəzɔɲø, -øz] **ADJ 1** *(travailleur)* plodding **2** *Littéraire (pauvre)* needy, poor

NM,F drudge

besoin [bəzwɛ̃] **NM 1** *(nécessité)* need; **un b. de chaleur humaine** a need for human warmth; **il a de gros besoins d'argent** he needs lots of money; **nos besoins en pétrole/ingénieurs** our oil/engineering requirements; **quels sont ses besoins?** what are his/her (basic) needs?; **tous vos besoins seront satisfaits** all your needs will be answered *or* satisfied; *Compta* **besoins de caisse** cash requirements; *Compta* **besoins de crédit** borrowing requirements; *Compta* **besoins en fonds de roulement** working capital requirements; **besoins (éducatifs) particuliers** special needs; **un enfant à besoins (éducatifs) particuliers** a child with special needs; *Compta* **besoins de trésorerie** cash requirements; **ressentir** *ou* **éprouver le b. de faire qch** to feel the need to do sth; **il n'est pas b. de vous le dire** you hardly need to be told; **si b. est** if necessary, if needs be; **si le b. s'en faisait sentir** if the need *or* necessity arose; **il n'est pas b. de mentir** there's no need to lie; **sans qu'il soit b. de prévenir les parents** without it being necessary to let the parents know; *Euph* **b. (naturel), petit b., b. pressant** call of nature; **faire ses besoins** *(personne)* to attend to *or* to answer the call of nature; *(animal)* to do its business; **être pris d'un b. pressant** to be taken *or* caught short; **avoir un b. pressant d'argent** to be pressed for money **2** *(pauvreté)* need; **dans le b.** in need; **ceux qui sont dans le b.** the needy; *Prov* **c'est dans le b. qu'on connaît le véritable ami** *ou* **ses vrais amis** a friend in need is a friend indeed **3** *(locutions)* **avoir b. de qn/qch** to need sb/sth; **avoir b. de faire qch** to need to do sth; **je n'en ai aucun b.** I have no need of it whatsoever; **il a b. qu'on s'occupe de lui** he needs looking after; **je n'ai pas b. de vous rappeler que...** I don't need to *or* I needn't remind you that...; **mon agenda a b. d'être mis à jour** my diary needs updating *or* to be updated; **avoir bien** *ou* **grand b. de qch** to be in dire need of sth, to need sth badly; **tu aurais bien b. d'un shampooing** your hair's badly in need of a wash; *Ironique* **un pneu crevé! on en avait bien b.** *ou* **on avait bien b. de ça!** a flat tyre, that's all we needed!

• **au besoin ADV** if necessary, if needs *or* need be

• **pour les besoins de PRÉP pour les besoins de la cause** for the purpose in hand; **pour les besoins du direct** for the purpose of the live broadcast

Bessemer [bɛsmɛr] **NM** *Métal* **convertisseur B.** Bessemer converter; **procédé B.** Bessemer process

bestiaire [bɛstjɛr] **NM 1** *(recueil)* bestiary **2** *Antiq* gladiator

bestial, -e, -aux, -ales [bɛstjal, -o] **ADJ** *(instinct, acte)* bestial, brutish

bestialement [bɛstjalmɑ̃] **ADV** bestially, brutishly

bestialité [bɛstjalite] **NF 1** *(brutalité)* bestiality, brutishness **2** *(zoophilie)* bestiality

bestiau, -x [bɛstjo] **NM** *Fam (animal)* beast❑, creature❑

• **bestiaux NMPL** *(d'une exploitation)* livestock; *(bovidés)* cattle; **traités/entassés comme des bestiaux** treated/penned in like cattle

bestiole [bɛstjɔl] **NF** *Fam (insecte)* creepy-crawly, *Am* creepy-crawler; *(petit animal)* creature❑

best of [bɛstɔf] **NM INV** greatest hits compilation; **un b. des Rolling Stones** a compilation of the greatest hits of the Rolling Stones

best-seller [bɛstsɛlœr] *(pl* **best-sellers**) **NM** best-seller

bêta, -asse [beta, -as] **ADJ** *Fam (stupide)* silly, *Br* daft

NM,F *Fam (idiot)* idiot, numbskull; **espèce de gros b.!** you idiot!

NM INV *(lettre)* beta

• **bêta ADJ INV** *Géol & Électron* beta *(avant n)*

bêtabloquant, -e [betablɔkɑ̃, -ɑ̃t] **ADJ** *Méd* beta-blocker *(avant n)*

NM beta-blocker

bêtacarotène [betakarɔtɛn] **NM** betacarotene

bétail [betaj] **NM** *Agr* **le b.** *(gén)* livestock; *(bovins)* cattle; **cent têtes de b.** a hundred head of cattle; **traiter les gens comme du b.** to treat people like cattle; **gros b.** (big) cattle; **petit b.** small livestock

bétaillère [betajɛr] **NF** *Br* cattle truck, *Am* stock car

bêtasse [betas] *voir* **bêta**

bêta-test [betatɛst] *(pl* **bêta-tests**) **NM** *Ordinat* beta test; **bêta-tests** *(procédure)* beta testing

bêtatron [betatrɔ̃] **NM** *Phys* betatron

bête [bɛt] **ADJ 1** *(peu intelligent)* stupid, idiotic; **ce que tu peux être b. parfois!** you can be really stupid sometimes!; **c'est encore moi qui vais payer, je suis bien b., tiens!** I'll end up paying again, like an idiot!; **mais oui, je me souviens maintenant, suis-je b.!** ah, now I remember, how stupid of me!; **je ne suis pas b. au point de...** I know better than to...; **il faudrait être b. pour dépenser plus** it would be foolish *or* you'd have to be an idiot to spend more; **loin d'être b.** far from stupid; **pas si b., j'ai pris mes précautions** I took some precautions, since I'm not a complete idiot; **pas si b., la petite!** she's no fool, that girl!; **ce n'est pas b., ton idée!** that's quite a good idea you've got there!; **être b. comme ses pieds** *ou* **comme une cruche** *ou* **comme une oie** *ou* **à manger du foin** *Br* to be as thick as two short planks, *Am* to be as dumb as the day is long; **c'est b. à pleurer** it's ridiculously stupid; **je suis b. et discipliné, moi, je fais ce qu'on me dit de faire!** I'm just carrying out orders!

2 *(regrettable)* **je n'ai pas su le retenir, comme c'est b.!** I didn't know how to keep him, what a pity *or* waste!; **c'est b. de ne pas y avoir pensé** it's silly *or* stupid not to have thought of it

3 *(simple)* **c'est tout b., il suffisait d'y penser!** it's so simple, we should have thought of it before!;

Fam **c'est b. comme tout** *ou* **chou** it's simplicity itself *or* easy as pie *or* easy as falling off a log
4 *(stupéfait)* **en être** *ou* **rester tout b.** to be struck dumb *or* dumbfounded
5 *Can (de mauvaise humeur)* grumpy; **avoir l'air b.** to look grumpy; **être b. comme ses (deux) pieds** to be a nasty piece of work
NF 1 *Zool (animal ▸ gén)* animal; *(▸ effrayant)* beast; **mener les bêtes aux champs** to take the herd off to graze; **aimer les bêtes** to be an animal-lover; *Antiq* **jeté** *ou* **livré (en pâture) aux bêtes** thrown to the lions; *Fig* **b. curieuse** strange-looking creature; **ils nous regardaient comme des bêtes curieuses** they were staring at us as if we were from Mars; **b. à cornes/poils/plumes** horned/furry/feathered animal; **b. fauve** *(gén)* wild animal *or* beast; *(félin)* big cat; **b. féroce** *ou* **sauvage** wild animal *or* beast; **b. de race** pedigree animal; **b. de somme** *ou* **de charge** beast of burden; **je ne veux pas être la b. de somme du service** I don't want to do all the dirty work in this department; **b. de trait** draught animal; *Fam* **malade comme une b.** sick as a dog; *Fam* **travailler comme une b.** to work like a slave *or* dog; *Fam* **s'éclater comme une b.** to have a great time; *Arch ou Hum* **faire la b. à deux dos** to make the beast with two backs
2 *(insecte)* **(petite) b.** insect, creature; **b. à bon Dieu** *Br* ladybird, *Am* ladybug
3 *(personne)* **grosse b., va!** you silly fool!; **tu n'es qu'une grande b.** you're a great fool; *Fam* **c'est une bonne** *ou* **brave b.** *(généreux)* he's a good sort; *(dupe)* he's a bit of a sucker
4 *Fam (expert)* **c'est une vraie b. en physique!** he's/she's brilliant at physics!◻; **b. à concours** *Br* swot, *Am* grind *(who sits many competitive exams)*; **b. de scène/télévision** great live/television performer◻
5 *Rel* **la b. de l'Apocalypse** the beast of the Apocalypse
6 *(locutions)* **ma b. noire** my bugbear *or* pet hate; **un ministre qui est la b. noire des étudiants** a minister students love to hate; **le latin, c'était ma b. noire** Latin was my pet hate; **se payer** *ou* **se servir sur la b.** to get one's payment in kind *(by docking it off a man's pay or by demanding a woman's sexual favours)*

bétel [betel] **NM** *Bot* betel

bêtement [bɛtmɑ̃] **ADV 1** *(stupidement)* foolishly, stupidly, idiotically; **rire b.** to giggle; **mourir b.** to die senselessly **2** *(simplement)* **tout b.** purely and simply, quite simply

Bethléem [betleem] **NF** *Géog & Bible* Bethlehem

bêtifiant, -e [betifjɑ̃, -ɑ̃t] **ADJ** idiotic, stupid

bêtifier [9] [betifje] **VI** to talk nonsense; **elle bêtifie quand elle parle à son enfant** she uses baby-talk to her child

bêtise [betiz] **NF 1** *(stupidité)* idiocy, foolishness, stupidity; **il est d'une rare b.** he's exceptionally stupid; **j'ai eu la b. de ne pas vérifier** I was foolish enough not to check; **c'est de la b. d'y aller seul** going there alone is sheer stupidity
2 *(remarque)* silly *or* stupid remark; **dire une b.** to say something stupid; **dire des bêtises** to talk nonsense
3 *(action)* stupid thing; **bêtises de jeunesse** youthful pranks; **ne recommencez pas vos bêtises** don't start your stupid tricks again; **faire une b.** to do something silly *or* stupid
4 *(vétille)* trifle, small detail; **pleurer pour des bêtises** to cry over the smallest thing; **on se dispute toujours pour des bêtises** we're always arguing over nothing; **dépenser tout son argent en bêtises** to fritter away one's money; **elle achète énormément de bêtises** she buys lots of rubbish *or Am* trash
5 *Culin* **b. de Cambrai** *Br* ≃ humbug, *Am* ≃ (hard) mint candy
6 *Can* **bêtises** *(injures)* insults

bêtisier [betizje] **NM** *(écrit)* collection of howlers; *(à la télévision)* collection of humorous TV out-takes; *Journ* **le b. de la semaine** gaffes of the week

béton [betɔ̃] **NM 1** *Constr* concrete; *Péj* **maintenant, il y a du b. partout** the place is just a vast expanse of concrete now; **b. armé/précontraint** reinforced/pre-stressed concrete **2** *Ftbl* **faire le b.** to pack the defence **3** *Fam (locution)* **laisse b.!** forget it!, drop it!
ADJ *Fam (solide ▸ argument)* cast-iron; **un dossier de candidature b.** an extremely thorough application◻
• **en béton ADJ 1** *Constr* concrete *(avant n)* **2** *Fam (solide ▸ estomac, alibi, argument)* cast-iron; *(▸ défense, garantie)* watertight, surefire; **la défense a un dossier en b.** the defence has a watertight case

bétonnage [betɔnaʒ] **NM 1** *Constr* concreting; *Fig Péj* **ils s'insurgent contre le b. du littoral** they are protesting against the way the coastline is being built up by property developers **2** *Ftbl* defensive play

bétonner [3] [betɔne] **VT 1** *Constr* to concrete; *Fig* **les promoteurs immobiliers qui bétonnent le littoral** the property developers who are building all along the coast **2** *Fam (préparer avec soin)* to work hard on◻; **il a bétonné son discours/dossier** he's worked really hard on his speech/application
VI *Ftbl* to pack the defence, to play defensively

bétonneur [betɔnœr] **NM** *Péj* = ruthless property developer who builds with no thought for the environment

bétonneuse [betɔnøz], **bétonnière** [betɔnjɛr] **NF** *Constr* cement mixer

bette [bɛt] **NF** *Bot* (Swiss) chard

betterave [bɛtrav] **NF** *Bot* **b. (potagère)** beet; **b. fourragère** mangel-wurzel; **b. (rouge)** *Br* beetroot, *Am* red beet; **b. sucrière** sugar beet

betteravier, -ère [bɛtravje, -ɛr] **ADJ** beet *(avant n)*
NM beet grower

beu [bø] **NF** *Fam Arg drogue* grass, weed, herb

beuglant [bøglɑ̃] **NM** *Fam Vieilli* sleazy nightclub

beuglante [bøglɑ̃t] **NF** *Fam (chanson)* song◻; *(cri)* yell; **pousser une b.** *(chanter)* to belt out a song; *(crier)* to give a yell

beuglement [bøgləmɑ̃] **NM 1** *(cri ▸ de la vache)* moo; *(▸ du taureau)* bellow; *(▸ d'une personne)* bellow, yell; **des beuglements** *(de vache)* mooing *(UNCOUNT)*, lowing *(UNCOUNT)*; *(de taureau)* bellowing *(UNCOUNT)*; *(d'une personne)* bellowing *(UNCOUNT)*, yelling *(UNCOUNT)*, bawling *(UNCOUNT)*; **pousser des beuglements** *(vache)* to moo, to low; *(taureau)* to bellow; *(personne)* to bellow, to yell, to bawl **2** *(bruit ▸ de la radio)* blaring noise

beugler [5] [bøgle] **VI 1** *(crier ▸ vache)* to moo, to low; *(▸ taureau)* to bellow; *(▸ chanteur, ivrogne)* to bellow, to bawl **2** *(être bruyant ▸ radio)* to blare
VT *(chanson)* to bawl out, to bellow out

beur [bœr] *Fam* **ADJ** *(culture, mode, musique)* = of people born in France of North African parents; *(personne)* = born in France of North African parents
• **Beur NMF** = person born in France of North African immigrant parents

Beurette [bœrɛt] **NF** *Fam* = young woman born in France of North African immigrant parents

beurk [bœrk] = **berk**

beurre [bœr] **NM** *Culin* **1** *(de laiterie)* butter; **au b.** *(biscuits)* (all-)butter *(avant n)*; **faire la cuisine au b.** to cook with butter; **du b. fondu** *Br* melted *or Am* drawn butter; **b. de baratte** butter from the churn; **b. clarifié** clarified butter; **b. demi-sel** slightly salted butter; **b. laitier** dairy butter; **b. non salé** unsalted butter; **b. salé** salted butter; **entrer dans qch comme dans du b.** to slice through sth like a hot knife through butter; *Fam* **faire son b.** to make money hand over fist; *Fam* **ça met du b. dans les épinards** it's a nice little earner; **vouloir le b. et l'argent du b.** to want to have one's cake and eat it; **il n'y en a pas plus que de b. en branche** *ou* **broche** *(inexistant)* there's no such thing; *(introuvable)* it's nowhere to be found **2** *(sauce, pâte)* **b. d'anchois** anchovy paste; **b. blanc/noir** white/black butter sauce; **b. de cacahuètes** peanut butter; **b. de cacao** cocoa butter; **b. composé** beurre composé; **b. d'escargot** = flavoured butter used in the preparation of snails; **b. manié** beurre manié **3** *Belg (locutions) Fam* **battre le b.** to get nowhere; *Fam* **le chat a mangé le b.** the game's up; *très Fam* **être le cul dans le b.** to be in clover

beurre-frais [bœrfrɛ] **ADJ INV** buttercup-yellow

beurrer [5] [bœre] **VT** *Culin (tartine, moule)* to butter
VI *Can Fam (exagérer)* to lay it on a bit thick
VPR se beurrer *très Fam* to get plastered, *Br* to get pissed

beurrerie [bœrri] **NF 1** *(laiterie)* (butter-producing) dairy **2** *(industrie)* butter industry

beurrier, -ère [bœrje, -ɛr] **ADJ** *(production, industrie)* butter *(avant n)*; *(région)* butter-producing
NM *(récipient)* butter dish

beuverie [bœvri] **NF** *Fam* drinking binge, bender

bévatron [bevatrɔ̃] **NM** *Phys* bevatron

bévue [bevy] **NF** *(gaffe)* blunder, gaffe; **commettre une b.** to make a gaffe

bey [bɛ] **NM** *Hist* bey

Beyrouth [berut] **NM** *Géog* Beirut, Beyrouth; **de B.** Beiruti; **B.-Est** East Beirut; **B.-Ouest** West Beirut

bézef [bezɛf] = **bésef**

BF [beef] **NF** *(abrév* **Banque de France***)* Bank of France

BFCE [beefseə] **NF** *(abrév* **Banque française du commerce extérieur***)* French foreign trade bank

Bhoutan, Bhutan [butɑ̃] **NM le B.** Bhutan; **vivre au B.** to live in Bhutan; **aller au B.** to go to Bhutan

bi- [bi] **PRÉF** bi-; **bilatéral** bilateral; **bipartisan** bipartisan

bi[1] [bi] **NM** *Can* **donner** *ou* **faire un bi** to lend a hand, to muck in

bi[2] [bi] **ADJ INV** *Fam (bisexuel)* bi

biacide [biasid] *Chim* **ADJ** diacidic
NM diacid

biais, -e [bjɛ, bjɛz] **ADJ** *(oblique)* slanting; **voûte biaise** skew arch
NM 1 *(obliquité)* slant; **le b. d'un mur** the slant of a wall
2 *Couture (bande)* bias binding; *(sens)* bias; **travailler dans le b.** to cut on the bias
3 *(moyen)* way; **j'ai trouvé un b. pour ne pas payer** I found a way of not paying; **par le b. de qch** through, via, by means of sth; **par le b. de qn** through sb
4 *(aspect)* angle; **je ne sais pas par quel b. le prendre** I don't know how *or* from what angle to approach him; **prendre le b.** to go off at a tangent
5 *(dans des statistiques)* bias
• **de biais ADV** *(aborder)* indirectly; **regarder qn de b.** to give sb a sidelong glance
• **en biais ADV** sideways, slantwise, at an angle; **regarder qn en b.** to give sb a sidelong glance; **traverser la rue en b.** to cross the street diagonally

biaiser [4] [bjeze] **VI** to prevaricate, to equivocate; **il va falloir b. pour avoir des places pour l'opéra** we'll have to be a bit clever to get tickets for the opera
VT *(résultats)* to distort

biathlon [biatlɔ̃] **NM** *Sport* biathlon

bibande [bibɑ̃d] *Tél* **ADJ** dual-band
NM *(téléphone portable)* dual-band *Br* mobile phone *or Am* cellphone

bibasique [bibazik] **ADJ** *Chim* dibasic

bibelot [biblo] **NM** *(précieux)* curio, bibelot; *(sans valeur)* trinket, knick-knack

biberon [bibrɔ̃] **NM** *Br* feeding *or Am* baby bottle; **l'heure du b.** feeding time; **donner le b. à un bébé/agneau** to bottle-feed a baby/lamb; **enfant nourri** *ou* **élevé au b.** bottle-fed baby; **il est encore au b.?** is he still being bottle-fed?; **prendre son b.** to have one's bottle; **il prend trois biberons par jour** he has three bottles *or* feeds a day; **prendre qn au b.** to start sb from the earliest possible age

biberonner [3] [bibrɔne] **VI** *Fam Hum* to tipple, to booze

bibi[1] [bibi] **NM** *Fam (chapeau)* (woman's) hat◻

bibi[2] [bibi] **PRON** *Fam Hum (moi)* yours truly; **les corvées, c'est pour b.** yours truly gets stuck *or Br* lumbered with the chores

bibine [bibin] NF *Fam* **c'est de la b.** *(boisson, bière)* it's dishwater; *(c'est facile)* it's a piece of cake

bibite [bibit] NF *Can Fam* **1** *(insecte)* bug; *(doryphore)* creepy-crawly, *Am* creepy-crawler; *(animal)* animal□ **2 il fait froid en b.** it's really cold□, it's freezing; **être en b. (contre qn)** to be teed off (with sb)

bible [bibl] NF **1** *Rel* **la B.** the Bible; **une b. de poche** a pocket Bible **2** *(référence)* bible; **la b. des mélomanes** the music lover's bible

bibliobus [biblijɔbys] NM *Br* mobile library, *Am* bookmobile

bibliographe [biblijɔgraf] NMF bibliographer

bibliographie [biblijɔgrafi] NF bibliography

bibliographique [biblijɔgrafik] ADJ bibliographic, bibliographical

bibliomane [biblijɔman] NMF book lover, *Spéc* bibliomaniac

bibliomanie [biblijɔmani] NF bibliomania

bibliophile [biblijɔfil] NMF book lover, *Spéc* bibliophile

bibliophilie [biblijɔfili] NF *(amour des livres)* bibliophily; *(science du bibliophile)* bibliophilism

bibliothécaire [biblijɔteker] NMF librarian

bibliothéconomie [biblijɔtekɔnɔmi] NF library science

bibliothèque [biblijɔtek] NF **1** *(lieu)* library; *(meuble)* bookcase; **b. de dépôt** legal copyright deposit library; **la B. de France** = the new French national library building; **b. municipale** public library; **la B. nationale** = the former French national library building, now containing only archive material and coins, medals etc; **la B. nationale de France** = French national library, comprising the "Bibliothèque de France" and the "Bibliothèque nationale"; **b. de prêt** lending library; **b. universitaire** university library
2 *(collection)* collection; **sa b. de livres d'art** his/her collection of art books; **c'est une b. ambulante** he's a walking encyclopedia; **b. de logiciels** software library; **la B. rose** = collection of books for very young children; **la B. verte** = collection of books for older children
3 *Ordinat (de programmes)* library
4 *Com* **b. de gare** station *Br* bookstall *or Am* newsstand

biblique [biblik] ADJ *Rel* biblical

Bi-bop® [bibɔp] NM *Tél* = mobile telephone system run by France Télécom

Bic® [bik] NM ballpoint (pen), *Br* ≃ Biro®, *Am* ≃ Bic®

bicaméral, -e, -aux, -ales [bikameral, -o] ADJ *Pol* two-chamber, *Sout* bicameral

bicaméralisme [bikameralism], **bicamérisme** [bikamerism] NM *Pol* two-chamber (political) system, *Sout* bicameralism

bicarbonate [bikarbɔnat] NM *Chim* bicarbonate; **b. de soude** bicarbonate of soda

bicentenaire [bisɑ̃tnɛr] ADJ bicentenary, bicentennial
NM bicentenary, bicentennial

bicéphale [bisefal] ADJ two-headed, *Sout* bicephalous

biceps [biseps] NM *Anat* biceps; *Fam* **avoir des b.** to have big biceps

biche [biʃ] NF **1** *Zool* doe, hind **2** *Fam (en appellatif)* **ma b.** darling, sweetheart

bicher [3] [biʃe] VI *Fam* **1** *(être satisfait)* to be tickled pink; **ça nous faisait b. de le voir s'empêtrer dans ses mensonges** it was really gratifying to see him getting tangled in his lies **2** *(tournure impersonnelle)* **ça biche?** how's it going?, how's things?

bichette [biʃɛt] NF **1** *Zool* hind calf, young hind *or* doe **2** *Fam (en appellatif)* **ma b.** darling, sweetheart

bichlorure [biklɔryr] NM *Chim* bichloride, dichloride

bichon, -onne [biʃɔ̃, -ɔn] NM,F *(chien)* Maltese (terrier)

bichonner [3] [biʃɔne] *Fam* VT **1** *(choyer)* to pamper□; **il aime se faire b.** he loves to be pampered **2** *(pomponner)* to spruce up
VPR **se bichonner** *(se pomponner)* to spruce oneself up

bichromate [bikrɔmat] NM *Chim* bichromate, dichromate

bichromie [bikrɔmi] NF *Typ* two-colour process

biclic [biklik] NM *Ordinat* double click

bicliquer [3] [biklike] VI *Ordinat* to double-click

biclo [biklo], **biclou** [biklu] NM *Fam* bike

bicolore [bikɔlɔr] ADJ two-coloured

biconcave [bikɔ̃kav] ADJ biconcave

biconvexe [bikɔ̃vɛks] ADJ biconvex

bicoque [bikɔk] NF shack

bicorne [bikɔrn] NM cocked *or* two-pointed hat

bicorps [bikɔr] *Aut* ADJ hatchback
NM hatchback (vehicle)

bicot [biko] NM **1** *Fam Zool (biquet)* kid□ **2** *très Fam* = offensive term used to refer to a North African Arab

bicross [bikrɔs] NM *Sport* cyclo-cross bicycle; **faire du b.** to do cyclo-cross

biculturalisme [bikyltyralism] NM biculturalism

biculturel, -elle [bikyltyrɛl] ADJ bicultural

bicyclette [bisiklɛt] NF **1** *(engin)* bicycle; **faire de la b.** to cycle; **apprendre à faire de la b.** to learn how to ride a bicycle; **monter à b.** to ride a bicycle; **allons-y à** *ou* **en b.** let's cycle, let's go there by bicycle; **b. de course** racer, racing bike; **b. de route** roadster, touring bike **2** *Sport* **la b.** cycling

bidasse [bidas] NM *Fam Mil (soldat) Br* squaddie, *Am* grunt

bide [bid] NM *Fam* **1** *(ventre)* belly, gut; **avoir/prendre du b.** to have/to develop a belly **2** *(échec)* flop, washout; **ça a été** *ou* **fait un b.** it was a complete flop *or* washout

bidet [bidɛ] NM **1** *(de toilette)* bidet **2** *Fam (cheval)* nag

bidimensionnel, -elle [bidimɑ̃sjɔnɛl] ADJ bidimensional

bidirectionnel, -elle, bi-directionnel, -elle [bidirɛksjɔnɛl] ADJ bidirectional

bidoche [bidɔʃ] NF *très Fam* meat□

bidon [bidɔ̃] ADJ INV *Fam (histoire, excuse, société)* phoney; *(numéro, adresse, information)* false□, bogus; *(élections)* rigged
NM **1** *(récipient)* can, tin; *Mil* water bottle, canteen; **b. d'essence** petrol can; **b. d'huile** oilcan; **b. de lait** *Br* milk churn, *Am* milk can **2** *Fam (ventre)* belly, gut **3** *Fam (mensonge)* **tout ça, c'est du b.** that's a load of garbage *or Br* rubbish; **je te jure que ce n'est pas du b.** I swear that's the honest truth
• **bidons** NMPL *Belg Fam (frusques)* togs, gear, threads; *(affaires)* things□, stuff

bidonnant, -e [bidɔnɑ̃, -ɑ̃t] ADJ *Fam* side-splitting, hysterical; **c'était b.** it was a scream *or* a hoot

bidonner [3] [bidɔne] **se bidonner** VPR *Fam* to kill oneself (laughing), to laugh one's head off; **qu'est-ce qu'on se bidonne avec eux!** it's a laugh a minute with them!

bidonville [bidɔ̃vil] NM shantytown

bidouillage [bidujaʒ] NM *Fam* tinkering; *Ordinat (d'un logiciel)* patching; **ce n'est pas vraiment réparé, c'est du b.** it hasn't really been fixed, it's just a patch-up job

bidouille [biduj] NF *Fam* quick fix

bidouiller [3] [biduje] VT *Fam* to tinker with; *Ordinat (logiciel)* to patch

bidouilleur, -euse [bidujœr, -øz] NM,F *Fam Ordinat* hacker, expert user□

bidule [bidyl] NM *Fam* **1** *(objet)* thingy, whatsit **2** *(personne)* thingy, what's-his-name, *f* what's-her-name; **eh, B., t'as pas vu ma sœur?** hey, you *or Am* buddy, seen my sister?

bief [bjɛf] NM *(de cours d'eau)* reach; *(de moulin)* race

bielle [bjɛl] NF *Tech* connecting rod; *Aut* **b. d'accouplement** coupling rod; *Aut* **b. de connexion** connecting rod; *Aut* **b. pendante** drop arm

biellette [bjɛlɛt] NF *Tech* rod

biélorusse [bjelɔrys] ADJ Belarusian, *Anciennement* Belorussian, Byelorussian
NM *(langue)* Belarusian, *Anciennement* Byelorussian
• **Biélorusse** NMF Belarusian, *Anciennement* Belorussian, Byelorussian

Biélorussie [bjelɔrysi] NF **la B.** Belarus, *Anciennement* Belorussia, Byelorussia

BIEN [bjɛ̃]

ADV
- well **1–3**
- right, correctly **4**
- really **6, 9**
- at least **12**
- good **1**
- very **6**
- a lot **8**
- quite a lot of **15**

ADJ
- good **1, 2**
- nice **3,4, 6**
- good-looking **3**
- well **5**

NM
- good **1, 2**
- possession, property **4, 5**
- good thing **3**

EXCLAM
- OK

ADV **1** *(de façon satisfaisante)* well; **tout allait b.** everything was going well *or* fine; **ça te va b.** *(aspect)* it suits you; *(taille)* it fits you; *Ironique* **ça te va b. de te plaindre!** you're a fine one to complain!; **il s'est b. remis de son opération** he recovered well *or* made a good recovery from his operation; **il s'en est b. tiré** he came out of it well; **elle se débrouille b. sans moi** she manages very well without me; **la pièce est très b. jouée** the acting in the play's very good; **il cuisine b.** he's a good cook; **elle écrit b.** *(style)* she writes well; *(calligraphie)* she has beautiful writing; **il parle b. (le) grec** his Greek is good, he speaks Greek well; **du travail b. fait** a job well done; **la pièce finit b.** the play has a happy ending; **ça commence b.!** it's got off to a good start!; *Ironique* here we go!; **on mange b. ici** the food is good here; **le grille-pain ne marche pas très b.** the toaster doesn't work very well; **la vis tient b.** the screw is secure *or* is in tight; **dors b.!** sleep well!; **il gagne b. sa vie** he earns a good living; **ils vivent b.** they have a comfortable life; **b. payé** well paid; **faire b.** to look good; **ce vase fait très b. sur la cheminée** the vase looks very good on the fireplace; **b. prendre qch** to take sth well; **il s'y est b. pris** he tackled it well; **il s'y est b. pris pour interviewer le ministre** he did a good job of interviewing the minister; **vivre b. qch** to have a positive experience of sth; **b. se tenir** to behave oneself; **tiens-toi b.!** *(à la rambarde)* hold on tight!; *(sur la chaise)* sit properly!; *(à table)* behave yourself!; **tu tombes b.!** you've come at (just) the right time!
2 *(du point de vue de la santé)* **aller** *ou* **se porter b.** to feel well *or* fine; **elle ne va pas très b. ces jours-ci** she's not very well at the moment; *Hum* **il se porte plutôt b.!** he doesn't look as if he's starving!
3 *(conformément à la raison, à la loi, à la morale)* well, decently; **b. agir envers qn** to do the proper *or* right *or* correct thing by sb; **b. se conduire** to behave well *or* decently; **tu as b. fait** you did the right thing, you did right; **tu fais b. de ne plus les voir** you're right not to see them any more; **il ferait b. de se faire oublier!** he'd be well advised to *or* he'd do well to *or* he'd better keep a low profile!; **tu ferais b. de partir plus tôt** you'd do well to leave earlier; **pour b. faire, nous devrions partir avant 9 heures** ideally, we should leave before 9
4 *(sans malentendu)* right, correctly; **si je vous comprends b.** if I understand you correctly *or* properly; **ai-je b. entendu ce que tu viens de dire?** did I hear you right?; **si je me souviens b.** if I remember right *or* correctly
5 *(avec soin)* **écoute-moi b.** listen (to me) carefully; **as-tu b. vérifié?** did you check properly?; **fais b. ce que l'on te dit** do exactly *or* just as you're told; **soigne-toi b.** take good care of yourself
6 *(suivi d'un adjectif) (très)* really, very; **c'est b. agréable** it's really *or* very nice; **b. déçu** really *or* terribly disappointed; **tu es b. sûr?** are you quite certain *or* sure?; **c'est b. bon** it's very *or* really good; **bois un thé b. chaud** have a nice hot cup of tea; **cette robe est b. chère** that dress is a bit on the expensive side *or* rather expensive

7 *(suivi d'un adverbe)* **tu habites b. loin** you live a long way away; **c'était il y a b. longtemps** it was a very long time ago; **embrasse-le b. fort** give him a big hug; **il est b. tard pour sortir** it's a bit late to go out; **b. souvent** (very) often; **b. avant/après** well before/after; **b. trop tôt** far *or* much too early; **c'est b. mieux** it's much better; **c'est b. plus joli comme ça** it looks much nicer like that

8 *(suivi d'un verbe) (beaucoup)* **on a b. ri** we had a good laugh, we laughed a lot; **hier soir, on a b. discuté** we had a good (long) discussion last night; **je t'aime b., tu sais** I like you a lot *or* I'm very fond of you, you know

9 *(véritablement)* **j'ai b. l'impression que...** I really have the feeling that...; **il a b. failli se noyer** he very nearly drowned; **sans b. se rendre compte de ce qu'il faisait** without being fully aware of *or* without fully realizing what he was doing

10 *(pour renforcer, insister)* **qui peut b. téléphoner à cette heure-ci?** who could that be calling at this hour?; **où peut-il b. être?** where on earth is he?; **je sais b. que tu dis la vérité** I know very well that you're not lying; **veux-tu b. te taire?** will you please be quiet?; **c'est b. lui** it IS him; **ce n'est pas lui, mais b. son associé que j'ai eu au téléphone** it wasn't him, but rather his partner I spoke to on the phone; **c'est b. ça** that's it, that's right; **c'est b. ce que je disais/pensais** that's just what I was saying/thinking; *Ironique* **c'est b. le moment d'en parler!** it's hardly the right time to talk about it!; **c'est b. ce qui me préoccupe!** that's (just) what's worrying me!; **vous vous appelez b. Anne, n'est-ce pas?** your name IS Anne, isn't it?; **j'ai pourtant b. entendu frapper** I'm sure I heard a knock at the door; **je le vois b. médecin** I can (quite) see him as a doctor; **je vais me plaindre – je comprends** *ou* **pense b.!** I'm going to complain – I should think so too!; **il ne m'aidera pas, tu penses b.!** he won't help me, you can be sure of that!; **c'est b. de lui, ça!** that's typical of him!, that's just like him!

11 *(volontiers)* **j'irais b. avec toi** I'd really like to go with you; **je te dirais b. quelque chose, mais je suis poli** I could say something rude but I won't; **je boirais b. quelque chose** I could do with *or* I wouldn't mind a drink; **je t'aurais b. accompagné, mais...** I'd have been happy to go with you, but...; **je l'aurais b. tué!** I could have killed him!

12 *(au moins)* at least; **ça fait b. 20 fois qu'on lui dit** he's/she's been told at least 20 times; **ils étaient b. 30** there were at least 30 of them; **il est b. 10 heures** it must be 10 o'clock at least; **il a b. 50 ans** he must be at least 50

13 *(exprimant la supposition, l'éventualité)* **tu verras b.** you'll see; **ça lui passera b.** he'll/she'll grow out of it; **ils pourraient b. refuser** they might well refuse; **ça se pourrait b.** it's perfectly possible

14 *(pourtant)* **mais il fallait b. le lui dire!** but he/she had to be told (all the same)!; **il faut b. le faire** it's got to be done

15 b. de, b. des *(suivi d'un nom)* quite a lot of; **j'ai eu b. du souci** I've had a lot to worry about; **b. des fois...** more than once...; **b. des gens** lots of *or* quite a lot of *or* quite a few people; **j'ai reçu b. des lettres** I received quite a lot of *or* a good many letters

16 *(dans la correspondance)* **b. à toi** love; **b. à vous** yours

ADJ INV 1 *(qui donne satisfaction)* good; **comment trouves-tu mon dessin? – très b.!** how do you like my drawing? – it's very nice *or* good!; **il est b., ton médecin?** is your doctor (any) good?; **elle serait b. dans le rôle de Turandot** she'd be *or* make a good Turandot; *Fam* **je recule? – non, vous êtes b. là** shall I move back? – no, you're all right *or* OK *or* fine like that; *Fam* **qu'est-ce qu'il est b. dans son dernier film!** he's great *or* really good in his new film!

2 *Scol (sur un devoir)* good; **assez b.** fair; **très b.** very good

3 *(esthétique ▸ personne)* good-looking, attractive; *(▸ chose)* nice, lovely; **je ne me trouve jamais de chaussures b.** I can never find (any) nice shoes; **tu es très b. en jupe** *(cela te sied)* you look very nice in a skirt; *(c'est acceptable pour l'occasion)* a skirt is perfectly all right; **elle est drôlement b., ta sœur!** *(jolie)* your sister's really good-looking!; **il est b. de sa personne** he's a good-looking man; **elle est b. de sa personne** she's a good-looking woman

4 *(convenable ▸ personne)* decent, nice; **ce ne sont pas des gens b.** they aren't decent people; **on ne rencontre pas que des gens b. par petites annonces** the people you meet through ads aren't always the right sort; *Fam* **ce serait b. de lui envoyer un peu d'argent** it'd be a good idea to send him/her some money; **ils se sont séparés et c'est b. comme ça** they've split up and it's better that way; **chacun a ses idées et c'est b. ainsi** everybody's got their own ideas and that's how it should be; **tout ça c'est très b., mais...** that's all well and good *or* all very well, but...; **c'est très b. à vous de n'avoir rien dit** it's very good of you not to have said anything; **ce n'est pas b. de tirer la langue** it's naughty *or* it's not nice to stick out your tongue; **ce n'est pas b. de tricher** you shouldn't cheat

5 *(en forme)* well; **elle n'est pas/est très b. en ce moment** she's not doing/she's doing well right now; **je n'étais pas b. hier** I wasn't feeling well yesterday; **se sentir b.** to feel fine *or* well; **se sentir b. dans sa peau** to feel at ease *or* happy with oneself; **vous ne vous sentez pas b.?** aren't you feeling well?; *(mentalement)* are you crazy?; *Fam* **il n'est pas b., celui-là!** he's got a problem, he has!; **me/te/***etc* **voilà b.!** NOW I'm/you're/*etc* in a fine mess!; *Fam* **là, on (n')est pas b.!** we're really in trouble now!

6 *(à l'aise)* **on est b. ici** it's nice here; **on est vraiment b. dans ce fauteuil** this armchair is really comfortable; **je suis b. avec toi** I like being with you

7 *(en bons termes)* **être b. avec qn** to be well in with sb; **ils sont b. ensemble** they're happy together; **se mettre b. avec qn** to get in with sb, to get into sb's good books

NM 1 *Phil & Rel* **le b.** good; **la différence entre le b. et le mal** the difference between good and evil *or* right and wrong; **faire le b.** to do good; **elle fait du b. autour d'elle** she does good (works) wherever she goes; **rendre le b. pour le mal** to return good for evil

2 *(ce qui est agréable, avantageux)* **c'est pour son b.** it's for his/her good; **c'est pour ton b. que je dis ça** I'm saying this for your own good *or* benefit; **c'est ton b. que je veux** I only want what's best for you; **en tout b. tout honneur** *(proposition, affaire)* (fair and) above-board; **le b. commun** *ou* **général** the common good; **c'est pour le b. de tous/de l'entreprise** it's for the common good/the good of the firm; **pour le b. public** in the public interest; **vouloir du b. à qn** to wish sb well; **elle ne te voulait pas que du b.** her motives weren't entirely honourable; **dire/penser du b. de** to speak/to think well of; **si tu savais le b. qu'on dit de toi** you should hear the wonderful things people say about you; **continue à me masser, ça fait du b.** carry on massaging me, it's doing me good; **cela fait du b. de se dégourdir les jambes** it's nice to be able to stretch your legs; *Fam* **les piqûres, ça ne fait pas de b.!** injections are no fun!; *Fam* **je me suis cogné l'orteil, ça fait pas du b.!** I banged my toe, it's quite painful!; **faire du b.** *ou* **le plus grand b. à qn** *(médicament, repos)* to do sb good, to benefit sb; **la promenade m'a fait du b.** the walk did me good; **le dentiste ne m'a pas fait du b.!** the dentist really hurt me!; **un peu de pluie ferait du b. aux plantes** some rain would do the plants good *or* wouldn't hurt the plants; **cela m'a fait du b. de te parler** it did me good to talk to you; **une subvention ferait du b. aux agriculteurs** a subsidy would be of great help to the farming community; *Fam* **laisser tomber les livres par terre, ça ne leur fait pas du b.** you don't do a book too much good by dropping it on the floor; **la séparation leur fera le plus grand b.** being apart will do them a lot *or* a world of good; **le repos m'a fait (un) grand b.** the rest did me the world *or* a power of good; *Ironique* **grand b. te/lui fasse!** much good may it do you/him/her!; **b. m'en a pris** it was just as well I did it; **b. leur en a pris de ne pas l'écouter** how right they were not to listen to him/her, it was just as well they didn't listen to him/her; *Fam* **ça fait du b. par où ça passe!** aah, I feel better for that!

3 *(bienfait)* good *or* positive thing, benefit; **la restructuration sera un b. pour l'entreprise** reorganization will be a positive move for the firm

4 *(propriété personnelle)* possession, piece *or* item of property; *(argent)* fortune; **mon b. t'appartient** what's mine is yours; **il a mangé tout son b. en trois mois** he squandered his fortune in three months; *Fam* **ils ont un petit b. en Ardèche** they have a bit of land in the Ardèche; **la jeunesse est un b. précieux** youth is a precious asset; **tous mes biens** all my worldly goods, all I'm worth; **les biens temporels** *ou* **de ce monde** material possessions, worldly goods; *Fam* **avoir du b. au soleil** to be well-off *or* rich

5 *Écon* possession; *Jur* assets; **biens** possessions, property; **biens capitaux** capital goods *or* items; **biens communs** marital property; **biens communaux** communal lands; **biens de consommation** consumer products, consumer goods; **biens de consommation courante** consumer goods; **biens de consommation durables** consumer durables; **biens de consommation non durables** disposable goods; **biens corporels** tangible assets; **biens dotaux** dowry; **biens durables** consumer durables, durable goods; **biens d'équipement** capital equipment *or* goods; **biens de famille** family property; **biens fonciers** (real) property, real estate; **biens immédiatement disponibles** off-the-shelf goods; **biens immeubles, biens immobiliers** real assets; **biens incorporels** intangible property; **biens en indivision** jointly-owned goods; **biens insaisissables** non-seizable property; **biens intermédiaires** intermediate goods; **b. marchand** commodity; **biens meubles, biens mobiliers** personal property *or* estate, movables; **biens d'occasion** second-hand goods; **biens personnels** personal property; **biens de première nécessité** staples; **biens présents et à venir** = all present and future property of an estate; **biens privés/publics** private/public property; **biens propres** = spouse's separate property; **biens de production** producer *or* capital goods; **biens saisis** distress; **biens et services** goods and services; *Compta* **biens sociaux** corporate assets *or* funds; **biens vacants** ownerless property

6 *Hist* **biens nationaux** = property confiscated from nobles during the Revolution and resold

EXCLAM 1 *(indiquant une transition)* OK, right (then); **b., je t'écoute** right *or* OK, I'm listening; **b.! où en étions-nous?** right! where were we?

2 *(marquant l'approbation)* **je n'irai pas! – b., n'en parlons plus!** I won't go! – very well *or* all right (then), let's drop the subject!; **c'est décidé! – b.!** we've decided! – good *or* fine!; **très b., je vais avec toi** fine *or* very well, I'll go with you; **fort b.** fine; **b., b., on y va** all right, all right *or* OK, OK, let's go

• **bien entendu ADV** of course; **tu m'aideras? – b. entendu!** will you help me? – of course *or* that goes without saying!

• **bien entendu que CONJ** of course; **b. entendu que j'aimerais y aller** of course I'd like to go

• **bien que CONJ** despite the fact that, although, though; **b. que je comprenne votre problème, je ne peux vous aider** although *or* though I understand your problem, I can't help you; **b. qu'ayant travaillé cette question, je serais en peine d'en parler** although I've studied this question, I would be hard put to speak about it; **sa maison, b. que petite, est agréable** small though it is, his/her house is nice

• **bien sûr ADV** of course; **viendras-tu? – b. sûr!** will you come? – of course (I will)!; **puis-je le prendre? – b. sûr** may I take it? – of course *or* please do *or* by all means

• **bien sûr que CONJ** of course; **b. sûr qu'elle n'avait rien compris!** of course she hadn't understood a thing!; **c'est vrai? – b. sûr que oui!** is it true? – of course it is!

bien-aimé, -e [bjɛ̃neme] *(mpl* **bien-aimés,** *fpl* **bien-aimées) ADJ** beloved

NM,F beloved

bien-être [bjɛ̃nɛtr] **NM INV 1** *(aise)* well-being; **une agréable sensation de b.** a wonderful feeling of well-being **2** *(confort matériel)* (material) well-being **3** *Can* **b. social** *Br* social security, *Am* welfare

bienfaisance [bjɛ̃fəzɑ̃s] **NF 1** *(charité)* charity **2** *Littéraire (générosité)* benevolence

• **de bienfaisance ADJ** *(bal)* charity *(avant n)*; **association** *ou* **œuvre de b.** charity, charitable organization; **travailler pour les œuvres de b.** to do charity work

bienfaisant, -e [bjɛ̃fəzɑ̃, -ɑ̃t] ADJ 1 *(bénéfique ▸ effet, climat)* beneficial, *Sout* salutary 2 *(indulgent ▸ personne)* kind, kindly, *Sout* beneficent

bienfait [bjɛ̃fɛ] NM 1 *Littéraire (acte de bonté)* kindness; **combler qn de bienfaits** to shower sb with kindness; *Prov* **un b. n'est jamais perdu** = a good deed will be rewarded 2 *(effet salutaire)* benefit; **les bienfaits d'un séjour à la montagne** the benefits *or* beneficial effects of a stay in the mountains

bienfaiteur, -trice [bjɛ̃fetœr, -tris] NM,F benefactor, *f* benefactress; **b. du genre humain** great man, *f* great woman

bien-fondé [bjɛ̃fɔ̃de] *(pl* **bien-fondés***)* NM *(d'une revendication)* rightfulness; *(d'un argument)* validity; **établir le b. de qch** to substantiate sth

bien-fonds [bjɛ̃fɔ̃] NM *Jur* real estate

bienheureux, -euse [bjɛ̃nørø, -øz] ADJ 1 *Rel* blessed 2 *(heureux ▸ personne, vie)* happy, blissful; *(▸ hasard)* fortunate, lucky
NM,F *Rel* **les b.** the blessed *or* blest; **dormir comme un b.** to sleep the sleep of the just

bien-jugé [bjɛ̃ʒyʒe] *(pl* **bien-jugés***)* NM *Jur* just and lawful decision

biennal, -e, -aux, -ales [bjenal, -o] ADJ biennial
• **biennale** NF biennial arts festival

bien-pensant, -e [bjɛ̃pɑ̃sɑ̃, -ɑ̃t] *(mpl* **bien-pensants,** *fpl* **bien-pensantes***)* *Péj* ADJ *(conformiste)* conservative, conformist
NM,F conservative person, conformist

bienséance [bjɛ̃seɑ̃s] NF decorum, propriety; **les bienséances** the proprieties

bienséant, -e [bjɛ̃seɑ̃, -ɑ̃t] ADJ decorous, proper, becoming; **il n'est pas b. d'élever la voix** it is unbecoming *or* it isn't proper *or* it isn't done to raise one's voice

bientôt [bjɛ̃to] ADV 1 *(prochainement)* soon, before long; **on est b. arrivés?** are we nearly there?, will we soon be there?; **à (très) b.!** see you soon!; **je reviens b.** I'll be back soon; **il sera b. de retour** he'll soon be back, he'll be back before long; **j'ai b. fini** I've almost finished; **il est b. midi** it's nearly midday; **b., ce ne sera plus qu'un mauvais souvenir** it'll soon be nothing but a bad memory; **l'accord de paix n'est pas pour b.** it is unlikely that the peace agreement will be signed soon; **c'est pour b.?** will it be long?; *(naissance)* is it *or* is the baby due soon?; *Fam* **c'est pas b. fini ce vacarme?** have you quite finished (making all that racket)? 2 *(rapidement)* soon, quickly, in no time; **il eut b. fait de reprendre ses esprits** he came around in no time; **cela est b. dit** that's easier said than done

bienveillance [bjɛ̃vejɑ̃s] NF 1 *(qualité)* benevolence, kindliness; **parler de qn avec b.** to speak favourably of sb 2 *(dans des formules de politesse)* **je sollicite de votre b. un entretien** I beg to request an interview

bienveillant, -e [bjɛ̃vejɑ̃, -ɑ̃t] ADJ *(personne)* benevolent, kindly; *(regard, sourire)* kind, kindly, gentle

bienvenu, -e [bjɛ̃vny] ADJ *(remarque)* opportune, apposite; *(repas, explication etc)* welcome
NM,F **être le b.** to be welcome; **soyez les bienvenus dans notre ville** welcome to our city; **tu seras toujours la bienvenue chez nous** you'll always be welcome here, we'll always be pleased to have you with us; **cet argent était vraiment le b.** that money was most welcome
• **bienvenue** NF welcome; **souhaiter la bienvenue à qn** to welcome sb EXCLAM welcome!; *Can (de rien)* you're welcome!; **bienvenue à toi, ami!** welcome to you, my friend!
• **de bienvenue** ADJ *(discours)* welcoming; *(cadeau)* welcome *(avant n)*

bière [bjɛr] NF 1 *(alcool)* beer; **b. blanche** wheat beer; **b. blonde** lager; **b. brune** *Br* brown ale, *Am* dark beer; **b. (à la) pression** draught beer; *Fam* **c'est de la petite b.** it's small beer; *Fam* **ce n'est pas de la petite b.** it's quite something 2 *(cercueil)* coffin, *Am* casket; **mettre qn en b.** to place sb in his/her *Br* coffin *or Am* casket; **assister à la mise en b.** to be present when the body is placed in the *Br* coffin *or Am* casket

biffe [bif] *Fam Arg mil* NF infantry
• **Biffe** NF **la B.** = nickname of the French infantry

biffer [3] [bife] VT to cross out, to score out; **tu peux b. ce nom de ta liste** you can cross *or* score this name off your list

biffeton [biftɔ̃] = **bifton**

biffin [bifɛ̃] NM 1 *Fam Arg mil* foot soldier, footslogger 2 *Fam (chiffonnier)* ragman, *Br* rag-and-bone man

biffure [bifyr] NF crossing out, stroke; **faire des biffures sur une lettre** to cross things out in a letter

bifide [bifid] ADJ bifid

bifidus [bifidys] NM *Biol* bifidus; **yaourt au b.** live yoghurt

bifocal, -e, -aux, -ales [bifɔkal, -o] ADJ *Opt* bifocal; **lunettes bifocales** bifocals

bifteck [biftɛk] NM 1 *(tranche)* (piece of) steak; **un b. dans le filet** a piece of fillet steak; **un b. haché** a beefburger; *Fam* **défendre/gagner son b.** to look after/to earn one's bread and butter 2 *(catégorie de viande)* steak; **du b. haché** *Br* (best) mince, *Am* lean ground beef

bifton [biftɔ̃] NM *Fam (billet de banque)* note□, *Am* greenback; *(de transport, de spectacle)* ticket□

bifurcation [bifyrkasjɔ̃] NF 1 *(intersection)* junction, turning 2 *(changement)* change (of course)

bifurquer [3] [bifyrke] VI 1 *(route)* to branch off, *Sout* to bifurcate; *(conducteur)* to turn off; **on a alors bifurqué sur Lyon** we then turned off towards Lyons; **b. à gauche** to turn left 2 *(changer)* **b. vers** to branch off into, to switch to; **il a bifurqué vers la politique** he branched out into politics

big(-)bang [bigbɑ̃g] NM *Phys & Fin* big bang

bigame [bigam] ADJ bigamous
NMF bigamist

bigamie [bigami] NF bigamy

bigarade [bigarad] NF *Bot* bitter *or* Seville orange

bigarré, -e [bigare] ADJ *(fleur)* variegated, multicoloured; *(vêtement)* multicoloured; *(foule)* colourful

bigarreau, -x [bigaro] NM *Bot (cerise)* bigarreau (cherry)

bigarrer [3] [bigare] VT *Littéraire (colorer)* to variegate, to colour in many shades

bigarrure [bigaryr] NF variegation, multicoloured effects

big band [bigbɑ̃d] *(pl* **big bands***)* NM *Mus* big band

bigle [bigl] *Fam Vieilli* ADJ *(myope)* short-sighted□; *(qui louche)* cross-eyed□
NMF *(myope)* short-sighted person□; *(qui louche)* cross-eyed person□

bigler [3] [bigle] *Fam* VI to squint
VT *(observer)* to eye, to check out, *Br* to clock
• **bigler sur** VT IND to eye (with greed)

bigleux, -euse [biglø, -øz] *Fam* ADJ *(myope)* short-sighted□; *(qui louche)* cross-eyed□
NM,F *(myope)* short-sighted person□; *(qui louche)* cross-eyed person□

bigophone [bigɔfɔn] NM *Fam (téléphone)* phone, *Br* blower, *Am* horn; **passe-moi un coup de b.** give me a buzz *or Br* a bell

bigophoner [3] [bigɔfɔne] VI *Fam* to make a phone call□; **b. à qn** to give sb a buzz *or Br* a bell

bigorneau, -x [bigɔrno] NM *Zool (mollusque)* periwinkle, winkle

bigorner [3] [bigɔrne] *très Fam* VT *(défoncer ▸ moto, voiture)* to smash up
VPR **se bigorner** to scrap, to fight□

bigot, -e [bigo, -ɔt] *Rel* ADJ *(dévot)* sanctimonious, holier-than-thou
NM,F religious zealot

> Il faut noter que le terme anglais **bigot** est un faux ami. Il se rapporte au sectarisme religieux et non à une attitude excessivement dévote.

bigoterie [bigɔtri] NF *Rel* (religious) bigotry

bigotisme [bigɔtism] NM *Rel* (religious) bigotry

bigoudi [bigudi] NM curler, roller; **(se) mettre des bigoudis** to put one's hair into curlers *or* rollers; **elle est sortie en bigoudis** she went out with her hair in curlers *or* rollers

bigre [bigr] EXCLAM *Fam Vieilli* gosh!, my!

bigrement [bigrəmɑ̃] ADV *Fam (très) Br* jolly, *Am* mighty; **il fait b. froid ici** it's *Br* jolly *or Am* mighty cold in here; **ça a b. changé** it has changed a heck of a lot

biguine [bigin] NF *Mus & (danse)* beguine

bihebdo [biɛbdo] NM biweekly

bihebdomadaire [biɛbdɔmadɛr] ADJ biweekly, twice-weekly

bijection [biʒɛksjɔ̃] NF *Math* bijection

bijou, -x [biʒu] NM 1 *(parure)* jewel; **bijoux** jewellery, jewels; **bijoux de famille** family jewels *or* jewellery; *très Fam Fig (sexe masculin)* family jewels, *Br* wedding tackle; **bijoux fantaisie** costume jewellery 2 *(fleuron)* gem; **un b. de l'art rococo** a gem of Rococo art; **cette montre est un b. de précision** this watch is a marvel of precision 3 *Fam (en appellatif)* **bonjour, mon b.** hello, precious *or* my love

bijouterie [biʒutri] NF 1 *(bijoux)* jewels, jewellery
2 *(magasin) Br* jeweller's (shop), *Am* jewelry store
3 *(industrie)* jewellery business
4 *(fabrication)* jewellery-making

bijoutier, -ère [biʒutje, -ɛr] NM,F jeweller

Bikini® [bikini] NM bikini

bilabiale [bilabjal] *Ling* ADJ F bilabial
NF bilabial (consonant)

bilan [bilɑ̃] NM 1 *Fin & Compta* statement (of accounts); *(de l'actif, des responsabilités)* schedule; *Banque (d'un compte)* balance; **dresser** *ou* **établir** *ou* **faire le b.** to draw up the balance sheet; **déposer le** *ou* **son b.** to file one's petition (in bankruptcy); **b. annuel** annual accounts; **b. commercial** market report; **b. (comptable)** balance sheet; **b. condensé** summary balance sheet; **b. consolidé** consolidated balance sheet; **b. de l'exercice** end-of-year balance sheet; **b. financier** financial statement; **b. de groupe** consolidated balance sheet; **b. intérimaire** interim statement; **b. de liquidation** statement of affairs; **b. d'ouverture** opening balance sheet; **b. prévisionnel** forecast balance sheet; **b. social** social report
2 *(appréciation)* appraisal, assessment; *(résultats)* results; **faire le b. de qch** to take stock of *or* to assess sth; **arrivé à 40 ans, on fait souvent le b.** you often stop to take stock when you reach 40; **b. de carrière** = summary of one's employment record; **b. de compétence** = summary of one's skills; **quel est le b. de ces discussions?** what is the end result of these talks?, what have these talks amounted to?; **le b. définitif fait état de 20 morts** the final death toll stands at 20; **un b. économique positif** positive economic results 3 *Méd* **b. (de santé)** (medical) check-up; **se faire faire un b. (de santé)** to have a check-up; *Fig* **faire le b. de santé d'une entreprise** to assess *or* to evaluate the state of a company

bilantiel [bilɑ̃sjɛl] ADJ balance-sheet

bilatéral, -e, -aux, -ales [bilateral, -o] ADJ bilateral, two-way

bilatéralisme [bilateralism] NM *Pol* bilateralism

bilboquet [bilbɔkɛ] NM 1 *(jeu)* cup-and-ball game 2 *Typ* small job

bile [bil] NF 1 *Physiol* bile; *Arch & Littéraire* choler 2 *Fam (locutions)* **se faire de la b.** to fret; **je me suis fait beaucoup de b. pour toi** I was worried sick about you; **te fais pas de b.** don't you fret *or* worry

bileux, -euse [bilø, -øz] ADJ *Fam* easily worried□; **je n'ai jamais été du genre b.** I never was one to worry about things, I never was much of a worrier

biliaire [biljɛr] ADJ *Physiol (vaisseaux)* biliary; *Méd* **calcul b.** gallstone, *Spéc* biliary calculus; *Anat* **vésicule b.** gall bladder; *Méd* **cirrhose b.** cirrhosis (of the liver)

bilieux, -euse [biljø, -øz] ADJ 1 *(pâle ▸ teint)* bilious, sallow, yellowish 2 *(colérique ▸ per-*

sonne, tempérament) testy, irascible **3** *(inquiet)* anxious

bilingue [bilɛ̃g] **ADJ 1** *(Ling)* bilingual **2** *Can Fam (bisexuel)* bi

NMF 1 *(Ling)* bilingual speaker **2** *Can Fam (bisexuel)* bi

bilinguisme [bilɛ̃gɥism] **NM** bilingualism

billard [bijar] **NM 1** *(jeu)* billiards *(singulier)*; **faire un b.** to play a game of billiards; **b. américain** pool; **b. anglais** snooker; **b. russe** bar billiards

2 *(salle ▸ gén)* billiard room; *(▸ pour billard anglais)* snooker room; *(▸ pour billard américain)* pool room

3 *(meuble ▸ gén)* billiard table; *(▸ pour billard anglais)* snooker table; *(▸ pour billard américain)* pool table; **b. électrique** *(jeu)* pinball; *(machine)* pinball machine

4 *Fam (table d'opération)* **monter** *ou* **passer sur le b.** to be operated (on)ᵓ, to have an operationᵓ; **faire passer qn sur le b.** to open sb up

bille¹ [bij] **NF 1** *(de verre)* marble; *Fig* **placer ses billes** to get oneself in; *Fig* **reprendre ses billes** to pull out *(of a deal)*; *Fam* **toucher sa b. en** to be *Br* bloody *or Am* darned good at; **en mécanique, je touche pas ma b.** I haven't got a clue about mechanics

2 *(de billard)* ball; **être chauve comme une b. de billard** to be bald *Br* as a coot *or Am* as an egg

3 *Ind & Tech* ball; **b. de roulement** ball bearing

4 *Fam (tête)* mug; **avoir une bonne b.** to look a good sort; **avoir une b. de clown** to have a funny face

5 *Fam (niais)* mug

• **à bille ADJ** *(crayon, stylo)* ballpoint *(avant n)*; *(déodorant)* roll-on *(avant n)*

• **bille en tête ADV** straight, straightaway; **il est allé b. en tête se plaindre à la direction** he went shooting off to complain to the management

bille² [bij] **NF** *(tronçon de bois)* saw log

billet [bijɛ] **NM 1** *(gén)* ticket; **b. d'avion/de train/de concert/de loterie** plane/train/concert/lottery ticket; **voyageurs munis de billets** ticket holders; **retenez** *ou* **réservez les billets à l'avance** book ahead; **b. aller** *ou* **simple** *Br* (single) ticket, *Am* one-way ticket; **b. aller-retour** *Br* return *or Am* roundtrip ticket; **b. circulaire** *Br* day return (ticket), *Am* roundtrip ticket; **b. électronique** e-ticket, electronic ticket; **b. de faveur** complimentary ticket; **b. de retour** return ticket

2 *(argent)* **b. (de banque)** *Br* note, banknote, *Am* bill; **le nouveau b. de 50 euros** the new 50-euro *Br* note *or Am* bill; *Vieilli* **un b.** *(dix francs)* ten francs; **le b. vert** the dollar, the US currency; **faux b.** forged banknote

3 *Com & Fin (effet)* note, bill; **b. de complaisance** accommodation bill; **b. à ordre** promissory note, note of hand; **b. au porteur** bearer bill; **b. de reconnaissance de dettes** IOU; **b. du Trésor** Treasury bill; *Banque* **b. de trésorerie** commercial paper

4 *(message)* note; **b. doux** *ou* **galant** billet doux, love letter; *Journ* **b. d'humeur** column

5 *Mil* **b. de logement** billet

6 *Fam (locutions)* **je te fiche mon b. que tu te trompes** I'd bet my bottom dollar *or* my boots that you're wrong; **elle est enceinte, je t'en fiche mon b.** I bet you anything she's pregnant

billétique [bijetik] **NF** *Banque & Ordinat* cash dispenser technology

billette [bijɛt] **NF 1** *(morceau de bois)* billet, piece of firewood **2** *(lingot d'acier)* billet **3** *Archit* billet

billetterie [bijɛtri] **NF 1** *(opérations)* ticket distribution; *(guichet)* ticket office; **b. automatique** ticket machine **2** *Banque (distributeur) Br* cashpoint, *Am* ATM

billettiste [bijɛtist] **NMF 1** *(vendeur)* ticket seller **2** *(journaliste)* columnist

billevesées [bijvəze] **NFPL** *Littéraire* nonsense, twaddle

billion [biljɔ̃] **NM 1** *(million de millions)* trillion, *Br Vieilli* billion **2** *Arch (milliard)* billion, *Br Vieilli* milliard

billot [bijo] **NM** *(de bourreau, d'enclume)* block; **finir** *ou* **périr sur le b.** to be beheaded

bilobé, -e [bilɔbe] **ADJ** bilobate, bilobed

bimane [biman] *Zool* **ADJ** bimanous

NMF bimane

bimbeloterie [bɛ̃blɔtri] **NF 1** *(babioles)* knick-knacks **2** *(commerce)* fancy goods business

bimbelotier, -ère [bɛ̃blɔtje, -ɛr] **NM,F 1** *(fabricant)* fancy goods manufacturer **2** *(vendeur)* fancy goods dealer

bimbo [bimbo] **NF** *Fam Péj* bimbo

bi-média [bimedja] **ADJ** bi-media

bimensuel, -elle [bimɑ̃sɥɛl] **ADJ** twice monthly, *Br* fortnightly, *Am* semimonthly

NM *(revue) Br* fortnightly, *Am* semimonthly

bimestriel, -elle [bimɛstrijɛl] **ADJ** bimonthly

NM *(revue)* bimonthly

bimétallique [bimetalik] **ADJ** bimetallic

bimétallisme [bimetalism] **NM** bimetallism

bimillénaire [bimilenɛr] **ADJ** bimillenary

NM bimillenary

bimoteur [bimɔtœr] *Aviat* **ADJ M** twin-engined

NM twin-engined plane *or* aircraft

binage [binaʒ] **NM** *Agr* hoeing

binaire [binɛr] **ADJ 1** *Math & Ordinat* binary; **langage b.** binary notation **2** *Littérature & Mus* binary

NF *Astron* binary (star)

biner¹ [3] [bine] **VT** *Agr* to hoe

biner² [3] [bine] **VI** *Rel* = to say mass twice a day

binette [binɛt] **NF 1** *Agr* hoe **2** *Fam (visage)* mug, faceᵓ **3** *Can Ordinat* smiley, emoticon

bineuse [binøz] **NF** *Agr* cultivator

bing [biŋ] **ONOMAT** thwack!, smack!

bingo [biŋgo] **NM 1** *(jeu)* bingo; **jouer au b.** to play bingo **2** *Can Fam (révolte)* prison riotᵓ

EXCLAM bingo!

biniou [binju] **NM 1** *Mus (instrument de musique)* (Breton) bagpipes **2** *Fam (téléphone)* phone, *Br* blower, *Am* horn; **filer un coup de b. à qn** to give sb a buzz *or Br* a bell

binoclard, -e [binɔklar, -ard] *Fam Péj* **ADJ être b.** to wear glassesᵓ *or Br* specs

NM,F four-eyes, *Br* speccy

binocle [binɔkl] **NM** *(lorgnon)* pince-nez

• **binocles NMPL OU NFPL** *Fam (lunettes)* glassesᵓ, *Br* specs

binoculaire [binɔkylɛr] **ADJ** *Opt* binocular

binôme [binom] **NM 1** *Math* binomial; **le b. de Newton** the binomial theorem **2** *Fam (étudiant)* partnerᵓ; **travailler en b.** to work in twosᵓ

binomial, -e, -aux, -ales [binɔmjal, -o] **ADJ** *Math* binomial

binouze [binuz] **NF** *Fam (bière)* beerᵓ; **on va se boire une b.?** *Br* fancy a pint?, *Am* want to go for a beer?

binz [bins] **NM 1** *(chose compliquée)* **quel b. pour trouver sa maison!** it was a real performance *or* hassle *or Br* carry-on finding his/her house! **2** *(désordre)* shambles *(singulier)*

bio [bjo] **ADJ INV** *(nourriture, aliment)* organic

NF *Fam* **1** *(abrév* **biographie***)* biog **2** *(abrév* **biologie***)* biologyᵓ; *Scol & Univ* **faire de la b.** to do biology

biocarburant [bjokarbyrɑ̃] **NM** *Écol* biofuel

biochimie [bjoʃimi] **NF** biochemistry

biochimique [bjoʃimik] **ADJ** biochemical

biochimiste [bjoʃimist] **NMF** biochemist

bioclimat [bjoklima] **NM** bioclimate

bioclimatique [bjoklimatik] **ADJ** bioclimatic

bioclimatologie [bjoklimatɔlɔʒi] **NF** bioclimatology

biodégradable [bjodegradabl] **ADJ** *Écol* biodegradable

biodiesel [bjodjezɛl] **NM** biodiesel

biodiversité [bjodivɛrsite] **NF** *Biol* biodiversity

bioénergétique [bjoenɛrʒetik] **ADJ** *Biol & Psy* bioenergetic

bioéthique [bjoetik] **NF** *Méd* bioethics *(singulier)*

biogenèse [bjoʒənɛz] **NF** *Biol* biogenesis

biographe [bjɔgraf] **NMF** biographer

biographie [bjɔgrafi] **NF** biography; **b. officielle** authorized biography; **b. romancée** fictionalized biography, biographical novel

biographique [bjɔgrafik] **ADJ** biographical

bio-industrie [bjoɛ̃dystri] **NF** biotechnology industry

bio-informatique [bjoɛ̃fɔrmatik] **NF** bioinformatics *(singulier)*

biologie [bjɔlɔʒi] **NF** biology

biologique [bjɔlɔʒik] **ADJ 1** *Biol* biological **2** *(naturel ▸ produit, aliment)* organic

biologiste [bjɔlɔʒist] **NMF** biologist

biomasse [bjomas] **NF** *Biol* biomass

biomatériau, -x [bjɔmaterjo] **NM** *Méd* biomaterial

biomédical, -e, -aux, -ales [bjɔmedikal, -o] **ADJ** biomedical

biométrie [bjɔmetri] **NF** *Biol & Math* biometry, biometrics *(singulier)*

biométrique [bjɔmetrik] **ADJ** biometric

biomoléculaire [bjɔmɔlekylɛr] **ADJ** *Biol* biomolecular

bionique [bjɔnik] **ADJ** bionic

NF bionics *(singulier)*

biophysicien, -enne [bjɔfizisjɛ̃, -ɛn] **NM,F** biophysicist

biophysique [bjɔfizik] **NF** biophysics *(singulier)*

biopsie [bjɔpsi] **NF** *Biol & Méd* biopsy

biopuce [bjopys] **NF** biochip

biorythme [bjɔritm] **NM** *Biol & Physiol* biorhythm

BIOS [bjɔs] **NM** *Ordinat (abrév* **Basic Input/Output System***)* BIOS

biosciences [bjɔsjɑ̃s] **NFPL** biosciences, life sciences

biosécurité [bjɔsekyrite] **NF** biosecurity

biosphère [bjɔsfɛr] **NF** *Biol* biosphere

biosynthèse [bjɔsɛ̃tɛz] **NF** *Biol & Chim* biosynthesis

biotechnique [bjɔtɛknik], **biotechnologie** [bjtɛknɔlɔʒi] **NF** *Biol* biotechnology

biotechnologique [bjɔtɛknɔlɔʒik] **ADJ** *Biol* biotechnological

bioterrorisme [bjɔterɔrism] **NM** bioterrorism

bioterroriste [bjɔterɔrist] **ADJ** bioterrorist

NMF bioterrorist

biothérapie [bjɔterapi] **NF** *Biol & Méd* biotherapy

biotope [bjɔtɔp] **NM** *Écol* biotope

biovigilance [bjovizilɑ̃s] **NF 1** *(en ce qui concerne les biotechnologies)* GM monitoring **2** *(en ce qui concerne les prélèvements biologiques)* = monitoring the health and safety of biological samples, removed organs etc

bioxyde [bjɔksid] **NM** *Chim* dioxide

bip [bip] **NM 1** *(signal sonore)* beep; **"parlez après le b. (sonore)"** "please speak after the beep *or* tone"; **faire b.** to bleep; **b. de censure** censor bleep **2** *(appareil)* pager, beeper

biparti, -e [biparti] **ADJ 1** *Bot* bipartite **2** *Pol* bipartite, two-party *(avant n)*

bipartisme [bipartism] **NM** *Pol* bipartism, two-party system

bipartite [bipartit] = **biparti**

bip-bip [bipbip] *(pl* **bips-bips***)* **NM** bleep, bleeping sound *or* tone; **faire b.** to bleep

• **Bip-Bip NM** *(personnage de dessin animé)* Road Runner

bipède [bipɛd] **ADJ** *(personne, animal)* biped

NM 1 *(deux pattes du cheval)* = any two legs of a horse **2** *Fam Hum (individu)* two-legged creature

biper [3] [bipe] **VT** to page

biphasé, -e [bifaze] **ADJ** *Élec* diphasic, two-phase *(avant n)*

biplace [biplas] **ADJ** two-seater *(avant n)*

NM two-seater

biplan [biplɑ̃] **NM** *Aviat* biplane

bipolaire [bipɔlɛr] **ADJ** bipolar

bipolarisation [bipɔlarizasjɔ̃] **NF** *Pol* bipolarization

bipolarité [bipɔlarite] **NF** bipolarity

biquadratique [bikwadratik] *Math* **ADJ** *(équation)* biquadratic

NF biquadratic (equation)

bique [bik] **NF 1** *Zool* nanny-goat **2** *Fam Péj (femme)* **vieille b.** old bag *or* cow

biquet, -ette [bikε, -εt] **NM,F 1** *Zool* kid **2** *Fam (en appellatif)* **mon b.** my pet

biquotidien, -enne [bikɔtidjɛ̃, -εn] **ADJ** twice-daily

bircher [birʃer] **NM** *Suisse* muesli

BIRD [bœrd] **NF** *Banque (abrév* **Banque internationale pour la reconstruction et le développement***)* IBRD

biréacteur [bireaktœr] **NM** *Aviat* twin-engined jet

biréfringence [birefrɛ̃ʒɑ̃s] **NF** *Opt* birefringence

biréfringent, -e [birefrɛ̃ʒɑ̃, -ɑ̃t] **ADJ** *Opt* birefringent

birman, -e [birmɑ̃, -an] **ADJ** Burmese

NM *(langue)* Burmese

• **Birman, -e NM,F** Burmese; **les Birmans** the Burmese

Birmanie [birmani] **NF la B.** Burma

biroute [birut] **NF 1** *Aviat* windsock, wind cone *or* sleeve **2** *Vulg (pénis)* cock, prick

bis[1] [bis] **ADV 1** *Mus* repeat, twice **2** *(dans une adresse)* **13 b.** 13A

EXCLAM *(à un spectacle)* encore!

bis[2], **-e**[1] [bi, biz] **ADJ** *(couleur)* greyish-brown; *(toile)* unbleached

bisaïeul, -e [bizajœl] **NM,F** great-grandfather, *f* great-grandmother

bisannuel, -elle [bizanɥεl] **ADJ** *(tous les deux ans)* biennial

bisbille [bizbij] *Fam* **NF** tiff

• **en bisbille ADV** at loggerheads *or* odds; **être en b. avec qn** to be at loggerheads with sb

Biscaye [biskaj] **NF** *Géog* Biscay

biscôme [biskom] **NM** *Suisse* = Swiss gingerbread

biscornu, -e [biskɔrny] **ADJ 1** *(irrégulier ▸ forme)* irregular, misshapen **2** *(étrange ▸ idée)* cranky, queer, weird; *(▸ esprit, raisonnement)* twisted, tortuous

biscoteaux [biskɔto] **NMPL** *Fam* biceps◻

biscotte [biskɔt] **NF** *Culin* = piece of toasted bread sold in packets and often eaten for breakfast

biscuit [biskɥi] **NM 1** *Culin (gâteau sec) Br* biscuit, *Am* cookie; **b. pour chien** dog biscuit; **b. à la cuiller** *Br* sponge finger, *Am* ladyfinger; **b. fourré** filled biscuit; **b. de mer** cuttlefish bone; **b. salé** cracker, *Br* savoury biscuit; **b. soda** soda cracker **2** *(gâteau)* **b. glacé** ice cream sandwich; **b. roulé** Swiss roll; **b. de Savoie** sponge cake **3** *(porcelaine)* biscuit, bisque

ADJ INV biscuit-coloured

biscuiterie [biskɥitri] **NF 1** *(usine) Br* biscuit *or Am* cookie factory **2** *(commerce) Br* biscuit *or Am* cookie trade **3** *(fabrication) Br* biscuit *or Am* cookie making

bise[2] [biz] **NF** *(vent)* North *or* northerly wind

bise[3] [biz] **NF** *(baiser)* kiss; **donner** *ou* **faire une b. à qn** to give sb a kiss; **se faire la b.** to kiss each other on both cheeks; **grosses bises** *(dans une lettre)* love and kisses

biseau, -x [bizo] **NM** *Tech (bord, outil)* bevel; **(taillé) en b.** bevelled

biseautage [bizotaʒ] **NM 1** *Tech (du bois, du verre)* bevelling **2** *(de cartes à jouer)* marking

biseauter [3] [bizote] **VT 1** *Tech (bois, verre)* to bevel **2** *Cartes* **b. les cartes** to mark the cards

biser[1] **[3]** [bize] **VI** *Agr (du grain)* to darken, to deteriorate

biser[2] **[3]** [bize] **VT** *Fam* to kiss◻

biset [bizε] **NM** *Orn* rock pigeon *or* dove

bisexualité [bisεksɥalite] **NF** bisexuality, *Am* bisexualism

bisexué, -e [bisεksɥe] **ADJ** *Biol* bisexual

bisexuel, -elle [bisεksɥεl] **ADJ** bisexual

NM,F bisexual

bismuth [bismyt] **NM** *Chim* bismuth

bison [bizɔ̃] **NM** *Zool* **1** *(d'Amérique)* American buffalo *or* bison **2** *(d'Europe)* European bison, wisent

Bison Futé [bizɔ̃fyte] **NM** = organization giving details of road conditions, traffic congestion etc

bisou [bizu] **NM** *Fam* kiss◻; **donner** *ou* **faire un b. à qn** to give sb a kiss

bisque [bisk] **NF** *Culin* bisque; **b. de homard** lobster bisque

bisquer [3] [biske] **VI** *Fam* to be riled *or* nettled; **bisque, bisque, rage!** I win! *(gloating exclamation of victory)*; **faire b. qn** to rile *or* nettle sb

bissecteur, -trice [bisεktœr, -tris] *Géom* **ADJ** bisecting

• **bissectrice NF** bisector, bisectrix

bissection [bisεksjɔ̃] **NF** *Géom* bisection, bisecting

bisser [3] [bise] **VT 1** *(sujet: artiste)* to do again; **b. qn** to ask sb to do an encore **2** *Belg Scol (redoubler)* to repeat

bissextile [bisεkstil] *voir* **année**

bissexué, -e [bisεksɥe] = **bisexué**

bissexuel, -elle [bisεksɥεl] = **bisexuel**

bistandard [bistɑ̃dar] **ADJ** *TV* dual-standard

bistouquette [bistukεt] **NF** *Fam Br* willy, *Am* peter

bistouri [bisturi] **NM** *Méd* bistoury, lancet

bistre [bistr] **ADJ INV** bistre; *(teint, peau)* swarthy, dark

NM bistre

bistré, -e [bistre] **ADJ** brownish; *(teint, peau)* swarthy, dark

bistro, bistrot [bistro] **NM** ≃ café, *Br* ≃ pub, *Am* ≃ bar; **chaise/table b.** bistrot-style chair/table

> **BISTROT**
>
> This word can refer either to a small café or to a cosy restaurant, especially one frequented by regulars. These establishments are not usually as upmarket as bistros in English-speaking countries. The "style bistrot" refers to a style of furnishing inspired by the chairs, tables and zinc countertops typical of the traditional "bistrot".

bisulfate [bisylfat] **NM** *Chim* bisulphate

bisulfite [bisylfit] **NM** *Chim* bisulphite

bisulfure [bisylfyr] **NM** *Chim* disulphide, bisulphide

BIT [beite] **NM** *(abrév* **Bureau international du travail***)* ILO

bit [bit] **NM** *Ordinat* bit; **bits par pouce/seconde** bits per inch/second; **b. d'arrêt** stop bit; **b. de contrôle** control bit; **b. de départ** start bit

bite [bit] **NF** *Vulg* prick, cock

biter [3] [bite] **VT** *Vulg* **j'y bite rien** I don't understand a fucking thing

biterrois, -e [biterwa, -az] **ADJ** of/from Béziers

• **Biterrois, -e NM,F** = inhabitant of or person from Béziers

bitmap [bitmap] *Ordinat* **ADJ** bitmap

NM bitmap

bitonal, -e, -aux, -ales [bitɔnal, -o] **ADJ** *Mus* bitonal; *Tél* **sonnerie bitonale** two-tone ring

bitoniau, -x [bitɔnjo] **NM** *Fam* thingy, whatsit

bitte [bit] **NF 1** *Naut* bitt; **b. d'amarrage** bollard **2** *Vulg (pénis)* prick, cock

bitter [biter] **NM** *(boisson)* bitters

bitture [bityr] **NF 1** *très Fam (soûlerie)* **prendre une b.** to get plastered; **il (se) tenait une de ces bittures!** he got really plastered! **2** *Naut* range of cable

bitturer [3] [bityre] **se bitturer VPR** *très Fam* to get plastered

bitumage [bitymaʒ] **NM** asphalting, bituminizing

bitume [bitym] **NM 1** *Chim & Constr* bitumen **2** *(revêtement)* asphalt, bitumen **3** *Fam (trottoir) Br* pavement◻, *Am* sidewalk◻; **arpenter le b.** to walk the streets; **sur le b.** *(sans abri)* out on the street; *(sans ressources)* on skid row

bitumer [3] [bityme] **VT** *Chim & Constr* to asphalt, to bituminize

bitumeux, -euse [bitymø, -øz], **bitumineux, -euse** [bityminø, -øz] **ADJ** *Chim* bituminous

biture [bityr] = **bitture**

biturer [bityre] = **bitturer**

biunivoque [biynivɔk] **ADJ** *Math* **correspondance b.** one-to-one mapping

bivalent, -e [bivalɑ̃, -ɑ̃t] **ADJ** *Chim* bivalent

bivalve [bivalv] *Bot & Zool* **ADJ** bivalve

NM bivalve

bivouac [bivwak] **NM** bivouac; **feu de b.** watch-fire

bivouaquer [3] [bivwake] **VI** to bivouac, to set up camp overnight

bizarre [bizar] **ADJ** *(comportement, personne, idée, ambiance)* odd, peculiar, strange; **tu ne le trouves pas b.?** don't you think he's strange?; **je l'ai trouvé b. ce matin-là** I thought he was behaving oddly that morning; *Fam* **c'est un type vraiment b.** he's a real weirdo; **c'est b., ce n'est pas ce qu'elle m'avait dit** that's odd *or* strange, that's not what she told me; **elle s'habille de manière b.** she has strange dress sense; **se sentir b.** to feel (a bit) funny

bizarrement [bizarmɑ̃] **ADV** oddly, strangely, peculiarly; **b., ce matin-là, il ne s'était pas rasé** for some strange reason, he hadn't shaved that morning

bizarrerie [bizarri] **NF 1** *(caractère bizarre)* strangeness; **la b. de son comportement** the strangeness of his/her behaviour **2** *(action bizarre)* eccentricity; **ses bizarreries ne me surprennent plus** his/her eccentricities no longer surprise me

bizarroïde [bizarɔid] **ADJ** *Fam* odd, weird, bizarre

bizou [bizu] = **bisou**

bizut [bizy] **NM** *Fam Arg scol Br* fresher, *Am* freshman

bizutage [bizytaʒ] **NM** *Fam Arg scol* = practical jokes played on new arrivals in a school or college, *Br* ≃ ragging, *Am* ≃ hazing

> **BIZUTAGE**
>
> In some French schools and colleges, students in fancy-dress take to the streets and play practical jokes, sometimes of a very cruel nature, on each other and on passers-by at the beginning of the school year. This is part of the traditional initiation ceremony known as "bizutage". As a consequence of the excessive behaviour to which it has often led, a law was passed in 1998 to make it an offence.

bizuter [3] [bizyte] **VT** *Fam Arg scol Br* ≃ to rag, *Am* ≃ to haze; **se faire b.** *Br* ≃ to be ragged, *Am* ≃ to be hazed

bizuth [bizy] = **bizut**

bla-bla(-bla) [blabla(bla)] **NM INV** *Fam* blah, claptrap; **arrête ton b.!** stop talking *Br* rubbish *or Am* garbage!; **c'est du b.** that's just a lot of baloney *or Br* waffle

blablater [3] [blablate] **VI** *Fam* to waffle on, *Br* to witter on

black [blak] *Fam* **ADJ** *(personne de race noire)* Black◻

NM travailler au b. *(clandestinement)* = to work without declaring one's earnings; *(en plus de son travail habituel)* to moonlight

Blackberry® [blakberi] **NM** Blackberry®

blackbouler [3] [blakbule] **VT** *(candidat ▸ dans des élections)* to blackball; *(▸ à un examen)* to fail; **se faire b.** *(dans des élections)* to be blackballed; *(à un examen)* to fail; **il s'est fait b. à son examen** they failed him at his exam

black-out [blakaut] **NM INV** blackout; **faire le b. sur qch** to hush up *or* cover up sth; **b. partiel** brownout

blad [blad] **NM** *Typ* blad

blafard, -e [blafar, -ard] **ADJ** pallid, wan

blague [blag] **NF 1** *(histoire)* joke; **il est toujours à dire des blagues** he's always joking

2 *(duperie)* hoax, *Br* wind-up; **c'est une b.?** are you kidding?, you can't be serious!; **raconter des blagues** to lie; **elle dit qu'elle va démissionner mais c'est de la b.** she says she'll resign but that's all guff *or* hot air; *Fam* **elle a eu des triplés – sans b.!** she had triplets – never *or* no kidding!; *Fam* **vous allez arrêter, non mais, sans b.!** will you PLEASE give it a rest!; **b. à part, c'est un homme très agréable** seriously though, *or* joking apart, he's a very nice man

3 *(farce)* (practical) joke, trick; **il m'a fait une mauvaise** *ou* **sale b.** he played a nasty trick on me

4 *(sottise)* silly *or* stupid thing (to do); **je vous laisse seuls deux minutes, pas de blagues!** I'm leaving you alone for two minutes, so no funny business!

• **blague à tabac** NF tobacco pouch

blaguer [3] [blage] *Fam* VI to joke; **je ne blague plus!** I'm serious!; **j'aime bien b.** I like a joke; **tu blagues?** you're kidding!

VT to tease

blagueur, -euse [blagœr, -øz] *Fam* ADJ *(enfant, expression)* joking, teasing; **il est très b.** he really likes a joke

NM,F joker

blair [blɛr] NM *Fam* nose, *Br* conk, *Am* schnozz

blaireau, -x [blɛro] NM **1** *Zool* badger

2 *(pour se raser)* shaving brush

3 *Beaux-Arts* (badger-hair) brush

4 *Fam (imbécile)* jerk, prat

blairer [4] [blɛre] VT *très Fam* **personne ne peut le b.** no one can stand *or Br* stick him

blâmable [blamabl] ADJ blameworthy

blâme [blam] NM **1** *(condamnation)* disapproval; **rejeter le b. sur qn** to put the blame on sb; **s'attirer** *ou* **encourir le b. de qn** to incur sb's disapproval **2** *Admin & Scol* reprimand; **recevoir un b.** to be reprimanded; **donner un b. à qn** to reprimand sb

blâmer [3] [blame] VT **1** *(condamner)* to blame; **je ne le blâme pas d'avoir agi ainsi** I don't blame him for having acted that way **2** *Admin & Scol (élève, fonctionnaire)* to reprimand

blanc, blanche [blɑ̃, blɑ̃ʃ] ADJ **1** *(couleur)* white; **avoir les cheveux blancs** to have grey hair, to be grey-haired; **un vieillard à cheveux blancs** a white-haired old man; **à 40 ans, j'étais déjà toute blanche** at 40 I was already grey *or* all my hair had already turned grey; **que tu es b.!** how pale you look!; **être b. de peau** to be white-skinned *or* pale-skinned; **être b. de rage** to be white *or* livid with rage; *Fam Hum* **être b. comme un cachet d'aspirine** *ou* **un lavabo** *(malade, de peur)* to be as white as a sheet; *(pas bronzé)* to be completely white; **b. comme un linge** white as a sheet; **b. comme le lis** lily-white; **b. comme neige** snow-white, (as) white as snow, (as) white as the driven snow; *Fig* (as) pure as the driven snow; **elle est sortie du procès blanche comme neige** she came out of the trial as pure as the driven snow *or* with her reputation intact

2 *(race)* white, Caucasian; *(personne)* white, white-skinned, Caucasian; **les quartiers blancs de la ville** the white areas of town

3 *(vierge)* blank; **elle a remis (une) copie blanche** she handed in a blank sheet of paper; **écrire sur du papier b.** to write on plain *or* unlined paper; **vote b.** blank vote

4 *(voix)* monotone

5 *(examen)* mock

6 *(innocent)* innocent, pure; **il n'est pas aussi b. qu'il en a l'air** he's not as innocent as he looks; **il n'est pas sorti tout b. de l'affaire** he hasn't come out of this business untarnished

7 *(verre)* plain

8 *Littérature (vers)* blank

NM **1** *(couleur)* white; **le b. lui va bien** he/she looks good in white; **b. cassé** off-white; **passer du b. au noir** to go from one extreme to the other

2 *(matière ▸ blanche) (fard)* white make-up powder; **b. de baleine** spermaceti; **b. de chaux** whitewash; **b. d'Espagne** *ou* **de Meudon** whiting

3 *(cornée)* **b. de l'œil** white of the eye; **regarder qn dans le b. de l'œil** *ou* **des yeux** to look sb straight in the face *or* eye

4 *Culin* **b. de poulet** chicken breast; **dans le poulet, je préfère le b.** when I have chicken, I like the white meat *or* the breast best; **b. d'œuf** egg white, white of an egg; **blancs d'œufs battus** beaten egg whites

5 *(linge)* **le b.** household linen; **un magasin de b.** a linen shop; **faire une machine de b.** to do a machine-load of whites

6 *(vin)* white wine; **boire du b.** to drink white wine; **un b. sec** a dry white wine; *Fam* **un petit b.** *(verre)* a (nice) little glass of white wine; **b. de blancs** blanc de blancs *(white wine from white grapes)*; **b. cassis** kir *(made with blackcurrant cordial rather than crème de cassis)*

7 *(espace libre)* blank space, blank, space; *(dans une conversation)* blank

8 *Bot* mildew

9 *Can & Suisse (trou de mémoire)* blank

ADV **il a gelé b. la semaine dernière** there was some white frost last week; **voter b.** to return a blank vote; **un jour il dit b., l'autre il dit noir** one day he says yes, the next day he says no; **l'un dit b., l'autre dit noir** one (of them) says one thing, the other says the opposite

• **Blanc, Blanche** NM,F **1** *(homme)* white man, Caucasian; *(femme)* white woman, Caucasian; **les Blancs** white people; **petit B.** poor white; *Péj* **les petits Blancs** white trash **2** *Hist (en Russie)* White Russian; *(en France)* Bourbon supporter *(in post-revolutionary France)*; **les Blancs et les Bleus** = Chouan insurgents and Republican soldiers during the French Revolution

• **blanche** NF **1** *Mus Br* minim, *Am* half note **2** *(bille)* white (ball) **3** *Fam Arg drogue (héroïne)* **la blanche** smack

• **à blanc** ADJ *(cartouche)* blank; **tir à b.** firing blanks ADV **1 tirer à b.** to fire blanks **2** *(à un point extrême)* **chauffer à b.** to make white-hot

• **en blanc** ADJ **1** *(chèque, procuration)* blank **2** *(personne)* **une mariée en b.** a bride wearing white; **les hommes en b.** (hospital) doctors ADV *(peindre, colorer)* white; *(s'habiller, sortir)* in white; **laisser une ligne/page en b.** to leave a line/page blank

blanc-bec [blɑ̃bɛk] *(pl* **blancs-becs***)* NM *Péj* greenhorn; **jeune b.** young whippersnapper

blanchaille [blɑ̃ʃaj] NF **1** *(poisson)* small fry, bait **2** *Culin* whitebait

blanchâtre [blɑ̃ʃatr] ADJ *(mur)* off-white, whitish; *(nuage)* whitish; *(teint)* pallid

blanche [blɑ̃ʃ] *voir* **blanc**

Blanche-Neige [blɑ̃ʃnɛʒ] NPR Snow White

blancheur [blɑ̃ʃœr] NF **1** *(couleur)* whiteness; **ces draps sont d'une b. douteuse** these sheets aren't very white **2** *Littéraire (pureté)* purity, innocence

blanchiment [blɑ̃ʃimɑ̃] NM **1** *(décoloration, nettoyage ▸ d'un mur)* whitewashing; *(▸ d'un tissu)* bleaching

2 *(d'argent)* laundering

3 *Hort* (industrial) blanching

4 *Culin (de légumes)* blanching

> Do not confuse with **blanchissement**.

blanchir [32] [blɑ̃ʃir] VT **1** *(couvrir de blanc)* to whiten, to turn white; **b. à la chaux** to whitewash; **le gel a blanchi les champs** the frost has turned the fields white

2 *(décolorer)* to turn white, to bleach; **le temps a blanchi ses cheveux** time has turned his/her hair white

3 *(linge ▸ nettoyer)* to launder; *(▸ à l'eau de Javel)* to bleach; **donner ses draps à b.** to take one's sheets to be laundered *or* cleaned; **être logé, nourri et blanchi** to get bed and board and to have one's laundry done

4 *(innocenter)* to exonerate, to clear; **il est sorti complètement blanchi des accusations portées contre lui** he was cleared of the charges laid against him

5 *(argent)* to launder; **b. l'argent de la drogue** to launder money made from drug trafficking; **ces sommes sont blanchies dans l'immobilier** this money is laundered by investing it in real estate

6 *Culin* to blanch; *Hort (légumes, salade)* to blanch (industrially)

7 *Typ (texte, page)* to space, to space out

VI *(barbe, cheveux)* to turn grey; **elle a blanchi très jeune** her hair turned grey when she was still very young; **b. de rage** to turn ashen-faced with rage

VPR **se blanchir** to exonerate oneself, to clear one's name; **se b. d'une accusation** to clear one's name of an allegation

blanchissage [blɑ̃ʃisaʒ] NM **1** *(nettoyage)* laundering; **porter ses draps au b.** to take one's sheets to the laundry **2** *(raffinage)* refining

blanchissant, -e [blɑ̃ʃisɑ̃, -ɑ̃t] ADJ **1** *(barbe, cheveux)* greying; *(peau etc)* paling; **l'aube blanchissante** the brightening dawn **2 agent b.** whitener

blanchissement [blɑ̃ʃismɑ̃] NM *(des cheveux)* whitening

> Do not confuse with **blanchiment**.

blanchisserie [blɑ̃ʃisri] NF *(laverie)* laundry

blanchisseur, -euse [blɑ̃ʃisœr, -øz] NM,F launderer, laundryman, *f* laundrywoman

blanchon [blɑ̃ʃɔ̃] NM *Can Zool* whitecoat *(baby seal)*

blanc-manger [blɑ̃mɑ̃ʒe] *(pl* **blancs-mangers***)* NM *Culin* = almond milk jelly

blanc-seing [blɑ̃sɛ̃] *(pl* **blancs-seings***)* NM *Jur* signature to a blank document; *aussi Fig* **donner son b. à qn** to give sb carte blanche

blanquette [blɑ̃kɛt] NF **1** *(vin)* **b. de Limoux** = sparkling white wine **2** *Culin* blanquette; **b. de veau** blanquette of veal

blasé, -e [blaze] ADJ blasé; **être b. de qch** to be indifferent to sth

NM,F blasé person; **jouer les blasés** to act as if one's seen it all

blaser [3] [blaze] VT to make blasé

VPR **se blaser** to become blasé

blason [blazɔ̃] NM **1** *(écu)* arms, blazon; *Fig* **salir** *ou* **ternir son b.** to tarnish one's reputation, *Br* to blot one's copy-book; **redorer son b.** *(ses finances)* to restore the family fortune *(by marrying into money)*; *(son prestige)* to polish up one's image **2** *(héraldique)* heraldry

blasonner [3] [blazɔne] VT to blazon

blasphémateur, -trice [blasfematœr, -tris] ADJ *(personne)* blaspheming; *(acte, parole)* blasphemous

NM,F blasphemer

blasphématoire [blasfematwar] ADJ blasphemous

blasphème [blasfɛm] NM blasphemy; **dire des blasphèmes** to blaspheme

blasphémer [18] [blasfeme] VI to blaspheme

VT *Littéraire* **b. le nom de Dieu** to take God's name in vain

blastoderme [blastɔdɛrm] NM *Biol* blastoderm

blatérer [18] [blatere] VI *(bélier)* to bleat; *(chameau)* to bray

blatte [blat] NF cockroach

blazer [blazɛr] NM blazer

bld *(abrév écrite* **boulevard***)* Blvd.

blé [ble] NM **1** *Bot* wheat; **b. dur** durum wheat; **b. d'hiver** winter wheat; *Can* **b. d'Inde** *Br* maize, *Am* (Indian) corn; **b. noir** buckwheat; **b. en herbe** wheat in the blade; *Fig* **manger son b. en herbe** to spend one's money as soon as one has it **2** *très Fam (argent)* dough, *Br* dosh

bled [blɛd] NM **1** *Fam (petit village)* small village; *Péj* dump, hole; **un petit b. paumé** a little place out in the sticks *or* the middle of nowhere **2** *(en Afrique du Nord)* **le b.** the interior of the country; **aller au b.** to go up-country

blême [blɛm] ADJ **1** *(personne)* pale, ashen-faced, wan; *(visage, teint)* pale, wan; **b. de peur/rage** ashen-faced with fear/rage; **elle est devenue b. quand je le lui ai dit** she went pale *or* she blanched when I told her **2** *(lueur)* pale, wan; *(matin)* pale

blêmir [32] [blemir] VI to blanch, to (turn) pale; **b. de peur/rage** to blanch *or* go white with fear/rage

> Il faut noter que le verbe anglais **to blemish** est un faux ami. Il ne signifie jamais **devenir pâle**.

blêmissement [blemismɑ̃] NM paling, blanching

blennorragie [blenɔraʒi] NF *Méd* blennorrhagia, gonorrhoea

blennorragique [blenɔraʒik] ADJ *Méd* blennorrhagic, gonorrhoeal

blépharite [blefarit] NF *Méd* blepharitis

blèsement [blɛzmɑ̃] NM lisping

bléser [18] [bleze] VI to lisp

blésité [blezite] NF lisping

blessant, -e [blɛsɑ̃, -ɑ̃t] ADJ *(propos)* hurtful, cutting; **se montrer b. envers qn** to hurt sb's feelings

blessé, -e [blese] ADJ **1** *(soldat)* wounded; *(accidenté)* injured; **b. au genou** hurt in the knee **2** *(vexé ▸ amour-propre, orgueil, personne)* hurt

NM,F *(victime ▸ d'un accident)* injured person; *(▸ d'une agression)* wounded person; **un mort et trois blessés** one dead and three wounded/injured; **les blessés de la route** road casualties; **b. léger/grave** slightly/severely injured person; **grand b.** severely injured person; **b. de la face** person with facial wounds/injuries; **b. de guerre** *(en service)* wounded soldier; *(après la guerre)* wounded veteran

blesser [4] [blese] VT **1** *(au cours d'un accident)* to injure, to hurt; *(au cours d'une agression)* to injure, to wound; **vous êtes blessé?** are you hurt?; **il a été blessé par balle** he was hit by a bullet, he sustained a bullet-wound; **b. qn avec un couteau** to wound sb with a knife, to inflict a knife-wound on sb; **être blessé d'un coup de couteau** to be stabbed *or* knifed; **elle est blessée à la jambe** she has a leg injury, her leg's hurt; **être blessé dans un accident de voiture** to be injured in a car accident; **il a été blessé à la guerre** he was wounded in the war, he has a war-wound **2** *(partie du corps)* to hurt, to make sore; **b. la vue** to offend the eye; **b. l'oreille** to grate on the ear **3** *(offenser)* to offend, to upset; **tu l'as blessé avec tes questions** you hurt his feelings with your questions; **b. qn dans son amour-propre** to hurt sb's pride

USAGE ABSOLU to hurt; **des chaussures qui blessent** *(par compression)* shoes that pinch; *(par frottement)* shoes that rub

VPR **se blesser** to injure *or* to hurt oneself; **elle s'est blessée au bras** she injured *or* hurt her arm

blessure [blesyr] NF **1** *Méd (dans un accident)* injury; *(par arme)* wound; **infliger une b. à qn** to wound sb; **b. grave/légère/mortelle** severe/slight/fatal injury; **b. par balle** gunshot wound; **b. pénétrante** puncture wound; **b. superficielle** flesh wound; **nettoyer une b.** to clean out a wound **2** *Fig (offense)* wound; **une b. d'amour-propre** a blow to one's pride *or* self-esteem

blet, -ette[1] [blɛ, -ɛt] ADJ *(fruit)* mushy, overripe

blette[2] [blɛt] NF *Bot* Swiss chard

blettir [32] [bletir] VI *(fruit)* to become mushy *or* overripe

blettissement [bletismɑ̃], **blettissure** [bletisyr] NM **pour empêcher le b. des poires** to stop pears going mushy *or* becoming overripe

bleu, -e [blø] ADJ **1** *(coloré)* blue; **avoir les yeux bleus** to have blue eyes, to be blue-eyed

2 *(meurtri, altéré)* blue, bruised; **avoir les lèvres bleues** *(meurtries)* to have bruised lips; *(de froid, de maladie)* to have blue lips; **son bras était tout b.** his arm was black and blue; *Méd* **enfant b.** blue baby, hole-in-the-heart baby; **b. de froid** blue with cold; *Can* **un froid b.** extreme cold; **il fait un froid b.** it's freezing (cold)

3 *Culin* very rare

4 *(locutions)* **j'en suis resté b.** I was flabbergasted; *Belg* **être b. de qn/qch** *(être passionné)* to be crazy about sb/sth

NM,F *(gén)* newcomer, greenhorn; *Mil* rookie, raw recruit; *Scol* new boy, *f* new girl

NM **1** *(couleur)* blue; **peindre un mur en b.** to paint a wall blue; **admirer le b. du ciel/de la mer** to admire the blueness of the sky/sea; **b. clair** light blue; **b. foncé** dark blue; **b. acier** steel blue; **b. ardoise** slate blue; **b. canard** peacock blue; **b. ciel** sky blue; **b. (de) cobalt** cobalt blue; **b. horizon** sky blue; **b. lavande** lavender blue; **b. marine** navy blue; *Méd* **b. de méthylène** methylene blue; **b. noir** blue black; **b. nuit** midnight blue; **b. outremer** ultramarine; **b. pastel** powder blue; **b. pervenche** periwinkle blue; **b. pétrole** petrol blue; **b. de Prusse** Prussian blue; **b. roi** royal blue; **b. turquoise** turquoise; **b. vert** blue green; *Fam* **il n'y a vu que du b.** he didn't notice a thing *or* was none the wiser

2 *(ecchymose)* bruise; **se faire un b.** to get a bruise; **se faire un b. à la cuisse** to bruise one's thigh; **être couvert** *ou* **plein de bleus** to be black and blue

3 *(vêtement)* **b. (de travail)** (worker's) overalls; **b. de chauffe** work overalls, *Br* boiler suit

4 *Suisse Fam (permis de conduire) Br* driving licence[□], *Am* driver's license[□]

5 *(fromage)* blue cheese

6 *Can Pol* Conservative

7 *(pour la lessive)* blue, blueing; **passer du linge au b.** to blue laundry

• **bleue** NF **1 la grande bleue** the Mediterranean (sea) **2** *Suisse (liqueur)* absinthe **3** *(locution)* **en voir de bleues** to go through a lot

• **bleus** NMPL *Can Fam* **1 avoir/prendre les bleus** *(être/devenir triste)* to have/get the blues; **prendre les bleus** *(voir rouge)* to go crazy **2 être dans les bleus** *(ivre)* to be wasted

• **au bleu** *Culin* ADJ **truite au b.** trout au bleu ADV **cuire** *ou* **faire un poisson au b.** to cook a fish au bleu

bleuâtre [bløatr] ADJ bluish, bluey

bleuet [bløɛ] NM *Bot* **1** *(fleur)* cornflower **2** *Can (fruit)* blueberry; *(buisson)* blueberry bush

bleuetière [bløetjɛr] NF *Can Hort* blueberry field

bleuir [32] [bløir] VI to turn *or* to go blue

VT to turn blue

bleuissement [bløismɑ̃] NM **empêcher le b. des chairs** to stop the flesh turning *or* going blue

bleuté, -e [bløte] ADJ *(pétale, aile)* blue-tinged; *(lentille, verre)* blue-tinted

blindage [blɛ̃daʒ] NM **1** *(revêtement)* armour plate *or* plating; *(fait de blinder)* armouring

2 *Élec* screening, shielding

3 *(d'une porte ▸ revêtement)* reinforcement; *(▸ fait de blinder)* reinforcing

4 *Mines* timbering

blinde [blɛ̃d] NF blind

• **à toute blinde** ADV *Fam* at full speed[□], like lightning, *Br* like the clappers

• **blindes** NFPL wooden frame *(to support planks, fascines)*

blindé, -e [blɛ̃de] ADJ **1** *(voiture, tank, train)* armoured, armour-clad, armour-plated; *(brigade, division)* armoured

2 *(renforcé ▸ paroi)* reinforced; **porte blindée** steel security door

3 *Élec* screened, shielded

4 *Fam (insensible)* hardened; **b. contre qch** hardened to sth

5 *très Fam (ivre)* blitzed, plastered

NM *Mil* **1** *(véhicule)* armoured vehicle; **les blindés** the armour **2** *(soldat)* = member of a tank regiment

blinder [3] [blɛ̃de] VT **1** *(contre les agressions)* to armour, to armour-plate

2 *(renforcer ▸ porte)* to reinforce

3 *Élec* to screen, to shield

4 *Mines* to timber

5 *Fam (endurcir)* to toughen (up), to harden; **b. qn contre qch** to harden sb to sth

VPR **se blinder** *Fam* **1** *(s'enivrer)* to get blitzed *or* plastered **2** *(s'endurcir)* to toughen oneself up; **se b. contre qch** to harden oneself to sth

bling bling [bliŋbliŋ] ADJ INV *Fam* bling (bling)

blini [blini] NM *Culin* blini

blister [blistɛr] NM blister pack; **marchandise vendue sous b.** goods sold in blister packs

blizzard [blizar] NM blizzard

bloblote [blɔblɔt] NF *Fam* **avoir la b.** to have the shakes

bloc [blɔk] NM **1** *(masse ▸ de pierre)* block; *(▸ de bois, de béton)* block, lump; **le fronton a été fait dans un seul b.** the pediment was hewn from a single block; **être tout d'un b.** *(en un seul morceau)* to be made of a single block; *(trapu)* to be stockily built; *(direct)* to be simple and straightforward; *(inflexible)* to be unyielding; **elle s'est retournée tout d'un b. et l'a giflé** she swivelled round and slapped him in the face

2 *(de papier)* pad; **b. de bureau** desk pad; **b. à dessin** sketch block; **b. à en-tête** headed notepad; **b. de papier** writing pad

3 *Ordinat* **b. d'alimentation secteur** mains power unit; **b. de calcul** arithmetic unit; **b. de données** data block; **b. de mémoire** memory bank; **b. de touches** keypad

4 *(installation)* **b. frigorifique** refrigeration unit; **b. opératoire** *(salle) Br* operating theatre, *Am* operating room; *(locaux)* surgical unit; **b. sanitaire** toilet block

5 *(maisons)* block

6 *(ensemble)* block; *(d'actions, de titres)* block, parcel; *(groupe d'actionnaires)* shareholding; **deux blocs adverses** two opposing factions *or* blocks; **former un b.** *(sociétés)* to form a grouping; *(amis, alliés)* to stand together; *(composants)* to form a single whole; **faire b.** to form a block; **faire b. avec/contre qn** to stand (together) with/against sb; *Fin* **b. de contrôle** controlling shareholding; **b. sièges** block of seats

7 *Suisse (immeuble)* block

8 *Géog, Écon & Fin (zone)* bloc; *Hist* **le b. des pays de l'Est** the Eastern bloc; **b. monétaire** monetary bloc; **le b. des pays de l'Ouest** *ou* **occidental** the Western Alliance; *Hist* **le b. soviétique** the Soviet bloc

9 *Géol* **b. erratique** erratic (block)

10 *Fam Arg crime (prison)* slammer, *Br* nick; **allez, au b.!** lock him/her up!

• **à bloc** ADV **visser une vis à b.** to screw a screw down hard; **serrer le frein à b.** to pull the brakes on hard; **gonfler un pneu à b.** to blow a tyre all the way up; **remonter une pendule à b.** to wind a clock all the way up; *Fam* **il est gonflé** *ou* **remonté à b.** he's on top form *or* full of beans; **ne le provoque pas, il est remonté à b.!** leave him alone, he's already wound up!

• **en bloc** ADV as a whole; **j'ai tout rejeté en b.** I rejected it lock, stock and barrel, I rejected the whole thing

blocage [blɔkaʒ] NM **1** *(arrêt ▸ des freins)* locking, jamming on; *(▸ d'un écrou)* tightening (up)

2 *Écon (des loyers, des tarifs, du crédit)* freeze; *(d'un compte bancaire)* freezing; **b. des prix/salaires** price/wage freeze

3 *Sport (de la balle)* trapping

4 *Psy* block, blockage; **avoir** *ou* **faire un b.** to have a (mental) block; **faire un b. sur qch** to block sth off

5 *Constr* rubble, infill

6 *Ordinat (dans réseau)* lockout; **b. majuscule** caps lock

7 *Pol* **b. institutionnel** institutional deadlock

bloc-appartement [blɔkapartəmɑ̃] *(pl* **blocs-appartements)** NM *Can Br* block of flats, *Am* apartment building

bloc-cuisine [blɔkkɥizin] *(pl* **blocs-cuisines)** NM kitchen unit

bloc-cylindres [blɔksilɛ̃dr] *(pl* **blocs-cylindres)** NM cylinder block

bloc-diagramme [blɔkdjagram] *(pl* **blocs-diagrammes)** NM *Géog* block diagram

bloc-évier [blɔkevje] *(pl* **blocs-éviers)** NM sink unit

blockhaus [blɔkos] NM **1** *Mil* blockhouse; *(de petite taille)* pillbox **2** *Naut* armoured tower

bloc-moteur [blɔkmɔtœr] *(pl* **blocs-moteurs)** NM *Aut* engine block

bloc-notes [blɔknɔt] *(pl* **blocs-notes)** NM notepad, memo pad, *Am* scratchpad; *Ordinat (pour texte supprimé)* clipboard; *Ordinat* **b. électronique** electronic notepad

blocus [blɔkys] NM *Mil* blockade; **faire le b. d'une ville** to blockade a city; **lever/forcer le b.** to raise/to run the blockade; **b. économique** economic blockade

blog [blɔg] NM *Ordinat (abrév* **weblog)** blog

bloggeur, -euse [blɔgœr, -øz] NM,F *Ordinat* blogger

blogging [blɔgiŋ] NM *Ordinat* blogging

blogosphère [blɔgɔsfɛr] NF blogosphere

bloguer [blɔge] VI *Ordinat* to blog, to write a blog; **elle blogue sur sa vie sentimentale** she blogs about her love life

blogueur, -euse [blɔgœr, -øz] **NM,F** *Ordinat* blogger

blond, -e [blɔ̃, blɔ̃d] **ADJ 1** *(chevelure)* blond, fair; *(personne)* blond, fair-haired; **b. platine** *ou* **platiné** platinum blond; **b. ardent** *ou* **roux** *ou* **vénitien** strawberry blond; **b. cendré** ash blond; **b. filasse** flaxen-haired; **b. comme les blés** golden-haired **2** *(jaune pâle)* pale yellow, golden, honey-coloured

NM,F blonde (person); **une blonde incendiaire** a blonde bombshell; **une blonde décolorée/platine** a peroxide/platinum blonde

NM *(couleur ▸ des cheveux)* blond colour; *(▸ du sable)* golden colour; **se teindre (les cheveux) en b.** to dye one's hair blond; **ses cheveux sont d'un b. très clair** she has light blond hair

• **blonde NF 1** *(cigarette)* Virginia cigarette **2** *(bière)* lager **3** *Can (amie)* girlfriend

blondasse [blɔ̃das] *Péj* **ADJ** *(cheveux)* yellowish; **elle est b.** she's blondish

NF *(personne)* brassy blonde

blondeur [blɔ̃dœr] **NF** *(des cheveux, d'une personne)* fairness, blondness, blondeness; *(du sable, des blés)* goldenness, gold

blondin[1], -e [blɔ̃dɛ̃, -in] **NM,F** fair-haired child

blondin[2] [blɔ̃dɛ̃] **NM** *Tech* cableway

blondinet, -ette [blɔ̃dinɛ, -ɛt] **ADJ** blond-haired, fair-haired

NM,F little blond-haired *or* fair-haired child

blondir [32] [blɔ̃dir] **VI 1** *(personne, cheveux)* to go fairer **2** *Culin* **faire b. des oignons** to sweat onions gently until transparent

VT to bleach; **b. ses cheveux** *(à l'eau oxygénée)* to bleach one's hair; *(par mèches)* to put (blonde) highlights in one's hair

bloquer [3] [blɔke] **VT 1** *(caler ▸ table)* to wedge, to stop wobbling; *(empêcher de fonctionner)* to jam; **bloque la porte** *(ouverte)* wedge the door open; *(fermée)* wedge the door shut; **c'est le tapis qui bloque la porte** the carpet's jamming the door; **b. une roue** *(avec une cale)* to put a block under *or* to chock a wheel; *(avec un sabot de Denver)* to clamp a wheel; **la roue est bloquée** the wheel is locked *or* jammed; **la porte est bloquée** the door is stuck *or* jammed

2 *(serrer fort ▸ vis)* to screw down hard, to overtighten; *(▸ frein)* to jam on, to lock

3 *(entraver)* **b. le passage** *ou* **la route** to block the way; **pousse-toi, tu me bloques le passage** move, you're (standing) in my way; **être bloqué dans l'ascenseur** to be stuck in the *Br* lift *or Am* elevator; **je suis bloqué à la maison avec un gros rhume** I'm stuck at home with a bad cold

4 *(empêcher l'accès à ▸ ville, point stratégique)* to block, to seal off; **la neige bloque les routes** the roads are blocked by the snow; **bloqué par la neige** snowbound

5 *Fam (retenir ▸ une personne)* to hold up

6 *Écon (loyers, prix, salaires, crédits)* to freeze; *Fin (compte bancaire)* to freeze, to stop; *(chèque)* to stop; *Pol (mesure, vote)* to block

7 *(réunir)* to group together; **les cours sont bloqués sur six jours** the classes are grouped together over six days

8 *Psy* to cause *or* to produce a (mental) block in; **ça la bloque** she has a mental block about it; **ça me bloque de me sentir observé** I get a (mental) block if I feel I'm being watched

9 *Ftbl* **b. la balle** to trap the ball

10 *Constr* to fill (with rubble)

VPR se bloquer 1 *(clef)* to jam, to stick, to get stuck; *(machine, mécanisme)* to jam, to get stuck; *(frein, roue)* to jam, to lock **2** *(personne ▸ ne pas communiquer)* to close in on oneself; *(▸ se troubler)* to have a mental block

blottir [32] [blɔtir] **VT 1** *(poser)* **b. sa tête contre l'épaule de qn** to lay one's head on sb's shoulder **2** *Fig* **une ferme blottie au fond de la vallée** a farmhouse nestling in the bottom of the valley; **blottis les uns contre les autres** huddled up *or* snuggled up together

VPR se blottir to curl up, to snuggle up; **se b. contre qn** to snuggle up to sb

blousant, -e [bluzɑ̃, -ɑ̃t] **ADJ** loose, loose-fitting

blouse [bluz] **NF 1** *(courte ▸ à l'école)* = smock formerly worn by French schoolchildren; *(▸ à l'ancienne, de paysan)* smock; *(▸ chemisier)* blouse **2** *(longue ▸ pour travailler)* overalls; *(▸ d'un médecin)* white coat; *(▸ d'un chimiste, d'un laborantin)* lab coat; **les blouses blanches** doctors and nurses **3** *(au billard)* pocket

blouser [3] [bluze] **VT** *Fam (tromper)* to con, to trick; **je me suis fait b.** I've been conned *or* had

VI to be loose-fitting, to fit loosely; **faire b. un chemisier** to pull a blouse out a bit at the waist

blouson [bluzɔ̃] **NM** (short) jacket; **b. d'aviateur** bomber jacket; *Vieilli* **les blousons noirs** = young louts in black leather jackets

blue-jean [bludʒin] *(pl* **blue-jeans***)* **NM**, **blue-jeans** [bludʒins] **NM INV** *Vieilli* (pair of) jeans

blues [bluz] **NM 1** *Mus (musique)* blues *(singulier)*; **chanter le b.** to sing the blues **2** *Fam (cafard)* **avoir le b.** to have the blues, to be feeling blue *or* down; **j'ai un coup de b.** I'm feeling a bit blue *or* down

bluff [blœf] **NM** bluff; **ne le crois pas, c'est du b.!** don't believe him, he's just bluffing!; **il faut y aller au b.** you'll have to try and bluff

bluffant, -e [blœfɑ̃, -ɑ̃t] **ADJ** *Fam* mind-blowing, *Br* gobsmacking

bluffer [3] [blœfe] **VT 1** *(tromper)* to bluff **2** *Fam (impressionner)* to blow away

VI to bluff

bluffeur, -euse [blœfœr, -øz] **ADJ il est très b.** he's always bluffing

NM,F bluffer

blush [blœʃ] **NM** blusher, blush

blutage [blytaʒ] **NM** *(tamisage)* bolting, boulting

bluter [3] [blyte] **VT** *(tamiser ▸ farine)* to bolt, to boult

BN [beɛn] **NF** *(abrév* **Bibliothèque nationale***)* = the former French national library building, now containing only archive material and coins, medals etc

BNF [beɛnɛf] **NF** *(abrév* **Bibliothèque nationale de France***)* = French national library, comprising the "Bibliothèque de France" and the "Bibliothèque nationale"

BO [beo] **NM** *Admin (abrév* **Bulletin officiel***)* = official listing of all new laws and decrees

NF *Cin (abrév* **bande originale***) (d'un film)* (original) soundtrack

boa [bɔa] **NM 1** *Zool* boa; **b. constricteur** boa constrictor **2** *(tour de cou)* boa

boat people [botpipœl] **NM INV** (South East Asian) refugee; **les b.** the boat people

bob [bɔb] **NM 1** *(chapeau)* sun hat **2** *Sport* bobsleigh, *Am* bobsled

bobard [bɔbar] **NM** *Fam* fib

bobet [bɔbe] **NM** *Suisse Fam* idiot

bobettes [bɔbɛt] **NFPL** *Can Fam (caleçon)* boxers

bobinage [bɔbinaʒ] **NM 1** *(enroulage)* winding, reeling **2** *Élec* coil

bobinard [bɔbinar] **NM** *très Fam* whorehouse, *Br* knocking shop

bobine [bɔbin] **NF 1** *(de ruban, de fil)* reel; *Couture (dans une machine à coudre)* bobbin

2 *Élec* coil; **b. d'allumage** ignition coil; **b. de dérivation** shunt coil; **b. d'induction** induction coil

3 *Cin & Phot* reel; **une b. de pellicule** a roll of film

4 *Fam (visage)* face[□], mug; **elle a fait une drôle de b.** she pulled a (funny) face

• **en bobine ADV rester en b.** to be left in the lurch

bobiner [3] [bɔbine] **VT 1** *Couture & Tex* to reel, to spool, to wind **2** *Élec* to coil **3** *Pêche* to reel in

bobineur, -euse [bɔbinœr, -øz] *Couture* **NM,F** winder, winding operative

NM *(d'une machine à coudre)* bobbin winder

• **bobineuse NF** winding machine, coiler

bobo[1] [bobo] **NM** *(en langage enfantin) (égratignure)* scratch, *Am* boo-boo; *(bosse)* bump; **faire b. (à qn)** to hurt (sb); **se faire b.** to hurt oneself; **j'ai un b. au doigt** my finger hurts

bobo[2] [bobo] *Fam (abrév* **bourgeois bohème***)*

ADJ bobo

NMF bobo

bobonne [bɔbɔn] **NF 1** *Fam Péj* the old lady, *Br* the missus; **il va partout avec b.** his old lady goes everywhere with him **2** *Belg Fam* grandma

bobsleigh [bɔbslɛg] **NM** *Sport* bobsleigh, *Am* bobsled

bobtail [bɔbtɛjl] **NM** *Zool (chien)* Old English sheepdog

bocage [bɔkaʒ] **NM 1** *Géog* bocage *(countryside with small fields and many hedges)* **2** *Littéraire (bois)* copse

bocager, -ère [bɔkaʒe, -ɛr] **ADJ pays/paysage b.** country/landscape of small fields and hedges

bocal, -aux [bɔkal, -o] **NM 1** *(pour les conserves)* jar, bottle; **mettre des haricots verts en bocaux** to preserve *or* to bottle green beans **2** *(aquarium)* fishbowl, bowl

bocard [bɔkar] **NM** *Métal* ore crusher, stamping mill

Boccace [bɔkas] **NPR** Boccaccio

BOCE [beoseə] **NM** *UE (abrév* **Bulletin officiel des communautés européennes***)* = official listing of all new EC directives

boche [bɔʃ] *très Fam Vieilli* **ADJ** Boche, Kraut

NMF Boche, Kraut, = offensive term used to refer to German people; **les boches** the Boche, the Krauts

bock [bɔk] **NM** *(récipient)* ≃ (half-pint) beer glass; *(contenu)* glass of beer

body [bɔdi] **NM** *(justaucorps)* bodystocking, body

body-building [bɔdibildiŋ] **NM le b.** body building; **faire du b.** to do body building

Boer [bur] **NM** Boer; **les Boers** the Boers

boëte, boette, boëtte [bwɛt] **NF** *Pêche* bait

bœuf [bœf, *pl* bø] **NM 1** *Zool (de trait)* ox; *(de boucherie)* bullock, steer; **b. musqué** musk ox; **il a un b. sur la langue** *(on l'a payé)* somebody's bought his silence; *(il ne veut rien dire)* he's keeping his own counsel; **fort comme un b.** as strong as an ox; **souffler comme un b.** to wheeze *or* to pant (heavily); *Fam* **on n'est pas des bœufs** you can't treat us like slaves **2** *Culin* beef; **b. bourguignon** bœuf *or* beef bourguignon; **b. gros sel** ≃ boiled beef and vegetables (with sea salt); **b. (à la) mode** beef à la mode **3** *Fam* jam session; **faire un b.** to have a jam session, to jam

ADJ INV *Fam* **elle a fait un effet b.** she made quite a splash; **il a eu un succès b.** he was incredibly successful[□]

bof [bɔf] **EXCLAM** = term expressing lack of interest or enthusiasm; **tu as aimé la pièce? – b.!** did you like the play? – it was all right, I suppose; **ça te dirait de venir avec nous? – b.** would you like to come with us? – I don't know *or* I'm not bothered

Bogota [bɔgɔta] **NM** *Géog* Bogota

bogue[1] [bɔg] **NF** *Bot* chestnut bur

bogue[2] [bɔg] **NM** *Ordinat* bug; **le b. de l'an 2000** the millennium bug; **b. de logiciel** software bug

bogué, -e [bɔge] **ADJ** *Ordinat* bug-ridden

bohème [bɔɛm] **ADJ** bohemian

NMF bohemian; **mener une vie de b.** to lead a bohemian *or* an unconventional life

NF la b. the bohemian *or* artistic way of life

Bohême [bɔɛm] **NF la B.** Bohemia

bohémien, -enne [bɔemjɛ̃, -ɛn] **ADJ** Bohemian

• **Bohémien, -enne NM,F 1** *(de Bohême)* Bohemian **2** *Péj (nomade)* gipsy, traveller

boire [108] [bwar] **VT 1** *(avaler)* to drink; **b. qch à petits coups** *ou* **à petites gorgées** to sip sth; **b. de l'eau/de la bière** to drink water/beer; *Fam* **b. un coup** *ou* **pot** *ou* **verre** to have a drink; **elle a tout bu d'un coup** she gulped it all down; **b. un coup de trop** to have one too many; **b. du lait** *ou* **du petit-lait** to lap it up; **il buvait ses paroles** he was lapping up everything he/she said; *Fam* **b. la tasse** *ou* **un bouillon** *(en nageant)* to swallow water; *(perdre de l'argent)* to lose a lot of money; *(faire faillite)* to go under

2 *(absorber)* to absorb, to soak up; **les géraniums ont bu toute l'eau** the geraniums soaked up *or* drank all the water

VI 1 *(s'hydrater)* to drink; **vous ne buvez pas assez** you don't drink enough liquids; **il buvait à petits**

coups *ou* **à petites gorgées** he was sipping his drink; **b. à la bouteille** to drink from the bottle; **commander à b.** to order a drink; **manger salé fait b.** eating salty things makes you thirsty; **fais-le b.** *(malade, enfant, animal)* give him a drink *or* something to drink; **faire b. les chevaux** to water the horses; **tant qu'elle a de la fièvre, faites-la b. abondamment** if she's feverish make sure she gets plenty of liquid; **il y a à b. et à manger là-dedans** *(dans un verre)* there are bits floating in the glass; *Fig* it's a bit of a mixed bag; **b. jusqu'à plus soif** to drink one's fill

2 *(pour fêter un événement)* **b. à** to toast, to drink to; **nous buvons à ta santé** we're drinking to *or* toasting your health

3 *(pour s'enivrer)* to drink; **il boit trop** he drinks too much, he has a drink problem; **il a toujours aimé b.** he's always enjoyed a drink; *Fam* **il boit bien** *ou* **sec** he's a rather heavy drinker; **elle l'a fait b. pour qu'il avoue** she got him drunk so that he'd confess; *Fam* **b. comme une éponge** *ou* **un tonneau** *ou* **un trou** to drink like a fish

4 *(plante)* to soak up *or* absorb water

5 *Can (bébé)* to feed

NM 1 le b. et le manger eating and drinking; **il en oublie** *ou* **perd le b. et le manger** he's becoming totally distracted **2** *Can* **le b. du bébé** the feeding of the baby

VPR se boire se boit frais/chambré should be drunk chilled/at room temperature; **ça se boit comme du petit-lait** it goes down like silk *or Br* a treat

bois [bwa] **NM 1** *(forêt)* *(▸ de grands arbres)* wood, wooded area; *(▸ de jeunes ou petits arbres)* thicket, copse, coppice; *(▸ d'arbres plantés)* grove; **un b. de pins** a pine grove; **un b. de chênes** an oak wood

2 *(matière)* wood *(UNCOUNT)*; *(pour la construction)* timber, *Am* lumber; **en b.** wooden; **b. blanc** whitewood; **b. à brûler** firewood; **b. de charpente** timber; **b. de chauffage**, *Can* **b. de corde** firewood; **b. debout** standing timber; **b. dur** hardwood; **b. d'ébène** ebony; *Fig* black gold; **b. exotique** imported wood; *Suisse* **b. de feu** firewood; **b. flottants** driftwood; *Can* **b. franc** hardwood; **b. des îles** tropical hardwood; **b. mort** deadwood; *Can* **b. mou** softwood; **b. de papeterie**, *Can* **b. de papier** pulpwood; **b. à pâte** pulpwood; *Can* **b. de poêle** firewood; *Can* **b. rond** log, roundwood; **une cabane en b. rond** a log cabin; **b. de rose** rosewood; **b. tendre** softwood; **b. de violette** kingwood; **petit b.** kindling; **il est du b. dont on fait les flûtes** he's very easy-going; **il est du b. dont on fait les héros** he's got the stuff of heroes; **faire feu** *ou* **flèche de tout b.** to use all available means; **touchons** *ou* **je touche du b.** *Br* touch wood, *Am* knock on wood; *Fam* **je vais leur montrer de quel b. je me chauffe!** I'll show them what I'm made of!; *Fam* **ça envoie le** *ou* **du b.** it rocks, *Br* it's the business

3 *(partie en bois ▸ d'une raquette)* frame; *Fam* **faire un b.** *(au tennis)* to hit the ball off the wood; **b. de lit** bedstead

4 *Beaux-Arts* **b. (gravé)** woodcut

5 *(club de golf)* wood

• **bois NMPL 1** *Zool* antlers **2** *Ftbl* goalposts **3** *Mus* woodwind section *or* instruments

• **de bois ADJ 1** *(charpente, jouet, meuble)* wooden **2** *(impassible)* **je ne suis pas de b.** I'm only human

boisage [bwazaʒ] **NM** *Mines (action)* timbering; *(soutènement)* timber work

boisé, -e [bwaze] **ADJ 1** *(région, terrain)* wooded, woody **2** *Constr* panelled

boisement [bwazmɑ̃] **NM** *Hort* afforestation

boiser [3] [bwaze] **VT 1** *Hort* to afforest **2** *Mines* to timber **3** *Constr* to panel

boiserie [bwazri] **NF** piece of decorative woodwork; **des boiseries** panelling

boisseau, -x [bwaso] **NM 1** *(mesure)* bushel; **garder** *ou* **mettre** *ou* **tenir qch sous le b.** to keep sth hidden *or* a secret **2** *Tech (tuyau)* drain tile; *(de cheminée)* chimney (flue) tile

boisson [bwasɔ̃] **NF 1** *(liquide à boire)* drink; **j'aimerais une b. fraîche** I'd like a cool drink; **je m'occupe de la b.** I'll take care of the drinks; **b. alcoolisée/non alcoolisée** alcoholic/soft drink; **b. chaude** hot drink; **b. gazeuse** *Br* fizzy drink, *Am* soda **2** *(alcool)* **la b.** drink, drinking; **c'est la b. qui l'a tué** it's the drink that killed him; **pris de b.** inebriated, intoxicated **3** *Can (spiritueux)* alcohol, alcoholic drinks; **être/se mettre en b.** to be/get drunk

boîte [bwat] **NF 1** *(récipient ▸ à couvercle, à fente)* box; **b. d'allumettes** *(pleine)* box of matches; *(vide)* matchbox; **b. à chaussures** shoebox; **b. à idées** suggestions box; *Can Joual* **b. à lunch** lunchbox; *Can Joual* **b. à malle** mailbox; **b. à ordures** *Br* dustbin, *Am* trash can; *aussi Ordinat* **b. à outils** tool box, toolkit; **b. à pain** bread bin; **b. à pharmacie** first aid box *or* kit; **b. à pilules** pillbox; **b. à thé** tea caddy; *Fam* **c'est dans la b.!** *(à un tournage de film)* it's in the can!; **b. de Pandore** Pandora's box; *Fam* **ferme ta b. (à camembert)** shut your trap *or* mouth

2 *(pour aliments)* **b. (de conserve)** can, *Br* tin; **acheter une b. de haricots** to buy a can *or Br* tin of beans; **il ne mange que des boîtes** he eats nothing but canned *or Br* tinned food

3 *(pour boissons)* can

4 *(contenu ▸ d'un récipient à couvercle, à fente)* box, boxful; *(▸ d'une conserve)* canful, *Br* tinful; **manger une b. de haricots** to eat a canful *or Br* tinful of beans; **dévorer une b. entière de chocolats** to eat one's way through a *or* to eat a whole box of chocolates

5 *(pour le courrier)* **b. à** *ou* **aux lettres** *(dans la rue)* *Br* postbox, *Br* letterbox, *Am* mailbox; *(chez soi)* *Br* letterbox, *Am* mailbox; **mettre qch à la b. aux lettres** to mail *or Br* to post sth; **servir de b. aux lettres** to be a go-between; *Ordinat* **b. de dialogue** dialogue box; *Ordinat* **b. aux lettres électronique** electronic mailbox, email; **b. postale** PO box; **b. vocale** voice mail

6 *Aviat & Aut* **b. noire** black box

7 *Fam (entreprise)* firm; **b. d'intérim** temping agency; **j'ai changé de b.** I got a job with a new firm

8 *Fam (discothèque)* **b. (de nuit)** club, nightclub; **aller** *ou* **sortir en b.** to go to a nightclub, to go clubbing; **b. de jazz** jazz club

9 *Fam (lycée)* school□; *Péj* **b. à bac** *ou* **à bachot** *Br* crammer

10 *Anat* **b. crânienne** cranium

11 *Aut* **b. à gants** glove compartment; **b. de vitesses** gearbox

12 *Élec* **b. de dérivation** junction box

13 *Mus* **b. à musique** musical box; **b. à rythmes** beatbox

• **en boîte ADJ** canned, *Br* tinned **ADV mettre des fruits en b.** to can *or Br* to tin fruit; *Fam* **mettre qn en b.** to pull sb's leg, *Br* to wind sb up

boîte-pont [bwatpɔ̃] *(pl* **boîtes-ponts***)* **NF** *Aut* transaxle

boiter [3] [bwate] **VI** *(en marchant)* to limp, to be lame; **b. du pied droit** *ou* **de la jambe droite** to have a lame right leg

boiterie [bwatri] **NF** lameness

boiteux, -euse [bwatø, -øz] **ADJ 1** *(cheval, personne)* lame; *(meuble)* rickety; **il est b.** he walks with a limp, he limps **2** *(imparfait ▸ paix, alliance)* fragile, shaky; *(▸ comparaison, raisonnement)* unsound, shaky; *(▸ traduction, phrase)* iffy; *(▸ vers)* limping

NM,F lame man, *f* woman

boîtier [bwatje] **NM 1** *(gén)* case, casing; *(d'une lampe de poche)* battery compartment; **b. de montre** watchcase

2 *Phot* camera body

3 *Ordinat* **b. de commande** command box; **b. commutateur** data switch

4 *Aut* **b. de direction** steering box; *Élec* **b. de raccordement** connecting box

boitillement [bwatijmɑ̃] **NM** slight limp, hobble

boitiller [3] [bwatije] **VI** to limp slightly, to be slightly lame, to hobble; **elle est rentrée/sortie en boitillant** she hobbled in/out

boit-sans-soif [bwasɑ̃swaf] **NMF INV** *Fam* drunk, lush

boitte [bwat] = **boëte**

boivent *etc voir* **boire**

bol [bɔl] **NM 1** *(récipient)* bowl

2 *(contenu)* bowl, bowlful; **prendre un b. d'air** *(se promener)* to (go and) get some fresh air; *(changer d'environnement)* to get a change of air

3 *Fam (chance)* luck□; **avoir du b.** to be a lucky devil; **pas de b.!** what rotten luck!

4 *Can Fam (tête)* nut, head□

• **au bol ADJ** *(coupe de cheveux)* bowl *(avant n)*, *Br* pudding-bowl *(avant n)*

• **bol alimentaire NM** bolus

bolchevik, bolchevique [bɔlʃəvik] **ADJ** Bolshevik, Bolshevist

NMF Bolshevik, Bolshevist

bolchevisme [bɔlʃəvism] **NM** Bolshevism

bolduc [bɔldyk] **NM** ribbon *(used for gift wrapping)*

bolée [bɔle] **NF b. de cidre** bowl *or* bowlful of cider *(in north-west France, cider is often served in bowls)*

boléro [bɔlero] **NM 1** *Mus & (danse)* bolero **2** *(veste)* bolero

bolet [bɔle] **NM** *Bot* boletus

bolide [bɔlid] **NM 1** *(voiture de course)* fast (racing) car; **entrer dans une/sortir d'une pièce comme un b.** to hurtle into a/out of a room **2** *Astron* meteor, fireball, *Spéc* bolide

bolivar [bɔlivar] **NM** *(monnaie)* bolivar

Bolivie [bɔlivi] **NF la B.** Bolivia

bolivien, -enne [bɔlivjɛ̃, -ɛn] **ADJ** Bolivian

• **Bolivien, -enne NM,F** Bolivian

bolognaise [bɔlɔɲɛz] **ADJ F** *Culin* **sauce b.** bolognese sauce; **spaghettis (à la) b.** spaghetti bolognese

Bologne [bɔlɔɲ] **NF** *Géog* Bologna

bolonais, -e [bɔlɔnɛ, -ɛz] **ADJ** Bolognese

• **Bolonais, -e NM,F** Bolognese; **les B.** the Bolognese

bombage [bɔ̃baʒ] **NM 1** *(action)* spray-painting; *(graffiti)* (aerosol) graffiti **2** *(en verrerie)* bending

bombance [bɔ̃bɑ̃s] **NF** feast; **faire b.** to feast

bombardement [bɔ̃bardəmɑ̃] **NM 1** *Mil (avec des obus)* shelling *(UNCOUNT)*; *(avec des bombes)* bombing *(UNCOUNT)*; **b. aérien** air raid; **le b. atomique d'Hiroshima** the dropping of the atomic bomb on Hiroshima **2** *(lancement de projectiles)* showering, pelting; *Fig (de questions)* flood; *Phys* **b. atomique** atomic bombardment

bombarder [3] [bɔ̃barde] **VT 1** *Mil (avec des obus)* to shell; *(avec des bombes)* to bomb **2** *(avec des projectiles)* to shower, to pelt; *Phys* to bombard; **être bombardé de boules de neige** to be pelted with snowballs; *Fig* **b. qn de questions** to bombard sb with questions; **être bombardé de coups de téléphone** to be bombarded *or* inundated with phone calls **3** *(suivi d'un nom) Fam (promouvoir)* **il a été bombardé responsable du projet** he found himself catapulted into the position of project manager; **il a réussi à la faire b. directrice** he managed to pitchfork her into the position of director

bombardier [bɔ̃bardje] **NM** *Aviat & Mil (avion)* bomber; *(pilote)* bombardier

bombe [bɔ̃b] **NF 1** *Mil & Nucl* bomb; **b. A** A bomb; **b. atomique** atom *or* atomic bomb; **la b. atomique** the Bomb; **b. à eau** water-bomb; **b. à fragmentation** fragmentation bomb; **b. H** H bomb; **b. à hydrogène** hydrogen bomb; **b. incendiaire** firebomb; **b. à neutrons** neutron bomb; **b. radioactive** radioactive *or* dirty bomb; *aussi Fig* **b. à retardement** time bomb; **b. sale** dirty bomb; **arriver comme une b.** to come like a bolt out of the blue; **la nouvelle est arrivée comme une** *ou* **a fait l'effet d'une b.** the news came like a bolt out of the blue

2 *Géol* **b. volcanique** volcanic bomb

3 *(aérosol)* spray; **en b.** in a spray can; **peinture en b.** spray paint; **déodorant en b.** deodorant spray; **chantilly en b.** aerosol cream; **b. insecticide** *Br* fly *or Am* bug spray; **b. lacrymogène** *ou Fam* **lacrymo** *(utilisée par la police)* tear-gas canister; *(pour l'auto-défense)* mace spray

4 *Équitation* riding hat *or* cap

5 *Culin* **b. glacée** bombe

6 *Méd* **b. au cobalt** cobalt bomb, cobalt therapy unit

7 *très Fam (personne)* **b. sexuelle** sex kitten *or* bomb

8 *Fam (fête)* feast, spree; **faire la b.** to whoop it up, to have a riotous old time

• **à toute bombe ADV** *Fam* at full speed□, like

lightning; **aller à toute b.** to belt along, *Br* to bomb along

bombé, -e [bɔ̃be] **ADJ 1** *(renflé ▸ paroi)* bulging; (▸ *front)* bulging, domed; (▸ *poitrine, torse)* thrown out, stuck out; (▸ *forme)* rounded **2** *(convexe ▸ route)* cambered

bombement [bɔ̃bmɑ̃] **NM 1** *(renflement)* bulge **2** *(convexité ▸ route)* camber

bomber **[3]** [bɔ̃be] **VT 1** *(rendre convexe ▸ route, chaussée)* to camber **2** *(gonfler)* **b. le torse** to stick out one's chest; *Fig* to swagger about **3** *(slogan)* to spray, to spray-paint

VI 1 *(route)* to camber **2** *Fam (se dépêcher)* to belt along, *Br* to bomb along

bombeur, -euse [bɔ̃bœr, -øz] **NM,F** graffiti artist *(who uses spray paint)*

bombinette [bɔ̃binɛt] **NF** *Fam* **1** *(petite bombe)* little bomb **2** *(petite voiture très nerveuse)* nippy little car

bombonne [bɔ̃bɔn] = **bonbonne**

bôme [bom] **NF** *Naut* boom

BON, BONNE[1] [bɔ̃, bɔn]

ADJ
- good **A1–5, B1–4, C3, D1–3, E1, 3**
- valid **A4**
- correct, right **C1**
- nice **B1, 2**
- right, appropriate **C2**
- OK **C4**
- kind **D2**

NM,F
- good person **1**
- right one **2**

NM
- goodie **1**
- voucher, coupon **5**
- bond **6**

ADV
- nice, warm **1**

EXCLAM
- so **1**
- right **1, 2**
- OK **2**

ADJ A. *QUI CONVIENT, QUI DONNE SATISFACTION* **1** *(en qualité ▸ film, récolte, résultat, connaissance)* good; **très bonne idée!** very good *or* excellent idea!; **viande de bonne qualité** good-quality meat; **de très bonne qualité** of superior *or* very good quality; **elle parle un b. espagnol** she speaks good Spanish, her Spanish is good; **il a un b. accent en russe** he has a good accent in Russian *or* a good Russian accent; *Scol* **de bonnes notes** good *or* high *Br* marks *or Am* grades; *Tennis* **il a un b. service** he has a good serve, his serve is good, he serves well

2 *(qui remplit bien sa fonction ▸ matelas, siège, chaussures)* good, comfortable; (▸ *éclairage, hygiène)* good, adequate; (▸ *freins)* good, reliable; (▸ *cœur, veines, charpente, gestion, investissement)* good, sound; **de bonnes jambes** a strong pair of legs; **une bonne vue, de bons yeux** good eyesight

3 *(au tennis)* good; **la balle est bonne** the ball's in *or* good; *Ftbl* **la remise en jeu n'était pas bonne** it was a foul throw

4 *(qui n'est pas périmé ▸ nourriture)* good; (▸ *document, titre de transport)* valid; **le lait n'est plus b.** the milk has turned *or Br* has gone off; **l'eau du robinet n'est pas bonne** the water from the *Br* tap *or Am* faucet isn't drinkable *or* isn't fit to drink; **ta carte d'identité n'est plus bonne** your identity card is no longer valid; **la colle n'est plus bonne** the glue isn't usable any more

5 *(compétent ▸ acteur, conducteur, comptable)* good; (▸ *politique)* fine, good; **b. père et b. époux** a good father and husband; **en b. professeur, il me reprend lorsque je fais des fautes** he corrects my mistakes, as any good teacher would; **être/ne pas être b. en musique** to be good/bad at music; **nos bons clients** our good *or* regular customers

6 b. à *(digne de)* **les poires/piles sont bonnes à jeter** the pears/batteries can go straight in the *Br* bin *or Am* trash can; **je ne suis bonne qu'à repasser tes chemises!** I'm only fit to iron your shirts!; **il y a un restaurant là-bas – c'est b. à savoir** there's a restaurant there – that's worth knowing *or* that's good to know; **à quoi b.?** what for?; **à quoi b. insister** there's no point in insisting; **je pourrais lui écrire, mais à quoi b.?** I could write to him/her but what would be the point?

7 *(condamné à)* **il est b. pour 15 ans (de prison)** he's going to get 15 years in prison; *Mil* **b. pour le service** fit for (national) service; *Fam* **on est bons pour une amende** we stand to get a fine; *Fam* **les motards nous suivent – on est bons!** the cops are following us – we've had it *or* we're in for it!

B. *PLAISANT* **1** *(pour les sens)* good, nice; **ton ragoût était très b.** your casserole was very good *or* nice; **il y a une bonne odeur de café ici** there's a nice smell of coffee in here; **avoir une bonne odeur** to smell good *or* nice; **viens te baigner, l'eau est bonne!** come for a swim, the water's lovely (and warm)!; **elle est bonne?** *(l'eau)* what's the water like?

2 *(atmosphère, compagnie, semaine)* good, nice, pleasant; **je me souviens des bons moments** I remember the good *or* happy times; **vous avez passé un b. Noël?** did you enjoy your Christmas?, did you have a good *or* nice Christmas?; **b. anniversaire!** happy birthday!; **bonne (et heureuse) année!** happy New Year!; **b. appétit!** enjoy your meal!, *Am* enjoy!; **bonne chance!** good luck!; **bonne journée!** have a nice day!; **b. voyage!** *(plaisant)* have a nice *or* good trip!; *(sans incident)* have a safe journey!; **passe une bonne soirée** enjoy yourself (tonight)

3 *(en intensif)* **un b. grog bien chaud** a nice hot toddy; **elle est bien bonne celle-là!** that's a good one (that)!; *Ironique* that's a bit much!; **se payer du b. temps** to have fun, to have a great *or* good time; **le b. vieux temps** the good old days; **c'était le b. temps!** those were the (good old) days!; **les bonnes vieilles méthodes** the good old methods

4 *(favorable, optimiste ▸ prévisions, présage)* good, favourable; (▸ *nouvelle)* good; **c'est (un) b. signe** it's a good sign

C. *JUSTE, ADÉQUAT* **1** *(correct ▸ numéro de téléphone)* right; (▸ *réponse, solution)* correct, right; **c'est la bonne rue** it's the right street

2 *(opportun)* right, convenient, appropriate; **ce n'est pas la bonne époque** it isn't the right time; **l'héritage est arrivé au b. moment pour elle** the inheritance came at the right time *or* at a convenient time for her; **je suis arrivé au b. moment pour les séparer** I got there in time to separate them; **ayez le b. geste** *(en sauvetage)* do the right thing; *(honnête)* do the decent thing; **juger** *ou* **trouver b. de** to think it appropriate *or* fitting to; **elle n'a pas jugé b. de s'excuser** she didn't see fit to apologize; **juger** *ou* **trouver b. que** to think it appropriate *or* fitting that; **il n'est pas toujours b. de dire ce que l'on pense** it's not always a good *or* wise thing to say what's on one's mind; **il serait b. de préciser l'heure de la réunion** it would be a good idea to say what time the meeting is; **il ne serait pas b. que l'on nous voie ensemble** it wouldn't be a good thing for us to be seen together; **il serait b. que tu te fasses oublier** you'd do well to keep *or* you'd better keep a low profile; **comme/où/quand/si b. vous semble** as/wherever/whenever/if you see fit

3 *(bénéfique, salutaire)* good, beneficial; **c'est b. pour les plantes** it's good for the plants; **c'est b. contre** *ou* **pour le mal de mer** it's good for seasickness; **b. pour la santé** good for you, good for your health; **le b. air de la campagne** the good *or* fresh country air

4 *Fam (locutions)* **c'est b.!** *(c'est juste)* that's right!; *(ça suffit)* that'll do!; *(c'est d'accord)* OK!; **c'est b., c'est b., je m'en occupe!** OK, OK, I'll do it!; **c'est b.?** OK?

D. *MORALEMENT* **1** *(décent, honnête ▸ conduite)* good, proper; (▸ *influence, mœurs)* good; **avoir de bonnes fréquentations** to mix with the right sort of people; **ils n'ont pas bonne réputation** they don't have a good reputation; **un b. Français n'aurait pas accepté la défaite** a good *or* proper Frenchman wouldn't have admitted defeat

2 *(bienveillant, amical ▸ personne)* good, kind, kindly; (▸ *sourire)* kind, warm; *Rel* **Dieu est b.** God is merciful; **avoir une bonne tête** *ou Fam* **bouille** to have a nice *or* a friendly face▫; **avoir l'air b.** to look kind *or* kindly; *Fam* **dites-lui plein de bonnes choses de ma part** give him/her my love; **avoir de bons rapports avec qn** to be on good terms with sb; **avoir b. cœur** to be kind-hearted; **de b. cœur** willingly; **tenez, prenez, c'est de b. cœur** please have it, I'd love you to; **le B. Dieu** the (good) Lord

3 *(brave)* good; **c'est un b. garçon** he's a good lad *or* sort; **c'est une bonne petite** she's a nice *or* good girl; **alors ma bonne dame, qu'est-ce qu'il vous faut aujourd'hui?** well, madam, what do you need today?

E. *EN INTENSIF* **1** *(grand, gros)* good; **un b. mètre de tissu** at least one metre *or* a good metre of material; **une bonne averse** a heavy shower (of rain); **une bonne tranche** a thick slice; **donnez-moi une bonne livre de raisin** give me a pound of grapes or a little over; **elle fait un b. 42** she's a 42 or a 44, she's a large 42; **ça a duré une bonne minute** it lasted a good minute or so; **une bonne cuillère à soupe de farine** a heaped tablespoon *or* tablespoonful of flour

2 *(fort, violent)* **un b. coup** *(heurt)* a hefty *or* full blow; **un b. coup de pied** a powerful kick; **un b. coup de bâton** a mighty crack with a stick; **une bonne fessée** a good *or* sound spanking; *Fam* **pleurer un b. coup** to have a good cry

3 *(complet, exemplaire)* good; **le mur a besoin d'un b. lessivage** the wall needs a good scrub; **arriver** *ou* **être b. dernier** to bring up the rear; **une bonne fois pour toutes** once and for all

ADJ F *Fam (belle)* gorgeous, stunning, *Br* fit; **elle est bonne, la sœur à Frédo** Frédo's sister is a real babe *or Br* cracker

NM,F 1 *(personne vertueuse)* good person; **les bons** the good

2 *(personne idéale, chose souhaitée)* right one; *Fam* **je crois que c'est enfin le b.** *(lors d'un recrutement)* I think we've got our man at last; *(lors d'une rencontre amoureuse)* I think it's Mr Right at last

3 *(personne, chose de qualité)* **c'est un b./une bonne!** he's/she's good!; **on m'en soumet beaucoup mais je ne publie que les bons** I get a lot of them sent to me but I only publish the good ones

4 *(par affection)* **mon b.** *(à un jeune homme)* my dear boy; *(à un homme mûr)* my dear man; **ma bonne** *(à une jeune femme)* my dear girl; *(à une femme mûre)* my dear

NM 1 *Cin (dans les films)* goody, goodie; **jouer le rôle du b.** to play the good guy; **les bons et les méchants** the goodies and the baddies, the good guys and the bad guys

2 *(chose de qualité)* **n'acheter que du b.** to buy only good quality; **il y a du b. et du mauvais dans ses propositions** his/her proposals have some good points *or* their merits; **avoir du b.** to have something good about it; **cette solution a cela de b. qu'elle est moins chère que les autres** this solution is interesting insofar as it is less expensive than the others

3 *(ce qui est moral)* **le b.** good

4 *(ce qui est plaisant)* **le b. de l'histoire, c'est que...** the funniest *or* best part of the story is that...

5 *(coupon)* voucher, coupon; **b. d'achat** discount voucher *(for future purchases)*; **b. de caisse** cash voucher; *Compta* interest-bearing note; **b. de commande** order form, purchase order; **b. d'expédition** dispatch note, consignment note; **b. de garantie** guarantee, guarantee slip; **b. de livraison** delivery note; *Fin* **b. à moyen terme négociable** medium term note; **b. de réduction** money-off coupon *or* voucher; **b. de remboursement** money-off voucher

6 *Bourse* **b. d'épargne** savings bond *or* certificate; **b. nominatif** registered bond; **b. de participation** participation certificate; **b. au porteur** bearer bond; **b. de souscription d'actions** equity *or* subscription warrant; **b. de souscription de parts de créateurs d'entreprise** = stock option in start-up company with tax privileges; **b. du Trésor** Treasury bill; *(obligation à terme)* Treasury bond

ADV 1 *Météo* **il fait b. ici** it's nice and warm here; **il fait b. ce soir** it's a nice evening

2 *(suivi d'un infinitif)* **il ne fait pas b. la déranger** you'll be ill-advised to disturb her; **il ne fait pas b. se promener seul dans les rues** walking the streets alone is not to be recommended; **il ne faisait pas b. être communiste alors** it wasn't advisable to be a communist in those days

EXCLAM 1 *(marque une transition)* right, so, well now; **b., eh bien je m'en vais** right, I'm off now; **b., où en étais-je?** right *or* so, where was I?

2 *(en réponse)* right, OK, fine; **sors d'ici! – b., b.,**

c'est pas la peine de crier! get out of here! – OK, OK, no need to shout!

• **bon à rien, bonne à rien** ADJ **1** *(inutile)* **je suis trop vieux, je ne suis plus b. à rien** I'm too old, I'm useless *or* no good now **2** *(incompétent)* useless, hopeless NM,F *(personne sans valeur)* good-for-nothing; *(personne incompétente)* useless individual

• **bon à tirer** NM press proof, final corrected proof; **donner le b. à tirer** to pass for press

• **bonne femme** NF *Fam* **1** *(femme)* woman□; **une vieille bonne femme** an old biddy **2** *(petite fille)* **une petite bonne femme adorable** a lovely little girl **3** *(épouse)* wife□, *Br* missus ADJ **1** *Culin* = cooking term used in the names of simple country dishes **2** *Couture* **des rideaux bonne femme** = old-fashioned curtains with tie-backs and frilled edges

• **bonnes feuilles** NFPL *(dans l'édition)* press proofs, final corrected proofs

bonapartisme [bɔnapartism] NM Bonapartism

bonapartiste [bɔnapartist] ADJ Bonapartist NMF Bonapartist

bonasse [bɔnas] ADJ *Péj* too easy-going, soft; **répondre d'un ton b.** to answer mildly

bonbon [bɔ̃bɔ̃] NM **1** *(sucrerie) Br* sweet, *Am* candy; **b. acidulé** acid drop; **b. anglais** fruit drop; **b. à la menthe** mint **2** *Belg (biscuit) Br* biscuit, *Am* cookie **3** *très Fam* **casser les bonbons à qn** to piss sb off, *Br* to get on sb's tits, *Am* to break sb's balls ADV *Fam* **coûter b.** to cost an arm and a leg *or* a packet *or Br* a bomb

bonbonne [bɔ̃bɔn] NF *(pour le vin)* demijohn; *(pour des produits chimiques)* carboy; **b. de gaz** gas canister

bonbonnière [bɔ̃bɔnjɛr] NF **1** *(boîte) Br* sweet *or Am* candy box **2** *(appartement)* bijou *Br* flat *or Am* apartment

bon-chrétien [bɔ̃kretjɛ̃] *(pl* **bons-chrétiens***)* NM *(poire)* William's (Bon Chrétien) pear

bond [bɔ̃] NM **1** *(d'une balle)* bounce; **prendre** *ou* **saisir la balle au b.** to catch the ball on the bounce *or* rebound; *Fig* to seize the opportunity **2** *(saut)* jump, leap; **faire un b.** *(d'effroi, de surprise)* to leap up; **faire des bonds** to jump up and down; *Fig* to go up and down; **faire un b. en avant** *(économie)* to boom; *(prix, loyer)* to soar; *(recherche)* to leap forward; **se lever d'un b.** to leap up; **franchir un ruisseau d'un b.** to clear a stream at one jump, to leap across a stream; **avancer** *ou* **progresser par bonds** to come on *or* to progress in leaps and bounds; *Hist* **le grand b. en avant** the Great Leap Forward

3 *Sport* jump

4 *(locution)* **faire faux b. à qn** *(ne pas se présenter)* to leave sb high and dry; *(décevoir)* to let sb down

bonde [bɔ̃d] NF **1** *(ouverture* ▸ *d'un tonneau)* bunghole; *(*▸ *d'un lavabo)* plughole **2** *(système de fermeture* ▸ *d'un tonneau)* bung, stopper; *(*▸ *d'un lavabo)* plug; *(*▸ *d'un bassin)* sluice gate

bondé, -e [bɔ̃de] ADJ packed, jam-packed; **le train était b.** the train was packed (with people)

bondieuserie [bɔ̃djøzri] NF *Fam Péj* **1** *(objet)* religious trinket□ **2** *(bigoterie)* religiosity□

bondir [32] [bɔ̃dir] VI **1** *(sauter)* to bounce, to bound, to leap (up); **le chat bondit sur la souris** the cat pounced *or* leapt on the mouse; **la moto bondit en avant** the motorbike leapt forward; **b. de joie** to leap for joy; **b. sur** *(pour importuner, semoncer)* to pounce on; **pareille inconscience me fait b.** such recklessness makes my blood boil; **ça va le faire b.** *(d'indignation, de colère)* he'll hit the roof, he'll go mad **2** *(courir)* to dash, to rush; **quand il a appris l'accident, il a bondi jusqu'à l'hôpital** when he heard about the accident, he rushed (over) to the hospital

bon enfant [bɔ̃nɑ̃fɑ̃] ADJ INV *(caractère, personne)* good-natured, easy-going; *(atmosphère)* relaxed, informal

bonheur [bɔnœr] NM **1** *(chance)* luck; **par b.** fortunately, luckily; **j'ai eu le b. de la connaître** I was lucky enough to know her; **tu ne connais pas ton b.!** you don't know when you're lucky *or* how lucky you are!; **porter b. à qn** to bring sb luck; **ça ne lui a pas porté b.!** he lived to regret it!, he had cause to bemoan the fact later! **2** *(contentement)* happiness; **quel b. de vous revoir!** how marvellous to see you again!; **b. total** bliss; **connaître le b.** to know what it's like to be happy, to experience happiness; **faire le b. de qn** *(le contenter)* to make sb happy, to bring sb happiness; **si cette robe peut faire ton b., prends-la** if this dress is any good *or* use to you, then take it; **trouver le b.** to find happiness; **as-tu trouvé ton b.?** did you find what you were looking for?

• **au petit bonheur (la chance)** ADV haphazardly

• **avec bonheur** ADV *Littéraire* **le salé et le sucré s'allient avec b.** savoury and sweet combine happily *or* are a happy combination

bonheur-du-jour [bɔnœrdyʒur] *(pl* **bonheurs-du-jour***)* NM escritoire, writing table

bonhomie [bɔnɔmi] NF geniality, bonhomie; **avec b.** good-naturedly

bonhomme [bɔnɔm] *(pl* **bonshommes** [bɔ̃zɔm]*)* *Fam* NM **1** *(homme)* fellow, *Br* chap; **un sale b.** a nasty piece of work

2 *(partenaire)* old man, *Vieilli* fellow; *(garçon)* lad; **allez viens, mon petit b.** come along, little man

3 *(figure)* man; **dessiner des bonshommes** to draw little men *or* people; **b. de neige** snowman; **le b. Noël** Father Christmas, Santa Claus; **(petit) b. de pain d'épice** gingerbread man

4 *(locutions)* **aller** *ou* **suivre son petit b. de chemin** to go *or* to carry on at one's own pace; **l'idée faisait son petit b. de chemin** the idea was slowly but surely gaining ground

ADJ *(air, caractère)* good-natured, good-tempered; **…, dit-il d'un ton b.** …, he said good-naturedly

boni [bɔni] NM *Com* **1** *(bénéfice)* profit; **faire un** *ou* **du b.** to make a profit; **b. de liquidation** liquidation surplus **2** *(dépense)* balance in hand **3** *(bonus, prime)* bonus

boniche [bɔniʃ] = **bonniche**

bonification [bɔnifikasjɔ̃] NF **1** *Agr* improvement

2 *Sport* bonus points; *(en cyclisme)* time bonus

3 *(somme allouée)* profit

4 *(rabais)* discount, reduction

5 *(prime)* bonus

bonifié, -e [bɔnifje] ADJ **1** *Agr* improved **2** *Banque (prêt)* soft, at a reduced rate of interest; *Fin (taux)* reduced

bonifier [9] [bɔnifje] VT **1** *Agr* to improve

2 *(adoucir* ▸ *caractère)* to improve

3 *(payer)* to pay as a bonus

4 *Écon* to credit

VPR **se bonifier** *(vin, caractère)* to improve

boniment [bɔnimɑ̃] NM **1** *Com* sales talk *or* patter; **faire du** *ou* **son b.** to deliver the sales patter *or* spiel; *Fam* **faire du b. à qn** *(pour convaincre)* to sweet-talk sb; *(pour séduire) Br* to chat sb up, *Am* to hit on sb **2** *Fam (mensonge)* tall story; **ce ne sont que des boniments** that's a load of claptrap *or* guff; **arrête tes boniments** stop fibbing

bonimenter [3] [bɔnimɑ̃te] VI *Fam* to deliver the sales talk *or* the patter

bonite [bɔnit] NF *Ich* bonito

bonjour [bɔ̃ʒur] NM **1** *(salutation* ▸ *gén)* hello; *(*▸ *le matin)* good morning; *(*▸ *l'après-midi)* good afternoon; *Can (au revoir* ▸ *pendant la journée)* goodbye, bye, see you later; **b., comment allez-vous?** hello, how are you?; **va dire b. à la dame** go and say hello to the lady; **vous lui donnerez le b.** *ou* **vous lui direz b. de ma part** say hello for me; **vous avez le b. de Martin** Martin sends his love **2** *Fam (exprime la difficulté)* **pour le faire aller à l'école, b.!** no way can you get him to go to school!; **b. l'odeur!** what a smell!□; **si mes parents l'apprennent, b. l'ambiance!** if my parents find out, there'll be one hell of an atmosphere!; **b. les dégâts!** what a mess!; *(ça va aller mal)* there'll be trouble!

bon marché [bɔ̃marʃe] ADJ INV cheap, inexpensive

bonnard [bɔnar] ADJ *Fam* great, *Am* neat; *(personne)* nice□

bonne[1] [bɔn] *voir* **bon**

bonne[2] [bɔn] NF **1** *(domestique)* maid; **b. d'enfants** nanny, nursemaid; **b. à tout faire** servant, maid of all work **2** *Fam (chose plaisante)* **il m'en a raconté une bien b.** he told me a good one **3** *(locutions)* **avoir qn à la b.** to like sb, *Am* to be in (solid) with sb; **le patron m'a à la b.!** I'm in the boss's good books!, the boss likes me!; **la petite Julie t'a à la b.!** Julie's really sweet on you!; **tu en as de bonnes!** are you kidding?

Bonne-Espérance [bɔnesperɑ̃s] *voir* **cap**[1]

bonne-maman [bɔnmamɑ̃] *(pl* **bonnes-mamans***)* NF *Vieilli* grand-mama

bonnement [bɔnmɑ̃] ADV **tout b.** (quite) simply

bonnet [bɔnɛ] NM **1** *(coiffe* ▸ *de femme, d'enfant)* hat, bonnet; *(*▸ *de soldat, de marin)* hat; *Fig* **gros b.** big shot, big wig; **b. d'âne** dunce's cap; **b. de bain** swimming cap; **b. de douche** shower cap; **b. de nuit** nightcap; *Fig Péj* wet blanket; **b. à poils** busby, bearskin; *Vieilli* **b. de police** forage cap; **b. phrygien** cap of liberty, Phrygian cap; **b. de ski** ski cap; **c'est b. blanc et blanc b.** it's six of one and half a dozen of the other, *Br* it's all much of a muchness; **prendre qch sous son b.** to take the initiative of doing sth; **il a pris sous son b. de le faire** he did it off his own bat; *Fam* **te casse pas le b.!** don't worry about it!□, don't let it bother you!□ **2** *Zool* reticulum **3** *(d'un soutien-gorge)* cup; **quelle profondeur de b.?** what cup size?

bonneterie [bɔnetri] NF **1** *(commerce)* hosiery business *or* trade

2 *(industrie)* hosiery-making (industry)

3 *(magasin)* hosier's (shop)

4 *(articles)* hosiery

bonnetier, -ère [bɔntje, -ɛr] NM,F **1** *(fabricant)* hosier **2** *(ouvrier)* hosiery worker

bonnette [bɔnet] NF *Tech (objectif)* positive supplementary lens; **b. (anti-vent)** *(d'un microphone)* windscreen, windshield

bonniche [bɔniʃ] NF *Fam Péj* maid□, *Br* skivvy; **je ne suis pas ta b.!** I'm not here to clean up your mess!

bonobo [bɔnɔbɔ] NM *Zool* bonobo

bon-papa [bɔ̃papa] *(pl* **bons-papas***)* NM *Vieilli* grand-papa

bonsaï [bɔnzaj] NM *Hort* bonsai

bonshommes [bɔ̃zɔm] *voir* **bonhomme**

bonsoir [bɔ̃swar] NM *(en arrivant* ▸ *le soir)* good evening; *(en partant* ▸ *le soir)* good night; *Can (en partant* ▸ *le soir)* goodbye; **viens dire b. à maman** come and say good night to mummy; **je vous souhaite le b.** I wish you a good night

bonté [bɔ̃te] NF *(bienveillance)* kindness, goodness; **une femme d'une grande b.** a very kind *or* good woman; **un sourire plein de b.** a kind(ly) *or* benevolent smile; **elle l'a fait par pure b. d'âme** she did it out of the goodness of her heart; **il a eu la b. de passer nous voir** he was kind enough to come for a visit; **ayez la b. de…** please be so kind as to…; **b. divine!, b. du ciel!** good gracious!

• **bontés** NFPL *Littéraire* kindness, kindnesses

bonus [bɔnys] NM **1** *Assur* no-claims bonus

2 *Mktg* bonus

3 *(sur un DVD)* special feature

4 *Fig* bonus

bonus-malus [bɔnysmalys] NM INV *Assur* no-claims bonus system

bonze [bɔ̃z] NM **1** *Rel* Buddhist monk, bonze **2** *Fam Fig Péj* big cheese; **un vieux b.** a pompous old fool

bonzerie [bɔ̃zri] NF *Rel* Buddhist monastery

bonzesse [bɔ̃zes] NF *Rel* Buddhist nun

boogie-woogie [bugiwugi] NM *Mus & (danse)* boogie-woogie

book [buk] NM pressbook, portfolio

bookmaker [bukmekœr] NM bookmaker

bookmark [bukmark] NM *Ordinat* bookmark

booléen, -enne [buleɛ̃, -ɛn], **boolien, -enne** [buljɛ̃, -ɛn] ADJ *Math & Ordinat* Boolean

boom [bum] NM **1** *(développement)* boom, expansion; **le b. de la natalité** the baby boom; **le b. des fours à micro-ondes** the booming microwave oven market **2** *Bourse* boom

boomerang [bumrɑ̃g] NM *(arme, jeu)* boomerang; *Fig* **faire b., avoir un effet b.** to boomerang

booster[1] [bustœr] **NM 1** *(d'une fusée)* booster **2** *(d'une radio, du son)* booster

booster[2] **[3]** [buste] **VT** *Fam (stimuler)* to boost

booter [3] [bute] **VI** *Ordinat* **b. (sur le lecteur B)** to boot (off the B drive)

boots [buts] **NMPL OU NFPL** (desert) boots

borate [bɔrat] **NM** *Chim* borate

borax [bɔraks] **NM** *Chim* borax, tincal

borborygme [bɔrbɔrigm] **NM 1** *(gargouillement)* rumble, gurgle, *Spéc* borborygmus **2** *Péj (paroles)* **borborygmes** mumbling

borchtch [bɔrtʃ] = **bortsch**

bord [bɔr] **NM 1** *(côté* ▸ *d'une forêt, d'un domaine)* edge; *(*▸ *d'une route)* side; **dessine sur le b. de ta feuille** draw on the edge of your paper; **sur le b. de la route** by the roadside; **sur les bords du fleuve** *(gén)* on the river bank; *(en ville)* on the waterfront; **sur les bords de Seine** on the embankment (in Paris), on the banks of the Seine; **regagner le b.** *(de la mer)* to get back to the shore *or* beach; *(d'une rivière)* to get back to the bank; *(d'une piscine)* to get back to the side; **le b. du trottoir** the kerb; **le b. de mer** the seafront; *Ordinat* **b. de reliure** inside margin

2 *(pourtour* ▸ *d'une plaie)* edge; *(*▸ *d'une assiette, d'une baignoire)* rim, edge; *(*▸ *d'un verre)* rim; **remplir un verre jusqu'au b.** to fill a glass to the brim *or* to the top

3 *Couture (non travaillé)* edge; *(replié et cousu)* hem; *(décoratif)* border; **chapeau à larges bords** wide-brimmed *or* broad-brimmed hat; **b. ourlé** rolled hem

4 *Naut (côté, bastingage)* side; **jeter qch/tomber par-dessus b.** to throw sth/to fall overboard; **tirer des bords** to tack; **les hommes du b.** the crew; **prendre qn à son b.** to take sb on board *or* aboard

5 *(opinion)* side; **nous sommes du même b.** we're on the same side

• **à bord ADV** *Aut* on board; *Aviat & Naut* aboard, on board; **il y avait toute une famille à b.** there was an entire family on board *or* in the vehicle; **avant de monter à b.** before boarding *or* going aboard; **être seul maître à b.** to be the one in charge

• **à bord de PRÉP** on board; **à b. d'un navire/d'une voiture** on board a ship/car; **monter à b. d'un bateau/avion** to board a boat/plane

• **au bord de PRÉP 1** *(en bordure de)* **une maison au b. de la mer** a house by the sea, a seaside house; **se promener au b. de l'eau/la mer** to walk at the water's edge/the seaside; **aller au b. de la mer** to go to the seaside; **je l'ai trouvé au b. de la rivière** I found it on the river bank; **s'arrêter au b. de la route** to stop by the roadside **2** *(à la limite de)* on the brink *or* verge of, very close to; **au b. des larmes/de la dépression** on the verge of tears/of a nervous breakdown; **au b. de la défaillance** very close to fainting

• **bord à bord ADV** edge to edge

• **de bord ADJ** *(journal, livre, commandant)* ship's

• **de haut bord ADJ** rated

• **sur les bords ADV** slightly, a touch; **il est un peu radin sur les bords** he's a bit tight-fisted

bordage [bɔrdaʒ] **NM 1** *Couture* edging **2** *Naut (en bois)* planking; *(en métal)* plating

bordé [bɔrde] **NM 1** *Naut (en bois)* planking; *(en fer)* plating **2** *Couture* (piece of) trimming

bordeaux [bɔrdo] **ADJ INV** *(grenat)* burgundy *(avant n)*, claret *(avant n)*

NM *(vin)* Bordeaux (wine); **un b. rouge** a red Bordeaux, a claret

bordée [bɔrde] **NF 1** *Naut (canons, salve)* broadside; *(distance)* tack; **lâcher une b.** to let fly a broadside; **tirer des bordées** to tack; *Fam Fig* **tirer une b.** to paint the town red; *Fam* **être en b.** to be on a binge; *Fig* **une b. d'insultes** a torrent *or* stream of abuse **2** *Naut (partie de l'équipage)* watch **3** *Can* **b. de neige** heavy snowfall

bordel [bɔrdɛl] *très Fam* **NM 1** *(hôtel de passe)* brothel, whorehouse, *Arch* bawdy-house **2** *(désordre)* shambles *(singulier)*, mess; **range ton b.!** clean up your (damn) mess!; **c'est toujours un vrai b. chez toi!** your place is always a shambles!; **foutre le b. dans une pièce/réunion** to turn a room into a pigsty/a meeting into a shambles; **ils sont venus foutre le b.** they only came to mess things up; **et tout le b.** and the whole damn lot **3** *(vacarme)* racket; **foutre le b.** to make a hell of a racket

EXCLAM shit!; **mais qu'est-ce qu'il fout, b.!** what is he doing, for Christ's sake?; *Vulg* **b. de merde!** fuck!, fucking hell!

bordelais, -e [bɔrdəle, -ez] **ADJ 1** *(de Bordeaux)* of/from Bordeaux **2** *(du Bordelais)* of/from the Bordeaux area

• **Bordelais, -e NM,F** = inhabitant of or person from Bordeaux

• **bordelaise NF** *(bouteille)* Bordeaux bottle; *(futaille)* = cask of about 225 litres

bordélique [bɔrdelik] **ADJ** *très Fam (chambre)* messy; *(écriture, esprit, réunion)* chaotic; **c'est plutôt b. chez toi** your place is a total shambles; **il est vraiment b.!** he leaves such a mess everywhere!

border [3] [bɔrde] **VT 1** *(garnir)* to edge, to trim; **b. qch de** to trim *or* to edge sth with; **un jupon bordé de dentelle** a lace-edged petticoat

2 *(en se couchant)* **as-tu bien bordé ton lit?** did you tuck the blankets in properly?; **va te coucher, je viendrai te b.** go to bed, I'll come and tuck you in

3 *(délimiter)* to line; **les troènes qui bordent la clôture** the privet lining the fence; **la route est bordée de haies** the road is lined with hedges

4 *Naut (de planches)* to plank; *(de tôles)* to plate; *(voile)* to haul on

bordereau, -x [bɔrdəro] **NM 1** *Fin & Com* note, slip; *(de marchandises)* invoice, account; *(formulaire)* form; **suivant b. ci-inclus** as per enclosed statement; **b. d'achat** purchase note; *Compta* **b. de caisse** cash statement; *Compta* **b. de compte** statement of account; **b. de dépôt** paying-in slip; *Banque* **b. d'encaissement** paying-in slip; **b. d'escompte** list of bills for discount; **b. d'expédition** *ou* **d'envoi** dispatch note, consignment note; **b. de livraison** delivery note; **b. (des) prix** price list; *Banque* **b. de remise (d'espèces** *ou* **de chèques)** paying-in slip; *Banque* **b. de retrait** withdrawal slip; *Compta* **b. de saisie** accounting entry sheet; **b. de salaire** salary advice, wages slip; **b. de vente** sales slip; *Banque* **b. de versement** *Br* paying-in slip, *Am* deposit slip **2** *Jur* **b. des pièces** docket

bordure [bɔrdyr] **NF 1** *(bord* ▸ *d'un évier)* edge; *(*▸ *d'un verre)* edge, rim; *(*▸ *d'une plate-bande)* border, edge; *(*▸ *d'une cheminée) Br* surround, *Am* border; **la b. du trottoir** *Br* the kerb, *Am* the curb

2 *(bande décorative)* border; **des assiettes à b. dorée** plates with a gold border *or* edged in gold

3 *(d'un vêtement)* border, edge; *(d'un chapeau)* brim; **foulard à b. bleue** scarf trimmed *or* edged with blue *or* with a blue border

4 *Typ & Ordinat (d'un paragraphe, d'une cellule)* border

• **en bordure de PRÉP en b. de mer** by the sea; **le parc est juste en b. de la ville** the park is on the edge of the town

bordurette [bɔrdyrɛt] **NF** = kerb separating a bus lane from the rest of the roadway

bore [bɔr] **NM** *Chim* boron

boréal, -e, -als *ou* **-aux, -ales** [bɔreal, -o] **ADJ** North *(avant n)*

borgne [bɔrɲ] **ADJ 1** *(personne)* one-eyed; **un homme b.** a one-eyed man, a man who's blind in one eye **2** *(fenêtre, mur)* obstructed **3** *(mal fréquenté* ▸ *hôtel)* shady

NMF one-eyed person

borique [bɔrik] **ADJ** *Chim* boracic, boric; **acide b.** boric acid

boriqué, -e [bɔrike] **ADJ** *Pharm* **pommade boriquée** boracic ointment; **compresse en coton b.** boracic lint compress

bornage [bɔrnaʒ] **NM** *Jur* boundary marking; **procéder au b. d'un terrain** to mark the boundaries of a plot

borne [bɔrn] **NF 1** *(pour délimiter)* boundary stone, landmark; **b. kilométrique** milepost; **ne reste pas planté là comme une b.!** don't just stand there!

2 *(point) Ordinat* **b. d'accès** *(à Internet)* access point; **b. d'appel d'urgence** emergency call box; **b. d'information** information point; **b. d'incendie** (fire) hydrant, *Am* fireplug; *Ordinat* **b. interactive** *ou* **multimédia** interactive terminal; *Ordinat* **b. Wi-Fi** hot spot

3 *(pour marquer un emplacement)* bollard; **b. d'amarrage** bollard

4 *Fam (kilomètre)* kilometre❑

5 *Élec* terminal

6 *Math* bound; **b. inférieure/supérieure** lower/upper bound

• **bornes NFPL** *Fig* bounds, limits; **sans bornes** *(patience, ambition)* boundless; **dépasser** *ou* **passer les bornes** to go too far; **son ambition n'a** *ou* **ne connaît pas de bornes** his/her ambition knows no bounds

borné, -e [bɔrne] **ADJ 1** *(individu)* narrow-minded; *(esprit)* narrow **2** *Math* bounded

borne-fontaine [bɔrnfɔ̃tɛn] *(pl* **bornes-fontaines) NF 1** *(fontaine)* public drinking fountain **2** *Can (bouche d'incendie)* (fire) hydrant, *Am* fireplug

borner [3] [bɔrne] **VT 1** *(délimiter* ▸ *champ, terrain)* to mark off *or* out, to mark the boundary of **2** *(restreindre)* to limit, to restrict

VPR se borner 1 se b. à *(se limiter à)* to be limited *or* restricted to; **son rôle se borne à recevoir les clients** his/her role is limited to welcoming the clients; **nos relations se sont bornées à quelques échanges sur le palier** our relationship was never more than the odd conversation on the landing **2 se b. à** *(se contenter de)* to limit *or* to restrict oneself to; **bornez-vous à l'essentiel** keep to the essentials; **se b. à faire qch** to limit *or* restrict oneself to doing sth; **je me bornerai à quelques commentaires** I'll just make a few comments

bortsch [bɔrtʃ] **NM** *Culin* borsch, borscht

bosco [bɔsko] **NM** *Fam Naut* bosun❑, boatswain❑

bosniaque [bɔsnjak] **ADJ** Bosnian

• **Bosniaque NMF** Bosnian

Bosnie [bɔsni] **NF la B.** Bosnia

Bosnie-Herzégovine [bɔsniɛrzegɔvin] **NF la B.** Bosnia-Herzegovina

bosnien, -enne [bɔsnjɛ̃, -ɛn] **ADJ** Bosnian

• **Bosnien, -enne NM,F** Bosnian

Bosphore [bɔsfɔr] **NM le B.** the Bosphorus, the Bosporus

bosquet [bɔskɛ] **NM** coppice, copse

boss [bɔs] **NM** *Fam* boss; **à la maison, c'est elle le b.!** she's the boss *or* she wears the trousers at home!

bossage [bɔsaʒ] **NM** *Archit & Tech* boss

bossa-nova [bɔsanɔva] *(pl* **bossas-novas) NF** *Mus* bossa nova

bosse [bɔs] **NF 1** *(à la suite d'un coup)* bump, lump; **se faire une b.** to get a bump

2 *Anat & Zool (protubérance)* hump; **b. de bison** dowager's hump; *Fam* **rouler sa b.** to knock about; *Fig* **avoir la b. des maths/du commerce** to be a born mathematician/businessman, *f* businesswoman

3 *(du sol)* bump; *(en ski)* mogul; **un terrain plein de bosses** a bumpy piece of ground

4 *Naut* painter

• **en bosse ADJ** *Beaux-Arts* embossed

bosselage [bɔslaʒ] **NM** *Beaux-Arts* embossing

bosseler [24] [bɔsle] **VT 1** *Beaux-Arts* to emboss **2** *(faire des bosses à)* to dent

bossellera *etc voir* **bosseler**

bosselure [bɔslyr] **NF** (irregular) bumps

bosser [3] [bɔse] *Fam* **VI** to work❑; **j'ai bossé toute la nuit pour cet examen** I stayed up all night working for that exam; **b. dur** to work hard❑, to graft

VT *Br* to swot up on, *Am* to bone up on; **tu ferais mieux de b. ta physique** you should *Br* swot up *or Am* bone up on your physics

bosseur, -euse [bɔsœr, -øz] *Fam* **ADJ être b.** to work hard❑, to be hardworking❑

NM,F hard worker❑, slogger

bossoir [bɔswar] **NM** *Naut (pour hisser un bateau)* davit; *(pour manœuvrer l'ancre)* cathead

bossu, -e [bɔsy] **ADJ** humpbacked, hunchbacked; **être b.** to be humpbacked, to have a hump *or* humpback

NM,F humpback, hunchback; *Fam* **rire comme un b.** to laugh fit to burst, to laugh oneself silly

bossuer [7] [bɔswe] **VT 1** *Beaux-Arts* to emboss **2** *(faire des bosses à)* to dent

boston [bɔstɔ̃] NM *Cartes, Mus & (danse)* boston

bot[1] [bɔt] NM *Ordinat* bot

bot[2], **-e** [bo, bɔt] ADJ **pied b.** club foot

botanique [bɔtanik] ADJ botanical
NF botany

botaniste [bɔtanist] NMF botanist

Botox® [bɔtɔks] NM *Pharm* Botox®; **se faire faire des injections de B.** to have Botox® (injections), *Fam* to get Botoxed

Botswana [bɔtswana] NM **le B.** Botswana

botte [bɔt] NF **1** *(chaussure)* (high) boot; **bottes en caoutchouc** *Br* wellington boots, *Am* rubber boots; **bottes de cavalier** riding boots; **bottes de cow-boy** cowboy boots; **bottes d'égoutier** waders; **bottes de sept lieues** seven-league boots; **être à la b. de qn** to be sb's puppet; **avoir qn à sa b.** to have sb under one's thumb; *Fam* **cirer** *ou* **lécher les bottes de qn** to lick sb's boots; **sous la b. de l'ennemi** beneath the enemy's heel; **être/se sentir droit dans ses bottes** to have an easy conscience **2** *(de fleurs, de radis)* bunch; *(de paille)* sheaf, bundle **3** *Escrime* thrust; **porter une b. à qn** to make a thrust at sb; *Fig* to hit out *or* to have a dig at sb; *Fig* **b. secrète** secret weapon

botter [3] [bɔte] VT **1** *(chausser ▸ enfant)* to put boots on; *(▸ client)* to provide boots for, to sell boots to; **botté de cuir** wearing leather boots **2** *Sport* to kick; **b. la balle en touche** to kick the ball into touch; *Fig* to dodge the issue **3** *(locutions) Fam* **ça me botte!** I like that!; **ça te botterait d'y aller?** do you want to go?▫, *Br* do you fancy going?; **b. le train** *ou* **les fesses** *ou* **le derrière** *ou très Fam* **le cul à qn** to kick sb in the pants; **se faire b. les fesses** *ou* **le derrière** *ou très Fam* **le cul** to get a kick up the *Br* arse *or Am* ass
VI *Sport* to kick the ball

bottier, -ère [bɔtje, -ɛr] NM,F *(fabricant ▸ de bottes)* bootmaker; *(▸ de chaussures)* shoemaker

bottillon [bɔtijɔ̃] NM ankle boot

Bottin® [bɔtɛ̃] NM telephone directory, phone book; **le B. mondain** = directory of famous people, ≃ Who's Who

bottine [bɔtin] NF ankle boot

botulisme [bɔtylism] NM *Méd* botulism

boubou [bubu] NM boubou, bubu

bouc [buk] NM **1** *Zool* goat, he-goat, billy goat; **sentir le b., puer comme un b.** to stink to high heaven; **b. émissaire** scapegoat **2** *(barbe)* goatee (beard)

boucan [bukɑ̃] NM *Fam* din, racket; **faire du b.** to kick up a din, to make a racket

boucane [bukan] NF *Can* smoke

boucaner [3] [bukane] VT *Culin (viande, poisson)* to smoke, to cure; **un teint boucané** a tanned *or* weatherbeaten complexion

boucanier [bukanje] NM buccaneer

bouchage [buʃaʒ] NM **1** *(d'une bouteille)* corking **2** *(d'une fuite)* plugging, stopping **3** *(d'un trou)* filling up

bouche [buʃ] NF **1** *(gén)* mouth; **j'ai la b. sèche** my mouth feels dry; **parler/avoir la b. pleine** to talk with/to have one's mouth full; **une pipe à la b.** with a pipe in his/her mouth; **ce n'est pas joli dans la b. d'un petit garçon!** that doesn't sound nice, coming from a little boy!; **il a six bouches à nourrir** he has six mouths to feed (at home); **je n'ai pas l'intention de nourrir des bouches inutiles** I won't have loafers around here; **ça c'est pour** *ou* **je le garde pour la bonne b.** *(nourriture)* I'm keeping this as a treat for later; *(nouvelle)* I'm keeping the best until last; **de b. en b.** from person to person; **b. à oreille** grapevine; **par le b. à oreille** through the grapevine, by word of mouth; **de b. à oreille** confidentially; **être** *ou* **rester b. bée** to stand open-mouthed; **rester b. cousue** to keep one's lips sealed; *Péj* **avoir la** *ou* **faire sa b. en cœur** to simper; **il m'a annoncé la b. en cœur qu'il ne venait plus** he blithely announced to me that he was no longer coming; **c'est une fine b.** he's/she's a gourmet; **faire la fine b.** to be fussy *or* choosy; **faire la b. en cul-de-poule** to purse one's lips; **ouvrir la b.** to open one's mouth; *Fig* **elle n'a pas ouvert la b. de la soirée** she didn't say a word *or* open her mouth all evening; **il n'a que ce mot/nom à la b.** he only ever talks about one thing/person; **son nom est sur toutes les bouches** his/her name is on everyone's lips, he's/she's the talk of the town
2 *(orifice ▸ d'un cratère)* mouth; *(▸ d'un canon)* muzzle; **b. d'aération** air vent; **b. d'air chaud** hot-air vent; **b. d'arrosage** water pipe, standpipe; **b. de chaleur** hot-air vent; **b. d'eau** fire hydrant, *Am* fireplug; **b. d'égout** manhole, inspection chamber; **b. d'incendie** fire hydrant, *Am* fireplug; **b. de métro** metro entrance, underground entrance
3 *(d'un vin)* full-bodiedness, richness; **un vin bien en b.** a full-bodied wine
• **bouches** NFPL *Géog (d'un fleuve, d'un détroit)* mouth

bouché, -e[1] [buʃe] ADJ **1** *(nez)* blocked, *Med* congested; *(oreilles)* blocked up; **j'ai le nez b.** my nose is blocked
2 *Météo (ciel, horizon, temps)* cloudy, overcast
3 *Fam (idiot)* stupid, *Br* thick
4 *(sans espoir ▸ avenir)* hopeless; *(▸ filière, secteur)* oversubscribed
5 *(bouteille)* corked; *(cidre, vin)* bottled

bouche-à-bouche [buʃabuʃ] NM INV mouth-to-mouth resuscitation; **faire du b. à qn** to give sb mouth-to-mouth resuscitation *or* the kiss of life

bouchée[2] [buʃe] NF **1** *(contenu)* mouthful; **il n'a fait qu'une b. du petit pain** he swallowed the roll whole; **elle n'a fait qu'une b. de ses rivales** she made short work of her rivals; **je n'en ferai qu'une b.!** I'll eat him for breakfast!; **mettre les bouchées doubles** to work twice as hard, to put on a spurt; **il a acheté ce tableau pour une b. de pain** he bought this painting for next to nothing **2** *Culin* (vol-au-vent) case; **b. à la reine** chicken vol-au-vent; *(friandise)* **b. (au chocolat)** chocolate bouchée

boucher[1] [3] [buʃe] VT **1** *(fermer ▸ trou)* to fill up; *(▸ fuite)* to plug, to stop; *(▸ bouteille)* to cork; *Fig* **b. un trou** to fill a gap; *Fam* **je parie que ça t'en bouche un coin!** I bet you're impressed! **2** *(entraver)* to obstruct, to block; **tu me bouches le passage** you're in *or* blocking my way; **la tour nous bouche complètement la vue** the tower cuts off *or* obstructs our view totally
VPR **se boucher 1** *(s'obstruer ▸ tuyau, narine)* to get blocked **2** *Météo (temps)* to become overcast **3** **se b. le nez** to hold one's nose; **se b. les oreilles** to put one's fingers in *or* to plug one's ears; *Fig* to refuse to listen; **se b. les yeux** to hide one's eyes; *Fig* to refuse to see

boucher[2], **-ère** [buʃe, -ɛr] NM,F butcher

boucherie [buʃri] NF **1** *(boutique)* butcher's *Br* shop *or Am* store; **b. chevaline** horse-butcher's (*Br* shop *or Am* store)
2 *(métier)* butchery
3 *Can & Suisse (abattage)* butchering *(of pigs)*
4 *Fig (massacre)* slaughter, butchery

bouche-trou [buʃtru] (*pl* **bouche-trous**) NM *Fam (personne)* stand-in, stopgap; *(objet)* makeshift replacement

bouchon [buʃɔ̃] NM **1** *(en liège)* cork; *(d'un bidon, d'une bouteille en plastique)* cap; *(d'une bouteille en verre, d'une carafe, d'un tonneau)* stopper; **vin qui sent le b.** corked wine; **b. (du réservoir) d'essence** petrol cap; *Aut* **b. de vidange** blow-off; *Fam* **tu pousses le b. un peu loin** you're going a bit far *or* pushing it a bit
2 *(bonde)* plug; **b. de cérumen** earwax plug
3 *(poignée de paille, de foin)* wisp
4 *Fam Aut (embouteillage)* traffic jam; *(à une intersection)* gridlock; **trois kilomètres de b.** a three-kilometre tailback
5 *Pêche* float
6 *(à Lyon)* = small restaurant serving traditional Lyonnaise food

bouchonné, -e [buʃɔne] ADJ *(vin)* corked

bouchonner [3] [buʃɔne] VT *(cheval)* to rub down
VI *Fam* **ça bouchonne à partir de 5 heures** traffic is heavy from 5 p.m. onwards

bouchot [buʃo] NM mussel bed

bouclage [buklaʒ] NM **1** *Journ (d'un article)* finishing off; *(d'un journal)* putting to bed; **c'est mardi le b.** the paper's going to bed *or* to press on Tuesday
2 *Fam (d'un coupable)* locking up▫; *(d'un quartier)* surrounding▫, sealing off▫
3 *(d'une ceinture)* fastening, buckling
4 *(des cheveux)* curling
5 *Tech* **b. acoustique** acoustic feedback

boucle [bukl] NF **1** *(de cheveux)* curl; **Boucles d'or** Goldilocks
2 *(d'une ceinture)* buckle; *(d'un lacet)* loop; *(d'un cours d'eau)* loop, meander; **elle ne fait pas de boucles à ses lettres** she doesn't put any loops on her letters; **faire une b. à un ruban** to loop a ribbon; **faire une b.** *(en marchant, en voiture)* to loop back
3 *Ordinat & Tél* loop
4 *Sport (en course)* lap; **la Grande b.** *(le Tour de France cycliste)* the Tour de France
• **boucle d'oreille** NF earring

bouclé, -e [bukle] ADJ *(cheveux, barbe)* curly; *(personne)* curly-haired

bouclement [bukləmɑ̃] NM **1** *(de taureau, de porc)* ringing **2** *Suisse (des comptes, d'un budget)* closing

boucler [3] [bukle] VT **1** *(fermer ▸ ceinture)* to buckle, to fasten; *(▸ chambre, maison etc)* to lock (up); **b. sa ceinture en voiture** to fasten one's seat belt; **b. sa valise** to shut one's suitcase; *Fig* to pack one's bags; *Fam* **toi, tu la boucles!** not a word out of you!
2 *(dans une opération policière)* **b. une avenue/un quartier** to seal off an avenue/area
3 *Fam (fermer ▸ porte)* to lock▫; *(enfermer)* to lock up▫; **il s'est fait b. pour six mois** he's been put away for six months
4 *(mettre un terme à ▸ affaire)* to finish off, to settle; *(▸ programme de révisions)* to finish (off); *Journ* **b. un journal/une édition** to put a paper/an edition to bed
5 *(équilibrer)* **b. son budget** to make ends meet; **il a du mal à b. ses fins de mois** he's always in the red at the end of the month
6 *Aviat* **b. la boucle** to loop the loop; *Fig* to come full circle; *Fig* **la boucle est bouclée, on a bouclé la boucle** we're back to square one
7 *(cheveux, mèches)* to curl
8 *(taureau, porc)* to ring
VI **1** *(cheveux)* to curl, to be curly; **il boucle naturellement** he has naturally curly hair **2** *Ordinat* to get stuck in a loop, to loop round and round
VPR **se boucler 1** *Fam* **se b. chez soi** to shut oneself away▫ **2** *Ordinat (lignes)* to wrap

bouclette [buklɛt] NF **1** *(de cheveux)* small curl; *(de laine, de moquette)* curl **2** *(comme adj) Tex (fil, laine)* bouclé

bouclier [buklije] NM **1** *(protection de soldat)* shield; *(de policier)* riot shield; *Fig* **elle lui a fait un b. de son corps** she shielded him/her with her body; **b. humain** human shield **2** *(protection)* shield; **b. antimissile** missile shield; **b. atomique** atomic shield; *Astron* **b. thermique** thermal *or* heat shield **3** *Géol* shield

Bouddha [buda] NPR Buddha

bouddhique [budik] ADJ *Rel* Buddhist, Buddhistic

bouddhisme [budism] NM *Rel* Buddhism

bouddhiste [budist] *Rel* ADJ Buddhist
NMF Buddhist

bouder [3] [bude] VI to sulk; **elle est partie b.** she's gone off in a sulk
VT *(ami)* to refuse to talk to; *(dessert)* to refuse; *(cadeau)* to refuse to accept; *(élection)* to refuse to vote in; *(fournisseur)* to stay away from; **le public a boudé son film** hardly anyone went to see his/her film; **en été les Parisiens boudent les salles de cinéma** Parisians stay away from *or* don't go to the cinema in summer; **b. son plaisir** to deny oneself
VPR **se bouder** not to talk to each other, to refuse to have anything to do with each other

bouderie [budri] NF sulking *(UNCOUNT)*

boudeur, -euse [budœr, -øz] ADJ sulky, sullen
NM,F sulky person
• **boudeuse** NF *(siège)* courting couch

boudin [budɛ̃] NM **1** *Culin* **b. (noir)** *Br* black pudding, *Am* blood sausage; **b. blanc** *Br* white pudding, *Am* white sausage; *Fam* **faire du b.** to sulk▫
2 *(cylindre)* roll

3 *Fam Péj (femme)* dog, *Br* boot, *Am* beast; **sa sœur est un vrai b.!** his sister looks like *Br* the back of a bus *or Am* a Mack truck!
4 *(doigt)* fat finger
5 *Belg (traversin)* bolster

boudiné, -e [budine] ADJ *(doigt, main) Br* podgy, *Am* pudgy; **je me sens boudinée dans cette robe** this dress is too tight for me; **il a l'air boudiné dans ses vêtements** he looks as though his clothes were a size too small

boudiner [3] [budine] VT **1** *(sujet: vêtement)* **cette jupe la boudine** this skirt shows all her bulges **2** *Ind (fil de métal)* to coil; *Tex* to rove; *(tuyau)* to extrude
VPR **se boudiner se b. dans une jupe** to squeeze oneself into a skirt (that is too tight)

boudoir [budwar] NM **1** *(pièce)* boudoir **2** *Culin (biscuit) Br* sponge finger, *Am* ladyfinger

boue [bu] NF **1** *Géol (terre détrempée)* mud; **couvert de b.** muddy **2** *(dépôt)* sludge; *Méd* **boues activées** activated sludge; **boues d'épuration** sewage sludge

bouée [bwe] NF **1** *Naut (en mer)* buoy; **b. d'amarrage** mooring buoy; **b. à cloche** bell buoy; **b. de corps-mort** anchor buoy; **b. lumineuse** light buoy, floating light; **b. sonore** sonobuoy **2** *(pour nager)* rubber ring; **b. de sauvetage** lifebelt, lifebuoy; **il s'est raccroché à elle comme à une b. de sauvetage** he hung onto her as if his life depended on it

bouette [bwet] = **boëte**

boueux, -euse [buø, -øz] ADJ **1** *(sale ▸ trottoir)* muddy; *(▸ tapis)* mud-stained **2** *Typ* smudged
NM *Fam Br* bin man, *Am* garbage collector

bouffant, -e [bufɑ̃, -ɑ̃t] ADJ *(coiffure)* bouffant; *(manche)* puffed out; *(pantalon)* baggy
NM *(d'une manche)* puff; *(des cheveux)* body

bouffarde [bufard] NF *Fam* pipe□

bouffe [buf] NF *Fam (aliments)* food□, grub, nosh; **aimer la bonne b.** to like one's food; **on se fait une b.?** do you fancy getting together for a meal?
ADJ **opéra b.** comic opera

bouffée [bufe] NF **1** *(exhalaison)* puff; **envoyer des bouffées de fumée** to puff (out) smoke; **tirer des bouffées d'une pipe** to draw on one's pipe; *aussi Fig* **une b. d'air frais** a breath of fresh air; **une b. de parfum** a whiff of perfume; **des odeurs de cuisine m'arrivaient par bouffées** the smell of cooking wafted over to me **2** *(accès)* fit, outburst; **une b. de colère** a fit of rage; **une b. de tendresse** a sudden burst of tenderness; *Méd* **avoir des bouffées de chaleur** to have hot *Br* flushes *or Am* flashes; *Psy* **b. délirante** delirious fit

bouffer [3] [bufe] VT *Fam* **1** *(manger)* to eat□; *(manger voracement)* to guzzle; *Fig* **je l'aurais bouffé!** I could have killed him!; **il ne va pas te b.** he won't eat you; **il a bouffé du lion aujourd'hui** he's full of beans today
2 *(gaspiller)* to be heavy on, to soak up; **b. de l'essence** to be heavy on *Br* petrol *or Am* gas; **il a bouffé toute sa fortune** he blew all his money
3 *(accaparer)* **les enfants me bouffent tout mon temps** the kids take up every minute of my time; **tu te laisses b. par ta mère** you're letting your mother walk all over you
4 *(locutions)* **b. du curé/communiste** to be a priest-hater/commie-basher; **b. des kilomètres** to eat up the miles
USAGE ABSOLU *Fam (manger)* **b. au restaurant** to eat out; **on a bien/mal bouffé** the food was great/terrible
VI *(gonfler)* to puff (out); **faire b. ses manches** to puff out one's sleeves; **faire b. ses cheveux** to give one's hair more volume
VPR **se bouffer** *Fam* **se b. le nez** *(une fois)* to have a go at one another; *(constamment)* to be at daggers drawn

bouffetance [buftɑ̃s] NF *très Fam (aliments)* food□, grub, nosh

bouffeur, -euse [bufœr, -øz] NM,F *Fam* guzzler; **un gros b. de viande** a great meat-eater□; **c'est un b. de curé** he's very anti-clerical□

bouffi, -e [bufi] ADJ *(yeux)* puffed-up, puffy; *(visage)* puffed-up, puffy, bloated; *Fig* **être b. d'orgueil** to be bloated with pride; **tu l'as dit, b.!** you said it!
NM *Culin (hareng)* bloater

bouffir [32] [bufir] VT **1** *(visage, yeux)* to puff up **2** *Culin (hareng)* to bloat
VI to become swollen *or* bloated, to puff up

bouffissure [bufisyr] NF *(d'un visage, d'un corps)* puffy *or* swollen state; *(d'un style)* turgidness

bouffon, -onne [bufɔ̃, -ɔn] ADJ *(scène)* comical, farcical
NM **1** *Théât* buffoon; *Hist* **le b. du roi** the king's jester **2** *Fam (personne ridicule)* buffoon, clown

bouffonnerie [bufɔnri] NF **1** *(acte)* piece of buffoonery; *(parole)* farcical remark; **faire des bouffonneries** to play *or* act the buffoon **2** *(caractère)* buffoonery

bougainvillée [bugɛ̃vile] NF *Bot* bougainvillaea

bougainvillier [bugɛ̃vilje] NM *Bot* bougainvillaea

bouge [buʒ] NM **1** *(logement)* hovel; *(café)* cheap *or* sleazy bar **2** *Naut* camber

bougeoir [buʒwar] NM candleholder, candlestick

bougeotte [buʒɔt] NF *Fam* fidgets; **avoir la b.** *(remuer)* to have the fidgets; *(voyager)* to have itchy feet

bouger [17] [buʒe] VI **1** *(remuer)* to move; **rien ne bouge** nothing's stirring; **j'ai une dent qui bouge** I have a loose tooth; **rester sans b.** to stay still; **ne bougeons plus!** hold it!; **le vent fait b. les branches des arbres** the branches of the trees are swaying in the wind; **il sait faire b. ses oreilles** he can wiggle his ears
2 *(se déplacer)* to move; **je n'ai pas bougé de la maison** I never stirred from the house; **un métier où on bouge beaucoup** a job involving a lot of travel
3 *(se modifier ▸ couleur d'un tissu)* to fade; **les prix n'ont pas bougé** prices haven't changed *or* altered
4 *(s'activer)* to move, to stir; **les syndicats commencent à b.** the unions are on the move; *Fam* **ça bouge pas mal, dans cette ville** there's a lot going on *or* happening in this town
VT to move, to shift
VPR **se bouger** *Fam* **bouge-toi de là!** shift yourself!; **si on se bougeait un peu?** come on, let's get moving!; **tu ne t'es pas beaucoup bougé pour trouver un nouveau boulot** you didn't try very hard to find a new job□

bougie [buʒi] NF **1** *(en cire)* candle; **s'éclairer à la b.** to use candles for lighting; **b. chauffe-plat** tea-light **2** *Aut Br* spark *or Am* sparking plug **3** *Méd (sonde)* bougie

bougnat [buɲa] NM *Vieilli* = owner of a small café also selling coal, usually from the Auvergne

bougnoul, bougnoule [buɲul] NM *Fam* = racist term used to refer to a North African

bougon, -onne [bugɔ̃, -ɔn] *Fam* ADJ grouchy, grumpy
NM,F grumbler, grouch

bougonnement [bugɔnmɑ̃] NM grouching *(UNCOUNT)*, grumbling *(UNCOUNT)*

bougonner [3] [bugɔne] VI *Fam* to grouch, to grumble

bougre [bugr] *Fam Vieilli* NM **1** *(homme)* chap, fellow; **un pauvre b.** a poor chap; **ce n'est pas un mauvais b.** he's not a bad sort **2** *Péj* **b. d'andouille!** you stupid idiot!
EXCLAM **1** *(marque la colère)* damn! **2** *(marque la surprise)* I'll be dashed!, cripes!

bougrement [bugrəmɑ̃] ADV *Fam Vieilli* damn, *Br* dashed; **il fait b. froid** it's damn cold

boui-boui [bwibwi] *(pl* **bouis-bouis***)* NM *Fam (restaurant)* greasy spoon, *Br* caff

bouillabaisse [bujabɛs] NF *Culin* bouillabaisse, = type of fish soup, typical of Provence

bouillant, -e [bujɑ̃, -ɑ̃t] ADJ **1** *(qui bout)* boiling; *(très chaud)* boiling hot **2** *(ardent)* fiery, passionate; **b. de colère** seething with anger; **b. d'impatience** bursting with impatience

bouille [buj] NF *Fam (figure)* face□, mug; **il a une bonne b.** *(sympathique)* he looks like a nice guy *or Br* bloke

bouilleur [bujœr] NM **1** *(distillateur)* distiller; **b. de cru** home distiller **2** *Tech (d'une chaudière)* heating *or* fire tube

bouilli, -e [buji] ADJ *Culin (eau, lait, viande)* boiled
NM *Culin (viande)* boiled meat; *(bœuf)* boiled beef; *Can* = stew of beans, cabbage, carrots, potatoes, salt pork and ham cooked together for several hours
• **bouillie** NF *(pour enfants)* baby food *or* cereal; *Hort* **bouillie bordelaise** Bordeaux mixture; **c'est de la bouillie pour chats** it's a dog's breakfast
• **en bouillie** ADV **réduire qch en bouillie** *(légumes, fruits)* to mash *or* to pulp sth; **mettre** *ou* **réduire qn en bouillie** to beat sb to a pulp; **les voitures ont été réduites en bouillie** the cars were completely smashed up

bouillir [48] [bujir] VI **1** *(arriver à ébullition)* to boil; **faire b. de l'eau/des légumes** to boil water/vegetables; **faire b. des instruments** *Méd* to sterilize *or* to boil instruments; **faire b. la marmite** to keep the pot boiling **2** *(s'irriter)* to boil; **ça me fait b.** it makes my blood boil; **b. d'impatience** to be bursting with impatience; **b. de colère** to seethe with anger
VT to boil; **b. du linge** to boil washing

bouilloire [bujwar] NF kettle

bouillon [bujɔ̃] NM **1** *Culin* broth, stock; **b. cube** stock cube; **b. gras/maigre** meat/clear stock; **b. de légumes** vegetable stock; **b. de onze** *ou* **d'onze heures** poisoned drink; *Fam* **boire** *ou* **prendre un b.** *(en nageant)* to swallow water; *Fig* to suffer heavy losses
2 *Biol* **b. de culture** culture medium; *Fig* **ces quartiers sont un véritable b. de culture pour la délinquance** these areas are a perfect breeding-ground for crime
3 *(remous)* **éteindre le feu dès le premier b.** turn off the heat as soon as it boils; **couler à gros bouillons** to gush out *or* forth; **bouillir à gros bouillons** to boil fast *or* hard; **cuire à gros bouillons** to bubble fiercely
4 *Couture* puff
5 *Journ* unsold copies
6 *(dans un métal)* blowhole

bouillonnant, -e [bujɔnɑ̃, -ɑ̃t] ADJ bubbling, foaming, seething; *Fig* **b. de vie/d'idées** bubbling over with life/ideas

bouillonnement [bujɔnmɑ̃] NM bubbling, foaming, seething; *Fig* **b. d'idées** ferment of ideas

bouillonner [3] [bujɔne] VI **1** *(liquide)* to bubble; *(source)* to foam, to froth; *Fig* **ils bouillonnent d'idées** they're full of ideas **2** *(s'agiter)* **b. d'impatience** to be bursting with impatience; **b. de colère** to seethe with anger

bouillotte [bujɔt] NF hot-water bottle

bouillotter [3] [bujɔte] VI to boil gently, to simmer

boulaie [bulɛ] NF *Bot* birch plantation

boulange [bulɑ̃ʒ] NF *Fam (métier)* bakery trade *or* business□; **il est dans la b.** he works as a baker

boulanger[1] [17] [bulɑ̃ʒe] VT **b. de la farine** to make bread
VI to make bread

boulanger[2], **-ère** [bulɑ̃ʒe, -ɛr] NM,F baker
ADJ bakery

boulangerie [bulɑ̃ʒri] NF **1** *(boutique)* bakery, baker's (*Br* shop *or Am* store); **b. pâtisserie** baker's and confectioner's, bread and cake *Br* shop *or Am* store **2** *(industrie)* bakery trade *or* business

boule [bul] NF **1** *(sphère)* ball; *(de machine à écrire)* golf ball; **b. de billard** billiard ball; **il a le crâne comme une b. de billard** he's (as) bald as a coot; *Ordinat* **b. de commande** trackball; **b. de cristal** crystal ball; **b. doseuse** *(pour la lessive)* detergent ball; **b. de feu** fireball; **b. de gomme** gumdrop; **b. de loto** lottery ball; **b. à neige** *(objet décoratif)* snowdome, snowglobe; **b. de neige** snowball; *Fig* **faire b. de neige** to snowball; **b. de poils** *(dans l'estomac d'un animal)* hairball; **une petite b. de poils** *(chaton)* a little ball of fluff; **b. puante** stinkbomb; **boules Quiès®** = earplugs made of wax; **b. à thé** tea ball; **avoir une b. dans la gorge** to have a lump in one's throat; **avoir une b. sur l'estomac** to have a heavy stomach
2 *Fam (tête)* head□, nut; **avoir la b. à zéro** to have

a shaved head; **coup de b.** headbutt□; **donner un coup de b. à qn** to headbutt□ *or* to nut sb; **perdre la b.** to crack up, to lose one's marbles, *Br* to lose the plot
3 *(jeux)* **b. (de pétanque)** = steel bowl used in playing boules; **jouer aux boules** to play boules *(popular French game played on bare ground with steel bowls)*
4 *Belg (bonbon)* boiled sweet
5 *Suisse (pâtisserie)* **b. de Berlin** doughnut
• **boules** NFPL *très Fam* **1** *(testicules)* balls, nuts **2** *(locutions)* **avoir les boules** *(être effrayé)* to be scared stiff; *(être furieux)* to be pissed off; *(être déprimé)* to be feeling down; **tu me fous les boules** *(tu me fais peur)* you're scaring me; *(tu me déprimes)* you're really getting me down; **les boules!** nightmare!
• **en boule** ADV **se mettre en b.** *(en rond)* to curl up into a ball; *Fam (en colère)* to fly off the handle, to go mad; *Fam* **ça me met en b.** it makes me mad *or* livid

bouleau, -x [bulo] NM *Bot* **1** *(arbre)* birch (tree) **2** *(bois)* birch

boule-de-neige [buldənɛʒ] *(pl* **boules-de-neige)** NF *Bot (arbuste)* guelder rose

bouledogue [buldɔg] NM *Zool (chien)* bulldog

bouler [3] [bule] VI to roll along; **b. au bas de l'escalier** to tumble down the stairs; *Fam* **envoyer b. qn** to send sb packing

boulet [bulɛ] NM **1** *(projectile)* cannonball; *(de prisonnier)* ball (and chain); *Fig* **c'est un b. qu'il traînera toute sa vie** it will be a millstone round his neck all his life; **tirer à boulets rouges sur qn** to lay into sb **2** *Mines* (coal) nut **3** *Zool* fetlock

boulette [bulɛt] NF **1** *Culin* **b. (de viande)** meatball; **b. (pour chien)** croquette; **b. empoisonnée** poison ball **2** *(de papier)* pellet **3** *Fam (erreur)* blunder, *Am* blooper; **faire une b.** to blunder, *Am* to goof

boulevard [bulvar] NM **1** *(avenue)* boulevard; **les grands boulevards** *(à Paris)* the main boulevards *(with many theatres, restaurants and nightclubs)*; **les boulevards extérieurs** *ou* **des maréchaux** the (Paris) outer boulevards *(following the old town wall)*; **le b. périphérique** the (Paris) *Br* ring road *or Am* beltway; *Fig* **ouvrir un b. à qn/qch** to leave the way open for sb/sth **2** *Théât* **le b.** light comedy
• **de boulevard** ADJ *Théât* **pièce de b.** light comedy

boulevardier, -ère [bulvardje, -jɛr] ADJ *Théât (humour)* facile

bouleversant, -e [bulvɛrsɑ̃, -ɑ̃t] ADJ *(émouvant)* deeply moving; *(pénible)* upsetting, distressing

bouleversement [bulvɛrsəmɑ̃] NM upheaval, upset; **son divorce a été un grand b. dans sa vie** his/her divorce drastically changed *or* was a great upheaval in his/her life; **le b. de toutes mes habitudes** the disruption of my entire routine; **des bouleversements politiques** political upheavals

bouleverser [3] [bulvɛrse] VT **1** *(émouvoir)* to move deeply; **bouleversé par la naissance de son fils** deeply moved by his/her son's birth **2** *(affliger)* to upset, to distress; **bouleversés par la mort de leur ami** shattered *or* very distressed by the death of their friend; **bouleversé par la souffrance des prisonniers** distressed *or* profoundly upset by the prisoners' suffering **3** *(désorganiser ▸ maison, tiroir)* to turn upside down; *(▸ habitudes, vie, plan)* to turn upside down, to disrupt, to change drastically

boulier¹ [bulje] NM abacus

boulier² [bulje] NM *Pêche* bag-net, wing-net

boulimie [bulimi] NF bulimia; **être atteint de b., faire de la b.** to be bulimic

boulimique [bulimik] ADJ bulimic
NMF bulimic

boulingrin [bulɛ̃grɛ̃] NM lawn *(in a formal garden)*

bouliste [bulist] NMF boules player

boulocher [3] [bulɔʃe] VI *Tex* to pill

boulodrome [bulɔdrom] NM bowling alley

boulon [bulɔ̃] NM bolt; **b. avec écrou** nut and bolt; **b. à vis** screw bolt; *Fam Fig* **serrer** *ou* **resserrer les boulons** to tighten the screws; *Fam* **il lui manque un b., à ce type!** that guy's got a screw loose!

boulonnage [bulɔnaʒ] NM *Tech* bolting (on)

boulonner [3] [bulɔne] VT *Tech* to bolt (on)
VI *Fam (travailler)* to work□, to plug away

boulonnerie [bulɔnri] NF **1** *(fabrique)* nut-and-bolt manufacture **2** *(industrie)* nut-and-bolt trade **3** *(dans une quincaillerie)* nut-and-bolt section

boulot¹ [bulo] NM *Fam* **1** *(fait de travailler)* **le b.** work□; *Péj* **elle est très b. b.** she's a workaholic
2 *(ouvrage réalisé)* piece of work□, job□; **il s'est coupé les cheveux tout seul, t'aurais vu le b.!** he cut his own hair, you should have seen the mess!
3 *(travail à faire)* **du b.** a lot of work□; **tout le monde au b.!** come on everybody, let's get cracking!
4 *(emploi, poste)* job□; **un petit b.** a casual job; **faire des petits boulots** to do casual work□
5 *(lieu)* work□; **aller au b.** to go to work; **je déjeune au b.** I have lunch at work

boulot², -otte [bulo, -ɔt] *Fam* ADJ plump, tubby
NM,F plump *or* tubby person

boulotter [3] [bulɔte] *Fam* VT *(manger)* to eat□
USAGE ABSOLU **elle n'arrête pas de b.** she just won't stop eating□
VI *Vieilli (travailler)* to work□, to slave away

boum [bum] EXCLAM bang!; **faire b.** to go bang; **ça a fait b.!** *(attentat)* it went bang!; *(ballon)* it went pop!; **bébé a fait b.** *(en langage enfantin)* baby's had a tumble
NM **1** *(bruit)* bang; **il y a eu un grand b.** there was a loud bang **2** *Fam (succès)* **le b. des portables** the *Br* mobile phone *or Am* cellphone boom, the boom in *Br* mobile phones *or Am* cellphones; **faire un b.** to be a great success story *or* a runaway success; **être en plein b.** *(dans une boutique, une entreprise)* to have a rush on; *(dans des préparations)* to be rushed off one's feet
NF *Fam* party□ *(for teenagers)*

boumer [3] [bume] VI *Fam* **alors, ça boume?** so, how's tricks?; **ça boume!** things are (going) fine!

bouquet [bukɛ] NM **1** *(fleurs ▸ gén)* bunch; *(▸ grand, décoratif)* bouquet; *(▸ petit)* sprig, spray; **le b. de la mariée** the wedding *or* bride's bouquet
2 *Bot (groupe ▸ d'arbres)* clump, cluster
3 *(dans un feu d'artifice)* **b. (final)** crowning *or* final piece, (grand) finale; *Fam* **alors ça, c'est le b.!** that's the limit!, that takes the *Br* biscuit *or Am* cake!
4 *Culin* **b. garni** bouquet garni
5 *(arôme ▸ d'un vin)* bouquet, nose
6 *Zool (crustacé)* (common) prawn
7 *TV* **b. numérique** *ou* **de programmes** multichannel digital TV package, multiplex; **b. satellite** satellite package

bouquetière [buktjɛr] NF flower girl

bouquetin [buktɛ̃] NM *Zool* ibex

bouquin [bukɛ̃] NM **1** *Fam (livre)* book□ **2** *Chasse & Zool (lapin)* buck rabbit; *(lièvre)* male hare **3** *Vieilli Zool (bouc)* (old) billy-goat

bouquiner [3] [bukine] *Fam* VT to read□
NM to read□

bouquiniste [bukinist] NMF secondhand bookseller

bourbe [burb] NF *(gén)* mud, *Littéraire* mire; *(dans l'eau)* sludge

bourbeux, -euse [burbø, -øz] ADJ muddy

bourbier [burbje] NM **1** *Géol (marécage)* quagmire **2** *Fig (situation difficile)* mess, quagmire

bourbillon [burbijɔ̃] NM *Méd (d'un abcès, d'un furoncle etc)* core

bourbon [burbɔ̃] NM *(alcool)* bourbon

bourdaine [burdɛn] NF *Bot* alder buckthorn

bourde [burd] NF *Fam* **1** *(bêtise)* blunder, *Br* bloomer, *Am* blooper; **faire une b.** *(gaffer)* to blunder, to put one's foot in it; *(faire une erreur)* to make a mistake□, to mess things up, *Am* to goof (up) **2** *Vieilli (mensonge)* fib; **raconter des bourdes** to tell fibs

bourdon [burdɔ̃] NM **1** *Entom* bumblebee; **faux b.** drone
2 *Mus (jeu d'orgue)* bourdon; *(son de basse)* drone
3 *(cloche)* great bell
4 *Typ* omission, out
5 *(bâton)* pilgrim's staff
6 *Fam (locution)* **avoir le b.** to feel down, to be down in the dumps

bourdonnement [burdɔnmɑ̃] NM *(vrombissement ▸ d'un insecte, d'une voix)* hum, buzz, drone; *(▸ d'un ventilateur, d'un moteur)* hum, drone; **j'ai des bourdonnements d'oreilles** my ears are ringing

bourdonner [3] [burdɔne] VI *(insecte, voix)* to hum, to buzz, to drone; *(moteur)* to hum; *(oreille)* to ring; *(lieu)* to buzz

bourg [bur] NM (market) town; **aller au b.** to go (up) to town

bourgade [burgad] NF (large) village, small town

bourge [burʒ] *Fam Péj* ADJ upper-class□, *Br* posh
NMF upper-class person□, *Br* toff; **chez les bourges** in upper-class circles□

bourgeois, -e [burʒwa, -az] ADJ **1** *(dans un sens marxiste)* of the bourgeoisie, bourgeois
2 *(dans un sens non marxiste)* middle-class
3 *Péj (caractéristique de la bourgeoisie)* bourgeois; **goûts b.** bourgeois taste
4 *(aisé, confortable)* **intérieur b.** comfortable middle-class home; **quartier b.** comfortable residential area; **cuisine bourgeoise** good plain home cooking
NM,F **1** *(dans un sens marxiste)* bourgeois
2 *(dans un sens non marxiste)* member of the middle class; **grand/petit b.** member of the upper middle/lower middle class
3 *Hist (au Moyen Âge)* burgher; *(avant la Révolution)* member of the third estate; *(roturier)* commoner
4 *Suisse (citoyen)* citizen; **les b.** the townspeople
5 *Péj (béotien)* Philistine
• **bourgeoise** NF *Fam* **ma bourgeoise** my old lady, *Br* the wife
• **en bourgeois** ADV *Vieilli* **habillé en b.** out of uniform, (dressed) in civvies

bourgeoisement [burʒwazmɑ̃] ADV **1** *(conventionnellement)* conventionally, respectably; **vivre b.** to lead a respectable life **2** *Jur* **occuper b. un local** to use premises for residential purposes only

bourgeoisie [burʒwazi] NF **1** *(dans un sens marxiste)* bourgeoisie; **la petite b.** the petty bourgeoisie **2** *(classe aisée, professions libérales)* middle class; **la petite/moyenne b.** the lower middle/the middle class; **la grande** *ou* **haute b.** the upper middle class; *(en France)* the haute bourgeoisie **3** *Hist (au Moyen Âge)* burghers; *(avant la Révolution)* bourgeoisie, third estate

bourgeon [burʒɔ̃] NM *Bot & Méd* bud; **en bourgeons** in bud; **b. gustatif** taste bud, *Spéc* gustatory bud

bourgeonnement [burʒɔnmɑ̃] NM **1** *Bot* budding **2** *Méd* granulation **3** *Biol* budding

bourgeonner [3] [burʒɔne] VI **1** *Bot* to bud **2** *(visage, nez)* to break out in spots

bourgmestre [burgmɛstr] NM *Belg* burgomaster

Bourgogne [burgɔɲ] NF **la B.** Burgundy

bourguignon, -onne [burgiɲɔ̃, -ɔn] ADJ **1** *Géog* Burgundian **2** *Culin (sauce)* bourguignonne
NM *(dialecte)* Burgundy dialect
• **Bourguignon, -onne** NM,F Burgundian

bourlingue [burlɛ̃g] NF *Fam (voyage)* perilous journey□; *(vie)* adventurous life□

bourlinguer [3] [burlɛ̃ge] VI **1** *Naut (voyager par mer)* to sail (around) **2** *Fam (se déplacer)* to get around, to kick about; **elle a bourlingué dans le monde entier** she's been all over the world **3** *Naut* to labour

bourlingueur, -euse [burlɛ̃gœr, -øz] ADJ *Fam* adventurous□
NM,F **1** *(marin)* old salt **2** *Fam (aventurier)* wanderer, rover; **c'est un b.** he's always on the move

bourrache [buraʃ] NF *Bot* borage

bourrade [burad] NF *(de la main)* push, shove; *(du coude)* poke, dig; **repousser qn d'une b.** to shove sb away

bourrage [buraʒ] NM **1** *(remplissage ▸ d'un coussin)* stuffing; *(▸ d'une chaise)* filling, padding; *(▸ d'une pipe, d'un poêle)* filling; *Fam* **b. de crâne** *(propagande)* brainwashing; *Scol* cramming **2** *Ordinat (dans une imprimante)* jam; **b. (de cartes)** (card) jam; *Cin* **b. du film** piling up *or* buckling of the film; **b. papier** paper jam **3** *(matériau)* stuffing, filling

bourrasque [burask] NF *(coup de vent)* squall, gust *or* blast (of wind); **b. de neige** snow flurry; **souffler en b.** to blow in gusts, to gust; *Fig* **une b. d'injures** a flurry of insults

bourrasser [3] [burase] VT *Can* to push around, to bully

bourratif, -ive [buratif, -iv] ADJ *Fam* filling[□], *Péj* stodgy; **des aliments bourratifs** stodge *(UNCOUNT)*

bourre[1] [bur] NM *Fam Arg crime* cop; **les bourres** the cops, the fuzz

bourre[2] [bur] NF **1** *(rembourrage)* filling, stuffing, wadding

2 *Tex* flock; **b. de laine** *(déchet)* flock of wool; *(rembourrage)* flock wool; **b. de papier** fluff; **b. de soie** flock *or* floss *or* waste silk

3 *Bot* down

4 *(de fusil, de cartouche)* wad

5 *(d'un animal)* underfur

6 *(locutions) Fam* **de première b.** great, excellent; *Fam* **le vendredi, c'est le coup de b. au bureau** Fridays are manic at work; *Vulg* **bonne b.!** hope you get your oats!

• **à la bourre** ADV *Fam* **être à la b.** *(être en retard)* to be late[□]; *(dans son travail)* to be behind; *(être pressé)* to be in a rush

bourré, -e[1] [bure] ADJ **1** *(plein ▸ théâtre, bus)* packed; *(▸ valise)* crammed; **le coffre est b.** the *Br* boot *or Am* trunk is crammed full; **les kiwis sont bourrés de vitamines** kiwi fruit are packed *or* crammed with vitamins; **un texte b. de fautes** a text full of *or* riddled with mistakes[□]; **être b. de complexes** to be full of *or* a mass of hang-ups; **b. à craquer** full to bursting **2** *très Fam (ivre) Br* pissed, *Am* bombed

bourreau, -x [buro] NM **1** *(exécuteur ▸ gén)* executioner; *(▸ qui pend)* hangman **2** *(tortionnaire)* torturer; *Fig* oppressor; **b. d'enfants** child beater; **b. des cœurs** heartbreaker; **b. de travail** workaholic

bourrée[2] [bure] NF *Suisse* **1** *(grande affluence)* crowd **2** *(grande quantité)* **une b. de** masses of, loads of

bourrée[3] [bure] NF *(danse)* bourrée

bourrelé, -e [burle] ADJ **b. de remords** full of remorse, racked with guilt

bourrelet [burlɛ] NM **1** *(isolant)* weather strip, *Br* draught excluder **2** *(de graisse)* fold; **b. de chair** roll of flesh; **des bourrelets autour de la taille** a spare tyre **3** *(petit coussin)* pad, cushion

bourrelier [burəlje] NM saddler

bourrellerie [burelri] NF saddlery

bourre-pif [burpif] *(pl* **bourre-pifs**) NM *Fam* punch on the nose[□]

bourrer [3] [bure] VT **1** *(rembourrer)* to fill, to stuff

2 *(remplir ▸ pipe)* to fill; *(▸ poche)* to fill, to cram, to stuff; *(▸ valise, tiroir)* to cram (full), to pack tightly; *Fam* **b. le crâne** *ou* **le mou à qn** *Br* to have *or Am* to put sb on

3 *(gaver ▸ sujet: aliment)* to fill up; **b. qn de** to cram *or* to stuff sb with; **tu le bourres de sucreries** you're stuffing him full of sweets

4 *(frapper) très Fam* **b. la gueule à qn** to kick sb's head *or* teeth in; **b. qn de coups** to beat sb (up)[□]

5 *Vulg (posséder sexuellement)* to hump, *Br* to shag

USAGE ABSOLU **les bananes, ça bourre** bananas are very filling *or* fill you up

VI *Fam (se hâter)* to hurry[□]; **allez, bourrez un peu!** come on, get a move on!

VPR **se bourrer 1** *Fam (manger)* to stuff oneself *or* one's face; **se b. de** to stuff one's face with **2** *très Fam (locution)* **se b. la gueule** to get *Br* pissed *or Am* bombed

bourrette [burɛt] NF *Tex* bourette

bourriche [buriʃ] NF **1** *(panier)* hamper, wicker case **2** *Pêche (filet)* keepnet

bourrichon [buriʃɔ̃] NM *Fam* **monter le b. à qn** *Br* to have *or Am* to put sb on; **se monter le b.** to get (all) worked up; **elle s'était monté le b.** she'd imagined all sorts of things[□]

bourricot [buriko] NM donkey, *Am* burro

bourrin, -e [burɛ̃, burin] *Fam* ADJ **1** *(qui manque de raffinement)* oafish[□]; **il est un peu b. avec ses blagues de cul, mon cousin** he's a bit of a Neanderthal, my cousin, what with his dirty jokes **2** *(agressif ▸ personne, méthode)* rough; *(▸ musique)* heavy, hardcore

NM **1** *(cheval)* (old) nag **2** *(policier)* cop

NM,F *(personne brusque)* brute[□]; **c'est de la musique de b.** it's real headbanging music

bourrique [burik] NF **1** *Zool* donkey **2** *Fam (personne obstinée)* pig-headed individual **3** *(locution)* **faire tourner qn en b.** to drive sb crazy *or* up the wall

bourru, -e [bury] ADJ **1** *(rude ▸ personne, manières)* gruff, rough; **d'un ton b.** gruffly **2** *Tex* rough **3** *(jeune ▸ vin)* fermented; *(▸ lait)* raw

Bourse [burs] NF **1** *(marché)* stock exchange, stock market; **la B. de Paris** the Paris Bourse *or* Stock Exchange; **B. de** *ou* **du commerce, B. de(s) marchandises** commodity *or* commodities exchange; **B. coulisse** unlisted market; **B. maritime** *ou* **des frets** shipping exchange; **B. du travail** ≃ (local or regional) trade union centre, *Br* ≃ trades' council; **la B. des valeurs** the stock exchange *or* market **2** *(cours)* market; **la B. est calme/animée/en hausse** the market is quiet/is lively/has risen

• **à la Bourse, en Bourse** ADV on the stock exchange *or* market; **jouer à la** *ou* **en B.** to speculate on the stock exchange *or* market; **entrer en B.** *(entreprise)* to go live

bourse [burs] NF **1** *(porte-monnaie)* purse; **avoir la b. bien garnie** to have money in one's pocket; **faire b. commune** to pool one's money; **faire b. à part** to keep one's money separate; **sans b. délier** without paying a penny *or Am* cent; **la b. ou la vie!** stand and deliver!, your money or your life!; **ouvrir sa b.** to put one's hand in one's pocket; **ouvrir sa b. à qn** to lend sb money **2** *Scol & Univ (allocation)* scholarship, grant; **b. d'études** bursary; **avoir une b.** to be on *or* to have a grant **3** *(vente d'occasion)* **b. aux vêtements/aux jouets** second-hand clothes/toy sale

• **bourses** NFPL *Anat* scrotum

boursicotage [bursikɔtaʒ] NM *Bourse* dabbling *or* speculating on the stock market

boursicoter [3] [bursikɔte] VI *Bourse* to dabble (on the stock market)

boursicoteur, -euse [bursikɔtœr, -øz], **boursicotier, -ère** [bursikɔtje, -ɛr] NM,F *Bourse* small-time investor

boursier, -ère [bursje, -ɛr] ADJ **1** *Scol & Univ* **un étudiant b.** a grant *or* scholarship holder **2** *(de la Bourse)* stock exchange *(avant n)*, (stock) market *(avant n)*

NM,F **1** *Scol & Univ* grant *or* scholarship holder **2** *Bourse* operator **3** *Suisse* treasurer

boursouflage [bursuflaʒ] NM *(gonflement ▸ du visage)* swelling, puffiness; *(▸ de la peinture)* blistering

boursouflé, -e [bursufle] ADJ **1** *(gonflé ▸ visage)* swollen, puffy; *(▸ peinture)* blistered; *(▸ plaie)* swollen **2** *(ampoulé)* bombastic, pompous, turgid

boursouflement [bursufləmɑ̃] = **boursouflage**

boursoufler [3] [bursufle] VT *(gonfler ▸ visage)* to swell, to puff up; *(▸ peinture)* to blister

VPR **se boursoufler** *(visage)* to become swollen *or* puffy; *(peinture)* to blister; *(surface)* to swell (up)

boursouflure [bursuflyr] NF **1** *(bouffissure)* swelling, puffiness; *(cloque)* blister **2** *(emphase)* pomposity, turgidity

bousculade [buskylad] NF **1** *(agitation)* crush, pushing and shoving; **pas de b.!** no jostling *or* shoving!; **une b. vers la sortie** a scramble *or* stampede towards the exit; **j'ai perdu mon parapluie dans la b.** I lost my umbrella in the confusion **2** *Fam (précipitation)* rush; **ç'a été la b. toute la journée** it's been one mad rush all day (long)

bousculer [3] [buskyle] VT **1** *(pousser ▸ voyageur, passant)* to jostle, to push, to shove; *(▸ chaise, table)* to bump *or* to knock into; **il l'a bousculée au passage** he bumped into her as he went past; **se faire b. par qn** to be jostled by sb **2** *Fig (changer brutalement)* to upset, to turn on its head, to turn upside down; **b. les habitudes de qn** to upset sb's routine **3** *(presser)* to rush, to hurry; **j'ai été très bousculé** I've had a lot to do *or* a very busy time; **laisse-moi le temps de réfléchir, ne me bouscule pas** don't rush me, I need time to think

VPR **se bousculer 1** *(dans une cohue)* to jostle, to push and shove **2** *(affluer)* to rush; **les idées se bousculaient dans sa tête** his/her head was a jumble of ideas; *Ironique* **ne vous bousculez surtout pas pour m'aider** don't all rush to help me at once, will you?; *Fam* **ça se bouscule au portillon!** *(il y a affluence)* there's a huge crowd trying to get in!; *(il/elle bafouille)* he/she can't get his/her words out; *Hum* **ça ne se bouscule pas au portillon** people aren't exactly turning up in droves

bouse [buz] NF **b. (de vache)** *(matière)* cow dung; *(motte)* cowpat

bouseux, -euse [buzø, -øz] NM,F *très Fam Péj* yokel, country bumpkin, *Am* hick; **les b. du coin** the local yokels

bousier [buzje] NM *Entom* dung beetle, dung chafer

bousillage [buzijaʒ] NM **1** *Fam (gâchis)* botch, botch-up **2** *Constr* cob

bousiller [3] [buzije] VT **1** *Fam (mal faire)* to bungle, to botch (up)

2 *Fam (casser)* to bust, to wreck; **ma montre est bousillée** my watch is bust

3 *Fam (gâcher)* to spoil, to ruin

4 *très Fam (tuer)* to bump off, to do in, to waste

VPR **se bousiller se b. les yeux/la santé** to ruin one's eyes/health[□]

bousilleur, -euse [buzijœr, -øz] NM,F *Fam* botcher, bungler

boussole [busɔl] NF **1** *(instrument)* compass; **b. de marine** mariner's compass; **b. de poche** pocket compass **2** *Fam (locution)* **il a complètement perdu la b.** *(vieillard)* he's lost his marbles, he's gone gaga; *(fou)* he's off his head *or* rocker

boustifaille [bustifaj] NF *très Fam* grub, *Br* nosh, *Am* chow

BOUT [bu]

- tip **1**
- end **1, 2**
- scrap **4**
- toe **1**
- piece **4**
- part, bit **4**

NM **1** *(extrémité ▸ d'un couteau, d'un crayon)* tip; *(▸ d'une botte, d'une chaussette)* toe; *(▸ d'une table, d'une ficelle)* end; **le b. est arrondi** it's got a round tip; **à bouts ronds/carrés** round-/square-tipped; **tiens bien ton b., je tire** hold on to your end while I pull; **b. du doigt** fingertip, tip of the finger; **b. du nez** tip of the nose; **b. du sein** nipple; **b. filtre** *(d'une cigarette)* filter tip; **à b. filtre** filter-tipped; *Fig* **prendre qch par le bon b.** to deal with sth in the right way; **prendre qn par le bon b.** to approach sb the right way; **plus que 40 pages à écrire, je tiens le bon b.** only another 40 pages to write, I can see the light at the end of the tunnel; **je ne sais pas par quel b. le prendre** *(personne)* I don't know how to handle *or* to approach him; *(article, travail)* I don't know how to tackle *or* to approach it; **voir les choses par le petit b. de la lorgnette** to take a narrow view of things; **il a accepté du b. des lèvres** he accepted reluctantly *or* half-heartedly; **je l'ai sur le b. de la langue** it's on the tip of my tongue; **il connaît** *ou* **sait ses verbes sur le b. des doigts** he knows his verbs by heart *or Br* off pat *or Am* down pat; **je connais son œuvre sur le b. des doigts** I know his/her work by heart *or* inside out; **s'asseoir du b. des fesses** to sit down gingerly; **enfin, on en voit le b.** at last, we're beginning to see the light at the end of the tunnel; **on n'en voit pas le b.** there's no end to it

2 *(extrémité ▸ d'un espace)* end; **le b. du tunnel** the end of the tunnel; *Fig* **on voit enfin le b. du**

tunnel at last we can see the light at the end of the tunnel; **le b. du monde** the back of beyond; **ce n'est pas le b. du monde!** it won't kill you!

3 *(portion de temps)* **un b. de temps** a while; *Fam* **ça fait un bon b. de temps de ça** it was quite a long time ago *or* a while back; **il faudra attendre un bon b. de temps** you'll have to wait for quite some time

4 *(morceau ▸ de pain, de bois, de terrain)* piece, a bit; *(▸ de papier)* scrap, piece; **un vieux b. de chewing-gum** an old piece of chewing gum; **un b. de ciel bleu** a patch of blue sky; **donne-m'en un b.** give me some *or* a piece *or* a bit; *Fam* **un (petit) b. d'homme/de femme** a little man/woman; *Fam* **b. de chou** *(enfant)* toddler; *(en appellatif)* sweetie, *Br* poppet; **b. d'essai** screen test; **ça fait un bon b. de chemin** it's quite some *or* a way; **faire un b. de chemin avec qn** to go part of the way with sb; *Théât & Cin* **b. de rôle** walk-on *or* bit part; *Fam* **discuter** *ou* **tailler le b. de gras** to chew the fat; *très Fam* **mettre les bouts** to make oneself scarce; **la vie avec lui était intolérable, alors elle a mis les bouts** life with him was intolerable, so *Br* she did a bunk *or Am* she split

5 *Naut* **être b. au vent** to be head to the wind

6 [but] *Can Fam* **dans mon b.** in my neck of the woods; *Fam* **c'est le b. du b.!** that takes *Br* the biscuit *or Am* the cake!

• **à bout** ADV **être à b.** to be at the end of one's tether; **ma patience est à b.!** I've run out of patience!; **mettre** *ou* **pousser qn à b.** to push sb to the limit; **ne me pousse pas à b.!** don't push me (too far)!

• **à bout de** PRÉP **1 être à b. de** *(ne plus avoir de)* **être à b. d'arguments/patience** to have run out of arguments/patience; **être à b. de course** to be worn out *or* done in; **il est à b. de forces** *(physiquement)* he's got no strength left in him; *(psychologiquement)* he can't cope any more; **être à b. de nerfs** to be on the verge of a breakdown **2** *(locutions)* **porter un paquet à b. de bras** to carry a parcel (in one's outstretched arms); *Fig* **porter qn/une entreprise à b. de bras** to carry sb/a business; **venir à b. de** *(adversaire, obstacle)* to overcome; *(travail)* to see the end of; **je ne suis pas venu à b. de ces taches** I couldn't get rid of these stains

• **à bout portant** ADV point-blank; **tirer (sur) qn/qch à b. portant** to shoot sb/sth at point-blank range

• **à tout bout de champ** ADV all the time, non-stop; **elle me pose des questions à tout b. de champ** she never stops asking me questions; **on cite son nom à tout b. de champ** his/her name is constantly being quoted

• **au bout** [but] *Can Fam* ADJ excellent, great ADV **bon au b.** excellent, great

• **au bout de** PRÉP **1** *(après)* after; **au b. d'un moment** after a while **2** *(à la fin de)* **j'arrive au b. de mon contrat** my contract's nearly up; **pas encore au b. de ses peines** not out of the woods yet **3** *(dans l'espace)* **au b. de la rue** at the bottom *or* end of the road; *Fig* **leur couple est arrivé au b. du chemin** the two of them have come to the end of the road; **la conclusion a dû rester au b. de sa plume** he must have forgotten to put in the conclusion; **être au b. de son** *ou* **du rouleau** *(épuisé)* to be completely washed out; *(presque mort)* to be at death's door

• **au bout du compte** ADV at the end of the day, in the end

• **bout à bout** ADV end to end; **disposez les montants b. à b. avant de les assembler** lay the struts end to end before assembling; **un ramassis de citations mises b. à b.** a whole mishmash of quotations

• **de bout en bout** ADV *(lire)* from cover to cover; **parcourir un couloir de b. en b.** to pace up and down a corridor; **tu as raison de b. en b.** you're completely *or* totally right; **elle a mené la course de b. en b.** she led the race from start to finish

• **d'un bout à l'autre** ADV **la pièce est drôle d'un b. à l'autre** the play's hilarious from beginning to end *or* from start to finish; **il m'a contredit d'un b. à l'autre** he contradicted me all the way

• **d'un bout de... à l'autre** PRÉP **d'un b. de l'année à l'autre** all year round; **d'un b. à l'autre du pays, les militants s'organisent** (right) throughout the country, the militants are organizing themselves

• **en bout de** PRÉP at the end of; **en b. de course** at the end of the race; *Fig* **le régime est en b. de course** the regime is running out of steam

• **jusqu'au bout** ADV to the very end; **il est resté jusqu'au b.** he stayed to the very end; **il va toujours jusqu'au b. de ce qu'il entreprend** he always sees things through to the very end; **jusqu'au b. du monde** to the end *or* ends of the earth; **il est toujours soigné jusqu'au b. des ongles** he's always immaculately turned out; **elle est artiste jusqu'au b. des ongles** she's an artist through and through

boutade [butad] NF *(plaisanterie)* joke, *Sout* sally; **faire une b.** to make *or* to crack a joke; **c'était une b.!** (I was) only joking!

bout-dehors [budɔɔr] *(pl* **bouts-dehors)** NM *Naut* boom

boute-en-train [butɑ̃trɛ̃] NM INV *(amuseur)* funny man, joker; **le b. de la bande** the life and soul of the group

bouteille [butɛj] NF **1** *(récipient ▸ pour un liquide)* bottle; *(▸ pour un gaz)* bottle, cylinder; **une b. de vin** *(pleine)* a bottle of wine; *(vide)* a wine bottle; **un casier à bouteilles** a bottle rack; **b. d'oxygène** cylinder of oxygen; **b. Thermos** Thermos® (*Br* flask *or Am* bottle); **avoir de la b.** to be an old hand; *Fam* **prendre de la b.** to be getting *or Br* knocking on a bit; **jeter** *ou* **lancer une b. à la mer** to send a message in a bottle; *Fig* to send out an SOS **2** *(contenu)* bottle, bottleful; **boire une bonne b.** to drink a good bottle of wine; **être porté sur** *ou* **aimer la b.** to like one's drink

• **bouteilles** NFPL *Naut* heads, toilets

• **en bouteille** ADJ *(gaz, vin)* bottled ADV **mettre du vin en b.** to bottle wine; **vieilli en b.** aged in the bottle

bouter [3] [bute] VT **1** *Littéraire Vieilli* **b. hors de France** to drive *or* chase out of France **2** *Belg & Suisse* **b. le feu à qch** to set fire to sth, to set sth on fire

bouteur [butœr] NM *Mil (engin)* bulldozer

boutiquaire [butikɛr] ADJ **niveau b.** *(dans un aéroport)* shopping level *or* concourse

boutique [butik] NF **1** *Com (magasin) Br* shop, *Am* store; **b. franchisée** franchise outlet; **b. hors taxe** duty-free shop; **b. de mode** boutique; **tenir b.** to have a shop **2** *Fam (lieu de travail)* place, dump; **changer de b.** to get a new job; **parler b.** to talk shop

boutiquier, -ère [butikje, -ɛr] NM,F *Br* shopkeeper, *Am* storekeeper

boutis [buti] NM **1** *(technique)* = Provençal embroidery style featuring embossed designs as in quilting **2** *(dessus de lit etc)* = bedspread, throw etc made using the Provençal "boutis" embroidery technique

boutoir [butwar] NM **1** *Zool (du sanglier)* snout **2** *(locution)* **coup de b.** cutting remark

bouton [butɔ̃] NM **1** *Bot* bud; **b. de rose** rosebud

2 *Couture* button; **b. de col/de bottine** collar/boot stud; **avoir des yeux en boutons de bottine** to have beady eyes; **b. de manchette** cuff link

3 *(poignée de porte, de tiroir)* knob

4 *(de mise en marche) & Ordinat* button; *(interrupteur)* switch; *TV* **b. de contraste** contrast button; *Ordinat* **b. de défilement** scroll button; *Ordinat* **b. de navigation** navigation button; *Ordinat* **b. d'option, b. radio** radio button; **b. de réglage** dial; **b. de réglage du volume** volume control; *Ordinat* **b. de réinitialisation** reset button; **b. de sonnette** bellpush; *Ordinat* **b. de souris** mouse button

5 *Méd* spot, pimple; **avoir des boutons** *(pustules)* to have spots; *(petits, rouges)* to have a rash; **b. d'acné** spot caused by acne; **b. de chaleur** heat bump; **b. de fièvre** fever blister, cold sore

6 *(bijou)* **b. d'oreille** stud (earring)

• **en bouton** ADJ *Bot* in bud

bouton-d'or [butɔ̃dɔr] *(pl* **boutons-d'or)** NM *Bot* buttercup

boutonnage [butɔnaʒ] NM **1** *(action de boutonner)* buttoning (up) **2** *(mode de fermeture)* buttons; **une veste à double b.** a double-buttoning jacket

boutonner [3] [butɔne] VT **1** *(vêtement)* to button (up), to do up **2** *Escrime* to button

VI *Bot* to bud (up)

VPR **se boutonner 1** *(se fermer)* to button (up) **2** *Fam (s'habiller)* to button oneself up

boutonneux, -euse [butɔnø, -øz] ADJ *(peau, visage, adolescent)* spotty, pimply

boutonnière [butɔnjɛr] NF **1** *Couture* buttonhole; **point de b.** blanket stitch **2** *Méd* buttonhole; **faire une b. à qn** to make a buttonhole in sb **3** *Fam (blessure)* gash

• **à la boutonnière** ADV on one's lapel; **avoir une fleur à la b.** to wear a flower on one's lapel *or* in one's buttonhole, to wear a *Br* buttonhole *or Am* boutonniere

bouton-poussoir [butɔ̃puswar] *(pl* **boutons-poussoirs)** NM push button

bouton-pression [butɔ̃presjɔ̃] *(pl* **boutons-pression)** NM snap (fastener), *Br* press stud

bouturage [butyraʒ] NM *Hort* propagation by cuttings

bouture [butyr] NF *Hort* cutting; **faire des boutures** to take cuttings

bouturer [3] [butyre] VT *Hort* **1** *(reproduire)* to propagate (by cuttings) **2** *(couper)* to take cuttings from

VI *Bot* to grow suckers

bouvet [buvɛ] NM *Menuis* grooving plane

bouvier, -ère [buvje, -ɛr] NM,F bullock driver, cowherd

NM *Zool (chien)* bouvier, sheepdog; **b. des Flandres** bouvier des Flandres

• **bouvière** NF *Ich* bitterling

bouvillon [buvijɔ̃] NM *Zool* young bullock

bouvreuil [buvrœj] NM *Orn* bullfinch

bovarysme [bɔvarism] NM romantic daydreaming

bovidé [bɔvide] NM *Zool* bovid; **les bovidés** the Bovidae

bovin, -e [bɔvɛ̃, -in] ADJ **1** *Zool (espèce)* bovine; *(élevage)* cattle *(avant n)* **2** *Péj (stupide)* bovine

NM bovine; **les bovins** *Zool* bovines; *Agr* cattle

boviné [bɔvine] NM *Zool* bovine; **les bovinés** bovines

bowling [buliŋ] NM **1** *(jeu)* (tenpin) bowling; **aller faire un b.** to go bowling **2** *(salle)* bowling alley

box[1] [bɔks] NM INV *(cuir)* box calf

box[2] [bɔks] *(pl inv ou* **boxes)** NM **1** *(enclos ▸ pour cheval)* stall, *Br* loose box

2 *(garage)* lock-up garage

3 *(compartiment ▸ à l'hôpital, au dortoir)* cubicle

4 *Jur* **b. des accusés** dock; *aussi Fig* **au b. des accusés** in the dock

boxe [bɔks] NF *Boxe* boxing; **gants/match de b.** boxing gloves/match; **faire de la b.** to box; **b. américaine** full-contact karate, full-contact kick boxing; **b. anglaise** boxing; **b. française** kick *or* French boxing; **b. thaï** Thai boxing

boxer[1] [bɔksɛr] NM *(chien)* boxer

boxer[2] [3] [bɔkse] VI *Boxe* to box, to fight; **b. contre qn** to box against *or* fight sb

VT *Fam* to punch⊐, to thump

boxeur, -euse [bɔksœr, -øz] NM,F *Boxe* boxer

box-office [bɔksɔfis] *(pl* **box-offices)** NM box office; **être en tête du b.** to be a box-office hit

boxon [bɔksɔ̃] NM *très Fam* **1** *(maison close)* brothel, whorehouse **2** *(désordre)* mess; **foutre le b. dans qch** to make a mess of sth; **il fout le b. en classe** he creates havoc in the classroom

boy [bɔj] NM **1** *(serviteur)* boy **2** *(danseur)* (music-hall) dancer

boyau, -x [bwajo] NM **1** *Culin* length of casing

2 *Mus* **b. (de chat)** catgut, gut

3 *(passage ▸ de mine)* gallery, tunnel; *(▸ souterrain)* narrow tunnel; *(▸ tranchée)* trench; *(▸ rue)* narrow alleyway

4 *(pneu)* racing bike tyre

5 *Can* **b. d'arrosage** (garden) hose, hosepipe

• **boyaux** NMPL *Zool* guts, entrails; *Fam (d'une personne)* innards, guts

boycott [bɔjkɔt], **boycottage** [bɔjkɔtaʒ] NM boycott, boycotting

boycotter [3] [bɔjkɔte] VT to boycott; **se faire b.** to be boycotted

boycotteur, -euse [bɔjkɔtœr, -øz] ADJ boycotting *(avant n)*
NM,F boycotter

BP [bepe] NF *(abrév* **boîte postale***)* PO Box

BPA [bepea] NM *Fin (abrév* **bénéfice par action***)* EPS

BPF *Anciennement Banque (abrév écrite* **bon pour francs***)* = abbreviation printed on cheques and invoices before amount to be written in figures

bpp [bepepe] NMPL *Ordinat (abrév* **bits par pouce***)* bpi

bps [bepeεs] NMPL *Ordinat (abrév* **bits par seconde***)* bps

brabançon, -onne [brabɑ̃sɔ̃, -ɔn] ADJ of/from Brabant
• **Brabançon, -onne** NM,F = inhabitant of or person from Brabant
• **Brabançonne** NF = Belgian national anthem

Brabant [brabɑ̃] NM **le B.** Brabant

bracelet [braslε] NM **1** *(gén)* bracelet; *(rigide)* bangle; **b. de cheville** anklet; **b. électronique** *ou* **de cheville** *ou* **de détention** electronic tag; **b. de montre** watchband, watchstrap **2** *(pour faire du sport)* wristband; **b. en éponge** sweatband; **b. de force** leather wristband **3** *(lien)* band
• **bracelets** NMPL *Fam Arg crime (menottes)* bracelets, cuffs

bracelet-montre [braslεmɔ̃tr] *(pl* **bracelets-montres***)* NM wristwatch

brachial, -e, -aux, -ales [brakjal, -o] ADJ *Anat* brachial

brachiopode [brakjɔpɔd] *Zool* NM brachiopod, lampshell
• **brachiopodes** NMPL Brachiopoda

brachycéphale [brakisefal] ADJ brachycephalic
NMF brachycephalic person

braconnage [brakɔnaʒ] NM *Chasse* poaching

braconner [3] [brakɔne] VI *Chasse* to poach

braconnier, -ère [brakɔnje, εr] NM,F *Chasse* poacher

bractée [brakte] NF *Bot* bract

bradé, -e [brade] ADJ cut-price

brader [3] [brade] VT *Com* to sell off cheaply; **on brade** *(sur vitrine)* clearance sale

braderie [bradri] NF *Com* **1** *(vente ▸ en plein air, dans une salle) Br* ≃ jumble sale, *Am* ≃ rummage sale **2** *(soldes)* clearance sale

braguette [bragεt] NF *Br* flies, *Am* fly *(on trousers)*

brahmane [braman] NM *Rel* Brahman

brahmanisme [bramanism] NM *Rel* Brahmanism

brahmine [bramin] NF *Rel* Brahmani

brai [brε] NM *(goudrons)* pitch

braillard, -e [brajar, -ard] *Péj* ADJ **un bébé b.** a bawler
NM,F bawler, squaller; **fais taire ton b.!** keep that squalling brat of yours quiet!

braille [braj] NM Braille; **lire en b.** to read Braille

braillement [brajmɑ̃] NM bawl, howl; **les braillements d'un bébé** the crying *or* howling of a baby

brailler [3] [braje] VI **1** *(pleurer bruyamment)* to wail, to bawl, to howl
2 *(crier ▸ mégère, ivrogne)* to yell, to bawl; *(▸ radio)* to blare (out)
3 *(chanter)* to roar, to bellow
4 *Can (pleurer)* to cry
VT to bawl (out), *Am* to holler (out)

brailleur, -euse [brajœr, -øz] = **braillard**

braiment [brεmɑ̃] NM *(d'un âne)* bray, braying

brainstorming [brεnstɔrmiŋ] NM brainstorming; **un b.** a brainstorming session

brain-trust [brεntrœst] *(pl* **brain-trusts***)* NM *Br* brains trust, *Am* brain trust

braire [112] [brεr] VI **1** *(âne)* to bray **2** *Fam (crier)* to yell, to bellow

braise [brεz] NF **1** *(charbons)* (glowing) embers; **cuire qch sur/sous la b.** to cook sth over/in the embers; *Fig* **un regard de b.** a smouldering look; *Fig* **être sur la b.** to be on tenterhooks **2** *Fam Arg crime (argent)* dough, moolah

braiser [4] [breze] VT *Culin* to braise

braisière [brezjεr] NF **1** *(cocotte)* braising-pan, stew-pan **2** *(étouffoir pour la braise)* extinguishing box *(for charcoal)*

bramement [brammɑ̃] NM **1** *(d'un cerf)* bell **2** *Fam (cri)* wail

bramer [3] [brame] VI **1** *(cerf)* to bell **2** *Fam (pleurer)* to wail

bran [brɑ̃] NM *(partie du son)* bran; **b. de scie** sawdust

brancard [brɑ̃kar] NM **1** *(civière)* stretcher **2** *(limon d'attelage)* shaft

brancardier [brɑ̃kardje] NM stretcher-bearer

branchage [brɑ̃ʃaʒ] NM *(ramure)* boughs, branches
• **branchages** NMPL (cut) branches

branche [brɑ̃ʃ] NF **1** *Bot (d'arbre)* branch, bough; *(de céleri)* stick; **grosse b.** limb, large branch; *Hum Vieilli* **vieille b.** old chum, old stick; *Fam* **se raccrocher** *ou* **se rattraper aux branches** to hang on by one's fingernails
2 *Anat* ramification
3 *Électron* leg, branch; **circuit à deux branches** two-legged circuit
4 *(tige ▸ de lunettes) Br* sidepiece, *Am* bow; *(▸ d'un compas, d'un aimant)* arm, leg; *(▸ de ciseaux)* blade; *(▸ de tenailles)* handle; *(▸ d'un chandelier)* branch
5 *(secteur)* field; **vous êtes dans quelle b.?** what's your line *or* field?; **les différentes branches de la physique** the different branches of physics
6 *(d'une famille)* side; **par la b. maternelle** on the mother's side (of the family); **la b. aînée de la famille** the senior branch of the family; *Vieilli* **avoir de la b.** to have breeding
7 *Suisse Univ* subject; **b. primaire** main subject, *Am* major; **b. secondaire** secondary subject, *Am* minor
8 *Suisse (chocolat)* = cylindrical bar of chocolate
• **en branches** ADJ *Bot (épinards)* leaf *(avant n)*; **céleri en branches** celery

branché, -e [brɑ̃ʃe] *Fam* ADJ trendy, hip; **être b. cinéma/jazz** to be into movies/jazz
NM,F trendy person; **tous les branchés viennent dans ce café** you get all the trendy people in this café

branchement [brɑ̃ʃmɑ̃] NM **1** *Élec & Électron (sur un réseau)* connection; *(sur une prise)* plugging in; **b. d'appareil** *(tuyau)* connecting branch; *(liaison)* connection, installation; **faire un b. d'égout** to be connected to the sewage system; **b. électrique** electric power supply; **b. au réseau électrique** network branch; **faire un b. au** *ou* **sur le réseau** to be connected to the mains (power supply) **2** *Rail Br* points, *Am* switch

brancher [3] [brɑ̃ʃe] VT **1** *Élec & Électron (sur un réseau)* to connect; *(sur une prise)* to plug in; **b. qch sur une prise** to plug sth in; *Fam* **je me branche où?** where is there a plug?; **être branché** *(appareil)* to be plugged in; *(canalisation)* to be connected to the system; **assurez-vous que l'appareil n'est pas branché** make sure the appliance is unplugged; **il faut que je fasse b. le téléphone** I've got to have the telephone installed
2 *Fam (faire parler)* **b. qn sur** to start sb off *or* to get sb going on; **je l'ai branché sur le reggae et il ne s'est plus arrêté** I got him into reggae and after that there was no stopping him
3 *Fam (mettre en rapport)* **b. qn avec** to put sb in touch with[□]; **je vais te b. avec ma sœur, elle sait ce qu'il faut faire** I'll put you in touch with my sister, she knows what to do
4 *Fam (intéresser)* **ça me branche bien!** that's great!; **ce type ne me branche pas des masses** that guy's really not my type; **il est très branché (sur les) voyages** he's really into travelling[□]; **ça vous brancherait d'y aller?** how do you fancy going there?
5 *Fam (séduire)* **se faire b. par qn** to be *Br* chatted up *or Am* hit on by sb
VI *(se percher)* to roost, to sit
VPR **se brancher 1** *Can Fam* to decide[□], to make up one's mind[□] **2 se b. sur** *(appareil)* to plug into; *Rad* to tune into; *(canalisation)* to connect up to; **se b. sur les grandes ondes** to tune in to long wave

branchette [brɑ̃ʃεt] NF *Littéraire* twig, sprig

branchial, -e, -aux, -ales [brɑ̃ʃjal, -o] ADJ *Zool* branchial

branchie [brɑ̃ʃi] NF *Zool* gill; **branchies** gills, *Spéc* branchiae

branchitude [brɑ̃ʃityd] NF *Fam* hipness, trendiness; **cette boîte est l'un des hauts lieux de la b. parisienne** this club is one of the coolest *or* hippest in Paris

branchouille [brɑ̃ʃuj] *Fam* ADJ hip, trendy
NMF trendy person

branchu, -e [brɑ̃ʃy] ADJ *Bot* branchy

brandade [brɑ̃dad] NF *Culin* **b. (de morue)** brandade, salt cod purée

brande [brɑ̃d] NF **1** *Bot (plantes)* heather, heath **2** *École (terrain)* heath, moor

Brandebourg [brɑ̃dbur] NM *Géog* Brandenburg; **la porte de B.** the Brandenburg Gate

brandebourg [brɑ̃dbur] *Couture* NM frog, frogging
• **à brandebourgs** ADJ frogged

brandir [32] [brɑ̃dir] VT *(arme)* to brandish; *(une menace)* to hold up

brandon [brɑ̃dɔ̃] NM *(pour allumer)* firebrand; **b. de discorde** *(objet, situation)* bone of contention; *(personne)* troublemaker
• **brandons, Brandons** NMPL *Suisse* **les brandons** *ou* **Brandons** = celebration of the end of winter in French-speaking Switzerland

brandy [brɑ̃di] NM *(alcool)* brandy

branlant, -e [brɑ̃lɑ̃, -ɑ̃t] ADJ **1** *(vieux ▸ bâtiment, véhicule)* ramshackle, rickety **2** *(instable ▸ pile d'objets)* unsteady, wobbly, shaky; *(▸ échelle, chaise)* rickety, shaky; *(▸ dent)* loose; *(▸ résolution, réputation)* shaky

branle [brɑ̃l] NM **1** *(mouvement)* pendulum motion **2** *(impulsion)* impulsion, propulsion; **donner le b. à qch** *(procédure, situation)* to set sth going *or* in motion; **être en b.** to be on the move; **mettre en b.** *(cloche)* to set going; *(mécanisme, procédure)* to set going *or* in motion; **se mettre en b.** *(voyageur)* to set off, to start out; *(mécanisme)* to start going, to start moving; *(voiture)* to start (moving) **3** *(danse)* branle

branle-bas [brɑ̃lba] NM INV **1** *(agitation)* pandemonium, commotion; **dans le b. du départ** in the commotion of setting off; *Naut & Fig* **b. de combat!** action stations!; **quand ma tante arrivait, c'était le b. de combat** when my aunt arrived, it was action stations all round **2** *Naut* clearing of the decks

branlée [brɑ̃le] NF *Fam* thrashing; **prendre** *ou* **recevoir une b.** to get a thrashing, to get thrashed

branlement [brɑ̃lmɑ̃] NM *(dodelinement)* wagging (of the head)

branler [3] [brɑ̃le] VI *(échelle, pile d'objets)* to be shaky *or* unsteady; *(fauteuil)* to be rickety; *(dent)* to be loose; **b. dans le manche** *(outil)* to have a loose handle; *Can Fam Fig* to hum and haw
VT **1 b. la tête** *(de haut en bas)* to nod; *(de droite à gauche)* to shake one's head **2** *Vulg (faire)* **j'en ai rien à b.** I don't give a (flying) fuck *or* a shit; **mais qu'est-ce qu'il branle?** *(il est en retard)* where the fuck is he?; *(il fait une bêtise)* what the fuck's he up to? **3** *Vulg (masturber) Br* to wank, *Am* to jerk off
VPR **se branler** *Vulg Br* to (have a) wank, *Am* to jerk off; *Fig* **je m'en branle** I don't give a shit *or* fuck

branlette [brɑ̃lεt] NF *Vulg* hand-job, *Br* wank; **se faire une (petite) b.** *Br* to have a wank, *Am* to jerk off

branleur, -euse [brɑ̃lœr, -øz] NM,F *Vulg* **1** *(bon à rien)* loser, *Br* waster, *Am* slacker **2** *(fanfaron)* show-off, *Am* hotshot

branque [brɑ̃k], **branquignol** [brɑ̃kiɲɔl] *Fam* ADJ *(fou)* crazy, nuts
NMF *(imbécile)* dope, jerk; *(fou)* headcase, *Br* nutter, *Am* wacko

braquage [brakaʒ] NM **1** *Aut* (steering) lock **2** *Aviat* deflection **3** *Fam (vol)* holdup, stickup

braque [brak] ADJ *Fam* crazy, nuts
NM *(chien)* pointer

braquemart [brakmar] NM **1** *Hist (épée)* cutlass **2** *très Fam* dick, prick, *Br* knob

braquer [3] [brake] **VT 1** *(pointer ▸ fusil)* to point, to aim, to level; *(▸ projecteur, télescope)* to train; **b. son revolver sur qn** to level *or* to point one's gun at sb; **b. une lunette sur** to train a telescope on
2 *(concentrer)* **son regard était braqué sur moi** she was staring straight at me, her gaze was fixed on me; **b. son attention sur qch** to fix one's attention on sth
3 *Aut & Aviat* to turn
4 *(rendre hostile)* to antagonize; **ne le braquez pas** don't antagonize him *or* put his back up; **b. qn contre** to set sb against; **elle est braquée contre ses collègues/ce mariage** she's totally opposed to her colleagues/dead set against this marriage
5 *Fam (attaquer ▸ banque)* to hold up; *(▸ caissier)* to hold at gunpoint
VI *(conducteur)* to turn the steering wheel; **b. bien/mal** to have a good/poor turning circle; **b. à droite/gauche** to turn hard to the right/left; **braque à fond!** *(vers la droite)* (turn) hard right!; *(vers la gauche)* (turn) hard left!
VPR se braquer to dig one's heels in; **il s'est braqué, il n'y a rien à faire** he's dug his heels in *or* he's set (his face) against it, there's nothing we can do

braquet [brakɛ] **NM** transmission ratio; **changer de b.** to change gear

braqueur, -euse [brakœr, -øz] **NM,F** armed robber

bras [bra] **NM 1** *(membre)* arm; *Anat* upper arm; **blessé au b.** wounded in the arm; **avoir qn à son b.** to have sb on one's arm; **son panier/épouse au b.** his basket/wife on his arm; **avoir qch dans les b.** to be carrying sth in one's arms; **porter un enfant dans les** *ou* **ses b.** to carry a child (in one's arms); **tomber dans les b. de qn** to fall into sb's arms; **ils sont tombés dans les b. l'un de l'autre** they fell into each other's arms; *Fig* **il l'a jetée dans les b. de Robert** he drove her into Robert's arms; **sous le b.** under one arm; **donner le b. à qn** to give sb one's arm; **prendre le b. de qn** to grab sb's arm; **offrir son b. à qn** to offer sb one's arm; **serrer qn dans ses b.** to hold sb in one's arms, to hug sb; **tendre** *ou* **allonger le b.** to stretch one's arm out; **les b. croisés** with one's arms folded, with folded arms; **rester les b. croisés** *(ne pas travailler)* to twiddle one's thumbs; *(être passif)* to stand idly by; **les b. en croix** (with) arms outstretched *or* outspread; *Fig* **b. droit** right-hand man, *f* woman; **faire un b. de fer avec qn** to arm-wrestle with sb; *Fig* to have a tussle with sb; **faire un b. d'honneur à qn** ≃ to give sb the finger; **jouer les gros b.** to throw one's weight around; *Fig Fam* **jouer petits b.** to hold back; **tomber à b. raccourcis sur qn** *(gén)* to lay into sb; *(physiquement)* to beat sb to a pulp; **avoir le b. long** to be influential; **se jeter dans les b. de qn** to throw oneself into sb's arms; *Fig* to fall an easy prey to sb; **les b. m'en tombent** I'm astounded, I'm flabbergasted; **lever les b.** *(d'impuissance)* to throw up one's arms (helplessly); **lever les b. au ciel** to throw up one's arms in indignation; **tendre les b. à qn** to hold out one's arms to sb; *Fig* to offer sb (moral) support; **tendre les b. vers qn** to hold out one's arms to sb; *Fig* to turn to sb for help
2 *Zool (du cheval)* arm; *(tentacule)* arm, tentacle
3 *(partie ▸ d'une ancre, d'un électrophone, d'un moulin)* arm; *(▸ d'une charrette)* arm, shaft; *(▸ d'une grue)* arm, jib; *(▸ d'un fauteuil)* arm, armrest; *(▸ d'une brouette)* handle; *(▸ d'une manivelle)* web, arm; *(▸ d'un brancard)* pole; *(▸ d'une croix)* arm; *Can* **b. d'escalier** banister; **b. de lecture** *(d'un électrophone)* pickup arm; **b. de levier** lever arm *or* crank; **b. manipulateur** computer-operated arm; *Can* **b. de vitesse** *Br* gear lever, *Am* stick shift
4 *(pouvoir)* **le b. séculier** the secular arm; **le b. de la justice** the long arm of the law
5 *Géog (d'un delta)* arm; **b. abandonné** *ou* **mort** dead channel; **b. de mer** sound, arm of the sea; **b. de rivière** arm *or Am* branch of a river
6 *Naut* (anchor) arm
7 b. de lumière sconce
NMPL *(main-d'œuvre)* workers; **on a besoin de b.** we're short-handed *or* short-staffed
• **à bras ouverts ADV** *(accueillir)* with open arms
• **au bras de PRÉP** on the arm of, arm in arm with
• **bras dessus, bras dessous ADV** arm in arm
• **sur les bras ADV avoir qn/qch sur les b.** to be stuck with sb/sth; **je me suis retrouvé avec le projet sur les b.** I got landed with the project; **les libraires craignent que cette anthologie ne leur reste sur les b.** booksellers are worried that this anthology might not sell

brasage [brazaʒ] **NM** *Métal* brazing, soldering

braser [3] [braze] **VT** *Métal* to solder

brasero [brazero] **NM** brazier

brasier [brazje] **NM 1** *(incendie)* blaze, fire; **la maison n'était plus qu'un b.** the house was now a blazing mass, the fire was now raging through the house **2** *(tumulte)* fire; **le b. de ses passions** the (consuming) fire of his/her passions; **le pays est maintenant un véritable b.** the whole country's ablaze

Brasilia [brazilja] **NM** *Géog* Brasilia

brasiller [3] [brazije] **VI** to glitter, to sparkle

bras-le-corps [bralkɔr] **à bras-le-corps ADV prendre** *ou* **saisir qn à b.** to catch hold of *or* to seize sb around the waist; *Fig* **prendre un problème à b.** to tackle a problem head on

brassage [brasaʒ] **NM 1** *(de la bière)* brewing; *(du malt)* mashing **2** *(de liquides)* mixing, swirling together; *(des cultures, des peuples)* intermixing, intermingling **3** *Naut (de la vergue)* bracing

brassard [brasar] **NM** armband; **b. de deuil** black armband

brasse [bras] **NF 1** *Sport* breaststroke; **tu sais nager la b.?** can you do the breaststroke?; **elle traverse la piscine en dix brasses** she can cross the swimming pool in ten strokes *(doing the breaststroke)*; **b. coulée** = breaststroke in which the face is submerged; **b. papillon** butterfly (stroke) **2** *(mesure)* = five feet; *Naut* fathom

brassée [brase] **NF** armful
• **par brassées ADV** by the armful

brasser [3] [brase] **VT 1** *(bière)* to brew; *(malt)* to mash
2 *Cartes* to shuffle
3 *(populations)* to intermingle
4 *(agiter ▸ air)* to fan; *(▸ feuilles mortes)* to toss about, to stir; *Fig* **b. de l'air** *ou* **du vent** to work without getting anything done
5 *(manier ▸ argent, sommes)* to handle; **b. des affaires** to handle a lot of business; **b. des millions** to handle millions
6 *Naut (vergue)* to brace
VPR se brasser 1 *(populations)* to intermingle **2** *(argent)* to be handled

brasserie [brasri] **NF 1** *(fabrique de bière)* brewery; *(industrie)* brewing, beer-making (industry) **2** *(café)* = large café serving light meals

brasseur, -euse [brasœr, -øz] **NM,F 1** *Sport* breaststroker; **c'est un bon b.** he's good at the breaststroke **2** *(fabricant de bière)* brewer
• **brasseur d'affaires NM** *Com* big businessman

brassière [brasjer] **NF 1** *(vêtement de bébé)* (baby's) *Br* vest *or Am* undershirt **2** *Naut* **b. de sauvetage** life jacket **3** *(soutien-gorge)* crop top; *Can Fam* bra ◻

brasure [brazyr] **NF** *Métal* **1** *(soudure)* soldering joint *or* surface *or* seam **2** *(alliage)* brazing alloy

Bratislava [bratislava] **NM** *Géog* Bratislava

bravache [bravaʃ] **ADJ** swaggering, blustering; **d'un air b.** blusteringly
NM swaggerer, *Littéraire* braggart; **faire le b.** to brag

bravade [bravad] **NF** *(ostentation)* bravado; *(défi)* defiance; **faire qch par b.** *(ostentation)* to do sth out of bravado; *(défi)* to do sth in a spirit of defiance

brave [brav] **ADJ 1** *(courageux)* brave, bold **2** *(avant le nom) (bon)* good, decent; **de braves gens** good *or* decent people; *Fam* **un b. type** a nice guy *or Br* bloke **3** *(ton condescendant)* **ma b. dame/mon b. monsieur, personne ne dit le contraire!** my dear lady/my dear fellow, nobody's saying anything to the contrary!; **il est bien b. mais il ne comprend rien** he means well but he doesn't understand a thing
NM 1 *(héros)* brave man, *f* woman; **faire le b.** to act brave **2** *Vieilli* **mon b.** my good man

> Il faut noter que l'adjectif anglais **brave** ne signifie jamais **gentil**.

bravement [bravmɑ̃] **ADV 1** *(courageusement)* bravely, courageously **2** *(sans hésitation)* boldly, resolutely; **il s'est b. mis au travail** he set to work with a will

braver [3] [brave] **VT 1** *(affronter ▸ danger, mort)* to defy, to brave; *(▸ conventions)* to go against, to challenge **2** *(défier ▸ autorité, personne)* to defy, to stand up to; *(▸ ordres, lois)* to go against, to defy

bravo [bravo] **EXCLAM 1** *(applaudissement)* bravo! **2** *(félicitations)* well done!, bravo!; **b.! bien parlé!** hear! hear!; **b., tu as raison!** good thinking!; *Ironique* **eh bien b., tu as réussi ton coup!** congratulations, you did a really great job there!
NM bravo; **un grand b. pour nos candidats** let's have a big hand for our contestants; **entrer/partir sous les bravos** to be cheered in/out

bravoure [bravur] **NF** bravery, courage; *Vieilli Mus* **air de b.** bravura; *Littérature* **morceau de b.** purple passage

Brazzaville [brazavil] **NM** *Géog* Brazzaville

break [brɛk] **NM 1** *Aut Br* estate car, *Am* station wagon
2 *Mus* break
3 *Sport* **faire le b.** to break away
4 *(au tennis)* **balle de b.** break point
5 *(à la boxe)* break

brebis [brəbi] **NF 1** *Zool* ewe; **lait de b.** ewe's milk; **fromage de b.** ewe's-milk cheese; **b. galeuse** black sheep **2** *Rel* sheep; **b. égarée** lost sheep; **les b. de Dieu** the faithful

brèche[1] [brɛʃ] **NF 1** *(ouverture)* breach, gap, break **2** *Mil* breach; **faire une b. dans un front** to break open *or* to breach an enemy line; *Fig* **être toujours sur la b.** to be always on the go **3** *Fig* hole, dent; **faire une b. à son capital** to make a hole *or* dent in one's capital

brèche[2] [brɛʃ] **NF** *Géol* breccia

bréchet [breʃɛ] **NM** *Orn* wishbone

bredouillage [brədujaʒ] **NM** mumbling, muttering

bredouille [brəduj] **ADJ** empty-handed; **rentrer b.** *Chasse & Pêche* to come home empty-handed *or* with an empty bag; *Fig* to come back empty-handed

bredouillement [brədujmɑ̃] **NM** mumbling, muttering

bredouiller [3] [brəduje] **VI** to mumble, to mutter
VT to mumble, to mutter

bredouilleur, -euse [brədujœr, -øz] **ADJ** mumbling, muttering
NM,F mumbler, mutterer

bref, brève [brɛf, brɛv] **ADJ 1** *(court ▸ moment, vision)* brief, fleeting; *(concis ▸ lettre, discours)* brief, short; **une brève histoire d'amour** a brief love affair; **soyez b.** be brief; **soyez plus b.** come to the point; **d'un ton b.** curtly **2** *Ling (syllabe, voyelle)* short
ADV in short, in a word; **enfin b., je n'ai pas envie d'y aller** well, basically, I don't want to go; **b., ce n'est pas possible** anyway, it's not possible
NM *Rel* (papal) brief
• **brève NF 1** *Ling (voyelle)* short vowel; *(syllabe)* short syllable **2** *Journ, Rad & TV* news in brief; **brèves de comptoir** bar talk
• **en bref ADV 1** *(en résumé)* in short, in brief **2** *Journ, Rad & TV* **les nouvelles en b.** the news in brief

bréhaigne [breɛɲ] **ADJ** *Zool (jument, biche)* barren

brelan [brəlɑ̃] **NM** *Cartes* = three of a kind; **b. de rois** three kings

brêle [brɛl] **NF** *Fam* **1** *(imbécile)* cretin, jerk, *Br* tosspot **2** *(personne médiocre)* **je suis une b. en anglais** *Br* I'm totally crap at English, *Am* I suck at English

breloque [brəlɔk] **NF 1** *(bijou)* charm **2** *Mil* break-off **3** *(locution)* **battre la b.** to sound the dismiss; *Fig (montre)* to be on the blink; *(intellectuellement)* to wander; **mon cœur bat la b.** *(bat* *vite)* my heart is racing; *(fonctionne mal)* my heart is playing me up

brème [brem] **NF 1** *Ich* bream **2** *Fam Arg crime* (playing) card□

Brême [brem] **NF** *Géog* Bremen

brent [brent] **NM** *(pétrole)* brent *(oil)*

Brésil [brezil] **NM le B.** Brazil

brésilien, -enne [breziljɛ̃, -ɛn] **ADJ** Brazilian; **maillot/slip b.** high-cut swimsuit/briefs
NM *(langue)* Brazilian Portuguese
• **Brésilien, -enne NM,F** Brazilian

brésiller [3] [brezije] **VT** *Littéraire & Tech* to break into small pieces; *(broyer)* to crumble, to pulverize
VI to crumble
VPR se brésiller *Littéraire & Tech* to crumble

Bretagne [brətaɲ] **NF la B.** Brittany

bretelle [brətɛl] **NF 1** *(bandoulière)* (shoulder) strap; **b. de fusil** gun sling; **porter l'arme à la b.** to carry one's weapon slung over one's shoulder
2 *(de robe)* shoulder strap; *(de soutien-gorge)* (bra) strap; **sans bretelles** strapless
3 *Rail* double crossover
4 *Transp* access road, *Br* slip road; **b. d'accès** access road; **b. d'autoroute** *Br* motorway slip road, *Am* highway on/off ramp; **b. de contournement** bypass; **b. de raccordement** *Br* motorway *or Am* highway junction; **b. de sortie** exit road
• **bretelles NFPL** *Br* braces, *Am* suspenders; *Fig* **se faire remonter les bretelles** to be told to pull one's socks up

breton, -onne [brətɔ̃, -ɔn] **ADJ** Breton
NM *(langue)* Breton
• **Breton, -onne NM,F** Breton

> **BRETON**
>
> Breton is a member of the Celtic family of languages and is related to Welsh and Gaelic. For many generations it was banned in favour of French before coming back into favour in recent decades with the revival of the Celtic identity and culture. However, despite efforts made to promote its use, Breton is still spoken principally by the older generations of Western Brittany.

bretonnant, -e [brətɔnɑ̃, -ɑ̃t] **ADJ** = relating to the preservation of Breton traditions and language

bretteler [24] [brətle] **VT** *(pierre etc)* to tool, to tooth; *(bijoux)* to hatch, to chase

bretzel [brɛtzɛl] **NM** *Culin* pretzel

breuvage [brœvaʒ] **NM 1** *(boisson)* beverage, drink; **un drôle de b.** a strange concoction **2** *(potion)* potion, beverage

brève [brɛv] *voir* **bref**

brevet [brəvɛ] **NM 1** *Jur* **b. (d'invention)** patent; **exploiter un b.** to work a patent; **prendre un b.** to take out a patent; **titulaire d'un b.** patentee; **(acte en) b.** contract delivered by a notary in the original
2 *Scol* diploma; **décerner** *ou* **délivrer un b. à qn** to award a diploma to sb; **le b. (des collèges)** = exam taken at 14 years of age; **b. d'aptitude aux fonctions d'animation** = diploma for youth leaders and workers; *Anciennement* **b. d'études du premier cycle** = former school certificate taken after four years of secondary education; **b. d'études professionnelles** = vocational diploma (taken after two years of study at a "lycée professionnel"); **brevets militaires** ≃ staff college qualifications; **b. professionnel** = vocational diploma; **b. de technicien** = vocational training certificate taken at 17 after three years' technical training; **b. de technicien supérieur** = advanced vocational training certificate (taken at the end of a two-year higher education course)
3 *Aviat* **b. de pilote** pilot's licence; **avoir son b. de pilote** to be a qualified pilot *or* qualified as a pilot
4 *(certificat)* certificate; **b. de secourisme** first-aid certificate

brevetabilité [brəvtabilite] **NF** patentability

brevetable [brəvtabl] **ADJ** patentable

breveté, -e [brəvte] **ADJ 1** *(diplômé)* qualified; **officier b. (d'état-major)** = officer who has passed staff college **2** *(invention)* patented; **inventeur b.** inventor holding letters patent
NM,F patentee

breveter [27] [brəvte] **VT** to patent; **faire b. qch** to take out a patent for sth

bréviaire [brevjer] **NM** *Rel* breviary; *Fig* bible; **dire son b.** to read one's breviary

briard, -e [brijar, -ard] **ADJ** of/from the Brie region
NM *(chien)* briard (dog)
• **Briard, -e NM,F** = inhabitant of or person from the Brie region

bribes [brib] **NFPL 1** *(restes ▸ d'un gâteau, d'un repas)* scraps, crumbs **2** *(fragments ▸ de discours, de conversation)* snatches, scraps; *(▸ d'information, de connaissances)* scraps, bits; **je ne connais que des b. de finlandais** I only know a few bits of Finnish
• **par bribes ADV** in snatches, bit by bit; **je connais l'histoire par b.** I've heard bits and pieces of the story

bric-à-brac [brikabrak] **NM INV 1** *(tas d'objets)* clutter, jumble, bric-à-brac; **c'est là que je mets tout mon b.** that's where I put all my odds and ends *or* bits and pieces **2** *(d'idées)* jumble, *Br* hotchpotch, *Am* hodgepodge **3** *(boutique) Br* junk shop, *Am* secondhand store

bric et de broc [brikedbrɔk] **de bric et de broc ADV** haphazardly; **meublé de b.** furnished with bits and pieces

bricheton [briʃtɔ̃] **NM** *Fam* bread□

brick [brik] **NM 1** *Naut* brig **2** *Culin* brik, = deep-fried filled filo-pastry parcel; **feuille de b.** = filo-type pastry used in North African cuisine **3** *(carton)* carton

bricolage [brikɔlaʒ] **NM 1** *(travail manuel)* do-it-yourself, *Br* DIY; **aimer le b.** to like do-it-yourself *or Br* DIY **2** *(réparation)* makeshift repair; **c'est du bon b.** it's good work **3** *(mauvais travail)* **c'est du b.** it's just been thrown together
• **de bricolage ADJ** *(magasin, manuel, rayon)* do-it-yourself *(avant n)*, *Br* DIY *(avant n)*

bricole [brikɔl] **NF 1** *(petit objet)* **des bricoles** things, bits and pieces
2 *(article de peu de valeur)* trifle; **je vais lui offrir une b.** I'm going to give him/her a little something; *Fam* **...et des bricoles** ...and a bit; **20 euros et des bricoles** 20-odd euros
3 *(chose sans importance)* piece of trivia; **des bricoles** trivia
4 *Fam (ennui)* trouble *(UNCOUNT)*; **il va t'arriver des bricoles** you're heading for trouble
5 *(harnais)* breast harness
6 *(bretelle)* carrying girth *or* strap

bricoler [3] [brikɔle] **VI 1** *(faire des aménagements)* to do odd jobs, *Br* to do DIY; **elle adore b.** she's a real do-it-yourself enthusiast; **j'ai passé la matinée à b. dans la maison** I spent the morning doing odd jobs about the house **2** *(avoir de petits emplois)* to do odd jobs; **jusqu'à 24 ans, j'ai bricolé** until I was 24, I never had a serious job **3** *Fam Péj (mauvais artisan, praticien ou étudiant)* to produce shoddy work
VT 1 *(confectionner)* to make; **c'est moi qui ai bricolé ça** it's all my own work **2** *(réparer)* to fix (up), to mend, to carry out makeshift repairs to; **j'ai bricolé la radio et elle a l'air de marcher** I've tinkered with the radio a bit and it seems to be working **3** *(manipuler)* to tinker *or* to tamper with; **qui a bricolé le grille-pain?** who's been tinkering with the toaster?; **b. un moteur** to soup up an engine

bricoleur, -euse [brikɔlœr, -øz] **NM,F 1** *(qui construit ou répare soi-même)* handyman, *f* handywoman, *Br* DIY enthusiast **2** *Péj (dilettante)* amateur, dilettante
ADJ il est très b. he's good with his hands; **il n'est pas b.** he's no handyman

bride [brid] **NF 1** *Équitation* bridle; **tenir son cheval en b.** to curb *or* to rein in a horse; *Fig* **tenir ses passions en b.** to keep a tight rein on one's emotions; **rendre la b. à un cheval** to give a horse its head; **à b. abattue, à toute b.** at full speed, like greased lightning; **avoir la b. sur le cou** to be given a free hand; **laisser la b. sur le cou à qn** to give sb a free rein; **tenir la b. haute à qn** to keep sb on a tight rein; **tourner b.** to turn tail
2 *Couture (de boutonnière)* bar; *(pour un bouton)* loop; *(en dentelle)* bride, bar
3 *Méd* adhesion; **b. amniotique** amniotic band *or* adhesion
4 *Tech* strap, tie; *(d'un cylindre, d'un tuyau)* flange, collar

bridé, -e [bride] **ADJ 1 yeux bridés** slanting eyes; **avoir les yeux bridés** to have slanting eyes **2** *Aut* **moteur b.** governed engine
NM,F *très Fam Br* slant-eye, *Am* gook, = offensive term used to refer to an Oriental

brider [3] [bride] **VT 1** *Équitation* to bridle
2 *(serrer)* to constrict; **ma veste me bride aux emmanchures** my jacket is too tight under the arms
3 *(émotion)* to curb, to restrain; *(personne)* to keep in check
4 *Couture* to bind
5 *Culin* to truss
6 *Naut* to lash together
7 *(tuyaux)* to flange, to clamp

bridge [bridʒ] **NM 1** *(dent)* bridge, bridgework **2** *Cartes* bridge; **faire un b.** to have *or* play a game of bridge; **b. contrat** contract bridge; **b. aux enchères** auction bridge

bridger [17] [bridʒe] **VI** *Cartes* to play bridge

bridgeur, -euse [bridʒœr, -øz] **NM,F** *Cartes* bridge player

bridon [bridɔ̃] **NM** *Équitation* snaffle (bridle)

brie [bri] **NM** *(fromage)* Brie

briefer [3] [brife] **VT** to brief

briefing [brifiŋ] **NM** briefing

brièvement [brijɛvmɑ̃] **ADV 1** *(pendant peu de temps)* briefly, fleetingly, for a short time **2** *(avec concision)* briefly, in a few words

brièveté [brijɛvte] **NF** *(courte durée)* brevity, briefness; *(du style, d'une réponse)* brevity

brigade [brigad] **NF 1** *Mil (détachement)* brigade; **b. aérienne** group, *Am* wing; **b. de gendarmerie** squad of gendarmes; **b. des sapeurs-pompiers** *Br* fire brigade, *Am* fire department
2 *(équipe d'ouvriers)* gang, team
3 *(corps de police)* squad; **b. anti-émeute** riot squad; **b. antigang** *ou* **de répression du (grand) banditisme** organized crime division; **b. des mineurs** juvenile division; **b. mobile** *ou* **volante** flying squad; **b. des mœurs** vice squad; *Fam* **b. des stupéfiants** *ou* **des stups** drug squad; *Hist* **les Brigades internationales** the International Brigades
4 *(en Italie)* **les Brigades rouges** the Red Brigades

brigadier [brigadje] **NM 1** *(de police)* sergeant **2** *Mil* corporal **3** *Hist* brigadier

brigadier-chef [brigadjeʃɛf] *(pl* **brigadiers-chefs) NM** *Mil* lance-sergeant

brigand [brigɑ̃] **NM 1** *(bandit)* bandit, *Littéraire* brigand **2** *(escroc)* crook, thief **3** *Fam (avec affection)* **b., va!** you rogue *or* imp *or* rascal!

brigandage [brigɑ̃daʒ] **NM 1** *(vol à main armée)* armed robbery **2** *(acte malhonnête)* **c'est du b.** it's daylight robbery

brigantin [brigɑ̃tɛ̃] **NM** *Naut* brigantine

brigantine [brigɑ̃tin] **NF** *Naut* spanker

brigue [brig] **NF** *Littéraire* intrigue; **avoir une place par (la) b.** to get a job by pulling strings

briguer [3] [brige] **VT** *(emploi)* to angle for; *(honneur)* to seek, to pursue, to aspire to; *(suffrage)* to seek

brillamment [brijamɑ̃] **ADV** brilliantly, magnificently; **réussir b. un examen** to pass an exam with flying colours

brillance [brijɑ̃s] **NF** *(du regard)* brilliance; *(des cheveux)* shine, sheen, gloss

brillant, -e [brijɑ̃, -ɑ̃t] **ADJ 1** *(luisant ▸ parquet)* shiny, polished; *(▸ peinture)* gloss *(avant n)*; *(▸ cheveux, lèvres, chaussures)* shiny, glossy; *(▸ soie)* lustrous; *(▸ pierre précieuse, cristal)* sparkling, glittering; *(▸ yeux)* bright, shining; **yeux brillants de malice/de fièvre** eyes sparkling with mischief/bright with fever **2** *(remarquable ▸ esprit, intelligence)* brilliant, outstanding; *(▸ personne)* outstanding; *(▸ succès, carrière, talent)* brilliant, dazzling, outstanding; *(▸ conversation)* brilliant, sparkling; *(▸ hommage)* superb, magnificent; (▸ *représentation, numéro)* brilliant, superb; **il a été b.** he did very well indeed *or* brilliantly; **il est promis à un b. avenir** he has a brilliant future ahead of him; **ce n'est pas b.** it's not brilliant; **sa santé n'est pas brillante** he's/she's not well, his/her health is not too good; **les résultats ne sont pas brillants** the results aren't too good *or* aren't all they should be

NM 1 *(éclat* ▸ *d'un métal, d'une surface)* gloss, sheen; (▸ *de chaussures, des cheveux)* shine; (▸ *d'une peinture)* gloss; (▸ *d'un tissu)* sheen; (▸ *d'un diamant, d'un regard)* sparkle **2** *(brio)* brio, sparkle; **malgré le b. de sa conversation/de son œuvre** in spite of his/her brilliant conversation/impressive work **3** *(diamant)* brilliant; **monté/taillé en b.** mounted/cut as a brilliant

• **brillant à lèvres NM** *(cosmétique)* lip gloss

brillantine [brijɑ̃tin] **NF** *(pour les cheveux)* brilliantine

briller [3] [brije] **VI 1** *(luire* ▸ *chaussure, soleil, lumière, regard)* to shine; (▸ *acier)* to glint, to gleam; (▸ *chandelle)* to glimmer; (▸ *étoile)* to twinkle, to shine; (▸ *lune)* to gleam, to shine; (▸ *diamant)* to shine, to glitter, to sparkle; (▸ *satin, soie)* to shimmer, to shine; (▸ *dents)* to sparkle; (▸ *eau)* to shimmer, to sparkle; (▸ *feuille)* to shine, to glisten; **tout brille dans sa cuisine** his/her kitchen's gleaming; **il a le nez qui brille** he's got a shiny nose; **la joie faisait b. ses yeux** his/her eyes were shining with joy; **faire b. ses chaussures** to shine one's shoes; **faire b. qch** to polish sth; **faire b. un meuble/l'argenterie** to polish a piece of furniture/the silver; **sa bague en diamant brillait de tous ses feux** his/her diamond ring glittered brightly; **des yeux qui brillent de colère/de fièvre** eyes ablaze with anger/bright with fever; **des yeux qui brillent de plaisir/d'envie** eyes sparkling with pleasure/glowing with envy; *Prov* **tout ce qui brille n'est pas (d')or** all that glitters is not gold **2** *(exceller)* to shine, to excel, to be outstanding; **b. à un examen** to do very well in an exam **3** *(se distinguer)* to stand out; **avoir le désir de b.** to be anxious to stand out; **b. en société** to be a social success; **b. dans une conversation** to shine in a conversation; **b. par son savoir/son intelligence** to be extraordinarily knowledgeable/intelligent; **b. par son absence** to be conspicuous by one's absence; **b. par son incompétence** to be remarkably incompetent; **elle ne brille pas par sa ponctualité** she's not noted for her punctuality; **faire b. les avantages d'une situation** to point out the advantages of a situation

brimade [brimad] **NF 1** *(vexation)* bullying (incident), (incident of) victimization; **faire subir des brimades à qn** to victimize sb, to bully sb **2** *Fam Arg scol* initiation ceremony[a], *Br* ragging, *Am* hazing

brimbaler [brɛ̃bale] = **bringuebaler**

brimborion [brɛ̃bɔrjɔ̃] **NM** *Littéraire* bauble, trinket

brimer [3] [brime] **VT 1** *(faire subir des vexations à)* to victimize; **il se sent brimé** he feels victimized **2** *Fam Arg scol* to initiate[a], *Br* to rag, *Am* to haze

brin [brɛ̃] **NM 1** *(filament)* strand; *Tex* fibre; **câble à un b.** single-strand *or* single-stranded cable; **corde/laine à trois brins** three-ply rope/wool

2 *(tige* ▸ *d'herbe)* blade; (▸ *d'osier)* twig; (▸ *de muguet, de persil, de bruyère, d'aubépine)* sprig

3 *(morceau* ▸ *de laine, de fil)* piece, length; **b. de paille** (piece of) straw

4 *(parcelle)* **un b. de** a (tiny) bit of; **un b. de génie** a touch of genius; **il n'a pas un b. de bon sens** he hasn't an ounce *or* a shred of common sense; **il n'y a pas un b. de vent** there isn't a breath of wind; **il n'y a pas un b. de vérité là-dedans** there isn't a grain of truth in it; **faire un b. de causette (à** *ou* **avec qn)** to have a quick chat (with sb); **faire un b. de cour à** to have a little flirt with; **faire un b. de toilette** to have a quick wash

5 *(locution)* **un beau b. de fille** a good-looking girl

• **un brin ADV** *Fam* a trifle, a touch; **il était un b. dépité** he was a trifle disappointed; **rigoler** *ou* **s'amuser un b.** to have a bit of fun

brindezingue [brɛ̃dzɛ̃g] **ADJ** *Fam* crazy, loopy

brindille [brɛ̃dij] **NF** *Bot* twig

bringue [brɛ̃g] **NF** *Fam* **1** *Péj (personne)* **une grande b.** a beanpole **2** *(noce)* **faire la b.** to live it up, to party **3** *Suisse (querelle)* row[a]; *(rengaine)* refrain[a]

bringuebaler [3] [brɛ̃gbale] **VT** to joggle, to jiggle, to shake

VI to rattle; **c'est fragile, il ne faut pas que ça bringuebale dans la valise** it's fragile, it mustn't rattle around in the suitcase

bringuer [3] [brɛ̃ge] *Suisse* **VI arrête de b.!** stop going on about it!

VT to go on at

VPR se bringuer ils se bringuaient they were having a row

brinquebaler [brɛ̃kbale] = **bringuebaler**

brio [brijo] **NM** brio, verve

• **avec brio ADV parler avec b.** *(en une occasion)* to make a brilliant speech; *(naturellement)* to be a dazzling speaker; **il s'en est tiré avec b.** he carried it off with style; **passer une épreuve avec b.** to pass an exam with flying colours

brioche [brijɔʃ] **NF 1** *Culin* brioche **2** *Fam (ventre)* paunch; **avoir de la b.** to be potbellied; **prendre de la b.** to be getting a paunch *or* potbelly

brioché [brijɔʃe] *voir* **pain**

brique [brik] **NF 1** *Constr* brick; **un mur de b.** *ou* **briques** a brick wall; **b. creuse/pleine** air/solid brick; **b. réfractaire** firebrick; *très Fam* **bouffer des briques** to have nothing to eat

2 *(morceau)* piece; **b. de jeu de construction** building block

3 *(emballage* ▸ *de lait, de jus de fruit)* carton

4 *Anciennement Fam (dix mille francs)* 10,000 francs[a]

5 *Suisse (fragment)* fragment, splinter

ADJ INV brick-red

• **en brique ADJ** brick *(avant n)*, made of brick

briquer [3] [brike] **VT** *(pont de navire)* to scrub; *(maison)* to clean from top to bottom

briquet [brike] **NM 1** *(appareil)* lighter; *(à amadou)* tinder box; **battre le b.** to strike a light **2** *(chien)* beagle

briquetage [briktaʒ] **NM** *Constr* **1** *(maçonnerie)* brickwork **2** *(enduit)* imitation brickwork

briqueter [27] [brikte] **VT 1** *Constr (pavement, surface)* to face in imitation brickwork **2** *(transformer en briquettes)* to briquette

briqueterie [briketri] **NF** brickworks *(singulier)*, brickyard

briqueteur [briktœr] **NM** *Constr* bricklayer

briquetier [briktje] **NM 1** *(ouvrier)* brickmaker **2** *(dirigeant)* brickyard manager

briquette [brikɛt] **NF 1** *Constr* small brick **2** *(de combustible)* briquette

bris [bri] **NM 1** *(fragment)* piece, fragment; **des b. de glace** shards, fragments of glass; **être assuré contre les b. de glace** to be insured for plate glass risk **2** *Jur* **b. de clôture** breach of close; **b. de scellés** breaking of seals

brisant, -e [brizɑ̃, -ɑ̃t] **ADJ explosif b.** high explosive; **obus b.** high-explosive shell

NM *(haut-fond)* reef, shoal

• **brisants NMPL** *(vagues)* breakers

brise [briz] **NF** breeze

brisé, -e [brize] **ADJ 1** *(détruit)* broken; **un homme b.** *(par la fatigue)* a run-down *or* worn-out man; *(par les ennuis, le chagrin)* a broken man; **b. de fatigue** exhausted, tired out; **b. de chagrin** crushed by grief, brokenhearted **2** *Géom* broken **3** *Archit (arc)* broken

NM *(danse)* brisé

brise-bise [brizbiz] **NM INV** half curtain *(on the bottom half of a window)*

brisées [brize] **NFPL 1** *Chasse* broken branches *(to mark the way)* **2** *(locutions)* **aller** *ou* **marcher sur les b. de qn** to poach on sb's territory; **suivre les b. de qn** to follow in sb's footsteps, to follow sb's lead *or* example

brise-fer [brizfer] **NM INV** *Fam Vieilli* vandal

brise-glace(s) [brizglas] **NM INV 1** *Naut* icebreaker **2** *(sur un pont)* icebreaker, ice apron *or* guard **3** *(outil)* hammer

brise-jet [brizʒɛ] **NM INV** tap swirl

brise-lames [brizlam] **NM INV** *Naut* breakwater, groyne, mole

brisement [brizmɑ̃] **NM** *Littéraire* breaking

brise-mottes [brizmɔt] **NM INV** harrow

briser [3] [brize] **VT 1** *(mettre en pièces* ▸ *verre, assiette)* to break, to smash; (▸ *vitre)* to break, to shatter, to smash; (▸ *motte de terre)* to break up; **b. qch en mille morceaux** to smash sth to pieces *or* smithereens, to shatter sth; **cela me brise le cœur** it breaks my heart; **la voix brisée par l'émotion** his/her voice choked with emotion; *Fig* **b. les tabous** to break taboos

2 *(séparer en deux* ▸ *canne, branche)* to break, to snap; (▸ *liens, chaînes)* to break; **b. la glace** to break the ice

3 *(assouplir)* **b. des chaussures** to break shoes in

4 *(défaire* ▸ *réputation, carrière)* to wreck, to ruin; (▸ *résistance, rébellion)* to crush, to quell; (▸ *contrat)* to break; (▸ *grève)* to break (up); **b. un mariage/une famille** to break up a marriage/family; **b. l'élan de qn** to make sb stumble; *Fig* to clip sb's wings

5 *(soumettre)* to break; **je le briserai** I'll break him

6 *(épuiser* ▸ *sujet: soucis, chagrin)* to break, to crush; (▸ *sujet: exercice, voyage)* to exhaust, to tire out; **brisé par la maladie** broken by illness

7 *très Fam* **tu me les brises!** you're really pissing me off!

• **briser avec VT IND** *(ami, tradition)* to break with

VPR se briser 1 *(se casser* ▸ *verre)* to shatter, to break; **se b. en mille morceaux** to break *or* to smash into pieces, to shatter

2 *(être altéré* ▸ *espoir)* to be shattered; (▸ *voix)* to break, to falter; **la voix brisée par l'émotion** his/her voice breaking with emotion

3 *(déferler* ▸ *vagues)* to break

4 *(échouer* ▸ *attaque, assaut)* to fail

brise-tout [briztu] **NM INV** *Fam Vieilli* vandal

briseur, -euse [brizœr, -øz] **NM,F 1** *Littéraire (casseur)* vandal **2** *Fig* **b. de grève** strikebreaker

brise-vent [brizvɑ̃] **NM INV** *Hort* windbreak

bristol [bristɔl] **NM 1** *(carton)* Bristol board **2** *(carte de visite) Br* visiting *or Am* calling card **3** *(fiche)* index card

brisure [brizyr] **NF 1** *(fêlure)* crack, break **2** *(fragment)* splinter, fragment **3** *(d'un gond)* break; *(d'un volet)* folding joint

• **brisures NFPL brisures de riz** broken rice

britannique [britanik] **ADJ** British

• **Britannique ADJ les îles Britanniques** the British Isles **NMF** Briton, *Am* Britisher; **les Britanniques** the British

broc [bro] **NM** *(gén)* pitcher; *(pour la toilette)* ewer

brocante [brɔkɑ̃t] **NF 1** *(objets)* **la b.** second-hand goods; **faire de la b.** to deal in second-hand goods **2** *Com (commerce)* second-hand trade; *(marché)* = market selling second-hand goods; **magasin de b.** second-hand *Br* shop *or Am* store; **il y a une b. près d'ici** there's a second-hand market near here

brocanter [3] [brɔkɑ̃te] **VI** *Com* to deal in second-hand goods

brocanteur, -euse [brɔkɑ̃tœr, -øz] **NM,F** *Com* second-hand dealer

brocarder [3] [brɔkarde] **VT** *Littéraire* to gibe at, to mock

brocart [brɔkar] **NM** *Tex* brocade

brochage [brɔʃaʒ] **NM 1** *Typ* stitching, sewing **2** *Tex* brocade **3** *Tech* broaching

broche [brɔʃ] **NF 1** *Culin* spit, skewer, broach

2 *(bijou)* brooch

3 *(en alpinisme)* piton; **b. à glace** ice screw

4 *Électron & Méd* pin

5 *Tech* broaching tool, broach

6 *Tex* spindle

7 *(d'une serrure)* broach, hinge pin

• **à la broche ADV** *Culin* on a spit; **cuit à la b.** roasted on a spit, spit-roasted

broché, -e [brɔʃe] **ADJ 1** *Tex* brocaded, broché **2** *(livre)* paperback *(avant n)*

NM 1 *(tissu)* brocade, broché *or* swivel fabric **2** *(procédé)* brocading, swivel weaving

brocher [3] [brɔʃe] **VT 1** *Typ* to stitch, to sew **2** *Tech* to broach **3** *Tex* to brocade, to figure; **tissu broché d'or** gold brocade

brochet [brɔʃɛ] **NM** *Ich* pike

brochette [brɔʃɛt] **NF 1** *Culin (broche)* skewer; *(mets)* brochette, kebab; **brochettes de mouton/de fruits de mer** lamb/seafood kebabs **2** *(assemblée)* lot; **une jolie b. d'hypocrites** a fine lot of hypocrites **3** *(ribambelle)* **b. de décorations** row of decorations

brocheur, -euse [brɔʃœr, -øz] **NM,F 1** *Typ* stitcher, sewer **2** *Tex* brocade weaver
NM brocade loom
• **brocheuse NF** *Typ* binding machine; **brocheuse automatique sans couture** perfect binder

brochure [brɔʃyr] **NF 1** *(livret)* pamphlet, booklet, brochure; **b. publicitaire/touristique** advertising/tourist brochure **2** *Typ (technique)* stitching, sewing **3** *Tex* brocaded design, figured pattern

brocoli [brɔkɔli] **NM** broccoli *(UNCOUNT)*; **des brocolis** broccoli; **b. violet** purple sprouting broccoli

brodequin [brɔdkɛ̃] **NM 1** *(chaussure)* (laced) boot **2** *Antiq (bottine)* brodekin, buskin; *Littéraire* **chausser le b.** *(écrire)* to write tragedies; *(jouer)* to tread the boards
• **brodequins NMPL** *(pour torture)* **les brodequins** the boot

broder [3] [brɔde] **VT 1** *Couture* to embroider; **brodé à la main** hand-embroidered; **brodé d'or** embroidered in gold thread **2** *Littéraire (embellir)* to embellish, to embroider
VI *(exagérer)* to use poetic licence; **b. sur qch** to embroider *or* to embellish sth

broderie [brɔdri] **NF 1** *Couture (technique)* embroidery; **b. à l'aiguille** needlework, embroidery; **faire de la b.** to do embroidery *or* needlework; **b. anglaise** broderie anglaise; **b. mécanique** machine embroidery **2** *(ouvrage)* (piece of) embroidery, embroidery work; **des broderies** embroidery **3** *(industrie)* embroidery trade

brodeur, -euse [brɔdœr, -øz] *Couture* **NM,F** embroiderer
• **brodeuse NF** embroidering machine

broie *etc voir* **broyer**

broiement [brwamɑ̃] = **broyage**

brol, broll [brɔl] **NM** *Belg (tas d'objets, bric-à-brac)* clutter, jumble, bric-à-brac

bromate [brɔmat] **NM** *Chim* bromate

brome [brom] **NM 1** *Chim* bromine **2** *Bot* brome grass, brome

bromure [brɔmyr] **NM** *Chim* bromide

bronca [brɔ̃ka] **NF 1** *(à une corrida)* = audience attending a bullfighting event **2** *(tollé)* outcry

bronche [brɔ̃ʃ] **NF** *Anat* bronchus; **les bronches** the bronchial tubes

broncher [3] [brɔ̃ʃe] **VI 1** *(réagir)* to react, to respond; **il n'a pas bronché** he didn't bat an eyelid; **tu n'as pas intérêt à b.!** not a word out of you!; **le premier qui bronche...** *(qui bouge)* the first one to move a muscle...; *(qui se plaint)* the first one to complain... **2** *(cheval)* to stumble
• **sans broncher ADV** without batting an eye *or* eyelid, without turning a hair *or* flinching

bronchiole [brɔ̃ʃjɔl] **NF** *Anat* bronchiole

bronchique [brɔ̃ʃik] **ADJ** bronchial

bronchite [brɔ̃ʃit] **NF** *Méd* bronchitis; **faire** *ou* **avoir une b.** to have bronchitis

bronchitique [brɔ̃ʃitik] *Méd* **ADJ** bronchitic; **être b.** to have chronic bronchitis
NMF chronic bronchitis patient

broncho-pneumonie [brɔ̃kɔpnømɔni] *(pl* **broncho-pneumonies**), **broncho-pneumopathie** [brɔ̃kɔpnømɔpati] *(pl* **broncho-pneumopathies**) **NF** *Méd* bronchopneumonia

bronchoscopie [brɔ̃kɔskɔpi] **NF** *Méd* bronchoscopy

brontosaure [brɔ̃tɔzɔr] **NM** *Zool* brontosaur, brontosaurus

bronzage [brɔ̃zaʒ] **NM 1** *(de la peau ▸ action)* tanning; *(▸ hâle)* suntan, tan; **b. intégral** all-over tan **2** *Tech (d'une statue)* bronzing; *(d'une surface métallique)* blueing

bronze [brɔ̃z] **NM** *Beaux-Arts & Métal* bronze; *Littéraire* **un homme au cœur de b.** a cold-hearted man
ADJ INV bronze, bronze-coloured

bronzé, -e [brɔ̃ze] **ADJ 1** *(hâlé)* suntanned, tanned **2** *Tech* bronze, bronzed

bronzer [3] [brɔ̃ze] **VT 1** *(hâler)* to tan **2** *(statue)* to bronze; *(surface métallique)* to blue
VI to tan, to go brown; **se faire b.** to sunbathe; **pour ceux qui ne veulent pas b. idiot** for those people who don't just want to lie on the beach

bronzette [brɔ̃zɛt] **NF** *Fam* sunbathing session[□]; **faire b.** to lie in the sun, to sunbathe for a while

bronzier, -ère [brɔ̃zje, -jɛr] **NM,F** *Beaux-Arts* bronzesmith

brook [bruk] **NM** *Courses de chevaux* water jump

broquette [brɔkɛt] **NF** *(clou)* (tin)tack

brossage [brɔsaʒ] **NM 1** *(de chaussures, de vêtements)* brushing **2** *(d'un cheval)* brushing down

brosse [brɔs] **NF 1** *(ustensile)* brush; **laver le sol à la b.** to give the floor a scrub, to scrub the floor; **donner un coup de b. à qch** *(pour dépoussiérer)* to brush sth; *(pour laver)* to give sth a scrub; **b. à chaussures** shoe brush; **b. à cheveux** hairbrush; **b. en chiendent** *Br* scrubbing *or Am* scrub brush; **b. à dents** toothbrush; **b. à habits** clothes brush; **b. métallique** wire brush; **b. à ongles** nailbrush; **b. à reluire** brush *(for buffing)*; *Fam* **passer la b. à reluire à qn** to butter sb up, to soft-soap sb
2 *Beaux-Arts (pinceau)* brush
3 *(coiffure)* brush cut; **se faire couper les cheveux en b.** to have a brush cut
4 *(d'un renard)* brush; *(d'une abeille)* scopa
5 *Can Fam (locutions)* **être/prendre en b.** to be/to get smashed *or* pissed
6 *Belg Fam (locution)* **faire b.** to draw a blank[□], to be out of luck[□]

brosser [3] [brɔse] **VT 1** *(épousseter ▸ miettes)* to brush (off); *(▸ pantalon, jupe)* to brush (down); *(▸ tapis, cheveux)* to brush
2 *(frictionner)* to brush, to scrub; **b. un cheval** to rub a horse down
3 *Beaux-Arts (paysage, portrait)* to paint; **b. le portrait de qn** to paint sb's portrait, *Fig* to describe sb; **il m'a brossé un tableau idéal de son travail** he painted me a glowing picture of his job; **je vais vous b. un tableau de la situation** I'll give you a brief outline of the situation
4 *Belg Fam* **b. un cours** to skip a class, *Br* to skive off, *Am* to cut a class
5 *Sport* to cut, to give spin to
VPR se brosser 1 *(se nettoyer)* to brush oneself (down); **se b. les dents/les cheveux** to brush one's teeth/hair **2** *Fam (locution)* **il peut toujours se b., il n'aura jamais mon livre** he can whistle for my book

brou [bru] **NM** *Bot* husk, *Am* shuck
• **brou de noix NM** walnut stain; **passer qch au b. de noix** to stain sth with walnut

broue [bru] **NF** *Can Fam* foam[□], froth[□]; *Fig* **péter de la b.** to talk big, to show off; *Fig* **avoir de la b. dans le toupet** to be rushed off one's feet

brouet [brue] **NM** *Hum ou Littéraire Culin* (coarse) gruel; **un noir b.** a foul brew

brouette [bruɛt] **NF** barrow, wheelbarrow

brouettée [bruete] **NF** barrowful, wheelbarrowful

brouetter [4] [bruete] **VT** to cart *(in a wheelbarrow)*, to barrow, to wheelbarrow

brouhaha [bruaa] **NM** hubbub, (confused) noise

brouillage [brujaʒ] **NM** *Rad (accidentel)* interference; *(intentionnel)* jamming; **b. électronique** electronic jamming

brouillard [brujar] **NM 1** *Météo (léger)* mist; *(épais)* fog; **il y a du b.** it's misty/foggy; **un b. à couper au couteau** a very thick fog, a peasouper; **b. givrant** freezing fog; **b. matinal** early-morning fog; *Fig* **il est dans le b.** he's not with it
2 *(voile)* mist; **avoir un b. devant les yeux** to have blurred vision; **voir à travers un b.** to see things through a haze *or* mist
3 *Phys* aerosol
4 *Compta (livre de comptes)* daybook; **b. de caisse** cash book

brouillasse [brujas] **NF** drizzle

brouillasser [3] [brujase] **V IMPERSONNEL il brouillasse** it's drizzling

brouille [bruj] **NF** tiff, quarrel; **leur b. dure toujours** they're still not speaking *or* on speaking terms; **leur b. est irrémédiable** they've fallen out (with each other) for good

brouillé, -e [bruje] **ADJ 1** *(terne)* **avoir le teint b.** to look off-colour
2 *(ciel)* cloudy
3 *Cartes* shuffled
4 *Culin* scrambled

brouille-ménage [brujmenaʒ] **NM** *Fam* red wine[□], *Br* plonk

brouiller [3] [bruje] **VT 1** *Culin (œuf)* to scramble
2 *(mélanger ▸ cartes)* to shuffle; *Fam* **b. la cervelle à qn** to get sb muddled *or* confused; **ça m'a brouillé les idées** it confused *or* befuddled me; *Fig* **b. les cartes** to confuse the issue; **b. les pistes** *(dans un roman)* to confuse the reader; *(dans une poursuite)* to cover one's tracks, to put sb off one's scent; *(dans un débat)* to put up a smokescreen
3 *(dérégler)* to jumble; **b. la combinaison d'un coffre** to jumble the combination of a safe
4 *(troubler ▸ liquide)* to cloud; **b. la vue à qn** to cloud *or* to blur sb's eyesight; **b. un miroir** to blur a mirror; **l'alcool brouille le teint** alcohol ruins your complexion; **les lettres étaient brouillées devant mes yeux** the letters were a blur before my eyes; **il avait les yeux brouillés par les larmes** his eyes were blurred with tears
5 *Rad (accidentellement)* to cause interference to; *(intentionnellement ▸ signal)* to scramble; *(▸ transmission, circuit)* to jam
6 *(amis, parents)* to turn against each other, to cause a disagreement between; **ça l'a brouillé avec sa famille** it's turned him against *or* estranged him from his family; *Fig* **ce professeur m'a brouillé avec les mathématiques** that teacher spoiled *or* ruined mathematics for me; **être b. avec qn** to be on bad terms with sb, to have fallen out with sb; **je suis brouillé avec les ordinateurs** I'm no good with computers
VPR se brouiller 1 *(se fâcher)* to quarrel, to fall out (with one another); **se b. avec qn** to fall out with sb **2** *(se mélanger ▸ idées)* to get confused *or* muddled *or* jumbled; *(se troubler ▸ vue)* to blur, to become blurred **3** *Météo (ciel)* to become cloudy, to cloud over; **le temps se brouille** it's clouding over

brouillerie [brujri] **NF** tiff

brouilleur [brujœr] **NM** *Rad & Ordinat* jammer

brouillon, -onne [brujɔ̃, -ɔn] **ADJ 1** *(travail)* untidy, messy **2** *(personne)* muddleheaded, unmethodical
NM,F muddler
NM 1 *(ébauche)* (rough) draft; **faire un b.** to make a (rough) draft; **faire une lettre au b.** to draft a letter, to write a first draft of a letter; **faire un exercice au b.** to do an exercise in rough; *Ordinat* **version b.** draft version **2 (papier) b.** rough paper, *Br* scrap *or Am* scratch paper

broum [brum] **EXCLAM** brum, brum!

broussaille [brusaj] **NF** *(touffe)* clump of brushwood
• **broussailles NFPL** *Géog (sous-bois)* undergrowth; *(dans un champ)* scrub
• **en broussaille ADJ** *(cheveux)* tousled, dishevelled; *(sourcils, barbe)* bushy, shaggy

broussailleux, -euse [brusajø, -øz] **ADJ 1** *Géog (terrain)* brushy, scrubby, covered with brushwood **2** *(sourcils, barbe)* shaggy, bushy; *(cheveux)* tousled, dishevelled

broussard, -e [brusar, -ard] **NM** bushman, *f* bushwoman

brousse [brus] **NF 1** *Géog (type de végétation)* **la b.** the bush **2** *(étendue)* **la b.** *(en Afrique)* the bush; *(en Australie)* the outback; *Fam Fig* **vivre en pleine b.** to live in the backwoods *or* out in the sticks *or Am* in the boondocks
• **de brousse ADJ 1** *(chaussures)* desert *(avant n)* **2** *(feux)* bush *(avant n)*

broutage [brutaʒ], **broutement** [brutmɑ̃] **NM 1** *(du bétail)* grazing; *(d'un animal sauvage)* browsing **2** *Tech (d'une machine, d'un outil)* jerking, *Br* juddering; *(d'un embrayage)* slipping

brouter [3] [brute] **VT 1** *(sujet: bétail)* to graze, to feed on; *(sujet: animal sauvage)* to browse, to feed on; **b. des feuilles** to nibble at leaves **2** *Vulg* **b. qn** to go down on sb; **il nous les broute** he's being a pain in the arse

VI 1 *(bétail)* to graze, to feed; *(animal sauvage)* to browse, to feed; **elle fait b. ses chèvres dans le pré du voisin** she grazes her goats in her neighbour's field **2** *Tech (machine-outil)* to chatter, to jerk, *Br* to judder; *(embrayage)* to slip

broutille [brutij] **NF** *(chose futile)* trifle, trifling matter; **il s'inquiète pour des broutilles** he's worrying over nothing

brownien [bronjɛ̃] **ADJ M** *Phys* Brownian

browning [broniŋ] **NM** Browning *(automatic rifle)*

broyage [brwajaʒ] **NM** *(des aliments par les dents)* crushing, grinding; *(pulvérisation ▸ d'une couleur)* grinding; *(▸ de la pierre, du sucre)* crushing; *(▸ d'une fibre)* breaking, crushing; *(▸ d'un grain)* milling, grinding, crushing

broyer [13] [brwaje] **VT 1** *(écraser ▸ couleur, matériau friable, nourriture)* to grind; *(▸ pierre, sucre, ail)* to crush; *(▸ grain)* to mill, to grind; *(▸ fibre)* to break, to crush; *(▸ main, pied)* to crush; **b. dans un mortier** to pound in a mortar; **se faire b.** to be *or* get crushed **2** *(locution)* **b. du noir** to be in the doldrums, to think gloomy thoughts

broyeur, -euse [brwajœr, -øz] **ADJ** grinding

NM,F grinder, crusher; *(de chanvre)* hemp braker *or* dresser

NM *(pulvérisateur ▸ à minerai, à sable)* grinder, crusher, mill; *(▸ à paille)* bruiser; *(▸ à fibre)* brake; *(▸ à déchets)* disintegrator, grinder; **b. d'ordures** *(dans un évier)* waste disposal unit; **b. sanitaire** Saniflo®, macerator unit

bru [bry] **NF** *Vieilli* daughter-in-law

bruant [bryɑ̃] **NM** *Orn* bunting; **b. jaune** yellowhammer

brucelles [brysel] **NFPL** *Suisse* (pair of) tweezers

brucellose [bryseloz] **NF** *Méd* brucellosis

bruche [bryʃ] **NM** *Entom* **b. des pois** pea beetle, weevil

brugnon [bryɲɔ̃] **NM** *Bot* nectarine

brugnonier [bryɲɔnje] **NM** *Bot* nectarine (tree)

bruine [brɥin] **NF** *Météo* drizzle; **petite b.** fine drizzle

bruiner [3] [brɥine] **V IMPERSONNEL** *Météo* **il bruine** it's drizzling

bruineux, -euse [brɥinø, -øz] **ADJ** *Météo* drizzly

bruire [105] [brɥir] **VI** *Littéraire (feuilles, vent)* to rustle, to whisper; *(étoffe)* to rustle; *(eau)* to murmur; *(insecte)* to hum, to buzz, to drone; **le vent faisait b. les arbres** the trees were rustling in the wind

bruissement [brɥismɑ̃] **NM** *(des feuilles, du vent, d'une étoffe)* rustle, rustling; *(de l'eau)* murmuring; *(d'un insecte)* hum, humming, buzzing; *(d'ailes)* flapping

bruissent *etc voir* **bruire**

bruit [brɥi] **NM 1** *(son)* sound, noise; **des bruits de pas** the sound of footsteps; **des bruits de voix** the hum of conversation; **les bruits de la maison/rue** the (everyday) sounds of the house/street; **un b. métallique** a clang; **un b. de vaisselle** a clatter of dishes; **un b. sec** a snap; **un b. sourd** a thud; **faire un b.** to make a sound *or* noise; **c'est très calme, il n'y a pas un b.** it's very quiet, there's not a sound; **b. blanc** white noise; **b. de fond** background noise; **en b. de fond** in the background

2 *(vacarme)* noise; **j'ai horreur d'expliquer quelque chose dans le b.** I hate explaining something against a background of noise; **lutte contre le b.** noise abatement campaign; **un b. d'enfer** a terrible racket; **faire du b.** to be noisy; **ne fais pas de b.** be quiet; **la machine ne fait pas de b.** the machine doesn't make any noise; **sans faire de b.** noiselessly; **il est entré sans (faire de) b.** he came in without (making) a sound; **faire beaucoup de b.** to be very loud *or* noisy; *Fig* **beaucoup de b. pour rien** much ado about nothing

3 *(retentissement)* sensation, commotion, furore; **ça va faire du b.** it'll cause a sensation, we haven't heard the last of it; **on a fait beaucoup de b. autour de cet enlèvement** the kidnapping caused a furore; **on a fait grand b. autour de sa déclaration** his/her statement caused a great sensation *or* commotion

4 *(rumeur)* rumour, piece of gossip; **le b. court que...** rumour has it *or* it is rumoured that...; **répandre** *ou* **faire courir un b.** to spread a rumour; **c'est un b. de couloir** it's a rumour; **faux b.** false rumour

5 *Méd* sound, bruit; **b. cardiaque** *ou* **du cœur** heart *or* cardiac sound; **b. respiratoire** rattle; **b. de souffle** (heart) murmur

6 *Rad & Tél* noise; **bruits ambiants** background noise; **bruits parasites** interference; **b. solaire** solar (radio) noise

• **sans bruit ADV** noiselessly, without a sound; **il s'avance sans b.** he moves forward without a sound

bruitage [brɥitaʒ] **NM** *Rad & Théât* sound effects; *Cin* foley

bruiter [3] [brɥite] **VT** *Cin, Rad & Théât* to do the sound effects for

bruiteur, -euse [brɥitœr, -øz] **NM,F** *Rad & Théât* sound effects engineer; *Cin* foley artist

brûlage [brylaʒ] **NM** *(des herbes)* burning; *(d'une peinture)* burning (off); *(des cheveux)* singeing; *(du café)* roasting; **se faire faire un b.** to have one's hair singed; **b. des terres** scorching

brûlant, -e [brylɑ̃, -ɑ̃t] **ADJ 1** *(chaud ▸ lampe, assiette)* burning (hot); *(▸ liquide)* burning *or* boiling (hot), scalding; *(▸ nourriture)* burning (hot), piping hot; *(▸ soleil, température)* blazing (hot), scorching, blistering; *(▸ personne, front)* feverish; **avoir les mains brûlantes** to have hot hands

2 *(animé)* **yeux brûlants de curiosité** eyes gleaming with curiosity; **un regard b. de désir** a look of burning desire

3 *(actuel, dont on parle)* **sujet/dossier b.** burning issue; **c'est dire l'actualité brûlante de ce livre** this shows how very topical this book is

4 *(ardent ▸ regard, sentiment)* ardent, impassioned; *(▸ imagination, récit, secret)* passionate

NM *Belg* **avoir le b.** to have heartburn

brûlé, -e [bryle] **ADJ 1** *(calciné)* burnt **2** *Fam* **être b.** *(être compromis)* to be finished, to have had it

NM,F *Méd* **un grand b.** a patient suffering from third-degree burns; **service pour les grands brûlés** burns unit

NM burnt part; *Can (d'une forêt)* burnt-out area, burn; **enlever le b. sur un gâteau** to scrape the burnt bits off a cake; **une odeur de b.** a smell of burning; **avoir un goût de b.** to taste burnt; **ça sent le b.** *(odeur)* there's a smell of burning; *Fam Fig* there's trouble brewing

brûle-parfum, brûle-parfums [brylparfœ̃] *(pl* **brûle-parfums)** **NM** perfume burner

brûle-pourpoint [brylpurpwɛ̃] **à brûle-pourpoint ADV 1** *(sans détour)* point-blank, without beating about the bush **2** *(inopinément)* out of the blue; **...demanda-t-elle à b.** ...she asked, out of the blue

brûler [3] [bryle] **VT 1** *(détruire ▸ feuilles, corps, objet)* to burn, to incinerate; **il a brûlé la moquette en jouant avec des allumettes** he burnt the carpet while playing with matches; **b. qn vif/sur le bûcher** to burn sb alive/at the stake; *Fig* **b. ce qu'on a adoré** to turn against one's former love *or* loves; **b. le pavé** to tear along; **b. les planches** to give an outstanding performance; **b. ses dernières cartouches** to shoot one's bolt

2 *(consommer ▸ électricité, fioul)* to burn (up), to use, to consume; **elle brûle un cierge à la Vierge deux fois par an** she lights a candle to the Virgin Mary twice a year; **b. la chandelle par les deux bouts** to burn the candle at both ends

3 *(trop cuire)* to burn; **mon gâteau est complètement brûlé** my cake is burnt to a cinder

4 *(trop chauffer ▸ tissu)* to burn, to scorch, to singe; *(▸ cheveux, poils)* to singe; *(▸ acier)* to spoil

5 *(irriter ▸ partie du corps)* to burn; **la fumée me brûle les yeux** the smoke is making my eyes smart *or* sting; **le froid me brûle les oreilles** the cold is making my ears burn; **le piment me brûle la langue** the chilli is burning my tongue; *Fig* **b. la cervelle à qn** to blow sb's brains out; *Fig* **l'argent lui brûle les doigts** money burns a hole in his/her pocket

6 *(endommager ▸ sujet: gel)* to nip, to burn; *(▸ sujet: acide)* to burn; **brûlé par le gel** frost-damaged; **le soleil brûle l'herbe** the sun scorches the grass; **un paysage brûlé par le soleil** a landscape scorched by the sun

7 *Fam (dépasser)* **b. son arrêt** *(bus, personne)* to go past *or* to miss one's stop; **b. un feu** to go through a red light; **b. un stop** to fail to stop at a stop sign; **b. la politesse à qn** *(passer devant lui)* to push in front of sb (in the queue); *(partir sans le saluer)* to leave without saying goodbye to sb; **b. les étapes** *(progresser rapidement)* to advance by leaps and bounds; *Péj* to cut corners, to take short cuts

8 *(café)* to roast

9 *(animer)* to burn; **le désir qui le brûle** the desire that consumes him

10 *Méd (verrue)* to burn off

VI 1 *(flamber)* to burn (up), to be on fire; *(lentement)* to smoulder; **le pin brûle bien** pine wood burns well; **b. sur le bûcher** to be burnt at the stake; **b. vif** to be burnt alive *or* to death; **la forêt a brûlé** the forest was burnt down *or* to the ground; **mon dîner a brûlé** my dinner's burnt; **ses vêtements brûlaient** his clothes were on fire

2 *(se consumer ▸ charbon, essence)* to burn; **laisser b. la lumière** to leave the light burning *or* on; **faire b. le rôti** to burn the roast

3 *(être chaud)* to be burning; **avoir le front/la gorge qui brûle** to have a burning forehead/a burning sensation in the throat; **ça brûle** *(plat, sol)* it's boiling hot *or* burning; *(eau)* it's scalding; *(feu)* it's burning; **les yeux me brûlent** my eyes are stinging *or* smarting

4 *Fig Littéraire* **b. pour qn** to be in love with sb, to have a burning passion for sb

5 *(jeux)* to be close; **je brûle?** am I getting warm?

• **brûler de VT IND 1** *(être animé de)* **b. de colère** to be burning *or* seething with anger; **b. d'impatience/de désir** to be burning with impatience/desire **2** *(désirer)* to be dying *or* longing to; **b. de parler à qn** to be dying to talk to sb; **je brûle de te revoir** I'm longing *or* I can't wait to see you again

VPR se brûler to burn oneself; **se b. avec du thé** to burn *or* to scald oneself with some tea; **se b. la main** to burn one's hand; *Fig* **se b. la cervelle** to blow one's brains out; *Fig* **se b. les ailes** to get one's fingers burnt

brûleur [brylœr] **NM** burner; **b. à gaz** gas burner *or* ring; **b. à mazout** oil burner

brûloir [brylwar] **NM** coffee roaster

brûlot [brylo] **NM 1** *Naut (bateau)* fireship

2 *(écrit)* fierce *or* blistering attack

3 *(eau-de-vie flambée)* burnt brandy

4 *Can Entom* (biting) midge

brûlure [brylyr] **NF 1** *(lésion)* burn; **se faire une b. au poignet** to burn oneself on the wrist; *Méd* **b. au premier/second/troisième degré** first-/second-/third-degree burn; **b. de cigarette** cigarette burn **2** *(sensation)* burning sensation; **brûlures d'estomac** heartburn **3** *(trace)* burnt patch

brume [brym] **NF 1** *Météo (brouillard)* mist; **b. de chaleur** heat haze; **b. de mer** sea mist **2** *Naut* fog **3** *(confusion)* daze, haze; **il est encore dans les brumes du sommeil** he's still half asleep; **être dans les brumes de l'alcool** to be in a drunken stupor

brumeux, -euse [brymø, -øz] **ADJ 1** *Météo* misty, foggy, hazy **2** *(vague)* hazy, vague; **un souvenir b.** a hazy *or* dim recollection

Brumisateur® [brymizatœr] **NM** = atomizer containing Evian® mineral water

brun, -e [brœ̃, bryn] **ADJ 1** *(au pigment foncé ▸ cheveux, peau)* brown, dark; *(▸ tissu, couleur)* brown; *Can (▸ yeux)* brown; **il est b. de peau** he's dark-skinned; **b. cuivré** tawny; *Can* **il fait b.** it's getting dark **2** *(bronzé)* brown, tanned

NM,F dark-haired man, *f* dark-haired woman, *f* brunette

NM brown (colour)

• **brune NF 1** *(cigarette)* brown tobacco cigarette **2** *(bière)* dark beer, *Br* ≃ brown ale

• **à la brune ADV** *Littéraire* at dusk

brunante [brynɑ̃t] **NF** *Can* dusk; **à la b.** at dusk

brunâtre [brynatr] **ADJ** brownish

brunch [brœntʃ] NM brunch

bruncher [3] [brœntʃe] VI to have brunch

brunet, -ette [brynɛ, -ɛt] NM,F brown-haired boy, *f* girl

brunir [32] [brynir] VI **1** *(foncer ▸ cheveux, couleur)* to get darker, to darken; *(▸ peau)* to get brown *or* browner; *(bronzer)* to tan **2** *Culin (sauce, oignons)* to brown; *(sucre)* to caramelize; **laissez b.** cook until golden; **faites b. les oignons** brown the onions

VT **1** *(hâler)* to tan; *(foncer ▸ cheveux)* to darken **2** *Tech (polir ▸ métal)* to burnish; *(▸ acier)* to brown, to burnish

brunissage [brynisaʒ] NM *Tech* burnishing

brunissement [brynismɑ̃] NM tanning

brunisseur, -euse [brynisœr, -øz] NM,F *Tech* burnisher

ADJ M **plat b.** browning dish

brunissoir [bryniswar] NM *Tech* burnisher, burnishing tool

brunissure [brynisyr] NF *Tex* burnish

Brushing® [brœʃiŋ] NM blow-dry; **faire un B. à qn** to blow-dry sb's hair; **se faire faire un B.** to have a blow-dry

brusque [brysk] ADJ **1** *(bourru ▸ ton)* curt, abrupt; *(▸ personne)* abrupt, brusque, blunt; *(▸ geste)* abrupt, rough; **un mouvement b.** a jerk, a sudden movement **2** *(imprévu)* abrupt, sudden; **un virage b.** a sharp bend; **une b. baisse de température** a sudden drop in temperature

brusquement [bryskəmɑ̃] ADV **1** *(soudainement)* suddenly, abruptly **2** *(sans ménagements)* abruptly, brusquely, curtly

brusquer [3] [bryske] VT **1** *(personne ▸ malmener)* to be rough with; *(▸ presser)* to rush **2** *(hâter ▸ dénouement)* to rush; *(▸ adieux)* to cut short; **b. les choses** to rush things

brusquerie [bryskəri] NF **1** *(brutalité)* abruptness, brusqueness, sharpness; **avec b.** abruptly **2** *(soudaineté)* abruptness, suddenness

brut, -e[1] [bryt] ADJ **1** *(non traité ▸ pétrole, métal)* crude, untreated; *(▸ laine, soie, charbon, brique)* untreated, raw; *(▸ bois)* undressed; *(▸ sucre, or)* unrefined; *(▸ pierre précieuse)* rough, uncut; *(▸ minerai)* raw; **bois b. de machine** machine-dressed timber; **b. de coulée** as cast; **b. de décoffrage** *(béton)* unsurfaced, exposed; *Fam (personne)* rough and ready; **b. de forge** as forged; **b. de laminage** as rolled

2 *Fig (non encore peaufiné)* rough and ready, no-frills *(avant n)*; *(personne)* unrefined

3 *(émotion, qualité)* naked, pure, raw; *(donnée)* raw; *(fait)* simple, plain; **à l'état b.** in the rough

4 *(sauvage)* brute; **la force brute** brute force

5 *Écon (bénéfice, marge, valeur, salaire)* gross

6 *(poids)* gross

7 *(champagne)* brut, dry; *(cidre)* dry

NM **1** *(salaire)* gross income **2** *(pétrole)* crude oil; **b. léger** light crude **3** *(champagne)* brut *or* dry champagne

ADV *Écon* gross; **gagner 2000 euros b.** to earn 2,000 euros gross

brutal, -e, -aux, -ales [brytal, -o] ADJ **1** *(violent ▸ personne)* brutal, violent; *(▸ enfant)* rough; *(▸ choc)* strong, violent; *(▸ coup)* brutal, savage; *(▸ force)* brute; *(▸ jeu)* rough; **être b. avec qn** to treat sb brutally, to be violent with sb

2 *(franc)* brusque, blunt; **il a été très b. en lui annonçant la nouvelle** he broke it to him/her very unfeelingly *or* harshly; **ils se parlèrent avec une franchise brutale** they had a very blunt and frank conversation

3 *(non mitigé)* brutal, raw; **cette vérité était trop brutale pour elle** the truth was too shocking for her

4 *(soudain ▸ changement, arrêt)* sudden, abrupt; *(▸ transition)* abrupt; *(▸ mort)* sudden; **cela a été très b.** it was very sudden

NM,F brute, violent individual

brutalement [brytalmɑ̃] ADV **1** *(violemment)* brutally, violently, savagely; **pousser qn b. contre qch** to shove sb brutally *or* roughly against sth **2** *(franchement)* brusquely, bluntly; **il lui annonça b. la nouvelle** he broke the news to him/her bluntly **3** *(tout d'un coup)* suddenly; **le vent peut changer b. de direction** the wind can change direction very suddenly; **s'arrêter b.** to come to an abrupt halt

brutaliser [3] [brytalize] VT **1** *(maltraiter)* to ill-treat; **b. qn** to knock sb about, to manhandle sb; **se faire b. par la police** to be manhandled by the police, to be a victim of police brutality **2** *(brusquer)* to rush; **il ne faut pas me b.** don't rush me

brutalité [brytalite] NF **1** *(violence, brusquerie)* brutality; **il lui a parlé avec b.** he spoke to him/her harshly *or* very aggressively; **brutalités policières** police brutality **2** *(soudaineté)* suddenness; **surpris par la b. de la crise** startled by the sudden onset of the crisis

brute[2] [bryt] NF **1** *(personne violente)* brute; **comme une b.** with all one's might, like mad; **frapper comme une b. sur qch** to hit sth with full force, to hammer away at sth; **ne tire pas comme une b., c'est fragile** don't pull so hard, it's delicate; **c'est une b. épaisse** he's nothing but a brute; **une grosse b.** a big brute (of a man) **2** *(personne fruste)* boor, lout **3** *Littéraire (animal)* brute

Bruxelles [brysɛl] NM *Géog* Brussels

bruyamment [brɥijamɑ̃] ADV *(parler, rire, protester)* loudly; *(manger, jouer)* noisily

bruyant, -e [brɥijɑ̃, -ɑ̃t] ADJ *(enfant, rue)* noisy; *(rire)* loud; **un quartier peu b.** a quiet neighbourhood

bruyère [brɥijɛr] NF **1** *Bot* heather; **(racine de) b.** briar; **b. cendrée** bell heather **2** *(lande)* moor, heath

bryone [brijɔn] NF *Bot* bryony

BSPCE [beɛspeseø] NM *Bourse (abrév* **bon de souscription de parts de créateurs d'entreprise***)* = stock option in a start-up company with tax privileges

BT[1] [bete] NM *Scol (abrév* **brevet de technicien***)* = vocational training certificate taken at 17 after three years' technical training

BT[2] *Élec (abrév écrite* **basse tension***)* LT

BTP [betepe] NMPL *Constr (abrév* **bâtiments et travaux publics***)* = building and public works sector

BTS [beteɛs] NM *Univ (abrév* **brevet de technicien supérieur***)* = advanced vocational training certificate (taken at the end of a two-year higher education course); **B. Action Commerciale** professional marketing qualification; **B. Force de Vente** professional sales qualification

bu, -e [by] *pp voir* **boire**

buanderie [byɑ̃dri] NF **1** *(pièce, local ▸ à l'intérieur)* laundry, utility room; *(▸ à l'extérieur)* washhouse **2** *Can (laverie)* (coin-operated) cleaner's, laundry

Buba [byba] NF *Banque (abrév* **Bundesbank***)* **la B.** the Bundesbank

bubon [bybɔ̃] NM *Méd* bubo

bubonique [bybɔnik] ADJ *Méd* bubonic

Bucarest [bykarɛst] NM *Géog* Bucharest

buccal, -e, -aux, -ales [bykal, -o] ADJ mouth *(avant n)*; *Spéc* buccal

bucco-dentaire [bykodɑ̃tɛr] ADJ mouth *(avant n)*; **hygiène b.** oral hygiene

bucco-génital, -e *(mpl* **buccogénitaux**, *fpl* **bucco-génitales***)* [bykoʒenital, -o] ADJ **rapports bucco-génitaux** oral sex

bûche [byʃ] NF **1** *(morceau de bois)* log

2 *Fam (personne apathique)* lump; **ne reste pas là comme une b.** don't just stand there *Br* like a lemon *or Am* like a lump on a log

3 *Culin & Hist* **b. glacée** Yule log *(with an ice-cream filling)*; **b. de Noël** Yule log

4 *Fam (locution)* **prendre** *ou* **ramasser une b.** to take a tumble, *Br* to come a cropper

bûcher[1] **[3]** [byʃe] VT **1** *Fam (travailler)* **b. un examen** to cram for an exam; **b. sa physique** to *Br* swot up on *or Am* bone up on one's physics **2** *Can (arbre)* to fell, to cut down

VI **1** *Fam (travailler) Br* to swot, *Am* to grind **2** *Can (couper du bois)* to fell trees

bûcher[2] [byʃe] NM **1** *(supplice)* **le b.** the stake; **être condamné au b.** to be sentenced to be burnt at the stake; **monter** *ou* **mourir sur le b.** to be burnt at the stake **2** *(funéraire)* pyre **3** *(remise)* woodshed

bûcheron, -onne [byʃrɔ̃, -ɔn] NM,F woodcutter, lumberjack

bûchette [byʃɛt] NF **1** *(petit bois)* twig, stick **2** *(pour compter)* stick

bûcheur, -euse [byʃœr, -øz] *Fam* ADJ hard-working□

NM,F *(étudiant)* hardworking student□, *Br Péj* swot, *Am Péj* grind; *(travailleur)* hard worker□

bucolique [bykɔlik] ADJ bucolic, pastoral

NF *Littérature* bucolic, pastoral poem

budget [bydʒɛ] NM **1** *(d'une personne, d'une entreprise)* budget; **avoir un petit b.** to be on a (tight) budget; **des prix pour les petits budgets** budget prices; **se fixer un b. loisirs** to decide on a budget for one's leisure activities; **b. temps** *(délai)* allowance; *(en sociologie)* time budget

2 *Fin, Compta & Pol* budget; **le B.** ≃ the Budget; **inscrire qch au b.** to budget for sth; **le b. de l'éducation** the education budget; **b. des approvisionnements** purchase budget; **b. des charges** overhead *or* cost budget; **b. commercial** sales budget; *UE* **b. communautaire européen** European Community budget; **b. des dépenses** expense budget; **b. équilibré** balanced budget; *Écon* **b. de l'État** state budget; **b. d'exploitation** *ou* **de fonctionnement** operating budget; **b. global** master *or* overall budget; **b. des investissements** capital budget; **b. marketing** marketing budget; **b. prévisionnel** provisional budget; **b. de production** production budget; **b. promotionnel** promotional *or* publicity budget; **b. publicitaire** *ou* **de publicité** advertising budget, publicity budget; **b. des recettes** revenue budget; **b. renouvelable** continuous budget; **b. de trésorerie** cash budget; **b. des ventes** sales budget

3 *(dans la publicité, dans le marketing)* account; **l'agence s'est assuré le b. Brook** the agency has secured the Brook account

budgétaire [bydʒetɛr] ADJ *(contrainte, dépenses, contrôle)* budgetary; budget *(avant n)*; *(année) Br* financial, *Am* fiscal

budgétisation [bydʒetizasjɔ̃] NF *Compta* budgeting

budgétiser [3] [bydʒetize] VT *Compta* to budget for

buée [bɥe] NF condensation; **il y a de la b. sur les carreaux** the windows are covered in condensation *or* misted up; **plein** *ou* **couvert de b.** misted *or* steamed up; **mes lunettes se couvrent de b.** my glasses are getting steamed up

buffet [byfɛ] NM **1** *(meuble ▸ de salle à manger)* sideboard; **b. (de cuisine)** kitchen cabinet *or* dresser

2 *(nourriture)* buffet; **il y aura un b. pour le déjeuner** there will be a buffet lunch; **b. campagnard** buffet *(mainly with country-style cold meats)*; **b. froid** (cold) buffet

3 *(salle)* **b. (de gare)** (station) café *or* buffet *or* cafeteria

4 *(comptoir roulant)* refreshment *Br* trolley *or Am* cart

5 *(d'un orgue)* case

6 *très Fam (ventre)* belly; **ne rien avoir dans le b.** *(être à jeun)* to have an empty belly; *(être lâche)* to have no guts; **se remplir le b.** to stuff one's face, to pig out

buffetier, -ère [byftje, -jɛr] NM,F *Fam Vieilli (d'un buffet de gare)* buffet manager□

buffle [byfl] NM **1** *Zool* buffalo **2** *(cuir)* buffalo hide **3** *(pour polir)* buffer

bufflesse [byflɛs], **bufflonne** [byflɔn] NF *Zool* cow buffalo

bug [bœg] NM *Ordinat* bug

bugle[1] [bygl] NM *Mus* bugle

bugle[2] [bygl] NF *Bot* bugle

building [bildiŋ] NM high-rise (building)

buire [bɥir] NF ewer, flagon

buis [bɥi] NM **1** *Bot* box, boxtree; *Rel* **b. bénit** (blessed) palm **2** *Menuis* box, boxwood

buisson [bɥisɔ̃] NM **1** *Bot* bush **2** *Culin* **b. d'écrevisses** crayfish en buisson **3** *Bible* **b. ardent** burning bush

buisson-ardent [bɥisɔ̃ardɑ̃] *(pl* **buissons-ardents***)* NM *Bot* pyracantha

buissonneux, -euse [bɥisɔnø, -øz] **ADJ 1** *Géog (terrain)* shrub-covered, covered with bushes **2** *(arbre, végétation)* bushy

buissonnier, -ère [bɥisɔnje, -jɛr] **ADJ 1** *(animal)* bush-dwelling **2** *voir* **école**

bulbe [bylb] **NM 1** *Bot* bulb, corm
2 *Anat* **b. pileux** hair bulb; **b. rachidien** medulla oblongata
3 *Archit* **b. (byzantin)** onion dome
4 *Naut* bulb

bulbeux, -euse [bylbø, -øz] **ADJ** *Bot* bulbous

bulgare [bylgar] **ADJ** Bulgarian
NM *(langue)* Bulgarian
• **Bulgare NMF** Bulgarian

Bulgarie [bylgari] **NF la B.** Bulgaria

bulldozer [byldozɛr] **NM 1** *(machine)* bulldozer **2** *Fam (fonceur)* bulldozer; **c'est un b., cette femme!** that woman bulldozes her way through life!

bulle [byl] **NF 1** *(d'air, de gaz, de bain moussant)* bubble; **b. d'air** *(dans un tuyau)* airlock; **b. de savon** soap bubble; **des bulles** bubbles, froth; **il n'y a plus de bulles dans le Coca®** the Coke® has gone flat; **faire des bulles** *(de savon)* to blow bubbles; *(bébé)* to dribble
2 *(de bande dessinée)* balloon, speech bubble; *Ordinat* **b. d'aide** help pop-up
3 *Fam Arg scol (zéro)* zero[a]; **j'ai eu la b. en maths** I got a zero in maths
4 *Méd (enceinte stérile)* bubble; **enfant b.** = child brought up in a sterile bubble
5 *(emballage)* blister
6 *Rel* bull
7 *Bourse* **b. boursière** stock market bubble, surge on the Stock Market; **b. spéculative** speculative bubble
NM (papier) b. Manila paper

buller [3] [byle] **VI** *très Fam* to laze about[a]

bulletin [byltɛ̃] **NM 1** *Rad & TV (communiqué)* bulletin; *(d'entreprise)* newsletter; **b. d'informations** news bulletin; **b. météorologique** weather forecast *or* report; **b. spécial** newsflash
2 *Admin* **b. de naissance** birth certificate; **le B. officiel** = official listing of all new laws and decrees; **B. officiel des communautés européennes** = official listing of all new EU directives; **b. de santé** medical report
3 *Scol* **b. (scolaire** *ou* **de notes)** *Br* (school) report, *Am* report card; **b. mensuel/trimestriel** monthly/end-of-term report; **avoir un bon/mauvais b.** to get a good/bad school report
4 *Bourse* **B. de la Cote Officielle** Stock Exchange Daily Official List; **b. des cours** official (Stock Exchange) price list
5 *Pol* **b. de vote** ballot paper; **b. blanc** blank ballot paper; **b. nul** spoiled ballot paper; **b. secret** secret ballot
6 *(revue)* bulletin, annals; (▸ *d'entreprise)* newsletter
7 *(ticket, formulaire)* form; *Com* **b. de commande** order form; **b. de consigne** *Am* checkroom *or Br* left luggage ticket; *Com* **b. d'expédition** dispatch note, consignment note; *Com* **b. de garantie** guarantee (certificate); *Com* **b. de paie** *ou* **de salaire** pay (advice) slip, salary advice note; **b. de participation** entry form; *Com* **b. de vente** sales note; *Suisse Banque* **b. de versement** money order

bulletin-réponse [byltɛ̃repɔ̃s] *(pl* **bulletins-réponse)** **NM** *(gén)* reply form *or* coupon; *(pour un concours)* entry form

bulleux, -euse [bylø, -øz] **ADJ** *Méd* blistered

bull-terrier [bultɛrje] *(pl* **bull-terriers) NM** *(chien)* bull-terrier

bungalow [bœ̃galo] **NM** *(maison ▸ sans étage)* bungalow; (▸ *de vacances)* chalet

bunker [bunkœr] **NM 1** *Sport* bunker, *Am* sand trap **2** *Mil* bunker

buraliste [byralist] **NMF** *(de bureau de tabac) Br* tobacconist, *Am* tobacco dealer *(licensed to sell stamps)*; *(de bureau de poste)* clerk; *(d'impôts)* receiver of taxes

bure[1] [byr] **NF 1** *Tex* homespun **2** *(vêtement)* frock, cowl; **la b. du moine** monk's habit

bure[2] [byr] **NM** *Mines* staple shaft

bureau, -x [byro] **NM 1** *(meuble ▸ gén)* desk; (▸ *à rabat)* bureau; *Can* (▸ *pour vêtements)* chest of drawers; **b. à cylindre** roll top desk; **b. ministre** pedestal desk
2 *(pièce d'une maison)* study; *(meubles de cette pièce)* set of furniture *(for a study)*
3 *(lieu de travail)* office; **aller au b.** to go to the office; **travailler dans un b.** to do office work; **elle est dans son b.** she's in her office; **b. informatisé** electronic office, paperless office; **b. paysager** open-plan office
4 *(agence)* office; **b. d'aide sociale** welfare office *or* centre; **b. de change** *(banque)* bureau de change, foreign exchange office; *(comptoir)* bureau de change, foreign exchange counter; **b. de cotation ou d'évaluation** credit *Br* agency *or Am* bureau; **b. de douane** customs house; **b. d'études** *(entreprise)* research consultancy; **b. d'expédition** forwarding office, shipping office; **b. d'exportation** export office; **b. des objets trouvés** *Br* lost property *or Am* lost-and-found office; **b. de perception** tax office; **b. de placement** employment agency *(for domestic workers)*; **b. de poste** post office; **b. de publicité** advertising agency; **b. de renseignements** information desk *or* point *or* centre; **b. de tabac** *Br* tobacconist's, *Am* tobacco dealer's; **b. de tri** sorting office; **b. de vote** polling station
5 *(service interne)* **b. d'achat** purchase department; **b. commercial** commercial department; **b. d'études** *(dans une entreprise)* research department *or* unit
6 *Théât* booking office; **jouer à bureaux fermés** to be fully booked
7 *(commission)* committee; **bureaux internationaux** international bureaux; **B. international du travail** International Labour Organization; **b. politique** Politburo; **B. de vérification de la publicité** = French advertising standards authority, *Br* ≃ ASA
8 *Journ* office (abroad)
9 *Ordinat (écran)* desktop; **b. actif** active desktop; **b. électronique** electronic desktop
10 *Jur* **b. de conciliation** *(prud'hommes)* conciliation panel; **b. de jugement** *(prud'hommes)* adjudication panel
• **bureaux NMPL** *(locaux)* office, offices; **nos bureaux sont transférés au 10, rue Biot** our office has *or* our premises have been transferred to 10 rue Biot; **les bureaux du ministère** the Ministry offices
• **de bureau ADJ** *(travail, heures)* office *(avant n)*; *(articles, fournitures)* office *(avant n)*; stationery *(avant n)*; *(employé)* office *(avant n)*, white-collar

> Il faut noter que le nom anglais **bureau** est un faux ami. Il ne s'emploie jamais pour désigner une pièce ou un meuble mais pour faire référence à une institution.

bureaucrate [byrokrat] **NMF** bureaucrat

bureaucratie [byrokrasi] **NF 1** *(système)* bureaucracy **2** *(fonctionnaires)* officials, bureaucrats **3** *(tracasseries)* red tape, bureaucracy

bureaucratique [byrokratik] **ADJ** bureaucratic, administrative

bureaucratisation [byrokratizasjɔ̃] **NF** bureaucratization

bureaucratiser [3] [byrokratize] **VT** to bureaucratize

Bureautique® [byrotik] **ADJ système/méthode B.** office IT system/method
NF 1 *(système)* office IT **2** *(matériel)* computerized office equipment

burette [byrɛt] **NF 1** *(bidon)* **b. (d'huile)** oilcan **2** *Chim* burette **3** *Rel* cruet
• **burettes NFPL** *Vulg* nuts, balls, *Br* bollocks; **il me casse les burettes** he's pissing me off, *Am* he's breaking my balls

burin [byrɛ̃] **NM 1** *Tech* cold chisel **2** *(outil de graveur)* burin, graver **3** *(gravure)* engraving, print

burinage [byrinaʒ] **NM** *Tech* chiselling, chipping

buriné, -e [byrine] **ADJ** *(traits)* strongly marked; *(visage)* craggy, furrowed

buriner [3] [byrine] **VT 1** *Beaux-Arts* to engrave **2** *Tech* to chisel

burineur [byrinœr] **NM** *Tech* chiseller, chipper

burka [burka] *voir* **burqa**

Burkina [byrkina] **NM le B.** Burkina

burkinabé [byrkinabe] **ADJ** of/from Burkina
• **Burkinabé NMF** = inhabitant of or person from Burkina

burlesque [byrlɛsk] **ADJ 1** *(très drôle ▸ accoutrement)* comic, comical, droll; (▸ *plaisanterie)* funny **2** *Péj (stupide ▸ idée)* ludicrous, ridiculous **3** *Cin, Littérature & Théât* burlesque
NM *Cin, Littérature & Théât* **le b.** the burlesque

burlingue [byrlɛ̃g] **NM** *Fam* office[a]

burnes [byrn] **NFPL** *Vulg* balls, nuts, *Br* bollocks; **casser les b. à qn** to piss sb off, *Am* to break sb's balls

burnous [byrnu] **NM** *(arabe)* burnous, burnouse; *(de bébé)* hooded coat

burqa [burka] **NF** burka, burkha, burqa

bus [bys] **NM 1** *Transp (véhicule)* bus; **on y va en b.** *ou* **par le b.** we're going there by bus; **il était dans le b.** he was on the bus; **monter dans le/descendre du b.** to get on/off the bus **2** *Ordinat* bus; **b. d'adresses** address bus; **b. de contrôle** control bus; **b. de données** data bus; **b. multimédia** multimedia bus

busard [byzar] **NM** *Orn* harrier; **b. Saint-Martin** hen harrier

buse [byz] **NF 1** *Orn* buzzard
2 *Fam Péj* fool, dolt; **quelle b.!** what a fool!
3 *(conduit)* duct; **b. d'aérage** ventilation duct, air shaft
4 *Aut* **b. de carburateur** choke tube; **b. d'injection** injector nozzle
5 *Belg (échec)* failure

business [biznɛs] **NM** *Fam* **1** *(affaires)* business; **parler b.** to talk business; **b. angel** *(commanditaire)* angel **2** *Vieilli (embrouillamini)* **qu'est-ce que c'est que ce b.?** what's this mess?; **c'est tout un b. pour démonter le moteur** it's a hell of a job taking the engine apart

businessman [biznɛsman] *(pl* **businessmen** [-mɛn] *ou* **businessmans) NM** businessman

businesswoman [biznɛswuman] *(pl* **businesswomans** *ou* **businesswomen** [-mɛn]) **NF** businesswoman

busqué, -e [byske] **ADJ** *(nez)* hook *(avant n)*, hooked

buste [byst] **NM 1** *Anat (haut du corps)* chest; *(seins)* bust **2** *Beaux-Arts (sculpture)* bust; **peindre qn en b.** to paint a half-length portrait of sb

bustier, -ère [bystje, -ɛr] **NM,F** *Beaux-Arts* bust sculptor
NM 1 *(soutien-gorge)* strapless bra **2** *(corsage)* bustier; **robe/maillot b.** strapless dress/swimming costume

but [byt] **NM 1** *(dessein)* aim, purpose; **je vous ai blessé, ce n'était pas mon b.** I've hurt you, but it wasn't my intention *or* I didn't mean to; **quel est le b. de votre visite?** what's the purpose *or* object of your visit?; **quel est le b. de la manœuvre** *ou* **de l'opération?** what's the point of such a move?; **j'aimerais vous voir – dans quel b.?** I'd like to see you – what for?; **avoir pour b. de** to aim to; **j'avais pour b. de vous connaître** I was aiming to *or* my aim was to get to know you; **la réforme a un b. bien précis** the purpose of the reform is quite precise; **dans un b. (bien) précis** with a specific aim in mind; **dans le b. de faire...** for the purpose of doing..., with the aim of doing...; **je lui ai parlé dans le seul b. de t'aider** my sole aim in talking to him/her was to help you; **dans ce b.** with this end *or* aim in view; **aller** *ou* **frapper droit au b.** to get straight to the point; **à b. industriel** industrial; **à b. lucratif** profit-making; **association à b. non lucratif** non profit-making organization, *Am* not-for-profit organization
2 *(ambition)* aim, ambition, objective; **ils n'ont aucun b. dans la vie** they have no aim *or* purpose in life; **je suis encore loin du b.** I still have a long way to go; **nous sommes tout près du b.** we don't have far to go; **toucher au** *ou* **le b.** to have nearly achieved one's aim, to have nearly finished; **on touche au b.** we're nearly there, we've nearly finished
3 *(destination)* **le b. de notre voyage leur était in-**

connu our destination was unknown to them; **aujourd'hui, le b. de la promenade sera le monastère** today, we'll walk as far as *or* to the monastery; **sans b.** aimlessly

4 *Sport (limite, point)* goal; *(cible)* target, mark; **jouer dans les buts** to be (the) goalkeeper; **gagner/perdre (par) 5 buts à 2** to win/to lose by 5 goals to 2; *Fam* **marquer un b.** to score a goal; **un b. égalisateur** an equalizer, an equalizing goal; **b. en argent/en or** silver/golden goal

5 *Gram* purpose

• **de but en blanc** ADV *(demander)* point-blank, suddenly; *(rétorquer)* bluntly; **répondre à qn de b. en blanc** to give sb a blunt answer, to answer sb bluntly; **demanda-t-elle de b. en blanc** she suddenly asked

butane [bytan] NM *Chim* **(gaz) b.** butane; *(dans la maison)* Calor® gas

butanier [bytanje] NM *Naut* tanker, butane carrier

buté, -e[1] [byte] ADJ stubborn; **elle est complètement butée** she's as stubborn as a mule

butée[2] [byte] NF 1 *Tech* stop; *(de ski)* toe-piece 2 *Archit* abutment, buttress

buter [3] [byte] VI 1 *(trébucher)* to stumble, to trip; **b. contre une pierre** to trip over a stone

2 **b. contre qch** *(cogner ▸ sujet: personne)* to walk *or* to bump into sth

3 *(achopper)* **b. sur une difficulté** to come across a problem; **b. sur un mot** *(en parlant)* to trip over a word; *(en lisant pour soi)* to have trouble understanding a word

4 *Constr* **b. contre** to rest against, to be supported by

VT 1 *(braquer)* **b. qn** to put sb's back up, to make sb dig his/her heels in 2 *(mur)* to prop up, to buttress, to shore up 3 *Fam Arg crime (tuer)* to bump off, to waste; **se faire b.** to be bumped off *or* done in

VPR **se buter** 1 *(se braquer)* to dig one's heels in 2 *(se heurter)* **se b. dans** *ou* **contre** to bump into

buteur, -euse [bytœr, -øz] NM,F 1 *Sport* striker; *(au rugby)* kicker 2 *Fam Arg crime (assassin)* killer□

butin [bytɛ̃] NM 1 *(choses volées ▸ par des troupes)* spoils, booty; *(▸ par un cambrioleur)* loot 2 *(trouvailles)* finds

butiner [3] [bytine] VI *(insectes)* to gather nectar and pollen

VT 1 *(pollen, nectar)* to gather; *(fleurs)* to gather pollen and nectar from 2 *(rassembler ▸ idées)* to glean, to gather

butineur, -euse [bytinœr, -øz] ADJ *Entom* pollen-gathering

NM *Ordinat* browser

butoir [bytwar] NM 1 *Rail* buffer 2 *(de porte)* door stop 3 **(date) b.** limit

butor [bytɔr] NM 1 *Péj (malotru)* boor, lout 2 *Orn* bittern

buttage [bytaʒ] NM *Hort & Agr* earthing *or* banking up

butte [byt] NF 1 *(monticule)* hillock, knoll; *Géog* **la B. (Montmartre)** Montmartre; **habiter sur la B.** to live up on the hill *(in Montmartre)*

2 *Mil* **b. de tir** butts

3 *Hort & Agr* mound

4 *Géog* **b. témoin** outlier

• **en butte à** PRÉP **être en b. à** to be exposed to, to be faced with; **en b. aux quolibets** exposed to *or* prey to jeers

butter [3] [byte] VT 1 *Hort & Agr* to earth *or* to bank up 2 *Fam Arg crime (tuer)* to bump off, to waste

buvable [byvabl] ADJ 1 *(qui n'est pas mauvais à boire)* drinkable; *Hum* **il est b., ce petit vin!** this is a very drinkable little wine! 2 *Pharm (ampoule)* to be taken orally

buvait *etc voir* **boire**

buvard [byvar] NM 1 *(morceau de papier)* piece of blotting paper; **(papier) b.** blotting paper 2 *(sous-main)* blotter

buvette [byvɛt] NF 1 *(dans une foire, une gare)* refreshment stall 2 *(de station thermale)* pump room

buveur, -euse [byvœr, -øz] NM,F 1 *(alcoolique)* drinker, drunkard; **c'est un gros b.** he's a heavy drinker 2 *(client de café)* customer 3 *(consommateur)* **nous sommes de grands buveurs de café** we're great coffee drinkers; **je ne suis pas un gros b. de lait** I don't drink much milk

BVP [bevepe] NM *(abrév* **Bureau de vérification de la publicité***)* = French advertising standards authority, *Br* ≃ ASA

by-pass [bajpas] NM INV 1 *Élec* bypass 2 *Méd* bypass operation; **b. gastrique** gastric bypass

byronien, -enne [bajrɔnjɛ̃, -ɛn] ADJ *(mélancolie, perspective)* Byronic; *(vers)* Byronian

Byzance [bizɑ̃s] NF 1 *Géog* Byzantium 2 *Fam (locutions)* **c'est B.!** it's the last word in luxury!; **c'est pas B.** it's not exactly luxurious

byzantin, -e [bizɑ̃tɛ̃, -in] ADJ 1 *Hist* Byzantine 2 *Péj* byzantine

• **Byzantin, -e** NM,F Byzantine

C[1], **c** [se] **NM INV 1** *(lettre)* C, c; **C comme Célestin** ≃ C for Charlie; **c cédille** c cedilla **2** *Mus (note)* C

C[2] *(abrév écrite* **Celsius, centigrade***)* C

c' [s] *voir* **ce**[2]

ç' [s] *voir* **ce**[2]

C++ [seplysplys] **NM** *Ordinat* C++

CA [sea] **NM 1** *Élec (abrév* **courant alternatif***)* AC

2 *Com (abrév* **chiffre d'affaires***)* turnover

3 *(abrév* **conseil d'administration***)* board of directors

4 *Mil (abrév* **corps d'armée***)* army corps

ça[1] [sa] **NM** *Psy* id

ÇA[2] [sa] **PRON DÉMONSTRATIF 1** *(désignant un objet ▸ proche)* this, it; *(▸ éloigné)* that, it; **donne-moi ça** give me that, give it to me; **ça se trouve où?** where is it *or* that?; **c'est qui/quoi ça?** who's/what's that?; **qu'est-ce que tu veux? – ça, là-bas** what do you want? – that, over there; **ça sent bon** that *or* it smells nice; **il y avait ça entre moi et l'autobus** there was this *or* that much between me and the bus; **il y a ça de différence de taille entre eux** there is this *or* that much difference in height between them; *Fam* **il ne m'a pas donné ça!** he didn't give me a thing *or* a bean!; *Fam* **regarde-moi ça!** just look at that!; *Fam* **écoute-moi ça!** just listen to this!; *Euph* **il ne pense qu'à ça!** he's got a one-track mind!

2 *(désignant ▸ ce dont on vient de parler)* this, that; *(▸ ce dont on va parler)* this; **qu'est-ce que tu dis de ça?** what do you say to that?; **je n'ai jamais dit ça!** I never said that *or* any such thing!; **la liberté, c'est ça qui est important** freedom, that's what matters; **pas de ça chez nous** we don't want any of that here; **à part ça, tout va bien** apart from that, everything's fine; **il est parti il y a un mois/une semaine de ça** he left a month/a week ago; **écoutez, ça va vous étonner...** this will surprise you, listen...

3 *Fam (servant de sujet indéterminé)* **et ton boulot, comment ça se passe?** how's your job going?; **je voudrais m'inscrire, comment ça se passe?** I'd like to join, what do I have to do *or* how do I go about it?; **ça souffle!** there's quite a wind (blowing)!; **ça fait deux kilos/trois mètres** that's two kilos/three metres; **ça vous fera 15 euros** that'll be 15 euros; **ça fait deux heures que j'attends** I've been waiting for two hours; **ça me fait de la peine de le voir malade** it upsets me to see him ill; **ça vaut mieux** it's just as well; **qu'est-ce que ça peut faire?** what does it matter?; **qu'est-ce que ça veut dire?** what does it *or* that mean?; *(c'est ridicule)* where's the sense in it?; *(ton menaçant)* what do you mean by that?, what's that supposed to mean?; **les enfants, ça comprend tout** children understand everything; **ça bavarde dans le fond de la classe** there's talking going on at the back of the classroom; *Péj* **et ça n'arrête pas de se plaindre!** and he's/they're/*etc* forever complaining!; **ça ira comme ça** that'll do; **ça y est, j'ai fini!** that's it, I'm finished!; **ça y est, ça commence!** here we go!; **ça y est, tu es prêt?** so are you ready now?; **ça y est, c'est de ma faute!** that's it, it's all my fault!; **c'est ça!** that's right; *Ironique* right!; **c'est ça, dites que je suis folle** so I'm crazy, is that it *or* am I?; **c'est ça, moquez-vous de moi!** that's right, have a good laugh at my expense!; **c'est ça les hommes!** that's men for you!

4 *(emploi expressif)* **pourquoi ça?** why?, what for?; **qui ça?** who?, who's that?; **où ça?** where?, whereabouts?; **quand ça?** when?; **comment ça, c'est fini?** what do you mean it's over?; **ah ça oui!** you bet!; **ah ça non!** certainly not!

çà [sa] **çà et là ADV** here and there

cabale [kabal] **NF 1** *(personnes)* cabal; *(intrigue)* cabal, intrigue; **monter une c. contre qn** to plot against sb **2** *Rel* cabala, cabbala, kabbala

cabaliste [kabalist] **NMF** *Rel* cabalist, cabbalist, kabbalist

cabalistique [kabalistik] **ADJ** *Rel (science)* cabalistic, cabbalistic, kabbalistic; *Fig (signes, formules)* arcane

caban [kabɑ̃] **NM** *(longue veste)* car coat; *(de marin)* reefer jacket; *(d'officier)* pea jacket

cabane [kaban] **NF 1** *(hutte)* hut, cabin; *(pour animaux, objets)* shed; **c. de** *ou* **en rondins** log cabin; **c. à outils** toolshed

2 *Fam (maison)* dump; **j'en ai marre de cette c.!** I'm fed up with this dump!

3 *Fam (prison)* clink; **il a fait huit ans de c.** he did *or* spent eight years in the clink *or* inside

4 *Can* **c. à sucre** sugar (and maple syrup) refinery, sap *or* sugar house

cabanon [kabanɔ̃] **NM 1** *(abri)* shed, hut; *(en Provence)* (country) cottage **2** *(chalet de plage)* beach hut **3** *Vieilli (pour fou)* padded cell; *Fam* **il est bon pour le c.** he should be put away

cabaret [kabare] **NM 1** *(établissement)* nightclub, cabaret

2 *(activité)* **le c.** cabaret; **un spectacle de c.** a floorshow

3 *(meuble)* liqueur cabinet

4 *Vieilli (auberge)* tavern

cabaretier, -ère [kabartje, -ɛr] **NM,F** *Vieilli* innkeeper

cabas [kaba] **NM 1** *(pour provisions)* shopping bag **2** *(pour figues, raisins)* basket

cabestan [kabɛstɑ̃] **NM** *Naut* capstan; **c. horizontal** windlass; **grand c.** main capstan; **virez au c.!** heave!

cabillaud [kabijo] **NM** *Ich* cod

cabine [kabin] **NF 1** *Naut* cabin

2 *Aviat (des passagers)* cabin; **c. (de pilotage)** cockpit; **personnel de c.** cabin crew

3 *(de laboratoire de langues)* booth; *(de piscine, d'hôpital)* cubicle; **c. (de bain)** *(hutte)* bathing *or* beach hut; *(serviette)* beach towel (for changing); **c. de bronzage** tanning booth; **c. de douche** shower cubicle; **c. d'essayage** *Br* changing *or* fitting room, *Am* dressing room; **c. Internet** Internet booth; *Cin* **c. de projection** projection room; **c. de régie** control room

4 *Tél* **c. téléphonique** phone booth *or Br* box

5 *(d'ascenseur)* cage, *Am* car; *(de camion, de tracteur, de grue, de train)* cab; **c. (de téléphérique)** cablecar

6 *Rail* **c. d'aiguillage** signal box, points control box

cabinet [kabinɛ] **NM 1** *(de médecin, de dentiste) Br* surgery, *Am* office; *(de magistrat)* chambers; *(d'avocat, de notaire)* firm; **c. de consultation** *(de médecin)* consulting room

2 *(réduit)* **c. de débarras** *Br* boxroom, *Am* storage room; **c. noir** walk-in cupboard

3 *(petite salle) Arch* **cabinets d'aisances** toilet, privy; **c. de lecture** reading room; **c. particulier** *(de restaurant)* private dining room; **c. de toilette** bathroom; **c. de travail** study

4 *(clientèle ▸ de médecin, de dentiste)* practice; **monter un c.** to set up a practice

5 *(agence)* **c. d'affaires** business consultancy; **c. d'architectes** firm of architects; **c. d'assurances** insurance firm *or* agency; **c. d'audit** firm of auditors; **c. conseil** consulting firm, consultancy firm; **c. de conseil en gestion** management consultancy; *Mktg* **c. d'études** market research firm; **c. d'expertise comptable** accounting firm; **c. d'experts-conseils** consultancy; **c. immobilier** *Br* estate agent's *or Am* realtor's office; **c. juridique** law firm; **c. de recrutement** recruitment agency; **c. de traduction** translation company

6 *Pol (gouvernement)* cabinet; *(d'un ministre)* departmental staff; **faire partie du c.** to be in *or* a member of the Cabinet; **le c. du Premier ministre** the Prime Minister's departmental staff; **c. fantôme** shadow cabinet; **c. ministériel** minister's advisers, departmental staff

7 *(d'un musée)* (exhibition) room; **c. des estampes/médailles** prints/medals room; **c. des dessins** prints and drawings room

8 *(meuble)* cabinet

• **cabinets NMPL** *Fam* toilet□, *Br* loo, *Am* bathroom□

câblage [kablaʒ] **NM 1** *TV (pose du réseau)* cable (TV) installation, cabling; **le c. d'une rue/ville** cabling a street/a town

2 *Élec (opération)* wiring; *(fils)* cables

3 *(torsion)* cabling

4 *(d'un message)* cabling

câble [kabl] **NM 1** *(cordage ▸ en acier)* cable, wire rope; *(▸ en fibres végétales)* line, rope, cable; *Aut* **c. d'accélérateur** accelerator cable; *Naut* **c. d'amarrage** mooring line *or* cable; *Aut* **c. de démarreur** *ou* **de démarrage** jump lead; *Aut* **c. de frein** brake cable; *Naut* **c. de halage** *ou* **de remorquage** towrope, towline

2 *Élec* cable; **c. d'alimentation** supply *or* feed *or* power cable; **c. coaxial** coaxial cable; **c. électrique** electric cable; *Tél* **c. hertzien** radio link *(by hertzian waves)*; *Ordinat* **c. d'imprimante** printer cable; *Ordinat* **c. modem** modem cable; **c. optique** optical fibre; **c. à paires** paired cable; **c. parallèle** parallel cable; **c. série** serial cable; *Fam* **péter un c.** *(craquer)* to crack up

3 *TV* **le c.** cable (TV); **avoir le c.** to have cable (TV); **transmettre par c.** to cablecast; **c. péritel®** SCART cable; **c. en fibres optiques** fibre-optic cable

4 *Tél (télégramme)* cable, cablegram

câblé, -e [kable] **ADJ 1** *TV (ville, région)* with cable (TV); *(émission)* cabled; **l'immeuble est c.** the building has cable (TV); **réseau c.** cable television network **2** *Ordinat* hard-wired **3** *Fam (à la mode)* switched on

câbler [3] [kable] **VT 1** *TV (ville, région)* to link to a cable television network, to wire for cable; *(émission)* to cable

2 *Élec* to cable

3 *Élec (fils)* to twist together (into a cable), to cable

4 *Tél (message)* to cable

câbleur, -euse [kablœr, -øz] NM,F *Élec* cable-layer

câbliste [kablist] NMF *Cin & TV (personne)* cable operator

câblodiffuseur [kablodifyzœr], **câblodistributeur** [kablodistribytœr] NM *TV* cable operator, cable company

câblodistribution [kablodistribysjɔ̃] NF *TV* cable television, cablevision

câblogramme [kablɔgram] NM *Tél* cablegram

câblo-opérateur [kablooperatœr] (*pl* **câblo-opérateurs**) NM *TV* cable operator, cable company

cabochard, -e [kabɔʃar, -ard] *Fam* ADJ pig-headed, stubborn□

NM,F **c'est un c.** he's pigheaded *or* as stubborn as a mule

caboche [kabɔʃ] NF **1** *Fam (tête)* nut, *Br* noddle; **mets-toi (bien) ça dans la c.!** get that into your thick head!; **avoir la c. dure** to be pigheaded **2** *(clou)* hob-nail

cabochon[1] [kabɔʃɔ̃] NM **1** *(pierre)* cabochon **2** *(de carafe à liqueur)* (glass) stopper **3** *(clou)* stud

cabochon[2], **-onne** [kabɔʃɔ̃, -ɔn] NM,F *Can (têtu)* stubborn person; *(incompétent)* bad worker

cabosser [3] [kabɔse] VT *(carrosserie, couvercle)* to dent; **une voiture cabossée** a battered *or* beat-up car; **un chapeau cabossé** a battered hat

cabot [kabo] NM **1** *Fam (chien)* dog□, *Péj* mutt **2** *Fam Arg mil* corporal□ **3** *(acteur)* ham (actor)

cabotage [kabɔtaʒ] NM *Naut* coastal navigation; *Naut* **petit/grand c.** inshore/seagoing navigation

caboter [3] [kabɔte] VI *Naut (gén)* to sail *or* to ply along the coast; *(ne pas s'éloigner)* to hug the shore

caboteur [kabɔtœr] NM *Naut (navire)* coaster, tramp

cabotin, -e [kabɔtɛ̃, -in] ADJ **1** *(manières, personne)* theatrical **2** *Péj (acteur)* ham

NM,F **1** *(personne affectée)* show-off, poseur **2** *Péj (acteur)* ham (actor)

cabotinage [kabɔtinaʒ] NM *(d'un poseur)* affectedness, theatricality; *(d'un artiste)* ham acting; **faire du c.** to ham it up

cabotiner [3] [kabɔtine] VI *Fam Péj* to play to the gallery, to showboat

caboulot [kabulo] NM *Fam* seedy pub, dive

cabrage [kabraʒ] NM **1** *(de cheval)* rearing (up) **2** *Aviat* nose-lift

cabré, -e [kabre] ADJ **1** *(cheval)* rearing **2** *Aviat (avion)* tail down

cabrer [3] [kabre] VT **1** *(cheval)* **il cabra son cheval** he made his horse rear up **2** *Aviat* to nose up **3** *(inciter à la révolte)* **c. qn** to put sb's back up; **c. qn contre qn** to turn *or* to set sb against sb

VPR **se cabrer 1** *(cheval)* to rear up **2** *Aviat* to nose up **3** *(se rebiffer)* to balk, to jib; **se c. contre** to rebel against

cabri [kabri] NM *Zool* kid

cabriole [kabrijɔl] NF **1** *(bond ▸ d'un enfant)* leap; *(▸ d'un animal)* prancing *(UNCOUNT)*, cavorting *(UNCOUNT)*; *(acrobatie)* somersault; **faire des cabrioles** *(clown)* to do somersaults; *(chèvre)* to prance *or* to cavort (about); *(enfant)* to dance *or* to jump about

2 *Fig (manœuvre)* clever manoeuvre; **il a éludé la question par une c.** he managed to dodge the question

3 *(danse)* cabriole

4 *Équitation* capriole

cabrioler [3] [kabrijɔle] VI *(enfant)* to leap (about); *(animal)* to prance *or* to cavort (about)

cabriolet [kabrijɔlɛ] NM **1** *Aut (véhicule ▸ automobile)* convertible; *(▸ hippomobile)* cabriolet **2** *(meuble)* cabriole chair

CAC, Cac [kak] NM **1** *Bourse (abrév* **cotation assistée en continu**) automated quotation; *Bourse* **l'indice C.-40, le C.-40** the CAC-40 (index) *(Paris Stock Exchange Index)* **2** *Fin (abrév* **Compagnie des agents de change**) Institute of stockbrokers

caca [kaka] NM *Fam* **du c.** *(excrément)* poo, poop; *Fig* **c'est du c.!** it's yucky!; **du c. de chien** some dog dirt *or* poo; **faire c.** to do *or Br* have a poo; **il nous fait un c. nerveux, l'autre!** he's having kittens!, he's having a fit!

• **caca d'oie** NM INV greenish-yellow ADJ INV greenish-yellow

cacahouète, cacahuète [kakawɛt] NF **1** *Bot* peanut **2** *Fam (locutions)* **ce film ne vaut pas une c.** the film's a load of garbage *or Br* rubbish; **il n'assure pas une c.** he hasn't got a clue

cacao [kakao] NM **1** *Bot (graine)* cocoa bean **2** *Culin* **(poudre de) c.** cocoa (powder); **au c.** cocoa-flavoured; *(boisson)* cocoa *(avant n)*

cacaoté, -e [kakaɔte] ADJ *Culin* cocoa-flavoured

cacaotier [kakaɔtje] NM *Bot* cocoa tree

cacaoui [kakawi], **cacaouite** [kakawit] NM *Can Orn* long-tailed duck

cacaoyer [kakaɔje] = **cacaotier**

cacatoès [kakatɔɛs] NM *Orn* cockatoo

cacatois [kakatwa] NM *Naut (voile)* royal; **grand/petit c.** main/fore royal; **(mât de) c.** royal mast

cachalot [kaʃalo] NM *Zool* sperm whale

cache [kaʃ] NF *(d'armes, de drogue)* cache

NM **1** *(pour œil, pour texte)* cover card; *(de machine à écrire)* cover **2** *Cin & Phot* mask **3** *Ordinat* cache; **c. du disque dur** hard disk cache; **c. externe** external cache

caché, -e [kaʃe] ADJ **1** *(dans une cachette ▸ butin, or)* hidden **2** *(secret ▸ sentiment)* secret; *(▸ signification)* hidden, secret; *(▸ talent)* hidden

cache-cache [kaʃkaʃ] NM INV hide-and-seek; *aussi Fig* **jouer à c. (avec qn)** to play hide-and-seek (with sb)

cache-col [kaʃkɔl] NM INV scarf

cachectique [kaʃɛktik] *Méd* ADJ cachectic

NMF person suffering from cachexia

Cachemire [kaʃmir] NM *Géog* **le C.** Kashmir

cachemire [kaʃmir] NM *Tex* **1** *(tissu, poil)* cashmere; **en c.** cashmere *(avant n)* **2** *(châle)* cashmere shawl; *(pullover)* cashmere sweater; *(gilet)* cashmere cardigan **3** *(comme adj) (motif, imprimé)* paisley *(avant n)*

cache-misère [kaʃmizɛr] NM INV **1** *(vêtement)* = coat or wrap hiding shabby appearance **2** *Fig (destiné à cacher des défauts)* **cette mesure n'est qu'un c.** this is just a cosmetic measure designed to distract attention from the real problem

cache-nez [kaʃne] NM INV scarf, *Br* comforter

cache-pot [kaʃpo] NM INV (flower *or* plant) pot holder

cache-poussière [kaʃpusjɛr] NM INV dust coat

cacher[1] [kaʃɛr] = **kascher**

cacher[2] [3] [kaʃe] VT **1** *(prisonnier, réfugié)* to hide; *(trésor, jouet)* to hide, to conceal

2 *(accroc, ride)* to hide, to conceal (from view); **il cache son jeu** he's not showing his hand; *Fig* he's playing his cards close to his chest

3 *(sujet: niche, grenier)* to hide, to conceal

4 *(faire écran devant)* to hide, to obscure; *Opt* **c. un œil** *(chez l'oculiste)* to cover one eye (with one's hand); **c. la lumière** *ou* **le jour à qn** to be in sb's light; **pousse-toi, tu caches ta sœur!** *(en prenant une photo)* get out of the way, you're right in front of your sister!; **tu me caches la vue!** you're blocking my view!

5 *(ne pas révéler ▸ sentiment, vérité)* to hide, to conceal, to cover up; **c. son âge** to keep one's age (a) secret; **c. qch à qn** to conceal *or* to hide sth from sb; **je ne cache pas que...** I must say *or* admit that...; **je ne (te) cacherai pas que je me suis ennuyé** to be frank with you, (I must say that) I was bored; **pour ne rien te c.** to be completely open with you

VPR **se cacher 1** *(aller se dissimuler ▸ enfant, soleil)* to hide; **se c. derrière des rideaux/dans un bois** to hide behind curtains/in the woods; **se c. de ses parents pour fumer, fumer en se cachant de ses parents** to smoke behind one's parents' back; **il me plaît, je ne m'en cache pas!** I like him, it's no secret!; **sans se c.** openly **2** *(être dissimulé ▸ fugitif)* to be hiding; *(▸ objet)* to be hidden; **le village se cache dans la vallée** the village lies tucked away at the bottom of the valley; **sa timidité se cache derrière une certaine rudesse** his/her shyness is hidden behind a bluff exterior **3** *(dissimuler quelque chose)* **je me cachais la tête sous les draps** I hid my head under the sheets; **cachez-vous un œil** cover one eye

cache-radiateur [kaʃradjatœr] NM INV radiator cover

cachère [kaʃɛr] = **kascher**

cache-sexe [kaʃsɛks] NM INV *(string)* G-string, thong; *(d'indigène)* apron

cachet [kaʃɛ] NM **1** *Pharm* tablet; **un c. d'aspirine** an aspirin (tablet)

2 *(sceau)* seal; *(empreinte)* stamp; **c. de la poste** *ou* **d'oblitération** postmark; **porter le c. de Nice** to be postmarked Nice, to bear a Nice postmark; **le c. de la poste faisant foi** date of postmark will be taken as proof of postage; *Mktg* **c. de fabrique** maker's trademark

3 *(rémunération d'un artiste)* fee

4 *(charme ▸ d'un édifice, d'une ville)* character; *(▸ d'un vêtement)* style; **avoir du c.** *(édifice, village)* to be full of character; *(vêtements)* to be stylish; **donner du c. à** *ou* **faire le c. de qch** to give sth its charm *or* character

cachetage [kaʃtaʒ] NM *(d'une lettre)* sealing

cache-tampon [kaʃtɑ̃pɔ̃] (*pl* **inv** *ou* **cache-tampons**) NM *(jeu)* ≃ hunt-the-thimble

cacheter [27] [kaʃte] VT *(enveloppe, vin)* to seal; **c. un billet à la cire** to seal a letter with wax; **vin cacheté** vintage wine

cacheton [kaʃtɔ̃] NM *Fam* **1** *(médicament)* tablet□, pill□; **il prend des cachetons pour dormir** he takes sleeping pills *or* tablets□ **2** *(cachet d'artiste)* fee□; **courir le c.** = to try to get little jobs here and there□

cachetonner [3] [kaʃtɔne] VI *Fam (artiste)* = to try to get little jobs here and there□

cachette [kaʃɛt] NF *(d'un enfant, pour un objet)* hiding place; *(d'un malfaiteur, d'un réfugié)* hide-out; **sors de ta c.!** *(à un enfant)* come out!; *Can* **jouer à la c.** to play hide-and-seek

• **en cachette** ADV *(fumer, lire, partir)* secretly, in secret; *(rire)* to oneself, up one's sleeve; **il me l'a donné en c.** he gave it to me secretly *or* without anybody noticing; **boire en c.** *(habituellement)* to be a secret drinker; **en c. de qn** *(boire, fumer)* behind sb's back, while sb's back is turned; *(préparer, décider)* without sb knowing, unbeknownst to sb

cachettera *etc voir* **cacheter**

cachexie [kaʃɛksi] NF **1** *Méd* cachexia **2** *Vét* rot

cachot [kaʃo] NM **1** *(cellule)* dungeon **2** *(isolement)* solitary confinement; **il a fait une semaine de c.** he spent a week in solitary (confinement)

cachotterie [kaʃɔtri] NF (little) secret; **elle aime faire des cachotteries** she likes to make a mystery of everything; **faire des cachotteries à qn** to keep secrets from sb

cachottier, -ère [kaʃɔtje, -ɛr] *Fam* ADJ secretive□; **il est c.** he's full of little mysteries *or* secrets

NM,F **c'est un c.** he's secretive; **tu ne me l'avais pas dit, petite cachottière!** you never told me, you secretive little thing!

cachou [kaʃu] NM **1** *(bonbon)* cachou **2** *(substance, teinture)* catechou, cachou, cutch

cacique [kasik] NM **1** *(notable)* cacique **2** *Fam Arg scol* **le c.** *(à un concours)* = student graduating in first place (especially from the "École normale supérieure") **3** *Fam (personne importante)* big shot, bigwig

cacochyme [kakɔʃim] *Littéraire* ADJ *Hum* doddery, doddering

NMF dodderer

cacophonie [kakɔfɔni] NF cacophony

cacophonique [kakɔfɔnik] ADJ cacophonous

cacou [kaku] NMF *Fam* **faire le c.** to act smart

cactus [kaktys] NM *Bot* cactus

CAD [seade] NM *(abrév* **Comité d'aide au développement**) DAC

c.-à-d. *(abrév écrite* **c'est-à-dire**) ie

cadastrage [kadastraʒ] NM *Admin* land registration

cadastral, -e, -aux, -ales [kadastral, -o] ADJ *Admin* cadastral

cadastre [kadastr] NM *Admin* **1** *(plans)* cadastral register, ≃ land register; **c. parcellaire** cadastral survey **2** *(service)* **le c.** cadastral survey (office), ≃ land registry

cadastrer [3] [kadastre] **VT** *Admin* ≃ to register with the land registry

cadavéreux, -euse [kadaverø, -øz] **ADJ** *(teint)* livid, deathly pale; *(fixité)* corpse-like

cadavérique [kadaverik] **ADJ 1** *(du cadavre)* of a corpse; **rigidité c.** rigor mortis **2** *(blancheur)* deathly, cadaverous; *(teint)* deathly pale; *(fixité)* corpse-like

cadavre [kadavr] **NM 1** *(d'une personne ▸ gén)* corpse, body; *(▸ à disséquer)* cadaver; *(d'un animal)* body, carcass; **c'est un c. ambulant** he's a walking corpse; *Fig* **il y a un c. entre eux** they share a guilty secret **2** *Fam Hum (bouteille)* empty, *Br* dead man

• **cadavre exquis NM** *(jeu)* ≃ consequences

caddie, caddy [kadi] **NM** *(au golf)* caddie, caddy

Caddie® [kadi] **NM 1** *(chariot) Br* (supermarket) trolley, *Am* (grocery) cart **2** *Ordinat (pour des achats en ligne) Br* shopping basket, *Am* shopping cart

cadeau, -x [kado] **NM 1** *(don)* present, gift; *Com* free gift, freebie; **recevoir un c. de qn** to get a present from *or* to be given a present by sb; **faire un c. à qn** to give sb a present; **faire c. de qch à qn** *(le lui offrir)* to make sb a present of sth, to give sb sth as a present; **je vous fais c. du kiwi** I'll give you *or* throw in the kiwi fruit for free; **je te dois cinq euros – je t'en fais c.!** I owe you five euros – forget it!; *Euph* **ils ne font pas c. des places!** the tickets aren't exactly cheap!; **il ne m'a pas fait de c.** *(dans une transaction, un match)* he didn't do me any favours; *(en me critiquant)* he didn't spare me; **dans la vie, on ne vous fait pas de c.** you can't expect things to be easy!; *Fam* **ce n'est pas un c.!** *(personne insupportable)* he's a real pain!; *(personne bête)* he's no bright spark!; *Hum* **tiens, c.!** here's a little present for you!; **c. d'anniversaire/de Noël** birthday/Christmas present; **c. empoisonné** poisoned chalice; **c. de noces** *ou* **de mariage** wedding present; **c. d'entreprise** giveaway *or* free gift; **c. publicitaire** free gift, freebie; *Prov* **les petits cadeaux entretiennent l'amitié** = gifts oil the wheels of friendship **2** *(comme adj; avec ou sans trait d'union)* **shampooing c.** free bottle of shampoo *(with a purchase)*

• **en cadeau ADV** *Com* free; **je l'ai eu en c.** I got it free *or* for nothing

cadenas [kadna] **NM** padlock; **fermer au c.** to padlock

cadenasser [3] [kadnase] **VT 1** *(fermer)* to padlock **2** *Fam (emprisonner)* to lock up[□], to put away

cadence [kadɑ̃s] **NF 1** *Mus & (en danse ▸ rythme)* rhythm; *(accords)* cadence; *(passage de soliste)* cadenza; **marquer la c.** to beat out the rhythm

2 *Littérature* cadence

3 *Sport (d'un marcheur)* pace; *(d'un rameur)* rate; **à une bonne c.** at quite a pace; **tenir la c.** to keep in step

4 *Ind* rate; **c. de production** rate of production; **c. de travail** work rate

5 *Mil* **c. de tir** rate of fire

• **à la cadence de PRÉP** at the rate of

• **en cadence ADV taper des mains en c.** to clap in time; **marcher en c.** to march

cadencé, -e [kadɑ̃se] **ADJ 1** *(marche, musique)* rhythmical; *(gestes, démarche)* swinging; *Mil* **au pas c.** in quick time **2** *Ordinat* **c. à** running at

cadencer [16] [kadɑ̃se] **VT** *(vers, phrase)* to give rhythm to; **c. son pas** to march in rhythm

cadet, -ette [kadɛ, -ɛt] **ADJ** *(plus jeune)* younger; *(dernier-né)* youngest; **la branche cadette** the younger branch

NM,F 1 *(dans une famille ▸ de deux)* younger (one); *(▸ de plus de deux)* youngest (one); **son c.** *(fils)* his/her youngest son *or* boy; *(frère)* his/her youngest brother

2 *(frère, sœur plus jeune)* **mon c.** my younger brother; **ma cadette** my younger sister

3 *(entre personnes non apparentées)* **être le c. de qn** to be younger than sb; **je suis son c. de quatre ans** I'm four years his/her junior *or* four years younger than he/she is

4 *Sport* junior *(16 to 18 years old)*

NM 1 *Mil (élève)* cadet **2** *Hist (futur militaire)* cadet **3** *(locution)* **c'est le c. de mes soucis** it's the least of my worries

Cadix [kadiks] **NM** *Géog* Cadiz

cadmium [kadmjɔm] **NM** *Chim* cadmium

cadogan [kadɔgɑ̃] = **catogan**

cador [kadɔr] **NM 1** *(chien)* mutt **2** *Fam (personne influente)* big cheese, big shot; *Fam Arg crime (d'une bande)* leader[□], boss

cadrage [kadraʒ] **NM 1** *Cin & Phot* centring; *(plan)* frame

2 *Mines* framing

3 *Typ (des dimensions)* cropping; *(des couleurs)* masking

4 *Ordinat (d'objets)* positioning; *(de caractères)* alignment

cadran [kadrɑ̃] **NM 1** *(d'une montre, d'une pendule)* face, dial; *(d'un instrument de mesure, d'une boussole)* face; *(d'un téléphone)* dial; **c. lumineux** luminous dial **c. solaire** sundial; **2** *Can Vieilli (réveille-matin)* alarm clock

cadrat [kadra] **NM** *Typ* quadrat, quad

cadratin [kadratɛ̃] **NM** *Typ* em quadrat, em quad; **demi-c.** en quad

CADRE [kadr]

• executive **A1**	• officer **A2**
• grade **B1**	• corps **B2**
• frame **C1, 4**	• setting **C2**
• scope **C3**	• box **C4**

NM A. 1 *(responsable ▸ dans une entreprise)* executive; *(▸ dans un parti, dans un syndicat)* cadre; **les cadres** the managerial staff, the management; **un poste de c.** an executive *or* a managerial post; **c. commercial** sales executive; **c. d'entreprise** executive manager; **c. moyen** middle manager; **c. supérieur** senior executive, member of (the) senior management; **l'école a été fondée pour les enfants des ouvriers et des cadres moyens** the school was founded for the children of working-class and lower middle-class families; **femme c.** woman executive; *Hum* **jeune c. dynamique** whizz kid

2 *Mil* officer, member of the officer corps; **les cadres** the (commissioned and non-commissioned) officers

B. 1 *Admin (catégorie)* grade, category *(within the Civil Service)*; **le c. (de la fonction publique)** *(toutes catégories)* the Civil Service

2 *Mil* corps; **c. d'active** ≃ active list; **c. de réserve** ≃ reserve list; **le C. noir** = military riding school in Saumur

C. 1 *(encadrement ▸ d'un tableau, d'une porte, d'une ruche etc)* frame; **c. de bicyclette** bicycle frame

2 *(environnement)* setting, surroundings; **habiter dans un c. agréable/de verdure** to live in pleasant surroundings/a leafy setting; **le c. de** the scene of; **c'était le c. de mes amours enfantines** it was the scene of my childhood loves; **c. de travail** working environment; **c. de vie** (living) environment

3 *(portée, limites ▸ d'accords, de réformes)* scope, framework; **loi c.** outline law; **plan c.** blueprint (project); **réforme c.** general outline of reform; **sortir du c. de ses fonctions** to exceed (the scope of) one's duties

4 *Typ* box, space; *Ordinat (pour graphique)* box; *(sur l'Internet)* frame; *Admin* **c. réservé à l'administration** *(dans un formulaire)* for official use only

5 *(emballage)* crate, packing case

6 *Élec (de radio)* frame aerial

7 *(d'un livre)* outline, skeleton, plan

8 *Naut* berth

• **cadres NMPL 1** *(contrainte)* **cadres sociaux** social structures; **cadres de la mémoire** structures of the memory **2** *Admin* staff list; **être sur les cadres** to be a member of staff; **rayé des cadres** dismissed; **hors c.** seconded, on secondment

• **dans le cadre de PRÉP** within the framework *or* scope of; **dans le c. de mes fonctions/de ce programme** as part of my job/of this programme; **s'inscrire dans le c. de** to come within the framework of; **cela n'entre pas dans le c. de mes fonctions** it falls outside the scope of my responsibilities

> **CADRE**
>
> In French companies, employees are divided into two categories, "employés" and "cadres". "Cadres", who are better qualified, tend to occupy more senior posts and consequently enjoy higher salaries, more benefits and more prestige. They are also expected to work longer hours.

cadré, -e [kadre] **ADJ** *Cin & Phot* in-frame, onframe

cadrer [3] [kadre] **VI** *(correspondre ▸ témoignages)* to tally, to correspond; **les deux notions ne cadrent pas ensemble** the two ideas don't go together; **c. avec** to be consistent with; **sa déposition cadre bien avec les premiers témoignages** his/her statement is consistent with the earlier testimonies; **les chiffres que vous nous avez communiqués ne cadrent pas avec les nôtres** the figures you gave us don't tally with *or* are not consistent with ours; **un suicide ne cadre pas du tout avec sa personnalité** he's/she's not the sort of person who would ever contemplate suicide

VT 1 *Cin & Phot* to centre; *(plan)* to frame **2** *Ordinat (objets)* to position; *(caractères)* to align

cadreur, -euse [kadrœr, -øz] **NM,F** *Cin & TV* cameraman, *f* camerawoman

caduc, caduque [kadyk] **ADJ 1** *Bot (feuille)* deciduous; **à feuilles caduques** deciduous

2 *Physiol (dent)* deciduous; *(membrane)* decidual

3 *Jur (accord, loi)* null and void; *(police d'assurances)* lapsed; **devenir c.** *(accord, contrat, loi)* to lapse; **rendre c.** *(accord, loi)* to make null and void

4 *(qui n'est plus fondé ▸ théorie)* outmoded, obsolete

caducée [kadyse] **NM** *(de médecin, de pharmacien)* caduceus, doctor's badge

caducité [kadysite] **NF** *Jur (d'un accord, d'une loi)* = state of being null and void

caduque [kadyk] *voir* **caduc**

cæcum [sekɔm] **NM** *Anat & Vét* caecum

CAF [kaf] **NF** *Admin (abrév* **Caisse d'allocations familiales**) *Br* Child Benefit office, *Am* Aid to Dependant Children office

ADJ INV & ADV *Com (abrév* **coût, assurance, fret**) cif; **vente C.** sale on cif basis

cafard[1] [kafar] **NM 1** *Entom* cockroach, *Am* roach **2** *Fam (locutions)* **avoir le c.** to feel low, to feel down; **donner le c. à qn** to get sb down; **j'ai eu un coup de c. hier** I felt a bit down yesterday

cafard[2]**, -e** [kafar, -ard] **NM,F** *Fam* **1** *(dénonciateur)* sneak, *Am* snitch **2** *(faux dévot)* (religious) hypocrite[□]

ADJ *(air)* hypocritical[□], sanctimonious[□]

cafardage [kafardaʒ] **NM** *Fam* sneaking, *Am* snitching

cafarder [3] [kafarde] *Fam* **VI 1** *(rapporter)* to sneak, *Am* to snitch **2** *(être déprimé)* to feel down; **l'arrivée de l'automne me fait toujours c.** the arrival of autumn always gets me down

VT to sneak on, to tell on, *Am* to snitch on

cafardeur, -euse[1] [kafardœr, -øz] **NM,F** *Fam* sneak, *Am* snitch

cafardeux, -euse[2] [kafardø, -øz] **ADJ** *Fam (air, tempérament)* gloomy[□]; *(endroit, temps)* miserable[□], depressing[□]; **je suis** *ou* **je me sens c. en ce moment** I'm feeling low *or* down at the moment

caf'conc' [kafkɔ̃s] **NM INV** *Fam* = café where music-hall performances are given

café [kafe] **NM 1** *(boisson, graine)* coffee; **faire du c.** to make coffee; **garçon, deux cafés** waiter, two coffees; **c. allongé** = coffee diluted with hot water; **c. crème** coffee with cream; **c. filtre** filter coffee; **c. frappé** *ou* **glacé** iced coffee; **c. en grains** coffee beans; **c. instantané** *ou* **soluble** *ou* **en poudre** instant coffee; **c. au lait** *Br* white coffee, *Am* coffee with milk; *Culin* **c. liégeois** coffee ice cream sundae; **c. moulu** ground coffee; **c. nature** *ou* **noir** black coffee; **c. turc** Turkish coffee; **c. vert** unroasted coffee; **c. viennois** Viennese coffee **2** *(fin du repas)* coffee, coffee-time; **venez pour le c.** come and have coffee with us *(after the meal)* **3** *(établissement)* (licensed) café; **c. tabac** = cafe

cum tobacconist's; *Péj* **quand on les entend parler, on se croirait au c. du Commerce** their conversation is nothing but bar-room philosophizing
ADJ INV c. (au lait) coffee-coloured
• **au café ADJ** *Culin (glace, entremets)* coffee, coffee-flavoured; **éclair au c.** coffee eclair

CAFÉ

In French cafés, a small cup of strong black coffee is called "un (petit) café", "un express" or, colloquially, "un petit noir". This may be served "serré" (extra-strong), "léger" (weak) or "allongé" (diluted with hot water). An "express" with a dash of milk added is called "une noisette". A large cup of black coffee is "un grand café", "un double express" or, colloquially, "un grand noir". Coffee with frothy, steam-heated milk is called "un (grand/petit) crème". The term "café au lait" is almost never used in cafés. Parisian cafés have traditionally played an important part in the intellectual and artistic life of the city. The Café de Flore, for example, was a favourite meeting place for the existentialists.

café-concert [kafekɔ̃sɛr] (*pl* **cafés-concerts**) **NM** = café where music-hall performances are given

caféier [kafeje] **NM** *Bot* coffee tree

caféière [kafejɛr] **NF** *Hort* coffee plantation

caféine [kafein] **NF** caffeine; **sans c.** decaffeinated, caffeine-free

caféiné, -e [kafeine] **ADJ** caffeinated

cafet [kafet] **NF** *Fam* cafeteria❑

cafetan [kaftɑ̃] **NM** caftan, kaftan

cafeter [28] [kafte] = **cafter**

cafétéria [kafeterja] **NF** cafeteria

café-théâtre [kafeteatr] (*pl* **cafés-théâtres**) **NM 1** *(café avec spectacle)* = café where theatre performances take place **2** *(petit théâtre)* alternative theatre

cafetier [kaftje] **NM** café owner

cafetière [kaftjɛr] **NF 1** *(machine)* coffee maker; *(récipient)* coffee pot; **c. à pression** percolator **2** *Fam (tête)* nut, *Br* noddle

cafouillage [kafujaʒ] **NM** *Fam* **1** *(désordre)* shambles *(singulier)*, muddle; **il y a eu un c. devant les buts** there was a scramble in front of the goal **2** *Aut* misfiring❑

cafouiller [3] [kafuje] **VI** *Fam* **1** *(projet, service)* to get into a muddle; *(décideur, dirigeant)* to dither around *or* about; *(présentateur, orateur)* to get mixed up *or* into a muddle; **il a cafouillé dans ses explications** he tied himself in knots (in his explanations); *Sport* **c. avec le ballon** to fumble the ball **2** *Aut* to misfire❑

cafouilleur, -euse[1] [kafujœr, -øz] *Fam* **ADJ** *(personne)* **il est c.** he's totally disorganized❑
NM,F bungler

cafouillis [kafuji] **NM** *Fam* **1** *(désordre)* shambles *(singulier)*, muddle **2** *Aut* misfiring❑

caftan [kaftɑ̃] = **cafetan**

cafter [3] [kafte] *Fam* **VI** to sneak, *Am* to snitch
VT c. qn to sneak *or Am* to snitch on sb; **elle a cafté que j'étais pas à l'école** she sneaked *or Am* snitched on me and said I wasn't at school

cafteur, -euse [kaftœr, -øz] **NM,F** *Fam* sneak, *Am* snitch
NM *Ordinat* cookie

cage [kaʒ] **NF 1** *(pour animaux)* cage; **un animal en c.** a caged animal; **mettre un animal en c.** to cage an animal; *Fig* **une c. dorée** a gilded cage; **c. à lapins** rabbit hutch; *Fig* **habiter dans des cages à lapins** to live in shoeboxes; **c. aux lions** lions' cage; **c. à oiseau** *ou* **oiseaux** birdcage; **c. à poules** hen coop; *Fig* **habiter dans une c. à poules** to live in a shoebox
2 *Anat* **c. thoracique** rib cage
3 *Constr* **c. d'ascenseur** *Br* lift *or Am* elevator shaft; **c. d'escalier** stairwell
4 *(structure, enceinte)* **c. d'écureuil** *Br* climbing frame, *Am* jungle gym; *Élec* **c. de Faraday** Faraday cage
5 *Fam Sport* goal❑; **dans la c.** in the net❑
6 *Fam (prison)* slammer, *Br* nick
7 *Ordinat* scroll box

cageot [kaʒo] **NM 1** *(contenant)* crate; *(contenu)* crate, crateful **2** *Fam Péj (laideron)* dog, *Br* boot, *Am* beast; **quel c., sa femme!** his wife looks like *Br* the back of a bus *or Am* a Mack truck

cagette [kaʒɛt] **NF** *(contenant)* crate; *(contenu)* crate, crateful

cagibi [kaʒibi] **NM** *Br* boxroom, *Am* storage room

cagna [kaɲa] **NF 1** *Fam Arg mil* dug-out❑ **2** *Fam Vieilli (logement)* digs

cagnard, -e [kaɲar, -ard] **ADJ** *Fam Vieilli* lazy❑, idle❑
NM,F *Fam Vieilli* lazybones
NM 1 *(dans le Midi ▸ endroit)* sunny and sheltered corner; *(▸ soleil)* blazing sunshine❑; **quel c.!** what a scorcher!, *Br* it's roasting!

cagne [kaɲ] = **khâgne**

cagneux, -euse [kaɲø, -øz] **ADJ** *(jambes)* crooked; *(cheval, personne)* knock-kneed; **genoux c.** knock knees
NM,F = **khâgneux**

cagnotte [kaɲɔt] **NF 1** *(caisse, somme)* jackpot; **la c. est maintenant de 2 millions d'euros** the jackpot is now 2 million euros **2** *Fam (fonds commun)* kitty **3** *Fam (économies)* nest egg

cagot, -e [kago, -ɔt] **ADJ** *Littéraire (air, personne)* sanctimonious, holier-than-thou
NM,F 1 *(hypocrite)* hypocrite **2** *Hist* outcast *(presumed descendant of lepers under the Ancien Régime)*

cagoule [kagul] **NF 1** *(capuchon ▸ d'enfant)* balaclava; *(▸ de voleur)* hood; *(▸ de pénitent)* hood, cowl **2** *(manteau ▸ de moine)* cowl **3** *Fam (préservatif)* condom❑, rubber

cahier [kaje] **NM 1** *Scol* notebook; **c. de maths/géographie** maths/geography copybook; **c. de brouillon** notebook *(for drafts)*, *Br* roughbook; **c. de correspondance** = notebook used by schoolteachers to write notes to pupils' parents, *Br* ≃ homework diary; **c. d'exercices** exercise book; **c. de textes** *(d'élève)* homework notebook; *(de professeur)* (work) record book; **c. de travaux pratiques** lab book
2 *(recueil) Compta* **c. des achats** purchase ledger; **c. des charges** *(de matériel)* specifications; *(dans un contrat)* terms and conditions; **c. de revendications** claims register
3 *(d'un journal)* section
4 *Typ* gathering
• **cahiers NMPL 1** *Littérature (mémoires)* diary, memoirs **2** *Hist* **cahiers de doléances** book of grievances **3** *Journ* review, journal

cahin-caha [kaɛ̃kaa] **ADV aller c.** *(marcheur)* to hobble along; *(entreprise, projet)* to struggle along; **comment va-t-il? – c.** how is he? – struggling along; **les affaires vont c.** business is slow *or* slack

cahot [kao] **NM** jolt, judder

cahotage [kaɔtaʒ] = **cahotement**

cahotant, -e [kaɔtɑ̃, -ɑ̃t] **ADJ** *(chemin)* bumpy, rough; *(voiture)* jolting, juddering

cahotement [kaɔtmɑ̃] **NM** *(fait de cahoter)* jolting, juddering; *(secousse)* jolt, judder

cahoter [3] [kaɔte] **VI** *(véhicule)* to jolt (along)
VT *(passagers)* to jolt, to bump about; *(voiture)* to jolt

cahoteux, -euse [kaɔtø, -øz] **ADJ** bumpy, rough

CAHT [seaaʃte] **NM** *Com (abrév* **chiffre d'affaires hors taxes)** pre-tax turnover

cahute [kayt] **NF 1** *(abri)* shack, hut **2** *Péj (foyer)* hovel

caïd [kaid] **NM 1** *Fam (dans une matière)* wizard; *(en sport)* ace; *(d'une équipe)* star **2** *Fam (chef ▸ de bande)* gang leader; *(▸ d'une entreprise, d'un parti)* big shot, bigwig; **un c. de la drogue** a drug(s) baron; **jouer au c., faire son c.** to act tough **3** *Hist* caid, local governor *(of indigenous origin, under French rule)*

caïdat [kaida] **NM 1** *(en Afrique du Nord)* caidship **2** *Fam (d'un chef de bande)* gang leadership

caillage [kajaʒ] **NM** *(du lait)* curdling; *Physiol (du sang)* coagulation, clotting

caillant, -e [kajɑ̃, -ɑ̃t] **ADJ** *Belg Fam* freezing (cold); **il fait c.** it's freezing (cold) *or Br* baltic

caillassage [kajasaʒ] **NM** *(acte de vandalisme)* throwing stones

caillasse [kajas] **NF 1** *(éboulis)* loose stones, scree
2 *Fam Péj (mauvais sol)* stones❑; **je ne peux rien planter, c'est de la c.** I can't plant anything, the ground's nothing but stones
3 *Géol* (gravelly) marl
4 *Fam (argent)* dough, *Br* dosh

caillasser [3] [kajase] **VT** to throw stones at

caille [kaj] **NF 1** *Orn* quail **2** *Fam (en appellatif)* **ma (petite) c.** pet, sweetheart

caillé [kaje] **NM** curds
ADJ M *(lait)* curdled

caillebotis [kajbɔti] **NM** *Tech* **1** *(grille)* grating **2** *(plancher)* duckboard

caillebotte [kajbɔt] **NF** curds

caillement [kajmɑ̃] **NM** *(du lait)* curdling; *Physiol (du sang)* coagulation, clotting

cailler [3] [kaje] **VI** *(lait)* to curdle; *Physiol (sang)* to coagulate, to clot; **faire c. du lait** to curdle milk
V IMPERSONNEL *Fam* **ça caille ici!** it's freezing *or Br* baltic here!
VT *(lait)* to curdle; *(sang)* to coagulate, to clot
VPR se cailler 1 *Fam (avoir très froid)* to be freezing **2** *très Fam* **se c. les miches, se les c.** to be freezing one's *Br* arse *or Am* ass off; **on se les caille dehors!** it's *Br* bloody *or Am* goddamn freezing outside!

caillera [kajra] **NF** *Fam Péj (verlan de* **racaille) 1** *(voyous)* trash, *Br* yobs **2** *(voyou)* lout, *Br* yob

caillette [kajɛt] **NF** *Zool & Vét* rennet stomach

caillot [kajo] **NM** *(de lait)* (milk) curd; *Physiol & Méd* **c. (de sang)** bloodclot

caillou, -x [kaju] **NM 1** *(gén)* stone
2 *Constr* **cailloux d'empierrement** road metal
3 *(en joaillerie)* stone; **c. du Rhin** rhinestone
4 *Fam (diamant)* rock, sparkler
5 *Fam (tête)* head❑, nut; **elle en a dans le c.** she's a smart cookie; **il n'a plus un cheveu** *ou* **un poil sur le c.** he's as bald as a coot
6 *Fam* **le C.** *(la Nouvelle-Calédonie)* New Caledonia ❑

cailloutage [kajutaʒ] **NM** *Constr* **1** *(empierrement ▸ d'une route)* metalling; *(▸ d'une voie ferrée)* ballasting **2** *(pierres ▸ d'une route)* road metal; *(▸ d'une voie ferrée)* ballast

caillouter [3] [kajute] **VT** *Constr (route)* to metal; *(voie ferrée)* to ballast

caillouteux, -euse [kajutø, -øz] **ADJ** *(chemin, champ)* stony; *(plage)* pebbly, shingly

cailloutis [kajuti] **NM** *Constr* gravel, *Br* chippings; *(de route)* road metal

caïman [kaimɑ̃] **NM** *Zool* caiman, cayman

Caïn [kaɛ̃] **NPR** *Bible* Cain

Caire [kɛr] **NM** *Géog* **Le C.** Cairo

cairn [kɛrn] **NM** cairn

cairote [kɛrɔt] **ADJ** of/from Cairo
• **Cairote NMF** Cairene

CAISSE [kɛs]

- case **A1, 2, B3**
- box **A1, 3**
- bodywork **C1**
- till **E1**
- cash **E3**
- fund **F**
- crate **A1**
- cylinder **B1**
- car **C2**
- check-out **E2**
- bank **E4**

NF A. 1 *(pour marchandises ▸ gén)* case; *(▸ à claire-voie)* crate; *(de rangement)* box, chest; *(à thé etc)* chest; **mettre en c.** to box; **c. américaine** cardboard box; **c. d'emballage** packing crate; **c. à outils** toolbox; *très Fam Fig* **lâcher** *ou* **larguer une c.** to fart, *Br* to let off, *Am* to lay one
2 *(boîte de 12 bouteilles)* case; **on a bu deux caisses de champagne** we drank two cases of champagne
3 *Hort* box, tub; **mettre un arbuste en c.** to plant a shrub in a tub
B. 1 *Mus (fût de tambour)* cylinder; **c. claire** side *or* snare drum; **c. de résonance** resonance chamber, resonating body; **c. roulante** side drum; **grosse c.** *(tambour)* bass drum; *(musicien)* bass drummer

2 *Mus (corps de violon)* belly, sounding board
3 *(d'horloge)* case, casing

C. 1 *(carrosserie)* body, bodywork
2 *Fam Aut (voiture)* car[□]; **vieille c.** old banger; **t'es venu en c.?** did you come by car?[□]
3 *Rail* water tank

D. 1 *Anat* **c. du tympan** middle ear, *Spéc* tympanic cavity
2 *Fam (locution)* **il part** *ou* **s'en va de la c.** his lungs are wearing out

E. 1 *(tiroir)* till; *(petit coffre)* cashbox; **c. (enregistreuse)** till *or* cash register; **tenir la c.** to be the cashier; **partir avec la c.** to run off with the takings; *aussi Fig* **on l'a pris en train de se servir dans la c.** he was caught helping himself from *or* with his hand in the till; **faire une c. commune** to put one's money together, to have a kitty; *Écon* **les caisses de l'État** the State coffers
2 *Com (lieu de paiement ▸ d'un supermarché)* check-out, till; *(▸ d'un cinéma, d'un casino, d'un magasin)* cash desk; *(▸ d'une banque)* cashier's desk; **c.** *(sur panneau)* please pay here; **passer à la c.** *(dans un magasin)* to go to the cash desk; *(dans un supermarché)* to go through the check-out; *(dans une banque)* to go to the cashier's desk; *(se faire payer)* to be paid; *(recevoir son salaire)* to collect one's wages; *Fam* **après ce qu'il a dit au patron, il n'a plus qu'à passer à la c.!** after what he said to the boss, he'll be getting his *Br* cards *or Am* pink slip!; *Com* **c. éclair** *(distributeur) Br* cashpoint, *Am* ATM; *Com* **c. rapide** *(dans un supermarché)* express checkout
3 *(argent ▸ d'un commerce)* cash (in the till), takings; **faire la** *ou* **sa c.** to balance the cash, to do the till, *Br* to cash up
4 *Banque* **c. de crédit** credit union; **c. d'épargne** ≃ savings bank; **c. d'épargne-logement** *Br* ≃ building society, *Am* ≃ savings and loan association; **C. nationale d'épargne** ≃ National Savings Bank; **c. régionale** ≃ local (bank) branch

F. 1 *Admin (organisme chargé de la gestion des fonds)* fund; *(bureau)* office; **C. d'allocations familiales** *Br* Child Benefit office, *Am* Aid to Dependant Children office; **c. d'amortissement** sinking fund; **c. de chômage** unemployment fund; **c. de compensation** = equalization fund for payments such as child benefit, sickness benefit, pensions; **la C. des dépôts et consignations** Deposit and Consignment Office *(national French savings and banking institution which manages National Savings Bank funds and local community funds)*; **c. des écoles** = local schools' fund for extra-curricular activities, school meals etc; **C. nationale d'assurance vieillesse** = French government department dealing with benefit payments relating to old age; *Can* **c. populaire** = type of credit union; **c. de prévoyance** provident fund; **c. primaire d'assurance maladie** = French Social Security department in charge of medical insurance; **c. de retraite** pension fund; **c. de Sécurité sociale** Social Security office
2 *(fonds)* fund, funds; **nous avons une c. pour les cas sociaux** we have a fund for needy individuals; **c. noire** slush fund

• **en caisse** ADJ **1** *Com* **argent en c.** cash **2** *Hort* **arbuste en c.** boxed shrub ADV **avoir 500 euros en c.** *Com* to have 500 euros in the till; *Fig* to have 500 euros in hand; **je n'ai plus rien en c.** *Com* my till's empty; *Fig* I'm broke

---

caissette [kesɛt] NF **1** *(contenant)* small box **2** *(contenu)* small boxful

caissier, -ère [kesje, -ɛr] NM,F *Com (d'une boutique, d'un casino, d'une banque)* cashier; *(d'un supermarché) Br* check-out operator *or Am* clerk; *(de cinéma)* cashier, *Br* box-office assistant

caisson [kɛsɔ̃] NM **1** *Constr (pour fondation)* caisson, cofferdam **2** *Archit (pour plafond)* coffer, caisson, lacunar **3** *Tech* **c. hyperbare** bathysphere; *Méd* **la maladie** *ou* **le mal des caissons** decompression sickness, the bends **5** *Tech* **c. de graves** subwoofer **6** *Nucl* (nuclear reactor) casing **7** *Hist & Mil* caisson, ammunition wagon **8** *Fam* **se faire sauter le c.** to blow one's brains out

cajoler [3] [kaʒɔle] VT *(enfant)* to cuddle

cajolerie [kaʒɔlri] NF *(manifestation de tendresse)* cuddle; **faire des cajoleries à qn** to cuddle sb

cajoleur, -euse [kaʒɔlœr, -øz] ADJ *(affectueux ▸ parent, ton)* affectionate, loving

cajou [kaʒu] *voir* **noix**

cake [kɛk] NM *Culin* fruit cake

cakos [kekɔs] NMF *Fam Péj* **1** *(ringard)* useless idiot, *Br* prat **2** *(locution)* **faire le c.** to show off, to pose[□]

cal¹ [kal] NM **1** *Méd (durillon ▸ à la main)* callus; *(▸ au pied)* corn **2** *Bot & Méd* callus

cal² *(abrév écrite* **calorie***)* cal

calabrais, -e [kalabrɛ, -ɛz] ADJ Calabrian
NM *(dialecte)* Calabrian dialect
• **Calabrais, -e** NM,F Calabrian

Calabre [kalabr] NF *Géog* **la C.** Calabria

calage [kalaʒ] NM *Tech* **1** *(de pied de chaise)* wedging; *(de roue)* chocking
2 *(fait d'appuyer)* propping (up)
3 *(de manivelle à un axe)* wedging, keying; *(de roue à un axe)* fixing; *(de valve)* jamming, locking
4 *Aut (de moteur)* stalling
5 *(réglage)* adjustment; *(de valve, moteur)* tuning; *Aut* **c. d'allumage** ignition timing
6 *Typ* setting

calamar [kalamar] = **calmar**

calamine [kalamin] NF **1** *Chim* calamine **2** *Aut* carbon deposit

calamistré, -e [kalamistre] ADJ *(cheveux)* brilliantined

calamité [kalamite] NF **1** *(événement)* calamity, catastrophe, disaster **2** *Fam Hum (personne)* walking disaster

calamiteux, -euse [kalamitø, -øz] ADJ disastrous, catastrophic

calancher [3] [kalɑ̃ʃe] VI *Fam* to croak, *Br* to snuff it

calandrage [kalɑ̃draʒ] NM *Tex & Typ* calendering

calandre [kalɑ̃dr] NF **1** *Aut* radiator grille **2** *Tex & Typ* calender

calandrer [3] [kalɑ̃dre] VT *Tex & Typ* to calender

calandreur, -euse [kalɑ̃drœr, -øz] N *Tex & Typ* calenderer

calanque [kalɑ̃k] NF *Géol* (Mediterranean) creek

calao [kalao] NM *Orn* hornbill

calbar [kalbar], **calbute** [kalbyt] NM *Fam Br* boxers, *Am* shorts, skivvies

calcaire [kalkɛr] ADJ *Géol & Chim (roche, relief)* limestone *(avant n)*; *(sol)* chalky, *Spéc* calcareous; *(sel)* calcium *(avant n)*; *(eau)* hard
NM **1** *Géol* limestone **2** *Chim (dans une casserole) Br* fur, *Am* sediment

calcanéum [kalkaneɔm] NM *Anat* calcaneum

calcédoine [kalsedwan] NF *Minér* chalcedony

calcif [kalsif] NM *Fam Br* boxers, *Am* shorts, skivvies

calcination [kalsinasjɔ̃] NF *Tech* calcination

calciner [3] [kalsine] VT **1** *(transformer en chaux)* to calcine **2** *(brûler)* to burn to a cinder, to char **3** *(chauffer ▸ brique, minerai)* to calcine; **désert calciné par le soleil** sun-baked desert
VPR **se calciner 1** *(viande)* to burn to a cinder **2** *(être chauffé ▸ brique, minerai)* to calcine

calcium [kalsjɔm] NM *Chim* calcium

calcul¹ [kalkyl] NM **1** *Math (suite d'opérations)* calculation; **faire un c.** to do *or* make a calculation; **je fais des calculs à longueur de journée** I handle figures all day long; **ça reviendra moins cher, fais le c.!** it'll be cheaper, just work it out!; **faire le c. de qch** to work sth out, to calculate sth; **le raisonnement est correct, mais le c. est faux** the method's right but the calculations are wrong; **erreur de c.** miscalculation; *Math* **c. algébrique** calculus; *Math* **c. différentiel/intégral/vectoriel** differential/integral/vector calculus; *Math* **c. des probabilités** probability theory
2 *Scol* **le c.** sums, arithmetic; **être mauvais en c.** to be bad at sums *or* arithmetic; **apprendre le c.** to learn (how) to count; **c. mental** *(matière)* mental arithmetic; *(opération)* mental calculation
3 *(estimation)* calculation, computation; **d'après mes calculs** according to my calculations; **tous calculs faits, le piano devrait pouvoir passer** if I've/we've/*etc* worked it out properly, we should get the piano through; **ça a été un bon c. de notre part** it was a good move on our part; **ce n'est pas un bon c.** it's not a good way of going about things; **un mauvais** *ou* **faux c.** a bad move
4 *Péj (manœuvre)* scheme; **par c.** out of (calculated) self-interest, from selfish *or* ulterior motives; **sans c.** without any *or* with no ulterior motive

calcul² [kalkyl] NM *Méd* stone, *Spéc* calculus; **c. biliaire** gall stone; **c. urinaire** *ou* **rénal** kidney stone

calculable [kalkylabl] ADJ *(prix)* calculable; *(dégâts)* estimable; **c'est c. de tête** you can work it out it in your head

calculateur, -trice [kalkylatœr, -tris] ADJ *Péj* calculating, scheming
NM,F **1** *(qui compte)* **c'est un bon/mauvais c.** he's good/bad at figures *or* sums **2** *Péj (personne intéressée)* **un fin c.** a shrewd operator; **un ignoble c.** a scheming character
NM **1** *Vieilli Ordinat (ordinateur)* computer; **c. digital** *ou* **numérique** digital computer; **c. électronique** electronic computer **2** *Aut* **c. embarqué** onboard computer
• **calculatrice** NF *Math (machine)* calculator; **calculatrice de bureau** desktop calculator; **calculatrice imprimante** print-out calculator; **calculatrice de poche** pocket calculator

calculé, -e [kalkyle] ADJ *(risque)* calculated; *(méchanceté)* premeditated, calculated; *(insolence)* deliberate; **"ça ne m'étonne pas de toi", lui dit-il avec une méchanceté calculée** "that doesn't surprise me coming from you," he said with deliberate malice; **sa générosité est calculée** his/her generosity is prompted by self-interest, he/she has an ulterior motive in being generous

calculer [3] [kalkyle] VT **1** *(dépenses, dimension, quantité etc)* to calculate, to work out; **c. qch de tête** *ou* **mentalement** to work sth out in one's head; **c. vite** to be quick at figures, to calculate quickly
2 *(avec parcimonie ▸ pourboire, dépenses)* to work out to the last penny, to budget carefully
3 *(évaluer ▸ avantages, inconvénients, chances, risque)* to calculate, to weigh up; **mal c. qch** to miscalculate sth; **c. que...** to work out *or* to calculate that...; **j'ai calculé qu'il me faudrait deux heures pour aller à Toulouse** I've worked out that it'll take me two hours to get to Toulouse; **tout bien calculé** taking everything into account
4 *(préparer ▸ gestes, effets, efforts)* to calculate, to work out; **j'ai tout calculé** I have it all worked out; *Sport* **c. son élan** to work out one's run-up; *Fam* **c. son coup** to plan one's moves carefully[□]; **tu as bien calculé ton coup!** you had it all figured out!; **tu as mal calculé ton coup!** you got it all wrong!
VI *Math* to calculate; **il calcule vite et bien** he's quick at arithmetic

calculette [kalkylɛt] NF **1** *Math* pocket calculator **2** *Fam (personne souffrant d'acné)* pizza-face

caldoche [kaldɔʃ] ADJ = relating to the white inhabitants of New Caledonia
• **Caldoche** NMF = white inhabitant of New Caledonia

cale [kal] NF **1** *(pour bloquer ▸ un meuble)* wedge; *(▸ une roue)* wedge, chock; **mettre une voiture sur cales** to put a car on blocks
2 *(sur rails)* chock
3 *Naut (d'un bateau)* hold; **c. à charbon** bunker
4 *Naut (d'un quai)* slipway; **mettre sur cales** to lay down; **le bateau est sur cales** the boat is on the stocks; **c. de construction** *ou* **de lancement** slip, slipway; **c. de radoub** graving *or* dry dock; **c. sèche** dry dock; **être en c. sèche** to be in dry dock

calé, -e [kale] ADJ *Fam* **1** *(instruit)* **il est c. en histoire/maths** he's brilliant at history/maths **2** *(difficile ▸ problème)* tough **3** *Belg (prêt)* ready[□]

calebasse [kalbas] NF **1** *Bot (fruit, récipient)* calabash, gourd **2** *Fam (tête)* nut, *Br* noddle

calèche [kalɛʃ] NF barouche, calash; **une promenade en c.** a ride in a horse-drawn carriage

calecif [kalsif] = **calcif**

caleçon [kalsɔ̃] NM **1** *(sous-vêtement)* boxer shorts; **c. long, caleçons longs** long johns **2** *(pour *nager)* **c. de bain** swimming trunks **3** *(pantalon)* leggings

calédonien, -enne [kaledɔnjɛ̃, -ɛn] **ADJ** Caledonian

• **Calédonien, -enne NM,F** Caledonian

calembour [kalɑ̃bur] **NM** play on words, pun; **faire un c.** to make a pun

calembredaine [kalɑ̃brədɛn] **NF** *(plaisanterie)* joke

• **calembredaines NFPL** *(sornettes)* balderdash, nonsense

calendes [kalɑ̃d] **NFPL 1** *Antiq* calends **2** *(locution)* **renvoyer** *ou* **remettre qch aux c. grecques** to put sth off *or* to postpone sth indefinitely

calendos [kalɑ̃dos] **NM** *Fam* Camembert

calendrier [kalɑ̃drije] **NM 1** *(tableau, livret, système)* calendar; *Hist* **c. grégorien/républicain** Gregorian/Republican calendar; **c. perpétuel/à effeuiller** perpetual/tear-off calendar **2** *(emploi du temps)* timetable, schedule; *(plan ► de réunions)* schedule, calendar; *(► d'un festival)* calendar; *(► d'un voyage)* schedule; **j'ai un c. très chargé** I have a very busy schedule *or* timetable; **établir un c.** to draw up a timetable *or* schedule; **c. de campagne** campaign schedule; *Mktg* media schedule; *Bourse* **c. des émissions** calendar of issues; *Bourse* **c. de remboursement** repayment schedule; *Sport* **c. des rencontres** *Br* fixture list, *Am* match schedule

cale-pied [kalpje] *(pl* **cale-pieds)** **NM** *Cyclisme* toe-clip

calepin [kalpɛ̃] **NM 1** *(carnet)* notebook **2** *Belg (serviette)* briefcase

caler [3] [kale] **VT 1** *(armoire, pied de chaise)* to wedge, to steady with a wedge; *(roue)* to chock, to wedge; *(chargement)* to secure; *Can (casquette, chapeau)* to jam on; **c. une porte** *(pour la fermer)* to wedge a door shut; *(pour qu'elle reste ouverte)* to wedge a door open

2 *(installer)* to prop up; **c. qn sur des coussins** to prop sb up on cushions; **bien calé dans son fauteuil** comfortably settled *or* ensconced in his/her armchair

3 *Fam (remplir)* **ça cale (l'estomac)** it fills you up, it's filling; **je suis calé** I'm full (up)

4 *(soupape)* to jam, to lock

5 *Naut (mât)* to house; *(voile)* to strike

VI 1 *Aut (moteur, voiture)* to stall; **j'ai calé** I've stalled

2 *(s'arrêter ► devant un problème)* to give up; *(► dans un repas)* to be full; **prends mon gâteau, je cale** have my cake, I'm full

3 *Naut* **c. 15 pieds** to draw 15 feet, to have a draught of 15 feet; **c. trop** to be too deep in water

4 *Can (enfoncer)* to sink

5 *Can (se dégarnir)* to have a receding hairline

VPR se caler 1 *(s'installer)* **se c. dans un fauteuil** to settle oneself comfortably in an armchair **2** *Fam (locution)* **se c. les joues, se les c.** *(bien manger)* to stuff one's face

caleter [28] [kalte] = **calter**

calfat [kalfa] **NM** *Naut (ouvrier)* calker, caulker

calfatage [kalfataʒ] **NM** *Naut* calking, caulking

calfater [3] [kalfate] **VT** *Naut* to calk, to caulk

calfeutrage [kalføtraʒ], **calfeutrement** [kalføtrəmɑ̃] **NM** *(d'une fenêtre, d'une porte)* draught-proofing; *(d'une ouverture)* stopping up, filling

calfeutrer [3] [kalføtre] **VT** *(ouverture)* to stop up, to fill; *(fenêtre, porte ► gén)* to make draught-proof; *(► avec un bourrelet)* to weather-strip

VPR se calfeutrer 1 *(s'isoler du froid)* to make oneself snug **2** *Fig (s'isoler)* to shut oneself up *or* away

calibrage [kalibraʒ] **NM 1** *(d'une pièce, d'un obus, d'un tube)* calibration

2 *Com (de fruits, d'œufs)* grading

3 *Phot (d'épreuve)* trimming

4 *Typ* cast-off

calibre [kalibr] **NM 1** *Ind & Tech* gauge; **c. d'épaisseur** feeler gauge, set of feelers

2 *Constr* template

3 *Mil (d'un canon, d'une arme)* bore, calibre; *(d'une balle)* calibre, size; **un canon de 70 calibres** a 70-millimetre gun; **fusil de c. 8 mm** 8-mm calibre rifle; *Sport* 8-mm gauge gun; **de gros c.** large-bore; **de petit c.** small-bore

4 *Com* grade, (standardized *or* standard) size

5 *Tech & Ind (pour la reproduction)* template

6 *Fam Arg crime (revolver) Br* shooter, *Am* rod

7 *Fig (type)* class, calibre; **de ce c.** of this calibre *or* class; **il est d'un autre c.** he's not in the same league

calibrer [3] [kalibre] **VT 1** *(usiner ► obus, revolver, tube)* to calibrate

2 *Com* to grade

3 *Phot (épreuve)* to trim

4 *Typ* to cast off

calibreur [kalibrœr] **NM** *Tech & Ind* calibrator; *Aut* **c. d'air** air bleed jet, air correction jet

calice [kalis] **NM 1** *Bot & Physiol* calyx **2** *Rel* chalice

calicot [kaliko] **NM 1** *Tex* calico **2** *(bande)* banner **3** *Vieilli (commis)* draper's assistant

califat [kalifa] **NM** caliphate

calife [kalif] **NM** caliph; **vouloir être c. à la place du c.** to want to be top dog

Californie [kalifɔrni] **NF** *Géog* **la C.** California

californien, -enne [kalifɔrnjɛ̃, -ɛn] **ADJ** Californian

• **Californien, -enne NM,F** Californian

californium [kalifɔrnjɔm] **NM** *Chim* californium

califourchon [kalifurʃɔ̃] **NM** *Can* crotch

• **à califourchon ADV** astride; **être à c. sur qch** to be astride sth, to bestride sth; **monter** *ou* **s'asseoir** *ou* **se mettre à c. sur qch** to sit astride *or* to straddle sth; *Équitation* **monter à c.** *(à cheval)* to ride astride

câlin, -e [kalɛ̃, -in] **ADJ 1** *(regard, voix)* tender **2** *(personne)* affectionate

NM cuddle; **faire un c. à qn** to give sb a cuddle; **faire des câlins à qn** to (kiss and) cuddle sb

câliner [3] [kaline] **VT** to (kiss and) cuddle, to pet; **se faire c.** to be cuddled

VPR se câliner to cuddle

câlinerie [kalinri] **NF** *(qualité)* tenderness; *(geste)* caress, cuddle; **faire des câlineries à qn** to kiss and cuddle sb

calisson [kalisɔ̃] **NM** *Culin* **c. (d'Aix)** = lozenge-shaped sweet made of iced marzipan

calleux, -euse [kalø, -øz] **ADJ** *(main, peau)* callous, horny

call-girl [kɔlgœrl] *(pl* **call-girls)** **NF** call girl

calligramme [kaligram] **NM** calligramme

calligraphe [kaligraf] **NMF** calligrapher

calligraphie [kaligrafi] **NF** calligraphy

calligraphier [9] [kaligrafje] **VT 1** to calligraph **2** *(écrire avec soin)* **c. qch** to write sth in a beautiful hand

calligraphique [kaligrafik] **ADJ** calligraphic

callosité [kalozite] **NF** *Physiol* callosity, callus

calmant, -e [kalmɑ̃, -ɑ̃t] **ADJ 1** *Pharm (contre l'anxiété)* tranquillizing, sedative; *(contre la douleur)* painkilling **2** *(propos)* soothing

NM *Pharm* **1** *(contre l'anxiété)* tranquillizer, sedative; **prendre des calmants** to be on tranquillizers **2** *(contre la douleur)* painkiller

calmar [kalmar] **NM** *Zool (mollusque)* squid

calme [kalm] **ADJ 1** *(sans agitation ► quartier, rue, moment)* quiet, peaceful; *(► sans tension)* calm; **nous avons passé trois jours calmes** we had three quiet days

2 *(sans mouvement ► eau, étang, mer)* still, calm; *(► air)* still; **par temps c.** when there's no wind

3 *(maître de soi)* calm, self-possessed; *(tranquille)* quiet; **parler d'une voix c.** to talk calmly

4 *Com (peu productif ► marché)* quiet, dull, slack; **les affaires sont calmes en ce moment** business is slack *or* quiet at the moment

NMF *(personne)* calm *or* placid person

NM 1 *(absence d'agitation)* peace, quiet, calm; *(de l'air, de la nuit)* stillness; **avec c.** calmly; **du c.!** *(ne vous agitez pas)* keep quiet!; *(ne paniquez pas)* keep cool!; **un moment de c.** a lull; **je n'ai pas eu un moment de c. de toute la journée!** I haven't had a minute's peace all day!; **le c.** peace and quiet; **être au c.** to have *or* to enjoy peace and quiet; **il faut rester au c.** you should avoid excitement; **manifester dans le c.** to hold a peaceful demonstration; **ramener le c.** *(dans une assemblée)* to restore order; *(dans une situation)* to calm things down; **c'est le c. avant la tempête** this is the calm before the storm

2 *(silence)* silence; **faire qch dans le c.** to do sth quietly; **allons les enfants, on rentre dans le c.!** come on children, let's go back in quietly now!

3 *(sang-froid)* composure, calm; **du c.!** calm down!; **une femme d'un grand c.** a very composed woman; **garder son c.** to keep calm; **perdre son c.** to lose one's composure; **retrouver son c.** to calm down, to regain one's composure

4 *(vent)* calm; **c'est le c. plat** *(en mer)* there's no wind; *(il ne se passe rien)* there's nothing happening; *(à la Bourse)* the Stock Exchange is in the doldrums; **c'est le c. plat dans ma vie sentimentale** my love life is in the doldrums, there's nothing happening in my love life

• **calmes NMPL** *Météo* **calmes équatoriaux** doldrums

> Attention: ne pas confondre **calm** et **quiet** lorsqu'on traduit **calme.** Le terme **calm** se rapporte généralement à la maîtrise de soi, alors que **quiet** désigne un comportement ou une situation paisible.

calmement [kalməmɑ̃] **ADV** calmly, quietly

calmer [3] [kalme] **VT 1** *(rendre serein ► enfant, opposant, foule)* to calm down; **essaie de c. les enfants** try and get the children to calm down; **nous devons c. les esprits** *(dans un groupe)* we must put everybody's mind at rest; *(dans la nation)* we must put the people's minds at rest; **c. le jeu** *Sport* to calm the game down; *Fig* to calm things down; *Fam* **je vais le c., moi!** I'll shut him up! **2** *(dépassionner ► mécontentement)* to soothe, to calm; *(► colère)* to calm, to appease; *(► querelle)* to pacify, to defuse; *(► débat)* to restore order to **3** *(diminuer ► fièvre, inflammation)* to bring down; *(► douleur)* to soothe, to ease; *(► faim)* to satisfy, to appease; *(► soif)* to quench; *(► désespoir, crainte)* to ease, to allay; *(► désir, passion, enthousiasme)* to dampen; *(► impatience)* to relieve; **pour c. sa frayeur** to dispel *or* to allay his fear; **ça devrait leur c. les nerfs** that should soothe their (frayed) nerves

VPR se calmer 1 *(devenir serein)* to calm down; **attends que les choses se calment** wait for things to calm down

2 *(se taire) Br* to quieten *or Am* to quiet down

3 *(s'affaiblir ► dispute, douleur)* to die down *or* away, to ease off *or* up; *(► fièvre)* to die *or* to go down; *(► anxiété)* to fade; *(► passion)* to fade away, to cool; *(► faim, soif)* to die down, to be appeased; **la douleur s'est calmée brusquement/peu à peu** the pain died away abruptly/eased up gradually

4 *Météo (averse)* to ease off; *(mer)* to become calm; *(vent)* to die down, to drop; *(tempête)* to die down, to blow over, to abate

calmos [kalmos] **EXCLAM** *Fam* chill (out)!, take it easy!

calomel [kalɔmɛl] **NM** *Chim & Pharm* calomel

calomniateur, -trice [kalɔmnjatœr, -tris] **ADJ** *(propos)* slanderous; *(écrit)* libellous

NM,F slanderer; *(par écrit)* libeller

calomnie [kalɔmni] **NF** *(oral)* slander, calumny; *(écrit)* libel; **ce ne sont que des calomnies** it's all lies; **répandre des calomnies sur qn** to cast aspersions on sb; **être en butte à la c.** to be a victim of slander/libel, to be slandered/libelled

calomnier [9] [kalɔmnje] **VT** *(dénigrer ► oralement)* to slander, *Sout* to calumniate; *(► par écrit)* to libel

calomnieuse [kalɔmnjøz] *voir* **calomnieux**

calomnieusement [kalɔmnjøzmɑ̃] **ADV** *(oralement)* slanderously; *(par écrit)* libellously

calomnieux, -euse [kalɔmnjø, -øz] **ADJ** *(propos)* slanderous; *(écrit)* libellous

caloporteur [kalɔpɔrtœr] *Tech & Ind* **ADJ M fluide** *ou* **liquide c.** coolant

NM coolant

calorie [kalɔri] **NF** *Phys & Physiol* calorie; **riche en calories** high in calories; **attention aux calories!** watch the calories!; **un régime basses calories** a low-calorie diet; **grande c.** kilocalorie, large calorie

calorifère [kalɔrifɛr] ADJ **1** *(produisant de la chaleur)* heat-giving **2** *(transportant de la chaleur)* heat-conveying

NM **1** *(poêle)* stove **2** *Can (radiateur)* heater

calorifique [kalɔrifik] ADJ *Phys (perte)* heat *(avant n)*; *Physiol (valeur)* calorific

calorifuge [kalɔrifyʒ] ADJ heat-insulating; **le bois est c.** wood is a poor conductor of heat

NM heat insulator; *(pour chaudière, pour tuyau)* lagging

calorifugeage [kalɔrifyʒaʒ] NM (heat) insulation; *(de chaudière, de tuyau)* lagging

calorifuger [17] [kalɔrifyʒe] VT to insulate; *(chaudière, tuyau)* to lag

calorimètre [kalɔrimɛtr] NM *Phys* calorimeter

calorimétrie [kalɔrimetri] NF *Phys* calorimetry

calorimétrique [kalɔrimetrik] ADJ *Phys* calorimetric, calorimetrical

caloriporteur [kalɔripɔrtœr] = **caloporteur**

calorique [kalɔrik] ADJ *Phys & Physiol* calorific, caloric; **ration c.** calorie intake

calorisation [kalɔrizasjɔ̃] NF *Métal* calorization

calot [kalo] NM **1** *Mil (coiffure militaire)* (forage) cap **2** *(bille)* big marble

• **calots** NMPL *Fam (yeux)* peepers

calotin [kalɔtɛ̃] NM *Fam Péj* holy Joe

calotte [kalɔt] NF **1** *(petit bonnet)* skullcap; *Rel (de prêtre)* calotte, skullcap; *(partie du chapeau)* crown; *Fam* **la c.** the clergy□

2 *Fam (tape)* clout; *(sur la joue)* slap□; **flanquer une c. à qn** to clout sb (in the face); *(sur la joue)* to give sb a slap; **(se) prendre** *ou* **recevoir une c.** to get a clout; *(sur la joue)* to get a slap

3 *Anat* **c. du crâne** *ou* **crânienne** top of the skull

4 *Astron* **c. polaire** polar region

5 *Littéraire* **la c. des cieux** the dome *or* vault of heaven

6 *Math* **c. sphérique** portion of a sphere

7 *Géog* **c. glaciaire** icecap

calotter [3] [kalɔte] VT *Fam* to clout; *(sur la joue)* to slap□

calquage [kalkaʒ] NM **1** *(reproduction)* tracing **2** *Fam (imitation ▸ d'une œuvre d'art)* imitating□

calque [kalk] NM **1** *(feuille)* piece of tracing paper; *(matériau)* tracing paper

2 *(dessin)* tracing, traced design; **prendre** *ou* **faire un c. de** to trace

3 *(copie ▸ d'un tableau, d'un texte)* exact copy, replica

4 *(répétition ▸ d'une attitude, d'une erreur)* carbon copy

5 *Ling* calque, loan translation

calquer [3] [kalke] VT **1** *(motif)* to trace **2** *(imiter ▸ manières, personne)* to copy exactly; **il calque sa conduite sur celle de son frère** he models his behaviour on his brother's **3** *Ling* to translate literally; **calqué sur** *ou* **de l'espagnol** translated literally from Spanish

calter [3] [kalte] *Fam* VI to beat it, *Br* to clear off, *Am* to split

VPR **se calter** to beat it, *Br* to clear off, *Am* to split

calumet [kalymɛ] NM peace pipe; **fumer le c. de la paix** to smoke the pipe of peace; *Fig* to make peace

calva [kalva] NM *Fam* Calvados□

calvados [kalvados] NM *(alcool)* Calvados

calvaire [kalvɛr] NM **1** *Rel (crucifixion)* **le C. (de Jésus)** the suffering of Jesus on the Cross; **le C.** (Mount) Calvary

2 *(monument ▸ à plusieurs croix)* calvary; *(▸ à une croix)* wayside cross

3 *Beaux-Arts* calvary, road to Calvary

4 *Fig (souffrance)* ordeal; **sa maladie a été un long c.** his/her illness was a long ordeal

5 *Can Joual (juron)* bastard; **mon c.!** you bastard!

EXCLAM *Can Joual* shit!

• **en calvaire** ADV *Can Joual* **1** *(beaucoup)* a lot□, very much□; **c'est beau en c.** it's really nice **2 être en c. (contre qn)** to be fuming mad (with sb)

calvinisme [kalvinism] NM *Rel* Calvinism

calviniste [kalvinist] *Rel* ADJ Calvinist, Calvinistic

NMF Calvinist

calvitie [kalvisi] NF **1** *(absence de cheveux)* baldness; **c. naissante** incipient baldness; **c. précoce** premature baldness **2** *Fam (emplacement)* bald spot□

calypso [kalipso] NM *Mus & (danse)* calypso

cama [kama] NM *Belg Fam (camarade)* pal, *Br* mate, *Am* buddy

camaïeu, -x [kamajø] NM *Beaux-Arts* **1** *(tableau)* monochrome painting

2 *(gravure)* monochrome engraving

3 *(technique)* **le c.** monochrome, monotint; **en c.** *(tableau)* monochrome

4 *(couleurs)* shades; **le c. du couchant** the shades of sunset

camail [kamaj] NM **1** *Zool (d'un cheval)* neck guard **2** *Rel (d'un ecclésiastique)* (ecclesiastical) cape, cope **3** *Orn (du coq)* neck feathers, hackles

camarade [kamarad] NMF **1** *(ami)* friend; **c. de chambre** roommate; **c. de classe** classmate; **c. d'école** schoolmate; **c. de jeu** playmate; **c. de régiment** comrade (in arms); **c. de travail** workmate, colleague **2** *Pol* comrade; **le c. Gorbatchev** comrade Gorbachev **3** *(en appellatif)* comrade

camaraderie [kamaradri] NF *(entre deux personnes)* good fellowship, friendship; *(dans un club, dans un groupe)* companionship, camaraderie

camard, -e [kamar, -ard] ADJ *Vieilli (nez)* pug; *(personne)* pug-nosed

• **Camarde** NF *Littéraire* **la Camarde** the Grim Reaper

camarguais, -e [kamargɛ, -ɛz] ADJ of/from the Camargue

• **Camarguais, -e** NM,F = inhabitant of or person from the Camargue

Camargue [kamarg] NF **la C.** the Camargue

cambiste [kɑ̃bist] *Fin & Banque* ADJ **banquier c.** = bank with a bureau de change or foreign exchange counter; **marché c.** currency *or* foreign exchange market

NMF **1** *Bourse* exchange broker **2** *(de bureau de change)* bureau de change *or* foreign exchange dealer

Cambodge [kɑ̃bɔdʒ] NM **le C.** Cambodia

cambodgien, -enne [kɑ̃bɔdʒjɛ̃, -ɛn] ADJ Cambodian

NM *(langue)* Cambodian

• **Cambodgien, -enne** NM,F Cambodian

cambouis [kɑ̃bwi] NM dirty oil *or* grease

cambrage [kɑ̃braʒ] NM *Tech (d'une barre, d'une poutre)* cambering

cambré, -e [kɑ̃bre] ADJ *Physiol (dos)* arched; *(pied)* with a high instep; *Zool (cheval)* bowlegged; **avoir la taille cambrée, être c.** to have a curved spine

cambrement [kɑ̃brəmɑ̃] NM *Physiol (du dos, du pied)* arching

cambrer [3] [kɑ̃bre] VT **1** *Physiol (pied)* to arch; **c. le dos** *ou* **les reins** to arch one's back **2** *Tech (barre, poutre)* to camber

VPR **se cambrer** to arch one's back

cambrien, -enne [kɑ̃brijɛ̃, -ɛn] *Géol* ADJ Cambrian

NM Cambrian (period)

cambriolage [kɑ̃brijɔlaʒ] NM **1** *(coup)* burglary, break-in **2** *(activité)* **le c.** burglary, housebreaking

cambrioler [3] [kɑ̃brijɔle] VT *(propriété)* *Br* to burgle, *Am* to burglarize; *(personne)* to burgle; **se faire c.** to be burgled

cambrioleur, -euse [kɑ̃brijɔlœr, -øz] NM,F burglar, housebreaker

cambrouse [kɑ̃bruz], **cambrousse** [kɑ̃brus] NF *Fam (campagne)* country□; **maison à la c.** *ou* **en pleine c.** house in the middle of nowhere *or* (out) in the sticks *or* at the back of beyond

cambrure [kɑ̃bryr] NF **1** *Physiol (posture ▸ du dos)* curve; *(▸ du pied, d'une semelle)* arch

2 *Physiol (partie ▸ du pied)* instep; *(▸ du dos)* small

3 *Tech (d'une chaussée, d'une pièce de bois)* camber

4 *(support de semelage)* instep; **des chaussures à forte c.** shoes with a high instep

cambuse [kɑ̃byz] NF **1** *Naut* storeroom **2** *Fam Péj (chambre, maison)* dump, *Br* tip

cambusier [kɑ̃byzje] NM *Naut* storekeeper

came [kam] NF **1** *Tech* cam **2** *Fam (drogue)* dope, stuff **3** *Fam (marchandises)* stuff, junk

camé, -e[1] [kame] *Fam* ADJ high; **elle est complètement camée** she's as high as a kite

NM,F junkie, druggie

camée[2] [kame] NM *(en joaillerie)* cameo

caméléon [kameleɔ̃] NM *Zool & Fig* chameleon

camélia, camellia [kamelja] NM *Bot* camellia

camelot [kamlo] NM **1** *(dans la rue)* street peddler, hawker **2** *Hist* **c. du roi** Royalist supporter *(in France)*

camelote [kamlɔt] NF *Fam* **1** *(marchandise)* stuff, goods; **c'est de la bonne c.** it's good stuff **2** *Péj (mauvaise qualité)* **c'est de la c.** it's junk *or* trash; **leurs bagues, c'est de la c.** their rings are cheap and nasty

camembert [kamɑ̃bɛr] NM **1** *Culin (fromage)* Camembert (cheese) **2** *(graphique)* pie chart

camer [3] [kame] **se camer** VPR *Fam* to do drugs; **se c. à la cocaïne** to be on coke; **il s'est jamais camé à l'héroïne** he's never done heroin

caméra [kamera] NF **1** *Cin & TV Br* film *or Am* movie camera; **il s'est expliqué devant les caméras** he gave an explanation in front of the (television) cameras; **c. cachée** hidden camera; **c. à l'épaule** hand-held camera; **c. espionne** spy camera; **c. grande vitesse** high-peed camera; **c. infrarouge** infrared camera; *Ordinat* **c. Internet** webcam; **c. invisible** hidden camera; **C. d'or** = important prize awarded at the Cannes Film Festival to a director's debut full-length film; **c. portative** press camera; **c. de reportage** hand-held camera; **c. sonore** sound camera; **c. super-8** super 8 camera; **c. de télévision** television camera; **c. thermique** thermal camera; **c. vidéo** video camera; **c. vidéo numérique** digital video camera **2** *Opt* **c. électronique** *ou* **électronographique** electronic camera

> Il faut noter que le mot anglais **camera** signifie également **appareil photo**.

caméra-film *(pl* **caméras-film***)* NF *Br* film *or Am* movie camera

cameraman [kameraman] *(pl* **cameramans** *ou* **cameramen** [-mɛn]*)* NM *Cin & TV* cameraman, camera operator

camérier [kamerje] NM *Rel (du Pape, d'un cardinal)* chamberlain

caméristе [kamerist] NF **1** *Hist (dame d'honneur)* lady-in-waiting **2** *Littéraire (femme de chambre)* lady's maid

Cameroun [kamrun] NM **le C.** Cameroon

camerounais, -e [kamrunɛ, -ɛz] ADJ Cameroonian

• **Camerounais, -e** NM,F Cameroonian

Caméscope® [kameskɔp] NM camcorder

camion [kamjɔ̃] NM **1** *Aut Br* lorry, *Am* truck; **interdit aux camions** *(sur panneau) Br* no HGVs, *Am* no trucks; **c. bâché** curtainsider; **c. de déménagement** *Br* removal van, *Am* moving van; **c. de dépannage** breakdown truck, *Am* wrecker; **c. des éboueurs** *Br* dustcart, *Am* garbage truck; **c. frigorifique** refrigerated *Br* lorry *or Am* truck; **c. à remorque** *Br* lorry *or Am* truck with trailer; **c. à semi-remorque** *Br* articulated lorry, *Am* trailer truck **2** *(de peintre)* (paint) pail

camion-benne [kamjɔ̃bɛn] *(pl* **camions-bennes***)* NM dumper truck

camion-citerne [kamjɔ̃sitɛrn] *(pl* **camions-citernes***)* NM *Br* tanker (lorry), *Am* tank truck

camionnage [kamjɔnaʒ] NM *Com (prix, service)* haulage, carriage, *Am* truckage; **une entreprise de c.** a haulage firm, *Am* a trucking business

camionner [3] [kamjɔne] VT *Com* to haul, to transport by *Br* lorry *or Am* truck

camionnette [kamjɔnɛt] NF *Aut* van; **c. de livraison** delivery van

camionneur [kamjɔnœr] NM **1** *(conducteur) Br* lorry *or Am* truck driver **2** *(entrepreneur)* (road) haulage contractor, (road) *Br* haulier *or Am* hauler

camisole [kamizɔl] NF 1 *Vieilli Can & Suisse (sous-vêtement féminin)* camisole; *Can & Suisse (sous-vêtement masculin) Br* vest, *Am* undershirt 2 *Psy* **c. chimique** chemical straitjacket *or* cosh; **c. de force** straitjacket

camomille [kamɔmij] NF 1 *Bot* camomile 2 *Culin (infusion)* camomile tea; **prendre une c.** to have a cup of camomile tea

camouflage [kamuflaʒ] NM 1 *Mil (procédé)* camouflaging; *(matériel)* camouflage 2 *(de la vérité)* hiding, concealing; *(d'une erreur)* covering up 3 *Zool* camouflage, mimicry

camoufler [3] [kamufle] VT 1 *Mil* to camouflage
2 *(cacher ▸ passage, gêne)* to conceal; *(▸ bavure)* to cover up; *(▸ vérité)* to hide, to conceal; **c. un bouton** to cover up *or* to camouflage a spot
3 *(déguiser)* **de nombreux crimes sont camouflés en suicides** murders are often made to look like suicide
4 *Compta* **c. un bilan** to window-dress the accounts
VPR **se camoufler** 1 *Mil* to camouflage oneself 2 *Zool* to camouflage itself

camouflet [kamuflɛ] NM *Littéraire (affront)* snub, insult, affront; **essuyer un c.** to be snubbed

camp [kɑ̃] NM 1 *Mil* (army) camp; **établir un c.** to set up *or* pitch camp; **c. de base** base camp; **c. militaire** military camp; **c. de prisonniers** prisoner of war camp; **c. volant** temporary camp; *Fig* **vivre en c. volant** *(en situation changeante)* to be always on the move; *(en déménageant souvent)* to live out of a suitcase; **lever le c.** to break camp; *Fig* to make tracks
2 *Hist & Pol* camp; **c. (de concentration)** concentration camp; **la vie dans les camps** life in the concentration camps; **c. de déportation** deportation camp; **c. d'extermination** *ou* **de la mort** death camp; **c. d'internement** internment camp; **c. de réfugiés** refugee camp; **c. de travail (forcé)** forced labour camp; *Hist* **C. David** Camp David
3 *(de loisirs) Br* campsite, camping site, *Am* campground; **je fais un c. à Pâques avec ma classe** I'm going on a camping trip at Easter with my class; **j'envoie les enfants en c. cet été** I'm sending the children off to summer camp this year; **c. de scouts** scout camp
4 *Sport & (dans un jeu)* team, side; **faire deux camps** to form two teams
5 *(faction)* camp, side; **il faut choisir son c.** you must decide which side you're on; **passer dans l'autre c., changer de c.** to change sides, to go over to the other side
6 *(locutions) Fam* **ficher le c.** to clear off, to beat it; *très Fam* **foutre le c.** *(personne)* to go to hell, *Br* to bugger off; **fous le c.!** go to hell!, *Br* bugger off!; **mon pansement fout le c.** my plaster's coming off[□]; **tout fout le c.!** what the hell is the world coming to?

campagnard, -e [kɑ̃paɲar, -ard] ADJ *(accent, charme, style, vie)* country *(avant n)*, rustic
NM,F countryman, *f* countrywoman; **les campagnards** countryfolk

campagne [kɑ̃paɲ] NF 1 *(habitat)* country; *(paysage)* countryside; **les travaux de la c.** farm *or* agricultural work; **la c. environnante** the surrounding country *or* countryside; **à la c.** in the country *or* countryside
2 *(activité)* campaign; **faire c. pour/contre** to campaign for/against; **lancer une c. pour/contre** to launch a campaign for/against
3 *Com & Pol* campaign; **c. d'affichage** poster campaign; **c. commerciale** sales campaign; *Mktg* **c. de dénigrement** countermarketing campaign; **c. de diffamation** smear campaign; **c. électorale** election campaign; *Mktg* **c. d'image de marque** branding campaign; **c. d'information** publicity campaign; *Mktg* **c. intensive** saturation campaign; **c. de presse** press campaign; **c. de prévention** public awareness campaign; **c. de prévention contre l'alcool au volant** anti-drink-driving campaign; **c. de promotion** promotional campaign; **c. publicitaire** *ou* **de publicité** advertising campaign; *Mktg* **c. de publicité directe** direct mail campaign; **c. de recrutement** recruitment drive; *Mktg* **c. de saturation** saturation campaign; **c. télévisée** *ou* **télévisuelle** television campaign; *Mktg* **c. de vente** sales drive
4 *Mil* campaign; **faire c.** to campaign, to fight; **les campagnes napoléoniennes** Napoleon's campaigns
• **de campagne** ADJ 1 *(rural ▸ chemin, médecin, curé)* country *(avant n)* 2 *Culin (pain, saucisson)* country *(avant n)* 3 *Mil (tenue, artillerie)* field *(avant n)*
• **en campagne** ADV in the field, on campaign; *Fig* **être en c.** to be on the warpath; *aussi Fig* **entrer** *ou* **se mettre en c.** to go into action

> Attention: ne pas confondre **country** et **countryside** lorsqu'on traduit **campagne**. On utilise **countryside** lorsqu'il risque d'y avoir confusion avec **country** dans le sens de **pays**, ou bien lorsqu'on parle de paysages campagnards.

campagnol [kɑ̃paɲɔl] NM *Zool* (field) vole

campanile [kɑ̃panil] NM *(d'une église)* bell-tower; *(isolé)* campanile

campanule [kɑ̃panyl] NF *Bot* bellflower, *Spéc* campanula

campé, -e [kɑ̃pe] ADJ **bien c.** *(robuste)* well-built; **bien c. sur ses jambes** standing firmly on his feet; *Littérature* **des personnages bien campés** *(bien décrits)* well-drawn characters; *Théât (bien interprétés)* well-played characters; **un récit bien c.** a well-constructed story

campement [kɑ̃pmɑ̃] NM *(installation)* camp, encampment; *(terrain)* camping place *or* ground; *(de bohémiens)* caravan site; **c. interdit** *(sur panneau)* no camping; **établir un c.** to set up camp; **replier le c.** to break camp

camper [3] [kɑ̃pe] VI 1 *(faire du camping)* to camp 2 *Mil* to camp (out); *aussi Fig* **c. sur ses positions** to stand one's ground 3 *(habiter temporairement)* **je campe chez un copain en attendant** meanwhile, I'm camping (out) at a friend's
VT 1 *Théât (personnage)* to play the part of
2 *Beaux-Arts (par un dessin ▸ silhouette)* to draw, to sketch out
3 *Littérature (par un écrit ▸ personnage)* to portray
4 *(placer)* **c. son chapeau sur sa tête** to stick one's hat on one's head
5 *Mil (troupes)* to encamp
VPR **se camper se c. devant qn** to plant oneself in front of sb

campeur, -euse [kɑ̃pœr, -øz] NM,F camper

camphre [kɑ̃fr] NM *Chim* camphor

camphré, -e [kɑ̃fre] ADJ *Chim* camphorated

camphrier [kɑ̃frije] NM *Bot* camphor tree

camping [kɑ̃piŋ] NM 1 *(activité)* camping; **on a fait du c. l'été dernier** we went camping last summer; **j'aime faire du c.** I like camping; **c. à la ferme** farm camping; **c. sauvage** *(non autorisé)* camping on non-authorized sites; *(en pleine nature)* camping in the open, wilderness camping 2 *(terrain) Br* camp *or* camping site, *Am* campground; *(pour caravanes) Br* caravan *or Am* trailer site; **c. aménagé** camp site with facilities

camping-car [kɑ̃piŋkar] *(pl* **camping-cars***)* NM camper, *Br* camper van

camping-caravaning [kɑ̃piŋkaravaniŋ] NM INV *Br* caravanning, *Am* trailer camping

Camping-Gaz® [kɑ̃piŋgaz] NM INV camping stove

campos [kɑ̃po] NM *Fam* **donner c. à qn** to give sb a day/an afternoon/*etc* off[□]

campus [kɑ̃pys] NM *Univ* campus; **sur le c.** on campus

camus, -e [kamy, -yz] ADJ *(nez)* pug *(avant n)*; *(personne)* pug-nosed

CAN [seaen] NM *(abrév* **convertisseur analogue-numérique***)* ADC

Canada [kanada] NM **le C.** Canada

Canadair® [kanadɛr] NM *Aviat* fire-fighting plane, *Am* tanker plane

canadianisme [kanadjanism] NM *Ling* Canadianism

canadien, -enne [kanadjɛ̃, -ɛn] ADJ Canadian
• **Canadien, -enne** NM,F 1 *(gén)* Canadian; **C. français** French Canadian 2 *Can (d'origine française)* = descendant of the original French (as opposed to British) settlers in Canada
• **canadienne** NF 1 *(tente)* (ridge) tent 2 *(veste)* sheepskin-lined jacket 3 *(pirogue)* (Canadian) canoe

canaille [kanaj] ADJ 1 *(polisson)* roguish 2 *(vulgaire)* coarse, vulgar
NF 1 *(crapule)* scoundrel, crook; *Vieilli* **la c.** the rabble 2 *(ton affectueux)* **petite c.!** you little devil *or* rascal!

canaillerie [kanajri] NF *Littéraire* 1 *(acte)* low trick 2 *(malhonnêteté)* crookedness 3 *(vulgarité)* coarseness, vulgarity

canal, -aux [kanal, -o] NM 1 *Naut & Géog* canal; *(bras de mer)* channel; **sur les canaux et rivières** on the inland waterways; **c. de dérivation** diversion *or* bypass channel; **c. maritime** *ou* **de navigation** ship canal; **le c. du Midi** = canal linking the Garonne estuary to the Mediterranean; **le c. de Panama** the Panama Canal; **le c. de Suez** the Suez Canal
2 *Constr* duct, channel; **c. d'amenée** feed *or* feeder channel; **c. de fuite** waste pipe
3 *Agr* channel; **c. de drainage/d'irrigation** drainage/irrigation canal
4 *Tél & Ordinat* channel; *Can (chaîne)* (TV) channel; **c. d'accès** access channel; **c. de dialogue en direct** IRC channel; **c. IRC** IRC channel; **C.+, C. Plus** = French TV pay channel
5 *Anat & Bot* duct, canal; **c. auditif** auditory canal; **c. biliaire** bile duct; **c. lacrymal** tear duct
6 *Com & Mktg* **c. de communication** communications channel; **c. de communication commerciale** marketing communications channel; **c. de distribution** distribution channel
7 *Astron* canal
• **par le canal de** PRÉP through, via

> **CANAL+**
>
> Canal+, France's first private television channel, was established in 1982 and started broadcasting in 1984. It broadcasts programmes that have to be unscrambled using a special decoding unit, although for part of the day its programmes can be seen without this device. Canal+ also plays a prominent role in funding international films.

canalisable [kanalizabl] ADJ *(eau, énergie, pensées, efforts)* which can be channelled

canalisation [kanalizasjɔ̃] NF 1 *Constr (conduit)* pipe; *Pétr (pour pétrole)* pipeline; **canalisations** *(système)* pipes, pipework, piping
2 *Élec* wiring
3 *Constr (travaux ▸ d'une rivière)* channelling; **la c. de la région** equipping the area with a canal system
4 *(rassemblement ▸ d'énergies, d'une foule, de pensées)* channelling

canaliser [3] [kanalize] VT 1 *Constr (cours d'eau)* to channel; *(région)* to provide with a canal system 2 *(énergies, foule, pensées, ressources)* to channel

cananéen, -enne [kananeɛ̃, -ɛn] *Bible* ADJ Canaanite
NM *(langue)* Canaanite
• **Cananéen, -enne** NM,F Canaanite

canapé [kanape] NM 1 *(siège)* settee, sofa; **c. deux places** two-seater sofa, *Am* loveseat; **c. trois places** three-seater sofa; **c. clic-clac** = spring-action *or* metal-action sofa bed; **c. convertible** sofa bed, bed settee 2 *Culin* canapé

canapé-lit [kanapeli] *(pl* **canapés-lits***)* NM sofa bed, bed settee

canaque [kanak] ADJ Kanak
• **Canaque** NMF Kanak *(native or inhabitant of New Caledonia who seeks independence from France)*

canard [kanar] NM 1 *Orn* duck; **c. mâle** drake; **c. sauvage** wild duck; *Fig* **c. boiteux** lame duck
2 *Culin* duck; **c. laqué** Peking duck; **c. à l'orange** duck in orange sauce, duck à l'orange
3 *(terme affectueux)* **mon petit c.** sweetie, sweetie-pie
4 *Fam Journ (journal)* paper, rag; *Presse* **le C. enchaîné** = French satirical weekly newspaper, famous for its investigative journalism
5 *Fam (informations)* rumour
6 *Mus (couac)* false note; **faire un c.** to hit a false note, to go off key

7 *Fam (sucre)* = sugar lump dipped in coffee/brandy/*etc*

8 *Can (bouilloire)* kettle

• **en canard** ADV **marcher en c.** to walk with one's feet turned out

canardeau, -x [kanardo] NM *Orn* duckling

canarder [3] [kanarde] VT *(avec une arme à feu)* to snipe at, to take potshots at; *(avec des projectiles)* to pelt; **se faire c.** *(au fusil)* to be sniped at; **se faire c. à coup de boules de neige** to be pelted with snowballs

VI **1** *Fam Mus (faire des fausses notes)* to sing off key; *(faire une fausse note)* to hit a false note, to go off key **2** *Naut (navire)* to pitch

canardière [kanardjer] NF **1** *(mare)* duck-pond **2** *Chasse (zone)* duck shoot; *(fusil)* punt gun

canari [kanari] NM *Orn* canary

ADJ INV **(jaune) c.** canary-yellow

Canaries [kanari] NFPL **les (îles) C.** the Canary Islands, the Canaries

canasson [kanasɔ̃] NM *Fam Zool* horse, *Péj* nag

canasta [kanasta] NF *Cartes* canasta

cancale [kɑ̃kal] NF *Ich* (Cancale) oyster

cancan [kɑ̃kɑ̃] NM **1** *(cri du canard)* quack **2** *(danse)* (French) cancan **3** *(bavardage)* piece of gossip; **des cancans** gossip *(UNCOUNT)*; **n'écoute pas les cancans** don't listen to gossip *or* to what people say

cancaner [3] [kɑ̃kane] VI **1** *(canard)* to quack **2** *(médire)* to gossip; **leur divorce a beaucoup fait c.** their divorce caused a lot of gossip

cancanier, -ère [kɑ̃kanje, -ɛr] ADJ gossipy

NM,F gossip

Cancer [kɑ̃sɛr] NM **1** *Astron* Cancer **2** *Astrol* Cancer; **être C.** to be Cancer *or* a Cancerian

cancer [kɑ̃sɛr] NM **1** *Méd* cancer; **avoir un c.** to have cancer; **mourir d'un c.** to die of cancer; **c. du foie/de la peau** liver/skin cancer **2** *(fléau)* cancer, canker

cancéreux, -euse [kɑ̃serø, -øz] *Méd* ADJ *(cellule, tumeur)* malignant, cancerous; *(malade)* cancer *(avant n)*

NM,F cancer victim *or* sufferer; **les c. en phase terminale** terminal cancer patients, people with terminal cancer

cancérigène [kɑ̃seriʒɛn] ADJ *Méd* carcinogenic; **produit c.** carcinogen

cancérisation [kɑ̃serizasjɔ̃] NF *Méd* **pour empêcher la c. des cellules** to prevent cells from becoming malignant

cancériser [3] [kɑ̃serize] **se cancériser** VPR *Méd* to become cancerous *or* malignant

cancérogène [kɑ̃serɔʒɛn] *Méd* ADJ carcinogenic; **produit c.** carcinogen

NM carcinogen

cancérologie [kɑ̃serɔlɔʒi] NF *Méd* oncology

cancérologue [kɑ̃serɔlɔg] NMF *Méd* cancerologist; *(médecin)* oncologist

cancéropôle [kɑ̃serɔpol] NM cancer research institute

cancre [kɑ̃kr] NM dunce

cancrelat [kɑ̃krəla] NM *Entom* cockroach, *Am* roach

cancroïde [kɑ̃krɔid] ADJ *Méd* cancroid

candélabre [kɑ̃delabr] NM **1** *(flambeau)* candelabra **2** *Vieilli (réverbère)* street lamp, lamppost

candeur [kɑ̃dœr] NF ingenuousness, naivety; **un regard plein de c.** a guileless look

> Il faut noter que le nom anglais **candour** est un faux ami. Il signifie **franchise**.

candi [kɑ̃di] ADJ M *Culin* **fruits candis** crystallized *ou* candied fruit; **sucre c.** sugar candy, rock candy

candidat, -e [kɑ̃dida, -at] NM,F **1** *Pol* candidate; **être c. aux élections** to be a candidate in the elections, to run *or Br* to stand in the elections; **être c. à la présidence** to run *or Br* to stand for president **2** *(à un examen, à une activité)* candidate; *(à un emploi)* applicant, candidate; **les candidats à l'examen d'entrée** entrance examination candidates; **être c. à un poste** to be a candidate for a post; **se porter c. à un poste** to apply for a post; **les candidats à l'aventure** adventure-seekers

candidature [kɑ̃didatyr] NF **1** *(gén)* candidature, candidacy; **poser sa c.** to declare oneself a candidate, *Br* to stand; **retirer sa c.** to stand down; **il a retiré sa c. à la présidence** he has stood down as a presidential candidate; **c. multiple** running *or Br* standing for election in several constituencies; **c. officielle** running *or Br* standing as official candidate **2** *(pour un emploi)* application; **poser sa c. (à)** to apply (for); **retirer sa c.** to withdraw one's application; **c. en-ligne** e-mail *or* on-line application; **c. spontanée** unsolicited application

candide [kɑ̃did] ADJ ingenuous, naive

> Il faut noter que l'adjectif anglais **candid** est un faux ami. Il signifie **franc**.

candidement [kɑ̃didmɑ̃] ADV ingenuously, naively

candidose [kɑ̃didoz] NF **1** *Biol (bactérie)* candida **2** *Méd (infection)* candidiasis

cane [kan] NF *Orn* (female) duck

cané, -e [kane] ADJ *Fam* dead

caner [3] [kane] VI *Fam* **1** *(de peur)* to chicken out **2** *(mourir)* to croak, to kick the bucket **3** *(s'enfuir)* to beat it, *Br* to leg it, *Am* to bug out

caneton [kantɔ̃] NM **1** *Orn* duckling **2** *Culin* **c. à l'orange** duckling à l'orange

canette[1] [kanɛt] NF *Orn* duckling

canette[2] [kanɛt] NF **1** *(bouteille)* (fliptop) bottle; **c. (de bière)** bottle (of beer) **2** *(boîte)* can

canevas [kanva] NM **1** *(d'un roman, d'un exposé)* framework **2** *Tex* canvas; **broderie sur c.** tapestry (work)

caniche [kaniʃ] NM **1** *Zool* poodle **2** *Péj (personne)* lapdog, poodle

caniculaire [kanikylɛr] ADJ *Météo* scorching, blistering

canicule [kanikyl] NF *(grande chaleur)* scorching heat; **la c.** *(en plein été)* the midsummer heat; **une semaine de c.** a weeklong heatwave; **quelle c.!** what a scorcher!

• **canicules** NFPL *Belg (grande chaleur)* scorching heat

canif [kanif] NM penknife, pocket knife; *Fam Fig* **donner un coup de c. dans le contrat** to have the occasional fling

canin, -e[1] [kanɛ̃, -in] ADJ *Zool* canine; **exposition canine** dog show; **société canine** kennel club

canine[2] [kanin] NF *Anat* canine tooth

caninette [kaninɛt] NF = motorized scooter with an attachment for cleaning up dog dirt in the street

canisse [kanis] = **cannisse**

caniveau, -x [kanivo] NM **1** *(le long du trottoir)* gutter **2** *(pour câbles)* trough, conduit

cannabis [kanabis] NM *Bot (chanvre, drogue)* cannabis

cannage [kanaʒ] NM **1** *(activité)* caning **2** *(produit)* canework

canne [kan] NF **1** *(d'un élégant)* cane; *(d'un vieillard)* walking stick; **c. (anglaise)** crutch; **marcher avec des cannes** to be on crutches; **c. blanche** white *Br* stick *or Am* cane; **les cannes blanches** the visually disabled

2 *Pêche* **c. à pêche** fishing rod

3 *Bot* **c. à sucre** sugar cane

4 *Suisse (au hockey sur glace) Br* ice hockey stick, *Am* hockey stick

5 *(rotin)* cane *(UNCOUNT)*

6 *Tech* **c. de souffleur** blowpipe

• **cannes** NFPL *Fam (jambes)* legs, *Br* pins; *Sport* ski sticks *or* poles

canné, -e [kane] ADJ **1** *(en rotin)* cane *(avant n)* **2** *très Fam (mort)* dead as a doornail

canneberge [kanbɛrʒ] NF *Bot* cranberry

canne-épée [kanepe] *(pl* **cannes-épées**) NF swordstick

cannelé, -e [kanle] ADJ **1** *(qui présente des cannelures ▸ colonne)* fluted; *(▸ pneu)* grooved; *(▸ ongle)* ridged **2** *(à gouttière)* grooved

canneler [24] [kanle] VT *(colonne)* to flute; *(pneu)* to groove

cannelier [kanəlje] NM *Bot* cinnamon tree

cannelle [kanɛl] NF **1** *(épice)* cinnamon **2** *(robinet)* spigot

ADJ INV pale brown *(avant n)*, cinnamon-coloured

• **à la cannelle** ADJ cinnamon-flavoured; **thé à la c.** cinnamon tea

cannelloni [kanelɔni] *(pl* **inv** *ou* **cannellonis)** NM *Culin* cannelloni

cannelure [kanlyr] NF **1** *Archit (d'un vase, d'un pilier)* flute, fluting **2** *(d'une vis, d'une pièce de monnaie)* groove, grooving **3** *Bot* stria; *Géol* **cannelures** striae

canner [3] [kane] VT *(chaise)* to cane

VI = **caner 2, 3**

Cannes [kan] NM *Géog* Cannes; *Cin* **le festival de C.** the Cannes film festival

cannette [kanɛt] = **canette**[2]

canneur, -euse [kanœr, -øz] NM,F cane worker

cannibale [kanibal] ADJ *(pratiques, rites)* cannibalistic; **tribu c.** tribe of cannibals

NMF *aussi Fig* cannibal

cannibalisation [kanibalizasjɔ̃] NF *Mktg & Tech (de machine, de produit)* cannibalization

cannibaliser [3] [kanibalize] VT *Mktg & Tech (machine, produit)* to cannibalize

cannibalisme [kanibalism] NM **1** *(anthropophagie)* cannibalism **2** *Mktg & Tech* cannibalization

cannisse [kanis] NF **1** *(coupe-vent)* rush fence **2** *Can Joual (bidon)* canister

canoë [kanɔe] NM *Sport* canoe; **faire du c.** to go canoeing; **ils ont remonté le fleuve en c.** they canoed up the river

canoéisme [kanɔeism] NM *Sport* canoeing

canoéiste [kanɔeist] NMF *Sport* canoeist

canoë-kayak [kanɔekajak] *(pl* **canoës-kayaks)** NM *Sport* **faire du c.** to go canoeing

canon [kanɔ̃] NM **1** *Mil (pièce ▸ moderne)* gun; *(▸ ancienne)* cannon; *(tube d'une arme à feu)* barrel; **à c. double** double-barrelled; **à c. scié** *Br* sawn-off, *Am* sawed-off; **c. antiaérien** anti-aircraft gun; **c. antichar** anti-tank gun; **c. automatique** machine-gun; **c. mitrailleur** heavy machine-gun

2 *Naut* **c. de chasse/retraite** fore/aft gun

3 *Électron* **c. électronique** *ou* **à électrons** electron gun

4 *Sport* **c. à neige** snow-making machine

5 *(de clé, de serrure)* barrel; *(de seringue)* body

6 *Mus* canon; **c. à trois voix** canon for three voices; **chanter en c.** to sing a *or* in canon

7 *(modèle)* model, *Sout* canon; **les canons de la beauté/du bon goût** the canons of beauty/good taste

8 *Rel* canon

9 *Arch (mesure)* = wine measure equivalent to 0.058 l.

10 *(verre ▸ de vin)* glass (of wine); *(▸ d'eau-de-vie)* shot (of spirits)

11 *Fam (personne très belle)* babe

ADJ INV **1** *Rel* **droit c.** canonic law **2** *Fam (beau)* gorgeous, stunning, *Br* fit

cañon [kanjɔn] = **canyon**

canonial, -e, -aux, -ales [kanɔnjal, -o] ADJ *Rel* **1** *(réglé par les canons)* canonic, canonical **2** *(du chanoine)* of a canon

canonique [kanɔnik] ADJ **1** *(conforme aux règles)* classic, canonic, canonical **2** *Rel* canonic, canonical

NF canon

canonisation [kanɔnizasjɔ̃] NF *Rel* canonization, canonizing

canoniser [3] [kanɔnize] VT *Rel* to canonize

canonnade [kanɔnad] NF *Mil* heavy gunfire, cannonade; **une c.** a burst of gunfire

canonner [3] [kanɔne] VT *Littéraire Mil* to shell, to cannonade

canonnier [kanɔnje] NM *Mil* gunner

canonnière [kanɔnjɛr] NF **1** *Naut* gunboat **2** *(meurtrière)* loophole

canot [kano] NM *Naut* **1** *(embarcation)* dinghy; **c. automobile** motorboat; **c. de pêche** fishing boat; **c. pneumatique** rubber *or* inflatable dinghy; **c. de sauvetage** lifeboat **2** *Can (canoë)* canoe

canotage [kanɔtaʒ] NM *Naut* boating; *Can Sport (en canoë)* canoeing; **faire du c.** to go boating; *Can Sport* to go canoeing

canoter [3] [kanɔte] VI **1** *Naut (se promener ▸ en canot)* to go boating; *Can Sport (▸ en canoë)* to go canoeing **2** *Naut (manœuvrer)* to handle a boat

canoteur, -euse [kanɔtœr, -øz] NM,F **1** *Naut* rower *(in a dinghy)* **2** *Can Sport (personne qui fait du canoë)* canoeist

canotier [kanɔtje] NM **1** *(chapeau)* (straw) boater **2** *Naut & Sport (rameur)* rower, oarsman

cantal [kɑ̃tal] NM Cantal (cheese)

cantaloup [kɑ̃talu] NM *Bot* cantaloup (melon)

cantate [kɑ̃tat] NF *Mus* cantata

cantatrice [kɑ̃tatris] NF *(d'opéra)* (opera) singer; *(de concert)* (concert) singer

cantharide [kɑ̃tarid] NF *Entom* blister beetle

cantilène [kɑ̃tilɛn] NF *Littérature & Mus* cantilena

cantilever [kɑ̃tilevœr] *Constr* ADJ *(poutre, pont)* cantilever

NM *(poutre)* cantilever

cantine [kɑ̃tin] NF **1** *(dans une école)* dining hall, canteen; *(dans une entreprise)* canteen **2** *(malle)* (tin) trunk

cantique [kɑ̃tik] NM *Rel & Mus* canticle; **c. de Noël** Christmas carol; **le C. des cantiques** The Song of Songs, The Song of Solomon

cantoche [kɑ̃tɔʃ] NF *Fam* canteen□

canton [kɑ̃tɔ̃] NM **1** *Admin (en France)* division of an "arrondissement", canton; *(en Suisse)* canton; *(au Luxembourg)* administrative unit, canton; *(au Canada)* township **2** *(de route, de voie ferrée)* section

cantonade [kɑ̃tɔnad] **à la cantonade** ADV **1** *(sans interlocuteur précis)* to all present, to the company at large; **crier qch à la c.** to call *or* to shout sth (out); **ce n'est pas la peine de le crier** *ou* **de l'annoncer à la c.** there's no need to shout it from the rooftops **2** *Théât* **parler à la c.** *(depuis les coulisses)* to speak off stage; *(à une personne qui est dans les coulisses)* to speak to the wings

cantonais, -e [kɑ̃tɔnɛ, -ɛz] ADJ Cantonese

NM *(langue)* Cantonese

• **Cantonais, -e** NM,F Cantonese; **les C.** the Cantonese

cantonal, -e, -aux, -ales [kɑ̃tɔnal, -o] *Pol* ADJ local

• **cantonales** NFPL = election held every six years for the "conseil général", ≃ local elections

cantonnement [kɑ̃tɔnmɑ̃] NM **1** *(à une tâche, à un lieu)* confinement, confining *(UNCOUNT)* **2** *Mil (lieu)* billet; *(action)* billeting *(UNCOUNT)*

cantonner [3] [kɑ̃tɔne] VT **1** *(isoler)* **c. qn dans un lieu** to confine sb to a place **2** *Fig* **c. qch à** *ou* **dans** *(activité, explication)* to limit *or* to confine sth to **3** *Mil* to billet; **c. un soldat chez qn** to billet a soldier on sb

VI to be billeted; **c. chez qn** to be billeted on sb

VPR **se cantonner 1 se c. dans** *(s'enfermer)* to confine oneself to; **il se cantonnait dans sa solitude** he took refuge in solitude **2 se c. à** *ou* **dans** *(être limité)* to be confined *or* limited *or* restricted to; *(se restreindre à)* to confine *or* to limit oneself to

cantonnier [kɑ̃tɔnje] NM **1** *Constr (sur une route)* roadman, road mender **2** *Rail Br* platelayer, *Am* trackman

cantonnière [kɑ̃tɔnjer] NF *(de lit)* valance; *(rideau)* pelmet

canular [kanylar] NM hoax; **faire un c. à qn** to play a hoax on sb; **monter un c.** to set up a hoax

canule [kanyl] NF *Méd* cannula

canuler [3] [kanyle] VT *Fam Vieilli* **1** *(agacer)* **c. qn** to drive sb mad *or* up the wall **2** *(tromper)* to hoax

canut, -use [kany, -yz] NM,F *Tex (à Lyon)* silk weaver *or* worker

canyon [kanjɔn, kanjɔ̃] NM canyon

canyoning [kanjɔniŋ], **canyonisme** [kanjɔnism] NM *Sport* canyoning

CAO [seao] NF *Ordinat (abrév* **conception assistée par ordinateur**) CAD

caoua [kawa] NM *Fam* coffee□

caoutchouc [kautʃu] NM **1** *(substance)* rubber; **c. Mousse** foam rubber; **c. synthétique** synthetic rubber

2 *Fam (élastique)* rubber *or* elastic band□

3 *(soulier)* galosh

4 *(manteau)* waterproof (coat), raincoat

5 *Bot (ficus)* rubber plant

• **de caoutchouc, en caoutchouc** ADJ rubber *(avant n)*

caoutchoutage [kautʃutaʒ] NM **1** *(processus)* coating with rubber, rubberizing **2** *(enduit)* rubberized coating

caoutchouter [3] [kautʃute] VT to cover *or* to overlay with rubber, to rubberize

caoutchouteux, -euse [kautʃutø, -øz] ADJ rubbery

CAP [seape] NM *Scol* **1** *(abrév* **certificat d'aptitude professionnelle**) = vocational training certificate (taken at secondary school), *Br* ≃ City and Guilds examination **2** *(abrév* **certificat d'aptitude pédagogique**) teaching diploma

cap[1] [kap] NM **1** *Géog* cape, headland, promontory; *Naut* **doubler** *ou* **passer un c.** to round a cape; **le c. de Bonne-Espérance** the Cape of Good Hope; **c. Canaveral** Cape Canaveral; **c. Cod** Cape Cod; **le c. Finisterre** Cape Finisterre; **le c. Horn** Cape Horn; **c. Kennedy** Cape Kennedy **2** *Aviat, Aut & Naut* course; *Naut* **c. au vent** head on to the wind; **changer de** *ou* **le c.** to alter one's *or* to change course; **mettre le c. sur** *Naut* to steer *or* to head for; *Aut* to head for; *Naut* **mettre le c. au large** to set out to sea; *Naut* **suivre un c.** to steer a course **3** *(étape)* milestone, hurdle; **passer** *ou* **franchir le c. de** *(dans une situation difficile)* to get over, to come through; *(dans une gradation, des statistiques)* to pass the mark of; **il a passé le c. de la cinquantaine** he's in his fifties; **la revue a dépassé le c. des 2000 lecteurs** the readership of the magazine has passed the 2,000 mark

cap[2] [kap] ADJ *Fam* **t'es pas c. de...!** bet you can't...!; **même pas c.!** bet you can't!

capable [kapabl] ADJ **1** *(compétent)* capable, competent, able **2** *Jur* competent **3 être c. de** *(physiquement)* to be able to, to be capable of; *(psychologiquement)* to be capable of; **c. de porter 30 kilos** capable of lifting *or* able to lift 30 kilos; **te sens-tu c. de te lever?** do you feel able to get up?; **il n'est pas c. de se maîtriser** he's unable to control himself; **je n'en suis pas c.** I can't do it; **c. de tout** capable of (doing) anything; **il est c. de nous oublier!** I wouldn't put it past him to forget us!

capacité [kapasite] NF **1** *(aptitude)* ability, capability; **avoir la c. de faire qch** to have the ability to do sth, to be capable of doing sth; **diriger? il n'en a pas la c.** managing? he hasn't got the ability for it; **avoir une grande c. de travail** to be capable of *or* to have a capacity for hard work; **c. de concentration** attention span

2 *(d'un récipient, d'une salle, d'un véhicule)* capacity; **sac d'une grande c.** roomy bag; **c. d'accueil** *(d'un hôtel)* accommodation capacity, available beds; *Mktg* **c. linéaire** shelf space; *Physiol* **c. vitale** *ou* **thoracique** vital capacity

3 *Phys* capacity; **c. calorifique** heat capacity

4 *Élec* capacitance

5 *Ordinat & Tél* capacity

6 *Jur* capacity; **avoir c. pour** to be (legally) entitled to; *Fig* **je n'ai pas c. pour vous répondre** it's not up to me to give you an answer; **c. de jouissance** legal entitlement (to a piece of property)

7 *Univ (diplôme)* **c. en droit** = law diploma leading to a degree course in law

8 *Écon* capacity; *Mktg* **c. d'achat** purchasing power; **c. de crédit, c. d'emprunter** borrowing power *or* capacity; **c. d'endettement** borrowing *or* debt capacity; **c. de financement** financing capacity; *Fin* **c. d'imposition** ability to pay tax; **c. de production** manufacturing capacity; **c. productrice** maximum possible output *or* capacity

9 *Ordinat* **c. d'adressage** address capability; **c. de disque/disquette** disk capacity; **c. de mémoire** memory capacity; **c. de stockage** storage capacity; **c. de traitement** throughput

• **capacités** NFPL ability; **un élève ayant des capacités mais paresseux** a pupil with ability but inclined to be lazy; **ses capacités d'organisateur** his/her abilities as an organizer; **capacités intellectuelles** intellectual capacity

caparaçon [kaparasɔ̃] NM caparison

caparaçonner [3] [kaparasɔne] VT **1** *(cheval)* to caparison **2** *(protéger)* to cover from top to bottom

VPR **se caparaçonner** to deck oneself out, to bedeck oneself

cape [kap] NF **1** *(pèlerine)* cloak, cape **2** *Naut* **être à la c.** to lie to; **mettre à la c.** to heave to

• **de cape et d'épée** ADJ swashbuckling; **une histoire/un film de c. et d'épée** a swashbuckler, a swashbuckling story/film

• **sous cape** ADV **rire sous c.** to laugh up one's sleeve

capeline [kaplin] NF wide-brimmed hat

capella [kapela] *voir* **a cappella**

CAPES, Capes [kapɛs] NM *Univ (abrév* **certificat d'aptitude au professorat de l'enseignement du second degré**) = secondary school teaching qualification, *Br* ≃ PGCE

> **CAPES**
>
> This is a required qualification for state teachers in France. Candidates who pass this competitive exam become "professeurs certifiés" and are entitled to teach in secondary education.

capésien, -enne [kapesjɛ̃, -ɛn] NM,F *Univ* **1** *(étudiant)* student preparing to take the "CAPES" **2** *(diplômé)* holder of the "CAPES"

CAPET, Capet [kapɛt] NM *Univ (abrév* **certificat d'aptitude au professorat de l'enseignement technique**) = secondary school teaching qualification for technical subjects

capétien[1]**, -enne**[1] [kapesjɛ̃, -ɛn] *Hist* ADJ Capetian *(dynasty of French kings, 987–1328)*

• **Capétien, -enne** NM,F Capetian

capétien[2]**, -enne**[2] [kapetjɛ̃, -ɛn] NM,F *Univ* **1** *(étudiant)* student preparing to take the "CAPET" **2** *(diplômé)* holder of the "CAPET"

capharnaüm [kafarnaɔm] NM *(chaos)* shambles *(singulier)*; **leur maison est un vrai c.** their house is a real shambles

cap-hornier [kapɔrnje] *(pl* **cap-horniers**) NM *Naut (marin)* sailor who has travelled the Cape Horn route, Cape Horner; *(navire)* ship that has sailed the Cape Horn route, Cape Horner

capillaire [kapilɛr] ADJ *Biol* **1** *(relatif aux cheveux)* hair *(avant n)* **2** *(très fin ▸ tube, vaisseau)* capillary *(avant n)*

NM **1** *Biol (vaisseau)* capillary **2** *Biol (tube)* capillary (tube) **3** *Bot* maidenhair (fern)

capillarité [kapilarite] *Phys* NF capillarity, capillary action

• **par capillarité** ADV by *or* through capillary action

capilliculture [kapilikyltyr] NF hair care

capilotade [kapilɔtad] **en capilotade** ADJ *(écrasé)* in a pulp; *(fatigué et douloureux)* aching; **j'ai les jambes en c.** my legs are aching; **mettre qch en c.** *(en morceaux)* to smash sth to pieces *or* to smithereens; *Fig* **la démocratie dans ce pays est en c.** democracy in this country is in ruins *or* tatters

capitaine [kapitɛn] NM **1** *Naut (dans la marine marchande)* captain, master; *(dans la navigation de plaisance)* captain, skipper; **oui, mon c.** yes, sir; *Mil* **c. de corvette** ≃ lieutenant commander; *Mil* **c. de frégate** ≃ commander; **c. au long cours** master mariner; *Admin & Naut* **c. de port** harbour master; *Mil* **c. de vaisseau** ≃ captain

2 *Mil (dans l'armée ▸ de terre)* captain; *(▸ de l'air) Br* ≃ flight lieutenant, *Am* ≃ captain; **c. de gendarmerie** = captain of the "gendarmerie"; **les capitaines d'industrie** the captains of industry

3 *Sport* captain

4 c. des pompiers *Br* chief fire officer, *Am* fire chief

capitainerie [kapitɛnri] NF *Admin & Naut* harbour master's office

capital[1]**, -e, -aux**[1]**, -ales** [kapital, -o] ADJ **1** *(détail)* vital; *(aide, témoignage)* vital, crucial; *(question, argument, point)* fundamental; **c'est c.**

it's essential *or* crucial; **c'est d'une importance capitale** it's of the utmost importance; **il est c. que nous prenions des mesures** it is absolutely essential that we take action

2 *(œuvre, projet)* major

3 *Typ (lettre ▸ imprimée)* capital; *(▸ manuscrite)* (block) capital

4 *Jur (crime, sentence)* capital; *Jur* **la peine capitale** capital punishment, the death penalty

• **capitale** NF **1** *Admin (ville)* capital (city); **la capitale** *(Paris)* the capital, Paris; **capitale régionale** regional capital; *Fig* **la capitale de la mode** the fashion capital **2** *Typ* capital (letter); **petite capitale** small capital

• **en capitales** ADV *Typ* in capitals, in block letters; **écrivez votre nom en capitales (d'imprimerie)** write your name in block capitals, print your name

capital², -aux² [kapital, -o] NM **1** *Écon & Fin (avoir ▸ personnel)* capital *(UNCOUNT)*; *(▸ d'une société)* capital *(UNCOUNT)*, assets; **une société au c. de 500 000 euros** a firm with assets of 500,000 euros; **il détient 5 pour cent du c. de la société** he has a 5 percent shareholding in the company, he holds 5 percent of the company's shares; **c. actions** share capital, equity (capital); **c. appelé** called-up capital; **c. d'apport** initial capital; **c. autorisé** authorized (share) capital; **c. circulant** circulating *or* floating capital; **c. déclaré** registered capital; **c. de départ** start-up capital; **c. disponible** available capital; *Bourse* **c. émis** issued capital; **c. d'emprunt** loan capital; **c. engagé** tied-up capital, capital employed; **c. d'établissement** invested capital; *Compta* **c. exigible** current liabilities; **c. existant** physical capital; **c. d'exploitation** *Br* working capital, *Am* operating capital; **c. financier** finance capital; **c. fixe** fixed *or* capital assets; **c. foncier** land; **c. humain** *(d'une entreprise)* manpower; **c. improductif** idle capital, unproductive capital; **c. initial** start-up capital; **capitaux investis** invested capital; **c. libéré** fully paid capital; **c. nominal** nominal capital; **c. d'origine** original capital; **c. réel** paid-up capital; **c. roulant** circulating capital; **c. de roulement** *Br* working capital, *Am* operating capital; *Bourse* **c. social** share capital; *Bourse* **c. social autorisé** authorized capital; **c. souscrit** subscribed capital; **c. technique** (technical) equipment; **c. variable** variable capital; **c. versé** paid-up capital

2 *(compensation)* **c. décès** death benefit; **c. départ** severance money *or* pay

3 *(monde de l'argent, des capitalistes)* **le c.** capital; **le grand c.** big business

4 *(ressources, accumulation)* **ces jeunes diplômés représentent un véritable c. pour notre entreprise** these qualified young people are an asset to our company; **un c. de connaissances** a fund of knowledge; **le c. culturel du pays** the nation's cultural wealth; **le c. intellectuel** intellectual resources; **le c. forêt de la planète** the forest reserves of the planet

• **capitaux** NMPL *Écon & Fin (valeurs disponibles)* capital; **circulation des capitaux** circulation of capital; **fuite des capitaux** flight of capital; **capitaux flottants** floating capital; **capitaux fébriles** hot money; **capitaux frais** new capital; **capitaux gelés** frozen assets; **capitaux permanents** capital employed, long-term capital; **capitaux propres** equity, shareholders' equity *or* funds

capitalisable [kapitalizabl] ADJ *Fin* capitalizable

capitalisation [kapitalizasjɔ̃] NF *Fin* capitalization; **c. boursière** market capitalization

capitaliser [3] [kapitalize] VT **1** *Fin (capital)* to capitalize; *(intérêts)* to add; *(revenu)* to turn into capital; **une fois que les intérêts ont été capitalisés** once the accrued interest has been calculated **2** *(amasser ▸ argent)* to save up, to accumulate **3** *(accumuler)* to accumulate

VI *(économiser)* to save

• **capitaliser sur** VT IND *Fam (tirer profit de)* to capitalize on□

capitalisme [kapitalism] NM *Écon* capitalism; **c. sauvage** ruthless capitalism

capitaliste [kapitalist] ADJ *Écon* capitalist, capitalistic

NMF capitalist

capitalistique [kapitalistik] ADJ *Fin* capital-intensive

capital-risque [kapitalrisk] *(pl* **capitaux-risques)** NM *Fin* venture capital

capital-risqueur [kapitalriskœr] *(pl* **capitaux-risqueurs)** NM *Fin* venture capitalist

capitation [kapitasjɔ̃] NF *Hist & Fin* capitation, poll tax

capiteux, -euse [kapitø, -øz] ADJ **1** *(fort ▸ alcool, senteur)* heady **2** *(excitant ▸ charme, blonde)* sensuous

Capitole [kapitɔl] NM **1** *(à Toulouse)* **le C.** = main square in Toulouse **2** *(à Rome)* **le C.** the Capitol **3** *(à Washington)* **le C.** Capitol Hill, the Capitol

capiton [kapitɔ̃] NM **1** *(matériau)* padding **2** *(section rembourrée)* boss, padded section

capitonnage [kapitɔnaʒ] NM padding

capitonner [3] [kapitɔne] VT to pad

capitulaire [kapitylɛr] ADJ *Rel* capitular; **salle c.** chapter house

NM *Jur & Hist* capitulary

capitulation [kapitylasjɔ̃] NF **1** *Mil (action)* surrender, capitulation; *(traité)* capitulation; **c. sans conditions** unconditional surrender **2** *Fig (fait de céder)* surrendering

capituler [3] [kapityle] VI **1** *Mil* to surrender, to capitulate **2** *Fig (céder)* to surrender, to give in

capon, -onne [kapɔ̃, -ɔn] *Fam Vieilli* ADJ cowardly□, yellow

NM,F coward□

caporal, -aux [kapɔral, -o] NM **1** *Mil (dans l'armée de terre) Br* ≃ lance corporal, *Am* ≃ private first class; *(dans l'armée de l'air) Br* ≃ senior aircraftman, *Am* ≃ airman first class; **c. d'ordinaire** mess corporal **2** *Hist* **le Petit C.** = nickname used to refer to Napoleon Bonaparte

caporal-chef [kapɔralʃɛf] *(pl* **caporaux-chefs** [kapɔroʃɛf]) NM *Mil (dans l'armée de terre)* ≃ corporal; *(dans l'armée de l'air) Br* ≃ corporal, *Am* ≃ senior airman

caporaliser [3] [kapɔralize] VT to set petty rules for

caporalisme [kapɔralism] NM **1** *(autoritarisme)* petty officiousness, bossiness **2** *(régime politique)* military rule

capot [kapo] NM **1** *Aut Br* bonnet, *Am* hood

2 *Naut (bâche)* tarpaulin; *(tôle)* cover; *(ouverture)* companion hatchway

3 *(d'une machine)* hood; *Ordinat* **c. d'imprimante** printer hood

4 *Can Vieilli (manteau)* loose woollen coat; *Fig* **virer** *ou* **changer son c. (de bord)** to switch allegiances; *Fam* **en avoir plein le c.** to be fed up, to have had it up to here

ADJ INV *Cartes* **être c.** to have made no tricks at all

capotage [kapɔtaʒ] NM **1** *(d'une machine, d'un moteur)* hooding **2** *(culbute ▸ d'une voiture)* overturning; *(▸ d'un bateau)* capsizing

capote [kapɔt] NF **1** *Fam (préservatif)* condom□, rubber; *Vieilli* **c. anglaise** condom□, *Br* French letter

2 *Aut (d'une voiture) Br* hood, *Am* top

3 *(manteau)* greatcoat

4 *(chapeau)* bonnet

capoter [3] [kapɔte] VT to fit with a *Br* hood *or Am* top

VI **1** *(voiture)* to overturn, to roll over; *(bateau)* to capsize, to turn turtle **2** *Fam (projet)* to fall through□, to collapse□; *(transaction)* to fall through□; **il a tout fait c.** he messed everything up **3** *Can Fam (perdre la tête)* to flip, to lose it; **c. sur qch/qn** to go mad for sth/sb

cappella [kapela] *voir* **a cappella**

cappuccino [kaputʃino] NM cappuccino

câpre [kapr] NF caper

caprice [kapris] NM **1** *(fantaisie)* whim; **elle lui passe tous ses caprices** she indulges his/her every whim; **il n'agit que par c.** he just acts on impulse; **par un c. du destin** by a whim of fate; **les caprices de la mode** the vagaries of fashion **2** *(colère)* tantrum; **faire des caprices** to throw tantrums **3** *(irrégularité)* **c'est un véritable c. de la nature** it's a real freak of nature

capricieuse [kaprisjøz] *voir* **capricieux**

capricieusement [kaprisjøzmɑ̃] ADV capriciously

capricieux, -euse [kaprisjø, -øz] ADJ **1** *(coléreux)* temperamental; **un enfant c.** a difficult child **2** *(fantaisiste)* capricious, fickle; *Fig (ruisseau)* meandering; **le vol c. d'un papillon** the flitting of a butterfly **3** *(peu fiable ▸ machine, véhicule)* unreliable, temperamental; *(▸ saison, temps)* unpredictable

NM,F capricious person; **un petit c.** a spoilt child

Capricorne [kaprikɔrn] NM **1** *Astron* Capricorn **2** *Astrol* Capricorn; **être C.** to be Capricorn *or* a Capricornean

capricorne [kaprikɔrn] NM **1** *Entom* capricorn beetle **2** *Zool* serow

câprier [kaprije] NM *Bot* caper (plant)

caprin, -e [kaprɛ̃, -in] ADJ *Zool* goat *(avant n)*, *Spéc* caprine

capsulage [kapsylaʒ] NM *(de bouteilles)* capping

capsule [kapsyl] NF **1** *(d'une bouteille)* top, cap

2 *Astron* **c. (spatiale)** (space) capsule

3 *Anat, Bot & Pharm* capsule

4 *Chim* dish

capsuler [3] [kapsyle] VT *(des bouteilles)* to put a cap *or* top on

captage [kaptaʒ] NM **1** *Rad & Tél* picking up, receiving **2** *Élec (du courant)* picking up **3** *(des eaux)* catchment; *(d'une source)* tapping

capteur, -trice [kaptœr, -tris] NM,F *Jur* inveigler; **c. de succession** legacy *or* inheritance hunter

captation [kaptasjɔ̃] NF *Jur* inveiglement

captatoire [kaptatwar] ADJ *Jur* inveigling

captatrice [kaptatris] *voir* **captateur**

capter [3] [kapte] VT **1** *(attention, intérêt)* to capture

2 *(eaux)* to collect, to catch; *(source)* to tap

3 *Rad & Tél* to pick up, to receive

4 *Élec (courant)* to pick up

5 *Jur* to inveigle

6 *Fam (comprendre)* to get; **répète, j'ai pas capté** say that again, I didn't get it

capteur [kaptœr] NM **1** *Écol* **c. (solaire)** solar panel **2** *(pour mesurer)* sensor; *(pour commander)* probe; *Ordinat* **c. photosensible** photosensitive *or* light-sensitive sensor

captieux, -euse [kapsjø, -øz] ADJ *Littéraire* specious, misleading

captif, -ive [kaptif, -iv] ADJ **1** *(emprisonné)* captive; *Fig Littéraire* **être c. de son propre plaisir** to be a slave to pleasure **2** *Écon (marché)* captive **3** *(ballon)* captive

NM,F *Littéraire* captive

captivant, -e [kaptivɑ̃, -ɑ̃t] ADJ *(personne)* captivating; *(spectacle, livre, histoire)* captivating, enthralling, riveting

captive [kaptiv] *voir* **captif**

captiver [3] [kaptive] VT *(personne)* to captivate; *(spectacle, livre, histoire)* to captivate, to enthral

captivité [kaptivite] NF captivity; **vivre en c.** to be in captivity; **garder un animal en c.** to keep an animal in captivity

capture [kaptyr] NF **1** *(de biens)* seizure, seizing, confiscation; *(d'un navire, d'un tank)* capture

2 *(arrestation)* capture

3 *(biens ou animaux capturés)* catch, haul

4 *Géog & Phys* capture

5 *Ordinat* **c. d'écran** screen capture, screen dump, screen shot; **c. vidéo** video capture

capturer [3] [kaptyre] VT **1** *(faire prisonnier)* to capture, to catch **2** *(navire, tank)* to capture **3** *Ordinat* to capture

capuche [kapyʃ] NF hood; **c. en plastique** rain hood; **une veste/un haut à c.** a hooded jacket/top

capuchon [kapyʃɔ̃] NM **1** *(bonnet)* hood; *(manteau)* hooded coat; *(de moine)* cowl **2** *(d'un stylo)* cap, top; *(d'un tube de dentifrice)* top **3** *(d'une cheminée)* cowl

• **à capuchon** ADJ hooded

capucin, -e [kapysɛ̃, -in] NM,F *Rel* Capuchin (Friar), *f* Capuchin nun

NM *Zool* capuchin (monkey)

• **capucine** NF *Bot* nasturtium

Cap-Vert [kapvɛr] **NM le C.** Cape Verde

caque [kak] **NF** herring barrel; *Prov* **la c. sent toujours le hareng** what is bred in the bone will come out in the flesh

caquelon [kaklɔ̃] **NM** *Culin* fondue pot

caquet [kakɛ] **NM 1** *(gloussement)* cackle, cackling **2** *Fam (bavardage)* yakking, prattle; **il a un de ces caquets!** he yaks on and on!; **rabattre** *ou* **rabaisser le c. à qn** to take sb down a peg or two, to put sb in his/her place

caquetage [kaktaʒ], **caquètement** [kakɛtmɑ̃] **NM 1** *(de poules)* cackle, cackling **2** *Fam (bavardage ▸ futile)* prattle; *(▸ indiscret)* gossip

caqueter [27] [kakte] **VI 1** *(poule)* to cackle **2** *(tenir des propos ▸ futiles)* prattle (on); *(▸ indiscrets)* to gossip

car[1] [kar] **NM 1** *(autobus)* bus, *Br* coach; **c. de police** police van; **c. de ramassage (scolaire)** school bus **2** *TV & Rad* **c. régie** *ou* **de reportage** mobile unit, *Br* outside broadcasting van, OB van; **c. de transmission** transmitter van **3** *TV* **c. monocaméra** single-camera unit; **c. multicaméra** multi-camera unit

> Il faut noter que le nom anglais **car** est un faux ami. Il signifie **voiture**.

car[2] [kar] **CONJ** because, for; **il est efficace, c. très bien secondé** he is efficient because he has very good back-up

carabe [karab] **NM** *Entom* ground beetle

carabin [karabɛ̃] **NM** *Fam Arg scol (étudiant en médecine)* medic

carabine [karabin] **NF** rifle; **c. à air comprimé** air rifle *or* gun

carabiné, -e [karabine] **ADJ** *Fam (note à payer, addition)* stiff, steep; *(rhume)* filthy, stinking; *(migraine)* blinding; *(fièvre)* violent, raging; **une grippe carabinée** a dreadful dose of the flu; **j'ai une gueule de bois carabinée** I've got one hell of a hangover

carabinier [karabinje] **NM 1** *(en Italie)* carabiniere, policeman **2** *(en Espagne)* carabinero, customs officer **3** *Hist & Mil* carabineer, carabinier

Carabosse [karabɔs] *voir* **fée**

Caracas [karakas] **NM** Caracas

caraco [karako] **NM** camisole

caracole [karakɔl] **NF** *Équitation & Archit* caracole; **escalier en c.** spiral staircase, caracole

caracoler [3] [karakɔle] **VI 1** *(sautiller)* to skip about, to gambol **2** *Équitation* to caracole **3** *Fig* **c. en tête** to be top dog, to be top of the league

caractère [karaktɛr] **NM 1** *(nature)* character, nature, temperament; **ce n'est pas dans son c. d'être agressif** it's out of character for him to be *or* it's not in his nature to be aggressive

2 *(tempérament)* temper; **quel c.!** what a temper!; *Fam* **quel fichu c.!** what a bad-tempered so-and-so!; **avoir bon c.** to be good-natured; **avoir mauvais** *ou* **(un) sale c.** to be bad-tempered; *Fam* **avoir un c. de chien** *ou* **de cochon** to have a foul temper

3 *(volonté, courage)* character; **avoir du c.** to have character; **elle manque de c.** she's not very strong-willed

4 *(type de personne)* character; **les caractères doux sont souvent mal compris** gentle people are often misunderstood

5 *(particularité)* nature, character; **le c. religieux de la cérémonie** the religious nature of the ceremony; **une maladie sans c. de gravité** an illness not considered to be serious; **à c. officiel** of an official nature

6 *(trait)* characteristic, feature, trait; *(dans des statistiques)* characteristic; **tous les caractères d'une crise économique** all the characteristics of an economic crisis

7 *(originalité)* character; **un édifice qui a du c.** a building with character; **sans aucun c.** characterless

8 *Biol* character; **c. acquis** acquired trait *or* characteristic; **c. héréditaire** hereditary trait *or* characteristic

9 *Typ* character; **le choix des caractères** the choice of typeface; **en gros/petits caractères** in large/small print; **caractères gras** bold (type); **en caractères gras** in bold (type); **caractères d'imprimerie** block letters; **écrivez en caractères d'imprimerie** please write in block letters; **caractères romains** roman (type); **en caractères romains** in roman (type)

10 *Ordinat* character; **caractères par pouce** characters per inch; **caractères par seconde** characters per second; **caractères alphanumériques** alphanumeric characters; **c. de changement de ligne** line feed character; **c. de changement de page** page break character; **c. de contrôle** control character; **c. d'effacement** delete character; **c. imprimable** printable character; **c. d'interruption** break character; **c. joker** wildcard character; **c. majuscule** upper-case character; **c. minuscule** lower-case character; **c. en mode point** bitmapped character, bitmap character; **c. de retour arrière** backspace character; **c. à sept bits** seven-bit character

• **de caractère ADJ appartement/maison de c.** flat/house with character; **une femme de c.** a woman of character

caractériel, -elle [karakterjɛl] **ADJ 1** *(d'humeur changeante)* moody **2** *Psy (adolescent)* maladjusted, (emotionally) disturbed; *(troubles)* emotional **3** *(du caractère)* character *(avant n)*

NM,F *(enfant)* problem child; *(adulte)* maladjusted person

caractérisation [karakterizasjɔ̃] **NF** characterization

caractérisé, -e [karakterize] **ADJ** *(méchanceté)* blatant; *(indifférence)* pointed; **une rougeole caractérisée** a clear *or* unmistakable case of measles

caractériser [3] [karakterize] **VT 1** *(constituer le caractère de)* to characterize; **avec la générosité qui le caractérise** with characteristic generosity; **les symptômes qui caractérisent cette maladie** the characteristic symptoms of this illness **2** *(définir)* to characterize, to define

VPR se caractériser se c. par to be characterized by

caractéristique [karakteristik] **ADJ** characteristic, typical; **observez la rougeur c.** note the characteristic red hue; **c'est c. de sa façon d'agir** it's typical of his/her way of doing things

NF *(trait)* characteristic, (distinguishing) feature *or* trait; **caractéristiques techniques** specifications

caractérologie [karakterɔlɔʒi] **NF** characterology

carafe [karaf] **NF 1** *(récipient ▸ ordinaire)* carafe; *(▸ travaillé)* decanter

2 *(contenu)* jugful; *(de vin)* carafe; **une demi-c.** half a carafe (of wine)

3 *Fam (tête)* nut

4 *Fam (locution)* **rester** *ou* **tomber en c.** *(véhicule)* to break down[□]; *(voyageur)* to be stranded[□]

carafon [karafɔ̃] **NM 1** *(récipient ▸ ordinaire)* small jug *or* carafe; *(▸ travaillé)* small decanter **2** *(contenu)* (small) jugful; *(de vin)* small carafe **3** *Fam (tête)* nut; **il a rien dans le c.!** he's got nothing between his ears, *Br* he's as thick as two short planks

caraïbe [karaib] **ADJ** *(personne)* Caribbean

NM *(langue)* Carib

• **Caraïbe NMF** Carib

• **Caraïbe NF** *(chaîne montagneuse)* **la C.** the Caribbean

• **Caraïbes NFPL les (îles) Caraïbes** the Caribbean, the West Indies; **la mer des Caraïbes** the Caribbean (Sea)

carambolage [karɑ̃bɔlaʒ] **NM 1** *(de voitures)* pile-up **2** *(au billard) Br* cannon, *Am* carom

caramboler [3] [karɑ̃bɔle] **VI** *(au billard) Br* to cannon, *Am* to carom

VT to crash into; **onze voitures carambolées** an eleven-car pile-up

VPR se caramboler dix voitures se sont carambolées sur l'autoroute there has been a ten-car pile-up on the *Br* motorway *or Am* freeway

carambouillage [karɑ̃bujaʒ] **NM** *Fam* fraudulent selling of goods bought on credit

caramel [karamɛl] **NM 1** *(pour napper)* caramel **2** *(bonbon)* toffee, caramel

ADJ INV caramel-coloured

caramélisation [karamelizasjɔ̃] **NF** caramelization

caraméliser [3] [karamelize] **VT 1** *(mets, moule)* to coat with caramel; *(glace)* to flavour with caramel **2** *(sucre)* to caramelize

VI to caramelize; **faire c. du sucre** to caramelize sugar

VPR se caraméliser *(sucre)* to caramelize; *(oignons)* to brown, to caramelize

carapace [karapas] **NF 1** *Zool* shell, *Spéc* carapace **2** *Fig* shell; **il est difficile de percer sa c.** it's difficult to get through to him/her; **la voiture était recouverte d'une c. de boue** the car was encrusted with mud

carapater [3] [karapate] **se carapater VPR** *Fam* to beat it, to make oneself scarce

carat [kara] **NM 1** *(d'un métal, d'une pierre)* carat; **or (à) 18 carats** 18-carat gold; **c. métrique** carat (weight); *Fam* **je te donne jusqu'à trois heures, dernier c.** I'll give you till three o'clock at the latest[□] *or* tops **2** *Fam (année)* **il a dépassé les 60 carats** he's over 60[□]

Caravage [karavaʒ] **NPR** *Beaux-Arts* **le C.** Caravaggio

caravanage [karavanaʒ] **NM** *Offic Br* caravanning, *Am* trailer camping; **faire du c.** *Br* to go caravanning, *Am* to go trailer camping

caravane [karavan] **NF 1** *(véhicule ▸ de vacancier) Br* caravan, *Am* trailer; *(▸ de nomade)* caravan **2** *(convoi)* caravan; **c. publicitaire** following vehicles

caravanier, -ère [karavanje, -ɛr] **NM,F 1** *(nomade)* caravanner **2** *(vacancier) Br* caravanner, *Am* camper *(in a trailer)*

ADJ chemin c. caravan route *or* track

caravaning [karavaniŋ] **NM** *Br* caravanning, *Am* trailer camping; **faire du c.** to go *Br* caravanning *or Am* trailer camping

caravansérail [karavɑ̃seraj] **NM** caravanserai, caravansary

caravelle [karavɛl] **NF** *Naut* caravel

carbochimie [karbɔʃimi] **NF** organic chemistry

carbonade [karbɔnad] **NF** *Culin* carbonade, carbonnade; **c. flamande** beef stew with beer

carbonate [karbɔnat] **NM** *Chim* carbonate

carbone [karbɔn] **NM 1** *(papier)* carbon paper; *(feuille)* sheet of carbon paper **2** *Chim* carbon; *Archéol* **c. 14** carbon-14; **dater qch au c. 14** to carbon-date sth, to date sth with carbon-14 **3** *École* carbon; **bilan du c.** carbon balance; **émissions de c.** carbon emissions

carbonifère [karbɔnifɛr] *Géol* **ADJ** carboniferous

NM Carboniferous (period)

carbonique [karbɔnik] **ADJ** *Chim (acide)* carbonic

carbonisation [karbɔnizasjɔ̃] **NF** *Chim* carbonization

carboniser [3] [karbɔnize] **VT 1** *(brûler ▸ viande)* to burn to a cinder; *(▸ édifice, forêt)* to burn to the ground; **des corps carbonisés** charred bodies **2** *Chim (transformer en charbon)* to carbonize, to turn into charcoal

carbonnade [karbɔnad] = **carbonade**

carbonyle [karbɔnil] **NM** *Chim* carbonyl

carburant [karbyrɑ̃] **ADJ M mélange c.** mixture of air and *Br* petrol *or Am* gas

NM fuel

carburateur [karbyratœr] **NM** *Tech* carburettor; **c. double corps** twin carburettor

carburation [karbyrasjɔ̃] **NF 1** *Tech* carburation **2** *Métal* carburization, carburizing

carbure [karbyr] **NM** *Chim* carbide; **c. de calcium** calcium carbide

carburé, -e [karbyre] **ADJ 1** *Métal* carburized **2** *Tech* carburetted

carburéacteur [karbyreaktœr] **NM** *Aviat* jet fuel

carburer [3] [karbyre] **VT 1** *Aut* to carburate **2** *Métal* to carburize

VI 1 *Aut* **le moteur carbure mal** the mixture is wrong

2 *Fam (aller vite)* **fais tes valises, et que ça carbure!** pack your bags, and be quick about it!

3 *Fam (travailler dur)* to work flat out; **alors, ça**

carbure? are you working hard, then?[a]

4 *Fam (fonctionner)* **ça carbure?** how are things?; **il carbure au whisky/au café** whisky/coffee keeps him going

carcajou [karkaʒu] **NM** *Zool* wolverine

carcan [karkɑ̃] **NM 1** *Hist (collier)* collar shackle; *Fig* **pris dans les règlements comme dans un c.** hemmed in by regulations **2** *(sujétion)* yoke, shackles; **le c. des horaires** scheduling constraints **3** *(pour bétail)* yoke

carcasse [karkas] **NF 1** *(d'un animal)* carcass

2 *Fam Fig* **amène ta c.!** get yourself over here!; **promener** *ou* **traîner sa (vieille) c.** to drag oneself along

3 *(armature ▸ d'un édifice, d'un bateau)* shell; *(▸ d'un meuble)* carcass; *(▸ d'un véhicule)* shell, body; *(▸ d'un parapluie)* frame

4 *(d'un pneu)* carcass; **c. diagonale** cross-ply carcass; **c. radiale** radial-ply carcass; **pneu à c. diagonale/radiale** cross-ply/radial-ply tyre

carcéral, -e, -aux, -ales [karseral, -o] **ADJ** prison *(avant n)*

carcinogène [karsinɔʒɛn] *Méd* **ADJ** carcinogenic; **produit c.** carcinogen

NM carcinogen

carcinologie [karsinɔlɔʒi] **NF** *Méd (étude du cancer)* oncology

carcinome [karsinom] **NM** *Méd* carcinoma; **c. glandulaire** glandular carcinoma

cardage [kardaʒ] **NM** *Tex* carding

cardan [kardɑ̃] **NM** *Tech & Aut* **(joint de) c.** universal joint

carde [kard] **NF 1** *Bot (d'une bette, d'un cardon)* leaf stalk **2** *Tex* card, carding brush

carder [3] [karde] **VT** *Tex* to card

cardeur, -euse [kardœr, -øz] *Tex* **NM,F** carder, carding operator

• **cardeuse NF** carding machine

cardiaque [kardjak] **ADJ** heart *(avant n)*, cardiac; **une maladie c.** a heart disease; **elle est c.** she has a heart condition

NMF cardiac *or* heart patient

cardigan [kardigɑ̃] **NM** cardigan

cardinal, -e, -aux, -ales [kardinal, -o] **ADJ 1** *Astrol & Math* cardinal **2** *(essentiel)* essential, fundamental; **vertus cardinales** cardinal virtues **3** *Géog* **points cardinaux** points of the compass

NM 1 *(apéritif)* = kir made with red wine

2 *Math* cardinal number, cardinal

3 *Rel* cardinal

4 *Orn* **c. (rouge)** cardinal

cardinalat [kardinala] **NM** *Rel* cardinalate, cardinalship

cardinalice [kardinalis] **ADJ** *Rel* of a cardinal

cardiogramme [kardjogram] **NM** *Méd* cardiogram

cardiographe [kardjograf] **NM** *Méd* cardiograph

cardiographie [kardjografi] **NF** *Méd* cardiography

cardiologie [kardjolɔʒi] **NF** *Méd* cardiology

cardiologue [kardjolɔg] **NMF** *Méd* heart specialist, *Spéc* cardiologist

cardio-respiratoire [kardjorespiratwar] *(pl* **cardio-respiratoires)** **ADJ** *Méd* cardiorespiratory; **maladie c.** disease of the heart and respiratory system

cardio-training [kardjotreniŋ] **NM INV** *Sport* cardio-training, CV training

cardio-vasculaire [kardjovaskylɛr] *(pl* **cardio-vasculaires)** **ADJ** *Méd* cardiovascular

cardite [kardit] **NF** *Méd* carditis

cardon [kardɔ̃] **NM** *Bot & Culin* cardoon

carême [karɛm] **NM** *Rel* **le c.** *(abstinence)* fasting; *(époque)* Lent; **faire c.** to fast for *or* to observe Lent; **face** *ou* **figure de c.** sad *or* long face

carême-prenant [karɛmprənɑ̃] *(pl* **carêmes-prenants)** **NM** *Arch* Shrovetide

carénage [karenaʒ] **NM 1** *Naut (opération, lieu)* careenage **2** *Aviat & Aut* streamlined body

carence [karɑ̃s] **NF 1** *Méd* deficiency; **c. en zinc** zinc deficiency; **avoir une c. alimentaire** to suffer from a nutritional deficiency

2 *(d'une administration, d'une œuvre, d'une méthode)* shortcoming, failing

3 *Psy* **c. affective** emotional deprivation

4 *Jur* insolvency

• **de carence, par carence ADJ** deficiency *(avant n)*

carencé, -e [karɑ̃se] **ADJ 1** *Méd* suffering from a nutritional deficiency **2** *Psy* emotionally deprived

carène [karɛn] **NF 1** *Naut* hull; **abattre un navire en c.** to careen a ship **2** *Aviat & Aut* streamlined body

caréner [18] [karene] **VT 1** *Naut* to careen **2** *Aut & Aviat* to streamline

carentiel, -elle [karɑ̃sjɛl] **ADJ** *Méd* deficiency-related

caressant, -e [karesɑ̃, -ɑ̃t] **ADJ 1** *(personne)* affectionate, loving; **un enfant c.** an affectionate child **2** *Littéraire (voix, sourire)* warm, caressing; *(vent)* caressing

caresse [karɛs] **NF 1** *(attouchement)* caress, stroke; **faire des caresses à** *(chat)* to stroke; *(personne)* to caress **2** *Littéraire (d'un sourire)* tenderness; *(du vent, du soleil)* caress, kiss; **sous la c. du soleil** kissed by the sun

caresser [4] [karese] **VT 1** *(toucher ▸ affectueusement)* to stroke; *(▸ sensuellement)* to caress; **c. un enfant** to pet a child; **c. les cheveux de qn** to stroke sb's hair; **c. qn des yeux** *ou* **du regard** to gaze lovingly at sb; *Fig* **c. qn dans le sens du poil** to stroke sb's ego; **il faut le c. dans le sens du poil** don't rub him (up) the wrong way

2 *Littéraire (effleurer ▸ tissu, papier)* to touch lightly

3 *(avoir, former)* **c. l'espoir de faire qch** to cherish the hope of doing sth; **c. le rêve de faire qch** to dream of doing sth

4 *Fam (battre)* **c. les oreilles à qn** to clout sb round the ear

VPR se caresser 1 *(emploi réfléchi)* to caress oneself **2** *(emploi réciproque)* to cuddle **3 se c. qch** to stroke sth

car-ferry [karferi] *(pl* **car-ferrys** *ou* **car-ferries** [-ri]) **NM** ferry, car-ferry

cargaison [kargɛzɔ̃] **NF 1** *(marchandises)* cargo, freight **2** *Fam (quantité)* load[a] **(de** of); **j'avais préparé toute une c. d'excuses** I had a whole load of excuses prepared

cargo [kargo] **NM** freighter; **c. mixte** cargo and passenger vessel

> Il faut noter que le nom anglais **cargo** est un faux ami. Il signifie **cargaison**.

cargue [karg] **NF** *Naut (de voile)* brail

carguer [3] [karge] **VT** *Naut (voile)* to take in, to brail (up)

cariant, -e [karjɑ̃, -ɑ̃t] **ADJ** *Méd* cariogenic

cariatide [karjatid] = **caryatide**

caribou [karibu] **NM** *Zool* caribou, reindeer

caricatural, -e, -aux, -ales [karikatyral, -o] **ADJ 1** *(récit, explication)* distorted; **un féminisme c.** a mockery *or* travesty of feminism **2** *(dessin, art)* caricatural **3** *(exagéré)* typical, caricature *(avant n)*

caricature [karikatyr] **NF 1** *(dessin)* caricature; **c. politique** (political) cartoon **2** *(déformation)* caricature; **c'est une c. de ce que j'ai dit** it makes a mockery of *or* it's a complete distortion of what I said **3** *(personne)* **c'est une vraie c.!** he/she's grotesque!

caricaturer [3] [karikatyre] **VT 1** *(dessiner)* to caricature **2** *(déformer)* to distort

caricaturiste [karikatyrist] **NMF** caricaturist

carie [kari] **NF 1** *Méd* caries; **c. dentaire** tooth decay, *Spéc* dental caries; **elle n'a pas de caries** she doesn't have any bad teeth **2** *Bot (du blé)* bunt, smut; *(des arbres)* blight

carié, -e [karje] **ADJ 1** *Méd (dent)* decayed, bad, *Spéc* carious; *(os)* decayed, *Spéc* carious **2** *Bot (blé)* smutty; *(arbre)* blighted

carier [10] [karje] *Méd* **VT** to decay, to cause decay in

VPR se carier to decay

carillon [karijɔ̃] **NM 1** *(cloches)* (set of) bells **2** *(sonnerie ▸ d'une horloge)* chime; *(▸ d'entrée)* chime; *(▸ de cloches)* (peal of) bells **3** *(horloge)* chiming clock

carillonnement [karijɔnmɑ̃] **NM 1** *(action)* ringing **2** *(son)* chiming

carillonner [3] [karijɔne] **VI 1** *(cloches)* to ring, to chime; **on a fait c. les cloches pour la victoire** the bells were sounded in celebration of the victory **2** *(à la porte)* to ring (the doorbell) loudly

VT 1 *(heures)* to chime **2** *Péj (rumeur)* to broadcast, to shout from the roof tops **3** *(festival)* to announce with a peal of bells

carillonneur, -euse [karijɔnœr, -øz] **NM,F** bell ringer

cariste [karist] **NM** forklift truck operator

caritatif, -ive [karitatif, -iv] **ADJ** charity *(avant n)*; **association caritative** charity

carlin [karlɛ̃] **NM** *Zool (chien)* pug (dog)

carlingue [karlɛ̃g] **NF 1** *Aviat* cabin **2** *Naut* keelson

carliste [karlist] *Pol* **ADJ** Carlist

NMF Carlist

carmagnole [karmaɲɔl] *Hist* **NF** *(veste)* carmagnole

• **Carmagnole NF la C.** the Carmagnole *(song and dance popular during the French Revolution)*

carme [karm] **NM** *Rel* Carmelite, White Friar

carmélite [karmelit] **NF** *Rel* Carmelite

carmin [karmɛ̃] **ADJ INV** crimson, carmine

NM crimson, carmine; *Littéraire* **lèvres de c.** ruby lips

carminé, -e [karmine] **ADJ** *Littéraire* crimson, carmine

carnage [karnaʒ] **NM** *(massacre)* slaughter, carnage; *Fig* **s'ils n'arrêtent pas, je fais un c.** if they don't stop, I'll kill them

carnassier, -ère [karnasje, -ɛr] **ADJ** *(animal)* carnivorous; *(dent)* carnassial; *Fig (regard, sourire)* predatory

NM carnivore

• **carnassière NF 1** *Zool (dent)* carnassial **2** *Chasse (sac)* game bag

carnation [karnasjɔ̃] **NF** *Littéraire (teint)* complexion; *(en peinture)* flesh tint

carnaval, -als [karnaval] **NM 1** *(fête)* carnival; **pendant le c.** during carnival, at carnival time **2** *(mannequin)* **(Sa Majesté) C.** King Carnival

carnavalesque [karnavalɛsk] **ADJ 1** *(de carnaval)* carnival *(avant n)* **2** *(burlesque)* grotesque

carne [karn] **NF** *Fam* **1** *(viande)* tough meat[a] **2** *Vieilli (cheval)* **(vieille) c.** old nag **3** *(terme d'injure)* swine; **petite c., va!** you little swine!; **vieille c.!** old bag!

carné, -e [karne] **ADJ 1** *(en diététique)* meat-based **2** *(rosé)* flesh-toned, flesh-coloured

carneau, -x [karno] **NM** *Tech* flue

carnet [karnɛ] **NM 1** *(cahier)* notebook; **c. à dessins** sketchbook

2 *(registre) aussi Ordinat* **c. d'adresses** address book; *Douanes* **c. ATA** ATA carnet; **c. de bord** logbook; **c. de route** logbook; **c. de santé** child's health record

3 *(à feuilles détachables)* **c. de chèques** cheque book; **c. à souches** counterfoil book; **c. de tickets (de métro)** = book of ten metro tickets; **c. de timbres** book of stamps

4 *Com* **c. de commandes** order book; **c. de dépenses** account book

5 *Journ (rubrique)* **c. blanc** marriages column; **c. mondain** court and social; **c. rose** births column

6 *Scol* **c. de correspondance** = school report book; **c. de notes** *Br* school report, *Am* report card; **elle a eu un bon c. (de notes)** she got *Br* a good report *or Am* good grades

7 *Banque* **c. de banque** bank book, *Br* savings book; **c. de dépôt** deposit book; **c. de versements** paying-in book; *Belg & Suisse* **c. (d'épargne)** savings account

carnier [karnje] **NM** *Chasse* game bag

carnivore [karnivɔr] **ADJ** carnivorous

NM carnivore, meat-eater

carnotzet, carnotset [karnɔtsɛ] **NM** *Suisse* = room set aside for drinking with friends, usually in a cellar

carolingien, -enne [karɔlɛ̃ʒjɛ̃, -ɛn] *Hist* ADJ Carolingian *(dynasty of Frankish kings, 751–987)*
• **Carolingien, -enne** NM,F Carolingian

caroncule [karɔ̃kyl] NF *Anat, Bot & Orn* caruncle; *(de dindon)* wattle

carotène [karɔtɛn] NM *Biol & Chim* carotene, carotin

carotide [karɔtid] NF *Anat* carotid

carottage [karɔtaʒ] NM **1** *Géol & Mines* core boring **2** *Fam (d'une somme)* pinching, *Br* nicking; *(d'une permission)* wangling; *(escroquerie)* swindling, diddling

carotte [karɔt] NF **1** *Bot* carrot; *Fam* **les carottes sont cuites** the game's up; *Suisse* **c. rouge** beetroot
2 *Fam (récompense)* carrot; **la c. et le bâton** the carrot and the stick
3 *Géol & Mines* core
4 *(tabac)* plug
5 *(enseigne)* tobacconist's sign
6 *Fam Vieilli* **tirer une c. à qn** to swindle *or* to diddle sb
ADJ INV **(rouge) c.** red, carrot-coloured, *Péj* carroty

carotter [3] [karɔte] VT **1** *Géol & Mines* to take a core (sample) of **2** *Fam (argent, objet)* to pinch, *Br* to nick; *(permission)* to wangle; **c. qch à qn** to swindle *or* to diddle sb out of sth

carotteur, -euse[1] [karɔtœr, -øz] NM,F *Fam (escroc)* crook

carotteuse[2] [karɔtøz] NF core drill

carottier, -ère [karɔtje, -ɛr] = **carotteur, -euse**

caroube [karub] NF *Bot* carob

caroubier [karubje] NM *Bot* carob (tree)

carpaccio [karpatʃjo] NM *Culin* carpaccio

Carpates [karpat] NFPL **les C.** the Carpathian Mountains, the Carpathians

carpe[1] [karp] NF *Ich* carp

carpe[2] [karp] NM *Anat* carpus

carpeau, -x [karpo] NM *Ich* young carp

carpette [karpɛt] NF **1** *(petit tapis)* (small) rug **2** *Fam Péj (personne)* doormat; **s'aplatir** *ou* **être (plat) comme une c. devant qn** to grovel in front of sb

> Il faut noter que le nom anglais **carpet** est un faux ami. Il signifie **moquette**.

carpiculture [karpikyltyr] NF carp farming

carpien, -enne [karpjɛ̃, -ɛn] ADJ *Anat* carpal

carquois [karkwa] NM quiver

carrare [karar] NM Carrara marble

carre [kar] NF **1** *Sport (d'un ski, d'un patin à glace)* edge; **lâcher les carres** to flatten the skis **2** *(d'une planche)* crosscut

carré, -e [kare] ADJ **1** *(forme, planche)* square; **avoir les épaules carrées** to be square-shouldered
2 *Géom & Math* square **3** *(sans détours)* straight, straightforward; **être c. en affaires** to have a forthright business manner; **il est un peu trop c.** he's a bit blunt
NM **1** *(gén) & Géom* square; **un petit c. de ciel bleu** a little patch of blue sky
2 *Math* square; **le c. de six** six squared, the square of six; **élever un nombre au c.** to square a number
3 *Hort* **c. de choux** cabbage patch
4 *(foulard)* (square) scarf
5 *(coiffure)* bob
6 *(viande)* **c. d'agneau/de mouton/de porc** loin of lamb/mutton/pork
7 *(fromage)* **c. de l'Est** = type of soft cheese
8 *Cartes* **c. d'as** four aces
9 *Mil* square; **former le c.** to get into square formation
10 *Naut* **c. (des officiers)** wardroom
11 *Fam Arg scol (élève)* = second year student in certain "grandes écoles"
• **carrée** NF *Fam* pad; **un peu d'ordre dans la carrée!** get this place tidied up!

carreau, -x [karo] NM **1** *(sur du papier)* square; *(sur du tissu)* check; **papier à carreaux** squared paper, graph paper; **veste à carreaux** check *or* checked jacket
2 *(plaque de grès, de marbre)* tile
3 *(sol)* tiled floor; *Fam* **se retrouver sur le c.** *(par terre)* to end up on the floor; *(pauvre)* to wind up on skid row; *Fam* **rester sur le c.** *(être assommé)* to be laid out; *(être tué)* to be bumped off; *(échouer)* *Br* to come a cropper, *Am* to take a spill; *Anciennement* **le c. des Halles** *(à Paris)* the (floor of the) market; **c. de mine** pithead
4 *(vitre)* window-pane; *(fenêtre)* window; **regarder à travers les carreaux** to look through the window; **un c. cassé** a broken window
5 *Cartes* **du c.** diamonds; **dame/dix de c.** queen/ten of diamonds
6 *Fam (locution)* **tiens-toi à c.!** watch your step!; **il s'est tenu à c.** he kept a low profile
• **carreaux** NMPL *Fam (lunettes)* specs; **t'as vu l'autre là-bas avec ses carreaux?** look at old four-eyes over there!

carreauté, -e [karɔte] ADJ *Can (chemise, nappe)* *Br* check(ed), *Am* checkered

carrefour [karfur] NM **1** *(de rues)* crossroads *(singulier)*, junction; *Fig* **nous arrivons à un c.** we've come to a crossroads; **c. ferroviaire** railway junction **2** *(point de rencontre)* crossroads *(singulier)*; **Hong Kong, c. de l'Asie** Hong Kong, crossroads of Asia; **un c. d'idées** a forum of ideas **3** *(rencontre)* forum, symposium

carrelage [karlaʒ] NM **1** *(carreaux)* tiles, tiling; **poser un c.** *(au sol)* to lay tiles *or* a tiled floor
2 *(opération)* tiling
3 *(sol)* tiled floor
4 *(mur)* tiled wall

carreler [24] [karle] VT **1** *(mur, salle de bains)* to tile **2** *(feuille de papier)* to draw squares on, to square

carrelet [karlɛ] NM **1** *Ich* plaice **2** *Pêche (filet)* square fishing net **3** *(règle)* square ruler

carreleur [karlœr] NM tiler

carrelle *etc voir* **carreler**

carrément [karemɑ̃] ADV **1** *(dire)* straight out, bluntly; *(agir)* straight; **elle a c. téléphoné au maire** she got straight on the phone to the mayor; **y aller c.** to get on with it **2** *Fam (en intensif)* downright[□]; **c. bête** downright stupid; **t'as c. raison** you're absolutely right[□]; **on gagne c. un mètre** you gain a whole metre[□]; **c'est c. du vol/de la corruption** it's daylight robbery/blatant corruption[□] **3** *(poser)* squarely, firmly

carrer [3] [kare] VT to square
VPR **se carrer 1** *(s'installer)* to settle (down) **2** *(locutions) très Fam* **tu peux te le c. où je pense!** you know what you can do with it!; *Vulg* **tu peux te le c. dans le cul** *ou* **dans l'oignon!** you can shove *or* stick it up your *Br* arse *or Am* ass!

carrier [karje] NM quarryman; **maître c.** quarry master

carrière [karjɛr] NF **1** *Mines (d'extraction)* quarry; **c. de craie** chalkpit; **c. à ciel ouvert** open quarry
2 *(profession)* career; **la C.** *(diplomatie)* the diplomatic service; **la c. des armes** a military career
3 *(parcours professionnel)* career; **faire c. dans** to pursue a career in; **en début/en fin de c.** at the beginning/end of one's career
4 *Littéraire (de la vie, du soleil)* course; **la c. de la gloire** the path to glory; **donner (libre) c. à** to give free rein to
• **de carrière** ADJ *(militaire)* regular; *(diplomate)* career *(avant n)*

carriérisme [karjerism] NM careerism

carriériste [karjerist] NMF careerist, career-minded person

carriole [karjɔl] NF **1** *(à deux roues)* cart **2** *Can (traineau)* (horsedrawn) sled, (horsedrawn) sleigh

carrossable [karɔsabl] ADJ suitable for motor vehicles

carrossage [karɔsaʒ] NM *Tech (angle)* camber

carrosse [karɔs] NM **1** *(véhicule)* coach; **c. d'apparat** state coach **2** *Can (voiture d'enfant)* *Br* pram, *Am* baby carriage

carrosser [3] [karɔse] VT **1** *(voiture)* to fit a body to **2** *très Fam (locution)* **elle est bien carrossée** she's got a good figure[□], she's got curves in all the right places

carrosserie [karɔsri] NF **1** *Aut (structure)* body; *(habillage)* bodywork; **atelier de c.** body shop **2** *très Fam (d'une personne)* **belle c.!** nice bod! **3** *(métier)* coachwork, coach-building

carrossier [karɔsje] NM coachbuilder

carrousel [karuzel, karusel] NM **1** *Équitation* carousel
2 *(de voitures, de personnes)* merry-go-round; **le c. ministériel** the comings and goings at the Ministry
3 *(à bagages)* carousel
4 *Phot (pour diapositives)* carousel
5 *Can, Belg & Suisse (manège)* merry-go-round, carousel

carrure [karyr] NF **1** *(corps)* build; **avoir une c. d'athlète** to have an athletic build **2** *(qualité)* stature, calibre; **une présidente d'une c. exceptionnelle** an exceptionally able chairwoman; **il a la c. d'un cadre supérieur** he's senior management material **3** *(d'un vêtement)* breadth across the shoulders

cartable [kartabl] NM **1** *(à bretelles)* satchel; *(à poignée)* schoolbag **2** *Can (classeur à anneaux)* ring binder

CARTE [kart]

• card **A1, 3–6 C**	• menu **A2**
• map **B**	• chart **B**

NF **A. 1** *(pour la correspondance)* card; *Can* **c. d'affaires** business card; **c. d'anniversaire** birthday card; **donner** *ou* **laisser c. blanche à qn** to give sb carte blanche *or* a free hand; **c. électronique** e-card; **c. d'invitation** invitation card; **c. de Noël** Christmas card; **c. postale** postcard; *Mktg* **c. de publicité** mailing card; *Mktg* **c. de publicité directe** self-mailer; *Mktg & Tél* **c. T** reply-paid card; **c. de visite** *(personnelle)* *Br* visiting *or Am* calling card; *(professionnelle)* business card; **laisser sa c. à qn** to leave one's card with sb; **c. de vœux** greetings card *(sent at Christmas and New Year)*
2 *(de restaurant)* menu; *(menu à prix non fixe)* à la carte menu; **c. des desserts** dessert menu; **c. des vins** wine list; **ils ont une belle/petite c.** they have an impressive/a limited menu; **choisissez dans la c.** choose one of the à la carte dishes
3 *(document officiel)* card; **il a la c. du parti écologiste** he's a card-carrying member of the green party; **fille** *ou* **prostituée en c.** registered prostitute; **c. d'abonnement** *Transp* season ticket *or* pass; *Mus & Théât* season ticket; **c. d'adhérent** membership card; **c. d'alimentation** ration card; **c. de débarquement** landing card; **c. de don d'organe** donor card; **c. d'électeur** voting *or Br* polling card, *Am* voter registration card; **c. d'embarquement** boarding card, boarding pass; **c. d'entrée** pass; **c. d'étudiant** student card; **c. européenne d'assurance maladie** European Health Insurance Card; **c. de famille nombreuse** discount card *(for families with at least three children)*; **c. de fidélité** loyalty card; **c. grise** car registration papers; **c. d'identité** identity card, ID card; **c. d'identité professionnelle** *(de représentant)* (official) ID card; **c. d'invalidité** = handicapped person's travel pass; **c. ISIC** ISIC card; **c. de lecteur** library *or Br* reader's card; **c. de membre** membership card; **c. nationale d'identité** national identity card *or* ID card; **c. (nationale) de priorité** = card giving priority in queues and on public transport; **C. Orange** = pass for travel on the Paris transport system; **c. de presse** press card; **c. de rationnement** ration card; **c. de réduction** discount card; **c. de représentant** = sales representative's official identity card; **c. de résident** (long term) residence permit; **c. sanitaire** prostitute's registration papers; **c. de Sécurité sociale** *ou* **d'assuré social** ≃ National Insurance Card; **c. de séjour (temporaire)** (temporary) residence permit; **C. Vermeil** = card entitling senior citizens to reduced rates in cinemas, on public transport etc; *Assur* **c. verte** green card; **c. VITALE** = smart card on which information about a patient is recorded, used when making payments to a doctor or chemist for purposes of reclaiming medical expenses
4 *Fin & Banque (autorisant une transaction)* card; **c. accréditive** charge card; **c. American Express®** American Express® card; **c. bancaire** bank card, cheque card; **c. bancaire à puce** smart card *(used as a bank card)*; **C. Bleue®** debit card; **c. de crédit** credit card; **c. de crédit professionnelle** corporate

(credit) card; **c. d'identité bancaire** bank card; **c. Mastercard®** Mastercard®; **c. de paiement** debit card; *Tél* **c. Pastel®** phone card *(use of which is debited to one's own phone number)*; **c. de retrait** bank card; *Tél* **c. SIM** SIM card; **c. de téléphone** phonecard; **c. Visa®** Visa® card

5 *Ordinat* (circuit) card, (circuit) board; **c. accélérateur graphique** graphics accelerator card; **c. accélératrice** accelerator card *or* board; **c. d'affichage** display card; **c. bus** bus board; **c. de circuits** circuit board; **c. de circuit(s) intégré(s)** integrated circuit board, IC board; **c. contrôleur de disque** disk controller card; **c. d'extension** expansion card; **c. d'extension mémoire** memory card; **c. fax** fax card; **c. graphique** graphics card; **c. graphique numérique** digital graphics card; **c. magnétique** magnetic card; **c. à mémoire** smart card; **c. mère** motherboard; **c. modem** modem card; **c. perforée** punch card; **c. à pistes magnétiques** magnetic stripe card; **c. à puce** smart card; **c. réseau** network card; **c. RNIS** ISDN card; **c. SCSI** SCSI card; **c. son** sound card; **c. de télécopie** fax card; **c. unité centrale** CPU board; **c. vidéo** video board, video card; **c. vidéo accélératrice** video accelerator card

6 *Com* **c. d'échantillons** sample card, showcard

7 *Belg (au football, au rugby)* **c. jaune** yellow card; **c. rouge** red card

B. *Géog & Géol* map; *Astron, Météo & Naut* chart; **dresser une c. de la région** to map (out) the area; **c. du ciel** sky *or* celestial chart; **c. cognitive** cognitive map; **c. d'état-major** *Br* ≃ Ordnance Survey map, *Am* ≃ Geological Survey map; *Biol* **c. du génome humain** map of the human genome; **c. marine** nautical chart; *Mktg* **c. perceptuelle** perceptual map; *Mktg* **c. de positionnement** positioning map;

c. routière road map; **c. topographique** contour map

C. *Cartes* **c. (à jouer)** (playing) card; **jouer aux cartes** to play cards; *Fam* **tirer** *ou* **faire les cartes à qn** to read sb's cards[□]; *Fam* **se faire tirer les cartes** to have one's cards read[□]; **jeu de cartes** *(activité)* card game; *(paquet)* pack *or* deck of cards; **c. forcée** forced card; *Fig* Hobson's choice; **c. maîtresse** master card; *Fig* master *or* trump card; *Fig* **une bonne c.** an asset; *aussi Fig* **montrer ses cartes** to show one's hand; *Fig* **jeter des cartes/une c. sur la table** to put proposals/a proposal on the table; *Fig* **jouer cartes sur table** to lay one's cards on the table; **il n'a pas joué toutes ses cartes** he hasn't played his last card; *Fig* he still has a trick *or* a card up his sleeve; *aussi Fig* **jouer sa dernière c.** to play one's last card; **jouons la c. de l'honnêteté/la qualité** let's go for honesty/quality

• **à cartes** ADJ card-programmed, card *(avant n)*

• **à la carte** ADJ **1** *(au restaurant)* à la carte **2** *(programme, investissement)* customized; *(horaire)* flexible; **horaires à la c.** flexitime; **vacances à la c.** customized *Br* holidays *or Am* vacation
ADV **manger à la c.** to eat à la carte

• **de grande carte** ADJ *(restaurant, établissement)* first-class

carte-adaptateur [kartadaptatœr] *(pl* **cartes-adaptateurs)** NF *Ordinat* adapter card; **c. réseau** network adaptor card

carte-clé [kartəkle] *(pl* **cartes-clés)** NF keycard; **c. électronique** electronic keycard

carte-guide [kartəgid] *(pl* **cartes-guides)** NF *(pour séparer des fiches)* file separator *or* divider

cartel [kartel] NM **1** *Écon* cartel; **c. de l'acier/de la drogue** steel/drug cartel; **se rassembler en c.** to form a cartel **2** *Pol* coalition, cartel **3** *(pendule)* (decorative) wall clock

carte-lettre [kartəletr] *(pl* **cartes-lettres)** NF letter card

cartellisation [kartelizasjɔ̃] NF *(d'entreprises)* cartelization

carter [karter] NM **1** *Élec* case, casing **2** *Aut* **c. d'engrenages** gearbox casing; **c. à l'huile** *Br* sump, *Am* oilpan; **c. du moteur** crankcase **3** *(de vélo)* chain guard

carte-réponse [kartrepɔ̃s] *(pl inv ou* **cartes-réponses)** NF reply card

Carterie® [kartəri] NF card shop

cartésianisme [kartezjanism] NM Cartesianism

cartésien, -enne [kartezjɛ̃, -ɛn] ADJ Cartesian
NM,F Cartesian

carte-vue [kartəvy] *(pl* **cartes-vues)** NF *Belg* (picture) postcard

carthaginois, -e [kartaʒinwa, -az] ADJ Carthaginian

• **Carthaginois, -e** NM,F Carthaginian

cartilage [kartilaʒ] NM **1** *Anat (substance)* cartilage *(UNCOUNT)* **2** *(du poulet)* gristle

cartilagineux, -euse [kartilaʒinø, -øz] ADJ **1** *Anat* cartilaginous **2** *(poulet)* gristly

cartographe [kartɔgraf] NMF cartographer

cartographie [kartɔgrafi] NF cartography; *Biol* **c. du génome** gene *or* genetic mapping

cartographier [9] [kartɔgrafje] VT to chart, to make a map of

cartographique [kartɔgrafik] ADJ cartographic

cartomancie [kartɔmɑ̃si] NF fortune-telling *(with cards)*

cartomancien, -enne [kartɔmɑ̃sjɛ̃, -ɛn] NM,F fortune-teller *(with cards)*

carton [kartɔ̃] NM **1** *(matière)* cardboard; *(feuille)* piece of cardboard, (piece of) card; **c. ondulé** corrugated cardboard

2 c. (d'invitation) invitation (card)

3 *(boîte ▸ grande)* cardboard box; *(▸ petite)* carton; **c. à chapeaux** hatbox; **c. à chaussures** shoebox; **faire des cartons** to pack one's things up in cardboard boxes

4 *(contenu ▸ d'une grande boîte)* cardboard boxful; *(▸ d'une petite boîte)* cartonful

5 *(rangement ▸ pour dossiers)* (box) file; *(▸ pour dessins)* portfolio; **c. à dessin** portfolio; *Fig* **le projet est resté dans les cartons** the project never saw the light of day, the project was shelved

6 *Beaux-Arts* sketch, cartoon

7 *Géog* inset map

8 *(au football, au rugby)* **c. jaune** yellow card; **c. rouge** red card

9 *Fam (locutions)* **taper le c.** to play cards[□]; **faire un c.** *(au ball-trap)* to take a potshot; *Fig (réussir)* to hit the jackpot; **faire un c. sur qn** to shoot sb down[□]; **prendre un c.** *(défaite)* to get thrashed; *(mauvaise note)* to get a bad mark[□]

10 *Cin & TV* **c. aide-mémoire** cue card

• **en carton** ADJ cardboard *(avant n)*

cartonnage [kartɔnaʒ] NM **1** *Typ (reliure)* boardbinding; **c. pleine toile** *(couverture)* cloth boards

2 *(boîte)* cardboard box

3 *(empaquetage)* cardboard packing

4 *(fabrication)* cardboard industry

cartonner [3] [kartɔne] VT *Typ (livre)* to bind in boards; **livre cartonné** hardback (book)
VI *Fam (réussir)* to hit the jackpot; *(avoir une bonne note)* to pass with flying colours; **ils ont cartonné avec leur dernier album** their last album was a huge hit

cartonnerie [kartɔnri] NF **1** *(industrie)* cardboard industry **2** *(commerce)* cardboard trade **3** *(usine)* cardboard factory

cartonneux, -euse [kartɔnø, -øz] ADJ cardboard-like; **du fromage c.** cheese that tastes like cardboard

cartonnier, -ère [kartɔnje, -ɛr] NM,F *(fabricant)* cardboard manufacturer
NM *Br* filing *or Am* file cabinet *(for cardboard files)*

carton-paille [kartɔ̃paj] *(pl* **cartons-pailles)** NM strawboard

carton-pâte [kartɔ̃pat] *(pl* **cartons-pâtes)** NM pasteboard; *Péj* **de c., en c.** *(décor)* cardboard *(avant n)*; *(personnage, intrigue)* cardboard cutout *(avant n)*

cartoon [kartun] NM *(dessin, film)* cartoon; *(bande dessinée)* comic strip, *Br* (strip) cartoon

cartouche [kartuʃ] NF **1** *Mil & Chasse (projectile, charge)* cartridge; **c. à blanc** blank cartridge

2 *(recharge ▸ de stylo)* cartridge; *Ordinat* **c. DAT** DAT cartridge; **c. d'encre** ink cartridge; **c. de polices** font cartridge; **c. de toner** toner cartridge; *Ordinat* **c. Zip®** zip® disk

3 *(de cigarettes)* carton

4 *Phot* cartridge, cassette, magazine

NM **1** *Antiq & Beaux-Arts* cartouche **2** *Typ (sur un plan)* box; *Presse* **c. de titre** masthead

cartoucherie [kartuʃri] NF **1** *(fabrique)* cartridge factory **2** *(dépôt)* cartridge depot

cartouchière [kartuʃjer] NF **1** *(de soldat)* cartridge pouch **2** *(de chasseur ▸ étui)* cartridge case; *(▸ ceinture)* cartridge belt

carvi [karvi] NM *Bot & Culin* caraway

caryatide [karjatid] NF *Archit* caryatid

caryotype [kariɔtip] NM *Biol* karyotype

CAS [ka] NM **1** *(hypothèse)* **dans le premier c.** in the first instance; **dans le meilleur des c.** at best; **dans le pire des c.** at worst; **dans l'un des c.** in one case; **dans certains c., en certains c.** in some *or* certain cases; **en aucun c.** under no circumstances, on no account; **en pareil c.** in such a case; **auquel c., en ce c., dans ce c.** in which case, in that case, this being the case; **dans un c. comme dans l'autre, dans l'un ou l'autre c., dans les deux c.** either way; **c. de figure** case, instance; **envisageons ce c. de figure** let us consider that possibility; **le c. échéant** if necessary, if need be, should the need arise; **selon le c.** as the case may be

2 *(situation particulière)* case, situation; **c'est également mon c.** I'm in the same situation; **j'ai expliqué mon c.** I stated my case *or* position; **certains animaux sont presque aveugles; c'est le c. de la taupe** some animals, such as the mole, are almost blind; **ce n'est pas le c.** that's not the case; **il parle plusieurs langues étrangères mais ce n'est pas mon c.** he speaks several foreign languages but I don't; **c'est un c. très rare** it's a very rare occurrence; **c. particulier** special case; **se mettre dans un mauvais c.** to paint oneself into a corner; **c. de conscience** matter of conscience; **poser un c. de conscience à qn** to put sb in a (moral) dilemma; **c. d'école** textbook case; **c. d'espèce** special *or* particular case; **c. de force majeure** *Jur* event of force majeure; *Fig* case of absolute necessity; *Jur* **c. fortuit** act of God; **c. limite** borderline case; **ce n'est pas un c. pendable** it's not a hanging offence; **c. urgent** emergency *or* urgent case; **c'est le c. de le dire!** you said it!, you can say that again!

3 *Méd* case; **il y a eu trois c. de varicelle** there have been three cases of chickenpox

4 *Fam (personne)* **ce garçon est un c.!** that boy is something else *or* a real case!

5 *Gram* case; **grammaire des** *ou* **de c.** case grammar; **langue à c.** inflected language; **les c. particuliers en grammaire française** exceptions in French grammar

6 *(locutions)* **faire grand c. de** *(événement)* to attach great importance to; *(argument, raison)* to set great store by; *(invité, ami)* to make a great fuss *or* much of; **on fit grand c. du jeune romancier** much was made of the young novelist; **ne faire aucun c. de** to pay no attention to, to take no notice of

• **au cas où** CONJ in case; **au c. où il ne viendrait pas** in case he doesn't come; *Fam* **prends un parapluie au c. où** take an umbrella just in case

• **dans le cas de** PRÉP **mettre qn dans le c. de faire** *ou* **d'avoir à faire qch** to put sb in the position of having to do sth

• **dans tous les cas** ADV in any case *or* event, anyway

• **en cas de** PRÉP in case of; **en c. de besoin** if need be, if the need should arise; **en c. d'incendie** in the event of a fire; **en c. d'urgence** in an emergency; **en c. de perte de la carte** should the card be lost

• **en tout cas** ADV in any case *or* event, anyway

• **cas social** NM = person needing social worker's assistance; **il y a beaucoup de c. sociaux dans son école** there are a lot of children from problem families at his/her school

casanier, -ère [kazanje, -ɛr] ADJ home-loving, *Péj* stay-at-home
NM,F homebody, *Péj* stay-at-home

casaque [kazak] NF *(d'un jockey)* silks; *(blouse)* paletot, short coat; *Fig* **tourner c.** *(fuir)* to turn and run; *(changer d'opinion)* to do a volte-face

casbah [kazba] NF **1** *(dans les pays arabes)* casbah, kasbah **2** *Fam (maison)* place, pad

cascade [kaskad] **NF 1** *(chute d'eau)* waterfall, *Littéraire* cascade **2** *(abondance)* **une c. de** *(tissu, boucles)* a cascade of; *(compliments)* a stream of; *(sensations)* a rush of, a gush of; **des cascades d'applaudissements** thundering applause **3** *(acrobatie ▸ au cinéma)* stunt; *(▸ au cirque)* acrobatic trick; **faire de la c.** *(au cinéma)* to do stunts; *(au cirque)* to do acrobatics

• **en cascade ADJ 1** *(applaudissements)* tumultuous; *(rires)* ringing; **ils ont connu des catastrophes en c.** they experienced a whole string *or* chain of disasters **2** *Élec* **montage en c.** cascade *or* tandem connection **ADV ses cheveux tombaient en c. sur ses épaules** his/her hair cascaded around his/her shoulders; *Ordinat* **ouvrir des fenêtres en c.** to cascade windows

cascader [3] [kaskade] **VI** *Littéraire* to cascade (down)

cascadeur, -euse [kaskadœr, -øz] **NM,F** *(au cinéma)* stuntman, *f* stuntwoman; *(au cirque)* acrobat

case [kaz] **NF 1** *(d'un damier, de mots croisés)* square; *(d'un formulaire)* box; **retournez ou retour à la c. départ** return to go; *Fig* **retour à la c. départ!** back to square one!

2 *(d'un meuble, d'une boîte)* compartment; *(pour le courrier)* pigeonhole; *Fam* **il a une c. (de) vide** *ou* **il lui manque une c.** he's not all there, he's got a screw loose

3 *Suisse* **c. (postale)** postbox

4 *Ordinat* button; *(en forme de boîte)* box; **c. d'aide** help button; **c. "annuler"** cancel button; **c. de dimensionnement** size box; **c. de fermeture** close box; **c. d'option** *ou* **de pointage** check box, option box; **c. de redimensionnement** size box; **c. de saisie** input box

5 *Rad & TV* slot

6 *(hutte)* hut

caséeux, -euse [kazeø, -øz] **ADJ** caseous

caséine [kazein] **NF** *Chim* casein

casemate [kazmat] **NF** *Mil* **1** *(d'une fortification)* casemate **2** *(ouvrage fortifié)* blockhouse

caser [3] [kaze] *Fam* **VT 1** *(faire entrer)* **c. qch dans qch** to fit sth in sth; **tu peux y c. un canapé** you can fit a sofa in

2 *(dire ▸ phrase, histoire)* to get in

3 *(loger ▸ invités)* to put up; **les enfants sont casés chez la grand-mère** the children are staying at their grandma's

4 *(dans un emploi)* to fix up; **elle est bien casée** she's fixed up nicely

5 *(marier)* to marry off; **il est enfin casé** he's settled down at last

VPR se caser 1 *(dans un emploi)* to get fixed up with a job **2** *(se marier)* to settle down❑ **3** *(se loger)* to find somewhere to live❑

caserne [kazɛrn] **NF 1** *Mil* barracks *(singulier ou pluriel)*; **c. de pompiers** fire station; **des plaisanteries de c.** barrack-room *or* locker-room jokes **2** *Péj (logements)* soulless high-rise *Br* flats *or Am* apartments

casernement [kazɛrnəmɑ̃] **NM 1** *(action)* quartering in barracks **2** *(locaux)* barrack buildings

caserner [3] [kazɛrne] **VT** to barrack

cash [kaʃ] **ADV** cash; **payer c.** to pay cash

cash and carry [kaʃɛndkari] **NM INV** cash-and-carry

casher [kaʃɛr] = **kasher**

cash-flow [kaʃflo] *(pl* **cash-flows***)* **NM** *Fin & Compta* cash flow; **c. actualisé** discounted cash flow; **c. courant** current cash flow; **c. disponible** operating cash flow; **c. marginal** incremental cash flow; **c. net** net cash flow

casier [kazje] **NM 1** *(case ▸ ouverte)* pigeonhole; *(▸ fermée)* compartment; *(▸ dans une consigne, dans un gymnase)* locker; **c. de consigne automatique** luggage locker

2 *(meuble ▸ à cases ouvertes)* pigeonholes; *(▸ à tiroirs) Br* filing *or Am* file cabinet; *(▸ à cases fermées)* compartment; *(▸ à cases fermant à clef)* locker

3 *(pour ranger ▸ des livres)* unit; *(▸ dans un réfrigérateur)* compartment; **c. à bouteilles** bottle rack

4 *Admin & Jur* record; **c. civil** civil register; **c. fiscal** tax record; **c. judiciaire** police *or* criminal record; **un c. judiciaire vierge** a clean (police) record; **maintenant, il a un c. (judiciaire)** now he's got a (criminal) record

5 *Pêche* pot

casino [kazino] **NM** casino

casinotier [kazinɔtje] **NM** casino operator

casoar [kazɔar] **NM 1** *Orn* cassowary **2** *(plumet)* plume *(on hats worn by Saint-Cyr cadets)*

Caspienne [kaspjɛn] **NF la (mer) C.** the Caspian Sea

casque [kask] **NM 1** *(pour protéger)* helmet; **le port du c. est obligatoire** *(sur un chantier)* hard hats must be worn; **c. colonial** pith helmet; **c. intégral** full face helmet; **c. de moto** crash helmet; **c. de protection** *(pour moto)* crash helmet; *(d'ouvriers)* hard hat; **c. bleu** member of the UN peace-keeping force, Blue Beret; **les casques bleus** the UN peace-keeping force, the Blue Berets

2 *(de coiffeur)* hood hairdrier

3 *(pour écouter)* **c. (à écouteurs)** headphones, headset, earphones; **écouter un disque au c.** to listen to a record on headphones

4 *Bot* helmet

5 *Zool* casque

casqué, -e [kaske] **ADJ** helmeted

casquer [3] [kaske] *Fam* **VT** *(payer)* to cough up **VI** to cough up, to come up with the cash

casquette [kaskɛt] **NF** cap; **c. d'officier** officer's peaked cap; *Fig* **avoir plusieurs casquettes** *(responsabilités)* to wear several hats; *Fam* **avoir la c. (de plomb)** to be hungover❑, to have a hangover❑

cassable [kasabl] **ADJ** breakable

Cassandre [kasɑ̃dr] **NPR** *Myth & Fig* Cassandra; **jouer les C.** to spread doom and gloom

cassant, -e [kasɑ̃, -ɑ̃t] **ADJ 1** *(cheveux, ongle)* brittle; *(métal)* short **2** *(réponse)* curt; **être c. avec qn** to be short *or* curt with sb **3** *Fam (fatigant)* tiring❑

cassate [kasat] **NF** *Culin* cassata

cassation [kasasjɔ̃] **NF 1** *Jur* annulment, *Spéc* cassation **2** *Mil* reduction to the ranks

casse¹ [kas] **NF** *Typ* case; **bas/haut de c.** lower/upper case; **lettre bas-/haut-de-c.** lower-case/upper-case letter

casse² [kas] **NF 1** *(bris, dommage)* breakage; **est-ce qu'il y a eu de la c.?** was anything broken?, were there any breakages? **2** *Fam (bagarre)* **de la c.** a fist-fight *or Br* punch-up; **il va y avoir de la c.** there's going to be trouble **3** *(de voitures)* scrapyard; **mettre** *ou* **envoyer à la c.** to scrap; **aller** *ou* **partir à la c.** to go for scrap; **vendre une voiture à la c.** to sell a car for scrap; *Fig* **une idéologie bonne pour la c.** an ideology fit for the scrapheap

casse³ [kas] **NF** *Bot (arbuste)* cassia

casse⁴ [kas] **NM** *Fam (d'une banque)* bank robbery❑; *(d'une maison)* break-in❑; **faire un c. chez un bijoutier** *Br* to do over *or Am* to boost a jeweller's

cassé, -e ADJ *Fam* **1** [kase] *(drogué)* stoned; *(ivre)* smashed, plastered; *(épuisé) Br* knackered, *Am* beat **2** [kɑse] *Can (sans argent)* broke; **c. comme un clou** flat *or Br* stony broke

casseau, -x [kɑso] **NM** *Typ* half-case

casse-bonbons [kasbɔ̃bɔ̃] *Fam* **ADJ INV être c.** to be a pain (in the neck)

NMF INV pain (in the neck)

casse-cou [kasku] **ADJ INV** *(personne)* daredevil; *(projet)* risky; *(endroit)* dangerous

NMF INV 1 *(personne)* daredevil **2** *(endroit)* danger *or* dangerous spot; **crier c. à qn** to warn sb *(of a danger)*

casse-couilles [kaskuj] *Vulg* **ADJ INV être c.** to be a pain in the *Br* arse *or Am* ass

NMF INV pain in the *Br* arse *or Am* ass

casse-croûte [kaskrut] **NM INV 1** *Fam (repas léger)* snack❑; *(sandwich)* sandwich❑, *Br* butty, sarnie **2** *Can (snack)* snack bar❑

casse-cul [kasky] *très Fam* **ADJ INV 1** *(sans intérêt)* boring as hell **2** *(agaçant)* **être c.** to be a pain in the *Br* arse *or Am* ass

NMF INV pain in the *Br* arse *or Am* ass

casse-dalle [kasdal] **NM INV** *Fam* sandwich❑, *Br* butty, sarnie

casse-graine [kasgrɛn] **NM INV** *Fam (repas léger)* snack❑

casse-gueule [kasgœl] *Fam* **ADJ INV** *(endroit)* dangerous❑, *Br* dodgy; *(projet)* risky❑, *Br* dodgy

NMF INV daredevil❑

NM INV *(endroit)* dangerous spot❑; *(entreprise)* risky undertaking❑

cassement [kasmɑ̃] **NM** *Fam Vieilli* **1 c. de tête** *(souci)* headache, worry❑ **2** *(cambriolage)* break-in❑, burglary❑

casse-noisettes [kasnwazɛt] **NM INV** *Br* (pair of) nutcrackers, *Am* nutcracker

casse-noix [kasnwa] **NM INV** *Br* (pair of) nutcrackers, *Am* nutcracker

casse-pieds [kaspje] *Fam* **ADJ INV** *(sans intérêt)* boring❑; *(agaçant)* annoying❑; **c'est c. à faire** it's a drag

NMF INV pain (in the neck)

casse-pipe, casse-pipes [kaspip] **NM INV** *Fam Mil* **le c.** the front❑; **aller au c.** to go to the front❑

CASSER [3] [kase]

VT
- to break **1, 2, 4**
- to demolish **3**
- to damage **5**

VI
- to break **1**
- to break up **2**

VPR
- to break **1, 5**
- to push off **2**
- to break down **3**
- to crack **4**

VT 1 *(mettre en pièces ▸ assiette, jouet, table)* to break; *(▸ porte)* to break down; *(▸ poignée)* to break off; *(▸ noix)* to crack (open); **c. qch en mille morceaux** to smash sth to bits *or* smithereens; **c. qch en deux** to break *or* to snap sth in two; *Fig* **un homme que la douleur a cassé** a man broken by suffering; **avoir envie de tout c.** to feel like smashing everything up; **c. sa tirelire** to break into one's piggybank; **c. du bois** to chop wood; *Fam Fig* to crash-land; *Fam* **c. du sucre sur le dos de qn** *Br* to bitch about sb, *Am* to badmouth sb; *très Fam* **c. de l'arabe** to beat up Arabs, *Br* ≃ to go Paki-bashing; *très Fam* **c. du pédé** to go gay-bashing; *aussi Fig* **c. la banque** to break the bank; *Fam* **c. la baraque** to bring the house down; *(faire échouer un plan)* to ruin it all; *Fam* **c. sa pipe** to kick the bucket; *Fam* **ça ne casse pas des briques, ça ne casse pas trois pattes à un canard** it's no great shakes *or* no big deal

2 *(interrompre ▸ fonctionnement, déroulement, grève)* to break; **le mécanisme est cassé** the mechanism is broken; **c. l'ambiance** to ruin *or* to spoil the atmosphere

3 *(démolir)* to demolish; **on a dû c. le mur** we had to knock down *or* to demolish the wall

4 *(en parlant de parties du corps)* to break; **avoue ou je te casse le bras!** own up or I'll break your arm!; **c.** *Fam* **la figure** *ou très Fam* **la gueule à qn** to smash sb's face in; *Fam* **c. les oreilles à qn** *(avec de la musique)* to deafen sb❑; *(en le harcelant)* to give sb a lot of hassle; *Fig* **c. les reins à qn** to put a stop to sb's career; *Fam* **c. les pieds à qn** to get on sb's nerves *or Br* wick; **ça fait deux mois qu'elle me casse les pieds pour que je t'en parle** she's been on at me for two months now to talk to you about it; *Vulg* **c. les bonbons** *ou* **les couilles à qn** *Br* to get on sb's tits, *Am* to break sb's balls; *très Fam* **tu nous les casses** you're a *Br* bloody *or Am* goddamn pain in the neck

5 *(abîmer ▸ voix)* to damage, to ruin; **ça m'a cassé la voix de chanter toute la nuit** I ruined my voice singing all night; **elle a la voix cassée** *(rauque)* she has a husky voice; *(éraillée)* she has a croaky voice

6 *(annihiler ▸ espoir)* to dash, to destroy; *(▸ moral)* to break, to crush; **la religion, la famille, ils veulent tout c.** religion, family values, they want to smash everything

7 *Jur (jugement)* to quash; *(arrêt)* to nullify, to annul; *(mariage)* to annul, to dissolve

8 *Com* **c. les prix** to slash prices; **c. le métier** to operate at unfairly competitive rates

9 *très Fam (cambrioler)* to do a job on, *Br* to do over

10 *Fam (voiture)* to take to bits *(for spare parts)*, to break, to cannibalize❑

VI 1 *(verre, chaise)* to break; *(fil)* to snap; *(poi-*

gnée) to break off; **la tige a cassé** *(en deux)* the stem snapped; *(s'est détachée)* the stem snapped off; **cela casse comme du verre** it's as fragile as glass

2 *Fam (se séparer)* to break up, to split up

VPR se casser 1 *(se briser ▸ assiette)* to break; *(▸ poignée)* to break off; **se c. net** *(en deux)* to snap in two; *(se détacher)* to break clean off

2 *très Fam (partir)* to push off, to clear off; **casse-toi!** get lost!, push off!; **le voilà, casse-toi!** he's coming, get the hell out of here!; **tu viens? on se casse** we're out of here, are you coming?; **elle s'est cassée de chez ses parents** she cleared out of her parents' place

3 *(cesser de fonctionner ▸ appareil, véhicule)* to break down

4 *(être altéré ▸ voix)* to crack, to falter

5 se c. qch to break sth; **elle s'est cassé la jambe** she's broken her leg; **se c. le cou** to break one's neck; *Fig* to take a tumble, *Br* to come a cropper; **se c.** *Vulg* **le cul** *ou Fam* **les reins** *(au travail)* to bust a gut, to kill oneself; **je me suis cassé le cul pour lui trouver cette adresse** I really went out of my way[□] *or* bust a gut to find him/her that address; **se c.** *Fam* **la figure** *ou très Fam* **la gueule** *(personne)* to take a tumble, *Br* to come a cropper; *(livre, carafe)* to crash to the ground; *(projet)* to bite the dust, to take a dive; *Fam* **se c. la tête** *ou* **la nénette** to rack one's brains; **ne te casse pas la tête, fais une omelette** don't put yourself out, just make an omelette; *Fam* **dis donc, tu ne t'es pas cassé la tête!** well, you didn't exactly strain yourself, did you!; *Fam* **se c. le nez** *(ne trouver personne)* to find no one in; *(échouer) Br* to come a cropper, *Am* to bomb; **tu vas te c. la voix si tu continues à crier** you'll ruin your voice if you keep shouting; *Fam* **ça vaut mieux que de se c. une jambe** it's better than a poke in the eye with a sharp stick

6 *Fam (se donner du mal)* **il ne s'est pas cassé pour m'aider** he didn't overstrain himself helping me

• **à tout casser** *Fam* **ADJ** *(endiablé ▸ fête)* fantastic; *(▸ succès)* runaway; **une soirée à tout c.** one hell of a party **ADV 1** *(tout au plus)* at the (very) most; **cela vaut 100 euros à tout c.** it's worth 100 euros at the very most[□] **2 applaudir à tout c.** to bring the house down

casserole [kasrɔl] **NF 1** *(ustensile, contenu)* pan, saucepan **2** *Fam (instrument de musique)* flat *or* off-key instrument; *(voix)* flat *or* off-key voice; **chanter comme une c.** to sing off key **3** *Cin* spot (light)

• **à la casserole ADJ** braised **ADV faire** *ou* **cuire à la c.** to braise; *Fam* **passer à la c.** *(être tué)* to get bumped off; *(subir une épreuve)* to go through it; *très Fam* **elle est passée à la c.** *(sexuellement)* she got screwed *or* laid, *Br* she got a good seeing-to

> Il faut noter que le nom anglais **casserole** est un faux ami. Il signifie **ragoût** ou **cocotte**, selon le contexte.

casse-tête [kastɛt] **NM INV 1** *(jeu)* puzzle, brainteaser; **c. chinois** Chinese puzzle; *Fig* **c'est un vrai c. chinois** it's totally baffling, it's a complete mystery **2** *(préoccupation)* headache; **ça a été un c. pour placer tout le monde à table** it was a headache seating everyone at the table **3** *(massue)* club

cassetin [kastɛ̃] **NM** *Typ* box

cassette [kasɛt] **NF 1** *(magnétique)* cassette, tape; **enregistrer qch sur c.** to tape sth; **c. audio** audio cassette *or* tape; **c. de démonstration** demo (tape); **c. pirate** pirate tape; **c. vidéo** video (cassette) **2** *Ordinat* cassette; **c. d'alimentation** *(de copieuse, d'imprimante)* paper tray; **c. compacte numérique** digital compact cassette; **c. de fontes** font cassette; **c. numérique** digital audio tape; **c. de polices de caractères** font cassette **3** *(coffret)* casket

cassettothèque [kasetɔtɛk] **NF** cassette library

casseur, -euse [kasœr, -øz] **NM,F 1** *(dans une manifestation)* rioting demonstrator

2 *Fam (cambrioleur)* burglar

3 *(ferrailleur)* scrap dealer, *Br* scrap merchant

4 c. de pierres stonebreaker

Cassin [kasɛ̃] *voir* **mont**

cassine [kasin] **NF** *Arch (petite maison)* small house

Cassiopée [kasjɔpe] **NPR** *Myth & Astron* Cassiopeia

cassis [kasis] **NM 1** *(baie)* blackcurrant

2 *(plante)* blackcurrant bush

3 *(liqueur)* blackcurrant liqueur, cassis

4 *Fam (tête)* nut

5 *(dos d'âne)* dip

cassolette [kasɔlɛt] **NF 1** *Culin* small baking dish **2** *(brûle-parfum)* incense-burner

cassonade [kasɔnad] **NF** light brown sugar

cassoulet [kasulɛ] **NM** *Culin* cassoulet, haricot bean stew *(with pork, goose or duck)*

cassure [kasyr] **NF 1** *(fissure)* crack

2 *(rupture dans la vie, dans le rythme)* break

3 *(d'un tissu)* fold

4 *Géol* break; *(faille)* fault

castagne [kastaɲ] **NF** *Fam (coup)* clout, wallop; **chercher la c.** to be looking for a fight[□]; **va y avoir de la c.** there's going to be a *Br* punch-up *or Am* fist fight

castagner [3] [kastaɲe] *Fam* **VT** to clout, to wallop

VPR se castagner to have a *Br* punch-up *or Am* fist fight

castagnettes [kastaɲɛt] **NFPL** castanets; **ses dents jouaient des c.** his/her teeth were chattering

caste [kast] **NF** caste; **esprit de c.** class consciousness; **avoir l'esprit de c.** to be class conscious

castel [kastɛl] **NM** *Littéraire* small castle

castillan, -e [kastijɑ̃, -an] **ADJ** Castilian

NM *(dialecte)* Castilian

• **Castillan, -e NM,F** Castilian

Castille [kastij] **NF la C.** Castile

casting [kastiŋ] **NM** *Cin & Théât (distribution)* casting; *(acteurs)* cast; **passer un c.** to go to an audition

castor [kastɔr] **NM** *(animal, fourrure)* beaver

castrat [kastra] **NM 1** *Mus* castrato **2** *(homme castré)* castrated man, eunuch

castrateur, -trice [kastratœr, -tris] **ADJ** *Psy* castrating; *Fig (autoritaire)* repressive

castration [kastrasjɔ̃] **NF 1** *(d'un homme, d'une femme)* castration; *Psy* **complexe de c.** castration complex; **c. chimique** chemical castration **2** *(d'un animal mâle)* castration; *(d'un cheval)* gelding; *(d'un animal domestique ▸ mâle)* neutering; *(▸ femelle)* spaying, neutering **3** *Bot* castration

castratrice [kastratris] *voir* **castrateur**

castrer [3] [kastre] **VT 1** *(homme, femme)* to castrate **2** *(animal mâle)* to castrate; *(cheval)* to geld; *(animal domestique ▸ mâle)* to neuter; *(▸ femelle)* to spay, to neuter **3** *Bot* to castrate

castrisme [kastrism] **NM** *Pol* Castroism

castriste [kastrist] *Pol* **ADJ** Castroist

NMF Castroist, Castro supporter

casuel, -elle [kazɥɛl] **ADJ 1** *(éventuel)* fortuitous **2** *Ling* case *(avant n)* **3** *Belg (fragile)* fragile

casuiste [kazɥist] **NM** casuist

casuistique [kazɥistik] **NF** casuistry

casus belli [kazysbeli] **NM INV** casus belli

CAT [seate] **NF 1** *(abrév* **Confédération autonome du travail**) = French trade union **2** *(abrév* **Centre d'aide par le travail**) = day centre which helps disabled people to find work and become more independent

cata[1] [kata] **NF** *Fam* **c'est la c.** it's a disaster[□]

cata[2] [kata] **NF** *(abrév* **catamaran**) cat

catabolisme [katabɔlism] **NM** *Biol & Chim* catabolism

catachrèse [katakrɛz] **NF** *Ling* catachresis

cataclysmal, -e, -aux, -ales [kataklismal, -o] **ADJ 1** *Géog* cataclysmal, cataclysmic **2** *(bouleversant)* catastrophic, disastrous, cataclysmic

cataclysme [kataklism] **NM 1** *Géog* natural disaster, cataclysm **2** *(bouleversement)* cataclysm, catastrophe, disaster

cataclysmique [kataklismik] **ADJ 1** *Géog* cataclysmal, cataclysmic **2** *(bouleversant)* catastrophic, disastrous, cataclysmic

catacombes [katakɔ̃b] **NFPL** catacombs

catadioptre [katadjɔptr] **NM 1** *(sur une voiture, sur un vélo)* reflector **2** *(sur une route)* cat's eye

catafalque [katafalk] **NM** catafalque

cataire [katɛr] **NF** *Bot* catmint

catalan, -e [katalɑ̃, -an] **ADJ** Catalan

NM *(langue)* Catalan

• **Catalan, -e NM,F** Catalan

catalepsie [katalɛpsi] **NF** *Méd* catalepsy; **tomber en c.** to have a cataleptic fit

cataleptique [katalɛptik] *Méd* **ADJ** cataleptic

NMF cataleptic

catalogage [katalɔgaʒ] **NM** cataloguing

Catalogne [katalɔɲ] **NF la C.** Catalonia

catalogue [katalɔg] **NM 1** *(liste ▸ de bibliothèque, d'exposition)* catalogue; **faire le c. des toiles exposées** to catalogue *or* to itemize the exhibits **2** *Com (illustré)* catalogue; *(non illustré)* price list; **c. d'échantillons** sample book; **c. électronique** electronic catalogue; **c. en ligne** on-line catalogue; **c. des prix** price list; **c. de vente par correspondance** mail-order catalogue; **je n'achète jamais rien sur c.** I never buy anything from a catalogue **3** *Péj (énumération)* (long) list

cataloguer [3] [katalɔge] **VT 1** *(livre)* to list, to catalogue; *(bibliothèque)* to catalogue; *(œuvre, marchandise)* to catalogue, to put into a catalogue **2** *Fam (juger)* to label, to categorize, to pigeonhole; **j'ai horreur d'être catalogué** I hate people putting labels on me; **il s'est fait c. comme dilettante** he was labelled a dilettante

catalpa [katalpa] **NM** *Bot* catalpa

catalyse [kataliz] **NF** *Chim* catalysis

catalyser [3] [katalize] **VT 1** *(provoquer ▸ forces, critiques)* to act as a catalyst for **2** *Chim* to catalyse

catalyseur [katalizœr] **NM 1** *(personne, journal)* catalyst; **il a été le c. de...** he acted as a catalyst for... **2** *Chim* catalyst

catalytique [katalitik] **ADJ** *Chim* catalytic

catamaran [katamarɑ̃] **NM** *Naut* **1** *(voilier)* catamaran **2** *(flotteurs)* floats

Cataphote® [katafɔt] **NM 1** *(sur une voiture, sur un vélo)* reflector **2** *(sur une route)* cat's eye

cataplasme [kataplasm] **NM** *Méd* poultice, cataplasm

catapultage [katapyltaʒ] **NM 1** *Aviat & Mil* catapulting **2** *Fig (d'un employé)* rapid promotion

catapulte [katapylt] **NF 1** *Aviat* catapult launcher **2** *Mil* catapult

catapulter [3] [katapylte] **VT 1** *Tech & Aviat* to catapult **2** *Fig (employé)* **il a été catapulté directeur** he was catapulted into the manager's job

cataracte [katarakt] **NF 1** *Méd* cataract; **se faire opérer de la c.** to have a cataract operation **2** *(chute d'eau)* waterfall, cataract

catarrhal, -e, -aux, -ales [kataral, -o] **ADJ** *Méd* catarrhal

catarrhe [katar] **NM** *Méd* catarrh

catarrheux, -euse [katarø, -øz] *Méd* **ADJ** catarrhal, catarrhous

NM,F catarrh sufferer

catastrophe [katastrɔf] **NF** *(désastre ▸ en avion, en voiture)* disaster; *(▸ dans une vie, dans un gouvernement)* catastrophe, disaster; **c. ferroviaire/aérienne** rail/air disaster; **c. naturelle** natural disaster; **frôler la c.** to come close to disaster; **ce n'est pas une c.** it's not the end of the world; **c'est la c.!** it's a disaster!; *Fam* **une c., ce type!** the guy's a walking disaster!; **c., il nous manque deux chaises!** disaster, we're two chairs short!

• **en catastrophe ADV partir en c.** to rush off; **s'arrêter en c.** to make an emergency stop; **atterrir en c.** to make a forced *or* an emergency landing

catastrophé, -e [katastrɔfe] **ADJ** *Fam* stunned; **il était c. de l'apprendre** he was stunned when he heard

catastropher [3] [katastrɔfe] **VT** to shatter, to stun

catastrophique [katastrɔfik] **ADJ** catastrophic, disastrous

catastrophisme [katastrɔfism] **NM 1** *(pessimisme)* pessimism; **ne fais pas de c.!** don't be so pessimistic! **2** *Géol* catastrophism

catatonie [katatɔni] **NF** *Psy* catatonia, catatonic schizophrenia

catatonique [katatɔnik] *Psy* **ADJ** catatonic
NMF catatonic

catch [katʃ] **NM** *Boxe* (all-in) wrestling; **faire du c.** to wrestle

catcher [3] [katʃe] **VI** *Boxe* to wrestle
VT *Can Joual* **1** *(attraper)* to catch **2** *(comprendre)* to get, to understand

catcheur, -euse [katʃœr, -øz] **NM,F** *Boxe* (all-in) wrestler

catéchèse [katefɛz] **NF** *Rel* catechesis

catéchisation [katefizasjɔ̃] **NF 1** *Rel* to catechization, catechizing **2** *Péj* indoctrination

catéchiser [3] [katefize] **VT 1** *Rel* to catechize **2** *Péj (endoctriner)* to indoctrinate; *(sermonner)* to preach at, to lecture

catéchisme [katefism] **NM 1** *Rel (enseignement, livre)* catechism; **aller au c.** to go to catechism, ≃ to go to Sunday school **2** *Fig* doctrine, creed; **cela fait partie de leur c.** it's Gospel truth to them

catéchiste [katefist] **NMF** *Rel (gén)* catechist; *(pour enfants)* Sunday-school teacher

catéchumène [katekymen] **NMF 1** *Rel* catechumen **2** *(que l'on initie)* novice

catégorie [kategɔri] **NF 1** *(pour classifier ▸ des objets, des concepts)* category, class, type; *(▸ des employés)* grade; **il appartient à cette c. de gens qui...** he belongs to that category *or* group of people who...; **c. d'âge** age group; **c. sociale** social class; **c. socio-économique** socioeconomic class; **c. socioprofessionnelle** socioprofessional group **2** *(qualité ▸ dans les transports, dans les hôtels)* class; **hôtel de seconde c.** second-class hotel; **morceau de première/deuxième/troisième c.** *(viande)* prime/second/cheap cut **3** *Sport* class; **premier dans sa c.** first in his class; **toutes catégories** for all comers

catégoriel, -elle [kategɔrjel] **ADJ 1** *(d'une catégorie)* category *(avant n)*; **classement c.** classification by category **2** *(d'une catégorie socioprofessionnelle)* **revendications catégorielles** sectional claims *(relating to one category of workers only)* **3** *Ling & Phil* category *(avant n)*

catégorique [kategɔrik] **ADJ 1** *(non ambigu ▸ refus)* categorical, point-blank; *(▸ réponse)* categorical **2** *(décidé)* adamant; **elle a été c. sur ce point** she was adamant *or* categorical on this point; **là-dessus, je serai c.** I'm not prepared to budge on that; **je suis c.** *(j'en suis sûr)* I'm positive **3** *Phil* categorical

catégoriquement [kategɔrikmɑ̃] **ADV** *(nettement ▸ affirmer)* categorically; *(▸ refuser)* categorically, point-blank

catégorisation [kategɔrizasjɔ̃] **NF** categorization

catégoriser [3] [kategɔrize] **VT** *(ranger)* to categorize

catelle [katel] **NF** *Suisse* ceramic tile

caténaire [katener] *Rail* **ADJ suspension c.** catenary
NF catenary

catgut [katgyt] **NM** *Méd* catgut

cathare [katar] *Rel & Hist* **ADJ** Cathar
• **Cathare NMF** Cathar

catharsis [katarsis] **NF** *Psy & Théât* catharsis

cathartique [katartik] **ADJ** *Psy & Théât* cathartic

cathédrale [katedral] **NF** cathedral

cathèdre [katedr] **NF** cathedra

Catherine [katrin] **NPR C. d'Aragon** Catherine of Aragon; **C. de Médicis** Catherine de Medici; **C. de Russie** Catherine the Great

catherinette [katrinet] **NF** = woman who is still single and aged 25 on St Catherine's Day

cathéter [kateter] **NM** *Méd* catheter, can(n)ula

cathétérisme [kateterism] **NM** *Méd* catheterization

catho [kato] *Fam* **ADJ** Catholic
NMF Catholic

cathode [katɔd] **NF** *Élec & Chim* cathode

cathodique [katɔdik] **ADJ** *Élec* cathodic; *Fig* **l'univers c.** the world of television

catholicisme [katɔlisism] **NM** (Roman) Catholicism

catholicité [katɔlisite] **NF** *(caractère)* catholicity; **la c.** *(église)* the (Roman) Catholic Church; *(fidèles)* the (Roman) Catholic community

catholique [katɔlik] **ADJ 1** *Rel* (Roman) Catholic; **une institution c.** a Catholic *or* an RC school **2** *Fam (locution)* **pas très c. comme façon de faire** *(peu conventionnel)* not a very orthodox way of doing things; *(malhonnête)* not a very kosher way of doing things; **un individu pas très c.** a rather shady individual
NMF (Roman) Catholic

catilinaire [katiliner] **NF** *Littéraire* diatribe, outburst

catimini [katimini] **en catimini ADV** on the sly *or* quiet; **arriver/partir en c.** to sneak in/out

catin [katɛ̃] **NF 1** *Vieilli (prostituée)* trollop **2** *Can (poupée)* doll **3** *Can (pansement)* finger bandage

cation [katjɔ̃] **NM** *Chim* cation

catogan [katɔgɑ̃] **NM** = large bow holding the hair at the back of the neck

Caton [katɔ̃] **NPR** Cato

Caucase [kokaz] **NM 1** *(montagnes)* **le C.** the Caucasus **2** *(région)* **le C.** Caucasia

caucasien, -enne [kokazjɛ̃, -en] **ADJ** Caucasian
• **Caucasien, -enne NM,F** Caucasian

cauchemar [koʃmar] **NM 1** *(mauvais rêve)* nightmare; **faire un c.** to have a nightmare; **ça me donne des cauchemars rien que d'y penser** it gives me nightmares just thinking about it **2** *(situation)* nightmare; **c'était un c. pour moi d'apprendre les verbes irréguliers** learning irregular verbs was a real nightmare for me; **une vision de c.** a nightmare vision **3** *(personne assommante)* nuisance

cauchemarder [3] [koʃmarde] **VI** to have nightmares; **la perspective d'une semaine avec eux me fait c.** the prospect of spending a week with them is a real nightmare

cauchemardesque [koʃmardesk], **cauchemardeux, -euse** [koʃmardø, -øz] **ADJ 1** *(sommeil)* nightmarish **2** *Fig (horrifiant)* nightmarish, hellish

caudal, -e, -aux, -ales [kodal, -o] **ADJ** *Zool* tail *(avant n)*, *Spéc* caudal

cauri [kori], **cauris** [koris] **NM** *Zool* cowrie (shell)

causal, -e, -als *ou* **-aux, -ales** [kozal, -o] **ADJ** *(lien) & Gram* causal

causalité [kozalite] **NF** causality; **rapport de c.** causal relation

causant, -e [kozɑ̃, -ɑ̃t] **ADJ** *Fam* chatty

CAUSE [koz] **NF 1** *(origine, motif)* cause, reason; **remonter jusqu'aux causes** to go back to the origins; **la c. profonde de sa tristesse** the underlying reason for his/her sadness; **on ne connaît pas la c. de sa mort** the cause of death is unknown; **être (la) c. de qch** to be the cause of sth, to cause sth; **les enfants sont souvent c. de soucis** children are often a cause of worry; **c'est elle qui en est la c.** it's her fault, she's to blame; **relation de c. à effet** causal relationship; *Prov* **à petite c. grands effets** great oaks from little acorns grow; **il s'est fâché, et non sans c.** he got angry, and with good reason; **et pour c.!** and for a very good reason!; **il n'est pas venu, et pour c.!** no wonder he didn't come!

2 *Phil* cause; **la c. première/seconde/finale** the first/secondary/final cause

3 *Jur (affaire ▸ gén)* case, (law)suit; *(▸ à plaider)* brief; *(motif)* cause; **un avocat sans causes** a briefless barrister; **la c. est entendue** each side has put forward its case; *Fig* it's an open and shut case; *aussi Fig* **c. célèbre** cause célèbre; **c. civile** civil action; **c. criminelle** criminal proceedings; **c. illicite** unjust cause; **c. licite** just cause; **plaider la c. de qn** to plead sb's case

4 *(parti que l'on prend)* cause; **la c. des mineurs** the miners' cause; **faire c. commune avec qn** to join forces with sb; **une c. perdue** a lost cause; **une bonne c.** a good cause; **je suis tout acquis à sa c.** I support him/her wholeheartedly

• **à cause de PRÉP 1** *(par la faute de)* because *or* on account of, due *or* owing to; **j'ai perdu mon temps à c. de toi** I wasted my time because of you **2** *(en considération de)* because *or* on account of, due *or* owing to; **acceptée à c. de ses diplômes** taken on on account of her qualifications **3** *(par égard pour)* for the sake *or* because of; **ils sont venus à c. de votre amitié** they came because of your friendship

• **en cause ADJ 1** *(concerné)* in question; **la voiture en c. était à l'arrêt** the car involved *or* in question was stationary; **la somme/l'enjeu en c.** the amount/the thing at stake **2** *(que l'on suspecte)* **les financiers en c.** the financiers involved **3** *(contesté)* **être en c.** *(talent)* to be in question; **votre honnêteté n'est pas en c.** your honesty is not in question *or* in doubt; *Jur* **affaire en c.** case before the court **ADV 1** *(en accusation)* **mettre qn en c.** to implicate sb; **mettre qch en c.** to call sth into question **2** *(en doute)* **remettre en c.** *(principe)* to question, to challenge; **son départ remet tout en c.** his/her departure reopens the whole question *or* debate

• **en tout état de cause ADV** in any case, whatever happens

• **pour cause de PRÉP** owing to, because of; **fermé pour c. de décès** *(magasin)* closed owing to bereavement

causer [3] [koze] **VT** *(provoquer ▸ peine, problème)* to cause; **c. des ennuis à qn** to make trouble for sb; **son départ nous a causé beaucoup de chagrin** his/her departure distressed us greatly *or* caused us great distress
VI *Fam* **1** *(bavarder)* **c. (à** *ou* **avec qn)** to chat (to sb); **je ne lui cause plus!** *(je suis fâché)* I'm not talking to him/her!; **c. de** to talk about; **c. de la pluie et du beau temps, c. de choses et d'autres** to talk about this and that; **cause toujours(, tu m'intéresses)!** *(je fais ce que je veux)* yeah, yeah, whatever!; *(tu pourrais m'écouter)* don't mind me!; **je l'avais prévenu, mais cause toujours!** I'd warned him but I might as well have been talking to the wall! **2** *(médire)* to gossip, to prattle; **ça a fait c. dans le quartier** it set tongues wagging in the neighbourhood **3** *(suivi d'un nom sans article) (parler)* **c. politique** to talk about politics, to talk politics

causerie [kozri] **NF 1** *(discussion)* chat, talk **2** *(conférence)* informal talk *(in front of an audience)*

causette [kozet] **NF 1** *Fam* **faire la c. à qn** to chat to sb; **faire un brin de c.** to chew the fat, *Br* to have a chinwag **2** *Offic Ordinat* chat

causeur, -euse [kozœr, -øz] **ADJ** chatty, talkative
NM,F talker, conversationalist
• **causeuse NF** love seat

causse [kos] **NM** *Géog* limestone plateau

causticité [kostisite] **NF** *Chim & Fig* causticity

caustique [kostik] **ADJ 1** *Chim* caustic **2** *Fig (mordant)* caustic, biting, sarcastic
NM *Chim* caustic
NF *Opt* caustic (curve)

cautèle [kotel] **NF** *Littéraire* wiliness, cunning

cauteleux, -euse [kotlø, -øz] **ADJ** *Littéraire* wily, cunning

cautère [koter] **NM 1** *Méd* cautery **2** *(locution)* **c'est un c. sur une jambe de bois** it's as much use as a poultice on a wooden leg

cautérisation [koterizasjɔ̃] **NF** *Méd* cauterization, cauterizing

cautériser [3] [koterize] **VT** *Méd* to cauterize

caution [kosjɔ̃] **NF 1** *Jur* bail; **se porter c. pour qn** to go *or* stand bail for sb; **payer la c. de qn** to bail sb out, *Am* to post bail for sb
2 *(garant)* surety, guarantor; **se porter c. pour qn** to stand security *or* surety *or* guarantee for sb; **les locataires étudiants doivent fournir une c. parentale** student tenants must provide proof that their parents will stand guarantor *or* surety for them
3 *(garantie morale)* guarantee; *(soutien)* support, backing; **avec la c. du ministre** with the support *or* the backing of the minister; **donner** *ou* **apporter sa c. à** to support, to back
4 *Com & Fin* (security) deposit; **verser une c. de 50 euros** to pay 50 euros as security, to put down

a 50-euro deposit (as security); **c. d'adjudication** bid bond; **c. bancaire** *ou* **de banque** bank guarantee; **c. de soumission** bid bond
• **sous caution** ADV *(libérer)* on bail

> Il faut noter que le nom anglais **caution** est un faux ami. Il signifie **prudence**.

cautionnement [kosjɔnmɑ̃] NM **1** *(contrat)* surety *or* security bond **2** *(somme)* security; *Jur* bail; **c. réel** collateral security **3** *(soutien)* support, backing

cautionner [3] [kosjɔne] VT **1** *Jur* **c. qn** *(se porter caution)* to bail sb out, *Am* to post bail for sb; *(se porter garant)* to stand *or* to go bail for sb **2** *(soutenir)* to support, to back; **je tiens à faire c. cette décision par le directeur des ventes** I want to get the sales director to back me up on this decision; **se faire c. par ses parents pour la location d'un appartement** to provide a parental guarantee when renting a flat

> Il faut noter que le verbe anglais **to caution** est un faux ami. Il signifie **mettre en garde**.

cavalcade [kavalkad] NF **1** *(défilé)* cavalcade **2** *(course)* stampede; **pas de c. dans l'escalier, s'il vous plaît!** please, no stampeding down the stairs!; **c'est tout le temps la c.** we're always in such a rush

cavalcader [3] [kavalkade] VI to scamper around

cavale [kaval] NF **1** *Littéraire (jument)* mare **2** *Fam Arg crime* jailbreak□; **être en c.** to be on the run

cavaler [3] [kavale] VI *Fam* **1** *(courir)* to run *or* to rush (around); **j'ai cavalé toute la journée pour trouver un cadeau** I ran around all day looking for a present **2** *(se hâter)* to get a move on; **il va falloir c. si tu veux avoir ton train** you'll have to get a move on if you want to catch your train **3** *(à la recherche de femmes)* to chase women; *(à la recherche d'hommes)* to chase men
VT *très Fam (agacer)* **il commence à me c.** *Br* he's starting to get right up my nose, *Am* he's starting to tick me off
VPR **se cavaler** *Fam* to clear off

cavalerie [kavalri] NF *Mil* cavalry; **c. légère** light (cavalry *or* horse) brigade; **c. lourde, grosse c.** armoured cavalry; *Fig* **la grosse c.** the run-of-the-mill stuff

cavaleur, -euse [kavalœr, -øz] *Fam* ADJ *(homme)* philandering□, womanizing; *(femme)* man-eating
NM philanderer□, womanizer
• **cavaleuse** NF man-eater

cavalier, -ère [kavalje, -ɛr] ADJ **1** *Équitation* **allée** *ou* **piste cavalière** bridle path, bridleway **2** *Péj (désinvolte ▸ attitude)* offhand, cavalier; *(▸ réponse)* curt, offhand; **agir de façon cavalière** to act in an offhand manner
NM,F **1** *Équitation* rider **2** *(danseur)* partner
NM **1** *Hist* Cavalier
2 *Mil* cavalryman, mounted soldier
3 *Bible* **les (quatre) Cavaliers de l'Apocalypse** the (Four) Horsemen of the Apocalypse
4 *(pour aller au bal)* escort; **faire c. seul** *(dans une entreprise)* to go it alone; *Pol* to be a maverick
5 *Échecs* knight
6 *Can (amoureux)* boyfriend
7 *(sur un dossier)* tab
8 *(clou)* staple
9 *(surcharge)* rider
10 *Ordinat* jumper

cavalièrement [kavaljɛrmɑ̃] ADV casually, in a cavalier *or* an offhand manner

cave[1] [kav] ADJ **1** *Littéraire (creux)* hollow, sunken **2** *Anat voir* **veine**

cave[2] [kav] NM **1** *Fam Arg crime (étranger au milieu)* outsider□ **2** *Fam (dupe)* sucker, *Br* mug
ADJ *Can Fam (idiot)* stupid□, *Am* dumb

cave[3] [kav] NF **1** *(pièce)* cellar; *Fig* **de la c. au grenier** *(ranger, nettoyer)* from top to bottom; **c. à charbon** coal cellar; **c. à vin** wine cellar
2 *(vins)* (wine) cellar; **avoir une bonne c.** to keep a good cellar
3 *Can (sous-sol)* basement, cellar
4 *(cabaret) Br* cellar *or Am* basement nightclub
5 *(coffret)* **c. à cigares** cigar box; **c. à liqueurs** cellaret

> Il faut noter que le nom anglais **cave** est un faux ami. Il signifie **grotte**.

cave[4] [kav] NF *Cartes (gén)* stake; *(au poker)* ante

caveau, -x [kavo] NM **1** *(sépulture)* vault, tomb, burial chamber **2** *(cabaret)* club *(in a cellar)*

caver[1] [3] [kave] VT *Littéraire (creuser)* to hollow *or* to dig (out)

caver[2] [3] [kave] *Cartes* VT to put up
VI to put up a sum of money; *Fig*; **c. sur la bêtise humaine** to count upon *or* bank on human stupidity

caverne [kavɛrn] NF **1** *(grotte)* cave, cavern; **une c. de brigands** a den of thieves; **la c. d'Ali Baba** Ali Baba's cave; *Fig* **c'est une véritable c. d'Ali Baba** it's a real treasure-trove **2** *Méd* cavity

caverneux, -euse [kavɛrnø, -øz] ADJ **1** *(voix)* sepulchral **2** *Anat (tissu)* cavernous

caviar [kavjar] NM **1** *Culin* caviar, caviare; **c. rouge** salmon roe; **c. d'aubergines** *Br* aubergine *or Am* eggplant caviar(e) **2** *Typ* blue pencil; **passer au c.** to blue-pencil, to censor

caviardage [kavjardaʒ] NM blue-pencilling, censoring

caviarder [3] [kavjarde] VT to blue-pencil, to censor

caviste [kavist] NM cellarman

cavité [kavite] NF **1** *(trou)* cavity; **une c. entre deux roches** a cavity *or* gap between two rocks **2** *Anat* cavity; **c. articulaire** socket; **c. buccale** oral cavity; **c. dentaire** pulp cavity

Cayenne [kajɛn] NF Cayenne

CB[1] [sibi] NF *Rad (abrév* **citizen's band, canaux banalisés***)* CB

CB[2] [sebe] NF *Banque (abrév écrite* **Carte Bleue®***)* = bank card with which purchases are debited directly from the customer's bank account, *Br* ≃ debit card

C/C [sese] NM *Banque & Compta (abrév* **compte chèque, compte courant***)* C/A

cc **1** *(abrév écrite* **cuillère à café***)* tsp **2** *(abrév écrite* **charges comprises***)* inclusive of maintenance costs

CCB [sesebe] NM *Banque (abrév* **compte de chèque bancaire***)* C/A

CCI [sesei] NF **1** *(abrév* **Chambre de commerce et d'industrie***)* CCI **2** *(abrév* **Chambre de commerce internationale***)* ICC

CCP [sesepe] NM *Banque (abrév* **compte chèque postal, compte courant postal***)* = post office account, *Br* ≃ Giro account, *Am* ≃ Post Office checking account

CCR [seseɛr] NM *Fin (abrév* **coefficient de capitalisation des résultats***)* p/e ratio

CD[1] [sede] NM *(abrév* **Compact Disc***)* CD; **CD audio** audio CD; **CD réinscriptible** CD-RW; **CD vidéo** CD video, CDV

CD[2] *(abrév écrite* **corps diplomatique***)* CD

CDD [sedede] NM *(abrév* **contrat à durée déterminée***)* fixed term contract; **elle est en C.** she's on a fixed term contract

CD-E [sedeə] NM *(abrév* **Compact Disc Erasable***)* CD-E

CDI [sedei] NM **1** *(abrév* **centre de documentation et d'information***)* ≃ school library **2** *(abrév* **contrat à durée indéterminée***)* permanent (employment) contract; **elle est en C.** she's got a permanent contract

CD-I NM *(abrév écrite* **Compact Disc interactif***)* CDI, interactive CD

CD-Photo [sedefoto] NM photo CD

CD-R [sedeɛr] NM *(abrév* **Compact Disc recordable***)* CD-R

CD-ROM, CD-Rom [sederɔm] NM INV *Ordinat (abrév* **Compact Disc read-only memory***)* CD-ROM; **C. d'installation** installation CD-ROM

CD-RW NM *Ordinat (abrév écrite* **Compact Disc Rewritable***)* CD-RW

CDthèque [sedetɛk] NF CD library

CDV [sedeve] NM *(abrév* **Compact Disc Video***)* CDV

CE [seə] NM **1** *(abrév* **comité d'entreprise***)* works council **2** *Scol (abrév* **cours élémentaire***)* = two-year subdivision of primary-level education in France (ages 7 to 9); **CE1** = second year of primary school, *Br* ≃ year 3; **CE2** = third year of primary school, *Br* ≃ year 4 **3** *UE (abrév* **conseil de l'Europe***)* Council of Europe
NF *UE (abrév* **Communauté européenne***)* EC

CE[1]**, CET, CETTE, CES** [sə, sɛt, se]

> **cet** is used before a masculine singular noun or adjective beginning with a vowel or mute h.

ADJ DÉMONSTRATIF **1** *(dans l'espace ▸ proche) (singulier)* this; *(pluriel)* these; *(▸ éloigné) (singulier)* that; *(pluriel)* those; **cet homme qui vient vers nous** the man (who's) coming towards us; **tiens, prends cette canne** here, take this walking-stick; **tu vois cet immeuble?** you see that building?; **regarde de ce côté-ci** look over here; **cette veste, là-bas en vitrine** that jacket, over there in the window; **cet homme qui gesticule là-bas** that man over there (who's) waving his arms about; **je ne connais pas cette région-là** I don't know that region
2 *(dans le temps ▸ à venir) (singulier)* this; *(pluriel)* these; *(▸ passé)* last; **vas-y ce matin** go this morning; **cette nuit nous mettrons le chauffage** tonight we'll turn *or* put the heating on; **cette nuit j'ai fait un rêve étrange** last night I had a strange dream; **cette semaine je n'ai rien fait** I haven't done a thing this *or* this past *or* this last week; **cette année-là** that year; **ces jours-ci** these days, lately; **un de ces jours** one of these days; **fait ce jour à Blois** witnessed by my hand this day in Blois
3 *(désignant ▸ ce dont on a parlé) (singulier)* this, that; *(pluriel)* these, those; *(▸ ce dont on va parler) (singulier)* this; *(pluriel)* these; **je t'ai déjà raconté cette histoire** I've told you that story before; **enfin, ces personnes se sont rencontrées** these people finally met; **cette remarque traduit son incompréhension** this *or* that remark shows that he/she doesn't understand; **écoute cette histoire et tu vas comprendre** listen to this story and you'll understand
4 *(suivi d'une proposition relative)* **voici ce pont dont je t'ai parlé** here's the *or* that bridge I told you about; **il était de ces comédiens qui…** he was one of those actors who…
5 *(emploi expressif)* **cette douleur dans son regard!** such grief in his/her eyes!; *Fam* **ce culot!** what a nerve!, the cheek of it!; **mais c'est qu'elle a grandi, cette petite!** hasn't she grown into a big girl!; *Fam* **et cette bière, elle vient?** so is that beer on its way or what?; *Fam* **et ces douleurs/cette grippe, comment ça va?** how's the pain/the flu doing?; **ce roquet n'entrera pas chez moi!** I won't have that nasty little dog in my house!; **et pour ces messieurs, ce sera?** now what will the *or* you gentlemen be having?; **ces dames sont au salon** the ladies are in the drawing room

CE[2] [sə]

> **ce** becomes **c'** before a vowel.

PRON DÉMONSTRATIF **1** *(sujet du verbe "être")* **c'est à Paris** it's in Paris; **c'était hier** it was yesterday; **demain c'est dimanche** tomorrow is Sunday, it's Sunday tomorrow; **ce n'est pas un hôtel ici!** this is not a hotel!; **c'est toi!** it's you!; **qui a dit ça? – c'est moi/lui** who said that? – me/him, I/he did; **c'est exact!** that's right!; **c'est un escroc** he's a crook; **ce sont mes frères** they are my brothers; **ce doit être son mari** it must be her husband; **dire oui, c'est renoncer à sa liberté** saying yes means *or* amounts to giving up one's freedom; **tes amis, ce sont** *ou Fam* **c'est des gens bien sympathiques** your friends are really nice people; **ce ne sont pas mes chaussures** they *or* these *or* those aren't my shoes; **c'est tout à fait possible** it's quite possible; **c'est encore loin, la mer?** is the sea still far away?, is it still a long way to the sea?; **c'est à toi, ce livre?** is this book yours?; **qui est-ce?**, *Fam* **c'est qui?** who is it?; **où est-ce?**, *Fam* **c'est où?** where is it?; **qu'est-ce que c'est?**, *Fam* **c'est quoi?** what is it?, what's that?; **à qui est-ce?**, *Fam* **c'est à qui?** whose is it?; **c'est à toi?** is this *or* is it yours?; **serait-ce que tu as oublié?** have you forgotten, by any chance?

2 *(pour insister)* **c'est la robe que j'ai achetée** this is the dress (that) I bought; **c'est l'auteur que je préfère** he's/she's my favourite writer; **c'est elles qui me l'ont dit** it was they who told me; **c'est toi qui le dis!** that's what you say!, says you!; **c'est à vous, monsieur, que je voudrais parler** it was you I wanted to speak to, sir; **c'est à lui/à toi de décider** it's up to him/you to decide

3 *("c'est que" introduisant une explication)* **s'il ne parle pas beaucoup, c'est qu'il est timide** if he doesn't say much, it's because he's shy; **c'est que maman est malade** Mum's ill, you see, the point is Mum's ill; **ce n'est pas qu'il n'y tienne pas** it's not that he isn't keen on it, it isn't that he's not keen on it

4 *(comme antécédent du pronom relatif)* **ce qui, ce que** what; **ce qui m'étonne, c'est que...** what surprises me is that...; **demande-lui ce qui lui ferait plaisir** ask him/her what he'd/she'd like; **voici ce que l'on me propose** here's what I've been offered; **je sais ce que c'est que la pauvreté** I know what poverty is; **il y a du vrai dans ce qu'il dit** there's some truth in what he says; **dis-moi ce que tu as fait** tell me what you did; **voici ce à quoi j'avais pensé** this is what I had thought of; **ce dont je ne me souviens pas, c'est l'adresse** what I can't remember is the address; **ce pour quoi j'ai démissionné** the reason (why) I resigned; **ce en quoi je croyais s'est effondré** the thing I believed in has collapsed

5 *(reprenant la proposition)* **ce qui, ce que** which; **cette action provoquerait une rupture, ce qui serait catastrophique** such an action would cause a split, which would be disastrous

6 *(introduisant une complétive)* **je m'étonne de ce qu'il n'ait rien dit** I'm surprised (by the fact that) he didn't say anything; **veille à ce que tout soit prêt** make sure everything's ready; **il insiste sur ce que le travail doit être fait en temps voulu** he insists that the work must be done in the specified time

7 *(emploi exclamatif)* **ce que tu es naïf!** you're so naive!, how naive you are!; **ce qu'elle joue bien!** she's such a good actress!, what a marvellous actress she is!; **ce que c'est (que) d'être instruit, tout de même!** it must be wonderful to be educated!

8 *(locutions) Littéraire ou Hum* **ce me semble** it seems to me, I think, *Littéraire ou Hum* methinks; **vous êtes pressé, ce me semble** it seems to me (that) *or* you look like you're in a hurry; **ce faisant** in so doing; **il l'a radiée de la liste, ce faisant il la prive de ses droits** he has struck her off the list, and in so doing he is depriving her of her rights; **ce disant** so saying, with these words; **il n'a rien dit, et ce malgré toutes les menaces** he said nothing, (and this) in spite of all the threats; **j'arrive et sur ce, le téléphone sonne** I arrive and just then the phone rings; **sur ce, je vous salue** and now, I take my leave; **sur ce, elle se leva** with that *or* thereupon *or* on that note, she got up; **pour ce faire** to this end, in order to do this; **ils veulent construire et pour ce faire ils ont pris contact avec des entrepreneurs** they want to start building and to this end they have contacted a firm of contractors

---

CEA [seəa] **NM** *(abrév* **Commissariat à l'énergie atomique**) = French atomic energy commission, *Br* ≃ AEA, *Am* ≃ AEC

CEAM [seəaem] **NF** *(abrév* **carte européenne d'assurance maladie**) EHIC

CECA, Ceca [seka] **NF** *UE (abrév* **Communauté européenne du charbon et de l'acier**) ECSC

ceci [səsi] **PRON DÉMONSTRATIF** this; **c. n'est pas très loin de nos préoccupations actuelles** this is not unrelated to our present concerns; **c. pour vous dire que...** all this to tell you that...; **c. (étant) dit** having said this *or* that; **à c. près que** except *or* with the exception that; **retenez bien c....** now, remember this...; **c. va vous étonner, écoutez...** this will surprise you, listen...; **son rapport a c. d'étonnant que...** his/her report is surprising in that...; **c. ne me concerne pas** this is nothing to do with me; **c. n'explique pas cela** one thing doesn't explain the other

cécité [sesite] **NF** blindness; **être frappé de c.** to be struck blind; **être atteint de c.** to be blind; **c. nocturne/des neiges/des rivières** night/snow/river blindness; **c. verbale** word blindness

cédant, -e [sedɑ̃, -ɑ̃t] **ADJ** *Jur* assigning, granting

NM,F assignor, grantor

céder [18] [sede] **VT 1** *(donner)* to give (up); **il est temps de c. l'antenne** our time is up; **nous cédons maintenant l'antenne à Mélanie** we're now going to hand over to Mélanie; **cédez le passage** *(sur panneau) Br* give way, *Am* yield; **c. le passage à qn** to let sb through, to make way for sb; **c. du terrain** *Mil* to give ground, to fall back; *Fig* to back down *or* off; **c. le pas à qn** to give way to sb; *Fig* to let sb have precedence; **c. sa place à qn** to give up one's seat to sb; *Fig* to give up one's place to sb; **il ne le cède à personne en ambition** as far as ambition is concerned, he's second to none **2** *(vendre)* to sell; *(faire cadeau de)* to give away, to donate; **c. qch à bail** to lease sth; **il a cédé son fonds de commerce pour rien** he gave up *or* sold his business for next to nothing; **à c.** *(dans une annonce, sur panneau)* for sale; **c. ses biens à une fondation** to donate *or* to transfer one's assets to a foundation **3** *Jur* to transfer, to make over, to assign; *(bail)* to dispose of, to sell

VI 1 *(à la volonté d'autrui)* to give in; **je ne céderai pas!** I won't give in!, I won't back down!; **tu n'arriveras jamais à le faire c.** you'll never get him to back down; **c. devant les menaces** to give in *or* to yield to threats **2** *Mil* **c. sous l'assaut de l'ennemi** to be overpowered *or* overwhelmed by the enemy **3** *(casser* ▸ *étagère, plancher)* to give way; *(*▸ *câble, poignée)* to break off; *(*▸ *couture)* to come unstitched

• **céder à VT IND 1** *(ne pas lutter contre* ▸ *sommeil, fatigue)* to succumb to; *(*▸ *tentation, caprice, menace, exigences)* to give in *or* to yield to; **la fièvre a cédé aux médicaments** the fever responded to medication **2** *(être séduit par)* **c. à la facilité** to take the easy way out; **c. à qn** to give in to sb

cédérom [sederɔm] **NM** *Ordinat* CD-ROM

cédétiste [sedetist] **ADJ** CFDT *(avant n)*

NMF member of the CFDT

CEDEX®, Cedex® [sedɛks] **NM** *(abrév* **courrier d'entreprise à distribution exceptionnelle**) = accelerated postal service for bulk users

cédille [sedij] **NF** *Ling* cedilla; **c c.** c cedilla

cédrat [sedra] **NM** *Bot & Culin* citron

cédratier [sedratje] **NM** *Bot* citron (tree)

cèdre [sɛdr] **NM 1** *(arbre)* cedar (tree); **c. blanc/bleu** white/blue cedar; **c. du Liban** cedar of Lebanon **2** *(bois)* cedar, cedarwood

CEE [seəə] **NF** *UE (abrév* **Communauté économique européenne**) EEC

CEG [seəʒe] **NM** *Scol (abrév* **collège d'enseignement général**) = former junior secondary school

CÉGEP, cégep [seʒɛp] **NM** *Can Scol (abrév* **collège d'enseignement général et professionnel**) = college of further education

cégétiste [seʒetist] **ADJ** CGT *(avant n)*

NMF member of the CGT

CEI [seəi] **NF** *(abrév* **Communauté des États indépendants**) CIS

ceindre [81] [sɛ̃dr] *Littéraire* **VT 1** *(entourer)* **son bras ceignant ma taille** his/her arm around my waist; **c. sa tête d'une couronne** to place a crown upon one's head; **la tête ceinte d'une couronne de lauriers** with his/her head crowned with a laurel wreath; **un château ceint de hautes murailles** a castle surrounded by high walls **2** *(porter)* **c. la couronne** to assume the crown; **c. l'écharpe tricolore** to don the mayoral (tricolour) sash

VPR se ceindre se c. les reins to gird one's loins

ceint, -e [sɛ̃, sɛ̃t] *pp voir* **ceindre**

ceinture [sɛ̃tyr] **NF 1** *(en cuir, en métal)* belt; *(fine et tressée)* cord; *(large et nouée)* sash; *(gaine, corset)* girdle; **c. cartouchière** cartridge belt; **c. de chasteté** chastity belt; **c. orthopédique** surgical corset; **c. de sauvetage** life belt; *Aut* **c. de sécurité** seat *or* safety belt; *Aut* **c. de sécurité à enrouleur** inertia-reel seat belt; *Aut* **c. de sécurité trois points** lap and shoulder belt, three-point seat belt; **attachez votre c.** fasten your seat belt; **faire c., se serrer la c.** *(se priver)* to tighten one's belt, to go without; *Fam* **on a trop dépensé ces derniers temps, maintenant c.!** we've been overspending lately, we're going to have to tighten our belts now

2 *Sport (à la lutte)* waistlock; *(au judo, au karaté)* belt; **elle est c. blanche/noire** she's a white/black belt; **il est c. noire de judo** he's a black belt in judo

3 *(taille)* waistband; *Anat* waist; **de l'eau jusqu'à la c.** with water up to one's waist; **nu jusqu'à la c.** naked from the waist up; *aussi Fig* **frapper au-dessous de la c.** to hit below the belt; **c'est un coup au-dessous de la c.!** that's a bit below the belt!

4 *Anat* **c. pelvienne/scapulaire** pelvic/pectoral girdle

5 *Transp* **chemin de fer de c.** circle line; **petite c.** *(à Paris* ▸ *périphérique)* = inner ring road in Paris that runs alongside the "boulevard périphérique"; *(*▸ *bus)* = bus that operates on this route; *(à Bruxelles)* = inner ring road; **grande c.** *(à Bruxelles)* outer ring road

6 *Archit* cincture

7 *(enceinte)* belt, ring; *(de fortifications)* circle; **une c. de peupliers** a belt of poplars; **c. verte** green belt

ceinturer [3] [sɛ̃tyre] **VT 1** *(porter avec une ceinture)* **vous pouvez la c.** *(robe)* you can wear it with a belt **2** *(saisir par la taille)* to grab round the waist **3** *(lieu)* to surround, to encircle

ceinturon [sɛ̃tyrɔ̃] **NM 1** *(ceinture)* (broad) belt **2** *Mil & Chasse (gén)* belt; *(à cartouches)* cartridge belt; *(à sabre)* sword belt

CEJ [seəʒi] **NF** *(abrév* **Cour européenne de justice**) ECJ

CEL [sɛl] **NM** *Banque (abrév* **compte épargne logement**) = savings account for purchasing a property

cela [səla] **PRON DÉMONSTRATIF 1** *(désignant un objet éloigné)* that; **regardez c., là-bas!** look at that (over there)!

2 *(désignant* ▸ *ce dont on vient de parler)* this, that; *(*▸ *ce dont on va parler)* this; **c. (étant) dit...** having said this *or* that...; **je n'ai pas dit c.** I didn't say that; **c., je ne pouvais pas le prévoir** I couldn't have foreseen that; **c. mérite qu'on s'y intéresse** that *or* this is worth studying; **je ne m'attendais pas à c.** I wasn't expecting that; **à part c.** apart from that; **après c., on n'en entendit plus parler** after that, nothing more was heard of it; **malgré c. il est resté fidèle à ses amis** in spite of (all) that, he remained loyal to his friends; **c'est pour c. que je viens** that's what I've come for *or* why I've come; **sans c. je ne serais pas venu** if it wasn't for that *or* otherwise I wouldn't have come; **qu'est-ce que c'est que c.?** what is that?; **c. n'explique pas ce qu'il a dit hier** this *or* that doesn't explain what he said yesterday; **il me l'a expliqué très clairement, et c. sans s'énerver le moins du monde** he explained it to me very clearly, and without getting the least bit annoyed; **il est parti il y a un mois/une semaine de c.** he left a month/a week ago; **c. va vous étonner, écoutez...** this'll surprise you, listen...; **son histoire a c. d'extraordinaire que...** his/her story is extraordinary in that...; *Ironique* **c'est c.!** that's right!; **c'est c., moquez-vous de moi!** that's right, have a good laugh (at my expense)!; **je suis folle, c'est (bien) c.?** so I'm out of my mind, is that it *or* am I?

3 *(remplaçant "ce")* **c. n'est pas très étonnant** that is not very surprising; **c. est mieux ainsi** it's better this way

4 *(dans des tournures impersonnelles)* it; **c. ne fait rien** it doesn't matter; **c. fait une heure que j'attends** I've been waiting for an hour; **c. fait longtemps que nous ne nous sommes vus** it's been a long time since we've seen each other

5 *(emploi expressif)* **pourquoi c.?** why?, what for?; **qui c.?** who?, who's that?; **où c.?** where?, whereabouts?; **quand c.?** when?

céladon [seladɔ̃] **ADJ INV** *(couleur)* pale green, celadon

célébrant, -e [selebrɑ̃, -ɑ̃t] *Rel* **ADJ** officiating

NM celebrant

célébration [selebrasjɔ̃] **NF** celebration

célèbre [selɛbr] **ADJ** famous; **c. par** *ou* **pour qch** famous for sth; **se rendre c. par qch** to become famous for sth; **tristement c.** notorious; **c. dans le monde entier** world-famous

célébrer [18] [selebre] **VT 1** *(fête)* to observe; *(anniversaire, messe, mariage)* to celebrate; *(rite)* to perform; *(funérailles)* to hold **2** *(glorifier ▸ personne)* to extol the virtues of; *(▸ exploit)* to toast, to celebrate; *(▸ courage)* to praise, to pay tribute to

célébrité [selebrite] **NF 1** *(gloire)* fame, celebrity **2** *(personne)* celebrity, personality

celer [25] [səle] **VT** *Arch & Littéraire* **c. qch à qn** to conceal sth from sb
VPR se celer *Littéraire* to hide

céleri [sɛlri] **NM** celery; **pied de c.** head of celery; **c. en branches** celery; **c. rémoulade** celeriac salad

céleri-rave [sɛlrirav] *(pl* **céleris-raves***)* **NM** celeriac

célérité [selerite] **NF** *Littéraire* swiftness, speed; **avec c.** swiftly, rapidly

célesta [selesta] **NM** *Mus* celesta

céleste [selɛst] **ADJ 1** *(du ciel)* celestial
2 *(du paradis)* celestial, heavenly; *Littéraire* **la voûte c.** the vault of heaven
3 *(de Dieu)* divine
4 *Littéraire (surnaturel ▸ beauté, voix, mélodie)* heavenly, sublime
5 *Hist* **le C. Empire** the Celestial Empire

célibat [seliba] **NM 1** *(vie de célibataire ▸ d'un prêtre)* celibacy; *(▸ d'un homme)* celibacy, bachelorhood; *(▸ d'une femme)* spinsterhood, celibacy; **elle a choisi le c.** she decided to remain single *or* not to marry; **vivre dans le c.** *(homme)* to remain a bachelor; *(femme)* to remain single; *(prêtre)* to be celibate **2** *(chasteté)* celibacy

> Il faut noter que l'adjectif anglais **celibate** est un faux ami. Il signifie **chaste**.

célibataire [selibatɛr] **ADJ 1** *(homme, femme)* single, unmarried; *(prêtre)* celibate **2** *Admin* single
NM single man; *Admin* bachelor; **un c. endurci** a confirmed bachelor; **un club pour célibataires** a singles club
NF single woman

celle [sɛl] *voir* **celui**

celle-ci [sɛlsi], **celle-là** [sɛlla] *voir* **celui**

cellérier, -ère [selerje, -ɛr] *Rel* **ADJ** = relating to the duties of a cellarer
NM,F cellarer

cellier [selje] **NM** *(pour nourriture)* storeroom, pantry; *(pour vin)* cellar

cello [selo] **NM** *Cin* cel

Cellophane® [selɔfan] **NF** Cellophane®; **sous C.** Cellophane®-wrapped

cellulaire [selylɛr] **ADJ 1** *Biol (de la cellule)* cell *(avant n)*; *(formé de cellules)* cellular
2 *Tech (béton)* cellular; *(matériau, mousse)* expanded
3 *(carcéral)* **emprisonnement** *ou* **régime c.** solitary confinement; **voiture c.** *Br* prison *or* police van, *Am* police wagon
4 *(gestion)* divisional
NM *Can Tél Br* mobile (phone), *Am* cellphone

cellule [selyl] **NF 1** *Biol* cell; **c. donneuse** donor cell; **c. nerveuse** nerve cell; **c. de peau** skin cell; **c. sanguine** blood cell; **c. somatique** somatic cell; **c. souche** stem cell; **c. souche embryonnaire** embryonic stem cell
2 *(d'un prisonnier, d'un religieux)* cell; *Mil* **dix jours de c.** ten days in the cells; *Hum* **il a passé la nuit en c. de dégrisement** he spent a night in the cells to sober up
3 *(élément constitutif)* basic element *or* unit; *Pol* cell; **c. du parti communiste** Communist party cell; *Com* **c. d'achat** purchasing unit; **c. (terroriste) dormante** *ou* **en sommeil** sleeper cell; **c. de crise** crisis centre; **c. familiale** family unit *or* group; **c. de réflexion** think tank
4 *(d'une ruche)* cell
5 *Aviat* airframe
6 *Phot* **c. photoélectrique** photoelectric cell
7 *(de tourne-disque)* cartridge
8 *Ordinat (dans un tableur)* cell; **c. (de) mémoire** storage cell

cellulite [selylit] **NF** *Physiol* cellulite

cellulitique [selylitik] **ADJ** *Physiol* cellulite *(avant n)*

Celluloïd® [selylɔid] **NM** celluloid®

cellulose [selyloz] **NF** *Chim* cellulose

cellulosique [selylozik] **ADJ** *Chim* cellulosic

celte [sɛlt] **ADJ** Celtic
• **Celte NMF** Celt

celtique [sɛltik] **ADJ** Celtic; **les langues celtiques** the Celtic languages
NM *Ling* Celtic

CELUI, CELLE [səlɥi, sɛl] *(mpl* **ceux** [sø], *fpl* **celles** [sɛl]) **PRON DÉMONSTRATIF 1** *(suivi de la préposition "de")* **le train de 5 heures est parti, prenons c. de 6 heures** we've missed the 5 o'clock train, let's get the 6 o'clock; **j'ai comparé mon salaire avec c. d'Ève** I compared my salary with Ève's; **les hommes d'aujourd'hui et ceux d'autrefois** the men of today and those of former times; **le robinet de la cuisine fuit et c. de la salle de bain aussi** the tap in the kitchen's leaking and so is the one in the bathroom; **ceux d'entre vous qui veulent s'inscrire** those of you who wish to register
2 *(suivi d'un pronom relatif)* **c., celle** the one; **ceux, celles** those, the ones; **prête-moi ceux que tu as lus** lend me those *or* the ones you have read; **c'est celle que j'ai achetée** that's the one I bought; **c'est c. qui a réparé ma voiture** he's the one who fixed my car; **tous les plats sont sales, prends c. qui est dans le lave-vaisselle** all the dishes are dirty, take the one in the dishwasher; **celle à qui j'ai écrit** the one I wrote to; **c. dont je t'ai parlé** the one I told you about
3 *(quiconque)* he, she; **heureux c. qui peut vivre de son art** happy (is) he who can make a living from his art
4 *(suivi d'un adjectif, d'un participe)* the one; **achetez celle conforme aux normes** buy the one that complies with the standard; **toutes les maisons sont en bois sauf celles voisines de l'église** all the houses are built of wood except the ones *or* those near the church; **tous ceux désirant participer à l'émission** all those wishing *or* who wish to take part in the show; **tous ceux ayant la même idée** all those with the same idea
• **celui-ci, celle-ci** *(mpl* **ceux-ci**, *fpl* **celles-ci***)* **PRON DÉMONSTRATIF 1** *(désignant une personne ou un objet proches)* **c.-ci, celle-ci** this one (here); **ceux-ci, celles-ci** these ones, these (here); **donne-moi c.-ci** give me this one (here); **c'est c.-ci que je veux** this is the one I want, I want this one; **passe-moi le pinceau, non, pas c.-là, c.-ci** pass me the brush, no, not that one, this one **2** *(désignant ce dont on va parler ou ce dont on vient de parler)* **son inquiétude était celle-ci...** his/her worry was as follows...; **elle voulait voir Anne, mais celle-ci était absente** she wanted to see Anne, but she was out; **ah c.-ci, il me fera toujours rire!** now he always makes me laugh!
• **celui-là, celle-là** *(mpl* **ceux-là**, *fpl* **celles-là***)* **PRON DÉMONSTRATIF 1** *(désignant une personne ou un objet éloignés)* **c.-là, celle-là** that one (there); **ceux-là, celles-là** those ones, those (over there); **donne-moi c.-là** give me that one (there); **c'est c.-là que je veux** that's the one I want, I want that one; **il n'y a aucun rapport entre les deux décisions, celle-ci n'explique pas celle-là** the two decisions are unconnected, the latter doesn't follow on from the former; **autre exemple, plus technique c.-là** another example, a more technical one this time **2** *(emploi expressif)* **il a toujours une bonne excuse, c.-là!** he's always got a good excuse, that one!

cément [semɑ̃] **NM 1** *Métal* carburizing powder **2** *Anat* cement, cementum

cémentation [semɑ̃tasjɔ̃] **NF** *Métal* case-hardening

cémenter [3] [semɑ̃te] **VT** *Métal* to case-harden

CEN [seəɛn] **NM** *UE (abrév* **Comité européen de normalisation***)* European Standards Commission

cénacle [senakl] **NM 1** *Rel* cenacle **2** *Littéraire (comité)* literary coterie *or* group; **admis au c.** admitted into the company of the select few

cendar [sɑ̃dar] **NM** *Fam* ashtray

cendre [sɑ̃dr] **NF 1** *(résidu ▸ gén)* ash, ashes; *(▸ de charbon)* cinders; **c. de bois/de cigarette** wood/cigarette ash; **faire cuire des marrons sous la c.** to roast chestnuts in the ashes *or* embers; **mettre** *ou* **réduire en cendres** *(objet)* to reduce to ashes; *(maison, ville)* to burn to the ground; *Littéraire* **les cendres d'une passion mourante** the embers of a dying passion **2** *Géol* (volcanic) ash; **cendres volcaniques** volcanic ash
• **cendres NFPL** *Littéraire (dépouille)* ashes, remains
• **Cendres NFPL** *Rel* **les Cendres, le mercredi des Cendres** Ash Wednesday

cendré, -e [sɑ̃dre] **ADJ 1** *(gris)* ashen, ash *(avant n)*, ash-coloured **2** *(couvert de cendres)* ash-covered; **fromage c.** cheese matured in wood ash
NM cheese matured in wood ash
• **cendrée NF 1** *Chasse & Pêche* dust shot **2** *(revêtement)* cinders; *(piste)* cinder track

cendrer [3] [sɑ̃dre] **VT** *(chemin, piste)* to cinder

cendreux, -euse [sɑ̃drø, -øz] **ADJ 1** *(plein de cendres)* full of ashes **2** *(gris ▸ écorce, roche)* ash-coloured; *(▸ teint)* ashen, ashy

cendrier [sɑ̃drije] **NM** *(de fumeur)* ashtray; *(de fourneau)* ash pit; *(de poêle)* ashpan

Cendrillon [sɑ̃drijɔ̃] **NPR** Cinderella

cène [sɛn] *Rel* **NF** *(communion)* Holy Communion, Lord's Supper
• **Cène NF la C.** the Last Supper

cenelle [sənɛl] **NF** *Bot (baie)* haw

cénobite [senɔbit] **NM** *Rel* coenobite

cénotaphe [senɔtaf] **NM** cenotaph

cénozoïque [senɔzɔik] **ADJ** *Géol* cenozoic

cens [sɑ̃s] **NM 1** *Antiq (recensement)* census **2** *Hist (féodal)* quitrent; **c. électoral** = minimum tax quota for voting rights

censé, -e [sɑ̃se] **ADJ** supposed to; **être c. faire qch** to be supposed to do sth; **tu n'es pas c. le savoir** you're not supposed to know (about it); **vous êtes c. arriver à 9 heures** *(indication)* you're supposed to arrive at 9 o'clock; *(rappel à l'ordre)* we expect you to arrive at 9 o'clock

censément [sɑ̃semɑ̃] **ADV** apparently, seemingly

censeur [sɑ̃sœr] **NM 1** *Anciennement Scol Br* deputy head (teacher), *Am* assistant principal
2 *(responsable de la censure)* censor
3 *(critique)* critic
4 *Antiq* censor

censitaire [sɑ̃sitɛr] *Hist* **ADJ** poll-tax based
NM eligible voter *(who has paid enough tax to gain voting rights)*

censurable [sɑ̃syrabl] **ADJ** censurable

censure [sɑ̃syr] **NF 1** *(interdiction, examen)* censorship; **la c.** *(commission)* the censors
2 *Pol* censure
3 *Rel* censure; **les censures de l'Église** the censure of the Church
4 *Psy & Antiq* censorship

censurer [3] [sɑ̃syre] **VT 1** *(film, livre)* to censor
2 *Pol* to pass a vote of censure *or* of no confidence; *Rel* to censure
3 *Psy* to exercise censorship on
4 *(critiquer)* to criticize, to censure

> Il faut noter que le verbe anglais **to censure** est un faux ami. Il signifie **critiquer**.

cent[1] [sɑ̃] **ADJ 1** *(gén)* a *or* one hundred; **c. mille** a hundred thousand; **deux cents filles** two hundred girls; **trois c. quatre rangs** three hundred and four rows; **elle est aux c. coups** *(affolée)* she's frantic; **je te l'ai dit c. fois** I've told you a hundred times; **elle a eu c. fois l'occasion de le faire** she's had every chance to do it; **tu as c. fois raison** you're a hundred percent right; **je préfère c. fois celle-ci** I prefer this one a hundred times over; **c. fois mieux** a hundred times better; **faire les c. pas** to pace up and down; **à c. pieds sous terre** dead and buried; *Fam* **il y a c. sept ans que...** it's been ages since...; *Fam* **je ne vais pas attendre c. sept ans** I'm not going to wait forever (and a day); *Fam* **je m'embête** *ou* **m'ennuie à c. sous de l'heure** I'm bored stiff *or* to death; *Fam* **on se faisait suer à c. sous de l'heure** it was as exciting as watching paint dry; *Hist* **les C.-Jours** the Hundred Days **2** *(dans des séries)* hundredth; **chambre c.** room one hundred; **page deux c. (six)** page two hundred (and six); **l'an neuf c.** the year nine hundred **3** *Sport* **le c. mètres** the hundred metres; **le quatre**

c. mètres haies the four hundred metres hurdle *or* hurdles; **le c. mètres nage libre** the hundred metres freestyle
PRON hundred
NM 1 *(gén)* hundred
2 *(numéro d'ordre)* number one hundred
3 *(chiffre écrit)* hundred
4 *(centaine)* hundred; **un c. d'huîtres** a hundred oysters
5 *Écon (unité divisionnaire de l'euro)* cent
6 *(locutions)* **pour c.** percent; **20 pour c.** 20 percent; *Chim* **une solution à 30 pour c.** a 30 percent solution; **c. pour c. coton** a *or* one hundred percent pure cotton; **il est c. pour c. anglais** he's a hundred percent English; **je suis c. pour c. contre** I'm a hundred percent against it; **je te le donne en c.** guess, I'll give you three guesses; *voir aussi* **cinquante**

cent[2] [sent] **NM** *(monnaie)* cent

centaine [sɑ̃tɛn] **NF 1** *(cent unités)* hundred; **la colonne des centaines** the hundreds column **2** *(quantité)* **une c.** around *or* about a hundred, a hundred or so; **une c. de voitures** around *or* about a hundred cars; **elle a une c. d'années** she's around *or* about a hundred (years old) **3** *(âge)* **avoir la c.** to be around *or* about a hundred
• **par centaines ADV** by the hundreds; **les gens arrivent par centaines** people are arriving by the hundreds *or* in their hundreds

centaure [sɑ̃tɔr] **NM** *Myth* centaur

centaurée [sɑ̃tɔre] **NF** *Bot* **c. (noire)** (common) knapweed; **petite c.** centaury

centenaire [sɑ̃tnɛr] **ADJ 1** *(qui dure cent ans)* hundred-year *(avant n)* **2** *(personne)* **ma grand-mère est c.** *(elle a cent ans)* my grandmother is a hundred (years old); *(elle a plus de cent ans)* my grandmother is over a hundred (years old) **3** *(bâtiment)* over a hundred years old
NMF *(vieillard)* centenarian
NM *(anniversaire)* centenary, *Am & Can* centennial

centésimal, -e, -aux, -ales [sɑ̃tezimal, -o] **ADJ** centesimal; *Méd* **dilution centésimale** dilution to one part per hundred

centiare [sɑ̃tjar] **NM** centiare, square metre

centième [sɑ̃tjɛm] **ADJ** hundredth
NMF 1 *(personne)* hundredth **2** *(objet)* hundredth (one)
NM 1 *(partie)* hundredth **2** *(étage) Br* hundredth floor, *Am* hundred and first floor **3** *(locution)* **je n'ai pas compris le c. de ce qu'il disait** I didn't understand a fraction of what he was saying
NF *Théât* hundredth performance; *voir aussi* **cinquième**

centigrade [sɑ̃tigrad] **ADJ** centigrade

centigramme [sɑ̃tigram] **NM** centigram

centilitre [sɑ̃tilitr] **NM** centilitre

centime [sɑ̃tim] **NM 1** *(centième d'euro)* cent; *Anciennement (centième de franc)* centime; **pas un c.** not a *Br* penny *or Am* cent; **ça ne m'a pas coûté un c.** it didn't cost me *Br* a penny *or Am* one cent; **je n'ai plus un c.** I haven't a penny to my name **2** *Fin* **centimes additionnels** additional tax

centimètre [sɑ̃timɛtr] **NM 1** *(unité de mesure)* centimetre; **c. carré/cube** square/cubic centimetre **2** *(ruban)* tape measure, *Am* tape line

centrafricain, -e [sɑ̃trafrikɛ̃, -ɛn] **ADJ** Central African; **République centrafricaine** Central African Republic
• **Centrafricain, -e NM,F** Central African

Centrafrique [sɑ̃trafrik] **NM** Central African Republic

centrage [sɑ̃traʒ] **NM** centring

central, -e, -aux, -ales [sɑ̃tral, -o] **ADJ 1** *(du milieu d'un objet)* middle *(avant n)*, central; **le trou c.** the central *or* middle hole
2 *(du centre d'une ville)* central; **mon bureau est très c.** my office is very central
3 *Admin & Pol* central, national
4 *(principal)* main, crucial; **le point c. de votre exposé** the main *or* crucial *or* key point in your thesis
5 *Ling* centre *(avant n)*
NM 1 *Tél* **c. (téléphonique)** (telephone) exchange; **c. numérique** digital exchange **2** *Sport (de tennis)* **(court) c.** centre court
• **centrale NF 1** *(usine)* **centrale (électrique)** power station; **centrale hydraulique/nucléaire/thermique** hydroelectric/nuclear/thermal station; **centrale surgénératrice** fast-breeder power station
2 *Pol* **centrale ouvrière** *ou* **syndicale** *Br* trade *or Am* labor union confederation
3 *(prison)* county jail, *Am* penitentiary
4 *Com* **centrale d'achat(s)** central purchasing office; *(au sein d'une entreprise)* central purchasing department; **centrale de réservation(s)** central reservations unit, central reservations office

Centrale [sɑ̃tral] **NF** *Univ* = "grande école" which trains engineers

centralien, -enne [sɑ̃traljɛ̃, -ɛn] **NM,F** *Univ* = student or ex-student of "Centrale"

centralisateur, -trice [sɑ̃tralizatœr, -tris] **ADJ** centralizing

centralisation [sɑ̃tralizasjɔ̃] **NF** centralization

centralisatrice [sɑ̃tralizatris] *voir* **centralisateur**

centraliser [3] [sɑ̃tralize] **VT** to centralize

centralisme [sɑ̃tralism] **NM** *Pol* centralism

centraliste [sɑ̃tralist] *Pol* **ADJ** centralist
NMF centralist

CENTRE [sɑ̃tr] **NM 1** *(milieu ▸ gén)* middle, centre; *(▸ d'une cible)* bull's eye, centre; **le c.** *(d'une ville) Br* the centre, *Am* downtown; **aller au c.** *Br* to go to the centre (of town), *Am* to go downtown; **elle était le c. de tous les regards** all eyes were fixed on her; **il se prend pour le c. du monde** *ou* **de l'univers** he thinks the world revolves around him
2 *(concentration)* **c. industriel** industrial area; **c. urbain** town; **les grands centres urbains** large conurbations
3 *(organisme)* centre; **c. d'accueil** reception centre; **c. d'accueil de jour** day care centre; **c. aéré** = holiday activity centre for schoolchildren; **c. d'affaires** business centre; *(dans un aéroport, dans un hôtel)* business lounge; **c. d'aide par le travail** = day centre which helps disabled people to find work and become more independent; *Compta* **c. d'analyse** cost centre; *Compta* **c. (d'analyse) auxiliaire/principal** secondary/main cost centre; *Compta* **c. d'analyse opérationnel** operational cost centre; *Com* **c. d'appels** call centre; **c. de chèques postaux** PO cheque account centre; **c. commercial** *Br* shopping centre, *Am* (shopping) mall; **c. de conférences** conference centre; **c. de contrôle** *(spatial)* mission control; *Fin* **c. de coût** cost centre; **c. culturel** art *or* arts centre; **c. de dépistage du cancer/SIDA** centre for cancer/Aids screening; **c. de documentation** information centre; **c. de documentation et d'information** ≃ school library; **c. pour femmes battues** women's refuge; **c. de formation continue** *ou* **permanente** = centre for continuing education; **c. d'hébergement pour les sans-abri** hostel for the homeless; **c. d'hébergement d'urgence** emergency refuge; **c. hospitalier** hospital (complex); **c. hospitalier spécialisé** psychiatric hospital; **c. hospitalo-universitaire** teaching hospital; **c. des impôts** tax centre *or* office; **c. d'information** information centre; **c. d'information et d'orientation** careers advisory centre; **c. d'instruction** military academy; **c. de loisirs** leisure *or* recreation centre; **c. médical** clinic; **c. médico-social** health centre; **C. national de la recherche scientifique** = French national organization for scientific research, *Br* ≃ Science Research Council; **C. national de transfusion sanguine** = national blood transfusion centre; *Fin* **c. de profit** profit centre; *Belg* **c. public d'aide sociale** welfare office *or* centre; **c. régional** = regional prison centre for prisoners serving three years or less; **c. régional de documentation pédagogique** = local centre for educational resources; **c. de renseignements (téléphoniques)** *Br* directory enquiries, *Am* information; *Fin* **c. de revenus** revenue centre; **c. social** social services office; **c. sportif** sports centre; **c. de tri** sorting office; **c. universitaire** university; **c. de vacances** holiday centre
4 *(point essentiel)* main *or* key point, heart, centre; **le c. du débat** the heart *or* crux of the matter; **être au c. de** to be the key point of, to be at the heart *or* centre of; **la sécurité est au c. de nos préoccupations** safety is at the centre of our concerns; **c. d'intérêt** centre of interest; **centres d'intérêt** *(sur un CV)* other interests; **c. d'intérêt touristique** tourist *or* visitor attraction
5 *Anat & Physiol* centre; *aussi Fig* **c. de gravité** centre of gravity; **c. nerveux** nerve centre; **c. vital** vital organs; *Fig* nerve centre
6 *Tech* **c. optique** optical centre
7 *Pol* middle ground, centre; **il est du c.** he's middle-of-the-road; **c. droit/gauche** moderate right/left; **il est (de) c. droit** he's right-of-centre; **il est (de) c. gauche** he's left-of-centre
8 *Sport (position ▸ au football)* centre-forward; *(▸ au rugby)* centre; *(▸ au basketball)* centre; *(passe ▸ au football)* centre
9 *Ind* **c. d'usinage** turning shop
• **Centre NM** *(région)* **le C.** Centre

centré, -e [sɑ̃tre] **ADJ** *Suisse (magasin, appartement)* central

centrer [3] [sɑ̃tre] **VT 1** *(gén) & Tech* to centre
2 *(orienter)* **centrons le débat** let's give the discussion a focus, let's concentrate on one issue; **être centré sur** to be centred *or* focused around; **le documentaire était centré sur l'enfance de l'artiste** the documentary was focused around the artist's childhood; **être trop centré sur soi-même** to be too self-centred
3 *Typ (texte)* to centre
4 *Sport (ballon)* to centre

centre-répéteur [sɑ̃trərepetœr] *(pl* **centres-répéteurs) NM** *TV & Rad* relay station

centre-ville [sɑ̃trəvil] *(pl* **centres-villes) NM** *Br* town centre, *Am* downtown; *(d'une grande ville) Br* city centre, *Am* downtown; **les boutiques du c.** *Br* the shops in the town/city centre, *Am* the downtown stores; **aller au c.** *Br* to go into the town/city centre, *Am* to go downtown

centrifugation [sɑ̃trifygasjɔ̃] **NF** *Tech* centrifugation

centrifuge [sɑ̃trifyʒ] **ADJ** *Tech* centrifugal

centrifuger [17] [sɑ̃trifyʒe] **VT** *Tech* to centrifuge

centrifugeur [sɑ̃trifyʒœr] **NM 1** *Méd & Tech* centrifuge **2** *Culin* juice extractor, juicer

centripète [sɑ̃tripɛt] **ADJ** *Phys* centripetal

centrisme [sɑ̃trism] **NM** *Pol* centrism

centriste [sɑ̃trist] *Pol* **ADJ** centrist
NMF centrist; **les centristes** the centre

centuple [sɑ̃typl] **ADJ 1000 est un nombre c. de 10** 1,000 is a hundred times 10
NM le c. de 20 est 2000 a hundred times 20 is 2,000
• **au centuple ADV** a hundredfold; **je te le rendrai au c.** I'll repay you a hundred times over *or* a hundredfold

centupler [3] [sɑ̃typle] **VT** to increase a hundredfold *or* a hundred times, to multiply by a hundred
VI to increase a hundredfold

centurion [sɑ̃tyrjɔ̃] **NM** *Antiq & Mil* centurion

CEP [seəpe] **NM** *Anciennement Scol (abrév* **certificat d'études primaires)** = basic examination taken at the end of primary education

cep [sɛp] **NM** *Bot* **c. (de vigne)** vine stock

cépage [sepaʒ] **NM** grape variety

cèpe [sɛp] **NM 1** *Bot* boletus **2** *Culin* cep

cependant [səpɑ̃dɑ̃] **CONJ 1** *(néanmoins)* however, nevertheless, yet; **il n'avait pas très envie de sortir ce soir-là; c. il se laissa entraîner** he didn't really want to go out that night, nevertheless he let himself be dragged along; **je suis d'accord avec vous, j'ai c. une petite remarque à faire** I agree with you, however I have one small comment to make; **il parle très bien, avec un léger accent c.** he speaks very well, albeit with a slight accent **2** *Littéraire (pendant ce temps)* meanwhile, in the meantime
• **cependant que CONJ** *Littéraire* while

céphalée [sefale], **céphalalgie** [sefalalʒi] **NF** *Méd* headache, *Spéc* cephalgia

céphalique [sefalik] **ADJ** *Anat* cephalic

Céphalonie [sefaloni] **NF** Cephalonia, Kefalonia

céphalopode [sefalɔpɔd] *Zool* NM *(mollusque)* cephalopod
• **céphalopodes** NMPL Cephalopoda

céramique [seramik] ADJ ceramic
NF **1** *(art)* ceramics *(singulier)*, pottery
2 *(objet)* piece of ceramic
3 *(matière)* ceramic; **des carreaux de c.** ceramic tiles
4 *Méd* dental ceramics *or* porcelain

céramiste [seramist] NMF ceramist

Cerbère [sɛrbɛr] NPR *Myth* Cerberus

CERC [sɛrk] NM *(abrév* **Centre d'études sur les revenus et les coûts)** = government body carrying out research into salaries and the cost of living

cerceau, -x [sɛrso] NM *(d'enfant, d'acrobate, de tonneau, de jupon)* hoop; *(de tonnelle)* half-hoop; **faire rouler un c.** to bowl a hoop

cerclage [sɛrklaʒ] NM **1** *(action de cercler)* hooping **2** *Méd* **c. (du col de l'utérus)** cerclage

cercle [sɛrkl] NM **1** *Géom* circle; *(forme)* circle, ring; **tracer un c.** to draw a circle; **décrire des cercles dans le ciel** *(avion, oiseau)* to fly around in circles, to wheel round, to circle; **faire c.** *ou* **former un c. autour de qn** to stand *or* to gather round sb in a circle; **entourer qch d'un c.** to put a ring round *or* to circle sth; **en c.** in a circle; **un village entouré d'un c. de collines** a village ringed with hills; **c. vicieux** vicious circle, catch-22; **se retrouver** *ou* **tomber dans un c. vicieux** to be caught in a vicious circle *or* in a catch-22 situation; **c. vertueux** virtuous circle; *Beaux-Arts* **le c. chromatique** the colour wheel
2 *(gamme, étendue* ▸ *d'activités, de connaissances)* range, scope
3 *(groupe)* circle, group; **c. d'amis** circle *or* group of friends; **c. de famille** family (circle); **c. de lecture** book club *or* group; **c. littéraire** literary circle
4 *(club)* club; **un c. militaire** an officer's club
5 *(objet circulaire)* hoop; **c. d'arpenteur** protractor; **c. de roue** (wheel) tyre
6 *Astron & Math* circle
7 *Géog* **c. polaire** polar circle; **c. polaire arctique/antarctique** Arctic/Antarctic Circle
8 *Mktg* **c. de qualité** quality circle

cercler [3] [sɛrkle] VT **1** *(emballage)* to ring; *(tonneau)* to hoop; **une caisse cerclée de fer** an iron-bound crate **2** *(entourer)* **des doigts cerclés d'or** gold-ringed fingers; **des lunettes cerclées d'écaille** horn-rimmed spectacles **3** *Méd* to wire

cercueil [sɛrkœj] NM *Br* coffin, *Am* casket

céréale [sereal] NF **1** *Bot & Agr* cereal; **ils cultivent des céréales** they grow cereals *or* grain **2** *Culin* **des céréales** (breakfast) cereal

céréalier, -ère [serealje, -ɛr] ADJ cereal *(avant n)*
NM *(producteur)* cereal farmer *or* grower

cérébelleux, -euse [serebelø, -øz] ADJ *Anat* cerebellar

cérébral, -e, -aux, -ales [serebral, -o] *(mpl* **cérébro-spinaux** [-o], *fpl* **cérébro-spinales)**
ADJ **1** *Anat* cerebral **2** *Méd* brain *(avant n)* **3** *(intellectuel* ▸ *activité, travail)* intellectual, mental; *(*▸ *film, livre, personne)* cerebral, intellectual
NM,F intellectual

cérébro-spinal, -e [serebrospinal] ADJ *Anat* cerebrospinal

cérémonial, -als [seremɔnjal] NM *(règles, livre)* ceremonial; **c. de cour** court etiquette

cérémonie [seremɔni] NF **1** *Rel* ceremony **2** *(fête)* ceremony, solemn *or* formal occasion; **c. nuptiale** wedding ceremony; **c. d'ouverture/de clôture** opening/closing ceremony; **la c. de remise des prix** the award ceremony **3** *(rituel)* ceremony, rites; **c. du thé** tea ceremony; **avant qu'il ne s'endorme, c'est tout une c.** it's quite a performance getting him to go to sleep
• **cérémonies** NFPL *Péj (manières)* fuss, palaver; **ne fais pas tant de cérémonies** don't make such a fuss
• **avec cérémonie** ADV ceremoniously
• **de cérémonie** ADJ *Mil (tenue)* ceremonial; **uniforme de c.** (full) dress uniform
• **en grande cérémonie** ADV *(apporter, présenter)* with great formality, very ceremoniously
• **sans cérémonie** ADV *(simplement)* casually, informally; **pas besoin de te changer, c'est sans c.** just come as you are, it's an informal occasion

cérémonieuse [seremɔnjøz] *voir* **cérémonieux**

cérémonieusement [seremɔnjøzmɑ̃] ADV ceremoniously, formally

cérémonieux, -euse [seremɔnjø, -øz] ADJ ceremonious, formal

cerf [sɛr] NM *Zool* stag; **jeune c.** staggard, young stag; **grand c., vieux c.** hart; **grand vieux c.** royal (stag *or* hart); **c. commun** *ou* **d'Europe** red deer

cerfeuil [sɛrfœj] NM *Bot* chervil

cerf-volant [sɛrvɔlɑ̃] *(pl* **cerfs-volants)** NM **1** *(jeu)* kite; **jouer au c.** to fly a kite **2** *Entom* stag beetle

cerisaie [s(ə)rizɛ] NF cherry orchard

cerise [s(ə)riz] NF **1** *(fruit)* cherry; *Fig* **la c. sur le gâteau** the icing on the cake **2** *Fam (tête)* head[□], nut
ADJ INV **(rouge) c.** cherry, cherry-red, cerise

cerisier [s(ə)rizje] NM **1** *(arbre)* cherry (tree); **c. acide** morello cherry, sour cherry **2** *(bois)* cherry (wood)

cérium [serjɔm] NM *Chim* cerium; **oxyde de c.** ceria

CERN, Cern [sɛrn] NM *(abrév* **Conseil européen pour la recherche nucléaire)** CERN

cerne [sɛrn] NM **1** *(sous les yeux)* shadow, (dark) ring *or* circle; **elle a des cernes** she's got dark rings *or* circles under her eyes
2 *Tex* ring; **faire un c.** to leave a ring
3 *Bot* (annual) ring
4 *Beaux-Arts* outline

cerné, -e [sɛrne] ADJ **avoir les yeux cernés** to have (dark) rings *or* circles under one's eyes

cerneau, -x [sɛrno] NM *(chair)* (shelled) walnut

cerner [3] [sɛrne] VT **1** *(entourer)* to surround, to lie around; **les lacs qui cernent la ville** the lakes dotted around the *or* surrounding the town
2 *(assiéger* ▸ *ville)* to surround, to seal off; *(*▸ *armée, population)* to surround; **rendez-vous, vous êtes cernés!** give yourselves up, you are surrounded!
3 *(définir* ▸ *question, problème)* to define, to determine; **ceci nous a permis de c. le problème de près** this has enabled us to home in on the problem
4 *(*▸ *comprendre)* **il est difficile à c.** it's hard to say what kind of person he is
5 *(ouvrir* ▸ *noix)* to crack open, to shell

cernier [sɛrnje] NM *Ich* wreck fish, stone bass

céroplastique [seroplastik] NF wax modelling

CERS [seəɛrs] NF *(abrév* **Commission européenne de recherches spatiales)** ESRO

CERTAIN, -E [sɛrtɛ̃, -ɛn]

ADJ
• definite **1** • certain **2–4**
• sure **3**
ADJ INDÉFINI
• certain **1, 2**

ADJ **1** *(incontestable* ▸ *amélioration)* definite; *(*▸ *preuve)* definite, positive; *(*▸ *avantage, rapport)* definite, clear; *(*▸ *décision, invitation, prix)* definite; **le médicament a des effets secondaires certains** the drug has definite side-effects; **avec un enthousiasme c.** with real *or* obvious enthusiasm; **tenir qch pour c.** to know sth for certain, to have no doubt about sth; **je tiens son accord pour c.** I have no doubt that he'll agree; **c'est c.** *(pour confirmer)* undoubtedly, that's for certain *or* sure; **le projet a beaucoup de retard – c'est c., mais…** the project is a long way behind schedule – that's certainly true but…; **il viendra, c'est c.** he'll definitely come; **il devrait venir, mais ce n'est pas c.** he should come, but it's not certain *or* definite; **une chose est certaine** one thing's for certain *or* sure
2 *(inéluctable* ▸ *échec, victoire)* certain; **devant un renvoi c./une mort certaine** faced with certain dismissal/death; **on nous avait présenté son départ comme c.** we'd been told he was certain to go
3 *(persuadé)* sure, certain; **être c. de ce qu'on avance** to be sure *or* certain about what one is saying; **il n'est pas très c. de sa décision** he's not sure he's made the right decision; **êtes-vous c. de votre bon droit?** are you sure (that) you're in the right?; **être c. d'avoir fait qch** to be sure *or* to be positive one has done sth; **il est c. de revenir** he's sure *or* certain to return; **si tu pars battu, tu es c. de perdre!** if you think you're going to lose, (then) you're bound *or* sure *or* certain to lose!; **êtes-vous sûr que c'était lui? – j'en suis c.!** are you sure it was him? – I'm positive!, I'm sure *or* certain (of it)!; **ils céderont – n'en sois pas si c.** they'll give in – don't be so sure; **j'étais c. que cela recommencerait** I was sure *or* I knew it would happen again
4 *Math* certain
ADJ INDÉFINI *(avant le nom)* **1** *(exprimant l'indétermination)* certain; **à remettre à une certaine date** to be handed in on a certain date; **à un c. moment** at one point; **un c. nombre d'entre eux** some of them; **je voudrais vous poser un c. nombre de questions** I'd like to ask you a number of *or* some questions; **j'y ai cru un c. temps** I believed it for a while; **un c. temps après/avant** a while later/earlier; **d'un c. point de vue, tu as raison** in some ways *or* in a sense, you're right; **d'une certaine façon** *ou* **manière** in a way; **dans** *ou* **en un c. sens** in a sense; **jusqu'à un c. point** up to a (certain) point
2 *(exprimant une quantité non négligeable)* certain; **il a fait preuve d'une certaine intelligence** he has shown a certain amount of *or* some intelligence; **il a un c. talent** he has a certain *or* some talent; **il a eu une certaine influence sur elle** he had some influence on her; **elle a un c. culot!** she's got some nerve!; **c'est quand même à une certaine distance d'ici** it is quite a distance away
3 *(devant un nom de personne)* **un c. Christophe a téléphoné** someone called Christophe phoned; **les dialogues sont l'œuvre d'un c.…** the dialogue is by someone called… *or* by one…; **si un c. M. Martin appelle, dites-lui que…** if a (certain) Mr Martin calls, tell him…; *Péj* **il voit souvent un c. Robert** he sees a lot of some character called Robert
NM *Bourse* fixed *or* direct rate of exchange; **le c. de la livre est de 1,46 euros** the rate of exchange for the pound is 1.46 euros
ADV *Can Fam* for sure, certainly[□]; **il va neiger aujourd'hui c.** it's going to snow today for sure
• **certains, certaines** ADJ INDÉFINI PL *(quelques)* some, certain; **certaines fois** sometimes, on some occasions; **dans certaines circonstances** in certain *or* some circumstances; **certains jours** sometimes, on some days; **certains indices retrouvés chez lui…** certain clues found at his home…; **on retrouve cette tradition dans certains pays** this tradition can be found in a number of *or* in certain countries; **j'ai certaines idées sur la question** I have some *or* a few ideas on the subject PRON INDÉFINI PL *(personnes)* some (people); *(choses)* some; *(d'un groupe)* some (of them); **certains pensent que…** some people think that…; *aussi Hum* **je travaille, moi, je ne suis pas comme certains!** I work, unlike some people!; **certains d'entre vous semblent ne pas avoir compris** some of you seem not to have understood; **parmi ces gens, certains n'avaient jamais navigué** some of these people had never sailed before; **il a de nombreux amis et certains sont très influents** he has a lot of friends and some of them are very influential

certainement [sɛrtɛnmɑ̃] ADV **1** *(sans aucun doute)* certainly, surely, no doubt; **il va c. échouer** he is bound to fail **2** *(probablement)* (most) probably; **il y a c. une solution à ton problème** there must be a way to solve your problem **3** *(dans une réponse)* certainly; **je peux? – c.!** may I? – certainly *or* of course!; **c. pas!** certainly not!

Il faut noter que l'adverbe anglais **certainly** est un faux ami. Il signifie **sans aucun doute**.

certes [sɛrt] ADV **1** *(assurément)* certainly, indeed; **c., je ne pouvais pas lui dire la vérité** certainly, I couldn't tell him/her the truth **2** *(servant de réponse)* certainly; **l'avez-vous lu? – c.!** did you read it? – I certainly did *or* I did indeed!; **m'en voulez-vous? – c. non!** are you angry with me? – of course not *or* certainly not! **3** *(indiquant la concession)* of course, certainly; **c., sa situation n'est pas enviable, mais que faire?** his/her situation is certainly not to be envied, but what can be done?; **je ne veux c. pas la décourager, mais...** I certainly wouldn't want to discourage her, but...; **il est beau, c., mais il n'est pas sympathique** he's handsome, I grant you, but he's not very nice

certificat [sɛrtifika] NM **1** *(attestation)* certificate; *Bourse* **c. d'actions provisoire** share certificate, (provisional) scrip; **c. d'arrêt de travail** *(pour cause de maladie)* medical certificate; **c. d'assurance** insurance certificate; *Jur* **c. de bonne vie et de bonnes mœurs** character reference; **c. de capacité** *(d'employé)* certificate of proficiency; **c. de concubinage** = official document stating that two people are cohabiting; *Com* **c. de dépôt** *(de marchandises)* warehouse warrant; *Bourse* **c. de dividende provisoire** scrip dividend; *Com* **c. d'entrepôt** warehouse warrant; *Com* **c. de garantie** certificate of guarantee, guarantee certificate, warranty; *Jur* **c. d'hérédité** proof of title; *Fin* **c. d'investissement** investment certificate; *Fin* **c. d'investissement privilégié** preferential investment certificate; *Com* **c. de jaugeage** tonnage certificate; **c. médical** medical certificate; *Admin* **c. de naissance** birth certificate; *Jur* **c. de nationalité** certificate of (French) nationality; **c. de navigabilité** *(aérienne)* certificate of airworthiness; *(maritime)* certificate of seaworthiness; *Bourse* **c. nominatif d'action(s)** registered share certificate; *Fin* **c. de non-paiement** *(de chèque)* notification of unpaid cheque; *(de lettre de change)* certificate of dishonour; *Com* **c. d'origine** certificate of origin; *Jur* **c. de propriété** title deed; *Bourse* **c. provisoire** share certificate, (provisional) scrip; *Assur* **c. provisoire d'assurance** cover note; *Com* **c. de qualité** certificate of quality; *Admin* **c. de résidence** certificate of residence; **c. sanitaire** health certificate; **c. de scolarité** *Scol* school attendance certificate; *Univ* university attendance certificate; *Ordinat* **c. de sécurité** security certificate; *Fin* **c. de titres** share certificate; *Jur* **c. de travail** attestation of employment, *Br* ≃ P45; *Fin* **c. de trésorerie** treasury bond; **c. de vaccination** vaccination certificate; *Com* **c. de valeur** certificate of value

2 *(diplôme)* diploma, certificate; **c. d'aptitude pédagogique** teaching diploma; *Jur* **c. d'aptitude à la profession d'avocat** = qualifying certificate required in order to be admitted as a trainee barrister; **c. d'aptitude professionnelle** = vocational training certificate (taken at secondary school), *Br* ≃ City and Guilds examination; **c. d'aptitude au professorat de l'enseignement secondaire** *ou* **du second degré** = secondary school teaching qualification, *Br* ≃ PGCE; **c. d'aptitude au professorat de l'enseignement technique** = secondary school teaching qualification for technical subjects; *Anciennement* **c. d'études (primaires)** = basic examination sat at the end of primary education; *Anciennement* **c. (d'études supérieures) de licence** *(unité de valeur)* = each of the four examinations for the "licence"; **c. de formation professionnelle** vocational training certificate

certificateur [sɛrtifikatœr] *Jur* ADJ M certifying, guaranteeing

NM *(gén)* certifier, guarantor; *(de caution)* counter-security

certification [sɛrtifikasjɔ̃] NF *Jur* **1** *(authentification)* certification, authentication; **c. conforme** certification **2** *(garantie)* (bank) guarantee **3** *(assurance, attestation)* attestation, witnessing; **c. de signature** *ou* **des signatures** witnessing of signatures

certifié, -e [sɛrtifje] *Scol* ADJ *(professeur)* holding the "CAPES"

NM,F "CAPES" holder, ≃ qualified *Br* secondary school *or Am* high school teacher

certifier [9] [sɛrtifje] VT **1** *(assurer)* to assure; **il m'a certifié que rien n'avait été vendu** he assured me nothing had been sold **2** *Jur (garantir ▸ caution)* to guarantee, to counter-secure; *(▸ signature)* to witness, to authenticate; *(▸ document)* to authenticate, to certify; **une copie certifiée conforme (à l'original)** a certified copy of the original document

certitude [sɛrtityd] NF certainty; **ce n'est pas une hypothèse, c'est une c.** it's not a possibility, it's a certainty; **avoir la c. de qch** to be convinced of sth; **il viendra, j'en ai la c.** I'm convinced *or* certain *or* quite sure he'll come; **je sais avec c. que...** I know for a certainty that...

cérumen [serymɛn] NM *Physiol* earwax, *Spéc* cerumen

céruse [seryz] NF ceruse; **blanc de c.** white lead

cerveau, -x [sɛrvo] NM **1** *Anat* brain; **c. antérieur** forebrain; **c. moyen** midbrain; **c. postérieur** hindbrain; *Fam* **il a le c. malade** *ou* **dérangé** *ou* **fêlé** he's got a screw loose, he's cracked

2 *(esprit)* mind, intellect, brains; **faire travailler son c.** to use one's brain

3 *Fam (génie)* brainy person, brain; **c'est un c.** he's got brains, he's a real brain

4 *(instigateur)* brains; **être le c. de qch** to be the brains behind sth

5 *Ordinat* **c. électronique** electronic brain

cervelas [sɛrvəla] NM *Culin* ≃ saveloy

cervelet [sɛrvəlɛ] NM *Anat* cerebellum

cervelle [sɛrvɛl] NF **1** *Anat* brain **2** *Fam (intelligence)* brain; **une fille sans c.** a brainless *or* dimwitted girl; **se mettre qch dans la c.** to get sth into one's head; **il n'a** *ou* **il n'y a rien dans sa petite c.** he's got nothing between his ears; **quand elle a quelque chose dans la c.** when she gets an idea into her head; **avoir une c. d'oiseau** *ou* **une tête sans c.** to be bird-brained; **se mettre la c. à l'envers** to rack one's brains **3** *Culin* brains; **de la c. de mouton** sheep's brains

cervical, -e, -aux, -ales [sɛrvikal, -o] ADJ *Anat* cervical

cervidé [sɛrvide] *Zool* NM member of the deer family *or Spéc* Cervidae, *Spéc* cervid

• **cervidés** NMPL Cervidae

Cervin [sɛrvɛ̃] NM **le (mont) C.** the Matterhorn

cervoise [sɛrvwaz] NF *Antiq* barley ale

CES [seəɛs] NM **1** *(abrév* **collège d'enseignement secondaire**) = former secondary school **2** *Anciennement (abrév* **contrat emploi-solidarité**) = short-term contract subsidized by the government

ces [se] *voir* **ce**[1]

César [sezar] NPR Caesar; **rendez à C. ce qui appartient à C.** render unto Caesar that which is Caesar's

césarien, -enne [sezarjɛ̃, -ɛn] ADJ *Antiq* Caesarean

• **césarienne** NF *Obst* Caesarean (section); **on lui a fait une césarienne** she had a Caesarean; **elle est née par césarienne** she was born by Caesarean

césium [sezjɔm] NM *Métal & Chim* caesium

cessant, -e [sɛsɑ̃, -ɑ̃t] *voir* **affaire**

cessation [sesasjɔ̃] NF **1** *Mil* **c. des hostilités** ceasefire **2** *(d'une activité)* cessation, stopping; **c. du travail** stoppage **3** *Com* **c. de paiement** suspension of payments; **être en c. de paiement** to have suspended (all) payments; **c. d'activité** termination of business; **pour cause de c. de commerce** due to closure

cesse [sɛs] NF **elle n'aura de c. qu'elle n'ait trouvé la réponse** she will not rest until she finds the answer

• **sans cesse** ADV continually, constantly; **elle se plaint sans c.** she's constantly complaining, she complains all the time

cesser [4] [sese] VI *(pluie, bruit, mouvement)* to stop, *Sout* to cease; *(vent)* to die down, to drop, *Sout* to abate; *(combat)* to (come to a) stop; **il y a trop d'absentéisme, il faut que cela cesse!** too many people are staying away from work, this must stop!; **faire c. qch** to put a stop to sth; **c. de faire qch** to stop doing sth; **cesse de pleurer** stop crying; **il ne cesse pas de gémir** he never stops moaning, he's always *or* forever moaning; **ne c. de faire qch** to keep doing, to persist in doing sth; **je ne cesse d'y penser** I can't stop thinking about it, I keep thinking about it; **les prix ne cessent d'augmenter** prices keep rising

VT **1** *(arrêter)* to stop, to halt; **c. le travail** to down tools, to walk out; **c. toutes relations avec qn** to break off all relations with sb; **cessez ces cris!** stop that shouting! **2** *Mil* **c. le combat** to stop fighting; **c. le feu** to cease fire

cessez-le-feu [seselfø] NM INV *Mil* ceasefire

cessible [sesibl] ADJ *Jur* assignable, transferable; *(pension, retraite)* negotiable

cession [sɛsjɔ̃] NF *Jur* assignment, transfer; **c. d'actifs** sale of assets; **c. de bail** lease transfer; *Jur* **c. de créance** assignment of receivables; *Jur* **c. de dettes** assignment of debts; *Com* **c. de licence** licensing; *Com* **c. de licence de marque** corporate licensing; *Com* **c. de licence de nom** name licensing; *Fin* **c. de parts** sale *or* disposal of securities

cession-bail [sɛsjɔ̃baj] *(pl* **cessions-bails** *ou* **cessions-baux**) NF *Jur* leaseback

cessionnaire [sɛsjɔnɛr] NMF *Jur (de biens)* assignee, transferee; *(d'un effet de commerce, d'une créance)* holder; *(d'un chèque)* endorser

c'est-à-dire [setadir] ADV **1** *(introduisant une explication)* that is (to say), i.e., in other words; **toute la famille, c. mes parents et mes sœurs** all the family, i.e. *or* that is, my parents and my sisters

2 *(pour demander une explication)* **c.?** what do you mean?

3 *(introduisant une rectification)* or rather; **il est venu hier, c. plutôt avant-hier** he came yesterday, I mean *or* or rather the day before yesterday

4 *(introduisant une hésitation)* **tu penses y aller? – eh bien, c....** are you thinking of going? – well, you know *or* I mean...

• **c'est-à-dire que** CONJ **1** *(introduisant une excuse, une hésitation)* actually, as a matter of fact; **voulez-vous nous accompagner? – c. que je suis un peu fatigué** do you want to come with us? – I'm afraid *or* actually I'm a bit tired; **elle m'en veut – c. qu'elle t'a attendue deux heures** she's annoyed with me – well, you DID keep her waiting for two hours **2** *(introduisant une explication)* which means; **il a acheté une maison, c. qu'il s'est endetté** he bought a house, which means he got himself into debt **3** *(introduisant une rectification)* or rather; **je ne sais pas ce qu'il veut, c. que je préfère ne pas le savoir** I don't know what he wants, or rather I don't want to know

césure [sezyr] NF **1** *Littérature* caesura **2** *Ordinat* break, hyphenation; **c. automatique** soft hyphen; **c. imposée** hard hyphen

CET [seəte] NM **1** *(abrév* **compte épargne temps**) = scheme which allows employees to save up the hours of overtime they accumulate under the "RTT" system for up to five years, eventually being compensated either financially or with additional holidays **2** *Anciennement (abrév* **collège d'enseignement technique**) = technical school

cet [sɛt] *voir* **ce**[1]

cétacé [setase] *Zool* NM cetacean

• **cétacés** NMPL Cetacea

cétane [setan] NM *Chim* cetane

cette [sɛt] *voir* **ce**[1]

ceux [sø] *voir* **celui**

ceux-ci [søsi], **ceux-là** [søla] *voir* **celui**

cévenol, -e [sevnɔl] ADJ of/from the Cévennes

• **Cévenol, -e** NM,F = inhabitant of or person from the Cévennes

Ceylan [selɑ̃] NM *Anciennement* Ceylon

cézig, cézigue [sezig] PRON *Fam* his lordship, *Br* his nibs

cf. *(abrév écrite* **confer**) cf

CFA [seɛfa] NF *(abrév* **Communauté financière africaine**) African Financial Community; **franc C.** = currency used in former French African colonies

NM *(abrév* **Centre de formation des apprentis**) = centre for apprenticeship training

CFAO [seɛfao] NF *(abrév* **conception et fabrication assistées par ordinateur**) CAD/CAM

CFC [seɛfse] NM **1** *Chim (abrév* **chlorofluorocarbure**) CFC **2** *(abrév* **centre de formation continue**) = centre for continuing education

CFDT [seɛfdete] NF *(abrév* **Confédération française démocratique du travail**) = French trade union

CFF [seɛfɛf] NMPL *Suisse (abrév* **Chemins de fer fédéraux**) = Swiss railways

CFP [seɛfpe] NF **1** *(abrév* **Compagnie française des pétroles**) = French oil company **2** *(abrév* **Communauté française du Pacifique**) **franc C.** = currency used in former French colonies in the Pacific area

NM 1 *(abrév* **Centre de formation permanente**) = centre for ongoing training and education **2** *(abrév* **Certificat de formation professionnelle**) vocational training certificate

CFR [seefer] *(abrév* **cost and freight**) CFR

CFTC [seeftese] **NF** *(abrév* **Confédération française des travailleurs chrétiens**) = French trade union

CGC [seʒese] **NF** *(abrév* **Confédération générale des cadres**) = French management union

CGI [seʒei] **NM** *Admin (abrév* **Code général des impôts**) general tax code

NF *Ordinat (abrév* **common gateway interface**) CGI

CGT [seʒete] **NF** *(abrév* **Confédération générale du travail**) = major association of French trade unions (affiliated to the Communist Party)

chablon [ʃablɔ̃] **NM** *Suisse (pochoir)* stencil

chabot [ʃabo] **NM** *Ich (de mer)* sea scorpion, bullhead; *(d'eau douce)* chub

chacal, -als [ʃakal] **NM 1** *Zool* jackal **2** *Péj (personne)* vulture, jackal

cha-cha-cha [tʃatʃatʃa] **NM INV** cha-cha, cha-cha-cha

chacone, chaconne [ʃakɔn] **NF** *Mus & (danse)* chaconne

chacun, -e [ʃakœ̃, -yn] **PRON INDÉFINI 1** *(chaque personne, chaque chose)* each; **c. à sa façon** each in his own way; **je les vends 15 euros c.** I'm selling them for 15 euros each *or* apiece; **ils ont pris c. son** *ou* **leur chapeau** each of them took their *or* his hat, they each took their hat; **ils sont partis c. de son** *ou* **de leur côté** they (each *or* all) went their separate ways; **c. de** each (one) of; **c. d'entre nous** each of us; **c. des employés a une tâche à remplir** each employee has a job to do; **nous y sommes allés c. à notre tour** we each went in turn **2** *(tout le monde)* everyone, everybody; **c. le dit** everyone says so; **à c. (selon) son dû** each according to his/her merits; **à c. ses goûts** to each his own; **à c. son métier** every man to his own trade; **c. pour soi** every man for himself; **tout un c.** everybody, each and every person

chaebol [kebɔl] **NM** *Écon* chaebol

chafouin, -e [ʃafwɛ̃, -in] **ADJ** *Péj (visage)* sly, cunning; **un homme à la mine chafouine** a sly-looking man

chagatte [ʃagat] **NF** *Vulg* pussy, snatch, *Br* fanny

chagrin[1] [ʃagrɛ̃] **NM** *(peine)* sorrow, grief; **avoir du c.** to be upset; **il a un gros c.** *(enfant)* he's very unhappy; **causer** *ou* **faire du c. à qn** to distress sb; **avoir un c. d'amour** to be disappointed in love

chagrin[2], -e [ʃagrɛ̃, -in] **ADJ** *Littéraire* **1** *(triste)* sad, sorrowful, woeful **2** *(revêche)* ill-tempered, quarrelsome; **esprits chagrins** malcontents

chagrin[3] [ʃagrɛ̃] **NM** *(cuir)* shagreen

chagrinant, -e [ʃagrinɑ̃, -ɑ̃t] **ADJ** grievous, distressing

chagriner[1] **[3]** [ʃagrine] **VT 1** *(attrister)* to grieve, to distress **2** *(contrarier)* to worry, to bother, to upset

VPR se chagriner *Can* **le temps se chagrine** it's clouding over, it's getting cloudy

chagriner[2] **[3]** [ʃagrine] **VT** *(cuir)* to shagreen, to grain

chah [ʃa] = **shah**

chahut [ʃay] **NM** *Fam* rumpus, uproar; **faire du c.** to kick up a rumpus, to cause an uproar

chahuter **[3]** [ʃayte] *Fam* **VI 1** *(être indiscipliné)* to kick up a rumpus, to cause an uproar **2** *(remuer)* **ça chahutait ferme sur le bateau!** it was a bit rough on the boat!

VT 1 *(houspiller ▸ professeur)* to rag, to bait; *(▸ orateur)* to heckle; **il se fait c. en classe** he can't keep (his class in) order; **le Premier ministre s'est fait c. à l'Assemblée** the Prime Minister was heckled in Parliament **2** *(remuer)* to knock about, to bash around

chahuteur, -euse [ʃaytœr, -øz] *Fam* **ADJ** rowdy, boisterous

NM,F rowdy (person); *(dans un meeting politique)* heckler

chai [ʃɛ] **NM** wine and spirits storehouse

chaînage [ʃenaʒ] **NM 1** *Constr (action)* clamping, tying; *(armature)* clamps, ties; *(mesurage)* chaining **2** *Ordinat* chaining; *(de commandes)* piping

chaîne [ʃɛn] **NF 1** *(attache, bijou)* chain; **le chien était attaché à sa niche par une c.** the dog was chained to its kennel; **une c. en or** a gold chain; **c. d'arpenteur** surveyor's chain; **c. de bicyclette** bicycle chain; **c. de montre** watch chain; **c. de sûreté** *(sur un bijou)* safety chain; *(sur une porte)* (door) chain; *Fig* **faire la c.** to form a (human) chain; **briser ses chaînes** to cast off one's chains *or* shackles

2 *(suite)* chain, series; **une c. d'événements** a chain of events; *École* **la c. alimentaire** the food chain; **c. de montagnes** (mountain) range; *Ling* **c. parlée** (speech) utterances; *Mktg* **c. de valeur** value chain

3 *TV* channel; **je regarde la première c.** I'm watching channel one; **c. à la carte** pay-per-view channel; **c. de cinéma** cinema channel, movie channel; **c. commerciale** commercial channel; **c. généraliste** general-interest channel; **c. hertzienne** terrestrial channel; **c. d'information continue** news channel; **c. musicale** music channel; **c. numérique** digital channel; **c. payante** *ou* **à péage** subscription *or* pay channel; **c. publique** public *or* state-owned channel; **c. par satellite** satellite channel; **c. de télé-achat** shopping channel; **c. de télévision** television channel; **c. thématique** specialized channel

4 *(stéréo)* hi-fi, music system; **c. compacte** compact system; **c. hi-fi** hi-fi; **c. laser** CD system; **c. stéréo** stereo

5 *Com (de restaurants, de supermarchés)* chain; **c. de détail** retail chain; **c. de journaux** newspaper group; **c. volontaire** voluntary chain; **c. volontaire de détaillants** voluntary retailer chain

6 *Ind* **c. de fabrication** production line; **c. du froid** cold chain; **c. de montage** assembly line

7 *Aut* **c. de distribution** timing *or* camshaft chain

8 *Ordinat* string; **c. vide/de caractères** nul/character string; **c. de recherche** search string

9 *Chim & Phys* chain; **à longue c.** long-chain

10 *Tex* warp

11 *Can* **c. du trottoir** kerb

• **chaînes NFPL** *Aut* (snow) chains

• **à la chaîne ADJ** *(travail)* assembly-line *(avant n)*, production-line *(avant n)* **ADV** *(travailler, produire)* on the production line; **faire qch à la c.** to mass-produce sth; **des objets produits à la c.** mass-produced items

• **en chaîne ADJ** *(réaction)* chain *(avant n)*; **des catastrophes en c.** a whole catalogue of disasters

chaîner **[4]** [ʃene] **VT 1** *Constr* to chain, to tie **2** *Aut (pneu)* to put chains on; *(voiture)* to fit with chains **3** *Ordinat* to chain; *(commandes)* to pipe

chaînette [ʃenɛt] **NF 1** *(bijou)* small chain **2** *Couture* **(point de) c.** chain stitch **3** *(attache)* **c. de sûreté** safety chain

chaînon [ʃɛnɔ̃] **NM 1** *(élément ▸ d'une chaîne, d'un raisonnement)* link; *aussi Fig* **le c. manquant** the missing link **2** *Géog* secondary chain *or* range (of mountains) **3** *Ordinat* **c. de données** data link

chair [ʃɛr] **NF 1** *(chez les humains, chez les animaux)* **la c., les chairs** the flesh; **c. à canon** cannon fodder; **il aime la c. fraîche** *(ogre)* he likes to eat children; **avoir la c. de poule** *(avoir froid, avoir peur)* to have goose pimples; **bien en c.** chubby; **un être de c. et de sang** a creature of flesh and blood; **voir qn en c. et en os** to see sb in the flesh; **c. à saucisse** sausage meat; *Fam Fig* **je vais en faire de la c. à saucisse** *ou* **à pâté!** I'm going to make mincemeat out of him/her! **2** *(de fruit)* flesh, pulp **3** *Rel & Littéraire* flesh; **souffrir dans sa c.** to suffer in the flesh; **la c. est faible** the flesh is weak; **la c. de sa c.** his/her own flesh and blood; **le péché de c.** the sin of the flesh

ADJ INV (couleur) c. flesh-coloured

• **chairs NFPL** *Beaux-Arts* flesh tones *or* tints

chaire [ʃɛr] **NF 1** *(estrade)* rostrum; **monter en c.** to go up on the rostrum; *Fig* to start one's speech **2** *Rel (siège)* throne, cathedra; *(tribune)* pulpit; **la c. apostolique** the Holy See **3** *Univ* chair; **être titulaire d'une c. de linguistique** to hold a chair in linguistics

chais [ʃɛ] = **chai**

chaise [ʃɛz] **NF 1** *(siège)* chair; **prenez donc une c.** have *or* take a seat; *Fig* **être assis entre deux chaises**, *très Fam* **avoir le cul entre deux chaises** to be in a difficult position; **c. à bascule**, *Can* **c. berçante** *ou* **berceuse** rocking chair; **c. de cuisine/de jardin** kitchen/garden chair; **c. haute** *ou* **d'enfant** *ou* **de bébé** highchair; **c. électrique** electric chair; **passer à la c. électrique** to go to the (electric) chair; **c. longue** *(d'extérieur)* deckchair; *(d'intérieur)* chaise longue; *Fam* **faire de la c. longue** to lounge about in a deckchair; **c. percée** commode; **c. pliante** folding chair; **c. à porteurs** sedan (chair); **c. de poste** post chaise; **c. roulante** wheelchair

2 *(jeu)* **chaises musicales** musical chairs

3 *Constr* wooden frame

4 *Naut* **nœud de c.** bowline

chaisier, -ère [ʃezje, -ɛr] **NM,F 1** *(fabricant)* chair maker **2** *(gardien)* chair attendant *(in gardens or church)*

chakra [ʃakra] **NM** chakra

chaland[1] [ʃalɑ̃] **NM** *Naut* barge

chaland[2], -e [ʃalɑ̃, -ɑ̃d] **NM,F** *Vieilli* regular customer; **attirer le c.** to attract customers *or* custom

chalandage [ʃalɑ̃daʒ] **NM** *Com* shopping

chalazion [ʃalazjɔ̃] **NM** *Méd* chalazion

chaldaïque [kaldaik] **ADJ** Chaldean

• **Chaldaïque NMF** Chaldean

Chaldée [kalde] **NF** *Anciennement* **la C.** Chaldea

chaldéen, -enne [kaldeɛ̃, -ɛn] **ADJ** Chaldean

NM *(langue)* Chaldee, Chaldean

• **Chaldéen, -enne NM,F** Chaldean

châle [ʃal] **NM** shawl

chalet [ʃalɛ] **NM 1** *(maison ▸ alpine)* chalet; *(▸ de plaisance)* wooden cottage **2** *Can* (holiday) cottage *(normally in the mountains or by the sea/lake)* **3** *Arch* **c. de nécessité** public convenience

chaleur [ʃalœr] **NF 1** *Météo* heat; **c. sèche/humide** dry/humid heat; **il fait une c. lourde** it's very muggy; **il fait une c. terrible dans ces dortoirs** it's terribly hot in these dormitories; **craint** *ou* **ne pas exposer à la c.** *(sur mode d'emploi)* store in a cool place; **c. animale** body heat

2 *Phys* heat; **c. atomique** atomic heat **c. latente** latent heat; **c. massique** *ou* **spécifique** specific heat;

3 *(sentiment)* warmth; **leur accueil manquait de c.** their welcome lacked warmth *or* wasn't very warm; **il y avait une certaine c. dans sa voix** his/her voice was warm (and welcoming); **c. humaine** human warmth

4 *Beaux-Arts (d'une couleur)* warmth

• **chaleurs NFPL 1** *Météo* **les grandes chaleurs** the hottest days of the summer **2** *Zool* heat; **la jument a ses chaleurs** the mare's *Br* on *or Am* in heat

• **en chaleur ADJ 1** *Zool Br* on heat, *Am* in heat **2** *Vulg (homme, femme)* horny

chaleureuse [ʃalœrøz] *voir* **chaleureux**

chaleureusement [ʃalœrøzmɑ̃] **ADV** warmly

chaleureux, -euse [ʃalœrø, -øz] **ADJ** *(remerciement, voix)* warm, sincere; *(accueil)* warm, cordial, hearty; *(applaudissements)* enthusiastic; *(approbation)* hearty, sincere; *(ami)* warm-hearted; **remercier qn en termes c.** to thank sb warmly

châlit [ʃali] **NM** bedstead

challenge [ʃalɑ̃ʒ, tʃalɑ̃ʒ] **NM 1** *(défi)* challenge **2** *Sport (épreuve)* sporting contest; *(trophée)* trophy

challenger, challengeur [ʃalɑ̃dʒœr, tʃalɛndʒœr] **NM** *Sport* challenger; *Mktg* (market) challenger

chaloir [ʃalwar] **V IMPERSONNEL** *Arch & Littéraire* **peu me** *ou* **peu m'en chaut** it matters (but) little to me, I care not

chaloupe [ʃalup] **NF 1** *Naut (à moteur)* launch; *(à rames) Br* rowing boat, *Am* rowboat; **c. de sauvetage** lifeboat **2** *Can (couvre-chaussure)* rubber overshoe, galosh

chaloupé, -e [ʃalupe] **ADJ 1** *(danse)* gliding, swaying **2** *(démarche)* rolling

chalumeau, -x [ʃalymo] **NM 1** *Tech Br* blowlamp, *Am* blowtorch; **chauffer un métal au c.** to heat a piece of metal with a *Br* blowlamp *or Am* blowtorch; **c. oxhydrique/oxyacétylénique** oxyhydrogen/oxyacetylene torch

2 *Mus* pipe
3 *Vieilli (paille)* straw
4 *Can* spout *(for collecting sap of maple tree)*

chalut [ʃaly] **NM** *Pêche* trawl; **pêcher au c.** to trawl

chalutage [ʃalytaʒ] **NM** *Pêche* trawling

chalutier [ʃalytje] **NM 1** *(pêcheur)* trawlerman **2** *(bateau)* trawler; **petit c.** dragger

chamade [ʃamad] **NF battre la c.** to beat *or* to pound wildly

chamailler [3] [ʃamaje] **se chamailler VPR** *Fam (emploi réciproque)* to bicker, to squabble; **se c. avec qn** to bicker with sb

chamaillerie [ʃamajri] **NF** *Fam* squabble, tiff; **des chamailleries** squabbling

chamailleur, -euse [ʃamajœr, -øz] *Fam* **ADJ** quarrelsome
NM,F bickerer, squabbler

chaman [ʃaman] **NM** shaman

chamanisme [ʃamanism] **NM** shamanism

chamarré, -e [ʃamare] **ADJ** richly-coloured, brightly-coloured; **c. d'or** with gold brocade

chamarrer [3] [ʃamare] **VT** to decorate, to adorn

chambard [ʃɑ̃bar] **NM** *Fam (bruit)* din, racket, rumpus; *(bouleversement)* upset, upheaval; **faire du c.** *(faire du bruit)* to kick up (a din), to cause a rumpus; *(protester)* to kick up (a fuss), to raise a stink

chambardement [ʃɑ̃bardəmɑ̃] **NM** *Fam* upheaval; **le grand c., le c. général** the revolution

chambarder [3] [ʃɑ̃barde] **VT** *Fam (endroit, objets)* to mess up, to turn upside down; *(projets)* to upset, to overturn, to turn upside down; *(société, conventions)* to turn upside down

chambellan [ʃɑ̃belɑ̃] **NM** chamberlain

chambouler [3] [ʃɑ̃bule] **VT** *Fam (endroit, objets)* to mess up, to turn upside down; *(projets)* to mess up; **cette réunion imprévue a chamboulé mon emploi du temps** this last-minute meeting has messed up my schedule

chambranle [ʃɑ̃brɑ̃l] **NM** *(de cheminée)* mantelpiece; *(de porte)* (door) frame *or* casing; *(de fenêtre)* (window) frame *or* casing

chambre [ʃɑ̃br] **NF 1** *(pièce)* bedroom; *(à l'hôtel)* room; **une maison de cinq chambres** a five-bedroomed house; **faire c. à part** to sleep in separate rooms; **faire c. commune** to share the same room *or* bedroom; **vous auriez une c. (de) libre?** do you have any vacancies?; **c. d'amis** guest *or* spare room; **c. de bonne** maid's room; *(louée à un particulier)* attic room; **c. à coucher** *(pièce)* bedroom; *(mobilier)* bedroom furniture; **c. double** *ou* **pour deux personnes** double room; **c. d'enfant** child's room; *(pour tout-petits)* nursery; **c. d'hôte** bed and breakfast; **chambres d'hôte** *(sur panneau)* rooms available; **c. d'hôtel** hotel room; **c. individuelle** *ou* **pour une personne** single (room); **chambres à louer** rooms available; **c. meublée** furnished room, *Br* bedsit; **c. avec ou sans pension** bed and breakfast or full board; **c. de service** servant's room; **camarade de c.** roommate

2 *(local)* **c. de décontamination** decontamination chamber; **c. forte** strongroom; **c. froide** cold room; **c. à gaz** gas chamber; *Suisse* **c. à lessive** laundry room

3 *Pol* House, Chamber; **la C.** the House; **siéger à la C.** to sit in the House; **la C. des communes** the House of Commons; *Anciennement* **la C. des députés** the (French) Chamber of Deputies; **la C. haute/basse** the Upper/Lower Chamber; **la C. des lords** *ou* **des pairs** the House of Lords; **la C. des représentants** the House of Representatives

4 *Jur (subdivision d'une juridiction)* chamber; *(section)* Court; **première c.** upper chamber *or* court; **deuxième c.** lower chamber *or* court; **c. d'accusation** *(à la cour d'appel)* Indictment Division; **c. des appels correctionnels** District Court; **c. civile** *(à la cour d'appel)* Civil Division; **c. commerciale** *(à la cour d'appel)* Commercial Division; **c. du conseil** court chambers; **c. correctionnelle** Criminal Division *(of the "tribunal de grande instance")*; **c. criminelle** *(à la Cour de cassation)* Criminal Division; **c. de discipline** = professional disciplinary panel; **c. de l'instruction** Investigative Division; **c. des mineurs** *(à la cour d'appel)* Juvenile Division; **c. des mises en accusation** Court of criminal appeal; **c. mixte** *(à la Cour de cassation)* joint bench, composite bench; **c. des requêtes** appeal court; **c. sociale** *(à la cour d'appel)* Social Division

5 *(organisme)* **c. d'agriculture** = farmers' association; *Fin* **c. de clearing** clearing house; **c. de commerce** Chamber of Commerce; **c. de commerce et d'industrie** Chamber of Commerce and Industry; **c. de commerce internationale** International Chamber of Commerce; *Fin* **c. de compensation** clearing house; *Fin* **c. de compensation automatisée** automated clearing house; **c. des métiers** Guild Chamber; **c. syndicale** Employer's Syndicate

6 *Naut (local)* **c. des cartes** *ou* **de navigation** chart house; **c. de chauffe** stokehold; **c. des machines** engine room; *(cabine)* cabin

7 *Mil* chamber

8 *Tech & Aut* chamber; **c. à air** inner tube; **sans c. à air** tubeless; **c. d'alimentation** feed chamber; **c. de carburation** mixing chamber; **c. de mélange** mixing chamber; **c. de résonance** resonating chamber; **c. de turbulence** swirl chamber, turbulence combustion chamber

9 *Phys* chamber; **c. à bulles** bubble chamber; **c. de combustion** combustion chamber

10 *Phot* **c. noire** darkroom

11 *Opt* **c. claire/noire** camera lucida/obscura

12 *Anat* **c. antérieure** *ou* **de l'œil** anterior chamber of the eye; **c. pulpaire (d'une dent)** (tooth) pulp chamber

13 *Belg & Suisse (pièce quelconque)* room; **une maison de six chambres** a six-roomed house

• **en chambre ADJ 1** *Hum (stratège, athlète)* armchair *(avant n)* **2** *(à domicile)* **couturière en c.** dressmaker working from home **ADV** *(travailler)* at *or* from home

chambré, -e [ʃɑ̃bre] **ADJ** *(vin)* at room temperature

chambrée [ʃɑ̃bre] **NF** *Mil* **1** *(pièce)* (barrack) room **2** *(soldats)* **toute la c.** all the soldiers in the barrack room

chambrer [3] [ʃɑ̃bre] **VT 1** *(vin)* to allow to breathe, to bring to room temperature **2** *Fam (se moquer de)* **c. qn** to make fun of sb$^{\square}$, *Br* to wind sb up, *Br* to take the mickey out of sb
VI *Can Joual* to rent a room, to room

chambrette [ʃɑ̃brɛt] **NF** small room

chambrière [ʃɑ̃brijɛr] **NF 1** *(servante)* chambermaid **2** *(fouet)* lunging whip **3** *(béquille)* cart-prop

chameau, -x [ʃamo] **NM 1** *(animal)* camel; **c. de Bactriane** Bactrian camel **2** *Fam Péj* **quel c.!** *(homme)* he's a real swine!; *(femme)* she's a real cow!
ADJ *Fam* **ce qu'il/elle est c.!** what a swine he is/cow she is!; **ce qu'il peut être c. avec elle!** he can be such a swine to her!

chamelier [ʃaməlje] **NM** camel driver

chamelle [ʃamɛl] **NF** *Zool* she-camel

chamois [ʃamwa] **NM 1** *(animal)* chamois **2** *Ski* = skiing proficiency grade
ADJ INV *(couleur)* buff, fawn

champ [ʃɑ̃] **NM 1** *Agr* field; **c. de blé** field of wheat; **c. de maïs** cornfield; **mener les bêtes aux champs** to take the herd to the fields; **en plein c.** *ou* **pleins champs** in the open (fields)

2 *(périmètre réservé)* **c. d'aviation** airfield; **c. de courses** racecourse; **c. de foire** fairground; *Mil & Sport* **c. de tir** *(terrain)* rifle range; *(portée d'une arme)* field of fire

3 *(domaine, étendue)* field, range; **le c. de la psychanalyse/conscience** the field of psychoanalysis/consciousness; **élargir le c. de ses activités** to widen the range *or* scope of one's activities; **un vaste c. d'action** a broad field of activity; **avoir le c. libre** to have a free hand; **laisser le c. libre à qn** to leave the field open for sb; **il a du c. devant lui** he's got an open field in front of him; **prendre du c.** *(pour observer)* to step back; *(pour réfléchir)* to stand back; *(pour sauter)* to take a run-up; *Mktg* **c. concurrentiel** competitive scope

4 *Cin & Phot* **être dans le c.** to be in shot; **sortir du c.** to go out of shot; **hors c.** off camera

5 *Opt (d'un télescope)* field

6 *Élec & Phys* field; **c. électrique/magnétique** electric/magnetic field; **c. de pesanteur** gravitational field

7 *Sport* **c. (de jeu)** playing area

8 *Ordinat* field; **c. d'action** sensitivity; **c. mémo** memo field; **c. numérique** numeric field; **c. de texte** text field; **c. variable** variable field

9 *Ling & Math* field; **c. lexical** lexical field; **c. sémantique** semantic field

10 *Méd* field; **c. opératoire/visuel** field of operation/view

11 *Mil* **aux champs** general salute; **c. de bataille** battlefield, battleground; *Fig* war zone; **c. clos** battleground; **c. d'honneur** field of honour; **il est mort** *ou* **tombé au c. d'honneur** he died for his country; **c. de manœuvre** parade ground; **c. de mines** minefield

12 *Myth* **les champs Élysées** *ou* **Élyséens** the Elysian Fields

• **champs NMPL** *(campagne)* country, countryside; **la vie aux champs** country life

• **sur le champ ADV** immediately, at once, right away

Champagne [ʃɑ̃paɲ] **NF la C.** Champagne

champagne [ʃɑ̃paɲ] **NM** Champagne; **c. brut/rosé** extra dry/pink Champagne
ADJ INV 1 *(couleur)* champagne *(avant n)* **2** *(alcool) voir* **voir** *nf*

champagnisation [ʃɑ̃paɲizasjɔ̃] **NF** sparkling wine production *(according to the Champagne method)*

champagniser [3] [ʃɑ̃paɲize] **VT c. le vin** to make sparkling wine *(by using the Champagne method)*; **vins champagnisés** Champagne method wines

champenois, -e [ʃɑ̃pənwa, -az] **ADJ** of/from Champagne; **méthode champenoise** Champagne method

• **Champenois, -e NM,F** = inhabitant of or person from the Champagne region

• **champenoise NF** = bottle designed for Champagne

champêtre [ʃɑ̃pɛtr] **ADJ** *Littéraire (vie, plaisirs, travaux)* country *(avant n)*, rustic; *(bal)* village *(avant n)*; **déjeuner c.** picnic in the country; **travaux champêtres** working in the fields

champignon [ʃɑ̃piɲɔ̃] **NM 1** *Bot* mushroom, fungus; *Culin* mushroom; **c. de Paris** *ou* **de couche** button mushroom; **c. hallucinogène** magic mushroom; **c. noir** dried mushroom; **c. vénéneux** poisonous mushroom, toadstool; **grandir** *ou* **pousser comme un c.** *(enfant)* to grow fast, to shoot up; *(ville, installations)* to mushroom

2 *Méd* **un c., des champignons** a fungus, a fungal infection

3 *(nuage)* **c. (atomique)** mushroom cloud

4 *Fam* accelerator (pedal)$^{\square}$; **appuyer sur le c.** to put one's foot down, to step on it

champignonnière [ʃɑ̃piɲɔnjer] **NF** mushroom bed

champignonniste [ʃɑ̃piɲɔnist] **NMF** mushroom grower

champion, -onne [ʃɑ̃pjɔ̃, -ɔn] **NM,F 1** *Sport* champion; **le c. du monde d'aviron** the world rowing champion; *Fam* **c'est un c. de la triche** he's a first-rate *or* prize cheat; **je suis vraiment le c. de la gaffe** I'm a great one for putting my foot in it **2** *(défenseur)* champion; **se faire le c. de qch** to champion sth
ADJ 1 *Sport* **l'équipe championne du monde** the world champions **2** *Fam* **pour les gaffes, il est c.!** he's a great one for putting his foot in it!; **c'est c.!** it's terrific!

championnat [ʃɑ̃pjɔna] **NM** championship; **c. du monde de course de fond** world cross-country running championship

Champs-Élysées [ʃɑ̃zelize] **NMPL les C.** *(avenue)* the Champs-Elysées

chançard, -e [ʃɑ̃sar, -ard] *Fam* **ADJ** lucky$^{\square}$, *Br* jammy
NM,F lucky dog *or* devil, *Br* jammy devil

chance [ʃɑ̃s] **NF 1** *(aléa, hasard)* luck; **bonne c.!** good luck!; **souhaiter bonne c. à qn** to wish sb good luck

2 *(hasard favorable)* (good) luck; **c'est une c. que je sois arrivée à ce moment-là!** it's a stroke of luck that I arrived then!; **quelle c. j'ai eue!** lucky me!; **avoir de la/ne pas avoir de c.** to be lucky/unlucky; **c'est bien ma c.!** just my luck!; **j'ai eu la c. de le ren-**

contrer I was lucky *or* fortunate enough to meet him; **votre génération aura peut-être plus de c. que la nôtre** your generation will perhaps have more luck than ours; **avec un peu de c., on pourra le faire** with a bit of luck, we'll be able to do it; **tenter sa c.** to try one's luck; *très Fam* **avoir une c. de cocu** *ou* **de pendu** to have the luck of the devil; *Fam* **c'est la faute à pas de c.** it's just bad luck; **pas de c.!** bad *or* hard luck!

3 *(sort favorable)* luck, (good) fortune; **la c. lui sourit** fortune favours him/her; **la c. a voulu que sa lettre se soit égarée** luckily his/her letter got lost; **la c. est avec nous** our luck's in; **jour de c.** lucky day; **sa c. tourne** his/her luck is changing; **porter c.** to bring (good) luck; **pousser sa c.** to push one's luck

4 *(possibilité)* chance; **tu n'as pas une c. sur dix de réussir** you haven't got a one-in-ten chance of succeeding; *Can* **participez et courez la c. de gagner une voiture** enter for your chance to win a car; **on pourrait lui donner encore une c.** we could give him/her another chance; **donner** *ou* **laisser sa c. à qn** to give sb his/her chance; **c'est ta dernière c.** it's your last chance; **négociations de la dernière c.** last-ditch negotiations; **ce qu'il dit a toutes les chances d'être faux** the chances are that what he is saying is wrong; **quelles sont mes chances d'être nommé à ce poste?** what are my chances of being appointed to this post?; **il y a peu de chances qu'on te croie** there's little chance (that) you'll be believed; **son projet a de fortes** *ou* **grandes chances d'être adopté** his/her plan stands a good chance of being adopted; **il a compris qu'il fallait mettre toutes les chances de son côté** he realised he had to leave nothing to chance; **je cherche à évaluer mes chances de succès** I'm trying to evaluate my chances of success; **n'hésite pas, tu as tes chances** don't hesitate, you've got *or* you stand a chance; *Fam* **tu assisteras au débat? – il y a des chances** will you be present at the debate? – maybe

• **par chance** ADV luckily, fortunately; **par c., le courant était coupé** luckily the current was turned *or* switched off

> Il faut noter que le nom anglais **chance** ne signifie jamais **bonne fortune**.

chancelant, -e [ʃɑ̃slɑ̃, -ɑ̃t] ADJ **1** *(vacillant ▸ démarche, pas)* unsteady, faltering; *(▸ pile)* wobbly, tottering **2** *(faiblissant ▸ santé)* failing, fragile; *(▸ mémoire)* shaky, failing; *(▸ courage, détermination)* wavering; *(▸ autorité)* faltering, flagging

chanceler [24] [ʃɑ̃sle] VI **1** *(vaciller ▸ personne)* to totter, to stagger; *(▸ pile d'objets)* to wobble, to totter; **avancer/sortir en chancelant** to stagger *or* to totter forward/out; **l'uppercut le fit c.** the uppercut sent him reeling **2** *(faiblir ▸ pouvoir, institution, autorité)* to falter, to flag; *(▸ santé, mémoire)* to be failing; **les émeutes ont fait c. le pouvoir** the riots rocked the government

chancelier [ʃɑ̃səlje] NM **1** *(d'ambassade)* (embassy) chief secretary, *Br* chancellor **2** *Pol (en Allemagne, en Autriche)* chancellor; *(en Grande-Bretagne)* **c. de l'Échiquier** Chancellor of the Exchequer **3** *Hist* chancellor

chancelière [ʃɑ̃səljɛr] NF **1** *(épouse)* chancellor's wife **2** *(chausson)* foot muff

chancelle *etc voir* **chanceler**

chancellerie [ʃɑ̃sɛlri] NF *Pol* chancery, chancellery

chanceux, -euse [ʃɑ̃sø, -øz] ADJ lucky, fortunate

NM,F lucky man, *f* woman

chanci [ʃɑ̃si] *Vieilli* ADJ mouldy

NM mould, mildew

chancre [ʃɑ̃kr] NM **1** *Méd* chancre, canker; **c. induré** *ou* **syphilitique** hard *or* infective *or* true chancre; **c. mou** chancroid, soft chancre; *Fam* **bouffer comme un c.** to stuff oneself *or* one's face **2** *Bot* canker

chancreux, -euse [ʃɑ̃krø, -øz] ADJ *Méd* cankerous

chandail [ʃɑ̃daj] NM **1** *(gén)* pullover, sweater **2** *Can* **c. (de hockey)** *Br* ice hockey shirt, *Am* hockey shirt

Chandeleur [ʃɑ̃dlœr] NF *Rel* **la C.** Candlemas

> **LA CHANDELEUR**
>
> This Catholic feast is celebrated on 2 February and commemorates the presentation of Jesus in the Temple after the completion of Mary's purification. Traditionally, crêpes with sweet fillings are eaten on this day, making it popular with children in particular.

chandelier [ʃɑ̃dəlje] NM *(à une branche)* candlestick; *(à plusieurs branches)* candelabrum, candelabra

> Il faut noter que le nom anglais **chandelier** est un faux ami. Il signifie **lustre**.

chandelle [ʃɑ̃dɛl] NF **1** *(bougie)* candle; **s'éclairer à la c.** to use candlelight; **le jeu n'en vaut pas la c.** the game's not worth the candle; **brûler la c. par les deux bouts** to burn the candle at both ends; **devoir une fière c. à qn** to be deeply indebted to sb; **tenir la c.** *Br* to play gooseberry, *Am* to be a fifth wheel *or* the third wheel

2 *(feu d'artifice)* **c. romaine** Roman candle

3 *Fam (morve)* trickle of snot

4 *Aviat* chandelle; **monter en c.** to chandelle, to climb vertically

5 *(au tir, au rugby)* up-and-under; *Ftbl* high ball; **faire une c.** *Tennis* to lob the ball; *Ftbl* to loft the ball; **botter une c.** *(au rugby)* to play an up-and-under

6 *(position de gymnastique)* **faire la c.** to do a shoulder stand

7 *Constr* prop, stay

• **aux chandelles** ADJ *(dîner, repas)* candlelit ADV *(dîner)* by candlelight

chanfrein [ʃɑ̃frɛ̃] NM **1** *Zool* nose, forehead **2** *Archit* chamfer, bevel edge

chanfreiner [4] [ʃɑ̃frene] VT *Archit* to chamfer, to bevel

change [ʃɑ̃ʒ] NM **1** *Fin (transaction)* exchange; *(taux)* exchange rate; **quel est le c.?** what's the rate of exchange *or* the exchange rate?; **faire le c.** to deal in foreign exchange; **c. du dollar** dollar exchange; **donner le c. à qn** *(le duper)* to hoodwink sb, to put sb off the track; **gagner/perdre au c.** to be better/worse off because of the exchange rate; *Fig* to come out a winner/loser on the deal

2 *(couche)* **c. complet** disposable *Br* nappy *or Am* diaper; **c. jetable** *Br* nappy *or Am* diaper liner

3 *Chasse* **donner le c.** to put hounds on the wrong scent; *Fig* **donner le c. à qn** to hoodwink sb, to put sb off the track

4 *Can Joual* **(petit) c.** *(monnaie)* change; **as-tu du c. pour un vingt?** have you got change for a twenty?

> Il faut noter que le nom anglais **change** signifie **petite monnaie** quand il se réfère à de l'argent.

changeable [ʃɑ̃ʒabl] ADJ *(caractère, ordre)* changeable, alterable

changeant, -e [ʃɑ̃ʒɑ̃, -ɑ̃t] ADJ **1** *(moiré)* shot **2** *(inconstant ▸ fortune, humeur)* fickle, unpredictable; **être d'humeur changeante** to be moody **3** *Météo (temps)* unsettled, changeable

changement [ʃɑ̃ʒmɑ̃] NM **1** *(substitution)* change (**de** of); **après le c. d'entraîneur/de régime** after the new trainer/regime came in; **c. d'adresse** change of address; **signaler son c. d'adresse** to give out one's new address; **en cas de c. de domicile** in case of a change of address; **c. de direction** *(dans une entreprise)* under new management; *Mktg* **c. de marque** brand switching; **c. de propriétaire** *(dans un magasin)* under new ownership

2 *(modification)* change; **un c. très net s'est produit** there's been a definite change; **apporter des changements à qch** to alter sth; **des changements sont intervenus** there have been changes; **comment va-t-il? – pas de** *ou* **aucun c.** how is he? – stable *or* no change; **c. de température/de temps** change in temperature/(the) weather; **c. de cap** *ou* **de direction** change of course; **c. de programme** *TV* change in the (published) schedule; *Fig* change of plan *or* in the plans; **c. de programme, on ne va plus chez Paul** there's been a change of plan, we're not going to Paul's any more; *Écon* **c. structurel** structural change

3 *(évolution)* **le c.** change; **je voudrais bien un peu de c.** I'd like things to change a little; **il va y avoir du c.** there are going to be some changes, things are going to change; **quand les enfants seront partis, ça fera du c.** things will be different after the children have gone

4 *Transp* change; **j'ai trois changements/je n'ai pas de c. pour aller chez elle** I have to change three times/I don't have to change to get to her place; **le voyage est sans c. jusqu'à Paris** the train goes straight through to Paris; **le c. est au bout du quai** change (lines) at the end of the platform

5 *Théât* **c. à vue** set change in full view of the audience; **c. de décor** scene change *or* shift; *Fig* **avoir besoin d'un c. de décor** to be in need of a change of scenery

6 *Sport* **c. de joueurs** change of players, changeover; *Tennis* **c. de balles!** new balls!

7 *Aut* **c. de vitesse** *(levier)* gear lever, *Am* gear shift; *(action ▸ en voiture)* gear change *or* shift; *(▸ à bicyclette)* gear change

8 *Ordinat* **c. de ligne** line feed; **c. de page** page break

9 *Cin & TV* **c. de plan** cutaway shot, cutaway

CHANGER [17] [ʃɑ̃ʒe] VT *(aux avoir)* **1** *(modifier ▸ apparence, règlement, caractère)* to change, to alter; *(▸ testament)* to alter; **cette expérience l'a beaucoup changée** the experience has changed her a lot; **on ne le changera pas** he'll never change; **cette coupe la change vraiment** that haircut makes her look really different; *Fam* **ça vous change un homme!** it changes a man!; **mais ça change tout!** ah, that changes everything!; **ça ne change rien** it makes no difference *or Br* odds; **qu'est-ce que ça change?** what difference does it make?; **je n'ai pas changé un mot à ton texte** I didn't alter a single *or* one word of your text; **il ne veut rien c. à ses habitudes** he won't alter his ways one jot *or* iota; **cela ne change rien au fait que...** that doesn't change *or* alter the fact that...; **tu n'y changeras rien** there's nothing you can do about it; **c. les règles du jeu** to alter the rules of the game; *Fig* to move the goalposts, to change the rules; **il est bien changé depuis son accident** he's changed a lot since his accident

2 *(remplacer ▸ installation, personnel)* to change, to replace; *(▸ roue, ampoule, draps)* to change; **ne change pas les assiettes** don't lay new plates; **j'ai fait c. les freins** I had new brakes put in; **c. l'eau d'un vase** to change the water in a vase; **le directeur a été changé** there's been a change of manager; *Théât* **c. le décor** to change the set

3 *Fin (en devises, en petite monnaie)* to change; **c. de l'argent** to change money; **c. un billet pour avoir de la monnaie** to change a *Br* note *or Am* bill in order to get small change; **c. des euros en dollars** to change euros into dollars

4 *(troquer)* **c. qch pour qch** to change *or* exchange sth for sth; **elle changerait bien sa place contre** *ou* **pour la tienne** she'd happily swap places with you

5 *(transformer)* **c. qch en qch** to turn sth into sth; **je veux bien être changé en pierre si...** I'll eat my hat if...

6 *(transférer)* **c. qch de place** to move sth; **c. les meubles de place** to change *or* move the furniture around; **c. une cassette de face** to turn a tape over; **c. qn de poste/service** to transfer sb to a new post/department; *Fig* **c. son fusil d'épaule** to have a change of heart

7 *Fam (désaccoutumer)* **pars en vacances, ça te changera un peu** you should go away somewhere, it'll make a change for you; **mets-toi en jupe, ça te changerait** wear a skirt for a change; **enfin un bon spectacle, ça nous change des inepties habituelles!** a good show at last, that makes a change from the usual nonsense!; **viens, ça te changera les idées** come along, it'll take your mind off things; **ça change de l'ordinaire** it makes a change

8 *(bébé)* to change

USAGE ABSOLU *(échanger)* **j'aime mieux ton écharpe, on change?** I like your scarf better, shall we swap?; *Fam* **je ne voudrais pas c. avec elle** I'd hate to be in her shoes

VI *(aux avoir)* **1** *(se modifier ▸ personne, temps, tarif etc)* to change; **sa personnalité a changé** he's/

she's become different; **tu n'as pas changé** you've not changed, you're still the same; **le corps change à ton âge** at your age, bodily *or* physical changes occur; **c. en bien/mal** to change for the better/worse; *Fam* **plus ça change plus c'est la même chose** the more things change the more they stay the same

2 *Transp (de métro, de train)* to change

3 *(être remplacé)* to change; **le président change tous les trois ans** there's a change of chairperson every three years

• **changer de** **VT IND c. d'adresse** *(personne)* to move to a new address; *(commerce)* to move to new premises; **c. de nom/nationalité** to change one's name/nationality; **c. de rouge à lèvres** to switch lipsticks, to use a different lipstick; **c. de fournisseur** to use a different supplier; **le magasin a changé de propriétaire** the shop is under new management; **c. de partenaire** *(en dansant, dans un couple)* to change partners; **c. de chaussettes** to change one's socks; **c. de vêtements** to get changed; **c. de coiffure** to get a new hairstyle, to change one's hairstyle; **c. de style** to adopt a new style; **c. de chaîne** *(une fois)* to change channels; *(constamment)* to zap; **je dois c. d'avion à Athènes** I have to get a connecting flight in Athens; **c. de vie** to embark on a new life; **c. d'avis** *ou* **d'idée** to change one's mind; **elle m'a fait c. d'avis** she changed *or* made me change my mind; **c. d'avis comme de chemise** to keep changing one's mind; **c. de sujet** to change the subject; **tu vas c. de ton, dis!** don't take that tone with me!; **c. de direction** *(gén)* to change direction; *(vent)* to change; **c. de place** to move; **c. de place avec qn** to change seats with sb; **changez de côté** *(au tennis, au ping-pong)* change *or* switch sides; *(dans un lit)* turn over; **c. d'aspect** to begin to look different; **c. de forme** to change shape; **le courant a changé d'intensité** the intensity of the current has changed; **c. de peau** *(serpent)* to change *or* to shed *or* to slough its skin; *Aut* **c. de vitesse** to change gear; **c. d'air** to have a break; *Théât* **c. de décor** to change the set; *Fig* **j'ai besoin de c. de décor** I need a change of scenery; *aussi Fig* **c. de cap** to change *or* alter course; *Fam* **c. de crémerie** to take one's custom *or* business elsewhere; *Fam* **change de disque!** give it a rest!, change the subject!

VPR se changer 1 *(emploi réfléchi ▸ s'habiller)* to get changed, to change (one's clothes) **2 se c. en** to change *or* to turn into; **la grenouille se changea en prince** the frog turned into a prince **3 je broie du noir, il faut que je sorte pour me c. les idées** I'm brooding, I must get out to take my mind off things

• **pour changer** **ADV** for a change

• **pour ne pas changer** **ADV** as usual; **et toi, tu ne fais rien, pour ne pas c.!** and you do nothing, as usual!

---

changeur [ʃɑ̃ʒœr] **NM 1** *(personne)* money changer **2** *(dispositif)* **c. de billets** change machine; **c. de disques** record changer; *Rad* **c. de fréquence** frequency changer; **c. de monnaie** change machine

Chang-hai [ʃɑ̃gaj] **NM** Shanghai

chanoine [ʃanwan] **NM** *Rel* canon

chanson [ʃɑ̃sɔ̃] **NF 1** *Mus* song; **la c. française** French songs; **c. d'amour/populaire** love/popular song; **c. à boire** drinking song; **c. enfantine** children's song, nursery rhyme; **c. de marins** *Br* sea shanty, *Am* sea chantey; *Fig* **c'est toujours la même c.** it's always the same old story; **ça va, on connaît la c.** enough of that, we've heard it all before; **ça, c'est une autre c.** that's another story **2** *Littérature* **c. courtoise** courtly love song; **c. de geste** chanson de geste, epic poem **3** *Vieilli* **chansons que tout cela!** nonsense!

chansonnette [ʃɑ̃sɔnɛt] **NF** ditty, simple song; *Fam* **pousser la c.** to sing a song

chansonnier, -ère [ʃɑ̃sɔnje, -ɛr] **NM,F** = satirical cabaret singer or entertainer

NM 1 *Vieilli* songwriter **2** *(recueil)* songbook

chant [ʃɑ̃] **NM 1** *(chanson)* song; *(mélodie)* melody; **c. funèbre** dirge; **c. grégorien** Gregorian chant; **c. de guerre** battle hymn; **c. de Noël** Christmas carol; **c. des sirènes** siren song

2 *(action de chanter)* singing

3 *(art de chanter)* singing; **apprendre le c.** to learn singing; **prendre des leçons de c.** to take singing lessons; **c. choral** choral singing

4 *(sons ▸ d'un oiseau)* singing, chirping; *(▸ d'un coq)* crowing; *(▸ d'un violon)* sound; **au c. du coq** at cockcrow; *Littéraire* **le c. des vagues/de la source** the song of the waves/of the spring; **son c. du cygne** his/her swan song

5 *(forme poétique)* ode, lyric; *(division de poème)* canto

6 *Constr* edge; **posés de c.** *ou* **sur c.** set edgewise *or* on edge

chantage [ʃɑ̃taʒ] **NM** blackmail; **faire du c. à qn** to blackmail sb; **il lui fait du c. au suicide** he's using suicide threats to blackmail him/her; **c. affectif** *ou* **au sentiment** emotional blackmail

chantant, -e [ʃɑ̃tɑ̃, -ɑ̃t] **ADJ 1** *(langue)* musical; *(voix, accent)* lilting, singsong **2** *(aisément retenu ▸ air)* tuneful; **un opéra très c.** an opera full of easily remembered tunes

chantepleure [ʃɑ̃tplœr] **NF** *Constr (de mur)* weephole; *(de gouttière)* spout

chanter **[3]** [ʃɑ̃te] **VI 1** *(personne)* to sing; **c. juste/faux** to sing in tune/out of tune; **c. à tue-tête** to sing at the top of one's voice; *Fam* **c'est comme si tu chantais** it's like talking to a brick wall, you're wasting your breath **2** *(oiseau)* to sing, to chirp; *(coq)* to crow; *(bouilloire)* to whistle; **écouter c. les oiseaux** to listen to the birds singing **3** *(locutions)* **faire c. qn** to blackmail sb; **si ça te chante** if you fancy it; **viens quand ça te chante** come whenever you feel like it; **ça te chante d'aller au concert?** how do you fancy (going to) a concert?

VT 1 *Mus (chanson, messe)* to sing; *Fig* **qu'est-ce que tu me chantes là?** what are you talking about?; **elle le chante sur tous les tons** she's always going on about it **2** *(célébrer)* to sing (of); **c. les exploits d'un héros** to sing (of) a hero's exploits; **c. victoire** to crow (over one's victory); **c. les louanges de qn** to sing sb's praises **3** *Can Fam (locution)* **c. la pomme à qn** *Br* to chat sb up, *Am* to hit on sb

> Il faut noter que le verbe anglais **to chant** est un faux ami. Il signifie **scander**.

chanterelle [ʃɑ̃trɛl] **NF 1** *Bot & Culin* chanterelle **2** *Mus* E-string **3** *Chasse* decoy (bird)

chanteur, -euse [ʃɑ̃tœr, -øz] **NM,F 1** singer; **c. de charme** crooner; **c. de rock** rock singer; **c. des rues** street singer **2** *Can Fam* **c. de pomme** flirt

ADJ oiseau c. songbird

chantier [ʃɑ̃tje] **NM 1** *(entrepôt)* yard, depot

2 *(terrain)* (working) site; *Can (en sylviculture)* tree felling site; **sur le c.** on the site; **c. d'équarrissage** rendering plant; *Naut* **c. naval** shipyard

3 *Constr* **c. (de construction)** building site; **c. de démolition** demolition site *or* area; **c. interdit au public** *(sur panneau)* no admittance to the public

4 *(sur la route)* roadworks

5 *(projet d'envergure)* major project *or* piece of work; **ce projet de dictionnaire est un de nos grands chantiers pour les années à venir** this dictionary will be one of our major projects over the next few years

6 *Fam (désordre)* mess, shambles *(singulier)*; **quel c.!** what a mess!, what a shambles!; **ta chambre, c'est un vrai c.** your bedroom is a total shambles *or* looks like a bomb's hit it

• **en chantier** **ADJ la maison est en c.** we're/they're/*etc* still doing up *or Am* fixing up the house **ADV il a plusieurs livres en c.** he has several books in the pipeline; **mettre un ouvrage en c.** to get a project started

chantilly [ʃɑ̃tiji] **ADJ INV** *voir* **crème**

NF INV sweetened chilled whipped cream, Chantilly cream

chantonnement [ʃɑ̃tɔnmɑ̃] **NM** crooning, singing softly; *(fredonnement)* humming

chantonner **[3]** [ʃɑ̃tɔne] **VT** to croon, to sing softly; *(fredonner)* to hum

VI to croon, to sing softly; *(fredonner)* to hum

chantoung [ʃɑ̃tuŋ] = **shantoung**

chantourner **[3]** [ʃɑ̃turne] **VT** *Tech* to jigsaw

chantre [ʃɑ̃tr] **NM 1** *Rel* cantor; **grand c.** precentor **2** *Littéraire (poète)* poet, bard; **les chantres des bois** the woodland chorus; **le c. de** the eulogist of *or* apologist for; **il s'était fait le c. de la république** he had championed the cause of the republic

chanvre [ʃɑ̃vr] **NM** *Bot & Tex* hemp; **c. indien** Indian hemp

chanvrier, -ère [ʃɑ̃vrije, -ɛr] **ADJ** hemp *(avant n)*

NM,F 1 *(cultivateur)* hemp grower **2** *(ouvrier)* hemp dresser

chaos [kao] **NM 1** *(confusion)* chaos; **un c. de ruines** a tangled heap of ruins **2** *Rel* **le C.** Chaos

chaotique [kaɔtik] **ADJ** chaotic

chapardage [ʃapardaʒ] **NM** *Fam* petty theft; **des chapardages répétés** pilfering *(UNCOUNT)*

chaparder **[3]** [ʃaparde] **VT** *Fam* to pinch, to swipe; **il s'est fait c. sa montre** he had his watch pinched *or Br* nicked

chapardeur, -euse [ʃapardœr, -øz] *Fam* **ADJ** sticky-fingered

NM,F (casual) thief[□]; **un c. invétéré** a habitual pilferer

chape [ʃap] **NF 1** *Rel (de prêtre)* cope

2 *Constr* screed; *(d'un pont, d'une chaussée)* coping; **comme une c. de plomb** like a lead weight

3 *(d'un pneu)* tread

4 *(d'une poulie)* shell; *(d'une bielle)* case; *(d'un cardan)* fork

chapeau, -x [ʃapo] **NM 1** *(couvre-chef)* hat; **c. cloche** cloche (hat); **c. de cow-boy** cowboy hat; **c. de feutre** felt hat; **c. de gendarme** paper hat; **c. haut-de-forme** top hat; **c. melon** *Br* bowler (hat), *Am* derby; **c. mou** *Br* trilby, *Am* fedora; **c. de paille** straw hat; **c. de pluie** rain hat; **c. de soleil** sunhat; **mettre** *ou* **porter la main au c.** to raise one's hat; *Fig* **faire porter le c. à qn** *Br* to force sb to carry the can, *Am* to leave sb holding the bag; *Fig* **si je me trompe je veux bien manger mon c.!** if I'm wrong I'll eat my hat!; *Fig* **tirer son c. à qn, donner un coup de c. à qn** to take one's hat off to sb; *Fig* **saluer qn c. bas** to doff one's hat to sb; **c. bas!** hats off!; **je te dis c.!** I'll take my hat off to you!, well done!, bravo!; *Fam* **travailler du c.** to have a screw loose, to be off one's rocker; *Can Fam* **parler à travers son c.** to talk through one's hat; *Can Fam* **faire le tour du c.** to score a hat-trick *(in an ice hockey game)*

2 *Bot (d'un champignon)* cap

3 *Culin (d'un vol-au-vent, d'une bouchée à la reine)* lid, top

4 *(de texte, d'article)* introductory paragraph; *Rad & TV* introduction

5 *(partie supérieure ▸ d'un tuyau de cheminée)* cowl; **c. de lampe** lampshade; **c. de roue** hubcap; **prendre un virage sur les chapeaux de roue** to take a turning on two wheels; **démarrer sur les chapeaux de roue** to shoot off; *(film, réception, relation)* to get off to a great start

• **chapeau chinois** **NM 1** *Mus* crescent **2** *Zool (mollusque)* limpet

chapeauter **[3]** [ʃapote] **VT 1** *Fam (superviser)* to oversee, to supervise; **il a décidé de faire c. les deux services par un secrétaire général** he decided to put both departments under the control of a general secretary **2** *(article, texte)* to write an introductory piece for

chapelain [ʃaplɛ̃] **NM** chaplain

chapelet [ʃaplɛ] **NM 1** *Rel (collier)* rosary, beads; *(prières)* rosary; **réciter** *ou* **dire son c.** to say the rosary, *Am* to tell one's beads; *Fam* **débiter** *ou* **dévider son c.** to tell all **2** *(d'îles, de saucisses)* string; *(d'insultes)* string, stream; **un c. de bombes** a stick of bombs

chapelier, -ère [ʃapəlje, -ɛr] **ADJ** *(commerce, industrie)* hat *(avant n)*

NM,F hatter

chapelle [ʃapɛl] **NF 1** *Rel (bâtiment)* chapel; *(chanteurs et musiciens)* choir and orchestra; *(objets liturgiques)* ornaments and plate; **c. ardente** chapel of rest **2** *Fig (cercle)* clique, coterie **3** *Belg (café)* café

chapellerie [ʃapɛlri] **NF 1** *(activité)* hat trade **2** *(industrie)* hat *or* hat-making industry **3** *(magasin)* hatshop

chapelure [ʃaplyr] **NF** breadcrumbs; **passer qch dans la c.** to coat sth with breadcrumbs

chaperon [ʃaprɔ̃] **NM 1** *(surveillant)* chaperon, chaperone; **servir de c. à qn** to chaperon *or* to chaperone sb **2** *Constr (d'un mur)* coping **3** *(de faucon)* hood

chaperonner [3] [ʃaprɔne] VT **1** *(jeune fille, groupe)* to chaperon, to chaperone **2** *Constr* to cope **3** *(faucon)* to hood

chapiteau, -x [ʃapito] NM **1** *Archit* capital, chapiter; *(d'une armoire)* cornice **2** *(cirque)* big top; **sous c.** in a marquee **3** *(d'un alambic)* head

chapitre [ʃapitr] NM **1** *(d'un livre)* chapter

2 *Fin & Compta (d'un budget)* item; **inscrire une somme au c. des recettes/dépenses** to enter a sum under (the heading of) revenue/expenditure

3 *(question)* matter, subject; **le c. est clos** that's the end of the matter, subject closed; **et maintenant, au c. des faits divers...** and now for the news in brief...; **il est exigeant sur le c. des vins** he's hard to please in the matter of *or* as regards wines; **tu as raison, au moins sur un c.** you're right, at least on one score

4 *Rel (assemblée)* chapter; *(lieu)* chapterhouse

chapitrer [3] [ʃapitre] VT *(sermonner)* to lecture; *(tancer)* to admonish; **je l'ai dûment chapitré sur ses responsabilités** I gave him the appropriate lecture about his responsibilities; **se faire c. par qn** to be *or* to get told off by sb

chapka [ʃapka] NF shapka *(round brimless fur hat worn in Russia)*

chaplinesque [ʃaplinɛsk] ADJ *(comique, personnage)* Chaplinesque

chapon [ʃapɔ̃] NM capon

chaptalisation [ʃaptalizasjɔ̃] NF chaptalization, chaptalizing

chaptaliser [3] [ʃaptalize] VT to chaptalize

chaque [ʃak] ADJ INDÉFINI **1** *(dans un groupe, dans une série)* each, every; **c. enfant a reçu un livre** each *or* every child received a book; **c. femme doit pouvoir travailler et élever ses enfants** every woman *or* all women should be able to work as well as bring up their children; **c. hiver** every *or* each winter; **la distance est de trois mètres entre c. poteau** there is a distance of three metres between each pole; **je pense à elle à c. instant** I think about her all the time; **c. chose en son temps!** all in good time! **2** *(chacun)* each; **on a gagné 200 euros c. au Loto** we won 200 euros each on the lottery; **les disques sont vendus 13 euros c.** the CDs are sold at 13 euros each

char [ʃar] NM **1** *Mil* tank; **c. léger/moyen/lourd** light/medium/heavy tank; **c. d'assaut** *ou* **de combat** tank; **fait comme un c. d'assaut** built like a tank

2 *(de carnaval)* float

3 *Sport* **c. à voile** sand yacht; **faire du c. à voile** to go sand yachting

4 *(voiture)* **c. à bancs** charabanc, = open wagon with seats for passengers; **c. à bœufs** ox cart; **c. funèbre** hearse

5 *Antiq* chariot; *Littéraire* **le c. de l'État** the ship of State; *Fam* **arrête ton c.(, Ben Hur)!** come off it!, yeah right!

6 *Can Fam (voiture)* car▫

charabia [ʃarabja] NM *Fam* gobbledegook, gibberish

charade [ʃarad] NF **1** *(devinette)* riddle **2** *(mime)* (game of) charades

> Il faut noter que le terme anglais **charade** est un faux ami.

charançon [ʃarɑ̃sɔ̃] NM *Entom* weevil, snout beetle

charançonné, -e [ʃarɑ̃sɔne] ADJ weevilled, weevily

charbon [ʃarbɔ̃] NM **1** *Mines* coal; **le rôti n'est plus qu'un morceau de c.** the roast is burnt to a cinder; **se passer le visage au c.** to black one's face; **chauffage au c.** coal-fired heating; **c. aggloméré** briquette; **c. de bois** charcoal; *Fam* **aller au c.** *(au travail)* to go to work; *(s'y mettre)* to do one's bit; **être** *ou* **marcher sur des charbons ardents** to be on tenterhooks, to be like a cat on *Br* hot bricks *or Am* a hot tin roof

2 *Beaux-Arts (crayon)* charcoal (pencil); **(dessin au) c.** charcoal drawing

3 *(maladie ▸ chez l'animal, chez l'homme)* anthrax; *(▸ des céréales)* smut, black rust

4 *Pharm* charcoal; **c. actif** *ou* **activé** active *or* activated carbon, activated charcoal

5 *Élec* carbon

charbonnage [ʃarbɔnaʒ] NM coalmining

• **charbonnages** NMPL coalmines, *Br* collieries; **les Charbonnages de France** the French Coal Board

charbonner [3] [ʃarbɔne] VT **1** *Beaux-Arts (croquis, dessin)* to (draw with) charcoal **2** *(noircir ▸ visage)* to charcoal

charbonneux, -euse [ʃarbɔnø, -øz] ADJ **1** *(noir)* coal-black

2 *(souillé)* sooty black; **un dépôt c.** a sooty deposit, a carbon deposit; *Péj* **avoir les yeux c.** to wear heavy black eye make-up

3 *(brûlé)* charred

4 *Méd* anthracoid; **mouche charbonneuse** anthrax-carrying fly

5 *Bot* smutty

charbonnier, -ère [ʃarbɔnje, -ɛr] ADJ *(commerce, industrie)* coal *(avant n)*; **navire c.** coaler, collier

NM,F *(vendeur)* coaler, coalman; *(fabricant de charbon de bois)* charcoal-burner; *Prov* **c. est maître dans sa maison** *ou* **chez soi** *Br* an Englishman's *or Am* a man's home is his castle

NM *Naut* coaler, collier

• **charbonnière** NF *(lieu)* charcoal kiln *or* stack

charcuter [3] [ʃarkyte] *Fam* VT *Péj* **1** *(opérer)* to butcher, to hack up; **se faire c.** to be hacked to pieces **2** *(couper ▸ volaille, texte)* to hack to pieces *or* about

VPR **se charcuter je me suis charcutée en essayant de m'enlever l'écharde** I made a real mess of my finger trying to get the splinter out

charcuterie [ʃarkytri] NF **1** *(magasin)* ≃ delicatessen **2** *(produits)* cooked meats; **assiette de c.** plate of assorted cooked meats **3** *(fabrication)* cooked meats trade

> **CHARCUTERIE**
>
> A "charcuterie" sells mainly food prepared with pork: sausages, pâtés, ham etc, collectively also known as "charcuterie". Ready-prepared dishes to take away are usually also sold.

charcutier, -ère [ʃarkytje, -ɛr] NM,F **1** *(commerçant)* pork butcher **2** *Fam Péj (chirurgien)* butcher

chardon [ʃardɔ̃] NM **1** *Bot* thistle **2** *(sur un mur)* spike

chardonneret [ʃardɔnrɛ] NM *Orn* goldfinch

charentais, -e [ʃarɑ̃tɛ, -ɛz] ADJ of/from the Charente

• **Charentais, -e** NM,F = inhabitant of or person from the Charente

• **charentaises** NFPL *(pantoufles)* carpet slippers

CHARGE [ʃarʒ]

NF	
• load **1, 2**	• burden **1, 3**
• responsibility **4**	• office **5**
• charge **6, 8, 13**	• cost **11**
NFPL	
• cost	

NF **1** *(cargaison ▸ d'un animal)* burden; *(▸ d'un camion)* load; *(▸ d'un navire)* cargo, freight; *Mil* payload; **plier sous une lourde c.** to be weighed down by a heavy burden; **camion en pleine c.** fully laden lorry; *Mil* **c. marchande** commercial payload; **c. utile** capacity load, payload; **c. à vide** empty weight

2 *(poussée)* load; *Aviat* **facteur de c.** load factor; **c. admissible** safe load; **c. de rupture** breaking *or* shearing stress; **c. de sécurité** safe load

3 *(gêne)* burden, *Fig* weight; **je ne veux pas devenir une c. pour eux** I don't want to become a burden to them

4 *(responsabilité)* responsibility; **à qui revient la c. de le faire?** who has *or* carries the responsibility for doing it?; **elle a (la) c. de réorganiser le service** she's got the job of reorganizing the department; **toutes les réparations sont à sa c.** he/she will pay for the repair work, all the repair work will be done at his/her cost; **à c. pour toi d'apporter le vin** you'll be responsible for bringing *or* it'll be up to you to bring the wine; **avoir c. d'âmes** *(prêtre)* to have the cure of souls; *(parent)* to have children in one's care; **nous prenons tous les frais médicaux en c.** we pay for *or* take care of all medical expenses; **elle a pris son neveu en c.** she took on responsibility for her nephew; **prendre un client en c.** *(taxi)* to pick up a fare; **être pris en c. à cent pour cent par la Sécurité sociale** to have one's medical expenses fully paid for by Social Security; **à ton âge, tu dois te prendre en c.** at your age, you should take yourself in hand *or* take responsibility for yourself; **enfants à c.** dependent children; **avoir qn à (sa) c.** *(gén)* to be responsible for supporting sb; *Admin* to have sb as a dependant; **ses enfants sont encore à sa c.** his/her children are still his/her dependants

5 *Admin (fonction)* office; **c. élective** elective office; **c. de greffier** registrarship; **c. de notaire** notary's office

6 *(d'une mine, d'explosifs)* charge; **il a reçu toute la c. dans la poitrine** his chest took the full impact of the blast; **c. creuse** hollow charge; **c. d'explosifs** explosive charge; **c. nucléaire** nuclear charge

7 *Élec* **mettre une batterie en c.** to charge a battery; **c. électrique** electric charge; **c. négative/positive** minus/positive charge; **c. spatiale** space charge

8 *Fin (d'une dette) Br* servicing, *Am* service

9 *(portée)* **c. affective** *ou* **émotionnelle** emotive power; **avoir une forte c. symbolique** to have strong symbolic power *or* resonance; **une c. psychologique impossible à supporter** an unbearable mental strain

10 *Jur (présomption)* serious suspicion; **de très lourdes charges pèsent sur lui** very serious suspicions are hanging over him; **c. de la preuve** burden of proof

11 *Fin (coût)* cost; **c. fictive** fictitious cost; **c. opérationnelle** operating cost; **c. à payer** sum payable

12 *Méd* **c. virale** viral load

13 *Mil (assaut)* charge; **donner la c.** to charge; **sonner la c.** to sound the charge; **au pas de c.** at the double; **retourner** *ou* **revenir à la c.** to mount a fresh attack; *Fig* to go back onto the offensive; **je t'ai déjà dit non, tu ne vas pas revenir à la c.!** I've already said no, don't keep on at me!

14 *Beaux-Arts & Littérature (d'un personnage, d'un portrait)* caricature, burlesque; *Théât (d'un rôle)* overacting; *(genre)* skit; **jouer un rôle en c.** to overact a part

• **charges** NFPL *(frais ▸ gén)* costs, expenses; *(▸ de locataire)* service or maintenance charges; *Compta* **charges constatées d'avance** prepaid expenses, prepayments; *Fin* **charges courantes** current expenses; **charges de famille** dependants; **charges financières** financial expenses; **charges fiscales** tax; **charges fixes** fixed costs; **charges (locatives)** maintenance charges; **charges du mariage** marital expenses; **charges patronales** employer's contributions; *Compta* **charges payées d'avance** prepaid expenses, prepayments; *Compta* **charges à payer** accrued expenses, accruals; **charges salariales** wage costs; **charges sociales** *Br* ≃ national insurance contributions *(paid by the employer)*, *Am* ≃ social security charges *(paid by the employer)*; *Compta* **charges terminales** terminal charges

• **à charge de** PRÉP **j'accepte, à c. de revanche** I accept, provided you'll let me do the same for you; **à c. de preuve** pending production of proof

> **CHARGES**
>
> Householders and tenants in blocks of flats are required to pay "charges", a monthly contribution to pay for the general upkeep of the building. In estate agencies, rent is expressed either including this sum ("charges comprises" or "cc") or excluding it ("hors charges" or "charges en sus"). Sometimes, the "charges" include heating costs.

chargé, -e [ʃarʒe] ADJ **1** *(occupé ▸ journée)* busy, full; *(▸ programme)* full

2 *(tissu, motif)* overelaborate; *(style)* (over) ornate

3 *Fig* **avoir la conscience chargée** to have a guilty conscience; **un gangster au passé c.** a gangster with a past; **il a un casier judiciaire c.** he has a long (criminal) record

4 *(plein)* **une pièce chargée de décorations de mau-**

vais goût a room cluttered with tasteless decorations; **un mur c. de tableaux** a wall covered in paintings; **l'air est c. du parfum des fleurs** the air is heavy with the scent of flowers; **un regard c. de reconnaissance** a look full of gratitude; *Littéraire* **c. d'ans** *ou* **d'années** stricken in years; **mourir c. d'ans** to die at a ripe old age, to die full of years

5 *Méd* **estomac c.** overloaded stomach; **avoir la langue chargée** to have a furred tongue

6 *Phys (particule)* charged; **particule chargée négativement/positivement** negatively-/positively-charged particle

7 *Fam (ivre)* loaded, wrecked, wasted

NM *(responsable)* **c. d'affaires** chargé d'affaires; **c. de budget** account executive; *Com* **c. de clientèle** account manager; **c. de comptes** account manager; *Univ* **c. de cours** ≃ part-time lecturer; **c. d'étude de marché** market researcher; **c. de famille** person supporting a family; **c. de mission** *Admin* project leader *or* manager; *Pol* ≃ (official) representative; *Com & Mktg* **c. de relations clients** customer relations manager; *Univ* **c. de TD** tutor

chargeable [ʃarʒabl] **ADJ** *Ordinat* loadable

chargement [ʃarʒəmɑ̃] **NM 1** *(marchandises ▸ d'un camion)* consignment, shipment; *(▸ d'un navire)* cargo, freight

2 *(fait de charger ▸ un navire, un camion)* loading; *(▸une chaudière)* stoking; *(▸une arme)* loading; **à c. automatique** self-loading; **machine à laver à c. frontal** front-loading washing machine

3 *Élec* charging (up)

4 *(de lettre, de colis)* registration; *(lettre)* registered letter; *(colis)* registered parcel

CHARGER [17] [ʃarʒe]

VT
- to load **1, 4**
- to pick up **2**
- to overload **3**
- to charge **4, 9**
- to put in charge of **5**
- to overdo **7**

VPR
- to load **2**
- to take care of **3**

VT 1 *(véhicule, marchandises)* to load (**dans/sur** into/onto); **tes livres chargent un peu trop l'étagère** the shelf is overloaded with your books; **être chargé** to be loaded; **il est entré, les bras chargés de cadeaux** he came in loaded down with presents; **les arbres sont chargés de fruits** the trees are loaded down *or* groaning with fruit; **table chargée de mets** table laden with food; **navire chargé de blé** ship laden with wheat; **la voiture est trop chargée** the car is overloaded; *Méd* **c. son estomac** to overload one's stomach; **être chargé comme un bourricot** *ou* **un mulet** *ou* **un baudet** to be weighed down

2 *(prendre en charge ▸ sujet: taxi)* to pick up

3 *(alourdir, encombrer)* to overload; **ces meubles chargent trop la pièce** this furniture makes the room look (too) cluttered; **c. qn de qch** to overload sb with sth; **c. sa mémoire de détails** to clutter up one's mind with details

4 *(arme, caméra, appareil photo)* to load (up); *Élec* to charge (up); *Ordinat* to load (up)

5 *(d'une responsabilité)* **c. qn de qch** to put sb in charge of sth; **on l'a chargée d'un cours à l'université** she was assigned to teach *or* given a class at the university; **je vous charge d'un travail important** I'm giving you *or* entrusting you with an important job; **il est chargé de l'entretien** he's in charge of *or* responsible for maintenance; **être chargé de famille** to have family responsibilities; **c. qn de faire qch** to give sb the responsibility for doing sth; **il m'a chargé de vous transmettre un message** he asked me to give you a message; **j'étais chargé de faire tout le courrier du service** I was in charge of *or* responsible for the department's mail

6 *(amplifier)* to inflate, to put up

7 *(exagérer ▸ rôle)* to camp up, to overdo; **ne charge pas ainsi ton rôle, joue plus en finesse** don't overact, be more subtle; **elle n'est pas si idiote, tu charges un peu la description!** she's not that stupid, you're overdoing it a bit!

8 *(incriminer)* **c. qn** to make sb appear guiltier; **certains témoins ont essayé de le c. au maximum** some witnesses tried to strengthen the prosecution's case against him

9 *(attaquer)* to charge (at); **chargez!** charge!; **la police n'a pas chargé (les manifestants)** the police didn't charge (at the demonstrators)

10 c. une lettre = to send valuables by post; *(l'affranchir)* to register a letter

11 *Banque (compte)* to overcharge (on)

VI *Can Joual* **c. cher** to charge a lot of money

VPR se charger 1 *(s'alourdir)* to weigh oneself down

2 *Ordinat* to load; **se c. automatiquement** to load automatically, to autoload

3 se c. de *(responsabilité)* to take on, to take care of; *(élève, invité)* to take care of, to look after; **je me charge de tout** I'll take care of everything; **quant à lui, je m'en charge personnellement** I'll personally take good care of him; **je me charge de le prévenir** I'll make sure to let him know; **je me charge de lui remettre votre lettre** I'll see to it personally that he/she gets your letter; **qui va se c. du travail?** who's going to take the job on?

chargeur [ʃarʒœr] **NM 1** *Phot* cartridge, magazine

2 *(d'arme)* cartridge clip

3 *Élec* charger

4 *(ouvrier)* loader

5 *Ordinat* feeder

chargeuse [ʃarʒøz] **NF 1** *(distributrice)* distributor **2** *Mines* loading machine **3** *Métal* charging *or* loading machine

charia [ʃarja] **NF** *Rel* sharia

chariot [ʃarjo] **NM 1** *(véhicule ▸ gén)* wagon, *Br* waggon; *(▸ dans un supermarché, à bagages)* *Br* trolley, *Am* cart; *(▸ d'hôpital)* *Br* (hospital) trolley, *Am* gurney; **le c. des desserts/à liqueurs** the dessert/drinks trolley; **c. élévateur** fork-lift truck; **c. élévateur à fourche** fork-lift truck

2 *Astron* **le Grand C.** *Br* the Great Bear, *Am* the Big Dipper; **le Petit C.** the Little *Br* Bear *or Am* Dipper

3 *(de machine à écrire)* carriage

4 *Cin & TV* dolly; **c. omnidirectionnel** crab *or* crabbing dolly

5 *Aviat* **c. d'atterrissage** landing gear, undercarriage

chariot-crabe [ʃarjɔkrab] *(pl* **chariots-crabes)** **NM** *Cin & TV* crab *or* crabbing dolly

charismatique [karismatik] **ADJ** charismatic; **être c.** to have charisma

charisme [karism] **NM** charisma

charitable [ʃaritabl] **ADJ 1** *(généreux)* charitable; **se montrer c. envers qn** to be charitable *or* to exercise charity towards sb; *Ironique* **avis** *ou* **conseil c.** so-called friendly piece of advice **2** *(association, mouvement)* charitable, charity *(avant n)*

charitablement [ʃaritabləmɑ̃] **ADV** charitably, generously

charité [ʃarite] **NF 1** *(altruisme)* charity, love; **aurais-tu la c. de leur rendre visite?** would you be kind enough to go and visit them?; **faites-moi** *ou* **ayez la c. d'écouter mon histoire** please be kind enough to listen to my story; *Prov* **c. bien ordonnée commence par soi-même** charity begins at home **2** *(aumône)* charity; **demander la c.** to beg (for charity); **faire la c. (à)** to give a handout (to), *Vieilli* to give alms (to); *Fig* **je n'ai nul besoin qu'on me fasse la c.** I don't need anybody's help, I'll manage on my own; **la c., s'il vous plaît!** can you spare some change, please?

• **de charité ADJ fête de c.** benefit event; **œuvres de c.** charities; **vente de c.** charity sale

charivari [ʃarivari] **NM** hurly-burly, hullabaloo

charlatan [ʃarlatɑ̃] **NM** *Péj* **1** *(médecin)* charlatan, quack; **remède de c.** quack remedy; **tous ces psys sont des charlatans** all these shrinks are quacks **2** *(vendeur)* conman, swindler **3** *(réparateur)* cowboy

charlatanerie [ʃarlatanri] **NF** *Péj* charlatanism

charlatanesque [ʃarlatanesk] **ADJ** *Péj* **1** *(médecine)* quackish **2** *(pratiques)* phoney, bogus

charlatanisme [ʃarlatanism] **NM** *Péj* charlatanism

Charles [ʃarl] **NPR C. Quint** Charles V, Charles the Fifth

charleston [ʃarlestɔn] **NM** charleston

charlot [ʃarlo] **NM** *Fam* clown, joker; **jouer les charlots** to fool around

charlotte [ʃarlɔt] **NF** *Culin* charlotte; **c. aux pommes** apple charlotte

charmant, -e [ʃarmɑ̃, -ɑ̃t] **ADJ** charming, delightful; **nous étions en charmante compagnie** we were in delightful company; **vous avez eu là une charmante attention** how very thoughtful of you; *Ironique* **charmante soirée!** what a great evening!; *Ironique* **c'est c.!** charming!

charme[1] [ʃarm] **NM 1** *(attrait)* charm; **faire le c. de qch** to be the most attractive *or* greatest asset of sth; **c'est ce qui fait tout son c.** that's what is so appealing *or* charming about him/her; **cette proposition ne manque pas de c.** the suggestion is not without a certain appeal

2 *(d'une femme, d'un homme)* charm, attractiveness; **elle a beaucoup de c.** she has great charm, she's very charming; **elle n'est pas belle, mais elle a du c.** she's not beautiful, but she is attractive; **les femmes lui trouvent du c.** women find him attractive; **faire du c. à qn** to try to charm sb

3 *(enchantement)* spell; **être/tomber sous le c. de** to be/to fall under the spell of; **tenir qn/un public sous le c.** to hold sb/an audience spellbound; **le c. est rompu** the spell's broken

4 *(locution)* **se porter comme un c.** to be in excellent health *or* as fit as a fiddle; **comment vous portez-vous? – comme un c.!** how do you feel? – never better!

• **charmes NMPL** *Euph (d'une femme)* charms; **vivre** *ou* **faire commerce de ses charmes** to trade on one's charms

• **de charme ADJ 1** *Mus* **chanson de c.** sentimental ballad **2** *Euph (érotique ▸ presse)* soft-porn; **magazine de c.** soft-porn magazine; **mannequin de c.** glamour model; **hôtesse de c.** escort (girl)

charme[2] [ʃarm] **NM** *Bot* hornbeam

charmer [3] [ʃarme] **VT 1** *(plaire à)* to delight, to enchant; **son sourire l'a charmé** he was enchanted by his/her smile **2** *(envoûter ▸ auditoire)* to cast *or* to put a spell on; *(▸serpent)* to charm **3** *(dans des formules de politesse)* **je suis charmé de vous revoir** I'm delighted to see you again; **charmé de vous avoir rencontré** (it's been) very nice meeting you

charmeur, -euse [ʃarmœr, -øz] **ADJ** *(air, sourire)* charming, engaging

NM,F *(séducteur)* charmer; **c. de serpents** snake charmer

charmille [ʃarmij] **NF 1** *(berceau de verdure)* bower, arbour **2** *(allée)* tree-covered walk *or* path

charnel, -elle [ʃarnɛl] **ADJ 1** *(sexuel)* carnal; **l'amour c.** carnal love **2** *(physique ▸ beauté)* physical, bodily; **nous parlons d'eux en tant qu'êtres charnels** we're talking about them as human beings made of flesh and blood

charnellement [ʃarnɛlmɑ̃] **ADV** carnally; **connaître qn c.** to have carnal knowledge of sb

charnier [ʃarnje] **NM 1** *(fosse)* mass grave **2** *(ossuaire)* charnel house **3** *(lieu de massacre)* scene of carnage

charnière [ʃarnjer] **NF 1** *Anat & Menuis* hinge

2 *(transition)* junction, turning point; **Goethe est à la c. du XVIIIème et du XIXème siècle** Goethe lived during the transition from the 18th to the 19th century; **marquer la c. entre deux périodes** to be a turning point between two eras

3 *Mil* (point of) junction

4 *(comme adj; avec ou sans trait d'union)* **moment/siècle c.** moment/century of transition

5 *(au rugby)* half-back partnership

charnu, -e [ʃarny] **ADJ 1** *(corps)* plump, fleshy; *(lèvres)* full, fleshy; *(fruit)* pulpy **2** *Anat* fleshy, flesh-covered; *Hum* **la partie charnue de son anatomie** his/her posterior

charognard [ʃarɔɲar] **NM 1** *Zool & Orn* carrion feeder **2** *Fam (exploiteur)* vulture

charogne [ʃarɔɲ] **NF 1** *(carcasse)* **une c.** a decaying carcass; **ces animaux se nourrissent de c.** these animals feed off carrion **2** *très Fam (homme)* bastard; *(femme)* bitch

Charon [karɔ̃] **NPR** *Myth* Charon

charpente [ʃarpɑ̃t] **NF 1** *Constr* skeleton, frame (work); **c. en bois** *Br* timber *or Am* lumber work; **maison à c. de bois** wood-frame house; **c. métallique** steel frame **2** *Anat* **il a la c. d'un boxeur** he's built like a boxer; **une c. d'athlète** an athlete's build **3** *(schéma ▸ d'un projet, d'un roman)* structure, framework

charpenté, -e [ʃarpɑ̃te] **ADJ bien** *ou* **solidement c.** *(personne)* well-built; *(film, argument)* well-structured

charpenter [3] [ʃarpɑ̃te] **VT 1** *Constr* to carpenter **2** *(structurer ▸ œuvre, discours)* to structure

charpenterie [ʃarpɑ̃tri] **NF** *(métier)* carpentry; *(chantier) Br* timberyard, *Am* lumber yard

charpentier [ʃarpɑ̃tje] **NM** *(ouvrier)* carpenter; *(entrepreneur)* (master) carpenter; **c. du bord** shipwright

charpie [ʃarpi] **NF** *(pansement)* lint

• **en charpie ADV mettre** *ou* **réduire qch en c.** to tear sth to shreds; *Fig* **je vais le mettre** *ou* **réduire en c.** I'll make mincemeat (out) of him; **il a servi de la viande en c.** he served meat that was cooked to shreds

charretée [ʃarte] **NF 1** *(contenu)* cartful, cartload; **par charretées entières** by the cartload **2** *Fam (grande quantité)* **une c. d'insultes** loads *or* a pile of insults

charretier, -ère [ʃartje, -ɛr] **ADJ** *(chemin, voie)* cart *(avant n)*

NM,F carter

charrette [ʃarɛt] **NF 1** *Agr* cart

2 *Hist* **la c. des condamnés** the tumbrel *or* tumbril

3 *Fam (travail intensif)* **se mettre en c.** to work against the clock

4 *(licenciements)* **faire partie de la première/dernière c.** to be included in the first/last wave of redundancies

6 *Belg (locution)* **ça ne veut pas dire c.** that's not saying much

ADJ INV *Fam* **être c.** to be working against the clock *or* flat out

EXCLAM *Suisse Fam* blast!, *Am* shoot!; **cette c. de Paul!** that *Br* blasted *or Am* darn Paul!

charriage [ʃarjaʒ] **NM 1** *Transp* carriage, haulage **2** *Géol* overthrust

charrier [10] [ʃarje] **VT 1** *(sujet: personne)* to cart *or* to carry (along) **2** *(sujet: fleuve, rivière)* to carry *or* to wash along; **la Néva charrie d'énormes glaçons** the Neva carries great blocks of ice **3** *Fam (railler)* **c. qn** *Br* to take the mickey out of sb, *Am* to goof with sb; **il s'est fait c.** he got made fun of, *Br* he got the mickey taken out of him

VI *Fam* **c. (dans les bégonias)** *(exagérer)* to go too far *or* (way) over the top; **cinq euros d'augmentation, ils charrient!** five euros on the price, they've got a nerve!; **je veux bien aider mais faut pas c.** I don't mind lending a hand, but this is a bit over the top

charroi [ʃarwa] **NM** cartage

charron [ʃarɔ̃] **NM 1** *(fabricant)* cartwright, wheelwright **2** *(réparateur)* wheelwright

charroyer [13] [ʃarwaje] **VT** to cart

charrue [ʃary] **NF 1** *(pour labourer)* plough; **c. polysoc** multiple plough; **mettre la c. avant les bœufs** to put the cart before the horse **2** *Can* snowplough

charte [ʃart] **NF 1** *(document)* charter; **c. commerciale** commercial charter; *Journ & Typ* **c. graphique** *ou* **rédactionnelle** house-style book; **C. sociale** Social Charter; **c. des valeurs** statement of principles **2** *Hist* charter; **la Grande C.** Magna Carta **3** *(plan)* **c. d'aménagement** development plan

• **chartes** *voir* **école**

charter [ʃartɛr] **NM** *(avion)* chartered plane; *(vol)* charter flight

chartérisation [ʃarterizasjɔ̃] **NF** chartering

chartisme [ʃartism] **NM** *Hist* chartism

chartiste [ʃartist] **NMF 1** *Pol (en Grande-Bretagne)* Chartist **2** *Univ* = student or former student of the "École des chartes" **3** *Bourse* chartist

ADJ 1 *Pol (en Grande-Bretagne)* Chartist **2** *Univ* = relating to the "École des chartes"

chartre [ʃartr] = **charte**

chartreux, -euse [ʃartrø, -øz] **NM,F** *Rel (moine)* Carthusian monk; *(religieuse)* Carthusian nun

NM *(chat)* British blue (cat)

• **chartreuse NF 1** *Rel (de moines)* Charterhouse, Carthusian monastery; *(de religieuses)* Carthusian convent **2** *(liqueur)* Chartreuse

Charybde [karibd] **NPR 1** *Myth* Charybdis **2** *(locution)* **tomber de C. en Scylla** to jump out of the frying pan into the fire

chas [ʃa] **NM** eye *(of a needle)*

chasse [ʃas] **NF 1** *(activité)* hunting; *(occasion)* hunt; **cette région a toujours été un pays de c.** this has always been a good area for hunting; **c. à courre** *(activité)* hunting (with hounds); *(occasion)* hunt; **c. au daim/renard/tigre** deer/fox/tiger hunting; **c. au faucon** falconry; **c. au furet** ferreting; **c. au lapin** rabbit shooting, rabbiting; **c. au lièvre** *(gén)* hare hunting; *(avec lévriers)* hare coursing; **c. aux papillons** butterfly catching; **c. au phoque** sealing, seal culling; **aller à la c.** *(à courre)* to go hunting; *(au fusil)* to go shooting; **dresser un chien pour la c.** *(à courre)* to train a dog for hunting *or* the hunt; *(au fusil)* to train a dog for shooting *or* the shoot; **c. sous-marine** underwater fishing; *Prov* **qui va à la c. perd sa place** = if somebody takes your place it serves you right for leaving it empty

2 *(domaine ▸ de chasse à courre)* hunting grounds; *(▸ de chasse au fusil)* shooting ground; **louer une c.** to rent a shoot; **les chasses du roi** the royal hunting grounds; **c. gardée** *(sur panneau)* private, poachers will be prosecuted; *Fam* **laisse-la tranquille, c'est c. gardée** leave her alone, she's spoken for

3 *(butin)* game; **la c. a été bonne** we got a good bag; **faire bonne c.** to get a good bag

4 *(période)* hunting season, shooting season; **la c. est ouverte/fermée** it's open/close(d) season, the shooting season has begun/is over

5 *(chasseurs)* hunters; **la c. vient de passer** the hunters have just gone by; *(à courre)* the hunt has just gone by

6 *(poursuite)* chase, hunt; **faire** *ou* **donner la c. à un cambrioleur** to chase after a burglar; **prendre en c. une voiture** to chase a car

7 *(recherche)* **c. à** search for; **c. à l'homme** manhunt; **c. au trésor** treasure hunt; **c. aux sorcières** witch hunt; **faire la c. à** to search for, to (try to) track down; **faire la c. aux abus** to root out abuses *(of a system)*; *Fam* **faire la c. au mari** to be looking for a husband; *Zool & Fig* **en c.** *Br* on *or Am* in heat; **se mettre en c. pour trouver qch** to go out hunting for sth

8 *Aviat* **la c.** fighter planes

9 *(d'eau)* flush; **tirer la c. (d'eau)** to flush the toilet

10 *Typ (épaisseur de la lettre)* width; *(d'une page)* overrun

11 *Aut* caster

> Il faut noter que le nom anglais **chase** est un faux ami. Il signifie **poursuite**.

châsse [ʃas] **NF 1** *(coffre)* shrine **2** *Opt (de lunettes)* frame **3** *(d'un bijou)* setting

chassé [ʃase] **NM** *(pas de danse)* chassé

chasse-clou [ʃasklu] *(pl* **chasse-clous***)* **NM** *Tech* nail punch, nail set

chassé-croisé [ʃasekrwaze] *(pl* **chassés-croisés***)* **NM 1** *(confusion)* **le c. ministériel/de limousines** the comings and goings of ministers/of limousines; **le c. des vacanciers sur les routes** the busy flow of holidaymakers on the roads **2** *(pas de danse)* set to partners

chasse-goupille [ʃasgupij] *(pl* **chasse-goupilles***)* **NM** *Tech* pin punch

chasselas [ʃasla] **NM** *(cépage)* **du c.** Chasselas grapes

chasse-marée [ʃasmare] **NM INV** *(bateau)* coasting lugger

chasse-mouches [ʃasmuʃ] **NM INV** flyswatter

chasse-neige [ʃasnɛʒ] **NM INV 1** *(véhicule)* snowplough **2** *Ski (position du skieur)* snowplough; **descendre/tourner en c.** to snowplough down/round; **virage en c.** snowplough turn

chasse-pierres [ʃaspjɛr] **NM INV** *Rail* cowcatcher

chasser [3] [ʃase] **VT 1** *(animaux)* to hunt; **il chasse le daim** he hunts deer

2 *(expulser)* to drive out, to expel; **c. qn du pays** to drive sb from the country; **il a été chassé de chez lui** he was made to leave home; **elle l'a chassé de la maison** she sent him packing; **c. qn/qch de son esprit** to dismiss sb/sth from one's mind *or* thoughts; **je ne veux pas vous c. mais il est tard** I'm not trying to get rid of you but it's getting late

3 *(congédier ▸ employé)* to dismiss

4 *(faire partir)* to dispel, to drive away, to get rid of; **le mauvais temps a chassé les touristes** the bad weather drove away the tourists; **pour c. les mauvaises odeurs** to get rid of bad smells; **sortez pour c. les idées noires** go out and forget your worries; **chassez le naturel, il revient au galop** the leopard can't change its spots

5 *(pousser)* to drive (forward); **c. une mouche (du revers de la main)** to brush away a fly; **le vent chasse le sable/les nuages** the wind is blowing the sand/the clouds along

VI 1 *(aller à la chasse ▸ à courre)* to go hunting; *(▸ au fusil)* to go shooting; **c. au furet** to ferret; *Fig* **c. sur les terres d'autrui** to poach on somebody's preserve *or* territory

2 *Naut (déraper)* to skid; **le navire chasse sur son ancre** the ship is dragging its anchor

3 *(venir)* to drive; **nuages qui chassent du nord** clouds driving from the north

4 *Typ (caractère)* to drive out; *(texte)* to overrun

> Il faut noter que le verbe anglais **to chase** est un faux ami. Il signifie **poursuivre**.

chasseresse [ʃasrɛs] **ADJ F** *Myth* **Diane c.** Diana the huntress

NF *Littéraire* huntress

châsses [ʃas] **NMPL** *Fam* peepers, eyes

chasseur, -euse [ʃasœr, -øz] **NM,F 1** *(d'animaux)* hunter, huntsman, *f* huntress; **un très bon c.** *(de gibier à plumes)* an excellent shot; **c. de daims** deerhunter **2** *(chercheur)* **c. d'autographes** autograph hunter; **c. d'images** (freelance) photographer; **c. de prime** bounty hunter; *aussi Fig* **c. de têtes** headhunter; **elle a été recrutée par un c. de têtes** she was headhunted

• **chasseur NM 1** *Aviat & Mil* fighter (plane); **c. à réaction** jet fighter; *Naut* **c. de sous-marins** submarine hunter **2** *Mil* chasseur; **c. alpin** Alpine chasseur **3** *(dans un hôtel)* messenger (boy), *Am* bellboy **ADJ INV** *Culin* chasseur

chasseur-bagagiste [ʃasbagaʒist] *(pl* **chasseurs-bagagistes***)* **NM** luggage porter, porter

chasseur-bombardier [ʃasbɔ̃bardje] *(pl* **chasseurs-bombardiers***)* **NM** *Mil* fighter-bomber

chassie [ʃasi] **NF** rheum; **avoir de la c. dans les yeux** to have rheumy eyes

chassieux, -euse [ʃasjø, -øz] **ADJ** *(œil)* rheumy; *(personne)* rheumy-eyed; **avoir les yeux c.** to have rheumy eyes

NM,F rheumy-eyed person

châssis [ʃasi] **NM 1** *Constr* frame; **c. dormant** fixed frame; **c. à guillotine** sash (frame); **c. mobile** sash

2 *Beaux-Arts* stretcher; *Phot* (printing) frame; *Typ* **c. d'imprimerie** chase

3 *Aut* chassis, steel frame; **c. treillis** box section chassis; **c. tubulaire** box section chassis, space frame chassis

4 *Hort (de jardin)* (cold) frame; **culture sous c.** forcing

5 *très Fam (corps féminin)* body[□], bod, chassis; *Hum* **quel beau c.!** what a bod!

chaste [ʃast] **ADJ** chaste, innocent; *Hum* **ce n'est pas une plaisanterie pour vos chastes oreilles** this joke isn't for your innocent *or* delicate ears

chastement [ʃastəmɑ̃] **ADV** chastely, innocently

chasteté [ʃastəte] **NF** chastity

chasuble [ʃazybl] **NF 1** *Rel* chasuble **2** *(vêtement)* **robe c.** *Br* pinafore dress, *Am* jumper

chat¹, chatte [ʃa, ʃat] **NM,F 1** *(animal ▸ gén)* cat; *(▸ mâle)* tomcat; *(▸ femelle)* she-cat; **un petit c.** a kitten; **c. angora** Angora cat; **c. de Birmanie** Burmese cat; **c. européen** tabby (cat); **c. de gouttière** alley cat; **c. pêcheur** fishing cat; **c. persan/siamois** Persian/Siamese cat; **c. sauvage** wildcat; **appeler un c. un c.** to call a spade a spade; **avoir un c. dans la gorge** to have a frog in one's throat; **acheter c. en poche** to buy a pig in a poke; **il n'y a pas de quoi fouetter un c.** it's nothing to make a fuss about; **j'ai d'autres chats à fouetter** I've got better things to do, I've got other fish to fry; *Fam* **il n'y avait pas un c.** there wasn't a soul about; *Prov* **il ne faut pas**

réveiller le c. qui dort let sleeping dogs lie; *Prov* **quand le c. n'est pas là, les souris dansent** when the cat's away, the mice will play; *Prov* **à bon c., bon rat** = it's tit for tat; *Prov* **c. échaudé craint l'eau froide** once bitten, twice shy

2 *Fam (terme d'affection)* **mon petit c., ma petite chatte** pussycat, sweetie, sweetheart

3 *(jeu)* tag, *Br* tig; **jouer à c.** to play tag *or Br* tig; **c'est Sonia le c.** Sonia's it; **jouer à c. perché** to play off-ground tag *or Br* tig; *Fig* **jouer au c. et à la souris avec qn** to play cat-and-mouse with sb

4 *(fouet)* **c. à neuf queues** cat-o'-nine-tails

• **chatte** NF *Vulg* pussy, *Br* fanny; **avoir de la chatte** to be lucky *or Br* jammy

chat[2] [tʃat] NM *Ordinat (sur l'Internet)* chat

châtaigne [ʃatɛɲ] NF **1** *Bot* chestnut; **c. d'eau** water chestnut **2** *très Fam (coup)* clout, thump; **il s'est pris une de ces châtaignes!** *(il a été frappé)* he got a real thump!; *(il s'est cogné)* he gave himself a nasty knock!; **je me suis pris une c.** *(choc électrique)* I got a shock

châtaigner [4] [ʃatɛɲe] *Fam* VT to whack, to clout

VPR **se châtaigner** to exchange blows□, to lay into each other

châtaigneraie [ʃatɛɲɔrɛ] NF chestnut grove

châtaignier [ʃateɲe] NM **1** *Bot* chestnut tree **2** *(bois)* chestnut

châtain [ʃatɛ̃] ADJ M *(cheveux)* chestnut (brown); **c. clair** light brown; **c. doré** *ou* **roux** auburn; **être c.** to have brown hair

NM chestnut brown

chataire [ʃatɛr] = **cataire**

château, -x [ʃato] NM **1** *(forteresse)* castle; **c. fort** fortified castle

2 *(palais)* castle, palace; *(manoir)* mansion, manor (house); **le c. de Versailles** the palace of Versailles; **les châteaux de la Loire** the Châteaux of the Loire; **c. de cartes** house of cards; **ses illusions se sont écroulées comme un c. de cartes** his/her illusions collapsed like a house of cards; **c. de sable** sandcastle; *Fig* **bâtir** *ou* **faire des châteaux en Espagne** to build castles in the air

3 *(exploitation vinicole)* château; **mis en bouteilles au c.** château bottled

4 *Naut* **c. d'arrière** *ou* **de poupe** aftercastle; **c. d'avant** *ou* **de proue** forecastle, fo'c's'le, fo'c'sle

• **château d'eau** NM water tower

chateaubriand, châteaubriant [ʃatobrijɑ̃] NM *Culin* Chateaubriand (steak)

Château-la-Pompe [ʃatolapɔ̃p] NM *Fam Hum* water□; **accompagné d'un verre de C.** washed down with a glass of good old tapwater

châtelain, -e [ʃatlɛ̃, -ɛn] NM,F **1** *(propriétaire)* lord of the manor, *f* lady of the manor, chatelaine **2** *Hist* (feudal) lord

• **châtelaine** NF *(chaîne de ceinture, bijou)* chatelaine

châtelet [ʃatlɛ] NM small (fortified) castle

chat-huant [ʃayɑ̃] *(pl* **chats-huants)** NM *Orn* brown owl

châtié, -e [ʃɑtje] ADJ *(style)* polished; **en langage c.** in refined language

châtier [9] [ʃatje] VT *Littéraire* **1** *(punir)* to chastise, to castigate; **c. son corps** to mortify the flesh; **c. l'audace de qn** to punish sb for his/her impudence **2** *(affiner)* to polish, to refine

chatière [ʃatjɛr] NF **1** *(pour un chat)* cat door *or* flap **2** *(dans un toit)* ventilation hole **3** *(passage étroit)* narrow underground passage

châtiment [ʃatimɑ̃] NM punishment, *Sout* chastisement; **c. corporel** corporal punishment; **il a reçu un c. sévère** he was severely punished

chatoie *etc voir* **chatoyer**

chatoiement [ʃatwamɑ̃] NM gleam, shimmer

chaton[1] [ʃatɔ̃] NM **1** *Zool* kitten

2 *Bot* catkin, *Spéc* ament, amentum

3 *(poussière)* ball of fluff, *Am* dust bunny

4 *(terme d'affection)* **mon c.** darling

chaton[2] [ʃatɔ̃] NM *(tête d'une bague)* bezel; *(pierre enchâssée)* stone

chatouille [ʃatuj] NF **1** *Fam* tickle; **faire des chatouilles à qn** to tickle sb; **elle craint les chatouilles** she's ticklish **2** *Belg (locution)* **avoir c. à la tête/aux jambes** to have an itchy head/legs

chatouillement [ʃatujmɑ̃] NM tickle

chatouiller [3] [ʃatuje] VT **1** *(pour faire rire)* to tickle; **ah! ça chatouille!** oh! that tickles!; *Fam* **c. les côtes à qn** to give sb a thrashing

2 *(irriter)* to tickle

3 *(exciter ▸ odorat, palais)* to titillate; *(▸ curiosité)* to arouse

4 *(heurter ▸ amour-propre, sensibilité)* to prick

VI *(démanger)* to itch

chatouilleux, -euse [ʃatujø, -øz] ADJ **1** *(physiquement)* ticklish **2** *(pointilleux)* sensitive, touchy; **il a un caractère c.** he's rather touchy; **elle est très chatouilleuse sur ce qu'elle appelle le bon goût** she's very sensitive *or* particular about what she calls good taste

chatouillis [ʃatuji] NM *Fam* tickle; **faire des c. à qn** to tickle sb

chatoyant, -e [ʃatwajɑ̃, -ɑ̃t] ADJ *(étoffe, plumage, couleur)* shimmering; *(pierre)* glistening, sparkling; *Fig (style)* sparkling

chatoyer [13] [ʃatwaje] VI *(étoffe, plumage, couleur)* to shimmer; *(pierre)* to glisten, to sparkle

châtrer [3] [ʃatre] VT **1** *(étalon, verrat)* to geld, to castrate; *(homme, taureau)* to castrate; *(chat)* to neuter, *Am* to fix **2** *(article)* to make innocuous

chatte [ʃat] *voir* **chat**[1]

chattemite [ʃatmit] NF *Littéraire Péj* **faire la c.** to be all sweetness and light

chatter [3] [tʃate] VI *Ordinat (sur l'Internet)* to chat

chatterie [ʃatri] NF **1** *(câlinerie)* coaxing; **faire des chatteries à qn** to pamper sb **2** *(friandise)* delicacy

chatterton [ʃatɛrtɔn] NM *Élec Br* insulating tape, *Am* friction tape

chat-tigre [ʃatigr] *(pl* **chats-tigres)** NM *Zool* tiger cat

CHAUD, -E [ʃo, ʃod] ADJ **1** *(dont la température est ▸ douce)* warm; *(▸ élevée)* hot; **climat/temps/vent c.** *(tempéré)* warm climate/weather/wind; *(tropical)* hot climate/weather/wind; **un bain c.** a hot bath; **une boisson chaude** a hot drink; **un repas c.** a hot meal; *Culin* **mettre à four c.** cook in a hot oven; **ton thé est à peine c.** your tea is barely warm; **son front est tout c.** his/her forehead is hot; **les nuits deviennent plus chaudes en juin** the nights become warmer in June; **au (moment le) plus c. de la journée** in the heat of the day; **marrons chauds** roasted chestnuts; **c. comme une caille** snug as a bug in a rug; **c. devant!** *(au restaurant)* excuse me! *(said by waiters carrying plates to clear the way)*

2 *(veste, couverture)* warm

3 *(qui n'a pas refroidi)* warm; **le lit est encore c.** the bed is still warm; *Fig* **la place du directeur est encore chaude** the manager's shoes are still warm

4 *(ardent ▸ ambiance)* warm; *(▸ partisan)* keen, ardent; *(▸ défenseur)* ardent; **avoir une chaude discussion sur qch** to debate sth heatedly; *Fam* **je ne suis pas très c. pour le faire** I'm not really keen to do it; **son accueil n'a pas été très c.** he/she didn't welcome us too warmly; **avoir un tempérament c.** to be hot-tempered

5 *(agité, dangereux)* hot; **les quartiers chauds** the rough areas; **les points chauds du monde** the world's hot spots *or* flash points; **le mois de septembre sera c.** there will be (political) unrest in September; **l'alerte a été chaude** it was a near *or* close thing

6 *Fam (récent)* hot (off the press); **une nouvelle toute chaude** an up-to-the-minute piece of news

7 *très Fam (sexuellement)* hot, horny; **c. lapin** randy devil

8 *(couleur, voix)* warm

9 *Can Fam (ivre)* wasted, *Br* pissed

NM **1** *(chaleur)* **le c.** the heat *or* hot weather

2 *Méd* **un c. et froid** a chill

ADV hot; **servir c.** serve hot; **j'aime manger c.** I like my food hot; **bois-le c.** drink it (while it's) hot; **avoir c.** *(douce chaleur)* to be warm; *(forte chaleur)* to be hot; **il fait c.** *(douce chaleur)* it's warm; *(forte chaleur)* it's hot; *Fam* **on a eu c. (aux fesses)!** that was a close *or* near thing!; **il fera c. le jour où tu l'entendras dire merci!** that'll be the day when you hear him/her say thank you!; **ça ne me fait ni c. ni froid** I couldn't care less

• **chaude** NF **1** *Métal* heat, melt; **chaude blanche/rouge** white/red heat **2** *Vulg* horny babe

• **à chaud** ADV **1** *(sans préparation)* **l'opération s'est faite à c.** it was emergency surgery; **ne lui pose pas la question à c.** don't just spring the question on him/her **2** *Métal* **souder à c.** to hot-weld; **étirer un métal à c.** to draw metal under heat; **travailler un métal à c.** to hot-work a metal

• **au chaud** ADV **restez bien au c.** *(au lit)* stay nice and cosy *or* warm in your bed; *(sans sortir)* don't go out in the cold; **mettre** *ou* **garder des assiettes au c.** to keep plates warm

chaudasse [ʃodas] *Vulg* ADJ hot, horny

NF horny bitch

chaudement [ʃodmɑ̃] ADV **1** *(contre le froid)* warmly; **se vêtir c.** to put on warm clothes, to dress warmly **2** *(chaleureusement ▸ gén)* warmly, warmheartedly; *(▸ recommander)* heartily; *(▸ féliciter)* warmly

chaude-pisse [ʃodpis] *(pl* **chaudes-pisses)** NF *Vulg* clap

chaud-froid [ʃofrwa] *(pl* **chauds-froids)** NM *Culin* chaudfroid

chaudière [ʃodjɛr] NF **1** *(de chauffage)* boiler; **c. à bois/charbon** wood-/coal-fired boiler; **c. accumulatrice de chaleur** heat storage vessel; **c. à eau chaude** hot water boiler; **c. à vapeur** steam boiler; **c. nucléaire** nuclear-powered boiler **2** *Arch (chaudron)* copper **3** *Can (seau)* bucket; **c. à sucre** = bucket for collecting maple sap

chaudron [ʃodrɔ̃] NM **1** *(récipient)* cauldron **2** *Can (marmite)* cooking pot

chaudronnerie [ʃodrɔnri] NF **1** *(profession)* boilermaking, boilerwork **2** *(marchandises ▸ de grande taille)* boilers; *(▸ de petite taille)* hollowware **3** *(usine)* boilerworks

chaudronnier, -ère [ʃodrɔnje, -ɛr] NM,F *(gén)* boilermaker; *(sur du cuivre)* coppersmith

ADJ **industrie chaudronnière** boilermaking

chauffage [ʃofaʒ] NM **1** *(d'un lieu)* heating; **système de c.** heating system **2** *(installation, système)* heating (system); *(dans une voiture)* heater; **installer le c.** to put heating in; **mettre le c.** to put *or* turn the heating on; **baisser/monter le c.** *(dans une maison)* to turn the heating down/up; *(en voiture)* to turn the heater down/up; **c. central/urbain** central/district heating; **c. électrique/solaire** electric/solar heating; **c. au gaz/au mazout** gas-fired/oil-fired heating; **c. par le sol** underfloor heating

chauffagiste [ʃofaʒist] NM heating engineer

chauffant, -e [ʃofɑ̃, -ɑ̃t] ADJ *(surface)* heating

chauffard [ʃofar] NM reckless driver; *(qui s'enfuit)* hit-and-run driver

chauffe [ʃof] NF **1** *(opération)* stoking; **chef de c.** head stoker **2** *(temps)* heating time; **pendant la c.** *(d'une machine)* while the machine's warming up; *(d'une chaudière)* while the boiler's heating

• **de chauffe** ADJ boiler *(avant n)*

chauffe-assiettes [ʃofasjɛt] NM INV plate warmer

chauffe-bain [ʃofbɛ̃] *(pl* **chauffe-bains)** NM water heater

chauffe-biberon [ʃofbibrɔ̃] *(pl* **chauffe-biberons)** NM bottle warmer

chauffe-eau [ʃofo] NM INV water heater; **c. électrique** immersion heater

chauffe-moteur [ʃofmɔtœr] *(pl* **chauffe-moteurs)** NM *Aut* (engine) block heater

chauffe-pieds [ʃofpje] NM INV footwarmer

chauffe-plat [ʃofpla] *(pl* **chauffe-plats)** NM chafing dish

chauffer [3] [ʃofe] VI **1** *(eau, plat, préparation)* to heat up; **mettre qch à c., faire c. qch** to heat sth up

2 *(dégager de la chaleur ▸ radiateur)* to give out heat; **ce radiateur chauffe bien/mal** this radiator gives out/doesn't give out a lot of heat; **en avril, le soleil commence à c.** in April, the sun gets hotter

3 *(surchauffer ▸ moteur)* to overheat; **faire c. sa voiture** to warm up one's car; **ne laissez pas c. l'élément** don't allow the element to overheat *or* to get too hot

4 *Fam (être agité)* **ça commence à c.** things are getting heated; **ça va c.!** there's trouble brewing!; **je**

te promets que ça va c. s'il est en retard! I promise you there'll be trouble if he's late!; **ça chauffe** *(à un concert)* things are really cooking

5 *(dans un jeu)* to get warm; **tu chauffes!** you're getting warmer!

6 *Can Fam (conduire)* to drive

VT 1 *(chambre, plat)* to warm *or* to heat up; **c. une maison à l'électricité** to have electric heating; **la chambre n'est pas chauffée** there's no heating in the bedroom, the bedroom's not heated; **piscine chauffée** heated swimming pool

2 *Métal* **c. un métal à blanc/au rouge** to make a metal white-hot/red-hot

3 *(moteur)* to warm up; *(chaudière, locomotive)* to fire, to stoke

4 *Fam (exciter)* **c. la salle** to warm up the audience; **il a chauffé la salle à blanc** *ou* **à bloc** he worked the audience up into a frenzy; **c. un étudiant pour un examen** to cram a student for an exam

5 *Fam (locution)* **tu commences à me c. les oreilles** you're starting to get my goat, *Br* you're getting up my nose

VPR se chauffer 1 *(se réchauffer)* to warm oneself (up); **viens te c. près du feu** come and warm yourself up *or* get warm by the fire **2** *(dans un local)* **ils n'ont pas les moyens de se c.** they can't afford heating; **se c. à l'électricité** to have electric heating **3** *(s'échauffer)* to warm up

chaufferette [ʃofrɛt] **NF** *(bouillotte, boîte)* foot-warmer

chaufferie [ʃofri] **NF 1** *(local)* boiler room **2** *Naut & Nucl* stokehold

chauffeur [ʃofœr] **NM 1** *(conducteur)* driver; **c. (routier), c. de camion** truck *or Br* lorry driver; **c. de taxi** taxi *or* cab driver; *Péj* **c. du dimanche** Sunday driver

2 *(employé)* chauffeur; **location de voiture avec c.** chauffeur-driven *Br* hire cars *or Am* rental cars; *Fam* **j'ai fait le c. de ces dames toute la journée** I drove the ladies around all day long; **c. de maître** chauffeur

3 *(d'une locomotive)* stoker

4 *TV* **c. de salle** warm-up man

chauffeuse [ʃoføz] **NF** low armless chair

chaulage [ʃolaʒ] **NM 1** *Agr* liming **2** *Constr* whitewashing

chauler [3] [ʃole] **VT 1** *Agr* to lime **2** *Constr* to whitewash

chaume [ʃom] **NM 1** *(sur un toit)* thatch; **recouvrir un toit de c.** to thatch a roof **2** *Littéraire (champ)* stubble field

chaumer [3] [ʃome] *Agr* **VT** *(champs)* to clear stubble from, to clear of stubble

VI to clear stubble

chaumière [ʃomjɛr] **NF** ≃ cottage; *(avec un toit de chaume)* thatched cottage; **faire causer** *ou* **jaser dans les chaumières** to give the neighbours something to talk about; **un roman à faire pleurer dans les chaumières** a tear-jerking novel

chaussant, -e [ʃosɑ̃, -ɑ̃t] **ADJ** *(botte, soulier)* well-fitting

chaussée [ʃose] **NF 1** *(d'une route)* roadway, *Am* pavement; **c. déformée** *(sur panneau)* uneven road surface; **c. glissante** *(sur panneau)* slippery road, slippery when wet **2** *(talus)* dyke, embankment; *(voie surélevée)* causeway; **la c. des Géants** the Giant's Causeway **3** *(écueil)* reef, line of rocks

chausse-pied [ʃospje] *(pl* **chausse-pieds) NM** shoehorn

chausser [3] [ʃose] **VT 1** *(escarpins, skis, palmes)* to put on; *Sport* **c. les étriers** to put one's feet into the stirrups; **elle était chaussée de pantoufles de soie** she was wearing silk slippers

2 *(enfant, personne)* **viens c. les enfants** come and put the children's shoes on for them

3 *(fournir en chaussures)* to provide shoes for, to supply with shoes; **je suis difficile à c.** it's hard for me to find shoes that fit

4 *(aller à)* to fit; **ce modèle te chausse mieux que l'autre** this style fits you better than the other one

5 *(lunettes)* to put *or* to slip on

6 *Aut* **la voiture est chaussée de pneus neige** the car has snow tyres on

7 *Hort (arbre, plante)* to earth up

VI voici un modèle qui devrait mieux c. this style of shoe should fit better; **ces chaussures chaussent petit** these shoes are small to size; **du combien chausses-tu?** what size shoes do you take?; **je chausse du 38** I take a size 38 (shoe)

VPR se chausser 1 *(emploi réfléchi)* **chausse-toi, il fait froid** put something on your feet, it's cold; **il se chausse tout seul maintenant** he can put his shoes on all by himself now **2** *(se fournir)* **je me chausse chez Lebel** I buy my shoes at *or* I get my shoes from Lebel's

chausses [ʃos] **NFPL** *Arch* hose, chausses

chausse-trape, chausse-trappe [ʃostrap] *(pl* **chausse-trapes** *ou* **chausse-trappes) NF** *aussi Fig* trap

chaussette [ʃosɛt] **NF 1** *(pièce d'habillement)* sock; **une paire de chaussettes** a pair of socks; **en chaussettes** in one's stockinged feet; *Fam* **laisser tomber qn comme une vieille c.** to ditch sb; **chaussettes de contention** support socks **2** *Fam Vieilli* **c. à clous** (policeman's) boot

chausseur [ʃosœr] **NM 1** *(fabricant)* shoemaker **2** *(vendeur)* shoemaker, footwear specialist; *(magasin) Br* shoe shop, *Am* shoe store

chausson¹ [ʃosɔ̃] **NM 1** *(d'intérieur)* slipper; *(de bébé)* bootee

2 *(de danseuse)* ballet shoe, pump; *(de gymnastique)* soft shoe; *(dans la chaussure de ski)* inner shoe

3 *Culin* turnover; **c. aux pommes** apple turnover

4 *Couture* **point de c.** blind hem stitch

chausson², -onne [ʃosɔ̃, -ɔn] **NM,F** *Can Fam* twit, idiot

chaussure [ʃosyr] **NF 1** *(gén)* shoe; **une paire de chaussures** a pair of shoes; **chaussures basses** shoes; **chaussures à lacets** lace-ups; **chaussures montantes** ankle boots; **chaussures plates** flat shoes, flats; **chaussures à semelles compensées** platform shoes; **chaussures à talons** (shoes with) heels; **chaussures de ville** town shoes; *Fig* **trouver c. à son pied** to find a suitable match; **elle a trouvé c. à son pied** she found her Mr Right **2** *Sport* **chaussures de marche** *ou* **de montagne** walking *or* hiking boots; **chaussures de ski** ski boots; **chaussures de sport** sports shoes, *Br* trainers, *Am* sneakers **3** *Com* shoe *or* footwear trade; *(industrie)* shoe *or* footwear industry

chaut *voir* **chaloir**

chauve [ʃov] **ADJ** *(crâne, tête)* bald; *(personne)* bald, baldheaded; *(montagne, pic)* bare; *Fam* **c. comme un œuf** *ou* **une bille** *ou* **un genou** as bald *Br* as a coot *or Am* as an egg

NMF bald person, bald man, *f* woman

chauve-souris [ʃovsuri] *(pl* **chauves-souris) NF** *Zool* bat

chauvin, -e [ʃovɛ̃, -in] **ADJ** chauvinistic, jingoist, jingoistic

NM,F chauvinist, jingoist

> Il faut noter que le nom anglais **chauvinist** est un faux ami. Il est désormais employé le plus souvent dans le sens de **phallocrate**.

chauvinisme [ʃovinism] **NM** chauvinism, jingoism

> Il faut noter que le nom anglais **chauvinism** est un faux ami. Il signifie le plus souvent **phallocratie**.

chaux [ʃo] **NF** lime; **mur passé** *ou* **blanchi à la c.** whitewashed wall; **c. éteinte** slaked lime; **c. vive** quicklime; **bâtir à c. et à sable** to build firmly *or* solidly; **être bâti à c. et à sable** *(personne)* to have an iron constitution

chavirer [3] [ʃavire] **VI 1** *Naut* to capsize, to keel over; **faire c.** to capsize; **arrête, tu vas faire c. la barque!** stop it, you'll tip the boat over! **2** *(se renverser)* to keel over, to overturn; **tout chavire autour de moi** everything around me is spinning **3** *(tourner ▸ yeux)* to roll; **avoir le cœur qui chavire** *(de dégoût)* to feel nauseated; *(de chagrin)* to be heartbroken

VT 1 *(basculer)* to capsize, to overturn **2** *(émouvoir)* to overwhelm, to shatter; **il a l'air tout chaviré** he looks devastated

chébran [ʃebrɑ̃] **ADJ INV** *Fam (verlan de* **branché**) hip, trendy

chèche [ʃɛʃ] **NM** North African scarf

chéchia [ʃeʃja] **NF** tarboosh, fez

check-list [tʃɛklist] *(pl* **check-lists) NF** *Aviat* checklist

check-point [tʃɛkpɔint] **NM INV** *Mil* checkpoint

check-up [tʃɛkœp] **NM INV** *Méd* check-up; **faire un c. à qn** to give sb a check-up; **le médecin me conseille de faire un c.** the doctor is advising me to have a check-up

chef [ʃɛf] **NM 1** *(responsable ▸ gén)* head; *(▸ d'une entreprise)* manager, boss; *(▸ d'un parti politique)* leader; *(▸ d'une tribu)* chief, chieftain; *Fam (patron)* boss; *Com* **c. des achats** purchasing manager; **c. d'antenne** programme supervisor; **c. d'atelier** shop foreman; **c. de bureau** head clerk; **c. de cabinet** *Br* minister's *or Am* secretary of state's principal private secretary; **c. de chantier** site foreman; **c. chasseur** head porter, *Am* bell captain; **c. de clinique** senior registrar; **c. comptable, c. de la comptabilité** *Br* chief accountant, *Am* chief financial officer; **c. de la diplomatie** foreign minister, *Br* ≃ Foreign Secretary, *Am* ≃ Secretary of State; *Scol* head of the family; **c. de l'Église** Head of the Church; **c. d'entreprise** company manager; **c. d'établissement** *Br* headmaster, *f* headmistress, *Am* principal; **c. de l'État** Head of the State; **chefs d'État** heads of state; **c. d'équipe** foreman; **c. de fabrication** production manager, manufacturing manager; **c. de famille** **c. de file** *Mktg (produit)* leader; *Banque & Bourse* lead manager; **c. du gouvernement** head of government; *Mktg* **c. de marque** brand manager; *TV & Cin* **c. opérateur** cinematographer; **c. du personnel** personnel manager, head of personnel; *TV* **c. de plateau** stage manager, floor boss; *Com* **c. de produit** product manager; **c. de projet** project manager; *Com* **c. de (la) publicité** publicity manager; **c. de rang** head waiter; **c. de rayon** *(dans un magasin)* department manager; *Com* **c. de service** *(dans une société)* department manager; *Ordinat* **c. des traitements** data processing manager; *Com* **c. des ventes** sales manager; *Com* **c. de zone** area manager

2 *Mil* **c. de bataillon** ≃ major; **c. d'état-major** chief of staff; **c. d'État-major de l'armée de l'air** *Br* ≃ Marshal of the Royal Air Force, *Am* ≃ General of the Air Force; **c. de patrouille** patrol leader; **c. de pièce** gun captain; **c. de section** platoon commander; *(Aviat)* flight commander

3 *Rail* **c. de gare** station master; **c. mécanicien** chief mechanic; **c. de train** guard, *Am* conductor

4 *Culin* **c. (cuisinier** *ou* **de cuisine)** (head) chef, chef de cuisine; **la spécialité du c. aujourd'hui** the chef's special today; **c. pâtissier** chef patissier, pastry chef

5 *Mus* **c. de pupitre** head of section; **c. des chœurs** choirmaster

6 *(en aviron)* **c. de nage** stroke; **être c. de nage** to row stroke

7 *(leader)* leader; **elle a toutes les qualités d'un c.** she has all the qualities of a leader; *Hum* **bravo, c'est toi le c.!** well done, boss!; *Hum* **c. de bande** gang leader; **c. de file** leader; *Péj* **petit c.** *(dans une famille)* domestic tyrant; *(au bureau, à l'usine)* slave driver; **une mentalité de petit c.** a petty-minded attitude to one's subordinates; *Fam* **elle s'est débrouillée comme un c.!** she did really well!

8 *(comme adj)* head *(avant n)*, chief *(avant n)*; **infirmière c.** head nurse; **ingénieur c.** chief engineer

9 *Littéraire & Hum (tête)* head; **opiner du c.** to nod

10 *Jur* **c. d'accusation** charge *or* count (of indictment)

NF *Fam (responsable)* **la c.** the boss

• **au premier chef ADV** above all, first and foremost; **leur décision me concerne au premier c.** their decision has immediate implications for me

• **de mon/son/***etc* **(propre) chef ADV** on my/their/*etc* own authority *or* initiative; **j'ai agi de mon propre c.** I acted on my own initiative

• **en chef ADJ commandant en c.** commander-in-chief; **ingénieur en c.** chief engineer **ADV commander en c.** to be commander-in-chief

• **chef d'orchestre NM 1** *Mus* conductor **2** *Fig* organizer, orchestrator

chefaillon [ʃefajɔ̃] **NM** *Fam* little Hitler

chef-d'œuvre [ʃedœvr] *(pl* **chefs-d'œuvre) NM** masterpiece; **un c. de la littérature** a literary masterpiece

chef-garde [ʃɛfgard] *(pl* **chefs-gardes) NM** *Belg Rail* ticket inspector

chef-lieu [ʃɛfljø] *(pl* **chefs-lieux) NM** *Admin* = in France, administrative centre of a "département", "arrondissement" or "canton"

cheftaine [ʃɛftɛn] **NF** *(de louveteaux) Br* cubmistress, *Am* den mother; *(chez les jeannettes) Br* Brown Owl, *Am* den mother; *(chez les éclaireuses)* captain

cheik, cheikh [ʃɛk] **NM** sheik, sheikh

chelem [ʃlɛm] **NM** *Sport & Cartes* slam; **grand c.** grand slam; **petit c.** small *or* little slam

chelou [ʃəlu] **ADJ INV** *Fam (verlan de* **louche)** shady, seedy, *Br* dodgy

chemin [ʃəmɛ̃] **NM 1** *(allée)* path, lane; **c. creux** sunken lane; **c. de halage** towpath; **c. de ronde** covered way; **c. de terre** rough *or* dirt track; **c. de traverse** path across the fields; *Fig* short cut; **c. vicinal** *ou* **départemental** minor road; **être toujours sur les (quatre) chemins** *ou* **par voies et par chemins** to be always on the move *or* road; *Prov* **tous les chemins mènent à Rome** all roads lead to Rome

2 *(parcours, trajet)* way; **faire** *ou* **abattre du c.** to go a long way; **le c. que nous avons fait** *ou* **abattu** the long way we've come *or* distance we've covered; *aussi Fig* **nous avons beaucoup de c. à faire** we've a long way to go; **nous avons fait la moitié du c. ensemble/à pied** we went half the way together/on foot; **nous avons déjà fait la moitié du c.** we're already halfway there; **il faut compter deux ou trois heures de c.** it takes two or three hours to get there; **on s'est retrouvés à mi-c.** *ou* **à moitié c.** we met halfway; **le c. de la gare** the way to the station; **suivre le c. de la balle** *(au tennis)* to follow the path of the ball; **demandons-lui notre c.** let's ask him/her the way *or* how to get there; **pas de problème, c'est sur mon c.** no problem, it's on my way; **c'est le c. le plus court/long** it's the shortest/longest way; **le plus court c. d'un point à un autre** the shortest distance between two points; **le c. de la gloire/réussite** the road to glory/success; **nous avons fait tout le c. à pied/en voiture** we walked/drove all the way; **se frayer** *ou* **s'ouvrir un c. dans la foule** to force one's way through the crowd; **barrer** *ou* **couper le c. à qn** to be in *or* to bar sb's way; *Vieilli* **passer son c.** to go on one's way; **passez votre c.!** on your way!; **prendre le c. de l'exil** to go into exile; *Fig* **prendre des chemins détournés pour faire qch** to use roundabout means in order to do sth; **par un c. détourné** by a roundabout route; *Fig* in a roundabout way; **prendre le c. des écoliers** to go the long way around; **je voudrais des petits-enfants mais ça n'en prend pas le c.** I'd like grandchildren but it doesn't seem to be on the agenda; *Littéraire* **le c. de velours** *ou* **de fleurs** *ou* **fleuri** the primrose path, the easy way

3 *(destinée, progression)* way; **barrer** *ou* **couper le c. à qn** to bar sb's way, to impede sb's progress; **ouvrir/montrer le c.** to open/to lead the way; **il va son c. sans se préoccuper des autres** he goes his own way without worrying about other people; **nos chemins se sont croisés autrefois** our paths crossed *or* we met a long time ago; **faire son c.** *(personne)* to make one's way in life; *(idée)* to gain ground, to catch on; **cet enfant fera du c., croyez-moi!** this child will go far *or* a long way, believe me!; **mettre un obstacle sur le c. de qn** to put an obstacle in sb's way; **se mettre sur le c. de qn** to stand in sb's way; **trouver qn sur son c.** *(ennemi)* to find sb standing in one's way; *Bible* **le c. de Damas** the road to Damascus; *Fig* **trouver son c. de Damas** to see the light; **le bon c.** the right track; **leur affaire est en bon c.** their business is off to a good start; **ne t'arrête pas en si bon c.** don't give up now that you're doing so well; **le droit c.** the straight and narrow

4 *Rel* **c. de croix** Way of the Cross

5 *(napperon)* **c. de table** table runner

6 *Ordinat* path; **c. d'accès** path; **c. d'accès aux données** data path; **c. du courrier électronique** mail path

7 *(en sciences)* **c. critique** critical path

8 *Tech* **c. de roulement** ball race

• **chemin faisant ADV** while going along; **nous en avons parlé c. faisant** we talked about it on our way there

• **en chemin ADV** on one's way, on the way; **ne t'amuse pas en c.** don't mess around on the way; **se mettre en c.** to set out *or* off

chemin de fer [ʃəmɛ̃dfɛr] *(pl* **chemins de fer) NM 1** *Rail Br* railway, *Am* railroad; **voyager en c.** to travel by train; **employé des chemins de fer** *Br* railwayman, rail worker, *Am* railroad worker **2** *Cartes* chemin de fer **3** *Typ* page plan

chemineau, -x [ʃəmino] **NM** *Vieilli* tramp, vagrant, *Am* hobo

cheminée [ʃəmine] **NF 1** *(gén)* shaft; *(de maison)* chimney (stack); *(dans un mur)* chimney; *(d'usine)* chimney (stack), smokestack; *(de paquebot)* funnel; **c. d'aération** ventilation shaft **2** *(âtre)* fireplace; *(chambranle)* mantelpiece; **viens te réchauffer près de la c.** come and get warm by the fire *or* fireplace; **un feu dans la c.** a fire in the grate **3** *Géol (d'un volcan)* vent; *(d'un massif)* chimney; **c. des fées** devil's chimney

cheminement [ʃəminmɑ̃] **NM 1** *(parcours)* movement; **le c. des eaux souterraines** the movement of underground water **2** *Fig (développement)* development, unfolding; **le c. de sa pensée** the development of his/her thought **3** *Mil* advance (under cover)

cheminer [3] [ʃəmine] **VI 1** *Littéraire (avancer ▸ marcheur)* to walk along; *(▸ eau, fleuve)* to flow; **la caravane chemine dans le désert** the caravan makes its way through the desert; **ils cheminaient avec difficulté à travers bois** they struggled through the woods **2** *Fig (progresser ▸ régulièrement)* to progress, to develop; *(▸ lentement)* to make slow progress *or* headway **3** *Mil* to advance (under cover)

cheminot [ʃəmino] **NM** *Rail Br* railwayman, *Am* railroad man

chemisage [ʃəmizaʒ] **NM** *Tech* **1** *(d'un projectile)* jacketing **2** *(d'un conduit, d'un moule)* lining

chemise [ʃəmiz] **NF 1** *(vêtement)* shirt; **c. à manches longues/courtes** long-/short-sleeved shirt; **c. américaine** vest, *Am* undershirt; **c. de nuit** *(de femme)* nightgown, nightdress; *(d'homme)* nightshirt; **en (bras** *ou* **manches de) c.** in shirt-sleeves; **il donnerait jusqu'à sa c.** he'd give the shirt off his back; *Fig* **ils ne lui ont laissé que sa c.** they took everything but what he stood up in; *Fam* **je m'en fiche** *ou* **soucie** *or* **moque comme de ma première c.** I couldn't care less about it; **perdre au jeu jusqu'à sa dernière c.** to gamble one's last *Br* penny *or Am* cent away

2 *Hist* **Chemises brunes** Brownshirts; **Chemises noires** Blackshirts; **Chemises rouges** Redshirts

3 *(de carton)* folder

4 *Tech (enveloppe ▸ intérieure)* lining; *(▸ extérieure)* jacket; *(▸ d'un mur)* facing; *Aut* **c. flottante/humide/sèche** slip/wet/dry liner

chemiser [3] [ʃəmize] **VT** *Tech (intérieurement)* to line; *(extérieurement)* to jacket

chemiserie [ʃəmizri] **NF 1** *(fabrique)* shirt factory **2** *(boutique) Br* men's outfitter's, *Am* haberdasher's **3** *(industrie)* shirt trade

chemisette [ʃəmizɛt] **NF** *(pour femme)* short-sleeved blouse; *(pour homme, pour enfant)* short-sleeved shirt

chemisier, -ère [ʃəmizje, -ɛr] **NM,F** *(fabricant) Br* shirtmaker, *Am* haberdasher; *(marchand) Br* men's outfitter, *Am* haberdasher

NM blouse

chênaie [ʃɛnɛ] **NF** stand of oak trees

chenal, -aux [ʃənal, -o] **NM 1** *(canal ▸ dans les terres)* channel; *(▸ dans un port)* fairway, channel **2** *Géol (sous la mer)* trench **3** *(de moulin)* millrace

chenapan [ʃənapɑ̃] **NM** *Hum* rascal, rogue, scoundrel

chêne [ʃɛn] **NM 1** *Bot* oak; **c. vert** holm oak, ilex; **fort** *ou* **solide comme un c.** as strong as an ox **2** *Menuis* oak; **une table en c. massif** a solid oak table

chéneau, -x [ʃeno] **NM** gutter *(on a roof)*

chêneau, -x [ʃeno] **NM** oak sapling

chêne-liège [ʃɛnljɛʒ] *(pl* **chênes-lièges) NM** *Bot* cork oak

chenet [ʃənɛ] **NM** andiron, firedog

chènevière [ʃɛnvjɛr] **NF** hemp field

chènevis [ʃɛnvi] **NM** hempseed

cheni, chenil[1] [ʃni] **NM** *Suisse Fam* **1** *(balayures)* sweepings; *(débris, déchets) Br* rubbish, *Am* garbage **2** *(désordre)* mess, shambles *(singulier)* **3** *(objets sans valeur)* junk, stuff

chenil[2] [ʃənil, ʃəni] **NM** *(établissement ▸ pour la reproduction)* breeding kennels; *(▸ pour la garde)* boarding kennels; *(▸ pour le dressage)* training kennels

chenille [ʃənij] **NF 1** *Entom* caterpillar; **c. processionnaire** processionary caterpillar **2** *Tech* caterpillar; **véhicule à chenilles** tracked vehicle **3** *Tex* chenille

chenillé, -e [ʃənije] **ADJ** *(engin, véhicule)* tracked

chenillette [ʃənijɛt] **NF** *Mil* small tracked vehicle; *(pour neige)* snowmobile

chenis, chenit [ʃni] = **cheni**

chenu, -e [ʃəny] **ADJ** *Littéraire* **1** *(vieillard)* hoary **2** *(arbre)* bald *or* leafless (with age), *Spéc* glabrous

cheptel [ʃɛptɛl] **NM 1** *(bétail)* stock, livestock; **le c. bovin de la France** France's national herd **2** *Jur* **c. (vif)** livestock; **c. mort** farm equipment

chèque [ʃɛk] **NM 1** *Fin & Banque Br* cheque, *Am* check; **faire** *ou* **remplir un c.** to write (out) *or* make out a cheque; **faire un c. de 100 euros à qn** to write sb a cheque for 100 euros; **tirer/toucher un c.** to draw/to cash a cheque; **établir** *ou* **libeller un c. à l'ordre de qn** to make a cheque out to sb; **faire opposition à un c.** to stop a cheque; **payer** *ou* **régler par c.** to pay by cheque; **refuser d'honorer un c.** to refer a cheque to drawer; **remettre** *ou* **déposer un c. à la banque** to pay a cheque into the bank; **c. bancaire** cheque; **c. de banque** banker's cheque, banker's draft, *Am* cashier's check; **c. barré** crossed cheque; **c. en blanc** blank cheque; *Fig* **donner un c. en blanc à qn** to give sb carte blanche; *Fam* **c. en bois** *Br* dud cheque, *Am* bad check; **c. certifié** certified cheque; **c. que hors-place** = cheque drawn on a bank in a different "département" from the bank in which it is cashed; **c. non barré** uncrossed cheque; **c. à ordre** cheque to order; **c. ouvert** open cheque; **c. périmé** out-of-date cheque; **c. au porteur** bearer cheque, cheque made payable to bearer; **c. postal** = cheque drawn on the postal banking system, *Br* ≃ Giro (cheque); **c. postdaté** post-dated cheque; **c. sans provision** bad cheque; **il a fait un c. sans provision** his cheque bounced; **c. de voyage** traveller's cheque **2** *(bon, coupon)* **un c. d'une valeur de 40 euros** a gift token to the value of 40 euros; **c. de caisse** credit voucher; **c. emploi-service** = special cheque used to pay casual workers such as part-time cleaners, babysitters etc

chèque-cadeau [ʃɛkkado] *(pl* **chèques-cadeaux) NM** *Br* gift token, gift voucher, *Am* gift certificate; **un c. d'une valeur de 40 euros** a gift *Br* token *or* voucher *or Am* certificate to the value of 40 euros

chèque-dividende [ʃɛkdividɑ̃d] *(pl* **chèques-dividende) NM** *Fin* dividend warrant

chèque-livre [ʃɛklivr] *(pl* **chèques-livre) NM** book token

chèque-repas [ʃɛkrəpa] *(pl* **chèques-repas) NM** *Br* ≃ luncheon voucher, *Am* ≃ meal ticket

chéquier [ʃekje] **NM** *Br* chequebook, *Am* checkbook

CHER, CHÈRE[1] [ʃɛr] **ADJ 1** *(aimé)* dear; **elle m'est plus chère qu'une sœur** she's dearer to me than a sister; **ceux qui vous sont chers** your loved ones, the ones you love; **un être c.** a loved one

2 *(dans des formules de politesse)* dear; **c. Monsieur, chère Madame** dear Sir, dear Madam; **bonjour, chère Madame** hello, my dear lady; **mon c. ami** my dear friend; **bien chers tous** dearest friends; *Hum ou Ironique* **le c. homme n'a pas compris** the dear man didn't understand; **cette chère Marie!** dear old Marie!

3 *(précieux)* dear, beloved; **il a retrouvé sa chère**

maison/son c. bureau he's back in his beloved house/office; **la formule si chère aux hommes politiques** the phrase beloved of politicians, that favourite phrase of politicians; **mon souhait le plus c.** my dearest *or* most devout wish

4 *(onéreux)* expensive, *Br* dear; **la vie est chère en ville** it's expensive living in town, the cost of living is high in town(s); **c'est plus c.** it's more expensive *or Br* dearer; **c'est moins c.** it's cheaper *or* less expensive; **un petit restaurant pas c.** an inexpensive little restaurant

NM,F mon c. my dear (fellow); **ma chère** my dear (girl); **ah ma chère! quel plaisir de vous voir!** how nice to see you, my dear!

ADV 1 *Com* **coûter c.** to cost a lot, to be expensive; **payer qch c./trop c.** to pay a high price/too much for sth; **est-ce que ça te revient c.?** does it cost you a lot?; **ça me revient trop c.** it's too expensive for me, I can't afford it; *Fam* **prendre c.** to charge a lot; **il te prend c.?** does he charge you a lot?; **tu ne prends pas assez c.** you don't charge enough; **il vaut c.** *(bijou de famille)* it's valuable *or* worth a lot; *(article en magasin)* it's expensive; *Fam* **je l'ai eu pour pas c.** I didn't pay much for it[□], I got it cheap; *Fam* **elle vend c.** her prices are high

2 *(locutions)* **je donnerais c. pour le savoir** I'd give anything to know; **je ne donne pas c. de sa vie** I wouldn't give much for his/her chances of survival; **il ne vaut pas c.** he's a good-for-nothing; **et toi, tu ne vaux pas plus c.** and you're no better

chérant, -e [ʃerɑ̃, -ɑ̃t] **ADJ** *Can* pricey, expensive

CHERCHER [3] [ʃɛrʃe]

VT
- to look for **1, 3**
- to search for **1, 2, 4, 5**
- to try to find **2**
- to fetch **6**
- to pick up **6**
- to get **6**

VPR
- to look for each other **1**
- to find oneself **2**

VT 1 *(dans l'espace)* to look for, to search for; **que cherches-tu?** what are you looking for?; **je l'ai cherché partout** I searched *or* looked for it high and low, I hunted for it everywhere; **cherche les clefs dans tes poches** look in your pockets for the keys; **c. un mot dans un dictionnaire** to look up a word in a dictionary; **c. qn du regard** *ou* **des yeux** to look around for sb; **c. qn/qch à tâtons** to fumble *or* to grope for sb/sth; *Fam* **c. la petite bête** to split hairs; *Fam* **c. des poux dans la tête de qn** to try and pick a fight with sb; **cherchez la femme** cherchez la femme

2 *(mentalement)* to try to find, to search for; **c. une solution** to try to find a solution; **je cherche son nom** I'm trying to think of *or* remember his/her name; **c. ses mots** to search for words; *Fam* **c. des crosses** *ou* **des histoires à qn** to try and cause trouble for sb; **c. chicane** *ou* **querelle à qn** to try and pick a quarrel with sb; *Fam* **c. midi à quatorze heures** to look for complications (where there are none); **pas besoin de c. midi à quatorze heures pour expliquer son départ** no need to look too far to understand why he/she left

3 *(essayer de se procurer)* to look for, to hunt for; **je cherche cette édition rare depuis longtemps** I've been hunting for this rare edition for years; **c. du travail** to look for work, to be job-hunting; **c. une maison** to look for a house, to be house-hunting; **il faut vite c. du secours** you must get help quickly; **il est parti c. fortune à l'étranger** he went abroad to look for fame and fortune; **c. refuge auprès de qn** to seek refuge with sb; *Vieilli* **c. femme** to look for a wife

4 *(aspirer à ▸ tranquillité, inspiration)* to look for, to search for, to seek (after); **il ne cherche que son intérêt** he thinks only of his own interests

5 *Fam (provoquer)* to look for; **tu l'as bien cherché!** you asked for it!; **tu me cherches, là?** do you want a fight?; **si tu me cherches, tu vas me trouver!** if you're looking for trouble, you've come to the right place, if you're looking for a fight, you'll get one!; **toujours à c. la bagarre!** always looking *or* spoiling for a fight!

6 *(avec des verbes de mouvement)* **aller c. qn/qch** to fetch sb/sth; **aller c. les enfants à l'école** to pick the children up from school; **aller c. qn à l'aéroport** to go and pick sb up at the airport; **allez me c. le directeur** *(client mécontent)* I'd like to speak to the manager; **aller c. du secours** to go for help, to get help; **envoyer c. qn/qch** to send for sb/sth; **monte/descends c. la valise** go up/down and fetch the suitcase; **viens me c. à 17 heures** come for me at 5 o'clock; *Fig* **que vas-tu c. là?** what on earth are you going on about?; **mais qu'est-ce que tu vas encore c., je n'ai rien dit de mal** now what are you thinking of? I didn't mean anything bad; **où va-t-il donc c. tout ça?** where on earth does he get that from?; **où as-tu été c. que j'avais accepté?** what made you think I said yes?; *Fam* **ça va bien c. dans les 60 euros** it's worth at least 60 euros; *Fam* **ça peut aller c. jusqu'à dix ans de prison** it could get you up to ten years in prison; *Fam* **ça va c. loin, cette histoire** this is a bad business

USAGE ABSOLU tu donnes ta langue au chat? – attends, je cherche give up? – wait, I'm still thinking *or* trying to think; **cherche!** *(à un chien)* fetch!; *Bible* **cherchez et vous trouverez** seek and ye shall find

• **chercher à VT IND** to try to, to attempt to, *Sout* to seek to; **je ne cherche qu'à t'aider** I'm only trying to help you; **c. à plaire** to aim to please; *Fam* **cherche pas à comprendre** don't even try to understand

• **chercher après VT IND** *Fam* to look for, to be *or* to chase after; **je cherche encore après ces maudites lunettes!** I'm still after those damn glasses!

VPR se chercher 1 *(emploi réciproque)* to look for each other; **ils se sont cherchés pendant longtemps** they spent a long time looking for each other **2** *(emploi réfléchi)* to find oneself; **il se cherche** he's trying to find himself

chercheur, -euse [ʃɛrʃœr, -øz] **ADJ** *(esprit, mentalité)* inquiring

NM,F 1 *Univ* researcher, research worker; **travailler comme c.** to be a researcher, to do research **2** *(aventurier)* **c. d'or** gold digger

NM *Astron* **c. de comètes** finder; **c. de fuites** gas leak detector

chère[1] [ʃɛr] **ADJ** *voir* **cher**

chère[2] **NF** *Littéraire ou Hum* food, fare; **la c. y est excellente** the food there is superb; **faire bonne c.** to eat well; **aimer la bonne c.** to be a lover of good food

chèrement [ʃɛrmɑ̃] **ADV 1** *(à un prix élevé)* dearly, at great cost; **la victoire fut c. payée** the victory was won at great cost; **il a payé c. sa liberté** his freedom cost him dearly, he paid a high price for his freedom **2** *Littéraire (tendrement)* dearly, fondly

chéri, -e [ʃeri] **ADJ** darling, dear, *Sout* beloved; **à notre grand-mère chérie** *(au cimetière)* to our beloved grandmother

NM,F 1 *(en appellatif)* darling, honey; **qu'y a-t-il, c.?** what's the matter, darling?; **mon c., je te l'ai dit cent fois** darling, I've already told you a hundred times **2** *(personne préférée)* **il a toujours été le c. de ses parents** he was always the darling of the family

chérif [ʃerif] **NM** *(prince arabe)* sherif, sharif

chérir [32] [ʃerir] **VT** *Littéraire (aimer ▸ personne)* to cherish, to love (dearly); *(▸ démocratie, liberté)* to cherish; *(▸ mémoire, souvenir)* to cherish, to treasure

chérot [ʃero] *Fam* **ADJ INV** pricey, on the pricey side

ADV il vend plutôt c.! his prices are on the stiff side!

cherra *etc voir* **choir**

cherry [ʃeri] *(pl* **cherrys** *ou* **cherries)** **NM** cherry brandy

cherté [ʃɛrte] **NF la c. des fraises** the high price of strawberries; **la c. de la vie** the high cost of living

chérubin [ʃerybɛ̃] **NM 1** *Rel* cherub **2** *(enfant)* cherub

chester [ʃɛstɛr] **NM** Cheshire cheese

chétif, -ive [ʃetif, -iv] **ADJ 1** *(peu robuste)* sickly, puny **2** *Bot* stunted **3** *Littéraire (peu riche ▸ récolte)* meagre, poor; *(▸ existence)* poor, wretched

chétivement [ʃetivmɑ̃] **ADV 1** *(d'une façon malingre)* punily, weakly **2** *(médiocrement, mal)* poorly, miserably

chevaine [ʃəvɛn] **NM** *Ich* chub

cheval, -aux [ʃəval, -o] **NM 1** *(animal)* horse; **c. d'attelage** carthorse, plough horse; **c. de bât** packhorse; *Fig* **c. de bataille** hobbyhorse, pet subject; **c. de chasse** hunter; **c. de cirque** circus horse; **c. de course** racehorse; **c. de labour** plough horse; **c. de manège** school horse; **c. marin** *(hippocampe)* sea horse; **c. pur sang** thoroughbred (horse); **c. de retour** *(récidiviste)* recidivist; **c. de rodéo** rodeo horse, bucking bronco; **c. de selle** saddle horse; **c. de trait** draught horse; **changer** *ou* **échanger** *ou* **troquer son c. borgne pour un aveugle** to jump out of frying pan into the fire; **travailler comme un c.** to work like a dog *or* slave; *Prov* **à c. donné on ne regarde pas la bouche** don't look a gift horse in the mouth; *Fig* **monter sur ses grands chevaux** to get on one's high horse; **ce n'est pas un** *ou* **le mauvais c.** he's not a bad guy *or* sort; **ça ne se trouve pas sous le pas** *ou* **sabot d'un c.** it doesn't grow on trees

2 *Équitation* (horseback) riding; **elle aime beaucoup le c.** she loves riding; **faire du c.** to ride, to go riding

3 *(loisirs)* **c. à bascule** rocking horse; **c. de bois** wooden horse; **faire un tour sur les chevaux de bois** to go on the roundabout *or* carousel; **jouer aux petits chevaux** ≃ to play ludo

4 *Aut & Admin* **c. fiscal** horsepower *(for tax purposes)*; *Fam* **une voiture de 20 chevaux, une 20 chevaux** a 20 horsepower car

5 *Antiq* **le c. de Troie** the Trojan horse

6 *(viande)* horsemeat

• **à cheval ADV 1** *Équitation* on horseback; **aller à c.** to ride; **aller au village à c.** to ride to the village, to go to the village on horseback; **traverser une rivière à c.** to ride across a river; **se tenir bien/mal à c.** to have a good/poor seat, to sit a horse well/badly **2** *(à califourchon)* **être à c. sur une chaise** to be sitting astride a chair; **l'étang est à c. sur deux propriétés** the pond straddles two properties; **mon congé est à c. sur février et mars** my period of leave starts in February and ends in March **3** *Fam (pointilleux)* **être à c. sur** to be particular about; **ils sont très à c. sur la tenue** they're very particular about dress **ADJ gendarme à c.** mounted policeman; **une promenade à c.** a ride; **faire une promenade à c.** to go for a ride, to go horseriding

• **de cheval ADJ 1** *Culin* horse *(avant n)*, horsemeat *(avant n)* **2** *Fam (fort)* **fièvre de c.** raging fever; **remède de c.** drastic remedy **3** *Péj (dents)* horsey, horselike

cheval-d'arçons [ʃəvaldarsɔ̃] **NM INV** *Gym* vaulting horse

chevaler [3] [ʃəvale] **VT** *Constr* to shore up

chevaleresque [ʃəvalrɛsk] **ADJ 1** *(généreux)* chivalrous; **agir de façon c.** to behave like a gentleman **2** *(des chevaliers)* **l'honneur/le devoir c.** a knight's honour/duty

chevalerie [ʃəvalri] **NF 1** *(ordre)* knighthood **2** *(institution)* chivalry; *Littérature* **roman de c.** romance of chivalry

chevalet [ʃəvalɛ] **NM 1** *(d'un peintre)* easel

2 *(support)* stand, trestle; **c. de scieur** sawbench, sawhorse

3 *Mus* bridge

4 *Hist (de torture)* rack

chevalier [ʃəvalje] **NM 1** *Hist* knight; **il a été fait c.** he was knighted; **c. errant** knight-errant; **c. d'industrie** wheeler-dealer; **c. servant** (devoted) escort; **les chevaliers de la Table ronde** the Knights of the Round Table

2 *(grade)* **c. de la Légion d'honneur** chevalier of the Legion of Honour

3 *Orn (Tringa hypoleucos)* sandpiper; *(Tringa nebularia)* greenshank

4 *Bourse* **c. blanc** white knight; **c. gris** grey knight; **c. noir** black knight

chevalière [ʃəvaljɛr] **NF** signet ring

chevalin, -e [ʃəvalɛ̃, -in] **ADJ 1** *(race)* equine **2** *(air, allure, visage)* horsey, horselike

cheval-vapeur [ʃəvalvapœr] *(pl* **chevaux-vapeur** [ʃəvovapœr]) **NM** horsepower

chevauchant, -e [ʃəvoʃɑ̃, -ɑ̃t] **ADJ** overlapping

chevauchée [ʃəvoʃe] **NF 1** *(course à cheval)* ride **2** *(personne)* cavalcade

chevauchement [ʃəvoʃmɑ̃] **NM 1** *(superposition)* overlap, overlapping; **pour éviter tout c. dans l'emploi du temps des élèves** to avoid clashes between subjects in the students' timetable
2 *Constr* spanning
3 *Géol* thrust fault
4 *Typ* falling *or* dropping out of place

chevaucher [3] [ʃəvoʃe] **VT 1** *(monter sur ▸ cheval, moto, balai)* to sit astride; *(▸ chaise)* to sit astride, to straddle; *(▸ vague)* to ride **2** *(recouvrir en partie)* to overlap
VI 1 *(se recouvrir en partie)* to overlap **2** *Typ* to fall *or* drop out of place **3** *Littérature* to ride (a horse)
VPR se chevaucher *(être superposé ▸ dents)* to grow into each other; *(▸ tuiles)* to overlap; **mon cours et le sien se chevauchent** my lesson overlaps with his/hers

chevau-léger [ʃəvoleʒe] *(pl* **chevau-légers)** **NM** *Hist & Mil* **1** *(soldat)* light horseman, *Br* ≃ member of the Household Cavalry **2** *(corps)* **les chevau-légers** light horse, *Br* ≃ Household Cavalry

chevêche [ʃəvɛʃ] **NF** *Orn* little owl

chevelu, -e [ʃəvly] **ADJ 1** *(ayant des cheveux)* hairy **2** *(à chevelure abondante)* long-haired
NM,F *Péj (personne)* long-haired man, *f* woman

chevelure [ʃəvlyr] **NF 1** *(cheveux)* hair; **son abondante c.** his/her thick hair; **une femme à la c. rousse/blonde** a red-haired/blonde woman **2** *Fig* **la c. des saules** the verdure of the willows **3** *Astron* tail

chevenne, chevesne [ʃəvɛn] = **chevaine**

chevet [ʃəvɛ] **NM 1** *(d'un lit)* bedhead **2** *Archit* chevet
• **au chevet de PRÉP** at the bedside of
• **de chevet ADJ** bedside *(avant n)*

cheveu, -x [ʃəvø] **NM 1** *(poil)* hair; **ses cheveux** his/her hair; **avoir les cheveux noirs/longs/frisés** to have black/long/curly hair; **aux cheveux blonds/noirs/frisés** blond-/black-/curly-haired; **une fille aux cheveux courts** a girl with short hair, a short-haired girl; **avoir les cheveux raides** to have straight hair; **les cheveux en désordre** *ou* **bataille** with unkempt *or* tousled hair; **(les) cheveux au vent** with his/her/*etc* hair blowing freely in the wind; **un c. blanc** a grey hair; **avoir les cheveux blancs** to have grey hair; **avoir des cheveux blancs** to have some grey hairs; **avoir le c. rare** to be thinning (on top); **s'il touche à un seul c. de ma femme...** if he dares touch a hair on my wife's head...; *Vieilli* **en cheveux** bare-headed; **une histoire à faire dresser les cheveux sur la tête** a story that makes your hair stand on end; **le coup l'a manqué d'un c.** the blow missed him by a hair's breadth; **il s'en est fallu d'un c. qu'on y reste** we missed death by a hair's breadth; **il s'en est fallu d'un c. qu'il ne soit renversé par une voiture** he very nearly got run over; **avoir un c. sur la langue** to (have a) lisp; **se faire des cheveux (blancs)** to worry oneself sick; **venir** *ou* **arriver comme un c. sur la soupe** to come at the wrong time; **sa question est tombée comme un c. sur la soupe** his/her question couldn't have come at a worse time; **saisir une occasion aux cheveux** to seize an opportunity; **c'est un peu tiré par les cheveux** it's a bit far-fetched; **se prendre aux cheveux** to come to blows; *Fam* **avoir mal aux cheveux** to have a hangover **2** *(coiffure)* hairstyle; **tu aimes mes cheveux comme ça?** how do you like my haircut *or* hairstyle?
• **à cheveux ADJ** hair *(avant n)*
• **à un cheveu de PRÉP** within a hair's breadth of
• **à un cheveu près ADV** by a hair's breadth; **à un c. près, je ratais mon train** I caught my train by a hair's breadth
• **cheveux d'ange NMPL 1** *(guirlande)* tinsel garland **2** *Culin* vermicelli

cheveu-de-Vénus [ʃəvødəvenys] *(pl* **cheveux-de-Vénus)** **NM** *Bot* maidenhair (fern)

chevillard [ʃəvijar] **NM** wholesale butcher

cheville [ʃəvij] **NF 1** *Anat* ankle; **ils avaient de la boue jusqu'aux chevilles, la boue leur arrivait aux chevilles** they were ankle-deep in mud, the mud came up to their ankles; *Fig* **son fils ne lui arrive pas à la c.** his/her son's hardly in the same league as him/her; **personne ne lui arrive à la c.** he's head and shoulders above everybody else; *Fam Péj* **tu as les chevilles qui enflent** you're getting too big for your boots *or Am* britches
2 *Menuis (pour visser)* plug; *(pour boucher)* dowel; **c. ouvrière** *(d'un véhicule)* kingpin; *Fig* **il est la c. ouvrière du mouvement** he's the mainspring *or* kingpin of the movement
3 *Mus* peg
4 *Littérature* cheville, expletive
5 *(de boucher)* hook; **vente à la c.** wholesale butchery trade
• **en cheville ADV être en c. avec qn** to be in cahoots with sb; **ils sont en c. tous les deux** they're in cahoots *or* in it together

cheviller [3] [ʃəvije] **VT** *Menuis* to peg; *Fig* **avoir l'âme chevillée au corps** to hang on grimly to life

cheviotte [ʃəvjɔt] **NF** *Tex* Cheviot wool

chèvre [ʃɛvr] **NF 1** *(animal ▸ mâle)* goat, billy-goat; *(▸ femelle)* goat, she-goat, nanny-goat; **fromage/lait de c.** goat's cheese/milk; *Fam* **devenir c.** to go up the wall *or* round the bend; *Fam* **rendre qn c.** to drive sb up the wall *or* round the bend **2** *(treuil)* hoist; *(chevalet)* trestle
NM goat's cheese

chevreau, -x [ʃəvro] **NM 1** *Zool* kid **2** *(peau)* kid; **des gants de c.** kid gloves

chèvrefeuille [ʃɛvrəfœj] **NM** *Bot* honeysuckle

chevrette [ʃəvrɛt] **NF 1** *Zool (chèvre)* kid, young nanny-goat *or* she-goat; *(femelle du chevreuil)* doe; *(crevette)* shrimp **2** *(fourrure)* goatskin **3** *(trépied)* tripod

chevreuil [ʃəvrœj] **NM 1** *Zool* roe deer **2** *Culin* venison

chevrier, -ère [ʃəvrije, -ɛr] **NM,F** goatherd
NM chevrier bean

chevron [ʃəvrɔ̃] **NM 1** *Constr* rafter
2 *Mil* chevron, V-shaped stripe
3 *(motif)* chevron; **veste à chevrons** *(petits)* herringbone jacket; *(grands)* chevron-patterned jacket
4 *Hér* chevron

chevronné, -e [ʃəvrɔne] **ADJ** seasoned, experienced, practised

chevrotain [ʃəvrɔtɛ̃] **NM** *Zool* chevrotain, mouse deer

chevrotant, -e [ʃəvrɔtɑ̃, -ɑ̃t] **ADJ** *(voix)* quavering

chevrotement [ʃəvrɔtmɑ̃] **NM** quavering; **avec des chevrotements dans la voix** with a quaver *or* a tremor in one's voice, in a quavering or trembling voice

chevroter [3] [ʃəvrɔte] **VI 1** *(voix)* to quaver; *(personne ▸ en parlant)* to speak in a quavering voice, to quaver; *(▸ en chantant)* to sing in a quavering voice, to quaver **2** *(chèvre)* to kid

chevrotine [ʃəvrɔtin] **NF** *Chasse* piece of buckshot; **de la c., des chevrotines** buckshot

chewing-gum [ʃwiŋgɔm] *(pl* **chewing-gums)** **NM** gum, chewing-gum; **un c.** a piece of gum

CHEZ [ʃe] **PRÉP 1** *(dans la demeure de)* **je rentre c. moi** I'm going home; **c. soi** at home; **rentrer c. soi** to go home; **rester c. soi** to stay at home *or* in; **est-elle c. elle en ce moment?** is she at home *or* in at the moment?; **il habite c. moi en ce moment** he's living with me *or* he's staying at my place at the moment; **elle l'a raccompagné c. lui** *(à pied)* she walked him home; *(en voiture)* she gave him a lift home; **je vais c. ma sœur/Nadine** I'm going to my sister's (house)/Nadine's (house); **puis-je venir c. vous?** may I come over (to your place)?; **les amis c. qui j'étais ce week-end** the friends I stayed with this weekend; **derrière c. moi** behind my house *(or Br* flat *or Am* apartment/*etc)*; **ça s'est passé pas loin de/devant c. nous** it happened not far from/right outside where we live; **elle arrive de c. lui** she's just come from his place; **on pourrait passer c. elle** we could drop by at her place *or* drop in on her; **c. M. Durand** *(dans une adresse)* care of Mr Durand; **il se sent partout c. lui** he's at home everywhere; **fais comme c. toi** make yourself at home; *Ironique* make yourself at home, why don't you; **c. nous** *(dans ma famille)* in my *or* our family; *(dans mon pays)* in my *or* our country; **c. nous, on ne fait pas de manières** we don't stand on ceremony in our family; **c. moi, ma mère disait toujours...** in my family *or* at home, my mother always used to say...; **chacun c. soi** everyone should look after his own affairs; **c'est une coutume/un accent bien de c. nous** it's a typical local custom/accent; **un bon vin bien de c. nous** one of our good local wines; *Hum* **une bonne tarte aux pommes bien de c. nous** a good old apple pie like mother used to make
2 *(dans un magasin, dans une société etc)* **aller c. le coiffeur/le médecin** to go to the hairdresser's/the doctor's; **il est c. le coiffeur/le médecin** he's at the hairdresser('s)/the doctor('s); **acheter qch c. l'épicier** to buy sth at the grocer's; **je l'ai acheté c. Denver & Smith** I bought it from Denver & Smith; **dîner c. Maxim's** to dine at Maxim's; **une robe de c. Dior** a Dior dress, a dress designed by Dior; **il a travaillé c. IBM** he worked at *or* for IBM
3 *(dans un pays, dans un groupe)* **c. les Russes** in Russia; **c'est une coutume c. les Suédois** it's a Swedish custom; **cette expression est courante c. les jeunes** this expression is widely used among young people; **c'est fréquent c. les mammifères** it's often the case in *or* with mammals
4 *(d'une personne)* **ce qui me gêne c. lui, c'est...** the problem with him is...; **c'est quand même curieux, c. un homme de son âge** it is strange, for *or* in a man of his age; **il y a quelque chose que j'apprécie particulièrement c. eux, c'est leur générosité** something I particularly like about them is their generosity
5 *(dans l'œuvre de)* in; **c. Molière/Giotto** in Molière's/Giotto's work
6 *Fam* **côté humour, ce film, c'est vraiment lourd de c. lourd** the humour in this film is SO in your face; **son nouveau petit copain, c'est le style blaireau de c. blaireau** her new boyfriend is a complete and utter jerk; **il est nul ton lecteur de CD, le son est carrément pourri de c. pourri!** your CD player's useless, the sound's as crap as you can get!

chez-moi [ʃemwa] **NM INV** *Fam* home▫; **mon petit c.** a home of my own

chez-soi [ʃeswa] **NM INV** *Fam* home▫; **son petit c.** a home of one's own

chez-toi [ʃetwa] **NM INV** *Fam* home▫; **ton petit c.** a home of your own

chiader [3] [ʃjade] **VT** *très Fam* **1** *(perfectionner)* to polish up; **il l'a vachement chiadée, sa lettre de candidature** he really took pains over his application letter **2** *Scol* to cram for, *Br* to swot (up)

chialer [3] [ʃjale] **VI** *très Fam* to blubber, to bawl

chialeur, -euse [ʃjalœr, -øz] *très Fam* **ADJ** blubbering, bawling
NM,F blubbering *or* bawling brat

chiant, -e [ʃjɑ̃, -ɑ̃t] **ADJ** *très Fam* **1** *(assommant ▸ personne, chose à faire, livre)* boring▫; **ce qu'elle est chiante avec ses histoires!** she's so boring when she gets going with her stories!; **c. comme la pluie** as boring as hell, dead boring **2** *(difficile ▸ chose à faire)* **c'est c. à mettre en service, cette imprimante!** this printer is a real pain *or Br* bugger to install! **3** *(contrariant ▸ personne, événement)* annoying▫; **c'est c., cette coupure de courant!** this power cut is a real pain in the *Br* arse *or Am* ass!

chianti [kjɑ̃ti] **NM** *(vin)* Chianti

chiard, -e [ʃjar, -ard] *Fam* **ADJ** *Suisse (peureux)* chicken, cowardly▫
NM,F *Suisse (peureux)* chicken, coward▫
NM *(enfant)* brat

chiasse [ʃjas] **NF 1** *Vulg (diarrhée)* **avoir la c.** to have the trots *or* runs **2** *très Fam (poisse)* **quelle c.!** what a pain in the *Br* arse *or Am* ass!

chiatique [ʃjatik] **ADJ** *très Fam* **t'es vraiment c.** you're a damn *or Br* bloody pain; **c'est vraiment c.!** it's a pain in the *Br* arse *or Am* ass!

chibre [ʃibr] **NM** *Suisse Cartes* = popular Swiss card game

chic [ʃik] **ADJ INV 1** *(élégant)* stylish, smart, classy; **c'est très c.!** very classy! **2** *(distingué)* smart; **il paraît que ça fait c. de...** it's considered smart (these days) to...; **les gens c.** the smart set **3** *(sympathique)* nice; **c'est un c. type!** he's a nice guy!; **c'est une c. fille!** she's really nice!; **être c. avec qn** to be nice to sb
NM 1 *(élégance ▸ d'une allure, d'un vêtement)*

style, stylishness, chic; **avoir du c.** to have style, to be chic; **une veste qui a du c.** a stylish jacket; **s'habiller avec c.** to dress smartly; *Fam* **bon c. bon genre** *Br* ≃ Sloaney, *Am* ≃ preppy **2** *Fam (locution)* **il a le c. pour dire ce qu'il ne faut pas** he has a gift for *or* a knack of saying the wrong thing

EXCLAM *Fam Vieilli* **c. (alors)!** great!, smashing!

• **de chic ADV** *Vieilli* off the cuff, impromptu

chicane [ʃikan] **NF 1** *(dans un procès)* quibble, pettifogging *(UNCOUNT)*, chicanery *(UNCOUNT)*

2 *(querelle)* quarrel, squabble; **chercher c. à qn** to try to pick a quarrel with sb

3 *Sport (de circuit)* chicane; *(de gymkhana)* zigzag

4 *Cartes* chicane

5 *Aut (de silencieux)* baffle

• **en chicane ADJ** zigzag *(avant n)*

chicaner [3] [ʃikane] **VT** to quibble with; **c. qn sur** to quibble with sb about

VI to quibble; **c. sur les frais** to haggle *or* to quibble over the expense

VPR se chicaner to squabble

chicanerie [ʃikanri] **NF** quibbling *(UNCOUNT)*; **arrête tes chicaneries!** stop quibbling!

chicaneur, -euse [ʃikanœr, -øz], **chicanier, -ère** [ʃikanje, -ɛr] **ADJ** quibbling

NM,F 1 *(au tribunal)* pettifogger **2** *(ergoteur)* quibbler

chiche [ʃiʃ] **ADJ 1** *(avare)* mean; **il n'a pas été c. de son temps/de ses efforts** he didn't spare his time/efforts; **il n'a pas été c. de compliments** he was generous with his compliments **2** *(peu abondant ▸ repas, dîner, récolte)* scanty, meagre **3** *Fam (capable)* **tu n'es pas c. de le faire!** I'll bet you couldn't do it!; **c.!** want to bet?; **c. que je mange tout!** bet you I can eat it all!; **je vais lui dire ce que je pense! – allez, c.!** I'm going to give him/her a piece of my mind! – go on, I dare you!

chiche-kebab [ʃiʃkebab] *(pl* **chiches-kebabs)** **NM** *Culin* kebab, shish kebab

chichement [ʃiʃmɑ̃] **ADV 1** *(de façon mesquine)* meanly, stingily **2** *(pauvrement)* scantily; **vivre c.** to lead a meagre existence

chichi [ʃiʃi] **NM** *Fam (simagrées)* airs (and graces); **faire des chichis** *(faire des simagrées)* to put on airs; *(faire des complications)* to make a fuss; **ce sont des gens à chichis** these people give themselves airs; **un dîner sans chichis** an informal dinner▫

chichiteux, -euse [ʃiʃitø, -øz] *Fam* **ADJ** affected▫

NM,F show-off, poseur

chichon [ʃiʃɔ̃] **NM** *Fam Arg drogue* hash, dope, *Br* blow

chicorée [ʃikɔre] **NF 1** *(salade) Br* endive, *Am* chicory **2** *(à café)* chicory

chicos [ʃikɔs] **ADJ** *Fam* classy, smart, chic

chicot [ʃiko] **NM** *(d'une dent)* stump; *(d'un arbre)* tree stump

chicoter [3] [ʃikɔte] **VI 1** *(souris)* to squeak **2** *Can (chipoter)* to quibble, to split hairs

VT *Can (tracasser)* to worry, to bother; **ça me chicote de voir qu'il n'est pas encore de retour** it worries me that he's not back yet

chié, -e [ʃje] *très Fam* **ADJ 1** *(réussi ▸ soirée, spectacle, livre)* shit-hot

2 *(culotté)* **il est c., lui!** he's got a nerve!

3 *(drôle)* **il est c.** he's a scream

4 *(difficile ▸ tâche)* hard▫; **alors là, c'est c. comme question!** well, that's a hell of a question!

• **chiée NF** *(grande quantité)* **une chiée de** a whole lot *or* loads of; **on a eu une chiée d'ennuis pendant le voyage** it was just one damn thing after another during the whole journey; **des gens serviables, y en a pas des chiées!** helpful people don't exactly grow on trees!

chien, -enne [ʃjɛ̃, ʃjɛn] **NM,F 1** *(animal)* dog, *f* bitch; **petit c.** puppy, pup; **c. d'appartement** lapdog; **c. d'arrêt** gun dog, pointing dog, pointer; **c. d'aveugle** *Br* guide dog, *Am* seeing eye dog; **c. de berger** sheepdog; **c. de chasse** hound, gun dog, retriever; **c. couchant** setter; **faire le c. couchant** to fawn, to crawl; **c. courant** hound; **c. errant** stray dog; **c. de garde** guard dog; *Fig* watchdog; **c. de manchon** lapdog; **c. méchant** *(sur panneau)* beware of the dog; **c. de meute** hound; **c. policier** police dog; **c. de prairie** prairie dog; **c. de race** pedigree dog; **c. de rapport** retriever; **c. savant** *(dans un cirque)* performing dog; *Péj (enfant)* performing monkey; **c. sauvage** wild dog; **c. sauveteur** rescue dog; **c. de traîneau** sled dog, husky; **un air de c. battu** a hangdog expression; **bon à jeter aux chiens** fit for the *Br* bin *or Am* garbage; **(rubrique des) chiens écrasés** minor news items; **se regarder en chiens de faïence** to glare at one another; **il est comme le c. du jardinier** he's a dog in the manger; **ils sont comme c. et chat** they fight like cat and dog; **comme un c.** like a dog; **comme un jeune c.** excitedly; **arriver comme un c. dans un jeu de quilles** to turn up at just the wrong moment; **entre c. et loup** at dusk *or* twilight; *Péj* **ce n'est pas fait pour les chiens** it's there for a good reason; *Fam* **et ta fourchette, c'est pour les chiens?** what do you think your fork's for?; *Hum* **merci mon c.!** I never heard you say thank you!; *Fam* **je ne suis pas ton c.!** don't order me about!; **je lui réserve** *ou* **garde un c. de ma chienne** I've got something up my sleeve for him/her that he's not going to like one bit; *Fam* **chienne de vie!** life's a bitch!; *Can Fam* **avoir la chienne** *(avoir peur)* to be scared stiff; *(être paresseux)* to be lazy▫; *Prov* **un c. regarde bien un évêque** a cat may look at a king; *Prov* **bon c. chasse de race** good breeding always tells; *Prov* **il menace beaucoup, mais c. qui aboie ne mord pas** his bark is worse than his bite; *Prov* **les chiens aboient, la caravane passe** = let the world say what it will **2** *très Fam (terme d'insulte ▸ homme)* bastard; *(▸ femme)* bitch

NM 1 *Astron* **le Grand/Petit C.** the Great/Little Dog

2 *(d'une arme)* hammer, cock

3 *Ich* **c. de mer** dogfish

4 *Naut* **coup de c.** squall

5 *Fam (locution)* **elle a du c.** she's quite sexy *or* horny, there's something quite sexy *or* horny about her; *Can Fam* **avoir du c. (dans le corps)** to be full of beans

• **chienne NF** *Belg* (long) fringe

• **chiens NMPL** (long) fringe **ADJ** *Fam* **être c.** to be rotten *or* nasty▫; *Can* **ce qu'il dit de ses concurrents, c'est pas mal c.** the stuff he says about his competitors is pretty nasty

• **à la chien ADV** *(coiffé)* with a long fringe

• **de chien ADJ** *Fam (caractère, temps)* lousy, rotten; **ça fait un mal de c.** it hurts like hell; **avoir un mal de c. à faire qch** to have a hard job doing sth

• **en chien ADV** *Fam (très) Br* dead, *Am* real; **il court vite en c.** he runs *Br* dead *or Am* real fast

• **en chien de fusil ADV** curled up

chien-chien [ʃjɛ̃ʃjɛ̃] *(pl* **chiens-chiens)** **NM** doggy

chiendent [ʃjɛ̃dɑ̃] **NM** *Bot* couch grass; **ça pousse comme du c.** it grows like weeds

chienlit [ʃjɑ̃li] **NF** *Fam* **1** *(désordre)* mess, shambles *(singulier)*; **c'est la c.** it's a shambles! **2** *(masque)* mask▫ **3** *(mascarade)* masquerade▫

chien-loup [ʃjɛ̃lu] *(pl* **chiens-loups)** **NM** wolfhound

chienne [ʃjɛn] *voir* **chien**

chiennerie [ʃjɛnri] **NF 1** *très Fam (saleté)* **cette c. de métier!** what a lousy job! **2** *Littéraire (comportement)* meanness

chier [9] [ʃje] **VI 1** *Vulg (déféquer)* to (*Br* have *or Am* take a) shit **2** *très Fam (locutions)* **si elle l'apprend, ça va c. (des bulles)!** the shit's really going to hit the fan *or* all hell's going to break loose if she ever finds out!; **c. dans les bottes de qn** *(l'ennuyer à l'excès)* to piss sb off; *(lui jouer un sale tour)* to play a dirty trick on sb; **c. dans la colle** to be *Br* bang *or Am* smack out of order; **en c. (des bulles** *ou* **des ronds de chapeau)** to have a hell of a time; **j'en ai chié pour le terminer à temps!** I've had a hell of a job getting this finished on time!; **envoyer c. qn** to tell sb to get stuffed; **faire c. qn** *(l'importuner, le contrarier)* to bug sb; *(l'ennuyer)* to bore the pants off sb; **fais pas c.!** give me a break!, don't be such a pain in the *Br* arse *or Am* ass!; **tu (me) fais c.** give me a break, will you?; **(ça) fait c., ce truc!** this thing's a real pain in the *Br* arse *or Am* ass!; **qu'est-ce qu'on s'est fait c. hier soir!** it was so damned boring last night!; **je vais pas me faire c. à tout recopier!** I'm not damned well writing it all out again!, I can't be bothered *or Br* arsed (with) writing it all out again!; **il se fait pas c., lui!** he's got a damn *or Br* bloody nerve!; **y a pas à c., faut que j'aie fini ce soir!** I've damned *or Br* bloody well got to finish by tonight and that's that!

VT *très Fam* **tu vas pas nous c. une pendule!** don't make such a fuss *or Br* a bloody song and dance about it!

• **à chier** *très Fam* **ADJ 1** *(très laid)* **son costard est à c.** his suit looks *Br* bloody awful *or Am* godawful **2** *(très mauvais)* crap; **ce film est à c.** this movie is (a load of) crap **3** *(insupportable)* **il est à c., ce prof!** that teacher is a pain in the *Br* arse *or Am* ass!

chierie [ʃiri] **NF** *très Fam* **quelle c.!** what a pain in the *Br* arse *or Am* ass!, *Br* what a bloody pain!

chiffe [ʃif] **NF 1** *Fam* **c'est une vraie c. molle** he's got no guts, he's totally spineless **2** *Vieilli* rag

chiffon [ʃifɔ̃] **NM 1** *(torchon)* cloth; **c. à poussière** *Br* duster, *Am* dust cloth **2** *(vieux tissu)* rag **3** *Péj (texte)* **qui est l'auteur de ce c.?** who's responsible for this mess?

• **chiffons NMPL** *Vieilli (vêtements)* clothes; **parler chiffons** to talk clothes *or* fashion

• **en chiffon ADJ** crumpled up (in a heap); **toutes ses affaires sont en c.** his/her things are all crumpled up **ADV mettre ses vêtements en c.** to leave one's clothes in a heap

chiffonnade [ʃifɔnad] **NF** *Culin* chiffonnade

chiffonnage [ʃifɔnaʒ] **NM** *(de vêtement)* creasing, crumpling; *(de papier)* crumpling

chiffonné, -e [ʃifɔne] **ADJ 1** *(froissé ▸ vêtements)* creased, crumpled; *(▸ papier)* crumpled **2** *(fatigué ▸ visage)* tired, worn **3** *(préoccupé ▸ air)* bothered, worried

chiffonner [3] [ʃifɔne] **VT 1** *(vêtement)* to crease, to crumple; *(papier)* to crumple **2** *Fam (préoccuper)* to bother, to worry▫ **quelque chose me chiffonne** something's bothering me

VI to do a bit of sewing

VPR se chiffonner to crease, to crumple; **ça se chiffonne facilement** it creases easily, it's easily creased

chiffonnier, -ère [ʃifɔnje, -ɛr] **NM,F** rag dealer, rag-and-bone man, *f* woman; **se battre** *ou* **se disputer comme des chiffonniers** to fight like cat and dog

NM *(meuble)* chiffonier, chiffonnier

chiffrable [ʃifrabl] **ADJ** quantifiable; **facilement/difficilement c.** easy/difficult to calculate

chiffrage [ʃifraʒ] **NM 1** *(d'un code)* ciphering **2** *(évaluation)* (numerical) assessment **3** *Mus* figuring

chiffre [ʃifr] **NM 1** *Math* figure, number; **nombre à deux/trois chiffres** two/three digit number; **inflation à deux chiffres** double-digit inflation; **jusqu'à deux chiffres après la virgule** up to two decimal points; **arrondi au c. supérieur/inférieur** rounded up/down; **écrivez la somme en chiffres** write the amount out in figures; **en chiffres ronds** in round figures; **c. arabe/romain** Arabic/Roman numeral

2 *(montant)* amount, sum; **le c. des dépenses s'élève à 500 euros** total expenditure amounts to 500 euros; **c. de diffusion** *(d'un magazine)* sales figures, circulation figures

3 *Écon (taux)* figures, rate; **les chiffres du chômage** the unemployment figures; **chiffres bruts** unweighted figures

4 *Com* **c. d'affaires** turnover; **faire un c. d'affaires de 2 millions d'euros** to have a turnover of 2 million euros; *Fam* **faire du c.** to run at a healthy profit▫; **c. d'affaires annuel** annual turnover; **c. d'affaires consolidé** group turnover; **c. d'affaires critique** breakeven point; **c. d'affaires à l'exportation** total export sales; **c. d'affaires global** total sales; **c. d'affaires hors taxes** pre-tax turnover; **c. d'affaires prévisionnel** projected turnover, projected sales revenue; **c. de vente** sales figures; **ils ont augmenté leur c. de vente** they have increased their sales

5 *Ordinat* digit; **c. ASCII** ASCII number; **c. binaire** bit, binary digit; **c. de contrôle** check digit; **chiffres numériques** numerics

6 *Tél* code, ciphering; *(service)* cipher (office)

7 *Biol* code

8 *(d'une serrure)* combination

9 *(initiales)* initials; *(à l'ancienne)* monogram; **du papier à lettres à son c.** (his/her) personalized *or* monogrammed stationery

10 *Mus* figure

chiffrement [ʃifrəmɑ̃] **NM** *(codage)* ciphering, (en)coding; *Ordinat* **c. de données** data encryption

chiffrer [3] [ʃifre] **VT 1** *(évaluer)* to assess, to estimate; **c. des travaux** to draw up an estimate (of the cost of work); **il est trop tôt pour c. le montant des dégâts** it's too early to put a figure to the damage

2 *(numéroter)* to number; **c. les pages d'un document** to number the pages of *or Spéc* to paginate a document

3 *Admin & Mil* to cipher, to code; *Ordinat* to encode, to encrypt

4 *(linge, vêtement* ▸ *marquer de ses initiales)* to mark *or* to inscribe with initials; (▸ *marquer d'un monogramme)* to monogram

5 *Mus* to figure

VI *Fam* to cost a packet; **ça chiffre!** it mounts up!

VPR se chiffrer 1 se c. à *(se monter à)* to add up *or* to amount to **2 se c. en** *ou* **par** to amount to, to be estimated at; **sa fortune se chiffre par milliards** his/her fortune amounts to billions

chiffreur, -euse [ʃifrœr, -øz] **NM,F** *(du service du chiffre)* coder, ciphering clerk

NM *Ordinat* encoder, encrypter

chignole [ʃiɲɔl] **NF 1** *(outil* ▸ *à main)* hand drill; (▸ *électrique)* electric drill **2** *Fam Péj (voiture)* heap

chignon [ʃiɲɔ̃] **NM 1** *(cheveux)* bun, chignon; **se faire un c.** to put one's hair in a bun; **porter un c.** to wear one's hair in a bun; **c. banane** French roll **2** *Can Fam (tête)* head[❑], nut

chihuahua [ʃiwawa] **NM** *(chien)* chihuahua

chiite [ʃiit] *Rel* **ADJ** Shiah, Shiite

• **Chiite NMF** Shiite

chikungunya [ʃikungunja] **NM** *Méd* chikungunya

Chili [ʃili] **NM le C.** Chile

chili [tʃili, ʃili] *(pl* **chiles)** **NM** *Bot & Culin* chili (pepper), chilli (pepper); **c. con carne** chilli con carne

chilien, -enne [ʃiljɛ̃, -ɛn] **ADJ** Chilean

• **Chilien, -enne NM,F** Chilean

chimère [ʃimɛr] **NF 1** *Myth* chimera **2** *(utopie)* dream, fantasy; **le pays des chimères** the land of fantasy *or* dreams; **se complaire dans des chimères** to live in a dream world; **je vous laisse à vos chimères** I'll leave you alone with your pipe dreams

chimérique [ʃimerik] **ADJ 1** *(illusoire)* fanciful; **des espoirs/projets chimériques** fanciful hopes/plans; **rêve c.** pipe dream **2** *(mythique* ▸ *animal)* mythical, fabled

chimie [ʃimi] **NF** chemistry; **c. biologique** biochemistry; **c. industrielle** chemical engineering; **c. inorganique** *ou* **minérale** inorganic chemistry; **c. nucléaire** nuclear chemistry; **c. organique** organic chemistry

chimio [ʃimjo] **NF** *Fam Méd* chemo; **faire une c.** to have chemo

chimiorécepteur [ʃimjɔreseptœr] **NM** *Biol* chemoreceptor

chimiothérapie [ʃimjɔterapi] **NF** *Méd* chemotherapy; **faire une c.** to have chemotherapy

chimique [ʃimik] **ADJ 1** *(de la chimie)* chemical **2** *Fam (artificiel)* chemical, artificial; **tous ces trucs chimiques qu'on trouve dans la nourriture** all these additives you find in food

chimiquement [ʃimikmɑ̃] **ADV** chemically

chimiquier [ʃimikje] **NM** chemical tanker

chimiste [ʃimist] **NMF** chemist; **ingénieur c.** chemical engineer

> Il faut noter que le sens le plus courant du mot anglais **chemist** est **pharmacien.**

chimpanzé [ʃɛ̃pɑ̃ze] **NM** chimpanzee; **c. pygmée** pygmy chimpanzee

chinchilla [ʃɛ̃ʃila] **NM** chinchilla; **une veste en c.** a chinchilla jacket

Chine [ʃin] **NF la C.** China

chine [ʃin] **NM 1** *(porcelaine)* china **2** *(papier)* rice paper

NF *(brocante)* second-hand goods trade

• **à la chine ADJ vente à la c.** hawking; **vendeur à la c.** hawker **ADV vendre qch à la c.** to hawk sth

chiner [3] [ʃine] **VT 1** *Tex* to mottle **2** *Fam (taquiner)* to kid, to tease

VI *(faire les boutiques)* to go round the second-hand shops

chinetoque [ʃintɔk] **ADJ** ≃ Chink, ≃ Chinky

NMF = racist term used to refer to Chinese people, ≃ Chink, ≃ Chinky

chineur, -euse [ʃinœr, -øz] **NM,F 1** *(amateur de brocante)* bargain hunter **2** *Vieilli (taquin)* teaser

chinois, -e [ʃinwa, -az] **ADJ 1** *(de Chine)* Chinese **2** *Fam (compliqué)* twisted

NM 1 *(langue)* Chinese; **c. du Nord** Mandarin (Chinese); **c. du Sud** Cantonese; **pour moi, c'est du c.** it's all Greek to me **2** *Culin (passoire)* (conical) strainer, chinois; **passer qch au c.** to sieve sth **3** *(orange)* candied kumquat

• **Chinois, -e NM,F** Chinese; **les C.** the Chinese

chinoiser [3] [ʃinwaze] **VI** to split hairs

chinoiserie [ʃinwazri] **NF 1** *Fam (complication)* complication[❑]; **chinoiseries administratives** red tape **2** *Beaux-Arts* chinoiserie

chintz [ʃints] **NM** *Tex* chintz; **des rideaux en c.** chintz curtains

chiot [ʃjo] **NM** puppy, pup

chiotte [ʃjɔt] *très Fam* **NF 1** *(désagrément)* **quelle c.!** what a pain in the *Br* arse *or Am* ass!; **quel temps de c.!** what shitty weather! **2** *(voiture)* car[❑], wheels; *(moto)* bike, *Am* hog; *(cyclomoteur)* (motor) scooter[❑], moped[❑]

• **chiottes NFPL** *Br* bog, *Am* john; **aux chiottes l'arbitre!** *Br* the referee's a wanker!, *Am* kill the umpire!; **il a un goût de chiottes** he's got shit taste

chiourme [ʃjurm] **NF** *Hist* **1** *(rameurs)* **la c.** the slaves *(on a galley)* **2** *(forçats)* **la c.** the convicts *(in a penitentiary)*

chiper [3] [ʃipe] **VT** *Fam* to pinch, to swipe; **elle me chipe tous mes pulls** she's always pinching my sweaters

chipeur, -euse [ʃipœr, -øz] *Fam* **ADJ** thieving[❑]

NM,F petty thief[❑]

chipie [ʃipi] **NF** minx

chipolata [ʃipɔlata] **NF** *Culin* chipolata

chipotage [ʃipɔtaʒ] **NM** *Fam* **1** *(en discutant)* quibbling, hairsplitting **2** *(en mangeant)* nibbling **3** *(marchandage)* haggling

chipoter [3] [ʃipɔte] **VI** *Fam* **1** *(discuter)* to quibble, to split hairs; **ne chipotons pas!** let's not quibble!; **c. sur les prix** to haggle over prices **2** *(sur la nourriture)* to pick at one's food **3** *Belg (bricoler)* to fiddle about

VT *Belg (tripoter)* to fiddle with

chipoteur, -euse [ʃipɔtœr, -øz] *Fam* **ADJ 1** *(en discutant)* quibbling; **ils sont chipoteurs** they quibble over everything **2** *(en mangeant)* fussy, finicky; **il est c.** he's a fussy eater, he's finicky

NM,F 1 *(ergoteur)* fault-finder, quibbler **2** *(mangeur)* picky eater

chips [ʃips] **NFPL (pommes) c.** (potato) *Br* crisps *or Am* chips

> Il faut noter qu'en anglais britannique **chips** est un faux ami. Il signifie **frites.**

chique [ʃik] **NF 1** *(tabac)* quid, chew (of tobacco); *Fam* **ça ne vaut pas une c.** it's not worth a bean *or Am* a red cent

2 *Fam (enflure de la joue)* swollen cheek[❑] *(due to toothache)*

3 *Entom (puce)* jigger

4 *Belg* sweet

5 *(locutions) Fam* **ça m'a coupé la c.** I was speechless *or Br* gobsmacked; *Belg* **mordre sur sa c.** to grit one's teeth

chiqué [ʃike] **NM** *Fam Péj* **c.!** *(dans un match)* that's cheating![❑]; **il n'a pas mal, c'est du** *ou* **il fait du c.** he's not in pain at all, he's putting it on

chiquement [ʃikmɑ̃] **ADV** *Fam* **1** *(avec élégance)* smartly[❑], stylishly[❑] **2** *(avec fair-play)* decently[❑]; **elle m'a c. invité** she was good *or* kind *or* decent enough to invite me[❑]

chiquenaude [ʃiknod] **NF** *(pichenette)* flick; **donner une c. à qn** to flick sb with one's finger; **d'une c.** with a flick of the finger; **d'une c., il envoya la boulette de papier sur le bureau du prof** he flicked the pellet of paper onto the teacher's desk

chiquer [3] [ʃike] **VT** to chew

VI 1 *(mâcher du tabac)* to chew tobacco **2** *très Fam (locution)* **y a pas à c.** there's no doubt about it[❑]

chiqueur, -euse [ʃikœr, -øz] **NM,F** tobacco chewer

chirographaire [kirɔgrafer] *Jur* **ADJ** *(créance, créancier)* unsecured; **obligation c.** simple contract

NM unsecured creditor

chirographie [kirɔgrafi] **NF** palmistry, *Sout* chiromancy

chiromancien, -enne [kirɔmɑ̃sjɛ̃, -ɛn] **NM,F** palmist, *Spéc* chiromancer

chiropracteur, -trice [kirɔpraktœr, -tris] **NM,F** *Méd* chiropractor

chiropractie [kirɔprakti] **NF** *Méd* chiropractic

chiropractrice [kirɔpraktris] *voir* **chiropracteur**

chiropraticien, -enne [kirɔpratisjɛ̃, -ɛn] **NM,F** *Méd* chiropractor

chiropraxie [kirɔpraksi] **NF** *Méd* chiropractic

chiroptère [kirɔptɛr] *Zool* **NM** chiropteran

• **chiroptères NMPL** Chiroptera

chirurgical, -e, -aux, -ales [ʃiryrʒikal, -o] **ADJ** *Méd* surgical

chirurgie [ʃiryrʒi] **NF** surgery; **petite/grande c.** minor/major surgery; **c. ambulatoire** day surgery; **c. cardiaque** cardiac *or* heart surgery; **c. à cœur ouvert** open-heart surgery; **c. de confort** elective surgery; **c. dentaire** dental surgery; **c. endoscopique** keyhole surgery; **c. esthétique** cosmetic surgery; **c. plastique** *ou* **réparatrice** plastic surgery

chirurgien, -enne [ʃiryrʒjɛ̃, -ɛn] **NM,F** surgeon

chirurgien-dentiste [ʃiryrʒjɛ̃dɑ̃tist] *(pl* **chirurgiens-dentistes)** **NM** dental surgeon

chirurgienne [ʃiryrʒjɛn] *voir* **chirurgien**

chistera [ʃistera] **NM** *Sport (à la pelote basque)* chistera

chiure [ʃjyr] **NF c. de mouche** fly speck

chlamydia [klamidja] *(pl* **chlamydiae** [-je]) **NF** *Méd* chlamydia

chlâsse [ʃlas] **ADJ** *très Fam* **1** *(ivre)* tanked-up, *Br* rat-arsed; **il était complètement c.** he was totally wasted *or Br* pissed out of his head **2** *(fatigué)* all in, *Br* knackered

chleuh, chleuhe [ʃlø] **ADJ & NM,F** *Fam Hist* = offensive term used to refer to German people; **les chleuhs** ≃ the Jerries, ≃ the Boche

chlinguer [3] [ʃlɛ̃ge] **VI** *très Fam* to stink, *Br* to pong

chloral, -als [klɔral] **NM** *Chim* chloral, trichloroethanol; **c. hydraté, hydrate de c.** chloral (hydrate)

chlorate [klɔrat] **NM** *Chim* chlorate

chlore [klɔr] **NM 1** *Chim* chlorine **2** *(Javel)* bleach, bleaching agent

chlorer [3] [klɔre] **VT** *Chim* to chlorinate; **eau chlorée** chlorinated water

chlorhydrate [klɔridrat] **NM** *Chim* hydrochloride

chlorhydrique [klɔridrik] **ADJ** *Chim* hydrochloric

chlorique [klɔrik] **ADJ** *Chim* chloric

chlorobutadiène [klɔrɔbytadjɛn] **NF** *Chim* chloroprene

chlorofluorocarbure [klɔrɔflyɔrɔkarbyr] **NM** *Chim* chlorofluorocarbon

chloroforme [klɔrɔfɔrm] **NM** *Chim & Méd* chloroform

chloroformer [3] [klɔrɔfɔrme] **VT 1** *Méd* to administer chloroform to **2** *(abrutir)* to stultify

chlorophylle [klɔrɔfil] **NF** *Bot* chlorophyll

chlorophyllien, -enne [klɔrɔfiljɛ̃, -ɛn] **ADJ** chlorophyll *(avant n)*

chloroprène [klɔrɔprɛn] **NM** *Chim* chloroprene

chloroquine [klɔrɔkin] **NF** *Pharm* chloroquine

chlorure [klɔryr] **NM** *Chim* chloride; **c. de chaux** chloride of lime, bleaching powder; **c. de calcium/sodium** calcium/sodium chloride

chlorurer [3] [klɔryre] **VT** *Chim* to chlorinate

chnoque [ʃnɔk] = **schnock**

chnouf [ʃnuf] = **schnouf**

choc [ʃɔk] **NM 1** *(heurt)* collision; **à l'épreuve des** *ou* **résistant aux chocs** shock-proof, shock-resistant; **l'essieu a subi un c.** the axle sustained a shock; **projeté dans le fossé par la violence du c.** thrown into the ditch by the force of the collision; **la poutre a cassé sous le c.** the beam snapped under the impact; *Fam* **tenir le c.** to withstand the impact

2 *Mil (affrontement)* clash

3 *(incompatibilité)* clash, conflict; **c. culturel** culture shock; **le c. des générations** the generation gap

4 *(émotion)* shock; **ça fait un c.!** it's a bit of a shock!; **ça m'a fait un sacré c. de les revoir** it was a great shock to see them again

5 *Élec* shock; *Phys* collision; **par chocs** by collision; **c. moléculaire** molecule collision; *Météo* **c. en retour** return shock

6 *Méd & Psy* shock; **être sous le c.** to be in shock; *Fig (bouleversé)* to be in a daze *or* in shock; **c. allergique/anaphylactique/anesthésique** allergic/anaphylactic/anaesthesia shock; **c. émotif** emotional *or* psychic shock; **c. opératoire** post-operative trauma *or* shock; **c. septique** septic shock; **c. thermique** thermal shock

7 *Mil* shock; **c. et stupeur** *(stratégie)* shock and awe

8 *Bourse* **c. boursier** market crisis; *Écon* **c. pétrolier** oil crisis

9 *(bruit ▸ métallique)* clang; *(▸ sourd)* thwack; *(▸ cristallin)* clink, tinkle

10 *(comme adj; avec ou sans trait d'union)* **argument/discours c.** hard-hitting argument/speech; **image-c.** shocking image; **mesures-chocs** hard-hitting measures; **des prix-chocs** rock-bottom prices

• **de choc** **ADJ 1** *Méd, Psy & Mil* shock *(avant n)*; **état de c.** state of shock; **être en état de c.** to be in a state of shock **2** *Fam (efficace)* super-efficient; **un patron de c.** a go-getting *or* whizz-kid manager **3** *Fam (d'avant-garde)* ultra-modern; **une mamie de c.** a glamorous granny

chochotte [ʃɔʃɔt] **NF** *Fam Péj* **quelle c. tu fais!** *(mijaurée)* don't be so stuck-up!; *(effarouchée)* don't be so squeamish!; **il ne supporte pas cette odeur, c.!** oh dear, his Lordship can't stand the smell!

ADJ *(douillet)* squeamish; *(efféminé)* camp, affected

chocolat [ʃɔkɔla] **NM 1** *(produit)* chocolate; **c. blanc** white chocolate; **c. à croquer** *ou* **noir** *Br* dark *or* plain chocolate, *Am* bittersweet chocolate; **c. à cuire** cooking chocolate; **c. au lait** milk chocolate; **c. de ménage** cooking chocolate; **c. aux noisettes** hazelnut chocolate; **c. de régime** diet chocolate **2** *(friandise)* chocolate; **c. fourré à la fraise** chocolate filled with strawberry cream; **c. glacé** *Br* choc ice, *Am* chocolate ice cream bar **3** *(boisson)* hot chocolate, cocoa; **un c. chaud** a (cup of) hot chocolate; **boire du c.** to drink a cup of hot chocolate *or* cocoa

ADJ INV 1 *(couleur)* chocolate (brown) **2** *Fam (locution)* **on est c.!** *(dupés)* we've been had!; *(coincés)* we've blown it!

• **au chocolat** **ADJ** chocolate *(avant n)*; **gâteau au c.** chocolate cake

• **en chocolat** **ADJ** chocolate *(avant n)*; **des œufs en c.** chocolate eggs

chocolaté, -e [ʃɔkɔlate] **ADJ** chocolate *(avant n)*, chocolate-flavoured

chocolaterie [ʃɔkɔlatri] **NF 1** *(fabrique)* chocolate factory **2** *(magasin)* chocolate shop

chocolatier, -ère [ʃɔkɔlatje, -ɛr] **NM,F 1** *(fabricant)* chocolate-maker **2** *(marchand)* confectioner

ADJ chocolate *(avant n)*

• **chocolatière** **NF** hot chocolate pot

chocottes [ʃɔkɔt] **NFPL** *très Fam* **avoir les c.** to be scared witless *or* stiff; **ça m'a donné** *ou* **filé les c.** it scared me out of my wits; **foutre les c. à qn** to scare sb witless *or* stiff, to put the wind up sb

chœur [kœr] **NM 1** *Mus (chorale)* choir, chorus; *(morceau)* chorus; **les chœurs** *(d'un opéra, d'un spectacle)* the chorus

2 *Fig (ensemble)* body, group; **le c. des critiques n'a pas ménagé ses louanges** the critics were unanimous in their praise

3 *Antiq* chorus

4 *Archit* choir

• **en chœur** **ADV 1** *Mus* **chanter en c.** to sing in chorus **2** *(ensemble)* (all) together; **tous en c.** all together!; **parler en c.** to speak in unison; **ils sont tous allés à la plage en c.** they all went to the beach together

choie *etc voir* **choyer**

choir [72] [ʃwar] **VI** to fall; **se laisser c. sur une chaise/dans un fauteuil** to flop onto a chair/down in an armchair; *Fig* **laisser c. qn** *(s'en séparer)* to drop sb; *(manquer à sa promesse)* to let sb down; *Fam* **tout laisser c.** to pack it all in, *Br* to jack it all in, *Am* to chuck everything

choisi, -e [ʃwazi] **ADJ 1** *(raffiné)* **une assemblée choisie** a select audience; **en termes choisis** in a few choice phrases; **il parle un langage c.** he chooses his words carefully **2** *(sélectionné)* selected, picked; **bien c.** well-chosen, appropriate; **mal c.** inappropriate

choisir [32] [ʃwazir] **VT 1** *(sélectionner)* to choose, to pick; **c. entre** *ou* **parmi** to choose from (among); **choisis ce que tu veux** take your pick; **à ta place, je choisirais celle-ci** if I were you, I'd choose this one; **voilà ce que/celui que j'ai choisi** this is/he's the one I've chosen; **j'ai choisi les pommes les plus mûres** I selected the ripest apples; *Ironique* **tu as choisi ton moment!** you really picked a good time! **2** *(décider)* to decide, to choose, *Sout* to elect; **ils ont choisi de rester** they decided *or* chose to stay; **à lui de c. quand il veut y aller** it's up to him to decide when he wants to go

USAGE ABSOLU **bien c.** to choose carefully, to be careful in one's choice; **je n'ai pas eu le temps de c.** I had no time to make my choice; **je n'ai pas choisi, c'est arrivé comme ça** it wasn't my decision, it just happened

choix [ʃwa] **NM 1** *(liberté de choisir)* choice; **donner le c. à qn** to give sb a *or* the choice; **avoir un** *ou* **le c.** to have a choice; **je n'avais pas le c.** I had no choice, I didn't have any choice; **nous n'avons pas d'autre c. que de…** we have no option *or* choice but to…; **ils ne nous ont pas laissé le c.** they left us no alternative *or* other option; **je vous laisse le c.** you choose; **tu as le c. entre rester et partir** you may choose either to stay or go; **avoir le c. de qch** to be able to choose sth; **vous avez le c. des moyens** you may use whatever means you choose

2 *(sélection)* choice; **faire un c.** to make a choice; **faire le bon c.** to make the right choice; **faites votre c.** take your pick; **arrêter** *ou* **fixer son c. sur** to decide on, to choose; **à c. multiples** *(question, questionnaire, enquête)* multiple-choice; **mon c. est fait** I've made up my mind; **nous allons procéder au c. des couleurs** we are going to choose the colour scheme; **chacun peut y trouver un article de son c.** everybody can find something that appeals to them; **la carrière de votre c.** your chosen career; *Com* **c. du marché** market choice

3 *(gamme)* **un c. de** a choice *or* range *or* selection of; **ils ont un bon/grand c. de robes** they have a good/large selection of dresses

4 *Com* **premier c.** top quality; **de premier c.** top-quality; **viande** *ou* **morceaux de premier c.** prime cuts; **de second c.** *(fruits, légumes)* standard *(avant n)*, grade 2 *(avant n)*; *(viande)* standard *(avant n)*; **articles de second c.** seconds, rejects

5 *Psy* **c. d'objet** object choice

• **au choix** **ADJ** *(question)* optional **ADV** **être promu au c.** to be promoted by selection; **prenez deux cartes au c.** choose *or* select (any) two cards; **vous avez fromage ou dessert au c.** you have a choice of either cheese or a dessert

• **de choix** **ADJ 1** *(de qualité)* choice *(avant n)*, selected; **des vins/mets de c.** choice wines/food **2** *(spécial)* special; **il gardera toujours une place de c. dans nos cœurs** he will always have a special place in our hearts

• **par choix** **ADV** out of choice

choléra [kɔlera] **NM** *Méd & Vét* cholera

cholériforme [kɔleriform] **ADJ** *Méd & Vét* choleriform

cholérique [kɔlerik] *Méd & Vét* **ADJ** choleraic

NMF cholera sufferer

cholestérol [kɔlɛsterɔl] **NM** *Méd* cholesterol; **avoir du c.** to have high cholesterol *or* a high cholesterol level

cholestérolémie [kɔlɛsterɔlemi] **NF** *Méd* cholesterol level (of the blood), *Spéc* cholesteraemia

chômable [ʃomabl] **ADJ** **jour c.** public holiday

chômage [ʃomaʒ] **NM 1** *(inactivité)* unemployment; **la montée du c.** the rise in unemployment; **le c. des femmes/des jeunes** female/youth unemployment, unemployment among women/young people; **mettre au c.** to lay off; **c. conjoncturel** cyclical unemployment; **c. déguisé** hidden unemployment; **c. frictionnel** frictional unemployment; **c. de longue durée** long-term unemployment; **c. partiel** short-time working; **être en c. partiel** to work short time; **c. récurrent** periodic *or* recurrent unemployment; **c. saisonnier** seasonal unemployment; **c. structurel** structural *or* long-term unemployment; **être mis au c. technique** to be laid off; **être en c. technique** to have been laid off **2** *Fam (allocation)* unemployment benefit, *Br* dole (money); **toucher le c.** to claim unemployment benefit, *Br* to be on the dole; **s'inscrire au c.** to register as unemployed, *Br* to sign on

• **au chômage** **ADJ** *(sans emploi)* unemployed, out of work; **être au c.** to be unemployed *or* out of work **ADV** **s'inscrire au c.** to register as unemployed, *Br* to sign on

chômedu [ʃomdy] **NM** *Fam* unemployment[□], *Br* dole; **être au c.** to be unemployed[□] *or* out of work[□]; **pointer au c.** to be *Br* on the dole *or Am* on welfare[□]

chômer [3] [ʃome] **VI 1** *(être sans emploi)* to be unemployed *or* out of work

2 *(être en arrêt d'activité ▸ entreprise, machine)* to stand idle, to be at a standstill

3 *(faire le pont)* **c. entre Noël et le jour de l'An** to take time off between Christmas and New Year

4 *(avoir du loisir)* to be idle, to have time on one's hands; **elle n'a pas le temps de c.** she hasn't got time to sit around and twiddle her thumbs; **il ne chôme pas** he's never short of something to do; **eh bien, vous n'avez pas chômé!** well, you certainly haven't been idle!

5 *(être improductif)* **laisser c. une terre** to allow land to lie fallow; **laisser c. son argent** to let one's money lie idle

VT *(jour férié)* to take off, not to work on

chômeur, -euse [ʃomœr, -øz] **NM,F** *(sans emploi)* unemployed person; **il est c.** he's unemployed *or* out of work; **les chômeurs** the unemployed; **un million de chômeurs** a million unemployed; **le nombre des chômeurs est très élevé** the unemployment *or* jobless figures are high; **les chômeurs de longue durée** the long-term unemployed

chope [ʃɔp] **NF** *(récipient)* beer mug, tankard; *(contenu)* mugful

choper [3] [ʃɔpe] *Fam* **VT 1** *(contracter)* to catch[□]; **j'ai chopé la grippe** I've caught the flu **2** *(intercepter)* to catch[□], to get[□], to nab; **tâche de la c. à sa descente du train** try to get hold of her when she gets off the train; **je l'ai chopé en train de fouiller dans mes affaires** I caught him rummaging through my things; **se faire c.** to be nicked *or* nabbed **3** *(voler)* to swipe, to pinch; **elle s'est fait c. son porte-monnaie, on lui a chopé son porte-monnaie** she had her *Br* purse nicked *or Am* change purse snatched

chopine [ʃɔpin] **NF 1** *Fam (bouteille)* bottle[□] **2** *Fam (verre)* glass[□]; **aller boire une c.** to go and have a drink *or Br* a jar **3** *Can (mesure)* pint

choquant, -e [ʃɔkɑ̃, -ɑ̃t] **ADJ 1** *(déplaisant ▸ attitude)* outrageous, shocking; **avec un mépris c. de la justice** with outrageous disregard for justice **2** *(déplacé ▸ tenue)* offensive, shocking; **tu trouves sa tenue choquante?** do you find the way she's dressed offensive?

choqué, -e [ʃɔke] **ADJ** shocked; **il les regardait d'un air profondément c.** he looked at them, visibly shocked; *Can* **être c. (contre qn)** to be angry (at sb), *Am* to be mad (at sb)

choquer [3] [ʃɔke] **VT 1** *(heurter)* to hit, to knock, to bump; **nous avons choqué nos verres** we clinked glasses

2 *(scandaliser)* to shock, to offend; **ça te choque qu'elle pose nue?** do you find it shocking *or* offensive that she should pose in the nude?; **ça ne me choque pas du tout** I don't see anything wrong with that; **être choqué (de/par qch)** to be shocked (at/by sth)

3 *(être désagréable à ▸ l'oreille)* to grate on, to offend; **c. la vue** *(couleur, saleté)* to offend the eye; *(bâtiment)* to be an eyesore

4 *(traumatiser)* **ils ont été profondément choqués par sa mort** they were devastated by his/her death; **j'ai été choqué de le voir tellement changé** I was shocked *or* it gave me a shock to see such a change in him; **la vue du sang l'a choqué** the sight of blood has shaken him; *Méd* **être choqué** to be in shock

USAGE ABSOLU *(scandaliser)* **son intention était de c.** he intended to be offensive *or* to shock; **ce qui choque le plus, dans ces images, c'est...** the most shocking thing about these pictures is...

VPR se choquer 1 *(se heurter ▸ véhicules)* to come into collision; *(▸ verres)* to knock against each other **2** *(être scandalisé)* to be shocked; **il n'y a pas de quoi se c.** there's nothing to be shocked at

choral, -e, -als *ou* **-aux, -ales** [kɔral, -o] *Mus & Rel* **ADJ** choral; **chants chorals** choral songs

• **choral, -als NM** choral, chorale

• **chorale NF** choir, choral society

chordé [kɔrde] = **cordé**

chorée [kɔre] **NF** *Méd* Saint Vitus' dance, *Spéc* chorea; **c. de Huntington** Huntington's chorea

chorégraphe [kɔregraf] **NMF** choreographer

chorégraphie [kɔregrafi] **NF** choreography; **faire la c. de** to choreograph

chorégraphier [9] [kɔregrafje] **VT** to choreograph

chorégraphique [kɔregrafik] **ADJ** choreographic

choria [ʃɔrja] **NF** *Rel* sharia

choriste [kɔrist] **NMF 1** *Rel* chorister **2** *(à l'opéra)* chorus singer; *(d'un chanteur de variétés)* backing singer; **les choristes** *(au cabaret)* the chorus line

chorizo [ʃɔrizo, tʃɔrizo] **NM** chorizo

chorus [kɔrys] **NM faire c.** to (all) agree, to speak with one voice; **faire c. avec qn** to voice one's agreement with sb

CHOSE [ʃoz] **NF A.** *SENS CONCRET* **1** *(bien matériel, nourriture, vêtement)* thing; **un livre et une table sont des choses** tables and books are things *or* objects; **il n'avait acheté que de bonnes choses** he had only bought good things to eat; **elle a eu trop de choses à Noël** she got too many things *or* presents for Christmas; **j'ai encore deux ou trois choses à acheter** I still have a couple of things to buy; **j'ai encore des choses à lui chez moi** I still have a few of his things *or* some of his belongings at home

2 *(objet ou produit indéterminé)* thing; **quelle est cette c. affreuse?** what is this hideous thing?; **tu sais faire marcher cette c.?** do you know how this thing works?

3 *Phil* thing; **la c. en soi** the thing in itself

B. *PERSONNE* creature, thing; **être la c. de qn** *(avoir été modelé par qn)* to be (like) putty in sb's hands; *(être la possession de qn)* to belong to sb; **elle me prend pour sa c.** she thinks she can do what she wants with me, she thinks she owns me

C. *SENS ABSTRAIT* **1** *(acte, fait)* **une c.** a thing, something; **les choses** things; **j'ai encore beaucoup de choses à faire** I've still got lots (of things) to do; **j'ai bien des choses à vous raconter** I've a lot (of things) to tell you; **elle fait beaucoup de choses pour les handicapés** she does a lot for handicapped people; **c'est une c. que je ne savais pas** that's something I didn't know; **il se passe des choses au ministère** there's something going on in the department; **ah, encore une c., je ne viendrai pas demain** oh, one more thing, I won't be coming tomorrow; **s'il y a bien une c. qui m'agace, c'est son manque de ponctualité** if there's one thing that annoys me (about him/her), it's that he's/she's never on time; **l'hypocrisie, c'est une c. que je ne supporte pas** hypocrisy is something I can't bear; **une c. est sûre, il perdra** one thing's (for) sure, he'll lose; *Littéraire* **y a-t-il une c.** *ou* **y a-t-il c. plus belle que l'amour?** is there anything more beautiful than love?; **c'est une bonne c. qu'elle soit restée** it's a good thing she stayed; **en avril, ce sera c. faite** *ou* **la c. sera faite** it will be done by April; **ce n'est pas la même c.** *(cela change tout)* it's a different matter; **je suis retourné à mon village, mais ce n'est plus la même c.** I went back to my village, but it's just not the same any more; **la fidélité est une c., l'amour en est une autre** faithfulness is one thing, love is quite another; **ce n'est pas la c. à dire/faire!** what a thing to say/do!; *Fam* **c'est pas des choses à dire/faire!** you just don't say/do that kind of thing!; **c'est la c. à ne pas faire** it's the wrong thing to do; **ce ne sont pas des choses à faire en société** that's just not done in polite circles; **c. extraordinaire/curieuse, il était à l'heure!** amazingly/strangely enough, he was on time!; **et, c. rare...** for once...; **ce n'est pas c. aisée que de...** it's no easy matter to...; **c. promise c. due** a promise is a promise; **je ne crois pas à toutes ces choses** I don't believe in all that; **ce sont des choses qui arrivent** it's just one of those things; **s'occuper de choses et d'autres** to potter about; **accomplir** *ou* **faire de grandes choses** to do great things; **faire bien les choses** *(savoir recevoir)* to do things in style; **il ne fait pas les choses à demi** *ou* **moitié** he doesn't do things by halves

2 *(parole)* thing; **il dit une c. et il en fait une autre** he says one thing and does something else; **la c. que je n'ai pas comprise** what *or* the thing I didn't understand; **je vais te dire une (bonne) c., ça ne marchera jamais** let me tell you something, it'll never work; **elle dit de ces choses parfois!** the things she comes out with sometimes!; **il est sorti de sa voiture et il m'a dit de ces choses!** he got out of his car and gave me a right mouthful!; **elle dit toujours des choses sur ses collègues** she's always saying things about the people she works with; **qu'a-t-il dit? – peu de choses en vérité** what did he say? – very little *or* nothing much, actually; **bavarder** *ou* **parler de choses et d'autres** to chat about this and that; **dites-lui bien des choses** give him/her my best regards

3 *(écrit)* thing; **elle a écrit de bonnes choses** she wrote some good things *or* stuff; **comment peut-on écrire des choses pareilles!** how can anyone write such things!

4 *(ce dont il est question)* **comment a-t-il pris la c.?** how did he take it?; **comment vois-tu la c.?** how do you see it *or* things *or* the matter?; **la c. est entendue** we're agreed on this; **la c. n'est pas faisable** it can't be done; **laisse-moi t'expliquer la c.** let me explain what it's all about; **la c. en question** the case in point; *Euph* **être porté sur la c.** to have a one-track mind

5 *Pol (affaires)* **la c. publique** the state

6 *Jur* **choses communes** common things *(which cannot be owned)*; **choses consomptibles** consumables; **choses corporelles** tangible assets; **choses fongibles** fungible assets; **choses frugifères** profit-yielding objects; **choses hors du commerce** non-negotiable objects; **c. jugée** res judicata

NM *Fam* **1** *(pour désigner un objet)* thingy, whatsit; **passe-moi le..., le c. bleu sur la table** give me the..., the blue thing on the table

2 *(pour désigner une personne)* **C.** *(homme)* what's-his-name, thingy; *(femme)* what's-her-name, thingy; **c'est une pièce avec C., tu sais, le grand blond!** it's a play with what's-his-name, you know, the tall blond guy!; **Madame C., elle devrait savoir ça** what's-her-name *or* Mrs thingy should know that

ADJ *Fam* funny, peculiar; **être** *ou* **se sentir un peu c.** to feel a bit peculiar; **ton fils a l'air tout c. aujourd'hui** your son looks a bit peculiar today

• **choses NFPL** *(situation)* things; **les choses de la vie** the things that go to make up life; **les choses étant ce qu'elles sont** as things stand, things being as they are; **au point où en sont les choses** as things now stand; **voilà où en sont les choses** this is how things stand (at the moment); **en mettant les choses au mieux/pire** looking on the bright/dark side (of things); **prendre les choses comme elles viennent** to take life as it comes; **prendre les choses à cœur** to take things to heart

• **de deux choses l'une ADV de deux choses l'une, tu es avec moi ou avec lui!** either you're on my side or you're on his!; **de deux choses l'une, ou tu m'obéis ou tu vas te coucher!** either you do as I tell you or you go to bed, it's up to you!

chosifier [9] [ʃozifje] **VT** to reify, to consider as a thing

chott [ʃɔt] **NM** *Géol* salt lake

chou[1], -x [ʃu] **NM 1** *Bot* cabbage; **c. (cabus)** white cabbage; **c. de Bruxelles** Brussels sprout; **c. chinois** Chinese cabbage *or* leaves; **c. frisé** (curly) kale; **c. de palmier** palm heart; **c. pommé** round cabbage; **c. romanesco** Romanesco; **c. rouge** red cabbage

2 *(pâtisserie)* **(petit) c.** chou; **c. à la crème** cream puff

3 *(ornement)* round knot, rosette

4 *Fam (locutions)* **être dans les choux** to be in a mess; **c'est dans les choux!** that's torn it!, that's the end of that!; **faire c. blanc** to draw a blank, to be out of luck; **faire ses choux gras de qch** to have a field day with sth; **rentrer dans le c. à qn** *(en voiture)* to slam into sb; *(agresser)* to go for sb; *Belg* **c'est c. vert et vert c.** it's six of one and half a dozen of the other, *Br* it's all much of a muchness

chou[2], choute [ʃu, ʃut] *Fam* **NM,F 1** *(en appellatif)* honey, sugar, sweetheart; **mon pauvre c.!** you poor little thing! **2** *(personne aimable)* darling, love; **c'est un c.** he's such a darling *or* love

ADJ INV *(gentil)* nice□, kind□; *(mignon)* cute; **tu es c.** *(en demandant un service)* there's a dear; *(pour remercier)* you're so kind, you're an absolute darling

chouan [ʃwɑ̃] **NM** *Hist* Chouan *(member of a group of counter-revolutionary royalist insurgents, one of whose leaders was Jean Chouan, in the Vendée area of western France from 1793 to 1800)*

chouannerie [ʃwanri] **NF** *Hist* **la c.** the Chouan uprising

choucas [ʃuka] **NM** *Orn* jackdaw

chouchou, -oute [ʃuʃu, -ut] **NM,F** *Fam Péj (préféré)* favourite□; **c'est le c. du prof** he's the teacher's pet; **le c. de sa grand-mère** his grandmother's blue-eyed boy

NM *(pour les cheveux)* scrunchie

chouchouter [3] [ʃuʃute] **VT** *Fam (élève)* to give preferential treatment to□; *(enfant, ami)* to mollycoddle□, to pamper□; **se faire c.** to let oneself be spoiled

choucroute [ʃukrut] **NF 1** *Culin (chou)* pickled cabbage; *(plat)* sauerkraut; **c. garnie** sauerkraut with meat **2** *Fam (coiffure)* beehive

chouette[1] [ʃwɛt] **NF 1** *Orn* owl; **c. blanche** snowy owl; **c. des bois** brown owl, wood owl; **c. des clochers, c. effraie** barn owl; **c. hulotte** tawny owl **2** *Fam Péj (femme)* **vieille c.** old bag

chouette[2] [ʃwɛt] *Fam* **ADJ 1** *(agréable)* fantastic, lovely, terrific; **il me reste 20 euros, c'est c.!** fantastic, I've got 20 euros left!; **c. journée, non?** lovely day, isn't it?; *Ironique* **ben il est c. avec ce chapeau!** doesn't he look great with that hat on! **2** *(gentil)* kind□; *(coopératif)* helpful□; **il est très c. avec nous** he's very good to us; **elle est drôlement c. avec les enfants** she's really good with the kids; **sois c., prête-moi ta voiture** oh go on, lend me your car

EXCLAM c. (alors)! great!

chou-fleur [ʃuflœr] *(pl* **choux-fleurs)** **NM** cauliflower; **oreille en c.** cauliflower ear

chouia, chouïa [ʃuja] **NM** *Fam* **un c. (de)** a little *or* tiny bit (of); **encore un c. de crème** just a drop more cream; **un c. trop à gauche** a tiny bit too much to the left

chouille [ʃuj] **NF** *Fam* party□, bash

chouiller [3] [ʃuje] **VI** *Fam* to party

chou-navet [ʃunavɛ] *(pl* **choux-navets)** **NM** *Bot Br* swede, *Am* rutabaga

choune [ʃun] **NF** *Vulg (sexe de la femme)* pussy, snatch, *Br* fanny; **avoir de la c.** to be fucking lucky *or Br* jammy

chou-palmiste [ʃupalmist] *(pl* **choux-palmistes)** **NM** *Bot* palm-heart, palm-cabbage

chou-rave [ʃurav] *(pl* **choux-raves***)* **NM** *Bot* kohlrabi

chouraver [3] [ʃurave], **chourer [3]** [ʃure] **VT** *très Fam* to swipe, to pinch; **c. qch à qn** to pinch sth from sb; **on m'a chouravé mon vélo** I've had my bike pinched

choute [ʃut] *voir* **chou² NM,F**

chow-chow [ʃoʃo] *(pl* **chows-chows***)* **NM** *(chien)* chow-chow, chow (dog)

choyer [13] [ʃwaje] **VT** to pamper, to make a fuss of; **se faire c.** to be pampered

chrême [krem] **NM** *Rel* chrism, consecrated oil

chrétien, -enne [kretjɛ̃, -ɛn] **ADJ** Christian **NM,F** Christian

chrétiennement [kretjenmɑ̃] **ADV vivre c.** to live as a good Christian

chrétienté [kretjɛ̃te] **NF** Christendom

Chris-Craft® [kriskraft] **NM INV** *Naut* Chris-Craft

Christ [krist] **NPR le C.** Christ
• **christ NM** *(crucifix)* (Christ on the) cross, crucifix

christiania [kristjanja] **NM** *Ski* christie, christy

christianisation [kristjanizasjɔ̃] **NF** Christianization, conversion to Christianity

christianiser [3] [kristjanize] **VT** to Christianize, to convert to Christianity

christianisme [kristjanism] **NM** Christianity

chromage [kromaʒ] **NM** *Tech* chromium plating

chromate [krɔmat] **NM** *Chim* chromate

chromatique [krɔmatik] **ADJ 1** *Mus* chromatic **2** *(relatif aux couleurs)* chromatic **3** *Biol* chromosomal

chromatiquement [krɔmatikmɑ̃] **ADV** *Mus* chromatically

chromatisme [krɔmatism] **NM** *Mus & Opt* chromaticism

chromatographique [krɔmatɔgrafik] **ADJ** *Chim* chromatographic

chrome [krom] **NM** *Chim & Métal* chromium
• **chromes NMPL** *(d'un véhicule)* chrome *(UNCOUNT)*, chromium-plated parts; **faire les chromes d'une voiture/bicyclette** to polish up the chrome on a car/bicycle

chromer [3] [krome] **VT** *Métal* **1** *(métal)* to chromium-plate **2** *(acier)* to chrome; **acier chromé** chrome steel

chrominance [krɔminɑ̃s] **NF** *TV* chrominance; **signal de c.** chrominance signal

chromo [kromo] **NM** *Péj* poor-quality colour print

chromosome [kromozom] **NM** *Biol* chromosome; **c. somatique** autosome; **jeu de chromosomes** set of chromosomes

chromosomique [kromozomik] **ADJ** *Biol & Méd (gén)* chromosomal, chromosomic, chromosome *(avant n)*; *(maladie)* chromosomal, genetic

chronicité [krɔnisite] **NF** *Méd* chronicity

chronique [krɔnik] **ADJ 1** *Méd* chronic **2** *(constant)* chronic; **chômage c.** chronic unemployment
NF 1 *Journ (rubrique)* column; **tenir la c. sportive** to write the sports column; **c. boursière** markets column; **c. financière** financial news; **c. judiciaire** court column; **c. littéraire** arts page; **c. mondaine** gossip column; **c. des spectacles** (entertainments) listings **2** *Littérature* chronicle **3** *Bible* **les Chroniques** Chronicles

chroniquement [krɔnikmɑ̃] **ADV 1** *Méd* chronically **2** *(constamment)* chronically, perpetually

chroniqueur, -euse [krɔnikœr, -øz] **NM,F 1** *(journaliste)* commentator, columnist; **c. boursier** market commentator; **c. financier** financial columnist; **c. judiciaire** court reporter; **c. littéraire** book editor, book reviewer; **c. mondain** gossip columnist **2** *(historien)* chronicler

chrono [krɔno] *Fam* **NM** stopwatch[▫]
ADV by the clock[▫]; **250 c.** recorded speed 250 kph

chronobiologie [krɔnobjɔlɔʒi] **NF** *Biol* chronobiology

chronogramme [krɔnɔgram] **NM** time-series chart

chronographe [krɔnɔgraf] **NM** *Astron* chronograph

chronologie [krɔnɔlɔʒi] **NF** chronology, time sequence; **c. des événements** calendar of events

chronologique [krɔnɔlɔʒik] **ADJ** chronological

chronologiquement [krɔnɔlɔʒikmɑ̃] **ADV** chronologically

chronométrage [krɔnɔmetraʒ] **NM** timing

chronomètre [krɔnɔmetr] **NM** *(pour le sport)* stopwatch; *(montre de précision)* chronometer

chronométrer [18] [krɔnɔmetre] **VT** to time *(with a stopwatch)*

chronométreur, -euse [krɔnɔmetrœr, -øz] **NM,F** *(en sport)* timekeeper; *(dans l'industrie)* time and motion (study) expert

chronométrique [krɔnɔmetrik] **ADJ** chronometric

Chronopost® [krɔnɔpɔst] **NM** = express mail service

chrysalide [krizalid] **NF** *Entom* chrysalis; *Fig* **sortir de sa c.** to come out of one's shell

chrysanthème [krizɑ̃tem] **NM** *Bot* chrysanthemum

> **CHRYSANTHÈME**
>
> Chrysanthemums are often associated with funerals in France, and so are never offered as gifts. They are traditionally used to decorate graves, especially on All Saints' Day.

chrysolithe [krizɔlit] **NF** *Minér* chrysolite, olivine

CHS [seaʃes] **NM** *(abrév* **centre hospitalier spécialisé***)* = psychiatric hospital

chtarbé, -e [ʃtarbe] **ADJ** *Fam* crazy, nuts, off one's rocker

ch'timi [ʃtimi] **ADJ** from the north of France
NMF northerner *(in France)*

chtouille [ʃtuj] **NF** *très Fam* **la c.** the clap

CHU [seaʃy] **NM 1** *(abrév* **centre hospitalo-universitaire***)* teaching hospital **2** *(abrév* **centre d'hébergement d'urgence***)* emergency refuge

chuchotement [ʃyʃɔtmɑ̃] **NM** whisper; **des chuchotements** whispering *(UNCOUNT)*

chuchoter [3] [ʃyʃɔte] **VI** to whisper
VT *(mot d'amour, secret)* to whisper; **c. qch à qn** to whisper sth to sb; **il lui a chuchoté quelques mots à l'oreille** he whispered a few words in his/her ear

chuchoterie [ʃyʃɔtri] **NF** whispers, whispered conversation

chuchoteur, -euse [ʃyʃɔtœr, -øz] **ADJ** whispering
NM,F whisperer

chuintant, -e [ʃɥɛ̃tɑ̃, -ɑ̃t] **ADJ** *(son)* hushing; *Ling* **consonne chuintante** palato-alveolar fricative
• **chuintante NF** *Ling* palato-alveolar fricative

chuintement [ʃɥɛ̃tmɑ̃] **NM 1** *Ling* = use of palato-alveolar fricatives instead of sibilants (characteristic of certain French regional accents) **2** *(sifflement)* hiss, hissing

chuinter [3] [ʃɥɛ̃te] **VI 1** *(d'une chouette)* to hoot **2** *(siffler)* to hiss **3** *Ling* to pronounce *or* articulate sibilants as fricatives

chut [ʃyt] **EXCLAM** hush!, sh!, shhh!

chute [ʃyt] **NF 1** *(perte d'équilibre)* fall; **faire une c.** to fall, to take a tumble; **faire une c. de cheval** to fall off one's horse; **il a fait une c. de neuf mètres** he fell nine metres; **attention, c. de pierres** *(sur panneau)* danger! falling rocks; **c. libre** free fall; **faire du saut en c. libre** to skydive; *Fig* **la livre est en c. libre** the pound's plummetting
2 *(perte)* fall; **la c. des cheveux** hair loss; **au moment de la c. des feuilles** when the leaves fall
3 *(baisse ▸ des prix, des températures)* drop, fall (de in); *Com* **c. des ventes** fall-off in sales; **c. de tension** *Méd* drop in blood pressure; *Élec & Phys* voltage drop; **c. de pression** pressure drop
4 *(effondrement ▸ d'un gouvernement, d'une institution)* collapse, fall; **entraîner qn dans sa c.** to drag sb down with one
5 *Mil* fall
6 *Bible* **la C.** the Fall
7 *Météo* **chutes de neige** snowfall; **chutes de pluie** rainfall
8 *(chute d'eau)* **les chutes du Niagara** (the) Niagara Falls; **les chutes Victoria** (the) Victoria Falls
9 *(fin ▸ d'une histoire)* punchline; *(▸ d'un roman, d'une pièce)* end; **j'ai été surpris par la c.** *(d'une situation)* I was surprised by the outcome; *Littéraire* **la c. du jour** nightfall, the day's end, eventide
10 *(inclinaison, pente)* **c. d'un toit** pitch of a roof; **c. d'une robe** hang of a dress; **c. de la voix** fall *or* cadence of the voice; *Anat* **c. des reins** small of the back
11 *(déchet ▸ de tissu)* scrap; *(▸ de bois, de métal)* offcut, trimming; **chutes de pellicule** film trims; **c'est une scène qui est restée parmi les chutes** that scene ended up on the cutting-room floor; **une couverture faite avec des chutes (de tissu)** a blanket made of remnants (of fabric)
12 *Constr (d'un toit)* pitch, slope
13 *Cartes* **avoir deux levées de c.** to be two tricks down
• **chute d'eau NF** waterfall

chuter [3] [ʃyte] **VI 1** *Fam (tomber)* to fall[▫]
2 *(ne pas réussir)* to fail, to come to grief; **c. sur** to fail on
3 *(baisser)* to fall, to tumble; **faire c. les ventes** to bring sales (figures) tumbling down
4 *Cartes* to go down

chyme [ʃim] **NM** *Physiol* chyme

Chypre [ʃipr] **NF** Cyprus

chypriote [ʃiprijɔt] = **cypriote**

CI [sei] **NM** *Fin (abrév* **certificat d'investissement***)* investment certificate

ci [si] **PRON DÉMONSTRATIF INV ci et ça** this and that; **faire ci et ça** to do this and that

CIA [seia] **NF** *(abrév* **Central Intelligence Agency***)* CIA

ciao [tʃao] **EXCLAM** *Fam* ciao!

ci-après [siapre] **ADV** *(gén)* below; *Jur* hereafter, hereinafter; **voir c.** see below

cibiche [sibiʃ] **NF** *Fam Vieilli* cig, ciggie

cibiste [sibist] **NMF** CB user

ciblage [siblaʒ] **NM** targeting; *Méd* **c. génique** gene targeting; **c. stratégique** strategic targeting

cible [sibl] **NF 1** *Mil & Phys* target; **c. fixe/mobile** stationary/moving target **2** *Fig (victime)* target; **prendre qn pour c.** to make sb the target of one's attacks; **servir de c. aux railleries de qn** to be the butt *or* the target for sb's jokes **3** *Com & Mktg* target; **c. commerciale** marketing target; **c. de communication** promotional target; **c. média** media target; **c. publicitaire** advertising target; **c. visée** intended target; **population c.** target population

ciblé, -e [sible] **ADJ** targeted

cibler [3] [sible] **VT** *(produit)* to define a target group for; *(public)* to target; **notre campagne publicitaire cible en priorité les jeunes** our advertising campaign is targeted principally at young people

ciboire [sibwar] **NM** *Rel* ciborium

ciboule [sibul] **NF** *Br* spring onion, *Am* scallion

ciboulette [sibulɛt] **NF** chives

ciboulot [sibulo] **NM** *Fam* head[▫], nut; **se creuser le c.** to rack one's brains; **il n'a rien dans le c.** he's got nothing between his ears; **elle en a dans le c.!** she's got a good head on her shoulders!; **travailler du c.** to be off one's rocker *or Br* trolley

cicatrice [sikatris] **NF 1** *Méd* scar, *Spéc* cicatrice **2** *Fig (marque)* mark, scar; **cette séparation a laissé une c. profonde en lui** the separation scarred him deeply *or* left a deep scar on him **3** *Bot* scar (of attachment)

cicatriciel, -elle [sikatrisjɛl] **ADJ** scar *(avant n)*, *Spéc* cicatricial

cicatrisant, -e [sikatrizɑ̃, -ɑ̃t] **ADJ** healing
NM healing agent, *Spéc* cicatrizant

cicatrisation [sikatrizasjɔ̃] **NF 1** *Méd* scarring, *Spéc* cicatrization; **la c. se fait mal** the wound is not healing *or* closing up properly **2** *(apaisement)* healing

cicatriser [3] [sikatrize] **VT 1** *Méd* to heal, *Spéc* to cicatrize; **cette pommade fera c. la plaie plus vite** this cream will help the wound heal up more quickly **2** *(adoucir)* to heal; **le temps cicatrise toutes les blessures** time heals all wounds
VI *(coupure)* to heal *or* to close up; *(tissus)* to form a scar
VPR se cicatriser *(coupure)* to heal *or* to close up; *(tissus)* to form a scar; *Fig* to heal

cicéro [sisero] **NM** *Typ* em

ciclée [sikle] **NF** *Suisse Fam* shriek

cicler [3] [sikle] **VI** *Suisse Fam* to shriek

ciclosporine [siklɔspɔrin] **NF** *Pharm* cyclosporin

ci-contre [sikɔ̃tr] **ADV** opposite; **illustré c.** as shown (in the picture) opposite; *Compta* **porté c.** as per contra

CICR [seiseɛr] **NM** *(abrév* **Comité international de la Croix-Rouge**) IRCC

> **SUFFIX**
>
> **-CIDE**
>
> • This suffix is found at the end of words such as **suicide**, **homicide**, **infanticide**, **génocide**, **ethnocide**, where it suggests the KILLING of human beings, but also in **herbicide**, **pesticide**, **fongicide** or **spermicide**, which are all products designed to kill undesirable micro-organisms.
>
> • Note that both the murder and the murderer are referred to by the same word in the case of **infanticide** (infanticide/child-killer), **régicide** (regicide), **fratricide** (fratricide), **matricide** (matricide), **parricide** (parricidal).
>
> • Note also that, where the French uses the same word for the adjective and the noun, the English has two different words: infanticid*al*/infanticide, homicid*al*/homicide, herbicid*al*/herbicide, etc.
>
> • In recent years, the adjective **liberticide**, originally considered literary in register, has become very widespread in the media, as in the following examples:
>
> **un projet de loi liberticide** a bill that will destroy civil liberty; **un député liberticide** a member of parliament intent on destroying one's civil liberty
>
> • Following the same pattern, adjectives like **démocraticide** (which threatens to destroy democracy) are being spontaneously coined, even if they don't appear in dictionaries.

ci-dessous [sidəsu] **ADV** below

ci-dessus [sidəsy] **ADV** above; **l'adresse c.** the above address

ci-devant [sidəvɑ̃] **ADV** *Vieilli* previously, formerly
NMF INV *Hist* former aristocrat

CIDEX, Cidex [sidɛks] **NM** *(abrév* **courrier individuel à distribution exceptionnelle**) = system grouping letter boxes in country areas

CIDJ [seideʒi] **NM** *(abrév* **centre d'information et de documentation de la jeunesse**) = careers advisory service

cidre [sidr] **NM** *Br* cider, *Am* hard cider; **c. bouché** bottled cider *(with a seal)*; **c. brut** dry cider; **c. doux** sweet cider

cidrerie [sidrəri] **NF** cider-house

Cie *(abrév écrite* **Compagnie**) Co

ciel [sjɛl] *(pl sens* **1, 3–5 cieux** [sjø], *pl sens* **2, 6, 7 ciels**) **NM 1** *(espace)* sky; **haut dans le c.** (high) up in the sky; **entre c. et terre** in the air, in midair; **une explosion en plein c.** a midair explosion; **jusqu'au c.** (up) to the skies; **c. pommelé** mackerel sky; **lever les bras au c.** to throw up one's hands *(in exasperation, despair etc)*; **lever les yeux au c.** *(d'exaspération)* to roll one's eyes; **tomber du c.** *(arriver opportunément)* to be heaven-sent *or* a godsend; *(être stupéfait)* to be stunned
2 *Météo* **c. clair/nuageux** clear/cloudy sky
3 *Astron* sky
4 *Rel* Heaven; **le c. m'en est témoin** (as) Heaven is my witness
5 *Littéraire (fatalité)* fate; *(providence)* **c'est le c. qui t'envoie** you're a godsend; **le c. soit loué** thank heavens
6 *Mines* roof; **carrière/mine à c. ouvert** opencast quarry/mine
7 *(plafond)* **c. de chambre** canopy; **c. de lit** canopy
EXCLAM *Vieilli* **(juste) c.!** heavens above!, (good) heavens!
• **ciels NMPL** *Littéraire (temps)* **les ciels changeants de Bretagne** the changing skies of Brittany; *Beaux-Arts* **les ciels tourmentés de Van Gogh** Van Gogh's tortured skies
• **cieux NMPL** *Littéraire (région)* climes, climate; **sous des cieux plus cléments** in milder climes
• **à ciel ouvert ADJ INV 1** *Mines Br* open-cast, *Am* open-cut **2** *(piscine, stade)* open-air

cierge [sjɛrʒ] **NM** *Rel (bougie)* altar candle; **brûler un c. à un saint** to burn a candle to a saint; **c. magique** sparkler

cieux [sjø] *voir* **ciel**

cigale [sigal] **NF** *Entom* cicada

cigare [sigar] **NM 1** *(à fumer)* cigar **2** *Fam (tête)* head, nut; **avoir mal au c.** to have a headache; **mets-toi ça dans le c.** get that into your thick skull

cigarette [sigarɛt] **NF 1** *(à fumer)* cigarette; **fumer une c.** to smoke a cigarette, to have a smoke; **la c. ce n'est pas bon pour la santé** smoking is bad for you *or* for your health; **c. filtre** filter-tipped cigarette **2** *(à manger)* **c. (russe)** = shortcake biscuit shaped like a brandy snap

cigarettier, -ère [sigarɛtje, -ɛr] **NM,F** cigarette manufacturer

cigarillo [sigarijo] **NM** cigarillo

cigogne [sigɔɲ] **NF 1** *Orn* stork; **c. blanche** white stork; **c. noire** black stork **2** *Tech (levier)* crank lever

ciguë [sigy] **NF** *Bot* **grande c.** hemlock; **petite c.** fool's-parsley

ci-inclus, -e [siɛ̃kly, -yz] *(mpl* **inv**, *fpl* **ci-incluses**) **ADJ** *(après le nom)* enclosed; **la copie ci-incluse** the enclosed copy
ADV (vous trouverez) c. vos quittances please find bill enclosed; **c. une copie du testament et les instructions du notaire** enclosures: one copy of the will and the solicitor's instructions

CIJ [seiʒi] **NF** *(abrév* **Cour internationale de justice**) ICJ

ci-joint, -e [siʒwɛ̃, -ɛ̃t] *(mpl* **ci-joints**, *fpl* **ci-jointes**) **ADJ** *(après le nom)* attached, enclosed; **après examen des pièces ci-jointes** on studying the enclosed documents
ADV *(avant le nom)* **c. photocopie** photocopy enclosed; **(veuillez trouver) c. la facture correspondante** please find enclosed *or* attached the invoice relating to your order

cil [sil] **NM 1** *Anat* eyelash, lash, *Spéc* cilium **2** *Biol* cilium

cilice [silis] **NM** hair shirt, *Spéc* cilice

cillement [sijmɑ̃] **NM** blinking, *Spéc* nictitation

ciller [3] [sije] **VI 1** *(battre des cils)* to blink **2** *(réagir)* **il n'a pas cillé** he didn't bat an eyelid *or* turn a hair

cimaise [simɛz] **NF 1** *Beaux-Arts* picture rail; **pendre un tableau aux plus hautes cimaises** to sky a painting **2** *Archit* cymatium

cime [sim] **NF 1** *Géog* peak, summit, top; *Littéraire* **les cimes** the mountain tops **2** *(d'un arbre, d'un mât)* crown, top

ciment [simɑ̃] **NM 1** *Constr* cement; **c. à prise lente/rapide** slow-setting/quick-setting cement; **c. armé** reinforced concrete; **c. dentaire** amalgam **2** *Fig (lien)* bond; **l'enfant fut le c. de leur amour** the child acted as a bond between them

cimentation [simɑ̃tasjɔ̃] **NF** *Constr & Fig* cementing

cimenter [3] [simɑ̃te] **VT 1** *Constr* to cement **2** *Fig (renforcer)* to consolidate

cimenterie [simɑ̃tri] **NF** cement factory, cement works *(singulier)*

cimeterre [simtɛr] **NM** *(sabre)* scimitar

cimetière [simtjɛr] **NM** cemetery, graveyard; *(autour d'une église)* churchyard; **le c. des éléphants** elephants' graveyard; **c. de voitures** scrapyard *(for cars)*

cimier [simje] **NM 1** *(d'un casque)* crest **2** *Culin (d'un cerf etc)* haunch; *(d'un bœuf)* rump

cinabre [sinabr] **NM 1** *Miner* cinnabar **2** *Beaux-Arts* vermilion

ciné [sine] **NM** *Fam* **1** *(spectacle)* **le c.** the cinema, the movies; **se faire un c.** to go and see a movie *or Br* film **2** *(édifice) Br* cinema, *Am* movie theater

cinéaste [sineast] **NMF** movie director, *Br* film director

ciné-club [sineklœb] *(pl* **ciné-clubs**) **NM** *Br* film society, *Am* movie club

cinéma [sinema] **NM 1** *(édifice) Br* cinema, *Am* movie theater; **aller au c.** to go to the movies *or Br* cinema; **c. d'art et d'essai** arthouse; **c. à domicile** home cinema; **c. multisalle** multiplex, multi-screen cinema; **c. permanent** continuous performance; **c. en plein air** *(dans les pays chauds)* open-air cinema; *(aux États-Unis)* drive-in (movie-theater); **un c. de quartier** a local cinema
2 *(spectacle, genre)* **le c.** the movies, the cinema; **des effets encore jamais vus au c.** effects never before seen on screen; **le c. de Pasolini** Pasolini's movies *or Br* films; **le c. d'animation** cartoons, animation; **le c. d'art et d'essai** arthouse movies *or Br* films; **c. d'auteur** independent film-making; **c. direct** direct cinema; **c. indépendant** independent cinema; **le c. muet** silent movies *or Br* films; **le c. parlant** talking pictures, talkies; **le c. en relief** three-dimensional *or* 3-D movies *or Br* films
3 *(métier)* **le c.** *Br* film-making, *Am* movie-making; **faire du c.** *(technicien)* to work in *Br* films *or Am* the movies; *(acteur)* to be a screen actor, *Br* to act in films; **étudiant en c.** student of *Br* film *or Am* movies; **école de c.** film school
4 *(industrie)* **le c.** the movie *or Br* film industry
5 *Fam (locutions)* **c'est du c.** it's (all) play acting; **faire du** *ou* **tout un c. (pour)** to kick up a huge fuss (about); **arrête (de faire) ton c.!** *(de faire des histoires)* stop making such a fuss!; *(de mentir)* stop winding us up!; *(de bluffer)* stop shooting your mouth off!; **se faire du c.** to fantasize
• **de cinéma ADJ** *(festival, revue, vedette)* movie *(avant n)*, *Br* film *(avant n)*

CinémaScope® [sinemaskɔp] **NM** *Cin* CinemaScope®

cinémathèque [sinematɛk] **NF** movie *or Br* film library; **la C. française** = the French film institute

> **LA CINÉMATHÈQUE FRANÇAISE**
>
> Founded in 1936, the Cinémathèque specializes in the conservation and restoration of films; it also screens films for public viewing.

cinématique [sinematik] **NF** kinematics *(singulier)*

cinématographe [sinematɔgraf] **NM** cinematograph

cinématographie [sinematɔgrafi] **NF** cinematography

cinématographier [9] [sinematɔgrafje] **VT** to film

cinématographique [sinematɔgrafik] **ADJ** cinematographic, movie *(avant n)*, *Br* film *(avant n)*; **les techniques cinématographiques** cinematic techniques; **une grande carrière c.** a great career in the cinema; **droits d'adaptation c.** film rights; **droits de reproduction c.** film printing rights

cinématophotographie [sinematɔfɔtɔgrafi] **NF** cinemaphotography

cinéma-vérité [sinemaverite] **NM INV** cinéma vérité

cinémomètre [sinemɔmɛtr] **NM** tachometer, speedometer

ciné-parc [sinepark] *(pl* **ciné-parcs**) **NM** *Can Br* drive-in cinema, *Am* drive-in (movie theater)

cinéphile [sinefil] **NMF** movie buff, *Br* film buff
ADJ être (très) c. to be a movie *or Br* film buff

cinéraire [sinerɛr] **ADJ** cinerary; **urne c.** funeral urn
NF *Bot* cineraria

Cinérama® [sinerama] **NM** Cinerama®

cinéroman [sinerɔmɑ̃] **NM** cinenovel

cinétique [sinetik] *Phys* **ADJ** kinetic
NF kinetics *(singulier)*

cinghalais, -e [sɛ̃galɛ, -ɛz] **ADJ** Singhalese, Sinhalese

NM *(langue)* Singhalese, Sinhalese
• **Cinghalais, -e NM,F** Singhalese, Sinhalese; **les C.** the Singhalese *or* Sinhalese

cinglant, -e [sɛ̃glɑ̃, -ɑ̃t] **ADJ 1** *(violent ▸ pluie)* lashing; *(▸ vent)* bitter, biting; *(▸ gifle)* stinging **2** *(blessant ▸ remarque, paroles)* biting, cutting, scathing; **d'un ton c.** scathingly

cinglé, -e [sɛ̃gle] *Fam* **ADJ** crazy, nuts; **t'es pas un peu c.!** are you crazy?
NM,F *Br* nutter, *Am* screwball; **les cinglés du volant/cinéma** car/movie fanatics

cingler [3] [sɛ̃gle] **VI 1** *Naut* **c. vers** to sail (at full sail) towards, to make for **2** *(tournure impersonnelle) Fam* **ça cingle** it's freezing *or Br* baltic
VT 1 *(fouetter)* to lash; **la pluie cingle les vitres** the rain is lashing the windowpanes **2** *(blesser)* to sting; **la grêle lui cinglait le visage** the hail was stinging his/her face

cinoche [sinɔʃ] **NM** *Fam* **1** *(bâtiment) Br* cinema❑, *Am* movie theater❑; **aller au c.** to go to the movies❑ *or Br* pictures; **je me ferais bien un petit c. ce soir** I quite fancy going to the movies❑ *or Br* pictures tonight **2** *(art)* movies❑, cinema❑

cinoque [sinɔk] *Fam* **ADJ** crazy, loopy
NMF nutcase, *Br* nutter, *Am* screwball

cinq [sɛ̃k] **ADJ 1** *(gén)* five; **c. livres de pommes** five pounds of apples; **c. cents/mille étoiles** five hundred/thousand stars; **c. pour cent** five per cent; **c. dixièmes** five tenths; **couper/partager qch en c.** to cut/divide sth into five; **c. par c.** five by five, in fives; **entrer (c.) par c.** to come in in fives *or* five at a time; **c. fois mieux** five times better; **elle a c. ans** *(fille)* she's five (years old *or* of age); *(voiture)* it's five years old; **une fille de c. ans** a five-year-old girl; *Euph* **les c. lettres** ≃ a four-letter word; **dire les c. lettres à qn** to tell sb where to go; **bouteille c. étoiles** = inexpensive wine bottle (with five stars embossed on the neck) for which a deposit is payable; *Aut* **une c. portes** a five-door model; *Journ* **c. colonnes à la une** a banner headline
2 *(dans des séries)* fifth; **à la page c.** on page five; **au chapitre c.** in chapter five, in the fifth chapter; **il arrive le c. novembre** he's arriving on November (the) fifth *or* the fifth of November; **quel jour sommes-nous? – le c. novembre** what's the date today? – the fifth of November; **Louis V** Louis the Fifth
3 *(pour exprimer les minutes)* **trois heures c.** five past three; **trois heures moins c.** five to three; *Fam* **elle est arrivée à c.** she arrived at five past; **c. minutes** *(d'horloge)* five minutes; *(un moment)* a short while; **c. minutes plus tard, il a changé d'avis** a few minutes later he changed his mind; **j'en ai pour c. minutes** it'll only take me a few minutes; **il doit s'absenter c. minutes pour changer sa voiture de place** he's got to go and move his car, it'll only take him a few minutes; **c'est à c. minutes (d'ici)** it's not very far from here
PRON five; **nous étions c. dans la pièce** there were five of us in the room; **j'en ai c.** I've got five; *Fam* **en serrer c. à qn** to shake hands with sb❑
NM INV 1 *(gén)* five; **c. est la moitié de dix** five is half of ten; **c. et c. font dix** five and five are ten; **deux fois c.** two times five, twice five
2 *(numéro d'ordre)* number five; **c'est le c. qui a gagné** number five wins; **allez au c.** *(maison)* go to number five
3 *(chiffre écrit)* five; **dessiner un c.** to draw a five
4 *(dans un jeu)* five; *(quille)* kingpin; *Cartes* **le c. de carreau/pique** the five of diamonds/spades
5 *TV* **La C., La 5** = former French television channel
• **cinq sur cinq ADV** *aussi Fig* **je te reçois c. sur c.** I'm reading *or* receiving you loud and clear; **t'as compris? – c. sur c.!** got it? – got it!
• **en cinq sec ADV** *Fam* in no time at all, in two shakes; **en c. sec, c'était fait** it was done in no time
• **cinq à sept NM INV** *Fam (réunion)* afternoon get-together; *(rendez-vous amoureux)* lovers' rendez-vous *(typically after work)*

cinquantaine [sɛ̃kɑ̃tɛn] **NF 1** *(quantité)* **une c.** around *or* about fifty, fifty or so; **une c. de voitures** around *or* about fifty cars; **elle a une c. d'années** she's around *or* about fifty (years old) **2** *(âge)* **avoir la c.** to be around *or* about fifty; **quand on arrive à** *ou* **atteint la c.** when you hit fifty

cinquante [sɛ̃kɑ̃t] **ADJ 1** *(gén)* fifty; **c. est la moitié de cent** fifty is half of one hundred; **c. et un** fifty-one; **c.-deux** fifty-two; **c. et unième** fifty-first; **c. mille habitants** fifty thousand inhabitants; *Fam* **deux billets de c.** two fifty-euro notes❑ *or* fifties; **dans les années c.** in the fifties; **la mode des années c.** fifties' fashions; **c. pour cent des personnes interrogées pensent que…** fifty per cent of *or* half the people we asked think that…; **il est mort à c. ans** he died at *or* when he was fifty
2 *(dans des séries)* fiftieth; **page/numéro c.** page/number fifty
3 *Sport* **le c. mètres** the fifty metres
4 *Fam (locutions)* **des solutions, il n'y en a pas c.** there aren't that many ways to solve the problem; **je te l'ai dit c. fois!** if I've told you once, I've told you a hundred times!
PRON fifty
NM INV 1 *(gén)* fifty; **c. est la moitié de cent** fifty is half of one hundred; **c. et c. font cent** fifty and fifty are a hundred; **deux fois c.** two times fifty **2** *(numéro d'ordre)* number fifty; **c'est le c. qui a gagné** number fifty wins; **allez au c.** *(maison)* go to number fifty **3** *(chiffre écrit)* fifty; **le c. n'est pas lisible** the fifty is illegible

cinquantenaire [sɛ̃kɑ̃tnɛr] **ADJ 1** *(qui dure cinquante ans)* fifty-year *(avant n)* **2** *(bâtiment)* over fifty years old
NM fiftieth anniversary, golden jubilee

cinquantième [sɛ̃kɑ̃tjɛm] **ADJ** fiftieth
NMF 1 *(personne)* fiftieth **2** *(objet)* fiftieth (one)
NM 1 *(partie)* fiftieth **2** *(étage) Br* fiftieth floor, *Am* fifty-first floor **3** *Naut* **les cinquantièmes hurlants** the Howling Fifties
NF *Théât* fiftieth performance; *voir aussi* **cinquième**

cinquième [sɛ̃kjɛm] **ADJ** fifth; **le c. volume de la collection** the fifth volume in the series; **le c. de la somme globale** the fifth part of the total sum; **le vingt-c. concurrent** the twenty-fifth competitor; **la quarante-c. année** the forty-fifth year; **arriver c.** to come fifth; **c. colonne** fifth column; *Méd* **c. maladie** fifth disease; *Fig* **être la c. roue du carrosse** *ou* **de la charrette** to be a fifth wheel
NMF 1 *(personne)* fifth; **je suis c.** *(dans une file)* I'm fifth; *(dans un classement)* I came fifth **2** *(objet)* fifth (one); **le c. était cassé** the fifth (one) was broken
NM 1 *(partie)* fifth **2** *(étage) Br* fifth floor, *Am* sixth floor **3** *(arrondissement de Paris)* fifth (arrondissement)
NF 1 *Scol Br* ≃ second year, *Am* ≃ seventh grade **2** *Aut* fifth gear; **en c.** in fifth (gear); **passer la c.** to go into fifth (gear)
3 *Mus* fifth
4 *(en danse)* fifth (position)

cinquièmement [sɛ̃kjɛmmɑ̃] **ADV** fifthly, in fifth place

cintrage [sɛ̃traʒ] **NM 1** *Métal* bending **2** *Archit* centring

cintre [sɛ̃tr] **NM 1** *(pour un habit)* (coat)hanger
2 *Archit* arch
3 *Métal* bend, curve
4 *Théât* rigging loft; **les cintres** the flies

cintré, -e [sɛ̃tre] **ADJ 1** *Couture* close-fitting *(at the waist)*, waisted **2** *(fenêtre)* arched; *(poutre)* bent, curved **3** *Fam (fou)* crazy, nuts

cintrer [3] [sɛ̃tre] **VT 1** *Archit* to arch, to vault **2** *(courber)* to bend, to curve **3** *Couture* to take in *(at the waist)*

CIO [seio] **NM 1** *(abrév* **Comité international olympique)** IOC **2** *(abrév* **centre d'information et d'orientation)** careers advisory centre

CIP [seipe] *Com (abrév* **carriage and insurance paid to)** CIP

cipaye [sipaj] **NM** *Mil* sepoy; *Hist* **la révolte des cipayes** the Indian Mutiny

cirage [siraʒ] **NM** *(cire)* shoe polish; *(polissage)* polishing; *Fam* **être dans le c.** to be flying blind; *Fig* to be a bit groggy

circadien, -enne [sirkadjɛ̃, -ɛn] **ADJ** *Biol* circadian

circlip [sirklip] **NM** *Tech* circlip

circoncire [101] [sirkɔ̃sir] **VT** to circumcise

circoncis [sirkɔ̃si] **ADJ** circumcised
NM *(garçon)* circumcised boy; *(homme)* circumcised man

circoncisait *etc voir* **circoncire**

circoncision [sirkɔ̃sizjɔ̃] **NF** circumcision

circonférence [sirkɔ̃ferɑ̃s] **NF 1** *Géom* circumference; **avoir dix centimètres de c.** to have a circumference of ten centimetres, to be ten centimetres in circumference **2** *(tour)* periphery

circonflexe [sirkɔ̃flɛks] **ADJ** *Ling* circumflex

circonlocution [sirkɔ̃lɔkysjɔ̃] **NF** *Péj* circumlocution; **que de circonlocutions!** what a roundabout way of putting it!; **parler par circonlocutions** to speak in a roundabout way; **après de longues circonlocutions…** after much beating about the bush…

circonscription [sirkɔ̃skripsjɔ̃] **NF 1** *Admin & Pol* area, district; **c. administrative** constituency; **c. électorale** *(aux municipales)* ward; *(aux législatives)* constituency **2** *Géom* circumscription, circumscribing

circonscrire [99] [sirkɔ̃skrir] **VT 1** *(limiter ▸ extension, dégâts)* to limit, to control; **c. un incendie** to bring a fire under control, to contain a fire **2** *(préciser ▸ sujet)* to define the limits *or* scope of **3** *Géom* to circumscribe

circonspect, -e [sirkɔ̃spɛ, -ɛkt] **ADJ** *(observateur, commentateur)* cautious, wary; *(approche)* cautious, *Sout* circumspect; **il était c. dans ses propos** he spoke cautiously

circonspection [sirkɔ̃spɛksjɔ̃] **NF** caution, cautiousness, wariness; **avec c.** cautiously, warily

circonstance [sirkɔ̃stɑ̃s] **NF 1** *(situation)* **circonstances** circumstances; **quelles étaient les circonstances?** what were the circumstances?; **étant donné les circonstances** given the circumstances *or* situation; **en pareille c.** under such circumstances, in such a case **2** *(conjoncture)* circumstance, occasion; **profiter de la c.** to seize the opportunity **3** *Jur* **circonstances aggravantes/atténuantes** aggravating/extenuating circumstances
• **de circonstance ADJ 1** *(approprié)* appropriate, fitting; **vers de c.** occasional verse; **ce ne serait pas de c.** it would not be appropriate **2** *Gram* **complément de c.** adverbial phrase
• **pour la circonstance ADV** for the occasion

circonstancié, -e [sirkɔ̃stɑ̃sje] **ADJ** detailed

circonstanciel, -elle [sirkɔ̃stɑ̃sjɛl] **ADJ 1** *Gram* adverbial **2** *Littéraire* circumstantial; **déclaration/mesure circonstancielle** declaration/measure dictated by the circumstances

circonvenir [40] [sirkɔ̃vnir] **VT** *(abuser ▸ juge, témoin)* to circumvent; **c. l'électorat** to trick the voters

circonvolution [sirkɔ̃vɔlysjɔ̃] **NF 1** *(enroulement)* circumvolution **2** *Anat* convolution, gyrus

circuit [sirkɥi] **NM 1** *Aut & Sport* circuit; **c. automobile** racing circuit
2 *(itinéraire)* tour, trip; **faire le c. des châteaux/vins** to do a tour of the chateaux/vineyards; **c. touristique** organized trip *or* tour
3 *(détour)* detour, circuitous route; **faire un long c. pour arriver quelque part** to make a long detour to get somewhere; *Fig* **par tout un c. de raisonnement** through a long and complicated thought process
4 *Élec & Électron* circuit; **couper le c.** to switch off; **mettre qch en c.** to connect sth, to switch sth on; **mettre qch hors c.** to disconnect sth; **c. basse tension** low-tension circuit; **c. haute tension** high-tension circuit; **c. d'induction** inductive circuit; **c. de retour à la masse** earth return circuit
5 *Ordinat* **c. de commande** command circuit; **c. ET** AND circuit; **c. imprimé** printed circuit; **c. intégré** integrated circuit; **c. de liaison** link circuit; **c. logique** logic circuit
6 *Tech & Aut* **c. d'allumage** ignition system; **c. d'allumage par bobine** coil-ignition system; **c. de carburant étanche** sealed fuel system; **c. de charge** *(de pile)* charging system; **c. de démarrage** starting circuit; **c. d'eau** water circuit; **c. de freinage** braking system; **c. de graissage** lubrication circuit; **c. hydraulique** hydraulic circuit; **c. d'injection d'essence** petrol-injection system; **c. de lubrification** lubrication system; **c. de préchauf-**

fage pre-heating system; **c. de refroidissement** cooling system

7 *(parcours)* progression, route

8 *Écon & Com* channel; **c. commercial** commercial channel; **c. de commercialisation** marketing network; **c. de distribution** distribution network; **circuits de vente** commercial channels

9 *Cin* network; **le film est fait pour le c. commercial** it's a mainstream movie

10 *Rad* **c. de cryptage** scrambling circuit

11 *(pourtour d'une ville)* circumference

12 *(locution)* **elle est encore dans le c.** she's still around; **quand je rentrerai dans le c.** when I'm back in circulation

• **en circuit fermé** ADJ *(télévision)* closed-circuit *(avant n)* ADV **1** *Électron* in closed circuit **2** *(discuter, vivre)* without any outside contact

circulaire [sirkylɛr] ADJ **1** *(rond)* circular, round

2 *(tournant ▸ mouvement, regard)* circular

3 *Transp Br* return *(avant n)*, *Am* round-trip *(avant n)*

4 *(définition, raisonnement)* circular

NF circular

circulairement [sirkylɛrmɑ̃] ADV *(marcher, rouler)* in a circle

circulant, -e [sirkylɑ̃, -ɑ̃t] ADJ *Fin (billets, devises)* in circulation; *(capitaux)* circulating

circulation [sirkylasjɔ̃] NF **1** *Transp* traffic; **la c. des camions est interdite le dimanche** *Br* lorries *or Am* trucks are not allowed to run on Sundays; **la c. est très difficile** the traffic is very heavy; **il y a de la/peu de c. aujourd'hui** the traffic is heavy/there isn't much traffic today; **une route à grande c.** a trunk road; **c. aérienne/ferroviaire/routière** air/rail/road traffic

2 *(du sang, de l'air, d'un fluide)* circulation; **avoir une bonne/mauvaise c.** to have good/bad circulation; **des problèmes de c.** circulation *or* circulatory problems

3 *(déplacement)* movement, circulation; **la libre c. des personnes/des biens/des capitaux** the free movement of people/goods/capital; **c. monétaire** circulation of money, money in circulation

4 *(circuit)* **enlever** *ou* **retirer de la c.** *Com* to take off the market; *Fig* to take out of circulation; **être en c.** to be on the market; **mettre en c.** *(argent)* to put into circulation; *Com* to bring out, to put on the market

> Il faut noter que le mot anglais **circulation** ne s'emploie jamais pour faire référence à la circulation routière.

circulatoire [sirkylatwar] ADJ *(appareil, troubles)* circulatory

circuler [3] [sirkyle] VI **1** *(se déplacer ▸ personne)* to move; **circulez, il n'y a rien à voir** move along now, there's nothing to see

2 *Transp (conducteur)* to drive; *(flux de voitures)* to move; *(train, bus)* to run; **rien ne circule ce matin** the traffic's at a standstill this morning; **on circule très mal à ce moment de la journée** it's very difficult to get anywhere at this time of day; **le bus 21 circule de nuit** the number 21 bus runs at night

3 *(air, fluide)* to circulate

4 *(passer de main en main)* to be passed around *or* round; *Fin (billets, devises)* to be in circulation; *Fin (capitaux)* to be circulating; **le rapport circule** the report's being circulated; **faites c. la bouteille** pass the bottle round; **faire c. des faux billets** to put forged banknotes into circulation; **faire c. une pétition** to circulate a petition; *Fin* **faire c. des effets** to keep bills afloat

5 *(se propager)* to circulate; **faire c. des bruits** to spread rumours; **c'est une rumeur qui circule** it's a rumour that's going around

circumnavigation [sirkɔmnavigasjɔ̃] NF circumnavigation

cire [sir] NF **1** *(pour le bois)* (wax) polish

2 *(plastique, dans une ruche)* wax; **un personnage en c.** a waxwork; **c. d'abeille** beeswax; **c. à cacheter** sealing wax

3 *(dans l'oreille)* earwax

4 *Pétr* mineral *or* earth wax

5 *(locution)* **c'est une c. molle** he's/she's got no will of his/her own

• **de cire** ADJ *(poupée, figurine)* wax *(avant n)*

ciré, -e [sire] ADJ *(meuble, parquet)* waxed, polished; *(chaussures)* polished

NM **1** *(vêtement ▸ gén)* oilskin; *(▸ de marin)* sou'-wester **2** *Tex* oilskin

cirer [3] [sire] VT **1** *(faire briller ▸ meuble, parquet)* to wax, to polish; *(▸ chaussure)* to polish; *Fam Fig* **c. les pompes à qn** to lick sb's boots **2** *très Fam (locution)* **il en a rien à c. (de tes histoires)** he doesn't give a damn (abour your stories)

cireur, -euse[1] [sirœr, -øz] NM,F *(de rue)* shoe-shiner; *Fam* **un c. de pompes** a bootlicker

• **cireuse** NF floor polisher

cireux, -euse[2] [sirø, -øz] ADJ **1** *(comme la cire)* waxy, wax-like, *Littéraire* waxen **2** *(jaunâtre)* wax-coloured, *Littéraire* waxen

cirque [sirk] NM **1** *(chapiteau)* circus, big top; *(représentation)* circus; **aller au c.** to go to the circus; **c. forain** *ou* **ambulant** travelling circus; *Fig* **c. médiatique** media circus

2 *Fam (agitation, désordre)* **c'est pas un peu fini ce c.?** will you stop fooling around?; **c'est un vrai c. ici!** it's chaos *or* pandemonium in here!

3 *Fam (complications)* **quel c. pour obtenir ces renseignements!** what a performance *or* carry-on just to get this information!; **arrête un peu ton c.!** stop making a fuss!; **tous les matins, elle fait son c. pour s'habiller** every morning she makes an awful fuss about getting dressed

4 *Géog* cirque, corrie; *(sur la Lune)* crater

cirrhose [siroz] NF *Méd* cirrhosis; **c. du foie** cirrhosis of the liver; **avoir une c. du foie** to have cirrhosis (of the liver)

cirrocumulus [sirɔkymylys] NM INV *Météo* cirrocumulus

cirrostratus [sirɔstratys] NM INV *Météo* cirrostratus

cirrus [sirys] NM INV *Météo* cirrus

cisaille [sizaj] NF **1** *Tech (outil)* **c., cisailles** (pair of) shears; **c. à bordures** edging shears; **c. à haies** hedge clipper(s); **c. à lame** guillotine **2** *Métal (rognures)* parings, cuttings

cisaillement [sizajmɑ̃] NM **1** *Métal* cutting **2** *Hort* pruning **3** *Tech (usure)* shearing, shear

cisailler [3] [sizaje] VT **1** *(barbelés, tôle)* to cut **2** *(branches)* to prune **3** *(couper grossièrement)* to hack (at)

VPR **se cisailler 1** *(métal)* to shear off **2** *(se couper)* **il s'est cisaillé la joue** he cut *or* slashed his cheek

cisalpin, -e [sizalpɛ̃, -in] ADJ Cisalpine; **la Gaule cisalpine** Cisalpine Gaul

ciseau, -x [sizo] NM **1** *Tech (outil)* chisel; **c. à froid** cold chisel **2** *Sport (prise de catch, de lutte)* scissors hold

• **ciseaux** NMPL **1** *(outil)* **(une paire de) ciseaux** (a pair of) scissors; **(une paire de) grands ciseaux** (a pair of) shears; **donner un coup de ciseaux dans un tissu** to cut a piece of material with scissors; **donner des coups de ciseaux dans un texte** to make cuts in a text; **ciseaux à bouts ronds** blunt- *or* round-ended scissors; **ciseaux de couturière** dressmaking scissors; **ciseaux à denteler** pinking shears; **ciseaux à ongles** nail scissors **2** *Sport* **saut en ciseaux** scissor jump; **sauter en ciseaux** to do a scissor jump **3** *Gym* **faire des ciseaux** to do the scissors

ciselage [sizlaʒ], **cisèlement** [sizɛlmɑ̃] NM *(d'une grappe de raisin)* shearing; *(du métal)* engraving; *(du cuir)* embossing

ciseler [25] [sizle] VT **1** *(métal ▸ en défonçant)* to engrave; *(▸ en repoussant)* to emboss; *(pierre)* to chisel; **un bracelet en or ciselé** an engraved gold bracelet; *Fig* **son nez délicatement ciselé** his/her finely chiselled nose **2** *Littéraire (texte)* to polish; **un sonnet délicatement ciselé** a delicately crafted sonnet **3** *(ciboulette)* to snip

ciseleur [sizlœr] NM engraver

ciselure [sizlyr] NF **1** *Métal (en défoncé)* engraving; *(en repoussé)* embossing; *(sur un bijou)* (engraved) design **2** *Beaux-Arts & Menuis* chiselling **3** *(de reliure)* embossing

Cisjordanie [sisʒɔrdani] NF **la C.** the West Bank

cisjordanien, -enne [sisʒɔrdanjɛ̃, -ɛn] ADJ of/from the West Bank

• **Cisjordanien, -enne** NM,F = inhabitant of or person from the West Bank

cistercien, -enne [sistɛrsjɛ̃, -ɛn] *Rel* ADJ Cistercian

NM,F Cistercian; **les cisterciens** the Cistercians

citadelle [sitadɛl] NF **1** *Constr* citadel; *Fig* **la ferme avait été transformée en c.** the farm had been made into a fortress **2** *(centre)* stronghold

citadin, -e [sitadɛ̃, -in] ADJ *(habitude, paysage)* city *(avant n)*, town *(avant n)*; *(population)* town-dwelling, city-dwelling

NM,F *(habitant d'une grande ville)* city-dweller, town-dweller; **les citadins** the townsfolk, the townspeople; **moi, je suis un c., je ne pourrais pas vivre à la campagne** I'm a real city person, I could never live in the country

citation [sitasjɔ̃] NF **1** *(extrait)* quotation; **fin de c.** unquote **2** *Jur* summons; **c. à comparaître** *(pour un témoin)* subpoena; *(pour un accusé)* summons; **il a reçu une c. à comparaître** *(témoin)* he was subpoenaed; *(accusé)* he was summonsed

3 *Mil* **c. à l'ordre du jour** mention in dispatches

cité [site] NF **1** *(ville)* city; *(plus petite)* town

2 *(dans des noms de lieux)* **la C. interdite** the Forbidden City; **la c. des Papes** Avignon; **la c. phocéenne** Marseille, Marseilles

3 *(résidence)* (housing) *Br* estate *or Am* development; **les cités de banlieue** suburban housing estates *(in France, often evocative of poverty and delinquency)*; **c. ouvrière** *Br* ≃ council estate, *Am* ≃ housing project; **c. de transit** transit *or* temporary camp; **c. universitaire,** *Fam* **c. U** *Br* hall of residence, halls of residence, *Am* dormitory

4 *Antiq* city-state

cité-dortoir [sitedɔrtwar] *(pl* **cités-dortoirs)** NF commuter town

cité-jardin [siteʒardɛ̃] *(pl* **cités-jardins)** NF garden city

citer [3] [site] VT **1** *(donner un extrait de)* to cite, to quote (from); **je vous ai cité dans mon article** I quoted you in my article; **il a dit, je cite:...** he said, and I quote...

2 *(mentionner)* to mention; **c. qn en exemple** to cite sb as an example

3 *(énumérer)* to name, to quote, to list

4 *Jur (témoin)* to subpoena; *(accusé)* to summons

5 *Mil* to mention; **c. un soldat à l'ordre du jour** to mention a soldier in dispatches

citerne [sitɛrn] NF **1** *(cuve)* tank; *(pour l'eau)* water tank, cistern; **c. à mazout** oil tank **2** *Naut* tank **3** *(camion)* tanker

cithare [sitar] NF *Antiq* cithara; *(instrument moderne)* zither

citizen band [sitizənbɑ̃d] *(pl* **citizen bands)** NF Citizens' Band, CB

citoyen, -enne [sitwajɛ̃, -ɛn] NM,F **1** *Hist & Pol* citizen; **les droits du c.** civic rights; **accomplir son devoir de c.** *(voter)* to do one's civic duty, to vote; **c. d'honneur** = freeman **2** *Fam (personnage)* **qu'est-ce que c'est que ce c.-là?** *(inquiétant)* he's a bit of *Br* a queer fish *or Am* an odd duck; *(amusant)* what an eccentric!

ADJ *(relatif à la citoyenneté)* civic; **il s'est produit une sorte de rassemblement c. contre l'extrême-droite** there was a sort of citizens' movement against the far right; **il faut encourager l'engagement c. au niveau local pour renforcer le tissu social** civic engagement on a local level should be encouraged as a way of strengthening the fabric of society; **on attend de nos élus un véritable projet c., pas une simple gestion de l'économie** we expect those we elected to come up with a manifesto which truly benefits society, not one which simply manages the economy; **cette société rêve de troquer sa réputation de pollueuse contre celle d'entreprise citoyenne** this company wants to banish its reputation as a polluter and instead to be known for being socially responsible

citoyen-expert [sitwajɛ̃ɛkspɛr] *(pl* **citoyens-experts)** NM = well-informed and politically aware citizen

citoyenneté [sitwajɛnte] NF citizenship; **prendre la c. française** to acquire French citizenship

citrate [sitrat] NM *Chim* citrate

citrique [sitrik] ADJ *Chim* citric

citron [sitrɔ̃] NM **1** *(fruit)* lemon; **c. givré** lemon *Br* sorbet *or Am* sherbet *(served inside the skin of a* *whole lemon)*; **c. pressé** freshly squeezed lemon juice; **c. vert** lime **2** *Fam (tête)* nut; **se presser** *ou* **se creuser le c.** to rack *or Am* cudgel one's brains **3** *Minér* brimstone

ADJ INV (jaune) c. lemon-yellow, lemon

• **au citron** **ADJ** lemon *(avant n)*; **parfumé au c.** lemon-scented

citronnade [sitrɔnad] **NF** *Br* lemon squash, *Am* lemonade

citronné, -e [sitrɔne] **ADJ** *(gâteau, sauce)* lemon-flavoured; *(pochette)* lemon-scented; *(eau de toilette, lotion)* lemon *(avant n)*

citronnelle [sitrɔnɛl] **NF 1** *(mélisse)* lemon balm

2 *(aromate tropical)* lemongrass

3 *(baume)* citronella oil

4 *(boisson)* lemon liqueur

citronnier [sitrɔnje] **NM** *Bot* lemon tree

citrouille [sitruj] **NF 1** *(fruit)* pumpkin; *Fam* **j'ai la tête comme une c.** my head is fit to burst **2** *Fam (tête)* nut

cive [siv] **NF** chives

civelle [sivɛl] **NF** elver

civet [sivɛ] **NM** civet, stew; **c. de lapin** rabbit stew; **c. de lièvre, lièvre en c.** civet of hare, ≃ jugged hare

civette [sivɛt] **NF 1** *Bot* chives **2** *(animal, parfum, fourrure)* civet; *Zool* **c. des palmiers** palm civet

civière [sivjɛr] **NF** *Méd* stretcher

civil, -e [sivil] **ADJ 1** *(non religieux)* civil; **mariage c.** civil marriage ceremony; **enterrement c.** non-religious burial

2 *(non militaire)* civilian; **porter des vêtements civils** to wear civilian clothes

3 *Admin* **jour c.** civil *or* calendar day

4 *(non pénal)* civil

5 *Littéraire (courtois)* courteous, civil

NM 1 *(non militaire)* civilian **2** *Jur* civil action; **porter une affaire au c.** to bring a case before the civil courts

• **dans le civil** **ADV** in civilian life

• **en civil** **ADJ** **être en c.** *(soldat)* to be wearing civilian clothes; **policier en c.** plain clothes policeman

> Attention: ne pas confondre **civil** et **civilian** lorsque l'on traduit le terme français **civil**. Le terme **civilian** signifie uniquement **non militaire**.

civilement [sivilmɑ̃] **ADV 1** *Jur* **se marier c.** to have a civil wedding, *Br* ≃ to get married in a registry office; **être enterré c.** to be buried without religious ceremony; **être c. responsable** to be legally responsible; **poursuivre qn c.** to bring a civil action against sb **2** *Littéraire (courtoisement)* courteously

civilisable [sivilizabl] **ADJ** civilizable

civilisateur, -trice [sivilizatœr, -tris] **ADJ** civilizing

NM,F civilizer

civilisation [sivilizasjɔ̃] **NF** *(culture)* civilization; **les grandes civilisations du passé** great civilizations of the past; *Hum* **nous sommes revenus à la c. après dix jours sous la tente** we got back to civilization after ten days under canvas

• **de civilisation** **ADJ** **langue de c.** language of culture; **maladie de c.** social disease

civilisatrice [sivilizatris] *voir* **civilisateur**

civilisé, -e [sivilize] **ADJ** *(nation, peuple)* civilized; *Fam* **on est chez des gens civilisés, ici!** we're not savages!

NM,F civilized person, member of a civilized society

civiliser [3] [sivilize] **VT** *(société, tribu)* to civilize, to bring civilization to; *Fig* **c. qn** to civilize sb, to have a civilizing influence on sb

VPR se civiliser to become civilized

civilité [sivilite] **NF** *Littéraire (qualité)* politeness, polite behaviour, *Sout* civility; **la plus élémentaire c. voudrait que l'on fasse** *ou* **serait de...** it would be only polite to...

• **civilités** **NFPL** *Littéraire (paroles)* polite greetings; **présenter ses civilités à qn** to pay one's respects to sb

civique [sivik] **ADJ** *(gén)* civic; *(droits)* civil; **avoir l'esprit c.** to be public-spirited; *Anciennement Scol* **éducation** *ou* **instruction c.** civics *(singulier)*

civisme [sivism] **NM** sense of citizenship, public-spiritedness

clabaudage [klabodaʒ] **NM** *Littéraire (médisance)* (spiteful) gossip, backbiting

clabauder [3] [klabode] **VI** *Littéraire* **1** *(chien de chasse)* to bark (a lot) **2** *Fig* **c. sur** *ou* **contre qn** to say nasty things about sb

clabauderie [klabodri] **NF** = **clabaudage**

clabaudeur, -euse [klabodœr, -øz] **ADJ 1** *(chien)* barking **2** *Fig* gossiping, backbiting

NM,F *Fig* gossip, scandalmonger

clac [klak] **EXCLAM** *(bruit ▸ de fouet)* crack!; *(▸ d'une fenêtre)* slam!

clafoutis [klafuti] **NM** clafoutis *(sweet dish made from cherries or other fruit cooked in batter)*

claie [klɛ] **NF 1** *(pour les fruits)* rack **2** *(barrière)* fence, hurdle **3** *(tamis)* riddle, screen

CLAIR, -E [klɛr]

ADJ	
• light **1, 4**	• clear **2, 5–8**
• thin **3**	• obvious **8**
NM	
• light colour **1**	
ADV	
• light	

ADJ 1 *(lumineux)* light; **la pièce est très claire le matin** the room gets a lot of light in the morning; **une nuit claire** a fine *or* cloudless night; **un ciel c.** a clear *or* cloudless sky; **par temps c.** in clear weather; **il a le regard c.** he's got bright eyes

2 *(limpide ▸ eau)* clear, transparent; **teint c.** *(frais)* clear complexion; *(pâle)* fair complexion

3 *(peu épais ▸ gén)* thin; *(▸ soupe)* clear; *(rare)* sparse; **des bois clairs** sparsely wooded area

4 *(couleur)* light; **porter des vêtements clairs** to wear light *or* light-coloured clothes; **vert/rose c.** light green/pink; **une robe bleu c.** a pale blue dress

5 *(bien timbré)* clear; **d'une voix claire** in a clear voice

6 *(précis ▸ compte-rendu)* clear; **un résumé c. de la situation** a clear *or* lucid account of the situation; **ce n'est pas très c., précisez** it's not very clear, be more precise; **il a été on ne peut plus c. (là-dessus)** he was perfectly clear (about it); **se faire une idée claire de** to form a clear *or* precise picture of; **vous pourriez être plus c.?** could you elucidate?

7 *(perspicace)* clear; **je n'ai plus les idées très claires** I can't see things clearly any more; **avoir l'esprit c.** to be clear-thinking

8 *(évident)* clear, obvious; **il est c. que nous irons** obviously we'll go; **c'est c. et net** it's obvious; **il n'a rien compris, c'est c. et net** he clearly hasn't understood a thing; **je veux une réponse claire et nette** I want a definite answer; **cette affaire n'est pas très claire** there's something fishy about all this; **c'est comme le jour** *ou* **comme de l'eau de roche** *ou* **comme deux et deux font quatre** it's crystal clear

NM 1 *(couleur)* light colour; *Beaux-Arts* **les clairs et les sombres** light and shade

2 *Astron* **c. de lune** moonlight; **il y a un beau c. de lune ce soir** it's a fine moonlit night tonight; **au c. de lune** in the moonlight; **c. de terre** earthlight

3 *(locution)* **le plus c. de** the best part of; **passer le plus c. de son temps à faire qch** to spend most *or* the best part of one's time doing sth

ADV il fait déjà c. dehors it's already light outside; **il ne fait pas très c. ici** there isn't much light here; **parlons c.** let's not mince words!; **il ne voit pas très c.** he can't see too clearly *or* well; **on n'y voit plus très c. à cette heure-ci** the light's not really good enough at this time of the day; **y voir c.** *(dans une situation)* to see things clearly; **j'aimerais y voir c.** I'd like to understand; **y voir c. dans le jeu de qn** to see right through sb, to see through sb's little game

• **au clair** **ADJ** *voir* **sabre** **ADV tirer du vin au c.** to decant wine; **mettre** *ou* **tirer qch au c.** to clarify sth; **il faut tirer cette affaire au c.** this matter must be cleared up; **mettre ses idées au c.** to get one's ideas straight; **mettre qch au c. avec qn** to sort sth out with sb, to get sth straight with sb

• **en clair** **ADV 1** *(sans code)* **envoyer un message en c.** to send an unscrambled message; *TV* **diffuser en c.** to broadcast unscrambled programmes; *TV* **en c. jusqu'à 20 heures** can be watched by non-subscribers until 8 o'clock **2** *(bref)* in plain language

• **claire** **NF 1** *(bassin)* oyster bed **2** *(huître)* fattened oyster

clairance [klɛrɑ̃s] **NF** *Méd* clearance

clairement [klɛrmɑ̃] **ADV** clearly; **il a répondu très c.** his answer was quite clear; **on le voit c. sur le tableau** it's clearly visible on the board

clairet, -ette [klɛrɛ, -ɛt] **ADJ 1** *(léger ▸ sauce, vin)* light, *Péj* thin **2** *(faible ▸ voix)* thin, reedy

NM = light red wine

• **clairette** **NF** = light sparkling wine

claire-voie [klɛrvwa] *(pl* **claires-voies***)* **NF 1** *(barrière)* lattice, open-worked fence **2** *Archit* clerestory, clearstory **3** *Naut* deadlight

• **à claire-voie** **ADJ** open-work

clairière [klɛrjɛr] **NF 1** *(dans une forêt)* clearing, glade **2** *Tex* thin place

clair-obscur [klɛrɔpskyr] *(pl* **clairs-obscurs***)* **NM 1** *Beaux-Arts* chiaroscuro **2** *(pénombre)* twilight, half-light

clairon [klɛrɔ̃] **NM** *Mus (instrument)* bugle; *(joueur)* bugler; *(d'orgue)* clarion stop

claironnant, -e [klɛrɔnɑ̃, -ɑ̃t] **ADJ** *(voix)* resonant, *Littéraire* stentorian; **...dit-il d'une voix claironnante** ...he said, his words ringing out

claironner [3] [klɛrɔne] **VI 1** *(crier)* to shout **2** *(jouer du clairon)* to sound the bugle

VT to proclaim far and wide, to broadcast (to all and sundry)

clairsemé, -e [klɛrsəme] **ADJ** *(barbe, cheveux)* sparse, thin; *(arbres)* scattered; *(public, gazon)* sparse; *(population)* scattered, sparse

clairvoyance [klɛrvwajɑ̃s] **NF 1** *(lucidité)* clear-sightedness; **faire preuve de c.** to be clear-sighted; **il l'avait analysé avec c.** he had analysed it perceptively **2** *(de médium)* clairvoyance

clairvoyant, -e [klɛrvwajɑ̃, -ɑ̃t] **ADJ 1** *(lucide ▸ personne)* clearsighted, perceptive; *(▸ esprit)* perceptive **2** *(non aveugle)* sighted **3** *(médium)* clairvoyant

NM,F 1 *(non aveugle)* sighted person; **les clairvoyants** the sighted **2** *(médium)* clairvoyant

clam [klam] **NM** clam

clamecer [16] [klamse] = **clamser**

clamer [3] [klame] **VT 1** *(proclamer)* **c. son innocence** to protest one's innocence; **clamant leur mécontentement** making their dissatisfaction known **2** *(crier)* to clamour, to shout

clameur [klamœr] **NF** clamour *(UNCOUNT)*; **pousser des clameurs** to shout; **la c. du marché montait** *ou* **les clameurs du marché montaient jusqu'à nos fenêtres** the hubbub of the market could be heard from our windows

clamser [3] [klamse] **VI** *très Fam* to kick the bucket, to croak

clan [klɑ̃] **NM 1** *(en sociologie)* clan; **chef de c.** clan chief **2** *Péj (coterie)* clan, coterie, clique

clandestin, -e [klɑ̃dɛstɛ̃, -in] **ADJ 1** *(secret)* secret, underground, clandestine; **un mouvement c.** an underground movement **2** *(illégal)* illegal, *Sout* illicit

NM,F *(passager)* stowaway; *(immigré)* illegal immigrant; *(travailleur)* illegal worker

clandestinement [klɑ̃dɛstinmɑ̃] **ADV 1** *(secrètement)* secretly, in secret, clandestinely **2** *(illégalement)* illegally, *Sout* illicitly

clandestinité [klɑ̃dɛstinite] **NF** secrecy, clandestine nature

• **dans la clandestinité** **ADV** underground; **entrer dans la c.** to go underground; **des armes sont fabriquées dans la c.** weapons are made clandestinely

clanique [klanik] **ADJ 1** *(en sociologie)* clan *(avant n)* **2** *Péj (coterie)* clannish

clanisme [klanism] **NM 1** *(en sociologie)* clan system **2** *Péj (comportement)* clannishness

clap [klap] **NM** *Cin* clapperboard; **c. de fin** tail slate

clapet [klapɛ] NM 1 *Tech (soupape)* valve; **c. d'admission/d'échappement** inlet/exhaust valve; **c. de dérivation** by-pass valve 2 *Tél* **téléphone à c.** flip-top phone 3 *Fam (bouche)* **elle a un de ces clapets!** she's a real chatterbox!, she can talk the hind legs off a donkey!; **ferme ton c.!** shut your mouth!

clapier [klapje] NM 1 *(à lapins)* hutch 2 *Péj (appartement)* **c'est un vrai c. ici!** it's like living in a shoe box in this place! 3 *Géol* scree

clapir [32] [klapir] VI *(lapin)* to squeal

clapotage [klapɔtaʒ] NM *(des vagues)* lapping

clapoter [3] [klapɔte] VI *(eau, vague)* to lap

clapotis [klapɔti] NM *(de l'eau)* lapping

clappement [klapmɑ̃] NM *(de la langue)* clicking; **des clappements de langue** clicks of the tongue

clapper [3] [klape] VI **c. de la langue** to click one's tongue

claquage [klakaʒ] NM 1 *Méd (muscle)* strained muscle; *(ligament)* strained ligament; **se faire** *ou* **avoir un c.** *(muscle)* to strain a muscle 2 *Élec* (electric) breakdown; **c. thermique** thermal breakdown

claquant, -e [klakɑ̃, -ɑ̃t] ADJ *Fam* killing, *Br* knackering

claque [klak] NM 1 *(chapeau)* opera hat 2 *Can (chaussure)* galosh, *Am* rubber 3 *très Fam (maison de passe) Br* knocking-shop, *Am* cathouse
NF 1 *(coup)* smack, slap; *Fam* **donner** *ou* **mettre une c. à qn** to give sb a slap *or* smack; *Fam* **tu vas recevoir** *ou* **prendre une c.!** you'll get a smack!; *Fig* **se prendre une c.** to get a slap in the face; **les centristes se sont pris une c. aux dernières élections** the last elections were a slap in the face for the centre party; **une bonne c.** a stinger; *très Fam* **une c. dans la gueule** a smack in the *Br* gob *or Am* kisser; *Fig* a slap in the face
2 *Théât* claque
3 *(d'une chaussure)* upper
4 *Can (chaussure)* rubber overshoe
5 *Fam (locution)* **j'en ai ma c.** I've had it up to here

claqué, -e [klake] ADJ 1 *Fam (éreinté) Br* shattered, *Am* bushed 2 *Méd* strained

claquement [klakmɑ̃] NM *(bruit violent)* banging, slamming; **le c. sec du fouet** the sharp crack of the whip; **un c. de doigts** a snap of the fingers; *Fig* **sur un c. de doigts** in the twinkling of an eye; **un c. de langue** a clicking of the tongue; **entendre un c. de portière** to hear a car door slam

claquemurer [3] [klakmyre] VT to shut in
VPR **se claquemurer** to shut oneself in *or* away

claquer [3] [klake] VT 1 *(fermer)* to bang *or* to slam (shut); **c. la porte** to slam the door; *Fig* to storm out; **c. la porte au nez à qn** to slam the door in sb's face; *Fig* to send sb packing; *Fam* **c. le beignet à qn** to shut sb up
2 *(faire résonner)* **c. sa langue** to click one's tongue; **c. des talons** to click one's heels
3 *Fam (dépenser)* to spend, to blow; **elle claque un fric fou en vêtements** she spends a fortune on clothes; **j'ai tout claqué** I blew the lot
4 *Fam (fatiguer)* to wear out; **ça m'a claqué** *Br* it was absolutely knackering, *Am* it wiped me out
5 *Fam (gifler)* to slap
VI 1 *(résonner ▸ porte)* to bang, to slam; *(▸ drapeau, linge)* to flap; **faire c. ses doigts** to snap one's fingers; **faire c. une porte** to slam a door; **faire c. sa langue** to click one's tongue; **le cocher fit c. son fouet** the coachman cracked his whip
2 *Fam (mourir)* to peg out; *(tomber en panne)* to conk out; *(griller ▸ ampoule électrique)* to go, to blow; **le frigo va c.** the fridge is on the way out; **elle lui a claqué dans les bras** she just died on him/her; **le projet lui a claqué dans les doigts** *(il a échoué)* his/her project fell through 3 *(céder avec bruit ▸ sangle)* to snap; *(▸ baudruche, chewing-gum)* to pop
• **claquer de** VT IND **il claque des dents** his teeth are chattering; **c. des doigts** to snap one's fingers; *Fam* **je claque du bec** I'm starving
VPR **se claquer** 1 *Fam (se fatiguer)* to wear oneself out 2 *(se blesser)* **se c. un muscle/ligament** to strain *or* to pull a muscle/ligament

claquette [klakɛt] NF *Cin* clapperboard
• **claquettes** NFPL 1 *(danse)* tap-dancing; **faire des claquettes** to tap-dance 2 *(tongs)* flipflops

claquoir [klakwar] NM clapperboard

clarification [klarifikasjɔ̃] NF 1 *(explication)* clarification 2 *(d'une suspension, d'une sauce, du beurre)* clarification; *(d'un vin)* settling

clarifier [9] [klarifje] VT 1 *(expliquer)* to clarify, to make clear 2 *(rendre limpide ▸ suspension, beurre, sauce)* to clarify; *(▸ vin)* to settle
VPR **se clarifier** 1 *(situation)* to become clearer 2 *(suspension, sauce)* to become clear 3 *Chim* to become clarified

clarine [klarin] NF cowbell

clarinette [klarinɛt] NF clarinet; **c. basse** bass clarinet

clarinettiste [klarinetist] NMF clarinettist, clarinet player

clarisse [klaris] NF Clarisse; **les clarisses** the Poor Clares

clarté [klarte] NF 1 *(lumière)* light; *(luminosité)* brightness; **la c. du jour** daylight; **à la c. de la lune** by the light of the moon, by moonlight 2 *(transparence ▸ gén)* clarity, limpidness, clearness; *(▸ du teint)* clearness 3 *(intelligibilité)* clarity, clearness; **manquer de c.** *(texte, devoir, argument)* to be unclear; **parler avec c.** to speak clearly; **voir avec c. que…** to see with great clarity *or* perfectly clearly that…
• **clartés** NFPL *Littéraire* knowledge; **avoir des clartés sur qch** to have some knowledge of sth

clash [klaʃ] *(pl* **clashs** *ou* **clashes)** NM *Fam* clash, conflict; **il y a eu un c. entre nous (à propos de)** we clashed (over)

classable [klasabl] ADJ classable; **cette musique est difficilement c.** it's hard to classify this kind of music

CLASSE [klas] NF A. *Scol* 1 *(salle)* classroom
2 *(groupe)* class; **sa c.** his/her class *or* classmates; **camarade de c.** classmate; **toute la c. riait** the whole class laughed; **c. de mer** = residential classes at the seaside for schoolchildren; **c. de nature** nature study trip; **c. de neige** = residential classes in the mountains for schoolchildren; **classes de niveau** *(groupes d'élèves)* classes segregated according to pupils' ability, *Br* streamed classes; *(pratique)* segregation of classes according to pupils' ability, *Br* streaming; **c. transplantée** = generic term referring to "classe de neige", "classe de mer" and "classe verte"; **c. unique** = class where pupils belonging to different years are taught together by one teacher; **c. verte** = residential classes in the countryside for urban schoolchildren
3 *(cours)* class, lesson; **c. de français** French class; **c. de perfectionnement** advanced class; **faire la c.** *(être enseignant)* to teach; *(donner un cours)* to teach *or* to take a class; **c'est moi qui leur fais la c.** I'm their teacher; **en sortant de c.** on coming out of school
4 *(niveau)* class, *Br* form, *Am* grade; **il y a plusieurs classes de sixième au collège** there are several *Br* first-year *or Am* sixth grade classes at high school; **dans les grandes/petites classes** in the upper/lower *Br* years *or* forms *or Am* grades; **passer dans la c. supérieure** to move up to the next *Br* year *or* form *or Am* grade; **refaire** *ou* **redoubler une c.** to repeat a year; **classes préparatoires** *(aux grandes écoles)* = preparatory classes for the entrance examinations for the "grandes écoles"
B. *DANS UNE HIÉRARCHIE* 1 *(espèce)* class, kind; *Math* class; *(dans des statistiques)* bracket, class, group; *Compta* group of accounts; **c. d'âge** age group; **c. de revenus** income bracket
2 *(rang)* class, rank; **former une c. à part** to be in a class *or* league of one's own
3 *Pol & (en sociologie)* class; **c. sociale** social class; **les classes moyennes/dirigeantes** the middle/ruling classes; **la c. ouvrière** the working class; **les classes populaires** *ou* **laborieuses** the working classes; **l'ensemble de la c. politique** the whole of the political establishment *or* class; **une société sans c.** a classless society
4 *Transp* class; **première/deuxième c.** first/second class; **billet de première/deuxième c.** first-/second-class ticket; **voyager en première c.** to travel first class; *Aviat* **c. affaires/économique** business/economy class; **c. club/touriste** club/tourist class; **voyager en c. affaires/club** to travel business/club class
5 *(niveau)* quality, class; **de grande c.** top-quality; **de première c.** first-class; **un hôtel de c. internationale** a hotel of international standing; **un sportif de c. internationale** a sportsman of international rank, a world-class sportsman
6 *(distinction)* class, style; **avec c.** smartly, with elegance; **avoir de la c.** to have class *or* style; *Fam* **la c.!** classy!
7 *Ling* class; **c. grammaticale** part of speech; **c. de mots** word class
C. *Mil* 1 *(de conscrits)* annual contingent; **la c. 70** the 1970 levy *or* draft
2 *(rang)* **(soldat de) deuxième c.** *(armée de terre)* private; *(armée de l'air) Br* aircraftman, *Am* airman basic; **(soldat de) première c.** *(armée de terre) Br* private, *Am* private first class; *(armée de l'air) Br* leading aircraftman, *Am* airman first class
ADJ INV *Fam (élégant)* classy
ADV *Fam* **s'habiller c.** to be a classy *or* stylish dresser
• **classes** NFPL **faire ses classes** *Mil* to go through training; *Fig* to learn the ropes
• **en classe** ADV **aller en c.** to go to school; **il a l'âge d'aller en c.** he's of school age; **rentrer en c.** *(pour la première fois)* to start school; *(à la rentrée)* to go back to school, to start school again

> **CLASSES PRÉPARATOIRES**
>
> This term refers to the two years of intensive preparation required for students who have passed their baccalauréat and wish to enter the "grandes écoles". These two years of study are extremely competitive and highly demanding. Students are completely immersed in their subject, which can be in humanities, economics or the sciences, and do little other than study for the "grandes écoles" exams. For students who are not successful in these exams, two years of "prépa" are considered equivalent to a **DEUG** (see box at this entry), and these students often go on to study at a university.

classé, -e [klase] ADJ 1 *(terminé)* closed, dismissed; **pour moi, c'est une affaire classée** all that's over and done with *or* the matter's closed as far as I'm concerned 2 *(protégé)* listed; **monument/château c.** listed *or* scheduled building/castle 3 *Sport* ranked, graded; *(au tennis)* seeded; **cheval non c.** also-ran

classement [klasmɑ̃] NM 1 *(tri ▸ de documents)* classifying, ordering, sorting; *(▸ d'objets)* sorting, grading; **faire un c. de livres** to sort out *or* to classify books; **c. alphabétique/chronologique** alphabetical/chronological order
2 *(rangement)* filing; **faire du c.** to do some filing; **faire une erreur de c.** to file something in the wrong place
3 *Chim* grading; **c. volumétrique** sizing
4 *(palmarès)* ranking, placing; **avoir un mauvais/bon c.** to do badly/well; **donner le c. d'un examen/d'une course** to give the results of an exam/of a race; **être troisième au c.** to be in third place; **c. général** overall classification; **premier au c. général** first overall; **c. des élèves** class list; **c. de sortie** pass list; **c. trimestriel** end of term results
5 *Ordinat* sequencing
6 *Admin* listing
7 *Jur (d'une affaire)* closing; **c. sans suite** discontinuing proceedings, dropping the case; **rendre une décision de c. sans suite** to discontinue proceedings, to drop the case

classer [3] [klase] VT 1 *(archiver ▸ vieux papiers)* to file (away); *(▸ affaire)* to close
2 *(agencer)* to arrange, to classify, to sort; **c. qch par ordre alphabétique** to put sth in alphabetical order; **ils sont classés par pays** they are classified according to country
3 *Ordinat* to sequence
4 *Admin (site)* to list, to schedule
5 *(définir)* **c. qn comme** to categorize *or Péj* to label sb as; **à sa réaction, je l'ai tout de suite classé** I could tell straight away what sort of person he was from his reaction; **ce chanteur, que l'on classe parmi les meilleurs ténors…** this singer, who is ranked among the best tenors…
VPR **se classer** 1 *(dans une compétition)* to finish, to rank; **se c. troisième** to rank third; **mon cheval**

s'est classé premier my horse came in *or* finished first; **il n'a pas réussi à se c.** *(au tennis)* he failed to get into the rankings **2** *(prendre son rang)* **se c. parmi** to rank among

classeur [klasœr] **NM 1** *(chemise)* binder, folder, *Am* jacket; **c. à anneaux** ring binder; **c. à feuilles mobiles** loose-leaf binder; **c. à levier** lever-arch file **2** *(tiroir)* filing drawer; *(meuble)* filing cabinet **3** *Ordinat* filer

classicisme [klasisism] **NM 1** *Beaux-Arts & Littérature* classicism **2** *(conformisme)* traditionalism

classieux, -euse [klasjø, -øz] **ADJ** *Fam* classy

classificateur, -trice [klasifikatœr, -tris] **ADJ** classifying

NM,F classifier

NM 1 *Ordinat* classifier **2** *Chim* screen, sizer

classification [klasifikasjɔ̃] **NF 1** *(répartition)* classification; **c. socio-économique** socio-economic classification; **c. du bois** lumber grading

2 *(système)* classification system; **c. décimale universelle** Dewey decimal system; **c. périodique des éléments** periodic table

3 *Naut (mode d'identification)* class logo

4 *Biol* classification; **c. des animaux/végétaux** animal/plant classification

classificatrice [klasifikatris] *voir* **classificateur**

classifier [9] [klasifje] **VT 1** *(ordonner)* to classify **2** *(définir)* to label **3** *Mil (documents)* to classify

classique [klasik] **ADJ 1** *Univ* classical; **faire des études classiques** to study classics

2 *Ling & Littérature* classical; **les auteurs classiques** the classical *or* seventeenth- and eighteenth-century authors

3 *Mus & (en danse ▸ traditionnel)* classical; *(▸ du XVIIIème siècle)* classical, eighteenth-century

4 *Antiq* classical

5 *(conventionnel)* conventional; **matériel/armement c.** conventional equipment/weapons; **vêtement de coupe c.** classically cut garment

6 *(connu ▸ sketch, plaisanterie, recette)* classic; **réaction c.** classic response; *Fam* **c'est le coup c.** *(ça arrive souvent)* that's typical!; *(une ruse connue)* that's a well-known trick!; **il m'a fait le coup c. de la panne** he gave me the old breakdown scenario

7 *Écon* classic

NM 1 *Littérature (auteur)* classical author; *(œuvre)* classic; **un c. du genre** a classic of its kind; **connaître ses classiques** to be well-read **2** *Mus (œuvre ▸ gén)* classic; *(▸ de jazz)* (jazz) standard; **le c.** *(genre)* classical music **3** *(style ▸ d'habillement, de décoration)* classic style

> Attention: ne pas confondre **classic** et **classical** lorsque l'on traduit l'adjectif **classique**. Le terme **classic** signifie généralement **typique**, **habituel**, alors que **classical** signifie **traditionnel** et s'oppose à **modern**.

classiquement [klasikmɑ̃] **ADV 1** *(avec classicisme)* classically **2** *(habituellement)* customarily; **méthode c. utilisée** customary *or* classic method

claudication [klodikasjɔ̃] **NF** limp, *Spéc* claudication

claudiquer [3] [klodike] **VI** *Littéraire* to limp

clause [kloz] **NF 1** *Jur* clause, stipulation; **c. abusive** unfair clause; **c. additionnelle** additional clause, rider; **c. d'annulation** cancellation clause; **c. d'arbitrage** arbitration clause; **c. attributive de compétence** jurisdiction clause; **c. compromissoire** arbitration clause; **c. conditionnelle** proviso; *Presse* **c. de conscience** conscience clause; **c. contractuelle** clause of a/the contract; **c. contraire** stipulation to the contrary; **c. dérogatoire** derogatory clause; **c. échappatoire** escape clause; *Com* **c. d'exclusivité** exclusivity clause, exclusive rights clause; **c. d'exonération** exemption clause; **c. de franchise** excess clause; *Compta* **c. d'indexation** escalation clause, indexation clause; **c. limitative** limiting clause; **c. de non-concurrence** non-competition clause; **c. pénale** penalty clause; *Fin* **c. au porteur** pay to bearer clause; *Fin* **c. de remboursement** refunding clause; **c. de réserve de propriété** retention of title clause; **c. de résiliation** termination clause, cancellation clause; **c. résolutoire** resolutive clause; **c. de retrait** withdrawal clause; **c. de sauvegarde** safeguard *or* safety clause; **c. de style** standard *or* formal clause; *Fig* **ce n'est qu'une c. de style** it's only a manner of speaking; **c. de variation** index clause **2** *Pol (d'un traité)* clause; **c. de la nation la plus favorisée** most-favoured-nation status

claustra [klostra] **NM** open-work partition *or* window

claustral, -e, -aux, -ales [klostral, -o] **ADJ 1** *(d'un cloître)* claustral, cloistral **2** *(retiré)* cloistered

claustration [klostrasjɔ̃] **NF** confinement

claustrer [3] [klostre] **VT** to confine; **vivre claustré** to lead the life of a recluse

VPR se claustrer to shut oneself away; **se c. dans le silence** to retreat into silence

claustrophobe [klostrɔfɔb] **ADJ** claustrophobic

NMF claustrophobe, claustrophobic

claustrophobie [klostrɔfɔbi] **NF** claustrophobia

clavardage [klavardaʒ] **NM** *Can Ordinat (sur l'Internet)* chat; **site de c.** chat room

claveau, -x [klavo] **NM 1** *(pierre taillée)* gauged stone **2** *(voussoir)* arch stone, voussoir **3** *Vét* sheep-pox

clavecin [klavsɛ̃] **NM** harpsichord

claveciniste [klavsinist] **NMF** harpsichordist, harpsichord player

claveter [27] [klavte] **VT** to key, to cotter

clavette [klavɛt] **NF** key, pin, cotter

clavicorde [klavikɔrd] **NM** clavichord

clavicule [klavikyl] **NF** collarbone, *Spéc* clavicle

clavier [klavje] **NM 1** *(d'une machine)* keyboard; *(d'un téléphone)* keypad; **c. alphanumérique** alphanumeric keyboard; **c. azerty** azerty keyboard; **c. dactylographique** alphanumeric keyboard; **c. étendu** expanded keyboard, extended keyboard; **c. de fonctions** function keyboard; **c. multifonction** multifunctional keyboard; **c. numérique** numeric keypad; **c. qwerty** qwerty keyboard **2** *Mus (d'un piano)* keyboard; *(d'un orgue)* manual; **c. main gauche** *(d'un accordéon)* fingerboard; **c. de pédales** pedal board **3** *(registre)* range; **tout le c. des émotions** the whole spectrum of emotions

• **claviers NMPL** *Mus* keyboards

claviste [klavist] **NMF** *Typ* typesetter; *Ordinat* keyboard operator, keyboarder

clayette [klɛjɛt] **NF 1** *(petite claie)* shelf, tray; **c. coulissante** *(d'un réfrigérateur)* slide-out shelf **2** *(cageot)* crate

clayon [klɛjɔ̃] **NM 1** *(petite claie)* wire stand **2** *Can (barrière)* fence

clé [kle] = **clef**

clean [klin] **ADJ** *Fam (homme)* clean-cut[□], wholesome-looking[□]; *(femme)* wholesome-looking[□]; **elle a un look c.** she's very wholesome-looking

clearing [kliriŋ] **NM** *Banque* clearing

clébard [klebar], **clebs** [klɛps] **NM** *très Fam* dog[□], mutt

clef [kle] **NF 1** *(de porte, d'horloge, de boîte de conserve)* key; *(d'un tuyau de poêle)* damper; **la c. est sur la porte** the key's in the lock *or* door; **mettre la c. sous la porte** *ou* **le paillasson** to shut up shop; *Fig* to disappear overnight; **prendre la c. des champs** to get away; **les clefs de saint Pierre** the papal authority; **fausse c.** picklock

2 *(outil) Br* spanner, *Am* wrench; **c. allen** Allen key, *Am* Allen wrench; **c. anglaise** monkey wrench, *Br* adjustable spanner; **c. à bougie** (spark)plug spanner; **c. BTR** Allen key, *Am* Allen wrench; **c. à douilles** socket wrench; **c. hexagonale** Allen key, *Am* Allen wrench; **c. à molette** monkey wrench, *Br* adjustable spanner; **c. à pipe** box spanner; **c. plate** (open) end wrench; **c. à six pans** Allen key, *Am* Allen wrench; **c. à tube** tube spanner; **c. universelle** monkey wrench, *Br* adjustable spanner

3 *Aut* **c. de contact** ignition key; **mes clefs de voiture** my car keys

4 *Élec* switch (key)

5 *Tél* **c. d'appel** call button; **c. d'écoute** audio-switch; **c. de réponse** reply key

6 *Ordinat* key; *(du DOS)* switch; **c. d'accès** enter key; **c. de chiffrement** encryption key; **c. électronique** electronic key; **c. gigogne** dongle; **c. de protection** data protection; **c. USB** memory stick, flash drive, pen drive

7 *Mus (signe)* clef, key; *(touche)* key; *(d'un instrument à cordes)* peg; **c. de sol** key of G, treble clef; **c. de fa** key of F, bass clef; **c. d'ut** key of C, C clef; **clefs de tension** screws

8 *(moyen)* **la c. de la réussite** the key to success; **la philosophie, c. de la connaissance** philosophy, the key to (all) knowledge

9 *(explication)* key; **l'histoire de son enfance nous livre quelques clés** the story of his/her childhood gives us a few clues; **la c. de l'énigme/du mystère** the key to the puzzle/mystery; **c. des songes** *(livre)* = how to interpret your dreams

10 *(influence déterminante)* **le parti écologiste détient la c. des élections** the green party holds the key to *or* is a key factor in the election results; **Gibraltar est la c. de la Méditerranée** he who holds Gibraltar holds the Mediterranean

11 *(introduction)* **clefs pour l'informatique/la philosophie** introduction to computer technology/philosophy

12 *(prise de lutte)* lock; **faire une c. au bras à qn** to have sb in an arm lock

13 *Archit* **c. d'arc** keystone; **c. de voûte** keystone, quoin; *Fig* linchpin, cornerstone

14 *Banque* **c. RIB** = two-digit security number allocated to account holders

15 *(comme adj; avec ou sans trait d'union) (essentiel)* key *(avant n)*; **mot/témoin c.** key word/witness

• **à clef ADV fermer une porte à c.** to lock a door

• **à clefs ADJ roman/film à clefs** novel/film based on real characters *(whose identity is disguised)*

• **à la clef ADV 1** *Mus* in the key signature; **il y a un bémol/dièse à la c.** the key signature has a flat/sharp **2** *(au bout du compte)* **avec... à la c.** *(récompense)* with... as a bonus; *(punition)* with... into the bargain; **une promenade dans la campagne, avec visite des vignobles à la c.** a ride in the country with a tour of the vineyards thrown in; **il y a une forte somme d'argent à la c.** there is a large sum of money at stake *or* involved

• **clef(s) en main,** *Belg* **clef sur porte ADJ 1** *Com* **prix c.** *ou* **clefs en main** *(d'un véhicule)* on-the-road price; *(d'une maison)* all-inclusive price **2** *Ind (usine)* turnkey *(avant n)* **ADV 1** *Com* **acheter une maison c.** *ou* **clefs en main** to buy a house with vacant *or* immediate possession; **acheter une voiture c.** *ou* **clefs en main** to buy a car ready to drive away **2** *Ind* on a turnkey basis

• **sous clef ADV 1** *(en prison)* behind bars; **mettre qn sous c.** to lock sb up, to put sb behind bars **2** *(à l'abri)* **mettre qch sous c.** to lock sth away, to put sth under lock and key

clématite [klematit] **NF** *Bot* clematis

clémence [klemɑ̃s] **NF 1** *Météo* mildness **2** *Littéraire (pardon)* leniency, mercy, clemency; **faire preuve de c. à l'égard de qn** to be lenient with sb; **s'en remettre à la c. de qn** to throw oneself on sb's mercy

clément, -e [klemɑ̃, -ɑ̃t] **ADJ 1** *Météo* mild; **temps c. sur toutes les régions** mild weather throughout the country; *Littéraire* **ciel c.** mild climate **2** *Littéraire (indulgent)* lenient, merciful, clement; **ils ont été cléments envers elle** they were lenient with her **3** *(favorable)* **à une époque moins clémente** in less happy times

clémentine [klemɑ̃tin] **NF** clementine

clenche [klɑ̃ʃ] **NF 1** *(loquet)* latch **2** *Belg (poignée)* doorhandle

Cléopâtre [kleɔpatr] **NPR** Cleopatra

cleptomane [klɛptɔman] = **kleptomane**

cleptomanie [klɛptɔmani] = **kleptomanie**

clerc [klɛr] **NM 1** *Rel* cleric **2** *(savant)* scholar; **il est grand c. en la matière** he's an expert on the subject; **point n'est besoin d'être grand c. pour deviner la fin de l'histoire** you don't need to be a genius to guess the end of the story **3** *(employé)* **c. de notaire** clerk; *Littéraire* **faire un pas de c.** to blunder

clergé [klɛrʒe] **NM** clergy

clérical, -e, -aux, -ales [klerikal, -o] **ADJ** *(du clergé)* clerical

cléricalisme [klerikalism] **NM** clericalism

clic [klik] NM *(gén) & Ordinat* click; **double c.** double click; **faire un c. (sur)** to click (on)
EXCLAM click!

clic-clac [klikklak] NM INV *(bruit ▸ d'un appareil photo, d'une ceinture de sécurité)* click; *(▸ des talons)* click-clack
ADJ INV *voir* **canapé**

cliché [kliʃe] NM **1** *Phot (pellicule)* negative; *(photo)* photograph, shot
2 *Typ* stereotype; *(de caractères)* plate; *(d'illustration)* block
3 *Ordinat* format, layout; **c. mémoire** dump
4 *Littérature* cliché
5 *Péj (banalité)* cliché; **tous ses gags sont des clichés** his/her gags are all so corny

clicheton [kliʃtɔ̃] NM *Fam* cliché□; **l'histoire est d'une banalité affligeante: tous les clichetons sont au rendez-vous** the story is as banal as can be and completely cliché-ridden

clicheur [kliʃœr] NM **1** *Typ* stereotyper, electrotyper, blockmaker **2** *Mines* cager, setter of hutches **3** *Ordinat* screen dump program

client, -e [klijɑ̃, -ɑ̃t] NM,F **1** *(d'un magasin, d'un restaurant)* customer; *(d'une banque)* customer, client; *(d'un hôtel)* guest; *(d'un médecin)* patient; *(d'un taxi)* passenger; *Mktg* account; **je suis c. chez eux** I'm one of their regular customers; *Fig* **désolé, je ne suis pas c.** sorry, I'm not interested; **ici, le c. est roi** the customer is always right; **c. actuel** existing customer; **c. douteux** doubtful debt, possible bad debt; *Mktg* **c. éventuel** prospective customer, prospect; **c. habitué** regular customer; **c. imprévu** chance customer; *Mktg* **c. mystère** mystery shopper; **c. de passage** passing customer; **c. potentiel** potential customer; *Mktg* **c. de référence** reference customer; **c. régulier** regular customer; **c. sans réservation** *(dans un hôtel)* chance guest, walk-in **2 les clients** *(la clientèle)* customers, the clientele; **les clients d'un médecin** a doctor's patients; **les clients d'un hôtel** hotel guests **3** *Fam Péj (individu)* **un drôle de c.** a dodgy customer; **chez eux, c'est à la tête du c.** they charge you what they feel like
NM *Ordinat* client; **c. de messagerie électronique** e-mail client, mail reader

clientèle [klijɑ̃tɛl] NF **1** *(clients ▸ gén)* clientele, customers; *(d'un médecin)* patients; *(d'un avocat)* clients, clientele; **acheter une c. à un confrère** to buy a practice from a colleague; **perdre sa c.** to lose one's customers; **avoir une grosse c.** to have a large clientele *or* customer base; **c. de passage** passing trade **2** *(fait d'acheter)* custom; **obtenir la c. de qn** to obtain sb's custom *or* business; **accorder sa c. à** to give one's custom to, to patronize **3** *Pol* **c. électorale** electorate, voters

clientélisme [klijɑ̃telism] NM *Péj* clientelism

clignement [kliɲəmɑ̃] NM **c. d'œil** *ou* **d'yeux** *(involontaire)* blink; *(volontaire)* wink; **des clignements d'œil** *ou* **d'yeux** blinking

cligner [3] [kliɲe] VT *(fermer)* **c. les yeux** to blink
VI *(paupières, yeux)* to blink
• **cligner de** VT IND **1** *(fermer involontairement)* **c. de l'œil** to blink; **c. des yeux** to blink **2** *(faire signe avec)* **c. de l'œil (en direction de qn)** to wink (at sb)

clignotant, -e [kliɲɔtɑ̃, -ɑ̃t] ADJ *(signal)* flashing; *(lampe défectueuse)* flickering; *(étoile)* twinkling; *(guirlande)* twinkling, flashing
NM **1** *Aut (lampe) Br* indicator, *Am* turn signal; **mettre son c. (à droite/gauche)** *Br* to indicate (to the right/left), *Am* to put on one's turn signal (to turn right/left) **2** *(signal)* warning light; *Sport* sequenced starting lights **3** *Écon (indice)* (key) indicator

clignotement [kliɲɔtmɑ̃] NM **1** *(lumière ▸ d'une guirlande, d'une étoile)* twinkling; *(▸ d'un signal)* flashing; *(▸ d'une lampe défectueuse)* flickering **2** *(mouvement ▸ des paupières)* flickering; *(▸ des yeux)* blinking

clignoter [3] [kliɲɔte] VI **1** *(éclairer ▸ étoile, guirlande)* to twinkle; *(▸ signal)* to flash (on and off); *(▸ lampe défectueuse)* to flicker **2** *(automobiliste) Br* to indicate, *Am* to put on one's turn signal **3** *Ordinat (d'un marqueur etc)* to flash, to blink

clignoteur [kliɲɔtœr] NM *Belg* **1** *Aut (lampe) Br* indicator, *Am* turn signal; **mettre son c. (à droite/gauche)** *Br* to indicate (to the right/left), *Am* to put on one's turn signal (to turn right/left) **2** *(signal)* warning light

clim [klim] NF *Fam* air-conditioning□, air-con

climat [klima] NM **1** *Géog* climate; **sous nos climats** in our country; **sous d'autres climats** in other countries; **partir vers des climats plus sereins** to travel to sunnier climes **2** *(ambiance)* climate, atmosphere; **un c. de méfiance** an atmosphere of suspicion; **le c. devient malsain!** things are turning nasty!; **c. économique** economic climate

climatique [klimatik] ADJ **1** *Météo* weather *(avant n)*, climatic; *École* **changement c.** climate change **2 centre/station c.** health centre/resort

climatisation [klimatizasjɔ̃] NF **1** *(dans un immeuble)* air-conditioning **2** *(dans une voiture)* heating and ventilation

climatiser [3] [klimatize] VT to air-condition, to install air-conditioning in; **restaurant climatisé** air-conditioned restaurant

climatiseur [klimatizœr] NM *(gén)* air-conditioner, air-conditioning unit; *Aut* climate control system

climatologie [klimatɔlɔʒi] NF climatology

climatologique [klimatɔlɔʒik] ADJ climatological

clin [klɛ̃] **à clin** ADJ **un pont à c.** a clapboard bridge; *Naut* **bordé à c.** *ou* **clins** clinker built

clin d'œil [klɛ̃dœj] *(pl* **clins d'œil***)* NM **1** *(clignement)* wink; **faire un c. à qn** to wink at sb **2** *(allusion)* allusion, implied reference; **un c. à...** an allusion *or* an implied reference to...
• **en un clin d'œil** ADV in the twinkling of an eye, in less than no time, in a flash

clinicien, -enne [klinisjɛ̃, -ɛn] NM,F **1** *Méd* clinician, clinical practitioner **2** *Psy* clinical psychologist

clinique [klinik] ADJ clinical; **médecine/psychologie c.** clinical medicine/psychology; **leçon c.** teaching at the bedside; **les signes cliniques de l'affection** the visible signs of the disease
NF **1** *(établissement)* (private) clinic; **c. d'accouchement** maternity hospital **2** *(service)* teaching department *(of a hospital)* **3** *(médecine)* clinical medicine

cliniquement [klinikmɑ̃] ADV clinically

clinquant, -e [klɛ̃kɑ̃, -ɑ̃t] ADJ **1** *(brillant)* glittering, *Péj* tinselly **2** *(superficiel ▸ style)* flashy; **le monde c. du show-business** the razzmatazz of show business
NM **1** *(faux éclat)* **le c. de leurs conversations** the superficial sparkle of their conversations **2** *(paillettes)* tinsel

clip [klip] NM **1** *(broche)* clip, brooch
2 *(boucle d'oreille)* clip-on earring
3 *(attache)* clamp, clip; **c. de blocage** lock clip; **clips de fixation** holders
4 *(film)* video; **c. vidéo** video (clip)

clipart [klipart] NM *Ordinat* clip art

clipper[1] [klipœr] NM **1** *Aviat* transport aircraft **2** *Naut* clipper

clipper[2] [3] [klipe] VT *(fixer)* to clip (**à** to *or* onto)

clippeur [klipœr] NM *Fam* video director

cliquable [klikabl] ADJ *Ordinat* clickable; **une icône c.** a clickable icon

clique [klik] NF **1** *Fam (coterie)* clique, gang; **et toute la c.** and the rest of the gang, and all the rest of them **2** *Mil (fanfare)* band
• **cliques** NFPL *Fam* **prendre ses cliques et ses claques** *(partir)* to up and leave; *(emporter ses affaires)* to pack one's bags (and go)

cliquer [3] [klike] VI *Ordinat* to click (**sur** on); **c. deux fois** to double-click; **c. avec le bouton gauche/droit de la souris** to left-click/right-click; **c. et glisser** to click and drag

cliquet [klikɛ] NM **1** *(mécanisme)* catch, dog, pawl **2** *(outil)* pawl; **à c.** pawl *(avant n)*

cliqueter [27] [klikte] VI *(clefs, bijoux)* to jangle; *(chaînes)* to rattle; *(épées, aiguilles à tricoter)* to click; *(pièces de monnaie)* to clink, to chink; *(machine à écrire)* to clack; *(assiettes)* to clatter; *(verres)* to clink; *(engrenage, moteur)* to pink, to knock

cliquetis [klikti] NM *(de clefs, de bijoux)* jangling *(UNCOUNT)*; *(de chaînes)* rattling *(UNCOUNT)*; *(d'épées, d'aiguilles à tricoter)* clicking *(UNCOUNT)*; *(de pièces de monnaie)* clinking *(UNCOUNT)*, chinking *(UNCOUNT)*; *(d'une machine à écrire)* clacking *(UNCOUNT)*; *(d'assiettes)* clatter, clattering *(UNCOUNT)*; *(de verres)* clinking *(UNCOUNT)*; *(d'un engrenage, d'un moteur)* pinking, knocking *(UNCOUNT)*

cliquette *etc voir* **cliqueter**

clisse [klis] NF **1** *(pour fromages)* wicker tray **2** *(pour bouteilles)* wicker casing

clitoridien, -enne [klitɔridjɛ̃, -ɛn] ADJ clitoral

clitoris [klitɔris] NM clitoris

clivage [klivaʒ] NM **1** *(de roche, de cristal)* cleavage, splitting; **plan de c.** cleavage plane **2** *(séparation)* divide, division; **c. idéologique** ideological divide; **clivages partisans** ideological divide, sectarianism; **dépasser les clivages partisans** to bridge the ideological divide; **c. social** social divide; **il y a un net c. entre les riches et les pauvres** there's a sharp divide between rich and poor **3** *Chim (de molécule)* cleavage

cliver [3] [klive] *Minér & Chim* VT to cleave, to split
VPR **se cliver** to cleave, to split

cloaque [klɔak] NM **1** *(égout)* cesspool, open sewer; **le grand C.** the Cloaca Maxima **2** *Littéraire (lieu sale)* cesspool, cloaca; *(lieu de corruption)* cesspit, cesspool **3** *Zool* cloaca

clochard, -e [klɔʃar, -ard] NM,F tramp, *Am* hobo; **si tu continues comme ça, tu vas finir c.** if you carry on like that, you're going to end up destitute

clochardisation [klɔʃardizasjɔ̃] NF **on observe une c. croissante chez les jeunes sans emploi** more and more young unemployed people are turning into vagrants *or* down-and-outs

clochardiser [3] [klɔʃardize] VT to make destitute; *(sans domicile)* to make homeless
VPR **se clochardiser** to become destitute; *(sans domicile)* to be made homeless

cloche [klɔʃ] ADJ *Fam (idiot)* stupid□, *Br* daft; **ce que tu peux être c.!** you can be such a dope!; **avoir l'air c.** to look stupid
NF **1** *(instrument, signal)* bell; **les enfants, c'est la c.!** *(à l'école)* children, the bell's ringing!; *Fam* **s'en mettre plein** *ou* **se taper la c.** to stuff one's face; *Fam* **déménager** *ou* **partir à la c. de bois** to leave without paying the rent□, *Br* to do a moonlight flit; **les cloches de Pâques** Easter bells *(traditionally believed to fly to Rome at Easter)*
2 *Hort* cloche
3 *Culin* dome, dish-cover; **c. à fromage** cheese dish *(with cover)*, cheese-bell
4 (chapeau) c. cloche (hat)
5 *Naut* **c. de plongée** *ou* **à plongeur** diving-bell
6 *Chim* **c. à vide** vacuum bell-jar; **c. de verre** bell glass
7 *Aut* **c. d'embrayage** clutch bell housing
8 *Fam (personne)* jerk, *Br* prat, *Am* geek; **quelle c., ce type!** what an idiot!; **salut, vieille c.!** hello, old thing!; **ne reste pas là à me regarder comme une c.!** don't just stand there gawping at me!
9 *Fam (vagabondage)* **la c.** vagrancy□; **être de la c.** to be of no fixed abode; **c'est la c. là-bas sous le pont** it's cardboard city over there under the bridge
10 *Belg Méd* blister
• **en cloche** ADJ bell-shaped; **courbe en c.** bell-shaped curve
• **sous cloche** ADV **mettre sous c.** *Hort* to put under glass, to cloche; *Fig* to mollycoddle

cloche-pied [klɔʃpje] **à cloche-pied** ADV **sauter à c.** to hop

clocher[1] [klɔʃe] NM **1** *(tour)* bell-tower, church tower **2** *(village)* **son c.** the place where he was born; **il n'a jamais quitté son c.** he knows nothing of the world
• **de clocher** ADJ **esprit de c.** parochialism, parish-pump mentality; **querelles de c.** petty bickering

clocher[2] [3] [klɔʃe] VI **1** *Fam (ne pas aller)* to be wrong□; **il y a quelque chose qui cloche** there's something wrong somewhere; **il y a quelque chose qui cloche dans son histoire** there's something not right about his/her story **2** *Arch (boiter)* to limp, to hobble

clocheton [klɔʃtɔ̃] NM *(petit clocher)* (small) steeple; *(ornement)* pinnacle turret

clochette [klɔʃɛt] NF **1** *(petite cloche)* small bell; **c. à vache/mouton** cow-/sheep-bell **2** *Bot (campanule)* bell-flower

clodo [klodo] NMF *Fam* tramp, *Am* bum

cloison [klwazɔ̃] NF **1** *Constr* partition; **mur de c.** dividing wall
2 *Aviat & Naut* bulkhead; **c. étanche** *Naut* watertight bulkhead; *Aviat* pressure bulkhead
3 *Anat & Bot* dissepiment, septum; **c. nasale** nasal septum
4 *Fig (sociale, raciale)* barrier

cloisonnage [klwazɔnaʒ] NM *Archit* partitioning

cloisonné, -e [klwazɔne] ADJ **1** *(pièce)* partitioned (off)
2 *Fig (divisé)* compartmentalized
3 *Anat & Bot* septated
4 *(en joaillerie)* cloisonné
NM *(en joaillerie)* cloisonné

cloisonnement [klwazɔnmɑ̃] NM **1** *(d'une pièce)* partitioning (off) **2** *Fig (division)* division; **le c. des services dans une entreprise** the excessive compartmentalization of departments in a firm **3** *Archit* partitioning

cloisonner [3] [klwazɔne] VT **1** *(pièce)* to partition off **2** *(séparer)* to compartmentalize

cloître [klwatr] NM **1** *(couvent)* convent, monastery **2** *Archit (d'un couvent)* cloister; *(d'une cathédrale)* close

cloîtrer [3] [klwatre] VT **1** *Rel* **c. qn** to shut sb up in a convent **2** *(enfermer)* to shut up *or* away; **nous sommes cloîtrés toute la journée/dans notre atelier** we're shut up all day/in our workshop
VPR **se cloîtrer** to shut oneself away; **se c. dans le silence** to retreat into silence

clonage [klonaʒ] NM *Biol* cloning; **c. reproductif/thérapeutique** reproductive/therapeutic cloning

clone [klon] NM *Biol & Fig* clone

cloner [3] [klone] VT to clone

clope [klɔp] NM OU NF *Fam Br* fag, *Am* smoke; **la c. ce n'est pas bon pour la santé** smoking is bad for you *or* for your health□

cloper [3] [klɔpe] VI *Fam* to smoke□

clopin-clopant [klɔpɛ̃klɔpɑ̃] ADV **1** *(en boitant)* **avancer/traverser c.** to hobble along/across **2** *(irrégulièrement)* **ça va c.** it has its ups and downs

clopiner [3] [klɔpine] VI *Fam* to hobble along

clopinettes [klɔpinɛt] NFPL *Fam* **des c.** (next to) nothing□; **gagner des c.** to earn peanuts; **des c.!** *(pas question)* nothing doing!, no way!

cloporte [klɔpɔrt] NM **1** *Zool* woodlouse **2** *Fam (individu répugnant)* creep

cloque [klɔk] NF **1** *Bot & Méd* blister **2** *(défaut)* raised spot, blister; **faire des cloques** to blister **3** *Fam (locution)* **être en c.** to have a bun in the oven, to be knocked up, *Br* to be up the duff; **mettre qn en c.** to knock sb up

cloqué, -e [klɔke] ADJ **1** *(tissu)* seersucker *(avant n)* **2** *Bot* blistered
NM seersucker

cloquer [3] [klɔke] VI **1** *(peinture, papier)* to blister **2** *Fam (peau)* to come up in a blister□, to blister□

clore [113] [klɔr] VT **1** *(fermer ▸ porte, volet)* to close, to shut; *(entourer ▸ parc)* to shut off
2 *Fin* **c. un compte** to close an account
3 *(conclure)* to conclude, to end, to finish; **c. les débats** *(s'arrêter)* to end the discussion, to bring the discussion to a close; *(reporter)* to adjourn (the discussion); **la scène qui clôt le film** the very last scene of the movie
4 *Ordinat* **c. une session** to log off, to log out

clos, -e [klo, kloz] ADJ **1** *(fermé)* closed, shut; **les yeux c.** with one's eyes shut; **garder** *ou* **rester la bouche close** to keep one's mouth shut; **trouver porte close** to find nobody at home
2 *(achevé)* finished, concluded; *Univ* **les inscriptions seront closes le lundi 15** the closing date for enrolment is Monday 15th; *Compta* **exercice c. le 31 décembre 2006** year ended 31 December 2006; **l'incident est c.** the matter is closed
3 *(enceint ▸ jardin)* walled
4 *Ling* closed
NM enclosure; **c. (de vigne)** vineyard

close-combat [klozkɔ̃ba] *(pl* **close-combats)** NM close combat

closent *etc voir* **clore**

closerie [klozri] NF enclosed garden

clôt *etc voir* **clore**

clôture [klotyr] NF **1** *(de bois)* fence; *(grille)* railings; **c. à claire-voie** split-rail fencing; **c. métallique** wire fence
2 *Rel* enclosure
3 *(fermeture ▸ gén)* closing; *(▸ d'un débat)* closure; **c. annuelle** *(d'un magasin)* closed for the season; **j'ai assisté à la c.** I attended the closing ceremony; *Univ* **c. des inscriptions le 20 décembre** the closing date for enrolment is 20 December; **la c. de la chasse** the close of the season
4 *Bourse* close; **à la c.** at the close
5 *Compta* **c. annuelle des livres** year-end closing of accounts; **c. de l'exercice** end of the financial year
6 *Ordinat* close; **c. de session** logging off
• **de clôture** ADJ *(gén) & Bourse & Com* closing
• **en clôture** ADV *Bourse* at closing; **combien valait l'euro en c.?** what was the closing price of the euro?

clôturer [3] [klotyre] VT **1** *(fermer)* to enclose, to fence (in) **2** *(terminer)* to close, to end; **c. les débats** to close the debate **3** *Fin (compte)* to close
VI *Bourse* to close; **le CAC 40 a clôturé en baisse/hausse de 9 points** the CAC 40 closed 9 points down/up; **la livre a clôturé à 1,76 dollars** the pound closed at 1.76 dollars

clou [klu] NM **1** *(pointe)* nail; **c. cavalier** staple; **c. à crochet** hook; **c. doré** brass-headed nail, stud; **c. à souliers** shoe tack; **c. (de) tapissier** (carpet) tack; **c. sans tête** brad; *Prov* **un c. chasse l'autre** one nail drives out another
2 *(d'un spectacle)* star turn, chief attraction; **le c. de la soirée** the climax *or* highlight of the evening
3 *Culin* **c. de girofle** clove
4 *Fam (furoncle)* boil□
5 *Fam Péj* **vieux c.** *(voiture)* old *Br* banger *or Am* crate; *(bicyclette)* old bike *or Br* boneshaker
6 *Fam (locutions)* **ça ne vaut pas un c.** it's not worth a bean; **il n'assure pas un c. avec les filles, il ne dit jamais ce qu'il faut** he hasn't got a clue when it comes to girls, he never says the right thing; **qu'est-ce qu'il a eu? – pas un c.!** what did he get? – *Br* not a sausage! *or Am* zilch!; **des clous!** no way!, nothing doing!; **pour des clous** for nothing
• **clous** NMPL *(passage piétons) Br* pedestrian *or* zebra crossing, *Am* crosswalk
• **à clous** ADJ *(chaussure)* hobnail *(avant n)*, hobnailed; *(pneu, ceinture)* studded
• **au clou** ADV *Fam* in the pawnshop□; **mettre qch au c.** to pawn sth□, to hock sth

clouer [6] [klue] VT **1** *(fixer)* to nail (down) **2** *(fermer)* to nail shut; *Fam* **c. le bec à qn** to shut sb up **3** *(immobiliser)* **c. qn au sol** to pin sb down; **il est resté cloué au lit pendant trois jours** he was laid up in bed for three days; **la peur le clouait sur place** he was rooted to the spot with fear

clouté, -e [klute] ADJ **1** *(décoré)* studded **2** *(renforcé ▸ chaussure, semelle)* hobnailed; *(▸ pneu)* studded

clouter [3] [klute] VT to stud

clovisse [klɔvis] NF clam

clown [klun] NM clown; **faire le c.** to clown, to fool around; *Fig* **quel c., ce gosse!** that kid's a clown!; **c. blanc** white-faced clown

clownerie [klunri] NF **1** *(pitrerie)* **des clowneries** clown's antics, clowning **2** *Péj (bêtise)* (stupid) prank; **faire des clowneries** to clown *or* to fool around

clownesque [klunɛsk] ADJ clownish, clownlike

club [klœb] NM **1** *(groupe ▸ de personnes)* club; *(▸ de nations)* group; **c. d'investissement** investment club
2 *(association)* **c. de gym** health club, gym; **c. de rencontres** dating agency; **c. sportif** sports club; **c. de vacances** travel club
3 *Sport (équipe)* club, team
4 *Golf* club
5 *Com* **c. de gros** warehouse club
6 *Can* **c. de nuit** nightclub

cluse [klyz] NF cluse, transverse valley

clystère [klistɛr] NM clyster

cm *(abrév écrite* **centimètre)** cm; **cm²** sq.cm., cm²; **cm³** cu.cm., cm³

CMJN *Ordinat (abrév écrite* **cyan, magenta, jaune, noir)** CMYK

CMP [seɛmpe] NM *Fin (abrév* **coût moyen pondéré)** weighted average cost

CMU [seɛmy] NF *Admin (abrév* **couverture maladie universelle)** = law introduced to ensure free health care for people on low incomes who have no social security cover

CNA [seɛna] NM *Tech (abrév* **convertisseur numérique-analogique)** DAC

CNAM [knam] NM *(abrév* **Conservatoire national des arts et métiers)** = science and technology school in Paris
NF *Admin (abrév* **Caisse nationale d'assurance maladie)** = French goverment department dealing with health insurance and sickness benefit

CNCE [seɛnseə] NM *(abrév* **Centre national du commerce extérieur)** = national export organization

CNIL [knil] NF *(abrév* **Commission nationale de l'informatique et des libertés)** = board which enforces data protection legislation

CNPF [seɛnpeɛf] NM *Anciennement (abrév* **Conseil national du patronat français)** = national council of French employers, *Br* ≃ CBI

CNRS [seɛnɛrɛs] NM *(abrév* **Centre national de la recherche scientifique)** = French national organization for scientific research, *Br* ≃ SRC

> **CO-** PREFIX
>
> The prefix **co-** is widely used in French to convey the idea of TOGETHERNESS OR COMMUNITY OF INTERESTS. It is worth noting three relatively recent coinages or uses:
>
> • **cohabitation**: although not a recent word in itself, **la cohabitation** has come to refer to three episodes in French political life, between 1986 and 2002, when a Prime Minister from one side of the political spectrum has had to share power with a president from the other side (see cultural box at the entry **cohabitation**)
>
> • **covoiturage**: this word was given particular prominence in 1995, when a national public transport strike forced commuters to resort to car-pooling
>
> • **cododo**: this is the colloquial equivalent of *sommeil partagé* (from the baby talk word *dodo*, meaning "sleep"), a practice where parents share a bed, or at least a bedroom, with their offspring

coaccusé, -e [koakyze] NM,F codefendant

coach [kotʃ] *(pl* **coachs** *ou* **coaches)** NM **1** *(entraîneur)* coach; *Sport* trainer; **c. personnel** life coach **2** *(voiture)* two-door car

coaching [kotʃiŋ] NM coaching; *Sport* training; **c. personnel** life coaching

coacquéreur [koakerœr] NM joint purchaser

coadjuteur [koadʒytœr] NM coadjutor

coadministrateur, -trice [koadministratœr, -tris] NM,F *Com* co-director; *Jur* co-trustee

coagulable [koagylabl] ADJ coagulable, liable to coagulate

coagulant, -e [koagylɑ̃, -ɑ̃t] ADJ coagulating
NM coagulant

coagulation [koagylasjɔ̃] NF *(du sang)* coagulation, coagulating *(UNCOUNT)*; *(du lait)* curdling *(UNCOUNT)*

coaguler [3] [koagyle] VT *(sang)* to coagulate; *(lait)* to curdle
VI *(sang)* to coagulate; *(lait)* to curdle
VPR **se coaguler** *(sang)* to coagulate; *(lait)* to curdle

coalescence [koalesɑ̃s] NF coalescence, coalescing *(UNCOUNT)*

coalisé, -e [koalize] ADJ allied
NM,F allied nation, ally

coaliser [3] [kɔalize] VT to make into a coalition
VPR **se coaliser** to form a coalition; *Fig* **ils se sont tous coalisés contre moi** they all ganged up on me *or* joined forces against me

coalition [kɔalisjɔ̃] NF *Pol* coalition; *Péj* conspiracy; **former une c. contre qn/qch** to join forces against sb/sth; **gouvernement de c.** coalition government

coaltar [kɔltar] NM coal tar; *Fam Fig* **être dans le c.** to be in a daze

coassement [kɔasmɑ̃] NM *(de grenouille)* croaking

coasser [3] [kɔase] VI *(grenouille)* to croak

coassocié, -e [kɔasɔsje] NM,F copartner

coassurance [kɔasyrɑ̃s] NF coinsurance

coassurer [3] [kɔasyre] VT to co-insure

coauteur [kootœr] NM **1** *Littérature* coauthor, joint author **2** *(d'un crime)* accomplice

coaxial, -e, -aux, -ales [kɔaksjal, -o] ADJ coaxial

COB, Cob [kɔb] NF *(abrév* **Commission des opérations de Bourse**) = French Stock Exchange watchdog, *Br* ≃ SIB, *Am* ≃ SEC

cobalt [kɔbalt] NM cobalt

cobaye [kɔbaj] NM guinea pig; *Fig* **servir de c.** to be used as a guinea pig

cobelligérant, -e [kɔbeliʒerɑ̃, -ɑ̃t] ADJ cobelligerent
NM,F cobelligerent

Coblence [kɔblɑ̃s] NM Koblenz

cobol [kɔbɔl] NM *Ordinat* Cobol, COBOL

cobra [kɔbra] NM *Zool* cobra

coca [kɔka] NF **1** *Bot* coca **2** *Pharm* coca extract
• **Coca®** NM INV *(boisson)* Coke®

cocagne [kɔkaɲ] **de cocagne** ADJ **époque de c.** years of plenty; **pays de c.** land of plenty

cocaïne [kɔkain] NF cocaine

cocaïnomane [kɔkainɔman] NMF cocaine addict

cocard [kɔkar] NM *Fam* black eye□, shiner

cocarde [kɔkard] NF **1** *(en tissu)* rosette; *Hist* cockade; **la c. tricolore** the revolutionary cockade **2** *(signe ▸ militaire, sur un avion)* roundel; *(▸ sur une voiture officielle)* official logo

cocardier, -ère [kɔkardje, -ɛr] ADJ *Péj* chauvinistic, jingoistic
NM,F chauvinist, jingoist

cocasse [kɔkas] ADJ comical

cocasserie [kɔkasri] NF *(d'une situation)* funniness; **c'était d'une c.!** it was a scream!

coccinelle [kɔksinɛl] NF **1** *Entom Br* ladybird, *Am* ladybug **2** *(voiture) Br* beetle, *Am* bug

coccyx [kɔksis] NM *Anat* coccyx

coche [kɔʃ] NF **1** *(encoche)* notch **2** *(symbole) Br* tick, *Am* check **3** *(truie)* sow
NM *(voiture)* stagecoach; *Fig* **manquer** *ou* **rater** *ou* **louper le c.** to miss the boat

cochenille [kɔʃnij] NF **1** *(insecte)* mealybug **2** *(teinture)* cochineal

cocher[1] [kɔʃe] NM coach driver; **c. de fiacre** cabman

cocher[2] [3] [kɔʃe] VT **1** *(marquer d'un trait) Br* to tick (off), *Am* to check (off) **2** *Vieilli (faire une entaille dans)* to nick, to notch

cochère [kɔʃɛr] ADJ F **porte c.** carriage entrance, porte cochère

cochet [kɔʃɛ] NM cockerel

cocheur [kɔʃœr] NM *Can Golf* **c. d'allée** pitching wedge; **c. de sable** sand wedge

Cochinchine [kɔʃɛ̃ʃin] NF **la C.** Cochin China

cochon, -onne [kɔʃɔ̃, -ɔn] ADJ *Fam* **1** *(sale)* dirty□, filthy□, disgusting□ **2** *(obscène)* smutty, dirty, filthy
NM,F *Fam* **1** *(vicieux)* lecher; **un vieux c.** a dirty old man; **tu es une petite cochonne!** you've got a filthy mind *or* a mind like a sewer! **2** *(personne sale)* (filthy) pig; **oh, le petit c.!** *(à un enfant)* you dirty thing!
NM **1** *Zool* pig; **c. de lait** suckling pig; **c. de mer** porpoise; **faire le c. pendu** to hang by one's legs; **sale comme un c.** filthy dirty; **manger comme un c.** to eat like a pig; **tu écris comme un c.** your writing is appalling; **copains comme cochons** as thick as thieves **2** *(homme méprisable)* dirty dog; **c. qui s'en dédit!** you've got a deal!; *Fam* **ben mon c.!** well, I'll be damned! **3** *Can (tirelire)* piggybank
• **de cochon** ADJ **1** *(mauvais ▸ temps)* foul, filthy; *(▸ caractère)* foul **2** *(yeux)* piggy
• **cochon d'Inde** NM guinea pig

cochonceté [kɔʃɔ̃ste] NF *Fam* **1** *(saleté)* **faire des cochoncetés** to make a filthy mess **2** *(nourriture)* junk food *(UNCOUNT)* **3** *(obscénité)* piece of smut; **dire des cochoncetés** to say dirty things; **allez faire vos cochoncetés ailleurs!** go and do that sort of thing somewhere else!

cochonnaille [kɔʃɔnaj] NF *Fam* pork products□

cochonne [kɔʃɔn] *voir* **cochon**

cochonner [3] [kɔʃɔne] VT *(dessin, chambre)* to make a mess of
VI *(truie)* to pig

cochonnerie [kɔʃɔnri] NF *Fam* **1** *(chose médiocre) Br* rubbish *(UNCOUNT)*, *Am* trash *(UNCOUNT)*; *(nourriture ▸ mal préparée)* pigswill *(UNCOUNT)*; *(▸ de mauvaise qualité)* junk food *(UNCOUNT)*; **on t'a vendu une c.** they sold you a piece of junk *or Br* rubbish; **il ne mange que des cochonneries** he only eats junk food
2 *(saleté)* mess *(UNCOUNT)*; **faire des cochonneries** to make a mess
3 *(obscénité)* smut *(UNCOUNT)*; **dire des cochonneries** to say filthy things
4 *(action déloyale)* dirty trick; **faire une c. à qn** to play a dirty trick on sb
5 *(dans des exclamations)* **c. de voiture/de brouillard!** damn this car/this fog!

cochonnet [kɔʃɔnɛ] NM **1** *Zool* piglet **2** *(aux boules)* jack

cocker [kɔkɛr] NM cocker spaniel

cockpit [kɔkpit] NM cockpit

cocktail [kɔktɛl] NM **1** *(boisson)* cocktail; *(réception)* cocktail party **2** *(mélange)* mix, mixture; **c. de fruits** fruit cocktail **3** *(bombe)* **c. Molotov** Molotov cocktail

coco [koko] NM **1** *(plante)* coconut; *(fibre)* coir
2 *Fam Vieilli ou Can (tête)* nut, head□
3 *Fam (estomac)* belly
4 *Fam (individu)* **un sacré c.** a bit of a lad; **un drôle de c.** a weirdo, an oddball
5 *Fam (en appellatif affectueux ▸ à un adulte)* sweetheart, honey; **toi mon c., je t'ai à l'œil** just watch it, *Br* mate *or* pal *or Am* buddy; **qu'est-ce qu'il y a, mon petit c.?** what's wrong, little man?
6 *(en langage enfantin ▸ œuf)* egg□
7 *(boisson)* = drink made from liquorice and water
NMF *Fam Péj (communiste)* commie
NF *Fam (cocaïne)* coke, snow
• **cocos** NMPL *(haricots)* = type of small white haricot bean

cocoler [3] [kɔkɔle] VT *Suisse* to cosset

cocon [kɔkɔ̃] NM cocoon; *Fig* **le c. familial** the family nest; *Fig* **vivre dans un c.** to live a cocooned *or* sheltered existence, to live in a cocoon; *Fig* **s'enfermer dans son c.** to stay in one's shell

cocontractant, -e [kɔkɔ̃traktɑ̃, -ɑ̃t] NM,F contracting partner

cocooning [kɔkuniŋ] NM cocooning; **on a fait du c. ce week-end** we had a quiet time at home this weekend

cocorico [kɔkɔriko] ONOMAT cock-a-doodle-doo; **faire c.** to crow
EXCLAM three cheers for France!
NM **1** *(chant du coq)* cock-a-doodle-doo **2** *Fig* = expression of French national pride; **les cocoricos qui ont salué leur victoire dans la presse** the national pride which their victory generated in the press

cocotier [kɔkɔtje] NM coconut palm; *Fig* **secouer le c.** to get rid of the dead wood

cocotte [kɔkɔt] NF **1** *(casserole)* casserole dish; **cuire à la c.** to casserole
2 *(en langage enfantin ▸ poule)* hen; **c. en papier** paper bird
3 *(en appellatif)* **ma c.** darling
4 *Péj (femme)* tart; **sentir** *ou* **puer la c.** to stink of cheap perfume
• **en cocotte** ADV **cuit en c.** casseroled; **(faire) cuire qch en c.** to casserole sth
ADJ *(œuf)* coddled

Cocotte-Minute® [kɔkɔtminyt] NF pressure cooker
• **à la Cocotte-Minute®** ADJ pressure-cooked ADV *(cuit)* in a pressure cooker

cocréancier, -ère [kokreɑ̃sje, -ɛr] NM,F *Fin* joint creditor

cocu, -e [kɔky] *Fam* ADJ **il est c.** his wife's cheated on him
NM,F **1** *(conjoint trompé)* cuckold□, deceived husband□, *f* wife□; **elle l'a fait c.** she cheated on him□, she was unfaithful to him **2** *(en appellatif)* sucker; **va donc, eh c.!** get lost, you sucker!

cocuage [kɔkɥaʒ] NM *Fam* cuckoldry□

cocufier [9] [kɔkyfje] VT *Fam* to cheat on, to be unfaithful to□, *Vieilli* to cuckold□

coda [kɔda] NF *Mus* coda

codage [kɔdaʒ] NM **1** *(chiffrement)* coding; **c. de données** data encryption **2** *Ling* encoding

code [kɔd] NM **1** *(ensemble de lois)* code; **le c. (civil)** the civil code; **c. de commerce** commercial law; **c. de déontologie** code of ethics; **c. général des impôts** general tax code; **c. maritime** navigation laws; **c. pénal** penal code; **c. de procédure civile/pénale** Code of Civil/Criminal Procedure; **c. de la route** *Br* Highway Code, *Am* rules of the road; **passer le c.** to sit the written part of a driving test; **c. du travail** Labour Code
2 *(normes)* code; **c. moral** moral code; **c. de la politesse** code of good conduct
3 *(ensemble de conventions)* code; *Naut* **c. international de signaux** International Code; **c. télégraphique** telegraphic code; **c. des transmissions** signal *or* signalling code
4 *(groupe de symboles)* code; **science des codes** cryptography; **c. alphanumérique** alphanumeric code; **c. assujetti TVA** VAT registration number; **c. (à) barres** bar code; **c. binaire** binary code; **c. client** customer code, customer reference number; **c. confidentiel** *(d'une carte bancaire)* personal identification number, PIN (number); **c. couleur** colour code; **c. d'entrée** *(sur une porte)* door code; **c. guichet** bank branch code; **c. à lecture optique** machine readable code line; **c. personnel** *ou* **porteur** *(pour carte bancaire)* personal identification number, PIN (number); **c. postal** *Br* post *or Am* zip code; **c. de routage** routing information
5 *Ordinat* code; **c. abrégé** shortcode; **c. d'accès** access code; **c. d'arrêt** stop code; **c. ASCII** ASCII code; **c. d'autorisation d'accès** access authorization code; **c. de caractère** character code; **c. de commande** command code; **c. de contrôle** control code; **c. de départ** start code; **c. d'erreur** error code; **c. d'imprimante** printer code; **c. machine** machine code; **c. malicieux** malware; **c. natif** source code; **c. objet** object code; **c. source** source code
6 *(manuel)* code-book; **c. de chiffrement** cipher book; **c. de déchiffrement** code-book
7 *Ling* language
8 *Biol* code; **c. génétique** genetic code
• **codes** NMPL *Aut Br* dipped headlights, *Am* low beams
• **en code** ADV *(sous forme chiffrée)* in code; **mettre qch en c.** to cipher *or Am* to code sth
• **en codes** ADV *Aut* **se mettre en codes** *Br* to dip one's headlights, *Am* to put on the low beams; **rouler en codes** *Br* to drive with dipped headlights, *Am* to drive with one's headlights on low beam

> **CODE POSTAL**
>
> In France, the first two numbers of a given post code correspond to the administrative code number of the relevant "département". Thus all postal codes for Paris begin with 75. This system also applies to vehicle registration numbers.

codé, -e [kɔde] ADJ encoded, coded; **caractère/programme c.** coded character/program; **message c.** cryptogram; **question codée** encoded question; **langage c.** secret language

code-barres [kɔdbar] *(pl* **codes-barres)** NM bar code

codébiteur, -trice [kɔdebitœr, -tris] NM,F joint debtor

codécision [kɔdesizjɔ̃] **NF** *UE* codecision (procedure)

codéine [kɔdein] **NF** codeine

codemandeur, -eresse [kɔdəmɑ̃dœr, -drɛs] **NM,F** joint plaintiff

codépendance [kɔdepɑ̃dɑ̃s] **NF** *Psy* codependency

coder [3] [kɔde] **VT 1** *(chiffrer)* to code, to encipher **2** *Ling* to encode

codétenteur, -trice [kɔdetɑ̃tœr, -tris] **NM,F** joint holder

codétenu, -e [kɔdetny] **NM,F** fellow prisoner

codeur, -euse [kɔdœr, -øz] **NM,F** coder
NM coding machine

codéveloppement [kodevlɔpmɑ̃] **NM** cooperative development

CODEVI, codevi, codévi [kɔdevi] **NM** *Banque* *(abrév* **compte pour le développement industriel***)* = type of instant-access savings account, money from which is invested in industrial development

codex [kɔdɛks] **NM** codex; **c. pharmaceutique** pharmacopoeia

codicillaire [kɔdisilɛr] **ADJ** *Jur* codicillary

codicille [kɔdisil] **NM** *Jur* codicil

codification [kɔdifikasjɔ̃] **NF 1** *(d'une profession, d'un système)* codification **2** *Jur (de lois)* codification **3** *Ordinat* **c. binaire** binary code; **c. décimale** decimal coding

codifier [9] [kɔdifje] **VT 1** *(pratique, profession)* to codify **2** *Jur (lois)* to codify

codirecteur, -trice [kɔdirɛktœr, -tris] **NM,F** joint manager

cododo [kododo] **NM** *Fam (sommeil partagé)* co-sleeping▫

coédition [kɔedisjɔ̃] **NF** *(procédé)* copublishing, coedition, joint publishing; *(livre)* joint publication

coefficient [kɔefisjɑ̃] **NM 1** *Math & Phys* coefficient; **c. de corrélation** correlation coefficient; *Tech* **c. de dilatation** coefficient of expansion; **c. d'élasticité** modulus of elasticity; **c. multiplicateur** multiplying factor; **c. numérique** numerical coefficient; *Aut* **c. de pénétration dans l'air** drag factor; *Math* **c. de pondération** weighting; *Aut* **c. de traînée** drag coefficient, drag factor **2** *(proportion)* rating, ratio; *Fin* **c. d'activité** activity ratio; *Fin* **c. de capital** output ratio; *Fin* **c. de capitalisation des résultats** price-earnings ratio; *Fin* **c. d'exploitation** operating ratio, performance ratio; **c. d'erreur** *ou* **d'incertitude** margin of error; *Compta* **c. d'exploitation** performance *or* operating ratio; *Compta* **c. de liquidité** liquidity ratio; **c. d'occupation des sols** plot ratio; *Fin* **c. de perte** loss ratio; *Compta* **c. de rotation** stock turnover ratio; *Compta* **c. de solvabilité** risk asset ratio, solvency coefficient; *Fin* **c. de trésorerie** cash ratio **3** *(valeur)* weight, weighting; **affecter qch d'un c.** to weight sth; **l'anglais est affecté du c. 3** English will be weighted at a rate equal to 300 percent

> **COEFFICIENT**
>
> In baccalauréat examinations, the grade for each subject is multiplied by a "coefficient" which is determined by the type of baccalauréat chosen. For a "bac S", which has a scientific bias, the "coefficient" for maths will be higher than the philosophy "coefficient", for example.

cœlacanthe [selakɑ̃t] **NM** *Ich* coelacanth

cœliaque [seljak] **ADJ** *Méd* coeliac

cœliochirurgie [seljɔʃiryrʒi] **NF** *Méd* laparotomy

cœlioscopie [seljɔskɔpi] **NF** *Méd* caelioscopy, laparoscopy

coentreprise [koɑ̃trəpriz] **NF** joint venture

coéquation [kɔekwasjɔ̃] **NF** proportional assessment

coéquipier, -ère [kɔekipje, -ɛr] **NM,F** team mate

coercible [kɔɛrsibl] **ADJ** coercible, which can be coerced

coercitif, -ive [kɔɛrsitif, -iv] **ADJ** coercive

coercition [kɔɛrsisjɔ̃] **NF** coercion

coercitive [kɔɛrsitiv] *voir* **coercitif**

CŒUR [kœr] **NM A.** *ORGANE* **1** *Anat* heart; **une balle en plein c.** a bullet through the heart; **il est malade du c.** he's got a heart condition; **c. droit/gauche** right/left side of the heart; **greffe du c.** heart transplant; **j'ai eu un coup au c.** it really made me jump; *Fig* **beau comme un c.** as pretty as a picture

2 *(poitrine)* heart, breast, *Littéraire* bosom; **serrer qn contre son c.** to hold sb close

3 *(estomac)* **avoir le c. au bord des lèvres** to feel queasy *or* sick; **avoir mal au c.** to feel sick; *Fig* **ça fait mal au c. de voir tout cet argent gaspillé** it makes you sick to see all that money wasted *or* go to waste; *Fam* **ça me ferait mal au c. de devoir le lui laisser!** I'd hate to have to leave it to him/her!; *Fam* **mettre le c. à l'envers à qn** *(le dégoûter)* to sicken sb▫, to turn sb's stomach; **lever** *ou* **soulever le c. à qn** to sicken sb, to turn sb's stomach; **un spectacle à vous lever** *ou* **soulever le c.** a nauseating *or* sickening sight; *Fam* **avoir le c. bien accroché** to have a strong stomach▫

B. *SYMBOLE DE L'AFFECTIVITÉ* **1** *(pensées, for intérieur)* heart; **ouvrir son c. à qn** to open one's heart to sb; **vider son c.** to pour out one's heart; **je veux en avoir le c. net** I want to know *or* to find out the truth; **je vais lui demander franchement, comme cela j'en aurai le c. net** I'll ask him/her straight out, that way, I'll get to the bottom of the matter

2 *(énergie, courage)* courage; **le c. lui a manqué** his/her courage failed him/her; **avoir le c. de faire qch** to have the heart to do sth; **avoir** *ou* **mettre du c. à l'ouvrage** to put one's heart into one's work; **il n'avait pas le c. à l'ouvrage** his heart wasn't in it; **avoir du c. au ventre** to be courageous; **donner du c. au ventre à qn** to give sb courage; **elle adore son travail, elle y met du c.** she loves her work, she really puts her heart (and soul) into it; **allez, haut les cœurs!** come on, chin up!

3 *(humeur)* **il est parti le c. joyeux** he left in a cheerful mood; **avoir le c. léger/triste** to be cheerful/heavy-hearted; **d'un c. léger** light-heartedly; **d'un c. content** contentedly; **avoir le c. à faire qch** to be in the mood to do *or* to feel like doing sth; **je n'ai plus le c. à rire** I don't feel like laughing any more; **ne plus avoir le c. à rien** to have lost heart; **si le c. t'en dit** if you feel like it, if the fancy takes you

4 *(charité, bonté)* **avoir du c.** *ou* **bon c.** to be kind *or* kind-hearted; **elle a du c.** *ou* **bon c.** her heart is in the right place; **tu n'as pas de c.!** you're heartless!, you have no heart!; **ton bon c. te perdra!** you're too kind-hearted for your own good!; **c'était un homme au grand c.** he was a good man; *Fam* **il a un c. gros comme ça** he'd give you the shirt off his back; **avoir le c. sur la main** to be very generous; **avoir un c. d'or** to have a heart of gold; **avoir le c. dur, avoir un c. de pierre** to have a heart of stone, to be hard-hearted; **à vot' bon c. (M'sieurs-Dames)** can you spare *Br* a few pence *or* *Am* a dime?

5 *(siège des émotions, de l'amour)* heart; **son c. se remplit de joie** his/her heart filled with joy; **son c. a parlé** he/she spoke from the heart; **laisser parler son c.** to let one's feelings come through; **venir du c.** to come (straight) from the heart; **des mots venus du (fond du) c.** heartfelt words; **vos paroles me sont allées droit au c.** your words went straight to my heart; **briser le c. à qn** *(par chagrin d'amour)* to break sb's heart; **cela me brise le c. de le voir dans cet état** it breaks my heart to see him in such a state; **c'était à vous fendre le c.** it was heartbreaking *or* heartrending; **cela réchauffe le c.** it warms the cockles of your heart, it's heart-warming; **avoir le c. serré** to have a lump in one's throat; **avoir le c. déchiré** *ou* **brisé** to be heartbroken; **avoir le c. gros** *ou* **lourd** to feel very sad, *Littéraire* to have a heavy heart; **avoir un c. sensible/pur** to be a sensitive/candid soul; **mon c. est libre** *ou* **à prendre** I'm fancy-free; **donner son c. à qn** to lose one's heart to sb; **comment trouver le chemin de** *ou* **gagner son c.?** how can I win his/her heart?; **ce sont des amis de c.** they're bosom friends; **une affaire de c.** a love affair, an affair of the heart; **ses problèmes de c.** the problems he/she has with his/her love life; *Fam* **je ne le porte pas dans mon c.** I'm not particularly fond of him

C. *PERSONNE* **1** *(personne ayant telle qualité)* **c'est un c. d'or** he's got a heart of gold; **c'est un c. sensible** he's a sensitive soul; **c'est un c. dur ou de pierre** he has a heart of stone, he's heartless; **c'est un c. de lion** he's a real lionheart; *Prov* **à c. vaillant rien d'impossible** where there's a will there's a way

2 *(terme affectueux)* darling, sweetheart; **mon (petit) c.** my darling; **tu viens, mon c.?** coming, darling?

D. *CENTRE* **1** *(d'un chou, d'une salade, d'un fromage)* heart; *(d'un fruit, d'un réacteur nucléaire)* core; *(d'une ville)* heart, centre; **enlever le c. d'une pomme** to core an apple; **c. d'artichaut** artichoke heart; *Fig* **c'est un vrai c. d'artichaut** he/she is always falling in love; *Mktg* **c. de cible** core market, core audience; **c. de laitue** lettuce heart; **c. de palmier** palm heart

2 *(partie la plus importante* ▸ *d'un débat)* central point; **le c. de mon argument est que…** the central point of my argument is that…; **le c. du problème** the heart of the matter

3 *Menuis* **c. de merisier/peuplier** heart of cherry/poplar

E. *OBJET EN FORME DE CŒUR* **1** *(bijou)* heart-shaped jewel

2 *Culin* heart-shaped delicacy; **petits cœurs à la crème** hearts of fromage frais with cream

3 *Cartes* **du c.** hearts; **dame/dix de c.** queen/ten of hearts; **jouer à** *ou* **du c.** to play hearts

• **à cœur ADV 1** *(avec sérieux)* **prendre les choses à c.** to take things to heart; **elle prend vraiment son travail à c.** she really takes her job seriously; **ce rôle me tient beaucoup à c.** the part means a lot to me; **avoir à c. de faire qch** to have one's heart set on doing sth; **2** *Culin* **fromage fait à c.** fully ripe cheese; **café grillé à c.** high roast coffee

• **à cœur de ADV** *Can* **à c. de jour/année** all day/year long

• **à cœur joie ADV** to one's heart's content; **s'en donner à c. joie** to have tremendous fun *or* a tremendous time

• **à cœur ouvert ADJ** *(opération)* open-heart *(avant n)* **ADV parler à c. ouvert à qn** to have a heart-to-heart (talk) with sb

• **au cœur de PRÉP au c. de l'été** at the height of summer; **au c. de l'hiver** in the depths of winter; **au c. de la forêt** deep in the forest; **au c. de la nuit** in the *or* at dead of night; **au c. du Morvan** in the heart of the Morvan region; **au c. de la ville** in the centre of town, in the town centre; **le sujet fut au c. des débats** the subject was central to the debate

• **cœur à cœur ADV** *Littéraire* **parler c. à c. avec qn** to have a heart-to-heart (talk) with sb

• **de bon cœur ADV 1** *(volontiers* ▸ *donner)* willingly; *(*▸ *parler)* readily; **ne me remerciez pas, c'est de bon c. (que je vous ai aidé)** no need to thank me, it was a pleasure (helping you) **2** *(énergiquement* ▸ *rire)* heartily; **y aller de bon c.** to get down to it

• **de tout cœur ADV** wholeheartedly; **être de tout c. avec qn** *(condoléances)* to sympathize wholeheartedly with sb; **je ne pourrai assister à votre mariage mais je serai de tout c. avec vous** I won't be able to attend your wedding but I'll be with you in spirit

• **de tout mon/son/***etc* **cœur ADV 1** *(sincèrement* ▸ *aimer, remercier)* with all my/his/*etc* heart, wholeheartedly, from the bottom of my/his/*etc* heart; *(*▸ *féliciter)* warmly, wholeheartedly; **je l'espère de tout mon c.** I sincerely hope so **2** *Fam (énergiquement)* **y aller de tout son c.** to go at it hammer and tongs, to give it all one's got; **rire de tout son c.** to laugh one's head off

• **en cœur ADJ** *(bouche, pendentif)* heart-shaped

• **par cœur ADV** *(apprendre)* by heart; **connaître qn par c.** to know sb inside out; **je connais toutes tes excuses par c.** I know all your excuses by heart **NM c'est du par c.** it's been learnt (off) by heart *or* parrot-fashion

• **sans cœur ADJ** heartless

• **sur le cœur ADV la mousse au chocolat m'est restée sur le c.** the chocolate mousse lay in the pit of my stomach; **ses critiques me pèsent sur le c.** I still haven't got over the way she criticized me; **avoir qch sur le c.** to have sth on one's mind;

dis ce que tu as sur le c. say what's (weighing) on your mind; **avoir un poids sur le c.** to have a heavy heart; *Fam* **en avoir gros sur le c.** to be really upset

coexistence [kɔegzistɑ̃s] **NF** coexistence; **c. pacifique** peaceful coexistence

coexister [3] [kɔegziste] **VI c. (avec)** to coexist (with)

COFACE [kɔfas] **NF** *(abrév* **Compagnie française d'assurances pour le commerce extérieur)** = export insurance company, ≃ ECGD

coffrage [kɔfraʒ] **NM 1** *Mines & (en travaux publics)* lagging, (plank) lining **2** *Constr (moule)* form, formwork, *Br* shuttering; *(pose de moule)* form *or* formwork preparation

coffre [kɔfr] **NM 1** *(caisse)* box, chest; **c. à jouets** toybox; **c. à linge** linen chest; **c. à outils** tool box

2 *Naut* locker; **c. d'amarrage** mooring buoy, trunk buoy

3 *Aut Br* boot, *Am* trunk; **c. à bagages** *(d'un autocar)* baggage *or* luggage compartment; **c. de rangement** *(d'un camion)* storage compartment

4 *(coffre-fort)* safe, strongbox; *(à la banque)* safe-deposit box; **les coffres de l'État** the coffers of the State; **c. de nuit** night safe

5 *(d'un piano)* case

6 *Aviat* **c. à parachute** parachute canister

7 *Fam (poitrine)* chest❑; *(voix)* (big) voice❑; **avoir du c.** *(du souffle)* to have a good pair of lungs; *(de la voix)* to have a powerful voice

coffre-fort [kɔfrfɔr] *(pl* **coffres-forts)** **NM** safe, strongbox

coffrer [3] [kɔfre] **VT 1** *Fam (emprisonner)* to put behind bars; **se faire c.** to be sent down, to get put inside *or* away *or* behind bars **2** *Mines* to lag **3** *Constr* to form

coffret [kɔfrɛ] **NM 1** *(petit coffre)* box, casket; **dans un c. cadeau** in a gift box; **un c. de cinq savons** a box set of five soaps; **vendu en c.** sold in a presentation box; **c. à bijoux** jewellery box

2 *(cabinet)* cabinet

3 *Ordinat* case

4 *Tél* **c. avec carte prépayée** prepay package

cogénération [koʒenerasjɔ̃] **NF** *Tech* cogeneration

cogérance [koʒerɑ̃s] **NF** joint management

cogérant, -e [koʒerɑ̃, -ɑ̃t] **NM,F** joint manager

cogérer [18] [koʒere] **VT** to manage jointly

cogestion [koʒestjɔ̃] **NF** joint management *or* administration

cogitation [kɔʒitasjɔ̃] **NF** *Hum* cogitation *(UNCOUNT)*, pondering *(UNCOUNT)*

cogiter [3] [kɔʒite] *Hum* **VI** to cogitate; **il faut que je cogite!** I must put my thinking cap on!; **c. sur qch** to ponder over sth

VT to think over, to ponder

cogito [kɔʒito] **NM INV** *Phil* cogito

cognac [kɔɲak] **NM** *(gén)* brandy; *(de Cognac)* Cognac

cognassier [kɔɲasje] **NM** *Bot* quince tree

cogne [kɔɲ] **NM** *Fam Arg crime (policier)* cop; **les cognes** the cops, *Br* the fuzz

NF *Fam (bagarre)* punch-up; **il va y avoir de la c.!** there's going to be trouble *or* a punch-up!

cognée [kɔɲe] **NF** axe, hatchet

cognement [kɔɲmɑ̃] **NM** *(gén)* knock, thump; *(d'un moteur)* knock

cogner [3] [kɔɲe] **VI 1** *(heurter)* to bang, to knock; **qu'est-ce qui cogne?** what's that banging?; **le moteur cogne** there's a knocking sound coming from the engine; **son cœur cognait dans sa poitrine** his/her heart was thumping; **c. à la fenêtre** *(fort)* to knock on the window; *(légèrement)* to tap on the window; **sa tête a cogné contre le bureau** he/she banged his/her head on the desk; **c. du poing sur la table** to bang (one's fist) on the table

2 *Fam (user de violence)* **mon père cognait** my father was handy with his fists; **il cogne dur** he knows how to use his fists; **c. sur qn** to beat sb up; **ça va c.** things are going to get rough

3 *Fam* **ça cogne** *(le soleil chauffe)* it's scorching *or Br* roasting

4 *Fam (puer)* to stink (to high heaven), *Br* to pong

VT 1 *(entrer en collision avec)* to bang *or* to knock *or* to smash into; **c. qn en passant** to bump into sb (in passing) **2** *Fam (battre)* to knock about; **se faire c.** to get knocked about

VPR se cogner 1 *(se faire mal)* **je me suis cogné** I banged into something; **se c. à** *ou* **contre qch** to bang into sth

2 *(heurter)* **se c. le coude** to hit *or* to bang one's elbow; *Fig* **se c. la tête contre les murs** to bang one's head against a brick wall

3 *Fam* **se c. qn/qch** *(corvée)* to get stuck *or Br* lumbered *or* landed with sb/sth

4 *très Fam (locution)* **il s'en cogne** he doesn't give a shit *or Br* a toss

cogneur [kɔɲœr] **NM** *Boxe & (gén)* hard hitter, bruiser

cogniticien, -enne [kɔgnitisjɛ̃, -ɛn] **NM,F** *Ordinat* knowledge engineer

cognitif, -ive [kɔgnitif, -iv] **ADJ** cognitive

cognition [kɔgnisjɔ̃] **NF** cognitive processes, cognition

cognitive [kɔgnitiv] *voir* **cognitif**

cohabitation [kɔabitasjɔ̃] **NF 1** *(vie commune)* cohabitation, cohabiting, living together **2** *Pol* = coexistence of an elected head of state and an opposition parliamentary majority

> **LA COHABITATION**
>
> Originally, this term refers to the period (1986–1988) during which the socialist President (François Mitterrand) had a right-wing Prime Minister (Jacques Chirac), following the victory of the RPR in the legislative elections and Mitterrand's decision not to resign as President. It has since been used to refer to the similar situation which arose following the 1993 elections (with Édouard Balladur as Prime Minister) and also after the 1997 elections (with the left-wing government of Lionel Jospin co-ruling with the President Jacques Chirac).

cohabiter [3] [kɔabite] **VI 1** *(partenaires)* to cohabit, to live together; *(amis)* to live together; **c. avec qn** to live with sb **2** *(coexister)* to coexist; **faire c. deux théories** to reconcile two theories

cohérence [kɔerɑ̃s] **NF 1** *(logique)* coherence; **manque de c.** incoherence **2** *(homogénéité)* consistency; **manque de c.** inconsistency **3** *Phys* coherence

cohérent, -e [kɔerɑ̃, -ɑ̃t] **ADJ 1** *(logique)* coherent

2 *(homogène)* consistent

3 *(fidèle à soi-même)* consistent

4 *Phys* coherent

cohéritier, -ère [koeritje, -ɛr] **NM,F** co-heir, *f* coheiress

cohésif, -ive [kɔezif, -iv] **ADJ** cohesive

cohésion [kɔezjɔ̃] **NF 1** *(solidarité)* cohesion, cohesiveness **2** *(d'un corps, de molécules)* cohesion

cohésive [kɔeziv] *voir* **cohésif**

cohorte [koɔrt] **NF 1** *Antiq* cohort **2** *Péj (foule)* **une c. de** hordes *or* droves of **3** *(en sociologie)* population

cohue [kɔy] **NF 1** *(foule)* crowd, throng **2** *(bousculade)* **dans la c.** amidst the general pushing and shoving, in the (general) melee

coi, coite [kwa, kwat] **ADJ** speechless; **en rester c.** to be speechless; **se tenir c.** to keep quiet

coiffage [kwafaʒ] **NM 1** *(de cheveux)* hairdressing; *(de ses cheveux)* doing one's hair **2** *(pour recouvrir)* covering

coiffe [kwaf] **NF 1** *(de costume régional)* (traditional) headdress; *(de nonne)* (nun's) headdress; *(garniture de chapeau)* lining

2 *Tech & Bot* cap

3 *(d'un livre relié)* head cap

4 *Anat* caul

coiffé, -e [kwafe] **ADJ 1** *(portant coiffure)* wearing a hat; **être c. de noir** to be wearing a black hat **2** *(avec les cheveux bien mis)* **être c.** to have combed/brushed one's hair; **je ne suis pas encore coiffée** I haven't done my hair yet; **elle était bien coiffée** her hair looked nice; **tu es très mal c.** your hair's all over the place; **il est c. en brosse** he's got a brush cut **3** *(locutions)* **être né c.** *(chanceux)* to be born lucky *or* under a lucky star

coiffer [3] [kwafe] **VT 1** *(peigner ▸ cheveux, frange)* to comb; *(▸ enfant, poupée)* to comb the hair of; **cheveux faciles/difficiles à c.** manageable/unmanageable hair

2 *(réaliser la coiffure de)* to do *or* to style the hair of; **elle s'est fait c. par Paolo** she had her hair done by Paolo; **qui vous coiffe d'habitude?** who normally does your hair?

3 *(chapeauter)* to cover the head of; **c. un enfant d'un bonnet** to put a bonnet on a child('s head)

4 *(aller à)* **un rien la coiffe** she suits any hat

5 *(mettre sur sa tête)* to put on; **c. la couronne** to be crowned

6 *Littéraire (couvrir)* **la neige coiffait les sommets** the mountain-tops were capped with snow

7 *(diriger)* to be in charge of, to head up; **elle coiffe plusieurs services** she's in charge of several departments

8 *(locution)* **c. qn (au** *ou* **sur le poteau)** *Br* to pip sb at the post, *Am* to pass sb up; **se faire c. au poteau** to be pipped at the post

VPR se coiffer 1 *(se peigner)* to comb one's hair; *(arranger ses cheveux)* to do one's hair **2** *(mettre un chapeau)* to put a hat on; **se c. d'une casquette** to put on a cap **3** *(acheter ses chapeaux)* **se c. chez les grands couturiers** to buy one's hats from the top designers

coiffeur, -euse [kwafœr, -øz] **NM,F** hairdresser, hairstylist; **aller chez le c.** to go to the hairdresser's; **c. pour hommes** gentlemen's hairdresser, barber; **c. pour dames** ladies' hairdresser

• **coiffeuse NF** dressing-table

coiffure [kwafyr] **NF 1** *(coupe)* hairdo, hairstyle; **se faire faire une nouvelle c.** to have one's hair styled *or* restyled; **c. à la garçonne** urchin cut, *Br* Eton crop; **c. à la Jeanne d'Arc** pageboy haircut **2** *(technique)* **la c.** hairdressing **3** *(chapeau)* headgear; *(de costume régional)* headdress

COIN [kwɛ̃]

> • corner **1, 2** • place **3**
> • patch **4** • die, stamp **5**
> • wedge **6**

NM 1 *(angle)* corner; **se cogner au c. de la table** to bang into the corner of the table; **le c. de la rue** the corner of the street; **la maison qui fait le c.** the house on the corner, the corner house; **à un c. de rue** on a street-corner; *Rail* **un c. couloir/fenêtre** an aisle/a window seat; **à tous les coins de rue** on every street corner, everywhere; **il n'y en a pas à tous les coins de rue** you don't see many of them about; **manger sur un c. de table** to eat a hasty meal; **travailler sur un c. de table** to bungle one's work; **au c. du feu** by the fireside; *Fig* **rester au c. du feu** to stay at home; **au c. d'un bois** somewhere in a wood; *Fig* in a lonely place; **on n'aimerait pas le rencontrer au c. d'un bois!** you wouldn't like to meet him on a dark night!

2 *(commissure ▸ des lèvres, de l'œil)* corner; **du c. de l'œil** *(regarder, surveiller)* out of the corner of one's eye

3 *(endroit quelconque)* place, spot; **dans un c. de la maison** somewhere in the house; **j'ai dû laisser mon livre dans un c.** I must have left my book somewhere or other; **dans un c. de sa mémoire** in a corner of his/her memory; **il connaît les bons coins** he knows all the right places; **un petit c. tranquille à la campagne** a quiet spot in the country; **un c. perdu** *(isolé)* an isolated spot; *Péj (arriéré)* a godforsaken place; *Fam* **c'est vraiment un c. pourri!** what a dump!; *Com* **le c. des bricoleurs** the do-it-yourself department; **c. enfants** *(au restaurant)* children's area; **chercher dans tous les coins et les recoins** to look in every nook and cranny; **connaître qch dans les coins** to know sth like the back of one's hand; *Fam Euph* **le petit c.** the smallest room in the house; **c. cuisine** kitchen recess; **c. repas** *ou* **salle à manger** dining area; **c. salon** lounge area; **c. travail** workspace, work area

4 *(parcelle)* patch, plot; **un c. de terre** a plot *or* patch of land; **le c. des fleurs** the flower plot; **il reste un c. de ciel bleu** there's still a patch of blue sky

5 *Typ (forme)* die; *(poinçon)* stamp, hallmark

6 *(cale)* wedge
• **au coin** ADV *(de la rue)* on *or* at the corner; **la boulangerie qui est au c.** the baker's on *or* at the corner; **mettre un enfant au c.** to make a child stand in the corner (as punishment)
• **dans le coin** ADV *(dans le quartier ▸ ici)* locally, around here; *(▸ là-bas)* locally, around there; **elle habite dans le c.** *(ici)* she lives (somewhere) around here; *(là-bas)* she lives somewhere around there; **et Victor? – il est dans le c.** where's Victor? – he's around somewhere; **je passais dans le c. et j'ai eu envie de venir te voir** I was in the area and I felt like dropping in (on you)
• **dans son coin** ADV **laisser qn dans son c.** to leave sb alone; **allons, ne laisse pas ton petit frère dans son c.** come on, make an effort to include your little brother; **rester dans son c.** to keep oneself to oneself; **elle reste toujours dans son c.** she doesn't mix
• **de coin** ADJ *(étagère)* corner *(avant n)*
• **du coin** ADJ *(du quartier ▸ commerce)* local; **la boucherie du c.** the butcher's just round the corner, the local butcher's; **les gens du c.** *(ici)* people who live round here, the locals; *(là-bas)* people who live there, the locals; **être du c.** to live locally *or* in the area; **désolé, je ne suis pas du c.** sorry, I'm not from around here
• **en coin** ADJ *(regard)* sidelong; **un sourire en c.** a half-smile ADV *(regarder, observer)* sideways; **sourire en c.** to give a half-smile

coinçage [kwɛ̃saʒ] NM *Tech* keying, wedging

coincé, -e [kwɛ̃se] ADJ *Fam* **1** *Péj (inhibé)* uptight, hung-up **2** *(mal à l'aise)* tense, uneasy

coincement [kwɛ̃smɑ̃] NM jamming

coincer [16] [kwɛ̃se] VT **1** *(immobiliser ▸ volontairement)* to wedge; *(▸ accidentellement)* to catch, to stick, to jam; **coince la roue avec une pierre** wedge the wheel with a stone; **mon manteau est coincé dans la portière** my coat's caught *or* stuck in the door; **j'ai coincé la fermeture de ma robe** I got the *Br* zip *or Am* zipper of my dress stuck; **il était coincé entre la voiture et le mur** he was jammed *or* trapped between the car and the wall; **la voiture est coincée entre deux camions** *(en stationnement)* the car is boxed in by two lorries
2 *Fam (attraper)* to corner, to nab, to collar; **se faire c.** to get nabbed; **je me suis fait c. dans le couloir par Darival** I got cornered by Darival in the corridor; **j'arriverai bien à le c. après le dîner** I'll corner him somehow after dinner
3 *Fam (retenir)* **je suis resté coincé dans un embouteillage** I got stuck in a traffic jam; **je suis coincé à Prague/dans l'ascenseur** I'm stuck in Prague/the *Br* lift *or Am* elevator; **il est coincé tout le weekend** he's tied up all weekend
4 *(mettre en difficulté ▸ par une question)* to put on the spot, *Br* to catch out; **là, ils t'ont coincé!** they've got you there!
VI **1** *(être calé)* **c'est la chemise bleue qui coince au fond du tiroir** the blue shirt at the back is making the drawer jam **2** *(être entravé)* to stick; **les négociations coincent** the negotiations are deadlocked; *Fam* **ça coince (quelque part)** there's a hitch somewhere **3** *très Fam (sentir mauvais)* to stink, *Br* to pong
VPR **se coincer 1** *(se bloquer ▸ clef, fermeture)* to jam, to stick **2 se c. le pied** to get one's foot caught; **il s'est coincé le doigt dans la serrure** he got his finger stuck in the lock; **se c. le doigt dans la porte** to catch one's finger in the door; **je me suis coincé le dos** my back's seized up; **il s'est coincé une vertèbre** he's got a trapped nerve

coïncidence [kɔɛ̃sidɑ̃s] NF **1** *(hasard)* chance; **quelle c. de vous voir ici!** what a coincidence seeing you here!; **c'est (une) pure c.** it's purely coincidental; **par une étrange c.** by a strange coincidence **2** *Math* coincidence

coïncident, -e [kɔɛ̃sidɑ̃, -ɑ̃t] ADJ **1** *(dans l'espace)* coextensive, coincident **2** *(dans le temps)* concomitant, simultaneous

coïncider [3] [kɔɛ̃side] VI **1** *(s'ajuster l'un sur l'autre)* to line up, to coincide, *Sout* to be coextensive; **faites c. les deux triangles** line up the two triangles (so that they coincide) **2** *(se produire ensemble)* to coincide; **nos anniversaires coïncident** our birthdays fall on the same day; **j'ai essayé de faire c. ma visite avec le début du festival** I tried to make my visit coincide with the beginning of the festival **3** *(concorder)* to coincide; **les deux témoignages coïncident** the two statements are consistent; **leurs intérêts coïncident** they have similar interests

coin-coin [kwɛ̃kwɛ̃] NM INV quacking; **des c.** quacks, quacking
ONOMAT quack quack; **faire c.** to go quack quack

coïnculpé, -e [kɔɛ̃kylpe] NM,F co-defendant

coing [kwɛ̃] NM quince; *Fam* **bourré comme un c.** plastered, *Br* legless

coït [kɔit] NM coitus; **c. interrompu** coitus interruptus

coite [kwat] *voir* **coi**

coke [kɔk] NM coke
NF *Fam (cocaïne)* coke

cokéfaction [kɔkefaksjɔ̃] NF coking

cokéfier [9] [kɔkefje] VT to coke

cokerie [kɔkri] NF coking plant

co-koter [3], cokoter [3] [kɔkɔte] VI *Belg Fam* to share a room[□]

co-koteur, -euse, cokoteur, -euse [kɔkɔtœr, -øz], **cokotier, -ère** [kɔkɔtje, -ɛr] NM,F *Belg Fam* (student) roommate[□], roomie

col [kɔl] NM **1** *Couture* collar; **c. blanc/bleu** white-collar/blue-collar worker; **c. camionneur** zipped rollneck; **c. cassé** wing collar; **c. châle** shawl collar; **c. cheminée** turtleneck; **c. chemisier** shirt collar; **c. Claudine** Peter Pan collar; **c. Mao** Mao collar; **c. marin** sailor's collar; **c. montant** turtleneck; **c. officier** mandarin collar; **c. rond** round neck; **c. roulé** polo neck; **c. en V** V-neck; **faux c.** detachable collar; *(de la bière)* head; **un demi sans faux c.** a glass of beer with as little froth as possible
2 *(d'une bouteille)* neck
3 *Anat* cervix, neck; **c. du fémur** neck of the femur; **c. de l'utérus** cervix, neck of the womb; **cancer du c. de l'utérus** cervical cancer
4 *Géog* pass, col

cola [kɔla] = **kola**

colback [kɔlbak] NM **1** *Hist* kalpak, (Napoleonic) busby **2** *Fam* **attraper/prendre qn par le c.** to catch/grab sb by the scruff of the neck

colbertisme [kɔlbɛrtism] NM = economic policy of state intervention and protectionism *(from Colbert, finance minister to Louis XIV)*

col-bleu [kɔlblø] *(pl* **cols-bleus***)* NM *Fam Vieilli* sailor[□], jack tar

colchique [kɔlʃik] NM *Bot* colchicum; **c. d'automne** autumn crocus, meadow saffron

cold-cream [kɔldkrim] *(pl* **cold-creams***)* NM cold cream

col-de-cygne [kɔldəsiɲ] *(pl* **cols-de-cygne***)* NM swan neck

colégataire [kɔlegatɛr] NMF joint legatee

coléoptère [kɔleɔptɛr] *Entom* NM member of the Coleoptera
• **coléoptères** NMPL Coleoptera

colère [kɔlɛr] NF **1** *(mauvaise humeur)* anger, rage; **passer sa c. sur qn** to take out one's anger on sb; **avec c.** angrily, in anger; **c. froide** cold fury; *Prov* **la c. est mauvaise conseillère** anger and haste hinder good counsel **2** *(crise)* fit of anger *or* rage; *(d'un enfant)* tantrum; **il avait des colères terribles** he was subject to terrible fits of anger; *Fam* **piquer une c.** *(adulte)* to fly into a temper; *(enfant)* to have *or* to throw a tantrum; **se mettre** *ou* **entrer dans une c. bleue** *ou* **noire** to fly into a towering rage **3** *Littéraire (des éléments, des dieux)* wrath; *Bible* **la c. de Dieu** the wrath of God
ADJ *Vieilli* **être c.** to be bad-tempered *or* choleric
• **en colère** ADJ angry, livid, mad; **être en c. contre qn** to be *Br* angry with sb *or Am* mad at sb; **mettre qn en c.** to make sb angry; **se mettre en c.** to flare up, to lose one's temper; **je vais me mettre en c.!** I'm going to get angry!

coléreux, -euse [kɔlerø, -øz], **colérique** [kɔlerik] ADJ *(personne)* irritable, quick-tempered

coleslaw [kɔlslo] NM *Culin* coleslaw

colibacille [kɔlibasil] NM *Biol* colibacillus, colon bacillus

colibacillose [kɔlibasiloz] NF *Méd* colibacillosis

colibri [kɔlibri] NM *Orn* hummingbird

colifichet [kɔlifiʃɛ] NM knick-knack, trinket; **vendre des colifichets** to sell fancy goods

colimaçon [kɔlimasɔ̃] NM snail; **escalier en c.** spiral staircase

colin [kɔlɛ̃] NM **1** *(lieu noir) Br* coley, coalfish, *Am* pollock; *(lieu jaune)* pollack; *(merlan)* whiting; *(merlu)* hake **2** *Orn* **c. de Californie** Californian quail

colinéaire [kɔlineɛr] ADJ *Math* collinear

colinéarité [kɔlinearite] NF *Math* collinearity

colin-maillard [kɔlɛ̃majar] *(pl* **colin-maillards***)* NM blind man's buff

colin-tampon [kɔlɛ̃tɑ̃pɔ̃] *(pl* **colin-tampons***)* NM drum beat; *Fam Vieilli* **il s'en moque** *ou* **il s'en soucie comme de c.** he doesn't give two hoots about it

colique [kɔlik] NF **1** *Fam (diarrhée)* diarrhoea[□], runs; **avoir la c.** to have the runs; *Fig* **ça me flanque la c.** it gives me the heebie-jeebies **2** *Méd (douleur)* colic *(UNCOUNT)*, stomach ache; *(chez le nourrisson)* colic *(UNCOUNT)*, gripes; **coliques hépatiques/néphrétiques** biliary/renal colic **3** *très Fam (contrariété)* hassle, drag; **quelle c.!** what a pain!
ADJ *Anat* colic

colis [kɔli] NM package, packet, parcel; **c. exprès** special delivery parcel; **c. piégé** *Br* parcel *or Am* package bomb; **c. postal** postal packet; **par c. postal** by parcel post; **c. contre remboursement** *Br* cash on delivery parcel, *Am* collect on delivery parcel; *Fam* **un joli petit c.** a knockout, a babe, *Br* a cracker

Colisée [kɔlize] NM **le C.** the Coliseum, the Colosseum

colis-épargne [kɔliepaɲ] NM INV *Com* saving stamps scheme

colistier, -ère [kɔlistje, -ɛr] NM,F fellow candidate *(on a list or platform)*

colite [kɔlit] NF *Méd* colitis

collabo [kɔlabo] NMF *Hist* collaborationist

collaborateur, -trice [kɔlabɔratœr, -tris] NM,F **1** *(assistant)* assistant
2 *(collègue)* associate; *(à une revue, un journal)* contributor
3 *(membre du personnel)* member of staff
4 *Hist* collaborator, collaborationist

collaboration [kɔlabɔrasjɔ̃] NF **1** *(aide)* collaboration, co-operation, help; **en c. étroite avec** in close co-operation with **2** *Hist (politique)* collaborationist policy; *(période)* collaboration

collaborationniste [kɔlabɔrasjɔnist] *Hist* NMF & ADJ collaborationist

collaboratrice [kɔlabɔratris] *voir* **collaborateur**

collaborer [3] [kɔlabɔre] VI **1** *(participer)* to participate; *(travailler ensemble)* to collaborate, to work together; **les deux services collaborent étroitement** the two departments work closely together; **c. à** to take part *or* to participate in; *Journ* to write for, to contribute to, to be a contributor to **2** *Hist* to collaborate

collage [kɔlaʒ] NM **1** *(fixation)* gluing, sticking; **c. d'affiches** billposting, bill sticking; **c. du papier peint** paperhanging
2 *Beaux-Arts* collage
3 *(en œnologie)* fining
4 *Ind* sizing

collagène [kɔlaʒɛn] NM *Biol* collagen; **crème de beauté au c.** collagen(-based) cream

collant, -e [kɔlɑ̃, -ɑ̃t] ADJ **1** *(adhésif)* adhesive, sticky; *(poisseux)* sticky **2** *(moulant)* tight-fitting, skintight; **un pull c.** a skintight sweater **3** *Fam Péj (importun)* limpet-like; **qu'il est c.!** *(importun)* he just won't leave you alone!; *(enfant)* he's so clingy!, he won't give you a minute's peace!
NM **1** *(bas)* (pair of) tights, *Am* pantyhose *(UNCOUNT)*; **c. de contention** support tights; **c. uni/fantaisie** self-coloured/patterned tights **2** *(de danse)* leotard
• **collante** NF *Fam Arg scol (convocation)* = letter asking a student to present him- or herself for an exam

collapsus [kɔlapsys] **NM** *Méd* collapse; **c. cardio-vasculaire** circulatory collapse

collatéral, -e, -aux, -ales [kɔlateral, -o] **ADJ 1** *(de chaque côté)* collateral; **les rues collatérales** *(les rues parallèles)* the streets that run parallel; *(les rues perpendiculaires)* the side streets **2** *Anat & Jur* collateral; **parents collatéraux** collaterals, collateral relatives **3** *Mil* collateral; **dommages** *ou* **dégâts collatéraux** collateral damage
NM 1 *Archit* aisle **2** *Jur* collateral (relative)

collation [kɔlasjɔ̃] **NF 1** *(repas)* light meal, snack **2** *Rel* collation, conferral, conferment **3** *(de textes)* collation

collationnement [kɔlasjɔnmɑ̃] **NM** checking, collation

collationner [3] [kɔlasjɔne] **VT 1** *(texte)* to collate **2** *(en reliure)* to collate

colle [kɔl] **NF 1** *(glu)* glue, adhesive; *(pour papier peint)* (wallpaper) paste; **de la c. en pot/stick/tube** a pot/stick/tube of glue; **c. blanche** paste; **c. à bois** wood glue; **c. forte** glue; **c. de poisson** fish glue, isinglass **2** *Fam (énigme)* trick question, poser, teaser; **poser une c. à qn** to set sb a poser; **là, vous me posez une c.!** you've got me there! **3** *Fam Arg scol (examen)* oral[□]; *(retenue)* detention[□]; **avoir une c.** to get detention, to be kept in *or* behind (after school); **mettre une c. à qn** to keep sb behind (in detention); **une heure de c.** an hour's detention
• **à la colle ADV** *Fam* **ils sont à la c.** they've shacked up together

collecte [kɔlɛkt] **NF 1** *(ramassage)* collection; **la c. des ordures ménagères** the *Br* rubbish *or Am* garbage collection; **faire la c. des vieux journaux** to pick up (bundles of) old newspapers set aside for collection
2 *Ordinat* **c. des données** data collection *or* gathering
3 *(quête)* collection; **c. de fonds** fundraising; **c. d'informations** data collection; *Journ* news gathering; **faire une c.** to collect money, to make a collection
4 *Rel (prière)* collect

collecter [4] [kɔlɛkte] **VT** *(argent)* to collect; *(lait, ordures)* to collect, to pick up

collecteur, -trice [kɔlɛktœr, -tris] **ADJ** *(gén)* collecting; *(égout)* main
NM,F *Admin* **c. d'impôts** tax collector
NM 1 *Élec (lames)* commutator; *Électron (d'un transistor)* collector
2 *Tech* manifold; *Aut* **c. d'admission** intake manifold; *Électron* **c. d'air** air-trap; **c. de dynamo** collector ring; *Aut* **c. d'échappement** exhaust manifold
3 *Culin* drip cup, juice collector cup
4 *(égout)* main sewer

collectif, -ive [kɔlɛktif, -iv] **ADJ 1** *(en commun)* collective, common; **une démarche collective serait plus efficace** collective representations would be more effective
2 *(de masse)* general, mass *(avant n)*, public; **suicide c.** mass suicide; **licenciements collectifs** mass redundancies; **terreur collective** general panic; **viol c.** gang rape
3 *Transp* group *(avant n)*
4 *Gram* collective
NM 1 *Gram* collective noun **2** *Fin* **c. budgétaire** interim budget, extra credits **3** *(équipe)* collective; **ouvrage rédigé par un c. sous la direction de Jean Dupont** by Jean Dupont et al

collection [kɔlɛksjɔ̃] **NF 1** *(collecte)* collecting; **il fait c. de timbres** he collects stamps
2 *(ensemble de pièces)* collection; **sa c. de timbres** his/her stamp collection; **c. privée** private collection; *Hum* **j'en ai toute une c.** I've got a whole collection *or* set of them
3 *Fam Péj (clique)* **une c. de** a bunch *or* crew of
4 *Com (série ▸ gén)* line, collection; *(▸ de livres)* collection, series; **toute la c.** *(de revues)* the complete set, all the back issues; **dans la c. jeunesse** in the range of books for young readers; **la c. complète des œuvres de Victor Hugo** the collected works of Victor Hugo
5 *(de mode)* collection; **les collections** *(présentations)* fashion shows; **pendant les collections** during the fashion show season

collectionner [3] [kɔlɛksjɔne] **VT** *(tableaux, timbres)* to collect; *Hum* **il collectionne les contraventions** he's been collecting parking tickets

collectionneur, -euse [kɔlɛksjɔnœr, -øz] **NM,F** collector

collective [kɔlɛktiv] *voir* **collectif**

collectivement [kɔlɛktivmɑ̃] **ADV** collectively; **ils se sont élevés c. contre la nouvelle loi** they protested as a group against the new law

collectivisation [kɔlɛktivizasjɔ̃] **NF** collectivization, collectivizing

collectiviser [3] [kɔlɛktivize] **VT** to collectivize

collectivisme [kɔlɛktivism] **NM** collectivism

collectiviste [kɔlɛktivist] **ADJ & NMF** collectivist

collectivité [kɔlɛktivite] **NF 1** *(société)* community; **dans l'intérêt de la c.** in the public interest; **la c. nationale** the nation, the country; **la vie en c.** community life *or* living **2** *Admin* **les collectivités locales** *(dans un État)* the local authorities; *(dans une fédération)* the federal authorities; **c. d'outre-mer** = French overseas collectivity; **c. publique** government organization; **c. territoriale** = administrative division with a higher degree of autonomy than a "département" **3** *(propriété en commun)* common ownership

collector [kɔlɛktœr] **NM** collector's piece

collectrice [kɔlɛktris] *voir* **collecteur**

collège [kɔlɛʒ] **NM 1** *Scol* school *(for pupils aged 11–15)*; **c. privé/technique** private/technical school; *Anciennement* **c. d'enseignement secondaire** = secondary school; *Anciennement* **c. d'enseignement technique** = technical school; **le C. de France** the Collège de France
2 *Rel* private school *(run by a religious organization)*; **le Sacré C.** the College of Cardinals
3 *(corps constitué)* college
4 *Admin* body; **c. électoral** body of electors, constituency

collégial, -e, -aux, -ales [kɔleʒjal, -o] **ADJ** collegial, collegiate; **exercer un pouvoir c.** to rule collegially
• **collégiale NF** *Rel* collegiate church

collégialité [kɔleʒjalite] **NF** collegiality, collegial structure *or* authority

collégien, -enne [kɔleʒjɛ̃, -ɛn] **NM,F** schoolboy, *f* schoolgirl *(aged 11-15)*; **rougir comme un c.** to blush like a schoolboy; **je me suis fait avoir comme un c.** I fell for it like a fool, I should have known better

collègue [kɔlɛg] **NMF 1** *(employé)* colleague, *Am* coworker **2** *(homologue)* opposite number, counterpart **3** *Fam Hum (camarade)* **demande au c. de se pousser** ask our friend here to move over; **salut, c.** how's things?

COLLER [3] [kɔle]

VT	
• to stick **1, 2, 7**	• to glue **1**
• to paste **1**	• to press **4**
• to follow closely **5**	• to put **7**
• to catch out **8**	
VI	
• to stick **1**	• to be sticky **2**
• to cling **3**	• to be OK, to be right **4**

VT 1 *(fixer ▸ étiquette, timbre)* to stick (down); *(▸ tissu, bois)* to glue (on); *(▸ papier peint)* to paste (up); *(▸ affiche)* to post, to stick up, to put up; *Ordinat* to paste; *TV & Cin (bande, film)* to splice; **il est resté collé à la télé toute la soirée** he was glued to the TV all evening
2 *(fermer ▸ enveloppe)* to close up, to stick down; **elle avait les paupières collées** her eyelids were stuck together
3 *(emmêler)* to mat, to plaster; **le poil du chien est tout collé** the dog's coat is all matted; **les cheveux collés par la pluie** his/her hair plastered flat by the rain
4 *(appuyer)* to press; **c. son nez à la vitre** to press one's face to the window; **c. son oreille contre le mur** to press one's ear against the wall; **elle a toujours l'oreille collée aux portes** she's always listening at doors; **c. qn au mur** to put sb against a wall
5 *Fam (suivre)* to follow closely[□], to tag along behind; **il me colle!** he sticks to me like glue!; **ne me colle pas comme ça!** stop following me everywhere!, just let go of me, will you!; **la voiture nous colle de trop près** the car's tailgating us
6 *Fam (punir)* to keep in; *(refuser)* to fail[□], *Am* to flunk; **se faire c.** *(punir)* to get a detention; **se faire c. à un examen** to fail *or Am* flunk an exam
7 *Fam (mettre ▸ chose)* to dump, to stick; *(▸ personne)* to put, to stick; **colle ton sac là** stick *or* dump your bag over there; **ils l'ont collée en pension/en prison** they packed her off to boarding school/threw her in jail; **je vais lui c. mon poing sur la figure!** I'm going to thump him/her on the nose!; **si tu continues, je t'en colle une!** if you don't stop, I'm going to thump you one!; **je vous colle une contravention!** I'm booking you!; **c. une punition/une amende à qn** to give sb a punishment/fine
8 *(poser une question difficile à)* to catch out
9 *(en œnologie)* to fine
10 *Ind* to size
VI 1 *(adhérer ▸ timbre)* to stick (à to); **ces vieilles étiquettes ne collent plus** these old labels don't stick any more; **les pâtes ont collé à la casserole** the pasta has stuck to the pan; *Fam* **c. aux basques** *ou* **aux semelles à qn** to stick to sb like glue; **c.** *Fam* **aux fesses** *ou très Fam* **au cul à qn** to stick to sb like a limpet; **ce rôle lui colle à la peau** he/she was made for that role, that role was tailor-made for him/her; **la peur qui lui collait à la peau** the fear that was ingrained in him/her; **la réputation qui lui colle à la peau** the reputation he/she carries around with him/her, the reputation he/she can't shake off
2 *(être poisseux)* to be sticky; **avoir les doigts qui collent** to have sticky fingers
3 *(vêtement)* to cling; **une robe qui colle au corps** a clingy dress
4 *Fam (aller bien)* **ça colle!** OK!, cool!; **ça ne colle pas** it doesn't work, something's wrong; **il y a quelque chose qui ne colle pas** there's something wrong somewhere; **ça ne colle pas pour demain soir** tomorrow night's off, it's no go for tomorrow night; **ça ne colle pas entre eux** they don't really see eye to eye; **c. avec** to match up to, to fit in with; **ça ne colle pas avec son caractère** it's just not like him; **leurs témoignages ne collent pas** their testimonies don't tally
• **coller à VT IND** *(respecter)* to be faithful to; **c. à son sujet** to stick to one's subject; **vous collez trop à l'original** you're too close to the original text; **c. à la réalité** to be true to life
VPR se coller 1 *(se blottir)* **se c. à qn** to snuggle up *or* to cling to sb, to hug sb; **les chatons se collaient les uns aux autres** the kittens were snuggling up to each other; **se c. à** *ou* **contre un mur pour ne pas être vu** to press oneself up *or* flatten oneself against a wall in order not to be seen
2 *Fam (s'installer)* **les enfants se sont collés devant la télé** the children plonked themselves down in front of the TV
3 *Fam (subir)* **se c. qch** to take sth on; **c'est moi qui me colle les gosses!** I'm the one who has to put up with the kids!; **il s'est collé tout Proust pour l'examen** he got through all of Proust for the exam
4 *(locutions) très Fam* **se c. ensemble** *(vivre ensemble)* to shack up together; *Fam* **s'y c.** *(s'atteler à un problème, une tâche)* to make an effort to do sth[□], to set about doing sth[□]; **je vais m'y c. sérieusement** I'm going to get down to it seriously

collerette [kɔlrɛt] **NF 1** *Couture* collar, collarette; *Hist* frill, ruff
2 *Culin* (paper) frill
3 *(sur une bouteille)* neck-band label
4 *Tech* flange
5 *Bot* annulus

collet [kɔlɛ] **NM 1** *(col)* collar; **mettre la main au c. à qn** to nab *or* to collar sb; **prendre qn au c.** to seize *or* to grab sb by the neck; *Fig* to nab sb in the act; **être c. monté** to be straight-laced
2 *Culin* neck
3 *(cape)* short cape
4 *(d'une dent)* neck
5 *Bot* annulus, ring
6 *Tech* flange
7 *(piège)* noose, snare; **prendre un lapin au c.** to snare a rabbit

colleter [27] [kɔlte] **VT** to seize by the collar; **se faire c.** to be collared *or* nabbed

VPR se colleter 1 *(emploi réciproque)* to fight **2 se c. avec** to struggle *or* to wrestle with

colleur, -euse[1] [kɔlœr, -øz] **NM,F 1 c. d'affiches** billsticker, bill poster **2** *Fam Scol* examiner
• **colleuse NF 1** *Cin & TV* splicer, splicing unit **2** *Typ* pasting machine **3** *Phot* mounting press

colleux, -euse[2] [kɔlø, -øz] **ADJ** *Can* cuddly

collier [kɔlje] **NM 1** *(bijou)* necklace, necklet; **c. de perles** string of pearls; **c. ras du cou** choker
2 *(parure)* collar; **c. de fleurs** garland of flowers
3 *(courroie ▸ pour chien, chat)* collar; **c. antipuces** flea collar; **c. de cheval** horse-collar; *Fig* **donner un coup de c.** to make a special effort; **reprendre le c.** to get back into harness *or Péj* on the treadmill
4 *Tech* clip, collar, ring; **c. de blocage** clamping ring; **c. de fixation** bracket, clip; **c. de serrage** clamp collar
5 *(de plumes, de poils)* collar, frill, ring; **pigeon à c.** ring-necked pigeon; **c. (de barbe)** short *or* clipped beard; **porter le c.** to be bearded, to have a beard
6 *Culin (de bœuf, mouton)* neck

collimateur [kɔlimatœr] **NM** *Astron & Opt* collimator; *(d'une arme à feu)* sight; **avoir qn dans le c.** *ou* **son c.** to have one's eye on sb

colline [kɔlin] **NF** hill; **les collines** *(au pied d'un massif)* the foothills; **au sommet de la c.** up on the hilltop

collision [kɔlizjɔ̃] **NF 1** *(choc)* collision, impact; *Aut* crash; **entrer en c. avec** to collide with; **c. en chaîne** *ou* **série** (multiple) pile-up; **c. frontale** head-on collision, frontal collision; **c. latérale** side-on collision, side impact **2** *(désaccord)* clash; **c. d'intérêts** clash of interests **3** *Géog & Phys* collision

collocation [kɔlɔkasjɔ̃] **NF 1** *Jur* = classification of creditors in order of priority **2** *Ling* collocation

collodion [kɔlɔdjɔ̃] **NM** *Chim* collodion

colloïdal, -e, -aux, -ales [kɔlɔidal, -o] **ADJ** colloidal

colloïde [kɔlɔid] **NM** colloid

colloque [kɔlɔk] **NM 1** *(conférence)* conference, seminar **2** *Hum (conversation)* confab

collusion [kɔlyzjɔ̃] **NF** collusion; **il y a c. entre eux** they're in collusion; **c. d'intérêts** merging of interests

collusoire [kɔlyzwar] **ADJ** collusive

collutoire [kɔlytwar] **NM** antiseptic throat preparation; **c. en aérosol** throat spray

collyre [kɔlir] **NM** *Méd* eyewash, antiseptic eye lotion

colmatage [kɔlmataʒ] **NM 1** *(de brèches, de trous)* filling-up, plugging
2 *Mil* consolidation
3 *Agr* warping
4 *(fait d'obstruer)* clogging, choking

colmater [3] [kɔlmate] **VT 1** *(boucher)* to fill in, to plug, to repair; *aussi Fig* **c. les brèches** to close the gaps **2** *Agr* to warp **3** *Mil* to consolidate

colo [kɔlo] **NF** *Br* (children's) holiday camp, *Am* summer camp□

colocataire [kɔlɔkatɛr] **NMF** *(dans un appartement) Br* flatmate, *Am* roommate; *(dans une maison) Br* housemate, *Am* roommate; *Admin* cotenant

colocation [kɔlɔkasjɔ̃] **NF** joint tenancy

Colomb [kɔlɔ̃] **NPR Christophe C.** Christopher Columbus

colombage [kɔlɔ̃baʒ] **NM** frame wall, studwork; *(pièce)* stud
• **à colombages ADJ** half-timbered

colombe [kɔlɔ̃b] **NF 1** *(oiseau) & Pol* dove **2** *(en appellatif)* **ma c.** my (little) dove

Colombie [kɔlɔ̃bi] **NF la C.** Colombia

Colombie-Britannique [kɔlɔ̃bibritanik] **NF la C.** British Columbia

colombien, -enne [kɔlɔ̃bjɛ̃, -ɛn] **ADJ** Colombian
• **Colombien, -enne NM,F** Colombian

colombier [kɔlɔ̃bje] **NM** dovecot, dovecote, pigeon house

colombin, -e [kɔlɔ̃bɛ̃, -in] **ADJ** reddish-purple
NM 1 *Orn* stock dove **2** *Cér* coil *(of clay)* **3** *très Fam Vieilli (étron)* turd

Colombine [kɔlɔ̃bin] **NPR** Columbine

colombophile [kɔlɔ̃bɔfil] **ADJ** pigeon-fancying
NMF pigeon fancier

colombophilie [kɔlɔ̃bɔfili] **NF** pigeon fancying

colon [kɔlɔ̃] **NM 1** *(pionnier)* colonist, settler
2 *(enfant)* boarder, camper *(at a "colonie de vacances")*
3 *Agr* farmer, smallholder
4 *Fam Arg mil* colonel□; *Fam Hum* **ben mon c.!** goodness me!, *Br* blimey!, *Am* gee (whiz)!

côlon [kolɔ̃] **NM** *Anat* colon; **c. transverse** transverse colon

colonel [kɔlɔnɛl] **NM** *(de l'armée ▸ de terre)* colonel; *(▸ de l'air) Br* ≃ group captain, *Am* ≃ colonel; **oui mon c.** yes Sir

colonelle [kɔlɔnɛl] **NF** *(épouse d'un colonel ▸ de l'armée de terre)* colonel's wife; *(▸ de l'armée de l'air) Br* ≃ group captain's wife, *Am* ≃ colonel's wife

colonial, -e, -aux, -ales [kɔlɔnjal, -o] **ADJ** colonial; **l'empire c.** the (colonial) Empire, the colonies
NM,F *(habitant)* colonial
NM *Mil* soldier of the colonial troops
• **coloniale NF** *Mil* **la coloniale** the colonial troops

colonialisme [kɔlɔnjalism] **NM** colonialism

colonialiste [kɔlɔnjalist] **ADJ** colonialistic
NMF colonialist

colonie [kɔlɔni] **NF 1** *(population)* settlement
2 *Pol (pays)* colony; **vivre aux colonies** to live in the colonies
3 *(fondation)* **c. pénitentiaire** penal colony
4 *(communauté)* community, (little) group; **la c. bretonne de Paris** the Breton community in Paris
5 *Zool* colony group; **une c. de fourmis** a colony of ants
6 c. (de vacances) *Br* (children's) holiday camp, *Am* summer camp; **envoyer ses enfants en c.** to send one's children to camp; **faire une c. de vacances** *(moniteur)* to be a camp leader *or* counsellor

COLONIE DE VACANCES

The "colonie de vacances", or "colo", is an integral part of childhood for many French people. The children's parents do not stay with them at the "colonie", the group being supervised by "moniteurs" or "animateurs" (group leaders), who organize games and activities.

colonisateur, -trice [kɔlɔnizatœr, -tris] **ADJ** colonizing
NM,F colonizer

colonisation [kɔlɔnizasjɔ̃] **NF 1** *(conquête, période)* colonization **2** *Péj (influence)* subjugation, colonization

colonisatrice [kɔlɔnizatris] *voir* **colonisateur**

coloniser [3] [kɔlɔnize] **VT 1** *Pol* to colonize **2** *Fam (envahir)* to take over□, to colonize□; **ne les laissez pas c. nos plages!** don't let them take over our beaches! **3** *Péj (influencer)* to subjugate, to influence

colonnade [kɔlɔnad] **NF** *Archit* colonnade

colonnage [kɔlɔnaʒ] **NM** *Presse & Typ* column space

colonnaire [kɔlɔnɛr] **ADJ** columnar
NM *Bot* columnar plant

colonne [kɔlɔn] **NF 1** *Archit* column, pilaster, pillar; **lit à colonnes** four-poster bed
2 *(monument)* column; *(colonnette)* pillar; **c. Morris** = dark green ornate pillar used to advertise forthcoming attractions in Paris
3 *Constr & (en travaux publics ▸ poteau)* column, post, upright; *(▸ conduite)* riser, pipe; **c. de distribution** standpipe; **c. montante** rising main, riser; **c. sèche** dry riser
4 *Anat* **c. (vertébrale)** backbone, *Spéc* spinal column; **avoir mal à la c.** to have backache
5 *Tech* column; **c. de direction** steering column
6 *(masse cylindrique)* **c. de liquide/mercure** liquid/mercury column
7 *(forme verticale)* column, pillar; **c. d'eau** column of water, waterspout; **c. de feu/fumée** pillar of fire/smoke
8 *(file)* column, line; *Mil* **c. de tête/queue** front/rear column; **c. d'assaut** attacking column; **c. de blindés** column of armoured vehicles; **c. de ravitaillement** supply column; **c. de secours** relief column; **c. de véhicules** vehicle column
9 *(d'un formulaire, d'une table, d'un tableur)* column; **c. créditrice/débitrice** credit/debit column
10 *Journ* column; **colonnes rédactionnelles** editorial columns; **écrire une c.** to write *or* have a column; **dans les colonnes de votre quotidien** in your daily paper; **comme je l'écrivais hier dans ces colonnes** as I wrote yesterday in these pages
• **en colonne ADV en c. par trois/quatre** in threes/fours; **les enfants étaient en c. par deux** the children formed a line two abreast

colonnette [kɔlɔnɛt] **NF** small column, colonnette

colopathie [kɔlɔpati] **NF** colonopathy

colophane [kɔlɔfan] **NF** colophony, rosin

colophon [kɔlɔfɔ̃] **NM** *Typ* colophon

coloquinte [kɔlɔkɛ̃t] **NF 1** *Bot* colocynth **2** *Fam (tête)* head□, nut

colorant, -e [kɔlɔrɑ̃, -ɑ̃t] **ADJ** colouring
NM colorant, dye, pigment; **c. alimentaire** food colouring *(UNCOUNT)*, edible dye; **sans colorants** *(sur emballage)* no artificial colouring

coloration [kɔlɔrasjɔ̃] **NF 1** *(fait de colorer)* colouring
2 *(couleur)* pigmentation, colouring
3 *(chez le coiffeur)* hair tinting *or* colouring; **se faire faire une c.** to have one's hair tinted *or* coloured
4 *(de la voix, d'un instrument)* colour; **la tristesse donnait une c. inhabituelle à sa voix** his/her voice had changed, there was a note of sadness in it
5 *(tendance)* **c. politique** political colour *or* tendency
6 *Biol* **c. de Gram** Gram staining

colorature [kɔlɔratyr] **NF** coloratura

coloré, -e [kɔlɔre] **ADJ 1** *(teinté)* coloured; *(vif)* brightly coloured; *(bariolé)* multicoloured; **une eau colorée** *(à la teinture)* water with dye in it; *(avec du vin)* water with just a drop of wine in it **2** *(expressif)* colourful, vivid, picturesque

colorer [3] [kɔlɔre] **VT 1** *(teinter ▸ dessin, objet)* to colour; *(▸ ciel, visage)* to tinge, to colour; **c. qch en rouge** to colour sth red
2 *(teindre ▸ tissu)* to dye; *(▸ bois)* to stain, to colour
3 *(oignons, viande)* to brown lightly
4 *(rendre plus pittoresque ▸ récit)* to lend colour to
VPR se colorer 1 *(visage)* to blush, to redden; **les pêches commencent à se c.** the peaches are beginning to ripen **2** *Fig* **se c. de** to be tinged with; **sa colère se colorait d'attendrissement** his/her anger was tinged with pity

coloriage [kɔlɔrjaʒ] **NM 1** *(technique)* colouring; **faire du c.** to colour (a drawing) **2** *(dessin)* coloured drawing

colorier [10] [kɔlɔrje] **VT** to colour in; **colorie le crocodile en vert** colour in the crocodile (in *or* with) green

coloris [kɔlɔri] **NM** *(couleur)* colour; *(nuance)* shade; **nous avons cette jupe dans d'autres c.** we have the same skirt in other colours

colorisation [kɔlɔrizasjɔ̃] **NF** colourization

coloriser [3] [kɔlɔrize] **VT** to colourize

coloriste [kɔlɔrist] **NMF 1** *Beaux-Arts* colourist **2** *Typ* colourer, colourist **3** *(coiffeur)* colourist

colossal, -e, -aux, -ales [kɔlɔsal, -o] **ADJ** huge, colossal

colossalement [kɔlɔsalmɑ̃] **ADV** hugely, colossally

colosse [kɔlɔs] **NM 1** *(statue)* colossus; **le c. de Rhodes** the Colossus of Rhodes; **un c. aux pieds d'argile** an idol with feet of clay **2** *(homme, institution)* giant

colostomie [kɔlɔstɔmi] **NF** *Méd* colostomy; **subir une c.** to have a colostomy

colostrum [kɔlɔstrɔm] **NM** colostrum

colportage [kɔlpɔrtaʒ] **NM 1** *(vente)* hawking, peddling **2** *(de nouvelles, de ragots)* spreading

colporter [3] [kɔlpɔrte] **VT 1** *(vendre)* to hawk, to peddle **2** *(nouvelles, ragots)* to spread

colporteur, -euse [kɔlpɔrtœr, -øz] **NM,F** hawker, pedlar; **c. de mauvaises nouvelles** bringer of bad tidings; **c. de ragots** scandalmonger

colposcopie [kɔlpɔskɔpi] **NF** *Méd* colposcopy

colt [kɔlt] **NM** gun *(revolver)*

coltinage [kɔltinaʒ] **NM** *(d'une charge sur le dos)* porterage, carrying

coltiner [3] [kɔltine] **VT** to carry

VPR se coltiner *Fam* **1** *(porter)* **se c. une valise** to lug a suitcase around **2** *(supporter ▸ corvée)* to take on, to put up with; *(▸ personne indésirable)* to put up with; **celui-là, faut se le c.!** you need the patience of a saint to put up with him!

coltineur [kɔltinœr] **NM** porter *(who carries heavy loads)*; **c. de charbon** coal heaver

columbarium [kɔlɔ̃barjɔm] **NM** columbarium

colvert [kɔlvɛr] **NM** *Orn* mallard

colza [kɔlza] **NM** *Bot* colza, rape

COM [kɔm] **NF** *(abrév* **collectivité d'outre-mer)** = French overseas collectivity

> **COM**
>
> There are four COMs or "collectivités d'outre-mer": French Polynesia, Mayotte (in the Indian Ocean), St Pierre and Miquelon (off Newfoundland) and Wallis and Futuna Islands (in the Pacific Ocean).

coma [kɔma] **NM** *Méd* **le c.** a coma; **être/tomber dans le c.** to be in/to go *or* to fall into a coma; **être dans un c. dépassé** to be brain dead

comarketing [komarkɛtiŋ] **NM** comarketing

comater [3] [kɔmate] **VI** *Fam* to veg (out); **j'ai passé la journée à c. devant la télé** I spent the day vegging (out) in front of theTV

comateux, -euse [kɔmatø, -øz] **ADJ** comatose

NM,F patient in a coma

combat [kɔ̃ba] *voir* **combattre**

NM 1 *Mil* battle, fight; **c. aérien** air battle; **c. naval** sea battle; *Belg (jeu)* battleships; *aussi Fig* **c. d'arrière-garde** rearguard action; **des combats de rue** street fighting; **quelques combats isolés dans les montagnes** some isolated skirmishes in the mountains; **les tanks ne sont jamais allés au c.** the tanks never went into battle; **il n'est jamais allé au c.** he never saw action

2 *(lutte physique)* fight; **c. corps à corps** hand-to-hand combat; **c. rapproché** close combat; **c. singulier** single combat; *Fig* **en c. singulier** on a one-to-one basis

3 *Sport* contest, fight; **c. de boxe** boxing match; **c. de coqs** cockfight

4 *(lutte morale, politique)* struggle, fight; **continuons le c.!** the struggle goes on!; **même c.!** we're fighting for the same thing!; **mener le bon c.** to fight for a just cause; **le c. contre la pauvreté** the fight against poverty

• **de combat ADJ 1** *Mil (zone)* combat *(avant n)*; *(réserves)* battle *(avant n)*, war *(avant n)*; **avion de c.** warplane, fighter plane; **navire de c.** battleship; **tenue de c.** battledress **2** *(de choc)* militant

combatif, -ive [kɔ̃batif, -iv] **ADJ** *(animal)* aggressive; *(personne)* combative, aggressive, *Littéraire* pugnacious; **être d'humeur combative** to be full of fight

combativité [kɔ̃bativite] **NF** combativeness, aggressiveness, *Littéraire* pugnacity

combattant, -e [kɔ̃batɑ̃, -ɑ̃t] **ADJ** fighting; **unité combattante** combatant *or* fighting unit

NM,F 1 *Mil* combatant, fighter, soldier **2** *(adversaire)* fighter **3** *Orn* ruff

combattre [83] [kɔ̃batr] **VT 1** *Mil* to fight (against); **c. l'ennemi** to fight the enemy, *Sout* to give battle to the enemy **2** *(s'opposer à ▸ inflation, racisme)* to combat, to fight, to struggle against; *(▸ politique)* to oppose, to fight; **il est difficile de c. son instinct** it's difficult to go against one's instincts; **il a longtemps combattu la maladie** he fought *or* struggled against the disease for a long time **3** *(agir contre ▸ incendie)* to fight; *(▸ effets)* to combat; **une crème qui combat l'acné** a cream for acne

VI 1 *Mil* to fight **2** *(en politique, pour une cause)* to fight, to struggle

combe [kɔ̃b] **NF** combe, valley

COMBIEN [kɔ̃bjɛ̃] **ADV 1** *(pour interroger sur une somme)* how much; **c'est c.?, ça fait c.?** how much is it?; **c. coûte ce livre?** how much is this book?, how much does this book cost?; **c. je vous dois?** how much do I owe you?; **c. te faut-il?** how much (money) do you need?; **je ne sais même pas c. il gagne** I don't even know how much he earns; **à c. se montent vos frais?** how much are your expenses?; **à c. cela vous est-il revenu?** how much did you pay for that?; **l'indice a augmenté de c.?** how much has the rate gone up by?; **de c. est le déficit?** how large is the deficit?

2 *(pour interroger sur le nombre)* how many; **c. serons-nous ce soir?** how many of us will there be this evening?; **c. sont-ils?** how many of them are there?; **c. se souviendront de lui?** how many will remember him?; **je me demande c. ils sont** I wonder how many of them there are

3 *(pour interroger sur la distance, la durée, la mesure etc)* **c. tu pèses?** how much do you weigh?; **c. tu mesures?** how tall are you?; **c. y a-t-il de Londres à Paris?** how far is it from London to Paris?; **c. dure le film?** how long is the movie?, how long does the movie last?; **il est arrivé c.?** where did he come?; *Fam* **c. ça lui fait maintenant?** how old is he/she now?ᵃ; **de c. votre frère est-il votre aîné?** how much older than you is your brother?; **elle est enceinte – de c.?** she's pregnant – how far gone is she?, how many months?

4 *(en emploi exclamatif)* how; **vous ne pouvez pas savoir c. il est distrait!** you wouldn't believe how absent-minded he is!; **j'ai pu constater c. tu avais changé** I could see how much you'd changed; **c. je regrette de ne pas vous voir plus souvent!** how I regret not seeing you more often!; **tu ne peux pas savoir c. je suis heureuse!** you can't imagine how happy I am!; **ces mesures étaient sévères mais c. efficaces** these measures were drastic but extremely effective; *Littéraire* **c. rares sont les gens sans ambition!** how few are those without ambition!; *Littéraire ou Hum* **elle a souffert, ô c.!** she suffered, oh how she suffered!

NM INV le c. sommes-nous? what's today's date?; **le bus passe tous les c.?** how often does the bus come?; **tu chausses du c.?** what's your shoe size, what shoe size do you take?

• **combien de DÉT 1** *(pour interroger ▸ suivi d'un nom indénombrable)* how much; *(▸ suivi d'un nom dénombrable)* how many; **c. d'argent avez-vous sur vous?** how much money have you got on *or* with you?; **c. de paquets reste-t-il?** how many packets are left?; **c. de fois par semaine vas-tu au cinéma?** how many times a week do you go to the movies?; **c. de fois faut-il que je te le répète?** how often *or* how many times do I have to tell you?; **tu en as pour c. de temps?** how long will it take you?, how long will you be?; **depuis c. de temps habitent-ils ici?** how long have they been living here for?; **c. de jours resterez-vous?** how many days *or* how long will you be staying?; **c. y a-t-il de pays en Europe?** how many countries are there in Europe? **2** *(emploi exclamatif)* **c. d'ennuis il aurait pu s'éviter!** he could have saved himself so much trouble!; **c. de gens furent tués pendant cette guerre!** what a lot of people were killed in that war!

combientième [kɔ̃bjɛ̃tjɛm] **ADJ INTERROGATIF c'est la c. fois que tu viens?** how often have you been now?; **c'est la c. fois que je te le dis?** how many times have I told you?; **tu es c. dans la liste?** where are you on the list?, what position are you in the list?

NMF 1 *(personne)* **c'est la c. qui demande à être remboursée depuis ce matin?** how many does that make wanting their money back since this morning?; **elle est arrivée la c.?** where did she come in?; **tu es le c. en math?** how high are you *or* where do you come in maths? **2** *(objet)* **prends le troisième – le c.?** have the third one – which one did you say?

combinaison [kɔ̃binezɔ̃] **NF 1** *Chim (action)* combining; *(résultat)* combination; *(composé)* compound

2 *(d'un cadenas, d'un coffre-fort)* combination; **la c. gagnante** *(au tiercé)* the winning combination (of numbers)

3 *Ordinat* **c. de code** password; **c. de touches** key combination

4 *Math* combination

5 *Pol* **c. ministérielle** composition of a cabinet

6 *(sous-vêtement)* slip; **c. de plongée** wetsuit; **c. de ski** ski suit; **c. spatiale** space suit; **c. de travail** *Br* overalls, *Am* coveralls; **c. de vol** flying suit

7 *(assemblage)* combination; **une heureuse c. de couleurs** a pleasing combination of colours *or* colour scheme

combinard, -e [kɔ̃binar, -ard] *Fam Péj* **ADJ** scheming; **il est vraiment c.** he's a real schemer

NM,F schemer

combinateur [kɔ̃binatœr] **NM 1** *Aut* selector switch **2** *Rail* controller

combinatoire [kɔ̃binatwar] **ADJ 1** *(capable d'agencer)* combinative **2** *Ling* combinatory **3** *Math* combinatorial

NF 1 *Ling* combinatorial rules **2** *Math* combinatorial mathematics *(singulier)*

combine [kɔ̃bin] **NF** *Fam (astuce, truc)* scheme, trick; **il a toujours des combines, lui!** he always knows some trick or other; **j'ai une c. pour entrer sans payer** I know a way of getting in for freeᵃ; **il a trouvé la c. pour voyager gratuitement** he's found a way of travelling for freeᵃ; **c'est simple, il suffit de connaître la c.** it's easy when you know howᵃ; **être dans la c.** to be in on it

combiné, -e [kɔ̃bine] **ADJ** joint, combined

NM 1 *(sous-vêtement)* corselet, corselette

2 *Tél* receiver, handset

3 *Chim* compound

4 *Sport* athletics event; *Ski* combined competition

combiner [3] [kɔ̃bine] **VT 1** *(harmoniser ▸ styles)* to combine, to match; *(▸ couleurs)* to match, to harmonize, to mix; *(▸ sons)* to harmonize, to mix; **c. son travail et ses loisirs** to combine business with pleasure

2 *(comprendre)* to combine; **un sentiment qui combine la crainte et le désir** a feeling of both fear and desire

3 *(planifier)* to plan, to work out; **bien combiné** well planned

4 *Fam Péj (manigancer)* to think upᵃ; **elle combine un sale coup** she's plotting something nasty, she's planning a dirty trick

5 *Chim* to combine

VPR se combiner 1 *(exister ensemble ▸ éléments)* to be combined

2 *(s'harmoniser ▸ couleurs)* to match, to harmonize, to mix; *(▸ sons)* to harmonize, to mix

3 *Chim* **se c. avec** to combine with

4 *Fam (se passer)* **ça se combine** *ou* **les choses se combinent bien** it's *or* things are working out very well; **ça s'est mal combiné** it didn't work out

combi-short [kɔ̃biʃɔrt] *(pl* **combi-shorts)** **NM** playsuit

comble [kɔ̃bl] **ADJ** packed, crammed

NM 1 *(summum)* **le c. de** the height *or* epitome of; **le c. du chic** the ultimate in chic; **le c. du snobisme est de…** the last word in snobbery is to…; **du champagne et, c. du luxe, du caviar** champagne and, luxury of luxuries, caviare; **c'est un** *ou* **le c.!** that beats everything!, that takes *Br* the biscuit *or Am* the cake!; **le c., c'est que…** to crown *or* to cap it all…; **le c., c'est qu'il est parti sans payer** and to crown it all *or* to add insult to injury, he left without paying **2** *(charpente ▸ en bois)* roof timbers *or* gable; *(▸ en métal)* roof structure; **c. brisé** curb roof; **faux c.** mansard roof deck; **elle loge sous les combles** she lives in the attic; **combles aménageables** attic suitable for conversion

• **à son comble ADV** at its height

• **au comble de PRÉP** at the height of, in a paroxysm of; **au c. du bonheur** deliriously happy; **au c. de la douleur** prostrate with *or* in a paroxysm of grief

• **pour comble de PRÉP et pour c. de malchance, la voiture est tombée en panne** and then, to cap it all, the car broke down; **pour c. d'hypocrisie, ils envoient leur fille chez les sœurs** then, to compound the hypocrisy, they send their daughter to a convent

comblé, -e [kɔ̃ble] **ADJ** *(personne)* happy, contented, satisfied; **il est c.** he has everything he could wish for

combler [3] [kɔ̃ble] VT **1** *(boucher ▸ cavité, creux)* to fill in

2 *(supprimer ▸ lacune, vide)* to fill; *(▸ silence)* to break; *(▸ perte, déficit)* to make up for; *(▸ découvert bancaire)* to pay off; **c. son retard** to make up for lost time

3 *(satisfaire ▸ personne)* to satisfy; *(▸ désir, vœu, besoin)* to satisfy, to fulfil; **vous me comblez!** you are too kind, I'm overwhelmed!

4 *Fig (couvrir, emplir)* **c. un enfant de cadeaux** to shower a child with gifts; **c. qn de joie** to fill sb with joy

comburant, -e [kɔ̃byrɑ̃, -ɑ̃t] ADJ comburent

NM oxidizer, oxidant

combustibilité [kɔ̃bystibilite] NF combustibility

combustible [kɔ̃bystibl] ADJ combustible

NM fuel; **c. fossile/liquide** fossil/liquid fuel; **c. nucléaire** nuclear fuel

combustion [kɔ̃bystjɔ̃] NF combustion; **à c. externe/interne** external-/internal-combustion *(avant n)*; **à c. lente/rapide** slow-/fast-combustion *(avant n)*; **mettre qch en c.** to set sth on fire

Côme [kom] NM Como; **le lac de C.** Lake Como

come-back [kɔmbak] NM INV comeback

comédie [kɔmedi] NF **1** *(art dramatique)* theatre; **jouer la c.** to act, to be an actor

2 *(pièce comique, genre)* comedy; **c. de caractères** character comedy; **c. dramatique** comedy drama; **c. de mœurs** comedy of manners; **c. musicale** musical; **c. de situation** situation comedy

3 *Péj (hypocrisie)* act; **cette réception, quelle c.!** what a farce that party was!; **jouer la c.** to put on an act; **il n'est pas vraiment malade, c'est de la c.** he's only play-acting *or* it's only an act, he's not really ill

4 *Fam (caprice, colère)* **faire une c.** to throw a tantrum, to make a fuss; **il m'a fait toute une c. pour que je lui achète le jouet** he kicked up a huge fuss to get me to buy the toy

5 *Fam (histoire)* **c'est toute une c. pour lui faire avaler sa soupe** you have to go through a whole rigmarole to get him/her to eat his/her soup; **pour avoir un rendez-vous, quelle c.!** what a palaver to get an appointment!

6 *Arch (pièce de théâtre)* play

• **de comédie** ADJ comic, comedy *(avant n)*; **personnage de c.** comedy character; *Fig* clown, buffoon

Comédie-Française [kɔmedifrɑ̃sɛz] NF **la C.** = French national theatre company

> **LA COMÉDIE-FRANÇAISE**
>
> This state-subsidized company dates back to the seventeenth century; the theatre itself, officially called "le Théâtre-Français" or "le Français", is situated in the rue Richelieu in Paris. Its repertoire consists mainly of classical works, although modern plays are sometimes staged. Actors who perform in the Comédie-Française fall into two categories: the "**sociétaires**" who are fully-fledged members of the company, and the "**pensionnaires**" who work with the company on a fixed salary but are not shareholders in it.

comédien, -enne [kɔmedjɛ̃, -ɛn] ADJ **1** *(acteur)* **être plus c. que tragédien** to be more of a comic than a tragic actor **2** *(qui exagère)* melodramatic

NM,F **1** *(acteur ▸ gén)* actor, *f* actress; *(▸ comique)* comic actor, *f* actress, comedian, *f* comedienne; **comédiens ambulants** strolling players **2** *(personne qui exagère)* **c'est une comédienne** she's a drama queen; **quel c.!** he can really overdo it!

> Il faut noter que le nom anglais **comedian** est un faux ami. Il signifie **comique**.

comédogène [kɔmedɔʒɛn] ADJ *Méd* comedogenic

comédon [kɔmedɔ̃] NM *Méd* blackhead, *Spéc* comedo

comestible [kɔmestibl] ADJ edible; **denrées comestibles** food, foodstuffs; **non c.** inedible

• **comestibles** NMPL food, foodstuffs

comète [kɔmɛt] NF **1** *Astron* comet **2** *(tranchefile)* headband

comice[1] [kɔmis] NF *(poire)* comice pear

comice[2] [kɔmis] NM **c. agricole** agricultural association

NM **1** *Antiq* comitia; *Hist (pendant la Révolution)* electoral meeting **2** *(foire)* **comices agricoles** agricultural fair

comics [kɔmiks] NMPL comic strips, cartoon strips, *esp Am Fam* funnies

coming out [kɔmiŋaut] NM *(d'un homosexuel)* coming out

comique [kɔmik] ADJ **1** *Littérature & Théât* comic, comedy *(avant n)*; *(acteur, auteur, rôle)* comic; **le genre c.** comedy **2** *(amusant)* comical, funny

NMF **1** *(artiste)* comic, comedian, *f* comedienne; **c'est un grand c.** he's a great comic actor **2** *(boute-en-train)* comic, comedian **3** *(auteur)* comic author, writer of comedies *or* comedy

NM **1** *(genre)* comedy; **le c. de caractères/situation** character/situation comedy; **le c. de répétition** comedy based on repetition; **le c. troupier** barrack-room comedy **2** *(ce qui fait rire)* **le c. de l'histoire, c'est que...** the funny part of it is that...

> Attention: ne pas confondre **comic** et **comical** lorsqu'on traduit l'adjectif **comique**. Le terme **comic** se rapporte au genre comique, alors que **comical** signifie **amusant**. En outre, l'adjectif **comic** ne s'utilise jamais comme attribut.

comiquement [kɔmikmɑ̃] ADV comically, funnily

comité [kɔmite] NM committee, board; **faire partie d'un c.** to sit on a committee; **c. d'action** action committee; **c. de conciliation** arbitration committee; **c. consultatif** advisory board; **c. de défense** defence committee; **c. directeur** steering committee; **c. d'enquête** board of enquiry; **c. d'entreprise** works council; **C. européen de normalisation** European Standards Commission; *Pol* **c. exécutif** executive committee *or* board; **c. de gestion** management board, managerial board; **c. d'hygiène et de sécurité** health and safety committee; **le C. international olympique** the International Olympic Committee; *Littérature & Théât* **c. de lecture** reading panel *or* committee; *Pol* **c. de quartier** local committee; **le C. de salut public** the Committee of Public Safety

• **en comité secret** ADV secretly

• **en petit comité, en comité restreint** ADV as a select group; **on a dîné en petit c.** the dinner was just for a select group; **pour leur anniversaire ils seront en petit c.** they'll celebrate their anniversary with just a few friends (and relations)

> **COMITÉ D'ENTREPRISE**
>
> The "CE" looks after the general welfare of company employees and organizes subsidized leisure activities, outings, holidays etc. It also deals with industrial problems.

commandant [kɔmɑ̃dɑ̃] NM **1** *Mil (de l'armée de terre)* ≃ major; **c. d'armes** garrison commander; **c. en chef** commander-in-chief

2 *Mil (de l'armée de l'air) Br* ≃ squadron leader, *Am* ≃ major

3 *Mil (de la marine)* ≃ commanding officer

4 *(de la marine marchande)* captain

5 *Aviat* **c. (de bord)** captain; **c. en second** second in command

6 *(de camp, base)* commandant

commande [kɔmɑ̃d] NF **1** *Com* order; *(marchandises)* order, goods ordered; **faire** *ou* **passer une c. (à qn/de qch)** to put in *or* to place an order (with sb/for sth); **passer c. de 10 véhicules** to order 10 vehicles; **exécuter/livrer une c.** to fill/deliver an order; **le garçon a pris la c.** the waiter took the order; **conformément à votre c.** as per (your) order; **c. d'essai** trial order; **c. export** export order; **c. ferme** firm order; **c. par ordinateur** teleorder; **c. par quantité** bulk order; **c. renouvelée** repeat order; **c. téléphonique, c. par téléphone** telephone order **2** *Tech (action)* control, operation; *(dispositif)* control mechanism; **la c. des essuie-glaces** the wiper mechanism; **une machine à c. électrique** an electrically-operated machine; **c. d'allumage** ignition control; **c. à distance** remote control; *Aut* **c. électronique du moteur** engine management system; **c. manuelle** hand *or* manual control; **à c. manuelle** manually controlled; **c. tactile** one-touch operation; *Aut* **c. de vitesse de croisière** cruise control **3** *Ordinat* command; **c. d'annulation** undo command; **c. à bascule** toggle switch; **c. binaire** bit command; **c. de copie** copy command; **c. du DOS** DOS command; **c. d'effacement** delete command; **c. erronée** *(message d'erreur)* bad command; **c. d'insertion** insert command; **c. numérique** digital control; **à c. numérique** digitally controlled *or* operated; **c. de recherche** search *or* find command; **c. système d'exploitation** operating system command; **à c. vocale** voice-activated

• **commandes** NFPL *(dispositif de guidage)* controls; **être aux commandes** to be at the controls; *Fig* to be in charge; **prendre les** *ou* **se mettre aux commandes** to take over at the controls; *Fig* to take charge

• **à la commande** ADV **payer à la c.** to pay while ordering; **payable à la c.** payment with order; **travailler à la c.** to work to order

• **de commande** ADJ **1** *Tech* control *(avant n)* **2** *Péj (factice ▸ enthousiasme, humour)* forced, unnatural

• **sur commande** ADV *Com & Fig* to order; **fait sur c.** made to order

commandement [kɔmɑ̃dmɑ̃] NM **1** *(ordre)* command, order; **donner un c.** to give an order; **obéir aux commandements de qn** to obey sb's orders; **à mon c., prêts, partez!** on my command, ready, go!

2 *(fait de diriger)* command; **prendre le c. d'une section** to take over command of a platoon; **avoir le c. de** *(armée, pays)* to be in command of, to lead

3 *(état-major)* command; **c. en chef** command-in-chief; **le haut c.** the High Command

4 *Jur* court order to pay

5 *Bible* commandment; **les Dix Commandements** the Ten Commandments

commander [3] [kɔmɑ̃de] VT **1** *(diriger ▸ armée, expédition, soldats, équipe)* to command; *(▸ navire)* to be in command of; **il commande hommes** he has men under his command; **sans vous c., est-ce que vous pourriez fermer la fenêtre?** I wonder if you'd mind closing the window; **c'est moi qui commande ici!** I'm the one who gives the orders around here!

2 *(ordonner)* **c. la retraite aux troupes** to order the troops back *or* to retreat; **c. à qn de faire** *ou* **qu'il fasse qch** to order sb to do sth

3 *Tech* to control; **l'ouverture des portes est commandée par une manette** the doors open by means of a lever

4 *Com (tableau, ouvrage)* to commission; *(objet manufacturé, repas)* to order; **c. qch chez qn/sur catalogue** to order sth from sb/from a catalogue; **c. qch par téléphone** to order sth by telephone; **c. qch en ligne** to order sth online; **on m'a commandé une affiche pour le festival** I was commissioned to do a poster for the festival; **vous avez commandé?** has somebody taken your order?

5 *(requérir)* to demand; **la prudence commande le silence absolu** prudence demands total discretion, total discretion is required for the sake of prudence

6 *(susciter)* to command; **c. le respect/l'attention** to command respect/attention

7 *Littéraire (maîtriser)* to control; **il ne commande plus ses nerfs** he is no longer in control of his emotions

8 *(dominer ▸ vallée, plaine)* to dominate, to command

9 *Ordinat* to drive; **commandé par menu** menu-driven; **commandé à la voix** voice-activated

• **commander à** VT IND **1** *(donner des ordres à ▸ armée)* to command **2** *Littéraire (maîtriser ▸ sentiments, désirs)* to control, to be in control *or* command of

VPR **se commander 1** *Fam (être imposé)* **je n'aime pas ces gens, ça ne se commande pas** I don't like those people, I can't help it; **l'amour ne se commande pas** you can't make love happen **2** *(être relié ▸ pièces d'un logement)* to be connected *or* interconnected, to connect, to interconnect

commanderie [kɔmɑ̃dri] NF commandery

commandeur [kɔmɑ̃dœr] **NM** commander

commanditaire [kɔmɑ̃ditɛr] **NM 1** *(d'une entreprise commerciale) Br* sleeping *or Am* silent partner; *(d'un tournoi, d'un spectacle)* backer, sponsor **2** *(d'un crime)* **nous ne savons pas qui sont les commanditaires de l'attentat** we don't know who is behind the attack **3** *(comme adj)* **associé c.** *Br* sleeping *or Am* silent partner

commandite [kɔmɑ̃dit] **NF 1** *Com (fonds)* capital invested by *Br* sleeping *or Am* silent partner(s) **2 (société en) c. simple** limited partnership, mixed liability company; **(société en) c. par actions** partnership limited by shares

commandité, -e [kɔmɑ̃dite] *Com* **ADJ** *(entreprise commerciale)* financed *(as a limited partner)*; *(tournoi, spectacle)* sponsored
NM,F (associé) c. active partner

commanditer [3] [kɔmɑ̃dite] **VT 1** *Com (entreprise commerciale)* to finance *(as a limited partner)*; *(tournoi, spectacle)* to sponsor **2** *(meurtre, attentat)* to be behind

commando [kɔmɑ̃do] **NM** commando

COMME [kɔm]

> **CONJ**
> • as **1, 2, 4, 7, 8** • like **1, 3**
> • since **7** • when **8**
> **ADV**
> • how

CONJ 1 *(introduisant une comparaison)* as, like; **c'est un jour c. les autres** it's a day like any other; **ce n'est pas un homme c. les autres** he's not like other men; **une maison pas c. les autres** a very unusual house; **ce fut c. une révélation** it was like a revelation; **il fait beau c. en plein été** it's like a beautiful summer's day; **nous nagerons c. quand nous étions en Sicile** we'll swim like when we were in Sicily; **c'est c. ta sœur, elle ne téléphone jamais** your sister's the same, she never phones; **je suis c. toi, j'ai horreur de ça** I'm like you, I hate that kind of thing; **fais c. moi, ne lui réponds pas** do as I do, don't answer him/her; **blanc c. neige** white as snow; **il parle c. un livre** he talks like a book; **je l'ai vu c. je vous vois** I saw it as sure as I'm standing here; **il sera dentiste, tout c. sa mère** he'll be a dentist, just like his mother; **elle a eu c. une hésitation avant de répondre** she seemed to hesitate before answering; **j'ai c. l'impression qu'on s'est perdus!** I've got a feeling we're lost!; *Fam* **il y a c. un défaut!** something seems to be wrong!; **c'est tout c.** as good as; **il ne m'a pas injurié, mais c'était tout c.** he didn't actually insult me, but it was close *or* as good as; **elle n'a pas encore le rôle, mais c'est tout c.** she hasn't got the part yet, but it's as good as *or* as near as makes no difference

2 *(exprimant la manière)* as; **fais c. il te plaira** do as you like *or* please; **fais c. je t'ai appris** do it the way I taught you; **tout s'est passé c. je l'ai dit** everything happened as I said (it would); **si, c. je le crois, il n'est pas trop tard** if, as I believe, it's not too late; **c. on pouvait s'y attendre, nos actions ont baissé** as could be expected, our shares have gone down; **c. je l'ai fait remarquer…** as I pointed out…; **ça s'écrit c. ça se prononce** it's written as it's pronounced; **la connaissant c. je la connais** knowing her as well as *or* like I do; **si, c. le dit Aristote…** if, as Aristotle says…; **je passerai vous prendre à 9 heures c. convenu** I'll pick you up at 9 as (we) agreed *or* planned; *Fam* **c. dirait l'autre, c. dit l'autre** as the saying goes, to coin a phrase, as they say; **c. on dit** as they say; **c. il se doit** as is fitting, in a fitting manner; **on le recevra c. il se doit** we'll receive him in a fitting manner; **c. il se doit en pareilles circonstances** as befits the circumstances, as is fitting in such circumstances; *Fam* **c. qui dirait** so to speak; **c'était c. qui dirait un gémissement** it was a sort of moan; **c. bon vous semble** as you think best; **fais c. bon te semble** do whatever you wish *or* like; *Fam* **c. ci c. ça** so-so

3 *(tel que)* like, such as; **une femme c. elle mérite mieux** a woman like her deserves better; **une grande fille c. toi ne pleure pas** a big girl like you doesn't cry; **des montres c. on n'en fait plus maintenant** the kind of watches they don't make anymore; **bête c. il est, il serait capable de lui dire** he's so stupid, he'd probably tell him/her; **les grands mammifères, c. l'éléphant…** large mammals, such as *or* like elephants…

4 *(en tant que)* as; **il vaut mieux l'avoir c. ami que c. ennemi** I'd sooner have him as a friend than as an enemy; **je l'ai eu c. élève** he was one of my students; **je l'ai eue c. professeur** I had her as my *or* a teacher; **elle a réussi c. actrice** she's a success as an actress; **qu'est-ce que vous avez c. vin?** what (kind of) wine do you have?; **qu'y a-t-il c. dessert?** what's for dessert?; **c'est plutôt faible c. excuse!** it's a pretty feeble excuse!; *Fam* **c'est pas mal c. clip** it's not a bad video; *Fam* **c. gaffeur, tu te poses là!** you really know how to put your foot in it!; **c'est tout ce que j'ai eu c. remerciements** that's all the thanks I got

5 *(pour ainsi dire)* **il restait sur le seuil, c. paralysé** he was standing on the doorstep, (as if he was) rooted to the spot; **ta robe est c. neuve!** your dress is as good as new!; **le village était c. mort** the village was dead; **il était c. fou** he was like a madman

6 *(et)* **l'un c. l'autre aiment beaucoup voyager** they both love travelling; **lui c. moi adorons les longues promenades** we both love long walks; **le règlement s'applique à tous, à vous c. aux autres** the rules apply to everybody, you included; **un spectacle que les parents, c. les enfants, apprécieront** a show which will delight parents and children alike; **elle sort tous les jours, été c. hiver** she goes out every day, summer and winter alike; **à la ville c. à la scène** in real life as well as on stage

7 *(indiquant la cause)* since, as; **c. j'ai bon cœur, je le lui ai donné** since *or* as I'm generous, I gave it to him/her; **c. il était en retard, on a raté le film** because he was late, we missed the film

8 *(au moment où)* as, when; *(pendant que)* while; **le pot de fleurs est tombé juste c. je passais** the flowerpot fell just as *or* when I was walking past; **c. le rôti cuisait, je préparais les légumes** while the joint was cooking, I prepared the vegetables

ADV 1 *(emploi exclamatif)* how; **c. c'est triste!** how sad (it is)!, it's so sad!; **c. tu es grande!** what a big girl you are now!, how tall you've grown!; **c. je regrette de l'avoir fait!** I'm so sorry I did it!, how I regret having done it!; **c. tu as de beaux cheveux!** what beautiful hair you have!; **c. je te comprends!** I know exactly how you feel!

2 *(indiquant la manière)* **tu sais c. il est** you know what he's like *or* how he is; **tu as vu c. elle m'a traité!** you saw how *or* the way she treated me!

• **comme ça ADJ 1** *(ainsi)* like that; **je suis c. ça** I'm like that; **il est c. ça, on ne le changera pas!** that's the way he is, you won't change him!; **c'est c. ça et pas autrement** that's the way it is and that's all there is to it; **je ne te dirai jamais plus rien, puisque** *ou* **si c'est c. ça** I'll never tell you anything ever again, if that's the way *or* how it is; **j'ai fait pousser une citrouille c. ça!** I grew a pumpkin THAT big!; **une petite femme haute c. ça** a little woman no taller than that *or* only so high **2** *(admirable)* great; **c'est une fille c. ça!** she's a great girl!; **il a un vin blanc c. ça!** he's got a fantastic white wine! **ADV 1** *(de cette manière)* like this *or* that; **je ne peux pas sortir c. ça** I can't go out (dressed) like this *or* that; **qu'as-tu à me regarder c. ça?** why are you looking at me like that?; *Fam* **il m'a répondu c. ça qu'il était majeur** I'm old enough, he says to me; **ne crie pas c. ça!** don't shout like that! **2** *(en intensif)* **alors c. ça, tu te maries?** (oh) so you're getting married?; **où vas-tu c. ça?** where are you off to? **3** *(de telle manière que)* that way, so that; **je te laisse la clef, c. ça tu pourras entrer** I'll leave you the key, so that you can let yourself in

• **comme il faut ADJ** respectable, proper; **une jeune fille c. il faut** a very well-bred girl; **des gens très c. il faut** very respectable people **ADV 1** *(correctement)* properly; **fais ton travail c. il faut** do your work properly; **tu ne t'y prends pas c. il faut** you're doing it the wrong way, you're not doing it properly; **elle est un peu maigre – et pourtant elle mange c. il faut!** she's a bit skinny – she eats well though *or* and yet she eats properly! **2** *Fam (emploi exclamatif)* **il s'est fait battre, et c. il faut (encore)!** he got well and truly thrashed!

• **comme quoi CONJ 1** *(ce qui prouve que)* which shows *or* (just) goes to show that; **c. quoi, on ne peut pas tout prévoir** which (just) goes to show that you can't foresee everything **2** *Fam (selon quoi)* **j'ai reçu des ordres c. quoi personne ne devait avoir accès au dossier** I've been instructed not to allow anybody access to the file; **c'est une lettre c. quoi je dois me présenter à leur bureau** it's a letter telling me to go to their office

• **comme si CONJ 1** *(exprimant la comparaison)* as if, as though; **il se conduit c. s'il était encore étudiant** he behaves as if he was still a student; **elle faisait c. si de rien n'était** she pretended (that) there was nothing wrong, she pretended (that) nothing had happened; **mais je n'y connais rien – fais c. si!** but I don't know anything about it – just pretend! **2** *(emploi exclamatif)* **c'est c. si c'était fait!** it's as good as done!; **c. s'il ne savait pas ce qu'il faisait!** as if *or* as though he didn't know what he was doing!

• **comme tout ADV** really, extremely, terribly; **tu es jolie c. tout!** you really are pretty!, aren't you pretty!; **il est malin c. tout** he's extremely cunning *or* as cunning as they come; **j'ai été malade c. tout sur le bateau** I was (as) sick as a dog on the boat

commémoratif, -ive [kɔmemɔratif, -iv] **ADJ** memorial *(avant n)*, *Sout* commemorative; **un monument c.** a memorial; **une plaque commémorative** a commemorative plaque

commémoration [kɔmemɔrasjɔ̃] **NF** commemoration; **en c. de** in commemoration of, in memory of

commémorative [kɔmemɔrativ] *voir* **commémoratif**

commémorer [3] [kɔmemɔre] **VT** to commemorate, to celebrate the memory of

commençant, -e [kɔmɑ̃sɑ̃, -ɑ̃t] **NM,F** beginner

commencement [kɔmɑ̃smɑ̃] **NM** beginning, start, early stages; **du c. jusqu'à la fin** from start to finish, from beginning to end; **commencements** *(période)* beginnings, early *or* initial stages; *Hum* **c'est le c. de la fin** it's the beginning of the end; **il y a un c. à tout** you have to start somewhere; *Jur* **c. d'exécution** = initial steps in the commission of a crime

• **au commencement ADV** in *or* at the beginning; *Bible* **au c. était le Verbe** in the beginning was the Word

COMMENCER [16] [kɔmɑ̃se] **VT 1** *(entreprendre ▸ ouvrage, jeu, apprentissage)* to start, to begin; **as-tu commencé le livre que je t'ai prêté?** have you started *or* begun (reading) the book I lent you?; **il a commencé le repas** he's started eating; **vous commencez le travail demain** you start (work) tomorrow; **c. le piano/la compétition très jeune** to start playing the piano/taking part in tournaments very young; **nous allons c. notre descente vers Milan** we are beginning our descent towards Milan

2 *(passer au début de ▸ journée, soirée)* to start, to begin; **j'ai bien/mal commencé l'année** I've made a good/bad start to the year

3 *(être au début de)* to begin; **la maille qui commence le rang** the first stitch in the row; **le mot qui commence la phrase** the word which starts the sentence *or* with which the sentence begins

USAGE ABSOLU à quelle heure tu commences? *(au lycée)* what time do you start school?; *(au travail)* what time do you start work?

VI 1 *(débuter)* to start; **tu ne vas pas c.!, ne commence pas!** don't start!; **ce n'est pas moi, c'est lui qui a commencé!** it wasn't me, HE started it!; *aussi Ironique* **ça commence bien!** that's a great start!; **c. à faire qch** to start *or* to begin doing sth; **elle a commencé à repeindre la cuisine** she started redecorating the kitchen; **je commençais à m'inquiéter** I was beginning to worry; **tu commences à m'énerver!** you're beginning to annoy me!, you're getting on my nerves!; **je commence à en avoir assez!** I've had just about enough!, I'm getting fed up with all this!; *Fam* **ça commence à bien faire!** enough is enough!, things have gone quite far enough!; **la pièce commence par un dialogue** the play starts *or* opens with a dialogue; **commençons par le commencement** let's begin at the beginning, first things first; **commence par enlever les couvertures** first, take the blankets off; **tu veux une moto? commence par réussir ton**

examen if you want a motorbike, start by passing your exam; **ça commence par un g** it begins with (a) g; **je ne sais par où c.** I don't know where to start; **il commence à pleuvoir/neiger** it's started to rain/to snow; *Fam* **il commence à se faire tard** it's getting late

2 *(avoir tel moment comme point de départ)* to start, to begin; **quand commence le trimestre?** when does term start?; **la séance commence à 20 heures** the session starts *or* begins at 8 pm; *Fam* **à quelle heure ça commence?** *(cours, spectacle, match)* what time does it start?; **les vendanges ont commencé tard cette année** the grape harvest started *or* is late this year

3 *(se mettre à travailler)* **c. dans la vie** to start off in life; **c. sur la scène/au cinéma** to make one's stage/screen debut; **j'ai commencé en 78 avec deux ouvrières** I set up *or* started (up) in '78 with two workers

4 *(dans un barème de prix)* to start; **les pantalons commencent à/vers 40 euros** trousers start at/at around 40 euros

• **à commencer par** PRÉP starting *or* beginning with

• **pour commencer** ADV **1** *(dans un programme, un repas)* first, to start with; **pour c., du saumon** to start the meal *or* as a first course, salmon **2** *(comme premier argument)* for a start, in the first place; **pour c., tu es trop jeune, et ensuite c'est trop cher!** for a start you're too young, and anyway, it's too expensive!

commensal, -e, -aux, -ales [kɔmɑ̃sal, -o] NM,F **1** *Littéraire (compagnon de table)* table companion; *(hôte)* guest **2** *Biol* commensal

commensurable [kɔmɑ̃syrabl] ADJ commensurable, measurable

comment [kɔmɑ̃] ADV **1** *(de quelle manière)* how; **c. lui dire que…?** how am I/are we/ *etc* going to tell him/her that…?; **c. t'appelles-tu?** what's your name?; **c. est-il, ce garçon?** what's this young man like?, what sort of young man is he?; **c. se fait-il qu'il n'ait pas appelé?** how come he hasn't called?; **c. est-ce possible?** how is it possible?; **c. faire?** what shall I/we do?; **je me demande c. tout cela va finir** I wonder how it's all going to end; **il faut voir c. elle lui parle** you should see *or* hear the way *or* how she speaks to him/her; **c. allez-vous?** how are you?; **et les enfants, c. ça va?** and how are the children? **2** *(pour faire répéter)* **c.?** sorry?, what (was that)?; **je pars – c.? – j'ai dit, je pars** I'm leaving – what (did you say)? – I said, I'm leaving **3** *(exprimant l'indignation, l'étonnement)* **c., c'est tout ce que tu trouves à dire?** what! is that all you can say?; **c. oses-tu me parler ainsi!** how dare you talk to me like this!; **c., ce n'est pas encore prêt?** you mean it's still not ready?; *Fam* **c. ça, tu pars?** what do you mean, you're leaving?; **le concert t'a plu? – et c.!** did you like the concert? – I certainly did!; **mais c. donc!** of course!, by all means!

NM **le c.** the how

commentaire [kɔmɑ̃tɛr] NM **1** *(remarque)* comment, remark, observation; **faire un c.** to make a remark *or* a comment; **il n'a pas fait de commentaires dans la marge** he didn't write any remarks in the margin; **je te dispense** *ou* **je me passe de tes commentaires** I can do without your remarks; *Fam* **c'est comme ça, et pas de c.!** that's how it is, and don't argue (with me)!; **cela se passe de c.** *ou* **commentaires** it speaks for itself; **sans c.!** no comment! **commentaires de presse** press comments

2 *Péj (critique)* comment; **son mariage a suscité bien des commentaires** his/her marriage caused a great deal of comment *or* gossip; **les commentaires vont bon train** comment is rife; **j'aurais des commentaires à faire sur ton attitude d'hier soir** I'd like to say something about your attitude last night

3 *Rad & TV* commentary; **c. en direct** live commentary; **c. sur image** voice-over, voice-over narration; **c. sportif** sports commentary; **c. en voix off** off-screen narration

4 *Scol & Univ* **un texte avec c.** an annotated text; **un c. de la Bible** a biblical commentary, *Sout* a biblical exegesis; **faire un c. de texte** to comment on a text; **un c. composé** a written commentary

5 *Ordinat* comment

6 *Ling* comment, theme

commentateur, -trice [kɔmɑ̃tatœr, -tris] NM,F **1** *(auteur ► d'un commentaire)* commentator, reviewer, critic **2** *(d'une cérémonie, d'un match)* commentator; *(d'un documentaire)* presenter; **c. du journal télévisé** newscaster, anchorman, *f* anchorwoman; **c. sportif** sports commentator

commenter [3] [kɔmɑ̃te] VT **1** *(expliquer ► œuvre)* to explain, to interpret; **veuillez c. ce dernier vers du poème** please write a commentary on the last line of the poem **2** *(donner son avis sur)* to comment on; **c. l'actualité** to comment on current events **3** *Rad & TV (cérémonie, match)* to cover, to do the commentary of *or* for

commérage [kɔmeraʒ] NM piece of gossip; **commérages** gossip; **faire des commérages** to gossip; **ce ne sont que des commérages** it's only gossip *or* hearsay

commerçant, -e [kɔmɛrsɑ̃, -ɑ̃t] ADJ **1** *(peuple, port, pays)* trading *(avant n)*; *(rue, quartier)* shopping *(avant n)* **2** *(qui a le sens du commerce)* **il a l'esprit c.** he's a born salesman, he could sell you anything; **il n'est pas très c.** he's not got much business sense; *Péj* **un sourire c.** a mercenary smile

NM,F *(négociant)* trader, merchant; *(qui tient un magasin) Br* shopkeeper, *Am* storekeeper; **tous les commerçants étaient fermés** all the *Br* shops *or Am* stores were closed; **c. de** *ou* **en détail** retail trader, retailer; **c. en gros** wholesale; **les petits commerçants** small *or* retail traders

commerce [kɔmɛrs] NM **1** *(activité)* **le c.** trade; **être dans le c.** to be in trade, to run a business; **faire du c. avec qn/un pays** to trade with sb/a country; **faire le c. de qch** to trade in sth; **c. bilatéral** bilateral trade; **c. de demi-gros** cash and carry; **c. de détail** retail trade; *Ordinat* **c. électronique** electronic commerce, e-commerce; **c. équitable** *ou* **éthique** fair trade; **c. d'exportation** export trade; **c. extérieur** foreign trade; **c. frontalier** border trade; **c. en gros** wholesale trade; **c. d'importation** import trade; **c. intérieur** domestic trade, home trade; **c. international** international trade; **c. mobile** m-commerce; **c. réciproque** reciprocal trade *or* trading; **c. de services** invisible trade; **c. transfrontalier** cross-border trade; **c. triangulaire** triangular trade; *Euph* **faire c. de ses charmes** to sell one's body

2 *(affaires)* business; **cela fait marcher le c.** it's good for business; **le c. marche mal** business is slow

3 *(commerçants)* **le petit c.** small *or* retail traders

4 *(magasin) Br* shop, *Am* store; **ouvrir** *ou* **monter un c.** to open *or* to start a business; **tenir un c.** to run a business; **c. de proximité** local *Br* shop *or Am* store; **on ne trouve pas encore ce produit dans le c.** this item is not yet available in the *Br* shops *or Am* stores

5 *Littéraire (relation, fréquentation)* company; **entretenir un c. d'amitié avec qn** to keep company with sb; **renoncer au c. des hommes** to renounce the company of one's fellow men; **être d'un c. agréable** to be easy to get on with *or* pleasant to deal with

• **de commerce** ADJ **1** *(opération)* commercial, business *(avant n)*; *(acte)* trade *(avant n)*; *(code, tribunal)* commercial; *(école)* business *(avant n)* **2** *Naut (marine, navire, port)* trading, merchant *(avant n)*

commercer [16] [kɔmɛrse] VI to trade, to deal; **c. avec un pays** to trade with a country

commercial, -e, -aux, -ales [kɔmɛrsjal, -o] ADJ **1** *(activité, attaché)* commercial; *(délégué, direction, service)* sales *(avant n)*; *(relation, embargo, tribunal)* trade *(avant n)*; **adressez-vous à notre service c.** please contact our sales department; **avoir des contacts commerciaux avec** to have trading *or* trade links with; **droit c.** commercial law; **l'anglais c.** business English; **un gros succès c.** *(film, pièce)* a big box-office success; *(livre)* a best-selling book, a best-seller **2** *Péj (sourire)* ingratiating; **vos anciens fans trouvent que vous êtes devenu c.** your old fans think you've sold out; **c'est une chanson très commerciale** it's a very commercial song

NM,F sales person

• **commerciale** NF *Fam* commercial vehicle

commercialement [kɔmɛrsjalmɑ̃] ADV commercially; **c. parlant** from a business point of view

commercialisable [kɔmɛrsjalizabl] ADJ marketable

commercialisation [kɔmɛrsjalizasjɔ̃] NF marketing

commercialiser [3] [kɔmɛrsjalize] VT **1** *Com* to market, to commercialize; **le modèle sera commercialisé en janvier** the model will be coming onto the market in January **2** *Jur (dette, lettre de change)* to market **3** *Fin (effet)* to negotiate

commère [kɔmɛr] NF **1** *(médisante)* gossip **2** *(bavarde)* chatterbox

commets *etc voir* **commettre**

commettant [kɔmetɑ̃] NM principal

commettre [84] [kɔmɛtr] VT **1** *(perpétrer ► erreur)* to make; *(► injustice)* to perpetrate; *(► meurtre)* to commit; **quand le crime a-t-il été commis?** when did the crime take place?; **c. une maladresse** to make a blunder, to make a gaffe; **c. une imprudence** to take an unwise step

2 *Jur (nommer ► arbitre, avocat, huissier)* to appoint; **commis d'office** appointed by the court

3 *Naut* to lay up

4 *Hum Péj (produire ► livre, émission)* to perpetrate; **il avait commis quelques articles dans les années 80** he had penned a few articles back in the eighties

5 *Vieilli (confier)* **c. qch à qn** to entrust sth to sb *or* to sb's care, to entrust sb with sth

VPR **se commettre** *Littéraire* to compromise oneself; **se c. avec qn** to associate *or* to consort with sb

comminatoire [kɔminatwar] ADJ **1** *Littéraire (menaçant)* threatening **2** *Jur* = involving a penalty for non-compliance

commis, -e [kɔmi, -iz] PP *voir* **commettre**

NM **1** *Jur* agent **2** *(employé ► de magasin) Br* sales assistant, *Am* sales clerk; *(► de banque)* runner, junior clerk; *(► de ferme)* lad, boy, farm hand; *Bourse* floor trader; **c. boucher** *ou* **de boucherie** butcher's boy; **c. aux comptes** government auditor; **c. de cuisine** commis chef; **c. aux écritures** accounting clerk; **c. greffier** assistant to the court clerk; **c. principal** senior clerk; *Vieilli* **c. voyageur** travelling salesman **3** *Admin* **grand c. de l'État** senior *or* higher civil servant

commisération [kɔmizerasjɔ̃] NF commiseration; **témoigner de la c. à qn** to show sb sympathy; **sans c.** ruthlessly, pitilessly

commissaire [kɔmisɛr] NM **1** *(membre d'une commission)* commissioner; **c. européen** European commissioner

2 *Sport* steward; **c. d'une course** race steward

3 *Admin* **c. divisionnaire** *Br* chief superintendent, *Am* police chief; **c. enquêteur** investigating commissioner; **c. du gouvernement** government commissioner; **c. de la Marine/de l'Air** chief administrator in the Navy/the Air Force; **c. de police** *Br* (police) superintendent, *Am* (police) captain, precinct captain; **bonjour, Monsieur le c.** good morning, *Br* Superintendent *or Am* Captain; **c. principal** *Br* chief superintendent, *Am* chief of police; **c. de la République** commissioner of the Republic

4 *Fin* **c. aux comptes** auditor

5 *(d'une exposition)* organizer

6 *Naut* **c. de** *ou* **du bord** purser

7 *Hist (en URSS)* commissar

commissaire-priseur [kɔmisɛrprisœr] *(pl* **commissaires-priseurs)** NM auctioneer

commissariat [kɔmisarja] NM **1** *(fonction)* commissionership; *Naut* **c. de** *ou* **du bord** pursership

2 *Admin* **c. de l'Air** Air Force staff; **C. à l'énergie atomique** = French atomic energy commission, *Br* ≃ AEA, *Am* ≃ AEC; **c. de la Marine** *Br* Admiralty Board, *Am* Naval Command

3 *Fin* **c. aux comptes** auditorship

4 *(local)* **c. (de police)** police station *or Am* precinct

commission [kɔmisjɔ̃] NF **1** *(groupe)* commission, committee; **c. de l'application des peines** sentence board; **c. d'arbitrage** arbitration committee; **C. d'accès aux documents administratifs** Commission for Access to Administrative Documents; **c. du budget** budget committee; **C. des communautés européennes** European Communities Commission; **c. de conciliation** arbitration committee; **c. de contrôle** supervisory committee; **C. du droit international** International Law Commission; **c. d'enquête** board *or* commission of enquiry; **la C. européenne** the European Commission; **C. européenne des droits de l'homme** European Human Rights Commission; **c. d'examen** examination board; **c. mixte paritaire** mixed joint commission; **c. de normalisation** standards commission; **C. des opérations de Bourse** = French Stock Exchange watchdog, *Br* ≃ SIB, *Am* ≃ SEC; **c. paritaire** joint commission; **c. parlementaire** parliamentary committee *or* commission; **c. permanente** standing committee; **être en c.** to be in committee; **renvoyer un projet de loi en c.** to commit a bill

2 *Jur (pouvoir)* commission; **c. rogatoire** letters rogatory

3 *Mil* **c. d'armistice** armistice council; **c. militaire** army exemption tribunal

4 *Fin (pourcentage)* commission, percentage; *(frais de courtage)* brokerage; **3 pour cent de c.** 3 percent commission; **il touche une c. de 5 pour cent sur chaque vente** he gets a commission of 5 percent on each sale; **travailler à la c.** to work on a commission basis *or* for a percentage; *Banque* **c. d'acceptation** acceptance fee; **c. d'affacturage** factoring charges; **c. de change** exchange commission; *Banque* **c. de compte** account fee; **c. d'endos** endorsement fee; **c. d'engagement** commitment fee; **c. de garantie** underwriting fee; **c. de gestion** agency fee; **c. immédiate** flat fee; **c. de placement** underwriting fee; *Bourse* **c. de rachat** redemption fee; *Bourse* **c. de souscription** front load; **c. de tenue de compte** account handling fee; **c. de vente** sales commission

5 *(course)* **faire une c.** to run an errand; **faire les commissions** to do the shopping; **n'oublie pas de lui faire la c.** *(de lui donner le message)* don't forget to give him/her the message

6 *Fam Euph* **faire la petite/grosse c.** to do a number one/two

7 *(perpétration)* **la c. d'un crime** the commission of a crime

commissionnaire [kɔmisjɔnɛr] **NMF 1** *Fin (intermédiaire)* commission agent, broker, agent; **c. en banque** outside broker; **c. en douane** customs agent *or* broker; **c. expéditeur** forwarding agent, carrier; **c. à l'export, c. exportateur** export agent; **c. en gros** factor; **c. à l'import, c. importateur** import agent; **c. de transport** forwarding agent **2** *(coursier)* commissionaire

commissionner **[3]** [kɔmisjɔne] **VT** to commission

commissure [kɔmisyr] **NF 1** *(dans le cerveau)* commissure **2** *(de la bouche)* corner

commode¹ [kɔmɔd] **ADJ 1** *(pratique ▸ moyen de transport)* useful, convenient; *(▸ outil)* useful, handy; **c'est bien c. d'avoir un marché dans le quartier** it's very handy *or* convenient having a market in the area; **les talons aiguilles ne sont pas très commodes pour marcher** high heels aren't very practical for walking (in) **2** *(facile)* easy; **ce n'est pas c. de concilier deux activités** combining two different jobs is not easy *or* a simple task **3** *(aimable)* **elle n'est pas c. (à vivre)** she's not easy to live with; **son patron n'est pas c.** his/her boss isn't an easy person to get along with; **il est peu c.** he's awkward *or* difficult

commode² [kɔmɔd] **NF** *(meuble)* chest of drawers

commodément [kɔmɔdemɑ̃] **ADV** *(confortablement)* comfortably

commodité [kɔmɔdite] **NF 1** *(facilité)* convenience; **pour plus de c.** for greater convenience, to make things more convenient **2** *(aspect pratique)* **la c. d'une maison** the comfort *or* convenience of a house

• **commodités** **NFPL 1** *(agréments)* conveniences; **les commodités de la vie moderne** the comforts *or* conveniences of modern life **2** *Vieilli (toilettes)* toilet, toilets

commodore [kɔmɔdɔr] **NM** *Can Mil Br* ≃ commodore, *Am* ≃ rear-admiral (lower half)

Commonwealth [kɔmɔnwɛls] **NM** *Pol* **le C.** the Commonwealth

commotion [kɔmɔsjɔ̃] **NF 1** *(choc)* shock; **être sous le coup de la c.** to be dazed by the shock **2** *Méd* **c. cérébrale** concussion **3** *(perturbation)* upheaval, agitation; **les commotions sociales/politiques** the social/political upheavals

commotionner **[3]** [kɔmɔsjɔne] **VT 1** *(choquer)* to shake (up); **la terrible nouvelle l'a commotionné** the appalling news gave him a shock **2** *Méd* to concuss; **il a été fortement commotionné** he was severely concussed, he had severe concussion

commuable [kɔmɥabl] **ADJ** commutable

commuer **[7]** [kɔmɥe] **VT** to commute; **c. une peine de prison en amende** to commute a prison sentence to a fine

commun, -e¹ [kɔmœ̃, -yn] **ADJ 1** *(non exclusif ▸ jardin, local)* shared, common; *(▸ ami)* mutual; **salle commune** common room; **hôtel avec salle de télévision commune** hotel with public TV lounge; **une langue commune à cinq millions de personnes** a language shared by five million people

2 *(fait ensemble ▸ travail, politique)* shared, common; *(▸ décision)* joint; **nous avons pris la décision commune de...** we took a joint decision to...; **la vie commune** *(conjugale)* conjugal life, the life of a couple; **ils vont reprendre la vie commune** they're going to live together again

3 *(identique ▸ caractère, passion, intérêts)* similar; *(▸ habitude)* common, shared, identical; **nous avons des problèmes communs** we share the same problems, we have similar problems; **il n'y a rien de c. entre eux** they've (got) nothing in common; **il n'y a pas de commune mesure entre...** there's no similarity whatsoever between...; **c'est sans commune mesure avec...** there's no comparison with...

4 *(courant ▸ espèce, usage, faute)* common, ordinary, run-of-the-mill; **il est d'un courage peu c.** he's uncommonly *or* exceptionally brave; **un nom peu c.** a very unusual name

5 *Péj (banal)* common, coarse; **il la trouvait commune** he thought she was common

6 *Ling* common

NM un homme hors du c. an exceptional *or* unusual man; **cela sort du c.** this is very unusual; **le c. des mortels** the common run of people; **le c. des mortels ne pourra sans doute pas comprendre** the man in the street won't be able to understand; **le c. des lecteurs** the average reader

• **communs** **NMPL** outbuildings, outhouses

• **d'un commun accord** **ADV** by mutual agreement, by common consent; **tous d'un c. accord ont décidé que...** they decided unanimously that...

• **en commun** **ADV** **avoir qch en c. (avec)** to have sth in common (with); **mettre qch en c.** to pool sth; **nous mettons tout en c.** we share everything; **on s'est mis en c. pour lui acheter un cadeau** we all clubbed together to buy him/her a present; **travailler en c.** to work together; **vivre en c.** to live communally

communal, -e, -aux, -ales [kɔmynal, -o] **ADJ 1** *Admin (en ville)* ≃ of the urban district; *(à la campagne)* ≃ of the rural district **2** *(du village ▸ fête)* local, village *(avant n)* **3** *Belg* **conseil c.** town council; **maison communale** town hall

• **communale** **NF** *Fam Br* primary school ▫, *Am* grade school ▫

• **communaux** **NMPL** *Belg (terres)* common land

communard, -e [kɔmynar, -ard] **ADJ** *Hist* of the (Paris) Commune

NM,F *Hist* Communard, member of the (Paris) Commune

NM = red wine mixed with crème de cassis liqueur

communautaire [kɔmynotɛr] **ADJ 1** *(vie, esprit)* communal, community *(avant n)*; **2** *UE* Community *(avant n)*; **droit c.** (European) Community law **3** *(lié à une communauté de personnes)* **des conflicts communautaires** conflicts between different communities; **on assiste à un repli c. au sein des quartiers sensibles** we're seeing ethnic communities withdrawing into themselves in sensitive areas; **réflexe c.** = tendency to see oneself as part of a particular community rather than part of society at large

communautariser **[3]** [kɔmynotarize] **VT 1** *UE* **c. la santé/la défense/le droit des travailleurs** to handle the issue of health/defence/workers' rights at EU level **2** *Belg Pol* = to devolve a political power to the French-, Flemish- and German-speaking Communities in Belgium

communautarisme [kɔmynotarism] **NM 1** *(tendance du multiculturalisme américain)* = emphasis on issues relating to minorities and ethnic communities within society **2** *(conception qui place la communauté avant l'individu)* communitarianism **3** *(dans le contexte des sociétés multiculturelles)* = tendency to withdraw into one's ethnic or religious community rather than seeing oneself as part of society at large

communauté [kɔmynote] **NF 1** *(similitude ▸ de vues, de pensées)* likeness, closeness; *(▸ d'intérêts)* community; *(▸ de sentiments)* commonness

2 *(groupe)* community; *(de hippies)* commune; **la C. (économique) européenne** the (European) Economic Community; **la C. des États indépendants** the Commonwealth of Independent States; **la C. européenne du charbon et de l'acier** the European Coal and Steel Community; **les Communautés européennes** the European Community; **la c. des fidèles** *(d'une paroisse)* the congregation; **c. internationale** international community; **c. linguistique** linguistic community; **c. religieuse** religious community; **la c. scientifique** the scientific community; **c. urbaine** = syndicate made up of a large town and surrounding "communes" responsible for the infrastructure of the area

3 *(public)* **la c.** the general public

4 *Jur* joint estate; **mariés sons le régime de la c.** married with a communal estate settlement; **c. des biens** community (of) property; **c. de vie** marital obligation to live together

• **en communauté** **ADV** *(vivre)* communally, as a community

commune² [kɔmyn] **ADJ** *voir* **commun**

NF 1 *(agglomération)* commune; **une jolie petite c. rurale** a nice little country village; **la c. et ses alentours** *(en ville)* the urban district; *(à la campagne)* the rural district

2 *(habitants)* **la c.** *(en ville)* people who live within the urban district; *(à la campagne)* people who live within the rural district

3 *(administrateurs)* **c'est la c. qui paie** the local authority *or Br* the council is paying

4 *Hist (ville autonome)* free town; **la C. (de Paris)** the (Paris) Commune *(in 1789 and 1871)*

5 *(en Grande-Bretagne)* **les Communes** the House of Commons

> COMMUNE
>
> There are over 36,000 "communes" or administrative districts in France, some with fewer than 25 inhabitants. Each "commune" has an elected mayor and a town council.

communément [kɔmynemɑ̃] **ADV** commonly, usually; **la torture est encore c. pratiquée là-bas** torture is still routinely practised there; **la renoncule terrestre, c. appelée bouton d'or** ranunculus, commonly known as *or* usually called the buttercup

communiant, -e [kɔmynjɑ̃, -ɑ̃t] **NM,F** communicant; **premier c., première communiante** first communicant

communicable [kɔmynikabl] **ADJ 1** *(exprimable)* communicable; **c'est une impression difficilement c.** it's a feeling difficult to put into words **2** *(transmissible ▸ données, informations)* communicable; **ces données ne sont pas communicables** this data is classified

communicant, -e [kɔmynikɑ̃, -ɑ̃t] **ADJ** communicating; **deux chambres communicantes** two *Br* connecting *or Am* adjoining rooms

communicateur, -trice [kɔmynikatœr, -tris] **ADJ** *(fil etc)* connecting

NM,F communicator

communicatif, -ive [kɔmynikatif, -iv] **ADJ 1** *(qui se répand ▸ rire, bonne humeur)* infectious **2**

(bavard) communicative, talkative; **peu c.** not very communicative, quiet

communication [kɔmynikasjɔ̃] **NF 1** *(annonce)* announcement, communication; **j'ai une c. importante à vous faire** I have an important announcement to make; **donner c. de qch** to communicate sth

2 *(exposé ▸ fait à la presse)* statement; *(▸ fait à des universitaires, des scientifiques)* paper; **faire une c. sur l'atome** to deliver a lecture *or* give a paper on the atom

3 *(transmission)* communicating, passing on, transmission; **pour éviter la c. de ces maladies** to stop the spread of these diseases; **avoir c. d'un dossier** to get hold of a file, to have a file passed on to one; **je n'ai pas eu c. de sa nouvelle adresse** his/her new address hasn't been passed on to me; **demander c. d'un dossier** to ask for a file (to be handed on to one); **donner c. d'un dossier (à qn)** to pass on a file (to sb); *Jur* **c. du dossier** discovery of documents; **c. de pièces** production of documents; **donner c. de pièces** to produce documents

4 *(contact)* communication, contact; **être en c. avec qn** to be in contact *or* touch with sb; **vous devriez vous mettre en c. avec elle** you should get in touch with her; **mettre deux personnes en c.** to put two people in touch *or* in contact with each other; **depuis l'explosion, nous n'avons plus de c. avec l'extérieur** we haven't been able to communicate with the outside world since the blast

5 *(échange entre personnes)* communication; **il a des problèmes de c. (avec les autres)** he has problems communicating with *or* relating to people

6 *(diffusion d'informations)* **les techniques de la c.** media techniques; **études de c.** media studies; **la c. de masse** the mass media; **c. commerciale** business correspondence; **c. interne** *(dans une entreprise)* interdepartmental communication

7 *Mktg (dans la publicité)* promotion; **c. événementielle** event promotion; **c. institutionnelle** corporate promotion; **c. sur le lieu de vente** point-of-sale promotion; **c. produit** product promotion

8 *(moyen de liaison)* (means of) communication; **toutes les communications entre les deux pays ont été interrompues** all communication between the two countries has been stopped

9 *Tél* **c. téléphonique** (phone) call; **je vous passe la c.** I'll put you through; **je prends la c.** I'll take the call; **vous avez la c.** you're through; **pour obtenir la c., faites le 12** dial 12 (in order) to get through; **mettez-moi en c. avec M. Martin** put me through to Mr Martin; **il est en c. avec...** he's speaking to…, he's on the phone to…; **la c. a été coupée** we were cut off; **la c. est mauvaise** the line is bad; **c. internationale** international call; **c. interurbaine** inter-city *or* long-distance call; **c. locale** local call; **c. longue distance** long-distance call; **c. en PCV** *Br* reverse-charge call, *Am* collect call

10 *Ordinat* **c. de données** data communications, datacomms; **c. homme-machine** man-machine dialogue; **c. en ligne** on-line communication; **c. télématique** datacommunications, datacomms

• **de communication ADJ 1** *(porte, couloir)* connecting **2** *(réseau, satellite)* communications *(avant n)*; **moyens de c.** means of communication **3** *(agence)* publicity *(avant n)*

communicative [kɔmynikativ] *voir* **communicatif**

communicatrice [kɔmynikatrice] *voir* **communicateur**

communier [9] [kɔmynje] **VI 1** *Rel* to communicate, to receive Communion **2** *Littéraire (s'unir spirituellement)* **c. avec qn** to share the same feelings as sb; **c. avec la nature** to be at one *or* to commune with nature

communion [kɔmynjɔ̃] **NF 1** *Rel* communion; *(partie de la messe)* (Holy) Communion; **donner la c. à qn** to give Communion to sb; **recevoir la c.** to receive *or* take Communion; **première c.** First Communion; **c. des saints** communion of saints; **c. solennelle** Solemn Communion **2** *Littéraire (accord)* **être en c. avec qn** to be at one *or* to commune with sb; **être en c. d'idées** *ou* **d'esprit avec qn** to share sb's ideas; **être en c. avec la nature** to commune with nature

communiqué [kɔmynike] **NM** communiqué; **un c. officiel** an official communiqué *or* announcement; **un c. de presse** a press release

communiquer [3] [kɔmynike] **VT 1** *(transmettre ▸ information)* to communicate, to give; *(▸ demande)* to transmit; *(▸ dossier, message)* to pass on; *(▸ savoir, savoir-faire)* to pass on, to hand down; **c. le goût de la lecture à ses enfants** to pass on one's love of reading to one's children; **c. qch par écrit à qn** to communicate *or* convey sth in writing to sb

2 *Phys (chaleur, lumière)* to transmit; *(mouvement, impulsion)* to impart

3 *(donner par contamination)* to transmit; **il leur a communiqué son fou rire/enthousiasme** he passed on his giggles/enthusiasm to them

4 *(annoncer)* to announce, to impart, to communicate; **j'ai une chose importante à vous c.** I have something important to say to you; **rien ne nous a été communiqué** we have heard nothing

VI 1 *(avoir des relations)* to communicate; **les dauphins communiquent entre eux** dolphins communicate with each other **2** *(être relié)* to interconnect; **la chambre communique avec la salle de bains** there's a connecting door between the bathroom and the bedroom; **toutes les chambres communiquent** all the bedrooms are interconnecting

VPR se communiquer 1 *(être transmis ▸ don, savoir, savoir-faire)* to be passed on, to be handed down; **le vrai talent ne se communique pas** you can't teach people how to be talented **2** *(se propager ▸ incendie)* to spread; *(▸ maladie)* to spread, to be passed on; **se c. à** to spread to

communisant, -e [kɔmynizɑ̃, -ɑ̃t] **ADJ** Communistic; **un journal c.** a paper with Communist sympathies

NM,F Communist sympathizer, fellow traveller

communisme [kɔmynism] **NM** Communism

communiste [kɔmynist] **ADJ** Communist

NMF Communist

commutable [kɔmytabl] **ADJ** commutable

commutateur [kɔmytatœr] **NM** *Élec & Électron (de circuits)* changeover switch, commutator; *(interrupteur)* switch; **actionner un c.** *(pour allumer)* to switch on; *(pour éteindre)* to switch off; *Ordinat* **c. de données** data switch; **c. téléphonique** exchange

commutatif, -ive [kɔmytatif, -iv] **ADJ 1** *Math* commutative **2** *Ling* commutable **3** *Jur* commutative

commutation [kɔmytasjɔ̃] **NF 1** *(substitution)* commutation, substitution; *Ling & Math* commutation

2 *Jur* **c. de peine** commutation of a sentence

3 *Élec & Électron* commutation, switching

4 *Ordinat & Tél* switch-over, switching; **c. de bande/circuits** tape/circuit switching; **c. de message/de paquets** message/packet switching

commutative [kɔmytativ] *voir* **commutatif**

commutatrice [kɔmytatris] **NF** rotary converter

commuté, -e [kɔmyte] **ADJ** *(réseau)* switched

commuter [3] [kɔmyte] **VT 1** *(gén)* to substitute **2** *Ling & Math* to commute; **c. A et B** to commute A and *or* with B **3** *Élec & Électron* to commutate

VI 1 *Math* to commute **2** *Ling* to substitute, to commute

Comores [kɔmɔr] **NFPL les C.** the Comoro Islands, the Comoros

comorien, -enne [kɔmɔrjɛ̃, -ɛn] **ADJ** Comoran, Comorian

• **Comorien, -enne NM,F** Comoran, Comorian

compacité [kɔ̃pasite] **NF** compactness

compact, -e [kɔ̃pakt] **ADJ 1** *(dense ▸ matière)* solid, dense; *(▸ foule)* dense, packed; *(▸ poudre)* pressed, compacted

2 *Fig (majorité)* large, solid

3 *Ski* short

4 *Aut, Phot & (disque)* compact

5 *Math* compact

NM 1 *Ski* short ski

2 *Vieilli (poudre)* pressed powder

3 *(disque)* compact disc, CD; **disponible en c.** available on CD

4 *(appareil photo)* compact (camera)

Compact Disc® [kɔ̃paktdisk] *(pl* **Compact Discs***)* **NM** compact disc, CD

compacter [3] [kɔ̃pakte] **VT** to compact; *Ordinat (base de données)* to pack

compacteur [kɔ̃paktœr] **NM 1** *(engin)* road roller, steamroller **2** *Ordinat* **c. d'exécutables** execute file compressor; **c. de données** data compressor

compagne [kɔ̃paɲ] **NF 1** *(camarade)* (female) companion; **c. de classe/jeux** (female) classmate/playmate; **mes compagnes de captivité** my fellow captives; **elle a été ma c. d'infortune** she suffered with me, she was my companion in misery **2** *(épouse)* wife; *(concubine)* partner **3** *(animal domestique)* companion

compagnie [kɔ̃paɲi] **NF 1** *(présence)* company; **sa c. m'est insupportable** I can't stand his/her company *or* being with him/her; **elle avait un chien pour toute c.** her dog was her only companion; **être d'une c. agréable/sinistre** to be a pleasant/gloomy companion; **être de bonne/mauvaise c.** to be good/bad company; **être en bonne/mauvaise c.** to be in good/bad company; **je te laisse en bonne c.** I leave you in good hands; **je l'ai trouvé en joyeuse/galante c.** I found him in cheerful company/in the company of a lady; **tenir c. à qn** to keep sb company; **il te faudrait de la c.** you need some company; **tu sais, je me passerais bien de c.!** I could do with being left alone, you know!

2 *(groupe)* party, company, gang; **toute la c. était là** the whole gang was there

3 *Com & Ind* company; **c. aérienne** airline (company); **c. d'assurances** insurance company; **c. maritime** shipping company *or* line; **c. pétrolière** oil company; **c. de transports** carrier; **Michel Darot et c.** Michel Darot and Company; *Fam Fig* **tout ça, c'est mensonge/arnaque et c.** that's nothing but a pack of lies/a swindle

4 *Théât* **c. (théâtrale)** (theatre) group *or* company *or* troupe

5 *Zool (de sangliers)* herd, sounder; *(de perdreaux)* covey, flock

6 *Mil* company; **c. de chars** tank brigade

7 *(dans des noms d'organisations)* **C. des agents de change** Institute of stockbrokers; **C. de Jésus** Society of Jesus; **Compagnies républicaines de sécurité** *Br* ≃ riot police, *Am* ≃ state troopers

• **de compagnie ADJ** *(animal)* domestic **ADV** *(voyager)* together

• **en compagnie de PRÉP** accompanied by, (in company) with

compagnon [kɔ̃paɲɔ̃] **NM 1** *(camarade)* companion; **c. d'armes** brother *or* comrade in arms; **c. de bord** shipmate; **c. de captivité** companion in captivity; **c. de cellule** cellmate; **c. d'exil** fellow exile; **c. d'infortune** companion in misfortune; **c. de jeux** playmate; **c. de route** *ou* **de voyage** travelling companion; *Pol* **c. de route** fellow traveller; **c. de table** table companion

2 *(époux)* husband, companion; *(ami, concubin)* partner

3 *(animal)* friend; **il a un chien pour tout c.** his only friend is a dog

4 *(franc-maçon)* Fellow of The Craft

5 *(artisan)* journeyman; *(membre d'un compagnonnage)* member of a trade guild

6 *Hist* **C. de la Libération** (French) Resistance fighter

7 *Ind* = workman who has finished his initial apprenticeship and is learning further skills from his employer

8 *Bot* **c. rouge/blanc** red/white campion

comparable [kɔ̃parabl] **ADJ** comparable, similar; **comparons ce qui est c.** let's compare like with like; **ce n'est pas c.** there's no comparison; **une fonction c. à celle de comptable** a function comparable with *or* similar to that of an accountant

comparais *etc voir* **comparaître**

comparaison [kɔ̃parezɔ̃] **NF 1** *(gén)* comparison; **faire la** *ou* **une c. entre deux qualités** to compare two qualities; **il n'y a pas de c. possible** there's no possible comparison; **c'est sans c. avec le mien** it cannot possibly be compared with mine; **elle est, sans c., la plus grande chanteuse du moment** she's by far our best contemporary singer; **aucune c.!** there's no comparison!; **point de c.** point of comparison; **comment décider sans avoir un point de c.?** how can you possibly make up your mind without some means of comparison?; **supporter** *ou* **soutenir la c. avec qch** to bear *or* to stand comparison with sth; *Prov* **c. n'est pas raison** comparisons are odious; *Mktg* **c. par paire** paired comparison **2** *(figure de style)* comparison, simile; **adverbe de c.** comparative adverb

• **en comparaison de, en comparaison avec** PRÉP in comparison *or* as compared with, compared to

• **par comparaison avec, par comparaison à** PRÉP compared with *ou* to

comparaître [91] [kɔ̃paretr] VI *Jur* to appear; **c. en justice** to appear before a court; **c. en personne** to appear in person; **c. par avoué** to be represented by counsel; **appelé** *ou* **cité à c.** summoned to appear; **faire c. qn devant un tribunal** to bring sb before a court

comparant, -e [kɔ̃parɑ̃, -ɑ̃t] *Jur*
ADJ appearing before the court
NM,F = person appearing before the court

comparateur [kɔ̃paratœr] NM comparator

comparatif, -ive [kɔ̃paratif, -iv] ADJ comparative
NM comparative; **c. de supériorité/d'infériorité** comparative of greater/lesser degree; **adjectif au c.** comparative adjective

comparatiste [kɔ̃paratist] NMF **1** *Ling* specialist in comparative linguistics **2** *Littérature* specialist in comparative literature

comparative [kɔ̃parativ] *voir* **comparatif**

comparativement [kɔ̃parativmɑ̃] ADV comparatively, by *or* in comparison; **c. à** compared with *or* to

comparé, -e [kɔ̃pare] ADJ *(littérature, anatomie, grammaire)* comparative

comparer [3] [kɔ̃pare] VT **1** *(confronter)* to compare; **c. deux tableaux** to compare two pictures; **c. un livre à** *ou* **avec un autre** to compare a book to *or* with another **2** *(assimiler)* **c. qn/qch à** to compare sb/sth to; **il compare les étoiles filantes à des cheveux** he compares *or* likens shooting stars to strands of hair; **comme artiste, il ne peut être comparé à Braque** as an artist, he cannot compare with Braque
VPR **se comparer 1** *(emploi passif)* **ce sont deux choses qui ne se comparent pas** there can be no comparison between these two things **2** *(soi-même)* **se c. à** to compare oneself with

• **comparé à** PRÉP compared to *or* with, in comparison to *or* with

comparse [kɔ̃pars] NMF **1** *Théât* extra, walk-on; **un rôle de c.** a walk-on part **2** *Péj (d'un brigand, d'un camelot)* stooge

compartiment [kɔ̃partimɑ̃] NM **1** *Rail* compartment; **c. de première classe** first-class compartment
2 *(case ▸ d'une boîte)* compartment; *(▸ d'un sac)* pocket; **c. à bagages** *(d'autocar)* luggage compartment; **c. à glace** freezer compartment
3 *(carreau)* square
4 *Naut* tank

• **à compartiments** ADJ *(tiroir, classeur)* divided into compartments

compartimentage [kɔ̃partimɑ̃taʒ] NM *(d'une caisse, d'une armoire)* partitioning; *(d'une administration, des connaissances)* compartmentalization, fragmenting

compartimenter [3] [kɔ̃partimɑ̃te] VT *(caisse, armoire)* to partition, to divide into compartments; *(administration, connaissances)* to compartmentalize, to split into small units

comparu, -e [kɔ̃pary] *pp voir* **comparaître**

comparution [kɔ̃parysjɔ̃] NF *Jur* appearance; **c. en conseil de discipline** appearance before a disciplinary committee; **c. en justice** court appearance; **c. immédiate** immediate hearing

compas [kɔ̃pa] NM **1** *Aviat & Naut* compass; **c. gyroscopique** gyrocompass; **c. de route** steering compass **2** *Géom* (pair of) compasses; **c. d'épaisseur** spring-adjusting callipers; **c. à pointes sèches** dividers; **c. quart de cercle** wing compasses; **c. de réduction** proportional compasses; *Fig* **avoir le c. dans l'œil** to be a good judge of distances/measurements/*etc*; **le placard tient juste, tu as eu le c. dans l'œil!** the cupboard just fits, you judged that well!

• **au compas** ADV **1** *Naut* by the compass **2** *(avec précision)* with military precision

compassé, -e [kɔ̃pase] ADJ stiff, strait-laced

compasser [3] [kɔ̃pase] VT **1** *(distances sur la carte etc)* to measure with compasses; *Naut (carte)* to prick **2** *Littéraire (ses actes etc)* to control, to regulate

compassion [kɔ̃pasjɔ̃] NF compassion, sympathy; **avec c.** compassionately

compatibilité [kɔ̃patibilite] NF *(gén) & Ordinat* compatibility; **c. sanguine** blood-group compatibility *or* matching

compatible [kɔ̃patibl] ADJ compatible; **leurs modes de vie ne sont pas compatibles** their lifestyles are totally incompatible; **cela n'est pas c. avec mon emploi du temps** this won't fit into my schedule; *Ordinat* **ces deux applications ne sont pas compatibles** these two applications are incompatible *or* not compatible; *Ordinat* **c. vers le haut/vers le bas** upward/downward compatible; *Ordinat* **c. avec les versions antérieures** backward compatible; *Ordinat* **c. IBM** IBM-compatible; *Ordinat* **c. Mac** Mac-compatible
NM *Ordinat* compatible

compatir [32] [kɔ̃patir] **compatir à** VT IND **je compatis à votre douleur** I sympathize with you in your grief, I share in your grief
USAGE ABSOLU **je compatis!** I sympathize!; *Ironique* my heart bleeds!

compatissant, -e [kɔ̃patisɑ̃, -ɑ̃t] ADJ sympathetic, compassionate

compatriote [kɔ̃patrijɔt] NMF compatriot, fellow countryman, *f* countrywoman

compensable [kɔ̃pɑ̃sabl] ADJ **1** *(perte)* that can be compensated, *Am* compensable **2** *(chèque)* clearable; **être c. à Paris** to be cleared at Paris, to be domiciled in Paris

compensateur, -trice [kɔ̃pɑ̃satœr, -tris] ADJ **1** *(indemnité)* compensating, compensatory **2** *(pendule)* compensation *(avant n)*
NM **1** *(appareil)* compensator; *Électron* equalizer; *Aut* **c. de frein** brake compensator **2** *Aviat* (trim) tab

compensation [kɔ̃pɑ̃sasjɔ̃] NF **1** *(dédommagement)* compensation; **je travaille dur mais il y a des compensations** I work hard but there are compensations
2 *Fin (de dette)* offsetting; *(de chèque)* clearing
3 *Jur* **c. des dépens** sharing of the costs *(among different parties)*
4 *Méd & Psy* compensation; **elle mange par c.** she eats for comfort
5 *École* **c. carbone** carbon offsetting
6 *Naut* correction, adjustment
7 *Aviat* tabbing
8 *Tech & Phys* balancing; *(de son)* equalization

• **en compensation** ADV as a *or* by way of (a) compensation

• **en compensation de** PRÉP by way of compensation *or* as compensation *or* to compensate for

compensatoire [kɔ̃pɑ̃satwar] ADJ **1** *(qui équilibre)* compensatory, compensating **2** *Fin* compensatory

compensatrice [kɔ̃pɑ̃satris] *voir* **compensateur**

compenser [3] [kɔ̃pɑ̃se] VT **1** *(perte, défaut)* to make up for, to compensate for
2 *Jur* **c. les dépens** to order each party to pay its own costs
3 *Méd* to compensate, to counterbalance; *Psy* to compensate
4 *Tech & Phys* to balance
5 *Naut* to adjust, to correct
6 *Fin (dette, pertes financières)* to offset; *(chèque)* to clear
USAGE ABSOLU **1** *(racheter)* **pour c., je l'ai emmenée au théâtre** to make up for it, I took her to the theatre **2** *Psy* **elle mange pour c.** she eats for comfort
VPR **se compenser** to make up for one another

compère [kɔ̃pɛr] NM **1** *(complice ▸ d'un camelot)* accomplice; *(▸ d'un artiste)* stooge **2** *Fam Vieilli (camarade)* comrade, crony; **un bon c.** a pleasant companion

compère-loriot [kɔ̃pɛrlɔrjo] *(pl* **compères-loriots)** NM **1** *Orn* golden oriole **2** *Méd (sur la paupière)* sty, stye

compète [kɔ̃pɛt] NF *Fam* competition[□]; **faire de la c.** to enter competitions

compétence [kɔ̃petɑ̃s] NF **1** *(qualification, capacité)* competence; **faire qch avec beaucoup de c.** to do sth very competently; **j'ai des compétences en informatique** I am computer literate; **ses compétences en traduction** his/her skills as a translator; **avoir recours aux compétences d'un expert** to refer to an expert; **cela n'entre pas dans mes compétences, ce n'est pas de ma c.** *(cela n'est pas dans mes attributions)* this doesn't come within my remit; *(cela me dépasse)* that's beyond my competence; **compétences transférables** transferable skills **2** *Jur* jurisdiction; **c. d'attribution** subject matter jurisdiction *(in civil law)*; **c. civile** civil jurisdiction; **c. commerciale** commercial jurisdiction; **c. de droit commun** ordinary jurisdiction; **c. exclusive** exclusive jurisdiction; **c. générale** omnicompetence; **c. internationale** international jurisdiction; **c. matérielle** subject matter jurisdiction *(in criminal law)*; **c. nationale** national jurisdiction; **c. territoriale** jurisdiction

compétent, -e [kɔ̃petɑ̃, -ɑ̃t] ADJ **1** *(qualifié)* competent, skilful, skilled; *Jur* who has jurisdiction; **un ouvrier c.** a competent worker; **les gens compétents en la matière** *(qui savent)* people who know about *or Sout* are conversant with this topic; **seul le maire est c. en la matière** *(habilité)* only the mayor is competent to act *or* has jurisdiction in this matter **2** *(approprié ▸ service)* relevant; **les services compétents** the relevant departments, the departments concerned

compétiteur, -trice [kɔ̃petitœr, -tris] NM,F **1** *(rival)* rival **2** *Com & Sport* competitor

compétitif, -ive [kɔ̃petitif, -iv] ADJ competitive; **leurs produits sont très compétitifs** their products are highly competitive *or* very competitively priced

compétition [kɔ̃petisjɔ̃] NF **1** *(rivalité)* competition, competing; **j'ai horreur de la c.** I hate having to compete (with others) **2** *(niveau d'activité sportive)* competition; **faire de la c.** *(athlétisme)* to take part in competitive events; *Aut & Naut* to race; **j'arrête la c.** I'm giving up competing; **elle a le niveau c. en aviron** she's a top-level oarswoman **3** *(concours ▸ en athlétisme, en natation)* competition, event; *(▸ au tennis)* tournament; *Aut & Naut* competition, race; **c. sportive** sports competition, sporting event

• **de compétition** ADJ **des skis de c.** *(de descente)* racing skis; *(de fond)* eventing skis; **sport de c.** competitive sport

• **en compétition** ADJ competing, in competition

• **en compétition avec** PRÉP competing *or* in competition with

compétitive [kɔ̃petitiv] *voir* **compétitif**

compétitivité [kɔ̃pétitivite] NF competitiveness

compétitrice [kɔ̃petitris] *voir* **compétiteur**

compilateur, -trice [kɔ̃pilatœr, -tris] NM,F **1** *(auteur)* compiler **2** *Péj (plagiaire)* plagiarist
NM *Ordinat* compiler; **c. croisé** cross-compiler

compilation [kɔ̃pilasjɔ̃] NF **1** *(fait de réunir des textes)* compiling; *(ensemble de textes, de morceaux de musique)* compilation **2** *Péj (plagiat)* plagiarizing, synthesizing; *(ouvrage)* (mere) compilation *or* synthesis **3** *Ordinat* compilation

compilatrice [kɔ̃pilatris] *voir* **compilateur**

compiler [3] [kɔ̃pile] VT **1** *(réunir)* to compile **2** *Péj (sujet: plagiaire)* to borrow from **3** *Ordinat* to compile

complainte [kɔ̃plɛ̃t] NF **1** *Mus, Littérature & Littéraire* lament, plaint **2** *Jur* complaint

complaire [110] [kɔ̃plɛr] **complaire à** VT IND *Littéraire* to please
VPR **se complaire 1 se c. dans qch** to revel *or* to delight *or* to take pleasure in sth; **il se complaît dans son malheur** he wallows in his own misery **2 se c. à dire/faire qch** to take great pleasure in saying/doing sth

complaisamment [kɔ̃plezamɑ̃] **ADV 1** *(avec amabilité)* kindly, obligingly **2** *Péj (avec vanité)* smugly, complacently, with self-satisfaction

complaisance [kɔ̃plezɑ̃s] **NF 1** *(amabilité)* kindness, obligingness; **auriez-vous la c. de le faire?** would you be so good *or* so kind as to do it?, would you oblige me by doing it?; **avec c.** kindly, obligingly **2** *(vanité)* complacency, smugness, self-satisfaction; **avec c.** smugly, complacently; **il s'écoute avec c.** he likes the sound of his own voice; **un ton plein de c.** a self-satisfied *or* smug tone **3** *(indulgence ▸ des parents)* laxity, indulgence; *(▸ d'un tribunal, d'un juge)* leniency, indulgence; *(▸ d'un mari)* connivance

• **complaisances NFPL** favours

• **de complaisance ADJ sourire de c.** polite smile; **certificat** *ou* **attestation de c.** phoney certificate *(given to please the person concerned)*; *Com* **billet de c.** accommodation bill

• **par complaisance ADV** out of kindness

complaisant, -e [kɔ̃plezɑ̃, -ɑ̃t] **ADJ 1** *(aimable)* kind; *(serviable)* obliging, complaisant **2** *(vaniteux)* smug, self-satisfied, complacent; **prêter une oreille complaisante aux éloges** to lap up praise **3** *(indulgent ▸ parents)* lax, indulgent; *(▸ juge, tribunal)* indulgent, lenient; **elle a un mari c.** her husband turns a blind eye to her infidelities

complaisons *etc voir* **complaire**

complément [kɔ̃plemɑ̃] **NM 1** *(supplément)* **un c. d'information est nécessaire** further *or* additional information is required; **demander un c. d'enquête** to order a more extensive inquiry

2 *(reste)* rest, remainder; **voici 70 euros, vous aurez le c. ce soir** here's 70 euros, you'll get the remainder tonight; **si on manque de crème brûlée, on fera le c. avec des yaourts** if we don't have enough crème brûlée to go round, we'll give the rest of them yoghurts

3 *Méd* complement

4 *Math* complement

5 *Gram* complement; **c. (d'objet) direct/indirect** direct/indirect object; **c. d'agent** agent; **c. circonstanciel de temps** adverbial phrase of time

6 *Admin* **c. (de) retraite** supplementary pension

complémentaire [kɔ̃plemɑ̃tɛr] **ADJ 1** *(supplémentaire ▸ information)* additional, further

2 *(industries, couleurs)* complementary

3 *Ling & Math* complementary

4 *Écon* complementary

5 *Scol* **cours c.** ≃ secondary modern school

6 *Compta (écriture)* supplementary

NM *Math* complementary

complémentarité [kɔ̃plemɑ̃tarite] **NF** complementarity

COMPLET, -ÈTE [kɔ̃plɛ, -ɛt]

ADJ	
• complete **1, 5, 6**	• full **1–4**
• thorough **2**	• total **6**
• wholemeal **8**	
NM	
• suit	

ADJ 1 *(qui a tous ses éléments ▸ série, collection, parure)* complete, full; *(▸ œuvre)* complete; **la panoplie n'est pas complète** there's something missing from the set; *Com* **café/thé c.** continental breakfast with coffee/tea; **change c.** disposable *Br* nappy *or Am* diaper

2 *(approfondi ▸ compte-rendu, description)* full, comprehensive; *(▸ analyse, examen)* thorough, full; **une lecture complète du manuscrit** a thorough *or* an in-depth reading of the manuscript

3 *(entier)* full; **nous resterons un mois c.** we'll stay a full month; **le ticket est valable pour la journée complète** the ticket is valid for the whole day

4 *(bondé ▸ bus, métro, stade)* full; **c.** *(sur panneau ▸ à l'hôtel)* no vacancies; *(▸ au parking)* full; **nous sommes complets** *(salle de concert, théâtre, restaurant)* we're (fully) booked

5 *(parfait ▸ homme, artiste)* all-round *(avant n)*, complete; **un sportif c.** an all-round athlete

6 *(total, absolu ▸ silence)* total, absolute; *(▸ repos)* complete; *(▸ échec)* total; **ils vivent dans la pauvreté la plus complète** they live in utter *or* absolute *or* abject poverty; **un fiasco c.** a complete (and utter) disaster; **c'est c.!** that's all we needed!, that's the last straw!, that caps it all!

7 *(fournissant tout le nécessaire)* **la natation est un sport c.** swimming is an all-round sport; **le lait est un aliment c.** milk is a complete food, milk contains all the necessary nutrients

8 *Culin (pain, farine, spaghettis)* wholemeal; *(riz)* brown

NM *(vêtement)* (man's) suit

• **au (grand) complet ADJ** *(toute)* **l'équipe au c.** the whole team; **mes amis étaient là au c.** all my friends showed up; **j'attends que l'assistance soit au c. pour commencer** I'm waiting for everyone to arrive before I begin

complètement [kɔ̃plɛtmɑ̃] **ADV 1** *(totalement)* completely, totally; **une maison c. refaite** a completely renovated house; **c. nu** stark naked; **il n'est pas c. responsable** he's not wholly to blame **2** *(vraiment)* absolutely; **je suis c. d'accord** I absolutely *or* totally agree; **il est c. fou d'elle** he's absolutely mad about her

compléter [18] [kɔ̃plete] **VT 1** *(ajouter ce qui manque à ▸ collection, dossier)* to complete; *(▸ somme, remboursement)* to make up; **il a complété sa collection par un Van Gogh** he completed his collection with a painting by Van Gogh; **c. une gamme de produits** to add to a range of products

2 *(approfondir ▸ analyse, notes, formation)* to complete; *(▸ enquête)* to finish, to complete

3 *(constituer le dernier élément de)* to complete, to finish *or* to round off; **un index complète le guide** the guide is completed by an index; **pour c. le tout** to cap *or* to crown it all

4 *(remplir ▸ formulaire)* to complete, to fill in *or* out

VPR se compléter 1 *(emploi passif)* **ma collection se complète peu à peu** my collection will soon be complete **2** *(personnes, caractères)* to complement (one another); **le vin et le fromage se complètent parfaitement** wine complements cheese perfectly

complétif, -ive [kɔ̃pletif, -iv] **ADJ proposition complétive** noun clause

• **complétive NF** noun clause

complet-veston [kɔ̃plɛvɛstɔ̃] *(pl* **complets-vestons)** **NM** (man's) suit

complexe [kɔ̃plɛks] **ADJ 1** *(compliqué ▸ processus, trajet)* complicated; *(▸ caractère, personne)* complex, complicated; **pour des raisons complexes** for complex reasons **2** *Ling & Math* complex

NM 1 *(gêne)* hang-up; *Psy* complex; **avoir des complexes** to have a lot of hang-ups; **ça me donne des complexes** it's giving me a complex; **c. d'infériorité/de supériorité/d'Œdipe** inferiority/superiority/Oedipus complex **2** *Constr & Écon* complex; **c. hospitalier/industriel** medical/industrial complex; **un grand c. hôtelier** a large hotel complex; *Cin* **c. multisalles** multiplex (*Br* cinema *or Am* theater), multiscreen *Br* cinema *or Am* theater; **un c. sportif** a sports centre *or* complex; **un c. touristique** a *Br* holiday *or Am* vacation resort **3** *Chim & Math* complex

• **sans complexe(s) ADJ 1** *(simple)* natural **2** *Péj (sans honte)* uninhibited; **elle est sans c., celle-là!** she's so brazen! **ADV 1** *(sans manières)* quite naturally *or* simply, uninhibitedly **2** *Péj (avec sans-gêne)* uninhibitedly; **elle s'est ruée sur le buffet sans c.** she went straight for the buffet quite unashamedly

complexé, -e [kɔ̃plɛkse] **ADJ** hung up; **il est très c.** he's got a lot of hang-ups; **elle est complexée par son poids** she has a complex about her weight

complexer [4] [kɔ̃plɛkse] **VT 1** *(personne)* **arrête, tu vas le c.** stop, you'll give him a complex **2** *Chim* to unite into a complex

complexifier [9] [kɔ̃plɛksifje] **VT** to complicate, to make more complex

VPR se complexifier to become more complex

complexion [kɔ̃plɛksjɔ̃] **NF 1** *Littéraire (constitution)* constitution; **être de c. robuste/délicate** to have a healthy/delicate constitution **2** *Vieilli (caractère)* temperament, disposition **3** *Vieilli (teint)* complexion

complexité [kɔ̃plɛksite] **NF** complexity

complication [kɔ̃plikasjɔ̃] **NF 1** *(problème)* complication; **elle aime les complications** she likes things to be complicated; **pourquoi faire des complications?** why make things more complicated than they need be? **2** *(complexité)* complicatedness, complexity

• **complications NFPL** *Méd* complications; **s'il n'y a pas de complications, il s'en sortira** if no complications set in *or* arise, he'll pull through

complice [kɔ̃plis] **ADJ** *(regard, sourire, silence)* knowing; **être c. de qch** to be (a) party to sth

NMF 1 *(malfrat)* accomplice; **c'est un de leurs complices** he's in league with them **2** *(ami, confident)* partner, friend; **sa femme et c. de tous les instants** his wife and constant companion **3** *(dans un spectacle, un canular)* partner

complicité [kɔ̃plisite] **NF 1** *Jur* complicity; **il a été accusé de c. de meurtre** he was accused of being an accessory to murder; **avec la c. de qn** with the complicity of sb, with sb as an accomplice **2** *(entente, amitié)* complicity; **un sourire de c.** a knowing smile; **on sent une grande c. entre eux** there is clearly a deep bond between them; **nous avons retrouvé ce très vieux film avec la c. du réalisateur** we've unearthed this very old footage, with the kind help of the director

• **en complicité avec PRÉP** in collusion with

complies [kɔ̃pli] **NFPL** complin, compline

compliment [kɔ̃plimɑ̃] **NM 1** *(éloge)* compliment; **faire un c. à qn** to pay sb a compliment, to pay a compliment to sb; **on m'a fait des compliments sur mon soufflé** I was complimented on my soufflé

2 *(félicitations)* congratulations; **adresser des compliments au vainqueur** to congratulate the winner; *Ironique* **(je vous fais) mes compliments!** congratulations!, well done!

3 *(dans des formules de politesse)* compliment; **mes compliments à votre épouse** my regards to your wife; **avec les compliments de l'auteur** with the author's compliments; *aussi Hum* **(mes) compliments au chef!** my compliments to the chef!

4 *(discours)* congratulatory speech

complimenter [3] [kɔ̃plimɑ̃te] **VT 1** *(féliciter)* to congratulate; **c. qn sur son succès** to congratulate sb on *or* for having succeeded **2** *(faire des éloges à)* to compliment; **Julie m'a complimentée sur** *ou* **pour ma robe** Julie complimented me on my dress

complimenteur, -euse [kɔ̃plimɑ̃tœr, -øz] *Littéraire* **ADJ** obsequious

NM,F flatterer

compliqué, -e [kɔ̃plike] **ADJ 1** *(difficile à comprendre ▸ affaire, exercice, phrase)* complicated; *(▸ jeu, langue, livre, problème)* difficult; *(▸ plan)* intricate; **elle avait un nom c.** she had a real tongue-twister of a name; **c'est trop c. à expliquer** it's too hard to explain; **regarde, ce n'est pourtant pas c.!** look, it's not so difficult to understand!; *Fam* **ce n'est pas c., si tu ne viens pas je n'y vais pas non plus** it's quite simple, if you don't come I'm not going either

2 *(ayant de nombreux éléments ▸ appareil, mécanisme)* complicated, complex, intricate

3 *(qui manque de naturel ▸ personne)* complicated; *(▸ esprit)* tortuous

4 *Méd* **fracture compliquée** compound fracture

compliquer [3] [kɔ̃plike] **VT** to complicate, to make (more) difficult *or* complicated; **ça risque de c. les choses** that may *or* might well complicate matters; **il me complique la vie** he makes things *or* life difficult for me

VPR se compliquer *(devenir embrouillé ▸ gén)* to become (more) complicated; *(▸ intrigue d'une pièce, d'un film)* to thicken; **ça se complique!** things are getting complicated!, *Hum* the plot thickens!; **se c. la vie** *ou* **l'existence** make life difficult for oneself

complot [kɔ̃plo] **NM 1** *Pol* plot **2** *(menées)* plot, scheme; **mettre qn dans le c.** to let sb in on the plot

comploter [3] [kɔ̃plɔte] **VT** to plot; **qu'est-ce que vous complotez tous les deux?** what are you two plotting?, what are you two up to?

VI to be part of a plot; **punis pour avoir comploté** punished for their part in the plot; **c. de tuer qn** to conspire to kill sb, to plot sb's murder

comploteur, -euse [kɔ̃plɔtœr, -øz] **NM,F** plotter

complu, -e [kɔ̃ply] *pp voir* **complaire**

compo [kɔ̃po] **NF** *Fam Scol* **1** *(dissertation)* essay□; *(examen)* test□; *(plus important)* exam□ **2** typesetting□, composition□

componction [kɔ̃pɔ̃ksjɔ̃] **NF** **1** *(gravité affectée)* gravity, solemnity; **avec c.** with solemnity **2** *Rel* compunction, contrition

comportement [kɔ̃pɔrtəmɑ̃] **NM** **1** *(attitude)* behaviour; **elle a un c. très bizarre avec les enfants** her behaviour towards children is very strange, she behaves very strangely towards children
2 *Aut & Phys (d'un véhicule)* performance, behaviour; *(de pneus)* performance; *(d'une molécule)* behaviour; *Aut* **c. en courbe** *ou* **en virage** cornering (ability)
3 *Mktg* **c. d'achat** buying *or* purchasing behaviour; **c. de l'acheteur** buyer *or* purchaser behaviour; **c. du consommateur** consumer behaviour; **c. post-achat** post-purchase behaviour
4 *Bourse & Fin (du marché, des cours, des actions)* performance

comportemental, -e, -aux, -ales [kɔ̃pɔrtəmɑ̃tal, -o] **ADJ** **1** *(relatif à la façon d'être)* behaviour *(avant n)*, behavioural **2** *Psy* behaviourist

comporter [3] [kɔ̃pɔrte] **VT** **1** *(être muni de)* to have, to include; **l'immeuble ne comporte pas d'escalier de secours** the building doesn't have a fire escape
2 *(être constitué de)* to be made up *or* to consist of; **la maison comporte trois étages** it's a three-storey house
3 *(contenir)* to contain; **le reportage comporte des interviews inédites** the report contains original interviews
4 *(entraîner)* to entail, to imply; **tout métier comporte des inconvénients** every profession has its disadvantages; **elle a choisi l'aventure, avec tout ce que cela comporte de dangers** she chose to lead a life of adventure with all the risks it entailed
5 *(permettre, admettre)* to allow, to admit; **la règle comporte quelques exceptions** there are one or two exceptions to this rule
VPR se comporter **1** *(réagir ▸ personne)* to act, to behave; **tâche de bien te c.** try to behave (yourself *or* well); **il s'est très mal comporté** he behaved very badly; **se c. en enfant/en adulte** to act childishly/like an adult **2** *(fonctionner ▸ voiture, pneus)* to behave, to perform; *(▸ molécule)* to behave; **la voiture se comporte très bien sur verglas** the car handles very well on ice; *Bourse & Fin* **ses actions se sont bien comportées** his/her shares have performed well

composant, -e [kɔ̃pozɑ̃, -ɑ̃t] **ADJ** **1** *(qui constitue)* constitutive **2** *Ling* compound *(avant n)*
NM **1** *(élément)* component, constituent **2** *Constr, Ind & Ling* component; **c. de base** base component
• **composante** **NF** *(gén) & Math & Phys* component

composé, -e [kɔ̃poze] **ADJ** **1** *(formé d'un mélange ▸ bouquet, salade)* mixed
2 *(affecté ▸ attitude)* studied; **un visage c.** a studied look
3 *Bot (feuille)* compound; *(inflorescence)* composite; **fleur composée** composite (flower)
4 *Archit* composite
5 *Ling (temps)* compound *(avant n)*; **mot c.** compound (word)
6 *Chim, Écon & Math* compound *(avant n)*; *Chim* **corps c.** compound
NM **1** *(ensemble)* **c. de** mixture *or* blend *or* combination of **2** *Chim & Math* compound **3** *Ling* compound (word)
• **composée** **NF** composite (flower)
• **composées** **NFPL** *Bot* Compositae

composer [3] [kɔ̃poze] **VT** **1** *(rassembler pour faire un tout ▸ équipe, cabinet)* to form, to select (the members of); *(▸ menu)* to prepare, to put together; *(▸ bouquet)* to make up
2 *(écrire ▸ roman, discours)* to write; *(▸ poème, symphonie)* to compose; *(▸ programme)* to draw up, to prepare
3 *(faire partie de)* to (go to) make up; **les personnes qui composent le gouvernement** the politicians who make up the government; **être composé de** to be made up of, to consist of
4 *Chim (combiner)* to compound
5 *Littéraire (apprêter)* **c. son visage** to compose one's features
6 *(numéro de téléphone)* to dial; *(code)* to key (in)
7 *Typ* to set
VI **1** *(transiger)* to compromise; **entre époux, il faut c.** there must be a certain amount of give and take between husband and wife; **c. avec qn** to come to a compromise with sb **2** *Scol* to take an exam; **c. en histoire** to take a history test *or* exam **3** *Mus* **il compose** he writes music
VPR se composer **1** **se c. un visage de circonstance** to assume an appropriate expression **2** **se c. de** to be made up *or* composed of; **l'équipe se compose de onze joueurs** the team is made up of *or* comprises eleven players

composeur [kɔ̃pozœr] **NM** *Tél* **c. de numéros** dialler

composeuse [kɔ̃pozøz] **NF** typesetter *(machine)*

composite [kɔ̃pozit] **ADJ** **1** *(mobilier, population)* heterogeneous, mixed, composite; *(foule, assemblée)* mixed; **matériau c.** composite (material) **2** *Archit & Tech* composite
NM *Archit* composite order

compositeur, -trice [kɔ̃pozitœr, -tris] **NM,F** **1** *Mus* composer **2** *Typ* compositor, typesetter

composition [kɔ̃pozisjɔ̃] **NF** **1** *(fabrication, assemblage ▸ d'un produit, d'un plat, d'un menu)* making up, putting together; *(▸ d'un bouquet)* making up, arranging; *(▸ d'une équipe, d'une assemblée, d'un gouvernement)* forming, formation, setting up; *(▸ d'un portefeuille d'actions)* building up; **c. florale** flower arrangement
2 *(écriture ▸ d'une symphonie)* composition; *(▸ d'un poème, d'une lettre)* writing; *(▸ d'un programme)* drawing up
3 *(éléments ▸ d'une assemblée, d'un plat, d'un corps chimique)* composition; *(▸ d'un programme)* elements; **la c. des équipes n'est pas encore connue** the teams haven't been announced yet; **c.: eau, sucre, fraises** ingredients: water, sugar, strawberries
4 *Beaux-Arts & Phot (technique, résultat)* composition
5 *Typ* typesetting, composition
6 *Chim* composition
7 *Ling* compounding
8 *Scol (dissertation)* essay, composition; *(examen)* test, exam, paper; **c. française** French paper
• **à composition** **ADV** **amener qn à c.** to lead sb to a compromise; **arriver** *ou* **venir à c.** to come to a compromise
• **de bonne composition** **ADJ** accommodating, good-natured, easy-going
• **de composition** **ADJ** *(rôle)* character *(avant n)*
• **de ma/sa/***etc* **composition** **ADJ** **il a chanté une petite chanson de sa c.** he sang a little song he'd written; **je vais servir une ratatouille de ma c.** I'm going to serve my own version of ratatouille
• **de mauvaise composition** **ADJ** difficult

compositrice [kɔ̃positris] *voir* **compositeur**

compost [kɔ̃pɔst] **NM** compost

compostage [kɔ̃pɔstaʒ] **NM** **1** *(pour dater)* datestamping **2** *(pour valider)* punching **3** *Agr* composting

composter [3] [kɔ̃pɔste] **VT** **1** *(pour dater)* to date stamp **2** *(pour valider)* to punch **3** *Agr* to compost

composteur [kɔ̃pɔstœr] **NM** **1** *(dateur)* datestamp
2 *(pour valider)* ticket-punching machine
3 *Typ* composing stick
4 *Hort* composter, compost bin

compote [kɔ̃pɔt] **NF** *Culin* **c. (de fruits)** stewed fruit, compote; **c. de pommes** stewed apples, apple compote, *Am* applesauce
• **en compote** **ADJ** **1** *(fruits)* stewed **2** *Fam (meurtri, détruit)* smashed up; **j'ai les pieds en c.** my feet are killing me; **il a la figure en c.** his face has been beaten to a pulp

compotée [kɔ̃pɔte] **NF** *Culin* **c. d'oignons** stewed onions; **c. de chou** stewed cabbage

compotier [kɔ̃pɔtje] **NM** fruit bowl

compréhensibilité [kɔ̃preɑ̃sibilite] **NF** intelligibility, comprehensibility

compréhensible [kɔ̃preɑ̃sibl] **ADJ** **1** *(intelligible)* intelligible, comprehensible; **c. de** *ou* **par tous** easy for anyone to understand, comprehensible to everyone **2** *(excusable, concevable)* understandable; **c'est tout à fait c. de sa part** it's altogether understandable on his/her part

> Attention: ne pas confondre **comprehensible** et **understandable** lorsqu'on traduit **compréhensible**. Le terme anglais **comprehensible** signifie **intelligible**, alors que **understandable** signifie **concevable, qui se comprend.**

compréhensif, -ive [kɔ̃preɑ̃sif, -iv] **ADJ** **1** *(disposé à comprendre)* understanding **2** *Phil* comprehensive

> Il faut noter que l'adjectif anglais **comprehensive** est un faux ami. Il signifie le plus souvent **complet, exhaustif.**

compréhension [kɔ̃preɑ̃sjɔ̃] **NF** **1** *(fait de comprendre)* comprehension, understanding; **des notes nécessaires à la c. du texte** notes that are necessary to understand the text **2** *(bienveillance)* sympathy, understanding; **être plein de c.** to be very understanding **3** *Ling & Math* comprehension

compréhensive [kɔ̃preɑ̃siv] *voir* **compréhensif**

COMPRENDRE [79] [kɔ̃prɑ̃dr]

VT	
• to understand **A**	• to see **A5**
• to comprise **B1**	• to include **B2, 3**
USAGE ABSOLU	
• to see	
VPR	
• to be understandable **1**	• to understand one another **2**

VT A. 1 *(saisir par un raisonnement)* to understand, *Sout* to comprehend; **je ne comprends pas ce que vous voulez dire** I don't understand what you mean; **ce que je n'arrive pas à c. c'est…** what I can't work out is…; **elle n'a pas compris la plaisanterie** she didn't get the joke; **vous m'avez mal compris** you've misunderstood me; **on ne te comprend pas** *(tu ne parles pas clairement)* nobody can understand *or* make out what you say; **c'est simple, qu'y a-t-il à c.?** it's very obvious, what is there to understand?; **ne cherche pas, il n'y a rien à c.** don't even try to understand; **va y c. quelque chose!** YOU try to make head or tail of it!, *Am* go figure!; **dois-je c. que…?** am I to understand *or* do you mean to say that…?; **je n'y comprends rien** I can't make head nor tail of it, it makes no sense to me; **c'est à n'y rien c.** it's just baffling; **il ne comprend rien à rien** he hasn't a clue about anything; **(c'est) compris?** *(vous avez suivi?)* is it clear?, do you understand?; *(c'est un ordre)* do you hear me!; **(c'est) compris!** all right!, OK!; **faire c. qch à qn** *(le lui prouver)* to get sb to understand sth; *(l'en informer)* to give sb to understand sth; **je lui ai bien fait c. que tout était fini** I gave him to understand that it was all over; **est-ce que je me fais bien c.?** *(mon exposé est-il clair?)* is my explanation clear enough?; *(ton menaçant)* do I make myself clear?
2 *(saisir grâce à ses connaissances ▸ théorie, langue)* to understand; **elle comprend parfaitement le russe** she understands Russian perfectly; **je n'arrive pas à c. cette phrase** I can't make sense of this sentence; **je n'arrive pas à me faire c. en allemand** I can't make myself understood in German
3 *(saisir par une intuition)* to understand, to realize; **il a compris qu'il était condamné** he understood *or* realized he was doomed; **comprends-tu l'importance d'une telle décision?** do you realize how important a decision it is?; **je commence à c. où il veut en venir** I'm beginning to realize what he's after; *Fig* **il a vite compris son malheur** *ou* **sa douleur!** it didn't take him long to understand that he was in trouble!; **quand j'ai vu la pile de dossiers, j'ai compris mon malheur** *ou* **ma douleur!** when I saw that great pile of files, I realized what I had let myself in for!
4 *(admettre)* to understand; **je comprends qu'on s'énerve dans les bouchons** it's quite understand-

able that people get irritable when caught in traffic jams; **je ne comprends pas qu'elle ne m'ait pas appelé** I don't understand why she didn't call me; **je n'arrive toujours pas à c. ce qui lui a pris** I still can't figure out what got into him/her

5 *(concevoir)* to understand, to see; **c'est ainsi que je comprends le rôle** this is how I understand *or* see the part; **comment c. ce poème?** what is one to make of this poem?

6 *(avoir les mêmes sentiments que)* to understand, to sympathize with; **je ne le comprendrai jamais** I'll never understand him; **il faut la c.** you have to put yourself in her shoes; **je vous comprends, cela a dû être terrible** I know how you feel, it must have been awful; **je la comprends, avec un mari pareil!** I don't blame her with the sort of husband she's got!

7 *(apprécier)* to have a feeling for, to understand; **un public qui comprend l'art abstrait** an audience that understands abstract art; **il ne comprend pas la plaisanterie** he can't take a joke

B. 1 *(être composé entièrement de)* to be composed *or* made up of, to comprise, to consist of; **la maison comprend cinq pièces** the house consists of five rooms; **l'examen comprend trois parties** the exam comprises *or* contains *or* is made up of three (different) sections

2 *(être composé en partie de)* to include, to contain; **l'équipe comprend trois joueurs étrangers** there are three foreign players in the team

3 *(englober ▸ frais, taxe)* to include; **le prix comprend tous les frais d'hébergement** the price is fully inclusive of accommodation

4 *(au passif) (se situer)* **l'inflation sera comprise entre 5 pour cent et 8 pour cent** inflation will be (somewhere) between 5 percent and 8 percent; **la partie comprise entre la table et le mur** the section between the table and the wall

USAGE ABSOLU ah! je comprends! oh! I see!; **elle a fini par c.** she finally got the message; **elle comprend vite** she's quick on the uptake, she catches on quickly; *Hum* **il comprend vite mais il faut lui expliquer longtemps!** he's a bit slow on the uptake!; **je l'ai fait sans trop c.** I did it without really knowing what I was doing; **tu comprends?** you see?, you know?; **tu comprends, ce qui me plaît c'est de vivre à la campagne** you see, what I like is living in the country

VPR se comprendre 1 *(être compréhensible)* to be understandable; **c'est une réaction/un motif qui se comprend** it's an understandable response/motive; **ça se comprend** that's quite understandable

2 *(l'un l'autre)* to understand one another; **nous nous sommes mal compris** we failed to understand *or* we misunderstood each other

3 *Fam* **je me comprends!** I know what I'm getting at *or* trying to say (even if nobody else does)!

comprenette [kɔ̃prənɛt] **NF** *Fam* **il n'a pas la c. facile, il a la c. dure** he's a bit slow (on the uptake)

comprenne *etc voir* **comprendre**

comprenure [kɔ̃prənyr] **NF** *Belg & Can Fam* **être dur de c.** to be slow (on the uptake)

compresse [kɔ̃prɛs] **NF** compress, pack

compresser **[4]** [kɔ̃prese] **VT** to pack (tightly) in, to pack in tight; *Ordinat (données)* to compress; *(fichier)* to compact, to compress, to zip

compresseur [kɔ̃presœr] **NM 1** *Tech (d'un réfrigérateur)* compressor; *(d'un moteur)* supercharger; *Aut* **c. centrifuge** centrifugal compressor; *Aut* **c. à palettes** palette compressor; *Aut* **c. Roots** Roots blower; *Aut* **c. sur vilebrequin** crankshaft compressor **2** *(en travaux publics)* **(rouleau) c.** steamroller **3** *Ordinat* **c. de données** data compressor

compressibilité [kɔ̃presibilite] **NF 1** *Tech & Phys* compressibility **2** *Fig (flexibilité)* **cela dépend de la c. des dépenses** it depends on how much expenditure can be cut down *or* reduced

compressible [kɔ̃presibl] **ADJ 1** *Tech & Phys* compressible **2** *Fig (réductible)* reducible; **commençons par les dépenses compressibles** let's begin with expenses that can be cut down *or* reduced

compressif, -ive [kɔ̃presif, -iv] **ADJ** *(bandage, appareil)* compressive

compression [kɔ̃presjɔ̃] **NF 1** *Tech & Phys* compression; **temps de c.** compression stroke

2 *(des dépenses, du personnel)* reduction, cutting down; **procéder à une c. des effectifs** to cut down the workforce; **des compressions budgétaires** cuts *or* reductions in the budget

3 *Méd* compression

4 *Ordinat (de données)* compression; *(d'un fichier)* compacting, compression, zipping; **c. des caractères** digit compression

• **à compression (de vapeur)** **ADJ** compression *(avant n)*

• **de compression** **ADJ** *Tech (pompe)* compression *(avant n)*

compressive [kɔ̃presiv] *voir* **compressif**

comprimable [kɔ̃primabl] **ADJ** compressible

comprimé, -e [kɔ̃prime] **ADJ** compressed

NM tablet, pill

comprimer **[3]** [kɔ̃prime] **VT 1** *(serrer ▸ air, vapeur, gaz)* to compress; *(▸ objets)* to pack (in) tightly; *(▸ foin, paille)* to compact, to press tight; **cette robe me comprime la taille** this dress is much too tight for me around the waist

2 *(diminuer ▸ dépenses)* to curtail, to trim, to cut down; *(▸ effectifs)* to trim *or* to cut down

3 *(contenir ▸ colère, joie, rire)* to hold back, to suppress, to repress; *(▸ larmes)* to hold back

4 *Ordinat* to compress

5 *Méd* to compress

compris, -e [kɔ̃pri, -iz] **PP** *voir* **comprendre**

ADJ *(inclus ▸ service, boisson)* included; *(▸ dans les dates)* inclusive; **450 euros de loyer, charges comprises** 450 euros rent, all maintenance charges included; **ils vivent à cinq, l'oncle c.** the five of them live together, the uncle included; **service non c.** service not included, not inclusive of the service charge; **y c.** included, including; **je travaille tous les jours y c. le dimanche** I work every day including Sundays *or* Sundays included; **je serai parti du premier au 15 c.** I'll be away from the first to the 15th inclusive

EXCLAM *Aviat & Tél* OK!

• **tout compris** **ADV** net, all inclusive, *Br* all in; **on a payé 600 euros tout c.** we paid 600 euros all inclusive *or* all in

compromets *etc voir* **compromettre**

compromettant, -e [kɔ̃prɔmetɑ̃, -ɑ̃t] **ADJ** *(document, action)* incriminating; *(situation)* compromising

compromettre **[84]** [kɔ̃prɔmɛtr] **VT 1** *(nuire à la réputation de)* to compromise; **ils ont tenté de la c.** they tried to compromise her; **compromis par une cassette** compromised *or* incriminated because of a tape; **il est compromis dans l'affaire** he's implicated *or* involved in the affair **2** *(mettre en danger ▸ fortune, avenir, santé)* to put in jeopardy, to jeopardize; **s'il pleut, notre sortie est compromise** if it rains, our outing is unlikely to go ahead

VI *Jur* to compromise

VPR se compromettre *(risquer sa réputation)* to compromise oneself, to jeopardize one's reputation; *(s'impliquer)* to commit oneself; **il s'est compromis dans une affaire de fausses factures** he became implicated in a scandal involving falsified invoices

compromis, -e [kɔ̃prɔmi, -iz] **PP** *voir* **compromettre**

NM 1 *(concession)* compromise; *(moyen terme)* compromise (solution); **faire des c.** to make compromises; **trouver un c., parvenir à un c.** to reach *or* to come to a compromise; **cette robe est un c. entre élégance et décontraction** this dress is neither too elegant nor too casual **2** *Jur* **mettre une affaire en c.** to submit a case for arbitration; **c. de vente** provisional sale agreement **3** *Assur* **c. d'avarie** average bond

compromission [kɔ̃prɔmisjɔ̃] **NF** base action, (piece of) dishonourable behaviour; **elle est prête à n'importe quelle c. pour réussir** she will stoop to anything in order to succeed

compta [kɔ̃ta] **NF** *Fam* accounting▫, accounts▫

comptabilisation [kɔ̃tabilizasjɔ̃] **NF 1** *Compta* posting, entering in the accounts; **faire la c. de qch** to enter sth in the accounts **2** *(dénombrement)* counting

comptabiliser **[3]** [kɔ̃tabilize] **VT 1** *Compta* to post, to enter in the accounts **2** *(compter)* to count

comptabilité [kɔ̃tabilite] **NF 1** *(profession)* accountancy, accounting; **faire de la c.** to work as an accountant

2 *(comptes)* accounts, books; **passer qch en c.** to put sth through the books *or* the accounts; **tenir la c.** to keep the books *or* the accounts; **faire sa c.** to do one's books *or* bookkeeping; **ma c. est à jour** my books are *or* my bookkeeping is up-to-date

3 *(technique)* accounting, book-keeping; **c. analytique** cost accounting; **c. budgétaire** budgeting; **c. de caisse** cash basis accounting; **c. commerciale** business accounting; **c. d'exploitation** cost accounting; **c. financière** financial accounting; **c. générale** general accounts; **c. de gestion** management accounting; **c. informatisée** computerized accounts; **c. en partie double/simple** double-/single-entry bookkeeping; **c. de prix de revient** cost accounting

4 *(service, bureau)* accounts (department); **adressez-vous à la c.** apply to the accounts department

5 *Écon & Fin* **c. nationale** national auditing; **c. publique** public finance

comptable [kɔ̃tabl] **ADJ 1** *Fin* accounting *(avant n)*, book-keeping *(avant n)* **2** *Ling* count *(avant n)*, countable **3** *(responsable)* **être c. (à qn) de qch** to be accountable *or* answerable (to sb) for sth

NMF accountant; *Can* **c. agréé** *Br* chartered accountant, *Am* certified public accountant; **c. du Trésor public** Treasury official

comptage [kɔ̃taʒ] **NM** counting; **faire le c. de** to count

comptant [kɔ̃tɑ̃] **ADJ M je lui ai versé 100 euros comptants** I paid him/her 100 euros in cash

ADV cash; **payer c.** to pay (in) cash; **payer 50 euros c.** to pay 50 euros in cash; **acheter/vendre (qch) c.** to buy/to sell (sth) for cash

NM cash; **c. contre documents** cash against documents, CAD

• **au comptant** **ADV** cash; **acheter/vendre (qch) au c.** to buy/to sell (sth) for cash; **payable au c.** *(lors d'un achat) Br* cash *or Am* collect on delivery; *(sur présentation de titre, de connaissement)* payable on presentation

COMPTE [kɔ̃t]

NM
- counting, count **A1**
- account **B1, 3**
- total **A2**
- bill, check **B2**

NMPL
- accounts, accounting

NM A. *CALCUL, SOMME CALCULÉE* **1** *(opération)* counting; *Boxe* count; **faire le c. (de)** *(personnes)* to count (up); *(dépenses)* to add up; **ils ont fait le c. des absents** they counted (up) the number of people absent; **faites le c. vous-même** work it out (for) yourself; **quand on fait le c....** when you add it all up...; **le c., les comptes** calculation; *aussi Fig* **c. à rebours** countdown

2 *(résultat)* (sum) total; **j'ai le c.** I've got the right money; **je vous remercie, monsieur, le c. est bon** *ou* **y est!** thank you sir, that's right!; **il n'y a pas le c.** *(personnes)* they're not all here *or* there, some are missing; *(dépenses)* it doesn't add up; **ça ne fait pas le c.** it doesn't come to the right amount, it doesn't add up; **cela fait un c. rond** that makes it a (nice) round sum *or* figure; **cela ne fait pas un c. rond** it comes to an odd figure; **faire bon c.** to be generous (when serving), to give generous helpings; **comment fais-tu ton c. pour te tromper à chaque fois?** how do you manage to get it wrong every time?; **mais comment il a fait son c.?** but how did he make such a mess of it?; **vous êtes loin du c.** you're wide of the mark

3 *(avantage)* **j'y trouve mon c.** I do well out of it, it works out well for me; **il n'y trouvait pas son c., alors il est parti** *(il ne gagnait pas assez d'argent)* he wasn't doing well enough out of it, so he left; *(dans une relation)* he wasn't getting what he wanted out of it, so he left

4 *(dû)* **demander son c.** to ask for one's wages; **donner son c. à qn** to give sb (his/her) notice; **avoir son c. (de)** to have more than one's fair share *or* more than enough (of); **je n'ai pas mon c. de sommeil** I don't get all the sleep I need *or* enough sleep; **avoir eu son c. d'ennuis** to have had one's fair share of trouble; *Fam* **il a déjà son c.** *(il a beaucoup bu)* he's had quite enough to drink already[a]; **recevoir son c.** to get one's (final) wages; *Fam Fig* to get one's marching orders *or Br* the sack; **régler son c. à qn** to pay sb off; *Fam Fig* to give sb a piece of one's mind; **je vais lui régler son c.!** I'm going to give him/her a piece of my mind!; **régler ses comptes** *(mettre en ordre ses affaires)* to put one's affairs in order; **régler ses comptes avec qn** *(le payer)* to settle up with sb; *(se venger)* to settle one's *or* old scores with sb; *Fam* **son c. est bon** he's had it, he's done for

B. *DANS LE DOMAINE FINANCIER ET COMMERCIAL* **1** *(de dépôt, de crédit)* account; **avoir/ouvrir un c. chez qn** to have/to open an account with sb; **déposer un montant sur son c.** to pay a sum into one's account; **régler un c.** to settle an account; **c. d'abonnement** budget account; *Ordinat* **c. d'accès par ligne commutée** dial-up account; **c. bancaire** *ou* **en banque** *Br* bank *or Am* banking account; **c. de caisse d'épargne** savings account; **c. chèques** *Br* current *or Am* checking account; **c. chèque postal** = account held at the Post Office, *Br* ≃ giro account; **c. commercial** office *or* business account; **c. de compensation** clearing account; **c. conjoint** joint account; **c. de contrepartie** contra account; **c. courant** *Br* current *or Am* checking account; *Ordinat* **c. de courrier électronique** e-mail account; **c. crédit** budget account; **c. à découvert** overdrawn account; **c. de dépôt** deposit account; **c. de dépôt à vue** drawing account; **c. des dépenses et recettes** income and expenditure account; **c. d'épargne** savings account; **c. d'épargne en actions** share savings account, savings and investment account; **c. épargne logement** savings account *(for purchasing a property)*; **c. épargne temps** *(dans le cadre de la réduction du temps de travail)* = scheme which allows employees to save up the hours of overtime they accumulate under the "RTT" system for up to five years, eventually being compensated either financially or with additional holidays; **c. inactif** dead account; **c. individuel** personal account; **c. d'intermédiaire** nominee account; *Ordinat* **c. Internet** Internet account; **c. d'investissement** investment account; **c. joint** joint account; **c. (sur) livret** savings account; **c. numéroté** numbered account; **c. ouvert** open account; **c. permanent** *Br* credit account, *Am* charge account; **c. de prêt** loan account; **c. professionnel** business account; *Bourse* **c. propre** personal account; **c. rémunéré** interest-bearing account; **c. de réserve** reserve account; *Bourse* **c. à terme** forward account; **c. des ventes** sales account

2 *(facture)* bill, *Am* check; **mettez-le** *ou* **inscrivez-le à mon c.** charge it to my account; **régler un c.** *(payer)* to settle a bill; *(mettre au net une situation)* to clear the air; *(se venger)* to settle a score *or* an old score; **pour règlement de tout c.** *(sur facture)* in full settlement

3 *(bilan)* account; **c. accréditif** charge account; **c. d'achats** purchase account; **c. d'agence** agency account; **c. bloqué** frozen account, *Am* escrow account; **c. de caisse** cash account; **c. de capital** capital account; **c. centralisateur** central account; **c. de charges** expense account; **c. client** customer account; **c. créditeur** account in credit, credit balance; **c. débiteur** account in debit, debit balance; **c. définitif** final accounts; **c. d'exploitation** profit and loss form, P&L; **comptes fournisseurs** book debts; **c. de pertes et profits, c. de résultat** profit and loss account; **c. de produits** income account; **c. des recettes et des dépenses** revenue account; **c. de régularisation** *(de l'actif)* prepayments and accrued income; *(du passif)* accruals and deferred income; **c. de résultat prévisionnel** interim profit and loss account, *Am* interim income statement; **c. de stock** inventory account

C. *LOCUTIONS* **reprendre à son c.** *(magasin)* to take over in one's own name; *(idée, écrit)* to adopt; **être** *ou* **travailler à son c.** to be self-employed; **il est à son c. maintenant** he's his own boss now, he's set up on his own now; **se mettre** *ou* **s'installer à son c.** to set up in business on one's own (account); **à c. d'auteur** at the author's own expense; **passer** *ou* **porter une somme en c.** *(recette)* to credit a sum; *(dépense)* to debit a sum; **je suis en c. avec ton frère** I've got some business to settle with your brother; **demander des comptes à qn** to ask sb for an explanation, to call sb to account; **rendre des comptes (à qn)** to give *or* to offer (sb) an explanation; **je n'ai de comptes à rendre à personne** I don't owe anybody any explanations, I don't have to justify my actions to anybody; **je n'ai pas de comptes à vous rendre** I don't have to justify myself to you; **rendre c. de qch à qn** *(s'en expliquer)* to justify sth to sb; *(faire un rapport)* to give an account of sth to sb; **si vous rencontrez des difficultés, rendez-en c. au chef d'équipe** if you have any difficulties, report to the team leader; **il est venu nous rendre c. de l'accident** he came to give us an account of the accident; **devoir des comptes à qn** to be responsible *or* accountable to sb; **il ne te doit pas de comptes** he doesn't owe you any explanations; **prendre qch en c.** *(prendre en considération)* to take sth into account *or* consideration; **se rendre c. de qch/que** to realize sth/that; **je ne me rendais pas c. de l'effort que cela lui avait coûté** I hadn't realized *or* appreciated the effort he'd/she'd put into it; **on lui a collé une étiquette dans le dos mais il ne s'en est pas rendu c.** somebody stuck a label on his back but he didn't notice; **non mais, tu te rends c.!** *(indignation)* can you believe it?; **tenir c. de qch** to take account of sth, to take sth into account; **ne tenir aucun c. de qch** to take no notice of sth, to disregard sth; **elle n'a pas tenu c. de mes conseils** she took no notice of *or* ignored my advice; **c. tenu de** in view of, bearing in mind, taking into account

• **comptes** NMPL accounts, accounting; **faire/tenir les comptes** to do/to keep the accounts; **elle tient bien ses comptes** she keeps her accounts in good order; **j'ai mal fait mes comptes** I've made a mistake in my accounts; *Prov* **les bons comptes font les bons amis** = pay your debts and you'll keep your friends; **comptes annuels** annual accounts; **comptes approuvés** certified accounts; **comptes clients** accounts receivable, *Am* receivables; **comptes consolidés** consolidated accounts; **comptes de gestion** management accounts; **comptes intégrés** consolidated accounts; **comptes de résultats courants/exceptionnels** above-the-line/below-the-line accounts; **comptes semestriels** interim accounts; **comptes sociaux** company accounts; **comptes trimestriels** interim accounts; **comptes de valeur** real accounts

• **à bon compte** ADV *(acheter)* cheap, cheaply; **s'en tirer à bon c.** *(sans frais)* to manage to avoid paying a fortune; *(sans conséquences graves)* to get off lightly

• **à ce compte, à ce compte-là** ADV *(selon ce raisonnement)* looking at it *or* taking it that way

• **pour compte** ADV **laisser des marchandises pour c.** to leave goods on a merchant's hands

• **pour le compte** ADV for the count; **il est resté à terre pour le c.** he was out for the count

• **pour le compte de** PRÉP for; **elle travaille pour le c. d'une grande société** she works for a large company

• **pour mon/son/***etc* **compte** ADV for my/his/*etc* part, as for me/him/*etc*; **pour son c., il la trouvait antipathique** as for him, he thought she was unpleasant

• **sur le compte de** PRÉP **1** *(à propos de)* on, about, concerning; **on a dit bien des bêtises sur son c.** people talked a lot of nonsense about him/her **2** *(locution)* **mettre qch sur le c. de qn** to attribute *or* ascribe sth to sb; **mettre qch sur le c. de qch** to put sth down to sth; **je mets ses excentricités sur le c. de sa jeunesse** I put his/her eccentric behaviour down to his/her youth

• **tout compte fait, tous comptes faits** ADV **1** *(en résumé)* all in all, on balance, all things considered **2** *(après tout)* thinking about it, on second thoughts

compte-chèques, compte chèques [kɔ̃tʃɛk] *(pl* **comptes-chèques** *ou* **comptes chèques)** NM *Br* current *or Am* checking account; **c. postal** = account held at the Post Office, *Br* ≃ giro account

compte-clé [kɔ̃tkle] *(pl* **comptes-clés)** NM key account

compte-gouttes [kɔ̃tgut] NM INV dropper

• **au compte-gouttes** ADV very sparingly; **payer qn au c.** to pay sb off in dribs and drabs; **distribuer qch au c.** to dole sth out

COMPTER [3] [kɔ̃te]

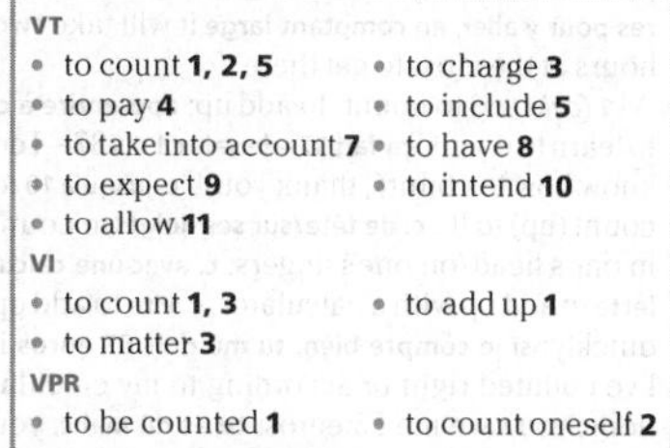

VT
- to count **1, 2, 5**
- to charge **3**
- to pay **4**
- to include **5**
- to take into account **7**
- to have **8**
- to expect **9**
- to intend **10**
- to allow **11**

VI
- to count **1, 3**
- to add up **1**
- to matter **3**

VPR
- to be counted **1**
- to count oneself **2**

VT 1 *(dénombrer ▸ objets, argent, personnes)* to count; **avez-vous compté l'argent de la caisse/les absents?** have you counted the money in the till/the people who are absent?; **il s'est mis à c. les billets** he started to count the notes; **on ne compte plus ses bévues** we've lost count of his/her mistakes; **j'ai compté qu'il restait 100 euros dans la caisse** according to my reckoning, there are 100 euros left in the till; **c. les heures/jours** *(d'impatience)* to be counting the hours/days; **on peut lui c. les côtes** he's/she's as thin as a rake; *Fam* **il m'a compté absent/présent** he marked me (down as) absent/present; *Fig* **c. les moutons** to count sheep; *aussi Fig* **c. les points** to keep score; **on peut les c. sur les doigts de la main** you can count them of the fingers of one hand; **il y a de cela 20 ans bien comptés** a good 20 years have passed since then

2 *(limiter)* to count (out); **le temps lui est compté, ses jours sont comptés** his/her days are numbered; **il ne comptait pas sa peine/ses efforts** he spared no pains/effort; **tu es toujours à c. tes sous!** you're always counting your pennies!

3 *(faire payer)* to charge for; **c. qch à qn** to charge sb for sth; **j'ai compté trois heures de ménage** I've charged for three hours' housework; **le serveur nous a compté trois euros de trop** the waiter has overcharged us by three euros, the waiter has charged us three euros too much

4 *(payer, verser)* to pay; **il m'a compté deux jours à 60 euros** he paid me (for) two days at 60 euros

5 *(inclure)* to count (in), to include; **dans le total nous n'avons pas compté le vin** wine has not been included in the overall figure

6 *(classer ▸ dans une catégorie)* **c. qn/qch parmi** to count sb/sth among, to number sb/sth among; **je compte ce livre parmi mes préférés** I count this book among my favourites

7 *(prendre en considération)* to take into account, to take account of; **on vous comptera vos années d'ancienneté** your length of service will be taken into account; **et je ne compte pas la fatigue!** and that's without mentioning the effort!

8 *(avoir ▸ membres, habitants)* to have; **notre musée compte quelques tableaux rares** our museum has *or* boasts several rare paintings; **la capitale compte deux millions d'habitants** the capital has two million inhabitants; **nous sommes heureux de vous c. parmi nous ce soir** we're happy to have *or* to welcome you among us tonight; **il compte beaucoup d'artistes au nombre de** *ou* **parmi ses amis** he can count many artists among his friends

9 *(s'attendre à)* to expect; **je compte recevoir les résultats cette semaine** I'm expecting the results this week

10 *(avoir l'intention de)* to intend; **c. faire qch** to intend to do sth, to mean to do sth, to plan to do sth; **que comptes-tu faire ce soir?** what are your plans for *or* what are you planning to do tonight?; **ils m'ont renvoyé – que comptes-tu faire maintenant?** I've been fired – what do you intend to do now?; **dis-lui ce que tu comptes faire** tell him what your intentions are *or* what you have in mind; **nous comptions aller en Grèce cet été** we'd planned to go to Greece this summer

11 *(prévoir)* to allow; **nous comptons une demi-bouteille de vin par personne** we allow half a bottle of wine per person; **il faut c. entre 15 et 20 euros pour un repas** you have to allow between 15 and 20 euros for a meal

12 *Sport (boxeur)* to count out

13 *Can (but)* to score

USAGE ABSOLU *(prévoir)* **c. juste** to skimp; **c. large** to be generous; **deux canards pour 10 personnes? c'est c. un peu juste!** two ducks between 10 people? that's cutting it a bit fine!; **il faudra deux heures pour y aller, en comptant large** it will take two hours at the most to get there

VI 1 *(calculer)* to count, to add up; **apprendre à c.** to learn to count; **ça fait 37 – je sais c.!** it's 37 – I do know how to count(, thank you)!; **c. jusqu'à 10** to count (up) to 10; **c. de tête/sur ses doigts** to count in one's head/on one's fingers; **c. avec une calculette** to add up with a calculator; **c. vite** to add up quickly; **si je compte bien, tu me dois 85 euros** if I've counted right *or* according to my calculations, you owe me 85 euros; **tu as dû mal c.** you must have got your calculations wrong, you must have miscalculated *or* miscounted

2 *(limiter ses dépenses)* to be careful (with money); **ils sont obligés de c. maintenant** they have to be careful with money now; **c'est quelqu'un qui n'a jamais compté** he has never been one to worry about money; **savoir c.** to be good at looking after one's money

3 *(importer)* to count, to matter; **ce qui compte, c'est ta santé/le résultat** the important thing is your health/the end result; **40 ans d'ancienneté, ça compte!** 40 years' service DOES count for something!; **une des personnes qui ont le plus compté dans ma vie** one of the most important people in my life; **tu comptes beaucoup pour moi** you mean a lot to me; **je prendrai ma décision seule! – alors moi, je ne compte pas?** I'll make my own decision! – so I don't count *or* matter, then?; **tu as triché, ça ne compte pas** you cheated, it doesn't count; **à l'examen, la philosophie ne compte presque pas** philosophy is a very minor subject in the exam; **c. double/triple** to count double/triple; **c. pour quelque chose/rien** to count for something/nothing; **et moi, je ne compte pour rien?** what about me then? don't I count for *or* mean anything?; *Fam* **c. pour du beurre** to count for nothing; **et moi, dans tout ça, je compte pour du beurre?** so I don't count, then?

4 *(figurer)* **c. parmi** to rank among, to be numbered among; **elle compte parmi les plus grands pianistes de sa génération** she is one of the greatest pianists of her generation

• **compter avec VT IND** to reckon with; **désormais, il faudra c. avec l'opposition** from now on, the opposition will have to be reckoned with; **dans une course, il faut toujours c. avec le vent** in a race, you always have to allow for the wind

• **compter sans VT IND** to fail to take into account, to fail to allow for; **il avait compté sans la rapidité de Jones** he had failed to take Jones's speed into account

• **compter sur VT IND** *(faire confiance à)* to count on, to rely on, to depend on; *(espérer ▸ venue, collaboration, événement)* to count on; **on ne peut pas c. sur lui** he can't be relied on, you can't count *or* rely *or* depend on him; **c'est quelqu'un sur qui tu peux c.** he's/she's a reliable person; **je compte sur son aide** I'm counting on his/her help; **ne compte pas trop sur la chance** don't count *or* rely too much on luck; **je vous le rendrai – j'y compte bien!** I'll give it back to you – I should hope so!; **je peux sortir demain soir? – n'y compte pas!** can I go out tomorrow night? – don't count *or* bank on it!; **compte sur lui pour aller tout répéter au patron!** you can rely on him to go and tell the boss everything!; **si c'est pour lui jouer un mauvais tour, ne comptez pas sur moi!** if you want to play a dirty trick on him/her, you can count me out!; **ne compte pas sur moi pour que j'arrange les choses!** don't count on me to patch things up!; *Fam Ironique* **compte là-dessus (et bois de l'eau fraîche)!** dream on!

VPR se compter 1 *(être compté)* to be counted; **les détournements de fonds se comptent par dizaines** there have been dozens of cases of embezzlement; **ses succès ne se comptent plus** his/her successes are innumerable *or* are past counting **2** *(se considérer)* to count *or* to consider oneself; *(s'inclure dans un calcul)* to count *or* to include oneself; **je ne me compte pas parmi les plus malheureux** I count myself as one of the luckier ones

• **à compter de PRÉP** as from, as of; **à c. du 7 mai** as from *or* of 7 May; **à c. de ce jour, nous ne nous sommes plus revus** from that day on, we never saw each other again

• **à tout compter ADV** all things considered, all in all

• **en comptant PRÉP** including; **il faut deux mètres de tissu en comptant l'ourlet** you need two metres of material including *or* if you include the hem

• **sans compter ADV** *(généreusement)* **donner sans c.** to give generously *or* without counting the cost; **dépenser sans c.** to spend money freely *or* like water; **se dépenser sans c.** to spare no effort **PRÉP** *(sans inclure)* not counting; *(sans parler de)* not to mention

• **sans compter que CONJ** quite apart from the fact that

• **tout bien compté ADV** all things considered, all in all

---

compte-titres [kɔ̃ttitr] *(pl* **comptes-titres***)* **NM** *Bourse* share account

compte-tours [kɔ̃ttur] **NM INV** rev counter, *Spéc* tachometer

compteur [kɔ̃tœr] **NM 1** *(appareil)* meter; *(affichage)* counter; **relever le c.** to read the meter; **mettre le c. à zéro** to set the counter on zero; **remettre le c. à zéro** to reset the counter; *Fig* **remettre les compteurs à zéro** to start from scratch, to go back to square one; **la voiture a 1000 kilomètres au c.** the car has 1,000 kilometres on the clock; **le c. marquait 16 euros** there was 16 euros on the meter; **c. à gaz/d'eau/d'électricité** gas/water/electricity meter; **c. Geiger** Geiger counter; **c. kilométrique** *Br* milometer, mileometer, *Am* odometer; **c. de vitesse** speedometer **2** *Ordinat* counter

comptine [kɔ̃tin] **NF** *(chanson)* nursery rhyme; *(formule)* counting-out rhyme

comptoir [kɔ̃twar] **NM 1** *(bar)* bar; **j'ai pris un café au c.** I had a coffee at the bar *or* counter

2 *Com (table)* counter, desk; **c. d'enregistrement** check-in desk; **c. d'information** information desk; **c. de réception** reception desk; **c. de vente** sales counter

3 *Hist* trading post

4 *Écon* trading syndicate

5 *Banque* bank branch; **c. d'escompte** discount house

6 *Suisse (foire)* fair *(where items are exhibited and sold)*

7 *Can* **c. de cuisine** *Br* worktop, *Am* kitchen counter

comptoir-caisse [kɔ̃twarkɛs] *(pl* **comptoirs-caisses***)* **NM** cash desk

compulser [3] [kɔ̃pylse] **VT** to consult, to refer to

compulsif, -ive [kɔ̃pylsif, -iv] **ADJ** *Psy* compulsive

compulsion [kɔ̃pylsjɔ̃] **NF** *Psy* compulsion

compulsive [kɔ̃pylsiv] *voir* **compulsif**

computation [kɔ̃pytasjɔ̃] **NF** computation (of time)

comte [kɔ̃t] **NM** count; *(en Grande-Bretagne)* earl

comté [kɔ̃te] **NM 1** *(territoire d'un comte)* earldom

2 *(division géographique)* county

3 *(fromage)* Comté (cheese)

4 *Can Pol* riding

comtesse [kɔ̃tɛs] **NF** countess

con, conne [kɔ̃, kɔn] **ADJ** *très Fam* **1** *(stupide) Br* bloody *or Am* goddamn stupid; *(irritant) Br* bloody *or Am* goddamn infuriating; **il est pas c.!** he's no fool!; **c'est pas c.!** that's pretty clever!; **qu'est-ce qu'elle est c.** *ou* **conne!** she's so *Br* bloody *or Am* goddamn stupid!; **c. comme un balai** *ou* **la lune** *ou* **un manche** *Br* daft as a brush, *Am* dumb as they come; **se retrouver tout c.** to look an idiot, to end up looking stupid **2** *(regrettable)* silly, stupid; **c'est vraiment c. que t'aies pas pu le prévenir!** it's really stupid that you weren't able to let him know in time!

NM,F *très Fam (imbécile) Br* arsehole, *Am* asshole; **pauvre c.!** you complete *Br* arsehole *or Am* asshole!; **pauvre conne!** silly bitch *or Br* cow!; **bande de cons!** what a bunch of *Br* arseholes *or Am* assholes!; **quel c., ce mec!** what a stupid bastard that guy is!; **le roi des cons** a complete and utter jerk; **jouer au c., faire le c.** *Br* to arse around, *Am* to screw around; *(faire semblant de ne pas comprendre)* to act dumb; **fais pas le c., ça va s'arranger** don't do anything stupid, it'll sort itself out; **fais pas le c. avec ce rasoir!** put that *Br* bloody *or Am* goddamn razor down!

NM *Vulg (sexe)* cunt

• **à la con ADJ** *très Fam* **1** *(stupide) Br* bloody *or Am* goddamn stupid; **c'est une histoire à la c.** it's a *Br* bloody *or Am* goddamn stupid story **2** *(de mauvaise qualité)* crappy, lousy; **j'en ai ras le bol de cette bagnole à la c.!** I'm fed up with this *Br* bloody *or Am* goddamn car!

conard [kɔnar] = **connard**

conasse [kɔnas] = **connasse**

concassage [kɔ̃kasaʒ] **NM** *(de la pierre, du sucre)* crushing, pounding; *(du poivre)* grinding

concasser [3] [kɔ̃kase] **VT** *(pierre, sucre)* to crush, to pound; *(poivre)* to grind

concasseur [kɔ̃kasœr] **ADJ M** crushing; **cylindre c.** crushing cylinder

NM crusher

concaténation [kɔ̃katenasjɔ̃] **NF** concatenation

concaténer [18] [kɔ̃katene] **VT** *Ordinat* to concatenate

concave [kɔ̃kav] **ADJ** concave

concavité [kɔ̃kavite] **NF 1** *(fait d'être concave)* concavity **2** *(creux)* hollow, cavity

concédant [kɔ̃sedɑ̃] **NM** *Fin* grantor

concéder [18] [kɔ̃sede] **VT 1** *(donner ▸ droit, territoire)* to concede, to grant; **on leur a concédé des terres** they were granted some land **2** *(admettre)* to admit, to grant; **je concède que j'ai tort** I admit that I'm wrong; **je te concède ce point** I grant you that point; **elle parle bien, ça je te le concède** I must admit that she's a good speaker, she's a good speaker, I grant you **3** *Sport (point, corner)* to concede, to give away

concélébrer [18] [kɔ̃selebre] **VT** to concelebrate

concentration [kɔ̃sɑ̃trasjɔ̃] **NF 1** *(attention)* **c. (d'esprit)** concentration; **l'exercice nécessite une grande c.** the exercise requires great concentration; **faire un effort de c.** to try to concentrate; **elle fait des erreurs par manque de c.** she makes mistakes because she doesn't concentrate enough

2 *(rassemblement)* concentration; **pour éviter la c. de tous les pouvoirs chez un seul homme** to make sure that all power isn't concentrated in the hands of one man; **une zone à haute c. de population** a high-density area; **c. urbaine** conurbation

3 *Chim, Culin & Pharm* concentration; **augmenter la c. en sucre d'un sirop** to increase the sugar content of a syrup

4 *Écon* concentration; **c. horizontale/verticale** horizontal/vertical concentration

concentrationnaire [kɔ̃sɑ̃trasjɔnɛr] **ADJ 1** *Hist* **l'univers c.** life in the (concentration) camps; **l'horreur c.** the horror of the (concentration) camps **2** *(rappelant les camps)* concentration camp-like

concentré, -e [kɔ̃sɑ̃tre] **ADJ 1** *(attentif)* **je n'étais pas assez c.** I wasn't concentrating hard enough **2** *Chim, Culin & Pharm* concentrated **3** *(concis ▸ style)* compact, taut

NM 1 *(de jus de fruit)* concentrate; **c. de tomate** tomato purée **2** *(de parfum)* extract **3** *(résumé)* summary, *Péj* boiled-down version

concentrer [3] [kɔ̃sɑ̃tre] **VT 1** *(rassembler ▸ troupes, foule, élèves)* to concentrate, to mass; **c'est là que l'on a concentré les malades** this is where all the sick people have been gathered together

2 *(intérêt, efforts)* to concentrate, to focus; **c. (toute) son attention sur** to concentrate (all) one's attention on

3 *Chim, Culin & Pharm* to concentrate

4 *Opt* to focus

VPR se concentrer 1 *(être attentif)* to concentrate; **la radio m'empêche de me c.** the radio is preventing me from concentrating *or* is ruining my concentration; **se c. sur qch** to concentrate *or* to focus on sth **2** *(se réunir ▸ foule)* to gather, to cluster, to concentrate; **la population se concentre de plus en plus dans les grandes villes** the population is concentrating more and more in the big cities **3** *(se canaliser)* to be concentrated *or* focused; **se c. sur un seul problème** to concentrate on a single issue

concentrique [kɔ̃sɑ̃trik] **ADJ** concentric

concentriquement [kɔ̃sɑ̃trikmɑ̃] **ADV** concentrically

concept [kɔ̃sɛpt] **NM** concept, notion; **c. publicitaire** advertising concept

concepteur, -trice [kɔ̃sɛptœr, -tris] **NM,F** designer; **c'est plutôt un c. qu'un gestionnaire** he's more of an ideas man than a manager; **c. graphiste** graphics designer; **c. multimédia** multimedia designer; **c. rédacteur** copywriter; *Ordinat* **c. de sites Web** web designer

conception [kɔ̃sɛpsjɔ̃] **NF 1** *(notion)* idea, concept, notion; **sa c. du socialisme** his/her idea of socialism; **nous avons la même c. des choses** we see things the same way; **elle a une c. originale de la vie** she has a unique way of looking at life **2** *Biol* conception **3** *(élaboration ▸ gén)* design; **produit de c. française** French-designed product; *Ordinat* **c. assistée par ordinateur** computer-aided *or* computer-assisted design; **c. graphique** graphic design; **c. du produit** product design

conceptrice [kɔ̃sɛptris] *voir* **concepteur**

conceptualisation [kɔ̃sɛptɥalizasjɔ̃] **NF** conceptualization

conceptualiser [3] [kɔ̃sɛptɥalize] **VT** to conceptualize

conceptuel, -elle [kɔ̃sɛptɥɛl] **ADJ** conceptual

concernant [kɔ̃sɛrnɑ̃] **PRÉP 1** *(relatif à)* concerning, regarding; **pour toutes questions c. nos nouveaux produits** for all questions concerning *or* regarding *or* relating to our new products **2** *(à propos de)* regarding, with regard to; **c. la réduction des impôts, voilà ce qu'il a dit** regarding *or* with regard to taxes, this is what he said

concerner [3] [kɔ̃sɛrne] **VT** to concern; **écoute un peu, cette discussion te concerne** listen, this discussion has implications for you *or* concerns you; **cette histoire ne nous concerne pas** this business doesn't concern us *or* is of no concern to us *or* is no concern of ours; **les salariés concernés par cette mesure** the employees concerned *or* affected by this measure; **veuillez passer me voir pour affaire vous concernant** please come and see me to discuss a matter which concerns *or* involves you; **se sentir concerné** to feel involved; **il ne se sent pas concerné** he's indifferent

• **en ce qui concerne PRÉP** concerning, as regards; **en ce qui me/le concerne** as far as I'm/he's concerned, from my/his point of view, as for me/him

concert [kɔ̃sɛr] **NM 1** *Mus* concert; **c. rock/de musique classique** rock/classical (music) concert; **aller au c.** to go to a concert; **il faut les voir en c.** you have to see them in concert *or* on stage **2** *Fig (ensemble)* chorus; **c. de louanges/protestations/sifflets** chorus of praises/protests/whistles **3** *(entente)* entente; **le c. des nations africaines** the entente between African nations

• **de concert ADV** together, jointly; **agir de c. avec qn** to act jointly *or* in conjunction with sb

concertant, -e [kɔ̃sɛrtɑ̃, -ɑ̃t] **ADJ** concertante

concertation [kɔ̃sɛrtasjɔ̃] **NF 1** *(dialogue)* dialogue; **une plus grande c. entre les pays industrialisés serait désirable** a greater dialogue between the industrialized countries would be welcome **2** *(consultation)* consultation; **sans c. préalable avec les syndicats** without consulting the unions

concerté, -e [kɔ̃sɛrte] **ADJ** *(plan, action)* concerted, joint

concerter [3] [kɔ̃sɛrte] **VT** to plan *or* to devise jointly

VPR se concerter to consult each other, to confer; **ils se concertèrent sur les moyens d'action** they consulted each other as to how to act

concertina [kɔ̃sɛrtina] **NM** *Mus* concertina

concertiste [kɔ̃sɛrtist] **NMF 1** *(gén)* concert performer *or* artist **2** *(soliste)* soloist *(in a concerto)*

concerto [kɔ̃sɛrto] **NM** concerto

concert-promenade [kɔ̃sɛrprɔmnad] *(pl* **concerts-promenades)** **NM** promenade concert

concessif, -ive [kɔ̃sesif, -iv] *Gram* **ADJ** concessive

• **concessive NF** concessive clause

concession [kɔ̃sesjɔ̃] **NF 1** *(compromis)* concession; **faire des concessions** to make concessions; **c'est un homme sans c.** he's an uncompromising man

2 *Jur (d'un privilège, d'un droit)* concession; **faire la c. d'un terrain à** to grant a piece of land to; **accorder une c. à** to grant a concession to; **retirer une c. à** to withdraw a concession from; **c. exclusive** tied outlet; **c. de franchise** grant of franchise; **c. immobilière** = concession of land for a minimum of 20 years; **c. de licence** licensing

3 *Com (dans l'automobile)* dealership

4 *(terrain)* concession; **c. funéraire** burial plot; **c. minière/pétrolière** mining/oil concession; **c. à perpétuité** plot held in perpetuity

• **de concession ADJ** *Gram* concessive

concessionnaire [kɔ̃sesjɔnɛr] **ADJ** concessionary

NMF 1 *Jur (détenteur ▸ d'une licence)* licensee; *(▸ d'une franchise)* franchisee **2** *Com* agent, dealer; **renseignez-vous auprès de votre c. (automobile)** see your (car) dealer; **c. agréé** approved dealer, authorized dealer; **c. exclusif** sole agent, sole dealer; **c. export** export agent

concessive [kɔ̃sesiv] *voir* **concessif**

concevable [kɔ̃səvabl] **ADJ** conceivable

concevoir [52] [kɔ̃səvwar] **VT 1** *(avoir une notion de)* to conceive of, to form a notion of; **c. l'infini** to form a notion of infinity

2 *(imaginer)* to imagine, to conceive of; **je ne conçois pas de repas sans vin** I can't imagine a meal without wine; **je ne conçois pas de ne jamais le revoir** I can't accept that I'll never see him again

3 *(comprendre)* to understand, to see; **c'est ainsi que je conçois l'amour** this is my idea of love *or* how I see love; **cela vous est difficile, je le conçois** I can (well) understand that it's difficult for you; **c. qch comme** to conceive *or* to see sth as

4 *Littéraire (ressentir ▸ haine, amitié)* to conceive, to develop; **il en conçut une vive amertume** he felt very bitter about it

5 *(créer ▸ meuble, décor, ouvrage)* to design; *(▸ plan, programme)* to conceive, to devise, to think up; **parc bien/mal conçu** well-/poorly-designed garden

6 *(rédiger ▸ message, réponse)* to compose, to couch; **une lettre conçue en ces termes** a letter written as follows *or* couched in the following terms

7 *Biol* to conceive

USAGE ABSOLU 1 la faculté de c. the ability to think **2** *(avoir des enfants)* to conceive; **les femmes qui ne peuvent pas c.** women who cannot have children *or* conceive

VPR se concevoir to be imagined; **une telle politique se conçoit en temps de guerre** such a policy is understandable in wartime; **cela se conçoit facilement** that is easy to understand *or* easily understood

conchyliculture [kɔ̃kilikyltyr] **NF** shellfish breeding

concierge [kɔ̃sjɛrʒ] **NMF 1** *(gardien ▸ d'immeuble)* caretaker, *Am* janitor; *(▸ en France)* concierge; *(▸ d'hôtel)* doorman; *(▸ d'une école)* caretaker, *Am & Scot* janitor **2** *Fam Péj (bavard)* gossip, blabbermouth; **c'est une vraie c.** she's a terrible gossip

conciergerie [kɔ̃sjɛrʒəri] **NF 1** *(loge)* caretaker's office, *Am* janitor's lodge **2** *Hist* **la C.** the Conciergerie prison *(in Paris)*

concile [kɔ̃sil] **NM** council; **c. œcuménique** ecumenical council; **le c. de Trente** the Council of Trent

conciliable [kɔ̃siljabl] **ADJ** reconcilable, compatible; **les études sont-elles conciliables avec le métier de chanteur?** is studying compatible with a singing career?; **des principes difficilement conciliables** principles difficult to reconcile

conciliabule [kɔ̃siljabyl] **NM 1** *(conversation)* confab; **les enfants étaient en grand c.** the children were having a big confab **2** *Arch (réunion)* secret meeting, secret assembly

conciliaire [kɔ̃siljɛr] **ADJ** conciliar

conciliant, -e [kɔ̃siljɑ̃, -ɑ̃t] **ADJ** *(personne)* conciliatory, accommodating; *(paroles, ton)* conciliatory, placatory

conciliateur, -trice [kɔ̃siljatœr, -tris] **ADJ** conciliatory, placatory

NM,F conciliator, arbitrator

conciliation [kɔ̃siljasjɔ̃] **NF 1** *(médiation)* conciliation; **esprit de c.** spirit of conciliation; **geste de c.** conciliatory gesture **2** *Jur* conciliation, arbitration; **comité de c.** arbitration committee **3** *Littéraire (entre deux personnes, deux partis)* reconciliation

conciliatoire [kɔ̃siljatwar] **ADJ** conciliatory

conciliatrice [kɔ̃siljatris] *voir* **conciliateur**

concilier [9] [kɔ̃silje] **VT 1** *(accorder ▸ opinions, exigences)* to reconcile; **c. travail et plaisir** to manage to combine work with pleasure **2** *(gagner ▸ faveurs, sympathie)* to gain, to win; **sa droiture lui a concilié l'admiration de tous les employés** his/her uprightness won *or* gained him/her the admiration of all the employees

VPR se concilier 1 *(être compatible)* to go together **2 se c. l'amitié de qn** to gain *or* to win sb's friendship; **se c. les électeurs** to win the voters over

concis, -e [kɔ̃si, -iz] **ADJ** *(style)* concise, tight; *(écrivain)* concise; **de manière concise** concisely; **soyez plus c.** come to the point

concision [kɔ̃sizjɔ̃] **NF** concision, conciseness, tightness; **avec c.** concisely; **style d'une extrême c.** extremely concise *or* tight style

concitoyen, -enne [kɔ̃sitwajɛ̃, -ɛn] **NM,F** fellow citizen

conclave [kɔ̃klav] **NM** conclave

concluant, -e [kɔ̃klyɑ̃, -ɑ̃t] **ADJ** *(essai, démonstration)* conclusive; **peu c.** inconclusive

conclure [96] [kɔ̃klyr] **VT 1** *(terminer ▸ discussion, travail)* to end, to conclude, to bring to a close *or* conclusion; *(▸ repas)* to finish *or* to round off **2** *(déduire)* to conclude; **que peut-on c. de cette expérience?** what conclusion can be drawn from this experience?; **n'ayant pas eu de réponse, j'en conclus que...** not having had an answer I conclude that... **3** *(accord)* to conclude; *(contrat)* to enter into, *Br* to conclude; *(traité)* to sign, to conclude; *(vente)* to close, to complete; **c. un marché** to strike *or* make a deal; **marché conclu!** it's a deal!

USAGE ABSOLU 1 *(terminer)* **c. par** to end *or* to conclude with; **elle a conclu par un appel à l'unité** she ended with a call for unity; **maintenant, vous devez c.** now you must come to a conclusion; **il faut savoir c.** you've got to know when to stop **2** *Fam (en matière amoureuse)* to get a result, to close the deal; **ce soir, je sens que je vais c.!** I'm going to close the deal tonight, I can feel it!

VI *Jur* **les témoignages concluent contre lui/en sa faveur** the evidence goes against him/in his favour

• **conclure à VT IND ils ont dû c. au meurtre** they had to conclude that it was murder; **le jury a conclu au suicide** the jury returned a verdict of suicide

• **pour conclure ADV** as a *or* in conclusion, to conclude

conclusion [kɔ̃klyzjɔ̃] **NF 1** *(fin)* conclusion **2** *(déduction)* conclusion; **nous en sommes arrivés à la c. suivante** we came to *or* reached the following conclusion; **gardons-nous des conclusions hâtives** let's not jump to conclusions; **tirer une c. de qch** to draw a conclusion from sth; *Fam* **c., la voiture est fichue** the upshot is that the car's a write-off[□] **3** *(d'un accord)* conclusion; *(d'un contrat)* entering into, *Br* conclusion; *(d'un traité)* signing, conclusion; *(d'un cessez-le-feu)* agreement; *(d'une vente)* closing, completion; *(d'un marché)* agreement; **la c. d'un accord de cessez-le-feu** the signing of a ceasefire agreement

• **conclusions NFPL** *(d'un rapport, d'une enquête)* findings; *Jur* submissions; **déposer** *ou* **signifier des conclusions** to file submissions with a court; **conclusions récapitulatives** final submissions, summation; **conclusions subsidiaires** accessory claims

• **en conclusion** ADV as a *or* in conclusion, to conclude

concocter [3] [kɔ̃kɔkte] VT to concoct

conçois *etc voir* **concevoir**

conçoivent *etc voir* **concevoir**

concombre [kɔ̃kɔ̃br] NM **1** *Bot* cucumber **2** *Can Fam Péj* idiot, twit **3** *Ich* **c. de mer** sea cucumber

concomitamment [kɔ̃kɔmitamɑ̃] ADV concomitantly

concomitance [kɔ̃kɔmitɑ̃s] NF concomitance

concomitant, -e [kɔ̃kɔmitɑ̃, -ɑ̃t] ADJ concomitant, attendant

concordance [kɔ̃kɔrdɑ̃s] NF **1** *(conformité)* agreement, similarity; **la c. des empreintes/dates** the similarity between the fingerprints/dates

2 *Gram* **c. des temps** sequence of tenses

3 *Géol* conformability

4 *(index)* concordance

• **en concordance avec** PRÉP in agreement *or* keeping *or* accordance with

concordant, -e [kɔ̃kɔrdɑ̃, -ɑ̃t] ADJ **1** *(correspondant)* **les versions sont concordantes** the stories agree *or* match **2** *Géol* conformable

concordat [kɔ̃kɔrda] NM **1** *Rel* concordat **2** *Jur* scheme of composition *or* arrangement

concorde [kɔ̃kɔrd] NF *Littéraire* concord, harmony

concorder [3] [kɔ̃kɔrde] VI *(versions, chiffres)* to agree, to tally; *(groupes sanguins, empreintes)* to match; **faire c. qch et** *ou* **avec qch** to make sth and sth agree

concourant, -e [kɔ̃kurɑ̃, -ɑ̃t] ADJ **1** *Géom* **droites concourantes** concurrent *or* convergent lines **2** *(actions, volontés)* joint, concerted, united

concourir [45] [kɔ̃kurir] VI **1** *(être en compétition)* to compete; **elle a refusé de c. cette année** she has refused to enter competitions *or* to compete this year; **c. avec qn** to compete with *or* against sb **2** *Géom* to converge **3** *Jur* to have concurrent claims

• **concourir à** VT IND to contribute to; **beaucoup de facteurs ont concouru à sa réussite** a number of factors contributed to his/her success; **tout concourt à me faire croire qu'il ment** everything leads me to believe that he's lying

concours [kɔ̃kur] NM **1** *(aide)* aid, help, support; **prêter son c. à** to lend one's support to; **grâce au c. du maire** thanks to the mayor's help *or* support; **c. financier** financial aid

2 *(combinaison)* **un heureux/un fâcheux c. de circonstances** a lucky/an unfortunate coincidence

3 *(épreuve)* competition, contest; **c. de beauté/de chant** beauty/singing contest; **c. agricole/hippique** agricultural/horse show

4 *Scol & Univ* competitive (entrance) exam; **le c. d'entrée à l'ENA** the entrance exam for the "ENA"; **c. interne/externe** in-house *or* internal/open competition; **c. administratifs** = examinations for entry into administrative posts in the government or civil service; **c. de la fonction publique** = examinations for entry into government or civil service jobs, including teaching; **le c. général** = competition in which the best pupils in the two upper forms at French "lycées" compete for prizes in a variety of subjects

5 *Arch & Littéraire (de personnes)* concourse, gathering

• **avec le concours de** PRÉP with the participation of, in association with

• **par concours, sur concours** ADV *(recruter, entrer)* on the results of a competitive entrance exam

CONCOURS

Unlike an ordinary examination, passing a "concours" does not lead to a degree, but rather to a teaching post in the state education system (for example the "CAPES" and "agrégation"), an appointment or promotion in the civil service, or a place in a "Grande École" ("ENA", "Centrale", "ENS" etc). "Concours" are extremely competitive examinations, and the quota of successful candidates is determined in advance. They are usually held over a period of several days, and comprise a series of written and oral examinations requiring a high level of preparation.

concouru [kɔ̃kury] *pp voir* **concourir**

concret, -ète [kɔ̃krɛ, -ɛt] ADJ **1** *(palpable)* concrete

2 *(non théorique)* concrete, practical; **faire des propositions concrètes** to make concrete *or* practical proposals; **je veux des résultats concrets** I want concrete *or* tangible results; **cas c.** actual case, concrete example

3 *(s'appuyant sur l'expérience)* concrete, empirical, experiential; **un esprit c.** a practical mind

4 *Ling & Mus* concrete

NM **le c.** that which is concrete, the concrete; **ce qu'il nous faut, c'est du c.** we need something we can get our teeth into

concrètement [kɔ̃krɛtmɑ̃] ADV concretely, in concrete terms; **je ne vois pas c. ce que ça peut donner** I can't visualize what it would be like; **c., qu'est-ce que cela va entraîner pour les usagers?** in real terms, what will that mean for the users?

concrétion [kɔ̃kresjɔ̃] NF *Chim, Géol & Méd* concretion; *Méd* **concrétions calcaires** chalk stones

concrétiser [3] [kɔ̃kretize] VT *(rêve)* to realize; *(idée, proposition)* to make concrete; **ils n'ont pas réussi à c. leur domination** *(équipe)* they were the stronger side but they didn't capitalize on it *or* they didn't manage to push their advantage home

VPR **se concrétiser** *(rêve)* to come true, to materialize; *(proposition, idée)* to be realized, to take concrete form *or* shape

conçu, -e [kɔ̃sy] *pp voir* **concevoir**

concubin, -e [kɔ̃kybɛ̃, -in] NM,F **1** *(amant)* concubine, partner **2** *Jur* partner, cohabitee

concubinage [kɔ̃kybinaʒ] NM **1** *(vie de couple)* **vivre en c.** to live together *or* as man and wife, to cohabit **2** *Jur* cohabitation, cohabiting; **c. notoire** common-law marriage

concupiscence [kɔ̃kypisɑ̃s] NF *(envers les biens)* greed; *(envers le sexe)* lust, *Littéraire* concupiscence

concupiscent, -e [kɔ̃kypisɑ̃, -ɑ̃t] ADJ *(envers les biens)* greedy; *(envers le sexe)* lustful, *Littéraire* concupiscent

concurremment [kɔ̃kyramɑ̃] ADV *(ensemble)* jointly, in conjunction *or Sout* concert; *(en même temps)* at the same time, concurrently

• **concurremment avec** PRÉP **1** *(de concert avec)* in conjunction *or Sout* concert with **2** *(en même temps que)* concurrently with

concurrence [kɔ̃kyrɑ̃s] NF **1** *(rivalité)* competition; **être en c. avec qn** to be in competition with sb; **entrer en c. avec qn** to compete with sb; **faire (de la) c. à** to be in competition *or* to compete with; **faire jouer la c.** to allow market forces to operate; **les Japonais nous livrent une c. acharnée** we're engaged in a cut-throat competition with the Japanese; **la libre c.** free *or* open competition; **c. déloyale** unfair competition *or* trading; **c. directe** direct competition; **c. imparfaite/parfaite** imperfect/perfect competition; **c. pure** pure competition **2** *(rivaux)* **la c.** the competition; **nos prix défient toute c.** our prices are unbeatable

• **à concurrence de, jusqu'à concurrence de** PRÉP up to, to the limit of; **vous pouvez être à découvert jusqu'à c. de 1000 euros** your overdraft limit is 1,000 euros

concurrencer [16] [kɔ̃kyrɑ̃se] VT to compete with; **leur nouvelle gamme ne peut c. la nôtre** their new line can't compete with ours; **ils nous concurrencent dangereusement** they're very dangerous competitors

concurrent, -e [kɔ̃kyrɑ̃, -ɑ̃t] ADJ **1** *(entreprises, produits)* competing, rival *(avant n)* **2** *Arch (actions, efforts)* joint, concerted, united

NM,F **1** *Com & Sport* competitor, rival; *Com* **c. principal** major competitor; *Mktg* **c. tardif** late entrant **2** *(à une épreuve, un poste)* candidate

concurrentiel, -elle [kɔ̃kyrɑ̃sjɛl] ADJ competitive; **ces marchandises sont vendues à des prix concurrentiels** these goods are competitively priced

concussion [kɔ̃kysjɔ̃] NF embezzlement, misappropriation of public funds

conçut *etc voir* **concevoir**

condamnable [kɔ̃danabl] ADJ blameworthy, reprehensible

condamnation [kɔ̃danasjɔ̃] NF **1** *Jur (action)* sentencing, convicting; *(peine)* sentence; **il a fait l'objet de trois condamnations pour vol** he's had three convictions for theft, he's been convicted three times for theft; **il a déjà quatre condamnations à son actif** he already has four convictions; **c. à mort** death sentence; **c. à la réclusion à perpétuité** life sentence, sentence of life imprisonment; **c. aux travaux forcés** sentence of hard labour; **c. par défaut/par contumace** decree by default/in absentia

2 *(blâme)* condemnation, blame; **c'est une c. sans appel de sa politique extérieure** it's an out-and-out condemnation of his/her foreign policy

3 *(fin ▸ d'un projet, d'une tentative)* end

4 *Aut (blocage)* locking; *(système)* locking device; **c. automatique des portes** automatic door locking; **c. centralisée des portes** central locking

condamné, -e [kɔ̃dane] NM,F *Jur* sentenced *or* convicted person; **c. à mort** prisoner under sentence of death; **c. à la réclusion perpétuelle** life prisoner, *Fam* lifer

condamner [3] [kɔ̃dane] VT **1** *Jur (accusé)* to sentence; **c. qn à mort/aux travaux forcés** to sentence sb to death/to hard labour; **condamné à trois mois de prison pour...** sentenced to three months' imprisonment for...; **c. qn à 2000 euros d'amende** to fine sb 2,000 euros; **condamné pour meurtre** convicted of murder; **c. qn par défaut/par contumace** to sentence sb by default/in absentia; **faire c. qn** to get *or* to have sb convicted

2 *(interdire ▸ magazine)* to forbid publication of; *(▸ pratique)* to forbid, to condemn; **la société condamne la bigamie** society forbids *or* condemns bigamy; **la loi condamne l'usage de stupéfiants** the use of narcotics is forbidden by law

3 *(désapprouver ▸ attentat, propos)* to express disapproval of; *(▸ personne)* to condemn, to blame; **c. qn pour avoir fait** *ou* **d'avoir fait qch** to blame sb for having done sth; **l'expression est condamnée par les puristes** the use of the phrase is condemned *or* is disapproved of by purists

4 *(accuser)* to condemn; **son silence la condamne** her silence condemns her

5 *(sujet: maladie incurable)* to condemn, to doom; **les médecins disent qu'il est condamné** the doctors say that there is no hope for him; **les malades condamnés sont renvoyés chez eux** terminally-ill patients are sent back home; *Fig* **ce projet est condamné par manque d'argent** the project is doomed through lack of money

6 *(murer ▸ porte, fenêtre)* to block up, to seal off; *(▸ pièce)* to close up; **c. toutes les fenêtres d'une maison** to board up the windows in a house; *Fig* **c. sa porte** to bar one's door

7 *(obliger)* **il était condamné à vivre dans la misère** he was condemned to live in poverty; **je suis condamnée à rester alitée pendant dix jours** I'm confined to bed for ten days; **je suis condamnée à l'attendre** I have to wait for him/her; **être condamné à la solitude** to be condemned to loneliness

condé [kɔ̃de] NM *Fam Arg crime (policier)* cop; **les condés** the cops, *Br* the fuzz

condensat [kɔ̃dɑ̃sa] NM *Phys* condensate

condensateur [kɔ̃dɑ̃satœr] NM **1** *Élec* condenser, capacitor **2** *Opt* **c. optique** condenser

condensation [kɔ̃dɑ̃sasjɔ̃] NF condensation; **une pièce où il y a beaucoup de c.** a very damp room

condensé [kɔ̃dɑ̃se] NM digest, summary, abstract

condenser [3] [kɔ̃dɑ̃se] VT **1** *Chim & Phys* to condense **2** *(raccourcir ▸ récit)* to condense, to cut down; **style condensé** terse style **3** *Ordinat (base de données)* to pack

VPR **se condenser** to condense

condenseur [kɔ̃dɑ̃sœr] NM condenser

condescendance [kɔ̃desɑ̃dɑ̃s] NF condescension; **avec c.** condescendingly; **traiter qn avec c.** to patronize sb

condescendant, -e [kɔ̃desɑ̃dɑ̃, -ɑ̃t] **ADJ** *(hautain ▸ regard, parole)* condescending, patronizing; **d'un air c.** patronizingly

condescendre [73] [kɔ̃desɑ̃dr] **condescendre à VT IND** to condescend to; *aussi Hum* **elle a condescendu à me recevoir** she condescended *or* deigned to see me

condiment [kɔ̃dimɑ̃] **NM** *(épices)* condiment; *(moutarde)* (mild) mustard

condisciple [kɔ̃disipl] **NMF** *Scol* classmate, schoolmate; *Univ* fellow student

condition [kɔ̃disjɔ̃] **NF 1** *(préalable)* condition; **une des conditions du progrès** one of the conditions of *or* requirements for progress; **c'est la c. de votre réussite** that's what will determine your success; **les conditions n'étaient pas réunies** the conditions weren't quite right; **il veut bien signer le contrat, mais il y met une c.** he's happy to sign the contract, but on one condition; **j'accepte mais à une c.** I accept but on one condition; **c. nécessaire/suffisante** necessary/sufficient condition; **c. préalable** prerequisite; **c. requise** requirement; **une c. sine qua non pour** an absolute prerequisite for

2 *(état ▸ de quelqu'un)* condition, shape; *(▸ de quelque chose)* condition; **c. physique/psychologique** physical/psychological shape; **être en bonne c. physique** to be in condition, to be fit; **en excellente c. physique** in excellent shape; **être en mauvaise c. physique** to be in poor physical shape, to be unfit; **les marchandises nous sont parvenues en bonne c.** the goods arrived in good condition

3 *(position sociale)* rank, station; **des gens de toutes conditions** people from all walks of life; **une femme de c. modeste** a woman from a modest background; **épouser qn de sa c.** to marry sb of one's own station *or* social background; **épouser qn au-dessous de sa c.** to marry beneath one's station; **pour améliorer leur c.** in order to improve their lot; **la c. féminine** the lives of women, women's status

4 *(destinée)* **la c. humaine** the human condition

5 *Jur* condition; **c. suspensive** condition precedent

• **conditions NFPL 1** *(environnement)* conditions; **conditions climatiques/économiques** weather/economic conditions; **voyager dans les meilleures conditions** to travel under the most favourable conditions; **conditions de vie/travail** living/working conditions; **conditions météo** weather conditions **2** *(termes)* terms; **les conditions d'un accord** the terms of an agreement; **aux conditions les plus avantageuses** on the most favourable terms; **quelles sont ses conditions?** what terms is he/she offering?; **conditions d'achat** terms of purchase; **conditions d'admission** admission requirements; **conditions générales de vente** general (terms and) conditions of sale; **conditions de livraison** terms of delivery; **conditions de paiement** terms of payment; **conditions particulières** *(d'un billet etc)* restrictions; **conditions de remboursement** terms of repayment; **conditions de vente** terms of sale

• **à condition ADV envoyer des marchandises à c.** to send goods on approval

• **à condition de PRÉP** on condition that, provided (that); **tu peux y aller à c. de ne pas rentrer tard** you may go on condition that *or* provided (that) you don't come back late

• **à (la) condition que CONJ** on condition that, provided (that); **je ne dirai rien à c. que tu en fasses autant** I won't say anything on condition that *or* provided (that) you do the same

• **dans ces conditions ADV** under these conditions; **dans ces conditions, j'accepte** under these conditions, I accept; **dans ces conditions, pourquoi se donner tant de mal?** if that's the case, why go to so much trouble?

• **en condition ADJ** *(en forme)* in shape **ADV 1** *(en forme)* in shape; **mettre en c.** *(athlète, candidat)* to get into condition *or* form; **se mettre en c.** to get (oneself) fit *or* into condition *or* into shape **2** *(dans un état favorable)* **mettre le public en c.** to condition the public **3** *Arch (dans la domesticité)* **entrer en c. chez qn** to enter sb's service

• **sans condition(s) ADV** unconditionally **ADJ** unconditional; **reddition sans conditions** unconditional surrender

• **sous condition ADV** conditionally; **acheter qch sous c.** to buy sth on approval

conditionnalité [kɔ̃disjɔnalite] **NF** *Écon* conditionality

conditionné, -e [kɔ̃disjɔne] **ADJ 1** *Psy* conditioned **2** *(climatisé ▸ bureau, autocar)* air-conditioned **3** *Com (emballé ▸ marchandise)* prepacked, prepackaged

conditionnel, -elle [kɔ̃disjɔnɛl] **ADJ 1** *(soumis à condition)* conditional, tentative; **notre soutien est c. et dépend de…** our support is conditional on… **2** *Psy* conditioned **3** *Gram* conditional

NM *Gram* conditional (mood); **c. présent/passé** present/perfect conditional tense

• **conditionnelle NF** *Gram* conditional clause

• **au conditionnel ADV 1** *Gram* in the conditional **2** *(comme une hypothèse)* **la nouvelle est à prendre au c.** the news has yet to be confirmed *or* checked

conditionnellement [kɔ̃disjɔnɛlmɑ̃] **ADV** conditionally, tentatively

conditionnement [kɔ̃disjɔnmɑ̃] **NM 1** *(fait d'emballer, emballage)* packaging

2 *Tex* conditioning

3 *Ind* processing

4 *Psy* conditioning; **c. instrumental** *ou* **opérant** instrumental learning

conditionner [3] [kɔ̃disjɔne] **VT 1** *(emballer ▸ marchandise, aliments)* to package

2 *Tex* to condition

3 *Ind* to process

4 *Psy (influencer)* to condition, to influence; **la publicité conditionne nos choix** advertising conditions *or* influences our choices; **notre départ est conditionné par son état de santé** our going away depends on *or* is conditional on his/her state of health

5 *(climatiser)* to air-condition

conditionneur, -euse [kɔ̃disjɔnœr, -øz] **NM,F** food-processing specialist

NM 1 *(climatiseur)* air conditioner **2** *Ind* packer

condo [kɔ̃do] **NM** *Can (abrév* **condominium)** condo

condoléances [kɔ̃dɔleɑ̃s] **NFPL** condolences; **lettre de c.** letter of condolence; **présenter ses c. (à qn)** to offer one's condolences (to sb); **veuillez accepter mes plus sincères c.** please accept my deepest sympathy *or* my most sincere condolences; **toutes mes c., Paul** with deepest sympathy *or* heartfelt condolences, Paul

condom [kɔ̃dɔm] **NM** condom, sheath

condominium [kɔ̃dɔminjɔm] **NM** condominium

condor [kɔ̃dɔr] **NM** *Orn* condor

conductance [kɔ̃dyktɑ̃s] **NF** conductance

conducteur, -trice [kɔ̃dyktœr, -tris] **ADJ 1** *Élec* conductive **2** *Fig (principal ▸ principe, fil)* guiding

NM,F 1 *Transp* driver; **c. d'autobus** bus driver; **c. de camions** truck *or Br* lorry driver **2** *Ind* operator; **c. de travaux** foreman, *f* forewoman, clerk of works

NM *Phys* conductor

> Il faut noter que le nom anglais **conductor** est un faux ami. Il signifie le plus souvent **chef d'orchestre** ou **contrôleur**, suivant le contexte.

conductibilité [kɔ̃dyktibilite] **NF** conductivity

conductible [kɔ̃dyktibl] **ADJ** conductive

conduction [kɔ̃dyksjɔ̃] **NF** conduction

conductivité [kɔ̃dyktivite] **NF** conductivity

conductrice [kɔ̃dyktris] *voir* **conducteur**

CONDUIRE [9] [kɔ̃dɥir]

VT	
• to take **1**	• to drive **1, 4**
• to lead **2, 3, 5**	• to run **5**
• to conduct **5, 7**	• to carry **8**
USAGE ABSOLU	
• to lead **1**	• to drive **2**
VPR	
• to drive, to be driven **1**	• to behave **2**

VT 1 *(emmener ▸ gén)* to take; *(▸ en voiture)* to drive, to take; **c. les enfants à l'école** to take *or* to drive the children to school; **je vais t'y c., si tu veux** I'll drive *or* take you there, if you like; **j'ai dû le c. chez le dentiste de toute urgence** I had to rush him to the dentist; **c. qn jusqu'à la porte** to see sb to the door, to show sb the way out; **on la conduisit à sa chambre** she was shown *or* taken to her room; **c. le troupeau à l'alpage** to drive the cattle to the high pastures

2 *(guider)* to lead; **c. un cheval par la bride** to lead a horse by the bridle; **c. un aveugle dans la rue** to lead a blind man along the street; **c. ses hommes au combat** to lead one's men into battle; **les empreintes m'ont conduit jusqu'au hangar** the footprints led me to the shed

3 *(mener)* **c. qn à** to lead sb to; **c. qn au désespoir** to drive sb to desperation; **cela va nous c. à la catastrophe/ruine** it's going to lead us to disaster/ruin; **ce qui nous conduit à la conclusion suivante** which leads *or* brings us to the following conclusion; **c. qn à la victoire** *(entraîneur, entraînement)* to lead sb (on) to victory

4 *Transp (véhicule)* to drive; *(hors-bord)* to steer

5 *(diriger ▸ État)* to run, to lead; *(▸ affaires, opérations)* to run, to conduct, to manage; *(▸ travaux)* to supervise; *(▸ recherches, enquête)* to conduct, to lead; *(▸ délégation, révolte)* to head, to lead

6 *(être en tête de)* **c. le deuil** to be at the head of the funeral procession, to be a chief mourner

7 *Mus (orchestre, symphonie)* to conduct

8 *(faire passer ▸ eau)* to carry, to bring; **l'oléoduc qui conduit le pétrole à travers le désert** the pipeline which carries the oil across the desert

9 *Phys (chaleur, électricité)* to conduct, to be a conductor of; **un corps qui conduit bien l'électricité** a good conductor of electricity

USAGE ABSOLU 1 *(mener)* **c. à** to lead to, to open out onto; **cet escalier ne conduit nulle part** this staircase doesn't lead anywhere; **la jalousie conduit aux pires excès** jealousy leads to *or* can cause extremes of bad behaviour

2 *(diriger un véhicule)* **qui conduisait?** who was driving?, who was behind the wheel?; **c. à droite/gauche** to drive on the right-/left-hand side of the road; **c. bien/mal/vite** to be a good/bad/fast driver

VPR se conduire 1 *(être piloté)* to be driven, to drive; **une voiture qui se conduit facilement** a car that's easy to drive

2 *(se comporter)* to behave, to conduct oneself; **ce n'est pas une façon de se c. avec une dame** that's no way to behave to a lady; **se c. bien** to behave (oneself) well; **tâche de bien te c.** try to behave (yourself); **se c. mal** to behave badly, to misbehave

conduit, -e [kɔ̃dɥi, -it] **PP** *voir* **conduire**

NM 1 *Tech* conduit, pipe; **c. d'aération** air duct; *Aut* **c. d'aspiration** suction pipe; *Aut* **c. de carburant** fuel pipe; *Aut* **conduits d'échappement** exhaust manifold; **c. de fumée** flue; **c. de ventilation** ventilation shaft **2** *Anat* canal, duct; **c. auditif** auditory canal; **c. lacrymal** tear *or Spéc* lachrymal duct; **c. urinaire** urinary canal

• **conduite NF 1** *(pilotage ▸ d'un véhicule)* driving; *(▸ d'un hors-bord)* steering; **conduite tout terrain** cross-country driving; **la conduite à droite/gauche** driving on the right-/left-hand side of the road; **avec conduite à droite/gauche** right-/left-hand drive *(avant n)*; **prendre des leçons de conduite** to take driving lessons; **conduite accompagnée** = driving practice accompanied by a qualified driver for learners who have passed their theory test; **conduite en état d'ivresse** *Br* drink-driving, *Am* drunk-driving

2 *(comportement)* conduct, behaviour; **je ne sais vraiment plus quelle conduite adopter avec elle** I really don't know what line to take with her *or* how to handle her any more; **avoir une conduite étrange** to behave oddly; **pour bonne conduite** *(libéré, gracié)* for good behaviour; **mauvaise conduite** misbehaviour, misconduct; *Psy* **conduite d'échec** defeatist behaviour

3 *(direction ▸ des affaires)* management, conduct, handling; *(▸ de la guerre)* conduct; *(▸ d'une armée, d'une flotte)* command; *(▸ d'un pays)* running; *(▸ des travaux)* supervision; **sous la conduite de qn** under sb's leadership

4 *(voiture)* **conduite intérieure** *Br* saloon (car), *Am* sedan

5 *Tech* pipe; *(canalisation principale)* main; **conduite d'eau/de gaz** water/gas pipe; *Aut* **conduite d'arrivée du combustible** supply pipe;

conduite forcée pressure pipeline; **conduite montante** flow pipe, rising main; **conduite souple** hose, flexible pipe

condyle [kɔ̃dil] NM condyle

cône [kon] NM 1 *Géom* cone; **en forme de c.** conical, cone-shaped
2 *Bot* **c. de pin** pine cone
3 *Géol* **c. de déjection** alluvial cone; **c. volcanique** volcanic cone
4 *Anat* **c. rétinien** retinal cone
5 *Zool (mollusque)* cone shell
6 *(glace)* cone, cornet
7 *Aut* **c. d'embrayage** clutch cone; **c. de friction** friction cone; **c. de synchronisation** synchromesh cone, baulking cone
8 *Astron* **c. d'ombre** umbra

confection [kɔ̃fɛksjɔ̃] NF 1 *Culin* preparation, making; **elle nous a offert des gâteaux de sa c.** she offered us some of her home-made cakes 2 *Couture (d'une robe)* making; *(d'un veston)* tailoring; *Ind* **la c.** the clothing industry *or* business
• **de confection** ADJ ready-to-wear, ready-made, *Br* off-the-peg

confectionner [3] [kɔ̃fɛksjɔne] VT 1 *(préparer ▸ plat, sauce)* to prepare, to make 2 *Couture (robe)* to make, to sew; *(veston)* to tailor

confectionneur, -euse [kɔ̃fɛksjɔnœr, -øz] NM,F clothes manufacturer

confédéral, -e, -aux, -ales [kɔ̃federal, -o] ADJ confederal

confédération [kɔ̃federasjɔ̃] NF 1 *(nation)* confederation, confederacy; **la C. helvétique** the Swiss Confederation 2 *Pol* **c. générale du travail** = major association of French trade unions (affiliated to the Communist Party); **c. paysanne** = militant French association that defends the rights of farmers and campaigns on rural and environmental issues

confédéré, -e [kɔ̃federe] ADJ confederate
NM,F *Suisse* = person from another canton
• **confédérés** NMPL *Hist* **les confédérés** the Confederates

confédérer [18] [kɔ̃federe] VT to confederate

confer [kɔ̃fɛr] VT *(à l'infinitif seulement)* **c. page 36** see page 36

conférence [kɔ̃ferɑ̃s] NF 1 *(réunion)* conference; **c. internationale sur la paix** international peace conference; **donner** *ou* **tenir une c.** to hold a meeting *or* conference; **ils sont en c.** they are in a meeting; **c. de presse** press conference; *Journ* **c. de rédaction** (editors') conference; **c. au sommet** summit conference 2 *(cours)* lecture; **il a fait une c. sur Milton** he gave *or* he delivered a lecture on Milton, he lectured on Milton 3 *Bot (poire)* conference pear

conférencier, -ère [kɔ̃ferɑ̃sje, -ɛr] NM,F speaker

conférer [18] [kɔ̃fere] VT 1 *(décerner ▸ titre, droit)* to confer, to bestow; **c. une médaille à qn** to confer a medal on *or* upon sb; **ils lui ont conféré les pleins pouvoirs** they invested him/her with *or* granted him/her full authority 2 *Fig (donner ▸ importance, prestance)* to impart
VI *(discuter)* to talk, to hold talks

confesse [kɔ̃fɛs] NF *(confession)* **aller à/revenir de c.** to go to/to come back from confession

confesser [4] [kɔ̃fese] VT 1 *Rel (péché)* to confess (to); *(foi)* to confess; *(personne)* to hear the confession of, to be the confessor of
2 *Fam (faire parler)* **c. qn** to make sb talk[□]
3 *Littéraire (foi, convictions)* to proclaim
4 *(reconnaître, admettre)* to admit, to confess; **j'ai eu tort, je le confesse** I admit *or* confess I was wrong
USAGE ABSOLU *Rel* **le Père Guérin ne confessera pas aujourd'hui** Father Guérin is not hearing confessions today
VPR **se confesser** 1 *Rel* to confess, to make one's confession; **se c. à un prêtre** to confess to a priest 2 **se c. à qn** *(se confier)* to confide in sb, to tell sb; **se c. de qch** to confess (to) sth

confesseur [kɔ̃fesœr] NM 1 *Rel* confessor 2 *(confident)* confidant, *f* confidante

confession [kɔ̃fesjɔ̃] NF 1 *Rel (aveu, rite)* confession; **entendre qn en c.** to hear sb's confession; *aussi Fig* **faire une c.** to make a confession, to confess; **je vais vous faire une c.** I've got a confession to make to you 2 *(appartenance)* faith, denomination; **des élèves de toutes confessions** pupils of all denominations; **être de c. luthérienne/anglicane** to belong to the Lutheran/Anglican faith 3 *Littéraire (proclamation)* proclaiming

confessionnal, -aux [kɔ̃fesjɔnal, -o] NM confessional

confessionnel, -elle [kɔ̃fesjɔnɛl] ADJ denominational

confetti [kɔ̃feti] NM (piece of) confetti; **des confettis** confetti; *Fam* **tu peux en faire des confettis!** *Br* you can chuck it out, you can throw it in the bin, *Am* you can throw it in the garbage

confiance [kɔ̃fjɑ̃s] NF 1 *(foi ▸ en quelqu'un, quelque chose)* trust, confidence; **avec c.** confidently; **envisager son avenir avec c.** to feel confident about one's future; **un climat de c. économique** a climate of economic confidence; **c. excessive** overconfidence; **avoir c. en qn/qch** to trust sb/sth, to have confidence in sb/sth; **faire c. à qn** to trust sb; **peut-on lui faire c.?** can he/she be trusted?, is he/she trustworthy *or* reliable?; **faites-moi c.** *(croyez-moi)* believe me; **elle va être en retard, tu peux lui faire c.!** she is absolutely guaranteed to be late!, you can rely on her to be late!; **elle a mon entière c.** I have complete confidence in her; **placer sa c. en qn** to put one's trust *or* to place one's confidence in sb; **j'ai c. en l'avenir de mon pays** I have faith in the future of my country 2 *Pol* **voter la c. au gouvernement** to pass a vote of confidence in the government; **vote de c.** vote of confidence 3 *(aplomb)* **c. en soi** confidence, self-confidence, self-assurance; **manquer de c. en soi** to lack self-confidence; **reprendre c. en soi** to regain one's self-confidence
• **de confiance** ADJ **poste de c.** position of trust; **personne de c.** reliable *or* trustworthy person; **les hommes de c. du président** the President's advisers
• **en confiance** ADV **mettre qn en c.** to win sb's trust; **se sentir** *ou* **être en c. (avec qn)** to feel safe (with sb)
• **en toute confiance** ADV with complete confidence; **tu peux l'acheter en toute c.** you can buy it with complete confidence, you needn't have any doubts or misgivings about buying it; **je vous parle en toute c.** I know this will go no further than ourselves, I know I can trust you (with what I have to say)

confiant, -e [kɔ̃fjɑ̃, -ɑ̃t] ADJ 1 *(qui fait confiance)* trusting, trustful 2 *(qui exprime la confiance)* trusting, confident 3 *(qui a confiance)* **être c. dans** *ou* **en** to have confidence in; **je suis c. dans la réussite de notre programme** I have confidence in the success of our programme, I'm confident that our programme will be a success; **il est c. (en lui-même)** he's self-assured *or* self-confident

confidence [kɔ̃fidɑ̃s] NF confidence; **faire une c. à qn** to confide something to sb, to trust sb with a secret; **faire des confidences à qn** to confide in sb; **mettre qn dans la c.** to take sb into one's confidence, to let sb into the secret; **être dans la c.** to be in on the *or* a secret; *Hum* **confidences sur l'oreiller** pillow talk; **c. pour c., je ne l'aime pas non plus** between ourselves, I don't like him/her either
• **en confidence** ADV in (strict) confidence

> Il faut noter que le nom anglais **confidence** signifie également **confiance**.

confident, -e [kɔ̃fidɑ̃, -ɑ̃t] NM,F confidant, *f* confidante

confidentialité [kɔ̃fidɑ̃sjalite] NF confidentiality; *Ordinat* **c. des données** data privacy

confidentiel, -elle [kɔ̃fidɑ̃sjɛl] ADJ 1 *(secret ▸ information)* confidential; *(▸ entretien)* private; *(sur document)* private and confidential; **à titre c.** in confidence, confidentially 2 *(limité)* **un tirage c.** a small print-run; **un livre un peu c.** a book that only appeals to a limited readership

confidentiellement [kɔ̃fidɑ̃sjɛlmɑ̃] ADV confidentially, in (strict) confidence

confier [9] [kɔ̃fje] VT 1 *(dire ▸ craintes, intentions)* to confide, to entrust; **est-ce que je peux te c. un secret?** can I tell you a secret?, can I share a secret (with you)?; **il m'a confié qu'il voulait divorcer** he confided to me that he wanted to get a divorce 2 *(donner)* to entrust; **c. ses clefs à un ami** to entrust one's keys to a friend; **c. une mission à qn** to entrust a mission to sb, to entrust sb with a mission; **la garde de Marie a été confiée à sa mère** Marie has been put in her mother's care; **c. qch aux soins de qn** to entrust sth to sb's care 3 *Littéraire (livrer)* to consign
VPR **se confier** 1 *(s'épancher)* to confide; **se c. à qn** to confide in sb; **je n'ai personne à qui me c.** I have nobody to confide in 2 **se c. à** *(s'en remettre à)* to trust to; **se c. à sa bonne étoile** to trust to one's lucky star

configurable [kɔ̃figyrabl] ADJ *Ordinat* configurable

configuration [kɔ̃figyrasjɔ̃] NF 1 *(aspect général)* configuration, general shape; **la c. des lieux** the layout of the place; **la c. du terrain** the lie of the land 2 *Chim & Ordinat* configuration; **c. par défaut** default setting; **c. matérielle** hardware configuration

configurer [3] [kɔ̃figyre] VT *Ordinat & (gén)* to configure

confiné, -e [kɔ̃fine] ADJ *(air)* stale; *(atmosphère)* stuffy; **vivre c. chez soi** to live shut up indoors

confinement [kɔ̃finmɑ̃] NM 1 *(enfermement)* confinement 2 *(d'une espèce animale)* concentration *(in a particular area)*

confiner [3] [kɔ̃fine] VT 1 *(reléguer)* to confine; **on le confine dans des rôles comiques** he's confined to comic parts 2 *(enfermer)* to confine, to shut away
• **confiner à** VT IND 1 *(être voisin de ▸ pays, maison)* to border on 2 *Fig (être semblable à)* to border *or* to verge on; **passion qui confine à la folie** passion bordering *or* verging on madness
VPR **se confiner** 1 *(s'enfermer)* **se c. dans son bureau** to confine oneself to one's study, to shut oneself away in one's study 2 **se c. à** *(se limiter à)* to confine oneself *or* to limit oneself *or* to keep to; **je préfère ne pas me c. aux auteurs que je connais bien** I'd rather not confine myself to *or* keep to those writers I'm familiar with

confins [kɔ̃fɛ̃] NMPL *(limites ▸ d'un pays)* borders; *(▸ d'un savoir, de l'intelligence)* confines, bounds; **les c. de l'Europe et de l'Asie** the borders of Europe and Asia
• **aux confins de** PRÉP on the borders of; *Fig* **aux c. du conscient et de l'inconscient** on the borders of the conscious and the unconscious

confiote [kɔ̃fjɔt] NF *Fam (confiture)* jam[□]

confire [101] [kɔ̃fir] VT *(dans du sucre)* to preserve, to candy; *(dans du vinaigre)* to pickle; *(dans de la graisse)* to preserve

confirmatif, -ive [kɔ̃firmatif, -iv] ADJ confirmative

confirmation [kɔ̃firmasjɔ̃] NF 1 *(attestation)* confirmation; **obtenir c. d'un résultat** to receive confirmation of a result, to have a result confirmed; **donnez-nous c. de votre rendez-vous** please give us confirmation of *or* please confirm your appointment; **c'est la c. de ce que je pensais** that (just) confirms what I thought; **en c. de** as a *or* in confirmation of, confirming 2 *Rel* confirmation; **recevoir la c.** to be confirmed; **donner la c. (à qn)** to confirm (sb) 3 *Jur* upholding

confirmative [kɔ̃firmativ] *voir* **confirmatif**

confirmer [3] [kɔ̃firme] VT 1 *(rendre définitif ▸ réservation, nouvelle)* to confirm; **c. par écrit** to confirm by letter *or* in writing
2 *(renforcer ▸ témoignage, diagnostic, impression)* to confirm, to bear out; **ceci confirme mes** *ou* **me confirme dans mes soupçons** this bears out *or* confirms my suspicions
3 *(affermir ▸ position, supériorité)* to reinforce; **c. qn dans ses fonctions** to confirm sb in office
4 *Rel* to confirm; **se faire c.** to be confirmed
VPR **se confirmer** 1 *(s'avérer ▸ rumeur)* to be confirmed; **son départ se confirme** it's been confirmed that he's leaving; **il se confirme que...** it has now been confirmed that... 2 *(être renforcé ▸ tendance, hausse)* to become stronger

confisait *etc voir* **confire**

confiscation [kɔ̃fiskasjɔ̃] NF 1 *(saisie)* confiscation, seizure, seizing 2 *Jur* forfeiture

confiserie [kɔ̃fizri] NF **1** *(produit) Br* sweet, *Am* candy; **acheter des confiseries** to buy confectionery, to buy *Br* sweets *or Am* candy **2** *(industrie)* confectionery (business *or* trade) **3** *(magasin)* confectioner's, *Br* sweet shop, *Am* candy store

confiseur, -euse [kɔ̃fizœr, -øz] NM,F confectioner

confisquer [3] [kɔ̃fiske] VT **1** *(retirer ▸ marchandises, drogue)* to confiscate, to seize; *(▸ sifflet, livre)* to take away, to confiscate; **c. qch à qn** to take sth away from *or* to confiscate sth from sb; **se faire c. qch par qn** to have sth confiscated by sb **2** *(supprimer)* to take away, to suppress; **le pouvoir a confisqué nos libertés** the authorities have taken away *or* suppressed our civil rights **3** *Jur* to seize, to confiscate

confit, -e [kɔ̃fi, -it] PP *voir* **confire**
ADJ **1** *(fruits)* candied, crystallized; *(cornichons)* pickled; **ailes de canards confites** confit of duck wings **2** *Littéraire* **être c. en dévotion** to be steeped in piety
NM conserve; **c. d'oie** goose confit *(goose cooked in its own fat to preserve it)*

confiture [kɔ̃fityr] NF jam, preserve; **c. de fraises/mûres** strawberry/blackberry jam; **c. d'oranges** (orange) marmalade; **tartine de c.** slice of bread with jam; **faire des confitures** to make jam; *Fig* **donner de la c. aux cochons** to cast pearls before swine
• **en confiture** ADV **mettre qch en c.** to reduce sth to a pulp

confiturerie [kɔ̃fityrri] NF **1** *(fabrication)* jam manufacture **2** *(fabrique)* jam factory

confiturier, -ère [kɔ̃fityrje, -ɛr] ADJ jam *(avant n)*
NM,F jam *or* preserve manufacturer
NM jam dish

conflagration [kɔ̃flagrasjɔ̃] NF **1** *(conflit)* conflagration, conflict **2** *(bouleversement)* major upheaval

conflictuel, -elle [kɔ̃fliktɥɛl] ADJ *(pulsions, désirs)* conflicting, clashing; **situation/relation conflictuelle** antagonistic situation/relationship

conflit [kɔ̃fli] NM **1** *Mil* conflict, war; **le c. irano-irakien** the Iran-Iraq war; **c. armé** armed conflict *or* struggle; **c. limité** limited conflict **2** *(heurt ▸ d'intérêts)* conflict, clash; **entrer en c. avec** to conflict with, to come into conflict with; **être en c. avec qn** to be in conflict with sb; **il y a beaucoup de conflits internes** there's a lot of infighting; **le c. des générations** the clash between generations **3** *Jur* conflict; **c. d'attribution** conflict of authority; **c. de juridictions** conflict of jurisdiction; **c. de lois** conflict of laws; **c. social** *ou* **du travail** labour *or* industrial *or* employment dispute; **c. salarial** wage dispute

confluence [kɔ̃flyɑ̃s] NF **1** *Géog* confluence **2** *(rencontre)* confluence, convergence; **à la c. de** at the junction of; **à la c. du marxisme et de la psychanalyse** where Marxism and psychoanalysis meet

confluent [kɔ̃flyɑ̃] NM **1** *Géog* confluence; **au c. du Rhône et de la Saône** at the confluence of the Saône and the Rhône **2** *(point de rencontre)* junction **3** *Anat* confluence

confluer [7] [kɔ̃flye] VI *Géog* to meet, to merge; **l'Oise conflue avec la Seine** the Oise flows into the Seine

confondant, -e [kɔ̃fɔ̃dɑ̃, -ɑ̃t] ADJ astonishing, astounding

confondre [75] [kɔ̃fɔ̃dr] VT **1** *(prendre pour un autre ▸ films, auteurs, dates)* to confuse, to mix up; **il a confondu la clef du garage et celle de la porte** he mistook the garage key for the door key, he mixed up the garage key and the door key; **j'ai confondu leurs voix** I got their voices mixed up; **c. qn/qch avec** to mistake sb/sth for; **on me confond avec ma cousine** I'm mistaken for *or* people mix me up with my cousin
2 *(réunir)* to merge, to mingle, to intermingle; **tous âges confondus** irrespective of age
3 *(démasquer ▸ menteur, meurtrier)* to unmask, to expose; **le misérable était enfin confondu!** at last the rogue was unmasked!
4 *(étonner)* to astound, to astonish; **une telle naïveté a de quoi vous c.** such naivety is truly astounding; **être** *ou* **rester confondu devant** to be speechless in the face of *or* astounded by
USAGE ABSOLU *(faire une confusion)* **on ne se connaît pas, vous devez c.** we've never met, you must be making a mistake *or* be mistaken; **attention, ce n'est pas ce que j'ai dit, ne pas c.** *ou* **ne confondons pas!** hey, let's get one thing straight, that's not what I said!
VPR **se confondre 1** *(se mêler ▸ fleuves)* to flow together, to merge; *(▸ formes, couleurs)* to merge; *(▸ intérêts, aspirations)* to merge, to be identical; **dans mon rêve, Marie et Sophie se confondaient en une seule personne** in my dream, Marie and Sophie merged into one person *or* were one and the same (person) **2** *(être embrouillé)* to be mixed up *or* confused; **les dates se confondaient dans mon esprit** the dates became confused *or* were all mixed up in my mind **3 se c. en excuses** to be effusive in one's apologies, to apologize profusely; **elle se confondit en remerciements** she thanked him/her/*etc* profusely

conformation [kɔ̃fɔrmasjɔ̃] NF **1** *(aspect physique)* build; **sa c. anatomique** its anatomical structure; **avoir une c. normale** to be of normal build **2** *Chim* conformation, configuration

conforme [kɔ̃fɔrm] ADJ **1** *(qui répond à une règle)* standard; **on ne peut pas brancher l'appareil, la fiche n'est pas c.** the machine can't be plugged in, the plug isn't standard; **ce n'est pas c. à la loi** this is not in accordance with the law **2** *(conventionnel ▸ pensée, idée)* conventional, orthodox; **non c.** unconventional, unorthodox **3** *(semblable)* identical; *Com* **c. à la demande** as per order; *Com* **c. à la description** as represented; **c. à l'original** true to the original; **ce n'est pas c. à l'esquisse** it bears little resemblance to *or* doesn't match the sketch; **la réalisation des travaux n'est pas c. à ce qui avait été prévu** the work is not being carried out in accordance with what was agreed

conformé, -e [kɔ̃fɔrme] ADJ **bien c.** *(fœtus)* well-formed; *(enfant)* well-built; **mal c.** *(fœtus)* malformed; **un enfant mal c.** a child with poor bone structure

conformément [kɔ̃fɔrmemɑ̃] **conformément à** PRÉP in accordance with, according to; **c. à la législation en vigueur** in accordance with (the) current legislation; **c. au souhait que vous avez exprimé** in accordance with your wish; **tout s'est déroulé c. au plan** everything went according to plan; **c. à l'article 26** in accordance with clause 26

conformer [3] [kɔ̃fɔrme] VT **1** *Com (standardiser)* to make standard, to produce according to the standards **2** *(adapter)* **c. qch à** to adapt *or* to match sth to; **c. ses envies à ses possibilités financières** to tailor *or* to match one's desires to one's financial means; **ils ont conformé leur tactique à la nôtre** they modelled their tactics on ours
VPR **se conformer se c. à** *(se plier à ▸ usage, habitudes)* to conform to; *(▸ ordre, décision)* to comply with, to abide by

conformisme [kɔ̃fɔrmism] NM **1** *(traditionalisme)* conventionality, conformism **2** *Rel* conformism, conformity

conformiste [kɔ̃fɔrmist] ADJ **1** *(traditionaliste)* conformist, conventional **2** *Rel* conformist
NMF **1** *(traditionaliste)* conformist, conventionalist **2** *Rel* conformist

conformité [kɔ̃fɔrmite] NF **1** *(ressemblance)* similarity; **être en c. de goûts avec qn** to have similar tastes to sb **2** *(obéissance)* **la c. à** *(gén)* conformity to; *(aux normes)* compliance with; **la c. aux usages sociaux** conformity to social customs **3** *(conventionnalisme)* conventionality
• **en conformité avec** PRÉP in accordance with, according to; **être en c. avec** to conform to

confort [kɔ̃fɔr] NM **1** *(commodités)* **le c.** *(d'un appartement, d'un hôtel)* modern conveniences; *(d'un aéroport)* modern facilities; **un cinq-pièces tout c.** a five-room apartment with all *Br* mod cons *or Am* modern conveniences **2** *(aise physique)* **le c.** comfort; **j'aime (avoir) mon c.** I like my (creature) comforts; **son petit c.** his/her creature comforts; **améliorer le c. d'écoute** to improve sound quality; **c. d'emploi** *(d'un ordinateur)* user-friendliness **3** *(tranquillité)* **le c. intellectuel** self-assurance

confortable [kɔ̃fɔrtabl] ADJ **1** *(douillet ▸ lit, maison)* comfortable, cosy, snug; **la chaise n'est pas très c.** the chair's rather uncomfortable
2 *(tranquillisant ▸ situation, routine)* comfortable; *aussi Fig* **être dans une position peu c.** to be in an awkward position
3 *(aisé ▸ vie, situation)* comfortable
4 *(important ▸ retraite, bénéfice, majorité)* comfortable
NM *Can (édredon) Br* quilt, *Am* comforter

confortablement [kɔ̃fɔrtabləmɑ̃] ADV comfortably; **installe-toi c.** make yourself comfortable; **vivre c.** *(dans l'aisance)* to lead a comfortable existence, to be comfortably off; **être c. rémunéré** to be on a good salary, to be well paid

conforter [3] [kɔ̃fɔrte] VT *(renforcer ▸ position, avance)* to reinforce, to strengthen; **cela la conforte dans la mauvaise opinion qu'elle a de moi** it confirms her poor opinion of me

confraternel, -elle [kɔ̃fratɛrnɛl] ADJ fraternal

confraternité [kɔ̃fratɛrnite] NF fraternity *or* brotherhood between colleagues

confrère [kɔ̃frɛr] NM *(professionnellement)* colleague, *Am* coworker; *(dans une société)* fellow member; **un c. de la BBC** a BBC colleague *or Am* coworker

confrérie [kɔ̃freri] NF **1** *(groupe professionnel)* fraternity **2** *Rel* confraternity, brotherhood

confrontation [kɔ̃frɔ̃tasjɔ̃] NF **1** *(face-à-face)* confrontation
2 *Jur* confrontation
3 *(comparaison)* comparison
4 *(conflit)* confrontation; **c. armée** armed confrontation *or* conflict

confronter [3] [kɔ̃frɔ̃te] VT **1** *(mettre face à face ▸ accusés, témoins)* to confront; **être confronté à** *ou* **avec qn** to be confronted with sb; *Fig* **être confronté à une difficulté** to be faced *or* confronted with a difficulty; **il n'est pas toujours facile d'être confronté à la réalité** it's not always easy to face up to reality **2** *(comparer ▸ textes, points de vue)* to compare

confucéen, -enne [kɔ̃fyseɛ̃, -ɛn] ADJ Confucian
NM,F Confucian

confucianisme [kɔ̃fysjanism] NM Confucianism

confus, -e [kɔ̃fy, -yz] ADJ **1** *(imprécis ▸ souvenir, impression)* unclear, confused, vague; *(▸ idées)* muddled; *(▸ situation, histoire)* confused, involved; *(▸ explication)* muddled, confused; *(▸ style, texte)* obscure, unclear; **c'est un esprit c.** he is muddleheaded **2** *(désordonné ▸ murmures, cris)* confused; *(▸ amas)* confused, disorderly; **des voix confuses** a confused babble of voices **3** *(embarrassé)* **c'est un cadeau magnifique, je suis c.** it's a wonderful present, I'm quite overwhelmed *or* I really don't know what to say; **je l'ai tellement regardé qu'il en est resté tout c.** I stared at him so much he didn't know what to do with himself; **c. de** ashamed at, embarrassed by; **être c. de sa propre ignorance** to be ashamed of one's (own) ignorance; **je suis c. de t'avoir fait attendre** I'm awfully *or* dreadfully sorry to have kept you waiting

> Il faut noter que l'adjectif anglais **confused** est un faux ami. Il signifie le plus souvent **désorienté, embrouillé**.

confusément [kɔ̃fyzemɑ̃] ADV **1** *(vaguement)* confusedly, vaguely; **sentir c. que** to have a vague feeling that; **j'entrevoyais c. la solution du problème** I was slowly beginning to see a solution to the problem **2** *(indistinctement)* unintelligibly, inaudibly

confusion [kɔ̃fyzjɔ̃] NF **1** *(méprise)* mix-up, confusion; **il y a eu c. entre deux personnes** they got two people mixed up *or* confused
2 *(désordre)* confusion, disarray, chaos; **la fête s'est terminée dans la c. générale** the party ended in total confusion; **semer** *ou* **répandre la c. dans une assemblée** to throw a meeting into confusion; **jeter la c. dans l'esprit de qn** to sow confu-

sion in sb's mind, to throw sb into confusion
3 *Psy* **c. mentale** mental confusion
4 *(gêne)* embarrassment, confusion; **rougir de c.** to blush (with shame); **à ma grande c.** to my great embarrassment
5 *Jur* **c. des peines** concurrent sentences; **avec c. des peines** the sentences to run concurrently
6 *Pol* **c. des pouvoirs** non-separation of legislative, executive and judiciary powers

congé [kɔ̃ʒe] NM 1 *(vacances) Br* holiday, *Am* vacation; *Admin & Mil* leave; **trois semaines de c.** three weeks off, three weeks' leave; **j'ai pris tous mes congés** I've used up all my holiday (entitlement); **j'ai c. le lundi** I have Mondays off, I'm off on Mondays, Monday is my day off; **c. d'adoption** = unpaid leave for an adopting parent; **c. annuel** *Br* annual leave *or* holiday, *Am* vacation leave; **c. pour convenance personnelle** compassionate leave; **c. de longue durée** extended leave; **c. de maladie** sick leave; **c. (de) maternité** maternity leave; **c. de naissance** (three-day) paternity leave; **c. parental (d'éducation)** = parent's right to take time off without pay (after a birth or an adoption); **c. de paternité** paternity leave; **congés payés** = annual paid leave (at least 30 days per year in France); **c. sabbatique** sabbatical (leave); **congés scolaires** school *Br* holidays *or Am* vacation; **c. sans solde** time off without pay, unpaid leave; **jour de c.** day off
2 *(avis de départ)* notice; **donner son c. à son patron** to hand in one's notice to one's boss; **donner son c. à son propriétaire** to give notice to one's landlord; **donner (son) c. à un employé** to give notice to *or* to dismiss an employee; **demander son c.** *(serviteur)* to ask to leave; **c. pour vente** notice to quit *(issued to tenants when the landlord wants to sell the property)*
3 *(adieu)* **donner c. à qn** to dismiss sb; **prendre c.** to (take one's) leave, to depart; **prendre c. de qn** to take one's leave of sb
4 *(autorisation)* authorization, permit; *(de vin en douane)* release; *Naut* **c. de navigation** clearance certificate
• **en congé** ADV **être en c.** *(soldat)* to be on leave; *(écolier, salarié)* to be on *Br* holiday *or Am* vacation; **je suis en c. demain jusqu'à lundi** I'm off (from) tomorrow till Monday

congédiable [kɔ̃ʒedjabl] ADJ liable to be dismissed *(at any time)*

congédier [9] [kɔ̃ʒedje] VT *(employé)* to dismiss, to discharge; *(locataire)* to give notice to; *(importun)* to send away; **se faire c.** to be dismissed

congelable [kɔ̃ʒlabl] ADJ freezable, suitable for freezing

congélateur [kɔ̃ʒelatœr] NM deep freeze, freezer

congélation [kɔ̃ʒelasjɔ̃] NF 1 *(technique)* freezing; *(durée)* freezing time; **sac de c.** freezer bag 2 *(solidification ▸ de l'eau)* freezing, turning to ice; *(▸ de l'huile)* congealing; **point de c.** freezing point

congeler [25] [kɔ̃ʒle] VT to freeze; **tarte/viande congelée** frozen pie/meat
VPR **se congeler** 1 *(emploi passif) (dans un congélateur)* to freeze; **la mayonnaise ne se congèle pas** you can't freeze mayonnaise (successfully), mayonnaise doesn't freeze well 2 *(eau)* to freeze

congélo [kɔ̃ʒelo] NM *Fam* freezer▫

congénère [kɔ̃ʒenɛr] ADJ *Biol* congeneric; *Anat (muscle)* congenerous; **c. à** congeneric with
NMF 1 *(animal)* congener 2 *Péj (personne)* **toi et tes congénères** you and your sort; **sans ses congénères, il se comporte correctement** away from his peers, he behaves well

congénital, -e, -aux, -ales [kɔ̃ʒenital, -o] ADJ congenital; *Hum* **il est bête, c'est c.!** he was born stupid!; **une maladie congénitale** a congenital illness

congère [kɔ̃ʒɛr] NF snowdrift

congestif, -ive [kɔ̃ʒɛstif, -iv] ADJ congestive

congestion [kɔ̃ʒɛstjɔ̃] NF *Méd* congestion; **il a eu une c.** he has had a stroke; **c. cérébrale** stroke; **c. pulmonaire** congestion of the lungs

congestionné, -e [kɔ̃ʒɛstjɔne] ADJ 1 *(visage)* flushed; *(route)* congested 2 *Méd (organe)* congested

congestionner [3] [kɔ̃ʒɛstjɔne] VT 1 *Méd (partie du corps)* to congest; *(visage)* to flush 2 *(encombrer ▸ réseaux routiers)* to congest, to clog up
VPR **se congestionner** 1 *Méd (partie du corps)* to congest, to become congested; *(visage)* to become flushed 2 *(être encombré)* to become clogged up *or* congested

congestive [kɔ̃ʒɛstiv] *voir* **congestif**

conglomérat [kɔ̃glɔmera] NM *Écon & Géol* conglomerate

conglomération [kɔ̃glɔmerasjɔ̃] NF conglomeration

conglomérer [18] [kɔ̃glɔmere] VT to conglomerate

Congo [kɔ̃go] NM **le C.** *(pays)* the Congo; **le C.** *(fleuve)* the Congo River, the River Congo; **le C. Belge** the Belgian Congo

congolais, -e [kɔ̃gɔlɛ, -ɛz] ADJ Congolese
NM *Culin* coconut cake
• **Congolais, -e** NM,F Congolese; **les C.** the Congolese

congratulations [kɔ̃gratylasjɔ̃] NFPL *Littéraire* felicitations

congratuler [3] [kɔ̃gratyle] *Littéraire* VT to congratulate
VPR **se congratuler** to congratulate each other

congre [kɔ̃gr] NM *Ich* conger (eel)

congrégation [kɔ̃gregasjɔ̃] NF *Rel* 1 *(ordre)* congregation, order 2 *(assemblée de prélats)* congregation

congrès [kɔ̃grɛ] NM congress; **c. médical/scientifique** medical/scientific conference *or* congress; **le C. (américain)** Congress; **membre du C.** member of Congress, Congressman, *f* Congresswoman; **C. national africain** African National Congress; **c. du parti** party conference

congressiste [kɔ̃gresist] NMF participant at a congress

congru, -e [kɔ̃gry] ADJ 1 *Math* congruent 2 *Arch (adéquat)* sufficient, adequate

congruence [kɔ̃gryɑ̃s] NF congruence

congruent, -e [kɔ̃gryɑ̃, -ɑ̃t] ADJ congruent

conifère [kɔnifɛr] ADJ coniferous
NM conifer

conique [kɔnik] ADJ 1 *(pointu)* conical, cone-shaped 2 *Math* conic 3 *Tech (tige, goupille)* coned, tapering; **engrenage c.** bevel gearing

conjectural, -e, aux, -ales [kɔ̃ʒɛktyral, -o] ADJ conjectural

conjecture [kɔ̃ʒɛktyr] NF conjecture, surmise; **se perdre en conjectures** to be perplexed; **nous en sommes réduits aux conjectures** we can only guess

conjecturer [3] [kɔ̃ʒɛktyre] VT to speculate about *or Sout* to conjecture; **je ne conjecture rien de bon de la situation** I can't see anything good coming out of the situation; **c. que** to surmise that
USAGE ABSOLU **que s'est-il passé? – on ne peut que c.** what happened? – one can but guess; **c. sur** to make guesses about

conjoint, -e [kɔ̃ʒwɛ̃, -ɛ̃t] ADJ 1 *(commun ▸ démarche)* joint
2 *(lié ▸ cas, problème)* linked, related
3 *(qui accompagne)* **note conjointe** attached note
4 *Mus* conjoint, conjunct
NM,F *Admin* spouse; **il faut l'accord des deux conjoints** the agreement of both husband and wife is necessary; **les conjoints n'ont pas été invités** partners weren't invited; **les futurs conjoints** the bride and groom, the future couple; *Jur* **c. survivant** surviving spouse

conjointement [kɔ̃ʒwɛ̃tmɑ̃] ADV jointly; **c. avec mon associé** together with my associate; **vous recevrez c. la facture et le catalogue** you'll find the invoice enclosed with the catalogue; *Jur* **c. et solidairement** jointly and severally

conjoncteur [kɔ̃ʒɔ̃ktœr] NM 1 *Élec* circuit breaker, cut-out 2 *Tél* telephone socket

conjoncteur-disjoncteur [kɔ̃ʒɔ̃ktœrdisʒɔ̃ktœr] *(pl* **conjoncteurs-disjoncteurs***)* NM *Élec* circuit breaker, cut-out

conjonctif, -ive [kɔ̃ʒɔ̃ktif, -iv] ADJ 1 *Gram* conjunctive 2 *Anat* connective
• **conjonctive** NF 1 *Gram* conjunctive clause 2 *Anat* conjunctiva

conjonction [kɔ̃ʒɔ̃ksjɔ̃] NF 1 *(union)* union, conjunction; **dû à la c. de deux facteurs** due to the conjunction of two factors 2 *Gram* conjunction; **c. de coordination/subordination** coordinating/subordinating conjunction 3 *Astron* conjunction
• **en conjonction avec** PRÉP in conjunction with

conjonctive [kɔ̃ʒɔ̃ktiv] *voir* **conjonctif**

conjonctivite [kɔ̃ʒɔ̃ktivit] NF *Méd* conjunctivitis; **faire** *ou* **avoir de la c.** to have conjunctivitis; **c. aiguë** contagious conjunctivitis

conjoncture [kɔ̃ʒɔ̃ktyr] NF 1 *(contexte)* situation, conditions; **dans la c. actuelle** under the present circumstances, at this juncture; **c. boursière** market trend 2 *Écon* **c. (économique)** economic situation, economic conditions; **attendre une amélioration de la c.** to wait for economic conditions to improve; **on assiste à une dégradation de la c. économique** the economic situation is deteriorating; **de c.** conjunctural; **crise de c.** economic crisis; **étude de c.** study of the (overall) economic climate

conjoncturel, -elle [kɔ̃ʒɔ̃ktyrɛl] ADJ *(chômage)* cyclical; **crise conjoncturelle** economic crisis *(due to cyclical and not structural factors)*; **prévisions conjoncturelles** economic forecasts; **test c.** economic test

conjoncturiste [kɔ̃ʒɔ̃ktyrist] NMF economic planner

conjugable [kɔ̃ʒygabl] ADJ which can be conjugated

conjugaison [kɔ̃ʒygɛzɔ̃] NF 1 *Biol, Chim & Gram* conjugation 2 *(union)* union, conjunction; **grâce à la c. de leurs efforts** thanks to their joint efforts

conjugal, -e, -aux, -ales [kɔ̃ʒygal, -o] ADJ *(devoir)* conjugal; **bonheur c.** wedded *or* married bliss; **vie conjugale** married life

conjugalement [kɔ̃ʒygalmɑ̃] ADV conjugally; **vivre c.** to live as a married couple *or* as husband and wife

conjugué, -e [kɔ̃ʒyge] ADJ 1 *(uni ▸ efforts)* joint, combined 2 *Chim, Math, Bot & Opt* conjugate 3 *Tech* paired, twin
• **conjugués** NMPL *Math* conjugate complex numbers

conjuguer [3] [kɔ̃ʒyge] VT 1 *(verbe)* to conjugate; **c. au futur** to conjugate in the future tense 2 *(unir ▸ efforts, volontés)* to join, to combine
VPR **se conjuguer** 1 *Gram* to conjugate, to be conjugated 2 *(s'unir)* to work together, to combine

conjuration [kɔ̃ʒyrasjɔ̃] NF 1 *(complot)* conspiracy 2 *(incantation)* conjuration

conjuré, -e [kɔ̃ʒyre] NM,F conspirator, plotter

conjurer [3] [kɔ̃ʒyre] VT 1 *Littéraire (supplier)* to beg, to beseech; **il la conjura de ne pas le dénoncer** he begged *or* besought her not to give him away; **ne le bats pas, je t'en conjure** don't hit him, I beseech you *or* I beg (of) you 2 *(écarter ▸ mauvais sort, danger, crise)* to ward off, to keep at bay 3 *Littéraire (manigancer)* to plot; **c. la perte de qn** to plot sb's downfall
VPR **se conjurer** *Littéraire* to conspire; **se c. contre** to plot *or* to conspire against

connais *etc voir* **connaître**

connaissable [kɔnɛsabl] ADJ knowable

connaissait *etc voir* **connaître**

connaissance [kɔnɛsɑ̃s] NF 1 *(maîtrise dans un domaine)* knowledge; **avoir une c. intuitive/empirique de** to have an intuitive/empirical knowledge of; **une c. approfondie de l'espagnol** a thorough knowledge *or* good command of Spanish; **la c. de soi** self-knowledge
2 *Phil* **la c.** knowledge; **toutes les branches de la c.** all areas of (human) knowledge
3 *(fait d'être informé)* **avoir c. de qch** to know *or* to learn about sth, to be aware of sth; **il n'en a jamais eu c.** he never learnt about it, he was never notified of it; **prendre c. des faits** to learn about *or* to hear of the facts; **prendre c. d'un dossier** to study *or* to examine a case, to familiarize oneself with a case; **il est venu à notre c. que...** it has come to

our attention that…; **porter qch à la c. de qn** to bring sth to sb's knowledge *or* attention; *Mktg* **c. de la marque** brand awareness

4 *(conscience)* consciousness; **avoir toute sa c.** to be fully conscious; **il gisait là, sans c.** he was lying there unconscious; **perdre c.** to lose consciousness; **reprendre c.** to come to, to regain consciousness; **faire reprendre c. à qn** to bring sb to *or* round

5 faire la c. de qn, faire c. avec qn to make sb's acquaintance, to meet sb; **on a fait c. à Berne** we met in Berne; **lier c. avec qn** to strike up an acquaintance with sb; **une fois que vous aurez mieux fait c.** once you've got to know each other better; **prendre c. d'un texte** to read *or* to peruse a text

6 *(ami)* acquaintance; **c'est une simple c.** he's a mere *or* nodding acquaintance; **c'est une vieille c.** I've known him/her for ages, he's/she's an old acquaintance; **faire de nouvelles connaissances** to make new acquaintances, to meet new people

7 *Jur* cognizance

• **connaissances** NFPL knowledge; **l'acquisition des connaissances** the acquisition of knowledge, the learning process; **avoir des connaissances** to be knowledgeable; **avoir de solides connaissances en** to have a thorough knowledge of *or* a good grounding in; **avoir des connaissances sommaires en** to have a basic knowledge of, to know the rudiments of; **connaissances informatiques** computer literacy; **avoir des connaissances en informatique** to be computer literate; **connaissances livresques** book-learning; **mes connaissances en chimie sont tout ce qu'il y a de rudimentaire** my knowledge of chemistry is extremely rudimentary

• **à ma/sa/***etc* **connaissance** ADV to (the best of) my/his/*etc* knowledge, as far as I know/he knows/*etc*; **pas à ma c.** not to my knowledge, not as far as I know, not that I know of; **il n'y avait pas, à sa c., de cas semblable dans la famille** there was, as far as he/she knew, no similar case in the family

• **de connaissance** ADJ **un visage de c.** a familiar face; **nous sommes entre gens de c. ici** we all know each other here; **être en pays de c.** *(dans un domaine)* to be on familiar ground; *(dans un milieu)* to be among familiar faces

• **de ma/sa/***etc* **connaissance** ADJ **une personne de ma c.** an acquaintance of mine, somebody I know

• **en connaissance de cause** ADV **faire qch en c. de cause** to do sth with full knowledge of the facts; **je souhaite que vous preniez la décision en toute c. de cause** I hope you're making an informed decision; **et j'en parle en c. de cause** and I know what I'm talking about

connaissement [kɔ̃nɛsmɑ̃] NM *Com* bill of lading, waybill; **c. aérien** air waybill; **c. clausé** dirty bill of lading; **c. direct** through bill; **c. net** clean bill of lading

connaisseur, -euse [kɔnɛsœr, -øz] ADJ *(regard, air)* expert *(avant n)*, knowledgeable; **je ne suis pas du tout c.** I'm by no means an expert

NM,F connoisseur; **un public de connaisseurs** a knowledgeable audience, an audience of experts; **parler de qch en c.** to speak knowledgeably about sth; **être c. en pierres précieuses** to be a connoisseur of *or* knowledgeable about gems

CONNAÎTRE [91] [kɔnɛtr]

VT
- to know **A1–4, B1, D1, 2**
- to recognize **A4**
- to feel **C1**
- to meet **B2**
- to have **D1**
- to experience **C1–3**

VPR
- to know **1**
- to be acquainted **2**
- to have met **2**
- to meet **3**

VT **A.** *AVOIR UNE IDÉE DE* **1** *(avoir mémorisé ▸ code postal, itinéraire, mot de passe)* to know; **connaistu le chemin pour y aller?** do you know how to get there *or* the way there?; **la cachette était connue d'elle seule** she was the only one who knew where the hiding place was; **c. les bonnes adresses** to know (all) the best places to go

2 *(être informé de ▸ information, nouvelle)* to know; **je suis impatient de c. les résultats** I'm anxious to know *or* to hear the results; **connaissez-vous la nouvelle?** have you heard the news?; *Fam* **tu connais celle du cheval qui ne voulait pas boire?** do you know *or* have you heard the one about the horse who wouldn't drink?; **tu ne connais pas ta chance** you don't know how lucky you are, you don't know your luck; **faire c.** *(avis, sentiment)* to make known; *(décision, jugement)* to make known, to announce; **je vous ferai c. ma décision plus tard** I'll inform you of my decision *or* I'll let you know what I've decided later; **je vous ferai c. mes intentions** I'll let you know what I intend to do; **je ne te connaissais pas ce manteau** I didn't know you had this coat, I've never seen you wearing this coat (before); **je ne lui connais aucun défaut** I'm not aware of him/her having any faults; **on ne lui connaissait aucun ennemi** he/she had no known enemies

3 *(avoir des connaissances sur ▸ langue, ville, appareil, œuvre)* to know, to be familiar with; *(▸ technique)* to know, to be acquainted with; *(▸ sujet)* to know (about); **je ne connais pas l'italien** I don't know *or* can't speak Italian; **je connais un peu l'informatique** I have some basic knowledge of computing; **apprenez à c. votre corps** learn to know your body; **je ne conduirai pas, je ne connais pas ta voiture** I won't drive, I'm not familiar with *or* I don't know your car; *aussi Ironique* **elle connaît tout sur tout** she knows everything there is to know; **il connaît bien les Alpes** he knows the Alps well; **je connais mal les dauphins** my knowledge of dolphins is patchy, I don't know much about dolphins; **faire c. un produit** to publicize a product; **son dernier film l'a fait c. dans le monde entier** his/her latest movie has brought him/her worldwide fame; **sa traduction a fait c. son œuvre en France** his/her translation has brought his/her work to French audiences; **cette émission est destinée à faire c. des artistes étrangers** this programme is aimed at introducing foreign artists; *Fam* **les bons vins, ça le connaît!** he knows a thing or two about *or* he's an expert on good wine!; **la mécanique, ça le connaît!** he's a whizz *or Br* a dab hand at mechanics!; **c. qch comme sa poche** to know sth inside out *or* like the back of one's hand; **y c. quelque chose en** to have some idea *or* to know something about; **tu y connais quelque chose en informatique?** do you know anything about computers?; **je n'y connais rien en biologie** I don't know a thing about biology; **c. son affaire** *ou* **métier** to know one's job; *Fam* **en c. un bout** *ou* **rayon sur** to know a thing or two about; *Fam* **c. la chanson** *ou* **musique** to have heard it all before; **il te remboursera – ouais, je connais la musique!** he'll pay you back – yeah, (I've) heard that one before!

4 *Littéraire (reconnaître)* to recognize, to know; **c. qn à qch** to recognize sb because of sth

B. *IDENTIFIER, ÊTRE EN RELATION AVEC* **1** *(par l'identité)* to know; **c. qn de vue/nom/réputation** to know sb by sight/name/reputation; **on la connaissait sous le nom de Louise Michel** she was known as Louise Michel; **se faire c.** *(révéler son identité)* to make oneself known; *(devenir une personne publique)* to make oneself *or* to become known; **notre auditeur n'a pas voulu se faire c.** our listener didn't want his name to be known *or* wished to remain anonymous; **la police ne le connaît que trop bien!** the police know him only too well!; **je suis patient, tu me connais** I'm patient, you know me; **la connaissant, ça ne me surprend pas** knowing her, I'm not surprised; **tu me connais mal!** you don't know me (at all)!; **elle a bien connu ton oncle** she knew your uncle well; **je la connais depuis toujours** I've always known her; **je t'ai connu plus enjoué** I've known you to be chirpier; **je l'ai connu enfant** I knew him when he was a child; **si tu fais ça, je ne te connais plus!** if you do that, I'll have nothing more to do with you!; *Fam* **je te connais comme si je t'avais fait!** I know you as if you were my own *or* like the back of my hand!; *Fam* **j'en connais un qui ne va pas être content!** I know at least one person who's not going to be happy!

2 *(rencontrer)* to meet; **j'aimerais le c.** I'd like to meet him; **ah, si je t'avais connu plus tôt!** if only I'd met you earlier!; **je l'ai connu au cours du tournage** I got to know him while we were shooting the movie; **j'aimerais vous faire c. mon frère** I would like to introduce you to my brother

3 *Bible (sexuellement)* to have carnal knowledge of, to know

C. *ÉPROUVER* **1** *(peur, amour)* to feel, to know, to experience; **dans ses bras, j'ai connu l'amour** in his/her arms, I understood what love was; **une famille où il pourra enfin c. la tendresse** a family where he will at last experience affection

2 *(faire l'expérience de)* to experience; **tu n'as pas connu les petits bars de Saint-Germain!** you never knew *or* experienced the little bars in Saint-Germain!; **elle n'a jamais connu la faim** she's never known hunger *or* what hunger means; **la tour avait connu des jours meilleurs** the tower had seen better days; **ah, l'insouciance de la jeunesse, j'ai connu ça!** I was young and carefree once!; *Fam* **ses promesses, je connais!** don't talk to me about his/her promises!; **faire c. qch à qn** to introduce sb to sth

3 *(obtenir ▸ succès, gloire)* to have, to experience; **enfin, elle connut la consécration** she finally received the highest accolade

4 *(subir ▸ crise)* to go *or* to live through, to experience; *(▸ épreuve, humiliation, guerre)* to live through, to suffer, to undergo; **il a connu bien des déboires** he has had *or* suffered plenty of setbacks; **il a connu un destin tragique** his was a tragic fate; **puis Rome connut la décadence** then Rome went through a period of *or* fell into decline; **sa carrière a connu des hauts et des bas** his/her career has had its ups and downs; **cette région connaît actuellement une famine** this region is now experiencing a famine

D. *ADMETTRE* **1** *(sujet: chose)* to have; *(au négatif)* to know; **son ambition ne connaît pas de bornes** *ou* **limites** his/her ambition is boundless *or* knows no bounds

2 *(sujet: personne) Littéraire* **il ne connaît pas de maître** he knows no master; **il ne connaît que le travail** work is the only thing he's interested in *or* he knows; *Fam* **les voitures, tu ne connais que ça!** cars, that's all you're interested in!; **il ne connaît que le mensonge** he is incapable of telling the truth; **contre les rhumes, je ne connais qu'un bon grog** there's nothing like a good old rum toddy to cure a cold

USAGE ABSOLU **tu sais comment ça marche? – oui, je connais** do you know how it works? – yes, I do

• **connaître de** VT IND *Jur* **ce tribunal ne connaît pas des fraudes fiscales** this court is not empowered to deal with tax fraud

VPR **se connaître 1** *(soi-même)* to know oneself, to be self-aware; **je n'oserai jamais, je me connais** I'd never dare, I know what I'm like; **connais-toi toi-même** know thyself

2 *(l'un l'autre)* to be acquainted, to have met (before); **vous vous connaissez?** have you met (before)?; **tout le monde se connaît?** has everybody met everybody else?; **ils se connaissent bien** they know each other well

3 *(se rencontrer)* to meet; **ils se sont connus en 1970** they met in 1970

4 s'y c. en architecture to know a lot about architecture; **je ne m'y connais pas en antiquités** I don't know anything about antiques; **je m'y connais peu en informatique** I don't know much about computers; *Fam* **ah ça, pour râler, il s'y connaît!** he's very good at grumbling!; *Fam* **pour les gaffes, tu t'y connais!** when it comes to putting you foot in it, you take some beating!; **c'est un escroc, ou je ne m'y connais pas!** I know a crook when I see one!

connard, -asse [kɔnar, -as] NM,F *très Fam* **1** *(homme stupide)* stupid bastard, prick; *(femme stupide)* stupid bitch **2** *(homme déplaisant)* bastard; *(femme déplaisante)* bitch

conne [kɔn] *voir* **con**

connecter [4] [kɔnɛkte] VT to connect; *Ordinat* **connecté** on line; *Ordinat* **connecté en anneau/bus/étoile** in a ring/bus/star configuration; *Ordinat* **connecté en série** series-connected; *Ordinat* **c. en boucle** to daisy-chain

VPR **se connecter** à *Ordinat (système)* to log on to; *(l'Internet)* to connect to

connecteur [kɔnɛktœr] NM *Ordinat* connector

connectivité [kɔnɛktivite] NF *Ordinat* connectivity

connement [kɔnmɑ̃] ADV *très Fam* stupidly; **il s'est fait c. piquer sa caisse** the stupid idiot got his car pinched; **et c. j'ai accepté** and like the idiot that I am, I said yes

connerie [kɔnri] NF *très Fam* **1** *(stupidité)* stupidity; **sa c. se lit sur sa figure** you can tell he's/she's a *Br* prat *or Am* schmuck just by looking at him/her **2** *(acte, remarque)* stupid thing; **raconter des conneries** to talk crap; **depuis qu'elle est arrivée, elle ne fait que des conneries** she's been an absolute *Br* bloody *or Am* goddamn liability since the day she arrived; **j'ai peur qu'il fasse une c.** *(un acte inconsidéré)* I'm afraid he might do something stupid

connétable [kɔnetabl] NM *Hist* constable

connexe [kɔnɛks] ADJ *(idées, problèmes)* closely related

connexion [kɔnɛksjɔ̃] NF connection

connivence [kɔnivɑ̃s] NF connivance, complicity; **être de c. avec qn** to be in connivance with sb, to connive with sb; **ils sont de c.** they're in league with each other; **un regard de c.** a conniving look

connotation [kɔnɔtasjɔ̃] NF **1** *Ling* connotation **2** *(nuance)* overtone

connoter [3] [kɔnɔte] VT **1** *Ling* to connote **2** *Physiol* to connote, to imply, to have overtones of

connu, -e [kɔny] PP *voir* **connaître**

ADJ **1** *(découvert ▸ univers)* known **2** *(répandu ▸ idée, tactique)* well-known, widely known; **c'est bien c.!** that's a well-known fact!, everyone knows that! **3** *(célèbre ▸ personnalité, chanteur)* famous, well-known; **peu c.** *(personne, œuvre)* little-known; *(lieu)* out-of-the-way; **un de ses tableaux les moins connus** one of his/her least well-known *or* least-known paintings; *Fam* **une blague connue** an old joke; **il est c. comme le loup blanc** everybody knows him

NM **le c. et l'inconnu** the known and the unknown

conque [kɔ̃k] NF **1** *Zool* conch **2** *Anat* external ear, *Spéc* concha

conquérant, -e [kɔ̃kerɑ̃, -ɑ̃t] ADJ **1** *Mil & Pol* conquering **2** *(hautain ▸ sourire)* domineering; *(▸ démarche)* swaggering; **il entra d'un air c.** he swaggered in

NM,F conqueror

conquérir [39] [kɔ̃kerir] VT **1** *Mil & Pol* to conquer **2** *(acquérir ▸ espace, pouvoir)* to gain control over, to capture, to conquer; *(▸ marché, part de marché)* to conquer; **c. de nouveaux marchés** to conquer new markets; **se comporter comme en pays conquis** to act as if one owns the place **3** *(séduire ▸ cœur, public)* to win (over), to conquer; *(▸ estime, respect)* to win, to gain; **c. un homme/une femme** to win a man's/a woman's heart; **être conquis** to be entirely won over

VPR **se conquérir** to be (hard) won *or* earned; **l'amitié ça se conquiert** friendship is something you have to work at

conquête [kɔ̃kɛt] NF **1** *(action)* conquest; **partir à la c. de l'Amérique** to set out to conquer America; **faire la c. d'un pays** to conquer a country; **il a fait la c. de ma cousine** he's made a conquest of my cousin, he's won my cousin's heart; **se lancer à la c. du pouvoir** to make a bid for power; **la c. de nouveaux marchés en Asie est une des priorités de l'entreprise** conquering new Asian markets is one of the company's priorities **2** *(chose gagnée)* conquest, conquered territory; **les conquêtes des premiers jours de la révolution** the conquests of the early days of the revolution **3** *(personne)* conquest; **sa dernière c. s'appelle Peter** her latest conquest is called Peter

conquiert *etc voir* **conquérir**

conquis, -e [kɔ̃ki, -iz] *pp voir* **conquérir**

conquistador [kɔ̃kistadɔr] NM conquistador

consacré, -e [kɔ̃sakre] ADJ **1** *Rel (hostie)* consecrated; *(terre)* hallowed **2** *(accepté ▸ rite, terme)* accepted, established; **c'est l'expression consacrée** it's the accepted way of saying it; **selon la formule consacrée** as the saying goes; **c. par l'usage** sanctioned by usage **3** *(célèbre ▸ artiste, cinéaste)* established, recognized

consacrer [3] [kɔ̃sakre] VT **1 c. qch à** *(réserver qch à)* to devote *or* to dedicate sth to; **combien de temps consacrez-vous à la lecture?** how much time do you devote to *or* spend reading?; **as-tu dix minutes à me c.?** can you spare me ten minutes?

2 *Rel (pain, église, évêque)* to consecrate; *(prêtre)* to ordain; **c. un temple à Jupiter** to consecrate *or* to dedicate a temple to Jupiter;

3 *(entériner ▸ pratique, injustice)* to sanction, to hallow; **expression consacrée par l'usage** expression that has become established by usage; **tradition consacrée par le temps** time-honoured tradition

4 *(couronner ▸ artiste, acteur)* to crown, to turn into a star; **le jury l'a consacré meilleur acteur de l'année** the jury voted him best actor of the year

VPR **se consacrer se c. à** to devote *or* to dedicate oneself to; **je ne peux me c. à mon fils que le soir** I can only find time for my son in the evenings; **se c. à Dieu** to consecrate one's life to the service of *or* to devote oneself to God

consanguin, -e [kɔ̃sɑ̃gɛ̃, -in] ADJ **sœur consanguine** half-sister *(on the father's side)*; **mariage c.** intermarriage, marriage between blood relatives

NM,F half-brother, *f* half-sister *(on the father's side)*; **les consanguins** blood relations *or* relatives

consanguinité [kɔ̃sɑ̃ginite] NF **1** *(parenté)* consanguinity **2** *(mariages consanguins)* intermarriage

consciemment [kɔ̃sjamɑ̃] ADV consciously, knowingly

conscience [kɔ̃sjɑ̃s] NF **1** *(connaissance)* consciousness, awareness; **avoir c. de qch/d'avoir fait qch** to be conscious *or* aware of sth/of having done sth; **j'ai c. de mes capacités** I'm aware of my abilities; **prendre c. de qch** to become aware of *or* to realize sth; **ça m'a fait prendre c. de la précarité du bonheur** it made me realize *or* aware (of) how precarious happiness is; **c. de classe** class consciousness; **c. collective/politique** collective/political consciousness; **c. de soi** self-awareness

2 *(sens de la morale)* conscience; **agir selon sa c.** to do as one thinks right; **libérer** *ou* **soulager sa c.** to relieve one's conscience; **avoir qch sur la c.** to have sth on one's conscience; **elle a un poids sur la c.** there is a heavy weight on her conscience; *Fam* **il a la c. large** *ou* **élastique** he has a very flexible sense of right and wrong; **avoir la c. tranquille** to have an easy conscience; **pour avoir la c. tranquille je vais vérifier que tout est bien fermé** to set my mind at rest, I'll just make sure everything's locked up; **je n'ai pas la c. tranquille de l'avoir laissé seul** I have an uneasy conscience *or* I feel bad about having left him alone; **avoir bonne c.** to have a clear conscience; **tu dis ça pour te donner bonne c.** you're saying this to appease your conscience; **avoir mauvaise c.** to have a guilty *or* bad conscience; **c'est une affaire** *ou* **un cas de c.** it's a matter of conscience; **crise de c.** crisis of conscience; **j'ai ma c. pour moi** my conscience is clear

3 *(lucidité)* consciousness; **perdre c.** to lose consciousness; **reprendre c.** to regain consciousness, to come to

4 *(application)* **c. professionnelle** conscientiousness; **faire son travail avec beaucoup de c. professionnelle** to do one's job very conscientiously, to be conscientious in one's work

• **en (toute) conscience** ADV in all conscience; **je ne peux, en c., te laisser partir seul** I can't in all conscience let you go on your own

> Attention: ne pas confondre **conscience** et **consciousness** lorsque l'on traduit le terme français **conscience**. Le terme anglais **conscience** se rapporte à la conscience morale, alors que **consciousness** se rapporte à la conscience psychologique et s'oppose à l'inconscience.

consciencieuse [kɔ̃sjɑ̃søz] *voir* **consciencieux**

consciencieusement [kɔ̃sjɑ̃sjøzmɑ̃] ADV conscientiously

consciencieux, -euse [kɔ̃sjɑ̃sjø, -øz] ADJ *(élève)* conscientious, meticulous; *(travail)* meticulous

conscient, -e [kɔ̃sjɑ̃, -ɑ̃t] ADJ **1** *(délibéré ▸ choix, geste, désir, haine)* conscious

2 *Phil* (self-)conscious

3 *(averti)* aware; **être c. du danger** to be aware *or* conscious of the danger; **es-tu c. que tu as failli tous nous tuer?** are you aware *or* do you realize that you nearly killed us all?

4 *(lucide ▸ blessé)* conscious

NM **le c.** the conscious (mind)

conscription [kɔ̃skripsjɔ̃] NF *Br* conscription, *Am* draft

conscrit [kɔ̃skri] NM *(qui a l'âge d'être inscrit)* person liable to conscription; *(qui fait son service) Br* conscript, *Am* draftee; **armée de conscrits** *Br* conscript *or Am* draft army; *Fam* **se faire avoir comme un c.** to be completely taken in

consécration [kɔ̃sekrasjɔ̃] NF **1** *Rel (du pain, d'une église, d'un évêque)* consecration; *(d'un prêtre)* ordination **2** *(confirmation ▸ d'une coutume)* establishment, sanctioning; *(▸ d'une injustice)* sanctioning **3** *(d'une carrière)* apotheosis, crowning point; **exposer dans cette galerie sera pour lui une c.** having an exhibition in that gallery will set the seal on his reputation *or* will establish his reputation once and for all

consécutif, -ive [kɔ̃sekytif, -iv] ADJ **1** *(successif)* consecutive; **dormir douze heures consécutives** to sleep for twelve consecutive hours *or* for twelve hours solid; **c'est la cinquième fois consécutive qu'il remet le rendez-vous** this is the fifth time running *or* in a row that he's postponed the meeting; **les dégâts consécutifs à l'incendie** the damage brought about *or* caused by the fire; **l'infarctus est souvent c. au surmenage** heart attacks are often the result of stress **2** *Gram & Math* consecutive

consécutivement [kɔ̃sekytivmɑ̃] ADV consecutively; **notre équipe a subi c. quatre défaites** our team has suffered four consecutive defeats *or* four defeats in a row; **les accidents se sont produits c.** the accidents happened one after another *or* the other

• **consécutivement à** PRÉP as a result of, following

conseil [kɔ̃sɛj] NM **1** *(avis)* piece of advice, *Sout* counsel; *(en marketing, finance etc)* consultancy; **un dernier petit c.** one last word *or* piece of advice; **un c. d'ami** a friendly piece of advice; **des conseils** *(d'ami)* advice; *(trucs)* tips, hints; **j'ai besoin de tes conseils** *ou* **ton c.** I need your advice; **conseils aux bricoleurs/jardiniers** hints for handymen/gardeners; **agir sur/suivre le c. de qn** to act on/to take sb's advice; **écouter le c. de qn** to listen to *or* to take sb's advice; **demander c. à qn** to ask sb's advice, to ask sb for advice; **donner un c. à qn** to advise sb; **si j'avais un c. à te donner** if I had one piece of advice to give you; **prendre c. auprès de qn** to take advice from sb; **suivre les conseils de qn** to follow *or Sout* to heed sb's advice; **c. conjugal** marriage guidance

2 *(conseiller)* adviser, consultant; **c. en communication** media consultant, PR consultant; **c. financier** financial consultant *or* adviser; **c. en gestion** management consultant; **c. judiciaire** guardian, trustee; **c. juridique** legal adviser; **c. en marketing** marketing consultant; **c. en organisation** organizational consultant; **c. en publicité** advertising consultant; **c. en recrutement** recruitment consultant; **ingénieur c.** consultant engineer

3 *(assemblée ▸ gén)* council, committee; *(▸ d'une entreprise)* board; *(réunion)* meeting; **tenir c.** to hold a meeting; **c. d'administration** *(d'une société)* board of directors; *(d'une organisation internationale)* governing body; **c. d'arbitrage** conciliation *or* arbitration board; **c. d'arrondissement** district council; **C. des Bourses de Valeurs** = regulatory body of the Paris Stock Exchange; **c. de cabinet** cabinet council, council of ministers; **le C. constitutionnel** = French government body ensuring that laws, elections and referenda are constitutional; **c. Ecofin** ECOFIN; **c. économique** economic council; **c. d'entreprise** works committee; **le C. d'État** the (French) Council of State; **le C. de l'Europe** the Council of Europe; *Can* **C. exécutif** ≃ Cabinet; **c. de famille** board of guardians; *Hum* family gathering; **c. général** ≃ county council; **c. de guerre** *(réunion)* council of war, ≃ War Cabinet; *(tribunal)* court-martial; **passer en c. de guerre** to be court-martialled; **faire passer qn en c. de guerre** to court-martial sb; **c. intermi-**

nistériel interministerial council; **le C. des ministres** ≃ the Cabinet; **c. municipal** *(en ville)* ≃ town council, ≃ local (urban) council; *(à la campagne)* ≃ local (rural) council, *Br* ≃ parish council; **C. national des autochtones du Canada** Native Council of Canada; *Jur* **c. national des barreaux** national Bar council; *Hist* **C. national de la Résistance** = central organization of the French Resistance founded in 1943; *Jur* **c. de l'ordre** = council of a professional body; *Jur* **c. de prud'hommes** industrial arbitration court, *Br* ≃ ACAS; **c. régional** regional council; *Mil* **c. de révision** recruiting board, *Am* draft board; **le C. de sécurité** the Security Council; **le C. supérieur de la magistrature** = French state body that appoints members of the judiciary; *Jur* **c. supérieur de la prud'homie** = industrial arbitration review board; **c. de surveillance** supervisory board

4 *Scol & Univ* **c. de classe** staff meeting *(concerning a class)*; **c. de discipline** disciplinary committee; **passer en c. de discipline** to appear before the disciplinary committee; **c. d'école** = committee responsible for internal organization of a primary school; **c. d'établissement** *Br* ≃ board of governors, *Am* ≃ board of education; **c. des maîtres** = teachers' committee at a primary school; **c. des professeurs** = meeting which takes place each term where teachers discuss progress made by individual pupils; **C. d'Université** *Br* ≃ university Senate, *Am* ≃ Board of Trustees

5 *Arch (résolution)* (firm) resolution; **ne savoir quel c. prendre** not to know what decision to make

• **de bon conseil** ADJ **un homme de bon c.** a man of sound advice, a wise counsellor; **demande-lui, elle est de bon c.** ask her, she's good at giving advice

CONSEIL DE CLASSE

The French school year is divided into three terms. In secondary schools, a "conseil de classe", or staff meeting, is held at the end of each term to discuss the progress made by pupils in a given class. A report containing the marks obtained during the term with teachers' comments is filled in for each pupil. The "conseil de classe" is initially held behind closed doors, attended by the teachers of a given class and the head teacher, and then with two elected class representatives present. During the last "conseil de classe" of the year, decisions are taken such as which pupils repeat a year and which should change courses.

conseiller[1] **[4]** [kɔ̃seje] VT **1** *(recommander ▸ livre, dentiste)* to recommend; **c. qn/qch à qn** to recommend sb/sth to sb **2** *(donner son avis à ▸ ami, enfant)* to advise, to give advice to; **elle conseille le président sur les questions économiques** she advises *or* counsels the President on economic matters; **on m'a bien/mal conseillé** I was given good/bad advice; **je vous conseille de réserver** I would advise you to make a reservation; **je ne vous le conseille pas** I wouldn't recommend it; **il n'est pas conseillé de conduire par ce temps** it's not advisable to drive in this weather; **beaucoup d'étudiants souhaitent se faire c. dans le choix d'une filière** many students want to be advised about choosing a field of study

conseiller[2]**, -ère** [kɔ̃seje, -ɛr] NM,F **1** *(guide)* adviser, counsellor; *(spécialiste)* adviser, consultant; **c'est un très bon c.** he gives very good advice; **c. de clientèle** consumer adviser; **c. commercial** marketing *or* sales consultant; **c. conjugal** marriage guidance counsellor; **c. économique** economic adviser; **c. financier** financial adviser *or* consultant; **c. fiscal** tax consultant; **c. en gestion (d'entreprise)** management consultant; **c. juridique** legal adviser; **c. en marketing** marketing consultant; **c. matrimonial** marriage guidance counsellor; *Fin* **c. en placements** investment adviser; **c. technique** technical adviser **2** *Scol* **c. d'éducation** = non-teaching staff member in charge of general discipline; **c. d'orientation** *Br* careers adviser, *Am* career *or* guidance counselor; **c. pédagogique** educational adviser **3** *Admin (membre d'un conseil)* council member, councillor; **c. d'État** member of the Conseil d'État; **c. général** regional councillor; **c. municipal** *(en ville)* ≃ local *or* town councillor; *(à la campagne)* ≃ local councillor

conseilleur, -euse [kɔ̃sejœr, -øz] NM,F *Péj* giver of advice; *Prov* **les conseilleurs ne sont pas les payeurs** = it's very easy to give advice when you're not going to suffer the consequences

consens *etc voir* **consentir**

consensualisme [kɔ̃sɑ̃sɥalism] NM mutual agreement

consensuel, -elle [kɔ̃sɑ̃sɥɛl] ADJ **1** *(contrat)* consensus *(avant n)*, consensual; **une politique consensuelle** a strategy of seeking the middle ground, consensus politics **2** *Anat* consensual

consensus [kɔ̃sɛ̃sys] NM consensus (of opinion); **il n'y a pas de c. là-dessus** there's no consensus of *or* generally agreed opinion on this

consentant, -e [kɔ̃sɑ̃tɑ̃, -ɑ̃t] ADJ **1** *(victime)* willing **2** *Jur* **les trois parties sont consentantes** the three parties are in agreement *or* are agreeable; **adultes consentants** consenting adults

consentement [kɔ̃sɑ̃tmɑ̃] NM consent; **donner son c. à** to (give one's) consent to; **avec/sans le c. de la famille** with/without the family's consent; *Jur* **c. exprès/tacite** formal/tacit consent; **c. éclairé** informed consent; **divorce par c. mutuel** divorce by mutual consent

consentir **[37]** [kɔ̃sɑ̃tir] VT *(délai, réduction)* to grant; **c. qch à qn** to grant *or* to allow sb sth; **on m'a consenti une remise de 10 pour cent** I was allowed a 10 percent discount

USAGE ABSOLU to consent

• **consentir à** VT IND to consent *or* to agree to; **c. à une hausse des salaires** to consent *or* to agree to a wage increase; **elle n'a pas consenti à m'accompagner** *(n'a pas été d'accord pour le faire)* she didn't agree to come with me; *(n'a pas daigné le faire)* she didn't deign to *or* stoop so low as to accompany me; **consentiront-ils à ce que tu épouses un étranger?** will they consent to your marrying a foreigner?

conséquemment [kɔ̃sekamɑ̃] ADV consequently; **c. à** as a result of, following (on *or* upon)

conséquence [kɔ̃sekɑ̃s] NF **1** *(résultat)* consequence, repercussion; **lourd de conséquences** with serious consequences; **ma gaffe a eu pour c. de les brouiller** my blunder resulted in their falling out (with each other); **cela ne tirera pas à c.** this won't have any repercussions *or* will be of no consequence; **une déclaration sans c.** *(sans importance)* a statement of no *or* little consequence; *(sans suite)* an inconsequential statement; **ton acte sera sans c. sur ton avenir** your action will have no effect on your future **2** *(conclusion)* inference, conclusion

• **de conséquence** ADJ **personne de c.** person of consequence *or* importance; **une affaire de c.** a matter of (some) consequence

• **en conséquence** ADV **1** *(par conséquent)* consequently, therefore **2** *(comme il convient)* accordingly

• **en conséquence de** PRÉP **1 en c. de quoi** as a result of which **2** *(conformément à)* according to

conséquent, -e [kɔ̃sekɑ̃, -ɑ̃t] ADJ **1** *(cohérent)* consistent; **être c. dans ses engagements** to be consistent in one's commitments **2** *Fam (important ▸ moyens, magasin)* sizeable; *(▸ somme)* tidy **3** *Géog* consequent

NM **1** *Phil & Gram* consequent **2** *Mus* answer

• **par conséquent** ADV consequently, as a result

conservateur, -trice [kɔ̃sɛrvatœr, -tris] ADJ **1** *(prudent ▸ placement, gestion)* conservative; **avoir un esprit c.** to be conservative-minded **2** *Pol (gén)* conservative; **le parti c.** *(en Grande-Bretagne)* the Conservative *or* Tory Party; *(au Canada)* the Progressive Conservative Party

NM,F **1** *Pol (gén)* conservative; *(en Grande-Bretagne)* Conservative, Tory **2** *(responsable ▸ de musée)* curator; *(▸ de bibliothèque)* librarian; **c. des Eaux et Forêts** *Br* ≃ Forestry Commissioner, *Am* ≃ member of the Forest Service; **c. des hypothèques** ≃ mortgage registrar; *Bourse* **c. de titres** custodian

NM *(additif)* preservative; **sans c.** preservative-free, free of preservatives

conservation [kɔ̃sɛrvasjɔ̃] NF **1** *(dans l'agroalimentaire)* preserving; **c. par le froid** cold storage; *(congélation)* freezing

2 *(maintien en bon état)* keeping, preserving, safeguarding

3 *Biol & Phys* **c. de l'énergie** conservation of energy

4 *(état)* state of preservation; **des bâtiments en bon état de c.** well-preserved buildings

5 *Admin* **c. des Eaux et Forêts** *Br* ≃ Forestry Commission, *Am* ≃ Forest Service; **C. des hypothèques** ≃ Land Registry

6 *Bourse* custody

conservatisme [kɔ̃sɛrvatism] NM **1** *(prudence)* conservatism **2** *Pol (gén)* conservatism; *(en Grande-Bretagne)* Conservatism

conservatoire [kɔ̃sɛrvatwar] ADJ protective

NM *(école)* school, academy; **c. de musique** conservatoire; **le C. (national supérieur d'art dramatique)** = national drama school in Paris; **le C. (national supérieur de musique)** the Conservatoire *(in Paris and Lyons)*; **c. national de région** = regional advanced music college; **le C. national des arts et métiers** = science and technology school in Paris

conservatrice [kɔ̃sɛrvatris] *voir* **conservateur**

conserve [kɔ̃sɛrv] NF *(en boîte)* item of canned *or Br* tinned food; *(en bocal)* bottled preserve; **les conserves** canned *or Br* tinned food; **c. de viande** canned *or Br* tinned meat; **conserves de fruits** conserves; **mettre en c.** to can, *Br* to tin; *Hum* **on ne va pas en faire des conserves!** we're not going to hang on to it forever!

• **de conserve** ADV **naviguer de c.** to sail in convoy; *Fig Littéraire* **aller de c.** to go (all) together; *Littéraire* **agir de c.** to act in concert

conservé, -e [kɔ̃sɛrve] ADJ **bien c.** well-preserved

conserver **[3]** [kɔ̃sɛrve] VT **1** *(aliment ▸ dans le vinaigre)* to pickle; *(▸ dans le sel, par séchage, en congelant)* to preserve; *(▸ dans le sucre)* to preserve, to conserve; *(▸ dans des boîtes)* to preserve, to can, *Br* to tin, *(▸ en bocal)* to bottle

2 *Archit, Constr & Écol (édifice, énergie)* to preserve

3 *(stocker)* to keep, to store, to stock; **c. à l'abri de l'humidité** *(sur mode d'emploi)* keep *or* store in a dry place

4 *(avoir en sa possession ▸ photos, relations)* to keep, to hang on to; **j'ai toujours conservé mes amis** I've always kept (up with) my friends; **c. qch précieusement** to treasure sth

5 *(garder ▸ charme, force, illusion, calme)* to keep, to retain; **c. (toute) sa tête** *(rester calme)* to keep one's head *or* self-control; *(être lucide)* to have all one's wits about one; **elle a conservé sa beauté** she's kept *or* retained her looks; *Fam* **le sport, ça conserve** sport keeps you young; **c. son amitié à qn** to stay friendly with sb

6 *(à la suite d'une expérience)* **c. des séquelles d'une maladie** to suffer the after-effects of a disease; **j'en ai conservé un excellent souvenir** I've retained very good memories of it; **j'en ai conservé la peur du noir** it left me with a fear of the dark

7 *Naut* **c. sa position** to hold one's position

8 *Mil* **c. ses positions** to hold fast

VPR **se conserver 1** *(être stocké)* to be kept; **les pommes doivent se c. sur des clayettes** apples must be stored on racks **2** *(durer ▸ aliment)* to keep; *(▸ poterie, parchemin)* to survive; **les truffes au chocolat ne se conservent pas longtemps** (chocolate) truffles don't keep long

conserverie [kɔ̃sɛrvəri] NF **1** *(industrie)* canning industry **2** *(technique)* canning **3** *(usine)* canning factory

considérable [kɔ̃siderabl] ADJ *(somme)* considerable, sizeable; *(changement)* significant; **cela représente un travail c.** that represents a considerable *or* significant amount of work; **un problème d'une importance c.** a major *or* serious problem

considérablement [kɔ̃siderabləmɑ̃] ADV considerably

considérant [kɔ̃siderɑ̃] NM *Jur* preamble

considération [kɔ̃siderasjɔ̃] NF **1** *(examen)* consideration, scrutiny; **la question mérite c.** the question is worth considering **2** *(préoccupation)* consideration, factor; **ce ne sont pas les seules considérations** these are not the only considerations; **ce sont des considérations bassement matérielles** these are very mundane preoccupations; **les considérations de temps** the time factor; **si l'on s'arrête à ce genre de considérations** if we pay too much attention to this kind of detail **3** *(respect)* regard, esteem; **par c. pour** out of respect *or* regard for; **jouir d'une grande c.** to be highly considered *or* regarded, to be held in great esteem; **quel manque de c.!** how inconsiderate!; **veuillez agréer l'assurance de ma c. distinguée** *(à quelqu'un dont on connaît le nom) Br* yours sincerely, *Am* sincerely (yours); *(à quelqu'un dont on ne connaît pas le nom) Br* yours faithfully, *Am* sincerely (yours)

• **considérations** NFPL *(remarques)* observations, reflections, thoughts; **se perdre en considérations inutiles** to get bogged down in idle considerations, to waste time on irrelevancies

• **en considération** ADV **faire entrer qch en c.** to bring sth into play *or* consideration; **prendre qch en c.** to take sth into account *or* consideration

• **en considération de** PRÉP **en c. de votre état de santé** because of *or* given *or* considering (the state of) your health; **en c. de vos services** in (full) recognition of your services

• **sans considération de** PRÉP **sans c. de personne** without taking individual cases into consideration *or* account; **sans c. du coût** regardless *or* heedless of *or* without considering (the) cost

considérer [18] [kɔ̃sidere] VT **1** *(regarder)* to gaze *or* to stare at; **c. qn avec hostilité** to stare at sb in a hostile manner; **considérons la droite AB** consider the line AB

2 *(prendre en compte ► offre, problème)* to consider, to take into consideration, to weigh up; **c. le pour et le contre** to weigh up the pros and cons; **nous devons c. l'intérêt de tous** we have to take everybody's interests into account *or* consideration

3 *(croire)* to consider, *Sout* to deem; **je la considère qualifiée pour ce travail** I consider her (to be) qualified for this job; **je considère ne pas en avoir le droit** *ou* **que je n'en ai pas le droit** I consider that I don't have any right to do so

4 *(juger)* **c. bien/mal** to hold in high/low esteem; **c. qn/qch comme** to regard *or* to consider sb/sth as; **elle me considère comme sa meilleure amie** she regards me as *or* looks upon me as *or* considers me to be her best friend; **je considère ta réponse comme un refus** I regard your answer as a refusal

5 *(respecter)* to respect, to hold in high esteem *or* regard; **un spécialiste hautement considéré** a highly-regarded *or* highly-respected expert

VPR **se considérer se c. comme responsable** to consider *or* hold oneself responsible; **il se considère comme un très grand artiste** he considers himself (as) a great artist

• **à tout bien considérer, tout bien considéré** ADV **1** *(en résumé)* all things considered, taking everything into consideration, considering; **elle s'est bien débrouillée, tout bien considéré** she managed rather well, considering **2** *(pour changer d'avis)* on second thoughts *or* further consideration

consignataire [kɔ̃siɲatɛr] NMF **1** *Com* consignee **2** *Naut* consignee, forwarding agent **3** *Jur* depositary

consignation [kɔ̃siɲasjɔ̃] NF **1** *Com* consignment; **en c.** on consignment; **envoyer qch à qn en c.** to consign sth to sb, to send sth to sb on consignment **2** *Jur* deposit **3** *(d'un emballage)* charging a deposit on; **la c. est de 10 centimes** there's a 10-cent refund on return

consigne [kɔ̃siɲ] NF **1** *(instruction)* orders, instructions; **c'est la c.** those are the orders; **observer la c.** to obey orders; **ils ont reçu pour c. de ne pas tirer** they've been given orders not to shoot; **je n'ai pas (reçu) de consignes** I have received no instructions; **elle avait pour c. de surveiller sa sœur** she'd been told to keep an eye on her sister; **consignes en cas d'incendie** fire notice, fire regulations

2 *(punition) Mil* confinement to barracks; *Scol* detention; *Fam* **on m'a filé deux heures de c.** I got two hours' detention

3 *Rail Br* left-luggage office, *Am* checkroom; **c. automatique** *(Br* left-luggage) lockers; **mettre qch à la c.** *(automatique)* to put sth in a *(Br* left-luggage) locker; *(manuelle)* to check sth in at the *Br* left-luggage office *or Am* checkroom

4 *(pour emballage)* deposit

consigner [3] [kɔ̃siɲe] VT **1** *(déposer ► valise)* to put in the *Br* left-luggage office *or Am* checkroom

2 *Fin (somme)* to deposit

3 *(emballage)* to put *or* to charge a deposit on; **la bouteille est consignée 20 centimes** there's a 20-cent deposit on the bottle, you get 20 cents back on the bottle

4 *Com (marchandises etc)* to consign

5 *(noter)* to record, to put down; **c. ses pensées dans un journal** to put *or* to write down one's thoughts in a diary; **c. qch par écrit** to put sth down in writing *or* on paper

6 *Mil* to confine to barracks; *Scol* to keep in (detention)

7 *(interdire)* **c. sa porte à qn** to bar one's door to sb, to refuse sb admittance; **être consigné à la troupe** to be out of bounds to troops

8 *Naut* to consign

consistance [kɔ̃sistɑ̃s] NF **1** *(état)* consistency; **c. crémeuse/dure** creamy/firm consistency; **donner de la c. à une sauce** to thicken a sauce; *Fig* **donner de la c. à un personnage** to flesh out *or* to give substance to a character; **prendre c.** *(sauce)* to thicken; *Fig* **le projet prend c.** the project is taking shape; *Fig* **sans c.** *(rumeur)* groundless, ill-founded; *(personne)* spineless; *(discours, raisonnement)* woolly **2** *(cohérence)* consistency

consistant, -e [kɔ̃sistɑ̃, -ɑ̃t] ADJ **1** *(épais ► sauce, peinture)* thick **2** *(substantiel ► plat, repas)* substantial **3** *(bien établi ► argument, rumeur)* well-founded, well-grounded

> Il faut noter que l'adjectif anglais **consistent** est un faux ami. Il signifie le plus souvent **cohérent**.

consister [3] [kɔ̃siste] **consister à** VT IND **c. à faire qch** to consist in doing sth

• **consister dans, consister en** VT IND to consist of; **en quoi consiste votre mission?** what does your mission consist of?, what is your mission all about?; **l'intérêt de la pièce consiste dans les effets scéniques** the interest of the play lies in *or* lies with its stage effects

consistoire [kɔ̃sistwar] NM *Rel* consistory

conso [kɔ̃so] NF *Fam (consommation)* drink[□]

consœur [kɔ̃sœr] NF **1** *(collègue)* (female) colleague; *(dans une société)* fellow member **2** *Rel* sister nun

consolable [kɔ̃sɔlabl] ADJ consolable

consolant, -e [kɔ̃sɔlɑ̃, -ɑ̃t] ADJ consoling, comforting; **ce qui est c., c'est que...** the comforting thing (about it) is that...

consolateur, -trice [kɔ̃sɔlatœr, -tris] ADJ comforting, consolatory

NM,F comforter

consolation [kɔ̃sɔlasjɔ̃] NF **1** *(soulagement)* consolation, comfort, *Littéraire* solace; **la compagnie de ses amis était une maigre c.** his/her friends were of little comfort to him/her; **chercher une c. dans qch** to seek consolation *or* solace *or* comfort in sth **2** *(personne ou chose qui réconforte)* consolation; **sa fille est sa seule c.** his/her daughter is his/her sole consolation

• **de consolation** ADJ *(épreuve, tournoi)* runners-up *(avant n)*; *(lot, prix)* consolation *(avant n)*; **des paroles de c.** words of comfort, comforting *or* consoling words

consolatrice [kɔ̃sɔlatris] *voir* **consolateur**

console [kɔ̃sɔl] NF **1** *(table)* console table

2 *Constr* cantilever, bracket

3 *Archit* console

4 *Mus (d'un orgue)* console; *(d'une harpe)* neck

5 *Ordinat* console; **c. de visualisation** (visual) display unit; **c. de jeux** games console

6 *(en audiovisuel)* **c. de mixage** sound mixer, mixing desk

consoler [3] [kɔ̃sɔle] VT to console, to comfort; **c. qn de sa peine** to comfort *or* console sb in his/her grief; **si cela peut te c.** if it's any consolation; **ça me console de voir que ça t'est déjà arrivé** it consoles me *or* is a consolation that it's happened to you too; **il avait besoin de se faire c.** he was in need of consolation

VPR **se consoler 1** *(emploi réfléchi)* to console oneself; **se c. dans l'alcool** to find solace in drink; **je me console en pensant que...** I console myself with the thought that... **2** *(emploi passif)* to console oneself, to be consoled; **il ne s'est jamais consolé de la mort de sa femme** he never got over losing his wife; **on dirait qu'elle s'est vite consolée!** it looks like she got over it fast! **3** *(emploi réciproque)* to console *ou* comfort each other

consolidation [kɔ̃sɔlidasjɔ̃] NF **1** *(d'un édifice, d'un meuble)* strengthening, reinforcement; *(d'un mur)* bracing, buttressing, reinforcement

2 *Couture (d'un bouton, d'un talon)* reinforcement

3 *(renforcement ► d'une amitié, d'une position, d'un pouvoir)* consolidation, strengthening

4 *Méd* setting

5 *Jur* consolidation

6 *Fin (d'une dette)* funding, financing; *(des bénéfices, des fonds, d'un bilan)* consolidation; *Mktg* **c. de ligne** line filling

7 *Géol & (en travaux publics)* bracing, strengthening

consolidé, -e [kɔ̃sɔlide] *Fin* ADJ *(bénéfices, fonds, bilan)* consolidated; *(dette)* funded, financed

• **consolidés** NMPL consols

consolider [3] [kɔ̃sɔlide] VT **1** *(renforcer ► édifice, meuble)* to strengthen; *(► mur, bouton, talon)* to reinforce

2 *(affermir ► position, majorité, amitié)* to consolidate, to strengthen

3 *Méd* to set

4 *Jur* to consolidate

5 *Fin (dette)* to fund, to finance; *(bénéfices, fonds, bilan)* to consolidate; **l'euro a consolidé son avance à la Bourse** the euro has strengthened its lead on the Stock Exchange

VPR **se consolider 1** *(s'affermir ► position, majorité, régime)* to be consolidated *or* strengthened; *(amitié)* to be strengthened **2** *Méd* to set

consommable [kɔ̃sɔmabl] ADJ **1** *(nourriture)* edible; *(boisson)* drinkable; **ce produit n'est c. que cru/cuit** this product can only be eaten raw/must be cooked before eating **2** *Chim* consumable

• **consommables** NMPL *Ordinat* consumables

consommateur, -trice [kɔ̃sɔmatœr, -tris] ADJ **système c. d'électricité** system that runs on electricity; **pays c.** consumer nation; **les pays fortement consommateurs de pétrole** the countries that consume large quantities of crude oil

NM,F **1** *(par opposition à producteur)* consumer; **mes collègues sont de grands consommateurs de café** my colleagues are great coffee drinkers; *Mktg* **c. cible** target consumer; *Mktg* **c. final** end-user **2** *(client ► d'un service)* customer, user

consommation [kɔ̃sɔmasjɔ̃] NF **1** *(absorption ► de nourriture, de boisson)* consumption; **viande impropre à la c.** meat unfit for (human) consumption

2 *(utilisation ► de gaz, d'électricité)* consumption; **elle fait une grande c. de parfum/papier** she gets through a lot of perfume/paper; **pour ma c. personnelle** for my own *or* personal use

3 *Écon* consumption; **la c. des ménages** household consumption; **c. intérieure** home consumption; **c. de masse** mass consumption; **biens/société de c.** consumer goods/society

4 *Aut* **c. (d'essence)** *(Br* petrol *or Am* gas) consumption; **la c. en ville** urban fuel consumption; **c. d'huile** oil consumption

5 *(au café)* drink; **prendre une c.** *(boire)* to have a drink

6 *Compta* **consommations de l'exercice** total annual expenses

7 *Littéraire (accomplissement ► d'un crime)* perpetration; *(► d'un mariage)* consummation; **jusqu'à la c. des siècles** until the end of time

consommatique [kɔ̃sɔmatik] NF consumer research

consommatrice [kɔ̃sɔmatris] *voir* **consommateur**

consommé, -e [kɔ̃sɔme] **ADJ** consummate
NM clear soup, consommé; **c. de poulet** chicken consommé

consommer [3] [kɔ̃sɔme] **VT 1** *(absorber ▸ nourriture)* to eat, *Sout* to consume; *(▸ boisson)* to drink, *Sout* to consume; **le pays où l'on consomme le plus de vin** the country with the highest wine consumption; **à c. avant (fin)...** *(sur emballage)* best before (end)...
2 *(utiliser ▸ combustible)* to use (up), to consume, to go through; **une voiture qui consomme beaucoup/peu (d'essence)** a car that uses a lot of/that doesn't use much petrol
3 *Jur (mariage)* to consummate
4 *Littéraire (accomplir ▸ crime)* to perpetrate; *(▸ ruine)* to bring about the completion of; **la rupture est consommée** they have broken up for good
USAGE ABSOLU toute personne attablée doit c. anyone occupying a table must order a drink; **c. sur place** *(dans un fast-food)* to eat in
VPR se consommer ça se consomme froid it's eaten cold, you eat it cold

consomption [kɔ̃sɔ̃psjɔ̃] **NF** *Vieilli Méd (amaigrissement)* wasting; *(tuberculose)* consumption

consonance [kɔ̃sɔnɑ̃s] **NF 1** *Littérature & Mus* consonance **2** *(sonorité)* sound; **de c. anglaise, aux consonances anglaises** English-sounding

consonant, -e [kɔ̃sɔnɑ̃, -ɑ̃t] **ADJ** *Littérature & Mus* consonant

consonantique [kɔ̃sɔnɑ̃tik] **ADJ 1** *Ling (des consonnes)* consonantal, consonant *(avant n)*; **le système c.** the consonant system **2** *(en acoustique)* consonant, resonant

consonne [kɔ̃sɔn] **NF** consonant; **c. occlusive** plosive *or* stop consonant; **c. labiale/dentale** labial/dental (consonant)

consort [kɔ̃sɔr] **ADJ M** consort
NM consort
• **consorts NMPL 1** *Jur* jointly interested parties **2** *Péj* **Paul et consorts** *(et sa bande)* Paul and company, Paul and his gang; *(et ceux de son espèce)* Paul and his kind, Paul and those like him

consortial, -e, -aux, -ales [kɔ̃sɔrsjal, -o] **ADJ** = relating to a consortium or a syndicate

consortium [kɔ̃sɔrsjɔm] **NM** consortium, syndicate; **c. de banques** banking consortium

conspirateur, -trice [kɔ̃spiratœr, -tris] **NM,F** conspirator, plotter, conspirer; **ils se donnaient des airs de conspirateurs** they had a conspiratorial air about them
ADJ conspiratorial

conspiration [kɔ̃spirasjɔ̃] **NF** conspiracy, plot

conspiratrice [kɔ̃spiratris] *voir* **conspirateur**

conspirer [3] [kɔ̃spire] **VI** to conspire, to plot, to scheme (**contre** against)
• **conspirer à VT IND** to conspire to; **tout conspire à la réussite de ce projet** everything conspires *or* combines to make this project a success

conspuer [7] [kɔ̃spɥe] **VT** to shout down; **se faire c.** *(orateur)* to be shouted down; *(comédien)* to be booed off the stage

constamment [kɔ̃stamɑ̃] **ADV 1** *(sans interruption)* continuously, continually **2** *(très fréquemment)* constantly

constance [kɔ̃stɑ̃s] **NF 1** *(persévérance)* constancy, steadfastness; **vous avez de la c.!** you don't give up easily!; **travailler avec c.** to work steadily
2 *Littéraire (fidélité)* constancy, fidelity, faithfulness; **manquer de c.** to be fickle; **faire preuve d'une grande c. en amitié** to be unswerving in one's friendships
3 *(de la température, d'un phénomène)* constancy, invariability
4 *Psy* invariability, constancy

constant, -e [kɔ̃stɑ̃, -ɑ̃t] **ADJ 1** *(invariable)* unchanging, constant; **c. dans ses amitiés** faithful to one's friends *or* in friendship; **être c. dans ses goûts** to be unchanging in one's tastes
2 *(ininterrompu)* continual, continuous, unceasing
3 *Math* constant
4 *Fin* constant; **en euros constants** in constant euros
• **constante NF 1** *Math & Phys* constant
2 *Élec* **constante diélectrique** (dielectric) permittivity, dielectric constant
3 *Météo* **constante solaire** solar constant
4 *(caractéristique)* stable *or* permanent trait
5 *Ordinat* constant

constat [kɔ̃sta] **NM 1** *(acte)* certified statement *or* report; **c. d'accident** accident statement; **faisons le c.** *(après un accident)* let's fill in the necessary papers (for the insurance); **c. d'adultère** adultery report; **c. (à l')amiable** = report of road accident agreed by the parties involved; **c. d'huissier** = affidavit drawn up by a bailiff **2** *(bilan)* review; **faire un c. d'échec** to acknowledge *or* to admit a failure

constatation [kɔ̃statasjɔ̃] **NF 1** *(observation)* noting, noticing; **la c. d'une fuite a entraîné une vérification de l'ensemble du système** the discovery of a leak led to a check-up of the entire system **2** *(remarque)* remark, comment, observation; **ce n'est pas un reproche, c'est une simple c.** this isn't a criticism, it's just an observation *or* I'm just stating a fact; **première c., le liquide vire au bleu** the first thing to note is that the liquid turns blue **3** *Compta* **c. de stock** stock take
• **constatations NFPL 1** *(d'une enquête)* findings; **procéder aux constatations** to establish the facts **2** *Assur* **c. des dommages** assessment of damages

constaté [kɔ̃state] **ADJ** *Fin (valeur)* registered; **c. d'avance** *(charge)* prepaid

constater [3] [kɔ̃state] **VT 1** *(remarquer ▸ gén)* to note, to observe, to notice; *(▸ erreur)* to discover, to find; **on constate une régression de la criminalité** a decline in criminality can be observed; **je constate que tu fumes toujours autant** I notice you still smoke just as much; **je suis forcé de c. que je ne peux te faire confiance** I am forced to the conclusion that I can't trust you; **vous pouvez c. vous-même qu'elle est partie** you can see for yourself that she's gone **2** *(enregistrer ▸ décès)* to certify; *(▸ faits)* to record, to list; **l'expert est venu c. les dégâts** the expert came to assess the damage
USAGE ABSOLU constatez par vous-même! just see for yourself!; **je ne critique pas, je ne fais que c.** I'm not criticizing, I'm just stating the facts

constellation [kɔ̃stelasjɔ̃] **NF 1** *Astron* constellation **2** *(ensemble ▸ de savants, de célébrités)* constellation, galaxy; **une c. de taches** stains all over

consteller [4] [kɔ̃stele] **VT** to spangle, to stud; **un ciel constellé d'étoiles** a star-studded sky; **une robe constellée de taches** a dress spattered with stains; **un visage constellé de taches de rousseur** a face covered in freckles
VPR se consteller le ciel se constella d'étoiles the stars came out in the sky

consternant, -e [kɔ̃sternɑ̃, -ɑ̃t] **ADJ** distressing; **d'une bêtise consternante** appallingly stupid; **la pièce est consternante** the play's dire *or* appallingly bad

consternation [kɔ̃sternasjɔ̃] **NF** consternation, dismay; **jeter la c. dans un groupe** to fill a group with consternation *or* dismay; **à la c. générale** to everyone's consternation *or* dismay

consterner [3] [kɔ̃sterne] **VT** to appal, to fill with consternation; **consterné par une nouvelle** appalled *or* dismayed by a piece of news; **regarder qch d'un air consterné** to look aghast *or* with consternation upon sth

constipation [kɔ̃stipasjɔ̃] **NF** constipation

constipé, -e [kɔ̃stipe] **ADJ 1** *Méd* constipated **2** *Fam (guindé)* **être** *ou* **avoir l'air c.** to look ill-at-ease *or* uncomfortable; **un style c.** a constipated style
NM,F 1 *Méd* constipated person **2** *Fam (personne guindée)* uptight *or* stuffy person; **quel c.!** he's so uptight!

constiper [3] [kɔ̃stipe] **VT** to constipate
USAGE ABSOLU les œufs constipent eggs cause constipation

constituant, -e [kɔ̃stitɥɑ̃, -ɑ̃t] **ADJ 1** *(élément)* constituent **2** *Jur & Pol* constituent; **pouvoir c.** constituent power
NM 1 *Jur & Pol* constituent; *Hist* = member of the 1789 Constituent Assembly **2** *Chim* component **3** *Ling* constituent
• **Constituante NF** *Hist* **la Constituante** the Constituent Assembly

constitué, -e [kɔ̃stitɥe] **ADJ 1** *(personne)* **un homme normalement c.** a (physically) normal man; **un enfant mal c.** a child of poor constitution; **un individu solidement c.** a sturdily-built individual; **bien c.** hardy **2** *Pol (autorité)* constituted; *(corps)* constituent

constituer [7] [kɔ̃stitɥe] **VT 1** *(créer ▸ collection)* to build up, to put together; *(▸ bibliothèque)* to build *or* to set up; *(▸ société anonyme, association, gouvernement)* to form, to set up; *(▸ équipe, cabinet)* to form, to select (the members of); *(▸ dossier)* to prepare; **c. des réserves/des stocks de qch** to stock up on sth; *Jur* **c. une dot/une rente à qn** to settle a dowry/a pension on sb
2 *(faire partie de)* to form, to constitute, to (go to) make up; **ces cinq pages constituent l'introduction** these five pages form the introduction; **les timbres qui constituent sa collection** the stamps that make up his collection; **être constitué de** to be made up of, to consist of; **l'eau est constituée de...** water consists *or* is composed of...; **un appartement constitué de six pièces** a six-roomed flat
3 *(être)* to be, to represent; **ce mobilier constitue tout mon bien** this furniture represents all my worldly goods, this furniture is all I own; **le vol constitue un délit** theft is *or* constitutes an offence
4 *Jur (nommer)* to name, to appoint; **c. qn président** to appoint sb as *or* to make sb chairman
VPR se constituer 1 se c. de *(être composé de)* to be made up of
2 *(se mettre en position de)* **se c. prisonnier** to give oneself up; *Jur* **se c. partie civile** to file a civil action in a criminal proceeding
3 *(se former)* to form, to be formed; **un nouveau comité s'est constitué** a new committee has formed *or* has been formed *or* has been created; **ils se sont constitués en association** they formed a society
4 se c. qch to build sth up *or* to amass sth (for oneself); **se c. une vidéothèque** to build up a video library; **se c. un patrimoine** to amass an estate

constitutif, -ive [kɔ̃stitytif, -iv] **ADJ 1** *(qui compose)* constituent, component; **les éléments constitutifs de l'eau** the elements which make up *or* the constituent elements of water **2** *(typique ▸ propriété)* constitutive **3** *Jur* constitutive

constitution [kɔ̃stitysjɔ̃] **NF 1** *(création ▸ d'une collection)* building up, putting together; *(▸ d'une bibliothèque)* building up, setting up; *(▸ d'une société anonyme, d'une association, d'un gouvernement)* forming, formation, setting up; *(▸ d'une équipe, d'un cabinet)* selection; *(▸ d'un dossier)* preparation, putting together
2 *(composition ▸ d'un groupe)* composition; *(▸ d'une substance)* make-up, composition
3 *Pol (lois)* constitution
4 *(santé)* constitution, physique; **une bonne/solide c.** a sound/sturdy constitution; **être de c. fragile** *(souvent malade)* to be susceptible to disease
5 *Pharm (en homéopathie)* composition
6 *Jur (d'une dot, d'une rente)* settling, settlement; *(d'un avocat) Br* briefing, *Am* hiring; **c. de partie civile** filing of a civil action in a criminal proceeding

constitutionnaliser [3] [kɔ̃stitysjɔnalize] **VT** to constitutionalize, to make constitutional

constitutionnalisme [kɔ̃stitysjɔnalism] **NM** *Pol* constitutionalism

constitutionnaliste [kɔ̃stitysjɔnalist] **NMF** *Jur* constitutional lawyer

constitutionnalité [kɔ̃stitysjɔnalite] **NF** constitutionality

constitutionnel, -elle [kɔ̃stitysjɔnel] **ADJ** constitutional

constitutionnellement [kɔ̃stitysjɔnelmɑ̃] **ADV** constitutionally

constitutive [kɔ̃stitytiv] *voir* **constitutif**

constricteur [kɔ̃striktœr] **ADJ M** *Anat & Zool* constrictor
NM 1 *Anat* constrictor **2** *Zool* boa constrictor

constriction [kɔ̃striksjɔ̃] **NF** constriction

constrictor [kɔ̃striktɔr] **ADJ M** *Anat & Zool* constrictor
NM *Zool* boa constrictor

constructeur, -trice [kɔ̃stryktœr, -tris] **ADJ 1** *(d'édifices, de bateaux)* building *(avant n)*; *(d'appareils, d'engins)* manufacturing *(avant n)* **2** *Zool* **animaux constructeurs** home-building animals
NM 1 *(d'édifices)* builder **2** *(d'appareils, d'engins)* manufacturer; **c. automobile** car manufacturer; **c. naval** shipbuilder **3** *Ordinat* handler, builder

constructible [kɔ̃stryktibl] **ADJ** constructible; **terrain c.** plot suitable for building on, building land

constructif, -ive [kɔ̃stryktif, -iv] **ADJ 1** *(qui fait progresser)* constructive, positive **2** *Constr* constructional, building *(avant n)*

construction [kɔ̃stryksjɔ̃] **NF 1** *(édification)* building, construction; **la c. de la tour a duré un an** it took a year to build *or* to erect the tower; **la maison est encore en c.** the house is still being built *or* still under construction; *Fig* **la c. européenne** European integration
2 *(édifice)* building, construction; **des constructions récentes** new buildings, recent constructions
3 *(fabrication)* building, manufacturing; **la c. aéronautique/automobile** aircraft/car manufacturing; **la c. mécanique** (mechanical) engineering; **appareil de c. française** French-built machine
4 *(entreprise)* **constructions navales** shipbuilding (industry); **constructions aéronautiques** aircraft industry
5 *(structure ▸ d'une œuvre)* structure; *(▸ d'une phrase)* construction, structure; *Fig* **ce n'est qu'une c. de l'esprit** it's purely hypothetical
6 *Gram* construction; **ce verbe a une c. passive** this verb is construed passively *or* has a passive construction
7 *Math* figure, construction
• **de construction ADJ 1** *(matériau)* building *(avant n)*, construction *(avant n)* **2 jeu de c.** set of building blocks

constructive [kɔ̃stryktiv] *voir* **constructif**

constructivisme [kɔ̃stryktivism] **NM** *Beaux-Arts & Phil* constructivism

constructiviste [kɔ̃stryktivist] *Beaux-Arts & Phil* **ADJ** constructivist
NMF constructivist

constructrice [kɔ̃stryktris] *voir* **constructeur**

construire [98] [kɔ̃strɥir] **VT 1** *(route, barrage)* to build, to construct; *(maison)* to build; **une maison récemment construite** a newly-built house; **se faire c. une maison** to have a house built
2 *Ind (fabriquer)* to build, to manufacture
3 *(structurer ▸ pièce, roman, phrase)* to structure, to construct; *(▸ théorie, raisonnement)* to build, to develop; *(▸ figure de géométrie)* to draw, to construct
4 *Gram* to construe; **on construit "vouloir" avec le subjonctif** "vouloir" takes the subjunctive *or* is construed with the subjunctive
USAGE ABSOLU leur rêve, c'est de pouvoir faire c. they dream of having their own house built
VPR se construire 1 *(être édifié)* to be built; **il s'est construit beaucoup de maisons** a lot of houses have been built; **la campagne environnante s'est construite** the surrounding countryside has become a built-up area **2** *Gram* **se c. avec** to take, to be construed with

consubstantiation [kɔ̃sypstɑ̃sjasjɔ̃] **NF** *Rel* consubstantiation

consubstantiel, -elle [kɔ̃sypstɑ̃sjɛl] **ADJ** *Rel* consubstantial

consul [kɔ̃syl] **NM 1** *(diplomate)* consul; **le c. de France** the French Consul; **c. général** consul general **2** *Hist* Consul *(in France from 1799 to 1804)* **3** *Antiq* consul

consulaire [kɔ̃sylɛr] **ADJ** consular

consulat [kɔ̃syla] **NM 1** *(résidence, bureaux)* consulate
2 *(fonction diplomatique)* consulship
3 *Hist* **le C.** the Consulate *(in France from 1799 to 1804)*
4 *Antiq* consulship

consultable [kɔ̃syltabl] **ADJ** *(ouvrage, fichier)* which may be consulted, available for reference *or* consultation

consultant, -e [kɔ̃syltɑ̃, -ɑ̃t] **ADJ** *voir* **avocat²**, **médecin**
NM,F consultant; **c. en gestion** management consultant

consultatif, -ive [kɔ̃syltatif, -iv] **ADJ** *(gén)* advisory; *(assemblée)* consultative; **à titre c.** in an advisory capacity

consultation [kɔ̃syltasjɔ̃] **NF 1** *(d'un plan, d'un règlement)* consulting, checking; **la c. d'un dictionnaire** looking words up in a dictionary; **après c. de mon emploi du temps** after checking my timetable
2 *Pol* **c. électorale** election; **c. populaire** consultation of the people
3 *(chez un professionnel)* consultation; **donner des consultations** *(gén)* to hold consultations; *(médecin)* to have one's *Br* surgery *or Am* office hours; **il est en c.** *(médecin)* he's with a patient; **horaires de c.** *(chez un médecin) Br* surgery *or Am* office hours; **il demande 80 euros pour la c.** he charges 80 euros for (his) professional services; **c. externe** out-patients' department
4 *Ordinat* **c. de table** table lookup; **c. de fichier** file browsing *or* browse

consultative [kɔ̃syltativ] *voir* **consultatif**

consulter [3] [kɔ̃sylte] **VT 1** *(médecin)* to visit, to consult; *(avocat, professeur)* to consult, to seek advice from; *(voyante)* to visit; **il ne m'a même pas consulté** he didn't even ask for my opinion; **c. qn du regard** to look questioningly at sb
2 *(livre, dictionnaire)* to refer to, to consult; *(plan, montre, baromètre, horaire)* to look at, to check; *(horoscope)* to read; **c. ses notes** to go over one's notes
3 *(au négatif) (prendre en compte)* **il ne consulte que son intérêt** he's guided only by self-interest
4 *Ordinat* to search
USAGE ABSOLU se décider à c. to decide to go to the doctor's; **lorsqu'il est venu c., j'ai prescrit des antibiotiques** when he came to see me, I prescribed some antibiotics
VI *(docteur)* to hold surgery, to see patients
VPR se consulter *(discuter)* to confer; **ils se sont consultés avant de m'annoncer la nouvelle** they conferred before giving me the news; **se c. du regard** to look questioningly at one another

consumer [3] [kɔ̃syme] **VT 1** *(brûler)* to burn, to consume; **le feu a consumé tous les livres** the fire destroyed all the books **2** *Littéraire (tourmenter)* **la jalousie la consume** she's consumed with jealousy; **il est consumé de chagrin** *ou* **par le chagrin** he is racked with grief **3** *Littéraire (fortune, énergie)* to waste
VPR se consumer 1 *(brûler)* to burn **2** *Littéraire* **il se consume de désespoir** he's consumed with despair; **se c. d'amour pour qn** to pine for sb; **se c. en efforts inutiles** to wear oneself out in useless efforts

consumérisme [kɔ̃symerism] **NM le c.** consumerism

consumériste [kɔ̃symerist] **ADJ** consumerist

contact [kɔ̃takt] **NM 1** *(toucher)* touch, contact; **maladies transmises par c.** diseases transmitted by (direct) contact
2 *Aut, Élec & Rad* contact, switch; **le c. ne se fait pas** there's no contact; **il y a un mauvais c.** there's a loose connection somewhere; **mettre/couper le c.** *Élec* to switch on/off; *Aut* to turn the ignition on/off; **nous avons perdu le c. radio avec eux** we're no longer in radio contact with them
3 *(lien)* contact; **avoir des contacts avec** to have contact with; **j'ai su qu'il m'était hostile dès le premier c.** I knew that he was hostile towards me from the moment we met; **il a perdu tout c. avec le réel** he's lost all contact with reality; **prendre des contacts** to establish some contacts; **prendre c. avec qn** to contact sb, to get in touch with sb; **j'ai gardé le c. avec mes vieux amis** I'm still in touch with my old friends; **il est d'un c. facile** he's easy to get on with
4 *(personne ▸ dans les affaires, l'espionnage)* contact, connection
5 *Géom* **(point de) c. de deux plans** intersection *or* meeting point of two planes
6 *Phot* contact (print)
7 *Équitation* contact
8 *Ordinat* **c. de page** *(sur l'Internet)* hit
• **au contact de PRÉP au c. de l'air** in contact with *or* when exposed to the air; **elle sursauta au c. de ma main sur son épaule** she jumped at the touch of my hand on her shoulder
• **de contact ADJ 1** *Aut* ignition *(avant n)* **2** *Rail (fil, ligne)* contact *(avant n)* **3** *Opt* contact *(avant n)*
• **en contact ADJ 1** *(reliés ▸ personnes)* in touch; **rester en c. avec qn** to keep *or* to stay in touch with sb **2** *(adjacents ▸ objets, substances)* in contact **3** *Élec* connected **ADV entrer en c. avec** *(toucher)* come into contact with; *(joindre)* to contact, to get in touch with; *Aviat & Mil* to make contact with; **mettre en c.** *(personnes)* to put in touch (with each other); *(objets, substances)* to bring into contact; *Aviat & Mil* to establish contact between

contacter [3] [kɔ̃takte] **VT** to contact, to get in touch with; **on peut me c. par téléphone au bureau** you can reach me by phone at the office

contacteur [kɔ̃taktœr] **NM** *Élec* contactor; *(du système d'allumage)* switch; **c. d'interdiction** inhibitor switch

contagieux, -euse [kɔ̃taʒjø, -øz] **ADJ** *(personne)* contagious; *(maladie, rire)* infectious, contagious; *(virus, enthousiasme)* catching
NM,F contagious patient

contagion [kɔ̃taʒjɔ̃] **NF 1** *Méd* contagion; **pour éviter tout risque de c.** to avoid any risk of infection *or* contagion **2** *(d'un rire, d'une peur)* contagiousness, infectiousness

contagiosité [kɔ̃taʒjozite] **NF** contagiousness; **à haute** *ou* **forte c.** highly contagious

container [kɔ̃tɛnɛr] **NM 1** *Ind & Com* container; **c. à gaz** gas tank; **mise en c.** containerization **2** *Hort* (large) plant holder

containérisation [kɔ̃tɛnerizasjɔ̃] **NF** containerization

containériser [3] [kɔ̃tɛnerize] **VT** to containerize

contaminateur, -trice [kɔ̃taminatœr, -tris] **ADJ** infectious
NM,F infectious carrier

contamination [kɔ̃taminasjɔ̃] **NF 1** *Méd* contamination, infection **2** *(de l'environnement, des aliments)* contamination; **c. radioactive** radioactive contamination **3** *Littéraire (corruption)* (moral) pollution

contaminatrice [kɔ̃taminatris] *voir* **contaminateur**

contaminer [3] [kɔ̃tamine] **VT 1** *Méd* to infect, to contaminate **2** *(environnement, aliments)* to infect, to contaminate **3** *Littéraire (corrompre ▸ personne)* to corrupt

conte [kɔ̃t] **NM 1** *(histoire)* story, tale; **c. de bonnes femmes** old wives' tale; *aussi Fig* **c. de fées** fairy tale; **elle vit un c. de fées** her life is a fairy tale **2** *Vieilli (histoire invraisemblable)* (tall) story, yarn; **c. à dormir debout** cock-and-bull story

contemplateur, -trice [kɔ̃tɑ̃platœr, -tris] **NM,F** contemplator

contemplatif, -ive [kɔ̃tɑ̃platif, -iv] **ADJ 1** *(pensif)* thoughtful, contemplative, meditative **2** *Rel* contemplative
NM,F contemplative; **c'est un c.** he likes to muse

contemplation [kɔ̃tɑ̃plasjɔ̃] **NF 1** *(admiration)* admiration; **elle est restée en c. devant le tableau** she stood gazing at the picture in admiration **2** *(méditation)* contemplation, reflection; **plongé dans la c. (de qch)** lost in contemplation (of sth) **3** *Rel* contemplation

contemplative [kɔ̃tɑ̃plativ] *voir* **contemplatif**

contemplatrice [kɔ̃tɑ̃platris] *voir* **contemplateur**

contempler [3] [kɔ̃tɑ̃ple] **VT** *(admirer)* to admire; *(regarder)* to gaze at; **d'ici, vous pouvez c. le superbe paysage** you can admire the superb view from here; **c. qn avec amour** to gaze lovingly at sb
VPR se contempler to gaze at oneself

contemporain, -e [kɔ̃tɑ̃pɔrɛ̃, -ɛn] **ADJ 1** *(de la même époque)* contemporary; **être c. de qn** to be

a contemporary of sb **2** *(moderne)* contemporary, modern, present-day
NM,F contemporary

contempteur, -trice [kɔ̃tɑ̃ptœr, -tris] **NM,F** *Littéraire* denigrator, despiser; **ses contempteurs** those who derided him/her

contenance [kɔ̃tnɑ̃s] **NF 1** *(attitude)* attitude, bearing; **il essayait de prendre** *ou* **se donner une c.** he was trying to put on a brave face; **faire qch pour se donner une c.** to do sth to give oneself an air of assurance; **faire bonne c.** to put up a bold *or* good front; **perdre c.** to lose one's composure **2** *(capacité ▸ d'un tonneau, d'un réservoir)* capacity; *(▸ d'un navire)* (carrying *or* holding) capacity; **d'une c. de 10 litres** capable of holding 10 litres, with a capacity of 10 litres

contenant [kɔ̃tnɑ̃] **NM** container

conteneur [kɔ̃tnœr] = **container**

conteneurisation [kɔ̃tnœrizasjɔ̃] = **containérisation**

conteneuriser [3] [kɔ̃tnœrize] = **containériser**

contenir [40] [kɔ̃tnir] **VT 1** *(renfermer)* to contain, to hold; **chaque boîte contient dix cigares** each box contains *or* holds ten cigars; **l'enveloppe contenait le reçu** the receipt was enclosed in the envelope
2 *(être constitué de)* to contain; **boissons qui contiennent de l'alcool** drinks containing alcohol
3 *(avoir telle capacité)* to hold; **le théâtre peut c. mille spectateurs** the theatre holds *or* seats a thousand
4 *(réprimer ▸ foule, larmes, sanglots)* to hold back; *(▸ poussée, invasion, ennemi)* to contain; *(▸ rire, colère)* to suppress; **une colère mal contenue** barely suppressed anger
VPR se contenir to control oneself; **ils ne pouvaient plus se c.** *(ils pleuraient)* they couldn't hold back their tears any longer; *(ils riaient)* they couldn't disguise their mirth any longer

content, -e [kɔ̃tɑ̃, -ɑ̃t] **ADJ 1** *(heureux)* happy, glad, pleased; **ils avaient l'air très contents** they looked very happy *or* pleased; **je suis très c. de vous voir** I'm very pleased to see you; **je suis c. que tu aies pu venir** I'm glad that you could make it; *Fam* **s'il n'est pas c., c'est pareil!** he can like it or lump it! **2** *(satisfait)* **être c. de qch** to be pleased with sth; **elle a l'air contente de sa nouvelle voiture** she seems pleased *or* happy with her new car; **je suis très c. de moi** I'm very pleased with myself; **tu peux être c. de toi, tu as vu ce que tu as fait!** I hope you're pleased with yourself *or* happy, just look what you've done!; **non c. d'être riche, il veut aussi être célèbre** not content *or* not satisfied with being rich, he wants to be famous as well
NM avoir (tout) son c. de qch to have (had) one's fill of sth; **manger tout son c.** to eat one's fill; **laisse-les s'amuser tout leur c.** let them play as much as they like

contentement [kɔ̃tɑ̃tmɑ̃] **NM** satisfaction, contentment; **avec c.** contentedly; **un sourire de c.** a satisfied *or* contented smile; **c. de soi** self-satisfaction

contenter [3] [kɔ̃tɑ̃te] **VT 1** *(faire plaisir à)* to please, to satisfy; **voilà qui devrait c. tout le monde** this should satisfy *or* please everybody **2** *(satisfaire ▸ curiosité, envie)* to satisfy
VPR se contenter se c. de qch/de faire qch to be content *or* to content oneself with sth/doing sth, to make do with sth/doing sth; **elle s'est contentée d'une modeste chambre** she contented herself *or* was satisfied with a modest room; **pour tout repas, elle s'est contentée de sandwiches** by way of a meal, she just had sandwiches; **il se contente de peu** he's easily satisfied; **en guise de réponse, elle s'est contentée de sourire** she merely smiled in reply; **je me contenterai de faire remarquer que…** I will merely point out that…

contentieux, -euse [kɔ̃tɑ̃sjø, -øz] **ADJ** contentious
NM 1 *(conflit)* dispute, disagreement; **avoir un c. avec qn** to be in dispute with sb **2** *Jur (service)* legal department *or* bureau **3** *Jur (affaire)* litigation; **c. administratif/électoral** procedure in contentious administrative/electoral matters; **c. fiscal** tax litigation

contention [kɔ̃tɑ̃sjɔ̃] **NF 1** *Littéraire* exertion, application; **c. d'esprit** concentration **2** *Méd (d'un os)* setting, reduction; *(d'un malade)* restraint; **moyen de c.** splint **3** *Psy (d'une personne)* restraint

contenu, -e [kɔ̃tny] **PP** *voir* **contenir**
NM 1 *(d'un récipient, d'un paquet)* content, contents
2 *(teneur ▸ d'un document)* content, text; **quel est le c. du texte?** what does the text say?; *Journ* **c. rédactionnel** editorial content
3 *Ling* (linguistic) content
4 *Psy* **c. latent/manifeste** latent/manifest content

conter [3] [kɔ̃te] **VT** *Can ou Littéraire* to relate, to tell; **je vais vous c. l'histoire de Barbe-Bleue** I'll tell you the story of Bluebeard; **que me contez-vous là?** what are you talking about?; **c. fleurette à qn** to murmur sweet nothings to sb; **elle ne s'en laisse pas c.** she's not easily taken in; *Can* **c. des peurs** to tell tall tales

contestable [kɔ̃testabl] **ADJ** debatable, questionable; **de manière c.** dubiously

contestataire [kɔ̃testatɛr] **ADJ** protesting *or* revolting *(against established values)*; **un journal c.** an anti-establishment newspaper
NMF anti-establishment protester; **c'est un c.** he's always calling things into question

contestation [kɔ̃testasjɔ̃] **NF 1** *(d'une loi, d'un testament, d'un document)* contesting, opposing; *(d'un récit, d'un droit)* contesting, questioning; *(d'une compétence)* questioning, challenging, doubting; **élever une c. sur qch** to raise an objection to sth; **il y a matière** *ou* **sujet à c.** there are grounds for dispute; **sans c. (possible)** beyond (all possible) dispute *or* question **2** *(litige)* dispute, controversy, debate **3** *Pol* **la c.** protests, protesting, the protest movement

conteste [kɔ̃test] **sans conteste ADV** indisputably, unquestionably

contester [3] [kɔ̃teste] **VT 1** *(testament)* to contest; *(récit, document, véracité)* to contest, to dispute, to question; *(compétence)* to question, to dispute, to throw into doubt; **je ne conteste pas que votre tâche ait été difficile** I don't dispute *or* doubt the fact that you had a difficult task; **je ne lui conteste pas le droit de…** I don't challenge *or* question his/her right to…; **être contesté** *(théorie)* to be a subject of controversy; **une personnalité très contestée** a very controversial personality **2** *Pol* to protest *or* to rebel against
VI 1 *(discuter)* **obéir aux ordres sans c.** to obey orders blindly *or* without raising any objections **2** *Pol* to protest

conteur, -euse [kɔ̃tœr, -øz] **NM,F 1** *(narrateur)* narrator, storyteller **2** *(écrivain)* storyteller

contexte [kɔ̃tekst] **NM 1** *(situation)* context; **il faut remettre cet événement dans son c.** we must put this event in its context; **dans le c. de l'économie européenne** (with)in the context of the European economy; **dans le c. actuel** under the present circumstances **2** *Ordinat* environment **3** *Ling* context; **hors c.** out of context
• **en contexte ADV** in context; **mettre qch en c.** to put sth into context, to contextualize sth

contextualiser [3] [kɔ̃tekstɥalize] **VT** to contextualize

contextuel, -elle [kɔ̃tekstɥel] **ADJ** contextual

contexture [kɔ̃tekstyr] **NF 1** *(d'un tissu, d'un matériel)* texture **2** *(d'une œuvre)* structure

contient *etc voir* **contenir**

contigu, -ë [kɔ̃tigy] **ADJ 1** *(bâtiments, terrains, objets)* adjacent, adjoining, *Sout* contiguous; **les maisons contiguës à la nôtre** *(accolées)* the houses joining on to ours **2** *(époques, sujets, domaines)* close, *Sout* contiguous

contiguïté [kɔ̃tigɥite] **NF 1** *(proximité ▸ de bâtiments, de terrains, d'objets)* adjacency, proximity, *Sout* contiguity **2** *(d'époques, de sujets, de domaines)* closeness, *Sout* contiguousness, contiguity **3** *Ordinat* adjacency

continence [kɔ̃tinɑ̃s] **NF 1** *(abstinence)* continence, (self-imposed) chastity; *(sobriété, discrétion)* restraint **2** *Méd* continence

continent[1] [kɔ̃tinɑ̃] **NM 1** *Géog* continent; **l'Ancien/le Nouveau C.** the Old/the New World **2** *(par opposition à une île)* **le c.** the mainland

continent[2]**, -e** [kɔ̃tinɑ̃, -ɑ̃t] **ADJ 1** *(chaste)* continent, chaste; *(discret)* discreet, restrained, reserved **2** *Méd* continent

continental, -e, -aux, -ales [kɔ̃tinɑ̃tal, -o] **ADJ 1** *(par opposition à insulaire)* mainland *(avant n)* **2** *Géog (climat, température)* continental
NM,F person who lives on the mainland; **les continentaux** people from the mainland

contingence [kɔ̃tɛ̃ʒɑ̃s] **NF** *Math & Phil* contingency
• **contingences NFPL** contingencies, eventualities; **les contingences de la vie quotidienne** everyday happenings *or* events; **prévoir toutes les contingences** to take unforeseen circumstances into consideration

contingent[1] [kɔ̃tɛ̃ʒɑ̃] **NM 1** *(quantité)* (allotted) share **2** *(quota)* quota; **contingents d'importation/d'exportation** import/export quotas **3** *(troupe)* contingent; *(ensemble des recrues) Br* call-up, *Am* draft; **le c., les soldats du c.** those conscripted, the conscripts, *Am* the draft

contingent[2]**, -e** [kɔ̃tɛ̃ʒɑ̃, -ɑ̃t] **ADJ 1** *Phil* contingent **2** *Littéraire (sans importance)* incidental

contingentement [kɔ̃tɛ̃ʒɑ̃tmɑ̃] **NM 1** *Écon* fixing of quotas, restriction; **le c. des importations** the fixing of import quotas **2** *Com* quota system, apportioning by quota

contingenter [3] [kɔ̃tɛ̃ʒɑ̃te] **VT 1** *Écon (importations)* to limit, to fix a quota on; *(produits de distribution)* to restrict the distribution of; **des produits contingentés** fixed quota products **2** *Com* to distribute *or* to allocate according to a quota

contint *etc voir* **contenir**

continu, -e [kɔ̃tiny] **ADJ 1** *(ininterrompu ▸ effort, douleur, bruit)* continuous, unremitting, relentless; *(▸ soins, attention)* constant; *(▸ ligne, trait)* continuous, unbroken; *(▸ sommeil)* unbroken
2 *Élec (courant)* direct
3 *Math* continuous
4 *Tex (métier)* throstle (frame)
NM *Math & Phil* continuum
• **continue NF** *Ling* continuant
• **en continu ADV 1** *(sans interruption)* continuously, uninterruptedly; **la nouvelle chaîne diffuse des informations en c.** the new channel gives non-stop *or* round-the-clock news coverage **2** *Typ* continuously **3** *Ordinat* **papier en c.** continuous paper

continuateur, -trice [kɔ̃tinɥatœr, -tris] **NM,F** *(de personne)* heir; *(de tradition)* continuator

continuation [kɔ̃tinɥasjɔ̃] **NF 1** *(suite)* continuation, extension; **notre politique doit être la c. de la vôtre** our policy must be a continuation of yours **2** *(fait de durer)* continuing, *Sout* continuance **3** *Fam (locution)* **bonne c.!** all the best!

continuatrice [kɔ̃tinɥatris] *voir* **continuateur**

continuel, -elle [kɔ̃tinɥel] **ADJ 1** *(ininterrompu)* continual **2** *(qui se répète)* constant, perpetual

continuellement [kɔ̃tinɥelmɑ̃] **ADV 1** *(de façon ininterrompue)* continually **2** *(de façon répétitive)* constantly, perpetually

continuer [7] [kɔ̃tinɥe] **VT 1** *(faire durer ▸ exposé)* to carry on; *(▸ conversation)* to carry on, to maintain, to keep up; *(▸ études)* to continue, to keep up, to go on with; **continuez le repas sans moi** go on with the meal without me; **je veux c. le chant** I want to keep up my singing
2 *(dans l'espace)* to continue, to extend; **continue le trait jusqu'au bout** continue the line to the end; **c. son chemin** *(sujet: voyageur)* to keep going; *(sujet: idée)* to keep gaining momentum
VI 1 *(dans le temps)* to go *or* to carry on; **son histoire a continué pendant tout le repas** his/her story went on throughout the meal; **si tu continues, ça va mal aller!** if you keep this up, you'll be sorry!; **"tu vois", continua-t-elle** "you see," she went on; **une telle situation ne peut c.** this situation cannot be allowed to continue; **c. à** *ou* **de faire qch** to continue to do *or* to keep on doing sth; **il continue de** *ou* **à pleuvoir** it keeps on raining; **malgré cela, il continue à fumer** in spite of this, he continues to smoke *or* carries on smoking; **je continue à me demander si…** I keep wondering if…
2 *(dans l'espace)* to continue, to carry on, to go

on; **la route continue jusqu'au village** the road runs straight on to the village; **arrête-toi ici, moi je continue** you can stop right here, I'm going on; **continue!** *(à avancer)* keep going!; **continue tout droit jusqu'au carrefour** keep straight on to the crossroads
3 *Ordinat (dans boîte de dialogue)* to proceed
VPR se continuer 1 *(dans le temps)* to carry on, to be carried on; **la fête se continua tard dans la nuit** the party went on late into the night **2** *(dans l'espace)* to extend

continuité [kɔ̃tinɥite] **NF 1** *(d'un effort, d'une tradition)* continuity; *(d'une douleur)* persistence; **assurer la c. d'une tradition** to carry on *or* to perpetuate a tradition **2** *Math* continuity **3** *Fin* **c. d'exploitation** going-concern status

continûment [kɔ̃tinymɑ̃] **ADV** *Littéraire* continually

continuum [kɔ̃tinɥɔm] **NM** continuum; **c. espace-temps** space-time continuum

contondant, -e [kɔ̃tɔ̃dɑ̃, -ɑ̃t] **ADJ** blunt

contorsion [kɔ̃tɔrsjɔ̃] **NF** *(d'acrobate)* contortion, acrobatic feat *(involving twisting the body)*

contorsionner **[3]** [kɔ̃tɔrsjɔne] **se contorsionner VPR** to twist one's body, to contort oneself; **se c. comme un ver** to squirm *or* to wriggle about like a worm

contorsionniste [kɔ̃tɔrsjɔnist] **NMF** contortionist

contour [kɔ̃tur] **NM 1** *(d'un objet, d'une silhouette)* contour, outline, shape; *Ordinat* **c. d'un caractère** character outline **2** *(arrondi ▸ d'un visage)* curve; *(▸ d'une rivière, d'un chemin)* winding part *or* section; **contours** *(méandres)* twists and turns **3** *Suisse (virage)* bend

contourné, -e [kɔ̃turne] **ADJ 1** *(avec des courbes)* **la balustrade contournée d'un balcon** the curved railing of a balcony **2** *(peu naturel)* overelaborate; **style c.** convoluted style

contournement [kɔ̃turnəmɑ̃] **NM 1** *(d'un obstacle ▸ à pied)* bypassing, walking round *or* around; *(▸ en voiture)* driving round *or* around **2** *(d'une difficulté)* bypassing, circumventing; *(d'une loi)* circumventing

contourner **[3]** [kɔ̃turne] **VT 1** *(faire le tour de ▸ souche, flaque)* to walk around; *(▸ ville)* to bypass, to skirt; *Mil (▸ position)* to skirt; **ayant contourné la forêt** *(à pied)* having walked round the forest; *(en voiture)* having driven round the forest **2** *(éluder ▸ loi, difficulté)* to circumvent, to get round **3** *Littéraire (modeler ▸ vase, piédestal)* to fashion *or* to shape (into complex curves)

contraceptif, -ive [kɔ̃traseptif, -iv] **ADJ** contraceptive
NM contraceptive, method of contraception; **c. local/oral** barrier/oral contraceptive

contraception [kɔ̃trasɛpsjɔ̃] **NF** contraception; **moyen de c.** method of contraception; **c. d'urgence** emergency contraception

contraceptive [kɔ̃traseptiv] *voir* **contraceptif**

contractant, -e [kɔ̃traktɑ̃, -ɑ̃t] *Jur* **ADJ** contracting
NM,F les contractants the contracting parties

contracté, -e [kɔ̃trakte] **ADJ 1** *Anat (muscle, voix)* taut, tense; **il avait les mâchoires contractées** his jaw was stiff **2** *(nerveux ▸ personne)* tense **3** *Ling* contracted

contracter **[3]** [kɔ̃trakte] **VT 1** *(se charger de ▸ dette)* to incur, to run up; *(▸ assurance, emprunt)* to take out; *(▸ obligation, engagement)* to take on; **c. une alliance** to enter into an alliance; **c. mariage avec qn** to contract a marriage with sb
2 *(acquérir ▸ manie, habitude)* to develop, to acquire; *(▸ maladie)* to catch, *Sout* to contract
3 *(réduire ▸ liquide, corps)* to contract
4 *(raidir ▸ muscle)* to contract, to tighten (up), to tauten; *(▸ visage, traits)* to tense (up), to tighten (up); **le visage contracté par la peur** his/her face taut with fear
5 *(rendre anxieux)* to make tense
6 *Ling* to contract
VPR se contracter 1 *(être réduit ▸ liquide, corps)* to contract, to reduce; *(▸ fibre)* to shrink **2** *(se raidir ▸ visage, traits)* to tense (up), to become taut; *(▸ muscle)* to contract, to tighten up; *(▸ cœur)* to contract; **ne vous contractez pas** don't tense up **3** *Ling (mot)* to contract, to be contracted

contractile [kɔ̃traktil] **ADJ** contractile

contraction [kɔ̃traksjɔ̃] **NF 1** *(raidissement ▸ d'un muscle)* contracting, tensing; *(▸ du visage, des traits, de l'estomac)* tensing, tightening (up); *(▸ des mâchoires)* clamping; *(raideur ▸ d'un muscle)* tenseness, tautness; *(▸ de l'estomac)* tightness; *(▸ des mâchoires)* stiffness
2 *Méd* **c. (utérine)** contraction
3 *Ling* contraction
4 *Scol* **c. de texte** summary
5 *Phys* contraction
6 *Écon (de l'activité, du crédit)* reduction (**de** in); **la c. de la demande** the fall in demand

contractuel, -elle [kɔ̃traktɥel] **ADJ** *(gén)* contractual, contract *(avant n)*; *(employé)* contract *(avant n)*; *(droits)* granted by contract
NM *Admin* contract public servant; *(agent de police) Br* (male) traffic warden, *Am* traffic policeman
• **contractuelle NF** *Admin* contract public servant; *(agent de police) Br* (female) traffic warden, *Am* traffic policewoman

contracture [kɔ̃traktyr] **NF 1** *Méd* contraction, cramp **2** *Archit* contracture

contradicteur [kɔ̃tradiktœr] **NM** contradictor; **il y avait de bruyants contradicteurs dans l'auditoire** there were some noisy hecklers in the audience

contradiction [kɔ̃tradiksjɔ̃] **NF 1** *(contestation)* contradiction; **elle ne supporte pas la c.** she can't stand contradiction *or* being contradicted; **porter la c. dans une discussion** to be a dissenter in a discussion
2 *(inconséquence)* contradiction, inconsistency; **il y a trop de contradictions dans son témoignage** there are too many contradictions *or* inconsistencies in his/her testimony; **il est plein de contradictions** he's full of contradictions
3 *Ling* contradiction
4 *Jur* allegation
• **en contradiction avec PRÉP** in contradiction with; **c'est en c. avec sa façon de vivre** it goes against his/her lifestyle; **être en c. avec soi-même** to be inconsistent

contradictoire [kɔ̃tradiktwar] **ADJ 1** *(opposé ▸ théories, idées)* contradictory, clashing; *(▸ témoignages)* conflicting; **débat/réunion c.** open debate/meeting; **c'est c. à** *ou* **avec ce que tu viens de dire** this contradicts what you've just said **2** *Ling* contradictory **3** *Jur* **jugement c.** = judgment rendered in the presence of the parties involved

contradictoirement [kɔ̃tradiktwarmɑ̃] **ADV 1** *(de façon opposée)* contradictorily **2** *Jur* = in the presence of the parties involved

contragestion [kɔ̃traʒɛstjɔ̃] **NF** postcoital contraception, *Spéc* contragestion

contraignait *etc voir* **contraindre**

contraignant, -e [kɔ̃trɛɲɑ̃, -ɑ̃t] **ADJ** *(occupation)* restricting; *(contrat)* restrictive; *(horaire)* restricting, limiting

contraindre **[80]** [kɔ̃trɛ̃dr] **VT 1** *(obliger)* **les grèves nous ont contraints à annuler notre voyage** the strikes forced us to cancel our trip; **je suis contraint de rester à Paris** I'm obliged *or* forced to stay in Paris
2 *Littéraire (réprimer ▸ désir, passion)* to constrain, to restrain, to keep a check on
3 *Littéraire (réprimer)* **c. une personne dans ses choix** to restrict sb's choice
4 *Jur* to constrain
VPR se contraindre 1 *(s'obliger)* **se c. à faire qch** to force oneself to do sth **2** *Littéraire (se retenir)* to restrain oneself

contraint, -e [kɔ̃trɛ̃, -ɛ̃t] **ADJ 1** *(emprunté ▸ sourire)* constrained, forced, unnatural; *(▸ politesse)* unnatural **2** *(obligé)* **c. et forcé** under duress
• **contrainte NF 1** *(obligation)* constraint, imposition; **les contraintes sociales** social constraints
2 *(force)* constraint; **obtenir qch par la contrainte** to get sth by force; **faire qch par contrainte** to be forced to do sth; **céder sous la contrainte** to give in under pressure
3 *(gêne)* constraint, embarrassment; **parler sans contrainte** to speak uninhibitedly
4 *Jur* **contrainte par corps** imprisonment for non-payment of debts
5 *Phys* stress; **contrainte de cisaillement** shearing stress; **contrainte en compression/flambage** compressive/bending stress; **contrainte de torsion/traction** torsional/tensile stress

contraire [kɔ̃trɛr] **ADJ 1** *(point de vue, attitude)* opposite; **ils ont des avis contraires** they hold opposite opinions; **sauf avis c.** unless otherwise informed
2 *(inverse ▸ direction, sens)* **fais le tour dans le sens c.** go the opposite way round; **dans le sens c. des aiguilles d'une montre** *Br* anticlockwise, *Am* counterclockwise
3 *(défavorable, nuisible)* unfavourable, *Sout* contrary
4 *Ling* contrary
5 *Mus* contrary
NM 1 *(inverse)* **le c.** the opposite; **j'avais raison, ne me dis pas le c.** I was right, don't deny it; **le c. de** the opposite of; **elle timide? c'est tout le c.!** her, shy? quite the opposite *or* contrary!; **elle dit toujours le c. de ce que disent les autres** she always says the opposite of what everyone else says; **dire tout et son c.** to contradict oneself **2** *Ling* opposite, antonym
• **au contraire, bien au contraire, tout au contraire,** *Belg* **que du contraire ADV** quite the reverse *or* opposite
• **au contraire de PRÉP** unlike
• **contraire à PRÉP c. à la règle** *ou* **aux règlements** against the rules, contrary to the rules; **c'est c. à mes principes** it's against my principles

contrairement [kɔ̃trɛrmɑ̃] **contrairement à PRÉP c. à ce qu'il m'a dit/aux prévisions** contrary to what he told me/to all expectations; **c. à son frère** unlike his/her brother

contralto [kɔ̃tralto] **NM** contralto

contrariant, -e [kɔ̃trarjɑ̃, -ɑ̃t] **ADJ** *(personne)* contrary; *(nouvelle)* annoying; **il n'est pas c.** he's really easy-going

contrarié, -e [kɔ̃trarje] **ADJ** *(amour)* frustrated, thwarted; *(projet)* disrupted; **tu as l'air c.** you look annoyed; **un gaucher c.** = a left-handed person forced to write with his/her right hand

contrarier **[10]** [kɔ̃trarje] **VT 1** *(ennuyer ▸ personne)* to annoy; **ça la contrarie de devoir arrêter de travailler** she's annoyed at having to stop work **2** *(contrecarrer ▸ ambitions, amour)* to thwart; *(▸ projets)* to disrupt; *(▸ mouvement, action)* to impede, to bar; **c. un gaucher** = to force a left-handed person to use his/her right hand **3** *(contraster)* **c. des couleurs** to use contrasting shades
VPR se contrarier 1 *(aller à l'encontre de ▸ forces)* to oppose one another **2** *(être en conflit ▸ personnes)* to clash **3** *(s'opposer ▸ formes, couleurs)* to contrast

contrariété [kɔ̃trarjete] **NF 1** *(mécontentement)* annoyance, vexation; **éprouver une c.** to be annoyed *or* upset; **elle doit avoir une grosse c.** something must have upset her a lot; **elle a dû avoir une petite c.** she must have had some minor setback **2** *(opposition)* clash; **c. d'humeur** clash of personalities

contrastant, -e [kɔ̃trastɑ̃, -ɑ̃t] **ADJ** contrasting

contraste [kɔ̃trast] **NM** contrast; **faire c. avec qch** to contrast with sth; **deux couleurs qui font c.** two contrasting shades; *TV* **réglage du c.** contrast control *or* adjustment
• **de contraste ADJ** *(substance)* contrast *(avant n)*; *(effet)* contrasting
• **en contraste ADV mettre deux choses en c.** to contrast two things
• **en contraste avec PRÉP 1** *(par opposition à)* by contrast to *or* with, in contrast to *or* with **2 mettre qch en c. avec** to contrast sth with
• **par contraste ADV** in contrast
• **par contraste avec PRÉP** by contrast to *or* with, in contrast to *or* with

contrasté, -e [kɔ̃traste] **ADJ 1** *(couleurs, situations)* contrasting
2 *(photo, image)* with strong contrast, *Spéc* contrasty
3 *Ordinat* highlighted
4 *(nuancé ▸ bilan, résultats)* uneven, mixed

contraster [3] [kɔ̃traste] VT *(caractères, situations, couleurs)* to contrast; *(photo)* to give contrast to

VI to contrast; **des couleurs qui contrastent** contrasting colours; **c. avec qch** to contrast with sth

contrat [kɔ̃tra] NM **1** *(acte, convention)* contract; **passer un c. avec qn** to enter into a contract with sb; **un c. de deux ans** a two-year contract; **un c. de plusieurs milliards de dollars** a contract worth several billion dollars; **remplir son c.** *Jur* to fulfil the terms of one's contract; *Fig (s'exécuter)* to keep one's promise; **c. d'adhésion** membership agreement; **c. administratif** public service contract; **c. d'agence** agency contract; **c. aléatoire** aleatory contract; **c. d'apprentissage** training contract; **c. d'assurance** insurance policy; **c. d'avenir** = short-term contract subsidized by the government to help people on benefits get back into part-time work; **c. de bail** lease contract; **c. bilatéral** bilateral contract; **c. collectif** group contract; **c. de concession** licence agreement; **c. à durée déterminée/indéterminée** fixed-term/permanent contract; **c. d'embauche** *Br* employment contract, contract of employment, *Am* labor contract; **c. emploi-solidarité** = short-term contract subsidized by the government; **c. d'entreprise** service contract; **c. exclusif** sole contract; **c. de licence** licensing agreement; **c. local de sécurité** = list of measures to increase public safety within a town, involving all the official bodies who work together with the residents; **c. de location-vente** hire purchase agreement; **c. de louage** rental contract; **c. de mariage** marriage contract; **c. de mission d'intérim** temporary contract; **c. notarié** notarized contract; **c. de prestation de service** service contract; **c. de prêt** loan agreement; **c. de promotion immobilière** property development contract; **c. de qualification** training contract; **c. de service** service contract; **c. de sponsoring** sponsorship deal; **c. synallagmatique** bilateral contract, synallagmatic contract; **c. temporaire** temporary contract; **c. à temps partiel/plein** part-/full-time contract; *Bourse* **c. à terme** forward contract, futures contract; **c. de transport** contract of carriage; **c. de travail** *Br* employment contract, contract of employment, *Am* labor contract; **c. de vente** bill of sale, sales contract; **c. verbal** verbal contract *or* undertaking

2 *(entente)* agreement, deal; **un c. tacite** an unspoken agreement

3 *Phil* **c. social** social contract

4 *Fam Arg crime (de tueur)* contract[□]

5 *Cartes* contract

contravention [kɔ̃travɑ̃sjɔ̃] NF **1** *(amende)* (parking) fine; *(avis)* (parking) ticket; **donner une c. à qn** to book sb, to give sb a (parking) ticket **2** *(infraction)* contravention, infraction, infringement; **être en c., se mettre en état de c.** to be in breach of the law

CONTRE [kɔ̃tr]

PREP
- against **1–3, 5, 6**
- on **1**
- for **4**
- to **5**

ADV
- against **2**

NM
- cons **1**
- block **2**

PRÉP 1 *(indiquant la proximité)* against, on; **s'appuyer c. un arbre/une palissade** to lean against a tree/a fence; **l'échelle était dressée c. le mur** the ladder was against the wall; **se frotter c. qch** to rub (oneself) against *or* on sth; **se blottir c. qn** to cuddle up to sb; **serrer qn c. son cœur** to hug sb, to clasp sb to one's breast; **joue c. joue** cheek to cheek; **pare-chocs c. pare-chocs** bumper to bumper; **tenir qn tout c. soi** to hold sb close; **allongé tout c. elle** lying right next to *or* beside her; **un coup c. la vitre** a knock on *or* at the window; **je me suis cogné la tête c. le radiateur** I hit my head on the radiator; **lancer une balle c. le mur** to throw a ball against *or* at the wall; **jeter des cailloux c. un carreau** to throw pebbles at a window; **mettez-vous c. le mur** stand (right) by the wall

2 *(indiquant l'opposition)* against; **nager c. le courant** to swim upstream *or* against the current; **notre équipe aura le vent c. elle** our team will play into the wind; **une attaque c. qn** an attack against *or* on sb; **agir c. qn** to act against sb; **être en colère c. qn** to be angry at *or* with sb; **nous avons des preuves c. lui** we have (some) evidence against him; **je suis c. l'intervention** I'm opposed to *or* against (the idea of) intervention; **voter c. qn/qch** to vote against sb/sth; *Jur* **Durier c. Chardin** Durier versus Chardin; **le match c. le Brésil** the Brazil match, the match against *or* with Brazil; **l'Angleterre c. l'Irlande** England against *or* versus Ireland; **jouer c. qn** to play against sb; **c'est c. ma religion/mes principes** it's against my religion/principles; **avoir quelque chose c. qn** to have something against sb; **je n'ai rien c. toi personnellement** it's nothing personal, I've nothing personal against you; **tout le monde est c. moi** everyone is against me; **je l'ai fait c. ma volonté** I did it against my will; **agir c. les ordres/son devoir** to act against orders/counter to one's duty; **pour une fois, j'irai c. mon habitude** for once, I'll break my habit; **ce serait aller c. sa nature** it would go *or* be against his/her nature

3 *(pour protéger de)* against; **pastilles c. la toux** cough lozenges; **bombe c. les acariens** spray against mites; **la loi c. l'avortement** the anti-abortion law; **lutter c. l'alcoolisme** to fight (against) alcoholism; **que faire c. l'inflation?** what can be done about *or* against *or* to combat inflation?; **s'assurer c. le vol** to take out insurance against theft

4 *(en échange de)* for, in exchange *or* return for; **j'ai échangé mon livre c. le sien** I swapped my book for his/hers; **il leur demande de l'argent c. son silence** he's asking them for money in return *or* exchange for his silence; **livraison c. remboursement** cash on delivery

5 *(indiquant une proportion, un rapport)* against, to; **parier à 10 c. 1** to bet at 10 to 1; **10 c. 1 qu'ils vont gagner!** 10 to 1 they'll win!; **156 voix c. 34** 156 votes to 34; **ils nous sont tombés dessus à trois c. un** there were three of them for every one of us, they were three to one against us; **la livre s'échange à 1,46 euros c. 1,62 hier** the pound is trading at 1.46 euros compared to *or* (as) against 1.62 yesterday

6 *(contrairement à)* **c. toute apparence** contrary to *or* despite all appearances; **c. toute attente** contrary to *or* against all expectations; **c. toute logique/prévision** against all logic/the odds

ADV 1 *(indiquant la proximité)* **le radiateur est allumé, mets-toi tout c.** the heater is on, stand right next to it; **approche-toi du mur, et appuie-toi c.** go up to the wall and lean against it

2 *(indiquant l'opposition)* against; **cette réforme ne passera pas, trop de gens sont c.** this reform won't get through, too many people are against it; **on partage? – je n'ai rien c.** *ou* **je ne suis pas c.** shall we share? – I've nothing against it *or* it's OK by me; **c'est l'instinct, tu ne pourras pas aller c.** it's instinctive, you won't be able to fight it

NM 1 *(argument opposé)* **le pour et le c.** the pros and cons; **il y a toujours du pour et du c.** there are two sides to everything

2 *Sport (au volley, au basket)* block; *(en escrime)* counter; *(au billard)* kiss; *(au bridge)* double; **faire un c.** to intercept the ball; *Ftbl* **marquer sur un c.** to score on a counter-attack

• **par contre** ADV on the other hand; **il est très compétent, par c. il n'est pas toujours très aimable** he's very competent, but (on the other hand) he's not always very pleasant

---

contre-accusation [kɔ̃trakyzasjɔ̃] *(pl* **contre-accusations)** NF *Jur* counter-charge

contre-alizé [kɔ̃tralize] *(pl* **contre-alizés)** NM *Météo* anti-trade (wind)

contre-allée [kɔ̃trale] *(pl* **contre-allées)** NF *(d'une avenue) Br* service *or Am* frontage road; *(d'une promenade)* side track *or* path

contre-amiral [kɔ̃tramiral] *(pl* **contre-amiraux** [-o]) NM *Mil Br* ≃ commodore, *Am* ≃ rear-admiral (lower half); *Can (grade) Br* ≃ rear-admiral, *Am* ≃ rear-admiral (upper half)

contre-analyse [kɔ̃tranaliz] *(pl* **contre-analyses)** NF second analysis, reanalysis

contre-appel [kɔ̃trapɛl] *(pl* **contre-appels)** NM *Mil* second roll call

contre-argument [kɔ̃trargymɑ̃] *(pl* **contre-arguments)** NM counterargument

contre-assurance [kɔ̃trasyrɑ̃s] *(pl* **contre-assurances)** NF reinsurance

contre-attaque [kɔ̃tratak] *(pl* **contre-attaques)** NF **1** *Mil (gén)* counterattack; *(à l'explosif)* counter-blast **2** *(dans une polémique)* counterattack, counter-blast

contre-attaquer [3] [kɔ̃tratake] VT to counter-attack, to strike back

contrebalancer [16] [kɔ̃trəbalɑ̃se] VT **1** *(poids)* to counterbalance **2** *(compenser ▸ inconvénients, efforts)* to offset, to make up for, to compensate; **les bénéfices ne contrebalancent plus les pertes** profits are no longer balancing losses

VPR **se contrebalancer 1** *(raisons, hypothèses)* to counterbalance each other; *(dépenses)* to cancel each other out **2** *Fam* **se c. de qch** *(se moquer)* not to give a damn about sth; **je m'en contrebalance** I couldn't give a damn; **je me contrebalance de perdre mon boulot** I don't give a damn about losing my job

contrebande [kɔ̃trəbɑ̃d] NF **1** *(trafic)* smuggling, contraband; **faire de la c.** to smuggle (in) goods **2** *(marchandises)* contraband, smuggled goods; *(alcool)* bootleg; **c. de guerre** wartime smuggling

• **de contrebande** ADJ *(marchandises)* smuggled, contraband *(avant n)*; *(alcool)* bootleg

• **en contrebande** ADV **faire entrer/sortir qch en c.** to smuggle sth in/out

contrebandier, -ère [kɔ̃trəbɑ̃dje, -ɛr] NM,F smuggler

contrebas [kɔ̃trəba] **en contrebas** ADV lower down, below

• **en contrebas de** PRÉP below; **le café est en c. de la rue** the café is below street level

contrebasse [kɔ̃trəbas] NF **1** *(instrument)* (double) bass, contrabass **2** *(musicien)* (double) bass player, double bassist

contrebassiste [kɔ̃trəbasist] NMF (double) bass player, double bassist

contrebasson [kɔ̃trəbasɔ̃] NM contrabassoon, double bassoon

contrebatterie [kɔ̃trəbatri] NF *Mil* counterbattery

contre-braquage [kɔ̃trəbrakaʒ] *(pl* **contre-braquages)** NM *Aut* opposite lock

contre-braquer [3] [kɔ̃trəbrake] VI *Aut* to drive into a skid

contrebuter [3] [kɔ̃trəbyte] VT *Constr* to buttress, to prop up, to shore up

contrecarrer [3] [kɔ̃trəkare] VT *(personne)* to thwart; *(projet, initiative)* to thwart, to block

contrechamp [kɔ̃trəʃɑ̃] NM *Cin* reverse shot

contre-chant [kɔ̃trəʃɑ̃] *(pl* **contre-chants)** NM counterpoint

contrecœur[1] [kɔ̃trəkœr] NM **1** *(d'un foyer)* fireback **2** *Rail* guardrail, *Br* checkrail

contrecœur[2] [kɔ̃trəkœr] **à contrecœur** ADV reluctantly, unwillingly, grudgingly

contrecoup [kɔ̃trəku] NM **1** *(répercussion)* repercussion, aftereffect; **subir le c. de qch** to suffer the aftershock *or* aftereffects of sth **2** *(ricochet)* rebound

contre-courant [kɔ̃trəkurɑ̃] *(pl* **contre-courants)** NM countercurrent

• **à contre-courant** ADV **1** *(d'un cours d'eau)* against the current, upstream **2** *(à rebours)* **aller à c.** to go against the grain

• **à contre-courant de** PRÉP **aller à c. de la mode** to go against the trend; **cela va à c. de ce que je voulais faire** that is the (exact) opposite of what I wanted to do

contredanse [kɔ̃trədɑ̃s] NF **1** *(danse)* contredanse, contradanse **2** *Fam (contravention)* ticket[□]

contredire [103] [kɔ̃trədir] VT *(personne, propos)* to contradict; **sa version contredit la tienne** his/her version is at variance with *or* contradicts yours

VPR **se contredire 1** *(personnes)* **ils se contredisent (l'un l'autre)** they contradict each other **2** *(témoignages, faits)* to be in contradiction (with each other), to contradict each other **3** *(emploi réfléchi)* **il se contredit** he contradicts himself

contredit [kɔ̃trədi] **sans contredit ADV** unquestionably, undoubtedly

contrée [kɔ̃tre] **NF** *Littéraire (pays)* country, land; *(région)* region, area; **dans une c. lointaine** in a faraway land

contre-écriture [kɔ̃trekrityr] *(pl* **contre-écritures)** **NF** *Compta* contra-entry

contre-écrou [kɔ̃trekru] *(pl* **contre-écrous)** **NM** locknut

contre-emploi [kɔ̃trɑ̃plwa] *(pl* **contre-emplois)** **NM** miscasting; **utiliser qn à c.** to miscast sb

contre-enquête [kɔ̃trɑ̃kɛt] *(pl* **contre-enquêtes)** **NF** counterinquiry

contre-épreuve [kɔ̃treprœv] *(pl* **contre-épreuves)** **NF 1** *Typ* counterproof **2** *(contre-essai)* repetition *or* second test, countercheck

contre-espionnage [kɔ̃trɛspjɔnaʒ] *(pl* **contre-espionnages)** **NM** counterespionage

contre-essai [kɔ̃trese] *(pl* **contre-essais)** **NM** repetition *or* second test, countercheck

contre-exemple [kɔ̃tregzɑ̃pl] *(pl* **contre-exemples)** **NM** *(illustration)* counterexample; **choisir un c.** to choose an example that goes against the rule; **il a donné un c.** he gave evidence to the contrary

contre-expertise [kɔ̃trɛkspertiz] *(pl* **contre-expertises)** **NF** second expert evaluation *or* opinion

contrefaçon [kɔ̃trəfasɔ̃] **NF 1** *(action d'imiter ▸ une signature, une écriture, une monnaie)* counterfeiting, forging; *(▸ un brevet)* infringement **2** *(copie ▸ d'un produit, d'un vêtement)* imitation, fake; *(▸ d'une signature, d'une écriture, de monnaie)* counterfeit, forgery; **méfiez-vous des contrefaçons** beware of imitations

contrefacteur, -trice [kɔ̃trəfaktœr, -tris] **NM,F** *(de produits)* copier, imitator, faker; *(de billets, d'une signature, d'une marque)* counterfeiter, forger

contrefaire **[109]** [kɔ̃trəfɛr] **VT 1** *(parodier)* to mimic, to take off

2 *(signature, écriture, argent)* to counterfeit, to forge; *(brevet)* to infringe; *(vidéo, enregistrement)* to pirate

3 *(déformer ▸ visage)* to distort; *(▸ voix)* to alter, to change, to distort

4 *Vieilli (feindre)* to feign

contrefait, -e [kɔ̃trəfe, -ɛt] **ADJ 1** *(déformé)* deformed, misshapen **2** *(falsifié ▸ signature, écriture, argent)* counterfeit, forged

contrefaites *voir* **contrefaire**

contrefera *etc voir* **contrefaire**

contre-feu [kɔ̃trəfø] *(pl* **contre-feux)** **NM 1** *(plaque)* fireback **2** *(incendie)* backfire

contrefiche [kɔ̃trəfiʃ] **NF 1** *(étai)* oblique prop *or* stay **2** *Archit (jambe de force)* brace, strut

contreficher **[3]** [kɔ̃trəfiʃe] **se contreficher VPR** *Fam* **se c. de** not to care less about; **je me contrefiche de ses problèmes** I couldn't care less about his/her problems; **je m'en contrefiche** I couldn't care less

contre-filet [kɔ̃trəfilɛ] *(pl* **contre-filets)** **NM** sirloin (steak)

contrefit *etc voir* **contrefaire**

contrefort [kɔ̃trəfɔr] **NM 1** *Archit* buttress, abutment **2** *(d'une chaussure)* stiffener **3** *Bot & Géog* spur

• **contreforts NMPL** *Géog* foothills

contrefoutre **[116]** [kɔ̃trəfutr] **se contrefoutre VPR** *très Fam* **se c. de qch** not to give a damn *or Br* a toss about sth; **je m'en contrefous** I don't give a damn *or Br* a toss (about it)

contre-haut [kɔ̃trəo] **en contre-haut ADV** (up) above

• **en contre-haut de PRÉP** (up) above

contre-indication [kɔ̃trɛ̃dikasjɔ̃] *(pl* **contre-indications)** **NF 1** *Méd* contra-indication **2** *(argument)* counter-argument; **je ne vois pas de c. à ce que nous construisions sur ce terrain** I see no reason why we shouldn't build on this piece of land

contre-indiquer **[3]** [kɔ̃trɛ̃dike] **VT** *Méd* to contra-indicate

contre-interrogatoire [kɔ̃trɛ̃terɔgatwar] *(pl* **contre-interrogatoires)** **NM** cross-examination

contre-jour [kɔ̃trəʒur] *(pl* **contre-jours)** **NM 1** *(éclairage)* backlighting; **un effet de c.** a backlit *or Spéc* contre-jour effect **2** *(photo)* backlit *or Spéc* contre-jour shot

• **à contre-jour, en contre-jour ADV** *(être placé ▸ personne)* with one's back to the light; *(▸ objet)* against the light *or* sunlight; **prendre une photo à c.** to take a photograph against the light

contre-la-montre [kɔ̃trəlamɔ̃tr] **NM INV** time trial

contre-lettre [kɔ̃trəlɛtr] *(pl* **contre-lettres)** **NF** *Jur* counter-letter, counter-deed

contremaître [kɔ̃trəmɛtr] **NM 1** *(dans un atelier)* foreman, supervisor **2** *Naut* petty officer

contre-manifestant, -e [kɔ̃trəmanifɛstɑ̃, -ɑ̃t] *(mpl* **contre-manifestants,** *fpl* **contre-manifestantes)** **NM,F** counterdemonstrator

contre-manifestation [kɔ̃trəmanifɛstasjɔ̃] *(pl* **contre-manifestations)** **NF** counterdemonstration

contremarche [kɔ̃trəmarʃ] **NF 1** *(d'escalier)* riser **2** *Mil* countermarch

contremarque [kɔ̃trəmark] **NF 1** *(billet ▸ au spectacle)* voucher *(exchanged for ticket at the entrance)*; *(▸ de transport)* extra portion (of ticket) **2** *Équitation* bishopping *(of horse's teeth)* **3** *Com & Hér* countermark

contremarquer **[3]** [kɔ̃trəmarke] **VT** *Com & Hér* to countermark

contre-mesure [kɔ̃trəməzyr] *(pl* **contre-mesures)** **NF 1** *(gén) & Mil* countermeasure; **c. électronique** jamming device **2** *Mus* **jouer à c.** to play against the beat *or* out of time

contre-offensive [kɔ̃trɔfɑ̃siv] *(pl* **contre-offensives)** **NF 1** *Mil* counteroffensive **2** *(réplique)* counteroffensive, counterblast **3** *Fin* counteroffer

contre-offre [kɔ̃trɔfr] *(pl* **contre-offres)** **NF** counter-offer

contre-OPA [kɔ̃trɔpea] **NF INV** *Fin* counterbid

contrepartie [kɔ̃trəparti] **NF 1** *(compensation)* compensation; **c. financière** financial compensation

2 *Compta (registre comptable)* duplicate register; *(entrée)* counterpart; **en c.** per contra

3 *(dans une transaction)* other party *or* side

4 *Bourse* market making, hedging; **faire (de) la c.** to operate against one's client

5 *(d'une opinion)* opposite view; *(d'un argument)* corollary, obverse, converse

• **en contrepartie ADV 1** *(en compensation)* in *or* by way of compensation **2** *(en revanche)* on the other hand **3** *(en retour)* in return

• **en contrepartie de PRÉP** (as a *or* in compensation) for; **service en c. duquel vous devrez payer la somme de…** for which services you will pay the sum of…

contre-passation [kɔ̃trəpasasjɔ̃] *(pl* **contre-passations)** **NF 1** *Compta* journal entry, contra-entry; *(d'un article, d'une entrée)* reversing, transferring **2** *Fin (d'un effet)* re-endorsement

contre-passer **[3]** [kɔ̃trəpase] **VT 1** *Compta (article, entrée)* to reverse, to contra, to transfer **2** *Fin (effet)* to endorse back, to re-endorse

contre-pente [kɔ̃trəpɑ̃t] *(pl* **contre-pentes)** **NF** reverse slope

contre-performance [kɔ̃trəpɛrfɔrmɑ̃s] *(pl* **contre-performances)** **NF** bad result, performance below expectation

contrepèterie [kɔ̃trəpetri] **NF** spoonerism

contre-pied [kɔ̃trəpje] *(pl* **contre-pieds)** **NM 1** *(d'une opinion)* opposite (view); *(d'un argument)* converse, obverse; **prenons le c. de sa position** let's take the (exact) opposite position to his/hers; **il prend toujours le c. de ce qu'on lui dit** *(en paroles)* he always says the opposite of what other people say; *(en actions)* he always does the opposite of what he's told **2** *Sport* **prendre un adversaire à c.** to catch an opponent off balance, to wrong-foot an opponent **3** *Chasse* backscent; **aller à c., prendre le c.** *(chien)* to run heel, to hunt counter; *Fig* to take the opposite view

contreplacage [kɔ̃trəplakaʒ] **NM 1** *(procédé)* plywood construction **2** *(feuille)* plywood panel

contreplaqué [kɔ̃trəplake] **NM** plywood

contre-plongée [kɔ̃trəplɔ̃ʒe] *(pl* **contre-plongées)** *Cin & Phot* **NF** low-angle shot

• **en contre-plongée ADV** from below; **prends-la en c.** get a low-angle shot of her, shoot her from below

contrepoids [kɔ̃trəpwa] **NM** *(gén)* counterbalance, counterweight; *(d'une horloge)* balance weight; *(d'un funambule)* balancing pole; *aussi Fig* **faire c. (à qch)** to provide a counterweight (to sth)

contre-poil [kɔ̃trəpwal] **à contre-poil ADV** the wrong way; *Fam* **prendre qn à c.** to rub sb up the wrong way

contrepoint [kɔ̃trəpwɛ̃] **NM** *Littérature & Mus* counterpoint

• **en contrepoint ADV 1** *Littérature & Mus* contrapuntally **2** *Littéraire (en même temps)* at the same time, concurrently

• **en contrepoint de PRÉP 1** *Littérature & Mus* as counterpoint to **2** *(avec)* as an accompaniment to

contrepoison [kɔ̃trəpwazɔ̃] **NM** antidote

contre-porte [kɔ̃trəpɔrt] *(pl* **contre-portes)** **NF** *(d'isolation)* inner door; *(de protection)* screen door

contre-pouvoir [kɔ̃trəpuvwar] *(pl* **contre-pouvoirs)** **NM** = challenge to established authority

contre-programmation [kɔ̃trəprɔgramasjɔ̃] *(pl* **contre-programmations)** **NF** *Cin & TV* counterprogramming

contre-projet [kɔ̃trəprɔʒɛ] *(pl* **contre-projets)** **NM** counterplan, counterproject; **y a-t-il des contre-projets?** are there any (other) projects to rival this one?

contre-proposition [kɔ̃trəprɔpozisjɔ̃] *(pl* **contre-propositions)** **NF** counterproposal

contre-publicité [kɔ̃trəpyblisite] *(pl* **contre-publicités)** **NF** *(qui concurrence)* knocking copy; *(qui manque son objectif)* adverse publicity; **cet article fait de la c. à son auteur** this article is a poor advertisement for its author

contrer **[3]** [kɔ̃tre] **VT 1** *(s'opposer à ▸ personne)* to block, to counter; *(▸ argument)* to counter, to refute; *(▸ attaque, initiative, interlocuteur)* to counter; **des mesures drastiques s'imposent pour c. la maladie** drastic measures must be taken to combat disease; **se faire c.** to come a cropper **2** *Cartes* to double **3** *Sport (au volley ▸ smash)* to block; *(au rugby ▸ coup de pied)* to block; *(à la boxe)* to counter

contre-rail [kɔ̃trəraj] *(pl* **contre-rails)** **NM** check-rail, *Br* guardrail

Contre-Réforme [kɔ̃trərefɔrm] **NF** *Hist* Counter-Reformation

contre-révolution [kɔ̃trərevɔlysjɔ̃] *(pl* **contre-révolutions)** **NF** counter-revolution

contre-révolutionnaire [kɔ̃trərevɔlysjɔnɛr] *(pl* **contre-révolutionnaires)** **ADJ** counter-revolutionary

NMF counter-revolutionary

contreseing [kɔ̃trəsɛ̃] **NM** counter-signature

contresens [kɔ̃trəsɑ̃s] **NM 1** *(mauvaise interprétation)* misinterpretation; *(mauvaise traduction)* mistranslation; **faire un c.** = to mistranslate a word or a phrase etc **2** *Tex* wrong way *(of fabric)*

• **à contresens ADV 1** *(traduire, comprendre, marcher)* the wrong way; **prendre une rue à c.** to go the wrong way down a street **2** *Tex* against the grain

contresignataire [kɔ̃trəsiɲatɛr] **NMF** countersigner

contresigner **[3]** [kɔ̃trəsiɲe] **VT** to countersign

contretemps [kɔ̃trətɑ̃] **NM 1** *(empêchement)* hitch, mishap, setback; **à moins d'un c.** unless there's a hitch; **voilà un c. bien fâcheux!** what an awful nuisance! **2** *Mus* offbeat

• **à contretemps ADV 1** *(inopportunément)* at the wrong time *or* moment **2** *Mus* off the beat

contre-terrorisme [kɔ̃trətɛrɔrism] *(pl* **contre-terrorismes)** **NM** counterterrorism

contre-terroriste [kɔ̃trəterɔrist] *(pl* **contre-terroristes)** ADJ counterterrorist
NMF counterterrorist

contre-torpilleur [kɔ̃trətɔrpijœr] *(pl* **contre-torpilleurs)** NM *Mil* destroyer

contre-transfert [kɔ̃trətrɑ̃sfɛr] *(pl* **contre-transferts)** NM *Psy* countertransfer, countertransference

contretype [kɔ̃trətip] NM duplicate

contre-ut [kɔ̃tryt] NM INV *Mus* top C, high C

contre-valeur [kɔ̃trəvalœr] *(pl* **contre-valeurs)** NF exchange value; **pour la c. de 20 euros** in exchange for 20 euros

contrevenant, -e [kɔ̃trəvnɑ̃, -ɑ̃t] NM,F offender

contrevenir [40] [kɔ̃trəvnir] **contrevenir à** VT IND to contravene, to infringe

contrevent [kɔ̃trəvɑ̃] NM **1** *(volet)* shutter **2** *Métal* back-draught **3** *Constr* strut, brace

contrevenu, -e [kɔ̃trəvny] PP *voir* **contrevenir**

contrevérité [kɔ̃trəverite] NF falsehood, untruth

contrevient *etc voir* **contrevenir**

contre-visite [kɔ̃trəvizit] *(pl* **contre-visites)** NF further consultation *(for a second medical opinion)*

contre-voie [kɔ̃trəvwa] *(pl* **contre-voies)** NF parallel track *(going in the opposite direction)*
• **à contre-voie** ADV **monter/descendre à c.** to get on/off on the wrong side of the train

contribuable [kɔ̃tribɥabl] NMF taxpayer; **petits contribuables** basic-rate taxpayers; **gros contribuables** people in high tax brackets

contribuer [7] [kɔ̃tribɥe] VI *(financièrement)* to contribute (money), to pay a share
• **contribuer à** VT IND **c. à qch** to have a part in *or* to contribute to sth; **c. à l'achat d'un cadeau** to contribute to (buying) a present; **c. au succès de** to contribute to *or* to have a part in the success of; **il a beaucoup contribué à...** he has made a great contribution to..., he has played a great part in...; **elle n'a pas contribué à la discussion** she took no part in the discussion; **c. à faire qch** to go towards doing sth; **cela contribue pour beaucoup à la rendre heureuse** that goes a long way towards making her happy

contributif, -ive [kɔ̃tribytif, -iv] ADJ contributory

contribution [kɔ̃tribysjɔ̃] NF **1** *(argent apporté)* contribution, sum contributed; **ma c. a été de 10 euros** I contributed 10 euros **2** *(aide)* contribution, help; **sa c. au spectacle se limite à la rédaction du programme** his/her only contribution to the show is the writing of the programme **3** *(impôt)* tax; **contributions** *(à l'État)* taxes; *(à la collectivité locale) Br* ≃ council tax, *Am* ≃ local taxes; **contributions directes/indirectes** direct/indirect taxation; **c. foncière** land tax; **les contributions sociales** social security contributions
• **Contributions** NFPL tax office, *Br* ≃ Inland Revenue, *Am* ≃ Internal Revenue Service
• **à contribution** ADV **mettre qn à c.** to get sb involved; **mets-le à c.** ask him to help

contributive [kɔ̃tribytiv] *voir* **contributif**

contrit, -e [kɔ̃tri, -it] ADJ contrite, chastened

contrition [kɔ̃trisjɔ̃] NF **1** *Littéraire (repentir)* contrition, remorse **2** *Rel* **acte de c.** act of contrition

contrôlable [kɔ̃trolabl] ADJ **1** *(maîtrisable)* that can be controlled, controllable; **des éléments difficilement contrôlables** elements that are hard to control **2** *(vérifiable)* that can be checked *or* verified, checkable, verifiable

contrôle [kɔ̃trol] NM **1** *(maîtrise)* control; **garder/perdre le c. de sa voiture** to keep/to lose control of one's car; **avoir le c. de** *(d'un secteur, de compagnies)* to have (owning) control of; *(d'un pays, d'un territoire, d'un match)* to be in control of; **prendre le c. d'une entreprise** to take over a company; **c. des naissances** birth control; **c. de soi(-même)** self-control
2 *(surveillance ▸ de personnes, de travail)* supervision, control; **exercer un c. sévère sur qn** to maintain strict control over sb, to keep sb under strict supervision; *Méd* **visite** *ou* **examen de c.** check-up; **c. aérien** flight control; *Sport* **c. antidopage** dope test; *Écon* **c. budgétaire** budgetary control; **c. des changes** exchange control; *Mktg* **c. continu** monitoring; **c. économique** *ou* **des prix** price control; *Écon* **c. de gestion** management control; **c. de (la) qualité** quality control; **c. des stocks** *Br* stock control, *Am* inventory control; *Aut* **c. de vitesse** speed trap
3 *(inspection ▸ d'actes, de documents)* control, check, checking; *(▸ des marchandises)* inspection; *(▸ d'un magasin)* audit; **c. bancaire** banking controls; *Compta* **c. du bilan** audit; **c. de la comptabilité** accounting control; **c. des comptes** *ou* **fiscal** audit; **il a un c. fiscal** ≃ the *Br* Inland Revenue *or Am* IRS is checking his returns; **c. de douane** customs control; **c. d'identité** *ou* **de police** identification papers control *or* check; **contrôles à l'importation** import controls; **c. de routine** routine check-up; **c. par sondage(s)** random check; *Aut* **c. technique** *Br* MOT (test), *Am* inspection
4 *(bureau)* check point
5 *Sport (de la balle)* control
6 *Scol* test; **avoir un c. en chimie** to have a chemistry test; **c. continu (des connaissances)** continuous assessment
7 *(poinçon)* hallmark; *(bureau)* hallmark centre
8 *Mil (liste)* list, roll; **rayer qn des contrôles de l'armée** to remove sb from the army list
9 *Ordinat* **touche c.** control key; **c. d'accès** access control; **c. croisé** cross-check; **c. du curseur** cursor control
10 *Tél* monitoring
11 *Jur* **c. de constitutionnalité** review of constitutionality; **c. judiciaire** ≃ probation; **placé sous c. judiciaire** ≃ put on probation; **c. juridictionnel, c. de légalité** judicial review

contrôler [3] [kɔ̃trole] VT **1** *(maîtriser ▸ émotions, sentiments)* to control, to master, to curb; *(▸ respiration, prix, naissances, personne)* to control; *(▸ discussion, match)* to control, to master; *(▸ véhicule)* to control, to be in control of; **contrôle tes nerfs!** get a grip on yourself!; **nous ne contrôlons plus la situation** the situation is out of our control
2 *(surveiller ▸ personnes, travail)* to supervise
3 *(vérifier ▸ renseignement, exactitude)* to check, to verify; *(▸ billet, papiers)* to check, to inspect; *(▸ marchandises)* to inspect; *(▸ magasin)* to audit; *(▸ qualité)* to control; *(▸ bon fonctionnement)* to check, to monitor; *(▸ traduction)* to check; *Compta (▸ comptes)* to check, to audit; **c. les livres** to check the books; **se faire c.** *(dans un bus, un train)* to have one's ticket checked; *(par un agent de police)* to have one's ID checked
4 *(avoir sous son autorité ▸ affaires, secteur)* to be in control of, to control; *(▸ territoire, zone)* to control, to be in command of
5 *Sport (ballon)* to have control of
6 *(argent, or)* to hallmark
7 *Tél* to monitor
8 *Fin (prix)* to control; *(dépenses, comptes)* to audit
9 *Ordinat* **contrôlé par le logiciel** software-controlled; **contrôlé par menu** menu-driven, menu-controlled; **contrôlé par ordinateur** computer-controlled
VPR **se contrôler** to control oneself, to be in control of oneself; **il ne se contrôlait plus** he'd lost his grip on himself, he was (totally) out of control

contrôleur, -euse [kɔ̃trolœr, -øz] NM,F **1** *Rail* ticket inspector **2** *Aviat* **c. aérien** air traffic controller **3** *Admin & Fin* **c. du crédit** credit controller; **c. (des impôts** *ou* **contributions)** (tax) inspector *or* assessor; **c. des douanes** customs inspector; **c. financier** financial controller; **c. de gestion** management controller; **c. aux liquidations** controller in bankruptcy
NM **1** *Ind* regulator **2** *(horloge)* time clock **3** *Ordinat* controller; **c. d'affichage** display *or* screen controller; **c. de bus** bus controller; **c. de disques** disk controller; **c. de transmission** transmission controller

contrordre [kɔ̃trɔrdr] NM countermand, counterorder; **il y a c., vous ne partez plus** orders have been countermanded *or* changed, you're not leaving; **à moins d'un** *ou* **sauf c.** unless otherwise informed

controuvé, -e [kɔ̃truve] ADJ *Littéraire* false, fabricated, concocted

controversable [kɔ̃trɔversabl] ADJ debatable, disputable

controverse [kɔ̃trɔvers] NF *(débat)* controversy; **donner lieu à c.** to be controversial

controversé, -e [kɔ̃trɔverse] ADJ *(décision, théorie, personne)* controversial; **une question controversée** a controversial *or* much debated question

contumace [kɔ̃tymas], **contumax** [kɔ̃tymaks] ADJ contumacious, defaulting
NF refusal to appear in court, contempt of court, *Sout* contumacy
• **par contumace** ADV in absentia

contusion [kɔ̃tyzjɔ̃] NF *Méd* bruise, *Spéc* contusion

contusionner [3] [kɔ̃tyzjɔne] VT *Méd* to bruise, *Spéc* to contuse

conurbation [kɔnyrbasjɔ̃] NF conurbation

convainc *etc voir* **convaincre**

convaincant, -e [kɔ̃vɛ̃kɑ̃, -ɑ̃t] ADJ convincing, persuasive; **de façon convaincante** convincingly; **peu c.** unconvincing; **un argument peu c.** a rather thin argument

convaincre [114] [kɔ̃vɛ̃kr] VT **1** *(persuader)* to convince, to persuade; **je n'ai pas su le c.** I couldn't convince him; **c. qn de faire qch** to persuade sb to do sth, to talk sb into doing sth; **se laisser c.** to let oneself be persuaded *or* convinced *or* won over; **votre dernier argument m'a convaincu** your last argument has won me over; **j'en suis convaincu** I'm convinced of it **2** *(prouver coupable)* **c. qn de mensonge** to force sb to admit he/she lied; **c. qn de vol** to convict sb of theft, to find sb guilty of theft
VPR **se convaincre** to realize, to accept; **il est difficile de s'en c.** it's difficult to accept it

convaincu, -e [kɔ̃vɛ̃ky] ADJ convinced; **un partisan c. du socialisme** a firm believer in socialism; **un végétarien c.** a committed vegetarian; **parler d'un ton c.** to talk with conviction
NM,F firm *or* great *or* strong believer *(in an idea)*

convainquait *etc voir* **convaincre**

convalescence [kɔ̃valesɑ̃s] NF **1** *Méd* convalescence; **être en c.** to be convalescing **2** *Mil* = army convalescence leave

convalescent, -e [kɔ̃valesɑ̃, -ɑ̃t] ADJ convalescent
NM,F convalescent

convecteur [kɔ̃vektœr] NM convector

convection [kɔ̃veksjɔ̃] NF convection

convenable [kɔ̃vnabl] ADJ **1** *(approprié ▸ moment, lieu)* suitable, appropriate **2** *(décent ▸ tenue)* decent, respectable; *(▸ comportement)* seemly, correct; **peu c.** improper; **de manière peu c.** inappropriately; **une famille très c.** a very respectable *or* decent *or* upstanding family; **ce n'est pas très c. de parler fort** it's not very polite to talk loudly **3** *(acceptable ▸ devoir)* passable, adequate; *(▸ logement, rémunération)* decent, adequate

convenablement [kɔ̃vnabləmɑ̃] ADV **1** *(de façon appropriée)* suitably, appropriately **2** *(décemment)* decently, properly; **habille-toi c.** dress decently *or* respectably; **se tenir c.** to behave properly **3** *(de façon acceptable)* **gagner c. sa vie** to earn a decent wage; **il travaille c. à l'école** his schoolwork is fairly good; **on y mange c.** the food is quite adequate there

convenance [kɔ̃vnɑ̃s] NF *Littéraire (adéquation)* appropriateness, suitability; **la c. de goût entre deux personnes** affinity of taste between two people; **mariage de c.** marriage of convenience
• **convenances** NFPL propriety, decorum, accepted (standards of) behaviour; **respecter les convenances** to respect *or* to observe the proprieties; **contraire aux convenances** unseemly, improper
• **à ma/sa/***etc* **convenance** ADV as suits me/him/*etc* (best); **je choisirai une couleur à ma c.** I'll choose a shade to suit me; **il n'a pas trouvé l'hôtel à sa c.** he didn't find the hotel to his liking *or* suitable
• **pour convenance(s) personnelle(s)** ADV for personal reasons

convenir [40] [kɔ̃vnir] **VT c'est convenu ainsi** it's been agreed this way; **comme (cela a été) convenu** as agreed; **c. que** to agree *or* to accept *or* to admit that; **tu dois bien c. qu'elle a raison** you must admit she's right
USAGE ABSOLU *(être approprié)* **dire les mots qui conviennent** to say the right words; **trouver le ton qui convient** to find the right *or* suitable tone
VPR se convenir to suit one another
• **convenir à VT IND 1** *(être approprié à)* to suit; **une robe qui convient à la circonstance** a dress that suits the occasion, a dress suitable for *or* befitting the occasion **2** *(plaire à)* to suit; **lundi matin me conviendrait assez** Monday morning would suit me fine; **dix heures, cela vous convient-il?** does ten o'clock suit you?; **ce travail ne lui convient pas du tout** this job's not right for him/her at all; **cette chaleur ne me convient pas du tout** this heat doesn't agree with me at all
• **convenir de VT IND 1** *(se mettre d'accord sur)* to agree upon; **nous avions convenu de nous retrouver à midi** we had agreed to meet at noon; **c. d'un endroit** to agree upon a place; **somme convenue** agreed sum; **comme convenu** as agreed **2** *(reconnaître)* **c. de qch** to admit sth; **je conviens d'avoir dit cela** I admit to having said that; **j'en conviens volontiers** I don't mind admitting it
• **il convient de V IMPERSONNEL 1** *(il est souhaitable de)* it is advisable *or* a good idea to; **il voudrait savoir ce qu'il convient de faire** he would like to know the right thing to do **2** *(il est de bon ton de)* it is proper *or* the done thing to; **il convient d'apporter des fleurs à la maîtresse de maison** it is the done thing to bring flowers for one's hostess
• **il convient que V IMPERSONNEL il convient que vous y alliez** you should *or* ought to go

convention [kɔ̃vɑ̃sjɔ̃] **NF 1** *(norme)* convention; **les conventions orthographiques** spelling conventions; **un système de conventions** an agreed system
2 *(règle de bienséance)* (social) convention; **respecter les conventions** to conform to accepted social behaviour *or* established conventions
3 *(accord ▸ tacite)* agreement, understanding; *(▸ officiel)* agreement; *(▸ diplomatique)* convention; *(clause)* article, clause; **c. écrite** written agreement; **C. européenne des droits de l'homme** European Convention on Human Rights; **c. collective (du travail)** collective agreement; **c. de crédit** credit agreement; **c. internationale** international convention *or* treaty; **c. signée entre le patronat et les syndicats** union *or* union–management agreement
4 *Pol (assemblée ▸ aux États-Unis)* convention; *(▸ en France)* assembly
5 *Hist* **la C.** the French National Convention *(1792–1795)*
• **de convention ADJ** *(gén)* conformist, conventional; *(amabilité, sourire)* superficial
• **par convention ADV par c., nous appellerons cet ensemble N** let us call this set N; **par c., on symbolise l'heure par un h** "hour" is usually symbolised by an "h", the generally-accepted abbreviation for "hour" is "h"

convention-cadre [kɔ̃vɑ̃sjɔ̃kadr] *(pl* **conventions-cadres)** **NF** framework convention

conventionné, -e [kɔ̃vɑ̃sjɔne] **ADJ 1** *(médecin, clinique)* subsidized, designated by the health system, *Br* ≃ National Health; **non c.** private **2** *(honoraires, prix)* set; **prêt c.** low-interest (subsidized) loan

conventionnel, -elle [kɔ̃vɑ̃sjɔnɛl] **ADJ 1** *(conformiste)* conventional, conformist; **formules conventionnelles** clichés, platitudes
2 *(arbitraire ▸ signe, valeur)* conventionally agreed; *(▸ langage)* conventional
3 *Pol* **accords conventionnels** agreements resulting from collective bargaining; **politique conventionnelle** policies relating to union–management agreements
4 *Jur* contractual
5 *(classique ▸ armement)* conventional
NM,F *(membre)* member *(of a convention)*
• **Conventionnel NM** *Hist* member of the French National Convention *(1792–1795)*

conventionnellement [kɔ̃vɑ̃sjɔnɛlmɑ̃] **ADV 1** *(sans originalité)* conventionally, *Péj* unoriginally **2** *Jur* by agreement

conventionnement [kɔ̃vɑ̃sjɔnmɑ̃] **NM** *Méd* medical care, *Br* ≃ National Health Service contract; **le c. d'une clinique** a clinic's adherence to a (public) medical care system

conventionner [3] [kɔ̃vɑ̃sjɔne] **VT** = to register with the state health system
VPR se conventionner = to register as a doctor within the state health system

conventuel, -elle [kɔ̃vɑ̃tɥɛl] *Rel* **ADJ** *(maison)* conventual; *(vie)* monastic

convenu, -e [kɔ̃vny] **PP** *voir* **convenir**
ADJ 1 *(décidé ▸ prix, somme)* agreed, stipulated; *(▸ date, moment)* agreed, appointed **2** *(sans originalité ▸ style)* conventional; **l'intrigue est très convenue** the plot is very obvious

convergence [kɔ̃vɛrʒɑ̃s] **NF 1** *(confluence ▸ de chemins, de lignes)* convergence, confluence; **point de c.** focal point **2** *(concordance)* **la c. de nos efforts** the convergence of our efforts (on a common goal); **la c. de nos conclusions** the fact that our conclusions lead to a single result; *UE* **c. économique** economic convergence **3** *Math & Opt* convergence

convergent, -e [kɔ̃vɛrʒɑ̃, -ɑ̃t] **ADJ** convergent

converger [17] [kɔ̃vɛrʒe] **VI 1** *(confluer)* to converge, to meet at a point; **tous les chemins convergent vers la clairière** all paths converge on the clearing; **nos efforts convergent vers le même but** all our efforts are focused on the same objective **2** *(aboutir au même point)* **nos conclusions convergent** we tend toward the same conclusions **3** *Math & Opt* to converge

convers, -e [kɔ̃vɛr, -ɛrs] **ADJ 1** *Rel* lay *(avant n)* **2** *Ling* converse

conversation [kɔ̃vɛrsasjɔ̃] **NF 1** *(discussion)* discussion, conversation, talk; **une c. animée** a heated discussion; **être en grande c. avec qn** to be deep in conversation with sb; **engager la c. (avec qn)** to start up a conversation (with sb); **faire la c. (à qn)** to make conversation (with sb); **suite à ma c. téléphonique avec votre secrétaire** following my phone conversation with your secretary; **interrompre sa c.** to break off in mid-conversation; **interrompre une c.** to interrupt a conversation; **détourner la c.** to change the subject; **amener la c. sur qch** to steer the conversation towards sth, to bring sth up in the conversation; **avoir de la c.** to be a good conversationalist; **il n'a aucune c.** he's a poor conversationalist **2** *Ling* **dans la c. courante** in everyday *or* ordinary speech **3** *(pourparlers)* **conversations diplomatiques** diplomatic talks *or* negotiations

conversationnel, -elle [kɔ̃vɛrsasjɔnɛl] **ADJ** interactive; **en mode c.** in interactive *or* conversational mode

converser [3] [kɔ̃vɛrse] **VI** to converse, to talk

conversion [kɔ̃vɛrsjɔ̃] **NF 1** *(de chiffres, de mesures)* conversion, converting; **c. des miles en kilomètres** converting of miles to kilometres; *Ordinat* **c. de fichier** file conversion
2 *Rel* conversion; **à cause de sa c. au judaïsme** because of his/her conversion *or* because he/she converted to Judaism
3 *(ralliement)* conversion
4 *Fin (d'argent, de devises étrangères, de titres, d'un emprunt)* conversion
5 *Naut* turning around
6 *Ski* kick turn
7 *Jur & Phys* conversion
8 *(changement d'activité ▸ d'un employé)* retraining; *(▸ d'une entreprise)* change in the line of business
9 *Biol & Méd* **c. génique** gene conversion

converti, -e [kɔ̃vɛrti] **ADJ** converted
NM,F convert

convertibilité [kɔ̃vɛrtibilite] **NF** convertibility

convertible [kɔ̃vɛrtibl] **ADJ 1** *(transformable)* convertible (**en** into); **canapé c.** sofa bed, *Br* bed-settee, *Am* convertible sofa **2** *Fin* convertible
NM 1 *(canapé)* sofa bed, *Br* bed-settee, *Am* convertible sofa **2** *Aviat* convertiplane, convertoplane

convertir [32] [kɔ̃vɛrtir] **VT 1** *(convaincre)* to convert; **c. qn à** *(religion)* to convert sb to; *(opinion, mouvement)* to win sb over *or* to convert sb to
2 *Fin & Math (mesure, grandeur, argent)* to convert; **c. des euros en dollars** to convert euros into dollars
3 *Ordinat (données)* to convert; **c. en numérique** to digitize
4 *(en logique)* to convert, to transpose
5 *(transformer)* to convert (**en** into); **ils ont converti la vieille gare en musée** they converted *or* transformed the old railway station into a museum
VPR se convertir 1 *(athée)* to become a believer; *(croyant)* to change religion **2** *(entreprise)* to change its line of business; *(employé)* to retrain **3 se c. à** *(religion, mouvement)* to be converted to, to convert to

convertissement [kɔ̃vɛrtismɑ̃] **NM** *Fin (de valeurs en espèces)* conversion (**en** into)

convertisseur, -euse [kɔ̃vɛrtisœr, -øz] **NM,F** *Rel* converter
NM 1 *Métal* converter; **c. Bessemer** Bessemer converter
2 *Élec* converter, convertor
3 *TV* converter; **c. d'images** image converter; **c. numérique de graphiques** graphics digitizer
4 *Tech* **c. catalytique** catalytic converter; **c. de couple** torque converter
5 *Ordinat* **c. analogique numérique** digitizer; **c. série-parallèle** staticizer; **c. de signal** converter
6 c. de monnaie currency converter

convexe [kɔ̃vɛks] **ADJ** convex

convexion [kɔ̃vɛksjɔ̃] = **convection**

convexité [kɔ̃vɛksite] **NF** convexity

conviction [kɔ̃viksjɔ̃] **NF** *(certitude)* conviction, belief; **j'ai la c. que…** it's my belief that…, I'm convinced that…; **avec/sans c.** with/without conviction; **sans grande c.** without much conviction; **manquer de c.** to lack conviction
• **convictions NFPL** *(credo)* fundamental beliefs; **avoir des convictions politiques** to have political convictions

convient *etc voir* **convenir**

convier [9] [kɔ̃vje] **VT** *Littéraire* **1** *(faire venir)* to invite; **c. qn à une soirée/un repas** to invite sb to a party/a meal **2** *(inciter)* **c. qn à faire qch** to invite *or* to urge sb to do sth

convint *etc voir* **convenir**

convive [kɔ̃viv] **NMF** guest *(at a meal)*; **combien y aura-t-il de convives?** how many guests will there be?

convivial, -e, -aux, -ales [kɔ̃vivjal, -o] **ADJ 1** *(ambiance, fête)* convivial **2** *Ordinat* user-friendly

convivialité [kɔ̃vivjalite] **NF 1** *(d'une société)* conviviality **2** *Ordinat* user-friendliness

convocation [kɔ̃vɔkasjɔ̃] **NF 1** *(d'une assemblée, de ministres)* calling together, convening; *(de témoins, d'un employé)* summoning **2** *(avis écrit)* notification; *Jur* summons *(singulier)*; **c. à un examen** notification of an examination; **vous recevrez bientôt votre c.** you'll be notified shortly

convoi [kɔ̃vwa] **NM 1** *Aut & Naut* convoy; **c. d'ambulances/de péniches** string of ambulances/of barges; **c. exceptionnel** *(sur panneau)* wide *or* dangerous load **2** *Rail* train; **c. de marchandises** goods *or* freight train; **c. postal** *Br* postal *or Am* mail train **3** *(cortège)* convoy; **un c. de prisonniers** a convoy of prisoners; **un c. de troupes** a convoy of troops; **c. funèbre** funeral procession
• **en convoi ADV** in convoy

convoie *etc voir* **convoyer**

convoiement [kɔ̃vwamɑ̃] **NM** *(gén)* escorting, convoying; *Aviat* = shuttling of new planes to operational zones

convoiter [3] [kɔ̃vwate] **VT 1** *(vouloir ▸ argent, héritage, poste)* to covet, to be after; **j'avais enfin le rôle tant convoité** at last, I had the role I had longed for **2** *Littéraire (par concupiscence)* to lust after

convoitise [kɔ̃vwatiz] **NF 1** *(désir ▸ d'un objet)* desire, covetousness; *(▸ d'argent)* greed, *Sout* cupidity; **agir par c.** to act out of greed; **regarder qch avec c.** to stare at sth greedily; **exciter les convoitises** to arouse envy *or* greed **2** *Littéraire (concupiscence)* **c. (de la chair)** lust

convoler [3] [kɔ̃vɔle] **VI** *Arch ou Hum* **c. en secondes noces** to re-marry; **c. en justes noces** to be wed

convoluté, -e [kɔ̃vɔlyte] ADJ convolute *(avant n)*, coiled

convoquer [3] [kɔ̃vɔke] VT *(assemblée, concile)* to convene; *(ministres, membres)* to convene, to call together; *(actionnaires)* to call to a meeting; *(témoin)* to summon to a hearing; *(employé, postulant)* to call in; *(journalistes, presse)* to invite; **c. une assemblée générale** to call a general meeting; **ils m'ont convoqué pour passer un entretien** they've called *or* invited me for an interview; **elle est convoquée chez le proviseur** she's been summoned to the *Br* head's *or Am* principal's office; **c. qn à un examen** to notify sb of an examination; **je suis convoqué à neuf heures au centre d'examens** I have to be at the examination centre at nine o'clock

convoyage [kɔ̃vwajaʒ] = **convoiement**

convoyer [13] [kɔ̃vwaje] VT *(accompagner ▸ gén)* to escort; *(▸ fonds)* to transport by armed guard; *Mil* to convoy

convoyeur, -euse [kɔ̃vwajœr, -øz] ADJ escort *(avant n)*

NM,F escort

NM **1** *(transporteur)* **c. de fonds** *(entreprise)* security firm *(transporting money)*; *(homme)* security guard **2** *Naut* convoy (ship) **3** *(tapis roulant)* conveyor belt; *Agr* grain elevator

convulser [3] [kɔ̃vylse] VT to convulse; **la peur convulsait son visage** his/her face was convulsed *or* contorted *or* distorted with fear

VPR **se convulser** *(personne)* to be convulsed; *(visage)* to become contorted *or* convulsed; **il se convulsait de douleur** he was convulsed with pain

convulsif, -ive [kɔ̃vylsif, -iv] ADJ **1** *Méd* convulsive **2** *(brusque)* **un mouvement c.** a sudden *or* uncontrolled movement

convulsion [kɔ̃vylsjɔ̃] NF **1** *Méd* convulsion; **avoir des convulsions** to have convulsions; **il fut soudain pris de convulsions** he suddenly went into convulsion *or* convulsions **2** *(agitation)* convulsion, upheaval, disturbance

convulsionner [3] [kɔ̃vylsjɔne] VT *Méd (visage)* to convulse, to distort; *(patient)* to send into convulsion *or* convulsions

convulsive [kɔ̃vylsiv] *voir* **convulsif**

convulsivement [kɔ̃vylsivmɑ̃] ADV *Méd* convulsively

coobligé, -e [kɔɔbliʒe] NM,F *Jur* joint debtor

cooccupant, -e [kɔɔkypɑ̃, -ɑ̃t] NM,F co-occupier

cookie [kuki] NM **1** *(gâteau) Br* biscuit, *Am* cookie **2** *Ordinat* cookie

cool [kul] *Fam* ADJ INV **1** *(détendu)* cool, laid-back; **ils sont c., ses parents** his/her parents are cool *or* laid-back; **c., mon vieux!** chill (out)!, take it easy! **2** *(bien)* cool; **il est c., son nouveau portable** his/her new *Br* mobile's *or Am* cell's really cool

coolie [kuli] NM coolie

coopé [kɔɔpe] NF *Fam (coopération ▸ aide aux PVD)* aid to developing countries; *Anciennement (service militaire)* = voluntary work overseas carried out as an alternative to national service

coopérant, -e [kɔɔperɑ̃, -ɑ̃t] ADJ cooperative

NM,F aid worker

NM *Anciennement (soldat)* = conscript doing voluntary work overseas as an alternative to national service

coopérateur, -trice [kɔɔperatœr, -tris] ADJ cooperative

NM,F *(collaborateur)* cooperator, collaborator; *(adhérent)* member of a cooperative

coopératif, -ive [kɔɔperatif, -iv] ADJ cooperative, helpful; **se montrer c.** to cooperate, to be cooperative

• **coopérative** NF *Écon (association)* cooperative, co-op; *(magasin)* cooperative store, co-op; **coopérative agricole** agricultural cooperative; **coopérative ouvrière** workers' cooperative; **coopérative de production** production cooperative

coopération [kɔɔperasjɔ̃] NF **1** *(collaboration)* cooperation; **il nous a offert sa c.** he offered to cooperate (with us); **en coopération avec** in collaboration with **2** *Admin & Mil (aide aux PVD)* aid to developing countries; *Anciennement (à la place du service militaire)* = voluntary work overseas carried out as an alternative to national service; **partir en c. en Afrique** *Br* ≃ to go off to do VSO in Africa, *Am* ≃ to go to Africa with the Peace Corps

coopératisme [kɔɔperatism] NM = doctrine encouraging the cooperative movement

coopérative [kɔɔperativ] *voir* **coopératif**

coopératrice [kɔɔperatris] *voir* **coopérateur**

coopérer [18] [kɔɔpere] VI to cooperate (à in)

cooptation [kɔɔptasjɔ̃] NF co-option; **élu par c.** elected by co-option

coopter [3] [kɔɔpte] VT to co-opt

coordinateur, -trice [kɔɔrdinatœr, -tris] ADJ coordinating

NM,F coordinator

coordination [kɔɔrdinasjɔ̃] NF **1** *(d'une opération, de mouvements)* coordination; **il manque de c.** he is uncoordinated **2** *(comité)* representative committee; **c. étudiante** student committee

coordinatrice [kɔɔrdinatris] *voir* **coordinateur**

coordonnateur, -trice [kɔɔrdɔnatœr, -tris] *Admin* ADJ coordinating

NM,F coordinator

coordonné, -née [kɔɔrdɔne] ADJ **1** *(harmonieux ▸ mouvements)* coordinated **2** *Ling* **propositions coordonnées** coordinate clauses **3** *(assorti)* matching; **veste et jupe coordonnées** matching *or* coordinating jacket and skirt

• **coordonnées** NFPL **1** *Géog & Math* coordinates **2** *(adresse)* (contact) details; **laissez-moi vos coordonnées** leave me your address and phone number, leave me your details; **je n'ai même pas ses coordonnées!** I don't even know where to reach him/her!

coordonner [3] [kɔɔrdɔne] VT to coordinate (à *ou* **avec** with)

copain, copine [kɔpɛ̃, kɔpin] *Fam* NM,F *(ami)* friend□, *Br* pal, *Am* buddy; **un c. d'école** a school friend, a friend from school; **être bons copains** to be good friends; **fais-en profiter les copains!** let everybody share it!; **(petit) c.** boyfriend; **(petite) copine** girlfriend; **soirée entre copines** *(à la maison)* girls' night in; *(en ville)* girls' night out

ADJ **être très copains** to be great friends *or Br* pals *or Am* buddies; *Péj* **être très c.-copain** to be very pally *or* buddy-buddy; *Fam* **être copains comme cochons** to be as thick as thieves

coparental, -e, -aux, -ales [kɔparɑ̃tal, -o] ADJ co-parental

coparentalité [kɔparɑ̃talite] NF co-parenthood

copartageant, -e [kɔpartaʒɑ̃, -ɑ̃t] NM,F *Jur* coparcener, parcener

coparticipant, -e [kɔpartisipɑ̃, -ɑ̃t] NM,F *Jur* copartner

coparticipation [kɔpartisipasjɔ̃] NF copartnership

copeau, -x [kɔpo] NM *(de bois, de métal)* shaving; **des copeaux de bois** wood shavings; *Culin* **des copeaux de chocolat** chocolate shavings

Copenhague [kɔpənag] NM Copenhagen

copiage [kɔpjaʒ] NM *Péj (plagiat)* copying; *Scol* cribbing

copie [kɔpi] NF **1** *(reproduction légitime ▸ d'un document)* copy, duplicate; *(▸ d'une lettre)* copy; **c'est la c. exacte de son père** he's/she's the (spitting) image of his/her father; **c. carbone** carbon copy, cc; *Admin* **c. certifiée conforme (à l'original)** certified copy; **pour copie conforme** certified accurate; **c. papier** paper copy

2 *(reproduction ▸ d'un tableau, d'une cassette, d'un produit)* copy, imitation, reproduction; **ce n'est pas un vrai Pollock, c'est une c.** it isn't a real Pollock, it's a copy; **ce n'est qu'une pâle c. de l'original** it's only a pale imitation of the original

3 *(feuille)* sheet; **des copies simples/doubles** = single-/double-width sheets of squared paper used for schoolwork

4 *Scol (devoir)* paper; **il m'a rendu une très bonne c.** he did a very good paper *or* piece of work for me; **rendre c. blanche** to hand in a blank paper; *Fig* to fail to come up with the solution *(for a problem)*; **le ministre va devoir revoir sa c.** the minister will need to have a rethink

5 *Cin & TV* print, copy; **c. antenne** broadcasting copy *or* print; **c. d'exploitation** release print; **c. de film** print; **c. de montage** first answer print, cutting copy, workprint; **c. positive** positive print; **c. standard** composite *or* combined print

6 *Journ* **être en mal de c.** to be short of copy

7 *Ordinat* copy; **c. archivée** archive (copy); **c. de bloc** copy block; **c. sur papier** hard copy, printout; **c. de sauvegarde** *ou* **de secours** backup (copy), security copy

copier [9] [kɔpje] VT **1** *(modèle)* to reproduce, to copy

2 *(bijou, tableau)* to fake, to copy

3 *(transcrire ▸ document, texte)* to copy (out), to make a copy of; *(punition)* to copy out; **c. un rapport au propre** to make a fair copy of a report; **vous me copierez dix fois cette phrase** write out this sentence ten times

4 *Ordinat* to copy; **c. qch sur le disque dur** to copy sth onto hard disk

5 *Scol (pour tricher)* to copy; **copier sur qn** to copy *or* to crib from sb; **arrête de copier!** stop copying *or* cribbing!

6 *(attitude, personne)* to copy, to imitate; **elle n'arrête pas de me copier** she copies everything I do, she copies me in everything

7 *Fam (locution)* **tu me la copieras!, vous me la copierez!** that's something that's going to stick with me for a while!

copier-coller [3] [kɔpjekɔle] *Ordinat* VT to copy and paste

VI to copy and paste

NM INV copy-and-paste; **faire un c. (sur qch)** to copy and paste (sth)

copieur, -euse[1] [kɔpjœr, -øz] NM,F *(plagiaire)* plagiarist; *Scol & Univ* cribber

NM *(photocopieuse)* copier

copieusement [kɔpjøzmɑ̃] ADV *(manger)* heartily; *(boire)* copiously; *(servir)* generously; **il s'est servi c.** he took a generous helping; **un repas c. arrosé** a meal washed down with copious *or* generous amounts of wine; *Hum* **il s'est fait c. insulter par sa femme** he got quite a mouthful from his wife

copieux, -euse[2] [kɔpjø, -øz] ADJ *(repas)* copious, hearty, lavish; *(ration)* lavish, big; *(pourboire)* generous

copilote [kɔpilɔt] NMF co-pilot

copinage [kɔpinaʒ] NM *Fam Péj* cronyism; **par c.** through cronyism *or* one's connections

copine [kɔpin] *voir* **copain**

copiner [3] [kɔpine] **copiner avec** VT IND *Fam* to to be *Br* pals *or Am* buddies with

copinerie [kɔpinri] NF *Fam* chumminess

copiste [kɔpist] NMF copyist, transcriber

coporteur [kɔpɔrtœr] NM *Fin* joint holder

coposséder [18] [kɔpɔsede] VT *Jur* to own jointly, to have joint ownership of

copossesseur [kɔpɔsesœr] NM *Jur* joint owner

copossession [kɔpɔsesjɔ̃] NF *Jur* joint ownership

copra(h) [kɔpra] NM copra; **huile de c.** coconut oil

copreneur, -euse [kɔprənœr, -øz] NM,F *Jur* colessee, co-tenant

coprésentateur, -trice [koprezɑ̃tatœr, -tris] NM,F co-presenter

coprésidence [koprezidɑ̃s] NF co-chairmanship, co-presidency

coprésident, -e [koprezidɑ̃, -ɑ̃t] NM,F co-chairman, co-president

coprocesseur [kɔprɔsesœr] NM *Ordinat* co-processor; **c. arithmétique** maths co-processor

coproducteur [kɔprɔdyktœr] NM co-producer

coproduction [kɔprɔdyksjɔ̃] NF coproduction; **ce film est une c. franco-allemande** this film was produced by France and Germany

coproduire [80] [kɔprɔdɥir] VT to coproduce, to produce jointly

coprophage [kɔprɔfaʒ] ADJ coprophagous

coprophagie [kɔprɔfaʒi] NF coprophagy

copropriétaire [kɔprɔprijetɛr] NMF co-owner, joint owner, coproprietor

copropriété [kɔprɔprijete] NF joint ownership, co-ownership; **acheter/posséder une maison en c.** to buy/own a house jointly

copte [kɔpt] ADJ Coptic
NM *(langue)* Coptic
• **Copte** NMF Copt

copulation [kɔpylasjɔ̃] NF copulation

copuler [3] [kɔpyle] VI to copulate

copyright [kɔpirajt] NM copyright

coq [kɔk] NM **1** *Orn (mâle ▸ de la poule) Br* cock, *Am* rooster; *(▸ des gallinacés)* cock, cockbird; **jeune c.** cockerel; **c. de bruyère** capercaillie; **c. de combat** fighting cock, gamecock; **c. faisan** cock pheasant; **être comme un c. en pâte** to be in clover; **avoir des mollets de c.** to be spindly-legged, to have legs like matchsticks; **passer** *ou* **sauter du c. à l'âne** to jump from one subject to another
2 *(figure, symbole)* **c. de clocher** weathercock, weather vane; **c. gaulois** = French national symbol (a cockerel)
3 *Culin* chicken; **c. au vin** coq au vin
4 *Fam* **le c. du village** the local Casanova
5 *Naut* (ship's) cook
ADJ *Sport (catégorie, poids)* bantam *(avant n)*

coq-à-l'âne [kɔkalan] NM INV *(dans la conversation)* sudden change of subject; **faire un c.** to go on to something completely different

coquard, coquart [kɔkar] NM *Fam* shiner, black eye□

coque [kɔk] NF **1** *(mollusque)* cockle
2 *(de noix, de noisette, d'amande)* shell; *Culin* **œuf à la c.** soft-boiled egg; *Fam* **c. de noix** *(embarcation)* cockleshell
3 *(châssis) & Naut* hull; *Aviat* hull, fuselage; *Aut* shell, body
4 chaussures à c. steel-capped shoes
5 *Tél (de téléphone portable)* cover, fascia

coquelet [kɔklɛ] NM young cockerel

coquelicot [kɔkliko] NM poppy

coqueluche [kɔklyʃ] NF **1** *Méd* whooping-cough; **avoir la c.** to have whooping-cough **2** *Fam Fig* **être la c. des adolescents** to be a teenage idol; **il est devenu la c. de ces dames** he has become a heart-throb

coquet, -ette [kɔkɛ, -ɛt] ADJ **1** *(soucieux de son apparence)* particular about one's appearance
2 *(élégant ▸ maison, mobilier)* pretty, charming; *(jardin)* trim
3 *Vieilli (qui cherche à séduire)* coquettish, flirtatious
4 *Fam* **une coquette somme** a tidy sum, a nice little sum
• **coquette** NF coquette, flirt

coquetel [kɔktɛl] NM *Can (boisson)* cocktail; *(réunion mondaine)* cocktail party

coquetier [kɔktje] NM eggcup; *Fam* **gagner le c.** to hit the jackpot; *Iron* **ça y est, j'ai gagné le c.!** that's it, I've really done it now!

coquette [kɔkɛt] *voir* **coquet**

coquettement [kɔkɛtmɑ̃] ADV *(décorer, meubler)* prettily, charmingly; *(s'habiller)* smartly, stylishly

coquetterie [kɔkɛtri] NF **1** *(goût de la toilette)* concern about one's appearance; **avec c.** *(décorer, meubler)* prettily, charmingly; *(s'habiller)* smartly, stylishly
2 *(fausse modestie)* affectation; **je vous le dis sans c. aucune** I'm saying that without any false modesty
3 *Littéraire (désir de plaire)* coquetry, flirtatiousness; **faire des coquetteries à qn** to flirt with sb
4 *Fam (locution)* **avoir une c. dans l'œil** to have a cast in one's eye *or* a slight squint

coquillage [kɔkijaʒ] NM **1** *(mollusque)* shellfish
2 *(coquille)* shell

coquillard [kɔkijar] NM *très Fam* **je m'en tamponne le c.** I don't give a damn *or* a monkey's

coquille [kɔkij] NF **1** *(de mollusque, d'œuf, de noix)* shell; **c. d'œuf** eggshell; *Fig* **rentrer dans sa c.** to withdraw *or* to retire into one's shell; *Fig* **sortir de sa c.** to come out of one's shell, to open up; **c. Saint-Jacques** *(mollusque)* scallop; *(enveloppe)* scallop shell
2 *(récipient)* shell, scallop, scallop-shaped dish
3 *Culin* **c. de beurre** butter curl
4 *(d'épée)* hand guard *or* shell
5 *Fam* **c. de noix** *(embarcation)* cockleshell
6 *Sport* box
7 *Typ (erreur ▸ en composition)* misprint; *(▸ d'une seule lettre)* literal; *(▸ en dactylographie)* typo

coquillettes [kɔkijɛt] NFPL pasta shells

coquin, -e [kɔkɛ̃, -in] ADJ **1** *(espiègle)* mischievous; **comme elle est coquine, cette petite!** what a little rascal *or* devil she is! **2** *(suggestif ▸ histoire)* risqué, naughty; *(▸ sous-vêtement)* sexy, naughty **3** *Vieilli* **c. de sort!** I'll be darned!
NM,F *(enfant)* (little) rascal *or* devil
NM *Arch (voyou)* rogue, scoundrel
• **coquine** NF *Arch* strumpet

coquinerie [kɔkinri] NF *Littéraire* **1** *(caractère malicieux)* mischievousness, roguishness **2** *(acte malicieux)* trick, prank; *(acte malfaisant)* dirty *or* mean trick; *(escroquerie)* swindle

cor [kɔr] NM **1** *Mus* horn; **c. (de chasse)** hunting horn; **c. anglais** cor anglais, English horn; **c. d'harmonie** French horn; **c. à piston** valve horn; *Fig* **réclamer qch à c. et à cri** to clamour for sth **2** *(au pied)* corn **3** *(d'un andouiller)* tine

corail, -aux [kɔraj, -o] NM **1** *Zool & (en bijouterie)* coral; *Littéraire* **lèvres de c.** coral lips **2** *Culin (d'une coquille Saint-Jacques)* coral, red part
• **corail** ADJ INV coral-red

corailleur, -euse [kɔrajœr, -øz] NM,F *(pêcheur)* coral gatherer; *(artisan)* coral worker

corallien, -enne [kɔraljɛ̃, -ɛn] ADJ *(île, récif)* coral *(avant n)*

Coran [kɔrɑ̃] NM **le C.** the Koran

coranique [kɔranik] ADJ *(texte, école)* Koranic

corbeau, -x [kɔrbo] NM **1** *Orn* crow; **c. freux** rook; **grand c.** raven
2 *Fam Péj (auteur anonyme)* = writer of poison-pen letters
3 *Vieilli Fam (prêtre)* priest□
4 *Archit* corbel, bracket

corbeille [kɔrbɛj] NF **1** *(contenant, contenu)* basket; **une c. de fruits** a fruit basket; **c. à courrier** desk tray; **c. de départ/d'arrivée** out-tray/in-tray; **c. à linge** laundry basket; **c. à ouvrage** workbasket; **c. à pain** breadbasket; **c. à papier** wastepaper basket *or* bin
2 *(massif de fleurs)* (round *or* oval) flower-bed
3 *Théât* dress circle
4 *Archit* bell
5 *Bourse (à Paris)* trading floor; **c. des obligations** bond-trading ring
6 *Ordinat (de Mac) Br* wastebasket, *Am* trash; *(dans Windows®)* recycle bin; **c. d'arrivée** *(pour courrier électronique)* inbox; **c. de départ** *(pour courrier électronique)* outbox
7 c. de mariage wedding presents; **mon père avait mis la voiture dans ma c. de mariage** the car was a wedding present from my father

corbeille-d'argent [kɔrbɛjdarʒɑ̃] *(pl* **corbeilles-d'argent**) NF *Bot* alyssum

corbillard [kɔrbijar] NM hearse

cordage [kɔrdaʒ] NM **1** *(lien)* rope; *Naut* **les cordages** the rigging **3** *(d'une raquette ▸ cordes)* strings; *(▸ action de corder)* stringing;

corde [kɔrd] NF **1** *(lien)* rope; *Fam* **tirer (un peu trop) sur la c.** *(profiter d'autrui)* to push one's luck, to go a bit too far; *Fam* **il tombe** *ou* **pleut des cordes** it's raining cats and dogs, it's bucketing down
2 *(câble tendu)* **c. à linge** clothes-line; *Fig* **être sur la c. raide** to walk a tightrope, to do a (difficult) balancing act
3 *(pour pendre)* (hangman's) rope; **il mérite la c.!** he deserves to be hanged *or* to hang!; **passer la c. au cou à qn** to send sb to the gallows; *Fig* **se mettre** *ou* **se passer la c. au cou** *(se marier)* to get hitched; *Prov* **il ne faut pas parler de c. dans la maison d'un pendu** talk not of ropes in a hanged man's house; **il ne vaut pas la c. pour le pendre** hanging's too good for him
4 *(matériau)* rope, cord; **semelle en c.** *ou* **de c.** rope sole; **échelle en c.** *ou* **de c.** rope ladder
5 *Mus* string; **instruments à cordes** stringed instruments; **toucher** *ou* **faire vibrer la c. sensible** to touch an emotional chord, to tug at the heartstrings
6 *Sport & (jeux)* rope; **c. lisse** climbing rope; **c. à nœuds** knotted climbing rope; **c. à sauter** *Br* skipping rope, *Am* jump rope; **sauter à la c.** *Br* to skip, *Am* to jump rope
7 *Boxe* **dans les cordes** on the ropes; *aussi Fig* **aller dans les cordes** to be on the ropes
8 *(d'une arbalète, d'une raquette)* string; *Fig* **avoir plus d'une c.** *ou* **plusieurs cordes à son arc** to have more than one string to one's bow
9 *Sport (intérieur d'une piste de course à pied)* inside lane; *Équitation* rails; **être à la c.** to be on the inside, to be on the rails; **tenir la c.** *(coureur)* to keep to the inside; **monter à la c.** *(coureur)* to move to the inside lane; **prendre un virage à la c.** *(voiture)* to hug a bend
10 *Anat* cord; **c. dorsale** dorsal cord, notochord; **c. du jarret** hamstring; **c. du tympan** chorda tympani; **cordes vocales** vocal cords
11 *(locutions)* **c'est dans ses cordes** it's right up his/her street, it's his/her line; **quelque chose qui soit dans vos cordes** something in your line
12 *Tex* thread; **il avait des manches qui montraient la c.** his sleeves were threadbare
13 *(mesure)* cord; *Can* **c. de bois** cord of wood *(128 cubic feet)*
14 *Math (d'un arc)* chord
• **cordes** NFPL *(instruments)* strings, stringed instruments

cordé, -e[1] [kɔrde] ADJ *(en forme de cœur)* heart-shaped, cordate

cordeau, -x [kɔrdo] NM **1** *(fil)* string, line; *aussi Fig* **tiré au c.** perfectly straight, straight as a die **2** *(mèche)* fuse; **c. Bickford** Bickford fuse; **c. détonant** detonator fuse **3** *(pour pêcher)* paternoster (line)

cordée[2] [kɔrde] NF *(alpinistes)* roped party

cordelette [kɔrdəlɛt] NF cord

cordelier, -ère [kɔrdəlje, -ɛr] NM,F **1** *Rel (religieux)* Franciscan friar, Cordelier; *(religieuse)* Franciscan nun **2** *Hist* **le Club des Cordeliers** = a left-wing club of the Revolutionary period
• **cordelière** NF *(de robe de chambre etc)* cord; *Archit* cable moulding

corder [3] [kɔrde] VT **1** *(lier ▸ valise, malle)* to rope up
2 *(tordre)* to twist (into ropes *or* a rope)
3 *(raquette)* to string
4 *(mesurer ▸ bois)* to cord

cordial, -e, -aux, -ales [kɔrdjal, -o] ADJ warm, cordial, friendly; **une haine/aversion cordiale pour…** a heartfelt hatred of/disgust for…
NM *(boisson)* tonic, pick-me-up

cordialement [kɔrdjalmɑ̃] ADV **1** *(saluer)* warmly, cordially; **ils se détestent c.** they heartily detest each other **2** *(dans la correspondance)* **c. vôtre** (best) regards; **(bien) c.** best wishes

cordialité [kɔrdjalite] NF warmth, cordiality

cordier [kɔrdje] NM **1** *Ind* ropemaker **2** *Mus (d'un violon etc)* tailpiece

cordillère [kɔrdijɛr] NF mountain range, *Spéc* cordillera; **la c. des Andes** the Andes (cordillera)

cordon [kɔrdɔ̃] NM **1** *(de rideaux)* cord; *(d'un bonnet, d'un sac)* string; **c. de sonnette** bellpull; **tenir les cordons de la bourse** to hold the purse strings
2 *(ligne ▸ de policiers)* row, cordon; *(▸ d'arbres)* row, line; **c. sanitaire** *Méd* cordon sanitaire; *Mil* cordon sanitaire, buffer zone
3 *Anat* **c. médullaire** spinal cord; **c. ombilical** umbilical cord; *Fig* **couper le c.** to cut the umbilical cord
4 *Géol* **c. littoral** offshore bar
5 *(insigne ▸ écharpe)* sash; *(▸ ruban)* ribbon; **avoir** *ou* **recevoir le grand c. de la Légion d'honneur** to be awarded the Grand Cross of the "Légion d'honneur"
6 *Archit* cordon
7 *(d'une pièce de monnaie)* milled edge

cordon-bleu [kɔrdɔ̃blø] *(pl* **cordons-bleus**) NM cordon bleu (cook), gourmet cook

cordonnerie [kɔrdɔnri] NF **1** *(boutique ▸ moderne)* heel bar, shoe repair *Br* shop *or Am* store; *(▸ artisanale)* cobbler's **2** *(activité ▸ de réparation)* shoe repairing, cobbling; *(▸ de fabrication)* shoemaking

cordonnet [kɔrdɔnɛ] NM **1** *(pour lier)* (piece of) cord **2** *(pour orner)* (piece of) braid

cordonnier, -ère [kɔrdɔnje, -ɛr] **NM,F** *(qui répare)* shoe repairer, cobbler; *(qui fabrique)* shoemaker; *Prov* **les cordonniers sont toujours les plus mal chaussés** the shoemaker's children are always the worst shod

Cordoue [kɔrdu] **NF** Cordoba

Corée [kɔre] **NF** Korea

coréen, -enne [kɔreɛ̃, -ɛn] **ADJ** Korean
NM *(langue)* Korean
• **Coréen, -enne NM,F** Korean

coreligionnaire [kɔrəliʒjɔnɛr] **NMF** coreligionist

Corfou [kɔrfu] **NM** Corfu

coriace [kɔrjas] **ADJ 1** *(viande)* tough **2** *(problème)* tough; *(personne)* tough, hard-headed; **être c. en affaires** to be hard-headed in business

coriandre [kɔrjɑ̃dr] **NF** coriander

coricide [kɔrisid] **NM** corn remover

corindon [kɔrɛ̃dɔ̃] **NM** corundum

Corinthe [kɔrɛ̃t] **NF** Corinth

corinthien, -enne [kɔrɛ̃tjɛ̃, -ɛn] **ADJ** Corinthian
• **Corinthien, -enne NM,F** Corinthian

cormoran [kɔrmɔrɑ̃] **NM** *Orn* cormorant

cornac [kɔrnak] **NM** elephant keeper, mahout

cornaline [kɔrnalin] **NF** *Minér* cornelian

cornaquer **[3]** [kɔrnake] **VT** *Fam* to show around

cornard [kɔrnar] **NM** *Fam Vieilli* cuckold

corne [kɔrn] **NF 1** *(d'un animal)* horn; **faire les cornes à qn** to mock sb *(by making a gesture with one's fingers shaped like horns)*; *Fam* **hou les cornes!** shame on you!; *Fam* **avoir** *ou* **porter des cornes** to be a cuckold; *Fam* **faire porter des cornes à qn** to cuckold sb
2 *(matériau)* horn; **lunettes à monture de c.** horn-rimmed glasses *or* spectacles
3 *(outil)* **c. à chaussures** shoehorn
4 *Mus* horn; **c. de brume** fog horn
5 *(récipient)* horn; **c. d'abondance** *(ornement)* horn of plenty, cornucopia; *Bot* horn of plenty
6 *(callosité)* **avoir de la c.** to have calluses
7 *(coin de page)* dog-ear; **faire une c. à** to turn down the corner of
8 *Géog* **la C. de l'Afrique** the Horn of Africa
9 *Culin* **c. de gazelle** = crescent-shaped cake, a North African speciality
• **à cornes ADJ 1** *(bête)* horned **2** *(chapeau)* cocked

corned-beef [kɔrnbif] **NM INV** corned beef

cornée [kɔrne] **NF** *Anat* cornea

cornéen, -enne [kɔrneɛ̃, -ɛn] **ADJ** corneal

corneille [kɔrnɛj] **NF** *Orn* crow; **c. mantelée** hooded crow; **c. noire** carrion crow

cornélien, -enne [kɔrneljɛ̃, -ɛn] **ADJ** *(héros, vers)* Cornelian; **choix** *ou* **dilemme c.** conflict of love and duty

cornemuse [kɔrnəmyz] **NF** bagpipes; **joueur de c.** bagpiper, piper

cornemuseur [kɔrnəmyzœr], **cornemuseux** [kɔrnəmyzø] **NM** bagpiper, piper

corner¹ [kɔrnɛr] **NM** *Ftbl* corner kick; **tirer un c.** to take a corner

corner² **[3]** [kɔrne] **VT 1** *(plier ▸ par négligence)* to dog-ear; *(▸ volontairement)* to turn down the corner *or* corners of **2** *(clamer ▸ nouvelle)* to blare out
USAGE ABSOLU *(hurler)* **c. aux oreilles** *ou* **dans les oreilles de qn** to deafen sb
VI 1 *Chasse* to sound a horn **2** *Arch Aut* to hoot, to sound one's horn **3** *(locution)* **les oreilles ont dû lui/te c.** his/her/your ears must have been burning

cornet [kɔrnɛ] **NM 1** *(papier)* cornet; *(contenu)* cornet, cornetful; **un c. de frites** a bag of *Br* chips *or Am* (French) fries
2 *Suisse (sac en papier)* paper bag; *(sac en plastique)* plastic bag
3 *Culin* **c. à la crème** cream horn; **c. de glace** *(gaufrette)* cone; *(gaufrette et glace)* ice cream cone, *Br* cornet
4 *(gobelet)* **c. à dés** dice cup
5 *Mus (d'un orgue)* cornet stop; **c. (à pistons)** *(instrument)* cornet
6 *Anat* **c. de nez** turbinate body
7 *(en acoustique)* **c. acoustique** ear trumpet; **mettre sa main en c.** to cup one's hand to one's ear
8 *Fam (locution)* **qu'est-ce qu'on s'est mis dans le c.!** we really stuffed ourselves *or* our faces!

cornette [kɔrnɛt] **NF 1** *(de religieuse)* cornet **2** *(salade)* endive **3** *Arch Mil (étendard)* pennant, standard
• **cornettes NFPL** *Suisse* (elbow) macaroni

cornettiste [kɔrnetist] **NMF** cornet player

corniaud [kɔrnjo] **NM 1** *(chien)* mongrel **2** *Fam (imbécile)* nitwit, twit

corniche [kɔrniʃ] **NF 1** *Géog (roche)* ledge; *(neige)* cornice **2** *(route)* corniche (road) **3** *Archit* cornice

cornichon [kɔrniʃɔ̃] **NM 1** *(légume)* gherkin, *Am* pickle; *(condiment)* (pickled) gherkin **2** *Fam (imbécile)* nitwit, twit **3** *Fam Arg scol* = student preparing for the entrance examination to Saint-Cyr

cornière [kɔrnjɛr] **NF 1** *Constr (sous les combles)* valley **2** *(pièce en équerre)* angle (iron *or* bar)

corniot [kɔrnjo] = **corniaud**

cornique [kɔrnik] *Ling* **ADJ** Cornish
NM Cornish

Cornouaille [kɔrnwaj] **NF la C.** Cornouaille *(part of Brittany)*

Cornouailles [kɔrnwaj] **NF la C.** Cornwall

cornouiller [kɔrnuje] **NM** dogwood

cornu, -e [kɔrny] **ADJ** horned
• **cornue NF 1** *Chim* retort **2** *Métal* steel converter

corollaire [kɔrɔlɛr] **NM** *(conséquence)* consequence; *Math* corollary; **le c. obligé de la hausse des prix** the inevitable consequence of the rise in prices

corolle [kɔrɔl] **NF** corolla

coron [kɔrɔ̃] **NM** *(quartier)* mining village; *(maison)* miner's cottage

coronaire [kɔrɔnɛr] *Anat* **ADJ** coronary
NF coronary artery

coronarien, -enne [kɔrɔnarjɛ̃, -ɛn] **ADJ** *Anat* coronary

coronavirus [kɔrɔnavirys] **NM** *Biol* coronavirus

corporatif, -ive [kɔrpɔratif, -iv] **ADJ** *(institution, système)* corporative; *(image, esprit)* corporate *(avant n)*

corporation [kɔrpɔrasjɔ̃] **NF 1** *(groupe professionnel)* corporate body; **dans notre c.** in our profession; **c. de droit public** public body **2** *Hist* (trade) guild

corporatisme [kɔrpɔratism] **NM 1** *Pol* corporatism **2** *Péj (esprit de caste)* professional protectionism

corporatiste [kɔrpɔratist] **ADJ** corporatist
NMF corporatist

corporative [kɔrpɔrativ] *voir* **corporatif**

corporel, -elle [kɔrpɔrɛl] **ADJ** *(fonction)* bodily; *(châtiment)* corporal; *(hygiène)* personal; **soins corporels** care of *or* caring for one's body; *Jur* **biens corporels** tangible assets

CORPS [kɔr] **NM 1** *Physiol* body; **tremblant de tout son c.** trembling all over; *Fig* **il faudra me passer sur le c.!** over my dead body!; *Fig* **elle te passerait sur le c. pour obtenir le poste** she'd trample you underfoot to get the job; **faire c. avec** to be at *or* as one with
2 *(cadavre)* body; **porter un c. en terre** to lay a body to rest
3 *(élément, substance)* body; **c. céleste** celestial *or* heavenly body; **c. composé** compound body; **c. conducteur** conductor; **c. étranger** foreign body; **c. gras** fatty substance; **c. noir** black body; **c. simple** simple body
4 *(groupe, communauté)* **grand c. de l'État** = senior civil servants recruited through the "École nationale d'administration"; **le c. de ballet** the corps de ballet; **c. constitué** constituent body; **le c. diplomatique** the diplomatic corps; **le c. électoral** the electorate, the body of voters; **le c. enseignant** the teaching profession; **c. d'état** building trade; **le c. exécutif** the executive; **c. législatif** legislative body; **c. de la magistrature** magistrature; **le c. médical** the medical profession; **c. de métier** building trade; **c. politique** body politic; **le c. professoral** the teaching profession *(excluding primary school teachers)*; **le c. professoral de l'université** the teaching staff of the university
5 *Mil* **c. d'armée** army corps; **c. de cavalerie** cavalry brigade; **c. expéditionnaire** task force; **c. franc** commando; **c. de garde** *(soldats)* guards; *(local)* guardroom; **chansons de c. de garde** ≃ rugby songs; **plaisanteries de c. de garde** barrack-room *or Am* locker-room jokes; **c. de troupes** unit of troops
6 *(partie principale ▸ d'un document)* body; *(▸ d'une machine)* main part; *(▸ d'un cylindre)* barrel; *(▸ d'une robe)* body, bodice; *(majorité)* bulk, greater part; **c. de bâtiment** main (part of a) building; **c. de logis** main (part of a) building
7 *(ensemble ▸ de lois, de textes)* body, corpus; *(▸ de preuves)* body; *Jur* **le c. du délit** corpus delicti
8 *(consistance ▸ d'un tissu, d'un arôme)* body; **un vin qui a du c.** a full-bodied wine; **donner c. à une idée/un plan** to give substance to an idea/a scheme; **prendre c.** *(sauce)* to thicken; *(projet)* to take shape
9 *Typ & Ordinat (de police de caractères)* point size, type size
10 *Anat* **c. jaune** yellow body; **c. caverneux** erectile tissue *(of the penis)*; **c. vitré** vitreous body
11 *Rel* **le c. mystique du Christ** the Body of Christ
• **à corps perdu ADV** with all one's might; **se jeter** *ou* **se lancer à c. perdu dans une aventure/entreprise** to throw oneself headlong into an affair/a task; **il se jeta** *ou* **lança à c. perdu dans son travail** he immersed himself in his work
• **à mon/son/etc corps défendant ADV** reluctantly
• **corps et âme ADV** body and soul; **il s'est donné à elle c. et âme** he gave himself to her body and soul; **être dévoué à qn c. et âme** to be devoted to sb body and soul
• **corps et biens ADV** *Naut* **perdu c. et biens** lost with all hands

corps à corps [kɔrakɔr] **NM INV** hand-to-hand combat *or* fight; *Fig* hard struggle
ADV *(lutter)* hand to hand

corpulence [kɔrpylɑ̃s] **NF 1** *(volume corporel)* build; **de forte c.** stoutly built, of stout build; **de faible c.** slightly built **2** *(embonpoint)* stoutness, corpulence; **avoir de la c.** to be stout *or* corpulent

corpulent, -e [kɔrpylɑ̃, -ɑ̃t] **ADJ** stout, corpulent, portly

corpus [kɔrpys] **NM** corpus

corpusculaire [kɔrpyskylɛr] **ADJ** *Anat & Phys* corpuscular

corpuscule [kɔrpyskyl] **NM** *Anat & Phys* corpuscle

corral, -als [kɔral] **NM** corral, enclosure

correct, -e [kɔrɛkt] **ADJ 1** *(sans fautes ▸ calcul, description)* correct, accurate; *(▸ déroulement)* correct, proper
2 *(tenue)* proper, correct, decent
3 *(courtois)* courteous, polite; **tu n'as pas été très c. en partant sans prévenir** it was rather ill-mannered *or* impolite of you to leave without warning; **elle a été correcte avec moi** she behaved correctly towards me
4 *(honnête ▸ somme, offre)* acceptable, fair; **200 euros, c'est c.** 200 euros, that's fair enough *or* acceptable; **il est c. en affaires** he's an honest businessman
5 *(peu remarquable ▸ repas, soirée)* decent, OK; **le concert était c., sans plus** the concert was all right but nothing special

correctement [kɔrɛktəmɑ̃] **ADV 1** *(sans fautes)* correctly, accurately
2 *(selon la décence, la courtoisie)* properly, correctly
3 *(comme il faut)* properly; **fais-le c.** do it properly
4 *(assez bien)* reasonably well; **on a mangé c.** we had a reasonable meal; **elle gagne c. sa vie** she makes a decent *or* reasonable living

correcteur, -trice [kɔrɛktœr, -tris] **ADJ** corrective
NM,F 1 *Scol & Univ* examiner **2** *Typ* proofreader; *Journ* copy reader
NM 1 *(dispositif)* corrector; *Ordinat* **c. grammatical** grammar checker; *Ordinat* **c. orthographique**

ou **d'orthographe** spellchecker **2** *(liquide)* **c. liquide** correction fluid

correctif, -ive [kɔʀɛktif, -iv] **ADJ** corrective

NM qualifying statement, corrective; **je voudrais apporter un c. à ce qu'a dit mon collègue** I'd like to qualify what my colleague said

correction [kɔʀɛksjɔ̃] **NF 1** *(rectificatif)* correction; *(action de rectifier)* correction, correcting; **apporter une c. à une déclaration** to qualify a statement

2 *Scol Br* marking, *Am* grading

3 *Typ* **c. d'auteur** author's corrections; **c. d'épreuves** proofreading

4 *(punition)* beating, thrashing; *(fessée)* spanking; **tu vas recevoir une bonne c.!** you're going to get a good beating *or* thrashing!

5 *(conformité)* accuracy; **la c. d'une traduction** the accuracy of a translation

6 *(comportement)* correctness, propriety; **apprenez-leur la c.** teach them manners *or* how to behave (properly); **c'est la plus élémentaire des corrections** it's basic good manners

7 *Aviat & Naut* **c. de compas** compass adjustment

correctionnel, -elle [kɔʀɛksjɔnɛl] *Jur* **ADJ peine correctionnelle** = penalty of more than five days' (but less than five years') imprisonment; **tribunal c.** *Br* ≃ magistrate's court, *Am* ≃ criminal court

• **correctionnelle NF la correctionnelle** *Br* ≃ magistrate's court, *Am* criminal court; **passer en correctionnelle** to go before a judge *or Br* magistrate

corrective [kɔʀɛktiv] *voir* **correctif**

correctrice [kɔʀɛktʀis] *voir* **correcteur**

corrélatif, -ive [kɔʀelatif, -iv] *Ling* **ADJ** correlative

NM correlative

corrélation [kɔʀelasjɔ̃] **NF** *(rapport)* correlation; **mettre en c.** to correlate; **être en c. étroite** to be closely connected *or* related

corrélative [kɔʀelativ] *voir* **corrétatif**

corrélativement [kɔʀelativmɑ̃] **ADV** correlatively

correspondance [kɔʀɛspɔ̃dɑ̃s] **NF 1** *(lettres)* letters, *Sout* correspondence; *(échange de lettres)* correspondence; **c. commerciale** business correspondence; **être en c. avec** *(par lettre)* to correspond with; **cours par c.** correspondence courses; **elle étudie l'anglais par c.** she's learning English through a correspondence course

2 *Transp* connection; *(vol)* connecting flight; **j'attends la c.** I'm waiting for my connection; **la c. est au bout du quai** change trains at the end of the platform; **la c. est assurée entre les aérogares** a shuttle service is provided between the air terminals

3 *(rapport)* correspondence

4 *Math* correspondence

correspondant, -e [kɔʀɛspɔ̃dɑ̃, -ɑ̃t] **ADJ** corresponding, relevant; **une commande et la facture correspondante** an order and the corresponding invoice *or* the invoice that goes with it; **il n'y a pas de terme grec c.** there's no equivalent *or* corresponding term in Greek

NM,F 1 *Tél* = person one is speaking to; **votre c. est en ligne** you're through; **nous recherchons votre c.** we're trying to connect you

2 *(par lettre)* correspondent; **le c. de mon fils** my son's pen-friend; **tous mes correspondants me disent que...** all the people who write to me tell me that...

3 *Journ* **c. (de presse)** (press) correspondent; **notre c. à Moscou** our Moscow correspondent; **c. à l'étranger** foreign correspondent; **c. financier** business correspondent; **c. de guerre** war correspondent; **c. permanent** permanent *or* resident correspondent

4 *Scol* guardian *(of a boarder)*

correspondre [75] [kɔʀɛspɔ̃dʀ] **VI 1 c. avec qn** *(par lettre)* to write to sb, *Sout* to correspond with sb; *(par téléphone)* to stay in touch with sb; **ils ont cessé de c.** they have stopped *or* are no longer writing (to each other) **2** *(communiquer ▸ pièces)* to communicate, to connect

USAGE ABSOLU *(être conforme)* **j'ai les vis, mais pas les écrous qui correspondent** I have the screws but I don't have the nuts that go with them *or* the corresponding nuts

• **correspondre à VT IND 1** *(équivaloir à)* to be equivalent to; **cela correspond à une centaine d'euros** it's roughly equivalent to a hundred euros; **mon rôle correspond à celui d'un de vos "tutors"** my function is equivalent *or* may be compared to that of what you call a tutor **2** *(être conforme à ▸ désir)* to correspond to; *(▸ vérité)* to correspond to, to tally with; *(▸ besoin)* to meet; **cela ne correspond pas à votre promesse** that wasn't what you promised **3** *(être lié à)* to correspond to

VPR se correspondre *(être en relation ▸ idées, mots)* to correspond

corrida [kɔʀida] **NF 1** *(de taureaux)* bullfight **2** *Fam* **cette c. pour la faire s'habiller!** what a performance trying to get her dressed!; **quelle c. hier soir, pour rentrer chez moi!** what a hassle *or Br* carry-on I had getting home last night!

corridor [kɔʀidɔʀ] **NM 1** *(d'un bâtiment)* corridor, passage **2** *(territoire)* corridor **3 c. humanitaire** *(voie de communication)* humanitarian corridor

corrigé [kɔʀiʒe] **NM** correct version; **faire un c. de qch** to give the correct version of sth; **un c. du problème de physique** a model answer to the physics problem

corriger [17] [kɔʀiʒe] **VT 1** *Scol (noter) Br* to mark, *Am* to grade; *(vérifier la justesse de)* to correct; **on va c. l'exercice ensemble** we'll correct the exercise together

2 *(vérifier ▸ texte)* to correct, to amend; *(▸ faute)* to correct; *Typ* to proofread; *Journ (article)* to sub-edit, to sub

3 *(punir)* to give a beating *or* a thrashing to; *(donner une fessée à)* to spank; **se faire c.** to get a beating *or* a thrashing

4 *(modifier ▸ vice)* to cure; *(▸ mauvaise habitude)* to break; *(▸ posture, myopie)* to correct; *(▸ situation)* to improve; **c. qch à la hausse/à la baisse** *(chiffre)* to round sth up/down; **en données corrigées des variations saisonnières** seasonally-adjusted

5 *(débarrasser)* **c. qn de** *(vice, mauvaise posture)* to cure sb of; *(mauvaise habitude)* to rid sb of

6 *(adoucir ▸ parole dure)* to soften; **l'ajout de miel corrige l'acidité du fruit** adding honey softens the acid taste of the fruit

7 c. le tir to adjust the firing; *Fig* to change one's approach

VPR se corriger 1 *(orateur, présentateur)* to correct oneself

2 *(devenir ▸ plus sage)* to improve (one's behaviour); *(▸ moins immoral)* to mend one's ways

3 *(se guérir)* **se c. de** *(avarice)* to cure oneself of; *(mauvaise habitude)* to rid oneself of

4 *(être rectifié)* to be put right; **la myopie se corrige avec une bonne paire de lunettes** short-sightedness can be corrected with a good pair of glasses

corrigible [kɔʀiʒibl] **ADJ** rectifiable

corroboration [kɔʀɔbɔʀasjɔ̃] **NF** corroboration

corroborer [3] [kɔʀɔbɔʀe] **VT** to corroborate, to confirm

corrodant, -e [kɔʀɔdɑ̃, -ɑ̃t] **ADJ** corrosive

corroder [3] [kɔʀɔde] **VT** *(métal)* to corrode, to eat into

VPR se corroder to corrode

corrompre [78] [kɔʀɔ̃pʀ] **VT 1** *(pervertir ▸ innocent, enfant)* to corrupt

2 *(soudoyer ▸ fonctionnaire)* to bribe

3 *(vicier ▸ denrée, air)* to taint

4 *Littéraire (faire dévier ▸ langue, sens)* to distort, to debase

corrompu, -e [kɔʀɔ̃py] **ADJ** corrupt; **des juges corrompus** corrupt judges

corrosif, -ive [kɔʀozif, -iv] **ADJ 1** *(satire, auteur)* corrosive, biting, caustic **2** *(acide)* corrosive

NM corrosive

corrosion [kɔʀozjɔ̃] **NF** *Chim, Géol & Métal* corrosion

corrosive [kɔʀosiv] *voir* **corrosif**

corroyage [kɔʀwajaʒ] **NM** *(du cuir)* currying; *(du métal)* welding; *(du bois)* rough-planing, trimming

corroyer [13] [kɔʀwaje] **VT 1** *(cuir)* to curry **2** *(métal)* to weld **3** *(bois)* to rough-plane, to trim

corroyeur [kɔʀwajœʀ] **NM** currier

corrupteur, -trice [kɔʀyptœʀ, -tʀis] **ADJ** corrupting

NM,F 1 *(qui soudoie)* briber **2** *Littéraire (qui débauche)* corrupter

corruptible [kɔʀyptibl] **ADJ** corruptible

corruption [kɔʀypsjɔ̃] **NF 1** *(vénalité)* corruption; *(fait de soudoyer)* corruption, bribing; *Jur* **c. de fonctionnaire** bribery and corruption *(of a civil servant)*

2 *(avilissement ▸ de la jeunesse, d'un innocent)* corruption

4 *Littéraire (déviation ▸ d'une langue, de termes)* distortion, debasement

corruptrice [kɔʀyptʀis] *voir* **corrupteur**

corsage [kɔʀsaʒ] **NM** *(blouse)* blouse; *(d'une robe)* bodice

corsaire [kɔʀsɛʀ] **NM 1** *(marin)* corsair **2** *(pantalon)* **c.** pedal pushers

Corse [kɔʀs] **NF la C.** Corsica

LA CORSE

Since the 1970s, the Corsican independence movement has become more radical and the FLNC (the Corsican Liberation Movement) is still engaged in sometimes violent struggle against the French government. In 1982, as part of the law on decentralization, Corsica was attributed a "statut spécial" (special statute) allowing for the election of its own assembly, and became a "collectivité locale" in 1991. However, in 1998 tension between the French authorities and the pro-independence movement reached new heights following the assassination of the prefect of Corsica. In 2003, Corsicans rejected offers of greater autonomy in a referendum, so the problem of the island's status is no nearer to a resolution.

corse [kɔʀs] **ADJ** Corsican

NM *(langue)* Corsican

• **Corse NMF** Corsican

corsé, -e [kɔʀse] **ADJ 1** *(café)* full-flavoured; *(vin)* full-bodied; *(mets, sauce)* spicy; *Fig* **l'addition était plutôt corsée!** the bill was a bit steep! **2** *(histoire, plaisanterie)* racy, spicy **3** *(problème, examen)* tough

corselet [kɔʀsəlɛ] **NM 1** *(d'une armure)* corselet, corslet **2** *Zool & (vêtement)* corselet

corser [3] [kɔʀse] **VT 1** *(compliquer ▸ problème)* to make harder to solve; *(▸ exercice)* to complicate **2** *(rendre ▸ plus intéressant)* to liven up; *(▸ plus osé)* to make racier **3** *Culin* to make spicier; *(boisson)* to spike; *(vin)* to strengthen

VPR se corser *(se compliquer)* to get complicated; **c'est là que l'histoire se corse** at this point the story gets really complicated; **l'affaire se corse, ça se corse** the plot thickens

corset [kɔʀsɛ] **NM 1** *(sous-vêtement)* corset **2** *Méd* **c. orthopédique** (orthopedic) corset

corseter [28] [kɔʀsəte] **VT** to fit with a corset; *Fig* to constrain, to constrict

corsetier, -ère [kɔʀsətje, -ɛʀ] **NM,F** corset maker

corso [kɔʀso] **NM c. fleuri** procession of flowered floats

cortège [kɔʀtɛʒ] **NM 1** *(d'un roi)* retinue; *(accompagnateurs)* cortege **2** *(série)* series, succession; **un c. d'échecs** a series of failures; **la guerre et son c. de malheurs** the war and its attendant tragedies **3** *(défilé)* procession; **c. (de voitures)** motorcade; **un c. de manifestants** a march (of protesters); **le c. allait de la Bastille à la République** the demonstration stretched from the Bastille to the Place de la République; **c. funèbre** funeral cortege *or* procession; **c. nuptial** bridal procession

cortex [kɔʀtɛks] **NM** cortex; **c. cérébral** cerebral cortex

cortical, -e, -aux, -ales [kɔʀtikal, -o] **ADJ** cortical

corticoïde [kɔʀtikɔid] **NM** corticoid

corticosurrénal, -e, -aux, -ales [kɔʀtikɔsyʀenal, -o] *Anat* **ADJ** adrenocortical

• **corticosurrénale NF** adrenal cortex

corticothérapie [kɔrtikɔterapi] NF corticotherapy

cortisol [kɔrtisɔl] NM *Biol & Chim* hydrocortisone, cortisol

cortisone [kɔrtizɔn] NF *Biol & Chim* cortisone

corvée [kɔrve] NF **1** *(activité pénible)* chore; **les corvées ménagères** the household chores; **c'est une vraie c. d'aller les voir** going to see them is a real chore

2 *(service)* duty; *Mil* fatigue; **être de c.** *(soldat)* to be on fatigue duty; *très Fam* **être de c. de chiottes** to be on latrine duty; *Fam* **on est de c. de vaisselle** we're on dishwashing duty; **c'est toujours moi qui suis de c.** I have to do everything around here

3 *Suisse (travaux d'intérêt public)* voluntary community work

4 *Hist* corvée

corvette [kɔrvɛt] NF corvette

coryphée [kɔrife] NM **1** *Antiq* coryphaeus **2** *(en danse)* coryphee

coryza [kɔriza] NM head cold, *Spéc* coryza

cosaque [kɔzak] NM Cossack

coscénariste [kosenarist] NMF *Cin* co-scriptwriter

cosécante [kɔsekɑ̃t] NF *Math* cosecant

cosignataire [kɔsiɲatɛr] NMF cosignatory

cosinus [kɔsinys] NM *Math* cosine

cosmétique [kɔsmetik] ADJ cosmetic

NM cosmetic

cosmétologue [kɔsmetɔlɔg] NMF cosmetics expert

cosmique [kɔsmik] ADJ *Astron* cosmic

cosmogonie [kɔsmɔgɔni] NF cosmogony

cosmographie [kɔsmɔgrafi] NF cosmography

cosmologie [kɔsmɔlɔʒi] NF cosmology

cosmonaute [kɔsmɔnot] NMF cosmonaut

cosmopolite [kɔsmɔpɔlit] ADJ cosmopolitan

cosmopolitisme [kɔsmɔpɔlitism] NM cosmopolitanism

cosmos [kɔsmos] NM *(univers)* cosmos; *(espace)* space, outer space

cossard, -e [kɔsar, -ard] *très Fam* ADJ lazy□

NM,F lazybones

cosse [kɔs] NF **1** *Bot* pod, husk; *(de pois)* shell

2 *Élec* cable terminal

3 *Naut* thimble, eyelet

4 *très Fam (locution)* **avoir la c.** to feel lazy

cossu, -e [kɔsy] ADJ *(famille)* affluent, well-off, wealthy; *(quartier)* affluent, moneyed; *(maison, intérieur)* luxurious

costal, -e, -aux, -ales [kɔstal, -o] ADJ rib *(avant n)*, *Spéc* costal

costard [kɔstar] NM *Fam* suit□

costard-cravate [kɔstarkravat] *(pl* **costards-cravates***)* NM *Fam (costume)* suit□; *(personne)* man in a suit□, suit

Costa Rica [kɔstarika] NM **le C.** Costa Rica

costaud, -e [kɔsto, -od] *Fam* ADJ **1** *(personne ▸ corpulent)* hefty, beefy; *(▸ fort)* strong□

2 *(meuble, arbre, tissu)* strong, tough, resilient; **c'est du c.** it's solid stuff

3 *(problème)* tough; **c'est c., comme bouquin!** it's pretty heavy stuff, that book!

4 *(alcool)* strong, robust; *(café)* strong

NM,F big guy, *f* girl

costume [kɔstym] NM **1** *(complet)* suit; **c. trois-pièces** three-piece suit **2** *(tenue spécifique)* costume; **en c. de cérémonie** in ceremonial costume *or* dress; **c. régional/national** regional/national dress; *Fam* **en c. d'Adam/d'Ève** in his/her birthday suit; *Vieilli & Can & Suisse* **c. de bain** *(de femme)* swimsuit, *Br* swimming costume; *(d'homme) Br* swimming trunks, *Am* swimming shorts **3** *Hist & Théât* costume

costumé, -e [kɔstyme] ADJ *(bal, soirée)* fancy dress; **des enfants costumés** children in fancy dress

costumer [3] [kɔstyme] VT **c. qn en Pierrot** to dress sb up as a Pierrot

VPR **se costumer** to wear fancy dress; **se c. en diable** to dress up as a devil

costumier, -ère [kɔstymje, -ɛr] NM,F **1** *(vendeur, loueur)* costumier, costumer **2** *Théât* wardrobe master, *f* mistress; *Cin* costume supervisor

cosy [kozi] ADJ INV cosy

NM *Vieilli* = bed with built-in shelves running along the headboard and down one side

cotangente [kɔtɑ̃ʒɑ̃t] NF *Math* cotangent

cotation [kɔtasjɔ̃] NF *Bourse* quotation, listing; **c. en continu** continuous trading; **c. à la criée** open-outcry trading

cote [kɔt] NF **1** *Bourse (valeur)* quotation; *(liste)* share (price) index; **inscrit à la c.** *(valeurs)* listed; **retirer de la c.** *(société, action)* to delist; **hors c.** *(actions)* unlisted; *(marché) Br* unofficial, *Am* over-the-counter; **c. de clôture** closing price; **c. officielle** official list; **c. des prix** official list, official share list

2 *Com* quoted value

3 *Courses de chevaux* odds

4 *(estime)* **c. d'amour** *ou* **de popularité** *(d'un homme politique)* standing with the electorate, (popular) rating, popularity; *(d'un film, d'une idée)* (popular) rating; *Fam* **avoir la c. (avec)** to be popular (with)

5 *Archit, Constr & (en travaux publics)* measurement

6 *Géog* height; **c. moins/plus 500** 500 below/above sea level; **la c. 304** hill 304; **c. d'alerte** flood *or* danger level; *Fig* crisis *or* flash point; **la c. d'alerte est atteinte** we're at flash point

7 *(taille)* (indication of) dimensions

8 *(dans une bibliothèque ▸ sur un livre)* shelf mark, *Am* call number; *(▸ sur un périodique)* serial mark

9 *Admin* assessment; **c. mobilière** property assessment *or* rate; *Fig* **c. mal taillée** awkward compromise

10 *Belg (note scolaire) Br* mark, *Am* grade

côte [kot] NF **1** *(hauteur)* slope, incline; *(à monter, à descendre)* hill; **monter la c.** to go uphill; **descendre la c.** to go downhill; **en haut de la c.** on the top of the hill

2 *(rivage)* coast; *(dans son ensemble)* coastline; **ils vivent sur la c.** they live on the coast; **on a fait toute la c.** we went all around the coast; **la C.** the (French) Riviera; **la C. d'Argent** = the Atlantic coast between the Gironde and Bidassoa estuaries; **la C. d'Azur** the French Riviera; **aller sur la C. d'Azur** to go to the south of France *or* the French Riviera; **la C. d'Émeraude** = part of the northern French coast, near Saint-Malo

3 *Anat* rib; **vraie/fausse c.** true/false rib; **c. flottante** floating rib; **on lui voit les côtes** he's/she's nothing but skin and bone; *Fam* **se tenir les côtes (de rire)** to be in stitches; *Fam* **caresser** *ou* **chatouiller les côtes à qn** to give sb a good hiding; *Fam* **avoir les côtes en long** to be bone idle

4 *(de porc, d'agneau, de veau)* chop; *(de bœuf)* rib; **côtes découvertes** middle neck; **c. première** *(de veau)* shoulder chop; *(d'agneau) Br* lamb chop, *Am* loin chop

5 *Archit, Bot & Tex* rib; **point de côtes** ribbing stitch; **un pull à côtes** a ribbed sweater

6 *Naut* **aller à la c.** to hug the coast

• **côte-à-côte** ADV *(marcher, s'asseoir)* side by side; *(travailler, lutter)* side by side, shoulder to shoulder

CÔTÉ [kote] NM **1** *(d'un tissu, d'une médaille)* side; **une feuille de papier écrite des deux côtés** a sheet of paper written on on both sides

2 *(d'un lieu)* side; **ton c. du lit** your side of the bed; **le c. sud de la ville** the south side *or* part of town; **il y a un arbre de chaque c.** there's a tree (on) each side; **la tour penche d'un c.** the tower leans to one side *or* leans sideways; *Théât* **c. cour** stage left, *Br* prompt side; *Théât* **c. jardin** stage right, *Br* opposite prompt side; **appartement c. jardin** *Br* flat *or Am* apartment overlooking the garden; *Rugby* **c. ouvert** open side; *Naut* **c. sous le vent** leeward side; *Naut* **c. du vent** windward side; *Fig* **voir de quel c. vient le vent** to see which way the wind blows

3 *(direction)* **de quel c. est-ce qu'il est allé?** which direction did he go in?; **allons de ce c.-ci** let's go this way

4 *(du corps)* side; **il a le c. gauche entièrement paralysé** his left side is completely paralysed; **dormir sur le c.** to sleep on one's side; **aux côtés de qn** at *or* by sb's side

5 *(parti)* side; **il s'est mis de mon c.** he sided with me; **se ranger du c. du plus fort** to side with the strongest; **je suis de ton c.** I'm on your side

6 *(aspect)* side; **c. repos, ça aurait pu être mieux** on the relaxation side *or* front, it could have been better; **de ce c. il n'y a rien à craindre** there's nothing to worry about on that score; *Fam* **c. travail** on the work front, workwise

7 *(facette ▸ d'une personnalité)* side, facet; *(▸ d'une situation)* side, aspect; **elle a un c. naïf** there's a naive side to her; **il a un c. méchant** there's a mean streak in him, there's a nasty side to him; **c'est son c. paternel qui ressort** it's the paternal streak in him *or* his paternal side coming out; **chaque emploi a ses bons et ses mauvais côtés** every job has its good and bad sides *or* points; **prendre qch du bon/mauvais c.** to take sth in good/bad part; **voir le bon c. des choses** to look on the bright side; **d'un c.** in a way, in some respects; **d'un c...., d'un autre c....** on the one hand..., on the other hand...

8 *(dans la famille)* side; **sa tante du c. maternel** his/her aunt on his/her mother's side

• **à côté** ADV **1** *(tout près)* next door; *(pas très loin)* nearby; **les voisins d'à c.** the next-door neighbours; **si vous voulez bien passer à c.** if you'd like to go that way **2** *(mal)* **passer** *ou* **tomber à c.** to miss; **elle a répondu à c.** *(exprès)* she avoided the question; *(involontairement)* her answer was not to the point

• **à côté de** PRÉP **1** *(pas loin)* next to; **le salon est à c. de la cuisine** the living room is next to the kitchen; **à c. de la cible** off target; **passer à c. de** *(chemin, difficulté, porte)* to miss; *(occasion)* to miss out on; **il est passé à c. du sujet** he missed the point; **à c. de ça** on the other hand; *Fam* **être à c. de la plaque** to have (got hold of) the wrong end of the stick **2** *(par rapport à)* by *or* in comparison with; **il fait plutôt avare à c. de son frère** he seems rather mean compared to his brother

• **de côté** ADJ *(regard)* sidelong ADV **1** *(regarder)* sideways; *(sauter, tomber)* aside, to one side; **la casquette posée de c.** the cap worn to *or* on one side **2** *(en réserve)* aside, to one side; **mettre qch de c.** to put sth aside *or* by; **j'ai 5000 euros de c.** I've got 5,000 euros put by; **laisser qch de c.** to put sth to one side; **laisser qn de c.** to leave sb out

• **de mon côté, de son côté** *etc* ADV **1** *(séparément)* **ils s'en allèrent chacun de son c.** they went their separate ways; **vivre chacun de son c.** to live separately **2** *(en ce qui concerne)* for my/his/*etc* part

• **de tous côtés** ADV **1** *(partout ▸ courir)* everywhere, all over the place; *(▸ chercher)* everywhere, high and low; *(▸ être cerné)* on all sides **2** *(de partout)* from all sides *or* directions

• **du côté de** PRÉP **1** *(dans l'espace)* **elle est partie du c. du village** she went towards the village; **du c. de chez toi** around where you live; **il habitait du c. de la rivière** he lived near the river; **le vent vient du c. de la mer** the wind's blowing from the sea **2** *(parmi)* **cherchons du c. des auteurs classiques** let's look among classical authors

coteau, -x [kɔto] NM **1** *(versant)* hillside, slope **2** *(colline)* hill

• **coteaux** NMPL vineyards *(on a hillside)*

Côte-d'Ivoire [kotdivwar] NF **la C.** Côte-d'Ivoire, the Ivory Coast

côtelé, -e [kotle] ADJ ribbed

côtelette [kotlɛt] NF **1** *(de viande)* chop, cutlet; **c. d'agneau/de porc** lamb/pork chop **2** *Fam (d'une personne)* rib□; **en plein dans les côtelettes** slap bang in the ribcage

coter [3] [kɔte] VT **1** *Bourse* to list (on the share index); **coté en Bourse** ≃ listed on the Stock Exchange; **être coté à 25 euros** to be trading at 25 euros

2 *Com* to price, to give a list price for; **ma voiture n'est plus cotée à l'argus** my car's not listed in the car buyer's guide any more

3 *(évaluer ▸ œuvre d'art)* to rate

4 *(dans une bibliothèque ▸ livre)* to assign a class *or* shelf mark to; *(▸ périodique)* to assign a serial mark to

5 *Géog* to write in the heights on

6 *Archit, Constr & (en travaux publics ▸ dessin)* to mark the dimensions on; *(▸ carte)* to put references on; **un croquis coté** a dimensioned sketch
VI les actions Rivetti cotaient autour de 22 euros Rivetti shares were listed at around 22 euros

coterie [kɔtri] **NF** *Péj* set, clique

côtier, -ère [kotje, -ɛr] **ADJ** *(région, navigation)* coastal; *(pêche)* inshore; *(chemin)* coast *(avant n)*; **un fleuve c.** a coastal river

cotillon [kɔtijɔ̃] **NM 1** *Arch ou Hum (jupon)* petticoat **2** *(farandole)* cotillion, cotillon
• **cotillons NMPL** party novelties

cotisant, -e [kɔtizɑ̃, -ɑ̃t] **ADJ** contributing
NM,F *(à une association)* subscriber; *(à une assurance)* contributor

cotisation [kɔtizasjɔ̃] **NF** *(à une association)* subscription, dues; *(pour la protection sociale)* contribution; **c. chômage** unemployment contribution; **cotisations maladie** health insurance contributions; **c. patronale** employer's contribution; **c. à la Sécurité sociale** ≃ National Insurance contribution; **cotisations sociales** ≃ National Insurance and National Health contributions; **c. syndicale** union dues; **c. vieillesse** pension contribution

cotiser [3] [kɔtize] **VI** *(à une association)* to subscribe; *(à la Sécurité sociale)* to pay one's contributions; **c. à une caisse de retraite** to contribute to a pension fund
VPR se cotiser *(pour acheter quelque chose)* to club together

côtoie *etc voir* **côtoyer**

côtoiement [kotwamɑ̃] **NM** contact (**de** with)

coton [kɔtɔ̃] **NM 1** *Bot (fibre, culture)* cotton; *(plante)* cotton plant
2 *Tex (tissu)* cotton; *(fil)* (cotton) thread, piece of cotton; **robe de** *ou* **en c.** cotton dress; **c. à broder** embroidery thread; **c. à repriser** darning thread *or* cotton
3 *(ouate)* **c. (hydrophile)** *Br* cotton wool, *Am* (absorbent) cotton; *Fam* **avoir du c. dans les oreilles** to be cloth-eared
4 *(tampon de ouate) Br* cotton wool pad, *Am* cotton pad
ADJ *Fam* tough, tricky; **c'est (plutôt) c.!** it's (pretty) tough *or* tricky!

cotonnade [kɔtɔnad] **NF** cotton fabric

cotonner [3] [kɔtɔne] **se cotonner VPR** *(tissu)* to fluff (up); *(fruit)* to go like cotton-wool

cotonneux, -euse [kɔtɔnø, -øz] **ADJ 1** *Bot* downy **2** *Littéraire (vaporeux ▸ nuages)* fleecy; **un ciel c.** a cotton-wool sky **3** *(sourd ▸ bruit)* muffled

cotonnier, -ère [kɔtɔnje, -ɛr] **ADJ** cotton *(avant n)*
NM cotton (plant)

Coton-Tige® [kɔtɔ̃tiʒ] *(pl* **Cotons-Tiges)** **NM** *Br* cotton bud, *Am* Q-tip®

côtoyer [13] [kotwaje] **VT 1** *(fréquenter)* to mix with; **ce travail me fait c. des gens intéressants** I meet some interesting people in this job **2** *(être confronté à)* to deal with; **elle côtoie le danger tous les jours** she faces danger every day; **cette expérience lui a fait c. la misère** this experience brought him/her face to face with poverty **3** *(sujet: chemin)* to skirt *or* to run alongside; *(sujet: fleuve)* to flow *or* to run alongside
VPR se côtoyer *(personnes)* to rub shoulders; **on se côtoie constamment au bureau** we see each other all the time at the office

cotre [kɔtr] **NM** *Naut* cutter

cottage [kɔtaʒ] **NM** (country) cottage

cotte¹ [kɔt] **NF 1** *Hist* **c. d'armes** coat of arms; **c. de mailles** coat of mail **2** *(bleu de travail) Br* overalls, *Am* coveralls; *(sans manches) Br* dungarees, *Am* overalls **3** *Arch (jupon)* petticoat

cotutelle [kotytɛl] **NF** *Jur* joint guardianship

cotuteur, -trice [kotytœr, -tris] **NM,F** *Jur* joint guardian

cotylédon [kɔtiledɔ̃] **NM** *Anat & Bot* cotyledon

cou [ku] **NM 1** *Anat* neck; **un pendentif autour du c.** a pendant round her neck; **sauter** *ou* **se jeter au c. de qn** to throw one's arms around sb's neck; **se casser** *ou* **se rompre le c.** to break one's neck; *Fig* **il a des problèmes jusqu'au c.** he's up to his neck in trouble; **endetté jusqu'au c.** up to one's eyes in debt **2** *(d'un vêtement)* neck **3** *(d'une bouteille, d'un vase)* neck

couac [kwak] **NM 1** *(note de musique)* wrong note; **faire un c.** to hit the wrong note **2** *Fig* dissension, disagreement; **il y a des couacs au sein du gouvernement à ce sujet** there is disagreement within the government on this issue
ONOMAT arrk, quack

couard, -e [kwar, -ard] *Littéraire* **ADJ** cowardly
NM,F coward, poltroon

couardise [kwardiz] **NF** *Littéraire* cowardice

couchage [kuʃaʒ] **NM** *(lit)* bed; *(préparatifs)* sleeping arrangements; **matériel de c.** bedding

couchant, -e [kuʃɑ̃, -ɑ̃t] **ADJ** *voir* **chien, soleil**
NM *(coucher de soleil)* sunset; *Littéraire (occident)* west

couche [kuʃ] **NF 1** *(épaisseur ▸ de peinture)* coat; *(▸ de maquillage)* layer; *(▸ de glace)* sheet; **passer une c. de peinture sur qch** to give sth a coat of paint; **étaler qch en couches épaisses/fines** to spread sth thickly/thinly; **c. d'apprêt** priming coat; **c. de fond** undercoat; *Fam* **avoir** *ou* **en tenir une c.** *Br* to be (as) thick as two short planks, *Am* to be as dumb as they come
2 *Astron & Géol* layer, stratum; **c. d'ozone** ozone layer; **préserve la c. d'ozone** *(sur emballage)* ozone-friendly
3 *(en sociologie)* **c. sociale** level, social stratum
4 *(de bébé) Br* nappy, *Am* diaper; **c. jetable** disposable *Br* nappy *or Am* diaper
5 *Littéraire (lit)* bed
• **couches NFPL** *Vieilli (accouchement)* confinement; **être en couches** to be in labour; **elle est morte en couches** she died in childbirth

couché, -e [kuʃe] **ADJ 1** *(allongé)* lying down; *(au lit)* in bed; **c.!** *(à un chien)* (lie) down! **2** *(écriture)* slanting, sloping

couche-culotte [kuʃkylɔt] *(pl* **couches-culottes)** **NF** disposable *Br* nappy *or Am* diaper

coucher¹ [kuʃe] **NM 1** *(action)* going to bed; **le c. d'un enfant** a child's bedtime routine **2** *(moment)* bedtime; **deux cachets au c.** *(sur mode d'emploi)* two tablets to be taken at bedtime *or* before bed; **c. de soleil** sunset; **au c. du soleil** at sunset, *Am* at sundown **3** *(gîte)* accommodation; **le c. et la nourriture** board and lodging

coucher² [3] [kuʃe] **VT 1** *(mettre au lit)* to put to bed; *(allonger)* to lay down; *Fam* **c. qn sur le carreau** to knock sb down, to lay sb out
2 *(héberger)* to put up, to accommodate; **on peut c. toute la famille** we can accommodate the entire family
3 *(poser ▸ par terre)* to lay down; **c. une bouteille/un vélo** to lay a bottle/a bicycle on its side; **la pluie a couché les herbes** the rain flattened the grasses; **des poteaux couchés en travers de la route** poles lying across the road; **le vent coucha le bateau** the wind made the boat keel over *or* keeled the boat over; **c. un fusil en joue** to aim a gun; **c. qn en joue** to (take) aim at sb
4 *(écrire)* to set down (in writing); **c. ses pensées sur le papier** to write down one's thoughts, *Sout* to commit one's thoughts to writing; **c. qn sur son testament** to name sb in one's will; **c. qn sur une liste** to include sb's name in a list
VI 1 *(aller dormir)* to go to bed; **cela va te faire c. tard** that will keep you up late **2** *(dormir)* to sleep; **on peut c. à cinq dans la caravane** the caravan can sleep five people; **on couchera à l'hôtel** *(une nuit)* we'll spend the night *or* we'll sleep in a hotel; *(plusieurs nuits)* we'll stay in a hotel; **tu restes c.?** are you staying overnight *or* the night?; **c. à la belle étoile** to sleep out in the open; **c. sous les ponts** to sleep rough; **la voiture couche dehors** the car stays in the street at night **3** *Fam (sexuellement)* to sleep around; **ils couchent ensemble** they're sleeping together
• **coucher avec VT IND** *Fam* to go to bed with, to sleep with
VPR se coucher 1 *(dans un lit)* to go to bed; **je ne veux pas vous faire c. tard** I don't want to keep you up; *Fam* **va te c.!** get lost *or Br* stuffed!; *Fam* **se c. avec les poules** to go to bed early[□]
2 *(s'allonger)* to lie down; **se c. en chien de fusil** to lie curled up *or* in the foetal position; **se c. à plat ventre** to lie face down *or* flat on one's stomach; **il se couchait sur sa copie pour que je ne puisse pas la lire** he was leaning over his work so I couldn't read it; **se c. sur son guidon** to lean hard against one's handlebars
3 *(soleil, lune)* to set, to go down
4 *Naut* to keel over

coucherie [kuʃri] **NF** *Fam* sleeping around, casual sex□

couchette [kuʃɛt] **NF** *(d'un train)* couchette; *(d'un bateau)* bunk

coucheur [kuʃœr] **NM** *Fam* **un mauvais c.** an awkward customer

couci-couça [kusikusa] **ADV** *Fam* so-so

coucou [kuku] **NM 1** *Orn* cuckoo
2 (pendule à) c. cuckoo clock
3 *Bot* cowslip
4 *Fam (avion)* crate, heap
EXCLAM 1 *(bonjour)* hi! **2** *(en langage enfantin)* peekaboo!, coo-ee!

coude [kud] **NM 1** *Anat* elbow; **coudes au corps** elbows in; **jusqu'au c.** up to one's elbow; **faire du c. à qn** to nudge sb; **jouer des coudes** to push and shove, to jostle; *Fig* to manoeuvre; **les gens jouaient des coudes pour atteindre le guichet** people were pushing and shoving to get to the kiosk; **j'ai dû jouer des coudes pour parvenir au bar** I had to elbow my way to the bar; **c. à c.** *(marcher, travailler)* shoulder to shoulder, side by side; **garder** *ou* **mettre** *ou* **tenir qch sous le c.** to keep sth shelved indefinitely, to keep sth on the back burner; *Fam* **lever le c.** to booze; **se serrer** *ou* **se tenir les coudes** to stick together **2** *(d'un vêtement)* elbow; *(pièce en cuir, en tissu)* elbow patch **3** *(d'un tuyau)* bend, elbow; *(d'une route)* bend; **le couloir fait un c.** there's a sharp bend in the passage

coudé, -e [kude] **ADJ** bent, angled
• **coudée NF 1** *Arch (mesure)* cubit **2** *(locutions)* **avoir les coudées franches** to have elbow room; **être à cent coudées au-dessus de qn** to be head and shoulders above sb

coude-à-coude [kudakud] **au coude-à-coude ADV** neck and neck

cou-de-pied [kudpje] *(pl* **cous-de-pied)** **NM** *Anat* instep

couder [3] [kude] **VT** to bend (at an angle)

coudoie *etc voir* **coudoyer**

coudoiement [kudwamɑ̃] **NM** *Sout (fréquentation)* rubbing shoulders; **le c. des stars lui a donné des idées** rubbing shoulders with the stars has given him/her ideas

coudoyer [13] [kudwaje] **VT** *(fréquenter)* to rub shoulders *or* to mix with

coudre [86] [kudr] **VT 1** *(ourlet)* to sew, to stitch; *(robe)* to make up; *(morceaux)* to sew *or* to stitch together; *(bouton)* to sew on; *(semelle)* to sew *or* to stitch on; **cousu (à la) main** hand-stitched; *Fam* **du cousu main** top-quality stuff **2** *(plaie)* to stitch up, to sew up **3** *(livre)* to stitch (together)
USAGE ABSOLU *Couture* **j'aime c.** I enjoy sewing; **machine à c.** sewing machine; **c. à la main/à la machine** to sew by hand/machine; *Fig* **être (tout) cousu d'or** to be extremely wealthy; *Fig* **c'est cousu de fil blanc** it's plain for all to see; **mensonge cousu de fil blanc** transparent lie

coudrier [kudrije] **NM** hazel tree

Coué [kwe] **NPR méthode C.** autosuggestion, Couéism; *Fig* self-persuasion

couenne NF 1 [kwan] *(de porc)* rind **2** [kwɛn] *Suisse (de fromage)* rind **3** [kwan] *Fam (peau)* skin□

couette [kwɛt] **NF 1** *(de cheveux)* **des couettes** bunches; **elle avait des couettes** she wore her hair in bunches; **se faire des couettes** to put *or* gather one's hair in bunches **2** *(édredon)* duvet, quilt

couffin [kufɛ̃] **NM** (straw) basket; *(pour bébé)* Moses basket

cougouar [kugwar], **couguar** [kug(w)ar] **NM** cougar, puma, mountain lion

couic [kwik] **ONOMAT** eek, squeak
• **que couic ADV** *très Fam* zilch, *Br* sod all

couille [kuj] **NF** *Vulg* **1** *(testicule)* nut, ball, *Br* bollock; **un coup de pied dans les couilles** a kick in the balls; **avoir des couilles (au cul)** to have balls; **il n'a**

pas de couilles he's got no balls; **casser** *ou* **peler les couilles à qn** *Br* to get on sb's tits, *Am* to break sb's balls; **se faire des couilles en or** to make a bundle *or Br* a packet **2** *(échec, erreur) Br* cock-up, balls-up, *Am* ball-up; **il m'est arrivé une c.** there's been a bit of a *Br* cock-up *or* balls-up *or Am* ball-up; **partir en c.** to cock up, to go down the tubes, *Br* to go tits-up **3** *(personne)* **une c. molle** a wimp

couillon [kujɔ̃] *très Fam* **NM** *(imbécile)* airhead, *Br* wally; *(dupe)* mug
ADJ damned stupid

couillonnade [kujɔnad] **NF** *très Fam* **dire des couillonnades** to talk crap *or* bull; **fais pas de couillonnades** don't do anything *Br* daft *or Am* dumb; **c'est de la c.** *(tromperie)* it's a con

couillonner [3] [kujɔne] **VT** *très Fam* to screw, to rip off; **te laisse pas c.** don't let yourself be screwed *or* ripped off; **se faire c.** to be screwed *or* ripped off

couillu, -e [kujy] **ADJ** *très Fam* ballsy

couinement [kwinmɑ̃] **NM 1** *(d'une souris)* squeak, squeaking; *(d'un lièvre, d'un porc)* squeal, squealing **2** *(d'un enfant)* whine, whining **3** *(d'un frein)* squeal, squealing

couiner [3] [kwine] **VI 1** *(souris)* to squeak; *(lièvre, porc)* to squeal **2** *(enfant)* to whine **3** *(frein)* to squeal

coulage [kulaʒ] **NM 1** *(d'une statue)* casting; *(d'un métal, de la cire, du verre)* pouring **2** *(gaspillage)* waste; *(chapardage)* shrinkage

coulant, -e [kulɑ̃, -ɑ̃t] **ADJ 1** *Fam (personne)* easy-going[□], **elle est plus coulante avec toi** she lets you get away with more
2 *(léger ▸ vin)* smooth; **il est c.** it slips down easily
3 *(style, prose)* free, free-flowing
4 *(fromage)* runny
NM 1 *(anneau)* sliding ring; *(d'une ceinture)* loop **2** *(d'une plante)* runner **3** *Fam (fromage)* = very ripe cheese, particularly Camembert

coule[1] [kul] **NF** *Fam* **être à la c.** to know the tricks of the trade, to know the ropes, to know what's what

coule[2] [kul] **NF** *(de religieux)* cowl

coulé, -e[1] [kule] **ADJ** *(mouvement)* smooth
NM 1 *Mus* slur **2** *(pas de danse)* glide **3** *(au billard)* follow-through

coulée[2] [kule] **NF 1** *(de sang, de peinture)* streak
2 *(chute)* **c. de boue** mudslide; **c. de lave** lava flow; **c. de neige** snowslide
3 *Métal* casting
4 *Chasse (d'un animal)* run, pass, path

coulemelle [kulmɛl] **NF** parasol mushroom

COULER [3] [kule]

VI	
• to flow **1, 2**	• to run **1, 4**
• to leak **3**	• to go under **5**
• to sink **5**	
VT	
• to sink **1**	• to pour **3**
• to cast **3, 4**	
VPR	
• to slip into **1**	

VI 1 *(fleuve, eau)* to run, to flow; *(larmes)* to run down, to flow; **la sueur coulait sur son visage** *(abondamment)* sweat was pouring down his/her face; *(goutte à goutte)* sweat was trickling down his/her face; **le vin coulait à flots** wine flowed freely; **le sang a coulé** there was bloodshed; **fais c. l'eau** turn on the water; **faire c. un bain** to run a bath; **il faisait c. du sable entre ses doigts** he was letting the sand run *or* trickle through his fingers; **fais c. un peu d'eau dessus** pour a little water over it; **avoir le nez qui coule** to have a runny nose; *Fig* **faire c. de la salive** to cause some tongue-wagging, to set the tongues wagging; *Fig* **faire c. beaucoup d'encre** to cause a lot of ink to flow; **il coulera de l'eau sous les ponts avant que...** there'll be a lot of water under the bridge before...
2 *(progresser facilement)* to flow; **depuis, sa vie a coulé, calme et tranquille** since then, he/she has enjoyed a calm and peaceful life; **c. de source** to follow (on naturally); **cela coule de source** *(c'est évident)* it's obvious; *(c'est une conséquence naturelle)* it follows naturally; *Fam* **laisse c.!** don't bother!, just drop it!
3 *(avoir une fuite ▸ robinet)* to leak, to drip; *(▸ stylo)* to leak
4 *(se liquéfier ▸ fromage, bougie)* to run
5 *(sombrer ▸ nageur)* to go under; *(▸ bateau)* to go down, to sink; *Fig (▸ entreprise)* to go under; **c. à pic** to sink straight to the bottom, to sink like a stone
VT 1 *(faire sombrer ▸ bateau)* to sink; *Fig (▸ entreprise, concurrent)* to sink, to bring down
2 *Littéraire (passer)* **c. des jours heureux** to spend some happy days
3 *(ciment)* to pour; *(métal)* to cast; **c. un bronze** *(métal)* to cast a bronze; *très Fam (déféquer)* to have a crap
4 *(fabriquer ▸ statue, cloche)* to cast
5 *(glisser)* **c. un sourire/regard à qn** to steal a smile/look at sb; **c. un mot à l'oreille de qn** whisper a word in sb's ear
6 *Aut* **c. une bielle** to run a rod
VPR se couler 1 *(se glisser)* **se c. dans** *(lit, foule)* to slip into; **elle se coula dans son lit et s'endormit aussitôt** she slipped into her bed and went straight to sleep; *Fig* **il s'est coulé dans le moule** he slipped into the mould; **se c. le long des murs** to hug the walls
2 *Fam* **se la c. douce** to have an easy time (of it)

couleur [kulœr] **NF 1** *(teinte)* colour; **de c. vive** brightly-coloured; **une maison de c. rose** a pink house; **de quelle c. est sa voiture?** what colour is his/her car?; *Fig* **je n'ai jamais vu la c. de son argent** I've never seen the colour of his/her money; **couleurs complémentaires** complementary colours; **couleurs primaires** *ou* **fondamentales** primary colours; *Fam* **en faire voir de toutes les couleurs à qn** to give sb a hard time; *Fam* **il nous en a fait voir de toutes les couleurs** he gave us a hard time; *Fam* **on en a vu de toutes les couleurs** we've been through some hard times
2 *(pour les cheveux)* tint, colour; **se faire faire une c.** to have one's hair tinted, to have a colour put through *or* in one's hair
3 *Cartes* suit
4 c. locale local colour; **un restaurant très c. locale** a restaurant with plenty of local colour; **pour faire c. locale** to add a bit of local colour
5 *(aspect)* light, colour; **voir la situation sous de nouvelles couleurs** to see the situation in a new light; **l'avenir m'apparaissait sous les couleurs les plus sombres/sous de belles couleurs** the future presented itself (to me) in an unfavourable/favourable light; **quelle sera la c. politique de votre nouveau journal?** what will be the political colour of your new newspaper?; **la c. du temps** the spirit of the times
6 *(d'une personne)* shade, colour; **c. de peau** skin colour; **changer de c.** to change colour; **passer par toutes les couleurs de l'arc-en-ciel** to go through all the colours of the rainbow
• **couleurs NFPL 1** *(linge)* coloureds
2 *(peintures)* coloured paints; **couleurs à l'huile** oil paints; **couleurs à l'eau** watercolours; **boîte de couleurs** box of paints, paintbox
3 *(bonne mine)* (healthy) glow, colour; **avoir des couleurs** to have a good colour; **tu as pris des couleurs** you've caught the sun, you've got some colour in your cheeks; **tu as repris des couleurs** you're getting your colour back, you're getting some colour (back) in your cheeks
4 *Sport (d'une équipe)* colours; *(d'un jockey, d'un cheval)* livery, colours; **elle a défendu les couleurs de la France** she defended the French flag
5 *(drapeau)* colours; *Mil* **envoyer** *ou* **hisser les couleurs** to hoist the colours *or* the flag
6 *Hér* colour
• **aux couleurs de PRÉP un maillot aux couleurs de son équipe préférée** a top in his favorite team's colours; **aux couleurs du propriétaire** *(yacht)* flying the owner's flag; *(cheval)* in the owner's colours
• **de couleur ADJ** coloured; **une personne de c.** a coloured person, a non-white
• **en couleur ADV** *(gén)* in colour; *(photo, télévision)* colour *(avant n)*; **tout en c.** in full colour; **haut en c.** very lively *or* colourful *or* picturesque
• **sous couleur de CONJ** under the pretext *or* guise of; **sous c. de me rendre service** under the pretext *or* guise of doing me a service

couleuvre [kulœvr] **NF** *Zool* garter snake, colubrid snake; **c. à collier** grass snake; **c. vipérine** viperine grass snake

coulis [kuli] **NM 1** *Culin (de fruits)* coulis **2** *(mortier)* grout; *(métal)* molten metal

coulissant, -e [kulisɑ̃, -ɑ̃t] **ADJ** sliding

coulisse [kulis] **NF 1** *Théât* **la c., les coulisses** the wings; **les coulisses du pouvoir** the corridors of power; **dans les coulisses, en c.** *Théât* in the wings; *Fig* behind the scenes; *Fig* **on murmure en c. que...** they say behind the scenes that...; **regard en c.** sidelong look
2 *(glissière)* runner
3 *Couture* hem *(through which to pass tape)*
4 *Bourse* outside market, kerb market
• **à coulisse ADJ** sliding

coulisseau, -x [kuliso] **NM** sliding block; *(de pièce de machine)* slide; *(de tiroir)* runner; *Aut* slider

coulisser [3] [kulise] **VI** to slide
VT 1 *(porte, tiroir)* to provide with runners **2** *Couture* to hem *(in order to run a tape through)*; **pantalon coulissé** trousers with a drawstring waist

coulissier [kulisje] **NM** *Bourse* outside broker, kerb broker

couloir [kulwar] **NM 1** *(d'un bâtiment)* corridor, passage; *(d'un wagon)* corridor; **les couloirs du métro** the corridors of the *Br* tube *or Am* subway; **intrigues de c.** backstage manoeuvring; **bruits de couloirs** rumours
2 *Transp* **c. (de circulation)** lane; **c. aérien** air traffic lane; **c. d'autobus** bus lane; **c. de navigation** sea lane; **c. à vélos** cycle lane
3 *(entre des régions, des pays)* corridor; **c. humanitaire** humanitarian corridor
4 *Géog* gully, *Spéc* couloir; **le c. rhodanien** the Rhône Corridor; **c. d'avalanche** avalanche corridor
5 *(d'un appareil de projection)* track
6 *(en athlétisme)* lane; *(au tennis) Br* tramlines, *Am* alley

couloiriste [kulwarist] **NM** *Journ* lobby correspondent

coulon [kulɔ̃] **NM** *Belg* pigeon

coulpe [kulp] **NF** *Littéraire* **battre sa c.** to beat one's breast

COUP [ku]

• blow **A1–3**	• punch **A1, 3**
• kick **A1**	• shock **A2**
• shot **A4, B3**	• knock **A5**
• stroke **A6, B3**	• *used with body part, or instrument* **B1, 2**
• knack **B4**	
• drink **B7**	• throw **B8**
• move **B9**	• go **B9, D**
• trick **C1**	• job **C2**
• coup **C4**	

NM A. HEURT, DÉFLAGRATION 1 *(gén)* blow, knock; *(avec le poing)* punch, blow; *(avec le pied)* kick; **un c. violent** a hard knock; **un c. brutal** a nasty blow; **frapper à coups redoublés** to hit twice as hard; **donner un petit c. à** *ou* **sur qch** to tap sth lightly; **donner un c. sec sur qch** to give sth a (hard *or* smart) tap; **il frappait sur la porte à grands coups/à petits coups** he banged on the door/knocked gently at the door; **donner un c. sur la table** *(avec le poing)* to thump the table, to bang one's fist (down) on the table; **en arriver** *ou* **en venir aux coups** to come to blows; **j'ai pris un c. sur la tête** I got a knock *or* a bang on the head; **prendre des coups** to get knocked about; **recevoir un c.** to get hit; **il a reçu un c. sur la tête** he was hit on the head; **j'en ai reçu des coups quand j'étais petit!** I was constantly knocked about when I was little!; *aussi Fig* **rendre c. pour c.** to hit back, to give as good as one gets; *Jur* **coups et blessures** grievous bodily harm; *Jur* **inculpé de coups et blessures** charged with inflicting grievous bodily harm; *aussi Fig* **porter un c. à qn** to deal sb a blow; **porter un c. mortel à qn** to strike sb a fatal blow; *Fig* **les grandes surfaces ont porté un (rude) c. au petit commerce** small traders have been dealt a (severe) blow by large retail chains; *aussi Fig* **le c. a porté** the blow struck home; **il a reçu un c. de gourdin sur la tête** he was clubbed on the head; **un c. de marteau** a blow with a hammer; **il s'est**

donné un c. de marteau sur le doigt he hit his finger with a hammer; **il a reçu un c. de marteau sur la tête** he was hit on the head with a hammer
2 *(attaque, choc)* blow, shock; **ça m'a fait un c.** *(émotion)* it gave me a shock; *(déception)* it was a blow; **les mauvais coups de la vie** the nasty blows that life deals you; *Fam* **sale c. (pour la fanfare)!** that's a bit of a blow *or* downer!; *Fam* **le buffet en a pris un c. pendant le déménagement** the dresser got a bit bashed in the move; **trois échecs d'affilée, son moral en a pris un c.** with three successive failures, his/her morale has taken a bit of a battering; **avec le krach boursier, l'économie en a pris un c.** the economy has suffered a great deal from the crash; **j'ai trop de travail, je ne sais pas si je tiendrai le c.** I've got too much work, I don't know if I'll be able to cope; **il faut que tu tiennes le c. jusqu'à la fin de la semaine** you'll have to keep going until the end of the week
3 *Boxe* punch, blow; *aussi Fig* **c. bas** blow *or* punch below the belt; **il m'a fait un c. bas** he played a lousy trick on me; *aussi Fig* **tous les coups sont permis** (there are) no holds barred; *aussi Fig* **compter les coups** to keep score
4 *(d'une arme à feu)* shot, blast; **un c. de revolver** a shot, a gunshot; **le c. est parti** *(revolver)* the gun went off; *(fusil)* the rifle went off; **tirer un c. de canon** to fire *or* to blast a cannon; **le c. est passé très près** the bullet just whistled past; **(revolver à) six coups** six-shot gun; **faire c. double** *Chasse* to kill two animals with one shot; *Fig* to kill two birds with one stone
5 *(bruit ▸ gên)* knock; *(▸sec)* rap; *(▸craquement)* snap; **des coups au carreau** knocking *or* knocks on the window
6 *(heure sonnée)* stroke; **c. de cloche** stroke of the bell; **l'horloge sonna trois coups** the clock struck three; **le dernier c. de trois heures** the last stroke of three; **les douze coups de minuit** the twelve strokes of midnight
7 *Vulg (éjaculation)* **tirer un** *ou* **son c.** to shoot one's load
B. *GESTE, ACTION* **1** *(mouvement d'une partie du corps)* **un c. de corne** a butt with the horn; **donner un c. de corne à qn** to butt sb; **un c. de langue** a lick; **elle nettoyait ses chatons à (grands) coups de langue** she was licking her kittens clean; **un c. de bec** a peck; *Fig* a cutting remark; **un c. de dent** a bite; *Fig* a cutting remark; **d'un grand c. de dent** with one snap of the jaws; **c. de griffe** *ou* **patte** swipe of the paw; *Fig* cutting remark
2 *(emploi d'un instrument)* **donner un (petit) c. de brosse/chiffon à qch** to give sth a (quick) brush/wipe; **passe un c. d'aspirateur au salon** give the living room a quick vacuum; **passe un c. d'éponge sur la table** give the table a wipe (with the sponge); *Fam* **passe un c. dans la salle de bains** give the bathroom a going-over; **en deux coups de rame nous pouvons traverser la rivière** we can cross the river in a couple of strokes; *Fam* **en donner** *ou* **ficher** *ou* **mettre un c.** to get down to business; **il va falloir qu'on en mette** *ou* **en mettre un c.** we'll have to get down to it *or* to get a move on; **mets-en un bon c.!** give it everything you've got!, go for it!; **il a fallu qu'ils en mettent un sacré c.** they really had to pull all out the stops
3 *Golf & (au billard)* stroke; *(au tennis)* shot, stroke; **c. droit** forehand stroke
4 *Fam (savoir-faire)* knack; **une fois que tu auras pris le c., ça ira tout seul!** you'll find it's very easy once you get used to it *or* once you've got the knack!; **pour la pâtisserie, il a le c.** he's *Br* a dab hand *or Am* a champ at baking cakes; **ah, tu as le c. pour mettre la pagaille!** you really have a gift *or* a knack for creating havoc, don't you!
5 *Météo* **c. de chaleur** heatwave; **c. de mer** heavy swell; **c. de vent** gust of wind; *Naut* **c. de roulis/tangage** sudden roll/dip; **il y a eu un petit c. de roulis/tangage** the boat started rolling/pitching a bit
6 *(effet soudain)* **j'ai un c. de cafard** I feel down all of a sudden; **j'ai eu un c. de fatigue** suddenly a wave of tiredness came over me; **il a eu un c. de folie et a acheté une Rolls** he had a moment of madness and bought himself a Rolls-Royce; **avoir un c. de chaleur** to get heatstroke
7 *Fam (boisson)* drink; **j'ai le hoquet – bois un c.** I've got (the) hiccups – drink something *or* have a drink; **tu me sers un c. (à boire)?** could you pour me a drink?; **tu boiras** *ou* **prendras bien un c. avant de partir?** you'll have a drink before you go *or* you'll have one for the road, won't you?; **boire un c. de trop** to have one too many; **avoir un c. dans le nez** to have had one too many; **un c. de rouge** a glass of red wine; **un c. de gnôle** a nip of brandy
8 *(lancer)* throw; *(aux dés)* throw (of the dice); **elle a renversé toutes les boîtes de conserve en un seul c.** she knocked down all the cans in one throw
9 *(action)* move; *Cartes* go; **la partie se joue dans les premiers coups** the game is won or lost in the opening moves; **c'est un c. pour rien** *(essai)* it's a trial run; *(échec)* it's a failure
C. *ACTE OU SITUATION EXCEPTIONNELS* **1** *Fam (mauvais tour)* trick; **il prépare un c.** he's up to something *or* some trick; **(faire) un mauvais** *ou* **sale c. (à qn)** (to play) a dirty trick (on sb); **je parie que c'est un c. de Julie!** I bet Julie's behind this!; **c'est encore un c. de ton ami** it's another of your friend's tricks; **c. en traître** blow below the belt, stab in the back; **monter un c. contre qn** to set sb up, to frame sb; **il nous a encore fait le c.** he's pulled the same (old) trick on us again; **il a essayé de me faire le c. de la panne** he tried to pull the old running-out-of-petrol trick on me; **ne me fais pas le c. de ne pas venir!** now don't stand me up, will you!; **c. monté** put-up job, frame-up; **l'accusé affirmait être victime d'un c. monté** the accused claimed it was a put-up job *or* claimed that he'd been framed; **elle a fait un c. en douce** she's cooked up something behind everybody's back; **il fait toujours ses coups en douce** he's always going behind people's backs
2 *Fam (vol, escroquerie)* job; **ils sont sur un gros c. avec le Balafré** they're on to a big job *or* number with Scarface; **il était sur le c. du supermarché** he was in on the supermarket job
3 *Fam (affaire)* **je suis sur un c.** I'm on to something; *Journ* I have a lead; **je veux l'acheter mais on est plusieurs sur le c.** I want to buy it but there are several people interested; **être dans tous les coups** to have a finger in every pie; **rattraper le c.** to sort things out; **il a manqué** *ou* **raté son c.** he didn't pull it off; **elle a réussi son c.** she pulled it off; **c'est un c. à avoir un accident, ça!** that's the sort of thing that causes accidents!; **combien crois-tu que ça va coûter? – oh, c'est un c. de 200 euros** how much do you think it will cost? – oh, about 200 euros
4 *(action remarquable, risquée)* coup; **faire un beau** *ou* **joli c.** to pull a (real) coup; **elle a décroché le contrat, quel joli c.!** she landed the contract, what a coup!; **tenter le c.** to have a go, to give it a try; **c'est un c. à tenter** it's worth trying *or* a try
5 *(circonstance marquante)* **marquer le c.** to mark the occasion; **un c. du ciel** *ou* **de la providence** a twist of fate; *Fam* **un c. de chance** *ou* **de pot** *ou* **de bol** a stroke of luck, a lucky break; **t'as vraiment eu un c. de chance** *ou* **pot** *ou* **bol!** you were a lucky devil!, you certainly got a lucky break there!
6 *Vulg (personne ▸ sexuellement)* **c'est un bon c.** he/she's a good lay
D. *FOIS* time, go; **du premier c.** first time, at the first attempt; **j'ai eu mon permis au deuxième c.** I passed my driving test at the second attempt; **au prochain c., tu vas y arriver** you'll do it next time *or* at your next go; **tu as encore droit à un c.** you've still got another go; **essaie encore un c.** have another go; **ce c.-ci, on s'en va** this time, we're off; **ce c.-là, je crois qu'elle a compris** I think she got the message that time; *Fam* **c'est ça, pleure un bon c.** that's it, have a good cry; **dites-le lui un bon c., qu'on n'en parle plus!** tell him once and for all, and let's not talk about it any more!; **vous devriez vous expliquer un bon c.!** you should have it out once and for all!; *Fam* **souffle un grand c.!** *(en se mouchant, sur des bougies)* blow!; **respire un grand c.** take a deep breath
• **à coups de** PRÉP **démolir qch à coups de marteau** to smash sth to pieces with a hammer; **il ne discute qu'à coups de statistiques** the only thing he puts forward is statistics; **faire une traduction à coups de dictionnaire** to do a translation with a dictionary in one hand
• **à coup sûr** ADV definitely, certainly, for sure; **tu vas à c. sûr rater ton train!** one thing's (for) sure, you'll miss your train!
• **après coup** ADV afterwards, later on; **ce n'est qu'après c. que j'ai compris ce qu'il voulait dire** it was only afterwards *or* later on that it dawned on me what he meant
• **à tous les coups** ADV *Fam* **1** *(chaque fois)* every time□; **ça marche à tous les coups** it never fails□; **à tous les coups l'on gagne** you win every time□ **2** *(sans aucun doute)* **à tous les coups, il a oublié** he's bound to have forgotten□
• **au coup par coup** ADV *Fam* bit by bit; **les avantages sociaux ont été obtenus au c. par c.** welfare benefits were won bit by bit; **négocier au c. par c.** to have piecemeal negotiations□
• **coup sur coup** ADV one after the other, in quick succession; **deux angines c. sur c.** two attacks of tonsillitis in quick succession
• **dans le coup** *Fam* ADJ **1** *(complice)* **elle est dans le c.** she's in on it *or* involved in it□; **je ne suis pas dans le c.** *(dans l'affaire)* it's nothing to do with me□, it doesn't involve me□ **2** *(à la mode)* **elle est dans le c.** she's hip *or* with it; **pour la pop, je ne suis plus dans le c.** I've not kept up with *or* I'm rather out of touch with the pop scene□ ADV **mettre qn dans le c.** *(faire participer qn)* to let sb in on the act; *(expliquer les choses à qn)* to put sb in the picture; **c'est Aglaée qui m'a mis dans le c.** Aglaée got me involved in it *or* in on it
• **du coup** ADV so, as a result; **alors, du c., tu ne pars plus!** so that means you're not going any more!; **elle ne pouvait pas venir, du c. j'ai reporté le dîner** she couldn't come so I put the dinner off
• **d'un (seul) coup** ADV **1** *(en une seule fois)* in one (go), all at once; **tu peux mettre toute la farine d'un seul c.** you can add the flour all at once; **avale-les d'un c.** swallow them down in one (go); **il a tout bu d'un c.** he drank the whole lot in one go **2** *(soudainement)* all of a sudden; *Fam* **j'ai eu envie de pleurer/de le gifler, ça m'a pris d'un c.** I got a sudden urge to cry/to slap him
• **pour le coup** ADV **pour le c., je ne savais plus quoi faire** at that point, I didn't know what to do next; *Fam* **j'ai aussi failli renverser le lait, c'est pour le c. qu'il aurait été en colère!** I nearly spilt the milk as well, he really would have been furious then!
• **sous le coup de** PRÉP **sous le c. de la colère, on dit des choses qu'on regrette après** when you're in a temper, you say things which you regret later; **sous le c. de l'excitation, il a trop promis** in the heat of the moment, he made promises he couldn't keep; **il est encore sous le c. de l'émotion** he still hasn't got over the shock; **être sous le c. d'une condamnation** to have a current conviction; **tomber sous le c. de qch** to come within the scope of sth; **tomber sous le c. de la loi** to be punishable by law
• **sur le coup** ADV **1** *(mourir)* instantly **2** *(à ce moment-là)* straight away, there and then; **je n'ai pas compris sur le c.** I didn't understand immediately *or* straight away; **sur le c., j'ai accepté, mais je le regrette aujourd'hui** I accepted straight away, but now I regret it
• **sur le coup de** PRÉP **sur le c. de six heures/de midi** roundabout six o'clock/midday
• **coup d'aile** NM **la cane a donné un petit c. d'aile** the duck flapped its wings; **tous les moineaux se sont envolés d'un c. d'aile** all the sparrows took wing suddenly; *Fig* **Paris-Amsterdam d'un c. d'aile** Paris-Amsterdam in one short hop; **on peut aller n'importe où dans le monde d'un c. d'aile** you can fly anywhere in the world in no time at all
• **coup de balai** NM **la cuisine a besoin d'un bon c. de balai** the kitchen needs a good sweep; **donner un c. de balai** to sweep (out) a room; *Fig* **le comité aurait besoin d'un bon c. de balai** the committee could do with a shake-up; *Fig* **donner un bon c. de balai dans la direction** to revamp the management
• **coup de barre** NM *Fam* sudden feeling of exhaustion□; **j'ai le c. de barre** I feel *Br* shattered *or Am* beat suddenly
• **coup de chapeau** NM praise; **donner un c. de chapeau à qn** to praise sb; **son livre mérite un c. de chapeau** his/her book deserves some recognition
• **coup de chien** NM **1** *Naut* sudden squall **2** *Fig* bolt from the blue
• **coup de cœur** NM **avoir un** *ou* **le c. de cœur pour qch** to fall in love with sth, to be really taken with

or by sth; **voici nos coups de cœur dans la collection de printemps** here are our favourite spring outfits; **des prix c. de cœur** special offers

• **coup de coude** NM **donner un c. de coude à qn** *(en signe)* to nudge sb; *(agressivement)* to dig one's elbow into sb

• **coup d'éclat** NM feat; **faire un c. d'éclat** to pull off a coup

• **coup d'État** NM *(putsch)* coup (d'état); *Fig* coup

• **coup de feu** NM **1** *(tir)* **tirer un c. de feu** to fire a shot, to shoot; **on a entendu des coups de feu** we heard shots being fired *or* gunfire **2** *Fig (dans un restaurant)* **c'est le c. de feu** there's a sudden rush on

• **coup de fil** = **coup de téléphone**

• **coup de filet** NM *(poissons)* draught, haul; *(suspects)* haul

• **coup de force** NM takeover by force

• **coup de foudre** NM **1** *Météo* flash of lightning **2** *Fig* love at first sight; **entre eux deux, ça a été le c. de foudre** it was love at first sight between (the two of) them

• **coup de fouet** NM **donner un c. de fouet à qn** to lash *or* to whip sb; *Fig* to give sb a boost; **le cocher a donné un c. de fouet aux chevaux** the coachman cracked his whip at the horses; *Fig* **ces vitamines te donneront un c. de fouet** these vitamins will give you a boost *or* a lift

• **coup fourré** NM **1** *Escrime* double hit **2** *Fig* low trick

• **coup franc** NM *Ftbl* free kick

• **coup de fusil** NM **1** *(acte)* shot; *(bruit)* shot, gunshot; **donner un c. de fusil à qn** to shoot sb (with a rifle); **on entendait des coups de fusil** you could hear shots being fired *or* gunfire; **j'ai entendu un coup de fusil** I heard a shot being fired; **recevoir un c. de fusil** to get shot; **il fut tué d'un c. de fusil** he was shot dead **2** *Fig* **on y mange bien, mais après c'est le c. de fusil!** it's a good restaurant, but the bill is a bit of a shock!

• **coup de grâce** NM *aussi Fig* coup de grâce, deathblow

• **coup du lapin** NM *(coup)* rabbit punch; *(dans un accident de voiture)* whiplash (injury) *(UNCOUNT)*

• **coup de main** NM **1** *(raid)* smash-and-grab (attack); *Mil* coup de main **2** *(aide)* **donner un c. de main à qn** to give *or* to lend sb a hand **3** *(savoir-faire)* **avoir le c. de main** to have the knack *or* the touch; **avoir le c. de main pour faire qch** to have the knack of doing sth

• **coup d'œil** NM **1** *(regard)* look, glance; **elle s'en rendit compte au premier c. d'œil** she noticed straight away *or* immediately *or* at a glance; **donner** *ou* **jeter un petit c. d'œil à** to have a quick look *or* glance at; **avoir le c. d'œil** to have a good eye; **pour repérer les coquilles, elle a le c. d'œil** she has a keen eye for misprints; **valoir le c. d'œil** to be (well) worth seeing **2** *(panorama)* view; **de là-haut, le c. d'œil est unique** the view up there is unique

• **coup de pied** NM *(d'une personne, d'un cheval)* kick; *Fig* **le c. de pied de l'âne** the parting shot; **donner un c. de pied à qn** to kick sb; **donner un c. de pied dans qch** to kick sth

• **coup de poing** NM punch; **donner un c. de poing à qn** to give sb a punch, to punch sb; **il a reçu un c. de poing** he was punched; **faire le c. de poing** to brawl, to fight ADJ INV **opération c. de poing** *(sur vitrine)* prices slashed

• **coup de poker** NM (bit of a) gamble; **on peut tenter la chose, mais c'est un c. de poker** we can try it but it's a bit risky

• **coup de pompe** NM *Fam* sudden feeling of exhaustion[□]; **j'ai un c. de pompe** I suddenly feel *Br* shattered *or Am* beat

• **coup de pouce** NM bit of help; **donner un c. de pouce à qn** to pull (a few) strings for sb; **donner un c. de pouce à qch** to give sth a bit of a boost; **il nous faudrait de la publicité pour donner un c. de pouce à nos ventes** we need some advertising to give our sales a bit of a boost

• **coup de sang** NM **1** *Méd* stroke **2** *Fig* angry outburst; **elle a eu un c. de sang** she exploded (with rage)

• **coup de soleil** NM sunburn *(UNCOUNT)*; **prendre** *ou* **attraper un c. de soleil** to get sunburnt

• **coup du sort** NM *(favorable)* stroke of luck; *(défavorable)* stroke of bad luck

• **coup de téléphone** NM (phone) call; **donner** *ou* **passer un c. de téléphone** to make a call; **donner** *ou* **passer un c. de téléphone à qn** to phone *or* to call *or Br* to ring sb; **recevoir un c. de téléphone** to receive *or* to get a phone call; **j'ai eu un c. de téléphone de Jean** I had a call from Jean

• **coup de tête** NM **1** *(dans une bagarre)* headbutt; **donner un c. de tête à qn** to headbutt sb **2** *Sport* header **3** *Fig* (sudden) impulse; **sur un c. de tête** on (a sudden) impulse

• **coup de théâtre** NM *Théât* coup de théâtre, sudden twist in the action; *Fig* sudden turn of events; **et alors, c. de théâtre, on lui demande de démissionner** and then, out of the blue, he/she was asked to resign

• **coup de torchon** NM *Fam (bagarre)* fist-fight; *(nettoyage)* clean-up, *Br* clear-out

• **coup de vent** NM **1** *(rafale)* gust (of wind) **2** *(locution)* **en c. de vent** in a flash *or* a whirl; **entrer/partir en c. de vent** to rush in/off; **elle est passée par Lausanne en c. de vent** she paid a flying visit to Lausanne; **je passe en c. de vent pour te dire...** I've just dropped in to tell you...; **manger en c. de vent** to grab something to eat

coupable [kupabl] ADJ **1** *(fautif)* guilty; **se sentir c.** to feel guilty; **prendre un air c.** to look sheepish *or* guilty; **c. de vol** guilty of theft **2** *(répréhensible ▸ amour, rêve, pensée)* sinful, reprehensible; *(▸ action)* culpable

NMF *Jur* guilty party

coupage [kupaʒ] NM *(mélange)* blending; *(avec de l'eau)* diluting, dilution, watering down

coupant, -e [kupɑ̃, -ɑ̃t] ADJ **1** *(tranchant ▸ ciseaux)* sharp; **herbe coupante** grass you can cut yourself on **2** *(caustique ▸ ton, remarque)* cutting, biting

NM cutting edge

coup-de-poing [kudpwɛ̃] *(pl* **coups-de-poing***)* NM **1 c. américain** knuckleduster **2** *(silex taillé)* hand axe

ADJ *(argument, publicité)* hard-hitting; *(politique)* tough and uncompromising

coupe [kup] NF **1** *(action)* cutting (out); *(coiffure)* **c. (de cheveux)** cut, haircut; **changer de c.** to have one's hair restyled; **c. au carré** (square) bob

2 *Couture (forme)* cut; *(action)* cutting; *(tissu)* length

3 *(dessin)* section; **c. longitudinale** longitudinal section; **c. transversale** cross-section; **la machine vue en c.** a section of the machine

4 *(au microscope)* section

5 *Cartes (séparation)* cut, cutting

6 *(sciage)* cutting (down); *(étendue)* felling area; *(entaille)* section; **c. sombre** thinning out; *Fig* drastic cut; **faire des coupes sombres dans un budget** to drastically cut a budget; **c. réglée** periodic felling; **mettre en c. réglée** to fell on a regular basis; *Fig* to bleed *or* to drain systematically; **coupes budgétaires** budget cuts

7 *Ling & Littérature* break, caesura; **c. syllabique** syllable break

8 *Cin* **c. sèche** jump cut

9 *Sport* cup; **la c. de l'America** the America's Cup; **la c. du monde** the World Cup; **la c. Davis** the Davis Cup

10 *(verre, contenu ▸ à boire)* glass; *(▸ à entremets)* dish; *(compotier)* dish, bowl; **c. de glace/fruits** *(dessert)* ice cream/fruit *(presented in a dish)*; **une c. à champagne** a champagne glass; **une c. de champagne** a glass of champagne; **c. à glace** sundae dish; **la c. est pleine** the cup is full

• **à la coupe** ADJ **fromage/jambon à la c.** cheese cut/ham sliced at the request of the customer

• **sous la coupe de** PRÉP *(soumis à)* **être sous la c. de qn** to be under sb's thumb; **tomber sous la c. de qn** to fall into sb's clutches

coupé [kupe] NM *Aut & (en danse)* coupé; **c. sport** sports coupé

coupe-choux [kupʃu] NM INV *Fam* **1** *(sabre)* sabre **2** *Hum* (cut-throat) razor

coupe-cigares [kupsigar] NM INV cigar cutter

coupe-circuit [kupsirkɥi] *(pl* **inv** *ou* **coupe-circuits***)* NM *Élec* cutout, circuit breaker

coupe-coupe [kupkup] NM INV machete

coupée [kupe] NF gangway

coupe-faim [kupfɛ̃] NM INV **1** *(gén)* snack **2** *Méd* appetite suppressant

coupe-feu [kupfø] NM INV **1** *(espace)* firebreak, fire line **2** *(construction)* fireguard

ADJ INV **porte c.** fire door

coupe-file [kupfil] *(pl* **coupe-files***)* NM pass

coupe-frites [kupfrit] NM INV chip-cutter *or* -slicer, *Am* French-fry-cutter *or* -slicer

coupe-gorge [kupgɔrʒ] NM INV *(quartier)* rough area; *(bistrot, boîte de nuit)* rough place

coupe-jarret [kupʒarɛ] *(pl* **coupe-jarrets***)* NM *Littéraire* cut-throat

coupe-légumes [kuplegym] NM INV vegetable cutter, vegetable slicer

coupelle [kupɛl] NF **1** *(petite coupe)* (small) dish **2** *Chim* cupel

coupe-ongles [kupɔ̃gl] NM INV nail clippers

coupe-papier [kuppapje] *(pl* **inv** *ou* **coupe-papiers***)* NM paper knife

COUPER [3] [kupe]

VT	
• to cut **1, 4–8, 11, 14, 16**	• to cut off **2, 5, 10, 12, 15**
• to cut up **3**	• to cut down **4**
• to cut out **5, 6**	• to interrupt **8**
• to intersect **10**	• to water down **13**
• to trump **16**	• to slice **17**
VI	
• to cut in **3**	• to cut **1**
• to interrupt **3**	

VT **1** *(entailler ▸ légèrement)* to cut; *(▸ gravement)* to slash; **c. la gorge à qn** to slit *or* to cut sb's throat; **c. le souffle** *ou* **la respiration à qn** to take sb's breath away; **beau à c. le souffle** breathtakingly beautiful; **le brouillard était à c. au couteau** the fog was so thick you couldn't see your hand in front of your face; **un accent à c. au couteau** a very strong accent; **un silence à c. au couteau** a silence you could cut with a knife; **le vent qui lui coupait le visage** the wind stinging his/her face

2 *(sectionner ▸ membre)* to cut off; *(▸ tête)* to cut off, to chop (off); **il a fallu lui c. un doigt** he/she had to have a finger cut off *or* amputated; **c. la tête** *ou* **le cou à qn** to cut off sb's head; *Fig* **c. bras et jambes à qn** *(surprise)* to stun sb; *Fig* **ça lui a coupé les jambes** *(de fatigue)* that's really tired him/her out

3 *(châtrer ▸ animal)* to neuter, to castrate; **il a fait c. son chat** he had his cat neutered

4 *(mettre en morceaux ▸ ficelle)* to cut; *(▸ gâteau)* to cut up; *(▸ saucisson)* to cut up, to slice (up); *(▸ bois)* to chop (up); **elle est obligée de lui c. sa viande** she has to cut up his/her meat (for him/her); **c. de la viande en morceaux** to cut up meat (into pieces); **c. une tomate en quartiers** to cut a tomato into quarters, to quarter a tomato; **c. en tranches** to cut up, to cut into slices, to slice; **c. qch en tranches fines/épaisses** to slice sth thinly/thickly, to cut sth into thick/thin slices; **elle se ferait c. en morceaux plutôt que de...** she'd rather die than...; *Fig* **c. la poire en deux** to meet halfway, to come to a compromise; **c. les ponts avec qn** to break all ties *or* to break off relations with sb; *Fig* **c. les cheveux en quatre** to split hairs

5 *(tailler ▸ fleurs)* to cut; *(▸ bordure)* to cut off; *(▸ arbre)* to cut down, to chop down, to fell; **c. les cheveux à qn** to cut *or* to trim sb's hair; **se faire c. les cheveux** to have one's hair cut; **c. la queue à un cheval** to dock a horse *or* a horse's tail; **c. le mal à la racine** to strike at the root of the evil

6 *Couture (robe)* to cut out; *(tissu)* to cut

7 *(écourter ▸ film, texte)* to cut; *(ôter ▸ remarque, séquence)* to cut (out), to edit out; **garde l'introduction mais coupe les citations latines** keep the introduction but edit *or* cut *or* take out the Latin quotations

8 *(arrêter ▸ crédit)* to cut; **c. l'eau** *(par accident)* to cut off the water; *(volontairement)* to turn *or* to switch off the water; **c. le courant** *ou* **l'électricité** to switch off the current; *(sujet: compagnie d'électricité)* to cut off the power; **son père va lui c. les vivres** his/her father will stop supporting him/her *or* will cut off his/her means of subsistence

9 *(interrompre ▸ fièvre)* to bring down; *(▸ appétit)* to spoil, to ruin; *(▸ relations diplomatiques, conversation)* to break off; **c. la parole à qn** to cut sb short; **ne coupe pas la parole comme ça!** don't cut in like that!; *Fam* **c. qn** to interrupt sb; **je vais à la gym à midi, ça (me) coupe la journée** I go to the gym at lunchtime, it helps to break up the day; **ces chaussettes sont trop serrées, elles me coupent la circulation** these socks are too tight, they're cutting off my circulation; *Fam* **c. la chique** *ou* **le sifflet à qn** to shut sb up; *Fam* **ça te la coupe, hein?** you weren't expecting that one, were you!, that shut you up, didn't it!; **c. ses effets à qn** to take the wind out of sb's sails; **c. le souffle à qn** to take sb's breath away; *(coup de poing)* to wind sb

10 *(barrer ▸ route)* to cut off; *(▸ retraite)* to block off, to cut off; **l'arbre nous coupait la route** the tree blocked our path; **la voiture nous a coupé la route** the car cut across in front of us

11 *(diviser ▸ surface)* to cut; *(▸ ligne)* to cut, to intersect; *(▸ voie)* to cross, to cut across; **le mur coupe la ville en deux** the wall cuts the town in two *or* bisects the town; **où le chemin de fer coupe la route** where the railway line cuts across *or* crosses the road; **la droite AB coupe le plan** the straight line AB cuts the plane; **la proue du navire coupait les vagues** the bow of the ship cut through the waves; *Fig* **depuis, la famille est coupée en deux** since then, the family has been split in two; **sur la question de l'euro, le pays est coupé en deux** the country is divided *or* split down the middle on the issue of the euro

12 *(séparer)* to cut off; **c. qn de qch** to cut sb off from sth; **c. l'ennemi de ses bases** to cut off the enemy from its base; **je me sens coupé de tout** I feel cut off from everything *or* totally isolated

13 *(diluer ▸ lait)* to add water to, to thin down, to water down; **coupé d'eau** diluted, watered down; **c. du vin** *(à l'eau)* to water wine down; *(avec d'autres vins)* to blend wine

14 *Cin* **coupez!** cut!

15 *Tél* to cut off

16 *Cartes (partager)* to cut; *(jouer l'atout)* to trump; **c'est à vous de c.** it's your turn to cut; **c. à carreau/à cœur** to trump with a diamond/heart

17 *Sport (balle)* to slice

VI 1 *(être tranchant)* to cut, to be sharp; **le couteau coupe bien** the knife cuts well; **attention, ça coupe!** careful, it's sharp!

2 *(prendre un raccourci)* **c. à travers champs** to cut across fields *or* country; **c. par une petite route** to cut through by a minor road; **coupons par le moulin** let's take a shortcut via the mill; **c. au plus court** to take the quickest way

3 *(interrompre)* to cut in, to interrupt; **"faux", coupa-t-elle** "not true," she cut in; *Tél* **ne coupez pas!** hold the line!

• **couper à VT IND c. court à qch** *(mettre fin à)* to cut sth short, to curtail sth; **c. à qch** *(se dérober)* to get out of sth; **tu ne couperas pas à la vaisselle!** you won't get out of doing the dishes!; **on n'y a pas coupé, à son sermon!** sure enough we got a lecture from him!; **tu dois y aller, tu ne peux pas y c.!** you've got to go, there's no way you can get out of it!

VPR se couper 1 to cut oneself; **se c. les ongles** to cut *or* to trim one's nails; **se c. les veines** to slit *or* to slash one's wrists; **se c. en quatre pour qn** to bend over backwards to help sb

2 *(lignes, routes)* to cut across one another, to intersect

3 *(se contredire)* to contradict oneself

4 se c. de qn *(interrompre le contact)* to cut oneself off from sb, to sever links with sb

coupe-racines [kuprasin] **NM INV** *Agr* root-slicer, root-cutter

couper-coller [3] [kupekɔle] *Ordinat* **VT & VI** to cut and paste

NM INV cut-and-paste; **faire un c. (sur qch)** to cut and paste (sth)

couperet [kuprɛ] **NM 1** *(d'une guillotine)* blade, knife **2** *(à viande)* cleaver, chopper

couperose [kuproz] **NF** red blotches (on the face), *Spéc* rosacea

couperosé, -e [kuproze] **ADJ** blotchy and red, *Spéc* affected by rosacea

coupeur, -euse [kupœr, -øz] **NM,F 1** *Couture* cutter **2** *(locution)* **un c. de cheveux en quatre** a nit-picker

coupe-vent [kupvɑ̃] **NM INV 1** *Br* windcheater, *Am* Windbreaker® **2** *Transp* V-shaped deflector

couplage [kuplaʒ] **NM** *Élec & Tech* coupling

couple [kupl] **NM 1** *(d'amoureux, de danseurs)* couple; *(de patineurs)* pair; *(d'animaux)* pair; **leur c. ne marche pas très fort** their relationship isn't going too well; **ils ont des problèmes de c.** they're having problems in their relationship; **vivre en c.** to live together (as a couple)

2 *Tech & Phys* couple; *Aut* **c. de démarrage** starting *or* cranking torque; **c. moteur** engine torque; *Phys* **c. thermoélectrique** thermocouple

3 *Math* pair

4 *Naut* frame; **interdiction de se mettre à c.** *(sur panneau)* no double-mooring

NF *Chasse (chiens)* couple; *(colliers)* brace

couplé [kuple] **NM** *(au tiercé)* double; **c. gagnant** forecast bet; **c. placé** each-way double

coupler [3] [kuple] **VT 1** *(mettre deux à deux)* to couple together, to pair up *or* off **2** *Élec & Tech* to couple **3** *Chasse* to leash together

couplet [kuplɛ] **NM 1** *(strophe)* verse; *(chanson)* song **2** *Péj (discours)* tirade; **il y est allé de son c. sur la jeunesse d'aujourd'hui** he gave his little set piece on the young people of today

coupleur [kuplœr] **NM 1** *Élec, Rail & Transp* coupler **2** *Aut* **c. hydraulique** fluid flywheel *or* coupling **3** *Ordinat* coupler; **c. acoustique** acoustic coupler

coupole [kupɔl] **NF 1** *Archit* dome; **petite c.** cupola; **la C.** *(Académie)* the "Académie française"; **être reçu sous la C.** to be made a member of the "Académie française" **2** *Mil* cupola

coupon [kupɔ̃] **NM 1** *(de tissu)* remnant

2 *(de papier)* coupon, voucher

3 *Fin (droit attaché à un titre)* coupon; **c. d'action** coupon; **c. attaché** cum dividend *or* coupon; **c. détaché** *ou* **échu** ex dividend *or* coupon

4 *Transp* **c. annuel/mensuel** yearly/monthly pass; *Belg* rail *or* train ticket

couponnage [kupɔnaʒ] **NM** *Mktg* couponing

coupon-réponse [kupɔ̃repɔ̃s] *(pl* **coupons-réponse)** **NM** reply coupon

coupure [kupyr] **NF 1** *(blessure)* cut; **se faire une c.** to cut oneself; **la c. est profonde** it's a deep cut, it's quite a gash

2 *(trêve, repos)* break; **une bonne c. dans la semaine** a good break during the week

3 *(rupture, changement)* break; **la Première Guerre mondiale marque une c. nette dans l'histoire du pays** the First World War represents a sharp break in the country's history

4 *Élec* **c. (de courant)** power cut, blackout; **il y a une c. de gaz/d'eau** the gas/the water has been cut off

5 *(suppression ▸ dans un texte)* deletion

6 *(article)* **c. de journal/presse** newspaper/press cutting

7 *Fin* note, *Am* bill; **grosses/petites coupures** large/small denominations; **2000 euros en petites coupures** 2,000 euros in small notes *or* denominations; **en coupures usagées** in used notes

8 *Typ* **c. automatique de fin de ligne** automatic line break *or* wrap; **c. de mots** word splits; **c. de page** page break

9 *Rad & TV* **c. publicitaire** commercial break

cour [kur] **NF 1** *(d'immeuble)* courtyard; *(de ferme)* yard, farmyard; **avec vue sur (la) c.** looking onto the inside of the building *or* onto the courtyard; **c. d'honneur** main courtyard; **c. intérieure** inner courtyard; *Scol* **c. de récréation** *Br* playground, *Am* schoolyard; *Fig* **jouer dans la c. des grands** to be up there with the leaders; *Hist* **c. des Miracles** = area in Paris where vagrants had the right of sanctuary; *Fig* **c'était la c. des Miracles dans la salle d'attente** the waiting room was full of sorry characters; *Fam* **n'en jetez plus, la c. est pleine!** please, no more!

2 *(d'un roi)* court; *Fig (admirateurs)* following, inner circle (of admirers); **vivre à la c.** to live at court; **être bien en c.** to be in favour; **être mal en c.** to be out of favour

3 *Jur (magistrats, tribunal)* court; **Messieurs, la C.!** all rise!, *Br* be upstanding in court!; **c. d'appel** court of appeal, *Am* court of appeals; **c. d'assises** *Br* ≃ Crown Court, *Am* ≃ Circuit Court; **C. de cassation** final Court of Appeal; **C. européenne des droits de l'homme** European Court of Human Rights; **C. internationale de justice** International Court of Justice; **C. de justice des Communautés européennes** Court of Justice of the European Communities; **c. martiale** court martial; **passer devant la c. martiale, passer en c. martiale** to be court-martialled; **c. pénale internationale** International Criminal Court; **c. de renvoi** = appellate court which can retry cases after a decision is quashed by the "Cour de Cassation"; *Can* **la C. suprême** the Supreme Court; **Haute c.** High Court *(for impeachment of president or ministers)*

4 *Admin* **C. des comptes** = the French audit office, *Br* ≃ controller and auditor general, *Am* ≃ General Accounting Office; *UE* **C. des comptes européenne** European Court of Auditors

5 *(locution)* **faire la c. à qn** *(chercher à séduire)* to court sb, to woo sb; *(flatter)* to curry favour with sb

courage [kuraʒ] **NM 1** *(bravoure)* courage, bravery; **avec c.** courageously, bravely; **je n'ai pas eu le c. de le lui dire** *(mauvaise nouvelle)* I didn't have the heart to tell him/her; **le c. me manqua** my courage failed me; **avoir le c. de ses opinions** to have the courage of one's convictions; **prendre son c. à deux mains** to muster all one's courage **2** *(énergie)* will, spirit; **travailler avec c.** to work with a will; **bon c.!** good luck!, hope it goes well!; *Ironique* good luck!; **c., la journée est bientôt finie** chin up *or* hang in there, the day's nearly over; **allez, c., les choses vont bien finir par s'arranger** don't worry, everything will be alright in the end; **un whisky pour te donner du c.** a whisky to buck you up; **prendre c.** to take heart; **perdre c.** to lose heart, to become discouraged; **je n'ai pas le c.** *ou* **je ne me sens pas le c. d'aller travailler** I don't feel up to going to work

courageuse [kuraʒøz] *voir* **courageux**

courageusement [kuraʒøzmɑ̃] **ADV 1** *(se battre, parler)* courageously, bravely **2** *(travailler)* with a will

courageux, -euse [kuraʒø, -øz] **ADJ 1** *(brave)* courageous, brave; **c. mais pas téméraire** brave but not reckless *or* foolhardy **2** *(énergique)* energetic; **il n'est pas très c. pour l'étude** he doesn't show much enthusiasm for studying; **je ne me sens pas très c. aujourd'hui** I don't feel up to much today

courailler [3] [kuraje] **VI** *Can Fam* to chase after women

courailleur [kurajœr] **NM** *Can Fam* womanizer

couramment [kuramɑ̃] **ADV 1** *(bien)* fluently; **elle parle danois c., elle parle c. le danois** she speaks Danish fluently *or* fluent Danish **2** *(souvent)* commonly; **objet employé c.** object in general use; **l'expression s'emploie c.** the expression is in common usage; **ça se dit c.** it's a common *or* an everyday expression; **cela se fait c.** it's common practice

courant[1] [kurɑ̃] **NM 1** *Élec* **c. (électrique)** (electric) current; **couper le c.** to cut the power off; **mettre le c.** to switch the power on; *Fam* **prendre le c.** to get a shock *or* an electric shock; **c. alternatif/continu** alternating/direct current; **le c. passe bien entre nous** we're on the same wavelength; **le c. passe bien entre lui et le public** he has a good rapport with the public

2 *(dans l'eau)* current, stream; **il y a trop de c.** the current is too strong; **suivre le c.** to go with the current; *Fig* to follow the crowd, to go with the tide; **remonter le c.** to swim against the current; *Fig* to go against the tide

3 *(dans l'air)* current; **c. (atmosphérique)** airstream, current; **c. d'air** draught; **il y a des courants d'air** it's draughty; *Hum* **se déguiser** *ou* **se transformer en c. d'air** to vanish into thin air

4 *(tendance)* current, trend; **les courants de l'opinion** currents *or* trends in public opinion; **un c. d'optimisme** a wave of optimism; **c. de pensée** way of thinking; **les différents courants de la gauche française** the various currents of the French left

5 *(masse mouvante)* movement, shift; **les courants de population** shifts of population

• **au courant ADJ** *(informé)* **personne/journal bien au c.** well-informed person/paper; **je n'en suis pas au c.** I don't know anything about it; **oui, je suis au c.** yes, I know; **tu veux dire que tu étais**

au c.? you mean you knew all about it? **ADV se tenir au c.** to keep abreast of things *or* oneself informed; **tiens-moi au c.** let me know how things are going; **mettre qn au c. (de qch)** to let sb know (about sth), to fill sb in (on sth); **tenir qn au c.** to keep sb up to date, to keep sb posted

• **au courant de** PRÉP *(informé de)* **tu es au c. de la panne?** do you know about the breakdown?; **je n'en suis pas au c.** I don't know anything about it; **être très au c. de ce qui se passe** to be very well-informed about what's happening; **on ne me tient jamais au c. de rien!** nobody ever tells me anything!; **il est très au c. des nouvelles méthodes** he is well up on new methods

• **dans le courant de** PRÉP in *or* during the course of

courant², -e [kurɑ̃, -ɑ̃t] **ADJ 1** *(quotidien ▸ vie, dépenses)* everyday; *(▸ travail)* everyday, routine; **en anglais c.** in everyday *or* conversational English

2 *(commun ▸ problème, maladie)* common; *(▸ incident)* everyday; **un mot d'usage c.** a word in current *or* common *or* general use, an everyday word

3 *(normal ▸ modèle, pointure)* standard

4 *(actuel)* current; **le mois c.** the current month; **votre lettre du 17 c.** your letter of the 17th of this month; **fin c.** at the end of this month

• **courante** **NF 1** *Fam (diarrhée)* **la courante** the runs **2** *(danse)* courante

> Il faut noter que l'adjectif anglais **current** est un faux ami. Il signifie **actuel**.

courbatu, -e [kurbaty] **ADJ** aching (and stiff)

courbature [kurbatyr] **NF** ache; **plein de courbatures** aching (and stiff) all over

courbaturé, -e [kurbatyre] **ADJ** aching (and stiff); **je me sens tout c.** I'm stiff *or* aching all over

courbe [kurb] **ADJ** curving, rounded, curved

NF 1 *Géom* curve, curved *or* rounded line; **la route fait des courbes** the road curves **2** *(sur un graphique)* curve; *(graphique)* graph; **tracer la c. de** to plot the curve of, to graph; **la c. d'apprentissage** the learning curve; **c. de croissance** growth curve; **c. de la demande** demand curve; **c. de l'offre** supply curve; **c. de popularité** popularity curve; **la c. des prix/des salaires** the price/salary curve; *Méd* **c. de température** temperature curve; **c. des ventes** sales chart **3** *Géog* **c. de niveau** contour line

courber [3] [kurbe] **VT 1** *(plier)* to bend; **arbre courbé par le poids des fruits** tree bending under *or* with the weight of the fruit **2** *(partie du corps)* **c. la tête** to bow *or* to bend one's head; **c. le front sur qch** to bend over sth; **marcher le dos courbé** to walk with a stoop; **c. l'échine** *ou* **le dos devant qn** to give in *or* to submit to sb **3** *Suisse Fam (cours)* to skip; **c. l'école** to skip school, *Br* to bunk off

VI c. sous le poids to bend beneath the weight

VPR se courber 1 *(ployer ▸ arbre, barre)* to bend **2** *(personne ▸ gén)* to bend down; *(▸ de vieillesse)* to stoop; *(▸ pour saluer)* to bow (down); **se c. en deux** to bend double; **se c. devant qch** *(par soumission)* to bow before sth, to submit to sth

courbette [kurbɛt] **NF 1** *(salut)* low bow; *Péj* **faire des courbettes à qn** to kowtow to sb, to bow and scrape to sb **2** *(d'un cheval)* curvet

courbure [kurbyr] **NF** *(d'une ligne, d'une surface, du dos)* curvature; *(d'une poutre)* sagging

courette [kurɛt] **NF** *(d'un immeuble)* small yard *or* courtyard, close; *(d'une ferme)* small yard *or* farmyard

coureur, -euse [kurœr, -øz] **ADJ 1** *(cheval)* racing **2** *Fam (séducteur)* **il est très c.** he's a womanizer *or* philanderer; **elle est très coureuse** she's always chasing men

NM,F 1 *Sport* runner; *(sauteur de haies)* hurdler; **c. automobile** racing driver; **c. cycliste** (racing) cyclist; **c. de fond/demi-fond** long-distance/middle-distance runner; **c. motocycliste** motorcycle *or Br* motorbike racer **2** *Fam (séducteur ▸ homme)* womanizer; *(▸ femme)* man-eater; **c. de jupons** womanizer, philanderer **3** *Can* **c. des bois** fur trader, trapper

courge [kurʒ] **NF 1** *Culin Br* (vegetable) marrow, *Am* squash; *(plante, fruit)* gourd, squash **2** *Fam (imbécile)* idiot, dope, twit

courgette [kurʒɛt] **NF** *Br* courgette, *Am* zucchini

COURIR [45] [kurir]

VI
- to run **1–3, 5, 6**
- to race **1, 2**
- to go round **4**

VT
- to run **1**
- to go round **3**
- to seek **4**

VI 1 *(gén)* to run; *(sportif, lévrier)* to run, to race; **entrer/sortir/traverser en courant** to run in/out/across; **monter/descendre l'escalier en courant** to run up/down the stairs; **partir en courant** to run off; **il arriva vers moi en courant** he ran up to me; **j'ai couru à fond de train** *ou* **à toutes jambes** I ran as fast as my legs could carry me; **il partit en courant à toutes jambes** he raced off; **c. ventre à terre** to run flat out; **c. tête baissée (vers)** to rush headlong (towards); **elle a fait c. son cheval dans le Grand Prix** she entered her horse in the Grand Prix; **il courra chez Renault l'année prochaine** he'll be driving for Renault next year; **c. comme le vent** to run like the wind; **l'assassin court toujours** the murderer is still on the run

2 *(se déplacer ▸ nuée)* to race along *or* by; *(▸ eau)* to rush, to run; **ses doigts couraient sur les touches** his/her fingers ran up and down the keyboard; **sa plume courait sur le papier** his/her pen was racing across the paper; **laisser c. sa plume** to let one's pen run freely; **des frissons couraient le long de son dos** shivers were running down his/her spine

3 *(se précipiter)* to rush, to run; **il est toujours en train de c. chez le médecin** he's always running to the doctor's; **cours acheter du pain** run out *or Br* nip out and get some bread; **j'ai couru le prévenir** I ran to warn him; **j'y cours** I'll rush over; **la pièce qui fait c. tout Paris** the play all Paris is flocking to see; *Fig* **qu'est-ce qui le fait c.?** what drives him?; **faire qch en courant** to do sth in a hurry; **j'ai couru toute la journée** I've been in a rush *or* I've been run off my feet all day

4 *(se propager ▸ rumeur, idée)* **un bruit qui court** a rumour that's going round; **faire c. des bruits sur qn** to spread rumours about sb; **le bruit court que...** rumour has it that...

5 *(temps)* to run; **l'année qui court** the current year; **la location court jusqu'au 25** it's rented until the 25th; **le bail n'a plus qu'un an à c.** the lease has only one more year to run; **par les temps qui courent** nowadays

6 *(s'étendre)* **c. le long de** *(rivière, voie ferrée)* to run *or* to stretch along; **le lierre court le long du mur** the ivy crawls *or* runs along the wall

7 *Fin (intérêt)* to accrue; **laisser c. des intérêts** to allow interest to accrue

8 *Naut* to sail; **c. au large** to stand out to sea; **c. à terre** to stand in for the land

9 *Fam (locutions)* **tu peux (toujours) c.!** no way!; **l'épouser? il peut toujours c.!** marry her? he doesn't have a hope in hell!; **laisse c.!** forget it!, drop it!; **c. sur le système** *ou* **le haricot à qn** *(l'énerver)* to get on sb's nerves *or Br* up sb's nose; **il commence à me c.!** he's beginning *Br* to get up my nose *or Am* to tick me off!

VT 1 *Sport (course)* to compete in, to run

2 *(sillonner ▸ ville, mers)* to roam, to rove; **c. le monde/la campagne** to roam the world/the countryside; *Fig* **c. les rues** to be run-of-the-mill *or* nothing unusual; **cela court les rues** *(idée, style)* it's run-of-the-mill; **quelqu'un comme ça, ça ne court pas les rues** people like that are hard to come by

3 *(fréquenter)* to go round; **elle court les musées** she's an inveterate museum-goer; **c. les filles/les garçons** to chase girls/boys; **c. le jupon** *ou* **le cotillon** to flirt with women, to womanize; *Hum & Vieilli* **c. la gueuse** *ou* **le guilledou** *ou* **la prétentaine** to chase women, to go wenching, to philander

4 *(rechercher ▸ honneurs, poste)* to seek; **acteur courant le cachet** actor desperate for work

5 *(encourir)* **c. un risque** to run a risk; **faire c. un risque** *ou* **danger à qn** to put sb at risk

6 *(tenter)* **c. sa chance** to try one's chance

7 *Chasse* to hunt; *Prov* **il ne faut pas c. deux lièvres à la fois** if you run after two hares you will catch neither

V IMPERSONNEL il court des bruits sur lui there are rumours going round about him

• **courir à** **VT IND** *(faillite, désastre)* to head for; **elle court à sa perte** she's heading for disaster, she's on the road to ruin

• **courir après** **VT IND 1** *(pour rattraper)* to run after **2** *Fam (rechercher)* **c. après qn** to chase *or* to run after sb; **il n'arrête pas de me c. après** he won't leave me alone, he's forever running after me; **c. après un poste** to be after a job; **c. après la célébrité** to strive for recognition; **elle ne court pas après l'argent** she's not after money; **il peut toujours c. après son argent!** he'll never see his money again!

• **courir sur** **VT IND** *(approcher de)* **c. sur ses 60 ans** to be approaching 60

VPR se courir le tiercé se court à Enghien aujourd'hui today's race is being run at Enghien

courlieu, -x [kurljø] **NM** *Orn* whimbrel

couronne [kurɔn] **NF 1** *(coiffure ▸ d'un souverain)* crown; *(▸ d'un pair)* coronet; *aussi Fig* **porter la c.** to wear the crown; **c. d'épines** crown of thorns; **c. de lauriers** crown of laurels, laurel wreath; **c. mortuaire** (funeral) wreath; **c. royale** royal crown

2 *Hist & Pol* **la C. d'Angleterre/de Belgique** the English/Belgian Crown; **prétendre à la C.** to lay claim to the throne; **les joyaux de la C.** the Crown jewels

3 *(cercle)* crown, circle; **une c. de nuages entourait la montagne** the mountain was surrounded by a ring of clouds

4 *(périphérie)* **la grande c.** = the area around Paris which takes in the "départements" of Seine-et-Marne, Yvelines, Essonne and Val-d'Oise; **la petite c.** = the suburbs adjacent to Paris in the "départements" of Seine-Saint-Denis, Val-de-Marne and Hauts-de-Seine

5 *(pain)* ring, ring-shaped loaf

6 *(prothèse dentaire)* crown; **se faire poser une c.** to have *or* to get a tooth crowned

7 *Aut* **c. dentée** crown wheel; **c. d'embrayage** clutch ring

8 *Archit, Astron & Bot* corona

9 *(monnaie)* crown; **c. danoise/norvégienne** krone; **c. suédoise** krona

10 *(d'un arbre)* crown

• **en couronne** **ADJ 1** *(en rond)* **fleurs en c.** wreath of flowers; **nattes en c.** plaits (worn) in a crown **2** *Culin* in a ring

couronné, -e [kurɔne] **ADJ** *(souverain)* crowned; **toutes les têtes couronnées d'Europe y assistaient** all the crowned heads of Europe were present

couronnement [kurɔnmɑ̃] **NM 1** *(cérémonie)* coronation, crowning

2 *(réussite)* crowning achievement

3 *(récompense)* **cette année a vu le c. de ses efforts** this year his/her efforts were finally rewarded

4 *(de jetée)* capping; *(de bâtiment, de colonne)* top; *(de mur)* coping; *(de toit)* ridge

couronner [3] [kurɔne] **VT 1** *(roi)* to crown; *Antiq & Hist (orateur, soldat)* to crown with a laurel wreath; **elle fut couronnée reine/impératrice** she was crowned queen/empress

2 *(entourer, couvrir)* **des pics couronnés de neige** snow-capped peaks

3 *(récompenser ▸ poète, chercheur)* to award a prize to; *(▸ œuvre, roman)* to award a prize for

4 *(conclure ▸ carrière, recherches, vie)* to crown; **sa nomination vient c. sa carrière** his/her nomination is the crowning achievement of his/her career; *Fam* **et pour c. le tout** and to crown it all, and on top of all that

5 *(dent)* to crown

VPR se couronner *(cheval)* to break its knee; *Fam* **se c. les genoux** to graze one's knees

courrai *etc voir* **courir**

course [kur] *voir* **chasse**

courriel [kurjɛl] **NM** *Ordinat (abrév* **courrier électronique)** e-mail

courrier [kurje] **NM 1** *(correspondance)* mail, letters, *Br* post; **j'ai beaucoup de c. en retard** I've got a lot of letters to write; **faire son c.** to write one's letters; **le c. est-il arrivé?** has the *Br* postman *or Am* mailman been yet?; **avec la grève, il y a du retard dans le c.** with the strike, there are delays in mail deliveries; **c. interne** internal mail

2 *(lettre)* **un c.** a letter; **en réponse à votre c. du** in answer to your letter of

3 *Admin & Pol (messager)* courier

4 *(chronique)* column; **c. du cœur** problem page, *Br* agony column, *Am* advice column; **c. des lecteurs** letters (to the editor)

5 *Ordinat* **c. électronique** e-mail; **envoyer un c. électronique à qn** to e-mail sb; **envoyer qch par c. électronique** to send sth by e-mail; *Fam* **c. escargot** snail mail

6 *Transp* mail; *Hist (homme)* messenger

courriériste [kurjerist] NMF columnist

courroie [kurwa] NF **1** *(gén)* belt strap **2** *Tech* belt; **c. de transmission** driving belt; *Aut* **c. de ventilateur** fan belt; *Aut* **c. d'entraînement** *ou* **de commande** drive belt

courroucé, -e [kuruse] ADJ *Littéraire* wrathful

courroucer [16] [kuruse] *Littéraire* VT to anger, to infuriate

VPR **se courroucer** to become infuriated

courroux [kuru] NM *Littéraire* anger, ire, wrath

COURS [kur]

• course **A1–3, C1, 2**	• rate **B1, 2**
• price **B2**	• class **C1, 3**
• lesson **C1**	• coursebook **C2**

NM **A.** *ÉCOULEMENT, SUCCESSION* **1** *Géog (débit)* flow; *(parcours)* course; **avoir un c. lent** to be slow-flowing; **avoir un c. rapide** to be fast-flowing; **descendre le c. de la Tamise** to go down the Thames; **dévier le c. d'une rivière** to divert the course of a river; **c. d'eau** *(gén)* waterway; *(ruisseau)* stream; *(rivière)* river; **au long c.** *(voyage)* long-haul; *Naut* **navigation au long c.** deep-sea navigation

2 *(déroulement ▸ des années, des saisons, de pensées)* course; *(▸ d'événements)* course, run; *(▸ de négociations, d'une maladie, de travaux)* course, progress; **donner** *ou* **laisser (libre) c. à** *(joie, indignation)* to give vent to; *(imagination, chagrin)* to give free rein to; **suivre le c. de ses idées** to follow one's train of thought; **suivre son c.** *(processus)* to continue; **ils ont voulu changer le c. de l'Histoire** they wanted to change the course of history; **la vie reprend son c.** life goes on

3 *Astron* course

4 *(dans des noms de rue)* avenue

B. *DANS LE DOMAINE FINANCIER* **1** *(de devises)* rate; **avoir c.** *(monnaie)* to be legal tender *or* legal currency; *(pratique)* to be common *or* current; **avoir c. légal** to be legal tender *or* legal currency; **ne plus avoir c.** *(monnaie)* to be out of circulation, to be no longer legal tender *or* legal currency; *(pratique, théorie)* to be obsolete; *(expression, terme)* to be obsolete *or* no longer in use; **c. du change** exchange rate; **c. des devises** foreign exchange rate

2 *Bourse (d'actions)* price, trading rate; **au c. du marché** at the market *or* trading price; **au c. (du jour)** at the today's rate, at the current daily price; **quel est le c. du sucre?** what is the price *or* quotation for sugar?; **le c. d'ouverture/de clôture de ces actions était de 3 euros** these shares opened/closed at 3 euros; **c. des actions** share prices; **c. en Bourse** official price; **les cours de la Bourse** Stock Exchange prices; **c. de clôture** closing price; **c. hors Bourse, c. hors cote** unofficial price; **c. légal** legal tender; **c. du marché** market price *or* rate; **c. officiel** official exchange rate; **c. d'ouverture** opening price

C. *DANS LE DOMAINE SCOLAIRE ET UNIVERSITAIRE* **1** *(classe) Scol* class, lesson; *Univ* class, lecture; *(ensemble des leçons)* course; **des heures de c.** teaching hours; **aller en c.** *(à un cours)* to go to one's class; *(à l'école)* to go to school; *(à l'université)* to attend lectures; **être en c.** to be in class; **suivre des c.** to attend *or* take a course; **suivre un c.** *ou* **des c. d'espagnol** to go to *or* to attend a Spanish class; **prendre des c.** to take lessons *or* a course; **j'ai c. tout à l'heure** *(élève, professeur)* I have a class later; **j'ai c. tous les jours** *(élève, professeur)* I have classes every day; **faire** *ou* **donner un c. d'histoire** to give a history lecture/lesson/course; **c'est moi qui vous ferai c. cette année** I'll be teaching you this year; **les professeurs ne font pas c. cet après-midi** there are no lessons this afternoon; **tu ne vas pas me faire un c. sur la politesse?** are you going to give me a lecture on how to be polite?; **c. par correspondance** correspondence *or* distance learning course; **c. magistral** lecture; **donner/prendre des c. particuliers** to give/to have private tuition; **je prends des c. particuliers de français** I get *or* have private tuition in French; **c. de perfectionnement** proficiency course; **c. du soir** evening class

2 *(manuel)* course, coursebook, textbook; *(notes)* notes

3 *(degré ▸ dans l'enseignement primaire)* **c. préparatoire** *Br* ≃ first-year infants class, *Am* ≃ nursery school; **c. élémentaire** = two-year subdivision of primary-level education in France (ages 8 to 9); **c. élémentaire 1** = second year of primary school, *Br* ≃ year 3; **c. élémentaire 2** = third year of primary school, *Br* ≃ year 4; **c. moyen** = two-year subdivision of primary-level education in France (ages 10 to 11); **c. moyen 1** = fourth year of primary school, *Br* ≃ year 5; **c. moyen 2** = fifth year of primary school, *Br* ≃ year 6

4 *(établissement)* school; **c. privé** private school

• **au cours de** PRÉP during, in *or* during the course of; **au c. du débat** in the course of *or* during the debate; **au c. des siècles** over the centuries; **au c. de notre dernier entretien** when we last spoke; **au c. des prochaines semaines** in the weeks to come

• **en cours** ADJ *(actuel)* **l'année/le tarif en c.** the current year/price; **affaire/travail en c.** business/work in hand; **être en c.** *(débat, réunion, travaux)* to be under way, to be in progress; **une enquête est en c.** investigations are taking place

• **en cours de** PRÉP in the process of; **c'est en c. d'étude** it's being examined; **en c. de construction** under construction, in the process of being built; **en c. d'investigation** being investigated, under investigation; **en c. de production** in production; **en c. de réparation** in the process of being repaired, undergoing repairs; **en c. de route** on the way

course [kurs] NF **1 faire la c.** to race; **on fait la c. jusqu'à la cabane!** race you *or* last (one) to the hut!; **faire la c. avec qn** to race (with) sb; *Fig* **c'est toujours la c. au bureau** we're always run off our feet at the office; **c. attelée/handicap** harness/handicap race; **c. de fond** *ou* **d'endurance** long-distance race; **c. automobile** motor *or* car race; **c. de chevaux** (horse) race; **c. à la cocarde** = traditional sport in Southern France in which rosettes are snatched from the horns of young cattle; **c. cycliste** cycle race; **c. de demi-fond** middle-distance race; *Équitation* **c. d'obstacles** steeplechase; **c. d'orientation** orienteering; **c. à pied** race; **c. de plat** flat race; **c. de relais** relay race; **c. en sac** sack race; **c. de taureaux** *(corrida)* bullfight; *(dans les rues)* bull-running; **c. de vaches landaises, c. de vachettes, c. landaise** = bullfight with young cows; **c. de vitesse** *Br* sprint, *Am* dash; **c. contre la montre** race against the clock, time-trial; *Fig* race against time; *Fam Fig* **rester dans la c.** to stay in *or* to be still in the race; **l'entreprise essaie de rester dans la c.** the company's trying to keep up with the competitors

2 *(activité, action)* **épuisé par sa c.** exhausted from his/her running; **la c.** *(à pied)* running; *(en voiture, à cheval)* racing; **je fais de la c. à pied tous les jours** I run every day; **la c. aux armements** the arms race; **la c. au pouvoir/à la présidence** the race for power/the presidency; *TV* **la c. à l'audimat** *ou* **à l'audience** the ratings war

3 *(randonnée)* **faire une c. en montagne** to go for a trek in the mountains

4 *(d'un taxi ▸ voyage)* journey; *(▸ prix)* fare; **payer (le prix de) la c.** to pay the fare

5 *(commission)* errand; **j'ai une c. à faire** I've got to buy something *or* to get something from the shops

6 *(trajectoire ▸ d'un astre, d'un pendule)* course, trajectory; *(▸ d'un missile)* flight; *(▸ d'un piston)* stroke

7 *Suisse (trajet)* trip *(by train or boat)*; *(excursion)* excursion

8 *Hist (d'un navire corsaire)* privateering

• **courses** NFPL **1** *(commissions)* shopping; **faire les/des courses** to do the/some shopping; **il est parti faire quelques courses** he went out to do a bit of shopping; **la liste des courses** the shopping list **2** *(de chevaux)* races; **jouer aux courses** to bet on the races *or* on the horses; **il a gagné 3000 euros aux courses** he won 3,000 euros on the races

courser [3] [kurse] VT *Fam* to chaseᵒ, to run afterᵒ; **il s'est fait c. par des voyous** he was chased by some thugs

coursier, -ère [kursje, -er] NM,F messenger, courier; *(à moto)* dispatch rider

NM *Littéraire (cheval)* steed

coursive [kursiv] NF **1** *Naut* gangway **2** *Constr* (raised) passageway

COURT, -E [kur, kurt]

ADJ	
• short **A1–3, B1, 2**	• small **C1**
• slender **C3**	
ADV	
• short **1–3**	
NM	
• court **1**	

ADJ **A.** *DANS L'ESPACE* **1** *(en longueur ▸ cheveux, ongles)* short; **il a les jambes courtes** he's got short legs; *Fam* **c. sur pattes** *(chien)* short-legged; *(personne)* short; **à manches courtes** short-sleeved, with short sleeves; **la jupe est trop courte de 3 centimètres** the skirt is 3 centimetres too short; **quel est le chemin le plus c. de Sens à Troyes?** what's the shortest route between Sens and Troyes?, what's the quickest way to get from Sens to Troyes?; **il y a un chemin plus c.** there's a shorter *or* quicker way

2 *Anat (os, muscle)* short

3 *Rad (ondes)* short

B. *DANS LE TEMPS* **1** *(bref ▸ discours, lettre, séjour, durée etc)* short, brief; **les jours sont de plus en plus courts** the days are getting shorter (and shorter) *or* are drawing in; **pendant un c. instant** for a brief *or* fleeting moment; **mon séjour a été plus c. que prévu** my stay was shorter than planned

2 *(proche)* **à c. terme** short-term *(avant n)*; **dette/emprunt à c. terme** short-term debt/loan; **j'ai des projets à c. terme** I have some plans in *or* for the short term

C. *FAIBLE, INSUFFISANT* **1** *(faible ▸ avance, avantage)* small; *(▸ majorité)* small, slender; **après sa courte victoire sur son compatriote** after a narrow victory over his fellow countryman; **il a mené la course sur une courte distance** he led the race over a short distance; **au virage, il avait une courte avance sur le peloton** in the bend, he was leading the bunch by a short distance; **gagner d'une courte tête** to win by a short head

2 *(restreint)* **avoir la respiration courte** *ou* **le souffle c.** to be short of breath *or* wind

3 *Fam (insuffisant ▸ connaissances)* slenderᵒ, limitedᵒ; *(▸ quantité, mesure)* meagreᵒ, skimpy; **10 sur 20, c'est un peu c.** 10 out of 20, it's a bit borderline; **deux bouteilles pour six, c'est un peu c.** two bottles for six people, that's a bit on the stingy side; **1500 euros pour refaire le toit, l'estimation me semble courte** 1,500 euros to redo the roof, the estimate seems on the low side to me; **l'avion décolle dans 30 minutes – c'est trop c. pour l'avoir** the plane takes off in 30 minutes – we won't make it in timeᵒ; **sa rubrique est amusante mais les idées sont courtes** his/her column is entertaining but short on ideas; **avoir la mémoire courte** to have a short memory

4 *(sans arguments)* **demeurer** *ou* **rester c.** to be at a loss

ADV **1** *(en dimension)* **je me suis fait couper les cheveux c.** I had my hair cut short; **des cheveux coupés** *ou* **taillés très c.** hair cut very short; **elle s'habille c.** she wears her skirts short

2 *Fam (en durée)* **pour faire c.** to cut a long story short

3 *(brusquement)* **s'arrêter c.** to stop short; **tourner c.** *(discussion, projet)* to come to an abrupt end

NM **1** *(terrain)* **c. (de tennis)** tennis court; **c. en gazon** grass court; **c. en terre battue** clay court

2 *Couture* **le c.** short fashions *or* hemlines *or* styles

3 *(locutions)* **aller au plus c.** to take the quickest course of action; **allons au plus c., qui a pris l'argent?** let's not beat about the bush, who took the money?

• **à court** ADV *Fam* short on cash, hard-up, a bit short
• **à court de** PRÉP **être à c. d'idées/de vivres** to have run out of ideas/food; **nous étions presque à c. d'eau** we were low on *or* running short of water; **être à c. d'argent** to be short of money; **à c. de personnel** short-staffed; **elle n'est jamais à c. d'arguments** she's never at a loss for an argument; *Belg* **être à c. d'haleine** to be out of breath
• **de court** ADV **prendre qn de c.** *(ne pas lui laisser de délai de réflexion)* to give sb (very) short notice; *(le surprendre)* to catch sb unawares *or* napping
• **tout court** ADV **appelez-moi Jeanne, tout c.** just call me Jeanne; **cela indigne les chrétiens démocrates et même les chrétiens tout c.** this is shocking to Christian Democrats and even to Christians *Br* full stop *or Am* period

courtage [kurtaʒ] NM *(profession)* brokerage; *(commission)* brokerage, commission; **vente par c.** selling on commission; **c. électronique** e-broking, on-line broking

courtaud, -e [kurto, -od] ADJ **1** *(personne)* short-legged, squat, dumpy **2** *Vét* docked and cropeared

court-bouillon [kurbujɔ̃] *(pl* **courts-bouillons***)* NM *Culin* court-bouillon; **faire cuire au** *ou* **dans un c.** to cook in a court-bouillon

court-circuit [kursirkɥi] *(pl* **courts-circuits***)* NM *Élec* short circuit; **faire c.** to short-circuit

court-circuitage [kursirkɥitaʒ] *(pl* **courts-circuitages***)* NM *Élec* short-circuiting

court-circuiter [3] [kursirkɥite] VT **1** *Élec* to short, to short-circuit **2** *Fam (assemblée, personnel)* to bypass

court-courrier [kurkurje] *(pl* **court-courriers***)* NM short-haul plane

courtepointe [kurtəpwɛ̃t] NF (quilted) bedspread, counterpane

courtier, -ère [kurtje, -ɛr] NM,F **1** *Bourse* broker; **c. de Bourse** stockbroker; **c. de change** exchange broker; **c. en valeurs mobilières** stockbroker **2** *Com* **c. en assurances** insurance broker; **c. maritime** ship *or* shipping broker; **c. en vins** wine broker

courtine [kurtin] NF curtain

courtisan [kurtizɑ̃] NM **1** *Hist* courtier **2** *(flatteur)* flatterer, sycophant

courtisane [kurtizan] NF *Littéraire* courtesan

courtiser [3] [kurtize] VT **1** *(femme)* to court, to woo, to pay court to **2** *(pays, puissants)* to woo; **c. le pouvoir/la gloire** to woo power/fame; **il le courtisait servilement** he fawned on him obsequiously

court-jus [kurʒy] *(pl* **courts-jus***)* NM *Fam Élec* short

court-métrage [kurmetraʒ] *(pl* **courts-métrages***)* NM short film, short

courtois, -e [kurtwa, -az] ADJ **1** *(poli ▸ personne, manières)* civil, courteous; **un homme c.** a courteous man; **d'un ton c.** civilly, courteously; **être c. envers qn** to be courteous *or* civil towards sb **2** *Hist & Littérature (roman, poésie, littérature)* about courtly love; **amour c.** courtly love

courtoisement [kurtwazmɑ̃] ADV courteously

courtoisie [kurtwazi] NF courtesy, courteousness; **avec c.** courteously

court-vêtu, -e [kurvety] *(mpl* **court-vêtus**, *fpl* **court-vêtues***)* ADJ **des femmes court-vêtues** women in short skirts

couru, -e [kury] PP *voir* **courir**
ADJ **1** *(populaire)* fashionable, popular; **les bars les plus courus** the most fashionable bars **2** *Fam (certain)* **c'est c. (d'avance)!** it's a sure thing!, *Br* it's a (dead) cert!; **c'était c.!** it was bound to happen!, it was a foregone conclusion!

cousait *etc voir* **coudre**

couscous [kuskus] NM *Culin* couscous

couscoussier [kuskusje] NM couscoussier, couscous steamer

cousin, -e [kuzɛ̃, -in] NM,F cousin; **c. germain** first *or* full cousin; **petit c., c. au second degré** second cousin; *Hum* **c. éloigné** *ou* **à la mode de Bretagne** distant relation
NM *Entom* (big) mosquito

cousinage [kuzinaʒ] NM *Vieilli* **1** *(parenté)* cousinhood **2** *(cousins)* **son c.** his/her kith and kin, his/her kinsfolk *or Am* kinfolk

cousine [kuzin] *voir* **cousin**

cousiner [3] [kuzine] VI **c. (avec qn)** to be on friendly terms (with sb)

coussin [kusɛ̃] NM **1** *(de siège, de meuble)* cushion; *Belg & Suisse (oreiller)* pillow **2** *Tech* **c. d'air** air cushion; **c. gonflable** Airbag

coussinet [kusinɛ] NM **1** *(petit coussin)* small cushion
2 *Zool* **c. plantaire** pad
3 *Tech* bearing; *Rail* chair; **c. de bielle** big end bearing; **c. de palier** bearing bush
4 *Archit* coussinet, cushion

cousu, -e [kuzy] PP *voir* **coudre**

coût [ku] NM **1** *(prix)* cost, price; **c. d'acquisition** acquisition cost; **coûts administratifs** administrative costs; **c. du crédit** credit charges *or* cost; **c. (total) de distribution** (total) distribution cost; **c. d'entretien** maintenance cost; **coûts d'exploitation** operational costs; **c. de fonctionnement** operating *or* running cost; **coûts indirects** indirect costs; **c. de la main-d'œuvre** labour costs; **coûts opérationnels** operational costs; **coûts prévisionnels** estimated costs; **c. de production** production cost; **c. réel** real cost; **c. de revient** cost price; **c. salarial** labour cost; **le c. de la vie** the cost of living **2** *Fig* cost; **le c. social de la privatisation** the social cost of privatization

coûtant [kutɑ̃] ADJ M cost *(avant n)*; **au** *ou* **à prix c.** at cost price

couteau, -x [kuto] NM **1** *(à main)* knife; *(d'une machine, d'un mixer)* blade; **il a ouvert le paquet avec un c.** he cut the parcel open with a knife; **il joue facilement du** *ou* **manie facilement le c.** he's quick with the knife; **coup de c.** stab (with a knife); **donner un coup de c. à qn** to stab sb (with a knife); *Fam* **prendre** *ou* **recevoir un coup de c.** to be knifed, to get stabbed; **ils l'ont tué à coups de c.** they stabbed *or* knifed him to death; *Fig* **enfoncer le c. dans la plaie** to dig the knife in; *Fig* **remuer** *ou* **retourner le c. dans la plaie** to twist the knife in the wound; *Fig* **mettre le c. sous** *ou* **sur la gorge à qn** to hold a gun to sb's head, to point a gun at sb's head; *Fig* **avoir le c. sous la gorge** to have a gun pointed at one's head; **jouer les seconds couteaux (dans une affaire)** to play a secondary role in a business, to play second fiddle; **être à couteaux tirés avec qn** to be at daggers drawn with sb; **c. à beurre/pain** butter/bread knife; **c. de chasse** hunting knife; **c. à cran d'arrêt** *Br* flick-knife, *Am* switchblade; **c. de cuisine/de table** kitchen/table knife; **c. à découper** carving knife; **c. à désosser** boning knife; **c. économe** *ou* **éplucheur** *ou* **à éplucher** potato peeler; **c. électrique** electric carving knife; **c. à fromage** cheese knife; **c. à mastiquer** *ou* **mastic** putty knife; **c. pliant** *ou* **de poche** pocket knife; **c. suisse** Swiss army knife; **c. à viande** carving knife
2 *(d'une balance)* knife edge
3 *Beaux-Arts* palette knife; **peinture au c.** knife painting
4 *Zool (mollusque)* razor *Br* shell *or Am* clam

couteau-scie [kutosi] *(pl* **couteaux-scies***)* NM serrated-edge knife

coutelas [kutla] NM **1** *(de cuisine)* large kitchen knife **2** *(sabre)* cutlass

coutelier, -ère [kutəlje, -ɛr] NM,F cutler, cutlery specialist

coutellerie [kutɛlri] NF **1** *(ustensiles)* cutlery
2 *(lieu de fabrication)* cutlery works
3 *(lieu de vente)* kitchenware *Br* shop *or Am* store *(specializing in cutlery)*
4 *(industrie)* cutlery industry

coûter [3] [kute] VT **1** *(somme)* to cost; *Fam* **combien ça coûte?** how much is it?, how much does it cost?; **cela coûte 100 euros** it costs 100 euros; **cela m'a coûté 20 euros** it cost me 20 euros; **je veux cette maison, ça coûtera ce que ça coûtera** I want that house no matter how much it costs; *Fam* **c. la peau des fesses** *ou* **une fortune** *ou* **les yeux de la tête** *ou Can* **un bras** to cost a fortune *or* the earth *or* an arm and a leg; **c. cher** *(produit, service)* to be expensive, to cost a lot of money; *Fig* **ça va lui c. cher!** he/she's going to pay for this!; **cela ne coûte pas cher** it's cheap *or* inexpensive
2 *(exiger ▸ efforts)* to cost; **ça ne coûte rien d'essayer** there's no harm in trying; **ça ne coûte rien d'être aimable!** it doesn't cost anything to be kind!; **ça te coûterait beaucoup d'être poli/de me répondre?** would it be asking too much for you to be polite/to answer me?; **cette démarche lui a beaucoup coûté** it was a very difficult *or* painful step for him/her to take; **ça me coûte de la quitter** it pains me to leave her; **tu peux bien l'aider, pour ce que ça te coûte!** it wouldn't be any trouble for you to help him/her!; **il m'en coûte de le dire** it pains me to have to say this
3 *(provoquer ▸ larmes)* to cost, to cause; **les nuits blanches que son roman lui a coûtées** the sleepless nights his/her novel cost him/her
4 *(entraîner la perte de ▸ carrière, membre, vote)* to cost; **ça a failli lui c. la vie** it nearly cost him/her his/her life; **un accident qui a coûté la vie à dix personnes** an accident which claimed the lives of ten people
USAGE ABSOLU *Fam* **une voiture, ça coûte!** a car is an expensive thing!
• **coûte que coûte** ADV at all costs, whatever the cost, no matter what

coûteuse [kutøz] *voir* **coûteux**

coûteusement [kutøzmɑ̃] ADV expensively

coûteux, -euse [kutø, -øz] ADJ **1** *(onéreux)* expensive, costly; **peu c.** cheap; **une guerre coûteuse en vies humaines** a war costing many human lives *or* with a high cost in human lives
2 *(lourd de conséquences)* costly; **il a pris une décision coûteuse pour son avenir** he made a decision which was to cost him dear

coutil [kuti] NM *(toile ▸ gén)* drill; *(▸ pour literie)* ticking

coutre [kutr] NM *(de charrue)* coulter

coutume [kutym] NF **1** *(tradition)* custom; **c'est une c. bretonne** it's a Breton custom; **comme c'est la c. en Alsace** as is the custom *or* is customary in Alsace; **d'après** *ou* **selon la c.** as custom dictates; **selon une c. ancienne** according to an age-old tradition **2** *(habitude, manie)* habit, custom; **selon** *ou* **comme c'était ma c.** as was my habit *or Littéraire* wont; **avoir (pour) c. de faire** to be in the habit of *or* accustomed to doing; **elle n'a pas c. de partir sans prévenir** she doesn't usually leave without warning; **comme de c.** as usual; **il pleuvait, comme de c.** as usual, it was raining; **plus que de c.** more than usual; **plus aimable que de c.** nicer than usual **3** *Jur* customary

coutumier, -ère [kutymje, -ɛr] ADJ **1** *(habituel)* customary, usual **2** *(habitué à)* **il ne m'a pas rendu toute ma monnaie – il est c. du fait!** he short-changed me – that wouldn't be the first time *or* that's one of his usual tricks!
NM *Jur* customary

couture [kutyr] NF **1** *(action de coudre, passe-temps)* **la c.** sewing; **elle fait de la c. dans le jardin** she's sewing in the garden; **la c. (artisanale)** dressmaking; **la haute c.** (haute) couture, fashion design
2 *(suite de points)* seam; **sans c.** seamless; **faire une c. à qch** to seam sth; **c. anglaise** French seam; **c. apparente** *ou* **sellier** top stitching, overstitching; **c. plate** *ou* **rabattue** flat seam
3 *(cicatrice)* scar; *(points de suture)* stitches
4 *(d'un moulage, d'une sculpture)* seam
ADJ INV designer *(avant n)*
• **à coutures** ADJ *(bas, collant)* seamed, with seams
• **à plate couture, à plates coutures** ADV *voir* **battre**
• **sans coutures** ADJ *(bas, collant)* seamless
• **sous toutes les coutures** ADV *(examiner)* from every angle, very closely, under a microscope

couturé, -e [kutyre] ADJ *(visage, joues)* scarred

couturier, -ère [kutyrje, -ɛr] NM **1** *(de haute couture)* **(grand) c.** fashion designer **2** *Anat* **grand c.** tailor's muscle *or Spéc* sartorius
• **couturière** NF **1** *(fabricant ▸ de robes)* dressmaker; *(en atelier)* dressmaker, seamstress **2** *Théât* = rehearsal preceding the final dress rehearsal, enabling last-minute alterations to costumes

couvain [kuvɛ̃] NM *(amas)* nest of insect eggs; *(rayon)* brood comb

couvaison [kuvezɔ̃] **NF 1** *(période)* incubation **2** *(action)* brooding

couvée [kuve] **NF 1** *(œufs)* clutch **2** *(oisillons)* brood, clutch; *Fig* **la nouvelle c. de jeunes cinéastes** the new generation *or* breed of young film-makers **3** *Fam (famille)* **sa c.** his/her brood

couvent [kuvɑ̃] **NM 1** *(de religieuses)* convent; *(de religieux)* monastery; **entrer au c.** to enter a convent **2** *(pensionnat)* convent school

couventine [kuvɑ̃tin] **NF** *(religieuse)* conventual; *(pensionnaire)* convent schoolgirl

couver [3] [kuve] **VT 1** *(sujet: oiseau)* to sit on; *(sujet: incubateur)* to hatch, to incubate

2 *(protéger ▸ enfant)* to overprotect; **c. des yeux** *ou* **du regard** *(personne aimée)* to gaze fondly at; *(friandise, bijou)* to look longingly at

3 *(maladie)* to be coming down with; **je crois que je couve quelque chose** I can feel something coming on, I think I'm coming down with something

4 *Littéraire (vengeance, revanche)* to plot

USAGE ABSOLU *(oiseau)* to brood, to sit on its eggs

VI 1 *(feu)* to smoulder **2** *(rébellion)* to be brewing (up); *(sentiment)* to smoulder; **la haine qui couvait en elle** the hatred that was smouldering inside her; **la révolte couvait chez les paysans** a peasant revolt was brewing (up); **c. sous la cendre** to be brewing (up), to bubble under the surface

couvercle [kuvɛrkl] **NM 1** *(qui se pose, s'enfonce)* lid, cover; *(qui se visse)* top, screw-top, cap **2** *Aut (de piston)* cover

couvert[1] [kuvɛr] **NM 1** *(cuillère, fourchette, couteau)* knife, fork and spoon; *(avec assiette et verre)* place setting; **des couverts en argent** silver cutlery; **couverts à salade** salad servers; **mettre le c.** to lay *or* to set the table; **j'ai mis trois couverts** I've laid three places *or* the table for three; **tu auras toujours ton c. chez moi** there'll always be a place for you at my table; *Fam Fig* **remettre le c.** *(faire quelque chose à nouveau)* to do it again; *(faire l'amour à nouveau)* to be at it again **2** *(prix d'une place au restaurant)* cover charge

couvert[2], **-e**[1] [kuvɛr, -ɛrt] **PP** *voir* **couvrir**

ADJ 1 *(abrité ▸ allée, halle, marché)* covered; *(▸ piscine, terrain de sports)* indoor *(avant n)* **2** *(vêtu ▸ chaudement)* warmly dressed, (well) wrapped-up *or* muffled-up; *(▸ décemment)* covered (up); **j'aime avoir les jambes couvertes** I like my legs to be covered up; **rester c.** *(garder son chapeau)* to keep one's hat on **3** *Météo (temps)* dull, overcast; *(ciel)* overcast, clouded-over; **attendez-vous à un après-midi c.** expect a cloudy afternoon

NM *Littéraire* leafy canopy

• **à couvert ADV être à c.** *(de projectiles)* to be under cover; *(de critiques, de soupçons)* to be safe; **se mettre à c.** *(de projectiles)* to get under *or* to take cover; *(de critiques, de soupçons)* to cover *or* to safeguard oneself; *Fin* **être à c.** *(pour un crédit)* to be covered

• **à couvert de PRÉP** protected against; **se mettre à c. de la pluie** to shelter from the rain

• **sous couvert de PRÉP** in the guise of; **sous le c. de l'amitié** under the cover *or* cloak *or* pretence of friendship

• **sous le couvert de PRÉP 1** *(sous l'apparence de)* in the guise of **2** *(sous la responsabilité de)* **il l'a fait sous le c. de son chef** he did it using his boss as a shield **3** *Littéraire (à l'abri de)* **sous le c. d'un bois** in the shelter of a wood

couverte[2] [kuvɛrt] **NF 1** *Cér* glaze; **peinture sous c.** underglaze painting **2** *(dans la fabrication du papier)* deckle frame

couverture [kuvɛrtyr] **NF 1** *(morceau de tissu)* blanket, cover; **sous les couvertures** under the blankets *or* covers; **c. chauffante** electric blanket; **c. de survie** space *or* survival blanket; *Fig* **amener** *ou* **tirer la c. à soi** *(après un succès)* to take all the credit; *(dans une transaction)* to get the best of the deal

2 *Constr (activité)* roofing; *(ouvrage)* (type of) roof

3 *Journ (activité)* coverage; *(page)* cover, front page; **assurer** *ou* **faire la c. d'un événement** to give coverage of *or* to cover an event; **c. médiatique** media coverage, media exposure

4 *(d'un livre)* cover; **première de c.** front cover; **deuxième de c.** inside front cover; **troisième de c.** inside back cover; **quatrième de c.** back cover; **c. cartonnée** case

5 *Com* coverage, exposure; **c. du marché** sales coverage

6 *(d'un besoin)* covering, catering for; **la c. des besoins en électricité n'est pas assurée** the electricity needed is not being provided

7 *(prétexte)* disguise, façade; **le financier/la société qui leur servait de c.** the financier/company they used as a front

8 *Mil* cover; **c. aérienne** air cover

9 *(d'une police d'assurance)* cover; **c. maladie universelle** = free health care for people on low incomes who have no Social Security cover; **c. santé** health cover; **c. sociale** Social Security cover; **avoir une c. sociale** to belong to a benefit scheme

10 *Fin* cover; *Bourse* margin, hedge; **opérer avec c.** to hedge

11 *Météo* **c. neigeuse** snow cover

• **de couverture ADJ** *Mil & Journ* cover *(avant n)*

couveuse [kuvøz] **NF 1** *(machine)* **c. (artificielle)** incubator; **il a été mis en c.** he was put in an incubator **2** *(oiseau)* brooder, sitter

couvrant, -e [kuvrɑ̃, -ɑ̃t] **ADJ** *(peinture, vernis)* that covers well

• **couvrante NF** *Fam* blanket[□]

couvre-chef [kuvrəʃɛf] *(pl* **couvre-chefs**) **NM** *Hum* hat[□], headgear[□]

couvre-feu [kuvrəfø] *(pl* **couvre-feux**) **NM** curfew

couvre-lit [kuvrəli] *(pl* **couvre-lits**) **NM** bedspread

couvre-livre [kuvrəlivr] *(pl* **couvre-livres**) **NM** dust jacket

couvre-nuque [kuvrənyk] *(pl* **couvre-nuques**) **NM 1** *(de casquette)* flap *(to protect back of neck from sun)* **2** *(de casque)* neck protector

couvre-pied, couvre-pieds [kuvrəpje] *(pl* **couvre-pieds**) **NM** quilt

couvre-plat [kuvrəpla] *(pl* **couvre-plats**) **NM** dish cover

couvreur [kuvrœr] **NM** roofer

COUVRIR [34] [kuvrir] **VT 1** *(d'une protection, d'une couche ▸ meuble)* to cover; *(▸ livre, cahier)* to cover, to put a dust cover on; *(d'un couvercle ▸ poêle)* to cover, to put a lid on; **c. avec** *ou* **de** *(protéger)* to cover with; **c. un toit d'ardoises/de tuiles/de chaume** to slate/to tile/to thatch a roof; **il avait couvert le mur de graffitis/posters** he'd covered the wall with graffiti/posters; **couvrez les fraisiers avec de la paille** cover *or* protect your strawberry plants with straw; **c. qn de son corps** to shield sb with one's body; **être couvert de poussière** to be covered with *or* in dust; **c. qn de cadeaux/d'injures/de louanges/de reproches** to shower sb with gifts/insults/praise/criticism; **c. qn de caresses/baisers** to stroke/to kiss sb all over; **c. qn de honte** to make sb feel ashamed; **c. qn d'or** to shower sb with gifts

2 *(vêtir)* to wrap up, to cover up, to muffle up; *(envelopper)* to cover; **il faut c. cet enfant** that child needs to be covered up *or* wrapped up; **couvre bien ta gorge!** make sure your throat is covered up!; **la jupe couvre tout juste le genou** the skirt barely covers the knee

3 *(dissimuler ▸ erreur)* to cover up; *(protéger ▸ complice)* to cover up for; **ils le couvrent** *(pour une erreur)* they're covering up for him; **il avance l'argent, mais en cas de difficulté, c'est moi qui le couvre** he puts up the money but if there's a problem, I step in

4 *(voix)* to drown (out); **les basses couvrent trop les ténors** the basses drown out the tenors

5 *(assurer ▸ dégâts, frais, personne)* to cover, to insure; *(▸ risques)* to insure against; **l'assurance me couvre contre l'incendie** the insurance policy covers me against fire

6 *(inclure)* to cover, to include; **le prix couvre la livraison et l'entretien** the price covers *or* includes delivery and maintenance

7 *(compenser)* to cover; **les recettes ne couvrent plus les dépenses** income no longer covers expenses

8 *Mil (retraite, soldat)* to cover, to give cover to; **on te couvre** we've got you covered; **c. ses arrières** to cover one's rear

9 *(parcourir)* to cover; **elle a couvert les 15 kilomètres en 52 minutes** she covered *or* ran the 15 kilometres in 52 minutes

10 *(englober ▸ dans l'espace)* to cover; *(▸ dans le temps)* to span; **leur propriété couvre dix hectares** their estate covers *or* occupies ten hectares; **le réseau couvre toute la région** the network covers the whole area; **ses recherches couvrent près de 30 ans** his research spans nearly 30 years

11 *(sujet: émetteur, représentant)* to cover

12 *Journ* to cover, to give coverage to; **c. entièrement un procès** to give full coverage to a trial

13 *Fin (emprunt)* to underwrite; **c. l'enchère de qn** to outbid sb, to bid higher than sb; **prière de nous c. par chèque** kindly remit by cheque

14 *Vét* to cover

15 *Cartes* to cover

VI cette peinture couvre bien this paint covers well

VPR se couvrir 1 *(se vêtir ▸ pour sortir)* to dress warmly, to wrap up (well); *(▸ pour cacher sa nudité)* to cover oneself up; **couvre-toi bien, il fait très froid dehors** wrap up well, it's very cold out

2 *(mettre un chapeau)* to put on one's hat

3 *Sport (en boxe, en escrime)* to cover oneself

4 *(se garantir)* to cover oneself

5 *(ciel)* to become overcast, to cloud over; **le temps se couvre, ça se couvre** it's *or* the sky is clouding over

6 se c. de qch *(honte, gloire)* to cover oneself with sth; **se c. de fleurs/bourgeons/feuilles** to come into bloom/bud/leaf; **le champ s'est couvert de coquelicots** poppies have come up all over the field; **se c. de boutons** to come out *or* to become covered in spots; **la place s'est couverte de monde** the square became crowded *or* swamped with people; **se c. de ridicule** to make oneself look ridiculous

covalent, -e [kɔvalɑ̃, -ɑ̃t] **ADJ** *Chim* covalent

cover-girl [kɔvœrgœrl] *(pl* **cover-girls**) **NF** cover girl

covoiturage [kovwatyraʒ] **NM** car-pooling, *Br* lift-sharing

cow-boy [kɔbɔj] *(pl* **cow-boys**) **NM** cowboy; **jouer aux cow-boys et aux Indiens** to play (at) cowboys and Indians

coxalgie [kɔksalʒi] **NF** coxalgia

coxarthrose [kɔksartroz] **NF** arthritis of the hip

coyote [kɔjɔt] **NM** coyote

CP [sepe] **NM** *(abrév* **cours préparatoire**) = first year of primary school

CPAM [sepeaɛm] **NF** *Admin (abrév* **caisse primaire d'assurance maladie**) = French Social Security department in charge of medical insurance

CPI [sepei] **NF** *Jur (abrév* **Cour pénale internationale**) ICC

cpl *Typ (abrév écrite* **caractères par ligne**) cpl

CPNT [sepeɛnte] **NF** *Pol (abrév* **Chasse, Pêche, Nature et Traditions**) = French political movement that promotes rural life, hunting, fishing and environmental protection

CQFD [sekyɛfde] **NM** *(abrév* **ce qu'il fallait démontrer**) QED; **et voilà, C.!** and there you have it!

crabe [krab] **NM** *Zool* crab; **marcher/se déplacer en c.** to walk/to move sideways

crabot [krabo] **NM** *Tech* dog clutch

crac [krak] **ONOMAT** *(de bois, d'os)* crack, snap; *(de tissu)* rip

EXCLAM *Fam (locution)* **et c.! il est tombé par terre** and bang! there he was on the floor

crac-crac [krakrak] **NM** *Fam (faire l'amour)* **faire c.** to do it

crachat [kraʃa] **NM 1** *(salive)* spit, *Méd* sputum; **un c.** a gob of spit; **des crachats** spit, spittle **2** *Fam (médaille)* medal, *Br* gong

craché [kraʃe] **ADJ INV** *Fam* **c'est son père tout c.!** he's the spitting image of his dad!; **c'est lui tout c.!** that's just like him!, that's him all over!

crachement [kraʃmɑ̃] **NM 1** *(fait de cracher)* spitting; *(crachat)* mucus, *Spéc* sputum; **crachements de sang** spitting blood **2** *(projection ▸ de flammes, de vapeur)* burst, shower; *(▸ de scories, d'étincelles)* shower **3** *(bruit ▸ d'un haut-parleur)* crackle, crackling

cracher [3] [kraʃe] **VI 1** *(personne)* to spit; **c. par terre** to spit on the ground; **c. sur qn** to spit at sb; *Fig* to spit on sb; *aussi Fig* **c. à la figure de qn** to spit in sb's face; *Fam* **c'est comme si on crachait en l'air!** it's like whistling in the wind!; **il ne faut pas c. dans la soupe** don't bite the hand that feeds you; *Fam* **il ne crache pas sur le champagne** he doesn't turn his nose up at champagne; **je ne cracherais pas sur 2000 euros!** I wouldn't turn my nose up at *or* say no to 2,000 euros!; **ce système a du bon, ne crache pas dessus!** there are things to be said for this system, don't knock it!; **c. au bassinet** to cough up

2 *(chat, marmotte)* to spit, to hiss

3 *(fuir ▸ stylo)* to splutter; *(▸ robinet)* to splutter, to splash

4 *(nasiller ▸ haut-parleur, radio)* to crackle

VT 1 *(rejeter ▸ sang)* to spit; *(▸ aliment)* to spit out; **c. du sang** to spit blood; *Fam* **c. ses poumons** to cough one's lungs up

2 *(sujet: volcan, canon)* to belch (forth) *or* out; **c. des flammes** *ou* **du feu** *(sujet: dragon)* to breathe fire

3 *(énoncer ▸ insultes)* to spit out, to hiss; **"racaille!" cracha-t-elle en sortant** "scum!" she hissed on her way out

4 *Fam (donner ▸ argent)* to cough up, to fork out; **grand-père ne les crache pas facilement!** grandpa's a real old skinflint!

cracheur, -euse [kraʃœr, -øz] **NM,F c. de feu** fire-eater

crachin [kraʃɛ̃] **NM** (fine) drizzle

crachiner [3] [kraʃine] **V IMPERSONNEL il crachine** it's drizzling

crachoir [kraʃwar] **NM** spittoon; *Fam* **tenir le c.** to go on and on, to monopolize the conversation; **je n'ai pas envie de lui tenir le c.!** I don't feel like listening to him/her rambling on for hours!

crachotement [kraʃɔtmɑ̃] **NM** *(d'une radio, d'un téléphone)* crackle, crackling; *(d'une personne, d'un robinet)* splutter, spluttering

crachoter [3] [kraʃɔte] **VI** *(radio, téléphone)* to crackle; *(personne, robinet)* to splutter

crack [krak] **NM 1** *Équitation* crack **2** *Fam (personne ▸ gén)* wizard; *(▸ en sport)* ace; **c'est un c. en ski** he's/she's an ace skier; **c'est un c. en latin** he's/she's brilliant at Latin **3** *(drogue)* crack

cracker [krakœr] **NM 1** *Culin* cracker **2** *Ordinat (pirate informatique)* cracker

cracking [krakiŋ] **NM** *Pétr* cracking

Cracovie [krakɔvi] **NF** Cracow

cracra [krakra] **ADJ INV** *Fam (personne, objet)* filthy□

cradingue [kradɛ̃g] **ADJ** *très Fam (personne, objet)* filthy□

craie [krɛ] **NF** chalk, limestone; **falaise de c.** chalk cliff; **une c.** a stick of chalk; **écrire qch à la c.** to write sth in chalk; **c. de tailleur** French chalk

craignait *etc voir* **craindre**

craignos [krɛɲos] **ADJ INV** *Fam* **c'est c.** *(louche)* it's shady, *Br* it's dodgy; *(ennuyeux)* it's a real pain; *(laid)* it's hideous; *(mauvais)* it's crap, it's the pits

craindre [80] [krɛ̃dr] **VT 1** *(redouter ▸ personne)* to fear, to be frightened *or* afraid of; *(▸ événement)* to fear, to be afraid *or* scared of; **c. Dieu** to go in fear of *or* to fear God; **il est très craint** he is greatly feared; **je ne crains personne!** I'm not afraid of anyone!; **sa grosse voix le faisait c. de tous ses élèves** his booming voice made all his pupils afraid of him; **elle sait se faire c. de ses subordonnés** she knows how to intimidate her subordinates; **qui ne craint pas la mort?** who isn't afraid of death *or* dying?; **c. le pire** to fear the worst; **ne crains rien** *(n'aie pas peur)* have no fear, never fear, don't be afraid; *(ne t'inquiète pas)* don't worry; **il n'y a rien à c.** there's nothing to fear, **il y a tout à c. d'une intervention militaire** one can expect the worst from a military intervention; **elle craignait toujours d'être en retard** she was always afraid of being late; **si je ne craignais pas de vous choquer** if I wasn't afraid of shocking you; **craignant de la réveiller, il retira ses chaussures** he took off his shoes, for fear of waking her up **2** *(tenir pour probable)* to fear; **alors, je suis renvoyé? – je le crains** so, I'm fired? – I'm afraid so; **elle pourrait nous dénoncer – c'est à c.** she might give us away – unfortunately, (I think) it's likely; **il n'y a pas à c. qu'il revienne** there is no fear of his coming back; **je crains de l'avoir blessée** I'm afraid I've hurt her; **je crains qu'il (n')ait oublié** I'm afraid that *or* I fear he might have forgotten; **je crains fort qu'il (ne) soit déjà trop tard** I fear *or* I'm very much afraid it's already too late; **je crains que oui/non** I fear *or* I'm afraid so/not **3** *(être sensible à)* **ça craint le froid** *(plante)* it's sensitive to cold, it doesn't like the cold; **je crains le froid** I can't stand *or* bear the cold; **c'est un bois qui craint les chocs** it's a fairly fragile kind of wood; **craint l'humidité** *(sur emballage)* keep *or* store in a dry place; **c'est une étoffe qui ne craint rien** it's a material that'll stand up to anything

VI *Fam (locution)* **ça craint** *(c'est louche)* it's shady, *Br* it's dodgy; *(c'est ennuyeux)* it's a real pain; *(c'est laid)* it's hideous; *(c'est mauvais)* it's crap, it's the pits; **elle craint** she's really awful

• **craindre pour VT IND c. pour qn/qch** to fear for sb/sth; **je crains pour sa santé** I fear for his/her health; **c. pour sa vie** to fear for *or* to go in fear of one's life

craint, -e [krɛ̃, -ɛ̃t] **PP** *voir* **craindre**

NF *(anxiété)* fear; **la crainte de l'échec** fear of failure *or* failing; **il vivait dans la crainte d'être reconnu** he lived *or* went in fear of being recognized; **n'aie (aucune) crainte** *ou* **sois sans crainte, tout se passera bien** don't worry *or* never fear, everything will be all right; **éveiller** *ou* **susciter les craintes de qn** to alarm sb; **avoir des craintes au sujet de qch** to have some fears *or* worries about sth; **par c. des représailles** for fear of reprisals; **je ne lui ai pas dit de crainte de la blesser** I didn't tell her for fear of hurting her; **de crainte qu'elle ne s'en aille** for fear that she might leave

craintif, -ive [krɛ̃tif, -iv] **ADJ 1** *(facilement effarouché ▸ personne)* timid, shy; *(▸ animal)* timid **2** *(qui reflète la peur ▸ regard, geste)* timorous, fearful

craintivement [krɛ̃tivmɑ̃] **ADV 1** *(timidement)* timidly, shyly **2** *(avec peur)* timorously, fearfully

cramé, -e [krame] *Fam* **ADJ** *(brûlé ▸ rôti)* burnt□, charred□; *(▸ tissu)* burnt□, scorched□; **la tarte est complètement cramée** the tart is burnt to a cinder

NM ça sent le c. there's a smell of burning□; **ne mange pas le c.** don't eat the burnt bits□

cramer [3] [krame] *Fam* **VI** *(rôti, tissu, immeuble)* to burn□; *(circuit électrique, prise)* to burn out□; **tout a cramé** everything went up in flames *or* in smoke; **il y a quelque chose qui crame dans la cuisine** there's something burning in the kitchen□; **faire c. qch** to burn sth□

VT *(rôti)* to burn (to a cinder□), to let burn□; *(vêtement)* to burn□, to scorch□

VPR se cramer se c. les doigts to burn one's fingers□

cramoisi, -e [kramwazi] **ADJ** *(velours)* crimson; *(visage)* flushed, crimson; **il est devenu c.** *(de honte, de colère)* his face turned crimson; **rouge c.** crimson red

NM crimson

crampant, -e [krɑ̃pɑ̃, -ɑ̃t] **ADJ** *Can Fam (amusant)* hysterical; **le film était c.!** the movie was hysterical!, *Br* the film cracked me up!

crampe [krɑ̃p] **NF 1** *Méd* cramp; **j'ai une c. au pied** I've got *Br* cramp *or Am* a cramp in my foot; **c. d'estomac** *(gén)* stomach cramp; *(de faim)* hunger pang; **la c. de l'écrivain** writer's cramp **2** *(pièce de serrage)* cramp **3** *Vulg* **tirer sa c.** *(coïter)* to screw, *Br* to have a shag; *(s'enfuir)* to beat it, *Br* to piss off, *Am* to book it

crampon [krɑ̃pɔ̃] **ADJ INV** *Fam (personne)* clingy; **un enfant un peu c.** a clingy child

NM 1 *(de chaussures ▸ de sport)* stud; *(▸ de montagne)* crampon; *(de fer à cheval)* calk

2 *Bot (de plante grimpante)* tendril; *(d'algue)* sucker

3 *(crochet)* cramp

4 *Fam (person)* **mais quel c.!** what a leech!

cramponner [3] [krɑ̃pɔne] **VT 1** *(s'accrocher à)* to cling to **2** *Fam (importuner)* to pester; **tu me cramponnes avec tes questions!** stop pestering me with your questions! **3** *Tech (pièces)* to cramp together

VPR se cramponner 1 *(s'agripper)* to hold on, to hang on; **cramponne-toi bien, on démarre!** hold on tight, here we go!; **se c. à** *(branche, barre)* to cling (on) *or* to hold on to; *(personne)* to cling (on) to **2** *Fam (s'acharner ▸ malade)* to cling *or* to hang on; *(▸ étudiant)* to stick with it; **il est distancé mais il se cramponne** he's lagging behind, but he's hanging (on) in there; **se c. à la vie** to cling to life; **il se cramponne à cet espoir** he's clinging to this hope

cran [krɑ̃] **NM 1** *(entaille ▸ d'une étagère, d'une crémaillère)* notch; *(trou ▸ d'une ceinture)* hole, notch; **il resserra/desserra sa ceinture d'un c.** he tightened/loosened his belt one notch; **baisser/monter d'un c.** *(dans une hiérarchie)* to come down/to move up a peg

2 *Couture (sur un ourlet)* notch; *(point de repère)* nick

3 *(mèche de cheveux)* wave

4 *Tech* catch; **c. de sûreté** *ou* **sécurité** safety catch; **c. d'arrêt** *(couteau) Br* flickknife, *Am* switchblade

5 *Fam (courage)* **allons, un peu de c.!** *(sois courageux)* come on, be brave!; *(ne te laisse pas aller)* come on, pull yourself together!; **avoir du c.** to have guts

• **à cran ADJ** *Fam (personne)* uptight, edgy, on edge; **être à c., avoir les nerfs à c.** to be edgy *or* uptight

crâne [kran] **NM 1** *Anat* skull, *Spéc* cranium **2** *Fam (tête)* **avoir mal au c.** to have a headache; **mets-toi bien ça dans le c.!** get that into your head!; **alors, c. d'œuf!** hey, baldy!

ADJ *Littéraire (air)* gallant

crânement [kranmɑ̃] **ADV** *Littéraire (fièrement)* gallantly

crâner [3] [krane] **VI** *Fam* to show off, *Br* to swank; **tu crânes moins maintenant!** you aren't so sure of yourself now, are you!

crâneur, -euse [kranœr, -øz] *Fam* **ADJ être c.** to be a bit of a show-off

NM,F show-off, *Am* hotshot; **faire le c.** to show off, *Br* to swank

crânien, -enne [kranjɛ̃, -ɛn] **ADJ** cranial

craniologie [kranjɔlɔʒi] **NF** *Méd* craniology

cranter [3] [krɑ̃te] **VT** *(ourlet)* to notch; *(roue)* to put notches on; *(cheveux)* to wave

crapahuter [3] [krapayte] **VI 1** *Fam (marcher)* to schlep *or* to traipse about **2** *Fam Arg mil* to yomp

crapaud [krapo] **NM 1** *Zool* toad; *Ich* **c. de mer** angler-fish

2 *Minér* flaw

3 *Mus* **(piano) c.** baby grand piano

4 (fauteuil) c. squat armchair

5 *Fam (gamin)* kid, *Br* sprog

crapaudine [krapodin] **NF 1** *(de gouttière)* strainer; *(de baignoire)* pop-up waste hole **2** *Constr* gudgeon **3** *Tech* pivot bearing *or* box *or* hole; *(de gond)* socket, gudgeon

• **à la crapaudine ADJ** *Culin* spatchcock *(avant n)*

crapette [krapɛt] **NF** = card game (played by two people)

crapoteux, -euse [krapɔtø, -øz] **ADJ** *Fam* filthy

crapule [krapyl] **NF 1** *(individu)* crook, villain; **petite c.!** you little rat! **2** *Littéraire (pègre)* **la c.** the riff-raff

ADJ roguish; **une expression/un air c.** a roguish phrase/look

crapuleux, -euse [krapylø, -øz] **ADJ** *(malhonnête)* crooked, villainous

> Il faut noter que l'adjectif anglais **crapulous** est un faux ami. Il signifie **intempérant**.

craquage [krakaʒ] **NM** *Chim* cracking

craquant, -e [krakɑ̃, -ɑ̃t] **ADJ 1** *(croustillant ▸ laitue)* crisp; *(▸ céréales)* crunchy **2** *Fam (personne)* irresistible

craque [krak] **NF** *Fam (mensonge)* fib, whopper, *Br* porky (pie); **et me raconte pas de craques!** and no fibbing!

craquelé, -e [krakle] **ADJ 1** *(fissuré)* cracked; **j'ai la peau des mains toute craquelée** my hands are badly chapped **2** *(décoré de craquelures)* crackled

craqueler [24] [krakle] **VT** *(fendiller)* to crack; *(poterie)* to crackle

VPR se craqueler *(peinture, peau)* to crack; *(poterie)* to crackle

craquelure [kraklyr] **NF 1** *(accidentelle)* crack; *Beaux-Arts* **les craquelures du tableau** the craquelure on *or* cracks in the painting **2** *(volontaire, pour décorer)* crackle

craquement [krakmɑ̃] **NM** *(d'un plancher)* creak; *(de bois qui casse)* snap, crack; *(d'herbes sèches)* crackle; *(de chaussures)* squeak, creak

craquer [3] [krake] **VI 1** *(plancher)* to creak; *(bois qui casse)* to snap, to crack; *(herbes sèches)* to crackle; *(chaussures)* to squeak, to creak; **faire c. ses doigts** to crack one's knuckles; **faire c. une allumette** to strike a match; **les branches craquaient dans la bourrasque** the branches were creaking in the gale

2 *(se déchirer, se fendre ▸ couture, tissu)* to split; *(▸ sac)* to split open; *(▸ fil, lacets)* to break, to snap off; *(▸ banquise)* to crack, to split (up); *(▸ collant)* to rip; **le pull a craqué aux emmanchures** the sweater split at the armholes

3 *Fam (psychologiquement)* to break down☐, to crack up; **ses nerfs ont craqué** she had a nervous breakdown☐, she cracked up; **ils ont essayé de me faire c. en fumant devant moi** they tried to make me crack by smoking in front of me

4 *Fam (s'effondrer ▸ institution, gouvernement, régime)* to founder, to be falling apart, to be on the verge of collapse

5 *Fam (être séduit)* to go wild; **je craque** I can't resist it/them/*etc*; **il me fait c.** I'm wild *or* crazy about him; **j'ai craqué pour cette robe** I really fell for that dress

6 *Can Fam* **riche à c.** loaded, rolling in it; **fou à c.** totally mad

VT 1 *(déchirer)* to split, to tear

2 *(allumette)* to strike

3 *Fam (dépenser)* to blow; **elle a craqué tout son argent au jeu** she blew all her money at the gambling tables

4 *Pétr* to crack

crash [kraʃ] **NM 1** *(accident)* crash **2** *(atterrissage forcé)* crash-landing

crasher [3] [kraʃe] **se crasher VPR** *Fam* **1** *Aviat (s'écraser)* to crash☐; *(atterrir accidentellement)* to crash-land☐ **2** *(conducteur, véhicule)* to crash☐; **il s'est crashé contre un arbre** he smashed *or* crashed into a tree; **il s'est crashé en voiture** he crashed his car

crasse [kras] **NF 1** *(saleté)* filth; **couvert de c.** filthy, covered in filth; **il vit dans la c.** he lives in squalor

2 *Fam (mauvais tour)* dirty *or* nasty trick; **faire une c. à qn** to play a dirty *or* nasty trick on sb

3 *Tech* **la c., les crasses** *(scories)* scum, dross, slag; *(résidus)* scale

4 *Can (personne malhonnête)* crook

ADJ *Fam (stupidité)* crass; **d'une ignorance c.** abysmally ignorant, pig-ignorant

crasseux, -euse [krasø, -øz] **ADJ** filthy, grimy; **une cuisinière toute crasseuse** a cooker caked with dirt

NM *Fam* comb☐

crassier [krasje] **NM** slag heap

cratère [kratɛr] **NM** *Antiq & Géog* crater

cravache [kravaʃ] **NF** riding-crop, horsewhip

• **à la cravache ADV** ruthlessly, with an iron hand

cravacher [3] [kravaʃe] **VT** *(cheval)* to use the whip on; *(personne)* to horsewhip

VI *Fam* **1** *(en voiture)* to belt along, to go at full tilt *or* speed **2** *(travailler dur) Br* to slog away, *Am* to plug away

cravate [kravat] **NF 1** *(de chemise)* tie, *Am* necktie; **en costume (et) c.** wearing a suit and tie; *Fam* **c. de chanvre** hangman's noose; *Fam* **s'en envoyer** *ou* **s'en jeter un derrière la c.** to knock back a drink

2 *(d'un drapeau)* bow and tassels

3 *(décoration)* insignia, ribbon

4 *(prise de lutte)* headlock

5 *Naut* sling

cravater [3] [kravate] **VT 1** *(homme)* to put a tie on **2** *(attraper par le cou)* to grab by the neck; *Sport* to get in a headlock, to put a headlock on **3** *Fam Arg crime (arrêter)* **se faire c.** to get nabbed

VPR se cravater to put on a tie

crawl [krol] **NM** crawl; **faire du** *ou* **nager le c.** to do *or* to swim the crawl

crawlé [krole] *voir* **dos**

crawler [3] [krole] **VI** to do *or* to swim the crawl

crayeux, -euse [krejø, -øz] **ADJ 1** *Géol* chalky **2** *(teint)* chalk-like; **d'un blanc c.** chalky-white

crayon [krɛjɔ̃] **NM 1** *(pour écrire, dessiner)* pencil; *(stylo)* pen; **c. gras** *ou* **à mine grasse** soft lead pencil; **c. à** *ou* **de papier** lead pencil; **c. sec** *ou* **à mine sèche** dry lead pencil; **c. de couleur** coloured pencil, crayon; **c. à lèvres** lip-liner, lip pencil; **c. noir** *(à papier)* (lead) pencil; **c. pour les yeux** eye *or* eyeliner pencil; **c. à sourcils** eyebrow pencil; **coup de c.** *(rature)* pencil stroke; *(d'un artiste)* drawing style; **avoir un bon coup de c.** to be good at drawing

2 *Beaux-Arts (œuvre)* pencil drawing, crayon-sketch; **c. lithographique** litho crayon, *Am* grease pencil

3 *Nucl* **c. (combustible)** fuel rod *or* pin

4 *Opt* **c. optique** *ou* **lumineux** electronic *or* light pen

5 *Pharm* **c. hémostatique** styptic pencil

• **au crayon ADJ** *(ajout, trait)* pencilled; *(dessin)* pencil *(avant n)* **ADV** *(dessiner, écrire)* in pencil; **écrire/dessiner qch au c.** to write/to draw sth in pencil; **faire ses yeux au c.** to outline one's eyes with eye pencil

crayon-feutre [krɛjɔ̃føtr] *(pl* **crayons-feutres)** **NM** felt-tip (pen)

crayon-lecteur [krɛjɔ̃lɛktœr] *(pl* **crayons-lecteurs)** **NM** electronic *or* light pen

crayonnage [krɛjɔnaʒ] **NM 1** *(action ▸ d'écrire)* scribbling; *(▸ de dessiner)* sketching **2** *(esquisse)* pencil sketch *or* drawing

crayonné [krɛjɔne] **NM** *Typ (avant-projet, maquette)* rough, rough layout

crayonner [3] [krɛjɔne] **VT 1** *(dessiner rapidement)* to sketch (in pencil) **2** *(gribouiller ▸ feuille, mur)* to scribble on **3** *(écrire ▸ au crayon)* to pencil; *(▸ rapidement)* to jot down

USAGE ABSOLU *(gribouiller)* **c. sur un bloc-notes** to doodle on a notepad

CRDS [seerdees] **NF** *(abrév* **contribution au remboursement de la dette sociale)** = income-based tax deducted at source as a contribution to paying off the French social security budget deficit

créance [kreɑ̃s] **NF 1** *Fin (dette)* debt; *(titre)* letter of credit; *Jur* claim; **c. douteuse** doubtful debt; **c. exigible** debt due; **c. irrécouvrable** bad debt; **c. litigieuse** contested debt **2** *Littéraire (foi)* credence; **donner c. à** *(ajouter foi à)* to give *or* to attach credence to; *(rendre vraisemblable)* to lend credibility to

créancier, -ère [kreɑ̃sje, -ɛr] **NM,F** creditor; **c. hypothécaire** mortgagee; **c. nanti** secured creditor; **c. privilégié** preferential *or* preferred creditor

créateur, -trice [kreatœr, -tris] **ADJ** creative; **imagination créatrice** creativity; **industrie créatrice d'emplois** job-creating industry

NM,F creator; *(de mode, d'un produit)* designer; **c. d'entreprise** *ou* **d'entreprises** entrepreneur

• **Créateur NM le C.** the Creator, our Maker

créatif, -ive [kreatif, -iv] **ADJ** *(esprit)* creative, imaginative, inventive; **une atmosphère créative** a creative atmosphere

NM,F creative person; *(de publicité)* designer, creative

création [kreasjɔ̃] **NF 1** *(œuvre originale ▸ bijou, parfum, vêtement)* creation; *Com & Ind* new product; **nos nouvelles créations** our new range

2 *Théât (d'un rôle)* creation; *(d'une pièce)* first production, creation; **il y aura de nombreuses créations au festival** a lot of new plays will be performed at the festival

3 *(fait de créer ▸ une mode, un style)* creation; *(▸ un vêtement, un produit)* designing, creating; *(▸ une entreprise)* setting up, founding; *(▸ une association)* founding, creating; *(▸ des emplois)* creating, creation; **je connais cette société depuis sa c.** I have known this firm since it was founded *or* set up; **c. d'emplois** job creation; **il y a eu 3000 créations d'emplois en mai** 3,000 new jobs were created in May

4 *(département, service)* **la c.** creative; **le département c.** creative, the creative department

5 *Rel* **la C.** the Creation; **les merveilles de la C.** the wonders of nature

créative [kreativ] *voir* **créatif**

créativité [kreativite] **NF** creativity

créatrice [kreatris] *voir* **créateur**

créature [kreatyr] **NF 1** *(personne ou bête)* creature; **c. humaine** human being

2 *(femme)* **c. de rêve** gorgeous creature

4 *Vieilli Péj (femme dissolue)* trollop

crécelle [kresɛl] **NF** rattle; **une voix de c.** a grating voice

crèche [krɛʃ] **NF 1** *(établissement préscolaire) Br* crèche, *esp Br* day nursery, *Am* child-care center; *(dans un centre sportif, un magasin) Br* crèche, *Am* day-care center; **c. parentale** = crèche run by parents **2** *(de la Nativité)* **c. (de Noël)** (Christ Child's) crib; **c. vivante** = nativity play **3** *Fam (chambre, maison)* pad

> **CRÈCHE**
>
> State-subsidized care for children under three years of age of working families is well established in France, although this is subject to the availability of places.

crécher [18] [kreʃe] **VI** *Fam* **1** *(habiter)* to live☐ **2** *(loger temporairement)* to crash, *Br* to doss (down); **il faut qu'on trouve un endroit où c.** we need to find somewhere to crash *or Br* to doss (down); **je peux c. chez toi ce soir?** can I crash *or Br* doss (down) at your place tonight?

crédence [kredɑ̃s] **NF 1** *(desserte d'église)* credence (table), credenza **2** *(buffet)* credenza

crédibilité [kredibilite] **NF** credibility; **perdre sa c.** to lose one's credibility; **il a perdu presque toute c.** his credibility (rating) is very low

crédible [kredibl] **ADJ** credible, believable; **son histoire n'est pas c.** his/her story is unconvincing *or* is hardly credible

crédit [kredi] **NM 1** *Banque (actif)* credit; *(en comptabilité)* credit, credit side; **porter 100 euros au c. de qn** to credit sb *or* sb's account with 100 euros, to credit 100 euros to sb *or* sb's account; **j'ai 156 euros à mon c.** I am 156 euros in credit

2 *Com (paiement différé, délai)* credit; *(somme allouée)* credit; **c. sur six mois** six months' credit; **faire c. à qn** to give sb credit; **il n'a pas voulu me faire c. pour la voiture** he wouldn't let me have the car on credit; **la maison ne fait** *ou* **nous ne faisons pas c.** *(sur panneau)* no credit given; **accorder/obtenir un c.** to grant/to obtain credit; **j'ai pris un c. sur 25 ans pour la maison** I've got a 25-year mortgage on the house; **c. acheteur** buyer credit; **c. bancaire, c. en banque** bank credit; **c. en blanc** blank credit, loan without security, unsecured loan; **c. à la consommation, c. au consommateur** consumer credit; **c. (à) court terme** short-term credit; *Bourse* **c. croisé** cross-currency swap; **c. à découvert** open credit; **c. documentaire** documentary credit; **c. fournisseur** supplier's credit, trade credit; **c. gratuit** interest-free credit; **c. immobilier** mortgage, home loan; **c. d'impôt** *(abattement)* tax rebate; *(report)* tax credit; **c. (à) long terme** long-term credit; **c. (à) moyen terme** medium-term credit; **c. permanent** *Br* revolving *or Am* revolver credit; **c. personnalisé** individual *or* personal credit arrangement; **c. relais** *Br* bridging loan, *Am* bridge loan; **c. renouvelable** *Br* revolving *or Am* revolver credit

3 *(établissement)* **c. foncier** = government-controlled building society; **c. municipal** pawnbroker

4 *(confiance, estime)* credibility, esteem; **jouir d'un grand c. auprès de qn** to be high in sb's esteem; **connaître un grand c.** *(idée, théorie)* to be widely accepted *or* held; **il n'a plus aucun c.** he's lost all credibility; **elle comptait sur son c. pour faire accepter l'idée** she was relying on her influence to get her idea accepted; **donner du c. aux propos de qn** to give credence to what sb says; **trouver c. auprès de qn** *(personne)* to win sb's confidence; *(histoire)* to find credence with *or* to be believed by sb

5 *Can Univ* credit

• **crédits NMPL 1** *(fonds)* funds; **l'enseignement a besoin de plus de crédits** education needs more funding; **on s'attend à une réduction des crédits**

pour les bibliothèques a reduction in funding for libraries is to be expected; **accorder des crédits** to grant *or* to allocate funds; **crédits de carbone** carbon credits; **crédits de développement** development loans; **crédits d'équipement** equipment financing; **crédits à l'exportation** export credit; **crédits à l'importation** import credit **2** *(autorisation de dépenses)* **voter des crédits** to vote supplies; **crédits budgétaires** supplies

• **à crédit** ADJ *voir* **achat**, **vente** ADV **acheter/vendre qch à c.** to buy/to sell sth on credit *or* on hire purchase *or Am* on the installment plan

• **à mon/son/*etc* crédit** ADV to my/her/*etc* credit; **c'est à mettre** *ou* **porter à son c.** one must credit him/her with it; **il faut dire à son c. qu'il a respecté les délais** it must be said to his credit that he met the deadlines

• **de crédit** ADJ *(agence, établissement)* credit *(avant n)*

crédit-acheteur [kredi aʃtœr] *(pl* **crédits-acheteurs)** NM buyer credit

crédit-bail [kredibaj] *(pl* **crédits-bails)** NM leasing

créditer [3] [kredite] VT **1** *Banque (somme)* to credit; **mon compte a été crédité** *ou* **j'ai été crédité de 500 euros** 500 euros were credited to my account; **les intérêts seront crédités sur votre compte à la fin de chaque mois** the interest will be credited to your account at the end of every month **2** *Fig* **c. qn de qch** to give sb credit for sth, to credit sb with sth

créditeur, -trice [kreditœr, -tris] ADJ *(solde)* credit *(avant n)*; **avoir un compte c.** to have an account in credit

NM,F customer in credit

crédit-fournisseur [kredifurnisœr] *(pl* **crédits-fournisseurs)** NM supplier credit

crédit-relais [kredirəle] *(pl* **crédits-relais)** NM *Br* bridging loan, *Am* bridge loan

créditrice [kreditris] *voir* **créditeur**

credo [kredo] NM INV **1** *(principe)* credo, creed; **c. politique** political creed *or* credo; **c'est mon c.** it's the thing I most fervently believe in **2** *Rel* **le C.** the (Apostles') Creed

Credoc [kredɔk] NM *Mktg (abrév* **Centre de recherche pour l'étude et l'observation des conditions de vie)** = large state-funded market research company in Paris

crédule [kredyl] ADJ gullible, credulous; **qu'est-ce que tu peux être c.!** you'll believe anything!, you're so gullible!

crédulité [kredylite] NF gullibility, credulity

créer [15] [kree] VT **1** *(inventer ▸ personnage, style)* to create; *(▸ machine)* to invent; *(▸ vêtement, produit)* to create, to design; *(▸ mot)* to invent, to coin; **c'est lui qui a créé la formule** he coined the phrase *or* expression; **écharpe/bague créée par Mélodie** scarf/ring created by Mélodie

2 *Théât (rôle)* to create, to play for the first time; *(pièce)* to produce for the first time

3 *(occasionner, engendrer ▸ emploi, différences, difficultés)* to create; *(▸ poste)* to create, to establish; *(▸ atmosphère)* to create, to bring about; *(▸ tension)* to give rise to; *(▸ précédent)* to set; **c. des ennuis** *ou* **difficultés à qn** to create problems for *or* to cause trouble to sb; **il ne nous a créé que des ennuis** he's given us nothing but trouble; **cela crée des jalousies** it causes jealousy; **elle a créé la surprise en remportant le match** she caused a sensation by winning the match

4 *(fonder ▸ association, mouvement)* to create, to found; *(▸ entreprise)* to set up; *(▸ État)* to establish, to create

VPR **se créer 1** *(être établi)* to be set up *or* created; **des associations se créent un peu partout** societies are being founded *or* set up almost everywhere **2** *(pour soi-même)* **se c. une image** to create an image for oneself; **il s'est créé un monde à lui** he's created a world of his own; **se c. des problèmes** to create problems for oneself; **se c. une clientèle** to build up a clientele

crémaillère [kremajɛr] NF **1** *(de cheminée)* trammel (hook) **2** *Tech, Aut & Rail* rack; *Aut* **c. de direction** steering rack **3** *(fête)* **(pendaison de) c.** housewarming (party); **pendre la c.** to have a housewarming (party)

• **à crémaillère** ADJ **engrenage/direction à c.** rack (and pinion) gearing/steering; **chemin de fer à c.** cog railway

crémant [kremɑ̃] ADJ M slightly sparkling

NM Crémant wine

crémation [kremasjɔ̃] NF cremation

crématoire [krematwar] ADJ crematory

NM *Br* cremator, *Am* cinerator

crématorium [krematɔrjɔm] NM *Br* crematorium, *Am* crematory

crème [krɛm] NF **1** *Culin (préparation)* cream; *(entremets)* cream (dessert); *(peau du lait)* skin; *Fig* **c'est la c. des maris** he's the perfect husband; **c. anglaise** custard; **c. au beurre** buttercream; **c. brûlée** crème brûlée; **c. (au) caramel** crème caramel; **c. Chantilly** sweetened chilled whipped cream, Chantilly cream; **c. au chocolat/citron** chocolate/lemon cream; **c. épaisse** *Br* ≃ double cream, *Am* ≃ heavy cream; **c. fleurette** *Br* ≃ single cream, *Am* ≃ light cream; **c. fouettée** whipped cream; **c. fraîche** crème fraîche; **c. glacée**, *Can* **c. à la glace** ice cream; **c. liquide** *Br* ≃ single cream, *Am* ≃ light cream; **c. de marrons** chestnut purée; **c. pâtissière** confectioner's custard; **c. renversée** ≃ crème caramel

2 *(potage)* **c. de brocoli/de poireaux** cream of broccoli/leek soup

3 *(boisson)* **c. de cassis** crème de cassis; **c. de cacao/menthe** crème de cacao/menthe

4 *(cosmétique)* cream; **c. antirides** anti-wrinkle cream; **c. de beauté** skin cream; **c. dépilatoire** hair removing cream; **c. hydratante** moisturizing cream, moisturizer; **c. de jour** day cream; **c. médicinale** treatment cream; **c. de nuit** night cream; **c. à raser** shaving cream; **c. (de soins) pour les mains/le visage** hand/face cream

5 *(produit d'entretien)* **c. pour chaussures** shoe cream *or* polish

ADJ INV cream, cream-coloured

NM **1** *(couleur)* cream **2** *Fam (café)* coffee with milk *or* cream, *Br* white coffee; **un grand/petit c.** a large/small cup of white coffee

• **à la crème** ADJ *(gâteau)* cream *(avant n)*; **framboises à la c.** raspberries and cream; **escalopes à la c.** escalopes with cream sauce

crémer¹ [18] [kreme] VT *(incinérer)* to cremate

crémer² [18] [kreme] VT *(sauce)* to add cream to

crémerie [kremri] NF **1** *(boutique)* = shop selling cheese and other dairy products **2** *Fam Fig* **changer de c.** to take one's custom *or* business elsewhere

crémeux, -euse [kremø, -øz] ADJ **1** *(onctueux)* creamy, unctuous, smooth **2** *(gras ▸ fromage)* soft

crémier, -ère [kremje, -ɛr] NM,F dairyman, *f* dairywoman

Crémone [kremɔn] NF *Géog* Cremona

crémone [kremɔn] NF *(espagnolette)* bolt on casement window, espagnolette

crénage [krenaʒ] NM *Ordinat* kerning

créneau, -x [kreno] NM **1** *Archit (creux)* crenel (embrasure), crenelle; *(bloc de pierre)* crenellation; **les créneaux** the crenellations *or* battlements; **à créneaux** crenellated

2 *(meurtrière)* slit, loophole; **c. de visée** aiming slit; *Fam* **monter au c.** to step into the breach

3 *Aut (espace)* gap, (parking) space; **faire un c.** to parallel park; **elle a raté son c.** she's parked badly *or* made a mess of parking the car

4 *(dans un emploi du temps)* slot, gap; *Rad & TV (temps d'antenne)* slot; **c. horaire/publicitaire** time/advertising slot; **l'émission occupera le c. 20–22 heures** the programme will take the 8 to 10 p.m. slot

5 *Écon* (market) niche, gap in the market; **trouver un bon c.** to find a niche in the market; **exploiter un nouveau c.** to fill a new gap *or* niche in the market; **c. porteur** potentially lucrative market

crénelage [krenlaʒ] NM **1** *(fait d'entailler)* milling (UNCOUNT) **2** *(entailles)* milled edge **3** *Typ (en PAO)* aliasing

crénelé, -e [krenle] ADJ **1** *Archit* crenellated **2** *Bot* crenate, scalloped **3** *Métal* notched; *(pièce de monnaie)* milled

créneler [24] [krenle] VT **1** *Archit* to crenellate **2** *Métal* to notch; *(pièce de monnaie)* to mill

crénelure [krenlyr] NF **1** *Archit* crenellation **2** *Métal* notch **3** *Bot* crenelling

créner [18] [krene] VT *Typ* to kern

crénom [krenɔ̃] EXCLAM *Fam Vieilli* **c. (de nom** *ou* **de Dieu)!** *(d'impatience)* for God's *or* Pete's sake!; *(de colère)* damn it!; *(de surprise) Br* blimey!, *Am* holy cow!

créole [kreɔl] ADJ creole

NM *(langue)* Creole

• **Créole** NMF Creole

• **créoles** NFPL hoop earrings

créosote [kreozɔt] NF creosote

créosoter [3] [kreozɔte] VT to creosote

crêpage [krɛpaʒ] NM **1** *(de tissu)* crimping; *(de papier)* cockling *or* crinkling (up) **2** *(des cheveux)* backcombing; *Fam* **c. de chignon** *(coups)* catfight; **attention au c. de chignon!** be careful the women don't come to blows!

crêpe¹ [krɛp] NM **1** *Tex* crepe, crêpe; **c. de Chine** crepe de Chine; **c. de deuil** *ou* **noir** black mourning crepe; **porter un c.** *(brassard)* to wear a black armband; *(au revers de la veste)* to wear a black ribbon; *(sur le chapeau)* to wear a black hatband **2** *(caoutchouc)* crepe rubber

• **de crêpe** ADJ **1** *(funéraire)* mourning; **voile de c.** mourning veil **2** *(chaussures, semelle)* rubber *(avant n)*

crêpe² [krɛp] NF *Culin* crepe; **c. au beurre/sucre** crepe with butter/sugar; **c. au jambon et aux champignons** crepe filled with ham and mushrooms; **c. dentelle** = very thin crepe; **c. Suzette** crepe suzette

crêpelé, -e [krɛple] ADJ *(cheveux)* frizzy

crêper [4] [krepe] VT **1** *(cheveux)* to backcomb **2** *Tex* to crimp, to crisp **3** *(papier)* to cockle *or* to crinkle (up)

VPR **se crêper se c. les cheveux** to backcomb one's hair; *Fam* **se c. le chignon** to have a catfight

crêperie [krɛpri] NF *(restaurant)* pancake restaurant, creperie; *(stand)* pancake *or* crepe stall

crépi, -e [krepi] ADJ roughcast *(avant n)*

NM roughcast

crêpier, -ère [krepje, -ɛr] NM,F *(d'un restaurant)* pancake *or* crepe restaurant owner; *(d'un stand)* pancake *or* crepe maker *or* seller

• **crêpière** NF *(poêle)* pancake *or* crepe pan; *(plaque)* griddle

crépine [krepin] NF **1** *Zool & Culin* caul **2** *Tech* strainer **3** *(de passementerie)* fringe

crépir [32] [krepir] VT to roughcast

crépissage [krepisaʒ] NM roughcasting

crépitation [krepitasjɔ̃] NF *Méd* **c. osseuse** crepitation, crepitus; **c. pulmonaire** lung crepitation

• **crépitations** NFPL *(d'un feu)* crackle, crackling

crépitement [krepitmɑ̃] NM *(d'un feu)* crackle, crackling; *(d'une fusillade)* rattle; *(d'une friture)* splutter; *(de la pluie)* pitter-patter; **les crépitements de la grêle sur les feuilles** the pattering of hail on the leaves

crépiter [3] [krepite] VI **1** *(feu, coups de feu)* to crackle; *(pluie)* to patter; *(friture)* to splutter; **les applaudissements crépitèrent** there was a ripple of applause **2** *Méd* to crepitate

crépon [krepɔ̃] NM **1** *(papier)* crepe paper **2** *Tex* crepon, seersucker

crépu, -e [krepy] ADJ *(cheveux)* frizzy

crépusculaire [krepyskylɛr] ADJ *Littéraire (lueur, moment)* twilight *(avant n)*; **lumière c.** twilight, half-light **2** *Zool* crepuscular

crépuscule [krepyskyl] NM **1** *(fin du jour)* twilight, dusk **2** *Astron (lumière ▸ du soir)* twilight; *(▸ du matin)* dawn light

• **au crépuscule de** PRÉP *Littéraire* **au c. de sa vie** in the twilight of his/her life; **au c. du siècle** in the closing years of the century

crescendo [kreʃendo, kreʃɛ̃do] NM **1** *Mus* crescendo; **faire un c.** to go crescendo; **ça se joue en c.** it must be played crescendo **2** *(montée)* escalation; **pour enrayer le c. de la violence** to stop the rising tide *or* the escalation of violence

ADV crescendo; **aller c.** *(notes)* to go crescendo; *(bruits, voix)* to grow louder and louder; *(violence, mécontentement)* to rise, to escalate

cresson [kresɔ̃] **NM** cress; **c. (d'eau** *ou* **de fontaine)** watercress; **c. des prés** lady's smock; **c. de terre** land cress

cressonnière [kresɔnjɛr] **NF** *Bot* watercress bed

Crésus [krezys] **NPR** Croesus; **il est riche comme C.** he's as rich as Croesus

Crésyl® [krezil] **NM** disinfectant *(containing cresol)*

crétacé, -e [kretase] **ADJ** Cretaceous

NM Cretaceous (period)

Crète [krɛt] **NF la C.** Crete

crête [krɛt] **NF 1** *(d'oiseau, de lézard)* crest; *(de volaille)* comb

2 *Mil (d'un casque)* crest

3 *(d'une montagne, d'un toit)* crest, ridge; *(d'un mur)* crest, top; *(d'une vague)* crest; *Géog* **c. de plage** *ou* **prélittorale** watershed

4 *Anat* **c. du tibia** *ou* **iliaque** edge *or* crest of the shin

5 *Élec & Électron* peak

crête-de-coq [krɛtdəkɔk] *(pl* **crêtes-de-coq)** **NF 1** *Bot* cockscomb **2** *Méd* venereal papilloma

crétin, -e [kretɛ̃, -in] **ADJ** *Fam* moronic; **vous êtes encore plus c. que lui** you're even more of a cretin *or* a moron *or* an idiot than he is

NM,F 1 *Fam (imbécile)* moron, cretin **2** *Méd & Vieilli* cretin

crétinerie [kretinri] **NF** *Fam* **1** *(caractère)* stupidity, idiocy **2** *(acte)* idiotic thing (to do); *(propos)* idiotic thing (to say)

crétinisation [kretinizasjɔ̃] **NF** dumbing down

crétiniser [3] [kretinize] **VT** *Fam (public)* to turn into morons; *(personne)* to turn into a moron

crétinisme [kretinism] **NM 1** *Fam (caractère)* stupidity, idiocy **2** *Méd & Vieilli* cretinism

crétois, -e [kretwa, -az] **ADJ** Cretan

• **Crétois, -e NM,F** Cretan

cretonne [krətɔn] **NF** *Tex* cretonne

cretons [krətɔ̃] **NMPL** *Can Culin* cretons, = type of pork pâté

creusage [krøzaʒ] **NM** *(d'un trou)* digging; *(d'un canal)* digging, cutting; *(d'un puits)* digging, sinking

creuse [krøz] *voir* **creux**

creusement [krøzmɑ̃] **NM 1** *(d'un trou)* digging; *(d'un canal)* digging, cutting; *(d'un puits)* digging, sinking **2** *(augmentation)* deepening, widening, growth; **le c. des inégalités dans la société** the widening inequalities in society

creuser [5] [krøze] **VT 1** *(excaver ▸ puits, mine)* to dig, to sink; *(▸ canal)* to dig, to cut; *(▸ tranchée)* to dig, to excavate; *(▸ sillon)* to plough; *(▸ passage souterrain, tunnel)* to bore, to dig; **c. un trou** *(à la pelle)* to dig a hole; *(en grattant)* to scratch a hole; **c. un terrier** to burrow; **ils ont creusé une piscine dans leur jardin** they've made *or* built a swimming pool in their garden; **la rivière a creusé son lit** the river has hollowed out its bed; *Fig* **c. sa propre tombe** to dig one's own grave; *Fig* **c. sa tombe avec ses dents** to eat oneself into an early grave; **ça a creusé un abîme** *ou* **fossé entre eux** this has opened up a gulf between them; **c. l'écart entre soi et le reste du peloton/de ses concurrents** to widen the gap between oneself and the rest of the bunch/and one's competitors

2 *(faire un trou dans ▸ gén)* to hollow (out); *(▸ avec une cuillère)* to scoop (out); **c. la terre** to dig (a hole in the earth)

3 *(ployer)* **c. les reins** *ou* **le dos** to arch one's back

4 *(marquer ▸ traits du visage)* **la maladie lui avait creusé les joues** illness had hollowed his/her cheeks; **il avait le visage creusé par la fatigue** his face was gaunt *or* haggard with fatigue; **il avait le front creusé de rides** his forehead was furrowed with wrinkles

5 *Fam (ouvrir l'appétit de)* to make hungry□; **la marche m'a creusé (l'estomac)** the walk gave me an appetite□

6 *(approfondir ▸ idée)* to look *or* to go into; *(▸ problème, question)* to look *or* to delve into; **tu n'as pas assez creusé l'aspect sociologique du problème** you didn't go into enough detail about the sociological aspect of the problem

USAGE ABSOLU *Hum* **toutes ces émotions, ça creuse!** all this excitement gives you an appetite!; *Hum* **il paraît intelligent, mais il vaut mieux ne pas c. (trop loin)** he seems intelligent, but it might be better not to scratch too far beneath the surface

VPR se creuser 1 *Fam (réfléchir)* **tu ne t'es pas beaucoup creusé pour écrire ce texte!** you didn't overtax yourself when you wrote this text!; **se c. la tête** *ou* **la cervelle** to rack one's brains **2** *(yeux, visage)* to grow hollow; *(joues)* to grow gaunt *or* hollow; *(fossettes, rides)* to appear **3** *(augmenter ▸ écart)* to grow bigger; **le fossé entre eux se creuse** the gap between them is widening

creuset [krøzɛ] **NM 1** *Pharm & Tech* crucible, melting pot; *(d'un haut-fourneau)* crucible, hearth **2** *(rassemblement)* melting pot, mixture; **un c. de cultures** a melting pot of cultures **3** *Littéraire (épreuve de purification)* crucible

creux, -euse [krø, krøz] **ADJ 1** *(évidé ▸ dent, tronc)* hollow; *Fig* **j'ai le ventre c.** my stomach feels hollow, I feel hungry; **je ne peux pas travailler quand j'ai le ventre c.** I can't work on an empty stomach

2 *(concave ▸ joues)* hollow, gaunt; *(▸ yeux)* sunken, hollow; **aux joues creuses** hollow-cheeked; **un chemin c.** a sunken lane

3 *Péj (inconsistant ▸ discours, phrases)* empty, meaningless; *(▸ argumentation)* weak; **il ne m'intéresse pas du tout, je le trouve très c.** he doesn't interest me at all, I find him very bland *or* insipid

4 *(sans activité)* **périodes creuses** *(au travail)* slack periods; *(dans une tarification)* off-peak periods; **pendant la saison creuse** *(pour le commerce)* during the slack season; *(pour les vacanciers)* during the off-peak season; **pendant les heures creuses le trajet ne vous coûtera que six euros** the journey will cost you only six euros off-peak

5 *Couture* **pli c.** box pleat, inverted pleat

NM 1 *(trou ▸ dans un roc)* hole, cavity; *(▸ d'une dent, d'un tronc)* hollow (part), hole, cavity; **la route est pleine de c. et de bosses** the road is bumpy *or* is full of potholes; *Fam* **avoir un c. (à l'estomac)** to feel a bit hungry□ *or Br* peckish; **j'ai un petit c.** I'm a bit hungry□ *or Br* peckish

2 *(concavité ▸ de la main, de l'épaule)* hollow; *(▸ de l'estomac)* pit; **tenir qch dans le c. de la main** to hold sth cupped in one's hand; **il a bu dans le c. de ma main** it drank out of my hand; **c'est si petit que ça tient dans le c. de la main** it's so small you can hold it in the palm of your hand; **j'ai mal dans le c. du dos** *ou* **des reins** I've got a pain in the small of my back

3 *(dépression ▸ d'une courbe, d'une vague)* trough; **il y avait des c. de dix mètres** *(sur la mer)* there were waves ten metres high

4 *(inactivité)* **une période de c., un c.** a slack period; **j'ai un c. dans mon emploi du temps entre deux et quatre** I've got a gap in my timetable between two and four

5 *Can (profondeur)* hole; **avoir 30 mètres de c.** to be 30 metres deep

6 *Beaux-Arts* mould

7 *Naut (d'une voile)* belly

ADV sonner c. to give *or* to have a hollow sound; *Fig* to ring hollow

• **au creux de PRÉP au c. de ses bras** (nestled) in his/her arms; **au c. de la vague** in the trough of the wave; *Fig* **être au c. de la vague** *(entreprise, personne)* to be at a low ebb, to be going through a bad patch

• **en creux ADJ 1** *Beaux-Arts* **gravure en c.** intaglio engraving **2** *Fig (sous-jacent)* indirect; **ce film est un portrait en c. de l'écrivain** this film is an indirect portrait of the writer

crevaison [krəvɛzɔ̃] **NF** *Br* puncture, flat tyre, *Am* flat; **avoir une c.** *Br* to have a puncture *or* a flat tyre, *Am* to have a flat

crevant, -e [krəvɑ̃, -ɑ̃t] **ADJ** *Fam* **1** *(fatigant ▸ travail, enfant)* exhausting□, *Br* knackering **2** *(drôle ▸ personne, histoire, spectacle)* hilarious, sidesplitting; **elle est crevante, leur gamine** their kid's a scream *or* riot

crevard, -e [krəvar, -ard] **NM,F** *Fam* **1** *(personne famélique)* half-starved wretch□ **2** *(personne affamée)* pig, *Br* gannet, *Am* hog

crevasse [krəvas] **NF 1** *Géog (dans le sol)* crevice, fissure, split; *(sur un roc)* crack, crevice, fissure; *(d'un glacier)* crevasse **2** *(sur les lèvres, sur les mains)* crack, split; **j'ai des crevasses aux doigts** my fingers are badly chapped

crevasser [3] [krəvase] **VT 1** *(sol)* to cause cracks *or* fissures in **2** *(peau)* to chap

VPR se crevasser 1 *(sol)* to become cracked **2** *(peau)* to become chapped

crève [krɛv] **NF** *Fam (rhume)* stinking cold; **j'ai la c.** I've got a stinking cold; **attraper** *ou* **choper la c.** to catch one's death

crevé, -e [krəve] **ADJ 1** *(pneu)* flat, punctured; *(tympan)* pierced; *(yeux)* gouged-out; *(ballon)* burst; **j'ai un pneu c.** I've got a *Br* puncture *or Am* flat **2** *(mort ▸ animal)* dead **3** *Fam (fatigué) Br* knackered, *Am* bushed

crève-cœur [krɛvkœr] **NM INV c'est un c. de les voir comme ça** it's a heartbreaking *or* heart-rending sight to see them like that; **c'est un c. d'entendre cela** it's heartbreaking *or* heart-rending to hear this

crève-la-faim [krɛvlafɛ̃] **NM INV** *Fam* half-starved wretch□

crever [19] [krəve] **VT 1** *(faire éclater ▸ abcès)* to burst (open); *(▸ bulle, ballon, sac)* to burst; *(▸ pneu)* to puncture, to burst; *(▸ tympan)* to puncture, to pierce; **un cri vint c. le silence** a cry pierced *or* rent the silence; **la pierre a crevé le pare-brise** the stone put a hole in the windscreen; **c. un œil à qn** *(agression)* to gouge *or* to put out sb's eye; *(accident)* to blind sb in one eye; **cela crève le cœur** it's heartbreaking *or* heart-rending; **ça me crève le cœur de devoir abandonner cette maison** I'm heartbroken about *or* it's heartbreaking having to leave this house; **tu me crèves le cœur!** you're breaking my heart!; *Fam* **ça crève les yeux** *(c'est évident)* it's as plain as the nose on your face, it sticks out a mile; *(c'est visible)* it's staring you in the face, it's plain for all to see; **c. le plafond** *(prix)* to go through the roof; **c. l'écran** *(acteur)* to have great screen presence

2 *Fam (fatiguer)* to wear out□, *Br* to knacker; **ce boulot/gosse me crève** this job/kid is killing me; **c'est ce rhume qui m'a crevé** that cold took it out of me; **ça vous crève, les transports en commun!** using public transport wears you out□ *or Br* is knackering!; **c. sa monture** to ride one's horse to death□

3 *Fam (locution)* **c. la faim** *(par pauvreté)* to be starving

VI 1 *(éclater ▸ pneu)* to puncture; *(▸ ballon, bulle, nuage, abcès)* to burst; *Fam* **on a crevé sur la rocade** we had *Br* a puncture *or Am* a flat on the bypass; *Culin* **faire c. du riz** to burst rice

2 *Fam (mourir)* to kick the bucket, *Br* to snuff it; **qu'il crève!** to hell with him!; **s'il veut que je l'aide, il peut toujours c. (la gueule ouverte)!** he can go to hell if he thinks I'm going to help him!; **ils me laisseraient c. comme un chien** they'd just let me die like a dog; **on monte jusqu'au sommet – tu veux me faire c.?** let's go up to the top – do you want to kill me?□; **il fait une chaleur à c.** it's stifling *or* boiling; **plutôt c.!** I'd rather die!, I'll die first!

3 *(mourir ▸ animal, végétal)* to die (off); **faire c. qch** to kill sth (off); **les moutons crevaient tous** the sheep were all dying

4 *Suisse Fam (voiture)* to stall□

• **crever de VT IND** *Fam* **1** *(éprouver)* **c. de faim** *(par pauvreté)* to be starving; *(être en appétit)* to be starving *or* famished; **c. de soif** to be parched; **je crève de chaud!** I'm baking *or* boiling!; **on crève de froid ici** it's freezing cold *or* you could freeze to death here; **faire c. qn de faim** to starve sb to death; **faire c. qn de soif/froid** to make sb die of thirst/cold; **c. d'ennui** to be bored to death; **c'est à c. de rire** it's a hoot *or* scream *or* riot; **c. de peur/d'inquiétude** to be scared/worried to death **2** *(être plein de)* **c. de jalousie** to be eaten up with jealousy; **c. d'orgueil** to be puffed up *or* bloated with pride; **je crève d'impatience de le voir** I can't wait to see him; **c. d'envie de faire qch** to be dying to do sth; **je ne veux pas y aller – mais si, tu en crèves d'envie** I don't want to go – oh yes you do, you're dying to go

VPR se crever *Fam* **se c. au boulot** *ou* **à la tâche** to work oneself to death; **je ne me suis pas crevé à faire des études pour gagner si peu!** I didn't kill myself studying to earn such a small salary!; *très Fam* **se c. le cul** *Br* to bust a gut, *Am* to bust one's ass

crevette [krəvɛt] NF prawn, *Am* shrimp; **c. grise** shrimp; **c. rose** (common) prawn

crevettier [krəvetje] NM *Pêche* **1** *(filet)* shrimping net **2** *(bateau)* shrimper, shrimp boat

CRF [seɛrɛf] NF *(abrév* **Croix-Rouge française***)* **la C.** the French Red Cross

cri [kri] NM **1** *(éclat de voix ▸ gén)* cry; *(▸ puissant)* shout, yell; *(▸ perçant)* shriek, scream; **un petit c. aigu** a squeak; **un c. perçant** a shriek; **un c. rauque** a squawk; **les cris des rues** street cries; **des cris me parvenaient du jardin** I could hear somebody shouting in *or* cries coming from the garden; **qu'est-ce que c'est que tous ces cris?** what is all this shouting *or* noise about?; **c. de douleur** cry *or* scream of pain; **c. de guerre** battle cry; **c. de joie** cry *or* shout of joy; **c. d'indignation** cry *or* scream of indignation; **c. d'horreur** shriek *or* scream of horror; **c. primal** primal scream; **jeter** *ou* **pousser un c.** to cry out; **pousser un c. de joie/douleur** to cry out with joy/in pain; **pousser des cris** to cry out, to shout; *Fig* to make loud protests; *Fig* **jeter** *ou* **pousser des hauts cris** to raise the roof, to raise a hue and cry, to kick up a fuss; **pousser des cris d'orfraie** *ou* **de paon** *(hurler)* to screech like a thing possessed; *(protester)* to raise the roof
2 *Zool* noise; *(d'un oiseau)* call; *(d'une souris)* squeak; *(d'un porc)* squeal; **quel est le c. de la chouette?** what noise does the owl make?
3 *(parole)* cry; **c. d'amour** cry of love; **c. d'avertissement** warning cry; **c. de détresse** cry of distress; **jeter** *ou* **lancer un c. d'alarme** to warn against the danger; **défiler au c. de "des subventions!"** to march chanting "subsidies!"; **c. du cœur** cry from the heart, *Littéraire* cri de coeur; **sa réaction a été un c. du cœur** his/her reaction was straight from the heart
• **à grands cris** ADV **appeler qn à grands cris** to shout for sb; **demander** *ou* **réclamer qch à grands cris** to cry out *or* to clamour for sth
• **dernier cri** ADJ *(machine, vidéo)* state-of-the-art; **il s'est acheté des chaussures de sport dernier c.** he bought the latest thing in *Br* trainers *or Am* sneakers NM INV **c'est le dernier c.** *(vêtement)* it's the (very) latest fashion *or* thing; *(machine, vidéo)* it's state-of-the-art

> Attention: ne pas confondre **shout** et **scream** lorsqu'on traduit **cri**. Le terme **scream** désigne le plus souvent un cri inarticulé de douleur ou de frayeur, alors que **shout** se rapporte plutôt à des éclats de voix ou à des paroles prononcées de façon autoritaire ou sous l'effet de la colère.

criailler [3] [kriaje] VI **1** *(crier sans cesse)* to screech, to shriek; **c. après qn** to shriek at sb **2** *(se plaindre)* to whine, to complain **3** *Orn (faisan)* to cry; *(oie)* to honk; *(paon)* to squawk, to screech

criailleries [kriajri] NFPL **1** *(cris)* screeching, shrieking **2** *(récriminations)* whining, complaining

criailleur, -euse [kriajœr, -øz] ADJ **1** *(qui crie)* screeching, shrieking **2** *(qui se plaint)* whining, complaining

criant, -e [krijɑ̃, -ɑ̃t] ADJ *(erreur)* glaring; *(mauvaise foi, mensonge)* blatant, glaring, rank; *(parti pris)* blatant; *(différence, vérité)* obvious, striking; *(injustice)* flagrant, blatant, rank; *(preuve)* striking, glaring; *(contraste)* striking; **être c. de vérité** *(témoignage, reportage)* to be obviously *or* patently true, to ring true; *(personnage, image)* to be extremely true to life; *(acteur)* to be extremely convincing

criard, -e [krijar, -ard] ADJ **1** *(voix)* shrill, piercing; **un enfant c.** a noisy child **2** *(couleur)* loud, garish; *(tenue)* garish, gaudy; **meublé avec un luxe c.** furnished ostentatiously

criblage [kriblaʒ] NM **1** *(tamisage ▸ de grains, de sable)* riddling, sifting; *(▸ de charbon, gravier, minerai)* screening **2** *(calibrage ▸ de fruits, d'œufs)* grading

crible [kribl] NM *(pour des grains, du sable)* riddle, sift; *(pour un charbon, un minerai)* screen; **passer au c.** *(charbon)* to riddle, to screen, to sift; *(grains, sable)* to riddle, to sift; *(fruits, œufs)* to grade; *(endroit)* to go over with a fine-tooth comb, to comb; *(preuves)* to sift *or* to examine closely; *(document)* to examine closely, to go over with a fine-tooth comb

cribler [3] [krible] VT **1** *(tamiser ▸ grains, sable)* to riddle, to sift; *(▸ minerai, charbon)* to screen
2 *(calibrer ▸ fruits, œufs)* to grade
3 *(trouer)* **c. qch de trous** to riddle sth with holes; **un tronc criblé de flèches** a trunk riddled with arrows; **la façade est criblée d'impacts de balles** the facade is riddled with bullet holes
4 *(assaillir)* **c. qn de coups** to rain blows on sb; **c. qn de questions** to bombard sb with questions, to fire questions at sb; **c. qn de reproches** to heap reproaches on sb
5 *(couvrir, accabler)* **être criblé de** to be covered in; **être criblé de dettes** to be crippled with debt, to be up to one's eyes in debt; **elle a le visage criblé de taches de rousseur** her face is covered with freckles; **un ciel c. d'étoiles** a sky studded with stars, a star-studded sky

cribleur [kriblœr] NM **1** *(personne)* screener, sifter **2** *(machine)* sifter, sifting machine

cribleuse [kribløz] NF *(machine)* sifter, sifting machine

cric[1] [krik] ONOMAT *(bruit de déchirement)* rip, crack; **c. (crac)!** *(tour de clé)* click!

cric[2] [krik] NM *Aut* (car) jack; **mettre une voiture sur** *ou* **élever une voiture avec un c.** to jack a car up; **c. hydraulique/à vis** hydraulic/screw jack

cricket [kriket] NM *Sport* cricket; **jouer au c.** to play cricket

cricri [krikri] NM **1** *Fam (grillon)* cricket **2** *(cri du grillon)* chirp, chirp-chirp

criée [krije] NF **1** *(lieu de vente)* fish market *(where auctions take place)* **2** *(vente)* auction; *(salle)* auction room **3** *Bourse* open outcry
• **à la criée** ADJ *voir* **vente** ADV by auction; **vendre du thon à la c.** to auction off tuna

crier [10] [krije] VI **1** *(gén)* to cry (out); *(d'une voix forte)* to shout, to yell; *(d'une voix perçante)* to scream, to screech, to shriek; **il n'a même pas crié quand on lui a fait la piqûre** he didn't even cry out when he got the injection; **ne crie pas, je ne suis pas sourd!** there's no need to shout *or* yell, I'm not deaf!; **ne fais pas c. ta mère!** don't get your mother angry!; *Fam* **ça crie, ta radio, baisse-la donc!** your radio's blaring, turn it down!; **c. de douleur** to scream with *or* to cry out in pain; **c. de joie** to shout for joy; **c. de plaisir** to cry out with pleasure; *Fam* **c. comme un sourd** to shout one's head off; *Fam* **c. comme un damné** *ou* **putois** *ou* **veau** *ou* **un cochon qu'on égorge** *(fort)* to shout *or* to yell at the top of one's voice; *(avec des sons aigus)* to squeal like a stuck pig; *(protester)* to scream blue murder; **c. à l'assassin** to cry blue murder; **c. à l'injustice** to call it an injustice; **c. à la trahison** to cry treason; **c. au loup** to cry wolf; **ils ont crié au miracle** they hailed it a miracle; **c. au scandale** to call it a scandal, to cry shame; **c. au voleur** to cry (stop) thief; **c. à l'aide** *ou* **au secours** to shout *or* to cry for help
2 *Zool (oiseau)* to call; *(souris)* to squeak; *(porc)* to squeal
3 *(freins, pneu)* to squeak, to screech; *(cuir, craie)* to squeak; *(charnière)* to creak
VT **1** *(dire d'une voix forte ▸ avertissement)* to shout *or* to cry (out); *(▸ insultes, ordres)* to bawl *or* to yell out; **il criait "arrêtez-le, arrêtez-le"** "stop him, stop him," he shouted; **elle nous cria de partir** she shouted at us to go; **quelqu'un criait "au feu!"** someone was shouting "fire!"; **sans c. gare** *(arriver)* without warning; *(partir)* without so much as a by-your-leave
2 *(faire savoir)* to proclaim; **c. son innocence** to proclaim *or* to protest one's innocence; **c. son dégoût/horreur** to proclaim one's disgust/indignation; **c. famine** to complain of hunger; **c. misère** *(se plaindre)* to complain of hardship; **c. victoire** to crow (over one's victory); **c. contre qch** to complain *or* to shout about sth; **ils crient contre la TVA** they're shouting about VAT; **c. qch sur les toits** *(le rendre public)* to shout *or* to proclaim sth from the rooftops; *(s'en vanter)* to let everyone know about sth; **ne va pas le c. sur les toits!** there's no need to publicize it!
3 *(demander)* **c. vengeance** to call for revenge; **c. grâce** to beg for mercy; *Fig* to cry for mercy
4 *(vendre)* to put up for auction, to auction
• **crier après** VT IND *Fam* **1** *(s'adresser à)* to shout *or* to yell at ▫ **2** *(réprimander)* to bawl out

> Il faut noter que le verbe anglais **to cry** signifie le plus souvent **pleurer**.

crieur, -euse [krijœr, -øz] NM,F **1** *(vendeur)* **c. (de journaux)** newspaper seller *or* vendor **2** *(dans une criée)* auctioneer **3** *Hist* **c. (public)** town crier

crime [krim] NM **1** *Jur (infraction pénale)* crime, (criminal) offence; **commettre un c.** to commit a crime; **un c. contre l'État** (high) treason *or* a crime against the state; **c. contre l'humanité** crime against humanity; **c. informatique** electronic crime; **c. contre la paix** crime against peace; **c. de guerre** war crime; **c. de lèse-majesté** act *or* crime of lèse-majesté; *Fig Hum* **il n'a pas salué le patron, c. de lèse-majesté!** he didn't say hello to the boss, what a heinous crime!
2 *(meurtre)* murder; **c'est le c. parfait** it's the perfect crime; **commettre un c.** to commit a murder; **c. crapuleux** heinous crime; **c. d'honneur** honour killing; **c. (à motif) sexuel** sex crime *or* murder; **c. passionnel** crime passionnel, crime of passion; **l'arme du c.** the murder weapon
3 *(acte immoral)* crime, act; **c'est un c. de démolir ces églises** it's a crime *or* it's criminal to knock down these churches; **son seul c. est d'avoir dit tout haut ce que chacun pensait** his/her only crime *or* fault was to say aloud what everybody was thinking; **ce n'est pas un c.!** it's not a crime!; *Littéraire* **faire à qn un c. de qch** to reproach sb with sth; **c. contre nature** act *or* crime against nature
4 *(criminalité)* **le c.** crime; **la lutte contre le c.** the fight against crime; **le c. organisé** organized crime; *Prov* **le c. ne paie pas** crime doesn't pay

Crimée [krime] NF **la C.** the Crimea

criminaliser [3] [kriminalize] VT to criminalize
VPR **se criminaliser** to become criminalized

criminaliste [kriminalist] NMF specialist in criminal law

criminalité [kriminalite] NF **1** *(ensemble des actes criminels)* crime; **lutter contre la c.** to fight crime; **la grande/petite c.** serious/petty crime; **c. en col blanc** white-collar crime; **c. informatique** computer crime; **c. organisée** organized crime, racketeering **2** *(caractère criminel)* criminality, criminal nature

criminel, -elle [kriminɛl] ADJ **1** *(répréhensible ▸ action, motif)* criminal; **acte c.** criminal offence, crime; **une organisation criminelle** a criminal organization, a crime syndicate **2** *(relatif aux crimes ▸ droit, enquête)* criminal; *(▸ brigade)* crime *(avant n)* **3** *(condamnable ▸ acte)* criminal, reprehensible; **c'est c. de...** it's criminal to..., it's a crime to...; **avoir des pensées criminelles** to think wicked thoughts
NM,F *(gén)* criminal; *(meurtrier)* murderer; **c. de guerre** war criminal
NM *Jur (juridiction criminelle)* **le c.** criminal law; **avocat au c.** criminal lawyer; **poursuivre qn au c.** to institute criminal proceedings against sb

criminellement [kriminɛlmɑ̃] ADV **1** *(répréhensiblement)* criminally **2** *Jur* **poursuivre qn c.** to institute criminal proceedings against sb

criminologie [kriminɔlɔʒi] NF criminology

criminologiste [kriminɔlɔʒist], **criminologue** [kriminɔlɔg] NMF criminologist

crin [krɛ̃] NM **1** *(de cheval)* hair **2** *(rembourrage)* horsehair **3** *Bot* **c. végétal** vegetable (horse)hair
• **à tout crin, à tous crins** ADJ out-and-out, diehard; **les conservateurs à tout c.** the diehard *or* dyed-in-the-wool conservatives
• **de crin, en crin** ADJ horsehair *(avant n)*

crincrin [krɛ̃krɛ̃] NM *Fam* (squeaky) fiddle; **il a joué un air sur son c.** he scraped out a tune on his fiddle

crinière [krinjɛr] NF **1** *Zool* mane **2** *Fam (chevelure)* mane, *Péj ou Hum* mop **3** *(d'un casque)* plume

crinoline [krinɔlin] NF **1** *Tex* crinoline **2** *(de jupe, de robe)* crinoline petticoat
• **à crinoline** ADJ *(de robe)* crinoline *(avant n)*

crinquer [3] [krɛ̃ke] VT *Can Joual* to wind up ▫

crique [krik] NF **1** *Géog* creek, inlet, (small) rocky beach **2** *Métal* tear, split

criquet [krikɛ] **NM** locust; **c. pèlerin** *ou* **migrateur** migratory locust

crise [kriz] **NF 1** *Psy (période, situation difficile)* crisis; **traverser une c.** to go through a crisis *or* a critical time; **c. d'adolescence** adolescent *or* teenage crisis; **il est en pleine c. d'adolescence** he's right in the middle of an adolescent *or* teenage crisis; **c. d'angoisse** anxiety attack; **c. de confiance** crisis of confidence; **c. de conscience** crisis of conscience; **c. d'identité** identity crisis; **la c. de la quarantaine** a mid-life crisis

2 *Écon & Pol* crisis; **c. du logement** housing shortage; **c. boursière** *(grave)* crisis *or* panic on the Stock Exchange; *(passagère)* blip on the Stock Exchange; **c. conjoncturelle** economic crisis *(due to cyclical and not structural factors)*; **c. diplomatique** diplomatic crisis; **c. économique** economic crisis *or* slump, recession; **c. politique** political crisis; **c. pétrolière** oil crisis; **la c. de 1929** the 1929 slump

3 *(accès)* outburst, fit; **c. de colère** fit of temper; **c. de désespoir** fit of despair; **c. de jalousie** fit of jealousy; **c. de larmes** crying fit; **c. de rage** angry outburst; *Fam* **quelle** *ou* **la c. (de rire)!** what a scream *or* hoot!; *Fam* **piquer une c.** to throw *or* to have a fit; *Fam* **pas besoin de nous faire une c. pour ça!** there's no need to kick up such a fuss!; **il a été pris d'une c. de rangement** he had the sudden urge to tidy up

4 *Méd* **c. d'apoplexie** apoplectic fit; **c. d'appendicite/d'arthrose** attack of appendicitis/arthritis; **elle a été prise d'une c. d'appendicite** she was struck down with appendicitis, she went down with appendicitis; **c. cardiaque** heart attack; **c. épileptique** *ou* **d'épilepsie** epileptic fit, seizure; **c. de foie** indigestion; *Fam* **tu vas attraper une c. de foie à manger tous ces chocolats** you'll make yourself sick if you eat all these chocolates; **c. de nerfs** fit of hysterics, attack of nerves; **elle a fait une c. de nerfs** she went into hysterics

• **en crise ADJ être en c.** to undergo a crisis; **la construction navale est un secteur en c.** the shipbuilding industry is in crisis

crispant, -e [krispɑ̃, -ɑ̃t] **ADJ** *(attente)* nerve-racking; *(stupidité, personne)* exasperating, irritating, infuriating; *(bruit)* irritating; **arrête de me dire comment jouer, c'est c. à la fin!** stop telling me how to play, it's getting on my nerves!; **ce que tu peux être c.!** you are SO infuriating!

crispation [krispasjɔ̃] **NF 1** *(du visage)* tension; *(des membres)* contraction; *(de douleur)* wince

2 *(tic)* twitch; **le médicament peut provoquer des crispations au niveau des mains** the drug can cause the hands to twitch

3 *(anxiété)* nervous tension

4 *(du cuir)* shrivelling; *(du papier)* cockling

crispé, -e [krispe] **ADJ 1** *(contracté ▸ sourire, rire)* strained, tense; *(▸ personne, visage, doigts)* tense; **le visage c. par la douleur** his/her face contorted *or* screwed up with pain; **les deux mains crispées sur la mallette** clutching the briefcase with both hands **2** *Fam (irrité)* irritated▫, exasperated▫

crisper [3] [krispe] **VT 1** *(traits du visage)* to contort, to tense; *(poings)* to clench; **ne crispez pas vos doigts sur le volant** don't grip the wheel too tightly; **le visage crispé par la souffrance** his/her face contorted *or* tense with pain **2** *Fam (irriter)* **c. qn** to get on sb's nerves; **ce bruit me crispe** this noise grates on my nerves **3** *(rider ▸ cuir)* to shrivel up

VPR se crisper 1 *(se contracter ▸ visage)* to tense (up); *(▸ personne)* to become tense; *(▸ doigts)* to contract; *(▸ sourire)* to become strained *or* tense; *(▸ poings)* to clench; **ses mains se crispèrent sur les barreaux** his/her hands tightened on the bars; **je me crispe dès que je suis sur des skis** I get all tensed up as soon as I put on skis; *Fig* **les relations entre les deux parties se sont crispées** tension has mounted between the two parties **2** *Fam (s'irriter)* to get irritated *or* exasperated▫

crispin [krispɛ̃] **NM** *(de gant)* gauntlet; **gants à c.** *(d'escrimeur, de motocycliste)* gauntlets

criss [kris] = **kriss**

crissement [krismɑ̃] **NM** *(de pneus, de freins)* squealing, screeching; *(de cuir)* squeaking; *(de neige, de gravillons)* crunching; *(d'une craie, d'une scie)* grating; **j'ai entendu le c. des pneus sur le gravier** I heard the crunch of tyres on the gravel

crisser [3] [krise] **VI** *(pneus, freins)* to squeal, to screech; *(cuir)* to squeak; *(neige, gravillons)* to crunch; *(craie, scie)* to grate; **la craie crissait sur le tableau** the chalk squeaked on the blackboard

cristal, -aux [kristal, -o] **NM 1** *Minér* crystal; **c. de roche** rock crystal **2** *Phys* **cristaux de givre** ice crystals; **cristaux liquides** liquid crystals; **cristaux de neige/sel** snow/salt crystals; **cristaux de sucre** sugar granules *or* crystals; **cristaux de soude** washing soda **3** *(objet)* piece of crystalware *or* of fine glassware; **des cristaux** crystalware, fine glassware; *(d'un lustre)* crystal droplets

• **de cristal ADJ 1** *(vase)* crystal *(avant n)* **2** *(pur ▸ eau)* crystal-like, crystalline; *(▸ voix)* crystal-clear, crystalline

cristallerie [kristalri] **NF 1** *(fabrication)* crystal-making **2** *(usine)* (crystal) glassworks **3** *(objets)* **de la c.** crystalware, fine glassware

cristallin, -e [kristalɛ̃, -in] **ADJ 1** *Littéraire (voix)* crystal-clear, crystalline; *(son, note)* ringing; *(eau)* crystal-like, crystalline **2** *Chim & Minér (massif, rocher)* crystalline

NM *Anat* crystalline lens

cristallisation [kristalizasjɔ̃] **NF** *Chim* crystallization, crystallizing

cristalliser [3] [kristalize] *Chim* **VT** to crystallize

VI to crystallize

VPR se cristalliser to crystallize

cristallographie [kristalɔgrafi] **NF** *Chim* crystallography

cristaux [kristo] *pl de* **cristal**

critère [kritɛr] **NM 1** *(principe)* criterion; **c. moral** moral criterion; **nos produits doivent remplir certains critères** our products must meet certain standards *or* comply with certain criteria; *UE* **critères d'adhésion** membership criteria; *UE* **critères de convergence** convergence criteria; *UE* **critères d'élargissement** enlargement criteria; **critères de sélection** selection criteria; *Ordinat* **c. de tri** sort criterion **2** *(référence)* reference (point), standard; **les résultats de l'année précédente nous servent de c.** we use the results of the previous year as a reference point *or* a benchmark; **ce n'est pas un c.** *(on ne peut rien en conclure)* that's nothing to go by, that doesn't mean anything

critérium [kriterjɔm] **NM** criterium; *Cyclisme & Natation* gala; *Équitation* **le grand c., le c. des deux ans** maiden race for two-year-olds

critiquable [kritikabl] **ADJ** which lends itself to criticism; **une décision peu c.** an uncontentious decision

critique [kritik] **ADJ 1** *(qui condamne ▸ article, personne)* critical; *Péj (personne)* fault-finding; **se montrer très c. envers** *ou* **à l'égard de** to be very critical towards; **elle est très c.** she's always finding fault, she's hypercritical; **examiner qch d'un œil c.** to examine sth critically *or* with a critical eye

2 *(plein de discernement ▸ analyse, œuvre, personne)* critical; **je souhaite que tu portes un regard c. sur mon texte** I'd like you to have a critical look at my text; **avoir l'esprit** *ou* **le sens c.** to have good judgement, to be discerning; **il n'a aucun esprit** *ou* **sens c.** he lacks discernment

3 *(crucial ▸ étape, période)* critical, crucial; *(▸ opération, seuil)* critical; **à un moment c.** at a critical moment

4 *(inquiétant ▸ état de santé, situation)* critical; **atteindre un stade c.** to reach a critical stage; **l'heure est c.** we are faced with a crisis, we have a crisis on our hands

5 *(en science)* critical

NMF *(commentateur)* critic, reviewer; **c. d'art** art critic; **c. de cinéma** movie *or Br* film critic *or* reviewer; **c. gastronomique** food and wine critic; **c. littéraire** book reviewer, literary critic; **c. musical** music critic; **c. de théâtre** theatre critic

NF 1 *Journ* review; *Univ* critique, appreciation; **je ne lis jamais les critiques** I never read reviews *or* what the critics write; **c. cinématographique** movie *or Br* film review; **c. littéraire** literary *or* book review; **c. musicale/théâtrale** music/theatre review

2 *(activité)* **la c.** criticism; **faire la c. de** *Journ* to review; *Univ* to write an appreciation *or* a critique of; **la c. gastronomique** food writing; **la c. littéraire** literary criticism; **la c. théâtrale** theatre criticism

3 *(personnes)* **la c.** the critics; **très bien/mal accueilli par la c.** acclaimed/panned by the critics; **l'approbation/le mépris de la c.** critical acclaim/scorn

4 *(blâme)* criticism; **ce n'est pas une c., mais…** don't take this as a criticism, but…

5 *(fait de critiquer)* **la c.** criticism, criticizing; **faire la c. de qch** to criticize sth; **la c. est aisée** *ou* **facile (mais l'art est difficile)** it's easy to be a critic (but hard to be an artist)

critiquer [3] [kritike] **VT 1** *(blâmer ▸ initiative, mesure, personne)* to criticize, to be critical of; **tu es toujours à me c.!** you're always criticizing me!, you find fault with everything I do!; **ce n'est pas pour te c., mais…** don't take this as a criticism, but…, I don't mean to criticize (you), but…; **il s'est déjà fait c. pour sa négligence** he has already been criticized for his negligence **2** *(analyser) Journ* to review; *Univ* to write an appreciation *or* a critique of

USAGE ABSOLU arrête de c.! stop criticizing!

critiqueur, -euse [kritikœr, -øz] **NM,F** *Péj* fault-finder; **les critiqueurs** those who carp *or* who find fault

croassement [krɔasmɑ̃] **NM** *(de corneille)* cawing; *(de corbeau)* croaking

croasser [3] [krɔase] **VI** *(corneille)* to caw; *(corbeau)* to croak

croate [krɔat] **ADJ** Croat, Croatian

NM *(langue)* Croat, Croatian

• **Croate NMF** Croat, Croatian

Croatie [krɔasi] **NF la C.** Croatia

croc [kro] **NM 1** *(de chien)* tooth, fang; *(d'ours, de loup)* fang; **montrer les crocs** *(animal)* to bare its teeth *or* fangs; *Fig* **la Prusse montrait les crocs** Prussia was showing its teeth **2** *Fam (dent)* (long) tooth; **j'ai les crocs** I could eat a horse **3** *(crochet ▸ de boucher)* butcher's *or* meat-hook; *(▸ de marinier)* hook, boat-hook

croc-en-jambe [krɔkɑ̃ʒɑ̃b] *(pl* **crocs-en-jambe)** **NM faire un c. à qn** to trip sb up; *Fig* to set sb up

croche [krɔʃ] **NF** *Mus Br* quaver, *Am* eighth note; **double c.** *Br* semiquaver, *Am* sixteenth note; **triple c.** *Br* demisemiquaver, *Am* thirty-second note; **quadruple c.** *Br* hemidemisemiquaver, *Am* sixty-fourth note

croche-patte [krɔʃpat] *(pl* **croche-pattes)**, **croche-pied** [krɔʃpje] *(pl* **croche-pieds)** **NM** *Fam* **faire un c. à qn** to trip sb up; *Fig* to set sb up

crocher [3] [krɔʃe] **VT 1** *Naut* to hook **2** *Suisse (accrocher)* to hang (**à** on)

crochet [krɔʃɛ] **NM 1** *(attache, instrument)* hook; *(pour volets)* catch; **c. d'arrêt** pawl, catch; **c. d'attelage** coupling hook; **c. à bottes** boot-hook; **c. de boucher** *ou* **boucherie** meat-hook, butcher's hook; **c. à boutons** buttonhook; **c. de bureau** spike file

2 *(de serrurier)* picklock, lockpick

3 *Couture (instrument)* crochet hook; *(technique)* crochet; *(ouvrage)* crochetwork; **faire du c.** to crochet; **au c.** *(nappe, châle)* crocheted; **faire un vêtement au c.** to crochet a garment; **terminer un vêtement au c.** to finish a garment with a crocheted trim

4 *Méd (instrument)* tenaculum

5 *Sport* hook; **il l'a envoyé à terre d'un c. à la tête** he knocked him down with a hook to the head; **c. du droit/gauche** right/left hook

6 *(détour)* detour, roundabout way; **faire un c.** to make a detour, to go a roundabout way

7 *(virage brusque ▸ d'une voie)* sudden *or* sharp turn; *(▸ d'une voiture)* sudden swerve; **faire un c.** *(rue)* to bend sharply; *(conducteur)* to swerve suddenly

8 *(concours)* **c. radiophonique** talent contest

9 *Typ* square bracket; **entre crochets** in square brackets

10 *Zool (d'un serpent)* fang; *(d'un chamois)* horn

• **crochets NMPL** *Vieilli (châssis)* frame; **vivres aux crochets de qn** to live off sb

crochetable [krɔʃtabl] **ADJ** *(serrure)* that can be picked, pickable

crochetage [krɔʃtaʒ] **NM** *(d'une serrure)* picking

crocheter [28] [krɔʃte] **VT 1** *(serrure)* to pick; *(porte)* to pick the lock on **2** *Couture* to crochet

crocheteur [krɔʃtœr] **NM** picklock

crocheur, -euse [krɔʃœr, -øz] *Suisse* **ADJ** *(tenace, travailleur)* dedicated and hard-working
NM,F *(personne tenace et travailleuse)* dedicated and hard-working person

crochu, -e [krɔʃy] **ADJ** *(nez)* hooked, hook *(avant n)*; *(doigts, mains)* claw-like; *Fig* **avoir les doigts crochus** *ou* **les mains crochues** to be tight-fisted *or Am* a tightwad

croco [krɔko] *Fam (abrév* **crocodile)** **NM** crocodile❑, crocodile skin❑
• **en croco** **ADJ** crocodile❑ *(avant n)*, crocodile skin❑

crocodile [krɔkɔdil] **NM 1** *(animal)* crocodile; **c. marin** saltwater *or* estuarine crocodile; **c. du Nil** Nile crocodile **2** *(peau)* crocodile, crocodile skin
• **en crocodile** **ADJ** crocodile *(avant n)*, crocodile skin

crocus [krɔkys] **NM** crocus

CROIRE [107] [krwar] **VT 1** *(fait, histoire, personne)* to believe; **tu crois son histoire?** do you believe what he/she says?; **je te crois sur parole** I'll take your word for it; **je te crois!** *(et comment)* you can say that again!; *Ironique* I believe you!, is that so?; **crois-moi, on n'a pas fini d'en entendre parler!** believe me, we haven't heard the last of this!; **je te prie de c. qu'il va entendre parler de nous!** believe me, we haven't finished with him!; **cela, je ne peux pas le c.** I can't believe that, I find that hard to believe; **je n'en crois pas un mot** I don't believe a word of it; **tu ne me feras pas c. que...** I refuse to believe that...; **on lui a fait c. que la réunion était annulée** they told him/her that the meeting had been cancelled; **croyez-en ceux qui ont l'expérience** take it from those who know; **à l'en c.** if he is to be believed; **si j'en crois cette lettre** if I go by what this letter says; **si vous m'en croyez** if you ask me *or* want my opinion; **n'en croyez rien!** don't believe (a word of) it!; **je n'en crois pas mes yeux/oreilles** I can't believe my eyes/ears; *Fam* **c. dur comme fer que...** to be firmly convinced that...❑; **ne va pas c. ça!** don't you believe it!; **ne va pas c. qu'il a toujours raison** don't think he's always right
2 *(penser)* to believe, to think; **je croyais pouvoir venir plus tôt** I thought *or* assumed I could come earlier; **j'ai cru bien faire** I thought *or* believed I was doing the right thing; **j'ai cru devoir le prévenir** I thought I ought to warn him; **j'ai cru nécessaire de...** I thought it necessary to...; **je crois que oui** I believe *or* think so; **il croit que non** he doesn't think so; **vous croyez?** do you really think so?; **à la voir on croirait sa sœur** to look at her, you'd think she was her sister; **on croirait qu'il dort** he looks as if he's asleep; **on croit rêver!** it's unbelievable!; **tu ne crois pas si bien dire** you don't know how right you are; **je vous croyais anglais/riche** I thought you were English/rich; **on l'a crue enceinte** she was believed *or* thought to be pregnant; **je n'aurais pas cru cela de lui** I wouldn't have *or* would never have believed *or* thought it of him; **elle en sait plus long que tu ne crois** she knows more than you think; **je ne suis pas celle que vous croyez** I'm not that kind of person; **il faut c. que tout lui réussit** seemingly, everything comes right for him/her; **il faut c. que tu avais tort** it looks like you were wrong; *Fam* **il faut c., faut c.** (it) looks like it❑, it would seem so❑; *Fam* **elle est intelligente, faut pas c.!** she may not look smart, but believe me, she is!
VI 1 *(sans analyser)* to believe; **on leur apprend à réfléchir et non à c.** they're taught to think and not simply to believe what they're told
2 *Rel* to believe; **il croit** he's a believer; **je ne crois plus** I've lost my faith
• **croire à** **VT IND 1** *(avoir confiance en)* to believe in; **c. à la paix** to believe in peace; **il faut c. à l'avenir** one must have faith in the future; **je ne crois pas à ses promesses** I don't believe *or* I have no faith in his/her promises
2 *(accepter comme réel)* to believe in; **c. aux fantômes** to believe in ghosts; **tu crois encore au Père Noël!** you're so naive!; **c'est à n'y pas c.!** you just wouldn't believe *or* credit it!; **franchement, je n'y crois pas** quite frankly, I don't believe it; **le médecin crut à une rougeole** the doctor thought it was measles; **elle voulait faire c. à un accident** she wanted it to look like an accident
3 *Rel* to believe in; **c. à la vie éternelle** to believe in eternal life; **il ne croit ni à Dieu ni au diable** he's a complete heathen
4 *(dans la correspondance)* **je vous prie de c. à mes sentiments les meilleurs** *(à quelqu'un dont on connaît le nom) Br* yours sincerely, *Am* sincerely (yours); *(à quelqu'un dont on ne connaît pas le nom) Br* yours faithfully, *Am* sincerely (yours)
• **croire en** **VT IND 1** *(avoir confiance en)* to believe in; **j'ai vraiment cru en lui** I really believed in him **2** *Rel* **c. en Dieu** to believe in God
VPR se croire 1 *(penser avoir)* **il se croit tous les droits** *ou* **tout permis** he thinks he can get away with anything; *Fam* **qu'est-ce qu'il se croit?** who does he think he is? **2** *(se juger)* **il se croit beau/intelligent** he thinks he's handsome/intelligent; **tu te crois malin?** think you're clever, do you?; **où te crois-tu?** where do you think you are?; **on se serait cru en octobre** it felt like October **3** *Fam (locutions)* **se c. sorti de la cuisse de Jupiter** to think one is God's gift (to mankind); **il s'y croit!** he really thinks a lot of himself!; **et ton nom en grosses lettres sur l'affiche, mais tu t'y crois déjà!** and your name in huge letters on the poster, you're letting your imagination run away with you!

crois *etc voir* **croître**

croisade [krwazad] **NF 1** *Hist* crusade; **les croisades** the (Holy) Crusades; **partir en c.** to go on a crusade **2** *Fig (campagne)* campaign, crusade; **partir en c. contre l'injustice** to go on a crusade *or* to mount a campaign against injustice

croisé, -e [krwaze] **ADJ 1** *(bras)* folded; *(jambes)* crossed; **il était debout, les bras croisés** he was standing with his arms folded; **ne reste pas là les bras croisés!** don't just stand there!; **assis les jambes croisées** sitting cross-legged
2 *Littérature (rimes)* alternate
3 *(hybride ▸ animal, plante)* crossbred
4 *(veste, veston)* double-breasted
5 *Écon* **détention** *ou* **participation croisée** cross-holding
NM 1 *Tex* twill **2** *Hist* crusader
• **croisée** **NF 1** *(intersection)* crossing; **être à la croisée des chemins** to be standing at the crossroads; *Fig* to be at the parting of the ways **2** *Archit* **croisée d'ogives** intersecting ribs; **croisée de** *ou* **du transept** transept crossing **3** *(châssis de fenêtre)* casement; *(fenêtre)* casement window

croisement [krwazmɑ̃] **NM 1** *(intersection)* crossroads, junction; **au c. de la rue et de l'avenue** at the intersection of the street and the avenue
2 *(hybridation)* crossbreeding, crossing; **faire des croisements (de races)** to crossbreed *or* to interbreed (animals); **c'est un c. entre un épagneul et un setter** it's a cross between a spaniel and a setter, it's a spaniel-setter crossbreed **3** *(rencontre)* **le c. de deux voitures/navires** two cars/boats passing each other

croiser [3] [krwaze] **VT 1** *(mettre en croix ▸ baguettes, fils)* to cross; **c. les jambes** to cross one's legs; **c. les bras** to cross *or* to fold one's arms; **je croise les doigts pour que tu réussisses** I've got my fingers crossed for you; *aussi Fig* **c. le fer** *ou* **l'épée avec qn** to cross swords with sb
2 *(traverser)* to cross, to intersect, to meet; **là où la route croise la voie ferrée** where the road and the railway cross, at the junction of the road and the railway; *Fig* **c. la route** *ou* **le chemin de qn** to come across sb
3 *(rencontrer)* to pass, to meet; **je l'ai croisé dans la rue** I passed him in the street; **je l'ai croisée en sortant de chez toi** I met her as I was leaving your place; **son regard a croisé le mien** her eyes met mine
4 *(hybrider)* to cross, to crossbreed, to interbreed
VI 1 *(vêtement)* to cross over; **ce manteau ne croise pas assez** this coat doesn't cross over enough **2** *Naut* to cruise
VPR se croiser 1 *(se rencontrer)* to come across *or* to meet *or* to pass each other; **nous nous sommes croisés chez ton frère** we saw each other briefly *or* met (each other) at your brother's; **leurs regards se sont croisés** their eyes met
2 *(aller en sens opposé ▸ trains)* to pass (each other); *(▸ lettres)* to cross; *(▸ routes)* to cross, to intersect; **nos chemins se sont croisés, nos routes se sont croisées** our paths met
3 se c. les bras to fold one's arms; *Fig (être oisif)* to twiddle one's thumbs
4 *Hist* to go off to the Crusades

croiseur [krwazœr] **NM** *Mil* cruiser

croisière [krwazjɛr] **NF** cruise; **faire une c. aux Bahamas** to go on a cruise to the Bahamas; **ils sont en c.** they're on a cruise

croisillon [krwazijɔ̃] **NM 1** *(d'une fenêtre)* cross bar; *(au dos d'un meuble)* strengthener; **fenêtre à croisillons** lattice window **2** *Archit* transept
• **croisillons** **NMPL** *(sur une tarte, d'une fenêtre, d'un meuble)* lattice pattern

croissait *etc voir* **croître**

croissance [krwasɑ̃s] **NF 1** *Physiol* growth; **elle est en pleine c.** she's growing fast **2** *(développement ▸ d'une plante)* growth; *(▸ d'un pays)* development, growth; *(▸ d'une entreprise)* growth, expansion; **facteur de c.** growth factor; **notre entreprise est en pleine c.** our company is growing rapidly; **c. démographique** demographic growth, population growth; **c. économique** economic growth *or* development; **c. du marché** market growth; **la c. zéro** zero growth

croissant[1] [krwasɑ̃] **NM 1** *Culin* croissant; **c. aux amandes** almond croissant; **c. au beurre** all-butter croissant; **c. ordinaire** croissant made without butter
2 *(forme incurvée)* crescent; **des boucles d'oreilles en c.** crescent-shaped earrings
3 *Astron* crescent; **c. de lune** crescent moon
4 *Hist & Géog* **le C. fertile** the Fertile Crescent

croissant[2]**, -e** [krwasɑ̃, -ɑ̃t] **ADJ 1** *(▸ grandissant ▸ gén)* growing, increasing; *(▸ ordre)* ascending; **tension croissante dans le sud du pays** increasing tension in the south of the country; **les jeunes diplômés arrivent en nombre c.** there's an increasing number of young graduates **2** *Math (nombre, fonction)* monotonic

Croissant-Rouge [krwasɑ̃ruʒ] **NM le C.** the Red Crescent

croître [93] [krwatr] **VI 1** *(augmenter)* to increase, to grow; *(▸ rivière)* to swell; *(▸ lune)* to wax; *(▸ vent)* to rise; **les jours croissent** the days are getting longer; **elle sentait c. en elle une violente colère** she could feel a violent rage growing within her; **ça ne fait que c. et embellir** it's getting better and better; *Ironique* it's getting worse and worse; **c. en volume/nombre** to increase in volume/number; **c. en beauté et en sagesse** to grow wiser and more beautiful; **aller croissant** to be on the increase; **le bruit allait croissant** the noise kept growing; *Bible* **croissez et multipliez** go forth and multiply **2** *(grandir, pousser)* to grow; **quelques fleurs croissent sur la berge** there are a few flowers growing on the bank

croix [krwa] **NF 1** *(gibet)* cross; **mettre qn sur la c.** *ou* **en c.** to crucify sb; **il est mort sur la c.** he died on the cross; *Rel* **la (Sainte) C.** the (Holy) Cross; *Fig* **porter sa c.** to have one's cross to bear
2 *(objet cruciforme)* cross; **une petite c. autour du cou** a small cross round his/her neck; **les (deux) poutres font une c.** the beams form a cross; **c'est la c. et la bannière pour le faire manger** it's an uphill struggle to get him to eat; **c. de bois, c. de fer, si je mens, je vais en enfer** cross my heart (and hope to die)
3 *(emblème)* cross; **c. de Malte/St André** Maltese/St Andrew's cross; **c. latine/grecque** Latin/Greek cross; **c. en tau** *ou* **de St-Antoine** tau *or* St Anthony's cross; **c. ansée** ansate cross; **c. gammée** swastika; **la c. de Lorraine** the cross of Lorraine *(cross with two horizontal bars, the symbol of the Gaullist movement)*
4 *(récompense)* cross, medal; *(de la Légion d'honneur)* Cross of the Legion of Honour; **la c. de guerre** the Military Cross
5 *(signe écrit)* cross; **signer d'une c.** to sign with a cross; **marquer qch d'une c.** to put a cross on sth; **faire une c. sur qch** to forget *or* to kiss goodbye to sth; **les vacances, j'ai fait une c. dessus** I've decided I might as well forget about going on holiday; **tu peux faire une c. là-dessus** you might as well kiss it goodbye *or* forget it
6 *Couture* **point de c.** cross-stitch

7 *Astron* **C. du Sud** Southern Cross
• **en croix** ADJ **les bras en c.** with one's arms stretched out to the sides; **les skis en c.** with skis crossed ADV **placer** *ou* **mettre deux choses en c.** to lay two things crosswise *or* across each other; **mettre les bras en c.** to stretch one's arms out to the sides

Croix-Rouge [krwaruʒ] NF **la C.** the Red Cross; **la C. française** the French Red Cross

cromlech [krɔmlɛk] NM cromlech

crooner [krunœr] NM crooner

croquant¹ [krɔkɑ̃] NM **1** *Hist* = name given to a peasant revolutionary during the reigns of Henry IV and Louis XIII **2** *Péj (paysan)* (country) bumpkin, yokel

croquant², -e [krɔkɑ̃, -ɑ̃t] ADJ crisp, crunchy
NM *Fam* **le c.** the crunchy part❑

croque-au-sel [krɔkosɛl] **à la croque-au-sel** ADV (raw) with salt; **manger des artichauts à la c.** to eat raw artichokes dipped in salt

croque-madame [krɔkmadam] NM INV = toasted cheese and ham sandwich with a fried egg on top

croquemitaine, croque-mitaine [krɔkmitɛn] *(pl* **croque-mitaines)** NM bogeyman

croque-monsieur [krɔkməsjø] NM INV = toasted cheese and ham sandwich

croque-mort [krɔkmɔr] *(pl* **croque-morts)** NM undertaker's assistant; **il a vraiment une allure de c.** he has a really funereal look about him

croquenot [krɔkno] NM *Fam* clodhopper, beetlecrusher

croquer [3] [krɔke] VT **1** *(pomme, radis etc)* to crunch; *Fam Fig* **il est (joli)** *ou* **mignon à c.** he looks good enough to eat
2 *Fam (dépenser ▸ héritage)* to squander❑; **elle va c. ta fortune** she'll squander all your money
3 *(esquisser)* to sketch; *(décrire)* to outline
4 *Fam* **c. le marmot** *(attendre)* to cool *or* to kick one's heels
VI to be crunchy; **des radis qui croquent (sous la dent)** crunchy radishes
• **croquer dans** VT IND to bite into

croquet [krɔkɛ] NM **1** *(jeu)* croquet; **faire une partie de c.** to have a game of croquet **2** *Couture* braid **3** *Culin* almond *Br* biscuit *or Am* cookie

croquette [krɔkɛt] NF *Culin* croquette; **c. de poisson** fishcake
• **croquettes** NFPL *(pour animal)* dry food

croqueuse [krɔkøz] NF *Fam* **c. de diamants** golddigger; **c. d'hommes** man-eater

croquignole [krɔkiɲɔl] NF = small crisp biscuit

croquignolet, -ette [krɔkiɲɔlɛ, -ɛt] ADJ *Fam Ironique* cutesy

croquis [krɔki] NM sketch; **faire un c. de qch** to sketch sth; **elle est partie faire des c. dans la vieille ville** she went to do some sketches in the old town; **c. coté** dimensional sketch

crosne [kron] NM Chinese artichoke

cross [krɔs], **cross-country** [krɔskuntri] *(pl* **cross-countrys** *ou* **cross-countries)** NM INV **1** *(sport ▸ à pied)* cross-country running; *(▸ à vélo)* mountain-biking; *(▸ à moto)* motocross; *(▸ à cheval)* cross-country riding; **faire du c.** *(à pied)* to go cross-country running; *(à vélo)* to go mountain-biking; *(à moto)* to do motocross; *(à cheval)* to go cross-country riding **2** *(épreuve ▸ à pied)* cross-country run *or* race; *(▸ à vélo)* mountain-bike race; *(▸ à moto)* motocross event; *(▸ à cheval)* cross-country horse trial

crosse [krɔs] NF **1** *Rel* crosier, crozier
2 *Sport (canne ▸ de hockey)* stick; *(▸ du jeu de crosse)* crosse
3 *Can (jeu)* lacrosse
4 *(extrémité ▸ d'une canne)* crook; *(▸ d'un violon)* scroll
5 *(partie ▸ d'un revolver)* grip, butt; *(▸ d'un fusil)* (butt) stock; *(▸ d'un canon)* trail; **ils l'ont tué à coups de c.** they beat him to death with their rifle butts; **lever** *ou* **mettre la c. en l'air** *(se révolter)* to refuse to fight; *(se rendre)* to surrender
6 *Bot (d'une fougère)* crosier
7 *Anat (de l'aorte)* arch
8 *Culin* **c. de bœuf** knuckle of beef
9 *Fam* **chercher des crosses à qn** to try to pick a fight with sb

cross-training [krɔstrejniŋ] NM *Sport* cross-training

crotale [krɔtal] NM *Zool (serpent à sonnette)* rattlesnake; *(famille)* pit viper

crotte [krɔt] NF **1** *(d'un animal)* dropping; *(d'un bébé)* poo; *Fam* **ton chien pourrait aller faire sa c. ailleurs!** your dog could do its business somewhere else!; *Fam* **c. (de bique)!** oh poo!, *Am* shoot!
2 *Fam Péj (chose ou personne méprisée)* **c'est de la c. (de bique)** it's a load of poo *or Br* rubbish *or Am* garbage; *Fam* **c'est pas de la c.!** it's none of your (cheap) *Br* rubbish *or Am* garbage!; **il se prend pas pour de la c.!** he thinks he's God's gift!, *Br* he really fancies himself!
3 *Arch (boue)* mud
4 *Culin* **c. en chocolat** chocolate
5 *(morve)* **c. de nez** *Br* bogey, *Am* booger
6 *Fam (par affection)* **ma petite c.!** you little sweetie you!

crotté, -e [krɔte] ADJ muddy, mucky

crotter [3] [krɔte] VT *(chaussures, voiture)* to dirty, to muddy
VI *Fam (chien)* to do its business
VPR **se crotter** to get dirty, to get covered in *or* with mud

crottin [krɔtɛ̃] NM **1** *(de cheval)* dung, manure **2** *Culin* crottin, = small round goat's milk cheese

crouille [kruj] NF *Suisse* **1** *(vaurien)* crook **2** *(farceur)* rascal
ADJ *Suisse* **1** *(de mauvaise qualité)* miserable **2** *(farceur)* playful
NM *très Fam* = racist term used to refer to a North African Arab

croulant, -e [krulɑ̃, -ɑ̃t] ADJ crumbling, tumbledown; **une vieille maison croulante** a tumbledown old house
NM,F *Fam Péj* **(vieux) c.** old fogey, old codger, *Br* wrinkly

crouler [3] [krule] VI **1** *(tomber ▸ édifice)* to collapse, to crumble, to topple; **le mur menace de c.** the wall is about to collapse; **l'étagère croule sous le poids des livres** the shelf is sagging under the weight of the books; **un arbre croulant sous les fruits** a tree laden with fruit; **un baudet qui croulait sous son chargement** a donkey weighed down with its load; *Fig* **c. sous le poids des ans/soucis** to be weighed down by age/worry; *Fig* **la salle croula sous les applaudissements** the auditorium thundered with applause; *Fig* **il croule sous le travail depuis deux mois** he's been buckling under his workload for the last two months **2** *(se désintégrer ▸ empire, société)* to be on the verge of collapse, to be crumbling; **le krach boursier a fait c. certaines entreprises** some firms collapsed *or* went under as a result of the Stock Market crash

croup [krup] NM *Méd* croup; **faux c.** false croup

croupade [krupad] NF *Équitation* curvet

croupe [krup] NF **1** *(de cheval)* croup, rump; **prendre qn en c.** to have sb ride pillion; **monter en c.** to ride pillion
2 *Fam (fesses)* behind
3 *(sommet ▸ d'une colline)* hilltop; *(▸ d'une montagne)* mountain top
4 *Archit (de toit)* hip

croupetons [kruptɔ̃] **à croupetons** ADV être **à c.** to crouch, to squat; **se mettre à c.** to squat down, to crouch (down)

croupi, -e [krupi] ADJ *(eau)* stagnant, foul

croupier [krupje] NM *(au jeu)* croupier

croupière [krupjɛr] NF *Équitation* crupper

croupion [krupjɔ̃] NM **1** *Orn* rump
2 *Culin Br* parson's *or Am* pope's nose
3 *Fam (fesses) Br* bum, *Am* butt
4 *(comme adj; avec ou sans trait d'union) Pol* **parti c.** rump of a party

croupir [32] [krupir] VI **1** *(eau)* to stagnate, to grow foul **2** *Fig (s'encroûter, moisir)* **c. dans un cachot** to rot in jail; **je ne vais pas c. ici toute ma vie** I'm not going to rot here all my life; **c. dans l'ignorance** to wallow in one's ignorance

croupissant, -e [krupisɑ̃, -ɑ̃t] ADJ *(eau, mare)* putrid, foul

crousille [kruzij] NF *Suisse* piggybank

croustade [krustad] NF *Culin* croustade

croustillant, -e [krustijɑ̃, -ɑ̃t] ADJ **1** *(biscuit, gratin)* crisp, crunchy; *(pain)* crusty **2** *(osé)* saucy

croustiller [3] [krustije] VI *(biscuit, gratin)* to be crisp *or* crunchy; *(pain)* to be crusty

croustilles [krustij] NFPL *Can Br* crisps, *Am* (potato) chips

croûte [krut] NF **1** *(partie ▸ du pain)* crust; *(▸ du fromage)* rind; **une c. de pain** a crust; *Fam* **casser la c.** to have a bite to eat; *Péj* **il ne reste que quelques croûtes** there are only a few (old) crusts left; *Suisse* **c. dorée** French toast
2 *(préparation)* pastry shell; **c. de vol-au-vent** vol-au-vent case
3 *Fam (nourriture)* grub; **t'as préparé la c.?** is the food ready?❑
4 *(dépôt)* layer; **c. de rouille/saleté** layer of rust/dirt
5 *Géol* **la c. terrestre** the earth's crust
6 *Can (de neige)* crust
7 *Méd* scab; **croûtes de lait** cradle cap
8 *Fam Péj (tableau)* (bad) painting❑, daub
9 *(de cuir)* hide
10 *Fam Péj (personne)* **quelle c.!** *(routinier)* what a stick-in-the-mud!; *(idiot)* what a dope!

croûter [3] [krute] VI *Fam* to eat❑

croûteux, -euse [krutø, -øz] ADJ scabby

croûton [krutɔ̃] NM **1** *Culin (frit)* crouton; *(quignon)* (crusty) end, crust *(of a baguette)* **2** *Fam Péj (personne)* **vieux c.** old fossil

croyable [krwajabl] ADJ believable, credible; **c'est à peine c.** it's hardly credible; **son histoire n'est pas c.** his/her story is incredible *or* unbelievable

croyait *etc voir* **croire**

croyance [krwajɑ̃s] NF **1** *(pensée)* belief; **les croyances populaires** popular beliefs, conventional wisdom **2** *(fait de croire)* faith; **la c. en Dieu** faith *or* belief in God; **la c. à** *ou* **en la démocratie** belief in democracy **3** *(religion)* faith, religion

croyant, -e [krwajɑ̃, -ɑ̃t] ADJ **il est/n'est pas c.** he's a believer/non-believer, he believes/he doesn't believe in God
NM,F believer

CRS [seɛrɛs] NM *(abrév* **compagnie républicaine de sécurité)** *(policier) Br* ≃ riot policeman, *Am* ≃ state trooper; **les C. ont chargé les manifestants** the riot police charged the demonstrators; **les C. responsables de la surveillance des plages** the security police responsible for keeping watch over the beaches

> **CRS**
>
> The CRS is the Minister of the Interior's police force, whose primary responsibility is to ensure public order at demonstrations and deal with riots. They have been criticized for certain strong-arm tactics.

cru¹ [kry] NM *(en œnologie ▸ terroir)* vineyard; *(▸ vin)* vintage, wine; **les grands crus de Bourgogne** the great wines of Burgundy
• **de mon/son/***etc* **cru** ADJ **une histoire de son c.** a story of his/her own invention
• **du cru** ADJ **un vin du c.** a local wine; **les gens du c.** the locals

cru², -e¹ [kry] ADJ **1** *(non cuit ▸ denrée)* raw, uncooked; *(▸ céramique)* unfired
2 *(non pasteurisé ▸ beurre, lait)* unpasteurized
3 *(sans préparation ▸ soie)* raw; *(▸ minerai)* crude; *(▸ bois)* untreated
4 *(aveuglant ▸ couleur)* crude, harsh, glaring; *(▸ éclairage)* harsh, blinding, glaring
5 *(net)* blunt, uncompromising; **c'est la vérité toute crue** it's the pure, unadorned truth
6 *(osé)* coarse, crude
7 *Belg, Can & Suisse (temps, bâtiment)* damp and cold
NM *Culin* **le c. et le cuit** the raw and the cooked
ADV **1** *(sans cuisson)* **manger qch c.** to eat sth raw; **avaler** *ou* **manger qn tout c.** to make mincemeat out of *or* to wipe the floor with sb; **je ne vais pas t'avaler tout c.!** I'm not going to eat you!, I don't bite! **2** *(brutalement)* **parler c.** to speak bluntly; **je vous le dis tout c.** I'm telling you it as it is
• **à cru** ADV **1** *Équitation* bareback **2** *Archit* without foundations

cru[3], **-e**[2] [kry] PP *voir* **croire**

crû, -ue[3] [kry] PP *voir* **croître**

cruauté [kryote] NF **1** *(dureté)* cruelty; **avec c.** cruelly; **c. mentale** mental cruelty **2** *(acte)* cruel act, act of cruelty **3** *Littéraire (rudesse)* harshness, (extreme) severity, cruelty; **la c. de l'hiver** the severity of the winter

cruche [kryʃ] NF **1** *(récipient)* jug, pitcher
2 *(contenu)* jugful
3 *Fam Péj (personne)* dope, *Br* plonker, *Am* goof
4 *Suisse (bouillotte)* hot-water bottle
ADJ *Fam Péj Br* thick, *Am* dumb; **ce que tu peux être c.!** you can be so *Br* thick *or Am* dumb!; **avoir l'air c.** to look stupid

cruchon [kryʃɔ̃] NM **1** *(récipient)* small jug **2** *(contenu)* small jugful

crucial, -e, -aux, -ales [krysjal, -o] ADJ **1** *(capital)* crucial, vital; **être d'une importance cruciale** to be crucially important, to be of crucial importance **2** *(en croix)* cross-shaped

crucifère [krysifɛr] *Bot* ADJ cruciferous
NF crucifer
• **crucifères** NFPL Cruciferea

crucifiement [krysifimɑ̃] NM crucifixion

crucifier [9] [krysifje] VT **1** *(mettre en croix)* to crucify **2** *Littéraire (humilier)* to crucify

crucifix [krysifi] NM crucifix

crucifixion [krysifiksjɔ̃] NF crucifixion

cruciforme [krysifɔrm] ADJ shaped like a cross, *Sout* cruciform

cruciverbiste [krysiverbist] NMF crossword (puzzle) enthusiast, *Spéc* cruciverbalist

crudité [krydite] NF **1** *(d'une couleur, de la lumière)* harshness **2** *(brutalité ▸ d'une réponse)* bluntness **3** *(vulgarité)* coarseness, crudeness
• **crudités** NFPL *Culin* (assorted) raw vegetables, crudités

crue[4] [kry] NF **1** *(élévation de niveau)* rise in the water level; **la rivière en c. a inondé la ville** the river burst its banks and flooded the town **2** *(inondation)* **la c. des rivières au printemps** the swelling of the rivers in the spring; **en période de c.** when there are floods

cruel, -elle [kryɛl] ADJ **1** *(méchant ▸ personne)* cruel; *(dur ▸ propos)* cruel, harsh **2** *(pénible ▸ destin)* cruel, harsh, bitter; *(▸ dilemme, choix)* cruel, painful; *(▸ perte)* cruel; **être dans un c. embarras** to be in a painfully difficult situation; **être dans une cruelle incertitude** to be horribly uncertain

cruellement [kryɛlmɑ̃] ADV **1** *(méchamment)* cruelly; **traiter qn c.** to be cruel to sb **2** *(péniblement)* sorely; **j'ai c. ressenti son absence** I missed him/her dreadfully; **être c. déçu** to be sorely *or* bitterly disappointed; **faire c. défaut** to be sorely lacking

cruiser [kruzœr] NM cruiser

crûment [krymɑ̃] ADV **1** *(brutalement)* bluntly; **laissez-moi vous dire c. ce que j'en pense** let me tell you quite frankly what I think about it; **pour parler c.** to put it bluntly **2** *(grossièrement)* coarsely; **il ne faut pas s'exprimer c. devant les enfants** you mustn't use coarse language in front of the children **3** *(vivement ▸ éclairé)* garishly

crustacé, -e [krystase] *Zool* ADJ crustacean, crustaceous
NM crustacean; *Culin* **des crustacés** shellfish
• **crustacés** NMPL Crustacea, Crustaceans

crut *etc voir* **croire**

crût *etc voir* **croître**

cryobiologie [krijobjɔlɔʒi] NF cryobiology

cryochirurgie [krijɔʃiryrʒi] NF cryosurgery

cryoconservation [krijokɔ̃sɛrvasjɔ̃] NF *Phys* cryoconservation

cryogène [krijɔʒɛn] ADJ *Phys* cryogenic; **mélange c.** freezing mixture

cryogénie [krijɔʒeni] NF *Phys* cryogenics *(singulier)*

cryogénisation [krijɔʒenizasjɔ̃] NF cryogenics *(singulier)*

cryogéniser [krijɔʒenize] VT to cryogenically freeze *or* preserve

cryothérapie [krijɔterapi] NF *Méd* cryotherapy

cryptage [kriptaʒ] NM **1** *(d'un message)* coding **2** *(d'une émission de télévision)* coding, scrambling

crypte [kript] NF *Archit & Anat* crypt

crypté, -e [kripte] ADJ **1** *(message)* coded **2** *(émission de télévision)* scrambled *(for non-subscribers)*, encrypted

crypter [3] [kripte] VT **1** *(message)* to encode **2** *(émission de télévision)* to scramble, to encrypt

cryptocommuniste [kriptɔkɔmynist] ADJ cryptocommunist
NMF cryptocommunist

cryptogramme [kriptɔgram] NM cryptogram

cryptographie [kriptɔgrafi] NF cryptography

cryptographique [kriptɔgrafik] ADJ cryptographic

cryptologie [kriptɔlɔʒi] NF cryptography

CSA [seɛsa] NM *(abrév* **Conseil supérieur de l'audiovisuel**) = French broadcasting supervisory body

CSCE [seɛsseə] NF *(abrév* **Conférence sur la sécurité et la coopération en Europe**) CSCE

CSG [seɛsʒe] NF *Fin (abrév* **contribution sociale généralisée**) = income-based tax deducted at source as a contribution to paying off the French social security budget deficit

Cte *(abrév écrite* **comte**) Count

Ctesse *(abrév écrite* **comtesse**) Countess

Cuba [kyba] NF Cuba

cubage [kybaʒ] NM **1** *(évaluation)* calculating the cubic volume **2** *(volume)* cubic volume, cubature, cubage

cubain, -e [kybɛ̃, -ɛn] ADJ Cuban
• **Cubain, -e** NM,F Cuban

cube [kyb] ADJ cubic; **centimètre c.** cubic centimetre
NM **1** *Géom & Math* cube; **quel est le c. de 4?** what's 4 cubed *or* the cube of 4?; **élever un nombre au c.** to cube a number
2 *(objet cubique)* cube; **couper de la viande en cubes** to cut meat into cubes; **la bâtisse ressemble à un gros c. de béton** the building's like a big concrete box
3 *(jeu)* (building) block
4 *Fam (cylindrée)* **un gros/petit c.** *(moto)* a big/small bike
5 *Fam Arg scol (en classe préparatoire)* = student repeating the second year of "classes préparatoires"

cuber [3] [kybe] VT to determine the cubic volume of
VI **1** *(contenir)* **le réservoir cube 100 litres** the tank has a cubic capacity of 100 litres **2** *Fam (être cher)* **tout ça finit par c.** it all adds up **3** *Fam Arg scol (redoubler ▸ en classe préparatoire)* = to repeat the second year of "classes préparatoires"

cubique [kybik] ADJ **1** *(en forme de cube)* cube-shaped, cubic **2** *Math & Minér* cubic
NF *Math* cubic

cubisme [kybism] NM *Beaux-Arts* Cubism

cubiste [kybist] *Beaux-Arts* ADJ Cubist, Cubistic
NMF Cubist

Cubitainer® [kybitenɛr] NM = large cubic plastic container *(for bulk purchase of wine etc)*

cubital, -e, -aux, -ales [kybital, -o] ADJ *Anat* ulnar

cubitus [kybitys] NM *Anat* ulna

cuchaule [kyʃol] NF *Suisse* brioche

cucu, cucul [kyky] ADJ INV *Fam* **c. (la praline)** *(personne, air)* cutesy, *Br* twee; *(film, livre)* corny

CUE [seyə] NM *(abrév* **Conseil de l'Union européenne**) CEU

cueillera *etc voir* **cueillir**

cueillette [kœjɛt] NF **1** *(ramassage ▸ de fruits)* gathering, picking; *(▸ de fleurs)* picking **2** *(récolte)* crop, harvest **3** *(en sociologie)* gathering; **une tribu qui vit de la c.** a tribe of gatherers

cueilleur, -euse [kœjœr, -øz] NM,F *(de fruits)* picker, gatherer; *(de fleurs)* picker

cueillir [41] [kœjir] VT **1** *(récolter ▸ fruits)* to gather, to pick; *(▸ fleurs)* to pick; *Fig* **c. des lauriers** to win laurels; *Littéraire* **cueillez le jour** seize the day
2 *(trouver)* to pick up, to collect; **il est venu me c. chez moi** he came to pick me up at my place; **où es-tu allé c. pareille idée?** where on earth did you get that idea?
3 *Fam (surprendre)* to catch, to grab; **si tu veux sa permission, cueille-la à son arrivée** if you want to get her permission, (make sure you) catch her as she comes in; **être cueilli à froid** to be caught off guard
4 *Fam (arrêter)* to nab, to collar
5 *(saisir au passage)* to snatch, to grab; **c. un baiser** to snatch a kiss; **la serveuse cueillit un menu au passage** the waitress grabbed a menu as she walked past

cuesta [kwesta] NF cuesta

cui-cui [kɥikɥi] NM INV tweet-tweet, twittering; **faire c.** to tweet, to go tweet-tweet

cuillère, cuiller [kɥijɛr] NF **1** *(instrument)* spoon; **c. à café** *ou* **à moka** teaspoon; *(plus petite)* coffee spoon; **c. en bois** wooden spoon; *Sport* **la c. de bois** the wooden spoon; **c. à dessert** dessert spoon; **c. parisienne** melon baller; **c. à soupe,** *Can* **c. à table** soup spoon; *(pour mesurer)* tablespoon; **petite c.,** *Can* **c. à thé** teaspoon; *Fam* **en deux** *ou* **trois coups de c. à pot** in a jiffy, in no time at all
2 *(contenu)* spoonful; **une c. à café de sucre** a teaspoonful of sugar; **deux cuillères à soupe de farine** two tablespoonfuls of flour; **une c., pour papa, une c., pour maman** *(à un enfant)* one (spoonful) for Daddy, one (spoonful) for Mummy
3 *Pêche* spoon, spoonbait
4 *(pièce d'amorçage d'une grenade)* safety catch
5 *très Fam (main)* mitt, paw
• **à la cuillère** ADJ **pêche à la c.** spinning, trolling
ADV **1** *(en mangeant)* **nourrir** *ou* **faire manger qn à la c.** to spoon-feed sb **2** *Pêche* **pêcher la truite à la c.** to spin *or* to troll for trout

cuillerée [kɥijere] NF spoonful; **une c. à café de sucre** a teaspoonful of sugar; **une c. à dessert** a dessertspoonful; **une c. à soupe de farine** a tablespoonful of flour

cuilleron [kɥijrɔ̃] NM *(d'une cuillère)* bowl

cuir [kɥir] NM **1** *(peau ▸ traitée)* leather; *(▸ brute)* hide; **le c.** *(vêtements en cuir)* leather clothes; *(objets en cuir)* leather goods; *Fam* **un c.** a leather jacket; **c. brut** *ou* **cru** *ou* **vert** rawhide; **c. bouilli** cuir-bouilli; **c. de Russie** Russia leather
2 *(peau humaine)* skin; **c. chevelu** scalp; *Fam* **tomber sur** *ou* **tanner le c. à qn** to tan sb's hide
3 *(lanière)* **c. à rasoir** strop
4 *Fam (faute de liaison)* incorrect liaison *(introducing an unwanted consonant between two words)*
• **de cuir, en cuir** ADJ leather *(avant n)*

cuirasse [kɥiras] NF **1** *Hist (armure)* breastplate, cuirass, corselet
2 *Fig* protective shell; **une c. de froideur** an air of aloofness
3 *Mil (d'un char, d'un navire de guerre)* armour
4 *(carapace)* cuirass

cuirassé, -e [kɥirase] ADJ *(char, navire)* armoured, armour-plated
NM battleship

cuirasser [3] [kɥirase] VT **1** *Mil* to armour, to armour-plate **2** *(endurcir)* to harden
VPR **se cuirasser 1** *Hist* to put on a breastplate **2** *(s'endurcir)* to harden oneself; **se c. contre qch** to harden oneself to sth

cuirassier [kɥirasje] NM *Hist* cuirassier

cuire [98] [kɥir] VT **1** *Culin (gén)* to cook; *(pain, gâteau, tarte)* to bake; **c. à l'eau** to boil; **c. à la vapeur** to steam; **c. au four** to cook in the oven; *(pain, gâteau, tarte)* to bake; **pain cuit au feu de bois** bread baked in a wood-burning oven **2** *(brûler ▸ peau)* to burn; **la canicule a cuit les prés** the fields are parched as a result of the heatwave **3** *Suisse (eau, lait)* to boil; *(vêtements, linge)* to boil-wash
VI **1** *Culin (aliment)* to cook; **c. à feu doux** *ou* **petit feu** to simmer; **c. à gros bouillons** to boil hard; **poulet prêt à c.** oven-ready chicken; **faire c. qch** to cook sth; **faire c. qch à feu doux** to simmer sth; **faire c. qch à feu vif** to cook sth over a high flame; **faire c. qch au four** to bake sth; **faire trop c. qch** to overcook sth; **j'ai trop fait c. les légumes** I've overcooked the vegetables; **tu n'as pas fait assez c. la viande** you've undercooked the meat; *Fam* **laisser qn c. dans son jus** to let sb stew in his/her own juice; *Fam* **va te faire c. un œuf!** go and take a running jump!, go and jump in a lake!;

Fam **je l'ai envoyé se faire c. un œuf** I sent him packing
2 *Fam (souffrir de la chaleur)* **je cuis!** I'm roasting!; **on cuit dans cette voiture!** it's boiling hot in this car!
3 *(brûler)* to burn, to sting; **les yeux me cuisent** my eyes are burning *or* stinging
4 il vous en cuira you'll regret it; **il pourrait t'en c.** you might regret it
• **à cuire** ADJ **chocolat à c.** cooking chocolate; **pommes à c.** cooking apples
cuisant, -e [kɥizɑ̃, -ɑ̃t] ADJ **1** *(douleur, sensation)* burning, stinging; **il ressentit une douleur cuisante à la jambe** he felt a burning pain in his leg **2** *(affront, injure)* stinging, bitter; *(défaite)* stinging; **déception cuisante** bitter disappointment
cuiseur [kɥizœr] NM large cooking pot
cuisine [kɥizin] NF **1** *(lieu)* kitchen; **c. roulante** field kitchen
2 *(activité)* cooking, *Br* cookery; **faire la c.** to cook; **elle fait très bien la c.** she's an excellent cook; **sais-tu faire la c.?** can you cook?; **c'est lui qui fait la c.** he does the cooking; **la c. au beurre/à l'huile** cooking with butter/oil; **c. bourgeoise** good plain home cooking
3 *(ensemble de mets)* cuisine, food, dishes; **c. fine et soignée** carefully prepared dishes *or* food; **j'apprécie la c. chinoise** I enjoy Chinese food; **c. allégée, c. minceur** cuisine minceur, lean cuisine; **nouvelle c.** nouvelle cuisine
4 *(cuisiniers)* **la c.** *(dans un château, dans un restaurant)* the kitchen staff; *(à la cantine)* the catering *or* kitchen staff
5 *(meubles)* kitchen (furniture); **c. américaine** = kitchen with a bar separating the cooking and eating areas; **c. intégrée,** *Suisse* **c. agencée** fitted kitchen; **c. en kit** kitchen units in kit form
6 *Fam Péj (malversations)* wheeling and dealing; **la c. électorale/parlementaire** electoral/parliamentary wheeling and dealing, electoral/parliamentary dirty tricks
• **cuisines** NFPL *(au restaurant)* kitchen; *Naut* galley
• **de cuisine** ADJ *(table, couteau)* kitchen *(avant n)*
cuisiné, -e [kɥizine] ADJ *voir* **plat**[1]
cuisiner [3] [kɥizine] VT **1** *(plat, dîner)* to cook; **spécialités cuisinées au vin rouge** specialities cooked in red wine; **qu'est-ce que tu nous as cuisiné pour ce soir?** what have you cooked for us tonight? **2** *Fam (interroger ▸ accusé, suspect)* to grill; **il s'est fait c. par la police** he was grilled by the police
VI to cook; **j'aime c.** I like cooking; **elle cuisine bien** she's a good cook
cuisinette [kɥizinɛt] NF *Offic & Can & Suisse* kitchenette
cuisinier, -ère [kɥizinje, -ɛr] NM,F cook
• **cuisinière** NF stove, *Br* cooker; **cuisinière électrique à gaz** electric gas stove *or Br* cooker; **cuisinière mixte** combined gas and electric stove *or Br* cooker
cuisons *etc voir* **cuire**
cuissage [kɥisaʒ] *voir* **droit**[3]
cuissard [kɥisar] NM **1** *(d'un cycliste)* cycling shorts **2** *(d'une armure)* cuisse, cuish
cuissardes [kɥisard] NFPL **1** *(de femme)* thigh boots **2** *(de pêcheur)* waders
cuisse [kɥis] NF **1** *(partie du corps)* thigh; *Fam Hum* **avoir la c. légère** to put it about; *très Fam* **il y a de la c.!** check out the babes *or Br* talent!; *Fam* **se croire sorti de la c. de Jupiter** to think a lot of oneself, to think one is the bee's knees *or* cat's whiskers **2** *Zool* leg **3** *Culin* leg; **cuisses de grenouille** frogs' legs; **c. de poulet** chicken leg
cuisseau, -x [kɥiso] NM *(de veau)* haunch
cuissettes [kɥisɛt] NFPL *Suisse* (sports) shorts
cuisson [kɥisɔ̃] NF **1** *(fait de cuire ▸ gén)* cooking; *(▸ pain, gâteau)* baking; *(▸ rôti)* roasting, cooking; **c. au grill** grilling; **c. à la vapeur** steaming; **temps de c.** cooking time; **quelle c.?** *(viande)* how would you like your meat cooked? **2** *(des briques, de la porcelaine)* burning, firing **3** *(brûlure)* burning, smarting
cuissot [kɥiso] NM *(de gibier)* haunch
cuistance [kɥistɑ̃s] NF *Fam* grub; **faire la c.** to make the grub
cuistot [kɥisto] NM *Fam* cook[□], chef[□]
cuistre [kɥistr] NM *(pédant)* pedant, prig
ADJ pedantic, priggish
cuistrerie [kɥistrəri] NF **1** *(pédanterie)* pedantry, priggishness **2** *(grossièreté)* boorishness
cuit, -e [kɥi, kɥit] ADJ **1** *(aliment)* cooked; **viande bien cuite** well-done meat; **viande cuite à point** medium-rare meat; **mal c., pas assez c.** undercooked; **trop c.** overcooked; **jambon c.** cooked ham; **attendre que ça tombe tout c. (dans le bec)** to wait for things to fall into one's lap
2 *(brûlé ▸ peau)* burnt, sunburnt; *(▸ jardin, champ)* parched
3 *Fam (usé)* worn out, threadbare; **elles sont cuites, mes bottes!** my boots have had it!
4 *Fam (perdu)* **je suis c.!** I'm done for!, I've had it!; **notre sortie de dimanche, c'est c.!** we can kiss our Sunday outing goodbye!
5 *très Fam (ivre)* loaded, plastered
NM **1** *Culin* **le c.** the cooked **2** *(locution)* **c'est du tout c.** it's as good as done (already); **ça n'a pas été du tout c.** it was no walkover
• **cuite** NF **1** *très Fam (beuverie)* **(se) prendre une cuite** to get loaded *or* plastered; **il tenait une de ces cuites!** he was totally loaded *or* plastered! **2** *(de céramiques)* baking, firing
cuiter [3] [kɥite] **se cuiter** VPR *très Fam* to get loaded *or* plastered
cuivre [kɥivr] NM **1** *Métal* copper; **de c., en c.** copper *(Avant n)*; **c. jaune** brass; **c. rouge** copper; **mine de c.** copper mine **2** *Beaux-Arts (planche)* copperplate
• **cuivres** NMPL **1** *(objets)* copperware; *(en cuivre jaune)* brasses; *(casseroles)* copper (pots and) pans; **faire (briller) les cuivres** to polish the brassware, to do the brasses **2** *Mus* brass instruments
cuivré, -e [kɥivre] ADJ **1** *Beaux-Arts & Métal* copperplated **2** *(rouge)* copper-coloured; **avoir le teint c.** *ou* **la peau cuivrée** *(par le soleil)* to be tanned; *(naturellement)* to have a ruddy complexion; **des cheveux aux reflets cuivrés** auburn hair **3** *(son, voix)* resonant
cuivrer [3] [kɥivre] VT **1** *Beaux-Arts & Métal* to copperplate **2** *(donner une teinte rougeâtre à)* to bronze, to tan
cuivreux, -euse [kɥivrø, -øz] ADJ cupreous, cuprous
cul [ky] NM **1** *très Fam (postérieur) Br* arse, *Am* ass; **un coup de pied au c.** a kick up the pants *or Br* backside; **être** *ou* **aller (le) c. nu** to go around *Br* bare-arsed *or Am* bare-assed; **en avoir plein le c. (de)** *(en avoir assez)* to be *Br* pissed off (with) *or Am* pissed (with); **en avoir plein le c.** *(être fatigué)* to be *Br* knackered *or Am* bushed; **plein le c., de leurs conneries!** I've had it up to here with their stupid tricks!; **avoir** *ou* **être le c. entre deux chaises** to have a foot in each camp; *Vulg* **l'avoir dans le c.** to have been shafted *or* screwed; *Vulg* **tu peux te le mettre au c.!** shove it up your *Br* arse *or Am* ass!; **avoir qn au c.** to have sb on one's tail; **on va lui foutre les flics au c.** let's get the cops on his/her tail; **pousser qn au c.** to be on sb's back; **tomber sur le c.** to fall on one's *Br* arse *or Am* ass; **en tomber** *ou* **en rester sur le c.** to be flabbergasted *or Br* gobsmacked; **je suis sur le c.!** *(fatigué) Br* I'm knackered!, *Am* I'm bushed!; *(surpris)* I can't believe it!, *Br* I'm gobsmacked!; **tirer au c.** *Br* to do sod all, *Am* to goldbrick; **faire la bouche en c. de poule** to purse one's lips, to pout; **avoir le c. bordé de nouilles** to be a lucky bastard; **et mon c., c'est du poulet?** *Br* you're taking the piss, aren't you!, *Am* gimme a break!; *Vulg* **parle à mon c., ma tête est malade** *(personne ne m'écoute)* I might as well talk to the fucking wall; *(laisse-moi tranquille)* fuck off!; *Vulg* **mon c.!** no fucking way!, my *Br* arse *or Am* ass!; **être comme c. et chemise** to be as thick as thieves; **il y a des coups de pied au c. qui se perdent** a kick in the *Br* arse *or Am* ass is too good for some people; *Can* **n'avoir rien que le c. et les dents** to be at rock bottom; **c. par-dessus tête** head over heels, *Br* arse over tit
2 *très Fam (sexe)* screwing, *Br* shagging; **leurs histoires de c. ne m'intéressent pas** what they get up to in the sack is of no interest to me; **un film de c.** a porn movie, *Am* a skin flick; **un magazine de c.** a porn *or* girlie mag, *Am* a skin mag ; **il s'intéresse qu'au c.** all he thinks about is screwing, *Br* he's got shagging on the brain
3 *très Fam (chance)* **avoir du c.** to be a lucky bastard
4 *très Fam Péj* **c. béni** Jesus freak
5 *très Fam (camion)* **un gros c.** *Br* a juggernaut, *Am* a semi, an eighteen-wheeler
6 *(fond d'une bouteille)* **un c. de bouteille** the bottom of a bottle; **faire c. sec** to down one's drink in one; **c. sec!** down in one!, *Br* bottoms up!
culasse [kylas] NF **1** *(d'une arme à feu)* breech; **c. mobile** *(de carabine)* bolt **2** *Tech* cylinder head
cul-blanc [kyblɑ̃] *(pl* **culs-blancs***)* NM *(oiseau)* wheatear
culbute [kylbyt] NF **1** *(galipette)* somersault; **faire des culbutes** to do somersaults **2** *(chute)* fall, tumble; **il a fait la c. dans l'escalier** he fell head over heels down the stairs **3** *Fam Fin* collapse[□]; **faire la c.** *(faire faillite)* to go bust *or* under; *(en revendant quelque chose)* to double one's money[□], to sell for double the cost price[□]; **le gouvernement a fait la c.** the government fell
culbuter [3] [kylbyte] VI *(à la renverse)* to tumble, to fall (over backwards); *(en avant)* to fall *or* to tumble (headfirst)
VT **1** *(faire tomber ▸ personne)* to knock over
2 *(venir à bout de ▸ régime)* to topple, to overthrow
3 *Mil* **c. l'ennemi** to overwhelm the enemy
4 *très Fam (femme)* to screw, to lay, *Br* to shag
culbuteur [kylbytœr] NM **1** *(jouet)* tumbler **2** *Mines* tippler, tipper **3** *Aut* rocker arm
cul-de-basse-fosse [kydbasfos] *(pl* **culs-de-basse-fosse***)* NM dungeon
cul-de-jatte [kydʒat] *(pl* **culs-de-jatte***)* NMF person with no legs
cul-de-lampe [kydlɑ̃p] *(pl* **culs-de-lampe***)* NM **1** *Typ* tailpiece **2** *Archit (dans une église)* cul-de-lampe, pendant; *(dans une maison)* bracket, corbel
cul-de-poule [kydpul] **en cul-de-poule** ADJ **une bouche en c.** a pouting little mouth; **faire la bouche en c.** to purse one's lips
cul-de-sac [kydsak] *(pl* **culs-de-sac***)* NM **1** *(rue)* dead end, cul-de-sac; *Fig* **être dans un c.** to have reached a dead end **2** *Anat* cul-de-sac
culée [kyle] NF abutment pier
culinaire [kylinɛr] ADJ culinary; **mes talents culinaires** my culinary skills; **les délices culinaires de la Bourgogne** the gastronomic delights of Burgundy
culminant, -e [kylminɑ̃, -ɑ̃t] *voir* **point**[2]
culminer [3] [kylmine] VI **1** *Géog* **les plus hauts sommets culminent à plus de 8000 mètres** the highest peaks are more than 8,000 metres high; **l'Everest culmine à 8848 mètres** Everest is 8,848 metres at its highest point **2** *(être à son maximum ▸ gén)* to reach its peak, to peak; *(▸ carrière)* to reach its height *or* peak; **la fréquentation culmine en juillet–août** the number of visitors peaks in July–August **3** *Astron* to culminate
culot [kylo] NM **1** *Fam (aplomb)* nerve, *Br* cheek; **tu as un sacré c.!** you've got a nerve *or* a cheek!; **il ne manque pas de c.** he's a cool customer
2 *(partie inférieure ▸ d'une lampe)* base, bottom; *(▸ d'une cartouche)* base, cap; *(▸ d'une ampoule)* base; *Aut (▸ d'une bougie)* body
3 *Métal (résidu)* residue, cinder, slag
4 *(d'une pipe)* dottle
• **au culot** ADV *Fam* **faire qch au c.** to bluff one's way through sth; **il faut y aller au c.** you've got to bluff it out *or* brazen it out
culottage [kylɔtaʒ] NM **1** *(d'une pipe)* seasoning **2** *(dépôt)* sooty layer
culotte [kylɔt] NF **1** *(sous-vêtement) Br* pants, *Am* panties; **petite c.** panties; *Fam* **faire dans sa c.** to dirty one's pants; *(avoir peur)* to be scared stiff; *Fam* **on a ri à en faire dans nos culottes** we wet *or* pissed ourselves laughing; *Fam* **poser c.** to *Br* have *or Am* take a dump *or* a crap
2 *(pantalon) Br* trousers, *Am* pants; *Hist* breeches; **culottes courtes** shorts; *Fig* **tu étais encore en c. courte** *ou* **culottes courtes** you were still in short *Br* trousers *or Am* pants; **des peintres/explorateurs en c. courte** *ou* **culottes courtes** young painters/explorers; **pour nos gastronomes en c. courte** *ou*

culottes courtes for our young gourmets; *Fam* **je m'en moque** *ou* **m'en fiche comme de ma première c.** I don't give a damn; **porter la c.** to wear the *Br* trousers *or Am* pants; **c. de cheval** riding breeches, jodhpurs; *Fig* jodhpur thighs; **c. de golf** plus-fours; **(vieille) c. de peau** (old) military type, *Br* Colonel Blimp

3 *(pièce de viande)* rump

4 *très Fam Sport & (à un jeu)* **prendre** *ou* **ramasser une c.** to get trounced

culotté, -e [kylɔte] **ADJ** *Fam (effronté) Br* cheeky, *Am* sassy; **il est drôlement c. en affaires!** he's a businessman who takes risks!

culotter [3] [kylɔte] **VT** *(pipe)* to season; *(théière)* to blacken

culpabilisation [kylpabilizasjɔ̃] **NF 1** *(action)* **la c. des victimes** making the victims feel guilty, putting the burden of guilt on the victims **2** *(sentiment)* (feeling of) guilt

culpabiliser [3] [kylpabilize] **VT c. qn** to make sb feel guilty

VI to feel guilty, to blame oneself; *Fam* **je culpabilise à fond** I'm on a real guilt-trip

VPR se culpabiliser to feel guilty, to blame oneself

culpabilité [kylpabilite] **NF 1** *(sentiment)* guilt, guilty feeling; **je ressens un certain sentiment de c. à son égard** I feel rather guilty about him/her **2** *Jur* guilt; **nier sa c.** to deny that one is guilty

culte [kylt] **NM 1** *(religion)* religion, faith; *(cérémonie)* service

2 *(dans le protestantisme)* **aller au c.** to go to church; **assister au c.** to attend church; **célébrer le c.** to worship

3 *(adoration)* cult, worship; **c. du soleil** sun worship; **le c. de la personnalité** personality cult; **elle a le c. du passé** she worships the past; **vouer un c. à qn** to worship sb; **il voue à son maître un véritable c.** he worships his master

4 *(comme adj)* cult; **film c.** cult movie *or Br* film

cul-terreux [kytɛrø] *(pl* **culs-terreux)** **NM** *Fam Péj* country bumpkin, yokel, *Am* hick

cultivable [kyltivabl] **ADJ** *(région, terre)* arable, farmable

cultivateur, -trice [kyltivatœr, -tris] **NM,F** farmer; **les petits cultivateurs** small farmers, smallholders

NM *(machine)* cultivator

cultivé, -e [kyltive] **ADJ 1** *Agr (terre, champs)* cultivated **2** *(éduqué)* cultured, educated, well-educated; **les gens cultivés** educated people

cultiver [3] [kyltive] **VT 1** *Agr (champ, terres)* to cultivate, to farm; *(plantes)* to grow

2 *Biol (virus, tissu)* to cultivate

3 *(conserver ▸ accent, image)* to cultivate; **elle cultive le paradoxe** she cultivates a paradoxical way of thinking

4 *(entretenir ▸ relations, savoir)* to keep up; **cultive ton russe** keep up your Russian; **c. sa mémoire** to work on one's memory; **cultivez l'ambassadeur** make sure you're in with the Ambassador

5 *(protéger)* to protect, to safeguard; **elle cultive son indépendance** she protects her independence

VPR se cultiver 1 *(accroître ses connaissances)* to educate oneself; **elle s'est cultivée par elle-même** she's self-taught **2 se c. l'esprit** to cultivate the mind

cultuel, -elle [kyltɥɛl] **ADJ** *(association, liberté)* religious; **édifice c.** place of worship

culture [kyltyr] **NF 1** *(production ▸ de blé, de maïs)* farming; *(▸ d'arbres, de fleurs)* growing; **faire de la c. commerciale** *ou* **de rapport** to specialize in cash crops; **c. biologique** organic farming; **c. intensive/extensive** intensive/extensive farming; **c. maraîchère** *Br* market gardening, *Am* truck farming; **c. sèche** dry farming

2 *(terrain)* **cultures** fields *or* lands (under cultivation); **ne passe pas à travers les cultures** don't walk across fields with crops

3 *(espèce)* crop

4 *(connaissance)* **la c.** culture; **parfaire sa c.** to improve one's mind; **un homme d'une grande c.** a highly cultured man; **c. générale** general knowledge; **avoir une bonne c. générale** *(candidat)* to have good general knowledge; *(étudiant)* to have had a broadly based education; **et maintenant, une question de c. générale** and now, a general knowledge question; **c. de masse** mass culture; **c. scientifique** scientific knowledge

5 *(civilisation)* culture, civilization; **c. d'entreprise** corporate culture

6 *Biol* culture; **faire une c. de cellules** to grow *or* to cultivate cells; **c. microbienne** bacterial culture; **c. de tissus** tissue culture

7 *Vieilli* **c. physique** physical education, PE; **elle fait de la c. physique tous les matins** she does exercises every morning

• **de culture** **ADJ** *Agr* farming *(avant n)*

• **en culture** **ADV** under cultivation; **combien avez-vous d'hectares en c.?** how many hectares do you farm *or* do you have under cultivation?

culturel, -elle [kyltyrɛl] **ADJ** cultural

culturisme [kyltyrism] **NM** bodybuilding

culturiste [kyltyrist] **NMF** bodybuilder

cumin [kymɛ̃] **NM** cumin; **c. des prés** caraway; **du pain au c.** caraway seed bread

cumul [kymyl] **NM 1 c. des fonctions, c. des mandats** plurality of offices, pluralism; **c. des traitements** *ou* **des salaires** drawing of more than one salary; *Fam* **faire du c.** *(directeur)* to wear several hats; *(artisan)* to moonlight **2** *Jur* plurality, combination; **c. d'actions** plurality of actions; **c. des peines** cumulative sentence

cumulable [kymylabl] **ADJ** *(fonctions)* which may be held concurrently; *(retraites, salaires)* which may be drawn concurrently; **ces deux réductions ne sont pas cumulables** the two discounts may not be claimed at the same time

cumulard, -e [kymylar, -ard] **NM,F** *Fam Péj* **1** *Pol* = politician with several mandates **2** *(directeur)* = person making money as the head of several companies **3** *(employé)* holder of several jobs

cumulatif, -ive [kymylatif, -iv] **ADJ** cumulative

cumuler [3] [kymyle] **VT 1** *(réunir ▸ fonctions)* to hold concurrently; *(▸ retraites, salaires)* to draw concurrently; **il cumule plusieurs emplois** he has several jobs **2** *(accumuler)* to pile up; **il cumule les erreurs depuis son arrivée** he's done nothing but make mistakes since he arrived **3** *Fin* to accrue; **intérêts cumulés** accrued interest

cumulo-nimbus [kymylɔnɛ̃bys] **NM INV** *Météo* cumulonimbus

cumulus [kymylys] **NM** *Météo* cumulus

cunéiforme [kyneifɔrm] **ADJ** cuneiform, wedge-shaped

NM cuneiform

cupide [kypid] **ADJ** *Littéraire* grasping, greedy; **il regardait l'argent d'un air c.** he was looking greedily at the money; **il est vraiment c.** he's a money grabber

cupidité [kypidite] **NF** *Littéraire* greed

Cupidon [kypidɔ̃] **NPR** *Myth* Cupid

cuprifère [kyprifer] **ADJ** cupriferous

cuprique [kyprik] **ADJ** cupric, cupreous

curable [kyrabl] **ADJ** curable, which can be cured; **la lèpre est c.** leprosy can be cured, leprosy is curable

curaçao [kyraso] **NM** curaçao

curage [kyraʒ] **NM** *(d'un égout, d'un fossé)* cleaning out

curare [kyrar] **NM** *Bot* curare, curari

curatelle [kyratɛl] **NF** *Jur* guardianship, trusteeship

curateur, -trice [kyratœr, -tris] **NM,F** *Jur* guardian, trustee

curatif, -ive [kyratif, -iv] **ADJ** healing

curatrice [kyratris] *voir* **curateur**

cure [kyr] **NF 1** *Méd (technique, période)* treatment; **c. d'amaigrissement** weight-loss *or Br* slimming course; **c. de désintoxication** detoxification programme; **faire une c. de désintoxication** to undergo treatment for alcoholism/drug addiction; **c. de repos** rest cure; **faire une c. de repos** to go on a rest cure; **c. de sommeil** sleep therapy; **faire une c. de sommeil** to have sleep therapy; **c. thermale** treatment at a spa

2 *Fig* **faire une c. de romans policiers** to go through a phase of reading nothing but detective stories; **faire une c. de fruits** to eat a lot of fruit

3 *Rel (fonction)* cure; *(paroisse)* parish; *(presbytère)* vicarage

4 *Littéraire (locution)* **n'avoir c. de** to care nothing about

curé [kyre] **NM** (Catholic) priest; **monsieur le c.** Father; **aller à l'école chez les curés** to be educated by priests; *Fam* **elle est toujours fourrée chez les curés** she's very churchy

cure-dent, cure-dents [kyrdɑ̃] *(pl* **cure-dents)** **NM** toothpick

curée [kyre] **NF 1** *Chasse* quarry, reward; *Fig* **il a provoqué les médias, et ç'a été la c.** he provoked the media and they were soon baying for his blood; *Fig* **ce fut la c. entre les héritiers** the heirs started to fight over the spoils **2** *(ruée)* (mad) scramble, rush; **à son départ ça a été la c. pour prendre sa place** people walked all over each other to get his/her job after he/she left

cure-ongle, cure-ongles [kyrɔ̃gl] *(pl* **cure-ongles)** **NM** nail-cleaner

cure-pipe, cure-pipes [kyrpip] *(pl* **cure-pipes)** **NM** pipe-cleaner

curer [3] [kyre] **VT** to scrape clean

VPR se curer se c. les ongles to clean one's nails; **se c. les dents** to pick one's teeth (clean); **se c. les oreilles** to clean (out) one's ears

curetage [kyrtaʒ] **NM** *Méd* curettage

cureter [27] [kyrte] **VT** to curette

cureton [kyrtɔ̃] **NM** *Fam Péj* priest

curette [kyrɛt] **NF** *Tech* scraper; *Méd* curette, curet

curie[1] [kyri] **NF 1** *Antiq* curia **2** *Rel* curia, Curia

curie[2] [kyri] **NM** *Phys (unité)* curie

curieuse [kyrjøz] *voir* **curieux**

curieusement [kyrjøzmɑ̃] **ADV 1** *(avec curiosité ▸ regarder)* curiously **2** *(étrangement ▸ s'habiller)* oddly, strangely; **c., il n'a rien voulu dire** strangely *or* funnily enough, he wouldn't say anything; **c., les valises avaient disparu** oddly enough, the suitcases had disappeared

curieux, -euse [kyrjø, -øz] **ADJ 1** *(indiscret)* curious, inquisitive **2** *(étrange)* curious, odd, strange; **c'est un c. personnage** he's a strange character; **il m'a répondu d'une manière curieuse** he gave me a strange answer **3** *(intéressé)* inquiring, inquisitive; **avoir un esprit c.** to have an inquiring mind; **je serais c. de voir cela** I'd be interested in seeing that

NM,F 1 *(badaud)* bystander, onlooker **2** *(indiscret)* inquisitive person; **je suis venu en c.** I just came to have a look

NM *(ce qui est étrange)* **c'est là le plus c. de l'affaire** that's what's so strange

curiosité [kyrjozite] **NF 1** *(indiscrétion)* curiosity, inquisitiveness; **par (pure) c.** out of (sheer) curiosity, just for curiosity's sake; *Prov* **la c. est un vilain défaut** curiosity killed the cat

2 *(intérêt)* curiosity; **c. intellectuelle** intellectual curiosity; **regarder qn avec c.** to look at sb curiously *or* enquiringly; **il faut éveiller la c. des enfants** it's a good thing to arouse children's curiosity

3 *(caractéristique)* oddity, idiosyncrasy; **c'est une des curiosités de son caractère** it's one of the odd things about him/her

4 *(objet)* curio, curiosity, oddity; **boutique** *ou* **magasin de curiosités** bric-à-brac *or Vieilli* curiosity shop

• **curiosités** **NFPL** **les curiosités de la ville** interesting and unusual things to see in the city

curiste [kyrist] **NMF** = person taking the waters at a spa

curling [kœrliŋ] **NM** *Sport* curling

curriculum vitae [kyrikylɔmvite] **NM INV** *Br* curriculum vitae, CV, *Am* résumé

curry [kyri] **NM 1** *(épice)* curry powder **2** *(plat)* curry

• **au curry** **ADJ** **poulet au c.** chicken curry, curried chicken

curseur [kyrsœr] **NM** cursor

cursif, -ive [kyrsif, -iv] **ADJ** *(écriture)* cursive; *(lecture, style)* cursory

• **cursive** **NF** cursive

cursus [kyrsys] **NM** degree course; **c. universitaire** degree course

curviligne [kyrviliɲ] ADJ curvilinear, curvilineal

custode [kystɔd] NF **1** *Aut* rear side panel **2** *Rel (pour hostie)* custodial

customiser [3] [kœstɔmize] VT to customize

cutané, -e [kytane] ADJ skin *(avant n)*, *Spéc* cutaneous; **maladie cutanée** skin disease

cuti [kyti] NF *Fam* skin test; **virer sa c.** to have a positive reaction to a skin test; *Fig* to have changed radically

cuticule [kytikyl] NF *Anat, Bot & Zool* cuticle

cuti-réaction [kytireaksjɔ̃] *(pl* **cuti-réactions***)* NF *Méd* skin test *(for detecting TB or allergies)*

cutter [kœtœr, kytɛr] NM Stanley® knife

cuvage [kyvaʒ] NM *(en œnologie)* fermentation in vats

cuvaison [kyvɛzɔ̃] NF = **cuvage**

cuve [kyv] NF **1** *(réservoir ▸ gén)* tank, cistern; *(▸ de machine à laver)* tub; *Phot* **c. à développement** developing tank **2** *(pour le blanchissage, la teinture)* vat **3** *(en œnologie)* vat, tank; **c. close** pressure tank

cuvée [kyve] NF **1** *(contenu)* tankful, vatful **2** *(en œnologie)* vintage; **la c. du patron** the house wine; **la c. 2005 était excellente** the 2005 vintage was excellent; **vin de première c.** wine of the first growth *or* vintage; *Hum* **la dernière c. de Polytechnique/du festival de Cannes** the latest batch of graduates from the "École Polytechnique"/ batch of movies *or Br* films from the Cannes film festival

cuver [3] [kyve] VI *(vin)* to ferment

VT *Fam* **c. son vin** to sleep off the booze; **c. sa colère** to simmer down

USAGE ABSOLU *Fam* **laisse-le c. en paix** leave him to sleep it off

cuvette [kyvɛt] NF **1** *(récipient ▸ gén)* basin, bowl, washbowl; *(▸ des W-C)* pan; *(▸ d'un lavabo)* basin

2 *(d'un thermomètre)* bulb

3 *Géog* basin

4 *Phot* **c. de fixage** fixing bath

CV[1] [seve] NM *(abrév* **curriculum vitae***)* *Br* CV, *Am* résumé; **ça fera bien dans ton CV** it'll look good on your *Br* CV *or Am* résumé

CV[2] *Aut (abrév écrite* **cheval-vapeur***)* hp

cyan [sjan] ADJ INV cyan

NM cyan

cyanhydrique [sjanidrik] ADJ *Chim* hydrocyanic

cyanose [sjanoz] NF *Méd* cyanosis

cyanure [sjanyr] NM *Chim* cyanide

cyberbanque [siberbɑ̃k] NF *Ordinat* Internet bank, online bank; *(activité)* online banking

cybercafé [siberkafe] NM cybercafé, internet café

cybercommerce [siberkɔmɛrs] NM *Ordinat* e-commerce

cybercrime [siberkrim] NM *Ordinat* cybercrime

cybercriminalité [siberkriminalite] NF *Ordinat* cybercrime

cyberculture [siberkyltyr] NF *Ordinat* cyberculture

cyberespace [siberespas] NM *Ordinat* cyberspace; **dans le c.** in cyberspace

cyberguerre [siberger] NF *Ordinat* cyberwar

cyberharcèlement [siberarselmɑ̃] NM *Ordinat* cyberstalking

cyberintimidation [siberɛ̃timidasjɔ̃] NF *Can* cyberbullying

cyberlibraire [siberlibrer] NM Internet *Br* bookshop *or Am* bookstore

cyberlibrairie [siberlibreri] NF Internet *Br* bookshop *or Am* bookstore

cybermonde [sibermɔ̃d] NM *Ordinat* cyberspace; **dans le c.** in cyberspace

cybernaute [sibernot] NM *Ordinat* Internet surfer, cybernaut

cybernéticien, -enne [sibernetisjɛ̃, -ɛn] *Ordinat & Biol* ADJ cybernetic

NM,F cybernetician, cyberneticist

cybernétique [sibernetik] *Ordinat & Biol* ADJ cybernetic

NF cybernetics *(singulier)*

cyberparesse [siberpares] NF *Ordinat* cyberslacking

cyberpirate [siberpirat] NM *Ordinat* cyberpirate

cyberpunk [siberpœnk] NM cyberpunk

cybersexe [siberseks] NM *Ordinat* cybersex

cybersquatter [siberskwater] NM *Ordinat* cybersquatter

cyberterrorisme [siberterɔrism] NM *Ordinat* cyberterrorism

cyclable [siklabl] ADJ **piste c.** cycle track, *Br* cycle path

cyclamen [siklamen] NM *Bot* cyclamen

cycle [sikl] NM **1** *(série ▸ gén)* cycle; *(▸ de conférences)* series; **le c. des saisons** the cycle of the seasons; *Astron* **c. lunaire/solaire** lunar/solar cycle

2 *(évolution)* cycle; **le c. d'un produit** the cycle of a product *(from manufacture to consumption)*; **c. économique** business *or* economic cycle; **c. d'exploitation** operating cycle

3 *Scol & Univ* cycle; **il suit un c. court/long** ≃ he'll leave school at sixteen/go on to higher education; **c. élémentaire** = term referring to the years spent at primary school between the ages of 7 and 9; **c. moyen** = term referring to the years spent at primary school between the ages of 9 and 11; **c. d'orientation** = final two years at a "collège"; **c. préparatoire** = first stage of primary school education (from the age of 6); **premier c.** *Scol Br* ≃ lower secondary school years, *Am* ≃ junior high school; *Univ Br* ≃ first and second years, *Am* ≃ freshman and sophomore years; **second c.** *Scol Br* ≃ upper school, *Am* ≃ high school; *Univ* = last two years of a degree course; **troisième c.** postgraduate studies; **être en troisième c.** to be a postgraduate student; **un étudiant de troisième c.** a postgraduate

4 *Littérature* cycle; **le c. d'Arthur** the Arthurian cycle

5 *Aut* **c. d'allumage** ignition cycle; **c. à deux temps** *Br* two-stroke cycle, *Am* two-cycle; **c. à quatre temps** *Br* four-stroke cycle, *Am* four-cycle

6 *(véhicule)* cycle; **magasin/fabricant de cycles** cycle shop/manufacturer

7 *Physiol* **c. menstruel** menstrual cycle; **c. œstral** oestrous cycle

8 *Chim* **le c. de l'azote** nitrogen cycle; **le c. du carbone** carbon cycle

9 *Biol & Météo* **c. de l'eau** water cycle

10 *Ordinat* **c. d'exécution** execute cycle

11 *Cin (de films)* season; **un c. Truffaut** a Truffaut season

> **CYCLES**
>
> The French education system is split into "cycles". The "cycle primaire" corresponds to the first five years of schooling (from age 6 to age 10). The "cycle secondaire" comprises the years spent both at "collège" (from age 11 to age 14) and at "lycée" (from age 15 to age 18). "Collège" education is split into three "cycles": "cycle d'adaptation" (the first year), "cycle central" (the next two years) and "cycle d'orientation" (the final year). "Second cycle des lycées" corresponds to the three years spent at the "lycée". French higher education comprises three "cycles": "premier cycle" corresponds to the first two years, up to "DEUG" level, and "deuxième cycle" to the third and fourth years, up to "licence" and "maîtrise"; "troisième cycle" corresponds to postgraduate study leading to a "doctorat".

cyclique [siklik] ADJ cyclic, cyclical

cyclisme [siklism] NM cycling; **il fait du c. tous les dimanches** he goes cycling every Sunday; **c. sur piste** track cycling; **c. sur route** road racing

cycliste [siklist] ADJ **coureur c.** *Br* racing cyclist, *Am* cycler; **course c.** cycle race

NMF *Br* cyclist, *Am* cycler

NM *(short)* (pair of) cycling shorts

cyclo-cross [siklɔkrɔs] NM INV cyclo-cross

cycloïdal, -e, -aux, -ales [sikloidal, -o] ADJ *Géom* cycloidal

cycloïde [sikloid] NF *Géom* cycloid

cyclomoteur [siklɔmɔtœr] NM moped, scooter

cyclomotoriste [siklɔmɔtɔrist] NMF scooter rider

cyclonal, -e, -aux, -ales [siklɔnal, -o] ADJ cyclonic, cyclonical, cyclonal

cyclone [siklon] NM *(dépression)* cyclone; *(typhon)* cyclone, hurricane; *Fig* **elle est entrée comme un c.** she came in like a whirlwind

cyclonique [siklɔnik] ADJ cyclonic

cyclope [siklɔp] NM *Zool (crustacé)* cyclops

• **Cyclope** NM *Myth* Cyclops

cyclopéen, -enne [siklɔpeɛ̃, -ɛn] ADJ *Littéraire (gigantesque)* Cyclopean, titanic, colossal

cyclopousse [siklopus] NM trishaw, rickshaw *(drawn by a bicycle)*

cyclorama [siklorama] NM *Cin & Théât* cyclorama

cyclothymie [siklɔtimi] NF *Psy* cyclothymia

cyclothymique [siklɔtimik] *Psy* ADJ cyclothymic, cyclothymiac

NMF cyclothymic, cyclothymiac

cyclotourisme [siklɔturism] NM cycle touring; **faire du c.** to go on a cycling *Br* holiday *or Am* vacation

cyclotron [siklɔtrɔ̃] NM *Phys* cyclotron

cygne [siɲ] NM *Orn* swan; **c. mâle** cob; **c. femelle** pen; **jeune c.** cygnet; **c. muet** *ou* **tuberculé** mute swan

• **Cygne** NM *Astron* **le C.** Cygnus, the Swan

cylindrage [silɛ̃draʒ] NM **1** *(en travaux publics)* rolling **2** *Tex* mangling

cylindre [silɛ̃dr] NM **1** *Aut & Géom* cylinder; **un moteur à quatre/six cylindres** a four-/six-cylinder engine; **une six cylindres** a six-cylinder car **2** *Tech* roller

cylindrée [silɛ̃dre] NF *Br* cubic capacity, *Am* capacity displacement; **une petite c.** a small *or* small-engined car; **grosse c.** a big *or* big-engined car

cylindrer [3] [silɛ̃dre] VT **1** *(en travaux publics)* to roll **2** *Tex* to mangle

cylindrique [silɛ̃drik] ADJ cylindric, cylindrical

cymbale [sɛ̃bal] NF cymbal; **coup de cymbales** crash of cymbals

cymbalier, -ère [sɛ̃balje, -ɛr] NM,F cymbalist

cynégétique [sineʒetik] ADJ hunting *(avant n)*

NF hunting

cynique [sinik] ADJ **1** *(gén)* cynical **2** *Phil* Cynic

NMF **1** *(gén)* cynic **2** *Phil* Cynic

cyniquement [sinikmɑ̃] ADV cynically

cynisme [sinism] NM **1** *(attitude)* cynicism **2** *Phil* Cynicism

cynodrome [sinɔdrom] NM greyhound track

cynophile [sinɔfil] ADJ *Mil* **unité** *ou* **équipe** *ou* **brigade c.** dog-training *or* dog-handling unit

NMF dog lover

cynorhodon, cynorrhodon [sinɔrɔdɔ̃] NM *(fruit)* rosehip; **confiture/tisane de c.** rosehip jam/tea

cyprès [siprɛ] NM *Bot* cypress

cypriote [siprijɔt] ADJ *(paysan, village)* Cypriot, Cypriote; *(paysage)* Cypriot, Cyprus *(avant n)*

• **Cypriote** NMF Cypriot, Cypriote

cyrillique [sirilik] ADJ Cyrillic

cystique [sistik] ADJ *Méd* cystic

cystite [sistit] NF *Méd* cystitis

cytise [sitiz] NM *Bot* laburnum, golden rain

cytologie [sitɔlɔʒi] NF *Biol* cytology

cytologique [sitɔlɔʒik] ADJ *Biol* cytologic, cytological

cytomégalovirus [sitomegalɔvirys] NM *Méd* cytomegalovirus, CMV

cytoplasme [sitɔplasm] NM *Biol* cytoplasm

cytoplasmique [sitɔplasmik] ADJ *Biol* cytoplasmic

czar [tsar] = **tsar**

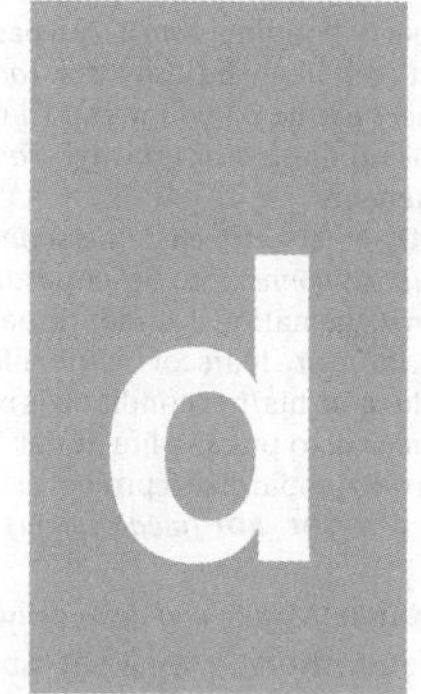

D[1], **d**[1] [de] **NM INV 1** *(lettre)* D, d; **D comme Désiré** ≃ D for dog **2** *Mus (note)* D

D[2] [de] **NF** *(abrév* **route départementale***)* = designation of secondary road

D[3] *Météo (abrév écrite* **dépression***)* cyclone, barometric depression, low

d' [d] *voir* **de**

DAB [dab] **NM** *(abrév* **distributeur automatique de billets***)* *Br* cashpoint, *Am* ATM

dab, dabe [dab] **NM** *Fam (père)* old man; **les dabs** *(parents)* folks, *Br* old dears, *Am* rents

dac, d'ac [dak] **ADV** *Fam (abrév* **d'accord***)* OK; **si t'es pas d.** *(si tu ne veux pas)* if you don't want to; **c'est la mieux des trois, si t'es pas d., tu n'as qu'à...** this is the best of the three, if you don't agree, then you should...

d'accord [dakɔr] *voir* **accord**

Dacron® [dakrɔ̃] **NM** *Br* Terylene®, *Am* Dacron®

dactyle [daktil] **NM** *Littérature* dactyl, dactylic

dactylo [daktilo] **NMF** *(personne)* typist

NF *(technique)* typing; **prendre des cours de d.** to learn how to type

dactylographe [daktilɔgraf] **NMF** typist

dactylographie [daktilɔgrafi] **NF** typing, typewriting; **prendre des cours de d.** to learn how to type

dactylographier **[9]** [daktilɔgrafje] **VT** to type (up)

dactylographique [daktilɔgrafik] **ADJ** typing

dactyloscopie [daktilɔskɔpi] **NF** fingerprinting, fingerprint identification

dactyloscopique [daktilɔskɔpik] **ADJ examen d.** fingerprint examination

dada [dada] **ADJ** *Beaux-Arts & Littérature* Dadaist, Dadaistic; **le mouvement d.** Dada, Dadaism

NM 1 *Beaux-Arts & Littérature* Dada, Dadaism **2** *(en langage enfantin) (cheval)* horsey, *Br* gee-gee; **à d.** on horseback **3** *Fam (passe-temps)* hobby[□]; *(idée)* hobby-horse[□]; **le voilà reparti sur** *ou* **il a enfourché son d.** he's off on his hobby-horse again; **c'est son nouveau d.** it's his/her latest obsession[□]

dadais [dadɛ] **NM** oaf; **grand d.** clumsy oaf

dadaïsme [dadaism] **NM** *Beaux-Arts & Littérature* Dada, Dadaism

dadaïste [dadaist] *Beaux-Arts & Littérature* **ADJ** Dadaist, Dadaistic

NMF Dadaist

DADS [deadeɛs] **NF** *Admin (abrév* **déclaration annuelle des données sociales***)* ≃ PAYE and NIC return

dague [dag] **NF** *(poignard)* dagger

daguerréotype [dagereɔtip] **NM** daguerreotype

dahlia [dalja] **NM** dahlia

dahu [day] **NM** imaginary animal *(featuring in stories told to the gullible)*

daigner **[4]** [deɲe] **VT d. faire qch** to deign to do sth

daim [dɛ̃] **NM 1** *Zool* (fallow) deer; **d. mâle** buck **2** *(cuir suédé)* suede; **de d., en d.** suede *(avant n)*

daine [dɛn] **NF** *Zool* doe *(female fallow deer)*

dais [de] **NM** canopy

Dakar [dakar] **NM** Dakar

dakin [dakɛ̃] **NM** *Chim* Dakin's solution

dal[1] *(abrév écrite* **décalitre***)* dal

dal[2] [dal] **que dal** = **que dalle**

dalaï-lama [dalailama] *(pl* **dalaï-lamas***)* **NM** Dalai Lama

dallage [dalaʒ] **NM** *(action)* paving; *(surface)* pavement

dalle [dal] **NF 1** *(plaque ▸ de pierre)* flagstone; *(▸ de moquette, de lino)* tile; *(de marbre)* slab; **d. funéraire** tombstone

2 *Constr* slab; **d. de béton** concrete slab; **d. pleine** reinforced concrete slab

3 *Fam (faim)* **avoir** *ou* **crever la d.** to be starving *or* famished; **je crève la d.** I could eat a horse

4 *Fam (locution)* **avoir la d. en pente** to be a boozer, to be fond of the bottle

• **que dalle ADV** *Fam* zilch, *Br* sod all; **j'y comprends que d.** I don't understand a damn *or Br* bloody thing

daller **[3]** [dale] **VT** to pave

dalleur [dalœr] **NM** paviour

dalmatien [dalmasjɛ̃] **NM** Dalmatian (dog)

dalot [dalo] **NM 1** *Naut* scupper **2** *Constr* culvert

daltonien, -enne [daltɔnjɛ̃, -ɛn] **ADJ** colour-blind

NM,F colour-blind person

daltonisme [daltɔnism] **NM** colour blindness

dam [dam] **NM** *Rel* **peine du d.** eternal damnation

• **au grand dam de PRÉP** *Littéraire (à son préjudice)* to the detriment of; *(à son mécontentement)* to the great displeasure of

damage [damaʒ] **NM** *(de la terre)* packing (down), ramming down; *(de la neige)* packing down; *(d'une piste)* grooming

damas [dama(s)] **NM 1** *Tex* damask **2** *Bot* damson

damasquinage [damaskinaʒ] **NM** *Métal* damascening

damasquiner **[3]** [damaskine] **VT** *Métal* to damascene

damassé, -e [damase] **ADJ** damask *(avant n)*

NM damask

damasser **[3]** [damase] **VT** to damask

damassine [damasin] **NF** *Suisse (fruit)* plum; *(eau de vie)* plum brandy

dame [dam] **NF 1** *(femme)* lady; **que prendront ces dames?** what will you have, ladies?; *Jur* **la d. Simon** Mrs Simon; **D. Nature** Mother Nature; *Fam* **ah, ma bonne** *ou* **pauvre d., les temps ont bien changé!** ah, my dear, times have changed!; *Fam* **qu'est-ce que je vous sers, ma petite d.?** what would you like, miss *or Br* love?; **d. de charité** Lady Bountiful; **d. de compagnie** lady's companion; **la D. de fer** the Iron Lady; **d. patronnesse** Lady Bountiful; *Fam* **d. pipi** toilet attendant[□]

2 *Fam (épouse)* **votre d.** your old lady

3 *(femme noble)* lady; **une grande d.** a (noble) lady; **les dames de France** the royal princesses of France; **la première d. de France** France's First Lady; **d. d'honneur** lady-in-waiting; *Péj* **faire** *ou* **jouer les grandes dames** to put on airs; **sa d., la d. de ses pensées** his ladylove

4 *(aux dames)* king; *Cartes & Échecs* queen; **aller à la** *ou* **mener un pion à d.** *(aux dames)* to crown a king; *Échecs* to queen a pawn; *Cartes* **la d. de cœur** the queen of hearts

5 *Constr (mur)* **d. de remblai** dam

EXCLAM *Vieilli* of course!

• **dames NFPL (jeu de) dames** *Br* draughts, *Am* checkers

• **de dames, pour dames ADJ** *(bicyclette)* ladies'

dame-d'onze-heures [damdɔ̃zœr] *(pl* **dames-d'onze-heures***)* **NF** *Bot* star-of-Bethlehem, star-flower

dame-jeanne [damʒan] *(pl* **dames-jeannes***)* **NF** demijohn

damer **[3]** [dame] **VT 1** *(tasser ▸ terre)* to ram down, to pack down; *(▸ neige)* to pack down; *(▸ piste)* to groom **2** *(pion ▸ aux dames)* to crown; *(▸ aux échecs)* to queen; *Fig* **d. le pion à qn** to outwit sb

dameuse [damøz] **NF** *Ski* piste basher

damier [damje] **NM** *Br* draughtboard, *Am* checkerboard; **un tissu à** *ou* **en d.** *Br* checked *or Am* checkered material

damnable [danabl] **ADJ** *Littéraire (qui mérite la damnation)* damnable; *(répréhensible)* to be condemned

damnation [danasjɔ̃] **NF** *Rel* damnation

EXCLAM *Arch* damnation!

damné, -e [dane] **ADJ 1** *Fam Péj (maudit)* cursed, damn, damned **2** *Rel* damned

NM,F *Rel* damned person *or* soul; **les damnés** the damned

damner **[3]** [dane] **VT** *Rel* to damn; *Littéraire* **dieu me damne!** damn!; *Fam Fig* **faire d. qn** to drive sb crazy *or Br* round the bend

VPR se damner to damn oneself; **je me damnerais pour un chocolat** I'd give anything for a chocolate

Damoclès [damɔklɛs] **NPR** *Myth* Damocles; **l'épée de D.** the sword of Damocles

damoiseau, -x [damwazo] **NM 1** *Hist (gentilhomme)* (young) squire **2** *Hum (jeune empressé)* (dashing) young blade

damoiselle [damwazɛl] **NF** *Hist* **1** *(fille noble)* damsel *(title given to an unmarried noblewoman)* **2** *(femme de damoiseau)* (young) squire's wife

damper [dampœr] **NM** *Aut* damper

dan [dan] **NM** dan

dancing [dɑ̃siŋ] **NM** dance hall

dandinement [dɑ̃dinmɑ̃] **NM** *(d'un canard, d'une personne)* waddling; **son d. a fait rire tout le monde** everybody was laughing at the way he/she waddled about

dandiner [dɑ̃dine] **se dandiner VPR** *(canard, personne)* waddle; **il est entré/sorti en se dandinant** he waddled in/out; **se d. d'un pied sur l'autre** to shift from foot to foot

dandy [dɑ̃di] **NM** dandy

dandysme [dɑ̃dism] **NM** dandyism

Danemark [danmark] **NM le D.** Denmark

danger [dɑ̃ʒe] **NM** danger; **attention d.!** danger!; **les dangers de la route** the hazards of the road; **en grand d. de** in great danger of; **en d. de mort** in danger of one's life; **il y a un d. d'inondation** there is a danger of flooding; *Fam* **il n'y a pas de d. qu'il dise oui** it's not likely he'll say yes; *Fam* **moi, t'accompagner? pas de d.!** you mean I'd have to go with you? no danger *or* no way!; *Fam* **d. public** public menace

• **en danger** ADJ **être en d.** *(personne)* to be in danger; *(paix, honneur)* to be jeopardized; **la patrie est en d.** the nation is under threat; **ses jours sont en d.** there are fears for his/her life; **ses jours ne sont plus en d.** his/her condition is now stable; **mettre qn en d.** to put sb's life at risk; **mettre un projet en d.** to jeopardize a project

• **sans danger** ADJ *(médicament)* safe ADV safely

dangereuse [dɑ̃ʒrøz] *voir* **dangereux**

dangereusement [dɑ̃ʒrøzmɑ̃] ADV dangerously, perilously

dangereux, -euse [dɑ̃ʒrø, -øz] ADJ **1** *(risqué)* dangerous, perilous, hazardous; **zone dangereuse** danger area *or* zone; **baignade/escalade dangereuse** *(sur panneau)* danger, no swimming/no climbing **2** *(nuisible)* dangerous, harmful; **les couleuvres ne sont pas dangereuses** grass snakes are harmless

dangerosité [dɑ̃ʒrozite] NF *Littéraire* dangerousness

danois, -e [danwa, -az] ADJ Danish
NM **1** *(langue)* Danish **2** *(chien)* Great Dane
• **Danois, -e** NM,F Dane; **les D.** the Danish

DANS [dɑ̃]

• in **1, 4–6**	• within **1, 4**
• into **1**	• out of **2**
• through **3**	• during **4**
• around, about **7**	

PRÉP **1** *(dans l'espace ▸ gén)* in; *(▸ avec des limites)* within; *(▸ avec mouvement)* into; **ils ont cherché partout d. la maison** they looked through the whole house, they looked everywhere in the house; **d. la rue** in the street; **d. le métro** *(wagon)* on the *Br* underground *orAm* subway; *(couloirs)* in the *Br* underground *orAm* subway; **d. le train/l'avion** on the train/the plane; **monte d. la voiture** get in *or* into the car; **partout d. le monde** all over the world, the world over; **habiter d. Paris** to live in (central) Paris; **d. l'espace** in space; **je suis bien d. ces chaussures** I feel comfortable in these shoes, these shoes are comfortable; **avoir mal d. le dos** to have backache; **ils se sont couchés d. l'herbe** they lay down in *or* on the grass; **elle avait des reflets d'or d. les cheveux** she had golden highlights in her hair; **prenant sa tête d. ses mains** holding his/her head in his/her hands; **d. ces murs** within these walls; **restez d. les limites du parc** stay within the boundaries of the estate; **entrer d. une pièce** to go into a room; **plonger d. une piscine** to dive into a swimming pool; **tomber d. l'escalier** to fall down the stairs; **mettre qch d. une boîte** to put sth in(to) a box; **prendre qn d. ses bras** to take sb in one's arms; **d. la brume/pénombre** in the mist/dark; **je n'arrivais pas à l'entendre d. ce vacarme** I couldn't hear him/her in all that noise; **elle a une profonde tristesse d. le regard** there is a great deal of sadness in her eyes; **d. son dernier film** in his/her last movie *or Br* film; **d. le journal** in the paper

2 *(à partir de ▸ prendre, boire, manger)* out of, from; **j'ai pris l'argent d. le tiroir** I took the money out of *or* from the drawer; **boire d. un verre** to drink out of *or* from a glass; **copier qch d. un livre** to copy sth out of *or* from a book; *Culin* **un morceau d. la poitrine** a cut off the breast

3 *(à travers)* through; **passe le doigt d. l'anneau** put your finger through the ring; **un murmure a couru d. la foule** a murmur ran through the crowd

4 *(dans le temps ▸ gén)* in; *(▸ insistant sur la durée)* during; *(▸ indiquant un délai)* within; **d. son enfance** in *or* during her childhood, when he/she was a child; **d. les années 50** in *or* during the 50s; **être d. sa vingt-cinquième année** to be in one's twenty-fifth year; **d. un déménagement, on casse toujours quelque chose** when you move house, something always gets broken; **les gaz qui se dégagent d. une réaction chimique** gases given off in a chemical reaction; **je n'ai qu'un jour de libre d. la semaine** I only have one day off during the week; **l'avion atterrit d. 25 minutes** the plane will be landing in 25 minutes *or* 25 minutes' time; **d. quelques minutes, la suite de notre programme** normal service will be resumed as soon as possible; **vous serez livré d. la semaine** you'll get the delivery within the week *or* some time this week; **je passerai d. l'après-midi** I'll call by in *or* during the afternoon; **à consommer d. les cinq jours** eat within five days of purchase; **arriver d. l'heure qui suit** to arrive within the next hour

5 *(indiquant l'appartenance à un groupe)* **il est d. le commerce** he's in business; **quelqu'un d. l'assistance** someone in the audience; **être d. l'Union européenne** to be in *or* a member of the European Union; **il est d. mon équipe** he's on *or* in my team; **d. nos rangs** within our ranks; **nous sommes d. le même club** we're in *or* we belong to the same club; **ministre de la Santé d. le dernier gouvernement** Minister of Health in the last government

6 *(indiquant la manière, l'état)* **d. son sommeil** in his/her sleep; **mettre qn d. l'embarras** to put sb in an awkward situation; **mourir d. la misère** to die in poverty; **tomber d. l'oubli** to sink into oblivion; **je ne suis pas d. le secret** I haven't been let in on *or* I'm not in on the secret; **il la voyait d. son délire** in his delirium he thought he could see her; **je ne peux pas travailler d. le bruit** I can't work when it's noisy; **d. le but de** in order to, with the aim of; **d. l'espoir de** in the hope of; **je l'aime bien d. ce rôle** I like him/her in this role; **une maison bâtie d. le style Régence** a house built in Regency style; **un contrat rédigé d. les formes légales** a contract drawn out *or* up in legal terms; **prendre un mot d. son sens littéral** to take a word in its literal sense *or* literally; **c'est quelqu'un d. ton genre** he's/she's like you

7 *(indiquant une approximation)* **d. les** around, about; **ça coûtera d. les 200 euros** it'll cost around 200 euros; **il était d. les cinq heures du soir** it was around five p.m.; **il doit avoir d. les 50 ans** he must be about 50

dansable [dɑ̃sabl] ADJ **cette musique n'est pas d.** you can't dance to this music

dansant, -e [dɑ̃sɑ̃, -ɑ̃t] ADJ **1** *(qui danse)* dancing; *Fig (reflet)* shimmering, dancing; *(lueur)* flickering **2** *(qui invite à danser)* **un rythme d.** a rhythm which makes you want to (get up and) dance **3** *(où l'on danse)* **soirée dansante** dance; **thé d.** tea dance

danse [dɑ̃s] NF **1** *(activité)* dancing; **il aime la d.** he likes dancing; **entrer dans la d.** to join in the dance; *Fig* to join in; **conduire** *ou* **mener la d.** to lead the dance; *Fig* to call the tune; *Can* **d. carrée** square dance; **d. classique** ballet (dancing), classical dancing; **d. folklorique** folk dancing; **d. sur glace** ice-dancing; **d. paysanne** country dancing; **d. de salon** ballroom dancing; **d. aux tables** table dancing; **d. du ventre** belly dancing

2 *(suite de pas ▸ dans un ballet, au bal)* dance; **jouer une d.** to play a dance (tune); **la d. des reflets sur le lac** reflections dancing on the surface of the lake; **la d. des hirondelles dans les airs** swallows swooping back and forth in the sky; **d. folklorique** folk dance; **d. de salon** ballroom dance

3 *(agitation)* **c'est la d. des valeurs ce mois-ci à la Bourse** share values are fluctuating this month on the Stock Exchange

4 *Méd* **d. de Saint-Guy** St Vitus' dance; *Fam* **tu as la d. de Saint-Guy, ou quoi?** can't you stop fidgeting?

5 *très Fam (correction)* hiding, thrashing, belting; **flanquer une d. à qn** to beat the living daylights out of sb

danser [3] [dɑ̃se] VI **1** *(évoluer)* to dance; **vous dansez?** would you like to dance?; **on danse?** shall we (have a) dance?; *Fig* **d. sur une corde raide** to walk a tightrope; **faire d. qn** *(sujet: cavalier)* to (have a) dance with sb; *(sujet: musicien)* to play dance tunes for sb; *Fam* **chez nous, on dansait devant le buffet** at home, the cupboard was always bare **2** *(bouger ▸ reflet, bouchon)* to move, to bob up and down; *(▸ mots, lignes)* to swim; *(▸ flamme)* to flicker

VT to dance; **d. une valse/un tango** to (dance a) waltz/tango; **d. 'Casse-Noisette'** to dance *or* to perform the 'Nutcracker Suite'

VPR **se danser un ballet qui se danse en costumes modernes** a ballet performed in contemporary dress; **le twist ne se danse plus** nobody dances the twist any more

danseur, -euse [dɑ̃sœr, -øz] NM,F **1** *(gén)* dancer; *(de ballet)* ballet dancer; **danseuse de cabaret** cabaret dancer; **d. de claquettes** tap-dancer; **d. de corde** tightrope walker; **d. étoile** principal dancer; **danseuse étoile** prima ballerina; **danseuse orientale** belly dancer; *Fig* **entretenir une danseuse** *(avoir une maîtresse)* to keep a mistress; *(avoir un passe-temps coûteux)* to indulge in an expensive hobby **2** *(cavalier)* **mon d.** my partner

NM **d. mondain** (male) escort

• **danseuse** ADJ F flexible, yielding

• **en danseuse** ADV **se mettre en danseuse** to stand up on the pedals; **monter la colline en danseuse** to cycle up the hill standing on the pedals

dantesque [dɑ̃tɛsk] ADJ *Littéraire* Dantean, Dantesque

Danube [danyb] NM **le D.** the (River) Danube

danubien, -enne [danybjɛ̃, -ɛn] ADJ Danubian

daphnie [dafni] NF *Entom* water flea, *Spéc* daphnia

dard [dar] NM **1** *(d'une abeille, d'une guêpe)* sting; *(d'un serpent)* forked tongue **2** *Pêche* spear, harpoon **3** *Vulg* dick, prick, cock

darder [3] [darde] VT **1** *(lancer)* to shoot; **le soleil du matin dardait ses rayons sur la plage** shafts of morning sunlight fell on the beach; **d. un regard furieux sur qn** to shoot sb an angry look **2** *(dresser)* to point; **une rose qui darde ses épines** a rose pointing its thorns

dare-dare [dardar] ADV *Fam* double-quick, on the double

darne [darn] NF steak, thick slice *(cut across the fish)*; **d. de saumon** salmon steak

dartre [dartr] NF *Méd* dry patch, *Spéc* dartre

dartreux, -euse [dartrø, -øz] ADJ *Méd* dartrous

darwinien, -enne [darwinjɛ̃, -ɛn] ADJ Darwinian

darwinisme [darwinism] NM Darwinism

darwiniste [darwinist] ADJ Darwinist, Darwinistic

NMF Darwinist

DAS [deaɛs] NM *Com & Mktg (abrév* **domaine d'activité stratégique***)* SBU

datable [databl] ADJ datable, dateable; **facilement/difficilement d.** easy to date/not easily dated

datation [datasjɔ̃] NF dating; **il y a eu une erreur de d. du fossile** the fossil was incorrectly dated; **d. au carbone 14** carbon dating; *Chim* **d. au potassium-argon** potassium-argon dating

date [dat] NF **1** *(moment précis)* date; **une lettre sans d.** an undated letter; **la lettre porte la d. du 5 mai** the letter is dated 5 May; **nous avons fixé la d. de la conférence au 13 juin** we have decided to hold the conference on 13 June; **à quelle d. arrivent-ils?** what date are they arriving on?; **se retrouver chaque année à d. fixe** to meet on the same day every year; *Com & Fin* **à 30 jours de d.** 30 days after date; **prenons d.** let's decide on a date; **d. d'achèvement** completion date, date of completion; **d. de base** base date; **d. butoir** deadline, cut-off date; **d. de clôture** closing date; **d. de départ** date of departure; *Fin* **d. d'échéance** *(de dû)* maturity date, due date; *(de terme)* expiry date; **d. d'émission** date of issue; **d. d'exécution** completion date; **d. d'exigibilité** due date; **d. d'expiration** expiry date; **d. de facturation** invoice date; *Banque & Fin* **d. de jouissance** date from which interest begins to run; **d. limite** *(pour un projet)* deadline; **d. limite de consommation** best-before date; **d. limite de paiement** deadline for payment; **d. limite de vente** sell-by date; **d. de livraison** delivery date; **d. de naissance** date of birth; *Fin* **d. d'ouverture de l'exercice** first day of the *Br* financial *or Am* fiscal year; **d. de péremption** *(d'un document)* expiry date; *(d'un aliment)* use-by date; **d. de remise** remittance date; *Banque* **d. de valeur** value date; **d. de validité** expiry date

2 *(période)* date; **à la d. dont tu me parles, j'étais encore aux États-Unis** at the time you're telling me about, I was still in the United States; **à cette**

d. j'étais déjà parti I'd already left by then; **les grandes dates de notre histoire** the most important dates in our history; **c'est une réalisation qui fera d. (dans l'histoire)** it's an achievement which will stand out (in history); **de longue d.** long-standing; **ils se connaissent de longue d.** they've known each other for a long time; **c'est une amitié de fraîche d.** they haven't been friends for very long

• **en date** ADV **qui est sa dernière conquête en d.?** who is his latest conquest?

• **en date du** PRÉP **lettre en d. du 28 juin** letter dated 28 June

dater [3] [date] VT **1** *(inscrire la date)* to date, to put a date on; **carte datée du 20** postcard dated the 20th **2** *(déterminer l'âge de ▸ fossile, manuscrit, édifice)* to date

VI **1** *(compter)* to stand out, to be a milestone **2** *(être désuet ▸ tenue)* to look dated *or* old-fashioned; *(▸ expression)* to sound old-fashioned; *(▸ film)* to show its age, to have aged, to be dated

• **dater de** VT IND to date from, to go back to; **un livre qui date du XVIIème siècle** a book dating back to the 17th century; **de quand date votre dernière visite?** when was your last visit?; **voilà une idée qui ne date pas d'hier** this idea's been around for quite some time; **ça date d'avant notre rencontre** it happened before we met

• **à dater de** PRÉP **à d. de ce jour** *(d'aujourd'hui)* from today; *(de ce jour-là)* from that day; **à d. du 1er mars, vous ne faites plus partie du service** as of *or* effective from 1 March, you are no longer on the staff

dateur [datœr] ADJ M *voir* **timbre**[1]

NM date stamp; **d. automatique de billets** ticket-dating machine

datif, -ive [datif, -iv] ADJ *Jur* **tuteur d.** guardian appointed by a court; **tutelle dative** trusteeship *or* guardianship ordered by a court

NM *Ling* dative; **au d.** in the dative

dation [dasjɔ̃] NF *(action de donner)* giving, conferring; **d. en paiement** accord and satisfaction

dative [dativ] *voir* **datif**

datte [dat] NF date *(fruit)*; **il n'en** *Fam* **fiche** *ou très Fam* **fout pas une d.** he doesn't do a damn thing, *Br* he does bugger all

dattier [datje] NM date palm

daube [dob] NF **1** *Culin* stew; **bœuf en d.** beef braised in red wine **2** *Fam* **c'est de la d.** it's (a load of) *Br* rubbish *orAm* garbage

dauber [3] [dobe] VT *Littéraire* to mock

VI **1** *Littéraire (se moquer)* to jeer, to scoff **2** *Fam (sentir mauvais)* to stink, *Br* to pong

daubière [dobjɛr] NF *Culin* = earthenware pot for braising

dauphin[1] [dofɛ̃] NM *Zool* dolphin; **grand d.** bottlenosed dolphin; **d. blanc** beluga (whale); **d. à gros nez, d. souffleur** bottlenosed dolphin

dauphin[2], **-e** [dofɛ̃, -fin] NM,F **1** *Hist* **le d.** the dauphin; **la dauphine** the dauphine **2** *(successeur)* heir apparent, successor; **qui est votre d.?** who's in line for your job?

dauphinois, -e [dofinwa, -az] ADJ of/from the Dauphiné

• **Dauphinois, -e** NM,F = inhabitant of or person from the Dauphiné

daurade [dɔrad] NF *Ich* sea bream

davantage [davɑ̃taʒ] ADV **1** *(plus)* more; **donne-m'en d.** give me some more; **tu devrais lire d.** you should read more; **vous êtes riche, mais il l'est bien d.** you're rich, but he's much richer; **je ne t'en dirai pas d.** I won't tell you any more; **je ne l'interrogerai pas d.** I won't question him/her any further; **le droit l'intéresse d. que l'économie** law interests him/her more than economics; **je ne lui ferai pas d. de reproches** I won't criticize him/her any more; **je voudrais d. de cerises** I'd like (some) more cherries; **il a eu d. de chance que les autres** he was luckier than the others **2** *(de plus en plus)* **chaque jour qui passe nous rapproche d.** each day that goes by brings us closer together; **je t'aime chaque jour d.** I love you more and more every day **3** *(plus longtemps)* **je n'attendrai pas d.** I won't wait any longer

davier [davje] NM **1** *Menuis* cramp **2** *(de dentiste)* forceps

Davis [devis] *voir* **coupe**

day time [detajm] *Rad & TV* ADJ daytime

NM daytime programming; **transmettre une émission en d.** to broadcast a programme as part of the daytime schedule

DBS [debeεs] NM *(abrév* **direct broadcasting satellite***)* DBS

DCA [desea] NF *Mil (abrév* **défense contre les aéronefs***)* AA, anti-aircraft

D^{chesse} *(abrév écrite* **duchesse***)* Duchess

DD [dede] *Ordinat* ADJ *(abrév* **double densité***)* DD

NM *(abrév* **disque dur***)* HD

DDASS, Ddass [das] NF *Admin (abrév* **Direction départementale d'action sanitaire et sociale***)* = Department of Health and Social Security; **un enfant de la D.** a state orphan

DDE [dedeə] NF *(abrév* **Direction départementale de l'équipement***)* = local offices of the Ministry of the Environment

NM *Ordinat (abrév* **dynamic data exchange***)* DDE

DDT [dedete] NM *Chim (abrév* **dichloro-diphényl-trichloréthane***)* DDT

DE [də]

PRÉP
- from **A1, 2, B1**
- during **B2**
- for **C**
- in **G**
- by **A3, D**
- with **C, D**
- of **G, H2, 3, I1–3, 6**

ART PARTITIF
- some **1**
- any **3**

ART INDÉFINI
- some **1**
- any **2**

de becomes **d'** before vowel and h mute; **de + le** is contracted to **du**, and **de + les** to **des**.

PRÉP **A.** *INDIQUANT L'ORIGINE, LE POINT DE DÉPART* **1** *(indiquant la provenance)* from; **il n'est pas d'ici** he's not from (around) here; **il vient de Paris** he comes from Paris; **la voiture venait de la gauche** the car was coming from the left; **l'express d'Aberdeen** the Aberdeen express; **un vin d'Alsace** an Alsace wine; **une boule s'est décrochée du sapin** a bauble fell off the Christmas tree; **vue de l'intérieur** seen from (the) inside; **il a sorti un lapin de son chapeau** he pulled a rabbit out of his hat; **sortir de table** to leave the table; **c'est un cadeau de mon oncle** it's a present from my uncle; **je l'ai oublié? c'est bien de moi** did I forget it? that's just like me

2 *(à partir de)* **de quelques fleurs des champs, elle a fait un bouquet** she made a posy out of *or* from a few wild flowers; **faire un drame de rien** to make a fuss over nothing

3 *(indiquant l'auteur)* by; **un roman de Mishima** a novel by Mishima; **une aria de Bach** a Bach aria; **la statue est de Rodin** the statue is by Rodin

4 *(particule)* **Madame de Sévigné** Madame de Sévigné; *Fam* **épouser un/une de quelque chose** ≃ to marry a man/woman with an aristocratic-sounding name

B. *DANS LE TEMPS* **1** *(à partir de)* from; **notre amitié date de cette époque** our friendship dates from that period; **de ce jour** from that day; **de pauvre, il devint riche** he went from rags to riches

2 *(indiquant le moment)* **de jour/nuit** during the *or* by day/night; **travailler de nuit** to work nights; **se lever de bonne heure** to get up early; **je ne l'ai pas vu de la soirée** I haven't seen him all evening; **je ne le vois pas de la semaine** I don't see him at all during the week; **le train de 9 heures 30** the 9.30 train; **le journal d'hier** yesterday's paper; **de longtemps, on n'avait vu cela** such a thing hadn't been seen for a long time

C. *INDIQUANT LA CAUSE* **rougir de plaisir** to blush with pleasure; **mourir de peur/de faim** to die of fright/of hunger; **trembler de froid** to shiver with cold; **sauter de joie** to jump for joy; **souffrir de rhumatismes** to suffer from rheumatism; **se tordre de douleur/de rire** to be doubled up in pain/with laughter; **puni de sa gourmandise** punished for his greed

D. *INDIQUANT L'AGENT, LE MOYEN, L'INSTRUMENT* **accompagné de ses amis** accompanied by his friends; **il est détesté de tous** everybody hates him; **faire signe de la main** to wave; **effleurer du doigt** to brush with one's finger; **d'un coup de fouet** with a crack of the whip; **il voit mal de l'œil gauche** he can't see properly with his left eye; **se nourrir de fruits** to eat fruit; **ce champ est entouré d'une palissade** this field is surrounded by a fence; **il a été tué d'une balle** he was killed by a bullet *or* shot dead; **armé de pierres** armed with stones; **poussez la porte du pied** push the door (open) with your foot

E. *INDIQUANT LA MANIÈRE* **manger de bon appétit** to eat heartily; **de toutes ses forces** with all his/her strength; **d'un air coupable** looking guilty, with a guilty look on his/her/*etc* face

F. *AVEC DES NOMBRES, DES MESURES* **1** *(emploi distributif)* **30 euros de l'heure** 30 euros per *or* an hour; **cinq euros du kilomètre** five euros per *or* a kilometre

2 *(introduisant une mesure)* **un appartement de** $60m^2$ a $60m^2$ *Br* flat, *orAm* apartment; **un homme d'1 m 80** a man who is 1 m 80 tall; **une hausse de 10 pour cent** a 10 percent increase; **une femme de 30 ans** a 30-year-old woman; **un cadeau de 200 euros** a gift worth 200 euros; **une pièce de 20 centimes** a 20-cent piece; **un chèque de 100 euros** a cheque for 100 euros; **il a été condamné à deux ans de prison** he was sentenced to two years' imprisonment; **une équipe de 15 personnes** a team of 15

3 *(indiquant une différence dans le temps, l'espace, la quantité)* **distant de cinq kilomètres** five kilometres away; **ma montre retarde de dix minutes** my watch is ten minutes slow; **il est plus grand que moi d'une tête** he's a head taller than I am

G. *INDIQUANT L'APPARTENANCE* of; **la maison de mes parents/Marie** my parents'/Marie's house; **la porte du salon** the living-room door; **le toit de la maison** the roof of the house; **les rues de Paris** the streets of Paris; **la chambre du second** the room on the *Br* second *orAm* third floor; **les clefs de la voiture** the car keys; **les pays de l'UE** the countries in the EU, the EU countries; **les membres du club** the members of the club *or* club members; **les élèves de sa classe** the pupils in his/her class

H. *MARQUANT LA DÉTERMINATION* **1** *(indiquant la matière, la qualité, le genre etc)* **un buffet de chêne** an oak dresser; **un bonhomme de neige** a snowman; **une robe de mariée** a wedding dress; **une équipe de spécialistes** a team of specialists; **une réaction d'horreur** a horrified reaction; **une pause de publicité** a commercial break; **la conférence de Berlin** the Berlin conference; **un hôtel de la rive gauche** a hotel on the left bank; **un livre d'un grand intérêt** a book of great interest; **des vêtements d'un goût contestable** clothes of questionable taste; **elle est d'un snob!** she is SO snobbish!, she's such a snob!

2 *(indiquant le contenu, le contenant)* **l'eau de la citerne** the water in the tank; **un verre d'eau** a glass of water; **un pot de fleurs** *(récipient)* a flowerpot; *(fleurs)* a pot of flowers; **une bouteille de whisky** a bottle of whisky; *(récipient)* a whisky bottle

3 *(dans un ensemble)* **la plupart de ses amis** most of his/her friends; **le plus jeune de la classe** the youngest pupil in the class; **le plus jeune des deux** the younger of the two

4 *(avec une valeur emphatique)* **l'as des as** the champ; **le fin du fin** the very latest thing

I. *SERVANT DE LIEN SYNTAXIQUE* **1** *(après un verbe)* **parler de qch** to speak about *or* of sth; **douter de qch** to doubt *or* to have doubts about sth; **se séparer de qn** *(conjoint)* to leave sb, to split up with sb; **cessez de faire qch** to stop doing sth; **se libérer du passé** to free oneself from the past; **se souvenir de qch** to remember sth; **traiter qn de menteur** to call sb a liar

2 *(après un substantif)* **l'amour de qch** the love of sth; **l'acquisition du langage** language acquisition; **troubles de l'audition** hearing problems; **sur présentation de votre carte** on presentation of your card; **la volonté de vaincre** the will to win

3 *(après un adjectif)* **sûr de soi** sure of oneself; **fier de son succès** proud of one's success; **il est facile de critiquer** it's easy to criticize

4 *(après un pronom)* **rien de nouveau** nothing new; **personne d'absent?** nobody missing?; **qui d'autre l'aurait fait?** who else would have done it?; **quoi de plus beau que la mer?** what is more beautiful than the sea?; **quelque chose de bon** something good

5 *(devant un adjectif, participe ou adverbe)* **c'est une heure de perdue** that's an hour lost; **encore un verre de cassé!** another glass broken!, another broken glass!; **j'ai quelques heures de libres** I have a few hours free; **restez une semaine de plus** stay (for) another *or* an extra week

6 *(introduisant un nom en apposition)* **la ville de Paris** the city of Paris; **le mois de janvier** the month of January; **cet imbécile de Pierre** that idiot Pierre

7 *(introduisant un infinitif) Littéraire* **de lire me fatigue** reading tires me; *Littéraire* **et tous de rire** they all burst into laughter; **j'aime mieux attendre que de me faire mouiller** I would rather wait than get wet

ART PARTITIF 1 *(dans une affirmation)* **j'ai acheté de la viande** I bought (some) meat; **il me faudra du courage** I'll need (some) courage; **respirer de l'air frais** to breathe fresh air; **c'est de la provocation!** it's sheer provocation!; **j'ai bu de ce vin** I drank some of that wine; **manger de tous les plats** to have some of everything; **écouter de la musique** to listen to music; **je ne bois que de l'eau** I only drink water; **lire du Proust** to read something by Proust *or* some Proust; **c'est du Bach, n'est-ce pas?** it's Bach, isn't it?

2 *(dans une interrogation)* **prends-tu du sucre dans ton café?** do you take sugar in your coffee?

3 *(dans une négation)* **il n'y a pas de place** there's no room, there isn't any room; **ils ne vendent pas de viande** they don't sell meat

4 *(exprimant une comparaison)* **il y a du prophète chez lui** he's a bit like a prophet; **ça c'est du Julien tout craché** *ou* **du pur Julien** that's Julien all over, that's typical of Julien

ART INDÉFINI 1 *(dans une affirmation)* **il a de bonnes idées** he has *or* he's got (some) good ideas; **de grands artistes se trouvaient là** there were some distinguished artists there

2 *(dans une négation)* **je n'ai pas de bouteilles à la cave** I have no *or* I haven't got any bottles in the cellar; **sans faire de fautes** without making any mistakes; **je ne veux pas qu'on lui mette de collier** I won't have a collar put on him/her

• **de... à PRÉP 1** *(dans l'espace)* from... to; **de Paris à Marseille** from Paris to Marseilles; **du Nord au Midi** from (the) North to (the) South

2 *(dans le temps)* from... to; **du 15 au 20 mars** from 15 to 20 March; **de Noël à Pâques** from Christmas to Easter; **ouvert du lundi au vendredi** open (from) Monday to Friday, *Am* open Monday through Friday; **d'un instant à l'autre** *(bientôt)* any minute *or* time now; **d'ici à demain** by tomorrow

3 *(dans une évolution)* from... to; **passer de la tristesse à la joie** to go from sadness to joy

4 *(dans une énumération)* from... to; **on y trouve tout, des chaussettes aux fours à micro-ondes** they've got everything from socks to microwave ovens

5 *(dans une évaluation)* **ça vaut de 50 à 60 euros** it's worth between 50 and 60 euros; **il y a de 4000 à 5000 emplois en jeu** there are between 4,000 and 5,000 jobs at stake

6 de vous à moi... between ourselves...

• **de... en PRÉP 1** *(dans l'espace)* from... to; **aller de ville en ville** to go from town to town **2** *(dans le temps)* **de jour en jour** from day to day; **d'heure en heure** as the hours go by; **d'année en année** every year *or* from one year to the next **3** *(dans une évolution)* **aller de mal en pis** to go from bad to worse; **aller de déception en déception** to go from one disappointment to the next; **un musée où vous irez de surprise en surprise** a museum where surprise after surprise awaits you

---

dé [de] **NM 1** *(pour jouer)* die, dice; **des dés** dice; **jouer aux dés** to play dice; **jeter les dés** to cast the dice; **coup de dé** *ou* **dés** throw of the dice; **jouer qch sur un coup de dés** to gamble sth away; *Fig* **les dés (en) sont jetés** the die is cast

2 *Culin* cube; **couper du lard en dés** to dice bacon, to cut bacon into dice

3 *Couture* **dé (à coudre)** thimble; **je prendrai un dé à coudre de cognac** I'll have a thimbleful of cognac

4 *Archit (de piédestal)* dado, die

PREFIX

DÉ-/DES-/DÉS-

• The prefix **dé-** (or its alternative forms **des-** and **dés-**) has three main functions: it can suggest DISTANCE, LOSS or an OPPOSITE EFFECT to that of the word – often a verb – it is added to, eg:

déplacer to move, to displace; **dévier** to swerve, to deviate, to divert; **détourner** to divert, to hijack; **désespoir** dispair; **décapiter** to decapitate; **débrancher** to disconnect, to unplug; **désinstaller** to uninstall; **dépourvu de** devoid of

Note that there are several equivalent English prefixes that can translate **dé-**: *dis-*, *de-* and *un-*.

• French slang is an area where **dé-** is often used, sometimes to amusing effect:

se défroquer (originally a term meaning "to leave the priesthood") to take one's trousers off; **se décalcifier** (a pun on the word *calcif* – slang for underpants – and the verb meaning "to become decalcified") to take one's trousers off; **ça te défrise?** (literally, "is it straightening your hair out?") do you have a problem with that?

DEA [deəa] **NM** *(abrév* **diplôme d'études approfondies***)* = postgraduate qualification which is a prerequisite for PhD candidates

deadline [dɛdlajn] **NM** deadline

deal [dil] **NM 1** *(accord)* deal **2** *Fam Arg drogue* (drug) deal; **il a fait de la taule pour d. d'héro** he did a stretch for dealing smack

dealer[1] [dilœr] **NM** *Fam Arg drogue* dealer

dealer[2] **[3]** [dile] *Fam Arg drogue* **VT** to deal
VI to deal

déambulateur [deɑ̃bylatœr] **NM** walking frame, *Br* Zimmer® (frame)

déambulatoire [deɑ̃bylatwar] **NM** ambulatory

déambuler [3] [deɑ̃byle] **VI** to stroll, to amble (along)

deb [dɛb] *Fam* **NMF** deb, debutante
ADJ *Br* daft, *Am* dumb

débâcher [3] [debaʃe] **VT** *(camion, toit)* to take the canvas sheet *or* the tarpaulin off

débâcle [debakl] **NF 1** *(d'une rivière)* breaking up (of ice); **nous sommes arrivés au moment de la d.** we arrived when the ice was starting to break up **2** *Mil* rout **3** *(faillite ▸ d'une institution, d'un système)* collapse; **c'est la d.!** it's absolute chaos!

débâillonner [3] [debajɔne] **VT d. qn** to remove sb's gag; **d. la presse** to end press censorship

déballage [debalaʒ] **NM 1** *(des bagages, de marchandises)* unpacking; **le d. de nos affaires nous a pris plusieurs heures** it took us several hours to unpack our things **2** *(exposition)* display; **je l'ai acheté au d. du marché Saint-Pierre** I bought it on display at the Marché St Pierre **3** *Fam (aveu)* outpouring; **un d. de sentiments** an outpouring of feeling

déballer [3] [debale] **VT 1** *(bagages, marchandises)* to unpack **2** *(exposer ▸ produits)* to display **3** *Fam (sentiments)* to unload, to pour out; *(vérité)* to admit
USAGE ABSOLU il déballe le dimanche aux Puces he has a stall on Sundays at the flea market

débandade [debɑ̃dad] **NF 1** *(déroute)* rout **2** *(panique)* panic, rush; **ce fut la d. générale** there was a mad rush

• **à la débandade ADV les enfants sortent de l'école à la d.** children are piling out of school

débander [3] [debɑ̃de] **VT 1** *(plaie)* to remove the bandages from, to take the bandages off; *(yeux)* to remove the blindfold from **2** *Tech (arc)* to unbend; *(ressort)* to slacken, to loosen
VI 1 *Vulg (ne plus avoir une érection)* to lose one's hard-on **2** *Fam (locution)* **sans d.** without letting up
VPR se débander 1 *(s'éparpiller)* to scatter, to disperse **2** *(ressort)* to recoil; *(arc)* to unbend

débaptiser [3] [debatize] **VT** *(place, rue)* to change the name of, to give another name to

débarbouillage [debarbujaʒ] **NM** *(du visage)* wash; **j'ai dû me contenter d'un rapide d.** I had to make do with giving my face a quick wash

débarbouiller [3] [debarbuje] **VT** *(visage)* to wash; **d. qn** to wash sb's face
VPR se débarbouiller *Fam* to wash one's face

débarbouillette [debarbujɛt] **NF** *Can Br* face flannel, facecloth, *Am* washcloth

débarcadère [debarkadɛr] **NM** *(de passagers)* landing stage; *(de marchandises)* wharf

débardage [debardaʒ] **NM** *(de marchandises)* unloading; *(de bois)* hauling

débarder [3] [debarde] **VT** *(marchandises)* to unload; *(bois)* to haul

débardeur [debardœr] **NM 1** *(ouvrier) Br* docker, *Am* longshoreman **2** *(tricot)* tank top; *(tee-shirt)* singlet, *Br* vest

débarqué, -e [debarke] **ADJ** *(passager)* disembarked
NM,F disembarked passenger; *Fig* **un nouveau d.** a new arrival

débarquement [debarkəmɑ̃] **NM 1** *(déchargement ▸ de marchandises)* unloading; *(▸ de passagers)* landing; **le d. des marchandises prendra plusieurs jours** it will take several days to unload the goods **2** *Mil* landing; *Hist* **le (jour du) d.** D-day, the Normandy landings; **troupes de d.** landing force; *Fig* **dès juillet c'est le d., toute la famille arrive** the invasion begins in July when the whole family arrives

• **de débarquement ADJ** *(quai)* arrival *(avant n)*; *(navire, troupe, fiche)* landing *(avant n)*

débarquer [3] [debarke] **VT 1** *(d'un bateau ▸ marchandises)* to unload; *(▸ voyageurs)* to land **2** *Fam (limoger)* to fire, *Br* to sack, *Am* to can; **il s'est fait d.** he got the boot *or Br* sack
VI 1 *(d'un bateau)* to disembark, to land; *(d'un avion)* to disembark; *(d'un train, d'un bus)* to get off, to alight
2 *Mil* to land
3 *Fam (arriver)* to turn up, to show up; **il a débarqué chez moi à minuit** he turned up at my place at midnight; **toute la famille débarque le week-end prochain** the whole family's descending on me/us next weekend
4 *Fam (être ignorant)* **tu débarques ou quoi?** where have you been?, what planet have you been on?; **mets-moi au courant, je débarque** give me an update, I haven't a clue what's going on

débarras [debara] **NM 1** *(dépôt)* storage room **2** *Fam (locution)* **bon d.!** good riddance!

débarrasser [3 [debarase] **VT 1** *(nettoyer ▸ table)* to clear; *(enlever ▸ assiette)* to clear (away); **ne débarrasse pas les verres** leave the glasses on the table; *Fam* **d. le plancher** to clear off; **je serai ravi quand ils auront débarrassé le plancher** I'll be delighted to see the back of them **2** *(désencombrer)* **je vais te d. de ta valise** I'll take your case; **il m'a demandé de le d. de sa vieille table** he asked me to take his old table off his hands; **d. la ville de ses voyous** to rid the city of its yobs; **l'arrivée du livreur m'a débarrassé de cette bavarde** the arrival of the deliveryman gave me the opportunity to get rid of that chatterbox; **d. la cave de vieilles bouteilles** to clear old bottles out of the cellar; **je fais le nettoyage maintenant pour en être débarrassé (plus tard)** I'll do the cleaning now to get it out of the way; **d. qn de ses mauvaises habitudes** to cure sb of his/her bad habits
VPR se débarrasser 1 se d. de *(se défaire de)* to get rid of; **je me suis débarrassé de mes vieux livres** I got rid of my old books
2 se d. de *(éloigner ▸ importun)* to get rid of; *(▸ serviteur)* to get rid of, to dismiss
3 *Euph* **se d. de** *(tuer)* to get rid of
4 se d. de *(veste, gants)* to take off, to remove; *(sac à main, éventail)* to put down
USAGE ABSOLU débarrasse-toi, tu vas avoir trop chaud take your coat *or* jacket off, you'll be too hot

débarrer [3] [debare] **VT 1** *(porte, fenêtre)* to unbar **2** *Can & (régional) (déverrouiller)* to unlock

débat [deba] **NM 1** *(controverse)* debate, discussion; **trancher un d.** to conclude a discussion; **d. télévisé** discussion programme; *(politique)* televised debate **2** *(conflit intérieur)* inner turmoil; **d.**

de conscience moral dilemma
• **débats** NMPL *Pol & Jur* proceedings

débâtir [32] [debatir] VT *Couture* to unpick the basting from

débattement [debatmɑ̃] NM *Aut & Tech* clearance; **d. de roue** wheel deflection

débattre [83] [debatr] VT *(discuter ▸ thème, question)* to discuss, to thrash out; **ils ont longtemps débattu le prix** they haggled at length over the price
• **débattre de, débattre sur** VT IND to debate, to discuss
VPR **se débattre 1** *(s'agiter ▸ victime)* to struggle; *(▸ poisson)* to thrash about; **se d. contre un voleur** to struggle with a thief; **se d. comme un forcené** *ou* **comme un beau diable** to struggle like a madman **2** *(lutter)* **se d. dans les problèmes financiers** to struggle against financial difficulties; **se d. contre l'angoisse** to wrestle *or* to grapple with anxiety
• **à débattre** ADJ **prix à d.** *(dans une annonce)* open to offers, negotiable; **300 euros à d.** *(dans une annonce)* 300 euros or nearest offer; **conditions à d.** conditions to be negotiated

débauchage [deboʃaʒ] NM **1** *(renvoi)* laying off, *Br* making redundant **2** *(d'employés d'autres entreprises)* poaching

débauche [deboʃ] NF **1** *(dévergondage)* debauchery; **inciter qn à la d.** to debauch sb; **vivre dans la d.** to live a life of debauchery; **lieu de d.** den of vice **2** *(profusion)* **une d. de mets rares** an abundance of rare delicacies; **une d. d'imagination** unbridled imagination; **une d. de couleurs** a riot of colour
• **de débauche** ADJ *(passé, vie)* dissolute

débauché, -e [deboʃe] ADJ *(personne)* debauched; *(vie)* dissolute
NM,F debauched person, libertine

débaucher [3] [deboʃe] VT **1** *(renvoyer)* to lay off, *Br* to make redundant
2 *(employés d'autres entreprises)* to poach; **d. les meilleurs cerveaux** to lure away *or* to poach the best brains
3 *(corrompre)* to corrupt
4 *Fam (détourner)* to lure *or* to tempt away; *Hum* **allez, je vous débauche!** I've come to drag you away!
5 *(inciter ▸ à la grève)* to incite to strike
USAGE ABSOLU *(licencier)* **on débauche dans le textile** there are lay-offs *or Br* redundancies in the textile industry

débecter [4] [debɛkte] VT *très Fam* **ça me débecte** it turns my stomach, it makes me feel sick; **t'es pas débecté!** you're a brave man, I wouldn't touch that with *Br* a bargepole *or Am* a ten-foot pole!

débet [debe] NM *Fin* balance due

débile [debil] ADJ **1** *Fam (inepte ▸ livre, film, décision) Br* daft, *Am* dumb; **il est complètement d.** he's a complete idiot; **c'est d., comment peux-tu dire ça?** how can you talk such nonsense? **2** *Littéraire (faible ▸ corps)* frail, weak, feeble; *(▸ intelligence)* deficient
NMF **1** *Fam (idiot)* dope, fool **2** *Psy* **d. léger/moyen/profond** mildly/moderately/severely retarded person; *Vieilli* **d. mental** retarded person

débilitant, -e [debilitɑ̃, -ɑ̃t] ADJ **1** *(affaiblissant)* debilitating, enervating **2** *(démoralisant)* demoralizing, discouraging **3** *Fam (abrutissant)* mind-numbing, soul-destroying

débilité [debilite] NF **1** *Fam (caractère stupide)* stupidity; **les films que tu regardes sont d'une d.!** you watch such *Br* daft films *or Am* dumb movies! **2** *Psy* **d. (mentale)** (mental) retardation **3** *Littéraire (faiblesse)* debility

débiliter [3] [debilite] VT **1** *(affaiblir)* to debilitate, to weaken **2** *(déprimer)* to drag down, to dishearten, to demoralize

débine [debin] NF *Fam* poverty□; **être dans la d.** to be hard up *or* broke; **c'est la d.!** times are hard!

débiner [3] [debine] *Fam* VT *Br* to bitch about, to slag off, *Am* to bad-mouth
VPR **se débiner 1** *(s'enfuir)* to take off, to make oneself scarce; **te débine pas, j'ai à te parler** stick around, I want to talk to you; *Fig* **n'essaie pas de te d., je veux une réponse** don't try to wriggle out of it, I want an answer **2** *(s'écrouler)* to come *or* to fall apart□

débineur, -euse [debinœr, -øz] NM,F *Fam* backbiter

débit [debi] NM **1** *(d'eau, de passagers)* flow; *(de vapeur)* capacity; *(de gaz)* output; *(de marchandises, de clients)* turnover; *(d'une machine)* output; *Géog* flow
2 *(élocution)* (speed of) delivery; *Fam* **il a un sacré d.** he talks nineteen to the dozen
3 *Ordinat & Tél* rate; **d. en bauds** baud rate; **d. binaire** bit rate; **d. de traitement** *ou* **de données** data throughput *or* speed; **d. de transmission** transmission rate; **haut d.** broadband
4 *Élec* output; **d. capacitif** charging capacity; **d. de courant** power output, delivery rate
5 *Com (ventes)* (retail) sale; **il n'y a pas beaucoup de d. dans ce magasin** this *Br* shop *or Am* store doesn't have a large turnover; **d. de boissons** bar; **d. de tabac** *Br* tobacconist, *Am* tobacco store
6 *Méd* output, rate; **d. cardiaque** cardiac output; **d. expiratoire de pointe** peak flow; **d. sanguin** circulation rate
7 *Fin & Compta* debit; *(sur un relevé)* debit side; **inscrire** *ou* **porter un article au d.** to debit an entry; **d. de caisse** cash debit; **d. cumulé** cumulative debit; **d. différé** deferred debit; **d. immédiat** immediate debit
8 *Com* bill; **je n'ai pas encore fait le d. (à la caisse)** I haven't rung it up yet
9 *(de bois)* cutting up
• **au débit de** PRÉP **inscrire une somme au d. d'un compte** to charge an amount of money to sb's account; **porter une somme au d. de qn** to debit sb *or* sb's account with an amount; **porter une somme au d. d'un compte** to debit an account; **520 euros à votre d.** 520 euros on the debit side (of your account)

débitable [debitabl] ADJ **1** *(bois)* good *or* ready for cutting up **2** *Banque* **compte d.** account one may draw money from, account with open access

débitant, -e [debitɑ̃, -ɑ̃t] NM,F **d. de boissons** *Br* publican, *Am* bar owner; **d. de tabac** *Br* tobacconist, *Am* tobacco dealer

débiter [3] [debite] VT **1** *(couper ▸ matériau, tissu, bœuf)* to cut up; *(▸ bois)* to cut *or* to saw up; **d. qch en tranches** to slice sth
2 *Com* to retail, to sell (retail)
3 *Ind (sujet: machine, usine)* to turn out, to produce; *Fam* **je ne veux pas d. du roman de gare** I don't want to churn out trashy novels
4 *(déverser ▸ pompe)* to discharge, to yield; *(▸ fleuve)* to have a flow rate of
5 *Péj (texte)* to reel off; *(sermon)* to deliver; *(banalité)* to trot out; **d. des mensonges/idioties** to come out with a lot of lies/nonsense; **d. ses leçons par cœur** to recite one's homework parrot-fashion
6 *Fin & Compta* to debit; **d. qn d'une somme** to debit sb with an amount; **d. une somme d'un compte** to debit an account with an amount, to debit an amount to an account; **votre compte sera débité (de 40 euros) à la fin du mois** your account will be debited (by 40 euros) at the end of the month
USAGE ABSOLU *Fam Ind* **pas de temps à perdre, il faut que ça débite!** there's no time to waste, we have to just churn the stuff out!

débiteur, -trice [debitœr, -tris] ADJ *(colonne, compte, solde)* debit *(avant n)*; *(personne, société)* debtor *(avant n)*; **mon compte est d. de plusieurs milliers d'euros** my account is several thousand euros overdrawn
NM,F **1** *Fin & Compta* debtor; **d. hypothécaire** mortgagor **2** *(obligé)* **être d. de qn** to be indebted to sb *or* in sb's debt

débitmètre [debimɛtr] NM flow meter; *Méd* **d. de pointe** peak flow meter

déblai [deblɛ] NM *(dégagement)* digging *or* cutting (out)
• **déblais** NMPL *(gravats)* debris, excavated material, rubble; *(terre)* (dug *or* excavated) earth
• **en déblai** ADJ *(route)* sunken

déblaie *etc voir* **déblayer**

déblaiement [deblɛmɑ̃] NM *(d'un terrain, d'une ruine)* clearing (out); **ils ont procédé au d. de la forêt après l'accident aérien** they cleared the forest of wreckage after the plane crash

déblatérer [18] [deblatere] **déblatérer contre** VT IND *Péj* to rant (and rave) about, to sound off about

déblayage [deblɛjaʒ] = **déblaiement**

déblayer [11] [debleje] VT **1** *(dégager ▸ neige, terre)* to clear away; *(▸ lieu)* to clear out; **d. la neige autour de la maison** to clear the snow from around the house; **d. un chantier des gravats** to clear rubble from a building site **2** *(en travaux publics)* to cut, to excavate, to dig **3** *Fig (travail)* to do the groundwork *or* spadework on; **d. le terrain** *(se débarrasser des détails)* to do the groundwork; *Fam* **allez, déblaie le terrain!** *(va-t'en)* go on, get out of here *or* get lost!

déblocage, débloquage [deblɔkaʒ] NM **1** *Tech (d'un écrou, d'un dispositif)* unblocking, releasing; *(de freins)* freeing
2 *(réouverture ▸ d'un tuyau)* clearing, freeing, unblocking; *(▸ d'une route)* clearing
3 *Écon (des salaires, des prix, de crédits)* unfreezing; *(de fonds)* releasing, making available; *Banque (d'un compte)* freeing
4 *Tél (de portable)* unlocking
5 *Psy* getting rid of inhibitions

débloquer [3] [deblɔke] VT **1** *Tech (écrou, dispositif)* to unblock, to release; *(freins)* to free
2 *(rouvrir ▸ tuyau)* to clear, to free, unblock; *(▸ route)* to clear; *Fig* **d. la situation** *(après un conflit)* to break the stalemate; *(la sortir de l'enlisement)* to get things moving again
3 *Écon (salaires, prix, crédits)* to unfreeze; *(fonds)* to release, to make available; *Banque (compte)* to free, to unfreeze
4 *Tél (portable)* to unlock
5 *Fam (décontracter)* **ça m'a débloqué** it got rid of some of my inhibitions
VI *Fam* **1** *(en parlant)* to talk nonsense *or Br* rubbish **2** *(être déraisonnable)* to be off one's rocker; **tu débloques!** you're out of your mind!; **son grand-père est vieux, il commence à d.** his/her grandfather is old and not all there **3** *(ne pas fonctionner correctement)* to be on the blink, *Am* to be on the fritz

débobiner [3] [debɔbine] VT to unwind, to unreel

débogage [debɔgaʒ] NM *Ordinat* debugging

déboguer [3] [debɔge] VT *Ordinat* to debug

débogueur [debɔgœr] NM **(programme) d.** debugger

déboires [debwar] NMPL disappointments, setbacks, (trials and) tribulations; **s'épargner** *ou* **s'éviter des d.** to spare oneself a lot of trouble; **elle a essuyé bien des d.** she suffered many disappointments *or* setbacks

déboisement [debwazmɑ̃] NM deforestation, clearing (of trees)

déboiser [3] [debwaze] VT *(couper les arbres de)* to deforest, to clear of trees; **il faudra d. le terrain avant de construire** we'll have to clear the area of trees before we can start building
VPR **se déboiser** *(terrain, région)* to lose its trees, to be deforested

déboîtement [debwatmɑ̃] NM **1** *(luxation ▸ de l'épaule, de la hanche)* dislocation; *(▸ de la rotule)* slipping **2** *(en voiture)* pulling out

déboîter [3] [debwate] VT **1** *(démonter ▸ tuyau)* to disconnect; *(▸ objet)* to unfasten, to release, to uncouple; *(▸ porte, fenêtre)* to take off its hinges **2** *Méd* to dislocate, to put out
VI *(véhicule)* to pull out
VPR **se déboîter 1** *(partie du corps)* **mon genou s'est déboîté** I've dislocated my knee **2** *(personne)* **se d. l'épaule** to dislocate one's shoulder

débonder [3] [debɔ̃de] VT to unplug
VPR **se débonder 1** *(tonneau)* to overflow **2** *(personne)* to pour out one's troubles, to open up

débonnaire [debɔnɛr] ADJ *(air)* kindly; *(personne)* good-natured, easy-going; **d'un ton d.** good-naturedly

débordant, -e [debɔrdɑ̃, -ɑ̃t] ADJ *(extrême ▸ affection)* overflowing; *(▸ activité)* tireless; *(▸ imagination)* wild, vivid; **d'un enthousiasme d.** bubbling with enthusiasm; **ressentir une joie débordante** to be bursting with joy; **être d. de** to be full of; **d. de santé/d'énergie** bursting with health/full of energy

débordé, -e [deborde] **ADJ 1** *(occupé)* snowed under **2** *(dépassé)* overwhelmed

débordement [debɔrdəmɑ̃] **NM 1** *(écoulement ▸ d'une rivière)* overflowing; *(▸ d'un liquide)* running over, overflowing

2 *(profusion ▸ de paroles)* rush, torrent; *(▸ d'injures, de joie, d'émotion etc)* outburst

3 *(manœuvre)* outflanking; **il y a eu d. des syndicats par la base** the rank and file have gone further than the union intended

4 *Ordinat* overflow

• **débordements NMPL** *(agitation)* wild *or* extreme behaviour; *Littéraire (débauche)* excesses

déborder [3] [debɔrde] **VI 1** *(rivière)* to overflow; *(bouillon, lait)* to boil over; **le fleuve a débordé de son lit** the river has burst its banks; **l'eau a débordé du lavabo** the sink has overflowed; **les papiers débordent de la corbeille** the papers are spilling out of the wastepaper basket; **j'ai fait d. le lait** I let the milk boil over; **son chagrin/sa joie débordait** he/she could no longer contain his/her grief/delight; *Fig* **d. de qch** to overflow *or* to be bursting with sth; **d. d'énergie** to be bursting with energy; **d. d'imagination** to have a wild *or* vivid imagination; **son cœur déborde de reconnaissance** his/her heart is brimming over with gratitude

2 *(récipient)* to overflow, to run over; *(tiroir, sac)* to be crammed, to spill over; **la casserole est pleine à d.** the saucepan's full to the brim *or* to overflowing; **laisser d. la baignoire** to let the bath overflow; **le train débordait de voyageurs** the train was crammed *or* overflowing with passengers

3 *(faire saillie)* to stick *or* to jut out, to project; **la pile de gravats débordait sur l'allée** the heap of rubble had spilled out into the lane; **d. en coloriant un dessin** to go over the edges while colouring in a picture

VT 1 *(dépasser)* to stick *or* to jut out from

2 *(s'écarter de)* **vous débordez le sujet** you've gone beyond the scope of the topic; **cela déborde le cadre de mes responsabilités** that exceeds my responsibilities

3 *(submerger ▸ troupe, parti, équipe)* to outflank; **le syndicat est débordé par la base** the rank and file are going further than the union intended; **être débordé de travail** to be up to one's eyes in *or* snowed under with work; **être débordé par les événements** to let things get on top of one; **je suis débordé par toutes ces nouvelles modes** I can't keep up with all these new fashions

4 *(tirer)* **d. les draps** to untuck the sheets

5 *(enlever les bords de)* to remove the edging from; *Tech* **d. une tôle** to trim the edges of an iron plate

USAGE ABSOLU nous débordons un peu, il est midi et deux minutes we're going slightly over time, it's two minutes past twelve

VPR se déborder se d. en dormant to throw off one's covers in one's sleep

débosselage [debɔslaʒ] **NM** *Can Aut* (car) bodywork repairs, *Br* panel beating

débosseleur, -euse [debɔslœr, -øz] **NM,F** *Can Aut* (car) bodywork repairer, *Br* panel beater

débotté, débotter[1] [debɔte] **au débotté ADV** *Littéraire* **prendre qn au d.** to pounce on sb, to take sb unawares; **répondre au d.** to answer off the cuff

débotter[2] **[3]** [debɔte] **VT** to remove the boots of

VPR se débotter to take one's boots off

débouchage [debuʃaʒ] **NM 1** *(d'un tuyau)* unblocking **2** *(d'une bouteille)* uncorking

débouché [debuʃe] **NM 1** *(possibilité d'emploi)* career prospect; **cette formation n'offre aucun d.** this training does not lead to any career openings **2** *(perspective de vente)* outlet, opening; *(marché)* market **3** *(issue ▸ d'un passage)* opening; *(▸ d'une vallée)* mouth; **avoir un d. sur la mer** to have an outlet to the sea

• **au débouché de PRÉP** at the end of; **au d. du défilé dans la vallée** where the pass opens out into the valley

déboucher [3] [debuʃe] **VT 1** *(ouvrir ▸ bouteille de bière, tube)* to take the top off, to open; *(▸ bouteille de vin)* to uncork, to open; *(▸ flacon)* to unstop, to remove the stopper from; **on débouche une bouteille pour fêter ça!** let's crack open a bottle to celebrate! **2** *(débloquer ▸ pipe, trou, gicleur)* to clear, to clean out; *(▸ lavabo)* to unblock, to unstop, to clear; *(▸ tuyau, conduit)* to clear, to unclog; *(▸ nez)* to unblock; *(▸ oreille)* to clean out

VI 1 *(aboutir)* **d. de** to emerge from, to come out of; **d. sur** to open into, to lead to; **la rue débouche sur l'avenue** the street leads to the avenue **2** *Fig* **d. sur** to lead to; **des études qui ne débouchent sur rien** a course that doesn't lead anywhere; **d. sur des résultats** to have positive results

VPR se déboucher 1 *(lavabo, tuyau)* to unblock; *(nez, oreilles)* to clear **2 se d. le nez** to clear one's nose

déboucheur [debuʃœr] **NM 1** *(produit)* drain clearing liquid **2** *(dispositif)* **d. à ventouse** plunger, *Am* plumber's friend

déboucler [3] [debukle] **VT 1** *(détacher ▸ ceinture)* to unbuckle, to undo, to unfasten **2** *(cheveux)* **la pluie avait débouclé ses cheveux** the rain had straightened his/her curly hair

déboulé [debule] **NM 1** *(en danse)* déboulé **2** *Sport* burst of speed

débouler [3] [debule] **VI 1** *Fam (surgir)* to shoot out, to burst out; *(arriver brusquement)* to show up, to turn up; **l'enfant a déboulé de derrière une voiture** the child shot out *or* emerged suddenly from behind a parked car; **elle a déboulé du coin de la rue** she came hurtling round the corner; **ils ont déboulé chez moi sans prévenir** they showed up at my place without any warning **2** *(tomber)* to tumble down

VT d. les escaliers *(en courant)* to race *or* to hurtle down the stairs; *(après être tombé)* to tumble down the stairs

déboulonnage [debulɔnaʒ], **déboulonnement** [debulɔnmɑ̃] **NM 1** *Tech* unbolting, removal of bolts **2** *Fam (fait de discréditer)* trashing; *(renvoi)* firing, *Br* sacking

déboulonner [3] [debulɔne] **VT 1** *Tech* to unbolt, to remove the bolts (from); **d. une statue** to take down a statue **2** *Fam (discréditer)* to trash; *(renvoyer)* to fire, *Br* to sack; **se faire d.** to get fired, *Br* to get the sack

débourber [3] [deburbe] **VT 1** *(nettoyer ▸ minerai, charbon)* to wash, to clean; *(▸ rivière)* to dredge **2** *(sortir de la boue)* to pull *or* to drag *or* to haul out of the mud

débourrer [3] [debure] **VT 1** *(trou)* to clear **2** *(cheval)* to break in **3** *(pipe)* to scrape out

débours [debur] **NM** expenditure, outlay

déboursement [debursəmɑ̃] **NM** spending, laying out

débourser [3] [deburse] **VT** to spend, to lay out; **je ne débourserai pas un centime** I won't pay a penny; **sans rien d.** without spending *or* paying a penny

déboussoler [3] [debusɔle] **VT** to confuse, to bewilder; **il est déboussolé depuis le départ de sa mère** his mother's departure has unsettled him

debout [dəbu] **ADV 1** *(en parlant des personnes ▸ en station verticale)* standing up; **manger d.** to eat standing up; **d.!** get *or* stand up!; **il était d. sur la table** he was standing on the table; **elle est d. toute la journée** she's on her feet all day; **ils l'ont mis d.** they helped him to his feet *or* helped him up; **se mettre d.** to stand (up), to rise; **je préfère rester d.** I'd rather stand; **je suis resté d. toute la journée** I was on my feet all day; **ne restez pas d.** (please) sit down; **tenez-le d.** keep him upright *or* in a standing position; **depuis l'opération elle a du mal à se tenir d.** she's been very unsteady on her feet since the operation; **on peut se tenir d. dans sa camionnette** his van is big enough to stand up in; **il ne tient plus d.** *(fatigué)* he's dead on his feet; *(ivre)* he can hardly stand

2 *(en parlant d'animaux)* **le poulain se tient déjà d.** the foal is already up on its feet; **le vieux chien s'est mis d.** the old dog got up *or* to its feet

3 *(en parlant d'objets)* upright, vertical; **mettre une échelle d. contre un mur** to stand a ladder against a wall; **mettre une chaise d.** to stand a chair up; *Fig* **mettre un projet d.** to set up a project; **ça ne tient pas d.** it doesn't make sense; **le raisonnement ne tient pas d.** the argument doesn't hold water *or* hold up

4 *(éveillé)* up; **d.!** get up!; **d. là-dedans!** get up, you lot!; **être d. à 5 heures** to be up at 5 o'clock; **il n'est pas encore d.** he's not up *or* out of bed yet; **je reste d. très tard** I stay up very late; **nous sommes restés d. toute la nuit** we stayed up all night

5 *(en bon état)* standing; **les murs sont encore d.** the walls are still standing; **la république ne restera pas longtemps d.** the republic won't hold out for long

6 *(guéri)* up on one's feet (again), up and about; *(sorti de chez soi, de l'hôpital)* out and about

7 *Littéraire (dignement)* uprightly, honourably; **mourir (tout) d.** to die with one's boots on

débouté, -e [debute] *Jur* **NM,F** severed plaintiff

NM *Br* nonsuit, *Am* dismissal

débouter [3] [debute] **VT** *Jur Br* to nonsuit, *Am* to dismiss; **être débouté de sa plainte** *Br* to be nonsuited, *Am* to have one's case dismissed

déboutonner [3] [debutɔne] **VT** to unbutton

VPR se déboutonner 1 *(pour se déshabiller)* to unbutton (oneself)

2 *(parler franchement)* to open up

3 *(vêtement)* to unbutton

4 *Can Fam (se montrer généreux)* to splash out

débraie *etc voir* **débrayer**

débraillé, -e [debraje] **ADJ** *(allure, vêtements, personne)* sloppy, scruffy; *(manières)* slovenly; *(conversation)* unrestrained

NM slovenliness; **être en d.** to be scruffy; **traîner en d.** to slop around

débrailler [3] [debraje] **se débrailler VPR** *Fam* to loosen one's clothing[□]; *Fig* **la conversation se débraille** the conversation is getting a bit out of hand

débranchement [debrɑ̃ʃmɑ̃] **NM 1** *(déconnexion ▸ d'un tuyau)* disconnecting; *(▸ d'un appareil électrique)* unplugging **2** *Rail* splitting up

débrancher [3] [debrɑ̃ʃe] **VT 1** *(déconnecter ▸ tuyau)* to disconnect; *(▸ appareil électrique)* to unplug; *Fam Hum* **débranchez-le!** shut him up, will you!; *Fam* **d. un malade** to turn off a patient's life support machine[□] **2** *Rail (train)* to split up

débrayage [debrɛjaʒ] **NM 1** *Aut* disengaging of the clutch, *Br* declutching **2** *(grève)* stoppage, walkout

débrayer [11] [debreje] **VT 1** *Aut* to disengage the clutch of, *Br* to declutch **2** *(machine)* to throw out of gear, to put out of operation

VI 1 *Aut* to disengage the clutch, *Br* to declutch; **débrayez!** take your foot off the clutch! **2** *(faire grève)* to stop work, to come out *or* to go on strike

débridé, -e [debride] **ADJ** unbridled, unrestrained, unfettered

débridement [debridmɑ̃] **NM 1** *(d'un cheval)* unbridling **2** *Littéraire (déchaînement)* unbridling, unleashing **3** *Méd (d'un abcès, d'une blessure)* incision

débrider [3] [debride] **VT 1** *(cheval)* to unbridle **2** *Méd (abcès, blessure)* to incise **3** *Culin (volaille)* to untruss

• **sans débrider ADV** nonstop, without stopping, at a stretch

débriefer [3] [debrife] **VT** to debrief

débris [debri] **NM 1** *(surtout au pl) (fragment ▸ de verre)* piece, splinter, shard; *(▸ de vaisselle)* (broken) piece *or* fragment; *(▸ de roche)* crumb, debris *(singulier)*; *(▸ de métal)* scrap; *(▸ d'un avion, d'une voiture)* remains, debris *(singulier)*, wreckage **2** *(surtout au pl) (nourriture)* scraps, crumbs; *(détritus)* litter, *Br* rubbish; *Littéraire (restes ▸ d'une fortune, d'un royaume)* last shreds, remnants **3** *très Fam (vieillard)* **(vieux) d.** old codger, *Am* geezer

débrouillard, -e [debrujar, -ard] **ADJ** resourceful

NM,F resourceful person

débrouillardise [debrujardiz] **NF** resourcefulness; **faire preuve de d.** to be resourceful

débrouiller [3] [debruje] **VT 1** *(démêler ▸ fils)* to unravel, to untangle, to disentangle; *(▸ énigme)* to puzzle out, to untangle, to unravel; **d. les affaires de qn** to sort out sb's business affairs **2** *Fam (enseigner les bases à)* to teach the basics to[□];

d. qn en gestion to give sb a grounding in management[a]
VPR se débrouiller 1 *(faire face aux difficultés)* to manage; **débrouille-toi** you'll have to manage by yourself; **comment vas-tu te d. maintenant qu'elle est partie?** how will you cope now that she's gone?; **elle se débrouille très bien dans Berlin** she really knows her way around Berlin; **tu parles espagnol? – je me débrouille** do you speak Spanish? – I get by; **se d. en anglais** to have a working knowledge of English; **je me suis débrouillé pour avoir des places** I managed to wangle some seats; *Fam* **donne cette casserole, tu te débrouilles comme un pied** give me that pan, you're all thumbs **2** *(subsister financièrement)* to make ends meet, to manage; **on se débrouille** we get by *or* manage

débroussailler [3] [debrusaje] **VT 1** *(terrain)* to clear **2** *Fig (travail, problème)* to do the groundwork *or* spadework on

débudgétisation [debydʒetizasjɔ̃] **NF** removing from the budget, debudgeting

débudgétiser [3] [debydʒetize] **VT** to remove from the budget, to debudget

débusquer [3] [debyske] **VT 1** *Chasse* to start, to flush **2** *(découvrir)* to hunt out; **le logiciel débusque la moindre faute d'orthographe** the software can track down the slightest spelling mistake

début [deby] **NM 1** *(commencement)* beginning, start; **le d. de la semaine** the beginning *or* start of the week; **le d. d'une maladie** the beginning *or* onset of an illness; **le d. d'un livre** the beginning *or* opening of a book; **salaire de d.** starting salary; **être en d. de carrière** to be at the start of one's career; **ce n'est pas mal pour un d.** it's quite good for a first try *or* attempt; **ce n'est qu'un d.** that's just the start *or* beginning; **il y a un d. à tout** you have to start sometime; **ressentir un d. de fatigue** to start feeling tired; **un d. de grippe** the first signs of flu **2** *(dans l'expression des dates)* **d. mars** at the beginning of *or* in early March **3** *Ordinat* home; **aller au d.** *(commande)* go top

• **débuts NMPL 1** *(dans une carrière)* start; *(dans le spectacle, en société)* debut; **il a eu des débuts difficiles** it wasn't easy for him at the start; **mes débuts dans le journalisme** my first steps *or* my early days as a journalist; **en être à ses débuts** *(projet)* to be in its early stages; *(personne)* to have just started (out); **faire ses débuts** to make one's debut **2** *(première période)* beginnings; **les débuts de l'aviation** the beginnings of aviation; **le rock à ses débuts** early rock music

• **au début ADV** at first, to begin with

• **au début de PRÉP au d. du printemps/de l'année** at the beginning of spring/of the year; **j'en suis encore au d. du livre** I've only just started the book; **il m'a aidé au d. de ma carrière** he started me (off) in my career

• **au tout début, tout au début ADV** at the very beginning, right at the beginning

• **dès le début ADV** from the outset *or* very start *or* very beginning

• **du début à la fin ADV** *(d'un livre, d'une histoire)* from beginning to end; *(d'une course, d'un événement)* from start to finish

débutant, -e [debytɑ̃, -ɑ̃t] **ADJ** *(dans un apprentissage)* novice *(avant n)*; *(dans une carrière)* young; **un professeur d.** a young teacher; **un conducteur d.** a newly qualified driver
NM,F 1 *(dans un apprentissage)* beginner, novice; *(dans une carrière)* beginner; **espagnol pour les débutants** beginner's Spanish; **grand d.** absolute beginner; *Fam* **se faire avoir comme un d.** to be taken in like a real greenhorn **2** *Cin & Théât* actor/actress making his/her debut

• **débutante NF** *(dans la haute société)* debutante

débuter [3] [debyte] **VI 1** *(commencer)* to start, to begin; **mal/bien d. dans la vie** to get off to a bad/good start in life; **d. par** to start (off) with; **l'histoire débute par un mariage** the story starts (off) *or* begins with a wedding
2 *(être inexpérimenté)* to be a beginner, to begin; **elle débute dans le métier** she's new to the job
3 *(commencer à travailler)* to start (out), to begin; **il a débuté comme serveur** he started out as a waiter
4 *(artiste)* to make one's debut
5 *(en société)* **d. (dans le monde)** to make one's debut
VT *Fam* **c'est nous qui débutons le concert** we're on first[a], we're opening the show[a]

déc [dɛk] **VI** *Fam* **sans d.!** *(je t'assure)* no kidding!, *Br* straight up!; **sans d.?** *(est-ce vrai?)* no kidding?, yeah?

déca [deka] **NM** *Fam* decaf

deçà [dəsa] **ADV** *Littéraire* **d. (et) delà** hither and thither

• **en deçà ADV** on this side

• **en deçà de PRÉP 1** *(de ce côté-ci de)* (on) this side of; **en d. de la frontière** on this side of the border; **en d. des Alpes** this side of the Alps **2** *Fig* **en d. d'un certain seuil** below a certain level; **rester en d. de la vérité** to be short of the truth; **ce travail est en d. de ses possibilités** this job doesn't exploit his/her potential to the full

décachetage [dekaʃtaʒ] **NM** *(en déchirant)* opening; *(en rompant le cachet)* unsealing

décacheter [27] [dekaʃte] **VT** *(ouvrir ▸ en déchirant)* to open, to tear open; *(▸ en rompant le cachet)* to unseal, to break open

décade [dekad] **NF 1** *(série de dix)* decade **2** *(dix jours)* period of ten days **3** *(dix ans)* decade

> Il faut noter que le nom anglais **decade** est un faux ami. Il signifie uniquement **décennie**.

décadenasser [3] [dekadnase] **VT** to remove the padlock from, to take the padlock off

décadence [dekadɑ̃s] **NF 1** *(état)* decadence; *(évolution)* decline, decay; **la d. romaine** Roman decadence; **la d. de l'Empire romain** the decline *or* fall of the Roman Empire **2** *Beaux-Arts & Littérature* decadence, decadent period

• **en décadence ADJ** declining, decaying, decadent **ADV tomber** *ou* **entrer en d.** to become decadent, to start to decline

décadent, -e [dekadɑ̃, -ɑ̃t] **ADJ 1** *(en déclin)* decadent, declining, decaying **2** *Beaux-Arts & Littérature* decadent
NM,F decadent; *Beaux-Arts & Littérature* **les décadents** the Decadents

décadrage [dekadraʒ] **NM** *Cin* off-centring

décadré, -e [dekadre] **ADJ** *Cin* off-centre

décaèdre [dekaɛdr] **ADJ** decahedral
NM decahedron

décaféiné, -e [dekafeine] **ADJ** decaffeinated
NM decaffeinated coffee

décagonal, -e, -aux, -ales [dekagɔnal, -o] **ADJ** decagonal

décagone [dekagɔn] **NM** decagon

décaissable [dekesabl] **ADJ** *(charge)* payable

décaissement [dekesmɑ̃] **NM 1** *Banque (retrait)* cash withdrawal; *(somme)* sum withdrawn; **faire un d.** to make a withdrawal **2** *(déballage)* unpacking **3** *Bot* planting out

• **décaissements NMPL** *Compta* outgoings

décaisser [4] [dekese] **VT 1** *Banque (retirer)* to withdraw **2** *(déballer)* to unpack, to take out of its container **3** *Bot* to plant out

décalage [dekalaʒ] **NM 1** *(dans l'espace)* space, interval, gap
2 *(dans le temps)* interval, time-lag, lag; **d. horaire** time difference; **souffrir du d. horaire** to have jet lag
3 *(manque de concordance)* discrepancy, gap
4 *(en audiovisuel)* shift, displacement; **d. de fréquence** frequency shift; **d. de l'image** image displacement
5 *Ordinat* shift; **introduire qch par d.** to shift sth in; **d. arithmétique/logique/de la virgule** arithmetic/logical/point shift

• **en décalage ADJ 1** *(dans le temps)* **nous sommes en d. par rapport à Bangkok** there's a time difference between here and Bangkok **2** *(sans harmonie)* **être en d. par rapport à qn** to be on a different wavelength from sb; **on est en complet d.** we're on completely different wavelengths

décalaminage [dekalaminaʒ] **NM 1** *(d'un moteur)* decarbonization, decoking, decarburization **2** *Métal* descaling

décalaminer [3] [dekalamine] **VT 1** *(moteur)* to decarbonize, to decoke, to decarburize **2** *Métal* to descale

décalcifiant, -e [dekalsifjɑ̃, -ɑ̃t] **ADJ** decalcifying

décalcification [dekalsifikasjɔ̃] **NF** decalcification, decalcifying

décalcifier [9] [dekalsifje] **VT** to decalcify
VPR se décalcifier to become decalcified

décalcomanie [dekalkɔmani] **NF 1** *(image)* transfer, *Am* decal, *Spéc* decalcomania; **faire des décalcomanies** to do transfers *or Am* decals **2** *(procédé)* transfer process, *Am* decal, *Spéc* decalcomania

décalé, -e [dekale] **ADJ** *(original)* offbeat, quirky

décaler [3] [dekale] **VT 1** *(dans l'espace)* to pull *or* to shift (out of line); **d. qch vers l'avant/l'arrière/la gauche** to shift sth forward/back/to the left; **les sièges sont décalés** the seats are staggered; **cette façade est légèrement décalée par rapport aux autres** this house is slightly out of line with the others
2 *(dans le temps ▸ horaire)* to shift; **l'horaire a été décalé d'une heure** *(avancé)* the schedule was brought forward an hour; *(reculé)* the schedule was brought *or* moved one hour back; **essaie de faire d. l'heure de ton départ** see if you can get your departure time changed
3 *(désorienter)* **être décalé par rapport à la réalité** to be out of phase with reality
4 *(ôter les cales de)* to unwedge
VPR se décaler to move (out of line); **décalez-vous à droite** move to the right; **décalez-vous d'un rang en avant/arrière** move forward/back a row

décalitre [dekalitr] **NM** decalitre

décalogue [dekalɔg] **NM** Decalogue

décalotter [3] [dekalɔte] **VT 1** *Méd* **d. le gland** to pull back the foreskin **2** *Fam* **d. une bouteille** to crack open a bottle

décalquage [dekalkaʒ] **NM** tracing, transferring

décalque [dekalk] **NM 1** *(reproduction)* tracing **2** *Fig (imitation)* copy

décalquer [3] [dekalke] **VT** to trace, to transfer

décamètre [dekamɛtr] **NM** decametre

décamper [3] [dekɑ̃pe] **VI** *Fam* to make oneself scarce, to take off; **décampe!** beat it!; **faire d. qn** to chase *or* to drive sb out

décan [dekɑ̃] **NM** decan

décanat [dekana] **NM** deanship

décaniller [3] [dekanije] **VI** *Fam* to clear off, to scram

décantation [dekɑ̃tasjɔ̃] **NF** *(d'un liquide)* settling, clarification; *(des eaux usées)* clarification; *(du vin)* decantation, settling; *(d'un produit chimique)* decantation

décanter [3] [dekɑ̃te] **VT 1** *(purifier ▸ liquide)* to allow to settle, to clarify; *(▸ eaux usées)* to clarify; *(▸ vin)* to decant, to allow to settle; *(▸ produit chimique)* to decant **2** *(éclaircir)* to clarify; **d. ses idées** to think things over
VPR se décanter 1 *(liquide)* to settle **2** *(situation)* to settle down

décapage [dekapaʒ] **NM** *(nettoyage ▸ en grattant)* scraping, scouring; *(▸ par un produit chimique)* stripping, pickling; *(▸ par la chaleur)* burning off; *(▸ au papier de verre)* sanding (down); *(▸ à la sableuse)* sandblasting

décapant, -e [dekapɑ̃, -ɑ̃t] **ADJ 1** *(nettoyant)* **agent** *ou* **produit d.** stripper **2** *(incisif ▸ remarque, humour)* caustic, vitriolic; *(▸ roman, article)* corrosive
NM stripper *(product)*

décaper [3] [dekape] **VT 1** *(nettoyer ▸ gén)* to clean off; *(▸ en grattant)* to scrape clean; *(▸ avec un produit chimique)* to strip; *(▸ à la chaleur)* to burn off; *(▸ au papier de verre)* to sand (down); *(▸ à la sableuse)* to sandblast **2** *Fam (racler)* to burn through[a], to scour[a]; **ça décape la gorge** it burns your throat

décapeuse [dekapøz] **NF** scraper

décapitation [dekapitasjɔ̃] **NF** beheading, decapitation

décapiter [3] [dekapite] **VT 1** *(personne)* **d. qn** *(le supplicier)* to behead sb, to cut sb's head off, to decapitate sb; *(accidentellement)* to cut sb's head off, to decapitate sb **2** *(arbre, fleur)* to top, to cut the top off **3** *(entreprise, gouvernement)* to decapitate, to deprive of leaders

décapode [dekapɔd] **NM** *Zool* decapod

décapotable [dekapɔtabl] **ADJ** convertible; **sa voiture est d.** his/her car has a folding top *or* is a convertible

NF convertible

décapoter [3] [dekapɔte] **VT 1** *(replier le toit de)* *Br* to fold back the roof of, *Am* to lower the top of **2** *(enlever le toit de)* to remove the *Br* roof *or Am* top of **3** *Can (ôter)* to take off

VPR se décapoter *Can* to take off one's outdoor clothes

décapsulage [dekapsylaʒ] **NM** opening

décapsuler [3] [dekapsyle] **VT** to uncap, to take the top off

décapsuleur [dekapsylœr] **NM** bottle opener

décapuchonner [3] [dekapyʃɔne] **VT** to take the cap off

décarcasser [3] [dekarkase] **se décarcasser VPR** *Fam* to sweat blood, to bust a gut (**pour qch** over sth; **pour faire qch** to do sth);

décarreler [24] [dekarle] **VT** *(sol, mur)* to take the tiles off

décarrer [3] [dekare] **VI** *Fam* **1** *(partir)* to make tracks, to hit the road **2** *(s'enfuir)* to beat it, to clear off

décartellisation [dekartelizasjɔ̃] **NF** decartelization

décasyllabe [dekasilab], **décasyllabique** [dekasilabik] **ADJ** decasyllabic

NM decasyllable

décathlon [dekatlɔ̃] **NM** decathlon

décathlonien, -enne [dekatlɔnjɛ̃, -ɛn] **NM,F** decathlete

décati, -e [dekati] **ADJ** *Fam (personne)* decrepit; *(corps)* decrepit, wasted; **un vieux tout d.** an old man gone all to seed *or* to pot

décatir [32] [dekatir] **VT** to hot-press, *Br* to decatize, *Am* to decate

VPR se décatir *Fam* to become decrepit□

décauser [3] [dekoze] **VT** *Belg* to malign

décavé, -e [dekave] *Fam* **ADJ** *(qui a perdu au jeu)* cleaned out; *(ruiné)* flat broke, *Br* skint

NM,F ruined gambler□

décédé, -e [desede] **ADJ** deceased

décéder [18] [desede] **VI** to die, *Euph* to pass away; **il est décédé dans la nuit** he passed away during the night; **personne décédée** deceased person; **s'il vient à d.** in the event of his death

décelable [deslabl] **ADJ 1** *(par analyse)* detectable **2** *(par observation)* discernible, detectable, perceivable

déceler [25] [desle] **VT 1** *(repérer ▸ erreur)* to detect, to spot, to discover; *(percevoir)* to detect, to discern, to perceive; **d. une fuite** to detect *or* to find *or* to trace a leak; **je n'ai rien décelé d'anormal** I've found nothing wrong **2** *(révéler)* to reveal, to betray, to give away

décélération [deselerasjɔ̃] **NF** deceleration, slowing down

décélérer [18] [deselere] **VI** to decelerate, to slow down

décembre [desɑ̃br] **NM** December; *voir aussi* **mars**

décemment [desamɑ̃] **ADV 1** *(comme il se doit)* decently, properly; **se tenir d.** to behave properly; **j'espère que tu te nourris d.** I hope you're feeding yourself properly **2** *(passablement)* reasonably, decently; **elle parle anglais d.** her English is reasonable *or* quite good, she speaks quite decent English **3** *(raisonnablement)* decently; **on ne peut pas d. lui raconter ça** we can't very well *or* we can hardly tell him/her that

décence [desɑ̃s] **NF** decency; **avoir la d. de faire qch** to have the (common) decency to do sth

décennal, -e, -aux, -ales [desenal, -o] **ADJ** decennial

décennie [deseni] **NF** decade

décent, -e [desɑ̃, -ɑ̃t] **ADJ 1** *(convenable)* decent; **être en tenue décente** to be appropriately dressed; **il serait plus d. de ne rien lui dire** it would be more appropriate *or* proper not to tell him/her anything **2** *(passable)* decent, reasonable; **faire qch d'une manière décente** to do sth reasonably well

décentrage [desɑ̃traʒ] **NM** off-centring

décentralisateur, -trice [desɑ̃tralizatœr, -tris] **ADJ** decentralization *(avant n)*, decentralist

NM,F decentralist, supporter of decentralization

décentralisation [desɑ̃tralizasjɔ̃] **NF** *(de l'administration)* decentralization, decentralizing; *(des entreprises, des écoles)* moving away from the capital

décentralisatrice [desɑ̃tralizatris] *voir* **décentralisateur**

décentraliser [3] [desɑ̃tralize] **VT** *(administration)* to decentralize; *(entreprise, école)* to move away from the capital

décentration [desɑ̃trasjɔ̃] **NF** *Phot* decentring, throwing off centre

décentrement [desɑ̃trəmɑ̃] **NM** *Phot* **d. vertical/horizontal** vertical/horizontal movement of the lens

décentrer [3] [desɑ̃tre] **VT** to bring out of centre; **être décentré** to be off-centre

VPR se décentrer to come *or* to move off centre

déception [desepsjɔ̃] **NF** disappointment; **la grande d. de sa vie** the great disappointment of his/her life; **quelle d.!** what a disappointment!; **d. sentimentale** disappointment in love

> Il faut noter que le nom anglais **deception** est un faux ami. Il signifie **tromperie**.

décérébrer [18] [deserebre] **VT** *Physiol* to decerebrate, to pith

décernement [desɛrnəmɑ̃] **NM** *(d'un prix etc)* award

décerner [3] [desɛrne] **VT 1** *(prix, médaille)* to award; *(titre, distinction)* to confer on; **se voir d. un prix** to be awarded a prize **2** *Jur* to issue

décès [desɛ] **NM** *Sout ou Jur* death

décevant, -e [desəvɑ̃, -ɑ̃t] **ADJ** disappointing

décevoir [52] [desəvwar] **VT** to disappoint; **elle attendait beaucoup mais elle a été très déçue** she was expecting a lot but she was very disappointed; **tu me déçois** I'm disappointed in you; **d. l'attente de qn** to disappoint sb, not to live up to sb's expectations; *Ironique* **il ne va pas être déçu (du voyage)!** he's going to get a shock!; *Ironique* **je croyais rencontrer l'homme idéal, je n'ai pas été déçue (du voyage)!** I thought I was meeting the ideal man, what a let-down!; *Suisse* **d. qn en bien** to give sb a pleasant surprise

> Il faut noter que le verbe anglais **to deceive** est un faux ami. Il signifie **tromper, abuser**.

déchaîné, -e [deʃene] **ADJ** *(tempête, mer, vent)* raging, wild; *(passions)* unbridled, raging; *(personne)* wild; *(public)* raving, delirious; *(opinion publique)* outraged; *(foule)* riotous, uncontrollable; *Fam* **tu es d., ce soir!** you're on top form tonight!

déchaînement [deʃɛnmɑ̃] **NM** *(des éléments, de la tempête)* raging, fury; *(de colère, de rage)* outburst

déchaîner [4] [deʃene] **VT 1** *(déclencher ▸ violence, colère)* to unleash, to arouse; *(▸ enthousiasme)* to arouse; *(▸ rires)* to trigger off; **d. l'hilarité générale** to cause general hilarity; **Greta Garbo a déchaîné les passions** Greta Garbo inspired many great passions **2** *(mettre en colère)* **c'est ce que j'ai dit qui l'a déchaîné** it was what I said that sent him wild; **il est déchaîné contre vous** he's ranting and raving about you

VPR se déchaîner 1 *(tempête, mer, vent)* to rage **2** *(hilarité, applaudissements)* to break *or* to burst out; *(instincts)* to be unleashed; **se d. contre qn** to rant at sb; **la presse s'est déchaînée contre le gouvernement** the press railed at the government; **elle s'est déchaînée contre son frère** she lashed out *or* let fly at her brother; **sa colère s'est déchaînée contre nous** he/she unleashed his/her anger on us

déchanter [3] [deʃɑ̃te] **VI** to be disillusioned, to become disenchanted; **il croyait avoir trouvé l'amour mais il a déchanté** he thought he'd found love but his illusions were shattered

décharge [deʃarʒ] **NF 1** *(tir)* shot; **il y a eu trois décharges** there were three shots; **prendre** *ou* **recevoir une d. en pleine poitrine** to get shot in the chest

2 *Élec* discharge; **d. électrique** electric *or* field discharge; *Fam* **prendre une d.** to get a shock *or* an electric shock

3 *(écrit)* discharge paper; *(reçu)* receipt; **je veux qu'on me signe une d.** I want a signed piece of paper saying I'm not responsible

4 *(dépotoir)* **d. (publique)** dump, *Br* rubbish tip, *Am* garbage dump; **d. interdite** *(sur panneau)* no dumping

5 *Fin* (tax) rebate; **porter une somme en d.** to mark a sum as paid

6 *Typ* set-off sheet, offset sheet

7 *Physiol* rush; **d. d'adrénaline** rush of adrenaline

• **à la décharge de PRÉP à sa d., il faut dire que...** in his/her defence, it has to be said that...

• **de décharge ADJ** *Géog* **courant de d.** discharge *or* discharging current

déchargement [deʃarʒəmɑ̃] **NM 1** *(d'une arme, d'un véhicule, d'une cargaison)* unloading **2** *Électron* dump

décharger [17] [deʃarʒe] **VT 1** *(débarrasser de sa charge ▸ véhicule, animal)* to unload; *(▸ personne)* to unburden; **je vais te d.** *(à un voyageur)* let me take your luggage; *(au retour des magasins)* let me take your parcels for you

2 *(enlever ▸ marchandises,cargaison)* to unload, to take off; *(▸ gravier d'un camion)* to tip, to dump; *(▸ passagers)* to set down

3 *(soulager)* to relieve, to unburden; **d. sa conscience** to relieve *or* to unburden one's conscience; **d. qn de qch** to relieve sb of sth; *(dette)* to discharge sb from sth; *(impôt)* to exempt sb from sth; **j'aimerais être déchargé de la comptabilité** I would like to be relieved of the accounting; **être déchargé de ses fonctions** to be discharged *or* dismissed

4 *(disculper)* to clear, to exonerate

5 *(tirer avec)* to fire, to discharge; **d. son arme sur qn** to fire one's gun at sb; *(ôter la charge de)* to unload

6 *Élec* to discharge

7 *Électron* to dump

8 *(laisser libre cours à)* to vent, to give vent to; **d. sa bile** to vent one's spleen; **d. sa mauvaise humeur sur qn** to vent one's temper on sb

VI 1 *(déteindre ▸ étoffe)* to run **2** *Vulg (éjaculer)* to shoot one's load

VPR se décharger 1 *Élec (batterie)* to run down, to go flat; *(accumulateur)* to run down, to lose its charge **2** *(se débarrasser)* **je vais essayer de me d. de cette corvée sur quelqu'un** I'll try to hand over the chore to somebody else; **tu te décharges toujours sur les autres** you're always shifting responsibility onto other people

décharné, -e [deʃarne] **ADJ 1** *(maigre ▸ personne, visage)* emaciated, gaunt, wasted; *(▸ main)* bony **2** *Fig (aride ▸ paysage, vallée)* bare, bald; *(▸ style)* bald

décharner [3] [deʃarne] **VT** *(personne)* to emaciate; *(os)* to strip the flesh off

déchaussé, -e [deʃose] **ADJ 1** *(sans chaussures ▸ pied)* bare, shoeless; *(▸ personne)* barefoot **2** *(branlant ▸ dent)* loose; *(▸ mur)* laid bare; **avoir les dents déchaussées** to have receding gums

déchaussement [deʃosmɑ̃] **NM** *(d'une dent)* loosening; *(d'un mur)* laying bare

déchausser [3] [deʃose] **VT 1** *(personne)* **d. qn** to take off sb's shoes **2** *(retirer ▸ skis)* to take off **3** *Constr (mur)* to lay bare

USAGE ABSOLU *Ski* to lose one's skis

VPR se déchausser 1 *(personne)* to take off one's shoes **2** *(dent)* to come loose; **avoir les dents qui se déchaussent** to have receding gums

dèche [dɛʃ] **NF** *Fam* dire poverty□; **je ne peux pas l'acheter, c'est la d.!** I can't afford it, I'm broke *or Br* skint; **être dans la d.** to be broke *or Br* skint

déchéance [deʃeɑ̃s] **NF 1** *(dégradation ▸ morale)* (moral) degradation, (moral) decline; *(▸ physique)* deterioration, decline; **tomber dans la d.** to go into (moral) decline

2 *(déclin social)* lowering of social standing
3 *Jur (d'un droit, d'un titre, d'un brevet)* forfeiture; *Assur (d'une police d'assurance)* expiry; **d. de l'autorité parentale** loss of parental authority
4 *Pol (d'un monarque)* deposition, deposing; *(d'un président)* removal *(after impeachment)*
5 *Compta* **tomber en d.** to lapse

déchet [deʃɛ] **NM 1** *(portion inutilisable)* **il y avait du d. parmi les fruits** some of the fruit was ruined; **dans un ananas il y a beaucoup de d.** there's a lot of waste in a pineapple **2** *Péj (personne)* (miserable) wretch **3** *Com* **d. de route** losses in transit
• **déchets NMPL 1** *(résidus)* waste; **déchets de fabrication** *ou* **production** waste products; **déchets de tissu** offcuts; **déchets de nourriture** food scraps; **déchets radioactifs/toxiques** radioactive/toxic waste **2** *Physiol* waste matter

déchetterie [deʃetri] **NF** dump, *Br* rubbish dump, tip

déchiffonner [3] [deʃifɔne] **VT** to smooth out, to smooth the creases out of

déchiffrable [deʃifrabl] **ADJ** decipherable; *(écriture)* legible

déchiffrage [deʃifraʒ] **NM 1** *(d'un texte codé, de hiéroglyphes)* deciphering **2** *(d'un morceau de musique)* sight-reading

déchiffrement [deʃifrəmɑ̃] **NM** deciphering; *Ordinat* decryption; **d. de données** data decryption

déchiffrer [3] [deʃifre] **VT 1** *(comprendre ▸ inscription, manuscrit)* to decipher; *(▸ langage codé)* to decipher, to decode; *Ordinat* to decrypt; **je déchiffre à peine son écriture** I can barely make out his/her handwriting
2 *(lire)* to spell out
3 *(morceau de musique)* to sight-read
4 *(élucider ▸ énigme)* to puzzle out, to make sense of; *(▸ sentiments, personnalité)* to fathom, to make out
USAGE ABSOLU *(lire)* **apprendre à d.** to start spelling out words

déchiffreur, -euse [deʃifrœr, -øz] **NM,F** *(gén)* decipherer; *(de messages codés)* decoder

déchiqueté, -e [deʃikte] **ADJ 1** *(irrégulier ▸ feuille)* jagged; *(▸ montagne, littoral)* jagged, ragged **2** *(tailladé)* torn to bits, hacked about **3** *Fam (ivre)* wasted, trashed; *(drogué)* stoned

déchiqueter [27] [deʃikte] **VT** *(papier, tissu)* to rip (to shreds), to tear (to bits); *(viande, proie)* to tear to pieces; **le chien a déchiqueté la couverture** the dog chewed the blanket to pieces *or* bits

déchiqueteuse [deʃiktøz] **NF** shredder

déchiqueture [deʃiktyr] **NF 1** *(partie déchiquetée)* shred **2** *(entaille)* tear, rip

déchirant, -e [deʃirɑ̃, -ɑ̃t] **ADJ** *(spectacle, adieux)* heartbreaking, heartrending; *(cri)* agonizing, harrowing; *(séparation)* unbearably painful

déchiré, -e [deʃire] **ADJ** *Fam (ivre)* wasted, trashed; *(drogué)* stoned

déchirement [deʃirmɑ̃] **NM 1** *(arrachement)* tearing, ripping, rending **2** *(souffrance)* wrench **3** *(désunion)* rift; **un pays en proie à des déchirements politiques** a country torn apart by internal strife

déchirer [3] [deʃire] **VT 1** *(lacérer)* to tear, to rip
2 *(mettre en deux morceaux)* to tear; *(mettre en morceaux)* to tear up *or* to pieces; **d. une page en deux** to tear a page into two; *Fig* **il s'est fait d. par la critique** he was torn apart *or* torn to shreds by the critics
3 *(arracher)* to tear off; **d. un ticket d'un carnet** to tear a ticket out of a book; *Fig* **d. le voile** to unmask the truth
4 *(ouvrir)* **d. une enveloppe** to tear open *or* to rip open an envelope
5 *(blesser)* to tear (the skin *or* flesh of), to gash; **le barbelé m'avait déchiré la jambe** I'd gashed my leg on the *Br* barbed wire *or Am* barbwire; **un bruit qui déchire les tympans** an earsplitting noise; **une douleur qui déchire la poitrine** a stabbing pain in the chest; *Littéraire* **d. qn** *ou* **le cœur de qn** to break sb's heart, to make sb's heart bleed; **être déchiré par la douleur** to be racked with pain
6 *Littéraire (interrompre ▸ nuit, silence)* to rend, to pierce; **un cri déchira la nuit** a scream pierced the night; **un éclair déchira le ciel** a flash of lightning rent the sky
7 *(diviser)* to tear apart; **le pays est déchiré par la guerre depuis dix ans** the country has been torn apart by war for ten years; **je suis déchiré entre eux deux** I'm torn between the two of them
VPR se déchirer 1 *(emploi réciproque) (se faire souffrir)* to tear each other apart
2 *(emploi passif)* to tear
3 *(vêtement, tissu, papier)* to tear, to rip; *(membrane)* to break; **mon gant s'est déchiré** my glove got torn; **mon cœur s'est déchiré** I was heartbroken
4 *Méd* **se d. un muscle/tendon/ligament** to tear a muscle/tendon/ligament

déchirure [deʃiryr] **NF 1** *(accroc)* tear, rip, split **2** *Littéraire (souffrance)* wrench **3** *Méd* tear; **d. musculaire** torn muscle

déchoir [71] [deʃwar] **VI 1** *(aux être)* **il est déchu de son rang** he has lost *or* forfeited his social standing **2** *(aux avoir) Littéraire (s'abaisser)* to demean oneself; **il croira d. en acceptant cela** he'll think he's demeaning himself if he agrees to this; **ce ne serait pas d. que de...** it wouldn't be demeaning to... **3** *Littéraire (diminuer ▸ fortune, prestige)* to wane
VT *(priver)* **d. qn d'un droit** to deprive sb of a right

déchristianisation [dekristjanizasjɔ̃] **NF** dechristianization, dechristianizing

déchristianiser [3] [dekristjanize] **VT** to dechristianize

déchu, -e [deʃy] **PP** *voir* **déchoir**
ADJ *(prince, roi)* deposed, dethroned; *(président)* deposed; *(ange, humanité)* fallen

déci [desi] **NM** *Suisse* = decilitre of wine

décibel [desibɛl] **NM** decibel; *Fam* **les décibels du festival de musique** the deafening noise coming from the music festival

décidé, -e [deside] **ADJ 1** *(résolu)* resolute, determined, decided; **d'un ton d.** decisively **2** *(réglé)* settled **3** *(déterminé)* **être d. à faire qch** to be determined *or* resolved to do sth

décidément [desidemɑ̃] **ADV d., ça ne marchera jamais** obviously it'll never work out; **d., c'est une manie** you're really making a habit of it, aren't you?; **d., tu exagères!** honestly, you are the limit!; **j'ai encore cassé un verre – d.!** I've broken another glass – it's not your day, is it!

> Il faut noter que l'adverbe anglais **decidedly** est un faux ami. Il signifie le plus souvent **vraiment, franchement**.

décider [3] [deside] **VT 1** *(choisir)* to decide (on); **ils ont décidé la guerre** they've decided to go to war; **d. de faire** to decide *or* to resolve to do; **ils ont décidé d'accepter/de ne pas accepter la proposition** they've decided in favour of/against the proposal; **il a décidé que nous irions demain** he's decided that we'll go tomorrow; **il fut décidé qu'on attendrait sa réponse** it was decided to wait for his/her reply, it was decided that we/they/*etc* should wait for his/her reply; **d. combien/quoi/comment/si** to decide how much/what/how/whether; **c'est décidé** it's settled; **c'est décidé, je reste** I'm staying, that's settled
2 *(entraîner)* **d. qn à faire qch** to convince *or* to persuade sb to do sth; **ce n'est pas cela qui m'a décidé à partir** that's not what convinced *or* persuaded me to go; **la pluie m'a décidé à ne pas sortir** I decided to stay in because of the rain
3 *(régler ▸ ordre du jour)* to decide, to set; *(▸ point de droit)* to resolve, to give a ruling on, to decide on
USAGE ABSOLU c'est toi qui décides it's your decision, it's up to you; **c'est moi qui décide ici** I'm the one who makes the decisions *or* who decides here; **je déciderai pour toi** I'll decide for you; **c'est le temps qui décidera** it will depend on the weather; **en cas de guerre, c'est la force de frappe qui décidera** if there's a war, the outcome will be decided solely by firepower; *Jur* **d. en faveur de qn** to give a ruling in favour of sb, to find for sb
• **décider de VT IND 1** *(influencer)* to determine; **leur intervention a décidé de la victoire** their intervention brought about the victory; **le résultat de l'enquête décidera de la poursuite de ce projet** the results of the survey will determine whether (or not) we carry on with the project
2 *(choisir ▸ lieu, date)* to choose, to determine, to decide on
3 *(juger)* **c'est le patron qui doit d. de son renvoi** it's the boss who'll have to decide (on) whether or not to fire him/her; **le sort en décida autrement** fate decreed otherwise
VPR se décider 1 *(être déterminé)* to be decided (on); **les choses se sont décidées très vite** things were decided very quickly; **la couleur des tissus se décide au printemps** fabric shades are decided on in the spring **2** *(faire son choix)* to make up one's mind; **décide-toi** make up your mind; **je n'arrive pas à me d.** I can't make up my mind; **se d. pour** to decide on; **elle s'est décidée pour un chat siamois** she decided on a Siamese cat; **elle s'est décidée à déménager** she's made up her mind to move house; **je ne me décide pas** *ou* **je ne peux pas me d. à le jeter** I can't bring myself to throw it out; **la voiture s'est enfin décidée à démarrer** the car finally decided to start; **il se décide à faire beau** it looks like the weather's trying to improve

décideur, -euse [desidœr, -øz] **NM,F** decision-maker

décigramme [desigram] **NM** decigramme, decigram

décilitre [desilitr] **NM** decilitre

décimal, -e, -aux, -ales [desimal, -o] **ADJ** decimal
• **décimale NF** decimal place; **nombre à trois décimales** number given to three decimal places

décimalisation [desimalizasjɔ̃] **NF** decimalization

décimaliser [3] [desimalize] **VT** to decimalize

décimation [desimasjɔ̃] **NF** decimation, decimating

décimer [3] [desime] **VT** to decimate

décimètre [desimɛtr] **NM** decimetre

décisif, -ive [desizif, -iv] **ADJ** *(déterminant ▸ influence, intervention)* decisive; *(▸ preuve)* conclusive; *(▸ élément, facteur, coup)* decisive, deciding; **il n'y a encore rien de d.** there's nothing conclusive *or* definite yet; **ça, c'est la question décisive!** that's the decider!; **de façon** *ou* **manière décisive** decisively, conclusively

décision [desizjɔ̃] **NF 1** *(résolution)* decision; **arriver à une d.** to come to *or* to reach a decision; **prendre une d.** to make a decision; **prendre la d. de faire qch** to decide to do sth; **je n'ai pas pris de d. là-dessus** I haven't made up my mind about it; **qui a pris cette d.?** whose decision was it?; **la d. t'appartient** the decision is yours, it's for you to decide; **soumettre qch à la d. d'un comité** to ask a committee to make a decision on sth; *Mktg* **d. d'achat** buying decision, purchasing decision
2 *Jur* **d. arbitrale** arbitration ruling; **d. autonome** autonomous decision; **d. collective** *ou* **commune** joint decision; **d. judiciaire** court ruling; **par d. judiciaire** by order of the court
3 *(fermeté)* decisiveness, resolution; **agir avec d.** to be decisive, to act decisively; **manquer de d.** to be hesitant *or* undecisive
4 *Ordinat* decision
• **de décision ADJ** *(organe, centre)* decision-making

décisionnaire [desizjɔnɛr] **NMF** decision-maker

décisionnel, -elle [desizjɔnɛl] **ADJ** decision-making *(avant n)*; **un poste d.** a job with decision-making responsibilities

décisive [desiziv] *voir* **décisif**

déclamateur, -trice [deklamatœr, -tris] *Péj* **ADJ** bombastic
NM,F declaimer

déclamation [deklamasjɔ̃] **NF 1** *(art de réciter)* declamation **2** *(emphase)* declamation, ranting

déclamatoire [deklamatwar] **ADJ 1** *(art)* declamatory **2** *Péj (style)* declamatory, bombastic

déclamatrice [deklamatris] *voir* **déclamateur**

déclamer [3] [deklame] **VT** to declaim
VI *Littéraire* **d. contre qn** to rail against sb

déclarable [deklarabl] ADJ *(marchandises)* liable to duty; *(revenu)* declarable; **marchandise non d.** duty-free goods

déclarant, -e [deklarɑ̃, -ɑ̃t] ADJ declaratory
NM,F declarant; **d. de TVA** VAT-registered person

déclaration [deklarasjɔ̃] NF **1** *(communication)* declaration, statement; **faire une d. à la presse** to issue a statement to the press; **j'ai une importante d. à faire** I have an important announcement to make; **je ne ferai aucune d.!** no comment!
2 *(témoignage)* declaration, statement; **faire une d. aux gendarmes** to make a statement to the police; **selon les déclarations du témoin** according to the witness's statement
3 *Admin* declaration; **faire une d. à la douane** to declare something at customs; **faire une d. à son assurance** to file a claim with one's insurance company; **d. d'accident** accident claim; **d. de changement de domicile** notification of change of address; **d. de décès** = official registration of death *(submitted to the Mairie)*; **d. d'entrée** declaration *or* clearance inwards; **d. d'exportation** export declaration; **d. d'importation** import declaration; **d. d'impôts** tax return; **remplir sa d. d'impôts** to *Br* make *or Am* file one's tax return; **d. d'intention** statement of intent; **d. de naissance** = official birth registration *(submitted to the Mairie)*; **d. de patrimoine** = official statement of net personal assets made by French politicians on being elected to office; **faire une d. de perte de passeport à la police** to report the loss of one's passport to the police; **d. de sinistre** damage claim; **d. sous serment** statement under oath; **d. de solvabilité** declaration of solvency; **d. de sortie** declaration *or* clearance outwards; **d. de succession** = official document naming the beneficiaries of a will; **d. de transit** transit entry; **d. de vol** report of theft; **faire une d. de vol** to report something stolen
4 *Compta* return; **d. annuelle de résultats** annual statement of results; **d. de faillite** declaration of bankruptcy; **d. fiscale** income tax return; **d. d'insolvabilité** declaration of insolvency; **d. de résultats** statement of results, financial statement; **d. de revenu** income tax return; **d. de solvabilité** declaration of solvency; **d. de TVA** VAT return
5 *Bourse* **d. de dividende** dividend announcement, declaration of dividend; **d. de valeur** declaration of value
6 *(aveu)* declaration; **faire une d. d'amour** *ou* **sa d. (à qn)** to declare one's love (to sb)
7 *(proclamation)* declaration, proclamation; **D. des Droits de l'Homme et du Citoyen** Declaration of Human and Civic Rights *(of 1789)*; **d. de guerre/d'indépendance** declaration of war/of independence; **d. de principe** declaration of principle
8 *Ordinat* **d. de champ** field definition

> **DÉCLARATION D'IMPÔTS**
>
> People in France are required to declare their taxable earnings at the beginning of the year. Thrice-yearly tax payments ("tiers provisionnels") are based on one third of the previous year's total, the final payment being adjusted according to the actual tax owed. It is also possible to pay tax on a monthly basis. This is known as "mensualisation".

déclaré, -e [deklare] ADJ **1** *(ennemi)* declared, sworn; *(intention, opinion)* declared; **un fasciste d.** a professed *or* self-confessed fascist **2** *Admin* **d. d'utilité publique** *(entreprise)* declared vital by the government despite public protest

déclarer [3] [deklare] VT **1** *(proclamer)* to declare, to announce, to assert; **le gouvernement a déclaré que...** the government announced *or* declared that...; **d. une séance ouverte** to declare a meeting open; **d. forfait** *Sport* to withdraw; *Fig* to throw in the towel; *aussi Fig* **d. la guerre à** to declare war on
2 *(juger)* **d. qn coupable** to find sb guilty; **on l'a déclaré incapable de gérer sa fortune** he was pronounced incapable of managing his estate
3 *(affirmer)* to profess, to claim; **elle déclare agir pour le bien de tous** she professes to work for the good of everyone; **il déclare être innocent** he claims to be innocent *or* protests his innocence
4 *(révéler ▸ intention, amour)* to declare
5 *(dire officiellement)* to declare; **d. ses employés** to declare one's employees; **d. ses revenus au fisc** to *Br* make *or Am* file one's tax return; **d. un enfant à la mairie** to register the birth of a child; **d. un vol** to report a theft; **rien à d.** nothing to declare; **si vous avez quelque chose à d. à la douane** if you have anything to declare at customs
6 *Ordinat (valeur)* to define
VPR **se déclarer 1** *(se manifester ▸ incendie, épidémie)* to break out; *(▸ fièvre, maladie)* to set in
2 *(se prononcer)* to take a stand; **se d. sur une question/un point** to take a stand on a question/a point; **elle ne veut pas se d. sur cette question** she refuses to state her opinion on the matter; **se d. pour/contre l'avortement** to come out in favour of/against abortion
3 *(se dire)* to say; **il s'est déclaré coupable** he said he was guilty; **elle s'est déclarée satisfaite de l'accord passé** she declared herself satisfied with the agreement that was reached
4 *Bourse* **se d. acheteur** to call the shares; **se d. vendeur** to put the shares

déclassé, -e [deklase] ADJ **1** *(personne)* déclassé **2** *(hôtel)* downgraded; *(joueur, équipe)* relegated **3** *Bourse (valeurs)* displaced
NM,F **c'est un d.** he has lost his social status *or* come down in the world

déclassement [deklasmɑ̃] NM **1** *(dans la société)* fall *or* drop in social standing
2 *(d'un hôtel)* downgrading; *(d'un joueur, d'une équipe)* relegation
3 *Bourse (de valeurs)* displacement
4 *Rail* change to a lower class
5 *Mil, Naut & Nucl* decommissioning

déclasser [3] [deklase] VT **1** *(déranger)* to put out of order
2 *(rétrograder ▸ hôtel)* to downgrade; *(▸ joueur, équipe)* to relegate
3 *(déprécier)* to demean; **ce travail le déclassait** he was lowering *or* demeaning himself in that job
4 *Rail* to change to a lower class
5 *Mil, Naut & Nucl* to decommission
VPR **se déclasser 1** *(dans l'échelle sociale)* to move one step down the social scale **2** *(dans un train)* to change to a lower-class compartment; *(dans un navire)* to change to lower-class accommodation

déclassifier [9] [deklasifje] VT *Mil* to declassify

déclenchement [deklɑ̃ʃmɑ̃] NM **1** *(début ▸ d'un événement)* starting point, start, trigger; *(▸ d'une attaque)* launching **2** *(d'un mécanisme)* triggering, activation; *(d'une sonnerie, d'une alarme)* setting off; *Tech (d'une pièce)* release; *Obst (de l'accouchement)* induction

déclencher [3] [deklɑ̃ʃe] VT **1** *(provoquer ▸ attaque)* to launch; *(▸ révolte, conflit)* to trigger (off), to bring about; *(▸ grève, émeute, rires)* to trigger *or* to spark off **2** *(mettre en marche ▸ mécanisme)* to trigger, to activate; *(▸ sonnerie, alarme)* to set off; *Tech (▸ pièce)* to release; *Obst (accouchement)* to induce
VPR **se déclencher 1** *(commencer ▸ douleur, incendie)* to start **2** *(se mettre en marche ▸ sirène, sonnerie, bombe)* to go off; *(▸ mécanisme)* to be triggered off *or* released

déclencheur [deklɑ̃ʃœr] NM **1** *Élec* release, circuit breaker **2** *Phot* shutter release; **d. automatique** time release, self-timer

déclic [deklik] NM **1** *(mécanisme)* trigger, releasing mechanism **2** *(bruit)* click; **se fermer avec un d.** to click shut; **s'enclencher avec un d.** to click into place **3** *(prise de conscience)* **il s'est produit un d. et elle a trouvé la solution** things suddenly fell into place *or* clicked and she found the answer; **pour moi, cette aventure a été le d.** what happened made me come to my senses

déclin [deklɛ̃] NM **1** *(diminution)* decline, waning; **le d. de la popularité d'un acteur** the decline of an actor's popularity; **le soleil à son d.** the setting sun **2** *Littéraire (fin)* close; **le d. du jour** nightfall, dusk; **le d. de la vie** the twilight years
• **en déclin** ADJ on the decline; **les adhésions sont en d.** membership is declining *or* falling off *or* on the decline
• **sur le déclin** ADJ *(prestige, puissance)* declining, on the wane; *(malade)* declining; **votre pauvre mère est sur le d.** your poor mother is getting worse; **un acteur sur le d.** an actor who's seen better days

déclinable [deklinabl] ADJ declinable; **une gamme d'ordinateurs d. en plusieurs configurations** a range of computers enabling several different configurations

déclinaison [deklinɛzɔ̃] NF **1** *Gram* declension **2** *Astron & Phys* declination; **d. magnétique** magnetic declination **3** *Mktg* **d. de gamme** range extension

déclinant, -e [deklinɑ̃, -ɑ̃t] ADJ *(force)* declining, deteriorating; *(influence, grandeur)* declining, waning, fading; *(société)* declining, decaying

décliner [3] [dekline] VT **1** *Gram* to decline; *Fig* **l'amour est décliné dans toutes les chansons** love is an ever-recurrent theme in songs; **un imprimé décliné dans plusieurs tons** a pattern available in several shades
2 *(énoncer ▸ identité)* to give, to state
3 *(refuser ▸ responsabilité, invitation)* to decline, to refuse; *(▸ offre)* to decline, to refuse, to reject; **d. toute responsabilité** to refuse all responsibilities; *(dans un contexte commercial)* to accept no liability; *Jur* **d. la compétence d'une juridiction** to refuse to acknowledge a jurisdiction
4 *Mktg* **d. une gamme** to extend a range
VI *(soleil)* to set; *(vieillard, jour)* to decline; *(malade)* to decline, to fade; *(santé, vue)* to deteriorate; *(prestige)* to wane, to decline
VPR **se décliner 1** *Gram* to be declined **2** *Com* **une robe qui se décline dans différentes couleurs** a dress available in different colours

déclive [dekliv] ADJ downward sloping
NF **en d.** sloping

déclivité [deklivite] NF **1** *(descente)* downward slope, incline **2** *(inclinaison ▸ d'une route, d'un chemin de fer)* gradient

décloisonnement [deklwazɔnmɑ̃] NM decompartmentalization, decompartmentalizing

décloisonner [3] [deklwazɔne] VT to decompartmentalize

déclouer [6] [deklue] VT *(planche)* to remove *or* to pull the nails out of; *(couvercle) Br* to prise *or Am* to pry open
VPR **se déclouer** to fall *or* to come apart

déco [deko] ADJ PL *(abrév* **décoratifs***)* **arts d.** art deco
NF *(abrév* **décoration***)* decor, decoration; *(métier)* (interior) decorating, interior design; **j'adore faire de la d.** I love decorating

décocher [3] [dekɔʃe] VT **1** *(flèche)* to shoot, to fire; *(coup)* to throw; **il m'a décoché un coup de pied** he kicked me; **le cheval lui a décoché une ruade** the horse lashed out *or* kicked at him/her **2** *(regard)* to shoot; *(sourire)* to flash; *(plaisanterie, méchanceté)* to fire, to shoot; **il lui a décoché un regard assassin** he shot him/her a murderous look; **elle lui a décoché une remarque acerbe** she bit his/her head off

décoction [dekɔksjɔ̃] NF *Pharm* decoction

décodage [dekɔdaʒ] NM **1** *(d'un texte)* decoding, deciphering **2** *Ordinat & TV* decoding, unscrambling

décoder [3] [dekɔde] VT **1** *(texte)* to decode **2** *Ordinat & TV* to decode, to unscramble

décodeur [dekɔdœr] ADJ M decoding
NM decoder; **d. numérique** set-top box, digibox

décoiffer [3] [dekwafe] VT **1** *(déranger la coiffure de)* **d. qn** to mess up *or Am* to muss up sb's hair; **elle est toute décoiffée** her hair's a mess **2** *(ôter le chapeau de)* **d. qn** to remove sb's hat **3** *Fam (locution)* **ça décoiffe** it's mind-blowing, it takes your breath away
VPR **se décoiffer 1** *(déranger sa coiffure)* to mess up *or Am* to muss up one's hair **2** *(ôter son chapeau)* to remove one's hat

décoinçage [dekwɛ̃saʒ], **décoincement** [dekwɛ̃smɑ̃] NM *(déblocage ▸ d'un objet)* unjamming, loosening

décoincer [16] [dekwɛ̃se] VT **1** *(débloquer ▸ objet)* to unjam, to free **2** *Fam (personne)* to loosen up
VPR **se décoincer 1** *(objet)* to unjam, to work loose **2** *Fam (personne)* to relax[□], to let one's hair down

déçoit *etc voir* **décevoir**

décolérer [18] [dekɔlere] **VI il ne décolérait pas** he was still fuming; **elle ne décolère jamais** she's permanently in a temper

décollage [dekɔlaʒ] **NM 1** *Aviat* takeoff; *Astron* lift-off, blast-off **2** *(d'une enveloppe, d'un papier)* unsticking **3** *Écon & (en sociologie)* takeoff

décollation [dekɔlasjɔ̃] **NF** *Arch* decollation

décollé, -e [dekɔle] **ADJ avoir les oreilles décollées** to have ears that stick out

décollement [dekɔlmɑ̃] **NM 1** *(d'un papier)* unsticking **2** *Méd* **d. de la rétine** detachment *or* separation of the retina

décoller [3] [dekɔle] **VI 1** *Aviat* to take off; *Astron* to lift *or* to blast off

2 *(quitter le sol ▸ skieur, motocycliste)* to take off

3 *Fam (partir)* to leave❑; **elle ne décolle pas de la bibliothèque** she never moves from *or* leaves the library; **j'ai eu du mal à le faire d. d'ici** I had trouble getting rid of him

4 *(progresser ▸ exportation, pays)* to take off; **au troisième trimestre, il a fini par d.** his work finally took off in the third term; **ces mesures n'ont pas réussi à faire d. l'économie** these measures failed to restart the economy

5 *(s'échapper)* to escape; **d. du réel** *ou* **de la réalité** to be in another world; **d. du peloton** *(coureur cycliste)* to peel away from the pack

6 *Fam (être distancé ▸ sportif, élève)* to fall *or* to drop behind

7 *Fam (maigrir)* to lose weight❑

VT 1 *(détacher ▸ papier)* to unstick, to unglue, to peel off; **d. à la vapeur** to steam off; **d. dans l'eau** to soak off; **d. une enveloppe** *(en tirant)* to open an envelope; *(à la vapeur)* to steam open an envelope

2 *Fam (faire partir)* to tear *or* to prise away; **on ne peut pas le d. de la télé** there's no prising him away from theTV

3 *Fam (quitter)* **il ne nous a pas décollés de la journée** he stuck to us like glue all day long

4 *(au billard)* to nudge away from the cushion

VPR se décoller 1 *(emploi passif)* to come off; **ça se décolle simplement en tirant dessus** just pull it and it comes off **2** *(se détacher)* to come *or* to peel off; **du papier peint qui se décolle** peeling wallpaper **3** *Méd* to become detached

décolletage [dekɔltaʒ] **NM** *(action)* cutting out of the neck; *(décolleté)* low-cut neckline, décolletage

décolleté, -e [dekɔlte] **ADJ 1** *(échancré)* low-cut, décolleté; **robe décolletée dans le dos** dress cut low in the back; **tu ne trouves pas que c'est trop d.?** you don't think it's too low? **2** *(femme)* décolleté, wearing a low-cut dress

NM 1 *(échancrure)* low neckline; **d. bateau** boat neck; **d. carré** square neck; **d. en pointe** *ou* **en V** V neck; **un d. plongeant** a plunging neckline; **en grand d.** *(en robe de soirée)* in full evening dress **2** *(d'une femme)* cleavage

décolleter [27] [dekɔlte] **VT** *(robe)* to give a low neckline to; *(personne)* to reveal the neck and shoulders of; **cette robe te décollette trop** this dress is too low(-cut)

décolonisation [dekɔlɔnizasjɔ̃] **NF** decolonization

décoloniser [3] [dekɔlɔnize] **VT** to decolonize

décolorant, -e [dekɔlɔrɑ̃, -ɑ̃t] **ADJ 1** *(gén)* decolorant, decolouring **2** *(pour cheveux)* decolorizing *(avant n)*, decolorant, bleaching *(avant n)*

NM 1 *(gén)* decolorant **2** *(pour cheveux)* bleaching agent, bleach

décoloration [dekɔlɔrasjɔ̃] **NF 1** *(atténuation de la couleur)* fading, discolouration **2** *(disparition de la couleur)* bleaching, discolouring **3** *(des cheveux)* bleaching; **faire une d. à qn** to bleach someone's hair; **se faire faire une d.** to have one's hair bleached

décolorer [3] [dekɔlɔre] **VT 1** *(affaiblir la couleur de)* to fade **2** *(éclaircir ▸ cheveux)* to bleach; **elle se fait d. (les cheveux)** she has her hair lightened *or* bleached

VPR se décolorer 1 *(emploi réfléchi) (personne)* to bleach one's hair **2** *(tissu, papier)* to fade, to lose its colour

décombres [dekɔ̃br] **NMPL 1** *(d'un bâtiment)* debris *(singulier)*, rubble, wreckage **2** *Littéraire (d'une civilisation)* ruins

décommander [3] [dekɔmɑ̃de] **VT** *(marchandise)* to cancel; *(invitation, rendez-vous)* to cancel, to call off; *(invité)* to put off

VPR se décommander *(à un rendez-vous)* to cancel (one's appointment); *(à un dîner, une soirée)* to cancel

décompacter [3] [dekɔ̃pakte] **VT** *Ordinat (données)* to unpack

décomplexer [4] [dekɔ̃plekse] **VT** to encourage, to reassure; **ça m'a décomplexé** it made me feel more confident

décomposable [dekɔ̃pozabl] **ADJ 1** *(corps chimique, matière)* decomposable **2** *(texte, idée)* analysable, that can be broken down

décomposer [3] [dekɔ̃poze] **VT 1** *Chim* to decompose, to break down

2 *Phys (force)* to resolve; *(lumière)* to disperse

3 *(analyser ▸ texte, idée)* to break down, to analyse; *(▸ mouvement, processus)* to decompose, to break up; *(▸ exercice, mélodie)* to go through (step by step); *Gram (▸ phrase)* to parse

4 *Compta (compte, résultats)* to analyse, to break down; *(dépenses)* to break down

5 *(pourrir ▸ terre, feuilles)* to decompose, to rot

6 *(altérer)* **l'horreur qui décomposait ses traits** the horror reflected in his/her contorted features; **un visage décomposé par la peur** a face distorted with fear; **être décomposé** to look stricken

VPR se décomposer 1 *(emploi passif) Gram (phrase)* to be parsed; **se d. en** to break down into; **le texte se décompose en trois parties** the text can be broken down *or* divided into three parts **2** *(pourrir)* to decompose, to decay, to rot **3** *(s'altérer ▸ visage)* to become distorted; **soudain son visage s'est décomposé** his/her face suddenly fell

> Il faut noter que le verbe anglais **to decompose** signifie uniquement **pourrir**.

décomposition [dekɔ̃pozisjɔ̃] **NF 1** *Chim* decomposition, breaking down

2 *Phys (de la lumière)* dispersion; *(d'une force)* resolution

3 *(analyse)* analysis, breaking down; *Gram* parsing; **faire la d. d'un planning/d'une tâche** to break down a schedule/a task; **faire la d. d'une phrase** to parse a sentence

4 *Compta (d'un compte, de résultats)* analysis, breakdown; *(des dépenses)* breakdown

5 *Ordinat* breakdown

6 *(pourrissement ▸ de la matière organique)* decomposition, decay, rot; *(▸ de la société)* decline, decay, decadence; **en (état de) d.** *(cadavre)* decomposing, decaying, rotting; *(société)* declining, decaying

7 *(altération ▸ des traits)* contortion

décompresser [4] [dekɔ̃prese] **VT 1** *Tech* to decompress **2** *Ordinat* to decompress

VI 1 *(plongeur)* to undergo decompression **2** *Fam (se détendre)* to relax❑, to unwind

décompresseur [dekɔ̃presœr] **NM** *Aut & Tech* decompressor

décompression [dekɔ̃presjɔ̃] **NF 1** *Méd & Tech* decompression; **avoir un accident de d.** *(plongeur)* to get the bends

2 *Fam (détente)* unwinding, relaxing

3 *Aut & Tech* decompression; **robinet de d.** *(dans un moteur)* compression tap; *(dans une machine à vapeur)* petcock

4 *Ordinat* decompression, unbundling

décomprimer [3] [dekɔ̃prime] **VT** to decompress

décompte [dekɔ̃t] **NM 1** *(calcul)* working out, calculation; **faire le d. des intérêts** to work out *or* to calculate the interest; **faire le d. des voix** to count the votes; **faire le d. des points** to add up the score

2 *(déduction)* deduction; **je vous fais le d. des deux fromages** I'll take the two cheeses off (your bill)

3 *(relevé)* detailed account, breakdown

4 *(solde)* balance

décompter [3] [dekɔ̃te] **VT 1** *(déduire)* to deduct **2** *(dénombrer)* to count

VI to strike the wrong time

déconcentration [dekɔ̃sɑ̃trasjɔ̃] **NF 1** *Admin* devolution

2 *Écon (décentralisation)* decentralization, dispersion

3 *(dilution)* dilution

4 *(manque d'attention)* lack of concentration

déconcentrer [3] [dekɔ̃sɑ̃tre] **VT 1** *(transférer ▸ pouvoir)* to devolve; *(▸ bureaux, entreprises)* to disperse **2** *(distraire)* **d. qn** to distract sb's attention; **le bruit l'a déconcentré** the noise distracted his attention **3** *Chim (diluer)* **d. une solution** to dilute a solution

VPR se déconcentrer to lose (one's) concentration

déconcertant, -e [dekɔ̃sertɑ̃, -ɑ̃t] **ADJ** disconcerting, off-putting

déconcerter [3] [dekɔ̃serte] **VT** to disconcert; **il ne faut pas te laisser d. par ses questions** you mustn't let yourself be disconcerted *or* put off by his/her questions

déconditionnement [dekɔ̃disjɔnmɑ̃] **NM** deconditioning

déconditionner [3] [dekɔ̃disjɔne] **VT** to decondition

déconfit, -e [dekɔ̃fi, -it] **ADJ** crestfallen

déconfiture [dekɔ̃fityr] **NF 1** *(échec)* collapse, defeat; *(d'une société)* collapse, failure, downfall; **tomber en d.** to collapse **2** *Jur* insolvency

décongélation [dekɔ̃ʒelasjɔ̃] **NF** defrosting, thawing

décongeler [25] [dekɔ̃ʒle] **VT** to defrost, to thaw

décongestif, -ive [dekɔ̃ʒestif, -iv] **ADJ** decongestant

NM decongestant

décongestionner [3] [dekɔ̃ʒestjɔne] **VT 1** *(dégager ▸ route, centre urbain)* to relieve congestion in; *(▸ aéroport, université)* to relieve congestion at **2** *Méd* to decongest

décongestive [dekɔ̃ʒestiv] *voir* **décongestif**

déconnecter [4] [dekɔnekte] **VT 1** *(débrancher ▸ tuyau, fil électrique)* to disconnect **2** *Fam Fig* to disconnect❑, to cut off❑; **il est totalement déconnecté de la réalité** he's totally cut off from reality

VPR se déconnecter *Ordinat* to go off-line

déconner [3] [dekɔne] **VI** *très Fam* **1** *(dire des bêtises)* to talk crap *or Br* bollocks; **arrête de d.** don't talk crap; **sans d.!** *(je t'assure)* no kidding!, *Br* straight up!; **sans d.?** *(est-ce vrai)* no kidding?, yeah?, *Br* straight up?

2 *(s'amuser)* to horse *or* to fool around

3 *(faire des bêtises)* to mess around; **déconne pas!** stop messing about!

4 *(mal fonctionner)* to be on the blink, *Am* to be on the fritz

5 *(ne plus avoir toute sa tête)* to be off one's rocker, to be not all there

6 *(ne pas être raisonnable)* **allez, déconne pas, viens avec nous!** come on, don't be like that, come with us!

déconneur, -euse [dekɔnœr, -øz] *très Fam* **ADJ être d.** to be a clown *or* a joker

NM,F clown, joker

déconseiller [4] [dekɔ̃seje] **VT** to advise against; **d. à qn de faire qch** to advise sb against doing sth; **un livre à d. aux jeunes** an unsuitable book for young people; **c'est déconseillé** it's not (to be) recommended, it's to be avoided

déconsidération [dekɔ̃siderasjɔ̃] **NF** *Littéraire* discredit; **tomber dans la d.** to fall into disrepute

déconsidérer [18] [dekɔ̃sidere] **VT** to discredit; **ces révélations l'ont déconsidéré** these revelations have cast a slur on *or* have discredited him

VPR se déconsidérer to discredit oneself, to lose one's credibility

déconsignation [dekɔ̃siɲasjɔ̃] **NF** *Com* deconsignment

déconsigner [3] [dekɔ̃siɲe] **VT 1** *(bagage)* to collect from the *Br* left-luggage office *or Am* checkroom **2** *(bouteille, emballage)* to return the deposit on

décontamination [dekɔ̃taminasjɔ̃] **NF** decontamination

décontaminer [3] [dekɔ̃tamine] VT to decontaminate

décontenancer [16] [dekɔ̃tnɑ̃se] VT to disconcert

VPR **se décontenancer** to lose one's composure

décontract [dekɔ̃trakt] ADJ INV *Fam* = **décontracté**

décontracté, -e [dekɔ̃trakte] ADJ 1 *(détendu ▸ muscle, corps, ambiance)* relaxed; *(▸ caractère)* easy-going, relaxed; *(▸ attitude)* relaxed, unworried; *(▸ style, vêtements)* casual; **en tenue décontractée** in casual dress, casually dressed 2 *Péj (désinvolte)* casual, off-hand

ADV *(s'habiller)* casually

décontracter [3] [dekɔ̃trakte] VT *(muscle)* to relax, to unclench; **elle sait d. les nouveaux venus** she knows how to put newcomers at ease

VPR **se décontracter** to relax

décontraction [dekɔ̃traksjɔ̃] NF 1 *(relâchement, détente)* relaxation, relaxing; **sa d. me sidère!** I'm amazed at how relaxed *or* laid back he/she is! 2 *(aisance)* coolness, collectedness

déconvenue [dekɔ̃vny] NF disappointment; **quelle ne fut pas ma d. lorsque...** I was so disappointed when...

décor [dekɔr] NM 1 *(décoration ▸ d'un lieu)* interior decoration, decor; *(▸ d'un objet)* pattern, design

2 *(environs)* setting, surroundings

3 *Cin, Théât & TV* set, scenery, setting; *(toile peinte)* backdrop, backcloth; **d. de cinéma** *Br* film *or Am* movie set; **d. en extérieur** outdoor set; **d. de théâtre** stage set; **tourné en décors naturels** shot on location; *Fig* **le d. est planté, le roman peut commencer** the scene is set, the novel can start

4 *(apparence)* façade, pretence

• **dans le(s) décor(s)** ADV *Fam* **aller** *ou* **entrer** *ou* **valser dans le d.** *(voiture, automobiliste)* to go off the road ◻; **envoyer dans le d.** *(voiture, automobiliste)* to force off the road ◻; **d'un coup de poing, elle l'a envoyé dans le d.** she sent him flying against the wall with a punch

décorateur, -trice [dekɔratœr, -tris] NM,F 1 *(d'appartement)* interior decorator *or* designer; **d. (de vitrines)** shopfitter 2 *Théât (créateur)* set designer *or* decorator; *(peintre)* set painter

décoratif, -ive [dekɔratif, -iv] ADJ *(gén)* decorative, ornamental; *(plante, arbre)* ornamental; *Fig* **n'avoir qu'un rôle d.** to have a purely decorative role

décoration [dekɔrasjɔ̃] NF 1 *(ornement)* decoration; **décorations de Noël** Christmas decorations 2 *(technique)* decoration, decorating; *Théât* set design, stage design; **faire de la d. (d'intérieur)** to do interior decorating 3 *(médaille)* medal, decoration

décorative [dekɔrativ] *voir* **décoratif**

décoratrice [dekɔratris] *voir* **décorateur**

décorer [3] [dekɔre] VT 1 *(orner ▸ intérieur, vase, assiette)* to decorate; *(▸ table, arbre)* to decorate, to adorn; **une table décorée de fleurs** a table adorned with flowers; **une tente décorée de drapeaux** a marquee decked out with flags 2 *(personne)* to decorate; **être décoré de la Légion d'honneur** to be awarded the Legion of Honour

décorner [3] [dekɔrne] VT 1 *(animal)* to dehorn 2 *(page)* to smooth out

décorticage [dekɔrtikaʒ] NM 1 *(d'une crevette)* peeling, shelling; *(du grain)* hulling, husking; *(d'une noix, d'une amande)* shelling 2 *(analyse)* dissection, thorough analysis

décortication [dekɔrtikasjɔ̃] NF 1 *Hort* decortication, barking 2 *Méd* decortication

décortiquer [3] [dekɔrtike] VT 1 *(éplucher ▸ crevette)* to peel, to shell; *(▸ grain)* to hull, to husk; *(▸ noix, amande)* to shell

2 *Hort (arbre)* to decorticate, to bark

3 *(analyser)* to dissect, to analyse; **d. un texte** to take a text to pieces *or* to dissect a text

4 *Méd* to decorticate

décorum [dekɔrɔm] NM 1 *(bienséance)* decorum, propriety; **observer le d.** to observe the proprieties 2 *(protocole)* etiquette, ceremonial

décote [dekɔt] NF 1 *(réduction d'impôt)* tax relief 2 *Bourse* below par rating; **d. en Bourse** *(d'une action)* discount 3 *(baisse)* depreciation, loss in value

découcher [3] [dekuʃe] VI to stay out all night

découdre [86] [dekudr] VT *(vêtement, couture)* to undo, to unpick; *(point)* to take out; *(bouton)* to take *or* to cut off; **mon bouton est décousu** my button has come off

VI **en d.** to fight; **vouloir en d.** to be spoiling for a fight; **en d. avec qn** to cross swords with sb

VPR **se découdre** *(vêtement)* to come unstitched; *(bouton)* to come off

découler [3] [dekule] **découler de** VT IND to stem from; **et tous les avantages qui en découlent** and all the ensuing benefits; **il découle de cette idée que...** it follows from this idea that...

découpage [dekupaʒ] NM 1 *(partage ▸ d'un tissu, d'un gâteau)* cutting (up); *(▸ d'une volaille, d'une viande)* carving; *(▸ en tranches)* slicing (up)

2 *(image ▸ à découper)* figure *(for cutting out)*; *(▸ découpée)* cut-out (picture); **faire des découpages dans un illustré** to cut things out of a comic

3 *Cin* shooting script

4 *Ordinat (d'un fichier, d'une image)* splitting; **d. du temps** time slicing

5 *Pol* **d. électoral** division into electoral districts, *Am* apportionment; **refaire le d. électoral** *Br* to review constituency boundaries, *Am* to redistrict

découpe [dekup] NF 1 *Couture* piece of appliqué work 2 *(de la viande)* (type of) cut 3 *(tronçonnage)* cutting (up); **faire la d.** to cut to length

découpé, -e [dekupe] ADJ 1 *(irrégulier ▸ côte)* indented, ragged; *(▸ montagne)* rugged, craggy, jagged 2 *(en morceaux)* cut

découper [3] [dekupe] VT 1 *(partager ▸ gâteau, papier, tissu)* to cut up; *(▸ viande, volaille)* to carve; **couteau à d.** carving knife

2 *(détacher ▸ image)* to cut out; **d. des articles dans le journal** to take cuttings out of the newspaper

3 *Ordinat (fichier, image)* to split; *(disque dur)* to partition

4 *(disséquer ▸ texte, film)* to dissect; *(▸ phrase)* to parse

5 *(échancrer)* **le temps a découpé la côte** over the years, the coast has become deeply indented

VPR **se découper** 1 *(emploi passif)* **ce poulet se découpe tout seul** this chicken practically carves itself 2 **se d. sur** to be outlined against

découpeur, -euse [dekupœr, -øz] NM,F *(ouvrier)* cutting machine operator; *Cin* cutter

• **découpeuse** NF cutting machine

découplé, -e [dekuple] ADJ **bien d.** well-built, strapping

découpler [3] [dekuple] VT 1 *Chasse & Élec* to uncouple 2 *Électron* to decouple

découpure [dekupyr] NF *(bord ▸ d'une dentelle, d'une guirlande)* edge; *(▸ d'une côte)* indentations

• **découpures** NFPL *(de papier)* clippings, shavings; *(de tissu)* cuttings, offcuts

décourageant, -e [dekuraʒɑ̃, -ɑ̃t] ADJ 1 *(nouvelle, situation)* discouraging, disheartening, depressing 2 *(personne)* hopeless

découragement [dekuraʒmɑ̃] NM discouragement, despondency, despondence; **le d. m'a envahi** I felt utterly discouraged *or* dispirited

décourager [17] [dekuraʒe] VT 1 *(abattre)* to discourage, to dishearten; **avoir l'air découragé** to look discouraged *or* dispirited; **ne te laisse pas d.** don't be discouraged 2 *(dissuader ▸ personne, familiarité)* to discourage; **d. qn de faire qch** to discourage sb from doing sth

VPR **se décourager** to get discouraged, to lose heart; **ne te décourage pas** don't give up; **il se décourage tout de suite** he gives up easily

découronner [3] [dekurɔne] VT *(roi)* to dethrone, to depose; *Fig (héros)* to debunk

décours [dekur] NM 1 *Astron* wane; **lune en d.** moon on the wane 2 *Méd* regression

décousait *etc voir* **découdre**

décousu, -e [dekuzy] PP *voir* **découdre**

ADJ 1 *Couture (défait ▸ vêtement, ourlet)* undone, unstitched 2 *(incohérent ▸ discours)* incoherent, disjointed; *(▸ conversation, style)* disjointed, rambling; *(▸ idées)* disjointed, disconnected, random; *(▸ travail)* unmethodical; **de manière décousue** disjointedly

découvert, -e[1] [dekuvɛr, -ɛrt] PP *voir* **découvrir**

ADJ *(terrain, allée, voiture)* open; *(tête, partie du corps)* bare, uncovered; **dormir d.** to sleep without any covers; **la tête découverte** bareheaded

NM 1 *Compta* deficit; **d. de la balance commerciale** trade gap 2 *Banque* overdraft; **avoir un d. de** to be overdrawn by; **demander une autorisation de d.** to apply for an overdraft; **accorder un d. à qn** to allow sb an overdraft; **d. en blanc** unsecured overdraft

• **à découvert** ADJ 1 *Fin (sans garantie)* uncovered, unsecured 2 *Bourse* without cover; **acheter à d.** to buy on margin; **vendre à d.** to go a bear, to sell short 3 *Banque* overdrawn; **être à d.** to be overdrawn, to have an overdraft; **votre compte est à d. de 200 euros** your account is overdrawn by 200 euros ADV 1 *(sans dissimuler)* openly 2 *(sans protection)* without cover; **cuire à d.** to cook without a lid; **sortir à d.** to break cover; **la marée laisse ces rochers à d.** the tide leaves these rocks exposed

découverte[2] [dekuvɛrt] NF 1 *(détection)* discovery, discovering; **faire la d. d'un gisement de pétrole** to strike oil; **faire la d. d'un vieux livre au grenier** to unearth an old book in the attic

2 *(chose détectée ▸ gén)* discovery, find; *(▸ scientifique)* discovery; *Hum* **ce n'est pas une d.!** that's nothing new!

3 *(prise de conscience)* discovery, discovering

4 *(personne de talent)* discovery, find

5 *Théât & TV* backcloth

• **à la découverte** ADV **aller** *ou* **partir à la d.** to explore, to go exploring

• **à la découverte de** PRÉP 1 *(en explorant)* on a tour of; **allez à la d. du Londres de Sherlock Holmes** discover London in the footsteps of Sherlock Holmes; **ils sont partis à la d. de la forêt amazonienne** they went exploring in the Amazon rainforest 2 *(à la recherche de)* in search of; **aller à la d. d'un trésor** to go in search of treasure

découvreur, -euse [dekuvrœr, -øz] NM,F discoverer

découvrir [34] [dekuvrir] VT 1 *(dénicher)* to discover, to find; **d. qch au fond d'un coffre** to find sth in the bottom of a trunk; **on a découvert l'arme du crime** the murder weapon has been found; **d. du pétrole/de l'or** to strike oil/gold; **j'ai découvert les lettres par accident** I came across the letters by accident; **d. l'Amérique** to discover America

2 *(apprendre à connaître)* to discover; **il découvrit l'amour/la musique baroque sur le tard** he discovered love/baroque music late in life; **elle m'a fait d. la région** she took me around the area

3 *(solution ▸ en réfléchissant)* to discover, to work out; *(▸ subitement)* to hit on *or* upon; *(virus, vaccin)* to discover; **soudain j'ai découvert la signification de son silence** suddenly I discovered why he/she had been keeping silent; **il ne parvint pas à d. qui elle était** he couldn't find out who she was

4 *(détecter)* to discover, to detect; **on lui a découvert une tumeur** they found he/she had a tumour

5 *(surprendre ▸ voleur, intrus)* to discover; *(▸ secret, complot)* to discover, to uncover; **et si l'on vous découvrait?** what if you were found out?; **on a découvert un passager clandestin** a stowaway has been found; **j'ai découvert que c'était faux** I found out (that) it wasn't true; *Fig* **d. le pot aux roses** to discover the truth; **c'est par hasard que j'ai découvert le pot aux roses** it was by chance that I found out what was going on

6 *(faire connaître)* to uncover, to disclose, to reveal; **d. ses projets à qn** to reveal *or* to disclose one's plans to sb; **d. son jeu** to show one's hand; *Littéraire* **d. son cœur à qn** to open one's heart to sb, to bare one's soul to sb

7 *(apercevoir)* to see; **du balcon on découvre la mer** from the balcony one has a view of the sea; **le rideau levé, on découvrit une scène obscure** the raised curtain revealed a darkened stage; **d. un ami dans la foule** to catch sight of *or* to spot a friend in a crowd

8 *(ôter ce qui couvre ▸ fauteuil)* to uncover; *(▸ statue)* to uncover, to unveil; *(▸ casserole)* to uncover, to take the lid off

9 *(exposer ▸ flanc, frontière)* to expose; *(▸ mur, pierre)* to uncover, to expose; *(▸ épaule, cuisse)* to uncover, to bare, to expose; *(▸ dents)* to bare; **sa robe lui découvrait le dos** her dress revealed her back

VI *(récif)* to uncover (at low tide)

VPR se découvrir 1 *(se déshabiller)* to take some layers off, to take off some clothes; *(au lit)* to throw off one's bedclothes

2 *(ôter son chapeau)* to take off one's hat

3 *(se connaître)* to (come to) understand oneself; **on se découvre avec l'âge** one comes to know oneself with age

4 *(s'exposer)* to expose oneself to attack; **un boxeur ne doit pas se d.** a boxer mustn't lower his guard

5 *(être révélé)* to emerge, to be discovered; **des scandales, il s'en découvre tous les jours** scandals come to light *or* are discovered every day; **la vérité se découvre toujours** the truth will out

6 *(l'un l'autre)* to discover each other

7 se d. qch to discover sth; **elle s'est découvert des amis partout** she discovered she had friends everywhere; **il s'est découvert un don pour la cuisine** he discovered (that) he had a gift for cooking

8 *Météo* **ça se découvre** it's clearing up; **les cimes se découvrent** the mist is lifting off the mountain tops

9 *Littéraire (se confier)* **se d. à** to confide in, to open up to; **il ne se découvre à personne** he doesn't confide in anyone

décrassage [dekrasaʒ], **décrassement** [dekrasmɑ̃] **NM 1** *Aut & Ind* scrubbing, cleaning out **2** *(du corps)* scrubbing; *(de l'esprit)* training, sharpening up

décrasser [3] [dekrase] **VT 1** *(nettoyer ▸ peigne, tête de lecture)* to clean; *(▸ poêle, casserole)* to scour, to clean out; *(▸ linge)* to scrub; *(▸ enfant)* to clean up

2 *Fam (dégrossir)* **d. qn** to give sb a basic grounding[◻], to teach sb the basics[◻]

3 *Aut & Ind* to clean out, to decoke

4 *Fam (remettre en forme)* to get back into shape, to tone up; **un peu d'exercice vous décrassera** a bit of exercise will get you back into shape

VPR se décrasser 1 *(se laver)* to clean up, to give oneself a good scrub; **décrasse-toi les mains** give your hands a scrub **2** *(se dérouiller)* to get some exercise

décrédibilisation [dekredibilizasjɔ̃] **NF** loss of credibility

décrédibiliser [3] [dekredibilize] **VT** to discredit, to take away the credibility of

décrément [dekremɑ̃] **NM** *Ordinat* decrement

décrêpage [dekrepaʒ] **NM** straightening

décrêper [4] [dekrepe] **VT** to straighten (out)

décrépir [32] [dekrepir] **VT** to strip the roughcast off

VPR se décrépir la façade se décrépit the roughcast is coming off the front of the house

décrépit, -e [dekrepi, -it] **ADJ** decrepit

décrépitude [dekrepityd] **NF 1** *(décadence)* decay; **tomber en d.** *(civilisation)* to decline, to decay; *(institution)* to become obsolete **2** *(mauvais état)* decrepitude, decrepit state

decrescendo [dekreʃendo] **NM INV** decrescendo

ADV jouer d. to decrescendo; *Fig* **aller d.** to be waning

décret [dekre] **NM** *Jur* decree, edict; **promulguer un d.** to issue a decree; **d. ministériel** = order to carry out legislation given by the Prime Minister; **d. présidentiel** *Br* ≃ Order in Council, *Am* ≃ executive order

• **décrets NMPL** *Littéraire* **les décrets du destin/de la Providence** what fate/Providence has decreed; **les décrets de la mode** the dictates of fashion

• **par décret ADV gouverner par d.** to rule by decree

décréter [18] [dekrete] **VT 1** *(ordonner ▸ nomination, mobilisation)* to order; *(▸ mesure)* to decree, to enact **2** *(décider)* **d. que** to decree that; **le patron a décrété qu'on ne changerait rien** the boss decreed *or* ordained that nothing would change; **elle a décrété qu'elle n'irait pas se coucher** she said categorically that she wasn't going to bed; **elle a décrété qu'elle n'aimait pas les glaces** she claims not to like ice-cream; **quand il a décrété quelque chose, il ne change pas d'avis** when he's made up his mind about something, he doesn't change it

décrier [10] [dekrije] **VT 1** *(collègues, entourage)* to disparage; *(livre, œuvre, théorie)* to criticize, to censure, *Sout* to decry; **ce genre de pratique est assez décrié** this kind of thing is generally frowned upon **2** *(monnaie)* to cry down, to depreciate by proclamation

décriminalisation [dekriminalizasjɔ̃] **NF** decriminalization

décrire [99] [dekrir] **VT 1** *(représenter)* to describe, to portray; **elle a très bien décrit son amie** she portrayed *or* described her friend very accurately; **l'histoire décrit une passion** the story depicts *or* describes a passion; **son exposé décrit bien la situation** his/her account gives a good picture of the situation **2** *(former ▸ cercle, ellipse)* to describe, to draw; *(▸ trajectoire)* to follow, to describe; **d. des cercles dans le ciel** to fly in circles; **d. des méandres** to follow a winding course, to meander (along); **la route décrit une courbe** the road curves *or* bends

décrispation [dekrispasjɔ̃] **NF** thaw, thawing; **la d. entre les deux pays** the easing of tension between the two countries

décrisper [3] [dekrispe] **VT 1** *(muscle)* to relax, to untense **2** *(relations)* to thaw; *(ambiance)* to ease; **pour d. la situation** to ease the situation; **la plaisanterie l'a décrispé** the joke made him relax *or* calmed him down

VPR se décrisper to relax, to unwind

décrit, -e [dekri, -it] **PP** *voir* **décrire**

décrochage [dekrɔʃaʒ] **NM 1** *(enlèvement ▸ d'un rideau, d'un tableau)* unhooking, taking down; *(▸ d'un wagon)* uncoupling

2 *Mil* disengagement

3 *Rad* break in transmission; **le d. a lieu à 19 heures** regional programming begins at 7 p.m.; **émettre en d.** to broadcast its own programmes

4 *Fam (désengagement)* **le d. par rapport à la réalité** being out of touch with reality

décrochement [dekrɔʃmɑ̃] **NM 1** *(fait de se décrocher)* slipping **2** *Géol* thrust fault

décrocher [3] [dekrɔʃe] **VT 1** *(dépendre)* to unhook, to take down; **d. un peignoir** to take a bathrobe off the hook *or* peg; *Fig* **il a décroché ses gants de boxe** he went back to boxing *or* into the ring again; **d. la lune** to do the impossible; **ne me demande pas de (te) d. la lune** don't ask me to do the impossible; *Fam* **d. la timbale** *ou* **le cocotier** *ou* **le pompon** to hit the jackpot

2 *(enlever ▸ chaîne, laisse)* to take off; *(▸ wagon)* to uncouple; **d. le fermoir d'un collier** to undo (the clasp of) a necklace

3 *Tél* **d. le téléphone** *(pour répondre)* to pick up the phone; *(le couper)* to take the phone off the hook; **le téléphone est décroché** the phone's off the hook

4 *Fam (obtenir)* to land, to get; **d. une grosse commande** to land a big order; **elle a décroché le boulot du siècle** she got *or* landed herself a plum job

5 *Fin* **d. le dollar de l'or** to take the dollar off the gold standard

USAGE ABSOLU elle a décroché au bout de dix sonneries she picked up the receiver *or* telephone after ten rings; **tu décroches?** could you answer it *or* get it?

VI 1 *Mil* to beat a retreat, to withdraw

2 *Fam (abandonner)* to opt out

3 *Fam (se déconcentrer)* to switch off; **j'ai complètement décroché** *(cessé de comprendre)* I was completely lost; *(cessé d'écouter)* I switched off completely

4 *(être distancé)* to drop *or* to fall behind

5 *Fam (se désintoxiquer)* to kick the habit; **ça fait trois mois qu'il a décroché** he's been clean for three months

6 *Can Fam (abandonner l'école)* to drop out (of school); **les étudiants qui décrochent** students who drop out

7 *Fin* **l'euro a décroché du dollar** the euro has lost against the dollar

VPR se décrocher 1 *(tableau)* to come unhooked; *(médaille)* to come unpinned **2 se d. qch** to dislocate sth; **il s'est décroché la mâchoire** he dislocated his jaw

décrocheur, -euse [dekrɔʃœr, -øz] **NM,F** *Can* (high school) dropout

décrois *etc voir* **décroître**

décroisement [dekrwazmɑ̃] **NM** *(de fibres)* uncrossing

décroiser [3] [dekrwaze] **VT d. les jambes/les bras** to uncross one's legs/one's arms

décroissait *etc voir* **décroître**

décroissance [dekrwasɑ̃s] **NF** *(diminution)* decrease, fall, decline

décroissant, -e [dekrwasɑ̃, -ɑ̃t] **ADJ** decreasing

décroissement [dekrwasmɑ̃] **NM** *Littéraire (diminution)* decrease, decline; *(de la lune)* waning

décroît [dekrwa] **NM la lune est sur** *ou* **dans son d.** the moon is in its last quarter

décroître [94] [dekrwatr] **VI** *(diminuer ▸ nombre, intensité, force)* to decrease, to diminish; *(▸ eaux)* to subside, to go down; *(▸ fièvre)* to abate, to subside; *(▸ bruit)* to die down, to decrease; *(▸ vent)* to let up, to die down; *(▸ intérêt, productivité)* to decline, to drop off; *(▸ vitesse)* to slacken off, to drop; *(▸ lumière)* to grow fainter, to grow dimmer, to fade; *(▸ influence)* to decline, to wane; **les jours décroissent** the days are drawing in *or* getting shorter; **il voyait leurs silhouettes d. à l'horizon** he could see their silhouettes getting smaller and smaller on the horizon; **aller en décroissant** to be on the decrease

décrottage [dekrɔtaʒ] **NM** scraping the mud off

décrotter [3] [dekrɔte] **VT 1** *(nettoyer)* to scrape the mud off **2** *Fam (dégrossir)* to refine[◻], to take the rough edges off; **elle n'arrivera jamais à le d.** she'll never get him to change[◻]

décrottoir [dekrɔtwar] **NM** *(pour chaussures)* (boot) scraper

décrue [dekry] **NF 1** *(de rivière etc)* fall, drop in level **2** *(en nombre etc)* decrease, decline, fall

décryptage [dekriptaʒ], **décryptement** [dekriptəmɑ̃] **NM 1** *(décodage)* deciphering, decoding **2** *(éclaircissement)* elucidation, working out

décrypter [3] [dekripte] **VT 1** *(décoder ▸ message, texte ancien)* to decode, to decipher **2** *(éclaircir)* to elucidate, to work out

DECS [deəseəs] **NM** *(abrév* **diplôme d'études comptables supérieures**) = postgraduate qualification in accounting

déçu, -e [desy] **PP** *voir* **décevoir**

ADJ 1 *(personne)* disappointed **2** *(amour)* disappointed, thwarted; *(espoir)* disappointed

décuiter [3] [dekɥite] **VI** *Fam* to sober up[◻]

déculottée [dekylɔte] **NF** *très Fam* thrashing, clobbering, hammering; **prendre une d.** to get thrashed *or* clobbered *or* hammered

déculotter [3] [dekylɔte] **VT d. qn** *(lui enlever sa culotte)* to take sb's underpants *or Br* pants off; *(lui enlever son pantalon)* to take sb's *Br* trousers *or Am* pants off

VPR se déculotter 1 *(emploi réfléchi) (enlever ▸ sa culotte)* to take one's underpants *or Br* pants down; *(▸ son pantalon)* to drop one's *Br* trousers *or Am* pants **2** *Fam (se montrer lâche)* to lose one's nerve *or Br* bottle **3** *très Fam (avouer)* to squeal

déculpabilisation [dekylpabilizasjɔ̃] **NF la d. de la sexualité** removing the guilt attached to sexuality

déculpabiliser [3] [dekylpabilize] **VT d. qn** to stop sb feeling guilty; **je suis déculpabilisée** I no longer feel guilty; **d. la sexualité** to remove the guilt attached to sexuality

VPR se déculpabiliser *(emploi réfléchi)* to get rid of one's guilt

déculturation [dekyltyrasjɔ̃] **NF** loss of cultural identity

décuple [dekyp] **NM le d. de ton salaire** ten times your salary

• **au décuple ADV** tenfold

décuplement [dekypləmɑ̃] **NM 1** *(d'une somme, d'un chiffre)* tenfold increase **2** *(augmentation)* **ceci permettra le d. de nos chances de succès** this will greatly increase our chances of success

décupler [3] [dekyple] VT **1** *(rendre dix fois plus grand)* to increase tenfold **2** *(augmenter)* to increase greatly
VI to increase tenfold

déçut *etc voir* **décevoir**

dédaignable [dedɛɲabl] ADJ **ce n'est pas d.** it's not to be sniffed at

dédaigner [4] [dedɛɲe] VT **1** *(mépriser ▸ personne)* to look down on, to despise, to scorn; *(▸ compliment, richesse)* to despise, to disdain **2** *(refuser ▸ honneurs, argent)* to despise, to disdain, to spurn; **une augmentation, ce n'est pas à d.** a salary increase is not to be sniffed at; **ne dédaignant pas la bonne chère** not being averse to good food **3** *(ignorer ▸ injure, difficulté)* to ignore, to disregard
• **dédaigner de** VT IND *Littéraire* **elle a dédaigné de parler** she didn't deign to speak; **il n'a pas dédaigné de goûter à ma cuisine** he was not averse to tasting my cooking

dédaigneuse [dedɛɲøz] *voir* **dédaigneux**

dédaigneusement [dedɛɲøzmɑ̃] ADV contemptuously, disdainfully

dédaigneux, -euse [dedɛɲø, -øz] ADJ **1** *(méprisant ▸ sourire, moue, remarque)* contemptuous, disdainful; **d'un ton d.** disdainfully **2 d. de** *(indifférent à)* disdainful *or* contemptuous of; **je n'ai jamais été d. de l'argent** I've never been one to spurn *or* to despise money
NM,F disdainful *or* scornful *or* contemptuous person

dédain [dedɛ̃] NM *(gén)* scorn, contempt, disdain; **avec d.** disdainfully
• **de dédain** ADJ disdainful, scornful, contemptuous

Dédale [dedal] NPR *Myth* Daedalus

dédale [dedal] NM maze; **un vrai d., ces greniers!** these attics are like a rabbit warren!; **dans le d. des rues/des lois** in the maze of streets/of the law

DEDANS [dədɑ̃] ADV *(reprenant "dans" + substantif)* inside, in it/them/*etc*; *(par opposition à "dehors")* inside, indoors; *(à partir de ▸ prendre, boire, manger)* out of, from; **tu m'attendras dehors ou d.?** will you wait for me outside or inside *or* indoors?; **de d., on ne voit rien** you can't see anything from inside; **une cabane, allons nous cacher d.** there's a hut, let's go and hide inside *or* in it; **prends les draps dans l'armoire, ils sont sûrement d.** take the sheets from the cupboard, I'm sure they're in there; **donne-moi mon sac, la lettre est d.** give me my bag, the letter is inside *or* in it; **il y a de l'anis d.** there's aniseed in it; **quand j'achète des chaussures, je veux me sentir bien d.** when I buy shoes, I want to feel comfortable in them; **quelle belle eau, cela donne envie de plonger d.** what lovely water, it makes you feel like diving into it *or* in; **le tiroir était ouvert, j'ai pris l'argent d.** the drawer was open, I took the money out of *or* from it; **ce verre est sale, ne bois pas d.** this glass is dirty, don't drink out of *or* from it; **on n'apprécie pas le luxe quand on vit d.** you don't appreciate luxury when you've got it; *Fam* **ne me parle pas de comptes, je suis en plein d.** don't talk to me about the accounts, I'm right in the middle of them *or* up to my eyeballs in them; *Fam* **mettre** *ou* **ficher qn d.** *(le tromper)* to confuse *or* to muddle sb□; *(en prison)* to put sb inside; *Fam* **je me suis fichu d.** I got it wrong□; **tomber en plein d.** to fall right into it; **le piège, il est tombé en plein d.** he fell right into the trap
NM inside; **agir du d.** to act on the *or* from inside
• **en dedans** ADV **c'est creux en d.** it's hollow inside; **marcher les pieds en d.** to be pigeon-toed; **en d. il n'était pas si calme** inwardly, he was not so calm
• **en dedans de** PRÉP within; **en d. d'elle-même, elle regrette son geste** deep down *or* inwardly, she regrets what she did

dédicace [dedikas] NF **1** *(formule manuscrite ▸ d'un ami)* (signed) dedication; *(▸ d'une personnalité)* autograph, (signed) dedication **2** *Rad* dedication **3** *Rel* dedication, consecration

dédicacer [16] [dedikase] VT **1** *(signer)* **d. un livre/une photo à qn** to autograph *or* to sign a book/photo for sb; **livre dédicacé par l'auteur** signed copy of a book **2** *Rad* to dedicate

dédicatoire [dedikatwar] ADJ dedicatory, dedicative; **formule** *ou* **inscription d.** dedication

dédié, -e [dedje] ADJ *Ordinat* dedicated

dédier [9] [dedje] VT **1** *(livre, symphonie)* to dedicate **2** *(église)* to dedicate, to consecrate **3** *Littéraire (vouer)* **dédiant toutes ses pensées à son art** dedicating *or* devoting all his/her thoughts to his/her art; **sans jamais lui d. une pensée** with never (so much as) a thought for him/her

dédire [103] [dedir] **se dédire** VPR **1** *(se rétracter ▸ délibérément)* to recant, to retract **2** *(manquer ▸ à sa promesse)* to go back on *or* to fail to keep one's word; *(▸ à son engagement)* to fail to honour one's commitment **3 se d. de** *(promesse)* to go back on, to fail to keep; *(engagement)* to fail to honour

dédit [dedi] NM **1** *(rétractation)* retraction; *(désengagement)* failure to keep one's word; **un engagement qui ne tolère aucun d.** a binding commitment, a commitment which must be honoured **2** *Jur (modalité)* default; *(somme)* forfeit, penalty

dédommagement [dedɔmaʒmɑ̃] NM compensation; **5000 euros de d.** 5,000 euros' compensation; **demander** *ou* **réclamer un d.** to claim compensation
• **en dédommagement** ADV as compensation; **il nous a offert une bouteille de champagne en d.** he gave us a bottle of champagne by way of *or* as compensation
• **en dédommagement de** PRÉP as a *or* in compensation for, to make up for; **tenez, en d. de votre dérangement** please take this for your trouble
• **à titre de dédommagement** ADV by way of *or* as compensation

dédommager [17] [dedɔmaʒe] VT **1** *(pour une perte)* to compensate, to give compensation to; **les paysans n'ont pas été dédommagés** the peasants have received no compensation; **d. qn d'une perte** to compensate sb for a loss, to make good sb's loss; **fais-toi d. pour le dérangement** claim compensation for the inconvenience; **j'ai réussi à me faire d.** *(en argent)* I managed to get reimbursed **2** *(pour un désagrément)* to compensate; **cela te dédommagera d'avoir attendu** this'll make up for your having had to wait

dédorer [3] [dedɔre] VT to remove the gilt from; **cadre dédoré** tarnished frame; *Fig* **aristocratie dédorée** faded aristocracy

dédouanage [dedwanaʒ], **dédouanement** [dedwanmɑ̃] NM *Admin (action)* clearing through customs; *(résultat)* customs clearance

dédouaner [3] [dedwane] VT **1** *Admin (marchandise)* to clear through customs **2** *(personne)* to clear (the name of)
VPR **se dédouaner** to make up for one's past misdeeds; **ne crois pas te d. en me signant des chèques** don't think you can get round me by signing cheques

dédoublage [dedublaʒ] NM **1** *(d'alcool)* diluting **2** *(d'un vêtement)* removing the lining

dédoublement [dedubləmɑ̃] NM **1** *(d'un groupe, d'une image)* splitting *or* dividing in two **2** *Psy* **d. de la personnalité** split *ou* dual personality **3** *Transp* **d. d'un train** putting on an extra train

dédoubler [3] [deduble] VT **1** *(diviser ▸ groupe, image)* to split *or* to divide in two; *(▸ brin de laine)* to separate into strands **2** *Transp* **d. un train** to put on *or* to run an extra train **3** *Couture* to remove the lining of
VPR **se dédoubler 1** *Psy* **sa personnalité se dédouble, il se dédouble** he suffers from a split *or* dual personality; *Hum* **je cuisine, viens ici, je ne peux pas me d.!** I'm cooking, come here, I can't be in two places at once! **2** *(se diviser ▸ convoi, image)* to be split *or* divided in two; *(▸ ongle)* to split

dédramatiser [3] [dedramatize] VT *(situation)* to make less dramatic

déductibilité [dedyktibilite] NF deductibility

déductible [dedyktibl] ADJ deductible; **non d.** non-deductible; **d. de l'impôt** tax-deductible

déductif, -ive [dedyktif, -iv] ADJ deductive

déduction [dedyksjɔ̃] NF **1** *(d'une somme)* deduction; **entrer en d. de qch** to be deductible from sth; **d. faite de** after deduction of, after deducting; **sous d. de 10 pour cent** less 10 percent; **sans d.** terms net cash; **d. fiscale** tax allowance; **d. forfaitaire** *(d'impôts)* standard allowance **2** *(conclusion)* conclusion, inference; **tirer des déductions de** to draw conclusions from **3** *(enchaînement d'idées)* deduction; **faire une d.** to go through a process of deduction
• **par déduction** ADV by deduction, through a process of deduction

déductive [dedyktiv] *voir* **déductif**

déduire [98] [dedɥir] VT **1** *(frais, paiement)* to deduct, to take off; **tous frais déduits** after deduction of expenses **2** *(conclure)* to deduce, to infer

déesse [deɛs] NF **1** *Myth & Rel* goddess **2** *(femme)* goddess

défaillance [defajɑ̃s] NF **1** *(évanouissement)* blackout; *(malaise)* feeling of faintness; **avoir une d.** *(s'évanouir)* to faint, to have a blackout; *(être proche de l'évanouissement)* to feel faint; **des défaillances dues à la chaleur** weak spells caused by the heat
2 *(faiblesse morale)* weakness; **dans un moment de d.** in a moment of weakness
3 *(lacune)* lapse, slip; **une d. de mémoire** a memory lapse; **une seule d. et vous êtes renvoyé** one single mistake and you're fired; **cet enfant a de sérieuses défaillances en lecture** the child has serious reading difficulties; **les défaillances du syndicat** the union's failings; **les défaillances du rapport** the weak spots in the report
4 *(mauvais fonctionnement)* failure, fault; **le moteur a régulièrement des défaillances** the engine is always breaking down; **d. mécanique** mechanical failure
5 *Méd* **d. cardiaque/rénale** heart/kidney failure
6 *Jur* default
7 *(faillite)* **d. d'entreprise** business failure
• **sans défaillance** ADJ *(mémoire)* faultless; *(attention, vigilance)* unflinching

défaillant, -e [defajɑ̃, -ɑ̃t] ADJ **1** *(près de s'évanouir)* **des spectateurs défaillants** spectators about to faint *or* on the verge of fainting
2 *(faible ▸ santé)* declining, failing; *(▸ cœur, poumon)* weak, failing; *(▸ force, mémoire)* failing; *(▸ détermination)* weakening, faltering; *(▸ voix)* faltering; **il avançait d'un pas d.** he walked with a faltering step
3 *(qui ne remplit pas son rôle ▸ appareil)* malfunctioning; **dû à l'organisation défaillante du concert** due to the poor organization of the concert
4 *Jur* defaulting

défaillir [47] [defajir] VI *Littéraire* **1** *(s'évanouir)* to faint **2** *(s'amollir)* **d. de** to swoon *or* to go weak at the knees with; **d. de plaisir** to swoon with pleasure **3** *(forces, mémoire)* to fail; *(détermination)* to weaken, to falter, to flinch; **j'accomplirai le travail sans d.** I'll do the job without flinching

défaire [109] [defer] VT **1** *(détacher ▸ nœud)* to untie, to unfasten; *(▸ fermeture)* to undo, to unfasten; *(▸ cravate)* to undo, to untie; **d. les lacets d'une botte** to unlace a boot; **d. ses cheveux** to let one's hair down; **avec les cheveux défaits** *(pas encore arrangés)* with his/her hair undone, with tousled hair; *(que l'on a dérangés)* with his/her hair messed up
2 *(découdre ▸ ourlet)* to undo, to unpick
3 *(démonter ▸ décor de théâtre)* to take down, to dismantle; *(▸ maquette, puzzle)* to take apart, to disassemble; *(▸ tente)* to take down
4 *(déballer ▸ paquet)* to open, to unwrap; **d. ses valises** to unpack
5 *(mettre en désordre)* **d. le lit** *(pour changer les draps)* to strip the bed; *(en jouant)* to rumple the bedclothes; **le lit défait** *(pas encore fait)* the unmade bed; **le lit n'a pas été défait** the bed hasn't been slept in
6 *Ordinat (opération)* to undo
7 *(détruire)* **faire et d. des gouvernements** to make and break governments
8 *Littéraire (délivrer)* **d. qn de** to rid sb of; **défaitesnous de ces sots!** deliver *or* save us from these fools!
9 *Littéraire (armée)* to defeat
VPR **se défaire 1** *(se détacher, se disloquer ▸ nœud)* to come loose *or* undone; *(▸ coiffure, paquet)* to come undone; *(▸ tricot)* to fray, to come

undone, to unravel; (► *viande à la cuisson*) to fall apart

2 (*être détruit* ► *gouvernement, amitié*) to break

3 (*se décomposer*) **son visage se défit** (*de chagrin*) he looked distraught; (*de déception*) his face fell

4 se d. de (*employé, dettes, meuble*) to get rid of, *Sout* to rid oneself of; (*idée*) to put out of one's mind; (*habitude*) to break; **il ne veut pas se d. de son vieux chien** he won't get rid of his old dog

défait, -e[1] [defɛ, -ɛt] **ADJ 1** (*accablé*) **être d.** to be broken **2** (*décomposé*) **il est arrivé à l'hôpital, complètement d.** he arrived at the hospital in total distress; **il se tenait là, le visage d.** he stood there, looking distraught

défaite[2] [defɛt] **NF** *Mil, Pol & Sport* defeat

défaites *voir* **défaire**

défaitisme [defetism] **NM** defeatism, negative attitude

défaitiste [defetist] **ADJ** defeatist

NMF defeatist

défalcation [defalkasjɔ̃] **NF** deduction; (*d'une mauvaise créance*) writing off; **d. faite des frais** after deduction of expenses

défalquer [3] [defalke] **VT** to deduct; (*mauvaise créance*) to write off

défasse *etc voir* **défaire**

défatigant, -e [defatigɑ̃, -ɑ̃t] **ADJ** relaxing, soothing

NM muscle relaxant

défatiguer [3] [defatige] **VT** to refresh, to relax

défaufiler [3] [defofile] **VT** to remove the tacking from

défausser [3] [defose] **VT** to straighten out again

VPR se défausser *Cartes* to discard an unwanted card; **se d. à cœur** to discard one's hearts; **se d. d'un valet** to discard a jack

défaut [defo] **NM 1** (*imperfection* ► *d'un visage, de la peau*) blemish, imperfection; (► *d'un tissu, d'un appareil*) defect, flaw; (► *d'un diamant, d'une porcelaine*) flaw; (► *d'une explication, d'une théorie*) flaw (**de** in); (► *d'un projet*) drawback, snag; **avoir un d.** (*machine*) to be defective; **cette école n'a qu'un d.: elle est trop loin** the school has only one drawback: it's too far away; **il y a un d. de fonctionnement** it doesn't work *or* work properly; *Fam* **le d. de ou avec ton attitude, c'est que…** the trouble with your attitude is that…; *Fam Hum* **il y a comme un d.!** there's something wrong somewhere!; *Com* **d. apparent/caché** visible/hidden defect; **d. d'élocution** *ou* **de prononciation** speech defect *or* impediment; **d. de fabrication** manufacturing defect

2 (*tache morale*) fault, failing; **son plus gros d., c'est qu'il est égoïste** his biggest fault is that he's selfish

3 (*manque*) **d. de** lack *or* want of; **d. de mémoire** memory lapse; **d. d'attention** lapse in concentration; **chèque refusé pour cause de d. de provision** cheque refused by the bank because of insufficient funds; **d. de provision** (*tampon sur chèque*) ≃ refer to drawer; **faire d.** to be lacking; **les provisions font d.** there is a shortage of supplies, supplies are short; **l'argent faisant d.** (*il y a peu d'argent*) money being short; (*il n'y a pas d'argent*) there being no money; **ses forces lui ont fait d.** his/her strength failed him/her; **le temps me fait d.** I don't have the time; **le bon sens lui fait cruellement d.** he/she is sadly lacking in common sense; **si ma mémoire ne me fait pas d.** if I'm not mistaken, if my memory serves me right; **notre fournisseur nous a fait d.** our supplier let us down

4 (*bord, lisière*) **au d. des côtes** under the ribcage; **le d. de la cuirasse** *ou* **de l'armure** the chink in one's *or* the armour

5 *Jur* default; **faire d.** to default; **d. de comparution** failure to appear; **d. de motif** lack of motive; **d. de paiement** default in payment, non-payment

6 *Ordinat* default setting

• **à défaut ADV** if not, failing that

• **à défaut de PRÉP** for lack *or* for want of; **un voyage reposant à d. d'être intéressant** a restful if not interesting trip

• **en défaut ADV être en d.** (*se tromper*) to be wrong; (*en faute*) to be at fault; **son pouvoir de réflexion est en d.** his/her ability to think is at fault; **prendre qn en d.** to catch sb out, to fault sb; **on ne le prend pas en d.** you can't fault him

• **par défaut ADJ** *Ordinat* default (*avant n*); **lecteur/clavier par d.** default drive/keyboard **ADV 1** (*sans agir*) by default; **avoir un poste par d.** to get a job by default **2** *Math* **total approché par d.** total rounded down **3** *Jur* by default **4** *Ordinat* by default; **sélectionner qch par d.** to default to sth

• **sans défaut ADJ** flawless

défaveur [defavœr] **NF** discredit, disfavour; **être en d. auprès de qn** to be in disfavour with sb; **c'est tombé en d.** it's gone out of favour *or* fashion; **cela a tourné à ma d.** it worked against me in the end

défavorable [defavɔrabl] **ADJ** unfavourable; **voir qch d'un œil d.** to view sth unfavourably; **en cas d'avis d. du jury** should the jury return an unfavourable verdict; **être d. à qn/qch** to be against sb/sth; **le taux de change nous est d.** the exchange rate is unfavourable

défavorablement [defavɔrabləmɑ̃] **ADV** unfavourably

défavorisé, -e [defavɔrize] **ADJ régions défavorisées** depressed areas; **classes défavorisées** underprivileged social classes

défavoriser [3] [defavɔrize] **VT** (*dans un partage*) to treat unfairly; (*dans un examen, une compétition*) to put at a disadvantage; **il est défavorisé par sa timidité** his shyness puts him at a disadvantage

défécation [defekasjɔ̃] **NF** *Physiol* defecation

défectif, -ive [defɛktif, -iv] **ADJ** *Gram* defective

défection [defɛksjɔ̃] **NF 1** (*fait de quitter*) abandonment, abandoning; **après la d. de son père** after his/her father walked out **2** (*désistement* ► *d'un allié, d'un partisan*) withdrawal of support; (► *d'un soldat*) defection, desertion; (► *d'un touriste, d'un client, d'un invité*) failure to appear; **cet été, nous avons eu beaucoup de défections** many tourists stayed away this summer; **faire d.** (*allié, partisan*) to withdraw support; (*espion*) to defect; (*soldat*) to defect, to desert; (*touriste, client, invité*) to fail to appear

défective [defɛktiv] *voir* **défectif**

défectueuse [defɛktyøz] *voir* **défectueux**

défectueusement [defɛktɥøzmɑ̃] **ADV** in a faulty manner

défectueux, -euse [defɛktɥø, -øz] **ADJ** (*appareil, produit*) faulty, defective; (*loi*) defective

défectuosité [defɛktɥozite] **NF 1** (*mauvaise qualité*) substandard quality, defectiveness **2** (*malfaçon*) imperfection, defect, fault

défendable [defɑ̃dabl] **ADJ 1** *Mil* defensible **2** (*justifiable* ► *position*) defensible; (► *comportement*) justifiable; (► *idée*) tenable, defensible; **des théories qui ne sont pas défendables** indefensible theories

défendeur, -eresse [defɑ̃dœr, -drɛs] **NM,F** defendant

défendre [73] [defɑ̃dr] **VT 1** (*interdire*) to forbid; **d. l'accès au jardin** to forbid access to the garden; **son père lui a défendu l'entrée de sa maison** his/her father has forbidden him/her to set foot in the house; **il défend qu'on passe par là** he forbids anyone to go that way; **d. à qn de faire qch** to forbid sb to do sth; **son père lui défend de sortir le soir** his/her father does not allow him/her to go out at night; **elle lui défend les bonbons** she doesn't allow him/her (to eat) sweets; **l'alcool lui est défendu** he's/she's not allowed (to drink) alcohol; **ce médicament est défendu aux enfants** this medicine must not be given to children; **c'est défendu** it's not allowed, it's forbidden; **il est défendu de fumer dans les classes** smoking is prohibited in the classrooms; **il est défendu de parler au chauffeur** (*dans autobus*) please do not speak to the driver; **il m'est défendu de fumer** I'm not allowed to smoke

2 (*protéger* ► *pays, population*) to defend; (► *forteresse*) to defend, to hold; **ville mal défendue** badly defended town; **d. chèrement sa vie** to fight for dear life; **la propriété est défendue par deux chiens** the estate is guarded by two dogs; *Ftbl* **Durant défendra les buts de l'équipe d'Aix** Durant will be the goalkeeper for Aix

3 (*donner son appui à* ► *ami*) to defend, to stand up for; (► *idée, cause*) to defend, to champion, to support; (► *droit, opinion*) to defend, to uphold; (► *intérêts*) to protect; **d. son honneur** to defend one's honour; **d. l'intérêt national** to defend *or* to safeguard the national interest

4 (*préserver*) **d. qn contre** *ou* **de qch** to protect sb from *or* against sth; **de lourdes tentures défendaient la pièce contre les regards indiscrets** heavy curtains shielded the room from prying eyes; **les fourrures défendent les esquimaux du froid** fur clothing protects the Eskimos from the cold

5 *Jur* to defend

6 *Sport* (*service*) to defend

VPR se défendre 1 (*en luttant* ► *physiquement*) to defend oneself (**contre** against); (► *verbalement*) to stand up for *or* to defend oneself (**contre** against); **se d. jusqu'au bout** to fight to the last

2 (*se protéger*) **se d. de** *ou* **contre** to protect oneself from *or* against; **se d. des microbes** to protect oneself against germs; **se d. des tentations** to steer clear of temptation; **se d. des agressions** to defend oneself against attack; **se d. de la pluie** to shelter from the rain

3 (*être plausible*) to make sense; **c'est une idée qui se défend** there is something to be said for the idea; **cela se défend** that makes sense

4 *Fam* (*être compétent*) to get by; **elle n'est pas la meilleure mais elle se défend** she's not the best but she gets by; **il se défend bien en maths** he's quite good at maths□; **il ne se défend pas trop bien avec les femmes** he doesn't have much success with women□; **pour un débutant il ne se défend pas mal!** he's not bad for a beginner!

5 se d. de faire qch (*s'interdire de*) to refuse to do sth; (*s'empêcher de*) to refrain from doing sth; **se défendant de penser du mal d'elle** refusing to think ill of her; **on ne peut se d. de l'aimer** you can't help liking him/her

6 se d. de qch (*nier*) to deny sth; **se défendant d'avoir dit cela** denying having said that; **il se défend de vouloir la quitter** he won't admit that he wants to leave her

défendu, -e [defɑ̃dy] **PP** *voir* **défendre**

défenestration [defənestrasjɔ̃] **NF** defenestration

défenestrer [3] [defənestre] **VT** to defenestrate, to throw out of the window

VPR se défenestrer to jump out of the window

défense [defɑ̃s] **NF 1** (*interdiction*) prohibition; **malgré la d. de sa mère** despite his/her mother having forbidden it; **mais d. expresse d'en parler!** but you're strictly forbidden to talk about it!; *Vieilli* **faire d. à qn de faire qch** to forbid sb to do sth; **d. d'entrer** (*sur panneau*) no admittance *or* entry; **danger, d. d'entrer** (*sur panneau*) danger, keep out; **d. d'afficher** (*sur panneau*) stick no bills; **d. de fumer** (*sur panneau*) no smoking; **d. de déposer des ordures** (*sur panneau*) no dumping

2 (*protection, moyen de protection*) defence; **la d. de la langue française** the defence of the French language; **association de d. du consommateur** *ou* **des consommateurs** consumer (protection) group; **pour la d. des institutions** in order to defend *or* to safeguard the institutions; **ne pas avoir de d.** to be unable to defend oneself; **sans d.** defenceless; *Mktg* **d. contre-offensive** counter-offensive defence; *Mktg* **d. mobile** mobile defence; *Mktg* **d. préventive** pre-emptive defence

3 (*dans un débat*) defence; **prendre la d. de qn/qch** to stand up for *or* to defend sb/sth

4 *Mil* defence; **d. contre avions** anti-aircraft defence; **la D. nationale** national defence; **d. opérationnelle du territoire** home defence; **d. passive** civil defence; **un secret D.** a military secret

5 *Physiol & Psy* defence; **les défenses de l'organisme** the body's defences; **défenses immunitaires** immune defences; **impossible de discuter, il est toujours en position de d.** there's no talking to him, he's always on the defensive

6 *Jur* defence; **assurer la d. de qn** to defend sb; **présenter la d.** to put the case for the defence

7 *Sport* **la d.** the defence; **jouer la d.** to play a defensive game

8 *Zool* tusk

• **défenses NFPL** *Mil* defences

• **de défense ADJ 1** *Mil voir* **ligne 2** *Psy* defence (*avant n*)

• **pour ma/sa/***etc* **défense ADV** in my/his/*etc* defence

• **sans défense** ADJ **1** *(animal, bébé)* defenceless, helpless **2** *Mil* undefended

défenseur [defɑ̃sœr] NM **1** *(partisan ▸ de la foi)* defender; *(▸ d'une cause)* supporter, advocate; **les défenseurs de ces idées** advocates *or* supporters of these ideas; **d. de l'art pour l'art** believer in art for art's sake; **jouer les défenseurs de la veuve et de l'orphelin** to play the champion of the poor and needy **2** *Jur Br* counsel for the defence, *Am* defense attorney; **l'accusé et son d.** the accused and his counsel **3** *Sport* defender; **d. droit/gauche** *(au hockey)* right/left defence

défensif, -ive [defɑ̃sif, -iv] ADJ *(armes, mesures)* defensive

• **défensive** NF **la défensive** the defensive; **être** *ou* **se tenir sur la défensive** to be (on the) defensive; **ne sois pas toujours sur la défensive** don't be so defensive

défensivement [defɑ̃sivmɑ̃] ADV defensively

déféquer [18] [defeke] VI to defecate

défera *etc voir* **défaire**

déférence [deferɑ̃s] NF respect, deference; **avec d.** deferentially; **par d. pour...** in *or* out of deference to...

déférent, -e [deferɑ̃, -ɑ̃t] ADJ *(employé, attitude, discours)* deferential, respectful

déférer [18] [defere] VT *(affaire)* to refer to a court; *(accusé)* to bring before a court; **d. qn à la justice** to hand sb over to the law; **il a été déféré au Parquet** he was sent to appear before the public prosecutor

• **déférer à** VT IND to defer to

déferlant, -e [deferlɑ̃, -ɑ̃t] ADJ *(vague)* breaking

• **déferlante** NF **1** *(vague)* breaker **2** *Fig (invasion)* tidal wave

déferlement [deferləmɑ̃] NM **1** *(de vagues)* breaking **2** *(invasion)* **d. de** *(soudain)* flood of; *(continu)* stream of; **on s'attend à un d. de visiteurs** crowds of visitors are expected **3** *(accès ▸ d'émotion, de colère)* wave

déferler [3] [deferle] VI **1** *(vague)* to break; *Fig* **une vague de violence/racisme déferla sur le pays** a wave of violence/racism spread through the country **2** *(se répandre)* to rush; **déferlant dans le parc** streaming into the park; **ils déferlaient dans la rue** they flooded into the streets; **les vacanciers déferlent sur les routes** holiday-makers are taking to the roads in droves **3** *(fuser ▸ émotion, applaudissements)* to erupt

VT *Naut (voile)* to unfurl; *(drapeau)* to break

défet [defɛ] NM *Typ* waste sheets

défi [defi] NM **1** *(appel provocateur)* challenge; **jeter** *ou* **lancer un d. à qn** to throw down the gauntlet to, to challenge sb; **relever un d.** to take up the gauntlet *or* a challenge **2** *(attitude provocatrice)* defiance; **refuser par d.** to refuse out of defiance **3** *(remise en question)* **un d. à** a challenge to; **c'est un d. à ma position de chef de famille** it's a challenge to my position as head of the family; **c'est un d. au bon sens** it defies common sense

• **au défi** ADV **mettre qn au d. (de faire)** to challenge sb (to do); **je mets quiconque au d. de comprendre leur formulaire** I challenge anybody to understand their form

• **de défi** ADJ *(attitude, air)* defiant

défiance [defjɑ̃s] NF **1** *(méfiance)* mistrust, distrust; **inspirer** *ou* **éveiller la d.** to arouse suspicion; **avec d.** mistrustfully, distrustfully; **mettre qn en d.** to make sb wary; **sans d.** unsuspecting **2** *(désapprobation)* **vote de d.** vote of no confidence

défiant, -e [defjɑ̃, -ɑ̃t] ADJ *(enfant, air)* mistrustful, distrustful

défibrillateur [defibrijatœr] NM *Méd* defibrillator

défibrillation [defibrijasjɔ̃] NF *Méd* defibrillation

déficeler [24] [defisle] VT *(paquet)* to untie, to take the string off; *(rôti)* to remove the string from, to take the string off

VPR **se déficeler** to come untied *or* undone

déficience [defisjɑ̃s] NF **1** *Méd* deficiency; **d. immunitaire** immune deficiency; **d. musculaire** muscle deficiency; **d. en vitamine B** vitamin B deficiency **2** *Psy* **d. mentale** *ou* **intellectuelle** mental retardation

déficient, -e [defisjɑ̃, -ɑ̃t] ADJ **1** *Méd* deficient **2** *(insuffisant ▸ théorie)* weak, feeble

NM,F **d. mental** person who is mentally deficient; **d. moteur** person with motor deficiency

déficit [defisit] NM **1** *Écon & Fin* deficit; **être en d.** to be in deficit; **accuser un d.** to show a deficit; **combler un d.** to make up a deficit; **société en d.** company in deficit; **d. de la balance commerciale** trade deficit; **d. budgétaire** budget deficit; **d. de caisse** cash deficit; **d. commercial** trade deficit *or* gap; **d. d'exploitation** operating deficit; **d. extérieur** external deficit, balance of payments deficit; **d. de financement** financing gap; **d. fiscal remboursable** negative income tax; **d. fiscal reportable** tax loss; **d. public** government deficit; *Compta* **d. reportable** loss carry forward; **d. du secteur public** public sector deficit; **d. social** public spending deficit; **d. de trésorerie** cash deficit **2** *Méd* **d. immunitaire** immunodeficiency; *Psy* **d. intellectuel** mental retardation **3** *(manque)* gap, lack

déficitaire [defisitɛr] ADJ **1** *Écon & Fin (entreprise)* loss-making; *(compte)* in debit; *(budget)* in deficit, adverse; *(bilan)* showing a loss **2** *(insuffisant ▸ production, récolte)* poor

défier [9] [defje] VT **1** *(dans un duel, un jeu)* to challenge; **d. qn du regard** to give sb a challenging look; **je te défie de trouver moins cher** I defy you to find a better price; **il m'a défié au tennis** he challenged me to a game of tennis **2** *(résister à ▸ danger)* to defy, to brave; **il ne craint pas de d. l'autorité paternelle** he's not afraid to stand up to his father; **d. l'imagination/les lois de l'équilibre** to defy the imagination/the laws of gravity; **prix/qualité défiant toute concurrence** absolutely unbeatable prices/quality

VPR **se défier** *Littéraire* **se d. de** to mistrust, to distrust; **elle se défie d'elle-même** she doesn't trust herself

défigurement [defigyrmɑ̃] NM *(d'une personne)* disfigurement; *(d'une statue)* defacement; *(de la vérité, du sens)* distortion

défigurer [3] [defigyre] VT **1** *(personne)* to disfigure; **l'accident/la maladie l'a défiguré** the accident/illness has disfigured him; **défiguré la colère** his face distorted with anger **2** *(ville, environnement)* to blight, to ruin **3** *(caricaturer ▸ vérité, faits)* to distort

défilé [defile] NM **1** *(procession ▸ pour une fête)* procession; *(▸ de militaires)* march, parade; *(▸ de manifestants)* march; **d. aérien** flypast; **un d. de mode** a fashion show **2** *(multitude ▸ d'invités, de pensées)* stream, procession; *(▸ de souvenirs)* string, procession **3** *Géog* defile, narrow pass

défilement [defilmɑ̃] NM *(d'un film, d'une bande)* unwinding; *Ordinat (d'un texte sur écran)* scrolling

> Il faut noter que le nom anglais **defilement** est un faux ami. Il signifie **souillure** ou **profanation**, selon le contexte.

défiler [3] [defile] VI **1** *(marcher en file)* to file (along); *(pour être vu)* to march, to parade; *(pour manifester)* to march; **les élèves défilent devant la statue** the pupils file past the statue; **d. dans la rue** to march through the streets; **les mannequins défilaient** the models were parading up and down the *Br* catwalk *or Am* runway **2** *(être nombreux)* **des centaines de voitures défilent vers la côte** hundreds of cars are streaming towards the coast; **les journalistes ont défilé au ministère toute la journée** the journalists were in and out of the ministry all day; **ses amis ont défilé à son chevet** his/her friends came to his/her bedside one after the other **3** *(se dérouler ▸ bande magnétique)* to unwind; *(▸ texte informatique)* to scroll; *(▸ souvenirs, publicité)* to stream past; **faire d.** *(bande, bobine)* to run; *(données sur écran)* to scroll; *Ordinat* **faire d. un document** to scroll through a document; *Ordinat* **d. vers le bas/haut** to scroll down/up; **les pâturages défilaient sans fin** the fields rolled past endlessly; *(rapidement)* the fields flashed by; **toute ma vie a défilé dans ma tête** my whole life flashed before my eyes

VT **1** *(perles)* to unthread; *(collier)* to unstring **2** *Mil* to put under cover, to defilade

VPR **se défiler** *Fam* **1** *(fuir)* to slip away **2** *(esquiver une responsabilité)* **n'essaie pas de te d.** don't try to get *or* wriggle out of it

défini, -e [defini] ADJ **1** *(qui a une définition)* defined; *(précis)* precise; **mal d.** ill-defined **2** *Gram* **article d.** definite article; **passé d.** preterite **3** *Ordinat* **d. par l'utilisateur** user-defined

NM **le d.** that which is defined

définir [32] [definir] VT **1** *(donner la définition de)* to define; **on définit le dauphin comme un mammifère** the dolphin is defined as a mammal **2** *(décrire ▸ sensation)* to define, to describe; *(▸ personne)* to describe, to portray **3** *(circonscrire ▸ objectif, politique, condition)* to define

VPR **se définir 1** *(concept)* **se d. comme** to be defined as **2** *(soi-même)* to describe oneself; **comment vous définissez-vous?** how would you describe yourself?

définissable [definisabl] ADJ definable; *Ordinat* **d. par l'utilisateur** user-definable

définitif, -ive [definitif, -iv] ADJ **1** *(irrévocable ▸ décision)* final; *(▸ acceptation)* definitive; **à titre d.** permanently; **leur séparation est définitive** they're splitting up for good; **soldes avant fermeture définitive** *(sur vitrine d'un magasin)* closing-down sale; **c'est non et c'est d.!** the answer's no and that's that!; **rien de d.** nothing definite **2** *(qui fait autorité ▸ œuvre)* definitive; *(▸ argument)* conclusive

NM **le d.** that which is definitive; **à ce stade de ma vie, je veux du d.** at my time of life I want something more definite

• **en définitive** ADV **1** *(somme toute)* finally, when all's said and done, in the final analysis **2** *(après tout)* after all

définition [definisjɔ̃] NF **1** *(d'une idée, d'un mot)* definition; **d. de poste** job description

2 *Ling* definition

3 *(de mots croisés)* clue

4 *Phot & Tél* definition

• **par définition** ADV by definition

définitive [definitiv] *voir* **définitif**

définitivement [definitivmɑ̃] ADV *(partir, s'installer)* for good; *(décider)* definitely; *(nommé)* permanently

défiscalisation [defiskalizasjɔ̃] NF tax exemption

défiscalisé, -e [defiskalize] ADJ tax free

défiscaliser [3] [defiskalize] VT to exempt from tax

défit *etc voir* **défaire**

déflagration [deflagrasjɔ̃] NF **1** *(explosion)* explosion; *(combustion)* deflagration **2** *(conflit)* clash; **une d. mondiale** a worldwide conflict

déflagrer [3] [deflagre] VI to deflagrate

déflation [deflasjɔ̃] NF *Fin & Géol* deflation

déflationniste [deflasjɔnist] ADJ *(principe)* deflationist; *(mesure)* deflationary

NMF deflationist

déflecteur [deflɛktœr] NM **1** *Aut Br* quarter light, *Am* vent **2** *Naut & Phys* deflector

défleurir [32] [deflœrir] *Littéraire* VT *(rose)* to deadhead, to take the heads off; *(arbre)* to remove the blossom from; *(paysage)* to remove the flowers from

VI *(arbre)* to shed its blossom; *(paysage)* to lose its flowers

déflexion [deflɛksjɔ̃] NF *Phys* deflection

déflocage [deflɔkaʒ] NM *Constr* removal of asbestos

défloraison [deflɔrɛzɔ̃] NF *Littéraire* falling of blossoms

défloration [deflɔrasjɔ̃] NF defloration

déflorer [3] [deflɔre] VT **1** *(fille)* to deflower **2** *Littéraire (sujet)* to corrupt, to spoil

défoliant [defɔljɑ̃] NM defoliant

défoliation [defɔljasjɔ̃] NF defoliation

défonçage [defɔ̃saʒ] NM *(destruction ▸ d'une porte)* breaking down; *(▸ d'un mur)* knocking down; *(▸ d'un tonneau, d'une caisse)* smashing open

défonce [defɔ̃s] NF *Fam* getting stoned; **son seul plaisir, c'est la d.** his/her only pleasure in life is getting stoned; **d. aux solvants** solvent abuse; **d. à l'acide** dropping acid; **d. aux amphétamines** taking speed, speeding

défoncé, -e [defɔ̃se] **ADJ 1** *(cabossé ▸ lit, sofa)* battered; *(▸ chemin)* rutted; **un matelas d.** a mattress with all the stuffing hanging out **2** *Fam (drogué)* stoned; **ils étaient complètement défoncés** they were stoned out of their minds

défoncement [defɔ̃smɑ̃] **NM** *(destruction ▸ d'une porte)* breaking down; *(▸ d'un mur)* knocking down; *(▸ d'un tonneau, d'une caisse)* smashing open

défoncer [16] [defɔ̃se] **VT 1** *(démolir ▸ porte)* to smash in, to knock down; *(▸ mur)* to knock down, to demolish; *(▸ lit)* to break (up), to smash (up); *(▸ chaussée)* to break up; *(▸ caisse, tonneau)* to smash in; **d. qch à coups de pied** to kick sth in; **le choc lui a défoncé trois côtes** the impact cracked three of his/her ribs; **les chars ont défoncé la route** the tanks have broken up the road surface; **il a eu le crâne défoncé** his skull was smashed; *Fam* **d. la gueule à qn** to smash sb's face in, *Br* to punch sb's lights out, *Am* to punch sb out **2** *Fam (sujet: drogue)* **d. qn** to get sb high; *Hum* **moi, c'est le café qui me défonce** I get my kicks from coffee

VPR se défoncer *Fam* **1** *(se démener ▸ au travail)* to work flat out, to sweat blood; *(▸ en se distrayant)* to have a wild time; **je me suis défoncé pour finir le manuscrit** I worked flat out to get the manuscript finished; **il s'est défoncé sur scène hier soir** he gave it all he had on stage last night **2** *(se droguer)* to get stoned; **elle se défonce tous les soirs** she gets stoned every night; **il se défonce à l'héroïne/à la colle** he does heroin/sniffs glue; *Hum* **moi je me défonce au café** I'm hooked on coffee

défont *voir* **défaire**

déforestation [defɔrɛstasjɔ̃] **NF** deforestation; **faire de la d.** to deforest

déformant, -e [defɔrmɑ̃, -ɑ̃t] **ADJ** distorting

déformation [defɔrmasjɔ̃] **NF 1** *(changement de forme ▸ gén)* putting out of shape; *(▸ par torsion)* bending out of shape; *(▸ en frappant)* knocking out of shape; *(▸ par la chaleur)* warping **2** *Méd* deformation; **avoir une d. du pied** to have a deformed foot; **il fume tellement qu'il souffre d'une d. du goût** he smokes so much that he's lost all sense of taste **3** *(travestissement ▸ d'une pensée, de la réalité)* distortion, misrepresentation; *(▸ d'une image)* distortion, warping; **elle pose toujours des questions, c'est une d. professionnelle** she's always asking questions because she's used to doing it in her job; *Hum* **ne fais pas attention, c'est de la d. professionnelle!** don't worry, it's just my job!

déformer [3] [defɔrme] **VT 1** *(changer la forme de ▸ planche)* to warp; *(▸ barre)* to bend (out of shape); *(▸ pare-chocs)* to knock out of shape, to buckle; *(▸ chaussure, pantalon)* to put out of shape, to ruin the shape of; **chapeau déformé** hat that's gone out of shape *or* lost its shape

2 *(transformer ▸ corps)* to deform; *(▸ visage, voix)* to distort; **les mains déformées par les rhumatismes** hands deformed by rheumatism; **traits déformés par la haine** features contorted with hatred

3 *(changer le comportement de)* **déformé par dix ans de journalisme** marked by ten years as a journalist; **l'enseignement l'a déformé** he's taken on all the mannerisms of the typical teacher

4 *(fausser ▸ réalité, pensée)* to distort, to misrepresent; *(▸ image)* to distort; *(▸ goût)* to warp; *(▸ paroles)* to misquote; *(▸ réalité, vérité)* to distort, to twist

VPR se déformer *(vêtement)* to become shapeless, to go out of shape, to lose its shape; *(planche)* to become warped; *(barre)* to become bent; **le pull ne s'est pas déformé** the sweater kept its shape

défoulement [defulmɑ̃] **NM** letting off steam; **crier par d.** to shout to let off steam *or* to release one's pent-up emotions

défouler [3] [defule] **VT** to liberate; **ça défoule** it helps you let off steam

VPR se défouler to let off steam, to unwind; **rien de tel que le sport pour se d.** there's nothing like sport for letting off steam; **se d. sur qn** to take it out on sb

défourner [3] [defurne] **VT** *(pain)* to take out (of the oven); *(poterie)* to take out (of the kiln)

défragmentation [defragmɑ̃tasjɔ̃] **NF** *Ordinat (de fichiers)* defragmentation

défragmenter [3] [defragmɑ̃te] **VT** *Ordinat* to defragment

défragmenteur [defragmɑ̃tœr] **NM** *Ordinat* defragmenter

défraîchi, -e [defreʃi] **ADJ** *Com (articles)* shopsoiled; *(usé ▸ vêtement)* shabby, past its best; *Fig (idées)* stale; **les fleurs sont défraîchies** the flowers are past their best

défraîchir [32] [defreʃir] **VT** *(rideau)* to give a worn look to; *(couleur)* to fade

VPR se défraîchir *(rideau, couleur)* to fade; *(vêtement)* to become shabby

défraiement [defremɑ̃] **NM** compensation; **je suis en droit d'attendre un d.** I'm entitled to compensation

défrayer [11] [defreje] **VT 1** *(indemniser)* **d. qn** to meet or pay sb's expenses; **d. qn de qch** to reimburse sb for sth **2** *(locutions)* **d. la chronique** to be the talk of the town; **d. la conversation** to be the main topic of conversation

défrichage [defriʃaʒ] **NM 1** *(d'un terrain)* clearing **2** *(approche)* **le d. d'un texte du programme** a first look at a book on the syllabus

défricher [3] [defriʃe] **VT 1** *(nettoyer ▸ terrain)* to clear; *Fig* **d. le terrain avant de négocier** to clear the way for negotiations **2** *(dégrossir ▸ texte)* to have a first look at; *(▸ domaine)* to pioneer; **mon assistant a défriché votre dossier** my assistant did some preliminary work on your file

défricheur, -euse [defriʃœr, -øz] **NM,F 1** *(agriculteur)* **les premiers défricheurs** the people *or* settlers who first cleared the land **2** *Fig (d'un nouveau domaine)* pioneer

défriper [3] [defripe] **VT** to smooth out, to take the creases out of

défriser [3] [defrize] **VT 1** *(cheveux, moustache)* to straighten out; **se faire d. (les cheveux)** to have one's hair straightened **2** *Fam (contrarier)* to bug; **ça me défrise, ce genre d'attitude!** that sort of attitude really bugs me *or* gets to me!; **et alors, ça te défrise?** have you got a problem with that?

défroisser [3] [defrwase] **VT** to smooth out, to take the creases out of

VPR se défroisser to lose its creases

défroque [defrɔk] **NF 1** *(vêtement)* (old) rag; **on lui passait les défroques de son frère** he used to get his brother's cast-offs **2** *(d'un religieux)* effects

défroqué, -e [defrɔke] **ADJ** defrocked, unfrocked

NM *(prêtre)* defrocked priest; *(moine)* defrocked monk

défroquer [3] [defrɔke] **VI** *(prêtre)* to leave the priesthood; *(moine)* to leave the order

VPR se défroquer 1 *(prêtre)* to leave the priesthood; *(moine)* to leave the order **2** *Fam (enlever son pantalon)* to take one's *Br* trousers *or Am* pants off[□], *Br* to get one's keks off

défunt, -e [defœ̃, -œ̃t] *Littéraire* **ADJ 1** *(décédé ▸ parent, mari)* late; **son d. cousin** her late cousin **2** *(terminé ▸ royauté)* defunct; *(▸ espoir, amour)* lost, extinguished

NM,F deceased person; **le d.** the deceased; **prière pour les défunts** prayer for the dead

dégagé, -e [degaʒe] **ADJ 1** *(vue)* open; *(pièce, passage)* cleared; **une allée dégagée** a treeless drive

2 *(épaules)* bare; **bien d. sur les oreilles, s'il vous plaît** *(chez le coiffeur)* nice and short over the ears, please; **je la préfère avec le front d.** I prefer her with her hair back

3 *(désinvolte ▸ air, ton)* casual; *(▸ mouvements, démarche)* swinging, free; **dit-elle d'un air d.** she said casually *or* trying to look casual

4 *Météo (ciel)* clear, cloudless

NM *(en danse)* dégagé

dégagement [degaʒmɑ̃] **NM 1** *(émanation ▸ d'odeur)* emanation; *(▸ de chaleur)* release, emission, emanation; **un d. de gaz** *(accidentel)* a gas leak; *(volontaire)* a release of gas

2 *(espace ▸ dans une maison)* passage, hall; *(▸ dans une ville)* open space; *(▸ dans un bois)* clearing; **un d. d'un mètre entre le pont et le véhicule** one metre headroom between the bridge and the vehicle

3 *(déblaiement)* opening out, digging out; **le d. du temple par les archéologues** the excavation of the temple by the archaeologists

4 *Mil & Pol* disengagement

5 *(au mont-de-piété)* redeeming *(from pawn)*

6 *Sport (d'un ballon)* clearance

7 *Fin (de fonds, de crédits)* release

dégager [17] [degaʒe] **VT 1** *(sortir)* to free; **il a essayé de d. sa main de la mienne** he tried to pull his hand away *or* to free his hand from mine; **il a fallu deux heures pour le d. de la voiture** it took two hours to free him from the car; **d. les blessés des décombres** to pull *or* to dig the injured out from the rubble

2 *(enlever ▸ arbres tombés, ordures)* to remove, to clear; **d. les branches de la route** to clear the branches off the road, to clear the road of branches; *Fam* **tu vas me d. toutes ces bricoles de tes étagères** I want you to clear all these odds and ends off your shelves

3 *(désencombrer ▸ couloir, table, salle)* to clear (out); *(▸ sinus)* to clear, to unblock; *(▸ poitrine, gorge)* to clear; *(▸ chemin, pont)* to clear; **ils ont dégagé une ouverture dans la haie** they made an opening in the hedge; **une coupe qui dégage la nuque** a hairstyle cut very short at the back; **la robe dégage les épaules** the dress leaves the shoulders bare; *Fam Fig* **dégagez la piste!** (get) out of the way!

4 *Fin (fonds, crédits)* to release; *(bénéfices, excédent)* to show

5 *(annuler)* **d. sa parole** to go back on one's word; **d. sa responsabilité** to deny responsibility; **d. qn de sa promesse** to release *or* to free sb from their promise; **d. qn de ses dettes** to cancel sb's debt; **il est dégagé des obligations militaires** he has completed his military service

6 *(émettre ▸ odeur)* to give off, to emit; *(▸ gaz)* to release, to emit; *(▸ chaleur)* to emit, to give out

7 *(manifester ▸ quiétude)* to radiate; **la bibliothèque dégageait une impression de sérénité** the library had an atmosphere of great calm

8 *(extraire ▸ règle, principe)* to draw; *(▸ vérité)* to draw, to bring out, to extract; **d. l'idée principale d'un texte** to identify the main idea of a text

9 *(du mont-de-piété)* to redeem *(from pawn)*

10 *Sport (ballon)* to clear; **d. le ballon en touche** to kick the ball into touch

USAGE ABSOLU 1 *(en danse)* to perform a dégagé **2** *Fam* **dégage!** clear off!, get lost! **3** *Sport* **d. en touche** to put the ball into touch

VI 1 *très Fam (sentir mauvais)* to stink, *Br* to pong, to hum **2** *Fam (produire un effet puissant ▸ musique)* to be mind-blowing, to kick ass; *(▸ plat, épice)* to blow the top of one's head off, to pack a punch

VPR se dégager 1 *(conclusion)* to be drawn; *(vérité)* to emerge, to come out; **il se dégage du rapport que les torts sont partagés** it appears from the report that both sides are to blame

2 *(s'extraire ▸ d'une voiture accidentée, d'un piège)* to free oneself (**de** from); **se d. d'une étreinte** to extricate oneself from an embrace; **le chien s'est dégagé de sa laisse** the dog's slipped its lead; **se d. du peloton** to leave the pack behind

3 *(se libérer ▸ d'un engagement)* **j'étais invité mais je vais me d.** I was invited but I'll get out of it; **il s'est dégagé en prétextant une indisposition** he cried off on the grounds of being unwell; **se d. d'une affaire** to drop out of a deal; **se d. d'une dette** to discharge *or* pay off a debt; **se d. d'une obligation** to free oneself from an obligation; **se d. de sa promesse** to go back on one's promise

4 *(se vider ▸ route, ciel)* to clear; *(▸ nez, sinus)* to become unblocked, to clear

5 *(émaner ▸ odeur, gaz, fumée)* to emanate, to be given off; *(se manifester ▸ quiétude)* to emanate, to radiate; **la tendresse qui se dégageait de sa lettre m'émut** the love which permeated his/her letter moved me; **le magnétisme qui se dégage d'elle** the magnetism she radiates

dégaine [degɛn] **NF** *Fam (démarche)* (peculiar) gait[□]; *(aspect ridicule)* strange appearance[□]; **tu parles d'une d.!** just look at that!; **il a vraiment une**

d. pas possible he looks like something from another planet!

dégainer [4] [degene] VT *(épée)* to unsheathe, to draw; *(revolver)* to draw

USAGE ABSOLU **avant que le gangster ait pu d.** before the gangster could draw his gun

déganter [3] [degɑ̃te] **se déganter** VPR to take off *or* to remove one's glove/gloves

dégarni, -e [degarni] ADJ **1** *(arbre, rayon, mur)* bare; **le placard est bien d.** the cupboard's rather empty *or* bare; **mon portefeuille est plutôt d.** I'm rather low on funds **2** *(personne, crâne)* balding; **il a le front d.** he has a receding hairline

dégarnir [32] [degarnir] VT **1** *(ôter les objets de ▸ salon, salle)* to empty; *(▸ collection)* to deplete; **j'ai complètement dégarni le mur** I've taken everything off the wall; **les devantures sont dégarnies de leurs mannequins** the dummies have been removed from the window displays; **l'autel est dégarni de ses bougies** the altar has been stripped of its candles

2 *(ôter l'argent de ▸ portefeuille)* to empty, to deplete; *(▸ compte en banque)* to drain, to draw heavily on

3 *(ôter les cheveux de ▸ crâne)* to cause to go bald; **un peu dégarni par les années** balding slightly with age

4 *(ôter les feuilles de)* to strip of its leaves; **l'hiver a dégarni les arbres** winter has stripped the trees of their leaves; **la rose, dégarnie de ses piquants** the rose, stripped of its thorns

VPR **se dégarnir 1** *(se vider ▸ boîte, collection, rayonnage)* to become depleted; *(▸ salle)* to empty; *(▸ groupe)* to become depleted, to thin out **2** *(devenir chauve)* to go bald, to start losing one's hair; **il commence à se d. sur le dessus (du crâne)** he's going thin on top; **son front se dégarnit** his hairline is receding; **son crâne se dégarnit** he's losing hair, he's thinning on top **3** *(arbre)* to lose its leaves; *(forêt)* to become depleted *or* thinner

dégât [dega] NM damage *(UNCOUNT)*; **il y a du d.** *ou* **des dégâts** there's some damage; *Fam* **il n'y a pas de dégâts?** *(après un accident)* no harm done?; *Fam* **si tu le perds, il va y avoir du d.** if you lose it, there'll be trouble; **faire des dégâts** to cause damage; **les chenilles ont fait des dégâts/de gros dégâts dans le verger** the caterpillars have caused some damage/wreaked havoc in the orchard; **dégâts des eaux** water damage; **dégâts collatéraux** collateral damage; **dégâts matériels** structural damage

dégauchir [32] [degoʃir] VT **1** *(redresser)* to straighten out **2** *(aplanir ▸ planche)* to plane; *(▸ pierre)* to trim

dégauchissage [degoʃisaʒ], **dégauchissement** [degoʃismɑ̃] NM **1** *(redressement)* straightening **2** *(fait d'aplanir ▸ une planche)* planing; *(▸ une pierre)* trimming

dégauchisseuse [degoʃisøz] NF surfacing machine, surfacer

dégazage [degazaʒ] NM **1** *Métal* (gas) extraction **2** *(d'un pétrolier, d'une mine de charbon)* degassing

dégazer [3] [degaze] VT *Métal* to extract gas from

VI *(pétrolier)* to degas

dégel [deʒɛl] NM **1** *Météo* thaw; **au d.** when the thaw comes **2** *(après un conflit)* thaw; *Pol* **une période de d.** a period of détente

dégelée [deʒle] NF *Fam* thrashing, hiding; **foutre une d. à qn** to give sb a thrashing *or* a hiding; **prendre une d.** to get a thrashing *or* a hiding

dégeler [25] [deʒle] VT **1** *(décongeler)* to defrost **2** *(réchauffer ▸ sol, étang)* to thaw (out); *(▸ tuyau)* to unfreeze

3 *Fam (mettre à l'aise)* to thaw (out), to relax□; **je n'arrive pas à d. mon collègue** I can't get my colleague to loosen up; **elle sait d. un auditoire** she knows how to warm up an audience

4 *(améliorer ▸ relations diplomatiques)* to thaw; **d. l'atmosphère** to make the atmosphere less chilly

5 *Fin (crédits)* to unfreeze

VI **1** *(se réchauffer ▸ banquise, étang)* to thaw **2** *(décongeler)* to defrost

V IMPERSONNEL **il dégèle** it's thawing

VPR **se dégeler 1** *(se décongeler)* to defrost **2** *(se réchauffer ▸ sol, étang)* to thaw (out)

3 *Fam (être moins timide)* to thaw (out), to relax□; **dégèle-toi un peu!** come on, relax *or* let your hair down!

4 *(s'améliorer ▸ relations)* to improve; **les relations entre les deux pays se dégèlent** there is a thaw in relations between the two countries

dégénératif, -ive [deʒeneratif, -iv] ADJ degenerative

dégénéré, -e [deʒenere] ADJ degenerate

NM,F degenerate

dégénérer [18] [deʒenere] VI **1** *(perdre ses qualités ▸ race, plante)* to degenerate; **ses gags ont beaucoup dégénéré** his/her jokes have really gone downhill

2 *(s'aggraver ▸ situation)* to worsen, to deteriorate; *(▸ discussion)* to get out of hand; **à chaque fois qu'on se voit, ça finit toujours par d.** every time we see each other it ends up getting out of hand

3 *Méd (tumeur)* to become malignant; *(infection)* to become severe

4 *(se changer)* **d. en** to degenerate into; **sa bronchite a dégénéré en pneumonie** his/her bronchitis developed into pneumonia

dégénérescence [deʒeneresɑ̃s] NF **1** *Biol* degeneration **2** *Littéraire (déclin)* degeneration, becoming degenerate; **d. morale** degeneration of moral standards

dégénérescent [deʒeneresɑ̃] ADJ *Méd* degenerating, degenerative

dégingandé, -e [deʒɛ̃gɑ̃de] ADJ gangling, lanky

dégivrage [deʒivraʒ] NM **1** *(processus ▸ d'un réfrigérateur)* defrosting; *Aviat & Aut* de-icing **2** *(dispositif ▸ d'un réfrigérateur)* defroster; *Aviat & Aut* **d. arrière** rear windscreen de-icer

dégivrer [3] [deʒivre] VT *(réfrigérateur)* to defrost; *Aviat & Aut* to de-ice

dégivreur [deʒivrœr] NM *(d'un réfrigérateur)* defroster; *Aviat & Aut* de-icer

déglaçage [deglasaʒ] NM **1** *Culin* deglazing **2** *(d'un bassin)* melting of the ice, thawing

déglacer [16] [deglase] VT **1** *Culin (poêle)* to deglaze **2** *(étang)* to remove the ice from, to melt the ice on

déglingue [deglɛ̃g] NF *Fam* **1** *Vieilli (physique, morale)* decline□ **2** *(d'un milieu)* decline□, deterioration□

déglinguer [3] [deglɛ̃ge] *Fam* VT **1** *(mécanisme)* to break□, to bust; **un vélo tout déglingué** a bike which is coming apart *or* falling to pieces **2** *(santé)* to wreck; **la fugue de son fils l'a déglingué** his son running away from home just broke him

VPR **se déglinguer 1** *(ne plus fonctionner)* to be bust; *(mal fonctionner) Br* to go on the blink, *Am* to go on the fritz; *(se détacher)* to come *or* to work loose **2** *(santé)* to get worse; *(poumons, reins)* to go to pieces; *Hum* **je me déglingue** I'm falling to pieces

déglutir [32] [deglytir] VI to swallow, to gulp

déglutition [deglytisjɔ̃] NF **1** *(de salive)* swallowing **2** *(d'aliments)* swallowing

dégobiller [3] [degɔbije] *Fam* VT to throw up, to puke up

VI to throw up, to puke

dégoiser [3] [degwaze] *Fam Péj* VT to spout, to come out with; **qu'est-ce que tu dégoises?** what are you going on *or* banging on about?

VI to bang on, to go on and on; **d. sur qn** *Br* to bitch about sb, to slag sb off, *Am* to bad-mouth sb

dégommage [degɔmaʒ] NM **1** *(d'un timbre)* removing the gum (**de** from) **2** *Fam (renvoi)* firing, *Br* sacking; *(destitution)* unseating□

dégommer [3] [degɔme] VT **1** *(timbre)* to remove the gum from

2 *Fam (tuer)* to blow away, to gun down□

3 *Fam (tirer sur)* to shoot at□

4 *Fam (évincer)* to kick out, to boot out

dégonflage [degɔ̃flaʒ] NM **1** *(d'un ballon, d'une bouée, d'un pneu)* letting air out of; **ajuster la pression par d.** to adjust the pressure by letting air out **2** *Fam (lâcheté)* chickening *or Br* bottling out; **dès qu'il a vu le patron, ça a été le d. total** as soon as he saw the boss he totally chickened out

dégonflard, -e [degɔ̃flar, -ard] NM,F *Fam* chicken *(person)*

dégonflé, -e [degɔ̃fle] ADJ **1** *(ballon)* deflated; *(pneu)* flat **2** *Fam (lâche)* chicken

NM,F *Fam* chicken *(person)*

dégonflement [degɔ̃fləmɑ̃] NM **1** *(d'un pneu, d'une bouée, d'un ballon)* deflation; **pour compenser le d. du pneu** in order to compensate for the amount of air that's been let out of the tyre **2** *Méd* **d. d'un doigt/pied** reduction of the swelling in a finger/foot **3** *(des dépenses)* cutback (**de** in)

dégonfler [3] [degɔ̃fle] VT **1** *(ballon, bouée, pneu)* to deflate, to let air out of

2 *Méd (jambes, doigt)* to bring down *or* to reduce the swelling in

3 *(prix)* to bring down

4 *(démystifier ▸ prétention, mythe)* to deflate, to debunk

VI *(jambes, doigt)* to become less swollen; **ma cheville dégonfle** the swelling in my ankle's going down

VPR **se dégonfler 1** *(ballon)* to go down, to deflate; *(pneu)* to go flat **2** *Méd (jambes, doigt)* to become less swollen; **ma cheville se dégonfle** the swelling in my ankle's going down **3** *Fam (perdre courage)* to chicken out, *Br* to bottle out, to lose one's bottle

dégorgement [degɔrʒəmɑ̃] NM **1** *(fait de déverser)* disgorging **2** *(fait de déboucher ▸ conduit, évier)* unblocking **3** *(décharge ▸ d'égout)* discharging, overflow

dégorger [17] [degɔrʒe] VT **1** *(déverser)* to disgorge; *Fig* **la rue a dégorgé un flot de gens** a crowd of people surged from the street **2** *(débloquer ▸ conduit, évier)* to clear, to unblock **3** *(vomir)* to vomit

VI **1** *(se déverser)* to empty **2** *Culin (ris de veau, cervelle)* to soak *(in cold water)*; *(concombre)* to drain *(having been sprinkled with salt)*; **faire d.** *(ris de veau, cervelle)* to (leave to) soak; *(concombre)* to drain of water *(by sprinkling with salt)*; *(escargot)* to clean *(by salting and starvation)*

VPR **se dégorger** *(se déverser)* to empty

dégoter, dégotter [3] [degɔte] VT *Fam (objet rare)* to unearth; *(idée originale)* to hit on; **où tu l'as dégoté, ce type?** where on earth did you find this guy?

dégoulinade [degulinad] NF *(coulée)* trickle, drip

dégoulinement [degulinmɑ̃] NM *(en traînées)* trickling; *(goutte à goutte)* dripping

dégouliner [3] [deguline] VI *(peinture, sauce)* to drip; *(larmes, sang)* to trickle down; *(maquillage)* to run; **la pluie me dégoulinait dans le cou** the rain was trickling down my neck; **je dégouline** I'm dripping, I'm soaking wet

dégoupiller [3] [degupije] VT *(grenade)* to take the pin out of

dégourdi, -e [degurdi] *Fam* ADJ **être d.** to be smart *or* on the ball; **il n'est pas très d.** he's a bit slow on the uptake

NM,F **c'est un petit d.!** there are no flies on him!

dégourdir [32] [degurdir] VT **1** *(ranimer ▸ membres)* to bring the circulation back to **2** *(réchauffer ▸ liquide)* to warm up **3** *Fam (rendre moins timide)* **d. qn** to teach sb a thing or two, to wise sb up

VPR **se dégourdir 1** *(remuer)* **se d. les jambes** to stretch one's legs; **se d. les doigts avant de jouer du piano** to warm up before playing the piano **2** *(en marchant)* to stretch one's legs **3** *Fam (devenir moins timide)* to learn a thing or two, to wise up

dégourdissement [degurdismɑ̃] NM *(d'un membre ▸ ankylosé)* bringing the circulation back (**de** to); *(▸ gelé)* warming up (**de** of)

dégoût [degu] NM **1** *(aversion)* disgust, distaste; **éprouver** *ou* **avoir du d. pour qn/qch** to have an aversion to sb/sth; **prendre qch en d.** to take a dislike to sth **2** *(lassitude)* weariness; **par d. de la vie** through world-weariness

dégoûtant, -e [degutɑ̃, -ɑ̃t] ADJ *(sale)* disgusting, disgustingly dirty; *(salace ▸ film, remarque)* disgusting, dirty; *(condamnable)* disgusting; **c'est d.!** *(injuste)* it's disgusting *or* awful!

NM,F 1 *(personne sale)* **petit d.!** you little pig! **2** *(vicieux)* **vieux d.!** you dirty old man! **3** *Fam (personne injuste)* **quelle dégoûtante!** that wretched woman!; **quel d.!** the swine!

dégoûtation [degutasjɔ̃] **NF** *Fam* **1** *(dégoût)* disgust❑ **2 quelle d.!** *(chose)* how disgusting!❑; *(situation)* what a disgusting state of affairs!❑

dégoûté, -e [degute] **ADJ 1** *(écœuré)* repulsed, disgusted; **elle m'a regardé d'un air d.** she gave me a look of utter disgust; *Hum* **il n'est pas d.!** he's not very fussy!
2 *(indigné)* outraged, revolted, disgusted
3 *Fam (découragé)* bummed (out), *Br* gutted
4 *(las)* **d. de** weary of; **d. de la vie** weary of life
NM,F faire le d. to be fussy, to make a fuss; **ne fais pas trop la dégoûtée, tu n'as pas d'autres propositions** you've had no other offers, so don't turn your nose up at it

dégoûter **[3]** [degute] **VT 1** *(écœurer)* to disgust, to repel, to be repugnant to; **son contact le dégoûta** his/her touch repulsed him, he found his/her touch repulsive **2** *(indigner)* to disgust, to outrage, to be (morally) repugnant to; **les égoïstes comme toi me dégoûtent** selfish people like you disgust me *or* make me sick **3** *(lasser)* to put off; **il gagne toujours, c'est à vous d.!** he always wins, it's enough to make you sick!; **la vie le dégoûtait** he was weary of life *or* sick of living; **d. qn de qch** to put sb off sth; **cela m'a dégoûté de la viande** that put me off meat; **c'est à vous d. d'être serviable** it's enough to put you (right) off being helpful
VPR se dégoûter 1 *(emploi réfléchi)* **je me dégoûte!** I disgust myself! **2 se d. de qn/qch** to get sick of sb/sth; **tu vas te d. des gâteaux** you're going to put yourself right off cakes

dégoutter **[3]** [degute] **VI** to drip; **son front dégoutte de sueur** his/her forehead is dripping with sweat, sweat is dripping off his/her forehead; **la pluie dégoutte de son chapeau** the rain is dripping from his/her hat

dégradant, -e [degradɑ̃, -ɑ̃t] **ADJ** degrading

dégradation [degradasjɔ̃] **NF 1** *(destruction naturelle ▸ d'un objet, d'un bâtiment)* wear and tear, deterioration; **les meubles en osier subissent la d. du temps** wicker furniture suffers wear and tear with time
2 *(destruction volontaire ▸ d'un monument)* defacement; *(▸ de matériel scolaire, de l'environnement)* damage (**de** to)
3 *(détérioration ▸ de rapports, d'une situation)* deterioration, worsening; *(▸ de l'environnement)* degradation
4 *(avilissement)* degradation; **d. morale** moral degradation
5 *Chim* degradation
6 *Phys* **d. de l'énergie** dissipation of energy
7 *Ordinat* **d. de données** corruption of data
8 *(d'une couleur)* toning down, gradation; *(de la lumière)* gradation
9 *(d'un officier)* ≃ dishonourable discharge; **d. civique** loss of civil rights

dégradé [degrade] **NM 1** *(technique)* shading off; *(résultat)* gradation; **un d. de verts** greens shading off into each other; *Ordinat* **d. de couleur** colour scale **2** *(d'une coiffure)* layered style; **se faire faire un d.** to have one's hair layered
• **en dégradé ADJ tons en d.** colours shading off (into one another); **coupe en d.** layered cut

dégrader **[3]** [degrade] **VT 1** *(abîmer ▸ gén)* to damage; *(▸ monument)* to deface; **quartier dégradé** run-down district
2 *(envenimer ▸ rapports humains)* to damage, to cause to deteriorate
3 *(avilir)* to degrade
4 *(couleurs)* to shade (into one another); *(lumières)* to reduce gradually
5 *(cheveux)* to layer
6 *Mil* **d. un officier** to strip an officer of his rank
7 *Ordinat (données)* to corrupt
VPR se dégrader 1 *(se détériorer ▸ meuble, bâtiment, rapports)* to deteriorate; *(▸ santé)* to decline; *(▸ langage)* to deteriorate, to become debased; *(▸ temps)* to get worse **2** *(s'avilir)* to degrade oneself **3** *Phys (énergie)* to dissipate

dégrafer **[3]** [degrafe] **VT** *(papiers)* to unstaple; *(col, robe)* to undo, to unfasten; *(ceinture)* to undo; *(bracelet)* to unclasp, to unhook; *Fam* **tu veux que je te dégrafe?** shall I undo your dress for you?❑
VPR se dégrafer 1 *(emploi passif) (robe)* to undo **2** *(emploi réfléchi) (ôter sa robe)* to undo *or* to unfasten one's dress; *(ôter son corset)* to undo *or* to unfasten one's corset **3** *(jupe)* to come undone; *(papiers)* to come unstapled; *(collier)* to come unhooked

dégraffitage [degrafitaʒ] **NM** graffiti removal

dégraissage [degrɛsaʒ] **NM 1** *(nettoyage)* removal of grease marks
2 *Fam (diminution du personnel)* downsizing❑
3 *Fam (élimination du surplus)* trimming❑; **faire du d. sur un manuscrit** to trim a manuscript down
4 *Culin (d'un bouillon)* skimming off the fat; *(d'une viande)* trimming off the fat

dégraisser **[4]** [degrese] **VT 1** *(ôter les taches de)* to remove grease marks from
2 *Fam (entreprise)* to downsize❑, to streamline❑; *(personnel)* to cut back❑, to shed❑
3 *Fam (dissertation, manuscrit)* to cut down❑, to trim down❑
4 *Culin (sauce)* to skim the fat off; *(viande)* to cut *or* to trim the fat off
USAGE ABSOLU *Fam* **il va falloir d.** we'll have to downsize❑

degré [dəgre] **NM 1** *(échelon ▸ d'une hiérarchie)* degree, grade; *(▸ d'un développement)* stage; **d'accord, il faut sévir, mais il y a des degrés** of course, you should be strict but there are degrees of strictness; **à un d. avancé de** at an advanced stage of; **cancéreux au dernier d.** in the last stages of cancer; *Scol* **le premier/second d.** primary/secondary education; **prendre une plaisanterie au premier d.** to take a joke seriously; **tu prends tout au premier d.** you take everything literally; **une remarque à prendre au second d.** a remark not to be taken literally; **c'est de l'humour au second d.** it's tongue-in-cheek humour
2 *(point)* degree; **un tel d. de dévouement** such a degree of devotion; **jusqu'à un certain d.** up to a point, to a degree; **intelligent au plus haut d.** of the highest intelligence; **courageux au plus haut d.** most courageous
3 *(unité)* degree; **du gin à 47,5 degrés** 83° proof gin, 47.5 degree gin *(on the Gay-Lussac scale)*; **d. alcoolique** *ou* **d'alcool** alcohol content; **d. Celsius/Fahrenheit** degree Celsius/Fahrenheit
4 *Astron, Géom & Math* degree; **un angle de 45 degrés** a 45-degree angle; **équation du premier/second d.** equation of the first/second degree; **d. zéro** degree zero; **son bouquin, c'est le d. zéro de la littérature** his book hardly deserves to be classed as literature
5 *Gram* degree
6 *(de parenté)* degree; **cousin au premier d.** first cousin
7 *Fin* **d. de liquidité** degree of liquidity, liquidity ratio; **d. de solvabilité** credit rating
8 *(surtout au pl) (d'un escalier)* step; *(d'une échelle)* rung; *Fig* **les degrés de l'échelle sociale** the rungs of the social ladder
• **par degrés ADV** by *or* in degrees, gradually

dégréer **[15]** [degree] **VT** *Naut* to unrig

dégressif, -ive [degresif, -iv] **ADJ** *(impôt, amortissement)* graded, graduated; *(tarif, taux)* tapering
NM discount; **d. sur le volume** bulk discount

dégressivité [degresivite] **NF** degression

dégrèvement [degrɛvmɑ̃] **NM** *Fin* **d. fiscal** *(d'une entreprise)* tax relief; *(d'un produit)* reduction of tax *or* duty

dégrever **[19]** [degrəve] **VT** *Fin & Jur (produit)* to reduce tax on; *(contribuable)* to grant tax relief to; *(industrie)* to derate; *(édifice)* to reduce the assessment on

dégriffé, -e [degrife] **ADJ** reduced *(and with the designer label removed)*
NM reduced (and unlabelled) designer item

dégringolade [degrɛ̃gɔlad] **NF** *Fam* **1** *(chute)* tumbling (down)❑ **2** *(baisse ▸ des prix)* slump❑ (**de** in); *(▸ des cours)* collapse❑; *(▸ d'une réputation)* plunge❑; **l'industrie est en pleine d.** the industry is in the middle of a slump; **il était si admiré, quelle d.!** he was so admired, what a comedown!

dégringoler **[3]** [degrɛ̃gɔle] *Fam* **VI 1** *(chuter)* to tumble down❑; *(bruyamment)* to crash down❑; **j'ai tout fait d.** I brought the whole lot down **2** *(baisser ▸ prix)* to slump❑, to tumble❑; *(▸ réputation)* to plunge❑; **ça a fait d. les prix** it sent prices plummeting❑ **3** *(pleuvoir)* **ça dégringole!** it's tipping it down!
VT d. l'escalier *(courir)* to run *or* to race down the stairs❑; *(tomber)* to tumble down the stairs❑

dégrippant [degripɑ̃] **NM** penetrating grease

dégripper **[3]** [degripe] **VT** to release *(parts which are stuck)*

dégrisement [degrizmɑ̃] **NM** *(désillusion)* coming back down to earth, sobering up; *(après l'ivresse)* sobering up

dégriser **[3]** [degrize] **VT** *(désillusionner)* to bring back down to earth, to sober up; *(après l'ivresse)* to sober up; **le lendemain, dégrisé, il réfléchit** the next day, having sobered up, he started to think
VPR se dégriser to sober up

dégrossir **[32]** [degrosir] **VT 1** *(apprenti, débutant)* to polish, to smooth the rough edges of; **des jeunes gens mal dégrossis** uncouth young men; **son séjour la dégrossira un peu** her stay will smooth off some of her rough edges **2** *(théorie, question)* to do the groundwork on; *(texte du programme)* to have a first look at **3** *(bloc de pierre)* to rough-hew; *(bloc de bois)* to trim

dégrossissage [degrosisaʒ], **dégrossissement** [degrosismɑ̃] **NM 1** *(d'une personne)* polishing, smoothing the rough edges **2** *(d'une théorie, d'une question)* sorting out (**de** of), doing the groundwork (**de** on); **faire le d. d'un projet** to do a first rough sketch for a project **3** *(d'un bloc de pierre)* rough-hewing; *(d'un bloc de bois)* trimming

dégrouiller **[3]** [degruje] **se dégrouiller VPR** *Fam* to get a move on, to hurry up❑; **dégrouillez-vous!** hurry up!, get a move on!

dégroupage [degrupaʒ] **NM** *Tél* unbundling

dégroupement [degrupmɑ̃] **NM** *(d'une classe)* dividing *or* splitting (up); *(d'objets)* splitting (up); **il va falloir procéder à un d. de la classe** the class will have to be divided up *or* split into groups

dégrouper **[3]** [degrupe] **VT** *(classe)* to divide (up), to split (up); *(objets)* to split (up)

déguenillé, -e [degənije] **ADJ** ragged, tattered; **tout d.** in rags, in tatters
NM,F ragamuffin

déguerpir **[32]** [degɛrpir] **VI** to run away, to decamp; **faire d. un intrus** to drive away an intruder

dégueu [degø] **ADJ INV** *très Fam (sale)* disgusting❑, gross; *(mauvais)* lousy, crappy; **c'est pas d.!** it's pretty good!; **trois millions, pas d.!** three million, not bad!

dégueulasse [degœlas] *très Fam* **ADJ 1** *(sale)* disgusting❑, filthy❑, gross
2 *(injuste)* disgusting❑, lousy
3 *(vicieux)* disgusting❑, filthy
4 *(sans valeur)* crappy, lousy; **c'est pas d. comme cadeau** it's not a bad present
NMF 1 *(personne sale)* filthy pig **2** *(pervers)* **un gros d.** a filthy lech **3** *(personne immorale)* *Br* swine, *Am* stinker

dégueulasser **[3]** [degœlase] **VT** *très Fam* to mess up

dégueuler **[5]** [degœle] *très Fam* **VI** to throw up, to puke
VT to throw up, to puke up

dégueulis [degœli] **NM** *très Fam* puke

déguiller **[3]** [degije] *Suisse* **VT** *(objet dressé)* to knock over; *(pommes, noix, cerises)* to get down; *(arbre)* to cut down
VI to tumble down

déguisé, -e [degize] **ADJ 1** *(pour une fête)* in fancy dress; *(pour duper)* in disguise, disguised
2 *Péj (mal habillé)* ridiculously dressed
3 *(changé ▸ voix)* disguised
4 *(caché ▸ intention)* disguised, masked, veiled; *(▸ impôt, chômage)* hidden; *(▸ agressivité)* veiled; **avec une joie non déguisée** with unconcealed delight

déguisement [degizmɑ̃] **NM** *(pour une fête)* fancy dress, costume; *(pour duper)* disguise

• **sans déguisement** ADV *Littéraire* plainly, openly

déguiser [3] [degize] VT 1 *(pour une fête)* to dress up; *(pour duper)* to disguise; **déguisé en pirate** dressed (up) as a pirate, wearing a pirate costume
2 *(mal habiller)* to dress ridiculously; **ne lui mets pas tous ces rubans, tu la déguises** don't put all those ribbons on her, you'll make her look ridiculous
3 *(changer ▸ voix)* to disguise
4 *(cacher ▸ intention, vérité)* to disguise, to mask, to veil; *(▸ honte)* to conceal; **parler sans d. sa pensée** to speak plainly *or* openly
VPR **se déguiser** *(pour une fête)* to dress up; *(pour duper)* to put on a disguise, to disguise oneself; **se d. en pompier** to dress up as a fireman; *Fam* **se d. en courant d'air** to vanish into thin air, to do a disappearing act

dégurgiter [3] [degyrʒite] VT 1 *(aliment)* to bring (back) up 2 *(leçon)* to regurgitate, to repeat parrot fashion

dégustateur, -trice [degystatœr, -tris] NM,F taster

dégustation [degystasjɔ̃] NF 1 *(par un convive)* tasting *(UNCOUNT)*; *(par un dégustateur)* tasting, sampling 2 *(dans une cave)* (free) tasting; **d. (de vins)** wine-tasting 3 *(à un étalage, dans un restaurant)* tasting; **d. de fruits de mer à toute heure** seafood served all day

dégustatrice [degystatris] *voir* **dégustateur**

déguster [3] [degyste] VT 1 *(goûter ▸ sujet: convive)* to taste; *(▸ sujet: dégustateur professionnel)* to taste, to sample; **venez d. nos spécialités** come and taste *or* try our specialities 2 *(savourer ▸ aliment, boisson, spectacle, musique)* to savour, to enjoy
VI *Fam (recevoir des coups)* to *Br* get *or Am* take a pasting; *(se faire réprimander)* to get a roasting; *(être éprouvé)* to have a rough time of it; **ils dégustent, les parents d'adolescents!** parents of teenagers go through hell!; **attends qu'il rentre, tu vas d.!** just wait till he gets home, you're really going to catch it!

déhanché, -e [deɑ̃ʃe] ADJ 1 *(balancé)* swaying 2 *(boiteux)* lop-sided

déhanchement [deɑ̃ʃmɑ̃] NM 1 *(démarche ▸ séduisante)* swaying walk; *(▸ claudicante)* lop-sided walk 2 *(posture)* = standing with one's weight on one leg

déhancher [3] [deɑ̃ʃe] **se déhancher** VPR 1 *(en marchant)* to sway (one's hips) 2 *(sans bouger)* to stand with one's weight on one leg

déharnacher [3] [dearnaʃe] VT to unharness

DEHORS [dəɔr] NM 1 *(surface extérieure d'une boîte, d'un bâtiment)* outside
2 *(plein air)* outside; **les bruits du d.** the noises from outside
3 *(étranger)* **menace venue du d.** threat from abroad
4 *Sport (en patinage)* outside edge; **faire un d.** to go on one's outside edge
NMPL *(apparences)* appearances; **sous des d. égoïstes** beneath a selfish exterior
ADV *(à l'extérieur)* outside; *(en plein air)* outside, outdoors, out of doors; *(hors de chez soi)* out; **manger d.** to eat outside; **dormir d.** to sleep outdoors *or* (out) in the open; **il passe tout son temps d.** he spends all his time outside *or* outdoors *or* out of doors; **on ne voit rien de d.** you can't see anything from the outside; **passe par d. pour aller dans la cuisine** go round the outside to get to the kitchen; **elle est toujours d.** she's always out (and about); **mettre qch d.** to put sth out; *Fam* **mettre qn d.** to kick sb out; *(renvoyer)* to sack sb; *très Fam* **si tu recommences je te fous d.** do it again and you're out (on your ear)
• **en dehors** ADV 1 *(à l'extérieur)* outside 2 *(vers l'extérieur)* **avoir** *ou* **marcher les pieds en d.** to walk with one's feet turned out
• **en dehors de** PRÉP 1 *(à l'extérieur de)* outside 2 *(excepté)* apart from; **en d. de toi** apart from you 3 *(à l'écart de)* **une petite auberge en d. des grands axes** a small inn off the beaten track; **il se tient toujours en d. des discussions** he always keeps out of discussions; **reste en d. de leur dispute** stay out of *or* don't get involved in their quarrel 4 *(au-delà de)* outside (of), beyond; **en d. de ses capacités** beyond his/her capabilities

déhoussable [deusabl] ADJ with loose *or* removable covers, with a loose *or* removable cover

déification [deifikasjɔ̃] NF deification

déifier [9] [deifje] VT to deify, to turn into a god

déisme [deism] NM deism

déiste [deist] ADJ deistic, deistical
NMF deist

déité [deite] NF deity, god

déj [deʒ] NM *Fam* **petit d.** breakfast▫, *Br* brekkie, brekky

DÉJÀ [deʒa]

- already **1, 2**
- ever **2**
- again **4**
- yet **1**
- as it is **3**

ADV 1 *(dès maintenant, dès lors)* already; **d. là!** here already!; **j'ai fini – d.!** I've finished – already!; **cela fait trois ans d.** it's been three years already; **est-ce qu'il est d. parti?** has he left yet?; *(exprimant la surprise)* has he left already?; **il doit être d. loin** he must be far away by now; **il savait d. lire à l'âge de quatre ans** he already knew how to read at the age of four; **enfant, il aimait d. les fleurs** even as a child he liked flowers; **d. en 1900** as early as 1900; **on serait d. riches!** we would be rich by now!
2 *(précédemment)* already; **je vous l'ai d. dit** I've told you already; **vous êtes d. allé au Canada?** have you ever been to Canada?; **il l'a d. vue quelque part** he's seen her somewhere before
3 *(emploi expressif)* **j'aurais dû le faire il y a d. trois jours** I should have done it three days ago as it is; **il est d'accord sur le principe, c'est d. beaucoup** he's agreed on the principle, that's something; **d. qu'il est en mauvaise santé** he's in poor health as it is; **elle est d. assez riche** she's rich enough as it is; **ce n'est d. pas si mal** you could do worse; **c'est d. quelque chose** it's better than nothing; **donne dix euros, ce sera d. ça** give ten euros, that'll be a start; **on a perdu une valise, mais ni l'argent ni les passeports, c'est d. ça!** we lost a case, but not our money or passports, which is something at least!; **il faut d. qu'il ait son examen** he needs to pass his exam first
4 *Fam (pour réitérer une question)* again▫; **tu as payé combien, d.?** how much did you pay again?

déjanté, -e [deʒɑ̃te] *Fam* ADJ wacko, *Br* mental
NM,F headcase, *Br* nutter

déjanter [3] [deʒɑ̃te] VT *(pneu)* to remove from its rim, to take the rim off
VI *Fam* to flip one's lid, to lose it

déjà-vu [deʒavy] NM INV 1 *(banalité)* commonplace; **c'est du d. comme idée** that idea's a bit banal 2 *(sensation)* **(sensation** *ou* **impression de) d.** (feeling of) déjà vu

déjection [deʒɛksjɔ̃] NF 1 *Physiol (action)* evacuation 2 *Géol (d'un volcan)* **déjections** ejecta
• **déjections** NFPL *Physiol* faeces

déjeté, -e [deʒte] ADJ 1 *Fam (diminué physiquement)* worn, worn-down; *Hum* **elle n'est pas déjetée!** she's pretty well preserved! 2 *(dévié ▸ mur, corps)* lop-sided, crooked; *(▸ colonne vertébrale)* twisted 3 *Belg Fam (en désordre)* messy; *(déformé)* deformed▫

déjeter [27] [deʒte] VT to make lop-sided

déjeuner[1] [5] [deʒœne] VI 1 *(le midi)* to (have) lunch; **invite-le à d.** invite him for *or* to lunch; **nous avons les Dupont à d. dimanche** the Duponts are coming for lunch on Sunday; **j'ai déjeuné d'une salade** I had a salad for lunch; **j'ai fait d. les enfants plus tôt** I gave the children an early lunch 2 *Belg, Can & Suisse & (régional en France) (le matin)* to have breakfast

déjeuner[2] [deʒœne] NM 1 *(repas de la mi-journée)* lunch; **prendre son d.** to have lunch; **un d. d'affaires** a business lunch; **d. sur l'herbe** picnic (lunch); **qu'est-ce qu'il y a pour le d.?** what's for lunch?
2 *Belg, Can & Suisse & (régional en France) (repas du matin)* breakfast
3 *(tasse et soucoupe)* (large) breakfast cup and saucer
4 *(locution)* **d. de soleil** *(sentiment)* short-lived feeling, flash in the pan

déjouer [6] [deʒwe] VT *(vigilance)* to evade, to elude; *(complot, machination, plan)* to thwart, to foil; *(feinte)* to outsmart

déjuger [17] [deʒyʒe] **se déjuger** VPR *(changer d'avis)* to go back on *or* to reverse one's decision

DEL [deəl] NF *Électron (abrév* **diode électroluminescente)** LED

delà [dəla] *voir* **deçà, au-delà, par-delà**

délabré, -e [delabre] ADJ 1 *(en ruine ▸ maison, mur)* dilapidated, crumbling 2 *(qui n'est plus florissant ▸ santé, réputation)* ruined

délabrement [delabrəmɑ̃] NM 1 *(d'un bâtiment)* disrepair, ruin, dilapidation 2 *(d'un esprit, d'un corps)* deterioration; **les patients étaient dans un état de d. total** the patients were in a state of total neglect 3 *(d'une réputation)* ruin; *(d'une fortune)* depletion

délabrer [3] [delabre] VT 1 *(bâtiment, meuble)* to ruin 2 *(santé)* to ruin; *(organe)* to damage 3 *(réputation)* to ruin
VPR **se délabrer** 1 *(bâtiment)* to go to ruins; *(meuble)* to become rickety, to fall apart 2 *(entreprise)* to collapse; *(santé)* to deteriorate

délacer [16] [delase] VT *(soulier, botte)* to undo (the laces of); *(corset, robe)* to unlace
VPR **se délacer** 1 *(emploi réfléchi) (ôter ses souliers)* to undo *or* to unlace one's shoes; *(ôter ses bottes)* to undo *or* to unlace one's boots; *(ôter son corset)* to unlace one's corset; *(ôter sa robe)* to unlace one's dress 2 *(soulier, botte)* to come undone; *(corset, robe)* to come unlaced

délai [dele] NM 1 *(répit)* extension (of time); **demande un d. pour trouver l'argent** ask for more time to find the money; **donner** *ou* **accorder un d. (supplémentaire) à qn** to grant sb an extension; **laissez-moi un d. de réflexion** give me time to think
2 *(temps fixé)* time limit; **dans le d. prescrit** *ou* **fixé** within the required *or* allotted time, on time; **quel est le d. à respecter?** what is the deadline?; **d. d'attente** waiting period; **d. de carence** waiting period; **d. de chargement** loading time; **d. de commercialisation** *(d'un produit)* launching period; **d. de congé** term of notice; **d. de crédit** credit period; **d. d'embarquement** loading time; **d. d'exécution** deadline; *(de livraison, de production)* lead time; **d. de garantie** guarantee period, term of guarantee; **d. garanti de livraison** guaranteed delivery period; **d. de grâce** period of grace; **un d. de grâce de dix jours** ten days' grace; **d. de livraison** delivery time; **d. de paiement** *(fixé par contrat)* term of payment; **demander un d. de paiement** to request a postponement of payment; **d. de préavis** term of notice; **d. de production** production lead time; **d. de réachat** repurchase period; **d. de recouvrement** break-even period; **d. de récupération du capital investi** payback period; **d. de réflexion** cooling-off period; **d. de règlement** settlement period; **d. de remboursement** payback period; **d. de rigueur** strict deadline; **avant le 20 février, d. de rigueur** by 20 February at the very latest; **d. de validité** period of validity
3 *(période d'attente)* waiting period; **il faut un d. de trois jours avant que votre compte soit crédité** the cheque will be credited to your account after a period of three working days
• **à bref délai** ADV shortly, soon
• **dans les délais** ADV within the required *or* allotted time, on time
• **dans les meilleurs délais, dans les plus brefs délais** ADV in the shortest possible time, as soon as possible
• **dans un délai de** PRÉP within (a period of); **livrable dans un d. de 30 jours** allow 30 days for delivery
• **sans délai** ADV without delay, immediately, forthwith

> Il faut noter que le nom anglais **delay** est un faux ami. Il signifie **retard**.

délai-congé [delɛkɔ̃ʒe] *(pl* **délais-congés)** NM *Jur* term of notice

délaie *etc voir* **délayer**

délaissement [delɛsmɑ̃] NM 1 *(abandon ▸ par un époux)* desertion; *(▸ par un ami)* neglecting

2 *(solitude)* loneliness
3 *(désengagement ▸ d'une activité)* neglecting, dropping
4 *Jur (d'un bien)* relinquishment; *(d'un droit)* relinquishing, renunciation

délaisser [4] [delese] **VT 1** *(quitter ▸ époux)* to desert; *(▸ ami)* to neglect **2** *(ne plus exercer ▸ temporairement)* to neglect; *(▸ définitivement)* to give up **3** *Jur (droit, succession)* to relinquish, to forego

délassant, -e [delasɑ̃, -ɑ̃t] **ADJ** *(bain, lotion)* relaxing, soothing; *(film, lecture)* light, entertaining

délassement [delasmɑ̃] **NM 1** *(passe-temps)* way of relaxing **2** *(état)* relaxation, rest; **avoir besoin de d.** to need to relax

délasser [3] [delase] **VT** *(physiquement)* to relax, to refresh, to soothe; *(mentalement)* to relax, to soothe
VPR se délasser to relax

délateur, -trice [delatœr, -tris] **NM,F** *Péj* informer

délation [delasjɔ̃] **NF** denouncing, informing; **mais ce serait de la d.!** but that would be tantamount to denunciation!

délatrice [delatris] *voir* **délateur**

délavage [delavaʒ] **NM 1** *(d'un tissu)* fading **2** *(de terres)* soaking, waterlogging

délavé, -e [delave] **ADJ 1** *(tissu)* faded; *(jean ▸ volontairement)* faded, stone-washed **2** *(terres)* waterlogged

délaver [3] [delave] **VT 1** *(tissu)* to fade **2** *(terre)* to soak (with water)

délayage [delejaʒ] **NM 1** *(mélange ▸ de farine, de poudre)* mixing; *(▸ de peinture)* thinning out **2** *Fig Péj (d'un discours)* padding out; *(d'une idee, d'un exposé)* watering down; **faire du d.** *Br* to waffle, *Am* to spout off; **elle fait du d. en attendant la liaison avec Moscou** she's filling in time while she waits for the Moscow link-up

délayer [11] [deleje] **VT 1** *(mélanger ▸ farine, poudre)* to mix; *(▸ peinture)* to thin **2** *Fig Péj (discours)* to pad *or* to spin out; *(idée, exposé)* to water down

Delco® [delko] **NM** *Aut* distributor

déleatur [deleatyr] **NM INV** *Typ* delete (mark), dele

délectable [delɛktabl] **ADJ** *Littéraire* delectable, delightful

délectation [delɛktasjɔ̃] **NF** *Littéraire* delight, delectation

délecter [4] [delɛkte] **se délecter VPR** *Littéraire* **se d. à qch/à faire qch** to take great delight in sth/in doing sth; **je me délecte à la regarder** I find her delightful to watch

délégalisation [delegalizasjɔ̃] **NF** *Jur* criminalization

délégaliser [3] [delegalize] **VT** *Jur* to criminalize

délégant, -e [delegɑ̃, -ɑ̃t] **NM,F** *Jur* delegant

délégataire [delegatɛr] **NMF** delegatee

délégateur, -trice [delegatœr, -tris] **NM,F** delegator

délégation [delegasjɔ̃] **NF 1** *(groupe envoyé)* delegation; **envoyé en d. (auprès de qn)** sent as a delegation (to sb); **les élèves sont allés trouver le directeur en d.** a delegation of pupils went to see the head teacher
2 *(commission)* commission
3 *(fait de mandater)* delegation; **agir par d. pour qn** to act on the authority of *or* as a proxy for sb; **d. de pouvoirs** delegation of powers; **d. de signature** power of attorney; **d. de vote** proxy voting
4 *(dans des noms d'organismes)* delegation
5 *Jur (de dette)* assignment, transfer

délégatrice [delegatris] *voir* **délégateur**

délégué, -e [delege] **NM,F** delegate, representative; **d. de classe** = pupil elected to represent his or her class at "conseils de classe", ≃ class rep; **d. commercial** sales representative; **d. des parents** parents' representative; **d. du personnel** staff representative; **d. syndical** union representative, shop steward

déléguer [18] [delege] **VT 1** *(envoyer ▸ groupe, personne)* to delegate; **j'ai délégué mon oncle pour voter à ma place** I have asked my uncle to cast my vote **2** *(transmettre ▸ pouvoir)* to delegate **3** *Jur (créance)* to assign, to transfer
USAGE ABSOLU il faut savoir d. you must learn to delegate

délestage [delɛstaʒ] **NM 1** *Aviat & Naut* unballasting **2** *Transp* relief; **itinéraire de d.** relief route; **opération de d.** scheme for relieving congestion **3** *Élec* selective power cut

délester [3] [deleste] **VT 1** *Fam Hum (voler)* **d. qn de qch** to relieve sb of sth
2 *(décharger)* **d. qn d'une valise/d'une obligation** to relieve sb of a suitcase/of an obligation
3 *Aviat & Naut* to unballast
4 *Transp* to relieve traffic congestion on
5 *Élec (secteur)* to cut off power from, to black out
VPR se délester se d. de to get rid of

délétère [deletɛr] **ADJ 1** *(gaz)* noxious, *Sout* deleterious **2** *(doctrine, pouvoir)* obnoxious, *Sout* deleterious

délibérant, -e [deliberɑ̃, -ɑ̃t] **ADJ** *(assemblée)* deliberative

délibératif, -ive [deliberatif, -iv] **ADJ** *(fonction)* deliberative; **avoir voix délibérative** to be entitled to speak and vote

délibération [deliberasjɔ̃] **NF 1** *(discussion)* deliberation; **le projet sera mis en d.** the project will be debated; **après d. du jury** after due deliberation by the jury **2** *(réflexion)* deliberation, consideration; **après (mûre) d.** after careful consideration
• **délibérations NFPL** *(décisions)* resolutions, decisions

délibérative [deliberativ] *voir* **délibératif**

délibéré, -e [delibere] **ADJ 1** *(intentionné)* deliberate, wilful **2** *(décidé)* resolute, determined, thought-out
NM deliberation of the court; **mettre en d.** to adjourn for further deliberation

délibérément [deliberemɑ̃] **ADV 1** *(intentionnellement)* deliberately, intentionally, wilfully **2** *(après réflexion)* after thinking it over (long and hard), after due consideration

délibérer [18] [delibere] **VI 1** *(discuter)* to deliberate; **le jury ayant délibéré** after due deliberation by the jury; **d. de** to deliberate **2** *Littéraire (réfléchir)* to ponder, to deliberate

délicat, -e [delika, -at] **ADJ 1** *(fragile ▸ tissu)* delicate; *(▸ peau)* sensitive; *(▸ santé)* delicate, frail; *(▸ intestin, estomac)* sensitive, delicate; *(▸ enfant, plante)* fragile
2 *(sensible ▸ palais)* discerning, delicate
3 *(subtil ▸ dentelle, aquarelle, nuance, travail)* delicate, fine; *(▸ doigts, traits)* delicate, dainty; *(▸ mets, saveur)* refined; *(▸ odeur)* delicate; **il posa le vase d'un geste d.** he put the vase down delicately *or* gently
4 *(difficile ▸ situation)* delicate, awkward, tricky; *(▸ opération chirurgicale, problème)* difficult, tricky; *(▸ question)* delicate, sensitive; **c'est d., je n'aurais pas voulu que cela se sache** it's tricky, I'd have preferred it to have remained a secret
5 *(courtois)* thoughtful, considerate; **c'est un geste d. que de téléphoner avant d'y aller** it's a considerate gesture to phone before going; **quelle délicate attention!** how thoughtful!, how considerate!
6 *(difficile à contenter)* fussy, particular; **être d. sur un point d'honneur** to be particular about a point of honour; **être d. sur la nourriture** to be fussy about one's food, to be a fussy eater
7 *(scrupuleux ▸ conscience, procédé)* scrupulous; **elle est peu délicate en affaires** she's rather unscrupulous when it comes to business
NM,F faire le d. *(devant un mets)* to be fussy; *(devant le sang, la malhonnêteté)* to be squeamish; **ne fais pas le d., tu en as entendu bien d'autres!** don't act so shocked, you've heard worse than that in your life!; **quel petit d.!** what a sensitive soul!

délicatement [delikatmɑ̃] **ADV 1** *(sans brusquerie ▸ poser, toucher)* delicately, gently; *(▸ travailler, orner)* delicately, daintily **2** *(agréablement et subtilement ▸ peindre, écrire)* delicately, finely; *(▸ parfumer)* delicately, subtly **3** *(avec tact)* delicately, tactfully

délicatesse [delikatɛs] **NF 1** *(subtilité ▸ d'une saveur, d'un coloris)* delicacy, subtlety; *(▸ d'une dentelle, d'un visage)* delicacy, fineness, daintiness; *(▸ d'un travail artisanal)* delicacy; *(▸ d'une mélodie)* subtlety; **elle posa les verres sur la table avec d.** she put the glasses down gently on the table; **avoir une grande d. de goût** to have very refined tastes
2 *(fragilité ▸ d'un tissu)* delicate texture, fragility; *(▸ de la peau)* sensitivity; *(▸ de la santé)* delicacy, frailty; *(▸ de l'intestin, de l'estomac)* sensitivity, delicacy; *(▸ d'un enfant, d'une plante)* fragility
3 *(honnêteté)* scrupulousness, punctiliousness; **agir en affaires avec une grande d.** to be scrupulously honest in business
4 *(tact)* delicacy, tact; **il n'en a rien dit, par d.** he kept quiet out of tact, he tactfully said nothing; **quelle d.!** how tactful!
5 *(difficulté ▸ d'une situation, d'une opération)* delicacy, sensitiveness, trickiness
• **délicatesses NFPL** *Littéraire (gestes aimables)* kind attentions; **elle a eu des délicatesses à notre égard** she showed consideration towards us
• **en délicatesse ADJ être en d. avec qn** to be on bad terms with sb; **nous sommes en d.** relations are a bit strained between us at the moment

délice [delis] **NM 1** *(source de plaisir)* delight; **c'est un d.** *(mets, odeur)* it's delicious; *(d'être au soleil, de nager)* it's sheer delight **2** *(ravissement)* delight, (great) pleasure; **ses paroles la remplissaient de d.** his/her words filled her with delight
• **délices NFPL** *(plaisirs)* delights, pleasures; **les délices de la campagne** the delights of the countryside; **faire les délices de qn** to delight sb, to give sb great pleasure; **faire ses délices de qch** to take delight in sth, to enjoy sth greatly
• **avec délice(s) ADV** with great pleasure, with delight

délicieuse [delisjøz] *voir* **délicieux**

délicieusement [delisjøzmɑ̃] **ADV 1** *(agréablement)* deliciously, delightfully, exquisitely; **elle était d. parfumée** her perfume was delightful *or* divine **2** *(en intensif)* **son repas était d. bon** his/her meal was absolutely delicious; **elle était d. bien dans ses bras** she was wonderfully happy in his arms; **il peint d. bien** he paints delightfully well

délicieux, -euse [delisjø, -øz] **ADJ 1** *(qui procure du plaisir ▸ repas, parfum, sensation)* delicious; *(▸ lieu, promenade, chapeau)* lovely, delightful **2** *(qui charme ▸ femme, geste)* lovely, delightful; **votre sœur est délicieuse!** your sister's a delight (to be with)!

délictuel, -elle [deliktɥɛl] **ADJ** *Jur (nature)* criminal

délictueux, -euse [deliktɥø, -øz] **ADJ** *Jur (fait, activité)* criminal

délié, -e [delje] **ADJ 1** *(sans épaisseur ▸ écriture)* fine; *(▸ cou)* slender; **avoir la silhouette déliée** to be slender **2** *(agile ▸ esprit)* sharp; *(▸ doigts)* nimble, agile; **avoir la langue déliée** to be chatty
NM *Typ* upstroke

délier [9] [delje] **VT 1** *(dénouer ▸ ruban, mains)* to untie; *(▸ gerbe, bouquet)* to undo **2** *(rendre agile)* **un exercice pour d. les jambes/les doigts** an exercise to warm up the leg muscles/the fingers; **le vin lui a délié la langue** the wine loosened his/her tongue **3** *(délivrer ▸ prisonnier)* to untie; **d. qn de** *(promesse, engagement)* to free *or* to release sb from
VPR se délier 1 *(se défaire)* to come undone *or* untied, to come loose
2 *(langue)* to loosen; **après quelques verres, les langues se délient** a few drinks help to loosen people's tongues
3 *(s'exercer)* **se d. les jambes/les doigts** to warm up one's leg muscles/one's fingers
4 se d. de to release oneself from; **se d. d'une obligation** to free oneself from an obligation

délimitation [delimitasjɔ̃] **NF 1** *(fait de circonscrire ▸ un terrain)* demarcation, delimitation; *(▸ un sujet, un rôle)* defining, delineating, delimitation **2** *(limites)* delimitation

délimiter [3] [delimite] VT *(espace, frontière)* to demarcate, to delimit, to circumscribe; *(sujet, rôle)* to define, to delineate

délimiteur [delimitœr] NM *Ordinat* delimiter; **d. de bloc** block delimiter, block marker; **d. de champ** field delimiter

délinquance [delɛ̃kɑ̃s] NF criminality; **d. juvénile** juvenile delinquency; **petite d.** petty crime

délinquant, -e [delɛ̃kɑ̃, -ɑ̃t] ADJ delinquent
NM,F offender; **jeune d., d. juvénile** juvenile delinquent; **d. mineur** juvenile offender; **d. primaire** first offender; **d. sexuel** sex offender

déliquescence [delikesɑ̃s] NF **1** *Chim* deliquescence **2** *(déclin)* gradual decay, creeping rot
• **en déliquescence** ADJ declining, decaying
ADV **tomber en d.** to be on the decline, to fall into decline

déliquescent, -e [delikesɑ̃, -ɑ̃t] ADJ **1** *Chim* deliquescent **2** *(déclinant)* declining, decaying

délirant, -e [delirɑ̃, -ɑ̃t] ADJ **1** *(malade)* delirious; **fièvre délirante** delirious fever **2** *Fam (insensé ▸ accueil, foule)* frenzied, tumultuous; *(▸ joie)* frenzied; *(▸ imagination)* frenzied, wild; *(▸ luxe, prix)* unbelievable, incredible; **une atmosphère complètement délirante** an atmosphere of total delirium; **c'est d. de travailler dans de telles conditions** working in such conditions is sheer madness *or* lunacy

délire [delir] NM **1** *Méd* delirium, delirious state; **avoir le d.** to be delirious *or* raving; **d. alcoolique** alcoholic dementia; *Psy* **d. de grandeur** delusions of grandeur; **d. hallucinatoire** hallucination
2 *(incohérences)* **un d. d'ivrogne** a drunkard's ravings
3 *Fam (moment amusant)* **le d.!** it was *Br* wicked *or Am* awesome!; **on s'est tapé un super d.!** we had a *Br* wicked *or Am* awesome time!
4 *Fam (locution)* **partout où il se produit, c'est le** *ou* **du d.** wherever he performs, audiences go wild *or* crazy; **sa nouvelle collection, c'est du d. total** his/her new collection is out of this world; **demander aux gens de payer 50 pour cent en plus, c'est du d.!** asking people to pay 50 percent over the odds is completely insane!
• **en délire** ADJ delirious, ecstatic; **des supporters en d.** delirious *or* frenzied supporters

délirer [3] [delire] VI **1** *(malade)* to be delirious, to rave; **d. de joie** to be delirious, to be mad with joy; *Fig* **tu délires!** you're out of your mind! **2** *Fam (s'amuser)* to have a great time, *Am* to have a blast

delirium tremens [delirjɔmtremɛ̃s] NM INV delirium tremens; **avoir une crise de d.** to have an attack of delirium tremens

délit [deli] NM **1** *Jur (infraction) Br* (nonindictable) offence, *Am* misdemeanor; **d. d'adultère** adultery; **d. civil** tort; **d. de fuite** = failure to stop after causing a road accident; **d. d'imprudence** negligence; **être incarcéré pour d. d'opinion** to be put in prison because of one's beliefs; **d. pénal** criminal offence; **d. politique** political offence; **d. de presse** press offence; **d. sans victime** victimless crime; *Fam* **ils l'ont arrêté pour d. de sale gueule** they arrested him because they didn't like the look of him **2** *Com* **d. d'initié** insider trading *or* dealing

délivrance [delivrɑ̃s] NF **1** *Littéraire (libération ▸ d'une ville)* liberation, deliverance; *(▸ d'un captif)* release
2 *(soulagement)* relief; **son départ fut une vraie d.** it was a real relief when he/she left; *Euph* **attendre la d.** to await death as a release from pain
3 *(d'un visa, d'un certificat, d'un brevet)* issue
4 *Méd (accouchement)* delivery; *(expulsion du placenta)* delivery of the afterbirth

délivrer [3] [delivre] VT **1** *(libérer ▸ prisonnier)* to release, to (set) free; **d. le peuple** to set the people free; **d. qn de ses liens** to free sb from his/her bonds
2 *(soulager)* to relieve; **se sentir délivré** to feel relieved; **ainsi délivré de ses incertitudes, il décida de...** thus freed from doubt, he decided to...; **tu me délivres d'un grand poids** you've taken a weight off my shoulders; *Bible* **délivre-nous du mal** deliver us from evil
3 *(visa, certificat, brevet)* to issue; *(ordonnance, autorisation)* to give, to issue
4 *(faire parvenir ▸ paquet, courrier)* to deliver; *(▸ signal)* to put out
VPR **se délivrer 1** *(se libérer)* to free oneself **2** *Fig* **se d. de** to get rid of

délocalisation [delɔkalizasjɔ̃] NF **1** *(dans le cadre de la décentralisation)* relocation **2** *Écon (d'entreprises vers l'étranger)* offshoring; **la d. des capitaux** the expatriation of capital

délocaliser [3] [delɔkalize] VT **1** *(dans le cadre de la décentralisation)* to relocate **2** *Écon (des entreprises vers l'étranger)* to offshore; **d. des capitaux** to expatriate capital
VPR **se délocaliser** to relocate

déloger [17] [delɔʒe] VT **1** *(congédier ▸ locataire)* to throw *or* to turn out, to oust; **après trois ans, comment d. les locataires?** after three years, how do you get the tenants out? **2** *(débusquer ▸ lapin)* to start **3** *(objet coincé)* to dislodge (**de** from)
VI **1** *(décamper)* to move out (hurriedly); *Fam* **allez, déloge!** *(pousse-toi)* come on, move (out of the way)!; **il finira bien par d.** he'll clear off eventually; **faire d. qn** to throw sb out, to get sb to move **2** *Belg (découcher)* to sleep out; **il a délogé hier** he didn't come home last night

déloquer [deloke] **se déloquer** VPR *Fam* to strip off, to get undressed

déloyal, -e, -aux, -ales [delwajal, -o] ADJ **1** *(infidèle ▸ ami)* disloyal, unfaithful, *Littéraire* untrue **2** *(malhonnête ▸ concurrence)* unfair; *(▸ méthode)* dishonest, underhand; *Sport* **un coup d.** a foul

déloyalement [delwajalmɑ̃] ADV *(agir ▸ d'un ami)* disloyally; *(▸ d'un concurrent)* unfairly; *(jouer aux cartes)* dishonestly

déloyauté [delwajote] NF **1** *(caractère perfide)* disloyalty, treacherousness **2** *(action)* disloyal act, betrayal; **commettre une d. envers qn** to play sb false, to be disloyal to sb

Delphes [dɛlf] NF Delphi

delta [dɛlta] NM INV *(lettre)* delta
NM *Géog* **d. (littoral)** delta; **le d. du Nil** the Nile Delta

deltaïque [dɛltaik] ADJ delta *(avant n)*, *Sout* deltaic

deltaplane, delta-plane [dɛltaplan] *(pl* **deltaplanes** *ou* **delta-planes)** NM **1** *(véhicule)* hang-glider **2** *(activité)* hang-gliding; **faire du d.** to go hang-gliding

deltiste [dɛltist] NMF hang-glider *(person)*

deltoïde [dɛltɔid] *Anat* ADJ deltoid
NM deltoid

déluge [delyʒ] NM **1** *(averse)* downpour, deluge **2** *Bible* **le D.** the Flood; *Fam* **ça remonte au d.** it's ancient history; **ne remonte pas au d.** *(en racontant une histoire)* give us the short version! **3** *(abondance ▸ de paroles, de larmes, de plaintes)* flood, deluge; *(▸ d'injures)* torrent; *(▸ de coups)* shower; **je reçois un d. de publicités par la poste** I'm inundated with junk mail; **le standard est submergé par un d. d'appels** the switchboard is jammed with calls

déluré, -e [delyre] ADJ **1** *(malin ▸ enfant, air)* quick, sharp, resourceful **2** *Péj (effronté ▸ fille)* forward, brazen
NM,F **un petit d.** a smart kid; **une petite délurée** a brazen little thing

délurer [3] [delyre] VT **1** *Littéraire (éveiller)* to awaken to the world around **2** *(dévergonder)* **d. qn** to open sb's eyes
VPR **se délurer 1** *(devenir éveillé)* to wake up; *Fig* to become aware **2** *(se dévergonder)* to become streetwise

délustrer [3] [delystre] VT *Tex* to take the lustre *or* gloss off

démagnétisation [demaɲetizasjɔ̃] NF *(d'une bande, d'une carte)* demagnetization

démagnétiser [3] [demaɲetize] VT *(bande, carte)* to demagnetize
VPR **se démagnétiser** to become demagnetized

démago [demago] *Fam* ADJ demagogic
NMF demagogue

démagogie [demagɔʒi] NF demagogy, demagoguery

démagogique [demagɔʒik] ADJ demagogic, demagogical

démagogue [demagɔg] ADJ rabble-rousing, *Sout* demagogic; **ils sont très démagogues** they're real rabble-rousers
NMF demagogue

démaillage [demajaʒ] NM **1** *(d'un tricot)* undoing, unravelling **2** *Naut* unlinking

démailler [3] [demaje] VT **1** *(défaire ▸ tricot)* to undo, to unravel; *(▸ bas, collant) Br* to ladder, *Am* to run; *(▸ chaîne)* to unlink **2** *Pêche* to take out of the net
VPR **se démailler** *(tricot)* to unravel, to fray, to come undone; *(bas, collant)* to run, *Br* to ladder

démailloter [3] [demajɔte] VT *(doigt blessé)* to take the bandage off; *(momie)* to unwrap; **d. un bébé** to take off a baby's *Br* nappy *or Am* diaper

demain [dəmɛ̃] ADV **1** *(le jour après aujourd'hui)* tomorrow; **d. matin/après-midi/soir** tomorrow morning/afternoon/evening *or* night; **à partir de d.** as from tomorrow, from tomorrow on, starting tomorrow; **pendant la journée de d.** tomorrow; **les journaux de d.** tomorrow's papers; **d. en huit** a week tomorrow, *Br* tomorrow week; **d. en quinze** two weeks tomorrow, *Br* a fortnight tomorrow; **salut, à d.!** bye, see you tomorrow!; *Fam* **avance, sinon on y sera encore d.!** come on, let's not stay here all night!; **d. il fera jour** tomorrow is another day; *Hum* **d. on rase** *ou* **rasera gratis** tomorrow never comes; **ce n'est pas d. la veille** it's not going to happen overnight *or* in a hurry; **ce n'est pas d. la veille que le système changera** the system's not going to change overnight; **l'égalité des salaires n'est pas pour d.** equal pay isn't just around the corner **2** *(à l'avenir)* in the future; **et si d. ils nous déclaraient la guerre?** what if in the future they were to declare war on us?
NM tomorrow
• **de demain** ADJ *(futur)* **les architectes/écoles de d.** the architects/schools of tomorrow

démanché, -e [demɑ̃ʃe] ADJ **1** *(membre)* dislocated **2** *(outil)* handleless, with no handle
NM *Mus* shift

démanchement [demɑ̃ʃmɑ̃] NM **1** *(d'un membre)* dislocation **2** *(d'un outil)* removal of the handle

démancher [3] [demɑ̃ʃe] VT *(couteau, marteau)* to remove the handle of; *(lame)* to work out of its handle
VI *Mus* to shift
VPR **se démancher 1** *(balai)* to lose its handle, to work loose in the handle **2** *Fam (se démener)* **se d. pour obtenir qch** to move heaven and earth *or* to bust a gut to get sth **3** *(se déboîter)* **se d. l'épaule/le bras** to put one's shoulder/arm out, to dislocate one's shoulder/arm

demande [dəmɑ̃d] NF **1** *(requête)* request; **d. d'argent** request for money; **adresser toute d. de renseignements à...** send all inquiries to...; **accéder à/refuser une d.** to grant/to turn down a request; **d. (en mariage)** (marriage) proposal; **faire sa d. en mariage (auprès de qn)** to propose (to sb); **d. de rançon** ransom demand
2 *Admin & Com* application; **faire une d. de bourse/visa** to apply for a scholarship/visa; **d. d'indemnité/de dommages-intérêts** claim for compensation/damages; **remplir une d.** to fill in an application (form); **d. d'emploi** *(candidature)* job application; *(petite annonce)* job wanted advertisement; **demandes d'emploi** *(dans un journal)* situations wanted
3 *Écon* demand; **l'offre et la d.** supply and demand; **répondre à la d.** to meet demand; **la d. est en hausse/en baisse** demand is up/down; **la d. croissante d'appareils photo numériques** the increasing demand for digital cameras; **il y a une forte d. de traducteurs** translators are in great demand, translators are very much sought after; **d. des consommateurs** consumer demand; **d. excédentaire** overdemand; **d. du marché** market demand; **d. prévisionnelle** projected demand; **d. primaire** primary demand; **d. soutenue** full demand
4 *Jur* **d. accessoire** related claim; **d. en justice** petition; **d. principale** main claim; **d. en renvoi** request for transfer of a case (to another court); **d. subsidiaire** subsidiary claim
5 *(expression d'un besoin)* need; **la d. doit venir du patient lui-même** the patient must express a need; **donne-leur de la tendresse, car il y a une d.**

de leur part be loving to them, they're in need of it

6 *École* **d. biochimique/biologique en oxygène** biochemical/biological oxygen demand

7 *Cartes* bid

• **à la demande** ADJ & ADV on demand

• **à la demande de, sur la demande de** PRÉP at the request of; **faire qch à** *ou* **sur la d. de qn** to do sth at sb's request

• **à la demande générale** ADV by popular request

> Il faut noter que le nom anglais **demand** est un faux ami. Il signifie **exigence**.

DEMANDER [3] [dəmɑ̃de]

VT	
• to ask **4**	• to ask for **1–3**
• to apply for **1**	• to claim **2**
• to demand **2**	• to want **3, 6**
• to send for **5**	• to require **6, 7**
• to need **7**	
USAGE ABSOLU	
• to ask	
VPR	
• to ask **1**	• to wonder **2**

VT 1 *(solliciter ▸ rendez-vous, conseil, addition)* to ask for, *Sout* to request; *(▸ emploi, visa)* to apply for; **d. un congé** to ask for leave; **le cuisinier a demandé son samedi** the cook has asked to have Saturday off; **qu'as-tu demandé pour Noël?** what did you ask for for Christmas?; **d. l'aumône** *ou* **la charité** to ask for charity, to beg for alms; *Fig* **je ne demande pas la charité** I'm not asking for any favours; **d. le divorce** to file *or* to petition for divorce; **d. la main de qn** to ask for sb's hand (in marriage); **d. qn en mariage** to propose to sb; **d. grâce** to ask *or* to beg for mercy; **d. pardon** to apologize; **je te demande pardon** I'm sorry; **il m'a demandé pardon de sa conduite** he apologized to me for his behaviour; **je vous demande pardon, mais c'est ma place** I beg your pardon, but this is my seat; **je vous demande pardon?** (I beg your) pardon?; **d. qch à qn** to ask sb for sth; **on nous a demandé nos passeports** we were asked for our passports; **d. une faveur** *ou* **un service à qn** to ask sb a favour; **d. son avis à qn** to ask sb's opinion; **d. un délai à son éditeur** to ask one's publisher for more time; **d. audience à qn** to request an audience with sb; **je ne t'ai jamais demandé quoi que ce soit** I never asked you for anything; **d. à qn de faire qch** to ask sb to do sth; **il m'a demandé de lui prêter ma voiture** he asked me to lend him my car

2 *(exiger ▸ indemnité, dommages)* to claim, to demand; *(▸ rançon)* to demand, to ask for; **nous demandons de meilleures conditions de travail** we want *or* we're asking for better working conditions; **d. l'ouverture d'une enquête** to call for an inquiry; **il demande qu'on lui rende justice** he wants justice; **il a demandé qu'on le laisse en paix** he asked to be left alone; **d. l'impossible** to ask (for) the impossible; **d. justice** to demand justice *or* fair treatment; **d. qch à qn** to ask sth of sb; **je ne peux pas faire ce que vous me demandez** I can't do what you're asking of me; **il ne demandait pas beaucoup à la vie** he didn't ask much of life; **combien demandez-vous de l'heure?** how much do you charge an hour?; **il en demande 50 euros** he wants *or* he's asking 50 euros for it; **il ne faut pas trop m'en d./leur en d.** you mustn't ask too much of me/them, you shouldn't expect too much of me/them; **c'est trop me d.** it's too much to ask of me, it's asking too much; **tout ce que je demande** *ou* **je ne demande qu'une chose, c'est qu'on me laisse seul** all I want *or* ask is to be left alone; **qui ne demande rien n'a rien** if you don't ask, you don't get; **je ne demande que ça** *ou* **pas mieux!** I'd be only too pleased!; **elle ne demande pas mieux que de t'héberger** she'll be only too pleased to put you up; *Fam* **ils ont tous les avantages possibles, que demande le peuple?** they've got all kinds of perks, what more could they want?; **partir sans d. son compte** *ou* **son reste** to leave without further ado *or* without so much as a by-your-leave

3 *(réclamer la présence de ▸ gén)* to want; *(▸ médecin, prêtre)* to ask for; **on te demande au téléphone** there's a call for you, you're wanted on the telephone; **il y a une demoiselle qui vous demande** there's a young lady wanting to see you; **M. Dubois est demandé au téléphone** *(annonce)* telephone for Mr Dubois; **qui demandez-vous?** *(au téléphone)* who would you like to speak to?; **demandez-moi le siège à Paris/M. Blanc** get me the head office in Paris/Mr Blanc

4 *(chercher à savoir)* to ask; **je n'ai pas compris ce qu'il m'a demandé** I didn't understand what he asked me; **d. l'heure à qn** to ask sb the time; **d. son chemin à qn** to ask sb for directions; **je lui ai demandé la raison de son départ** I asked him/her why he/she (had) left; **il y a des choses qu'il vaut mieux ne pas d.** some things are better left unasked; **d. des nouvelles de qn** to ask after sb; **j'ai demandé de tes nouvelles à Marie** I asked for news of you from Marie, I asked Marie about you; **demande-lui comment il s'appelle et d'où il vient** ask him what his name is and where he comes from; **je lui demanderai s'il peut t'aider** I'll ask him whether he can help you; **on ne t'a rien demandé (à toi)!** nobody asked YOU, nobody asked for YOUR opinion!; *Fam* **je ne te demande pas l'heure qu'il est, est-ce que je t'ai demandé si ta grand-mère fait du vélo?** mind your own business!, who asked your opinion?; *Fam* **à quoi sert la police, je vous le demande** *ou* **je vous demande un peu!** what are the police for, I ask you?; *Fam* **il avait tout peint en noir, je te demande un peu!** he'd painted everything black, I ask you!

5 *(faire venir ▸ ambulance, taxi)* to send for, to call (for)

6 *(chercher à recruter ▸ vendeur, ingénieur)* to want, to require; **on demande un livreur** *(petite annonce)* delivery boy wanted *or* required; **on demande beaucoup de secrétaires** there's a great demand for secretaries, secretaries are in great demand

7 *(nécessiter)* to require, to call for, to need; **cela demande une patience que je n'ai pas** this requires *or* needs the kind of patience I don't have; **cela demande une explication** this calls for an explanation; **cette plante demande un arrosage quotidien** this plant needs to be watered every day; **une manipulation qui demande une grande précision** an experiment that calls for the utmost precision; **ce travail demande toute votre attention** the work demands all your attention; **ce livre a demandé beaucoup de recherches** the writing of this book required much research

USAGE ABSOLU **il suffisait de d.** you only had to *or* all you had to do was ask; **il n'y a qu'à d.** you/he/*etc* only have/has to ask; **demandez à votre agent de voyages** ask your travel agent

• **demander à** VT IND to ask to; **je n'ai pas demandé à naître** I never asked to be born; **il demande à voir le chef de rayon** he wants to see the department supervisor; **je demande à parler** may I speak, please let me speak; **d. à manger/boire** to ask for something to eat/drink; **il demande à ce qu'on lui rende son argent** he's asking for *or* he wants his money back; *Fam* **demande à ce qu'on vienne te chercher** ask someone to come and collect you[□]; **ce vin demande à être bu frais** this wine should be drunk chilled; *Fam* **je demande à voir!** I'll believe it when I see it!; **je ne demande qu'à vous embaucher/aider** I'm more than willing to hire/help you; **ce pauvre petit ne demande qu'à vivre** this poor little mite's only asking for a chance to live

• **demander après** VT IND **ils ont demandé après toi** *(ils t'ont réclamé)* they asked for you; *(pour avoir de tes nouvelles)* they asked how you were, they asked after you

VPR **se demander 1** *(être demandé)* **des choses comme ça, ça ne se demande pas!** you don't ask that sort of question!; **cela ne se demande pas!** *(c'est évident)* need you ask! **2** *(s'interroger sur)* to wonder, to ask oneself; **c'est ce que je me demande** that's what I'm wondering, that's what I'd like to know; **je me demande bien pourquoi/ce que/où...** I wonder why/what/where..., I really can't think why/what/where...; **on est en droit de se d. pourquoi/comment/si...** one may rightfully ask oneself why/how/whether...; **c'est à se d. s'il n'est pas fou** one may well wonder if he isn't mad

> Il faut noter que le verbe anglais **to demand** est un faux ami. Il signifie **exiger**.

demandeur¹, -eresse [dəmɑ̃dœr, -ərɛs] NM,F *Jur* plaintiff, claimant; **d. en appel** appellant

demandeur², -euse [dəmɑ̃dœr, -øz] NM,F **1 d. d'asile** asylum-seeker; **d. d'emploi** job seeker; **je suis d. d'emploi** I'm looking for a job; **2** *Tél* caller

ADJ **les Français sont très demandeurs de ce produit** there is an enormous demand for this product in France

démangeaison [demɑ̃ʒɛzɔ̃] NF **1** *(irritation)* itch; **j'ai des démangeaisons partout** I'm itching all over; **donner des démangeaisons à qn** to make sb itch; **où ressentez-vous cette d.?** where does it *or* do you itch? **2** *Fam (envie)* itch

démanger [17] [demɑ̃ʒe] VT **ce pull le démange** that jumper makes him itch; *Fam* **ça le démangeait de dire la vérité** he was itching *or* dying to tell the truth

VI to itch; **ce pull lui démange** that jumper makes him/her itch; *Fam Fig* **la langue lui démangeait** he/she was itching *or* dying to say something

démantèlement [demɑ̃tɛlmɑ̃] NM **1** *(démolition)* demolition, pulling *or* taking to pieces **2** *(d'un réseau, d'une secte)* breaking up, dismantling **3** *Com* **d. d'entreprise** asset stripping

démanteler [25] [demɑ̃tle] VT **1** *(démolir ▸ rempart)* to demolish, to tear down **2** *(désorganiser ▸ réseau, secte)* to break up; *(▸ entreprise, service)* to dismantle

démantibuler [3] [demɑ̃tibyle] VT to demolish, to take to bits *or* pieces

VPR **se démantibuler** *Fam (se rompre)* to fall apart[□], to come to pieces[□]

démaquillage [demakijaʒ] NM make-up removal; **gel/lotion pour le d. des yeux** eye make-up removing gel/lotion

démaquillant, -e [demakijɑ̃, -ɑ̃t] ADJ **crème/lotion démaquillante** cleansing cream/lotion

NM cleanser, make-up remover; **d. pour les yeux** eye make-up remover

démaquiller [3] [demakije] VT *(yeux, visage)* to remove the make-up from; **d. qn** to remove sb's make-up

VPR **se démaquiller** to remove *or* to take off one's make-up; **se d. les yeux** to remove one's eye make-up

démarcage [demarkaʒ] = **démarquage**

démarcatif, -ive [demarkatif, -iv] ADJ demarcating

démarcation [demarkasjɔ̃] NF **1** *(limite)* demarcation, dividing line **2** *(fait de démarquer)* boundary-defining, demarcating

démarcative [demarkativ] *voir* **démarcatif**

démarchage [demarʃaʒ] NM *Com (porte-à-porte)* door-to-door selling; *(prospection)* canvassing; **faire du d. (à domicile)** to do door-to-door selling, to sell door-to-door; **d. à distance** telephone canvassing; **d. téléphonique** telephone prospecting; **d. interdit** *(sur panneau)* no hawkers; *Pol* **d. électoral** canvassing

démarche [demarʃ] NF **1** *(allure)* gait, walk; **avoir une d. gracieuse** to have a graceful gait, to walk gracefully **2** *(initiative)* step, move; **faire toutes les démarches nécessaires** to take all the necessary steps; **faire une d. auprès d'un organisme** to approach an organization; **démarches administratives/juridiques** administrative/legal procedures **3** *(approche ▸ d'un problème)* approach; **d. intellectuelle/philosophique** intellectual/philosophical approach

démarcher [3] [demarʃe] VT *(client, entreprise)* to visit

VI *(faire du porte-à-porte)* to do door-to-door selling, to sell door-to-door

démarcheur, -euse [demarʃœr, -øz] NM,F **1** *Com (représentant)* door-to-door salesman, *f* saleswoman; **d. en assurances** insurance agent **2** *(prospecteur)* canvasser; **d. en publicité** advertisement canvasser

démariage [demarjaʒ] NM *Agr* thinning out

démarketing [demarketiŋ] NM demarketing; **politique de d.** demarketing policy

démarquage [demarkaʒ] NM **1** *Com* markdown, marking down
2 *(fait d'ôter la marque)* **le d. des vêtements** *(pour les vendre moins cher)* removing the designer labels from clothes
3 *(plagiat)* copying, plagiarizing; **la pièce n'est qu'un habile d.** the play is nothing but a clever copy
4 *Sport* **le d. d'un joueur** shaking off a marker

démarque [demark] NF **1** *Com* marking down, markdown; **d. inconnue** shrinkage *(losses through shoplifting and pilfering)* **2** *Sport* freeing

démarquer [3] [demarke] VT **1** *(enlever la marque de)* **d. des vêtements** to remove the designer labels from clothes
2 *Com* to mark down
3 *(plagier)* to copy, to plagiarize
4 *Sport* to free
VPR **se démarquer 1** *Sport* to shake off one's marker **2 se d. de** to distinguish oneself *or* to be different from

démarrage [demaraʒ] NM **1** *Aut & Tech (mouvement)* moving off; **faire un d. en trombe** to shoot off
2 *(mise en marche)* starting; **le d. de la voiture** starting the car; **d. en côte** hill-start; *Ordinat* **d. automatique** autostart; *Ordinat* **d. à chaud/froid** warm/cold start
3 *(commencement)* start; **le d. d'une campagne publicitaire** the start of an advertising campaign
4 *Sport* spurt
5 *Naut* casting off, unmooring

démarrer [3] [demare] VT to start; *Ordinat* to boot (up), to start up; **on a démarré cette affaire avec très peu d'argent** we started this business with very little money
VI **1** *Aut & Tech (se mettre à fonctionner)* to start (up); *(s'éloigner ▸ voiture)* to move off; *(▸ conducteur)* to drive away *or* off; **je n'arrive pas à faire d. la voiture** I can't get the car started
2 *(débuter)* to start; **le feuilleton démarre le 18 mars** the series starts on 18 March; **faire d. un projet** to get a project off the ground
3 *(dans une progression ▸ économie)* to take off, to get off the ground; **les ventes ont bien démarré** sales have got off to a good start; **l'association a mis du temps à d.** the association got off to a slow start
4 *Sport (coureur)* to put a spurt on
5 *Naut* to cast off, to unmoor
6 *Fam (s'en aller)* to budge, *Br* to shift

démarreur [demarœr] NM *Aut & Tech* starter; **d. automatique** self-starter

démasquer [3] [demaske] VT **1** *(ôter le masque de)* to unmask
2 *(confondre ▸ traître, menteur)* to unmask, to expose; **se faire d.** to be unmasked
3 *(dévoiler ▸ hypocrisie)* to unmask, to reveal; *(▸ complot, mensonge)* to expose
4 *(locution)* **d. ses batteries** to unmask one's guns; *Fig* to show one's hand
VPR **se démasquer 1** *(ôter son masque)* to take off one's mask, to unmask oneself **2** *Fig* to throw off *or* to drop one's mask

démassification [demasifikasjõ] NF *(des médias)* demassification

démassifier [9] [demasifje] VT *(médias)* to demassify
VPR **se démassifier** to demassify

dématage [demataʒ] NM dismasting

démâter [3] [demate] VT to dismast
VI to lose its mast/masts, to be dismasted

démêlage [demelaʒ] NM *(des cheveux)* detangling, untangling

démêlant, -e [demelɑ̃, -ɑ̃t] ADJ *(baume)* conditioning
NM *(pour les cheveux)* conditioner, detangler

démêlé [demele] NM *(querelle)* quarrel; **démêlés** problems, trouble; **avoir des démêlés avec qn** to have a bit of trouble *or* a few problems with sb; **elle a eu des démêlés avec l'administration** she's had some trouble *or* problems with the authorities

démêler [4] [demele] VT **1** *(cheveux)* to untangle, to detangle, to comb out; *(nœud, filet)* to disentangle, to untangle **2** *(éclaircir ▸ mystère, affaire)* to clear up, to disentangle, to see through; **d. les intentions de qn** to fathom (out) sb's intentions; **d. la vérité du mensonge** *ou* **le vrai du faux** to disentangle truth from falsehood, to sift out the truth from the lies **3** *Littéraire (locution)* **avoir quelque chose à d. avec qn** to have a bone to pick with sb
VPR **se démêler 1** *(cheveux)* to comb out, to be disentangled; **ses cheveux se démêlent tout seuls** his/her hair combs out beautifully **2** *Vieilli* **se d. de** to extricate oneself from; **se d. de ses affaires de famille** to extricate oneself from one's family problems

démêloir [demɛlwar] NM large-toothed comb

démembrement [demɑ̃brəmɑ̃] NM *(d'un empire)* breaking up; *(d'une propriété agricole)* division

démembrer [3] [demɑ̃bre] VT *(empire)* to break up; *(propriété agricole)* to divide

déménagement [demenaʒmɑ̃] NM **1** *(changement de domicile)* move; **c'est mon quatrième d.** it's my fourth move, it's the fourth time I've moved (*Br* house); **on les a aidés à faire leur d.** we helped them to move (*Br* house); **camion de d.** *Br* removal *or Am* moving van; **entreprise de d.** *Br* removal company *or* firm, *Am* mover **2** *(déplacement des meubles)* **le d. du salon est fini** we've finished moving the furniture out of the living room **3** *(mobilier)* furniture; **le d. est arrivé** the furniture has arrived

déménager [17] [demenaʒe] VT *(salon)* to move the furniture out of, to empty of its furniture; *(piano, meubles)* to move; **j'ai tout déménagé dans ma chambre** I moved everything into my bedroom; *Fam* **qui est-ce qui vous déménage?** which *Br* removal company *or Am* movers are you using?❑
VI **1** *(changer de maison)* to move (*Br* house); **il déménage, tu veux reprendre son appartement?** he's moving out, do you want to rent his *Br* flat *or Am* apartment?; **où déménage-t-il?** where's he moving to?
2 *(changer de lieu)* to move
3 *Fam (partir)* to clear off; **il est dans mon bureau? je vais le faire d. vite fait!** in my office, is he? I'll have him out of there in no time!
4 *très Fam (déraisonner)* to be off one's nut *or* rocker, to have lost it
5 *très Fam (faire de l'effet ▸ musique)* to be mind-blowing; *(▸ plat, épice)* to blow the top of one's head off, to pack a punch; **t'as vu la blonde? elle déménage!** did you see that blonde? she's a knockout!

déménageur [demenaʒœr] NM **1** *(ouvrier) Br* removal man, *Am* (furniture) mover; *(entrepreneur) Br* furniture remover, *Am* mover **2** *Fam (homme)* great hulk (of a man); **ses gardes du corps, c'est des vrais déménageurs!** his/her bodyguards are built like barn doors!

démence [demɑ̃s] NF **1** *(gén)* insanity, madness **2** *Méd* dementia; **d. précoce** dementia praecox; **d. présénile** presenile dementia **3** *Fam (conduite déraisonnable)* **c'est de la d.!** it's madness!

démener [19] [demne] **se démener** VPR **1** *(s'agiter)* to thrash about, to struggle; **se d. comme un beau diable** to thrash about, to struggle violently **2** *(faire des efforts)* **se d. pour** to exert oneself *or* to go out of one's way (in order) to; **il faut se d. pour trouver un emploi** you have to put yourself out if you want to find a job

démens *etc voir* **démentir**

dément, -e [demɑ̃, -ɑ̃t] ADJ **1** *(gén)* mad, insane
2 *Méd* demented
3 *Fam (remarquable)* fantastic, *Br* wicked, *Am* awesome
4 *Fam Péj (inacceptable)* incredible, unbelievable
NM,F *Méd* dementia sufferer, demented person

démenti [demɑ̃ti] NM denial; *Journ* disclaimer; **publier un d.** to issue a denial; *Journ* to publish a disclaimer; **opposer un d. formel à une rumeur** to deny a rumour categorically; **le témoignage reste sans d.** the testimony remains uncontradicted

démentiel, -elle [demɑ̃sjɛl] ADJ **1** *Psy* insane **2** *Méd* dementia *(avant n)* **3** *Fig (excessif, extravagant)* insane

démentir [37] [demɑ̃tir] VT **1** *(contredire ▸ témoin)* to contradict **2** *(nier ▸ nouvelle, rumeur)* to deny, to refute; **les autorités démentent avoir envoyé des troupes** the authorities deny having sent troops; **son regard démentait ses paroles** the look in his/her eyes belied his/her words; *Littéraire* **il a démenti nos espérances** he has not come up to our expectations, he has disappointed us
VPR **se démentir son amitié pour moi ne s'est jamais démentie** his/her friendship has been unfailing; **des méthodes dont l'efficacité ne s'est jamais démentie** methods that have proved consistently efficient

démerdard, -e [demerdar, -ard] *très Fam* ADJ resourceful❑; **toi qui es d., trouve-nous des places pour demain soir** you always seem to be able to wangle this kind of thing, find us some seats for tomorrow night; **il est d., il s'en sortira** he's always got some trick up his sleeve, he'll make it; **il n'est pas d. pour deux sous** he hasn't got a clue
NM,F **c'est un sacré d.** *(il est ingénieux)* he knows a trick or two; *(il sait se tirer d'un mauvais pas)* he can always wriggle his way out of a tricky situation

démerde [demerd] NF *très Fam* **dans ce pays, tout marche à la d.** you have to use your wits to get anything done in this country

démerder [3] [demerde] **se démerder** VPR *très Fam* **1** *(se débrouiller)* to get by, to manage❑; **il se démerde pas mal pour un débutant** he's not bad for a beginner; **t'inquiète pas, je me démerderai** don't worry, I'll manage somehow; **elle se démerde pas mal en cuisine/tennis** she's not a bad cook/tennis player; **elle se démerde pas mal en anglais** she gets by quite well in English **2** *(se dépêcher)* to get a move on, *Am* to get it in gear

démerdeur, -euse [demerdœr, -øz] = **démerdard**

démérite [demerit] NM *Littéraire* fault, flaw, demerit; **il n'y a aucun d. à avoir agi ainsi** there's nothing wrong in having acted this way

démériter [3] [demerite] VI *(s'abaisser)* **d. aux yeux de qn** to come down in sb's esteem; **il n'a jamais démérité** he has never proved unworthy of the trust placed in him; **il n'a démérité en rien** he has incurred no blame, he has in no way demeaned himself

démesure [deməzyr] NF *(d'un personnage)* excessiveness, immoderation; *(d'une passion, d'une idée)* outrageousness; **donner dans la d.** to (tend to) be excessive; **la d. absurde de ses projets** the absurdity of his/her grandiose projects

démesuré, -e [deməzyre] ADJ **1** *(énorme ▸ empire)* vast, enormous; **d'une longueur démesurée** interminable **2** *(exagéré ▸ orgueil)* inflated, inordinate; *(▸ ambition)* excessive, enormous; *(▸ appétit)* huge, enormous; **cette affaire a pris une importance démesurée** this affair has been blown up out of all proportion

démesurément [deməzyremɑ̃] ADV excessively, immoderately, inordinately; **des yeux d. ouverts** eyes as round as saucers

démet *etc voir* **démettre**

démettre [84] [demetr] VT **1** *Méd (os, bras)* to dislocate, to put out of joint **2** *(destituer)* to dismiss; **d. qn de ses fonctions** to dismiss sb from his/her duties **3** *Jur (débouter)* **d. qn de son appel** to dismiss sb's appeal
VPR **se démettre 1** *Méd* **se d. le poignet** to dislocate one's wrist, to put one's wrist out of joint **2** *(démissionner)* to resign, to hand in one's resignation; **se d. de ses fonctions** *(directeur)* to resign one's post *or* from one's job; *(député, président)* to resign from office

demeurant [dəmœrɑ̃] **au demeurant** ADV *(du reste)* for all that, notwithstanding; **photographe de talent et très joli garçon au d.** a talented photographer and very good-looking with it

demeure [dəmœr] NF **1** *(maison)* residence **2** *(domicile)* dwelling-place, abode **3** *Jur* delay; **mettre qn en d. de payer** to give sb notice to pay; **mettre qn en d. de témoigner/de s'exécuter** to order sb to testify/to comply
• **à demeure** ADV **il s'est installé chez elle à d.** he moved in with her permanently *or* for good

demeuré, -e [dəmœre] **ADJ** *Vieilli* mentally retarded; *Fam Péj* halfwitted; **il est complètement d., ce mec** the guy's a complete halfwit
NM,F *Vieilli* mentally retarded person; *Fam Péj* halfwit

demeurer [5] [dəmœre] **VI 1** *(aux être) (rester ▸ dans tel état)* to remain; **d. silencieux/inconnu** to remain silent/unknown; **l'affaire en est demeurée là** the matter rested there; **il vaut mieux en d. là pour aujourd'hui** we'd better leave it at that for today **2** *(aux être) (subsister)* to remain, to be left; **peu de traces demeurent** there are few traces left; **d. à qn** *(rester sa propriété)* to be left to sb; **cette épée nous est demeurée de notre père** this sword was left to us by our father **3** *(aux avoir) Sout (habiter)* to live, to stay; **il demeure toujours à la même adresse** he's still living at the same address

demi, -e [dəmi] **ADJ INV** *(devant le nom, avec trait d'union)* **1** *(moitié de)* half; **une d.-pomme** half an apple; **plusieurs d.-pommes** several halves of apple; **une d.-livre de pommes** a half-pound of *or* half a pound of apples **2** *(incomplet)* **cela n'a été qu'un d.-succès** it wasn't a complete *or* it was only a partial success
NM,F *(moitié)* half; **j'achète un pain? – non, un d.** shall I buy a loaf? – no, just half a one
NM 1 *(bière)* **un d. (de bière)** a beer, *Br* ≃ a half, a half-pint; **prends deux demis** get two beers **2** *Sport* **d. droite** *(au football)* right half *or* half-back; **d. de mêlée** *(au rugby)* scrum half; **d. d'ouverture** *(au rugby)* fly *or* stand-off half **3** *Suisse (vin)* = half a litre of wine
• **demie NF la demie** half past; **à la demie** at half past; **on va attendre la demie** we'll wait till half past; **à la demie de chaque heure** every hour on the half hour; **à la demie de 4 heures** at half past 4
• **à demi ADV 1** *(avec un adjectif)* **à d. mort** half-dead; **être à d. convaincu** to be half-convinced **2** *(avec un verbe)* **ouvrir la porte à d.** to half-open the door; **faire les choses à d.** to do things by halves; **ne croire qn qu'à d.** to only half-believe sb
• **et demi, et demie ADJ 1** *(dans une mesure)* and a half; **quinze mètres et d.** fifteen and a half metres; **ça dure deux heures et demie** it lasts two and a half hours; **boire une bouteille et demie** to drink a bottle and a half **2** *(en annonçant l'heure)* **à trois heures et demie** at three thirty, at half past three

demiard [dəmjar] **NM** *Can* half-pint, = 0.284 litres

demi-bas [dəmiba] **NM INV** knee-length sock; *(pour femmes)* knee-high, popsock

demi-botte [dəmibɔt] *(pl* **demi-bottes)** **NF** half-boot

demi-bouteille [dəmibutej] *(pl* **demi-bouteilles)** **NF** half-bottle, half a bottle

demi-canton [dəmikɑ̃tɔ̃] *(pl* **demi-cantons)** **NM** *Suisse* = state of the Swiss confederation which is one half of a divided canton

demi-centre [dəmisɑ̃tr] *(pl* **demi-centres)** **NM** *Sport* centre-half

demi-cercle [dəmiserkl] *(pl* **demi-cercles)** **NM** half-circle, semicircle
• **en demi-cercle ADV** in a semicircle

demi-circulaire [dəmisirkylɛr] *(pl* **demi-circulaires)** **ADJ** *(canal)* semicircular

demi-clef [dəmikle] *(pl* **demi-clefs)** **NF** half hitch

demi-deuil [dəmidœj] *(pl* **demi-deuils)** **NM** *(tenue)* half-mourning

demi-dieu [dəmidjø] *(pl* **demi-dieux)** **NM** demigod

demi-douzaine [dəmiduzɛn] *(pl* **demi-douzaines)** **NF 1** *(six)* half-dozen, half-a-dozen; **deux demi-douzaines** two half-dozens; **une d. de tomates** half-a-dozen tomatoes **2** *Fam (environ six)* **une d. de gens attendaient** half-a-dozen people were waiting

demi-droite [dəmidrwat] *(pl* **demi-droites)** **NF** half-line, half-ray

demi-écrémé [dəmiekreme] **ADJ M** *Br* semi-skimmed, *Am* part skim

demi-fin, -e [dəmifɛ̃, -in] *(mpl* **demi-fins,** *fpl* **demi-fines)** **ADJ** *Com* **petits pois demi-fins** garden peas; **haricots demi-fins** green beans

demi-finale [dəmifinal] *(pl* **demi-finales)** **NF** semifinal; **les demi-finales femmes/hommes** the women's/men's semifinals

demi-finaliste [dəmifinalist] *(pl* **demi-finalistes)** **NMF** semi-finalist

demi-fond [dəmifɔ̃] **NM INV 1** *(activité)* middle-distance running; **faire du d.** to do middle-distance running **2** *(course)* middle-distance race

demi-frère [dəmifrɛr] *(pl* **demi-frères)** **NM** half-brother

demi-gros [dəmigro] **NM INV** wholesale *(dealing in retail quantities)*

demi-heure [dəmijœr] *(pl* **demi-heures)** **NF** half-hour; **une d.** half an hour; **il y en a un toutes les demi-heures** there's one every half-hour; **laisser mijoter une d.** allow to simmer for half an hour

demi-jour [dəmiʒur] *(pl* **demi-jours)** **NM** *(clarté)* half-light; *(crépuscule)* twilight, dusk

demi-journée [dəmiʒurne] *(pl* **demi-journées)** **NF** half-day, half a day; **une d. de travail** half a day's work, a half-day's work; **travailler trois demi-journées par semaine** to work three half-days a week

démilitarisation [demilitarizasjɔ̃] **NF** demilitarization

démilitariser [3] [demilitarize] **VT** to demilitarize

demi-litre [dəmilitr] *(pl* **demi-litres)** **NM** half-litre, half a litre; **un d. de lait, s'il vous plaît** half a litre of milk, please

demi-longueur [dəmilɔ̃gœr] *(pl* **demi-longueurs)** **NF** half-length, half a length; **une d. d'avance** a half-length's lead; **gagner d'une d.** to win by half a length

demi-lune [dəmilyn] *(pl* **demi-lunes)** **NF 1** *(ouvrage fortifié)* demi-lune, half-moon **2** *(place urbaine)* crescent
ADJ INV half-moon *(avant n)*, half-moon-shaped
• **en demi-lune ADJ** half-moon *(avant n)*, half-moon-shaped

demi-mal [dəmimal] *(pl* **demi-maux** [-mo]) **NM il n'y a que d.** there's no great harm done

demi-mesure [dəmiməzyr] *(pl* **demi-mesures)** **NF 1** *(compromis)* half measure; **elle ne connaît pas les demi-mesures** *ou* **ne fait pas de demi-mesures** she doesn't do things by halves **2** *(moitié d'une mesure)* half measure

demi-monde [dəmimɔ̃d] *(pl* **demi-mondes)** **NM** demi-monde

demi-mot [dəmimo] **à demi-mot ADV il comprend à d.** he doesn't need to have things spelled out for him; **j'ai compris à d.** I took the hint; **on se comprend à d.** we know how each other's mind works

déminage [deminaʒ] **NM** *(sur la terre)* mine clearance; *(en mer)* mine sweeping

déminer [3] [demine] **VT** to clear of mines

déminéralisation [demineralizasjɔ̃] **NF 1** *(de l'eau)* demineralization **2** *Physiol* mineral deficiency

déminéraliser [3] [demineralize] **VT 1** *(eau)* to demineralize **2** *Physiol* to deprive of minerals
VPR se déminéraliser *(malade)* to become deficient in essential minerals

démineur [deminœr] **ADJ M** bomb-disposal *(avant n)*
NM bomb-disposal expert, member of a bomb-disposal unit

demi-pause [dəmipoz] *(pl* **demi-pauses)** **NF** *Br* minim *or Am* half-note rest

demi-pension [dəmipɑ̃sjɔ̃] *(pl* **demi-pensions)** **NF** *(à l'hôtel)* half-board; **sept jours en d.** seven days' half-board; *Scol* **être en d.** to have school lunches *or Br* dinners

demi-pensionnaire [dəmipɑ̃sjɔnɛr] *(pl* **demi-pensionnaires)** **NMF** = pupil who has school lunches *or Br* dinners

demi-place [dəmiplas] *(pl* **demi-places)** **NF 1** *(au spectacle)* half-price ticket *or* seat **2** *Transp* half-fare

demi-pointe [dəmipwɛ̃t] *(pl* **demi-pointes)** **NF** *(position)* demi-point; **(chausson de) d.** demi-point shoe

demi-portion [dəmipɔrsjɔ̃] *(pl* **demi-portions)** **NF 1** *(moitié de portion)* half-portion **2** *Fam Hum (personne)* weed, squirt

demi-produit [dəmiprɔdɥi] *(pl* **demi-produits)** **NM** *Écon* semi-finished product

demi-queue [dəmikø] *(pl* **demi-queues)** **ADJ un piano d.** a baby grand (piano)
NM baby grand (piano)

demi-reliure [dəmirəljyr] *(pl* **demi-reliures)** **NF** quarter-binding; **d. à (petits) coins** half-binding

démis, -e [demi, -iz] **PP** *voir* **démettre**

demi-saison [dəmisɛzɔ̃] *(pl* **demi-saisons)** **NF** *(printemps)* spring; *(automne)* autumn, *Am* fall; **un temps de d.** the sort of mild weather you get in spring or autumn

demi-salaire [dəmisalɛr] *(pl* **demi-salaires)** **NM** half-pay

demi-sang [dəmisɑ̃] **NM INV** half-breed *(horse)*

demi-sel [dəmisɛl] **ADJ INV** slightly salted
NM INV 1 *(beurre)* slightly salted butter **2** *(fromage)* = slightly salted cream cheese **3** *Fam Arg crime (souteneur)* small-time pimp; *(voyou)* small-time gangster

demi-sœur [dəmisœr] *(pl* **demi-sœurs)** **NF** half-sister

demi-solde [dəmisɔld] *(pl* **demi-soldes)** *Mil* **NF** half-pay
NM INV half-pay officer

demi-sommeil [dəmisɔmɛj] *(pl* **demi-sommeils)** **NM** half-sleep, doze; **dans mon d., j'ai entendu…** while I was half asleep, I heard…
• **en demi-sommeil ADJ** half-asleep; **entreprise/marché en d.** sluggish business/market

demi-soupir [dəmisupir] *(pl* **demi-soupirs)** **NM** *Br* quaver *or Am* eighth note rest

démission [demisjɔ̃] **NF 1** *(départ)* resignation; **donner sa d.** to resign, to hand in *or Sout* to tender one's resignation **2** *(irresponsabilité)* abdication of responsibility; **la d. face au terrorisme** the abdication of responsibility in the face of terrorism; **à cause de la d. des parents** because of the refusal of parents to shoulder their responsibilities

démissionnaire [demisjɔnɛr] **ADJ 1** *(qui quitte son poste)* resigning, outgoing **2** *(irresponsable)* who has abdicated his/her responsibilities
NMF person resigning; **les démissionnaires** those who have resigned

démissionner [3] [demisjɔne] **VI 1** *(quitter son emploi)* to resign, to hand in one's resignation *or* notice; **qu'est-ce qui t'a fait d.?** what made you resign?; **d. de son poste de directeur** to resign (one's position) as manager **2** *(refuser les responsabilités)* to fail to shoulder one's responsibilities; **d. devant qn** to give in to sb; **d. devant qch** to give in when faced with sth; **c'est trop difficile, je démissionne** it's too hard, I give up
VT *Fam (renvoyer)* **d. qn** to talk sb into resigning▫; **ils l'ont démissionné?** did he resign or was he fired?

démit *etc voir* **démettre**

demi-tarif [dəmitarif] *(pl* **demi-tarifs)** **NM** *(billet)* half-price ticket; *(carte)* half-price card; *(abonnement)* half-price subscription; **voyager à d.** to travel at half-fare; **enfants d.** *(billet)* children half-price

demi-teinte [dəmitɛ̃t] *(pl* **demi-teintes)** **NF** half-tone
• **en demi-teinte ADJ 1** *Phot* half-tone **2** *(subtil)* subtle, delicate

demi-ton [dəmitɔ̃] *(pl* **demi-tons)** **NM** *Br* semitone, *Am* half-step

demi-tour [dəmitur] *(pl* **demi-tours)** **NM 1** *(pivotement)* about-face, about-turn; **faire un d.** *(gén) & Mil* to about-face, to about-turn; *Mil* **d., droite!** (right) about face! **2** *Aut* U-turn; **faire un d.** to do *or* to pull a U-turn; **faire d.** *(piéton)* to retrace one's steps; *(conducteur)* to turn back

démiurge [demjyrʒ] **NM** demiurge, creator

demi-volée [dəmivɔle] *(pl* **demi-volées)** **NF** half-volley

démo [demo] **NF** *Fam (d'un appareil, d'un objet)* demo

démobilisateur, -trice [demɔbilizatœr, -tris] ADJ *(démotivant)* demobilizing

démobilisation [demɔbilizasjɔ̃] NF **1** *Mil* demobilization; **à la d.** when demobilization time comes/came **2** *(démotivation)* growing apathy; **on constate une d. de l'opinion publique sur ces questions** public opinion has become apathetic about *or* has turned away from these issues

démobilisatrice [demɔbilizatris] *voir* **démobilisateur**

démobiliser [3] [demɔbilize] VT **1** *Mil* to demobilize **2** *(démotiver)* to cause to lose interest, to discourage

VPR **se démobiliser** to lose interest, to become discouraged

démocrate [demɔkrat] ADJ **1** *(gén)* democratic **2** *(dans des noms de partis)* Democratic

NMF **1** *(gén)* democrat **2** *(aux États-Unis)* Democrat

démocrate-chrétien, -enne [demɔkratkretjɛ̃, -ɛn] *(mpl* **démocrates-chrétiens,** *fpl* **démocrates-chrétiennes)** ADJ Christian Democrat

NM,F Christian Democrat

démocratie [demɔkrasi] NF **1** *(système)* democracy; **d. directe/représentative** direct/representative democracy; **d. populaire** people's democracy **2** *(pays)* democracy, democratic country; **vivre en d.** to live in a democracy; *Fam* **on est en d., non?** this is a free country, as far as I know! **3** *Pol* **d. chrétienne** Christian Democracy

démocratique [demɔkratik] ADJ **1** *Pol* democratic **2** *(respectueux des désirs de tous)* democratic; **tu as pris une décision pas très d.** your decision was biased; **notre groupe est très d.** in our group, everyone gets a chance to have their say

démocratiquement [demɔkratikmɑ̃] ADV democratically

démocratisation [demɔkratizasjɔ̃] NF **1** *Pol* democratization **2** *(mise à la portée de tous)* **la d. du ski** putting skiing holidays within everyone's reach

démocratiser [3] [demɔkratize] VT **1** *Pol* to democratize, to make more democratic **2** *(mettre à la portée de tous)* **d. les voyages à l'étranger** to put foreign travel within everyone's reach

VPR **se démocratiser 1** *Pol* to become more democratic **2** *(devenir accessible)* to become available to anyone

démodé, -e [demɔde] ADJ *(style, technique, idée, théorie)* old-fashioned, out-of-date; *(parents)* old-fashioned

démoder [3] [demɔde] **se démoder** VPR to go out of fashion *or* vogue, to become old-fashioned

démodulation [demɔdylasjɔ̃] NF demodulation

démographe [demɔgraf] NMF demographer, demographist

démographie [demɔgrafi] NF *(science)* demography; *(croissance de la population)* population growth

démographique [demɔgrafik] ADJ demographic, population *(avant n)*; **poussée/explosion d.** population increase/explosion

demoiselle [dəmwazɛl] NF **1** *(jeune femme)* young lady; **d. d'honneur** *(d'une mariée)* bridesmaid; *(d'une souveraine)* lady-in-waiting; **d. de compagnie** lady's companion

2 *Vieilli (célibataire)* maiden lady; **j'ai une tante qui est encore d.** I have an aunt who is still unmarried; **les demoiselles Dupin** the Misses Dupin

3 *(fille)* **votre d.** your daughter

4 *Entom (libellule)* dragonfly

démolir [32] [demɔlir] VT **1** *(détruire ▸ immeuble, mur)* to demolish, to pull *or* to tear down; *(▸ jouet, voiture)* to wreck, to smash up; **d. une porte à coups de pied** to kick a door down

2 *(anéantir ▸ argument, théorie)* to destroy, to demolish; *(▸ projet)* to ruin, to play havoc with; *(▸ réputation, autorité)* to shatter, to destroy; **l'alcool lui a démoli la santé** alcohol ruined *or* wrecked his/her health; **ces piments m'ont démoli l'estomac** those chillis played havoc with my stomach; *Fam* **la mort de son père l'a démolie** she was shattered by her father's death

3 *Fam (causer la ruine de ▸ auteur, roman)* to pan; **la presse peut d. un homme politique** the press can break a politician

4 *Fam (battre)* to beat up; **il s'est fait d.** he got beaten up; **d. le portrait à qn** to smash sb's face in

5 *Fam (épuiser)* to wipe out, *Br* to shatter

VPR **se démolir se d. la santé** to ruin one's health; **se d. la santé à faire qch** to kill oneself doing sth; **te démolis pas la santé à les chercher** don't wear yourself out looking for them

démolissage [demɔlisaʒ] NM *Fam (critique)* panning

démolisseur [demɔlisœr] NM **1** *(ouvrier)* demolition worker, *Am* wrecker **2** *(entrepreneur)* demolition contractor **3** *(détracteur)* destructive critic

démolition [demɔlisjɔ̃] NF **1** *(d'un bâtiment)* demolition, pulling *or* tearing down **2** *Fig (d'une théorie)* destruction

• **démolitions** NFPL *(matériaux)* debris, rubble

• **de démolition** ADJ **chantier/entreprise de d.** demolition site/contractors; *Fig* **une campagne de d. systématique** a systematic campaign of destruction

• **en démolition** ADJ being demolished, under demolition

démon [demɔ̃] NM **1** *Rel* **le d.** the Devil; **être possédé du d.** to be possessed by the Devil; **comme un d.** like a thing possessed

2 *Myth* daemon, daimon; *Fig* **son d. intérieur** *(mauvais)* the evil *or* demon within (him); *(bon)* the good spirit within (him)

3 *(tentation)* demon; **le d. de la curiosité/du jeu** the demon of curiosity/gambling; **le d. de midi** midlife crisis

4 *(enfant turbulent)* **(petit) d.** (little) devil

5 *Can* **être en d.** to be furious

démonétisation [demɔnetizasjɔ̃] NF **1** *Fin* demonetization, demonetarization **2** *(discrédit)* discrediting

démonétiser [3] [demɔnetize] VT **1** *Fin* to demonetize, to demonetarize **2** *(discréditer)* to discredit, to bring into disrepute

démoniaque [demɔnjak] ADJ *(ruse, rire)* diabolical, fiendish, *Sout* demonic

NMF person possessed by the devil

démonstrateur, -trice [demɔ̃stratœr, -tris] NM,F *Com* demonstrator, salesperson *(in charge of demonstrations)*

démonstratif, -ive [demɔ̃stratif, -iv] ADJ **1** *(expressif)* demonstrative, expressive, effusive; **peu d.** reserved, undemonstrative **2** *(convaincant)* demonstrative, conclusive **3** *Gram* demonstrative

NM *Gram (pronom)* demonstrative pronoun; *(adjectif)* demonstrative adjective

démonstration [demɔ̃strasjɔ̃] NF **1** *Ling & Math (preuve)* demonstration, proof; *(ensemble de formules)* demonstration; **faire la d. de qch** to demonstrate *or* to prove sth; *Fig* **la d. n'est plus à faire** it has been proved beyond all doubt; **d. par l'absurde** reductio ad absurdum

2 *Com (d'article)* demonstration; **faire la d. d'un aspirateur** to demonstrate a vacuum cleaner; **je ne peux pas vous vendre cet appareil, il est en d.** I can't sell you this appliance, it's a demonstration model; **d. sur le lieu de vente** in-store demonstration

3 *(prestation)* display, demonstration; **d. aérienne** air display; **faire une d. aérienne** to put on an air display; **faire une d. de karaté** to give a karate demonstration; **d. de force** display *or* show of force

4 *(fait de manifester)* demonstration, show; **faire une d. de force** to display one's strength; **faire la d. de son talent** to show one's talent

• **démonstrations** NFPL *(effusions)* (great) show of feeling, gushing; *(crises)* outbursts; **démonstrations de tendresse/joie/colère** show of tenderness/joy/anger; **toutes ces démonstrations ne te mèneront nulle part** these outbursts will get you nowhere

démonstrative [demɔ̃strativ] *voir* **démonstratif**

démonstratrice [demɔ̃stratris] *voir* **démonstrateur**

démontable [demɔ̃tabl] ADJ which can be dismantled *or* taken to pieces

démontage [demɔ̃taʒ] NM dismantling; **pour faciliter le d.** to make it easier to dismantle

démonté, -e [demɔ̃te] ADJ **1** *(mécanisme etc)* dismantled, taken to pieces, taken apart

2 *(déconcerté)* disconcerted, *Fam* thrown; *(troublé)* upset

3 *(mer)* raging, stormy; **par une mer démontée** in heavy seas

4 *Équitation (cavalier)* thrown

démonte-pneu [demɔ̃tpnø] *(pl* **démonte-pneus)** NM *Br* tyre lever, *Am* tire iron

démonter [3] [demɔ̃te] VT **1** *(désassembler ▸ bibliothèque, machine, tente)* to dismantle, to take down; *(▸ moteur)* to strip down, to dismantle; *(▸ fusil, pendule)* to dismantle, to take to pieces, to take apart; *(▸ manche de vêtement, pièce rapportée)* to take off

2 *(détacher ▸ pneu, store, persienne)* to remove, to take off; *(▸ rideau)* to take down

3 *(décontenancer)* to take aback; **ma question l'a démontée** she was taken aback *or* flummoxed by my question; **ne te laisse pas d. par son ironie** don't be flustered by his/her ironic remarks

4 *Équitation* to unseat, to unhorse

5 *Can (décourager)* to discourage

VPR **se démonter 1** *(emploi passif)* to be taken to pieces, to be dismantled; **ça se démonte facilement** it can be easily dismantled **2** *(se troubler)* to lose countenance, to get flustered

démontrable [demɔ̃trabl] ADJ demonstrable, provable; **facilement/difficilement d.** easy/difficult to prove

démontrer [3] [demɔ̃tre] VT **1** *Math* to prove; **démontrez que c'est une bijection** prove *or* demonstrate that it's a bijection; **d. qch par A plus B** to prove sth conclusively; **je ne peux pas te le d. par A plus B** I can't quote you chapter and verse **2** *(montrer par raisonnement)* to prove, to demonstrate; **d. son erreur à qn** to prove sb wrong **3** *(révéler)* to show, to reveal, to indicate; **un geste qui démontre notre bonne volonté** a gesture that shows *or* demonstrates our goodwill

démoralisant, -e [demɔralizɑ̃, -ɑ̃t] ADJ *(remarque, nouvelle)* demoralizing, disheartening, depressing

démoralisateur, -trice [demɔralizatœr, -tris] ADJ demoralizing

démoralisation [demɔralizasjɔ̃] NF demoralization; **ne nous laissons pas gagner par la d.!** let's not become disheartened *or* demoralized!

démoralisatrice [demɔralisatris] *voir* **démoralisateur**

démoralisé, -e [demɔralize] ADJ **il était complètement d.** he was completely demoralized *or* downcast

démoraliser [3] [demɔralize] VT to demoralize, to dishearten; **il ne faut pas te laisser d.** you mustn't let it get you down

VPR **se démoraliser** to become demoralized, to lose heart

démordre [76] [demɔrdr] **démordre de** VT IND **ne pas d. de** to stick to, to stand by; **il ne démord pas de son idée** he won't budge from his position; **rien ne m'en fera d.** I'll stick to my guns come what may; **elle n'en démord pas, elle ne veut pas en d.** she won't have it any other way

démotivation [demɔtivasjɔ̃] NF demotivation, loss of motivation; **il ne faut pas laisser s'installer la d. au sein de l'équipe** we mustn't let the team become demotivated

démotiver [3] [demɔtive] VT to demotivate, to discourage; **les salaires les ont démotivés** the salary levels have discouraged *or* demotivated them

démoulage [demulaʒ] NM *(d'une statuette)* removal from the mould; *(d'un gâteau)* turning out; *(tarte)* removal from its tin

démouler [3] [demule] VT *(statuette)* to remove from the mould; *(gâteau)* to turn out; *(tarte)* to remove from its tin

démoustication [demustikasjɔ̃] NF clearing of mosquitoes

démoustiquer [3] [demustike] VT to rid of mosquitoes

démultiplicateur [demyltiplikatœr] ADJ *(dispositif)* reducing, reduction *(avant n)*
NM reduction system

démultiplication [demyltiplikasjɔ̃] NF *(action)* gearing down, (gear) reduction; **(rapport de) d.** reduction ratio

démultiplier [9] [demyltiplije] VT **1** *Tech* to reduce, to gear down **2** *(multiplier)* to increase

démuni, -e [demyni] ADJ **1** *(pauvre)* destitute; **des mesures d'aide aux plus démunis** an aid package to help those who need it most **2** *(sans défense)* powerless, resourceless

démunir [32] [demynir] VT to deprive; **d. qn de qch** to deprive *or* to divest sb of sth
VPR **se démunir se d. de** to part with, to give up

démuseler [24] [demyzle] VT *(animal)* to unmuzzle, to remove the muzzle from; **d. la presse** to lift restrictions on the freedom of the press

démystifiant, -e [demistifjɑ̃, -ɑ̃t] ADJ **1** *(qui détrompe)* eye-opening **2** *(qui rend moins mystérieux)* demystifying

démystificateur, -trice [demistifikatœr, -tris] ADJ **1** *(qui détrompe)* eye-opening **2** *(qui rend moins mystérieux)* demystifying
NM,F demystifier

démystification [demistifikasjɔ̃] NF **1 la d. de qn** opening sb's eyes **2** *(d'un mystère, d'un phénomène)* demystification

démystificatrice [demistifikatris] *voir* **démystificateur**

démystifier [9] [demistifje] VT **1** *(détromper)* to open the eyes of **2** *(rendre plus clair)* to explain, to demystify

démythification [demitifikasjɔ̃] NF demythologization; **on assiste à la d. de l'ordinateur** computers are no longer regarded with awe *or* are losing their mystique

démythifier [9] [demitifje] VT to demythologize, to make less mythical *or* into less of a myth; **il faut d. le génie génétique** we must remove the mystique that surrounds genetic engineering

dénatalité [denatalite] NF fall *or* drop in the birth rate

dénationalisation [denasjɔnalizasjɔ̃] NF denationalization, denationalizing

dénationaliser [3] [denasjɔnalize] VT to denationalize

dénatter [3] [denate] VT *(cheveux) Br* to unplait, *Am* to unbraid

dénaturalisation [denatyralizasjɔ̃] NF denaturalization

dénaturaliser [3] [denatyralize] VT to denaturalize

dénaturant, -e [denatyrɑ̃, -ɑ̃t] ADJ adulterating
NM denaturant

dénaturation [denatyrasjɔ̃] NF denaturation

dénaturé, -e [denatyre] ADJ **1** *(alcool)* denatured **2** *(pervers ▸ goût)* unnatural, perverted; **quelle mère dénaturée je fais!** what a bad mother I am!

dénaturer [3] [denatyre] VT **1** *(modifier ▸ alcool)* to adulterate, to denature; *(▸ saveur)* to alter, to adulterate **2** *(fausser ▸ propos, faits, intention)* to distort, to misrepresent, to twist; **vous dénaturez mes propos!** you're twisting my words *or* putting words into my mouth!; **c'est d. nos efforts!** it's making a mockery of our efforts!

dénazification [denazifikasjɔ̃] NF denazification

dénazifier [9] [denazifje] VT to denazify

dénégation [denegasjɔ̃] NF **1** *(contestation)* denial **2** *Psy* denial
• **de dénégation** ADJ *(geste, attitude)* denying, of denial; **en signe de d.** as a sign of disagreement

déneigement [denɛʒmɑ̃] NM snow clearance; **le d. des cols** clearing the cols of snow

déneiger [23] [deneʒe] VT to clear of snow, to clear snow from

déneigeuse [deneʒøz] NF snowplough; *(pour souffler la neige)* snowblower; *(pour fondre la neige)* snow remover

dengue [dɑ̃g] NF *Méd* dengue fever, breakbone fever

déni [deni] NM **1** *Jur* denial; **d. de justice** denial of justice **2** *Psy* **d. de réalité** denial

déniaiser [4] [denjeze] VT **1** *(dépuceler)* **d. qn** to take away sb's innocence; **j'ai été déniaisé à 15 ans** I lost my innocence when I was 15 **2** *(rendre moins naïf)* to open the eyes of
VPR **se déniaiser** *(devenir moins naïf)* to learn the ways of the world

dénicher [3] [deniʃe] VT **1** *Fam (trouver ▸ collier, trésor)* to find, to unearth; *(▸ informations)* to dig up *or* out; *(▸ chanteur, cabaret)* to discover, to spot; **d. de jeunes acteurs** to scout for young actors; **j'ai déniché un chouette petit restaurant** I've found a great little restaurant; **elle a l'art de d. des antiquités intéressantes** she has a talent for hunting out interesting antiques **2** *(oiseau)* to remove from the nest
VI *(oiseau)* to leave the nest, to fly away

dénicheur, -euse [deniʃœr, -øz] NM,F **1** *(d'oiseaux)* bird's nester **2** *(découvreur)* **d. de bibelots rares** curio-hunter; **d. de talents, d. de vedettes** talent scout *or* spotter

dénicotinisation [denikɔtinizasjɔ̃] NF reduction of nicotine

dénicotiniser [3] [denikɔtinize] VT to denicotinize; **du tabac dénicotinisé** low-nicotine tobacco

denier [dənje] NM **1** *Hist (monnaie ▸ romaine)* denarius; *(▸ française)* denier; **le d. du culte** the contribution to parish costs **2** *Tex* denier; **bas de 20 deniers** 20-denier stockings
• **deniers** NMPL money, funds; **je l'ai payé de mes deniers** I paid for it out of my own pocket; **j'en suis de mes deniers** I had to pay with my own money; **les deniers publics** *ou* **de l'État** public money *or* funds

dénier [9] [denje] VT **1** *(rejeter ▸ responsabilité)* to deny, to disclaim **2** *(refuser)* to deny, to refuse; **d. qch à qn** to deny *or* to refuse sb sth

dénigrement [denigrəmɑ̃] NM denigration, disparagement; **le mot ne s'emploie que par d.** the word is only used disparagingly
• **de dénigrement** ADJ **esprit/paroles de d.** disparaging spirit/remarks; **campagne de d.** smear campaign

dénigrer [3] [denigre] VT to disparage, to denigrate, to run down
VPR **se dénigrer** to do oneself down

dénivelé [denivle] NM difference in level *or* height

dénivelée [denivle] NF difference in level *or* height

déniveler [24] [denivle] VT to make uneven, to put out of level

dénivellation [denivɛlasjɔ̃] NF **1** *(action)* making uneven, putting out of level **2** *(écart)* difference in level *or* height; **les dénivellations d'une route** the gradients *or* ups and downs of a road

dénivelle [denivɛl] = **dénivelée**

dénivellement [denivɛlmɑ̃] NM = **dénivellation**

dénombrable [denɔ̃brabl] ADJ countable; **non d.** uncountable

dénombrement [denɔ̃brəmɑ̃] NM counting (out), count; **le d. des animaux** counting the animals; **faire un d. de la population** to do a population count

dénombrer [3] [denɔ̃bre] VT to count (out); **on dénombre 130 morts à ce jour** at the latest count there were 130 dead; **d. les habitants d'une ville** to count the population of a town

dénominateur [denɔminatœr] NM *Math* denominator; **d. commun** common denominator; **plus grand d. commun** highest common denominator; **avoir comme** *ou* **en d. commun** to have as a common denominator; **avoir un d. commun** *(personnes)* to have something in common, to share (some) common ground

dénominatif [denɔminatif] NM *Gram* denominative

dénomination [denɔminasjɔ̃] NF **1** *(fait de nommer)* naming, *Sout* denomination **2** *(nom)* designation, denomination, name; *Pharm* **d. commune** generic name; *Com* **d. sociale** company name

dénommer [3] [denɔme] VT **1** *(donner un nom à)* to name, to call **2** *Jur* to name

dénoncer [16] [denɔ̃se] VT **1** *(complice, fraudeur)* to denounce, to inform on; *(camarade de classe)* to tell on; **d. qn aux autorités** to denounce sb *or* to give sb away to the authorities
2 *(condamner ▸ pratiques, dangers, abus)* to denounce, to condemn
3 *(annuler ▸ armistice, traité)* to denounce, to renege on; *(▸ contrat)* to terminate
4 *(dénoter)* to indicate, to betray
VPR **se dénoncer** to give oneself up

dénonciateur, -trice [denɔ̃sjatœr, -tris] ADJ denunciatory; **lettre dénonciatrice** letter of denunciation
NM,F informer; **les dénonciateurs de ses méfaits** those who exposed his/her wrongdoings

dénonciation [denɔ̃sjasjɔ̃] NF **1** *(accusation)* denunciation; **arrêté sur la d. de son frère** arrested on the strength of his brother's denunciation; **d. calomnieuse** false accusation **2** *(révélation ▸ d'une injustice)* exposure, denouncing, castigating **3** *(rupture ▸ d'un traité)* denunciation; *(▸ d'un contrat)* termination

dénonciatrice [deɔ̃sjatris] *voir* **dénonciateur**

dénotation [denɔtasjɔ̃] NF *Ling & Phil* denotation

dénoter [3] [denɔte] VT **1** *Ling & Phil* to denote **2** *(être signe de)* to denote, to indicate

dénouement [denumɑ̃] NM *(d'un film, d'une histoire, d'une pièce)* dénouement; *(d'une crise, d'une affaire)* outcome, conclusion; **un heureux d.** a happy ending, a favourable outcome

dénouer [6] [denwe] VT **1** *(défaire ▸ ficelle, lacet)* to undo, to untie; *(▸ cheveux)* to let down, to loosen **2** *(résoudre ▸ intrigue)* to unravel, to untangle
VPR **se dénouer 1** *(cheveux)* to come loose *or* undone; *(lacet)* to come undone *or* untied **2** *(crise)* to end, to be resolved **3 se d. les cheveux** to let one's hair down

dénoyautage [denwajotaʒ] NM **1** *(d'un fruit) Br* stoning, *Am* pitting **2** *Fig (d'une entreprise)* = removal of officials appointed for reasons of political influence

dénoyauter [3] [denwajote] VT **1** *(fruit) Br* to stone, *Am* to pit **2** *Fig* **d. une entreprise** = to remove officials appointed by politicians from a company

dénoyauteur [denwajotœr] NM *Br* stoner, *Am* pitter

denrée [dɑ̃re] NF commodity; *(aliment)* foodstuff; **denrées alimentaires** food products, foodstuffs; **denrées de base** basic commodities; **denrées coloniales** exotic produce; **denrées de consommation courante** basic consumer goods; **denrées du pays** domestic products; **denrées périssables** perishable goods, perishables; **denrées de première nécessité** staple foods, staples; **une d. rare** a scarce commodity; **c'est une d. rare que la générosité** generosity is hard to come by

dense [dɑ̃s] ADJ **1** *(épais ▸ brouillard, végétation)* thick, dense
2 *(serré ▸ foule)* thick, tightly packed; *(▸ circulation)* heavy; **population peu d.** sparse population
3 *(concis ▸ style)* compact, condensed
4 *Phys* dense

densité [dɑ̃site] NF **1** *Phys* density; *Élec* **d. de charge/courant** charge/current density
2 *(du brouillard, de la foule)* denseness, thickness; **selon la d. de la circulation** depending on how heavy the traffic is; **d. de population** population density; **pays à faible/forte d. de population** sparsely/densely populated country
3 *Phot* density
4 *Ordinat* **d. d'enregistrement** packing *or* recording *or* data density; **à double d.** double-density; **haute d.** high density; **simple d.** single density

dent [dɑ̃] NF **1** *Anat* tooth; **faire** *ou* **percer ses dents** to cut one's teeth, to teethe; **faire une d.** to cut a (new) tooth; **avoir les dents en avant** to have protruding teeth; **dents du bas/haut** lower/upper teeth; **dents de devant/du fond** front/back teeth; *Fam Fig* **avoir les dents du fond qui baignent** to have stuffed oneself *or* one's face, to have pigged out; **d. barrée** impacted tooth; **d. de lait** baby *or Br* milk tooth; **d. permanente** permanent *or* second tooth; **d. à pivot** post; **d. de sagesse** wisdom tooth; **fausses dents** false teeth; *Fam* **avoir la d.** to be ravenous *or* starving; *Fam* **avoir** *ou* **garder une d. contre qn** to have a grudge against sb, to bear sb a grudge; **avoir la d. dure** to be scathing; **avoir les dents longues** to be extremely ambitious, to set one's sights high; *Fam* **être sur les dents** *(occupé)* to be frantically busy; *(anxieux)* to be stressed out; **la police est sur les dents** the police are on red alert; *Fam* **il n'y a pas de quoi remplir une d. creuse** this wouldn't keep a sparrow alive; *aussi Fig* **montrer les dents** to bare one's teeth; **parler entre ses dents** to mutter; **se faire les dents** to cut one's teeth; **le jeune ténor s'est fait les dents sur 'la Bohème'** the young tenor cut his teeth on 'La Bohème'; **se mettre qch sous la d.** to find sth to eat; **on n'avait rien à se mettre sous la d.** we didn't have a thing to eat; **tout ce qui lui tombe sous la d.** anything he can get his teeth into; **sourire toutes dents dehors** to give a beaming smile

2 *(de roue, d'engrenage)* cog; *(de courroie)* tooth

3 *(pointe ▸ d'une scie, d'un peigne)* tooth; *(▸ d'une fourchette)* tine, prong; *(▸ d'un timbre)* perforation; **à deux dents** two-pronged; **à trois dents** three-pronged

4 *Géog* (jagged) peak, jag

• **à belles dents** ADV **déchirer qch à belles dents** to tear into sth; **mordre dans** *ou* **croquer** *ou* **manger qch à belles dents** to eat one's way through sth; *Fig* **mordre dans** *ou* **croquer la vie à belles dents** to live (one's) life to the full

• **en dents de scie** ADJ *(couteau)* serrated; **évolution en dents de scie** uneven development; **elle a eu une scolarité en dents de scie** her education was a very uneven business

dentaire [dɑ̃tɛr] ADJ *(hygiène)* oral, dental; *(cabinet, études, école)* dental

NF *Fam (école)* dental school❑; **faire d.** to study dentistry❑

dental, -e, -aux, -ales [dɑ̃tal, -o] *Ling* ADJ dental

• **dentale** NF dental (consonant)

dent-de-lion [dɑ̃dəljɔ̃] *(pl* **dents-de-lion**) NF dandelion

denté, -e [dɑ̃te] ADJ *(courroie)* toothed; *(feuille)* serrate, dentate

dentelé, -e [dɑ̃tle] ADJ *(contour)* jagged, indented; *(feuille)* dentate, serrate; *(timbre)* perforated

denteler [24] [dɑ̃tle] VT *(gén)* to indent the edge of, to give a jagged outline to; *(timbre)* to perforate; **machine/ciseaux à d.** pinking machine/shears

dentelle [dɑ̃tɛl] NF **1** *(tissu)* lace, lacework; **faire de la d.** to do lacework; **des gants de** *ou* **en d.** lace gloves; **d. à l'aiguille** *ou* **au point** lace, needlepoint; **d. de Chantilly** Chantilly lace; **d. au fuseau** *ou* **aux fuseaux** pillow lace; **d. de papier** paper doily; **d. au point** point lace, needlepoint; *Fam* **il ne fait pas dans la d.** he's completely unsubtle *or* in-your-face **2** *(morceau de tissu)* piece of lacework

ADJ INV **1 bas d.** lace stocking **2** *Culin* **crêpes d.** paper-thin pancakes

• **de dentelle, en dentelle** ADJ lace *(avant n)*

dentellier, -ère [dɑ̃təlje, -ɛr] ADJ *(industrie)* lace(making) *(avant n)*

NM,F lacemaker, laceworker

• **dentellière** NF *(machine)* lacemaking machine

dentelure [dɑ̃tlyr] NF *(d'un rivage)* indentation; *(d'une montagne)* jagged summit; *(d'une feuille)* serration; *(d'un timbre)* perforations

dentier [dɑ̃tje] NM dentures

dentifrice [dɑ̃tifris] ADJ **eau d.** mouthwash; **pâte d.** toothpaste; **poudre d.** tooth powder

NM toothpaste

dentine [dɑ̃tin] NF dentin, dentine

dentiste [dɑ̃tist] NMF dentist

dentition [dɑ̃tisjɔ̃] NF **1** *(dents)* teeth, *Spéc* dentition; **avoir une bonne d.** to have good teeth; **d. adulte** *ou* **définitive** adult teeth, *Spéc* secondary dentition; **d. lactéale** *ou* **de lait** baby *or Br* milk teeth, *Spéc* primary dentition **2** *(poussée)* tooth growth

denture [dɑ̃tyr] NF **1** *Anat & Zool* set of teeth, *Spéc* dentition **2** *Tech* teeth, cogs

> Il faut noter que le nom anglais **dentures** est un faux ami. Il signifie **dentier**.

dénucléarisation [denyklearizasjɔ̃] NF denuclearization

dénucléariser [3] [denyklearize] VT *(région)* to denuclearize

dénudation [denydasjɔ̃] NF **1** *Méd* stripping **2** *Littéraire (d'un arbre)* baring, laying bare

dénudé, -e [denyde] ADJ *(dos, corps)* bare, unclothed; *(crâne)* bald; *(terrain)* bare, bald; *(fil électrique)* bare

dénuder [3] [denyde] VT *(dos, épaules)* to leave bare; *(sol, câble, os, veine)* to strip

VPR **se dénuder 1** *(se déshabiller)* to strip (off) **2** *(se dégarnir ▸ crâne)* to be balding; *(▸ arbre, colline)* to become bare; *(▸ fil électrique)* to show through

dénué, -e [denɥe] ADJ **d. de** lacking in, devoid of; **d. d'intérêt** utterly uninteresting, devoid of interest; **d. de bon sens** devoid of common sense; **d. d'humanité** inhuman, devoid of human feeling; **d. d'ambiguïté** unambiguous; **une accusation dénuée de tout fondement** a completely unfounded accusation; **être d. de tout** to be destitute

dénuement [denymɑ̃] NM destitution; **être dans le d. le plus complet** to be utterly destitute

dénutrition [denytrisjɔ̃] NF malnutrition

déodorant [deɔdɔrɑ̃] ADJ M deodorant *(avant n)*

NM deodorant

déodoriser [3] [deɔdɔrize] VT to deodorize

déontologie [deɔ̃tɔlɔʒi] NF professional code of ethics, deontology; **la d. médicale** the medical code of ethics; **code de d.** *(écrit)* code of practice; **d. professionnelle** business ethics

déontologique [deɔ̃tɔlɔʒik] ADJ ethical, deontological; **règles déontologiques** rules of ethics

dépannage [depanaʒ] NM **1** *(réparation)* repair job; *(remorquage)* recovery; *Ordinat* troubleshooting; **SOS dépannages** = emergency breakdown service; **faire un d.** to fix a breakdown **2** *Fam (aide)* helping out❑, bailing out; **merci pour le d.** thanks for bailing me out

• **de dépannage** ADJ **voiture de d.** *Br* breakdown lorry, *Am* tow truck; **service de d.** breakdown service

• **en dépannage** ADV *Fam* **prête-moi 20 euros en d.** lend me 20 euros just to tide me over *or* bail me out; **j'ai pris une intérimaire en d.** I got a temp in to help us out

dépanner [3] [depane] VT **1** *(réparer ▸ voiture, mécanisme)* to repair, to fix; **d. qn sur le bord de la route** to help sb who's broken down on the side of the road; **il m'a dépanné** he fixed the problem for me **2** *Fam (aider ▸ gén)* to help out; *(▸ financièrement)* to tide over, to bail out; **elle m'a dépanné en me prêtant sa voiture** she helped me out by lending me her car; **est-ce que 50 euros pourraient te d.?** would 50 euros bail you out *or* tide you over?; **est-ce que tu peux me d. de cinq euros?** can you give me five euros to bail me out?

USAGE ABSOLU **nous dépannons 24 heures sur 24** we have a 24-hour breakdown service

dépanneur, -euse [depanœr, -øz] NM,F *(d'appareils)* repairman, *f* repairwoman; *(de véhicules)* breakdown mechanic

NM *Can Br* ≃ corner shop, *Am* ≃ convenience store

• **dépanneuse** NF *Br* breakdown lorry, *Am* tow truck

dépaquetage [depaktaʒ] NM unpacking, unwrapping

dépaqueter [27] [depakte] VT to unpack, to unwrap

déparasiter [3] [deparazite] VT *Électron & Rad* **1** *(débarrasser des parasites)* to eliminate the interference in **2** *(munir d'un dispositif antiparasite)* to fit with a suppressor

dépareillé, -e [depareje] ADJ **1** *(mal assorti ▸ serviettes, chaussettes)* odd; **mes draps sont tous dépareillés** none of my sheets match; *Com* **articles dépareillés** oddments

2 *(incomplet ▸ service, collection)* incomplete

3 *(isolé)* **un volume d. d'une collection** a single volume (that used to be part) of a collection

4 *Can (sans pareil)* **c'est un mari d.** he's a husband in a million

dépareiller [4] [depareje] VT **1** *(désassortir)* **d. des draps** to put unmatched *or* non-matching sheets together **2** *(ôter des éléments à)* to leave gaps in; **en cassant cette assiette, tu as dépareillé mon service de table** my dinner service is incomplete now that you've broken that plate

déparer [3] [depare] VT *(paysage)* to disfigure, to spoil, to be a blight on; *(visage)* to disfigure; **les fenêtres déparent la façade** the windows detract from the beauty of *or* spoil the façade; **un CD qui ne dépare pas ma collection** a CD well worthy of my collection; **le petit chapeau ne dépare pas du tout l'ensemble** the little hat goes very nicely with the rest

déparier [10] [deparje] VT **1** *(gants, chaussettes, chaussures)* to split **2** *(animaux)* to uncouple

dépars *etc voir* **départir**

départ [depar] NM **1** *Transp* departure; **le d. du train est à 7 heures** the train leaves at 7 a.m.; **le d. est dans une heure** we're leaving in an hour; **départs grandes lignes** *(dans une gare)* main-line departures; **départs banlieue** suburban *or* local departures; **hall des départs** *Rail* (departure) concourse; *Aviat & Naut* departure lounge

2 *(fait de quitter un lieu)* departure, leaving; **on en a parlé après son d.** we discussed it after he/she left; **le d. de la navette spatiale** the launch of the space shuttle; **le d. du courrier a été retardé** the post was collected late; **les grands départs** = the mass exodus of people from Paris and other major cities at the beginning of the holiday period, especially in August; **le grand d.** the big departure; *Fig (la mort)* the final journey; **être sur le d.** to be ready to go

3 *(d'une course)* start; **donner le d. d'une course** to start a race, to give the signal to start a race; **12 chevaux/voitures/coureurs ont pris le d. (de la course)** there were 12 starters; **d. arrêté/lancé/décalé** standing/flying/staggered start; *Fig* **prendre un bon/mauvais d.** to get off to a good/bad start; **prendre un nouveau d. dans la vie** to make a fresh start in life, to turn over a new leaf

4 *(de son travail)* departure; *(démission)* resignation; **au d. du directeur** when the manager left *or* quit (the firm); **d. en préretraite** early retirement; **d. volontaire** voluntary redundancy

5 *(origine)* start, beginning; **au d.** at first, to begin with

6 *Com* **d. entrepôt** ex warehouse; **d. usine** ex works; **prix d. usine** factory price, ex works price

7 *(d'un compte)* opening date

8 *(distinction)* distinction, separation, differentiation; **faire le d. entre** to draw a distinction between, to distinguish between; **une thèse où le d. n'a pas été bien fait entre causes et conséquences** a thesis which makes no attempt to distinguish *or* to differentiate between causes and effects

• **au départ de** PRÉP **visites au d. des Tuileries** tours departing from the Tuileries; **au d. du Caire, tout allait encore bien entre eux** when they left Cairo, everything was still fine between them

• **de départ** ADJ **1** *(gare, quai, heure)* departure *(avant n)* **2** *(initial)* **l'idée de d.** the initial *or* original idea; **prix de d.** *(dans une enchère)* upset *or* asking price; **salaire de d.** initial *or* starting salary

départager [17] [departaʒe] VT **1** *(séparer ▸ ex æquo)* to decide between; **d. l'un de l'autre** to decide between one and the other **2** *Admin & Pol* **d. les votes** to settle the voting, to give the casting vote

département [departəmɑ̃] NM **1** *(du territoire français)* département, department; **les départements d'outre-mer** French overseas departments **2** *(service ▸ d'une société)* department, service, division; *(▸ d'une université)* department; *(▸ d'un musée)* section; **le d. du contentieux** the legal department **3** *(ministère)* department, ministry;

d. ministériel ministry; **le D. d'État** the State Department, the Department of State

DÉPARTEMENT

A "département" is the chief administrative division of France. There are 95 "départements" in metropolitan France and 4 overseas (Guadeloupe, Martinique, Guiana and Réunion) and each is administered by a "conseil général" and a "préfet". The number of the "département" corresponds to the first two figures in a postcode and the last two figures on a car registration number.

départemental, -e, -aux, -ales [departəmɑ̃tal, -o] **ADJ 1** *(des départements français)* of the département, departmental **2** *(dans une entreprise, une organisation)* departmental, sectional **3** *(ministériel)* ministerial

• **départementale** **NF** *(route)* secondary road, *Br* ≃ B-road

départir **[32]** [departir] **VT** *Littéraire (tâches)* to assign, to apportion; *(faveurs)* to distribute, to dispense, to deal out

VPR se départir se d. de to depart from, to abandon, to lose; **sans se d. de sa bonne humeur** without losing his/her good humour; **elle ne se départit pas de son calme** she remained unruffled; **il s'est départi de ses sarcasmes habituels** he abandoned his usual sarcasm

dépassé, -e [depase] **ADJ** *(mentalité, technique)* outdated, old-fashioned; **c'est d. tout ça!** all that's old hat!; **tu es d., mon pauvre!** you're behind the times, my friend!

dépassement [depasmɑ̃] **NM 1** *Aut Br* overtaking, *Am* passing

2 *(excès)* exceeding, excess; *Fin* **d. budgétaire** *ou* **de budget** overspending; **être en d. budgétaire** to be over budget; *Ordinat* **d. de capacité** overflow; **d. de coûts** cost overrun; *Fin* **d. de crédit** overspending; **il y a un d. de crédit de plusieurs millions** the budget has been exceeded by several million; **un d. d'horaire de 15 minutes** an overrun of 15 minutes

3 *(surpassement)* **d. (de soi-même)** surpassing oneself, transcending one's own capabilities

4 *Admin* = charging, by a medical practitioner, of more than the standard fee recognized by the social services; **pratiquer le d. d'honoraires** to charge more than will be reimbursed by Social Security

dépasser **[3]** [depase] **VT 1** *(doubler ▸ voiture) Br* to overtake, *Am* to pass; *(▸ coureur)* to outrun, to outdistance; **se faire d.** *(en voiture)* to be overtaken

2 *(aller au-delà de ▸ hôtel, panneau)* to pass, to go *or* to get past; *(▸ piste d'atterrissage)* to overshoot; **attention de ne pas d. le tournant!** be careful you don't miss the turn-off!

3 *(être plus grand que)* to stand *or* to be taller than; **d. qch en hauteur** to be higher than sth; **notre immeuble dépasse les autres** our building stands higher *or* is taller than the others; **elle me dépasse d'une tête** she's a head taller than me

4 *(déborder sur)* to go over *or* beyond; **ne dépasse pas la ligne** don't go over the line; **il a dépassé son temps de parole** he talked longer than had been agreed, he went over time; **d. la date limite** to miss the deadline; **votre renommée dépasse les frontières** your fame has spread abroad

5 *(excéder)* to exceed, to go beyond; **ne pas d. la dose prescrite** *(sur mode d'emploi)* do not exceed the stated dose; **d. la limite de vitesse** to exceed the speed limit; **montants dépassant 500 euros** amounts in excess of *or* exceeding 500 euros; **les socialistes nous dépassent en nombre** the socialists outnumber us, we're outnumbered by the socialists; **l'exposé ne doit pas d. 20 minutes** the talk must not last longer than *or* exceed 20 minutes; **les ventes ont dépassé le chiffre de l'an dernier** sales figures have overtaken last year's; **d. le budget de 15 millions** to go 15 million over budget; **l'addition dépasse rarement 40 euros** the bill is seldom more than *or* seldom goes over 40 euros; **elle a dépassé la trentaine** she's turned thirty, she's over thirty; **ça dépasse mes moyens** it's beyond my means, it's more than I can afford

6 *(surpasser ▸ adversaire)* to surpass, to do better than, to be ahead of; **elle veut d. sa sœur aînée** she wants to do better than her elder sister; **d. l'attente** *ou* **les espérances de qn** to surpass *or* to exceed sb's expectations; **cela dépasse tout ce que j'avais pu espérer** this is beyond all my hopes *or* my wildest dreams; **d. qn/qch en drôlerie/stupidité** to be funnier/more stupid than sb/sth; **ça dépasse tout ce que j'ai vu en vulgarité** for sheer vulgarity, it beats everything I've ever seen; **elle nous dépassait tous en musique** she was a far better musician than any of us

7 *(outrepasser ▸ ordres, droits)* to go beyond, to overstep; **cela dépasse l'entendement** it is beyond comprehension; **la tâche dépasse mes forces** the task is beyond me; **les mots ont dépassé ma pensée** I got carried away and said something I didn't mean; *Fam* **d. les limites** *ou* **la mesure** *ou* **les bornes** to go too far, to overstep the mark; *Fam* **cette fois, ça dépasse la mesure** *ou* **les bornes** this time it's gone too far

8 *(dérouter)* **être dépassé par les événements** to be overtaken *or* swamped by events; **une telle ignorance me dépasse** such ignorance defeats me; **les échecs, ça me dépasse!** chess is (quite) beyond me!

9 *(surmonter)* **avoir dépassé un stade/une phase** to have gone beyond a stage/a phase

VI 1 *Aut Br* to overtake, *Am* to pass; **interdiction de d.** *(panneau sur la route) Br* no overtaking, *Am* no passing **2** *(étagère, balcon, corniche)* to jut out, to protrude; **notre perron dépasse par rapport aux autres** our front steps stick out further than the others **3** *(chemisier, doublure)* to be hanging out, to be untucked; **ta combinaison dépasse** your slip's showing; **d. de** to be sticking out *or* protruding from/under; **pas une mèche ne dépassait de son chignon** her chignon was impeccable *or* hadn't a hair out of place; **un revolver dépassait de son sac** a gun was sticking out of his/her bag

VPR se dépasser 1 *(l'un l'autre)* to pass one another; **les voitures cherchent toutes à se d.** the cars are all jostling for position **2** *(se surpasser)* to surpass *or* to excel oneself

dépassionner **[3]** [depasjɔne] **VT** *(débat)* to take the heat out of, to calm *or* to cool down

dépatouiller **[3]** [depatuje] **se dépatouiller VPR** *Fam* to manage▫, to get by▫; **se d. d'une situation** to get out of *or* to wriggle one's way out of a situation

dépaver **[3]** [depave] **VT** to remove the cobblestones from

dépaysement [depeizmɑ̃] **NM 1** *(changement de cadre)* change of scene *or* scenery; **un petit d. ne te ferait pas de mal** you could do with a change of scene; **à Moscou, on a une extraordinaire impression de d.** when you're in Moscow everything feels totally unfamiliar **2** *(malaise)* feeling of unfamiliarity; **les enfants n'aiment pas le d.** children don't like changes in environment

dépayser **[3]** [depeize] **VT 1** *(changer de cadre)* to give a change of scenery *or* surroundings to; **mes vacances m'ont beaucoup dépaysé** my holiday provided a great change of scene **2** *(désorienter)* to disorientate; **se sentir dépaysé** to feel like a stranger; **on fait tout pour que le touriste ne soit pas dépaysé** we do everything possible to make the tourist feel at home

dépeçage [depəsaʒ], **dépècement** [depɛsmɑ̃] **NM 1** *(de volaille)* cutting *or* carving up **2** *(d'un pays)* dismembering, carving up

dépecer **[29]** [depəse] **VT 1** *(démembrer ▸ proie)* to tear limb from limb; *(▸ volaille)* to cut up **2** *(détruire ▸ empire)* to dismember, to carve up

dépeceur, -euse [depəsœr, -øz] **NM,F** cutter-up; *Com* **d. d'entreprise** asset-stripper

dépêche [depɛʃ] **NF 1** *Admin* dispatch; **d. diplomatique** diplomatic dispatch **2** *Tél* **d. (télégraphique)** telegram, wire; **envoyer une d. à qn** to wire *or* to telegraph sb **3** *(nouvelle)* news item *(sent through an agency)*; **une d. vient de nous arriver** a news item *or* some news has just reached us; **d. d'agence** agency copy

dépêcher **[4]** [depeʃe] **VT 1** *(enquêteur)* to send, to dispatch **2** *Arch ou Littéraire* **d. qn d'un coup d'épée** to dispatch sb *or* to put sb to death with the sword

VPR se dépêcher to hurry (up); **pas besoin de se d.** there's no (need to) hurry; **mais dépêche-toi donc!** come on, hurry up!; **se d. de faire qch** to hurry to do sth; **dépêche-toi de finir cette lettre** hurry up and finish that letter; **on s'est dépêchés de rentrer** we hurried home

dépeignait *etc* **1** *voir* **dépeindre 2** *voir* **dépeigner**

dépeigner **[4]** [depeɲe] **VT d. qn** to mess up *or* to muss *or* to ruffle sb's hair; **elle est toujours dépeignée** her hair's always untidy *or* dishevelled

dépeindre **[81]** [depɛ̃dr] **VT** to depict, to portray

dépenaillé, -e [depənaje] **ADJ** scruffy; **un mendiant tout d.** a beggar in rags

dépénalisation [depenalizasjɔ̃] **NF** decriminalization

dépénaliser **[3]** [depenalize] **VT** to decriminalize

dépendance [depɑ̃dɑ̃s] **NF 1** *(rapport)* dependence

2 *(subordination)* dependence; **être dans** *ou* **sous la d. de qn** to be subordinate to sb; **vivre dans la d.** to be dependent

3 *(d'un drogué)* addiction

4 *(annexe)* outhouse, outbuilding

5 *(territoire)* dependency

dépendant, -e [depɑ̃dɑ̃, -ɑ̃t] **ADJ 1** *(lié, subordonné)* dependent; **être d. de qn/qch** to be dependent on sb/sth **2** *(drogué)* dependent (**de** on)

dépendre **[73]** [depɑ̃dr] **VT** *(décrocher ▸ tableau, tapisserie)* to take down

USAGE ABSOLU ça dépend! it (all) depends!

• **dépendre de VT IND 1** *(sujet: employé, service)* to be answerable to; **il dépend du chef de service** he's answerable *or* he reports to the departmental head

2 *(sujet: propriété, domaine, territoire)* to be a dependency of, to belong to; **le parc dépend du château** the park is part of the castle property

3 *(financièrement)* to depend on *or* upon, to be dependent on; **d. (financièrement) de qn** to be financially dependent on *or* upon sb; **je ne dépends que de moi-même** I'm my own boss; **d. d'un pays pour le pétrole** to be dependent on a country for one's oil supply

4 *(sujet: décision, choix, résultat)* to depend on; **ça dépend de la couleur que tu veux** it depends on what shade you want; **notre avenir en dépend** our future depends *or* rests on it; **ça ne dépend pas que de moi** it's not entirely up to me; **ces événements ne dépendent pas de nous** such events are beyond our control; **ça dépend des fois** it depends

5 *(tournure impersonnelle)* **il dépend de toi que ce projet aboutisse** whether this project succeeds depends on *or* is up to you; **il dépend de toi de rester ou de partir** it's up to you whether you stay or not

dépens [depɑ̃] **NMPL** *Jur* costs; **être condamné aux d.** to be ordered to pay costs

• **aux dépens de PRÉP** at the expense of; **rire aux d. de qn** to laugh at sb's expense; **s'amuser aux d. de sa santé** to have a good time at the expense of one's health; **je l'ai appris à mes d.** I learnt it to my cost

dépense [depɑ̃s] **NF 1** *(frais)* expense, expenditure; **occasionner de grosses dépenses** to entail a lot of expense; **c'est une grosse d.** it's a lot of money; **je ne peux pas me permettre cette d.** I can't afford to spend so much money; **faire des dépenses** to incur expenses; **faire trop de dépenses** to overspend; *Compta* **dépenses de caisse** cash expenditure; **dépenses en capital** capital expenditure *or* outlay; **dépenses de consommation** consumer spending; **dépenses courantes** current expenditure; **dépenses de création** above-the-line costs; **dépenses d'entretien** maintenance (costs); **dépenses d'équipement** capital expenditure; **dépenses de l'État** public spending, government spending; **dépenses d'exploitation** operating costs; **dépenses fiscales** tax expenditure; **dépenses de fonctionnement** operating costs; **dépenses d'investissement** capital expenditure; **dépenses des ménages** household expenditure; **dépenses publicitaires, dépenses de la publicité** publicity expenses; **dépenses publiques** public *or* government spending; **dépenses**

de santé *(de l'État)* health expenditure; **dépenses sociales** welfare expenditure; *Écon & Fin* **dépenses et recettes** expenditure and income
2 *(fait de dépenser)* spending; **faire la d. de qch** to lay out *or* to spend money on sth; **regarder à la d.** to watch what one spends, to watch every penny; **ne regardez pas à la d.** spare no expense
3 *(consommation)* consumption; **d. physique** physical exertion; **d. de temps/d'énergie** expenditure of time/energy; **c'est une d. de temps inutile** it's a waste of time; **d. de carburant** fuel consumption

dépenser [3] [depɑ̃se] **VT 1** *(argent)* to spend; **à quoi dépenses-tu ton argent?** what do you spend your money on?; **d. son salaire en cadeaux** to spend one's salary on gifts; **les enfants me font d. beaucoup d'argent** I spend a lot because of the children; **voilà de l'argent bien** *ou* **utilement dépensé** it's money well spent; **mal** *ou* **inutilement dépensé** wasted **2** *(consommer ▸ mazout, essence)* to use **3** *(employer ▸ temps)* to spend; *(▸ énergie)* to expend; **d. toute son énergie/ses forces à faire qch** to use up all one's energy/one's strength in doing sth
USAGE ABSOLU d. sans compter to spend (money) lavishly
VPR se dépenser 1 *(se défouler)* to let off steam; **il se dépense beaucoup physiquement** he uses up a lot of energy; **elle a besoin de se d.** she needs an outlet for her (pent-up) energy **2** *(se démener)* to expend a lot of energy, to work hard; **tu t'es beaucoup dépensé pour cette soirée** you've worked hard for (the success of) this party; **se d. en efforts inutiles** to waste one's energies in useless efforts; **se d. sans compter pour qch** to put all one's energies into sth, to give sth one's all

dépensier, -ère [depɑ̃sje, -ɛr] **ADJ** extravagant; **j'ai toujours été d.** I've always been a big spender, money has always slipped through my fingers
NM,F spendthrift; **un grand d.** a big spender

déperdition [depɛrdisjɔ̃] **NF** *(de chaleur, de matière)* loss

dépérir [32] [deperir] **VI** *(malade)* to fade *or* to waste away; *(de tristesse)* to pine away; *(plante)* to wilt, to wither; *(industrie)* to decline

dépérissement [deperismɑ̃] **NM** *(affaiblissement ▸ d'un malade)* fading *or* wasting away; *(▸ de tristesse)* pining away; *(▸ d'une plante)* wilting, withering; *(déclin ▸ d'une industrie)* decline

dépersonnalisation [depɛrsɔnalizasjɔ̃] **NF** *(gén) & Psy* depersonalization

dépersonnaliser [3] [depɛrsɔnalize] **VT** *(gén) & Psy* to depersonalize
VPR se dépersonnaliser *(individu)* to become depersonalized, to lose one's personality; *(lieu, œuvre)* to become anonymous

dépêtrer [4] [depetre] **VT d. qn/qch de** to extricate sb/sth from; **d. qn d'une situation** to extricate sb from *or* to get sb out of a situation
VPR se dépêtrer 1 se d. de *(de filets, de pièges)* to free oneself from; **le bouvreuil n'arrivait pas à se d. du filet** the bullfinch couldn't free itself from *or* find its way out of the net **2 se d. de** *(d'un gêneur)* to shake off; *(d'une situation)* to get out of; **il nous a dit tant de mensonges qu'il ne peut plus s'en d.** he's told us so many lies that he can no longer extricate himself from them

dépeuplement [depœpləmɑ̃] **NM 1** *(d'un pays, d'une région)* depopulation **2** *(désertion)* **le d. de la forêt** *(déboisement)* clearing *or* thinning (out) the forest; *(absence d'animaux)* the disappearance of animal life from the forest; **le d. des rivières** *(volontaire)* destocking the rivers; *(par la pollution)* the destruction of the fish stocks of the rivers

dépeupler [5] [depœple] **VT 1** *(pays, région)* to depopulate **2** *(volontairement ▸ étang)* to empty (of fish), to destock; *(▸ forêt)* to clear (of trees), to thin out the trees of; *(involontairement ▸ étang)* to kill off the fish stocks in; *(▸ forêt)* to kill off the trees in
VPR se dépeupler 1 *(pays, région)* to become depopulated **2** *(rivière)* to lose its stock; *(forêt)* to thin out **3** *(salle, rues)* to empty

déphasage [defazaʒ] **NM 1** *Élec* phase difference; **d. en avant** (phase) lead; **d. en arrière** lag **2** *(décalage)* difference; *Psy* loss of contact with reality; **le d. entre le P-DG et le conseil d'administration est de plus en plus important** the chairman is getting increasingly out of touch with the board

déphasé, -e [defaze] **ADJ 1** *Élec* out-of-phase; **d. en arrière** lagging; **d. en avant** leading **2** *(désorienté)* disorientated; **être d. par rapport à la réalité** to be out of touch with reality

déphaser [3] [defaze] **VT 1** *Élec* to cause a phase difference in **2** *(désorienter)* **son séjour prolongé à l'hôpital l'a déphasé** his long stay in hospital made him lose touch with reality

dépiauter [3] [depjote] **VT** *Fam* **1** *(enlever la peau de ▸ lapin, poisson)* to skin; *(▸ fruit)* to peel **2** *(analyser)* **d. un texte** to dissect a text

dépigmentation [depigmɑ̃tasjɔ̃] **NF** depigmentation, loss of pigmentation

dépilation [depilasjɔ̃] **NF 1** *Méd* hair loss **2** *(épilation)* hair removal

dépilatoire [depilatwar] **ADJ** depilatory; *(crème)* hair-removing, depilatory
NM hair-removing *or* depilatory cream

dépiler [3] [depile] **VT** *Méd* to cause hair loss to

dépiquer [3] [depike] **VT 1** *(repiquer)* to transplant **2** *(égrener ▸ blé)* to thresh; *(▸ riz)* to hull **3** *Couture* to unstitch, to unpick

dépistage [depistaʒ] **NM 1** *Méd* screening; **le d. du cancer** cancer screening; **le d. du sida** Aids testing; **d. précoce** early screening **2** *(recherche)* detection, unearthing; **l'auteur se livre à un travail de d. sur des documents historiques** the author is doing some detective work on historical documents **3** *(d'un criminel, de gibier)* tracking down

dépister [3] [depiste] **VT 1** *Méd* to screen for; **des techniques pour d. le cancer** cancer screening techniques; **il a été dépisté séropositif** he tested HIV-positive **2** *(criminel, gibier)* to track down; *(source, ruse)* to detect, to unearth **3** *(perdre ▸ poursuivant)* to throw off; *(▸ chien de chasse)* to put off the scent

dépit [depi] **NM** pique; **faire qch par d.** to do sth in a fit of pique *or* out of spite; **ressentir du d. contre qn** to be annoyed with sb; **j'en ai conçu un peu de d.** I was a little piqued *or* vexed at it; **d. amoureux** heartache, unrequited love; **faire qch par d. amoureux** to do sth out of unrequited love; **se marier par d. amoureux** to marry on the rebound
• **en dépit de PRÉP** despite, in spite of; **faire qch en d. du bon sens** *(sans logique)* to do sth with no regard for common sense; *(n'importe comment)* to do sth any old how

dépité, -e [depite] **ADJ** (greatly) vexed, piqued

dépiter [3] [depite] **VT** to pique, to vex
VPR se dépiter *(concevoir du dépit)* to feel piqued

déplacé, -e [deplase] **ADJ 1** *(malvenu ▸ démarche, remarque, rire)* inappropriate, uncalled-for **2** *(de mauvais goût ▸ plaisanterie)* indelicate, shocking **3** *(personne)* displaced

déplacement [deplasmɑ̃] **NM 1** *(mouvement)* moving, shifting; **le d. du piano n'a pas été facile** moving the piano wasn't easy; **le d. de l'aiguille sur le cadran** the movement of the hands around the clock face; **le d. à gauche de l'électorat** the swing to the left by the electorate; **d. d'air** displacement of air; *Ordinat* **d. du curseur** cursor movement; *Ordinat* **d. entre fichiers** movement between files
2 *(sortie)* moving about; *(voyage d'affaires)* (business) trip; **Josie me remplace pendant mes déplacements** Josie steps in for me when I'm away on business; **le docteur m'a interdit tout d.** the doctor said I mustn't move about; **merci d'avoir fait le d.** thanks for coming all this way; *Fam* **joli panorama, ça vaut le d.!** what a lovely view, it's definitely worth going out of your way to see it!
3 *(mutation ▸ d'un employé)* transfer
4 *Naut* displacement; **d. en charge** displacement loaded, load displacement
5 *Méd* displacement; **d. de vertèbre** slipped disc
6 *Psy* displacement
7 *Chim & Phys* displacement
8 *Fin (de fonds)* movement
• **de déplacement ADJ 1** *Transp* **moyen de d.** means *or* mode of transport **2** *Psy* displacement *(avant n)*
• **en déplacement ADV** away; **la directrice est en d.** the manager's away (on business); *Sport* **Bordeaux est en d. à Marseille** Bordeaux are playing away against Marseilles

déplacer [16] [deplase] **VT 1** *(objet, pion, voiture)* to move, to shift; **déplace-le vers la droite** move *or* shift it to the right; *Fam Hum* **d. de l'air** *(en parlant)* to talk big *or* a lot of hot air; **la délégation déplaçait beaucoup d'air** the delegation looked as though it was taking itself very seriously indeed
2 *(élève, passager)* to move; *(population)* to displace
3 *(infléchir)* **d. la discussion** to shift the emphasis of the discussion; **ne déplacez pas le problème** *ou* **la question** don't change the question
4 *Méd (os)* to displace, to put out of joint; *(vertèbre)* to slip
5 *(muter ▸ fonctionnaire)* to transfer; **d. qn par mesure disciplinaire** to transfer sb for disciplinary reasons
6 *(faire venir ▸ médecin, dépanneur)* to send for; **ils ont déplacé l'ambulance pour cela?** did they really get the ambulance out for that?; **son concert a déplacé des foules** crowds flocked to his concert; **on avait déplacé des sommités** experts had been summoned
7 *(dans le temps ▸ festival, rendez-vous)* to change, to shift, to move; **d. une date** *(l'avancer)* to move a date forward; *(la reculer)* to put back a date
8 *Chim & Phys* to displace
9 *Naut* to have a displacement of
10 *Pol* **d. des voix (en faveur de)** to shift votes (towards)
11 *Fin (fonds)* to move
VPR se déplacer 1 *(masse d'air, nuages)* to move, *Spéc* to be displaced; *(aiguille d'horloge)* to move **2** *(marcher)* to move about *or* around, to get about *or* around; **se d. à l'aide de béquilles** to get about on crutches; **ne pas se d. pendant le spectacle** do not move around during the show; **faites vos courses sans vous d.** do your shopping from home; *Fam* **cela ne vaut pas/vaut le coup de se d.** it's not worth/it's worth the trip
3 *(voyager)* to travel, to get about
4 se d. une vertèbre to slip a disc

déplafonnement [deplafɔnmɑ̃] **NM d. des cotisations** removal of the upper limit for contributions

déplafonner [3] [deplafɔne] **VT** to raise the ceiling on, to remove the upper limit for; *Fin* **d. un crédit** to raise the ceiling on a credit, to raise a credit limit

déplaire [110] [deplɛr] **déplaire à VT IND 1** *(rebuter)* to put off; **son attitude m'a (souverainement) déplu** his/her attitude put me off (completely), I didn't like his/her attitude (at all); **il m'a tout de suite déplu** I took an instant dislike to him; **je lui déplais tant que ça?** does he/she dislike me as much as that?; **un café? voilà qui ne me déplairait pas** *ou* **ne serait pas pour me d.** a coffee? I wouldn't say no!; **il m'a parlé franchement, ce qui n'a pas été pour me d.** he was frank with me, which I liked; **il ne lui déplairait pas de vivre à la campagne** he/she wouldn't object to living in the country; *Littéraire* **il me déplaît d'avoir à vous dire ceci, mais…** I hate to tell you this but… **2** *(contrarier)* to annoy, to offend; **ce que je vais dire risque de vous d.** I'm afraid you may not like what I'm going to say; *Littéraire ou Hum* **ne vous (en) déplaise** whether you like it or not; **n'en déplaise à Votre Majesté** may it please your Majesty; **n'en déplaise aux libéraux** whatever the liberals may say
VPR se déplaire 1 *(ne pas se plaire l'un à l'autre)* to dislike each other *or* one another **2** *(être mal à l'aise)* to be unhappy *or* dissatisfied; **ils se sont déplu chez leur tante** they disliked staying with their aunt, they were unhappy at their aunt's; **je ne me suis pas déplu ici** I quite enjoyed *or* liked it here

déplaisant, -e [deplɛzɑ̃, -ɑ̃t] **ADJ 1** *(goût, odeur, atmosphère)* unpleasant, nasty **2** *(personne, comportement)* unpleasant, offensive

déplaisir [deplezir] **NM 1** *Littéraire (tristesse)* unhappiness **2** *(mécontentement)* displeasure, disapproval; **elle me verrait sans d. accepter** she'd be quite pleased if I accepted; **je fais les corvées mé-**

nagères sans d. I don't mind doing the housework; **ils constatèrent sa présence avec un vif d.** they were most displeased to see him/her; **à mon grand d.** much to my chagrin

déplaisons *etc voir* **déplaire**

déplantage [deplɑ̃taʒ] **NM le d. des arbustes** taking up *or* uprooting the shrubs; **le d. de la forêt** clearing the forest

déplanter [3] [deplɑ̃te] **VT** *(arbuste)* to uproot, to take up; *(forêt)* to clear; *(jardin)* to clear (of plants), to remove the plants from; *(piquet)* to dig out, to remove

déplantoir [deplɑ̃twar] **NM** hand-fork

déplâtrage [deplatraʒ] **NM 1** *Constr* removal of the plaster; **le d. d'un mur** stripping the plaster off a wall **2** *Méd* removal of the plaster cast

déplâtrer [3] [deplatre] **VT 1** *Constr* to strip of plaster, to remove the plaster from **2** *Méd* to take out of a plaster cast; **on le déplâtre demain** his plaster cast comes off tomorrow

dépliage [deplijaʒ] **NM** unfolding, spreading out

dépliant, -e [deplijɑ̃, -ɑ̃t] **ADJ** folding

NM 1 *(brochure)* brochure, leaflet; **d. publicitaire** advertising leaflet; **d. touristique** travel brochure **2** *Typ* foldout (page)

dépliement [deplimɑ̃] **NM** unfolding, spreading out

déplier [9] [deplije] **VT 1** *(journal, lettre, carte)* to open out *or* up, to unfold; *(mouchoir)* to unfold; *(tissu)* to spread out; **dépliant ses dentelles devant les clientes** spreading his pieces of lace before the customers **2** *(bras, jambes)* to stretch; **les rangées étaient si serrées que je ne pouvais d. mes jambes** the rows of seats were so close (together) that I couldn't stretch my legs **3** *(mètre pliant, canapé)* to open out

VPR se déplier 1 *(journal, lettre, carte)* to unfold, to open out **2** *(canapé, mètre pliant)* to open out; **un canapé qui se déplie** a foldaway sofa-bed

déplissage [deplisaʒ] **NM 1** *(d'un tissu plissé)* unpleating **2** *(défroissage)* smoothing out

déplisser [3] [deplise] **VT 1** *(vêtement plissé)* to unpleat; **d. une jupe** to take the pleats out of a skirt **2** *(défriper)* to smooth out; **d. une écharpe au fer** to iron the creases out of a scarf

VPR se déplisser *(vêtement plissé)* to come unpleated, to lose its pleats

déploie *etc voir* **déployer**

déploiement [deplwamɑ̃] **NM 1** *(des ailes d'un oiseau)* spreading out, unfolding; *(d'un drapeau, des voiles)* unfurling **2** *Mil* deployment; **un grand d.** *ou* **tout un d. de police** a large deployment of police **3** *(manifestation)* **d. de** show *or* demonstration *or* display of; **un grand d. de force** a great show of strength; **un d. d'affection** a display of affection; *Péj* a gush of affection

déplombage [deplɔ̃baʒ] **NM 1** *(d'une dent)* removing the filling (**de** from) **2** *(ouverture)* removal of the seal *or* seals; **la douane a procédé au d. des wagons** the customs officials proceeded to remove the seals from the trucks **3** *Ordinat* cracking

déplomber [3] [deplɔ̃be] **VT 1** *(dent)* to remove the filling from **2** *(ouvrir)* to take the seals off, to remove the seals from **3** *Ordinat* to crack

déplorable [deplɔrabl] **ADJ 1** *(regrettable)* deplorable, regrettable, lamentable **2** *(mauvais ▸ résultat)* appalling; *(▸ plaisanterie)* awful, terrible, appalling; **elle s'habille avec un goût d.** she dresses with appallingly bad taste, she has appalling taste in clothes

déplorablement [deplɔrabləmɑ̃] **ADV** deplorably, lamentably

déplorer [3] [deplɔre] **VT 1** *(regretter)* to object to, to regret, to deplore; **nous déplorons cet incident** we regret this incident; **je déplore que vous n'ayez pas compris** I find it regrettable that you didn't understand; **il est à d. que vous ayez eu cette conduite** your behaviour was regrettable **2** *(constater)* **nous n'avons eu que peu de dégâts à d.** fortunately, we suffered only slight damage; **on déplore la mort d'une petite fille dans l'accident** sadly, a little girl was killed in the accident **3** *Littéraire (pleurer sur)* to lament, to mourn; **d. le départ de qn** to mourn sb's departure; **d. la mort d'un ami** to grieve over the death of a friend

déployer [13] [deplwaje] **VT 1** *(déplier)* to spread out, to unfold, to unroll; *Naut* **d. les voiles** to unfurl *or* to extend the sails **2** *(faire montre de)* to display, to exhibit; **d. un luxe impressionnant** to indulge in a great display of luxury; **il m'a fallu d. des trésors de persuasion auprès d'elle** I had to work very hard at persuading her **3** *Mil* to deploy

VPR se déployer 1 *Naut* to unfurl **2** *(foule)* to extend, to stretch out **3** *Mil* to be deployed

déplu, -e [deply] **PP** *voir* **déplaire**

déplumé, -e [deplyme] **ADJ 1** *(sans plumes)* moulting; **des tourterelles déplumées** turtledoves that have lost their feathers **2** *Fam (chauve)* bald□, balding□; **un nounours tout d.** a balding teddy bear

déplumer [3] [deplyme] **se déplumer VPR 1** *(perdre ses plumes)* to lose *or* to drop its feathers **2** *Fam (devenir chauve)* **il** *ou* **son crâne se déplume** he's going bald *or* thinning on top□

déplut *etc voir* **déplaire**

dépoitraillé, -e [depwatraje] **ADJ** *Fam Péj* bare-chested□; **tout d.** with his shirt open almost down to his navel

dépolarisant, -e [depɔlarizɑ̃, -ɑ̃t] **ADJ** depolarizing

NM depolarizer

dépolarisation [depɔlarizasjɔ̃] **NF** depolarization

dépolariser [3] [depɔlarize] **VT** to depolarize

dépoli, -e [depɔli] **ADJ** frosted, ground

NM *(verre)* ground glass

dépolir [32] [depɔlir] **VT** *(surface)* to dull, to tarnish; *(verre)* to frost, to grind

VPR se dépolir to lose its shine, to become tarnished

dépolissage [depɔlisaʒ], **dépolissement** [depɔlismɑ̃] **NM** *(du verre)* frosting, grinding

dépolitisation [depɔlitizasjɔ̃] **NF** *(d'une personne, d'un thème)* depoliticization

dépolitiser [3] [depɔlitize] **VT** to depoliticize; **faut-il d. le sport?** should politics be kept out of sport?

dépolluer [7] [depɔlɥe] **VT** to cleanse, to clean up

dépollution [depɔlysjɔ̃] **NF** cleaning up, decontamination; **d. de l'eau** water purification

déponent, -e [depɔnɑ̃, -ɑ̃t] *Gram* **ADJ** deponent

NM deponent verb

dépopulation [depɔpylasjɔ̃] **NF** depopulation

déportation [depɔrtasjɔ̃] **NF 1** *(exil)* transportation, deportation **2** *Hist (en camp de concentration)* deportation, internment; **pendant mes années de d.** during my years in a concentration camp; **mort en d.** *(sur plaque)* died in Nazi concentration camp **3** *Hist & Jur (peine)* deportation

déporté, -e [depɔrte] **NM,F 1** *(prisonnier)* deportee, internee **2** *Hist (en camp de concentration)* concentration camp prisoner **3** *Hist & Jur* convict *(sentenced to deportation)*

déportement [depɔrtəmɑ̃] **NM** *(embardée)* swerve, swerving

• **déportements NMPL** *Littéraire* misbehaviour, misconduct

déporter [3] [depɔrte] **VT 1** *(prisonnier)* to transport, to deport

2 *Hist (dans un camp de concentration)* to deport, to send to a concentration camp

3 *Hist & Jur* to deport

4 *(déplacer)* **la voiture a été déportée sur la gauche** the car swerved to the left

VPR se déporter *(doucement)* to move aside; *(brusquement)* to swerve; **se d. vers la droite/gauche** to veer (off) to the right/left

déposant, -e [depozɑ̃, -ɑ̃t] **NM,F 1** *Banque* depositor **2** *Jur* deponent, witness **3** *(d'un brevet, d'une marque)* applicant

dépose [depoz] **NF** removal; **d. gratuite de vos anciens appareils** your old appliances removed free of charge

déposer [3] [depoze] **VT 1** *(poser ▸ gén)* to lay *or* to put down; **d. un bébé dans un landau** to lay a baby down in a *Br* pram *or Am* baby carriage; **d. un bébé dans une poussette** to put *or* to sit a baby in a *Br* pushchair *or Am* stroller

2 *(laisser ▸ gerbe)* to lay; *(▸ objet livré)* to leave, to drop off; *(▸ valise)* to leave

3 *(faire descendre d'un véhicule)* to drop (off); *(décharger ▸ matériel)* to unload, to set down; **je te dépose?** can I drop you off?, can I give you a lift?

4 *(argent, valeurs)* to deposit; **d. de l'argent en banque** to deposit money with a bank; **d. de l'argent sur son compte** to pay money into one's account; **d. des titres en garde** to deposit securities in safe custody; **d. une caution** to leave a deposit

5 *Admin* **d. son bilan** to file for bankruptcy, to go into (voluntary) liquidation; **d. un brevet** to file a patent application, to apply for a patent; **d. sa candidature** to apply; **d. une plainte (contre qn)** to lodge a complaint (against sb); **d. un projet de loi** to introduce *or* to table a bill

6 *(destituer ▸ roi)* to depose

7 *Littéraire (donner)* **d. un baiser sur le front de qn** to kiss sb's forehead gently

8 *(démonter ▸ radiateur, étagère)* to remove; *(tapis, moquette)* to lift, to take up

9 *(laisser s'accumuler ▸ limon, sédiments)* to deposit

VI 1 *Jur* to give evidence, to testify **2** *Chim* to form a deposit, to scale **3** *(en œnologie)* to settle, to form a sediment

VPR se déposer to settle

dépositaire [depoziter] **NMF 1** *Jur* depositary, trustee; **être le d. d'une lettre** to hold a letter in trust; **il n'est que le d. de la fortune de son frère** he is merely the trustee of his brother's fortune; **d. de valeurs** holder of securities on trust

2 *Com (de produits)* agent; **d. agréé** authorized agent; **d. exclusif** sole agent; **d. d'une marque** agent for a brand; **d. de journaux** newsagent

3 *Admin* **d. de l'autorité publique** = officer of the State; **d. public** = government official with responsibility for the management of public funds

4 *Littéraire (confident)* repository; **faire de qn le d. d'un secret** to entrust sb with a secret

déposition [depozisjɔ̃] **NF 1** *(témoignage)* deposition, evidence, statement; **faire une d.** to testify; **recueillir une d.** to take a statement **2** *(destitution ▸ d'un roi)* deposition

dépositionner [3] [depozisjɔne] **VT** *Mktg* to deposition

déposséder [18] [depɔsede] **VT** to dispossess; **sa famille a été dépossédée** his/her family was stripped of all its possessions; **d. qn de** to deprive sb of

dépossession [depɔsesjɔ̃] **NF** deprivation, dispossessing

dépôt [depo] **NM 1** *(remise ▸ d'un rapport)* handing in, submission; *(▸ d'un paquet, d'un télégramme)* handing in

2 *(pose ▸ d'une gerbe)* laying

3 *Admin (inscription)* application, filing; *(enregistrement)* filing, registration; **d. d'une liste électorale** presentation of a list of candidates; **d. de bilan** petition in bankruptcy; **d. de brevet** patent registration; **d. légal** copyright deposit *(in France, copies of published or recorded documents have to be deposited at the Bibliothèque nationale)*; **numéro de d. légal** book number; **d. d'une marque** registration of a trademark; **d. d'une plainte** lodging of a complaint; **d. d'un projet de loi** introduction *or* tabling of a bill

4 *Fin (démarche)* depositing; *(somme)* deposit; **faire un d.** to make a deposit; **d. bancaire** bank deposit; **d. en coffre-fort** safe-deposit; **d. à échéance fixe** fixed deposit; **d. d'espèces** cash deposit; *Bourse* **d. de garantie** margin deposit; **d. interbancaire** interbank deposit; **d. à terme** short-term deposit; **d. à terme fixe** fixed deposit; **d. à vue** demand *or* sight deposit

5 *Géol* deposit; **d. alluvial/de cendres/de carbone** alluvial/ash/carbon deposit

6 *(couche)* layer; *(sédiment)* deposit, sediment; **d. calcaire** *ou* **de tartre** *(dans une bouilloire, un chauffe-eau)* layer of scale *or* fur; **d. marin** silt; **d. de poussière** layer of dust

7 *(en œnologie)* sediment

8 *Métal* depositing, deposition; **d. métallique** sputtering

9 *(entrepôt)* store, depot; **d. de charbon** coal depot; **d. de distribution** distribution depot; **d. d'expédition** shipping depot; **d. des machines** engine house; **d. de marchandises** goods depot, warehouse; **d. de matériel** storage yard; **d. mortuaire** mortuary; **d. d'ordures** *Br* rubbish dump *or* tip, *Am* garbage dump
10 *Mil* depot; **d. de munitions** ammunition dump
11 *Transp* depot, *Am* station
12 *(boutique)* retail outlet; **d. de pain** ≃ bread shop; **l'épicier fait d. de pain** the grocer sells bread
13 *(prison)* (police) cells *(in Paris)*; **au d.** in the cells; **écroué au d.** committed to the cells
• **en dépôt** ADV *Fin* in trust, in safe custody; **confier qch en d. à qn** to entrust sb with sth; **avoir en d.** to have on bond; **mettre en d.** to bond

dépotage [depɔtaʒ], **dépotement** [depɔtmɑ̃] NM **1** *Hort* transplanting **2** *Chim* decanting **3** *(vidage)* discharging, dumping

dépoter [3] [depɔte] VT **1** *Hort* to plant out, to transplant **2** *Chim* to decant **3** *(vider)* to discharge, to dump

dépotoir [depɔtwar] NM **1** *(décharge)* dump; *(usine)* disposal plant, sewage works **2** *Péj (lieu sale)* pigsty; **ta chambre est un vrai d.** your bedroom's a complete pigsty; **il faut empêcher la Manche de devenir un d.** we must prevent the Channel becoming an open sewer **3** *Fam (débarras)* dumping ground

dépôt-vente [depovɑ̃t] *(pl* **dépôts-ventes***)* NM = second-hand shop which gives the original owner a percentage of the profits on goods sold, *Am* consignment store; **mettre qch en d.** to put sth *Br* on sale or return *or Am* on consignment

dépouille [depuj] NF **1** *(cadavre)* **d. (mortelle)** (mortal) remains; **les dépouilles des victimes ont été rapatriées hier** the bodies of the victims were repatriated yesterday **2** *(peau ▸ d'un mammifère)* hide, skin; *(▸ d'un reptile)* slough
• **dépouilles** NFPL *(trophée)* booty, plunder, spoils

dépouillé, -e [depuje] ADJ **1** *(sans peau)* skinned; *(sans feuilles)* bare, leafless
2 *(sans ornement)* plain, simple, uncluttered; **un style d.** a concise *or* terse style
3 *(dénué)* **d. de** lacking in
4 vin d. = wine that has lost its alcohol content

dépouillement [depujmɑ̃] NM **1** *(analyse)* breakdown, collection and analysis; **d. des données** data reduction; **d. du scrutin** tally *or* counting of the votes
2 *(ouverture ▸ du courrier)* opening; *(▸ d'appels d'offres)* checking
3 *(simplicité ▸ d'un décor)* bareness, soberness
4 *(concision)* conciseness, terseness
5 *(dénuement)* dispossession, destitution; **ils ont choisi de vivre dans le d. le plus complet** they chose to live an ascetic life

dépouiller [3] [depuje] VT **1** *(lapin)* to skin
2 *(câble)* to strip; **la bise a dépouillé les arbres de leurs feuilles** the north wind has stripped the trees bare *or* of their leaves
3 *(voler)* to rob; **d. un héritier** to deprive *or* rob an heir of his inheritance; **d. qn de qch** *(terres, droits)* to deprive *or* to dispossess sb of sth; **d. qn de ses droits** to strip sb of his/her rights; **ils m'ont dépouillé de tout ce que j'avais sur moi** they stripped me of *or* took everything I had on me; **il s'est fait d. de tout ce qu'il avait sur lui** he was robbed of everything he was carrying
4 *(priver)* **dans le film, le personnage est dépouillé de tout son charme** all the character's charm is lost in the movie *or Br* film
5 *(lire ▸ journal, courrier, inventaire)* to go through; *(analyser ▸ questionnaire, réponses)* to analyse, to study, to scrutinize; *(▸ données)* to process; *(▸ appels d'offres)* to check; *Pol* **d. le scrutin** to count the votes
6 *(quitter)* to cast aside, to strip off; **d. ses vêtements** to throw off *or* to strip off one's clothes; *Zool* **les reptiles dépouillent leur peau** reptiles slough off *or* shed their skin
VPR **se dépouiller 1** *(arbre, végétation)* **les arbres se dépouillent peu à peu** the trees are gradually losing *or* shedding their leaves
2 *Zool* to slough off its skin
3 se d. de *(se défaire de)* to rid oneself of; **se d. de ses vêtements** to strip off; **se d. de tous ses biens** to give away all one's property
4 *Littéraire* **se d. de** *(se départir de)* to cast off; **il ne s'est pas dépouillé un seul instant de son arrogance** he didn't depart from his arrogant attitude for a single moment

dépourvu, -e [depurvy] ADJ **1** *(misérable)* destitute **2** *(manquant)* **d. de** devoid of, lacking in; **c'est d. de tout intérêt** it is of *or* holds no interest at all; **chambre dépourvue de confort** room lacking in comfort; **totalement d. de scrupules** totally unscrupulous; **sa remarque n'était pas entièrement dépourvue de bon sens** his/her remark was not entirely devoid of common sense; **paysage d. d'arbres** treeless countryside
• **au dépourvu** ADV **prendre qn au d.** to catch sb off guard *or* unawares; **ils ont été pris au d. par cette information** the news caught them unawares

dépoussiérage [depusjeraʒ] NM dusting

dépoussiérant, -e [depusjerɑ̃, -ɑ̃t] ADJ dust-removing
NM dust remover

dépoussiérer [18] [depusjere] VT **1** *(nettoyer)* to dust **2** *(rajeunir)* to rejuvenate, to give a new lease of life to

dépravation [depravasjɔ̃] NF depravity, perversion

dépravé, -e [deprave] ADJ depraved, perverted
NM,F degenerate, pervert

dépraver [3] [deprave] VT **1** *(corrompre)* to deprave, to corrupt, to pervert **2** *Littéraire (altérer ▸ goût, jugement)* to corrupt, to spoil
VPR **se dépraver** to become depraved *or* perverted

dépréciateur, -trice [depresjatœr, -tris] ADJ disparaging, deprecatory, depreciative
NM,F depreciator, disparager

dépréciatif, -ive [depresjatif, -iv] ADJ derogatory, disparaging

dépréciation [depresjasjɔ̃] NF depreciation, drop *or* fall in value; **la d. des propriétés foncières** the drop in property values; *Compta* **d. annuelle** annual depreciation; *Compta* **d. de créances** write-down of accounts receivable; *Compta* **d. fonctionnelle** *(du matériel)* wear and tear

dépréciative [depresjativ] *voir* **dépréciatif**

dépréciatrice [depresjatris] *voir* **dépréciateur**

déprécier [9] [depresje] VT **1** *Fin* to depreciate, to cause to drop in value **2** *(dénigrer)* to run down, to belittle, to disparage **3** *(mal évaluer)* to undervalue
VPR **se déprécier 1** *(se déconsidérer)* to belittle *or* to disparage oneself, to run oneself down **2** *Fin* to depreciate, to fall in value

déprédateur, -trice [depredatœr, -tris] ADJ plundering, *Sout* depredatory
NM,F *(pilleur)* plunderer, *Sout* depredator; *(escroc)* swindler, embezzler

déprédation [depredasjɔ̃] NF **1** *(pillage)* pillaging; *(dégâts)* (wilful) damage; **commettre des déprédations sur qch** to cause wilful damage to sth **2** *(détournement)* **d. de biens** misappropriation of property; **d. des finances publiques** embezzlement of public funds

déprédatrice [depredatris] *voir* **déprédateur**

dépressif, -ive [depresif, -iv] ADJ *(personne, caractère)* depressive; **avoir des tendances dépressives** to be depressive
NM,F depressive

dépression [depresjɔ̃] NF **1** *Méd & Psy* depression; **d. nerveuse** nervous breakdown; **avoir** *ou* **faire une d. (nerveuse)** to have a nervous breakdown; **tu ne vas pas nous faire une d., au moins?** you're not going to get depressed, are you?; **d. hivernale** seasonal affective disorder, SAD
2 *Géog* depression
3 *(absence de pression)* vacuum; *(différence de pression)* suction
4 *Météo* cyclone, barometric depression
5 *Écon* depression, slump

dépressionnaire [depresjɔnɛr] ADJ **1** *Écon* slump *(avant n)*; **le marché a des tendances dépressionnaires** the market's sliding towards a slump
2 *Météo* low pressure *(avant n)*; **zone d.** area of low pressure

dépressive [depresiv] *voir* **dépressif**

dépressurisation [depresyrizasjɔ̃] NF depressurization

dépressuriser [3] [depresyrize] VT to depressurize

déprimant, -e [deprimɑ̃, -ɑ̃t] ADJ *(démoralisant)* depressing, disheartening, demoralizing

déprime [deprim] NF *Fam* **faire une d.** to be depressed; **tu ne vas pas nous faire une d. pour si peu?** you're not going to get depressed over such a small thing?; **avoir un (petit) coup de d.** to be (a bit) depressed; **il est en pleine d.** he's really down at the moment

déprimé, -e [deprime] ADJ **1** *(abattu)* dejected, depressed; **je suis plutôt d. aujourd'hui** I feel a bit down today **2** *(aplati)* depressed, flattened **3** *Bourse (marché)* depressed

déprimer [3] [deprime] VT **1** *(abattre)* to depress, to demoralize **2** *(enfoncer)* to push in, to press down; **le choc a déprimé l'aile avant** the front wing was dented in the crash
VI *Fam* to be depressed

déprogrammation [deprɔgramasjɔ̃] NF *Rad & TV* withdrawal *or* removal from the schedule

déprogrammer [3] [deprɔgrame] VT **1** *Rad & TV* to withdraw *or* to remove from the schedule
2 *Ordinat* to remove from a program
3 *Fam (déconditionner)* to debrief□
4 *(annuler ▸ rendez-vous)* to cancel

déprotection [deprɔteksjɔ̃] NF *Ordinat* unprotecting

DEPS [deəpeɛs] NM *Com & Compta (abrév* **dernier entré premier sorti***)* LIFO

dépucelage [depyslaʒ] NM *Fam (d'une fille)* deflowering□; *(d'un garçon)* loss of virginity□

dépuceler [24] [depysle] VT *Fam (fille)* to deflower□, to take the virginity of□; *(garçon)* to take the virginity of□; **c'est elle qui l'a dépucelé** he lost his virginity to her□; **se faire d.** to lose one's virginity□

DEPUIS [dəpɥi]

PRÉP	
• since **1**	• for **2**
• from **3**	
ADV	
• since	

PRÉP **1** *(à partir d'une date ou d'un moment précis)* since; **il est là d. hier** he has been here since yesterday; **je ne suis pas sorti d. hier** I haven't been out since yesterday; **d. le 10 mars** since 10 March; **d. le début** from the very beginning, right from the beginning; **elle est aveugle d. l'âge de cinq ans** she has been blind since she was five *or* from the age of five; **je ne l'ai/l'avais pas vu d. son mariage** I haven't/hadn't seen him since he got married; **d. son accident, il boite** he's walked with a limp since his accident; **il nous suit d. Tours** he's been following us since (we left) Tours; **je ne fais du golf que d. cette année** I only started to play golf this year
2 *(exprimant une durée)* for; **d. dix ans** for ten years; **il est parti d. plus d'un mois** he's been gone now for over a month; **je ne l'avais pas vu d. un an quand je l'ai rencontré** I hadn't seen him for a year when I met him; **il n'est pas en forme d. quelques jours** he hasn't been on form for the last few days; **d. longtemps** for a long time; **d. quelque temps** of late; **il ne joue plus d. quelque temps** he hasn't been playing of late *or* lately, he hasn't played for some time; **d. peu** recently, not long ago; **la piscine n'est ouverte que d. peu** the pool opened only recently; **d. toujours** always; **les hommes font la guerre d. toujours** men have always waged war; **nous répétons la pièce d. trois mois** we've been rehearsing the play for three months; **d. combien de temps le connais-tu?** how long have you known him for?; **et tu ne sais toujours pas t'en servir d. le temps!** and you still don't know how to use it after all this time!; **comment vas-tu, d. le temps?** how have you been all this time?; **ça devait casser, d. le temps!** it was bound to break sometime!; **il me l'a rendu hier – d. le temps!** he gave it back to me yesterday – it took

him long enough *or* and not before time! **3** *(dans l'espace, un ordre, une hiérarchie)* from; **il lui a fait signe d. sa fenêtre** he waved to him/her from his window; **téléphoner d. chez soi** to ring from home; **concert retransmis d. Londres** concert broadcast from London; **un embouteillage d. La Rochelle** a traffic jam all the way from La Rochelle; **d. le sommet, le village paraissait si petit** from the top of the hill, the village seemed so small; **des matelas d. 60 euros** mattresses from 60 euros (upwards); **toutes les tailles d. le deux ans** all sizes from two years upwards

ADV je ne l'ai rencontré qu'une fois, je ne l'ai jamais revu d. I only met him once and I've not seen him again since (then); **trois lettres en janvier et rien d.** three letters in January and nothing since (then); **je l'ai connu d.** I made his acquaintance after that *or* later

• **depuis… jusqu'à 1** *(dans le temps)* from… to; **d. le début jusqu'à la fin** from the beginning to the end; **d. 12 heures jusqu'à 20 heures** from 12 to *or* till 8; **d. le matin jusqu'au soir** from morning till night **2** *(dans l'espace, un ordre, une hiérarchie)* from… to; **d. le premier jusqu'au dernier** from the first to the last; **ils vendent de tout, d. les parapluies jusqu'aux sandwiches** they sell everything, from umbrellas to sandwiches

• **depuis le temps que CONJ d. le temps que tu me le promets…** you've been promising me that for such a long time…; **d. le temps que tu le connais, tu pourrais lui demander** considering how long you've known him you could easily ask him; **d. le temps que tu voulais y aller!** you've been wanting to go there for ages now!

• **depuis lors ADV** since then; **il n'est pas retourné au village d. lors** he hasn't been back to the village since then; **d. lors, plus rien** since then, nothing more

• **depuis quand ADV 1** *(pour interroger sur la durée)* how long; **d. quand m'attends-tu?** how long have you been waiting for me?; **d. quand travaillait-il pour vous?** how long had he been working for you? **2** *(exprimant l'indignation, l'ironie)* since when; **d. quand est-ce que tu me donnes des ordres?** since when do you give me orders?

• **depuis que CONJ** since; **je ne l'ai pas revu d. qu'il s'est marié** I haven't seen him since he got married; **je veux être danseuse d. que j'ai cinq ans** I've wanted to be a dancer (ever) since I was five; **d. qu'il sait qu'il va la voir, il ne tient plus en place** he hasn't been able to keep still since he found out he was going to see her; **d. que j'ai arrêté de fumer, je me sens mieux** I feel better since I stopped smoking

dépuratif, -ive [depyratif, -iv] **ADJ** cleansing, depurative

NM depurative

dépuration [depyrasjɔ̃] **NF** *Méd (du sang)* cleansing, depuration

dépurative [depyrativ] *voir* **dépuratif**

dépurer [3] [depyre] **VT 1** *Méd* to cleanse, to depurate **2** *Chim* to purify

députation [depytasjɔ̃] **NF 1** *(envoi)* deputation, mandating **2** *(groupe)* delegation, deputation **3** *Pol* office of Deputy, membership of the Assemblée Nationale; **se présenter à la d.** to stand for the position of Deputy

député [depyte] **NM 1** *(représentant)* delegate, representative **2** *Pol (en France)* deputy; *(en Grande-Bretagne)* member of Parliament; *(aux États-Unis)* Congressman, *f* Congresswoman; **un d. européen** a member of the European Parliament, an MEP, a Euro-MP; **femme d.** *(en Grande-Bretagne)* woman MP; *(aux États-Unis)* Congresswoman

député-maire [depytemer] *(pl* **députés-maires***)* **NM** = deputy who also holds the post of mayor

députer [3] [depyte] **VT** to send, to delegate; **d. qn auprès du ministre** to send sb (as delegate) *or* to delegate sb to speak to the Minister

déqualification [dekalifikasjɔ̃] **NF** *(liée à la technologie)* deskilling; **la d. (professionnelle) est de plus en plus fréquente** more and more people are overqualified for their jobs *or* for the work they do; **cette catégorie de travailleur subit une rapide d.** workers who fall into this category quickly lose the professional skills needed to compete on the job market

déqualifier [9] [dekalifje] **VT** *(emploi, employé ▸ à cause de la technologie)* to deskill; **en élevant le niveau d'exigence par rapport aux postes offerts, on déqualifie les diplômes** the rising threshold of qualifications being required of job applicants means that degrees are being devalued; **le chômage de longue durée déqualifie les travailleurs** people lose their professional skills as a result of long-term unemployment

der [dɛr] **NM INV OU NF INV la d. des d.** the war to end all wars

déracinable [derasinabl] **ADJ** eradicable, easy to suppress *or* to uproot

déraciné, -e [derasine] **ADJ** *Bot & Fig* uprooted; **ils se sentent déracinés** they feel cut off from their roots

NM,F person without roots; **les déracinés** people without roots

déracinement [derasinmɑ̃] **NM 1** *Bot* uprooting; *Fig (exil)* uprooting (from one's environment); **ce fut pour eux un d. complet** it was a complete change of environment for them **2** *(extirpation)* eradication, suppression; **le d. des préjugés** eradicating prejudice

déraciner [3] [derasine] **VT 1** *Bot & Fig* to uproot **2** *(détruire ▸ vice, racisme)* to root out; **ces habitudes sont difficiles à d.** these habits die hard

déraidir [32] [derɛdir] **VT** *(membre, tissu etc)* to take the stiffness out of; *Fig (caractère de quelqu'un)* to soften

VPR se déraidir *(membre, tissu etc)* to lose its stiffness; *(personne)* to unbend, to thaw

déraillement [derajmɑ̃] **NM 1** *Rail* derailment; **il y a eu un d. à Foissy** a train came off the track *or* was derailed at Foissy **2** *(d'un disque)* groove jumping

dérailler [3] [deraje] **VI 1** *Rail* to go off *or* to leave the rails; **faire d. un train** to derail a train **2** *Fam (fonctionner mal)* to be on the blink, *Am* to be on the fritz; **elle déraille, cette radio!** this radio's on the blink *or Am* on the fritz!; **faire d. les négociations** to derail the talks **3** *Fam (dire des sottises)* to talk nonsense; *(divaguer)* to rave; **tu dérailles complètement!** you're talking utter nonsense!

dérailleur [derajœr] **NM** derailleur (gear)

déraison [derɛzɔ̃] **NF** *Littéraire* foolishness, folly

déraisonnable [derɛzɔnabl] **ADJ** foolish, senseless; **une attente/attitude d.** irrational expectation/behaviour; **il serait d. de partir si tard** it wouldn't be wise to leave so late

déraisonnablement [derɛzɔnabləmɑ̃] **ADV** foolishly, senselessly, unwisely

déraisonner [3] [derɛzɔne] **VI 1** *(dire des sottises)* to talk nonsense **2** *(divaguer)* to rave

dérangé, -e [derɑ̃ʒe] **ADJ 1** *Fam (fou)* deranged; **t'es pas un peu d.?** have you gone out of your mind?; **il a l'esprit un peu d.** he's lost his marbles, *Br* he's lost the plot **2** *(malade)* upset; **il a l'estomac** *ou* **il est d.** he's got an upset stomach **3** *(en désordre ▸ coiffure)* dishevelled, messed-up; *(▸ tenue)* untidy; **en rentrant j'ai trouvé le salon/tiroir d.** when I got home I found the living room/drawer in a mess

dérangeant, -e [derɑ̃ʒɑ̃, -ɑ̃t] **ADJ 1** *(qui fait réfléchir)* thought-provoking **2** *(qui crée un malaise)* distressing, upsetting

dérangement [derɑ̃ʒmɑ̃] **NM 1** *(désordre)* disarrangement, disorder

2 *(gêne)* trouble, inconvenience; **je peux le recevoir sans grand d.** it won't be any trouble for me to put him up; **causer du d. à qn** to inconvenience sb, to put sb to trouble; **je ne veux surtout pas vous causer de d.** I don't want to inconvenience you *or* put you to any trouble

3 *Méd* disturbance, upset; **d. de l'esprit** insanity, mental derangement; **d. gastrique** *ou* **intestinal** *ou* **de l'intestin** stomach upset

4 *(déplacement)* trip; **cela m'épargnera le d.** it'll save me having to go; **cela ne vaut pas/vaut le d.** it isn't/it's worth the trip

• **en dérangement ADJ** out of order, faulty

déranger [17] [derɑ̃ʒe] **VT 1** *(mettre en désordre ▸ objets)* to mix *or* to muddle up, to make a mess of; *(▸ pièce)* to make untidy, to make a mess in; **ne dérange pas mes papiers!** don't get my papers mixed up *or* in a muddle!; **rien n'a été dérangé** nothing was touched; **d. la coiffure de qn** to mess up sb's hair

2 *(gêner)* to bother, to disturb; **ne pas d.** *(sur panneau)* do not disturb; **si cela ne vous dérange pas** if you don't mind; **est-ce que cela vous dérange si** *ou* **que…?** do you mind if…?; **ça ne te dérange pas de poster ma lettre?** would you mind posting my letter for me?; *Fam* **et alors, ça te dérange?** so, what's it to you?; *Ironique* **je ne te dérange pas trop, au moins?** am I in your way?; *Fam* **ça te dérangerait d'être poli?** would it be too much trouble for you to be polite?

3 *(interrompre)* to interrupt, to intrude upon; **allô, Marie, je te dérange?** hello Marie, is this a good time to call?; **désolé de vous d.** sorry to disturb you; **je ne peux pas travailler, je suis sans arrêt dérangé** I can't work with all these interruptions

4 *(perturber ▸ projets)* to interfere with, to upset; **d. l'esprit de qn** to affect the balance of sb's mind

5 *(estomac)* to upset

VI ses livres dérangent his/her books are challenging

VPR se déranger 1 *(venir)* to come; *(aller)* to go out; **il a refusé de se d.** he wouldn't come (out); **je refuse de me d.** I refuse to go; **s'est-elle dérangée pour la réunion?** did she put in an appearance at the meeting?; **ce coup de fil m'a évité de me d.** that phone call saved me a useless journey; **grâce à l'ordinateur, faites vos courses sans vous d.** thanks to computers, you can shop without leaving the house; **se d. pour rien** to have a wasted journey **2** *(se pousser)* to move (aside); **ne te dérange pas, je passe très bien** stay where you are, I can get through **3** *(se donner du mal)* to put oneself out; **ne te dérange pas** (please) don't put yourself out; **ne vous dérangez pas, je reviendrai** please don't go to any trouble, I'll come back later

dérapage [derapaʒ] **NM 1** *Sport & Ski* side-slipping; *(en moto)* skidding; *Ski* **faire du d.** to sideslip

2 *Aviat & Aut* skid; **d. contrôlé** controlled skid

3 *(dérive)* (uncontrolled) drifting; **le d. des prix** the uncontrolled increase in prices; **le d. de l'économie** the downward spiral of the economy; **il y a déjà eu plusieurs dérapages dans cette émission** there have already been several inappropriate outbursts in the programme; **un d. verbal** a verbal faux pas, a gaffe

4 *(erreur)* mistake, slip-up

déraper [3] [derape] **VI 1** *(gén)* to skid

2 *Ski* to sideslip

3 *Aviat* to skid sideways

4 *Fig (prix)* to rise uncontrollably; *(situation)* to go wrong; **il faut éviter que les négociations ne dérapent** the talks must not go wrong; **dommage que son article dérape à deux pages de la fin** it's a pity his/her article starts to go off at a tangent two pages before the end; **la conversation a vite dérapé sur la politique** the conversation soon got round to politics

5 *Naut (ancre)* to drag

dératé, -e [derate] **NM,F courir comme un d.** to run like lightning

dératisation [deratizasjɔ̃] **NF** rodent control; **la d. de l'immeuble est prévue le 10 décembre** the building will be cleared of rodents on 10 December

dératiser [3] [deratize] **VT** to clear of rats *or* rodents

dérayage [derejaʒ] **NM** *Cin & TV* polishing out

dérayer [11] [dereje] **VT** *Cin & TV* to polish out

derby [dɛrbi] *(pl* **derbys** *ou* **derbies***)* **NM 1** *Équitation* derby; **le d. d'Epsom** the Derby **2** *(match)* local derby **3** *(chaussure)* derby shoe

derche [dɛrʃ] **NM** *très Fam* butt, *Br* bum, *Am* fanny; **se magner le d.** to move one's butt *or Br* bum; **un faux d.** a two-faced *Br* swine *or Am* stinker

derechef [dərəʃɛf] **ADV** *Hum* once again, one more time

déréférencement [dereferɑ̃smɑ̃] **NM** *Mktg (d'un produit)* delisting

déréférencer [16] [dereferɑ̃se] **VT** *Mktg (produit)* to delist; **certains produits ont été déférencés par le distributeur** some products have been delisted by the distributor

dérèglement [dereglǝmɑ̃] **NM 1** *(d'une machine, d'une horloge)* malfunctioning **2** *(du temps)* unsettled state; *(du pouls)* irregularity; **d. de l'esprit** mental derangement; **d. hormonal** hormone disorder
• **dérèglements NMPL** *(écarts)* dissoluteness, debauchery

déréglementation [dereglǝmɑ̃tasjɔ̃] **NF** deregulation

déréglementer [3] [dereglǝmɑ̃te] **VT** to deregulate

dérégler [18] [deregle] **VT 1** *Tech (mécanisme)* to disturb; *(carburateur)* to put *or* to throw out of tuning; **le compteur est déréglé** the meter's not working properly; **l'orage a déréglé la pendule électrique** the storm has sent the electric clock haywire **2** *(perturber)* to unsettle, to upset; **d. son sommeil** to disturb one's sleep pattern
VPR se dérégler 1 *Tech* to go wrong, to start malfunctioning; **le carburateur s'est déréglé** the carburettor's out; **ma fixation s'est déréglée** my binding's come loose **2** *(de pouls)* to be irregular; *(d'estomac)* to be upset; **son esprit se dérègle** his/her mind is going; **elle s'est déréglé le système digestif** she's ruined her digestive system

déridage [deridaʒ] **NM** *Méd* facelift

dérider [3] [deride] **VT 1** *(détendre)* to cheer up; **je n'ai pas réussi à le d.** I couldn't get a smile out of him **2** *(déplisser)* to unwrinkle
VPR se dérider to brighten, to cheer up

> Il faut noter que le verbe anglais **to deride** est un faux ami. Il signifie **ridiculiser**.

dérision [derizjɔ̃] **NF 1** *(moquerie)* derision, mockery; **avec d.** mockingly, derisively; **dire qch par d.** to say sth derisively *or* mockingly; **un geste de d.** a derisive gesture; **tourner qn/qch en d.** to scoff at *or* to mock sb/sth; **sur le ton de la d.** mockingly **2** *(ironie)* irony; **quelle d.!** how ironic!

dérisoire [derizwar] **ADJ 1** *(risible)* ridiculous, laughable **2** *(piètre ▸ salaire, prix)* derisory, ridiculous **3** *(sans effet)* inadequate, pathetic

dérisoirement [derizwarmɑ̃] **ADV** ridiculously, preposterously

dérivatif, -ive [derivatif, -iv] **ADJ 1** *(activité, occupation)* derivative **2** *Ling* derivative
NM distraction, escape; **le travail sert de d. à son chagrin** work is an outlet for his/her grief; **le sport est un excellent d.** sport is an excellent way of taking your mind off things

dérivation [derivasjɔ̃] **NF 1** *(d'un cours d'eau)* diversion
2 *Élec* shunt, branch circuit; **monté en d.** shunt connected
3 *Chim, Ling & Math* derivation
4 *Naut* drift
5 *Méd* **d. gastrique** gastric bypass
• **de dérivation ADJ 1** *(détourné)* **canal de d.** headrace; **conduite de d.** by-pass **2** *Élec* dividing

dérivative [derivativ] *voir* **dérivatif**

dérive [deriv] **NF 1** *(dérapage)* drifting, drift; **la d. de l'économie** the downward spiral of the economy; **sa d. vers l'alcoolisme** his/her drifting *or* slipping into alcoholism; **une d. totalitaire est à craindre dans ce pays** this country is in danger of drifting into totalitarianism; **aller à la d.** to drift, to go adrift; *Fig* to go downhill
2 *Naut (déplacement)* drift, drifting off course; *(quille)* centreboard, keel; **partir à la d.** to drift; **un navire en d.** a drifting vessel
3 *Aviat (trajectoire)* drift, drifting off course; *(empennage)* fin, stabilizer; **d. d'empennage** tailfin; **d. de queue** vertical fin; **d. ventrale** lower vertical fin
4 *(en artillerie)* deflection
5 *Géog* **d. des continents** continental drift; **d. des vents d'ouest** west wind drift; **d. latérale** leeway
• **en pleine dérive ADJ** on the decline; **ayant eu son heure de gloire, le chanteur est en pleine d.** after a successful spell, the singer's popularity is fading fast

dérivé, -e [derive] **ADJ 1** *Ling & Math* derived **2** *Élec* diverted, shunt *(avant n)*; **circuit d.** branch circuit
NM 1 *Chim* derivative **2** *Ling* derivation **3** *(sous-produit)* by-product
• **dérivée NF** *Math* derivative

dériver [3] [derive] **VI** *Naut* to drift, to be adrift
VT 1 *(détourner ▸ rivière)* to divert (the course of)
2 *Élec* to shunt
3 *Chim, Ling & Math* to derive
4 *Tech* to unrivet
• **dériver de VT IND 1** *(être issu de)* to derive *or* to come from **2** *Chim* to be produced from **3** *Ling* to derive from, to be derived from

dériveur [derivœr] **NM** *(bateau)* sailing dinghy *(with a centreboard)*; *(voile)* storm sail

dermatite [dermatit] **NF** *Méd* dermitis, dermatitis

dermato [dermato] **NMF** *Fam (abrév* **dermatologiste***)* dermatologist, skin specialist

dermatologie [dermatɔlɔʒi] **NF** *Méd* dermatology

dermatologique [dermatɔlɔʒik] **ADJ** *Méd* dermatological, skin *(avant n)*

dermatologiste [dermatɔlɔʒist], **dermatologue** [dermatɔlɔg] **NMF** *Méd* dermatologist, skin specialist

dermatose [dermatoz] **NF** *Méd* dermatosis, skin disease

derme [derm] **NM** *Anat* dermis

dermique [dermik] **ADJ** *Anat* dermic, dermal

dermite [dermit] **NF** *Méd* dermitis, dermatitis

DERNIER, -ÈRE [dernje, -er]

ADJ	
• last **A1, 3, 4, B3, C1, 2**	• final **A1, 2**
• latest **A4**	• previous **A3**
• highest **C3**	• bottom **B1, 2**
	• utmost **D1**
NM,F	
• last **1, 3–5**	• final **1**
• youngest **2**	• latter **6**
NM	
• top floor **1**	• last **2**
NF	
• final performance **1**	• last edition **2**

ADJ A. *DANS LE TEMPS* **1** *(avant le nom) (qui vient après tous les autres ▸ avion, bus, personne)* last; *(▸ détail, préparatif)* final; **la dernière femme à être condamnée à mort** the last woman to be sentenced to death; **un d. mot/point!** one final word/point!; **le d. jour des soldes** the last day of the sales; **le d. lundi d'avril** the last Monday in April; **il vient de terminer ses derniers examens** *(en fin de cycle d'études)* he's just taken his final exams *or* finals; **le d. enchérisseur** the highest bidder; **un Warhol dernière période** a late Warhol; **les dernières années de sa vie** the last years of his/her life; **jusqu'à son d. jour** to his/her dying day, until the day he/she died; **ses dernières paroles/volontés** his/her last *or* dying words/wishes; **d. arrivant** *ou* **arrivé** *ou* **venu** latecomer; **je résume pour les derniers venus** *ou* **arrivés** *ou* **arrivants** I'll sum up for those of you who've just got here; **sa dernière demeure** his/her final resting place; **la dernière édition** the late edition; **la dernière séance** the last *or* late performance; **il faut toujours qu'il ait le d. mot** he always has to have the last word; **rendre les derniers devoirs** *ou* **honneurs** *ou* **un d. hommage à qn** to pay a final tribute *or* one's last respects to sb
2 *(avant le nom) (ultime)* final; **c'est mon d. prix** *(vendeur)* it's the lowest I'll go; *(acheteur)* that's my final offer; **c'est le d. avertissement!** it's your last *or* final warning!; **d. rappel** *(de facture)* final reminder; **faire un d. effort** to make a final *or* one last effort; **les derniers mètres de l'ascension** the final metres of the climb; **en dernière analyse** in the final analysis; *Bourse* **d. cours** closing price
3 *(précédent)* last, previous; **mon d. patron était anglais** my last boss was English; **la nuit dernière** last night; **lundi d.** last Monday; **l'été/le mois d.** last summer/month; **la dernière fois, la fois dernière** last time; **où ont eu lieu les derniers jeux Olympiques?** where did the previous *or* last Olympic Games take place?; **ces dix dernières années** these last ten years
4 *(avant le nom) (le plus récent)* last, latest; **achète-moi la dernière biographie de Proust** get me the latest biography of Proust; **les derniers développements d'une affaire** the latest developments of an affair; **le d. modèle** the latest model; **une décision prise à la dernière seconde** *ou* **minute** a last-minute decision; **je ferai mes valises au d. moment** I'll pack at the last minute *or* last possible moment; **on nous apprend/ils apprirent en dernière minute que...** we've just heard this minute/at the last minute they heard that...; **ces derniers temps** lately, of late; **les derniers temps de** the last stages *or* days of, the end of; **pendant les derniers temps de son mandat** towards the end of his/her mandate; **tu connais la dernière nouvelle?** have you heard the latest?; **aux dernières nouvelles, le mariage aurait été annulé** the last I heard, the wedding's off; **de dernière heure** *(changement)* last-minute; **une information de dernière heure** *ou* **minute** a late newsflash
B. *DANS L'ESPACE* **1** *(du bas)* bottom; **le d. tiroir** the bottom drawer; **la dernière marche de l'escalier** the bottom step of the stairs
2 *(du haut)* top; **au d. étage** on the top floor; **la dernière marche de l'escalier** the top step of the stairs
3 *(du bout)* last; **un siège au d. rang** a seat in the back (row); **sur la photo, c'est la dernière personne à droite** in the picture, he's/she's the last person on the right
C. *DANS UN CLASSEMENT, UNE HIÉRARCHIE* **1** *(dans une série)* last; **la dernière lettre de l'alphabet** the last letter of the alphabet; **suite à la dernière page** continued on the back page; **quelqu'un vient d'acheter le d. billet** someone's just bought the last ticket; *Typ* **dernières épreuves** press proofs
2 *(le plus mauvais)* last, bottom; **en dernière position** in last position, last; **en dernière position du championnat** (at the) bottom of the league (table); **le d. élève de la classe** the pupil at the bottom of the class; **je suis d. à l'examen** I came last *or Br* bottom in the exam; **arriver bon d.** to come in last
3 *(le meilleur)* top, highest; **le d. échelon** the highest level
D. *EN INTENSIF* **1** *(avant le nom) (extrême, sens positif)* **de la dernière importance** of paramount *or* of the utmost importance; **du d. chic** extremely smart; **nos fauteuils sont du d. confort** our armchairs are the ultimate in comfort; **atteindre le d. degré de la perfection** to attain the summit of perfection; **le d. degré de la bêtise** the height of stupidity; **être du d. bien avec qn** to be extremely friendly with sb, to be great friends with sb
2 *(avant le nom) (extrême, sens négatif)* **le d. degré de la misère** the depths of poverty; **être du d. égoïsme** to be extraordinarily selfish; **un acte de la dernière lâcheté** the most cowardly of acts; **traiter qn avec le d. mépris** to treat sb with the greatest contempt; **c'est de la dernière impolitesse** it's extremely rude; **du d. mauvais goût** in appalling bad taste; **c'est la dernière chose à faire** it's the last thing one should do; **un couteau électrique! c'est bien le d. appareil que j'achèterais!** an electric knife! that's the last thing I'd buy!; **c'est le d. métier qu'on puisse imaginer** it's the lowest job you could imagine; **se livrer aux derniers excès** to indulge in the most abominable excesses; *Euph* **faire subir les derniers outrages à une femme** to violate a woman
NM,F 1 *(dans le temps)* last *or* final one; **je suis partie la dernière** I left last, I was the last one to leave; **je suis arrivé dans les derniers** I was among the last ones to arrive; **le d. à l'avoir vue en vie** the last person to see her alive; **le d./la dernière en date** the latest (one)
2 *(dans une famille)* youngest; **le d.** the youngest *or* last (boy); **la dernière** the youngest *or* last (girl); **ses deux derniers** his two youngest (children); **le petit d.** the youngest son; **la petite dernière** the youngest daughter
3 *(dans l'espace ▸ celui du haut)* top one; *(▸ celui du bas)* last *or* bottom one; *(▸ celui du bout)* last one; **son dossier est le d. de la pile** her file is at the bottom of the pile; **où es-tu sur la photo? – je suis le d. sur la gauche** where are you in the picture? – I'm the last one on the left
4 *(dans une hiérarchie ▸ le pire)* **j'étais toujours le d. en classe** I was always (at the) bottom of the class; **il est le d. de sa promotion** he is bottom of his year; **tu arrives le d. avec 34 points** you come last with 34 points; **dans les derniers** among the last; **les six derniers** the last six; **elle est la dernière**

à qui je le dirais she's the last person I'd tell; *Fam* **le d. des derniers** the lowest of the low; *Fam* **tu es le d. des imbéciles** you're a complete idiot; *Fam* **le d. des lâches n'aurait pas fait ça** even the worst coward wouldn't have done that; *Fam* **je serais vraiment le d. des idiots!** I'd be a complete fool!; *Fam* **c'est le d. des maris** he's a terrible husband

5 *(dans une série)* last one; **allez, on en prend un d.!** *(verre)* let's have a last one (for the road)!; **ils les ont tués jusqu'au d.** every single *or* last one of them was killed

6 *(dans une narration)* **ce d., cette dernière** *(de deux)* the latter; *(de plusieurs)* this last, the last-mentioned; **il attendait la réponse de Luc, mais ce d. se taisait** he was waiting for Luc's answer but the latter kept quiet; **Myriam, Annie et Joëlle étaient parties et on avait retrouvé la voiture de cette dernière sur une plage** Myriam, Annie and Joëlle had left and Joëlle's car had been found on a beach

NM 1 *(étage)* top floor

2 *(dans une charade)* **mon d. est/a...** my last is/has...

• **dernière NF 1** *Théât* last night, final performance **2** *Presse (édition)* last edition; *(page)* back page **3** *Fam (nouvelle)* **tu connais la dernière?** have you heard the latest?; **je te raconte la dernière de Fred** let me tell you the latest about Fred

• **au dernier degré, au dernier point ADV** extremely, to the highest *or* last degree; **j'étais excédé au d. point** I was utterly furious; **c'est un alcoolique au d. degré** he's a complete alcoholic; **drogué au d. degré** drugged to the eyeballs

• **au dernier degré de PRÉP au d. degré de la misère/du désespoir** in the depths of poverty/despair

• **dernier délai ADV** at the latest

• **en dernier ADV** last; **entrer en d.** to go in last, to be the last one to go in; **il sort toujours en d.** he's always last out; **son nom a été mentionné en d.** his/her name was mentioned last; **en d., je mangerais bien une glace** I wouldn't mind an ice cream to finish; **ajoute le sel en d.** add the salt last *or* at the end

dernièrement [dɛrnjɛrmɑ̃] **ADV** lately, not long ago, (quite) recently

dernier-né, dernière-née [dɛrnjene, dɛrnjɛrne] *(mpl* **derniers-nés**, *fpl* **dernières-nées)** **NM,F 1** *(benjamin)* last-born (child), youngest child **2** *Com* **le d. de notre gamme d'ordinateurs** the latest addition to our range of computers

dérobade [derɔbad] **NF 1** *(fuite)* avoidance, evasion; **il a pris mon silence pour une d.** when I said nothing, he thought I was trying to avoid answering **2** *Équitation* jib, refusal

dérobé, -e [derɔbe] **ADJ 1** *(caché)* hidden, concealed, secret **2** *(volé)* stolen

• **à la dérobée ADV** secretly, on the sly, furtively; **regarder qn à la dérobée** to steal a glance at sb; **il la surveillait à la dérobée** he was watching her furtively; **ils sont sortis à la dérobée** they stole out

dérober [3] [derɔbe] **VT 1** *(voler)* to steal; **d. qch à qn** to steal sth from sb; **on lui a dérobé son argent** he/she has been robbed of his/her money; *Littéraire* **d. un baiser (à qn)** to steal a kiss (from sb) **2** *(cacher)* **d. qch à la vue** to hide *or* to conceal sth from view; **ce mur dérobe la vue** the wall hides the view

VPR se dérober 1 *(éluder la difficulté)* to shy away; **n'essaie pas de te d.** don't try to be evasive

2 *Équitation* to jib, to refuse; **se d. devant l'obstacle** to refuse at the jump

3 *(s'effondrer)* to collapse, to give way; **ses jambes se sont dérobées sous lui** his legs gave way under him; **le sol s'est dérobé brusquement** the ground suddenly caved in

4 se d. à to avoid, to evade; **se d. aux regards** to conceal oneself, to hide; **se d. à ses obligations** to evade *or* to shirk one's responsibilities

dérogation [derɔgasjɔ̃] **NF** (special) dispensation *or* exemption; **consentir une d.** to grant an exemption; **d. aux usages** departure from custom; **par d. à la réglementation** notwithstanding the rules; **sauf d. explicite** unless otherwise specified

dérogatoire [derɔgatwar] **ADJ** dispensatory; *Jur* **clause d.** waiver, *Spéc* derogatory clause

déroger [17] [derɔʒe] **VI** to demean oneself; **en se mêlant à nous, il croirait d.** he thinks it's beneath him to associate with people like us

• **déroger à VT IND 1** *(manquer à)* to depart from; **d. à la loi/ses principes** to depart from the law/one's principles **2** *Hist* **d. à son rang** to lose caste *(after working at a demeaning occupation)*

dérougir [32] [deruʒir] **VI 1** *Vieilli (perdre de sa rougeur)* to stop blushing **2** *Can Fam* **ne pas d.** *(travail)* not to let up; *(être bondé)* to be jam-packed; *(être en colère)* to be always fuming; *(être soûl)* to be permanently plastered

dérouillée [deruje] **NF** *très Fam* thrashing, hammering; **je vais lui mettre une d.!** I'll give him/her what for!; **prendre une d.** to get thrashed *or* hammered

dérouiller [3] [deruje] **VT 1** *(enlever la rouille sur)* to remove the rust from **2** *(assouplir ▸ doigts, esprit)* to loosen up; *(▸ jambes)* to stretch **3** *Fam (battre)* to beat up

VI *Fam* **1** *(être battu)* to get it; **tu vas d.!** you're for it *or* going to get it! **2** *(souffrir)* to be in agony[□]; **qu'est-ce que j'ai dérouillé avec mon entorse!** when I sprained my ankle, it was total agony!

VPR se dérouiller se d. les doigts to loosen up one's fingers; **se d. les jambes** to stretch one's legs; **se d. l'esprit** to exercise one's mind

déroulement [derulmɑ̃] **NM 1** *(débobinage)* unreeling, unwinding **2** *(cours ▸ d'une cérémonie, d'un discours)* course; **le d. des événements** the course *or* sequence of events; **il a surveillé tout le d. des opérations** he monitored operations from start to finish; **pendant tout le d. de la cérémonie** throughout the ceremony

dérouler [3] [derule] **VT 1** *(débobiner ▸ câble)* to unroll, to unwind, to uncoil; *(▸ tapis, rouleau)* to unroll; *(▸ store)* to let down; *Fig* **d. le tapis rouge pour qn** to roll out the red carpet for sb **2** *Ordinat (menu)* to pull down

VPR se dérouler 1 *(se déployer ▸ câble, bande)* to unwind, to uncoil, to unroll; *(▸ store)* to come down; *(▸ serpent)* to uncoil; **le paysage se déroule sous nos yeux** the landscape unfolds before our eyes **2** *(avoir lieu)* to take place, to be going on; **les spectacles qui se déroulent en ce moment** the shows currently running; **les deux opérations se déroulent en même temps** the two operations are concurrent; **les épreuves se sont déroulées conformément au règlement** the exams were conducted in accordance with the rules **3** *(progresser)* to develop, to progress

dérouleur [derulœr] **NM 1** *(de papier)* holder; *(de bande)* winder **2** *(de cuisine)* kitchen roll dispenser **3** *Ordinat* **d. de bande magnétique** tape unit, magnetic tape drive; **d. de film magnétique** magnetic film handler

déroutage [derutaʒ] **NM** rerouting

déroutant, -e [derutɑ̃, -ɑ̃t] **ADJ** perplexing, disconcerting

déroute [derut] **NF 1** *Mil* retreat, rout; **mettre qn en d.** to rout sb, to put sb to rout *or* flight; **le loup a mis le troupeau en d.** the wolf scattered the flock **2** *(débâcle)* ruin; **l'entreprise est en pleine d.** the company is heading for ruin

déroutement [derutmɑ̃] **NM** rerouting

dérouter [3] [derute] **VT 1** *(changer l'itinéraire de)* to reroute **2** *(étonner)* to disconcert, to perplex; **la question l'a dérouté** the question threw him off balance

derrick [derik] **NM** derrick

DERRIÈRE [dɛrjɛr]

PRÉP	
• behind **1, 2**	• beneath **3**
• under **3**	
ADJ	
• behind **1, 4**	• at the back **2, 3**
NM	
• back **1**	• bottom, behind **2**
• rump **3**	

PRÉP 1 *(en arrière de)* behind, *Am* in back of; **ça s'est passé d. chez moi** it happened behind my house; **d. la colline, il y a une forêt** on the other side of the hill *or* beyond the hill there is a forest; **il s'est caché d. le rideau** he hid behind the curtain; **reste au coin, les mains d. la tête** remain standing in the corner with your hands behind your head; **regarde d. toi!** look behind you!; *Fig* **il a l'impression que ses plus belles années sont d. lui** he feels his best years are behind him; **avec une telle expérience d. elle, elle n'aura pas de mal à retrouver un emploi** with that kind of experience behind her she'll have no trouble finding a job; **être d. qn** *(le soutenir)* to support sb; **il sait que le public est d. lui** he knows that the public supports him *or* is behind him; **ne sois pas toujours d. moi!** *(à me surveiller)* stop breathing down my neck all the time!; **je sais bien ce qu'elle dit d. mon dos** I'm quite aware of what she says behind my back; **il faut toujours être d. lui** *ou* **d. son dos** he has to be watched all the time, you have to be at his back all the time

2 *(à la suite de)* behind; **un motard roulait d. le convoi** a policeman was riding behind the convoy; **l'un d. l'autre** one behind the other; **le Kenyan est en première place, avec loin d. lui le Jamaïcain** the Kenyan is in first place with the Jamaican a long way behind; **leur équipe est passée d. nous au classement** their team has dropped behind us in the league; **les Italiens sont d. nous en matière d'électronique** as far as electronics is concerned, the Italians are lagging behind us

3 *(sous)* beneath, under; **d. son indifférence apparente** beneath his/her apparent indifference; **c'est lui qui est d. tout ça** he's the one behind all this; **qu'y a-t-il d. tout ça?** what's behind all this?, what's all this really about?

ADV 1 *(en arrière)* behind; **tu vois le bureau de poste? la bibliothèque est juste d.** do you see the post office? the library's just behind it; **laisser qn d.** to leave sb behind; **regarde d. avant de tourner** look behind you before you turn; **passe d., tu verras mieux** come through, you'll get a better view; **restez d. et suivez notre voiture** stay behind and follow our car

2 *(du côté arrière)* at the back; *(sur la face arrière)* on the back; **ça se boutonne d.** it buttons up at the back; **écris le nom de l'expéditeur d.** write the sender's name on the back

3 *(dans le fond)* at the rear *or* back; **le jardin est d.** the garden is at the rear *or* back (of the house); **installe-toi d.** *(dans une voiture)* sit *Br* in the back *or Am* in back; **hé, taisez-vous d.!** *(dans une voiture)* hey, be quiet there *Br* in the back *or Am* in back!; *(dans une pièce)* hey, be quiet at the back!

4 *Fig* behind; **elle est loin d.** she's a long way behind

NM 1 *(d'un objet, d'un espace)* back

2 *Fam (fesses)* bottom, behind, butt; **pousse ton d.!** shift your backside!; **avoir le d. à l'air** to be bare-bottomed; **coup de pied au d.** kick up the backside *or Am* in the pants; **être** *ou* **tomber sur le d.** *ou* **tomber le d. par terre** to be stunned *or* flabbergasted

3 *Zool* rump, hindquarters; **le chien assis sur son d.** the dog sitting on its haunches

• **de derrière ADJ** *(dent, jardin, roue etc)* back *(avant n)*; **la porte de d.** the back door; **voici une vue de d.** here's a rear view; **pattes de d.** hind legs **PRÉP** *(par l'arrière de)* from behind; **il est arrivé de d. la maison** he arrived from behind the house

dérushage [deræʃaʒ] **NM** *Cin & TV* film editing

dérusher [3] [deræʃe] **VT** *Cin & TV* to edit

derviche [dɛrviʃ] **NM** dervish; **d. tourneur** whirling dervish

des [de] **ADJ** *voir* **un**

PRÉP *voir* **de**

des-, dés- *voir* **dé-**

dès [dɛ] **PRÉP 1** *(dans le temps)* from; **d. son arrivée, j'ai compris que quelque chose n'allait pas** from the moment *or* as soon as he/she arrived, I realised that there was something wrong; **d. son retour, il faudra y penser** as soon as he/she comes back, we'll have to think about it; **d. le début** from the beginning; **d. la première fois** right from the start; **d. les premiers jours d'avril** from early April onwards; **prêt d. 8 heures** ready by 8 o'clock; **d. le quinzième siècle** as far back as the fifteenth century; **d. Noël** from Christmas onwards; **je vais le faire d. aujourd'hui** I'm going to do it this very day; **d. maintenant** from now on; **vous pouvez réserver vos places d. maintenant** booking is now open; **pouvez-vous commencer d. maintenant?** can you start straight away?; **il y pensait d. avant sa retraite** he was thinking of it even before he retired **2** *(dans un ordre, une hiérarchie)* **d. la sixième, on apprend l'anglais** English is studied from the first year onwards; **d. la seconde année** from the second year onwards; **d. sa nomination** as soon as he/she was appointed; **d. l'entrée en vigueur de la loi** as soon as the law comes into force; **d. le troisième verre, il ne savait plus ce qu'il disait** after his third glass he started talking nonsense **3** *(dans l'espace)* **d. la frontière** on reaching the border; **d. la sortie du village commence la forêt** the woods lie just beyond the village

• **dès lors** ADV **1** *(à partir de là)* from then on, since (then); **il a quitté la ville; d. lors, on n'a plus entendu parler de lui** he left the town and he's never been heard of since **2** *(en conséquence)* consequently, therefore; **tu es d'accord avec lui: d. lors, je n'ai plus rien à dire** you agree with him: in which case *or* consequently I have nothing more to say

• **dès lors que** CONJ **1** *(étant donné que)* as, since; *(du moment où)* from the moment (that); **d. lors qu'il a renoncé à ce poste, il ne peut prétendre à une augmentation** given that *or* since *or* as he refused that job, he can't expect a rise; **d. lors qu'il a été déclaré coupable, rien ne saurait le sauver** from the moment he was found guilty, nothing could possibly save him **2** *(dès que)* as soon as; **d. lors que la loi entre en vigueur, il faut s'y conformer** as soon as the law comes into force, it must be respected

• **dès que** CONJ **1** *(aussitôt que)* as soon as; **d. que possible** as soon as possible; **nous partirons d. que tout le monde sera prêt** we'll go once *or* (just) as soon as everybody's ready **2** *(chaque fois que)* whenever; **d. qu'il peut, il part en vacances** whenever he can, he goes off on holiday

désabonnement [dezabɔnmɑ̃] NM cancellation of subscription

désabonner [3] [dezabɔne] VT to cancel the subscription of

VPR **se désabonner** to stop subscribing, to cancel *or* to withdraw *or* to discontinue one's subscription; **se d. à une revue** to stop taking a magazine

désabusé, -e [dezabyze] ADJ **1** *(déçu)* disillusioned, disenchanted **2** *(amer)* embittered

désabuser [3] [dezabyze] VT to disabuse; **je la croyais honnête mais l'enquête m'a désabusé** I thought she was honest but the inquiry opened my eyes

désacclimater [3] [dezaklimate] VT to disacclimatize

désaccord [dezakɔr] NM **1** *(litige)* conflict, disagreement, dissension *(UNCOUNT)*; **s'il y a d.** if there's any disagreement **2** *(contraste)* discrepancy

• **en désaccord** ADJ **les parties en d.** the dissenting parties; **ils sont en d. en ce qui concerne l'éducation de leurs enfants** they disagree about their children's education; **être en d. avec qn sur qch** to be in conflict with sb over sth; **sa conduite est en d. avec ses principes** his/her behaviour is not consistent with his/her principles

désaccorder [3] [dezakɔrde] *Mus* VT to detune; **le piano est désaccordé** the piano's out of tune

VPR **se désaccorder** to go out of tune

désaccoupler [3] [dezakuple] VT to uncouple

désaccoutumance [dezakutymɑ̃s] NF **1** *(perte d'une habitude)* loss of a habit **2** *Méd & Psy* end of a dependency; **la d. du tabac** breaking tobacco dependency; **la d. à la drogue** overcoming drug addiction

désaccoutumer [3] [dezakutyme] VT **1** *(déshabituer)* to disaccustom, to cause to lose a habit; **d. qn de faire qch** to get sb out of the habit of doing sth **2** *Méd & Psy* **d. qn** to end sb's dependency

VPR **se désaccoutumer 1** *(se déshabituer)* **se d. de faire qch** to get out of the habit of doing sth **2** *Méd & Psy* **se d. de qch** to lose one's dependency on sth; **se d. du tabac** to kick the tobacco habit

désacralisation [desakralizasjɔ̃] NF deconsecration; *Fig* demythologization

désacraliser [3] [desakralize] VT to deconsecrate; *Fig* to demythologize

désactivation [dezaktivasjɔ̃] NF **1** *Nucl* decontamination, cleaning up **2** *Ordinat* deactivation

désactiver [3] [dezaktive] VT **1** *Nucl* to decontaminate, to clean up **2** *Ordinat* to deactivate, to disable

désadaptation [dezadaptasjɔ̃] NF loss of adaptability

désadapter [3] [dezadapte] VT **d. qn de qch** to wean sb away from sth; **le risque de les d. à** *ou* **de leur vie quotidienne** the danger of creating a gulf between them and their everyday life

désaffectation [dezafektasjɔ̃] NF *(d'une église)* deconsecration, secularization, secularizing; *(d'une gare)* closing down

désaffecté, -e [dezafekte] ADJ *(église)* deconsecrated, secularized; *(gare, entrepôt)* disused

désaffecter [4] [dezafekte] VT *(église)* to deconsecrate, to secularize; *(entrepôt)* to close down, to put out of use *or* commission; **il a désaffecté son garage pour en faire un atelier** he turned his garage into a workshop

désaffection [dezafeksjɔ̃] NF disaffection, loss of interest; **manifester une certaine d. pour qch** to lose interest in *or* to turn one's back on sth; **expliquer la d. du public à l'égard de la religion** to explain why people turn their backs on religion

désagrafer [dezagrafe] VT *(vêtement)* to unfasten, to undo

VPR **se désagrafer** to unfasten *or* undo one's dress/*etc*

désagréable [dezagreabl] ADJ **1** *(déplaisant)* disagreeable, unpleasant; **caractère d.** disagreeableness; **d. à voir** unsightly; **une odeur d.** a nasty smell; **ce n'est pas d.** it's rather pleasant *or* nice; **ce petit vent n'est pas d.** this gentle breeze is (very) welcome **2** *(peu sociable)* bad-tempered, rude

désagréablement [dezagreabləmɑ̃] ADV unpleasantly, offensively; **un bruit qui résonne d. aux oreilles** a noise that grates on the ears

désagrégation [dezagregasjɔ̃] NF **1** *(d'un tissu, d'un béton)* disintegration **2** *(d'une équipe)* break-up, breaking *or* splitting up, disbanding

désagréger [22] [dezagreʒe] VT **1** *(effriter)* to break up, to cause to disintegrate *or* to crumble; **la bombe a complètement désagrégé l'immeuble** the bomb completely destroyed the building **2** *(désunir ▶ équipe)* to break up, to disband

VPR **se désagréger 1** *(s'effriter)* to disintegrate, to break up **2** *(groupe, équipe)* to break up, to disband

désagrément [dezagremɑ̃] NM trouble *(UNCOUNT)*, inconvenience *(UNCOUNT)*; **causer du d.** *ou* **des désagréments à qn** to cause trouble for sb, to inconvenience sb; **les désagréments du travail à domicile** the disadvantages of working from home

désaimantation [dezemɑ̃tasjɔ̃] NF demagnetization, demagnetizing

désaimanter [3] [dezemɑ̃te] VT to demagnetize

désaisonnalisé, -e [desezɔnalize] ADJ seasonally adjusted

désaligné [dezaliɲe] ADJ out of alignment, out of line

désalinisateur [desalinizatœr] NM desalinator

désalinisation [desalinizasjɔ̃] NF desalination

désaltérant, -e [dezalterɑ̃, -ɑ̃t] ADJ refreshing, thirst-quenching

désaltérer [18] [dezaltere] VT *(apaiser la soif de)* to refresh, to quench the thirst of

USAGE ABSOLU **le thé désaltère mieux qu'une boisson glacée** tea is more thirst-quenching than an ice-cold drink

VPR **se désaltérer** to quench one's thirst; **se d. de sang** to sate *or* to slake one's thirst for blood

désambiguïsation [dezɑ̃bigɥizasjɔ̃] NF clarification

désambiguïser [3] [dezɑ̃bigɥize] VT to disambiguate; **un mot est souvent désambiguïsé par un contexte** a word in context is rarely ambiguous

désamiantage [dezamjɑ̃taʒ] NM removal of asbestos

désamorçage [dezamɔrsaʒ] NM **1** *(d'une bombe)* defusing; *(d'une arme)* unpriming **2** *Élec* running down, de-energization **3** *(d'une situation)* defusing

désamorcer [16] [dezamɔrse] VT **1** *(bombe)* to defuse; *(arme)* to unprime

2 *Élec* to run down, to de-energize

3 *Tech* **d. une pompe** to draw off the water from a pump

4 *(contrecarrer)* to defuse, to forestall, to inhibit; **des mesures d'urgence pour d. la grève** emergency measures to defuse the strike

désamour [dezamur] NM **1** *(cessation de l'amour)* falling out of love **2** *(désillusion)* disenchantment, disillusionment

désaper [3] [desape] **se désaper** VPR *Fam* to strip off

désapparier [10] [dezaparje] VT **1** *(objets)* to remove one of a pair of **2** *(animaux)* to uncouple

désappointement [dezapwɛ̃tmɑ̃] NM *Littéraire* disappointment, dissatisfaction

désappointer [3] [dezapwɛ̃te] VT *Littéraire* to disappoint

désapprendre [79] [dezaprɑ̃dr] VT *(involontairement)* to forget; *(volontairement)* to unlearn; **il a désappris l'italien** he can't speak Italian any more; **ce n'est pas facile de d. à mentir** it's not easy to get out of the habit of lying; **l'enfant avait désappris à sourire** the child no longer knew how to smile; *Littéraire* **d. de faire qch** to lose the habit of doing sth

désapprobateur, -trice [dezaprɔbatœr, -tris] ADJ disapproving; **d'un ton d.** disapprovingly

désapprobation [dezaprɔbasjɔ̃] NF disapproval; **exprimer ouvertement sa d.** to disapprove openly; **un regard/murmure de d.** a look/murmur of disapproval

désapprobatrice [dezaprɔbatris] *voir* **désapprobateur**

désapprouver [3] [dezapruve] VT **1** *(condamner)* to disapprove of; **un mariage civil? sachez que je désapprouve!** a registry office wedding? let me say that I thoroughly disapprove *or* I do not approve! **2** *(s'opposer à ▶ projet, idée)* to object to, to reject; **la commission désapprouvera cette solution** this solution will be unacceptable to the committee; **nous désapprouvons le concept de discrimination** we strongly oppose the notion of discrimination

désapprovisionné, -e [dezaprɔvizjɔne] ADJ *(compte)* overdrawn

désarçonner [3] [dezarsɔne] VT **1** *Équitation* to unseat, to unhorse **2** *(déconcerter)* to throw, to put off one's stride; **son intervention a désarçonné l'orateur** his/her remark threw the speaker off balance

désargenté, -e [dezarʒɑ̃te] ADJ *Fam* penniless; **une famille désargentée** a family fallen on hard times; **je suis plutôt d. ces jours-ci** I'm a bit short (of money) at the moment

désarmant, -e [dezarmɑ̃, -ɑ̃t] ADJ **1** *(touchant)* disarming; **de façon désarmante** disarmingly; **elle est désarmante de gentillesse** she is disarmingly sweet **2** *(confondant)* amazing, breathtaking

désarmé, -e [dezarme] ADJ **1** *(personne ▶ qui n'a plus d'arme)* disarmed; *(▶ qui n'a jamais eu d'arme)* unarmed, defenceless

2 *(arme, mine)* uncocked

3 *Naut* laid up

4 *(surpris)* dumbfounded

5 *(privé de moyens)* **être d. devant la vie** to be ill-equipped to cope with life

désarmement [dezarməmɑ̃] NM **1** *Mil & Pol* disarmament; **d. nucléaire** nuclear disarmament; **d. unilatéral** unilateral disarmament **2** *(d'une arme, d'une mine)* uncocking **3** *Naut* laying-up, release

désarmer [3] [dezarme] VT **1** *Mil & Pol* to disarm

2 *(arme, mine)* to uncock

3 *(attendrir)* to disarm; **être désarmé par la bonne volonté de qn** to find sb's willingness disarming; **ce genre de remarque vous désarme** this kind of remark takes the wind out of your sails

4 *Naut* to lay up, to put out of commission
VI 1 *Mil* to disarm **2** *(locution)* **il ne désarme pas** he won't give in, he keeps battling on; **sa haine ne désarme pas** his/her hatred is unrelenting; **les journaux ne désarmeront pas** the press stories will go on and on

désarrimage [dezarimaʒ] **NM 1** *Naut* shifting, slipping *(of cargo)* **2** *(sur un véhicule)* **à cause du d. de la cargaison** *(accidentel)* because the load came off; *(volontaire)* because the load was unfastened

désarrimer [3] [dezarime] **VT 1** *Naut* to cause to move about **2** *(sur un véhicule)* to unfasten
VPR se désarrimer 1 *Naut* to come loose **2** *(sur un véhicule)* to come off *or* loose

désarroi [dezarwa] **NM** confusion; **être dans le d. le plus profond** to be completely at a loss; **jeter qn dans le d.** to throw sb into utter confusion

désarticulation [dezartikylasjɔ̃] **NF 1** *(torsion)* dislocation, disjointing **2** *Écon* disarticulation

désarticuler [3] [dezartikyle] **VT** to disjoint, to dislocate
VPR se désarticuler 1 *(se contorsionner)* to twist *or* to contort oneself **2** *(par accident)* **se d. un doigt/le genou** to put a finger/one's knee out of joint

désassembler [3] [dezasɑ̃ble] **VT** to dismantle, to take apart *or* to pieces, to disassemble

désassembleur [dezasɑ̃blœr] **NM** *Ordinat* disassembler

désassortir [32] [dezasɔrtir] **VT 1** *(série, collection etc)* to spoil, to break up; **service de table désassorti** dinner service made up of odd pieces **2** *(magasin)* to clear (of stock)

désastre [dezastr] **NM 1** *(calamité)* calamity, catastrophe, disaster; **ils ne purent que constater l'ampleur du d.** they could only record the extent of the damage **2** *(échec)* disaster, failure; **le gâteau fut un d.** the cake was a complete disaster; **courir au d.** to be heading for disaster

désastreuse [dezastrøz] *voir* **désastreux**

désastreusement [dezastrøzmɑ̃] **ADV** disastrously, catastrophically

désastreux, -euse [dezastrø, -øz] **ADJ 1** *(catastrophique)* calamitous, disastrous, catastrophic; **des conditions de vie désastreuses** wretched living conditions **2** *(résultat, effet)* disastrous, awful, terrible; **des résultats d. en physique** appalling results in physics; **le spectacle/pique-nique a été d.** the show/picnic was a complete disaster

désatellisation [desatelizasjɔ̃] **NF 1** *(d'une station spatiale)* de-orbit **2** *(d'un pays)* making more autonomous

désatomisation [dezatɔmizasjɔ̃] **NF** nuclear disarmament

désatomiser [dezatɔmize] **VT** to undertake the nuclear disarmament of

désavantage [dezavɑ̃taʒ] **NM 1** *(inconvénient)* disadvantage, drawback; **avoir tous les désavantages de qch** to get the worst of sth, to bear the brunt of sth **2** *(infériorité)* disadvantage, handicap; **avoir un d. par rapport à qn** to be at a disadvantage compared with sb
• **au désavantage de PRÉP c'est à ton d.** it's not to your advantage; **se montrer à son d.** to show oneself in an unfavourable light; **tourner au d. de qn** to go against sb

désavantager [17] [dezavɑ̃taʒe] **VT** *(défavoriser)* to (put at a) disadvantage, to penalize; **d. un concurrent** to put a competitor at a disadvantage; **être désavantagé par rapport à qn** to be at a disadvantage compared with sb; **il est désavantagé par son jeune âge** his youth is against him; **elle est désavantagée simplement parce que c'est une femme** she's at a disadvantage simply because she is a woman

désavantageuse [dezavɑ̃taʒøz] *voir* **désavantageux**

désavantageusement [dezavɑ̃taʒøzmɑ̃] **ADV** disadvantageously

désavantageux, -euse [dezavɑ̃taʒø, -øz] **ADJ** detrimental, disadvantageous; **vendre à des conditions moins désavantageuses** to sell at a better price; **c'est d. pour les petites entreprises** this works against the interests of small businesses

désaveu, -x [dezavø] **NM 1** *(reniement)* disavowal, retraction; **contraindre qn au d.** to force sb to retract; **faire un d. public** to make a public retraction
2 *(condamnation)* repudiation; **encourir le d. de ses supérieurs** to incur the disapproval of one's superiors; **il n'a pas supporté ce d. public** he couldn't stand the idea of being condemned in public
3 *Jur* **d. de paternité** repudiation of paternity
4 *Psy* denial

désavouer [6] [dezavwe] **VT 1** *(renier ▸ propos)* to disavow, to repudiate; *(▸ dette)* to repudiate; **d. sa promesse** to go back on one's word, to break one's promise
2 *(refuser de reconnaître ▸ représentant, candidat)* to challenge the authority *or* legitimacy of; **elle avait un si bon accent qu'un autochtone ne l'aurait pas désavouée** her accent was so good that she could have passed for a native
3 *(condamner ▸ personne, comportement)* to disapprove of
4 *Jur* to disclaim, to repudiate
VPR se désavouer to retract

désaxé, -e [dezakse] **ADJ 1** *Tech* out of alignment; **cylindre d.** offset cylinder; **roue désaxée** dished wheel **2** *(dérangé)* mentally deranged, unhinged
NM,F psychopath

désaxer [3] [dezakse] **VT 1** *Tech* to offset, to throw out of alignment **2** *(perturber)* to unhinge; **ils ont été désaxés par la guerre** the war unhinged them *or* left them psychologically disturbed

descellement [deselmɑ̃] **NM à cause du d. des dalles** *(accidentel)* because the flagstones have worked loose; *(volontaire)* because the flagstones have been loosened

desceller [4] [desele] **VT 1** *(ouvrir)* to unseal, to take the seal off **2** *(détacher)* to loosen; **les briques sont descellées** the bricks have worked loose *or* are loose
VPR se desceller to work loose

descendance [desɑ̃dɑ̃s] **NF 1** *Jur* descent, lineage **2** *(progéniture)* descendants

descendant, -e [desɑ̃dɑ̃, -ɑ̃t] **ADJ** down *(avant n)*, downward, descending; **escalator d.** down escalator; **mouvement d.** downward movement
NM,F 1 *(dans une famille)* descendant **2** *(partisan)* follower; **un d. des pointillistes** a latter-day pointillist

descendeur, -euse [desɑ̃dœr, -øz] **NM,F** *(skieur)* downhill skier, downhiller; *(cycliste)* downhill racer; **d. en rappel** *(alpiniste)* abseiler
NM *(en alpinisme)* descender

DESCENDRE [73] [desɑ̃dr]

VI	
• to go down **A1–3, 7, B1, 2, C3**	• to come down **A1, 2, B2, C1**
• to climb down **A1**	• to get down **A1**
• to get off **A1, 4**	• to stay **A6**
• to raid **A5**	• to fall **C1**
• to drop **C1**	
VT	
• to go down **1**	• to lower **2**
• to take down **3, 4**	• to bring down **3**
• to shoot down **5**	• to slate **6**
• to knock back **7**	

VI *(aux être)* **A. 1** *(personne, mécanisme, avion ▸ vu d'en haut)* to go down; *(▸ vu d'en bas)* to come down; *(oiseau)* to fly *or* to swoop down; **d. à la cave** to go down to the cellar; **tu peux d.? j'ai besoin de toi à la cuisine** can you come down (stairs)? I need you in the kitchen; **j'ai rencontré la concierge en descendant** I met the caretaker on my way down; **d. en courant** to run down; **aide-moi à d.** help me down; **ils descendront par la face nord** they'll climb down *or* make their descent via the North face; **je descends toujours par l'escalier** I always go down by the stairs *or* take the stairs down; **dès qu'ils ont 15 ans, ils descendent dans la mine** as soon as they're 15 they go down the mine; **les plongeurs descendent jusqu'à 60 mètres** the divers go down to *or* reach depths of 60 metres; **quand les saumons descendent vers la mer** when the salmon go *or* swim downriver to the sea; **notre équipe est descendue à la huitième place** our team moved down *or* dropped to eighth place; **d. en seconde division** to move down to the second division; **le premier coureur à d. au-dessous de dix secondes au 100 mètres** the first runner to break ten seconds for the 100 metres; **l'ascenseur ne descend pas plus bas** the *Br* lift *or Am* elevator doesn't go down any further; **la pièce de monnaie ne voulait pas d. (dans la fente)** the coin wouldn't go down (the slot); **le store ne veut pas d.** the blind won't come down; **le yo-yo monte et descend** the yo-yo's going up and down; **son chapeau lui descendait jusqu'aux yeux** his/her hat came down over his/her eyes; **mes chaussettes descendent** my socks are coming down *or* slipping down; **fais d. la malade** help the patient down; **qu'il soit prêt ou non, fais-le d.** get him to come down, whether he's ready or not; **cette défaite fait d. notre équipe à la septième place** this defeat means that our team will move down *or* drop to seventh place; **je vais faire d. l'ascenseur** I'll call the *Br* lift *or Am* elevator (down); **c'est ce mécanisme qui fait d. la plate-forme** this mechanism brings the platform down *or* lowers the platform; **d. de** *(échafaudage, échelle)* to come *or* to climb down from, to get down from; *(arbre)* to climb *or* to come down out of; *(balançoire)* to get off; *(colline)* to come down; **les marins descendent de la mâture** the sailors climb down the rigging; **descends de cette échelle!** get down from that ladder!; **peux-tu faire d. les enfants de cet arbre?** can you get the children down out of *or* down from that tree?; **descends de là, tu vas tomber** get down from there or you'll fall; *Fig* **descends de ton nuage!** come down to earth!; **d. dans la rue** to take to the streets; **d. en soi-même** to take a close look at oneself
2 *(air froid, brouillard)* to come down; *(soleil)* to go down; **la nuit** *ou* **le soir descend** night is closing in *or* falling; **on sent la fraîcheur du soir d.** you can feel the cool of the evening coming down; **le soleil descend sur l'horizon** the sun is sinking *or* going down below the horizon
3 *(se rendre ▸ dans un lieu d'altitude inférieure, dans le Sud, à la campagne)* to go down; **je descends au marché** I'm going to the market; **d. en ville** to go into town, *Am* to go downtown; **je suis descendu à Bordeaux en voiture/en auto-stop** I drove/hitched down to Bordeaux; **les voiliers descendront le long de la côte atlantique** the yachts will sail south along the Atlantic coast; **les réfugiés continuent à d. vers le sud** the refugees are still travelling south; **samedi, je descends chez mes parents** I'll go down to my parents' on Saturday
4 *(poser pied à terre ▸ d'un véhicule)* to get off, *Sout* to alight; **ne pas d. avant l'arrêt complet du train** please do not attempt to alight until the train has come to a complete standstill; **tout le monde descend!** *(au terminus)* all change!; **d. à terre** to go ashore; **d. de bateau** to get off a boat, to land; **d. de voiture** to get out of a car; **il descendait de l'avion** he was getting off *or* out of the plane; **d. de cheval** to get off one's horse, to dismount; **d. de vélo** to get off one's bike; **d. du train** to get off the train; **descends vite!** *(d'une voiture, d'un train)* get *or* jump out, quick!; **à quelle station descendez-vous?** where do you get off?; **aider une vieille dame à d.** to help an old lady off
5 *(faire irruption)* **la police est descendue chez elle/dans son bar** the police raided her place/his/her bar
6 *(se loger)* to stay; **nous descendons toujours à l'Hôtel de la Gare** we always stay at the Hôtel de la Gare
7 *Fam (repas, boisson)* to go down, to slip down; **ton petit vin rouge descend bien** your red wine goes down very easily; **les saucisses ne descendent pas** the sausages aren't going down very well; **bois un café pour faire d. tout ça** have a coffee to wash it all down; **qu'est-ce qu'il descend!** *(il boit)* he certainly knows how to knock it back!; *(il mange)* he certainly knows how to put it away!
B. 1 d. à *ou* **jusqu'à** *(cheveux, vêtement)* to come down to; *(puits)* to go down to; **des robes qui descendent jusqu'au genou/jusqu'aux chevilles** knee-length/ankle-length dresses; **la jupe doit d. jusqu'au-dessous du genou** the skirt must cover the knee; **le puits descend jusqu'à 150 mètres** the well

is 150 metres deep *or* goes down to 150 metres

2 *(suivre une pente ▸ rivière)* to flow down; *(▸ route)* to go down *or* downwards; *(▸ toit)* to slope down; **le sentier descendait parmi les oliviers** the path threaded its way down through the olive grove; **le fleuve descend vers la mer** the river flows down to the sea; **le jardin descend en pente douce jusqu'à la plage** the garden slopes gently down to the beach; **d. en pente raide** *(route, terrain, toit)* to drop sharply; **la route descend brusquement** the road suddenly dips; **la route descend en lacets** the road winds down

C. 1 *(baisser ▸ marée, mer)* to go out, to ebb; *(▸ prix)* to come down, to fall; **les eaux sont enfin descendues** the floods have subsided at last; **la température est descendue au-dessous de zéro** the temperature has dropped *or* fallen below zero; **les températures ne descendent jamais au-dessous de 10°** temperatures never go below 10°; *Fam* **le thermomètre descend** the weather's *or* it's getting colder; **ses notes n'arrêtent pas de d. depuis mars** his/her marks have been getting worse since March; **les taux d'intérêt sont descendus brusquement** interest rates fell sharply *or* dropped suddenly; **le pain est descendu à un euro** bread's gone down to one euro; **faire d.** *(cours, fièvre, notes)* to bring down; *(inflation, prix)* to bring *or* to push down; **j'ai essayé de lui faire d. son prix** I tried to get him/her to lower his/her price; **ça a fait d. les prix** it brought prices down

2 *(s'abaisser moralement)* to stoop; **je ne descendrai jamais jusqu'à la supplier** I'll never stoop to begging her; **d. dans l'estime de qn** to go down in sb's estimation

3 *Mus* to go down, to drop down; **d. d'une octave** to go down *or* to drop an octave; **les altos descendent très bas dans la deuxième mesure** the altos go down very low in the second bar

VT *(aux avoir)* **1** *(parcourir ▸ escalier, montagne)* to go down; **d. une pente** to go down a hill; **d. un escalier quatre à quatre** to race downstairs; **elle a descendu toute la pente sur le dos** she went *or* slid all the way down the slope on her back; **d. le courant** *(détritus, arbre)* to float downstream; **d. un fleuve** *(en nageant)* to swim downstream; *(en bateau)* to sail down a river; **ils ont descendu le Mississippi en radeau** they went down the Mississippi on a raft; *Ftbl* **il a descendu tout le terrain balle au pied** he ran the length of the field with the ball

2 *(placer plus bas ▸ tableau)* to lower; *(▸ store)* to pull down, to lower; **il faudrait d. le cadre de deux centimètres** the frame should be taken down two centimetres

3 *(porter vers le bas)* to take down, to get down; *(porter vers soi)* to bring down; **d. la poubelle** to take the rubbish down; **aide-moi à d. la valise du filet** help me take *or* lift *or* get the suitcase (down) from the rack; **tu pourrais me d. une veste, s'il te plaît?** could you bring me down a jacket, please?; **ils ont descendu le sauveteur au bout d'une corde** they lowered the rescuer on the end of a rope

4 *(amener en voiture)* to take down, to drive down

5 *Fam (abattre ▸ gangster)* to gun down[□], to shoot down[□]; *(▸ avion)* to bring down[□], to shoot down[□]; **se faire d.** to get shot; **tu aurais pu te faire d.!** you could have got shot!

6 *Fam (critiquer)* to slate, to pan; **il s'est fait d. par le jury** he was slated by the jury

7 *Fam (boire ▸ bouteille)* to down, to knock back

8 *Mus* **d. la gamme** to go *or* run down the scale

• **descendre de VT IND** *(être issu de)* to be descended from; **l'homme descend du singe** man is descended from the apes

descente [desɑ̃t] **NF 1** *(pente)* slope, hill; **d. dangereuse** steep gradient; **courir/déraper dans la d.** to run/to skid down; **on ira vite, il n'y a que des descentes** we'll do it in no time, it's all downhill

2 *(chute)* drop, fall

3 *(sortie d'un véhicule)* getting off, alighting; *Rail* **station en courbe, attention à la d.** *(sur panneau)* mind the gap; **à sa d. d'avion** as he/she got off the plane; **à sa d. du bateau** as he/she landed *or* disembarked; **accueillir qn à la d. du train** to meet sb off the train

4 *Mines* **d. de mine** descending shaft

5 *Ski* downhill race; **être bon en d.** *(cycliste)* to be good downhill *or* on the downhill sections; **d. en rappel** *(en alpinisme)* abseiling, *Am* rappeling; **faire une d. en rappel** to abseil down, *Am* to rappel down

6 *Aviat* descent; **d. en piqué** dive; **d. en spirale** spinning dive, spiral descent; **d. en vol plané** glide, gliding fall

7 *Méd* **d. d'organe** *ou* **d'organes** prolapse

8 *Constr* **d. d'antenne** downlead; **d. de gouttière** rainwater pipe, downpipe; **d. de paratonnerre** down inductor

9 *(contrôle)* inspection; *(attaque)* raid; **faire une d.** *Admin* to carry out a (surprise) inspection; *Mil* to mount a raid; *Fam Fig* to make an unexpected visit[□]; *Fig Hum* **faire une d. sur qch** to raid sth; **il a encore fait une d. sur le chocolat!** he's been raiding *or* he's been at the chocolate again!; *Jur* **d. sur les lieux** visit to the scene *(of a crime etc)*; **d. de police** police raid

10 *Fam (locution)* **il a une bonne d.** *(il boit beaucoup)* he can really knock it back

• **descente de lit NF 1** *(tapis)* bedside rug **2** *Fam Péj (personne)* toady

déscolarisation [deskɔlarizasjɔ̃] **NF** *(action)* removal from school; *(résultat)* lack of schooling *or* education; **les impératifs des travaux agricoles conduisent à la d. des enfants des milieux ruraux** children in rural areas are taken out of school because of the demands of farm work; **on assiste à une d. massive des jeunes gitans** the level of school attendance among young gipsies is falling drastically

déscolariser [3] [deskɔlarize] **VT** to take out of the school system

descripteur, -trice [dεskriptœr, -tris] **NM,F** describer

NM *Ordinat* descriptor

descriptible [dεskriptibl] **ADJ** describable; **sa joie n'était pas d.** his/her joy was beyond description *or* words

descriptif, -ive [dεskriptif, -iv] **ADJ 1** *(présentation, texte)* descriptive **2** *Géom* solid

NM *(d'un appartement)* description; *(de travaux)* specification

description [dεskripsjɔ̃] **NF 1** *(fait de décrire)* description, depiction; **d. de poste** job description; **d. de brevet** patent specification; **faire la d. de qch** to describe *or* to depict sth **2** *Littérature* description, descriptive passage

descriptive [dεskriptiv] *voir* **descriptif**

descriptrice [dεskriptris] *voir* **descripteur**

désectorisation [desεktɔrizasjɔ̃] **NF** freedom of choice *(by virtue of the fact that parents no longer need to send their children to the school designated for their area)*; **la d. de l'école primaire se fera plus vite que celle de l'école secondaire** freedom of choice will come about in primary schools sooner than in secondary schools

désectoriser [3] [desεktɔrize] **VT d. le primaire/secondaire** = to allow parents to choose which primary/secondary school they send their children to, regardless of where they live

désembourber [3] [dezɑ̃burbe] **VT** to pull *or* to get out of the mud

désembourgeoiser [3] [dezɑ̃burʒwaze] **VT** *(personne)* to free from bourgeois habits; *(quartier)* to make less bourgeois

VPR se désembourgeoiser *(personne)* to lose one's bourgeois mentality; *(quartier, profession)* to become less bourgeois

désembouteiller [4] [dezɑ̃buteje] **VT 1** *Aut* to unblock; **d. les grandes villes** to ease the traffic in the big cities **2** *Tél* **d. le standard** to unjam the exchange

désembrouiller [3] [dezɑ̃bruje] **VT 1** *(gén)* to disentangle, to make less complicated **2** *Ordinat* to unscramble

désembrouilleur [dezɑ̃brujœr] **NM** *(de signaux etc)* descrambler

désembuage [dezɑ̃bɥaʒ] **NM** *(processus)* demisting; *(dispositif)* demister; **d. arrière** rear demister

désembuer [7] [dezɑ̃bɥe] **VT** to demist

désemparé, -e [dezɑ̃pare] **ADJ 1** *(perdu)* **être tout d.** to be lost; **sans argent dans cette ville étrangère, il était complètement d.** in a foreign town with no money, he had no idea what to do **2** *Aviat & Naut* crippled

désemparer [3] [dezɑ̃pare] **VT** *(navire, avion)* to disable

VI sans d. without a pause *or* break; **lire des heures sans d.** to read for hours on end

désemplir [32] [dezɑ̃plir] **VI leur maison ne désemplit pas** their house is always full

VPR se désemplir to empty

désencadrement [dezɑ̃kadrəmɑ̃] **NM 1** *(d'un tableau)* removal from its frame **2** *Écon (des crédits)* unblocking

désenchaîner [4] [dezɑ̃ʃene] **VT** *Littéraire* to unchain, to take out of *or* to free from one's chains

désenchanté, -e [dezɑ̃ʃɑ̃te] **ADJ** *(personne)* disenchanted, disillusioned; *(sourire)* wistful

NM,F disenchanted *or* disaffected person; **les désenchantés du socialisme** those who have become disenchanted with socialism

désenchantement [dezɑ̃ʃɑ̃tmɑ̃] **NM 1** *Littéraire (désensorcellement)* removal of a spell **2** *(déception)* disillusionment, disenchantment, disillusion

désenchanter [3] [dezɑ̃ʃɑ̃te] **VT 1** *Littéraire (désensorceler)* to release *or* to free from a spell **2** *(décevoir)* to disillusion, to disappoint

désenclavement [dezɑ̃klavmɑ̃] **NM** *(d'une région, d'un quartier)* opening up

désenclaver [3] [dezɑ̃klave] **VT** *(région, quartier)* to open up

désencombrement [dezɑ̃kɔ̃brəmɑ̃] **NM** clearing, unblocking

désencombrer [3] [dezɑ̃kɔ̃bre] **VT** to clear (**de** of), to unblock

désencrasser [3] [dezɑ̃krase] **VT** *(ustensile, four)* to clean out; *(moteur)* to decarbonize, to decoke

désencroûter [3] [dezɑ̃krute] **VT d. qn** to get sb out of his/her rut

VPR se désencroûter to get out of the *or* one's rut; **j'ai besoin de me d.** I need to get out of this rut I'm in *or* out of my rut

désendettement [dezɑ̃dεtmɑ̃] **NM** clearing of debts, degearing; **le d. des pays africains se fera progressivement** African countries will gradually be relieved of their debt burden

désendetter [4] [dezɑ̃dete] **VT d. qn** to free sb of *or* to release sb from debt

VPR se désendetter to get out of debt, to clear one's debts

désenfiler [3] [dezɑ̃file] **VT** *(aiguille)* to unthread; *(perles)* to unstring

VPR se désenfiler *(aiguille)* to come unthreaded; *(perles)* to come unstrung

désenflammer [3] [dezɑ̃flame] **VT** to reduce the inflammation in

VPR se désenflammer to become less inflamed

désenfler [3] [dezɑ̃fle] **VT** to bring down *or* to reduce the swelling of

VI to become less swollen; **ma cheville désenfle** the swelling in my ankle's going down; **la pommade a fait d. ma cheville** the cream made my swollen ankle go down *or* eased the swelling in my ankle

désenfumer [3] [dezɑ̃fyme] **VT** to clear of smoke

désengagement [dezɑ̃gaʒmɑ̃] **NM** disengagement, backing out

désengager [17] [dezɑ̃gaʒe] **VT 1** *(libérer d'un engagement)* to free *or* to release from a commitment; **d. qn d'une obligation** to free *or* to release sb from an obligation **2** *Mil* to withdraw, to pull out

VPR se désengager 1 *(se dépolitiser)* to give up one's political commitment **2** *(se décommander)* to back out of a commitment; **se d. d'une obligation** to free oneself of an obligation; **je ne peux pas me d.** I can't get out of it **3** *Mil* to withdraw, to pull out

désengorger [17] [dezɑ̃gɔrʒe] **VT** *(tuyau, rue)* to unblock, to clear; *Écon* **d. le marché** to reduce the overload on the market

désenivrer [3] [dezɑ̃nivre] **VT** to sober up

VI to sober up; **il ne désenivre pas** he's never sober

VPR se désenivrer to sober up

désennuyer [14] [dezɑ̃nɥije] VT to dispel the boredom of
VPR **se désennuyer** to dispel one's boredom
désensabler [3] [dezɑ̃sable] VT **1** *(extraire)* to get out of *or* to extract from the sand **2** *(nettoyer)* to free *or* to clear of sand
VPR **se désensabler** *(chenal)* to become clear of sand
désensevelir [dezɑ̃səvlir] VT *(objet)* to dig up; *(cadavre)* to disinter, to exhume
désensibilisation [desɑ̃sibilizasjɔ̃] NF **1** *Méd & Phot* desensitizing, desensitization **2** *(perte d'intérêt)* loss of interest (**à** in) **3** *(perte de la sensibilité)* desensitization; **la d. est l'une des conséquences de l'exposition répétée à la violence télévisuelle** viewers become desensitized to violence through repeated exposure to violent images on television
désensibiliser [3] [desɑ̃sibilize] VT **1** *Méd & Phot* to desensitize **2** *(désintéresser)* **d. qn à qch** to make sb lose interest in sth **3** *(rendre insensible)* to desensitize; **la violence à l'écran tend à d. les téléspectateurs** viewers become desensitized to violence through seeing so much of it on television
VPR **se désensibiliser** *(devenir insensible)* to become desensitized (**à** to)
désensorceler [24] [dezɑ̃sɔrsəle] VT to free *or* to release from a spell
désentortiller [3] [dezɑ̃tɔrtije] VT **1** *(détordre)* to untwist **2** *(démêler)* to disentangle, to sort out
désentraver [3] [dezɑ̃trave] VT to unchain
désenvaser [3] [dezɑ̃vaze] VT **1** *(extraire)* to get out of *or* to extract from the mud **2** *(nettoyer)* to clear (of mud)
désenvoûtement [dezɑ̃vutmɑ̃] NM removal of a/the spell; **procéder au d. de qn** to remove a/the spell from sb
désenvoûter [3] [dezɑ̃vute] VT to remove a/the spell from
désépaissir [32] [dezepesir] VT *(sauce)* to thin (down); *(cheveux)* to thin (out)
déséquilibre [dezekilibr] NM **1** *(inégalité)* imbalance; **il y a un d. dans les programmes de la chaîne** the channel's schedule is unbalanced
2 *Écon* disequilibrium, imbalance; **d. de la balance commerciale** unfavourable trade balance; **d. financier** financial imbalance
3 *(perte d'équilibre)* loss of balance
4 *Psy* **d. mental** *ou* **psychique** derangement
5 *Physiol* imbalance
• **en déséquilibre** ADJ *(mal posé)* off balance; *(branlant)* unsteady, wobbly
déséquilibré, -e [dezekilibre] ADJ *(personne, esprit)* unbalanced, mentally disturbed
NM,F unbalanced *or* mentally disturbed person
déséquilibrer [3] [dezekilibre] VT **1** *(faire perdre l'équilibre à)* to throw off balance; *(faire tomber)* to tip over **2** *(déstabiliser ▸ système, économie)* to throw off balance, to destabilize **3** *(faire déraisonner)* **d. qn** to disturb the balance of sb's mind
désert, -e [dezer, -ert] ADJ *(abandonné)* deserted, empty; *(inhabité)* desolate, uninhabited
NM **1** *Géog* desert; **d. de sable** sandy desert; **le d. du Sahara** the Sahara Desert **2** *(lieu inhabité)* desert, wilderness, wasteland; **c'est le d. ici!** it's deserted here!; **un d. de béton** a concrete desert; **il crie** *ou* **parle** *ou* **prêche dans le d.** his words fall on deaf ears **3** *Littéraire (monotonie)* vacuity; **le d. de ma vie** my vacuous *or* empty life

> Do not confuse with the adjective **désertique**.

déserter [3] [dezerte] VI *Mil* to desert
VT **1** *(quitter sans permission)* to desert; **pour avoir déserté son poste** for having deserted his post
2 *(abandonner ▸ parti, cause)* to abandon, to give up on
3 *(sujet: touristes, clients)* to desert; **un village déserté** a deserted *or* an abandoned village
4 *Littéraire (amant, ami)* to abandon, to forsake
déserteur [dezertœr] NM deserter
désertification [dezertifikasjɔ̃] NF **1** *(transformation en désert)* desertification **2** *(dépeuplement)* depopulation
désertion [dezersjɔ̃] NF **1** *Mil* desertion **2** *(fait de quitter)* **la d. des campagnes** the rural exodus **3** *(d'une cause, d'un parti)* deserting, abandoning
désertique [dezertik] ADJ *(du désert)* desert *(avant n)*; *(sans végétation)* infertile

> Do not confuse with the adjective **désert**.

désertisation [dezertizasjɔ̃] NF *(transformation en désert)* desertification; *(dépeuplement)* depopulation
désescalade [dezeskalad] NF **1** *Mil* de-escalation **2** *(diminution progressive)* decline; **le conflit semble désormais en phase de d.** the conflict now seems to be winding down
désespérance [dezesperɑ̃s] NF *Littéraire* despair
désespérant, -e [dezesperɑ̃, -ɑ̃t] ADJ **1** *(navrant)* hopeless; **d'une paresse désespérante** hopelessly lazy; **il ne sait toujours pas compter, c'est d.!** he still can't count, it's hopeless!; **toujours pas de lettre, c'est d.!** still no letter, it's enough to drive you to despair! **2** *(très mauvais ▸ temps, nourriture)* appalling, dreadful **3** *(douloureux)* appalling, distressing, terrible; **le spectacle d. des enfants affamés** the heartbreaking sight of starving children
désespéré, -e [dezespere] ADJ **1** *(au désespoir ▸ personne)* in despair, distressed
2 *(qui exprime le désespoir ▸ regard, cri)* desperate
3 *(extrême ▸ tentative)* desperate, reckless; *(▸ mesure, situation)* desperate
4 *(sans espoir)* hopeless; **c'est un cas d.** *(incorrigible)* it's a hopeless case; *(gravement malade)* the patient is critical; **être dans un état d.** *(malade)* to be in a critical condition
NM,F **1** *(personne sans espoir)* desperate person **2** *(suicidé)* suicide
désespérément [dezesperemɑ̃] ADV **1** *(avec désespoir, avec acharnement)* desperately; **on entendait appeler d. à l'aide** desperate cries for help could be heard **2** *(extrêmement)* hopelessly, desperately; **ce train est d. lent** this train is desperately slow; **je suis d. seul** I'm desperately *or* horribly lonely
désespérer [18] [dezespere] VI to despair, to give up hope; **il ne faut jamais d.!** you should never give up hope!, *Hum* never say die!
VT **1** *(exaspérer)* to drive to despair; **tu me désespères!** what am I going to do with you? **2** *(décourager)* to drive *or* to reduce to despair; **elle en a désespéré plus d'un** she's driven more than one (suitor) to despair
• **désespérer de** VT IND **d. de qch** to have lost faith in sth; **d. de qn** to despair of sb; **je désespère de ses capacités** I no longer believe he's/she's capable of anything; **d. de faire qch** to despair of doing sth; **ils désespéraient d'atteindre la côte** they despaired of reaching the shore; **je ne désespère pas d'obtenir le poste** I still think I may get *or* I haven't yet given up on the idea of getting the job
VPR **se désespérer** to (be in) despair
désespoir [dezespwar] NM **1** *(détresse)* despair; **faire le d. de qn** to drive *or* to reduce sb to despair; **à mon grand d., il n'a pu venir** to my despair, he was unable to come; **avec d.** despairingly, in despair; **cette sauce est mon d.** I despair of ever being able to make this sauce **2** *Bot* **d. des peintres** London pride
• **au désespoir** ADJ **être au d.** *(être désespéré)* to be desperate, to have lost all hope; **je suis au d. de ne pouvoir vous aider** I'm deeply *or* desperately sorry that I am unable to help you ADV **mettre qn au d.** to drive *or* to reduce sb to despair; **tu me mets au d.** I despair of you
• **en désespoir** ADV *Can Fam (beaucoup) Br* dead, *Am* real; **je suis fatigué en d.** I'm *Br* dead *or Am* real tired
• **en désespoir de cause** ADV in desperation, as a last resort
désétatisation [dezetatizasjɔ̃] NF denationalization
désétatiser [3] [dezetatize] VT to denationalize
désexualiser [3] [deseksɥalize] VT to desex
déshabillage [dezabijaʒ] NM **1** *(d'une personne)* undressing; **une cabine pour le** *ou* **de d.** a cubicle (for undressing) **2** *(dégarnissage ▸ d'une pièce)* emptying (of ornaments); *(▸ d'un fauteuil)* stripping of upholstery (**de** from)
déshabillé [dezabije] NM négligé
déshabiller [3] [dezabije] VT **1** *(dévêtir)* **d. qn** to undress sb, to take sb's clothes off; **d. qn du regard** to undress sb with one's eyes; **c'est d. saint Pierre pour habiller saint Paul** it's robbing Peter to pay Paul **2** *(vider ▸ pièce)* to empty (of ornaments); *(dégarnir ▸ fauteuil)* to strip the upholstery from
VPR **se déshabiller 1** *(se dénuder)* to strip (off), to take one's clothes off **2** *(ôter son manteau etc)* **déshabille-toi** take off your coat
déshabituer [7] [dezabitɥe] VT **d. qn du tabac/de l'alcool** to wean sb off cigarettes/alcohol; **d. qn de faire qch** to get sb out of the habit of doing sth
VPR **se déshabituer il s'est déshabitué du tabac/de l'alcool** he got out of the habit of smoking/drinking; **se d. de faire qch** to get oneself out of the habit of doing sth
désherbage [dezerbaʒ] NM weeding
désherbant, -e [dezerbɑ̃, -ɑ̃t] ADJ weed-killing *(avant n)*
NM weedkiller
désherber [3] [dezerbe] VT to weed
déshérence [dezerɑ̃s] NF escheat
• **en déshérence** ADJ *(succession)* escheated ADV **tomber en d.** to escheat
déshérité, -e [dezerite] ADJ **1** *(pauvre)* underprivileged, deprived **2** *(région)* poor *(lacking natural advantages)* **3** *(privé d'héritage)* disinherited
NM,F deprived person; **les déshérités** the destitute
déshéritement [dezeritmɑ̃] NM disinheritance
déshériter [3] [dezerite] VT **1** *(priver d'héritage)* to cut out of one's will, to disinherit; *Hum* **si tu continues, je te déshérite!** carry on like this and I'll cut you off without a penny! **2** *(défavoriser)* **il se croit déshérité** he feels hard done by
déshonnête [dezɔnet] ADJ *Littéraire* immodest, improper, indecent
déshonneur [dezɔnœr] NM **1** *(perte de l'honneur)* disgrace, dishonour; **vivre dans le d.** to live in dishonour **2** *(honte)* disgrace; **il n'y a aucun d. à travailler de ses mains** there's no disgrace in working with your hands; **c'est le d. de sa famille** he's a disgrace to his family
déshonorant, -e [dezɔnɔrɑ̃, -ɑ̃t] ADJ **1** *(qui prive de l'honneur)* dishonourable, disgraceful **2** *(humiliant)* degrading, shameful; **cela n'a rien de d.** there's nothing shameful about it
déshonorer [3] [dezɔnɔre] VT **1** *(nuire à l'honneur de)* to dishonour, to bring shame upon, to bring into disrepute; **cette attitude déshonore la profession tout entière** such behaviour brings the whole profession into disrepute; **il a déshonoré le nom de ses ancêtres** he has dishonoured the family name **2** *Littéraire (abuser de ▸ femme, jeune fille)* to ruin **3** *Littéraire (lieu, monument)* to spoil *or* to ruin the look of
VPR **se déshonorer** to bring disgrace upon oneself
déshuiler [3] [dezɥile] VT to de-oil, to remove oil from
déshumaniser [3] [dezymanize] VT to dehumanize
VPR **se déshumaniser** to become dehumanized
déshumidification [dezymidifikasjɔ̃] NF dehumidification
déshydratation [dezidratasjɔ̃] NF **1** *Physiol* dehydration; *(de la peau)* loss of moisture, dehydration; **évitez la d.** avoid dehydration *or* becoming dehydrated; **être dans un état de d.** to be dehydrated **2** *Chim & Tech* dehydration
déshydrater [3] [dezidrate] VT **1** *Physiol* to dehydrate; *(peau)* to dehydrate, to dry (out) **2** *Chim & Tech* to dehydrate **3** *(aliment)* to dehydrate, to desiccate; **noix de coco déshydratée** desiccated coconut
VPR **se déshydrater** *(personne)* to get dehydrated; *(peau)* to lose moisture, to become dehydrated; **on se déshydrate beaucoup en avion** you get very dehydrated when you fly
déshydrogénation [dezidrɔʒenasjɔ̃] NF *Chim* dehydrogenation, dehydrogenization

déshydrogéner [18] [dezidrɔʒene] VT *Chim* to dehydrogenate, to dehydrogenize

déshypothéquer [18] [dezipɔteke] VT to free from mortgage

desiderata [deziderata] NMPL requirements, wishes; **les d. du personnel** the wishes of the staff; *Hum* **le menu est-il conforme à tes d.?** does the menu meet with your requirements?

design [dizajn] NM **1** *(création)* design; **d. industriel** industrial design **2** *(comme adj inv)* designer *(avant n)*; **mobilier d.** modern *or* contemporary furniture

désignation [deziɲasjɔ̃] NF **1** *(appellation)* designation; *(de marchandises)* description **2** *(nomination)* appointment, nomination; **d. de nouveaux membres d'une commission** appointment of new members of a committee **3** *Jur* **d. du défendeur/requérant** name of the defendant/plaintiff

designer [dizajnœr] NM designer; **d. graphiste** graphic designer

désigner [3] [deziɲe] VT **1** *(montrer)* to indicate, to point at *or* to, to show; **d. qn du doigt** to point at sb

2 *(choisir)* to choose, to single out; **d. qn comme héritier** to name sb as one's heir

3 *(nommer ▸ expert, président)* to appoint; *(▸ représentant)* to nominate; *(élire)* to elect; **d. qn pour un poste** to appoint sb to a post; **le président de séance a été désigné à la majorité des voix** the chairperson was elected by a majority of votes

4 *(nommer, s'appliquer à)* to refer to; **d. qn par son nom** to refer to sb by name; **d. qn par un surnom** to call sb by a nickname; **le mot "félin" désigne de nombreux animaux** the word "feline" refers to many animals

5 *Admin (répertorier)* to list, to set out; **les conditions désignées à l'annexe ii** the specifications set out in Annex ii

6 *(destiner)* **sa compétence la désigne pour cet emploi** her ability makes her the right person for the job

7 *(exposer)* **un geste qui vous désignera à sa fureur** a gesture which will surely unleash his/her fury on you; **d. qch à l'attention de qn** to call *or* draw sb's attention to sth

VPR **se désigner 1** *(se proposer)* to volunteer; **se d. pour une mission** to volunteer for a mission **2 se d. à l'attention générale** to draw attention to oneself

désillusion [dezilyzjɔ̃] NF disappointment, disillusionment, disillusion; **connaître des désillusions** to be disillusioned *or* disenchanted

désillusionnement [dezilyzjɔnmɑ̃] NM disillusionment

désillusionner [3] [dezilyzjɔne] VT to disillusion; **être désillusionné** to be disenchanted *or* disillusioned

désincarcération [dezɛ̃karserasjɔ̃] NF freeing; **sa d. a pris une heure** it took an hour to free him/her

désincarcérer [18] [dezɛ̃karsere] VT *(des débris d'une voiture etc)* to free

désincarné, -e [dezɛ̃karne] ADJ **1** *(sans corps)* disembodied **2** *(irréel)* insubstantial, unreal

désincarner [3] [dezɛ̃karne] **se désincarner** VPR to become disembodied

désincrustant, -e [dezɛ̃krystɑ̃, -ɑ̃t] ADJ **1** *(pour la peau)* cleansing; **masque d.** face pack *or* mask **2** *(détartrant)* descaling

NM **1** *(pour la peau)* cleanser **2** *(détartrant)* scale solvent

désincrustation [dezɛ̃krystasjɔ̃] NF **1** *(de la peau)* cleansing **2** *(détartrage)* descaling

désincruster [3] [dezɛ̃kryste] VT **1** *(peau)* to cleanse **2** *(détartrer)* to descale

désindexation [dezɛ̃dɛksasjɔ̃] NF removal of index-linking (**de** from), deindexing (**de** of)

désindexer [4] [dezɛ̃dɛkse] VT to stop index-linking, to de-index; **ces retraites ont été désindexées** these retirement schemes are no longer index-linked

désindustrialisation [dezɛ̃dystrijalizasjɔ̃] NF deindustrialization

désindustrialiser [3] [dezɛ̃dystrijalize] VT to deindustrialize

désinence [dezinɑ̃s] NF *Gram* inflection, ending

désinfectant, -e [dezɛ̃fɛktɑ̃, -ɑ̃t] ADJ disinfecting *(avant n)*

NM disinfectant

désinfecter [4] [dezɛ̃fekte] VT to disinfect

désinfection [dezɛ̃fɛksjɔ̃] NF disinfection, disinfecting

désinflation [dezɛ̃flasjɔ̃] NF deflation, disinflation

désinformation [dezɛ̃fɔrmasjɔ̃] NF disinformation

désinformer [3] [dezɛ̃fɔrme] VT to disinform

désinscription [desɛ̃skripsjɔ̃] NF unsubscription

désinscrire [99] [desɛ̃skrir] **se désinscrire** VPR *Ordinat* to unsubscribe

désinsectisation [dezɛ̃sɛktizasjɔ̃] NF insect control; **la d. de l'immeuble aura lieu demain** the building will be cleared of insects tomorrow

désinsectiser [3] [dezɛ̃sɛktize] VT to clear of insects

désinstallateur [dezɛ̃stalatœr] NM *Ordinat* deinstaller

désinstallation [dezɛ̃stalasjɔ̃] NF *Ordinat* deinstallation

désinstaller [3] [dezɛ̃stale] VT *Ordinat* to deinstall

désintégration [dezɛ̃tegrasjɔ̃] NF **1** *(d'un matériau, d'un groupe)* disintegration, breaking-up, splitting **2** *Nucl* disintegration; **d. radioactive** radioactive decay

désintégrer [18] [dezɛ̃tegre] VT **1** *(matériau)* to crumble, to disintegrate; *(groupe, famille)* to break up, to split (up) **2** *Nucl* to disintegrate

VPR **se désintégrer 1** *(exploser)* to disintegrate **2** *(groupe, famille, théorie)* to disintegrate, to collapse **3** *Hum (disparaître)* to vanish into thin air

désintéressé, -e [dezɛ̃terese] ADJ **1** *(impartial ▸ conseil, jugement)* disinterested, objective, unprejudiced **2** *(généreux ▸ personne)* selfless, unselfish

désintéressement [dezɛ̃teresmɑ̃] NM **1** *(impartialité)* disinterestedness, impartiality, absence of bias

2 *(générosité)* selflessness

3 *(désintérêt)* **d. pour** lack of interest in, indifference to

4 *Fin (d'un créancier)* paying off; *(d'un actionnaire, de partenaire)* buying out

> Do not confuse with **désintérêt**.

désintéresser [4] [dezɛ̃terese] VT *(créancier)* to pay off; *(actionnaire, partenaire)* to buy out

VPR **se désintéresser se d. de** *(ignorer)* to be uninterested in; *(perdre son intérêt pour)* to lose interest in

désintérêt [dezɛ̃tere] NM indifference, lack of interest; **manifester du d. pour** to show indifference to *or* no interest in

> Do not confuse with **désintéressement**.

désintermédiation [dezɛ̃termedjasjɔ̃] NF *Écon* disintermediation

désintoxication [dezɛ̃tɔksikasjɔ̃] NF *Méd* detoxification; *Fig* **la d. idéologique d'un pays** ridding a country of pernicious ideological influences

désintoxiquer [3] [dezɛ̃tɔksike] VT *Méd* to detoxify; **se faire d.** *(drogué)* to be weaned off drugs; *(alcoolique)* to be weaned off alcohol; *Fig* **l'association s'efforce de d. les ex-adeptes de la secte** the association is trying to wean the ex-members away from the influence of the sect; *Fam* **c'est un drogué de la télé, il faut le d.!** he's a complete TV addict, we need to get him out of the habit!

VPR **se désintoxiquer** *(drogué)* to kick the habit; *(alcoolique)* to dry out; *Fig (se remettre en forme)* to detox

désinvestir [32] [dezɛ̃vestir] VT **1** *Écon* to disinvest in **2** *Mil* **d. une ville** to raise the blockade of a town

VI to become less involved

désinvestissement [dezɛ̃vestismɑ̃] NM **1** *Écon* disinvestment; **d. marginal** marginal disinvestment **2** *Psy* withdrawal of involvement

désinvolte [dezɛ̃vɔlt] ADJ **1** *(sans embarras ▸ personne)* casual, nonchalant; *(▸ mouvements)* easy, free; **d'un ton d.** casually **2** *Péj (trop libre)* offhand

désinvolture [dezɛ̃vɔltyr] NF **1** *(légèreté ▸ d'une personne)* casualness, nonchalance; *(▸ des mouvements)* ease **2** *Péj (négligence)* offhandedness; **avec d.** offhandedly; **elle le traite avec d.** she's rather offhand with him

désir [dezir] NM **1** *(aspiration)* want, wish, desire; *(souhait exprimé)* wish; **il a le d. de plaire** he aims to please; **ses désirs ont été satisfaits** his/her wishes have been met; **j'ai toujours eu le d. d'écrire** I've always wanted to *or* had a desire to write; **tu prends tes désirs pour des réalités!** wishful thinking!; **selon le d. de qn** following sb's wishes; **il sera fait selon votre d.** it shall be done as you wish; **à l'encontre des désirs de qn** against sb's wishes; *Hum* **tes désirs sont des ordres** your wish is my command **2** *(motivation)* desire, drive; *Psy* urge; **d. de mort** death wish **3** *(appétit sexuel)* desire; **rempli de d.** *(personne)* consumed with desire; *(regard)* lustful

désirabilité [dezirabilite] NF desirability

désirable [dezirabl] ADJ **1** *(souhaitable)* desirable; **peu d.** undesirable **2** *(séduisant)* desirable, (sexually) exciting

désirer [3] [dezire] VT **1** *(aspirer à ▸ paix, bonheur)* to wish for; **d. ardemment qch** to crave sth, to long for sth; **je ne désire pas leur perte** I do not wish to ruin them; **je n'ai plus rien à d.** I have nothing left to wish for; **il a tout ce qu'il peut d.** he has everything he could wish for; **elle a toujours désiré posséder un piano** she's always wanted to own a piano; **d. vivement rencontrer qn** to be eager to meet sb; **ton père se fait d.!** where could your father have got to?; **fais-toi d.** let them wait for you; **cette bière se fait d.!** how long's that beer going to take?; **laisser à d.** to leave a lot to be desired, to fail to come up to expectations; **ça laisse à d.** it leaves a lot to be desired

2 *(vouloir)* **d. faire** to want *or* to wish to do; **désirez-vous ouvrir un compte?** do you want *or* wish to open an account?; **les enfants désirent rester avec leur père** the children would prefer to stay with their father; **il ne désirait pas vous faire de la peine** he didn't mean to hurt you; **je désire que tu restes** I want *or Sout* wish you to stay

3 *(dans un achat, une prestation de service)* **vous désirez?** can I help you?; **quelle couleur désirez-vous?** which colour would you like?

4 *(sexuellement)* to desire; **désirez-vous toujours votre mari?** do you still find your husband (sexually) attractive?

USAGE ABSOLU **tu ne peux d. mieux** you couldn't wish for anything better

désireux, -euse [dezirø, -øz] ADJ **d. de faire** inclined *or* willing to do; **d. de plaire** anxious *ou* eager to please; **assez peu d. de le suivre** reluctant to follow him; **il était peu d. de poursuivre la discussion** he was not willing to continue the discussion

désistement [dezistəmɑ̃] NM **1** *Pol* withdrawal, standing down **2** *Jur (d'une poursuite)* withdrawal; *(d'une demande)* waiver

désister [3] [deziste] **se désister** VPR **1** *Pol* to stand down, to withdraw **2** *Jur* **se d. d'une poursuite** to withdraw a suit; **se d. d'une demande** to waive a claim

desk [dɛsk] NM *Journ* desk

deskman [dɛskman] NM *Journ* deskman

désobéir [32] [dezɔbeir] VI **1** *(être désobéissant)* to be disobedient **2** *(enfreindre un ordre)* to disobey; **d. à** to disobey, to fail to obey; **d. aux ordres/à ses parents** to disobey orders/one's parents; **tu m'as désobéi!** you disobeyed me!, you didn't do as you were told!; **d. aux lois** to break the law; **d. à un code** to disregard a code

VT *(au passif uniquement)* **elle n'accepte pas d'être désobéie** she will not stand for disobedience

désobéissance [dezɔbeisɑ̃s] NF disobedience (**à** qn to sb); **d. à une règle** disregard for *or* breaking of a rule; **d. civile** civil disobedience

désobéissant, -e [dezɔbeisɑ̃, -ɑ̃t] ADJ *(enfant)* disobedient, rebellious; *(chien)* disobedient

désobligeance [dezɔbliʒɑ̃s] NF disagreeableness

désobligeant, -e [dezɔbliʒɑ̃, -ɑ̃t] ADJ **1** *(personne ▸ désagréable)* disagreeable, unkind; *(▸ impoli)* rude; **d'un ton d.** sharply **2** *(propos ▸ blessant)* invidious; *(▸ méchant)* nasty

désobliger [17] [dezɔbliʒe] VT to offend, to hurt, to upset; **sans vouloir vous d.** no offence (meant)

désobstruer [7] [dezɔpstrye] VT **1** *(tuyau)* to clear **2** *Méd* to remove an obstruction from

désodé, -e [desɔde] ADJ sodium-free, salt-free

désodorisant, -e [dezɔdɔrizɑ̃, -ɑ̃t] ADJ deodorizing *(avant n)*

NM air freshener

désodoriser [3] [dezɔdɔrize] VT to deodorize

désœuvré, -e [dezœvre] ADJ **être d.** to have nothing to do; **d., il errait dans le parc** having nothing (better) to do, he would roam about the park; **je ne supporte pas de rester d. plus de cinq minutes** I can't bear to be idle for more than five minutes

NM,F idle person

désœuvrement [dezœvrəmɑ̃] NM idleness; **ils ne le font que par d.** they only do it because they have nothing better to do

désolant, -e [dezɔlɑ̃, -ɑ̃t] ADJ **1** *(triste ▸ spectacle)* wretched, pitiful, awful **2** *(contrariant)* annoying, irritating

désolation [dezɔlasjɔ̃] NF **1** *(chagrin)* desolation, grief; **être plongé dans la d.** to be disconsolate; **après son départ, ce fut la d.** when he'd/she'd gone, gloom descended **2** *(cause de chagrin)* **cet enfant est ma d.** I despair of this child **3** *Littéraire (d'un lieu, d'un paysage)* desolation, desolateness, bleakness

désolé, -e [dezɔle] ADJ **1** *(contrit)* apologetic, contrite; **à sa mine désolée, j'ai compris qu'il l'avait cassé** when I saw him looking so apologetic, I gathered he'd broken it

2 *(pour s'excuser)* sorry; **je suis vraiment d.** I am awfully *or* really sorry; **d. de vous déranger** sorry to disturb you; **il est d. de ne pas vous avoir vu** he's sorry he missed you; **d., je n'ai pas le temps** sorry, I haven't got the time; *Ironique* **d., j'étais là avant vous!** excuse me *or* sorry, (but) I was here before you!; **ah, je suis d., ces deux notions ne sont pas identiques** excuse me *or* I'm sorry, but these two concepts are not the same

3 *Littéraire (triste)* disconsolate, sorrowful

4 *Littéraire (aride)* desolate, bleak

désoler [3] [dezɔle] VT **1** *(attrister)* to distress, to sadden; **l'état de la maison le désole** he's distressed about the state of the house **2** *(irriter)* **tu me désoles!** I despair (of you)!

VPR **se désoler** to be sorry; **ne te désole pas pour une petite tache** there's no need to be sorry about a little stain; **se d. de qch** to be disconsolate *or* in despair about *or* over sth; **ses parents se désolent de la voir si malheureuse** it grieves her parents to see her so unhappy

désolidariser [3] [desɔlidarize] VT **1** *(personnes)* to divide **2** *(objets, pièces d'un ensemble)* to separate

VPR **se désolidariser se d. de** to dissociate oneself from

désopilant, -e [dezɔpilɑ̃, -ɑ̃t] ADJ hilarious, hysterically funny

désordonné, -e [dezɔrdɔne] ADJ **1** *(désorganisé ▸ dossier, esprit)* confused, untidy

2 *(personne)* untidy

3 *(lieu)* untidy, messy

4 *(irrégulier)* helter-skelter *(avant n)*; **courir de façon désordonnée** to run helter-skelter *or* pell-mell; **le chien faisait des bonds désordonnés** the dog was leaping about all over the place

5 *Littéraire (immoral)* disorderly, disordered

désordre [dezɔrdr] NM **1** *(fouillis)* mess; **quel d. là-dedans!** what a mess *or* it's chaos in there!; **mettre le d. dans une pièce** to mess up a room; **c'est un peu le d. dans ses papiers** his/her papers are not altogether in order; *Fig* **ça fait d.!** *(ça ne se fait pas)* it's just not done!; *(ce n'est pas sérieux)* that's a laugh!

2 *(manque d'organisation)* muddle, confusion, disarray; **d. des idées** confused ideas

3 *(agitation)* disorder, disturbance; **semer le d.** to cause a disturbance, to wreak havoc; **lorsque le chat sauta, ce fut un beau d. parmi les poules** when the cat jumped, the hens went into a panic; *Jur* **d. sur la voie publique** disorderly conduct

4 *Méd* disorder; **d. nerveux/fonctionnel/hormonal** nervous/functional/hormone disorder

5 *Littéraire (immoralité)* dissoluteness, dissipation; **vivre dans le d.** to live a dissolute life

ADJ messy, untidy

• **désordres** NMPL **1** *(émeutes)* riots **2** *Littéraire (débauche)* dissolute *or* disorderly behaviour; **se livrer à des désordres** to lead a disorderly life

• **en désordre** ADJ *(lieu)* messy, untidy; *(cheveux)* unkempt, dishevelled; **une chambre en d.** an untidy room; **mon bureau était tout en d.** my desk was in a terrible mess ADV **mettre qch en d.** to mess sth up; **il a mis mes dossiers en d.** he got my files all muddled up

désorganisation [dezɔrganizasjɔ̃] NF disorganization, disruption

désorganisé, -e [dezɔrganize] ADJ disorganized

désorganiser [3] [dezɔrganize] VT *(service)* to disorganize, to disrupt; *(fiches)* to disrupt the order of; *(projets)* to upset

désorientation [dezɔrjɑ̃tasjɔ̃] NF **1** *(perplexité)* disorientation, confusion **2** *Psy* **d. spatiale/temporelle** spatial/temporal disorientation

désorienté, -e [dezɔrjɑ̃te] ADJ **1** *(perplexe)* confused, disorientated **2** *(égaré)* lost

désorienter [3] [dezɔrjɑ̃te] VT **1** *(faire s'égarer)* to disorientate **2** *(déconcerter)* to confuse, to throw into confusion *or* disarray, to disorientate

désormais [dezɔrmɛ] ADV *(à partir de maintenant)* from now on, *Sout* henceforth; *(dans le passé)* from that moment on, from then on; **je ferai attention d.** I'll pay attention from now on; **d. nous étions amis** from then on we were friends

désorption [dezɔrpsjɔ̃] NF *Chim* desorption

désossé, -e [dezɔse] ADJ *(viande, poisson)* boned; *(gigot, jambon)* off the bone; *Fig (personne)* supple

désossement [dezɔsmɑ̃] NM *(de viande, poisson)* boning

désosser [3] [dezɔse] VT **1** *(viande, poisson)* to bone **2** *Fam (étudier)* to go over with a fine-tooth comb **3** *Fam (démonter)* to take to bits

VPR **se désosser** *(se désarticuler)* to contort oneself

désoxydant [dezɔksidɑ̃] NM *Chim* deoxidizer

désoxyder [3] [dezɔkside] VT *Chim* to deoxidize, to deactivate

desperado [desperado] NM desperado

despote [despɔt] NM **1** *Pol* despot, tyrant **2** *(personne autoritaire)* tyrant, bully

ADJ **mari/femme d.** despotic husband/wife

despotique [despɔtik] ADJ **1** *Pol* despotic, tyrannical, dictatorial **2** *(autoritaire)* despotic, domineering, bullying

despotiquement [despɔtikmɑ̃] ADV *Pol & Fig* despotically, tyrannically, dictatorially

despotisme [despɔtism] NM **1** *Pol* despotism **2** *(autorité)* tyranny, bullying

desquamation [deskwamasjɔ̃] NF *(de la peau)* flaking, *Spéc* desquamation; *(des écailles)* scaling off

desquamer [3] [deskwame] VI *(peau)* to flake off, *Spéc* to desquamate; *(écailles)* to scale off

VPR **se desquamer** *(peau)* to flake (off), *Spéc* to desquamate; *(écailles)* to scale off

desquels, desquelles [dekɛl] *voir* **lequel**

DESS [deəɛsɛs] NM *(abrév* **diplôme d'études supérieures spécialisées***)* = postgraduate diploma lasting one year

dessaisir [32] [desezir] VT *Jur* **d. qn de** to deny sb jurisdiction over; **d. un tribunal d'une affaire** to remove a case from a court

VPR **se dessaisir 1 se d. de** *(se départir de)* to part with, to relinquish **2** *Jur* **se d. d'une affaire** to decline (to exercise) jurisdiction over a case

dessaisissement [desezismɑ̃] NM **1** *Jur (d'un tribunal)* removal of a case from **2** *(renoncement)* relinquishment

dessalage [desalaʒ] NM **1** *Chim* desalination **2** *Culin* removal of salt (**de** from)

dessalaison [desalezɔ̃] NF **1** *Chim* desalination **2** *Culin* removal of salt (**de** from)

dessaler [3] [desale] VT **1** *Chim* to desalinate **2** *Culin* to remove the salt from; **d. du poisson** to freshen fish **3** *Fam (dégourdir)* **d. qn** to teach sb a thing or two; **elle est très dessalée** she knows a thing or two

VI *Naut* to overturn, to capsize

VPR **se dessaler** *Fam* to learn a thing or two, to wise up; **il s'est drôlement dessalé depuis qu'il travaille!** he's learnt a thing or two since he started working!

dessangler [3] [desɑ̃gle] VT *(cheval)* to ungirth

dessaouler [3] [desule] = **dessoûler**

desséchant, -e [deseʃɑ̃, -ɑ̃t] ADJ **1** *(asséchant)* drying, withering; **un vent d.** a searing wind **2** *(activité, études)* soul-destroying **3** *Chim* desiccating

desséché, -e [deseʃe] ADJ **1** *(peau, cheveux)* dry; *(pétale, feuille)* withered; *(bois)* seasoned, dried; *(gorge)* parched **2** *(décharné)* emaciated, wasted **3** *(cœur, personne)* hardened; **un vieux solitaire d.** a hardened old recluse

dessèchement [deseʃmɑ̃] NM **1** *(de peau, de cheveux)* drying (up); *(de pétale, de feuille)* withering; *(de bois)* seasoning, drying

2 *(amaigrissement)* emaciation, wasting away

3 *(procédé)* desiccation, drying (out)

4 *(stérilité ▸ du cœur)* hardening; *(▸ de la créativité)* drying up

dessécher [18] [deseʃe] VT **1** *(peau, cheveux)* to dry out; *(pétale, feuille)* to wither; *(bois)* to season, to dry; **trop de soleil dessèche la peau** too much sun dries the skin; **la bouche desséchée par la peur** his/her mouth dry *or* parched with fear **2** *(amaigrir)* to emaciate, to waste; **son corps desséché par la maladie** his/her body wasted by illness **3** *(endurcir)* **d. le cœur de qn** to harden sb's heart

VPR **se dessécher 1** *(peau, cheveux)* to go dry; *(pétale, feuille)* to wither; *(bois)* to dry out **2** *(maigrir)* to waste away **3** *(s'endurcir ▸ cœur)* to harden; *(▸ personne)* to become hardened

dessein [desɛ̃] NM **1** *Littéraire* intention, goal, purpose; **son d. est de prendre ma place** his/her intention is to *or* he/she has determined to take my place; **former le d. de faire qch** to determine to do sth; **avoir le d. de faire qch** to intend to do sth **2 d. intelligent** intelligent design

• **à dessein** ADV deliberately, purposely; **c'est à d. que je n'ai pas répondu** I deliberately didn't answer

• **dans ce dessein** ADV with this intention, with this in mind

• **dans le dessein de** PRÉP in order *or* with a view to

desseller [4] [desele] VT to unsaddle

desserrage [deseraʒ], **desserrement** [desɛrmɑ̃] NM **1** *(processus)* loosening, slackening **2** *(résultat)* looseness

desserrer [4] [desere] VT **1** *(vis, cravate, ceinture)* to loosen **2** *(relâcher ▸ étreinte, bras)* to relax; *(▸ poings, dents)* to unclench; *Fig* **il n'a pas desserré les dents** *ou* **lèvres** he didn't utter a word, he never opened his mouth **3** *(frein)* to release

VPR **se desserrer 1** *(vis, cravate, ceinture)* to come loose **2** *(se relâcher ▸ étreinte)* to relax

dessers *etc voir* **desservir**

dessert [desɛr] NM dessert, *Br* pudding, sweet; **veux-tu un d.?** will you have some dessert?; **qu'est-ce qu'il y a comme** *ou* **au d.?** what's for dessert?; **au d.** at the end of the meal

desserte [desɛrt] NF **1** *(meuble)* sideboard; *(table roulante) Br* tea-trolley, *Am* tea wagon **2** *Transp* service; **d. aérienne** air service; **la d. du village est très mal assurée** the village is poorly served by public transport **3** *Rel* ministry

dessertir [32] [desɛrtir] VT to unset

VPR **se dessertir** to come unset

desservant [desɛrvɑ̃] NM *Rel* incumbent

desservir [38] [desɛrvir] VT **1** *(débarrasser)* to clear (away)

2 *(désavantager)* to be detrimental *or* harmful to, to go against; **son intervention m'a desservi** he/she did me a disservice by intervening; **son perfectionnisme la dessert** the fact that she's such a perfectionist goes against her

3 *Transp* to serve; **le village est mal desservi** public transport to the village is poor; **l'hôpital est desservi cinq fois par jour** there is a bus (service)

to the hospital five times a day; **ce train dessert les gares suivantes** this train stops at the following stations

4 *Rel (paroisse)* to serve

5 *(donner accès à)* to lead to; **une allée dessert la maison** a drive leads up to the house; **un couloir dessert les chambres** a corridor leads off to the bedrooms

USAGE ABSOLU *(débarrasser)* **puis-je d.?** may I clear the table?

dessiccation [desikasjɔ̃] **NF** *(gén)* desiccation, drying; *(du bois)* drying

dessiller [3] [desije] *Littéraire* **VT d. les yeux de** *ou* **à qn** to cause the scales to fall from sb's eyes, to open sb's eyes

VPR se dessiller mes yeux se dessillent the scales have fallen from my eyes

dessin [desɛ̃] **NM 1** *(croquis)* drawing; **les dessins de Michel-Ange** Michelangelo's drawings; **des dessins d'enfants** children's drawings; **d. humoristique** *ou* **de presse** cartoon *(in a newspaper)*; **d. animé** cartoon; **d. à main levée** free hand drawing; **d. à la plume** pen and ink drawing; **d. au trait** *ou* **linéaire** outline drawing; *Fam* **tu veux que je te fasse un d.?** do you want me to spell it out for you?; *Fam* **pas besoin d'un** *ou* **de faire un d., elle a compris!** you don't have to spell it out for her, she's got the message!

2 *(art)* **le d.** drawing; **apprendre le d.** to learn (how) to draw; **être bon en d.** to be good at drawing, to be a good drawer

3 *(technique)* **la vigueur de son d.** the firmness of his/her drawing technique

4 *Tech* **d. assisté par ordinateur** computer-aided design; **d. coté** dimensioned drawing; **d. industriel** draughtsmanship, industrial design; **d. par ordinateur** computer art

5 *(forme, ligne)* line, outline; **pour donner à vos sourcils un d. parfait** to give your eyebrows the perfect shape

6 *(ornement)* design, pattern; **un tissu à d.** a patterned fabric; **un tissu à dessins géométriques** a fabric with geometric patterns

• **de dessin ADJ cours/école de d.** art class/school

dessinateur, -trice [desinatœr, -tris] **NM,F 1** *(technicien)* **d. (industriel)** draughtsman, *f* draughtswoman **2** *(concepteur)* designer; **d. de mode** fashion designer **3** *Beaux-Arts* **il est meilleur d. que peintre** he draws better than he paints; **d. de bande dessinée** cartoonist; **d. d'études** design draughtsman; **d. humoristique** cartoonist

dessinateur-cartographe [desinatœrkartograf] *(pl* **dessinateurs-cartographes)** **NM** cartographer

dessinatrice [desinatris] *voir* **dessinateur**

dessiner [3] [desine] **VT 1** *Beaux-Arts* to draw; **d. qch sur le vif** to draw sth from life

2 *(former)* to delineate; **menton/visage bien dessiné** firmly delineated chin/face; **bouche finement dessinée** finely drawn *or* chiselled mouth

3 *(concevoir ▸ meuble, robe, bâtiment)* to design; *(▸ paysage, jardin)* to landscape

4 *(souligner)* to emphasize the shape of; **un vêtement qui dessine bien la taille** a garment that shows off the waist

USAGE ABSOLU il dessine bien he's good at drawing; **d. à la plume/au crayon/au fusain** to draw in pen and ink/in pencil/in charcoal

VPR se dessiner 1 *(devenir visible)* to stand out; **un sourire se dessina sur ses lèvres** a smile formed on his/her lips; **les douces collines du Perche se dessinent au lointain** the gentle slopes of the Perche hills stand out in the far distance **2** *(apparaître ▸ solution, tendance)* to emerge

dessouder [3] [desude] **VT 1** *Tech* to unsolder **2** *Fam Arg crime (tuer)* to do in, to waste

VPR se dessouder *Tech* to become unsoldered

dessoûler [3] [desule] **VT** to sober up

VI to sober up; **il ne dessoûle pas de la journée** he's drunk all day

dessous [dəsu] **ADV** underneath; **les prix sont marqués d.** the prices are marked underneath; **mets-toi d.** get under it

NM *(d'un meuble, d'un objet)* bottom; *(d'une feuille)* underneath; **le d. de l'assiette est sale** the bottom of the plate is dirty; **les gens du d.** the people downstairs, the downstairs neighbours; **les d. de la politique/de la finance** the hidden agenda in politics/in finance; **le d. des cartes** *ou* **du jeu** the hidden agenda; **avoir le d.** to come off worst, to get the worst of it; **être dans le trente-sixième d.** to be down in the dumps

NMPL *(sous-vêtements)* underwear; **des d. coquins** sexy underwear

• **de dessous PRÉP** from under, from underneath; **enlève ça de d. la table** pick that up from under *or* underneath the table

• **en dessous ADV** underneath; **la feuille est verte en d.** the leaf is green underneath; *Fam* **les gens qui habitent en d., les gens d'en d.** the people downstairs, the downstairs neighbours; **agir en d.** to act in an underhand way; **rire en d.** to laugh up one's sleeve

• **en dessous de PRÉP** below; **en d. de zéro** below zero; **vous êtes très en d. de la vérité** you're very far from the truth

• **par en dessous ADV** *(prendre, saisir)* from underneath; *Fig* **regarder qn par en d.** to steal a glance at sb

dessous-de-bouteille [dəsudbutɛj] **NM INV** coaster *(for a bottle)*

dessous-de-bras [dəsudbra] **NM INV** dress shield

dessous-de-plat [dəsudpla] **NM INV** table mat *(to protect the table from hot dishes)*, *Am* hot pad

dessous-de-table [dəsudtabl] **NM INV** *Péj* bribe

dessous-de-verre [dəsudvɛr] **NM INV** coaster

dessus [dəsy] **ADV** *(placer, monter)* on top; *(marcher, écrire)* on it/them; *(passer, sauter)* over it/them; **écrivez l'adresse d.** write the address on it; **monte d., tu verras mieux** get on top (of it), you'll get a better view; **assieds-toi d.** sit on it; **avec du chocolat d.** with chocolate on top; **ils lui ont tiré d.** they shot at him/her; **ils lui ont tapé d.** they hit him/her; **ne compte pas trop d.** don't count on it too much; **je suis d. depuis un moment** *(affaire, travail)* I've been (working) on it for a while; **ça nous est tombé d. à l'improviste** it was like a bolt out of the blue; **il a fallu que ça me tombe d.!** it had to be me!; **qu'est-ce qui va encore me tomber d.?** what next?

NM 1 *(d'un objet, de la tête, du pied)* top; *(de la main)* back; **prends la nappe du d., elle est repassée** take the tablecloth on the top, it's been ironed; **avoir/prendre le d.** to have/to get the upper hand; **après 15 minutes de jeu, l'équipe marseillaise a nettement pris le d. sur ses adversaires** after 15 minutes of play the Marseilles team gained a definite advantage over their opponents; **reprendre le d.** *(gagner)* to get back on top (of the situation), to regain the upper hand; **elle a bien repris le d.** *(après une maladie)* she was soon back on her feet again; *(après une dépression)* she got over it quite well; **le d. du panier** *(personnes)* the cream, the elite; *(choses)* the top of the pile *or* heap **2** *(étage supérieur)* **les voisins du d.** the people upstairs, the upstairs neighbours; **l'appartement du d.** the *Br* flat *or Am* apartment above

• **dessus NMPL** *Théât* flies

• **de dessus PRÉP enlève ça de d. la table!** take it off the table!; **elle ne leva pas les yeux de d. son ouvrage** she didn't look up from *or* take her eyes off her work

• **en dessus ADV** on top

dessus-de-cheminée [dəsydʃəmine] **NM INV** mantleshelf runner

dessus-de-lit [dəsydli] **NM INV** bedspread

déstabilisant, -e [destabilizɑ̃, -ɑ̃t], **déstabilisateur, -trice** [destabilizatœr, -tris] **ADJ** *(pour un pays, un régime)* destabilizing; *(pour une personne)* unsettling

déstabilisation [destabilizasjɔ̃] **NF** *(d'un pays, d'un régime)* destabilization; *(d'une personne)* unsettling

déstabilisatrice [destabilizatrice] *voir* **déstabilisant**

déstabiliser [3] [destabilize] **VT** *(pays, régime)* to destabilize; *(personne)* to unsettle

déstalinisation [destalinizasjɔ̃] **NF** destalinization

déstaliniser [3] [destalinize] **VT** to destalinize

destin [dɛstɛ̃] **NM 1** *(sort)* fate, destiny; **le d. a voulu que...** fate decreed that... **2** *(vie personnelle)* life, destiny, fate; **il a eu un d. tragique** his destiny was tragic; **maître de son d.** master of one's (own) fate **3** *(évolution)* destiny, fate; **son roman a connu un d. imprévu** his/her novel had an unexpected fate; **leur union devait avoir un d. malheureux** their marriage was destined to be unhappy

destinataire [destinatɛr] **NMF** *(d'une lettre)* addressee; *(de produits)* consignee; *(d'un mandat postal)* payee; *Ordinat (d'un message électronique)* recipient

destination [dɛstinasjɔ̃] **NF 1** *(lieu)* destination; **arriver à d.** to reach one's destination **2** *(emploi)* purpose, use; **quelle d. lui donneras-tu?** what do you plan to use it for?; **détourné de sa d. primitive** diverted from its original purpose

• **à destination de PRÉP avion/vol à d. de Nice** plane/flight to Nice; **les voyageurs à d. de Paris** passengers for Paris, passengers travelling to Paris; **le train de 15h30 à d. de Bordeaux** the 3.30 train to Bordeaux

destinée [dɛstine] **NF 1** *(sort)* **la d.** fate; **la d. de qn/qch** the fate in store for sb/sth **2** *(vie)* destiny; **il tient ma d. entre ses mains** he holds my destiny in his hands; *Littéraire* **unir sa d. à celle de qn** to unite one's destiny with sb's

• **destinées NFPL les dieux qui président à nos destinées** the gods who decide our fate (on earth); **promis à de hautes destinées** destined for great things; **de hautes destinées l'attendaient** he/she was destined to achieve great things

destiner [3] [dɛstine] **VT 1** *(adresser)* **d. qch à qn** to intend sth for sb; **cette remarque ne t'est pas destinée** this remark isn't meant *or* intended for you; **voici le courrier qui lui est destiné** here is his/her mail *or* the mail for him/her; **festival destiné aux enfants** children's festival, festival for children

2 *(promettre)* **d. qn à** to destine sb for; **rien ne/tout me destinait au violon** nothing/everything led me to become a violinist; **nous étions destinés l'un à l'autre** we were meant for each other; **on la destine à quelque gros industriel** her family wants to marry her off to some rich industrialist; **il avait destiné son fils au barreau** he had intended his son for the bar; **il était destiné à mourir jeune** he was fated to die young; **son idée était destinée à l'échec dès le départ** his/her idea was bound to fail *or* doomed (to failure) from the very start

3 *(affecter)* **d. qch à** to set sth aside for; **d. des fonds à** to allocate funds to, to set aside *or* to earmark funds for; **marchandises destinées à l'exportation** goods intended for export; **cette somme a été destinée à l'achat d'un microscope** this sum has been set aside to buy a microscope; **cette salle est destinée aux répétitions** this room is for rehearsing in

VPR se destiner se d. à qch to want to take up sth; **se d. au journalisme** to want to become a journalist

destituable [dɛstitɥabl] **ADJ** *(fonctionnaire)* dismissible; *(roi)* deposable; **il n'est pas d.** *(fonctionnaire)* he cannot be dismissed (from his post); *(officier)* he cannot be stripped of his rank

destituer [7] [dɛstitɥe] **VT** *(fonctionnaire)* to relieve from duties, to dismiss; *(roi)* to depose; *(officier)* to demote; **d. un général de son commandement** to relieve a general of his command

destitution [dɛstitysjɔ̃] **NF** *(d'un fonctionnaire)* dismissal; *(d'un roi)* deposition, deposal; *(d'un officier)* demotion

déstockage [destɔkaʒ] **NM** destocking, reduction in stocks; *Compta* **d. de production** *(poste de bilan)* decrease in stocks

déstocker [3] [destɔke] **VT** to destock, to reduce stocks of

VI to reduce stocks

déstresser [4] [destrese] **VI** to destress, to unwind

VT to relax

destrier [dɛstrije] **NM** *Arch* charger, steed

destroy [dɛstrɔj] **ADJ** *Fam* **1** *(personne)* wasted-looking□; *(jean)* ripped□; **il avait l'air complète-**

ment d. he looked a complete wreck, he looked totally wasted **2** *(style, esthétisme)* subversive; *(musique)* loud and aggressive **3** *(en mauvais état ▸ voiture)* beat up, wrecked, *Br* knackered

destroyer [destrwaje, destrɔjœr] **NM** *Mil* destroyer

destructeur, -trice [dɛstryktœr, -tris] **ADJ** destructive; **caractère d.** destructiveness

NM,F destroyer

NM d. de documents document shredder

destructible [destryktibl] **ADJ** destructible; **facilement d.** easy to destroy; **difficilement d.** virtually indestructible

destructif, -ive [destryktif, -iv] **ADJ** *(action, croyance)* destructive

destruction [dɛstryksjɔ̃] **NF 1** *(fait d'anéantir ▸ gén)* destroying, destruction; *(▸ des rats, des insectes)* extermination; **la d. des récoltes** the destruction of the crops; **après la d. de la ville par le feu/les bombardements** after the town had been gutted by fire/destroyed by bombing **2** *(dégâts)* damage

destructive [destryktiv] *voir* **destructif**

destructrice [destryktris] *voir* **destructeur**

déstructuration [destryktyrasjɔ̃] **NF** deconstruction, taking apart

déstructuré, -e [dɛstryktyre] **ADJ** *(vêtement)* unstructured

déstructurer **[3]** [destryktyre] **VT** to remove the structure from

VPR se déstructurer to lose (its) structure, to become destructured

désuet, -ète [dezɥɛ, -ɛt] **ADJ** *(mot, vêtement)* outdated, old-fashioned, out-of-date; *(technique)* outmoded, obsolete; *(charme)* old-fashioned

désuétude [dezɥetyd] **NF** obsolescence; **tomber en d.** *(mot)* to fall into disuse, to become obsolete; *(technique, pratique)* to become obsolete; *Jur (droit)* to lapse; *(loi)* to fall into abeyance; **d. calculée** planned *or* built-in obsolescence

désuni, -e [dezyni] **ADJ** *(brouillé ▸ famille, ménage)* disunited, divided

désunion [dezynjɔ̃] **NF** division, dissension *(UNCOUNT)*

désunir **[32]** [dezynir] **VT 1** *(séparer)* **des amants que le temps a désunis** lovers who grew apart with the passage of time **2** *(brouiller ▸ famille)* to split, to divide; **ils sont désunis** they don't get on (with each other) any more **3** *(disjoindre)* **d. les éléments d'un ensemble** to separate the elements of a set (from each other), to split up a set

VPR se désunir *(athlète)* to lose one's stride

désyndicalisation [desɛ̃dikalizasjɔ̃] **NF** declining level of unionization (**de** among)

désyndicaliser **[3]** [desɛ̃dikalize] **VT** *(entreprise)* to de-unionize

détachable [detaʃabl] **ADJ** *(feuillet, capuchon)* removable, detachable

détachage [detaʃaʒ] **NM** *(nettoyage)* stain removal

détachant, -e [detaʃɑ̃, -ɑ̃t] **ADJ** *(produit)* stain-removing

NM stain remover

détaché, -e [detaʃe] **ADJ 1** *(ruban, animal)* untied **2** *(air, mine)* detached, casual, offhand **3** *Admin* **fonctionnaire d.** civil servant *Br* on secondment *or Am* on a temporary assignment

détachement [detaʃmɑ̃] **NM 1** *(désintéressement)* detachment; **prendre un air de d.** to look detached *or* casual; **il montrait un certain d. vis-à-vis des biens de ce monde** he was quite unworldly **2** *(troupe)* detachment; **d. précurseur** advance party **3** *Admin Br* secondment, *Am* temporary assignment

• **en détachement** **ADV** *Br* on secondment, *Am* on a temporary assignment; **en d. auprès de** *Br* seconded to, *Am* on a temporary assignment with

détacher **[3]** [detaʃe] **VT 1** *(libérer)* to untie; **d. un animal** to untie an animal; **d. ses cheveux** to untie one's hair, to let one's hair down; **d. les mains d'un prisonnier** to untie a prisoner's hands; **d. une guirlande** to take down a garland; **d. une caravane** to unhitch *or* to unhook a caravan; **d. une barque** to detach a boat from its moorings

2 *(séparer)* **d. une photo d'une lettre** *(enlever le trombone)* to unclip a photo from a letter; *(enlever l'agrafe)* to unstaple a photo from a letter; **d. une recette d'un magazine/un timbre d'un carnet** to tear a recipe out of a magazine/a stamp out of a book; **d. les pétales d'une fleur** to pick *or* to pluck the petals off a flower

3 *(défaire ▸ ceinture)* to unfasten; *(▸ col)* to unfasten, to loosen; *(▸ chaîne)* to undo

4 *(détourner)* **d. ses yeux** *ou* **son regard de qn** to take one's eyes off sb; **d. son attention d'une lecture** to stop paying attention to one's reading; **d. qn de** *(affectivement)* to take sb away from; **être détaché de** to be detached from *or* indifferent to; **il est détaché des biens de ce monde** he has renounced all worldly goods

5 *Admin* to send *Br* on secondment *or Am* on a temporary assignment; *Mil* to detach; **je vais être détaché auprès du ministre** I will be sent *Br* on secondment *or Am* on a temporary assignment to the Ministry; **d. un officier auprès de qn** to detach an officer to serve with sb; **il faut d. quelqu'un de votre service pour m'aider** you must assign *or Br* second somebody from your department to help me

6 *(faire ressortir)* to separate (out); **détachez bien chaque mot/note** make sure every word/note stands out (clearly)

7 *(nettoyer)* to clean; **j'ai donné ton costume à d.** I took your suit to the cleaner's

USAGE ABSOLU *(séparer)* **d. suivant le pointillé** tear (off) along the dotted line

VPR se détacher 1 *(se libérer ▸ personne)* to untie *or* to free oneself; *(▸ animal)* to break loose

2 *(sandale, lacet)* to come undone; *(étiquette)* to come off; *(page)* to come loose; **l'écorce se détache** the bark is peeling off, the bark is coming away from the tree

3 *Sport (se séparer ▸ du peloton)* to break away

4 se d. les cheveux *(enlever ce qui les attache)* to let one's hair down

5 *(se profiler)* to stand out; **le mont Blanc se détache à l'horizon** Mont Blanc stands out against the horizon

6 se d. de *(se décrocher de)* to come off

7 se d. de qn *(en devenant adulte)* to break away from sb; *(par manque d'intérêt)* to grow apart from sb; **se d. de qch** to turn one's back on sth; **il a eu du mal à se d. d'elle** he found it hard to leave her behind; **puis je me suis détachée de ma famille/de l'art figuratif** later, I grew away from my family/from figurative art

• **à détacher** **ADJ fiche/recette à d.** tear-off card/recipe

détacheur [detaʃœr] **NM** stain remover

détail [detaj] **NM 1** *(exposé précis)* breakdown, detailed account, itemization; **faire le d. de qch** *(dépenses, travaux)* to break sth down, to itemize sth; **faites-moi le d. de ce qui s'est passé** tell me in detail what happened; *Fam* **il n'a pas fait le d.!** he was a bit heavy-handed!; *Fam* **ici, on ne fait pas le d.!** we make no distinctions here!

2 *(élément ▸ d'un récit, d'une information)* detail, particular; **les détails croustillants de l'histoire** the juicy details of the story; **donner des détails sur qch** to enlarge on sth, to go into more detail about sth; **je te passe les détails** *(ennuyeux)* I won't bore you with the detail *or* details; *(horribles)* I'll spare you the (gory) details; **jusque dans les moindres détails** down to the smallest detail; **soigner les détails** to pay attention to detail; **pour plus de détails...** for further details...

3 *(point sans importance)* detail, minor point; **je trouve l'article longuet mais ce n'est qu'un d.** I think the article's a bit long, but that's a mere detail; **c'est un d. de l'Histoire** it is a mere footnote of history; **ne nous arrêtons pas à ces détails** let's not worry about these minor details

4 *Beaux-Arts* detail

5 *Com* retail

6 *(petite partie ▸ d'un meuble, d'un édifice)* detail; **il a été vendu plus cher à cause du d. Art nouveau** it was sold for a higher price because of the Art nouveau detail

• **au détail** **ADJ** *(vente)* retail *(avant n)* **ADV vendre qch au d.** to sell sth retail, to retail sth; **vous vendez les œufs au d.?** do you sell eggs individually?

• **de détail** **ADJ 1** *(mineur)* **faire quelques remarques de d.** to make a few minor comments **2** *Com* retail *(avant n)*; **commerce de d.** retailing

• **en détail** **ADV** in detail

détaillant, -e [detajɑ̃, -ɑ̃t] **NM,F** retailer, shopkeeper; **d. indépendant** independent retailer; **d. spécialisé** specialist retailer

détaillé, -e [detaje] **ADJ** *(récit)* detailed; *(facture, relevé de compte)* itemized

détailler **[3]** [detaje] **VT 1** *Com* to retail, to sell retail; **nous détaillons cet ensemble pull, jupe et pantalon** we sell the sweater, skirt and trousers separately; **nous ne le détaillons pas** *(service à vaisselle)* we don't sell it separately; *(fromage, gâteau)* we only sell it whole **2** *(dévisager)* to scrutinize, to examine; **d. qn de la tête aux pieds** to look sb over from head to foot, to look sb up and down; **d. qn effrontément** to stare insolently at sb **3** *(énumérer ▸ faits, facture)* to itemize, to detail

détaler **[3]** [detale] **VI** *(animal)* to bolt; *(personne)* to decamp, *Am* to cut and run; **les gamins ont détalé comme des lapins** the kids scattered like rabbits; **tu aurais vu comme il a détalé!** you couldn't see him for dust!

détartrage [detartraʒ] **NM** *(des dents)* scaling; *(d'une bouilloire, d'une chaudière)* descaling; **se faire faire un d. (des dents)** to have one's teeth cleaned

détartrant, -e [detartrɑ̃, -ɑ̃t] **ADJ** *(produit, substance)* descaling; **dentifrice d.** toothpaste for tartar removal

NM descaling agent

détartrer **[3]** [detartre] **VT** *(dents ▸ sujet: dentiste)* to scale; *(▸ sujet: dentifrice)* to remove the tartar from; *(bouilloire, chaudière)* to descale

détartreur [detartrœr] **NM** *(pour chaudière)* scaler

détaxation [detaksasjɔ̃] **NF la d. des livres** *(réduction)* the reduction of duty *or* tax on books; *(suppression)* the lifting of duty *or* tax on books

détaxe [detaks] **NF 1** *(levée)* **la d. des tabacs** *(réduction)* the reduction of duty *or* tax on tobacco; *(suppression)* the lifting of tax *or* duty on tobacco; **vendus en d.** duty-free; **la d. des marchandises à l'exportation** the lifting of duty on exports **2** *(remboursement)* refund; **cela m'a fait 200 euros de d.** I got 200 euros in duty refunded

détaxé, -e [detakse] **ADJ** *(produits, articles)* duty-free

détaxer **[3]** [detakse] **VT** *(supprimer)* to lift the tax *or* duty on; *(diminuer)* to reduce the tax *or* duty on

détectable [detektabl] **ADJ** detectable; **le signal est à peine d.** the signal is almost undetectable

détecter **[4]** [detekte] **VT** to detect, to spot

détecteur [detɛktœr] **NM** detector; *Aut* **d. d'anomalie** fault warning sensor; *Aut* **d. anti-pincement** anti-pinch sensor; *Aut* **d. de choc** crash sensor; *Aut* **d. de cognement** knock sensor; *Aut* **d. de collision** crash sensor; **d. de faux billets** forged banknote detector; **d. de fumée** smoke detector, smoke alarm; **d. d'incendie** fire detector; **d. de mensonges** lie detector, polygraph; **d. de mines** mine detector; **d. d'ondes** wave detector; **d. de particules** particle detector; **d. de radar** radar detector; **d. transistorisé** solid-state sensor; *Ordinat* **d. de virus** virus detector

détection [deteksjɔ̃] **NF** *(gén)* detection, detecting, spotting; **d. électromagnétique** radio location; *Ordinat* **d. d'erreurs** error detection; **d. des mines** mine detection; **d. à ultrasons** ultrasound detection; *Ordinat* **d. virale** virus detection

détective [detektiv] **NMF** detective; **jouer les détectives** to play detective; **d. privé** private detective *or* investigator

déteindre **[81]** [detɛ̃dr] **VI 1** *(se décolorer)* to fade; **d. au lavage** to run in the wash; **le noir va d. sur le rouge** the black will run into the red **2** *Fam (humeur, influence)* **on dirait que la mauvaise humeur, ça déteint!** bad temper is catching, it seems!; **d. sur qn** to rub off on sb, to influence sb; **sa gentillesse a déteint sur tout le monde** his/her kindness has rubbed off on everybody

VT *(linge)* to discolour; *(tenture, tapisserie)* to fade

dételage [detlaʒ] **NM** *(d'un cheval)* unharnessing, unhitching; *(d'un bœuf)* unyoking; *(d'une voiture)* unhitching; *(de wagons)* uncoupling

dételer [24] [detle] **VT 1** *(cheval)* to unharness, to unhitch; *(bœuf)* to unyoke **2** *(caravane, voiture)* to unhitch; *(wagon)* to uncouple

VI *Fam (s'arrêter)* to ease off[□]; **on dételle!** time for a break!, let's call it a day!

• **sans dételer ADV** *Fam* without a break[□], nonstop[□]

détendeur [detɑ̃dœr] **NM** *Tech* pressure-reducing valve

détendre [73] [detɑ̃dr] **VT 1** *(relâcher ▸ corde)* to ease, to loosen, to slacken; *(▸ressort)* to release; *(▸arc)* to unbend **2** *(décontracter)* to relax; **la musique me détend** music relaxes me; **il a réussi à d. l'atmosphère avec quelques plaisanteries** he made things more relaxed by telling a few jokes **3** *(gaz)* to depressurize

VPR se détendre 1 *(corde, courroie)* to ease, to slacken; *(ressort)* to uncoil

2 *(se décontracter)* to relax; **détends-toi!** relax!; **j'ai besoin de me d. après une journée au bureau** I need to unwind *or* relax after a day at the office

3 *(s'améliorer ▸ ambiance)* to become more relaxed

4 *(gaz)* to be reduced in pressure

détendu, -e [detɑ̃dy] **ADJ 1** *(calme)* relaxed **2** *(corde, courroie)* slack

détenir [40] [detnir] **VT 1** *(posséder ▸ record)* to hold, to be the holder of; *(▸ actions, pouvoir, secret)* to hold; *(▸ document, bijou de famille)* to hold, to have (in one's possession); **d. un monopole** to have a monopoly; **société détenue à 50 pour cent** 50 percent-owned company; **ils détiennent 30 pour cent des parts de marché** they have a 30 percent market share; **détenu par des intérêts privés** privately-held **2** *Jur (emprisonner)* to detain; **d. qn préventivement** to hold sb on remand

détente [detɑ̃t] **NF 1** *(relaxation)* relaxation; **j'ai besoin de d.** I need to relax; **une heure de d. après une journée d'école** an hour's relaxation *or* break after a day at school

2 *Pol* **la d.** détente

3 *(d'une horloge)* catch; *(d'un ressort)* release mechanism

4 *(d'une arme)* trigger; *Fam* **il est dur à la d.** *(il est pingre)* he's tight-fisted *or* stingy; *(il ne comprend pas vite)* he's slow on the uptake

5 *Sport* spring; **avoir de la d., avoir une belle d.** to have a powerful spring

6 *(d'un gaz)* expansion; *(dans un moteur)* explosion *or* power stroke

7 *Écon (des taux d'intérêt)* lowering, easing

détenteur, -trice [detɑ̃tœr, -tris] **NM,F** holder; **le d. du record** the record holder; **le d. du titre** the titleholder; **d. d'actions** *ou* **de titres** *Br* shareholder, *Am* stockholder

détention [detɑ̃sjɔ̃] **NF 1** *(emprisonnement)* detention; **être maintenu en d.** to be detained; **d. criminelle** imprisonment; **d. criminelle à perpétuité** life imprisonment; **d. criminelle à temps** imprisonment for a fixed term; **d. illégale** unlawful imprisonment; **d. préventive** *ou* **provisoire** remand; **en d. préventive** *ou* **provisoire** in detention awaiting trial, on remand; **mettre qn en d. préventive** *ou* **provisoire** to remand sb in custody **2** *(possession ▸ gén)* possession; *(▸ d'actions)* holding; **arrêté pour d. d'armes** arrested for illegal possession of arms

détentrice [detɑ̃tris] *voir* **détenteur**

détenu, -e [detny] **PP** *voir* **détenir**

ADJ *(accusé, prisonnier)* imprisoned

NM,F prisoner

détergence [detɛrʒɑ̃s] **NF** detergency

détergent, -e [detɛrʒɑ̃, -ɑ̃t] **ADJ** detergent

NM *(gén)* detergent; *(en poudre)* washing powder; *(liquide)* liquid detergent

déterger [17] [detɛrʒe] **VT** to clean

détérioration [deterjɔrasjɔ̃] **NF** *(de la santé, des relations)* worsening, deterioration; *(des locaux)* deterioration

détériorer [3] [deterjɔre] **VT** to cause to deteriorate, to damage, to harm

VPR se détériorer *(temps, climat social)* to deteriorate, to worsen; *(denrée)* to go bad

déterminable [determinabl] **ADJ** determinable; **facilement/difficilement d.** easy/difficult to determine

déterminant, -e [determinɑ̃, -ɑ̃t] **ADJ** deciding, determining; **le prix a été l'élément d.** the price was the deciding factor

NM 1 *Math* determinant **2** *Ling* determiner

déterminatif, -ive [determinatif, -iv] **ADJ** determinative; *(proposition)* defining

NM determiner, determinative

détermination [determinasjɔ̃] **NF 1** *(ténacité)* determination, resoluteness

2 *(résolution)* determination, decision; **agir avec d.** to act determinedly

3 *(de causes, de termes)* determining, establishing; **la d. des causes de l'accident sera difficile** it will be difficult to determine the cause of the accident

4 *(des prix)* fixing, setting

5 *Ling & Phil* determination

6 *Biol* determination, determining; **d. des sexes** sex determination; **d. du groupe sanguin** blood typing

déterminative [determinativ] *voir* **déterminatif**

déterminé, -e [determine] **ADJ 1** *(défini)* determined, defined, circumscribed; **non encore d.** to be specified (later); **il n'a pas d'opinion déterminée à ce sujet** he doesn't really have a strong opinion on the matter; **dans un but bien d.** for a definite reason; **à un prix bien d.** at a set price **2** *(décidé)* determined, resolute; **avoir l'air d.** to look determined; **être d. à faire qch** to be determined to do sth **3** *Ling & Phil* determined

déterminer [3] [determine] **VT 1** *(définir)* to ascertain, to determine; *(fixer ▸ lieu, heure)* to fix, to decide on; *(▸ prix)* to fix

2 *(inciter)* to incite, to encourage; **d. qn à faire qch** to encourage sb to do sth; **qu'est-ce qui vous a déterminé à partir?** what made you (decide to) leave?; **est-ce lui qui vous a déterminé à agir ainsi?** did you act in this way because of him?

3 *(causer)* to determine; **qu'est-ce qui détermine l'achat?** what determines whether somebody will buy or not?

4 *Ling & Phil* to determine

5 *Biol (sexe)* to determine; *(groupe sanguin)* to type

VPR se déterminer to decide, to make a decision, to make up one's mind; **se d. à faire qch** to make up one's mind to do sth

déterminisme [determinism] **NM** determinism

déterministe [determinist] **ADJ** determinist, deterministic

NMF determinist

déterré, -e [detere] **NM,F avoir l'air d'un d.** *ou* **une mine de d.** *ou* **une tête de d.** to look like death warmed up

déterrer [4] [detere] **VT 1** *(os, trésor)* to dig up, to unearth; *(arbre)* to uproot **2** *(exhumer ▸ cadavre)* to dig up, to disinter **3** *(dénicher ▸ secret, texte)* to dig out, to unearth

détersif, -ive [detersif, -iv] **ADJ** detergent

NM *(gén)* detergent; *(en poudre)* washing powder; *(liquide)* liquid detergent

détersion [detersjɔ̃] **NF** *(nettoyage au détergent)* cleaning with a detergent; *Méd* cleansing

détersive [detersiv] *voir* **détersif**

détestable [detestabl] **ADJ** dreadful, detestable, foul

détestablement [detestabləmɑ̃] **ADV** appallingly, dreadfully

détester [3] [deteste] **VT** to hate, to detest, to loathe; **il me déteste cordialement** he hates me with a passion; **il va se faire d.** he's going to make himself really unpopular, people are really going to hate him; **il déteste devoir se lever tôt** he hates having to get up early; **je déteste qu'on me mente** I hate *or* I can't stand being lied to; **je ne déteste pas une soirée tranquille à la maison** I'm quite partial to a quiet evening at home; **je ne détesterais pas dîner au restaurant ce soir** I wouldn't mind eating out tonight; **il m'a fait d. les maths** he put me off maths completely

déthéiné, -e [deteine] **ADJ** decaffeinated

détient *etc voir* **détenir**

détint *etc voir* **détenir**

détonant, -e [detɔnɑ̃, -ɑ̃t] **ADJ** *(substance)* explosive; **explosif d.** high explosive

NM explosive

détonateur [detɔnatœr] **NM 1** *(d'une bombe, d'une charge)* detonator **2** *Fig (déclencheur)* detonator, trigger; **servir de d. à qch** to trigger off sth

détonation [detɔnasjɔ̃] **NF 1** *(bruit ▸ d'explosion)* explosion; *(▸ de coup de feu)* shot; *(▸ d'un canon)* boom, roar **2** *Aut* backfiring

détoner [3] [detɔne] **VI** to detonate; **faire d. qch** to detonate sth

> Do not confuse with **détonner.**

détonner [3] [detɔne] **VI 1** *Mus (instrument, personne)* to be out of tune *or* off key **2** *(contraster ▸ couleurs, styles)* to clash; *(▸ personne)* to be out of place; **la remarque détonne dans ce texte** the remark jumps out in this text *or* looks really out of place in this text

> Do not confuse with **détoner.**

détordre [76] [detɔrdr] **VT** *(câble, corde, linge)* to untwist

VPR se détordre to come untwisted, to untwist

détortiller [3] [detɔrtije] **VT** *(câble, corde, linge)* to untwist; *(cheveux)* to disentangle

détour [detur] **NM 1** *(tournant)* bend, curve, turn; *(méandre)* wind, meander; **la route fait de nombreux détours jusqu'au bout de la vallée** the road winds all the way through the valley; **faire un brusque d.** to make a sharp turn **2** *(crochet)* detour, diversion; **faire un d. par un village** to make a detour through a village; **elle nous a fait faire un d. pour venir ici** she brought us a roundabout way; *Fig* **faisons un petit d. par la psychanalyse** let's go off at a tangent for a minute and talk about psychoanalysis; **valoir le d.** *(restaurant, paysage)* to be worth the detour; *Fam* **tu verrais son nouveau copain, il vaut le d.!** her new boyfriend is really something! **3** *(faux-fuyant)* roundabout way; **un discours plein de détours** a roundabout way of speaking

• **au détour de PRÉP 1** *(en cheminant le long de)* **je l'ai aperçue au d. du chemin** I spotted her at the bend in the path **2** *(en consultant, en écoutant)* **au d. de votre œuvre, on devine vos préoccupations** glancing through your work, one gets an idea of your main concerns; **au d. de la conversation** in the course of the conversation

• **sans détour ADV** *(parler, répondre)* straightforwardly, without beating about the bush

détourage [deturaʒ] **NM** *Tech* routing

détourné, -e [deturne] **ADJ 1** *(route, voie)* roundabout *(avant n)*, *Sout* circuitous **2** *(façon, moyen)* indirect, roundabout *(avant n)*, *Sout* circuitous; **par des moyens détournés** in a roundabout way; **apprendre qch de façon détournée** to learn sth indirectly; **agir de façon détournée** to behave deviously

détournement [deturnəmɑ̃] **NM 1** *(dérivation ▸ de la circulation)* redirection, diversion, rerouting; *(▸ d'une rivière)* diverting, diversion

2 *Aviat* **d. d'avion** hijacking; **faire un d. d'avion** to hijack a plane

3 *Fin* misappropriation; **d. d'actif** embezzlement of assets; **d. de fonds** misappropriation of funds, embezzlement

4 *Jur* **d. de mineur** corruption of a minor; **d. de pouvoir** abuse of power

5 *Ordinat* **d. de modem** modem hijacking

détourner [3] [deturne] **VT 1** *(circulation)* to redirect, to divert, to reroute; *(rivière)* to divert; **il a fallu d. le convoi par le village** the convoy had to be rerouted through the village

2 *(avion, autocar)* to hijack

3 *(éloigner ▸ coup)* to parry; *(▸ arme)* to turn aside *or* away; **d. les yeux** *ou* **le regard** to avert one's eyes, to look away; **d. la tête** to turn one's head away; **d. l'attention de qn** to divert sb's attention; **d. la conversation** to change the subject; **d. les soupçons** to divert suspicion (away from oneself); **d. les soupçons sur qn** to divert suspicion towards sb

4 *(déformer ▸ paroles, texte)* to distort, to twist; **il sait comment d. le sens du contrat à son profit** he knows how to make the wording of the contract work to his advantage

5 *(écarter)* to take away; **d. qn de sa route** to take sb out of his/her way; **d. qn de son devoir** to divert sb from his/her duty; **d. qn du droit chemin** to lead sb astray
6 *(extorquer)* to misappropriate; **d. des fonds** to embezzle *or* to misappropriate funds
7 *Jur (mineur)* to corrupt
VPR se détourner 1 *(tourner la tête)* to turn (one's head), to look away **2 se d. de** to turn away from; **se d. de ses études** to turn away from one's studies; **en grandissant, je me suis détourné de la natation** I got tired of swimming as I grew older

détoxication [detɔksikasjɔ̃] **NF** detoxication, detoxification

détoxifier [9] [detɔksifje] *Méd* **VT** to detoxify
VPR se détoxifier to detox

détoxiquer [3] [detɔksike] **VT** to detoxicate, to detoxify

détracter [3] [detrakte] **VT** *Littéraire* to denigrate, to disparage

détracteur, -trice [detraktœr, -tris] **ADJ** disparaging, detractory
NM,F detractor, critic

détraqué, -e [detrake] **ADJ 1** *(cassé)* broken; **ma montre/la télé est détraquée** my watch/the TV isn't working properly **2** *Fam (dérangé)* **le temps est d.** the weather's gone haywire; **ma santé est détraquée** my health is wrecked; **elle a les nerfs complètement détraqués** she's a nervous wreck **3** *Fam (désaxé)* crazy, psycho; **il est complètement d.** he's totally cracked; **il a le cerveau d.** his mind is unhinged
NM,F *Fam* maniac, psycho; **d. sexuel** sex maniac

détraquement [detrakmɑ̃] **NM depuis le d. de ma montre** *(elle fonctionne mal)* since my watch started going wrong; *(elle est cassée)* since my watch stopped working

détraquer [3] [detrake] **VT 1** *(appareil)* to damage; *(mécanisme)* to throw out of gear **2** *Fam (déranger)* **ça va te d. l'estomac** that'll upset your stomach; *Hum* **toutes ces études lui ont détraqué le cerveau** all that studying has addled his/her brain
VPR se détraquer 1 *(mal fonctionner)* to go wrong; *(cesser de fonctionner)* to break down **2** *Fam (temps)* to become unsettled▫; *(l'estomac)* to be upset▫ **3** *Fam* **se d. le foie/le système** to wreck one's liver/health

détrempe [detrɑ̃p] **NF 1** *Métal* softening, annealing **2** *(produit ▸ à base de lait, d'eau)* distemper; *(▸ à base d'œuf)* tempera; *(œuvre)* distemper painting; **peindre un tableau à la** *ou* **en d.** to distemper a painting

détremper [3] [detrɑ̃pe] **VT 1** *Métal* to soften, to anneal **2** *(mouiller ▸ chiffon, papier)* to soak (through); *(▸ chaux)* to slake; *(▸ mortier)* to mix with water; **détrempé** *(champ, terre)* sodden, waterlogged **3** *Beaux-Arts* to distemper

détresse [detres] **NF 1** *(désespoir)* distress, anxiety; **pousser un cri de d.** to cry out in distress **2** *(pauvreté)* distress; **les familles dans la d.** families in dire need *or* dire straits; **tomber dans une grande d.** to fall on hard times, to encounter hardship **3** *Méd* **d. respiratoire** respiratory distress
• **en détresse ADJ** *(navire, avion)* in distress

détriment [detrimɑ̃] **NM** *Littéraire* detriment
• **au détriment de PRÉP** to the detriment of; **je l'ai appris à mon d.** I found out to my cost

détritus [detrity(s)] **NM** piece of *Br* rubbish *or Am* garbage; **des d.** refuse, detritus

détroit [detrwa] **NM** *Géog* strait; **le d. de Gibraltar** the Strait of Gibraltar

détromper [3] [detrɔ̃pe] **VT** to disabuse
VPR se détromper détrompez-vous! don't be so sure!; **si tu crois qu'il va venir, détrompe-toi!** if you think he's coming, you'd better think again!

détrôner [3] [detrone] **VT** *(roi)* to dethrone, to depose; *(champion)* to dethrone; *(rival, produit)* to oust, to push into second position; **les biofuels vont-ils d. l'essence?** will petrol be ousted by biofuels?; **se faire d.** to be dethroned; *Fig* to be ousted

détrousser [3] [detruse] **VT** *Littéraire* to rob

détrousseur [detrusœr] **NM** *Littéraire* **d. de grands chemins** highwayman

détruire [98] [detrɥir] **VT 1** *(démolir, casser)* to destroy; **le village a été détruit** the village was destroyed *or* razed to the ground; **les deux véhicules sont détruits** both cars are write-offs; **détruisez cette lettre** destroy this letter; **l'enfant construit un château, puis le détruit** the child builds a castle, then demolishes it; **ma vie est détruite** my life is in ruins; **d. par le feu** *(maison)* to burn down; *(objet, documents)* to burn **2** *(éliminer ▸ population, parasites)* to destroy, to wipe out; *(tuer ▸ ennemi)* to kill; *(▸ animal malade, chien errant)* to destroy **3** *(porter préjudice à ▸ santé, carrière)* to ruin, to destroy, to wreck; **tu as détruit la confiance que j'avais en toi** you have destroyed the trust I had in you; **tous ses espoirs ont été détruits en un instant** all his/her hopes were shattered in an instant
VPR se détruire *Vieilli* to do away with oneself

dette [dɛt] **NF 1** *(d'argent)* debt; **avoir une d.** to have run up a debt; **avoir 1000 euros de dettes** to be 1,000 euros in debt; **avoir des dettes** to be in debt; **avoir de plus en plus de dettes** to get deeper and deeper into debt; **avoir des dettes vis-à-vis de qn** to be in debt to sb; **être couvert** *ou* **criblé** *ou* **perdu de dettes** to be up to one's *Br* eyes *or Am* ears in debt; **faire des dettes** to get *or* to run into debt; **je n'ai plus de dettes** I've cleared my debts; *Compta* **dettes actives** accounts receivable, assets; **dettes bancaires** bank debts; **d. caduque** debt barred by the Statute of Limitations; **dettes compte** book debts; *Écon & Fin* **d. consolidée** consolidated *or* funded debt; *Compta* **dettes à court terme** current liabilities; **d. de l'État** national debt; **d. exigible** debt due for (re)payment; **dettes d'exploitation** trade debt; **d. extérieure** external *or* foreign debt; **d. flottante** floating debt; **d. foncière** property charge; **dettes fournisseurs** accounts payable; **d. d'honneur** debt of honour; *(hypothécaire)* mortgage debt; **d. inexigible** unrecoverable debt; **d. inscrite** consolidated debt; **d. de jeu** gambling debt; **d. liquide** liquid debt; *Compta* **dettes à long terme** long term liabilities; *Compta* **dettes à moyen terme** medium-term liabilities; *Fin* **d. négociable** assignable debt; *Compta* **dettes passives** *(en comptabilité)* accounts payable, liabilities; **d. privilégiée** preferred *or* privileged debt; **d. publique** national debt; **d. en souffrance** outstanding debt; **d. véreuse** bad debt **2** *(obligation morale)* debt; **régler sa d. envers la société** to pay one's debt to society; **être en d. envers qn** to be indebted to sb, to be under an obligation to sb; **avoir une d. de reconnaissance envers qn** to be in sb's debt, to owe sb a debt of gratitude

deuche [dœʃ], **deudeuche** [dødœʃ] **NF** *Fam* Citroën 2CV▫

DEUG [dœg] **NM** *(abrév* **diplôme d'études universitaires générales**) = university diploma taken after two years

> **DEUG, DEUST**
>
> In French universities, students take the "DEUG" or the "DEUST" after two years of courses. They may then take further courses leading to the "licence" (the equivalent of a bachelor's degree). Most students who obtain the "DEUG" choose to do this, while the majority of students who obtain the "DEUST" leave university and go straight into employment.

deuil [dœj] **NM 1** *(chagrin)* grief, mourning; *Fam* **j'en ai fait mon d.** I've resigned myself to not having it; **ta nouvelle voiture, tu peux en faire ton d.** you might as well kiss your new car goodbye
2 *(décès)* bereavement; **il y a eu un d. dans la famille** there was a bereavement *or* death in the family
3 *(tenue conventionnelle)* mourning; **porter/prendre le d. (de qn)** to be in/to go into mourning (for sb); *Fig* **elle porte le d. de sa jeunesse/de sa fortune** she is mourning the loss of her youth/fortune; **quitter le d.** to come out of mourning
4 *(période)* mourning; **son d. n'aura pas duré longtemps** he/she didn't mourn for very long; **il l'a rencontrée pendant son d.** he met her when he was still in mourning; **une journée de d. national** a day of national mourning
5 *(convoi)* funeral procession; **conduire** *ou* **mener le d.** to be the chief mourner
• **de deuil ADJ** *(vêtement)* mourning *(avant n)*; **brassard de d.** black armband
• **en deuil ADJ** bereaved; **une femme en d.** a woman in mourning; *Fig* **la Bretagne est en d.** the whole of Brittany is in mourning
• **en deuil de PRÉP être en d. de** to mourn for
• **en grand deuil ADJ** in deep mourning

DEUST [døst] **NM** *(abrév* **diplôme d'études universitaires scientifiques et techniques**) = university diploma taken after two years of science courses; *voir aussi encadré sous* **DEUG**

deutérium [døterjɔm] **NM** *Chim* deuterium

Deutéronome [døterɔnɔm] **NM** *Bible* **le D.** Deuteronomy

DEUX [dø] **ADJ 1** *(gén)* two; **on a dû lui enlever les d. pieds** they had to remove both his/her feet; **des d. côtés** on both sides; **d. fois** twice; **d. fois plus de livres** twice as many books; **d. fois moins de livres** half as many books; **j'ai d. mots à te dire** I want a word with you, I've a bone to pick with you; **je reviens dans d. minutes** I'll be back in a minute; **tu peux venir? – d. secondes!** can you come here? – just a minute!; **d. ou trois** a couple of, a few, one or two; **écris-moi d. ou trois lignes de temps en temps** drop me a line from time to time; **ça s'écrit avec d. g** it's spelt with a double g *or* two g's; **une personne à d. visages** a two-faced individual; **à d. pas** close by, not far away; **à d. pas de** close by, not far away from; **à d. doigts de** close to, within an inch of; **à d. doigts de mourir** *ou* **de la mort** within an inch of death *or* dying; **j'ai été à d. doigts de le renvoyer** I came very close to *or* I was within inches of firing him; **je suis à d. doigts d'avoir terminé** I've very nearly finished; **entre d. âges** middle-aged; *Mil & Fig* **pris entre d. feux** caught in the crossfire; **nager entre d. eaux** to sit on the fence; **je l'ai vu entre d. portes** I only saw him briefly; **il n'a pas d. sous de jugeote** he hasn't got a scrap of common sense; *Fam* **en d. temps trois mouvements** in no time at all, in a jiffy; *très Fam* **de mes d.** *Br* bloody, *Am* goddamn; **t'as vu ce chauffard de mes d.!** did you see that *Br* bloody *or Am* goddamn idiot driving that car?; **avoir d. poids d. mesures** to apply double standards; **d. avis valent mieux qu'un** two heads are better than one; *Prov* **d. précautions valent mieux qu'une** better safe than sorry; **de d. maux, il faut choisir le moindre** one must choose the lesser of two evils
2 *(dans des séries)* second; **page/numéro/chapitre d.** page/number/chapter two; **Charles D.** Charles the Second
PRON two; **casser qch en d.** to break sth in two; **venez, tous les d.** come along, both of you; **eux/nous d.** both of them/us, the two of them/us; **à nous d.!** right, let's get on with it!; *(à un adversaire)* let's fight it out!; *Fam* **lui et le dessin, ça fait d.!** he can't draw to save his life!; **les maths/les ordinateurs et moi, ça fait d.** I just don't get on with maths/computers; **elle et la propreté, ça fait d.!** she doesn't know the meaning of the word "clean"!; *Fam* **comme pas d.** as anything; **les d. font la paire** they're two of a kind
NM INV 1 *(gén)* two; *(date)* second; **d. fois d. font quatre** two times two *or* twice two is four; **aujourd'hui nous sommes le d.** today is the second, it's the second today; **en moins de d.** in no time at all, in the twinkling of an eye; *Fam* **je n'ai fait ni une ni d.** I didn't think twice
2 *(numéro d'ordre)* number two
3 *(chiffre écrit)* two
4 *Cartes* two; **le d. de cœur** the two of hearts; *Can Fam* **un d. de pique** *(personne)* a loser; *voir aussi* **cinq**
• **à deux ADV** *(vivre)* as a couple, together; *(travailler)* in pairs; **il faudra s'y mettre à d.** it'll take two of us
• **deux à deux ADV** in twos *or* pairs
• **deux par deux ADV** in twos *or* pairs; **les enfants, mettez-vous d. par d.** children, get into twos *or* pairs

deux-chevaux *(pl* **inv)** [døʃ(ə)vo] **NF** *Aut* deux-chevaux, 2CV

2G [døʒe] **ADJ** *Ordinat & Tél* 2G

deuxième [døzjɛm] **ADJ** second; *Gram* **la d. personne du singulier/pluriel** the second person singular/plural; **de d. choix, de d. qualité** *(marchandises, articles)* inferior; *Cin & TV* **d. équipe** second unit

NMF 1 *(personne)* second **2** *(objet)* second (one); *Typ* **d. de couverture** inside front cover, IFC; *Typ* **d. épreuve** revise proof

NM 1 *(partie)* second

2 *(étage) Br* second floor, *Am* third floor

3 *(arrondissement de Paris)* second (arrondissement)

4 *Fin* **d. de change** second of exchange; *voir aussi* **cinquième**

deuxièmement [døzjɛmmɑ̃] **ADV** secondly, in second place

deux-mâts [døma] **NM INV** two-master

deux-pattes [døpat] **NF INV** *Fam* Citroën 2CV◻

deux-pièces [døpjɛs] **NM INV 1** *(maillot de bain)* two-piece **2** *(costume)* two-piece **3** *(appartement)* two-room *Br* flat *or Am* apartment

deux-points [døpwɛ̃] **NM INV** colon

deux-ponts [døpɔ̃] **NM INV** double-decker

deux-quatre [døkatr] **NM INV** *Mus* two-four time

deux-roues [døru] **NM INV** two-wheeled vehicle

deux-temps [døtɑ̃] **NM INV** *(moteur)* two-stroke; **(mélange) d.** two-stroke mixture

deuz, deuze [døz] *Fam (abrév* **deuxième***)* **ADJ** second◻; **je suis d.!** I'm second!

NMF second◻

dévaler [3] [devale] **VT** *(en courant)* to run *or* to race *or* to hurtle down; *(en roulant)* to tumble down

VI 1 *(personne)* to hurry *or* to hurtle down; *(torrent)* to gush down; *(animal)* to run down **2** *(s'abaisser ▸ terrain)* to fall *or* to slope away **3** *(rouler)* to tumble *or* to bump down; **le chariot a dévalé tout seul** the trolley ran off on its own

dévaliser [3] [devalize] **VT 1** *(cambrioler ▸ banque, diligence)* to rob; *(▸ maison)* to burgle; *(dépouiller ▸ personne)* to rob; **il s'est fait d.** he was robbed **2** *Fam (vider)* to raid; **ils ont dévalisé le frigo** they raided the fridge; **tous les marchands de glaces ont été dévalisés** all the ice-cream sellers have sold out◻

dévalorisation [devalɔrizasjɔ̃] **NF 1** *Fin (de la monnaie)* depreciation; *(de marchandises)* markdown **2** *(perte de prestige)* devaluing, loss of prestige

dévaloriser [3] [devalɔrize] **VT 1** *(discréditer ▸ personne, talent)* to depreciate, to devalue **2** *Fin (monnaie)* to devalue; *(marchandises)* to mark down

VPR se dévaloriser 1 *(se discréditer)* to put oneself down; **se d. aux yeux de qn** to discredit oneself in the eyes of sb **2** *Fin (monnaie)* to become devalued; *(marchandises)* to lose value; **ce diplôme s'est dévalorisé** this degree has lost its prestige

dévaluation [devalɥasjɔ̃] **NF** *Écon & Fin* devaluation, devaluing; **d. compétitive** competitive devaluation

dévaluer [7] [devalɥe] **VT 1** *Fin* to devalue **2** *(déprécier)* to devalue; **il l'a fait pour te d. à tes propres yeux** he did it to make you feel cheap

VPR se dévaluer to drop in value

devancement [dəvɑ̃smɑ̃] **NM 1** *Mil* **d. d'appel** enlistment before call-up **2** *Fin (d'une échéance)* payment before the due date, prepayment

devancer [16] [dəvɑ̃se] **VT 1** *(dans l'espace ▸ coureur, peloton)* to get ahead of, to outdistance; **je la devançais de quelques mètres** I was a few metres ahead of her; *Fig* **sur ce marché, nous ne sommes plus devancés que par les Japonais** only the Japanese are ahead of us in this market

2 *(dans le temps ▸ personne)* to arrive ahead of; *(▸ demande, désirs)* to anticipate; **elle m'avait devancé de deux jours** she had arrived two days before me; **d. son siècle** *ou* **époque** to be ahead of one's time; **d. l'appel** *Mil* to enlist before call-up; *Fig* to jump the gun

3 *(agir avant ▸ personne)* **tu m'as devancé, c'est justement ce que je voulais lui dire** you beat me to it, that's just what I wanted to say to them; **il s'est fait d. par les autres** the others got there before him

4 *Fin* **d. une échéance** to make a payment before it falls due

devancier, -ère [dəvɑ̃sje, -ɛr] **NM,F 1** *(précurseur)* precursor, forerunner **2** *(qui précède)* predecessor

DEVANT [dəvɑ̃]

PRÉP	
• in front of **1–3**	• past **1**
• ahead of **2**	• in the face of **4**
• given **4**	
ADV	
• in front **1, 2**	• ahead **3**
• before **4**	
NM	
• front	

PRÉP 1 *(en face de)* in front of; *(avec mouvement)* past; **il s'est garé d. la maison** he parked in front of the house; **il a déposé le paquet d. la porte** he left the parcel outside the door; **tricoter d. la télévision** to knit in front of the TV *or* while watching TV; **toujours d. la télé!** always glued to the TV!; **assis d. un verre de vin** sitting over a glass of wine; **il faut mettre un zéro d. le code** you have to put a zero in front of *or* before the code; **elle est passée d. moi sans me voir** she walked right past (me) without seeing me; **la voiture est passée/un lièvre a détalé d. moi** the car drove/a hare bolted past me

2 *(en avant de)* in front of; *(en avance sur)* ahead of; **il marchait d. nous** he was walking in front of us; **nous passerons d. lui pour lui montrer le chemin** we'll go ahead of him to show him the way; **passe d. moi, tu verras mieux** go in front of me, you'll get a better view; **il est loin d. nous** he is a long way in front of *or* ahead of us; **l'ère de la communication est d. nous** the age of communication lies ahead of *or* before us; **ils sont d. nous en matière d'électronique** their electronics industry's ahead of ours; **aller droit d. soi** to go straight on *or* ahead; *Fig* to carry on regardless; **regardez d. vous** look where you're going; **j'ai une heure d. moi** I have an hour to spare; **elle avait une belle carrière d. elle** she had a promising career ahead of her; **tu as la vie d. toi** you've got your whole life ahead of you; **avoir quelques économies d. soi** to have some savings put by

3 *(en présence de)* in front of; **pleurer d. tout le monde** *(devant les gens présents)* to cry in front of everyone; *(en public)* to cry in public; **il vaudrait mieux ne pas en parler d. lui** it would be better not to mention it in front of him; **d. témoins** in front of *or* in the presence of witnesses; **ils comparaîtront d. le tribunal demain** they will appear in court tomorrow; **porter une affaire d. la justice** to bring a case before the courts *or* to court; **je jure d. Dieu…** I swear to God…

4 *(face à)* in the face of, faced with; *(étant donné)* given; **nos troupes ont reculé d. leur puissance de feu** our troops withdrew in the face of their (superior) fire power; **je n'ai su que faire d. cette petite fille en pleurs** I didn't know what to do when faced *or* confronted with this little girl in tears; **son attitude d. le malheur** his/her attitude to *or Littéraire* in the face of disaster; **d. des preuves accablantes** in the face of overwhelming evidence; **d. son hésitation…** as he/she was *or* seeing that he/she was reluctant…, given his/her reluctance…; **d. la gravité de cette affaire** given the serious nature of this matter; **égaux d. la loi** equal in the eyes of the law *or* before the law

ADV 1 *(à l'avant)* **mettez les plus petits de la classe d.** put the shortest pupils at the *or* in front; **avoir des places d.** to have seats at the front; **installe-toi d.** *(en voiture)* sit *Br* in the front *or Am* in front; **ça se boutonne d.** it buttons up *Br* at the front *or Am* in front; **écris le nom du destinataire d.** write the addressee's name on the front; **faites passer la pétition d.** pass the petition forward; **d. derrière** back to front, the wrong way round; **tu as mis ton pull d. derrière** you've put your jumper on back to front *or* the wrong way round

2 *(en face)* **tu es juste d.** it's right in front of you; **tu peux te garer juste d.** you can park (right) in front; **je suis passé d. sans faire attention** I went past without paying attention

3 *(en tête)* **elle est loin d.** she's a long way ahead; **tu n'as pas vu Martin? – je crois qu'il est d.** have you seen Martin? – I think he's up ahead; **passe d., tu verras mieux** come *or* go through, you'll get a better view; **marche d.** walk in front; **pars d., je te rattraperai** go ahead, I'll catch you up

4 *Vieilli & Littéraire* **il revint plus effaré que d.** he came back more scared than before; **comme d.** as before

NM *(gén)* front; *Naut* bow, bows, fore; **avec cuisine sur le d. (de l'immeuble)** with a kitchen at the front (of the building); **la figure B indique le d.** figure B shows the front; **la jupe est plus longue sur le d.** the skirt is longer at the front; *Fig* **sur le d. de la scène** in the limelight; **prendre les devants** to make the first move, to be the first to act; **d. de caisse** check-out display

• de devant ADJ *(dent, porte)* front; **pattes de d.** forelegs **PRÉP va-t-en de d. la fenêtre** move away from the window; **sors de d. la télé** don't stand in front of the TV

devanture [dəvɑ̃tyr] **NF 1** *(vitrine) Br* shop window, *Am* store window

2 *(étalage)* (window) display

3 *(façade) Br* shopfront, *Am* storefront

4 *Can Fam (seins)* boobs, rack

• en devanture ADV in the window; **nous l'avons en d.** it's in the window

dévastateur, -trice [devastatœr, -tris] **ADJ** devastating; **de manière dévastatrice** devastatingly

NM,F wrecker

dévastation [devastasjɔ̃] **NF** devastation, havoc

dévastatrice [devastatris] *voir* **dévastateur**

dévaster [3] [devaste] **VT 1** *(pays, ville)* to devastate, to lay waste; *(récolte)* to ruin, to destroy; **des villages dévastés** destroyed villages **2** *Littéraire (cœur)* to ravage; **l'âme dévastée par ces morts successives** devastated by this succession of bereavements; **la souffrance a dévasté son visage** his/her looks have been ravaged by suffering

déveine [devɛn] **NF** bad luck; **avec ma d. habituelle** with my (usual) luck; **être dans la d.** to be down on one's luck; **quelle d.!** (what) hard luck!

développé [devlɔpe] **NM 1** *(en danse)* developpé **2** *Sport* press

développement [devlɔpmɑ̃] **NM 1** *(fait de grandir)* development; *(fait de progresser)* development, growth; **le d. normal de l'enfant/du chêne** a child's/an oak's normal development; **pour aider au d. du sens des responsabilités chez les jeunes** in order to foster a sense of responsibility in the young; **d. du marché** market development; **d. des ventes** sales expansion

2 *Écon* **le d.** development; **une région/entreprise en plein d.** a fast-developing area/business; **d. durable** sustainable development; **d. outre-mer** overseas development

3 *(exposé)* exposition; **faire un d. sur qch** to develop the theme of sth; **entrer dans des développements superflus** to go into unnecessary detail

4 *(perfectionnement)* developing; **nous leur avons confié le d. du prototype** we asked them to develop the prototype for us; **payé 5000 euros pour le d. du scénario** paid 5,000 euros for script development

5 *Phot (traitement complet)* processing, developing; *(étape du traitement)* developing; **une heure pour le d. des photos** one hour to develop *or* process the pictures; **appareil photo à d. instantané** instant camera

6 *Tech* gear; **bicyclette avec un d. de six mètres** bicycle with a six metre gear

7 *Math* development

8 *(déploiement ▸ d'une banderole)* unrolling

9 *Mus, Beaux-Arts & Littérature (d'un thème)* development

• développements NMPL *(prolongements ▸ d'une affaire)* developments

développer [3] [devlɔpe] **VT 1** *(faire croître ▸ faculté)* to develop; *(▸ usine, secteur)* to develop, to expand; *(▸ pays, économie)* to develop; **pour d. les muscles** for muscle development; **un jeu qui**

développe l'intelligence a game which develops the player's intelligence

2 *(exposer ▸ argument, plan)* to develop, to enlarge on

3 *(symptôme, complexe, maladie)* to develop

4 *Phot (traiter)* to process; *(révéler)* to develop; **faire d. une pellicule** to have a film processed; **faire d. des photos** to have some photos developed

5 *Math* to develop

6 *Tech* **une bicyclette qui développe cinq mètres** a bicycle with a five-metre gear

7 *(déballer ▸ coupon)* to unfold, to open out; *(▸ paquet)* to unwrap; *(▸ banderole)* to unroll

8 *Mus, Beaux-Arts & Littérature (thème)* to develop

VPR se développer 1 *(croître ▸ enfant, plante)* to develop, to grow; *(▸usine, secteur)* to develop, to expand; *(▸ pays, économie)* to develop, to become developed; **une région qui se développe** a developing area; **ça se développe beaucoup dans la région** the region is developing quickly; **il s'est beaucoup développé sur le plan physique** he has grown quite a lot; **elle n'est pas très développée pour son âge** she's physically underdeveloped for her age

2 *(apparaître ▸ membrane, moisissure)* to form, to develop

3 *(se déployer ▸ armée)* to be deployed; *(▸ cortège)* to spread out; *(▸ argument, récit)* to develop, to unfold; **la plaine se développe à perte de vue** the plain extends *or* stretches out as far as the eye can see

4 *(se diversifier ▸ technique, science)* to improve, to develop

5 *(s'aggraver ▸ maladie)* to develop

développeur [devlɔpœr] **NM** *Ordinat* software developer

devenir[1] [dəvnir] **NM** *Littéraire* **1** *(évolution)* evolution **2** *(avenir)* future; **quel est le d. de l'homme?** what is the future of mankind?

• **en devenir ADJ** *Littéraire (société, œuvre)* evolving, changing; **en perpétuel d.** constantly changing, ever-changing

devenir[2] **[40]** [dəvnir] **VI 1** *(acquérir telle qualité)* to become; **d. professeur** to become a teacher; **d. la femme de qn** to become sb's wife; **tu es devenue une femme** you're a woman now; **d. réalité** to become a reality; **d. vieux** to get *or* to grow old; **d. rouge/bleu** to go red/blue; **l'animal peut d. dangereux lorsqu'il est menacé** the animal can be dangerous when threatened; *Fam* **d. chèvre** *(s'énerver)* to blow one's top; *Fam* **à (vous faire) d. dingue, à (vous faire) d. fou, à (vous faire) d. chèvre** enough to drive you round the bend *or* up the wall *or* to make you scream

2 *(avoir tel sort)* **que sont devenus tes amis de jeunesse?** what happened to your childhood friends?; **que sont devenues tes belles intentions?** what has become of your good intentions?; **et moi, qu'est-ce que je vais d.?** what's to become of me?; **et moi, qu'est-ce que je deviens dans tout ça?** and where do I fit into all this?; **je ne sais pas ce que je deviendrais sans toi** I don't know what I'd do without you; **qu'est-ce que tu es devenu, il y a une heure qu'on t'attend!** where have you been *or* what have you been doing, we've been waiting for you for an hour!

3 *Fam (pour demander des nouvelles)* **que devenez-vous?** how are you getting on?, what have you been up to?; **et lui, qu'est-ce qu'il devient?** what's he up to these days?

4 *(tournure impersonnelle)* **il devient difficile de...** it's getting difficult to...; **il devient inutile de...** it's now pointless to...

dévergondage [devergɔ̃daʒ] **NM 1** *(immoralité)* licentiousness, licentious *or* immoral behaviour **2** *(fantaisie ▸ du style, de l'imagination)* extravagance

dévergondé, -e [devergɔ̃de] **ADJ** licentious, shameless

NM,F shameless person; **quel d.!** he's a wild one!; **petite dévergondée** little hussy

dévergonder [3] [devergɔ̃de] **VT** to corrupt, to lead astray; *Hum* **j'ai décidé de te d., tu ne vas pas travailler aujourd'hui** I've decided to lead you astray, you're staying off work today

VPR se dévergonder to go off the rails; *Hum* **dis donc, tu te dévergondes!** you're letting your hair down!

dévernir [32] [devernir] **VT** to strip the enamel off

déverrouillage [deveruјaʒ] **NM 1** *Ordinat & (d'une arme)* unlocking **2** *(d'une porte)* unbolting **3** *Aut* **d. du capot/du hayon par l'intérieur** internal bonnet/hatchback release

déverrouiller [3] [deveruje] **VT 1** *Ordinat & (arme)* to unlock; *(majuscules)* to lock off; **d. un fichier en écriture** to unlock a file, to remove the read-only lock on a file **2** *(porte)* to unbolt

dévers [dever] **NM 1** *(en travaux publics)* banking **2** *(d'un mur)* inclination, slope **3** *Rail* bank, banking, camber

déversement [deversəmɑ̃] **NM 1** *(écoulement)* flowing **2** *(déchargement ▸ d'eaux usées)* pouring, discharging; *(▸ de passagers)* offloading, discharging; *(▸ d'ordures)* dumping, *Br* tipping

déverser [3] [deverse] **VT 1** *(répandre ▸ liquide)* to pour, to discharge; **le canal déverse ses eaux dans un bassin** the canal discharges its water into a pool **2** *(décharger)* to discharge; **les paysans ont déversé des tonnes de fruits sur la chaussée** the farmers dumped tons of fruit on the road; *Fig* **le train déversa des centaines de vacanciers sur le quai** the train deposited hundreds of holidaymakers on the platform **3** *(exprimer ▸ chagrin, rage, plainte)* to vent, to let *or* to pour out; **d. des flots de larmes** to be in floods of tears; **d. des flots d'injures** to come out with a stream of abuse; **d. sa colère sur qn** to take one's anger out on sb

VPR se déverser 1 *(couler)* to flow; **se d. dans la mer** to flow into the sea **2** *(tomber)* **le chargement s'est déversé sur la route** the load tipped over *or* spilled onto the road

déversoir [deverswar] **NM 1** *(d'un barrage)* spillway, *Br* wasteweir **2** *Fig (exutoire)* outlet, safety valve

dévêtir [44] [devetir] **VT** to undress; **dévêts-le** take his clothes off, undress him

VPR se dévêtir to undress oneself, to get undressed, to take one's clothes off

déviance [devjɑ̃s] **NF** deviance, deviancy

déviant, -e [devjɑ̃, -ɑ̃t] **ADJ** deviant

NM,F deviant

déviation [devjasjɔ̃] **NF 1** *Transp* detour, *Br* diversion

2 *(écart)* swerving, deviating; **il ne se permet aucune d. par rapport à la ligne du parti** he will not deviate from *or* be deflected away from the party line

3 *Méd (de la colonne vertébrale)* curvature; *(de l'utérus)* displacement

4 *Électron* deflection

5 *Naut (d'un compas)* deviation

> Il faut noter que le nom anglais **deviation** ne s'utilise jamais dans un contexte routier.

déviationnisme [devjasjɔnism] **NM** deviationism

déviationniste [devjasjɔnist] **ADJ** deviationist

NMF deviationist

dévidage [devidaʒ] **NM 1** *(d'une bobine)* unwinding; *(d'un câble, d'une corde)* uncoiling **2** *(mise en écheveau)* reeling

dévider [3] [devide] **VT 1** *(mettre en écheveau)* to reel **2** *(dérouler ▸ bobine)* to unwind; *(▸ câble, corde)* to uncoil; **d. son rosaire** to say the rosary

dévideur [devidœr] **NM** *Ordinat* streamer

dévidoir [devidwar] **NM 1** *Tex* reel, spool **2** *(de tuyau d'incendie)* reel; *(pour câbles)* drum

devient *etc voir* **devenir**

dévier [9] [devje] **VI 1** *(s'écarter)* to swerve, to veer; **le bus a brusquement dévié sur la droite/gauche** the bus suddenly veered off to the right/left; **le vent a fait d. la voiture** the wind blew the car off course; **d. de** to move away from, to swerve from; **nous n'irons pas, cela nous ferait d. de notre chemin** we won't go, it would mean making a detour **2** *(être tordu ▸ colonne vertébrale)* to be out of alignment, not to be straight **3** *(dans un débat, un projet)* to diverge, to deviate; **faire d. la conversation** to change the subject; **la conversation dévie** the conversation is getting out of hand; **l'association ne doit pas d. par rapport à son but premier** the association must not be diverted from its original purpose; **d. de** to move away from, to stray off

VT 1 *(balle, projectile)* to deflect, to turn away *or* aside; *(coup)* to parry; *(circulation)* to divert, to redirect, to reroute; **le planeur a été dévié par le vent** the glider was blown off course *or* deflected by the wind; **les appels sont déviés vers le standard** calls are diverted *or* rerouted to the switchboard **2** *Phys* to refract **3** *(distraire ▸ attention)* to divert

devin, devineresse [dəvɛ̃, dəvinrɛs] **NM,F** soothsayer; **il n'est pas d.!** he's not a mind-reader!; **(il n'y a) pas besoin d'être d. pour comprendre** you don't need to be a genius to understand

devinable [dəvinabl] **ADJ 1** *(énigme)* solvable; *(secret)* guessable **2** *(prévisible ▸ avenir)* foreseeable

deviner [3] [dəvine] **VT 1** *(imaginer ▸ gén)* to guess, to work out, to figure (out); *(▸ la pensée de quelqu'un)* to read; **devine qui est là!** guess who's here!; **je n'ai fait que d.** it was sheer guesswork; **à toi de d. la suite** I'll leave it to you to figure out what happened next; **je ne pouvais pas d.!** how was I supposed to know!

2 *(découvrir ▸ énigme, mystère)* **il a tout de suite deviné ses intentions** he saw through him/her right away; **il devine toujours ce que je pense** he can read me like a book; **tu ne devineras jamais ce qui m'est arrivé** you'll never guess what happened to me; **je n'arrive pas à d. où il veut en venir** I can't work out what he's driving at; **j'ai deviné qu'il y avait quelque chose de bizarre** I guessed there was something strange

3 *(prédire ▸ avenir)* to foresee, to foretell

4 *(apercevoir)* **on devinait son soutien-gorge sous son chemisier** her bra showed through slightly under her blouse

5 *Littéraire (percer à jour)* **d. qn** to see through sb

VPR se deviner 1 *(être aperçu)* **sa tête se devine derrière le rideau** you can just make out his/her head behind the curtain; **la propriété se devine derrière les hauts murs** the property can just be made out behind the high walls **2** *(transparaître ▸ sentiment)* to show (through); **sa détresse se devine derrière son extérieur enjoué** his/her distress can be seen through his/her apparent jollity; **son attachement se devine à de petits détails** his/her love shows through in the little things he/she does

devineresse [dəvinrɛs] *voir* **devin**

devinette [dəvinɛt] **NF** riddle; **poser une d. (à qn)** to ask (sb) a riddle; **jouer aux devinettes** to play (at) riddles; *Fig* to speak in riddles

devint *etc voir* **devenir**

devis [dəvi] **NM** estimate, quotation; **faire** *ou* **établir un d.** to draw up an estimate; **il m'a fait un d. de 8000 euros** he quoted me 8,000 euros (in his estimate); **sur d.** on the basis of an estimate; **d. appréciatif** estimate, quotation; **d. descriptif** specification; **d. estimatif** estimate, quotation

dévisager [17] [devizaʒe] **VT** to stare (persistently) at; **on ne dévisage pas les gens** it's rude to stare

devise [dəviz] **NF 1** *Hér* device **2** *(maxime)* motto; **laisser faire les autres, c'est sa d.!** let the others do the work, that's his/her motto!; **la d. de notre maison** our company motto **3** *Fin* currency; **acheter des devises** to buy foreign currency; **d. contrôlée** managed currency; **d. convertible** convertible currency; **devises étrangères** foreign currency; **d. faible** soft currency; **d. flottante** floating currency; **d. forte** hard currency; **d. internationale** international currency; **d. non convertible** nonconvertible currency; **d. solide** strong currency

deviser [3] [dəvize] **VI** *Littéraire* to converse, to talk

VT *Suisse (projet de construction)* to draw up an estimate *or* a quotation for; **travaux devisés à 100 000 euros** work estimated to cost 100,000 euros

devise-titre [dəviztitr] *(pl* **devises-titres***)* **NF** *Fin* foreign security, exchange currency

dévissage [devisaʒ] **NM 1** *(d'un écrou, d'une vis)* unscrewing **2** *(en montagne)* fall

dévisser [3] [devise] **VT 1** *(desserrer ▸ écrou, vis)* to loosen; *(détacher)* to undo, to unscrew; **dévis-**

sez le bouchon unscrew the top of the bottle **2** *(tordre ▸ bras, cou)* to twist

VI *(en montagne)* to fall *or* to come off

VPR se dévisser 1 *(être amovible)* to unscrew; **le bouchon se dévisse facilement** the top twists off the bottle easily **2** *(se détacher)* to come unscrewed **3** *Fig* **se d. le cou/la tête** to screw one's neck/one's head round

de visu [devizy] **ADV je l'ai constaté d.** I saw it for myself *or* with my own eyes

dévitalisation [devitalizasjɔ̃] **NF** root canal treatment (**de** on)

dévitaliser [3] [devitalize] **VT** to carry out root canal work *or* treatment on; **se faire d. une dent** to have root canal work *or* treatment done on a tooth

dévitaminé, -e [devitamine] **ADJ** lacking in vitamins

dévoie *etc voir* **dévoyer**

dévoiement [devwamɑ̃] **NM** *(d'un conduit etc)* canting, tilting

dévoilement [devwalmɑ̃] **NM 1** *(d'un visage, d'une statue)* unveiling **2** *(d'un secret, d'une intention, d'un sentiment)* disclosing, revealing; *(d'une conspiration)* unmasking; *(d'une fraude)* uncovering

dévoiler [3] [devwale] **VT 1** *(dénuder ▸ visage, statue)* to unveil, to uncover; *Euph* **d. ses charmes** to reveal all **2** *(révéler ▸ secret, intention, sentiment)* to disclose, to reveal, to unveil; *(▸ conspiration)* to unmask; *(▸ fraude)* to uncover; **il a dévoilé ses pensées les plus secrètes** he laid bare his innermost thoughts; **d. ses batteries** to reveal one's true intentions

VPR se dévoiler 1 *(ôter son voile)* to unveil one's face *or* oneself **2** *(se manifester)* to be disclosed *or* revealed, to show up, to come to light

devoir[1] [dəvwar] **NM 1** *Scol (en classe ▸ exercice)* exercise; *(▸ épreuve)* test; *(à la maison)* homework; *(dissertation)* essay, paper; **j'ai un d. de maths à rendre pour lundi** I've got maths homework *or* a maths exercise to hand in by Monday; **faire ses devoirs** to do one's homework; **d. sur table** (written) class test; **devoirs de vacances** *Br* holiday *or Am* vacation homework

2 *(impératifs moraux)* duty; **le d. m'appelle** duty calls; **je ne l'ai prévenu que par d.** I warned him only because I thought it was my duty

3 *(tâche à accomplir)* duty, obligation; **les devoirs d'une mère** a mother's duties; **faire** *ou* **accomplir** *ou* **remplir son d.** to carry out *or* to do one's duty; **merci – je n'ai fait que mon d.** thank you – I only did my duty; **avoir le d. de** to have the duty to; **vous avez le d. de le signaler** it's your duty to *or* you must report it; **se faire un d. de faire qch** to make it one's duty to do sth; **se mettre en d. de faire qch** to set about (doing) sth; **je me suis mis en d. de l'éclairer** I set about enlightening him; **d. conjugal** conjugal duties; *Pol* **d. d'ingérence** duty to intervene; **d. de mémoire** duty to remember *(historical tragedies etc)*; **avoir un d. de réserve** to be bound by professional secrecy

• **devoirs NMPL rendre les derniers devoirs à qn** to pay sb a final homage *or* tribute; **rendre ses devoirs à qn** to pay one's respects to sb

• **de devoir ADJ homme/femme de d.** man/woman with a (strong) sense of duty

• **du devoir de PRÉP il est du d. de tout citoyen de voter** it is the duty of every citizen to vote; **j'ai cru de mon d. de l'aider** I felt duty-bound to help him; **je l'ai rendu, comme il était de mon d.** I gave it back, as it was my duty to do *or* as was my duty

• **en devoir ADJ** *Can Joual* on duty□

DEVOIR[2] **[53]** [dəvwar]

V AUX	
• to have to **1, 5**	• should **2, 3**
• must **1, 4**	• to be supposed to **3**
• ought **2**	
VT	
• to owe	
VPR	
• must **1, 2**	

V AUX 1 *(exprime l'obligation)* **il doit** he has to, he needs to, he must; **je dois partir à midi** I must leave at midday; **dois-je être plus clair?** do I need *or* have to be more explicit?; **je dois admettre que...** I must admit that...; **si vous deviez donner une définition du bonheur, quelle serait-elle?** if you had to give a definition of happiness, what would it be?; **il ne doit pas** he must not, he mustn't; **on ne doit pas fumer** smoking is forbidden *or* is not allowed; **tu ne dois pas le punir** you mustn't punish him

2 *(dans des conseils, des suggestions)* **il devrait** he ought to, he should; **tu ne devrais pas boire** you shouldn't drink

3 *(indique une prévision, une intention)* **il doit m'en donner demain** he's due to *or* he should give me some tomorrow; **c'est une pièce que l'on doit voir depuis un an!** it's a play we've supposedly been going to see *or* we've been planning to see for a year!; **il devait venir mais je ne l'ai pas vu** he was supposed to come *or* to have come but I didn't see him

4 *(exprime une probabilité)* **il/cela doit** he/it must, he's/it's got to; **il doit savoir** he's bound to *or* he must know; **mais si, tu dois connaître son frère, un petit gros** but you must know *or* I'm sure you know his/her brother, a short fat man; **il doit être fatigué** he must be tired, he's probably tired; **il n'y a qu'une explication, elle a dû garder les clefs** there's only one explanation, she must have kept the keys; **il ne devait pas beaucoup l'aimer pour écrire cela** he can't have really loved him/her to write this; **il doit y avoir** *ou* **cela doit faire un an que je ne l'ai pas vu** it must be a year since I (last) saw him; **une offre qui devrait les intéresser** an offer which should interest them

5 *(exprime l'inévitable)* **nous devons tous mourir un jour** we all have to die one day; **il devait mourir à 20 ans** he was to die when he was 20; **la maison où elle devait écrire 'Claudine'** the house where she was to write 'Claudine'

6 *(exprime une norme)* **un bon chanteur doit savoir chanter en direct** a good singer should be able to sing live; **le four ne devrait pas faire ce bruit** the oven isn't supposed to *or* shouldn't make that noise

7 dût-il refuser even if he should have to refuse; **je l'aiderai, dussé-je aller en prison/y passer ma vie** I'll help him/her, even if it means going to prison/devoting my life to it

VT 1 *(avoir comme dette)* to owe; **d. qch à qn** to owe sb sth, to owe sth to sb; **tu me dois 60 euros** you owe me 60 euros; **d. de l'argent** to owe money, to have debts; **je te dois l'essence** I owe you for the *Br* petrol *or Am* gas; **j'ai perdu, je te dois le repas** I lost, I'll buy the meal for you; **combien vous dois-je?** how much do I owe you?; **je ne demande que ce qui m'est dû** I'm only asking for my due; **ainsi, je ne te dois plus rien** that way, I've cleared my debt with you *or* I don't owe you anything now

2 *(être moralement obligé de fournir)* **d. qch à qn** to owe sb sth; **je te dois des excuses/une explication** I owe you an apology/explanation; **je vous dois cet aveu** I've got this to confess to you, I owe you this confession; **je te dois bien ça** that's the least I can do for you; **traiter qn avec le respect qu'on lui doit** to treat sb with due respect; **selon les honneurs dus à sa fonction** with such pomp as befits his/her office

3 *(être redevable de)* **d. qch à qn** to owe sth to sb; **je lui dois tout/beaucoup/la vie** I owe him/her everything/a lot/my life; **c'est à Guimard que l'on doit cette découverte** we have Guimard to thank *or* we're indebted to Guimard for this discovery; **on lui doit un remarquable 'Christ en croix'** he's/she's the creator of a remarkable 'Christ on the Cross'; **c'est à lui que je dois d'avoir trouvé du travail** it's thanks to him that I found a job; **le son doit sa qualité à des enceintes très performantes** the good sound quality is due to excellent speakers; **sa victoire ne doit rien au hasard** his/her victory has nothing to do with luck

VPR se devoir 1 *(avoir comme obligation mutuelle)* **les époux se doivent fidélité** spouses *or* husbands and wives must be faithful to each other

2 se d. à qn/qch to have to devote oneself to sb/sth; **il se doit aux siens** he must spend time with his family; **je me dois à mon public** I must attend to my fans

3 se d. de to have it as one's duty to; **tu es grand, tu te dois de donner l'exemple** you're a big boy now, it's your duty to set a good example

dévoisé, -e [devwaze] **ADJ** *Ling* devoiced

dévoisement [devwazmɑ̃] **NM** *Ling* devoicing *(UNCOUNT)*

dévoltage [devɔltaʒ] **NM** *Élec* reduction of voltage

dévolter [3] [devɔlte] **VT** *Élec (courant)* to reduce the voltage of

dévolu, -e [devɔly] **ADJ** *(somme, responsabilités)* assigned (**à** to); **argent d. à cet usage** money assigned to that purpose; **la tâche qui vous a été dévolue** the task which has been assigned to you; **part dévolue à la ligne paternelle** share that falls to the heirs on the father's side; **c'est le terrain qui lui a été d.** the land went to him/her

NM jeter son d. sur *(chose)* to go for, to choose; *(personne)* to set one's cap at

dévoluer [7] [devɔlɥe] **VT** to devolve

dévolutif, -ive [devɔlytif, -iv] **ADJ** devolutive

dévolution [devɔlysjɔ̃] **NF** devolution

dévolutive [devɔlytiv] *voir* **dévolutif**

dévorant, -e [devɔrɑ̃, -ɑ̃t] **ADJ 1** *(faim)* gnawing; *(soif)* burning; **avoir une faim dévorante** to be ravenous; **avoir une soif dévorante** to be dying of thirst **2** *(amour, passion)* (all-)consuming, burning, powerful; **éprouver une jalousie dévorante** to be consumed *or* devoured by jealousy **3** *Littéraire (feu)* all-consuming

dévorer [3] [devɔre] **VT 1** *(manger ▸ sujet: animal, personne)* to devour; **d. son repas à belles dents** to eat heartily; **les sauterelles dévorent les récoltes** the locusts eat away at the crops; *Fig* **dévoré par les moustiques** eaten alive by mosquitoes; **une voiture qui dévore les kilomètres** a car which eats up the miles; **d. qn/qch des yeux** *ou* **du regard** to stare hungrily at sb/sth; **d. qn de baisers** to smother sb with kisses

2 *(lire)* to devour, to read avidly; **j'ai dévoré tout Tolstoï** I devoured (the whole of) Tolstoy; **depuis le scandale, il dévore les journaux** since the scandal he reads the papers avidly

3 *(consommer)* to use (up); **dans mon métier, je dévore du papier/de la pellicule** in my job I use (up) huge quantities of paper/of film; **mon salaire est en grande partie dévoré par les impôts** my salary is swallowed up to a large extent by tax; **ne te laisse pas d. par ton travail** don't let your work monopolize your time

4 *(consumer ▸ sujet: flammes)* to devour

5 *(tenailler)* to devour; **l'ambition le dévore** he's eaten up *or* devoured by ambition; **être dévoré par l'envie/la curiosité** to be eaten up with envy/curiosity; **être dévoré de remords** to be eaten up with remorse; **elle n'est pas dévorée par les scrupules** she isn't hampered by scruples

USAGE ABSOLU *(manger)* **il dévore!** he eats like a horse!

dévoreur, -euse [devɔrœr, -øz] **NM,F** *Fam* **c'est une dévoreuse de romans/de pellicule** she's an avid reader of novels/a keen photographer□

dévot, -e [devo, -ɔt] **ADJ** devout

NM,F 1 *(qui croit)* staunch believer **2** *Péj (bigot)* sanctimonious individual; **faux d.** pharisee

dévotement [devɔtmɑ̃] **ADV** devoutly, religiously

dévotion [devosjɔ̃] **NF 1** *Rel* devoutness, religiousness, piety; *Péj* **fausse d.** false piety; **avec d.** devoutly **2** *Littéraire (attachement)* devotion; **il voue une véritable d. à sa mère** he worships his mother; **être à la d. de qn** to be devoted to sb; **avec d.** devotedly

• **dévotions NFPL** *(prières)* devotions

Do not confuse with **dévouement**.

dévoué, -e [devwe] **ADJ 1** *(fidèle)* devoted, faithful; **être d. à ses amis** to be devoted to one's friends; **nous vous remercions de votre appui d.** we thank you for your staunch support **2** *(dans des formules de politesse)* **votre (tout) d.** *Br* yours sincerely, *Am* sincerely (yours); **votre d. serviteur** your humble servant; **je vous prie de croire à mes sentiments les plus dévoués** *Br* yours sincerely, *Am* sincerely (yours)

dévouement [devumɑ̃] **NM 1** *(abnégation)* dedication, devotedness, devotion; **soigner qn avec d.** to look after sb devotedly; **avoir l'esprit de d.** to be self-sacrificing **2** *(loyauté)* devotion; **son d. à la cause** his/her devotion to the cause

> Do not confuse with **dévotion**.

dévouer [6] [devwe] **VT** *Littéraire* **d. qch à** to dedicate *or* to devote sth to; **d. sa vie à ses parents/à l'aide aux pays du tiers-monde** to dedicate one's life to one's parents/to helping Third World countries

VPR se dévouer 1 *(proposer ses services)* to volunteer; **qui va se d. pour faire le ménage?** who's going to volunteer to clean up?; *Hum* **vous voulez que je finisse la tarte? bon, je me dévoue!** you want me to finish up the tart? oh well, if I must! **2 se d. à** *(se consacrer à)* to dedicate oneself to

dévoyé, -e [devwaje] **ADJ** perverted, corrupted

NM,F corrupt individual

dévoyer [13] [devwaje] **VT** *Littéraire* to lead astray

VPR se dévoyer to go astray

dextérité [dɛksterite] **NF** dexterity, deftness; **avec d.** dexterously, deftly

dextre [dɛkstr] **ADJ** *Hér* dexter

NF *Vieilli, Hum & Littéraire* right hand; **veux-tu t'asseoir à ma d.?** will you sit on my right?

dextrine [dɛkstrin] **NF** *Chim & Ind* dextrin

dézinguer [3] [dezɛ̃ge] **VT** *Fam* **1** *(démolir)* to pull down▫ **2** *(critiquer)* to pull to pieces, to slam **3** *(tuer)* to bump off

dézipper [3] [dezipe] **VT** *Ordinat (fichier)* to unzip

DG [deʒe] **NM** *(abrév* **directeur général***)* *Br* GM, *Am* CEO

NF *(abrév* **direction générale***)* general management, senior management

DGA [deʒea] **NF** *(abrév* **Délégation générale pour l'armement***)* = section of the French armed forces responsible for building and testing armaments

NM *(abrév* **directeur général adjoint***)* *Br* deputy managing director, *Am* vice-president

DGSE [deʒeesə] **NF** *(abrév* **Direction générale de la sécurité extérieure***)* = arm of the Defence Ministry in charge of international intelligence, *Br* ≃ MI6, *Am* ≃ CIA

DHEA [deaʃəa] **NF** *(abrév* **déhydroépiandrostérone***)* DHEA

DI [dei] **NF** *Mil (abrév* **division d'infanterie***)* infantry division

diabète [djabɛt] **NM** diabetes; **avoir du d.** to have diabetes; **d. sucré** diabetes mellitus

diabétique [djabetik] **ADJ** diabetic

NMF diabetic; **chocolat/confiture pour diabétiques** diabetic chocolate/jam

diable [djabl] **NM 1** *Rel* devil; **le d.** the Devil; **les Diables** = nickname of Belgian national football team; **aller au d.** to go to hell; **envoyer qn au d.** to send sb packing; **au d. l'avarice!** hang the expense!; **nous partons en vacances, au d. les soucis!** we're off on holiday, let's leave our worries behind us *or* at home!; **au d. les convenances!** to hell with propriety!; *Fam* **avoir le d. au corps** to be a real handful; **comme un beau d.** *(courir, sauter)* like the (very) devil, like a thing possessed; *(hurler)* like a stuck pig; **se démener** *ou* **s'agiter comme un beau d.** to thrash about, to struggle violently; **comme un d. dans un bénitier** like a cat on a hot tin roof; **comme s'il avait le d. à ses trousses** *(courir, partir)* like greased lightning, as if his life depended on it; **faire le d. à quatre** *(faire du bruit)* to make a din; *(se démener)* to raise hell and high water; **habiter au d. vauvert** *ou* **vert** to live miles away; **tirer le d. par la queue** to live from hand to mouth; **c'est le d. pour lui faire entendre raison** it's the devil of a job making him see reason; **ce serait bien le d. s'il refusait!** I'd be very surprised if he refused!; **ce n'est pourtant pas le d.!** it's really not that difficult!; **c'est bien le d. si je ne récupère pas mon argent!** I'll be damned if I don't get my money back!; *Can* **le d. est aux vaches** there is internal strife; *Arch* **le d. soit de ces gens-là/tes principes** the devil take these people/your principles; **le d. m'emporte si j'y comprends quelque chose!** I'll be hanged *or* damned if I understand (it)!; *Prov* **c'est le d. qui bat sa femme et marie sa fille** = it's rainy and sunny at the same time

2 *(enfant)* (little) devil

3 *(homme)* **un bon d.** a good sort; **un grand d.** a great tall fellow; **un mauvais d.** a bad sort; **un pauvre d.** a wretched man, a poor wretch; **un petit d.** *(enfant)* a little devil

4 *(chariot)* trolley

5 *(jouet)* jack-in-the-box

6 *(casserole)* earthenware (cooking) pot

7 *Zool* **d. (de Tasmanie)** Tasmanian devil; *Ich* **d. de mer** devil fish, manta (ray)

ADJ 1 *(espiègle)* **que tu es d.!** stop being such a little devil! **2** *Culin (sauce)* devilled

ADV qui/que/comment d.? who/what/how the devil?, who/what/how on earth?; **pourquoi d. est-il allé si loin?** why the devil *or* on earth did he go so far?

EXCLAM my goodness!, goodness me!; **d., voilà une histoire bien compliquée!** goodness me, what a complicated story!; **que d.!** for heaven's *or* goodness' sake!

• **à la diable ADV 1** *(vite et mal)* **un repas préparé à la d.** a meal thrown together quickly; **elle est sortie coiffée à la d.** she went out, after hastily running a comb through her hair **2** *Culin* **œufs à la d.** devilled eggs

• **diable de ADJ ce d. de rhumatisme!** this damned rheumatism!

• **du diable, de tous les diables ADJ** *Fam* **faire un boucan du d.** *ou* **de tous les diables** to kick up a hell of a racket; **il a eu un mal du d.** *ou* **de tous les diables pour finir à temps** he had a devil of a job to finish in time; **il fait un froid/une chaleur du d.** *ou* **de tous les diables** it's dreadfully cold/hot

• **en diable ADV** devilishly; **difficile en d.** devilishly *or* fiendishly difficult; **jolie en d.** pretty as a picture; **retors en d.** sly as a fox **ADJ** *Can Fam* **être en d.** to be fed up, *Br* to be cheesed off

diablement [djabləmɑ̃] **ADV** *Fam Vieilli* damned; **c'est d. bon!** it's damn *or* damned good!; **il était d. intéressé** he was awfully keen

diablerie [djabləri] **NF 1** *(farce)* piece of mischief, trick; **avec leurs petits cousins, ce ne sont que diableries** they get up to all sorts of mischief with their little cousins **2** *(sortilège)* piece of devilry

diablesse [djablɛs] **NF 1** *Rel* she-devil **2** *(femme méchante)* witch **3** *(fillette)* **petite d.!** you little devil!

diablotin [djablɔtɛ̃] **NM 1** *Myth* small *or* little devil **2** *(enfant)* imp **3** *(pétard)* cracker

diabolique [djabɔlik] **ADJ** diabolic, diabolical, devilish; **il a agi de façon d.** he acted diabolically

diaboliquement [djabɔlikmɑ̃] **ADV** diabolically, devilishly

diabolisation [djabɔlizasjɔ̃] **NF** demonization

diaboliser [3] [djabɔlize] **VT** to demonize

diabolo [djabɔlo] **NM 1** *(jouet)* diabolo **2** *(boisson)* **d. menthe/fraise** mint/strawberry syrup and lemonade

diachromie [djakrɔmi] **NF** *Phot* screen-plate colour-photography

diachronie [djakrɔni] **NF** diachrony

diachronique [djakrɔnik] **ADJ** diachronic

diaconesse [djakɔnɛs] **NF** deaconess

diacre [djakr] **NM** deacon

diacritique [djakritik] **ADJ** diacritic; **signe d.** diacritic

NM diacritic

diadème [djadɛm] **NM** tiara

diagnostic [djagnɔstik] **NM** diagnosis; **établir** *ou* **faire un d.** to make a diagnosis; **ce médecin a un d. très sûr** this doctor makes very reliable diagnoses; *Ordinat* **d. d'autotest** self-test diagnosis; **d. financier** financial healthcheck, diagnostic audit

diagnostique [djagnɔstik] **ADJ** diagnostic

diagnostiquer [3] [djagnɔstike] **VT** to diagnose; **on lui a diagnostiqué un diabète** he's been diagnosed as suffering from diabetes

diagnostiqueur [djagnɔstikœr] **NM** *Méd* diagnostician; **elle n'est pas bon d.** she's not a good diagnostician, diagnosis is not her strong point

diagonal, -e, -aux, -ales [djagɔnal, -o] **ADJ** diagonal

• **diagonale NF** diagonal (line)

• **en diagonale ADV 1** *(en biais)* diagonally **2** *(vite)* **lire** *ou* **parcourir un livre en diagonale** to skim through a book

diagonalement [djagɔnalmɑ̃] **ADV** diagonally

diagramme [djagram] **NM** diagram; *(graphique)* graph, chart; **d. à bâtons** *ou* **à barres** bar chart; **d. de circulation** flow chart; **d. polaire** polar diagram; **d. à secteurs** pie chart

dialectal, -e, -aux, -ales [djalɛktal, -o] **ADJ** dialectal

dialecte [djalɛkt] **NM 1** *(gén)* dialect **2** *Suisse* Swiss German

dialecticien, -enne [djalɛktisjɛ̃, -ɛn] **NM,F** dialectician

dialectique [djalɛktik] **ADJ** dialectic, dialectical

NF dialectic, dialectics *(singulier)*

dialectiquement [djalɛktikmɑ̃] **ADV** dialectically

dialogue [djalɔg] **NM 1** *(discussion)* dialogue; **d. Nord-Sud** dialogue *or* talks between North and South; **entre eux, c'était un véritable d. de sourds** they were not on the same wavelength at all **2** *Cin & Théât* dialogue; **écrire les dialogues d'un film** to write the dialogue for a movie *or Br* film **3** *Ordinat* **d. en direct** Internet Relay Chat, IRC; **d. d'établissement de liaison** handshaking; **d. homme-machine** interactive use (of a computer)

dialoguer [3] [djalɔge] **VI 1** *(converser)* to converse **2** *(négocier)* to have *or* to hold talks; **les syndicats vont de nouveau d. avec le ministre** the unions are to resume talks *or* their dialogue with the minister **3** *Ordinat* **d. avec un ordinateur** to interact with a computer

VT *Littérature (roman)* to write in dialogue form

dialoguiste [djalɔgist] **NMF** dialogue writer

dialyse [djaliz] **NF** dialysis; **se faire faire une d.** to undergo dialysis; **être sous d.** to be on dialysis

dialyser [3] [djalize] **VT** to dialyse

dialyseur [djalizœr] **NM** dialyser

diam [djam] **NM** *Fam (diamant)* sparkler, rock; **diams** ice, sparklers

diamant [djamɑ̃] **NM** diamond; **d. brut** rough diamond; **d. de la guerre** blood diamond, conflict diamond; **d. de vitrier** glass cutter, *Spéc* glazier's diamond, diamond point

diamantaire [djamɑ̃tɛr] **ADJ** *(pierre)* diamond-like, sparkling

NMF 1 *(vendeur)* diamond merchant **2** *(tailleur)* diamond cutter

diamantifère [djamɑ̃tifɛr] **ADJ** diamantiferous

diamétral, -e, -aux, -ales [djametral, -o] **ADJ** diametral, diametric, diametrical

diamétralement [diametralmɑ̃] **ADV** diametrically; **d. opposé** diametrically opposed

diamètre [djamɛtr] **NM** diameter; **le fût fait 30 cm de d.** the barrel is 30 cm across *or* in diameter; *Aut* **d. de braquage hors tout** overall turning circle

diane [djan] **NF** *Arch ou Littéraire* reveille; **battre** *ou* **sonner la d.** to sound reveille

diantre [djɑ̃tr] *Arch ou Littéraire* **EXCLAM** ye gods!

ADV qui d. a dit cela? who the deuce *or* the devil said that?; **que d....!** what the devil...?; **décidezvous, que d.!** make up your mind, for heaven's sake!

diapason [djapazɔ̃] **NM 1** *(instrument ▸ métallique)* tuning fork; *(▸ à vent)* pitch pipe **2** *(ton)* pitch, diapason **3** *(registre)* range, diapason

• **au diapason ADV** in tune; *Fig* **il n'est plus au d.** he's out of touch; **se mettre au d. (de qn)** to fall *or* to step into line (with sb)

diaphane [djafan] **ADJ** diaphanous

diaphonie [djafɔni] **NF** diaphony

diaphragme [djafragm] **NM 1** *Anat & Tech* diaphragm

2 *(contraceptif)* diaphragm, (Dutch) cap

3 *(d'un télescope)* diaphragm; *(d'un objectif photographique)* stop, diaphragm; **d. iris** iris diaphragm

4 *(d'une enceinte)* soundbox

diaphragmer [3] [djafragme] *Phot* **VT** to stop down

VI to stop down; **diaphragmez à 11** stop down to 11, use stop number 11

diaphyse [djafiz] NF diaphysis

diapo [djapo] NF *Fam Phot* slide

diaporama [djaporama] NM slide show

diapositive [djapozitiv] NF *Phot* slide

diapré, -e [djapre] ADJ *Littéraire* shimmering, iridescent

diaprer [3] [djapre] VT *Littéraire* to make shimmer, to make iridescent

diaprure [djapryr] NF *Littéraire* shimmering *or* iridescent colours; **la d. de ses ailes** the rainbow colours of its wings

diariste [djarist] NMF *Littérature* diarist

diarrhée [djare] NF diarrhoea; **avoir la d.** to have diarrhoea; *Fig* **d. verbale** verbal diarrhoea

diarrhéique [djareik] ADJ diarrhoeal, diarrhoeic

NMF person subject to diarrhoea

diaspora [djaspɔra] NF diaspora; **la D.** the Diaspora

diastole [djastɔl] NF *Physiol* diastole

diatomée [djatɔme] NF diatom

diatomique [djatɔmik] ADJ *Chim* diatomic

diatonique [djatɔnik] ADJ diatonic

diatoniquement [djatɔnikmɑ̃] ADV diatonically

diatribe [djatrib] NF (vicious) attack, *Sout* diatribe

dichotomie [dikɔtɔmi] NF dichotomy

dichotomique [dikɔtɔmik] ADJ dichotomous; *Psy* **test d.** yes/no test, true/false test

dichromatique [dikrɔmatik] ADJ *Méd* dichromatic

dico [diko] NM *Fam* dictionary

dicotylédone [dikɔtiledɔn] *Bot* ADJ dicotyledonous

NF dicotyledon

• **dicotylédones** NFPL Dicotyledonae

Dictaphone® [diktafɔn] NM Dictaphone

dictateur [diktatœr] NM dictator

dictatorial, -e, -aux, -ales [diktatɔrjal, -o] ADJ dictatorial

dictatorialement [diktatɔrjalmɑ̃] ADV dictatorially

dictature [diktatyr] NF dictatorship; **d. militaire** military dictatorship; **la d. du prolétariat** the dictatorship of the proletariat; **il fait de la d. intellectuelle** he tells people what to think

dictée [dikte] NF **1** *Scol* dictation; **d. musicale** musical dictation **2** *(à une secrétaire, un assistant)* dictating; **j'ai écrit le rapport sous sa d.** he dictated the report to me; *Fig* **agir sous la d. de son cœur/de sa conscience** to follow the dictates of one's heart/one's conscience

dicter [3] [dikte] VT **1** *Scol* to read out as dictation **2** *(courrier, lettre, résumé)* to dictate

3 *(imposer ▸ choix)* to dictate, to impose, to force; *(▸ conditions)* to dictate; **on lui a dicté ses réponses** his replies had been dictated to him

4 *(conditionner)* to dictate; **ses actes sont dictés par la haine** his actions are driven *or* motivated by hatred; **ces mesures ont été dictées par la conjoncture économique** these measures were dictated by the economic situation

diction [diksjɔ̃] NF diction; **avoir une d. parfaite** to have perfect diction; **professeur de d.** elocutionist

• **de diction** ADJ speech *(avant n)*

dictionnaire [diksjɔnɛr] NM **1** *(livre)* dictionary; **d. analogique** thesaurus; **d. bilingue** bilingual dictionary; **d. anglais-français** English-French dictionary; **d. de la musique/des beaux-arts** dictionary of music/of art; **d. encyclopédique/de langue** encyclopedic/language dictionary; **d. électronique** electronic dictionary; **d. de synonymes** thesaurus; *Fam* **traduire un livre à coup de d.** to translate a book with a dictionary in one hand; **c'est un d. ambulant** he's a walking encyclopedia **2** *Ordinat* dictionary

dicton [diktɔ̃] NM (popular) saying, *Sout* dictum; **comme dit le d.** as they say, as the saying goes

didacthèque [didaktɛk] NF *Ordinat* set of educational software *or Am* teachware

didacticiel [didaktisjɛl] NM *Ordinat* tutorial, courseware, *Am* teachware

didactique [didaktik] ADJ **1** *(de l'enseignement)* didactic

2 *(instructif)* didactic, educational

3 *(spécialisé ▸ mot, langage)* technical

4 *Psy* **analyse d.** training analysis

NF didactics *(singulier)*

didactiquement [didaktikmɑ̃] ADV didactically

didactyle [didaktil] ADJ didactyl, didactylous

didgeridoo, didjeridoo [didʒeridu] NM *Mus* didgeridoo

dièdre [djɛdr] ADJ dihedral

NM **1** *Géom* dihedron **2** *(en montagne)* corner, dièdre

diélectrique [djelɛktrik] ADJ dielectric

NM dielectric

diérèse [djerɛz] NF *Ling & Littérature* diaeresis, dieresis

dies academicus [djesakademikys] NM INV *Suisse* = annual public ceremony in universities marking the start of the new academic year and the conferment of honorary doctorates

dièse [djɛz] ADJ *Mus* **la d.** A sharp

NM *Mus* sharp; *Typ & Ordinat* hash; **double d.** double sharp

diesel [djezɛl] NM **1 (moteur) d.** diesel engine *or* motor **2** *(véhicule, camion)* **c'est un d.** it's a diesel **3** *(combustible)* diesel (oil)

NF *(voiture)* **c'est une d.** it's a diesel

diéséliste [djezelist] NM *Tech* diesel fitter

diéser [18] [djeze] VT *Mus* to sharpen, to make sharp

diète [djɛt] NF **1** *(régime)* diet **2** *(absence de nourriture)* fasting *(for health reasons)* **3** *Hist (assemblée)* diet

• **à la diète** ADV **1** *(au régime)* on a diet **2** *(sans nourriture)* **mettre qn à la d.** to prescribe a fast for sb

diététicien, -enne [djetetisjɛ̃, -ɛn] NM,F dietician, dietitian, nutritionist

diététique [djetetik] ADJ *(aliment)* health *(avant n)*; *(magasin)* health food *(avant n)*

NF nutrition science, *Spéc* dietetics *(singulier)*; **conseils de d.** nutritional advice

dieu, -x [djø] NM **1** *(divinité)* god; **le d. de la Guerre/l'Amour** the god of war/love; **une vie sans d.** a godless life; **comme un d.** divinely, like a god; *Littéraire* **grands dieux!** good heavens *or* gracious!; **jurer ses grands dieux** to swear to God; **il a juré ses grands dieux qu'il n'en savait rien** he swore to God *or* to heaven that he didn't know about it; *Hum* **vingt dieux!** strewth! **2** *(héros)* god, idol; **les dieux du stade** the gods *or* idols of sport **3** *(objet de vénération)* god; **l'argent/l'art est son d.** money/art is his god, he idolizes money/art

• **Dieu** NM **1** *(gén)* God; **le D. vivant** the living God; **D. le père** God the father; *Péj* **il se prend pour D. le père** he thinks he's God (Himself); **vivre en D.** to live with God; **le bon D.** the good Lord; **recevoir le bon D.** to receive the Holy Sacrament; **apporter le bon D. à un malade** to bring the Holy Sacrament to a sick person; **tous les jours** *ou* **chaque jour que (le bon) D. fait** every blessed day; **il n'y a pas de bon D.!** there's no justice!; **on lui donnerait le bon D. sans confession** he looks as if butter wouldn't melt in his mouth; **comme le bon D. l'a fait** in his birthday suit; **il vaut mieux s'adresser à D. qu'à ses saints** it's better to talk to the organ-grinder than the monkey; *Vieilli* **comme D. en France** *(vivre)* exceedingly well, comfortably; **si D. le veut** God willing; **si D. me prête vie** if I'm still alive (by then)

2 *(dans des exclamations) Littéraire* **D. me damne** *ou* **maudisse (si...)!** may God strike me dead (if...)!; *Littéraire* **D. m'est témoin** as God is my witness; *Littéraire* **D. me pardonne!** (may) God forgive me!; **D. nous protège** God *or* Lord protect us; *Littéraire* **D. veuille que tout se passe bien!** God willing, all will be well; *Littéraire* **D. vous bénisse/entende!** may God bless/hear you!; *Littéraire* **D. vous garde** God be with you; **D. sait** God *or* (the) Lord knows; **D. sait combien il l'a aimée!** God knows he loved her!; **D. sait où je l'ai mis!** God only knows where I put it!; **et il est parti à l'étranger, D. sait où, chercher du travail** he's gone abroad, God knows where, to look for work; **D. seul le sait!** God (only) knows!; *Littéraire* **à D. va** *ou* **vat!** it's in God's hands!, in God's hands be it!; *Littéraire* **à D. ne plaise!** God forbid!; *Littéraire* **grand D.!** good God *or* Lord!; *Fam* **bon D.!** for God's sake!, for Pete's sake!; *Fam* **bon D. de...** blasted..., blessed...; *Fam* **ce bon D. de cabot a encore réveillé le gosse!** that blasted dog's woken up the kid again!; **bon D. de bon D.!** for crying out loud!; *Littéraire* **D. ait son âme!** God rest his soul!; *Littéraire* **D. le veuille!** God willing!; *Littéraire* **D. merci!** thank God *or* the Lord!; **mon D.!** my God!, my goodness!, good Lord!; **mon D.** *(dans des prières)* Lord, God

• **des dieux** ADJ *(festin)* sumptuous, princely; *(plaisir)* divine, exquisite

diffamant, -e [difamɑ̃, -ɑ̃t] ADJ *(texte)* defamatory, libellous; *(geste, parole)* slanderous; **des propos diffamants** slander

diffamateur, -trice [difamatœr, -tris] ADJ *(texte)* defamatory, libellous; *(geste, parole)* slanderous

NM,F *(par écrit)* libeller; *(en paroles)* slanderer

diffamation [difamasjɔ̃] NF **1** *(accusation ▸ gén)* defamation; *(▸ par un texte)* libelling; *(▸ par des discours)* slandering **2** *(texte)* libel; *(gestes, paroles)* slander

• **de diffamation** ADJ *(campagne)* smear *(avant n)*

• **en diffamation** ADJ **intenter un procès en d. à qn** *(pour un texte injurieux)* to bring an action for libel against sb; *(pour des paroles injurieuses)* to bring an action for slander against sb

diffamatoire [difamatwar] ADJ *(texte)* defamatory, libellous; *(geste, parole)* slanderous; **parler/agir de façon d.** to speak/to act slanderously

diffamatrice [difamatris] *voir* **diffamateur**

diffamer [3] [difame] VT *(par écrit)* to defame, to libel; *(oralement)* to slander

différé, -e [difere] ADJ **1** *(paiement, rendez-vous, réponse)* deferred, postponed **2** *Rad & TV* prerecorded **3** *Phot & Tech* **à action différée** delayed-action

• **en différé** ADJ *Rad & TV* prerecorded; *Ordinat (traitement)* off-line

différemment [diferamɑ̃] ADV differently; **il agit d. des autres** he's not behaving like the others, he's behaving differently from the others

différence [diferɑ̃s] NF **1** *(distinction)* difference, dissimilarity; **il y a une d. entre A et B** there's a difference between A and B, A and B are different, A is different from B; **faire la d. entre** to make the distinction between, to distinguish between; **les électeurs indécis feront la d.** the don't-knows will tip the balance; **je ne fais aucune d. entre eux deux** I make no distinction between the two of them; **c'est ce qui fait toute la d.!** that's what makes all the difference!; **intéressé ou désintéressé? il y a une d.!** uninterested or disinterested? it's not the same thing at all *or* there's quite a difference between the two!; *Fam* **ça fait une sacrée d.!** there's a big difference!; **il s'est excusé – cela ne fait aucune d.** he apologized – it doesn't make any *or* it makes no difference; **faire des différences entre ses enfants** to treat one's children differently from each other; **toute la d. est là** it makes all the difference

2 *(écart)* difference; **d. d'âge** age difference *or* gap; **d. de caractère** difference in characters; **d. de taille** difference in size; **il y a deux ans de d. entre eux** there are two years between them

3 *Math (d'une soustraction)* result; *(ensemble)* difference; **je paierai la d.** I'll make up *or* pay the difference

4 *Bourse (entre le cours offert et le cours demandé)* spread

• **à la différence de** PRÉP unlike

• **à cette différence (près) que, à la différence que** CONJ except that; **j'ai accepté son offre à cette d. près que, cette fois, je sais ce qui m'attend** I accepted his/her offer but this time I know what to expect

différenciateur, -trice [diferɑ̃sjatœr, -tris] ADJ differentiating

NM *Psy* **d. sémantique** semantic differentiator

différenciation [diferɑ̃sjasjɔ̃] NF **1** *(distinction)* differentiation; *Mktg* **d. de ligne** line differentiation; **d. du produit** product differentiation **2** *Biol* **d. des sexes** sex determination

différenciatrice [diferɑ̃sjatris] *voir* **différenciateur**

différencier [9] [diferɑ̃sje] VT **1** *(distinguer)* to distinguish, to differentiate; **d. A et B** to differentiate between A and B; **rien ne les différencie** it's impossible to tell them apart **2** *Biol & Math* to differentiate

VPR **se différencier 1** *(se distinguer)* to be different, to differ (**de** from); **ils se différencient (l'un de l'autre) par leur manière de parler** they're different from one another in the way they speak **2** *Biol* to differentiate

différend [diferɑ̃] NM disagreement, dispute; *Jur* dispute; **avoir un d. avec qn (sur qch)** to be in dispute with sb (over sth), to have a difference of opinion with sb (over sth)

différent, -e [diferɑ̃, -ɑ̃t] ADJ **1** *(distinct)* different; **d. de** unlike, different *Br* from *or Am* than; **très différente de sa sœur** very unlike her sister; **ils sont très différents** they're very unlike each other *or* different; **il n'est pas désagréable, il est timide, c'est d.** he isn't unpleasant, he's shy, there's a difference **2** *(original)* different; **un week-end un peu d.** a weekend with a difference; **nous avons voulu faire un film d.** we wanted to make a different kind of movie *or Br* film

ADJ INDÉFINI *(devant un nom au pluriel)* different, various; **différentes personnes ont protesté** various people complained; **elle a écrit sous différents noms** she wrote under various names

différentiation [diferɑ̃sjasjɔ̃] NF *Math* differentiation

différentiel, -elle [diferɑ̃sjɛl] ADJ differential

NM **1** *(pourcentage)* differential; **d. d'inflation** inflation differential; **d. de prix** price differential; **d. de taux (d'intérêt)** interest rate differential **2** *Aut* differential (gear)

• **différentielle** NF *Math* differential

différer [18] [difere] VT *(repousser* ▸ *rendez-vous, réponse, réunion)* to defer, to postpone; *(*▸ *départ)* to postpone, to put off; *Littéraire* **d. de faire qch** to defer doing sth

VI **1** *(se différencier* ▸ *personnes, choses)* to differ, to vary; **d. de** to differ from; **nous différons en tout** we differ on everything; **les coutumes diffèrent d'un endroit à un autre** customs vary from one place to another; **les traitements diffèrent du tout au tout** treatments vary quite drastically; **ils diffèrent par la taille** they differ in height, they are of different heights **2** *(s'opposer* ▸ *dans un débat)* to differ, to be at variance; **ils diffèrent sur ce point** they differ on this point

difficile [difisil] ADJ **1** *(route, montée)* difficult, hard; **la noire est la piste la plus d.** the toughest *or* most difficult ski run is the black one

2 *(tâche)* difficult, hard; **ce sera un livre d. à vendre** this book will be hard to sell; **ce n'est pourtant pas d.!** it's not that difficult!; **ce n'est pas d., je ne lui confierai plus rien!** it's quite simple, I won't confide in him again!; **il est d. de dire si...** it's hard to say whether...; **il s'en sortira? – d. à dire** will he manage? – it's hard to say

3 *(douloureux)* difficult, hard, tough; **il traverse une période d.** he's going through a bad *or* tough time; **il m'est d. de lui parler de son père** it's difficult *or* hard for me to talk to him about his father

4 *(personne* ▸ *d'un tempérament pénible)* difficult, demanding; *(*▸ *pointilleuse)* particular, awkward, fussy; **un enfant d.** a demanding child; **être d. (sur la nourriture)** to be a fussy eater; **il est si d. à satisfaire!** he's so hard to please!; **elle est d. à vivre** she is difficult to get on with

5 *(moralement)* difficult, tricky; *(financièrement)* difficult, tough; **la génétique pose des questions difficiles** genetics raises difficult *or* tricky questions; **connaître des années/moments difficiles** *(financièrement)* to go through years/a time of penury

6 *(impénétrable* ▸ *œuvre, auteur)* difficult, abstruse

NMF *Br* fusspot, *Am* fussbudget; **ne fais pas le d.!** don't be so awkward *or* fussy!

NM **le d. dans cette affaire est de plaire à tous** the difficult part of this business is knowing how to please everyone

ADV *Belg* **avoir d. à/de faire qch** to have problems *or* difficulty doing sth

difficilement [difisilmɑ̃] ADV with difficulty; **il s'endort d.** he has a hard time getting to sleep; **je peux d. accepter** I can't possibly accept

difficulté [difikylte] NF **1** *(caractère ardu)* difficulty; **nous ne nous cachons pas la d. de l'entreprise** we're aware of the difficulty of the task; **exercices d'une d. croissante** increasingly difficult exercises; **aimer la d.** to enjoy a challenge; **chercher la d.** to look for problems

2 *(gêne)* difficulty; **avoir de la d. à faire qch** to find it difficult to do sth; **avoir de la d. à marcher** to have difficulty walking, to walk with difficulty

3 *(problème)* problem, difficulty; **il abandonne dès qu'il rencontre une d.** he gives up as soon as he comes up against a problem; **il a des difficultés en maths** he has problems with maths; **faire des difficultés** to create problems, to make a fuss; **avoir des difficultés à faire qch** to have problems *or* difficulty doing sth; **avoir des difficultés avec qn** to have difficulties *or* problems with sb

4 *(point difficile)* difficulty; **les difficultés du français** the difficulties of the French language; **cela ne présente aucune d.** that doesn't present any difficulty

5 *(impénétrabilité* ▸ *d'une œuvre, d'un auteur)* difficult *or* abstruse nature

6 *Jur* **d. d'exécution** legal obstacle

• **en difficulté** ADJ *(nageur)* in difficulties; *(navire, avion)* in distress; *(entreprise, économie, secteur)* in difficulties *or* trouble; **un enfant en d.** *(scolairement)* a child with learning difficulties; *(psychologiquement)* a child with behavioural problems; **un couple en d.** *(sur le plan affectif)* a couple who are having problems; *(financièrement)* a couple with money problems ADV **mettre qn en d.** to put sb in a difficult *or* an awkward situation; **la crise a mis plusieurs banques en d.** the crisis put several banks in a difficult position

• **sans difficulté** ADV easily, with no difficulty

difforme [difɔrm] ADJ deformed, misshapen

difformité [difɔrmite] NF deformity

diffracter [3] [difrakte] VT to diffract

diffraction [difraksjɔ̃] NF diffraction

diffus, -e [dify, -yz] ADJ *(gén) & Bot* diffuse; *(souvenir)* vague; *(style)* loose; **il ressentait une douleur diffuse dans la poitrine** he felt a dull pain in his chest; **une sensation diffuse de bien-être** a general *or* overall feeling of well-being

diffusément [difyzemɑ̃] ADV diffusely

diffuser [3] [difyze] VT **1** *(répandre* ▸ *chaleur, lumière)* to spread, to diffuse, *Sout* to disseminate; **la lumière diffusée par une petite lampe de chevet** the (soft) light coming from a small bedside lamp

2 *Rad & TV* to broadcast; **émission diffusée en direct/différé** live/prerecorded broadcast

3 *(propager* ▸ *nouvelle, rumeur)* to spread

4 *(distribuer* ▸ *tracts)* to hand out; *(*▸ *produits)* to distribute; *(*▸ *rapport)* to circulate; *(dans l'édition)* to distribute, to sell; **des affiches antitabac ont été diffusées dans les cabinets médicaux** antismoking posters have been distributed *or* circulated to doctors' *Br* surgeries *or Am* offices; **leurs produits sont diffusés sur une grande échelle** their products are widely available

VPR **se diffuser** *(information, racontars, chaleur, lumière)* to spread

diffuseur [difyzœr] NM **1** *Com* distributing agent, distributor; *TV & Rad* broadcaster; **d. hertzien** terrestrial broadcaster; **d. public** public broadcaster

2 *Élec, Tech & (en acoustique)* diffuser

3 *(de parfum, de sèche-cheveux)* diffuser

4 *(conduit)* diffuser

diffusion [difyzjɔ̃] NF **1** *(en acoustique)* diffusion, diffusivity

2 *Phys (d'une particule)* diffusion

3 *Opt* diffusion

4 *Méd* spreading

5 *Rad & TV* broadcasting; **d. audionumérique** digital audio broadcasting; **d. directe par satellite** direct satellite broadcasting, DSB; **d. hertzienne** terrestrial broadcasting; **d. numérique** digital broadcasting; **d. satellite** satellite broadcasting; **d. simultanée** simulcasting; **d. terrestre** terrestrial broadcasting

6 *(propagation* ▸ *du savoir, d'une théorie)* spreading

7 *(distribution* ▸ *de tracts)* distribution, distributing; *(*▸ *de livres)* distribution, selling; **d. de masse** *(d'un journal)* mass circulation

8 *(exemplaires vendus)* number of copies sold, circulation

• **en deuxième diffusion, en seconde diffusion** ADJ *TV* repeated, repeat *(avant n)*

digérer [18] [diʒere] VT **1** *Physiol* to digest; **je ne digère pas le lait** milk doesn't agree with me, I can't digest milk **2** *(assimiler* ▸ *connaissances, lecture)* to digest, to assimilate; **des notions de psychologie mal digérées** half-understood ideas on psychology **3** *Fam (supporter)* to stomach, to take; **je n'ai pas digéré le coup qu'il m'a fait** I'm still not about to forgive him for what he did to me; **des vérités dures à d.** unpalatable truths

USAGE ABSOLU *Physiol* **je digère mal** my digestion isn't very good, I have poor digestion; **prendre qch pour d.** to take sth to help one's digestion

digest [diʒɛst, daidʒɛst] NM digest

digeste [diʒɛst] ADJ **un aliment d.** an easily digested foodstuff; *Fig* **ce livre est vraiment peu d.** this book is indigestible

digestibilité [diʒɛstibilite] NF digestibility

digestible [diʒɛstibl] ADJ digestible

digestif, -ive [diʒɛstif, -iv] ADJ *(de la digestion)* digestive; *(substance, pastille)* which aids digestion

NM after-dinner drink; *(liqueur)* liqueur *(taken after dinner)*; *(cognac, eau-de-vie etc)* brandy *(taken after dinner)*

digestion [diʒɛstjɔ̃] NF digestion; **avoir une d. lente** to digest one's food slowly; **ne te baigne pas pendant la d.** don't go swimming right after a meal

digestive [dizestiv] *voir* **digestif**

Digicode® [diʒikɔd] NM door code *(for entrance to a building)*

digit [diʒit] NM *(chiffre)* digit; *(caractère)* character

digital, -e[1]**, -aux, -ales** [diʒital, -o] ADJ **1** *Anat* digital **2** *(numérique)* digital

digitale[2] [diʒital] NF *Bot* digitalis; **d. pourprée** foxglove

digitaline [diʒitalin] NF *Chim* digitalin

digitaliser [3] [diʒitalize] VT to digitalize, to digitize

digitaliseur [diʒitalizœr] NM digitizer

digne [diɲ] ADJ **1** *(noble)* dignified; **rester d. dans la douleur** to carry one's grief with dignity **2 d. de** *(qui mérite)* worthy *or* deserving of; **un détail d. de votre attention** a detail worthy of your attention; **elle est d. du premier prix** she deserves first prize; **je ne suis pas d. de toi** I am not worthy of you, you're too good for me; **toute amie d. de ce nom aurait accepté** a true friend would have accepted; **je n'ai pas eu de vacances dignes de ce nom depuis une éternité** I haven't had any holidays as such for ages; **d. de confiance** trustworthy; **d. de foi** credible; **d. d'être mentionné** worth mentioning; **une pièce d. d'être vue** a play worth seeing; **il n'est pas d. d'être notre représentant** he does not deserve *or* he is not fit to be our representative **3 d. de** *(en conformité avec)* worthy of; **ce n'est pas d. de toi** it's unworthy of you; **il me faut une tenue d. de cette occasion** I need an outfit worthy of this occasion; *aussi Hum* **il est le d. fils de son père** like father like son

dignement [diɲmɑ̃] ADV **1** *(noblement)* with dignity, in a dignified manner; **il s'en est allé d.** he left with dignity **2** *Littéraire (justement)* **d. récompensé** justly rewarded

dignitaire [diɲitɛr] NM dignitary

dignité [diɲite] NF **1** *(noblesse)* dignity; *(maintien)* poise; **manquer de d.** to lack dignity, to be undignified

2 *(respect)* dignity; **la d. de la personne humaine** human dignity
3 *(amour-propre)* pride, self-respect; **ah non, j'ai ma d.!** no, I have my pride!
4 *(fonction)* dignity
5 *(honneur)* honour

digramme [digram] NM *Ling* digraph

digraphie [digrafi] NF *Compta* double-entry bookkeeping

digression [digresjɔ̃] NF digression; **faire une d.** to digress; **tomber** *ou* **se perdre dans des digressions** to digress (endlessly)

digue [dig] NF **1** *(mur)* dyke, seawall; *(talus)* embankment; **d. de retenue** flood barrier **2** *Fig (protection)* safety valve, barrier **3** *Can (de billes de bois)* logjam; *(de glace)* ice jam

diktat [diktat] NM diktat

dilapidateur, -trice [dilapidatœr, -tris] ADJ spendthrift, wasteful
NM,F squanderer, spendthrift; **d. de fonds publics** embezzler of public funds

dilapidation [dilapidasjɔ̃] NF wasting, frittering away, squandering; **d. de fonds publics** embezzlement of public funds

dilapidatrice [dilapidatris] *voir* **dilapidateur**

dilapider [3] [dilapide] VT *(gén)* to waste, to fritter away, to squander; *(fonds publics)* to embezzle

dilatateur, -trice [dilatatœr, -tris] ADJ dilatator *(avant n)*, dilator *(avant n)*
NM dilatator, dilator

dilatation [dilatasjɔ̃] NF **1** *Phys* expansion **2** *(des narines, des pupilles)* dilation; *(de l'estomac)* distension; *(du col de l'utérus)* dilation, opening; *Méd* **d. et curetage** dilatation and curettage, D and C

dilatatrice [dilatatris] *voir* **dilatateur**

dilater [3] [dilate] VT **1** *Phys* to cause to expand **2** *(remplir d'air ▸ tuyau, pneu)* to inflate, to blow up **3** *(élargir ▸ narine, pupille, veine)* to dilate; *(▸ estomac)* to distend; *(▸ col de l'utérus)* to dilate, to open; *(▸ poumons)* to expand; **il a les pupilles dilatées** his pupils are dilated; *Fam* **d. la rate à qn** to have sb in stitches
VPR **se dilater 1** *Phys* to expand
2 *(être gonflé ▸ tuyau, pneu)* to blow up, to inflate
3 *(être élargi ▸ narine, pupille, veine)* to dilate; *(▸ estomac)* to become distended; *(▸ col de l'utérus)* to dilate, to open; *(▸ poumons)* to expand
4 se d. les poumons to fill one's lungs; *Fam* **se d. la rate** to kill oneself laughing

dilatoire [dilatwar] ADJ delaying, *Sout* dilatory, procrastinating; *Jur* dilatory; **user de moyens dilatoires** to play for time; **donner une réponse d.** to answer evasively *(so as to play for time)*

dilemme [dilɛm] NM **1** *(situation)* dilemma; **être devant un d.** to face a dilemma; **être aux prises avec un d.** to be (caught) on the horns of a dilemma **2** *Mktg (produit)* problem child

dilettante [diletɑ̃t] NMF dilettante, dabbler
ADJ dilettantish, amateurish
• **en dilettante** ADV **il fait de la peinture en d.** he dabbles in painting

dilettantisme [diletɑ̃tism] NM **1** *(attitude dilettante)* dilettantism **2** *(amateurisme)* amateurishness

diligemment [diliʒamɑ̃] ADV *Littéraire* **1** *(soigneusement)* diligently, conscientiously **2** *(rapidement)* hastily, promptly, with dispatch

diligence [diliʒɑ̃s] NF **1** *(véhicule)* stagecoach **2** *Littéraire (rapidité)* haste, dispatch; **avec d.** hastily, promptly, with dispatch; **faire d.** to make haste **3** *(soin)* diligence, conscientiousness; *Jur* **d. normale** due care
• **à la diligence de** PRÉP *Jur* at the request *or* behest of

diligent, -e [diliʒɑ̃, -ɑ̃t] ADJ *Littéraire* **1** *(actif)* prompt, speedy, active **2** *(assidu ▸ soins)* constant, assiduous; *(▸ élève)* diligent; *(▸ employé)* conscientious, scrupulous

diluant [dilɥɑ̃] NM thinner, *Spéc* diluent

diluer [7] [dilɥe] VT **1** *(allonger ▸ d'eau)* to dilute, to water down; *(▸ d'un liquide)* to dilute
2 *(délayer)* to thin down
3 *Péj (discours, exposé)* to pad *or* to stretch out; *(idée, argument)* to dilute
4 *Fin & Bourse (capital, actions)* to dilute; **d. le bénéfice par action** to dilute equity
VPR **se diluer 1** *(se mélanger)* to become diluted; *(sel, sucre)* to dissolve **2** *Fig (se disperser)* to become attenuated

dilutif, -ive [dilytif, -iv] ADJ *Fin & Bourse* dilutive

dilution [dilysjɔ̃] NF **1** *(mélange de liquides)* dilution, diluting; *(ajout d'eau)* dilution, watering down
2 *(désépaississement)* thinning down
3 *(dissolution ▸ d'un comprimé)* dissolving
4 *Péj (d'un discours)* padding *or* stretching out
5 *Fin (du capital, des actions)* dilution; **d. du bénéfice par action** dilution of equity

dilutive [dilytiv] *voir* **dilutif**

diluvien, -enne [dilyvjɛ̃, -ɛn] ADJ **1** *Bible* diluvial, diluvian **2** *(pluie)* torrential

dimanche [dimɑ̃ʃ] NM Sunday; **le d. de Pâques** Easter Sunday; **le d. des Rameaux** Palm Sunday
• **du dimanche** ADJ **1** *(journal, promenade)* Sunday *(avant n)* **2** *Fam Péj (amateur)* **chauffeur du d.** Sunday driver; **un peintre du d.** a weekend painter; *voir aussi* **mardi**

dîme [dim] NF tithe; **payer une d.** to (pay a) tithe; **prélever une d. (sur qch)** to levy a tithe (on sth); *Fig* to take one's cut (of sth)

dimension [dimɑ̃sjɔ̃] NF **1** *(mesure)* dimension, measurement; **quelles sont les dimensions de la pièce?** what are the measurements *or* dimensions of the room?; **coupé dans sa plus grande/plus petite d.** cut lengthways/crossways; **prendre les dimensions de qch** to measure sth (up); **prendre les dimensions d'un événement** to get the measure of an event
2 *(taille)* size, dimension; **une pièce de petite/grande d.** a small-size(d)/large-size(d) room
3 *(importance)* dimension; **cela donne une nouvelle d. au problème** this gives a new dimension to the problem; **une erreur de cette d.** an error of this magnitude; **lorsque l'information prend les dimensions d'une tragédie** when news assumes tragic proportions
4 *(aspect)* dimension, feature; **le suspens est une d. prépondérante de son œuvre** suspense is a significant feature of his work; **à la lumière des récents événements, les manifestations anti-américaines prennent une nouvelle d.** the anti-American demonstrations have taken on a whole new dimension *or* significance in the light of recent events
5 *Math & Phys* dimension
• **à deux dimensions** ADJ two-dimensional
• **à la dimension de** PRÉP corresponding *or* proportionate to; **un salaire à la d. du travail requis** wages proportionate to *or Sout* commensurate with the work involved
• **à trois dimensions** ADJ three-dimensional

dimensionner [3] [dimɑ̃sjɔne] VT to size; **un appartement bien dimensionné** a well laid-out apartment

diméthyle [dimetil] NM *Chim* dimethyl

diminué, -e [diminɥe] ADJ **1** *(affaibli)* **il est très d.** *(physiquement)* his health is failing; *(mentalement)* he's losing his faculties
2 *Mus* diminished
3 *Archit* tapering
4 *(rang de tricot)* decreased

diminuer [7] [diminɥe] VT **1** *(réduire ▸ prix, impôts, frais, ration)* to reduce, to cut; *(▸ longueur)* to shorten; *(▸ taille, effectifs, volume, vitesse, consommation)* to reduce; *(▸ autorité, pouvoir, crédibilité)* to lessen, to diminish; **d. le chauffage** *(pour qu'il fasse moins chaud)* to turn down the heating; *(pour économiser l'énergie)* to cut down on the heating; **d. les impôts de 5 pour cent** to reduce tax by 5 percent; **montant net diminué du prix de vente** net amount less purchase price; **cela ne diminue en rien votre mérite** this doesn't detract from *or* lessen your merit at all
2 *(atténuer ▸ douleurs, souffrance)* to alleviate, to lessen
3 *(personne ▸ affaiblir)* to affect; *(▸ humilier)* to belittle, to cut down to size; **la maladie l'a beaucoup diminué** his illness has affected him very badly; **sortir diminué d'une attaque** to suffer from the after-effects of an attack; **elle sort diminuée de cette affaire** her reputation has been badly damaged by this business
4 *(en tricot)* to decrease
5 *Mus* to diminish
VI **1** *(pression)* to fall, to drop; *(volume)* to decrease; *(prix)* to fall, to come down; *(profits, ventes, recettes)* to fall (off), to drop; *(chômage, accidents, criminalité)* to fall, decrease; **le prix des ordinateurs a diminué de 20 pour cent** the price of computers has fallen by 20 percent; **le chiffre d'affaires a diminué de 10 pour cent par rapport à l'année dernière** turnover is 10 percent down on last year's figure; **d. de valeur** to drop in value **2** *(s'affaiblir ▸ forces)* to ebb away, to wane, to lessen; *(▸ peur, douleur)* to lessen; *(▸ fièvre)* to abate; *(▸ intérêt, attention)* to drop, to lessen, to dwindle **3** *(raccourcir)* **les jours diminuent** the days are getting shorter *or* drawing in
VPR **se diminuer** *(se rabaisser)* to lower *or* demean oneself

diminutif, -ive [diminytif, -iv] ADJ *Ling* diminutive
NM **1** *(nom)* diminutive; **Greg est le d. de Gregory** Greg is short for Gregory **2** *Ling* diminutive

diminution [diminysjɔ̃] NF **1** *(réduction ▸ de prix, d'impôts, des frais, des rations)* reduction (**de** in); *(▸ de longueur)* shortening (**de** in); *(▸ de taille)* reduction (**de** in); *(▸ de volume)* decrease (**de** in); *(▸ de pression)* fall (**de** in); *(▸ de vitesse, de consommation)* reduction (**de** in); *(▸ du chômage, de la violence)* drop, decrease (**de** in); **une d. des effectifs** a reduction in the number of staff; **être en d.** *(effectifs)* to be dwindling *or* decreasing; *(naissances, ventes)* to be falling
2 *(affaiblissement ▸ d'une douleur)* alleviation; *(▸ des forces)* waning, lessening; *(▸ de la fièvre)* abatement; *(▸ de l'intérêt, de l'attention)* drop, lessening; *(▸ de l'appétit)* decrease
3 *Mus* diminution
4 *(en tricot)* decrease; **faire une d.** to decrease; **faites trois diminutions** decrease three stitches

diminutive [diminytiv] *voir* **diminutif**

dimorphe [dimɔrf] ADJ dimorphic, dimorphous

dimorphisme [dimɔrfism] NM dimorphism

dinanderie [dinɑ̃dri] NF **1** *(technique)* sheet metal craft **2** *(objets)* objects made from sheet metal

dinar [dinar] NM dinar

dînatoire [dinatwar] ADJ **buffet d.** buffet-dinner; **goûter d.** early supper, *Br* (high) tea

dinde [dɛ̃d] NF **1** *Orn* turkey (hen) **2** *Culin* turkey **3** *(sotte)* **quelle petite d.!** what a silly little goose!

dindon [dɛ̃dɔ̃] NM **1** *Orn* turkey (cock) **2** *(sot)* fool; **être le d. de la farce** *(dupe)* to be taken for a ride; *(victime de railleries)* to end up a laughing stock

dindonneau, -x [dɛ̃dɔno] NM *Orn* poult, young turkey

dîner[1] [dine] NM **1** *(repas du soir)* dinner; *(réception)* dinner party; **d. dansant** dinner dance; **d.-débat** dinner-debate; **d.-concert** dinner-concert **2** *Belg, Can & Suisse (déjeuner)* lunch

dîner[2] **[3]** [dine] VI **1** *(faire le repas du soir)* to dine, to have dinner; **dînons au restaurant** let's eat out, let's go out for dinner; **avoir des amis à d.** to have friends to dinner *or* round for dinner; **il est resté à d.** he stayed for dinner; **nous avons dîné d'un simple potage** we just had soup for dinner; **j'ai fait d. les enfants plus tôt** I gave the children an early dinner **2** *Belg, Can & Suisse (déjeuner)* to have lunch

dînette [dinɛt] NF **1** *(jouet)* toy *or* doll's tea set; **jouer à la d.** to have a doll's tea-party **2** *Fam (repas)* light *or* quick meal ▫; **faire la d.** to have a bite to eat

dîneur, -euse [dinœr, -øz] NM,F diner

ding [diŋ] ONOMAT ding; **d. dong!** ding-dong!

dingo [dɛ̃go] ADJ *Fam* nuts, crazy; **il est complètement d.** he's completely nuts, he's got a screw loose
NMF *Fam* nutcase, *Am* wacko
NM *(chien)* dingo

dingue [dɛ̃g] *Fam* ADJ **1** *(fou)* nuts, crazy; **elle est vraiment d. de rouler aussi vite** she's got to be nuts to drive so fast; **il a signé, faut être d.!** he signed, how crazy can you get! **2** *(incroyable ▸ prix, histoire)* crazy, mad; *(extravagant ▸ vêtements, soi-*

rée) great, terrific; **c'est d. ce qu'il peut faire chaud ici** it's hot as hell here; **en ce moment j'ai un boulot d.!** the amount of work I have at the moment is unreal *or* crazy

NMF nutcase, *Am* wacko; **il conduit comme un vrai d.** he drives like a complete maniac; **c'est une maison de dingues!** this place is a real loony bin!; **envoyer qn chez les dingues** to send sb to the loony bin *or* funny farm; **c'est un d. de motos** he's a motorbike freak

dinguer **[3]** [dɛ̃ge] **VI** *Fam Vieilli* **les assiettes dinguaient dans la cuisine!** plates were flying all over the kitchen!; **il m'a attrapé, j'ai dingué** he grabbed me and I went flying; **sa voiture est allée d. contre un mur** his/her car went crashing *or* flying into a wall; **envoyer d. qn** *(l'éconduire)* to tell sb where to go, *Br* to send sb packing

dinguerie [dɛ̃gri] **NF** *Fam* stupidity; **ce livre est d'une d.!** this is an incredibly stupid book; **voilà sa dernière d.: s'acheter une moto!** you know what his latest mad *or* crazy idea is? to buy a motorbike!; **ils ne savent faire que des dingueries** they get up to all sorts of nonsense; **il est capable des pires dingueries** he's capable of doing the most idiotic things

dinosaure [dinozɔr] **NM** *Zool & Fig* dinosaur

dinucléotide [dinykleɔtid] **NM** *Biol & Chim* dinucleotide

diocésain, -e [djɔsezɛ̃, -ɛn] **ADJ** diocesan

NM,F diocesan

diocèse [djɔsez] **NM** diocese

diode [djɔd] **NF** diode; **d. électroluminescente** light-emitting diode

dionysiaque [djɔnizjak] **ADJ** Dionysiac, Dionysian

• **dionysiaques NFPL** *Antiq* Dionysia

diorama [djɔrama] **NM** diorama

dioxine [diɔksin] **NF** *Chim* dioxin

dioxyde [diɔksid] **NM** *Chim* dioxide; **d. de carbone** carbon dioxide

diphasé, -e [difaze] **ADJ** diphase, diphasic, two-phase *(avant n)*

diphtérie [difteri] **NF** diphtheria; **avoir la d.** to have diphtheria

diphtérique [difterik] **ADJ** diphtherial, diphtheric, diphtheritic

NMF diphtheria sufferer

diphtongue [diftɔ̃g] **NF** *Ling* diphthong

diphtonguer **[3]** [diftɔ̃ge] **VT** to diphthongize, to make into a diphthong

diplodocus [diplɔdɔkys] **NM** *Zool* diplodocus

diplômant, -e [diplomɑ̃, -ɑ̃t] **ADJ** diploma-level; **une formation diplomante** a diploma-level course

diplomate [diplɔmat] **ADJ** diplomatic

NMF *Pol & Fig* diplomat

NM *Culin* = dessert made of sponge cake pieces covered with custard and glacé fruits, ≃ trifle

diplomatie [diplɔmasi] **NF 1** *Pol (relations, représentation)* diplomacy; **la d.** *(corps)* the diplomatic corps *or* service **2** *(tact)* diplomacy, tact; **avec d.** diplomatically, tactfully

diplomatique [diplɔmatik] **ADJ 1** *Pol* diplomatic **2** *(adroit)* diplomatic, tactful; **faire un mensonge d.** to tell a white lie; **avoir une maladie d.** to pretend to be indisposed

diplomatiquement [diplɔmatikmɑ̃] **ADV 1** *Pol* diplomatically **2** *(adroitement)* diplomatically, courteously, tactfully

diplôme [diplom] **NM 1** *(titre)* diploma, qualification; **un d. d'ingénieur** an engineering diploma; **elle a des diplômes** she's highly qualified; **d. d'État** recognized qualification; **d. d'études approfondies** = postgraduate qualification which is a prerequisite for PhD candidates; **d. d'études supérieures spécialisées** = postgraduate diploma lasting one year; **d. d'études universitaires générales** = university diploma taken after two years; **d. d'études universitaires scientifiques et techniques** = university diploma taken after two years of science courses; **d. universitaire d'études littéraires** = university diploma gained after two years of arts courses, still existing in some French-speaking countries but replaced in France in 1973; **d. universitaire d'études scientifiques** = university diploma gained after two years of science courses, still existing in some French-speaking countries but replaced in France in 1973; **d. universitaire de technologie** = diploma taken after two years at an institute of technology **2** *(examen)* exam; **il a raté son d. de programmeur** he failed his computer programming exam

diplômé, -e [diplome] **ADJ** *(gén)* qualified; *(de l'université ou équivalent)* graduate; **un ingénieur d. de l'École Polytechnique** an engineering graduate of the "École Polytechnique"

NM,F *(gén)* holder of a qualification; *(de l'université ou équivalent)* graduate; **les hauts diplômés** highly qualified people; **embaucher des diplômés** to take on people with qualifications

diplômer **[3]** [diplome] **VT** to award a diploma to, to confer a diploma (up)on

diplopie [diplɔpi] **NF** *Méd* double vision, *Spéc* diplopia

dipode [dipɔd] *Zool* **ADJ** biped

NM biped

dipsomane [dipsɔman], **dipsomaniaque** [dipsɔmanjak] **ADJ** dipsomaniac

NMF dipsomaniac

dipsomanie [dipsɔmani] **NF** dipsomania

diptère [dipter] **ADJ 1** *Archit* dipteral **2** *Entom* dipteran, dipterous

NM *Entom* dipteran, dipteron

• **diptères NMPL** Diptera

diptyque [diptik] **NM 1** *Beaux-Arts* diptych **2** *(œuvre)* = literary or artistic work in two parts

dirco [dirko] **NMF** *Fam* marketing manager; *(en chef)* marketing director

dircom [dirkɔm] *Fam* **NF** *(service)* communications department□

NMF *(responsable)* head of communications□

dire¹ [dir] **NM** *Jur (mémoire)* statement

• **dires NMPL** statement; **je tiens à confirmer les dires de M. Leblanc** I can confirm what Mr Leblanc said; **d'après** *ou* **selon les dires de son père** according to his/her father *or* to what his/her father said; **selon les dires de son professeur, il était bon élève** according to his teacher, he was good at school

• **au dire de PRÉP** according to; **au d. de la mère, il a fallu trois hommes pour le tenir** according to the mother, it took three men to restrain him

DIRE² **[102]** [dir]

VT
- to say **A1, 2, B1, 3, 8, 9, 12, D1, 2**
- to give **B4**
- to claim **B10**
- to look/smell/*etc* like **C2**
- to recite **A2**
- to express **B2**
- to tell **B1, 5, 6, 7**
- to think **C1**
- to show **D1**
- to be in the mood for **D4**

USAGE ABSOLU
- to say **3**

VPR
- to tell each other **1**
- to say **2, 4, 5, 6**
- to claim **5, 6**
- to be in use **3**
- to think **4**

VT A. *ARTICULER, PRONONCER* **1** *(énoncer)* to say; **dis "ah!"** say "ah!"; **dites "je le jure"** say "I swear by Almighty God"; **quel nom dis-tu? Castagnel?** what name did you say *or* what's the name again? Castagnel?; **il n'arrive pas à d. ce mot** he cannot pronounce that word; **une poupée qui dit "oui"** a doll which says "yes"; **"je t'attendais", dit-elle** "I was waiting for you," she said; **vous avez dit "démocratie"?** "democracy", did you say?; *Fam* **je te dis zut!** get lost!; *très Fam* **je te dis merde!** *(pour porter bonheur)* break a leg!; *(pour insulter)* get lost!; **comment dit-on "pain" en breton?** how do you say "bread" in Breton?, what's the Breton for "bread"?; **je ne dirais pas qu'il est distant, je dirais plutôt effarouché** I wouldn't say he's haughty, rather that he's been frightened off; **je n'ai pas dit "oublier", j'ai dit "pardonner"** I said "forgive", not "forget"; **une honte, que dis-je, une infamie!, une honte, pour ne pas d. une infamie!** a shame, not to say an infamy!; **en ce temps-là, qui disait vol disait galère** in those days, theft meant the gallows; **qui dit fatigue dit inattention et qui dit inattention dit accident** when you're tired you're less vigilant and therefore more likely to have an accident; **si (l')on peut d.** in a way, so to speak; **disons-le, disons le mot** let's not mince words; **c'est, disons le mot, une trahison** it's a betrayal, let's not mince words; **je me sens humilié, disons-le** I must admit *or* confess I feel humiliated, to be honest *or* frank (about it), I feel humiliated; **d. non** to say no, to refuse; **d. non au nucléaire** to say no to nuclear energy; **tu veux un gin? – je ne dis pas non** would you like a gin? – I wouldn't say no; **si on lui proposait le poste, il ne dirait pas non** if he was offered the job, he wouldn't say no *or* wouldn't refuse; **d. oui** *(gén)* to say yes; *(à une proposition)* to accept; *(au mariage)* to say I do; **l'impôt sur les grandes fortunes, moi je dis oui!** I'm all in favour of a supertax on the rich!; **d. bonjour de la main** to wave (hello); **d. oui de la tête** to nod; **d. non de la tête** to shake one's head; *Fam* **obéissant? il faut le d. vite** obedient? I'm not so sure about that; *Fam* **déménager, c'est vite dit!** move? that's easier said than done; *Fam* **menteur! – c'est celui qui (le) dit qui y est** *ou* **qui l'est!** liar! – it takes one to know one!

2 *(réciter ▸ prière, table de multiplication)* to say; *(▸ texte)* to say, to recite, to read; *(▸ rôle)* to speak; **d. la/une messe** to say mass/a mass; **d. son chapelet** to say the rosary, to tell one's beads

B. *EXPRIMER* **1** *(oralement)* to say; **que dis-tu là?** what did you say?, what was that you said?; **tu ne sais pas ce que tu dis** you don't know what you're talking about; **elle dit tout ce qui lui passe par la tête** she says anything that comes into her head; **dis quelque chose!** say something!; **c'est juste pour d. quelque chose** it was just for the sake of saying something; **qu'est-ce que tu veux que je dise?** what do you expect me to say?; **j'ai l'habitude de d. ce que je pense** I always speak my mind *or* say what I think; **bon, bon, je n'ai rien dit!** OK, sorry I spoke!; **pourquoi ne m'as-tu rien dit de tout cela?** why didn't you speak to me *or* tell me about any of this?; **dis-moi où il est** tell me where he is; **ne me dis pas que c'est brûlé!** don't tell me it's burnt!; *Fam* **il me dit comme ça, "t'as pas le droit"** so he says to me, "you can't do that"; *Fam* **je suis un raté? tu sais ce qu'il te dit, le raté?** so I'm a loser, am I? well, do you want to hear what this loser's got to say to you?; **je te l'ai dit une fois, je ne te le redirai pas** *ou* **je ne te le dirai pas deux fois** I've told you before and I won't tell you again; **combien de fois faut-il que je te le dise?** how many times do I have to tell you?; **impossible de lui faire d. l'âge de sa sœur** he/she won't say *or* give his/her sister's age; **impossible de lui faire d. la vérité** he/she just refuses to tell the truth; **ne me fais pas d. ce que je n'ai pas dit!** don't put words into my mouth!; **laisser qn d. qch** to let sb say sth; **laissez-moi d. ceci** let me say this; **laissez-la d.!** let her speak!; **je peux d. que tu m'as fait peur!** you certainly frightened me!; **j'ai failli faire tout rater! – ça, tu peux le d.!** I nearly messed everything up – you can say that again!; **ce disant** with these words, so saying; **ce qui est dit est dit** there's no going back on what's been said (before); **c'est (te/vous) d. s'il est riche!** that gives you an idea how wealthy he is!; **c'est d. si je l'aimais!** so you see how much I loved him/her!; **il ne m'a même pas répondu, c'est tout d.** he never even answered me, that says it all; **pour tout d.** in fact, to be honest; **je ne te le fais pas d.** you said it, I couldn't have put it better myself; **de l'escroquerie, je ne vous le fais pas d.** a swindle, you said it! *or* as you so rightly say!; **il va sans d. que…** needless to say…; **ça va sans d.** it goes without saying; *Fam* **ça va sans d. mais ça va encore mieux en le disant** it doesn't hurt to overstate it; *Fam* **ce n'est pas pour d., mais à sa place j'aurais réussi** though I say it myself, if I'd been him I'd have succeeded; **ce n'est pas pour d. mais elle se débrouille bien** she's doing well, you've got to give her that, give her her due, she's doing well; *Fam* **alors j'ai parlé de racisme, ce que j'avais pas dit là!** then I mentioned racism and that really set the cat among the pigeons!; **il en est incapable, enfin (moi), ce que j'en dis…** he's not capable of it, at least that's what I'd say…; *Fam* **je ne dis pas** maybe; **je ne dis pas, mais…** that's as may be but…; *Fam* **il a un petit manoir, je ne te dis que ça!** he owns a lovely little country house, what (more) can I say!; *Fam* **voici une confiture maison, je ne te dis que ça** here's some homemade jam that's out of this world; *Fam* **il y avait un monde, je te dis pas!** you wouldn't have believed the crowds!; *Fam* **je te dis pas la pagaille qu'il y avait!** you should've seen the chaos!

2 *(symboliquement)* to express, to tell of; **je voudrais d. mon espoir** I'd like to express my hope; **un journal où elle dit son dégoût de la vie** a diary in which she tells of her disgust for life; **comment d. mon amour?** how can I express my love?; **toute cette haine que je n'avais jamais dite** all my unexpressed hatred; **une lettre où il me disait sa surprise** a letter telling me how surprised he was; **un sculpteur qui n'a plus rien/qui a encore beaucoup à d.** a sculptor who has nothing left to say/ who still has a lot left to say; **vouloir d.** *(signifier)* to mean; **un haussement d'épaules dans ce cas-là, ça dit bien ce que ça veut d.** in a situation like that, a shrug (of the shoulders) speaks volumes **est-ce à d. que...?** does this mean that...?; *Arch* **vous partez, madame, qu'est-ce à d.?** Madam, what mean you by leaving?

3 *(écrire)* to say; **dans sa lettre, elle dit que...** in her letter she says that...

4 *(annoncer ▸ nom, prix)* to give; **cela t'a coûté combien? – dis un prix!** how much did it cost you? – have a guess!; **dites un** *ou* **votre prix, je l'achète** name your price; **le général vous fait d. qu'il vous attend** the general has sent me to tell you he's waiting for you; **on m'a fait d. qu'elle était sortie** I was told she'd gone out; **faire d. à qn de venir** to send for sb; **je lui ai fait d. qu'on se passerait de lui** I let him know that we'd manage without him

5 *(prédire)* to foretell, to tell; **tu verras ce que je te dis!** you just wait and see if I'm right!; **qui aurait dit que je l'épouserais?** who would have said that I'd marry him/her?; **je te l'avais bien dit** I told you so; *Fam* **tu vas le regretter, moi je te le dis!** you'll be sorry for this, let me tell you *or* mark my words!

6 *(ordonner)* to tell; **il m'a dit d'arrêter** he told me to stop; **on ne me le dira pas** *ou* **je ne me le ferai pas d. deux fois** I don't need to be told twice; **il ne se l'est pas fait d. deux fois** he didn't have to be told twice

7 *(conseiller)* to tell; **tu me dis d'oublier, mais...** you tell me I must forget, but...

8 *(objecter)* to say, to object; **sa mère ne lui dit jamais rien** his/her mother never tells him/her off; **toi, on ne peut jamais rien te d.!** you can't take the slightest criticism!; **quand on lui a fait le vaccin, il n'a rien dit** when they gave him the injection he never said a word; **mais, me direz-vous, il n'est pas majeur** but, you will object *or* I hear you say, he's not of age; **as-tu quelque chose à d. sur la façon dont j'élève nos enfants?** have you got any objections to *or* anything to say about the way I bring up our children?; **c'est tout ce que tu as trouvé à d.?** is that the best you could come up with?; **Pierre n'est pas d'accord – il n'a rien à d.** Pierre doesn't agree – he's in no position to make any objections; **il n'a rien trouvé à d. sur la qualité** he had no criticisms to make about the quality; *Fam* **elle est maligne, il n'y a pas à d.** *ou* **on ne peut pas d. (le contraire)** she's shrewd, there's no denying it *or* and no mistake

9 *(affirmer)* to say, to state; **le diriez-vous à la barre des témoins?** would you swear to it?; **si c'est vous qui le dites, si vous le dites, du moment que vous le dites** if you say so; **puisque je vous le dis!** I'm telling you!, you can take it from me!; **d. que** to say *or* to state that; **elle dit que ce n'est pas vrai** she says it's not true; **c'est le bon train? – je te dis que oui!** is it the right train? – yes it is! *or* I'm telling you it is!; **il va neiger – la météo a dit que non** it looks like it's going to snow – the weather forecast said it wouldn't; **je n'ai jamais dit que j'étais spécialiste!** I never claimed to be *or* said I was an expert!; **tu étais content, ne me dis pas le contraire!** you were pleased, don't deny it *or* don't tell me you weren't!; **on dit qu'il a un autre fils** rumour has it that *or* it's rumoured that *or* it's said that he has another son; **loin des yeux, loin du cœur, dit-on** out of sight, out of mind, so the saying goes *or* so they say; **je ne les laisserai pas d. que mon fils est un fainéant** I won't allow them to *or* let them say that my son's an idler; **on le disait lâche** he was said *or* alleged *or* reputed to be a coward; **qui (me) dit que tu n'es pas un espion?** how can I tell *or* who's to say (that) you're not a spy?; *Fam* **ça ne coûtera pas grand-chose – que tu dis!** it won't cost much – that's what you think *or* say!; *Fam* **elle trouvera bien une place – qu'elle dit** she'll find a job, no problem – that's what she thinks!; **on dira ce qu'on voudra, mais l'amour ça passe avant tout** whatever people say, love comes before everything else; **on ne dira jamais assez l'importance d'un régime alimentaire équilibré** I cannot emphasize enough the importance of a balanced diet

10 *(prétendre)* to claim, to allege; **elle disait ne pas savoir qui le lui avait donné** she claimed *or* alleged that she didn't know who'd given it to her

11 *(dans des jeux d'enfants)* **on dirait qu'on serait des rois** let's pretend we're kings

12 *(admettre)* to say, to admit; **tu ne m'aimes plus, dis-le** you don't love me any more, say *or* admit it; **je dois d. qu'elle est jolie** I must say *or* admit she's pretty; **il a beaucoup travaillé, on doit le d.** it's got to be said that he's worked hard; **il faut bien d. qu'il n'est plus tout jeune** he's not young any more, let's face it; **il faut d. qu'elle a des excuses** (to) give her her due, there are mitigating circumstances; **disons que...** let's say (that)...

13 *(décider)* **il est dit que...** fate has decreed that...; **il ne sera pas dit que...** let it not be said that...; **rien n'est dit** *(décidé)* nothing's been decided yet; *(prévisible)* nothing's for certain (yet); **tout est dit** *(il n'y a plus à discuter)* the matter is closed; *(l'avenir est arrêté)* the die is cast; **tout n'est pas encore dit** nothing's final yet; **aussitôt dit, aussitôt fait** no sooner said than done

C. *PENSER, CROIRE* **1** *(penser)* to say, to think; **que disent les médecins?** what do the doctors say?; **que dis-tu de ma perruque?** what do you think of *or* how do you like my wig?; **que d. de ce geste?** what is one to make of this gesture?; **et comme dessert? – que dirais-tu d'une mousse au chocolat?** and to follow? – what would you say to *or* how about a chocolate mousse?; **d. que...** to think that...; **d. qu'elle était si jolie étant petite!** to think that she was so pretty as a child!

2 *(introduit une comparaison, une impression)* **si livide qu'on eût dit un fantôme** so pale he looked like a ghost; **quand il parle, on dirait son père** he sounds just like his father; **on dirait du thé** *(au goût)* it tastes like tea; *(à l'odeur)* it smells like tea; *(d'apparence)* it looks like tea; **on dirait de la laine** *(au toucher)* it feels like wool; **on dirait que je te fais peur** you behave as if *or* as though you were scared of me

3 *(pour exprimer une probabilité)* **on dirait sa fille, au premier rang** it looks like her daughter there in the front row; **on dirait qu'ils vont passer avec trois pour cent de marge** it looks like they'll get through with a three percent lead

D. *INDIQUER, DONNER DES SIGNES DE* **1** *(indiquer ▸ sujet: instrument)* to say; *(▸ sujet: attitude, regard)* to say, to show; **que dit le baromètre?** what does the barometer say?; **l'horloge de l'école disait 5 heures** it was five o'clock according to the *or* by the school clock; **ses yeux disaient sa détresse** you could see *or* read the distress in his eyes; **un geste qui disait sa peur** a gesture that betrayed his fear; **sa réponse te dira tout sur elle** her answer will tell you all you need to know about her; *Fam* **à la voir, quelque chose me dit qu'elle va nous laisser en plan** something about her tells me that she'll leave us in the lurch; **mon intuition** *ou* **quelque chose me dit qu'il reviendra** I have a feeling (that) he'll be back; *Fam* **que dit ton épaule?** how's your shoulder doing?; *Fam* **ça dit quoi, ce rosbif?** how's that joint of beef doing?

2 *(stipuler par écrit)* to say; **que dit la Bible/le dictionnaire à ce sujet?** what does the Bible/dictionary say about this?; **écoute ce que dit mon horoscope** listen to what my horoscope says; **la loi ne dit rien sur la vente de ces produits** the law says nothing about the sale of these products

3 *(faire penser à)* **son visage me dit quelque chose** I've seen her face before, her face seems familiar; **ce nom vous dit-il quelque chose?** have you come across *or* heard the name before?; **Lambert, cela ne vous dit rien?** Lambert, does that mean anything to you?; **cela ne me dit rien de bon** *ou* **qui vaille** I'm not sure I like (the look of) it

4 *(tenter)* **ta proposition me dit de plus en plus** your suggestion's growing on me; **tu viens? – ça ne me dit rien** are you coming? – I'm not in the mood *or* I don't feel like it; **la viande ne me dit rien du tout en ce moment** I'm off meat at the moment; **j'ai tellement attendu que maintenant ça ne me dit plus grand-chose** I waited so long that now I've lost interest in it; **ça te dirait d'aller à Bali?** (how) would you like a trip to Bali?; **ça te dirait d'aller jouer au tennis?** are you in the mood for a game of tennis?

USAGE ABSOLU 1 nul n'a oublié à quel point elle disait juste nobody can forget how accurate her rendering was

2 *Cartes* **à vous de d.!** your call!

3 c'est idiot – dis toujours it's silly – say it anyway; **j'ai une surprise – dis vite!** I have a surprise – let's hear it *or* do tell!; **comment d.** *ou* **dirais-je?** how shall I put it *or* say?; **bien dit!** well said! **dites donc, pour demain, on y va en voiture?** by the way, are we driving there tomorrow?; *Fam* **dis donc** *ou* **dis-moi, faut pas se gêner!** hey, do you mind?; *Fam* **tu te fiches de moi, dis!** you're pulling my leg, aren't you?; *Fam* **tu me le sers, dis** *ou* **dis-moi, ce café?** am I getting that coffee or not?; *très Fam* **merde! – dis donc, sois poli!** shit! – hey, (mind your) language!; *Fam* **dis donc, t'as pas une gomme?** hey, have you got a rubber?; **je peux y aller, dis?** can I go, please?; **vous lui parlerez de moi, dites?** you will talk to her about me, won't you?; *Fam* **c'est beau – eh dis, j'y ai mis le prix!** that's beautiful – so it should be, I paid enough for it!; **tu es bien habillé, ce soir, dis donc!** my word, aren't you smart tonight!; **ah dis donc, la belle moto!** wow, get a load of that bike!; **il nous faut, disons, deux secrétaires** we need, (let's) say, two secretaries; **j'ai, disons, de bonnes raisons de ne pas te croire** let's say I've got good reasons not to believe you; **il a, disons, la cinquantaine bien sonnée** let's say he's on the wrong side of fifty; *Hum* **j'ai dit!** I have spoken!

VPR se dire 1 *(échanger ▸ secrets, paroles)* to tell each other *or* one another; **nous n'avons plus rien à nous d.** we've got nothing left to say to each other; **ils se disaient des injures/des mots doux** they were exchanging insults/sweet nothings; **nous nous disions tout** we had no secrets from each other; *Arch* **qu'on se le dise** let this be known; *Hum* **je n'emmène personne au cirque si ce bruit continue, qu'on se le dise!** I'm not taking anyone to the circus if this noise doesn't stop, believe you me!

2 *(être formulé)* **comment se dit "bonsoir" en japonais?** how do you say "goodnight" in Japanese?, what's the Japanese for "goodnight"?; **il est vraiment hideux – peut-être, mais ça ne se dit pas** he's really hideous – maybe, but it's not the sort of thing you say; **cela ne se dit pas à table/devant les enfants** such things shouldn't be said at the table/in front of the children; **se dit de** *(pour définir un terme)* (is) said of, (is) used for, describes; **se dit d'une personne affaiblie par la maladie** said of a person weakened by ill-health

3 *(être en usage)* to be in use, to be accepted usage; **cela se dit encore par ici** it's still in use *or* they still say it around here; **cela ne se dit plus guère** it's not really accepted usage now *or* used any more

4 *(penser)* to think (to oneself), to say to oneself; **maintenant, je me dis que j'aurais dû accepter** now I think I should have accepted; *Fam* **il est malin, que je me dis** he's cunning, I thought to myself; **je me suis dit comme ça que je ne risquais rien en essayant** I thought *or* said to myself there was no harm in giving it a go; **dis-toi bien que tu n'auras rien!** you can be sure you won't get a thing!; **dis-toi bien que je ne serai pas toujours là pour t'aider** you must realize that *or* get it into your head that I won't always be here to help you

5 *(estimer être)* to say; **il se dit flatté de l'intérêt que je lui porte** he says he's *or* he claims to be flattered by my interest in him

6 *(se présenter comme)* to say, to claim; **elle se dit mannequin** she claims to be *or* she says she's a model; **ils se disent attachés à la démocratie** they claim to care *or* (that) they care about democracy

Attention: ne pas confondre **to say** et **to tell** lorsqu'on traduit **dire**. Le verbe **to tell** est toujours suivi d'un complément d'objet désignant la personne à qui l'on s'adresse.

direct, -e [dirɛkt] ADJ **1** *(sans détour ▸ voie, route, chemin)* direct, straight
2 *Transp* direct, without a change; **c'est d. en métro jusqu'à Pigalle** the metro goes direct to Pigalle; **un vol d. Paris-New York** a direct *or* nonstop flight from Paris to New York
3 *(franc ▸ question)* direct; *(▸ langage)* straightforward; *(▸ personne)* frank, straightforward; **il y a fait une allusion directe** he made a direct reference to it, he referred to it directly
4 *(sans intermédiaire ▸ cause, conséquence)* immediate; *(▸ supérieur, descendant)* direct; **un rapport d. entre deux événements** a direct connection between two events; **mettez-vous en relation directe avec Bradel** get in touch with Bradel himself; **être en rapport d.** *ou* **contact d.** *ou* **relations directes avec qn** to be in direct contact with sb
5 *Astron, Gram & Tech* direct
NM **1** *Sport* straight punch; **un d. du gauche** a straight left **2** *Rail* through *or* nonstop train **3** *TV* live; **il préfère le d. au playback** he prefers performing live to lipsynching
ADV *Fam ou Suisse* straight; **je pars d. vers Grenoble** I'm going to Grenoble direct; **s'il recommence, je vais d. chez le proviseur** if he starts again, I'm going straight to the headmaster
• **directe** NF *(ascension)* direct route
• **en direct** ADJ live ADV live
• **en direct de** PRÉP live from

directement [dirɛktəmɑ̃] ADV **1** *(tout droit)* straight; **rentre d. à la maison** go straight home; **va d. au lit** go straight to bed; **la route mène d. à Deauville** the road goes straight to Deauville
2 *(franchement)* **entrer d. dans le sujet** to broach a subject immediately; **allez d. au fait** come straight to the point
3 *(inévitablement)* straight, inevitably; **cela vous mènera d. à la faillite** this will lead you inevitably to bankruptcy
4 *(sans intermédiaire)* direct; **adresse-toi d. au patron** go straight to the boss; **vendre d. au public** to sell direct to the public; **d. du producteur au consommateur** direct *or* straight from the producer to the consumer; **il descend d. des du Mail** he's a direct descendant of the du Mail family
5 *(personnellement)* **adressez-moi d. votre courrier** address your correspondence directly to me; **cela ne vous concerne pas d.** this doesn't affect you personally *or* directly

directeur, -trice [dirɛktœr, -tris] ADJ **1** *(principal ▸ force)* controlling, driving; *(▸ principe)* guiding; *(▸ idée, ligne)* main, guiding **2** *Aut (roue)* front *(avant n)*
NM,F **1** *(d'un magasin, d'un service)* manager; *(qui fait partie du conseil d'administration)* director; **d. des achats** purchasing manager; **d. administratif** executive director; **d. administratif et financier** administrative and financial manager; **d. d'agence** *(dans une banque)* bank manager; **d. de banque** bank manager; **d. de la clientèle** customer relations manager; **d. commercial** sales director/manager; **d. de la communication** head of communications; **d. des comptes-clients** account director; **d. de la création** creative director; **d. du crédit** credit manager; **d. de division** *(au siège)* divisional director; **d. d'exploitation** operations director/manager; **d. export** export director/manager; **d. des exportations** export manager; **d. financier** financial manager; **d. général** *(d'une entreprise) Br* managing director, *Am* chief executive officer; *(d'une organisation internationale)* director general, general manager; **d. général adjoint** *Br* deputy managing director, *Am* vice-president; **d. gérant** executive director; **d. (de l') informatique** computer manager; **d. intérimaire** acting manager; **d. de marché** market manager; **d. du marketing** marketing director/manager; **d. de marque** brand manager; **d. du personnel** personnel manager; **d. de production** production manager; **d. de produit** product manager; **d. de projet** project director/manager; **d. de la publicité** advertising director/manager; **d. de recherche et développement** research and development director/manager; **d. de recherche marketing** marketing research director/manager; **d. régional** regional manager; **d. des relations publiques** public relations director/manager; **d. des ressources humaines** human resources manager; **d. de service** head of department; **d. des services techniques** technical director; **d. de succursale** branch manager; **d. technique** technical manager; **d. des ventes** sales director/manager; **d. de la vente-marketing** sales and marketing director/manager
2 *Admin & Pol* director; **d. de prison** prison *Br* governor *or Am* warden; **d. de cabinet** *Br* ≃ principal private secretary, *Am* ≃ chief of staff
3 *Scol Br* head teacher, *Am* principal
4 *Univ (d'un département)* head of department; **d. de recherche** supervisor; **d. de thèse** (thesis) supervisor
5 *Cin, Théât & TV* director; **d. d'antenne** station director; **d. artistique** artistic director; **d. de casting** casting director; **d. musical** musical director; **d. de la photographie** cinematographer, director of photography; **d. des programmes** director of programming, programme controller; **d. de scène** stage director; **d. du son** sound director
6 *Journ* **d. éditorial** publishing manager; **d. de la fabrication** production manager; **d. de la rédaction** managing editor
NM **1** *Hist* Director **2** *Rel* **d. spirituel** *ou* **de conscience** spiritual director
• **directrice** NF *Math* directrix

directif, -ive [dirɛktif, -iv] ADJ **1** *(entretien, méthode)* directive **2** *(antenne, micro)* directional **3** *(personne)* authoritarian; **elle est très directive** she's always giving orders
• **directive** NF *Admin, Mil & Pol* directive
• **directives** NFPL orders, instructions

direction [dirɛksjɔ̃] NF **1** *(fonction de chef ▸ d'une entreprise)* management, managing; *(▸ d'un parti)* leadership; *(▸ d'un orchestre)* conducting, *Am* direction; *(▸ d'un journal)* editorship; *(▸ d'une équipe sportive)* captaincy; **prendre la d. de** *(société, usine)* to take over the running *or* management of; *(journal)* to take over the editorship of; **se voir confier la d. d'une société/d'un journal/d'un lycée** to be appointed manager of a firm/chief editor of a newspaper/head of a school; **avoir la d. d'une entreprise** to manage a company; **orchestre (placé) sous la d. de** orchestra conducted by; **d. commerciale** sales management; **d. des crédits** credit management; **d. des entreprises** business management; **d. export** export management; **d. financière** financial management; **d. générale** general management, senior management; **d. de la production** production control; **d. par objectifs** management by objectives; **d. des ventes** sales management
2 *(organisation ▸ de travaux)* supervision; *(▸ d'un débat)* chairing, conducting; *(▸ de la circulation, des opérations)* directing; **c'est lui qui a pris la d. des opérations** he took charge of operations
3 *(maîtrise, cadres)* **la d.** the management; **la d. refuse toute discussion avec les syndicats** (the) management refuses to talk to the unions; *Admin* **d. centrale** = headquarters of a branch of the civil service
4 *(bureau)* manager's office
5 *(sens)* direction, way; **dans la même d.** the same way, in the same direction; **dans la d. opposée** in the opposite direction; **il est parti dans la d. de la gare** he went towards the station; **il a lancé la balle dans ma d.** he threw the ball towards me; **vous êtes dans la bonne d.** you're going the right way; **engagé dans une mauvaise d.** heading the wrong way; **vous allez dans quelle d.?** which way are you going?, where are you heading for?; **quelle d. ont-ils prise?** which way did they go?; **prenez la d. Nation** *(dans le métro)* take the Nation line; **toutes/autres directions** *(panneau sur la route)* all/other directions; **partir dans toutes les directions** *(coureurs, ballons)* to scatter; *(pétards)* to go off in all directions; *(conversation)* to wander; **la discussion a pris une tout autre d.** the discussion took a different turn *or* shifted to another subject
6 *Cin, Théât & TV* **d. (d'acteurs)** directing, direction
7 *Aut & Tech* steering; **la d. du vélo est faussée** the bicycle's handlebars are out of true; **d. assistée** power steering; **d. à crémaillère** rack and pinion steering; **d. mécanique** manual steering
8 *(service)* department; **d. du contentieux** legal department; **D. départementale de l'action sanitaire et sociale** = office administering health and social services at regional level; **D. départementale de l'équipement** = local government body responsible for public works; **d. de l'exploitation** operations department; **D. générale des Impôts** *Br* ≃ Inland Revenue, *Am* ≃ Internal Revenue; *Admin* **D. générale de la santé** = central administrative body for health and social services; *Admin* **D. des hôpitaux** = central government office for hospital administration; **d. marketing** marketing department; **d. du personnel** personnel department; **D. régionale de l'environnement** = local government body in charge of environmental issues; **d. du trésor** finance department
9 *Ordinat* **d. systématisée** systems management
• **de direction** ADJ *(équipe)* managerial
• **en direction de** PRÉP in the direction of, towards; **embouteillages en d. de Paris** holdups for Paris-bound traffic; **les trains/avions/vols en d. de Marseille** trains/planes/flights to Marseilles; **jeter un regard en d. de qn** to cast a glance at *or* towards sb; **il a tiré en d. des policiers** he fired at the policemen

directionnel, -elle [dirɛksjɔnɛl] ADJ directional

directive [dirɛktiv] *voir* **directif**

directoire [dirɛktwar] NM *Admin & Com* directorate, board of directors
• **Directoire** NM **le D.** the (French) Directory; **meuble D.** piece of Directoire furniture

directorial, -e, -aux, -ales [dirɛktɔrjal, -o] ADJ **1** *(fonction, pouvoir)* managerial, executive, directorial; **le bureau d.** the executive suite *or* manager's office **2** *Hist* Directory *(avant n)*, of the Directory

directrice [dirɛktris] *voir* **directeur**

dirham [diram] NM dirham

dirigé, -e [diriʒe] ADJ *(monnaie)* managed, controlled; *(économie)* controlled, planned

dirigeable [diriʒabl] ADJ dirigible
NM airship, dirigible

dirigeant, -e [diriʒɑ̃, -ɑ̃t] ADJ *(classes)* ruling; *(cadres)* managing
NM,F *Pol (d'un parti)* leader; *(d'un pays)* ruler, leader; *(d'une entreprise)* manager; **d. syndical** union leader; **les dirigeants d'une entreprise** the management of a company

DIRIGER [17] [diriʒe]

VT	
• to run **1**	• to manage **1, 2**
• to be in charge of **1**	• to supervise **2**
• to direct **1–4, 6, 7**	• to steer **4**
• to send **5**	• to aim **8**
VPR	
• to head for **1**	• to find one's way **2**

VT **1** *(être à la tête de ▸ usine, entreprise)* to run, to manage; *(▸ personnel, équipe)* to manage; *(▸ service, département)* to be in charge of, to be head of; *(▸ école)* to be head of; *(▸ orchestre)* to conduct, *Am* to direct; *(▸ journal)* to edit; *(▸ pays)* to run; *(▸ parti, mouvement)* to lead; **une société bien dirigée** a well-managed *or* well-run firm; **mal d. une société** to mismanage a company
2 *(superviser ▸ travaux)* to supervise, to manage, to oversee; *(▸ débat)* to conduct; *(▸ thèse, recherches)* to supervise, to oversee, to direct; *(▸ circulation)* to direct; *(▸ opérations)* to direct, to oversee; **ceux qui veulent d. les consciences** those who would influence other people's moral choices
3 *Cin, Théât & TV* to direct
4 *(piloter ▸ voiture)* to steer; *(▸ bateau)* to navigate, to steer; *(▸ avion)* to fly, to pilot; *(▸ cheval)* to drive; *(guider ▸ aveugle)* to guide; *(▸ dans une démarche)* to direct, to steer; **d. qn vers la sortie** to direct sb to the exit; **on vous a mal dirigé** you were misdirected; **d. les troupes vers le front** to move the troops up to the front; **un véhicule difficile à d. sur route verglacée** a vehicle which is hard to handle on an icy road; **d. un étranger**

dans le dédale administratif to guide *or* to help a foreigner through the red tape; **elle a été mal dirigée dans son choix de carrière** she had poor career guidance; **d. un élève vers un cursus littéraire** to guide *or* to steer a student towards an arts course; *Fig* **l'appât du gain dirige tous ses actes** the lure of gain motivates everything he does

5 *(acheminer ▸ marchandises)* to send; *(▸ investissements, fonds)* to channel (**vers** to); **d. des colis sur** *ou* **vers la Belgique** to send parcels to Belgium; **je fais d. mes appels sur mon autre numéro** I have my calls redirected *or* rerouted to my other number

6 *(orienter ▸ pensée)* to direct; **d. son regard vers qn** to look in the direction of sb; **tous les yeux étaient dirigés sur elle** everyone was staring at her; **d. la conversation sur un autre sujet** to steer the conversation on to *or* to switch the conversation to a new subject; **d. ses espoirs vers qn** to pin one's hopes on *or* to vest one's hopes in sb; *aussi Fig* **d. ses pas vers** to head for

7 *(adresser hostilement)* to level, to direct; **d. des accusations contre qn** to level accusations at sb; **leurs moqueries étaient dirigées contre lui** he was the butt of their jokes

8 *(braquer ▸ arme)* to aim; **il dirigea son télescope sur la lune** he trained his telescope on the moon; **une antenne dirigée vers la tour Eiffel** an aerial trained on the Eiffel tower; **lorsque la flèche est dirigée vers la droite** when the arrow points to the right; **d. un canon vers** *ou* **sur une cible** to aim *or* to level *or* to point a cannon at a target; **d. une arme sur qn** to aim a weapon at *or* to train a weapon on sb

USAGE ABSOLU **savoir d.** to be a good manager

VPR **se diriger 1** *(aller)* **se d. sur** *ou* **vers** *(frontière)* to head *or* to make for; **se d. vers la sortie** to make one's way to the exit; **les voitures se dirigent vers la ligne d'arrivée** the cars are heading for the finish; *Fig* **les pourparlers se dirigent vers un compromis** the discussions are moving towards a compromise; *Fig* **nous nous dirigeons vers le conflit armé** we're headed for armed conflict

2 *(trouver son chemin)* to find one's way; **l'avion a réussi à se d. dans la tempête** the plane found its way through the storm; **un animal qui sait se d. dans le noir** an animal which can find its way in the dark; **savoir se d. dans une ville** to be able to find one's way round a city; **on apprend aux élèves à se d. dans leurs études** pupils are taught to take charge of their own studies

---

dirigisme [diriʒism] NM state control, state intervention

dirigiste [diriʒist] ADJ interventionist

NMF partisan of state control

dirlo [dirlo] NMF *Fam Arg scol Br* head◻, *Am* principal◻

disait *etc voir* **dire**[2]

discal, -e, -aux, -ales [diskal, -o] ADJ discal

discernable [disɛrnabl] ADJ discernible, perceptible

discernement [disɛrnəmɑ̃] NM **1** *(intelligence)* (good) judgement, *Sout* discernment; **il a agi avec d.** he showed (good) judgement in what he did **2** *(distinction)* distinguishing; **il est difficile de faire le d. entre ce qui est juste et ce qui ne l'est pas** it's difficult to distinguish between what is just and what is unjust

discerner [3] [disɛrne] VT **1** *(voir)* to discern, to distinguish, to make out; **on discernait à peine les contours** you could just make out the outline

2 *(deviner)* to discern, to perceive, to detect; **j'ai cru d. une certaine colère dans sa voix** I thought I could detect a hint of anger in his voice **3** *(différencier)* **d. le bien du mal** to distinguish between right and wrong, to tell *or* distinguish right from wrong

disciple [disipl] NM **1** *Rel & Scol* disciple **2** *(partisan)* follower, disciple

disciplinable [disiplinabl] ADJ disciplinable, liable to be disciplined

disciplinaire [disiplinɛr] ADJ disciplinary

discipline [disiplin] NF **1** *(règlement)* discipline

2 *(obéissance)* discipline; **avoir de la d.** to be disciplined; **maintenir la d.** to maintain discipline; **faire grève par d. syndicale** to join an official strike; **d. de vote** voting discipline

3 *Scol & Univ (matière)* subject, discipline

4 *(fouet)* discipline, whip, scourge

discipliné, -e [disipline] ADJ **1** *(personne)* obedient, disciplined **2** *(cheveux)* neat (and tidy), well-groomed

discipliner [3] [disipline] VT **1** *(faire obéir ▸ élèves, classe)* to discipline, to (bring under) control

2 *(maîtriser ▸ instincts)* to control, to master; *(▸ pensée)* to discipline, to train

3 *(endiguer ▸ rivière)* to control

4 *(coiffer ▸ cheveux)* to groom

VPR **se discipliner** to discipline oneself

disc-jockey [diskʒɔkɛ] *(pl* **disc-jockeys***)* NMF disc jockey

disco [disko] ADJ disco; **musique d.** disco (music)

NM *(musique)* disco (music); *(danse, chanson)* disco number

NF *Fam Vieilli (discothèque)* disco

discobole [diskɔbɔl] NM *Antiq* discobolus, discobolos

discographie [diskɔgrafi] NF discography

discographique [diskɔgrafik] ADJ *(rubrique, production)* record *(avant n)*

discoïde [diskɔid], **discoïdal, -e, -aux, -ales** [diskɔidal, -o] ADJ discoid, discoidal

discompte [diskɔ̃t] = **discount**

discompter [diskɔ̃te] = **discounter**[1]

discompteur [diskɔ̃tœr] = **discounter**[2]

discontinu, -e [diskɔ̃tiny] ADJ **1** *(ligne)* broken; *(effort)* discontinuous, intermittent; **le bruit est d.** the noise comes on and off **2** *Ling & Math* discontinuous

NM **le d.** that which is discontinuous

discontinuer [7] [diskɔ̃tinɥe] VT *Littéraire* to stop, to cease

VI *Littéraire* to stop, to cease

• **sans discontinuer** ADV nonstop, continuously; **il peut parler des heures sans d.** he can talk for hours nonstop *or* on end

discontinuité [diskɔ̃tinɥite] NF *(gén) & Math* discontinuity

disconvenir [40] [diskɔ̃vənir] **disconvenir de** VT IND **je ne disconviens pas de son utilité** I don't deny that it's useful *or* its usefulness; **vous avez raison, je n'en disconviens pas** I don't deny that you're right

discophile [diskɔfil] NMF record collector, *Spéc* discophile

discordance [diskɔrdɑ̃s] NF **1** *Mus* discord, discordance, disharmony **2** *(disharmonie ▸ de couleurs, de sentiments)* lack of harmony, clash; *(▸ entre des personnes, idées)* clash, conflict, disagreement **3** *(écart)* contradiction, inconsistency; **il existe certaines discordances entre les deux récits** the two stories contain several inconsistencies

discordant, -e [diskɔrdɑ̃, -ɑ̃t] ADJ **1** *(son ▸ faux)* discordant; *(▸ criard)* harsh, grating **2** *(opposé ▸ styles, couleurs, avis, diagnostics)* clashing; **ils ont présenté des témoignages discordants** their testimonies were at variance with each other

discorde [diskɔrd] NF discord, dissension, dissention

discorder [3] [diskɔrde] VI *(couleurs, témoignages)* to clash (**avec** with); **sa voix discorde dans l'orchestre** his/her voice clashes with the orchestra

discothèque [diskɔtɛk] NF **1** *(collection)* record collection

2 *(meuble)* record case *or* holder

3 *(établissement de prêt)* record *or* music library

4 *(boîte de nuit)* disco, discotheque, night club

discount [diskunt, diskaunt] NM **1** *(rabais)* discount; **un d. de 20 pour cent** 20 percent discount, 20 percent off **2** *(technique)* discount selling; **magasin de d.** discount *Br* shop *or Am* store

ADJ INV discount *(avant n)*

discounter[1] [3] [diskunte, diskaunte] VT to sell at a discount

VI to sell at a discount

discounter[2] [diskuntœr, diskaunter] NM *(commerçant)* discounter

discoureur, -euse [diskurœr, -øz] NM,F *Péj* speechifier; **méfie-toi, c'est un grand d.** watch out, he loves the sound of his own voice

discourir [45] [diskurir] VI **1** *Littéraire (bavarder)* to talk **2** *Péj (disserter)* to speechify

discours [diskur] NM **1** *(allocution)* speech, address; **faire un d.** to make a speech; **d. de bienvenue** welcoming speech *or* address; **d. de clôture** closing speech; **d. d'inauguration** inaugural lecture *or* speech; **d.-programme** keynote speech; **d. de réception** acceptance speech; *Pol* **d. du trône** inaugural speech *(of a sovereign before a Parliamentary session)*, *Br* ≃ King's/Queen's Speech; **le d. sur l'État de l'Union** the State of the Union Speech

2 *Péj (bavardage)* chatter; **se perdre en longs d.** to talk *or* to chatter endlessly; **tous ces (beaux) d. ne servent à rien** all this fine talk doesn't get us anywhere; **rien de concret, que des d.!** nothing concrete, just (a lot of) words!

3 *Ling (langage réalisé)* speech; *(unité supérieure à la phrase)* discourse; *Gram* **d. direct** direct speech; *Gram* **d. indirect** reported *or* indirect speech; **d. rapporté** reported speech

4 *Phil* discourse

5 *(expression d'une opinion)* discourse; **le d. des jeunes** the sorts of things young people say; **tenir un d. de droite** to talk like a right-winger

discourtois, -e [diskurtwa, -az] ADJ discourteous, impolite

discourtoisement [diskurtwazmɑ̃] ADV discourteously, impolitely

discourtoisie [diskurtwazi] NF discourtesy

discouru, -e [diskury] PP *voir* **discourir**

discrédit [diskredi] NM discredit, disrepute; **le d. attaché à cette entreprise** this firm's discredited reputation; **être en d. auprès de qn** to be in disfavour with sb; **jeter le d. sur qn/qch** to discredit sb/sth; **tomber dans le d.** to fall into disrepute

discréditer [3] [diskredite] VT to discredit, to bring into disrepute

VPR **se discréditer 1** *(personne)* to bring discredit upon oneself; **se d. auprès du public** to lose one's good name **2** *(idée, pratique)* to become discredited (**auprès de** in the eyes of)

discret, -ète [diskrɛ, -ɛt] ADJ **1** *(réservé ▸ personne, attitude)* reserved, discreet; **de manière discrète** discreetly

2 *(délicat ▸ personne)* tactful, discreet; *(▸ allusion)* subtle

3 *(qui garde le secret)* discreet; **sois sans inquiétude, je serai d.** don't worry, I'll be discreet

4 *(effacé ▸ personne, manières)* unobtrusive, unassuming

5 *(dissimulé)* **sous emballage d.** in a plain wrapper

6 *(neutre ▸ toilette, style)* plain, sober, understated; *(▸ couleur)* subtle; *(▸ lumière)* subdued, soft; *(▸ parfum)* subtle; *(▸ maquillage)* light, subtle

7 *(isolé ▸ lieu)* quiet, secluded

8 *Math* discrete

discrètement [diskrɛtmɑ̃] ADV **1** *(sans être remarqué)* quietly, discreetly, unobtrusively; **entrer/sortir d.** to slip in/out (unobtrusively); **je lui en parlerai d.** I'll have a quiet word with him/her **2** *(se maquiller, se parfumer)* discreetly, lightly, subtly; *(s'habiller)* discreetly, quietly, soberly

discrétion [diskresjɔ̃] NF **1** *(réserve)* discretion, tact, tactfulness; **manquer de d.** to be tactless

2 *(modestie)* unobtrusiveness, self-effacement

3 *(sobriété ▸ d'un maquillage)* lightness, subtlety; *(▸ d'une toilette)* soberness; **s'habiller avec d.** to dress soberly

4 *(silence)* discretion; **comptez sur ma d.** you can count on my discretion; **d. assurée** *(dans une petite annonce)* write in confidence

• **à discrétion** ADV **vous pouvez manger à d.** you can eat as much as you like; **champagne à d.** unlimited champagne

• **à la discrétion de** PRÉP at the discretion of; **pourboire à la d. du client** gratuities at the discretion of the customer

discrétionnaire [diskresjɔnɛr] ADJ discretionary

discrètos [diskretos] ADV *Fam* on the quiet

discriminant, -e [diskriminɑ̃, -ɑ̃t] ADJ distinguishing, discriminating

NM discriminant

discrimination [diskriminasjɔ̃] **NF 1** *(ségrégation)* **d. positive** *Br* positive discrimination, *Am* affirmative action; **d. raciale/sexuelle** racial/sexual discrimination; **sans d. de race ni de sexe** regardless of race or sex, without discrimination on the grounds of race or sex **2** *Littéraire (distinction)* discrimination, distinction

discriminatoire [diskriminatwar] **ADJ** discriminatory

discriminer **[3]** [diskrimine] **VT** *Littéraire* to distinguish between

disculpation [diskylpasjɔ̃] **NF** exoneration; **sa d. n'a pas été facile à obtenir** it was not easy to clear him/her *or* to prove him/her innocent

disculper **[3]** [diskylpe] **VT** to exonerate (**de** from)

VPR se disculper pour se d. il invoqua l'ignorance to vindicate *or* to exonerate himself, he pleaded ignorance; **se d. de qch** to exonerate oneself from sth

discursif, -ive [diskyrsif, -iv] **ADJ 1** *(raisonné)* discursive **2** *Ling* discourse *(avant n)*

discussion [diskysjɔ̃] **NF 1** *(négociation)* talk, discussion; **avec lui la d. est impossible** he's incapable of compromise

2 *(querelle)* quarrel, argument; **pas de d.!** no arguing!, don't argue!; **il s'exécuta sans d.** he complied without arguing

3 *(débat)* debate, discussion; **ils sont en pleine d.** they're in the middle of a debate; **le projet de budget est en d.** the budget proposal is under discussion

4 *(conversation)* discussion, conversation; **dans la d., il m'a dit que…** during our conversation, he told me that…

discutable [diskytabl] **ADJ** *(fait, théorie, décision)* debatable, questionable; *(sincérité, authenticité)* questionable, doubtful; *(goût)* dubious

discutailler **[3]** [diskytaje] **VI** *Fam Péj* to quibble

discuté, -e [diskyte] **ADJ 1** *(débattu)* debated, discussed; **très d.** hotly debated **2** *(contesté ▸ nomination)* controversial, disputed; **une œuvre à l'authenticité discutée** a work of art whose authenticity is the subject of controversy *or* is disputed

discuter **[3]** [diskyte] **VT 1** *(débattre ▸ projet de loi)* to debate, to discuss; *(▸ sujet, question)* to discuss, to argue, to consider; *Fam* **d. le coup** to have a chat **2** *(contester ▸ ordres)* to question, to dispute; *(▸ véracité)* to debate, to question; *(▸ prix)* to haggle over; **un penalty qu'on discute encore** a penalty which they're still arguing about

USAGE ABSOLU suis-moi sans d. follow me without any arguments, follow me and don't argue; **tu discutes?** *Br* no ifs and buts!, *Am* no ifs, ands or buts!; **inutile de d., je ne céderai pas** it's no use arguing, I'm not going to give in

VI 1 *(parler)* to talk, to have a discussion; **on ne peut pas d. avec toi** it's impossible to have a discussion with you; **d. de** *ou* **sur** to talk about, to discuss; **nous en avons longuement discuté** we've had a long discussion about it; **d. de choses et d'autres** to talk about this and that; **2** *(négocier)* to negotiate

VPR se discuter 1 *(sujet, question)* to be debated; **le projet de loi se discute actuellement à l'Assemblée** the bill is being debated *or* is under discussion in the Assembly **2** *(point de vue)* **ça se discute** that's debatable

dise *etc voir* **dire**[2]

disert, -e [dizer, -ert] **ADJ** *Littéraire* articulate, eloquent, fluent

disette [dizet] **NF 1** *(pénurie ▸ gén)* shortage, dearth; *(▸ de nourriture)* scarcity of food, food shortage **2** *Littéraire (manque)* **d. d'argent** want *or* lack of money; **d. d'eau** drought

diseur, -euse [dizœr, -øz] **NM,F d. de bons mots** wit; **fin d.** fine talker

• **diseuse NF diseuse de bonne aventure** fortuneteller

disgrâce [disgras] **NF 1** *(défaveur)* disgrace, disfavour; **la d. d'un homme politique** a politician's disgrace; *Littéraire* **encourir la d. de qn** to incur sb's displeasure; **tomber en d.** to fall into disfavour, to fall from grace **2** *Littéraire (manque de grâce)* inelegance, awkwardness

disgracié, -e [disgrasje] **ADJ 1** *(laid)* ungraceful, ugly **2** *(en disgrâce)* disgraced

disgracier **[9]** [disgrasje] **VT** *Littéraire* to disgrace

disgracieux, -euse [disgrasjø, -øz] **ADJ 1** *(laid ▸ visage)* ugly, unattractive; *(▸ geste)* awkward, ungainly; *(▸ comportement)* uncouth; *(▸ personne)* unattractive, unappealing; *(▸ objet)* unsightly **2** *Littéraire (discourtois)* ungracious, discourteous

> Il faut noter que l'adjectif anglais **disgraceful** est un faux ami. Il signifie **honteux, scandaleux.**

disjoindre **[82]** [disʒwɛ̃dr] **VT 1** *(planches)* to break up **2** *(causes, problèmes)* to separate, to consider separately; **il faudrait d. ces deux questions** these two questions should be considered separately

VPR se disjoindre to come apart

disjoint, -e [disʒwɛ̃, -ɛ̃t] **ADJ 1** *(planches)* disjointed

2 *(causes, problèmes)* unconnected, separate

3 *Math* disjoint

4 *Mus* disjunct

disjoncter **[3]** [disʒɔ̃kte] **VT** *(circuit)* to break

VI to short-circuit; **ça a fait d. tout le circuit** it blew the whole circuit; *Fam* **il disjoncte complètement** he's cracking up, he's losing it

disjoncteur [disʒɔ̃ktœr] **NM** circuit breaker, cutout (switch), trip switch

disjonctif, -ive [disʒɔ̃ktif, -iv] **ADJ** disjunctive

NM disjunctive

disjonction [disʒɔ̃ksjɔ̃] **NF 1** *Biol* disjunction **2** *Jur* **d. d'instance** disjoinder of proceedings

disjonctive [disʒɔ̃ktiv] *voir* **disjonctif**

dislocation [dislɔkasjɔ̃] **NF 1** *(d'une caisse)* breaking up; *(d'un empire)* dismantling; *(d'un parti)* breaking up, disintegration; *(d'une manifestation)* breaking up, dispersal

2 *Méd & Phys* dislocation

3 *(contorsion)* contorsion

4 *Géol* fault

disloqué, -e [dislɔke] **ADJ 1** *(machine)* dismantled **2** *(empire, État etc)* dismembered, broken up **3** *Méd* dislocated

disloquer **[3]** [dislɔke] **VT 1** *(caisse)* to take to pieces, to break up; *(corps)* to mangle **2** *(faire éclater ▸ empire)* to dismantle; *(▸ parti)* to break up **3** *Méd* to dislocate

VPR se disloquer 1 *(meuble)* to come *or* to fall apart, to fall to pieces

2 *(fédération)* to disintegrate, to break up; *(empire)* to break up

3 *(se disperser ▸ manifestation)* to disperse, to break up

4 *Méd (articulation)* to be dislocated; **se d. l'épaule** to dislocate one's shoulder

5 *(se contorsionner)* to contort oneself

disneylandisation [disnelɑ̃dizasjɔ̃] **NF** *(d'un lieu, de l'histoire, de la culture)* Disneyfication

disneylandiser **[3]** [disnelɑ̃dize] **VT** *(lieu, histoire, culture)* to Disneyfy

disparaître **[91]** [disparetr] **VI 1** *(se dissiper ▸ peur, joie)* to evaporate, to fade, to disappear; *(▸ douleur, problème, odeur)* to disappear; *(▸ bruit)* to stop, to subside; *(▸ brouillard)* to clear, to vanish; **faire d. qch** *(gén)* to remove sth; *(supprimer)* to get rid of sth; **ce médicament a fait d. ma migraine** the medicine got rid of my migraine; **fais-moi d. cette horreur!** get that revolting thing out of my sight!; **il a fait d. tous mes doutes** he dispelled all my doubts; *Com* **tout doit d.** everything must go

2 *(devenir invisible ▸ soleil, lune)* to disappear; *(▸ côte, bateau)* to vanish, to disappear; **les rues ont disparu sous la neige** the roads have disappeared under the snow; **elle a disparu dans la foule** she vanished into the crowd; *Fam* **disparais, je t'ai assez vu** clear off, I've had enough of you

3 *(être inexplicablement absent)* to disappear, to vanish; **le temps que j'arrive, la clef/ma sœur avait disparu** by the time I got there, the key/my sister had disappeared; **la petite fille a disparu il y a une semaine** the little girl disappeared *or* went missing a week ago; **d. sans laisser de traces** to disappear *or* vanish without trace; **faire d. qn/qch** to conceal sb/sth; *Hum* **où est-ce que tu as encore fait d. les clés?** where have you hidden the keys now?; *Fam* **d. de la circulation** *ou* **dans la nature** to vanish into thin air

4 *(ne plus exister ▸ espèce, race)* to die out, to become extinct; *(▸ langue, coutume)* to die out, to disappear; *(mourir)* to pass away, to die; *Euph* **faire d. qn** to eliminate sb, to have sb removed; **d. en mer** to be lost at sea

disparate [disparat] **1** *(hétérogène ▸ objets, éléments)* disparate, dissimilar **2** *(mal accordé ▸ mobilier)* ill-assorted, non-matching; *(▸ couleurs)* clashing; *(▸ couple)* ill-assorted, ill-matched; **deux chaises disparates** two chairs that don't match

disparité [disparite] **NF** disparity (**de** in); **une d. entre deux éléments** a disparity between two elements

disparition [disparisjɔ̃] **NF 1** *(du brouillard)* lifting, clearing; *(du soleil)* sinking, setting; *(d'une côte, d'un bateau)* vanishing; *(de la peur, du bruit)* fading away; *(du doute)* disappearance; **à prendre jusqu'à d. de la douleur** to be taken until the pain disappears *or* stops

2 *(absence ▸ d'une personne, d'un porte-monnaie)* disappearance; **depuis la d. du bébé** since the baby went missing *or* disappeared; **j'ai remarqué la d. de ma carte de crédit deux jours plus tard** I first missed my credit card two days later

3 *(extinction ▸ d'une espèce)* extinction; *(▸ d'une langue, d'une culture)* dying out, disappearance

4 *(mort)* death, disappearance; **après sa d.** after his death

disparu, -e [dispary] **PP** *voir* **disparaître**

ADJ 1 *(mort)* dead; **porté d.** *(soldat)* missing (in action); *(marin)* lost at sea; *(passager, victime)* missing believed dead **2** *(espèce)* extinct; *(langue)* dead; *(coutume, culture)* vanished, dead; *(ère, époque)* bygone

NM,F 1 *(défunt)* dead person; **les disparus** the dead; **les disparus en mer** *(marins)* men lost at sea; **nos chers disparus** our dear departed **2** *(personne introuvable)* missing person

dispatcher[1] [dispatʃœr] **NM** dispatcher

dispatcher[2] **[3]** [dispatʃe] **VT** *(produits)* to distribute; *(personnes)* to spread out

dispatching [dispatʃiŋ] **NM** *(du courrier)* routing

dispendieuse [dispɑ̃djøz] *voir* **dispendieux**

dispendieusement [dispɑ̃djøzmɑ̃] **ADV** *Littéraire* extravagantly, expensively

dispendieux, -euse [dispɑ̃djø, -øz] **ADJ** *Littéraire* expensive, costly

dispensaire [dispɑ̃sɛr] **NM** clinic

dispensateur, -trice [dispɑ̃satœr, -tris] **NM,F** dispenser

dispense [dispɑ̃s] **NF 1** *(exemption)* exemption; **d. d'oral/du service militaire** exemption from an oral exam/from military service

2 *(certificat)* exemption certificate

3 *(autorisation spéciale)* **d. d'âge** = special permission for people under or over the age limit

4 *Rel* dispensation

dispenser **[3]** [dispɑ̃se] **VT 1** *(exempter)* **d. qn de qch/de faire qch** to exempt sb from sth/from doing sth; **il est dispensé de service militaire** he is exempt *or* exempted from military service; **se faire d. de gymnastique** to be excused (from) gym; **cela ne te dispense pas de payer** this doesn't exempt you from paying; **je vous dispense de vos commentaires** you can keep your remarks to yourself **2** *Rel* **d. qn de qch** to release sb from sth **3** *(donner ▸ charité)* to dispense, to administer; *(▸ parole)* to utter; **d. des soins aux malades** to provide patients with medical care

VPR se dispenser se d. de *(obligation)* to get out of; **je me dispenserais bien de cette corvée!** I could do without this chore!; **peut-on se d. de venir à la répétition?** is it possible to skip the rehearsal?; **un élève qui peut se d. de travailler en français** a pupil who can afford not to work at his French

dispersal, -als [dispersal] **NM** *Aviat* apron

dispersant, -e [dispersɑ̃, -ɑ̃t] **ADJ** dispersive

NM dispersant

dispersé, -e [disperse] **ADJ 1** *(famille, peuple)* scattered; *(habitations)* scattered, spread out **2**

Fig **dans mon ancien poste j'étais trop d.** in my old job, I had too many different things to do

disperser **[3]** [disperse] **VT 1** *(répandre ▸ cendres, graines)* to scatter
2 *(brume, brouillard)* to disperse, to lift
3 *(efforts)* to dissipate; *(attention)* to divide
4 *(foule, manifestants)* to disperse, to break up, to scatter; *(collection)* to break up, to scatter
5 *(troupes, policiers)* to spread out
VPR se disperser 1 *(brume, brouillard)* to lift, to disperse; *(nuages)* to disperse, to break up **2** *(manifestation, foule)* to disperse, to break up **3** *(dans son travail)* to tackle too many things at once; **la production s'est (trop) dispersée** the firm has overdiversified

dispersion [dispersjɔ̃] **NF 1** *(de cendres, de graines)* scattering
2 *(de la brume, du brouillard)* dispersal, lifting
3 *(de troupes, de policiers)* spreading out
4 *(d'une foule, de manifestants)* dispersal
5 *(des forces, de l'énergie)* waste; *(de l'attention)* dividing; **une trop grande d. de la production** over-diversification in manufacturing
6 *Chim & Phys* dispersion

disponibilité [disponibilite] **NF 1** *(d'une fourniture, d'un service)* availability
2 *(liberté)* availability *(for an occupation)*; **d. d'esprit** open-mindedness, receptiveness; **avoir une grande d. d'esprit** to be very open-minded
3 *Admin* **mise en d.** (extended) leave; **professeur en d.** teacher on (extended) leave; **se mettre en d.** to take leave of absence
4 *Mil* **la d.** the reserve; **mettre qn en d.** to release sb temporarily from duty
5 *Jur* **d. des biens** (owner's) free disposal of property
• **disponibilités NFPL** *Fin* available funds, liquid assets; **disponibilités en caisse** cash in hand; **disponibilités monétaires** money supply; **disponibilités du stock** items available in stock

disponible [disponibl] **ADJ 1** *(utilisable ▸ article, service)* available; **il n'y avait plus un siège (de) d.** there weren't any seats left, no seats were available; **ces articles sont disponibles en magasin** these items can be supplied from stock; *Ordinat* **d. pour Mac/PC** available for the Mac/PC; **revenu d.** disposable income
2 *(libre ▸ personne)* free, available; **êtes-vous d. ce soir?** are you free tonight?
3 *(ouvert ▸ personne)* receptive, open-minded; **mon père a toujours été quelqu'un de d.** my father has always been ready to listen
4 *Admin* on leave of absence; *Mil* **officier d.** unattached officer, half-pay officer
5 *Fin* available
NMF *Admin* civil servant on (extended) leave of absence; *Mil* reservist
NM *Com* stock items; *Fin* liquid *or* available assets

dispos, -e [dispo, -oz] **ADJ** *(personne)* in good form *or* shape; *(esprit)* alert

disposé, -e [dispoze] **ADJ 1** *(arrangé)* **bien/mal d.** well/poorly laid out **2** *(personne)* **bien/mal d.** in a good/bad mood; **être bien/mal d. à l'égard de** *ou* **envers qn** to be well-disposed/ill-disposed towards sb

disposer **[3]** [dispoze] **VT 1** *(arranger ▸ verres, assiettes)* to lay, to set; *(▸ fleurs)* to arrange; *(▸ meubles)* to place, to arrange; **d. des convives autour d'une table** to seat guests at a table; **j'ai disposé la chambre autrement** I've changed the layout of the bedroom **2** *(inciter)* **d. qn à** to incline sb to *or* towards; **l'isolement me disposait à l'écriture** being on my own induced me to write **3** *(préparer)* **d. qn à** to prepare sb for; **ses études ne le disposent pas à la recherche** his course of studies does not prepare him for research *or* to do research; **être disposé à faire qch** to feel disposed *or* to be willing to do sth; **être peu disposé à faire qch** to be disinclined to do sth
VI *(partir)* **vous pouvez d.** you may leave *or* go
• **disposer de VT IND 1** *(avoir)* to have (at one's disposal *or* available); **je ne dispose que de très peu d'argent liquide** I don't have much cash (available); **les renseignements dont je dispose** the information at my disposal; **le directeur va vous recevoir, mais sachez qu'il ne dispose que de trente minutes** the manager can see you now, but he only has half an hour **2** *(utiliser)* to use; **puis-je d. de votre téléphone?** may I use your phone?; **disposez de moi comme il vous plaira** I am at your service **3** *Jur* **d. de ses biens** to dispose of one's property
VPR se disposer se d. à faire qch to prepare to do sth; **je me disposais à partir** I was preparing to leave

> Il faut noter que le verbe anglais **to dispose of** est un faux ami. Il signifie **se débarrasser de**.

dispositif [dispozitif] **NM 1** *(appareil, mécanisme)* machine, device; **d. d'alarme/de sûreté** alarm/safety device; *Ordinat* **d. d'alimentation** *(électrique)* power unit; *(pour papier)* sheet feed; *Ordinat* **d. d'alimentation feuille à feuille** *(d'une imprimante)* cut sheet feed, stacker; *Ordinat* **d. d'alimentation papier** *(d'une imprimante)* sheet *or* paper feed; *Aut* **d. antidémarrage** engine immobilizer; *Rad* **d. antiparasite** suppressor; *Électron* **d. de balayage** scanning device; **d. de commande/de manœuvre** operating/controlling gear *or* mechanism; **d. de coupure** cut-out (device); *Ordinat* **d. externe** external device; *Aut* **d. de préchauffage** pre-heater; *Tél* **d. de renvoi automatique d'appels** call-forwarding device; *Ordinat* **d. de sortie** output device; *Ordinat* **d. de stockage** storage device; *Ordinat* **d. de visualisation** display unit **2** *(mesures)* plan, measure; **il s'agit d'un d. gouvernemental pour favoriser l'emploi des jeunes** it's a government plan to stimulate youth employment; **un important d. policier sera mis en place** there will be a large police presence **3** *Mil* plan; **d. d'attaque** plan of attack; **d. de défense** defence system

disposition [dispozisjɔ̃] **NF 1** *(arrangement ▸ de couverts)* layout; *(▸ de fleurs, de livres, de meubles)* arrangement; **la d. du terrain** the lie of the land; **la d. des pièces dans notre maison** the layout of the rooms in our house; **la d. de la vitrine** the window display; *Ordinat* **d. de texte/de clavier** text/keyboard layout
2 *(fait d'arranger ▸ des couverts)* laying out, setting; *(▸ des meubles)* placing, arranging; *(▸ des fleurs)* arranging
3 *(tendance ▸ d'une personne)* tendency; **avoir une d. à la négligence/à grossir** to have a tendency to carelessness/to put on weight
4 *Jur (clause)* clause, stipulation; **les dispositions testamentaires de...** the last will and testament of...; **d. fiscale** tax provision
5 *Jur (jouissance)* disposal; **d. à titre gratuit** provision free of charge; **avoir la d. de ses biens** to be free to dispose of one's property
6 *Admin* **mise à la d.** *Br* secondment, *Am* temporary transfer
• **dispositions NFPL 1** *(humeur)* mood; **être dans de bonnes/mauvaises dispositions** to be in a good/bad mood; **attends qu'il soit dans** *ou* **revenu à de meilleures dispositions** wait until he's in a better mood; **être dans de bonnes dispositions pour faire qch** to be in the right mood to do *or* for doing sth; **être dans de bonnes/mauvaises dispositions à l'égard de qn** to be well-disposed/ill-disposed towards sb **2** *(mesures)* measures; **prendre des dispositions** *(précautions, arrangements)* to make arrangements, to take steps; *(préparatifs)* to make preparations; **prends tes dispositions pour être libre ce jour-là** make arrangements *or* arrange to be free that day **3** *(aptitude)* aptitude, ability, talent; **avoir des dispositions pour** to have a talent for
• **à la disposition de,** *Suisse* **à disposition de PRÉP** at the disposal of; **avoir qch à sa d.** to have sth at one's disposal; **mettre** *ou* **tenir qch à la d. de qn** to place sth at sb's disposal, to make sth available to sb; **se tenir à la d. de** to make oneself available for; **je suis** *ou* **me tiens à votre entière d. pour tout autre renseignement** should you require further information, please feel free to contact me

disproportion [disprɔpɔrsjɔ̃] **NF** disproportion

disproportionné, -e [disprɔpɔrsjɔne] **ADJ** *(inégal)* disproportionate; **d. à** out of (all) proportion to; **avoir des jambes disproportionnées** to have disproportionately long legs

dispute [dispyt] **NF** quarrel, argument

disputé, -e [dispyte] **ADJ une question très disputée** a very controversial *or* hotly disputed matter; **un match très d.** a very hard-fought match; **ce poste sera très d.** there will be a lot of competition for the position; **c'est un héritage d. par tous les membres de la famille** the entire family is quarrelling over the inheritance

disputer **[3]** [dispyte] **VT 1** *(participer à ▸ match, tournoi)* to play; *(▸ course)* to run; *(▸ combat)* to fight; **d. le terrain** *Mil* to dispute every inch of ground; *Fig* to fight tooth and nail
2 *(tenter de prendre)* **d. qch à qn** to fight with sb over sth; **d. la première place à qn** to contend *or* to vie with sb for first place
3 *Fam (réprimander)* to scold, to tell off; **tu vas te faire d.!** you're in for it!
4 *Littéraire (contester)* to deny; **je ne vous dispute pas le succès de votre opération** I don't deny the success of your operation
VI *Arch (se quereller)* to quarrel, to argue, to fight
• **disputer de VT IND** *Littéraire* to debate, to discuss
VPR se disputer 1 *(avoir lieu)* to take place; **le tournoi se disputera demain** the tournament will take place *or* will be played tomorrow
2 *(se quereller)* to quarrel, to argue, to fight
3 se d. qch to fight over sth; **ils se disputent le même poste** they are fighting over the same job
4 se d. avec to have an argument *or* a row with; **je me suis disputé avec Anne pour une question d'argent** I had an argument *or* a row with Anne about money

disquaire [diskɛr] **NMF 1** *(commerçant)* record dealer; **tu trouveras ça chez un d.** you'll find this in a record shop **2** *(vendeur)* record salesman, *f* saleswoman

disqualification [diskalifikasjɔ̃] **NF** disqualification

disqualifier **[9]** [diskalifje] **VT 1** *Sport* to disqualify; **l'équipe s'est fait d.** the team was disqualified **2** *(discréditer)* to discredit, to bring discredit on
VPR se disqualifier to lose credibility

disque [disk] **NM 1** *(cercle plat)* disc; **d. de stationnement** parking disc
2 *Anat, Astron & Math* disc
3 *Sport* discus
4 *Aut* **d. d'embrayage** clutch plate
5 *(enregistrement)* record, disc; **mettre un d.** to play a record; **d. audionumérique** compact disc; **d. compact** compact disc; **d. compact interactif** interactive CD, CD-I; **d. compact vidéo** video compact disc; **d. laser** laser disc; **d. vidéo** videodisc; **d. vidéo numérique** digital video disk
6 *Ordinat* disk; **d. amovible** removable disk; **d. cible** target disk; **d. de démarrage** boot disk; **d. de destination** destination disk; **d. dur** hard disk; **d. fixe** fixed disk; **d. magnétique** magnetic disk; **d. maître** master disk; **d. optique** optical disk; **d. optique compact** CD-ROM; **d. optique numérique** digital optical disk; **d. souple, mini d.** floppy disk; **d. source** source disk; **d. système** system disk
7 *Rail* disc signal

disquette [diskɛt] **NF** floppy (disk), diskette; **sur d.** on diskette, on floppy; **d. cible** target disk; **d. de copie** copy disk; **d. de démarrage** boot disk, start-up disk; **d. de démonstration,** *Fam* **d. démo** demo disk; **d. de destination** destination disk; **d. de diagnostic** diagnostic disk; **d. (à) double densité** double density disk; **d. haute densité** high-density disk; **d. d'installation** installation disk, installer; **d. magnétique** magnetic disk; **d. optique** optical disk, floptical disk; **d. programme** program disk; **d. (à) simple densité** single density disk; **d. source** source disk; **d. système** system disk; **d. vierge** blank unformatted disk

disruptif, -ive [disryptif, -iv] **ADJ** *Élec* disruptive

dissection [disɛksjɔ̃] **NF 1** *Méd* dissection **2** *(analyse)* (close *or* minute) analysis, dissection

dissemblable [disɑ̃blabl] **ADJ** different, dissimilar

dissemblance [disɑ̃blɑ̃s] **NF** dissimilarity, difference

dissémination [diseminasjɔ̃] **NF** *(de graines)* scattering; *(de troupes)* scattering, spreading, dispersion; *(de maisons, des habitants)* scattering; *(d'idées)* spread, dissemination

disséminer **[3]** [disemine] **VT** *(graines)* to scatter; *(idées)* to spread, to disseminate; **quelques maisons disséminées** a few scattered houses; **les écoles sont très disséminées** the schools are very thin on the ground; **sa famille est disséminée dans le monde** her family is scattered all over the world
VPR se disséminer *(graines)* to scatter; *(personnes)* to spread (out)

dissension [disɑ̃sjɔ̃] **NF** disagreement, difference of opinion

dissentiment [disɑ̃timɑ̃] **NM** *Littéraire* disagreement

disséquer **[18]** [diseke] **VT 1** *Méd* to dissect **2** *(analyser)* to dissect, to carry out a close *or* minute analysis of

dissert [disɛrt] **NF** *Fam Scol & Univ (abrév* **dissertation**) essay

dissertation [disɛrtasjɔ̃] **NF 1** *Scol & Univ* essay **2** *Péj (discours)* (long and boring) speech; **on a eu droit à une d. sur la politesse** we were treated to a lecture on politeness

disserter **[3]** [disɛrte] **VI 1 d. sur** *(à l'écrit)* to write an essay on; *(à l'oral)* to discourse on **2** *Fig Péj* to hold forth on *or* about

dissidence [disidɑ̃s] **NF 1** *(rébellion)* dissidence; **un mouvement de d.** a rebel movement **2** *(dissidents)* dissidents, rebels

dissident, -e [disidɑ̃, -ɑ̃t] **ADJ 1** *(rebelle)* dissident *(avant n)*, rebel *(avant n)*; **un groupe d.** a splinter *or* breakaway group **2** *Rel* dissenting
NM,F 1 *(rebelle)* dissident, rebel **2** *Rel* dissenter, nonconformist

dissimilation [disimilasjɔ̃] **NF** *Ling* dissimilation

dissimilitude [disimilityd] **NF** dissimilarity

dissimulateur, -trice [disimylatœr, -tris] **ADJ** dissembling
NM,F dissembler

dissimulation [disimylasjɔ̃] **NF 1** *(fait de cacher)* concealment **2** *(hypocrisie)* deceit, dissimulation, hypocrisy **agir avec d.** to act in an underhand way **3** *Jur* **d. d'actif** (fraudulent) concealment of assets

dissimulatrice [disimylatris] *voir* **dissimulateur**

dissimulé, -e [disimyle] **ADJ 1** *(invisible ▸ haine, jalousie)* concealed; **avec un plaisir non d.** with unconcealed delight **2** *Péj (fourbe)* deceitful, hypocritical

dissimuler **[3]** [disimyle] **VT 1** *(cacher à la vue)* to hide (from sight); **des arbres dissimulaient la maison** the house was hidden by trees **2** *(ne pas révéler ▸ identité)* to conceal; *(▸ sentiments, difficultés)* to hide, to conceal, to cover up; *(▸ faute)* to cover up; **n'essaie pas de me d. les faits** don't try to conceal the facts from me; **je ne vous dissimulerai pas que...** I won't hide from you (the fact) that...
VPR se dissimuler 1 *(se cacher)* to hide (oneself); **se d. derrière un rideau** to hide (oneself) behind a curtain **2 se d. qch** to hide sth from oneself; **ne nous dissimulons pas la difficulté de l'entreprise** let us not delude ourselves as to the difficulties involved in the venture

dissipateur, -trice [disipatœr, -tris] *Littéraire* **ADJ** wasteful, spendthrift
NM,F squanderer, spendthrift

dissipation [disipasjɔ̃] **NF 1** *(de nuages)* dispersal, clearing; *(du brouillard)* lifting; *(de craintes, de soupçons)* dispelling; *(d'un malentendu)* clearing up; **après d. des brouillards matinaux** after the morning mist lifts *or* clears
2 *(d'un héritage)* wasting, squandering
3 *Littéraire (débauche)* dissipation
4 *(indiscipline)* lack of discipline, misbehaviour
5 *Phys (de l'énergie)* dissipation

dissipatrice [disipatris] *voir* **dissipateur**

dissipé, -e [disipe] **ADJ 1** *(indiscipliné ▸ classe)* unruly, rowdy, undisciplined **2** *(débauché)* dissolute

dissiper **[3]** [disipe] **VT 1** *(brouillard, fumée)* to disperse, to clear away; *(nuages)* to break up, to disperse; *(malentendu)* to clear up; *(crainte, soupçons)* to dispel **2** *(dilapider ▸ héritage, patrimoine)* to dissipate, to squander **3** *(distraire)* to distract, to divert; **il se laisse facilement d.** he is easily distracted
VPR se dissiper 1 *(orage)* to blow over; *(nuages)* to break up, to disperse; *(brouillard)* to lift, to clear; *(fumée)* to clear **2** *(craintes, soupçons, malentendu)* to disappear, to vanish; *(migraine, douleurs)* to go, to disappear **3** *(s'agiter ▸ enfant)* to misbehave, to be undisciplined *or* unruly; **il se dissipe vite** his attention soon wanders

dissociable [disɔsjabl] **ADJ 1** *(questions, chapitres)* separable **2** *Chim* dissociable

dissociatif, -ive [disɔsjatif, -iv] **ADJ** dissociative

dissociation [disɔsjasjɔ̃] **NF 1** *(de questions, de chapitres, d'une famille)* separation **2** *Chim* dissociation

dissociative [disɔsjativ] *voir* **dissociatif**

dissocier **[9]** [disɔsje] **VT 1** *(questions, chapitres)* to separate; *(famille)* to break up **2** *Chim* to dissociate
VPR se dissocier 1 *(personnes)* to break up **2 se d. de** to dissociate oneself from

dissolu, -e [disɔly] **ADJ** *Littéraire* dissolute

dissolubilité [disɔlybilite] **NF** *(d'une assemblée)* dissolubility

dissoluble [disɔlybl] **ADJ** *(assemblée)* which can be dissolved, dissoluble

dissolution [disɔlysjɔ̃] **NF 1** *(d'un produit, d'un comprimé)* dissolving; **remuer jusqu'à d. du sucre** stir until the sugar has dissolved
2 *(d'une société)* winding-up, dissolution; *(d'un groupe)* splitting up, breaking up
3 *Jur & Pol (d'un mariage, d'une association, d'un parlement)* dissolution; *(d'un contrat)* dissolution, termination
4 *(pour pneus)* rubber solution
5 *Littéraire (débauche)* dissoluteness, debauchery

dissolvait *etc voir* **dissoudre**

dissolvant, -e [disɔlvɑ̃, -ɑ̃t] **ADJ 1** *(substance)* solvent, dissolvent **2** *Littéraire (climat)* enervating; *(doctrine)* corrupt
NM 1 *(détachant)* solvent **2** *(de vernis à ongles)* **d. (gras)** nail polish remover

dissonance [disɔnɑ̃s] **NF 1** *(cacophonie)* dissonance, discord
2 *Littéraire (de couleurs, d'idées)* discord, clash, mismatch
3 *Psy & Mktg* **d. cognitive** cognitive dissonance
4 *Mus* dissonance

dissonant, -e [disɔnɑ̃, -ɑ̃t] **ADJ 1** *(sons, cris)* dissonant, discordant, jarring; *Littéraire (couleurs)* discordant, clashing **2** *Mus* discordant

dissoudre **[87]** [disudr] **VT 1** *(diluer ▸ sel, sucre, comprimé)* to dissolve; **faites d. le comprimé** dissolve the tablet **2** *(désunir ▸ assemblée, mariage)* to dissolve; *(▸ contrat)* to dissolve, to terminate; *(▸ parti)* to break up, to dissolve; *(▸ association)* to dissolve, to break up, to bring to an end; *(▸ entreprise)* to wind up, to dissolve
VPR se dissoudre 1 *(sel, sucre, comprimé)* to dissolve **2** *(groupement)* to break up, to come to an end

dissuader **[3]** [disɥade] **VT d. qn de faire qch** to dissuade sb from doing sth; **je l'ai dissuadé d'acheter une voiture** I dissuaded him from *or* talked him out of buying a car

dissuasif, -ive [disɥazif, -iv] **ADJ 1** *(qui décourage)* dissuasive, discouraging **2** *Mil* deterrent

dissuasion [disɥazjɔ̃] **NF** dissuasion; **d. nucléaire** nuclear deterrent
• de dissuasion ADJ *(puissance)* dissuasive

dissuasive [disɥaziv] *voir* **dissuasif**

dissyllabe [disilab] **ADJ** disyllabic
NM disyllable

dissyllabique [disilabik] **ADJ** disyllabic

dissymétrie [disimetri] **NF** dissymmetry

dissymétrique [disimetrik] **ADJ** dissymmetrical

distance [distɑ̃s] **NF 1** *(intervalle ▸ dans l'espace)* distance; **la d. entre Pau et Tarbes** *ou* **de Pau à Tarbes** the distance between Pau and Tarbes *or* from Pau to Tarbes; **on ne voyait rien à cette d.** you couldn't see anything at that distance; **on les entend à une d. de 100 mètres** you can hear them (from) 100 metres away *or* at a distance of 100 metres; **à quelle d. sommes-nous de l'hôtel?** how far are we from the hotel?; **nous habitons à une grande/courte d. de la ville** we live far (away)/a short distance (away) from the city; *Hum* **il a mis une d. respectueuse entre lui et le fisc** he made sure he stayed well out of reach of the taxman; **garder ses distances** to stay aloof, to remain distant; **prendre ses distances** *Sport* to space out; *Mil* to spread out in *or* to form open order; **prendre ses distances envers** *ou* **à l'égard de qn** to hold oneself aloof *or* to keep one's distance from sb; *Aut* **d. d'arrêt/de freinage** stopping/braking distance
2 *(parcours)* distance; **la jument est excellente sur cette d.** the mare is particularly suited to that distance; *aussi Fig* **tenir la d.** to go the distance, to stay the course
3 *(intervalle ▸ dans le temps)* **ils sont nés à deux mois de d.** they were born within two months of each other; **il l'a revue à deux mois de d.** he saw her again two months later
4 *(écart, différence)* gap, gulf; **ce malentendu a mis une certaine d. entre nous** we've become rather distant from each other since that misunderstanding
5 *(recul)* **prendre de la d. (par rapport à un événement)** to stand back (in order to assess an event)
6 *Géom* distance
7 *Opt* **d. focale** focal length
• à distance ADV 1 *(dans l'espace)* at a distance, from a distance; **cette chaîne peut se commander à d.** this stereo has a remote control; **tenir qn à d.** to keep sb at a distance *or* at arm's length; **se tenir à d. (de)** to keep one's distance (from) **2** *Ordinat* **à d.** remote **3** *(dans le temps)* with time
• de distance, en distance ADV at intervals, in places

distancement [distɑ̃smɑ̃] **NM** *(de cheval)* disqualification

distancer **[16]** [distɑ̃se] **VT 1** *Sport* to outdistance; **se laisser d.** to drop away, to fall *or* to lag behind **2** *(surclasser)* to outdistance, to outstrip; **le parti socialiste distance la droite de deux points** the socialists are two points ahead of the conservatives; **se laisser d.** to fall behind; **se faire d. économiquement** to lag behind economically **3** *Courses de chevaux* to disqualify

distanciation [distɑ̃sjasjɔ̃] **NF 1** *(gén)* detachment **2** *Théât* **l'effet de d.** the alienation effect

distancier **[9]** [distɑ̃sje] **se distancier VPR se d. de qn/qch** to distance oneself from sb/sth

distant, -e [distɑ̃, -ɑ̃t] **ADJ 1** *(dans l'espace)* far away, distant; **être d. de qch** to be far *or* some distance from sth; **les deux écoles sont distantes de cinq kilomètres** the (two) schools are five kilometres away from each other **2** *(dans le temps)* distant; **ces événements sont distants de plusieurs années** these events took place several years apart **3** *(personne)* aloof, distant; *(air, sourire)* remote, distant; *(rapports)* distant, cool; **elle est très distante avec moi** she's being very distant towards me

distendre **[73]** [distɑ̃dr] **VT 1** *(étirer ▸ ressort)* to stretch, to overstretch; *(▸ peau)* to stretch, to distend; *(▸ muscle)* to strain; *(▸ estomac)* to distend **2** *(rendre moins intime ▸ liens)* to loosen
VPR se distendre 1 *(s'étirer ▸ ressort)* to stretch; *(▸ peau, estomac)* to stretch, to become distended **2** *(devenir moins intime ▸ liens)* to loosen

distension [distɑ̃sjɔ̃] **NF** *(▸ d'un ressort)* slackening (off); *(▸ de la peau)* stretching; *(▸ d'un muscle)* straining; *(étirage ▸ de l'estomac)* distension

distillat [distila] **NM** *Chim* distillate

distillateur [distilatœr] **NM** *(personne)* distiller

distillation [distilasjɔ̃] **NF** distillation, distilling; *Pétr* **d. fractionnée** fractional distillation

distiller **[3]** [distile] **VT 1** *(alcool, pétrole, eau)* to distil **2** *Littéraire (ennui, tristesse)* to exude
VI *Chim* to distil

distillerie [distilri] **NF 1** *(usine, atelier)* distillery **2** *(activité)* distilling

distinct, -e [distɛ̃, -ɛ̃kt] **ADJ 1** *(clair, net)* distinct, clear **2** *(différent)* distinct, different; **un résultat d. du précédent** a result different from the previous one

distinctement [distɛ̃ktəmɑ̃] **ADV** distinctly, clearly

distinctif, -ive [distɛ̃ktif, -iv] ADJ *(qui sépare)* distinctive, distinguishing

distinction [distɛ̃ksjɔ̃] NF **1** *(différence)* distinction; **faire une d. entre deux choses** to make *or* to draw a distinction between two things **2** *(élégance, raffinement)* refinement, distinction; **avoir de la d.** to be distinguished **3** *(honneur)* honour; *(décoration)* decoration

• **sans distinction** ADV indiscriminately, without exception; **il a renvoyé tout le monde sans d.** he fired everybody without exception

• **sans distinction de** PRÉP irrespective of

distinctive [distɛ̃ktiv] *voir* **distinctif**

distinguable [distɛ̃gabl] ADJ distinguishable

distingué, -e [distɛ̃ge] ADJ **1** *(élégant ▸ personne)* distinguished; *(▸ manières, air)* refined, elegant, distinguished; **ça ne fait pas très d.** it's not very elegant **2** *(brillant, éminent)* distinguished, eminent **3** *(dans une lettre)* **veuillez croire en l'assurance de mes sentiments distingués** *(à quelqu'un dont on connaît le nom) Br* yours sincerely, *Am* sincerely yours; *(à quelqu'un dont on ne connaît pas le nom) Br* yours faithfully, *Am* sincerely yours

distinguer [3] [distɛ̃ge] VT **1** *(voir)* to distinguish, to make out; **on distingue à peine leur contour** you can hardly distinguish their outline

2 *(entendre)* to hear, to distinguish, to make out; **je ne distingue pas les aigus** I can't make out *or* hear high notes

3 *(percevoir)* **je commence à d. ses mobiles** I'm beginning to understand his motives; **j'ai cru d. une certaine colère dans sa voix** I thought I detected a note of anger in his/her voice

4 *(différencier)* to distinguish; **il est facile à d. de son jumeau** he and his twin brother are easy to tell apart; **je n'arrive pas à les d.** I can't tell which is which, I can't tell them apart; **je n'arrive pas à d. ces deux arbres** I can't tell the difference between these two trees; **comment d. le diamant du zircon?** how can you tell the difference between diamond and zircon?

5 *(honorer)* to single out (for reward), to honour

USAGE ABSOLU *(voir)* **on distingue mal dans le noir** it's hard to see in the dark

VPR **se distinguer 1** *(être vu)* to be seen *or* distinguished

2 se d. de qn/qch (par) *(se différencier)* to be distinguishable from sb/sth (by); **le safran se distingue du curcuma par l'odeur** you can tell the difference between saffron and turmeric by their smell

3 *(se faire remarquer)* to distinguish oneself; **son fils s'est distingué en musique** his son has distinguished himself *or* done particularly well in music

4 *(devenir célèbre)* to become famous; **elle devait se d. sur la scène de l'opéra** she was to become a famous opera singer

5 se d. de *(être supérieur à)* to stand out from; **il se distingue de tous les autres poètes** he stands out from all other poets

distinguo [distɛ̃go] NM distinction

distique [distik] NM *Littérature* distich

distordre [76] [distɔrdr] VT to twist

VPR **se distordre** to twist, to distort

distorsion [distɔrsjɔ̃] NF **1** *(déformation)* distortion; *Électron* **d. de fréquence** frequency distortion; **d. de l'image** *ou* **d'image** image *or* picture distortion; *Mktg* **d. sélective** selective distortion **2** *(déséquilibre)* imbalance

distraction [distraksjɔ̃] NF **1** *(caractère étourdi)* absent-mindedness; *(acte)* lapse in concentration; **par d.** inadvertently; **excusez ma d.** forgive me, I wasn't concentrating

2 *(détente)* **il te faut de la d.** you need to have your mind taken off things

3 *(activité)* source of entertainment; **la lecture et le cinéma sont mes distractions préférées** reading and going to the cinema are my favourite forms of recreation *or* what I like doing best in my spare time; **il n'y a pas assez de distractions le soir** there's not enough to do at night

4 *Jur* appropriation; **d. des dépens** award of costs

distraire [112] [distrɛr] VT **1** *(déranger)* to distract; **d. qn de ses travaux** to distract sb from his work **2** *(amuser)* to entertain, to divert; **j'aime bien que tu viennes me voir, ça me distrait** I like you to visit me, it gives me something else to think about **3** *(détourner)* **d. un ami de ses soucis** to take a friend's mind off his worries

VPR **se distraire 1** *(s'amuser)* to have fun, to enjoy oneself **2** *(se détendre)* to relax, to take a break **3 se d. de qch** to take one's mind off sth

distrait, -e [distre, -ɛt] ADJ *(gén)* absent-minded; *(élève)* inattentive; **d'un air d.** absent-mindedly; **excusez-moi, j'étais d.** sorry, I wasn't paying attention

NM,F absent-minded person; **j'ai oublié ma montre, quel d.!** I forgot my watch, how absent-minded of me!

> Il faut noter que l'adjectif anglais **distracted** est un faux ami. Il signifie **préoccupé**.

distraitement [distrɛtmɑ̃] ADV absent-mindedly

distrayait *etc voir* **distraire**

distrayant, -e [distrejɑ̃, -ɑ̃t] ADJ amusing, entertaining

distribanque [distribɑ̃k] NM *Br* cashpoint, *Am* ATM

distribuer [7] [distribɥe] VT **1** *(donner ▸ feuilles, cadeaux, bonbons)* to distribute, to give *or* to hand out; *(▸ cartes)* to deal; *(▸ secours)* to dispense, to distribute; *(▸ courrier)* to deliver; *(▸ vivres)* to dispense, to share out, to distribute; *(▸ argent)* to apportion, to distribute, to share out; *Fin (▸ dividendes)* to pay; *(▸ actions, bénéfices)* to distribute; *Fam* **mon père n'hésitait pas à d. les coups** my father had no qualms about handing out punishment; **d. des sourires à tout le monde** to bestow smiles on everybody

2 *(attribuer ▸ rôles)* to allocate, to assign; *(▸ tâches, travail)* to allot, to assign

3 *(répartir)* to distribute, to divide (out); **la richesse est mal distribuée à travers le monde** wealth is unevenly distributed throughout the world

4 *(approvisionner)* to supply; **un réseau qui distribue le courant** a network that supplies *or* provides power; **l'eau est distribuée dans tous les villages** water is supplied *or* carried to all the villages

5 *Cin & Théât (rôle)* to cast; *Cin (film)* to distribute

6 *Com* to distribute

distributaire [distribytɛr] ADJ distributional

NMF distributee

distributeur, -trice [distribytœr, -tris] NM,F distributor, dealer

NM **1** *(machine non payante)* dispenser; **d. de savon/gobelets** soap/cup dispenser; **d. automatique de billets** *Br* cashpoint, *Am* ATM; **d. de monnaie** change machine

2 *(machine payante)* **d. (automatique)** vending *or* slot machine; **d. de cigarettes/de timbres** cigarette/stamp machine

3 *Aut & Élec* distributor; **d. de vapeur** steam distributor *or* regulator, steam valve

4 *Agr* **d. d'engrais** muckspreader

5 *Com (vendeur)* distributor, dealer; *(grande surface)* retailer; *(de films)* (film) distributor; **d. agréé** authorized distributor *or* dealer; **d. en détail** retailer; **d. en gros** wholesaler

distributif, -ive [distribytif, -iv] ADJ distributive

distribution [distribysjɔ̃] NF **1** *(remise ▸ de feuilles, de cadeaux, de bonbons)* distribution, giving *or* handing out; *(▸ de cartes)* dealing; *(▸ de secours)* dispensing, distributing; *(▸ de tâches, du travail)* allotment, assignment; *(▸ du courrier)* delivery; *Fin (▸ de dividendes)* payment; *(▸ de produits, de mailings)* distribution; **assurer la d. du courrier** to deliver the mail; *Scol* **la d. des prix** prizegiving day; *Mktg* **d. à domicile** door drop; *Mktg* **d. d'échantillons** sampling

2 *(répartition dans l'espace ▸ de pièces)* layout; *(▸ de joueurs)* positioning

3 *(approvisionnement)* supply; **d. d'eau/de gaz** water/gas supply

4 *Bot & (en sociologie ▸ classement)* distribution

5 *Cin, Théât & TV (des rôles ▸ choix)* casting; *(▸ liste)* cast; **une brillante d.** an all-star cast

6 *Com* distribution; *(par des grandes surfaces)* retail; **la grande d.** mass distribution; **d. à flux tendus** just-in-time distribution; **d. en gros** wholesale distribution; **d. juste à temps** just-in-time distribution; **d. de masse** mass distribution; **d. physique** physical distribution

7 *Écon, Jur & Math* distribution; **d. des richesses** distribution of wealth; **d. sélective** selective distribution; **d. valeur** weighted distribution

8 *Aut* timing

distributionnel, -elle [distribysjɔnɛl] ADJ distributional

distributive [distribytiv] *voir* **distributif**

distributivement [distribytivmɑ̃] ADV distributively

distributivité [distribytivite] NF distributiveness

distributrice [distribytris] *voir* **distributeur**

district [distrikt] NM **1** *(région)* district, region; **le d. fédéral de Columbia** the District of Columbia **2** *(d'une ville)* district

dit, -e [di, dit] PP *voir* **dire**[2]

ADJ **1** *(surnommé ▸ personne)* (also) known as; **Louis XIV, d. le Roi-Soleil** Louis XIV, (also) known as the Sun King; **la zone dite tempérée** the temperate zone, as it is called **2** *(fixé)* appointed, indicated; **à l'heure dite** at the appointed time, at the time indicated; **le jour d.** on the agreed *or* appointed day

NM **1** *Psy* **le d. et le non-d.** the spoken and the unspoken **2** *Littérature* traditional story *(usually in verse)*

dites *voir* **dire**[2]

dithyrambe [ditirɑ̃b] NM **1** *Antiq* dithyramb **2** *(panégyrique)* panegyric, eulogy

dithyrambique [ditirɑ̃bik] ADJ **1** *Antiq* dithyrambic **2** *(paroles)* eulogistic, laudatory

dito [dito] ADV ditto

diurèse [djyrez] NF *Méd* diuresis

diurétique [djyretik] *Méd*

ADJ diuretic

NM diuretic

diurne [djyrn] ADJ diurnal

diva [diva] NF **1** *Mus* diva, (female) opera singer **2** *(célébrité)* star

divagation [divagasjɔ̃] NF *(d'une rivière)* shifting from its course

• **divagations** NFPL *(propos)* ramblings, meanderings

divaguer [3] [divage] VI **1** *(malade)* to ramble, to be delirious; **la soif le fait d.** he's delirious with thirst **2** *Fam Péj (déraisonner)* to talk nonsense **3** *(rivière)* to shift its course

divan [divɑ̃] NM **1** *(meuble)* divan, couch **2** *Hist* **le d.** the divan

divergence [divɛrʒɑ̃s] NF **1** *(différence)* **d. (d'idées** *ou* **de vues)** difference of opinion **2** *Opt & Phys* divergence

divergent, -e [divɛrʒɑ̃, -ɑ̃t] ADJ **1** *(opinions, interprétations, intérêts)* divergent, differing **2** *Opt & Phys* divergent

diverger [17] [divɛrʒe] VI **1** *(intérêts, opinions)* to differ, to diverge (**de** from) **2** *Opt & Phys* to diverge (**de** from)

divers, -e [divɛr, -ɛrs] ADJ **1** *(variés ▸ éléments, musiques, activités)* diverse, varied; **nous avons abordé les sujets les plus d.** we talked about a wide range of topics; **à usages d.** multipurpose *(avant n)*; *Com* **articles d.** miscellaneous items **2** *(dissemblables ▸ formes, goûts, motifs)* different, various **3** *(multiple ▸ sujet)* complex; *(▸ paysage)* varied, changing

ADJ INDÉFINI *(plusieurs)* various, several; **pour diverses raisons** for a variety of reasons

diversement [divɛrsəmɑ̃] ADV **1** *(différemment)* in different ways; **les participants ont d. compris la question** the contestants understood the question in different ways **2** *(de façon variée)* in diverse *or* various ways

diversification [divɛrsifikasjɔ̃] NF diversification; **l'entreprise a adopté une stratégie de d.** the company has adopted a policy of diversification; *Bourse* **d. de portefeuille** portfolio diversification

diversifier **[9]** [divɛrsifje] **VT 1** *(production, tâches)* to diversify **2** *(varier)* to make more varied
VPR se diversifier *(entreprise, économie, centres d'intérêt)* to diversify; *(produits)* to become diversified

diversion [divɛrsjɔ̃] **NF 1** *(dérivatif)* diversion, distraction; **faire d.** to create a distraction; **faire d. à la douleur de qn** to take sb's mind off his/her suffering **2** *Mil* diversion

diversité [divɛrsite] **NF 1** *(richesse)* diversity, variety; **un paysage étonnant dans sa d.** an amazingly varied landscape **2** *(pluralité ▸ de formes, d'opinions, de goûts)* diversity

divertir **[32]** [divɛrtir] **VT 1** *(amuser ▸ sujet: clown, spectacle, lecture)* to entertain, to amuse **2** *Jur* to divert, to misappropriate **3** *Littéraire (éloigner)* **d. qn de qch** to turn sb away *or* to distract sb from sth
VPR se divertir 1 *(se distraire)* to amuse *or* to entertain oneself; **que faire pour se d. ici?** what do you do for entertainment around here? **2** *(s'amuser)* to enjoy oneself, to have fun; **nous nous sommes beaucoup divertis à 'Cyrano'** we enjoyed 'Cyrano' very much **3 se d. de qn/qch** to make fun of sb/sth

divertissant, -e [divɛrtisɑ̃, -ɑ̃t] **ADJ** amusing, entertaining

divertissement [divɛrtismɑ̃] **NM 1** *(jeu, passe-temps)* distraction; *(spectacle)* entertainment; *(type d'émission de télévision)* light entertainment show
2 *(amusement)* entertaining, distraction; **pour le d. de la Cour** to amuse *or* to entertain the Court
3 *Mus (intermède)* divertissement; *(divertimento)* divertimento
4 *Jur (de fonds)* misappropriation

dividende [dividɑ̃d] **NM** *Fin & Math* dividend; **toucher** *ou* **recevoir un d.** to draw a dividend; **avec d.** cum div(idend), *Am* dividend on; **sans d.** ex div (idend), *Am* dividend off; **dividendes accrus** accrued dividends; **d. par action** dividend per share; **d. anticipé** advance dividend; **d. brut** gross dividend; **d. cumulatif** cumulative dividend; **d. définitif** final dividend; **d. en espèces** cash dividend; **d. final** final dividend; **d. intérimaire, d. par intérim** interim dividend; **d. prioritaire, d. de priorité** preference dividend; **d. privilégié** preference dividend

divin, -e [divɛ̃, -in] **ADJ 1** *Rel* divine; *Antiq* **le d. Auguste** the Divine Augustus; **le d. enfant** the Holy Child; **le d. Sauveur** the Holy *or* Heavenly Saviour **2** *(parfait ▸ beauté, corps, repas, voix)* divine, heavenly
NM le d. the divine

divinateur, -trice [divinatœr, -tris] **ADJ** divining, clairvoyant; **puissance divinatrice** power of divination
NM,F diviner

divination [divinasjɔ̃] **NF** divination, divining

divinatoire [divinatwar] **ADJ** divinatory

divinatrice [divinatris] *voir* **divinateur**

divinement [divinmɑ̃] **ADV** divinely, exquisitely

divinisation [divinizasjɔ̃] **NF** deification, deifying

diviniser **[3]** [divinize] **VT** to deify

divinité [divinite] **NF 1** *(dieu)* deity, divinity **2** *(qualité)* divinity, divine nature

diviser **[3]** [divize] **VT 1** *(fragmenter ▸ territoire)* to divide up, to partition; *(▸ somme, travail)* to divide up; *(▸ cellule, molécule)* to divide, to split; **d. un domaine entre des héritiers** to divide up an estate between heirs; **les bénéfices ont été divisés en huit** the profits were divided into eight parts; **la classe est divisée en trois groupes** the class is divided up into three groups
2 *Math* to divide; **d. 9 par 3** to divide 9 by 3; **9 divisé par 3 égale 3** 9 divided by 3 makes *or* is 3
3 *(opposer)* to divide, to set against each other; **les dissensions qui nous divisent** the disagreements that divide us; **l'association est divisée en deux sur le problème de l'intégration** the association is split down the middle on the problem of integration; **c'est d. pour (mieux) régner** it's (a case of) divide and rule
4 *Fin & Bourse (actions)* to split
VPR se diviser 1 *Math* to be divisible **2** *(cellule)* to divide *or* to split (up); *(branche, voie)* to divide, to fork; **se d. en** to be divided into; **le texte se divise en cinq parties** the text is divided into five parts; **l'équipe s'est divisée en deux** the team divided itself *or* split up into two groups **3** *(opposition, parti)* to split

diviseur [divizœr] **NM 1** *Math* divisor; **plus grand commun d.** highest common factor **2** *Tech* divider

divisibilité [divizibilite] **NF** divisibility; *(d'une créance, d'une dette)* divisibility, severability

divisible [divizibl] **ADJ** divisible; **8 n'est pas d. par 3** 8 cannot be divided *or* is not divisible by 3

division [divizjɔ̃] **NF 1** *Math* division; **j'ai des divisions à faire** I've got some division to do; **d. à un chiffre** simple division; **d. à plusieurs chiffres** long division
2 *(fragmentation ▸ d'un territoire)* splitting, division, partition; *(▸ d'une cellule, d'une molécule)* splitting; *Écon* **la d. du travail** the division of labour; *Biol* **d. cellulaire** cell division; *Écon* **d. du marché** market division
3 *(désaccord)* division, rift; **le problème de la défense nationale crée des divisions au sein du parti** the party is divided over the defence issue
4 *Ftbl* division; **la première d. du championnat** the first league division; **un club de première/deuxième/troisième d.** a first-/second-/third-division club; **d. d'honneur** ≃ fourth division
5 *(en base-ball)* league; **première/deuxième d.** major/minor league
6 *Mil & Naut* division; **d. blindée** armoured division
7 *Bourse (des actions)* splitting

divisionnaire [divizjɔnɛr] **ADJ** *Admin (service)* divisional
NM 1 *Mil* major general **2** *(commissaire) Br* ≃ chief superintendent, *Am* ≃ police chief

divorce [divɔrs] **NM 1** *Jur* divorce; **demander le d.** to ask for *or* to petition for a divorce; **obtenir le d. d'avec qn** to get a divorce from sb; **d. à l'amiable** *ou* **par consentement mutuel** divorce by mutual consent, *Am* no-fault divorce **2** *(divergence)* gulf

divorcé, -e [divɔrse] **ADJ** divorced
NM,F divorcee

divorcer **[16]** [divɔrse] **VI** *Jur* to get a divorce, to get divorced; **elle a déjà divorcé une fois** she has already been divorced (once) before; **il veut d.** he wants a divorce; **d. de qn** *ou* **d'avec qn** to get divorced from *or* to divorce sb

divulgateur, -trice [divylgatœr, -tris] **NM,F** divulger

divulgation [divylgasjɔ̃] **NF** divulgation, disclosure

divulgatrice [divylgatris] *voir* **divulgateur**

divulguer **[3]** [divylge] **VT** to divulge, to disclose, to reveal

dix [dis] **ADJ 1** *(gén)* ten; **il ne sait rien faire de ses d. doigts** he can't do anything with his hands; *Bible* **les d. commandements** the Ten Commandments **2** *(dans des séries)* tenth; **page/numéro d.** page/number ten
PRON ten
NM INV 1 *(gén)* ten
2 *(numéro d'ordre)* number ten
3 *(chiffre écrit)* ten
4 *Cartes* ten; *voir aussi* **cinq**

dix-huit [dizɥit] **ADJ 1** *(gén)* eighteen **2** *(dans des séries)* eighteenth; **page/numéro d.** page/number eighteen
PRON eighteen
NM INV 1 *(gén)* eighteen **2** *(numéro d'ordre)* number eighteen **3** *(chiffre écrit)* eighteen; *voir aussi* **cinq**

dix-huitième [dizɥitjɛm] *(pl* **dix-huitièmes***)* **ADJ** eighteenth
NMF 1 *(personne)* eighteenth **2** *(objet)* eighteenth (one)
NM 1 *(partie)* eighteenth **2** *(étage) Br* eighteenth floor, *Am* nineteenth floor **3** *(arrondissement de Paris)* eighteenth (arrondissement)
NF *Mus* eighteenth; *voir aussi* **cinquième**

dixième [dizjɛm] **ADJ** tenth
NMF 1 *(personne)* tenth **2** *(objet)* tenth (one)
NM 1 *(partie)* tenth **2** *(étage) Br* tenth floor, *Am* eleventh floor **3** *(arrondissement de Paris)* tenth (arrondissement)
NF 1 *Anciennement Scol Br* = second year of primary school, *Am* ≃ second grade **2** *Mus* tenth; *voir aussi* **cinquième**

dixièmement [dizjɛmmɑ̃] **ADV** tenthly, in tenth place

dixit [diksit] **il faudra tout ranger après, d. Papa** we must tidy everything up afterwards (so) Dad says

dix-neuf [diznœf] **ADJ 1** *(gén)* nineteen **2** *(dans des séries)* nineteenth; **page/numéro d.** page/number nineteen
PRON nineteen
NM INV 1 *(gén)* nineteen **2** *(numéro d'ordre)* number nineteen **3** *(chiffre écrit)* nineteen; *voir aussi* **cinq**

dix-neuvième [diznœvjɛm] *(pl* **dix-neuvièmes***)* **ADJ** nineteenth
NMF 1 *(personne)* nineteenth **2** *(objet)* nineteenth (one)
NM 1 *(partie)* nineteenth **2** *(étage) Br* nineteenth floor, *Am* twentieth floor **3** *(arrondissement de Paris)* nineteenth (arrondissement)
NF *Mus* nineteenth; *voir aussi* **cinquième**

dix-sept [diset] **ADJ 1** *(gén)* seventeen **2** *(dans des séries)* seventeenth; **page/numéro d.** page/number seventeen
PRON seventeen
NM INV 1 *(gén)* seventeen **2** *(numéro d'ordre)* number seventeen **3** *(chiffre écrit)* seventeen; *voir aussi* **cinq**

dix-septième [disetjɛm] *(pl* **dix-septièmes***)* **ADJ** seventeenth
NMF 1 *(personne)* seventeenth **2** *(objet)* seventeenth (one)
NM 1 *(partie)* seventeenth **2** *(étage) Br* seventeenth floor, *Am* eighteenth floor **3** *(arrondissement de Paris)* seventeenth (arrondissement)
NF *Mus* seventeenth; *voir aussi* **cinquième**

dizain [dizɛ̃] **NM** *Littérature* ten-line poem

dizaine [dizɛn] **NF une d.** around *or* about ten, ten or so; **une d. de voitures** around *or* about ten cars; **elle a une d. d'années** she's around *or* about ten (years old)

dizygote [dizigɔt] *Biol* **ADJ** fraternal, *Spéc* dizygotic
NM,F fraternal twin, *Spéc* dizygotic twin

DJ [didʒi, didʒe] **NM** *(abrév* **disc-jockey***)* DJ

djellaba [dʒelaba] **NF** djellaba

djembé [dʒembe] **NM** *Mus* djembe drum

djeune [dʒœn] *Fam Ironique* **ADJ** young and hip
NMF hip young person

Djibouti [dʒibuti] **NM 1** *(république)* Djibouti **2** *(ville)* Djibouti City

djihad [dʒiad] **NM** jihad

djihadiste [dʒiadist] **NM** jihadi

djinn [dʒin] **NM** jinn

DLC [deɛlse] **NF** *(abrév* **date limite de consommation***)* best-before date

DNS [deɛnɛs] **NM** *Ordinat (abrév* **Domain Name System***)* DNS

do[1] [do] **NM INV** C; *(chanté)* doh

do[2] *(abrév écrite* **dito***)* do

doberman [dɔbɛrman] **NM** Doberman (pinscher)

doc [dɔk] **NF** *Fam (abrév* **documentation***)* literature□, info; **est-ce que tu as de la d. sur les ordinateurs?** do you have any literature *or* info about computers?

docile [dɔsil] **ADJ** *(animal)* docile; *(enfant, nature)* docile, obedient; *(cheveux)* manageable

docilement [dɔsilmɑ̃] **ADV** docilely, obediently

docilité [dɔsilite] **NF** *(d'un animal, d'une personne)* docility; **avec d.** docilely

dock [dɔk] **NM 1** *(bassin)* dock; **d. de carénage/flottant** dry/floating dock **2** *(bâtiments, chantier)* **les docks** the docks, the dockyard; **entrer aux docks** *(bateau)* to dock **3** *(entrepôt)* warehouse; **d. frigorifique** cold storage dock

docker [dɔkɛr] **NM** docker

docte [dɔkt] **ADJ** *Littéraire* learned, erudite

doctement [dɔktəmɑ̃] **ADV** *Littéraire* knowledgeably

docteur [dɔktœr] **NM 1** *(médecin)* **le d. Jacqueline R.** Dr Jacqueline R.; **faites venir le d.** send for the doctor; **d. en médecine** doctor (of medicine) **2**

Univ Doctor; **d. en histoire/physique** doctorate *or* PhD in history/physics; **Paul Vuibert, d. ès lettres** Paul Vuibert, PhD **3** *Rel* **d. de l'Église** Doctor of the Church; **d. de la loi** Doctor of the Law

doctoral, -e, -aux, -ales [dɔktɔral, -o] **ADJ 1** *(pédant)* pedantic **2** *Univ* doctoral

doctoralement [dɔktɔralmɑ̃] **ADV** pedantically

doctorat [dɔktɔra] **NM** doctorate, PhD; **d. en droit/chimie** doctorate *or* PhD in law/chemistry; **d. d'État** doctorate *(leading to high-level research)*; **d. de troisième cycle** doctorate, PhD *(awarded by a specific university)*

doctoresse [dɔktɔrɛs] **NF** *Vieilli* (woman) doctor

doctrinaire [dɔktrinɛr] **ADJ** doctrinaire, dogmatic

NMF doctrinaire

doctrinal, -e, -aux, -ales [dɔktrinal, -o] **ADJ** doctrinal

doctrine [dɔktrin] **NF** doctrine

docudrame [dɔkydram] **NM** *TV* docudrama, dramatized documentary

docu-fiction [dɔkyfiksjɔ̃] *(pl* **docu-fictions)** **NM OU NF** docufiction, fictional documentary

document [dɔkymɑ̃] **NM 1** *Jur & Com* document; **d. administratif unique** unique data folder; **documents contre acceptation** documents against acceptance; **documents contre paiement** documents against payment; **d. d'embarquement** shipping document; **d. d'expédition** shipping document; **d. interne à l'entreprise** internal company document; **d. maître** master document; **documents maritimes** shipping documents; **d. d'offre** tender document; *Mktg* **d. de publicité directe** direct mail; **d. source** source document; *Compta* **d. de synthèse** financial statement; **d. de tendre** tender document; **d. transmissible** transferable document; **d. de transport** transport document; **d. de transport combiné** combined transport document; **d. de travail** working document; **d. type** standard document; **documents de voyage** travel documents

2 *Ordinat* document; **d. de base, d. source** source document; **d. transmissible** transferable document; **d. type** standard document

3 *(d'un service de documentation)* document

4 *(de travail)* document, paper; **des documents sont tombés de sa valise** documents *or* papers fell out of her case

documentaire [dɔkymɑ̃tɛr] **ADJ 1** *(de témoignage ▸ livre, intérêt)* documentary **2** *(de documentation)* document *(avant n)*; **ce rapport vous est fourni à titre d.** this report is supplied for information only

NM *Cin & TV* documentary

documentaliste [dɔkymɑ̃talist] **NMF 1** *(gén)* archivist; **d. iconographique** picture researcher **2** *Admin* information officer **3** *Scol* (school) librarian

documentariste [dɔkymɑ̃tarist] **NMF** documentary maker

documentation [dɔkymɑ̃tasjɔ̃] **NF 1** *(publicités)* literature, information, documentation; *(instructions)* instructions, specifications; **voulez-vous recevoir notre d.?** would you like us to send you our literature?; **se référer à la d.** please refer to the instructions

2 *(informations)* (written) evidence; **réunir une d. sur qch** to gather evidence on sth

3 *(technique)* documentation (technique); **d. iconographique** picture research

4 *(service)* **la d.** the research department

5 *Journ* **d. de presse** press kit

documenter [3] [dɔkymɑ̃te] **VT** *(thèse)* to document; *(avocat)* to supply *or* to provide with documents, to document

VPR se documenter to inform oneself; **se d. sur qn/qch** to gather information *or* material about sb/sth

dodécaèdre [dɔdekaɛdr] **NM** dodecahedron

dodécagonal, -e, -aux, -ales [dɔdekagɔnal, -o] **ADJ** twelve-sided, dodecagonal

dodécagone [dɔdekagɔn] **NM** dodecagon

dodécaphonique [dɔdekafɔnik] **ADJ** dodecaphonic

dodécaphonisme [dɔdekafɔnism] **NM** dodecaphonism

dodelinement [dɔdəlinmɑ̃] **NM** nodding

dodeliner [3] [dɔdəline] **dodeliner de VT IND d. de la tête** to nod gently

dodo [dodo] **NM 1** *(en langage enfantin ▸ sommeil)* beddy-byes; *(▸ lit)* bed; **faire d.** to sleep; **c'est l'heure d'aller au d.!** time to go to beddy-byes! **2** *(oiseau)* dodo

dodu, -e [dɔdy] **ADJ** *(oie)* plump; *(personne, visage)* plump, fleshy, chubby; *(bébé)* chubby

doge [dɔʒ] **NM** doge

dogmatique [dɔgmatik] **ADJ** dogmatic

NMF dogmatic person

NF dogmatics *(singulier)*

dogmatiquement [dɔgmatikmɑ̃] **ADV** dogmatically

dogmatiser [3] [dɔgmatize] **VI** to pontificate, to dogmatize

dogmatisme [dɔgmatism] **NM** dogmatism

dogme [dɔgm] **NM** dogma

dogue [dɔg] **NM** mastiff; **d. allemand/anglais** German/English mastiff

doigt [dwa] **NM 1** *(partie du corps)* finger, *Spéc* digit; **des doigts fins/boudinés** slender/podgy fingers; **le d. sur la bouche** with one's finger on one's lips; **lever le d.** to put one's hand up; **manger avec ses doigts** to eat with one's fingers; **mettre ses doigts dans** *ou* **se mettre les doigts dans le nez** to pick one's nose; **mettre son d. dans l'œil de qn** to poke sb in the eye; **le d. de Dieu** the hand of God; **d. de pied** toe; *Fam* **les doigts de pied en éventail** with one's feet up; **une couturière aux doigts de fée** a seamstress with skilful hands; **petit d.** little finger, *Am & Scot* pinkie; **ils sont comme les (deux) doigts de la main** they're like brothers, they're as thick as thieves; **glisser** *ou* **filer entre les doigts de qn** to slip through sb's fingers; **mettre le d. dans l'engrenage** to get involved; *Fam* **se fourrer** *ou très Fam* **se foutre le d. dans l'œil (jusqu'au coude)** to be barking up the wrong tree; **mener** *ou* **faire marcher qn au d. et à l'œil** to have sb toe the line, to rule sb with a rod of iron; **il lui obéit au d. et à l'œil** he/she rules him with a rod of iron; *Fam* **tu pourrais le faire? – les doigts dans le nez!** could you do it? -- standing on my head!; *Fam* **gagner les doigts dans le nez** to win hands down; **mettre le d. sur qch, toucher qch du d.** to identify sth precisely; **tu as mis le d. dessus!** that's precisely it!, you've put your finger on it!; **il faut lui faire toucher le problème du d.** he has to have the problem spelt out for him; **c'est mon petit d. qui me l'a dit** a little bird told me; **il ne bougera** *ou* **lèvera pas le petit d. pour faire…** he won't lift a finger to do…; **le petit d. sur la couture du pantalon** standing to attention; *Fam* **faire un d. d'honneur à qn** *Br* to give sb the finger, *Am* to flip sb the bird

2 *(mesure)* little bit; **raccourcir une jupe de deux doigts** to take a skirt up a little bit; **servez-m'en un d.** just pour me out a drop; **deux doigts de whisky** two fingers of whisky

• **à un doigt de, à deux doigts de PRÉP** within an inch *or* a hair's breadth of

doigté [dwate] **NM 1** *Mus (annotation, position)* fingering; *(technique)* fingering technique; **exercices de d.** five-finger exercises **2** *(adresse)* dexterity **3** *(tact)* tact, diplomacy; **avoir du d.** to be tactful; **manquer de d.** to be tactless

doigter [3] [dwate] **VT** *Mus* to finger

doigtier [dwatje] **NM** fingerstall

doit[1] *voir* **devoir**[2]

doit[2] [dwa] **NM** *Fin* debit, liability; *(d'un compte)* debit side; **d. et avoir** debits and credits; *(personnes)* debtors and creditors

doive *etc voir* **devoir**[2]

dol [dɔl] **NM** *Jur* fraud

Dolby® [dɔlbi] **NM** Dolby®; **en D. stéréo** in Dolby® stereo

dôle [dol] **NF** *Suisse* = red wine from the Valais canton

doléance [dɔleɑ̃s] **NF** complaint, grievance; **faire** *ou* **présenter ses doléances** to air one's grievances

dolent, -e [dɔlɑ̃, -ɑ̃t] **ADJ** *Littéraire (plaintif ▸ personne)* doleful, mournful; *(▸ voix)* plaintive, mournful

doline [dɔlin] **NF** doline, dolina

dollar [dɔlar] **NM 1** *(en Amérique du Nord)* dollar; **d. américain** US dollar **2** *UE* **d. vert** green dollar

dollarisation [dɔlarizasjɔ̃] **NF** dollarization

dollariser [3] [dɔlarize] **VT** to dollarize

dolman [dɔlmɑ̃] **NM** dolman

dolmen [dɔlmɛn] **NM** dolmen

dolomie [dɔlɔmi], **dolomite** [dɔlɔmit] **NF** dolomite

Dolomites [dɔlɔmit] **NFPL les D.** the Dolomites

dolomitique [dɔlɔmitik] **ADJ** dolomitic

dolosif, -ive [dɔlɔzif, -iv] **ADJ** *Jur* fraudulent

domaine [dɔmɛn] **NM 1** *(propriété)* estate, (piece of) property; **entretenir les arbres du d.** to look after the trees on the estate; **vous êtes ici sur mon d.** you're on my land *or* property; **mis en bouteille au d.** *(dans le Bordelais)* chateau-bottled; **le d. forestier** the national forests; **le d. royal** ≃ Crown lands *or* property; *Hist (en France)* the property of the Kings of France; **d. skiable** area developed for skiing *(within a commune or across several communes)*; **d. vinicole** domaine

2 *(lieu préféré)* domain; **étant enfant, le grenier était mon d.** when I was a child, the attic was my domain *or* kingdom

3 *Jur* **le D.** State property; **d. privé** private ownership; **d. public** public ownership (of rights); **être dans le d. public** to be out of copyright; **tomber dans le d. public** to come into the public domain

4 *(secteur d'activité)* field, domain, area; **le d. musical/scientifique** the musical/scientific field; **dans le d. de la prévention, il y a encore beaucoup à faire** as far as preventive action is concerned, there's still a lot to do; **dans tous les domaines** in every field *or* domain; **dans tous les domaines de la recherche** in all research areas; *Com* **d. d'activité stratégique** strategic business unit; *Mktg* **d. concurrentiel** competitive scope

5 *(compétence, spécialité)* field; **c'est du d. du service commercial** that's for the marketing department to deal with; **ce n'est pas de mon d.** that's not my field *or* my line; **l'art oriental, c'est son d.** she's a specialist in oriental art

6 *Math & Ordinat* domain

• **Domaines NMPL** *Admin* **cet étang appartient aux Domaines** this pond is State property

domanial, -e, -aux, -ales [dɔmanjal, -o] **ADJ** *Jur* **1** *(de l'État)* national, state *(avant n)* **2** *(privé)* belonging to a private estate

dôme [dom] **NM 1** *(en Italie ▸ cathédrale)* cathedral; *(▸ église)* church

2 *Archit* dome, *Spéc* cupola

3 *Littéraire (voûte)* vault, canopy

4 *Géol* dome

domestication [dɔmɛstikasjɔ̃] **NF** *(d'un animal, d'une plante)* domestication; *(d'une énergie)* harnessing

domesticité [dɔmɛstisite] **NF la d.** *(dans une maison)* the (domestic *or* household) staff; **avoir une nombreuse d.** to have a large staff *or* many servants

domestique [dɔmɛstik] **ADJ 1** *(familial ▸ problème, vie, querelle)* family *(avant n)*; *(▸ dieu)* household *(avant n)*

2 *(du ménage ▸ affaires, devoirs, tâches)* household *(avant n)*, domestic; **les travaux domestiques** household work, domestic chores; **personnel d.** domestic staff, (domestic) servants

3 *Écon (consommation, marché)* domestic, home *(avant n)*

4 *(animal)* domesticated; **les animaux domestiques** pets

NMF domestic, servant

domestiquer [3] [dɔmɛstike] **VT** *(animal)* to domesticate; *(plante)* to turn into a cultivated variety; *(personne)* to subjugate, to bring to a state of subjection; *(énergie)* to harness

domicile [dɔmisil] **NM 1** *(lieu de résidence)* home, *Sout* place of residence; *Admin & Jur* domicile; *(adresse)* (home) address; **dernier d. connu** last known address; **le chéquier sera renvoyé à votre d.** the chequebook will be sent to your home address; **nos représentants se rendent à votre d.** our representatives make house calls; **un(e) sans d. fixe** a homeless person; **être sans d. fixe** to be homeless; *Admin & Jur* to be of no fixed abode; **d. conjugal** marital home; **d. fiscal** tax domicile; **d. légal** address for legal purposes; **d. permanent** permanent place of residence **2** *(d'une entreprise)* registered address

• **à domicile** ADJ **soins à d.** domiciliary care, home care; **vente à d.** door-to-door selling; *Sport* **match à d.** home game *or Br* match ADV *(chez soi)* at home; **travailler à d.** to work from home; **nous livrons à d.** we deliver to your home; *Sport* **jouer à d.** to play *or* be at home; **le P.S.G. joue à d. contre Lille** PSG are at home to Lille

domiciliaire [dɔmisiljɛr] ADJ *(visite)* home *(avant n), Sout* domiciliary

domiciliataire [dɔmisiljatɛr] NMF *Banque* paying agent

domiciliation [dɔmisiljasjɔ̃] NF *(d'une société)* domiciliation; **d. (bancaire)** payment (by banker's order)

domicilié, -e [dɔmisilje] ADJ *(salaire)* paid directly into one's bank account; **être fiscalement d. dans un pays** to be liable to pay tax in a country; **d. à Tokyo/en Suède** resident *or Sout* domiciled in Tokyo/in Sweden

domicilier [9] [dɔmisilje] VT **1** *Admin* to domicile **2** *Banque & Com* to domicile

domien, -enne [dɔmjɛ̃, -ɛn] ADJ of/from the French overseas "départements"

• **Domien, -enne** NM,F = inhabitant of or person from the French overseas "départements"

dominance [dɔminɑ̃s] NF **1** *Biol & Physiol* dominance, dominant nature **2** *Zool* dominance, dominant behaviour

dominant, -e [dɔminɑ̃, -ɑ̃t] ADJ **1** *(principal ▸ facteur, thème, trait de caractère)* dominant, main; *(▸ espèce)* dominant; *(▸ couleur)* dominant, main, predominant; *(▸ intérêt)* main, chief; *(▸ idéologie)* prevailing; *(▸ position)* commanding **2** *Biol (caractère, gène)* dominant **3** *Météo (vent)* dominant, prevailing

• **dominante** NF **1** *(aspect prépondérant)* dominant *or* chief *or* main characteristic

2 *(teinte)* predominant colour; **j'ai choisi une tapisserie à dominante jaune** I chose wallpaper that is mainly yellow

3 *Mus* dominant; **cinquième/septième de dominante** dominant fifth/seventh

4 *Univ Br* main subject, *Am* major; **un cursus à dominante linguistique** a course with *Br* linguistics as the main subject *or Am* linguistics major

dominateur, -trice [dɔminatœr, -tris] ADJ **1** *(puissant ▸ esprit, force, nation)* dominating; *(▸ passion)* ruling **2** *(autoritaire ▸ personne)* domineering, overbearing; *(▸ ton)* imperious **3** *Zool* dominant

NM,F **1** *Pol* ruler **2** *(personne autoritaire)* tyrant, despot

domination [dɔminasjɔ̃] NF **1** *(politique, militaire)* domination (**sur** of), dominion, rule (**sur** over); **maintenir une île sous sa d.** to have control over an island; **territoires sous d. allemande** territories under German domination *or* rule

2 *(prépondérance ▸ d'un facteur)* preponderance, domination

3 *(ascendant personnel, influence)* domination, influence; **il exerçait sur eux une étrange d.** he had a strange hold over them; **subir la d. de qn, être sous la d. de qn** to be dominated by sb

4 *(contrôle ▸ de sentiments)* control; **d. de soi-même** self-control

dominatrice [dɔminatris] *voir* **dominateur**

dominer [3] [dɔmine] VT **1** *Pol (nation, peuple)* to dominate, to rule

2 *(contrôler ▸ marché)* to control, to dominate; **ils ont dominé le match** they controlled *or* dominated the match

3 *(influencer ▸ personne)* to dominate; **se laisser d. par qn** to let oneself be dominated by sb

4 *(surclasser)* to outclass; **il s'est fait d. pendant les premiers rounds** his opponent had the upper hand during the early rounds; **elle domine toutes les autres danseuses** she outclasses all the other dancers

5 *(colère)* to control; *(complexe, dégoût, échec, timidité)* to overcome; *(passion)* to master, to control; *(matière, question)* to master; **elle domine son sujet** she has a thorough knowledge *or* grasp of her subject; **d. la situation** to be in control of the situation

6 *(prédominer dans ▸ œuvre, style, débat)* to predominate in, to dominate; **sa voix dominait le brouhaha de la salle** his/her voice rose above the noise of the room; **le thème qui domine la campagne électorale** the main theme in *or* the theme which dominates the electoral campaign

7 *(surplomber)* to overlook, to dominate; **de la tour, on domine tout le village** from the tower you have a view over the whole valley; **d. qn de la tête et des épaules** to be taller than sb by a head; *Fig* to tower above sb, to be head and shoulders above sb

VI **1** *(être prédominant ▸ couleur, intérêt)* to predominate, to be predominant; *(▸ caractéristique)* to dominate, to be dominant; *(▸ idéologie, opinion)* to prevail; **chez lui, c'est l'égoïsme/la gentillesse qui domine** selfishness/kindness is his dominant characteristic; **les femmes dominent dans l'enseignement** women outnumber men in teaching **2** *(l'emporter)* to dominate; **notre équipe a dominé tout le long du match** our team dominated the entire match *or* was in control throughout the match; **notre entreprise domine largement dans ce secteur** our company has the biggest share of the market *or* is the market leader in this sector

VPR **se dominer** to control oneself; **fou de rage, il ne se dominait plus** he was so angry, he could no longer control himself; **ne pas savoir se d.** to have no self-control

dominicain[1], -e[1] [dɔminikɛ̃, -ɛn] ADJ *Rel* Dominican

NM,F Dominican

dominicain[2], -e[2] [dɔminikɛ̃, -ɛn] ADJ *(de Saint-Domingue)* Dominican

• **Dominicain, -e** NM,F Dominican

dominical, -e, -aux, -ales [dɔminikal, -o] ADJ Sunday *(avant n), Sout* dominical

dominion [dɔminjɔ̃] NM dominion

Dominique [dɔminik] NF **la D.** Dominica

domino [dɔmino] NM **1** *(jeu)* domino; **jouer aux dominos** to play dominoes **2** *Élec* connecting block **3** *(vêtement)* domino

dommage [dɔmaʒ] NM **1** *Jur (préjudice)* harm, injury; **causer un d. à qn** to cause *or* to do sb harm; **il s'en est tiré sans d.** he came out of it unscathed; **d. corporel** physical injury; **dommages de guerre** war damage; **dommages et intérêts, dommages-intérêts** damages; **poursuivre qn en dommages-intérêts** to sue sb for damages, to bring an action for damages against sb; **verser/obtenir des dommages-intérêts** to pay/to be awarded damages; **dommages punitifs** punitive damages **2** *(gén pl) (dégât matériel)* **d. matériel, dommages matériels** (material) damage; **le d. n'était pas bien grand** there wasn't much harm done; **causer des dommages à** to cause damage to; *Mil* **dommages collatéraux** collateral damage **3** *(expression d'un regret)* **(quel) d.!** what a shame *or* pity!; **c'est vraiment d. de devoir abattre ce chêne** it's a real shame to have to cut down this oak; **ça ne m'intéresse pas! – d.!** I'm not interested! – pity!; **d. que tu n'aies pas pu venir!** what a pity *or* shame you couldn't come!; *Fam* **le plus d., c'est que...** the worst of it is that...

• **beau dommage** EXCLAM *Can* of course!, you bet!

dommageable [dɔmaʒabl] ADJ detrimental, damaging (**à** to)

domotique [dɔmɔtik] NF home automation

domptable [dɔ̃tabl] ADJ tameable; **facilement/difficilement d.** easy/difficult to tame

domptage [dɔ̃taʒ] NM *(apprivoisement)* taming; *(dressage ▸ de cheval)* breaking in

dompter [3] [dɔ̃te] VT **1** *(apprivoiser)* to tame; *(dresser ▸ cheval)* to break in **2** *Littéraire (révoltés)* to quash; *(peuple)* to subjugate **3** *(énergie, vent, torrent)* to master; *(rébellion)* to break, to put down; *(sentiments, passions)* to subdue, to overcome

dompteur, -euse [dɔ̃tœr, -øz] NM,F *(d'animaux sauvages)* tamer; **d. de chevaux** horse-breaker

DOM-TOM [dɔmtɔm] NMPL *Anciennement (abrév* **départements et territoires d'outre-mer)** = French overseas "départements" and territories

DON [dɔn] NM *Ordinat (abrév* **disque optique numérique)** digital optical disk

don [dɔ̃] NM **1** *(aptitude naturelle)* talent, gift; **c'est un d. chez elle** it's a talent *or* a gift she has; **avoir le d. de voyance** to be clairvoyant; **avoir le d. des langues** to have a gift for languages; **elle a un d. pour la danse** she has a talent for dancing, she's a gifted dancer; **elle a le d. de trouver des vêtements pas chers** she has a flair for finding cheap clothes; **mes initiatives ont le d. de la contrarier** I seem to have a knack for upsetting her

2 *(cadeau)* gift, donation; **faire d. de qch** to give sth as a present *or* gift; **la collection dont elle m'a fait d.** the collection she gave me as a present; **ceux qui ont fait d. de leur vie pour leur pays** those who have laid down *or* sacrificed their lives for their country; *Fig* **les dons de la terre** the fruits of the earth; *Fig* **d. du ciel** godsend; **le d. de soi** *ou* **de sa personne** self-denial, self-sacrifice; **d. en espèces** cash donation; **d. en nature** donation in kind

3 *Jur* donation; **faire d. d'un bien à qn** to donate a piece of property to sb; **d. de...** *(dans un musée)* gift of..., donated by...

4 *Méd* donation, donating; **faire d. d'un organe** to donate an organ; **d. du sang/de sperme** blood/sperm donation

donataire [dɔnatɛr] NMF donee, recipient

donateur, -trice [dɔnatœr, -tris] NM,F donor

donation [dɔnasjɔ̃] NF *(gén)* donation, disposition; *(d'argent)* donation; **faire une d. à un musée** to make a donation to a museum; *Jur* **d. entre époux** donation between spouses; **d. entre vifs** donation inter vivos; **donations parents-enfants** donations from parents to children

donation-partage [dɔnasjɔ̃partaʒ] *(pl* **donations-partages)** NF *Jur* = distribution of estate during one's lifetime to avoid inheritance tax

donatrice [dɔnatris] *voir* **donateur**

donc [dɔ̃k] CONJ **1** *(par conséquent)* so; **je n'en sais rien, inutile d. de me le demander** I don't know anything about it, so there's no use asking me; **elle est tombée malade et elle a d. annulé son voyage** she fell ill, so she cancelled her trip; **nous devrions d. aboutir à un accord** we should therefore reach an agreement

2 *(indiquant une transition)* so; **nous disions d. que...** so, we were saying that...; **d., vous n'avez rien entendu?** so, you didn't hear anything?

3 *(indiquant la surprise)* so; **c'était d. toi!** so it was you!; **c'est d. pour ça!** so that's why!

4 *(renforçant une interrogation, une assertion, une injonction)* **mais qu'y a-t-il d.?** what's the matter, then?; **mais pourquoi ris-tu d.?** what are you laughing at *or* about?; **que voulez-vous d.?** what do you want, then?; **fermez d. la porte!** shut the door, will you!; **viens d. avec nous!** come on, come with us!; **tais-toi d.!** just shut up, will you?; **range d. tes affaires!** why don't you put your things away?; **allons d., je ne te crois pas!** come off it, I don't believe you!; **comment d. est-ce possible?** how can that be possible?; **eh ben dis d.!** well, really!; **essaie d.!** go on, try!; *Ironique* **essaie d. pour voir!** just (you) try it!, go on then!; **tiens d.!** well, well, well!; **ben, voyons d.!** *(évidemment)* naturally!, what else!; *(ne vous gênez pas)* don't mind me!; **dites d., pour qui vous vous prenez?** hold on, who do you think you are?; **dis d., à propos, tu l'as vue hier soir?** oh, by the way, did you see her yesterday evening?

dondon [dɔ̃dɔ̃] NF *Fam Péj* **une grosse d.** a big fat lump

donf [dɔ̃f] **à donf** ADV *Fam (verlan de* **à fond)** *(vite) Br* like the clappers, *Am* like sixty; *(très fort)* at full blast; *(beaucoup)* really, like crazy; **je la kiffe à d., cette nana** she really gives me the horn

donjon [dɔ̃ʒɔ̃] NM keep, donjon

don Juan [dɔ̃ʒɥɑ̃] *(pl* **dons Juans)** NM *(séducteur)* Don Juan, lady's man

donjuanesque [dɔ̃ʒɥanɛsk] ADJ *(attitude, manières)* of a Don Juan

donjuanisme [dɔ̃ʒɥanism] NM donjuanism, philandering

donne [dɔn] NF *Cartes* deal; **faire la d.** to deal; **à moi la d.** it's my (turn to) deal; **il y a eu fausse** *ou* **mauvaise d.** there was a misdeal; *Fig* **nouvelle d.** *(situation)* new state of affairs; *(réorganisation)* new deal

donné, -e [dɔne] ADJ **1** *(heure, lieu)* fixed, given; **à une distance donnée** at a certain distance; **il doit improviser sur un thème d.** he must improvise on a given theme **2** *(particulier, spécifique)* **sur ce point d.** on this particular point; **à cet instant d.** at this (very) moment; **à un moment d.** *(dans le passé)* at one point; *(dans l'avenir)* at some point **3** *(bon marché)* **c'est d.!** it's dirt cheap!
NM *Phil* given

• **donnée** NF **1** *Ordinat & Math* piece of data, *Sout* datum; **données** data; **fichier/saisie/transmission de données** data file/capture/transmission; *Écon* **en données corrigées des variations saisonnières** with adjustments for seasonal variations, seasonally adjusted; *Ordinat* **données numériques** digital data **2** *(information)* piece of information; **données** facts, information; **je ne connais pas toutes les données du problème** I don't have all the information about this question; **données brutes** raw data; **données démographiques** demographic data; **données primaires** primary data; **données secondaires** secondary data; **données de style de vie** lifestyle data

DONNER [3] [dɔne]

VT
- to give **A1–3, A5–13, B1, 3, C1–4, D1–3, 5**
- to give away **A1, D4**
- to give out **A1**
- to leave **A2, 5**
- to donate **A2**
- to hand out **A3**
- to pass on **A12**
- to produce **C1, 2**
- to cause **C2**
- to yield **C1, 4**
- to show **D3**

USAGE ABSOLU
- to give

VI
- to yield **1**
- to deal **2**
- to charge **3**

VT **A.** *CÉDER, ACCORDER* **1** *(offrir)* to give; *(se débarrasser de)* to give away; *(distribuer)* to give out; **d. qch à qn** to give sth to sb, to give sb sth; **d. sa vie/son sang pour la patrie** to give (up) one's life/to shed blood for one's country; **d. qch à qn pour son anniversaire** to give sb sth (as a present) for his/her birthday; **d. qch en cadeau à qn** to make sb a present of sth; **d. qch en souvenir à qn** to give sb sth as a souvenir; **il est joli, ce tableau! – je te le donne** what a lovely picture! – please have it; **à ce prix-là, ma petite dame, je vous le donne!** at that price, dear, I'm giving it away!; **d. sa place à qn dans le train** to give up one's seat to sb on the train; **d. des timbres contre des disques** to swap stamps for records; **d. à boire à un enfant** to give a child a drink *or* something to drink; **d. à manger aux enfants/chevaux** to feed the children/horses; *Fam* **c'était donné, l'examen, cette année!** the exam was a piece of cake this year!; *Hum* **dis donc, on te l'a donné, ton permis de conduire!** how on earth did you pass your driving test!

2 *Jur (léguer)* to leave; *(faire don public de ▸ argent, œuvre d'art, organe)* to donate, to give; **d. une collection à la ville** to donate a collection to the town

3 *(accorder ▸ subvention)* to give, to hand out; *(▸ faveur, interview, liberté)* to give, to grant; *(▸ prix)* to give, to award; *(▸ récompense)* to give; **d. sa fille en mariage à qn** to marry one's daughter to sb; **d. la permission à qn de faire qch** to allow sb to do sth, to give sb permission to do sth; **d. rendez-vous à qn** *Admin* to make an appointment with sb; *(ami, amant)* to make a date with sb; **d. à qn l'occasion de faire qch** to give sb the opportunity to do sth *or* of doing sth; **d. son soutien à qn** to give one's support to sb, to support sb; **d. son accord à qn** to give sb one's consent

4 *(tournure impersonnelle)* **il m'a été donné de voir l'original** I was privileged to see the original; **il n'est pas donné à tout le monde de partir en vacances** not everybody is fortunate enough to be able to go on *Br* holiday *or Am* vacation

5 *(laisser ▸ délai)* to give, to leave; **ça me donne cinq jours pour le finir** that gives *or* leaves me five days to finish it; **il m'a donné trois heures/jusqu'en janvier pour le faire** he gave me three hours/until January to do it

6 *(confier)* to give; **donne-moi ta lettre, je vais la poster** let me have *or* give me your letter, I'll post it; **d. une tâche à qn** to entrust sb with a job; **d. son manteau au teinturier** to take one's coat to the dry cleaner's; **elle m'a donné sa valise à porter** she gave me her suitcase to carry; **d. qch à faire** *(à un professionnel)* to have sth done; **d. ses enfants à garder** to have one's children looked after; **d. son manteau à nettoyer** to have one's coat cleaned

7 *(remettre ▸ gén)* to give; *(▸ devoir)* to give, to hand in; **donne la balle, Rex, donne!** come on Rex, let go (of the ball)!; **donnez vos papiers** hand over your papers

8 *(vendre ▸ sujet: commerçant)* to give; **donnez-moi un beau rôti** I'd like a nice joint; *Fam* **des pêches, combien je vous en donne?** how many peaches would you like?

9 *(payer)* to give; **je lui donne 15 euros de l'heure** I give *or* pay her 15 euros an hour; **et la table, combien m'en donnez-vous?** how much *or* what will you give me for the table?; **combien t'en a-t-on donné?** how much did you get for it?; **je vous en donne 25 euros** I'll give you 25 euros for it; **je donnerais cher pour le savoir** I'd give a lot to know that; **je donnerais n'importe quoi pour le retrouver** I'd give anything to find it again

10 *(administrer ▸ médicament, sacrement)* to give, *Sout* to administer; *(▸ bain)* to give; **d. 15 ans de prison à qn** to give sb a 15-year prison sentence; **d. une punition à qn** to punish sb; **ne pas d. aux enfants de moins de trois ans** *(sur mode d'emploi)* not suitable for *or* not to be given to children under three

11 *(appliquer ▸ coup, baiser)* to give; **d. une claque à qn** to give sb a slap; **d. une fessée à qn** to smack sb's bottom, to spank sb; **d. un coup à qn** to hit sb; **d. un coup de pied/poing à qn** to kick/to punch sb; **d. un coup de rabot/râteau/pinceau à qch** to go over sth with a plane/rake/paintbrush

12 *(passer, transmettre)* to give, to pass on; **donnez-moi le sel** pass *or* hand me the salt; **d. son rhume à qn** to give sb one's cold, to pass one's cold on to sb; **son père lui a donné le goût du théâtre** he/she she got his/her love of the theatre from his/her father

13 *(organiser ▸ dîner, bal)* to give, to throw; **l'association donnera un goûter** the association will give a small party

14 *Fam (locution)* **je vous le donne en cent** *ou* **mille** you'll never guess in a month of Sundays *or* in a million years

B. *CONFÉRER* **1** *(assigner)* to give; **d. un nom à qn** to give sb a name, to name sb; **d. un titre à qn** to confer a title on sb; **je donne peu d'importance à ces choses** I attach little importance to these things; **on donne au verbe la valeur d'un substantif** the verb is given noun status

2 *(attribuer)* **on ne lui donnerait pas son âge** he/she doesn't look his/her age; **on lui donne facilement son âge** he/she looks his/her age; **quel âge me donnez-vous?** how old would you say I am *or* was?

3 *(prédire)* to give; **je ne lui donne pas trois mois** *(à vivre)* I give him/her less than three months to live; *(avant d'échouer)* I'll give it three months at the most

C. *GÉNÉRER* **1** *(sujet: champ)* to yield; *(sujet: arbre fruitier)* to give, to produce; **la graine donne une nouvelle plante** the seed produces a new plant; **le vieux noyer donne encore des kilos de noix** the old walnut tree still gives *or* produces masses of nuts; **les sources d'énergie qui donnent de l'électricité** the energy sources which produce electricity

2 *(susciter, provoquer ▸ courage, énergie, espoir)* to give; *(▸ migraine)* to give, to cause; *(▸ sensation)* to give, to create; *(▸ impression)* to give, to produce; **d. des forces à qn** to give sb strength; **cela m'a donné une belle frayeur** it gave me a real fright; **d. du souci à qn** to worry sb; **les enfants donnent du travail** children are a lot of work; **la promenade m'a donné de l'appétit** the walk has given me an appetite; **d. des boutons à qn** to make sb come out in spots; *Fig* **faire la vaisselle me donne des boutons** I'm allergic to washing up; **la maladie peut d. des complications** the illness may have complications; **ça donne la diarrhée** it gives you *or* causes diarrhoea; **le poisson, ça donne de la mémoire** fish is good for your memory; **les tilleuls donnent de l'ombre** the lime trees give shade; **d. chaud/froid/faim/soif à qn** to make sb hot/cold/hungry/thirsty; **d. mal au cœur à qn** to make sb (feel) sick *or* nauseous

3 *(conférer ▸ prestige)* to confer, to give; *(▸ aspect, charme)* to give, to lend; **le procédé donne au tissu l'aspect du velours** this process gives the material a velvety look; **le grand air t'a donné des couleurs** the fresh air has brought colour to your cheeks; **ton maquillage te donne bonne mine** your make-up makes you look well; **d. de l'ampleur à une veste** to let a jacket out; **pour d. meilleur goût à la sauce** to make the sauce taste better; **pour d. de la vitalité à vos cheveux** to give bounce to your hair; **pour d. plus de mystère à l'histoire** to make the story more mysterious

4 *(aboutir à ▸ résultats)* to give, to yield; *(▸ effet)* to result in; **en ajoutant les impôts, cela donne la somme suivante** when you add (in *or* on) the tax, it comes to the following amount; **j'espère que vos efforts donneront des résultats** I hope your efforts will give *or* yield results; **le deuxième tour a donné la majorité aux écologistes** the second ballot resulted in a majority for the green party; **la combinaison de l'acide et du gaz donne un polymère** a polymer is obtained from combining the acid with the gas; **et ta candidature, ça donne quelque chose?** have you heard anything about your application?; **les recherches n'ont rien donné** the search was fruitless; **la robe ne donne pas grand-chose comme cela, essaie avec une ceinture** the dress doesn't look much like that, try it with a belt; **j'ai ajouté du vin à la sauce – qu'est-ce que ça donne?** I've added some wine to the sauce – what's it like now?; **et la fac, qu'est-ce que ça donne?** how's university going?; **et ton épaule, qu'est-ce que ça donne?** how's your shoulder doing?

D. *EXPRIMER, COMMUNIQUER* **1** *(présenter, fournir ▸ garantie, preuve, précision)* to give, to provide; *(▸ explication)* to give; *(▸ argument)* to put forward; *(▸ ordre, consigne)* to give; **d. un conseil à qn** to give sb a piece of advice, to advise sb; **d. une réponse** to give *or* to provide an answer; **d. son avis** to give one's opinion; **ceux qui ont donné la combinaison gagnante** those who had the winning numbers; **d. ses sources** to quote one's sources; **d. une certaine image de son pays** to show one's country in a particular light; **d. à entendre** *ou* **comprendre que…** to let it be understood that…; **ces faits nous ont été donnés comme vrais** we were led to believe that these facts were true; **d. qch pour certain** to give sth as a certainty; **on le donnait pour riche** he was said *or* thought to be rich; **dans le village, on la donnait pour une sorcière** in the village, she was rumoured to be a witch

2 *(dire)* to give; **d. son nom** to give one's name; **donnez la date de la bataille de Crécy** give the date of the battle of Crécy; **qui peut me d. la racine carrée de 196** who can give *or* tell me the square root of 196?, who can tell me what the square root of 196 is?; **d. des nouvelles à qn** to give sb news; **d. des nouvelles de qn** to give news of sb; **donnez-moi de ses nouvelles** tell me how he/she is; *Fam* **je te le donne pour ce que ça vaut** that's what I was told, for what it's worth

3 *(indiquer ▸ sujet: instrument)* to give, to indicate, to show; **l'altimètre donne l'altitude** an altimeter gives *or* shows the altitude

4 *Fam (dénoncer)* to give away, to rat on, *Br* to shop

5 *(rendre public ▸ causerie, cours)* to give; *(▸ œuvre, spectacle)* to put on; **l'année où j'ai donné 'Giselle'** *(dit par le metteur en scène)* the year I put on 'Giselle'; *(dit par le danseur)* the year I performed 'Giselle'; **elle donnera au printemps une édition critique de Proust** she has a critical edition of Proust coming out in the spring; **qu'est-ce qu'on donne au Rex?** what's on at the Rex?; **ce soir, on donne 'Médée' sur la deuxième chaîne** 'Medea' is on channel two tonight

USAGE ABSOLU to give; **tu as donné à la quête?** did you give anything to the collection?; **d. aux pauvres** to give to the poor; **d. de son temps** to give up one's time; **d. de sa personne** to give of oneself; *Fam* **j'ai déjà donné!** I've been there *or* through that already!

VI 1 *(produire ▸ arbre)* to bear fruit, to yield; *(▸ potager, verger, terre)* to yield; **le cerisier ne donnera pas avant deux ans** the cherry tree won't bear *or* have any fruit for a couple of years; **la vigne a bien/mal donné cette année** the vineyard had a good/bad yield this year; *Fam* **ça donne!** it's something else!, it's wicked *or Br* mental!; *Fam* **dis donc, elle donne, ta chaîne hi-fi!** that's a mean sound system you've got there!; **d. à plein** *(radio)* to be on full blast, to be blaring (out); *(campagne de publicité, soirée)* to be in full swing; **le soleil donne à plein** the sun is beating down

2 *Cartes* to deal; **à toi de d.** your deal

3 *(attaquer)* to charge; **la police va d.** the police are about to charge; **faire d. la garde/troupe** to send in the guards/troops

• **donner dans VT IND 1** *(tomber dans)* **d. dans une embuscade** to be ambushed; **sans d. dans le mélodrame** without becoming too melodramatic; **votre essai donne trop souvent dans le lyrisme** your essay lapses too frequently into lyricism; **on peut s'en réjouir, mais ne donnons pas dans l'excès d'optimisme** we may feel pleased about it, but let's not be over-optimistic **2** *(se cogner contre)* **l'enfant est allé d. dans la fenêtre** the child crashed into the window **3** *(déboucher sur)* to give out onto; **la porte donnait dans un couloir** the door opened *or* gave out onto a corridor; **l'escalier donne dans une petite cour** the staircase gives out onto *or* leads to *or* leads into a small courtyard

• **donner de VT IND 1** *(cogner avec)* **d. du coude/de la tête contre une porte** to bump one's elbow/one's head against a door

2 *(utiliser)* **d. du cor** to sound the horn; **d. de l'éperon à son cheval** to spur one's horse; **d. de la voix** to raise one's voice **d. de la tête** *(animal)* to shake its head; *Fig* **ne plus savoir où d. de la tête** to be run off one's feet

3 *Naut* **d. de la bande** to list

4 *(locution)* **elle lui donne du "monsieur"** she calls him "Sir"

• **donner sur VT IND 1** *(se cogner contre)* **la barque alla d. sur le rocher** the boat crashed into the rock; **d. sur les écueils** to strike the rocks **2** *(être orienté vers)* **la chambre donne sur le jardin/la mer** the room overlooks the garden/the sea; **chambre donnant sur la mer** room with a sea view

• **donnant donnant ADV** that's fair, fair's fair; **je te prête mon costume si tu me passes ta voiture, c'est donnant donnant** I'll lend you my suit if you lend me your car, fair's fair *or* you can't say fairer than that; **d'accord, mais c'est donnant donnant** OK, but I want something in return

VPR se donner 1 *(film, pièce)* to be on; **sa pièce se donne à l'Odéon** his play is being staged *or* is on at the Odéon

2 *(employer son énergie)* **monte sur scène et donne-toi à fond** get on the stage and give it all you've got; **se d. à une cause** to devote oneself *or* one's life to a cause; **elle s'est donnée à fond** *ou* **complètement dans son entreprise** she put all her effort into her business

3 *(sexuellement)* **se d. à qn** to give oneself to sb

4 *(donner à soi-même)* **se d. un coup de marteau sur les doigts** to hit one's fingers with a hammer; **se d. les moyens de faire qch** to give oneself the means to do sth; **se d. du bon temps** *(gén)* to have fun; *Euph* to give oneself a good time

5 *(s'accorder ▸ délai)* to give *or* to allow oneself; **je me suis donné six mois pour finir ma thèse** I've given *or* allowed myself six months to finish my thesis; **donne-toi un peu de repos** allow yourself to rest for a while

6 *(échanger)* to give one another *or* each other; **se d. un baiser** to give each other a kiss, to kiss; **se d. des coups** to exchange blows; **ils se sont donné leurs impressions** they swapped views

7 *(se doter de)* to give oneself; **se d. un chef** to give oneself a leader; **la capitale vient de se d. un second opéra** the capital has been given a second opera house

8 *(prétendre avoir)* **il se donne 30 ans** he claims to be 30

9 *Fam* **se la d.** to show off, to pose

10 se d. pour to pass oneself off as, to claim to be; **elle se donne pour l'amie du ministre** she claims to be the minister's friend

11 *(locutions)* **les enfants s'en sont donné au square** the children had the time of their lives in the park; **avec les crêpes, ils s'en sont donné à cœur joie** they really tucked into their pancakes

donneur, -euse [dɔnœr, -øz] **NM,F 1** *Méd* donor; **d. d'organes** organ donor; **d. de sang** blood donor; **d. universel** universal blood donor

2 *Cartes* dealer

3 je ne veux pas me transformer en d. de leçons, mais... I don't want to lecture you, but...; **c'est un d. de leçons** he likes lecturing *or* sermonizing people

4 *Fam (délateur)* squealer, informer

NM 1 *Écon & Fin* **d. d'aval** backer, referee; **d. de caution** guarantor; **d. d'ordre** principal **2** *Chim* donor **3** *Méd* donor; **d. de sperme** sperm donor

donquichottisme [dɔ̃kiʃɔtism] **NM** quixotism

DONT [dɔ̃] **PRON RELATIF 1** *(exprimant le complément du nom ▸ personne)* whose; *(▸ chose)* whose, *Sout* of which; **le club d. je suis membre** the club I belong to, the club to which I belong *or Sout* of which I'm a member; **un projet d. vous pouvez voir les grandes lignes** a plan whose general outline you can see, *Sout* a plan, the general outline of which you can see; **un buffet d. le bois est vermoulu** a sideboard with woodworm; **cette femme, d. le charme les avait captivés** this woman whose charm had captivated them; **l'hôtel d. nous avons apprécié la tranquillité** the hotel whose quietness we appreciated, *Sout* the hotel of which we appreciated the quietness

2 *(exprimant la partie d'un tout ▸ personnes)* of whom; *(▸ choses)* of which; **il y a 95 candidats, d. 33 Canadiens** there are 95 candidates, of whom 33 *or* 33 of whom are Canadians; **des livres d. la plupart ne valent rien** books, most of which are worthless; **deux personnes ont téléphoné, d. ton frère** two people phoned, including your brother; **les invités étaient arrivés, d. nos amis marseillais** the guests had arrived, amongst whom were *or* including our friends from Marseilles

3 *(exprimant le complément de l'adjectif)* **le service d. vous êtes responsable** the service for which you are responsible; **c'est la seule photo d. je sois fier** it's the only photograph I'm proud of *or Sout* of which I'm proud

4 *(exprimant l'objet indirect)* **celui d. je vous ai parlé** the one I spoke to you about; **ce d. nous avons discuté** what we talked about; **explique-moi ce d. il s'agit** tell me what it's about; **une corvée d. je me passerais bien** a chore (which) I could well do without; **il n'y a rien là d. on puisse se féliciter** there's nothing to congratulate ourselves about; **une affaire d. il s'occupe** a matter which he is dealing with; **les vacances d. tu rêves** the holidays which you dream of *or* about

5 *(exprimant le complément du verbe ▸ indiquant la provenance, l'agent, la manière etc)* **le mal d. il souffre** the illness which he suffers from; **une personne d. on ne sait rien** a person nobody knows anything about; **cette femme d. je sais qu'elle n'a pas d'enfants** that woman who I know doesn't have any children; **la famille d. je viens** the family (which) I come from; **le nectar d. les abeilles tirent le miel** the nectar from which bees make honey, the nectar which bees make honey from; **les amis d. il est entouré** the friends he is surrounded by; **les cadeaux d. il a été comblé** the many presents (which) he received; **la façon d. elle s'y prend** the way (in which) she goes about it; **la manière d. il joue** the way (in which) he plays, his way of playing

donzelle [dɔ̃zɛl] **NF** *Fam Hum* little madam

dopage [dɔpaʒ] **NM 1** *(des sportifs)* drug use *(in competitive sport)* **2** *Fig (de l'économie, des ventes)* boosting, artificial stimulation

dopant, -e [dɔpɑ̃, -ɑ̃t] **ADJ produit d.** drug

NM drug *(used as stimulant in competitive sport)*

dope [dɔp] **NF** *très Fam Arg drogue* dope, stuff, *Br* gear

doper [3] [dɔpe] **VT 1** *(droguer)* to dope *(in competitive sport)* **2** *(économie, ventes)* to boost **3** *Chim* to dope

VPR se doper to take drugs *(in competitive sport)*

dope sheet [dɔpʃit] **NM** *Cin & TV* dope sheet

doping [dɔpiŋ] **NM** drug use *(in competitive sport)*

Doppler [dɔplɛr] **NPR** *Phys* **effet D.** Doppler effect

dorade [dɔrad] = **daurade**

doré, -e [dɔre] **ADJ 1** *(bouton, robinetterie)* gilt, gilded; **d. sur tranche** *(livre)* gilt-edged, with gilded edges **2** *(chevelure, lumière, blés)* golden; *(peau, gâteau, viande)* golden (brown); **ses cheveux étaient d'un blond d.** he had golden hair **3** *(idéal ▸ jours, rêves)* golden

NM 1 *(dorure)* gilt **2** *Can Ich* yellow *or* wall-eyed pike

• **dorée NF** *Ich* John Dory, dory

dorénavant [dɔrenavɑ̃] **ADV** *(à partir de maintenant)* from now on, *Sout* henceforth, henceforward; *(dans le passé)* from then on

dorer [3] [dɔre] **VT 1** *(couvrir d'or)* to gild; **d. un cadre à la feuille** to gild a frame with gold leaf; *Fam* **d. la pilule à qn** to sugar the pill for sb **2** *(brunir ▸ peau)* to give a golden colour to, to tan; *(▸ blés, poires)* to turn golden; *(▸ paysage)* to shed a golden light on; **le couchant dorait les roseaux** the setting sun tipped the reeds with gold **3** *Culin* **d. une pâte à l'œuf/au lait** to glaze pastry with egg yolk/with milk

VI 1 *Culin* to turn golden; **faire d. la viande** to brown the meat; **faites d. la tarte** bake the pie until golden **2 se faire d. au soleil** to sunbathe

VPR se dorer to sunbathe; **se d. les jambes au soleil** to tan one's legs in the sun; *Fam* **se d. la pilule** *(bronzer)* to sunbathe▫, to lie in the sun▫; *(ne rien faire)* to do *Br* sweet FA *or Am* zilch

doreur, -euse [dɔrœr, -øz] **NM,F** gilder

dorique [dɔrik] **ADJ** *(ordre)* Doric; **une colonne d'ordre d.** a Doric column

NM le d. the Doric order

dorlotement [dɔrlɔtmɑ̃] **NM** coddling, pampering

dorloter [3] [dɔrlɔte] **VT** to coddle, to pamper; **il adore se faire d.** he loves being looked after

VPR se dorloter to pamper oneself

dormance [dɔrmɑ̃s] **NF** dormancy

dormant, -e [dɔrmɑ̃, -ɑ̃t] **ADJ 1** *(eau)* still

2 *Littéraire (passion, sensualité)* dormant

3 *Biol* dormant, latent

4 *Constr (bâti, chassis)* fixed

5 *Fin (compte)* dormant; *(marché, capital)* unproductive, lying idle

NM *Constr (bâti)* fixed frame, casing; *(vitre)* fixed pane

dormeur, -euse [dɔrmœr, -øz] **ADJ** *(poupée, poupon)* sleeping

NM,F sleeper; **c'est un grand** *ou* **gros d.** he likes his sleep

NM *(crabe)* (common *or* edible) crab

• **dormeuse NF** *(boucle d'oreille)* stud earring

dormir [36] [dɔrmir] **VI 1** *(gén)* to sleep; *(à un moment précis)* to be asleep, to be sleeping; **tu as bien dormi?** did you sleep well?; **dors bien!** sleep well!; **j'ai dormi tout l'après-midi** I was asleep *or* I slept all afternoon; **il dort tard le dimanche** he sleeps late on Sundays; **on dort mal dans ce lit** you can't get a good night's sleep in this bed; **tu as pu d. dans le train?** did you manage to get some sleep on the train?; **parler en dormant** to talk in one's sleep; **je n'ai pas dormi de la nuit** I didn't sleep a wink all night; **la situation m'inquiète, je n'en dors pas** *ou* **plus (la nuit)** the situation worries me, I'm losing sleep over it; **prends ce comprimé, ça te fera d.** take this, it'll help you sleep; **le thé m'empêche de d.** tea keeps me awake; **avoir envie de d.** to feel sleepy; **d. d'un sommeil léger** *(habituellement)* to be a light sleeper; *(à tel moment)* to be dozing; **d. d'un sommeil profond** *ou* **lourd** *ou* **de plomb** *(habituellement)* to be a heavy sleeper; *(à tel moment)* to be fast asleep, to be sound asleep, to be in a deep sleep; **d. à poings fermés** to be fast asleep, to be sleeping like a baby; **d. comme un ange** *(bébé)* to be sound asleep; *(adulte)* to sleep like a baby; **d. comme une bûche** *ou* **un loir** *ou* **une marmotte** *ou* **une souche** *ou* **un sabot** to sleep like a log; **il est là-haut, et dort comme une marmotte** he's upstairs, sound asleep *or* dead to the world; **tu dors debout** you can't (even) keep awake, you're dead on your feet; **elle a raconté au juge une his-**

toire à d. debout she told the judge a pack of lies; **d. du sommeil du juste** to sleep the sleep of the just; **tu peux d. sur tes deux oreilles** there's no reason for you to worry, you can sleep soundly in your bed at night; **je ne dors que d'un œil** *(je dors mal)* I can hardly sleep, I hardly get a wink of sleep; *(je reste vigilant)* I sleep with one eye open; *Prov* **qui dort dîne** he who sleeps forgets his hunger

2 *(être sans activité ▸ secteur)* to be dormant *or* asleep; *(▸ volcan)* to be dormant; *(▸ économies personnelles)* to lie idle; *(▸ économie nationale)* to be stagnant; **ils ont laissé d. le projet** they left the project on the back burner

3 *(être inattentif)* **dépêche-toi, tu dors!** come on, wake up!; **ce n'est pas le moment de d.!** now's the time for action!

VT *Littéraire* **d. un bon sommeil** to sleep peacefully

dormitif, -ive [dɔrmitif, -iv] ADJ **1** *Arch (qui fait dormir)* sleep-inducing, soporific **2** *Hum (ennuyeux)* soporific

dorsal, -e, -aux, -ales [dɔrsal, -o] ADJ **1** *Anat & Zool* dorsal, back *(avant n)*; **la face dorsale de la main** the back of the hand **2** *Ling* dorsal

NM *Anat* **grand d., long d.** latissimus dorsi

• **dorsale** NF **1** *Ling* dorsal consonant

2 *Zool* dorsal fin

3 *Géol (élévation)* ridge; *(montagne)* mountain range

4 *Météo* **dorsale barométrique** ridge of high pressure

dort *etc voir* **dormir**

dort-en-chiant [dɔrɑ̃ʃjɑ̃] NM INV *Fam Br* slowcoach, *Am* slowpoke

dortoir [dɔrtwar] NM dormitory

dorure [dɔryr] NF **1** *(couche ▸ d'or)* gilt; *(▸ artificielle)* gold-effect finish; **bureau couvert de dorures** desk covered in gilding; **uniforme couvert de dorures** gold-braided uniform **2** *(processus)* gilding; **d. à la feuille** gold leaf gilding; **d. industrielle** foil blocking, gold blocking

doryphore [dɔrifɔr] NM *Entom* Colorado *or* potato beetle

DOS, Dos [dɔs] NM *Ordinat (abrév* **Disk Operating System**) DOS

DOS [do] NM **1** *(partie du corps)* back; **le bas de son d.** the small of his/her back; **avoir le d. rond** to be hunched up *or* round-shouldered; **avoir le d. voûté** to have a stoop; **j'ai mal au d.** my back hurts, I've got backache; **j'avais le soleil dans le d.** the sun was behind me *or* on my back; **quand vous aurez l'église dans le d., tournez à droite** when you've passed the church, turn right; **être sur le d.** to be (lying) on one's back; **mets-toi sur le d.** lie on your back; **tourner le d. à qn** *(assis)* to sit with one's back to sb; *(debout)* to stand with one's back to sb; *(l'éviter)* to turn one's back on sb; **je ne l'ai vu que de d.** I only saw him from behind *or* the back; **j'étais d. à la fenêtre** I had my back to the window; **où est la gare? – vous lui tournez le d.** where is the station? – you're going away from it; **dès que j'ai le d. tourné, il fait des bêtises** as soon as my back is turned, he gets up to mischief; **partir sac au d.** to set off with one's rucksack on one's back *or* with one's backpack; **comme d'habitude, j'ai bon d.!** as usual, I get the blame!; *Ironique* **il a bon d., le mauvais temps!** (why not) blame the bad weather!; **j'ai le d. large mais il ne faut pas exagérer!** I can take a lot *or* I may be resilient, but there are limits!; *Fam* **ce gosse n'a rien sur le d.!** that kid's not dressed warmly enough!; *Fam* **elle a pas mal de dettes sur le d.** she's up to her *Br* eyes *or Am* ears in debt; *Fam* **c'est moi qui ai tous les préparatifs sur le d.** I've been saddled with all the preparations; **il est toujours derrière mon d.** he's always breathing down my neck; **faire qch dans** *ou* **derrière le d. de qn** to do sth behind sb's back; *Fam* **elle lui a fait un enfant dans le d.** she deliberately got pregnant[□]; *Fam* **être tombé sur le d. et se casser le nez** to be damned unlucky, to have rotten luck; *Fam* **tu es toujours sur le d. de ce gosse, laisse-le un peu!** you're always nagging the kid, leave him alone!; *Fam* **vous aurez les syndicats sur le d.** the unions will be breathing down your necks; **faire le gros d.** *(chat)* to arch its back; *Fig* to lie low; *Fam* **ils ont bâti leur empire sur le d. des indigènes** they built their empire at the expense of the natives; *Fam* **il l'a dans le d.!** he's been had *or* done!; *Fam* **fais gaffe, tu vas l'avoir dans le d.!** watch out or you'll get done!; **se mettre qn à d.** to put sb's back up; **je ne veux pas l'avoir** *ou* **me le mettre à d.** I don't want him to turn against me *or* to get his back up; **il les avait tous à d.** they were all after him; *Fam* **mettre qch sur le d. de qn** *(crime, erreur)* to pin sth on sb; **ils lui ont tout mis sur le d.!** they blamed *or* pinned everything on him; **c'est les flics qui m'ont mis ça sur le d.** I was set up by the cops!; **je n'ai rien/pas grand-chose à me mettre sur le d.** I've got nothing/virtually nothing to wear; **il s'est mis toute la responsabilité sur le d.** he shouldered the responsibility for the whole business; *Fig* **tirer dans le d. de qn** to shoot *or* to stab sb in the back; *Fam* **si le fisc lui tombe sur le d., ça va lui coûter cher!** if the *Br* Inland Revenue *or Am* IRS gets hold of *or* catches him, it'll cost him!; *Fig* **avoir le d. au mur** to have one's back to the wall

2 *(d'une fourchette, d'un habit)* back; *(d'un couteau)* blunt edge; *(d'un livre)* spine; **corsage décolleté dans le d.** low-backed blouse; *Fam* **il n'y est pas allé avec le d. de la cuillère!** *(dans une action)* he didn't go in for half-measures!; *(dans une discussion)* he didn't mince his words!

3 *Natation* **d. crawlé** backstroke; **on va jusqu'à la bouée en d. crawlé?** let's do the backstroke all the way to the buoy

• **à dos de** PRÉP on the back of; **aller à d. d'âne/d'éléphant** to ride (on) a donkey/an elephant; **le matériel est transporté à d. de lamas/d'hommes** the equipment is carried by llamas/men

• **au dos** ADV *(d'une feuille)* on the other side *or* the back, overleaf; **voir au d.** see over *or* overleaf

• **au dos de** PRÉP *(feuille)* on the back of; **signer au d. d'un chèque** to endorse a cheque, to sign the back of a cheque

• **dos à dos** ADV with their backs to one another; **mettez-vous d. à d.** stand back to back *or* with your backs to one another; *Fig* **mettre** *ou* **renvoyer deux personnes d. à d.** to refuse to get involved in an argument between two people

dosage [dozaʒ] NM **1** *(détermination)* measurement, measuring; **faire un d.** to determine a quantity

2 *(dose précise de médicaments)* (prescribed) dose

3 *(proportions)* proportions; **le d. de ce cocktail est...** the (correct) proportions for this cocktail are...

4 *Méd* **d. hormonal** test to determine hormone levels; **d. immunologique** immunoassay; **d. radio-immunologique** radioimmunoassay

dos-d'âne [dodan] NM INV speed bump, *Br* sleeping policeman; **pont en d.** humpback bridge

dose [doz] NF **1** *Pharm* dose; *Méd* dose, dosage; **une forte d. de ce médicament peut être mortelle** in large doses, this drug can be fatal; **ne pas dépasser la d. prescrite** *(sur mode d'emploi)* do not exceed the prescribed dose

2 *Com (quantité prédéterminée ▸ gén)* dose, measure; *(▸ en sachet)* sachet; **mesurez trois doses de lait en poudre** take three measures of powdered milk; **une d. de désherbant pour dix doses d'eau** one part weedkiller to ten parts water

3 *(quantité ▸ d'un aliment, d'un composant)* amount, quantity; **je ne connais pas les doses pour la vinaigrette** I don't know the right proportions *or* quantities to use when making vinaigrette; **ses documentaires ont tous une petite d. d'humour** there's a touch of humour in all his/her documentaries; **il a une d. de paresse peu commune** he's uncommonly lazy; **il faut une sacrée d. de bêtise/naïveté pour le croire** you have to be pretty stupid/naive to believe him; **du moment qu'il a sa d. journalière de télévision, il est content** as long as he gets his daily dose of television, he's happy

4 *Fam (locutions)* **il a sa d.** *(lassé, ivre)* he's had a bellyful *or* as much as he can stand; **j'ai eu ma d. de problèmes!** I've had my (fair) share of problems!; **sa mère, j'en ai eu ma d.!** I've seen quite enough of his/her mother!

• **à faible dose** ADV in small doses *or* quantities

• **à forte dose** ADV in large quantities *or* amounts

• **à haute dose** ADV in large doses *or* quantities; *Fam* **travailler à haute d.** to work like a dog

• **à petite dose, à petites doses** ADV in small doses *or* quantities; **j'aime bien le sport/ma sœur, mais à petites doses** I like sport/my sister, but (only) in small doses

doser [3] [doze] VT **1** *(médicament)* to measure a dose of; *(composant, ingrédient)* to measure out **2** *(équilibrer ▸ cocktail, vinaigrette)* to use the correct proportions for; **comment doses-tu ta vinaigrette?** what proportions do you use for your vinaigrette? **3** *(utiliser avec mesure)* **d. ses forces** *ou* **son effort** to pace oneself; **il faut savoir d. ses critiques** you have to know how far you can go in your criticism

dosette [dozɛt] NF individual sachet; *(de café)* capsule; *(de détergent lave-linge)* doser

doseur [dozœr] NM **1** *(appareil)* measure **2** *(comme adj)* **bouchon/gobelet d.** measuring cap/cup

doseur-distributeur [dozœrdistribytœr] *(pl* **doseurs-distributeurs**) NM *(de carburant)* fuel distributor

dossard [dosar] NM *Sport* number *(worn by player or competitor)*

dossier [dosje] NM **1** *(d'une chaise, d'un canapé)* back; **chaise à d. droit** straight-backed chair

2 *(documents)* file; **avoir un d. sur qn** to keep a file on sb, to keep sb on file; **constituer** *ou* **établir un d. sur qn/qch** to build up a file on sb/sth; **il connaît** *ou* **possède son d.** he knows what he's talking about; **d. d'appel d'offres** tender documents; **d. de candidature** application; **d. client** client file; **d. crédit** credit file; **d. de demande d'introduction en Bourse** listing agreement; **d. de demande de prêt** loan application form; **d. de domiciliation** domiciliation papers, domiciliation file; **d. de douane** customs papers *or* file; *Univ* **d. d'inscription** registration forms; **d. de lancement** *(d'un produit)* product launch file; **d. médical** medical file *or* records; *Scol* **d. scolaire** *Br* school record, *Am* student file

3 *Jur (d'un prévenu)* record; *(d'une affaire)* case; *Admin (d'un cas social)* case file; **ouvrir/fermer un d.** to open/to close a case file

4 *Journ, Rad & TV* **numéro spécial avec un d. sur le Brésil** special issue with an extended report on Brazil; **d. de presse** press pack

5 *(sujet)* question, matter; **c'est lui qui est chargé du d. environnement** he's in charge of environmental matters, he has special responsibility for the environment; **c'est un d. brûlant** it's a highly sensitive *or* topical issue

6 *(chemise cartonnée)* folder, file; **d. suspendu** suspension file

7 *Ordinat (répertoire)* folder; *(fichier)* file; **d. actif** active file; **d. archivé** archive file; **d. clos** closed file; **d. ouvert** open file; **d. sauvegardé** saved file; **d. système** system file

dot [dɔt] NF *(d'une mariée)* dowry; *(d'une religieuse)* (spiritual) dowry

• **en dot** ADV as a dowry; **apporter qch en d.** to bring sth as one's dowry, to bring a dowry of sth

dotal, -e, -aux, -ales [dɔtal, -o] ADJ dotal; *Arch Jur* **régime d.** (marriage) settlement in trust

dotation [dɔtasjɔ̃] NF **1** *(fonds versés ▸ à un particulier, à une collectivité)* endowment; *(▸ à un service public)* grant, funds

2 *(revenus ▸ du président)* (personal) allowance, emolument; *(▸ d'un souverain)* civil list

3 *(attribution ▸ de matériel)* equipment; **la somme est réservée pour la d. du service en ordinateurs** the sum has been earmarked for providing *or* equipping the department with computers; *Can* **d. en personnel** staffing

4 *Compta* provision; **d. aux amortissements** depreciation provision, allowance for depreciation; **d. en capital** capital contribution; **d. aux provisions** charge to provisions

doter [3] [dɔte] VT **1** *(équiper)* **d. qch de qch** to provide *or* to equip sth with sth; **cette machine est dotée de mémoire** this machine is equipped with a memory

2 *(gratifier)* **la nature l'avait dotée d'une beauté exceptionnelle** nature had endowed her with exceptional beauty; **quand on est doté d'une bonne santé** when you enjoy good health

3 *(donner une dot à)* to give a dowry to; **ses filles sont richement dotées** his daughters have large dowries

4 *(financer ▸ particulier, collectivité)* to endow; *(▸ service public)* to fund

VPR se doter se d. de to acquire

douaire [dwɛr] **NM** dower

douairière [dwɛrjɛr] **NF 1** *(veuve)* dowager (lady) **2** *Péj (femme)* rich old woman

douane [dwan] **NF 1** *(à la frontière)* **(poste de) d.** customs; **passer à la d.** to go through customs; **d. volante** mobile customs and excise unit **2** *(administration)* **la d., les douanes, le service des douanes** *(gén)* the Customs (service); *(en Grande-Bretagne)* Customs and Excise (department); **entreposer qch en d.** to put sth in *or* into bond **3** *(taxe)* **(droits de) d.** customs duty; **exempté de d.** duty-free, non-dutiable; **s'acquitter des droits de d.** to clear customs

douanier, -ère [dwanje, -ɛr] **ADJ** *(tarif, visite)* customs *(avant n)*

NM,F customs officer

doublage [dublaʒ] **NM 1** *Cin (d'un film, d'une voix)* dubbing; *(par une doublure)* doubling; **il n'y a pas de d. pour les cascades** there's no body double for the stunts **2** *(habillage d'un coffre)* lining **3** *Couture* lining

double [dubl] **ADJ 1** *(deux fois plus grand ▸ mesure, production)* double; **les profits seront doubles cette année** profits will be double *or* will have doubled this year; **un d. whisky** a double whisky; **chambre/lit d.** double room/bed; *Ordinat* **disquette d. densité/d. face** double-density/double-sided disk; **d. imposition** double taxation; **d. menton** double chin

2 *(à deux éléments identiques)* double; **contrat en d. exemplaire** contract in duplicate; **d. deux/cinq** *(à un jeu)* double two/five; **d. allumage** dual ignition; **en d. aveugle** double-blind; **d. commande** dual controls; **à d. commande** dual-control; **faire un d. débrayage** *Br* to double-declutch, *Am* to double-clutch; *Sport* **d. faute** *(au tennis)* double fault; **faire une d. faute** to serve a double fault, to double-fault; **stationner en d. file** to double-park; **je suis en d. file** I'm double-parked; **à d. fond** *(mallette)* double-bottomed, false-bottomed; **d. liaison** double bond; **d. nœud** double knot; **d. page** double-page spread; **à d. revenu** *(foyer, ménage)* two-income; **d. vitrage** double glazing; **faire poser un d. vitrage à une fenêtre** to double-glaze a window; **faire d. emploi** to be redundant; **faire d. emploi avec qch** to replicate sth

3 *(à éléments différents ▸ avantage, objectif)* double, twofold; *(▸ fonction, personnalité, tarification)* dual; **le préjudice est d.** the damage is of two kinds *or* is twofold; **avoir la d. nationalité** to have dual nationality; **mener une d. vie** to lead a double life; **à d. emploi** *ou* **usage** dual-purpose; **d. contrainte** double bind; *Com* **d. affichage des prix** dual pricing; *Fin* **d. circulation** *(de monnaies)* dual circulation; **à d. effet** double acting; *Fig* **d. jeu** double-dealing; *Bourse* **d. marché des changes** dual exchange market; *Bourse* **d. option** double option, put and call option; **jouer** *ou* **mener (un) d. jeu** to play a double game; **faire coup d.** *Chasse* to kill two animals with one shot; *Fig* to kill two birds with one stone

4 *Bot* double; **lilas d.** double lilac

5 *Jur* **d. degré de juridiction** double degree of jurisdiction; **avoir le droit à un d. degré de juridiction** to have the right to appeal; **d. peine** double punishment *(consisting of a prison sentence followed by expulsion from the country)*

NM 1 *(en quantité)* **six est le d. de trois** six is twice three *or* two times three; **coûter le d. de qch** to cost twice as much as sth; **j'ai payé le d.** I paid double that price *or* twice as much; **je croyais que ça coûtait 40 euros – c'est plus du d.** I thought it was 40 euros – it's more than twice that *or* double that price

2 *(exemplaire ▸ d'un document)* copy; *(▸ d'un timbre de collection)* duplicate, double; **tu as un d. de la clé?** have you got a spare *or* duplicate key?; **je garde des doubles de toute ma correspondance** I keep copies of all the letters I send; **faites un d.** *(d'un document)* make a copy; **j'ai fait faire un d. de la clé** I had a duplicate key made; **d. original** double original

3 *(sosie)* double, doppelgänger

4 *Sport* **jouer un d.** to play doubles *or* a doubles match; **c'est un bon joueur de d.** he's a good doubles player; **d. messieurs/dames/mixte** men's/women's/mixed doubles

ADV *(compter)* twice as much, double; *(voir)* double

• **à double sens ADJ un mot à d. sens** a double-entendre; **une phrase à d. sens** a double-entendre **ADV on peut prendre la remarque à d. sens** you can interpret *or* take that remark two ways

• **à double tour ADV fermer à d. tour** to double lock; **enfermer qn à d. tour** to lock sb up

• **à double tranchant ADJ** *(couteau, action)* double-edged, two-edged; **c'est un argument à d. tranchant** the argument cuts both ways; **la mondialisation est un phénomène à d. tranchant** globalization is a double-edged sword

• **en double ADV les draps sont pliés en d.** the sheets are folded double *or* doubled over; **mettre qch en d.** *(corde)* to double sth over; *(couverture)* to double sth over, to fold sth double; **j'ai une photo en d.** I've got two of the same photograph; *Sport* **jouer en d.** to play (a) doubles (match)

doublé, -e [duble] **ADJ 1** *Couture* lined (**de** with) **2** *Cin* dubbed

NM 1 *Chasse* right and left **2** *(succès)* double; **vainqueur du 100 et du 200 m, c'est un beau d.** he's won both the 100 and 200 m races, that's a nice double **3** *(en joaillerie)* **d. (or)** rolled gold; **d. argent** silver plate

double-bande [dubləbɑ̃d] *(pl* **doubles-bandes***)* **NF** *TV* double head

double-blanc [dubləblɑ̃] *(pl* **doubles-blancs***)* **NM** *(aux dominos)* double blank

double-clic [dubləklik] *(pl* **doubles-clics***)* **NM** *Ordinat* double-click; **faire un d. (sur)** to double-click (on)

double-cliquer [3] [dubləklike] **VI** *Ordinat* to double-click

double-corde [dubləkɔrd] *(pl* **doubles-cordes***)* **NF** *Mus (sur un violon etc)* double-stopping

double-crème [dubləkrɛm] *(pl* **doubles-crèmes***)* **NM** ≃ cream cheese

double-croche [dubləkrɔʃ] *(pl* **doubles-croches***)* **NF** *Br* semi-quaver, *Am* sixteenth note

double-décimètre [dublədesimɛtr] *(pl* **doubles-décimètres***)* **NM** ruler

double-fenêtre [dubləfənɛtr] *(pl* **doubles-fenêtres***)* **NF** double window

doublement[1] [dubləmɑ̃] **NM 1** *(augmentation ▸ des bénéfices, du personnel, d'une quantité, d'un prix, d'une production)* doubling *(UNCOUNT)*, twofold increase; **ils demandent le d. de leur prime** they want their bonus to be doubled

2 *(d'un coureur, d'un véhicle)* passing, *Br* overtaking

3 *(d'une couverture, d'un papier, d'un tissu)* doubling, folding; *(d'une corde, d'un fil)* doubling

4 *(d'une consonne)* doubling

doublement[2] [dubləmɑ̃] **ADV** doubly; **c'est d. ironique** there's a double irony there; **je suis d. déçu/surpris** I'm doubly disappointed/surprised

doubler [3] [duble] **VT 1** *(dépasser ▸ coureur, véhicule) Br* to overtake, *Am* to pass; **défense de d.** *(sur panneau)* no overtaking, no passing

2 *(porter au double ▸ bénéfices, personnel, quantité, prix, production)* to double; **d. l'allure** *ou* **le pas** to quicken one's pace; **d. la mise** *(à un jeu)* to double the stake; *Fig* to raise the stakes

3 *(garnir d'une doublure ▸ coffret, jupe, tenture)* to line (**de** with)

4 *Cin (film, voix)* to dub; *(acteur)* to stand in for, to double; **il se fait d. pour les cascades** he's got a stand-in *or* a double for his stunts

5 *(mettre en double ▸ corde, fil)* to double; *(▸ couverture, papier, tissu)* to fold (in half), to double (over); **les enfants, doublez les rangs** children, walk in twos

6 *Fam* **d. qn** *(trahir)* to pull a fast one on sb, to double-cross sb; *(devancer) Br* to pip sb at the post, *Am* to beat sb out

7 *Mus (parties)* to split

8 *Naut (cap)* to double, to round; *Fig* **d. le cap de la trentaine** to turn thirty

9 *Vieilli ou Belg, Can & Suisse Scol* to repeat; **il a doublé sa troisième** he had to do his fourth year again

VI 1 *(bénéfices, poids, quantité)* to double, to increase twofold **2** *(au tennis)* to double bounce **3** *Vieilli ou Belg, Can & Suisse Scol* to repeat a year

VPR se doubler se d. de to be coupled with; **une mauvaise foi qui se double d'agressivité** insincerity coupled with aggressiveness

doublet [dublɛ] **NM 1** *Ling, Phys & (en joaillerie)* doublet **2** *Opt* doublet (lens)

doubleur[1]**, -euse** [dublœr, -øz] **NM,F** *Belg* = pupil repeating a year

doubleur[2] [dublœr] **NM** *Ordinat* **d. de fréquence** clock speed doubler

doublon [dublɔ̃] **NM 1** *(pièce)* doubloon **2** *Typ* doublet

doublonner [3] [dublɔne] **doublonner avec VT IND** to duplicate

doublure [dublyr] **NF 1** *(garniture)* lining **2** *Cin* stand-in, double; *Théât* understudy

douce [dus] *voir* **doux**

douce-amère [dusamer] *(pl* **douces-amères***)* **NF** *Bot* woody nightshade, bittersweet

ADJ *voir* **doux-amer**

douceâtre [dusatr] **ADJ** *(odeur, goût, saveur)* sweetish; *(sourire, ton, voix)* sugary

doucement [dusmɑ̃] **ADV 1** *(avec délicatesse, sans brusquerie ▸ caresser, poser, prendre)* gently; *(▸ manier)* gently, with care; *(▸ démarrer)* smoothly; **d. gently!, careful!**; **d. avec les verres!** careful *or* go gently with the glasses!; **d. avec le champagne/poivre!** (go) easy on the champagne/pepper!

2 *(lentement ▸ marcher, progresser, rouler)* slowly

3 *(graduellement ▸ augmenter, s'élever)* gently, gradually; **le champ descend d. jusqu'à la rivière** the field slopes gently down to the river

4 *(sans bruit ▸ chantonner)* softly; **parle plus d., il dort** lower your voice *or* keep your voice down, he's sleeping

5 *Fam (discrètement)* **ça me fait d. rigoler, son projet de créer une entreprise** his idea of setting up a company is a bit of a joke

6 *(pour calmer, contrôler)* **d., d., vous n'allez pas vous battre, tout de même!** calm down, you don't want to fight, do you?; *Fam* **d. les basses!** hey, hold on!

7 *Fam (moyennement)* so-so; **comment va ton commerce? – d.** how's your business doing? – so-so *or* it's just about keeping afloat

doucereux, -euse [dusrø, -øz] **ADJ** *(goût, liqueur)* sweetish; *Péj* sickly sweet; *(voix, ton, paroles)* sugary, honeyed; *(manières, personne)* suave, smooth

doucet, -ette [duse, -ɛt] **ADJ** *Arch* meek, mild

• **doucette NF** corn salad, lamb's lettuce

douceur [dusœr] **NF 1** *(toucher ▸ d'une étoffe, d'une brosse)* softness; *(▸ des cheveux, de la peau)* softness, smoothness

2 *(goût ▸ d'un vin, du miel)* sweetness; *(▸ d'un fromage)* mildness

3 *(délicatesse ▸ de caresses, de mouvements, de manières)* gentleness; *(▸ d'une voix)* softness; **manipuler qch avec d.** to handle sth gently; **parler avec d.** to speak softly; **prendre qn par la d.** to use the soft approach with sb; **la d. de vivre** the gentle pleasures of life

4 *(bonté ▸ d'une personne)* sweetness, gentleness; *(▸ d'un regard, d'un sourire)* gentleness

5 *(d'un relief)* softness; **la d. de ses traits** his soft features

6 *Tech (de l'eau)* softness

7 *(du temps, du climat)* mildness; **j'étais surpris par la d. du soir** I was surprised by how mild an evening it was

8 *(friandise)* sweet

• **douceurs NFPL 1** *(agréments)* pleasures; **les douceurs de la vie** the pleasures of life, the pleasant things in life **2** *(propos agréables)* sweet words; *Ironique* **les deux conducteurs échangeaient des douceurs** the two drivers were swapping insults

• **en douceur ADJ** *(décollage, démarrage)* smooth **ADV** *(sans brusquerie ▸ gén)* gently; *(▸ dé-*

marrer, atterrir) smoothly; **allez-y en d.!** gently does it!, easy does it!

douche [duʃ] **NF 1** *(jet d'eau)* shower; **prendre une d.** to have *or* to take a shower; **il est sous la d.** he's in the shower; **d. écossaise** hot and cold shower *(taken successively)*; **ce mélangeur ne marche pas, c'est la d. écossaise!** that mixer tap's not working, you get scalded one minute and frozen the next!; **c'est la d. écossaise avec lui!** he blows hot and cold!
2 *(bac, cabine)* shower (unit); **les douches** the showers
3 *Fam (averse)* **recevoir** *ou* **prendre une bonne d.** to get drenched□ *or* soaked□
4 *Fam (choc, surprise)* shock□; *(déception)* letdown, anticlimax□; **ça m'a fait l'effet d'une d. (froide)** it came as a shock to me; **lui qui croyait être nommé directeur, quelle d.!** he thought he was going to be appointed manager, what a letdown for him!
5 *Fam (reproches)* telling-off, dressing-down

doucher [3] [duʃe] **VT 1** *(laver)* to shower, to give a shower to; *Méd* to douche; *Fam* **je me suis fait d.** *(par la pluie)* I got drenched□ *or* soaked□ **2** *Fam (décevoir ▸ personne)* to deflate **3** *Fam (réprimander)* **d. qn** to tell sb off, to give sb a good telling-off
VPR se doucher to have *or* to take a shower

douchette [duʃɛt] **NF** shower head

doudou¹ [dudu] **NF** *(aux Antilles) (en appellatif)* honey, babe

doudou² [dudu] **NM** *Fam (tissu)* security blanket; *(objet fétiche)* = any object carried round by small children to make them feel secure

doudoune [dudun] **NF** (thick) quilted jacket *or* anorak

doué, -e [dwe] **ADJ** *(acteur, musicien)* gifted, talented; **être d. en dessin/pour les langues** to have a gift for *or* to be good at drawing/languages; **tu es vraiment d. pour envenimer les situations!** you've got a real knack for stirring things up!; *Fam* **je n'arrive pas à brancher le tuyau – tu n'es pas d.!** I can't connect the hose – you're hopeless!

douer [6] [dwe] **VT d. qn de qch** to endow sb with sth; **la nature l'a doué d'une mémoire étonnante** nature has endowed *or* blessed him with an exceptional memory; **être doué de** *(intelligence, raison)* to be endowed with; *(mémoire)* to be gifted *or* blessed *or* endowed with

douille [duj] **NF 1** *(de cuisine)* piping nozzle
2 *(d'une cartouche)* (cartridge) case
3 *(d'une ampoule)* (lamp) socket
4 *(de cylindre)* casing

douiller [3] [duje] **VI** *Fam (payer)* to cough up, to fork out; **la bouffe est super, mais ça douille!** the food is great but it costs a packet *or* an arm and a leg!

douillet, -ette [duje, -ɛt] **ADJ 1** *(très sensible à la douleur)* oversensitive; *(qui a peur de la douleur)* afraid of getting hurt; *Péj* **que tu es d.!** don't be such a wimp! **2** *(confortable ▸ vêtement, lit, appartement)* (nice and) cosy, snug
• **douillette NF 1** *(robe de chambre)* quilted dressing gown **2** *(de prêtre)* quilted overcoat **3** *Can (couvre-lit) Br* quilted bedspread, *Am* comforter

douillettement [dujɛtmɑ̃] **ADV** cosily, snugly; **vous êtes d. installé ici!** you're nice and cosy here!; **il a été élevé trop d.** he was coddled too much as a child

douleur [dulœr] **NF 1** *(physique ▸ gén)* pain; *(▸ diffuse)* ache; **vous ne ressentirez aucune d.** you won't feel any pain; **une d. fulgurante/sourde** a searing/dull pain; **douleurs abdominales** stomach ache *or* pains; **douleurs rhumatismales** rheumatic pains; **j'ai une d. à la cuisse** my thigh hurts, my thigh's sore, I've got a pain in my thigh; **quand mes vieilles douleurs se réveillent** when my old pains *or* aches and pains come back **2** *(psychologique)* grief, sorrow, pain; **à notre grande d., il s'est éteint hier** to our great sorrow, he passed away yesterday; **j'ai eu la grande d. de perdre ma femme il y a deux ans** I suffered the grief of losing my wife two years ago; **nous avons la d. de vous faire part du décès de...** it is with great *or* deep sorrow (and regret) that we have to announce the death of...; *Fam* **si je le chope, il va comprendre sa d.** if I catch him, he'll get what's coming to him *or* his worst nightmares will come true

douloureuse [duluroz] *voir* **douloureux**

douloureusement [dulurøzmɑ̃] **ADV 1** *(physiquement)* painfully **2** *(moralement)* painfully, grievously; **la disparition de sa sœur l'a d. frappée** her sister's death was a great blow to her; **d. éprouvé par le départ de sa femme** wounded *or* deeply hurt by his wife's leaving him

douloureux, -euse [dulurø, -øz] **ADJ 1** *(brûlure, coup, coupure)* painful; *(articulation, membre)* painful, sore; **mes jambes sont très douloureuses le soir** my legs are very sore *or* hurt a lot at night **2** *(humiliation, souvenirs)* painful; *(circonstances, sujet, période)* painful, distressing; *(nouvelle)* grievous, painful, distressing; *(poème, regard)* sorrowful
• **douloureuse NF** *Fam Hum (au restaurant) Br* bill□, *Am* check□; *(facture)* bill□; **on va bientôt recevoir la douloureuse** we'll soon get the bad news

Douro [duro] **NM** *Géog* **le D.** the Douro

doute [dut] **NM 1** *(soupçon)* doubt; **avoir des doutes sur** *ou* **quant à** *ou* **au sujet de qch** to have (one's) doubts *or* misgivings about sth; **je n'ai pas le moindre d. là-dessus** I haven't the slightest doubt about it; **il n'y a aucun d. (possible), c'est lui** it's him, (there's) no doubt about it; **sa responsabilité ne fait pratiquement aucun d.** there's little doubt (about the fact) that he's/she's responsible; **il n'y a aucun d. que c'est lui le coupable** there's no doubt that he is the culprit; **de gros doutes pèsent sur lui** heavy suspicion hangs over him; **il y a des doutes quant à l'identité du peintre** there is some doubt as to the identity of the painter **2** *(perplexité, incertitude)* doubt, uncertainty; *Phil* doubt; **il ne connaît pas le d.** he never has any doubts; **le d. persiste sur ses motifs** there's still some doubt about his/her motives; **jeter le d. sur qch** to cast *or* to throw doubt on sth; **tu as semé** *ou* **mis le d. dans mon esprit** you've made me doubtful; **d. de soi** self-doubt
• **dans le doute ADV être dans le d.** to be doubtful *or* uncertain; **je suis toujours dans le d. quant à sa sincérité** I'm still in doubt *or* doubtful *or* uncertain about his honesty; **laisser qn dans le d.** *(sujet: personne, circonstances)* to leave sb in a state of uncertainty
• **en doute ADV mettre en d.** *(sujet: personne)* to question, to challenge; *(sujet: circonstances, témoignage)* to cast doubt on; **je ne mets pas votre sincérité en d.** I don't question your sincerity
• **sans doute ADV 1** *(probablement)* no doubt; **sans d. vous êtes-vous déjà rencontrés** you've no doubt met before; **comme elle te l'a sans d. appris** as she has no doubt told you **2** *(assurément)* **sans aucun** *ou* **nul d.** without (a) doubt, undoubtedly, *Sout* indubitably **3** *(certes)* **tu me l'avais promis – sans d., mais...** you'd promised me – that's true *or* I know, but...

douter [3] [dute] **douter de VT IND 1** *(ne pas croire à ▸ succès, victoire)* to be doubtful of; *(▸ fait, éventualité)* to doubt; **d. de l'existence/la véracité de qch** to doubt the existence/truth of sth; **je n'ai jamais douté de ton talent** I never doubted your talent; **tu viendras? – j'en doute fort** will you come? – I very much doubt it; **elle ne doute de rien** she has no doubts about anything **2** *(traiter avec défiance ▸ ami, motivation)* to have doubts about; **elle semble d. de mes sentiments** she seems to doubt my feelings; **d. de la parole de qn** to doubt sb's word; **d. de soi** *(habituellement)* to have doubts about *or* to lack confidence in oneself; *(à un moment)* to have doubts about oneself **3** *Rel* to have doubts about
USAGE ABSOLU j'étais prête à me marier, mais maintenant je doute I was going to get married, but now I've got doubts about it; **je doute que le projet voie le jour** I have (my) doubts about the future of the project, I doubt whether the project will ever see the light of day
VPR se douter 1 se d. de *(s'attendre à)* to know, to suspect; **j'aurais dû m'en d.** I should have known; **je me doutais un peu de sa réaction** I half expected him/her to react the way he/she did, his/her reaction didn't surprise me; **comme tu t'en doutes sûrement** as you've probably guessed; **il a eu très peur – je m'en doute** he got quite a fright – I can (well) imagine that; **il faudra que tu viennes me chercher – je m'en doute!** *(avec irritation)* you'll have to come and fetch me – well, yes, I expected that! **2 se d. de** *(soupçonner)* to suspect; **son mari ne s'est douté de rien pendant des années** her husband suspected nothing for years; **j'étais loin de me d. que...** little did I know that...; **tu te doutes bien que je te l'aurais dit si je l'avais su!** you know very well that I would have told you if I'd known!

douteux, -euse [dutø, -øz] **ADJ 1** *(non certain, non assuré ▸ authenticité, fait)* doubtful, uncertain, questionable; *(▸ avenir, issue, origine etc)* doubtful, uncertain; *(▸ signature)* doubtful; **il est d. qu'il vienne** it's doubtful whether he will come; **il n'est pas d. que...** there's no doubt that...
2 *Péj (inspirant la méfiance ▸ individu)* dubious-looking; *(▸ comportement, manœuvres, passé etc)* dubious, questionable; **d'une manière douteuse** dubiously; **le portrait/ta plaisanterie était d'un goût d.** the portrait/your joke was in dubious taste **3** *(sale, dangereux)* dubious; **du linge d.** *ou* **d'une propreté douteuse** clothes that are none too clean; **jetez toujours une viande douteuse** always throw away any meat you're not sure of; **il s'est présenté sous un jour d.** he showed himself in a dubious *or* uncertain light

douve [duv] **NF 1** *Équitation* water jump **2** *(fossé ▸ dans les champs)* trench, ditch; *(▸ d'un château)* moat **3** *(d'un fût)* stave

Douvres [duvr] **NM** Dover

doux, douce [du, dus] **ADJ 1** *(au toucher ▸ cheveux, peau)* soft, smooth; *(▸ brosse à dents)* soft; **le d. contact de la soie** the soft touch of silk
2 *(au goût ▸ vin)* sweet; *(▸ fromage)* mild
3 *(détergent, savon, shampooing)* mild; *(énergie, technique)* alternative; *(drogue)* soft; **médecines douces** alternative medicine
4 *(sans brusquerie ▸ geste, caresse, personne)* gentle; *(▸ pression)* soft, gentle; *(▸ balancement, pente)* gentle; *(▸ accélération)* smooth; *(▸ véhicule)* smooth-running; **il a eu une mort douce** he died peacefully
5 *(bon, gentil ▸ personne, sourire, tempérament)* gentle; **d. comme un agneau** meek as a lamb
6 *(modéré ▸ châtiment)* mild; *(▸ reproche)* mild, gentle; *(▸ éclairage, teinte)* soft, subdued; *(▸ chaleur, campagne, forme)* gentle
7 *Météo (air, climat)* mild; *(chaleur, vent)* gentle
8 *(harmonieux ▸ intonation, mélodie, voix)* soft, sweet, gentle
9 *(plaisant ▸ rêves, souvenir)* sweet, pleasant; *(▸ paix, succès)* sweet; *Littéraire* **ton amour m'était alors si d.** how sweet it was, being loved by you then
10 *Ling* soft
NM,F *(par affection)* **ma douce** my sweet
ADV 1 *(tiède)* **il fait d.** it's mild out **2** *(locution)* **tout d.!** *(sans brusquerie)* gently (now)!; *(pour calmer)* calm down!, easy now!; **vas-y tout d. avec elle** be careful with her
• **douce NF** *Vieilli* **sa douce** *(sa fiancée)* his beloved
• **en douce ADV** *Fam (dire, donner, partir etc)* on the quiet, sneakily

doux-amer, douce-amère [duamer, dus-] **ADJ** *aussi Fig* bittersweet

douzain [duzɛ̃] **NM** *Littérature* twelve-line poem

douzaine [duzɛn] **NF 1** *(douze)* dozen; **une d. d'escargots/d'œufs** a dozen snails/eggs **2** *(environ douze)* **une d. de** a dozen or so, about twelve; **une d. de pages** about *or* roughly twelve pages, a dozen or so pages; **il y a une d. d'années** about twelve years ago, a dozen or so years ago
• **à la douzaine ADV** *(acheter, vendre)* by the dozen; **il y en a à la d.** *Br* they're ten a penny, *Am* they're a dime a dozen; *Fam* **des chanteurs comme lui, il y en a à la d.!** you'll find dozens of singers like him!

douze [duz] **ADJ 1** *(gén)* twelve **2** *(dans des séries)* twelfth; **page/numéro d.** page/number twelve
PRON twelve
NM INV 1 *(gén)* twelve **2** *(numéro d'ordre)* number twelve **3** *(chiffre écrit)* twelve; *voir aussi* **cinq**

douzième [duzjɛm] **ADJ** twelfth
NMF 1 *(personne)* twelfth **2** *(objet)* twelfth (one)
NM 1 *(partie)* twelfth **2** *(étage) Br* twelfth floor,

Am thirteenth floor **3** *(arrondissement de Paris)* twelfth (arrondissement)

NF *Mus* twelfth; *voir aussi* **cinquième**

douzièmement [duzjɛmmɑ̃] **ADV** in twelfth place

doyen, -enne [dwajɛ̃, -ɛn] **NM,F 1** *(d'un club, d'une communauté)* most senior member; *(d'un pays)* eldest *or* oldest citizen; *(d'une profession)* doyen, *f* doyenne; **d. (d'âge)** oldest person **2** *Univ* dean

NM *Rel* dean

doyenné [dwajene] **NM 1** *(district, demeure)* deanery **2** *(fonction)* deanship

NF d. (du comice) comice (pear)

DPI [depei] **NM** *Méd (abrév* **diagnostic préimplantatoire)** PGD

dpi [depei] *(abrév* **dots per inch)** dpi

drache [draʃ] **NF** *Belg (averse)* shower

dracher [3] [draʃe] **V IMPERSONNEL** *Belg* to pour with rain

drachme [drakm] **NF 1** *Anciennement* drachma **2** *Pharm* dram, drachm

draconien, -enne [drakɔnjɛ̃, -ɛn] **ADJ** *(mesure)* drastic, draconian, stringent; *(règlement)* harsh, draconian; *(régime)* strict

dragage [dragaʒ] **NM** *(pour prélèvement)* dragging, dredging; *(pour nettoyage)* dredging; **d. de mines** minesweeping

dragée [draʒe] **NF 1** *(confiserie)* sugared almond; *Pharm* (sugar-coated) pill; **tenir la d. haute à qn** *(dans une discussion, un match)* to hold out on sb **2** *(balle)* lead shot **3** *Agr* dredge

dragéifier [9] [draʒeifje] **VT** *Pharm (pilule)* to coat with sugar, to sugar; **comprimé dragéifié** sugar-coated pill

drageon [draʒɔ̃] **NM** *Bot* sucker

dragon [dragɔ̃] **NM 1** *Myth* dragon

2 *(gardien)* dragon; *Hum* **c'est un d. de vertu** she claims to be such a paragon of virtue

3 *Vieilli (mégère)* dragon

4 *Hist & Mil* dragoon

5 *Zool* **d. de Komodo** Komodo dragon *or* lizard; **d. volant** flying lizard

dragonne [dragɔn] **NF** *(de bâton de ski, de piolet, de parapluie)* wrist-loop; *(d'épée)* sword-knot

drague [drag] **NF 1** *(en travaux publics)* dredge; **d. flottante** *ou* **hydrographique** dredger; **d. à godets** bucket dredger; **d. suceuse** pump dredger **2** *Pêche* dragnet **3** *Fam (flirt)* **pour la d., il est doué!** he's always *Br* on the pull *or Am* on the make!; **ce mec-là, c'est un pro de la d.** he's a bit of a pro at *Br* chatting up *or Am* hitting on women, that guy; **c'est un lieu de d. idéal** it's an ideal place for *Br* chatting people up *or Am* hitting on people

draguer [3] [drage] **VT 1** *(nettoyer ▸ fleuve, canal, port)* to dredge; *(en cherchant)* to drag

2 *(retirer ▸ mine)* to sweep; *(▸ ancre)* to drag (anchor)

3 *(pêcher ▸ coquillages)* to dredge for

4 *Fam (fille, garçon) Br* to chat up, *Am* to hit on; *(en voiture)* to cruise; **je me suis fait d. par le serveur** I got *Br* chatted up *or Am* hit on by the waiter

VI *Fam* to be *Br* on the pull *or Am* on the make

dragueur, -euse [dragœr, -øz] **ADJ il n'a jamais été très d.** he's never been one for *Br* chatting up *or Am* hitting on women

NM,F *Fam* **c'est un d.** he's always *Br* on the pull *or Am* on the make; **sa sœur est une sacrée dragueuse** his/her sister's always chasing after men

NM 1 *(navire)* dredger; **d. de mines** minesweeper **2** *(matelot)* dredgerman **3** *Pêche* dragnet fisherman

drain [drɛ̃] **NM** *Méd & Tech* drain

drainage [drɛnaʒ] **NM 1** *(d'une plaie, d'un sol)* drainage **2** *(de capital, de ressources)* tapping **3** *(massage)* **d. lymphatique** lymph *or* lymphatic drainage

drainer [4] [drene] **VT 1** *(assécher)* to drain **2** *(rassembler ▸ capital, ressources)* to tap; **d. des auditeurs/des téléspectateurs** to draw listeners/viewers **3** *(canaliser ▸ foule)* to channel; **d. la circulation vers une voie de dégagement** to channel the traffic towards a relief road

Dralon® [dralɔ̃] **NM** Dralon®

DRAM [dram] **NF** *Ordinat (abrév* **dynamic random access memory)** DRAM

dramatique [dramatik] **ADJ 1** *Théât (musique, œuvre)* dramatic **2** *(grave ▸ conséquences, issue, période, situation)* horrendous, appalling; **elle ne comprend rien aux équations, c'est d.!** she hasn't got a clue about equations, it's appalling!; **j'ai raté mon permis de conduire – ce n'est pas d.!** I've failed my driving test – it's not the end of the world! **3** *(tragique ▸ dénouement, événement)* tragic

NF *TV* television play *or* drama; *Rad* radio play *or* drama

> Il faut noter que l'adjectif anglais **dramatic** ne signifie jamais **terrible** ni **tragique**.

dramatiquement [dramatikmɑ̃] **ADV** tragically; **encore une soirée qui se termine d.** yet another party with a tragic ending

> Il faut noter que l'adverbe anglais **dramatically** est un faux ami. Il signifie le plus souvent **radicalement**.

dramatisation [dramatizasjɔ̃] **NF** over-dramatization

dramatiser [3] [dramatize] **VT 1** *(exagérer ▸ histoire)* to over-dramatize **2** *Théât (œuvre)* to dramatize, to turn into a play

USAGE ABSOLU ne dramatise pas! don't be so melodramatic!

dramaturge [dramatyrʒ] **NM** playwright, dramatist

dramaturgie [dramatyrʒi] **NF** dramatic art, drama

drame [dram] **NM 1** *Théât (œuvre)* drama; *Arch (pièce)* play; *(genre)* drama; **d. lyrique** opera **2** *Rad & TV* drama, play; **d. judiciaire** courtroom drama; **d. télévisé** television drama **3** *(événement)* drama; **il a raté son examen, mais ce n'est pas un d.** he failed his exam, but it's not the end of the world; **faire un d. de qch** to make a drama out of sth; **le d., c'est que personne ne le croit** the sad thing is that nobody believes him; **je lui ai emprunté son appareil photo, le d.!** I borrowed his/her camera and he/she made such a fuss!; **l'excursion a tourné** *ou* **viré au d.** the trip ended tragically

dramédie [dramedi] **NF** *TV* dramedy

drap [dra] **NM 1** *(pour lit)* **d. (de lit)** (bed) sheet; **des draps** sheets, bedlinen; **d. de dessus/dessous** top/bottom sheet; **se mettre dans** *ou* **entre les draps** to get between the sheets; **se retrouver** *ou* **se trouver dans de beaux draps** to find oneself up the creek (without a paddle); **nous voilà dans de beaux** *ou* **de vilains draps!** we're in a fine mess!

2 *(serviette)* **d. de bain** bath sheet; **d. de plage** beach towel

3 *Belg* towel; **d. de maison** tablecloth

4 *Tex* woollen cloth; **d. fin** broadcloth; **gros d.** coarse woollen cloth; **d. d'or/de soie** gold/silk brocade

drapé [drape] **NM** *(plis, tombé)* **la jupe a un beau d.** the skirt hangs beautifully

drapeau, -x [drapo] **NM 1** *(pièce d'étoffe)* flag; *Mil* flag, colours; **saluer le d.** to salute the colours; **le d. blanc** the white flag, the flag of truce; **le d. britannique** the British flag, the Union Jack; **le d. noir** the black flag; **le d. rouge** the red flag; **le d. tricolore** the French flag, the tricolour (flag); **combattre/se ranger sous le d. de qn** to fight under/to rally round sb's flag **2** *aussi Hum (patrie)* **pour le d.** *ou* **l'honneur du d.** *Br* ≃ for King/Queen and country, *Am* ≃ for the red, white and blue **3** *Aviat* **mettre en d.** *(hélice)* to feather

• **sous les drapeaux ADV être sous les drapeaux** *(au service militaire)* to be doing one's military service; *(en service actif)* to serve in one's country's armed forces

drapement [drapmɑ̃] **NM** draping

draper [3] [drape] **VT 1** *(couvrir ▸ meuble)* to drape, to cover with a sheet **2** *(arranger ▸ châle, rideaux)* to drape **3** *Tex (laine)* to process

VPR se draper se d. dans qch to drape oneself in sth; **se d. dans sa dignité** to stand on one's dignity

draperie [drapri] **NF 1** *(tissu disposé en grands plis)* drapery, hanging **2** *(industrie)* cloth trade; *(fabrique)* cloth manufacture **3** *Beaux-Arts* drapery

drap-housse [draus] *(pl* **draps-housses) NM** fitted sheet

drapier, -ère [drapje, -ɛr] **ADJ marchand d.** *Br* draper, *Am* clothier; **ouvrier d.** cloth worker

NM,F *(fabricant)* cloth manufacturer; *(vendeur) Br* draper, *Am* clothier

DRASS [dras] **NF** *Admin (abrév* **Direction Régionale des Affaires Sanitaires et Sociales)** = office administering health and social services at regional level

drastique [drastik] **ADJ 1** *(mesure)* harsh, drastic; *(règlement)* strict **2** *Pharm* drastic

NM *Méd* drastic purgative

drave [drav] **NF** *Can (flottage)* transport *(of floating logs)*

draver [3] [drave] **VT** *Can* to float

draveur [dravœr] **NM** *Can* driver

drawback [drobak] **NM** *Com* drawback

dreadlocks [drɛdlɔks] **NFPL** dreadlocks

drelin [drəlɛ̃] **EXCLAM** *Fam Vieilli* ting-a-ling!

Dresde [drezd] **NM** Dresden

dressage [dresaʒ] **NM 1** *(d'un fauve)* taming *(UNCOUNT)*; *(d'un cheval sauvage)* breaking in *(UNCOUNT)*; *(d'un chien de cirque, de garde)* training *(UNCOUNT)*; *(d'un cheval de parade)* dressage **2** *(d'un mât, d'un monument, d'un échafaudage)* erection, raising; *(d'une tente)* pitching

dresser [4] [drese] **VT 1** *(ériger ▸ mât, pilier)* to put up, to raise, to erect; *(▸ statue)* to put up, to erect; *(▸ tente, auvent)* to pitch, to put up; **d. une échelle contre un mur** to put up *or* to set up a ladder against a wall

2 *(construire ▸ barricade, échafaudage)* to put up, to erect; *(▸ muret)* to erect, to build; **d. des obstacles devant qn** to put obstacles in sb's way, to raise difficulties for sb

3 *(installer ▸ autel)* to set up; **d. un camp** to set up camp; **d. le couvert** *ou* **la table** to lay *or* to set the table; **d. un buffet** to set out a buffet; *Fig* **d. ses batteries** to lay one's plans

4 *(lever ▸ bâton)* to raise, to lift; *(▸ menton)* to stick out; *(▸ tête)* to raise, to lift; **d. les oreilles** *(chien)* to prick up *or* to cock its ears; **d. l'oreille** *(personne)* to prick up one's ears

5 *(dompter ▸ fauve)* to tame; *(▸ cheval sauvage)* to break in; *(▸ cheval de cirque, chien de garde)* to train; **d. un chien à attaquer** to train a dog to attack

6 *Fam (mater ▸ soldat)* to drill, to lick into shape; **ce gamin aurait besoin d'être dressé!** that kid needs to be taught his place!; **je vais le d., moi!** I'll make him toe the line!

7 *(établir ▸ liste, inventaire)* to draw up, to make out; *(▸ bilan)* to draw up, to prepare; **d. le bilan d'une situation** to take stock of a situation; **d. (une) contravention** to give a ticket *(for a driving offence)*

8 *(opposer)* **d. qn contre qn/qch** to set sb against sb/sth

9 *Menuis* to dress

VPR se dresser 1 *(se mettre debout)* to stand up, to rise; **se d. sur la pointe des pieds** to stand on tiptoe; **l'ours se dressa sur ses pattes de derrière** the bear rose *or* reared *or* stood up on its hind legs; **se d. sur son séant** to sit up straight

2 *(oreille de chien)* to prick up; **à ce nom, ses oreilles se sont dressées** *(chien)* when he/she heard that name, he/she pricked up his/her ears; **un film à faire se d. les cheveux sur la tête** *ou* **à vous faire d. les cheveux sur la tête** a hair-raising movie *or Br* film; **c'est à vous faire d. les cheveux sur la tête!** it's enough to make your hair stand on end!

3 *(être vertical ▸ montagne, tour)* to stand, to rise; *(dominer)* to tower; **un paravent se dresse entre le salon et la chambre** a screen stands between the lounge and the bedroom

4 *(surgir ▸ obstacles)* to rise, to stand; *(▸ objet)* to loom; **on vit soudain se d. les miradors** the watchtowers loomed up suddenly

5 *(manifester son opposition)* **se d. contre** to rise up *or* to rebel against

dresseur, -euse [dresœr, -øz] **NM,F** *(de fauves)* tamer; *(de chiens de cirque, de garde)* trainer; *(de chevaux sauvages)* horsebreaker

dressing [dresiŋ], **dressing-room** [dresiŋrum] (*pl* **dressing-rooms**) NM dressing room *(near a bedroom)*

dressoir [dreswar] NM sideboard

dreyfusard, -e [drefyzar, -ard] NM,F supporter of Dreyfus

DRH [deerɑʃ] NF *(abrév* **direction des ressources humaines**) human resources department

NM *(abrév* **directeur des ressources humaines**) human resources manager

dribble [dribl] NM *Sport* dribble; **faire un d.** to dribble

dribbler [3] [drible] *Sport* VT *(ballon)* to dribble; *(joueur)* to dribble round

VI to dribble

dribbleur, -euse [driblœr, -øz] NM,F *Sport* dribbler

dribbling [dribliŋ] NM *Sport (au rugby)* forward ruck

drill [dril] NM *(singe)* drill

drille[1] [drij] NM *voir* **joyeux**

drille[2] [drij] NF *Tech* hand drill

driller [3] [drije] VT *Tech* to drill, to bore

dring [driŋ] EXCLAM ding!, ding-a-ling!

drink [driŋk] NM *Fam* drink

drisse [dris] NF halyard

drive [drajv] NM *Ordinat & Sport* drive

drive-in [drajvin] (*pl* **drive-ins**) NM *(restauration rapide)* drive-through; *(cinéma)* drive-in

driver[1] [drajvœr] NM *Équitation & Golf* driver

driver[2] [3] [drajve] *Sport* VT to drive

VI to drive

drogman [drɔgmɑ̃] NM *Hist* dragoman

drogue [drɔg] NF **1** *(narcotique)* drug; **le jeu était devenu une d. pour lui** gambling had become a drug for him; *Fam* **le travail est ma d.** I'm a workaholic; *Fam* **moi, ma d., c'est le chocolat** I'm addicted to chocolate, I'm a chocaholic; **la télévision est une d. pour eux** they're television addicts; **d. douce/dure** soft/hard drug; **d. de synthèse** synthetic drug **2** *(usage)* **la d.** drug-taking, drugs; **la d. est un fléau** drugs are a scourge of society **3** *Vieilli (médicament)* drug; *Péj* nostrum, quack remedy

drogué, -e [drɔge] NM,F drug addict; *Fam* **c'est une droguée du café** she's addicted to coffee; *Fam* **les drogués du travail** workaholics; *Fam* **les drogués de l'information** information addicts

droguer [3] [drɔge] VT **1** *(prisonnier)* to drug; *(chien, cheval)* to dope **2** *(malade)* to dose with drugs; **on m'a complètement drogué pendant deux semaines** I was given massive doses of drugs for two weeks **3** *(boisson)* to drug, to lace with a drug; *(repas)* to put a drug in

VPR **se droguer 1** *(prendre des stupéfiants)* to take drugs, to be on drugs; **je ne me drogue pas** I don't take drugs; **se d. à l'héroïne** to be on heroin **2** *(prendre des médicaments)* to take drugs

droguerie [drɔgri] NF **1** *(boutique)* hardware *Br* shop *or Am* store **2** *(activité)* hardware trade

droguet [drɔgɛ] NM *Vieilli Tex* drugget

droguiste [drɔgist] NMF keeper of a hardware *Br* shop *or Am* store

droïde [drɔid] NM *(en science-fiction)* droid

droit[1]**, -e**[1] [drwa, drwat] ADJ *(ailier, jambe, œil)* right; **le côté d.** the right-hand side

NM right; **crochet du d.** right hook; **direct du d.** straight right

• **droite** NF **1** *(côté droit)* **la droite** the right (side), the right-hand side; **à ma droite, le château** to *or* on my right is the castle; **à la droite de Dieu** *ou* **du Père** on God's right hand; **sur la droite** on the right; *Aut* **tenir sa droite** to keep to the right; **de droite et de gauche** from all quarters *or* sides **2** *Pol* **la droite** the right (wing); **droite dure** hard right; **droite modérée** soft right

• **à droite** ADV **1** *(du côté droit)* **conduire à droite** to drive on the right-hand side; **tourne à droite** turn right; **le poster est trop à droite** the poster's too far to the right; *Fig* **à droite et à gauche** here and there, all over the place **2** *Mil* **à droite, droite!** right wheel!; **à droite, alignement!** right, dress! **3** *Pol* **être à droite** to be right-wing *or* on the right; **être très à droite** to be very right-wing *or* on the far right; **voter à droite** to vote for the right

• **à droite de** PRÉP to *or* on the right of

• **de droite** ADJ **1** *(du côté droit)* **la porte de droite** the door on the right, the right-hand door **2** *Pol* right-wing; **les gens de droite** right-wingers, people on the right; **l'électorat de droite** right-wing electorate; **être de droite** to be right-wing

droit[2]**, -e**[2] [drwa, drwat] ADJ **1** *(rectiligne ▸ allée, bâton, nez)* straight; **après le village, la route redevient droite** after the village, the road straightens out again; **ta raie n'est pas droite** your *Br* parting *or Am* part isn't straight *or* is crooked; *Fig* **le d. chemin** the straight and narrow; **rentrer dans le d. chemin** to mend one's ways; **rester dans le d. chemin** to keep to the straight and narrow

2 *(vertical, non penché ▸ mur)* upright, straight, *Spéc* plumb; *(▸ dossier, poteau)* upright, straight; **restez le dos bien d.** keep your back straight; **être** *ou* **se tenir d.** *(assis)* to sit up straight; *(debout)* to stand up straight; **d. comme un cierge** *ou* **un i** *ou* **un piquet** (as) stiff as a poker *or* a ramrod *or* a post

3 *(d'aplomb)* straight; **tiens le plat d.** hold the dish straight *or* level *or* flat; **mettre d.** *(casquette, cadre)* to set straight, to put straight, to straighten

4 *(loyal ▸ personne)* upright, honest

5 *(sensé ▸ raisonnement)* sound, sane

6 manteau/veston d. single-breasted coat/jacket; **col d.** stand-up collar; **jupe droite** straight skirt

ADV **1** *(écrire)* in a straight line; *(couper, rouler)* straight; **après le carrefour, c'est toujours tout d.** after the crossroads, keep going straight on *or* ahead; **il s'est dirigé d. vers moi** he walked straight towards me; **j'irai d. au but** I'll come straight to the point, I won't beat about the bush; **il est allé d. à l'essentiel** *ou* **au fait** he went straight to the point; **aller d. à la catastrophe/l'échec** to be heading straight for disaster/a failure; **aller d. à la ruine** to be on the road to ruin; **ça m'est allé d. au cœur** it went straight to my heart **2** *Suisse (exactement)* exactly; *(tout à fait)* completely, absolutely; *(tout juste)* just; **c'est d. son père** he's the spitting image of his father; **elle est d. arrivée** she's just arrived

• **droite** NF *Géom* straight line

DROIT[3] [drwa]

• law **1**	• right **2, 3**
• tax **4**	• duty **4**
• fee **5**	

NM **1** *Jur* **le d.** *(lois, discipline)* law; **faire son d.** to study law; **étudiant en d.** law student; **en d., ça s'appelle "contrefaçon"** the legal term for that is "infringement"; **avoir le d. pour soi** to have right *or* the law on one's side; **d. administratif** administrative law; **d. des affaires** corporate law; **d. bancaire** banking law; **d. de brevet** patent law; **d. cambiaire** law of negotiable instruments; **d. civil** civil law; **d. commercial** business law; **d. commun** common law; **d. communautaire** Community law; **d. de la concurrence** *Br* competition law, *Am* antitrust law; **d. constitutionnel** constitutional law; **d. coutumier** customary law; **d. des contrats** contract law; **d. douanier** customs legislation; **d. écrit** statute law; **d. de l'environnement** environmental law; **d. fiscal** tax law; **d. international** international law; **d. judiciaire** (law of) procedure; **d. maritime** maritime law; **d. des obligations** law of contract; **d. pénal** criminal law; **d. positif** statute law; **d. privé** private law; **d. de procédure** (law of) procedure; **d. public** public law; **d. social** employment law; **d. des sociétés** corporate law; **d. du travail** labour law

2 *(prérogative)* right; **connaître/défendre ses droits** to know/to defend one's rights; **nos droits en tant que consommateurs** our rights as consumers; **avoir des droits sur qch** to have rights to sth; **tu n'as aucun d. sur moi** you have no power over me; **avoir d. de vie et de mort sur qn** to have the power of life and death over sb; **d. d'accès aux documents administratifs** = right of access to government documents; **d. d'aînesse** primogeniture; **d. d'asile** right of asylum; **d. d'association** right of (free) association; **d. de chasse** hunting rights; **droits civiques** civil rights; **d. à la couronne** entitlement to the crown; *Hist* **d. de cuissage** droit de seigneur; *Fig* **le patron exerçait un d. de cuissage sur les jeunes employées** the boss forced the young female employees to have sex with him; **d. divin** divine right; **droits extrapatrimoniaux** non-pecuniary rights; **d. de grâce** right of reprieve; **d. de grève** right to strike; **les droits de l'homme** human rights; **d. incorporel** intangible right; **d. de licenciement** right to dismiss; **d. de passage** right of *Br* way *or Am* easement; **d. patrimonial** pecuniary right; **le d. des peuples à disposer d'eux-mêmes** the right of peoples to self-determination; **d. de préemption** right of first refusal; **d. de préférence** pre-emptive right; **d. préférentiel de souscription** pre-emptive right; *Fin* **d. de rachat** repurchase right, buyback right; **d. de retention** tax lien; *Bourse* **d. de souscription (d'actions)** subscription right; *Fin* **droits de tirage** drawing rights; *Fin* **droits de tirage spéciaux** special drawing rights; **d. d'usage** right of user; **droits de visite** *Br* access rights, *Am* visitation rights; **d. de voirie** = tax paid by businesses who wish to place displays, signs etc on the public highway; **le d. de vote** the franchise, the right to vote; **avoir d. de cité** *(idéologie)* to be established, to have currency; *Fam* **ce gosse a tous les droits dans la maison** that kid lords it over the whole household; **ils se croient tous les droits, ces gens-là!** these people think they can do what they like!

3 *(autorisation sociale ou morale)* right; **j'ai ouvert ton courrier – de quel d.?** I opened your mail – who gave you permission?; **de quel d. l'a-t-il lue?** what gave him the right to read it?, what right had he to read it?; **le billet donne d. à une consommation gratuite** the ticket entitles you to a free drink; **son rang lui donne d. à des privilèges particuliers** his/her rank entitles him/her to certain privileges; **donner le d. à qn de faire qch** to give sb the right to *or* to entitle sb to do sth; **être en d. de faire qch** to be entitled *or* to have the right to do sth; **je suis en d. d'obtenir des explications** I'm entitled to an explanation; **faire d. à une demande** to comply with *or Sout* accede to a request; **reprendre ses droits** *(idée, habitude, nature)* to reassert itself; **après Noël, la politique reprend ses droits** after the Christmas break, politics returns to centre stage; **avoir d. à** *(explications)* to have a right to; *(bourse, indemnité)* to be entitled to, to be eligible for; *(reconnaissance, respect)* to deserve; **je n'ai pas d. à une retraite** I'm not entitled to a pension; **et moi, je n'y ai pas d. au gâteau?** don't I get any cake then?; **on a encore eu d. à ses souvenirs de guerre!** we were regaled with his war memories as usual!; *Fam* **on va avoir d. à une bonne saucée!** we'll get well and truly soaked!; *Fam* **ils parlent de licencier 300 personnes, je sens que je vais y avoir d.** they're talking about laying off 300 people and I think that's going to include me; **avoir d. de regard sur** *(comptabilité, dossier)* to have the right to examine *or* to inspect; *(activités)* to have the right to control; **avoir le d. de faire qch** *(gén)* to be allowed *or* to have the right to do sth; *(officiellement)* to have the right *or* to be entitled to do sth; **tu n'as pas le d. de parler ainsi!** you've no right to talk like that!; *Hum* **tu as le d. de te taire** you can shut up; **j'ai bien le d. de me reposer!** I'm entitled to some rest, aren't I?; **tu n'as pas le d.! – je le prends!** you can't do that! – who says I can't!; **le d. à la différence** the right to be different; **d. de réponse** right of reply

4 *(imposition)* duty; *(taxe)* tax; **payer des droits sur les alcools** to pay duty on alcohol; **exempt de droits** duty-free; **soumis à des droits** dutiable; **d. au bail** = tax on rented accommodation (usually included in the rent); **droits de douane** customs duties; **d. d'entrée** import duty; **d. d'exportation** export duty; **d. d'importation** import duty; **droits de port** harbour dues; **d. de sortie** export duty; **droits de succession** death duties, inheritance tax; **d. de timbre** stamp duty; *Bourse* **d. de transfert** transfer duty

5 *(frais)* fee; **droits à la charge du vendeur/de l'acheteur** duty to be paid by the seller/purchaser; **d. de courtage** brokerage (fee); **d. d'enregistrement** registration fee *(for legal documents)*; **d. d'entrée** entrance fee; **d. fixe** fixed fee; *Banque* **droits de garde** custody account charges; **droits d'inscription** registration fee *or* fees

6 *(locutions)* **à bon d.** quite rightly, with good reason; **à qui de d.** *(sur un document)* to whom it may concern; **s'adresser à qui de d.** to apply to the

proper quarter *or* to an authorized person; **être dans son (bon) d.** to be within one's rights; **de (plein) d.** by rights, as a right; **c'est de plein d. qu'il l'a repris** he had every right to take it back; **membre de plein d.** ex officio member
• **droits** NMPL **droits (d'auteur)** *(prérogative)* rights, copyright; *(somme)* royalties; **avoir les droits exclusifs pour qch** to have (the) sole rights for sth; **tous droits (de reproduction) réservés** copyright *or* all rights reserved; **tous droits réservés pour le Canada** all rights reserved for Canada; **droits d'achat** purchasing rights; **droits de distribution, droits de diffusion** distribution rights; **droits étrangers** foreign rights; **droits exclusifs, droits d'exclusivité** sole rights, exclusive rights; **droits d'exclusivité** exclusive rights; **droits statutaires** statutory rights; **droits de traduction** translation copyright; **droits de vente exclusifs** exclusive selling rights; *Bourse* **droits de vote** *(des actionnaires)* voting rights

droitement [drwatmɑ̃] ADV uprightly, honestly

droitier, -ère [drwatje, -ɛr] ADJ **1** *(qui utilise la main droite)* right-handed **2** *Pol* right-wing
NM,F right-handed person

droitiser [3] [drwatize] *Pol* VT to shift to the right
VPR **se droitiser** to shift to the right

droiture [drwatyr] NF *(d'une personne)* uprightness, honesty; *(d'intentions, de motifs)* uprightness

drolatique [drɔlatik] ADJ funny

drôle [drol] ADJ **1** *(amusant ▸ personne, film, situation etc)* funny, amusing; **sa sœur est très d.** his/her sister's very funny *or* good fun; **le plus d. c'est que...** the funny thing is that...; *Ironique* **très d.!** very funny *or* droll *or* amusing!; **ce n'est pas toujours d. au bureau!** life at the office isn't always a barrel of laughs!; **la grand-mère n'est pas toujours d.** grandma isn't always easy!; *Fam* **tu aurais dû le laisser faire – tu es d., il se serait fait mal!** you should have let him – are you kidding? he'd have hurt himself!
2 *(étrange)* strange, funny, peculiar; **je l'ai trouvé d. hier** he was behaving rather oddly *or* strangely yesterday; **c'est d., il était ici il y a un instant** that's strange *or* funny *or* peculiar, he was here a minute ago; *Fam* **ça me fait (tout) d. de revenir ici** it feels really strange *or* funny to be back; **se sentir (tout) d.** to feel (really) funny *or* weird; **en voilà une d. d'idée!** what a strange *or* funny *or* weird idea!; **ça fait un d. de bruit** it makes a strange *or* funny noise; **tu en fais une d. de tête!** you look as if something's wrong!; *Hist* **la d. de guerre** the phoney war
3 *Fam (en intensif)* **il a de drôles de problèmes en ce moment** he's got some real problems at the moment; **il faut un d. de courage pour faire ça!** you need a hell of a lot of courage to do that!; **j'ai eu une d. de grippe!** I had a really bad case of flu
NM **1** *Littéraire (voyou)* rascal, rogue; *(enfant déluré)* little rascal *or* rogue
2 *Arch (enfant)* child
• **drôles** NFPL *Fam (histoires)* **il en a entendu/raconté de drôles!** he heard/told some very weird stories!▫

drôlement [drolmɑ̃] ADV **1** *Fam (vraiment)* **d. ennuyeux** deadly boring; **les prix ont d. augmenté** prices have gone up an awful lot▫; **il fait d. chaud ici!** it's really hot in here!; **j'ai d. eu peur** I got a real fright; **je me suis d. fait mal** I really hurt myself▫ **2** *(bizarrement ▸ regarder, parler)* in a strange *or* funny *or* peculiar way▫ **3** *(de façon amusante)* amusingly▫

drôlerie [drolri] NF **1** *(d'une personne, d'un spectacle, d'une remarque)* drollness, funniness **2** *(acte)* funny *or* amusing thing (to do); *(remarque)* funny *or* amusing thing (to say)

drôlesse [drolɛs] NF **1** *Vieilli (femme)* (brazen) hussy **2** *Arch (fille)* lass

DROM [drom] NM *(abrév* **Département et Région d'outre-mer***)* = French overseas department and region

> **DROM**
>
> The acronym **DROM** replaced the acronym **DOM** in 2003 (see also entries **DOM-TOM** and **COM**). The "départements et régions d'outre-mer" are Guadeloupe, Martinique, French Guiana and La Réunion.

dromadaire [drɔmadɛr] NM *Zool* dromedary

drop [drɔp], **drop-goal** [drɔpgɔl] *(pl* **drop-goals***)* NM *Sport (au rugby)* drop goal

droppage [drɔpaʒ] NM *Aviat* (parachute) drop; **zone de d.** drop zone

drosophile [drozɔfil] *Entom*
NF fruit fly, *Spéc* drosophila
• **drosophiles** NFPL fruit flies, *Spéc* Drosophilae

drosser [3] [drɔse] VT *Naut* to drive

dru, -e [dry] ADJ *(cheveux)* thick; *(végétation)* dense, thick; *(barbe)* bushy, thick; *(pluie)* heavy
ADV *(croître, pousser)* densely, thickly; *(pleuvoir)* heavily; **les mauvaises herbes ont poussé d.** there has been a thick growth of weeds; **la pluie tombe d.** it's raining heavily; *Fig* **les coups pleuvaient d.** blows rained down (on all sides)

drugstore [drœgstɔr] NM small shopping *Br* centre *or Am* mall

druide, -esse [drɥid, -ɛs] NM,F druid, *f* druidess

druidique [drɥidik] ADJ druidic, druidical

druidisme [drɥidism] NM druidism

drummer [drœmœr] NM *(batteur)* drummer

drupe [dryp] NF *Bot* drupe

dry [draj] ADJ INV *(apéritif, champagne)* dry; *(whisky)* neat, straight
NM INV dry Martini®

dryade [drijad] NF **1** *Myth* dryad **2** *Bot* dryas, mountain avens

DST [deɛste] NF *(abrév* **Direction de la surveillance du territoire***)* = internal state security department, *Br* ≃ MI5, *Am* ≃ CIA

DTP [detepe], **DT-Polio** [detepɔljo] NM *Méd (abrév* **diphtérie, tétanos, polio***)* = vaccine against diphtheria, tetanus and polio

DTS [detees] NMPL *Fin (abrév* **droits de tirage spéciaux***)* SDRs

du [dy] *voir* **de**

dû, due [dy] PP *voir* **devoir**[2]
ADJ **1** *(à payer)* owed; **quelle est la somme due?** what's the sum owed *or* due? **2 dû à** *(causé par)* due to; **sa maladresse est due à sa timidité** his/her clumsiness is caused by *or* is due to his/her shyness; **son licenciement est dû aux difficultés économiques de l'entreprise** he/she was made redundant because of *or* due to the company's economic difficulties
NM due; **je ne fais que lui réclamer mon dû** I'm only asking for what he/she owes me
• **en bonne et due forme** ADV *Jur* in due form
• **jusqu'à due concurrence de** PRÉP up to (a limit of); **jusqu'à due concurrence de 2000 euros** up to 2,000 euros

dualisme [dɥalism] NM dualism

dualiste [dɥalist] ADJ dualistic
NMF dualist

dualité [dɥalite] NF duality

dubitatif, -ive [dybitatif, -iv] ADJ dubious, sceptical

dubitativement [dybitativmɑ̃] ADV dubiously, sceptically

Dublin [dyblɛ̃] NM Dublin

dublinois, -e [dyblinwa, -az] ADJ of/from Dublin
• **Dublinois, -e** NM,F Dubliner

duc [dyk] NM **1** *(titre)* duke **2** *Orn* horned owl

ducal, -e, -aux, -ales [dykal, -o] ADJ ducal; **un titre d.** a duke's title

duché [dyʃe] NM duchy, dukedom

duchesse [dyʃɛs] NF **1** *(titre)* duchess; *Péj* **faire la d.** to play the fine lady **2** *(fruit)* **(poire) d.** duchess pear **3** *(meuble)* duchesse

Duchnoque [dyʃnɔk] NM *Fam Br* pal, matey, *Am* bud, buddy

Ducon [dykɔ̃], **Ducon-la-joie** [dykɔ̃laʒwa] NM *très Fam* shit-for-brains, *Br* dick features

ducroire [dykrwar] NM *Com* del credere; *(agent)* del credere agent

ductile [dyktil] ADJ ductile

ductilité [dyktilite] NF ductility

duègne [dɥɛɲ] NF duenna

duel [dɥɛl] NM **1** *(entre deux personnes)* duel; **se battre en d. avec qn** to fight a duel *or* to duel with sb; **provoquer qn en d.** to challenge sb to a duel
2 *(conflit ▸ entre États, organisations)* battle; **d. d'artillerie** artillery battle
3 *(compétition)* **d. oratoire** verbal battle
4 *Ling* dual

duelliste [dɥelist] NMF duellist

duettiste [dɥetist] NMF duettist

duffle-coat *(pl* **duffle-coats***)*, **duffel-coat** *(pl* **duffel-coats***)* [dœfœlkot] NM duffel coat

dulcinée [dylsine] NF *Hum* ladylove, dulcinea

dum-dum [dumdum] *voir* **balle**

dûment [dymɑ̃] ADV duly; **d. expédié/reçu** duly dispatched/received

dumping [dœmpiŋ] NM *Écon* dumping; **faire du d.** to dump (goods); **d. social** social dumping

dune [dyn] NF dune

dunette [dynɛt] NF *Naut* poop

Dunkerque [dœ̃kɛrk] NM Dunkirk

duo [dyo, dɥo] NM **1** *(spectacle ▸ chanté)* duet; *(▸ instrumental)* duet, duo; **chanter en d.** to sing a duet **2** *(dialogue)* exchange

duodécimal, -e, -aux, -ales [dɥɔdesimal, -o] ADJ duodecimal

duodénal, -e, -aux, -ales [dɥɔdenal, -o] ADJ *Anat* duodenal

duodénite [dɥɔdenit] NF *Méd* duodenitis

duodénum [dɥɔdenɔm] NM *Anat* duodenum

duopole [dɥɔpɔl] NM duopoly

dupe [dyp] NF dupe; **prendre qn pour d.** to dupe sb, to take sb for a ride; **jeu de dupes** fool's game
ADJ **elle a été d. de ses promesses** she was fooled by his promises; **elle ment, mais je ne suis pas d.** she's lying but it doesn't fool me

duper [3] [dype] VT *Littéraire* to dupe, to fool
VPR **se duper** to fool oneself

duperie [dypri] NF dupery

dupeur, -euse [dypœr, -øz] NM,F *Littéraire* duper

duplex [dyplɛks] NM **1 (appartement en) d.** *Br* maisonnette *(on two floors)*, *Am* duplex **2** *Tél* duplex; **(émission en) d.** linkup

duplexer [4] [dyplɛkse] VT *Tél* to set up a linkup to

duplicata [dyplikata] NM duplicate

duplicateur [dyplikatœr] NM duplicator

duplication [dyplikasjɔ̃] NF **1** *(fait de copier)* duplication, duplicating; **d. de logiciel** software copying *(UNCOUNT)*
2 *(d'un enregistrement sonore)* linking up
3 *Biol* doubling
4 *Mktg* **d. d'audience** audience duplication

duplicité [dyplisite] NF duplicity, falseness, hypocrisy

dupliquer [3] [dyplike] VT *(document)* to duplicate
VPR **se dupliquer** *Biol* to be replicated; *Ordinat (virus informatique)* to spread

duquel [dykɛl] *voir* **lequel**

DUR, -E [dyr]

> **ADJ**
> • hard **1–4, 6–9** • tough **1, 6**
> • difficult **2** • harsh **3, 5**
> **NM,F**
> • tough cookie **1** • tough guy **2**
> • hardliner **3**
> **NM**
> • train
> **ADV**
> • hard **1**

ADJ **1** *(ferme ▸ viande)* tough; *(▸ muscle)* firm, hard; *(▸ lit, mine de crayon)* hard; **bois d.** hardwood; **d. comme du bois** *ou* **le marbre** *ou* **le roc** rock-hard
2 *(difficile)* hard, difficult; **la route est dure à monter** it's a hard road to climb; *Fam* **c'est plutôt d. à digérer, ton histoire!** your story's rather hard to take!; **il est parfois d. d'accepter la vérité** accepting the truth can be hard *or* difficult; **le plus d. dans l'histoire, c'est de comprendre ce qui s'est passé** the hardest part of the whole business is

understanding what really happened

3 *(pénible à supporter ▸ climat)* harsh; **les conditions de vie sont de plus en plus dures** life gets harder and harder; **nous avons eu de durs moments** we've been through some hard times; **le plus d. est passé maintenant** the worst is over now; **les temps sont durs** these are hard times; *Fam* **pas de congé? d. d.!** no time off? bad luck!

4 *(cruel)* **il m'est d. de t'entendre parler ainsi** it's hard for me to hear you talk like this; **dis donc, tu es dure!** don't be so hard-hearted!; **ne sois pas d. avec lui** don't be nasty to *or* tough on him

5 *(rude, froid)* harsh; **d'une voix dure** in a harsh voice; **des couleurs dures** harsh colours; **des yeux d'un bleu très d.** steely blue eyes

6 *(endurci)* tough; **elle est dure, elle ne se plaint jamais** she's tough, she never complains; **il est d. à la douleur** he's tough, he can bear a lot of pain; **il est d. au travail** *ou* **à l'ouvrage** he's a hard worker; **avoir le cœur d.** to have a heart of stone, to be hard-hearted; *Fam* **il est d. à cuire** he's a hard nut to crack; *Fam* **d. à la détente** *(avare)* tight-fisted; *(peu vif)* slow on the uptake; *Fam* **être d. d'oreille** *ou* **de la feuille** to be hard of hearing▫

7 *(intransigeant)* hard; **la droite/gauche dure** the hard right/left

8 *Ling* hard

9 *Phys* hard

10 *Métal* **fer d.** chilled iron

11 *Can Fam* **faire d.** to look awful▫

NM,F *Fam* **1** *(personne sans faiblesse)* toughie, tough cookie *or Br* nut; **un d. en affaires** a hard-nosed businessman; **c'est un d. à cuire** he's a hard nut to crack

2 *(voyou)* tough guy, toughie; **un d. de d.** a real tough guy *or Br* tough nut

3 *Pol* hardliner, hawk; **les durs du parti** the hard core in the party

NM *Fam (train)* train▫

ADV 1 *(avec force)* hard; **il a tapé** *ou* **frappé d.** he hit hard; **il travaille d. sur son nouveau projet** he's working hard *or* he's hard at work on his new project; **croire** *ou* **penser d. comme fer que...** to be firm in the belief that...

2 *(avec intensité)* **le soleil tape d. aujourd'hui** the sun is beating down today

• **dures NFPL** *Fam (histoires, moments)* **il lui en a fait voir de dures** he gave him/her a hard time; **il nous en a dit de dures** he told us some really nasty things

• **à la dure ADV élever ses enfants à la dure** to bring up one's children the hard way; **ils ont toujours vécu à la dure** they always had a tough life

• **en dur ADJ construction/maison en d.** building/house built with non-temporary materials

• **sur la dure ADV coucher sur la dure** *(sur le plancher)* to sleep on the floor; *(dehors)* to sleep on the ground

durabilité [dyrabilite] **NF** *(qualité)* durableness, durability

durable [dyrabl] **ADJ 1** *(permanent)* enduring, lasting, long-lasting; **caractère d.** durability; **faire œuvre d.** to create a work of lasting significance

2 *Écon* **biens durables** durable goods, durables

durablement [dyrabləmɑ̃] **ADV** durably, enduringly, for a long time

duraille [dyraj] **ADJ** *Fam* hard▫; **il était d., le problème de maths** the maths question was a real stinker; **se faire piquer son mec par sa meilleure copine, c'est plutôt d.** it's a bit of a bummer *or* downer when your best friend steals your man

Duralumin® [dyralymɛ̃] **NM** Duralumin®

durant [dyrɑ̃] **PRÉP 1** *(avant le nom) (au cours de)* during, in the course of; **il est né d. la nuit** he was born during *or* in the middle of the night; **fermé d. les travaux** *(sur panneau ou vitrine)* closed for alterations **2** *(avant le nom) (exprime la durée)* for; **d. quelques instants, j'ai cru qu'il allait la frapper** for a few moments I thought he was going to hit her **3** *(après le nom) (pour insister)* for; **il peut parler des heures d.** he can speak for hours (on end); **toute sa vie d.** his/her whole life through, throughout his/her whole life

Durban [dœrban] **NM** Durban

durcir [32] [dyrsir] **VT** *(rendre plus dur)* to harden, to make firmer; *Fig* to harden, to toughen; **la colère durcissait son regard** his/her eyes were set in anger; **d. ses positions** to take a tougher stand

VI *(sol, plâtre, pain)* to harden, to go hard

VPR se durcir *(personne)* to harden oneself; *(traits)* to harden; *(cœur)* to become hard; *(opposition)* to take a tougher stance

durcissement [dyrsismɑ̃] **NM 1** *(raffermissement ▸ du sol, du plâtre)* hardening **2** *(renforcement)* **le d. de l'opposition** the tougher stance taken by the opposition; **le d. de la résistance ennemie** the stiffening of enemy resistance

dure [dyr] **à la dure, sur la dure** *voir* **dur**

durée [dyre] **NF 1** *(période)* duration, length; *Fin (de crédit)* term; *(d'un prêt)* life; **quelle est la d. de votre congé?** how long is your leave?, how long does your leave last?; **pendant la d. de** during, for the duration of; **vente promotionnelle pour une d. limitée** special sale for a limited period; **disque longue d.** long-playing record; *Compta* **d. d'amortissement** depreciation period; **d. de conservation** best-before date; **d. d'écoute** *Rad* listening time; *TV* viewing time; **d. de vie** *(d'une personne)* lifespan; *(d'une pile)* life; *(d'une machine)* useful life; **d. (utile) de vie** *(d'un produit)* life expectancy, shelf-life; **d. de vol** flight time

2 *(persistance)* lasting quality

3 *Mus, Ling & Littérature* length

4 *Ordinat* **d. de connexion** on-line time

• **de courte durée ADJ** short-lived

• **de longue durée ADJ** *(chômeur, chômage)* long-term

durement [dyrmɑ̃] **ADV 1** *(violemment ▸ frapper)* hard; **je suis tombé d.** I had a hard fall, I fell really hard

2 *(avec sévérité)* harshly, severely; **elle a élevé ses enfants d.** she brought up her children strictly

3 *(douloureusement)* deeply; **d. éprouvé par la mort de** deeply distressed by the death of; **son absence est d. ressentie** he's/she's sorely missed

4 *(méchamment ▸ répondre)* harshly

durer [3] [dyre] **VI 1** *(événement, tremblement de terre)* to last, to go *or* to carry on; **la situation n'a que trop duré** the situation has gone on far too long; **ça ne peut plus d.!** it can't go on like this!; **ça fait longtemps/trois ans que ça dure** it's been going on for a long time/for three years; **il pleure quand sa mère le quitte mais cela ne dure pas** he cries when his mother leaves him but it doesn't last *or* he doesn't carry on for long; **ça a duré toute la journée** it lasted all day; *Fam* **ça durera ce que ça durera!** it might last and then it might not!

2 *(rester, persister)* to last; **ce soleil ne va pas d.** this sunshine won't last (long); **cela ne durera pas** it can't *or* won't last; **faire d. les provisions** to stretch supplies, to make supplies last; **faire d. le plaisir** to spin things out

3 *(moteur, appareil)* to last; *(œuvre)* to last, *Sout* to endure; *Fam* **mon manteau m'a duré dix ans** my coat lasted me ten years, I got ten years' wear out of my coat; **voici une nouvelle montre, essaie de la faire d., celle-là** here's a new watch, try to make this one last

4 *(peser)* **le temps me dure** time is lying heavy (on my hands) *or* hangs heavily on me

5 *(vivre)* to last; **il ne durera plus longtemps** he won't last *or* live much longer

6 *(en Afrique francophone ▸ rester)* to stay; *(▸ habiter)* to live

dureté [dyrte] **NF 1** *(du sol, du plâtre)* hardness, firmness

2 *(du climat, de conditions)* harshness

3 *(d'un maître, d'une règle)* severity, harshness; *(d'une grève)* bitterness, harshness; **traiter qn avec d.** to be harsh to *or* tough on sb

4 *(d'une teinte, d'une voix, d'une lumière)* harshness

5 *Chim (de l'eau)* hardness

6 *Phys* hardness

durillon [dyrijɔ̃] **NM** callus

Durit® [dyrit] **NF** flexible pipe; **D. de radiateur** radiator hose; *Fam* **péter une D.** *(se mettre en colère)* to hit the *Br* roof *or Am* ceiling

DUT [deyte] **NM** *(abrév* **diplôme universitaire de technologie**) = diploma taken after two years at an institute of technology

dut *etc voir* **devoir**[2]

duvet [dyvɛ] **NM 1** *(poils)* down, downy hairs; *(d'un animal)* underfur

2 *(plumes)* down; **un oreiller en d.** a down pillow

3 *(sac de couchage)* sleeping bag

4 *Belg & Suisse* duvet, (continental) quilt

duveté, -e [dyvte] **ADJ** downy

duveter [28] [dyvte] **se duveter VPR** to go *or* to become downy, to get covered in down

duveteux, -euse [dyvtø, -øz] **ADJ** downy

DVD [devede] **NM** *(abrév* **Digital Versatile Disk, Digital Video Disk**) DVD; **D. réenregistrable** rerecordable DVD

DVD-R [devedeer] **NM** *(abrév* **Digital Versatile Disk-recordable**) DVD-R

DVD-ROM, DVD-Rom [devederɔm] **NM INV** *(abrév* **Digital Versatile Disk read-only memory**) DVD-ROM

DVD-RW [devedeerdubləve] **NM** *Ordinat (abbr* **Digital Video Disk-rewritable**) DVD-RW

dwell [dwel] **NM** *Aut* dwell

dynamique [dinamik] **ADJ 1** *(énergique)* dynamic, energetic **2** *(non statique)* dynamic

NF 1 *Mus & Tech* dynamics *(singulier)* **2** *(mouvement)* dynamics *(singulier)*, dynamic; **la d. du marché** market dynamics **3** *Psy* **d. de groupe** group dynamics

dynamiquement [dinamikmɑ̃] **ADV** dynamically

dynamisant, -e [dinamizɑ̃, -ɑ̃t] **ADJ** motivating, stimulating

dynamisation [dinamizasjɔ̃] **NF** *(excitation)* **responsable de la d. de l'équipe** responsible for making the team more dynamic

dynamiser [3] [dinamize] **VT** *(équipe)* to dynamize, to make more dynamic

dynamisme [dinamism] **NM 1** *(entrain)* energy, enthusiasm **2** *Phil* dynamism

dynamiste [dinamist] *Phil* **ADJ** dynamistic

NM,F dynamist

dynamitage [dinamitaʒ] **NM** blowing up *or* blasting *(with dynamite)*

dynamite [dinamit] **NF** dynamite; *Fam Fig* **c'est de la d.!** it's dynamite!

dynamiter [3] [dinamite] **VT 1** *(détruire à l'explosif)* to blow up *or* to blast with dynamite **2** *(abolir ▸ préjugé)* to explode

dynamiteur, -euse [dinamitœr, -øz] **NM,F 1** *(à l'explosif)* dynamiter, dynamite expert **2** *(démystificateur)* destroyer of received ideas

dynamo [dinamo] **NF** dynamo, generator

dynamoélectrique [dinamoelektrik] **ADJ** dynamoelectric, dynamoelectrical

dynamogène [dinamoʒen], **dynamogénique** [dinamoʒenik] **ADJ** dynamogenic

dynastie [dinasti] **NF 1** *(de rois)* dynasty **2** *(famille)* **la d. des Rothschild** the Rothschild dynasty

dynastique [dinastik] **ADJ** dynastic, dynastical

dyne [din] **NF** dyne

dysenterie [disɑ̃tri] **NF** dysentery

dysentérique [disɑ̃terik] **ADJ** dysenteric

NMF dysentery sufferer

dysferline [disferlin] **NF** *Physiol* dysferlin

dysfonction [disfɔ̃ksjɔ̃] **NF** *Méd (d'un organe)* dysfunction, malfunction

dysfonctionnement [disfɔ̃ksjɔnmɑ̃] **NM** *Méd (d'un organe)* dysfunction, malfunction; *(d'une institution, d'un service)* malfunctioning

dyslexie [disleksi] **NF** dyslexia

dyslexique [disleksik] **ADJ** dyslexic

NMF dyslexic

dysménorrhée [dismenɔre] **NF** *Méd* dysmenorrhoea

dysmorphophobie [dismɔrfofobi] **NF** *Psy* body dysmorphic disorder

dyspepsie [dispepsi] **NF** *Méd* dyspepsia

dyspepsique [dispepsik], **dyspeptique** [dispeptik] *Méd* **ADJ** dyspeptic

NMF dyspeptic

dysphasie [disfazi] **NF** *Méd* dysphasia

dyspraxie [dispraksi] **NF** *Méd* dyspraxia

dyspraxique [dispraksik] **ADJ** *Méd* dyspraxic

dystrophie [distrɔfi] **NF** *Méd* dystrophy; **d. musculaire progressive** muscular dystrophy

E[1]**, e** [ə] **NM INV 1** *(lettre)* E, e; **E comme Eugène** ≃ E for Eric **2** *Mus (note)* E **3** *Math & Phys* e

E[2] *(abrév écrite* **est***)* E

EAO [əao] **NM** *(abrév* **enseignement assisté par ordinateur***)* CAL

EARL [əaerɛl] **NF** *Écon (abrév* **Exploitation agricole à responsabilité limitée***)* = farm registered as a limited company

eau, -x [o] **NF 1** *(liquide incolore)* water; **les fougères ont besoin d'e.** ferns need water; **cloque** *ou* **ampoule pleine de d'e.** water blister; **prendre l'e.** *(chaussure, tente)* to leak, to let in water; **mettre un navire à l'e.** to launch a ship; **se mettre à l'e.** *(pour se baigner)* to go in the water (for a swim); **tomber à l'e.** to fall into the water; **passer qch à l'e.** to rinse sth; **il est tombé beaucoup d'e.** a lot of rain fell; **dans l'e. de votre bain** in your bathwater; *Rel* **e. bénite** holy water; **e. calcaire** hard water; **e. courante** running water; **avoir l'e. courante** to have running water; **e. déminéralisée** demineralized water; **e. distillée** distilled water; **e. douce** *(non salée)* fresh water; *(sans calcaire)* soft water; **d'e. douce** freshwater, river *(avant n)*; **e. dure** hard water; **eaux d'égout** waste water; **e. de jouvence** waters of youth; **e. de mer** seawater; **e. de pluie** rainwater; **e. de refroidissement** cooling water; **e. de roche** spring water; **eaux de ruissellement** runoff; **e. de source** spring water; **e. de vaisselle** dishwater; **e. de la ville** main(s) water; **e. vive** (fresh) running water; **sports d'e. vive** whitewater sports; **descente en e. vive** whitewater rafting; **jet d'e.** *ou* **d'eaux** fountains; *Fig* **pêcher en e. trouble** to fish in troubled waters; *Fig* **nager** *ou* **naviguer en e. trouble** to sail close to the wind; *Fig* **nager entre deux eaux** *(ne pas s'engager)* to keep a foot in both camps; *(hésiter)* to hum and haw; *Fig* **être** *ou* **naviguer dans les eaux de qn** *(rallier ses opinions)* to take the same line as sb; **il navigue dans les eaux de plusieurs peintres en vue** he hangs around several well-known painters; **comme l'e. et le feu** as different *Br* as chalk and cheese *or Am* as night and day; *Fam* **ça doit valoir 3000 euros, enfin, c'est dans ces eaux-là!** it costs 3,000 euros or thereabouts; **cela amène de l'e. à son moulin** it's (all) grist to his/her mill; **tu apportes de l'e. à mon moulin** you're adding weight to my argument; **il est passé beaucoup d'e. sous les ponts** a lot of water has gone under the bridge; *Fam* **il y a de l'e. dans le gaz** there's trouble brewing; **porter de l'e. à la rivière** *ou* **à la mer** to take *or* to carry coals to Newcastle; **il ne trouverait pas d'e. à la rivière** *ou* **au lac** *ou* **à la mer** he can't find anything even if it's staring him in the face; **j'en ai l'e. à la bouche** my mouth is watering; **ça me donne** *ou* **ça me met l'e. à la bouche** it makes my mouth water

2 *(boisson)* water; **e. gazeuse** soda *or* fizzy water; **e. minérale** mineral water; **e. plate** still water; **e. du robinet** tap water; **e. rougie** = water with a drop of wine in it; **e. de Seltz** soda water, *Am* club soda; **e. de source** spring water; **point d'e.** *(pour les animaux)* watering hole; *(dans un village)* standpipe; **mettre de l'e. dans son vin** to water down one's wine; *Fig* to climb down, to back off

3 *Culin* water; *(d'un melon)* juice; **les concombres rendent beaucoup d'e.** cucumbers give out a lot of water; **e. de cuisson** cooking water; **des légumes/melons pleins d'e.** watery vegetables/melons; **e. de fleur d'oranger** orange flower water; **e. sucrée** sugar water; *Fam* **finir** *ou* **partir** *ou* **tourner** *ou* **s'en aller en e. de boudin** *(mal se terminer)* to end in tears; *(échouer)* to go down the tubes

4 *(parfum) & Pharm* **e. de Cologne** (eau de) Cologne; **e. dentifrice** mouthwash; **e. de lavande** lavender water; **e. de mélisse** = liqueur made from lemon balm; **e. de parfum** perfume; **e. de rose** rose water; **e. de toilette** toilet water

5 *Chim* **e. écarlate** stain-remover; **e. de Javel** bleach, *Am* Clorox®; **nettoyer une tache à l'e. de Javel** to bleach a stain out; **e. lourde** heavy water, *Spéc* deuterium oxide; **e. oxygénée** hydrogen peroxide

6 *(limpidité ▸ d'un diamant)* water; *aussi Fig* **de la plus belle e.** of the first water; *Littéraire* **dans l'e. claire de ses yeux** *ou* **de son regard** in his/her limpid eyes, in the pools of his/her eyes

7 *Naut* **faire de l'e.** *(s'approvisionner)* to take on water; **faire e.** *(avoir une fuite)* to take on water; *Fig* **faire e. de toutes parts** to go under

• **eaux NFPL 1** *(masse)* water; **les eaux se retirent** *(mer)* the tide's going out; *(inondation)* the (flood) water's subsiding; **eaux de fonte** meltwater; *Écol* **eaux grasses** swill; *(pour les porcs)* slops; **eaux ménagères** waste water; **eaux usées** sewage; *Géog* **hautes/basses eaux** high/low water; **les grandes eaux de Versailles** the fountains of Versailles; **dimanche: grandes eaux à Versailles** the fountains will play at Versailles on Sunday; *Fam Fig* **on a eu droit aux grandes eaux (de Versailles)** he/she turned on the waterworks

2 *Naut (zone)* waters; **eaux internationales/territoriales** international/territorial waters; **eaux côtières** inshore waters; **dans les eaux de** in the wake of

3 *Obst (d'une accouchée)* waters; **elle a perdu les eaux** her waters have broken; **poche des eaux** amniotic sac

4 *(thermes)* **eaux thermales** thermal *or* hot springs; **prendre les eaux** to take the waters, to stay at a spa *(for one's health)*

5 *Admin* **les Eaux et Forêts** *Br* ≃ the Forestry Commission, *Am* ≃ the Forest Service

• **à grande eau ADV laver à grande e.** *(au jet)* to hose down; *(dans un évier, une bassine)* to wash in a lot of water

• **à l'eau ADJ 1** *Culin* boiled **2** *(perdu)* **mon week-end est à l'e.** bang goes my weekend **ADV 1** *Culin* **cuire à l'e.** *(légumes)* to boil; *(fruits)* to poach **2** *(locutions)* **se jeter** *ou* **se lancer à l'e.** to take the plunge; **tomber à l'e.** to fall through, to come to nothing; *Can* **s'en aller à l'e.** to be going bankrupt

• **à l'eau de rose ADJ** *Péj* sentimental

• **de la même eau ADJ** *Péj* of the same ilk; **ces deux-là sont de la même e.** they're two of a kind, they're tarred with the same brush

• **en eau ADJ** sweating profusely; **ils étaient en e.** the sweat was pouring off them, they were dripping with sweat

• **en eau profonde ADV** *Naut* in deep (sea) waters

eau-de-vie [odvi] *(pl* **eaux-de-vie***)* **NF** eau de vie

eau-forte [ofɔrt] *(pl* **eaux-fortes***)* **NF 1** *Chim* aqua fortis, nitric acid **2** *Beaux-Arts* etching

eaux-vannes [ovan] **NFPL** effluent, sewage (water)

ébahi, -e [ebai] **ADJ** astounded, dumbfounded, stunned; **regard é.** a look of blank astonishment

ébahir [32] [ebair] **VT** to astound, to dumbfound, to stun

VPR s'ébahir to be dumbfounded; **s'é. de** *ou* **devant** *(s'étonner de)* to be dumbfounded at

ébahissement [ebaismɑ̃] **NM** amazement, astonishment

ébarbage [ebarbaʒ] **NM 1** *Métal (d'une surface métallique)* deburring

2 *(d'un livre)* trimming the pages; *(d'une feuille de papier)* trimming

3 *Agr* clipping, trimming; *(d'une haie, d'une pelouse)* clipping

4 *Culin (du poisson)* trimming

ébarber [3] [ebarbe] **VT 1** *Métal (surface métallique)* to deburr

2 *(livre)* to trim the pages of; *(feuilles de papier)* to trim

3 *Agr* to clip, to trim; *(haie, pelouse)* to clip

4 *Culin (poisson)* to trim

ébarbure [ebarbyr] **NF** *Ind (de métal)* burr, paring; *(de papier)* trimming

ébat *etc voir* **ébattre**

ébats [eba] **NMPL** frolics, frolicking; **é. amoureux** lovemaking

ébattre [83] [ebatr] **s'ébattre VPR** to frolic; *(animaux)* to gambol

ébaubi, -e [ebobi] **ADJ** *Vieilli* dumbfounded, stunned

ébauchage [eboʃaʒ] **NM 1** *(façonnement ▸ gén)* outlining; *(▸ d'un tableau)* roughing out, sketching out; *(▸ d'un roman etc)* outlining **2** *Métal* roughing out

ébauche [eboʃ] **NF 1** *(première forme ▸ d'un dessin)* rough sketch *or* draft; *(▸ d'une lettre, d'une traduction)* draft; *(▸ d'un plan)* outline; **projet à l'état d'é.** project in its early stages; **faire l'é. de** *(tableau)* to make a rough sketch of, to sketch out; *(roman, lettre, traduction)* to draft; *(projet)* to outline **2** *(fait de préparer ▸ un dessin)* roughing *or* sketching out; *(▸ un plan)* outlining; **j'ai travaillé trois mois à l'é. de mon scénario** I spent three months on the drafting of my scenario **3** *(début)* **l'é. d'un sourire** the beginning of a smile, an incipient smile; **une é. de réconciliation** the first steps towards reconciliation; **il eut l'é. d'un geste vers elle puis se ravisa** he started moving towards her then stopped; **je n'ai réussi à avoir avec lui qu'une é. de conversation** I managed only a rather stilted conversation with him

ébaucher [3] [eboʃe] **VT 1** *(esquisser ▸ dessin, portrait)* to rough *or* to sketch out; *(▸ lettre)* to draft, to make a draft of; *(▸ plan)* to outline; **é. une traduction** to make a draft *or* rough translation, to draft a translation; **c'est un portrait qu'il a juste ébauché** it's a portrait he's just begun working on **2** *(commencer)* to begin, to start; **é. des négociations/une réconciliation** to start the process of negotiation/reconciliation; **elle ébaucha un vague sourire** she made as if to smile; **elle ébaucha un geste de bienvenue** she made a vague gesture of welcome **3** *Constr & Ind* to rough-hew

VPR s'ébaucher to (take) form, to start up

ébène [ebɛn] NF *Bot* ebony; **une table en é.** an ebony table; **(d'un) noir d'é., d'é.** ebony black; *Hist* **(bois d')é.** slaves; **marchand d'é.** slave-trader

ébénier [ebenje] NM *Bot* ebony (tree)

ébéniste [ebenist] NM *Menuis* cabinetmaker

ébénisterie [ebenistəri] NF *Menuis* **1** *(métier)* cabinetmaking **2** *(placage)* veneer; **une table en é.** a veneered table **3** *(meuble)* cabinet work

éberlué, -e [ebɛrlɥe] ADJ *Fam* dumbfounded, flabbergasted

EBIT [ebit] NM *Fin* (*abrév* **earnings before interest and tax**) EBIT

EBITDA [ebitta] NM *Fin* (*abrév* **earnings before interest, tax, depreciation and amortization**) EBITDA

éblouir [32] [ebluir] VT **1** *(aveugler)* to dazzle **2** *(impressionner)* to dazzle, to stun; **nous avons été éblouis par son talent** we were dazzled by his/her talent

éblouissant, -e [ebluisɑ̃, -ɑ̃t] ADJ **1** *(aveuglant ▸ lumière)* dazzling, blinding; *(▸ couleur)* dazzling **2** *(impressionnant ▸ femme, performance)* dazzling, stunning; **d'une beauté éblouissante** dazzlingly *or* stunningly beautiful; **mise en scène éblouissante d'ingéniosité** stunningly ingenious staging

éblouissement [ebluismɑ̃] NM **1** *(fait d'être aveuglé)* being dazzled **2** *(vertige)* dizziness; **être pris d'éblouissements** to feel dizzy *or* faint; **avoir un é.** to have a dizzy spell **3** *(enchantement)* dazzlement, bedazzlement; **quand on arrive chez eux, c'est un véritable é.** their place is dazzling

ébonite [ebɔnit] NF *Chim* ebonite, vulcanite

e-book [ibuk] NM e-book

éborgner [3] [ebɔrɲe] VT **1 é. qn** to blind sb in one eye, to put sb's eye out; **attention, tu vas m'é.!** hey, watch my eyes! **2** *Hort (arbre fruitier)* to disbud

VPR **s'éborgner** to put one's eye out

éboueur [ebwœr] NM *Br* dustman, *Am* garbage collector

ébouillanter [3] [ebujɑ̃te] VT *Culin* to scald

VPR **s'ébouillanter** to scald oneself; **s'é. la main/le pied** to scald one's hand/foot

éboulement [ebulmɑ̃] NM **1** *(chute)* crumbling, subsiding, collapsing; **un é. de terrain** a landslide; **l'é. de la falaise/carrière a fait deux morts** two people were killed when the cliff collapsed/the quarry fell in; **il y a eu un é. dans la mine** there has been a cave-in at the mine; **si vous allez vers la carrière, méfiez-vous des éboulements** if you're going in the direction of the quarry, watch out for falling rocks **2** *(éboulis ▸ de terre)* mass of fallen earth; *(▸ de rochers)* mass of fallen rocks, rock slide; *(▸ en montagne)* scree

> Do not confuse with **éboulis**.

ébouler [3] [ebule] VT to break *or* to bring down; **un vieux mur éboulé** a crumbling old wall

VPR **s'ébouler** *(falaise, côte ▸ petit à petit)* to crumble; *(▸ brutalement)* to collapse; *(mine)* to cave in; **le talus s'est éboulé** there has been a landslide

éboulis [ebuli] NM *(de terre)* mass of fallen earth; *(de rochers)* mass of fallen rocks, rock slide; *(en montagne)* scree

> Do not confuse with **éboulement**.

ébourgeonnage [eburʒɔnaʒ], **ébourgeonnement** [eburʒɔnmɑ̃] NM *Hort* disbudding

ébourgeonner [3] [eburʒɔne] VT *Hort* to disbud

ébouriffant, -e [eburifɑ̃, -ɑ̃t] ADJ *Fam* amazing, stunning

ébouriffé, -e [eburife] ADJ **1** *(décoiffé)* tousled, dishevelled; **je suis tout é.** my hair is all tousled *or* dishevelled **2** *Fam (ébahi)* amazed, stunned

ébouriffer [3] [eburife] VT **1** *(décoiffer)* **é. qn** to ruffle *or* tousle sb's hair; **tu m'as tout ébouriffé** you've made my hair all tousled **2** *Fam (ébahir)* to amaze, to stun

ébranchage [ebrɑ̃ʃaʒ], **ébranchement** [ebrɑ̃ʃmɑ̃] NM *Hort (d'un arbre)* lopping the branches off

ébrancher [3] [ebrɑ̃ʃe] VT *Hort (arbre)* to lop the branches off

ébranchoir [ebrɑ̃ʃwar] NM *Hort* billhook

ébranlement [ebrɑ̃lmɑ̃] NM **1** *(départ, mise en route ▸ d'un train, d'une procession, d'un convoi)* departure, setting off **2** *(tremblement ▸ d'une vitre)* shaking; **l'é. fut si violent que les murs se sont lézardés** the walls shook so violently that they cracked; *Fig* **causer l'é. du gouvernement** to shake *or* rock the government **3** *(choc)* shock

ébranler [3] [ebrɑ̃le] VT **1** *(faire trembler)* to shake, to rattle; *(▸ édifice, mur)* to shake, to rock; *(▸ vitres)* to shake **2** *(affaiblir)* to shake, to weaken; **le scandale a ébranlé le gouvernement** the government was shaken by the scandal; **é. la confiance de qn** to shake *or* to undermine sb's confidence; **é. la foi de qn** to shake sb's faith; **é. les nerfs de qn** to make sb very nervous **3** *(atteindre moralement)* to shake; **ta gentillesse a fini par l'é.** your kindness finally touched him/her; **il ne faut pas te laisser é. par ses critiques** don't let his/her criticism get to you; **très ébranlé par la mort de son fils** shattered by the death of his son; **il a été très é. par l'annonce de cet accident** he was very shaken *or* upset by the news of the accident

VPR **s'ébranler** *(cortège)* to move *or* to set off; *(train)* to pull away, to start, to move off

Èbre [ɛbr] NM **l'È.** the Ebro

ébréché, -e [ebreʃe] ADJ chipped

ébrécher [18] [ebreʃe] VT **1** *(assiette, vase)* to chip; *(couteau, lame)* to nick, to notch **2** *(fortune, héritage)* to make a hole in, to deplete; *Fig (réputation)* to damage; *Fig* **é. la confiance de qn** to dent sb's confidence

VPR **s'ébrécher** to chip

ébréchure [ebreʃyr] NF *(sur un plat)* chip; *(sur une lame)* nick, notch

ébriété [ebrijete] NF *Jur* intoxication; **être en état d'é.** to be under the influence (of drink); **arrêté pour conduite en état d'é.** arrested for *Br* drink-driving *or Am* drunk-driving

ébrouement [ebrumɑ̃] NM **1** *(d'un cheval)* snort, snorting *(UNCOUNT)*; *(dans l'eau)* splashing about **2** *(d'ailes)* flap, flapping

ébrouer [6] [ebrue] **s'ébrouer** VPR **1** *(cheval)* to snort; *(dans l'eau)* to splash about **2** *(personne, chien)* to shake oneself **3** *(ailes)* to flap

ébruitement [ebrɥitmɑ̃] NM disclosing, spreading

ébruiter [3] [ebrɥite] VT to disclose, to spread; *(nouvelle)* to spread; *(secret)* to give away; *(accord, pourparlers)* to leak

VPR **s'ébruiter** to spread

EBS [əbees] NF *Vét* (*abrév* **encéphalopathie bovine spongiforme**) BSE

ébullition [ebylisjɔ̃] NF *Phys* boiling; **la température d'é. de l'eau est de 100°C** the boiling point of water is 100°C, water boils at 100°C

• **à ébullition** ADV **porter du lait à é.** to bring milk to the boil; **arriver à é.** to come to the boil

• **en ébullition** ADJ *(liquide)* boiling; *Fig* in turmoil; **maintenir en é. pendant cinq minutes** boil for five minutes; *Fam* **il a le cerveau en é.** he's bubbling over with excitement; **tout le pays est en é. depuis qu'ils l'ont arrêté** the whole country has been in turmoil since they arrested him

écaillage [ekajaʒ] NM **1** *(du poisson)* scaling; *(des huîtres)* opening, shucking **2** *(d'une peinture)* flaking *or* peeling *or* scaling off; *(d'un vernis)* chipping off; *(d'émail)* scaling off, chipping

écaille [ekaj] NF **1** *Zool (de poisson, de serpent)* scale; *(de tortue)* shell; *(matière)* tortoiseshell; **lunettes à monture d'é.** tortoiseshell-rimmed spectacles; *Fig Littéraire* **les écailles lui tombèrent des yeux** the scales fell from his/her eyes **2** *(fragment ▸ gén)* chip; *(▸ de peinture)* flake; *(▸ d'émail)* chip

• **en écaille** ADJ tortoiseshell *(avant n)*

écailler[1] [3] [ekaje] VT **1** *Culin (poisson)* to scale; *(huître)* to open, to shuck **2** *(plâtre, vernis)* to cause to flake off *or* to chip **3** *(chaudière)* to scale

VPR **s'écailler** *(vernis, plâtre)* to flake off; *(peinture)* to peel off

écailler[2]**, -ère** [ekaje, -ɛr] NM,F *(vendeur)* oyster seller; *(dans un restaurant)* = restaurant employee who opens oysters and prepares seafood platters

• **écaillère** NF *(instrument)* oyster knife

écailleux, -euse [ekajø, -øz] ADJ **1** *Ich (poisson)* scaly **2** *Géol (ardoise, schiste)* flaky

écale [ekal] NF *(d'une noix)* hull, husk; *(d'une châtaigne)* shuck

écaler [3] [ekale] VT *(noix)* to hull, to husk; *(châtaignes)* to shuck; *(œuf dur)* to shell

écarlate [ekarlat] ADJ scarlet; **devenir é.** to blush, to go *or* to turn scarlet

NF scarlet

écarquiller [3] [ekarkije] VT **é. les yeux** to open one's eyes wide, to stare (wide-eyed); **les yeux écarquillés par la peur** eyes wide with fear

ÉCART [ekar]

> • difference **1** • swerving **3** • gap **2** • margin **7**

NM **1** *(variation)* difference, discrepancy (**de** in); **on constate de grands écarts dans ses résultats** his/her results are very uneven; **il y a des écarts de niveau trop importants dans cette classe** ability differs *or* varies too much in the class; *Mktg* **é. de performance** gap level; *Com* **é. de poids/température** difference in weight/temperature; **é. d'opinions/de points de vue** difference of opinions/points of view; **é. de prix/salaires** price/wage differential; **é. technologique** technology gap; *Com* **é. entre le prix de vente et le coût** margin between cost and selling price; *Tech* **é. admissible** tolerance, permissible deviation

2 *(intervalle)* gap, distance; **un é. de huit ans les sépare** there's an eight-year gap between them; **réduire** *ou* **resserrer l'é. entre** to close *or* to narrow the gap between; **l'é. entre chaque soldat doit être de...** there must be (a distance of)... between each soldier, soldiers must be... apart

3 *(déviation)* swerving; *Tech (de l'aiguille d'une boussole)* deflection; **é. par rapport à la norme** deviation from the norm; **faire un é.** *(cheval)* to shy; *(voiture, vélo)* to swerve; *(piéton)* to step aside, to swerve

4 *(excès)* **é. de conduite** misdemeanour, misbehaviour *(UNCOUNT)*; **faire des écarts de langage** to use bad language; **écarts de jeunesse** youthful indiscretions; **j'ai fait un petit é. aujourd'hui: j'ai mangé deux gâteaux** I broke my diet today: I ate two cakes

5 *Cartes (action)* discarding; *(carte)* discard

6 *(en danse, en gymnastique)* **faire le grand é.** to do the splits

7 *Compta* margin; *(en statistique)* deviation; *Bourse* spread; *Mktg* gap; *(stratégie d'attaque)* bypass attack; **il y a un é. de cent euros entre les deux comptes** there is a discrepancy of a hundred euros between the two accounts; *Bourse* **é. d'acquisition** goodwill; *Fin* **écarts de conversion** exchange adjustments; *Bourse* **écarts de cours** price spreads; **é. des coûts** cost variance; *Compta* **é. net** net variance; *Compta* **écarts de réévaluation** revaluation reserve

• **à l'écart** ADV **1** *(de côté)* aside; **j'ai mis mes verres en cristal à l'é.** I've put my crystal glasses out of the way; **je mets mes sentiments personnels à l'é. dans cette histoire** I'm setting my personal feelings aside in this matter; **mettre qn à l'é.** to put sb on the sidelines; **prendre qn à l'é.** to draw sb aside; **tenir qn à l'é.** to keep sb out of things; **rester** *ou* **se tenir à l'é.** *(dans une réunion, dans la société)* to remain an outsider, to stay in the background; *(du monde, de la foule etc)* to keep oneself apart, to hold oneself aloof; **se sentir à l'é.** to feel isolated *or* out of things **2** *(loin des habitations)* **vivre à l'é.** to live in a remote spot

• **à l'écart de** PRÉP **un terrain à l'é. de la ville** a piece of land outside the town; **tenir qn à l'é. de qch** to keep sb away from sth; **il essaie de la tenir à l'é. de tous ses problèmes** he's tryingto keep her away from all his problems; **se tenir à l'é. de la vie politique** to keep out of politics

écarté, -e [ekarte] ADJ **1** *(isolé)* isolated, remote **2** *(loin l'un de l'autre)* **mettez-vous debout les jambes écartées** stand up with your legs wide apart; **gardez les bras écartés** keep your arms outspread; **avoir les dents écartées** to be gap-toothed; **avoir les yeux écartés** to have widely-spaced eyes

écartelé, -e [ekartəle] ADJ *Hér* quartered, quarterly

écarteler [25] [ekartəle] VT 1 *(torturer)* to quarter 2 *(partager)* to tear apart; **écartelé entre le devoir et l'amour** torn between duty and love 3 *Hér* to quarter

écartement [ekartəmɑ̃] NM 1 *(distance ▸ entre des barres etc)* space, gap, clearance; *Rail* **é. (des rails** *ou* **de voie)** gauge; *Aut* **é. des électrodes** spark *or* plug *or* electrode gap; *Aut* **é. des roues** tracking 2 *(fait d'ouvrir)* spreading (open), opening; *Tech* **pièce d'é.** spacer 3 *(évincement ▸ d'un directeur)* dismissing, removing; *(▸ d'un obstacle)* setting aside; **depuis l'é. des gêneurs, la société va beaucoup mieux** things have been much better in the company since it got rid of the troublemakers

écarter [3] [ekarte] VT 1 *(séparer ▸ objets)* to move apart; *(▸ branches)* to part; *(▸ personnes)* to separate; **é. les pinces d'un crabe** to prise open a crab's pincers; **é. les rideaux** *(le matin)* to open the curtains; *(pour observer)* to move the curtain aside; **ils écartèrent la foule pour passer** they pushed their way through the crowd; **é. les bras** to open *or* to spread one's arms; **é. les jambes/doigts/orteils** to spread one's legs/fingers/toes; **é. les coudes** to square one's elbows

2 *(éloigner ▸ objet)* to move away *or* aside; *(▸ personne)* to pull away *or* aside; *(▸ obstacle)* to move out of the way; *(▸ danger)* to ward off, to avert; **é. les soupçons** to divert suspicion; **é. les obstacles de son chemin** to brush aside the obstacles in one's path

3 *(détourner)* to divert; **cette route vous écarte un peu** that road takes you a little bit out of your way; **ses interventions nous ont écartés de notre sujet** his/her interruptions caused us to stray *or* wander from the subject *or* to digress

4 *(refuser ▸ idée, solution,)* to dismiss, to set aside, to rule out; *(▸ candidat, proposition)* to turn down

5 *(tenir à distance)* **é. qn de qch** *(succession, conseil d'administration)* to keep sb out of sth; **é. qn du pouvoir** *(aspirant)* to cut sb off from the road to power; *(homme d'État)* to manoeuvre sb out of power

6 *Cartes* to discard

VPR **s'écarter** 1 *(se séparer ▸ personnes)* to move apart; *(▸ routes)* to diverge; **la foule s'est écartée sur le passage des pompiers** the crowd parted *or* drew aside to let the firemen through 2 *(s'éloigner ▸ personne)* to move away *or* out of the way, to step *or* to draw aside; *(▸ piéton)* to move *or* to step aside; *(▸ voiture, vélo)* to swerve; *(dévier)* to deviate, to stray **(de** from); **écarte-toi!** move *or* get out of the way!; **s'é. de sa trajectoire** *(fusée)* to deviate from its trajectory; *(pilote)* to deviate from one's course; **s'é. du droit chemin** to go off the straight and narrow (path); **s'é. du sujet** to stray *or* to wander from the subject; **ne vous écartez pas de la route** keep to the road 3 *Can (s'égarer)* to get lost, to go astray

écarteur [ekartœr] NM *Méd* retractor; *Aut* **é. de mâchoire** shoe expander

ecchymose [ekimoz] NF *Méd* bruise, *Spéc* ecchymosis

Ecclésiaste [eklezjast] NM *Bible* **(le Livre de) l'E.** Ecclesiastes

ecclésiastique [eklezjastik] *Rel* ADJ *(devoir)* ecclesiastic, ecclesiastical; *(habitude)* priestly, priestlike

NM ecclesiastic, clergyman

écervelé, -e [eservəle] ADJ scatterbrained

NM,F scatterbrain

ECG [əseʒe] NM *Méd (abrév* **électrocardiogramme)** *Br* ECG, *Am* EKG

échafaud [eʃafo] NM 1 *(lieu d'exécution)* scaffold; **finir sur l'é.** to die on the scaffold 2 *Vieilli (estrade)* stand, platform

échafaudage [eʃafodaʒ] NM 1 *Constr* scaffolding; **é. pour caméra** (camera) tower 2 *(pile d'objets)* heap, pile, stack 3 *(élaboration ▸ de systèmes)* elaboration, construction; *Fig (assemblage, structure)* structure, fabric

échafauder [3] [eʃafode] VT 1 *(entasser)* to stack *or* to heap *or* to pile (up) 2 *(construire ▸ systèmes, théories)* to devise, to construct; *(▸ argumentation)* to put together, to construct; **é. des projets** to make plans

VI *Constr* to put up scaffolding, to scaffold

échalas [eʃala] NM 1 *(perche)* pole, stake; **être droit** *ou* **raide** *ou* **sec comme un é.** to be as stiff as a poker *or* ramrod 2 *Fam (personne)* beanpole; **c'est un grand é.** he's a real beanpole

échalier [eʃalje] NM 1 *(clôture)* gate 2 *(échelle)* stile

échalote [eʃalɔt] NF *Bot* shallot

échancré, -e [eʃɑ̃kre] ADJ 1 *Couture* low-necked; **une robe échancrée dans le dos** a dress cut low in the back, a dress with a low back; **une robe très échancrée sur le devant** a dress with a plunging neckline 2 *Géog (côte, littoral)* indented, jagged

échancrer [3] [eʃɑ̃kre] VT 1 *Couture* to cut a low neckline in 2 *(entailler)* to indent; *(planche)* to notch

échancrure [eʃɑ̃kryr] NF 1 *Couture* low neckline; *(découpe de veste)* vent, slit; **é. en pointe** *ou* **en V dans le dos** V neckline in the back 2 *Géog* indentation 3 *(d'une planche)* notch

échange [eʃɑ̃ʒ] NM 1 *(troc)* swap, exchange; **faire un é.** to swap, to do a swap; *(dans un magasin)* to exchange; **ils ont fait l'é. de leurs bicyclettes** they swapped bicycles; **on fait (l')é.?** do you want to swap?, do you want to do a swap?; **é. de prisonniers** exchange of prisoners; **é. standard** replacement *(of a spare part)*; *Pol* **é. de voix** vote-trading

2 *(aller et retour)* exchange; **avoir un é. de vues** to exchange opinions; **échanges culturels** cultural exchanges; **il y a eu plusieurs échanges de coups de feu** there were exchanges of gunfire; **de violents échanges entre la police et les manifestants** *(physique)* violent clashes between the police and demonstrators; *(verbal)* violent exchanges between the police and demonstrators; **c'est un é. de bons procédés** one good turn deserves another; **nous faisons des échanges de bons procédés** we do favours for each other, we help each other out

3 *(visite)* **é. (linguistique)** (language) exchange

4 *Sport* **é. de balles** *(avant un match)* knocking up; *(pendant le match)* rally; **on va faire quelques échanges?** shall we knock a few balls about?; **quel bel é.!** what a beautiful rally!

5 *Biol* **échanges gazeux** gaseous interchange

6 *Ordinat* **é. de données** data exchange *or* swap; **é. de données informatisé** electronic data interchange; **É. électronique de données** Electronic Data Interchange

7 *Bourse* **é. d'actions** share swap; *Fin* **é. de créances** debt swap; **é. de devises** currency swap; *Fin* **é. financier** swap; **é. de taux d'intérêt** interest-rate swap; **é. à terme** forward swap

• **échanges** NMPL *Fin* exchange; *Écon* trade; **les échanges entre la France et l'Allemagne** trade between France and Germany; **le volume des échanges** the volume of trade; **échanges commerciaux** trade; **échanges industriels** industrial trade; **échanges internationaux/intracommunautaires** international/intra-Community trade

• **en échange** ADV in exchange, in return; **recevoir/donner qch en é.** to receive/give sth in exchange *or* in return

• **en échange de** PRÉP in exchange *or* return for

échangeable [eʃɑ̃ʒabl] ADJ exchangeable

échanger [17] [eʃɑ̃ʒe] VT 1 *(troquer)* to exchange, to swap, *Vieilli* to barter **(contre** for); **é. un stylo contre** *ou* **pour un briquet** to exchange *or* to swap a pen for a lighter 2 *(se donner mutuellement)* to exchange; **é. un regard/sourire** to exchange glances/smiles; **é. des impressions** to exchange *or* compare impressions; **é. des coups/des injures/des idées avec qn** to exchange blows/insults/ideas with sb; **é. quelques mots avec qn** to exchange a few words with sb 3 *Sport* **é. des balles** *(avant le match)* to knock up

VPR **s'échanger** 1 *(emploi passif) (être troqué)* to be swapped; *Bourse* to trade; **le dollar s'échange aujourd'hui à 1,12 euros** today the dollar is trading at 1.12 euros 2 *(emploi réciproque)* **s'é. des disques** to swap records with each other

échangeur [eʃɑ̃ʒœr] NM 1 *Transp (sur une autoroute)* interchange; *(donnant accès à l'autoroute)* feeder 2 *Phys* **é. (de chaleur)** heat exchanger 3 *Aut* **é. air/air** air-to-air exchanger

échangisme [eʃɑ̃ʒism] NM *(sexuel)* partner-swapping, swinging

échangiste [eʃɑ̃ʒist] ADJ partner-swapping, swinging

NMF 1 *Jur* exchanger 2 *(sexuellement)* swinger

échanson [eʃɑ̃sɔ̃] NM *Hist* cupbearer; *Hum* wine waiter

échantillon [eʃɑ̃tijɔ̃] NM 1 *Com & Mktg (petite quantité)* sample; **é. de tissu/d'étoffe** swatch; **é. gratuit** free sample; **catalogue d'échantillons** *(gén)* sample *or* pattern book; *(d'étoffe)* swatch book; **(non) conforme à l'é.** (not) up to sample; **é. publicitaire** free sample

2 *Méd (prélèvement)* sample, specimen; **prélever** *ou* **prendre des échantillons de qch** to take samples of sth, to sample sth

3 *Fig (cas typique)* example, sample; **voici un é. de son œuvre** here is an example of his/her work

4 *(de population)* cross-section; *(pour un sondage)* sample; **é. aléatoire** random sample; **é. normal** average sample; **é. représentatif** cross-section, *Spéc* true sample; **é. stratifié** stratified sample; **é. type** representative sample

5 *Ordinat, Mus & Tél* sample

6 *Vieilli* **brique/tuile d'é.** standard brick/tile

échantillonnage [eʃɑ̃tijɔnaʒ] NM 1 *Com & Mktg (action)* sampling; **l'é. se fait sur un produit sur cent** one product in a hundred is sampled *or* tested; **un é. est effectué systématiquement** sampling is done systematically; **é. aléatoire** random sampling; **é. stratifié** stratified sampling

2 *(personnes)* sample

3 *(série d'échantillons)* range of samples; *(de parfum)* selection; *(de papier peint, de moquette)* swatch *or* sample book; *Fig* **un é. de ce que je sais faire/de mes capacités** a sample of what I can do/of my ability

4 *Ordinat, Mus & Tél* sampling

échantillonner [3] [eʃɑ̃tijɔne] VT 1 *Com* to sample; *(préparer des échantillons de)* to prepare samples of; *(tissus)* to take a sample of

2 *(population)* to take a cross-section of, to take a sample of

3 *(vin)* to sample, to taste

4 *Vieilli (étalonner ▸ articles)* to make according to sample

échantillonneur, -euse [eʃɑ̃tijɔnœr, -øz] NM,F *Com (personne)* tester, sampler

NM *Mus* sampler

échappatoire [eʃapatwar] NF loophole, way out; **ne cherche pas d'é., réponds-moi!** don't avoid the issue, answer me!; **je n'ai pas d'é. possible** I can't get out of it; **le sommeil est mon é.** sleep is my escape mechanism; **é. fiscale** tax loophole

ADJ **clause é.** escape clause

échappé, -e [eʃape] NM,F 1 *Sport (sportif)* = competitor who has broken away; **les échappés du peloton** the breakaway group 2 *Vieilli (évadé)* escaped prisoner, escapee; *Hum* **un é. de l'asile** *(fou)* a lunatic

• **échappée** NF 1 *Sport* breakaway; **être dans l'échappée** to be part of the breakaway group

2 *(espace ouvert à la vue)* vista, view; **échappée (de vue) (sur)** vista (over); **échappée de lumière** shaft of light

3 *(dans un escalier)* headroom

4 *(passage)* space, gap; *(pour véhicules)* turning space; **l'échappée d'un garage** a garage entrance

• **par échappées** ADV every now and then, in fits and starts

échappement [eʃapmɑ̃] NM 1 *Aut & Tech* exhaust; *(tuyau)* exhaust (pipe)

2 *Tech (d'horloge)* escapement; **montre à é.** lever watch

3 *(d'un escalier)* headroom

4 *Ordinat* escape

échapper [3] [eʃape] VT 1 *Can (laisser échapper)* to let go; **le pêcheur a échappé le poisson** the fisherman let the fish go 2 *Can (laisser tomber)* to drop 3 *(locutions)* **nous l'avons échappé belle** we had a narrow escape; **ouf, on l'a échappé belle!** phew, that was close!

VI 1 *(s'enfuir)* **faire é.** *(animal)* to let out; *(détenu)* to help to escape; **laisser é.** *(personne, animal)* to let escape; *(de l'air d'un ballon)* to let out; *(vapeur)* to let off; **il a laissé é. le chien** he let the dog loose 2 *(sortir)* **laisser é. qch** *(secret)* to let sth slip, to let sth out; *(soupir, cri, grossièreté)* to let sth out; *(larme)* to let sth fall

3 *(glisser)* to slip; **le vase lui a échappé des mains** the vase slipped out of his/her hands

4 *(erreur, occasion)* **j'ai pu laisser é. quelques fautes** I may have overlooked a few mistakes; **laisser é. une occasion** to miss an opportunity, to let an opportunity go by

• **échapper à VT IND 1** *(se soustraire à)* to avoid, to evade; **é. de justesse à une amende** to narrowly avoid being fined *or* having to pay a fine; **é. à ses obligations** to evade one's duties; **é. aux recherches** *(criminel, animal)* to evade capture; **é. à la règle** to be an exception to the rule; **tu n'échappes pas à la règle** you're no exception to the rule; **é. à tout contrôle** to be out of control; **cet enfant/ce chien échappe à notre contrôle** this child/dog has got out of hand *or* is beyond our control; **é. à toute définition** to defy definition; **je n'échapperai pas à une leçon de morale** I'm in for a lecture; **il n'y a pas moyen d'y é.** there is no escaping it *or* getting away from it

2 *(éviter)* to escape from, to get away from; *(grippe, punition)* to escape; *(corvées)* to get out of, to dodge; **il n'a pas pu é. à ses ennemis** he couldn't escape from his enemies; **le prisonnier nous a échappé** the prisoner got away from us *or* escaped; **é. à la mort** to escape death

3 *(être dispensé de)* **é. à l'impôt** *(officiellement)* to be exempt from taxation; *(en trichant)* to evade income tax

4 *(être oublié par)* **rien ne lui échappe** he/she doesn't miss a thing; **rien n'échappe à son regard** he/she sees everything; **l'enfant a échappé à la vue de sa mère cinq minutes seulement** the child was out of his/her mother's sight for only five minutes; **ce fait a échappé à mon attention** this fact escaped *or* slipped my attention; **ce détail m'a échappé** that detail escaped me; **quelques erreurs ont pu m'é.** I may have overlooked a few mistakes; **son nom m'échappe** his/her name escapes me *or* has slipped my mind; **je me souviens de l'air mais les paroles m'échappent** I remember the tune but I forget the lyrics; **il ne vous aura pas échappé que...** it will not have escaped your attention that...

5 *(être enlevé à)* **la victoire lui a échappé** victory eluded him/her; **la fortune de leur tante leur a échappé** they couldn't get their hands on their aunt's money

6 *(être prononcé par)* **la phrase lui aura échappé** the remark must have slipped out; **je n'aurais pas dû le dire mais ça m'a échappé** I shouldn't have said it but it just slipped out; **un sanglot/une injure lui échappa** he/she let out a sob/an oath

VPR s'échapper 1 *(s'enfuir)* to escape, to get away (**de** from); **s'é. de prison** to escape from prison, to break out of prison; **le chat s'est échappé** the cat ran away *or* escaped

2 *(se rendre disponible)* to get away; **je ne pourrai pas m'é. avant midi** I won't be able to get away *or* escape before noon; **je n'arriverai jamais à m'é. de cette réunion de famille** I'll never manage to get out of this family reunion; **il faut que je m'échappe pendant quelques minutes** I've got to go somewhere (else) for a few minutes

3 *(jaillir)* to escape, to leak; **le gaz s'échappe** the gas is leaking; **la lave s'échappe du volcan** lava is coming out of the volcano; **un cri s'échappa de ses lèvres** a cry burst from his/her lips; **de hautes flammes s'échappaient de tous côtés** great flames were shooting from every side

4 *(disparaître)* to disappear, to vanish; **sa dernière chance s'est échappée** his/her last chance slipped away *or* disappeared

5 *Sport (coureur)* to break *or* to draw away

écharde [eʃard] **NF** splinter

écharpe [eʃarp] **NF 1** *(vêtement)* scarf; *(d'un député, d'un maire)* sash; **l'é. tricolore** = sash worn by French mayors at civic functions **2** *(pansement)* sling

• **en écharpe ADV 1 avoir le bras en é.** to have one's arm in a sling **2** *(locution)* **prendre qch en é.** to hit sth sideways on

écharper [3] [eʃarpe] **VT** to tear to pieces; **vous allez vous faire é.!** you'll get torn to pieces!

échasse [eʃas] **NF 1** *(bâton)* stilt; **marcher** *ou* **être monté sur des échasses** to walk *or* to be on stilts; *Fam (avoir de longues jambes)* to have long legs□ **2** *Orn* stilt

échassier [eʃasje] **NM** *Orn* wader, wading bird

échauder [3] [eʃode] **VT 1** *(ébouillanter ▸ volaille)* to scald; *(▸ vaisselle)* to run boiling water over; *(▸ théière)* to warm **2** *(décevoir)* **l'expérience de l'année dernière m'a échaudé** my experience last year taught me a lesson; **il a déjà été échaudé une fois** he's had his fingers burned once already

échauffement [eʃofmɑ̃] **NM 1** *(réchauffement ▸ du sol, d'une planète)* warming (up)

2 *Sport (processus)* warming-up; *(exercices, période)* warm-up

3 *(excitation)* over-excitement; **dans l'é. de la discussion** in the heat of the argument

4 *Tech (d'une pièce, d'un moteur)* overheating; *(d'une corde)* chafing

5 *Fin (de l'économie)* overheating

6 *Agr* fermenting

échauffer [3] [eʃofe] **VT 1** *(chauffer)* to heat (up), to warm up

2 *(exciter)* to heat, to fire, to stimulate; **discussion qui échauffe les esprits** discussion that gets people worked up; **les esprits sont échauffés** feelings are running high; *Fam* **il m'échauffe la bile** *ou* **les oreilles** *ou* **les sangs** he really gets my goat *or* on my nerves

3 *Tech* to overheat

4 *Agr (céréales, foin)* to cause fermentation in

5 *Sport* to warm up

VPR s'échauffer 1 *Sport* to warm up

2 *(s'exciter)* to become heated; **il s'échauffe pour un rien** he blows up *or* flares up at the slightest provocation; **ne vous échauffez pas** don't get excited

3 *(moteur, machine)* to become *or* get overheated, *Tech* to run hot

4 *Agr (de céréales, du foin)* to ferment

échauffourée [eʃofure] **NF** clash, skirmish

échéance [eʃeɑ̃s] **NF 1** *Fin (date ▸ de paiement)* date of payment; *(▸ de maturité)* date of maturity; *(▸ de péremption)* expiry date; **avant é.** *(paiement, règlement)* before the due date; **venir à é.** to fall due; **payable à l'é.** payable at maturity; **payable à quinze jours d'é.** payable in two weeks' time; **l'intérêt n'a pas été payé à l'é.** the interest is overdue; **é. à court/long/moyen terme** short-/long-/medium-term maturity; **é. fixe** fixed maturity; **é. moyenne** average due date; *Bourse* **é. proche** short maturity, near month; **é. à vue** sight bill *or* maturity **2** *Fin (somme d'argent)* financial commitment; **faire face à ses échéances** to meet one's financial commitments; **avoir de lourdes échéances** to have a lot of bills to pay each month, to have a lot of monthly payments to make; **é. commune** equation of payment **3** *(moment)* term; **l'é. électorale** election day, the elections; **nous sommes à trois mois de l'é. électorale** there are three months to go before the date set for the election

• **à brève échéance, à courte échéance ADJ** short-term; **billet à courte é.** short-dated bill **ADV** in the short term; **emprunter/prêter à courte é.** to borrow/to lend short

• **à longue échéance** *Banque & Fin* **ADJ** long-term; **billet à longue é.** long-dated bill **ADV** in the long run; **emprunter/prêter à longue é.** to borrow/to lend long

échéancier [eʃeɑ̃sje] **NM 1** *(livre)* bill book, *Am* tickler; *Compta* due date file, aged debtor schedule; *Com* **é. de paiement** payment schedule **2** *(délais)* schedule of repayments

échéant, -e [eʃeɑ̃, -ɑ̃t] **ADJ 1** *Fin* falling due **2** *voir* **cas**

échec [eʃɛk] **NM 1** *(revers)* failure; **l'é. des discussions** the failure *or* breakdown of the negotiations; **subir un é.** to suffer a setback; **reconnaître son é.** to admit defeat *or* failure; **la réunion s'est soldée par un é.** nothing came out of the meeting; **faire é. à qn** to foil sb, to frustrate sb; **faire é. à qch** *(projet)* to foil sth, to prevent sth; *(activités, agissements)* to put a stop to sth; **faire é. à un coup d'État** to foil *or* to defeat a coup; **l'é. scolaire** academic failure, poor performance at school; **les problèmes familiaux sont très souvent à l'origine de l'é. scolaire** family problems are often the reason why children do badly at school **2** *(défaite)* defeat; **son é. au championnat** his/her defeat in the championship **3** *Échecs* **é. (au roi)!** check!; **é. et mat!** checkmate!; **faire é.** to check; **faire é. au roi** to check the king; **faire é. et mat** to checkmate

• **échecs NMPL** *Échecs* chess; **jouer aux échecs** to play chess; **une partie d'échecs** a game of chess; **joueur d'échecs** chess player

• **en échec ADV mettre/tenir qn en é.** to put/to hold sb in check; **il a tenu toutes les polices d'Europe en é.** he thwarted the entire European police network

échelle [eʃɛl] **NF 1** *(outil)* ladder; **é. de corde** rope ladder; **é. coulissante** extension ladder; **é. double** (high) stepladder; **é. d'incendie** *ou* **de pompiers** fireman's ladder; **é. de marée** tide gauge; **é. de meunier** straight wooden staircase; **é. de sauvetage** fire (escape) ladder; *Fig* **l'é. sociale** the social ladder; **faire la courte é. à qn** to give sb a leg up *or Am* a boost; *Fig* to give sb a leg up, to help sb better his/her prospects; *Fig* **monter dans l'é. sociale** to climb the social ladder; *Fig* **être en haut** *ou* **au sommet de l'é.** to be at the top of the tree *or* the ladder; *Fam* **il n'y a plus qu'à tirer l'é.** we might as well just give up; *Fam* **monter à l'é.** to be taken in; **vous voulez me faire monter à l'é.** you're having *or Am* putting me on

2 *(mesure)* scale; **une carte à l'é. 1/10000** a map on a scale of 1/10,000; **ton train électrique est à quelle é.?** what scale is your electric train?; **réduire l'é. d'un dessin** to scale a drawing down

3 *Géol* scale; **sur l'é. de Richter** on the Richter scale

4 *Météo* **l'é. de Beaufort** the Beaufort scale

5 *Ordinat* **é. des gris** levels of grey

6 *(dimension)* scale; **des évènements à l'é. mondiale** great world events; **à l'é. nationale** nationwide; **des villes à l'é. humaine** cities (built) on a human scale; *Fig* **faire les choses sur une grande é.** to do things in a big way *or* on a large scale

7 *Jur & Admin (hiérarchie)* scale; *Écon* **é. mobile** *(des prix, des salaires)* sliding scale; **é. (mobile) des salaires** *ou* **traitements** (sliding) salary scale; **é. des valeurs** scale of values; **é. des êtres** evolutionary ladder; **dans l'é. des êtres** on the evolutionary ladder; *Mktg* **é. d'attitude** attitude scale; *Mktg* **é. de classement** rating scale; *Mktg* **é. d'importance** scale of importance; **é. des prix** price scale

8 *Mus* **é. diatonique/chromatique/harmonique** diatonic/chromatic/harmonic scale; **é. des sons** scale

9 *Beaux-Arts* **é. des couleurs** range of colours

10 *Naut* **é. de commandement** *ou* **d'honneur** companion ladder; **é. de coupée** accommodation ladder; **é. de revers** Jacob's ladder; **é. de tirant d'eau** water *or* draught marks, *Am* immersion scale

11 *Hist* **les Échelles du Levant** the Ports of the Levant; **les échelles de Barbarie** the Barbary ports

12 *Rel* **é. de Jacob** Jacob's ladder

13 **é. animale** evolutionary ladder

14 *(dans un collant)* run, *Br* ladder; **j'ai fait une é. à mon collant** I've laddered my tights, *Am* I have a run in my pantihose

• **à grande échelle ADJ 1** *(dessin)* large-scale **2** *(projet)* ambitious **3** *Ordinat* **intégration à grande é.** large-scale integration **ADV** on a big scale

• **à l'échelle ADV 1** *Tech* **la façade n'est pas à l'é.** the façade isn't (drawn) to scale; **dessiner une carte à l'é.** to scale a map **2** *(suivi d'un adjectif)* **à l'é. régionale/internationale** on a regional/an international level

• **à l'échelle de PRÉP** at the level *or* on a scale of; **à l'é. de la région/planète** on a regional/world scale *or* level; **à l'é. de l'homme** on a human scale; **à l'é. de temps humain** on a human time scale

• **à petite échelle ADJ 1** *(dessin, modèle)* small-scale **2** *Ordinat* **intégration à petite é.** small-scale integration

échelon [eʃlɔ̃] **NM 1** *(barreau)* rung

2 *Admin* grade; **le dernier/premier é.** the bottom/top grade *or* step; **j'en suis au dernier é.** I'm at *or* I've reached the top of my grade; **grimper d'un é.** to go up one step *or* grade; **il a gravi rapidement tous les échelons** he climbed the ladder rapidly; **monter par échelons** to rise by degrees *or* by successive stages

3 *(niveau)* level; **à l'é. local** at local level; **à l'é. ré-**

gional/national on a regional/national level; **à tous les échelons** at all levels, at every level
4 *Mil* echelon
5 *Bourse* **é. de cotation** tick size
• **à l'échelon de** PRÉP at the level of; **à l'é. du ministère** at Ministry level

échelonnement [eʃlɔnmɑ̃] NM **1** *(dans l'espace)* spreading out, placing at regular intervals **2** *(dans le temps ▸ d'un paiement)* spreading (out); *(▸ de congés)* staggering; **l'é. des travaux se fera sur plusieurs mois** the work will be spread out over several months **3** *(graduation ▸ de difficultés)* grading

échelonner [3] [eʃlɔne] VT **1** *(dans l'espace ▸ arbres, poteaux)* to space out, to place at regular intervals
2 *(dans le temps ▸ livraisons, remboursements, publication)* to spread (out), to stagger, to schedule at regular intervals; *(▸ congés, vacances)* to stagger; **paiements échelonnés** payments in instalments, staggered payments; **les versements sont échelonnés sur dix ans** the instalments are spread (out) over ten years
3 *(graduer ▸ difficultés, problèmes)* to grade, to place on a sliding scale
4 *Mil* to echelon
VPR **s'échelonner 1 s'é. sur** *(dans le temps ▸ sujet: projet, travaux, remboursement)* to be spread out over; *(▸ sujet: vacances, congés)* to be staggered over **2 s'é. sur** *(dans l'espace)* to be spaced out; **le cours s'échelonne sur dix niveaux** there are ten levels of difficulty in the course

écheniller [3] [eʃnije] VT **1** *Hort* to rid of caterpillars, to worm **2** *Fig (histoire, récit)* to trim

écheveau, -x [eʃvo] NM **1** *Tex* hank, skein **2** *(labyrinthe de rues)* maze **3** *(embrouillamini)* tangle; **l'é. d'une intrigue** the intricacies *or* complexities of a plot; **démêler l'é. d'une intrigue** to untangle a plot

échevelé, -e [eʃəvle] ADJ **1** *(ébouriffé)* dishevelled, tousled **2** *(effréné)* frantic, wild, unbridled; **une danse échevelée** a wild dance **3** *Littéraire (arbre)* windswept

échevin [eʃvɛ̃] NM **1** *Hist* municipal magistrate *(under the Ancien Régime)*, ≃ alderman **2** *Belg* deputy burgmaster *or* burgomaster

échine [eʃin] NF **1** *Anat & Zool* backbone, spine; **courber** *ou* **plier l'é. devant qn** to submit to sb; **avoir l'é. souple** to be obsequious *or* subservient
2 *Culin* chine, loin; **une côte de porc dans l'é.** a pork loin chop **3** *Archit* echinus

échiné, -e [eʃine] ADJ *Can* tired out, exhausted

échiner [3] [eʃine] **s'échiner** VPR **s'é. à faire qch** *(se fatiguer)* to wear *or* to tire oneself out doing sth; *(se donner du mal)* to go to great lengths *or* to make a great effort to do sth

échiquier [eʃikje] NM **1** *Échecs* chessboard; *Fig* **le rôle que nous jouons sur l'é. européen/mondial** the part we play on the European/world scene **2** *Pol* **l'É.** the (British) Exchequer
• **en échiquier** ADV in a *Br* check *or Am* checkered pattern

écho [eko] NM **1** *(acoustique)* echo; **faire é.** to echo (back); **il y a de l'é.** there is an echo; **échos parasites** clutter; *Électron* **suppresseur d'é.** echo suppressor
2 *Fig* **j'en ai eu des échos** I heard something about it; **j'en ai eu de bons échos** I've had positive feedback about it; **trouver un é.** to get a response; **sa proposition est restée sans é.** his/her offer wasn't considered; **se faire l'é. d'une information** to spread a piece of news; **se faire l'é. des opinions de qn** to echo *or* to repeat sb's opinions
3 *TV* ghosting; **à cause des arbres, nous avons de l'é.** we get ghosting because of the trees
4 *(rubrique de journal)* **échos** news in brief; **échos mondains** gossip column
5 *Ordinat* echo
• **à tous les échos** ADV in all directions

échocardiographie [ekokardjɔgrafi] NF *Méd* echocardiography

échographe [ekɔgraf] NF *Méd* (ultrasound) scanner

échographie [ekɔgrafi] NF *Méd* (ultrasound) scan; **passer une é.** to have a scan *or* an ultrasound scan

échoir [70] [eʃwar] VI *Fin (dette)* to fall due; *(investissement)* to mature; **intérêts à é.** accruing interest, interest falling due; **abonnement échu** expired subscription; **billets échus** bills (over) due; **intérêts échus** outstanding interest, interest due; **le terme échoit le 20 de ce mois** the date for payment is the 20th of this month; **le délai est échu** the deadline has expired
• **échoir à** VT IND **é. à qn** to fall to sb; **c'est à moi qu'il échoit d'annoncer la mauvaise nouvelle** it falls to me to announce the bad news; **le sort qui lui est échu n'est guère enviable** one can hardly envy his/her lot

échoppe [eʃɔp] NF **1** *Tech (outil)* burin **2** *(magasin)* booth, stall; *(de cordonnier)* small workshop

échosondeur [ekosɔ̃dœr] NM *Tech* echo sounder

échotier, -ère [ekɔtje, -ɛr] NM,F *Journ (journaliste)* gossip columnist

échouage [eʃwaʒ], **échouement** [eʃumɑ̃] NM *Naut (d'un navire)* grounding, running aground; *(sur la plage)* beaching

échouer [6] [eʃwe] VI **1** *(rater ▸ projet, tentative)* to fail, to fall through; *(▸ personne)* to fail; **ils ont échoué dans leur tentative de coup d'État** their attempted coup failed; **é. à un examen** to fail an exam; **faire é.** *(projet)* to thwart, to frustrate; *(complot)* to foil **2** *Fam (finir)* to end *or* to wind up; **ils ont échoué dans un bar vers minuit** they ended *or* wound up in a bar around midnight **3** *Naut* to ground, to run aground; *(baleine)* to beach
VT *Naut (accidentellement)* to ground, to run aground; *(volontairement)* to beach; **navire échoué** ship aground, stranded vessel *or* ship; **échoué à sec** high and dry; **quelques caisses échouées sur la plage** a few boxes washed up on the beach
VPR **s'échouer** *Naut* to run aground; *(baleine)* to beach

échu, -e [eʃy] PP *voir* **échoir**
ADJ *Fin* **payer un loyer à terme é.** to pay at the end of the rental term

écimage [esimaʒ] NM *Hort* pollarding

écimer [3] [esime] VT *Hort* to pollard

éclaboussement [eklabusmɑ̃] NM splashing, spattering

éclabousser [3] [eklabuse] VT **1** *(asperger)* to splash, to spatter; **éclaboussé de boue** mud-spattered; **les cheveux éclaboussés de peinture** hair spattered with paint **2** *(nuire à la réputation de)* **é. qn** to malign sb, to tarnish sb's reputation **3** *Littéraire (impressionner)* **é. qn de son luxe/sa richesse** to flaunt one's luxurious lifestyle/one's wealth at sb

éclaboussure [eklabusyr] NF **1** *(tache ▸ de boue, de peinture)* splash, spatter; **des éclaboussures de sang** bloodstains **2** *(retombée)* smear; **atteint par les éclaboussures d'un scandale financier** implicated in a financial scandal

éclair [eklɛr] NM **1** *Météo* flash of lightning; **éclairs** lightning; **éclairs de chaleur** heat lightning; **éclairs en zigzag** forked lightning; **entrer/sortir/traverser comme un é.** to dart in/out/across; **le peloton est passé comme un é.** the pack of cyclists flashed past; **cette pensée traversa mon esprit comme un é.** the thought flashed through my mind; **rapide** *ou* **vif comme l'é.** (as) quick as lightning *or* a flash
2 *(lueur ▸ d'un coup de feu, d'un flash)* flash; **jeter** *ou* **lancer des éclairs** *(diamant, yeux etc)* to flash; **la lame jetait des éclairs dans la pénombre** the blade flashed *or* glinted in the shadows
3 *(bref instant)* **un é. de** a flash *or* spark of; **un é. de lucidité/génie** a flash of lucidity/inspiration
4 *Culin* éclair; **é. au chocolat** chocolate éclair
5 *(comme adj)* lightning *(avant n)*; **grève é.** lightning strike; **guerre é.** blitzkrieg; **visite é.** lightning *or* flying visit; **il a fait un passage é. au sein de la rédaction** he had a very brief spell on the editorial team
• **en un éclair** ADV in a flash *or* an instant; **tout lui est revenu à la mémoire en un é.** everything came back to him/her in a flash

éclairage [eklɛraʒ] NM **1** *(illumination artificielle)* lighting; **é. d'ambiance** background light; **é. d'appoint** fill light; **é. en contre-jour** backlighting; **é. direct/indirect** direct/indirect *or* concealed lighting; **é. doux** soft lighting; **é. à l'électricité/au gaz** electric/gas lighting; **é. public** street lighting
2 *(intensité de lumière)* light; **l'é. est faible au premier étage** the first floor is badly lit
3 *(installation)* **l'é., les éclairages** the lighting; **les éclairages sont de Y. Dumais** lighting effects by Y. Dumais; **é. sur batterie** sungun; *Aut* **é. intérieur** courtesy light; *Cin & TV* **é. de plateau** stage lighting; **é. aux projecteurs** floodlighting; *Aut* **é. de route** full-beam headlights; **é. de sécurité** emergency lighting; *Aut* **é. de ville** dipped headlights
4 *Beaux-Arts* use of light; *Phot* light; **é. clair-obscur** Rembrandt *or* chiaroscuro lighting; **é. à la Rembrandt** Rembrandt lighting
5 *(aspect)* light, perspective; **sans cet é. historique, le problème ne peut pas être analysé** without this historical perspective the problem cannot be analysed; **vu sous cet é.** seen in this light; **apporter à qch un é. nouveau** to throw new light on sth
6 *Mil* scouting expedition

éclairagiste [eklɛraʒist] NMF **1** *Cin, Théât & TV* lighting engineer **2** *Com* dealer in lights and lamps

éclairant, -e [eklɛrɑ̃, -ɑ̃t] ADJ **1** *(lumineux)* lighting **2** *(édifiant ▸ commentaire, conclusion)* enlightening

éclaircie [eklɛrsi] NF **1** *Météo* sunny spell, bright interval **2** *(amélioration)* improvement **3** *(de forêt)* clearing

éclaircir [32] [eklɛrsir] VT **1** *(rendre moins sombre)* to make lighter; **ce papier éclaircit la pièce** this wallpaper brightens up the room *or* makes the room feel lighter; **é. ses cheveux** to lighten one's hair; *(par mèches)* to put highlights in one's hair; **é. le teint** to clear the complexion
2 *(rendre plus audible)* **des pastilles pour é. la voix** *ou* **gorge** lozenges to clear the throat
3 *Culin (sauce, soupe)* to thin (down)
4 *(forêt)* to thin; *(jeunes plantes)* to thin out
5 *(élucider ▸ affaire, mystère)* to clear up; *(▸ situation)* to clarify
VPR **s'éclaircir 1** *Météo* to clear (up), to brighten up; *(brouillard)* to clear (up); *(teint, voix)* to clear, to become clear(er); **le ciel s'est éclairci** the sky's cleared (up) *or* brightened up; *Fig* **l'avenir semble s'é.** the future seems to be getting brighter; *Fam* **ça s'éclaircit** it's brightening up; **son visage s'éclaircit** his/her face brightened up *or* lit up
2 *(pâlir ▸ cheveux)* to go lighter *or* paler *or* blonder; **s'é. les cheveux** to lighten one's hair
3 *(se raréfier)* to thin (out); *(cheveux)* to grow thin, to be thinning; **ses cheveux s'éclaircissent** his hair's getting thinner, he's going bald
4 *(être clarifié ▸ mystère)* to be solved; *(▸ situation)* to become clearer
5 s'é. la voix *ou* **gorge** to clear one's throat

éclaircissage [eklɛrsisaʒ] NM **1** *Vieilli (du verre)* polishing **2** *(de forêt)* thinning; *Hort (de plantes)* thinning out

éclaircissant, -e [eklɛrsisɑ̃, -ɑ̃t] ADJ *(lotion, shampooing)* lightening, highlighting

éclaircissement [eklɛrsismɑ̃] NM **1** *(d'une peinture)* lightening
2 *(de cheveux)* lightening; **je me suis fait faire un é.** I had my hair lightened
3 *(élucidation)* clarification, *Sout* elucidation; **l'é. de ce mystère a pris des mois** it was months before the mystery was cleared up
4 *(explication)* explanation; **demander des éclaircissements** to ask for further information *or* an explanation; **je voudrais des éclaircissements sur ce point** I would like some further clarification on this point

éclairé, -e [eklere] ADJ **1** *(lumineux)* **une pièce bien/mal éclairée** a well-/badly-lit room **2** *(intelligent)* enlightened

éclairement [eklɛrmɑ̃] NM **1** *Littéraire* lighting, brightening **2** *Phys* illumination

éclairer [4] [eklere] VT **1** *(chemin, lieu)* to light (up); *(personne)* to light the way for; **les phares éclairent la route** the road is lit by beacons; **une bougie éclairait la pièce** the room was lit by a candle; **é. une cuisine au néon** to use fluorescent lighting in a kitchen; **cafés éclairés au néon** cafés with neon lights, neon-lit cafés; **é. un stade avec des projecteurs** to floodlight a stadium

2 *(égayer)* to brighten up, to light up, to illuminate; **un sourire éclairait son visage** a smile lit up his/her face

3 *(rendre compréhensible)* to clarify, to throw light on; **é. qch d'un jour nouveau** to shed *or* throw new light on sth

4 *(informer)* to enlighten; **j'ai besoin qu'on m'éclaire sur ce point** I need someone to explain this point to me *or* to enlighten me on this point; *Fam* **é. la lanterne de qn** to put sb in the picture

5 *Mil* to scout out; **é. le terrain** *ou* **la marche** to reconnoitre the ground, to scout

VI 1 *(diffuser de la lumière)* **la lampe n'éclaire plus** the lamp's gone out; **cette ampoule éclaire bien/mal** this bulb throws out a lot of/doesn't throw out much light **2** *Can (lors d'un orage)* to flash (lightning)

VPR s'éclairer 1 *(emploi réfléchi)* **s'é. au gaz/à l'électricité** to have gaslight/electric lighting; **s'é. à la bougie** to use candlelight; *(pour se diriger)* to light one's way with a candle; **il s'éclaire toujours au pétrole** he still has *or* uses oil lamps; **tiens, prends ma lampe électrique pour t'é.** here, take my *Br* torch *or Am* flashlight to let you see where you're going

2 *(s'allumer)* to be lit; **les fenêtres s'éclairent une à une** the windows light up one by one

3 *(visage, regard)* to brighten up, to light up

4 *(se résoudre)* to get clearer; **enfin, tout s'éclaire!** it's all clear (to me) now!

éclaireur, -euse [eklɛrœr, -øz] **NM,F** *(scout)* boy scout, *f* girl scout, *Br* girl guide; **les Éclaireurs de France** the (French) Scout Association; **chef é.** scoutmaster, *f* guide captain

NM 1 *Mil* scout; *Naut* scouting vessel, scout; *Aviat* **avion é.** reconnaissance aircraft **2** *Aut* **é. de coffre** *Br* boot *or Am* trunk light

• **en éclaireur ADV envoyer qn en é.** to send sb scouting; *aussi Fig* **partir en é.** to go (off) and scout around; *Fig* **parti en é. chercher un restaurant** scouting around for a restaurant; *Fig* **il part un mois avant, en é.** he's leaving a month in advance to check things out

éclampsie [eklɑ̃psi] **NF** *Obst* eclampsia

ÉCLAT [ekla]

- splinter **1**
- scandal **3**
- glamour **6**
- burst **2**
- brightness **4, 5**

NM 1 *(fragment ▸ de métal)* splinter, shard; *(▸ de bois)* splinter, sliver; *(▸ de pierre)* chip; *(▸ de mica)* flake; **un é. de verre** a fragment *or* splinter of glass; **éclats de verre** *(bris)* broken glass; *(projeté)* flying glass; **é. d'obus** piece of shrapnel; **des éclats d'obus** shrapnel

2 *(bruit)* burst; **é. de rire** burst *or* roar of laughter; **é. de colère** outburst of anger; **on entendait des éclats de voix** loud voices could be heard

3 *(scandale)* scandal; **faire un é. en public** to cause a public scandal *or* embarrassment; **il adore provoquer** *ou* **faire des éclats dans les soirées mondaines** he loves creating a commotion at society parties; **sans é.** quietly, without any fuss

4 *(de la lumière, du jour)* brightness; *(du soleil, de projecteur)* glare; **l'é. d'un diamant** the sparkle of a diamond; **le soleil brille de son plus vif é.** the sun is (shining) at its brightest *or* most brilliant

5 *(du regard, d'un sourire)* brightness; *(d'une couleur)* vividness, brilliance; *(du teint)* radiance, bloom; *(d'un diamant)* glitter, lustre; **l'é. de ses yeux** the sparkle in his/her eyes; **sans é.** dull; **elle a perdu tout son é.** *(vivacité)* she has lost all her sparkle; *(physiquement)* she has lost her bloom

6 *(splendeur)* glamour, glitter; *(de style etc)* brilliance; **l'é. de la conversation** the brilliant *or* scintillating conversation; **l'é. de la jeunesse** the bloom *or* freshness of youth; **l'é. de son intelligence** his/her brilliant mind; **aimer faire les choses avec é.** to like doing things in style

éclatant, -e [eklatɑ̃, -ɑ̃t] **ADJ 1** *(soleil, couleur, sourire)* dazzling, brilliant; *(miroir, surface)* sparkling; *(dents)* gleaming; **draps d'une blancheur éclatante** dazzling white sheets; **aux couleurs éclatantes** *(tissus)* flamboyant; **écharpe d'un rouge é.** bright red scarf

2 *(excellent ▸ santé, teint)* radiant, glowing; **être dans une forme éclatante** to be on brilliant *or* dazzling form; **éclatante de beauté** radiantly beautiful; **é. de santé** glowing *or* blooming with health

3 *(spectaculaire ▸ revanche)* spectacular; *(▸ triomphe, victoire)* resounding

4 *(bruyant)* loud, resounding

éclate [eklat] **NF** *Fam* **c'est l'é.** it's a laugh *or* a hoot; **c'est pas l'é.** it's not exactly a barrel of laughs

éclaté, -e [eklate] **ADJ** *(groupe)* scattered, dispersed; *(programme, mesures)* fragmented, fragmentary; **paysage politique é.** fragmented political landscape; **avoir une vision éclatée des choses** to have a fragmented view of things

NM *Tech* exploded drawing

éclatement [eklatmɑ̃] **NM 1** *(déflagration ▸ d'une bombe)* explosion; *(▸ d'un pneu, d'un tuyau, d'un fruit)* bursting; *(▸ d'un verre)* shattering; *(▸ du foie, de la rate)* rupture; *Aut* **é. de l'étincelle** jump spark **2** *(rupture ▸ d'un parti)* breakup; *(▸ d'un convoi, d'un groupe)* dispersal

éclater [3] [eklate] **VI 1** *(exploser)* to explode, to blow up, to burst; *(obus)* to burst, to explode; *(arme)* to explode; *(mine)* to blow up; *(pneu, ballon)* to burst; *(verre)* to shatter; **faire é. qch** to burst/explode/shatter sth; **faire é. un pétard** to set off a firework; **j'ai l'impression que ma tête va é.** I feel as if my head is going to burst

2 *(se fractionner)* to split, to break up; **notre département a éclaté en plusieurs services** our department was broken up into several subdivisions

3 *(retentir)* **l'orage a enfin éclaté** the thunderstorm finally broke; **un coup de tonnerre a soudain éclaté** there was a sudden thunderclap; **des applaudissements éclatèrent** there was a burst of applause; **des coups de feu ont éclaté** shots rang out; **é. de rire** to burst out laughing; **é. en sanglots** to burst into tears, to burst out sobbing

4 *(se déclencher ▸ guerre, scandale)* to break out; *(▸ scandale)* to break; *(▸ colère)* to burst out; **quand la guerre éclata** at the outbreak of the war, when war broke out

5 *(apparaître)* to stand out; **son talent éclate à chaque page** his/her talent stands out on each page; **l'indignation éclatait dans ses yeux** his/her eyes were blazing with indignation

6 *(de colère)* to explode

VT *Fam (pneu)* to burst[□]; *très Fam Fig* **je vais l'é., je vais lui é. la tête** *ou* **la gueule** I'll smash his/her head in

VPR s'éclater *Fam* to have a great time, to have a ball; **s'é. comme une bête** to freak out

éclateur [eklatœr] **NM** *Tech* spark gap, spark discharger

éclectique [eklɛktik] **ADJ** eclectic, varied

NMF eclectic, person with eclectic tastes

éclectisme [eklɛktism] **NM** eclecticism

éclipse [eklips] **NF 1** *Astron* eclipse; **é. de Soleil/Lune** solar/lunar eclipse; **é. annulaire/totale/partielle** annular/total/partial eclipse **2** *(éloignement)* eclipse, decline; **après une longue é.** after a long absence; *Fig* **é. totale de la raison/mémoire** total loss of reason/memory **3** *Méd* blackout

éclipser [3] [eklipse] **VT 1** *Astron* to eclipse **2** *Fig (surclasser ▸ personne)* to eclipse, to overshadow, to outshine; *(▸ événement, exploit etc)* to eclipse, to overshadow

VPR s'éclipser 1 *Fam (s'esquiver)* to slip away *or* out, to sneak off **2** *Astron* to be eclipsed; *(être voilé)* to be obscured

écliptique [ekliptik] *Astron* **ADJ** ecliptic

NM ecliptic

éclisse [eklis] **NF 1** *(plaque de bois)* (wooden) wedge

2 *(éclat)* piece of split wood

3 *Méd* splint

4 *Rail* fishplate

éclisser [3] [eklise] **VT** *Méd (membre)* to put in splints, to splint

éclopé, -e [eklɔpe] **ADJ** lame, limping

NM,F person with a limp; *Mil* temporarily disabled soldier

éclore [113] [eklɔr] **VI** *(aux être ou avoir)* **1** *(œuf, poussin)* to hatch (out); **faire é. un œuf** to hatch (out) an egg **2** *Littéraire (fleur)* to open out; *Fig (talent)* to be born, to appear; **des roses fraîches écloses** newly-opened roses; *Fig* **faire é. un talent** to nurture *or* develop a talent **3** *Littéraire (apparaître ▸ jour, amour)* to dawn; **le jour est près d'é.** dawn is near

éclosion [eklozjɔ̃] **NF 1** *(d'un œuf)* hatching; **jusqu'à leur é.** until they hatch **2** *Littéraire (d'une fleur)* opening (out); *Fig (d'un talent)* birth **3** *Littéraire (d'un amour)* dawning

écluse [eklyz] **NF 1** *(gén)* lock; **(porte d')é.** lock *or* sluice gate; **é. de moulin** mill dam; **lâcher** *ou* **ouvrir les écluses** to open the sluice gates; *Fig* to turn on the waterworks **2** *(d'un dock)* tide gate **3** *Ordinat* firewall

éclusée [eklyze] **NF** lockage water

écluser [3] [eklyze] **VT 1** *Naut (canal, voie d'eau)* to lock; *(bateau, péniche)* to lock, to sluice **2** *très Fam (boire)* to down, to knock back

VI *très Fam* to booze, to knock back the booze; **qu'est-ce qu'il écluse!** he can really knock it back!

éclusier, -ère [eklyzje, -ɛr] **NM,F** lockkeeper

> **ÉCO-** PREFIX
>
> In recent years, growing interest and concern over the environment have given rise, in French as well as in English, to a string of new words including the prefix **éco-** (from the Greek *oikos* meaning "house"), with or without a hyphen:
>
> **écolabel** ecolabel; **éco-recharge** eco-refill; **éco-produit** eco-friendly product; **éco-industrie** eco-friendly industry; **éco(-)certification** ecocertification

éco(-)quartier [ekɔkartje] **NM** green neighbourhood

écobilan [ekɔbilɑ̃] **NM** *Écol & Écon* life cycle assessment *or* analysis

écobobo [ekɔbobo] **NMF** *Fam* bobo environmentalist

éco-chic [ekɔʃik] **ADJ** eco-chic

écocitoyen, -enne [ekɔsitwajɛ̃, -ɛn] **NM,F** green *or* eco-friendly citizen

écocitoyenneté [ekɔsitwajɛnte] **NF** green *or* eco-friendly citizenship

écoemballage [ekɔɑ̃balaʒ] **NM** eco-packaging, eco-friendly packaging

écœuramment [ekœramɑ̃] **ADV** *Can Joual* really[□], *Am* real; **c'est é. bon** *(plat, gâteau)* it's absolutely delicious!, it's divine!; *(musique, film)* it's *Br* wicked *or Am* awesome!

écœurant, -e [ekœrɑ̃, -ɑ̃t] **ADJ 1** *(nauséeux ▸ nourriture)* nauseating, sickly; *(▸ personne)* disgusting, sickening; **la seule vue de ce gâteau est écœurante** just looking at that cake *or* the mere sight of that cake makes me feel sick

2 *(indigne)* disgusting; **j'ai trouvé son comportement é.** his/her behaviour sickened me, I found his/her behaviour disgusting

3 *Fam (démoralisant)* sickening, disheartening[□]; **elle réussit tout, c'est é.** she's good at everything, it's sickening *or* it makes you sick; **tu as une chance écœurante!** what disgusting luck!

4 *Can Joual* **c'est é. comme il fait chaud** it's absolutely boiling!, *Br* it's a scorcher!; **c'est é. (comme c'est bon)** it's *Br* wicked *or Am* awesome!

NM,F *Can Joual* pig *(unpleasant person)*

écœuranterie [ekœrɑ̃tri] **NF** *Can Fam* **1** *(saleté)* filth[□] **2** *(coup bas)* dirty trick; **elle m'a fait une é.** she played a dirty trick on me

écœurement [ekœrmɑ̃] **NM 1** *(nausée)* nausea; *(dégoût)* disgust, loathing; **manger des chocolats jusqu'à é.** to make oneself sick eating chocolates; *Fig* **j'ai jardiné jusqu'à é.** I've done so much gardening I'm sick (and tired) of it *or* I'm fed up **2** *(aversion)* disgust, aversion, distaste; **sa cruauté a provoqué l'é. général** everyone was disgusted *or* nauseated by his/her cruelty, his/her cruelty turned everyone's stomach; **on ne peut le regarder agir sans é.** it's impossible to watch him at work without feeling disgust **3** *Fam (découragement)* discouragement[□]; **ça a été l'é. dans toute la classe** the entire class lost heart[□]

écœurer [5] [ekœre] **VT 1** *(donner la nausée à)* **é. qn** to nauseate sb, to make sb feel sick *or Am* nauseous; *(dégoûter)* to disgust sb, to make sb feel sick

2 *(inspirer le mépris à)* to disgust, to sicken; **sa mauvaise foi m'écœure** I'm disgusted by his/her insincerity; **ça m'écœure que...** it sickens me *or* makes me sick that...

3 *Fam (décourager)* to dishearten, to discourage; **l'attitude de son patron l'écœure tellement que...** he/she finds his/her boss's attitude so disheartening *or* discouraging that...

4 *Can Fam (donner envie à)* **é. qn** to make sb green with envy

Ecofin [ekofin] **NM** *UE (abrév* **Economic Council of Finance Ministers**) Ecofin

écoguerrier, -ère [ekogɛrje, -ɛr] **NM,F** *Écol* eco-warrior

écoinçon [ekwɛ̃sɔ̃] **NM** *Constr* corner piece *or* stone

écolabel [ekolabɛl] **NM** *Écol* eco-label

écolage [ekɔlaʒ] **NM 1** *Suisse (frais de scolarité)* school fees **2** *Belg (formation)* training

école [ekɔl] **NF 1** *Scol (établissement)* school; **aller à l'é.** *(tous les matins)* to go to school; *(à six ans)* to start school, to reach school age; **reprendre l'é.** *(après les vacances)* to go back to school; **é. communale** local primary school; *Vieilli ou Can* **é. élémentaire** primary school; **é. libre** private school; **é. maternelle,** *Fam* **petite é.,** *Suisse* **é. enfantine** nursery school, kindergarten; **é. primaire,** *Fam* **grande é.** primary school; **é. privée** private school; **é. publique** *Br* state school, *Am* public school; *Can & Suisse* **é. secondaire** *Br* secondary school, *Am* high school; **é. de filles/garçons** girls'/boys' school; **faire l'é. buissonnière** to play truant *or Am Fam* hooky; *Fig Hum* **tu peux retourner à l'é.** what did they teach you at school?

2 *(cours)* school; **faire l'é.** to teach; **l'é. recommencera le 9 septembre** school will reopen on 9 September; **l'é. est obligatoire jusqu'à 16 ans** schooling is compulsory up to the age of 16; *Fam* **je n'ai pas é. aujourd'hui** I don't have any classes today; *Fig* **à l'é. de la vie** in the university of life

3 *(système)* **l'é. laïque** secular education; **l'é. obligatoire** compulsory schooling

4 *(lieu spécialisé)* school; **é. de l'air** flying school; **é. des Beaux-Arts** art school; **é. de commerce** business school; **é. de conduite** driving school; **é. de danse** ballet school; **é. de dessin** art school; **é. d'équitation** riding school; **é. hôtelière** hotel school; **é. de journalisme** school of journalism; **é. militaire** military academy; **é. de musique** music school; **é. navale** naval college; **é. de police** police college *or Am* academy; **é. de secrétariat** secretarial college; **é. de ski** ski school; **é. de voile** sailing school

5 *(collège supérieur)* **grande école** = higher education establishment with competitive entrance, specializing in professional training; **É. des Arts et Métiers** = university-level engineering college; **É. (centrale) des arts et manufactures, É. centrale** = prestigious engineering school; **É. nationale d'administration** = prestigious university-level college preparing students for senior posts in the civil service and public management; **É. (nationale) des chartes** = "grande école" for archivists and librarians; **l'É. nationale d'ingénieurs** = one of five prestigious engineering schools throughout France; **É. nationale de la magistrature** = "grande école" for the judiciary; *Anciennement* **É. normale (d'instituteurs)** = primary school teachers' training college; **É. normale supérieure** = prestigious "grande école" for teachers and researchers; **É. supérieure des sciences économiques et commerciales** = "grande école" for management and business studies

6 *(pédagogie)* **l'é. active** the active method of teaching

7 *(disciples)* school; **l'é. de Pythagore** the Pythagorean school; **il est de la vieille é.** he's one of the old school; **faire é.** to attract a following

8 *Fig* **une é. de courage** a lesson in courage; **être à bonne é.** to be in good hands; **avec lui, j'ai été à bonne é.** he taught me a lot; **être à rude é.** to learn the hard way

9 *Équitation* **basse/haute é.** basse/haute école

10 *Mil (exercice)* drill, training; **é. du soldat** drill; **é. de tir** rifle drill, knotting and splicing; *Aviat* **appareil d'é.** training aircraft

> **GRANDES ÉCOLES**
>
> These are highly selective establishments which exist in parallel to the universities. Admission is usually only possible after two years of intensive preparatory studies ("**écoles préparatoires**") and a competitive examination ("**concours**"). Graduates from these institutions typically go on to work in senior and executive posts in the civil service or the private sector. The "grandes écoles" include HEC (management), Polytechnique, Centrale, the École des Mines and the École des Ponts et Chaussées (engineering), the ENA (senior civil service) and the École normale supérieure (humanities or science). Having been to a "grande école" is comparable in prestige to having an Oxbridge degree in Britain or a degree from Harvard or Yale in the US.

écolier, -ère [ekɔlje, -ɛr] **NM,F** *Scol* schoolboy, *f* schoolgirl

écolo [ekɔlo] *Fam* **ADJ** *(abrév* **écologique, écologiste**) green

NMF *(abrév* **écologiste**) environmentalist

écologie [ekɔlɔʒi] **NF** ecology

écologique [ekɔlɔʒik] **ADJ** *(gén)* ecological, environmental; *(politique)* green

écologisme [ekɔlɔʒism] **NM** ecology

écologiste [ekɔlɔʒist] **ADJ** *(parti)* green, ecology *(avant n)*; *(politique)* green, environmentalist

NMF 1 *(expert)* ecologist, environmentalist **2** *(partisan)* ecologist, green

e-commerce [ikɔmɛrs] **NM** e-commerce

écomusée [ekɔmyze] **NM** ecomuseum

éconduire [98] [ekɔ̃dɥir] **VT 1** *(importun, vendeur)* to get rid of **2** *(refuser ▸ soupirant)* to turn down, to reject; *(▸ suppliant, requérant) (en personne)* to turn away; *(par lettre)* to turn down

éconocroques [ekɔnɔkrɔk] **NFPL** *Fam Vieilli* savings

économat [ekɔnɔma] **NM 1** *(service ▸ dans un collège, un hôpital)* bursarship; *(▸ dans un club)* stewardship

2 *(bureau ▸ dans un collège, un hôpital)* bursar's office; *(▸ dans un club)* steward's office

3 *(coopérative)* staff co-op

4 *(fonction d'économe ▸ dans une institution, un hôpital)* bursarship; *(▸ dans un club, un collège)* stewardship

économe [ekɔnɔm] **ADJ 1** *(avec l'argent)* thrifty **2** *(parcimonieux)* **é. de** economical *or* sparing with; **être é. de ses paroles/gestes** to be sparing with one's words/gestures; **être é. de son temps** to give of one's time sparingly

NMF *(d'une institution, d'un hôpital)* bursar; *(d'un club, d'un collège)* steward

NM *(couteau)* (vegetable) peeler

> Note that **économe** means **thrifty** and cannot be used to translate **economic**, for which the correct translation is always **économique.**

économètre [ekɔnɔmɛtr] **NMF** *Écon* econometrist, econometrician

économétrie [ekɔnɔmetri] **NF** *Écon* econometrics *(singulier)*

économétrique [ekɔnɔmetrik] **ADJ** *Écon* econometric

économie [ekɔnɔmi] **NF 1** *Écon (système)* economy; **la nouvelle é.** the new economy; **é. du bien-être** welfare economy; **é. capitaliste** capitalist economy; **é. à deux vitesses** two-speed economy; **é. dirigée** planned economy; **é. éthique** caring economy; **é. illégale** illegal economy; **é. immergée** underground economy; **é. industrielle** industrial organization; **é. informelle** informal economy; **é. libérale** free-market economy; **é. de libre entreprise** free-enterprise economy; **é. de marché** market economy; **é. mixte** mixed economy; **é. mondiale** world economy; **é. noire** black economy; **é. ouverte** open economy; **é. parallèle** black economy, underground economy; **é. planifiée** planned economy; **é. de rente** rent economy; **é. salariale** wage economy; **é. sociale** social economy; **é. solidaire** economy of solidarity, socially responsible economy; **é. souterraine** black economy, underground economy; **é. de subsistance** subsistence economy; **é. de transition** transition economy; **é. de troc** barter economy

2 *Écon (discipline)* economics *(singulier)*; **é. (politique)** economics; **é. de la demande** demand-side economics; **é. domestique** home economics; **é. d'entreprise** business *or* managerial economics; **é. de l'environnement** environmental economics; **é. keynésienne** Keynesian economics; **é. de l'offre** supply-side economics

3 *(gain)* economy, saving; *(vertu)* economy, thrift; **avoir le sens de l'é.** to be thrifty, to be good with money; **elle n'a aucun sens de l'é.** she's no good at managing money, she's got no idea about money; **nous avons fait une é. de trois euros par livre** we saved three euros on each book; **ce sera une é. de temps/d'argent/de vingt pour cent** it'll save time/money/twenty percent; **avec une grande é. de moyens** with very limited means; **je ferai l'é. d'un voyage** it'll save me a trip; **je vais faire l'é. d'un coup de fil** I'll save myself a phone call; *Fam* **une é. de bouts de chandelles** cheese-paring; **ce mariage a vraiment été fait à l'é.** the wedding was really done on the cheap

4 *(structure)* arrangement, structure

• **économies NFPL** savings; **faire des économies** to save money; **prendre sur ses économies** to break into *or* to draw on one's savings; **les économies d'énergie** energy conservation; **faire des économies d'énergie** to conserve *or* to save energy; **économies d'échelle** economies of scale; *Fam* **économies de bouts de chandelle** cheeseparing (economy); *Prov* **il n'y a pas de petites économies** take care of the pennies and the pounds will take care of themselves

économique [ekɔnɔmik] **ADJ 1** *Écon* economic **2** *(peu coûteux)* economical, cheap, inexpensive; **classe é.** economy class; **cycle é.** *(d'un lave-vaisselle etc)* economy cycle; **voiture é.** economy car

NM l'é. the economic situation

> Attention: ne pas confondre **economic** et **economical** lorsque l'on traduit **économique. Economic** signifie **qui se rapporte à l'économie** alors que **economical** signifie **qui permet d'économiser.**

économiquement [ekɔnɔmikmɑ̃] **ADV 1** *Écon* economically, from an economic point of view; **les é. faibles** the lower-income groups **2** *(à moindre frais)* inexpensively; *(frugalement)* frugally

économiser [3] [ekɔnɔmize] **VT 1** *(épargner ▸ richesse, argent)* to economize, to save; *(▸ temps)* to save; **économisez 10 euros** 10 euros off, save 10 euros **2** *(ménager ▸ force)* to save; *(▸ ressources)* to husband; **é. ses paroles** to be sparing of one's words; **é. sa salive** to save one's breath **3** *(énergie, électricité, denrée)* to save, to conserve

VI to save money, to economize; **é. sur l'électricité** to save on *or* economize on electricity

économiseur [ekɔnɔmizœr] **NM** *Aut* fuel-saving device; *Ordinat* **é. d'écran** screen saver

économiste [ekɔnɔmist] **NMF** *Écon* economist

écope [ekɔp] **NF** bailer

écoper [3] [ekɔpe] **VT** *(barque, bateau)* to bail out; **é. l'eau d'une embarcation** to bail out a boat *or* the water out of a boat

VI *Fam (recevoir une sanction, une réprimande)* to take the rap; **j'en ai marre d'é. pour les autres** I'm sick of getting the blame for what other people do

• **écoper de VT IND** *Fam* to get, *Br* to cop; **il a écopé de cinq ans de prison** he got five years inside

écoproduit [ekɔprɔdɥi] **NM** *Écol* eco-friendly *or* environmentally-friendly product, eco-product

écorçage [ekɔrsaʒ] **NM** *(d'arbres)* barking; *(d'oranges)* peeling; *(de riz)* husking

écorce [ekɔrs] **NF 1** *(d'un arbre)* bark; *(d'un fruit)* peel; *(d'une orange)* rind, peel; *(de riz)* husk; *(de châtaigne)* skin

2 *Bot* cortex

3 *Géog* **l'é. terrestre** the earth's crust

4 *Fig (extérieur)* exterior, outward appearance

écorcer [16] [ekɔrse] **VT** *(arbre)* to bark; *(fruit)* to peel; *(riz)* to husk

écorché, -e [ekɔrʃe] **NM,F c'est un é. vif/une écorchée vive** he's/she's hypersensitive

NM 1 *Beaux-Arts* écorché **2** *(dessin)* cutaway

écorchement [ekɔrʃəmɑ̃] **NM** *(d'un animal)* skinning

écorcher [3] [ekɔrʃe] **VT 1** *(animal)* to skin

2 *(torturer)* to flay; **é. vif** to flay alive; *Fig* **se faire é. vif** to be skinned alive

3 *(blesser)* to scratch, to graze; *(jambe, peau etc)* to graze, to scrape; *(la gorge ▸ sujet: l'alcool, plat pimenté)* to burn; *(▸ sujet: bonbon)* to scratch; **elle a eu les mains écorchées par les épines** her hands were scratched by the thorns; *très Fam* **ça t'écorcherait la bouche de dire merci?** it wouldn't actually hurt to say thank you, would it?

4 *Fig (mal prononcer ▸ mot)* to mispronounce; **il écorche toujours mon nom** he always mispronounces my name; **é. une langue** to murder *or* to massacre a language

VPR s'écorcher to scrape *or* to scratch oneself; **s'é. le genou** to graze *or* scrape one's knee

écorcheur [ekɔrʃœr] **NM 1** *(d'animaux)* flayer, skinner **2** *Fam (escroc)* swindler, crook; **ce sont de véritables écorcheurs** they rob you blind

écorchure [ekɔrʃyr] **NF** scratch, graze; **se faire une é.** to scratch oneself

éco-recharge [ekorəʃarʒ] *(pl* **éco-recharges)** **NF** eco-refill

écorner [3] [ekɔrne] **VT 1** *(endommager ▸ cadre, meuble)* to chip a corner off; *(▸ livre, page)* to fold down the corner of, to dog-ear; **un livre tout écorné** a dog-eared book **2** *(fortune, héritage)* to make a dent in **3** *Can (animal)* to dehorn; *Fig* **un vent à é. les bœufs** a fierce gale

écornifler [3] [ekɔrnifle] **VT** *Fam* **1** *Vieilli (grappiller)* to scrounge **2** *Can (être indiscret)* to snoop, to pry□

écornifleur, -euse [ekɔrniflœr, -øz] *Fam* **ADJ** *Can* snooping, prying□

NM,F 1 *Vieilli (profiteur)* scrounger **2** *Can (personne indiscrète)* snoop

écossais, -e [ekɔse, -ez] **ADJ 1** *Géog (coutume, lande)* Scottish; *(personne)* Scottish, Scots; **whisky é.** Scotch (whisky) **2** *Tex* tartan

NM 1 *Ling (dialecte de l'anglais)* Scots; *(langue celtique)* (Scots) Gaelic **2** *Tex* tartan

• **Écossais, -e NM,F** Scot, Scotsman, *f* Scotswoman; **les É.** Scottish people, the Scots

Écosse [ekɔs] **NF l'É.** Scotland; **vivre en É.** to live in Scotland; **aller en É.** to go to Scotland

écosser [3] [ekɔse] **VT** *(petits pois)* to shell, to pod; *(fèves, haricots)* to shell

écosystème [ekɔsistɛm] **NM** *Écol* ecosystem

écot [eko] **NM** share; **payer chacun son é.** to pay one's share

écotaxe [ekɔtaks] **NF** ecotax

écotourisme [ekɔturism] **NM** *Écol* ecotourism

écoulement [ekulmɑ̃] **NM 1** *(d'un liquide)* flow, outflow; *Constr (du toit etc)* run-off; **l'é. se fait mal** it's not flowing very well; **système d'é. des eaux** drainage system; **(tube d')é.** *(d'une baignoire)* waste pipe; *Aviat* **é. (des filets) d'air** air flow

2 *Méd* discharge

3 *(mouvement ▸ de la foule, de la circulation)* flow

4 *(passage ▸ du temps)* passage, passing; **vous n'avez pas le droit de répondre après é. du temps** you must answer before the time is up

5 *(vente)* selling, sale; *(distribution)* distributing, distribution; **marchandises d'é. facile/difficile** fast-/slow-moving goods

écouler [3] [ekule] **VT 1** *(vendre ▸ marchandises, stocks)* to sell (off); **é. qch à perte** to sell sth at a loss **2** *(se débarrasser de)* to dispose *or* to get rid of; **é. des faux billets** to put forged notes into circulation

VPR s'écouler 1 *(se déverser ▸ liquide)* to flow out (**de** of); *(▸ foule, circulation)* to flow; **l'eau s'écoule peu à peu** the water trickles out; **faire s'é. l'eau** to run off *or* to drain off the water **2** *(passer ▸ année, temps)* to go by, to pass (by) **3** *(se vendre ▸ marchandises, stocks)* to sell

écourter [3] [ekurte] **VT 1** *(rendre plus court)* to shorten, to cut short; *(visite, discours)* to curtail, to cut short; *(barbe, moustache)* to trim **2** *Vét* to dock

écoute [ekut] **NF 1** *Rad* listening; **dès la première é....** *(d'un disque, d'un morceau)* the first time you hear it...; **se mettre** *ou* **se porter à l'é., prendre l'é.** to listen in, to tune in; **heure** *ou* **période de grande é.** *Rad* peak listening time; *TV* peak viewing time, prime time; **cette émission bénéficie d'une grande é.** the programme has a large audience *or* stands high in the ratings

2 *(détection)* listening (in); **é. clandestine** wiretapping; **é. électronique** electronic listening; **é. sous-marine** sonar; **écoutes (téléphoniques)** phone tapping; **mettre** *ou* **placer qn sur é.** *ou* **écoutes** to tap sb's phone; **elle est sur é.** *ou* **écoutes** her phone's been tapped; **poste d'é.** listening post; **table d'é.** wiretapping set

3 *(attention)* ability to listen; **avoir une bonne é.** to be good at listening *or* a good listener

4 *Naut (d'une voile)* sheet

5 *Zool (d'un sanglier)* **écoutes** ears

• **à l'écoute ADV 1** *Mil & Rad* **être à l'é. (de)** to be listening (to); *Rad* **restez à l'é. de nos programmes de nuit** stay tuned to our late-night programmes **2** *(attentif à)* **être à l'é. de** to be attentive to; *(électeurs, opinion publique)* to be in touch with; *(enfants)* to be attentive to the needs of

• **aux écoutes ADV être** *ou* **se tenir aux écoutes** *Fam Vieilli* to listen□, to eavesdrop□; *Fig* to keep one's ears open; **être aux écoutes derrière la porte** to be listening at the door

écouter [3] [ekute] **VT 1** *(entendre ▸ chanson, discours, émission)* to listen to; **je vais te faire é. un truc génial** I'm going to play you something really great; *Rad* **vous écoutez France Inter** you are listening *or* tuned to France Inter; **é. la messe** to hear Mass; **é. qn jusqu'au bout** to hear sb out

2 *(être attentif à)* to listen to; **écoutez-moi avant de vous décider** listen to what I have to say before you make up your mind

3 *(obéir à)* to listen to; **il faut é. ses parents** you must do as your parents tell you

4 *(suivre ▸ personne, avis)* to listen to, to pay attention to; **é. sa conscience** to listen to *or* to be guided by one's conscience

5 *(à l'impératif, à valeur d'insistance)* **écoutez, nous n'allons pas nous disputer!** listen *or* look, let's not quarrel!; **écoute, ça suffit maintenant!** listen *or* look here, that's enough now!

USAGE ABSOLU je n'écoutais que d'une oreille I was only half listening; **é. de toutes ses oreilles** to be all ears; **é. aux portes** to eavesdrop; **il sait é.** he's a good listener

VPR s'écouter 1 *(emploi passif)* **c'est le genre de musique qui s'écoute dans le recueillement** this is the kind of music one should listen to with reverence **2** *(emploi réfléchi)* **il s'écoute trop** he's a bit of a hypochondriac; **si je m'écoutais, je le mettrais dehors** if I had any sense, I'd throw him out; **s'é. parler** to love the sound of one's own voice

écouteur [ekutœr] **NM 1** *Tél* earpiece; **prendre l'é.** to listen in **2** *(pour écouter de la musique)* earphone; *TV & Rad* **é. auriculaire** earpiece; **écouteurs** earphones, headphones

écoutille [ekutij] **NF** *Naut* hatch, hatchway

écouvillon [ekuvijɔ̃] **NM 1** *Méd & Mil* swab **2** *(goupillon)* bottlebrush

écouvillonner [3] [ekuvijɔne] **VT** *(bouteille)* to clean out; *Méd (cavité)* to swab

écovillage [ekɔvilaʒ] **NM** ecovillage

écrabouillage [ekrabujaʒ], **écrabouillement** [ekrabujmɑ̃] **NM** *Fam* crushing□, squashing□

écrabouiller [3] [ekrabuje] **VT** *Fam* to crush□, to squash□; **se faire é.** to get squashed; **se faire é. par une voiture** to get flattened by a car

écran [ekrɑ̃] **NM 1** *(d'une console, d'un ordinateur)* screen; **à l'é.** on screen; **é. antireflets** antiglare screen; **é. couleur** colour screen *or* display; **é. à cristaux liquides** liquid crystal screen; **é. haute résolution** high-resolution screen; **é. LCD** LCD screen; **é. (à) plasma** (gas) plasma screen; **é. plat** flat screen; **é. protecteur** *ou* **de protection** shield; **é. tactile** touch *or* touch-sensitive screen; **é. de visualisation** visual display unit, VDU

2 *Ordinat (page visualisée)* screen; **é. d'accueil** start-up screen; **é. d'aide** help screen; **é. de dialogue** dialog(ue) screen; **é. divisé** split screen; **é. à fenêtres** split screen; **é. pleine page** full-page display; **é. de saisie** input screen; **é. de travail** working *or* work screen

3 *Cin* screen; **é. de cinéma** cinema *or Am* movie screen; **porter un roman à l'é.** to adapt a novel for the screen; **à l'é.** *ou* **sur les écrans, cette semaine** what's on this week (at the *Br* cinema *or Am* movies); **le grand é.** the big screen; *Cin & Phot* **é. (de projection)** screen; **é. panoramique** wide screen

4 *TV* screen; **é. de télévision** TV screen; **le petit é.** television; **é. cathodique** cathode ray tube screen; **é. de contrôle** control monitor; **é. plat** flat-faced screen; **téléviseur à é. plat** flat-screen TV; **é. de prévisualisation** preview monitor; **é. de vision** review screen; **é. de visualisation** display screen

5 *(protection)* screen, shield; **il se fit un é. de sa main** he shielded his eyes with his hand; **il m'a fait é. de son corps pour me protéger** he shielded me with his body; **elle se cachait derrière l'é. de ses cheveux** she was using her hair as a screen to hide behind; *aussi Fig* **é. de fumée** smoke screen; **é. anti-bruit** noise barrier; **é. de cheminée** fire screen; **é. pare-fumée** smoke deflector; **é. de protection** shield; **é. solaire** sunscreen, sunblock; **crème é. total** total sunblock, total protection sun cream

6 *Beaux-Arts* silk screen

7 *Rad & TV* **é. publicitaire, é. de publicité,** *Fam* **é. de pub** commercial break

écran-mosaïque [ekrɑ̃mɔzaik] *(pl* **écrans-mosaïques)** **NM** multi-screen, multi-split screen

écrasant, -e [ekrazɑ̃, -ɑ̃t] **ADJ 1** *(insupportable ▸ gén)* crushing, overwhelming; *(▸ chaleur)* unbearable; *(▸ responsabilité)* weighty, burdensome; *(▸ charge de travail)* overwhelming; *(▸ travail)* backbreaking **2** *(manifeste ▸ proportion, preuve, majorité, victoire)* overwhelming

écrasé, -e [ekraze] **ADJ** squashed; **nez é.** flat nose

écrasement [ekrazmɑ̃] **NM 1** *(de fruits, de graines, d'ail)* crushing; *(de pommes de terre)* mashing

2 *(d'un membre)* crushing

3 *(anéantissement ▸ d'une révolte)* crushing; *(▸ d'un peuple)* oppression; *(▸ d'une armée, d'une équipe)* crushing defeat

4 *Aviat* **é. (au sol)** crash

5 *Ordinat (de données, d'un fichier)* overwriting

écrase-merdes [ekrazmerd] **NMPL** *Fam* clodhoppers, beetle-crushers

écraser [3] [ekraze] **VT 1** *(appuyer sur)* to crush; *(accidentellement)* to squash; *(boîte, membre, ail)* to crush; *(carton)* to flatten; *Fam* **é. l'accélérateur** *ou* **le champignon** to step on it, *Am* to step on the gas; **é. le frein** to slam on the brake

2 *(fruit, pomme de terre, œuf dur)* to mash; *(cafard)* to squash; *(mouche, moustique)* to swat; **é. une cigarette** to stub a cigarette out; *Fam Fig* **je compte sur toi pour é. le coup** I'm relying on you to keep your mouth shut

3 *(piéton, animal)* to run over; **il s'est fait é.** he was run over

4 *(faire mal à)* to crush, to squash; **tu m'écrases les pieds** you're treading on my feet

5 *(accabler)* to crush; **é. un pays d'impôts** to overburden a country with taxes; **écrasé d'impôts** crushed by taxation, staggering under the burden of taxation; **être écrasé de chaleur** to be dropping with the heat

6 *(anéantir ▸ adversaire, troupes etc)* to crush; **se faire é. par l'équipe adverse** to get crushed by the opposing team; **il écrase tout le monde en latin** he is much better than everyone else at Latin

7 *(réduire considérablement)* **é. les prix** to slash prices

8 *(dominer)* to outdo; **essayer d'é. qn** to try and beat sb at his/her own game; **il écrase tout le monde de son luxe** he flaunts his luxurious lifestyle everywhere

9 *Ordinat (fichier)* to overwrite

VI *très Fam* **1** *(se taire)* **écrase, tu veux bien!** shut up, will you! **2** *(locution)* **en é.** to sleep like a log

VPR s'écraser 1 *(emploi passif)* to be crushed; **les tomates s'écrasent facilement** tomatoes are crushed easily

2 *(fruit, légume)* to get crushed *or* mashed *or* squashed; **les fraises se sont écrasées dans mon sac** the strawberries got squashed inside my bag **3** *(se fracasser ▸ aviateur, avion)* to crash; *(▸ alpiniste)* to crash to the ground; **l'avion s'est écrasé au sol** the plane crashed

4 *Fam (se presser)* to be *or* to get crushed; **les gens s'écrasent pour entrer** there's a great crush to get in
5 *très Fam (se taire)* to shut up, to pipe down; **toi, tu t'écrases!** just shut up, will you!

écraseur, -euse [ekrazœr, -øz] **NM,F** *Fam* road hog

écrémage [ekremaʒ] **NM 1** *Culin* skimming, creaming **2** *Mktg* **é. du marché** market skimming **3** *Fig* **ce lycée n'aurait pas de si bons résultats sans un sévère é. des élèves** the school wouldn't get such good results if it didn't choose only the very best pupils *or* if it didn't pick and choose its pupils; **le recrutement de leurs élèves passe par un sacré é.** they only take the crème de la crème

écrémer [18] [ekreme] **VT 1** *Culin* to skim **2** *Mktg (marché)* to skim **3** *(sélectionner)* to cream off

écrémeuse [ekremøz] **NF** *(mécanique)* skimmer; *(centrifugeuse)* cream separator

écrêter [4] [ekrete] **VT 1** *(coq)* to remove the comb of **2** *Fig (revenus, prix)* to even out

écrevisse [ekrəvis] **NF** *Zool* crayfish, *Am* crawfish

écrier [10] [ekrije] **s'écrier VPR** to cry *or* to shout (out), to exclaim; **"j'arrive", s'écria-t-elle** "I'm coming," she cried

écrin [ekrɛ̃] **NM** *(gén)* box, case; *(à bijoux)* casket

écrire [99] [ekrir] **VT 1** *(tracer ▸ caractère, mot)* to write; **é. qch à** *ou* **avec de l'encre** to write sth in ink; *Ordinat* **é. qch sur un disque** to write sth to disk
2 *(rédiger ▸ lettre, livre)* to write; *(▸ chèque, ordonnance)* to write (out); **é. une lettre à la machine** to type a letter; **é. un mot à la hâte** to scribble a note; **é. un mot à qn** to drop sb a line; **je veux que cela soit écrit dans le contrat** I want it written into the agreement; *Fig* **c'est écrit noir sur blanc** *ou* **en toutes lettres** it's written (down) in black and white; **c'est écrit sur sa figure** you can tell from his/her face, it's written all over his/her face; **c'était écrit** it was bound to happen; **il était écrit qu'ils se retrouveraient** they were bound to find each other again
3 *(noter)* to write down; **é. ses dépenses dans la marge** to write down one's expenses in the margin
4 *(épeler)* to spell; **tu écris ça comment?** how do you spell it?; **tu as mal écrit le mot "apéritif"** you spelled the word "apéritif" wrong
USAGE ABSOLU to write; **il écrit bien** his (hand) writing is good, he has good handwriting; *(écrivain)* he's a good writer, he writes well; **ce stylo écrit très bien** this pen writes very well; **tu écris mal** *(illisiblement)* your handwriting is bad; **é. à l'encre** to use ink; **é. à qn** to write to sb; **é. pour demander des renseignements** to write in *or* off for information
VPR s'écrire 1 *(s'épeler)* to be spelled; **ça s'écrit comment?** how do you spell it? **2** *(échanger des lettres)* to write to each other

écrit, -e [ekri, -it] **ADJ** written; **bien é.** well-written; **mal é.** poorly written; **é. à la main** hand-written
NM 1 *(document)* document; **signer un é.** to sign a document; *Journ* **é. diffamatoire** libel **2** *(œuvre)* written work **3** *Scol & Univ (examen)* written examination *or* papers; *(partie)* written part (of the examination)
• **par écrit ADV** in writing; **mettre qch par é.** to put sth down in writing

écriteau, -x [ekrito] **NM** board, notice, sign

écritoire [ekritwar] **NF** *(coffret)* writing case

écriture [ekrityr] **NF 1** *(calligraphie)* writing; *(façon d'écrire)* (hand)writing; **avoir une é. élégante** to have elegant handwriting
2 *(système)* writing; **é. abrégée** speedwriting; **é. phonétique** phonetic script; *Tél* **é. prédictive** predictive texting, predictive text (input)
3 *Typ (type de caractère)* script; **é. cursive** cursive; **é. droite/en italique** upright/italic script; **é. grasse** bold typeface, bold face
4 *(création, style)* writing; *TV & Cin* **é. de scénarios** scriptwriting, screenwriting
5 *Compta* entry; **passer une é.** to make an entry; **é. comptable** accounting *or* journal entry; **é. de régularisation** adjusting entry
6 *Jur* written document
7 *Bible & Rel* **l'É. sainte, les (saintes) Écritures** the Scriptures, Holy Scripture
• **écritures NFPL** *Compta* accounts; **tenir les écritures** to keep the accounts *or* the books; **employé aux écritures** accounts *or* ledger clerk; **écritures en partie double/simple** double-/single-entry bookkeeping

écrivailler [3] [ekrivaje] **VI** *Péj* to scribble

écrivailleur, -euse [ekrivajœr, -øz] **NM,F** *Péj (gén)* scribbler; *(journaliste)* hack

écrivain [ekrivɛ̃] **NM** writer

écrivait *etc voir* **écrire**

écrivasser [3] [ekrivase] **VI** *Péj* to scribble

écrivassier, -ère [ekrivasje, -ɛr] **NM,F** *Péj* scribbler

écrou[1] [ekru] **NM** *Tech* nut; **é. à ailettes** *ou* **à oreilles** wing nut; **é. crénelé** *ou* **à créneaux** *ou* **à encoches** castellated nut; **é. de réglage** adjusting *or* adjuster nut

écrou[2] [ekru] **NM** *Jur* committal; **sous é.** detained, in detention

écrouelles [ekruɛl] **NFPL** *Arch* scrofula, king's evil

écrouer [6] [ekrue] **VT** to imprison, to jail

écroulement [ekrulmɑ̃] **NM** *(d'un édifice, d'une théorie, d'un empire)* collapse; *(de terre, roche)* fall

écrouler [3] [ekrule] **s'écrouler VPR 1** *(tomber ▸ mur)* to fall (down), to collapse; *(▸ plafond, voûte)* to cave in
2 *(être anéanti ▸ empire, monnaie)* to collapse; **tous ses espoirs se sont écroulés** all his/her hopes vanished
3 *(défaillir ▸ personne)* to collapse; **le témoin s'est écroulé devant le juge** the witness broke down in front of the judge; **s'é. de sommeil/fatigue** to be overcome by sleep/weariness; **s'é. sur une chaise** to drop *or* flop onto a chair; **écroulé dans un fauteuil** slumped in an armchair
4 *Fam (locution)* **s'é. (de rire)** to kill oneself laughing

écru, -e [ekry] **ADJ 1** *Tex* raw; **soie écrue** raw silk; **toile écrue** holland **2** *(couleur)* ecru

ecsta [ɛksta] **NF** *Fam Arg drogue* E

ecstasy [ɛkstazi] **NM** ecstasy *(drug)*; **e. liquide** liquid ecstasy

ectoplasme [ɛktɔplasm] **NM** *Biol* ectoplasm

ÉCU, écu[1] [eky] **NM** *Anciennement UE (abrév* **European Currency Unit)** ECU, ecu; **É. dur** hard ECU

écu[2] [eky] **NM 1** *Hist (bouclier)* shield; *Hér* escutcheon, coat of arms **2** *(ancienne monnaie)* crown

écubier [ekybje] **NM** *Naut* hawsehole

écueil [ekœj] **NM 1** *Naut* reef; **donner sur les écueils** *(bateau)* to strike the rocks **2** *Littéraire (difficulté)* pitfall, danger, hazard; *Fig* **se heurter à un é.** to hit a snag

écuelle [ekɥɛl] **NF** *(assiette creuse)* bowl; **une é. de soupe** a bowlful of soup

éculé, -e [ekyle] **ADJ 1** *(botte, chaussure)* down-at-heel, worn down at the heel **2** *(plaisanterie)* hackneyed, well-worn

écumage [ekymaʒ] **NM 1** *Culin* skimming **2** *(pillage ▸ gén)* scouring; *(▸ d'une région)* plundering

écume [ekym] **NF 1** *(de la bière, de la bouche)* foam, froth; *(de la mer)* foam, spume; *(sur la soupe, la confiture)* scum; **il avait l'é. à la bouche** he was foaming at the mouth
2 *Minér* **é. de mer** meerschaum
3 *Littéraire (de la société)* scum, dross
4 *Métal* dross

écumer [3] [ekyme] **VI** *(vin, bouche etc)* to foam, to froth; *(mer)* to foam; *(soupe, confiture, métal fondu etc)* to form a scum; *(cheval)* to lather; **é. (de rage** *ou* **colère)** to be foaming at the mouth (with rage), to foam with anger
VT 1 *Culin (confiture)* to remove the scum from; *(bouillon)* to skim **2** *Métal* to scum **3** *(piller)* to plunder; *Fig* to go through; **é. les mers** to scour the seas; **j'ai écumé tout le quartier pour trouver une boulangerie** I scoured the whole area to find a bakery

écumeur [ekymœr] **NM 1** *Hist* **é. des mers** pirate **2** *(escroc)* plunderer

écumeux, -euse [ekymø, -øz] **ADJ** *Littéraire* foamy, frothy, spumy; *(mer, vagues)* foaming; *(bière)* foamy, frothy; *(confiture etc)* scummy

écumoire [ekymwar] **NF** *Culin* skimmer, skimming ladle; *Fam* **transformer qn en é.** to pump sb full of lead

écureuil [ekyrœj] **NM** *Zool* squirrel; **é. gris/roux** grey/red squirrel; **é. volant** flying squirrel

écurie [ekyri] **NF 1** *(local à chevaux, mulets, ânes)* stable; **é. (de courses)** *(de chevaux, voitures)* racing) stable; **mettre à l'é.** to stable; *Myth* **les écuries d'Augias** the Augean stables **2** *Fam (endroit sale)* pigsty **3** *(chevaux)* stable; *Sport* stable, team

écusson [ekysɔ̃] **NM 1** *(écu)* badge; *Mil* tab, badge, (collar) patch **2** *Hist* escutcheon, coat of arms **3** *(de serrure)* key-plate, keyhole escutcheon

écuyer, -ère [ekɥije, -ɛr] **NM,F 1** *(acrobate de cirque)* circus rider **2** *Équitation (cavalier)* rider
NM 1 *Hist (d'un chevalier)* squire; *(d'un souverain)* (royal) equerry; *Hist* **grand é.** Master of the Horse **2** *(professeur d'équitation)* riding teacher

eczéma [egzema] **NM** *Méd* eczema; **avoir** *ou* **faire de l'e.** to have eczema

eczémateux, -euse [egzematø, -øz] **ADJ** *Méd* eczema *(avant n)*, *Spéc* eczematous

édam [edam] **NM** *Culin* Edam (cheese)

edelweiss [edɛlvɛs] **NM** *Bot* edelweiss

éden [eden] **NM 1** *Bible* **l'É., le jardin d'É.** (the Garden of) Eden **2** *Littéraire* **un é.** an earthly paradise

édénique [edenik] **ADJ** Edenic

édenté, -e [edɑ̃te] **ADJ** *(vieillard, peigne, sourire ▸ totalement)* toothless; *(▸ partiellement)* gap-toothed; *Biol* edentulous

édenter [3] [edɑ̃te] **VT** *(peigne, scie, lame)* to break the teeth of

EDF [ədeɛf] **NF** *(abrév* **Électricité de France)** = French national electricity company

EDI [ədei] **NM** *Ordinat (abrév* **échange de données informatisé)** EDI

édicter [3] [edikte] **VT** *(loi)* to decree, to enact; *(peine)* to decree, to prescribe

édiction [ediksjɔ̃] **NF** *(d'une loi)* decree, enactment

édicule [edikyl] **NM** *(toilettes)* public lavatory; *(abri)* shelter

édifiant, -e [edifjɑ̃, -ɑ̃t] **ADJ 1** *(lecture)* instructive, edifying **2** *Hum (révélateur)* edifying, instructive

édification [edifikasjɔ̃] **NF 1** *(construction)* erection, construction; *Fig (d'un empire, d'une fortune)* building up **2** *(instruction)* edification, enlightenment; **pour votre é.** for your edification

édifice [edifis] **NM 1** *Constr* edifice, building; **é. public** public building **2** *(structure)* structure, edifice, system; **l'é. social** the social fabric **3** *(assemblage)* heap, mound, pile

édifier [9] [edifje] **VT 1** *(construire ▸ temple)* to build, to construct, to erect; **faire é. qch** to have sth built **2** *(rassembler ▸ empire, fortune)* to build up, to accumulate; *(▸ théorie)* to construct, to develop **3** *(instruire)* to edify, to enlighten; **vous voilà édifiés sur ses intentions** now you know what his/her (true) intentions are; *Ironique* **ces dernières révélations nous ont tous édifiés** these latest revelations were an education for us all

édile [edil] **NM 1** *Antiq* aedile, edile **2** *Hum (magistrat municipal)* town councillor, local worthy *(on the town council)*

Édimbourg [edɛ̃bur] **NF** *Géog* Edinburgh

édimbourgeois, -e [edɛ̃burʒwa, -az] **ADJ** of/from Edinburgh
• **Édimbourgeois, -e NM,F** = inhabitant of or person from Edinburgh

édit [edi] **NM** edict, decree

éditer [3] [edite] **VT 1** *Com (roman, poésie)* to publish; *(disque)* to produce, to release; *(meuble, robe)* to produce, to present **2** *(commenter ▸ texte)* to edit **3** *Ordinat* to edit; **pouvant être édité** editable

Il faut noter que le verbe anglais **to edit** ne s'emploie jamais pour dire **publier.**

éditeur, -trice [editœr, -tris] ADJ publishing; **société éditrice** publishing company

NM,F **1** *(maison d'édition)* publisher; *(personne, métier)* editor; **é. de disques** record producer; **é. de film** film releasing company; **é. de logiciels** software producer; **é. de presse** newspaper publisher; **é. de vidéo** video publisher **2** *(commentateur)* editor

NM *Ordinat (de programme)* editor; **é. HTML** HTML editor; **é. d'icônes** icon editor; **é. de liens** linker, link editor; **é. de texte** text editor

édition [edisjɔ̃] NF **1** *(activité, profession)* publishing; **le monde de l'é.** the publishing world; **travailler dans l'é.** to be in publishing *or* in the publishing business; **é. électronique** electronic publishing

2 *(livre)* edition; **une é. critique de 'Hamlet'** a critical edition of 'Hamlet'; **é. augmentée** enlarged edition; **é. de luxe** library edition; **é. originale** first edition; **é. de poche** paperback edition, *Am* pocket book; **é. revue et corrigée** revised edition; **é. entièrement revue et corrigée** major new edition; **é. scolaire** school edition

3 *(disque ▸ classique)* edition, release; *(▸ de rock)* release; **é. de disques** record production

4 *(de journaux)* edition; **l'é. du matin/soir** the morning/evening edition; **é. exceptionnelle** extra; **é. locale** local edition; **é. spéciale** *(de journal)* special edition; *(de revue)* special issue; *Journ* **dernière é.** final edition; *Hum* **où est le sucre? – dans le placard, troisième é.!** where's the sugar? – for the third time, it's in the cupboard!

5 *TV* **é. du journal télévisé** (television) news bulletin; **é. spéciale en direct de Budapest** special report live from Budapest

6 *(action de commenter)* editing

7 *Ordinat* editing; **é. de liens** linking; **é. pleine page** full page editing

Il faut noter que le terme anglais **edition** est un faux ami. Il ne désigne jamais **l'industrie du livre.**

éditique [editik] NF *Ordinat* electronic publishing

édito [edito] NM *Fam Journ* editorial[□], *Br* leader

éditorial, -e, -aux, -ales [editɔrjal, -o] ADJ editorial

NM *Journ (de journal)* editorial, *Br* leader

éditorialiste [editɔrjalist] NMF *Journ* editorial *or Br* leader writer

éditrice [editris] *voir* **éditeur**

Édouard [edwar] NPR *(roi)* Edward; **É. le Confesseur** Edward the Confessor

édredon [edrədɔ̃] NM eiderdown, quilt

éducable [edykabl] ADJ teachable

éducateur, -trice [edykatœr, -tris] ADJ educational, educative

NM,F *(gén)* teacher; *(pour jeunes)* youth leader; **é. spécialisé** special needs worker

éducatif, -ive [edykatif, -iv] ADJ educational; **le système é.** the education system

éducation [edykasjɔ̃] NF **1** *Scol & Univ (instruction)* education; **faire l'é. de qn** to educate sb; **il n'a aucune é. musicale** *(technique)* he has no musical training; *(connaissances générales)* he has no musical education; **avoir reçu une bonne é.** to be well-educated; **é. manuelle et technique** handicraft classes; **l'É. nationale** *(ministère)* the (French) Ministry *or* Department of Education; *(system)* state education *(in France)*; **é. permanente** lifelong learning; **é. physique (et sportive)** physical education, PE; **é. professionnelle** vocational training; **é. religieuse** religious instruction; **é. sexuelle** sex education **2** *(d'un enfant)* upbringing; *(bonnes manières)* good manners; **avoir de l'é.** to be well-bred *or* well-mannered; **manquer d'é.** to be ill-bred *or* ill-mannered; **manque d'é.** bad manners; **sans é.** ill-bred, uncouth; *Hum* **en rock, toute mon é. est à faire** I know absolutely nothing *or* I'm totally ignorant about rock music **3** *Fig (de la volonté, de l'esprit)* training

Il faut noter que le nom anglais **education** ne fait référence qu'à l'instruction scolaire et à l'enseignement et non à la façon dont on est élevé.

éducative [edykativ] *voir* **éducatif**

éducatrice [edykatris] *voir* **éducateur**

édulcorant, -e [edylkɔrɑ̃, -ɑ̃t] ADJ sweetening

NM sweetener, sweetening agent; **é. de synthèse** artificial sweetener

édulcorer [3] [edylkɔre] VT **1** *(sucrer)* to sweeten **2** *Fig (modérer ▸ propos, texte, compte rendu)* to tone down, to water down

éduquer [3] [edyke] VT **1** *Scol & Univ (instruire ▸ élève, masses)* to teach, to educate **2** *(exercer ▸ réflexe, volonté)* to train **3** *(élever ▸ enfant)* to bring up, to raise; **être bien/mal éduqué** to be well/badly brought up, to be well-/ill-mannered

EED [əəde] NM *Ordinat (abrév* **Échange électronique de données***)* EDI

EEE [əəə] NM *Pol (abrév* **Espace économique européen***)* EEA

EEG [əəʒe] NM *Méd (abrév* **électro-encéphalogramme***)* EEG

effaçable [efasabl] ADJ **1** *(encre, crayon, inscription)* erasable **2** *Ordinat (mémoire)* erasable

efface [efas] NF *Can Fam* eraser[□], *Br* rubber[□]

effacé, -e [efase] ADJ **1** *(couleur)* faded, discoloured **2** *(personne)* self-effacing, retiring; *(rôle)* small, insignificant; **mener une vie très effacée** to live very quietly **3** *(épaules)* sloping; *(menton)* receding; *(poitrine)* flat

effacement [efasmɑ̃] NM **1** *(annulation ▸ d'une faute)* erasing; *(d'un mot ▸ en gommant)* erasure; *Ordinat* deletion; *(d'une tache)* removal; *(par les éléments ▸ d'une inscription)* wearing away

2 *(oubli ▸ d'un cauchemar, d'un souvenir)* fading

3 *(modestie)* **e. (de soi)** self-effacement

4 *(d'une bande magnétique)* erasing, wiping

effacer [16] [efase] VT **1** *(ôter ▸ graffiti)* to erase, to remove, to clean off; *(gommer ▸ mot)* to erase, *Br* to rub out; *(nettoyer ▸ tableau noir)* to clean, to wipe; *Ordinat* to delete; **e. une tache** to remove a stain; *(en lavant)* to wash out a stain; *(avec un chiffon)* to wipe off a stain; **e. toutes traces de son passage** to remove *or* to eliminate all traces of one's presence; *Ordinat* **e. l'écran** to clear the screen; **e. des imperfections** to smooth out imperfections

2 *(cassette, disquette, enregistrement)* to erase, to wipe

3 *Fig (occulter ▸ rêve, image)* to erase; *(▸ bêtise)* to erase, to obliterate; **e. un mauvais souvenir** to erase *or* wipe out *or* blot out an unhappy memory; **e. qch de sa mémoire** to blot sth out of *or* to erase sth from one's memory; **on efface tout et on recommence** *(on se pardonne)* let bygones be bygones, let's wipe the slate clean; *(on reprend)* let's go back to square one, let's start afresh

4 *(éclipser ▸ adversaire)* to eclipse, to outshine

5 e. le corps to stand side-on; **e. les épaules** to throw back one's shoulders

VPR **s'effacer 1** *(emploi passif)* **le crayon à papier s'efface très facilement** pencil rubs out easily *or* is easily erased; **cela s'effacera à l'eau** it will wash off; **la tache ne s'est pas effacée au lavage** the stain didn't come out in the wash; *Fig* **avec le temps, tout s'efface** everything fades with time

2 *(encre, lettres)* to fade, to wear away; *(couleur)* to fade

3 *(s'écarter)* to move *or* to step aside; **s'e. pour laisser passer qn** to step out of sb's way; *Fig* **il a dû s'e. au profit de son frère** he had to step aside in favour of his brother; *Fig* **il a tendance à s'e. derrière elle** he tends to hide behind her

4 *(disparaître ▸ souvenir, impression)* to fade, to be erased

effaceur [efasœr] NM **e. (d'encre)** ink eraser *or Br* rubber

effarant, -e [efarɑ̃, -ɑ̃t] ADJ frightening, alarming; *(cynisme, luxe)* outrageous, unbelievable; *(étourderie, maigreur)* unbelievable, stunning; **ils pratiquent des prix effarants** their prices are frightening *or* shocking; **il y avait un monde e. sur les plages** there were an awful lot of people on the beach; **d'une naïveté effarante** alarmingly *or* shockingly naive

effaré, -e [efare] ADJ **1** *(effrayé)* alarmed **2** *(troublé)* bewildered, bemused

effarement [efarmɑ̃] NM **1** *(peur)* alarm **2** *(trouble)* bewilderment, bemusement

effarer [3] [efare] VT **1** *(effrayer)* to alarm **2** *(troubler)* to bewilder, to bemuse; **son hypocrisie m'effare!** his/her hypocrisy astounds me!; **je suis effaré par les prix!** the prices are frightening *or* shocking!, I'm astounded at the prices!

effarouchement [efaruʃmɑ̃] NM frightening off *or* away, scaring off *or* away

effaroucher [3] [efaruʃe] VT **1** *(effrayer)* to scare, to alarm; *(intimider)* to frighten away *or* off, to scare away *or* off **2** *(choquer)* to shock

VPR **s'effaroucher 1** *(prendre peur)* to take fright; **s'e. de** to shy at, to take fright at; **elle s'effarouche pour un rien** she gets frightened at the least little thing, the least little thing frightens her **2** *(s'offusquer)* to be shocked (**de** by *or* at)

effectif, -ive [efektif, -iv] ADJ **1** *Fin (coût, monnaie, taux)* effective; *(valeur, revenu)* real; *(circulation)* active; *(rendement)* actual **2** *(efficace ▸ méthode, raisonnement)* effective **3** *(règlement, mesures)* in effect; **cette loi sera effective au 1er janvier** this law will come into effect on 1 January

NM *(employés)* manpower, (number of) employees, staff; *(d'un lycée)* size, (total) number of pupils; *(d'un parti)* size, strength; *(d'une armée)* strength; *Naut* complement; **réduction de l'e. des classes** reduction in the number of pupils per class; **à e. réduit** under *or* below strength; **l'e. est au complet, nos effectifs sont au complet** we are at full strength; **e. budgétaire** budgetary strength, *Am* authorized strength

• **effectifs** NMPL *Mil* numbers, strength; **crise d'effectifs** manpower crisis

effectivement [efɛktivmɑ̃] ADV **1** *(efficacement)* effectively, efficiently; **contribuer e. au processus de paix** to make a real contribution to the peace process **2** *(véritablement)* actually, really; **cela s'est e. produit** that actually *or* really happened **3** *(en effet)* actually; **je suis e. sorti dans l'après-midi** I DID actually go out in the afternoon; **j'ai dit cela, e.** I did indeed say so; **c'est pratique, hein? – e.!** it's practical, isn't it? – (yes) indeed! *or* indeed it is!; **e., on aurait pu prévoir un parapluie** we should have thought about bringing an umbrella

Il faut noter que l'adverbe anglais **effectively** est un faux ami. Il signifie **efficacement.**

effectuer [7] [efektɥe] VT *(expérience, essai)* to carry out, to perform; *(trajet, traversée)* to make, to complete; *(voyage, calcul) & Mil (retraite)* to make; *(saut, pirouette)* to make, to execute; *(mouvement, geste)* to execute; *(service militaire)* to do; *(retouche, enquête)* to carry out; *(opération)* to execute, to carry out; *(réconciliation)* to bring about; *(paiement)* to make, *Sout* to effect; **e. des démarches** to take steps; **e. une réservation** to make a reservation; *Com* **e. une commande** to place an order

VPR **s'effectuer 1** *(avoir lieu)* to take place **2** *(mouvement, opération)* to be executed; *(paiement, voyage)* to be made; *(réconciliation)* to be brought about; **l'aller-retour s'effectue en une journée** the *Br* return trip *or Am* round trip can be made in one day

efféminé, -e [efemine] ADJ effeminate

NM *(garçon)* effeminate boy; *(homme)* effeminate man

efféminer [3] [efemine] VT *Littéraire* to make effeminate

effervescence [efervesɑ̃s] NF **1** *Chim* effervescence **2** *(agitation)* agitation, turmoil; *(excitation)* excitement

• **en effervescence** ADJ bubbling *or* buzzing with excitement; **le pays était en e.** the whole country was buzzing with excitement; **il avait l'esprit en e.** his mind was in turmoil

effervescent, -e [efervesɑ̃, -ɑ̃t] ADJ **1** *Chim (comprimé, aspirine)* effervescent **2** *(excité)* agitated

EFFET [efɛ]

- effect **1, 3, 5, 7**
- impression **2, 4**
- spin **8**
- result **1**
- bill **6**

NM 1 *(résultat)* effect, result, outcome; **c'est un e. de la pesanteur** it's a result of gravity; **c'est bien l'e. du hasard si...** it's really quite by chance that...; **les mesures du gouvernement n'ont eu aucun e.** the government's measures have had no effect; **cela n'a pas eu l'e. escompté** it didn't have the desired *or* intended effect; **ton insistance n'aura pour e. que de l'agacer** the only thing you'll achieve *or* do by insisting is (to) annoy him/her; **cela a eu pour e. de le mettre en colère** it had the effect of making him angry; **ce poison a pour e. de paralyser le système nerveux** this poison results in the paralysis of the nervous system; **le whisky lui fait toujours cet e.** whisky always has this effect on him/her; **attends que le médicament fasse son e.** wait for the medicine to take effect; **tes somnifères ne m'ont fait aucun e.** your sleeping pills didn't work on me *or* didn't have any effect on me; **faire de l'e.** to have an effect, to be effective; **faire de l'e. sur** to have an effect on; **faire e.** to take effect; **sans e.** ineffective, ineffectual; **mettre à e.** to bring into effect, to put into operation; **à quel e.?** to what end?; *Mktg* **e. de halo** halo effect; *Fin* **e. de levier** gearing, leverage; **e. pervers** undesired effect; *Méd* side effect; **e. placebo** placebo effect; **e. en retour** backlash; *Méd* **e. secondaire** side effect; **relation de cause à e.** cause and effect relationship

2 *(impression)* impression; **faire beaucoup d'e./peu d'e.** to be impressive/unimpressive; **les pleurs de sa femme ne lui firent aucun e.** his wife's tears had no effect on him; **sa réponse a fait l'e. d'une bombe** his/her answer came as *or* was a bombshell; **cela fait mauvais e. de le faire attendre** it looks bad to keep him waiting; **faire bon/mauvais e. à qn** to make a good/bad impression on sb; **son discours a fait (très) bon/mauvais e. sur l'auditoire** the audience was (most) favourably impressed/(extremely) unimpressed by his/her speech; **ça m'a fait un drôle d'e.** it gave me a funny *or* strange feeling, it made me feel all funny *or* strange; **à chaque fois qu'il me parle, ça me fait un drôle d'e.** I feel all funny inside whenever he talks to me; **ça fait un drôle d'e. de penser que...** it's funny *or* strange to think that...; **il me fait l'e. d'un jeune homme sérieux** he strikes me as (being) a reliable young man; **faire de l'e.** to make a show, to attract attention; **dès que je l'ai vu, il m'a fait de l'e.** I fancied him the minute I saw him; **eh bien! elle te fait de l'e.!** she's got quite an effect on you, I see!; **son départ précipité a fait de l'e.** his/her hurried departure caused a stir; *Fam* **je t'assure que ça fera un e. bœuf** I bet you it will make a terrific impression; *Fam* **faire** *ou* **produire son petit e.** to cause a bit of a stir; **c'est l'e. que cela m'a fait** that's how it impressed *or* struck me; **ça m'a fait un sale e.** it gave me a nasty turn; **ça m'a fait un drôle d'e. de le revoir** it felt strange seeing him again; **quel e. ça te fait qu'elle revienne?** how do you feel about her coming back?

3 *(procédé)* effect; **e. de contraste/d'optique** contrasting/visual effect; *Cin & TV* **effets optiques** camera effects; **e. (de) domino** domino effect; **e. de style** stylistic effect; **e. de perspective** 3-D *or* three-dimensional effect; **rechercher l'e.** to strive for effect; **manquer** *ou* **rater son e.** *(magicien)* to spoil one's effect; **créer un e. de surprise** to create a surprise, to cause a stir; **nous ne gagnerons cette bataille qu'en créant un e. de surprise** we won't win this battle unless we can take the enemy by surprise; *Théât* **e. de lumière** lighting effect; *Théât* **effets scéniques** stage effects; *Cin, Rad & TV* **effets sonores** sound effects; *Cin* **effets spéciaux** special effects; *Ordinat & TV* **e. de transition** melt; *TV* **effets vidéo** video effects; *Cin & TV* **effets visuels** visual effects

4 *(but recherché, force artistique)* **manquer son e.** *(discours)* not to have the desired effect; *(plaisanterie)* to misfire, to fall flat; **il fit une pause pour mieux juger de l'e. de ses paroles** he paused to see what effect his words were having; **soigner ses effets** to work hard to make the right impression; **rechercher les effets** to try to make an impression; **ménager ses effets** to have a sense of the dramatic; **faire des effets de jambes** to show off one's legs, to draw attention to one's legs; **faire des effets de voix** to make dramatic use of one's voice; **ça m'a coupé tous mes effets** it stole my thunder; *Littéraire* **phrases à e.** words used for effect

5 *(application)* effect; **mettre un projet à e.** to put a plan into action *or* into effect; **prendre e. à partir de** to take effect *or* to come into operation as of; *Jur* **e. rétroactif d'une loi/d'un accord** retroactive effect of a law/an agreement; **augmentation avec e. rétroactif au 1er avril** rise retroactive *or* backdated to 1 April

6 *Com & Fin* bill; **e. accepté** accepted bill; **e. bancaire** bill, draft; **e. de commerce** bill of exchange; **e. à courte échéance** short *or* short-dated bill; **e. à date fixe** fixed-term bill; **e. domicilié** domiciled bill; **effets à encaisser** accounts receivable; **e. à l'encaissement** bill for collection; **e. endossé** endorsed bill; **e. libre** clean bill; **e. à longue échéance** long *or* long-dated bill; **e. négociable** negotiable bill; *Bourse* **effets nominatifs** registered stock; **e. à ordre** promissory note; **e. payable à vue** sight bill; **effets à payer** bills payable; **e. au porteur** bill payable to bearer; **effets publics** government securities; **e. en souffrance** overdue bill; **e. à terme** period *or* term bill; **e. à vue** sight bill, demand bill *or* draft

7 *(en sciences)* effect; *Phys* **e. Doppler/Joule** Doppler/Joule effect; *Écol & Météo* **e. de serre** greenhouse effect; *Tech* **e. utile** efficiency; **à simple/double e.** single-/double-action, single-/double-acting; **e. Edison** Edison effect; *Phys* **e. tunnel** tunnel effect

8 *Sport* spin; **donner de l'e. à une balle** to put spin on a ball; **mettre trop d'e.** to put on too much spin; **e. de côté** *(au billard)* side (screw)

• **effets NMPL** *(affaires)* things; *(vêtements)* clothes; *Jur* **effets mobiliers** chattels; **effets personnels** personal effects *or* belongings

• **à cet effet ADV** to that effect *or* end *or* purpose; **cet appareil n'a pas été conçu à cet e.** the machine was not designed for that purpose *or* with that in mind

• **en effet ADV 1** *(effectivement)* actually, in (actual) fact; **en e., tu avais raison** you were right after all; **oui, je m'en souviens en e.** yes, I do remember; **c'est ce que je me suis en e. demandé** that's just what I wondered; **c'est en e. la meilleure solution** it's actually *or* in fact the best solution **2** *(introduisant une explication)* **il n'a pas pu venir; en e., il était malade** he was unable to come since he was ill **3** *(dans une réponse)* **drôle d'idée! – en e.!** what a funny idea! – indeed *or* isn't it!; **mais c'est monstrueux! – en e.!** it's abominable! – isn't it just!

• **sous l'effet de PRÉP être sous l'e. d'un calmant** to be under the effect of a tranquillizer; **être sous l'e. de l'alcool/la drogue** to be under the influence of alcohol/drugs; **j'ai dit des choses regrettables sous l'e. de la colère** anger made me say things which I later regretted; **je suis encore sous l'e. de la colère** I'm still angry, I still haven't calmed down; **les feuilles sont tombées sous l'e. de la chaleur** the leaves dropped off with the heat

effeuillage [efœjaʒ] **NM 1** *Hort* leaf removal **2** *Fam (déshabillage)* striptease[□]

effeuillaison [efœjezɔ̃] **NF** shedding of leaves

effeuiller [5] [efœje] **VT** *Hort (arbre)* to thin out (the leaves of); *(fleurs)* to pull the petals off; *(sujet: vent ▸ arbre)* to blow off the leaves of; **e. la marguerite** *(fille)* to play "he loves me, he loves me not"; *(garçon)* to play "she loves me, she loves me not"

VPR s'effeuiller *(arbre)* to shed *or* to lose its leaves; *(fleur)* to shed *or* to lose its petals

effeuilleuse [efœjøz] **NF** *Fam* **1** *(strip-teaseuse)* stripper[□] **2** *Suisse (ouvrière)* = woman employed to strip vines of unwanted leaves

efficace [efikas] **ADJ** *(politique, intervention)* effective; *(remède, prière)* effective, *Sout* efficacious; *(employé, machine)* efficient

> Attention: ne pas confondre **effective** et **efficient** lorsqu'on traduit **efficace**. **Effective** signifie **qui fait de l'effet** alors que **efficient** signifie **compétent**.

efficacement [efikasmɑ̃] **ADV** *(avec succès)* effectively; *(de façon productive)* efficiently

efficacité [efikasite] **NF** *(d'une politique, d'une intervention)* effectiveness; *(d'un remède, d'une prière)* effectiveness, *Sout* efficacy; *(d'un employé, d'une machine)* efficiency; **manque d'e.** inefficiency; **manquer d'e.** to be inefficient; *Écon* **e. économique** economic efficiency; *Écon* **e. marginale du capital** marginal efficiency of capital; *Mktg* **e. publicitaire** advertising effectiveness; *Mktg* **e. des ventes** sales effectiveness

efficience [efisjɑ̃s] **NF** efficiency

efficient, -e [efisjɑ̃, -ɑ̃t] **ADJ** efficient

effigie [efiʒi] **NF** effigy

• **à l'effigie de PRÉP** bearing the effigy *or* image of

• **en effigie ADV** in effigy

effilage [efilaʒ] **NM 1** *Tex* fraying **2** *(des haricots)* stringing **3** *(des cheveux)* feathering

effilé, -e [efile] **ADJ 1** *(mince ▸ doigt)* slender, tapering; *(▸ main)* slender; *(▸ silhouette)* rangy; *(▸ carrosserie)* streamlined; *(▸ outil)* tapered, pointed; *(▸ cheveux)* thinned; *Culin* **amandes effilées** flaked almonds **2** *(effiloché)* frayed; *(frange)* ragged **3** *Culin (poulet)* dressed, drawn

NM *Couture* fringe

effilement [efilmɑ̃] **NM 1** *(des doigts)* tapering **2** *Littéraire (de tissu)* fraying

effiler [3] [efile] **VT 1** *(tissu)* to fray, to unravel **2** *(allonger ▸ ligne, forme)* to streamline; **e. sa moustache** to trim one's moustache into a point **3** *(cheveux)* to thin out

VPR s'effiler 1 *(s'effilocher)* to fray, to unravel **2** *(s'allonger)* to taper (off)

effilochage [efilɔʃaʒ] **NM** fraying; *Tex (en peignant)* teasing out

effiloche [efilɔʃ] **NF** *Tex (de fils laissés libres)* fringe

effilocher [3] [efilɔʃe] **VT** to fray, to unravel; *(avec un peigne)* to tease out

VPR s'effilocher to fray, to unravel

efflanqué, -e [eflɑ̃ke] **ADJ** *(animal)* raw-boned; *(homme)* lanky, tall and skinny

effleurement [eflœrmɑ̃] **NM 1** *(contact)* light touch; *(de l'eau)* skimming **2** *(caresse)* light touch, gentle stroke *or* caress; *Ordinat* **touche à e.** touch-sensitive key

effleurer [5] [eflœre] **VT 1** *(frôler)* to touch lightly; *(accidentellement)* to brush (against); *(cime, eau)* to skim, to graze; **il m'a effleuré en passant** he brushed past me **2** *(égratigner ▸ peau)* to graze **3** *(aborder ▸ sujet)* to touch on *or* upon; **ça ne m'a même pas effleuré** it didn't even occur to me *or* cross my mind

efflorescence [eflɔresɑ̃s] **NF 1** *Chim* efflorescence **2** *Littéraire (épanouissement)* blooming, flowering; **être en pleine e.** to be flourishing **3** *(sur les fruits)* bloom

efflorescent, -e [eflɔresɑ̃, -ɑ̃t] **ADJ** *Chim* efflorescent

effluent, -e [eflyɑ̃, -ɑ̃t] **ADJ** effluent

NM *(eaux ▸ de ruissellement)* drainage water; *(▸ usées)* (untreated) effluent; **e. radioactif** radioactive waste

effluve [eflyv] **NM 1** *(émanation)* emanation; **effluves** *(bonnes odeurs)* fragrance, exhalations; *(mauvaises odeurs)* effluvia, miasma **2** *Phys* **e. électrique** discharge

effondrement [efɔ̃drəmɑ̃] **NM 1** *(chute ▸ d'un toit, d'un pont)* collapse, collapsing, falling down; *(▸ d'un plafond, d'une voûte)* falling *or* caving in; *(▸ d'une mine)* caving in; *Géol* subsidence; *Fig (▸ d'un plan)* falling through **2** *(chute importante ▸ d'une monnaie)* collapse, slump; *(▸ des prix, du marché, de la demande)* slump (**de** in); *(▸ d'un empire)* collapse **3** *(abattement)* dejection; **être dans un état d'e. complet** to be in a state of utter dejection

effondrer [3] [efɔ̃dre] **VT 1** *Agr* to subsoil **2** *(briser ▸ toit)* to bring down; *(▸ mur)* to break down; *Fig* **après la mort de sa femme, il était effondré** he was prostrate with grief after his wife's death

VPR s'effondrer 1 *(tomber ▸ mur, pont, bâtiment)* to fall (down), to collapse; *(▸ plafond, voûte)* to collapse, to fall *or* to cave in; *(▸ mine)* to cave in **2** *(chuter ▸ monnaie)* to collapse, to plummet, to slump; (▸ *prix, marché, demande, cours, bénéfices*) to slump; (▸*empire*) to collapse, to crumble, to fall apart; (▸ *rêve, projet*) to collapse, to fall through; (▸*raisonnement*) to collapse; **le marché s'est effondré** the bottom has fallen out of the market **3** (*défaillir*) to collapse, to slump; **s'e. en larmes** to break down and cry, to dissolve into tears; **s'e. dans un fauteuil** to slump *or* to sink into an armchair

efforcer [16] [efɔrse] **s'efforcer VPR s'e. de faire qch** to try hard *or* to endeavour to do sth; **s'e. de maigrir** to try hard *or* to do one's best to lose weight; **s'e. de sourire** to force oneself to smile; **s'e. à la clarté** to try to be as clear as possible; **je m'y efforce** I'm doing my best *or* utmost

effort [efɔr] **NM 1** (*dépense d'énergie*) effort; **e. physique/intellectuel** physical/intellectual effort; **e. de volonté** effort of (the) will; **e. financier** financial outlay; **e. de guerre** war effort; *Mktg* **e. de marketing** marketing effort; *Mktg* **e. de promotion** promotional campaign; **son médecin lui a interdit tout e.** his/her doctor has forbidden any exertion; **cela va te demander un certain e.** you'll need to exert yourself a bit; **après bien des efforts** after a great deal of effort; **avec e.** with an effort; **sans e.** effortlessly; **encore un (petit) e.!** one more try!; **fournir un gros e.** to make a great deal of effort; **il a fourni un gros e. au dernier trimestre** he worked very hard *or* he put in a great deal of work in the last term; **il est partisan du moindre e.** he doesn't do any more than he has to; **faire l'e. de faire qch** to make the effort to do sth; **tu aurais pu faire l'e. d'écrire/de comprendre** you could (at least) have tried to write/to understand; **faire un e.** to make an effort; **a progressé mais doit encore faire des efforts** has made progress but still needs to make an effort; **chacun doit faire un petit e.** everybody must do their share; **faire un e. sur soi-même** to exercise self-control; **faire un e. d'imagination** to try to use one's imagination; *Ironique* **cela demande un sacré e. d'imagination** it takes an awful lot of imagination, it puts quite a strain on the imagination; **faire un (gros) e. de mémoire** to try hard to remember; **faire un e. pour faire qch** to make an effort to do sth; **faire tous ses efforts pour obtenir qch** to do one's utmost *or* all one can to obtain sth; *Fam* **après l'e., le réconfort** after all that hard work I/you/*etc* deserve this!

2 *Tech* stress, strain; **e. de cisaillement/torsion** shearing/torsional stress; **e. de rupture** breaking strain; **e. de tension** tensile stress; **e. de torsion** torque; **e. de traction** pull, tractive effort, tensile stress; *Aut* **efforts en virage** cornering force

3 *Fam Vieilli Méd* strain❑, rick❑; **se donner** *ou* **attraper un e.** to rick one's back❑

effraction [efraksjɔ̃] **NF** *Jur* breaking and entering, housebreaking; **entrer par e.** to break in; **entrer par e. dans une maison** to break into a house; **il n'y a pas eu e.** there was no sign of a burglary

effraie[1] *voir* **effrayer**

effraie[2] [efrɛ] **NF** *Orn* barn owl

effranger [17] [efrɑ̃ʒe] **VT** to fray into a fringe

VPR s'effranger to fray

effrayant, -e [efrɛjɑ̃, -ɑ̃t] **ADJ 1** (*qui fait peur*) frightening, fearsome **2** (*extrême* ▸ *chaleur, charge de travail*) frightful, appalling; (▸*prix, bêtise, laideur*) frightening

effrayer [11] [efreje] **VT 1** (*faire peur à*) to frighten, to scare; (*inquiéter*) to alarm **2** (*décourager*) to put *or* to frighten off; **l'énormité de la tâche ne m'effrayait pas** the magnitude of the task didn't put me off

VPR s'effrayer 1 (*avoir peur*) to become frightened, to take fright; **s'e. de qch** to be frightened *or* scared *or* afraid of sth **2** (*s'alarmer*) to become alarmed; **je m'effraie de la lenteur avec laquelle elle travaille** I'm alarmed by how slowly she works

effréné, -e [efrene] **ADJ** (*poursuite, recherche*) wild, frantic; (*orgueil, curiosité, luxe*) unbridled, unrestrained; (*vie, rythme*) frantic, hectic; (*efforts*) frantic; (*galop*) frantic, mad

effritement [efritmɑ̃] **NM 1** (*désagrégation* ▸ *d'une roche, de bas-relief*) crumbling away; (▸*du plâtre, d'un revêtement*) crumbling, disintegration **2** (*affaiblissement* ▸ *d'une autorité, d'une majorité, de la popularité*) erosion **3** *Bourse* (*des valeurs, des cours*) crumbling; *Fin* (*de fonds*) erosion

effriter [3] [efrite] **VT** to cause to crumble

VPR s'effriter 1 (*se désagréger* ▸ *roche, bas-relief*) to crumble away; (▸ *plâtre, revêtement*) to crumble, to disintegrate **2** (*s'affaiblir* ▸ *autorité, majorité, popularité*) to erode **3** *Bourse* (*valeurs, cours*) to crumble; *Fin* (*fonds*) to erode

effroi [efrwa] **NM** *Littéraire* terror, dread; **regard plein d'e.** frightened look; **inspirer de l'e. à qn** to fill sb with terror; **un spectacle qui inspire l'e.** an awe-inspiring sight; **je fus saisi d'e.** I was seized by terror, I was terror-stricken

effronté, -e [efrɔ̃te] **ADJ** (*enfant, manières, réponse*) impudent, *Br* cheeky; (*menteur, mensonge*) shameless, barefaced, brazen

NM,F (*enfant*) impudent *or Br* cheeky child; (*homme*) impudent fellow; (*femme*) brazen hussy; **petite effrontée!** you *Br* cheeky *or Am* sassy little girl!

effrontément [efrɔ̃temɑ̃] **ADV** impudently, *Br* cheekily; **mentir e.** to lie shamelessly *or* barefacedly *or* brazenly

effronterie [efrɔ̃tri] **NF** (*d'un enfant, d'une attitude*) insolence, impudence, *Br* cheek; (*d'un mensonge*) shamelessness, brazenness; **il a eu l'e. de me répondre** he had the nerve to *or* he was impudent enough to answer me back

effroyable [efrwajabl] **ADJ 1** (*épouvantable*) frightening, appalling, horrifying **2** (*extrême* ▸ *maigreur, misère, erreur*) dreadful, frightful

effroyablement [efrwajabləmɑ̃] **ADV** awfully, terribly; **s'ennuyer e.** to be bored to death

effusion [efyzjɔ̃] **NF 1 e. de sang** bloodshed; **sans e. de sang** without any bloodshed **2** (*de sentiments*) effusion, outpouring, outburst; (*exubérance*) effusiveness; **effusions de joie/tendresse** demonstrations of joy/affection; **remercier qn avec e.** to thank sb effusively

égaie *etc voir* **égayer**

égaiement [egemɑ̃] **NM** cheering up, enlivenment, brightening up

égailler [3] [egaje] **s'égailler VPR** to disperse, to scatter

égal, -e, -aux, -ales [egal, -o] **ADJ 1** (*identique* ▸ *part, poids etc*) equal; **partager qch en parts égales** to divide sth up into equal parts; **deux mannequins de taille égale** two models of the same height; **ils sont de force/d'intelligence égale** they are equally strong/intelligent; **à travail é. salaire é.** equal pay for equal work; **à prix é., tu peux trouver mieux** for the same price, you can find something better; **à égale distance de A et de B** equidistant from A and B, an equal distance from A and B; **la partie n'est pas égale (entre les deux joueurs)** the players are unevenly matched; **toutes choses égales d'ailleurs** all (other) things being equal; **faire jeu é.** to have an equal score, to be evenly matched (in the game); *Fig* to be neck and neck; **être é. à** to be equal to, to equal; **être** *ou* **rester é. à soi-même** to remain true to form, to be still one's old self; **é. à lui-même, il n'a pas dit un mot** typically, he didn't say a word

2 *Math* **3 est é. à 2 plus 1** 3 is equal to 2 plus 1

3 (*régulier* ▸ *terrain*) even, level; (▸*souffle*) even, regular; (▸ *pas*) even, regular, steady; (▸ *pouls*) steady, regular; (▸ *allure*) steady; (▸ *climat*) equable, unchanging; **être de caractère é.** *ou* **d'humeur égale** to be even-tempered

4 (*locutions*) **ça m'est (bien/complètement) é.** (*ça m'est indifférent*) I don't care either way, it's all the same to me; (*ça ne m'intéresse pas*) I don't care at all, I couldn't care less; **tout lui est é.** he/she doesn't feel strongly about anything; **tout lui est é. désormais** he/she doesn't care about anything now; **c'est é., tu aurais pu téléphoner** all the same, you could have phoned

NM,F (*personne*) equal; **nos égaux** our equals; **la femme est l'égale de l'homme** woman is equal to man; **il n'a pas son é. pour animer une fête** he's second to none when it comes to livening up a party; **son arrogance n'a d'égale que sa sottise** his/her arrogance is only equalled by his/her foolishness

• **à l'égal de PRÉP** *Littéraire* **je l'aimais à l'é. d'un fils** I loved him like a son

• **d'égal à égal ADV** (*s'entretenir*) on equal terms; (*traiter*) as an equal; **nous avons eu une discussion d'é. à é.** we had a discussion as equals *or* on equal terms *or* on an equal footing

• **sans égal ADJ** matchless, unequalled, unrivalled; **elle est d'une malhonnêteté sans é.** she is incredibly dishonest

égalable [egalabl] **ADJ** which can be equalled *or* matched; **un exploit difficilement é.** a feat difficult to match

également [egalmɑ̃] **ADV 1** (*autant*) equally; **servir tout le monde é.** to give everyone an equal serving; **je crains é. le froid et la chaleur** I dislike the cold as much as the heat **2** (*aussi*) also, too, as well; **je l'ai vu é.** I saw him as well *or* too; **elle m'a é. dit que…** she also told me that…

égaler [3] [egale] **VT 1** (*avoir la même valeur que*) to equal, to match (**en** for); **é. le record mondial** to equal the world record; **rien n'égale sa beauté** her beauty is unequalled

2 *Math* **3 fois 2 égale 6** 3 times 2 equals 6; **deux et deux égalent quatre** two and two equal *or* make four; **si X égale Y** let X equal Y

3 *Arch* (*comparer*) to rank; (*rendre égal*) to make equal; **é. Milton à Shakespeare** to rank Milton with Shakespeare; **la douleur égale les hommes** grief makes all men equal

4 (*niveler*) to level (out), to make flat

égalisateur, -trice [egalizatœr, -tris] **ADJ** equalizing, levelling; *Sport* **but/point é.** *Br* equalizer, *Am* tying goal/point

égalisation [egalizasjɔ̃] **NF 1** (*nivellement* ▸ *des salaires, d'un terrain*) levelling **2** (*équilibrage*) equalization, equalizing; *Math* **é. à zéro** equating to zero **3** *Sport* **le but/point de l'é.** *Br* the equalizer, *Am* the tying goal/point; **réussir l'é.** to score the *Br* equalizer *or Am* tying goal/point

égalisatrice [egalizatris] *voir* **égalisateur**

égaliser [3] [egalize] **VT** (*sentier*) to level (out); (*cheveux, frange*) to trim; (*conditions, chances, salaire*) to make equal, to balance (out); *Math* **é. une expression à zéro** to equate an expression to zero

VI *Sport* to tie, *Br* to equalize

VPR s'égaliser to become more equal, to balance out

égaliseur [egalizœr] **NM** *Tech* **é. graphique** graphic equalizer

égalitaire [egalitɛr] **ADJ** egalitarian

égalitarisme [egalitarism] **NM** egalitarianism

égalitariste [egalitarist] **ADJ** egalitarian

égalité [egalite] **NF 1** (*entre des quantités, des personnes*) equality; *Jur* **é. des armes** right to a fair trial; **é. des chances** equal opportunities; **é. devant l'impôt** equality of taxation; **é. des salaires/droits** equal pay/rights; **l'é. des citoyens devant la loi** the equality of citizens before the law; **être sur un pied d'é. avec qn** to be on an equal footing *or* on equal terms with sb

2 *Math* equality; **(signe d')é.** equal *or* equals sign

3 *Géom* **é. de deux triangles** isomorphism of two triangles

4 *Tennis* deuce; *Ftbl* draw, tie

5 (*uniformité* ▸ *du pouls, de la respiration*) regularity, steadiness; (▸ *d'une allure*) steadiness; (▸ *du sol*) evenness, levelness; (▸ *du tempérament*) evenness; **être d'une grande é. d'humeur** to be very even-tempered

• **à égalité ADV** (*au tennis*) at deuce; (*dans des jeux d'équipe*) drawn, in a draw *or* tie; *Golf* all square; *Sport* **être à é.** (*équipes*) to be level; **ils ont fini le match à é.** they tied; **ils sont à é. avec Riom** they're lying equal with Riom; *Fig* **maintenant, nous sommes à é.** now we're even; *Courses de chevaux* **parier à é. sur un cheval** to lay evens on a horse

égard [egar] **NM** (*point de vue*) **à bien des égards** in many respects; **à cet/aucun é.** in this/no respect; **n'ayez aucune crainte à cet é.** don't worry about that, don't have any worries on that score; **à certains égards** in some respects

• **égards NMPL** (*marques de respect*) consideration; **être plein d'égards** *ou* **avoir beaucoup d'égards pour qn** to show great consideration for *or* to be very considerate towards sb; **manquer d'égards envers qn** to show a lack of consideration for *or* to be inconsiderate towards sb;

elle est toujours accueillie avec les égards dus à son rang she is always greeted with the respect due to her rank; **il nous a reçus avec beaucoup d'égards** he received us very warmly
• **à l'égard de** PRÉP **1** *(envers)* towards; **être dur/tendre à l'é. de qn** to be hard on/gentle with sb; **être injuste à l'é. de qn** to be unjust to(wards) sb; **il a été très gentil à mon é.** he has been very kind to me; **ils ont fait une exception à mon é.** they made an exception for me *or* in my case **2** *(à l'encontre de)* against; **prendre des sanctions à l'é. de qn** to impose sanctions against *or* to apply sanctions to sb **3** *(quant à)* with regard to; **elle émet des réserves à l'é. de ce projet** she's putting up some resistance with regard to the project
• **à tous égards** ADV in all respects *or* every respect
• **eu égard à** PRÉP in view of, considering; **eu é. à son âge** in view of *or* given his/her age
• **par égard pour** PRÉP out of consideration *or* respect for
• **sans égard pour** PRÉP with no respect *or* consideration for, without regard for

égaré, -e [egare] ADJ **1** *(perdu ▸ dossier, personne)* lost; *(▸ animal)* lost, stray **2** *(affolé ▸ esprit)* distraught; *(▸ regard)* wild, distraught; *(▸ yeux)* wild; **avoir le regard é.** to be wild-eyed

égarement [egarmɑ̃] NM **1** *(folie)* distraction, distractedness; **dans son é., il a oublié de…** he was so distracted he forgot to…; **dans un moment d'é.** in a moment of panic *or* confusion **2** *(perte)* loss
• **égarements** NMPL *Littéraire (dérèglements de conduite)* wild behaviour, wildness; **revenir de ses égarements** to see the error of one's ways

égarer [3] [egare] VT **1** *(perdre ▸ bagage, stylo)* to lose, to mislay; *(en donnant de mauvaises indications ▸ personne)* to mislead; **il jouait à é. les nouveaux arrivants** it amused him to get the newcomers lost; **é. les soupçons** to avert suspicion **2** *(tromper ▸ opinion, lecteur)* to mislead, to deceive; *(▸ jeunesse)* to lead astray; **un électorat égaré par des promesses fallacieuses** voters misled by fraudulent promises **3** *Littéraire (affoler)* to make distraught, to drive to distraction; **la douleur vous égare** you're distraught with pain
VPR **s'égarer 1** *(se perdre ▸ promeneur)* to lose one's way, to get lost; *(▸ dossier, clef)* to get lost *or* mislaid; *(▸ colis)* to get lost, to go astray; **s'é. dans des considérations secondaires** to get bogged down in minor considerations; **s'é. hors du droit chemin** to go off the straight and narrow **2** *(sortir du sujet)* to wander; **ne nous égarons pas!** let's not wander off the point!, let's stick to the subject!; **son esprit s'égare** his/her mind is wandering

égayer [11] [egeje] VT *(personne)* to cheer up; *(chambre, robe, vie)* to brighten up; *(ambiance, récit)* to brighten up, to liven up
VPR **s'égayer** *(s'amuser)* to have fun, to enjoy oneself; *(s'animer)* to cheer up

Égée [eʒe] NPR *Myth* Aegeus
NF *Antiq & Géog* **la mer É.** the Aegean Sea

égéen, -enne [eʒeɛ̃, -ɛn] ADJ *Antiq & Géog* Aegean

e-génération [iʒenerasjɔ̃] NF e-generation

Égérie [eʒeri] NPR *Antiq & Myth* Egeria
• **égérie** NF *(inspiratrice)* muse; **elle est l'é. du groupe** she's the driving force of the group

égide [eʒid] NF *Myth* aegis
• **sous l'égide de** PRÉP *Littéraire* under the aegis of; **prendre qn sous son é.** to take sb under one's wing; **se mettre sous l'é. des lois** to take refuge in the law

églantier [eglɑ̃tje] NM *Bot* wild *or* dog rose (bush)

églantine [eglɑ̃tin] NF *Bot* wild *or* dog rose

églefin [egləfɛ̃] NM *Ich* haddock

Église [egliz] NF *Rel* **l'É.** the Church; **l'É. anglicane** the Church of England, the Anglican Church; **l'É. catholique (romaine)** the (Roman) Catholic Church; **l'É. orthodoxe** the Orthodox Church; **l'É. protestante** the Protestant Church; **l'É. réformée** the Reformed Church; **l'É. de scientologie** the Church of Scientology; **l'É. et l'État** Church and State
• **église** NF *Rel (édifice)* church; **aller à l'é.** *(pratiquer)* to go to church, to be a churchgoer; **se marier à l'é.** to get married in church, to have a church wedding; **l'é. Saint-Pierre** St Peter's (church)
• **d'Église** ADJ **homme d'É.** clergyman; **gens d'É.** priests, clergymen

églogue [eglɔg] NF *Littérature* eclogue

ego [ego] NM *Psy* ego

égocentrique [egɔsɑ̃trik] ADJ egocentric, self-centred
NMF egocentric *or* self-centred person

égocentrisme [egɔsɑ̃trism] NM egocentricity, self-centredness; *Psy* egocentrism

égoïne [egɔin] NF handsaw

égoïsme [egɔism] NM selfishness

égoïste [egɔist] ADJ selfish
NMF selfish man, *f* woman

égoïstement [egɔistəmɑ̃] ADV selfishly

égorgement [egɔrʒəmɑ̃] NM cutting *or* slitting the throat

égorger [17] [egɔrʒe] VT **1** *(couper la gorge de)* to cut *or* to slit the throat of **2** *Fam Vieilli (ruiner)* to bleed white *or* dry
VPR **s'égorger** to butcher each other

égorgeur, -euse [egɔrʒœr, -øz] NM,F cut-throat

égosiller [3] [egozije] **s'égosiller** VPR **1** *(crier)* to shout oneself hoarse; **mais je m'égosille à vous le dire!** I've told you so till I'm blue in the face *or* I'm hoarse! **2** *(chanter fort)* to sing at the top of one's voice

ego-surfing [egɔsœrfiŋ] NM *Fam Ordinat* ego-surfing

égotisme [egɔtism] NM egotism

égotiste [egɔtist] ADJ egotistic, egotistical
NMF egotist

égout [egu] NM sewer; **les égouts** the sewers; **é. collecteur** main sewer; **eaux d'é.** sewage; **rat d'é.** sewer rat

égoutier [egutje] NM sewer worker

égouttage[1] [eguta̠ʒ], **égouttement** [egutmɑ̃] NM *(du linge)* leaving to drip-dry; *(de légumes, de la vaisselle)* draining; **é. des légumes dans une passoire** straining vegetables in a sieve

égouttage[2] [egutaʒ] NM *Belg* **1** *(installation)* installation of a sewerage system (**de** in) **2** *(réseau d'égouts)* sewers, sewerage system

égoutter[1] [3] [egute] VT *(linge)* to leave to drip; *(vaisselle, fromage frais, pâtes)* to drain; **é. des légumes dans une passoire** to strain vegetables in a sieve
VI *(vaisselle)* to drain; *(linge)* to drip; **laisser é. la vaisselle** to leave the dishes to drain; **faire é. les haricots** to strain the beans
VPR **s'égoutter** *(linge)* to drip; *(légumes, fromage frais, vaisselle)* to drain

égoutter[2] [3] [egute] VT *Belg* to install a sewerage system in

égouttoir [egutwar] NM **1** *(passoire)* strainer, colander; **panier é.** *(d'une friteuse)* basket **2** *(pour la vaisselle ▸ élément de l'évier)* draining board; *(▸ mobile)* drainer, draining rack

égrappage [egrapaʒ] NM *Agr (de raisins, de baies)* destalking, stemming

égrapper [3] [egrape] VT *Agr (raisins, baies)* to destalk, to stem

égratigner [3] [egratiɲe] VT **1** *(jambe, carrosserie)* to scratch, to scrape; *(peau)* to graze **2** *Fam (critiquer)* to have a dig *or* a go at; **ils l'ont bien égratigné dans 'Le Monde'** they had a good go at him in 'Le Monde'
VPR **s'égratigner s'é. le genou** to scrape *or* to scratch *or* to graze one's knee

égratignure [egratiɲyr] NF **1** *(écorchure)* scratch, scrape, graze; *Fig (remarque)* dig, gibe; **il s'en est sorti sans une é.** he escaped without a scratch **2** *(rayure)* scratch; **faire une é. à un panneau peint** to scratch a painted panel

égrenage [egrənaʒ] NM *Agr (du blé, du maïs)* shelling; *(de pois)* shelling, podding; *(du coton)* ginning; *(des graines fourragères)* threshing; *(de raisins, de baies)* picking off

égrènement [egrenmɑ̃] NM *(de lumières, d'habitations)* string

égrener [19] [egrəne] VT **1** *Agr (blé, maïs)* to shell; *(pois)* to shell, to pod; *(coton)* to gin; *(graines fourragères)* to thresh; *(raisins, baies)* to pick off; **des groseilles égrenées** redcurrants off the stalk **2** *(faire défiler)* **é. son chapelet** *Br* to say one's rosary, *Am* to tell one's beads; **pendule qui égrène les heures** clock marking out the hours **3** *Can (pain)* to break into crumbs, to crumble
VPR **s'égrener 1** *(grappe de raisin)* to drop off the stalk; *(blé)* to seed **2** *(se disperser ▸ famille, foule)* to scatter *or* to disperse slowly, to trickle away **3** *Littéraire (heures)* to tick by; *(notes)* to be heard one by one; **des lumières s'égrenaient le long du quai** a string of lights stretched along the quay

égrillard, -e [egrijar, -ard] ADJ *(histoire)* bawdy, ribald; *(personne, ton)* ribald, lewd; **en société, il a des manières égrillardes** he tends to be bawdy in company

Égypte [eʒipt] NF **l'É.** Egypt; **la Basse-É.** Lower Egypt; **la Haute-É.** Upper Egypt

égyptien, -enne [eʒipsjɛ̃, -ɛn] ADJ Egyptian
NM *(langue)* Egyptian
• **Égyptien, -enne** NM,F Egyptian
• **égyptienne** NF *Typ* egyptian

égyptologie [eʒiptɔlɔʒi] NF *Antiq* Egyptology

égyptologue [eʒiptɔlɔg] NMF *Antiq* Egyptologist

eh [e] EXCLAM hey!; **eh vous, là-bas!** hey you, over there!; **eh quoi, on n'a plus le droit de se reposer?** so can't we even have a rest any more?; **eh! que voulez-vous que j'y fasse?** well what do you want me to do about it?
• **eh bien** ADV **1** *(au début d'une histoire)* well, right **2** *(en interpellant)* hey; **eh bien, que faites-vous là-bas?** hey, what are you up to, over there?; **eh bien, comment ça va aujourd'hui?** so how are you today? **3** *(pour exprimer la surprise)* well, well; **eh bien, te voilà riche maintenant** well, well, you're rich now; **eh bien, je ne sais pas** well I don't know; **eh bien, je vais m'en occuper** oh well, I'll deal with it
• **eh non** ADV well no; **eh non, justement ce jour-là je ne peux pas** no, that's the one day I can't do it
• **eh oui** ADV well, (actually,) yes; **c'est fini? – eh oui!** is it over? – I'm afraid so!

éhonté, -e [eɔ̃te] ADJ *(menteur, tricheur)* barefaced, brazen, shameless; *(mensonge, hypocrisie)* brazen, shameless

eider [edɛr] NM *Orn* eider (duck)

Eiffel [efɛl] NPR **la tour E.** the Eiffel Tower

> **LA TOUR EIFFEL**
>
> The Eiffel Tower is France's best known monument and has become a symbol for France itself. Standing 324 metres high, it was built in 1889 for the Universal Exhibition in Paris by engineer Gustave Eiffel (whose other achievements include designing the structural frame of the Statue of Liberty in 1886). At first the tower was supposed to be dismantled after the exhibition, but the decision was taken to keep it and it has since become the most distinctive feature of the Paris landscape. It remained the tallest building in the world for 40 years, until New York's Chrysler Building was built in 1930.

einsteinien, -enne [enstenjɛ̃, -ɛn] ADJ Einsteinian

éjaculateur, -trice [eʒakylatœr, -tris] ADJ ejaculatory
NM **é. précoce** man who suffers from premature ejaculation

éjaculation [eʒakylasjɔ̃] NF *Physiol* ejaculation; **é. nocturne** nocturnal emission, wet dream; **é. précoce** premature ejaculation

éjaculatrice [eʒakylatris] *voir* **éjaculateur**

éjaculer [3] [eʒakyle] VI *Physiol* to ejaculate
VT to ejaculate

éjectable [eʒɛktabl] *voir* **siège**

éjecter [4] [eʒɛkte] VT **1** *(sujet: arme)* to eject **2** *Aviat & Aut* to eject **3** *Fam (renvoyer)* to kick *or* to chuck *or* to boot out (**de** of); **elle s'est fait é.** she was *or* got thrown *or* kicked out; **il s'est fait é. de l'équipe** he was kicked out of the team
VPR **s'éjecter** *Aviat* to eject

éjection [eʒɛksjɔ̃] **NF 1** *Aviat & Aut* ejection; **éjections volcaniques** ejecta **2** *Fam (expulsion)* kicking *or* chucking *or* booting out

élaboration [elabɔrasjɔ̃] **NF 1** *(d'une théorie, d'une idée)* working out; *(d'un plan, d'une stratégie)* development; *(d'une constitution, d'une loi, d'un budget etc)* drawing up; *Mktg* **é. de concept/produit** concept/product development

2 *Physiol* elaboration

3 *Métal* processing

4 *Psy* **é. psychique** working out repressed emotions

élaboré, -e [elabɔre] **ADJ 1** *(complexe ▸ dessin)* elaborate, intricate, ornate; *(▸ style littéraire)* studied; *(perfectionné ▸ système)* elaborate, sophisticated; *(détaillé ▸ carte, schéma)* elaborate, detailed; *(▸ plan)* elaborate **2** *Bot (sève)* elaborated

élaborer [3] [elabɔre] **VT 1** *(préparer ▸ plan, système)* to develop, to design, to work out; *(▸ constitution, loi, budget etc)* to draw up **2** *Physiol* to elaborate

VPR s'élaborer *(système, théorie)* to develop

élagage [elagaʒ] **NM** *(d'un arbre) & Fig (d'un film, d'un roman etc)* pruning; *Mktg* **é. de la ligne** line pruning

élaguer [3] [elage] **VT 1** *(arbre) & Fig (film, roman etc)* to prune **2** *(ôter ▸ phrase, scène)* to edit out, to cut

élagueur [elagœr] **NM** *Hort* tree-trimmer

élan[1] [elɑ̃] **NM 1** *(dans une course)* run-up, impetus; **prendre son é.** to take a run-up; **saut avec/sans é.** running/standing jump; **mal calculer son é.** to misjudge one's run-up; **d'un seul é.** *(en sautant)* at one bound; *(en courant)* in one burst; *Fig* **elle courut chez sa mère d'un seul é.** she ran all the way to her mother's without stopping

2 *(énergie)* momentum; **prendre de l'é.** to gather speed *or* momentum; *aussi Fig* **être emporté par son (propre) é.** to be carried along by one's own momentum; **emportée par son é. la voiture alla au fossé** gathering momentum, the car went into the ditch; **emporté par son é., il a tout raconté à sa mère** he got carried away and told his mother everything

3 *(impulsion)* impulse, impetus; **donner de l'é. à une campagne** to give an impetus to *or* to provide an impetus for a campaign; **donner de l'é. à l'industrie** to give a boost to industry

4 *(effusion)* outburst, surge, rush; **élans de tendresse** surges *or* rushes of affection; **é. de l'imagination** flight of fancy; **avoir des élans d'énergie** to have sudden fits *or* surges *or* bursts of activity; **é. de générosité** generous impulse; **contenir les élans du cœur** to check the impulses of one's heart; **l'é. créateur** creative drive; **l'é. patriotique/nationaliste** patriotic/nationalistic fervour; **avec é.** eagerly, keenly, enthusiastically; **dans un é. amoureux** in a surge of love; **il ne connaissait plus aucun des élans de sa jeunesse** he no longer felt the impulses of his youth

5 *(ferveur)* fervour; **parler avec é.** to speak with fervour *or* fervently

6 *(accent)* **sa voix avait des élans lyriques** his/her voice had a lyrical ring; **le violon avait des élans plaintifs** the violin had plaintive tones

7 *Golf* swing

8 *Phil* **l'é. vital** the life force

élan[2] [elɑ̃] **NM** *Zool* elk; **é. du Canada** moose

élancé, -e [elɑ̃se] **ADJ** *(silhouette, personne, arbre)* slim, slender; **à la taille élancée** slim-waisted; **à la silhouette élancée** willowy; **aux formes élancées** *(bateau, voiture)* streamlined

élancement [elɑ̃smɑ̃] **NM** sharp *or* shooting *or* stabbing pain

élancer [16] [elɑ̃se] **VI mon bras m'élance** I've got a shooting pain in my arm

VT la cathédrale élance ses flèches vers le ciel the cathedral's spires soar skywards

VPR s'élancer 1 *(courir)* to rush *or* to dash forward; **s'é. à la poursuite de qn** to dash after sb; **s'é. au secours de qn** to rush to sb's aid, to rush to help sb; **s'é. dans une course effrénée** to break into a mad dash; **s'é. sur qn** to rush *or* make a rush at sb; **le chat s'élança sur moi** the cat flew at me; **s'é. à l'assaut d'une forteresse** to launch an attack on a fortress; **s'é. à l'assaut des vagues** *(navire, surfeur)* to take to the water, *Littéraire* to brave the seas **2** *Sport* to take a run-up; **les coureurs s'élancent sur la piste** the athletes set off at a sprint **3** *Littéraire (se dresser ▸ tour, flèche)* to soar upwards; **s'é. vers le ciel** to soar skywards; *Archit* **le vaisseau de la nef s'élance vers la voûte** the nave soars up to the vaulting

élargir [32] [elarʒir] **VT 1** *(rendre moins étroit ▸ veste, robe)* to let out; *(▸ chaussure)* to stretch, to widen; *(▸ route, rue)* to widen; *(▸ tube)* to expand; *(▸ trou)* to enlarge; *(▸ propriété)* to enlarge, to extend, to add to; **le miroir élargit la pièce** the mirror makes the room look wider

2 *(connaissance, débat)* to broaden, to widen; *(groupe, gamme de produits)* to expand; **é. le cercle de ses relations** to broaden *or* to widen the circle of one's acquaintances; **é. son horizon** to broaden *or* to widen one's outlook; **é. un marché** to broaden a market

3 *(renforcer)* **le gouvernement cherche à é. sa majorité** the government is seeking to increase its majority

4 *Jur (libérer ▸ détenu)* to free, to release

VI *Fam* to get broader□, to get bigger *(across the shoulders)*□

VPR s'élargir 1 *(être moins étroit ▸ sentier, rivière, rue, route)* to widen, to get wider, to broaden (out); *(▸ sourire)* to widen; *(▸ hanches, épaules)* to broaden (out) **2** *(se relâcher ▸ vêtement)* to stretch; **le col de l'utérus s'élargit** the neck of the womb opens *or* stretches **3** *(groupe)* to expand; *(horizon, débat)* to broaden out, to widen; **le cercle de mes amis s'est élargi** my circle of friends has broadened *or* grown wider; **ses idées se sont élargies au contact des jeunes** he/she became more broadminded through being in contact with young people

élargissement [elarʒismɑ̃] **NM 1** *(agrandissement ▸ d'une route, d'une rue)* widening; *(▸ d'une robe)* letting out; *(▸ de chaussures)* stretching; *(▸ d'une propriété)* extension, enlargement **2** *(extension ▸ d'un débat)* broadening, widening; *(▸ d'un groupe, des connaissances, d'activités)* expansion; *UE* **l'é. de l'Union européenne** the enlargement *or* expansion of the EU; *Mktg* **é. du marché** market expansion **3** *Jur (libération ▸ d'un prisonnier)* freeing, release

élasticité [elastisite] **NF 1** *(extensibilité)* stretchiness, stretch, elasticity; **la ceinture a perdu toute son é.** there's no stretch left in the waistband

2 *Anat (d'un corps, de la peau)* elasticity

3 *(souplesse ▸ d'un geste)* suppleness; *(▸ d'un pas)* springiness

4 *Fig Péj (laxisme ▸ d'une conscience, d'un règlement)* accommodating nature□

5 *(variabilité)* flexibility; **l'é. de l'offre/de la demande** the elasticity of supply/of demand; **é. des prix** price elasticity

élastine [elastin] **NF** *Biol* elastin

élastique [elastik] **ADJ 1** *(ceinture, cuir, tissu)* stretchy, elastic; *(badine)* supple; **gomme é.** india rubber; **balle é.** bouncy ball

2 *(agile ▸ démarche)* springy, buoyant; **elle a un corps é.** she's got a supple body

3 *Fig Péj (peu rigoureux ▸ conscience)* accommodating□, elastic; *(règlement, principes)* flexible□, elastic

4 *(variable ▸ horaire)* flexible; *(▸ demande, offre, prix)* elastic

5 *Anat (tissu)* elastic

NM 1 *Couture* elastic **2** *(de bureau)* rubber band, *Br* elastic band **3** *(jeu)* **jouer à l'é.** to play at elastics

élastiqué, -e [elastike] **ADJ** elasticated

élastomère [elastɔmɛr] *Chim* **ADJ** elastomeric

NM elastomer

Elbe [ɛlb] **NF 1** *(fleuve)* **l'E.** the (River) Elbe **2 l'île d'E.** Elba

eldorado [ɛldɔrado] **NM** Eldorado; **il veut faire de son pays un véritable e. pour les investisseurs étrangers** he wants to turn his country into a land of opportunity for foreign investors

électeur, -trice [elɛktœr, -tris] **NM,F 1** *Pol* voter; **les électeurs** the voters, the electorate; **mes électeurs** the people who voted for me; **é. flottant** *ou* **indécis** floating voter **2** *Hist* Elector; **Électrice** Electress; **le Grand É.** the Great Elector

électif, -ive [elɛktif, -iv] **ADJ 1** *Pol* elective **2** *(douleur, traitement)* specific

élection [elɛksjɔ̃] **NF 1** *Pol (procédure)* election, polls; **procéder à une é.** to hold an election; **remporter les élections** to win the election; **annuler l'é. de qn** to unseat sb; **jour des élections** election *or* polling day; **se présenter aux élections** *Br* to stand *or Am* to run as a candidate; **élections européennes** European elections; **élections législatives** general elections; **élections municipales** = elections held every six years to elect members of the "Conseil municipal"; **é. partielle** by-election; **é. présidentielle** presidential election; **élections régionales** = elections held every six years to elect members of the "Conseil régional"; **élections sénatoriales** = elections held every three years to elect one third of the members of the "Sénat"

2 *(nomination)* election; **son é. à la présidence** his/her election as president *or* to the presidency

3 *Littéraire (choix)* choice

4 *Jur* **é. de domicile** address for service; **faire é. de domicile** to state an address for service

• **d'élection ADJ** *(choisi ▸ patrie, famille)* of (one's own) choice *or* choosing, chosen

> **ÉLECTIONS**
>
> All French citizens of 18 or over are entitled to vote in elections, which take place on a Sunday. Polling stations are often set up in local schools. Voters collect leaflets (each corresponding to the different political parties or candidates), go to a booth and put their chosen leaflet into the envelope provided, which is then placed in the ballot box ("l'urne") supervised by an "assesseur", who then utters the words "a voté!" Unlike Britain with its first-past-the-post system, the French electoral system is based on a type of proportional representation. Presidential elections and general elections take place every five years.

élective [elɛktiv] *voir* **électif**

électoral, -e, -aux, -ales [elɛktɔral, -o] **ADJ** *Pol (liste)* electoral; *(succès)* electoral, election *(avant n)*; *(campagne, promesses)* election *(avant n)*; **en période électorale** at election time; **nous avons le soutien é. des syndicats** we can rely on the union vote

électoralisme [elɛktɔralism] **NM** *Péj Pol* electioneering

électoraliste [elɛktɔralist] **ADJ** *Péj Pol (promesse, programme)* vote-catching

électorat [elɛktɔra] **NM 1** *Pol (électeurs)* electorate; **l'importance de l'é. féminin/noir** the importance of the women's/the black vote; **é. flottant** *ou* **indécis** floating voters **2** *Pol (droit de vote)* franchise **3** *Hist* electorate

Électre [elɛktr] **NPR** *Myth* Electra

électrice [elɛktris] *voir* **électeur**

électricien, -enne [elɛktrisjɛ̃, -ɛn] **NM,F 1** *(artisan)* electrician **2** *(commerçant)* electrical goods dealer

électricité [elɛktrisite] **NF 1** *(phénomène)* electricity; **é. atmosphérique** atmospherics; **é. statique** static (electricity)

2 *(installation domestique)* wiring; **faire installer l'é. dans une maison** to have a house wired; **refaire l'é. dans une maison** to rewire a house; **nous n'avons pas l'é. dans notre maison de campagne** there's no electricity in our country cottage

3 *(consommation)* electricity (bill); **payer son é.** to pay one's electricity bill

4 *Fam (tension)* tension, electricity; **il y a de l'é. dans l'air!** there's a storm brewing!

électrification [elɛktrifikasjɔ̃] **NF 1** *(d'une ligne de chemin de fer)* electrification, electrifying **2** *(d'une région)* **l'é. des campagnes reculées** bringing electricity to remote villages

électrifier [9] [elɛktrifje] **VT 1** *(ligne de chemin de fer)* to electrify **2** *(région, village)* to bring electricity to

électrique [elɛktrik] **ADJ 1** *Tech (moteur, radiateur, guitare, train, courant)* electric; *(appareil, équipement)* electric, electrical; *(système, éner-*

gie) electrical; *Fig* **atmosphère é.** highly-charged atmosphere **2** *(par l'électricité statique)* static; *Fam* **elle a les cheveux électriques** her hair is full of static □ **3** *(couleur)* **bleu é.** electric-blue

électriquement [elɛktrikmɑ̃] **ADV** electrically; **commandé é.** working off electricity

électrisant, -e [elɛktrizɑ̃, -ɑ̃t] **ADJ 1** *Tech* electrifying **2** *(exaltant)* electrifying, exciting

électrisation [elɛktrizasjɔ̃] **NF** electrifying, charging; **à é. positive** positively charged, charged with positive electricity

électriser [3] [elɛktrize] **VT 1** *Tech* to electrify, to charge; **fil électrisé** live wire **2** *Fig (stimuler)* to electrify, to rouse

électro- [elɛktrɔ] **PRÉF** electro-

électro-acousticien, -enne [elɛktroakustisjɛ̃, -ɛn] *(mpl* **électro-acousticiens,** *fpl* **électro-acousticiennes)** *Élec* **ADJ** electroacoustics *(avant n)*

NM,F electroacoustics expert

électroaimant [elɛktrɔɛmɑ̃] **NM** *Élec* electromagnet

électrocardiogramme [elɛktrɔkardjɔgram] **NM** *Méd* electrocardiogram

électrocardiographe [elɛktrɔkardjɔgraf] **NM** *Méd* electrocardiograph

électrocardiographie [elɛktrɔkardjɔgrafi] **NF** *Méd* electrocardiography

électrochimie [elɛktrɔʃimi] **NF** electrochemistry

électrochimique [elɛktrɔʃimik] **ADJ** electrochemical

électrochoc [elɛktrɔʃɔk] **NM** *Méd* electric shock *(for therapeutic purposes)*; **(traitement par) électrochocs** electroconvulsive *or* electroshock therapy; **faire des électrochocs à qn** to give sb electroconvulsive therapy

électrocuter [3] [elɛktrɔkyte] **VT** to electrocute; **se faire é.** to be electrocuted

VPR s'électrocuter to electrocute oneself, to be electrocuted; **attention, on peut s'é.** careful, you could get a fatal (electric) shock; **il a failli s'é.** he got a very bad electric shock

électrocution [elɛktrɔkysjɔ̃] **NF** electrocution; **vous risquez l'é.** you're at risk *or* in danger of being electrocuted

électrode [elɛktrɔd] **NF** *Élec & Chim* electrode; **é. de masse** earth electrode

électrodomestique [elɛktrɔdɔmɛstik] **ADJ appareils électrodomestiques** household electrical appliances, *Am* electricals

NM l'é. *(appareils)* household electrical appliances, *Am* electricals; *(secteur)* electrical goods, *Am* electricals

électrodynamique [elɛktrɔdinamik] *Phys* **ADJ** electrodynamic

NF electrodynamics *(singulier)*

électroencéphalogramme [elɛktrɔɑ̃sefalɔgram] **NM** *Méd* electroencephalogram

électroencéphalographie [elɛktrɔɑ̃sefalɔgrafi] **NF** *Méd* electroencephalography

électrogène [elɛktrɔʒɛn] **ADJ 1** *Ich* electric; **organe é.** *(d'un poisson)* electric organ **2** *Élec* electricity-generating

électroluminescent, -e [elɛktrɔlyminesɑ̃, -ɑ̃t] **ADJ** *Phys* electroluminescent

électrolyse [elɛktrɔliz] **NF** *Chim & Méd* electrolysis

électrolyser [3] [elɛktrɔlize] **VT** *Chim* to electrolyse

électrolyte [elɛktrɔlit] **NM** *Chim* electrolyte

électrolytique [elɛktrɔlitik] **ADJ** *Chim* electrolytic

électromagnétique [elɛktrɔmaɲetik] **ADJ** *Phys* electromagnetic

électromagnétisme [elɛktrɔmaɲetism] **NM** *Phys* electromagnetism

électromécanicien, -enne [elɛktrɔmekanisjɛ̃, -ɛn] **NM,F** electrical engineer

électromécanique [elɛktrɔmekanik] *Élec* **ADJ** electromechanical

NF electromechanical engineering

électroménager [elɛktrɔmenaʒe] **ADJ** *(domestic or household)* electrical; **appareils électroménagers** domestic *or* household appliances, *Am* electricals

NM l'é. *(appareils)* domestic *or* household electrical appliances; *(secteur)* the domestic *or* household electrical appliance industry; **le petit é.** small household appliances

électrométallurgie [elɛktrɔmetalyrʒi] **NF** *Métal* electrometallurgy

électrométallurgique [elɛktrɔmetalyrʒik] **ADJ** *Métal* electrometallurgical

électromètre [elɛktrɔmɛtr] **NM** electrometer

électromoteur, -trice [elɛktrɔmɔtœr, -tris] *Élec & Tech* **ADJ** electromotive

NM electric motor

électron [elɛktrɔ̃] **NM** *Phys* electron; **é. célibataire** lone electron; **é. libre** free electron; *Fig* maverick; **é. lié** bound electron; **é. négatif** negatron; **é. positif** positron

électronégatif, -ive [elɛktrɔnegatif, -iv] **ADJ** *Chim* electronegative

électronicien, -enne [elɛktrɔnisjɛ̃, -ɛn] **NM,F** electronics engineer; **ingénieur é.** electronics engineer

électronique [elɛktrɔnik] **ADJ 1** *Électron (équipement)* electronic; *(microscope, télescope)* electron *(avant n)*; *(industrie)* electronics *(avant n)*

2 *(de l'électron ▸ flux, faisceau)* electron *(avant n)*

3 *Mus* electronic

4 *(réservation, traitement de données, point de vente, argent)* electronic

NF electronics *(singulier)*; **l'é. grand public** the consumer electronics industry; **é. aérospatiale** avionics *(singulier)*

électroniquement [elɛktrɔnikmɑ̃] **ADV** electronically

électronucléaire [elɛktrɔnykleɛr] **ADJ** *(centrale, industrie)* nuclear *(avant n)*; **énergie é.** nuclear power

NM nuclear energy production

électronvolt [elɛktrɔ̃vɔlt] **NM** *Phys* electronvolt

électrophone [elɛktrɔfɔn] **NM** record player

électropositif, -ive [elɛktrɔpozitif, -iv] **ADJ** *Chim* electropositive

électroscope [elɛktrɔskɔp] **NM** *Élec* electroscope

électrosensible [elɛktrɔsɑ̃sibl] **ADJ** *Élec* electrosensitive

électrostatique [elɛktrɔstatik] *Phys* **ADJ** electrostatic

NF electrostatics *(singulier)*

électrotechnique [elɛktrɔtɛknik] **ADJ** electrotechnical

NF electrotechnics *(singulier)*, electrical engineering

électrothérapie [elɛktrɔterapi] **NF** *Méd (pratique)* electrotherapy; *(étude)* electrotherapeutics *(singulier)*

électrovalve [elɛktrɔvalv] **NF** *Tech* electromagnetic valve; *Aut* solenoid; **é. de starter** starter solenoid

électrovanne [elɛktrɔvan] **NF** *Tech* electrical solenoid, solenoid valve

élégamment [elegamɑ̃] **ADV** *(s'habiller)* elegantly, smartly; *(maquillée)* smartly; *(écrire, parler)* stylishly, elegantly; *(agir)* courteously; **coiffée é.** with an elegant *or* smart hairstyle

élégance [elegɑ̃s] **NF 1** *(chic)* elegance, smartness; **s'habiller avec é.** to dress elegantly *or* smartly

2 *(délicatesse ▸ d'un geste, d'un procédé)* elegance; *(▸ d'une méthode, d'une solution)* neatness; **savoir perdre avec é.** to be a good *or* graceful loser; **elle a eu l'é. de ne pas protester** she had the courtesy not to protest

3 *(harmonie)* grace, elegance, harmoniousness; **l'é. du chat siamois** the elegance *or* grace of a Siamese cat

4 *(d'un style littéraire)* elegance; *(tournure)* elegant *or* well-turned phrase; *Péj* **style plein d'élégances** over-ornate style

élégant, -e [elegɑ̃, -ɑ̃t] **ADJ 1** *(chic ▸ personne, mobilier, vêtement, restaurant, style)* elegant, smart, stylish **2** *(courtois ▸ procédé, excuse)* handsome, graceful; *(geste, comportement)* courteous; **c'était une façon élégante de me dire que...** it was a polite *or* diplomatic way of telling me that... **3** *(harmonieux ▸ architecture, proportions)* elegant, harmonious, graceful; *(▸ démonstration)* elegant, neat; *(▸ méthode, solution)* neat

NM,F *Vieilli (homme)* dandy; *(femme)* elegant *or* smart woman; **vouloir faire l'é.** to try to look fashionable

élégiaque [eleʒjak] **ADJ 1** *Littérature* elegiac **2** *Littéraire (mélancolique)* melancholy

élégie [eleʒi] **NF 1** *Antiq* elegy **2** *Littérature (poème, œuvre)* elegy, lament

ÉLÉMENT [elemɑ̃]

- component **1**
- element **1–5**
- cell **5**
- item **9**
- ingredient **1**
- factor **2**
- unit **6, 8**

NM 1 *(partie ▸ d'un parfum, d'une œuvre)* component, ingredient, constituent; *(▸ d'une structure, un problème)* element, component, constituent; *(▸ d'un médicament)* ingredient; **les éléments d'un ensemble** the elements *or* parts of a whole; *Aut* **é. filtrant en papier** paper filtering element; *Ordinat* **é. de menu** menu item; *Tech* **é. mobile** working part; *Électron* **é. de calculateur** *ou* **de calculatrice** *ou* **électronique** computer unit; *Tech* **é. chauffant** heating unit *or* element

2 *(donnée)* element, factor, fact; **éléments** data, information; **l'é. décisif** the deciding factor; **éléments d'information** facts, information; **j'apporte un é. nouveau au dossier** I have new material to add to the file; **aucun é. nouveau à signaler** nothing new to report; **d'après les premiers éléments de l'enquête** according to the initial findings of the inquiry

3 *(personne)* element; **des éléments étrangers se sont infiltrés dans le mouvement** foreign elements have infiltrated the movement; **éléments indésirables** undesirable elements, undesirables; **l'é. féminin** the female element *or* contingent; **l'é. féminin est faiblement représenté dans cette société** there are few women in the company; **c'est un des meilleurs éléments de mon service** he's one of the best people in my department; **il y a de bons éléments dans ma classe** there are some good students in my class

4 *Chim* element; **l'é. oxygène** the element oxygen; **é. radioactif** radioactive element

5 *Élec (de pile, d'accumulateur)* cell; *(de bouilloire, de radiateur)* element; **batterie de cinq éléments** five-cell battery

6 *(de mobilier)* **é. (de cuisine)** kitchen unit; **éléments préfabriqués** prefabricated *or* ready-made units; **éléments de rangement** storage units

7 *(milieu)* element; **l'é. liquide** water; **les quatre éléments** the four elements; **lutter contre les éléments (naturels)** to struggle against the elements; **être dans son é.** to be in one's element; **je ne me sens pas dans mon é. ici** I don't feel at home *or* I feel like a fish out of water here

8 *Mil* unit; **éléments blindés/motorisés** armoured/motorized units; *Mil* **é. de tir** piece of firing *or* range data

9 *Compta (d'un compte)* item

• **éléments NMPL 1** *(notions)* elements, basic principles; **j'en suis resté aux premiers éléments de latin** I've never had more than an elementary knowledge of Latin; **'Éléments de géométrie'** 'Elementary Geometry' **2** *Biol* **éléments figurés du sang** formed elements of blood

élémentaire [elemɑ̃tɛr] **ADJ 1** *(facile ▸ exercice)* elementary; **c'est é.!** it's elementary!

2 *(fondamental ▸ notion, principe)* basic, elementary; *(▸ habitation)* basic, rudimentary; **c'est la politesse la plus é.** it's only common courtesy

3 *Chim & Phys (relatif à un élément chimique)* elemental; *(relatif à une analyse chimique, à une particule d'atome)* elementary

4 *Scol* primary, *Am* elementary

éléphant [elefɑ̃] **NM** *Zool* elephant; **é. mâle/femelle** bull/cow elephant; **é. d'Asie/d'Afrique** Indian/African elephant; **é. de mer** sea elephant,

elephant seal; **comme un é. dans un magasin de porcelaine** like a bull in a china shop

éléphanteau, -x [elefɑ̃to] **NM** *Zool* elephant calf; *(très jeune)* baby elephant

éléphantesque [elefɑ̃tɛsk] **ADJ** *Fam* elephantine, colossal, mammoth

éléphantiasis [elefɑ̃tjazis] **NM** *Méd* elephantiasis

élevage [ɛlvaʒ] **NM** *Agr & Écon* **1** *(activité)* animal husbandry, breeding *or* rearing (of animals); **l'é.** stock breeding; **faire de l'é.** to breed animals; **é. de poulets/volaille** chicken/poultry farming; **é. des animaux à fourrure** fur farming; **é. intensif/en batterie** intensive/battery farming; **é. des bovins** cattle-rearing; **é. des chevaux** horse-breeding; **é. industriel** factory farming; **é. des lapins** rabbit-breeding; **é. des moutons** sheep-farming **2** *(entreprise)* farm, *Br* (stock) farm, *Am* ranch, *Austr* station; **un é. de vers à soie/de visons** a silkworm/mink farm; **un é. de porcs** a pig farm **3** *(en œnologie)* élevage *(stage in the wine-producing process between fermentation and bottling)*

• **d'élevage ADJ 1** *(poulet)* battery-reared **2** *(région)* **pays d'é.** *(bovin)* cattle-rearing country; *(ovin)* sheep-farming country

élévateur, -trice [elevatœr, -tris] **ADJ 1** *Anat* elevator *(avant n)*; **muscle é.** elevator **2** *Tech (appareil, matériel)* lifting *(avant n)*

NM 1 *Anat* elevator

2 *(en manutention)* elevator, hoist; **é. (à fourche)** fork-lift truck; **é. à bascule** tip; **é. à augets** *ou* **à godets** bucket elevator

3 *Élec* **é. de tension** step-up transformer

4 *Can Joual (ascenseur) Br* lift☐, *Am* elevator☐

élévation [elevasjɔ̃] **NF 1** *(action d'élever ▸ d'un mur, de la voix etc)* raising; *(▸ de la température, des prix etc)* raising, increasing; *(▸ d'une statue etc)* erection, setting up

2 *(augmentation)* rise; *(de la température, des prix etc)* rise, increase (**de** in); **é. du niveau de vie** rise in the standard of living; **é. du pouls** quickening of the pulse

3 *Math* **é. d'un nombre au carré** squaring of a number; **é. d'un nombre à une puissance** raising a number to a power

4 *Archit (construction)* erection, putting up; *(plan, projection)* elevation; *(tertre)* rise (in the ground), mound

5 *(promotion)* raising; **l'é. à la dignité de...** being elevated to the rank of...

6 *(noblesse ▸ de style)* elevation; *(▸ des sentiments, du caractère)* nobility; **é. d'âme** *ou* **d'esprit** high-mindedness; **lire Platon contribue à l'é. de l'esprit** reading Plato improves the mind

7 *Rel* **l'É. (de l'hostie)** *(moment, geste)* the Elevation *(of the Host)*

élévatoire [elevatwar] **ADJ** lifting *(avant n)*, hoisting *(avant n)*, elevator *(avant n)*

élévatrice [elevatris] *voir* **élévateur**

élève [elɛv] **NMF 1** *Scol (enfant)* pupil; *(adolescent)* student; **é. infirmière** student nurse; **é. pilote** trainee pilot; **é. professeur** student *or* trainee teacher

2 *(disciple)* disciple, pupil

3 *Mil* cadet; **é. officier** officer cadet *(in the Merchant Navy)*; **é. officier de réserve** military cadet

4 *Agr* young stock animal

5 *Hort* seedling

élevé, -e [elve] **ADJ 1** *(fort ▸ prix, niveau de vie)* high; **le nombre é. des victimes** the high number of victims; **taux peu é.** low rate; **pouls é.** rapid pulse

2 *(étage)* high; *(arbre, montagne)* tall

3 *(important ▸ position)* high, high-ranking; *(▸ rang, condition)* high, elevated; **de rang é.** high-ranking; **l'officier ayant le grade le plus é.** the senior *or* highest-ranking officer; **il occupe un rang é. dans ce parti** he ranks high in the party

4 *Littéraire (noble ▸ inspiration, style)* elevated, noble, lofty; **un sens é. du devoir** a strong sense of duty

5 *(éduqué)* **bien é.** well-mannered, well-bred, well brought-up; **mal é.** bad-mannered, ill-mannered, rude; **c'est très mal é. de répondre** it's very rude *or* it's bad manners to answer back; **c'est un mal é., ce garçon** he has bad manners, that boy

ÉLEVER [19] [elve]

VT	
• to bring up **1**	• to raise **1–8, 10**
• to breed **2**	• to erect **4**
• to elevate **8, 9**	
VPR	
• to rise **1, 4, 6**	• to soar **3**
• to arise **5**	• to add up to **7**

VT 1 *(éduquer ▸ enfant)* to bring up, to raise; **nous avons été élevés ensemble** we were brought up *or* raised together; *Fig* **é. qn dans du coton** to overprotect sb, to mollycoddle sb; **bébé élevé au sein/au biberon** breast-/bottle-fed baby

2 *Agr (nourrir ▸ bétail)* to breed, to raise; *(▸ chevaux)* to rear, to breed; *(▸ moutons, chiens, lapins)* to breed; *(▸ abeilles, volaille)* to keep

3 *(hisser ▸ fardeau)* to raise, to lift (up)

4 *(dresser ▸ statue, monument, chapiteau)* to erect, to raise, to put up; *(▸ les bras, le poing, les yeux)* to raise; *Fig* **é. des autels à qn** to praise sb to the skies

5 *(rehausser ▸ immeuble, mur etc)* to raise, to make higher; *(▸ plafond, plancher)* to raise

6 *(augmenter ▸ niveau, volume)* to raise; *(▸ prix, température)* to increase, to raise; **é. la voix** *ou* **le ton** to raise one's voice

7 *(manifester ▸ objection, protestation)* to raise; *(▸ critique)* to make

8 *(promouvoir)* to elevate, to raise; *(porter à un rang supérieur)* to promote (**au rang de** to); **é. qn au grade d'officier** to promote *or* to raise sb to (the rank of) officer

9 *(ennoblir)* to elevate, to uplift; **une lecture qui élève l'esprit** an elevating *or* uplifting read; **é. le débat** to raise the tone of the debate

10 *Géom* **é. une perpendiculaire** to raise a perpendicular; *Math* **é. un nombre au carré/cube** to square/to cube a number; **é. un nombre à la puissance 3** to raise a number to the power of 3

VPR s'élever 1 *(augmenter ▸ taux, niveau, prix)* to rise, to go up; **la température s'est élevée de 10 degrés** the temperature has risen by *or* has gone up 10 degrees

2 *(se manifester)* **on entend s'é. des voix** you can hear voices being raised; **un cri s'éleva** a shout went up; **s'é. contre** *(protester contre)* to rise up against; *(s'opposer à)* to oppose

3 *(monter ▸ oiseau)* to soar, to fly *or* to go up, to ascend; *(▸ cerf-volant)* to go up, to soar

4 *(être dressé ▸ falaise, tour)* to rise; *(▸ mur, barricades)* to stand; **là où s'élève maintenant l'école** where the school now stands

5 *(paraître ▸ doutes, difficultés)* to arise

6 *Fig (moralement, socialement)* to rise; **s'é. à force de travail** to work one's way up; **s'é. socialement** to climb the social ladder; **s'é. au-dessus de** *(jalousies, passions, préjugés)* to rise above; **s'é. au-dessus de sa condition** to rise above one's condition; **votre âme s'élèvera par des prières constantes** your soul will be elevated by constant prayer; **des lectures qui permettent à l'âme de s'é.** spiritually uplifting reading matter

7 s'é. à *(facture, bénéfices, pertes)* to add up to, to total, to amount to; **la note s'élève à 300 euros** the bill comes to *or* amounts to 300 euros; **le bilan s'élève à 10 morts et 12 blessés** the number of casualties is 10 dead and 12 injured

éleveur, -euse [elvœr, -øz] *Agr* **NM,F** stockbreeder; **é. de bétail** cattle breeder *or* farmer, *Am* cattle rancher; **é. de chevaux/chiens** horse/dog breeder; **é. de moutons/poulets/volaille** sheep/chicken/poultry farmer

• **éleveuse NF éleveuse à poussins** brooder

elfe [ɛlf] **NM** elf, spirit of the air

élider [3] [elide] *Ling* **VT** to drop, *Spéc* to elide

VPR s'élider to be dropped, to disappear, *Spéc* to elide

éligibilité [eliʒibilite] **NF** *Pol* eligibility

éligible [eliʒibl] **ADJ** *Pol* eligible

élimé, -e [elime] **ADJ** worn, threadbare

élimer [3] [elime] **VT** to wear thin

VPR s'élimer to wear thin, to become threadbare

élimination [eliminasjɔ̃] **NF 1** *Physiol* eliminating, voiding, expelling **2** *(exclusion)* elimination, eliminating, excluding; **procéder par é.** to use a process of elimination; **en procédant par é.** by a process of elimination; *Ind* **é. des déchets** waste disposal

éliminatoire [eliminatwar] **ADJ** *(note, épreuve)* eliminatory; *(condition, vote)* disqualifying; **cinq est une note é.** five counts as a fail; **il a eu une note é.** he didn't get a *Br* pass mark *or Am* passing grade

NF *(souvent pl) Sport* preliminary heat

éliminer [3] [elimine] **VT 1** *(se débarrasser de)* to remove, to get rid of; *Physiol (déchets, urine)* to void, to expel; **é. les kilos en trop** to get rid of excess weight

2 *Sport* to eliminate, to knock out; **ils ont tous été éliminés pour dopage** they were all disqualified for drug-taking

3 *(rejeter ▸ hypothèse, théorie, possibilité)* to rule out, to eliminate; *(▸ candidat, suspect)* to eliminate; **é. un nom d'une liste** to strike *or* to cross a name off a list; **se faire é.** to be eliminated; **être éliminé** *(candidat)* to be knocked out *or* eliminated

4 *(tuer)* to eliminate, to liquidate

5 *Math* to eliminate

USAGE ABSOLU *Physiol* to get rid of *or* eliminate body wastes; **il faut boire pour é.** you have to drink to clean out your system

élire [106] [elir] **VT 1** *Pol (candidat, représentant)* to elect; **é. un député** ≃ to elect *or* to return a Member of Parliament; **être élu à une assemblée** to be elected to an assembly; **é. un nouveau président** to elect *or* to vote in a new president; **é. qn président** to elect sb president, to vote sb in as president **2** *Littéraire (choisir)* to elect, to choose; **é. qn pour confident** to choose sb as one's confidant **3** *(locution)* **é. domicile à** to take up residence *or* to make one's home in; *Jur* to elect domicile in; **une souris a élu domicile dans notre grenier** a mouse has moved into *or* taken up residence in our attic

élisabéthain, -e [elizabetɛ̃, -ɛn] **ADJ** Elizabethan

• **Élisabéthain, -e NM,F** Elizabethan

élisait *etc voir* **élire**

élision [elizjɔ̃] **NF** *Ling* elision; **il y a é. du "e"** the "e" elides

élite [elit] **NF 1** *(groupe)* elite; **une é.** an elite; **l'é. de** the elite *or* cream of; **l'é. de la haute couture** top fashion designers; **les élites** the élite **2** *Suisse Mil* = section of the Swiss army for reservists aged between 20 and 42 (before 1996, between 20 and 32)

• **d'élite ADJ** elite *(avant n)*, top *(avant n)*; **personnel d'é.** select *or* hand-picked personnel; *Mil* **régiment/tireur d'é.** crack regiment/shot

élitisme [elitism] **NM** elitism

élitiste [elitist] **ADJ** elitist

NMF elitist

élixir [eliksir] **NM 1** *Myth & Pharm* elixir; **é. d'amour/de longue vie** elixir of love/life; **é. parégorique** paregoric (elixir) **2** *Arch (quintessence)* quintessence, substance

elle [ɛl] *(pl* **elles***)* **PRON 1** *(sujet d'un verbe ▸ personne)* she; *(▸ chose)* it; *(▸ animal de compagnie, bébé, nation)* she, it; **elles** they; **e. chante** she sings; **elles dansent** they dance; **eh bien, ta cousine, e. n'est pas près de me revoir** well, your cousin isn't likely to see me again in a hurry; **e. arrivée, la fête a pu commencer** once she had arrived the party was able to start; **e., e. n'aurait même pas levé le petit doigt** she wouldn't have lifted a finger; **e., se marier? tu ne la connais pas!** her get married? you don't know her!; **qui a fait ça? – c'est e.** who did that? – she did *or* her; **ah!, e. est bien bonne, celle-là!** that's a good one!

2 *(emphatique ▸ dans une interrogation)* **ta mère est-e. rentrée?** has your mother come back?; **Sophie a-t-e. appelé?** has Sophie called?; **la télévision est-e. toujours en panne?** is the television still not working?

3 *(emphatique ▸ avec "qui" et "que")* **c'est e. qui est partie la première** she left first; **c'est e. qui me l'a dit** she's the one who told me, it was she who told me; **ce sont elles qui ont voulu partir** they were the ones who wanted to leave, it was they who wanted to leave; **c'est à e. qu'il veut avoir affaire** it's her he wants to talk to; **c'est à e. de dire si**

e. veut venir it's up to her to say if she wants to come or not

4 *(complément ▸ personne)* her; *(▸ animal, chose)* it; *(▸ animal de compagnie, bébé, nation)* her, it; **elles** them; **je suis content d'e./d'elles** I am pleased with her/them; **dites-le-lui à e.** tell it to her, tell her it; **ce n'est pas à moi, c'est à e.** it's not mine, it's hers; **e. possède une entreprise à e.** she has her own company; **je l'ai entendu dire par une relation à e.** I heard it from a relation of hers; **il n'aime qu'e.** he loves only her; **e. ne pense qu'à e.** she thinks only of herself; **il aimait sa patrie et mourut pour e.** he loved his country and died for it; **et e., tu l'oublies?** and are you forgetting HER?; **tu la connais, e.?** do you know her?; **tu les imagines, e. et lui, sur des skis!** imagine the pair of them on skis!

5 *(dans les comparaisons)* **il est mieux qu'e.** he is better than she is *or* than her; **il boit plus qu'e.** he drinks more than she does *or* than her; **je fais comme e.** I do what she does

ellébore [elebɔr] = **hellébore**

elle-même [elmɛm] **PRON** *(désignant une personne)* herself; *(désignant une chose)* itself; *(désignant un bébé, un animal, une nation)* itself, herself; **elles-mêmes** themselves; **mais e. n'est pas sans défauts** but she's no paragon herself; **c'est e. qui me l'a dit** she told me so herself, she herself told me so

elles [ɛl] *voir* **elle**

ellipse [elips] **NF 1** *Math* ellipse **2** *Ling* ellipsis; **parler par ellipses** *(allusivement)* to hint at things, to express oneself elliptically

ellipsoïdal, -e, -aux, -ales [elipsɔidal, -o] **ADJ** *Géom* ellipsoidal

ellipsoïde [elipsɔid] *Géom* **ADJ** ellipsoidal

NM ellipsoid

elliptique [eliptik] **ADJ 1** *Math* elliptic, elliptical **2** *Ling* elliptical

elliptiquement [eliptikmɑ̃] **ADV** elliptically

élocution [elɔkysjɔ̃] **NF 1** *(débit)* delivery; *(diction)* diction, elocution; **avoir une é. claire** to have clear diction, to enunciate clearly; **avoir une é. trop rapide** to speak too quickly **2** *Belg Scol (exposé)* talk, presentation

éloge [elɔʒ] **NM 1** *(compliment)* praise; **couvrir qn d'éloges** to shower sb with praise; **digne d'éloges** praiseworthy; **faire l'é. de** to speak highly of *or* in praise of; **faire son propre é.** to sing one's own praises, to blow one's own *Br* trumpet *or Am* horn **2** *Littéraire (panégyrique)* eulogy; **faire l'é. d'un écrivain** to eulogize a writer; **é. funèbre** eulogy, funeral oration; **prononcer l'é. funèbre de qn** to deliver a eulogy *or* funeral oration in praise of sb

• **à l'éloge de PRÉP** (much) to the credit of; **il fait du bénévolat et c'est tout à son é.** to his credit, he does volunteer work; **c'est tout à votre é. d'avoir accepté** it's to your credit that you accepted

élogieuse [elɔʒjøz] *voir* **élogieux**

élogieusement [elɔʒjøzmɑ̃] **ADV** highly, favourably; **il a décrit é. leur demeure** he was full of praise for their house

élogieux, -euse [elɔʒjø, -øz] **ADJ** laudatory, complimentary, eulogistic; **parler en termes é. de** to speak very highly of, to be full of praise for

éloigné, -e [elwaɲe] **ADJ 1** *(loin de tout ▸ province, village)* distant, remote, faraway

2 *(distant)* **la ville est très éloignée** the town is a long way away *or* off, the town is very far away; **la ville est éloignée de cinq kilomètres** the town is five kilometres away; **les deux villes sont éloignées de 50 kilomètres** the two towns are 50 kilometres apart; **maintenant que tout danger est é.** now that there is no further risk, now that the danger is past; **le point le plus é.** the furthest *or* furthermost point; **maison éloignée de la gare** house a long way from the station; **rien ne me tiendra é. de toi** nothing will keep me away from you; **se tenir é. du feu** to keep away from the fire; **se tenir é. de la politique** to keep away from *or* to steer clear of politics; **je ne suis plus é. de croire que…** I'm coming round to believe that *or* to the belief that…

3 *(dans le temps)* distant, remote, far-off; **notre mariage est encore à une date éloignée** our wedding is still a long way off; **tout cela me semble si é. maintenant** all this seems so distant *or* far away now; **dans un passé/avenir pas si é. que ça** in the not-too-distant past/future

4 *(par la parenté)* distant; **nous sommes parents éloignés** we're distantly related; **nous sommes cousins éloignés** we're distant cousins *or* cousins several times removed

5 *(différent)* **é. de** far removed *or* very different from; **rien n'est plus é. de ma pensée** nothing could be *or* nothing is further from my thoughts

éloignement [elwaɲmɑ̃] **NM 1** *(distance dans l'espace)* distance, remoteness; *(dans le temps)* remoteness; **l'é. du village ne facilite pas l'organisation des secours** the remoteness of the village makes rescue work more difficult; **l'é. de nos deux bureaux ne favorise pas la communication** the distance between our two offices does not help communication; **avec l'é. on arrive mieux à comprendre ce qui s'est passé** with the benefit of hindsight *or* the passage of time it is easier to understand what happened **2** *(fait d'être éloigné)* absence; **l'é. est difficile à vivre** it is difficult to be apart *or* separated; **l'é. de la vie politique m'a fait réfléchir** being away from politics made me do some thinking **3** *(mise à distance)* taking away, removing, removal; **le tribunal a ordonné l'é. de mes enfants** the court has ordered that my children be taken away from me

éloigner [3] [elwaɲe] **VT 1** *(mettre loin ▸ dans l'espace)* to move *or* to take away; **é. sa chaise de la table** to move one's chair away from the table; **é. qn du feu/de la voiture** to move sb away from the fire/car; **ce trajet nous éloigne du centre ville** this route takes us away from the centre of town; **ça nous éloignerait du sujet** that would take us away from the point

2 *(dans le temps)* **chaque jour m'éloigne un peu plus de cette époque** that time recedes with each day that passes

3 *(séparer)* **é. qn de** to take sb away from; **mon travail m'a éloigné de ma famille** my work's kept me away from my family; **elle a tout fait pour l'é. de moi** she tried everything to take him/her away from me; **tes parents cherchent à m'é. de toi** your parents are trying to keep me away from you; **é. qn du pouvoir** to keep sb out of power

4 *(repousser ▸ insectes, bêtes féroces, mauvaises odeurs)* to keep off, to keep at bay

5 *(dissiper ▸ idée, souvenir)* to banish, to dismiss; *(▸ danger)* to ward off; **é. les soupçons de qn** to avert suspicion from sb; **é. une crainte/une pensée** to banish a fear/dismiss a thought

6 *(reporter ▸ échéance)* to postpone, to put off

VPR s'éloigner 1 *(partir ▸ tempête, nuages, orage)* to pass, to go away; *(▸ véhicule)* to move away (**de** from); *(▸ personne)* to go away (**de** from); **les bruits de pas s'éloignèrent** the footsteps grew fainter; **s'é. à la hâte** to hurry away; **ne vous éloignez pas trop, les enfants** don't go too far (away), children; **éloignez-vous du bord de la falaise** move away *or* get back from the edge of the cliff; **j'ai fait s'é. les enfants de la fenêtre** I told the children to come away from the window; *Fig* **s'é. du sujet** to wander away from *or* off the point

2 *(s'estomper ▸ souvenir, rêve)* to grow more distant *or* remote; *(▸ crainte)* to go away; *(▸ danger)* to pass

3 *(s'isoler)* to move *or* to grow away; **s'é. du monde des affaires** to move away from *or* to abandon one's involvement with the world of business; **s'é. de tout le monde** to distance oneself from everybody

4 *(se détourner)* **s'é. de la réalité** to lose touch with reality; **s'é. de la vérité** to stray *or* to wander from the truth; **s'é. de son devoir** to neglect one's duty

5 *(affectivement)* **s'é. de qn** to grow away from sb; **il la sentait qui s'éloignait de lui** he could feel that she was growing away from him *or* becoming more and more distant; **il s'est lentement éloigné de nous** he slowly drifted away from us; **peu à peu ils se sont éloignés l'un de l'autre** they gradually drifted apart

6 *(dans le temps)* **plus on s'éloigne de cette période…** the more distant that period becomes…

élongation [elɔ̃gasjɔ̃] **NF 1** *Méd (d'un muscle)* strained *or* pulled muscle; *(d'un ligament)* pulled ligament; **se faire une é.** *(d'un muscle)* to strain *or* to pull a muscle; *(d'un ligament)* to pull a ligament **2** *Phys* displacement **3** *Astron* elongation

éloquemment [elɔkamɑ̃] **ADV** eloquently

éloquence [elɔkɑ̃s] **NF 1** *(art de parler)* eloquence, fine oratory **2** *(expressivité)* eloquence, expressiveness; **avec é.** eloquently **3** *(persuasion)* persuasiveness, eloquence

éloquent, -e [elɔkɑ̃, -ɑ̃t] **ADJ 1** *(parlant bien)* eloquent; **il est très é.** he's a fine speaker **2** *(convaincant ▸ paroles)* eloquent, persuasive; *(▸ chiffres, réaction)* eloquent **3** *(expressif)* eloquent, expressive; **le geste était très é.** the gesture said it all; **ces images sont éloquentes** these pictures speak volumes *or* for themselves; **52 à 0, le score est é.** 52 nil: the score speaks for itself

élu, -e [ely] **PP** *voir* **élire**

ADJ 1 *Rel* chosen **2** *Pol* elected; **président é.** president elect

NM,F 1 *Pol (député)* elected representative; *(conseiller)* elected representative, councillor; **les élus locaux** local councillors **2** *Hum (bien-aimé)* **qui est l'heureux é.?** who's the lucky man?; **l'é. de mon/ton cœur** my/your beloved **3** *Rel* **les élus** the chosen ones, the elect

élucidation [elysidasjɔ̃] **NF** elucidation

élucider [3] [elyside] **VT** *(mystère)* to elucidate, to explain, to clear up; *(problème, texte)* to elucidate, to clarify

élucubrations [elykybrasjɔ̃] **NFPL** *Péj Littéraire* ravings, rantings

élucubrer [3] [elykybre] **VT** *Péj Littéraire* to dream up

éluder [3] [elyde] **VT** to elude, to evade; **é. le paiement de l'impôt** to evade payment of tax

élusif, -ive [elyzif, -iv] **ADJ** elusive

élut *etc voir* **élire**

Élysée [elize] **NM 1** *Myth* Elysium **2** *Pol* **(le palais de) l'É.** the Élysée Palace *(the official residence of the French President)*

> **L'ÉLYSÉE**
>
> This eighteenth-century palace near the Champs-Élysées in Paris is the official residence of the French President. The name is often used to refer to the presidency itself.

élyséen, -enne [elizeɛ̃, -ɛn] **ADJ 1** *Myth* Elysian **2** *Pol* of/from the Élysée Palace, presidential

émaciation [emasjasjɔ̃] **NF** emaciation

émacié, -e [emasje] **ADJ** emaciated, wasted

émacier [9] [emasje] **VT** to emaciate

VPR s'émacier to become emaciated *or* wasted

e-mail [imɛl] *(pl* **e-mails)** **NM** *Ordinat* e-mail; **envoyer qch par e.** to send sth by e-mail; **envoyer un e. à qn** to e-mail sb

émail [emaj] *(pl sens* **1, 2 émaux** [emo], *pl sens* **3 émails)** **NM 1** *(matière)* enamel; *Cér (sur porcelaine)* glaze **2** *(objet)* piece of enamelware *or* enamelwork **3** *Anat* enamel

• **émaux NMPL** coloured enamels; **faire des émaux** to do enamel work

• **d'émail, en émail ADJ** enamel *(avant n)*, enamelled

émaillage [emajaʒ] **NM 1** *(en décoration)* enamelling **2** *Cér* glazing

émailler [3] [emaje] **VT 1** *(en décoration)* to enamel; **émaillé au four** stove-enamelled **2** *Cér (porcelaine)* to glaze **3** *(parsemer)* to dot, to scatter, to speckle; **le pré est émaillé de coquelicots** the field is scattered *or* dotted *or* speckled with poppies; **é. un discours de citations** to pepper *or* to sprinkle a speech with quotations; **texte émaillé de métaphores** text littered with *or* full of metaphors; **une lettre émaillée de fautes** a letter riddled with mistakes; **un ciel émaillé d'étoiles** a star-studded sky

émailleur, -euse [emajœr, -øz] **NM,F** enamel worker

émaillure [emajyr] **NF** enamelling, enamel work

émanation [emanasjɔ̃] **NF** *(expression)* expression; **l'é. de la volonté populaire** the expression of the people's will; **être l'é. de qch** to emanate from sth

• **émanations** NFPL *(vapeurs)* smells, emanations; **des émanations de gaz** a smell of gas; **émanations pestilentielles** miasmas, foul emanations; **émanations volcaniques** volatiles; **émanations toxiques** toxic fumes

émancipateur, -trice [emɑ̃sipatœr, -tris] ADJ emancipatory, liberating
NM,F emancipator, liberator

émancipation [emɑ̃sipasjɔ̃] NF **1** *(libération ▸ gén)* emancipation; *(▸ de la femme)* emancipation, liberation; *Fig (▸ de l'esprit, de la pensée etc)* liberation, freeing **2** *Jur* emancipation

émancipatrice [emɑ̃sipatris] *voir* **émancipateur**

émancipé, -e [emɑ̃sipe] ADJ *(peuple)* emancipated; *(femme)* emancipated, liberated
NM,F *(sans préjugés)* free spirit

émanciper [3] [emɑ̃sipe] VT **1** *(libérer ▸ gén)* to emancipate; *(▸ femmes)* to emancipate, to liberate; **é. qn de** to liberate *or* to free sb from **2** *Jur* to emancipate
VPR **s'émanciper 1** *(se libérer ▸ gén)* to become emancipated; *(▸ femme)* to become emancipated *or* liberated; **s'é. de** to become free from; **elle n'a jamais réussi à s'é. de l'éducation stricte qu'elle a reçue** she never managed to break free from her strict upbringing **2** *Péj (devenir trop libre)* to become rather free in one's ways; **elle s'est drôlement émancipée** she's become very liberated

émaner [3] [emane] **émaner de** VT IND *(sujet: odeur, lumière, ordre)* to emanate from, to come from; *(sujet: demande, mandat)* to come from, to be issued by; *(sujet: autorité, pouvoir)* to issue from

émargement [emarʒəmɑ̃] NM **1** *Admin (fait de signer)* signing; **é. d'un contrat** initialling a contract; **feuille d'é.** *(de présence)* attendance sheet; *(de paie)* pay sheet
2 *Admin (signature)* signature
3 *(annotation)* marginal note
4 *Typ (de pages)* trimming

émarger [17] [emarʒe] VT **1** *Admin (document, compte etc)* to initial (in the margin); *(signer)* to sign; *(courrier)* to sign for; *(annoter)* to annotate **2** *(réduire la marge de)* to trim
• **émarger à** VT IND to draw one's salary from; **il émarge aux fonds secrets** he's paid out of the secret funds

e-marketing [imarketiŋ] NM *Ordinat* e-marketing

émasculation [emaskylasjɔ̃] NF **1** *(castration)* emasculation, emasculating **2** *Littéraire (affaiblissement ▸ gén)* emasculation, weakening; *(▸ d'une œuvre)* weakening; **l'é. d'une politique** taking all the teeth out of a policy

émasculer [3] [emaskyle] VT **1** *(castrer)* to emasculate **2** *Littéraire (affaiblir ▸ politique, directive)* to weaken; *(▸ œuvre)* to weaken

émaux [emo] *voir* **émail**

embâcle [ɑ̃bakl] NM *(obstruction dans un cours d'eau)* blockage; *(par un bloc de glace)* ice block *or* jam

emballage [ɑ̃balaʒ] NM **1** *Mktg & Tech (gén)* packaging; *(papier)* wrapper; *(matière)* wrapping *or* packing materials; **e. consigné** returnable packaging; **l'e. est consigné** there is a deposit on the packaging; **e. compris** packaging included; **e. gratuit** packaging free of charge; **e. récupérable** recoverable packaging; **e. sous vide** vacuum-pack; **emballages vides** empty packaging; **e. bulle** blister pack; **e. d'origine** original packaging; **e. de présentation, e. présentoir** display pack; **e. transparent** blister pack **2** *Tech (processus ▸ gén)* packing *or* wrapping (up), packaging; *(▸ dans du papier)* wrapping (up) **3** *Vieilli Cyclisme* final sprint
• **d'emballage** ADJ *(papier)* wrapping; **toile d'e.** canvas wrapper

emballé, -e [ɑ̃bale] ADJ *Fam* (mad) keen, enthusiastic□; **il était complètement e. par l'idée** he was completely bowled over by the idea

emballement [ɑ̃balmɑ̃] NM **1** *(d'un cheval)* bolting; *(d'un moteur)* racing; **l'e. des cours à la Bourse** the Stock Market boom; **cela aboutirait certainement à l'e. de l'économie** that would definitely lead to the economy spiralling out of control **2** *(enthousiasme)* sudden passion, flight *or* burst of enthusiasm **3** *(emportement)* **dans un moment d'e.** without thinking; **pas d'e.!** *(par enthousiasme)* let's not get carried away!; *(par colère)* let's not get worked up!

emballer [3] [ɑ̃bale] VT **1** *Mktg & Tech (empaqueter ▸ marchandises)* to pack (up); *(dans du papier ▸ marchandises)* to package; *(▸ cadeau)* to wrap (up); **emballé sous vide** vacuum-packed
2 *(moteur)* to race
3 *Fam (enthousiasmer ▸ sujet: projet, livre)* to grab, to thrill (to bits); **ça l'a vraiment emballé** he was really taken with it; **ça n'a pas l'air de l'e.** he/she doesn't seem mad keen on the idea; **ça ne m'emballe pas vraiment de les voir** I'm not exactly thrilled about seeing them *or* mad keen to see them
4 *très Fam (arrêter ▸ truand) Br* to nick, *Am* to bust
5 *très Fam (partir avec ▸ partenaire sexuel) Br* to pull, to get off with, *Am* to pick up
6 *très Fam (embrasser)* to French kiss, *Br* to snog
VPR **s'emballer 1** *(cheval)* to bolt; *(moteur)* to race; *(cours, taux)* to take off
2 *Fam (s'enthousiasmer)* to get carried away; **ne t'emballe pas trop vite!** don't get carried away!; **s'e. pour qch** to get excited about sth□
3 *(s'emporter)* to flare *or* to blow up
4 *Bourse (cours, monnaie)* to spiral out of control

emballeur, -euse [ɑ̃balœr, -øz] NM,F packer

embarbouiller [3] [ɑ̃barbuje] *Fam* VT to confuse□, to muddle□, to befuddle□
VPR **s'embarbouiller** to get mixed *or* muddled up□

embarcadère [ɑ̃barkadɛr] NM landing stage, pier

embarcation [ɑ̃barkasjɔ̃] NF (small) boat *or* craft

embardée [ɑ̃barde] NF *(d'une voiture)* swerve, lurch; *(d'un bateau)* yaw, lurch; **faire une e.** *(voiture)* to swerve, to lurch; *(bateau)* to yaw, to lurch

embargo [ɑ̃bargo] NM **1** *Naut* embargo; **mettre l'e. sur un navire** to lay *or* to put an embargo on a ship, to embargo a ship **2** *Écon* embargo; **mettre un e. sur** to enforce an embargo on, to embargo; **lever l'e. sur les ventes d'armes** to lift *or* to raise the embargo on arms sales; **e. commercial/économique** trade/economic embargo

embarqué, -e [ɑ̃barke] ADJ **1** *Aut & Aviat* onboard **2** *Journ (journaliste, reporter)* embedded

embarquement [ɑ̃barkəmɑ̃] NM **1** *(action d'embarquer ▸ de marchandises)* loading; *(▸ à bord d'un navire)* shipping; *Rail & Mil (▸ de troupes)* entrainment; *Rail* **quai d'e.** departure platform; *(de chargement)* loading platform **2** *(action de s'embarquer ▸ sur un navire)* embarkation, boarding; *(▸ dans un avion, un train)* boarding; **le vol 123 est prêt pour l'e.** flight 123 is ready for boarding *or* is now boarding; **e. immédiat porte 16** now boarding at gate 16

embarquer [3] [ɑ̃barke] VT **1** *Transp (matériel, troupeau)* to load; *(passagers)* to embark, to take on board; *(dans un navire ▸ marchandises)* to ship; *Rail & Mil (troupes)* to entrain
2 *Naut* **e. de l'eau** to take in *or* to ship water
3 *Fam (emporter ▸ voiture, chien)* to cart off *or* away; **m'embarque pas mon blouson!** don't walk *or* waltz off with my jacket!
4 *Fam (voler)* to pinch, *Br* to nick; **les voleurs avaient tout embarqué dans le salon** the burglars had walked off with everything there was in the living room
5 *Fam (arrêter ▸ gang, manifestant)* to pull in; **se faire e. par les flics** to get pulled in by the police
6 *Fam (entraîner)* to drag off; **c'est un chemin non carrossable, où nous embarques-tu?** this is a dirt track, where are you taking us (off) to?□; **c'est eux qui l'ont embarqué dans cette affaire** they're the ones who got him involved *or* mixed up in this business□; **son divorce l'a embarqué dans un procès sans fin** his divorce got him involved *or* embroiled in an endless lawsuit□
7 *Fam (commencer)* **la réunion est bien/mal embarquée** the meeting's got off to a flying/lousy start
VI **1** *(aller à bord)* to board, to go aboard *or* on board; **e. (sur un navire)** to go on board *or* to board (a ship); **e. (dans un train/un autobus)** to get on *or* to board (a train/bus) **2** *(partir en bateau)* to embark (**pour** for); **nous embarquons demain pour Rio** we're embarking *or* sailing for Rio tomorrow **3** *Naut* **l'eau embarquait dans les cales** the holds were taking in *or* shipping water
VPR **s'embarquer 1** *(aller à bord)* to embark, to go on board, to board; *(partir)* to embark (**pour** for); **s'e. pour une croisière** to embark on a cruise; **s'e. sur un navire** to go on board *or* to board a ship **2** *(s'engager)* **s'e. dans une aventure financière** to embark on *or* to launch oneself into a business venture; **dans quelle histoire me suis-je embarqué!** what sort of a mess have I got myself into!; **je ne savais pas dans quoi je m'embarquais en acceptant** I didn't know what I was walking into *or* getting mixed up in when I said yes

embarras [ɑ̃bara] NM **1** *(malaise)* embarrassment, confusion; **répondre avec e.** to reply with embarrassment, to reply embarrassedly *or* in confusion; **plonger qn dans l'e.** to embarrass sb
2 *(souci)* **l'e., les e.** trouble; **tout l'e. que tu me causes** all the trouble you give me; **avoir des e. financiers** *ou* **d'argent** to be in financial difficulties, to have money problems; **être dans l'e.** *(dans la pauvreté)* to be short of money
3 *(cause de souci)* nuisance, cause of annoyance; **être un e. pour qn** to be a nuisance to sb
4 *(position délicate)* predicament, awkward position *or* situation; **être dans l'e.** *(mal à l'aise)* to be in a predicament *or* in an awkward position; *(face à un dilemme)* to be in a *or* caught on the horns of a dilemma; **ma question l'a mis dans l'e.** my question put him on the spot; **tirer un ami d'e.** to help a friend out of a predicament; **l'e. du choix** an embarrassment of riches; **on les a en dix teintes, vous avez** *ou* **vous n'avez que l'e. du choix** they come in ten different shades, you're spoilt for choice
5 *Péj (simagrées)* **faire des e.** to make a fuss
6 *Méd* **e. gastrique** upset stomach, stomach upset
7 *Vieilli* **les e. de la circulation** traffic congestion

embarrassant, -e [ɑ̃barasɑ̃, -ɑ̃t] ADJ **1** *(gênant ▸ silence, situation)* embarrassing, awkward **2** *(difficile ▸ problème, question)* awkward, thorny, tricky **3** *(encombrant ▸ colis, vêtement)* cumbersome

embarrassé, -e [ɑ̃barase] ADJ **1** *(gêné ▸ personne)* embarrassed; *(▸ sourire, regard)* embarrassed, uneasy; *(▸ gestes)* hampered; **avoir l'air e.** to look embarrassed *or* awkward; **me voilà bien e.** I'm in a really awkward situation, I'm really embarrassed
2 *(confus ▸ explication)* confused, muddled; *(▸ style)* awkward; **explications embarrassées** involved *or* confused explanations
3 *(encombré ▸ table, pièce etc)* cluttered; **avoir les mains embarrassées** to have one's hands full
4 *(pauvre)* short (of money)
5 *Méd* **avoir l'estomac e.** to have an upset stomach; **avoir la langue embarrassée** to have a coated *or* furred tongue

embarrasser [3] [ɑ̃barase] VT **1** *(mettre mal à l'aise)* to embarrass; **ça m'embarrasse de lui demander son âge** I'm embarrassed to ask him/her how old he/she is; **tu m'embarrasses beaucoup en me demandant ce service** you really embarrass me *or* put me in a very awkward situation by asking me this favour
2 *(rendre perplexe)* **ce qui m'embarrasse le plus c'est l'organisation du budget** what I find most awkward is how to organize the budget; **je serais bien embarrassé de dire qui a raison** I'd be hard put *or* at a loss to decide who was right
3 *(encombrer ▸ gén)* to clutter up, to obstruct; *(▸ personne)* to hamper; *(▸ table, pièce etc)* to clutter up (**de** with); **des colis embarrassaient le couloir** packages were cluttering up *or* obstructing the corridor; **cette valise t'embarrasse, laisse-moi la porter** that suitcase is cumbersome for you, let me carry it; **je peux poser mon manteau? il m'embarrasse** can I put my coat down? it's a bit of a nuisance
4 *Méd* **e. l'estomac** to cause a stomach upset
VPR **s'embarrasser 1 s'e. dans qch** *(s'empêtrer dans)* to trip over sth, to get tangled up in sth; *Fig* **s'e. dans ses mensonges/explications** to get tangled up in one's lies/explanations **2 s'e. de**

qn/qch *(s'encombrer de)* to burden oneself with sb/sth **3** *(s'inquiéter de)* **pour réussir dans ce métier, il ne faut pas s'e. de scrupules** you mustn't trouble *or* burden yourself with scruples if you want to succeed in this job; **sans s'e. de présentations** without bothering with the (usual) introductions

embastiller **[3]** [ɑ̃bastije] **VT 1** *Hist* to imprison in the Bastille **2** *(emprisonner)* to imprison, to incarcerate

embauchage [ɑ̃boʃaʒ] **NM** hiring

embauche [ɑ̃boʃ] **NF 1** *(action)* hiring **2** *(emploi)* employment; **il n'y a pas d'e. (chez eux)** they're not hiring anyone, there are no vacancies; **quelle est la situation de l'e.?** are companies taking on *or* hiring staff?

embaucher **[3]** [ɑ̃boʃe] **VT** *(recruter)* to take on, to hire; **e. qn pour le poste de** *ou* **comme** to engage *or* recruit sb as; *Fam* **je me suis encore fait e. pour faire la vaisselle** I got roped into doing the washing-up again

USAGE ABSOLU to recruit, to hire people

embaucheur, -euse [ɑ̃boʃœr, -øz] **NM,F** employer

embauchoir [ɑ̃boʃwar] **NM** *Tech* shoetree

embaumement [ɑ̃bommɑ̃] **NM** embalming

embaumer **[3]** [ɑ̃bome] **VT 1** *(parfumer ▸ air)* to make fragrant; **l'encens embaume l'église** the scent of incense fills the church **2** *(dégager une odeur de ▸ parfum)* to be fragrant with the scent of; *(▸ aliment, épice etc)* to be fragrant with the aroma of; **air embaumé** fragrant *or* balmy air; **l'église embaume l'encens** the church is heavy with (the scent of) incense **3** *(momifier)* to embalm

VI *(femme)* to be fragrant; *(mets)* to fill the air with a pleasant smell *or* a delicious aroma; *(fleur, plante)* to fill the air with a lovely fragrance *or* a delicate scent

embaumeur, -euse [ɑ̃bomœr, -øz] **NM,F** embalmer

embellie [ɑ̃beli] **NF 1** *Météo (de soleil)* bright interval; *(du vent)* lull; **courte e.** bright interval **2** *Fig (amélioration ▸ de l'économie, d'une situation etc)* improvement; **une e. dans sa vie** a happier period in his/her life

embellir **[32]** [ɑ̃belir] **VT 1** *(enjoliver ▸ rue, parc)* to make prettier; *(▸ pièce)* to decorate, to adorn; *(▸ personne)* to make look (more) beautiful, to improve the looks of; **la maternité l'embellit** pregnancy is making her look more beautiful **2** *(exagérer ▸ histoire)* to embellish, to embroider on, to add frills to; **e. la réalité** to make things seem more attractive than they really are

VI to grow prettier *or* more beautiful

embellissement [ɑ̃belismɑ̃] **NM 1** *(fait d'améliorer)* embellishment, embellishing **2** *(apport ▸ à un décor)* embellishment, improvement; *(▸ à une histoire)* embellishment, frill; **il faudra apporter des embellissements à l'appartement** the *Br* flat *or Am* apartment needs improving *or* needs a few embellishing touches; **il y a beaucoup d'embellissements dans son récit** there's a lot of poetic licence in his/her story

emberlificoter **[3]** [ɑ̃bɛrlifikɔte] *Fam* **VT 1** *(tromper ▸ personne)* to hoodwink; **se laisser e.** to let oneself be hoodwinked **2** *(compliquer)* to muddle up[□]; **quelle histoire emberlificotée!** what a muddle *or* mix-up of a story! **3** *(empêtrer)* to tangle up[□]

VPR s'emberlificoter s'e. les pieds dans to get (one's feet) tangled up in; **s'e. dans** *(tissu, câbles, récit, mensonges)* to get tangled up in

embêtant, -e [ɑ̃bɛtɑ̃, -ɑ̃t] **ADJ** *Fam* **1** *(lassant ▸ travail)* tiresome[□], boring[□] **2** *(importun ▸ enfant)* annoying[□]; **tu es e. avec tes questions** you're a real pain with all these questions; **c'est drôlement e.!** it's really annoying! **3** *(gênant)* tricky[□], awkward[□]; **c'est e. d'inviter son ex-femme?** would it be awkward to invite his ex-wife *or* if we invited his ex-wife?

embêtement [ɑ̃bɛtmɑ̃] **NM** *Fam* problem[□]; **embêtements** hassle[□]; **va les voir au commissariat, sinon tu peux avoir des embêtements** go and see them at the police station or you could get into trouble; **faire des embêtements à qn** to cause *or* to make trouble for sb

embêter **[4]** [ɑ̃bete] *Fam* **VT 1** *(importuner)* to annoy[□], to bother[□]; **n'embête pas ce pauvre animal** stop tormenting that poor creature; **ça m'embête d'y aller** I wish I didn't have to go[□]; **se faire e. par qn** to be hassled by sb **2** *(lasser)* to bore[□]; **ça m'embête d'y aller** I can't be bothered going *or* to go **3** *(mettre mal à l'aise)* to bother[□], to annoy[□]; **cela m'embête d'avoir oublié** it annoys *or* bothers me that I forgot; **ça m'embête d'arriver en retard** I don't like being late[□]; **je suis drôlement embêté avec ma fille** I'm having a lot of hassle with my daughter

VPR s'embêter 1 *(s'ennuyer)* to be bored[□]; **s'e. à mourir** to be bored to death *or* tears **2** *(se donner la peine)* **s'e. à faire qch** to go to the trouble of doing sth; **je ne vais pas m'e. à les éplucher** I'm not going to bother peeling them **3** *(locutions)* **il s'embête pas!** *(il est sans scrupules)* he's got a nerve!; *(il est riche)* he does pretty well for himself!; **s'e. avec** *(des histoires d'argent, des scrupules, sa belle-mère)* to bother oneself about *or* with

emblée [ɑ̃ble] **d'emblée ADV** straightaway, right away; *(réussir)* at the first attempt

emblématique [ɑ̃blematik] **ADJ** emblematic; *Fig* symbolic; **figure e.** *(légendaire)* legendary figure; *(marquant)* symbol

emblème [ɑ̃blɛm] **NM 1** *(blason)* emblem **2** *(insigne)* emblem, symbol; **les emblèmes de la profession** the insignia of the trade; *Mktg* **e. de marque** brand mark

embobiner **[3]** [ɑ̃bɔbine] **VT 1** *Fam (tromper)* to take in; *(manipuler)* to get round; **ne vous laissez pas e.** don't let yourself be taken in; **je l'ai embobiné** I've got him where I want him; **tu ne m'embobineras pas avec toutes ces belles paroles** you won't get round me by sweet-talking me **2** *Tex (fil)* to wind round a bobbin

emboîtable [ɑ̃bwatabl] **ADJ** *(chaise)* stacking *(avant n)*, stackable; **cubes/tuyaux emboîtables** cubes/pipes fitting into each other; **des tables emboîtables** a nest of tables

emboîtage [ɑ̃bwataʒ] **NM 1** *(action d'empiler ▸ de chaises, de boîtes, de tables)* stacking; *Constr (▸ de tuyaux, de poutres etc)* jointing

2 *(action d'envelopper ▸ d'un livre)* casing

3 *(rangement en boîte)* packing (into boxes)

4 *(étui)* case, casing; *(d'un livre)* slipcase

emboîtement [ɑ̃bwatmɑ̃] **NM l'e. de deux tuyaux/os** the interlocking of two pipes/bones; **à l'e. des deux pièces** at the join between the two parts, where the two parts fit into each other

emboîter **[3]** [ɑ̃bwate] **VT 1** *(empiler ▸ chaises, boîtes, tables)* to stack; *Constr (▸ tuyaux, poutres etc)* to joint; *(▸ poupées russes)* to fit into each other **2** *(envelopper ▸ livre)* to case **3** *(locution)* **e. le pas à qn** to follow close behind sb; *Fig* to follow sb, to follow sb's lead

VPR s'emboîter to fit together *or* into each other; *(chaises, boîtes, tables)* to stack; **des tables qui s'emboîtent les unes dans les autres** a nest of tables

embolie [ɑ̃bɔli] **NF** *Méd* embolism; **e. gazeuse/pulmonaire** air/pulmonary embolism; **e. cérébrale** clot on the brain, *Spéc* cerebral embolism

embonpoint [ɑ̃bɔ̃pwɛ̃] **NM** stoutness, portliness; **avoir de l'e.** to be stout *or* corpulent; **prendre de l'e.** to flesh out, to become stout, to put on weight

embouché, -e [ɑ̃buʃe] **ADJ** *Fam* **mal e.** *(grossier)* foul-mouthed; *(de mauvaise humeur)* in a foul mood

emboucher **[3]** [ɑ̃buʃe] **VT 1** *Mus* to put to one's mouth; *Fig* **e. la trompette** to wax lyrical; **il a allégrement embouché la trompette du libéralisme** he trumpeted *or* extolled the virtues of the free market **2** *Équitation* **e. un cheval** to put the bit in a horse's mouth

embouchure [ɑ̃buʃyr] **NF 1** *Géog* mouth

2 *Mus* mouthpiece, embouchure

3 *Équitation* mouthpiece

4 *(d'un sac, d'un vase)* opening, mouth

embourber **[3]** [ɑ̃burbe] **VT** *(enliser)* to stick

VPR s'embourber *(dans la boue)* to get bogged down *or* stuck in the mud; **il s'est embourbé dans des explications compliquées** he got bogged down in complicated explanations

embourgeoisement [ɑ̃burʒwazmɑ̃] **NM** *(d'un groupe, d'un milieu, d'une profession)* becoming (more) bourgeois *or* middle-class; *(d'un quartier)* gentrification

embourgeoiser **[3]** [ɑ̃burʒwaze] **s'embourgeoiser VPR 1** *(quartier)* to become gentrified; *(parti politique)* to become (more) bourgeois *or* middle-class **2** *Péj (personne)* to become fonder and fonder of one's creature comforts

embout [ɑ̃bu] **NM** *(d'un parapluie)* tip, ferrule; *(d'un tuyau)* nozzle; *(d'une seringue)* adapter; *(d'un câble)* terminal; *(d'un tirant, d'un fil etc)* connector

embouteillage [ɑ̃butɛjaʒ] **NM 1** *Aut* traffic jam; *(à un carrefour)* gridlock; **tomber dans les embouteillages** to get caught in traffic **2** *Fam (au téléphone)* logjam (of calls); **il y a un e. sur la ligne** the line is jammed with calls **3** *Naut (de navires)* bottling up

embouteiller **[4]** [ɑ̃buteje] **VT 1** *Aut* to jam (up); **les routes sont embouteillées** the roads are congested *or* jammed; **e. un carrefour** to gridlock a junction **2** *(mettre en bouteilles)* to bottle

emboutir **[32]** [ɑ̃butir] **VT 1** *(heurter)* to crash into; **je me suis fait e. par un bus** I was hit by a bus; **l'aile est toute emboutie** the wing's all dented; **tout l'arrière de ma voiture est embouti** the entire rear end of my car is bashed in **2** *Métal* to stamp; **châssis en tôle emboutie** pressed steel frame **3** *(arrondir)* to stamp, emboss

emboutissage [ɑ̃butisaʒ] **NM 1** *Métal* stamping **2** *(fait d'arrondir)* stamping, embossing **3** *Aut (de voitures)* collision; **l'e. d'une voiture par un autobus** the collision between a bus and a car

embraie *etc voir* **embrayer**

embranchement [ɑ̃brɑ̃ʃmɑ̃] **NM 1** *Transp (carrefour ▸ routier)* fork; *(▸ ferroviaire)* junction; *(voie annexe ▸ routière)* side road; *(▸ ferroviaire)* branch line

2 *(d'égout)* junction

3 *(dans un arbre)* **un nid dans l'e.** a nest built where the trunk branches out

4 *Biol & Bot* subkingdom, *Spéc* phylum

embrancher **[3]** [ɑ̃brɑ̃ʃe] **VT** *(route, conduite etc)* to connect up, to join up **(à** to)

VPR s'embrancher s'e. (sur) to join (up with)

embrasement [ɑ̃brazmɑ̃] **NM** *Littéraire* **1** *(incendie)* blaze **2** *(rougeoiement)* **l'e. du couchant** the blaze of the setting sun **3** *(exaltation ▸ de l'âme)* kindling; *(▸ de l'imagination)* firing; **il ne pouvait pas lutter contre l'e. de son cœur** he could not fight against the love that flared up in his heart

embraser **[3]** [ɑ̃braze] **VT** *Littéraire* **1** *(incendier)* to set ablaze *or* on fire, to set fire to; *Fig* **la soif qui lui embrasait la gorge** the thirst burning his/her throat

2 *(illuminer)* to set ablaze *or* aglow; **le soleil levant embrasait le ciel** the rising sun set the sky aglow

3 *(rendre brûlant)* to make burning hot; **le soleil de midi embrasait la route** the road was burning hot under the midday sun

4 *(exalter ▸ imagination)* to fire; *(▸ âme)* to kindle, to set aflame; *(▸ foule)* to fire, to set alight, *Péj* to inflame; **ces projets d'aventure l'embrasaient** this talk of adventure fired his/her imagination

VPR s'embraser *Littéraire* **1** *(prendre feu)* to catch fire, to blaze *or* to flare up

2 *(s'illuminer)* to be set ablaze; *(rougeoyer)* to glow

3 *(devenir brûlant)* to become burning hot

4 *(s'exalter ▸ âme, imagination)* to be set on fire, to be kindled; *(▸ opprimés)* to rise up; **dès que je l'ai vu, mon cœur s'est embrasé** the mere sight of him kindled a flame; **les esprits s'embrasaient** *(par enthousiasme)* imaginations were fired; *(par colère)* passions were running high

embrassade [ɑ̃brasad] **NF une e.** a hug and a kiss; **des embrassades** hugging and kissing, hugs and kisses

embrasse [ɑ̃bras] **NF** *(de rideau)* tieback

embrasser **[3]** [ɑ̃brase] **VT 1** *(donner un baiser à)* to kiss; **l'embrassant sur le front** kissing him/her on the forehead, kissing his/her forehead; **e. qn sur la bouche/joue** to kiss sb on the lips/cheek;

embrasse Mamie, on s'en va! kiss Granny goodbye!; **elle l'embrassait avant qu'il ne s'endorme** she used to kiss him goodnight; **vous embrasserez vos parents pour moi** (kind) regards to your parents; **embrasse Lucie pour moi!** give Lucie a big kiss *or* hug for me!; **je t'embrasse** *(dans une lettre)* with love; *(au téléphone)* take care

2 *Littéraire (serrer dans ses bras)* to embrace, to hug; *Prov* **qui trop embrasse, mal étreint** = one shouldn't spread oneself too thinly

3 *(adopter ▸ idée, foi)* to embrace, to take up; *(▸ carrière)* to take up; *(▸ cause)* to embrace, to take up; **e. la carrière diplomatique** to enter the diplomatic service

4 *(saisir)* **e. du regard** to behold; **e. d'un seul coup d'œil** to take in at a single glance; **il embrassa toute sa famille d'un regard satisfait** he cast a satisfied eye over his family

5 *(comprendre)* to grasp; **e. les données complexes d'un problème** to grasp the complex elements of a problem

6 *(englober)* to encompass, to embrace

VPR s'embrasser to kiss (one another)

> Il faut noter que le verbe anglais **to embrace** ne signifie jamais **donner un baiser**.

embrasure [ɑ̃brazyr] **NF 1** *(cadre ▸ de porte)* door-frame, door-jamb; *(▸ de fenêtre)* window-frame; **dans l'e. de la porte/fenêtre** in the door/window recess; **se tenir dans l'e. d'une porte/fenêtre** to be framed in a doorway/window **2** *Archit* embrasure **3** *Mil* gun port

embrayage [ɑ̃brejaʒ] **NM 1** *(mécanisme) Aut* clutch; *Tech* coupling (gear); **e. à diaphragme** diaphragm spring *or* DS clutch; **e. électromagnétique** magnetic clutch; **e. à friction** friction clutch; **e. monodisque** single-plate *or* disc clutch; **e. multidisque** multi-disc clutch pack **2** *Aut & Tech (pédale)* clutch (pedal); **pédale d'e.** clutch pedal **3** *Aut (fait d'embrayer)* putting in the clutch; *Tech (de pièces de moteur)* coupling, engaging; **voiture à e. automatique** automatic car

embrayer [11] [ɑ̃breje] **VT** *Aut* to put in the clutch of; *Tech (pièces de moteur)* to couple, to engage

VI 1 *Aut* to put in *or* to engage the clutch; **embraye!** clutch in! **2** *Fam (commencer)* to get cracking, to go into action; **e. sur** to get straight into; **on pourrait peut-être e. sur un autre sujet** maybe we could change the subject□ **3** *Can Fam (se dépêcher)* **embraye!** get a move on!

embrigadement [ɑ̃brigadmɑ̃] **NM 1** *Mil (dans une brigade)* brigading; *(enrôlement forcé)* dragooning (into the army) **2** *Fig Péj (adhésion forcée)* press-ganging

embrigader [3] [ɑ̃brigade] **VT 1** *Mil (dans une brigade)* to brigade; *(de force)* to dragoon into the army, to press into service **2** *Fig Péj (faire adhérer)* to press-gang; **je ne veux pas être embrigadé dans leur mouvement** I won't let myself be press-ganged into joining their movement

embringuer [3] [ɑ̃brɛ̃ge] *Fam* **VT e. qn dans** to drag sb into; **il ne veut pas se laisser e. dans cette histoire** he doesn't want to get mixed up in this affair

VPR s'embringuer to get mixed up (**dans** in)

embrocation [ɑ̃brɔkasjɔ̃] **NF** embrocation

embrocher [3] [ɑ̃brɔʃe] **VT 1** *Culin (un animal)* to spit, to spit-roast; *(en brochettes)* to skewer **2** *Fam (transpercer)* **e. qn avec qch** to run sth through sb□

embrouillage [ɑ̃brujaʒ] = **embrouillement**

embrouillamini [ɑ̃brujamini] **NM** *Fam* (hopeless) muddle *or* mix-up; **sa vie sentimentale est un tel e. que…** his/her love life is so complicated *or* involved that…□; **comment veux-tu que je m'y retrouve dans cet e. de papiers?** how can I be expected to know what I'm doing when these papers are in such a muddle?

embrouillé, -e [ɑ̃bruje] **ADJ 1** *(fils, câbles)* tangled up, entangled, snarled up **2** *(situation)* muddled, confusing; *(style, affaire)* complicated, involved; **des idées embrouillées** confused ideas

embrouillement [ɑ̃brujmɑ̃] **NM 1** *(de fils ▸ action)* tangling; *(▸ état)* tangle **2** *Fig (d'une situation, d'idées etc ▸ action)* muddling, confusing; *(▸ état)* muddle, confusion; **l'e. de la situation est tel que…** the situation is so confused that…

embrouiller [3] [ɑ̃bruje] **VT 1** *(emmêler)* to tangle up **2** *Fig* **e. qn** to muddle sb, to confuse sb; **il a réussi à m'e.** he managed to confuse me; *Fam* **ni vu ni connu je t'embrouille** hey presto; *Fam* **…alors qu'il était avec une autre: ni vu ni connu je t'embrouille** …while all the time he was with another woman: talk about a con artist *or* about being conned! **3** *(compliquer)* to complicate; **e. la situation** *ou* **les choses** to confuse matters

VPR s'embrouiller to get muddled (up), to get confused; **je me suis embrouillé dans mes rendez-vous** I got my appointments muddled (up), I got into a muddle with my appointments

embroussaillé, -e [ɑ̃brusaje] **ADJ** *(jardin)* overgrown; *(sentier, jardin, dunes etc)* covered with *or* in bushes; *(cheveux, barbe)* bushy, shaggy

embrumé, -e [ɑ̃bryme] **ADJ** *(temps)* misty; *(horizon)* hazy; *Fig (esprit ▸ par l'alcool)* fuddled, fogged; **il avait l'esprit e. par toutes ces paroles** all that talking had left him feeling less than clear-headed

embrumer [3] [ɑ̃bryme] **VT 1** *Météo* to cover in mist; **la ligne embrumée des cimes** the misty mountain tops **2** *Fig Littéraire* to cloud; **le sommeil lui embrumait encore les yeux** his/her eyes were still heavy *or* blurred with sleep; **intelligence embrumée par la boisson** mind clouded with drink; **tous ces discours lui ont embrumé l'esprit** his/her mind is less than clear after all those speeches

VPR s'embrumer 1 *Météo* to mist over; *(ciel)* to become misty *or* hazy; *(paysage, ville, île)* to become covered with mist *or* haze **2** *(esprit, intelligence)* to become clouded

embruns [ɑ̃brœ̃] **NMPL les e.** the sea spray *or* spume

embryologie [ɑ̃brijɔlɔʒi] **NF** *Biol* embryology

embryologique [ɑ̃brijɔlɔʒik] **ADJ** *Biol* embryologic, embryological

embryologiste [ɑ̃brijɔlɔʒist] **NMF** *Biol* embryologist

embryon [ɑ̃brijɔ̃] **NM 1** *Biol & Bot* embryo **2** *Fig (commencement)* embryo, beginning; **un e. de projet** an embryonic project

embryonnaire [ɑ̃brijɔnɛr] **ADJ 1** *Biol & Bot* embryonic; **sac e.** embryo sac **2** *Fig (non développé)* embryonic, incipient; **idée encore à l'état e.** idea still at the embryonic stage; **le projet en est encore à un stade e.** the project is still at a very early stage *or* in its very early stages

embryotomie [ɑ̃brijɔtɔmi] **NF** *Obst* embryotomy

embu, -e [ɑ̃by] *Beaux-Arts* **ADJ** *(couleur, tableau)* flat, dull

NM *(d'une couleur)* flatness, dullness

embûche [ɑ̃byʃ] **NF 1** *(difficulté)* pitfall, hazard **2** *(piège)* trap; **tendre** *ou* **dresser des embûches à qn** to set traps for sb; **sujet plein d'embûches** tricky subject; **examen semé d'embûches** exam paper full of trick questions; **la vie est semée d'embûches** life is full of pitfalls

embuer [7] [ɑ̃bɥe] **VT** to mist (up *or* over); **des lunettes embuées** misted-up spectacles; **les yeux embués de larmes** eyes misty with tears

VPR s'embuer to steam up

embuscade [ɑ̃byskad] **NF** ambush; **attirer qn dans une e.** to ambush sb; **se tenir en e.** to lie in ambush; *Fig* **tomber dans une e.** to be caught in an ambush; *Fig* **tendre une e. à qn** to set up an ambush for sb

embusqué, -e [ɑ̃byske] **NM,F 1** *Péj & Mil* shirker, dodger; **les embusqués de l'arrière** the troops that keep behind the lines **2** *Sport* **les embusqués** the back row of forwards

embusquer [3] [ɑ̃byske] *Mil* **VT 1** *(placer en embuscade)* to place in ambush **2** *(affecter loin du front)* to find a cushy posting for

VPR s'embusquer 1 *(pour attaquer)* to lie in ambush **2** *Péj (pendant la guerre)* to avoid active service

éméché, -e [emeʃe] **ADJ** *Fam* tipsy

émeraude [emrod] **NF** *Minér* emerald

NM *(couleur)* emerald green

ADJ INV emerald *(avant n)*, emerald-green

émergence [emɛrʒɑ̃s] **NF 1** *(apparition ▸ d'une idée)* (sudden) appearance *or* emergence; **on assiste à cette époque à l'é. de nouvelles théories politiques** at the time new political theories were emerging *or* were coming to the fore **2** *Géog (d'une source)* source; **c'est là que se trouve le point d'é. de la source** the spring emerges here **3** *Opt* **point d'é.** point of emergence

émergent, -e [emɛrʒɑ̃, -ɑ̃t] **ADJ 1** *(idée)* emerging, developing; *(pays, économie, maladie)* emerging **2** *Opt* emergent

émerger [17] [emɛrʒe] **VI 1** *(soleil)* to rise, to come up

2 *(dépasser)* **é. de** *(eau)* to float (up) to the top of, to emerge from; **une bonne copie/un bon élève qui émerge du lot** a paper/pupil standing out from the rest

3 *Fig (apparaître ▸ vérité, fait)* to emerge, to come to light; *(▸ nouvel écrivain)* to emerge

4 *Fam (d'une occupation, du sommeil)* to emerge; **é. de** to emerge from, to come out of; **le dimanche, il n'émerge jamais avant midi** he never surfaces before noon on Sundays

émeri [emri] **NM** emery; **papier** *ou* **toile (d')é.** emery paper; **bouchon à l'é.** (ground glass) stopper

émerillon [emrijɔ̃] **NM 1** *Orn* merlin **2** *Pêche* swivel

émeriser [3] [emrize] **VT** *Tech (recouvrir de poudre)* to coat with emery; *(gratter)* to grind with emery

émérite [emerit] **ADJ 1** *(éminent)* (highly experienced and) skilled, expert *(avant n)* **2** *Belg Univ* **professeur é.** emeritus professor

émerveillement [emɛrvejmɑ̃] **NM 1** *(émotion)* wonder, *Littéraire* wonderment; **il découvrait la mer avec é.** he discovered the sea with wonder **2** *(chose merveilleuse)* wonder; **c'était un é.** it was amazing *or* wonderful; **un é. perpétuel** a constant source of amazement

émerveiller [4] [emɛrveje] **VT** to fill with wonder *or Littéraire* wonderment; **être émerveillé par** to marvel at, to be filled with wonder by; **elle fixait la poupée d'un regard émerveillé** she gazed at the doll in wonder

VPR s'émerveiller to be filled with wonder, to marvel; **s'é. de** *ou* **devant** *(s'étonner de)* to be amazed by; *(s'enchanter de)* to marvel at; **il s'émerveillait d'un rien** he marvelled at the smallest thing

émet *etc voir* **émettre**

émétique [emetik] *Med & Pharm* **ADJ** emetic

NM emetic

émetteur, -trice [emetœr, -tris] **ADJ 1** *Rad* transmitting; **poste é.** transmitter; **station émettrice** transmitting *or* broadcasting station **2** *Fin* issuing

NM,F 1 *Fin (de billets, d'actions, d'une carte)* issuer; *(d'un chèque)* drawer **2** *Ling* speaker

NM 1 *Rad (appareil)* transmitter; **é. monophonique/stéréo** monoaural/stereo transmitter; **é. terrestre** ground transmitter **2** *(élément)* emitter

émetteur-récepteur [emetœrreseptœr] *(pl* **émetteurs-récepteurs)** **NM** *Rad* transmitter-receiver, transceiver; **é. (portatif)** walkie-talkie

émettre [84] [emetr] **VT 1** *(produire ▸ rayon, son)* to emit, to give out; *(▸ odeur)* to give off, to produce; *(▸ chaleur)* to give out *or* off; *(▸ lumière)* to give (out); **mon ordinateur émet un bruit bizarre** my computer is making a funny noise

2 *(exprimer ▸ hypothèse, opinion)* to venture, to put forward, to volunteer; *(▸ doute, réserve)* to express; *(▸ objection)* to voice, to raise, to put forward

3 *Fin (billets, actions, chèque, timbres)* to issue; *(emprunt)* to float; *(lettre de crédit)* to open

4 *Rad & TV* to broadcast, to transmit; *(onde, signal)* to send out

5 *Jur (monnaie)* to utter

USAGE ABSOLU *Rad & TV* to transmit, to broadcast; **é. sur grandes ondes** to broadcast on long wave

émettrice [emetris] *voir* **émetteur**

émeu [emø] **NM** *Orn* emu

émeut *etc voir* **émouvoir**

émeute [emøt] NF riot; **il y a eu des émeutes** there has been rioting; **tourner à l'é.** to turn into a riot

émeutier, -ère [emøtje, -ɛr] NM,F rioter

émeuvent *etc voir* **émouvoir**

émiettement [emjɛtmɑ̃] NM **1** *(d'un gâteau)* crumbling **2** *(dispersion ▸ des efforts)* frittering away, dissipating; *(▸ du pouvoir)* fragmentation

émietter [4] [emjete] VT **1** *(mettre en miettes ▸ gâteau)* to crumble, to break up (into crumbs) **2** *(morceler ▸ propriété)* to break up **3** *Littéraire (gaspiller ▸ efforts)* to fritter away, to disperse, to dissipate

VPR **s'émietter** *(gâteau)* to crumble; *(pouvoir)* to fragment; *(fortune)* to gradually disappear; *(domaine, empire)* to crumble away

émigrant, -e [emigrɑ̃, -ɑ̃t] NM,F emigrant

émigration [emigrasjɔ̃] NF **1** *(d'une personne, population)* emigration, emigrating; **pays à forte/faible é.** country with high/low emigration **2** *Zool* migration

émigré, -e [emigre] ADJ migrant; **travailleurs émigrés** migrant workers

NM,F emigrant; *Hist* emigré

émigrer [3] [emigre] VI **1** *(s'expatrier)* to emigrate **2** *Zool* to migrate

émincé [emɛ̃se] NM *Culin* **1** *(plat)* émincé; **é. de veau** émincé of veal, veal cut into slivers *(and served in a sauce)* **2** *(tranche)* thin slice *(of meat)*

émincer [16] [emɛ̃se] VT *Culin* to slice thinly, to cut into thin strips

éminemment [eminamɑ̃] ADV eminently

éminence [eminɑ̃s] NF **1** *Géog* hill, hillock, knoll **2** *Anat* protuberance; **l'é. du pouce** the ball of the thumb

3 *Arch (excellence)* eminence

4 *(locutions)* **é. grise** éminence grise; **c'est l'é. grise du patron** he's/she's the power behind the throne

éminent, -e [eminɑ̃, -ɑ̃t] ADJ eminent, prominent, noted; **mon é. collègue** my learned colleague; **il nous a rendu d'éminents services** he rendered us outstanding service

émir [emir] NM emir, amir

émirat [emira] NM *Géog & Pol* emirate; **les Émirats arabes unis** the United Arab Emirates

émis, -e [emi, -iz] PP *voir* **émettre**

émissaire[1] [emisɛr] NM *Pol (envoyé)* emissary, envoy

émissaire[2] [emisɛr] NM *Géog (d'un lac)* outlet, drainage channel

émission [emisjɔ̃] NF **1** *Phys (de son, de lumière, de signaux, de gaz)* emission; **é. de particules** particle emission; **tuyau d'é.** discharge pipe

2 *Rad & TV (transmission de sons, d'images)* transmission, broadcasting; *(programme)* programme; **é. d'actualités** current affairs programme; **é. en différé** prerecorded broadcast; **é. en direct** live broadcast; **é. diffusée simultanément** simultaneous broadcast; **émissions pour enfants** children's television; **é. pilote** pilot; **é. en public** audience show; **é. de radio** radio programme; **é. radiotélévisée** simulcast; **é. relayée** relay; **émissions scolaires** schools broadcasting; **émissions à sensation** tabloid television, tabloid TV; **émissions de service public** public-service broadcasting; **é. spéciale** special programme; **é. de télévision** television programme, *Spéc* telecast; **é. de variétés** variety show; **l'é. de nos programmes sera interrompue à 22 heures** transmission of our programmes will be interrupted at 10 p.m.; **é. d'expression directe** live debate programme; **é. d'expression directe (de formation politique)** party political broadcast; **poste d'é.** transmitter; **station d'é.** transmitting *or* broadcasting station

3 *Fin (de billets, d'actions, d'un chèque, de timbres)* issue; *(d'un emprunt)* flotation; *(d'une lettre de crédit)* opening; *Bourse* **é. boursière** *ou* **d'actions** share issue; *Bourse* **é. d'actions gratuites** scrip issue; *Bourse* **é. de conversion** conversion issue; *Banque* **é. fiduciaire** fiduciary *or* note issue; *Bourse* **é. obligataire** *ou* **d'obligations** bond issue; *Bourse* **é. par séries** block issues; *Bourse* **é. des valeurs du Trésor** tap issue

4 *(de sons articulés)* **é. de voix** utterance

5 *Physiol* emission

6 *Électron* **é. électronique** electron emission

7 *Jur (d'une monnaie)* uttering

emmagasinage [ɑ̃magazinaʒ] NM **1** *Com (dans une arrière-boutique)* storage; *(dans un entrepôt)* warehousing **2** *(d'électricité, de chaleur)* storing up, accumulation

emmagasiner [3] [ɑ̃magazine] VT **1** *Com (marchandises ▸ dans une arrière-boutique)* to store; *(▸ dans un entrepôt)* to warehouse **2** *(accumuler ▸ connaissances)* to store up, to accumulate; *(▸ provisions)* to stock up on, to stockpile; *(▸ électricité, chaleur)* to store up, to accumulate

emmailloter [3] [ɑ̃majɔte] VT *(bébé)* to swaddle; *(membre)* to wrap up

emmanchement [ɑ̃mɑ̃ʃmɑ̃] NM **1 l'e. d'un outil** fitting a handle on a tool **2** *(d'une pièce à une autre)* fitting; **cela rendait l'e. des deux pièces impossible** it made it impossible to fit the two parts together

emmancher [3] [ɑ̃mɑ̃ʃe] VT **1** *(ajuster ▸ tête de râteau, lame)* to fit into a handle **2** *(tuyaux)* to fit together, to joint; *(pièce dans une autre)* to fit (**dans** to)

VPR **s'emmancher 1** *(de deux pièces)* to fit together **2** *Fam* **s'e. bien/mal** *(commencer)* to be off to a good/bad start; **l'affaire était mal emmanchée** the business got off to a bad start

emmanchure [ɑ̃mɑ̃ʃyr] NF **1** *Couture (de vêtement)* armhole; **la veste me serre aux emmanchures** the jacket's too tight at the armpits **2** *Belg (combine)* scheme, trick

emmêlement [ɑ̃mɛlmɑ̃] NM *(de cheveux, de fils, de laine ▸ action)* tangling; *(▸ état)* tangle; *Fig (de faits, d'une histoire ▸ action)* mixing up, muddling; *(▸ état)* mix-up, muddle

emmêler [4] [ɑ̃mele] VT **1** *(mêler ▸ cheveux, fils, laine)* to entangle, to tangle (up), to get into a tangle; **complètement emmêlé** all tangled up **2** *(rendre confus, confondre)* to mix up; **j'emmêle les dates** I'm getting the dates confused; **des explications emmêlées** confused *or* muddled explanations

VPR **s'emmêler 1** *(être mêlé)* to be tangled *or* knotted *or* snarled up **2** *(être confus ▸ faits, dates)* to get mixed up **3 s'e. les pieds dans** to get one's feet caught in; *Fam Fig* **s'e. les pieds** *ou* **pédales** *ou* **pinceaux dans qch** to get sth all muddled up

emménagement [ɑ̃menaʒmɑ̃] NM moving in; **nous avons dû remettre notre e. à plus tard** we had to put off moving in *or* we had to put our move off to later; **comment s'est passé ton e.?** how did the move go?

emménager [17] [ɑ̃menaʒe] VI to move in; **e. dans** to move into

VT *(meubles, personne)* to move in; **e. qn/qch dans** to move sb/sth into

emmener [19] [ɑ̃mne] VT **1** *(inviter à aller)* to take along; **je t'emmène en montagne** I'll take you (with me) to the mountains; **je vous emmène avec moi** I'm taking you with me; **cette année nous emmenons les enfants** we're taking the children away this year; **e. qn dîner** to take sb out to dinner; **e. promener qn** to take sb for a walk

2 *(sujet: bateau, avion etc ▸ passagers)* to take, to carry

3 *(forcer à aller)* to take away

4 *(accompagner)* **e. qn à la gare** to take sb to the station; *(en voiture)* to give sb a lift to *or* to drop sb off at the station; **il m'a emmené à l'aéroport en voiture** he drove me to the airport

5 *Fam (emporter)* to take (away)[□]; **emmène la fourchette à la cuisine** take the fork into the kitchen

6 *Sport & Mil (sprint, peloton, équipe, soldat)* to lead

emmenthal, emmental [emɛtal] NM *Culin* Emmenthal, Emmental

emmerdant, -e [ɑ̃mɛrdɑ̃, -ɑ̃t] ADJ *très Fam* **1** *(importun)* **ce que tu peux être e.!** you can be a real pain (in the neck *or Am* butt)!; **il est e.** he's a pain (in the neck *or Am* butt) **2** *(gênant)* damn *or Br* bloody awkward; **c'est e. d'avoir à laisser la porte ouverte** having to leave the door open is a real pain *or Br* a bloody nuisance **3** *(ennuyeux) Br* bloody *or Am* godawful boring

emmerde [ɑ̃mɛrd] NF *très Fam* hassle; **en ce moment j'ai que des emmerdes** it's just one frigging hassle after another at the moment; **faire des emmerdes à qn** to make trouble *or* to cause hassle for sb

emmerdement [ɑ̃mɛrdəmɑ̃] NM *très Fam* hassle; **en ce moment j'ai que des emmerdements** it's just one frigging hassle after another at the moment; **être dans les emmerdements jusqu'au cou** to be up the creek; **avoir des emmerdements** to have a hell of a lot of trouble; **j'ai encore eu un e. avec la bagnole** I had trouble with the car again

emmerder [3] [ɑ̃mɛrde] *très Fam* VT **1** *(gêner)* **e. qn** *(contrarier)* to get up sb's nose *or* on sb's nerves; *(ennuyer)* to bore sb stiff *or* silly *or* rigid; **elle va m'e. longtemps?** when is she going to stop hassling me?; **m'emmerde pas** stop bugging me; **plus j'y pense, plus ça m'emmerde** the more I think about it, the more it bugs me; **avoir l'air/être emmerdé** to look/be in a bit of a mess; **se faire e. par qn** to be hassled by sb **2** *(mépriser)* **je t'emmerde!** *Br* sod off!, *Am* screw you!; **je l'emmerde!** *Br* he can sod off!, *Am* screw him!; **dis-lui que je l'emmerde!** tell him/her from me he/she can (go and) get stuffed!

VPR **s'emmerder 1** *(s'ennuyer)* to be bored stiff *or* rigid; **on s'emmerde (à cent sous de l'heure) ici!** it's so damn boring here! **2** *(se donner la peine)* **je vais pas m'e. à les éplucher** I can't be bothered *or Br* arsed to peel them; **et moi qui me suis emmerdé à tout recopier!** to think I went to the trouble of copying the whole damn thing out! **3** *(locution)* **il s'emmerde pas!** *(il est sans scrupules)* he's got a (damn) nerve!; *(il est riche)* he does pretty well for himself!

emmerdeur, -euse [ɑ̃mɛrdœr, -øz] NM,F *très Fam (qui contrarie)* damn *or Br* bloody pain; *(qui ennuie)* helluva *or Br* bloody bore

emmitoufler [3] [ɑ̃mitufle] VT to wrap up (well) (**dans** in)

VPR **s'emmitoufler** to wrap up well; **s'e. dans une cape** to wrap oneself up in a cape

emmurer [3] [ɑ̃myre] VT **1** *(enfermer)* to wall up *or* in **2** *Fig Littéraire (isoler)* to immure

VPR **s'emmurer** *Littéraire* **s'e. dans le silence** to retreat into silence

emo [emo] NM *Mus* emo

émoi [emwa] NM *Littéraire (émotion)* agitation; *(tumulte)* commotion; *(plaisir)* excitement; **elle était tout en é.** she was all in a fluster; **la population est en é.** there's great agitation among the population; **toute la ville était en é.** the whole town was in a commotion; **non sans é.** in some agitation

émollient, -e [emɔljɑ̃, -ɑ̃t] *Pharm* ADJ emollient

NM emollient

émolument [emɔlymɑ̃] *Jur* NM **1** *(part d'actif)* portion of inheritance **2** *(rémunération)* basic fee

• **émoluments** NMPL *(d'un employé)* salary, wages; *(d'un notaire)* fees; **percevoir des émoluments** to receive payment

émondage [emɔ̃daʒ] NM *Hort (d'arbuste, de buisson)* pruning; *(d'arbre)* trimming (the top of)

émonder [3] [emɔ̃de] VT *Hort (arbuste, buisson)* to prune; *(arbre)* to trim (the top of); *Fig (livre, texte)* to prune, to trim

émondeur, -euse [emɔ̃dœr, -øz] NM,F *Hort* pruner

émondoir [emɔ̃dwar] NM *Hort* pruning hook

émoticon [emotikɔ̃] NM *Ordinat* smiley, emoticon

émoticone [emotikon] NF = **émoticon**

émotif, -ive [emɔtif, -iv] ADJ *(personne)* emotional, sentimental; *(trouble, choc)* psychological

NM,F **c'est un grand é.** he's very emotional

émotion [emosjɔ̃] NF **1** *(sensation)* feeling; *Fam (inquiétude)* fright, shock; **une é. indicible** an indescribable feeling, a feeling that can't be put into words; **vive é.** strong emotion; *(exaltation)* excitement, thrill; **le meurtre de l'enfant a provoqué une vive é.** people were shocked by the child's murder; **l'atterrissage mouvementé a provoqué une vive é. parmi les passagers** the bumpy landing frightened the passengers; **ressentir une vive é.** *(attendrissement)* to be greatly moved; *(exaltation)* to be thrilled; **émotions fortes** strong feelings; **quelle é. de l'avoir revu!** seeing him again was quite a shock! **2** *(affectivité)* emotion, emotionality; **chargé d'é.** emotional, charged with emotion; **se laisser gagner par l'é.** to become emotional; **parler avec é.** to speak emotionally **3** *(qualité ▸ d'une œuvre)* emotion; **l'é. qui se dégage de ces lignes/cet oratorio** the emotion emanating from these lines/this oratorio

• **émotions** NFPL *Fam* **j'ai eu des émotions** I got a fright; **donner des émotions à qn** to give sb a (nasty) turn *or* a fright

émotionnel, -elle [emosjɔnel] ADJ *(réaction)* psychological

émotionner [3] [emosjɔne] *Fam* VT *(émouvoir)* to upset□, to shake up; **tout émotionné** very upset *or* shaken□

VPR **s'émotionner** *(s'émouvoir)* **il s'émotionne pour un rien** he gets worked up about the slightest little thing

émotive [emɔtiv] *voir* **émotif**

émotivité [emɔtivite] NF emotionalism; **être d'une trop grande é.** to be too emotional

émoulu, -e [emuly] *voir* **frais²**

émoussé, -e [emuse] ADJ blunt; *Fig (sentiment, qualité etc)* blunted, diminished; **une patience émoussée par le temps** patience diminished *or* worn thin by time; **il a l'appétit é. par la maladie** illness has blunted *or* taken the edge off his appetite

émousser [3] [emuse] VT **1** *(rasoir, épée)* to blunt, to take the edge off **2** *(affaiblir ▸ appétit, goût, peine)* to dull, to take the edge off; *(▸ curiosité)* to temper; *(▸ sens, passions etc)* to dull, to blunt

VPR **s'émousser 1** *(couteau)* to become blunt, to lose its edge **2** *(faiblir ▸ appétit, peine)* to dull; *(▸ curiosité)* to become tempered; *(▸ des sens, passions)* to become blunted *or* dulled

émoustillant, -e [emustijɑ̃, -ɑ̃t] ADJ exhilarating; *(sexuellement)* titillating

émoustiller [3] [emustije] VT **1** *(animer)* to excite, to exhilarate; **le champagne les avait tous émoustillés** they'd all got merry on champagne **2** *(sexuellement)* to turn on

émouvant, -e [emuvɑ̃, -ɑ̃t] ADJ moving, touching; **de façon émouvante** movingly; **un moment é.** an emotional moment

émouvoir [55] [emuvwar] VT **1** *(attendrir)* to touch, to move; **é. qn (jusqu')aux larmes** to move sb to tears **2** *(perturber)* to disturb, to unsettle; **encore tout ému de la rencontre** still very upset by the meeting; **nullement ému par ces accusations** quite undisturbed *or* unperturbed by these accusations; **cela ne m'émeut pas le moins du monde** that doesn't upset me in the least; **ça n'a pas eu l'air de l'é.** he/she seemed quite unsympathetic; **se laisser é.** to let oneself be affected

VPR **s'émouvoir 1** *(s'attendrir)* to be touched *or* moved; **s'é. à la vue de** to be affected by the sight of **2** *(être perturbé)* to be disturbed *or* perturbed; **ce qu'il me déclara sans s'é. le moins du monde** which he announced to me with perfect composure **3** *Fig* **s'é. de** to pay attention to; **le gouvernement s'en est ému** it came to the notice *or* attention of the government; *Fam* **pas de quoi s'é.** it's nothing to get worked up about

empaffé [ɑ̃pafe] NM *Vulg* dickhead, prick, *Br* wanker

empagement [ɑ̃paʒmɑ̃] NM *Ordinat & Typ* text area, text block

empaillage [ɑ̃pajaʒ] NM **1** *(d'animaux)* taxidermy; **e. d'un animal** stuffing **2** *(d'une chaise)* bottoming with straw **3** *Hort* covering with straw

empaillé, -e [ɑ̃paje] ADJ *(animal)* stuffed; *Fam* **avoir l'air e.** to look self-conscious□ *or* awkward□

NM,F *Fam Péj* fat lump

empailler [3] [ɑ̃paje] VT **1** *(animal)* to stuff

2 *(chaise)* to bottom with straw

3 *Hort* to mulch

4 *(produit)* to pack in straw

VPR **s'empailler** *Fam (se quereller)* to lay into each other

empailleur, -euse [ɑ̃pajœr, -øz] NM,F **1** *(d'animaux)* taxidermist **2** *(de chaises)* chair caner

empalement [ɑ̃palmɑ̃] NM impalement

empaler [3] [ɑ̃pale] VT **1** *(supplicier)* to impale **2** *(embrocher)* to put on a spit

VPR **s'empaler s'e. sur une fourche/un pieu** to impale oneself on a pitchfork/stake

empanacher [3] [ɑ̃panaʃe] VT to plume, to deck out *or* to decorate with plumes; **casque empanaché** plumed helmet

empannage [ɑ̃panaʒ] NM *Naut* gybing

empanner [3] [ɑ̃pane] VT *Naut* to gybe

empapaouter [3] [ɑ̃papaute] VT *très Fam* to bugger, to take up the *Br* arse *or Am* ass; **va te faire e.!** go to hell!, *Br* bugger off!, sod off!

empaquetage [ɑ̃paktaʒ] NM **1** *Com (action)* packing, packaging; *(emballage)* packaging **2** *(confection d'un paquet-cadeau)* wrapping up; *(enveloppe)* wrapping

empaqueter [27] [ɑ̃pakte] VT **1** *Com* to pack, to package **2** *(envelopper)* to wrap up

empaqueteur, -euse [ɑ̃paktœr, -øz] NM,F packer

emparer [3] [ɑ̃pare] **s'emparer** VPR **1 s'e. de** *(avec la main ▸ gén)* to grab (hold of), to grasp, to seize; *(▸ vivement)* to snatch

2 s'e. de *(prendre de force ▸ territoire)* to take over, to seize; *(▸ véhicule)* to commandeer; *(▸ ville, otage, butin, pouvoir)* to seize; *Sport (▸ ballon)* to take possession of, to get hold of; **la grande industrie s'est emparée des médias** big business has taken over the media; **s'e. de la conversation** to monopolize the conversation

3 s'e. de *(tirer parti de ▸ prétexte, idée)* to seize (hold of); **la presse s'est emparée de cette histoire** the press got hold of the story

4 s'e. de *(envahir ▸ sujet: doute, obsession, jalousie etc)* to take hold of; **la colère s'est emparée d'elle** anger swept over her; **l'émotion s'est emparée d'elle** she was seized by a strong emotion; **le doute s'est emparé de moi** *ou* **mon esprit** my mind was seized with doubt; **depuis que cette idée s'est emparée de mon esprit** since the idea took hold of me

empâté, -e [ɑ̃pate] ADJ *(voix)* slurred; *(langue)* coated; *(visage)* fleshy, bloated

empâtement [ɑ̃patmɑ̃] NM **1** *Agr (de la volaille)* fattening (up) **2** *(obésité)* fattening out; *(épaississement ▸ des traits)* coarsening; *(▸ de la taille)* thickening **3** *Beaux-Arts* impasto

empâter [3] [ɑ̃pate] VT **1** *Agr (engraisser ▸ volaille)* to fatten (up)

2 *(bouffir)* to make podgier; *(visage)* to bloat, to coarsen; **la vie à la campagne l'a empâtée** she's put on weight in the country

3 *(rendre pâteux ▸ langue)* to coat, to fur up; **le vin lui a empâté la langue** his/her speech has become slurred from drinking wine

4 *Beaux-Arts* impaste

VPR **s'empâter** to put on weight; *(visage)* to coarsen; **sa taille/figure s'est empâtée** he's/she's grown fatter round the waist/in the face

empattement [ɑ̃patmɑ̃] NM **1** *Constr (de planches)* tenoning; *(d'un mur)* footing; *(d'une grue)* base plate

2 *(d'un arbre, d'une branche)* (wide) base

3 *Aut* wheelbase

4 *Typ* serif

empatter [3] [ɑ̃pate] VT *Constr (mur)* to give footing to

empaumer [3] [ɑ̃pome] VT **1** *(au jeu de paume ▸ attraper)* to catch in the palm of the hand; *(▸ frapper)* to strike with the palm of the hand **2** *Fam Vieilli (duper)* to con; **se laisser** *ou* **se faire e.** to be tricked *or* taken in **3** *(sujet: magicien etc ▸ carte, pièce etc)* to palm

empêché, -e [ɑ̃peʃe] ADJ **il a été e.** *(par un problème)* he hit a snag; *(il n'est pas venu)* he couldn't make it; *(il a été retenu)* he was held up

empêchement [ɑ̃peʃmɑ̃] NM **1** *(obstacle)* snag, hitch; **si tu as un e., téléphone** *(si tu as un problème)* if you hit a snag, phone; *(si tu ne viens pas)* if you can't make it, phone; *(si tu es retenu)* if you're held up, phone; **j'ai eu un e.** I got held up *or* detained, something came up at the last minute **2** *Jur* **e. à mariage** impediment to a marriage

empêcher [4] [ɑ̃peʃe] VT **1** *(ne pas laisser)* **e. qn de faire qch** to prevent sb (from) *or* to keep sb from *or* to stop sb (from) doing sth; **il m'a empêché de partir** he prevented me from leaving; **pousse-toi, tu m'empêches de voir!** move over, I can't see!; **il sera difficile de l'en e.** it will be difficult to stop *or* prevent him/her; **je ne vous empêche pas de partir/dîner, au moins?** I hope I'm not keeping you from leaving/your dinner?; **e. qn d'entrer/de sortir/d'approcher** to keep sb out/in/away; **e. que qn/qch (ne) fasse** to stop sb/sth from doing, to prevent sb/sth from doing; **le café m'empêche de dormir** coffee keeps me awake; *Fig* **ce n'est pas ça qui va l'e. de dormir!** he's/she's not going to lose any sleep over that!

2 *(pour renforcer une suggestion)* to stop, to prevent; **cela ne t'empêche pas** *ou* **rien ne t'empêche de l'acheter à crédit** you could always buy it in instalments; **il n'y a rien qui t'empêche de lui téléphoner** there's nothing to stop you phoning him/her; **qu'est-ce qui nous empêche de le faire?** what's to prevent us (from) doing it?; **qu'est-ce qui vous empêche d'écrire à ses parents?** why don't you write to his/her parents?

3 *(prévenir ▸ mariage, famine)* to prevent, to stop; *(▸ action, événement etc)* to prevent; *(▸ mouvement, progrès etc)* to obstruct, to impede; **pour e. l'hémorragie** to prevent a haemorrhage; **e. l'extension d'un conflit** to stop a conflict spreading; *Fam* **ça n'empêche pas** *ou* **rien!** it makes no difference!

V IMPERSONNEL **il n'empêche que** nevertheless; **il n'empêche que cela nous a coûté cher** all the same *or* nevertheless it has cost us dear; **il n'empêche qu'elle ne l'a jamais compris** the fact remains that she's never understood him

• **n'empêche** ADV *Fam* all the same□, though□; **il a été assez gentil, n'empêche!** he was kind, though!; **n'empêche, tu aurais pu (me) prévenir!** all the same *or* even so, you could have let me know!

• **n'empêche que** CONJ *Fam* **on ne m'a pas écouté, n'empêche que j'avais raison!** they didn't listen to me, even though I was right!

VPR **s'empêcher s'e. de faire** to refrain from *or* to stop oneself doing; **je ne pouvais pas m'e. de rire** I couldn't help laughing, I had to laugh; **je ne peux pas m'e. de penser qu'il a raison** I can't help thinking he's right; **il n'a pas pu s'e. de le dire** he just had to say it; **elle ne peut pas s'e. de se ronger les ongles** she can't stop (herself) biting her nails; **je ne peux pas m'en e.** I can't help it, I can't stop myself

empêcheur, -euse [ɑ̃peʃœr, -øz] NM,F *Fam* **un e. de danser** *ou* **tourner en rond** a spoilsport

empeigne [ɑ̃pɛɲ] NF *Tech* upper *(of a shoe)*; *Fam* **gueule d'e.** ugly mug

empennage [ɑ̃pɛnaʒ] NM **1** *Aviat* empennage **2** *(d'un obus, d'une bombe)* tail fins; *(d'une arbalète, d'une flèche)* feathers; *(d'une torpille)* fins

empenner [3] [ɑ̃pene] VT *(flèche)* to feather

empereur [ɑ̃prœr] NM emperor; *Hist* **l'E.** Napoleon (Bonaparte *or* the First)

emperlousé, -e [ɑ̃perluze] ADJ *très Fam* dripping with pearls

empesage [ɑ̃pəzaʒ] NM starching

empesé, -e [ɑ̃pəze] ADJ **1** *(tissu)* starched **2** *(discours, style)* starchy

empeser [19] [ɑ̃pəze] VT to starch

empester [3] [ɑ̃peste] VT **1** *(empuantir ▸ pièce, réfrigérateur)* to make stink, *Br* to stink out; *(▸ personne)* to stink out; **le fromage empeste le frigo** the cheese is making the fridge stink *or Br* is stinking out the fridge; **e. qn (avec sa fumée)** to stink sb out (with one's smoke) **2** *(dégager une forte odeur de)* to stink of; **e. l'alcool/le parfum** to reek *or* stink of alcohol/perfume; **le frigo empeste le fromage** the fridge stinks of cheese

VI *(sentir très mauvais)* to stink

empêtrer [4] [ɑ̃petre] VT **1** *(entortiller ▸ personne)* to trap, to entangle; *(▸ jambes, chevilles)* to trap, to catch; **empêtrée dans sa grosse veste** hampered by her bulky jacket; **empêtré dans ses couvertures** all tangled up in his blankets **2** *(embarrasser)* to bog down; **être empêtré dans ses explications** to be bogged down *or* muddled up in one's explanations

VPR **s'empêtrer 1** *(s'entortiller)* to become

tangled up *or* entangled; **elle s'est empêtrée dans la corde** she got tangled up in the rope; **s'e. les pieds dans les broussailles** to get one's feet caught in the undergrowth **2** *(s'enferrer)* **s'e. dans** *(mensonges, explications)* to get bogged down *or* tied up in; **s'e. dans une sale affaire** to get involved *or* mixed up in a bad business

emphase [ɑ̃faz] **NF 1** *Péj (grandiloquence)* pomposity, bombast; **un discours plein d'e.** a pompous speech; **avec e.** pompously, bombastically; **solennel mais sans e.** solemn but not pompous **2** *Ling* emphasis

emphatique [ɑ̃fatik] **ADJ 1** *Péj (grandiloquent)* pompous, bombastic **2** *Ling* emphatic

> Il faut noter que l'adjectif anglais **emphatic** est un faux ami. Il signifie **énergique** ou **catégorique**.

emphatiquement [ɑ̃fatikmɑ̃] **ADV** pompously, bombastically

> Il faut noter que l'adverbe anglais **emphatically** est un faux ami. Il signifie **énergiquement** ou **catégoriquement**.

emphysémateux, -euse [ɑ̃fizematø, -øz] *Méd* **ADJ** emphysematous

NM,F person suffering from emphysema

emphysème [ɑ̃fizem] **NM** *Méd* emphysema

empiècement [ɑ̃pjesmɑ̃] **NM** *Tex* yoke

empierrement [ɑ̃pjermɑ̃] **NM 1** *(couche de pierres)* gravel, *Br* road metal; *Rail* ballast **2** *(pour le drainage)* lining with stones **3** *(action ▸ d'une route)* macadamization, *Br* metalling; *Rail* ballasting; **procéder à l'e. d'une route** to macadamize *or Br* to metal a road

empierrer [4] [ɑ̃pjere] **VT 1** *(route)* to macadamize, *Br* to metal; *Rail* to ballast **2** *(pour le drainage)* to line with stones

empiétement, empiètement [ɑ̃pjetmɑ̃] **NM** encroachment, encroaching *(UNCOUNT)* (**sur** on); **c'est un e. sur ma vie privée** it's an encroachment on my private life; **cette barrière est un e. sur mon terrain** that fence encroaches on my land; **e. sur les droits de qn** infringement of sb's rights

empiéter [18] [ɑ̃pjete] **empiéter sur VT IND 1** *(dans l'espace, le temps)* to encroach on *or* upon, to overlap with; **cette affiche empiète sur l'autre** this poster overlaps the other **2** *(droit, liberté, pouvoir)* to encroach on *or* upon, to infringe; **mon travail empiète de plus en plus sur mes loisirs** my work encroaches more and more upon my leisure time; **son collègue essaie d'e. sur ses attributions** his/her colleague is trying to trespass on his/her territory; **e. sur les droits de qn** to infringe sb's rights; **empiétant peu à peu sur nos privilèges** gradually eating away at our privileges

empiffrer [3] [ɑ̃pifre] **s'empiffrer VPR** *Fam* to stuff oneself *or* one's face, to pig out; **s'e. de gâteaux** to stuff oneself with cakes

empilable [ɑ̃pilabl] **ADJ** stackable

empilage [ɑ̃pilaʒ], **empilement** [ɑ̃pilmɑ̃] **NM 1** *(action ▸ de boîtes)* piling *or* stacking up; *(▸ de chaises)* stacking up **2** *(pile ▸ ordonnée)* stack; *(▸ désordonnée)* heap, pile, mound

empiler [3] [ɑ̃pile] **VT 1** *(mettre en tas)* to pile *or* to heap up; *(ranger en hauteur)* to stack (up) **2** *(thésauriser)* to amass (large quantities of) **3** *Fam (tromper)* to screw, to fleece; **se faire e. (par qn)** to get screwed *or* fleeced (by sb)

VPR s'empiler 1 *(emploi passif)* to be stacked up; **ces chaises s'empilent** the chairs are stackable **2** *(s'entasser)* to pile up; *(former une pile)* to be piled up; **s'e. dans** *(entrer nombreux dans)* to pile *or* to pack into

Empire [ɑ̃pir] **NM l'E., le premier E.** the (Napoleonic) Empire; **sous l'E.** during the Napoleonic era; **noblesse de l'E.** nobility created by Napoleon (Bonaparte); **le Second E.** the Second Empire; **meubles E.** Empire furniture, furniture in the French Empire style; **l'E. du Milieu** the Middle Kingdom, the Celestial Empire

empire [ɑ̃pir] **NM 1** *Hist (régime, territoire)* empire; **je ne m'en séparerais pas pour (tout) un e.!** I wouldn't be without it for the world!; **l'e. d'Occident** the Western Empire; **l'e. d'Orient** *(romain)* the Eastern (Roman) Empire; *(byzantin)* the Byzantine Empire; **l'e. du Soleil Levant** the Land of the Rising Sun

2 *Myth & Rel* **l'e. céleste** the kingdom of heaven; **l'e. des ténèbres** hell; **l'e. des morts** the realm of the dead; **l'e. de Neptune** Neptune's empire

3 *(groupe d'états)* empire

4 *Com & Ind* empire

5 *(influence)* influence; **avoir de l'e. sur qn** to have a hold on *or* over sb; **avoir de l'e. sur soi-même** to be self-controlled; **quand j'ai bu, je n'ai plus aucun e. sur moi-même** I lose all self-control when I drink; **prendre de l'e. sur qn** to gain influence over sb; **user de** *ou* **exercer son e. sur qn** to use one's power over sb

• **sous l'empire de PRÉP 1** *(poussé par)* **sous l'e. de l'alcool** under the influence of alcohol; **sous l'e. de la jalousie** in the grip of jealousy; **sous l'e. du désir** possessed *or* consumed by desire; **faire qch sous l'e. de la colère** to do sth in a fit of anger; **elle s'est enfuie sous l'e. de la peur** she fled in fear **2** *(soumis à)* **sous l'e. d'un tyran** ruled by a tyrant, under the rule *or Littéraire* sway of a tyrant; **sous l'e. d'un mari brutal** under the sway of a brutal husband

empirer [3] [ɑ̃pire] **VI** *(santé)* to become worse, to worsen, to deteriorate; *(mauvais caractère)* to become worse; *(problème, situation)* to get worse

VT to make worse, to cause to deteriorate

empirique [ɑ̃pirik] **ADJ 1** *Phil* empirical **2** *Péj (non rigoureux)* empirical, purely practical

empirisme [ɑ̃pirism] **NM 1** *Phil* empiricism **2** *Péj (pragmatisme)* empiricism, charlatanry

empiriste [ɑ̃pirist] *Phil* **ADJ** empiricist

NMF empiricist

emplacement [ɑ̃plasmɑ̃] **NM 1** *(pour véhicule)* (parking) space

2 *(position ▸ d'un édifice, d'un monument, d'une tente)* site, location; *(▸ d'une démarcation)* position, place; *(▸ sur un marché)* space; **à l'e. d'un ancien tombeau** on the site of an old tomb; *Naut* **e. de chargement** loading berth

3 *Mktg (site)* site, location; *(dans un journal, à la télé)* space; **e. d'affichage** billboard site, *Br* hoarding site; **e. publicitaire** advertising space

4 *Ordinat* slot; **e. pour carte** card slot; **e. pour carte d'extension** expansion slot; **e. d'évolutivité** upgrade slot; **e. (pour) périphériques** extension slot

emplafonner [3] [ɑ̃plafɔne] **VT** *Fam* to crash into; **elle s'est fait e. par mon voisin** my neighbour crashed into her

emplâtre [ɑ̃platr] **NM 1** *Pharm* plaster; *Fig* **c'est un e. sur une jambe de bois** it's like putting a plaster on a wooden leg **2** *Fam (aliment)* **un véritable e., leur purée!** their mashed potatoes go down like a lead weight! **3** *Fam (personne) Br* waster, *Am* klutz

emplette [ɑ̃plet] **NF 1** *(fait d'acheter)* **faire ses/des emplettes** to do one's/some shopping; **faire l'e. de** to purchase **2** *(objet acheté)* purchase

emplir [32] [ɑ̃plir] **VT** *(récipient)* to fill (up) (**de** with); *(salle)* to fill (**de** with); **la foule emplissait les rues** the crowd filled the streets; **cette nouvelle m'emplit de joie** the news fills me with delight; **les enfants emplissaient la cour de leurs rires** the playground was filled with children's laughter

VPR s'emplir to fill up (**de** with); **s'e. d'air** to inflate, to fill with air

emploi [ɑ̃plwa] **NM 1** *(travail)* job; *(embauche)* employment; **être sans e.** to be out of work *or* out of a job, to be unemployed; **chercher un e.** to be looking for work *or* a job; **avoir un e.** to have a job, to be in work; **emplois de proximité** = employment in the community *(as a way of reducing unemployment)*; **e. saisonnier** seasonal job; **e. à temps partiel** part-time job

2 *(fait d'employer)* employing; **l'e. de spécialistes coûte cher** employing experts is expensive

3 *Écon* **l'e.** employment; **la crise de l'e.** the employment crisis; **le marché de l'e.** the labour market; **le partage de l'e.** job-sharing; **la sécurité de l'e.** job security

4 *(au spectacle)* part; **limitée à des emplois de soubrette** restricted to playing chambermaids; **on le cantonne dans des emplois de grand amoureux** he's typecast as the great lover; **danser/jouer à contre-e.** to be miscast; *Fam* **avoir le physique** *ou* **la tête** *ou* **la gueule de l'e.** to look the part

5 *(utilisation)* use; **il n'en a pas l'e.** he has no use for it; **d'un e. facile** easy to use; **faire bon/mauvais e. de qch** to make good/bad use of sth, to put sth to good/bad use; **faire mauvais e. de son argent** to misuse one's money; **faire double e.** to be redundant; **quel e. vas-tu faire de tout cet argent/ce temps?** what are you going to do with all that money/time?; **prêt à l'e.** ready to use

6 *Scol* **e. du temps** *(de l'année)* timetable; *(d'une journée, des vacances)* timetable, schedule; **un e. du temps chargé** a busy timetable *or* schedule; **quel est mon e. du temps aujourd'hui?** what's my schedule for today?

7 *(cas d'utilisation ▸ d'un objet)* use; *(▸ d'une expression)* use, usage; **les divers emplois d'un verbe** the different uses of a verb; **ce mot est d'un e. rare** the word is rarely used

8 *Compta* entry

emploie *etc voir* **employer**

emploi-jeunes [ɑ̃plwaʒœn] *(pl* **emplois-jeunes**) **NM** = job, usually in the public sector or in education, created for a young person as part of a programme to combat unemployment

employabilité [ɑ̃plwajabilite] **NF** employability

employé, -e [ɑ̃plwaje] **NM,F** employee; **généreux avec leurs employés** generous to their staff *or* their employees; **e. de banque** bank clerk; **e. de bureau** office worker; **e. de chemin de fer** railway employee; **employés communaux** local authority employees; **e. aux écritures** accounts *or* ledger clerk; **j'attends un e. du gaz** I'm expecting someone from the gas *Br* board *or Am* company; **e. de maison** servant; **employés de maison** domestic staff; **être e. de maison** to do domestic work; **e. de mairie** town hall employee; **être e. de mairie** to work at the town hall; **e. occasionnel** casual worker; **e. des postes** postal worker; **être e. des postes** to work for the Post Office

employer [13] [ɑ̃plwaje] **VT 1** *(professionnellement)* to employ; **nous employons 200 personnes** we employ 200 people, we have 200 people on our staff, we employ a staff of 200; **la ganterie emploie 300 personnes dans la région** the glove trade provides jobs for *or* employs 300 local people; **e. qn à faire qch** *(l'assigner à une tâche)* to use sb to do sth; **e. qn comme secrétaire** to employ sb as secretary; **e. qn à des petits travaux** to employ sb to do odd jobs; **employé à plein temps/à temps partiel** employed full-time/part-time

2 *(manier ▸ instrument, machine)* to use

3 *(mettre en œuvre ▸ méthode, ruse)* to employ, to use; **e. la force** to use force; **e. beaucoup d'énergie à faire qch** to expend a lot of energy doing sth; **e. son énergie à faire qch** to devote *or* to apply one's energy to doing sth; **de l'argent bien employé** money well spent, money put to good use; **des fonds mal employés** misused funds; **à quoi vas-tu e. cette somme?** what are you going to spend the money on?

4 *(expression)* to use; **mal e. un mot** to misuse a word, to use a word incorrectly

5 *(temps, journée)* to spend; **bien e. son temps** to make good use of one's time; **mal e. son temps** to misuse one's time, to use one's time badly, to waste one's time; **e. son temps à nettoyer/étudier** to spend one's time cleaning/studying; **il ne sait à quoi e. son temps** he doesn't know what to do with his time

6 *Compta* to enter

VPR s'employer 1 *(mot)* to be used; **ce verbe ne s'emploie plus** that verb is no longer in common usage **2** *(outil, machine)* to be used **3 s'e. à** *(se consacrer à)* to devote *or* to apply oneself to; **je m'y emploie** I'm working on it; *Vieilli* **s'e. pour** *ou* **en faveur de** *(s'activer)* to exert oneself on behalf of

employeur, -euse [ɑ̃plwajœr, -øz] **NM,F** employer

emplumer [3] [ɑ̃plyme] **VT** to decorate with feathers

empocher [3] [ɑ̃pɔʃe] **VT 1** *(mettre dans sa poche)* to pocket **2** *(s'approprier)* to snap up **3** *(au billard)* to pot

empoignade [ɑ̃pwaɲad] NF *Fam* **1** *(coups)* brawl, set-to **2** *(querelle)* row, set-to

empoigne [ɑ̃pwaɲ] *voir* **foire**

empoigner [3] [ɑ̃pwaɲe] VT **1** *(avec les mains)* to grab, to grasp **2** *(émouvoir)* to grip

VPR **s'empoigner** to set to; **ils se sont tous empoignés** there was a general mêlée *or* a free-for-all

empois [ɑ̃pwa] NM starch

empoisonnant, -e [ɑ̃pwazɔnɑ̃, -ɑ̃t] ADJ *Fam* **1** *(exaspérant)* annoying□; **ce que tu peux être e.!** you can be such a pain sometimes! **2** *(ennuyeux)* tedious□, boring□

empoisonné, -e [ɑ̃pwazɔne] ADJ *(trait, paroles)* poisonous, vicious

empoisonnement [ɑ̃pwazɔnmɑ̃] NM **1** *Physiol* poisoning; **e. par le plomb** lead poisoning **2** *Fam (souci, ennui)* problem□

empoisonner [3] [ɑ̃pwazɔne] VT **1** *(tuer)* to poison; **il pensait qu'il s'était fait e.** he thought he'd been poisoned

2 *École* to contaminate, to poison

3 *(mettre du poison sur* ▸ *flèche)* to poison

4 *(empester)* **des odeurs de cuisine empoisonnaient la pièce** the room was full of cooking smells

5 *(dégrader* ▸ *rapports)* to poison, to taint, to blight; *(*▸ *esprit)* to poison; **e. l'existence** *ou* **la vie à qn** to make sb's life a misery

6 *Fam (importuner)* to bug; **tu m'empoisonnes avec tes questions!** you're being a real pain with your questions!

VPR **s'empoisonner 1** *(se tuer)* to poison oneself

2 *Physiol* to get food poisoning

3 *Fam (s'ennuyer)* to be bored stiff; **s'e. l'existence** *ou* **la vie** to make one's life a misery

4 s'e. à faire qch *(se donner du mal pour)* to go to the trouble to do sth; **on va s'e. à peindre deux couches?** is it worth (going to) the trouble *or* bother of painting two coats?

empoisonneur, -euse [ɑ̃pwazɔnœr, -øz] NM,F **1** *Fam (importun* ▸ *qui lasse)* nuisance, bore; *(*▸ *qui gêne)* nuisance, pain (in the neck) **2** *(assassin)* poisoner

empoissonner [3] [ɑ̃pwasɔne] VT to stock with fish

emporté, -e [ɑ̃pɔrte] ADJ *(coléreux* ▸ *personne)* quick-tempered; *(*▸ *ton)* angry; **d'un ton e.** irascibly

NM,F quick-tempered person

emportement [ɑ̃pɔrtəmɑ̃] NM **1** *(colère)* anger *(UNCOUNT)*; *(accès de colère)* fit of anger; **avec e.** angrily **2** *Littéraire ou Vieilli (passion)* transport; **aimer qn avec e.** to love sb passionately; **dans l'e. de la discussion** in the heat of the debate

emporte-pièce [ɑ̃pɔrtəpjɛs] NM INV *Tech* punch; *Culin Br* pastry cutter, *Am* cookie cutter; **découper qch à l'e.** to stamp *or* to punch sth out; *Culin* to cut out (with a *Br* pastry cutter *or Am* cookie cutter)

• **à l'emporte-pièce** *Fig* ADJ incisive; **style à l'e.** incisive style ADV incisively; **répondre à l'e.** to reply incisively *or* trenchantly

emporter [3] [ɑ̃pɔrte] VT **1** *(prendre avec soi)* to take; **n'oubliez pas d'e. vos pilules** don't forget to take your tablets (with you); **en randonnée, je n'emporte que le strict minimum** I only ever carry the lightest possible load on a hike; *Fig* **e. un secret dans la** *ou* **sa tombe** to take *or* to carry a secret to the grave; **il ne l'emportera pas au paradis!** he's not getting away with that!

2 *(transporter* ▸ *stylo, parapluie, animal)* to take; *(*▸ *bureau, piano, blessé)* to carry (off *or* away); **emporte tout ça au grenier/à la cave** take these things (up) to the attic/(down) to the cellar; **e. un malade sur un brancard** to carry off a sick person on a stretcher; **l'avion qui nous emporte vers le soleil** the plane taking *or* carrying us off to sunny climes

3 *(retirer* ▸ *livre, stylo)* to take (away), to remove; *(*▸ *malle, piano)* to carry away, to remove; **qui a emporté la clef?** who removed the key?; **feuilles emportées par le vent** leaves carried away *or* swept along by the wind; **le vent emporta son chapeau** the wind blew his/her hat off *or* away; **autant en emporte le vent** promises are cheap, talk is easy

4 *(voler)* to take, to go off with; **ils ont tout emporté!** they took everything!

5 *(endommager)* to tear off; *(sujet: courant, lave)* to sweep *or* carry away; **l'ouragan a emporté les toits des maisons** the hurricane blew the roofs off the houses; **il a eu le bras emporté par l'explosion** he lost an arm in the explosion, the explosion blew his arm off; **cette sauce emporte** *Fam* **la bouche** *ou très Fam* **la gueule** this sauce takes the roof of your mouth off

6 *(émouvoir* ▸ *sujet: amour, haine)* to carry (along); *(*▸ *sujet: élan)* to carry away; **se laisser e. par** *(la colère, l'enthousiasme, l'imagination, les sentiments)* to get *or* let oneself be carried away by; **il s'est laissé e. par son imagination** he let his imagination run away with him

7 *(tuer* ▸ *sujet: maladie)* **il a été emporté par un cancer** he died of cancer

8 *(gagner* ▸ *victoire)* to win, to carry off; *(*▸ *fort, ville etc)* to take (by assault); *(*▸ *marché)* to close; *(*▸ *contrat)* to land; **e. la victoire (contre)** to be victorious (over), to be the victor (over); **e. la décision** to win *or* to carry the day; **e. tous les suffrages** *Pol* to get all the votes; *Fig* to win general approval; *Fam* **e. le morceau** to have the upper hand; **l'e.** *(argument)* to win *or* to carry the day; *(attitude, méthode)* to prevail; **la raison a fini par l'e.** reason finally triumphed *or* prevailed; **le plus fort l'emportera** *(boxeurs)* the stronger man will win; *(concurrents)* the best competitor will come out on top *or* carry the day; **l'équipe nantaise l'a emporté par deux buts à zéro** the Nantes team won (by) two goals to nil; **Cendrillon l'emportait en beauté (sur les autres)** Cinderella's beauty far outshone the others; **l'e. sur** to win *or* to prevail over; **considérations qui l'emportent sur toutes les autres** considerations that override *or* outweigh all others; **ce dossier/ce candidat/ce prototype l'emporte sur tous les autres** this file/candidate/prototype stands head and shoulders above the others *or* is streets ahead of the others; **ici, le rugby l'emporte sur le foot** rugby is more important *or* popular than football here

VPR **s'emporter 1** *(personne)* to lose one's temper, to fly into a rage (**contre qn** with sb) **2** *(cheval)* to bolt

• **à emporter,** *Suisse* **à l'emporter** ADJ *Br* to take away, *Am* to go; **plats à e.** *Br* takeaway *or Am* takeout food; **nous faisons des plats à e.** we have a *Br* takeaway *or Am* takeout service

empoté, -e [ɑ̃pɔte] *Fam* ADJ clumsy□, awkward□

NM,F clumsy oaf, *Am* klutz

empoter [3] [ɑ̃pɔte] VT *Hort* to pot

empourprer [3] [ɑ̃purpre] *Littéraire* VT **1** *(horizon)* to (tinge with) crimson **2** *(de honte, de plaisir)* to make flush (bright crimson)

VPR **s'empourprer 1** *(horizon)* to turn crimson **2** *(joues, personne)* to flush (bright crimson)

empoussiérer [18] [ɑ̃pusjere] VT to cover with dust, to make dusty

empreindre [81] [ɑ̃prɛ̃dr] *Littéraire* VT *(dans la cire)* to impress, to imprint, to stamp; *(pensée)* to mark, to stamp; *(cœur, comportement)* to mark; **empreint d'un amour véritable** marked by true love; **d'un ton empreint de gravité** in a grave tone of voice; **article empreint d'un certain sérieux** article with serious overtones; **des histoires empreintes d'onirisme** stories with a dreamlike quality

VPR **s'empreindre s'e. de qch** to be tinged with sth

empreint, -e [ɑ̃prɛ̃, -ɛ̃t] PP *voir* **empreindre**

• **empreinte** NF **1** *(du pas humain)* footprint; *(du gibier)* track; **les loups ont laissé des empreintes dans la neige** the wolves left tracks *or* footprints in the snow; **empreinte de pas** footprint; **empreinte de doigt** fingermark; **empreintes (digitales)** fingerprints; **prendre** *ou* **relever les empreintes de qn** to take sb's fingerprints, to fingerprint sb; **relever les empreintes sur un revolver** to fingerprint a revolver

2 *(d'un sceau)* imprint; *(sur une médaille)* stamp; **(frappé) à l'empreinte du roi** stamped with the king's head

3 *(d'une serrure)* impression; **prendre l'empreinte de** to take the impression of; **empreinte en plâtre** plaster cast

4 *(influence)* mark, stamp; **marquer qn/qch de son empreinte** to put one's stamp *or* mark on sb/sth; **être marqué de l'empreinte de qn** to bear sb's stamp *or* mark

5 *École* **empreinte carbone** carbon footprint; **empreinte écologique** ecological footprint

6 *Psy* imprint

7 *(en dentisterie)* **empreintes dentaires** dental impression

8 *Géol* imprint

9 *Biol* **empreinte génétique** genetic fingerprint; **empreinte génomique** genetic imprinting; **empreinte vocale** voiceprint

empressé, -e [ɑ̃prese] ADJ **1** *(fiancé)* thoughtful, attentive; *(vendeur)* eager, willing; *(serveuse, garde-malade)* attentive; *Péj* overzealous; **des soins empressés** assiduous attention; **ils m'ont entouré de soins empressés** they gave me every care and consideration; **il lui fait une cour empressée** he is courting her assiduously **2** *Littéraire Vieilli (pressé)* **il est e. à vous revoir** he is eager to see you again

NM,F **faire l'e. auprès de qn** to fawn over sb

empressement [ɑ̃presmɑ̃] NM **1** *(zèle)* assiduousness, attentiveness; *(d'un vendeur)* eagerness, willingness (**à faire qch** to do sth); **montrer de l'e.** to be eager to please; **son e. auprès des femmes est presque gênant** he is almost embarrassingly attentive to women **2** *(hâte)* enthusiasm, eagerness, keenness; **avec e.** eagerly; **il est allé les chercher avec e./sans (aucun) e.** he went off to get them enthusiastically/(very) reluctantly; **il montre peu d'e. à faire les travaux** he doesn't seem to be very eager *or* keen to do the work

empresser [4] [ɑ̃prese] **s'empresser** VPR **1 s'e. autour** *ou* **auprès de qn** *(s'activer)* to bustle around sb; *(être très attentif)* to attend to sb's needs; **les hommes s'empressent autour d'elle** she always has men hovering around her, men are always dancing attendance on her **2 s'e. de faire qch** to hasten to do sth; **il s'est empressé de mettre l'argent dans sa poche** he hastily put the money in his pocket; **il s'empressa de répondre à ma lettre** he lost no time in answering my letter

emprise [ɑ̃priz] NF **1** *(intellectuelle, morale)* hold; **l'e. du désir** the ascendancy of desire; **sous l'e. de la peur** in the grip of fear; **sous l'e. de mon amour pour elle** swayed by my love for her; **c'est sous l'e. de la colère qu'il l'a mise à la porte** he fired her in a fit of anger; **être sous l'e. de qn** to be under sb's thumb; **avoir de l'e. sur qn** to have a hold over sb **2** *Admin & Jur* expropriation

emprisonnement [ɑ̃prizɔnmɑ̃] NM imprisonment; **peine d'e.** prison sentence; **condamné à cinq ans d'e.** *ou* **à une peine d'e. de cinq ans** sentenced to five years in prison, given a five-year sentence; **e. à perpétuité** life imprisonment

emprisonner [3] [ɑ̃prizɔne] VT **1** *Jur (incarcérer* ▸ *malfaiteur)* to imprison, to jail, to put in prison *or* jail **2** *(immobiliser)* to trap; *(esprit)* to imprison; **le cou emprisonné dans une minerve** his/her neck tightly held in *or* constricted by a surgical collar **3** *(psychologiquement)* **e. qn dans une morale** to put sb in a moral straitjacket; **emprisonné dans des habitudes dont il ne peut pas se défaire** trapped in habits he is unable to break

emprunt [ɑ̃prœ̃] NM **1** *Banque & Fin (procédé)* borrowing; *(argent)* loan; **faire un e.** to borrow money, to take out a loan; **faire un e. de 10000 euros** to raise a loan of *or* to borrow 10,000 euros; **faire un e. à qn** to borrow (money) from sb; **e. à 11 pour cent** loan at 11 percent; **contracter un e.** to raise a loan; **couvrir un e.** to cover a loan; **rembourser un e.** to repay a loan; **souscrire un e.** to subscribe a loan; **émettre un e.** to float a loan; **e. consolidé** consolidated loan; **e. de conversion** conversion loan; **e. à court terme** short-term loan; **e. à découvert** unsecured loan; **e. en devises** currency loan; **e. d'État** government loan; **e. forcé** forced loan; **e. garanti** secured loan; **e. indexé** indexed loan; **e. à long terme** long-term loan; **e. à lots** lottery loan; **e. obligataire** bond issue, loan stock; *(titre)* debenture bond; **e. obligataire convertible** convertible loan stock; **e. public** public loan; **e. public d'État** government loan; **e. de remboursement** refunding loan; **e. à risques** nonaccruing loan; **emprunts à taux fixe** fixed-rate borrowing; **e. à terme (fixe)** term loan; **e. sur titres** loan on securities *or* stock

2 *(d'un vélo, d'un outil)* borrowing; **ce n'est pas à moi, c'est un e.** it's not mine, it's borrowed
3 *Ling (processus)* borrowing (**à** from); *(mot)* loan (word)
4 *(fait d'imiter)* borrowing; *(élément imité)* borrowing
• **d'emprunt** ADJ *(nom)* assumed

emprunté, -e [ɑ̃prœ̃te] **ADJ 1** *(peu naturel ▸ façon)* awkward; *(▸ personne)* awkward, self-conscious; **dit-elle d'un ton e.** she said self-consciously *or* awkwardly **2** *Littéraire (factice ▸ gloire)* usurped; *(▸ sentiments)* feigned; **un air de bonté e.** a feigned air of goodness

emprunter [3] [ɑ̃prœ̃te] **VT 1** *Banque & Fin* to borrow (**à** from)
2 *(outil, robe)* to borrow (**à** from); **est-ce que je peux t'e. ton fiancé pour cette danse?** can I borrow your fiancé for this dance?
3 *(nom)* to assume
4 *(imiter ▸ élément de style)* to borrow, to take; **des coiffures empruntées aux punks** hairstyles borrowed from punk
5 *(route)* to take; *(circuit)* to follow; **le cortège emprunta la rue de Rivoli** the procession took *or* went down the Rue de Rivoli; **vous êtes priés d'e. le souterrain** you are requested to use the underpass
6 *Ling* to borrow; **mot emprunté** loan (word); **mot emprunté à l'anglais** word borrowed from English, English loan word
USAGE ABSOLU *Banque & Fin* to take out a loan, to borrow; **la société a dû e. pour s'acquitter de ses dettes** the company had to borrow to pay off its debts; **e. sur hypothèque/titres** to borrow on mortgage/securities; **e. à long/court terme** to borrow long/short; **e. à intérêt** to borrow at interest

emprunteur, -euse [ɑ̃prœ̃tœr, -øz] **ADJ** borrowing
NM,F borrower

empuantir [32] [ɑ̃pɥɑ̃tir] **VT** *(salle)* to make stink, *Br* to stink out; *(air)* to fill with a foul smell

ému, -e [emy] **PP** *voir* **émouvoir**
ADJ *(de gratitude, de joie, par une musique, par la pitié)* moved; *(de tristesse)* affected; *(d'inquiétude)* agitated; *(d'amour)* excited; **é. (jusqu')aux larmes** moved to tears; **parler d'une voix émue** to speak with (a voice full of) emotion; **trop é. pour parler** too overcome by emotion to be able to speak; **je garde d'elle un souvenir é.** I have fond memories of her; **j'en suis encore tout é.** I still haven't got over it

émulateur [emylatœr] **NM** emulator; *Ordinat* **é. de terminal** terminal emulator; **é. graphique** graphics emulator

émulation [emylasjɔ̃] **NF 1** *(compétition)* emulation **2** *Ordinat* emulation; **é. de terminal** terminal emulation

émule [emyl] **NMF** emulator; **le dictateur et ses émules** the dictator and his followers; **j'ai fait des émules** people followed my lead *or* example

émuler [3] [emyle] **VT** *Ordinat* to emulate

émulseur [emylsœr] **NM** *Chim (appareil)* emulsifier

émulsif, -ive [emylsif, -iv] **ADJ** *Pharm* emulsive; *Chim* emulsifying
NM *Chim* emulsifier

émulsifiable [emylsifjabl] **ADJ** *Chim* emulsifiable

émulsifiant, -e [emylsifjɑ̃, -ɑ̃t] **ADJ** *Pharm* emulsive; *Chim* emulsifying
NM *Chim* emulsifier

émulsifier [9] [emylsifje] **VT** *Chim* to emulsify

émulsion [emylsjɔ̃] **NF** *Chim, Culin & Phot* emulsion

émulsionner [3] [emylsjɔne] **VT 1** *Chim (produit)* to emulsify **2** *Phot* to coat with emulsion

émulsive [emylsiv] *voir* **émulsif**

émut *etc voir* **émouvoir**

EN[1] [əen] **NF** *Anciennement Scol (abrév* **École normale)** = primary school teachers' training college

EN[2] *(abrév écrite* **Éducation Nationale)** *(ministère)* (French) Ministry *or* Department of Education; *(system)* state education *(in France)*

EN [ɑ̃]

> **PRÉP**
> • in **A, B, C, E1, 2, G** • during **A**
> • to **B1** • made of **D**
> • into **E3** • by **E4**
> • + ing **F1–3** • if **F4**
> **PRON**
> • some/any **A3** • about it **A5**
> • of it/them **B, C**

PRÉP A. *DANS LE TEMPS (indiquant le moment)* in; *(indiquant la durée)* in, during; **en 1992** in 1992; **en été** in summer; **en avril** in April; **en soirée** in the evening; **je l'ai fait en dix minutes** I did it in ten minutes; **en deux heures c'était fini** it was over in two hours; **en quarante ans de carrière…** in my forty years in the job…; **il a plu une fois en trois mois** it rained once in three months; **je n'ai pas le temps en semaine** I have no time *or* I don't have the time during the week

B. *DANS L'ESPACE* **1** *(indiquant la situation)* in; *(indiquant la direction)* to; **habiter en montagne/en Turquie** to live in the mountains/in Turkey; **habiter en Arles/en Avignon** to live in Arles/in Avignon; **se promener en forêt/en ville** to walk in the forest/around the town; **faire une croisière en Méditerranée** to go on a cruise around the Mediterranean; **aller en Espagne** to go to Spain; **partir en mer** to go to sea; **partir en forêt** to go off into the forest
2 *Fig* **en moi-même, j'avais toujours cet espoir** deep down *or* in my heart of hearts, I still had that hope; **trouver en soi la force de faire qch** to find in oneself the strength to do sth; **en mon âme et conscience…** in all honesty…; **ce que j'apprécie en lui** what I like about him

C. *INDIQUANT LE DOMAINE* **bon en latin/physique** good at Latin/physics; **j'ai eu 18 sur 20 en chimie** I got 18 out of 20 in chemistry; **je ne m'y connais pas en peinture** I don't know much about painting; **il fait de la recherche en agronomie** he's doing research in agronomy; **en cela il n'a pas tort** and I have to say he's right *or* not wrong there; **elle est intraitable en affaires** she's very tough in business matters *or* when it comes to business; **malheureux en amour** unlucky in love; **je suis fidèle en amitié** I'm a faithful friend; **être expert en la matière** to be an expert on *or* in the subject

D. *INDIQUANT LA COMPOSITION* **chaise en bois/fer** wooden/iron chair; **table en marbre** marble table; **jupe en velours/coton** velvet/cotton skirt; *Fam* **c'est en quoi?** what's it made of?

E. *INDIQUANT LA MANIÈRE, LE MOYEN* **1** *(marquant l'état, la forme, la manière)* **être en colère/en rage** to be angry/in a rage; **être en forme** to be on (good) form; **être en sueur** to be covered in *or* with sweat; **être en transe** to be in a trance; **le pays est en guerre** the country is at war; **les arbres sont en fleurs** the trees are in blossom; **se conduire en gentleman** to behave like a gentleman; **mourir en héros** to die like a hero; **en gage de ma bonne foi** as a token of my goodwill; **je suis venu en ami** I came as a friend; **je l'ai eu en cadeau** I was given it as a present; **il m'a envoyé ces fleurs en remerciement** he sent me these flowers to say thank you; **peint en bleu** painted blue; **je la préfère en vert** I prefer it in green; **un policier en uniforme** a policeman in uniform; **on ne te voit pas souvent en robe** you don't wear dresses very often, it's not often we see you in a dress; **il était en pyjama** he was in his pyjamas, he had his pyjamas on; **couper qch en deux** to cut sth in two *or* in half; **on nous a répartis en deux groupes** we were divided into two groups; **ils étaient disposés en cercle** they were in a circle; **en (forme de) losange** diamond-shaped; **il est en réunion** he's in a meeting; **j'ai passé Noël en famille** I spent Christmas with my family; **faire qch en cachette/en vitesse/en douceur** to do sth secretly/quickly/smoothly; **faire une photo en noir et blanc** to take a black-and-white picture *or* photo; **c'est vendu en sachets** it's sold in sachets; **du sucre en morceaux** sugar cubes; **du lait en poudre** powdered milk; **un château en ruines** a ruined castle; **une rue en pente** a street on a slope *or* a hill
2 *(introduisant une mesure)* in; **je veux le résultat en dollars** I want the result in dollars; **je vous ai donné l'équivalent de 150 euros en livres** I've given you the equivalent of 150 euros in pounds; **auriez-vous la même robe en 38?** do you have the same dress in a 38?; **la chanson est en sol** the song's in (the key of) G
3 *(indiquant une transformation)* into; **convertir des euros en yens** to convert euros into yen; **l'eau se change en glace** water turns into ice; **se déguiser en fille** to dress up as a girl; **la citrouille se transforma en carrosse** the pumpkin turned into a coach; **son chagrin s'est mué en amertume** his/her grief turned into bitterness
4 *(marquant le moyen)* **j'y vais en bateau** I'm going by boat; **ils ont fait le tour de l'île en voilier** they sailed round the island (in a yacht); **elle est venue en taxi** she came in a *or* by taxi; **en voiture/train** by car/train; **avoir peur en avion** to be scared of flying; **ils ont descendu le fleuve en canoë** they canoed down the river; **payer en liquide** to pay cash

F. *AVEC LE GÉRONDIF* **1** *(indiquant la simultanéité)* **il est tombé en courant** he fell while running; **il chantait tout en dansant** he was singing and dancing at the same time; **nous en parlerons en prenant un café** we'll talk about it over a cup of coffee; **c'est en le voyant que j'ai compris** when I saw him I understood; **rien qu'en le voyant, elle se met en colère** she gets angry just seeing him, the mere sight of him makes her angry; **tout en marchant, elles tentaient de trouver une réponse** while walking *or* as they walked, they tried to find an answer
2 *(indiquant la concession, l'opposition)* **tout en se plaignant, il a fini par faire ce qu'on lui demandait** although he complained about it *or* for all his complaining, in the end he did what was asked of him
3 *(indiquant la cause, le moyen, la manière)* **en ne voulant jamais la croire, tu l'as blessée** you hurt her by never believing her; **il marche en boitant** he walks with a limp; **il est parti en courant** he ran off; **retapez en changeant toutes les majuscules** type it out again and change all the capitals; **en s'entraînant tous les jours on fait des progrès** you can make progress by training every day; **ce n'est pas en criant que l'on résoudra le problème** shouting won't solve the problem; **vous y arriverez en persévérant** through perseverance you will succeed
4 *(introduisant une condition, une supposition)* if; **en travaillant avec plus de méthode, tu réussirais** if you worked more methodically, you would succeed; **en prenant un cas concret, on voit que…** if we take a concrete example, we can see that…; **en supposant que…** supposing that…; **bon, en admettant que vous ayiez raison…** OK, supposing you're right…

G. *INTRODUISANT LE COMPLÉMENT DU VERBE* in; **croire en Dieu** to believe in God; **croire en qn/qch** to believe in sb/sth; **espérer en qch** to put one's hope in sth

PRON A. *COMPLÉMENT DU VERBE* **1** *(indiquant le lieu)* **il faudra que tu ailles à la poste – j'en viens** you'll have to go to the post office – I've just got back from *or* just been there; **il partit à la guerre et n'en revint pas** he went off to war and never came back
2 *(indiquant la cause, l'agent)* **on en meurt** you can die of *or* from it; **je n'en dors plus** it's keeping me awake at nights; **il en a beaucoup souffert** he has suffered a lot because of it; **elle était tellement fatiguée qu'elle en pleurait** she was so tired (that) she was crying; **j'en suis étonné** that surprises me
3 *(complément d'objet)* **voilà des fraises/du lait, donne-lui-en** here are some strawberries/here's some milk, give him/her some; **passe-moi du sucre – il n'en reste plus** give me some sugar – there's none left; **si tu n'aimes pas la viande/les olives, n'en mange pas** if you don't like meat/olives, don't eat any; **et du vin, tu n'en bois jamais?** what about wine? don't you ever drink any?; **tous les invités ne sont pas arrivés, il en manque deux** all the guests haven't arrived yet, two are missing; **j'ai ces deux cassettes – je voudrais en écouter une** I've got these two tapes – I'd like to listen to one of them; **j'en ai vu plusieurs/certains** I saw several/some of them; **tu en as acheté beaucoup** you've bought a lot (of it/of them); **on en a trop**

entendu *(des mensonges)* we've heard too many of them; *(d'un secret)* we've heard too much about it; **tu n'en as pas dit assez** you haven't said enough about it

4 *(avec une valeur emphatique)* **elle en a, de l'argent!** she's got plenty of money, she has!; **tu en as de la chance!** you really are lucky, you are!; **j'en ai chanté des chansons!** I've sung lots of songs, I have!

5 *(complément d'objet indirect)* about it; **parlez-m'en** tell me about it; **nous en reparlerons plus tard** we'll talk about it again later; **ne vous en souciez plus** don't worry about it any more; **j'en aviserai le directeur** I'll inform the manager about it

6 *(comme attribut)* **les volontaires? – j'en suis!** any volunteers? – me!; **c'en est** that's what it is; *Fam* **en être** *(être homosexuel)* to be one of them

B. *COMPLÉMENT DU NOM OU DU PRONOM* **j'en garde un bon souvenir** I have good memories of it; **j'aime beaucoup cette chanson – tu en connais les paroles?** I like this song a lot – do you know the lyrics *or* words?; **vous pouvez lui faire confiance, je m'en porte garant** you can trust him/her, take it from me *or* take my word for it; *Belg* **je n'en peux rien** I can't help it

C. *COMPLÉMENT DE L'ADJECTIF* **sa maison en est pleine** his/her house is full of it/them; **j'en suis très satisfait** I'm very satisfied with it/them; **tu en es sûr?** are you sure (of that)?; **elle en est convaincue** she's convinced of it; **elle n'en est pas fière** she's not proud of it

D. *DANS DES LOCUTIONS VERBALES* **il en va de même pour lui** the same goes for him; **s'en prendre à qn** to blame *or* to attack sb; **s'en tenir à** to limit oneself to, to content oneself with; **si l'on en croit les journaux** if we are to believe the newspapers, if the newspapers are to be believed

---

ENA [ena] **NF** *Admin & Pol (abrév* **École nationale d'administration***)* = prestigious university-level college in France preparing students for senior posts in the civil service and public management

enamouré, -e [ɑ̃namure], **énamouré, -e** [enamure] **ADJ** *Vieilli ou Hum (regard, sourire)* amorous; **être e. de qn** to be enamoured of sb

enamourer **[3]** [ɑ̃namure] **s'enamourer** **VPR** *Vieilli ou Hum* to become enamoured (**de** of)

énarchie [enarʃi] **NF** = network of graduates of the "ENA"

énarque [enark] **NMF** = student or former student of the "ENA"

énarthrose [enartroz] **NF** *Anat* ball-and-socket joint, *Spéc* enarthrosis

en-avant [ɑ̃navɑ̃] **NM INV** *Sport (au rugby)* knock-on

en-but [ɑ̃byt] **NM INV** *Sport (au rugby)* in-goal

encabaner **[3]** [ɑ̃kabane] **VT** *(vers à soie)* to put into trays

VPR s'encabaner *Can* to shut oneself up *or* away (at home)

encablure [ɑ̃kablyr] **NF** *Naut* cable, cable's length *(120 fathoms)*; *Fig* **à une e. de** a stone's throw away from; **à deux encablures de** not very far from

encadré, -e [ɑ̃kadre] **ADJ** *Typ* panelled-in, boxed

NM *Typ* box; *(presse écrite)* boxed article; *Ordinat* **e. graphique/texte** graphics/text box

encadrement [ɑ̃kadrəmɑ̃] **NM 1** *(mise sous cadre)* framing; *(cadre)* frame

2 *(embrasure* ▸ *d'une porte)* door frame; *(*▸ *d'une fenêtre)* window frame; **il apparut dans l'e. de la porte** he appeared (framed) in the doorway; *Tech* **e. en caoutchouc** rubber seal

3 *(responsabilité* ▸ *de formation)* training; *(*▸ *de surveillance)* supervision; *(*▸ *d'organisation)* backing; *Mil (*▸ *d'une unité)* officering; **fonctions d'e.** executive functions

4 *(personnel* ▸ *pour former)* training staff; *(*▸ *pour surveiller)* supervisory staff; *Sport (*▸ *pour entraîner)* coaching staff; *Mil* officers; **personnel d'e.** management, managerial staff

5 *Écon* **e. des prix** price controls; **e. du crédit** credit control; **diminuer l'e. du crédit** to reduce credit restrictions, to loosen the credit squeeze; **e. des loyers** rent control

encadrer **[3]** [ɑ̃kadre] **VT 1** *(dans un cadre)* to (put into a) frame; **son frère, alors, il est à e.!** his/her brother's really priceless!

2 *(border)* to frame, to surround; **un dessin encadré de bleu** a drawing with a blue border

3 *(entourer* ▸ *des mots, une phrase)* to circle; *(flanquer)* to flank; **encadré par deux gendarmes** flanked by two policemen; **encadré de ses gardes du corps/de jolies filles** surrounded by his bodyguards/by pretty girls

4 *(surveiller, organiser)* to lead, to organize, to supervise; *(personnel, équipe)* to manage; *(groupe d'enfants, de handicapés, d'étudiants)* to supervise; *Mil (unité)* to officer; **les guides qui encadrent l'expédition** the guides leading the expedition; **nous sommes bien encadrés** our management is good

5 *Écon (prix, loyers, crédit)* to control

6 *Fam (percuter)* to smash *or* to slam into; **je me suis fait e. au carrefour** I had an accident at the crossroads▫

7 *Fam (supporter* ▸ *personne)* **je ne peux pas l'e.** I can't stand (the sight of) him/her, *Br* I can't stick him/her

VPR s'encadrer 1 *Littéraire (apparaître)* to be framed (**dans** in) **2** *Fam (heurter)* to crash; **s'e. dans un arbre** to crash one's car into a tree

encadreur, -euse [ɑ̃kadrœr, -øz] **NM,F** picture framer

encager **[17]** [ɑ̃kaʒe] **VT** *(mettre en cage)* to cage, to put in a cage; *(emprisonner)* to cage; **tenir qn encagé** *(en cage, en prison)* to keep sb caged up; **tenir un oiseau/un animal encagé** to keep a bird/an animal in a cage *or* caged up

encagoulé, -e [ɑ̃kagule] **ADJ** hooded, wearing a hood

encaissable [ɑ̃kesabl] **ADJ** *Fin (chèque)* cashable; *(argent, traite)* collectable, receivable; **ce chèque est e. à la banque** this cheque can be cashed at the bank

encaisse [ɑ̃kɛs] **NF** *Compta & Fin* cash in hand, cash balance; **e. de 100 euros** cash balance of 100 euros; **e. disponible** cash in hand; **e. métallique** gold and silver reserves, bullion; *Banque* **pas d'e.** no funds

encaissé, -e [ɑ̃kese] **ADJ** *(vallée)* deep, steep-sided; *(rivière)* deeply embanked; *(route)* sunken

encaissement [ɑ̃kesmɑ̃] **NM 1** *(d'une vallée)* steep-sidedness, depth; *(d'une rivière)* deep embankment; **dans l'e. de la route** in the deep cutting made by the road

2 *Fin (d'argent)* collection, receipt; *(d'un chèque)* cashing; *(d'une traite)* collection; **donner un chèque à l'e.** to cash a cheque; **encaissements et décaissements** cash inflows and outflows

3 *(de marchandises)* boxing, packing (in boxes)

4 *Hort* tubbing, planting in tubs

encaisser **[4]** [ɑ̃kese] **VT 1** *Fin (argent)* to receive; *(chèque)* to cash; *(traite)* to collect; **e. de l'argent** *(sur son compte)* to pay in cash; *Bourse* **e. un premium** to receive a premium

2 *Fam (gifle, injure, échec, critiques)* to take▫; *Sport* **e. un coup** to take a blow; **il n'a pas encaissé que tu lui mentes/ce que tu lui as dit** he just can't stomach the fact that you lied to him/what you told him

3 *Fam (tolérer)* **je ne peux pas l'e.** I can't stand him/her, *Br* I can't stick him/her

4 *(marchandises)* to box, to pack in boxes

5 *Bot (planter* ▸ *arbuste)* to plant (out) in a box *or* tub

6 *(resserrer* ▸ *sujet: collines)* to hem in; *Tech (rivière etc)* to embank

USAGE ABSOLU *Fam* **ne dis rien, encaisse!** take it, don't say anything!▫; **il faut pouvoir e.** you have to be able to take a few hard knocks; **e. sans broncher** to grin and bear it

VPR s'encaisser *(rivière, route etc)* to be hemmed in; **la route s'encaisse profondément entre les montagnes** mountains tower above the road on both sides

encaisseur, -euse [ɑ̃kesœr, -øz] *Fin* **ADJ** *(banque, établissement)* collecting

NM *(d'un chèque)* payee; *(de l'argent, d'une traite)* collector, receiver

encan [ɑ̃kɑ̃] **NM** *Com* **vente à l'e.** auction; **vendre qch à l'e.** to sell sth by *or* at auction; *Fig Littéraire* **mettre qch à l'e.** to sell sth to the highest bidder; *Fig* **la loi semble mettre la justice à l'e.** the law seems to put a low price on justice

encanaillement [ɑ̃kanajmɑ̃] **NM** *(d'une personne)* mixing with the riff-raff, slumming it; *(du langage, d'un comportement)* increasing coarseness

encanailler **[3]** [ɑ̃kanaje] **s'encanailler** **VPR** to mix with the riff-raff, to slum it; **il faudrait qu'elle s'encanaille un peu** she ought to loosen up a bit; **la mode s'encanaille** fashion is becoming less inhibited

encapuchonner **[3]** [ɑ̃kapyʃɔne] **VT 1** *(personne, tête)* to put a hood on; **la tête encapuchonnée** hooded; **enfants encapuchonnés** children with their hoods on *or* up **2** *(stylo)* to put the cap on

VPR s'encapuchonner 1 *(personne)* to put on a/one's hood **2** *Équitation (cheval)* to curve *or* arch the neck

encart [ɑ̃kar] **NM** insert; *(mobile)* (loose) insert; *Journ* slip sheet; **e. publicitaire** advertising insert; *TV & Rad* commercial break

encartage [ɑ̃kartaʒ] **NM 1** *Typ* insetting **2** *(fixation sur un carton)* carding

encarté, -e [ɑ̃karte] **ADJ** *(membre)* card-carrying; **il est e. au PC** he's a card-carrying *or* paid-up member of the communist party

encarter **[3]** [ɑ̃karte] **VT 1** *Typ* to insert, to inset **2** *(fixer sur un carton)* to card **3** *Tex* to card

en-cas, encas [ɑ̃ka] **NM INV** snack; **j'ai un petit e. dans mon sac** I have something to eat in my bag

encaserner **[3]** [ɑ̃kazerne] **VT** to barrack; **être encaserné à** to be barracked at

encastrable [ɑ̃kastrabl] **ADJ** *(machine à laver, cuisinière)* that can be built in *or* fitted

encastré, -e [ɑ̃kastre] **ADJ** *(machine à laver, cuisinière)* built-in, fitted; *(four, baignoire)* built-in; *(interrupteur)* flush-fitting, set-in

encastrement [ɑ̃kastrəmɑ̃] **NM 1** *(d'un placard* ▸ *action)* building in, recessing; *(placard, étagères)* built-in fitting; *(d'une machine à laver, d'une cuisinière* ▸ *action)* fitting, building in **2** *(d'un interrupteur* ▸ *action)* flushing in; *(interrupteur)* flush fitting **3** *(espace prévu)* recess

encastrer **[3]** [ɑ̃kastre] **VT 1** *(placard)* to build in, to slot in; *(machine à laver, cuisinière)* to build in, to fit; *(four, baignoire)* to build in; *(interrupteur)* to recess, to fit flush; *(coffre-fort)* to recess **2** *(dans un boîtier, un mécanisme)* to fit

VPR s'encastrer *(deux éléments)* to fit together; **s'e. dans** *(machine à laver, cuisinière)* to fit into; **la voiture s'est encastrée sous un camion** the car embedded itself under a lorry

encaustiquage [ɑ̃kostikaʒ] **NM** *Beaux-Arts* polishing, waxing

encaustique [ɑ̃kostik] *Beaux-Arts* **ADJ** *(peinture)* encaustic

NF 1 *(cire)* polish, wax **2** *(technique)* encaustic (painting)

encaustiquer **[3]** [ɑ̃kostike] **VT** *Beaux-Arts* to polish, to wax

encavage [ɑ̃kavaʒ] **NM** *Suisse (du vin)* cellarage, cellaring; *(du fromage, de légumes, de fruits)* storage in a cellar

encavement [ɑ̃kavmɑ̃] **NM** *(du vin)* cellarage, cellaring

encaver **[3]** [ɑ̃kave] **VT** to store in a a cellar, to cellar

encaveur [ɑ̃kavœr] **NM 1** *(ouvrier)* cellarman **2** *Suisse (négociant)* wine-maker, wine producer

enceindre **[81]** [ɑ̃sɛ̃dr] **VT** *Littéraire* **e. la ville de murs** to encircle *or* to surround the city with walls

enceinte[1] [ɑ̃sɛ̃t] **NF 1** *(mur)* (surrounding) wall; *(palissade)* fence; **mur d'e.** surrounding wall

2 *(ceinture)* enclosure, fence; *Courses de chevaux* ring; **protégé par une e. de fossés** closed in by a circular moat

3 *Chasse (fourré)* cover

4 *(pour haut-parleur)* **e. (acoustique)** speaker

• **dans l'enceinte de PRÉP** within (the boundary of); **dans l'e. du parc** within *or* inside the park; **il est interdit de pénétrer en voiture dans l'e. du parc** cars may not enter the park, cars are not allowed into the park; **dans l'e. de l'école** on school premises; **en dehors de l'e. de l'école** outside school

enceinte² [ɑ̃sɛ̃t] **ADJ F** *Biol & Physiol (femme)* pregnant; **femme e.** pregnant woman, expectant mother; **e. de son premier enfant/d'une fille** expecting her first child/a little girl; **e. de trois mois** three months pregnant; **elle est e. de Paul** she's pregnant by Paul, she's expecting Paul's child; **mettre qn e.** to make *or* to get sb pregnant

encens [ɑ̃sɑ̃] **NM 1** *(résine)* incense; **bâtonnet d'e.** incense stick, joss stick **2** *Fig Littéraire* sycophancy, flattery

encensement [ɑ̃sɑ̃smɑ̃] **NM 1** *(d'un écrivain)* praising to the skies **2** *Rel* incensing

encenser [3] [ɑ̃sɑ̃se] **VT 1** *(louer ▸ mérites)* to praise to the skies; *(▸ écrivain, œuvre)* to praise to the skies, to shower *or* to heap praise upon **2** *Rel* to incense

VI *(cheval)* to toss its head up and down

> Attention: le verbe anglais **to incense** est un faux ami. Il signifie **rendre furieux**.

encenseur, -euse [ɑ̃sɑ̃sœr, -øz] **NM,F 1** *Rel* thurifer, censer bearer **2** *Vieilli (flatteur)* sycophant

encensoir [ɑ̃sɑ̃swar] **NM 1** *Rel* censer **2** *Fam (locutions)* **un coup d'e.** a piece of flattery□; **manier l'e., donner des coups d'e.** to use flattery

encéphale [ɑ̃sefal] **NM** *Anat* encephalon

encéphalite [ɑ̃sefalit] **NF** *Méd* encephalitis; **e. léthargique** sleeping sickness; *Vét* **e. bovine spongiforme** bovine spongiform encephalopathy, BSE

encéphalogramme [ɑ̃sefalɔgram] **NM** *Méd* encephalogram

encéphalographie [ɑ̃sefalɔgrafi] **NF** *Méd* encephalography

encéphalomyélite [ɑ̃sefalɔmjelit] **NF** *Méd* encephalomyelitis

encerclement [ɑ̃sɛrkləmɑ̃] **NM** surrounding; **après l'e. de l'ennemi** after the enemy was surrounded *or* encircled

encercler [3] [ɑ̃sɛrkle] **VT 1** *(marquer)* to ring, to draw a ring round, to encircle; **encerclé d'un trait rouge** circled in red **2** *(entourer)* to surround, to encircle, to form a circle around; **la barrière qui encercle la propriété** the fence encircling the property **3** *Mil (cerner)* to surround, to encircle, to hem in; **village encerclé par des soldats** village surrounded by troops

enchaîné [ɑ̃ʃene] **NM** *TV & Cin* dissolve

enchaînement [ɑ̃ʃɛnmɑ̃] **NM 1** *(série)* sequence, series; **raconte-moi l'e. des événements** tell me what the sequence of events was

2 *(lien)* (logical) link; *TV & Cin (entre deux vues)* melt; **faire un e.** *(dans un raisonnement)* to link up two ideas; *(dans un exposé)* to link up two items

3 *(structure)* structure, logical sequence; **l'e. des paragraphes est très important** the way in which the paragraphs follow on from each other *or* the paragraphs are linked is very important

4 *(en danse)* enchaînement, sequence of steps, linked-up steps

5 *Sport* linked-up movements; **un bel e. à la poutre** a fluid sequence of movements on the beam; **faire un e.** to perform a sequence

6 *Mus* **e. des accords** chord progression

7 *(dans un spectacle)* filler

8 *Ordinat* concatenation

enchaîner [4] [ɑ̃ʃene] **VT 1** *(lier ▸ personne)* to put in chains, to chain; *(▸ animal)* to chain up; **e. à** to chain (up) to; **un chien enchaîné à un arbre** a dog chained (up) to a tree

2 *(attacher ensemble ▸ prisonniers)* to chain (up) together; *(▸ maillons)* to link (up)

3 *(asservir ▸ média)* to trammel, to shackle; *(▸ personne)* to enslave; *(▸ libertés)* to put in chains *or* shackles

4 *(relier ▸ idées, mots, phrases)* to link (up), to link *or* to string together; **vos arguments ne sont pas bien enchaînés** your arguments aren't presented in logical sequence *or* don't follow on from each other; **ils enchaînaient les sujets très vite** they moved very quickly from one subject to another; **e. le tournage de plusieurs épisodes** to shoot several episodes one after the other; **pour la répétition de ce soir, on enchaîne toutes les scènes** at this evening's rehearsal we'll run through all the scenes one after the other without a break

5 *(dans une conversation)* **"c'est faux", enchaîna-t-elle** "it's not true," she went on

6 *(en danse)* to link; *Sport (mouvements)* to run together *or* into each other, to link up (together); **la séquence est bien/mal enchaînée** the sequence flows naturally/feels jerky

VI 1 *(poursuivre)* to move *or* to follow on; **enchaîne avec les diapositives** follow on with the slides; **on enchaîne avec les nouvelles internationales** we'll move on to the international news; **elle a enchaîné sur les élections** she went on to talk about the election **2** *Rad & TV* to link up two items of news; **enchaînons** let's go on to the next item **3** *Cin* to fade; *Théât* to carry straight on; **e. sur une scène** to fade into a scene

VPR s'enchaîner *(idées)* to be connected, to follow on (from one another); *(images, épisodes)* to form a (logical) sequence; *(événements)* to be linked together; **tes paragraphes s'enchaînent mal** your paragraphs don't hang together well *or* are a bit disjointed; **les événements se sont enchaînés très vite** things moved *or* happened very quickly

enchanté, -e [ɑ̃ʃɑ̃te] **ADJ 1** *(magique)* enchanted **2** *(ravi)* delighted, pleased; **être e. de qch** to be enchanted by *or* delighted with sth; **e.!** pleased to meet you!; **je suis (vraiment) e. de vous rencontrer** I am (really) delighted *or* (very) pleased to meet you; **e. de faire votre connaissance!** how do you do!, pleased to meet you!

enchantement [ɑ̃ʃɑ̃tmɑ̃] **NM 1** *(en magie)* (magic) spell, enchantment; **c'est par e. qu'elle s'est transformée en princesse** she was magically turned into a princess; **comme par e.** as if by magic **2** *(merveille)* delight, enchantment; **la soirée fut un véritable e.** the evening was absolutely delightful *or* enchanting; **être dans l'e. (de)** to be enchanted *or* delighted (by)

enchanter [3] [ɑ̃ʃɑ̃te] **VT 1** *(faire plaisir à)* to enchant, to charm, to delight; **elle nous a enchantés par son humour** we were charmed *or* delighted by her sense of humour; **cela ne l'enchante pas beaucoup** *ou* **guère** he's/she's none too pleased *or* happy (at having to do it) **2** *(par la magie)* to bewitch, to cast a spell on

enchanteur, -eresse [ɑ̃ʃɑ̃tœr, -trɛs] **ADJ** *(sourire)* enchanting, bewitching; *(discours, endroit)* enchanting, delightful

NM 1 *(magicien)* enchanter, sorcerer **2** *(séducteur)* charmer

• **enchanteresse NF 1** *(magicienne)* enchantress, witch **2** *(séductrice)* charmer, enchantress

enchâssement [ɑ̃ʃasmɑ̃] **NM** *(en joaillerie)* setting

enchâsser [3] [ɑ̃ʃase] **VT 1** *(en joaillerie)* to set **2** *(insérer ▸ mot)* to insert **3** *Rel (relique)* to enshrine

VPR s'enchâsser to fit together exactly

enchâssure [ɑ̃ʃasyr] **NF** *(d'un bijou)* setting, mount

enchère [ɑ̃ʃɛr] **NF 1** *Com (vente)* auction; **enchères publiques** public auction; **vendre qch aux enchères** to sell sth by auction; **acheter qch aux enchères** to buy sth at an auction; **mettre qch aux enchères** to put sth up for auction **2** *Com (offre d'achat)* bid; **les enchères** the bidding; **faire une e.** to bid, to make a bid; **faire monter les enchères** to raise the bidding; *Fig* to raise the stakes; **couvrir une e.** to make a higher bid, to bid higher; **couvrir l'e. de qn** to bid higher than sb, to outbid sb; **commencer les enchères à 400 euros** to start the bidding at 400 euros **3** *Cartes* bid; **système des enchères** *(au bridge)* bidding system

enchérir [32] [ɑ̃ʃerir] **VI 1** *Com (dépasser)* to make a higher bid; **e. de dix euros** to bid another ten euros **2** *Vieilli ou Littéraire (devenir cher)* to become dearer *or* more expensive, to go up in price

• **enchérir sur VT IND 1** *Com (dans une enchère)* **e. sur une offre** to make a higher bid; **e. sur une somme** to go over and above an amount; **e. sur qn** to bid higher than sb; *Fig* to go one better than sb **2** *Littéraire (aller au-delà de)* to go (over and) beyond; **e. sur son devoir** to go above and beyond the call of duty

enchérissement [ɑ̃ʃerismɑ̃] **NM** *Littéraire* **l'e. de** the rise in the price of

enchérisseur, -euse [ɑ̃ʃerisœr, -øz] **NM,F** *Com* bidder; **au plus offrant et dernier e.** to the highest bidder

enchevaucher [3] [ɑ̃ʃəvoʃe] **VT** *Constr* to overlap

enchevêtré, -e [ɑ̃ʃəvetre] **ADJ** *(écheveau, fils)* tangled, in a tangle; *(style, idées)* confused; **un amas de branches enchevêtrées** a tangle of branches; **une intrigue enchevêtrée** a complicated *or* muddled plot

enchevêtrement [ɑ̃ʃəvɛtrəmɑ̃] **NM 1** *(objets emmêlés)* tangle, tangled mass; **dans un e. de draps et de couvertures** in a tangle of sheets and blankets **2** *(confusion)* tangle, tangled state, confusion; **l'e. de ses idées est tel que...** he/she is so confused that...

enchevêtrer [4] [ɑ̃ʃəvetre] **VT 1** *(mêler ▸ fils, branchages)* to tangle (up), to entangle **2** *(embrouiller ▸ histoire)* to confuse, to muddle

VPR s'enchevêtrer 1 *(être emmêlé ▸ fils)* to become entangled, to get into a tangle; *(▸ branchages)* to become entangled **2** *(être confus ▸ idées, événements)* to become confused *or* muddled

enchifrené, -e [ɑ̃ʃifrəne] **ADJ** *Vieilli (nez)* blocked; **une voix enchifrenée** a voice thick with catarrh

enclave [ɑ̃klav] **NF 1** *(lieu)* enclave; **une e. de maisons isolées parmi les lotissements** an enclave of detached houses surrounded by housing developments **2** *(groupe, unité)* enclave; **notre petite e. culturelle perpétue les traditions de notre pays d'origine** within our little group of expatriates we uphold our native country's traditions **3** *Géol* inclusion, xenolith

enclaver [3] [ɑ̃klave] **VT 1** *(région, pays etc)* to cut off, to isolate; **pays enclavé** *(sans accès maritime)* landlocked country **2** *(terrain, jardin etc)* to enclose, to hem in **3** *(deux éléments)* to fit into each other, to interlock

enclenchement [ɑ̃klɑ̃ʃmɑ̃] **NM** *Tech* **1** *(action)* engaging; *(résultat)* engagement; **avant l'e. du loquet** before the catch engages **2** *(dispositif)* interlock

enclencher [3] [ɑ̃klɑ̃ʃe] **VT 1** *Tech* to engage; *(pièces)* to interlock **2** *(commencer ▸ démarche, procédure)* to set in motion, to get under way, to set off

VPR s'enclencher 1 *Tech* to engage; *(pièces)* to interlock **2** *(démarche, procédure)* to get under way, to get started; **bien/mal s'e.** to get off to a good/bad start

enclin, -e [ɑ̃klɛ̃, -in] **ADJ e. à qch/à faire qch** inclined to sth/to do sth; **elle est encline à la paresse/à la panique** she is inclined *or* tends to be lazy/to panic; **il est e. à l'alcoolisme** he is inclined to drink, he has alcoholic tendencies; **peu e. au bavardage** not very talkative; **peu e. à partager ses secrets** reluctant to share his secrets

enclitique [ɑ̃klitik] **NM** *Ling* enclitic

enclore [113] [ɑ̃klɔr] **VT** to enclose; *(sujet: palissade)* to fence in; *(sujet: mur)* to wall in; **enclos d'une haie** hedged in; **enclos d'un mur** walled in

enclos [ɑ̃klo] **NM 1** *Agr (terrain)* enclosed plot of land; *(à moutons)* pen, fold; *(à chevaux)* paddock

2 *(muret)* wall

3 *(grillage)* (wire) fence

4 *Hist (en Bretagne)* **e. paroissial** church precincts

enclosons *etc voir* **enclore**

enclume [ɑ̃klym] **NF 1** *(du forgeron)* anvil; *(du couvreur)* (slater's) iron; *(du cordonnier)* last; *Fig* **entre l'e. et le marteau** between the devil and the deep blue sea **2** *Anat* anvil

encoche [ɑ̃kɔʃ] **NF 1** *(entaille)* notch

2 *(d'une flèche)* nock

3 *(d'un livre)* thumb index; **avec encoches** thumb-indexed, with a thumb index

4 *Ordinat* **e. de protection contre l'écriture** write-protect notch

5 *Élec* **armature à encoches** slotted armature

encochement [ɑ̃kɔʃmɑ̃] **NM** notching

encocher [3] [ɑ̃kɔʃe] **VT 1** *(faire une entaille à)* to notch **2** *(flèche)* to nock **3** *(livre)* to thumb-index

encodage [ɑ̃kɔdaʒ] NM encoding

encoder [3] [ɑ̃kɔde] VT to encode

encodeur, -euse [ɑ̃kɔdœr, -øz] NM,F encoder

encoignure [ɑ̃kwaɲyr, ɑ̃kɔɲyr] NF 1 *(angle)* corner 2 *(table)* corner table; *(placard)* corner cupboard; *(siège)* corner chair

encollage [ɑ̃kɔlaʒ] NM *(à l'aide de colle ▸ de papier)* pasting; (▸ *de bois)* gluing; *(à l'aide d'apprêt ▸ de papier, tissu, plâtre etc)* sizing; *Typ* perfect binding

encoller [3] [ɑ̃kɔle] VT *(papier)* to paste; *(bois etc)* to glue, to apply glue to; *(à l'aide d'apprêt ▸ papier, tissu, plâtre etc)* to size

encolure [ɑ̃kɔlyr] NF 1 *Anat* neck; *(tour de cou)* neck size; **homme de forte e.** thickset *or* stocky man 2 *Zool & Équitation* neck; **à une e. du vainqueur** a neck behind the winner; **gagner d'une e.** to win by a neck 3 *Couture (de vêtement)* neck; **e. carrée** square neck

encombrant, -e [ɑ̃kɔ̃brɑ̃, -ɑ̃t] ADJ 1 *(volumineux)* bulky, cumbersome; **j'ai dû m'en débarrasser, c'était trop e.** I had to get rid of it, it was taking up too much space *or* it was getting in the way 2 *(importun)* inhibiting, awkward; **un témoin e.** an unwanted witness

NMPL *(régional)* **les encombrants passent demain** the bulk refuse disposal people are coming tomorrow; **mettre qch aux encombrants** to put sth out for collection

encombre [ɑ̃kɔ̃br] **sans encombre** ADV safely, without mishap; **tu es rentré sans e.?** did you get home safely?

encombrement [ɑ̃kɔ̃brəmɑ̃] NM 1 *(embouteillage)* traffic jam

2 *(fait d'obstruer)* jamming, blocking; **par suite de l'e. des lignes téléphoniques/de l'espace aérien** because the telephone lines are overloaded/the air space is overcrowded

3 *(entassement)* clutter, cluttered state; **il y a un tel e. de livres dans son bureau** his/her office is so cluttered up with books

4 *(dimension)* size

5 *Méd* **e. des voies respiratoires** congestion of the respiratory system

6 *Ordinat* footprint; **faible e. sur le disque dur** low use of hard disk space

7 *Com (de marchandises)* glut

encombrer [3] [ɑ̃kɔ̃bre] VT 1 *(remplir)* to clutter (up), to fill *or* to clog up; **e. qch de** to clutter sth (up) with; **table encombrée de papiers** table littered with papers; **j'ai l'esprit encombré de souvenirs** my mind's cluttered up with memories

2 *(obstruer ▸ couloir)* to block (up); (▸ *route)* to block *or* to clog up; (▸ *circulation)* to hold up; **une ville très encombrée** a congested city, a city choked with traffic; **sentier encombré de ronces** path overgrown with brambles

3 *(saturer ▸ lignes téléphoniques)* to jam, to block; (▸ *marché)* to glut, to flood; **les logiciels encombrent le marché** there's a glut *or* surplus of software packages on the market; **une profession encombrée** an overcrowded profession

4 *(charger ▸ sujet: objet lourd)* to load (down), to encumber; **e. qn de** to load sb down with

5 *(sujet: objet gênant)* **tiens, je te donne ce vase, il m'encombre** here, have this vase, I don't know what to do with it; **que faire de ces sacs qui nous encombrent?** what shall we do with these bags that are in the way?

6 *(gêner)* to burden, to encumber; **son enfant l'encombre** his/her child's a burden to him/her; **encombré d'une famille nombreuse** encumbered *or* burdened with a large family

VPR **s'encombrer** *(avoir trop de bagages, de vêtements)* to be loaded *or* weighed down; **s'e. de** *(colis, équipement etc)* to load oneself down with; *Fig (obligations, enfants etc)* to burden oneself *or* saddle oneself with, to be overburdened with; **je ne m'encombre pas de biens matériels** I don't allow myself to become encumbered with material possessions; **il ne s'encombre pas de scrupules** he's not exactly overburdened with scruples; *Fig* **s'e. l'esprit de qch** to fill one's mind *or* to cram one's head with sth

encontre [ɑ̃kɔ̃tr] **à l'encontre** ADV in opposition; **je n'ai rien à dire à l'e.** I have no objections

• **à l'encontre de** PRÉP **aller à l'e. de** to go against, to run counter to; **cette décision va à l'e. du but recherché** this decision is self-defeating *or* counterproductive; **cela va à l'e. de la loi** that's against the law; **cela va à l'e. de ce qu'il proposait la semaine dernière** that's the opposite of *or* contradicts what he was saying last week; **ces nouvelles méthodes vont à l'e. de tout ce qu'on m'a toujours appris** these new methods go against *or* are contrary to *or* run counter to everything I've been taught; **cela va à l'e. du bon sens** it goes against common sense

encorbellement [ɑ̃kɔrbɛlmɑ̃] NM corbelled construction; *(d'un mur etc)* corbelling; *(d'un étage supérieur)* overhang; **balcon en e.** corbelled balcony; **fenêtre en e.** oriel window

encorder [3] [ɑ̃kɔrde] *Sport* VT to rope up

VPR **s'encorder** to rope up (together)

ENCORE [ɑ̃kɔr]

- still **1**
- yet **3**
- more **5**
- only **2**
- again **4**
- even **6**

ADV 1 *(toujours)* still; **il travaillait e. à minuit** he was still working at midnight; **la banque sera e. ouverte à 19 heures** the bank will still be open at 7 p.m.; **tu es e. là?** so you're still here?, are you still here?; **j'ai e. faim** I'm still hungry; **ils en sont e. à taper tout à la machine** they're still using typewriters

2 *(pas plus tard que)* only; **ce matin e., il était d'accord** only this morning he was in agreement; **hier e., je lui ai parlé** I spoke to him/her only yesterday

3 *(dans des phrases négatives)* **pas e.** not yet; **je n'ai pas e. fini** I haven't finished yet; **e. rien** still nothing, nothing yet; **je n'ai e. rien écrit** I haven't written anything (down) yet, I still haven't written anything (down); **vous n'avez e. rien vu!** you haven't seen anything yet!; **elle n'est e. jamais** *ou* **e. pas venue me voir** she hasn't come to see me yet, she still hasn't come to see me; **je n'avais e. jamais vu ça!** I'd never seen anything like it before!

4 *(de nouveau)* again; **il est e. venu la voir** he came to see her again; **voilà e. la pluie!** here's the rain again!; **tu manges e.!** you're not eating again, are you!; **e. toi!** (not) you again!; **je me suis coupé – e.!** I've cut myself – not again!; **e. une fois, c'est non!** the answer's still no!; **si tu fais ça e. une fois...** if you do that again *or* one more time *or* once more...; **nous l'avons e. vu hier** we saw him again yesterday; **e. de la glace?** some more *or* a little more ice-cream?; **je te sers e. un verre?** will you have another drink?; **e. une panne!** not another breakdown!; **il y a e. eu un meurtre d'enfant** another child has been murdered; **qui e.?** who else?; **quoi e.?** *(dans une énumération)* what else?; *Fam (ton irrité)* now what?; **et puis quoi e.?** *(dans une énumération)* what else?; *Ironique* will that be all?; *(marquant l'incrédulité)* whatever next?; **que faut-il que je prenne e.?** what else do I need to take?; **qu'est-ce qu'il y a e.?** what is it this time?; **qu'est-ce qu'il a e. fait?** now what's he done?, what's he done now *or* this time?; **elle est bien élevée, charmante, mais e.?** she's well brought-up and charming, and (apart from that)?; **il a dit qu'il avait bien aimé – mais e.?** he said he liked it – but what exactly did he say?; **elle est sympa – mais e.?** she's nice – yes, go on!; **e. un qui ne sait pas ce qu'il veut!** another one who doesn't know what he wants!

5 *(davantage)* more; **il va grandir e.** he's still got a bit more growing to do; **réduisez-le e.** reduce it even more; **il faudra e. travailler cette scène** that scene still needs more work on it; **e. un mot** (just) one word more; **en voulez-vous e.?** would you like some more?; **e. du vin, s'il vous plaît!** some more wine please!; **e. une tasse de café** another cup of coffee; **pendant e. trois mois** for three months longer, for another three months; **réduire e. le prix** to reduce the price still *or* even further *or* more

6 *(devant un comparatif)* **il est e. plus gentil que je n'imaginais** he is even nicer than I'd imagined (he'd be); **ses affaires vont e. mieux que l'an dernier** his/her business is even more successful than it was last year, his/her business is going even better than it was last year; **elle travaille e. plus qu'avant** she works even harder than before; **e. autant** as much again; **e. pire** even *or* still worse

7 *(introduisant une restriction)* **il ne suffit pas d'être beau, il faut e.** *ou* **e. faut-il être intelligent** it's not enough to be good-looking, you need to be intelligent too; **c'est bien beau d'avoir des projets, e. faut-il les réaliser** it's all very well having plans, but the important thing is to put them into practice; **si e. il** *ou* **e. s'il était franc, on lui pardonnerait** if only *or* if at least he was honest, you could forgive him; **je t'en donne 20 euros, et e.!** I'll give you 20 euros for it, if that!; **il aura peut-être une chance là-bas, et e.!** perhaps he'll have a chance over there, but only just *or* but not much of one!; **et e., on ne sait pas tout!** and even then we don't know the half of it!; **e. heureux!** thank goodness for that!; **e. une chance qu'il n'ait pas été là!** thank goodness *or* it's lucky he wasn't there!; **(mais) e. faudrait-il qu'elle accepte!** she has to agree first!

• **encore que** CONJ (al)though, even though; **j'aimerais y aller, e. qu'il soit tard** I'd like to go even though it's late; **temps agréable e. qu'un peu froid** pleasant if *or* though rather cold weather; **on a assez d'argent, e. que, avec l'assurance à payer...** we've enough money, although with the insurance still to be paid...; **e. que...!** but then again...!

encorné, -e [ɑ̃kɔrne] ADJ *Littéraire (animal)* horned

encorner [3] [ɑ̃kɔrne] VT to gore; **se faire e.** to be gored

encornet [ɑ̃kɔrnɛ] NM *Zool (mollusque)* squid

encoubler [3] [ɑ̃kuble] **s'encoubler** VPR *Suisse* to trip over

encourageant, -e [ɑ̃kuraʒɑ̃, -ɑ̃t] ADJ *(paroles, personne)* encouraging; *(succès, résultat)* encouraging, promising

encouragement [ɑ̃kuraʒmɑ̃] NM encouragement, support; **e. à la vertu/au crime** incentive to virtue/to crime; **quelques mots d'e.** a few encouraging words *or* words of encouragement; **recevoir peu d'encouragements à faire qch** to receive little encouragement *or* little inducement to do sth

• **encouragements** NMPL incentives; **encouragements fiscaux/à l'exportation** tax/export incentives

encourager [17] [ɑ̃kuraʒe] VT 1 *(inciter)* to encourage; **e. qn du geste** to wave to sb in encouragement; **e. qn de la voix** to cheer sb (on); **elle l'a encouragé d'un sourire** she gave him an encouraging smile; **e. qn à faire qch** to encourage sb to do sth; **être encouragé par qn** to be encouraged by sb, to receive *or* to get encouragement from sb; **encouragé par les premiers résultats** encouraged *or* heartened by the first results 2 *(favoriser)* to encourage, to promote; **l'oisiveté encourage le vice** idleness encourages *or* promotes vice

VPR **s'encourager** 1 *(emploi réfléchi)* to spur oneself on 2 *(emploi réciproque)* to cheer each other on

encourir [45] [ɑ̃kurir] VT *(dédain, reproche, critique)* to incur, to bring upon oneself; **faire e. des risques à qn** to put sb at risk; **il sait qu'il encourt une lourde punition** he knows he risks being severely punished; **le coupable encourt une peine de cinq ans d'emprisonnement** the guilty party is liable to *or* faces five years in prison

encours, en-cours [ɑ̃kur] NM INV 1 *Banque* loans outstanding; **l'e. de la dette** the outstanding debt; **e. de crédit** outstanding credits; **e. débiteur autorisé** authorized overdraft facility 2 *Compta* **e. de production de biens** work-in-progress 3 **e. de fabrication** material undergoing processing

encrage [ɑ̃kraʒ] NM *Typ* inking

encrassé, -e [ɑ̃krase] ADJ *(filtre)* clogged (up); *(tuyau)* clogged (up), fouled (up); *(arme)* fouled (up); *Aut (bougie)* sooted-up; *(chaudière)* scaled-up

encrassement [ɑ̃krasmɑ̃] NM *(d'un filtre)* clogging (up); *(d'un tuyau)* clogging (up), fouling (up); *(d'une arme)* fouling (up); *Aut (d'une bougie)* fouling, sooting up; *(d'une chaudière)* sealing (up)

encrasser [3] [ɑ̃krase] VT **1** *(obstruer ▸ filtre)* to clog (up); *(▸ tuyau)* to clog *or* to foul (up); *(▸ arme)* to foul (up); *Aut (▸ bougie)* to soot up; *(chaudière)* to scale up **2** *(salir)* to dirty, to muck up

VPR **s'encrasser 1** *(s'obstruer ▸ filtre)* to become clogged (up); *(▸ tuyau)* to become clogged (up), to become fouled (up); *(▸ arme)* to become fouled (up); *Aut (▸ bougie)* to soot up; *(chaudière)* to scale up **2** *(se salir)* to get dirty

encre [ɑ̃kr] NF **1** *(pour écrire)* ink; **écrire à l'e.** to write in ink; **e. de Chine** Indian ink; **e. d'impression** *ou* **d'imprimerie** printing ink, printer's ink; **e. indélébile** indelible ink; **e. en poudre** toner; **e. sympathique** invisible ink; **doigts couverts d'e.** inky fingers, fingers covered in ink; **noir comme de l'e.** inky black, black as ink; *Fig* **nuit d'e.** inky black night; **cela a fait couler beaucoup d'e.** a lot has been written about it **2** *(style)* **écrire de sa plus belle e.** to write in one's best style **3** *Zool* ink; *Culin* **calmars à l'e.** squid in its ink

encrer [3] [ɑ̃kre] VT *Typ* to ink

encreur [ɑ̃krœr] ADJ M inking; **ruban e.** (typewriter) ribbon; *Typ* **rouleau e.** inker

encrier [ɑ̃krije] NM *(pot)* inkpot; *(accessoire de bureau)* inkstand; *(récipient encastré)* inkwell

encroûté, -e [ɑ̃krute] *Fam* ADJ **être e.** *(dans ses préjugés)* to be a fuddy-duddy *or* stick-in-the-mud; *(dans sa routine)* to be stuck in a rut; **vieux bonhomme e.** old fogey *or* stick-in-the-mud

NM,F **1** *(personne ayant des préjugés)* **un vieil e.** an old fuddy-duddy *or* stick-in-the-mud **2** *(personne routinière)* **mener une vie d'e.** to be in a rut

encroûtement [ɑ̃krutmɑ̃] NM **1** *Fam (d'une personne)* rut, mundane routine□; **sortir** *ou* **tirer qn de son e.** to get sb out of his/her rut **2** *(d'une paroi)* encrusting **3** *(d'une plaie)* scabbing

encroûter [3] [ɑ̃krute] VT **1** *(couvrir ▸ de terre, de sang)* to encrust; *(▸ de calcaire)* to fur up **2** *(rendre routinier)* to be (stuck) in a rut; **la retraite l'a encroûté** retirement has made him set in his ways *or* got him into a rut **3** *Fam (abêtir)* to turn into a vegetable

VPR **s'encroûter 1** *(s'encrasser ▸ vêtement)* to become encrusted; *(▸ bouilloire)* to fur up **2** *Fam (devenir routinier)* to get into a rut; **il s'encroûte dans ses habitudes** he's got into a rut

encrypter [3] [ɑ̃kripte] VT *Ordinat (données)* to encrypt

enculé, -e [ɑ̃kyle] NM,F *Vulg* bastard, *Br* arsehole, *Am* asshole; **quelle bande d'enculés!** what a load of bastards!

enculer [3] [ɑ̃kyle] VT *Vulg* **1** *(sodomiser)* to bugger, to fuck up the *Br* arse *or Am* ass; **va te faire e.!** fuck off!, go (and) fuck yourself! **2** *(duper)* to screw, to shaft **3 e. les mouches** to split hairs, to nit-pick

encuver [3] [ɑ̃kyve] VT *Tech* to vat

encyclique [ɑ̃siklik] *Rel* ADJ encyclical

NF encyclical

encyclopédie [ɑ̃siklɔpedi] NF encyclopedia; *Fam* **une e. vivante** a walking encyclopedia

encyclopédique [ɑ̃siklɔpedik] ADJ **1** *(d'une encyclopédie)* encyclopedic **2** *(connaissances)* exhaustive, extensive, encyclopedic; **un esprit/une mémoire e.** a mind/memory that retains every detail

encyclopédiste [ɑ̃siklɔpedist] NMF **1** *(auteur)* encyclopedist **2** *Hist* **les encyclopédistes** *ou* **Encyclopédistes** Diderot's Encyclopedists, the contributors to the "Encyclopédie"

endéans [ɑ̃deɑ̃] PRÉP *Belg* within

endémie [ɑ̃demi] NF *Méd* endemic disease

endémique [ɑ̃demik] ADJ *(gén) & Écol & Méd* endemic; **e. en Malaisie/dans notre société** endemic to Malaysia/our society

endémisme [ɑ̃demism] NM *Écol* endemism

endenter [3] [ɑ̃dɑ̃te] VT **1** *(roue)* to tooth, to cog **2** *(assembler ▸ roues)* to mesh

endetté, -e [ɑ̃dete] ADJ *Fin* in debt; *Fig* in debt, indebted (**envers** to); **très e.** deep(ly) *or* heavily in debt

endettement [ɑ̃detmɑ̃] NM **1** *Fin (état)* indebtedness, debt; *(action)* running *or* getting into debt; **e. des consommateurs** consumer debt; **e. extérieur/intérieur** foreign/internal debt; **l'e. des pays du tiers-monde** the debt burden of Third World countries; **e. public** public debt; **cela a provoqué l'e. des pays de l'Est** this caused the Eastern countries to get into debt; **ratio d'e.** debt ratio; **facilité d'e.** borrowing capacity **2** *Compta* indebtedness, gearing

endetter [4] [ɑ̃dete] VT **1** *Fin* to get into debt; **il est lourdement endetté** he's heavily in debt; **l'acquisition de nouvelles machines a endetté la société** the purchase of new machinery has got the company into debt **2** *Fig* **être endetté envers qn** to be indebted to sb

VPR **s'endetter** *Fin* to get *or* to run into debt; **ne vous endettez pas davantage** don't get any further into debt; **je me suis endetté de 10000 euros** I got 10,000 euros in debt; **s'e. trop lourdement** to take on too many debts

endeuiller [5] [ɑ̃dœje] VT **1** *(famille, personne)* to plunge into mourning; **maison endeuillée** house in mourning **2** *(réception, course)* to cast a tragic shadow over

endiablé, -e [ɑ̃djable] ADJ **1** *(danse, musique, poursuite)* wild, frenzied; **se lancer dans une ronde endiablée** to begin to dance wildly *or* frenziedly in a circle **2** *(enfant)* boisterous, unruly

endiguement [ɑ̃digmɑ̃] NM **1** *(d'un cours d'eau)* dyking (up) **2** *(d'émotions, d'un développement)* holding back, checking; *(du chômage, de dettes)* curbing; **tenter l'endiguement de la violence/de la hausse des prix** to attempt to contain violence/price increases **3** *Bourse & Fin* hedging

endiguer [3] [ɑ̃dige] VT **1** *(cours d'eau)* to dyke (up) **2** *(émotion, développement)* to hold back, to check; *(chômage, excès)* to curb; *(violence)* to contain

endimanché, -e [ɑ̃dimɑ̃ʃe] ADJ in one's Sunday best; **avoir l'air e.** to be overdressed

endimancher [3] [ɑ̃dimɑ̃ʃe] **s'endimancher** VPR to put on one's Sunday best, to get all dressed up

endive [ɑ̃div] NF *Bot* chicory, French endive; *Fam* **pâle comme une e.** as white *or* pale as a sheet

endocarde [ɑ̃dɔkard] NM *Anat* endocardium

endocardite [ɑ̃dɔkardit] NF *Méd* endocarditis

endocarpe [ɑ̃dɔkarp] NM *Bot* endocarp

endocrine [ɑ̃dɔkrin] ADJ *Physiol* endocrine

endocrinien, -enne [ɑ̃dɔkrinjɛ̃, -ɛn] ADJ *Physiol* endocrinal, endocrinous

endocrinologie [ɑ̃dɔkrinɔlɔʒi] NF *Méd* endocrinology

endoctrinement [ɑ̃dɔktrinmɑ̃] NM indoctrination

endoctriner [3] [ɑ̃dɔktrine] VT to indoctrinate

endogame [ɑ̃dɔgam] ADJ endogamous

NMF endogamous man, *f* woman

endogamie [ɑ̃dɔgami] NF endogamy

endogène [ɑ̃dɔʒɛn] ADJ **1** *Biol, Bot & Méd* endogenetic, endogenous **2** *Géol* endogenetic

endolori, -e [ɑ̃dɔlɔri] ADJ painful, aching; **le corps tout e.** aching all over; **mon pied était e.** my foot hurt *or* was aching

endolorir [32] [ɑ̃dɔlɔrir] VT to make painful

endolorissement [ɑ̃dɔlɔrismɑ̃] NM **1** *(action)* hurting **2** *(douleur)* ache, aching

endommagement [ɑ̃dɔmaʒmɑ̃] NM *(action)* damaging (**de** of); *(result)* damage (**de** to)

endommager [17] [ɑ̃dɔmaʒe] VT **1** *(bâtiment)* to damage; *(environnement, récolte)* to damage, to harm **2** *Ordinat* to corrupt; **fichier endommagé** damaged *or* corrupt file

endomorphine [ɑ̃dɔmɔrfin] NF *Biol & Chim* endorphin

endormant, -e [ɑ̃dɔrmɑ̃, -ɑ̃t] ADJ **1** *(professeur, film)* boring **2** *(massage, tisane)* sleep-inducing

endormi, -e [ɑ̃dɔrmi] ADJ **1** *(sommeillant)* sleeping; **il est e.** he's asleep *or* sleeping; **à moitié e.** half asleep; **avoir l'air e.** to look sleepy

2 *(apathique)* sluggish, lethargic

3 *(calme ▸ ville)* sleepy, drowsy

4 *(faible ▸ désir)* dormant; *(▸ vigilance)* lulled

5 *(ankylosé)* **une jambe endormie** a leg which has gone to sleep

NM,F *(personne apathique)* good-for-nothing, ne'er-do-well

> Attention: le terme **asleep** n'est jamais utilisé comme épithète.

endormir [36] [ɑ̃dɔrmir] VT **1** *(d'un sommeil naturel)* to put *or* to send to sleep; *(avec douceur)* to lull to sleep

2 *(anesthésier)* to put to sleep

3 *(ennuyer)* to send to sleep, to bore

4 *(tromper ▸ électeurs, public)* to lull into a false sense of security

5 *(affaiblir ▸ douleur)* to deaden; *(▸ scrupules)* to allay; **e. les soupçons** to allay suspicion; **e. la vigilance de qn** to get sb to drop his/her guard

VPR **s'endormir 1** *(d'un sommeil naturel)* to drop off *or* to go to sleep, to fall asleep

2 *(sous anesthésie)* to go to sleep

3 *(mourir)* to pass away *or* on

4 *(se relâcher)* to let up, to slacken off; **s'e. sur ses lauriers** to rest on one's laurels

5 *(devenir calme ▸ maisonnée, pays)* to grow calm

6 *(s'affaiblir ▸ douleur)* to subside, to die down; *(▸ scrupules)* to be allayed; *(▸ vigilance)* to slacken

endormissement [ɑ̃dɔrmismɑ̃] NM **1 au moment de l'e.** when falling asleep; **qui aide à l'e.** sleep-inducing **2** *Ordinat* hibernation, sleep mode

endorphine [ɑ̃dɔrfin] NF *Biol & Chim* endorphin

endort *etc voir* **endormir**

endos [ɑ̃do] NM *Banque & Fin* endorsement

endoscope [ɑ̃dɔskɔp] NM *Méd* endoscope

endoscopie [ɑ̃dɔskɔpi] NF *Méd* endoscopy

endossable [ɑ̃dosabl] ADJ *Banque & Fin* endorsable

endossataire [ɑ̃dosatɛr] NMF *Banque & Fin* endorsee

endossement [ɑ̃dosmɑ̃] NM *Banque & Fin* endorsement; **e. en blanc** blank endorsement

endosser [3] [ɑ̃dose] VT **1** *(revêtir)* to put *or* to slip on, to don

2 *(assumer)* to assume; **e. la responsabilité de qch** to shoulder *or* to assume the responsibility for sth; **il lui a fait e. la responsabilité de l'accident** he made him/her take responsibility for the accident

3 *Banque & Fin* to endorse; **e. en blanc** to blank endorse

4 *(livre)* to back

endosseur [ɑ̃dosœr] NM *Banque & Fin* endorser

endroit [ɑ̃drwa] NM **1** *(emplacement)* place; **à l'e. de sa chute** where he/she fell; **à quel e. tu l'as mis?** where *or* whereabouts did you put it?; **ce n'est pas au bon e.** it's not in the right place; **il est assis au même e. depuis une heure** he's been sitting in the same place *or* spot for the last hour; **j'ai besoin d'un e. pour ranger mes affaires** I need a place *or* space to store my things; **l'e. de la réunion** the place for *or* the venue of the meeting; **rire au bon e.** to laugh in the right place

2 *(localité)* place, spot; **il y a de belles églises à cet e.** there are some beautiful churches in this area; **un e. tranquille** a quiet place *or* spot; **l'e.** the locality, the area; **les gens de l'e. sont très accueillants** the local people *or* the locals are very friendly

3 *(partie ▸ du corps, d'un objet)* place; *(▸ d'une œuvre, d'une histoire)* place, point; **cela fait mal à quel e.?** where does it hurt?; **en plusieurs endroits** in several places; **c'est l'e. le plus drôle du livre** it's the funniest part *or* passage in the book; **j'ai arrêté ma lecture à cet e.** this is where I stopped reading, I stopped reading here; **on va reprendre au même e.** we'll start again at the same point; *Fig* **toucher à un e. sensible** to touch a sore spot *or* a nerve

4 *(d'un vêtement)* right side

5 *Euph* **petit e.** smallest room in the house; **aller au petit e.** to go and powder one's nose, *Br* to go and spend a penny

6 *Géog* south-facing slope

• **à l'endroit** ADV **1** *(le bon côté en haut)* right side up; *(le bon côté à l'extérieur)* right side out; *(le bon côté devant)* right side round; **ton pull n'est pas à l'e.** your sweater's on the wrong way round; *(les coutures ne sont pas à l'intérieur)* your sweater's on inside out; **remets la bouteille à l'e.** turn the bottle the right way up **2** *Couture (dans les explications)* **deux mailles à l'e.** two plain, knit two; **un rang à l'e.** knit one row
• **à l'endroit de** PRÉP *Littéraire (personne)* towards; *(événement, objet)* regarding, with regard to, in regard to
• **par endroits** ADV in places, here and there; **il y a de l'herbe par endroits** there's some grass here and there *or* in places

enduire [98] [ɑ̃dɥir] VT **1** *(recouvrir)* **e. de** *(peinture, ciment, colle etc)* to coat *or* to cover with; *(crème, boue etc)* to smear with; **e. de beurre le fond d'un plat** to grease the bottom of a dish with butter; **e. qch de colle** to apply glue to sth; **il enduisait ses jambes de crème solaire** he was rubbing suntan cream on his legs **2** *Constr* **e. un mur** to plaster a wall over, to face a wall *(with finishing plaster)*
VPR **s'enduire s'e. de crème solaire** to cover oneself with suntan cream

enduit [ɑ̃dɥi] NM **1** *Constr (revêtement)* coat, coating; **e. au ciment** cement rendering
2 *Constr (plâtre)* plaster; **e. de lissage/de rebouchage** finishing/sealing plaster; **e. étanche** sealant; **e. imperméable** proofing
3 *Cér* glaze, glazing
4 *Méd* coating, fur *(on the tongue, the stomach)*

endurable [ɑ̃dyrabl] ADJ endurable, bearable

endurance [ɑ̃dyrɑ̃s] NF **1** *(d'une personne ▸ physique)* endurance, stamina; *(▸ morale)* endurance, powers of resistance; **il n'a pas eu l'e. nécessaire pour résister à la pression** he wasn't tough enough to stand up to the pressure; **e. à la chaleur** tolerance of heat; **e. à la douleur** pain threshold **2** *(d'une matière, d'une machine)* endurance, resilience; **e. à la flexion** bending endurance, stress fatigue limit **3** *Sport (discipline)* endurance; **épreuve/course d'e.** endurance test/race

endurant, -e [ɑ̃dyrɑ̃, -ɑ̃t] ADJ **1** *(résistant)* resistant, tough **2** *Fam Vieilli (patient)* enduring☐, long-suffering☐

endurci, -e [ɑ̃dyrsi] ADJ **1** *(invétéré)* hardened, inveterate; **célibataire e.** confirmed bachelor **2** *(insensible ▸ âme, caractère)* hardened; **des cœurs endurcis** hard-hearted people

endurcir [32] [ɑ̃dyrsir] VT **1** *(rendre résistant ▸ corps, personne)* to harden, to toughen; **son séjour dans l'armée l'a endurci** his time in the army toughened him up **2** *(rendre insensible)* to harden; **être endurci à la fatigue** to be inured *or* hardened to fatigue
VPR **s'endurcir 1** *(devenir résistant)* to harden oneself, to become tougher; **je me suis endurci avec l'âge** age has made me tougher *or* has toughened me up **2** *(devenir insensible)* to harden one's heart; **il s'est beaucoup endurci** he has become very hard

endurcissement [ɑ̃dyrsismɑ̃] NM **1** *(endurance)* hardening, toughening **2** *(insensibilité)* **son e. au fil des années** his/her increasing hard-heartedness over the years; **l'e. du cœur** the hardening of the heart

endurer [3] [ɑ̃dyre] VT to endure, to bear, to stand; **comment peut-il e. qu'on lui parle ainsi?** how can he tolerate being spoken to in that way?; **il a dû e. beaucoup d'épreuves** he had to put up with *or* to suffer a lot of trials and tribulations; **le bourreau faisait e. à ses victimes des supplices épouvantables** the executioner subjected his victims to horrific torture; **je ne vois pas pourquoi je devrais e. cela** I can't see why I should put up with that

enduro [ɑ̃dyro] NM *Sport* cross-country motorcycle race

Énée [ene] NPR *Myth* Aeneas

Énéide [eneid] NF *Littérature* **l'É.** the Aeneid

énergétique [enɛrʒetik] ADJ **1** *Écol & Écon* energy *(avant n)* **2** *(boisson, aliment)* energy-giving; *(besoins, apport)* energy *(avant n)*; **dépense é.** expenditure of energy
NF energetics *(singulier)*

> Note that **énergétique** means **energy-giving**: it should not be confused with **énergique** which means **energetic**.

énergie [enɛrʒi] NF **1** *(dynamisme)* energy; **parler avec é.** to speak vigorously; **se mettre au travail avec é.** to start work energetically; **avoir de l'é.** to have a lot of energy; **je n'ai pas assez d'é. pour sortir ce soir** I haven't got the energy to go out this evening; **je ne me sens pas beaucoup d'é.** I'm not feeling very energetic; **donner de l'é. à qn** to invigorate *or* to energize sb; **être sans** *ou* **manquer d'é.** to lack energy, to be listless; **mettre toute son é. à** to devote *or* to apply all one's energies to
2 *(force)* energy, vigour, strength; **il faudrait dépenser trop d'é.** it would be too much of an effort; **avec l'é. du désespoir** with the strength born of desperation; **avec é.** energetically; *(refuser, répondre)* forcefully, vigorously; **il a fait face à la situation avec é.** he faced up to the situation with spirit
3 *Tech* energy, power; **la crise de l'é.** the energy crisis; **les énergies nouvelles** new energy sources; **les énergies renouvelables** renewable energy sources; **é. électrique/solaire** electrical/solar energy; **é. potentielle/cinétique** potential/kinetic energy; **é. des vagues/hydraulique** wave/water power; **é. atomique** atomic power; **é. éolienne** wind power; **é. nucléaire** nuclear power *or* energy; **é. propre** clean energy; *Astron* **é. sombre** dark energy; **é. thermique** thermal power
4 *Psy* **é. psychique** psychic energy
• **énergies** NFPL **rassembler les énergies d'un pays** to mobilize the people of a country; **nous aurons besoin de toutes les énergies** we'll need all the help we can get

énergique [enɛrʒik] ADJ **1** *(fort ▸ mouvement, intervention)* energetic, vigorous; *(▸ mesure)* energetic, drastic, extreme; *(▸ paroles)* emphatic; *(▸ traitement)* strong, powerful **2** *(dynamique ▸ personne, caractère)* energetic, forceful, active; *(▸ visage)* determined-looking; **une jeune femme é.** a young woman with plenty of spirit *or* drive

> Note that **énergique** means **energetic**: it should not be confused with **énergétique** which means **energy-giving**.

énergiquement [enɛrʒikmɑ̃] ADV *(bouger, agir, parler)* energetically; *(refuser)* emphatically; *(répondre, condamner)* vigorously

énergisant, -e [enɛrʒizɑ̃, -ɑ̃t] ADJ energizing, energy-giving
NM energizer

énergumène [enɛrgymɛn] NMF wild-eyed fanatic *or* zealot, *Littéraire* energumen; **c'est un drôle d'é.** he's a queer fish

énervant, -e [enɛrvɑ̃, -ɑ̃t] ADJ irritating, annoying, trying

énervé, -e [enɛrve] ADJ **1** *(irrité)* irritated, annoyed **2** *(tendu)* edgy; **il est souvent é.** he's often edgy *or* on edge **3** *(agité)* agitated, restless

énervement [enɛrvəmɑ̃] NM **1** *(agacement)* irritation, annoyance; **notre départ s'est fait dans l'é. général** everyone was getting irritated with everyone else when we left **2** *(tension)* edginess **3** *(agitation)* restlessness

énerver [3] [enɛrve] VT **1** *(irriter)* to annoy, to irritate; **ça m'énerve quand il dit des idioties** it gets on my nerves when he says stupid things; **son attitude m'énerve** I find his/her behaviour annoying *or* irritating
2 *(agiter)* to make restless, to excite, to overexcite; **n'énerve pas le petit avant son coucher** don't excite the little one before he goes to bed
3 *Méd* to denervate
4 *Vieilli ou Littéraire (débiliter)* to enervate, to weaken
VPR **s'énerver 1** *(être irrité)* to get worked up *or* annoyed *or* irritated **2** *(être excité)* to get worked up *or* excited *or* overexcited; **il ne faut pas laisser les enfants s'é. avant de se coucher** the children mustn't get worked up *or* excited before going to bed

> Il faut noter que le verbe anglais **to unnerve** est un faux ami. Il signifie **troubler.**

enfaîteau, -x [ɑ̃feto] NM *Constr* ridge tile

enfaîtement [ɑ̃fɛtmɑ̃] NM *Constr* ridge tiling

enfaîter [4] [ɑ̃fete] VT *Constr* to top with ridge tiles

enfance [ɑ̃fɑ̃s] NF **1** *(période de la vie ▸ gén)* childhood; *(▸ d'un garçon)* boyhood; *(▸ d'une fille)* girlhood; **dans mon e.** in my childhood, when I was a child; **depuis mon e.** ever since I was a child; **dès sa plus tendre e.** from a very tender age; **dès sa première e.** in his/her infancy; **dès son e.** from an early age; **retomber en e.** to regress; **il retombe en e.** he's in his second childhood; **la petite e.** infancy, babyhood, early childhood **2** *(enfants)* children; **l'e. délinquante/malheureuse** delinquent/unhappy children **3** *(commencement)* infancy, start, early stage; **l'e. d'une civilisation** the dawn *or* beginning of a civilization; **c'est l'e. de l'art** it's child's play
• **d'enfance** ADJ childhood *(avant n)*

enfant [ɑ̃fɑ̃] ADJ **1** *(jeune)* **il était encore e. quand il comprit, tout e. encore, il comprit** he was still a child when he understood; **je l'ai connu e.** I have known him since he was a child **2** *(naïf)* childlike; **il est resté très e.** he's still a child at heart
NMF **1** *(jeune ▸ gén)* child; *(▸ garçon)* little boy; *(▸ fille)* little girl; **c'est une belle e.** she's a beautiful child; **un e. à naître** an unborn child *or* baby; **e. en bas âge** infant; **faire l'e.** to act like a child; **ne fais pas l'e.!** act your age!, don't be such a baby!, grow up!; **il n'y a plus d'enfants!** children are so precocious these days!; **prendre qn pour un e.** to treat sb like a child; **elle me parle comme à un e.** she talks to me as if I was a child; *Méd* **e. bleu** blue baby; *Rel* **e. de chœur** altarboy; *Fig* **comme un e. de chœur** like an angel *or* a cherub; **ce n'est pas un e. de chœur** he's no angel; **prendre qn pour un e. de chœur** to think sb is still wet behind the ears; **e. gâté** spoilt child; *Rel* **l'e. Jésus** Baby Jesus; **e. légitime** legitimate child; **e. à naître** unborn child; **e. naturel, e. illégitime** illegitimate child; **e. prodige** child prodigy; **e. sauvage** *(vivant à l'état sauvage)* wolf child; **e. soldat** child soldier; **e. surdoué** exceptionally gifted child; **e. terrible** enfant terrible; **e. trouvé** foundling; **grand e.** overgrown child; **ce sont de grands enfants** they're very naive; **petit e.** infant, little child, small child; *Bible* **laissez venir à moi les petits enfants** suffer the little children to come unto me; **dormir comme un e.** to sleep like a baby; **comme l'e. qui vient de naître** (as) innocent as a new-born babe
2 *(descendant)* child; **faire un e.** to have a child; **faire un e. à une femme** to get a woman pregnant; **il lui a fait un e.** she had a child by him; **avoir de jeunes enfants/de grands enfants** to have a young family/grown-up children; **un couple sans enfants** a childless couple; **être en mal d'e.** to be broody; **mourir sans enfants** to die childless *or* *Jur* without issue; **un e. de la crise/des années 80** a child of the depression/of the 80s; **la chorale, c'est son e.** the choir is his/her brainchild, he/she was the one who set up the choir; **e. de l'amour** love child; **je suis un e. de la balle** *(théâtre)* I was born into the theatre; *(cirque)* I was born under the big top; *Can très Fam* **être en e. de chienne** to be fuming, to be hopping mad; *Can très Fam* **cet e. de chienne m'a fait perdre mon boulot** I lost my job because of that son-of-a-bitch!; *Rel* **e. de Marie** child of Mary; *Fig* **ce n'est pas une e. de Marie** she's no saint; **un e. de Paris** a native of Paris; **e. du pays** *(homme)* son of the soil; *(femme)* daughter of the soil; **un e. du peuple** a child of the people; *Bible* **l'e. prodigue** the prodigal son; *Hist* **e. de troupe** = soldier's child who lives in barracks or in a special military school and whose education is paid for by the government; **les enfants d'Israël** the children of Israel
3 *(en appellatif)* child; **mon e.** my child; **belle e.** dear girl *or* child; *Fam* **alors, les enfants, encore un peu de champagne?** a bit more champagne, boys and girls *or* folks?; *Fam* **bon, les enfants, on y va?** come on you lot, let's go!; *Vulg* **e. de putain** *ou* **de salaud** son-of-a-bitch
• **bon enfant** ADJ INV good-natured; **tenez, je suis bon e., je ne vous fais pas payer les intérêts** look, I'll be good to you, I won't charge you any interest; **d'un ton bon e.** good-naturedly
• **d'enfant** ADJ **1** *(des enfants ▸ dessin, imagination)* child's *(avant n)* **2** *Péj (puéril)* childish, babyish

enfant-bulle [ɑ̃fɑ̃byl] (*pl* **enfants-bulles**) NM *Méd* = child who has to stay in a sterile tent

enfantement [ɑ̃fɑ̃tmɑ̃] NM *Littéraire* **1** *(création)* birth, bringing forth **2** *(accouchement)* childbirth

enfanter [3] [ɑ̃fɑ̃te] VT *Littéraire* **1** *(produire)* to give birth to, to create, to bring forth; **les héros que notre pays a enfantés** the heroes that our country has brought forth; **la discorde enfante le crime** discord begets crime **2** *(sujet: mère)* to give birth to

enfantillage [ɑ̃fɑ̃tijaʒ] NM **1** *(comportement)* infantile *or* childish behaviour; **arrête ces enfantillages!** don't be so childish!, do grow up! **2** *(chose sans importance)* trifle, trifling matter

enfantin, -e [ɑ̃fɑ̃tɛ̃, -in] ADJ **1** *(de l'enfance)* childlike; *(littérature)* children's *(avant n)*; **voix enfantine** child's *or* childlike voice; **avoir un sourire e.** *(homme)* to have a boyish smile; *(femme)* to have a girlish smile **2** *(simple)* easy; **c'est e.** there's nothing to it, it's child's play; **c'est d'une simplicité enfantine** it's childishly simple **3** *(puéril)* childish, infantile, puerile

enfarger [17] [ɑ̃farʒe] *Can Fam* VT to trip up[□]
VPR **s'enfarger** to trip up[□]; *Fig* **s'e. dans les fleurs du tapis** to get bogged down in too much detail, to lose sight of the big picture

enfariné, -e [ɑ̃farine] ADJ *(visage, cheveux etc ▸ de farine)* covered with flour; *(▸ de poudre)* smothered in powder; *Fam* **il est arrivé à 4 heures, la gueule enfarinée** *ou* **le bec e.** he breezed in at 4 o'clock as if nothing was the matter; *Fam* **je suis arrivée, la gueule enfarinée, demander mon augmentation** I arrived in all innocence *or* quite unsuspecting to ask for my pay rise[□]

enfer [ɑ̃fɛr] NM **1** *Rel* hell; *Fig* **aller en e.** to go to hell; *Hum* **e. et damnation!** (hell and) damnation!, heck!; *Prov* **l'e. est pavé de bonnes intentions** the road to hell is paved with good intentions; **l'E. de Dante** Dante's Inferno **2** *(lieu, situation désagréable)* hell; **sa vie est un véritable e.** his/her life is absolute hell; **il fait de ma vie un e.** he's making my life hell; **c'est vraiment l'e. à la maison** it's sheer hell at home; **quelquefois c'est l'e. pour se garer ici** it can be hell trying to park here; **l'e. de la drogue/de la prostitution/du chômage** the living hell of drug addiction/of prostitution/of unemployment; **l'e. de la guerre** the inferno of war **3** *(d'une bibliothèque)* = section where books forbidden to the public are stored
• **enfers** NMPL *Myth* **les enfers** the underworld; **descendre aux enfers** to go down into the underworld; *Fig* **descente aux enfers** descent into hell
• **d'enfer** ADJ **1** *(très mauvais ▸ vie)* hellish; *(▸ bruit)* deafening; *(▸ feu)* blazing, raging; **jouer un jeu d'e.** to play for high stakes; **une vision d'e.** a vision of hell; **aller un train d'e.** to go at top speed *or Fam* hell for leather **2** *Fam (très bien)* great, wicked, cool; **il est d'e. ton blouson!** what a cool jacket!

enfermement [ɑ̃fɛrməmɑ̃] NM **1** *(action d'enfermer)* shutting *or* locking up **2** *(fait d'être enfermé)* seclusion

enfermer [3] [ɑ̃fɛrme] VT **1** *(mettre dans un lieu clos ▸ personne, animal)* to shut up *or* in; **e. qn/qch (à clef)** to lock sb/sth up; **la nuit, on enferme le chien** at night we shut the dog up *or* in; **e. qn dans un placard** to lock sb in a cupboard; **e. qn dehors** to shut *or* lock sb out; **il s'est fait e.** *(chez lui)* he got locked in
2 *(emprisonner ▸ criminel)* to lock up *or* away, to put under lock and key; *(▸ fou)* to lock up; **e. qn dans une cellule** to shut sb up in a cell; **ce type-là, il faudrait l'e.!** *ou* **il est bon à e.!** *(dangereux)* that guy ought to be locked up!; *(fou)* that guy needs his head examined!; **faire e. qn** to have sb locked away; **il s'est fait e.** *(dans un asile)* he was put away
3 *(ranger)* to put *or* to shut away; *(en verrouillant)* to lock up *or* away
4 *(confiner)* to confine, to coop up; **enfermé dans une petite pièce toute la journée** cooped up in a small room all day; **ne restez pas enfermés, voilà le soleil!** don't stay indoors, the sun's come out!; *Fig* **e. qn dans un rôle** to typecast sb; **être enfermé dans ses contradictions** to remain trapped *or* bound by one's own contradictions
5 *(entourer)* to enclose; **les murailles enferment la ville** the walls enclose the town
6 *(contenir ▸ allusion, menace)* to contain; **un triangle enfermé dans un cercle** a triangle circumscribed by *or* in a circle
7 *(maintenir ▸ dans des règles)* to confine, to restrict; **e. la poésie dans des règles strictes** to confine poetry within strict rules
8 *Sport* to hem in
VPR **s'enfermer 1** *(se cloîtrer ▸ dans un couvent)* to shut oneself up *or* away **2** *(verrouiller sa porte)* to shut oneself up *or* in, to lock oneself in; **s'e. dehors** to lock *or* to shut oneself out **3** *(s'isoler)* to shut oneself away; **elle s'enferme à la bibliothèque toute la journée** she spends all day in the library; **s'e. dans le silence** to retreat into silence; **s'e. dans un rôle** to stick to a role

enferrer [4] [ɑ̃fere] VT *(avec une lame)* to run through, to transfix
VPR **s'enferrer 1** *(s'enfoncer)* to make matters worse; **s'e. dans ses explications** to get tangled up *or* muddled up in one's explanations; **s'e. dans ses mensonges** to be caught *or* trapped in the mesh of one's lies **2** *(s'embrocher)* to spike *or* to spear oneself **3** *Pêche (poisson)* to hook itself

enfichable [ɑ̃fiʃabl] ADJ *Élec* that can be plugged in; *Ordinat* slot-in

enficher [3] [ɑ̃fiʃe] VT *Élec* to plug in; *Ordinat* to slot in

enfiévré, -e [ɑ̃fjevre] ADJ *(front, imagination)* fevered; *(atmosphère)* feverish; *(foule)* in a fever (of excitement), at fever pitch

enfiévrer [18] [ɑ̃fjevre] VT **1** *(exalter)* to fire, to stir up; **e. les esprits** to stir people up; **e. l'imagination** to fire the imagination **2** *Vieilli Méd* to make feverish
VPR **s'enfiévrer** to get excited; **s'e. pour une idée nouvelle** to get very excited over a new idea

enfilade [ɑ̃filad] NF **1** *(rangée)* row, line; **une e. de peupliers** a row of poplars; **je me suis perdu dans l'e. des couloirs** I got lost in the maze of corridors *or* the endless corridors **2** *Mil* enfilade; **tir d'e.** raking *or* enfilading fire
• **en enfilade** ADJ **des pièces en e.** a suite of adjoining rooms; **le salon et la salle à manger sont en e.** the living room opens into *or* adjoins the dining room; **maisons en e.** *(toutes mitoyennes)* a row of *Br* terraced houses *or Am* townhouses, *Br* a terrace; *(mitoyennes deux à deux)* a row of semi-detached houses; *(isolées)* a row of houses ADV *Mil* **prendre en e.** to enfilade; **prendre les rues en e.** to follow along in a straight line from one street to the next

enfiler [3] [ɑ̃file] VT **1** *(faire passer)* **e. un élastique dans un ourlet** to thread a piece of elastic through a hem
2 *(disposer ▸ sur un fil)* to thread *or* to string (on); *(▸ sur une tige)* to slip on; **e. une aiguille** to thread a needle; **elle enfila ses bagues** she slipped her rings on; **e. des tomates sur une brochette** to slide tomatoes onto a skewer, to skewer tomatoes; *Fam Fig* **e. des perles** to waste one's time with trifles
3 *(mettre ▸ vêtement)* to pull *or* to slip on, to slip into; **e. ses gants** to put *or* to pull one's gloves on; **e. son collant** to slip on one's *Br* tights *or Am* pantihose
4 *(suivre)* to take; **la voiture a enfilé la rue jusqu'au carrefour** the car drove up the street to the crossroads
5 *Mil (troupes etc)* to enfilade, to rake
6 *Vulg (sexuellement)* to screw, *Br* to shag
VPR **s'enfiler 1** *(gants, bottes)* to pull on, to go on; *(étui)* to slide on
2 s'e. dans to go into; **s'e. dans un couloir/une rue** to go along a corridor/street; **s'e. sous un porche** to disappear into a doorway
3 *Fam (avaler ▸ boisson)* to knock back, to down; *(▸ nourriture)* to guzzle, to gobble up, to put away; **s'e. un bon dîner** to have a slap-up meal; **je me suis enfilé un sandwich en vitesse** I grabbed a sandwich, I had a quick sandwich
4 *Fam (faire ▸ corvée)* to get lumbered *or* landed with

enfin [ɑ̃fɛ̃] ADV **1** *(finalement)* at last; **les voilà! – ah, e.!** here they are! – ah, at last!; **vous voilà e.** here *or* there you are at last!; **j'y suis e. arrivée** I finally managed, I managed it at last; **e.! depuis le temps!** and not before time!, and about time too!; **e. seuls!** alone at last!; **e. bref...** *(à la fin d'une phrase)* anyway...; **e. bref, je n'ai pas envie d'y aller** well, basically, I don't want to go
2 *(en dernier lieu)* finally; **e., j'aimerais vous remercier de votre hospitalité** finally, I would like to thank you for your hospitality; **je vais en Suisse, en Allemagne et e. en Grèce** I'll go to Switzerland, Germany and finally to Greece
3 *(en un mot)* in short, in brief, in a word; **il est brutal, instable, e. c'est un homme dangereux** he's violent, unstable, in short *or* in a word (he's) a dangerous man
4 *(cependant)* still, however, after all; **ce sera difficile, e., on peut essayer** it'll be difficult, still we can try; **oui mais e., c'est peut-être vrai** after all it might well be true
5 *(avec une valeur restrictive)* well, at least; **blonde, e. châtain clair** blond, well, light brown; **il était malade, e. c'est ce qu'il dit** he was sick, at least that's what he says; **e., n'en parlons plus!** let's forget it; **mais e. bon, c'est son problème** oh well, that's HIS/HER problem!; **e.! ce qui est fait est fait** what's done is done; **e. je ne dis pas non, mais...** well, I'm not saying no, but...
6 *(emploi expressif)* **e.! c'est la vie!** oh well, such is life!; **ce n'est pas la même chose, e.!** oh come on, it's not the same thing at all!; **e., qu'est-ce qui t'a pris?** what on earth possessed you?; **e., reprends-toi!** come on, pull yourself together!; **c'est son droit, e.!** it's his/her right, after all!; **mais e., si elle est heureuse!** but as long as she's happy!; **tu ne peux pas faire ça, e.!** you can't DO that!; **e. quoi, tu n'as plus dix ans!** after all, you're not ten any more!; **mais e. je te l'avais déjà dit!** I already TOLD you!; **e., lâche-moi un peu!** give me some peace!, give it a rest!

enfirouâper [3] [ɑ̃firwape] VT *Can Fam* **1** *(tromper)* to fool[□], to hoodwink; **se faire e.** *(se faire avoir)* to get taken for a ride, to be had; *(être enjôlé)* to be taken in; *(se faire mettre enceinte)* to get knocked up **2** *(nourriture)* to gulp down, to wolf down

enflammé, -e [ɑ̃flame] ADJ **1** *(allumette, torche)* lighted, burning; *(bûche)* burning
2 *Littéraire (visage)* burning; *(regard)* fiery
3 *(passionné ▸ discours, déclaration)* impassioned, fiery; *(▸ nature)* fiery, hot-blooded
4 *Méd* inflamed

enflammer [3] [ɑ̃flame] VT **1** *(mettre le feu à ▸ bois)* to light, to kindle, to ignite; *(▸ branchages)* to ignite; *(▸ allumette)* to light, to strike; *(▸ papier)* to ignite, to set on fire, to set alight
2 *Littéraire (rougir)* to flush; **la fièvre enflammait ses joues** his/her cheeks were burning *or* flushed with fever; **la colère enflamme son regard** his/her eyes are blazing with anger
3 *(exalter ▸ imagination, passion)* to kindle, to fire; *(▸ foule)* to inflame
4 *Méd* to inflame
VPR **s'enflammer 1** *(prendre feu ▸ forêt)* to go up in flames, to catch fire, to ignite; *(▸ bois)* to burst into flame, to light
2 *Littéraire (rougir ▸ visage, ciel)* to flush; **le ciel s'enflammait au soleil levant** the rising sun set the sky ablaze
3 *(s'intensifier ▸ passion)* to flare up
4 *(s'enthousiasmer)* to be fired with enthusiasm; **chaque jour, il s'enflamme pour une cause nouvelle** he develops a passion for a new cause every day

enfle [ɑ̃fl] ADJ *Suisse (cheville, joue)* swollen

enflé, -e [ɑ̃fle] ADJ *(cheville, joue, paupière)* swollen; *Fig (style)* bombastic, turgid, pompous
NM,F *très Fam* fathead, jerk

enfléchure [ɑ̃fleʃyr] NF *Naut* ratline

enfler [3] [ɑ̃fle] VT **1** *(gonfler ▸ forme)* to cause to swell, to make swell; *(▸ voix)* to make louder, to raise; **e. les joues** to puff out *or* to blow out one's cheeks; **e. les voiles** *(vent)* to fill the sails **2** *(majorer ▸ calcul, budget)* to inflate; *Fam* **e. le nombre/la dépense** to swell *or* to add to the number/the expense **3** *Littéraire (exagérer ▸ difficulté, prestige)* to overestimate; **e. son style** to inflate one's style
VI *(augmenter de volume ▸ cheville)* to swell (up); *(▸ voix)* to boom (out)
VPR **s'enfler** *(voix)* to boom (out); *(voile)* to bil-

low *or* to swell *or* to fill out; *(rivière etc)* to swell, to rise; *(style)* to become inflated *or* turgid

enflure [ɑ̃flyr] **NF 1** *(partie gonflée)* swelling **2** *(emphase)* bombast, turgidity, pompousness; **il donne dans l'e.** he tends to be pompous **3** *très Fam (personne détestable)* jerk

enfoiré, -e [ɑ̃fware] **NM,F** *très Fam* bastard

enfoncé, -e [ɑ̃fɔ̃se] **ADJ** *(yeux)* sunken, deep-set; *(cavité, ravin etc)* sunken, deep

enfoncement [ɑ̃fɔ̃smɑ̃] **NM 1** *(destruction ▸ d'un mur)* breaking down; *(▸ d'une porte)* breaking down, bashing in

2 *(fait de faire pénétrer)* driving in

3 *(profondeur)* (penetration) depth

4 *(creux)* depression, hollow; *(dans un mur)* alcove, recess

5 *Méd* fracture; **e. de la boîte crânienne** skull fracture; **e. du thorax** flail chest

6 *Naut* difference of draught

enfoncer [16] [ɑ̃fɔ̃se] **VT 1** *(faire pénétrer ▸ piquet, aiguille)* to push in; *(▸ vis)* to drive *or* to screw in; *(▸ clou)* to drive *or* to hammer in; *(▸ épingle, punaise)* to push *or* to stick in; *(▸ couteau)* to stick *or* to thrust in; **e. un clou dans une planche** to drive a nail into a plank; **e. un couteau dans** to thrust *or* plunge *or* stick a knife into; **e. la clef dans la serrure** to insert the key in the lock; **e. la main dans sa poche** to thrust one's hand into one's pocket; **e. au marteau** to hammer in; **il a enfoncé le pieu d'un seul coup** he drove *or* stuck the stake home in one; **elle lui a enfoncé un revolver dans le dos** she thrust *or* jabbed a gun into his/her back; *Fig* **il faut e. le clou** it's important to ram the point home

2 *(faire descendre)* to push *or* to ram (on); **il enfonça son chapeau jusqu'aux oreilles** he rammed his hat onto his head

3 *(briser ▸ côte, carrosserie)* to stave in, to crush; *(▸ porte)* to break down, to force open; *(▸ barrière, mur)* to smash, to break down; *(voiture)* to smash in; **e. une porte à coups de pied** to kick a door in *or* down; **la voiture a enfoncé la barrière** the car crashed through the fence; *Fig* **e. une porte ouverte** *ou* **des portes ouvertes** to labour the point

4 *(vaincre ▸ armée, troupe)* to rout, to crush; **e. un front** to break through a frontline; *Fam* **e. un adversaire** to crush an opponent

5 *(condamner)* **son témoignage n'a fait que l'e.** he/she just dug himself/herself into a deeper hole with that statement

6 *Fam (humilier)* to humiliate▫; **tu n'étais pas obligé de l'e. comme ça!** you didn't have to be so hard on him/her!

VI to sink; **nous avons enfoncé jusqu'aux genoux** we sank into it up to our knees

VPR s'enfoncer 1 *(dans l'eau, la boue, la terre)* to sink (in); *(clou, couteau etc)* to sink *or* go in; **le navire s'enfonçait lentement** the boat was slowly going down *or* sinking; **s'e. jusqu'aux genoux** to sink up to one's knees; **ils s'enfoncèrent dans la neige jusqu'aux genoux** they sank knee-deep into the snow; **les vis s'enfoncent facilement dans le bois** screws go *or* bore easily through wood; **la balle s'enfonça dans le mur** the bullet embedded itself in the wall

2 *(se lover)* **s'e. dans un fauteuil** to sink into an armchair; **s'e. sous une couette** to burrow *or* to snuggle under a quilt; *Péj* **s'e. dans son chagrin** to bury oneself in one's grief

3 *(s'engager)* **s'e. dans l'ombre/dans la nuit** to disappear into the darkness/night; **s'e. dans une rue/dans un bois** to go down a street/plunge into a wood; **plus on s'enfonce dans la forêt plus le silence est profond** the further you go into the forest the quieter it becomes

4 *(s'affaisser ▸ plancher, terrain)* to give way, to cave in

5 *(aggraver son cas)* to get into deep *or* deeper waters, to make matters worse; **plus tu t'excuses, plus tu t'enfonces** you're only making matters worse (for yourself) by apologizing so much

6 *(se mettre)* **s'e. une épine dans le doigt** to get a thorn (stuck) in one's finger; *Fam* **s'e. une idée dans la tête** to get an idea into one's head; *Fam* **je ne reviendrai pas, enfonce-toi bien ça dans la tête!** and I won't be back, just get that into your thick head!

enfonceur, -euse [ɑ̃fɔ̃sœr, -øz] **NM,F c'est un e. de portes ouvertes** he's a great one for stating the obvious

enfonçure [ɑ̃fɔ̃syr] **NF** hollow *or* sunken part

enfouir [32] [ɑ̃fwir] **VT 1** *(mettre sous terre ▸ os, trésor)* to bury (**dans/sous** in/beneath *or* under); *Agr (fumier)* to plough in **2** *(blottir)* to nestle; **les mains enfouies dans ses poches** with his/her hands buried in his/her pockets; **elle a enfoui sa tête dans l'oreiller** she buried her head in the pillow **3** *(cacher)* to stuff, to bury; **la lettre était enfouie sous une pile de dossiers** the letter was buried under a pile of files

VPR s'enfouir 1 *(s'enterrer)* to bury oneself **2** *(se blottir)* to burrow; **s'e. sous les couvertures** to burrow under the blankets

enfouissement [ɑ̃fwismɑ̃] **NM** burying

enfourcher [3] [ɑ̃furʃe] **VT** *(bicyclette, cheval)* to mount, to get on; *(chaise)* to straddle; **e. son cheval de bataille** *ou* **son dada** to get on one's hobby-horse

enfourchure [ɑ̃furʃyr] **NF** *Couture* crotch

enfournage [ɑ̃furnaʒ], **enfournement** [ɑ̃furnəmɑ̃] **NM 1** *Cér* setting **2** *(mise dans un four)* putting into the kiln

enfourner [3] [ɑ̃furne] **VT 1** *Culin* to put into the oven; *(briques, poteries)* to put into the kiln **2** *Fam (entasser)* to shove *or* to cram *or* to push (in); **e. du linge dans une machine à laver** to cram laundry into a washing machine **3** *Fam (manger)* to put away, to wolf down

VPR s'enfourner *Fam* **1 s'e. qch** *(le manger)* to wolf sth down **2 s'e. dans** *(entrer dans)* to rush into, to pile into; **l'équipe s'enfourna dans le car** the team piled into the bus

enfourneur [ɑ̃furnœr] **NM** *(en boulangerie)* oven man; *Cér* kiln man

enfreindre [81] [ɑ̃frɛ̃dr] **VT** to infringe; *(ordres)* to disobey; *(vœu)* to break; **e. la loi** to break *or* to infringe the law; **e. le règlement** to fail to comply with *or* to break the rules; **e. un contrat** to violate a contract

enfuir [35] [ɑ̃fɥir] **s'enfuir VPR** *(se sauver)* to run away, to flee; *(s'échapper)* to run away, to escape; **s'e. avec qn** *(pour échapper à des sanctions)* to run away *or* off with sb; *(pour se marier)* to elope with sb; **s'e. de prison** to break out of *or* to escape from jail; **s'e. de chez soi** to run away from home; **s'e. d'un pays** to flee a country; **à mesure que les jours s'enfuyaient** as the days flew by; *Littéraire* **pleurer son bonheur enfui** to mourn one's lost happiness

enfumé, -e [ɑ̃fyme] **ADJ** *(pièce)* smoky, smoke-filled; *(paroi)* sooty

enfumer [3] [ɑ̃fyme] **VT 1** *(abeille, renard)* to smoke out **2** *(pièce)* to fill with smoke; *(paroi)* to soot up

enfûtage [ɑ̃fytaʒ] **NM** barrelling, casking

enfutailler [3] [ɑ̃fytaje], **enfûter [3]** [ɑ̃fyte] **VT** to barrel, to cask

enfuyait *etc voir* **enfuir**

engagé, -e [ɑ̃gaʒe] **ADJ 1** *(artiste, littérature)* politically, politically committed, engagé **2** *Archit* engaged **3** *(inscrit)* **les concurrents engagés dans la course** the competitors who are signed up to take part in the race

NM,F 1 *Mil* **e. (volontaire)** volunteer **2** *Courses de chevaux & Cyclisme* **la liste des engagés** the list of starters

> Il faut noter que l'adjectif anglais **engaged** est un faux ami. Il ne s'utilise jamais dans un contexte politique.

engageant, -e [ɑ̃gaʒɑ̃, -ɑ̃t] **ADJ** *(manières, sourire)* engaging, winning; *(regard)* inviting; *(perspective)* attractive, inviting; **un restaurant bien peu e.** a less than inviting restaurant

engagement [ɑ̃gaʒmɑ̃] **NM 1** *(promesse)* commitment, undertaking, engagement; **contracter un e.** to enter into a commitment; **faire honneur à** *ou* **tenir** *ou* **respecter ses engagements** to honour *or* meet *or* fulfil one's commitments; **manquer à ses engagements** to fail to honour one's commitments; **passer un e. avec qn** to come to an agreement with sb; **prendre l'e. de** to undertake *or* to agree to; **respecter ses engagements envers qn** to fulfil one's commitments *or* obligations towards sb; **sans e. de date** date subject to change; **sans e. de votre part** with no obligation on your part; *(dans une publicité)* no obligation to buy; **faire face à ses engagements** to meet one's commitments; *Com* **e. d'achat** purchase agreement

2 *Fin (de capital, d'investissements)* tying up, locking up; *(de dépenses, de frais)* incurring; *(dette)* (financial) commitment, liability; **e. à court terme** short-term undertaking; **e. bancaire** (bank) commitment; **e. de dépenses** commitment of funds; **e. hors bilan** contingent liabilities

3 *(embauche)* appointment, hiring; *(d'un musicien etc)* booking; *Cin & Théât* job; **e. à l'essai** appointment for a trial period; **se trouver sans e.** to be out of work; *Théât* to be resting; **acteur sans e.** out-of-work actor

4 *(début)* beginning, start; **l'e. des travaux** the start *or* beginning of the work; **l'e. des négociations ne pourra se faire avant le mois prochain** negotiations cannot begin *or* start before next month

5 *(introduction ▸ d'une clé)* fitting, inserting; *(▸ d'un véhicule)* driving (**dans** into)

6 *Mil (combat)* engagement, action, clash; *(recrutement)* enlistment; **e. d'une troupe** *(mise en action)* committing troops to action

7 *(encouragement)* encouragement; **c'est un e. à poursuivre votre effort** it's an encouragement to continue your effort

8 *(prise de position)* commitment (**à** to); **c'est de cette époque que date son e.** he/she started getting involved politically from that point on, his/her political commitment dates from that time

9 *(mise en gage ▸ au mont-de-piété)* pawning; *(▸ auprès de créanciers)* pledging

10 *Obst* engagement; **l'e. de la tête** engagement of the head

11 *Sport (participation)* entry; *Ftbl* kick-off; *(au hockey)* bully-off; *Escrime* engagement; **son e. dans le tournoi** his/her entry into *or* entering the competition

ENGAGER [17] [ɑ̃gaʒe]

VT
- to insert **1**
- to invest **3**
- to advise **5**
- to hire **7**
- to enter **9**
- to pawn **10**
- to put into gear **12**
- to commit **2**
- to involve **4**
- to start **6**
- to commit to military action **8**
- to entangle **11**

VPR
- to start **1**
- to enlist **3**
- to hire onself out **4**
- to commit oneself **2, 6, 7**
- to go into **8**

VT 1 *(insérer ▸ clef, disquette)* to insert, to put *or* to slot in; **e. une vitesse** to put a car into gear; **e. la clef dans la serrure** to fit *or* insert the key in the lock; **e. un véhicule dans une allée** to drive a vehicle into a lane

2 *(lier)* to bind, to commit; **cela vous engage à vie** it's a lifetime commitment; **voilà ce que je pense, mais ça n'engage que moi** that's how I see it, but it's my own view; **cela ne t'engage à rien** it doesn't commit you to anything

3 *(mettre en jeu ▸ énergie, ressources)* to invest, to commit; *(▸ fonds)* to put in; *Fin (argent)* to lock up, to tie up; *(dépenses)* to incur; **e. sa parole** to give one's word (of honour); **e. sa responsabilité** to accept responsibility; **votre responsabilité est engagée dans cette affaire** you have certain responsibilities in this matter; **e. sa fortune/des capitaux dans une affaire** to lock up *or* tie up one's fortune/capital in a deal

4 *(entraîner)* to involve (**dans** in); **e. qn dans une querelle** to involve sb in *or* draw sb into a quarrel

5 *(conseiller)* **e. qn à faire qch** to advise sb to do sth; **je vous engage à la prudence/modération** I advise you to be prudent/moderate

6 *(commencer)* to open, to start, to begin; **e. la conversation avec qn** to engage sb in conversation, to strike up a conversation with sb; **l'affaire est mal engagée** the whole thing is off to a bad start; **e. le match** *Ftbl* to kick off; *Sport* to begin; **la partie est maintenant bien engagée** the match is now well under way

7 *(embaucher)* to take on, to hire; *(pianiste)* to book

8 *Mil (envoyer)* to commit to military action; *(recruter)* to enlist; *(mercenaire)* to hire; **e. le combat** to join battle, to engage; *aussi Fig* **e. les hostilités** to open hostilities

9 *Sport (inscrire sur liste des concurrents)* to enter; **cet entraîneur a deux chevaux engagés dans cette course** this trainer has two horses entered in the race

10 *(mettre en gage ▸ au mont-de-piété)* to pawn; *(▸ auprès de créanciers)* to pledge; *(▸ propriété)* to mortgage

11 *(entraver ▸ corde)* to catch, to foul, to entangle; *(▸ machinerie)* to jam; *Naut* **e. une ancre** to foul an anchor; *Naut* **e. un aviron** to catch a crab; *Naut* **e. un vaisseau** to run a ship aground

12 *Tech (engrenage)* to engage, to put into gear; *Aut* **e. la première** to change into first (gear)

VPR s'engager 1 *(commencer ▸ négociations, procédure, tournoi)* to start, to begin; **une conversation s'est engagée entre les voyageurs** the passengers struck up a conversation

2 *(prendre position)* to commit oneself; **elles n'ont pas peur de s'e.** they're not afraid of taking a stand; **s'e. contre la peine de mort** to campaign against *or* to take a stand against the death penalty

3 *Mil* to enlist; **s'e. avant l'appel** to volunteer before conscription

4 *(auprès d'un employeur)* to hire oneself out; **s'e. chez qn** to be *or* to get taken on by sb; **s'e. comme jeune fille au pair** to get taken on as an au pair

5 *(corde, hélice)* to foul, to become fouled; *(machine)* to jam

6 s'e. à faire qch *(promettre)* to commit oneself to doing sth, to undertake to do sth; **sais-tu à quoi tu t'engages?** do you know what you're letting yourself in for?; **je m'engage à vous payer dans les 30 jours** I promise to pay you within 30 days

7 s'e. vis-à-vis de qn to commit oneself to sb; **je ne veux pas m'e.** *(sentimentalement)* I don't want to get involved

8 s'e. dans *(avancer dans ▸ sujet: véhicule, piéton)* to go *or* to move into; **la voiture s'est engagée dans une rue étroite** the car drove *or* turned into a narrow street; **la voiture s'engagea dans le rond-point** the car pulled out onto the roundabout

9 s'e. dans *(se loger)* to fit; **un tube s'engage dans l'ouverture** a pipe fits into the opening

10 s'e. dans *(entreprendre)* to enter into, to begin; **s'e. dans une aventure/un combat/une affaire** to get involved in an adventure/a fight/a deal; **le pays s'est engagé dans la lutte armée** the country has committed itself to *or* has entered into armed struggle

11 *Sport* **s'e. dans une course/compétition** to enter a race/an event

engazonnement [ɑ̃gazɔnmɑ̃] **NM** *(par plaques)* turfing; *(par semis)* grassing

engazonner [3] [ɑ̃gazɔne] **VT** *(par plaques)* to turf; *(par semis)* to grass

engeance [ɑ̃ʒɑ̃s] **NF** *Péj* scum, *Am* trash; **ils feraient n'importe quoi pour se procurer de l'argent, quelle (sale) e.!** they'd do anything for money, what scum!

engelure [ɑ̃ʒlyr] **NF** *Méd* chilblain

engendrement [ɑ̃ʒɑ̃drəmɑ̃] **NM 1** *(procreation)* fathering; *Bible* begetting **2** *(de chaleur)* generation; *(de maladie, pauvreté)* breeding

engendrer [3] [ɑ̃ʒɑ̃dre] **VT 1** *(procréer)* to father; *Bible* to beget; *(sujet: étalon etc)* to sire; **les fils qu'il a engendrés** the sons he fathered; **les fils qu'elle a engendrés** the sons she bore; **les fils qu'ils ont engendrés** the sons they brought into the world **2** *(provoquer ▸ sentiment, situation)* to generate, to create, *Péj* to breed; *(▸ maladie, pauvreté)* to breed; *(▸ chaleur)* to generate, to develop; *Hum* **il n'engendre pas la mélancolie** he's great fun **3** *Ling & Math* to generate

engin [ɑ̃ʒɛ̃] **NM 1** *Tech (appareil)* machine, appliance; **e. agricole** piece of farm machinery; **engins de levage** lifting gears; **e. de manutention** conveyor, handling equipment; **engins de pêche** fishing tackle; **e. prohibé** illegal hunting/fishing device; **e. de terrassement** earthmover; **attention: passage d'engins** *(sur panneau)* heavy plant crossing

2 *Astron* **e. spatial** spacecraft

3 *Mil* weaponry; **e. blindé** armoured vehicle; **e. blindé de reconnaissance** armoured car; **e. amphibie** amphibious craft *or* vehicle; **e. de mort** deadly weapon; **engins de guerre** engines of war

4 *Fam (chose)* contraption, thingamabob, thingamajig

5 *très Fam (pénis)* tool

> Il faut noter que le nom anglais **engine** est un faux ami. Il signifie **moteur**.

engineering [ɛnʒiniriŋ] **NM** engineering

englober [3] [ɑ̃glɔbe] **VT 1** *(réunir)* to encompass; **son livre englobe tout ce qui est connu sur le sujet** his/her book encompasses *or* covers the whole range of knowledge on the subject **2** *(inclure)* to include; **e. un texte dans un recueil** to include a piece in an anthology **3** *(annexer)* to merge; **ces états furent englobés dans l'Empire** these states were merged into the Empire

engloutir [32] [ɑ̃glutir] **VT 1** *(faire disparaître)* to swallow up, to engulf; **une île engloutie par la mer** an island swallowed up by the sea

2 *(manger)* to gobble up, to gulp *or* to wolf down

3 *(dépenser)* to squander; **il a englouti son capital dans son agence** he sank all his capital into his agency

4 *Fig* to swallow up; **les travaux ont englouti tout mon argent** the work swallowed up all my money

VPR s'engloutir *(vaisseau)* to be swallowed up *or* engulfed, to sink

engloutissement [ɑ̃glutismɑ̃] **NM 1** *(d'un navire, d'une ville)* swallowing up, engulfment **2** *(d'une fortune)* squandering

engluage [ɑ̃glyaʒ], **engluement** [ɑ̃glymɑ̃] **NM 1** *Chasse* liming, birdliming **2** *(enduit)* (bird)lime

engluer [7] [ɑ̃glye] **VT 1** *Chasse (oiseau, branche)* to lime, to birdlime **2** *(rendre collant)* to make sticky; **des doigts englués de colle** fingers sticky with glue

VPR s'engluer 1 *(se couvrir de glu)* to become gluey **2 s'e. les doigts** to get sticky fingers **3** *Fig* **s'e. dans qch** to get bogged down in sth; **s'e. dans une vie médiocre** to become bogged down in a life of mediocrity

engoncer [16] [ɑ̃gɔ̃se] **VT** to cramp, to restrict; **e. qn** *(vêtement)* to make sb look hunched up; **être engoncé dans ses vêtements** to be restricted by one's clothes

engorgement [ɑ̃gɔrʒəmɑ̃] **NM 1** *(d'un tuyau)* flooding; *(d'un sol)* saturation; **l'e. des grandes villes** congestion in the big cities; **l'e. du marché automobile** saturation in the car industry, the glut of cars on the market **2** *Méd* **e. mammaire** engorgement

engorger [17] [ɑ̃gɔrʒe] **VT** *(canalisation)* to flood; *(route)* to congest, to jam; *(organe)* to engorge; *(sol)* to saturate; *(marché)* to saturate, to glut

VPR s'engorger 1 *(tuyau etc)* to become choked (up) *or* blocked (up) *or* clogged **2** *Méd (organe)* to become engorged *or* congested **3** *(route, carrefour)* to become blocked up *or* congested

engouement [ɑ̃gumɑ̃] **NM 1** *(pour une activité, un type d'objet)* keen interest; **un e. pour le jazz** a keen interest in jazz; **d'où te vient cet e. soudain pour la politique?** how come you're so smitten with politics all of a sudden? **2** *(élan amoureux)* infatuation; **avoir un e. pour** to be infatuated with **3** *Méd (d'une hernie)* obstruction

engouer [6] [ɑ̃gwe] **VT** *Méd* to obstruct

VPR s'engouer s'e. de, s'e. pour *(activité, objet)* to have a craze *or* a sudden passion for; *(personne)* to become infatuated with

engouffrement [ɑ̃gufrəmɑ̃] **NM 1** *(consommation ▸ de nourriture)* wolfing, cramming; *(▸ d'argent)* sinking, squandering **2** *(entrée ▸ du vent)* rushing *or* sweeping *or* blowing in; *(▸ de la foule)* rushing in; *(▸ de la mer)* surging *or* rushing in

engouffrer [3] [ɑ̃gufre] **VT 1** *(avaler)* to wolf *or* to shovel (down), to cram (in); *(bateau etc)* to engulf, to swallow up **2** *(entasser)* to cram *or* to stuff (in) **3** *(dépenser)* to swallow up; **ils ont engouffré des sommes énormes dans la maison** they sank vast amounts of money into the house

VPR s'engouffrer *(foule)* to rush, to crush; *(personne)* to rush, to dive; *(mer)* to surge, to rush; *(vent)* to blow, to sweep, to rush; *(bateau etc)* to be engulfed *or* swallowed up; **le vent s'engouffra par la porte** the wind swept in through the door

engoulevent [ɑ̃gulvɑ̃] **NM** *Orn* **e. (d'Europe)** nightjar; **e. (d'Amérique)** nighthawk

engourdi, -e [ɑ̃gurdi] **ADJ 1** *(doigt, membre)* numb, numbed; **j'ai les doigts engourdis** my fingers have gone numb; **à force d'être resté dans cette position, j'ai la jambe engourdie** I have been sitting like this so long that my leg has gone to sleep **2** *(esprit, imagination)* slow, lethargic

engourdir [32] [ɑ̃gurdir] **VT 1** *(insensibiliser ▸ doigt, membre)* to numb, to make numb; *(▸ sens)* to deaden; **être engourdi par le froid** to be numb with cold **2** *(ralentir ▸ esprit, faculté)* to blunt, to dull; **la fatigue lui engourdissait l'esprit** he/she was so tired he/she couldn't think straight

VPR s'engourdir 1 *(se rouiller)* to go numb; **mes doigts commençaient à s'e.** my fingers were starting to go numb **2** *Fig (l'esprit)* to become dull *or* sluggish **3** *(animal qui hiberne)* to become dormant

engourdissement [ɑ̃gurdismɑ̃] **NM 1** *(insensibilité physique)* numbness

2 *(torpeur)* drowsiness, sleepiness

3 *(d'un animal qui hiberne)* torpor

4 *(action ▸ d'un membre etc)* numbing; *(▸ de l'esprit, des facultés)* blunting, dulling

engrais [ɑ̃grɛ] **NM 1** *Agr (fertilisant)* fertilizer; **e. (animal)** manure; **e. azotés** nitrate fertilizers, nitrates; **e. chimique** artificial fertilizer; **e. verts** *ou* **végétaux** green *or* vegetable manure **2** *(locution)* **mettre une bête à l'e.** to fatten (up) an animal

engraissage [ɑ̃grɛsaʒ], **engraissement** [ɑ̃grɛsmɑ̃] **NM** *Agr* fattening (up)

engraisser [4] [ɑ̃grese] **VT 1** *Agr (bétail)* to fatten (up) **2** *(personne)* to make fat **3** *(terre)* to feed

VI to grow fat *or* fatter, to put on weight; *Hum* **ta fille a besoin d'e. un peu** your daughter needs fattening up *or* feeding up a bit

VPR s'engraisser to get fat; *Fig* **il s'engraisse sur le dos de ses employés** he lines his pockets by underpaying his employees

engrangement [ɑ̃grɑ̃ʒmɑ̃] **NM 1** *Agr* gathering in, storing **2** *(de documents)* storing, collecting

engranger [17] [ɑ̃grɑ̃ʒe] **VT 1** *Agr* to gather in, to store **2** *(documents)* to store (up), to collect; *(connaissances)* to amass, to store (up)

engrenage [ɑ̃grənaʒ] **NM 1** *Tech (roues dentées)* gears; *(disposition du système)* gearing; **les engrenages d'une machine** the wheelwork *or* train of gears *or* gearing of a machine; **système** *ou* **jeu d'engrenages** train *or* set of gears; **e. à chevrons** herringbone *or* double-helical gear; **e. conique** bevel gear pair; *Aut* **e. de démarrage** starter gear; **e. en prise constante** constant-mesh gear; **e. à train planétaire** planetary gearing; **e.** *ou* **engrenages de transmission** driving gear; **e. à variations progressives** gradually variable gear; **e. à vis sans fin** worm gears **2** *Fig* trap; **l'e. de la violence/de l'agressivité** the spiral of violence/aggression; **mettre le doigt dans l'e.** to get caught up in it; **être pris dans l'e. du jeu** to be trapped in the vicious circle of gambling

engrènement [ɑ̃grɛnmɑ̃] **NM 1** *Tech* meshing **2** *Agr (d'un moulin etc)* feeding with grain

engrener [19] [ɑ̃grəne] **VT 1** *Tech* to gear, to mesh; **e. dans** to engage into, to mesh with; *Fam* **e. une affaire** to set a thing going **2** *Agr* to feed with grain, to fill with grain

VI to gear, to mesh

VPR s'engrener to gear (**dans** into), to mesh (**dans** with)

engrenure [ɑ̃grənyr] **NF** *Tech* gearing

engrosser [3] [ɑ̃grose] **VT** *très Fam* to knock up; **se faire e. (par)** to get oneself knocked up (by)

engueulade [ɑ̃gœlad] **NF** *très Fam* **1** *(réprimande)* bawling out; **passer une e. à qn** to give sb a bawling out, to bawl sb out; **se prendre une e.** to get bawled out **2** *(querelle)* run-in, *Br* slanging match

engueuler [5] [ɑ̃gœle] *très Fam* **VT e. qn** to bawl sb out; **ce n'est pas la peine de m'e.** there's no need to have a go at me; **je vais l'e.** I'm going to give him/her what for; **se faire e.** to get bawled out

VPR s'engueuler to have a row *or Br* slanging

match; **on ne va tout de même pas s'e. pour ça** we're not going to have a row over this, are we?

enguirlander **[3]** [ɑ̃girlɑ̃de] **VT 1** *(décorer)* to garland, to deck with garlands; *Fig (discours)* to dress up **2** *Fam (réprimander) Br* to tick off, *Am* to chew out; **se faire e.** to get *Br* a ticking-off *or Am* a chewing-out

enhardir **[32]** [ɑ̃ardir] **VT** to embolden, to make bolder, to encourage
VPR s'enhardir to become bold(er); **s'e. à faire qch** to pluck up the courage to do sth

enharmonie [ɑ̃narmɔni] **NF** *Mus* enharmonic change

enharmonique [ɑ̃narmɔnik] **ADJ** *Mus* enharmonic

enharnacher **[3]** [ɑ̃arnaʃe] **VT** *Équitation* to harness

énième [enjɛm] **ADJ** umpteenth, nth; **pour la é. fois** for the umpteenth time; **après une é. tentative** after countless attempts
NMF nth

énigmatique [enigmatik] **ADJ** enigmatic, mysterious, puzzling; **d'un air é.** enigmatically

énigmatiquement [enigmatikmɑ̃] **ADV** enigmatically

énigme [enigm] **NF 1** *(mystère)* riddle, enigma, puzzle; **trouver la clé de l'é.** to find the answer to the riddle, to guess *or* solve the riddle; **les enquêteurs tentent de résoudre l'é. de sa disparition** the police are trying to solve the riddle of his/her disappearance; **ce garçon est une é. pour moi** I can't make the boy out; **ça, c'est une é. pour moi** it's a mystery to me **2** *(devinette)* riddle; **le Sphinx parle par énigmes** the Sphinx talks in riddles

enivrant, -e [ɑ̃nivrɑ̃, -ɑ̃t] **ADJ 1** *(qui rend ivre)* intoxicating **2** *(exaltant)* heady, exhilarating

enivrement [ɑ̃nivrəmɑ̃] **NM 1** *Vieilli (par l'alcool)* intoxication, inebriation **2** *Fig* elation, exhilaration; **dans l'e. de** intoxicated *or* exhilarated by

enivrer **[3]** [ɑ̃nivre] **VT 1** *(soûler ▸ sujet: vin)* to make drunk, to intoxicate **2** *Fig (exalter)* to intoxicate, to exhilarate, to elate; **le succès l'enivrait** he/she was intoxicated by his/her success
VPR s'enivrer to get drunk; *Fig* **s'e. de** to become intoxicated with

enjambée [ɑ̃ʒɑ̃be] **NF** stride; **marcher à grandes enjambées** to stride along

enjambement [ɑ̃ʒɑ̃bmɑ̃] **NM 1** *Littérature* enjambment **2** *Biol* crossing-over

enjamber **[3]** [ɑ̃ʒɑ̃be] **VT** *(muret, rebord)* to step over; *(fossé)* to stride across *or* over; *(tronc d'arbre)* to stride *or* to step over; **le pont enjambe le Gard** the bridge spans the river Gard

enjeu, -x [ɑ̃ʒø] **NM 1** *(ce que l'on peut gagner ou perdre ▸ dans un jeu)* stake, stakes; *Fig* **l'e. d'une guerre** the stakes of war; **quel est l'e. de cette élection?** what is at stake in this election?; **c'est un e. important** the stakes are high **2** *(sujet)* issue; *(défi)* challenge; **l'environnement est un e. primordial dans ces élections** the environment is a key issue in this election; **cela représente un e. économique majeur pour les entreprises** this represents a major economic challenge for companies

enjoindre **[82]** [ɑ̃ʒwɛ̃dr] **VT** *Littéraire* **e. à qn de faire qch** to enjoin sb to do sth

enjôlement [ɑ̃ʒolmɑ̃] **NM** wheedling, cajoling

enjôler **[3]** [ɑ̃ʒole] **VT** to cajole, to wheedle; **se faire e.** to be taken in

enjôleur, -euse [ɑ̃ʒolœr, -øz] **ADJ** cajoling, wheedling
NM,F cajoler, wheedler

enjolivement [ɑ̃ʒɔlivmɑ̃] **NM** embellishment, embellishing

enjoliver **[3]** [ɑ̃ʒɔlive] **VT 1** *(décorer ▸ vêtement)* to embellish, to adorn; **enjolivé de** adorned with **2** *(travestir ▸ histoire, récit, vérité)* to embellish, to embroider

enjoliveur, -euse [ɑ̃ʒɔlivœr, -øz] **NM,F c'est un e.** he likes to embellish *or* embroider his stories
NM *Aut* hubcap; **e. de phare** headlamp rim

enjolivure [ɑ̃ʒɔlivyr] **NF** embellishment, ornament

enjoué, -e [ɑ̃ʒwe] **ADJ** *(personne, caractère)* cheerful, jolly, genial; *(remarque, ton)* playful, cheerful, jolly

enjouement [ɑ̃ʒumɑ̃] **NM** cheerfulness, playfulness

enkystement [ɑ̃kistəmɑ̃] **NM** *Méd* encystment, encystation

enkyster **[3]** [ɑ̃kiste] **s'enkyster VPR** *Méd* to encyst, to turn into a cyst

enlacement [ɑ̃lasmɑ̃] **NM 1** *(entrecroisement)* intertwining, interlacing, entwinement **2** *(embrassement)* (lovers') embrace

enlacer **[16]** [ɑ̃lase] **VT 1** *(étreindre)* to clasp; **e. qn** to embrace sb (tenderly); **ils étaient tendrement enlacés** they were locked in a tender embrace **2** *(mêler)* to interweave, to intertwine, to interlace; **initiales enlacées** interwoven initials; **les doigts enlacés** fingers entwined
VPR s'enlacer 1 *(amoureux)* to embrace, to hug; **amants enlacés** lovers (clasped) in an embrace **2** *(s'entrelacer)* to intertwine, to interlace

enlaidir **[32]** [ɑ̃ledir] **VT** *(personne)* to make ugly; *(paysage, ville etc)* to disfigure; **cette robe l'enlaidit** that dress makes her look ugly
VI to become ugly
VPR s'enlaidir to make oneself (look) ugly

enlaidissement [ɑ̃ledismɑ̃] **NM** *(de personne ▸ par accident)* disfigurement; *(▸ naturel)* growing ugly *or* plain, loss of good looks; *(de paysage, ville etc)* disfigurement; **les nouvelles constructions ont contribué à l'e. du quartier** the area has been disfigured partly by the new buildings

enlevage [ɑ̃lvaʒ] **NM 1** *(en teinturerie)* bleaching, decolorizing **2** *Sport (dans une course d'aviron)* spurt

enlevé, -e [ɑ̃lve] **ADJ** *(style, rythme)* lively, spirited; *(danse, sonate etc)* performed in a lively *or* spirited fashion; **ses dialogues sont enlevés** he/she writes quickfire dialogues; **une caricature enlevée** a rapidly drawn caricature

enlèvement [ɑ̃lɛvmɑ̃] **NM 1** *(rapt)* abduction, kidnapping, *Littéraire* ravishment; *Jur* **e. de mineur** abduction of a minor; *Jur* **e. d'enfant** child abduction
2 *(fait d'ôter)* removal, taking away; *Com* **e. et livraison** collection and delivery
3 *Admin (ramassage)* **e. des ordures** *Br* rubbish collection, *Am* garbage disposal
4 *Mil (d'une position)* taking, storming, carrying
5 *Hist* **l'e. des Sabines** the rape of the Sabine women

enlever **[19]** [ɑ̃lve] **VT 1** *(ôter ▸ couvercle, housse, vêtement)* to remove, to take off; *(▸ étagère)* to remove, to take down; **e. les pépins** to take the pips out; **ne mets pas ta voiture là, elle va être enlevée** don't park your car here, it'll get towed away *or* removed; **ils ont enlevé le reste des meubles ce matin** they took away *or* collected what was left of the furniture this morning
2 *(arracher)* to remove, to pull out; **e. les mauvaises herbes** to pull out the weeds; **e. un clou avec des tenailles** *Br* to prise *or Am* to pry a nail out with a pair of pliers; **une bombe lui a enlevé les jambes** a bomb took off *or* blew off his/her legs; *Littéraire* **enlevé par la mer** carried away *or* washed away by the sea
3 *(faire disparaître)* to remove; **e. une tache** *(gén)* to remove a stain; *(en lavant)* to wash out a stain; *(en frottant)* to rub out a stain; *(à l'eau de Javel)* to bleach out a stain; **e. les plis d'une chemise** to take the creases out of a shirt; **e. un passage d'un texte** to remove a passage from *or* to cut a passage out of a text
4 *Méd* **se faire e. une dent** to have a tooth pulled out *or* extracted; **se faire e. un grain de beauté** to have a mole removed
5 *(soustraire)* **e. qch à qn** to take sth away from sb; **enlève-lui ces allumettes des mains** take those matches off him/her; **cela m'a enlevé tout mon courage/toute ma bonne humeur** it has drained me of all courage/of my good humour; **e. à qn la garde d'un enfant** to remove *or* take a child from sb's care *or* custody; **e. à qn le goût de qch** to take away sb's taste for sth; **ça lui a enlevé le goût des mathématiques** it put him/her off mathematics
6 *(obtenir ▸ récompense)* to carry off, to win; *(▸ course, victoire, prix)* to win; **il a enlevé la victoire** he ran away with the victory; **e. un marché/un contrat** to get *or* to secure a deal/a contract; **e. les suffrages** *Pol* to win *or* to capture votes; *Fig* to be liked by everyone, to be universally liked
7 *(soulever)* to lift; **e. 10 kilos sans effort** to lift 10 kilos easily; **e. son cheval** *(le faire bondir)* to lift one's horse; *(le faire partir)* to set one's horse at full gallop
8 *Littéraire (faire mourir)* to carry off; **c'est un cancer qui nous l'a enlevé** cancer took him from us
9 *Mil* to carry, to seize
10 *(morceau de musique)* to play brilliantly
11 *(kidnapper)* to abduct, to kidnap, to snatch; **il a été enlevé à son domicile** he was snatched from his home; **se faire e.** to be kidnapped; **se faire e. par son amant** to elope (with one's lover)
VPR s'enlever 1 *(vêtement, étiquette)* to come off; *(écharde)* to come out; **le costume s'enlève par le haut** you slip the costume off over your head; **le costume s'enlève par le bas** you step out of the costume; **ça s'enlève en arrachant/décollant** it tears/peels off; **comment ça s'enlève?** how do you take it off?
2 *(s'effacer ▸ tache)* to come out *or* off; **le vernis ne s'enlève pas** the varnish won't come off
3 *(marchandises)* to sell quickly, to be snapped up
4 *(ballon etc)* to rise; *(cheval)* to take off
5 *Fam* **enlève-toi de là!** get out of there!
6 *(retirer)* **s'e. une écharde du doigt** to pull a splinter out of one's finger; *Fig* **s'e. une épine du pied** to get rid of a niggling problem

enlisement [ɑ̃lizmɑ̃] **NM 1** *(enfoncement)* sinking **2** *(stagnation)* stagnation; **le manque de coopération a entraîné l'e. des pourparlers** due to a lack of cooperation, the talks have reached a stalemate

enliser **[3]** [ɑ̃lize] **VT** *(voiture, roue etc ▸ dans la boue, le sable etc)* to get stuck; **e. ses roues** to get one's wheels stuck
VPR s'enliser 1 *(s'embourber)* to get bogged down *or* stuck, to sink; **s'e. dans des sables mouvants** to sink *or* to get sucked (down) into quicksand **2** *Fig* to get bogged down; **s'e. dans la routine** to get *or* to be bogged down in routine

enluminer **[3]** [ɑ̃lymine] **VT 1** *(manuscrit, livre)* to illuminate **2** *(colorer ▸ gravure, carte etc)* to colour **3** *Fig* **visage enluminé** flushed *or* glowing face

enlumineur, -euse [ɑ̃lyminœr, -øz] **NM,F** illuminator

enluminure [ɑ̃lyminyr] **NF 1** *(art, lettre)* illumination **2** *Fig (d'un visage)* colour

enneigé, -e [ɑ̃neʒe] **ADJ** *(champ, paysage)* snow-covered; *(pic)* snow-capped; *(village, route etc)* snowbound, snowed up; **la campagne est enneigée** the countryside's covered in snow

enneigement [ɑ̃nɛʒmɑ̃] **NM** *Météo* snow cover; **l'e. annuel** yearly *or* annual snowfall; **bulletin d'e.** snow report

ennemi, -e [enmi] **ADJ 1** *Mil* enemy *(avant n)*, hostile; **l'armée ennemie** the hostile army, *Littéraire* the foe; **le camp e.** the enemy('s) camp; **en pays e.** in enemy country
2 *(inamical)* hostile, unfriendly
3 *(adverse)* **familles/nations ennemies** feuding families/nations
4 e. de *(opposé à)* opposed to; **être e. du changement** to be opposed *or* averse to change
NM,F 1 *Mil* enemy, *Littéraire* foe; **passer à l'e.** to go over to the enemy **2** *(individu hostile)* enemy; **on ne lui connaissait aucun e.** he/she had no known enemy; **se faire des ennemis** to make enemies; **se faire un e. de qn** to make an enemy of sb; **e. mortel** mortal enemy; **e. public (numéro un)** public enemy (number one) **3** *(antagoniste)* **le bien est l'e. du mal** good is the enemy of evil; **les ennemis de la liberté** the enemies of freedom

ennoblir **[32]** [ɑ̃nɔblir] **VT 1** *(personne)* to ennoble; *(caractère, esprit)* to ennoble, to elevate; *(physique)* to lend dignity to **2** *Tex (tissu, fil)* to finish

> Do not confuse with **anoblir**, which means **to raise to the peerage**.

ennui [ɑ̃nɥi] **NM 1** *(problème)* problem, difficulty; **des ennuis** trouble, troubles, problems; **attirer des ennuis à qn** to get sb into trouble; **avoir des ennuis** *(soucis)* to be worried *or* anxious; *(problèmes)* to have problems; **avoir de gros en-**

nuis to be in serious trouble; **tu vas avoir des ennuis** you're going to get into trouble; **avoir des ennuis d'argent/de santé** to have money/health problems; **avoir des ennuis avec la police** to be in trouble with the police; **avoir des ennuis de voiture** to have problems with one's car; **avoir des ennuis de moteur** to have engine trouble; **faire des ennuis à qn** to get sb into trouble; **c'est ça l'e.!** that's the trouble!; **l'e., c'est qu'il ne peut pas venir** the problem *or* trouble is that he can't come; *Prov* **un e. ne vient jamais seul** it never rains but it pours **2** *(lassitude)* boredom; **c'était à mourir d'e.** it was dreadfully *or* deadly boring; **ils me font mourir d'e.** they bore me to death *or* stiff; **sa conversation est d'un e.!** his/her conversation is so boring! **3** *Littéraire (mélancolie)* ennui

ennuyant, -e [ɑ̃nɥijɑ̃, -ɑ̃t] *Vieilli ou Belg & Can* = **ennuyeux, -euse**

ennuyé, -e [ɑ̃nɥije] **ADJ** *(contrarié)* annoyed, bothered (**de** about); **je suis très e. de la savoir fâchée** it bothers *or* upsets me a lot to know that she is angry

ennuyer [14] [ɑ̃nɥije] **VT 1** *(contrarier)* to worry, to bother; **ce contretemps m'ennuie beaucoup** this complication worries me a great deal; **avoir l'air ennuyé** to look bothered *or* worried; **ça m'ennuie de les laisser seuls** I am loath to *or* I don't like to leave them alone; **ça m'ennuie de te le dire mais...** I'm sorry to have to say this to you but...; **cela m'ennuierait d'être en retard** I'd hate to be late

2 *(déranger)* to bother, to annoy; **si cela ne vous ennuie pas** if you don't mind; **cela vous ennuierait-il d'attendre?** would you mind waiting?; **je ne voudrais pas vous e. mais...** I don't *or* wouldn't like to bother you but...; **sa sœur l'ennuie tout le temps** his/her sister keeps bothering him/her

3 *(agacer)* to annoy; **tu l'ennuies avec tes questions** you're annoying him/her with your questions

4 *(lasser)* to bore; **les jeux de cartes m'ennuient** I find card games boring; **il m'ennuie à mourir** he bores me to death

VPR s'ennuyer *(être lassé)* to be bored; **elle s'ennuie toute seule** she gets bored on her own; *Hum* **avec lui on ne s'ennuie pas!** you're never bored with him!, he's great fun!; **je m'ennuie à ne rien faire** *(maintenant)* I'm bored *or Fam* fed up with doing nothing; *(en général)* I get bored if I have nothing to do; **s'e. de qn/qch** to miss sb/sth

> Il faut noter que le verbe anglais **to annoy** signifie **importuner** ou **irriter** et non **lasser**.

ennuyeux, -euse [ɑ̃nɥijø, -øz] **ADJ 1** *(lassant ▸ travail, conférencier, collègue)* boring, dull; **e. à mourir** *ou* **comme la pluie** (as) dull as *Br* ditchwater *or Am* dishwater, deadly boring **2** *(fâcheux)* annoying, tiresome; **c'est e. qu'il ne puisse pas venir** *(regrettable)* it's a pity (that) he can't come; *(contrariant)* it's annoying *or* a nuisance that he can't come; **comme c'est e.!** what a nuisance!

énoncé [enɔ̃se] **NM 1** *(libellé ▸ d'un sujet de débat)* terms; *(▸ d'une question d'examen, d'un problème d'arithmétique, d'un contrat, d'une loi)* wording **2** *(lecture)* reading, declaration; **é. des faits** statement of the facts; **à l'é. des faits** when the facts were stated; **é. du jugement** pronouncement of the verdict; **écouter l'é. du jugement** to listen to the verdict being read out **3** *Ling* utterance

énoncer [16] [enɔ̃se] **VT** *(formuler)* to formulate, to enunciate, to express; **cela peut être énoncé plus simplement** it can be formulated *or* expressed *or* put in simpler terms

VPR s'énoncer *(opinion)* to be stated; **énoncez-vous plus clairement** express yourself more clearly

énonciation [enɔ̃sjasjɔ̃] **NF 1** *(exposition)* statement, stating **2** *Ling* enunciation

enorgueillir [32] [ɑ̃nɔrgœjir] *Littéraire* **VT** to make proud

VPR s'enorgueillir s'e. de qch/d'avoir fait qch to be proud of sth/having done sth

énorme [enɔrm] **ADJ 1** *(gros)* enormous, huge **2** *(important)* huge, enormous, vast; **une somme é.** a huge *or* vast amount of money; **ça fait une différence é.** that makes all the difference; **20 euros, ce n'est pas é.** 20 euros isn't such a huge amount; **il n'est pas mort, c'est déjà é.** he's still alive, which is incredible **3** *(exagéré ▸ mensonge)* outrageous

énormément [enɔrmemɑ̃] **ADV** enormously, hugely; **le spectacle m'a é. plu** I liked the show very much indeed; **s'amuser é.** to enjoy oneself immensely *or* tremendously; **je le regrette é.** I'm extremely *or* awfully sorry; **elle a é. changé** she has changed enormously *or* a great deal; **é. de** *(argent, bruit)* an enormous *or* a huge *or* a tremendous amount of; **il y avait é. de monde dans le train** the train was extremely crowded; **ils ont mis é. de temps à comprendre** it took them ages to understand

énormité [enɔrmite] **NF 1** *(ampleur ▸ d'une difficulté)* enormity; *(▸ d'une tâche, d'une somme, d'une population)* enormity, size

2 *(taille démesurée ▸ d'une personne, d'un édifice)* vastness, hugeness; **l'é. du gaspillage** the huge *or* enormous amount wasted

3 *(extravagance)* outrageousness, enormity; **l'é. de son crime** the enormity of his/her crime

4 *(propos)* piece of utter *or* outrageous nonsense; **dire des énormités** to say the most outrageous things

enquérir [39] [ɑ̃kerir] **s'enquérir VPR s'e. de** to inquire about *or* after; **s'e. du prix** to ask the price; **s'e. de la santé de qn** to inquire *or* to ask after sb's health

enquête [ɑ̃kɛt] **NF 1** *Jur (investigation)* investigation, inquiry; **faire** *ou* **mener sa petite e.** to make discreet inquiries; **il a fait l'objet d'une e.** he was the subject of an investigation; *Jur* **faire** *ou* **procéder à une e. sur qch** to hold *or* to conduct an inquiry into sth; *(police)* to carry out *or* to conduct an investigation into sth; **mener une e. sur un meurtre** to investigate a murder; **l'inspecteur mène l'e.** the inspector is leading the investigation(s) *or* inquiries; **ouvrir/conduire une e.** to open/to conduct an investigation; *Jur* **e. administrative** public inquiry; **e. judiciaire (suite à un décès)** inquest; **e. officielle** official *or* public inquiry; **e. préliminaire** preliminary investigation *or* inquiry; **e. d'utilité publique** public inquiry

2 *(étude)* survey, investigation; *Mktg* survey; **faire une e.** to conduct a survey; **notre e. a porté sur l'alcoolisme** the topic of our survey was alcoholism; *Mktg* **e. d'attitude** attitude survey; **e. auprès des consommateurs** consumer survey; **e. fiscale** tax survey; **e. de marché** market survey; *Mktg* **e. omnibus** omnibus survey; **e. d'opinion** opinion poll; *Mktg* **e. pilote** pilot survey; **e. postale** postal survey; **e. sur les prix** price survey; **e. par questionnaire** questionnaire survey; **e. par sondage** opinion poll, sample survey; **e. par téléphone, e. téléphonique** telephone survey; **e. sur le terrain** field study

3 *Presse* (investigative) report, exposé

enquêter [4] [ɑ̃kete] **VI** to investigate; *Jur* to hold an inquiry; *(police)* to make investigations; *(faire un sondage)* to conduct a survey (**sur** into); **c'est elle qui enquête** she's in charge of the investigation; **e. sur un meurtre** to carry out an investigation into *or* to investigate a murder

enquêteur, -euse *ou* **-trice** [ɑ̃ketœr, -øz, -tris] **ADJ** *Jur* **commissaire e.** investigating commissioner

NM,F 1 *(de police)* officer in charge of investigations, investigator **2** *(de sondage)* & *Journ* interviewer **3** *(sociologue)* researcher

enquiert *etc voir* **enquérir**

enquiller [3] [ɑ̃kije] *Fam* **VT** *(but)* to let in; **on a enquillé l'autoroute** we took the motorway

VPR s'enquiller s'e. une boisson to knock back a drink; **s'e. des kilomètres** ≃ to clock up the miles

enquiquinant, -e [ɑ̃kikinɑ̃, -ɑ̃t] **ADJ** *Fam (agaçant)* irritating[□]; *(lassant)* boring[□]; **elle est enquiquinante à toujours se plaindre** the way she complains all the time is a real pain

enquiquinement [ɑ̃kikinmɑ̃] **NM** *Fam* **des enquiquinements** hassle; **je n'ai eu que des enquiquinements avec cette voiture** I've had nothing but hassle with this car

enquiquiner [3] [ɑ̃kikine] *Fam* **VT 1** *(ennuyer)* to bore (stiff) **2** *(irriter)* to bug; **il m'enquiquine** he bugs me **3** *(importuner)* **se faire e.** to be hassled

VPR s'enquiquiner *(s'ennuyer)* to be bored (stiff); **je ne vais pas m'e. à tout recopier** I can't be bothered *or Br* arsed to copy it out again

enquiquineur, -euse [ɑ̃kikinœr, -øz] **NM,F** *Fam* pain, drag, nuisance

enquis, -e [ɑ̃ki, -iz] **PP** *voir* **enquérir**

enraciné, -e [ɑ̃rasine] **ADJ bien e.** *(idée)* firmly implanted *or* entrenched; *(habitude)* deeply ingrained; *(croyance)* deep-seated, deep-rooted

enracinement [ɑ̃rasinmɑ̃] **NM 1** *Bot* rooting **2** *Fig (d'une opinion, d'une coutume)* deep-rootedness

enraciner [3] [ɑ̃rasine] **VT 1** *Bot* to root **2** *(fixer ▸ dans un lieu, une culture)* to root; **se sentir profondément enraciné dans une culture** to feel deeply rooted in a culture **3** *(fixer dans l'esprit)* to fix, to implant

VPR s'enraciner 1 *Bot* to root, to take root **2** *Fig (personne)* to put down roots; *(sentiments, habitudes, coutume)* to take root, to become established *or* deeply rooted; **s'e. profondément dans une culture/l'esprit** to become deeply rooted in a culture/the mind

enragé, -e [ɑ̃raʒe] **ADJ 1** *Méd* rabid **2** *(furieux)* enraged, livid **3** *Fam (passionné ▸ partisan, supporter etc)* rabid, out-and-out

NM,F *Fam (passionné)* fanatic; **un e. de football/musique** a football/music fanatic

• **enragés NMPL** *Hist* **les enragés** the Enragés *(faction of militant Parisian extremists during the French Revolution); (en 1968)* leftist militants

enrageant, -e [ɑ̃raʒɑ̃, -ɑ̃t] **ADJ** *Fam* maddening, infuriating

enrager [17] [ɑ̃raʒe] **VI** *(être en colère)* to be furious *or* infuriated; **j'enrage de m'être laissé prendre** I'm enraged *or* furious at having been caught; **faire e. qn** *(l'irriter)* to annoy sb; *(le taquiner)* to tease sb mercilessly

enraie *etc voir* **enrayer**

enrayage [ɑ̃rɛjaʒ] **NM 1** *(blocage ▸ d'une roue)* locking; *(▸ d'un mécanisme, d'une arme)* jamming **2** *(montage des rayons ▸ d'une roue)* spoking

enrayer [11] [ɑ̃reje] **VT 1** *(bloquer ▸ roue)* to lock; *(▸ arme, mécanisme)* to jam **2** *Fig (empêcher la progression de)* to check, to stop, to call a halt to; **e. la crise** to halt the economic recession; **e. l'inflation** to check *or* to control *or* to curb inflation; **e. une maladie/un fléau** to arrest *or* to check a disease/scourge; **l'épidémie est enrayée** the epidemic has been halted **3** *(équiper de rayons ▸ roue)* to spoke

VPR s'enrayer 1 *(arme, mécanisme)* to jam **2** *Fig (épidémie)* to abate

enrégimenter [3] [ɑ̃reʒimɑ̃te] **VT 1** *Mil* to form into regiments **2** *(dans un parti, une organisation)* to press-gang; **je déteste être enrégimenté!** I hate being regimented!

enregistrable [ɑ̃rəʒistrabl] **ADJ 1** *Admin & Jur* receivable **2** *(sur une bande magnétique)* recordable

enregistrement [ɑ̃rəʒistrəmɑ̃] **NM 1** *Jur (fait de déclarer)* registration, registering; *(entrée)* entry; **faire l'e. d'une société** to register a company; *Admin* **l'E.** the Registration department; **droit d'e.** stamp duty

2 *Com (fait d'inscrire)* booking; *(d'une commande)* booking, entering (up); *(entrée)* booking, entry; **e. comptable** accounting entry

3 *Transp (à l'aéroport)* check-in; *(à la gare)* registration; **procéder à l'e. de ses bagages** *(à l'aéroport)* to check one's luggage in; *(à la gare)* to register one's luggage; **e. anticipé** advanced check-in; **guichet d'e.** *(à l'aéroport)* check-in (desk)

4 *(de son)* recording; **e. magnétique** tape recording; **e. audio/vidéo** audio/video recording; **e. sur bande/cassette** tape/cassette recording; **e. haute fidélité** hi-fi recording; **e. laser** *(procédé)* laser recording; *(disque)* laser disc; **e. numérique** digital recording; *TV & Rad* **e. son** *ou* **sonore** audio *or* sound recording; *TV* **camion d'e. (du son)** sound van; **e. vocal** voice recording

5 *Ordinat (article, informations)* record; *(action)* recording, logging

6 *(diagramme)* trace

• **d'enregistrement ADJ 1** *Com* registration *(avant n)* **2** *Ordinat (clef, tête, structure)* format *(avant n)*; *(densité, support)* recording *(avant n)*; *(unité)* logging *(avant n)* **3** *(dans l'audiovisuel)* **tête d'e.** recording head

enregistrer [3] [ɑ̃rəʒistre] VT **1** *(inscrire ▸ opération, transaction, acte)* to enter, to record; *(▸ déclaration)* to register, to file; *(▸ naissance, acte etc)* to register; *(▸ note, mention)* to log; *(▸ commande)* to enter up; **société enregistrée** registered company

2 *(constater)* to record, to note; **l'entreprise a enregistré un bénéfice de…** the company showed a profit of…; **les meilleures ventes enregistrées depuis des mois** the best recorded sales for months

3 *(réaliser une copie de ▸ cassette audio, disque, émission)* to record, to tape; *(▸ sur un magnétoscope)* to record, to video, to video-tape; *Ordinat (▸ données)* to store; *(▸ CD)* to write; **musique enregistrée** taped *or* recorded music; *Ordinat* **programme enregistré** stored programme

4 *(pour commercialiser ▸ émission, dialogue)* to record; **e. un disque** to make a record

5 *(afficher)* to register, to record, to show; **l'appareil n'a rien enregistré** nothing registered on the apparatus, the apparatus did not register anything

6 *Fam (retenir)* to take in□; *(mémoriser)* to note□, to memorize□; **d'accord, c'est enregistré** all right, I've got that; **je n'ai rien enregistré de ce que j'ai lu** I haven't taken in any of what I read

7 *Transp (à l'aéroport)* to check in; *(à la gare)* to register

USAGE ABSOLU **1 ils sont en train d'e.** they're doing *or* making a recording; **e. sur bande** to tape, to record on tape; **e. au magnétoscope** to video, to record on video **2** *Fam (retenir)* **je lui ai dit mais il n'a pas enregistré** I told him but it didn't register *or* he didn't take it in□

enregistreur, -euse [ɑ̃rəʒistrœr, -øz] ADJ recording *(avant n)*

NM recorder, recording device; *Belg (magnétophone)* tape recorder; **e. à bande** (strip) chart recorder; *Belg* **e. à cassettes** cassette recorder; **e. de pression** pressure recorder; **e. de son** *ou* **sonore** sound recorder; **e. à tambour** drum recorder; *Ind* **e. de temps** time clock *or* recorder; **e. de vol** flight recorder

enrhumer [3] [ɑ̃ryme] VT **1 e. qn** to give sb a cold **2** *Fam* to overtake at top speed

VPR **s'enrhumer** to catch cold, to get a cold

enrichi, -e [ɑ̃riʃi] ADJ **1** *Péj (personne)* nouveau riche **2** *(amélioré)* enriched; **il est sorti e. de ses voyages** his travelling has enriched his mind; **céréales enrichies en vitamines** cereals with added vitamins, vitamin-enriched cereals **3** *Ordinat & Typ (texte)* enriched

enrichir [32] [ɑ̃riʃir] VT **1** *(en argent)* to enrich, to make rich *or* richer **2** *(améliorer ▸ savon, minerai, culture) & Phys* to enrich; *(▸ esprit)* to enrich, to improve; **e. la terre** to enrich the soil; **cette expérience m'a enrichi** I'm all the richer for that experience; **édition enrichie de nombreuses cartes** edition to which many new maps have been added **3** *Ordinat & Typ (texte)* to enrich

VPR **s'enrichir 1** *(devenir riche)* to grow rich *or* richer, to become rich *or* richer **2** *(se développer ▸ collection)* to increase, to develop; *(▸ esprit)* to be enriched, to grow; *(▸ langue)* to grow *or* become richer (**de/en** with/in); **s'e. à force de lectures/de voyages** to enrich one's mind through reading/travel

enrichissant, -e [ɑ̃riʃisɑ̃, -ɑ̃t] ADJ enriching; *(travail)* rewarding

enrichissement [ɑ̃riʃismɑ̃] NM **1** *(en argent)* becoming rich *or* richer; *(d'une entreprise)* increase in capital; **l'e. personnel du dirigeant de l'association a fait scandale** the personal fortune *or* wealth accrued by the head of the organization caused a scandal; *Jur* **e. sans cause** unjust enrichment

2 *(développement ▸ de l'esprit, d'une collection)* enriching, enrichment; *Fig* **l'ultime objectif est l'e. personnel** the ultimate objective is personal development

3 *(amélioration ▸ d'un minerai, d'un sol)* improvement, improving

4 *Nucl* enrichment

5 *Ordinat & Typ (de texte)* enriching

enrobage [ɑ̃rɔbaʒ] NM *(action, enveloppe)* coating; **e. de chocolat** chocolate coating

enrobé, -e [ɑ̃rɔbe] ADJ *(personne)* plump, chubby

NM *(revêtement)* surfacing

• **enrobés** NMPL coated materials; **enrobés à froid/chaud** cold/hot mix

enrober [3] [ɑ̃rɔbe] VT **1** *Culin (enduire)* to coat; **e. de chocolat** to coat with chocolate **2** *(adoucir)* to wrap *or* to dress up; **il a enrobé son reproche de mots affectueux** he wrapped his criticism in kind words

enrôlé [ɑ̃role] NM enlisted private

enrôlement [ɑ̃rolmɑ̃] NM **1** *Mil* enlistment **2** *Admin & Jur* enrolment

enrôler [3] [ɑ̃role] VT **1** *Mil* to enrol, to enlist; *Hist* **e. de force** to press-gang, to impress; **il s'est fait e. dans l'armée à 16 ans** he was enlisted at the age of 16; *Fig* **je vois que tu t'es fait e. pour faire la vaisselle** I see you've been dragooned into doing the washing up; **e. qn dans un parti/groupe** to recruit sb into a party/group **2** *Admin & Jur* to enrol, to record

VPR **s'enrôler 1** *Mil* to enlist, to sign up **2** *(dans un groupe, dans un parti)* to enrol, to sign up

enroué, -e [ɑ̃rwe] ADJ hoarse; **d'une voix enrouée** hoarsely

enrouement [ɑ̃rumɑ̃] NM hoarseness

enrouer [6] [ɑ̃rwe] VT *(voix, personne)* to make hoarse

VPR **s'enrouer** *(de froid)* to get hoarse; *(en forçant sa voix)* to make oneself hoarse; **je me suis enroué à force de crier/chanter** I shouted/sang myself hoarse

enroulable [ɑ̃rulabl] ADJ windable; *Aut* **ceinture de sécurité e.** inertia-reel seat belt

enroulement [ɑ̃rulmɑ̃] NM **1** *(mise en rouleau ▸ de carte, de tissu, de tapis etc)* rolling up; *(▸ de câble, de ruban)* winding up **2** *(volute)* whorl, scroll **3** *Élec (bobinage)* winding; *(bobine)* coil; **e. du champ d'excitation** field winding; **e. en série** series winding

enrouler [3] [ɑ̃rule] VT **1** *(mettre en rouleau ▸ carte, tissu, tapis etc)* to roll up; *(▸ câble, ruban)* to wind up; *(▸ ressort)* to coil; **lierre enroulé autour d'un arbre** ivy twined *or* wound round a tree **2** *(envelopper)* **e. dans** to roll *or* to wrap in; **e. un corps dans un drap** to wrap a body in a sheet

VPR **s'enrouler** *(corde, fil)* to be wound *or* to wind (up); *(serpent)* to coil (itself); **s'e. dans une couverture** to wrap oneself up in a blanket; **le papier s'enroule autour de ce cylindre** the paper winds round this cylinder

enrouleur, -euse [ɑ̃rulœr, -øz] ADJ winding, coiling

NM **1** *(tambour)* drum, reel **2** *(galet)* idle pulley, idler, roller; *Aut* **e. de ceinture automatique** automatic seat belt winder, inertia reel

• **à enrouleur** ADJ self-winding; *Aut* **ceinture de sécurité à e.** inertia-reel seat belt

enrubanner [3] [ɑ̃rybane] VT **1** *(orner de rubans)* to decorate *or* to adorn with ribbons **2** *Agr* to bale

ENS [əenes] NF *Scol & Univ (abrév* **École normale supérieure***)* = prestigious "grande école" for teachers and researchers

ensablement [ɑ̃sabləmɑ̃] NM **1** *Naut (d'un bateau)* running aground; *(d'un tuyau)* choking (up) with sand; *(d'une route)* sanding over; *(d'un port)* silting up **2** *(dépôt ▸ amené par l'eau)* sandbank, sand bar; *(▸ amené par le vent)* sand dune

ensabler [3] [ɑ̃sable] VT **1** *(couvrir de sable)* **être ensablé** *(port, estuaire)* to be silted up; *(route, piste)* to be covered in sand (drifts) **2** *Naut (enliser ▸ bateau)* to strand, to run aground; *(▸ véhicule)* to get stuck in the sand; **une voiture ensablée** a car stuck in the sand

VPR **s'ensabler 1** *(chenal)* to silt up **2** *(véhicule)* to get stuck in the sand **3** *(poisson)* to bury itself in the sand

ensachage [ɑ̃saʃaʒ] NM *Ind* bagging (up), sacking

ensacher [3] [ɑ̃saʃe] VT *Ind* to bag (up), to sack

ensanglanter [3] [ɑ̃sɑ̃glɑ̃te] VT **1** *(tacher)* to bloody; **un mouchoir ensanglanté** a bloodstained handkerchief; **mains ensanglantées** bloodstained *or* bloody hands; **il entra, le visage ensanglanté** he came in with his face covered in blood **2** *(sujet: troubles, guerre, crime)* to bathe in blood; **les émeutes qui ont ensanglanté la capitale** the riots which have brought bloodshed to the streets of the capital; **un festival ensanglanté par un attentat** a festival marred by the bloody violence of an attempted murder

enseignant, -e [ɑ̃sɛɲɑ̃, -ɑ̃t] ADJ *voir* **corps**

NM,F *Scol & Univ* teacher

enseigne [ɑ̃sɛɲ] NM **1** *Mil* **e. de vaisseau 1er classe** *Br* sub-lieutenant, *Am* lieutenant junior grade; **e. de vaisseau 2ème classe** *Br* midshipman, *Am* ensign **2** *Hist (porte-drapeau)* ensign

NF **1** *(panneau)* sign; *Mktg* brand name; **e. lumineuse** *ou* **au néon** neon sign; **à l'e. du Lion d'or** at the (sign of the) Golden Lion; *Fam Fig* **nous sommes tous logés à la même e.** we're all in the same boat; *Prov* **à bon vin point d'e.** good wine needs no bush **2** *Littéraire (étendard)* ensign

• **à telle(s) enseigne(s) que** CONJ so much so that

enseignement [ɑ̃sɛɲmɑ̃] NM *Scol & Univ* **1** *(instruction)* education; **e. assisté par ordinateur** computer-assisted learning; **e. pour adultes** adult education; **e. par correspondance** correspondence courses

2 *(méthodes d'instruction)* teaching (methods); **méthode d'e.** teaching method; **l'e. des langues est excellent dans mon collège** languages are taught very well at my school

3 *(système scolaire)* **e. primaire/supérieur** primary/higher education; **e. privé** private education; **e. professionnel** vocational education; **e. programmé** programmed learning; **e. public** *Br* state *or Am* public education *or* schools; **l'e. du second degré** *ou* **secondaire** secondary education; **e. technique** technical education

4 *(profession)* **l'e.** teaching, the teaching profession; **entrer dans l'e.** to go into teaching; **il est dans l'e.** he is a teacher, he teaches

5 *(leçon)* lesson, teaching; **tirer un e. de qch** to learn (a lesson) from sth; **quel e. en avez-vous tiré?** what did you learn from it?; **les enseignements d'un maître** the teachings of a master

enseigner [4] [ɑ̃seɲe] VT **1** *(apprendre)* to teach; **e. qch à qn** to teach sb sth *or* sth to sb; **e. à qn à faire qch** to teach sb (how) to do sth **2** *Vieilli (indiquer)* to show, to point out; **e. à qn son devoir** to point out his/her duty to sb

USAGE ABSOLU **elle enseigne depuis trois ans** she's been teaching for three years

ensemble [ɑ̃sɑ̃bl] ADV **1** *(l'un avec l'autre)* together; **ils y sont allés e.** they went together; **mettre e.** to put together; **nous en avons parlé e.** we spoke *or* we had a talk about it; **on pourrait partir tous e.** we could all go together *or* in a group; **aller bien e.** *(vêtements, couleurs)* to go well together; *(personnes)* to be well-matched; **ils vont mal e.** *(vêtements)* they don't match; *(couple)* they're ill-matched; **être bien/mal e.** to be on good/bad terms

2 *(en même temps)* at once, at the same time; **ne parlez pas tous e.** don't all speak at once; **ils sont arrivés tous les deux e.** they both arrived at the same time

NM **1** *(collection ▸ d'objets)* set, collection; *(▸ d'idées)* set, series; *(▸ de données, d'informations, de textes)* set, body, collection; **la table et la chaise forment un e.** the table and chair are part of the same set; **un e. de conditions** a set of conditions; *Mktg* **e. de besoins** need set; *Mktg* **e. de considérations** consideration *or* product choice set; *Aut* **e. moteur-boîte** power unit

2 *(totalité)* whole; **la question dans son e.** the question as a whole; **la classe, prise dans son e., a un bon niveau** the class, (taken) as a whole, is of a good standard; **l'e. des joueurs** all the players; **l'e. du travail est bon** the work as a whole is good; **il s'est adressé à l'e. des employés** he spoke to all the staff *or* the whole staff

3 *(simultanéité)* unity; **avec e.** all together, in unison, as one; **manquer d'e.** to lack unity; **ils ont protesté dans un e. parfait** they protested unanimously

4 *(groupe)* group; **e. de chanteurs** group of singers; **e. instrumental** (instrumental) ensemble; **e. vocal** vocal group

5 *(vêtement)* suit, outfit; **e. de plage** beach outfit; **e. pantalon** trouser suit

6 *(d'habitations)* block; **grand e.** residential estate

7 *Math* set
8 *Ordinat (de caractères, d'informations)* set
• **dans l'ensemble** ADV on the whole, by and large, in the main; **dans l'e. tout va bien** on the whole *or* by and large *or* in the main everything's fine
• **d'ensemble** ADJ **1** *(général)* overall, general; **mesures d'e.** comprehensive *or* global measures; **vue d'e.** overall *or* general view **2** *Mus* **faire de la musique d'e.** to play in an ensemble

ensemblier [ɑ̃sɑ̃blije] NM **1** *(décorateur)* interior designer **2** *Cin & TV* props assistant

ensemencement [ɑ̃səmɑ̃smɑ̃] NM **1** *Agr* seeding, sowing **2** *Pêche* stocking **3** *Biol* culturing

ensemencer [16] [ɑ̃səmɑ̃se] VT **1** *Agr* to sow, to seed; **champ ensemencé de tournesols** field seeded *or* sown with sunflowers **2** *Pêche* to stock **3** *Biol* to culture

enserrer [4] [ɑ̃sere] VT **1** *(agripper)* to clutch, to grasp, to grip; **e. qn dans ses bras** to clasp sb in one's arms, to embrace *or* to hug sb **2** *(être autour de ▸ sujet: col, bijou)* to fit tightly around; **un bracelet lui enserrait le bras** she wore a tightly-fitting bracelet around her arm; **des fortifications enserrent la vieille ville** fortified walls form a tight circle around the old town

ensevelir [32] [ɑ̃səvlir] VT **1** *Littéraire (dans un linceul)* to shroud, to enshroud; *(dans la tombe)* to entomb **2** *(enfouir)* to bury; **l'éruption a enseveli plusieurs villages** the eruption buried several villages
VPR **s'ensevelir** *aussi Fig* **s'e. dans** to bury oneself in

ensevelissement [ɑ̃səvlismɑ̃] NM **1** *Littéraire (mise ▸ dans un linceul)* enshrouding; *(▸ au tombeau)* entombment **2** *(disparition ▸ d'une ruine, d'un souvenir)* burying

ensilage [ɑ̃silaʒ] NM *Agr* **1** *(méthode)* ensilage, silaging **2** *(produit)* silage

ensiler [3] [ɑ̃sile] VT *Agr* to ensile, to silage

en-soi [ɑ̃swa] NM INV *Phil* **l'e.** the thing in itself

ensoleillé, -e [ɑ̃sɔleje] ADJ sunny, sunlit; **très e.** sundrenched

ensoleillement [ɑ̃sɔlejmɑ̃] NM (amount of) sunshine, *Spéc* insolation; **la pièce n'a pas un bon e.** the room doesn't get much sun *or* sunlight; **l'e. annuel** the number of days of sunshine per year; **cinq journées/heures d'e.** five days/hours of sun(shine)

ensoleiller [4] [ɑ̃sɔleje] VT **1** *(donner du soleil à)* to bathe in *or* to fill with sunlight **2** *Fig* to brighten (up); **cet enfant ensoleillait leur existence** that child was like a ray of sunshine in their lives

ensommeillé, -e [ɑ̃sɔmeje] ADJ sleepy, drowsy, dozy; *(yeux, visage)* sleepy; **les yeux tout ensommeillés** eyes heavy with sleep; **il était encore tout e.** he was still half-asleep

ensorcelant, -e [ɑ̃sɔrsəlɑ̃, -ɑ̃t] ADJ bewitching, entrancing, spellbinding

ensorcelé, -e [ɑ̃sɔrsəle] ADJ bewitched, under a spell

ensorceler [24] [ɑ̃sɔrsəle] VT **1** *(envoûter)* to bewitch, to cast a spell over; **elle m'a ensorcelé** I fell under her spell **2** *Fig (personne)* to bewitch, to captivate

ensorceleur, -euse [ɑ̃sɔrsəlœr, -øz] ADJ bewitching, entrancing, spellbinding
NM,F **1** *(sorcier)* enchanter, *f* enchantress, sorcerer, *f* sorceress **2** *(charmeur)* charmer

ensorcelle *etc voir* **ensorceler**

ensorcellement [ɑ̃sɔrsɛlmɑ̃] NM *(action)* bewitching; *(état)* bewitchment, enchantment; *Fig (charme)* charm, spell

ensuit *etc voir* **ensuivre**

ensuite [ɑ̃sɥit] ADV **1** *(dans le temps ▸ puis)* then, next; *(▸ plus tard)* later, after, afterwards; **qu'est-ce que vous prendrez e.?** what will you have to follow?; **et e., que s'est-il passé?** and what happened next?, and then what happened?; **d'abord, c'est très cher, et e. ça ne te va pas du tout** for one thing it's very expensive and for another it doesn't at all suit you; **ils ne sont arrivés qu'e.** they didn't arrive until later; **ils se sont disputés, e. de quoi on ne l'a jamais revu** they fell out, after which we didn't see him again **2** *(dans l'espace)* then, further on; **la porte d'entrée donnait sur le salon et e. venait la chambre** the front door opened into the living room and then came the bedroom

ensuivre [89] [ɑ̃sɥivr] **s'ensuivre** VPR to follow, to ensue; **sa maladie et toutes les conséquences qui s'en sont suivies** his/her illness and all the ensuing consequences; **il ne s'ensuit pas forcément que tu as raison** it doesn't necessarily follow that you are right; **il s'ensuit qu'il est sans emploi** the consequence is he's out of a job; **il s'en est suivi que…** it ensued that…; **jusqu'à ce que mort s'ensuive** *(battre quelqu'un etc)* to death; **et tout ce qui s'ensuit** and so on (and so forth)

ensuqué, -e [ɑ̃syke] ADJ *Fam (dans le sud de la France)* dazed, in a daze

entablement [ɑ̃tabləmɑ̃] NM *Archit* entablature

entaché, -e [ɑ̃taʃe] ADJ **e. de nullité** *(contrat, texte)* voidable

entacher [3] [ɑ̃taʃe] VT **1** *(souiller)* to sully, to soil; **ce scandale a entaché son honneur** the scandal has sullied his/her reputation **2** *(marquer)* to mar; **une attitude entachée d'hypocrisie** an attitude marred by hypocrisy

entaille [ɑ̃taj] NF **1** *(encoche)* notch, nick **2** *(blessure)* gash, slash, cut; **petite e.** nick; **se faire une e. au front** to gash one's forehead

entailler [3] [ɑ̃taje] VT **1** *(fendre)* to notch, to nick **2** *(blesser)* to gash, to slash, to cut; **la lame lui a entaillé l'arcade sourcilière** the blade slashed his/her face above the eye **3** *Can* to tap; **e. un érable** to tap a maple tree
VPR **s'entailler s'e. le doigt** to cut one's finger

entame [ɑ̃tam] NF **1** *Culin (morceau ▸ de viande)* first slice *or* cut; *(▸ de pain)* crust **2** *Cartes (début)* opening; **dès l'e. de qch** from the start *or* beginning of sth

entamer [3] [ɑ̃tame] VT **1** *(jambon, fromage)* to start; *(bouteille, conserve)* to open; *(pot de confiture etc)* to start on, to open
2 *(durée, repas)* to start, to begin; *(négociation)* to launch, to start, to initiate; **e. une conversation** to strike up a conversation; **e. des démarches** to begin to take steps, to initiate steps; *Jur* **e. des poursuites (contre qn)** to initiate *or* to institute proceedings (against sb); **nous avons entamé une longue procédure** we have started *or* launched a long procedure
3 *(réduire ▸ fortune, économies)* to make a dent *or* hole in; *(▸ capital, profits)* to eat into; *(▸ résistance)* to lower, to deal a blow to; *(▸ ligne ennemie)* to break through
4 *(ébranler)* to shake; **rien ne peut e. sa confiance en lui** nothing can shake *or* undermine his self-confidence
5 *(user)* to damage; **l'acide entame le fer** acid eats into *or* corrodes metal; **le coin a été entamé** the corner was damaged *or* chipped
6 *(écorcher ▸ peau)* to graze
7 *Cartes* to open; **e. trèfle** to open clubs

entartrage [ɑ̃tartraʒ] NM **1** *Tech (d'une chaudière, d'un tuyau)* scaling, *Br* furring (up) **2** *Méd (d'une dent ▸ processus)* scaling; *(▸ état)* scale, tartar deposit

entartrer [3] [ɑ̃tartre] VT **1** *Tech (chaudière, tuyau)* to scale, *Br* to fur (up) **2** *Méd (dent)* to cover with tartar *or* scale
VPR **s'entartrer 1** *Tech (chaudière, tuyau)* to scale, *Br* to fur (up) **2** *Méd (dent)* to become covered in tartar *or* scale

entassement [ɑ̃tasmɑ̃] NM **1** *(amas)* heap, pile, stack; *(mise en tas)* heaping *or* piling up, stacking **2** *(fait de s'agglutiner)* crowding; **l'e. des voyageurs dans le wagon** the crowding of passengers into the carriage

entasser [3] [ɑ̃tase] VT **1** *(mettre en tas)* to heap (up), to pile (up), to stack (up); **e. de la terre** to heap up *or* to bank up earth
2 *(accumuler ▸ vieilleries, journaux)* to pile (up), to heap (up)
3 *(thésauriser ▸ fortune, argent)* to pile up, to heap up
4 *(serrer)* to cram (in), to pack (in); **ils vivent entassés à quatre dans une seule pièce** the four of them live in one cramped room
VPR **s'entasser** *(neige, terre)* to heap up, to pile up, to bank; *(vieilleries, journaux)* to heap up, to pile up; *(personnes)* to crowd (in) *or* together, to pile in; **s'e. dans une voiture** to pile into a car

ente [ɑ̃t] NF **1** *Agr (greffon)* scion; *(greffe)* graft **2** *(de pinceau)* handle

entendement [ɑ̃tɑ̃dmɑ̃] NM comprehension, understanding; **cela dépasse l'e.** it's beyond all comprehension *or* understanding

entendeur [ɑ̃tɑ̃dœr] NM *Prov* **à bon e. salut** a word to the wise is enough

ENTENDRE [73] [ɑ̃tɑ̃dr]

VT	
• to hear **1, 2, 4, 5, 7**	• to listen to **2**
• to agree to **3**	• to understand **6**
• to mean **8**	• to intend **9**
USAGE ABSOLU	
• to hear **1**	• to understand **2**
VPR	
• to be heard **1, 2**	• to be understood **3**
• to hear each other **4**	• to agree **5**
• to reach an agreement **5**	• to get on **6**
• to be good at **8**	• to hear oneself **7**

VT **1** *(percevoir par l'ouïe)* to hear; **parlez plus fort, on n'entend rien (de ce que vous dites)** speak up, we can't hear a word (you're saying); **on l'entend à peine** you can hardly hear him/her/it, he/she/it is scarcely audible; **on n'entend que toi, ici! c'est lassant à la fin!** yours is the only voice we can hear, it's so annoying!; **silence, je ne veux pas vous e.!** quiet, I don't want to hear a sound from you!; **tu entends ce que je te dis?** do you hear me?; **tu entends ce que tu dis?** do you know what you're saying?; **elle a dû m'e. le lui dire** she must have overheard me telling him/her; **j'entends pleurer à côté** I can hear someone crying next door; **je l'entendis rire** I heard him/her laugh *or* laughing; **e. dire** to hear; **j'ai entendu dire qu'il était parti** I heard that he had left; **c'est la première fois que j'entends (dire) ça** that's the first I've heard of it; **on entend dire beaucoup de choses sur son compte** one hears many things about him/her; **e. qn dire qch** to hear sb say sth; **e. parler de** *(connaître l'existence de)* to hear of; *(être au courant de)* to hear about; **je ne veux pas en e. parler!** I don't want to hear (a word) about it!; **il ne veut pas e. parler d'informatique** he won't hear of computers; **j'ai entendu parler de leur maison** I've heard about their house; **je ne veux plus e. parler de lui** I don't want to hear him mentioned again; **on entend beaucoup parler de lui ces temps-ci à la radio** we hear a lot about him on the radio at the moment; **on n'entend parler que de lui/de sa pièce** he's/his play's the talk of the town; **vous n'avez pas fini d'en e. parler!** you haven't heard the last of this!; **celui-là, il va e. parler de moi** *ou* **du pays!** he'll get a piece of my mind!; **je l'entends d'avance** *ou* **d'ici!** I can hear it already!; **on entendrait/on aurait entendu voler une mouche** you could hear/could have heard a pin drop; **j'aurai tout entendu!** whatever next?; *Fam* **j'en ai entendu de belles** *ou* **de bonnes** *ou* **des vertes et des pas mûres sur son compte** I've heard a thing or two about him/her; *Fam* **ce qu'il faut e.!, ce qu'il faut pas e.!** the things some people come out with!, the things you hear!; *Fam* **qu'entends-je, qu'ouïs-je, qu'acoustiqué-je?** *ou* **qu'entends-je, qu'ouïs-je, rêvé-je ou dors-je?** I can't believe my ears!
2 *(écouter)* to hear, to listen to; **aller e. un concert** to go to a concert; **essayer de se faire e.** to try to make oneself heard; **un bruit se fit e.** a noise was heard; **il ne veut rien e.** he won't listen; **à les e. tout serait de ma faute** to hear them talk *or* according to them it's all my fault; **à vous e., il a eu tort** judging from *or* going by what you say, he was in the wrong; **e. raison** to see sense; **faire e. raison à qn** to make sb listen to reason, to bring sb to his/her senses; **il va m'e.!** I'll give him hell!
3 *(accepter ▸ demande)* to agree to; *(▸ vœu)* to grant; **nos prières ont été entendues** our prayers were answered
4 *Rel* **e. la messe** to attend *or* to hear mass; **e. une confession** to hear *or* to take a confession
5 *Jur (témoin)* to hear, to interview
6 *(comprendre)* to understand; **entend-il la plaisanterie?** can he take a joke?; **c'est comme ça que j'entends la vie!** this is the life!; **ce n'est pas ainsi qu'il l'entend** he doesn't see it that way *or* like

that; **comment entendez-vous cette remarque?** how do you interpret this remark?; **il doit être bien entendu que…** it must be properly understood that…; **laisser e. qch** to insinuate *or* to imply sth; **elle m'a laissé** *ou* **donné à e. que…** *(m'a fait croire)* she led me to believe that…; *(m'a fait comprendre)* she gave me to understand that…; **y entendez-vous quelque chose?** do you know anything about it?; **il ne l'entend pas de cette oreille** he won't have any of it

7 *(apprendre)* to hear; **qu'est-ce que j'entends, tu n'as pas été sage?** what's this I hear *or* what did I hear, you didn't behave yourself?

8 *(vouloir dire)* to mean; **qu'entendez-vous par là?** what do you mean by that?; *Vieilli* **sans y e. malice** without meaning any harm (by it)

9 *(vouloir)* to want, to intend; **e. faire qch** to intend *or* mean to do sth; **fais comme tu l'entends** do as you wish *or* please; **j'entends qu'on m'obéisse** I intend to *or* I mean to *or* I will be obeyed; **j'entends que vous veniez** I expect you to come; **je n'entends pas être exploité** I have no intention of being *or* I won't be exploited; **il entend bien partir demain** he's determined to go tomorrow; **elle voulait trouver du travail, mais lui ne l'entendait pas ainsi** she wanted to get a job, but he wouldn't hear of it

USAGE ABSOLU 1 *(percevoir par l'ouïe)* **est-ce qu'il entend?** can he hear properly?; **il entend mal** he is hard of hearing; **j'entends mal de l'oreille droite** my hearing's bad in the right ear; *Fam* **attends, j'ai mal entendu!** hold on, I don't think I heard you right!; **tu entends!** *(menace)* do you hear (me)!

2 *(comprendre)* **j'entends bien** I (do) understand; **certes, j'entends, mais…** certainly, I do understand, but…

VPR s'entendre 1 *(être perçu)* to be heard; **cela s'entend de loin** you can hear it *or* it can be heard from far off

2 *(être utilisé ▸ mot, expression)* to be heard; **cela s'entend encore dans la région** you can still hear it said *or* used around here

3 *(être compris)* to be understood; **ces chiffres s'entendent hors taxes** these figures do not include tax; **(cela) s'entend** *(c'est évident)* obviously, it's obvious, that much is clear; **après l'hiver, (cela) s'entend** when the winter is over, of course *or* it goes without saying

4 *(pouvoir s'écouter)* to hear each other *or* one another

5 *(s'accorder)* to agree; **s'e. avec** to reach an agreement with; **parvenir à s'e. avec qn sur qch** to come to an understanding *or* to reach an agreement with sb about sth; **s'e. directement avec qn** to come to a direct understanding with sb; **s'e. pour commettre un crime** to conspire to commit a crime; **s'e. sur un prix** to agree on a price; **entendons-nous bien** let's get this straight

6 *(sympathiser)* to get on; **s'e. avec** to get on with; **ils ne s'entendent pas** they don't get on; **je crois que nous sommes faits pour nous e.** I think we were made to get on well together; **nous n'étions pas faits pour nous e.** we weren't suited to each other; **s'e. comme chien et chat** to fight like cat and dog; **s'e. comme larrons en foire** to be as thick as thieves

7 *(percevoir sa voix)* to hear oneself; **on ne s'entend plus tellement il y a de bruit** there's so much noise, you can't hear yourself think; **tu ne t'entends pas!** you should hear yourself (talking)!, if (only) you could hear yourself!

8 *(s'y connaître)* **il s'y entend en mécanique** he's good at *or* he knows (a lot) about mechanics; **s'y e. pour réparer un vélo** to know how to fix a bicycle; **elle s'y entend pour tout embrouiller!** she's a great one for getting into a mess!; **s'e. aux affaires** to have a good head for business

9 *(locution)* **quand je dis qu'il est grand, je m'entends, il est plus grand que moi** when I say he's tall I really mean he's taller than me

entendu, -e [ɑ̃tɑ̃dy] **ADJ 1** *(complice ▸ air, sourire)* knowing; **hocher la tête d'un air e.** to nod knowingly **2** *(convenu)* agreed; **(c'est) e., je viendrai** all right *or* very well, I'll come; **c'est une affaire entendue** that's agreed *or* settled

entente [ɑ̃tɑ̃t] **NF 1** *(harmonie)* harmony; **entre eux c'est l'e. parfaite** they're in complete harmony (with each other); **il y a une bonne e. entre eux** they're on good terms (with each other); **la bonne/mauvaise e. qui règne dans la famille** the good/bad feeling that prevails in the family; **vivre en bonne e. avec** to live in harmony with

2 *Pol* agreement, understanding; **arriver à une e. sur** to come to an understanding *or* agreement over

3 *Écon* agreement, accord; **e. entre producteurs** agreement between producers; **e. industrielle** cartel, combine

4 *Hist* **l'E. cordiale** the Entente Cordiale

• à double entente ADJ ambiguous; **une expression à double e.** *(ambiguë)* an ambiguous expression; *(à connotation sexuelle)* a double entendre

enter [3] [ɑ̃te] **VT 1** *Constr* to scarf **2** *Hort* to graft

entérinement [ɑ̃terinmɑ̃] **NM 1** *Jur* ratification **2** *(approbation ▸ d'un usage)* adoption; *(▸ d'un état de fait, d'une situation)* acceptance

entériner [3] [ɑ̃terine] **VT 1** *Jur* to ratify, to confirm **2** *(approuver ▸ usage)* to adopt; *(▸ état de fait, situation)* to go along with, to accept

entérique [ɑ̃terik] **ADJ** *Méd* enteric

entérite [ɑ̃terit] **NF** *Méd* enteritis

enterrement [ɑ̃tɛrmɑ̃] **NM 1** *(funérailles)* funeral; *Fig* **cette soirée, c'était un e. de première classe** it was like watching paint dry, that party

2 *(ensevelissement)* burial

3 *(cortège)* funeral procession

4 *(abandon ▸ d'une idée, d'une dispute)* burying; *(▸ d'un projet)* shelving, laying aside; **e. de vie de garçon** *Br* stag night *or* party, *Am* bachelor party; **e. de vie de jeune fille** *Br* hen night *or* party, *Am* bachelorette party

• d'enterrement ADJ *(mine, tête)* gloomy, glum; **faire une tête d'e.** to wear a gloomy *or* long expression

enterrer [4] [ɑ̃tere] **VT 1** *(ensevelir)* to bury; **être enterré vivant** to be buried alive **2** *(inhumer)* to bury, to inter; **vous nous enterrerez tous** you'll outlive us all; **e. sa vie de garçon** to have a *Br* stag night *or* party *or Am* bachelor party; **e. sa vie de jeune fille** to have a *Br* hen night *or* party *or Am* bachelorette party **3** *(oublier ▸ scandale)* to bury, to hush up; *(▸ souvenir, passé, querelle)* to bury, to forget (about); *(▸ projet)* to shelve, to lay aside; **elle désire e. toute cette affaire** she wants the whole thing buried and forgotten

VPR s'enterrer to bury oneself; *Fig* to hide oneself away; **aller s'e. en province** to hide oneself away in the country

entêtant, -e [ɑ̃tɛtɑ̃, -ɑ̃t] **ADJ** heady

en-tête [ɑ̃tɛt] *(pl* **en-têtes***)* **NM 1** *(sur du papier à lettres)* letterhead, heading **2** *Typ* head, header; **e. de facture** billhead; *Journ* **e. de colonne** column header **3** *Ordinat* header

• à en-tête ADJ *(papier, bristol)* headed; **papier à e. de la compagnie** company notepaper

• en en-tête de PRÉP at the head *or* top of; **mettez l'adresse en e. de la lettre** put the address at the top of the letter; **je veux le logo en e. de la feuille** I want the sheet headed with the logo

entêté, -e [ɑ̃tete] **ADJ** obstinate, stubborn

NM,F stubborn *or* obstinate person

entêtement [ɑ̃tɛtmɑ̃] **NM** stubbornness, obstinacy; **e. à faire qch** persistence in doing sth

entêter [4] [ɑ̃tete] **VT** to make dizzy; **ce parfum m'entête** I find this perfume quite intoxicating

VPR s'entêter to persist, to be persistent; **s'e. à faire qch** to persist in doing sth; **elle s'entête à vouloir/à ne pas vouloir venir** she's set her mind on/against coming; **s'e. dans l'erreur/dans une opinion** to persist in one's error/in an opinion

enthousiasmant, -e [ɑ̃tuzjasmɑ̃, -ɑ̃t] **ADJ** exciting, thrilling

enthousiasme [ɑ̃tuzjasm] **NM** enthusiasm, keenness; **être plein d'e., déborder d'e.** to be full of *or* to be bubbling with enthusiasm; **avec e.** enthusiastically; **parler de qch avec e.** to enthuse over sth; **faire qch sans e.** to do sth half-heartedly *or* without enthusiasm

enthousiasmer [3] [ɑ̃tuzjasme] **VT** to fill with enthusiasm; **cela n'avait pas l'air de l'e.** he/she didn't seem very enthusiastic (about it); **il est revenu enthousiasmé** he came back full of *or* fired with enthusiasm

VPR s'enthousiasmer to be/become enthusiastic, to enthuse (**pour** about); **il s'enthousiasme facilement** he's easily carried away

enthousiaste [ɑ̃tuzjast] **ADJ** enthusiastic, keen; **trop e.** overenthusiastic

NMF enthusiast; **c'est un grand e.** he's very keen!

entiché, -e [ɑ̃tiʃe] **ADJ être e. de** to be wild about

enticher [3] [ɑ̃tiʃe] **s'enticher VPR s'e. de qn** *(s'amouracher de)* to become infatuated with sb; **s'e. de qch** *(s'enthousiasmer pour)* to become very keen on sth

ENTIER, -ÈRE [ɑ̃tje, -ɛr]

ADJ	
• whole **1, 5**	• entire **1**
• absolute **2**	• complete **2**
• intact **3**	• intense **4**
NM	
• integer	

ADJ 1 *(complet)* whole, entire; **une semaine entière** a whole *or* an entire week; **la France entière** the whole of France; **pendant des journées/des heures entières** for days/hours on end; **manger un camembert e.** to eat a whole camembert; **dans le monde e.** in the whole world, throughout the world; **payer place entière** *(à un spectacle)* to pay the full price; *(en train ou en avion)* to pay full fare; **il a mangé le gâteau tout e.** he ate the whole (of the) cake; **je le voulais tout e. pour moi** I wanted him all to myself; **être tout e. à son travail** to be completely wrapped up *or* engrossed in one's work; **se donner tout e. à son travail** to devote oneself entirely to one's work

2 *(avant le nom) (en intensif)* absolute, complete; **il a mon entière confiance** I have complete confidence in him; **donner entière satisfaction à qn** to give sb complete satisfaction

3 *(après le verbe) (intact)* intact; **conserver sa réputation entière** to keep one's reputation intact; **le problème reste e.** the problem is no nearer solution *or* remains unsolved

4 *(absolu ▸ personne)* intense; **c'est quelqu'un de très e.** he's/she's very intense

5 *Culin (lait)* whole, *Br* full-cream

NM *Math (nombre)* integer, whole number

• dans son entier ADV as a whole; **l'industrie automobile dans son e.** the car industry as a whole; **raconter une histoire dans son e.** to relate a story in its entirety

• en entier ADV manger un gâteau en e. to eat a whole *or* an entire cake; **je l'ai lu en e.** I read all of it, I read the whole of it, I read it right through; **il a fait ses devoirs en e.** he has done all (of) his homework

entiercement [ɑ̃tjɛrsəmɑ̃] **NM** *Jur* escrow

entièrement [ɑ̃tjɛrmɑ̃] **ADV** entirely, completely; **tu as e. raison** you're quite *or* absolutely right; **ce n'est pas e. faux** it's not completely *or* entirely wrong, there's some truth in it; **il n'est pas e. mauvais** he's not all bad

entièreté [ɑ̃tjɛrte] **NF** entirety

entité [ɑ̃tite] **NF 1** *(abstraction)* entity

2 *Méd* **e. morbide** morbid entity

3 *Jur* entity; **Largal est une e. juridique à part entière** Largal is a company in its own right

4 *Compta* item

entoilage [ɑ̃twalaʒ] **NM 1** *(technique ▸ renforcement)* mounting on canvas; *(▸ recouvrement)* covering with canvas; *Couture* stiffening with canvas **2** *(toile)* canvas cover

entoiler [3] [ɑ̃twale] **VT** *(renforcer)* to mount on canvas; *(recouvrir)* to cover with canvas; *Couture* to stiffen with canvas; **carte entoilée** canvas-mounted map

entôler [3] [ɑ̃tole] **VT** *très Fam* to fleece *(prostitute's client)*

entomologie [ɑ̃tɔmɔlɔʒi] **NF** *Entom* entomology

entomologique [ɑ̃tɔmɔlɔʒik] **ADJ** *Entom* entomologic, entomological

entomologiste [ɑ̃tɔmɔlɔʒist] **NMF** *Entom* entomologist

entonner [3] [ɑ̃tɔne] **VT 1** *(hymne, air)* to strike up, to start singing; **e. les louanges de qn** to start singing sb's praises **2** *(vin)* to barrel, to cask

entonnoir [ɑ̃tɔnwar] **NM 1** *(ustensile)* funnel **2** *Géog* sinkhole, swallow hole **3** *(trou d'obus)* shell-hole, crater **4** *Fam (locution)* **avoir un bon e.** to have hollow legs

entorse [ɑ̃tɔrs] **NF 1** *Méd (foulure)* sprain; **se faire une e. au poignet** to sprain one's wrist **2** *(exception)* infringement (**à** of); **faire une e. au règlement** to bend the rules; **faire une e. à la vérité** to twist *or* to distort the truth; **faire une e. à son régime** to break one's diet; **tu peux bien faire une petite e. à tes habitudes** surely you can make an exception

entortillement [ɑ̃tɔrtijmɑ̃], **entortillage** [ɑ̃tɔrtijaʒ] **NM 1** *(action)* twisting, winding; *(d'un fil, du papier etc)* twisting, wrapping; *(d'un serpent, du lierre etc)* twisting, twining, coiling **2** *(état)* entwinement

entortiller [3] [ɑ̃tɔrtije] **VT 1** *(enrouler ▸ ruban, papier)* to twist, to wrap (**autour de** round); *(▸ bonbon etc)* to wrap (up) (**dans** in); **e. une mèche de cheveux autour de son doigt** to wind *or* to twist a strand of hair round one's finger **2** *(compliquer)* **être entortillé** to be convoluted; **e. une demande dans des explications fumeuses** to wrap up a request in woolly explanations **3** *Fam (tromper)* to hoodwink, to con; **il essaie de t'e.** he's trying to con you; **se faire e.** to be taken in

VPR s'entortiller 1 *(s'enrouler ▸ lierre)* to twist, to wind (**autour de** round) **2** *(être empêtré)* to get caught *or* tangled up (**dans** in); **s'e. dans ses explications** to get tangled up in one's explanations **3 il s'est entortillé les pieds dans le tapis** he got his feet entangled *or* tangled (up) in the carpet

entour [ɑ̃tur] **NM** *Vieilli* **à l'e. de** round (about); *Littéraire* **les entours de** the environs *or* surroundings of

entourage [ɑ̃turaʒ] **NM 1** *(d'une personne)* circle; *(d'un roi, d'un président)* entourage; **e. familial** family circle; **on dit dans l'e. du Président que…** sources close to the President say that… **2** *(bordure ▸ d'une ouverture, d'un parterre de fleurs etc)* border; *(▸ d'un bijou)* setting; **miniature avec un e. de perles** miniature set in pearls

entourer [3] [ɑ̃ture] **VT 1** *(encercler ▸ terrain, mets)* to surround; *(armée)* to encircle, to surround; **un châle entourait ses épaules** a shawl was wrapped around her shoulders; **e. un champ de barbelés** to surround a field with barbed wire, to put barbed wire around a field; **e. un mot de** *ou* **en rouge** to circle a word in red

2 *(être autour de)* to surround; **le monde qui nous entoure** the world around us *or* that surrounds us; **les gens qui vous entourent** the people around *or* about you; **un rang de perles entourait son cou** a string of pearls encircled her neck, she had a string of pearls round her neck

3 *(graviter autour de ▸ sujet: foule, conseillers)* to surround, to be around

4 *(soutenir ▸ malade, veuve)* to rally round; **au moment de son divorce, sa famille l'a beaucoup entouré** his family rallied round *or* supported him at the time of his divorce; **e. un ami de son affection** to surround a friend with affection; **e. qn de soins/respect** to lavish attention on sb/show respect to sb

VPR s'entourer s'e. d'objets d'art/d'excellents musiciens to surround oneself with works of art/with excellent musicians

USAGE ABSOLU savoir s'e. to know all the right people

entourloupe [ɑ̃turlup] **NF** *Fam* nasty *or* dirty trick; **faire une e. à qn** to play a dirty trick on sb; *Br* to do the dirty on sb, *Am* to do sb dirty

entourlouper [3] [ɑ̃turlupe] **VT** *Fam* **e. qn** to play a dirty trick on sb; *Br* to do the dirty on sb, *Am* to do sb dirty

entourloupette [ɑ̃turlupɛt] = **entourloupe**

entournure [ɑ̃turnyr] **NF** *Couture* armhole

> **PREFIX**
>
> **ENTR-, ENTRE-**
>
> This prefix, which has no equivalent in English, has several distinct uses.
>
> • Added to a verb or a noun, it can convey the idea of RECIPROCITY. The verbal use is often translated by *each other* or *one another*, eg:
>
> **ils s'entraident** they help each other; **ils se sont presque entretués** they almost killed one another; **une entrevue** a meeting, an interview
>
> • Added to a verb, **entr-** or **entre-** can mean HARDLY, SLIGHTLY or CURSORILY, eg:
>
> **la porte était entrebâillée** *ou* **entrouverte** the door was ajar, the door was half-open; **je l'ai entraperçue dans la rue** I caught a glimpse of her in the street
>
> • Added to a noun, the prefix refers to something IN THE MIDDLE OF two things, eg:
>
> **l'entrejambe** the crotch; **une entrecôte** an entrecôte steak (from between the ribs); **à l'entresol** on the mezzanine floor (between the ground and first floors)

entracte [ɑ̃trakt] **NM 1** *Cin & Théât Br* interval, *Am* intermission; **à** *ou* **pendant l'e.** *Br* in the interval, *Am* during the intermission; **un e. de 15 minutes** a 15-minute *Br* interval *or Am* intermission **2** *(spectacle)* interlude, entr'acte **3** *(pause)* break, interlude

entraide [ɑ̃trɛd] **NF** mutual aid; *Admin* **comité d'e.** support committee

entraider [4] [ɑ̃trede] **s'entraider VPR** to help one another *or* each other

entrailles [ɑ̃traj] **NFPL 1** *Anat & Zool* entrails, guts; **être pris aux e.** *(être ému)* to be stirred to the depths of one's soul; **ne pas avoir d'e.** to be heartless **2** *Littéraire (ventre)* womb **3** *(profondeur ▸ de la terre)* depths, bowels; *(▸ d'un piano, d'un navire)* innards

entrain [ɑ̃trɛ̃] **NM 1** *(fougue)* spirit; **avoir beaucoup d'e., être plein d'e.** to be full of life *or* energy; **il faut y mettre un peu plus d'e.** you need to put a little more spirit into it **2** *(animation)* liveliness; **musique pleine d'e.** lively music

• **avec entrain ADV** with gusto, enthusiastically; **manger avec e.** to eat with gusto; **travailler avec e.** to work with a will

• **sans entrain ADV** half-heartedly, unenthusiastically

entraînant, -e [ɑ̃trɛnɑ̃, -ɑ̃t] **ADJ** *(chanson)* catchy, swinging; *(rythme)* swinging, lively; *(style, éloquence)* rousing, stirring

entraînement [ɑ̃trɛnmɑ̃] **NM 1** *Sport (d'un sportif)* training, coaching; *(d'un cheval)* training; **un e.** a training session, a work-out; **suivre un e.** to follow a training programme; **avoir de l'e.** to be well trained; **manquer d'e.** to be out of training; **se blesser à l'e.** to hurt oneself while training *or* during a training session

2 *(habitude)* practice; **il ne faut pas de technique spéciale, juste un peu d'e.** there's no need for any special skills, just some practice; **toi qui as de l'e., fais-le** you've had a lot of practice at this type of thing, you do it

3 *Tech* drive; **e. à chaîne/par courroie** chain/belt drive; **e. du papier** *(d'une imprimante)* paper advance

4 *Littéraire (des passions)* force; **céder à des entraînements** to get carried away

• **d'entraînement ADJ 1** *Équitation & Sport (séance, matériel)* training *(avant n)*; **match d'e.** practice game; **terrain d'e.** training *or* practice ground; **camp d'e. militaire** military training camp **2** *Tech* drive *(avant n)*; **arbre d'e.** drive shaft

entraîner [4] [ɑ̃trene] **VT 1** *(emporter)* to carry along, to sweep along; *Fig* to carry away; **le torrent entraînait tout sur son passage** the torrent swept everything along with it; **entraînés par la foule** swept along by the crowd; **se laisser e. par la musique** to let oneself be carried away by the music

2 *(tirer ▸ wagons)* to pull, to haul; *(actionner ▸ bielle)* to drive; **poulie entraînée par une courroie** belt-driven pulley

3 *(conduire)* to drag (along); **e. qn quelque part** to drag *or* to take sb off somewhere; **il m'a entraîné au fond de la salle** he dragged me (off) to the back of the room; **un étranger peut vous e. dans les bois** a stranger might entice you into the woods; **e. qn dans un piège** to lure sb into a trap; **c'est lui qui m'a entraîné dans cette affaire** he's the one who dragged me into this mess; **se laisser e.** to allow oneself to be led astray; **il a entraîné son associé dans sa faillite** he dragged his partner down with him when he went bankrupt; **ce sont les grands qui les entraînent à faire des bêtises** it's the older children who encourage them to be naughty; **e. qn dans sa chute** to pull *or* to drag sb down in one's fall; *Fig* to drag sb down with one

4 *(occasionner)* to bring about, to lead to, to involve; **cela risque d'e. de gros frais** this is likely to involve heavy expenditure; **sa victoire entraînerait la fin de la démocratie** his/her victory would lead to *or* mean the end of democracy

5 *Équitation & Sport (équipe, boxeur, sportif)* to train, to coach; *(cheval)* to train; **e. qn à la natation** to coach sb in swimming; **e. qn à faire qch** to train sb to do sth

VPR s'entraîner *Sport* to train; **je m'entraîne tous les matins** I train every morning; **s'e. au saut à la perche** to be in training *or* to train for the pole vault; **s'e. à faire qch** *(gén)* to teach oneself to do sth; *Sport* to train oneself to do sth

entraîneur, -euse [ɑ̃trɛnœr, -øz] **NM,F 1** *(d'un cheval)* trainer; *(d'un sportif)* trainer, coach; *(d'une équipe de foot)* manager, coach; *Fig* **e. d'hommes** leader of men **2** *(d'un cycliste)* pacemaker

• **entraîneuse NF entraîneuse (de bar)** hostess *(in a bar)*

entrant, -e [ɑ̃trɑ̃, -ɑ̃t] **ADJ** incoming; *(fonctionnaire)* newly appointed; *(représentant parlementaire)* newly elected; **les élèves entrants** the new pupils

NM,F 1 *Sport* substitute **2** *(celui qui entre)* **les entrants et les sortants** those who go in and those who come out

entrapercevoir, entr'apercevoir [52] [ɑ̃trapɛrsəvwar] **VT** to catch a (fleeting) glimpse of

entrave [ɑ̃trav] **NF 1** *(obstacle)* hindrance, obstacle; **e. à la circulation** hindrance to traffic; **e. à la liberté/à la bonne marche de la justice** interference with freedom/with the due process of the law; **cette mesure est une e. au libre-échange** this measure is an obstacle *or* a hindrance to free trade **2** *(chaîne ▸ d'esclave)* chain, fetter, shackle; *(▸ de cheval)* hobble, shackle, fetter; **mettre des entraves à un cheval** to fetter a horse

• **sans entraves ADJ** unfettered

entravé, -e [ɑ̃trave] **ADJ 1** *Couture* hobble *(avant n)* **2** *Ling* checked

entraver [3] [ɑ̃trave] **VT 1** *(gêner ▸ circulation)* to hold up

2 *(contrecarrer ▸ initiative, projet)* to hinder, to hamper, to get in the way of; **e. une négociation** to hamper negotiations

3 *(attacher ▸ esclave)* to put in chains, to shackle; *(▸ cheval)* to hobble, to fetter, to shackle

4 *très Fam (comprendre)* to understand[□], to get; **j'entrave que dalle** it beats me, I don't get it at all

ENTRE [ɑ̃tr] **PRÉP 1** *(dans l'espace)* between; *(dans)* in; *(à travers)* through, between; **la distance e. la Terre et la Lune** the distance between the Earth and the Moon; **e. ces murs** within these walls; **serrer qn e. ses bras** to clasp sb in one's arms, to hug sb; **tenir qch e. ses mains** to hold sth in one's hands; **une phrase e. crochets** a sentence in square brackets; **ce sont deux moitiés de génoise avec du chocolat e.** it's two halves of sponge cake with chocolate in between; **il passa la main e. les barreaux** he put his hand through the bars; **l'aiguille glissa e. ses doigts** the needle slipped through his/her fingers

2 *(dans le temps)* between; **e. deux et trois (heures)** between two and three (o'clock); **e. 1830 et 1914** between 1830 and 1914; **j'ai réussi à le voir e. deux réunions** I managed to see him between two meetings; **e. le travail et le transport, je n'ai plus de temps à moi** between work and travel, I haven't any time left for myself

3 *(indiquant un état intermédiaire)* **une couleur e. le jaune et le vert** a colour between yellow and green; **elle était e. le rire et les larmes** she didn't know whether to laugh or cry; **pris e. le désir de le frapper et celui de l'embrasser** wanting both to hit him and kiss him; **le cidre est doux ou sec? – e. les deux** is the cider sweet or dry? – it's between the two *or* in between; *Fam* **c'était bien? – e. les deux** was it good? – so-so

4 *(exprimant une approximation)* between; **il y a e. 10 et 12 kilomètres** it's between 10 and 12 kilometres; **les températures oscilleront e. 10° et 15°** temperatures will range from 10° to 15°; **ils ont invité e. 15 et 20 personnes** they've invited 15 to 20 people

5 *(parmi)* among; **hésiter e. plusieurs solutions/routes/robes** to hesitate between several solutions/roads/dresses; **choisir une solution e. plusieurs autres** to choose one solution among *or* from several others; **partagez le gâteau e. les enfants** *(entre deux)* share the cake between the children; *(entre plusieurs)* share the cake among the children; **l'un d'e. vous** one of you; **plusieurs d'e. nous** several of us; **certains d'e. eux** some of them *or* among them; **ceux d'e. vous qui désireraient venir** those among you *or* of you who'd like to come; **lequel est le plus âgé d'e. vous?** who is the oldest amongst you?; **d'e. toutes ses sonates, c'est celle que je préfère** of all his sonatas, that's the one I like most; **tu as le choix e. trois réponses** you've got a choice of three answers; **choisir e. plusieurs candidats** to choose among *or* between several candidates; **un jour e. mille** a day in a thousand; **je me souvenais de ce jour e. tous** I remembered that day above all others; **je le reconnaîtrais e. tous** *(personne)* I'd know him anywhere; *(objet)* I couldn't fail to recognize it; **un homme dangereux e. tous** a most dangerous man; **brave e. les braves** bravest of the brave

6 *(dans un groupe)* **passer une soirée e. amis** to spend an evening among friends; **nous ferons une petite fête, juste e. nous** *(à deux)* we'll have a small party, just the two of us; *(à plusieurs)* we'll have a party, just among ourselves; **nous dinerons e. nous** we'll have dinner alone *or* by ourselves; **ils ont tendance à rester e. eux** they tend to keep themselves to themselves; **e. nous, il n'a pas tort** *(à deux)* between you and me, he's right; *(à plusieurs)* between us, he's right; **e. vous et moi** between you and me

7 *(indiquant une relation)* between; **le combat e. les deux adversaires a été sanglant** the fight between the two enemies was bloody; **les clans se battent e. eux** the clans fight (against) each other, there are fights between the clans; **ils se sont mis d'accord e. eux** they agreed among(st) themselves; **qu'y a-t-il e. vous?** what is there between you?; **mais qu'y a-t-il e. eux, exactement?** but what's (going on) between them exactly?; **il n'y a plus rien e. nous** there's nothing between us any more

• **entre autres** ADV among others; **sa fille, e. autres, n'est pas venue** his daughter, for one *or* among others, didn't come; **sont exposés, e. autres, des objets rares, des œuvres de jeunesse du peintre, etc** the exhibition includes, among other things, rare objects, examples of the artist's early work, etc

• **entre quat'z'yeux** ADV *Fam* **il faut que je te parle e. quat'z'yeux** I've got to talk to you in private□

entre- *voir* **entr-**

entrebâillement [ɑ̃trəbajmɑ̃] NM **dans/par l'e. de la porte** in/through the half-open door

entrebâiller [3] [ɑ̃trəbaje] VT *(porte, fenêtre)* to half-open; **laisse la porte entrebâillée** leave the door half-open *or* ajar; **la porte était entrebâillée** the door was ajar *or* half-open

entrebâilleur [ɑ̃trəbajœr] NM door chain

entrechat [ɑ̃trəʃa] NM **1** *(en danse)* entrechat **2** *Hum (bond)* leap, spring; **faire des entrechats** to leap about

entrechoquer [3] [ɑ̃trəʃɔke] VT to knock *or* to bang together; **e. des verres** to chink glasses

VPR **s'entrechoquer 1** *(se heurter)* to knock *or* bang against one another; *(verres)* to clink (together); *(épées)* to clash (together); *(dents)* to chatter **2** *(affluer ▸ images, mots)* to jostle together; **elle parle tellement vite que les mots s'entrechoquent** the words come tumbling out when she speaks

entrecôte [ɑ̃trəkot] NF *Culin* entrecôte (steak)

entrecoupé, -e [ɑ̃trəkupe] ADJ *(voix)* broken; **d'une voix entrecoupée** with a catch in one's voice, in a broken voice

entrecouper [3] [ɑ̃trəkupe] VT **1** *(interrompre ▸ discours, voyage, représentation etc)* to interrupt (**de** by *or* with); **la conversation a été entrecoupée de sonneries de téléphone** the phone kept interrupting the conversation; **une voix entrecoupée de sanglots** a voice broken by sobs **2** *(émailler)* **e. qch de** to intersperse *or* to pepper sth with

VPR **s'entrecouper** to intersect

entrecroisement [ɑ̃trəkrwazmɑ̃] NM *(de lignes)* intersecting, (criss)crossing; *(de fils)* intertwining, interlacing

entrecroiser [3] [ɑ̃trəkrwaze] VT *(lignes)* to intersect, to (criss)cross; *(fils)* to intertwine, to interlace

VPR **s'entrecroiser** *(de lignes, de routes)* to intersect, to (criss)cross; *(de fils)* to intertwine, to interlace

entre-déchirer [3] [ɑ̃trədeʃire] **s'entre-déchirer** VPR *aussi Fig* to tear one another to pieces

entre-deux [ɑ̃trədø] NM INV **1** *(dans l'espace)* space between, interspace

2 *(dans le temps)* intervening period, period in between

3 *Sport* jump ball

4 *Couture* **e. de dentelle** lace insert

entre-deux-guerres [ɑ̃trədøgɛr] NM INV OU NF INV *Hist* **l'e.** the interwar period

entre-dévorer [3] [ɑ̃trədevɔre] **s'entre-dévorer** VPR to devour one another; *Fig* to tear one another to pieces

ENTRÉE [ɑ̃tre]

• entrance **1, 4, 5**	• entry **1–4, 13, 14**
• admission **2, 3**	• hall **5**
• ticket **6**	• starter **7**
• input **8**	• cue **11**

NF **1** *(arrivée)* entrance, entry; **l'e. au port du navire** the ship's entry into the port; **l'e. en gare du train** the entry of the train into the station; **à l'e. en Italie** when crossing into Italy; **à son e., tout le monde s'est levé** everybody stood up as he/she walked in *or* entered; **faire une e. triomphale/discrète** to enter triumphantly/discreetly; **faire son e. dans une pièce** to make one's entrance into a room; **faire son e. dans le monde** *(demoiselle)* to come out into society, to make one's debut; **e. en action** coming into play; **l'e. en guerre de la France** France's entry into *or* France's joining the war; **depuis l'e. en guerre du pays** since the country entered the war; **il a marqué un but dès son e. en jeu** he scored a goal as soon as he entered the game; **e. en matière** *(d'un livre)* introduction; **e. en scène** entrance; **au moment de mon e. en scène** as I made my entrance *or* as I walked onto the stage; *Jur* **l'e. en vigueur d'une loi** the promulgation of a law; **date d'e. en vigueur** commencement

2 *(adhésion)* entry, admission; **l'e. de la Finlande dans l'Union européenne** Finland's entry into the European Union; **au moment de l'e. à l'université** when students start university; **e. dans l'armée/le club/le parti** joining the army/club/party; **depuis mon e. au parti** since I joined *or* became a member of the party; **son e. dans les ordres** his being ordained *or* taking holy orders

3 *(accès)* entry, admission; **e. à l'hôpital** admission into hospital; **se voir refuser l'e. d'une discothèque** to be refused admission *or* entry to a nightclub; **l'e. est gratuite pour les enfants** there is no admission charge for children; **e.** *(sur panneau)* way in; **e. libre** *(dans un magasin)* no obligation to buy; *(dans un musée)* free admission; **e. interdite** *(dans un local)* no entry, keep out; *(pour empêcher le passage)* no way in, no access; *(dans un bois)* no trespassing; **e. réservée au personnel** *(dans une entreprise)* staff only; **avoir ses entrées auprès de qn** to have (privileged) access to sb; **avoir ses entrées dans un club** to be a welcome visitor to a club

4 *(voie d'accès ▸ à un immeuble)* entrance (door) (**de** to); *(▸ à un tunnel, une grotte)* entry, entrance, mouth; **e. des artistes** stage door; **e. des fournisseurs** tradesmen's entrance; **e. principale** main entrance; **e. de service** service *or* tradesmen's entrance

5 *(vestibule ▸ dans un lieu public)* entrance (hall), lobby; *(▸ dans une maison)* hall, hallway

6 *(billet)* ticket; *(spectateur)* spectator; *(visiteur)* visitor; **je te paie ton e.** I'll pay for you *or* buy your ticket; **nombre d'entrées par salle** number of tickets sold per auditorium; **le film a fait deux millions d'entrées** two million people have seen the film; **on n'a fait que 300 entrées** we sold only 300 tickets

7 *Culin* first course, starter; *(dans un repas de gala)* entrée; **je prendrai une salade en e.** I'll have a salad to start with

8 *Ordinat (processus)* input, entry; *(information)* entry; *(touche)* enter (key); *(de caractère etc)* entering; **e. des données** *(gén)* inputting of data, data input; *(par saisie)* keying in *or* keyboarding of data; **données d'e.** input (data); **e. (par le) clavier** keyboard input; **e. (à partir du) scanneur** scanned input; **e. de données à distance** remote data entry; **e. de gamme** entry level; **e. opérateur** operator input **e. de papier** paper input;

9 *(inscription)* entry; *(dans un dictionnaire)* headword, *Am* entry word; **faire une e. dans un registre** to enter an item into a register

10 *Com & Douanes* entry; *(de marchandises)* importation, import; **droit d'e.** import duty; **e. en douane** inward customs clearance; **e. en franchise** free import

11 *(réplique)* cue; **ne rate pas ton e.** don't miss your cue

12 *Tech (ouverture)* **e. d'air** air inlet; **e. de clef** keyhole; *Rad* **e. de poste** lead-in

13 *Mus* entry

14 *Compta (dans un livre de comptes)* entry

• **entrées** NFPL *Compta* takings, receipts; **entrées d'argent** cash inflow, cash received

• **à l'entrée de** PRÉP **1** *(dans l'espace)* at the entrance *or* on the threshold of; **à l'e. de la grotte** at the entrance *or* mouth of the cave **2** *Littéraire (dans le temps)* at the beginning of; **à l'e. du printemps** at the beginning of spring; **à l'e. de la vie** at the dawn of life

• **d'entrée, d'entrée de jeu** ADV from the outset, right from the beginning

entrefaites [ɑ̃trəfɛt] NFPL **sur ces e.** at that moment *or* juncture

entrefilet [ɑ̃trəfile] NM *Journ* short piece, paragraph *(in a newspaper)*; **l'affaire a eu droit à un e.** there was a paragraph *or* there were a few lines in the newspaper about it

entregent [ɑ̃trəʒɑ̃] NM **avoir de l'e.** to know how to handle people

entr'égorger [17] [ɑ̃tregɔrʒe] **s'entr'égorger** VPR to cut one another's throats

entrejambe [ɑ̃trəʒɑ̃b] NM crotch; **hauteur de l'e.** inside leg measurement

entrelacement [ɑ̃trəlasmɑ̃] NM intertwining, interlacing

entrelacer [16] [ɑ̃trəlase] VT to intertwine, to interlace; **initiales entrelacées** intertwined initials; **les mains entrelacées** with one's fingers entwined; *Ordinat* **écran entrelacé** interlaced screen

VPR **s'entrelacer** to intertwine, to interlace

entrelacs [ɑ̃trəla] NM *Archit* tracery

entrelarder [3] [ɑ̃trəlarde] VT **1** *Culin* to lard **2** *(entrecouper)* **e. qch de** to intersperse *or* to interlard sth with

entremêlement [ɑ̃trəmɛlmɑ̃] NM intermingling *(UNCOUNT)*, entanglement

entremêler [4] [ɑ̃trəmele] VT **1** *(mêler ▸ rubans, fleurs)* to intermingle, to mix together **2** *(entrecouper)* **paroles entremêlées de sanglots** words broken with sobs

VPR **s'entremêler** *(fils, cheveux)* to become entangled; *(idées, intrigues)* to become intermingled

entremet *etc voir* **entremettre**

entremets [ɑ̃trəmɛ] NM *Culin* entremets

entremetteur, -euse [ɑ̃trəmɛtœr, -øz] NM,F **1** *Vieilli (intermédiaire)* mediator, go-between **2** *Péj (dans des affaires galantes)* procurer, *f* procuress

entremettre [84] [ɑ̃trəmɛtr] **s'entremettre** VPR **1** *(à bon escient)* to intervene; **s'e. dans une querelle** to intervene in a quarrel **2** *(à mauvais escient)* to interfere

entremise [ɑ̃trəmiz] NF intervention, intervening *(UNCOUNT)*; **offrir son e.** to offer to act as mediator

• **par l'entremise de** PRÉP through

entremit *etc voir* **entremettre**

entrepont [ɑ̃trəpɔ̃] **NM** *Naut* 'tweendecks; **voyager dans l'e.** to travel steerage *or* in steerage class

entreposage [ɑ̃trəpozaʒ] **NM** *(gén)* storing, storage, warehousing; *(douane)* bonding

entreposer [3] [ɑ̃trəpoze] **VT 1** *(mettre en entrepôt)* to store, to put in a warehouse, to warehouse **2** *(en douane)* to bond, to put in bond **3** *(déposer)* to leave; **e. des livres chez un ami** to leave some books with a friend

entrepositaire [ɑ̃trəpozitɛr] **NMF** *(gén)* warehouse keeper; *(douane)* bonder

entrepôt [ɑ̃trəpo] **NM 1** *(bâtiment)* warehouse; **marchandises en e.** warehoused goods, goods in storage; *Douanes* goods in bond; **mettre des marchandises en e.** to put goods into storage; *Douanes* to bond goods; *Douanes* **e. de douane** bonded warehouse; **e. frigorifique** cold store; **e. de stockage** warehouse; **e. privé/public** private/public bonded warehouse **2** *(ville, port)* entrepôt, free port

entreprenait *etc voir* **entreprendre**

entreprenant, -e [ɑ̃trəprənɑ̃, -ɑ̃t] **ADJ 1** *(dynamique)* enterprising **2** *(hardi)* forward

entreprenariat [ɑ̃trəprənarja] **NM** entrepreneurship

entreprenaute [ɑ̃trəprənot] **NM** dotcom entrepreneur

entreprendre [79] [ɑ̃trəprɑ̃dr] **VT 1** *(commencer ▸ lecture, étude)* to begin, to start (on); *(▸ croisière, carrière)* to set out on *or* upon; *(▸ projet)* to undertake, to set about; **e. la rédaction d'une thèse** to begin *or* to start writing a thesis; **e. de faire qch** to undertake to do sth **2** *(séduire ▸ femme)* to make (amorous) advances towards **3** *(interpeller ▸ passant)* to buttonhole; **e. qn sur qch** to engage sb in conversation about sth

entrepreneur, -euse [ɑ̃trəprənœr, -øz] **NM,F 1** *Constr* contractor; **e. en bâtiment** *ou* **construction** (building) contractor, builder **2** *(chef d'entreprise)* entrepreneur; **petit e.** small businessman; **e. de roulage, e. de transport** haulage contractor, carrier; **e. de pompes funèbres** funeral director, undertaker

entrepreneurial, -e, -aux, -ales [ɑ̃trəprənœrjal, -o] **ADJ** entrepreneurial

entrepreneuriat [ɑ̃trəprənœrja] **NM** entrepreneurship

entreprennent *etc voir* **entreprendre**

entrepris, -e[1] [ɑ̃trəpri, -iz] **PP** *voir* **entreprendre**

entreprise[2] [ɑ̃trəpriz] **NF 1** *Com & Écon (société)* company, business, firm; **monter une e.** to set up a business; **e. agricole** farm; **e. commerciale** business concern; **e. commune** joint venture; *Mktg* **e. dominante** dominant firm; **e. d'économie sociale** social enterprise; **e. d'État** state-owned *or Br* public company; **e. exportatrice** export company; **e. familiale** family business *or* firm; **e. industrielle** industrial concern; *Mktg* **e. innovatrice** innovator, innovating company; **e. d'investissement** investment company; **e. de messageries** parcel delivery company; **e. multinationale** multinational company; **e. en participation** joint venture; **e. privée** private company; **e. publique** public corporation; **e. de pompes funèbres** funeral director's, undertaker's; **e. de services** service company; *Mktg* **e. à la traîne** trailing firm; **e. de transports** transport company; **e. de travail intérimaire** temp agency; **e. de travaux publics** civil engineering firm; **e. unipersonnelle à responsabilité limitée** trader with limited liability; **e. d'utilité publique** public utility company; **e. de vente par correspondance** mail-order company; **junior e.** = company set up by students to gain experience in business; **petite/moyenne/grosse e.** small/medium-sized/large firm

2 *(monde des affaires)* **l'e.** business, the business world

3 *(régime économique)* enterprise; **l'e. publique/privée** public/private enterprise

4 *(initiative)* undertaking, initiative

5 *Jur (louage)* contracting; **travail à l'e.** contract work, work by *or* on contract; **mettre qch à l'e.** to put sth out to contract *or* tender

• **entreprises NFPL** *Hum (avances)* (amorous) advances

• **d'entreprise ADJ** *(matériel, véhicule)* company *(avant n)*

ENTRER [3] [ɑ̃tre]

> **VI**
> • to enter **A1, 3, 6, 7** • to go to **A2**
> • to fit **A4** • to sink in **A5**
> • to log in **A8** • to start **B**
> **VT**
> • to bring in **1** • to input **4**

VI *(aux être)* **A.** *PÉNÉTRER* **1** *(personne ▸ gén)* to enter; *(▸ vu de l'intérieur)* to come in; *(▸ vu de l'extérieur)* to go in; *(▸ à pied)* to walk in; *(▸ à cheval, à bicyclette)* to ride in; *(véhicule)* to drive in; **toc, toc! – entrez!** knock, knock! – come in!; **entrez, entrez!** do come in!, come on in!; **la cuisine est à droite en entrant** the kitchen is on the right as you come/go in; **empêche-les d'e.** keep them out, don't let them in; **entrez sans frapper** go (straight) in; **il m'invita à e.** he invited me in; **il me fit signe d'e.** he beckoned me in; **les visiteurs sont contrôlés en entrant et en sortant** visitors are checked on the way in and out; **je suis simplement entré en passant** I just popped in; **il n'a fait qu'e. et sortir** he just popped in for a moment; **e. en gare** to pull in (to the station); **e. au port** to come into *or* to enter harbour; **qui vous a permis d'e. chez moi?** who allowed you (to come) in?; **et voici les joueurs qui entrent sur le terrain/court** here are the players coming onto the field/court; **faire e. qn** to let sb in; **faites-la e.** *(en lui montrant le chemin)* show her in; *(en l'appelant)* call her in; **laisser e. qn** to let sb in; **le vent entrait par rafales** the wind was blowing in in gusts; **par où entre l'eau?** how does the water penetrate *or* get in?; **ce genre de fenêtre laisse e. plus de lumière** this kind of window lets more light in

2 *(adhérer)* **e. à l'université** to go to university; **elle entre à la maternelle/en troisième année** she's going to nursery school/moving up into the third year; **e. au barreau** to become a lawyer; **quand elle est entrée au ministère de l'Agriculture** when she was appointed to the Ministry of Agriculture; **e. au service de qn** to enter sb's service; **il a fait e. sa fille comme attachée de presse** he got a job for his daughter as a press attaché

3 *Écon (devises)* to enter; *(marchandises)* to enter, to be imported; **faire e. des marchandises** *(gén)* to get goods in; *(en fraude)* to smuggle goods in; **pour faire e. plus de devises étrangères** to attract more foreign currencies

4 *(tenir, trouver sa place)* **ton morceau de puzzle n'entre pas là** your jigsaw piece doesn't fit in here *or* doesn't belong here; **je peux faire e. un autre sac sous le siège** *(gén)* I can fit another bag under the seat; *(en serrant)* I can squeeze another bag under the seat

5 *Fam (connaissances, explication)* to sink in; **la chimie n'entre pas du tout** I just can't get the hang of chemistry; **l'informatique, ça entre tout seul avec elle** learning about computers is very easy with her as a teacher

6 *Rel* **e. en religion** to enter the religious life; **e. au couvent** to enter a convent

7 *Théât* **la Reine entre** enter the Queen; **les sorcières entrent** enter the witches

8 *Ordinat* to log in *or* on

B. *DÉBUTER* **e. en pourparlers** to start *or* to enter negotiations; **e. en conversation avec qn** to strike up a conversation with sb; **e. en concurrence** to enter into competition; **e. en ébullition** to reach boiling point, to begin to boil; **e. en guerre** to go to war

VT *(aux avoir)* **1** *(produits ▸ gén)* to bring in; *(▸ marchandises)* to import; *(▸ en fraude)* to smuggle in

2 *(enfoncer)* to dig; **elle lui entrait les ongles dans le bras** *(volontairement)* she was digging her nails into his arm; *(involontairement)* her nails were digging into his arm

3 *(passer)* **entre la tête par ce trou-là** get your head through that hole

4 *Ordinat (données)* to enter, to input; *(au clavier)* to key in

• **entrer dans VT IND 1** *(pénétrer dans ▸ lieu)* to enter *(venir)* to come into, *(aller)* to go into; *(à pied)* to walk into; **e. dans l'eau** to get into the water; **elle entra lentement dans son bain** she slowly lowered herself into the bath; **y a-t-il un autre moyen d'e. dans cette pièce?** is there another way into this room?; **comment entre-t-on dans ce parc?** where's the way into this park?; **le premier coureur à e. dans le stade** the first runner to enter the stadium; **ils nous ont fait e. dans une cellule** they got us into a cell; **il ne les laisse jamais e. dans la chambre noire** he never lets *or* allows them into the darkroom; **un rayon de soleil entra dans la chambre** a ray of sunlight entered the room

2 *(adhérer à ▸ club, association, parti)* to join, to become a member of; *(▸ entreprise)* to join; **e. dans l'Union européenne** to enter *or* to join *or* to become a member of the European Union; **e. dans le monde du travail** to start work; **e. dans la magistrature** to become a magistrate, to enter the magistracy; **e. dans un marché** to enter a market; **e. dans une famille** *(par mariage)* to marry into a family; **il l'a fait e. dans la société** he got him/her a job with the firm

3 *(heurter ▸ pilier, mur)* to crash into, to hit; *(▸ voiture)* to collide with

4 *(constituant)* **e. dans la composition de** to go into; **l'eau entre pour moitié dans cette boisson** water makes up 50 percent of this drink

5 *(se mêler de)* to enter into; **je ne veux pas e. dans vos histoires** I don't want to have anything to do with *or* to be involved in your little schemes

6 *(se lancer dans)* **sans e. dans les détails** without going into details; **elle est entrée dans des explications sans fin** she launched into endless explanations

7 *(être inclus dans)* **c'est entré dans les mœurs** it's become accepted; **e. dans l'usage** *(terme)* to come into common use, to become part of everyday language; **la TVA n'entre pas dans le prix** *Br* VAT *or Am* sales tax isn't included in the price

8 *(s'enfoncer, pénétrer dans)* **les éperons entraient dans son poitrail** the spurs were digging into its breast; **l'écharde est entrée profondément dans sa cuisse** the splinter has gone deep into his/her thigh; **la balle/flèche est entrée dans son bras** the bullet/arrow lodged itself in his/her arm; **faire e. qch de force dans** to force sth into; **faire e. un clou dans une planche** *(avec un marteau)* to hammer a nail into a plank; **faire e. une sonde dans l'estomac** to have a tube inserted into one's stomach

9 *(tenir dans)* to get in, to go in, to fit in; **tout n'entrera pas dans la valise** we won't get everything in the suitcase, everything won't fit in the suitcase; **mais son pied n'entrait pas dans le soulier de verre** but the glass slipper didn't fit her; **la clé est trop grosse pour e. dans la serrure** the key is too big to get in the keyhole

10 *(période)* to enter; **nous entrons dans une ère de changement** we're entering a time of change; **elle entre dans sa 97ème année** she's entering her 97th year; **quand on entre dans l'âge adulte** when one becomes an adult

11 *(relever de ▸ rubrique)* to fall into, to come into; *(▸ responsabilités)* to be part of; **cela n'entre pas dans mes attributions** this is not within my responsibilities; **nos réformes entrent dans le cadre d'un grand projet social** our reforms are part of a large social scheme; **j'espère ne pas e. dans cette catégorie de personnes** I hope I don't belong to that category of people

12 *Fam (connaissances, explication)* **faire e. qch dans la tête de qn** to put sth into sb's head; *(à force de répéter)* to drum *or* to hammer sth into sb's head; **elle lui fait e. de telles idées dans la tête!** she puts such wild ideas into his/her head!; **les professeurs leur en font e. dans la tête!** the teachers fill their heads with all sorts of ideas!; **tu ne lui feras jamais e. dans la tête que c'est impossible** you'll never get it into his/her head *or* convince him/her that it's impossible

entre-rail [ɑ̃trəraj] *(pl* **entre-rails***)* **NM** *Rail* gauge

entresol [ɑ̃trəsɔl] **NM** mezzanine, entresol; **à l'e.** on the mezzanine, at mezzanine level

entre-temps [ɑ̃trətɑ̃] **ADV** meanwhile, in the meantime

NM INV *Arch* **dans l'e.** in the meantime

entretenir [40] [ɑ̃trətnir] **VT 1** *(tenir en bon état ▸ locaux, château)* to maintain, to look after, to see to the upkeep of; *(▸ argenterie, lainage)* to look after; *(▸ matériel, voiture, route)* to maintain; *(▸ santé, beauté)* to look after, to maintain; **e. sa forme** *ou* **condition physique** to keep oneself fit *or* in shape; **e. sa santé/sa beauté** to look after *or* take care of one's health/beauty; **e. son français** to keep up one's French; **facile à e.** *(maison, voiture)* easy to maintain; *(moquette, plante, jardin)* easy to look after

2 *(maintenir ▸ feu)* to keep going *or* burning; *(▸ querelle, rancune)* to foster, to feed; *(▸ enthousiasme)* to foster, to keep alive; *(▸ espoirs, illusions)* to cherish, to entertain; *(▸ fraîcheur, humidité)* to maintain; **e. des soupçons/des craintes** to entertain *or* harbour suspicions/fears; **e. une correspondance avec qn** to keep up *or* to carry on a correspondence with sb; **e. de bonnes relations avec** *(personne)* to remain on good terms with; *(pays)* to maintain good relations with

3 *(encourager)* **e. qn dans l'ignorance** to keep sb in ignorance; **e. qn dans l'idée que...** to keep sb believing that...

4 *(payer les dépenses de ▸ enfants)* to support; *(▸ maîtresse)* to keep, to support; *(▸ troupes)* to keep, to maintain; **entretenu à ne rien faire** paid to do nothing; **se faire e. par qn** to be kept by sb

5 e. qn de *(lui parler de)* to converse with sb about; **e. qn d'un projet** to speak to sb about a project

6 *Compta (comptes)* to keep in order

VPR s'entretenir 1 *(emploi réciproque)* to have a discussion, to talk; **ils se sont longuement entretenus de...** they had a lengthy discussion about...

2 *(emploi passif)* **le synthétique s'entretient facilement** man-made fabrics are easy to look after

3 *(emploi réfléchi) (se maintenir en forme)* to keep fit

4 *(parler avec)* **s'e. avec** to converse with, to speak to; **s'e. avec qn au téléphone** to speak to sb on the phone; **s'e. de qch avec qn** to have a discussion with sb about sth

> Il faut noter que le verbe anglais **to entertain** est un faux ami. Il signifie le plus souvent **divertir**.

entretenu, -e [ɑ̃trətny] **ADJ 1** *(personne)* kept **2** *(lieu)* **maison bien entretenue** *(où le ménage est fait)* well-kept house; *(en bon état)* house in good repair; **maison mal entretenue** *(sale et mal rangée)* badly kept house; *(en mauvais état)* house in bad repair; **jardin bien/mal e.** well-kept/neglected garden **3** *Rad (oscillations)* sustained; *(ondes)* undamped, continuous

entretien [ɑ̃trətjɛ̃] **NM 1** *(maintenance)* maintenance, upkeep; **facile/difficile d'e., d'e. facile/difficile** easy/difficult to maintain; **sans e.** *(appareil)* maintenance-free; **personnel d'e.** maintenance staff; **manuel d'e.** service manual

2 *(subsistance ▸ d'une famille, armée etc)* support, maintenance

3 *(discussion ▸ entre employeur et candidat)* interview; *(colloque)* discussion; **solliciter/accorder un e.** to request/to grant an interview; **j'ai réussi à décrocher un e.** *(pour une embauche)* I managed to get myself an interview; **avoir des entretiens avec le patronat** to hold talks *or* discussions with the employers; **e. d'embauche** job interview

4 *Rad & TV (questions)* interview

5 *Mktg* interview; **e. assisté par ordinateur** computer-assisted interview; **e. centré** structured interview; **e. directif** guided interview; **e. de groupe** group interview; *(activité)* group interviewing; **e. libre** *ou* **non structuré** unstructured interview; **e. non directif** unguided interview; **e. organisé** arranged interview; **e. en profondeur** in-depth interview; **e. spontané** intercept interview; **e. structuré** structured interview; **e. par téléphone, e. téléphonique** telephone interview

entretient *etc voir* **entretenir**

entretoile [ɑ̃trətwal] **NF** *Couture* (lace) insertion

entretoise [ɑ̃trətwaz] **NF** crosspiece, brace; *Aut* spacer; *(étai)* strut; **e. de réglage** distance piece

entre-tuer [7] [ɑ̃trətɥe] **s'entre-tuer VPR** to kill one another

entreverra *etc voir* **entrevoir**

entrevit *etc voir* **entrevoir**

entrevoie [ɑ̃trəvwa] **NF** *Rail* **l'e.** the space between the tracks

entrevoir [62] [ɑ̃trəvwar] **VT 1** *(apercevoir)* to catch sight *or* a glimpse of; **je n'ai fait que l'e.** I only caught a glimpse of him/her *or* saw him/her briefly **2** *(pressentir ▸ solution, vie meilleure)* to glimpse; *(▸ difficultés, issue)* to foresee, to anticipate; **il entrevoyait la vérité** he had an inkling of the truth; **le directeur lui a fait e. des possibilités de promotion** the director hinted at a possible promotion

entrevue [ɑ̃trəvy] **NF** *(réunion)* meeting; *(tête-à-tête)* interview; **avoir/fixer une e. avec qn** to have/to arrange a meeting/an interview with sb

entrisme [ɑ̃trism] **NM** *Pol* entryism, entrism

entriste [ɑ̃trist] *Pol* **ADJ** entryist

NMF entryist

entropie [ɑ̃trɔpi] **NF** *Phys* entropy

entrouvert, -e [ɑ̃truvɛr, -ɛrt] **ADJ** *(porte)* half-open, ajar; **dormir la bouche entrouverte** to sleep with one's mouth slightly open; **laissez la porte entrouverte** leave the door ajar

entrouvrir [34] [ɑ̃truvrir] **VT** to half-open

VPR s'entrouvrir *(porte)* to half-open; *(rideau)* to draw back (slightly); *(lèvres)* to part

entuber [3] [ɑ̃tybe] **VT** *Vulg* to screw, to rip off; **se faire e.** to get screwed, to get ripped off

enturbanné, -e [ɑ̃tyrbane] **ADJ** turbaned

énucléation [enykleasjɔ̃] **NF 1** *(d'un œil)* enucleation **2** *(d'un fruit)* stoning, pitting

énucléer [15] [enyklee] **VT 1** *(œil)* to enucleate **2** *(fruit)* to stone, to pit

énumératif, -ive [enymeratif, -iv] **ADJ** enumerative

énumération [enymerasjɔ̃] **NF 1** *(énonciation)* enumeration, enumerating **2** *(liste)* list, catalogue

énumérative [enymerativ] *voir* **énumératif**

énumérer [18] [enymere] **VT** to enumerate, to itemize, to list

énurésie [enyrezi] **NF** *Méd* bedwetting, *Spéc* enuresis

énurétique [enyretik] *Méd* **ADJ** bedwetting *(avant n)*, *Spéc* enuretic

NMF bedwetter, *Spéc* enuresis sufferer

envahir [32] [ɑ̃vair] **VT 1** *(occuper ▸ pays, palais)* to invade, to overrun

2 *(se répandre dans)* to overrun; **les touristes envahissent les plages** the beaches are overrun with tourists; **plate-bande envahie par les mauvaises herbes** border overrun with weeds; **cette mode ne va pas tarder à e. la France** it won't be long before this fashion sweeps France; *Com* **e. le marché** to flood the market

3 *Fam (déranger)* **e. qn** to intrude on sb□; **se laisser e. par les tâches quotidiennes** to let oneself be swamped by daily duties

4 *(sujet: sensation, crainte)* to sweep over, to seize; **il a été envahi par le doute** he was seized with doubt

envahissant, -e [ɑ̃vaisɑ̃, -ɑ̃t] **ADJ 1** *(qui s'étend ▸ végétation)* overgrown, rampant; *(▸ ambition, passion)* invasive; *(▸ odeur)* overwhelming **2** *(importun ▸ voisin, ami)* interfering, intrusive

envahissement [ɑ̃vaismɑ̃] **NM** invasion

envahisseur [ɑ̃vaisœr] **NM** invader

envapé, -e [ɑ̃vape] **ADJ** *Fam* out of it, *Br* off one's face

envasement [ɑ̃vazmɑ̃] **NM** silting up

envaser [3] [ɑ̃vaze] **VT** to silt up

VPR s'envaser *(canal)* to silt up; *(barque)* to get stuck in the mud

enveloppant, -e [ɑ̃vlɔpɑ̃, -ɑ̃t] **ADJ 1** *(couvrant)* **regard e.** look that takes everything in; *Aut* **pare-chocs e.** wrapround bumper **2** *(voix, paroles)* enticing, seductive

enveloppe [ɑ̃vlɔp] **NF 1** *(pour lettre)* envelope; **prière de joindre une e. affranchie** please enclose a stamped addressed envelope; **e. autoadhésive** *ou* **autocollante** self-seal envelope; **e. à fenêtre** window envelope; **e. gommée** stick-down envelope; **e. matelassée** *ou* **rembourrée** padded envelope, Jiffy bag®; **e. premier jour** first-day cover; **e. de réexpédition** = special envelope used for forwarding several items at once; **e. timbrée** stamped envelope; **e. timbrée avec nom et adresse** stamped addressed envelope, SAE; **e. T** ≃ business reply *or* reply-paid envelope

2 *(d'un colis etc)* wrapper, wrapping

3 *Biol (membrane)* envelope, membrane; **e. nucléaire** nuclear envelope *or* membrane

4 *Bot (membrane)* covering membrane; *(cosse)* husk

5 *Tech (revêtement ▸ d'un pneu)* cover, casing; *(▸ d'un tuyau)* lagging *(UNCOUNT)*, jacket; **e. calorifuge** lagging

6 *Fin (don)* sum of money, gratuity; *(don illégal)* bribe; *(crédits)* budget; **nous disposons d'une e. de 1000 euros pour la maintenance** we have a budget of *or* we've been allocated 1,000 euros for maintenance; **il a touché une e.** *(pot-de-vin)* he got a backhander; **e. budgétaire** budget (allocation); **l'e. (budgétaire) du ministère de la Culture** the Arts budget; **e. fiscale** = savings scheme with tax advantages; **e. salariale** wages bill

7 *(aspect)* exterior, outward appearance; **sous une e. de rudesse** beneath a rough exterior

8 *Littéraire (corps)* **e. mortelle** *ou* **charnelle** earthly *or* mortal frame

• **sous enveloppe ADV mettre/envoyer sous e.** to put/to send in an envelope; **envoyer un magazine sous e.** *(pour le dissimuler)* to send a magazine under plain cover

enveloppé, -e [ɑ̃vlɔpe] **ADJ** *Fam (personne)* well-padded, plump□

enveloppement [ɑ̃vlɔpmɑ̃] **NM 1** *(emballage)* wrapping, packing *(UNCOUNT)* **2** *Mil* encirclement, surrounding; **manœuvre d'e.** pincer movement, envelopment **3** *Méd* packing; **e. froid** cold pack

envelopper [3] [ɑ̃vlɔpe] **VT 1** *(empaqueter)* to wrap (up); **e. qch dans un journal** to wrap sth up in a newspaper

2 *(emmailloter)* to wrap (up); **e. un enfant dans une couverture** to wrap a child in a blanket *or* a blanket around a child; **enveloppé dans des bandages** swathed in bandages; *Fig* **e. des remarques désagréables dans des phrases gentilles** to wrap up unpleasant remarks in kind words

3 *(entourer)* **e. qn de sa sollicitude** to lavish one's attention on sb; **e. qch du regard** to take sth in with one's gaze; **il enveloppa le paysage du regard** he took in the landscape; **e. qn du regard** to gaze at sb

4 *(voiler ▸ sujet: brume, obscurité)* to shroud, to envelop; **la nuit nous enveloppa** darkness closed in on us; **enveloppé de mystère/brume** shrouded in mystery/in mist

5 *Mil* to encircle, to surround

VPR s'envelopper s'e. dans *(vêtement)* to wrap oneself in; *Fig* **s'e. dans son silence** to immure oneself in silence

enveloppe-réponse [ɑ̃vlɔprepɔ̃s] *(pl* **enveloppes-réponses) NF** *Com* reply-paid envelope

envenimé, -e [ɑ̃vnime] **ADJ** *(plaie)* poisoned, septic; *Fig (discussion)* acrimonious

envenimement [ɑ̃vnimmɑ̃] **NM** worsening; *Fig (d'une querelle, d'une discussion)* embittering; *(d'une situation)* aggravation

envenimer [3] [ɑ̃vnime] **VT 1** *Méd* to poison, to infect **2** *(aggraver ▸ conflit)* to inflame, to fan the flames of; *(▸ situation)* to aggravate; *(▸ rapports)* to poison, to spoil; **tu n'as fait qu'e. les choses** you've only made things *or* matters worse

VPR s'envenimer 1 *Méd* to fester, to become septic **2** *(empirer ▸ relation)* to grow more bitter *or* acrimonious; *(▸ situation)* to get worse, to worsen; *(▸ querelle, discussion)* to grow acrimonious

envergure [ɑ̃vɛrgyr] **NF 1** *(d'un oiseau, d'un avion)* wingspan, wingspread

2 *Naut* breadth

3 *(importance ▸ d'une manifestation, d'une œuvre)* scale, scope; **de petite** *ou* **faible e.** small; **de grande e.** *(réforme, rapport, question)* far-reaching, wide-ranging; *(opération, firme)* large-scale; **son entreprise a pris de l'e.** his/her company has expanded

4 *(d'un savant, d'un président)* calibre; **homme d'e./de cette e.** man of calibre/of this calibre; **il manque d'e.** he doesn't have a strong personality

enverra *etc voir* **envoyer**

envers [ɑ̃vɛr] **PRÉP** *(à l'égard de)* towards, to; **elle est loyale e. ses amis** she's loyal to her friends; **être cruel/juste e. qn** to be cruel/fair to *or* towards sb; **son attitude e. moi** his/her attitude towards me; **leur devoir e. leur patrie** their duty to *or* towards their country; **ma dette e. vous** my indebtedness to you; **avoir une dette e. qn** to be indebted to sb; **e. et contre tout** *ou* **tous** in the face of *or* despite all opposition; **on a maintenu notre décision, e. et contre tout** we kept to our decision, despite all opposition *or* everything

NM 1 *(autre côté)* **l'e.** *(d'un papier)* the other side, the back; *(d'une feuille d'arbre)* the underside; *(d'une médaille, d'un tissu)* the reverse side; *(d'une peau)* the inside **2** *(mauvais côté)* wrong side; *Fig* **l'e. du décor** *ou* **tableau** the other side of the coin **3** *Géog* cold northern slope *(of valley)*

• **à l'envers ADV 1** *(dans le mauvais sens)* **mettre à l'e.** *(chapeau)* to put on the wrong way round, to put on back to front; *(chaussettes)* to put on inside out; *(portrait)* to hang upside down *or* the wrong way up **2** *(mal, anormalement)* **tout va** *ou* **marche à l'e.** everything is upside down *or* topsy-turvy; **tu as tout compris à l'e.** you misunderstood the whole thing; **il a l'esprit** *ou* **la tête à l'e.** his mind is in a whirl, he doesn't know whether he's coming or going **3** *(dans l'ordre inverse)* backwards, in reverse; **faire les mouvements à l'e.** to do the movements backwards

envi [ɑ̃vi] **à l'envi ADV** *Littéraire* **ils se sont déchaînés contre moi à l'e.** they vied with one another in venting their rage on me; **trois sketches féroces à l'e.** three sketches, each more corrosive than the last

enviable [ɑ̃vjabl] **ADJ** enviable; **peu e.** unenviable

envie [ɑ̃vi] **NF 1** *(souhait, désir)* desire; **contenter** *ou* **passer son e.** to satisfy one's desire; **l'e. de qch/de faire qch** the desire for sth/to do sth; **avoir e. de qch** to want sth; **j'avais (très) e. de ce disque** I wanted that record (very much); **j'ai des envies de fraises** I have cravings for strawberries; *Fam* **j'ai une de ces envies de champagne!** I've got a real craving for champagne!, I could really go some champagne!; **avoir e. de faire qch** to want to do sth; **avoir e. de rire/pleurer** to feel like laughing/crying; **avoir e. de vomir** to feel sick; **j'avais e. de dormir/boire/manger** I felt sleepy/thirsty/hungry; **je n'ai pas e. de passer ma vie à ça** I don't want to spend the rest of my life doing that; **j'ai presque e. de ne pas y aller** I have half a mind not to go; **je le ferai quand j'en aurai e.** I'll do it when I feel like it; **brûler d'e. de faire qch** to be burning *or* dying to do sth; *Fam* **mourir** *ou* **crever d'e. de faire qch** to be dying to do sth; **ça m'a donné e. de les revoir** it made me want to see *or* feel like seeing them again; **elle n'a pas e. que tu restes** she doesn't want you to stay; **je n'ai pas e. que ça se sache** I don't want it to be known; **la robe beige me fait vraiment e.** I'm really tempted by the beige dress; **l'e. lui prend de** *ou* **il lui prend l'e. de faire...** he/she feels like *or* fancies doing...; **voilà qui lui ôtera l'e. de revenir** this'll make sure he's/she's not tempted to come back; **je vais lui ôter** *ou* **faire passer l'e. de s'amuser** I'll stop his/her messing around; **e. de femme enceinte** (pregnant woman's) craving

2 *(désir sexuel)* desire; **j'ai e. de toi** I want you

3 *(besoin)* urge; **être pris d'une terrible e. de rire** to have a terrible urge to laugh; **être pris d'une e. (pressante** *ou* **naturelle)** to feel the call of nature, *Br* to be caught short; *très Fam* **ça l'a pris comme une e. de pisser** he felt a sudden urge for it *or* to do it[□]

4 *(jalousie)* envy; **regarder qch avec e.** to look enviously at sth; **tant de luxe, ça (vous) fait e.** such luxury makes one *or* you envious

5 *Anat (tache)* birthmark; *(peau)* hangnail

envier [9] [ɑ̃vje] **VT e. qch à qn** to envy sb sth; **on lui envie sa fortune** people envy him/her his/her wealth; **elle n'a rien à e. à personne** she has no cause to be envious of anyone; **e. qn d'avoir fait qch** to envy sb for having done sth; **je t'envie de ne jamais avoir faim!** I envy your never being hungry!

envieux, -euse [ɑ̃vjø, -øz] **ADJ** envious; **être e. de** to be envious of, to envy

NM,F envious person; **faire des e.** to arouse *or* to excite envy

environ [ɑ̃virɔ̃] **ADV** about, around; **il y a e. six mois** about six months ago; **il était e. midi** it was around *or* about midday; **ça vaut e. 300 euros** it costs around *or* about 300 euros; **il habite à e. 100 m** *ou* **à 100 m e. d'ici** he lives about 100 m from here

environnant, -e [ɑ̃virɔnɑ̃, -ɑ̃t] **ADJ** surrounding; **la campagne environnante** the surrounding countryside, the country round about

environnement [ɑ̃virɔnmɑ̃] **NM 1** *(lieux avoisinants)* environment, surroundings, surrounding area; **l'e. immédiat de l'école est agréable** the school's immediate surroundings are pleasant

2 *(milieu)* background; **l'e. culturel/familial** the cultural/family background; **e. commercial** business environment; **e. du marché** market environment; *Com* **e. institutionnel** corporate environment

3 *École* **l'e.** the environment; **un produit qui respecte l'e.** an environment-friendly product; **pollution/politique de l'e.** environmental pollution/policy

4 *Ordinat* environment; **e. partagé** shared environment

environnemental, -e, -aux, -ales [ɑ̃virɔnmɑ̃tal, -o] **ADJ** *Écol* environmental

environnementalisme [ɑ̃virɔnmɑ̃talism] **NM** *Écol* environmentalism

environnementaliste [ɑ̃virɔnmɑ̃talist] **NMF** *Écol & Psy* environmentalist

environner [3] [ɑ̃virɔne] **VT** to surround, to encircle; **être environné de** to be surrounded with

VPR s'environner s'e. d'artistes to surround oneself with artists

environs [ɑ̃virɔ̃] **NMPL** surroundings, surrounding area; **les e. de Paris** the area around Paris

• **aux environs de PRÉP 1** *(dans l'espace)* near, close to; **aux e. de Nantes** in the vicinity of *or* near Nantes **2** *(dans le temps)* around, round about; **aux e. de Noël** around *or* round about Christmas time, at Christmas or thereabouts; **aux e. de 20 heures** around 8 p.m. **3** *(avec un chiffre)* **aux e. de cent euros** in the region *or* vicinity of a hundred euros, about *or* around a hundred euros

• **dans les environs ADV** in the local *or* surrounding area

• **dans les environs de PRÉP** in the vicinity of, near; **elle habite dans les e. d'Amiens** she lives near Amiens

envisageable [ɑ̃vizaʒabl] **ADJ** conceivable

envisager [17] [ɑ̃vizaʒe] **VT 1** *(examiner)* to consider; **essayez d'e. le problème autrement** try to look at *or* consider the problem differently; **le cas que nous envisageons** the case under consideration; **il n'envisageait pas de partir** he wasn't thinking of leaving, he wasn't considering leaving **2** *(prévoir)* to envisage, to contemplate, to consider; **e. des licenciements/réparations** to consider lay-offs/repairs; **e. de faire qch** to consider *or* to contemplate doing sth; **j'envisage d'aller vivre là-bas** I'm contemplating going *or* I'm thinking of going to live there

envoi [ɑ̃vwa] **NM 1** *(de marchandises, d'argent)* sending; **faire un e.** *(colis)* to send a parcel; *(lettre)* to send a letter; *(marchandises)* to send goods; **contre e. de** on receipt of

2 *(d'un messager, de soldats)* sending in, dispatching, dispatch; **décider l'e. des troupes** to decide to send in (the) troops; **demander l'e. de troupes** to ask for troops to be dispatched

3 *(colis)* parcel, consignment; *(lettre)* letter; *(marchandises)* consignment (**de** of); **j'ai bien reçu votre e. du 10 octobre** I acknowledge receipt of your consignment of 10 October; **e. postal** postal delivery; **e. exprès** express delivery; **e. franco de port** postage-paid consignment; **e. recommandé** *(colis)* registered parcel; *(lettre)* registered letter; **e. recommandé avec accusé de réception** *(colis)* *Br* recorded delivery parcel, *Am* registered package with return receipt; *(lettre)* *Br* recorded delivery letter, *Am* registered letter with return receipt; **e. contre paiement** cash with order; **e. contre remboursement** *Br* cash on delivery, *Am* collect on delivery; **e. en groupage, e. groupé** grouped consignment; **e. en nombre** mass mailing

4 *Ordinat* **e. multiple** crossposting; **faire un e. multiple de qch** to cross-post sth

5 *Sport* **coup d'e.** kick-off; **donner le coup d'e. d'un match** *(arbitre)* to give the sign for the match to start; *(joueur)* to kick off; *Fig* **donner le coup d'e. d'une campagne** to get a campaign off the ground

6 *Littérature* envoi

7 *Jur* **e. en possession** writ of possession

envoie *etc voir* **envoyer**

envol [ɑ̃vɔl] **NM 1** *(d'un oiseau)* taking flight; **l'aigle prit son e.** the eagle took flight **2** *Aviat* taking off *(UNCOUNT)*, takeoff

envolée [ɑ̃vɔle] **NF 1** *(élan)* flight; **e. de l'imagination** flight of fancy; **e. lyrique** flight of lyricism; *Hum* **il s'est lancé dans une grande e. lyrique** he waxed lyrical **2** *(augmentation)* sudden rise; **l'e. de l'euro** the sudden rise of the euro

envoler [3] [ɑ̃vɔle] **s'envoler VPR 1** *(oiseau)* to fly off *or* away; **faire s'e. des oiseaux** to put birds to flight

2 *(avion)* to take off; **je m'envole pour Tokyo demain** I'm flying (off) to Tokyo tomorrow; **mon avion s'envole** *ou* **je m'envole dans une heure** my plane takes off *or* my flight leaves in an hour

3 *(passer ▸ temps)* to fly

4 *(augmenter ▸ cours, prix)* to soar; **s'e. dans les sondages** to rise rapidly in the opinion polls

5 *(être emporté ▸ écharpe)* to blow off *or* away; *(▸ chapeau)* to blow off; *(▸ papiers)* to blow away; **le vent a fait s'e. tous les papiers** the wind sent all the documents flying (everywhere)

6 *(disparaître ▸ voleur, stylo)* to disappear, to vanish (into thin air); **il n'a pourtant pas pu s'e., ce livre!** the book can't just have vanished into thin air!

envoûtant, -e [ɑ̃vutɑ̃, -ɑ̃t] **ADJ** spellbinding, bewitching, entrancing

envoûtement [ɑ̃vutmɑ̃] **NM** *aussi Fig* bewitchment, spell; **cette région me fait l'effet d'un e.** this region has a bewitching *or* captivating effect on me

envoûter [3] [ɑ̃vute] **VT** *aussi Fig* to bewitch, to cast a spell on; *Fig* **être envoûté par une voix/femme** to be under the spell of a voice/woman

envoûteur, -euse [ɑ̃vutœr, -øz] **NM,F** sorcerer, *f* sorceress

envoyé, -e [ɑ̃vwaje] **ADJ** *aussi Fam Fig* **bien e.** well-aimed; *Fam Fig* **c'est e.!** well said!

NM,F *(gén)* messenger; *Pol* envoy; *Presse* correspondent; **de notre e. spécial à Londres** from our special correspondent in London

envoyer [30] [ɑ̃vwaje] **VT 1** *(expédier ▸ gén)* to send (off); *(▸ message radio)* to send out; *(▸ lettre, colis)* to send, to dispatch; *(▸ marchandises)* to send, to consign; *(▸ invitation)* to send (out); *(▸ vœux, condoléances)* to send; *(▸ CV, candidature)* to send (in); *(▸ argent, mandat)* to send, to remit; **e. une lettre à qn** to send sb a letter, to send a letter to sb; **e. un (petit) mot à qn** to drop sb a line; **tu peux te faire e. la documentation** you can have the information sent to you; **e. qch par courrier** *ou* **par la poste** to mail sth, *Br* to post sth; **e. qch par fax/télex** to fax/telex sth; **e. qch par bateau** to ship sth, to send sth by ship; **e. des fleurs à qn** to send sb flowers; *Fig* to give sb a pat on the back; **Fred t'envoie ses amitiés** Fred sends you his regards

2 *(personne)* to send; **e. un homme dans** *ou* **sur la Lune** to send a man to the moon; **e. un enfant à l'école** to send a child (off) to school; **on les envoie à la mer/chez leur tante tous les étés** we send them (off) to the seaside/to their aunt's every summer; **on m'a envoyé aux nouvelles** I've been sent to find out whether there's any news; **e. un criminel en prison** to send a criminal to jail; *Euph* **e. qn dans l'autre monde** to send sb to meet his/her maker; **e. des soldats à la mort** to send soldiers to their deaths; **e. chercher qn** to have sb picked up; **je l'ai envoyé la chercher à la gare** I sent him to the station to pick her up *or* to fetch her; **e. chercher un médecin** to send for a doctor; **j'ai envoyé (quelqu'un) prendre de ses nouvelles** I sent someone to ask after him/her; **elle ne le lui a pas envoyé dire** she told him/her straight *or* to his/her face; *Fam* **e. promener** *ou* **balader** *ou* **paître**

ou **bouler qn, e. qn au diable, e. qn sur les roses** to send sb packing; **je l'ai envoyé promener** I told him where to get off; *Fam* **j'avais envie de tout e. promener** *ou* **valser** *ou* **dinguer** I felt like chucking the whole thing in; **j'ai envoyé promener la famille/ma thèse** I sent my family packing/packed in my thesis; **je me suis fait e. balader quand je leur ai demandé des explications** they sent me packing when I asked for an explanation; *Fam* **e. dinguer qn** *(le repousser)* to send sb sprawling; *(l'éconduire)* to send sb packing

3 *(projeter)* **e. qn par terre** to knock sb to the ground; **e. un adversaire à terre** *ou* **au tapis** to knock an opponent down *or* to the ground; *Fam* **e. qn dans le décor** to send sb flying; *Fam* **e. une voiture dans le décor** to send a car skidding off the road□

4 *(lancer ▸ projectile)* to throw, to fling; *(▸ ballon)* to throw; *(▸ balle de tennis)* to send; **e. la balle hors du court** to send the ball out of court; **envoie-moi ma chemise** throw me my shirt; **e. sa fumée dans les yeux de qn** to blow smoke into sb's eyes; **e. des baisers à qn** to blow sb kisses

5 *(donner ▸ coup) Fam* **e. des gifles** *ou* **baffes à qn** to slap sb (in the face)□; **e. des coups de pied/poing à qn** to kick/to punch sb; *Fam* **il le lui a envoyé dans les dents** he really let him/her have it

6 *(hisser ▸ pavillon)* to hoist; *Naut* **e. les couleurs/une vergue** to hoist the colours/to send up a yard; *Naut* **envoyez!** about ship!

7 *Fam (locution)* **ça envoie le** *ou* **du bois** it's the business

VI *Fam* **ce guitariste envoie grave** that guitarist really rocks; **elle envoie, ta moto** your motorbike goes like a bomb

VPR s'envoyer 1 *(emploi réciproque)* to send one another; **ils s'envoient des cartes postales régulièrement** they regularly send postcards to each other; **s'e. des lettres** to write to one another

2 *Fam (subir ▸ corvée)* to get saddled with

3 *Fam (consommer ▸ bière, bouteille)* to knock back, to down; *(▸ gâteau)* to wolf down; *très Fam* **s'e. qn** *(sexuellement)* to screw sb, *Br* shag sb

4 *Fam (se donner)* **je m'enverrais des gifles** *ou* **baffes!** I could kick myself!

5 *très Fam (locution)* **s'e. en l'air** to screw, *Br* shag

envoyeur, -euse [ɑ̃vwajœr, -øz] **NM,F** sender

enzyme [ɑ̃zim] **NF OU NM** *Biol & Chim* enzyme; **produit de lavage aux enzymes** cleaning product with biological action

éocène [eɔsɛn] *Géol* **ADJ** eocene

NM Eocene (period)

éolien, -enne [eɔljɛ̃, -ɛn] **ADJ** wind *(avant n)*, *Spéc* aeolian; **moteur é.** wind-powered engine

• **éolienne NF** windmill, wind pump

épagneul [epaɲœl] **NM** spaniel; **é. breton** Brittany spaniel

épais, -aisse [epɛ, -ɛs] **ADJ 1** *(haut ▸ livre, strate, tranche)* thick; *(▸ couche de neige)* thick, deep; **peu é.** thin; **une planche épaisse de 10 centimètres** a board 10 centimetres thick

2 *(charnu ▸ lèvres, cheville, taille)* thick; *(▸ corps)* thickset, stocky; **avoir la taille épaisse** to be thickset; *Fam* **il n'est pas (bien) é.** he's thin (as a rake)

3 *(dense ▸ fumée, sauce, foule, cheveux)* thick; *(▸ sourcil)* thick, bushy; *(▸ feuillage, brouillard)* dense, thick

4 *(profond ▸ silence, sommeil)* deep; *(▸ nuit)* pitch-black

5 *Péj (non affiné ▸ esprit, intelligence)* dull, coarse

NM au plus é. de la foule in the thick of the crowd; **au plus é. de la forêt** deep in the heart of the forest

ADV *(tartiner, semer, pousser)* thick, thickly; *Fam* **il n'y en avait pas é., de la viande** there wasn't a ton of meat; *Fam* **en avoir é. (sur le cœur)** to have a heavy heart□

épaisseur [epɛsœr] **NF 1** *(d'un mur, d'un tissu, d'une strate)* thickness; **un mur de 30 centimètres d'é.** a wall 30 centimetres thick; **ça fait quelle é.?** how thick is it?

2 *(couche)* layer, thickness; **plusieurs épaisseurs de vêtements** several layers of clothing

3 *(densité ▸ du brouillard, d'une soupe, d'un feuillage)* thickness

4 *(intensité ▸ du silence, du sommeil)* depth; *(▸ de la nuit)* darkness, depth

5 *(substance)* depth; **les personnages manquent d'é.** the characters lack depth

épaissir [32] [epesir] **VT 1** *(sauce, enduit)* to thicken (up) **2** *(grossir)* to thicken; **les traits épaissis par l'alcool** his/her features bloated with alcohol **3** *(ombre, mystère)* to deepen

VI 1 *(fumée, peinture, mayonnaise)* to thicken, to get thicker; **faire é.** *(sauce)* to thicken **2** *(grossir ▸ taille)* to get thicker *or* bigger; *(▸ traits du visage)* to get coarser, to coarsen

VPR s'épaissir 1 *(fumée, brouillard, crème)* to thicken, to get thicker **2** *(grossir ▸ traits)* to get coarse *or* coarser; *(▸ taille)* to get thicker *or* bigger; *(▸ personne)* to grow stout *or* stouter **3** *Fig (mystère, ténèbres)* to deepen; **le mystère s'épaissit** *(dans un fait divers)* the mystery deepens; *(dans un roman)* the plot thickens

épaississant, -e [epesisɑ̃, -ɑ̃t] **ADJ** thickening *(avant n)*

NM thickening agent

épaississement [epesismɑ̃] **NM** thickening

épanchement [epɑ̃ʃmɑ̃] **NM 1** *(confidences)* outpouring **2** *Méd* extravasation; **é. de synovie** water on the knee

épancher [3] [epɑ̃ʃe] **VT 1** *(tendresse, craintes)* to pour out; *(colère)* to vent, to give vent to; **é. sa bile sur qn** to vent one's spleen on sb; **é. son cœur** to open one's heart, to pour out one's feelings **2** *Méd* to extravasate **3** *Arch ou Littéraire (liquide)* to pour out, to discharge

VPR s'épancher 1 *(se confier)* **s'é. auprès d'un ami** to open one's heart to *or* to pour out one's feelings to a friend **2** *Arch ou Littéraire (couler)* to pour out

épandage [epɑ̃daʒ] **NM** *Agr* muck spreading; **champ d'é.** sewage farm

épandeur [epɑ̃dœr] **NM** *Agr* muck spreader

épandre [74] [epɑ̃dr] **VT** to spread

VPR s'épandre *Littéraire* to spread (**sur** over)

épanoui, -e [epanwi] **ADJ** *(rose, jeunesse)* blooming; *(sourire)* beaming, radiant; *(personne)* radiant; **une jeune femme épanouie** a young woman in full bloom

épanouir [32] [epanwir] **VT 1** *Littéraire (fleur)* to open (up); *(voiles)* to spread **2** *(détendre ▸ visage)* to light up; **un large sourire lui épanouit le visage** his/her face broadened into a grin

VPR s'épanouir 1 *(fleur)* to bloom, to open **2** *(visage)* to light up **3** *(personne)* to blossom; **une atmosphère où les enfants s'épanouissent** an atmosphere where children can blossom

épanouissant, -e [epanwisɑ̃, -ɑ̃t] **ADJ** fulfilling

épanouissement [epanwismɑ̃] **NM 1** *(d'une plante)* blooming, opening up **2** *(d'un visage)* lighting up; *(d'un enfant, d'une personnalité)* fulfilment, self-fulfilment; **elle a trouvé son é. dans le mariage** she's found fulfilment in marriage, she's blossomed since she got married; **une civilisation en plein é.** a civilization in full bloom

épargnant, -e [eparɲɑ̃, -ɑ̃t] **NM,F** *Banque, Écon & Fin* saver, investor; **petits épargnants** small investors

épargne [eparɲ] **NF 1** *Banque, Écon & Fin (économies)* **l'é.** savings; **é. salariale** save as you earn scheme, SAYE **2** *(fait d'économiser)* saving; **encourager l'é.** to encourage saving **3** *(épargnants)* **l'é. privée** private investors

épargner [3] [eparɲe] **VT 1** *(économiser ▸ argent, essence)* to save; *(▸ beurre, sel etc)* to be sparing with; **é. ses forces** to save one's strength; **épargnez l'eau!** save *or* don't waste water!; **n'é. ni sa peine ni son temps** to spare neither time nor trouble **2** *(éviter)* **é. qch à qn** to spare sb sth; **tu m'as épargné un déplacement inutile** you spared *or* saved me a wasted journey; **je vous épargnerai les détails** I'll spare you the details; **é. à qn la honte/vue de qch** to spare sb the shame/sight of sth; **é. à qn la peine de faire qch** to save sb the trouble of doing sth; **épargne-moi tes commentaires!** spare me your comments! **3** *(ménager ▸ vieillard, adversaire)* to spare; **personne ne sera épargné** nobody *or* no life will be spared; **l'incendie a épargné l'église** the church was spared by the fire; **elle a toujours tenté d'é. ses enfants** she has always tried to shield her children

VI *Banque, Écon & Fin* to save (money), to put money aside; *Péj* **é. sur qch** to save on sth; **é. sur les loisirs** to save on leisure activities

VPR s'épargner s'é. qch to save oneself sth

épargne-retraite [eparɲərətrɛt] *(pl* **épargnes-retraites)** **NF** pension fund

éparpillement [eparpijmɑ̃] **NM 1** *(de papiers, de graines)* scattering; *(état)* scattered state **2** *(de la pensée, des efforts)* dissipation

éparpiller [3] [eparpije] **VT 1** *(disperser ▸ papiers, graines)* to scatter; *(▸ troupes, famille)* to disperse; **éparpillés un peu partout dans le monde** scattered about the world **2** *(dissiper ▸ attention, forces)* to dissipate

VPR s'éparpiller 1 *(se disperser ▸ foule, élèves)* to scatter, to disperse **2** *(disperser son énergie)* to dissipate one's energies

épars, -e [epar, -ars] **ADJ** scattered; *(végétation, population, informations)* sparse

éparvin [eparvɛ̃] **NM** *Vét* spavin

épatant, -e [epatɑ̃, -ɑ̃t] **ADJ** *Fam Vieilli* splendid; **c'est un type é.!** he's a splendid fellow!

épate [epat] **NF** *Fam Péj* showing off; **faire de l'é.** to show off

épaté, -e [epate] **ADJ 1** *Fam (étonné)* amazed□ **2** *(aplati ▸ nez, forme)* flat, snub

épatement [epatmɑ̃] **NM 1** *Fam (étonnement)* amazement□ **2** *(du nez)* flatness

épater [3] [epate] **VT 1** *Fam (étonner)* to amaze□; **ça t'épate, hein?** how about that, then? **2** *Fam Péj (impressionner)* to impress□; **pour é. la galerie** in order to cause a sensation□; **pour é. le bourgeois** in order to shock□ *(middle-class values)* **3** *(rendre plat)* to flatten out the base of

épaulard [epolar] **NM** *Zool* killer whale

épaule [epol] **NF 1** *Anat* shoulder; **être large d'épaules** to be broad-shouldered; *Fam* **avoir les épaules tombantes** to be round-shouldered□; *Mil* **l'arme sur l'é.** with rifle at the slope; **la réussite du projet repose sur ses épaules** the project's success rests on his/her shoulders **2** *Culin* shoulder; **é. d'agneau** shoulder of lamb

épaulé-jeté [epoleʒəte] *(pl* **épaulés-jetés) NM** *Sport* clean-and-jerk

épaulement [epolmɑ̃] **NM 1** *Constr* retaining wall

2 *(rempart)* breastwork

3 *Menuis* shouldering

4 *Géog* escarpment

épauler [3] [epole] **VT 1** *(fusil)* to raise (to the shoulder)

2 *(aider)* to support, to back up; **il a besoin de se sentir épaulé** he needs to feel that people are supporting him *or* are behind him; **j'aurais besoin de me faire é. dans ce travail** I could do with some support *or* help in this job

3 *Couture* to put shoulder pads into; **veste très épaulée** jacket with big shoulder pads

4 *(mur)* to retain, to support

USAGE ABSOLU *(viser)* to take aim

VI *(en danse)* to shoulder

épaulette [epolɛt] **NF 1** *Mil* epaulette **2** *Couture* shoulder pad **3** *(bretelle)* shoulder strap

épave [epav] **NF 1** *(débris)* piece of flotsam (and jetsam); **épaves flottantes** flotsam; **épaves rejetées** jetsam

2 *(véhicule, bateau)* wreck

3 *Jur (objet perdu)* abandoned object

4 *(personne)* (human) wreck

épeautre [epotr] **NM** *Agr & Bot* spelt

épée [epe] **NF 1** *Mil* sword; *Escrime* épée; **coup d'é.** swordthrust; **l'é. de Damoclès** the sword of Damocles; **c'est un coup d'é. dans l'eau** it's a waste of time; **mettre l'é. dans les reins de qn** to chivy sb **2** *(escrimeur)* swordsman, *f* swordswoman

épeiche [epɛʃ] **NF** *Orn* great spotted woodpecker

épeichette [epɛʃɛt] **NF** *Orn* lesser spotted woodpecker

épéiste [epeist] **NMF** *Escrime* épéeist

épeler [24] [eple] **VT** *(mot)* to spell (out)

épépiner [3] [epepine] **VT** to seed, to de-seed; **tomates épépinées** de-seeded tomatoes

éperdu, -e [epɛrdy] **ADJ 1** *(fou ▸ regard, cri)* wild, distraught; **une fuite éperdue** a headlong flight; **é. de** overcome with; **é. de bonheur** overcome with happiness; **é. de douleur** frantic *or* distraught with grief **2** *(intense ▸ gratitude)* boundless; *(▸ besoin)* violent, intense; *(▸ résistance)* desperate

éperdument [epɛrdymɑ̃] **ADV 1** *(à la folie)* madly, passionately; **aimer qn é.** to love sb madly, to be madly in love with sb **2** *(en intensif)* *Fam* **je m'en moque** *ou* **fiche é.** I couldn't care less *or* give a damn

éperlan [epɛrlɑ̃] **NM** *Ich* smelt

éperon [eprɔ̃] **NM 1** *Équitation & Tech* spur; **donner de l'é. à son cheval, piquer de l'é.** to spur (on) one's horse; **gagner ses éperons** to win one's spurs

2 *(d'une fleur, d'une montagne, d'un coq)* spur; **é. rocheux** rocky spur

3 *Naut* cutwater

4 *Hist (d'un vaisseau de guerre)* ram

éperonner [3] [eprɔne] **VT 1** *Équitation* to spur (on)

2 *(munir d'éperons)* to put spurs on

3 *(stimuler)* to spur on; **éperonné par la volonté de réussir** spurred on by the will to succeed

4 *Hist (vaisseau de guerre)* to ram

épervier [epɛrvje] **NM 1** *Orn* sparrowhawk **2** *Pêche* cast *or* casting net

e-pétition [ipetisjɔ̃] **NF** *Ordinat* e-petition

éphèbe [efɛb] **NM** *Antiq* ephebe; *Fig Hum* **(jeune) é.** Adonis

éphémère [efemɛr] **ADJ** *(gloire, sentiment)* short-lived, ephemeral, transient; *(mode)* short-lived; *(regret)* passing; **ce chanteur n'a connu qu'un succès é.** this singer enjoyed only a short-lived *or* brief success

NM *Entom* mayfly, dayfly, *Spéc* ephemera

éphéméride [efemerid] **NF** *(calendrier)* tear-off calendar

• **éphémérides NFPL** *Astron* ephemeris

Éphèse [efez] **NF** *Antiq* Ephesus

épi [epi] **NM 1** *Bot (de fleur)* spike; *(de céréale)* ear; **é. de maïs** corncob; *Culin* corn on the cob **2** *(de cheveux)* tuft; **il a un é.** his hair's sticking up **3** *(dans les travaux publics)* spur, groyne

• **en épi ADV 1** *Agr* **blés en é.** wheat in the ear **2** **voitures stationnées en é.** cars parked at an angle to the kerb

épicarpe [epikarp] **NM** *Bot* epicarp

épice [epis] **NF** spice

épicé, -e [epise] **ADJ 1** *Culin* highly spiced, hot, spicy; **ce n'est pas très é.** it's quite mild, it's not very hot **2** *(grivois ▸ histoire)* spicy, juicy

épicéa [episea] **NM** *Bot* spruce

épicentre [episɑ̃tr] **NM** epicentre

épicer [16] [epise] **VT 1** *Culin* to spice **2** *(corser ▸ récit)* to spice up

épicerie [episri] **NF 1** *(magasin)* grocery *Br* shop *or Am* store; **é. fine** delicatessen **2** *(profession)* grocery trade **3** *(aliments)* provisions, groceries

épicier, -ère [episje, -ɛr] **NM,F** grocer

• **d'épicier ADJ** *Péj (idées, littérature etc)* common-or-garden; *(mentalité)* small-town, parochial

épicurien, -enne [epikyrjɛ̃, -ɛn] **ADJ 1** *Phil* Epicurean **2** *(hédoniste)* epicurean

NM,F 1 *Phil* Epicurean **2** *(bon vivant)* epicure, bon viveur

épicurisme [epikyrism] **NM 1** *Phil* Epicureanism **2** *(hédonisme)* hedonism, epicureanism

épidémie [epidemi] **NF** *Méd* epidemic; **é. de typhus** epidemic of typhus, typhus epidemic; *aussi Fig* **c'est devenu une véritable é.** it has reached epidemic proportions

épidémiologie [epidemjɔlɔʒi] **NF** *Méd* epidemiology

épidémiologique [epidemjɔlɔʒik] **ADJ** *Méd* epidemiological

épidémiologiste [epidemjɔlɔʒist] **NMF** *Méd* epidemiologist

épidémique [epidemik] **ADJ** *Méd* epidemic; *Fig* contagious

épiderme [epidɛrm] **NM** *Anat* skin, *Spéc* epidermis; **avoir l'é. sensible** to have a sensitive *or* a delicate skin; *Fig* to be thin-skinned *or* touchy

épidermique [epidɛrmik] **ADJ 1** *Anat* skin *(avant n)*, *Spéc* epidermic, epidermal; *(blessure)* surface *(avant n)*; *(greffe)* skin *(avant n)* **2** *(immédiat ▸ sentiment, réaction)* instant; **je ne peux pas le sentir, c'est é.** I don't know why, I just can't stand him

épier [9] [epje] **VT 1** *(espionner)* to spy on **2** *(réaction, mouvement)* to watch closely; *(bruit)* to listen out for; *(signe, occasion)* to be on the look-out for, to watch (out) for

épigastre [epigastr] **NM** *Anat* epigastrium

épigastrique [epigastrik] **ADJ** *Anat* epigastric

épiglotte [epiglɔt] **NF** *Anat* epiglottis

épigone [epigɔn] **NM** *Littéraire* epigone

épigramme [epigram] **NF** *Littérature (poème)* epigram; *(mot)* witticism

épigraphe [epigraf] **NF** epigraph; **mettre une citation en é.** to use a quotation as an epigraph

épigraphie [epigrafi] **NF** epigraphy

épilation [epilasjɔ̃] **NF** hair removal; **é. des sourcils** plucking the eyebrows; **é. à la cire** waxing; **é. définitive** permanent hair removal; **é. au laser** laser hair removal, laser depilation

épilatoire [epilatwar] **ADJ** depilatory, hair-removing *(avant n)*

épilepsie [epilɛpsi] **NF** *Méd* epilepsy

épileptique [epilɛptik] *Méd*

ADJ epileptic

NMF epileptic

épiler [3] [epile] **VT** *(aisselles, jambes)* to remove unwanted hair from; *(sourcils)* to pluck; **se faire é. les jambes à la cire** to have one's legs waxed

VPR s'épiler to remove unwanted hair; **s'é. les jambes à la cire** to wax one's legs

épilogue [epilɔg] **NM 1** *Littérature & Théât* epilogue **2** *(issue)* conclusion, dénouement

épiloguer [3] [epilɔge] **VI c'est fini, on ne va pas é.!** it's over and done with, there's no point going on about it!; **é. sur qch** to hold forth about *or* to go over (and over) sth

épinard [epinar] **NM** *Bot (plante)* spinach; *Culin* **épinards** spinach; **épinards en branches** leaf spinach

épine [epin] **NF 1** *(de fleur)* thorn, prickle; *(de hérisson)* spine, prickle; **couvert d'épines** *(plante)* prickly; *(animal)* spiny; *Fig* **tirer** *ou* **ôter une é. du pied à qn** *(tirer d'embarras)* to get sb out of a mess *or* a spot; *(soulager)* to relieve sb's mind; **tu m'a tiré une belle é. du pied!** you've saved my life! **2** *(buisson)* thorn bush; **é. blanche** hawthorn; **é. noire** blackthorn; **é. de rat** butcher's broom, knee holly **3** *Anat & Ordinat* **é. dorsale** backbone

épinette [epinɛt] **NF 1** *Mus* spinet **2** *Can Bot (épicéa)* spruce; **é. blanche** white spruce; **é. noire** black spruce; **é. rouge** tamarack, red spruce **3** *(cage)* hen coop

épinettière [epinɛtjɛr] **NF** *Can* spruce grove, spruce stand

épineux, -euse [epinø, -øz] **ADJ 1** *(fleur)* thorny, prickly; *(poisson)* spiny **2** *(délicat ▸ problème, contexte)* thorny, tricky; *(▸ situation)* tricky

NM *Bot* thorn bush

épinglage [epɛ̃glaʒ] **NM** pinning

épingle [epɛ̃gl] **NF 1** *Couture* pin; **é. à nourrice** *ou* **de sûreté** *Br* safety pin, *Am* babby pin; **é. à chapeau** hatpin; **é. à cheveux** hairpin; **é. à linge** clothes *Br* peg *or Am* pin; **é. de cravate** tiepin; **monter qch en é.** to blow sth out of all proportion; **tirer** *ou* **retirer son é. du jeu** to pull out **2 é. de signalisation** *(d'une fiche)* marker tag

épingler [3] [epɛ̃gle] **VT 1** *(attacher ▸ badge, papier)* to pin (on); **é. une robe** *(pour l'assembler)* to pin a dress together; *(pour l'ajuster)* to pin a dress up **2** *Fam (arrêter)* to nab; **se faire é.** to get nabbed

épinière [epinjɛr] *voir* **moelle**

épinoche [epinɔʃ] **NF** *Ich* stickleback

épiphanie [epifani] **NF** *Rel* **l'É.** *(du Christ)* the Epiphany

• **Épiphanie NF l'É.** *(fête)* Twelfth Night, the Epiphany

épiphénomène [epifenɔmɛn] **NM** *Méd & Phil* epiphenomenon; *Fig* side-effect

épiphyse [epifiz] **NF** *Anat (os)* epiphysis; *(glande)* epiphysis (cerebri), pineal gland

épique [epik] **ADJ 1** *Littérature* epic; **poème é.** epic (poem) **2** *(extraordinaire ▸ discussion, scène)* epic; **pour retrouver sa trace, ça a été é.!** finding out where he/she was was quite a saga!

épiscopal, -e, -aux, -ales [episkɔpal, -o] **ADJ** *Rel* episcopal

épiscopat [episkɔpa] **NM** *Rel (fonction, évêques)* episcopate, episcopacy

épiscope [episkɔp] **NM 1** *Opt Br* episcope, *Am* opaque projector **2** *Mil* periscope *(of a tank)*

épisiotomie [epizjɔtɔmi] **NF** *Méd* episiotomy

épisode [epizɔd] **NM 1** *(partie)* episode, instalment; **feuilleton en six épisodes** six-part serial; *Fig Fam* **j'ai dû rater un é.** I must have missed something **2** *(circonstance)* episode; **un é. heureux de ma vie** a happy episode in my life **3** *Méd (trouble passager)* phase

• **à épisodes ADJ** serialized

épisodique [epizɔdik] **ADJ 1** *(ponctuel)* occasional; **de manière é.** occasionally; **le caractère é. de leur relation** the on-off nature of their relationship **2** *(secondaire)* minor, secondary

épisodiquement [epizɔdikmɑ̃] **ADV** occasionally

épisser [3] [epise] **VT** *Élec & Naut* to splice

épissure [episyr] **NF** *Élec & Naut* splice

épistémologie [epistemɔlɔʒi] **NF** *Phil* epistemology

épistémologique [epistemɔlɔʒik] **ADJ** *Phil* epistemological

épistolaire [epistɔlɛr] **ADJ** *Littérature (roman)* epistolary; *(style)* letter-writing *(avant n)*; **être en relations épistolaires avec qn** to have a correspondence with sb; **nous n'avons que des relations épistolaires** our only contact is by letter

épistolier, -ère [epistɔlje, -ɛr] **NM,F** *Littéraire Littérature* letter writer

épitaphe [epitaf] **NF** epitaph

épithélium [epiteljɔm] **NM** *Biol & Bot* epithelium

épithète [epitɛt] **ADJ** attributive; **adjectif é.** attributive adjective

NF 1 *Gram* attribute **2** *(qualificatif)* epithet

épitoge [epitɔʒ] **NF 1** *(écharpe)* sash **2** *Antiq* cloak *(worn over the toga)*

épître [epitr] **NF 1** *Rel* epistle; *Bible* **l'É. aux Corinthiens** the Epistle to the Corinthians; **Épîtres des Apôtres** Epistles; **côté de l'é.** *(de l'autel)* Epistle side **2** *Littérature* epistle; *Hum* **quand j'ai reçu son é.** when I received his/her missive **3** *Antiq* epistle

éploré, -e [eplɔre] **ADJ** *(parent, veuve)* tearful, weeping; *(voix)* tearful; *(visage)* bathed *or* covered in tears

épluchage [eplyʃaʒ] **NM 1** *(de légumes, de fruits)* peeling; *(de poireaux)* stripping the outer leaves; *(d'une laitue)* picking out the best leaves; *(de crevettes)* peeling, shelling **2** *(examen)* dissection, critical examination

épluche-légumes [eplyʃlegym] **NM INV** potato *or* vegetable peeler

éplucher [3] [eplyʃe] **VT 1** *(peler ▸ légumes, fruits)* to peel; *(▸ poireau)* to strip the outer leaves off; *(▸ crevettes)* to peel, to shell; **é. une laitue** to pick the best leaves out of a lettuce **2** *(analyser ▸ texte, comptes)* to dissect, to go over with a fine-tooth comb; *(▸ liste, statistiques)* to go through; **ma mère épluche mon emploi du temps** my mother checks up on how I spend my time

épluchette [eplyʃɛt] **NF** *Can* **é. de blé d'Inde** = party at which corn is husked and eaten

éplucheur, -euse [eplyʃœr, -øz] **NM,F** peeler

NM *(couteau)* potato *or* vegetable peeler

• **éplucheuse NF** *(appareil)* automatic potato *or* vegetable peeler

épluchure [eplyʃyr] **NF** piece of peeling; **épluchures** peelings; **épluchures de pommes de terre** potato peelings

EPO [əpeo] **NF** *Physiol (abrév* **érythropoïétine)** EPO

épointer [3] [epwɛ̃te] **VT** *(en cassant ▸ crayon)* to break the point of; *(en usant ▸ aiguille, crayon, outil etc)* to blunt

éponge [epɔ̃ʒ] **NF 1** *Zool* sponge
2 *(pour nettoyer)* sponge; **é. métallique** scouring pad, scourer; **d'un coup d'é.** with a sponge; *Fig* **jeter l'é.** to throw in the sponge *or* towel; **passer l'é.** to let bygones be bygones; **passer l'é. sur qch** to forget all about sth; **je passe l'é. pour cette fois** this time, I'll overlook it; **boire comme une é., avoir une é. dans le gosier** *ou* **l'estomac** to drink like a fish
3 *Bot* **é. végétale** loofah, vegetable sponge
4 *Fam (poumon)* lung□

épongeage [epɔ̃ʒaʒ] **NM 1** *(d'un liquide)* sponging (up) **2** *(d'une surface)* wiping, sponging (down)

éponger [17] [epɔ̃ʒe] **VT 1** *(absorber ▸ liquide)* to soak *or* to sponge (up); **il épongea la sueur de son front** he wiped the sweat off his forehead **2** *(nettoyer ▸ surface)* to wipe, to sponge (down); **é. le front à qn** to mop sb's brow **3** *(déficit)* to mop up, to absorb; **é. ses dettes** to pay off one's debts
VPR s'éponger s'é. le front to mop one's brow

épontille [epɔ̃tij] **NF** *Naut (de pont)* shore, prop

éponyme [epɔnim] **ADJ** eponymous

épopée [epɔpe] **NF** *Littérature (poème)* epic (poem); *(récit)* epic (tale); *Fig (saga)* saga

époque [epɔk] **NF 1** *(moment, date)* time; **les savants de l'é.** the scientists of the time *or* day; **ça n'existait pas à l'é.** it didn't exist at the time *or* in those days; **à cette é.-là** at that time, in those days; **à l'é., elle était très connue** at the time she was very well known; **à l'é. où j'étais étudiant** when I was a student; **être de** *ou* **vivre avec son é.** to move with the times; **quelle é. (nous vivons)!** what times we live in!; **on vit une drôle d'é.** we live in strange times; **avec cette musique, c'est toute une é. qui lui revenait en mémoire** the music brought memories of an entire era flooding back to him/her
2 *(période historique)* age, era, epoch; **l'é. victorienne** the Victorian era *or* age; *Hist* **la Belle É.** the Belle Epoque; **faire é.** *(invention, déclaration etc)* to leave its mark on history; **découverte qui fait é.** epoch-making discovery
3 *(style)* period; **la Haute é.** *(Moyen Âge)* the Middle Ages; *(XVIème siècle)* the High Renaissance
4 *Géol* period
5 *Astron* epoch
• **d'époque ADJ** period *(avant n)*; **meubles d'é.** period furniture, (genuine) antique furniture; **documents d'é.** archive documents; **la pendule est d'é.** it's a period clock

épouillage [epujaʒ] **NM** delousing

épouiller [3] [epuje] **VT** to delouse

époumoner [3] [epumɔne] **s'époumoner VPR** to shout oneself hoarse; **j'avais beau m'é., il n'entendait pas** even though I was yelling at the top of my voice, he still didn't hear me; **c'est ce que je m'époumone à te dire!** I've told you so until I'm hoarse

épousailles [epuzaj] **NFPL** *Arch* nuptials

épouse [epuz] **NF** wife, spouse; **voulez-vous prendre Marguerite Leblanc pour é.?** do you take Marguerite Leblanc to be your lawful wedded wife?

épousée [epuze] **NF** *Arch ou Littéraire* bride

épouser [3] [epuze] **VT 1** *(se marier avec)* to marry; **veux-tu m'é.?** will you marry me?; **é. une grosse dot** *ou* **fortune** to marry into money *or* into a rich family; **elle cherche à se faire é.** she's looking for a husband **2** *(adopter ▸ idées)* to espouse, to embrace; *(▸ cause)* to take up **3** *(suivre)* **é. la forme de qch** to take on the exact shape of sth; **une robe qui épouse la forme du corps** a figure-hugging *or* close-fitting dress

époussetage [epustaʒ] **NM** dusting

épousseter [27] [epuste] **VT 1** *(nettoyer)* to dust; *(vêtements)* to brush (the dust from) **2** *(enlever ▸ poussière)* to dust *or* to flick off

époustouflant, -e [epustuflɑ̃, -ɑ̃t] **ADJ** *Fam* stunning, astounding, staggering

époustoufler [3] [epustufle] **VT** *Fam* to stun, to astound, to flabbergast

épouvantable [epuvɑ̃tabl] **ADJ 1** *(très désagréable)* awful, horrible, terrible; **il fait un temps é.** the weather's abominable; **elle a un caractère é.** she has a foul temper **2** *(effrayant)* frightening, dreadful

épouvantablement [epuvɑ̃tabləmɑ̃] **ADV** frightfully, terribly, dreadfully

épouvantail [epuvɑ̃taj] **NM 1** *(pour oiseaux)* scarecrow **2** *(menace)* bogey, bogeyman; **agiter l'é. de la drogue** to use the threat of drugs as a bogey **3** *Péj (personne ▸ laide)* fright; *(▸ mal habillée)* mess, sight; *(▸ terrifiante)* bogey; **elle a l'air d'un é. habillée comme ça** she looks a real sight dressed like that

épouvante [epuvɑ̃t] **NF** horror, dread; **être glacé** *ou* **saisi d'é.** to be terror-struck *or* terror-stricken; **penser à qch avec é.** to think of sth with horror
• **d'épouvante ADJ** *(film, roman)* horror *(avant n)*; *(cris)* terrified, terror-stricken

épouvanté, -e [epuvɑ̃te] **ADJ** horror-sticken, horrified; **regarder qn d'un air é.** to look at sb in horror; **prendre un air é.** to look horror-stricken *or* horrified

épouvanter [3] [epuvɑ̃te] **VT** to terrify, to fill with terror

époux [epu] **NM** husband, spouse; **voulez-vous prendre Paul Hilbert pour é.?** do you take Paul Hilbert to be your lawful wedded husband?; **les é.** the married couple, the husband and wife; *Jur* **les é. Bertier** Mr and Mrs Bertier; **les futurs é.** the engaged couple; **les jeunes é.** the newly-weds

éprendre [79] [eprɑ̃dr] **s'éprendre VPR** *Littéraire* **s'é. de qn** to fall for sb, to become enamoured of sb; *Littéraire* **s'é. d'une idée** to fall in love with *or* to become passionate about an idea

épreuve [eprœv] **NF 1** *(test)* test; **l'é. du temps** the test of time; **é. de force** trial of strength; **l'é. de vérité pour...** the critical test for...
2 *(obstacle)* ordeal, trial; **vie remplie d'épreuves** life of hardship
3 *Littéraire (adversité)* **l'é.** adversity, hardship; **rester digne dans l'é.** to retain one's dignity in the face of adversity
4 *Scol & Univ (examen)* test, examination; *(copie)* paper, script; **é. écrite** paper, written test; **é. orale** oral (test); **corriger des épreuves** to *Br* mark *or Am* grade exam papers
5 *Sport* event; **épreuves d'athlétisme** track events; **é. éliminatoire** heat; **é. contre la montre** time trial; **épreuves sur piste** track events
6 *Typ* proof; **corriger** *ou* **revoir les épreuves d'un livre** to proofread a book; **dernière/première é.** final/galley *or* first proof; **épreuves d'imprimerie** printer's proofs
7 *Phot* print; **é. par contact** contact (print); **é. négative/positive** negative/positive print; *Cin* **épreuves de tournage** rushes
8 *Hist* ordeal; **épreuves judiciaires** trial by ordeal; **l'é. du feu** ordeal by fire
• **à l'épreuve ADV mettre qn/qch à l'é.** to put sb/sth to the test
• **à l'épreuve de PRÉP** proof against; **à l'é. des balles** bulletproof; **à l'é. du feu** fireproof; **à l'é. de l'eau** waterproof
• **à rude épreuve ADV mettre qch à rude é.** to put sth to the test; **mettre les nerfs de qn à rude é.** to put sb's nerves to the test; **être mis à rude é.** *(personne, patience, honneur etc)* to be severely tested; *(jouets etc)* to be roughly treated *or* handled; **les bateaux ont été mis à rude é. par la tempête** the boats took a battering from the storm
• **à toute épreuve ADJ** *(mécanisme)* foolproof; *(patience, bonne humeur, courage)* unfailing

épris, -e [epri, -iz] **PP** *voir* **éprendre**
ADJ *Littéraire* **être é. de qn** to be in love with sb; **ils sont très é. (l'un de l'autre)** they're very much in love (with one another); **é. de qch** passionate about sth; **être é. de liberté** to be in love with freedom

éprouvant, -e [epruvɑ̃, -ɑ̃t] **ADJ** trying, testing; **un climat é.** a difficult climate

éprouvé, -e [epruve] **ADJ 1** *(sûr ▸ méthode, matériel)* well-tested, tried and tested, proven; *(▸ compétence, courage)* proven **2** *(mis à rude épreuve ▸ famille)* stricken; *(▸ région)* hard-hit

éprouver [3] [epruve] **VT 1** *(ressentir ▸ douleur, haine)* to feel, to experience; **les sentiments qu'il éprouve pour moi** the feelings that he has for me; **je n'éprouve plus rien pour lui** I don't feel anything for him any more; **é. une grande honte/déception** to feel deeply ashamed/disappointed; **é. le besoin de** to feel the need to
2 *(tester ▸ procédé)* to try *or* to test (out); *(▸ courage, personne)* to test; **é. la résistance d'un matériau** to test (out) the resilience of a material; **é. la patience de qn** to try sb's patience, to put sb's patience to the test
3 *(subir ▸ pertes)* to suffer, to sustain; *(▸ difficultés)* to meet with
4 *(faire souffrir)* to try, to test; **son divorce l'a beaucoup éprouvée** her divorce was a very trying experience for her; **une région durement éprouvée par la crise** an area that has been hard hit by the recession; **le gel a durement** *ou* **fortement éprouvé les récoltes** the crops have suffered greatly *or* have sustained severe damage from the frost

éprouvette [epruvɛt] **NF** test tube; **é. graduée** burette

EPS [əpeɛs] **NF** *Scol (abrév* **éducation physique et sportive***)* PE

epsilon [ɛpsilɔn] **NM** epsilon

épucer [16] [epyse] **VT** to rid of fleas

épuisant, -e [epɥizɑ̃, -ɑ̃t] **ADJ** exhausting

épuisé, -e [epɥize] **ADJ 1** *(fatigué)* exhausted, worn out, tired out; **être é. de fatigue** to be exhausted *or* wornout; **être é. nerveusement** to be emotionally drained **2** *(sol, mine)* exhausted, worked out; *Nucl* **uranium é.** depleted *or* impoverished uranium **3** *Com (article)* sold out; *(marchandises)* sold out, out of stock; *(livre)* out of print; *(ressources, réserves, stocks)* exhausted, depleted

épuisement [epɥizmɑ̃] **NM 1** *(fatigue)* exhaustion; **mourir d'é.** to die of exhaustion; **être dans un état d'é. total** to be completely *or* utterly exhausted, to be in a state of complete *or* utter exhaustion; **danser/marcher jusqu'à l'é.** to dance/to walk until one drops **2** *Com & Ind* exhaustion; *(de ressources)* depletion; *(de marchandises)* selling out; *(de stocks)* exhaustion, depletion; *(d'une citerne)* draining, emptying; **exploiter une mine jusqu'à é.** to exhaust a mine; **jusqu'à é. des stocks** while stocks last; **jusqu'à é. des provisions** until supplies run out

épuiser [3] [epɥize] **VT 1** *(fatiguer)* to exhaust, to wear *or* to tire out; *Fam* **tu m'épuises avec tes questions** you're wearing me out with your questions **2** *(exploiter ▸ puits)* to work dry; *(▸ gisement, veine)* to exhaust, to work out; *(▸ sol, sujet)* to exhaust; **cette marche a épuisé toute mon énergie** that walking has used up all my energy **3** *(consommer ▸ vivres, ressources)* to exhaust, to use up; *(▸ stocks)* to exhaust; *(▸ marchandises)* to sell out
VPR s'épuiser 1 *(être très réduit ▸ provisions, munitions)* to run out, to give out; *(▸ source)* to dry up; *(▸ filon)* to be worked out **2** *(se fatiguer ▸ athlète)* to wear oneself out, to exhaust oneself; *Fam* **s'é. à faire qch** *(s'évertuer)* to wear oneself out doing sth; **je me suis épuisé à le lui faire comprendre** I wore myself out trying to make him/her understand; **mais oui, il viendra, puisque je m'épuise à te le répéter!** of course he'll come, I'm tired of telling you so!□ *or* I've told you so until I'm blue in the face!

épuisette [epɥizɛt] **NF 1** *(filet)* landing net **2** *(pelle)* bailer

épurateur [epyratœr] **NM** *Tech* filter, purifier; **é. d'air** air filter; **é. d'eau** water filter; **é. de gaz** gas purifier, (gas) scrubber

épuration [epyrasjɔ̃] **NF 1** *(de l'eau)* purification, filtering; *(du gaz)* purification, scrubbing; *(du pétrole, d'un minerai)* refining; **é. biologique** biological treatment
2 *(du style)* refinement, refining
3 *Pol* purge; *Hist* **l'É.** = period after the Second World War during which collaborators were tried and punished
4 é. ethnique ethnic cleansing

épure [epyr] **NF** *Beaux-Arts* working drawing

épurer [3] [epyre] **VT 1** *(liquide)* to filter; *(eau)* to purify; *(gaz)* to purify, to scrub; *(pétrole, minerai)* to refine **2** *(style, langue)* to refine, to make purer **3** *Pol (administration)* to purge

équarrir [32] [ekarir] **VT 1** *(bois, pierre)* to square (off) **2** *(animal)* to cut up

équarrissage [ekarisaʒ] **NM 1** *(du bois, de la pierre)* squaring (off) **2** *(d'un animal)* cutting up; **chantier d'é.** knacker's yard

équarrisseur [ekarisœr] **NM 1** *(de bois, de pierre)* squarer **2** *(aux abattoirs)* (meat) renderer

équarrissoir [ekariswar] **NM 1** *(couteau)* knacker's knife **2** *(abattoir)* knacker's yard

Équateur [ekwatœr] **NM** *Géog* **(la république de) l'É.** (the Republic of) Ecuador

équateur [ekwatœr] **NM** *Géog* equator; **sous l'é.** at the equator; *Astron* **é. céleste** celestial equator

équation [ekwasjɔ̃] **NF 1** *Math* equation; **é. du premier/second degré** simple/quadratic equation **2** *Chim* **é. chimique** chemical equation **3** *Psy* **é. personnelle** personal equation

équatorial, -e, -aux, -ales [ekwatɔrjal, -o] **ADJ** *Astron & Géog* equatorial
NM equatorial (telescope)

équatorien, -enne [ekwatɔrjɛ̃, -ɛn] **ADJ** Ecuadoran, Ecuadorian
• **Équatorien, -enne NM,F** Ecuadoran, Ecuadorian

équerre [eker] **NF 1** *(instrument)* **é. (à dessin)** set square; **é. en T, double é.** T-square; **é. à coulisse** (sliding) calliper gauge **2** *(pièce métallique)* corner plate
• **d'équerre ADJ** *(mur)* straight; *(pièce)* square; **mettre qch d'é.** to square sth
• **à l'équerre ADJ 1** *(mur)* straight; *(pièce)* square; **mettre qch à l'é.** to square sth **2** *Sport* with one's legs straight out *or* outstretched
• **en équerre ADJ** *Sport* with one's legs straight out *or* outstretched

équestre [ekestr] **ADJ** *(statue, peinture)* equestrian; *(exercice, centre)* horseriding *(avant n)*; **le sport é.** (horse)riding

équeuter [3] [ekøte] **VT** *(fruit)* to pull the stalk off, to remove the stalk from

équidé [ekide] *Zool* **NM** member of the horse family *or Spéc* of the Equidae
• **équidés NMPL les équidés** the horse family, *Spéc* the Equidae

équidistance [ekɥidistɑ̃s] **NF** equidistance
• **à équidistance de PRÉP à é. de Moscou et de Prague** halfway between Moscow and Prague

équidistant, -e [ekɥidistɑ̃, -ɑ̃t] **ADJ** equidistant (**de** from)

équilatéral, -e, -aux, -ales [ekɥilateral, -o] **ADJ** *Math* equilateral; *Hum* **ça m'est é.!** I really couldn't care less!

équilibrage [ekilibraʒ] **NM** *Aut* balancing, counterbalancing; **faire faire l'é. des roues** to have the wheels balanced

équilibrant, -e [ekilibrɑ̃, -ɑ̃t] **ADJ** balancing *(avant n)*; **lotion équilibrante** ≃ cream that restores the skin's natural balance; **shampooing é.** ≃ shampoo that restores the hair's natural balance; **poids é.** counterweight; *Psy* **c'est un facteur é. dans la vie d'un enfant** it's a stabilizing factor in a child's life

équilibre [ekilibr] **NM 1** *(stabilité du corps)* balance; *(d'un avion)* stability; **avoir (le sens) de l'é.** to have a good sense of balance; **garder/perdre l'é.** to keep/to lose one's balance; **faire perdre l'é. à qn** to throw sb off balance; **cet acrobate fait de l'é.** *ou* **des tours d'é.** this acrobat does balancing tricks
2 *(rapport de force)* balance; **établir un é. entre** to strike a balance between; **rétablir l'é.** to restore the balance; **l'é. des forces** *ou* **du pouvoir** the balance of power; **é. instable** unstable equilibrium; **l'é. de la terreur** the balance of terror; **l'é. naturel** the natural balance
3 *(des éléments d'un ensemble)* balance, harmony; *TV & Cin* **é. des couleurs** colour balance
4 *Écon & Fin* **é. budgétaire** balance in the budget; **é. économique** economic equilibrium
5 *Psy* **é. (mental)** (mental) balance *or* equilibrium; **manquer d'é.** to be (mentally *or* emotionally) unbalanced
6 *Écol* **é. biologique/écologique** biological/ecological balance
7 *Chim & Phys* equilibrium; *Phys* **é. indifférent/stable** unstable/stable equilibrium
• **en équilibre ADJ** *(plateau, pile de livres)* stable; *(budget)* balanced; **la chaise est en é. instable** the chair is precariously balanced **ADV marcher en é. sur un fil** to balance on a tightrope; **mettre qch en é.** to balance sth; **le clown tenait un verre en é. sur son nez** the clown was balancing a glass on his nose

équilibré, -e [ekilibre] **ADJ 1** *(mentalement)* balanced, stable **2** *(chargement, budget)* balanced; *(alimentation, repas, emploi du temps)* balanced, well-balanced; *(vie)* regular, stable; **mal é.** unbalanced, unstable; **vie peu équilibrée** irregular *or* unstable life

équilibrer [3] [ekilibre] **VT 1** *(contrebalancer ▸ poids, forces)* to counterbalance; *(▸ roues)* to balance; **faire é. ses roues** to have the wheels balanced **2** *(rendre stable)* to balance; **é. ses comptes** to break even, to reach break-even point; **é. son alimentation** to eat a more balanced diet
VPR s'équilibrer to counterbalance each other *or* one another, to even out

équilibreur [ekilibrœr] **NM** *Aviat* stabilizer

équilibriste [ekilibrist] **NMF** *(acrobate)* acrobat; *(funambule)* tightrope walker

équille [ekij] **NF** *Ich* launce, sand eel *or* lance

équin, -e [ekɛ̃, -in] **ADJ** *Méd* equine

équinoxe [ekinɔks] **NM** *Géog* equinox; **é. de printemps/d'automne** spring/autumn equinox

équinoxial, -e, -aux, -ales [ekinɔksjal, -o] **ADJ** *Géog* equinoctial

équipage [ekipaʒ] **NM 1** *Aviat & Naut* crew; **membres de l'é.** members of the crew, crew members; **homme d'é.** crew member; *Naut* **maître d'é.** boatswain
2 *Arch (escorte ▸ d'un prince)* retinue, suite; *Hum* **aller en** *ou* **mener grand é.** to live in grand style; **arriver en grand é.** to arrive in state
3 *(matériel) Mil* equipment; *Tech* equipment, gear
4 *Hist (voiture, chevaux etc)* equipage
5 *Chasse* **l'é.** the hunt
6 *Vieilli (tenue)* attire

équipe [ekip] **NF 1** *(groupe ▸ de travailleurs)* team; *(▸ à l'usine)* shift; **travailler en é.** to work as a team; **travailler en** *ou* **par équipes** *(à l'usine)* to work in shifts; **faire é. avec qn** to team up with sb; **se mettre en** *ou* **par équipes** to get into *or* form teams; venture team; **é. commerciale** marketing team; **é. gouvernementale** Government, *Br* ≃ Cabinet, *Am* ≃ Administration; **é. de jour/nuit** day/night shift; **é. ministérielle** ministerial team; **é. de secours** *ou* **de sauveteurs** rescue team
2 *Sport (gén)* team; *(sur un bateau)* crew; **jouer en** *ou* **par équipes** to play in teams; **l'é. de France de rugby/football** the French rugby/football team; **é. d'amateurs/de professionnels** amateur/professional team; **é. de reserve** reserve team
3 *(bande)* crew, gang; **on formait une joyeuse é.** we were a happy lot
4 *Cin & TV* **é. de prise de vue** camera crew; *Cin & TV* **é. de production** production team; **é. de télévision** television crew
• **d'équipe ADJ 1** *(collectif)* **esprit d'é.** team *or* group spirit; **travail d'é.** teamwork **2** *(sport, jeu)* team *(avant n)*

équipée [ekipe] **NF 1** *(aventure)* escapade; **une folle é.** a mad escapade **2** *Hum (promenade)* jaunt

équipement [ekipmɑ̃] **NM 1** *(matériel ▸ léger)* equipment, supplies; *(▸ lourd)* equipment; **renouveler l'é. d'une usine** to refit a factory; **é. de bureau** office supplies; **é. industriel** industrial plant; *Aut* **é. intérieur** internal fittings; *Aut* **équipements spéciaux** *(pneus)* snow tyres; *(chaînes)* chains
2 *(panoplie)* kit, gear; **un é. de ski** a set of skiing equipment *or* gear; **é. de survie** survival kit
3 *(infrastructure)* **équipements collectifs** public amenities; **équipements sportifs/scolaires** sports/educational facilities; **l'é. routier/ferroviaire du pays** the country's road/rail infrastructure; **(le service de) l'É.** ≃ local government department responsible for road maintenance and issuing building permits
4 *(fait de pourvoir ▸ atelier, cuisine)* equipping, equipment, fitting out (**de** with); **procéder à l'é. d'un régiment** to equip a regiment
5 *Aviat* **é. embarqué** *ou* **de bord** on-board equipment

équipementier [ekipmɑ̃tje] **NM** *Ind* manufacturer of components

équiper [3] [ekipe] **VT 1** *(pourvoir en matériel ▸ armée, élève, skieur)* to kit out, to fit out (**de** *ou* **en** with); *(▸ salle, atelier, cuisine)* to equip, to fit out (**de** with); *(▸ usine)* to equip, to tool up (**de** *ou* **en** with); *(▸ navire)* to equip, to fit out; *(pourvoir en hommes ▸ navire)* to man; **cuisine entièrement équipée** fully-equipped kitchen; **é. une voiture pour la neige** to equip a car for the snow; **être bien équipé pour une expédition** to be all set up *or* kitted out for an expedition; **é. une maison d'un système d'alarme** to install a burglar alarm in a house; *Fam* **comme vous voilà équipé!** what a get-up! **2** *(pourvoir d'une infrastructure)* **é. une ville d'un réseau d'égouts** to equip a town with a sewage system; **é. une ville en terrains de sport** to provide a town with sports grounds
VPR s'équiper to equip oneself, *Br* to kit oneself out; **sa société s'est équipée en ordinateurs** his/her company has equipped itself with computers

équipier, -ère [ekipje, -ɛr] **NM,F** *Sport* team member; *Naut* crew member; **son é.** his team mate *or* fellow team member; *Naut* **mené par 14 équipiers** manned by a crew of 14, with a 14-man crew

équitable [ekitabl] **ADJ 1** *(verdict, répartition)* fair, equitable **2** *(personne)* fair, fair-minded, even-handed

équitablement [ekitabləmɑ̃] **ADV** fairly, equitably

équitation [ekitasjɔ̃] **NF** *Sport* horseriding, riding; **faire de l'é.** to go horseriding; **école/professeur d'é.** riding school/instructor

équité [ekite] **NF** equity, fairness, fair-mindedness; **en toute é.** very equitably *or* fairly

équivalence [ekivalɑ̃s] **NF 1** *(gén) & Math* equivalence **2** *Univ* **avoir une é.** to have an equivalent diploma; **quels sont les diplômes étrangers admis en é.?** which foreign diplomas are recognized?

équivalent, -e [ekivalɑ̃, -ɑ̃t] **ADJ** *(gén) & Math* equivalent (**à** to); **le prix de vente est é. au prix de revient** the selling price is equivalent to the cost price
NM *(élément comparable)* equivalent; **sans é.** without equal, unequalled; **l'é. de 300 dollars en euros** the equivalent of 300 dollars in euros; **il n'y a pas d'é. anglais de ce mot** there is no English equivalent for this word

équivaloir [60] [ekivalwar] **équivaloir à VT IND** *(être égal à)* to be equal *or* equivalent to; *(revenir à)* to amount to; **le prix de cette voiture équivaut à un an de salaire** this car costs the equivalent of a year's salary; **ça équivaut à s'avouer vaincu** it amounts to admitting defeat; **cela équivaut à dire que…** that amounts to *or* is tantamount to *or* is equivalent to saying that…; **cela équivaut à un refus** that amounts to a refusal
VPR s'équivaloir to be equivalent

équivoque [ekivɔk] **ADJ 1** *(ambigu ▸ terme, réponse, attitude)* equivocal, ambiguous; *(▸ compliment)* double-edged, back-handed; **de manière é.** equivocally **2** *(suspect ▸ fréquentation, comportement)* questionable, dubious; *(▸ personnage)* shady
NF 1 *(caractère ambigu)* ambiguity; **sans é.** *(adj)* unequivocal; *(adv)* unequivocally **2** *(malentendu)* misunderstanding; **afin d'éviter toute é.** in order to avoid any possibility of misunderstanding; **cela pourrait prêter à é.** this could be misinterpreted *or* misconstrued; **pour lever** *ou* **dissiper l'é. sur mes intentions** so as to leave no doubt as to my intentions

SUFFIX

-ER

• This very productive suffix is used in French to create verbs from nouns, other verbs or adjectives, eg:

dégueulasser to mess up; **positiver** to think positively
Note that the final consonant of the adjective can be changed (positif ▸ *positiver)*
• In recent years, this suffix has often been added to English nouns or verbs to create gallicized verbs, eg:
faxer to fax; **mailer** to e-mail; **zapper** to channel-hop; **tchater** to chat online (from *tchat*, a gallicized form of "chat", ie an online forum); **relooker quelqu'un** to give somebody a makeover

érable [erabl] NM *Bot* maple; **é. à sucre** *ou* **du Canada** sugar maple; **é. champêtre** field maple

érablière [erablijɛr] NF *Bot* maple grove, *Am* sugar bush

éradication [eradikasjɔ̃] NF eradication, rooting out

éradiquer [3] [eradike] VT to eradicate, to root out

érafler [3] [erafle] VT **1** *(écorcher ▸ peau, genou)* to scrape, to scratch, to graze **2** *(rayer ▸ peinture, carrosserie)* to scrape, to scratch; (▸ *bois, meuble)* to scratch
VPR **s'érafler** to scratch oneself, to graze oneself; **s'é. les mains** to graze one's hands

éraflure [eraflyr] NF scratch, scrape; *(au genou etc)* scratch, graze; *(sur cuir etc)* scuff (mark); *(sur bois, meuble)* scratch (mark); **se faire une é. au coude** to scrape *or* to graze one's elbow

éraillé, -e [eraje] ADJ *(rauque)* rasping, hoarse; **avoir la voix éraillée** to be hoarse

éraillement [erajmɑ̃] NM *(de voix)* hoarseness

érailler [3] [eraje] VT **1** *(peau, surface etc)* to scratch **2** *(voix)* to make hoarse
VPR **s'érailler** *(voix)* to become hoarse; **s'é. la voix** to make oneself hoarse

erbium [ɛrbjɔm] NM *Chim* erbium

ère [ɛr] NF **1** *Hist (époque)* era; **l'é. chrétienne** the Christian era; **è. de prospérité** period of prosperity; **une nouvelle è. commence** it's the beginning of a new era, a new era has begun; **270 ans avant notre è.** 270 BC; **en l'an 500 de notre è.** in the year AD 500, in the year of our Lord 500 **2** *Géol* era

érecteur, -trice [erektœr, -tris] ADJ *Physiol* erector

érectile [erɛktil] ADJ *Physiol* erectile

érection [erɛksjɔ̃] NF **1** *Physiol* erection; **avoir une é.** to have an erection; **être en é.** *(personne)* to have an erection; *(organe)* to be erect **2** *Littéraire (édification ▸ d'une statue, d'une église)* erection, raising **3** *Vieilli (établissement ▸ d'un tribunal)* establishment, setting up

érectrice [erɛktris] *voir* **érecteur**

éreintant, -e [erɛ̃tɑ̃, -ɑ̃t] ADJ *Fam* gruelling, backbreaking

éreinté, -e [erɛ̃te] ADJ exhausted, worn out

éreintement [erɛ̃tmɑ̃] NM **1** *Fam (d'un auteur)* panning, *Br* slating **2** *(fatigue)* exhaustion

éreinter [3] [erɛ̃te] VT **1** *(épuiser)* to exhaust, to wear out **2** *Fam (critiquer ▸ pièce, acteur)* to pan, *Br* to slate; **son spectacle s'est fait é. par la critique** all the critics panned *or Br* slated his/her show
VPR **s'éreinter** to wear oneself out; **s'é. à faire qch** to wear oneself out doing sth

érémiste [eremist] NMF *Fam* = person receiving the "RMI" benefit

Erevan [erevan] NF *Géog* Yerevan

erg [ɛrg] NM *Géog, Phys* erg

ergol [ɛrgɔl] NM *Astron* propellant

ergonome [ɛrgɔnɔm] NMF *Tech* ergonomist

ergonomie [ɛrgɔnɔmi] NF *Tech* ergonomics *(singulier)*; **ce téléphone portable est doté d'une excellente e.** this *Br* mobile phone *or Am* cellphone is very ergonomic; **il ont amélioré l'e. de leur nouveau modèle** their new model is more ergonomically designed

ergonomique [ɛrgɔnɔmik] ADJ *Tech* ergonomic

ergot [ɛrgo] NM **1** *Zool (de coq)* spur; *(de chien)* dewclaw; *Fig* **monter** *ou* **se dresser sur ses ergots** to get on one's high horse **2** *Bot* ergot **3** *Tech* lug; **e. d'arrêt** stop lug; **e. de tracteur** *(d'imprimante)* tractor pin

ergotage [ɛrgɔtaʒ] NM quibbling

ergoter [3] [ɛrgɔte] VI to quibble; **e. sur des détails** to quibble about details

ergoteur, -euse [ɛrgɔtœr, -øz] ADJ quibbling
NM,F quibbler

ergothérapeute [ɛrgɔterapøt] NMF *Méd* occupational therapist

ergothérapie [ɛrgɔterapi] NF *Méd* occupational therapy

-ERIE — SUFFIX

This is a multifunctional suffix that is used to form feminine words.
• When added to an adjective, **-erie** can refer to a TRAIT OF CHARACTER and as such can often be translated by the English suffix *-ness*, eg:
étourderie carelessness; **sournoiserie** slyness; **galanterie** courteousness; **mesquinerie** meanness
• When added to a noun or a verb, the idea is that of an ACTION, often with derogatory undertones:
tromperie deception; **moquerie** jeering; **flatterie** flattery; **ânerie** stupid remark, stupid mistake; **faire des cochonneries** to make a mess
• At the end of a noun, the suffix **-erie** can refer to an ACTIVITY. When this activity is a trade, the French word can sometimes be translated by an English noun ending in *-ing*. As well as the activity, some of the words created by the addition of the suffix can also refer to the PLACE where it is practised – often a shop, hence the translation of some of the following items:
parfumerie perfume trade, perfume shop; **bijouterie** jewellery-making, jeweller's (shop); **ébénisterie** cabinet-making; **plomberie** plumbing; **boucherie** butcher's shop; **carterie** card shop; **sandwicherie** sandwich bar

Érié [erje] NM *Géog* **le lac É.** Lake Erie

ériger [17] [eriʒe] VT **1** *(édifier ▸ statue, temple)* to erect, to raise **2** *(instituer ▸ comité, tribunal)* to set up, to establish **3** *Fig* **é. qn en** to set sb up as, to elevate sb to the status of; **é. qch en** to elevate sth to the status of, to present sth as; **le cynisme érigé en art** cynicism raised to the status of fine art
VPR **s'ériger s'é. en moraliste/censeur** to set oneself up as a moralist/a censor

ermitage [ɛrmitaʒ] NM **1** *(d'un ermite)* hermitage **2** *(retraite)* retreat

ermite [ɛrmit] NM **1** *Rel* hermit **2** *(reclus)* hermit, recluse; **vivre comme un e.** *ou* **en e.** to live like *or* as a hermit, to lead the life of a recluse

éroder [3] [erɔde] VT *(côte, rochers etc)* to erode, to wear away; *(métaux etc)* to corrode, to eat away

érogène [erɔʒɛn] ADJ erogenous, erogenic

éros [eros] NM *Psy* **l'é.** Eros

érosif, -ive [erozif, -iv] ADJ erosive

érosion [erozjɔ̃] NM **1** *Géog & Méd* erosion; **é. côtière** coastal erosion; **é. dentaire** dental erosion **2** *(dégradation)* erosion; *Écon & Fin* **é. monétaire** monetary erosion

érosive [eroziv] *voir* **érosif**

érotique [erɔtik] ADJ erotic

érotiquement [erɔtikmɑ̃] ADV erotically

érotisation [erɔtizasjɔ̃] NF eroticization, eroticizing

érotiser [3] [erɔtize] VT to eroticize

érotisme [erɔtism] NM eroticism

érotomane [erɔtɔman] NMF *Psy* erotomaniac

errance [erɑ̃s] NF wandering, roaming

errant, -e [erɑ̃, -ɑ̃t] ADJ wandering, roaming; **mener une vie errante** to lead the life of a wanderer

errata [erata] *voir* **erratum**
NM INV *(liste)* list of errata

erratique [eratik] ADJ **1** *Géol & Méd* erratic **2** *(variation)* erratic

erratum [eratɔm] *(pl* **errata** [-ta]) NM *Presse* erratum

erre [ɛr] NF *Naut* headway; *(lancée)* way
• **erres** NFPL *Chasse (traces)* track, trail; *Fig* **suivre les erres de qn** to follow in sb's footsteps
• **sur son erre** ADV **aller/continuer sur son e.** to coast (along), to freewheel

errements [ɛrmɑ̃] NMPL *Littéraire* erring ways, bad habits; **retomber dans** *ou* **revenir à ses errements passés** to fall back into one's bad old ways

errer [4] [ɛre] VI **1** *(marcher)* to roam, to wander; **e. par les rues** to wander about *or* roam the streets; **e. comme une âme en peine** to wander about like a lost soul **2** *(imagination, pensées)* to wander, to stray; *(regard)* to wander, to rove; **un sourire errait sur ses lèvres** a smile played on *or* over his/her lips **3** *Littéraire (se tromper)* to err

erreur [erœr] NF **1** *(faute)* mistake, error; **il doit y avoir une e.** there must be a *or* some mistake; **il y a e. sur la personne** you've got the wrong person, it's a case of mistaken identity; **il n'y a pas d'e. (possible)** there's no doubt about it; **e.!** wrong!; **c'est lui, pas d'e.!** that's him all right!; **ce serait une e. (que) de penser cela** it would be wrong *or* a mistake to believe this; **être dans l'e.** to be wrong *or* mistaken; **faire** *ou* **commettre une e.** to make a mistake *or* an error; **faire e.** to be wrong *or* mistaken; **e. de calcul** miscalculation; **e. de jugement** error of judgement; **e. de traduction** mistake in translation, mistranslation; **e. typographique** *ou* **d'impression** misprint, printer's error; *Prov* **l'e. est humaine** to err is human
2 *(errement)* error; **des erreurs de jeunesse** youthful indiscretions; **retomber dans les mêmes erreurs** to lapse back into the same old bad habits
3 *Jur* **e. judiciaire** miscarriage of justice; **e. sur la personne** mistaken identity
4 *Ordinat* error; **e. de programmation** programming error; **e. de saisie** keying error; **e. de syntaxe** syntax error
• **par erreur** ADV by mistake
• **sauf erreur** ADV **je crois, sauf e., qu'il est venu hier** I believe, if I'm not mistaken, that he came yesterday; **sauf e. de ma part, ce lundi-là est férié** unless I'm (very much) mistaken, that Monday is a public holiday
• **sauf erreur ou omission** ADV *Com & Jur* errors and omissions excepted

erroné, -e [erɔne] ADJ erroneous, mistaken

erronément [eronemɑ̃] ADV erroneously

ersatz [ɛrzats] NM ersatz, substitute; **un e. de café** ersatz coffee; **un e. d'aventure/d'amour** a substitute for adventure/for love

erse[1] [ɛrs] ADJ & NM *Ling* Erse

erse[2] [ɛrs] NF *Naut* grummet, grommet

éructation [eryktasjɔ̃] NF belch, *Spéc* eructation

éructer [3] [erykte] VI to belch, *Spéc* to eructate
VT **é. des injures** to belch (forth) insults

érudit, -e [erydi, -it] ADJ erudite, learned, scholarly
NM,F scholar, erudite *or* learned person

érudition [erydisjɔ̃] NF erudition, scholarship

éruptif, -ive [eryptif, -iv] ADJ *Géol & Méd* eruptive

éruption [erypsjɔ̃] NF **1** *Astron & Géol* eruption; **entrer en é.** to erupt; **volcan en é.** erupting volcano **2** *Méd* outbreak; **é. de boutons** outbreak of spots; **é. cutanée** rash; **é. dentaire** *ou* **des dents** cutting of teeth **3** *Fig (crise)* outbreak; **é. de colère** fit of anger, angry outburst

Do not confuse with **irruption**.

éruptive [eryptiv] *voir* **éruptif**

érysipèle [erizipɛl] NM *Méd* erysipelas, Saint Anthony's fire

érythème [eritɛm] NM *Méd* erythema; **é. fessier** *Br* nappy *or Am* diaper rash; **é. solaire** sunburn

Érythrée [eritre] NF *Géog* **l'É.** Eritrea

érythréen, -enne [eritreɛ̃, -ɛn] ADJ *Géog* Eritrean
• **Érythréen, -enne** NM,F *Géog* Eritrean

E/S *Ordinat (abrév écrite* **entrée/sortie**) I/O

es *voir* **être**[1]

ès [ɛs] PRÉP **licencié ès lettres** ≃ Bachelor of Arts, ≃ BA; **licencié ès sciences** ≃ Bachelor of Sciences, ≃ BSc; **docteur ès lettres** ≃ Doctor of Philosophy, ≃ PhD; *Admin & Jur* **ès qualités** ex officio

ESB [əɛsbe] NF *Vét (abrév* **encéphalopathie spongiforme bovine**) BSE

esbigner [3] [ɛzbiɲe] **s'esbigner** VPR *Fam Vieilli (s'enfuir)* to skedaddle, to make *or* to clear off

esbroufe [ɛzbʀuf] *Fam* NF showing off; **faire de l'e.** to show off

• **à l'esbroufe** ADV **il l'a fait à l'e.** he bluffed his way through it; **avoir qn à l'e.** to bluff sb

esbroufeur, -euse [ɛzbʀufœʀ, -øz] NM,F *Fam* smooth talker, bluffer

escabeau, -x [ɛskabo] NM **1** *(tabouret)* stool **2** *(échelle)* stepladder

escadre [ɛskadʀ] NF **1** *Naut* squadron; **chef d'e.** squadron commander **2** *Aviat* **e. aérienne** wing; **chef d'e.** wing commander

escadrille [ɛskadʀij] NF **1** *Naut* flotilla **2** *Aviat* flight, squadron; **e. de chasse** fighter squadron

escadron [ɛskadʀɔ̃] NM **1** *(dans la cavalerie, les blindés)* squadron; *(dans la gendarmerie)* company; **e. de chars** armoured squadron; *Pol* **e. de la mort** death squad **2** *Aviat* squadron; **e. de chasse/bombardement** fighter/bomber squadron **3** *Fam Hum (groupe)* bunch, gang

escagasser [3] [ɛskagase] VT **1** *(dans le Sud) (objet)* to smash, to wreck **2** *(en Provence) (personne ▸ éreinter)* to wear out; *(▸ agacer)* to annoy, to pester

VPR **s'escagasser** to wear oneself out

escalade [ɛskalad] NF **1** *Sport (activité)* (rock) climbing; *(ascension)* climb; **faire de l'e.** to go (rock) climbing; **e. artificielle** artificial climbing; **e. libre** free climbing

2 *(d'un mur, d'une grille)* climbing, scaling

3 *(parcours)* climb

4 *(aggravation)* escalation; **l'e. de la violence** the escalation of violence; **à cause de l'e. des prix/taux d'intérêt** because of escalating prices/interest rates

escalader [3] [ɛskalade] VT *(montagne)* to climb; *(portail)* to climb, to scale, to clamber up; *(grille)* to climb over; *(muret)* to scramble up; *Hist & Mil (forteresse)* to escalade

Escalator® [ɛskalatɔʀ] NM escalator, moving staircase

escale [ɛskal] NF **1** *(lieu) & Naut* port of call; *Aviat* stop **2** *(halte) & Naut* call; *Aviat* stop, stopover; **faire e.** *Naut* to put into port; *Aviat* to touch down; **faire e. à** *Naut* to call at, to put in at; *Aviat* to stop over at; **l'avion a fait une e. forcée à Rio** the plane was forced to stop over at Rio; **visiter une ville pendant l'e.** *Naut* to visit a town while the ship is in port; *Aviat* to visit a town during a stopover; **e. technique** refuelling stop

• **sans escale** ADJ nonstop, direct

escalier [ɛskalje] NM *(marches)* (flight of) stairs; *(cage)* staircase; **les escaliers** the staircase *or* stairs; **être dans l'e.** *ou* **les escaliers** to be on the stairs; **rencontrer qn dans l'e.** *ou* **dans les escaliers** to meet sb on the stairs; *Ski* **monter en e.** to sidestep; *Fig* **avoir des escaliers dans les cheveux** to have unevenly cut hair; **e. en colimaçon** *ou* **en vrille** spiral staircase; **e. dérobé** hidden staircase; **e. d'honneur** main staircase; **e. mécanique** *ou* **roulant** escalator; **e. de secours** fire escape; **e. de service** backstairs, service stairs

escalope [ɛskalɔp] NF *Culin* escalope; **e. de veau/de poulet** veal/chicken escalope; **e. panée** escalope in breadcrumbs

escamotable [ɛskamɔtabl] ADJ *(antenne, train d'atterrissage, phares)* retractable; *(lit, table)* collapsible, foldaway

escamotage [ɛskamɔtaʒ] NM **1** *Aviat (d'un train d'atterrissage)* retraction

2 *(disparition)* conjuring *or* spiriting away; **tour d'e.** vanishing trick

3 *(vol)* filching

4 *(action d'éluder ▸ de problèmes, questions)* dodging; *(▸ de difficultés)* evading; *(▸ de mot, note)* skipping

escamoter [3] [ɛskamɔte] VT **1** *(faire disparaître ▸ mouchoir, carte)* to conjure *or* to spirit away; *(▸ placard, lit)* to fold away

2 *(voler)* to filch

3 *Fig (éluder ▸ difficultés)* to evade, to skirt round; *(▸ mot, note)* to skip; *(▸ problème, question)* to dodge

4 *Aviat (train d'atterrissage)* to retract

escamoteur, -euse [ɛskamɔtœʀ, -øz] NM,F *(prestidigitateur)* conjurer

escampette [ɛskɑ̃pɛt] *voir* **poudre**

escapade [ɛskapad] NF **1** *(fugue)* running off *or* away; **faire une e.** to run off *or* away **2** *(séjour)* jaunt; **une e. de deux jours à Deauville** a two-day visit *or* jaunt to Deauville

escarbille [ɛskaʀbij] NF piece of soot

escarboucle [ɛskaʀbukl] NF *(pierre)* carbuncle

escarcelle [ɛskaʀsɛl] NF *Arch* moneybag; **tomber** *ou* **rentrer dans l'e. de qn** *(argent, collection de tableaux etc)* to come sb's way; *Hum* **200 euros vont tomber** *ou* **rentrer dans mon e.** I'm about to have a little windfall of 200 euros

escargot [ɛskaʀgo] NM *Zool* snail; **avancer comme un e.** *ou* **à une allure d'e.** to go at a snail's pace; **opération e.** slowing down of the traffic *(by protesting truck drivers)*

escargotière [ɛskaʀgɔtjɛʀ] NF **1** *(parc)* snailery, snail farm **2** *(plat)* snail dish

escarmouche [ɛskaʀmuʃ] NF skirmish

escarpé, -e [ɛskaʀpe] ADJ steep; *(falaise)* sheer

escarpement [ɛskaʀpəmɑ̃] NM **1** *(pente)* steep slope **2** *Géog* escarpment; **e. de faille** fault scarp

escarpin [ɛskaʀpɛ̃] NM pump, *Br* court shoe; *(pour danser)* pump

escarpolette [ɛskaʀpɔlɛt] NF *Arch (balançoire)* swing

escarre [ɛskaʀ] NF *Méd* scab; *(due à l'alitement)* bedsore

Escaut [ɛsko] NM *Géog* **l'E.** the (River) Scheldt

eschatologie [ɛskatɔlɔʒi] NF *Rel* eschatology

Eschyle [eʃil] NPR Aeschylus

escient [ɛsjɑ̃] NM **à bon e.** advisedly, judiciously; **à mauvais e.** injudiciously, unwisely

esclaffer [3] [ɛsklafe] **s'esclaffer** VPR to burst out laughing, to guffaw

esclandre [ɛsklɑ̃dʀ] NM scene, scandal; **faire** *ou* **causer un e., faire de l'e.** to make a scene

esclavage [ɛsklavaʒ] NM **1** *(pratique)* slavery; **réduire qn en e.** to reduce sb to slavery, to make a slave out of sb **2** *(contrainte)* slavery, *Littéraire* bondage; **c'est un véritable e.!** it's slave labour! **3** *(dépendance)* **vivre dans l'e. de** to be a slave to; **subir l'e. de la drogue** to be a slave to drugs

esclavagisme [ɛsklavaʒism] NM **1** *(pratique)* slavery; *(doctrine)* pro-slavery **2** *Zool* helotism

esclavagiste [ɛsklavaʒist] NMF supporter of slavery; *Fig* slavedriver

ADJ **État e.** slave state

esclave [ɛsklav] ADJ *(asservi)* enslaved; *Fig (assujetti)* **être e. de ses habitudes** to be a slave to *or* the slave of one's habits; **être e. de l'alcool/du tabac** to be a slave to drink/to tobacco; **je refuse d'être e. du ménage!** I won't be a slave to housework!

NM **1** *(personne réduite en esclavage)* slave; **marchand d'esclaves** slave trader **2** *Fig* slave; **elle en a fait son e.** she has made him/her (into) her slave, she has enslaved him/her; **elle est l'e. de sa famille** she is a slave to her family; **être l'e. de son travail/de ses passions** to be a slave to one's work/one's passions

escogriffe [ɛskɔgʀif] NM **un grand e.** a beanpole

escomptable [ɛskɔ̃tabl] ADJ *Compta* discountable

escompte [ɛskɔ̃t] NM **1** *Com* discount; **à e.** at a discount; **e. de caisse** cash discount; **2** *Fin* discount; **prendre à l'e. un effet de commerce** to discount a bill of exchange; **présenter une traite à l'e.** to have a bill discounted; **e. de banque** bank discount **3** *Can (remise)* discount; **50 pour cent d'e. sur toute la marchandise** 50 percent discount on all goods

escompter [3] [ɛskɔ̃te] VT **1** *(espérer)* to expect, to anticipate (**que** that); **e. une hausse** to anticipate an increase; **c'est mieux que ce que j'escomptais** it's better than what I expected; **obtenir le succès escompté** to be as successful as expected *or* anticipated **2** *Fin (traite)* to discount

escorte [ɛskɔʀt] NF **1** *Aviat, Mil & Naut* escort; **faire e. à qn** to escort sb; **un avion d'e.** an escort plane **2** *(personne, groupe)* escort; **servir d'e. à qn** to escort sb; **il arriva avec toute son e. de photographes** he arrived escorted by a whole bunch of photographers

• **sous bonne escorte** ADV under escort

escorter [3] [ɛskɔʀte] VT **1** *(ami, président, célébrité)* to escort; *(femme)* to escort, to be the escort of; **escortée de ses admirateurs** surrounded by her admirers **2** *Aviat, Mil & Naut* to escort

escorteur [ɛskɔʀtœʀ] NM *Mil & Naut* escort ship

escouade [ɛskwad] NF **1** *Mil* squad **2** *(équipe ▸ de balayeurs, de contrôleurs)* squad, gang; *(▸ de touristes, de jeunes gens etc)* group

ESCP [əɛssepe] NF *Scol & Univ (abrév* **École supérieure de commerce de Paris**) = prestigious business and management school

escrime [ɛskʀim] NF *Sport* fencing *(UNCOUNT)*; **faire de l'e.** to fence

escrimer [3] [ɛskʀime] **s'escrimer** VPR **s'e. à faire qch** to strive to do sth; **il s'escrimait à faire démarrer la voiture** he was struggling to get the car started; *Fig* **s'e. sur qch** to plug away at sth

escrimeur, -euse [ɛskʀimœʀ, -øz] NM,F *Sport* fencer

escroc [ɛskʀo] NM swindler, crook

escroquer [3] [ɛskʀɔke] VT *(voler ▸ victime, client)* to swindle, to cheat; *(▸ argent, milliard)* to swindle; **e. de l'argent à qn** to swindle money out of sb, to swindle sb out of (his/her) money; **se faire e. de qch** to be swindled out of sth

escroquerie [ɛskʀɔkʀi] NF **1** *(pratique malhonnête)* swindle; *(action)* swindling; *Fam* **10 euros le kilo, c'est de l'e.!** 10 euros a kilo, it's *Br* daylight *or Am* highway robbery! **2** *Jur* fraud

escudo [ɛskydo] NM escudo

esgourde [ɛsguʀd] NF *Fam* ear□, *Br* lug, lughole

e-signature [isiɲatyʀ] NF *Ordinat* e-signature

eskimo [ɛskimo] = **esquimau**

Ésope [ezɔp] NPR Aesop

ésotérique [ezɔteʀik] ADJ esoteric

ésotérisme [ezɔteʀism] NM esotericism

espace[1] [ɛspas] NM **1** *(gén) & Astron* **l'e.** space; **voyager dans l'e.** to travel through space

2 *(place, volume)* space, room; **as-tu assez d'e.?** do you have enough space *or* room?; **manquer d'e.** to be cramped; **la plante verte prend trop d'e.** the pot plant takes up too much space *or* room; **e. vital** living space; *Pol* lebensraum; *Fig (d'une personne)* personal space

3 *(distance ▸ physique)* space, gap; *(▸ temporelle)* gap, interval, space; **il y a un petit e. entre la cuisinière et le placard** there's a small gap between the stove and the unit; **laissez un e. d'un mètre entre les deux arbres** leave (a gap of) one metre between the two trees; **laisser un e. entre deux mots** to leave a space between two words; **l'e. d'un instant** just for a second; **il a relâché son attention l'e. d'un instant et il est rentré dans le véhicule de devant** he let his attention wander just for a second and crashed into the car in front; **en l'e. de** *(dans le temps)* within (the space of); **malade cinq fois en l'e. d'un mois** sick five times within (the space of) a month

4 *(surface)* space, stretch; **e. désertique** desert area

5 *(lieu)* **e. de rangement** storage space; **un e. vert** a park; **des espaces verts** parkland

6 *Géom & Math* space; **e. euclidien** Euclidean space; **e. à trois/quatre dimensions** three-/four-dimensional space

7 *Aviat* **e. aérien** airspace; **dans l'e. aérien allemand** in German airspace

8 *UE* **e. économique européen** European economic area; **e. social européen** common European social legislation

9 *Ordinat* **e. disque** disk space; **e. mémoire** memory space; **e. de stockage** storage space

10 *Mktg* **e. publicitaire** advertising space; **e. de vente** sales area

espace[2] [ɛspas] **NF** *Typ* space; **e. fine/moyenne/forte** hair/middle/thick space

espacement [ɛspasmɑ̃] **NM 1** *(dans le temps ▸ action)* spreading *or* spacing out; *(résultat)* spacing; **l'e. des paiements** staggering of payments; **l'e. de nos rencontres/tes visites** the growing infrequency of our meetings/your visits **2** *(distance)* space; **l'e. entre les tables** the space between the tables **3** *Typ (entre deux lettres)* space; *(interligne)* space (between the lines), spacing; **e-constant** monospace

espacer **[16]** [ɛspase] **VT 1** *(séparer ▸ lignes, mots, arbustes)* to space out; **e. des chaises d'un mètre** to space chairs out a metre apart **2** *(dans le temps)* to space out; **vous devriez e. vos rencontres** you should meet less often *or* less frequently; **j'ai espacé mes visites** my visits became less frequent

VPR s'espacer 1 *(dans le temps ▸ visites)* to become less frequent **2** *(s'écarter)* **espacez-vous** move further away from each other

espace-temps [ɛspastɑ̃] *(pl* **espaces-temps)** **NM** *Math & Phys* space-time (continuum)

espadon [ɛspadɔ̃] **NM** *Ich* swordfish

espadrille [ɛspadrij] **NF** espadrille

Espagne [ɛspaɲ] **NF** *Géog* **l'E.** Spain; **la guerre d'E.** the Spanish Civil War

espagnol, -e [ɛspaɲɔl] **ADJ** Spanish

NM *(langue)* Spanish

• **Espagnol, -e** **NM,F** Spaniard; **les Espagnols** the Spanish

espagnolette [ɛspaɲɔlɛt] **NF** window catch *(long vertical bar with pivoting central catch)*; **fermer une fenêtre à l'e.** to leave a window on the latch *or* ajar

espalier [ɛspalje] **NM 1** *Hort* espalier; **(mur d')e.** espalier wall; **(arbre en) e.** espalier **2** *Sport* gym ladder, wall bars

espar [ɛspar] **NM** *Mil & Naut* spar

espèce [ɛspɛs] **NF 1** *Biol, Bot & Zool* species *(singulier)*; **l'e. humaine** the human race, mankind; **des espèces animales/végétales** animal/plant species; **e. protégée** protected species; **e. en voie de disparition** endangered species **2** *(sorte)* sort, kind; **différentes espèces d'arbres** different sorts *or* kinds *or* species of trees; **il y a plusieurs espèces de café** there are various sorts of coffee; **de son e.** like him/her, of his/her kind; **des escrocs de ton/son e.** crooks like you/him/her; **des gens de leur e.** their sort, the likes of them; **un escroc/menteur/avare de la pire e.** a crook/liar/miser of the worst sort *or* kind, the worst sort *or* kind of crook/liar/miser; **ça n'a aucune e. d'importance!** that is of absolutely no importance!; *aussi Péj* **c'était une e. de ferme** it was a sort of farm *or* a farm of sorts; *Péj* **l'e. de blonde qui lui sert de femme** that blonde he calls his wife; *Fam Péj* **e. d'idiot!** you idiot!; *Fam Péj* **e. de snob!** you're such a snob! **3** *Jur* particular *or* specific case; **cas d'e.** specific case

• **espèces** **NFPL 1** *Fin (argent)* cash; *Hist (monnaie métallique)* coin; **payer en espèces** to pay in cash; **espèces sonnantes et trébuchantes** hard cash **2** *Rel* species

• **en l'espèce** **ADV** in this particular case; **j'avais de bons rapports avec mes employés mais en l'e. l'affaire a fini au tribunal** I always had good relations with my employees but in this instance, the matter finished up in court

espérance [ɛsperɑ̃s] **NF 1** *(espoir)* hope, expectation; **dans l'e. que...** in the hope that...; **au-delà de nos espérances** beyond our expectations, beyond expectation; **répondre aux espérances de qn** to live up to sb's expectations; **contre toute e.** contrary to (all) *or* against all expectations **2 e. de vie** life expectancy **3** *Rel* hope

• **espérances** **NFPL** *Euph (espoir d'hériter)* expectations, prospects of inheritance; **j'ai des espérances du côté maternel** I have great expectations on my mother's side

espérantiste [ɛsperɑ̃tist] **ADJ & NMF** Esperantist

espéranto [ɛsperɑ̃to] **NM** Esperanto

espérer **[18]** [ɛspere] **VT 1** *(souhaiter)* to hope for; **e. le succès** to hope for success, to hope to succeed; **e. faire qch** to hope to do sth; **j'espère vous revoir bientôt** I hope to see you soon; **j'espère arriver à la convaincre** I hope (that) I will be able to sway her; **j'espère que vous viendrez** I hope (that) you will come; **je l'espère** I hope so; **j'espère que non** I hope not **2** *(escompter)* to expect; **n'espère pas qu'elle te rembourse** don't expect her to pay you back; **je n'en espérais pas tant de lui** I didn't expect that much of him; **le médecin leur avait fait e. une guérison rapide** the doctor had led them to hope for a fast recovery **3** *(attendre)* to expect, to wait for; **on ne vous espérait plus!** we'd given up on you!

USAGE ABSOLU *(souhaiter)* **j'espère (bien)!** I (do *or* certainly) hope so!; **espérons!** let's hope so!; **il est encore permis d'e.** there's still cause *or* room for hope

• **espérer en** **VT IND** to have faith in; **e. en Dieu** to have faith *or* to trust in God; **il faut e. en des temps meilleurs** we must live in hope of better times

esperluette [ɛspɛrlɥɛt] **NF** ampersand

espiègle [ɛspjɛgl] **ADJ** *(personne)* impish, mischievous; *(regard, réponse)* mischievous; **d'un air e.** mischievously

NMF (little) rascal, imp

espièglerie [ɛspjɛgləri] **NF 1** *(caractère)* impishness, mischievousness; **par pure e.** out of pure mischief **2** *(farce)* prank, trick, piece of mischief

espion, -onne [ɛspjɔ̃, -ɔn] **NM,F** spy

NM *(comme adj; avec ou sans trait d'union)* spy *(avant n)*; **avion e.** spy plane; **satellite e.** spy satellite

espionnage [ɛspjɔnaʒ] **NM 1** *(action)* spying; **être accusé d'e.** to be accused of spying; **film/roman d'e.** spy film/novel **2** *(activité)* espionage; **faire de l'e. (au profit de)** to spy (for); **e. industriel** industrial espionage

espionner **[3]** [ɛspjɔne] **VT** to spy on; **faire e. qn** to have sb spied on *or* watched; **e. au profit de** *ou* **pour le compte de** to spy for; **elle est toujours là, à e.** she's always snooping (around)

espionnite [ɛspjɔnit] **NF** spymania

esplanade [ɛsplanad] **NF** esplanade

espoir [ɛspwar] **NM 1** *(espérance)* hope; **être plein d'e.** to be very hopeful; **avoir l'e. de faire qch** to have hopes of *or* to be hopeful of doing sth; **nous avons encore bon e.** we remain confident; **j'ai bon e. qu'il va gagner** *ou* **de le voir gagner** I'm confident that he'll win; **reprendre e.** to be *or* become hopeful again; **mettre (tout) son e. en qn/qch** to put one's hopes in *or* to pin one's hopes on sb/sth; **nourrir l'e. de faire qch** to live in hope of doing sth; **il n'y a plus d'e.** there's no hope left, all hope is lost; **tous les espoirs sont permis** things look hopeful; *Prov* **l'e. fait vivre** hope springs eternal **2** *(cause d'espérance)* hope; **tu es mon dernier e.** you're my last hope; **c'est un des espoirs du tennis français/de la chanson française** he's one of France's most promising young tennis players/singers

• **dans l'espoir de** **PRÉP** in the hope of; **dans l'e. d'un succès immédiat** hoping for immediate success **CONJ** in the hope of + *gérondif*; **dans l'e. de vous voir bientôt** hoping to see you soon

• **sans espoir** **ADJ** hopeless

ESPRIT [ɛspri]

• mind **1, 2, 7**	• head **2**
• sense **3**	• spirit **4, 9, 10, 12**
• mood **5**	• wit **8**

NM 1 *(manière de penser)* mind; **avoir l'e. clair** to be clear-thinking; **avoir l'e. critique** to have a critical mind; **avoir l'e. étroit/large** to be narrow-minded/broad-minded; **avoir l'e. lent/vif** to be slow-witted/quick-witted; *Fam* **avoir l'e. mal tourné** to have a dirty mind; **avoir l'e. scientifique/mathématique** to have a scientific/mathematical (turn of) mind; **avoir l'e. d'analyse** to have an analytical mind, to be analytical; **avoir l'e. d'aventure** to be adventurous; **avoir l'e. d'à-propos** to be quick off the mark; **avoir l'e. de contradiction** to be contrary *or* argumentative; **avoir l'e. de système** to systematize things; **avoir l'e. de synthèse** to be good at drawing ideas together *or* at synthesizing information; **il a l'e. de l'escalier** he always thinks of the perfect retort too late; **un e. sain dans un corps sain** a healthy mind in a healthy body

2 *(facultés, cerveau)* mind, head; **avoir l'e. libre** to have a clear mind; **avoir l'e. tranquille** to be easy in one's mind; **où avais-je l'e.?** what was I thinking of?; **elle avait l'e. ailleurs** her thoughts were *or* her mind was elsewhere, she was miles away; **il n'a pas l'e. à ce qu'il fait** his mind is elsewhere *or* is not on what he's doing; **dites-moi ce que vous avez à l'e.** tell me what you have in mind; **ça m'a traversé l'e.** it occurred to me, it crossed my mind; **une pareille idée ne me serait jamais venue à l'e.** such an idea would never have occurred to me *or* crossed my mind *or* entered my head; **ça m'est sorti de l'e.** it slipped my mind, it went clean out of my head; **perdre l'e.** to lose one's mind

3 *(idée)* sense; **il a eu le bon e. de ne pas téléphoner** he had the sense not to call

4 *(mentalité)* spirit; **nous n'avons pas travaillé dans le même e.** we haven't worked in the same spirit; **avoir un e. positif** to have a positive outlook; **je déplore le mauvais e. qui règne ici** I hate the bad atmosphere that reigns here; **s'attacher à l'e. de la loi plutôt qu'à la lettre** to go by the spirit of the law rather than the letter; **e. de chapelle** *ou* **de clan** *ou* **de clocher** *ou* **parti** parochial attitude; **avoir l'e. de clocher** to be parochial; **e. de caste** class consciousness; **e. de compétition/d'équipe** competitive/team spirit; **(avoir l') e. de corps** (to have) esprit de corps; **avoir l'e. d'entreprise** to be enterprising; **avoir l'e. de famille** to be family-minded; **e. de sacrifice** spirit of sacrifice; **c'est un mauvais e.** he's a troublemaker; **c'est du mauvais e.** he's/they're/*etc* just trying to make trouble; **faire du mauvais e.** to be negative

5 *(humeur)* **je n'ai pas l'e. à rire** I'm not in the mood for laughing

6 *(interprétation)* **dans son e., nous devrions voter** according to him we should vote; **dans mon e., la chambre était peinte en bleu** in my mind's eye, I saw the bedroom painted in blue; **dans mon e., ils arrivaient demain** I thought they were coming tomorrow

7 *(personne)* mind; **un des esprits marquants de ce siècle** one of the great minds *or* leading lights of this century; *Péj* **esprits chagrins** faultfinders; **un e. fort** a freethinker; **un e. libre** a freethinker; **un bel e.** a wit; *Hum* **les grands esprits se rencontrent** great minds think alike

8 *(humour)* wit; **une remarque pleine d'e.** a witty remark, a witticism; **une femme (pleine) d'e.** a witty woman; *Péj* **faire de l'e.** to try to be witty *or* funny; **avoir de l'e.** to be witty

9 *Rel* spirit; **E.** *(ange)* Spirit; **Esprits célestes** Celestial *or* Heavenly Spirits; **l'E. malin, l'E. des ténèbres** the Evil Spirit, the Evil One; **E. Saint** Holy Spirit *or* Ghost; **l'e. est fort mais la chair est faible** the spirit is willing but the flesh is weak; *Hum* **je ne suis pas un pur e., il faut bien que je mange** I'm flesh and blood, I do have to eat; *Littéraire* **rendre l'e.** to give up the ghost

10 *(fantôme)* ghost, spirit; **e. frappeur** poltergeist; **croire aux esprits** to believe in ghosts *or* spirits; **e., es-tu là?** is there anybody there?

11 *Ling* breathing; **e. doux/rude** smooth/rough breathing

12 *Chim (partie volatile)* spirit; **e. de bois** wood alcohol, wood spirit; **e. de sel** spirits of salt; **e. de vin** spirits of wine

• **esprits** **NMPL** senses; **reprendre ses esprits** *(après un évanouissement)* to regain consciousness, to come to; *(se ressaisir)* to get a grip on oneself; **reprends tes esprits!** get a grip on yourself!

• **dans un esprit de** **PRÉP** **dans un e. de conciliation** in an attempt at conciliation; **dans un e. de justice** in a spirit of justice, in an effort to be fair

SUFFIX

-ESQUE

This suffix is added to nouns or proper nouns to form adjectives with a notion of LIKENESS (hence the use of *-like* in some of the possible English translations).

• It is added to nouns as follows:

éléphantesque elephantine, colossal; **simiesque** (from the Latin word for "monkey") monkey-like; **hippopotamesque** hippo-like; **clownesque** clownish, clown-like

As this is a suffix of Italian origin, some common adjectives ending in **-esque** are actually directly derived from an Italian word rather than based on a French word with suffix attached. This is the case of **gigantesque** (gigantic), **grotesque** (ridiculous, ludicrous), **romanesque** (novelistic/romantic) or **burlesque** (comical/burlesque).

• Some adjectives based on proper nouns are in common usage and appear in dictionaries, eg:

dantesque (from the XIIIth-century Italian writer Dante Alighieri) Dantean, Dantesque; **gargantuesque** (from Garguantua, a character in a novel by XVIth-century writer Rabelais) gargantuan; **donjuanesque** (from don Juan, a legendary Spanish seducer) of a Don Juan; **rocambolesque** (from Rocambole, a character in XVIIIth-century serialized novels) fantastic, incredible; **grand-guignolesque** (from the name of a XIXth-century theatre specialized in gruesome dramas) gruesome.

But new adjectives are constantly being created using the suffix **-esque** at the end of a proper noun. They often refer to current public figures such as writers, artists or politicians, eg:

raffarinesque of Jean-Pierre Raffarin, former French Prime Minister 2002–2005; **talibanesque** of the Taliban; **dylanesque** of the American singer Bob Dylan; **woody allenesque** of the American film director Woody Allen

• Note that the use of the suffix can sometimes have a humorous effect, possibly because of the discrepancy between a rather formal ending and a proper noun taken from modern culture.

esquif [ɛskif] NM *Littéraire* skiff; **frêle e.** frail barque *or* vessel

esquille [ɛskij] NF *(de bois)* splinter; *Méd (d'os)* bone splinter

esquimau, -aude, -aux, -audes [ɛskimo, -od] ADJ Inuit, Eskimo; **chien e.** husky

NM *(langue)* Eskimo

• **Esquimau, -aude, -aux, -audes** NM,F Inuit, Eskimo

Esquimau® [ɛskimo] NM *Culin Br* choc-ice on a stick, *Am* Eskimo

esquimautage [ɛskimotaʒ] NM *Sport* Eskimo roll

esquintant, -e [ɛskɛ̃tɑ̃, -ɑ̃t] ADJ *Fam* killing, backbreaking

esquinter [3] [ɛskɛ̃te] *Fam* VT **1** *(endommager ▸ chose)* to wreck; *(▸ voiture)* to smash up; *(▸ santé)* to ruin; **tout l'avant est esquinté** the front is totally smashed up; **n'esquinte pas cette lampe!** don't break that lamp!

2 *(amocher)* to do in; **il s'est drôlement fait e.** he got really badly smashed up

3 *(épuiser ▸ personne)* to exhaust, to knock out

4 *(dénigrer ▸ livre, film)* to pan, to slam, *Br* to slate

VPR **s'esquinter 1** *(s'épuiser)* to kill oneself (**à faire** doing); **ne t'esquinte pas au travail** don't work yourself to death *or* into the ground **2** *(s'abîmer)* **s'e. la santé/la vue (à faire qch)** to ruin one's health/eyesight (doing sth) **3** *(se blesser)* **elle s'est esquinté le dos** she's done her back in; **je me suis esquinté la jambe en tombant** I did my leg in when I fell

esquisse [ɛskis] NF **1** *Beaux-Arts* sketch

2 *Typ (de page)* rough layout

3 *(d'un projet, d'un discours, d'un roman)* draft, outline

4 *(d'un sourire, d'un geste)* hint; **sans l'e. d'un regret** with no regrets at all, without the slightest regret

esquisser [3] [ɛskise] VT **1** *Beaux-Arts* to sketch **2** *(projet, histoire)* to outline, to draft **3** *Fig (geste, mouvement)* to give a hint of; **e. un sourire** to give a faint *or* slight smile

VPR **s'esquisser** *(sourire)* to appear, to flicker; *(solution, progrès)* to appear; **un sourire s'esquissa sur son visage** he/she gave a slight smile, he/she half-smiled; **un plan commençait à s'e. dans mon esprit** a plan started to take shape in my mind

esquive [ɛskiv] NF dodge, sidestep; *Fig (d'une question, d'un problème etc)* dodging, evasion; *Boxe* **e. de la tête** dodge

esquiver [3] [ɛskive] VT **1** *(éviter ▸ coup)* to dodge **2** *(se soustraire à ▸ question)* to evade, to avoid, to skirt; *(▸ difficulté)* to skirt, to avoid, to side step; *(▸ démarche, obligation)* to shirk, to evade

VI **e. (de la tête)** to dodge

VPR **s'esquiver** to slip *or* to sneak out (unnoticed)

essai [esɛ] NM **1** *(vérification ▸ d'un produit, d'un appareil)* test, testing, trial; *(▸ d'une voiture)* test, testing, test-driving; **e. nucléaire** nuclear test; *Aviat* **essais en vol** test flights; *Aut* **e. sur route** test drive; **essais comparatifs** comparative tests; **faire l'e. de qch** to test sth

2 *(tentative)* attempt, try; **au deuxième e.** at the second try; **nous avons fait plusieurs essais** we had several tries, we made several attempts; **après notre e. de vie commune** after our attempt at living together; **des essais de lancement** trial launches; **coup d'e.** first attempt *or* try

3 *(expérimentation)* **faire l'e. de qch** to try sth (out); **faites un e. avant de vous décider** try it out before you decide; **e. gratuit** free trial

4 *Littérature* essay

5 *Chim & Pharm* assay; **e. biologique** bioassay

6 *Mines* assaying; **fourneau d'e.** assay furnace

7 *Sport (au rugby)* try; **marquer un e.** to score a try; **transformer un e.** to convert a try

• **à l'essai** ADV **1** *(à l'épreuve)* **mettre qn/qch à l'e.** to put sb/sth to the test **2** *Com & Jur* on a trial basis; **engager** *ou* **prendre qn à l'e.** to appoint sb for a trial *or* probationary period; **prendre/acheter qch à l'e.** to take/buy sth on approval

• **d'essai** ADJ **1** *Aviat* **pilote d'e.** test pilot **2** *(période)* trial *(avant n)* **3** *Cin* **bout d'e., e. de caméra** screen test

essaie *etc voir* **essayer**

essaim [esɛ̃] NM **1** *Entom* swarm **2** *(foule)* **un e. de** *(supporters, admirateurs)* a throng *or* swarm of; *(adolescentes)* a bevy *or Péj* gaggle of

essaimage [esɛmaʒ] NM **1** *Entom* swarming; *(époque)* swarming time **2** *Littérature (d'un peuple)* dispersion; *(d'une firme)* expansion

essaimer [4] [eseme] VI **1** *Entom* to swarm **2** *Littéraire (se disperser ▸ groupe)* to spread, to disperse; *(▸ firme)* to expand

VT *(sujet: firme ▸ usines, filiales etc)* to spread

essayage [esejaʒ] NM *Couture (séance)* fitting; *(action)* trying on

essayer [11] [eseje] VT **1** *(tenter)* to try; **essaie ce numéro** try this number; **e. de faire** to try to do, to try and do; **essaie d'être à l'heure** try to be on time, try and be on time; **as-tu essayé d'arrêter de fumer?** have you tried to stop smoking?; *Fam* **j'essaierai que la soirée soit réussie** I'll do my best to make the party a success

2 *(utiliser pour la première fois)* to try (out); *(vin, plat etc)* to try, to taste; **e. un (nouveau) restaurant** to try a new restaurant; **e. une (nouvelle) marque de lessive** to try out a new brand of washing powder

3 *(mettre ▸ vêtement, chaussures)* to try on; **faire e. qch à qn** to give sb sth to try on

4 *(expérimenter)* to try (out), to test; **e. un nouveau médicament** to test a new drug; **e. une voiture** *(pilote, client)* to test-drive a car; **e. les agences de rencontres** to try dating agencies; **e. sa force** to test one's strength; **l'e. c'est l'adopter** = publicity slogan indicating that a product is sure to please (sometimes used ironically)

5 *Mines* to assay

USAGE ABSOLU to try; **d'accord, je vais e.** alright, I'll try; **laissez-moi e.** let me (have a) try; *Fam* **essaie un peu (pour voir)!** just you try!

VPR **s'essayer s'e. à qch/à faire qch** to try one's hand at sth/at doing sth

essayeur, -euse [esejœr, -øz] NM,F **1** *Couture* fitter **2** *Mines* assayer **3** *(d'une machine, d'un produit etc)* tester

essayiste [esejist] NMF *Littérature* essayist, essay writer

esse [ɛs] NF **1** *(crochet)* (s-shaped) hook; *(cheville)* linchpin **2** *(de violon)* (s-shaped) sound hole

-ESSE — SUFFIX

• The use of the suffix **-esse** in WOMEN'S JOB TITLES is currently falling into disuse as it seems to have acquired over the years a pejorative connotation. (The same trend can be observed in English, where words such as *manageress* and *actress* have largely fallen out of favour.) It is thus advisable to use **la maire** (the mayor) instead of **la mairesse**, **la poète** (the poet) instead of **la poétesse**, **la docteur(e)** (the doctor) instead of **la doctoresse**

• The suffix **-esse** is also added to adjectives to form feminine nouns expressing a QUALITY linked to that adjective, be it physical or moral. The English equivalent *-ness* can often be used in translation, eg:

gentillesse kindness; **finesse** subtlety/fineness; **jeunesse** youth; **richesse** wealth/richness; **rudesse** roughness/harshness; **vieillesse** old age

ESSEC, Essec [esɛk] NF *Scol & Univ (abrév* **École supérieure des sciences économiques et commerciales**) = "grande école" for management and business studies

essence [esɑ̃s] NF **1** *(liquide pétrolier) Br* petrol, *Am* gas, gasoline; **à e.** petrol-powered; *Fam* **prendre de l'e.** to fill up; **e. ordinaire** *Br* two-star petrol, *Am* regular gas; **e. sans plomb** unleaded *Br* petrol *or Am* gas

2 *Chim* spirit, spirits; **e. de térébenthine** spirit *or* spirits of turpentine, turps

3 *Culin* essence; **e. de café** coffee essence

4 *Pharm (cosmétique)* (essential) oil, essence; **e. de citron** lemon oil; **e. de roses** rose oil, essence of roses

5 *Bot* species; **essences résineuses** resinous trees, conifers

6 *Phil* essence

7 *(contenu fondamental)* essence, gist

8 *Can (parfum)* flavour; **tu veux une sucette à quelle e.?** what flavour lollipop would you like?

• **par essence** ADV essentially, in essence

essentiel, -elle [esɑ̃sjɛl] ADJ **1** *(indispensable)* essential (**à/pour** to/for); **e. à la vie** essential to life; **il est e. d'avoir compris ce point** it is essential *or* necessary to have understood this point

2 *(principal)* main, essential; *(raison)* basic, main; **le point e. du débat** the main point of the debate

3 *Phil* essential

4 *Pharm* idiopathic

NM **1** *(l'indispensable)* **l'e.** the basic essentials; **n'apportez que l'e.** bring only the (bare) essentials *or* the basics **2** *(le plus important)* **vous avez la santé, c'est l'e.** you're healthy, that's the main *or* important thing; **l'e., c'est que tu comprennes** the most important *or* the main thing is that you should understand; **l'e. de l'article se résume en trois mots** the bulk of the article can be summed up in three words **3** *(la plus grande partie)* **l'e. de la conversation** most of the conversation; **elle passe l'e. de son temps au téléphone** she spends most of her time on the phone; **l'e. des effectifs est resté à la base** the greater part *or* most of the men stayed at base

essentiellement [esɑ̃sjɛlmɑ̃] ADV **1** *(par nature)* in essence, essentially **2** *(principalement)* mainly, essentially

esseulé, -e [esœle] ADJ *Littéraire* **1** *(délaissé)* forsaken **2** *(seul)* forlorn, lonely

essieu, -x [esjø] NM axle, axletree; **e. avant/arrière** front/rear axle

essor [esɔr] NM **1** *(d'un oiseau)* flight; **prendre son e.** to soar **2** *Fig (d'une entreprise, d'une industrie)* rise, rapid growth; **e. économique** (rapid) economic expansion, economic boom; **industrie en plein e.** booming *or* fast-growing industry; **un nouvel e.** a new lease of life; **prendre son e.** *(adolescent)* to fend for oneself, to become self-sufficient; *(économie, entreprise)* to take off

essorage [esɔraʒ] NM *(à la machine)* spinning; *(à l'essoreuse à rouleaux)* mangling; *(à la main)* wringing; **pas d'e.** *(sur l'étiquette d'un vêtement)* do not spin; **l'e. de la salade** drying *or* spin-drying lettuce

essorer [3] [esɔre] **VT** *(sécher)* **e. le linge** *(à la machine)* to spin-dry the laundry; *(à l'essoreuse à rouleaux)* to put the laundry through the mangle; *(à la main)* to wring the laundry; **e. la salade** to dry *or* to spin-dry the lettuce

essoreuse [esɔrøz] **NF 1** *(pour le linge)* **e. (à tambour)** spin-drier; **e. (à rouleaux)** mangle **2** *(pour la salade)* salad spinner

essoufflement [esufləmɑ̃] **NM** breathlessness; *Fig* **en raison de l'e. de l'économie** because the economy is running out of steam

essouffler [3] [esufle] **VT** to make breathless; **être (tout) essoufflé** to be breathless *or* out of breath; **ce sont les marches qui m'ont essoufflé** climbing the steps has left me breathless

VPR s'essouffler 1 *Physiol* to get breathless; **s'e. à faire qch** to struggle to do sth **2** *(s'affaiblir ▸ moteur)* to get weak; *(▸ économie)* to run out of steam; *(▸ production)* to lose momentum; *(▸ inspiration, écrivain)* to dry up

essuie[1] *voir* **essuyer**

essuie[2] [esɥi] **NM** *Belg (essuie-mains)* hand towel; *(torchon)* dish towel, *Br* tea towel; *(serviette de bain)* bath towel

essuie-glace [esɥiglas] *(pl* **essuie-glaces***)* **NM** *Aut Br* windscreen *or Am* windshield wiper; **e. arrière** back wiper

essuie-mains [esɥimɛ̃] **NM INV** hand towel

essuie-meubles [esɥimœbl] **NM INV** duster

essuie-phare [esɥifar] *(pl* **essuie-phares***)* **NM** headlamp wiper

essuie-pieds [esɥipje] **NM INV** doormat

essuie-tout [esɥitu] **NM INV** kitchen paper

essuie-verre, essuie-verres [esɥivɛr] **NM INV** dish towel, *Br* tea towel

essuyage [esɥijaʒ] **NM 1** *(séchage)* wiping, drying up **2** *(nettoyage)* wiping

essuyer [14] [esɥije] **VT 1** *(sécher ▸ vaisselle)* to wipe, to dry (up); *(▸ liquide, sueur)* to wipe, to mop up, to wipe (off); *(▸ surface)* to wipe (down); *(▸ sol)* to wipe, to dry; *(▸ main)* to dry, to wipe; **essuie tes mains** wipe your hands; **e. une larme** to wipe away a tear; **e. les larmes de qn** to dry sb's tears; *Fam* **e. les plâtres** to have to endure initial problems; **les premiers acheteurs de cette voiture ont essuyé les plâtres** the first purchasers of this car had to put up with a few teething troubles **2** *(nettoyer ▸ surface poussiéreuse)* to dust (down); *(▸ tableau noir)* to wipe (clean), to clean; **tes mains sont pleines de farine, essuie-les** wipe your hands, they're covered in flour; **essuie tes pieds sur le paillasson** wipe your feet on the doormat **3** *(subir ▸ reproches)* to endure; *(▸ refus)* to meet with; *(▸ défaite, échec, pertes)* to suffer; *(▸ tempête)* to weather, to bear up against; **e. le feu de l'ennemi** to come under enemy fire

VPR s'essuyer *(se sécher)* to dry oneself; **s'e. les mains/pieds/yeux** to dry *or* to wipe one's hands/feet/eyes; **essuie-toi les mains** dry your hands

est[1] [ɛ] *voir* **être**[1]

est[2] [ɛst] **NM INV 1** *(point cardinal)* east; **à l'e.** in the east; **où est l'e.?** which way is east?; **le vent vient de l'e.** it's an east *or* easterly wind, the wind is coming from the east; **un vent d'e.** an easterly wind; **aller à** *ou* **vers l'e.** to go east *or* eastwards; **les trains qui vont vers l'e.** trains going east, eastbound trains; **rouler vers l'e.** to drive east *or* eastwards; **la cuisine est plein e.** *ou* **exposée à l'e.** the kitchen faces due east; **le soleil se lève à l'e.** the sun rises in the east

2 *(partie d'un pays, d'un continent)* east, eastern area *or* regions; *(partie d'une ville)* east; **l'e. de l'Italie** eastern Italy, the east of Italy; **dans l'e. de la France** in eastern France, in the east of France; **les gens de l'e. (de la France)** people from eastern France; **elle habite dans l'e.** she lives in the East; **il habite dans l'e. de Paris** he lives in the east of Paris

ADJ INV east *(avant n)*, eastern; *(▸ côte, face)* east; *(▸ banlieue, partie, région)* eastern; **la façade e. d'un immeuble** the east-facing wall of a building; **la côte e. des États-Unis** the East coast *or* Eastern seaboard of the United States; **suivre la direction e.** to head *or* to go eastwards

• **Est ADJ INV** East **NM 1** *Géog* **l'E.** the East **2** *Pol & Hist* **l'E.** Eastern Europe, Eastern European countries; **l'Europe de l'E.** Eastern Europe; **les pays de l'E.** the countries of Eastern Europe, Eastern European countries; *Hist* **le bloc de l'E.** the Eastern bloc

• **à l'est de PRÉP** (to the) east of; **il habite à l'e. de Paris** he lives to the east of Paris

establishment [establiʃment] **NM l'e.** *(gén)* the dominant *or* influential group *or* body; *(en Grande-Bretagne)* the Establishment

estacade [ɛstakad] **NF** byre; *Naut (pieux)* stockade; *(jetée)* pier *(on piles)*

estafette [ɛstafɛt] **NF 1** *Hist (courrier)* courier **2** *Mil (agent de liaison)* liaison officer **3** *Aut (camionnette)* van

estafilade [ɛstafilad] **NF** slash, gash

est-allemand, -e [ɛstalmɑ̃, -ɑ̃d] *Anciennement* **ADJ** East German

• **Est-Allemand, -e NM,F** East German

estaminet [ɛstaminɛ] **NM** *Vieilli* small café, bar; *Littéraire* estaminet

estampage [ɛstɑ̃paʒ] **NM 1** *Tech (façonnage)* stamping; *(empreinte)* stamp **2** *Fam (action d'escroquer)* swindling, fleecing; *(résultat)* swindle

estampe [ɛstɑ̃p] **NF 1** *(image)* engraving, print; *Hum* **et alors comme ça, il t'a invitée à aller voir ses estampes japonaises?** so he invited you up to see his etchings, did he? **2** *Tech (outil)* stamp

estamper [3] [ɛstɑ̃pe] **VT 1** *Tech (façonner, marquer)* to stamp **2** *Fam (escroquer)* to swindle, to con; **e. qn de 20 euros** to con sb out of 20 euros

estampeur, -euse [ɛstɑ̃pœr, -øz] **NM,F** *Fam (escroc)* swindler, con-man

NM *Tech* stamper

estampillage [ɛstɑ̃pijaʒ] **NM** *(d'un document)* stamping; *(d'une marchandise)* marking

estampille [ɛstɑ̃pij] **NF** *(sur un document)* stamp; *(sur une marchandise)* mark, trademark

estampiller [3] [ɛstɑ̃pije] **VT** *(document)* to stamp; *(marchandise)* to mark

est-ce que [ɛskə] **ADV INTERROGATIF 1** *(suivi d'un verbe plein)* **e. je/tu/nous/vous...?** *(au présent)* do I/you/we/you...?; **est-ce qu'il/qu'elle...?** *(au présent)* does he/she...?; **e. vous aimez le thé?** do you like tea?; **e. vous avez acheté la maison?** did you buy the house?; **e. vous dormiez bien?** did you (use to) sleep well?; **e. tu iras?** will you go? **2** *(suivi d'un auxiliaire) (au présent)* **e. je suis...?** am I...?; **e. tu as une enveloppe?** do you have *or* have you got an envelope?; **e. je dois...?** must I...?; **e. tu peux...?** can you...?; *(au passé)* **e. tu y étais?** were you there?; **est-ce qu'il devait signer?** should he have signed?; *(au futur)* **e. tu seras là?** will you be there?; *(au futur proche)* **e. tu vas lui téléphoner?** are you going to *or* will you phone him/her? **3** *(avec un autre adverbe interrogatif)* **quand est-ce qu'il arrive?** when does he arrive?; **qui e. tu as vu?** who did you see?; **pourquoi e. tu ris?** why are you laughing?

este [ɛst] **NM** *(langue)* Estonian

ester[1] [ɛste] **VI** *(à l'infinitif seulement) Jur* **e. en justice** to go to court

ester[2] [ɛstɛr] **NM** *Chim* ester

esthète [ɛstɛt] **NMF** aesthete; **cela ne plaira sûrement pas aux esthètes** this will offend some people's aesthetic sense

esthéticien, -enne [ɛstetisjɛ̃, -ɛn] **NM,F 1** *(en institut de beauté)* beautician **2** *Beaux-Arts & Phil* aesthetician

esthétique [ɛstetik] **ADJ 1** *Beaux-Arts & Phil* aesthetic **2** *(joli)* beautiful, aesthetically pleasing; **ce chantier devant la maison n'est pas très e.** *ou* **n'a rien d'e.** this building site in front of the house is rather unsightly

NF 1 *Beaux-Arts & Phil (science)* **l'e.** aesthetics *(singulier)*; *(code)* aesthetic **2** *(harmonie)* beauty, harmony; *(beauté)* aesthetic quality, attractiveness; **ça ne sert à rien, c'est uniquement pour l'e.** it doesn't have any use, it's just there to look nice; **ça manque d'e.** it's not very attractive, it's not aesthetically pleasing **3** *Ind* **e. industrielle** industrial design

esthétiquement [ɛstetikmɑ̃] **ADV 1** *Beaux-Arts & Phil* aesthetically **2** *(harmonieusement)* harmoniously, beautifully **3** *(du point de vue de la beauté)* aesthetically, from an aesthetic point of view; **e., ce n'est pas réussi** aesthetically, it's a failure

esthétisme [ɛstetism] **NM** aestheticism

estimable [ɛstimabl] **ADJ 1** *(digne de respect ▸ personne)* respectable **2** *(assez bon ▸ ouvrage, film)* decent **3** *(calculable ▸ frais, perte)* assessable

estimatif, -ive [ɛstimatif, -iv] **ADJ** *(valeur, état)* estimated; **devis e.** estimate, quotation

estimation [ɛstimasjɔ̃] **NF 1** *(évaluation ▸ d'une marchandise, d'une œuvre d'art)* appraisal, valuation; *(▸ de dégâts, de besoins, d'un poids)* estimation, assessment; *(▸ d'une distance)* gauging; **faire une e.** to give an estimation/a valuation/an assessment; *Mktg* **e. des besoins** needs assessment **2** *(montant)* estimate, estimation; **d'après mon e.** according to my estimate *or* estimation **3** *(prévision)* projection; **le score réalisé par le candidat sortant dépasse toutes les estimations** the outgoing candidate's score surpasses all the pollsters' projections

estimative [ɛstimativ] *voir* **estimatif**

estime [ɛstim] **NF** esteem, respect; **avoir de l'e. pour qn/qch** to have a great deal of respect for sb/sth, to hold sb/sth in high esteem; **baisser/monter dans l'e. de qn** to go down/up in sb's esteem; **il force l'e. par son intégrité** one cannot but respect his integrity; **tenir qn en grande** *ou* **haute e.** to hold sb in high esteem

• **à l'estime ADV 1** *Naut* by dead reckoning; **navigation à l'e.** dead reckoning **2** *(approximativement)* roughly; **j'ai tracé les plans à l'e.** I drew the plans blind; **faire un budget à l'e.** to work out a budget roughly

estimer [3] [ɛstime] **VT 1** *(expertiser ▸ valeur, prix)* to appraise, to evaluate, to assess; *(marchandises)* to value, to appraise; **faire e. un tableau** to have a painting valued; **ce tableau a été estimé à 2 millions d'euros** this painting has been estimated at 2 million euros

2 *(évaluer approximativement ▸ quantité, poids)* to estimate; *(▸ distance)* to gauge; *(dégâts, besoins)* to estimate, to assess; **les dégâts ont été estimés à 500 euros** the damage was estimated at 500 euros; *Naut* **longitude estimée** longitude by dead reckoning

3 *(apprécier ▸ ami, écrivain, collègue)* to regard with esteem, to esteem, to think highly of; **elle était estimée de tous** she was highly thought of *or* was esteemed by everyone; **je l'estime trop pour ça** I respect him/her too much for that; **e. qn à sa juste valeur** to judge sb correctly

4 *(juger)* to think, to consider, to believe (**que** that); **j'estime qu'il a eu tort** I think *or* believe (that) he was wrong; **si tu estimes que tu peux le faire** if you believe you can do it; **j'estime qu'il est de mon devoir de parler** I consider *or* think it (is) my duty *or* that it is my duty to speak; **il n'a pas estimé nécessaire de me prévenir** he didn't consider *or* think it (was) necessary to warn me

5 *Naut* to reckon

VPR s'estimer *(suivi d'un adj)* **s'e. heureux** to count oneself lucky; **s'e. satisfait de/que** to be happy with/that

estivage [ɛstivaʒ] **NM** *Agr* mountain summering

estival, -e, -aux, -ales [ɛstival, -o] **ADJ** summer *(avant n)*; **station estivale** summer resort

estivant, -e [ɛstivɑ̃, -ɑ̃t] **NM,F** summer tourist, *Br* holidaymaker, *Am* vacationer

estiver [3] [ɛstive] **VT** *Agr* to summer on mountain pastures

estoc [ɛstɔk] **NM** *Escrime* rapier; **coup d'e.** thrust; **frapper d'e. et de taille** to cut and thrust

estocade [ɛstɔkad] **NF 1** *(lors d'une corrida)* final sword thrust, death-blow; **donner** *ou* **porter l'e. à un taureau** to deal the death-blow to a bull **2** *Littéraire (locutions)* **donner** *ou* **porter l'e. à qn** to deal the death-blow to sb

estomac [ɛstɔma] **NM 1** *Anat* stomach; **j'ai mal à l'e.** I have stomach ache; *Fam* **il a pris de l'e.** he's developed a paunch *or* potbelly; *Fam* **avoir l'e. bien accroché** to have a strong stomach; *Fam* **ça m'est resté sur l'e.** it weighed on my stomach; *Fig* it stuck in my craw; **avoir l'e. vide** *ou* **creux** to have an empty stomach; **avoir l'e. plein** *ou* **bien rempli** to be full (up); **avoir l'e. lourd** to feel bloated; *Fam* **avoir l'e. dans les talons** to be famished *or* ravenous; *Méd* **cancer de l'e.** stomach cancer **2** *Fam (hardiesse)* **avoir de l'e.** to have a nerve *or Br* a cheek; **manquer d'e.** to lack guts

• **à l'estomac** ADV *Fam* **ils y sont allés à l'e.** they bluffed their way through it; **avoir qn à l'e.** to intimidate sb

estomaquer [3] [ɛstɔmake] VT *Fam* to stagger, to flabbergast

estompe [ɛstɔ̃p] NF *Beaux-Arts* stump, tortillon; **(dessin à l')e.** stump drawing

estompé, -e [ɛstɔ̃pe] ADJ blurred; *Ordinat* dimmed; **les contours estompés des immeubles** the dim outline of buildings

estomper [3] [ɛstɔ̃pe] VT **1** *Beaux-Arts* to stump, to shade off **2** *(silhouette, contours)* to dim, to blur; *(contraste)* to tone down **3** *(souvenir, sentiment)* to dim, to blur; **le temps estompera la douleur** time will ease the pain

VPR **s'estomper 1** *(disparaître ▸ contours)* to become blurred; *(▸ couleurs)* to fade; *(▸ rides)* to be smoothed out **2** *(s'affaiblir ▸ souvenir)* to fade away; *(▸ douleur, rancune)* to diminish, to die down; *(▸ peine)* to ease

Estonie [ɛstɔni] NF *Géog* **l'E.** Estonia

estonien, -enne [ɛstɔnjɛ̃, -ɛn] ADJ Estonian

NM *(langue)* Estonian

• **Estonien, -enne** NM,F Estonian

estoquer [3] [ɛstɔke] VT *(taureau)* to deal the death blow to

estouffade [ɛstufad] NF *Culin* **e. de bœuf** ≃ beef stew

estourbir [32] [ɛsturbir] VT *Fam Vieilli* **1** *(assommer)* to knock out, to lay out **2** *(tuer)* to do in **3** *(étonner)* to astound

estrade [ɛstrad] NF platform

estragon [ɛstragɔ̃] NM *Bot* tarragon

estran [ɛstrɑ̃] NM *Géog* strand, foreshore

estrapade [ɛstrapad] NF *Hist (supplice)* strappado

estrogène [ɛstrɔʒɛn] = **œstrogène**

estropié, -e [ɛstrɔpje] ADJ crippled, maimed; **il en restera e.** he'll be left a cripple

NM,F cripple, disabled *or* maimed person

estropier [9] [ɛstrɔpje] VT **1** *(personne)* to cripple, to maim **2** *Fig (en prononçant)* to mispronounce; *(à l'écrit)* to misspell; *(texte)* to mutilate; *(morceau de musique)* to murder; **e. une citation** to misquote a text

estuaire [ɛstɥɛr] NM *Géog* estuary

estudiantin, -e [ɛstydjɑ̃tɛ̃, -in] ADJ *Littéraire* student *(avant n)*

esturgeon [ɛstyrʒɔ̃] NM *Ich* sturgeon

et [e] CONJ **1** *(reliant des termes, des propositions)* and; **noir et blanc** black and white; **le père et le fils** the father and the son; **une belle et brillante jeune fille** a beautiful, clever girl; **ils jouent au tennis et au hand-ball** they play tennis and handball; **une robe courte et sans manches** a short sleeveless dress; **toi et moi, nous savons ce qu'il faut faire** you and I know what should be done; **2 et 2 font 4** two and two make four, two plus two makes four; **il y a mensonge et mensonge** there are lies, and then there are lies; **un livre ancien et qui n'est plus en librairie** an old book which is out of print; **il connaît l'anglais, et très bien** he speaks English, and very well at that

2 *(exprimant une relation de simultanéité, de succession ou de conséquence)* **il s'est levé et il a quitté la pièce** he got up and left the room; **j'ai bien aimé ce film, et toi?** I really liked the film, how *or* what about you?; **il travaille et ne réussit pas** he works but he's not successful; **c'est un jeune homme de grande énergie, et qui réussira dans la vie** he is a young man of great energy, who will succeed

3 *(reliant des propositions comparatives)* **plus ça va, et plus la situation s'aggrave** as time goes on, the situation just gets worse; **moins je le vois et mieux je me porte!** the less I see him the better I feel!; **moins il travaille et moins il a envie de travailler** the less he works the less he feels like working

4 *(avec une valeur emphatique)* **je ne peux pas et répondre au téléphone et ouvrir la porte** I can't answer the phone AND open the door; **j'ai dû supporter et les enfants et les parents!** I had to put up with both the parents and the children *or* with the parents AND the children!; **et d'un, je n'ai pas faim, et de deux, je n'aime pas ça** for one thing I'm not hungry and for another I don't like it; **je l'ai dit et répété** I've said it over and over again, I've said it more than once; **c'est fini et bien fini!** that's the end of that!; **et moi alors?** (and) what about me?; **et les dix euros que je t'ai prêtés?** and (what about) the ten euros I lent you?; **et si on lui disait tout?** what if we told him everything?; **et les bagages?** what about the luggage?; **et pourquoi pas?** (and) why not?; **je n'ai pas envie d'y aller – et pourquoi?** I don't want to go – and why not?; **et voilà!** there you are!, there you go!; **et moi je vous dis que je n'irai pas!** and I'm telling you that I won't go!; **et vous osez me proposer cela!** and you dare (to) suggest that!; **et tout à coup il se mit à courir** and suddenly he started running; **et c'est ainsi que se termine mon histoire…** and that is how my story ends…; **et on a ri!** how we laughed!; *Littéraire* **et le garçon de se sauver** at this the boy ran off

5 *(dans les nombres composés, les horaires, les poids et les mesures)* **vingt et un** twenty one; **vingt et unième** twenty-first; **deux heures et demie** half past two; **cinq heures et quart** five fifteen, a quarter past five; **deux kilos et demi** two and a half kilos

NM **1 et commercial** ampersand **2** *Ordinat* **ET** AND; **circuit ET** AND gate

> **SUFFIX**
>
> **-ET, -ETTE**
>
> • When added to nouns, this suffix denotes SMALLNESS, eg:
>
> **un bâtonnet** a small stick; **un jardinet** a small garden; **une maisonnette** a small house; **un garçonnet** a little boy; **une fillette** a little girl; **une gouttelette** a droplet; **un porcelet** a piglet
>
> One interesting recent coinage is **la mesurette**, which is used to describe an inadequate or half-hearted measure taken by politicians.
>
> • When added to adjectives, **-et** carries an idea of EXCESS and it is often (though not always) slightly derogatory, eg:
>
> **le roman est un peu longuet** the novel is a bit on the long side; **il est un peu jeunet pour être nommé directeur** he's a bit young to be appointed director; **c'est un film gentillet, sans plus** it's a nice enough little film, nothing special; **elle est bien maigrelette** she's really skinny; **un petit jardin bien propret** a neat little garden
>
> • As it denotes smallness, the suffix **-et** sometimes has positive connotations of endearment (as in **mignonnet** pretty, **propret** neat and tidy, **mon biquet** my pet), but in other contexts it takes on derogatory connotations associated with weakness (as in **une femmelette, une mauviette** a wimp).
>
> • Note that an **l** is often insterted when adding the suffix **-et** to words ending with a vowel, as in **gouttelette** and **maigrelet**.

ETA [əteɑ] NF *Pol (abrév* **Euskadi Ta Askatasuna***)* ETA

étable [etabl] NF cowshed

> Il faut noter que le nom anglais **stable** est un faux ami. Il signifie **écurie**.

établi[1] [etabli] NM workbench

établi[2]**, -e** [etabli] ADJ established; **bien é.** well-established; **avoir une réputation bien établie** to have a well established reputation; **l'ordre é.** the established order

établir [32] [etablir] VT **1** *(implanter ▸ usine, filiale, locaux, quartier général)* to establish, to set up; *(▸ camp)* to pitch; *(▸ taxe, tribunal)* to institute, to create; **é. son domicile à Paris** to take up residence in Paris

2 *(dresser ▸ organigramme)* to set out; *(▸ liste)* to draw up; *(▸ devis)* to provide; *(▸ chèque)* to make out; *(▸ programme, prix)* to fix; *(▸ plan, proposition, facture, bilan, budget)* to draw up; *(▸ objectifs)* to determine; **é. une moyenne** to work out an average; **é. un parallèle entre** to establish *or* draw a parallel between

3 *(instaurer ▸ règlement)* to introduce; *(▸ usage)* to pass; *(▸ ordre, relation, système de gouvernement)* to establish; *(▸ principe)* to lay down; **é. un précédent** to set a precedent; **é. des liens d'amitiés** to establish friendly relations

4 *(bâtir ▸ réputation, autorité)* to establish; *(▸ empire)* to build; **é. sa fortune sur** to establish *or* build up one's fortune on

5 *(duplex, liaison téléphonique)* to set up, to establish

6 *(prouver)* to establish, to prove; **é. l'innocence de qn** to establish sb's innocence, to vindicate sb; **é. l'identité de qn** to establish sb's identity; **é. la vérité** to establish the truth; **nous cherchons à é. qu'à 18 h notre client était chez lui avec son épouse** we are trying to establish that at 6 p.m., our client was at home with his wife

7 *Vieilli (pourvoir d'une situation)* to set up in business; **j'attendrai d'avoir établi mes enfants** I'll wait until my children are settled in life; **elle est établie comme pharmacienne** she's set up as a chemist

8 *Vieilli (marier)* to marry off; **il lui reste une fille à é.** he still has a daughter at home

9 *Sport* **é. un record** to set a record

VPR **s'établir 1** *(s'installer)* **ils ont préféré s'é. en banlieue** they chose to settle in the suburbs **2** *(professionnellement)* to set oneself up (in business); **elle n'a pas assez d'argent pour s'é.** she doesn't have enough funds to start up on her own; **s'é. à son compte** to set oneself up in business, to become self-employed **3** *(être instauré ▸ coutume, idée)* to become established; **une atmosphère plus détendue finit par s'é.** the atmosphere eventually became more relaxed; **une relation stable s'est établie entre nous** a stable relation has developed between the two of us

établissement [etablismɑ̃] NM **1** *(institution)* establishment, institution; *(école)* school; **é. d'enseignement primaire/secondaire** primary/secondary school; *(université)* university; **é. hospitalier** hospital; **é. pénitentiaire** prison, *Am* penitentiary; **é. privé** private school; **é. religieux** *(monastère)* monastery; *(couvent)* convent; *(collège)* religious *or* denominational school; *(séminaire)* seminary; **é. scolaire** school; **é. thermal** hydropathic establishment, spa

2 *(institution commerciale)* business, firm; **les établissements Leroy** Leroy and Co; **les établissements Fourat et fils** Fourat and Sons; **é. bancaire** bank; **é. classé** = potentially dangerous industrial premises (having to conform to strict safety regulations); **é. commercial** commercial establishment *or* institution; *Fin* **é. de crédit** credit institution; *Fin* **é. financier** financial institution; **é. industriel** factory, manufacturing firm; *Admin* **é. public** state-owned company; *Fin* **é. payeur** paying bank; **é. d'utilité publique** public utility

3 *(construction ▸ d'un barrage, d'une usine)* building, construction; *(▸ d'un camp)* pitching

4 *(instauration ▸ d'un empire)* setting up, establishing; *(▸ d'un régime)* installing; *(▸ d'un usage)* establishing; *(▸ d'un règlement)* prescribing, laying down; *(▸ d'un principe)* laying down; *(▸ d'objectifs)* determining; *(▸ de la paix)* establishment; *(▸ d'un prix)* fixing; *(▸ d'une taxe, d'un tribunal)* institution, creation; *Fin* **é. d'un compte** opening an account, setting up an account; *Com* **é. des prix** pricing; **é. des prix de revient** costing

5 *(préparation ▸ d'un devis, d'une liste, d'un plan, d'une proposition)* drawing up; *(▸ d'un organigramme)* laying out, drawing up

6 *(installation)* settling, fixing; *Hist* **établissements** *(colonies)* settlements, colonies; **l'é. des Français en Afrique** the settlement of the French in Africa

7 *Vieilli (dans une profession)* setting up; **son é. dans la profession médicale** his/her setting up in medical practice; **l'é. de sa fille** *(par le mariage)* his marrying off his daughter

8 *(preuve ▸ de la vérité)* establishment; **rien n'est possible sans l'é. de son identité** nothing can be done if his identity cannot be established

étage [etaʒ] NM **1** *(dans une maison)* floor, *Br* storey, *Am* story; *(dans un parking, un aéroport)* level; **au troisième é.** *(maison) Br* on the third floor; *Am* on the fourth floor; **habiter au premier**

é. *Br* to live on the first floor, *Am* to live on the second floor; **au dernier é.** on the top floor; **elle est dans les étages** she's upstairs somewhere; **à deux étages** *Br* two-storeyed, *Am* two-storied; **un immeuble de cinq étages** a five-storey building

2 *(division ▸ d'une pièce montée)* tier; *(▸ d'un buffet, d'une bibliothèque)* shelf; **dans le placard, sur l'é. du haut** in the cupboard on the top shelf

3 *Géol* stage, layer; *(d'un terrain)* level; *(d'un jardin)* terrace

4 *Bot* **é. de végétation** level of vegetation

5 *Aviat & Tech* stage; **fusée à trois étages** three-stage rocket

6 *Mines* level

7 *Arch & Littéraire* degree, rank; **étages de la société** strata *or* levels of society

• **étages** NMPL *(escaliers)* **grimper/monter les étages** to climb/to go upstairs; **dévaler les étages** to race down the stairs; **monter les étages à pied/en courant** to walk/to run up the stairs

• **à l'étage** ADV upstairs, on the floor above

• **de bas étage** ADJ *Péj* **1** *Vieilli (inférieur ▸ personne)* low-born **2** *(vulgaire ▸ cabaret)* sleazy; *(▸ plaisanterie)* cheap

étagement [etaʒmɑ̃] NM *(de collines, de vignobles)* terracing

étager [17] [etaʒe] VT *(mettre par étages)* to stack, to set out *or* to range in tiers; **jardin étagé** terraced garden; **vignes étagées** vines arranged in terraces

VPR **s'étager les maisons s'étageaient le long de la pente** the houses rose up the slope in tiers

étagère [etaʒɛr] NF *(planche)* shelf; *(meuble)* (set of) shelves; **é. encastrée** built-in shelves *or* shelving

étai[1] [etɛ] NM *Naut (cordage)* stay; **voile d'é.** staysail

étai[2] [etɛ] NM *Constr* stay, prop, strut; *Mines* **é. de mine** pit prop

étaie *etc voir* **étayer**

étaiement [etemɑ̃] NM **1** *Constr (d'un mur)* propping-up, shoring-up **2** *(d'un raisonnement)* support, supporting, shoring-up

étain [etɛ̃] NM **1** *(métal blanc)* tin **2** *(vaisselle)* piece of pewterware; **des étains** pewter (pieces), pewterware; **vaisselle d'é.** pewter (plate)

• **en étain** ADJ pewter *(avant n)*

était *etc voir* **être**[1]

étal, -als [etal] NM **1** *(au marché)* (market) stall **2** *(pour découper la viande)* block

étalage [etalaʒ] NM **1** *(des marchandises)* display; *(vitrine)* (display) window; *(stand)* stall; **il y a un bel é. de poisson le vendredi** there is a nice display of fish on Fridays; **faire un é.** *(vitrine)* to dress a window; *(stand)* to set up a stall; **mettre qch à l'é.** to display sth for sale; **é. publicitaire** display advertising

2 *Péj (démonstration)* display, show, parading; **un é. de luxe** a display *or* show of wealth; **faire é. de ses bijoux/son savoir/sa richesse** to show off *or* to parade one's jewels/knowledge/wealth; **faire é. de ses succès** to show off one's success; **faire é. de son argent** to flaunt one's wealth; **faire é. de sa force** to show one's strength; **elle fait é. de sa vie privée** she flaunts her private life

3 *(impôt)* tax paid by street trader

4 *Tex* roving (of flax)

• **étalages** NMPL *Métal* bosh

étalager [17] [etalaʒe] VT *Com* to display, to put on display

étalagiste [etalaʒist] NMF *Com* **1** *(dans un magasin)* window dresser **2** *(marchand)* street trader

étale [etal] ADJ *Géog (mer, marée, fleuve)* slack; *(navire)* becalmed; *(vent)* steady

NM OU NF *Géog* **é. du flot** slack water

étalement [etalmɑ̃] NM **1** *(déploiement ▸ de papiers, d'objets)* spreading (out); *(▸ de marchandises)* displaying **2** *(des vacances, des horaires, des paiements)* staggering, spreading out (**sur** over); *(de travaux)* spreading (out) (**sur** over) **3** *(de connaissances)* showing off, flaunting

étaler [3] [etale] VT **1** *(exposer ▸ marchandise)* to display, to lay out

2 *(exhiber ▸ richesse, luxe)* to flaunt, to show off; **é. ses malheurs** to parade one's misfortunes; **é. ses connaissances** to show off one's knowledge; **é. sa vie privée** to flaunt *or* parade one's private life; **é. une affaire au grand jour** to make a matter public

3 *(disposer à plat ▸ tapis, tissu)* to spread (out); *(▸ plan, carte, journal)* to open *or* to spread (out); *(▸ papiers)* to spread out, to lay out; *(▸ pâte à tarte)* to roll out; **é. ses cartes** *ou* **son jeu** to show one's hand

4 *(appliquer en couche ▸ beurre, miel)* to spread; *(▸ pommade, fond de teint)* to rub *or* to smooth on; *(▸ enduit, peinture)* to apply (**sur** to); **une peinture facile à é.** paint which is easy to apply

5 *(échelonner ▸ dates, rendez-vous)* to spread out; *(▸ vacances, envoi du courrier)* to stagger (**sur** over); *(▸ paiements)* to stagger, to spread out (**sur** over); *(▸ travaux, cours)* to spread (**sur** over); **é. les remboursements (sur plusieurs exercices)** to spread (out) the repayments (over several financial years)

6 *Fam Arg scol* **se faire é. (à un examen)** to flunk an exam

7 *Naut (orage)* to weather out; *(courant, vent)* to stem

VPR **s'étaler 1** *(s'appliquer)* to spread; **une peinture qui s'étale facilement** a paint which goes on easily

2 *(s'étendre ▸ ville, plaine)* to stretch *or* to spread out

3 *(être exhibé)* **son nom s'étale à la une de tous les journaux** his/her name is in *or* is splashed over all the papers

4 *Fam (s'affaler)* **s'é. dans un fauteuil/sur un canapé** to sprawl in an armchair/on a sofa

5 *Fam (tomber)* to take a tumble, to fall (down)

6 *Fam Péj (prendre trop de place)* to spread oneself out; **si tu t'étalais moins, j'aurais la place de m'asseoir** if you didn't take up so much room, I might be able to sit down

7 s'é. sur *(sujet: vacances, paiements)* to be spread over; **les vacances s'étalent sur trois mois** the holiday is spread over three months; **mon crédit s'étale sur cinq ans** my credit extends over five years; **ses rendez-vous s'étalent sur toute la semaine** he has appointments the whole week

étalon[1] [etalɔ̃] NM *Zool (cheval)* stallion, stud; *(âne, taureau)* stud

étalon[2] [etalɔ̃] NM *(référence)* standard; *Fig (modèle)* standard, yardstick; **é. de change-or** gold exchange standard; **é. monétaire** monetary standard; **mètre é.** standard metre

étalonnage [etalɔnaʒ], **étalonnement** [etalɔnmɑ̃] NM **1** *Tech (graduation)* calibration, calibrating

2 *Cin, Phot* calibration

3 *(vérification)* standardization, standardizing; *(d'un instrument)* gauging, testing

4 *Psy (d'un test)* standardization

étalonner [3] [etalɔne] VT **1** *Tech (graduer)* to calibrate

2 *Cin, Phot* to calibrate

3 *(vérifier)* to standardize

4 *Psy (test)* to standardize, to set the standards for

étamage [etamaʒ] NM **1** *Métal (de cuivre)* tinning; *(d'une tôle de fer)* tinplating **2** *(d'une glace)* silvering

étambot [etɑ̃bo] NM *Naut* stern post

étamer [3] [etame] VT **1** *Métal (cuivre etc)* to tin; *(tôle de fer)* to tinplate **2** *(glace)* to silver

étameur [etamœr] NM **1** *Métal* tinsmith **2** *(en miroiterie)* silverer

étamine[1] [etamin] NF *Bot* stamen

étamine[2] [etamin] NF **1** *Tex* challis; *(pour drapeaux)* bunting; *(en tapisserie)* tammy **2** *Culin (pour filtrer)* cheese muslin *or* cloth, butter muslin; **passer qch à** *ou* **par l'é.** *(liquide)* to filter; *(farine)* to sift

étanche [etɑ̃ʃ] ADJ *(chaussure, montre)* waterproof; *(réservoir, toit)* watertight; *(surface)* water-resistant, water-repellent; **é. à l'eau/à l'air/à la poussière** watertight/airtight/dustproof

étanchéité [etɑ̃ʃeite] NF *(d'une montre, de chaussures)* waterproofness; *(d'un réservoir, d'un toit)* watertightness; *(d'un revêtement)* water-resistance; **é. à l'eau/à l'air** watertightness/airtightness; **vérifier l'é. (de)** to check for leaks (in)

étancher [3] [etɑ̃ʃe] VT **1** *(rendre étanche)* to make watertight **2** *(arrêter ▸ sang)* to stanch, to staunch, to stem; *(▸ liquide)* to check the flow of; *(▸ voie d'eau)* to stop up; *(▸ larmes)* to dry; **é. sa soif** to quench *or* to slake one's thirst

étançon [etɑ̃sɔ̃] NM *Constr & Mines* stanchion, strut, post

étançonner [3] [etɑ̃sɔne] VT *Constr & Mines* to shore *or* to prop up, to strut, to stanchion

étang [etɑ̃] NM pond; *(plus grand)* lake

étant [etɑ̃] *voir* **être**[1]

étape [etap] NF **1** *(arrêt)* stop, stopover; **faire é. en chemin** to make a stop, to stop en route; **nous avons fait é. à Lille** we stopped off *or* over at Lille; **brûler une é.** *(train, autobus)* to go past *or* to miss a stop, to fail to stop (at a scheduled stop); *Fig* **brûler les étapes** *(dans son métier)* to move up the ladder very quickly; *(dans une tâche)* to cut corners

2 *(distance)* stage; **un voyage en deux étapes** a trip in two stages; **nous avons fait une é. de 500 kilomètres hier** we covered *or* did 500 kilometres yesterday

3 *Cyclisme* stage; **dans la prochaine é. du Tour de France** in the next stage of the Tour de France

4 *Fig (phase)* phase, stage, step; **les différentes étapes de la vie** the different stages *or* phases of life; **une procédure en deux étapes** a two-stage *or* -step procedure; **par étapes** in stages; **nous allons procéder par étapes** we'll do it in stages *or* step by step

ÉTAT [eta]

• state **A1–4, B**	• condition **A1, 2**
• profession **C1**	• social position **C1**
• account **D1**	• statement **D1, 2**

NM **A.** *MANIÈRE D'ÊTRE PHYSIQUE* **1** *(d'une personne ▸ condition physique)* state, condition; *(▸ apparence)* state; **le malade est dans un é. grave** the patient's condition is serious; **son é. empire/s'améliore** his/her condition is worsening/improving; **tu t'es mis dans un drôle d'é.!** look at the state of you!; **te voilà dans un triste é.!** you're in a sorry *or* sad state!; **être dans un é. second** *(drogué)* to be high; *(en transe)* to be in a trance; **être en é. d'ivresse** *ou* **d'ébriété** to be under the influence (of alcohol), to be inebriated; **être en é. de faire qch** to be fit to do sth; **être hors d'é. de, ne pas être en é. de** to be in no condition to *or* totally unfit to; **tu n'es pas en é. de conduire** you're in no condition to drive *or* not in a fit state to drive; **mettre qn hors d'é. de nuire** *(préventivement)* to make sb harmless; *(après coup)* to neutralize sb; **é. général** general state of health; **é. de santé** (state of) health, condition; *Méd* **é. végétatif chronique** persistent vegetative state; **é. de veille** waking state

2 *(d'un appartement, d'une route, d'une machine, d'un colis)* condition, state; **être en bon/mauvais é.** *(meuble, route, véhicule)* to be in good/poor condition; *(bâtiment)* to be in a good/bad state of repair; *(colis, marchandises)* to be undamaged/damaged; **le mauvais é. des pneus a pu causer l'accident** the bad condition of the tyres might have caused the accident; **vendu à l'é. neuf** *(dans petites annonces)* as new; **réduit à l'é. de cendres/poussière** reduced to ashes/a powder; **en é. de marche** in working order; *Aut* **en é. de rouler** roadworthy; *Naut* **en é. de naviguer** seaworthy; *Aviat* **en é. de voler** airworthy; **être hors d'é. (de fonctionner)** to be out of order; **laisser une pièce en l'é.** to leave a room as it is; **remettre en é.** *(appartement)* to renovate, to refurbish; *(véhicule)* to repair; *(pièce de moteur)* to recondition; **maintenir qch en é.** *(bâtiment, bateau, voiture)* to keep sth in good repair

3 *(situation particulière ▸ d'un développement, d'une technique)* state; **dans l'é. actuel des choses** as things stand at the moment, in the present state of affairs; **dans l'é. actuel de nos connaissances/de la science** in the present state of our knowledge/science; **l'é. de mes finances** my financial situation; **quand il est encore à l'é. larvaire** *ou* **de larve** when it's still a larva *or* in a larval state; **le chat était retourné à l'é. sauvage** the cat had gone back to its wild state; **(en) é. d'alerte/d'urgence** (in a) state of alarm/emergency; **être**

en é. d'arrestation to be under arrest; **je me suis renseigné sur l'é. d'avancement des travaux** I enquired about the progress of the work; **é. de choses** state of things; **é. de fait** (established) fact; **é. de guerre** state of war; **é. de non-droit** = situation in which law and order have broken down; **être en é. de siège** to be under siege

4 *Chim & Phys* state; **é. gazeux/liquide/solide** gaseous/liquid/solid state; **à l'é. brut** *(pétrole)* crude, unrefined, raw; **c'est de la bêtise à l'é. brut** it's plain stupidity; **à l'é. naturel** in its natural state; **à l'é. pur** *(gemme, métal)* pure; **c'est du racisme à l'é. pur** it's out-and-out racism

5 *Ling* **verbe d'é.** stative verb

B. *MANIÈRE D'ÊTRE MORALE, PSYCHOLOGIQUE* state; **être dans un é. de grande excitation** to be in a state of great excitement *or* very excited; **parfois, il tombait dans un é. de grand abattement** sometimes, he would fall into a state of utter dejection; **elle n'est pas dans son é. normal** she's not her normal *or* usual self; **qu'as-tu dit pour la mettre dans cet é.?** what did you say to put her in such a state?; **ne te mets pas dans cet é.!** *(à une personne inquiète, déprimée)* don't worry!; *(à une personne énervée)* don't get so worked up!; **é. de conscience** state of consciousness; **é. d'esprit** state *or* frame of mind; **é. limite** borderline state; *Fam* **être dans tous ses états** *(d'anxiété)* to be beside oneself with anxiety; *(de colère)* to be beside oneself (with anger); *Fam* **son fils n'est pas rentré de l'école, elle est dans tous ses états** her son hasn't returned from school, she's in a terrible state; *Fam* **se mettre dans tous ses états** *(en colère)* to go off the deep end, to go spare

C. *CONDITION SOCIALE* **1** *(profession)* trade, profession; *(statut social)* social position, standing, station; **il avait choisi l'é. ecclésiastique** he had chosen to become a clergyman; **il est cordonnier de son é.** he's a shoemaker by trade

2 *Admin* **(bureau de l')é. civil** registry office; **é. civil** *(d'une personne)* (civil) status

3 *Hist* **les états généraux** the States *or* Estates General; *Fig* **organiser les états généraux de l'enseignement** to organize a conference *or* convention on education

D. *DOCUMENT COMPTABLE OU LÉGAL* **1** *(compte rendu)* account, statement; *(inventaire)* inventory; *(rapport)* form; *(des paiements, des marchandises)* list; **l'é. des dépenses/des recettes** statement of expenses/takings; **figurer sur les états d'une entreprise** to be on a company's payroll; **états de service** *Mil* service record; *(professionnellement)* professional record; **é. des lieux** inventory (of fixtures); **dresser** *ou* **faire un é. des lieux** to draw up an inventory of fixtures; *Fig* to take stock of the situation

2 *Compta* statement; **é. de caisse** cash statement; **états comptables** accounting records; **é. de compte** bank statement, statement of account; *Compta* statement of account; **é. financier** *(rapport)* financial statement; *(situation)* financial standing *or* situation; **é. néant** nil return

3 *(locution)* **faire é. de** *(sondage, témoignages, thèse)* to put forward; *(document)* to refer to; *(fait)* to mention; *(préoccupations)* to mention; **les premières estimations font é. de plusieurs centaines de victimes** according to the initial estimates, several hundred people have been killed; **s'il y a eu un témoin, le rapport de police devrait en faire é.** if there was a witness, the police report should mention *or* state this

• **État** NM *(nation, territoire aux États-Unis)* state; **l'É.** *(autorité centrale)* the State; **É. croupion** rump state; **É. membre** member state; **É. paria** rogue state; **É. paternaliste** nanny state; **É. providence** welfare state

• **état d'âme** NM mood; **elle ne me fait pas part de ses états d'âme** she doesn't confide in me; *Fam* **je me fiche de vos états d'âme!** I don't care whether you're happy about it or not!; **avoir des états d'âme** to suffer from angst; **faire qch sans états d'âme** to do sth without any qualms

• **état de grâce** NM *Rel* state of grace; *Pol* honeymoon period; **être en é. de grâce** to be in a state of grace; **le président est en é. de grâce** the President can do no wrong

---

étatique [etatik] ADJ *Écon & Pol* under state control, state-controlled; **l'appareil é.** the machinery of state

étatisation [etatizasjɔ̃] NF *Écon & Pol* **1** *(gestion par l'État ▸ de l'économie, d'un secteur d'activité)* establishment of state control (**de** of) **2** *(nationalisation ▸ d'une industrie)* nationalization (**de** over) **3** *(dirigisme étatique)* state control

étatisé, -e [etatize] ADJ *Écon & Pol* state-controlled, state-run

étatiser [3] [etatize] VT *Écon & Pol* to bring under state control; **une firme étatisée** a state-owned company

étatisme [etatism] NM *Écon & Pol* state control

étatiste [etatist] ADJ state-control *(avant n)*; **système é.** system of state control

NMF supporter of state control

état-major [etamaʒɔr] *(pl* **états-majors)** NM **1** *Mil (officiers)* general staff; *(locaux)* headquarters; **officier d'é.** staff officer **2** *(direction ▸ d'une entreprise)* management; *(▸ d'un parti politique)* leadership; **le président et son é.** the president and his advisers

États-Unis [etazyni] NMPL **les É. (d'Amérique)** the United States (of America)

étau, -x [eto] NM **1** *Tech* vice; **é. d'établi** bench vice **2** *Fig* stranglehold; **être pris dans un é.** to be in a stranglehold; **l'é. se resserre (sur les terroristes)** the noose is tightening around the terrorists; *Fam* **avoir la tête comme dans un é.** to have a splitting headache

étayage [etejaʒ], **étayement** [etejmɑ̃] NM **1** *Constr (d'un mur)* propping-up, shoring-up **2** *(d'un raisonnement)* support, supporting, shoring-up

étayer [11] [eteje] VT **1** *Constr (mur)* to prop *or* to shore up **2** *(raisonnement, théorie)* to support, to back up; *(thèse, argument)* to support; **pour é. ses allégations** in support of his allegations

VPR **s'étayer s'é. sur** *(s'appuyer sur)* to be based on

etc. *(abrév écrite* **et cetera, et cætera)** etc

et cætera, et cetera [etsetera] ADV et cetera, and so on (and so forth)

été[1] [ete] PP *voir* **être**[1]

été[2] [ete] NM summer; **en é.** in (the) summer *or* summertime; **pendant l'é. 2004** in the summer of 2004; **l'é. prochain** next summer; **é. comme hiver, j'habite la campagne** I live in the country winter and summer alike; **l'é. est ma saison préférée** summer *or* summertime is my favourite season; **é. indien** *ou Can* **des Indiens** Indian summer; **l'é. de la Saint-Martin** Saint Martin's summer

• **d'été** ADJ **robe d'é.** summer dress; **nuit/journée d'é.** summer's night/day; **temps d'é.** summer weather; **heure d'é.** summer time, *Am* daylight (saving) time

éteignait *etc voir* **éteindre**

éteignoir [etɛɲwar] NM **1** *(instrument)* extinguisher; **en é.** conical **2** *Fam (rabat-joie)* wet blanket, spoilsport, killjoy

éteindre [81] [etɛ̃dr] VT **1** *(arrêter la combustion de ▸ cigarette, incendie)* to put out, to extinguish; *(▸ bougie)* to put *or* to blow out; *(▸ gaz, chauffage)* to turn off; *Ordinat* to power down, to shut down

2 *(phare, lampe, lumière)* to turn *or* to switch off; *(radio, télévision)* to turn off; *Fam* **va é. la chambre** switch off the light in the bedroom

3 *(faire perdre son éclat à ▸ couleur)* to fade, to soften

4 *Compta & Fin (annuler ▸ dette, rente)* to wipe out

5 *Littéraire (soif)* to quench, to slake; *(désirs, sentiments)* to kill; *(querelle)* to put an end to

USAGE ABSOLU to switch off (the lights) (**dans** in)

VPR **s'éteindre 1** *(feu, gaz, chauffage)* to go out; *(bougie)* to blow out; *(cigarette)* to burn out; *(volcan)* to die down; **laisser s'é. le feu** to let the fire go out

2 *(lampe, lumière)* to go out; *(radio, télévision)* to go off

3 *Fig (s'affaiblir ▸ couleur)* to fade; *(▸ son, rires)* to die away, to subside; *(▸ voix)* to die away; **le jour s'éteint** daylight is failing *or* fading

4 *Littéraire (se dissiper ▸ ardeur, amour)* to fade away; *(▸ colère)* to abate, to cool down

5 *Euph (mourir ▸ personne)* to pass away

6 *(race)* to die out, to become extinct

éteint, -e [etɛ̃, -ɛ̃t] ADJ **1 être é.** *(incendie, cigarette, lampe)* to be out; *(électricité, radio)* to be off; **c'était é. chez les voisins** the neighbours' lights were out

2 *(race, famille, volcan)* extinct

3 *(sans éclat ▸ regard)* dull, *Littéraire* lacklustre; *(▸ visage, esprit)* dull; *(▸ couleur)* faded; **d'une voix éteinte** faintly

4 *(chaux)* slaked

étendard [etɑ̃dar] NM **1** *Mil* standard; *Fig* **lever l'é. de la révolte** to raise the standard of revolt; *Fig* **se ranger sous l'é. de qn** to join sb's camp **2** *Bot* standard, *Spéc* vexillum

étendoir [etɑ̃dwar] NM **1** *(corde)* clothes line; *(dispositif pliable)* clotheshorse **2** *(lieu)* drying shed

étendre [73] [etɑ̃dr] VT **1** *(beurre, miel)* to spread; *(pommade, fond de teint)* to rub *or* to smooth on

2 *(tapis, tissu)* to unroll; *(nappe)* to spread (out); *(plan, carte, journal)* to open *or* to spread (out); *(pâte à tarte)* to roll out; **é. le bras** to stretch out *or* reach out (one's arm); **é. les bras/jambes** to stretch (out) one's arms/legs

3 *(faire sécher)* **é. du linge** *(dehors)* to put the washing out to dry, to hang out the washing; *(à l'intérieur)* to hang up the washing

4 *(allonger ▸ personne)* to stretch out; **é. un blessé sur une civière** to place an injured person on a stretcher; **il m'a fait é. sur le sol** he made me lie down on the ground; *Fam* **é. qn (par terre) d'un coup de poing** to knock sb down *or* flat, to deck sb

5 *(élargir ▸ pouvoir, propriété)* to extend; *(▸ recherches)* to broaden, to extend; *(▸ cercle d'amis)* to extend, to widen; **é. son vocabulaire** to increase *or* to extend one's vocabulary; **la société cherche à é. ses activités** the company is trying to branch out; **é. une grève au secteur privé** to extend a strike to the private sector

6 *(diluer ▸ peinture)* to dilute, to thin down; *(▸ sauce)* to thin out *or* down, to water down; *(▸ vin)* to water down; **é. d'eau une boisson** to water down a drink

7 *Fam (vaincre)* to thrash; **se faire é.** *(à un match de boxe)* to get knocked *or* laid out; *(aux élections)* to be trounced; *(à un examen)* to be failed

8 *Ordinat (mémoire)* to upgrade

VPR **s'étendre 1** *(dans l'espace)* to extend, to stretch; **la zone pluvieuse s'étendra du nord au sud** the rainy zone will stretch from North to South; **la ville s'étendait à l'infini** the city stretched out endlessly; **notre parc s'étend sur plusieurs hectares** our grounds spread over several acres; **mes connaissances ne s'étendent pas jusque-là** my knowledge doesn't stretch that far

2 *(dans le temps)* to extend; **les vacances s'étendent sur trois mois** the *Br* holiday *or Am* vacation stretches over three months

3 *(se développer ▸ épidémie, grève, incendie)* to spread; *(▸ cercle d'amis)* to widen; *(▸ culture, vocabulaire)* to increase, to broaden; *(▸ fortune, entreprise)* to expand, to grow larger; *(▸ influence)* to spread, to widen, to increase

4 *(s'allonger ▸ malade)* to stretch out, to lie down

5 s'é. sur *(évoquer en détail)* to enlarge on; **je ne m'étendrai pas davantage sur ce sujet** I won't discuss this subject at any greater length; **il ne s'est pas étendu sur les raisons de son absence** he didn't enlarge *or* expand on the reasons for his absence

étendu, -e[1] [etɑ̃dy] ADJ **1** *(vaste ▸ territoire)* big, wide, spread-out; *(▸ banlieue)* sprawling; **la ville/banlieue est très étendue** the town/suburb is very spread-out *or* covers a large area

2 *(considérable ▸ pouvoir, connaissances)* extensive, wide-ranging; *(▸ vocabulaire)* wide, extensive; *(▸ influence)* far-reaching, widespread; *(▸ dégâts)* extensive

3 *(étiré)* **les bras étendus** with outstretched arms; **les jambes étendues** with legs stretched out; **é. sur un divan** stretched out *or* lying on a couch; **é. sur le dos** lying (flat) on one's back

4 *(dilué ▸ gén)* diluted (**de** with); *(▸ vin, sauce)* watered-down; *(▸ peinture, couleur)* thinned-down

étendue[2] [etɑ̃dy] NF **1** *(surface)* area, stretch; *(d'eau, de sable)* expanse, stretch; *(de terre)* expanse, tract; **la forêt occupe une grande** *ou* **vaste**

é. dans cette région the forest covers a huge area in this region; **une é. désertique** a stretch of desert

2 *(dimension)* area; **un domaine d'une grande é.** a large estate; **quelle est l'é. de ce terrain?** how large is this piece of land?; **sur toute l'é. du pays** throughout the country; **sur toute l'é. du champ** over the entire field; **sur une grande é.** over a wide area

3 *(durée)* **l'é. d'un discours** the length of a speech; **sur une é. de dix ans** over a period of ten years

4 *(ampleur ▸ gén)* extent; *(▸ de connaissances, de vocabulaire, d'un pouvoir)* extent, scope; **pour évaluer** *ou* **mesurer l'é. du désastre** to assess the extent of the disaster; **ses propos révèlent l'é. de sa culture/de son ignorance** his/her remarks show the extent of his/her knowledge/of his/her ignorance; **te rends-tu compte de l'é. de ton erreur?** do you realize the extent *or* the magnitude of your error?

5 *Mus (d'une voix, d'un instrument)* range

6 *Phil* extension

éternel, -elle [etɛrnɛl] **ADJ 1** *Phil & Rel* eternal; *(vie)* eternal, everlasting; *(jeunesse)* eternal; **neiges éternelles** eternal snows **2** *Fig (regrets)* eternal, endless; *(amour)* eternal, undying; **je lui voue une reconnaissance éternelle** I'll be for ever *or* eternally grateful to him/her; **je ne suis pas é.** I won't live forever; *Fig Littéraire* **dans la nuit éternelle** in the endless night **3** *(avant le nom) (invariable)* **c'est un é. mécontent** he's perpetually discontented, he's never happy *or* satisfied; **leurs éternelles discussions politiques** their endless *or* interminable political discussions; **avec son éternelle petite robe noire** with her inevitable little black dress

NM l'é. féminin the eternal feminine

• **Éternel NM l'É.** the Eternal; *Fam* **grand voyageur/menteur devant l'É.** great *or* inveterate traveller/liar

éternellement [etɛrnɛlmɑ̃] **ADV 1** *Phil & Rel* eternally **2** *(durer, rester)* for ever; **je l'aimerai é.** I will always love him/her, I'll love him/her forever; **je ne l'attendrai pas é.** I'm not going to wait for him/her for ever; **avec ses cheveux é. ébouriffés** with his/her perpetually tousled hair; **je vous en serais é. reconnaissant** I would be eternally grateful (to you)

éterniser [3] [etɛrnize] **VT 1** *Péj (prolonger ▸ discussion, crise)* to drag *or* to draw out **2** *Littéraire (perpétuer)* **é. le nom/la mémoire de qn** to immortalize *or* to perpetuate sb's name/memory

VPR s'éterniser *Péj* **1** *(durer ▸ crise, discussion)* to drag on **2** *Fam (s'attarder)* **les invités se sont éternisés, j'ai cru qu'ils n'allaient jamais partir!** the guests overstayed their welcome, I thought they'd never leave!; **on ne va pas s'é. ici** we're not going to stay here for ever

éternité [etɛrnite] **NF 1** *Phil & Rel* eternity **2** *(longue durée)* eternity; **il y avait une é. que je ne l'avais vu** I hadn't seen him for ages *or* an eternity; **j'ai attendu pendant une é.** I waited an eternity, I waited for ages; **la construction du stade va durer une é.** it will take forever to build the stadium

• **de toute éternité ADV** *Littéraire* from time immemorial

éternuement [etɛrnymɑ̃] **NM** sneeze

éternuer [7] [etɛrnɥe] **VI** to sneeze

êtes *voir* **être**[1]

étêtage [etetaʒ], **étêtement** [etɛtmɑ̃] **NM** *Hort* pollarding

étêter [4] [etete] **VT** *Hort (arbre)* to pollard; *Culin (poisson)* to cut off the head of; *(clou, épingle)* to knock the head off

éthane [etan] **NM** *Chim* ethane

éthanol [etanɔl] **NM** *Chim* ethanol

éther [etɛr] **NM** *Littéraire & Chim* ether

éthéré, -e [etere] **ADJ** *Littéraire & Chim* ethereal

Ethernet® [etɛrnɛt] **NM** *Ordinat* Ethernet®

éthéromane [eterɔman] *Méd* **ADJ** addicted to ether

NMF ether addict

éthicien, -enne [etisjɛ̃, -ɛn] **NM,F** ethicist

Éthiopie [etjɔpi] **NF** *Géog* **l'É.** Ethiopia

éthiopien, -enne [etjɔpjɛ̃, -ɛn] **ADJ** Ethiopian

• **Éthiopien, -enne NM,F** Ethiopian

éthique [etik] **ADJ** ethic, ethical

NF 1 *Phil* ethics *(singulier)* **2** *(code moral)* ethic; **é. biomédicale** bioethics

ethnie [ɛtni] **NF** ethnic group

ethnique [ɛtnik] **ADJ** ethnic

ethnocentrisme [ɛtnɔsɑ̃trism] **NM** *Pol* ethnocentrism

ethnographe [ɛtnɔgraf] **NMF** *Hist* ethnographer

ethnographie [ɛtnɔgrafi] **NF** *Hist* ethnography

ethnographique [ɛtnɔgrafik] **ADJ** *Hist* ethnographic, ethnographical

ethnolinguistique [ɛtnɔlɛ̃gɥistik] *Ling* **ADJ** ethnolinguistic

NF ethnolinguistics *(singulier)*

ethnologie [ɛtnɔlɔʒi] **NF** ethnology

ethnologique [ɛtnɔlɔʒik] **ADJ** ethnologic, ethnological

ethnologue [ɛtnɔlɔg] **NMF** ethnologist

éthologie [etɔlɔʒi] **NF** *Zool* ethology

éthologique [etɔlɔʒik] **ADJ** *Zool* ethological

éthologiste [etɔlɔʒist], **éthologue** [etɔlɔg] **NMF** ethologist

éthyle [etil] **NM** *Chim* ethyl

éthylène [etilɛn] **NM** *Chim* ethylene

éthylique [etilik] *Chim* **ADJ** ethyl *(avant n)*, ethylic; **alcool é.** ethyl alcohol

NMF alcoholic

éthylisme [etilism] **NM** *Méd* alcoholism

éthylomètre [etilɔmɛtr], **éthylotest** [etilɔtɛst] **NM** *Br* breathalyser, *Am* Breathalyzer®

étiage [etjaʒ] **NM** *Géog* low water level *or* mark

étincelant, -e [etɛ̃slɑ̃, -ɑ̃t] **ADJ 1** *(brillant ▸ diamant, étoile)* sparkling, gleaming, twinkling; *(▸ métal, lac)* sparkling, glittering; *(▸ soleil)* brightly shining; *(bien lavé ▸ vaisselle)* shining, sparkling, gleaming; **un diamant plus é. que celui-là** a diamond that sparkles more than that one; **la mer étincelante** the sparkling sea; **le lac était é. sous le soleil** the lake sparkled in the sunlight; **sapin de Noël é.** Christmas tree glittering with lights; **é. de propreté** gleaming **2** *(vif ▸ regard, œil)* sparkling, twinkling; **les yeux étincelants de joie/de plaisir** eyes sparkling *or* twinkling with joy/pleasure; **les yeux étincelants de colère/de haine** eyes glinting with rage/with hate **3** *(plein de brio ▸ conversation, esprit, style)* brilliant, sparkling; *(personne)* dazzling, brilliant

étinceler [24] [etɛ̃sle] **VI 1** *(diamant)* to sparkle, to glitter; *(étoile)* to sparkle, to gleam, to twinkle; *(mer, lac)* to sparkle, to glitter; *(soleil)* to shine brightly; *(vaisselle)* to shine, to sparkle, to gleam; *(métal, lame)* to gleam; **la mer étincelait** the sea was sparkling; **le sapin de Noël étincelait** the Christmas tree was glittering with lights; **é. de propreté** to be gleaming, to be sparkling clean; **é. de blancheur** to be gleaming white **2** *(regard, œil)* to sparkle, to glitter; **ses yeux étincelaient de colère/jalousie/passion** his/her eyes glittered with anger/jealousy/passion; **ses yeux étincelaient de convoitise** his/her eyes gleamed with envy **3** *(conversation, style)* to sparkle, to be brilliant

étincelle [etɛ̃sɛl] **NF 1** *(parcelle incandescente)* spark; **é. électrique** electric spark; **faire des étincelles** to throw off sparks; *Fig (avoir du succès)* to cause a huge sensation, to be a big success; *Hum* **on ne peut pas dire qu'il ait fait des étincelles pendant son mandat** he didn't exactly set the world on fire during his term of office; **c'est l'é. qui a mis le feu aux poudres** it was this which sparked everything off **2** *(lueur)* spark, sparkle; **jeter** *ou* **lancer des étincelles** to sparkle; **ses yeux jetaient des étincelles** *(de joie)* his/her eyes shone with joy; *(de colère)* his/her eyes flashed with rage **3** *(bref élan)* **é. d'intelligence** spark of intelligence; **il a eu une é. de génie** he had a stroke of genius, he had a brilliant idea

étincellement [etɛ̃sɛlmɑ̃] **NM** *(d'un diamant)* sparkle, glitter; *(d'une étoile)* sparkle, gleam, twinkle; *(d'un métal, d'une lame)* gleam; *(de la mer, d'un lac)* glittering *(UNCOUNT)*, sparkling *(UNCOUNT)*; *(des yeux ▸ de joie)* sparkle, twinkle; *(▸ de colère)* glint

étincellera *etc voir* **étinceler**

étiolement [etjɔlmɑ̃] **NM 1** *Agr & Bot* bleaching, blanching, *Spéc* etiolation; **pour empêcher l'é. de vos plantes** to stop your plants going leggy *or* straggly **2** *(affaiblissement ▸ d'une personne)* decline, weakening

étioler [3] [etjɔle] **VT 1** *Agr & Bot (plante)* to make leggy; *Agr (intentionnellement)* to bleach, to blanch, *Spéc* to etiolate **2** *(personne)* to make weak *or* pale *or* sickly

VPR s'étioler 1 *Agr & Bot* to wilt, to blanch, *Spéc* to etiolate **2** *(s'affaiblir ▸ personne)* to decline, to become weak

étiologie [etjɔlɔʒi] **NF** *Méd* aetiology

étique [etik] **ADJ** *Littéraire* skinny, emaciated, scrawny

étiquetage [etiktaʒ] **NM** *Com (d'une marchandise)* labelling; *(d'un colis, de bagages)* ticketing, labelling; **é. de la composition** ingredient labelling; **é. préventif** precautionary labelling; **é. du prix** price marking *or* labelling

étiqueter [27] [etikte] **VT 1** *Com (marchandise)* to mark, to label; *(colis, bagages)* to ticket, to label **2** *Péj (cataloguer)* to label; **j'ai été étiqueté comme écologiste** I was labelled as a green

étiqueteur, -euse [etiktœr, -øz] **NM,F** labeller

• **étiqueteuse NF** *(machine)* labelling machine

étiquette [etikɛt] **NF 1** *(marque ▸ de colis, de bagages)* label; *(▸ portant le prix)* ticket; **coller une é. sur un paquet** to label a parcel, to stick a label on a parcel; **é. autocollante** *ou* **gommée** sticky label, sticker; **é. de prix** price ticket, price tag, price label

2 *(appartenance)* label; **mettre une é. à qn** to label sb; **on a collé cette é. socialiste à notre journal** our paper has been labelled as socialist; **é. politique** political affiliation; **sans é. politique** *(candidat, journal)* independent

3 *Ordinat* label

4 *(protocole)* **l'é.** etiquette; **é. de Cour** court etiquette

étirable [etirabl] **ADJ** stretchable

étirage [etiraʒ] **NM 1** *Tech (du verre, du métal, du fil)* drawing **2** *(du tissu, des peaux)* stretching

étirement [etirmɑ̃] **NM** *(des membres, du corps)* stretching; **faire des étirements** to do stretching exercises

étirer [3] [etire] **VT 1** *(allonger ▸ membres, cou)* to stretch **2** *Tech (verre, métal)* to draw (out) **3** *Tex* to stretch

VPR s'étirer 1 *(personne, animal)* to stretch (out)

2 *(s'allonger ▸ tissu, vêtement)* to stretch

3 *(s'éterniser ▸ journée, récit)* to drag on (forever)

4 *(▸ peloton, convoi)* to stretch out

étoffe [etɔf] **NF 1** *Tex* material, fabric; **acheter de l'é.** to buy material; **des étoffes somptueuses** rich fabrics **2** *(calibre ▸ d'un professionnel, d'un artiste)* calibre; **il est d'une autre/de la même é.** he's in a different/the same league; **manquer d'é.** *(personne)* to lack calibre; *(film, roman)* to lack substance, to be thin *or* insubstantial; **avoir l'é. de** to have the makings of; **il a l'é. d'un héros** he has the makings of a hero, he's the stuff heroes are made of; **avoir l'é. d'un chef** to be leadership material

étoffé, -e [etɔfe] **ADJ 1** *(roman, récit)* full of substance, well-rounded; *(discours)* weighty **2** *(voix)* deep, sonorous **3** *(personne)* **il est é. maintenant** he has filled out

étoffer [3] [etɔfe] **VT 1** *(faire grossir)* to put weight on; **son séjour à la campagne l'a étoffé** his spell in the country has made him fill out a bit **2** *(renforcer ▸ effectifs, équipe)* to beef up **3** *(développer ▸ roman, personnage)* to flesh *or* to fill out, to give substance to

VPR s'étoffer to fill out, to put on weight

étoile [etwal] **NF 1** *Astron* star; **contempler** *ou* **observer les étoiles** to stargaze; **ciel parsemé d'étoiles** starry sky, sky studded with stars; **une nuit/un ciel sans étoiles** a starless night/sky; **à la clarté des étoiles** in the starlight; *Fam* **voir les étoiles en plein midi** to see stars; **é. géante/naine** giant/dwarf star; **é. du matin/soir** morning/evening star; **é. du berger** morning star; **é. filante** shooting star; **é. Polaire** pole star

2 *(insigne)* star; **hôtel trois/quatre étoiles** three-star/four-star hotel; **c'est un deux étoiles** it has a two-star rating; **général à quatre étoiles** four-star general; *Hist* **l'É. jaune** the yellow star; *Rel* **l'É. de David** the Star of David

3 *(destin)* stars, fate; **son é. blanchit** *ou* **pâlit** her fortunes are waning, her star is fading; **né sous une bonne/mauvaise é.** born under a lucky/an unlucky star; **croire** *ou* **avoir foi en son é.** *ou* **en sa bonne é.** to believe in *or* trust to luck

4 *Vieilli (célébrité)* star; **une é. du cinéma** a movie star; **c'est une é. montante** he's/she's a rising star; **elle est l'é. du spectacle** she's the star of the show

5 *(en danse)* prima ballerina

6 *Typ* star, asterisk

7 *(au ski)* badge (of achievement); **première/deuxième/troisième é.** beginners/intermediate/advanced badge of proficiency

8 *Zool* **é. de mer** starfish

• **à la belle étoile** ADV *(coucher, dormir)* (out) in the open, outside

• **en étoile** ADV **disposé en é.** star-shaped; **carrefour en é.** multi-road junction; *Ordinat* **connecté en é.** in a star configuration

étoilé, -e [etwale] ADJ **1** *(ciel)* starry, star-studded; *(nuit)* starry **2** *(fêlé ▸ pare-brise)* starred

étoiler [3] [etwale] VT *(fêler ▸ vitre)* to craze, to crack

VPR **s'étoiler 1** *Littéraire (ciel)* to become starry **2** *(vitre)* to crack

étole [etɔl] NF *(gén) & Rel* stole

étonnamment [etɔnamɑ̃] ADV surprisingly; *(plus fort)* amazingly, astonishingly

étonnant, -e [etɔnɑ̃, -ɑ̃t] ADJ **1** *(remarquable ▸ personne, acteur, mémoire)* remarkable, astonishing; *(▸ roman)* great, fantastic **2** *(surprenant)* surprising; *(plus fort)* amazing, astonishing; **c'est é. de sa part** it's quite amazing, coming from him/her; **ce n'est pas é. qu'il soit malade** it's not surprising *or* it's no wonder that he's ill; **rien d'é. à ce qu'il ait divorcé** no wonder he got divorced; **ça n'a rien d'é.** it's no wonder; **chose étonnante, il est arrivé à l'heure** astonishingly *or* amazingly *or* surprisingly (enough), he arrived on time

NM **l'é. est qu'il soit venu** the astonishing *or* amazing *or* surprising thing is that he came

étonné, -e [etɔne] ADJ surprised; *(plus fort)* astonished, amazed (**de qch** at sth; **de voir** to see); **prendre un air é., faire l'é.** to act surprised; **il avait l'air é.** he looked surprised; **un regard é.** a surprised look; *(plus fort)* a look of astonishment *or* amazement, an astonished look

étonnement [etɔnmɑ̃] NM surprise; *(plus fort)* astonishment, amazement; **je fus frappé d'é. en apprenant la nouvelle** I was astonished when I heard the news; **à mon grand é.** to my great surprise; **imaginez (quel a été) mon é. quand...** imagine my surprise *or* astonishment when...

étonner [3] [etɔne] VT to surprise; *(plus fort)* to amaze, to astonish; **je suis étonné de ses progrès** I'm amazed at the progress he's/she's made; **cet enfant m'étonne de plus en plus** this child never ceases to amaze me; **tu m'étonneras toujours!** you never cease to astonish me!; **ce que je vais vous dire va probablement vous é.** what I have to say may come as a surprise; **ça m'étonne qu'elle ne t'ait pas appelé** I'm surprised she didn't call you; **plus rien ne m'étonne** nothing surprises me anymore; **cela m'étonnerait** I'd be surprised; *Fam* **alors ça, ça m'étonnerait** that'll be the day; **cela ne m'étonnerait pas** it wouldn't surprise me, I wouldn't be the least bit surprised; **ça ne m'étonne pas du tout** it doesn't surprise me in the least, I'm not the least bit surprised; **ça ne m'étonne pas de toi!** you do surprise me!; *Ironique* **tu m'étonnes!** you DO surprise me!, you don't say!

VPR **s'étonner** to be surprised (**de** at); **ne t'étonne pas si elle te quitte** don't be surprised if she leaves you; **je ne m'étonne plus de rien** nothing surprises me any more; **je m'étonne qu'il ne soit pas venu** I'm surprised he didn't show up; **comment s'é. qu'il ait refusé?** is it any wonder that he refused?

étouffant, -e [etufɑ̃, -ɑ̃t] ADJ **1** *(oppressant ▸ lieu, climat, ambiance)* stifling; *(▸ temps)* oppressive, sultry; **une journée étouffante** a stifling hot day **2** *(indigeste ▸ mets)* stodgy, heavy

étouffe-chrétien [etufkretjɛ̃] *Fam* ADJ heavy[□], stodgy[□]; **c'est un peu é., sa quiche** his/her quiche is a bit stodgy

NM INV heavy *or* stodgy food[□]

étouffée [etufe] **à l'étouffée** ADJ steamed *(in a tightly shut saucepan)*

ADV **cuire à l'é.** to steam *(in a tightly shut saucepan)*

étouffement [etufmɑ̃] NM **1** *(asphyxie)* suffocation; **mourir d'é.** to die of *or* from suffocation **2** *(respiration difficile)* breathlessness; *(crise)* fit of breathlessness **3** *(d'une rumeur)* stifling; *(d'un scandale)* hushing-up, covering-up

étouffer [3] [etufe] VT **1** *(asphyxier ▸ personne, animal)* to suffocate, to smother; **é. qn de baisers** to smother sb with kisses; **le bébé a été étouffé** *(accident)* the baby suffocated to death; *(meurtre)* the baby was smothered; **mourir étouffé** to die of suffocation; **ne le serre pas si fort, tu l'étouffes!** don't hug him so hard, you'll smother him!; *Fam Hum* **ce n'est pas la politesse qui l'étouffe** politeness isn't exactly his/her strong point; *Fam Hum* **ce ne sont pas les scrupules qui l'étouffent** he's/she's not exactly over-scrupulous; *Fam* **ça t'étoufferait de dire bonjour?** would it kill you to say hello?

2 *(oppresser ▸ sujet: famille, entourage)* to smother; *(▸ sujet: ambiance)* to stifle; **le milieu familial l'étouffait** he/she found the family circle stifling; **cette chaleur m'étouffe** the heat is stifling (me)

3 *(émouvoir fortement)* **la colère/l'émotion l'étouffe** he's/she's choking with anger/emotion

4 *(arrêter, atténuer ▸ feu)* to put out, to smother; *(▸ bruit)* to muffle, to deaden; *(▸ cris, pleurs, sentiment, rire)* to stifle, to hold back; *(▸ bâillement)* to stifle, to smother, to suppress; *(▸ sanglot)* to stifle, to choke back; *(▸ voix)* to lower; *(▸ révolte, rumeur)* to quash; *(▸ scandale)* to hush *or* to cover up; *Mus* to damp; *Élec (étincelle)* to quench; **il a réussi à faire é. l'affaire** he managed to get the affair hushed up

VI **1** *(s'asphyxier)* to choke; **j'ai failli é. en avalant de travers** I almost choked on my food; **é. de colère/jalousie/rire** to choke with anger/jealousy/laughter **2** *(avoir chaud)* to suffocate, to be gasping for air **3** *(être oppressé)* to feel stifled; **j'étouffe dans ce milieu** this atmosphere stifles me

VPR **s'étouffer** to suffocate; *(en mangeant)* to choke; **une sardine et une demi-tomate, on ne risque pas de s'é.!** a sardine and half a tomato! there's no fear of us choking on that!; **arrête de la faire rire, tu vas la faire s'é.!** stop making her laugh, you'll make her choke *or* she'll choke!

étouffoir [etufwar] NM **1** *(pour la braise)* charcoal extinguisher **2** *Mus* damper **3** *Fam (lieu)* oven; **c'est un é. ici!** it's like an oven in here!

étourderie [eturdəri] NF **1** *(faute)* careless mistake **2** *(caractère)* carelessness; **il est d'une é. incroyable** he is incredibly scatterbrained *or Fam* scatty; **faute d'é.** foolish mistake

• **par étourderie** ADV carelessly, without thinking

étourdi, -e [eturdi] ADJ *(personne)* careless *(acte, réponse)* thoughtless

NM,F scatterbrain

étourdiment [eturdimɑ̃] ADV thoughtlessly, carelessly, foolishly

étourdir [32] [eturdir] VT **1** *(assommer)* to stun, to daze; **le coup l'avait un peu étourdi** he was slightly dazed by the blow **2** *(griser ▸ sujet: vertige, sensation, alcool)* to make dizzy *or* light-headed; *(▸ sujet: odeur)* to overpower; **le succès l'étourdissait** success had gone to his/her head; **je suis tout étourdi** my head's spinning **3** *(abasourdir ▸ sujet: bruit)* to deafen

VPR **s'étourdir s'é. dans le plaisir** to live a life of pleasure; **s'é. de paroles** to get drunk on words

étourdissant, -e [eturdisɑ̃, -ɑ̃t] ADJ **1** *(bruit)* deafening, ear-splitting **2** *(extraordinaire ▸ beauté, créativité, activité)* stunning; **il est é. de beauté** he's stunningly handsome; **nous roulions à une vitesse étourdissante** we were driving at breakneck speed

étourdissement [eturdismɑ̃] NM **1** *(vertige)* fit of giddiness *or* dizziness, dizzy spell; *Méd* fainting fit, blackout; **avoir un é.** to feel giddy *or* dizzy; **cela me donne des étourdissements** it makes me feel giddy *or* dizzy, it makes my head spin *or* swim **2** *Littéraire (griserie)* exhilaration

étourneau, -x [eturno] NM **1** *Orn* starling **2** *Fam (étourdi)* birdbrain

étrange [etrɑ̃ʒ] ADJ strange, odd; **quelle é. coïncidence!** what a strange coincidence!; **chose é., elle a dit oui** strangely enough, she said yes; **aussi é. que cela puisse paraître...** strange as it may seem...

étrangement [etrɑ̃ʒmɑ̃] ADV **1** *(bizarrement)* oddly, strangely; **elle était é. habillée** she was oddly dressed; **ressembler é. à qn/qch** to look suspiciously like sb/sth **2** *(inhabituellement)* strangely; **il est é. silencieux** he's strangely silent

étranger, -ère [etrɑ̃ʒe, -ɛr] ADJ **1** *(d'un autre pays)* foreign

2 *(extérieur à un groupe)* **des éléments étrangers se sont introduits dans l'enceinte de l'école** outsiders entered the school premises; **je suis é. à leur communauté** I'm not a member of *or* I don't belong to their community; **elle est étrangère au projet** she isn't involved in the plan; **des personnes étrangères au service** non-members of staff; **entrée interdite à toute personne étrangère au service** no entry to unauthorized personnel

3 *(non familier ▸ voix, visage, région, sentiment)* unknown, unfamiliar (**à** to); **ce sentiment/visage ne m'est pas é.** that feeling/face is not unknown to me; **la haine lui est étrangère** he/she doesn't know what hatred is

4 *(sans rapport)* **je suis complètement é. à cette affaire** I'm in no way involved in *or* I have nothing to do with this business

NM,F **1** *(habitant d'un autre pays)* foreigner, alien **2** *(inconnu)* stranger; **je suis devenu un é. pour elle** I'm like a stranger to her now

NM **l'é.** *(pays)* foreign countries; **ça vient de l'é.** it comes from abroad

• **à l'étranger** ADV abroad; **aller/vivre à l'é.** to go/live abroad; **voyages à l'é.** foreign travel

> Attention: ne pas confondre **foreigner** et **stranger** lorsqu'on traduit le nom **étranger**. **Foreigner** s'applique uniquement à quelqu'un venant d'un autre pays, alors que **stranger** désigne quelqu'un d'extérieur à un groupe donné.

étrangeté [etrɑ̃ʒte] NF *(singularité ▸ d'un discours, d'un comportement)* strangeness, oddness

étranglé, -e [etrɑ̃gle] ADJ **1** *(rauque ▸ voix, son)* tight, strangled **2** *(resserré ▸ rue, passage)* narrow; *(taille)* nipped-in **3** *Méd (hernie)* strangulated

étranglement [etrɑ̃gləmɑ̃] NM **1** *(strangulation)* strangling, strangulation; *(à la lutte)* stranglehold

2 *(étouffement, resserrement)* tightening, constriction; *(de la taille)* narrowing; **j'ai compris à l'é. de sa voix que...** the tightness in his/her voice told me that...

3 *(passage étroit)* bottleneck; *(d'une rivière)* narrow part, narrows; **grâce à l'é. du tuyau** owing to the narrower section of the pipe

4 *Littéraire (restriction ▸ des libertés)* stifling

5 *Méd* strangulation; **é. herniaire** strangulated hernia

6 *Aut & Tech* throttling; **soupape d'é.** throttle valve

étrangler [3] [etrɑ̃gle] VT **1** *(tuer ▸ intentionnellement)* to strangle; *(▸ par accident)* to strangle, to choke; **elle a été étranglée par son écharpe** she was strangled by her scarf

2 *(serrer)* to choke, to constrict; **ce col roulé m'étrangle** this turtleneck is choking me *or* is too tight around my neck; **une grosse ceinture lui étrangle la taille** she wears a wide belt pulled in tight around the waist

3 *(faire balbutier ▸ sujet: colère, peur)* to choke; **la colère l'étrangle** he/she is choking with rage; **il répondit d'une voix étranglée par l'émotion** he replied in a voice choking *or* tight with emotion

4 *(ruiner)* to decimate, to squeeze out of existence; **les supermarchés ont étranglé le petit commerce** supermarkets have decimated small businesses

5 *Littéraire (restreindre ▸ libertés)* to stifle

6 *Tech (vapeur etc)* to throttle; *Aut* **é. le moteur** to throttle (down) the engine

VPR s'étrangler 1 *(personne)* to choke; **s'é. avec un os** to choke on a bone; **s'é. de rire/colère** to choke with laughter/anger; **s'é. d'indignation** to be speechless with indignation **2** *(voix)* to choke; **un sanglot s'étrangla dans sa gorge** a sob caught *or* died in his/her throat; **les mots se sont étranglés dans sa gorge** the words died on his/her lips, he/she couldn't get the words out **3** *(chemin, rue, vallée)* to form a bottleneck, to narrow (down); *(rivière)* to narrow

étrangleur, -euse [etrɑ̃glœr, -øz] **NM,F** strangler
NM *Aut & Tech* throttle

étrave [etrav] **NF** *Naut* stem

ÊTRE[1] **[2]** [etr]

VI	
• to be **A, B**	• to exist **A1**
• to go **C**	
V IMPERSONNEL	
• there is/are **1**	• to be **2, 3**
V AUX	
• to have **1**	• to be **2**

VI A. *EXPRIME L'EXISTENCE, LA RÉALITÉ* **1** *(exister)* to be, to exist; **si Dieu est** if God exists; **si cela est** if (it is) so; *Littéraire* **il n'est plus** he is no more, he passed away; **le prof le plus patient qui soit** the most patient teacher that ever was *or* in the world; **le plus petit ordinateur qui soit** the tiniest computer ever; **ê. ou ne pas ê.** to be or not to be; **on ne peut pas ê. et avoir été** you only live once; **ne nie pas ce qui est** don't deny the facts

2 *Math* **soit une droite AB** let AB be a straight line

B. *RELIE L'ATTRIBUT, LE COMPLÉMENT AU SUJET* **1** *(suivi d'un attribut)* to be; **le boa est un serpent** the boa is a snake; **elle est professeur** she's a teacher; **le sac est trop lourd** the bag is too heavy; **ê. malade/déprimé** to be ill/depressed; *Fam* **je ne te le prêterai pas! – comment** *ou* **comme tu es!** I won't lend it to you! – you see what you're like!; **je suis comme je suis** I am what I am; **comment es-tu ce matin?** how are you feeling this morning?; **elle n'est plus rien pour lui** she no longer matters to him; **elle n'est plus ce qu'elle était** she's not what she used to be; **qui était-ce?** who was it?

2 *(suivi d'une préposition)* **ê. à l'hôpital** to be in hospital; **je suis à la gare** I'm at the station; **où sommes-nous?** where are we?; **le propriétaire? il est au troisième étage** the owner? he lives on the third floor; **j'y suis, j'y reste** here I am and here I stay; **je n'y suis pour personne** *(à la maison)* I'm not at home for anyone; *(au bureau)* I won't see anybody; **je suis à vous dans un instant** I'll be with you in a moment; **je suis à vous** *(je vous écoute)* I'm all yours; **tout le monde est à la page 15/au chapitre 9?** is everybody at page 15/chapter 9?; **vous êtes (bien) au 01.40.06.24.08** this is 01 40 06 24 08; **nous ne sommes qu'au début du tournoi** the tournament has just started; **ce livre est à moi** the book's mine; **il est tout à son travail** he's busy with his work; **il est toujours à me questionner** he's always asking me questions; **ê. contre** to be against; **ê. de** *(provenir de)* to be from, to come from; **je suis de la Martinique** I come from *or* was born in Martinique; **l'église est du XVIème** the church is from *or* dates back to the 16th century; **la lettre est du 12** the letter's dated the 12th; **ê. de** *(appartenir à)* to belong to, to be a member of; **êtes-vous du club?** do you belong to the club?, are you a member of the club?; **le lys est de la famille des liliacées** the lily belongs to the family Liliaceae; **qui est de corvée de vaisselle?** who's on washing-up duty?; **ê. en prison/en France** to be in prison/in France; **la table est en chêne** the table is made of oak; **ê. en bonne santé** to be in good health; **ê. en forme** to be fit; **vous n'êtes pas sans savoir que...** I'm sure you're aware that...; **les joueurs en sont à deux sets partout** the players are two sets all; **le projet n'en est qu'au début** the project has only just started; **où en es-tu avec Michel?** how is it going with Michel?; **où en es-tu dans le livre?** how far have you got into the book?; **j'en suis au moment où il découvre le trésor** I've got to the part *or* the bit where he discovers the treasure; **où en étais-je?** *(après une interruption dans une conversation)* where was I?; **où en sont les travaux?** how's the work coming along?; **j'en suis à me demander si...** I'm beginning to wonder if...; **tu en es encore à lui chercher des excuses! – oh non, je n'en suis plus là!** you're still trying to find excuses for him/her! – oh no, I'm past that!; **je ne sais plus du tout où j'en suis dans tous ces calculs** I don't know where I am any more with all these calculations; **j'ai besoin de faire le point, je ne sais plus où j'en suis** I've got to take stock, I've completely lost track of everything; **tout le monde y est?** *(tout le monde est prêt?)* is everyone ready?; **vas-y, j'y suis** go on, I'm ready; **tu te souviens bien de Marie, une petite brune! – ah, oui, j'y suis maintenant!** but you must remember Marie, a brunette! – oh yes, I'm with you now!; **je n'y suis pas du tout!** I'm lost!; **mais non, vous n'y êtes pas du tout!** you don't understand!; *Fam* **en ê.** *(être homosexuel)* to be one of them

3 *(dans l'expression du temps)* to be; **nous sommes le 8/jeudi** today is the 8th/Thursday; **quel jour sommes-nous?** what day is it today?; **on était en avril** it was April; **on n'est qu'en février** it's only February; **imaginez, nous sommes en 1804** imagine it's (the year) 1804; **le mariage est en août** the wedding is in August

C. *SUBSTITUT DE "ALLER", "PARTIR"* to go; **tu y as déjà été?** have you already been there?; *Littéraire* **elle s'en fut lui porter la lettre** she went to take him/her the letter

V IMPERSONNEL 1 *(exister)* **il est** *(il y a ▸ suivi d'un singulier)* there is; *(▸ suivi d'un pluriel)* there are; *Littéraire* **il est une île où...** there's an island where...; *Littéraire* **il est des romanciers qui...** there are novelists who..., some novelists...; **il était une fois un prince...** once (upon a time) there was a prince...; **un escroc s'il en est** a crook if ever there was one

2 *(pour dire l'heure)* **il est 5 heures** it's 5 o'clock; **quelle heure est-il?** what time is it?

3 *(locutions)* **il en est ainsi** that's how it is; **on a dit que vous vouliez démissionner – il n'en est rien** it was rumoured you wanted to resign – that's not true; **il n'est que de lire les journaux pour s'en rendre compte** you only have to read the newspapers to be aware of it

V AUX 1 *(sert à former les temps composés)* **je suis/j'étais descendu** I came/had come down; **dès qu'elle est apparue** as soon as she appeared; **serais-tu resté?** would you have stayed?; **la tour s'est écroulée** the tower collapsed

2 *(sert à former le passif)* **des arbres ont été déterrés par la tempête** trees were uprooted during the storm

3 *(sert à exprimer une obligation)* **ce dossier est à préparer pour lundi** the file must be ready for Monday; **cela est à prouver** we have no proof of that yet

• **cela étant ADV** *(dans ces circonstances)* things being what they are; *(cela dit)* having said that

• **étant donné PRÉP** given, considering; **étant donné les circonstances** given *or* in view of the circumstances

• **étant donné que CONJ** since, given the fact that; **étant donné qu'il pleuvait...** since *or* as it was raining...

être[2] [ɛtr] **NM 1** *Biol & Phil* being; *Phil* **l'ê.** being; **des êtres venus d'ailleurs** beings *or* creatures from outer space; **des êtres étranges** strange creatures; **ê. humain** human being; **ê. vivant** living thing; *Littéraire* **un ê. de feu/lumière/ténèbres** a creature of fire/light/darkness **2** *(personne)* person; **c'est un ê. cruel** he's/she's a cruel person; **c'est un ê. hors du commun** he/she is someone out of the ordinary *or* is no common mortal; **c'est un ê. méprisable** he's/she's a despicable creature; **il était tout ému de tenir ce petit ê. dans ses bras** he was very moved holding the little thing in his arms; **nul ê. au monde ne t'a aimé plus que moi** no one in the world loved you more than I; **un ê. cher** a loved one; **l'ê. aimé** the beloved **3** *(cœur, âme)* being, heart, soul; **tout mon ê. se révolte à cette idée** my entire being rebels at the idea; **au fond de son ê.** deep down in his/her heart; **il a été bouleversé jusqu'au fond de son ê.** he was profoundly moved; **il tremblait de tout son ê.** his whole being quivered *or* shuddered

étreindre [81] [etrɛ̃dr] **VT 1** *(serrer entre ses bras ▸ ami, amant)* to hug, to clasp; *(▸ lutteur, adversaire)* to clasp, to grapple **2** *(oppresser ▸ sujet: émotion, colère, peur)* to seize, to grip

VPR s'étreindre *(amis, amants)* to hug (each other), to embrace each other; *(lutteurs)* to grip each other, to have each other in a tight grip

étreinte [etrɛ̃t] **NF 1** *(embrassade)* hug, embrace **2** *(d'un boa)* constriction; *(d'un lutteur)* grip; **les troupes ennemies resserrent leur é. autour de la ville** the enemy troops are tightening their grip *or* stranglehold on the city **3** *Littéraire (oppression)* grip, grasp; **l'é. de la douleur se faisait sentir de plus en plus** the pain was strengthening its grip *or* hold

étrenner [4] [etrene] **VT** *(machine)* to use for the first time; *(robe, chaussures)* to wear for the first time

VI *(souffrir)* **c'est toi qui vas é.!** YOU'RE going to get *or* catch it!

étrennes [etrɛn] **NFPL** *(cadeau)* New Year's Day present; **qu'est-ce que tu veux pour tes étrennes?** what would you like as a present for New Year's Day?; **les étrennes du facteur/de l'éboueur** New Year's tip *(given to postmen, dustmen, delivery men etc in the weeks running up to the New Year)*, *Br* ≃ Christmas box, *Am* ≃ Christmas bonus

étrier [etrije] **NM 1** *Équitation* stirrup; **tenir l'é. à qn** to help sb mount; *Fig* to give sb a leg up; **vider les étriers** to be thrown; *Fig* to be thrown *or* disconcerted; *Fig* **avoir le pied à l'é.** *(être sur le départ)* to be on the point of leaving; *(être en bonne voie pour réussir)* to be off to a good start; *Fig* **mettre le pied à l'é. à qn** to give sb a helping hand; **boire** *ou* **prendre le coup de l'é.** to have one for the road

2 *Anat* stirrup, stirrup-bone

3 *Méd* **é. (de soutien)** stirrup, leg rest; **é. (de traction** *ou* **de réduction)** calliper

4 *(d'escalade)* *Br* étrier, *Am* stirrup

5 *Constr* stirrup

6 *Aut* stirrup, shackle; *(de frein)* caliper

étrille [etrij] **NF 1** *(peigne)* currycomb **2** *Zool* swimming crab

étriller [3] [etrije] **VT 1** *(cheval)* to curry, to currycomb

2 *Fam (vaincre)* to crush, to trounce

3 *Fam (critiquer)* to pan, *Br* to slate

4 *Fam (escroquer)* to swindle, to con

étripage [etripaʒ] **NM 1** *Culin (d'un poisson)* gutting; *(d'une volaille, d'un gibier)* drawing, cleaning **2** *Fam (tuerie)* slaughter[□]

étriper [3] [etripe] **VT 1** *Culin (poisson)* to gut; *(volaille, gibier)* to draw, to clean out **2** *Fam (tuer)* **je vais l'é., celui-là!** I'm going to make mincemeat of him *or Br* to have his guts for garters!

VPR s'étriper *Fam* to tear each other to pieces; **ils allaient s'é.** they were at each other's throats

étriqué, -e [etrike] **ADJ 1** *(trop petit ▸ vêtement)* skimpy **2** *(mesquin ▸ vie, habitudes, caractère)* mean, petty; *(▸ perspective, esprit, vie)* narrow; *(▸ avenir)* limited; **un point de vue très é.** a very narrow outlook

étriquer [3] [etrike] **VT** *(vêtement)* to make too tight; **cette robe vous étrique** that dress is too tight on you

étrivière [etrivjɛr] **NF** stirrup leather

étroit, -e [etrwa, -at] **ADJ 1** *(rue, bande, sentier, épaules, hanches)* narrow; *(vêtement)* tight

2 *(logement)* poky, cramped

3 *(mesquin ▸ esprit)* narrow; *(▸ idées)* limited; **être é. d'esprit, avoir l'esprit é.** to be narrow-minded

4 *(liens, rapport, complicité, collaboration)* close; **je suis en rapport é. avec sa sœur** I am in close contact *or* touch with his/her sister; **travailler en étroite collaboration avec** to work closely *or* in close co-operation with

5 *(surveillance)* close, strict, tight; **sous étroite surveillance** under close surveillance; **un mot dans son sens le plus é.** the strictest sense of a word

• **à l'étroit ADV on est un peu à l'é. ici** it's rather cramped in here; **ils vivent** *ou* **sont logés à l'é.** they haven't much living space; **je me sens trop à l'é. dans ce jean** these jeans feel too tight, I'm bursting out of these jeans

étroitement [etrwatmɑ̃] **ADV 1** *(nouer, tenir)* tightly; **tenir qn/qch é. serré contre sa poitrine** to clasp sb/sth to one's breast

2 *(strictement ▸ respecter)* strictly; **surveiller qn é.**

to watch sb closely, to keep a close watch on sb
3 *(intimement ▸ relier, collaborer)* closely; **être é. unis** to be closely allied, to have close links; **ces problèmes sont é. liés** these problems are closely *or* intimately linked
4 *(à l'étroit)* **être é. logé** to live in cramped conditions

étroitesse [etrwatεs] **NF 1** *(d'une route, d'un couloir, d'épaules, de hanches)* narrowness **2** *(d'un logement, d'une pièce)* pokiness, lack of space **3** *(mesquinerie)* **é. d'esprit** *ou* **de vues** narrow-mindedness

étron [etrɔ̃] **NM** piece of excrement

étrusque [etrysk] **ADJ** Etruscan, Etrurian
NM *(langue)* Etruscan, Etrurian
• **Étrusque NMF** Etruscan, Etrurian

Ets *Com (abrév écrite* **établissements)** **E. Legrand** Legrand (& Co)

-ette *voir* **-et**

étude [etyd] **NF 1** *(apprentissage)* study; **l'é. des langues** the study of languages; **aimer l'é.** to like studying; **elle a le goût de l'é.** she likes studying
2 *(analyse, essai)* study, paper; *Constr* survey; **une é. sur les mollusques** a study of *or* paper on molluscs; **procéder à l'é. d'une question, mettre une question à l'é.** to study *or* investigate *or* go into a question; **é. des besoins** needs study *or* analysis; **é. de cas** case study; *Mktg* **é. client** customer survey; **é. du comportement** behavioural study; **é. sur le terrain** field study; *Scol* **é. de texte** textual analysis
3 *(travail préparatoire)* study; **ce projet est à l'é.** this project is under study *or* being studied; *Mktg* **é. de faisabilité** feasability study; *Mktg* **é. d'impact** impact study; **é. de marché** market survey, market study; **é. préliminaire** preliminary study
4 *Scol (salle)* study *or Br* prep room; *(période)* study-time; **(salle d')é.** (private) study room, *Br* prep room; **pendant l'é.** during study-time; **elle reste à l'é. le soir** she stays on to study in the evenings; **je laisse mes enfants à l'é. jusqu'à 5 heures** ≃ I leave the children in homework class until 5 o'clock
5 *(bureau ▸ gén)* office; *(▸ d'un avocat, d'un notaire)* office, *Br* chambers; *(charge ▸ d'un avocat, d'un notaire)* practice
6 *Mus* study, étude; **é. pour violon** violin study
7 *Beaux-Arts* study
• **études NFPL** *Scol & Univ* studies; **faire des études** to study; **faire des études de français/de droit** to study *or Br* to read French/law; **faire de brillantes études** to do extremely well at university; **il a fait ses études à Eton/la Sorbonne** he was educated at Eton/he went to *or* studied at the Sorbonne; **j'ai arrêté mes études à 16 ans** I left school when I was 16; **payer ses études** to pay for one's education; **études du développement** development studies; **études secondaires** secondary education; **études supérieures** higher education

étudiant, -e [etydjɑ̃, -ɑ̃t] **ADJ** student *(avant n)*
NM,F *Univ (avant la licence)* undergraduate, student; *(après la licence)* postgraduate, student; **é. en droit/médecine** law/medical student; **é. de première année** first-year (student), *Am* freshman

étudié, -e [etydje] **ADJ 1** *(bien fait ▸ plan, dessin)* specially *or* carefully designed; *(▸ discours)* carefully composed; *(▸ tenue)* carefully selected **2** *Com (prix)* reasonable **3** *(affecté ▸ gestes)* studied; *(manières, sourires)* affected; **avoir un comportement é.** to have a studied manner

étudier [9] [etydje] **VT 1** *Scol & Univ (apprendre ▸ matière)* to learn, to study; *(▸ leçon)* to learn; *(▸ instrument)* to learn (to play), to study; *(▸ auteur, période, rôle)* to study; *(observer ▸ insecte)* to study; **é. l'histoire** *Scol* to study history; *Univ* to study *or Br* to read history; **é. une matière en vue d'un examen** to read up a subject for an examination
2 *(examiner ▸ contrat, théorie)* to study, to examine; *(▸ proposition)* to consider, to examine; *(▸ liste, inventaire)* to go through, to check over; **nous étudierons votre suggestion** we'll consider your suggestion; **il faut é. toutes les éventualités** we have to look at *or* to examine all possible angles; **sa demande mérite d'être étudiée** his/her application merits examination; **é. le terrain** to survey the land
3 *(observer ▸ passant, adversaire)* to watch, to observe; *(▸ visage)* to study
4 *(concevoir ▸ méthode)* to devise; *(▸ modèle, maquette)* to design; **être très étudié** to be specially designed; *Fam* **c'est étudié pour** that's what it's for
5 *Péj (son apparence etc)* to study; **elle étudie ses poses** she strikes poses
VI 1 *(faire ses études)* to study, to be a student **2** *(réviser, apprendre)* to study
VPR s'étudier 1 *(se regarder soi-même)* to gaze at *or* to study oneself
2 *Péj (s'observer avec complaisance)* to admire oneself
3 *(se regarder l'un l'autre)* to observe each other; **ils se sont longuement étudiés** they took careful stock of each other
4 *(se donner une attitude)* to behave affectedly

étui [etɥi] **NM 1** *(gén)* case; *(de parapluie)* cover; **é. à cigarettes** cigarette case; **é. à lunettes** glasses case; **é. de revolver** holster; **é. à violon** violin case **2** *Mil* **é. de cartouche** cartridge case

étuve [etyv] **NF 1** *(sauna)* steam room **2** *Tech (pour stériliser)* sterilizer, autoclave; *(pour sécher)* drier **3** *Fam (lieu où il fait trop chaud)* oven; **quelle é.** *ou* **c'est une vraie é. ici!** it's like an oven in here!

étuvée [etyve] **à l'étuvée ADJ** steamed *(in a tightly shut saucepan)*
ADV cuire à l'é. to steam *(in a tightly shut saucepan)*

étuver [3] [etyve] **VT 1** *Culin* to steam
2 *(sécher)* to dry, to heat
3 *Tech* to bake, to stove; *(stériliser)* to sterilize
4 *Méd* to foment

étymologie [etimɔlɔʒi] **NF 1** *(discipline)* etymology, etymological research **2** *(origine)* etymology, origin; **l'é. d'un terme** the etymology *or* origin of a term

étymologique [etimɔlɔʒik] **ADJ** *Ling* etymological

étymologiquement [etimɔlɔʒikmɑ̃] **ADV** *Ling* etymologically

étymologiste [etimɔlɔʒist] **NMF** *Ling* etymologist

étymon [etimɔ̃] **NM** *Ling* etymon

eu, -e [y] **PP** *voir* **avoir**[2]

eucalyptus [økaliptys] **NM** *Bot* eucalyptus

Eucharistie [økaristi] **NF l'E.** the Eucharist, Holy Communion

eucharistique [økaristik] **ADJ** Eucharistic

Euclide [øklid] **NPR** Euclid

euclidien, -enne [øklidjε̃, -εn] **ADJ** *Math* Euclidean, Euclidian; **non e.** non-Euclidean

eugénique [øʒenik] *Biol* **ADJ** eugenic
NF eugenics *(singulier)*

euh [ø] **EXCLAM** er

eunuque [ønyk] **NM** eunuch

euphémique [øfemik] **ADJ** euphemistic

euphémiquement [øfemikmɑ̃] **ADV** euphemistically

euphémisme [øfemism] **NM** *(pour éviter de déplaire ou de choquer)* euphemism; *(litote)* understatement; **je dis "pas très gentil" mais c'est un e.** I say "not very nice" but it's an understatement
• **par euphémisme ADV** euphemistically

euphonie [øfɔni] **NF** *Ling* euphony

euphonique [øfɔnik] **ADJ 1** *(harmonieux)* euphonic, euphonious, harmonious **2** *Gram* **un "t" e.** a euphonic "t"

euphorbe [øfɔrb] **NF** *Bot* spurge, *Spéc* euphorbia; **e. des bois** wood spurge

euphorie [øfɔri] **NF** euphoria

euphorique [øfɔrik] **ADJ** euphoric; **rendre e.** to make euphoric

euphorisant, -e [øfɔrizɑ̃, -ɑ̃t] **ADJ 1** *(médicament, drogue)* euphoriant **2** *(atmosphère, succès)* heady
NM *(médicament)* anti-depressant; *(drogue)* euphoriant

Euphrate [øfrat] **NM** *Géog* **l'E.** the (River) Euphrates

> SUFFIX
> **-EUR, -EUSE**
> • This suffix appears in adjectives and nouns derived from a verb and gives the idea of a person WHO PERFORMS THE ACTION described by the verb and can often be translated by the English suffix *-er*. It mostly refers to occupations or social activities, as well as traits of character, eg:
> **un danseur, une danseuse** a dancer; **un professeur, une professeur(e)** a teacher; **un serveur, une serveuse** a waiter, a waitress; **il est râleur, c'est un râleur** he never stops moaning; **elle est très bagarreuse** she's always ready for a scrap
> • Note that not all names of occupations ending in **-eur** in the masculine have a feminine ending in **-euse**. The official recommendation for feminization of those nouns is the following:
> When there is a verb in direct semantic relation to the noun, the feminine is **-euse**:
> **chercheur, chercheuse** (from *chercher*); **enquêteur, enquêteuse** (from *enquêter*); **programmeur, programmeuse** (from *programmer*)
> When there is no corresponding verb or when the verb doesn't have a direct semantic link with the noun, the noun can either stay the same in the feminine or take an ending in **-e**. In both cases, the feminine article is used:
> **une ingénieur(e); une professeur(e); une proviseur(e)**
> See also **-TEUR, -TRICE**

eurafricain, -e [ørafrikε̃, -εn] **ADJ** Afro-European

Eurasie [ørazi] **NF l'E.** Eurasia

eurasien, -enne [ørazjε̃, -εn] **ADJ** Eurasian
• **Eurasien, -enne NM,F** Eurasian

-eure [œr] *voir* **-eur, -euse**

eurêka [øreka] **EXCLAM** eureka!

eurent [yr] *voir* **avoir**[2]

Euripide [øripid] **NPR** Euripides

EURL [əyerel] **NF** *Com (abrév* **entreprise unipersonnelle à responsabilité limitée)** trader with limited liability

euro- [øro] **PRÉF** Euro-

euro [øro] **NM** *UE (monnaie)* euro

eurobanque [ørobɑ̃k] **NF** *Banque & Fin* Eurobank

eurocentrisme [ørosɑ̃trism] **NM** *Pol* Eurocentrism

eurochèque [ørɔʃεk] **NM** *Banque & Fin* Eurocheque

eurocommunisme [ørokɔmynism] **NM** Eurocommunism

Eurocorps [ørokɔr] **NM** *Mil* Eurocorps

eurocrate [ørokrat] **NMF** Eurocrat

eurodéputé, -e [ørodepyte] **NMF** *Pol* Euro MP

eurodevise [ørodəviz] **NF** eurocurrency

eurodollar [ørodɔlar] **NM** eurodollar

eurofranc [ørofrɑ̃] **NM** *Anciennement Banque & Fin* Eurofranc

Euroland, Eurolande [ørolɑ̃d] **NF** Euroland

euromarché [øromarʃe] **NM** Euromarket

euromissile [øromisil] **NM** euromissile

euro-obligation [øroɔbligasjɔ̃] *(pl* **euro-obligations) NF** *Fin* eurobond

Europe [ørɔp] **NF 1** *Géog* **l'E.** Europe; **l'E. centrale** Central Europe; **l'E. continentale** mainland Europe; **l'E. de l'Est** East *or* Eastern Europe; **l'E. du Nord** Northern Europe; **l'E. du Sud** Southern Europe; **l'E. sociale** social Europe *(a united Europe committed to a progressive social and welfare policy)*; **l'E. verte** European (community) agriculture; **l'E. des 25** the European Union *(comprising 25 member states)* **2** *Rad* **E. 1** = radio station broadcasting popular entertainment and general interest programmes; **E. 2** = radio station broadcasting mainly music

européanisation [ørɔpeanizasjɔ̃] **NF** Europeanization, Europeanizing *(UNCOUNT)*

européaniser [3] [øʀɔpeanize] **VT** to Europeanize, to make European
VPR s'européaniser to become Europeanized

européen, -enne [øʀɔpeɛ̃, -ɛn] **ADJ** European; **les (élections) européennes** the European elections
• **Européen, -enne NM,F** European

europhile [øʀɔfil] **NMF** Europhile

europhobe [øʀɔfɔb] **NMF** Europhobe

europudding [øʀopudiŋ] **NM** *Cin* europudding

euroscepticisme [øʀɔseptisism] **NM** Euroscepticism

eurosceptique [øʀɔseptik] **NMF** Eurosceptic

Eurostat [øʀɔstat] **NM** *UE* Eurostat

eurostratégique [øʀostʀateʒik] **ADJ** *Mil* Eurostrategic

Eurotunnel® [øʀotynɛl] **NM** Eurotunnel®

Eurovision® [øʀɔvizjɔ̃] **NF** Eurovision®; **le concours E. de la chanson** the Eurovision® Song Contest

eurozone [øʀozon] **NF** Euro zone

-euse *voir* **-eur** *et* **-eux**

eusse, eut *etc voir* **avoir**[2]

euthanasie [øtanazi] **NF** euthanasia; **e. active/passive** voluntary/passive euthanasia

eutrophisation [øtʀɔfizasjɔ̃] **NF** *Écol* eutrophication

eux [ø] **PRON 1** *(sujet)* they; **e. l'ignorent encore** they still don't know about it; **ils le savent bien, e.** they know it all right; **nous sommes invités, e. pas** *ou* **non** we are invited but they aren't *or* but not them; **ce sont e. les responsables** they are the ones *or* it is they who are responsible; **e. seuls connaissent la réponse** they alone *or* only they know the answer; **e., voter? cela m'étonnerait!** them? vote? I doubt it very much!; **nous sommes plus satisfaits qu'e.** we're happier than they are
2 *(après une préposition)* them; **nous irons sans e.** we'll go without them; **ne t'occupe pas d'e.** don't pay any attention to them; **c'est à e.** it's theirs; **à e. seuls, ils n'y arriveront pas** they'll never manage on their own
3 *(en fonction de pronom réfléchi)* themselves; **ils ne pensent qu'à e.** they only think of themselves
4 *(suivi d'un nombre)* **e. deux** both *or* the two of them; **e. quatre/cinq** the four/five of them

> **-EUX, -EUSE** SUFFIX
>
> • Adjectives and nouns ending in **-eux** or **-euse** refer to a QUALITY or PROPERTY. They are mostly derived from a noun, but also, rarely, from a verb. Possible variants are **-ieux, -ieuse** and **-ueux, -ueuse**, eg:
> **paresseux(euse)** lazy/lazy person; **frileux (euse)** who feels the cold; **joyeux(euse)** joyful, merry; **boiteux(euse)** lame, who has a limp; **glamoureux(euse)** glamorous; **pâteux (euse)** doughy; **graisseux(euse)** greasy, fatty; **boueux(euse)** muddy; **capricieux (euse)** temperamental/fickle; **classieux (euse)** classy; **luxueux(euse)** luxurious
> Note the use of the suffix *-y* in English to translate the French suffix when it refers to a natural property or texture.
>
> • MEDICAL VOCABULARY in particular contains numerous examples of words ending in **-eux** and **-euse**. Adjectives can often be translated by an equivalent ending in *-ous*, eg:
> **cancéreux(euse)** cancerous; **les cancéreux** cancer victims; **un lépreux** a leper; **nerveux(euse)** nervous; **veineux(euse)** venous
>
> • There is a recent use of **-eux** and **-euse** in the creation of nouns applied to people who have as an OCCUPATION the thing described by the noun base. Those nouns are, as a rule, informal in register. They are usually found in the plural, as a generic and derogatory way of referring to a whole group of people, eg:
> **les modeux** fashionistas; **les journaleux** hacks; **les théâtreux** luvvies, thespians; **les footeux** footballers

eux-mêmes [ømɛm] **PRON** themselves

évacuateur, -trice [evakɥatœʀ, -tʀis] **ADJ** evacuative, evacuation *(avant n)*; *(tuyau)* drainage
NM é. (des eaux) sluice

évacuation [evakɥasjɔ̃] **NF 1** *Physiol (de toxines)* elimination, eliminating *(UNCOUNT)*; *(du pus)* draining off
2 *(écoulement)* draining; **une conduite assure l'é. des eaux usées** the waste water drains out through a pipe
3 *(d'une ville, d'un lieu)* evacuation; *(d'une salle)* evacuation, clearing; *Méd* **é. sanitaire** medical evacuation
4 *(sauvetage)* evacuation, evacuating; **organiser/procéder à l'é. des habitants** to evacuate the local people

évacuatrice [evakɥatʀis] *voir* **évacuateur**

évacué, -e [evakɥe] **ADJ personne évacuée** evacuee
NM,F evacuee

évacuer [7] [evakɥe] **VT 1** *Physiol (toxine)* to eliminate; *(excrément)* to evacuate; *(pus)* to drain off
2 *(faire s'écouler)* to drain; **les eaux usées sont évacuées par cette canalisation** the waste water drains out through this channel
3 *Mil (terrain)* to move off; *(position)* to retreat from; *(forteresse, ville)* to evacuate, to vacate
4 *(navire, hôpital)* to evacuate; **évacuez la salle!** please leave the room!; **ils ont fait é. la salle d'urgence** they had the room evacuated immediately; **faire é. un bâtiment** to evacuate *or* to clear a building; *Naut* **é. le bâtiment** to abandon ship
5 *(personne, population)* **é. qn de** to evacuate sb from; **faire é. tous les habitants** to evacuate all the inhabitants
6 *Fig (problème)* to get rid of, to solve; **c'est une question que je préférerais é. le plus vite possible** it's a matter I'd like to dispose of as soon as possible

évadé, -e [evade] **ADJ** escaped
NM,F escaped prisoner, escapee; **un é. de l'asile/de Fresnes** an escapee from the mental hospital/from Fresnes prison

évader [3] [evade] **s'évader VPR 1** *(s'enfuir)* **s'é. de** to escape from, to break out of; **il les a fait s'é.** he helped them to escape **2** *(pour oublier ses soucis)* to escape, to get away from it all; **s'é. à la campagne** to get out of town for a break; **j'ai besoin de m'é.** I need to get away from it all

> Il faut noter que le verbe anglais **to evade** est un faux ami. Il signifie **éviter**.

évaluation [evalɥasjɔ̃] **NF 1** *(estimation)* evaluation, assessment; *(d'une propriété, d'un bien)* valuation, appraisal; *(des dommages)* assessment; *(d'un poids, d'un nombre, des risques)* estimation; **faire l'é. d'un tableau** to estimate the value of *or* to value a painting; **é. des performances** *(d'un employé)* performance appraisal; **é. des risques** risk assessment **2** *(quantité évaluée)* estimation; *(d'une propriété, d'un bien)* valuation; *(des dommages)* assessment; *(d'un poids, d'un nombre, des risques)* estimate

évaluer [7] [evalɥe] **VT 1** *(estimer ▸ bijou, tableau)* to appraise, to assess; **faire é. qch** to have sth valued; **la propriété a été évaluée à trois millions d'euros** the estate has been valued at *or* the value of the estate has been put at three million euros
2 *(mesurer ▸ volume, débit)* to estimate; *(▸ dégâts, coût, besoin)* to assess, to estimate; **é. qch à** to estimate *or* to evaluate sth at; **à combien évalue-t-on le nombre des victimes?** what is the estimated number of victims?; **on évalue à 12000 le nombre des victimes** the number of victims is estimated at 12,000
3 *(estimer approximativement ▸ distance)* to gauge; *(poids, nombre)* to estimate; **on évalue sa fortune à trois millions de dollars** his/her fortune is estimated at three million dollars
4 *(juger ▸ qualité)* to evaluate, to gauge, to assess; **bien é. la difficulté d'un projet** to make a realistic assessment of the difficulty of a project; **as-tu évalué les risques?** have you weighed up the risks?

évanescent, -e [evanesɑ̃, -ɑ̃t] **ADJ** *Littéraire* evanescent

évangélique [evɑ̃ʒelik] **ADJ 1** *(de l'Évangile)* evangelic, evangelical **2** *(protestant)* evangelical; **les chrétiens évangéliques** evangelical Christians

évangélisateur, -trice [evɑ̃ʒelizatœʀ, -tʀis] **ADJ** evangelistic
NM,F evangelist

évangélisation [evɑ̃ʒelizasjɔ̃] **NF** evangelization, evangelizing

évangélisatrice [evɑ̃ʒelizatʀis] *voir* **évangélisateur**

évangéliser [3] [evɑ̃ʒelize] **VT** to evangelize

évangélisme [evɑ̃ʒelism] **NM** evangelism

évangéliste [evɑ̃ʒelist] **NM** *(prédicateur)* evangelist; *(auteur de l'un des Évangiles)* Evangelist

évangile [evɑ̃ʒil] **NM 1** *Rel* **l'É.** the Gospel; **les Évangiles** the Gospels; **l'É. selon saint…** the Gospel according to Saint…; **l'é. du jour** the gospel for the day **2** *(credo)* gospel

évanoui, -e [evanwi] **ADJ** unconscious; **tomber é.** to fall down in a faint; **on l'a trouvé é.** he was found unconscious *or* in a (dead) faint

évanouir [32] [evanwiʀ] **s'évanouir VPR 1** *Méd* to faint, to pass out; **la chaleur l'a fait s'é.** he/she fainted in the heat **2** *(disparaître ▸ personne, apparition, ombre)* to vanish (into thin air); *(▸ craintes, illusions, doutes)* to vanish, to disappear; *(▸ souvenir, rêve)* to fade (away); *(▸ son)* to die away, to fade away; **s'é. dans la nature** to fade into the background

évanouissement [evanwismɑ̃] **NM 1** *Méd (syncope)* fainting *(UNCOUNT)*, blackout; **avoir un é.** to (go into a) faint **2** *(disparition)* disappearance, disappearing, vanishing; *(d'un souvenir, d'un rêve)* fading **3** *Tél* fading

évaporation [evapɔʀasjɔ̃] **NF** evaporation

évaporé, -e [evapɔʀe] **ADJ** *(écervelé)* scatterbrained, birdbrained; **une blonde évaporée** a dumb blonde; **elle prend toujours des airs évaporés** she always acts like an airhead
NM,F dimwit

évaporer [3] [evapɔʀe] **VT** to evaporate
VI faire é. un liquide to evaporate a liquid
VPR s'évaporer 1 *(liquide)* to evaporate **2** *(colère, crainte)* to vanish, to disappear, *Littéraire* to evaporate **3** *Fam (disparaître)* to vanish (into thin air); **ces lunettes n'ont pas pu s'é.!** these glasses can't just have vanished (into thin air)!; **je me suis retourné et hop, il s'était évaporé!** I turned round and he'd gone *or* vanished, just like that!

évasé, -e [evaze] **ADJ** *(vêtement, manche)* flared; *(ouverture, tuyau)* funnel-shaped, splayed; *(récipient)* tapered; **la jupe a une jolie forme évasée** the skirt flares out nicely

évasement [evazmɑ̃] **NM** *(d'une ouverture, d'un tuyau)* splay; *(d'un entonnoir)* widening-out; *(d'un vêtement)* flare

évaser [3] [evaze] **VT** *(jupe)* to flare; *(ouverture, tuyau)* to splay (out)
VPR s'évaser to widen, to open out; *(chenal)* to open out, to broaden; *(forme, vêtement)* to flare; *(tuyau)* to splay (out)

évasif, -ive [evazif, -iv] **ADJ** evasive, noncommittal; **d'un air é.** evasively

évasion [evazjɔ̃] **NF 1** *(d'un prisonnier)* escape (**de** from); **il a raté son é.** he didn't manage to escape; **le roi de l'é.** the master escaper
2 *(distraction)* **l'é.** getting away from it all; **j'ai besoin d'é.** I need to get away from it all
3 *Fin & Jur* **é. fiscale** tax avoidance
4 *Écon* **é. de capitaux** flight of capital
• **d'évasion ADJ** escapist; **cinéma d'é.** escapist films

> Il faut noter que le nom anglais **evasion** est un faux ami. Il signifie le plus souvent **dérobade**.

évasive [evaziv] *voir* **évasif**

évasivement [evazivmɑ̃] **ADV** evasively

Ève [ɛv] **NPR** *Bible* Eve; **je ne le connais ni d'È. ni d'Adam** I don't know him from Adam; **en costume** *ou* **en tenue d'È.** naked, in the altogether, in her birthday suit

évêché [eveʃe] **NM** *Rel* **1** *(territoire)* bishopric, diocese **2** *(demeure)* bishop's palace *or* house **3** *(ville)* cathedral town

éveil [evɛj] **NM 1** *(fin du sommeil)* awakening **2** *(déclenchement)* **l'é. de** the awakening *or* early development *or* first stirrings of; **l'é. des sens/de la sexualité** the awakening of the senses/of sexuality; **l'é. de qn à qch** sb's awakening to sth; **l'auteur raconte l'é. à l'amour d'une jeune fille** the author recounts the dawning of love in a young girl's heart

3 *Scol* **activité** *ou* **matière d'é.** non-core subject *(covering subjects such as arts, history, geography or biology)*

4 *(alerte)* **donner l'é.** to raise the alarm; **donner l'é. à qn** to arouse sb's suspicions, to put sb on their guard

• **en éveil ADV 1** *(sur ses gardes)* **être en é.** *(personne)* to be on the alert; *(esprit)* to be alert **2** *(actif)* **maintenant que ses soupçons sont en é.** now that his/her suspicions have been aroused

éveillé, -e [eveje] **ADJ 1** *(vif ▸ enfant, esprit)* alert, bright, sharp; *(▸ intelligence)* sharp **2** *(en état de veille)* awake; **tout é.** wide awake; **se tenir é.** to stay awake

éveiller [4] [eveje] **VT 1** *Littéraire (tirer du sommeil)* to awaken, to waken, to arouse **2** *(susciter ▸ désir, jalousie, passion)* to kindle, to arouse; *(▸ amour, méfiance)* to arouse; *(▸ curiosité, soupçons)* to arouse, to awaken; *(▸ espoir)* to awaken; *(▸ attention, intérêt)* to attract **3** *(stimuler ▸ intelligence)* to stimulate, to awaken

VPR s'éveiller 1 *(animal, personne)* to awaken, to wake up, to waken

2 *(s'animer ▸ campagne, village)* to come to life, to wake up

3 *(se révéler ▸ intelligence, talent)* to reveal itself, to come to light

4 *(naître ▸ curiosité, jalousie, méfiance)* to be aroused; *(▸ amour)* to dawn, to stir

5 *Littéraire* **s'é. à un sentiment** *(le ressentir)* to wake up to *or* to discover a feeling

événement, évènement [evɛnmɑ̃] **NM 1** *(fait)* event, occurrence, happening; **plus tard, les événements lui ont donné raison** what happened later *or* the later events proved him/her right; **vacances riches en événements** *Br* eventful holidays, *Am* an eventful vacation; **être dépassé par les événements** to be overtaken by events; **attendre la suite des événements** to await the course of events **2** *Pol* **les événements d'Algérie** the Algerian War of Independence; **les événements de mai 68** the events of May 68 **3** *(fait important)* event; **quand le cirque venait au village, c'était un (grand) é.** when the circus came to our village, it was quite an event *or* a big occasion; *Hum* **quand il fait la vaisselle, c'est (tout) un é.,** when he does the dishes it's a cause for celebration *or* it's quite an event; **un é. historique** a historic event; **l'é. sportif de l'année** this year's main sporting event; **faire** *ou* **créer l'é.** to be news *or* a major event; **sa démission fait l'é. dans tous les quotidiens** his/her resignation is making headlines in all the daily newspapers; **nous vous rappelons l'é. de la journée** here's the main news of the day again

événementiel, -elle, évènementiel, -elle [evɛnmɑ̃sjɛl] **ADJ** purely descriptive; *(histoire, programme télévisé)* factual

évent [evɑ̃] **NM 1** *Zool* blowhole, *Spéc* spiracle **2** *Tech* vent hole

éventail [evɑ̃taj] **NM 1** *(accessoire)* fan **2** *(gamme)* range; **é. des prix** price range; **é. des salaires** salary range *or* spread; **l'é. politique** the political spectrum **3** *Com (de produits)* range

• **en éventail ADJ** fan-shaped; *(queue)* spread-out; *Fam Fig* **elle est restée les doigts de pied en é. toute la matinée** she lazed around all morning

éventaire [evɑ̃tɛr] **NM 1** *(étalage)* stall **2** *(plateau)* (street vendor's) tray

éventé, -e [evɑ̃te] **ADJ 1** *(altéré ▸ bière, limonade)* flat, stale; *(▸ parfum, vin)* musty, stale **2** *(connu ▸ complot)* discovered; *(▸ secret)* well-known

éventer [3] [evɑ̃te] **VT 1** *(avec un éventail, un magazine)* to fan **2** *(révéler ▸ secret)* to disclose, to give away; **le secret est éventé** the secret is out

VPR s'éventer 1 *(pour se rafraîchir)* to fan oneself; **s'é. avec un magazine** to fan oneself with a magazine **2** *(être divulgué ▸ plan d'attaque, secret)* to get out, to become public knowledge **3** *(s'altérer ▸ parfum, vin)* to go musty *or* stale; *(▸ bière, limonade)* to go flat *or* stale

éventration [evɑ̃trasjɔ̃] **NF** ventral rupture

éventrer [3] [evɑ̃tre] **VT 1** *(personne)* to disembowel, to eviscerate; **il a été éventré par le taureau** he was gored by the bull **2** *(canapé, outre, oreiller, sac)* to rip (open); *(boîte en carton)* to tear open **3** *(immeuble)* to rip apart

VPR s'éventrer 1 to disembowel oneself **2** *(se fendre ▸ oreiller, sac)* to burst open; **la barque s'est éventrée sur un récif** the boat hit a reef ripping a hole in its hull

éventreur [evɑ̃trœr] **NM** ripper; **Jack l'É.** Jack the Ripper

éventualité [evɑ̃tɥalite] **NF 1** *(possibilité)* possibility, contingency; **cette é. ne m'avait pas effleuré** this possibility hadn't occurred to me **2** *(circonstance)* eventuality, possibility, contingency; **pour parer** *ou* **être prêt à toute é.** to be ready for anything that might crop up; **il faut envisager toutes les éventualités** we must consider all the possibilities; **dans cette é.** in such an *or* in this event, if this should happen

• **dans l'éventualité de PRÉP** in the event of; **dans l'é. d'une guerre** should a war break out, in the event of a war

éventuel, -elle [evɑ̃tɥɛl] **ADJ** possible; *(client)* potential, prospective

> Il faut noter que l'adjectif anglais **eventual** est un faux ami. Il signifie **final.**

éventuellement [evɑ̃tɥɛlmɑ̃] **ADV** *(peut-être)* possibly; **tu me le prêterais? – é.** would you lend it to me? – maybe *or* possibly; **il viendra avec sa cousine et é. avec sa tante** he'll come with his cousin and possibly with his aunt; **faites cet exercice en vous servant é. d'un dictionnaire** do this exercise using a dictionary if necessary; **j'aurais é. besoin de votre concours** I may need your help (later)

> Il faut noter que l'adverbe anglais **eventually** est un faux ami. Il signifie **finalement.**

évêque [evɛk] **NM** *Rel* bishop

évertuer [7] [evɛrtɥe] **s'évertuer VPR s'é. à faire qch** to strive *or* to make every effort to do sth, to do one's utmost to do sth

éviction [eviksjɔ̃] **NF 1** *Jur (d'un locataire)* eviction; **procéder à l'é. d'un locataire** to evict a tenant **2** *(expulsion ▸ d'un rival, d'un leader)* ousting; **depuis son é. du parti** since his/her ousting *or* since being ousted from the party; **é. scolaire** exclusion, expulsion

évidage [evidaʒ] **NM** hollowing out

évidement [evidmɑ̃] **NM 1** *(d'un fruit, d'un bloc de pierre, d'un tronc)* hollowing *or* scooping out *(UNCOUNT)* **2** *Méd* scraping out

évidemment [evidamɑ̃] **ADV 1** *(bien entendu)* of course; *(manifestement)* obviously; **bien é.!** of course!; **tu me crois? – é.!** do you believe me? – of course (I do)! **2** *(avec colère, irritation)* needless to say, predictably enough; **é., elle n'a rien préparé!** needless to say she hasn't prepared a thing!; **j'ai oublié mes clés – é.!** *(ton irrité)* I've forgotten my keys – you would!

> Il faut noter que l'adverbe anglais **evidently** est un faux ami. Il signifie **manifestement, à l'évidence.**

évidence [evidɑ̃s] **NF** *(caractère certain)* obviousness; *(fait manifeste)* obvious fact; **c'est une é., c'est l'é. même** it's obvious; **il n'a dit que des évidences** he just stated the obvious; **accepter** *ou* **se rendre à l'é.** to face facts; **c'est l'é. même!** it's quite obvious *or* evident!; **refuser** *ou* **nier l'é.** to deny the facts *or* the obvious

• **à l'évidence, de toute évidence ADV** evidently, obviously

• **en évidence ADV** *(chose, personne)* **j'ai laissé le message bien en é. sur la table** I left the message on the table in a place where it couldn't be missed; **être en é.** *(objet)* to be in a prominent position, to be conspicuous; **mettre en é.** *(exposer)* to display (prominently); *(détail, talent)* to highlight, to bring out; **les chercheurs ont mis en é. l'existence du virus** the researchers revealed the existence of the virus; **se mettre en é.** *(se faire remarquer)* to make oneself conspicuous

> Il faut noter que le nom anglais **evidence** est un faux ami. Il signifie le plus souvent **preuve.**

évident, -e [evidɑ̃, -ɑ̃t] **ADJ 1** *(manifeste)* obvious, evident, self-evident; **il était d'une mauvaise foi évidente** he was obviously *or* clearly insincere; **la réponse/solution me paraît évidente** the reply/solution seems obvious to me **2** *(certain)* obvious, certain; **il est bien é. que...** it's quite obvious *or* evident that...; **c'est é.!** of course!, obviously!, that's obvious!; **il viendra? – pas é.!** will he come? – I wouldn't bet on it!; **l'issue du match semblait évidente** it seemed fairly certain what the result of the match would be; *Fam* **je suis sûr que c'est lui le coupable – c'est pas é.** I'm sure he did it – don't be so sure **3** *Fam (facile)* easy□, simple□; **ce n'est pas é.** *(difficile)* it's not that easy; *(problématique)* it's a bit of a problem; **ce n'est pas une décision évidente à prendre** it's not such an easy decision to make

évider [3] [evide] **VT** *(fruit, bloc de pierre, tronc)* to hollow *or* to scoop out

évier [evje] **NM** (kitchen) sink

évincer [16] [evɛ̃se] **VT 1** *(concurrent, rival)* to oust (**de** from); **é. qn d'un emploi** to oust sb from a job; **être évincé d'un comité** to be thrown off a committee; **se faire é.** to be ousted **2** *Jur (locataire)* to evict

> Il faut noter que le verbe anglais **to evince** est un faux ami. Il signifie **faire preuve de, manifester.**

éviscération [eviserasjɔ̃] **NF** *Méd* evisceration, eviscerating *(UNCOUNT)*

éviscérer [18] [evisere] **VT** *Méd* to eviscerate

évitable [evitabl] **ADJ** *(obstacle)* avoidable; *(accident)* preventable

évitage [evitaʒ] **NM** *Naut* **1** *(mouvement ▸ d'un bateau)* swinging; **bassin d'é.** turning basin **2** *(espace)* room to swing, sea room

évitement [evitmɑ̃] **NM 1** *(action d'éviter)* avoidance; **faire une manœuvre d'é.** to take evasive action; *Biol, Psy* **réaction d'é.** avoidance reaction **2** *Rail* shunting; **voie** *ou* **gare d'é.** siding; **ligne d'é.** loop line **3** *Belg Transp* diversion

éviter [3] [evite] **VT 1** *(ne pas subir ▸ coup)* to avoid, to dodge; *(▸ danger)* to avoid, to steer clear of; *(▸ corvée)* to avoid, to shun; **on ne pourra é. la guerre** war cannot be avoided; **pour é. que le vent n'entre dans la maison** to prevent the wind getting into the house, to keep the wind out of the house; **évite que ça se sache** don't let it get out, prevent it getting out

2 *(ne pas heurter ▸ ballon)* to avoid, to dodge, to stay out of the way of; *(▸ obstacle)* to avoid; **je n'ai pas pu vous é.** I couldn't avoid you

3 *(regard, personne)* to avoid, to shun; **é. le regard de qn** to avoid sb's eyes; **depuis notre querelle, il m'évite** since we quarrelled he's been avoiding me

4 *(lieu, situation, aliment)* to avoid; **en passant par là, on évite le carrefour** that way, you miss *or* avoid the junction; **elle évite la foule** she shies away from crowds; **é. l'alcool/le sucre** to avoid *or* keep off alcohol/sugar

5 *(maladresse, action)* to avoid; **é. de faire qch** to avoid doing sth, to try not to do sth; **évite de laisser tes livres par terre** try not to leave your books on the floor; **j'évite de me baisser** I avoid bending *or* I try not to bend down; **évite de recommencer!** don't start again!

6 *(épargner)* **é. qch à qn** to spare sb sth; **é. des ennuis à qn** to save *or* to spare sb trouble; **cela lui évitera d'avoir à sortir** that'll save him/her having to go out

VI *Naut* **é. sur l'ancre** to swing at anchor

VPR s'éviter 1 *(mutuellement)* to avoid each other *or* one another, to stay out of each other's way **2 s'é. qch** to save *or* to spare oneself sth; **s'é. des tracas** to spare *or* to save oneself trouble

évocateur, -trice [evɔkatœr, -tris] **ADJ** evocative, suggestive (**de** of)

évocation [evɔkasjɔ̃] **NF 1** *(rappel ▸ du passé, d'une personne, d'un paysage etc)* evocation, recalling; **la simple é. de cette scène la faisait pleurer**

just recalling this scene made her weep; **le pouvoir d'é. d'un lieu/mot** the evocative power of a place/word **2** *(fait de mentionner)* mention; **l'é. d'un sujet/d'un problème** the mention of a topic/problem **3** *(par la magie ▸ d'un esprit)* evocation, calling forth, conjuring up

évocatrice [evɔkatris] *voir* **évocateur**

évolué, -e [evɔlɥe] **ADJ 1** *(civilisé ▸ peuple, société)* advanced, sophisticated
2 *(progressiste ▸ personne)* broadminded, enlightened; *(▸ idées)* progressive
3 *(méthode, technologie)* advanced, sophisticated
4 *(espèce animale)* evolved
5 *Ordinat (langage)* high-level

évoluer [7] [evɔlɥe] **VI 1** *(changer ▸ maladie)* to develop; *(▸ mœurs, société, circonstances)* to change; **la position du syndicat a évolué depuis hier** the union's position has changed since yesterday; **les choses ont beaucoup évolué depuis le mois dernier** there have been many developments since last month; **ils cherchent à faire é. la situation** they are trying to get things to progress, they are trying to make some headway in the situation; **une maladie qui évolue lentement/rapidement** an illness which develops slowly/rapidly
2 *(progresser ▸ pays)* to develop; *(▸ civilisation, technique)* to develop, to advance; *(▸ personne)* to mature
3 *(se déplacer ▸ personne)* to move about; *(▸ avion)* to fly around; *(▸ poisson)* to swim (about); **elle évolue sur scène avec grâce** she glides across the stage; **é. dans la haute société** to move in high society; **les cercles dans lesquels elle évoluait** the circles in which she moved
4 *Mil & Naut* to manoeuvre
5 *Biol* to evolve
6 *Ordinat* **faire é.** to upgrade

évolutif, -ive [evɔlytif, -iv] **ADJ 1** *(poste)* with career prospects; **une situation évolutive** a changing situation **2** *Méd (maladie)* progressive **3** *Ordinat* upgradable

évolution [evɔlysjɔ̃] **NF 1** *(changement ▸ de mœurs, de société)* change; *(▸ d'une institution, de la mode)* evolution; *(▸ d'idées, d'événements)* development; *(▸ d'une situation, d'un conflit)* evolution, development
2 *(progrès ▸ d'un pays)* development; *(▸ d'une technique, d'une science)* development, advancement, evolution; **suivre une lente é.** to evolve *or* develop slowly
3 *Méd (d'une maladie)* development, progression; *(d'une tumeur)* growth; **à é. lente/rapide** slow/rapidly developing
4 *Biol* **(la théorie de) l'é.** (the theory of) evolution
5 évolutions *(d'un joueur, d'un patineur)* movements; *(des troupes)* manoeuvres

évolutionnisme [evɔlysjɔnism] **NM** *Biol* evolutionism, evolutionary theory

évolutionniste [evɔlysjɔnist] *Biol* **ADJ 1** *(théorie etc)* evolutionist **2** *(biologie)* evolutionary
NMF evolutionist

évolutive [evɔlytiv] *voir* **évolutif**

évolutivité [evɔlytivite] **NF** *Ordinat* upgradability

évoquer [3] [evɔke] **VT 1** *(remémorer ▸ image, journée)* to conjure up, to evoke; *(▸ souvenirs)* to call up, to recall, to evoke; **é. qch à qn** to remind sb of sth; **le nom ne lui évoquait rien** the name didn't ring any bells with *or* meant nothing to him/her
2 *(recréer ▸ pays, atmosphère)* to call to mind, to conjure up, to evoke
3 *(rappeler par ressemblance)* to be reminiscent of; **un goût qui évoque un peu le romarin** a taste slightly reminiscent of rosemary
4 *(aborder ▸ affaire, question)* to refer to, to mention; **nous n'avons fait qu'é. le sujet** we've only touched on the subject
5 *(appeler ▸ démon, fantôme)* to call up
6 *Jur* = to transfer from a lower to a higher court

ex- [ɛks] **PRÉF** ex-; **mon ex-mari** my ex-husband *or* former husband; **l'ex-champion du monde** the ex-world *or* former world champion

ex [ɛks] **NMF INV** *Fam* ex; **un de mes ex** one of my exes

exacerbation [ɛgzasɛrbasjɔ̃] **NF** *(d'une douleur)* exacerbation, aggravation; *(d'une tension)* exacerbation, heightening

exacerber [3] [ɛgzasɛrbe] **VT** *(douleur)* to exacerbate, to aggravate, to sharpen; *(colère, curiosité, désir, tension)* to exacerbate, to heighten; *(mépris, remords)* to deepen; **des mesures qui vont e. la concurrence** measures which will sharpen *or* heighten competition
VPR s'exacerber to intensify; **sa jalousie n'a fait que s'e.** he/she has become even more jealous

exact, -e [ɛgzakt] **ADJ 1** *(conforme à la réalité ▸ description, information, rapport)* exact, accurate; *(▸ copie, réplique)* exact, true; *(▸ prédiction, réponse)* correct, accurate; **il est e. que j'ai dit cela** it's quite true that I said that; **c'est e.** *(vrai)* it's quite true, it's a fact; **vous vous appelez bien Martin? – e.!** your name is Martin? – correct!
2 *(précis ▸ mesure, poids, quantité)* exact, precise; *(▸ expression, mot)* exact, right; **le lieu e. où cela s'est passé** the precise *or* exact place where it happened; **l'heure/la date exacte à laquelle…** the exact time/date when…; **as-tu l'heure exacte?** have you got the right *or* correct time?; **au moment e. où…** at the exact *or* precise *or* very moment when…; **pour être e., disons que…** to be accurate, let's say that…
3 *Math* right, correct, accurate; **l'addition n'est pas exacte** the figures don't add up (properly) *or* aren't right
4 *(fonctionnant avec précision ▸ balance, montre)* accurate
5 *(ponctuel)* punctual, on time; **elle n'est jamais exacte à ses rendez-vous** she's never on time for her appointments
6 *Littéraire (strict ▸ discipline, obéissance etc)* strict, rigorous

exactement [ɛgzaktəmɑ̃] **ADV 1** *(précisément ▸ calculer, placer)* exactly, precisely; *(fidèlement ▸ rapporter, reproduire)* exactly, accurately; **je ne sais pas e. où ça se trouve** I don't exactly know where it is; **ce n'est pas e. ce que je cherchais** it's not exactly *or* quite what I was looking for; **mais c'est e. le contraire!** but it's exactly *or* precisely the opposite!; **il est très e. 2 heures 13** it is 2.13 precisely **2** *(tout à fait)* **e.!** exactly!, precisely!

exaction [ɛgzaksjɔ̃] **NF** exaction
• **exactions NFPL** violent acts, acts of violence *or* brutality; **se livrer à** *ou* **commettre des exactions (contre qn)** to perpetrate *or* to commit acts of violence (against sb)

exactitude [ɛgzaktityd] **NF 1** *(conformité à la réalité)* exactness, accuracy; **je me souviens avec e. des mots de sa lettre** I can remember the precise *or* exact words he/she used in his/her letter
2 *(expression précise ▸ d'une mesure)* exactness; **calculer/mesurer avec e.** to calculate/measure exactly *or* precisely
3 *(d'un instrument de mesure)* accuracy
4 *(justesse ▸ d'une traduction, d'une réponse)* exactness, correctness
5 *(ponctualité)* punctuality; **avec e.** punctually; *Prov* **l'e. est la politesse des rois** punctuality is the politeness of kings
6 *(minutie)* punctiliousness, meticulousness; **faire son travail avec e.** to be punctilious in one's work

ex aequo, ex æquo [ɛgzeko] **ADV** placed equal; **être e. (avec)** to tie *or* to be placed equal (with); **être troisième e.** to tie for third place, to be placed equal third; **être e. avec qn** to tie with sb, to be placed equal with sb; **on trouve Lille et Nantes e. à la troisième place** Lille and Nantes come joint third; **elle est première e. avec la joueuse suédoise** she's placed equal first with the Swedish player; **premiers e., Maubert et Vuillet** *(à un concours)* the joint winners are Maubert and Vuillet; *(à l'école) Br* top marks *or Am* highest grades have been awarded to Maubert and to Vuillet
NMF INV il y a deux e. pour la troisième place there's a tie for third place; **séparer** *ou* **départager les e.** to break the tie

exagération [ɛgzaʒerasjɔ̃] **NF 1** *(amplification)* exaggeration, overstating *(UNCOUNT)*; **tomber dans l'e.** to exaggerate **2** *(écrit, parole)* exaggeration, overstatement **3** *(outrance ▸ d'un accent, d'une attitude)* exaggeration
• **avec exagération ADV** exaggeratedly, excessively
• **sans exagération ADV on peut dire sans e. que…** it is no exaggeration to say *or* one can say without exaggeration that…

exagéré, -e [ɛgzaʒere] **ADJ 1** *(excessif ▸ dépense, prix)* excessive; *(▸ éloge, critique)* exaggerated, overblown; *(▸ optimisme, prudence)* excessive, exaggerated; *(▸ hâte)* undue; *(▸ ambition, confiance en soi)* excessive, overweening; **confiance exagérée** overconfidence; **accorder une importance exagérée à qch** to attach too much importance to sth, to exaggerate the importance of sth; **50 euros par personne, c'est un peu e.!** 50 euros per person, that's a bit much!; **dire qu'il est bête, c'est un peu e.** it's a bit much *or* a bit excessive to say that he's stupid **2** *(outré ▸ accent, attitude)* exaggerated, overdone

exagérément [ɛgzaʒeremɑ̃] **ADV** excessively, exaggeratedly; **e. optimiste** over-optimistic; **e. méticuleux** over-meticulous

exagérer [18] [ɛgzaʒere] **VT 1** *(amplifier ▸ importance, dangers, difficultés)* to exaggerate, to overemphasize, to overstate; *(▸ mérites, pouvoir)* to exaggerate, to overstate; *(▸ proportions, richesse, valeur)* to exaggerate; **on a beaucoup exagéré l'importance de ce fait** the significance of this fact has been overstated *or* greatly exaggerated, too much importance has been attached to this fact; **il ne faut rien e., n'exagérons rien** let's not get carried away **2** *(outrer ▸ accent, attitude)* to overdo, to exaggerate
USAGE ABSOLU *(amplifier)* **il faut toujours que tu exagères!** you always exaggerate!; **sans e.** without any exaggeration; **sans e., elle mesurait bien deux mètres** I'm not kidding, she was at least two metres tall
VI *(abuser)* **ça fait deux heures que j'attends, il ne faut pas e.!** I've been waiting for two hours, that's a bit much!; *Fam* **ça fait ton troisième cake, tu exagères!** that's your third pastry, aren't you overdoing it a bit?; **cette fois ils exagèrent, j'appelle la police!** this time they've really gone too far, I'm calling the police!; *Fam* **j'étais là avant vous, faut pas e.!** I was there before you, you've got a nerve!
VPR s'exagérer s'e. qch to overestimate sth; **s'e. les mérites de qn** to exaggerate sb's merits

exaltant, -e [ɛgzaltɑ̃, -ɑ̃t] **ADJ** stirring, thrilling

exaltation [ɛgzaltasjɔ̃] **NF 1** *(excitation)* (intense) excitement; *(joie)* elation; **e. mystique** exaltation
2 *(célébration ▸ d'un talent, du travail)* extolling, glorification
3 *Psy (d'un malade mental)* overexcitement
4 *Rel* **E. de la sainte Croix** Exaltation of the Cross

exalté, -e [ɛgzalte] **ADJ 1** *(intense ▸ désir, passion)* inflamed **2** *(excité ▸ personne)* elated, (very) excited; *(▸ esprit)* excited, inflamed; *(▸ imagination)* wild; *(▸ discours)* wild, impassioned
NM,F *Péj* fanatic, hothead

exalter [3] [ɛgzalte] **VT 1** *(intensifier ▸ désir)* to excite, to kindle; *(▸ enthousiasme)* to fire, to excite; *(▸ ressentiment, orgueil)* to intensify; *(▸ imagination)* to fire, to stimulate **2** *(exciter ▸ foule, partisan)* to excite; **exalté à l'idée de** carried away by the idea of **3** *Littéraire (faire l'éloge de ▸ beauté, bienfaits, talent)* to glorify, to extol, to exalt
VPR s'exalter to become excited

exam [ɛgzam] **NM** *Fam (abrév* **examen***)* exam ▫

examen [ɛgzamɛ̃] **NM 1** *Scol & Univ* examination, exam; **passer un e.** *(série d'épreuves)* to take *or Br* to sit an exam; **être reçu/refusé à un e.** to pass/to fail an exam; **e. blanc** *Br* mock exam, *Am* practice test; **e. écrit** written exam; **e. d'entrée** entrance exam; **e. final** final exam; **e. oral** oral (exam), *Br Univ* viva; **e. partiel** *(année)* half-year exam; *(semestre, trimestre)* half-term exam, mid-term exam; **e. de passage** end-of-year *or Br* sessional exam, *Am* final exam *(for admission to the year above)*
2 *Méd (auscultation)* **e. (médical)** (medical) examination; *(analyse)* test; **e. médical complet** complete checkup; **e. prénuptial** premarital checkup; **e. préopératoire** preoperative examination, *Fam* preop; **se faire faire un e./des examens** to have a test/some tests done; **faire faire des examens à un patient** to send *or* to refer a patient

for (further) tests; **e. de laboratoire** test *(of blood, urine etc)*; **e. de la vue** eye test, sight test

3 *(inspection)* inspection, examination; **après e. du corps de la victime** having examined the body of the victim; **je viens faire l'e. de l'installation électrique** I've come to inspect the wiring

4 *(de documents, d'un dossier, d'un projet de loi)* examination; *(d'une requête)* examination, consideration; *(d'un texte)* study; *(d'une comptabilité)* checking, inspection; **son argumentation ne résiste pas à l'e.** his/her arguments don't stand up to examination *or* under scrutiny; **après un e. attentif de la situation/du problème** after careful examination of the situation/problem; **e. de conscience** examination of (one's) conscience; **faire son e. de conscience** *(réfléchir)* to do some soul-searching, to search one's conscience

5 *Jur* **mettre qn en e.** to indict sb; **mise en e.** indictment

• **à l'examen** ADV under consideration; **mettre une question à l'e.** to put a topic on the table for discussion

examinateur, -trice [ɛgzaminatœr, -tris] NM,F examiner

examiner [3] [ɛgzamine] VT **1** *(réfléchir sur ▸ dossier, documents)* to examine, to go through; *(▸ requête, demande)* to examine, to consider; *(▸ affaire)* to investigate, to examine, to go into; *(▸ comptes)* to inspect, to go through

2 *(regarder de près ▸ meuble, signature etc)* to examine; **e. l'horizon** to scan the horizon; **e. les lieux** to inspect the premises; **nous allons e. la question** we're going to examine *or* look into the matter; **e. une question de près** to look at sth in detail; **e. qch à la loupe** to look at sth through a magnifying glass; *Fig* to have a very close look at sth, to scrutinize sth; **elle m'a examiné de la tête aux pieds** she eyed me from head to toe *or* looked me up and down

3 *Méd (lésion, malade)* to examine; **se faire e. par un médecin** to have oneself *or* be examined by a doctor; **tu devrais te faire e.** you should go and see a doctor; **se faire e. les yeux** to have one's eyes tested

4 *Scol & Univ (candidat)* to examine

VPR **s'examiner 1** *(emploi réfléchi)* to examine oneself; **s'e. dans un miroir** to examine oneself *or* to look (closely) at oneself in the mirror **2** *(emploi réciproque)* to scrutinize one another *or* each other; **ils s'examinaient avec méfiance** they were eyeing each other up

exanthème [ɛgzɑ̃tɛm] NM *Méd* exanthema

exaspérant, -e [ɛgzasperɑ̃, -ɑ̃t] ADJ exasperating, infuriating

exaspération [ɛgzasperasjɔ̃] NF **1** *(colère)* extreme annoyance, exasperation **2** *Littéraire (d'une douleur)* aggravation, worsening

exaspérer [18] [ɛgzaspere] VT **1** *(irriter)* to infuriate, to exasperate; **être exaspéré contre qn** to be exasperated with sb **2** *(intensifier ▸ dépit, désir)* to exacerbate; *(▸ douleur, tension)* to aggravate

exaucement [ɛgzosmɑ̃] NM fulfilment, granting

exaucer [16] [ɛgzose] VT **1** *(vœu)* to grant, to fulfil; *(prière)* to answer, to grant **2** *(personne)* to grant the wish of; **Dieu m'avait exaucé** God had answered *or* heard my prayer

ex cathedra [ɛkskatedra] ADV **1** *Rel* ex cathedra **2** *(doctement)* solemnly, with authority

excavateur, -trice [ɛkskavatœr, -tris] NM,F *Tech* excavator, digger

excavation [ɛkskavasjɔ̃] NF **1** *(trou ▸ artificiel)* excavation, hole; *(▸ naturel)* hollow, cave **2** *(creusement)* excavation, excavating

excavatrice [ɛkskavatris] *voir* **excavateur**

excaver [3] [ɛkskave] VT to excavate

excédant, -e [ɛksedɑ̃, -ɑ̃t] ADJ exasperating, infuriating

excédent [ɛksedɑ̃] NM **1** *(surplus)* surplus, excess; **e. de blé/main-d'œuvre** wheat/labour surplus; **il y a un e. de personnel dans le service** the department is overstaffed; **e. de bagages** excess luggage *or* baggage; **payer 30 euros d'e.** to pay 30 euros excess (charge); **e. de poids** excess weight **2** *Écon & Fin (d'un budget)* surplus; **dégager un e.** to show a surplus; **excédents et déficits** overs and shorts; **e. budgétaire** budget(ary) surplus; *Compta* **e. de caisse** cash overs; **e. commercial** trade surplus; **e. d'exploitation** operating profit

• **en excédent** ADJ surplus *(avant n)*, excess; **la balance commerciale est en e.** the trade balance shows a surplus, there is a trade surplus; **vous avez deux kilos en e.** your luggage is two kilos overweight *or* over

excédentaire [ɛksedɑ̃tɛr] ADJ *(budget)* surplus *(avant n)*; *(solde)* positive; *(poids)* excess; *(production)* excess, surplus; **balance commerciale e.** trade surplus; **la production est e.** production is over target

excéder [18] [ɛksede] VT **1** *(dépasser ▸ poids, prix)* to exceed, to be over, to be in excess of; *(▸ durée)* to exceed, to last more than; *(▸ limite)* to go beyond; *(▸ quantité, somme, période)* to exceed; **les recettes excèdent les dépenses** income is in excess of expenditure; **nos pertes excèdent nos bénéfices** our losses are greater than our profits; **e. les moyens de qn** to be beyond sb's means

2 *(outrepasser ▸ pouvoirs, responsabilités)* to exceed, to go beyond, to overstep; *(▸ compétences)* to be beyond

3 *(exaspérer)* to exasperate, to infuriate

4 *(épuiser)* **excédé de fatigue** exhausted, overtired; **excédé de travail** overworked

excellemment [ɛkselamɑ̃] ADV excellently

excellence [ɛkselɑ̃s] NF **1** *(qualité ▸ d'une prestation, d'un produit)* excellence **2** *(titre)* **E.** Excellency; **Son/Votre E.** His/Your Excellency

• **par excellence** ADV par excellence, archetypal; **c'est le macho par e.** he's the archetypal male chauvinist, he's the male chauvinist par excellence

excellent, -e [ɛkselɑ̃, -ɑ̃t] ADJ excellent

exceller [4] [ɛksele] VI to excel, to shine (**en** at *or* in); **pose-lui des questions en botanique, c'est là qu'il excelle** ask him questions on botany, that's where he shines; **e. dans** to excel in *or* at; **elle excelle dans la pâtisserie** she excels at baking, she's an excellent pastry cook

excentré, -e [ɛksɑ̃tre] ADJ **1** *Tech* thrown off centre, set over **2** *(quartier, stade)* outlying; **c'est très e.** it's quite a long way out

excentricité [ɛksɑ̃trisite] NF **1** *(attitude, acte)* eccentricity; **qu'est-ce que c'est encore que ces excentricités?** what's all this eccentric behaviour? **2** *Astron & Math* eccentricity **3** *(d'un quartier)* remoteness (from the town centre)

excentrique [ɛksɑ̃trik] ADJ **1** *(bizarre)* eccentric **2** *Math* eccentric **3** *(quartier, habitation)* outlying

NMF *(personne)* eccentric

excentriquement [ɛksɑ̃trikmɑ̃] ADV eccentrically

excepté[1] [ɛksɛpte] PRÉP except, apart from; **tous les enfants ont eu les oreillons, e. le plus petit** all the children had the mumps, except *or* apart from the youngest; **tous les jours e. quand il pleut** every day except *or* apart from *or* with the exception of when it rains

• **excepté que** CONJ except for *or* apart from the fact that; **tout s'est bien passé, e. qu'on a attendu trois heures** everything went well except for *or* apart from the fact that we had to wait three hours

excepté[2], -e [ɛksɛpte] ADJ *(après le nom)* **les femmes exceptées** except for *or* apart from the women; **vous deux exceptés** you two aside, except *or* apart from you two

excepter [4] [ɛksɛpte] VT to except (**de** from); **si l'on excepte Marie, elles sont toutes là** with the exception of *or* except for Marie they are all here

exception [ɛksɛpsjɔ̃] NF **1** *(chose, être ou événement hors norme)* exception; **ils sont tous très paresseux, à une e./quelques exceptions près** all of them with one exception/a few exceptions are very lazy; **faire e.** to be an exception; **être l'e.** to be the *or* an exception; **son cas est une** *ou* **fait e.** his/her case is an exception *or* is exceptional; **l'e. confirme la règle, c'est l'e. qui confirme la règle** the exception proves the rule; **sauf e.** almost without exception; **sauf e., ils n'ont pas le droit de regarder la télé** they are only very rarely allowed to watch television; **e. culturelle** cultural exception; **l'e. française** the French exception **2** *(dérogation)* exception (**à** to); **faire une e. pour qn/qch** to make an exception for sb/sth; **faire une e. à une règle** to make an exception to a rule; **faire e. de** *(exclure)* to make an exception of, to except; **si l'on fait e. des enfants** the children excepted, if you except the children **3** *Jur* plea; **e. d'illégalité/d'incompétence** plea of illegality/incompetence; **e. péremptoire** peremptory plea

• **à l'exception de, exception faite de** PRÉP except (for), with the exception of

• **d'exception** ADJ **1** *(mesure)* exceptional; *(loi)* emergency *(avant n)* **2** *(remarquable)* remarkable, exceptional; **c'est un être d'e.** *(homme)* he's an exceptional man; *(femme)* she's an exceptional woman

• **sans (aucune) exception** ADV without (any) exception; **sortez tous, sans e.!** out, every (single) one of you!

> **EXCEPTION FRANÇAISE**
>
> "L'exception française" is used to describe France's individual status in terms of economic development. It is characterized by a large public sector, by a larger degree of state intervention in the economy than in Britain or the US and by the persistence of a relatively generous welfare State coupled with greater investment in public services, all of which goes against the principles of market-driven economics. France is also keen to safeguard its film industry and has been campaigning in favour of "l'exception culturelle" – the notion that cultural products should not be treated in the same way as other commercial products and that consequently governments should be authorized to subsidize their film industries.

exceptionnalité [ɛksɛpsjɔnalite] NF exceptional character; **l'e. de ces mesures reflète l'e. de la situation** these exceptional *or* special measures reflect the exceptional situation

exceptionnel, -elle [ɛksɛpsjɔnɛl] ADJ **1** *(très rare ▸ faveur, chance, circonstances)* exceptional; *(▸ accident, complication)* exceptional, rare; *(▸ mesure)* exceptional, special; *(unique ▸ concert)* special, *Br* one-off; *(▸ offre, promotion)* special; **congé e.** special leave; **à titre e.** exceptionally **2** *(remarquable ▸ intelligence, œuvre)* exceptional; *(▸ personne)* remarkable, exceptional; **ne rien avoir d'e.** to be nothing special **3** *Pol (assemblée, conseil, mesures)* special, emergency *(avant n)*

NM **l'e.** the exceptional

exceptionnellement [ɛksɛpsjɔnɛlmɑ̃] ADV **1** *(beau, doué)* exceptionally, extremely **2** *(contrairement à l'habitude)* exceptionally; **e., le square est fermé ce soir** for one night only, the park is closed this evening; **e. tu peux partir maintenant** just this once you can leave now

excès [ɛksɛ] NM **1** *(surabondance)* surplus, excess; **e. de poids/calories** excess weight/calories; **un e. de sucre dans le sang** an excess of sugar in the blood; **c'est un peu un e. de précautions** these are rather excessive precautions; **e. de l'offre sur la demande** excess of supply over demand; **e. de zèle** overzealousness; **faire de l'e. de zèle, pécher par e. de zèle** to go beyond the call of duty, to be overzealous

2 *Transp* **e. de vitesse** speeding; **faire un e. de vitesse** to exceed *or* to break the speed limit, to speed

3 *(abus)* excess; **évitez tout e.** avoid overdoing things; *(alimentaire)* avoid overeating; **e. de langage** immoderate language; **se livrer à** *ou* **commettre des e. de langage** to use strong language; *Jur* **e. de pouvoir** abuse of power, *Spéc* action ultra vires

4 *(manque de mesure)* **tomber dans l'e.** to go to extremes, to overdo it; **tomber dans l'e. inverse** to go to the opposite extreme; *Prov* **l'e. en tout est un défaut** moderation in all things

NMPL **1 e. (de table)** overindulgence; **faire des e. (de table)** to eat and drink too much, to overindulge **2** *(violences, débauche)* excesses; **des e. de conduite** loose living

• **à l'excès** ADV to excess, excessively; **jusqu'à l'e.** to excess, excessively; **gentil/scrupuleux à l'e.** kind/scrupulous to a fault, overkind/overscrupulous

• **avec excès** ADV to excess, excessively, immoderately; **manger avec e.** to overeat, to eat excessively *or* to excess; **dépenser avec e.** to overspend

• **sans excès** ADV with moderation, moderately

excessif, -ive [ɛksesif, -iv] ADJ **1** *(chaleur, sévérité, prix, quantité)* excessive; *(colère)* undue; *(enthousiasme, optimisme)* undue, excessive; *(langage)* immoderate; *(opinion, idée)* extreme; **50 euros, ce n'est pas e.** 50 euros is quite a reasonable amount to pay; **des mois de travail e. l'ont rendu malade** he has become ill through months of overwork **2** *(personne)* extreme; **c'est quelqu'un de très e.** he's given to extremes of behaviour; **elle est excessive dans ses critiques** she overdoes her criticism

excessivement [ɛksesivmɑ̃] ADV **1** *(trop ▸ raffiné)* excessively; **e. cher** overpriced **2** *(extrêmement)* extremely; **il fait e. froid** it's hideously cold

exciper [3] [ɛksipe] **exciper de** VT IND **1** *Jur* **e. de l'inconstitutionnalité d'une loi** to claim that a law is unconstitutional, to challenge the constitutionality of a law **2** *Littéraire* **e. de son ignorance/sa bonne foi** to plead ignorance/one's good faith

excipient [ɛksipjɑ̃] NM *Pharm* excipient, binder

exciser [3] [ɛksize] VT *Méd* to excise

exciseur, -euse [ɛksizœr, -øz] NM,F *Méd* excisionist, excisor

excision [ɛksizjɔ̃] NF *Méd* excision

excitabilité [ɛksitabilite] NF excitability

excitable [ɛksitabl] ADJ **1** *(facilement irrité)* **il est très e.** he gets worked up quickly *or* annoyed easily **2** *Physiol* excitable

excitant, -e [ɛksitɑ̃, -ɑ̃t] ADJ **1** *(stimulant ▸ boisson)* stimulating **2** *(aguichant ▸ femme, homme, tenue)* arousing **3** *(passionnant ▸ aventure, projet, vie)* exciting, thrilling; *(▸ film, roman)* exciting; **le match devient un peu plus e.** the match is warming up; **ce n'est pas très e.!** it's not very exciting!

NM stimulant

excitation [ɛksitasjɔ̃] NF **1** *(exaltation)* excitement; **ils étaient dans un état d'e.!** they were in such a state of excitement *or* such an excited state!; **dans l'e. du moment** in the heat of the moment

2 *(stimulation ▸ d'un sens)* excitation; **e. (sexuelle)** (sexual) arousal *or* excitement

3 *(incitation)* incitement (**à** to); **e. à la révolte** incitement to rebellion; **e. des mineurs à la débauche** incitement of minors to commit immoral acts

4 *Physiol* excitation, stimulation

5 *Électron & Phys* excitation

excité, -e [ɛksite] ADJ **1** *(enthousiasmé)* excited, thrilled; **nous étions tout excités à l'idée de la revoir** we were really excited at *or* thrilled by the idea of seeing her again

2 *(stimulé ▸ sens, curiosité, imagination)* aroused, fired

3 *(agité ▸ enfant, chien)* excited, restless; **un jeune homme, passablement e., lançait des injures à la police** a young man, who was rather worked up, was shouting abuse at the police

4 *(sexuellement ▸ organe, personne)* aroused, excited

NM,F *Péj* hothead; **les excités du volant** dangerous drivers

exciter [3] [ɛksite] VT **1** *(exalter)* to excite, to exhilarate; **la vitesse l'excite** speed exhilarates him/her; *Fam* **les malheurs des autres, ça l'excite!** other people's misfortunes turn him/her on!

2 *(rendre agité ▸ drogue, café)* to overstimulate, to stimulate; **n'excite pas les enfants avant le coucher** don't get the children excited before bed

3 *(pousser)* to urge on; **e. qn à la révolte** to urge sb to rebel, to incite sb to rebellion; **e. qn contre qn** to set sb against sb, to work sb up against sb

4 *(attiser ▸ admiration, envie)* to provoke; *(▸ curiosité, intérêt, soupçons)* to arouse, to stir up; *(▸ amour, jalousie)* to arouse, to inflame, to kindle

5 *(intensifier ▸ appétit)* to whet; *(▸ rage)* to whip up; *(▸ désir)* to increase, to sharpen; *(▸ douleur)* to intensify

6 *(sexuellement)* to excite, to arouse

7 *Fam (enthousiasmer)* to excite, to thrill, to get worked up; **cette perspective ne m'excite pas vraiment!** I can't say I'm thrilled *or* wild about the idea!

8 *Fam (mettre en colère)* to bug, to annoy; **tu commences à m'e.!** you're beginning to bug me!

9 *Physiol (nerf, muscle)* to excite, to stimulate; *Biol* to stimulate

10 *Électron* to excite

USAGE ABSOLU *(rendre agité)* **le café/le tabac excite** coffee/tobacco acts as a stimulant

VPR **s'exciter 1** *Fam (se mettre en colère)* to get worked up; **t'excite pas!** don't get worked up!, keep your shirt on! **2** *Fam (s'acharner)* **j'ai commencé à m'e. sur la serrure** I was losing my patience with the lock **3** *(s'exalter)* to get carried away *or* excited *or* overexcited; **ne t'excite pas trop, ce n'est qu'un petit rôle** don't get carried away, it's only a small part

exclamatif, -ive [ɛksklamatif, -iv] ADJ exclamatory

exclamation [ɛksklamasjɔ̃] NF **1** *(cri)* exclamation, cry; **des exclamations de joie/surprise** cries of joy/surprise **2** *Ling* exclamation

exclamative [ɛksklamativ] *voir* **exclamatif**

exclamer [3] [ɛksklame] **s'exclamer** VPR to exclaim, to cry out; **"toi!" s'était-il exclamé** "you!" he had cried out *or* exclaimed; **s'e. de surprise/colère** to cry out in surprise/anger; **tous s'exclamaient sur le nouveau-né** they were all admiring the new-born baby; **s'e. sur la montée du chômage/de la violence** to make a lot of noise about rising unemployment/violence

exclu, -e [ɛkskly] ADJ **1** *(non compris)* excluded, left out; **du 15 au 30 e.** from the 15th to the 30th exclusive; **le mois d'août jusqu'au 31 e.** the month of August excluding the 31st; **prix des travaux, TVA exclue** the cost of the work, excluding *Br* VAT *or Am* sales tax **2** *(rejeté ▸ hypothèse, solution)* ruled out, dismissed, rejected; **une victoire de la gauche n'est pas exclue** a victory of the left is not to be ruled out; **il est e. que...** it's out of the question *or* impossible that...; **il est e. qu'il vienne avec nous** it's out of the question for him to come with us, *Fam* there's no way he's coming with us; **il n'est pas e. qu'on les retrouve** it's not impossible that they might be found **3** *(renvoyé ▸ définitivement)* expelled, excluded; *(▸ provisoirement)* suspended

NM,F **le grand e. du palmarès à Cannes** the big loser in the Cannes festival

• **exclus** NMPL **les exclus (de la société)** the underprivileged; **les exclus du progrès** those whom progress has ignored *or* passed by

exclure [96] [ɛksklyr] VT **1** *(expulser ▸ membre, élève)* to expel, to exclude; *(▸ sportif)* to ban, to expel; **e. qn de** *(parti, école, comité)* to expel sb from; *(équipe, compétition)* to ban *or* to expel sb from; *(fonction publique)* to remove from; *(salle, réunion)* to eject from; **elle s'est fait e. de l'école pour trois jours** she's been suspended from school for three days

2 *(écarter)* to exclude (**de** from); **ils l'excluaient de leurs jeux** they used to exclude him/her from their games; **e. le pain de son régime** to exclude *or* to cut out bread from one's diet

3 *(mettre à part)* to exclude, to leave aside *or* out; **si l'on exclut le mois de mars** March excluded; **si l'on exclut de petits incidents techniques** apart from a few minor technical hitches

4 *(être incompatible avec)* to exclude, to preclude; **la chimiothérapie n'exclut pas d'autres formes de traitement** chemotherapy doesn't preclude other forms of treatment; **l'un n'exclut pas l'autre** they're not mutually exclusive; **cela n'exclut pas que vous puissiez enseigner** that doesn't rule out the possibility of your teaching

5 *(rejeter ▸ hypothèse)* to exclude, to rule out, to reject; **e. l'hypothèse d'un suicide** to rule out suicide; **cette solution est à e.** this solution is out of the question

VPR **s'exclure 1** *(solutions, traitements)* to exclude *or* to preclude one another, to be incompatible *or* mutually exclusive **2** *(s'exposer au rejet)* to cut oneself off; **s'e. de** to cut oneself off from

exclusif, -ive [ɛksklyzif, -iv] ADJ **1** *(droit, modèle, privilège)* exclusive; *(agent, droits de reproduction, usage)* exclusive, sole; *(dépositaire, concessionnaire)* sole; **avoir la jouissance exclusive de** to be the sole user *or* possessor of; **avoir un intérêt e. pour qch** to be solely interested in sth; **vente exclusive en pharmacie** sold exclusively in pharmacies; **propriété exclusive de l'auteur** exclusive property of the author

2 e. de *(incompatible avec)* exclusive of, incompatible with

3 *(absolu ▸ amour, relation)* exclusive; **les jumeaux ont une relation exclusive** the twins relate to nobody outside each other; **il est e. en amour** he stays faithful to his partner, he believes in monogamy; **avoir un goût e. pour qch** to only like sth; **dans le but e. de faire qch** with the sole aim of doing sth

4 *(sélectif)* selective; **être e. dans ses goûts/amitiés** to be selective *or* discriminating in one's tastes/choice of friends

5 *(dossier, image, reportage)* exclusive; **une interview exclusive** an exclusive (interview)

6 *Ling & Math* disjunctive; **le "ou" e. de l'expression "ouvert ou fermé"** the disjunctive "or" in the phrase "open or shut"

• **exclusive** NF *(exclusion)* debarment; **frapper qn/un pays d'exclusive** to debar sb/a country; **jeter** *ou* **prononcer l'exclusive contre qn** to debar sb; **sans exclusive** without exception

exclusion [ɛksklyzjɔ̃] NF **1** *(renvoi)* expulsion (**de** from); *(de la fonction publique)* removal (**de** from); *(d'une salle, d'une réunion)* ejection (**de** from); **demander l'e. de qn** to ask for sb to be expelled; **son e. du club** his/her expulsion from the club; **e. temporaire** suspension **2** *(dans la société)* **l'e. (sociale)** social exclusion **3** *Math* exclusion

• **à l'exclusion de** PRÉP to the exclusion of; *(à l'exception de)* except, apart from, with the exception of; **tous les jours à l'e. de jeudi** every day apart from Thursday *or* Thursday excluded

exclusive [ɛksklyziv] *voir* **exclusif**

exclusivement [ɛksklyzivmɑ̃] ADV **1** *(uniquement)* exclusively, solely; **ouvert le lundi e.** open on Mondays only; **parking e. réservé aux clients de l'hôtel** customer parking only **2** *(non inclus)* **du 1er au 10 e.** from the 1st to the 10th exclusive **3** *(aimer)* exclusively, in an exclusive way; **il aime e. les opéras de Verdi** he likes Verdi's operas to the exclusion of all others

exclusivisme [ɛksklyzivism] NM exclusivism

exclusivité [ɛksklyzivite] NF **1** *Com (droit)* sole *or* exclusive rights; **avoir l'e. de** to have the exclusive rights to; **c'est notre journal qui a eu l'e. de son interview** our paper had an exclusive with him/her; **nous avons l'e. de la vente de ce produit** we have the (sole) rights for this product; **avoir un contrat d'e.** to have an exclusive contract

2 *(chose unique ▸ article)* exclusive (article); *(▸ interview)* exclusive (interview), scoop; *(▸ film)* exclusive film; **ce modèle est une e.** this is an exclusive design

3 *TV (de film)* first run; *Cin* movie on general release

4 *(privilège exclusif)* **il n'a pas l'e. du talent** he doesn't have a monopoly on talent

• **en exclusivité** ADV **1** *Com* exclusively; **ce modèle se trouve en e. chez...** this model is exclusive to *or* can only be found at... **2** *(diffusé, publié)* exclusively; **en e. sur notre chaîne** exclusively on our channel; **en e. dans 'le Figaro'** a 'Figaro' exclusive; **ses lettres ont été publiées en e. par le magazine 'Aujourd'hui'** his/her letters were published as an exclusive by 'Aujourd'hui' magazine **3** *Cin* **film en e.** movie on general release; **film en première e.** first showing

excommunication [ɛkskɔmynikasjɔ̃] NF *Rel* excommunication

excommunier [9] [ɛkskɔmynje] VT *Rel* to excommunicate; **se faire e.** to be excommunicated

excrément [ɛkskremɑ̃] NM excrement

• **excréments** NMPL excrement, faeces

excrémentiel, -elle [ɛkskremɑ̃sjɛl] ADJ excremental

excréter [18] [ɛkskrete] VT to excrete

excréteur, -trice [ɛkskretœr, -tris] ADJ excretory

excrétion [ɛkskresjɔ̃] *Physiol* NF excretion

• **excrétions** NFPL *(substance)* excreta

excrétoire [ɛkskretwar] ADJ excretory

excrétrice [ɛkskretris] *voir* **excréteur**

excroissance [ɛkskrwasɑ̃s] NF **1** *Méd* growth, *Spéc* excrescence **2** *Fig* excrescence

excursion [ɛkskyrsjɔ̃] **NF 1** *(voyage ▸ en car)* excursion, trip; *(▸ à pied)* ramble, hike; *(▸ à bicyclette)* ride, tour; *(▸ en voiture)* drive; **faire une e., partir en e.** *(avec un véhicule)* to go on an excursion; *(à pied)* to go on *or* for a hike; **excursions de deux jours au pays de Galles** two-day tours *or* trips to Wales; **e. en car** coach trip; **e. en mer** boat trip; **e. en montagne** hill walk **2** *(sortie ▸ scolaire)* outing, trip; **l'e. annuelle de l'école** the annual school outing *or* trip

excursionner [3] [ɛkskyrsjɔne] **VI** *(faire une excursion ▸ en car)* to go on an excursion *or* trip; *(▸ à pied)* to go hiking *or* walking

excursionniste [ɛkskyrsjɔnist] **NMF 1** *(d'un jour)* day-tripper **2** *(randonneur)* hiker, rambler

excusable [ɛkskyzabl] **ADJ** excusable, forgivable; **ce n'est absolument pas e.** it's absolutely inexcusable *or* unforgivable; **allons, c'est e.!** come on, it's understandable!

excuse [ɛkskyz] **NF 1** *(motif allégué)* excuse; **j'étais fatigué – ce n'est pas une e.!** I was tired – that's no excuse!; **il a toujours une bonne e. pour ne pas téléphoner** he always has a good excuse for not phoning; **tu n'as aucune e.** you have no excuse; **trouver une e. à qch/pour faire qch** to find an excuse for sth/for doing sth; **trouver des excuses à qn** to find excuses for *or* to excuse sb; *Ironique* **la belle e.!** what an *or* that's some excuse!; *Fam* **faites e.!** *(regrets)* I do apologize!; *(objection)* excuse me!; **mot d'e.** absence note **2** *Jur* **e. absolutoire** excuse involving acquittal; **e. légale** legal excuse **3** *(au tarot)* excuse

• **excuses NFPL** apology; **exiger des excuses** to demand an apology; **faire** *ou* **présenter ses excuses à qn** to offer one's apologies *or* to apologize to sb; **je vous fais mes plus plates excuses** *ou* **mes excuses les plus plates** you have my humble apologies; **tu me dois des excuses** you owe me an apology; **lettre d'excuses** letter of apology; **mille excuses!** *(dans une conversation)* I'm so sorry!; *(dans une lettre)* please accept my apologies!

excuser [3] [ɛkskyze] **VT 1** *(pardonner ▸ conduite)* to excuse, to forgive; *(▸ personne)* to forgive; **excusez ma curiosité mais…** excuse *or* forgive my curiosity but…; **excusez mon indiscrétion mais…** excuse my being indiscreet *or* forgive me for being indiscreet but…; **excuse-moi d'appeler si tard** forgive me *or* I do apologize for phoning so late; **excuse-moi de te déranger** I'm sorry to disturb you, excuse me for disturbing you; **excuse-moi de ne pas t'avoir téléphoné** I'm sorry I didn't phone you; **excusez-moi de vous le faire remarquer** excuse me for saying so, I hope you don't mind my mentioning it; **excusez-moi** *(regret)* forgive me, I'm sorry, I do apologize; *(interpellation, objection, après un hoquet)* excuse me; **oh, excusez-moi, je vous ai fait mal?** oh, sorry, did I hurt you?; **excusez-moi mais je suis pressé** excuse me *or* I'm sorry but I'm in a hurry; **je vous prie de** *ou* **veuillez m'e.** I (do) beg your pardon, I do apologize; **tu es tout excusé** you're forgiven, please don't apologize; *Ironique* **excusez du peu!** would you believe!, if you please!

2 *(justifier ▸ attitude, personne)* to excuse, to find excuses *or* an excuse for; **tu l'excuses toujours!** you're always finding excuses for him/her!; **l'ignorance n'excuse rien** ignorance is no excuse

3 *(accepter l'absence de)* to excuse; **se faire e.** to ask to be excused; **liste des présents, absents, excusés** list of those present, those absent and those from whom apologies have been received; **e. un juré** to excuse a juror (from attendance)

4 *(présenter les excuses de)* **excuse-moi auprès de lui** apologize to him for me

VPR s'excuser 1 *(demander pardon)* to apologize; **ne vous excusez pas** (please) don't apologize; *Ironique* **surtout ne t'excuse pas!** an apology wouldn't go amiss!; **tu pourrais t'e.!** it wouldn't hurt you to say sorry!; **s'e. auprès de qn** to apologize to sb; **s'e. de qch/de faire qch** to apologize for sth/for doing sth; **je m'excuse de mon retard/de vous interrompre** sorry for being late/for interrupting you; *Fam* **je m'excuse!** sorry!, excuse me!; *Prov* **qui s'excuse, s'accuse** he who excuses himself accuses himself **2** *(ton indigné)* **je m'excuse (mais…)!** excuse me *or* I'm sorry (but…)!; **je m'excuse mais je n'ai jamais dit ça!** excuse me but I never said that!

exécrable [ɛgzekrabl] **ADJ 1** *(mauvais ▸ dîner, goût, spectacle)* abysmal, awful, foul; *(▸ temps)* awful, rotten, wretched; *(▸ travail)* abysmal; **il est d'une humeur e. aujourd'hui** he's in a foul *or* filthy mood today; **avoir un caractère e.** to be foul-tempered; **elle a été e. avec moi** she was horrible to me **2** *(crime)* heinous

exécrablement [ɛgzekrabləmɑ̃] **ADV** abominably, abysmally

exécration [ɛgzekrasjɔ̃] **NF** *Littéraire (dégoût, horreur)* execration; **avoir qch en e.** to loathe *or* to abhor sth

exécrer [18] [ɛgzekre] **VT** *Littéraire* to loathe, to abhor

exécutable [ɛgzekytabl] **ADJ 1** *(réalisable)* possible, feasible; **être facilement/difficilement e.** to be easy/difficult to do **2** *Ordinat (programme)* executable

exécutant, -e [ɛgzekytɑ̃, -ɑ̃t] **NM,F 1** *(musicien)* performer **2** *Péj (subalterne)* subordinate, underling; **je ne suis qu'un simple e.** I only carry out orders

exécuter [3] [ɛgzekyte] **VT 1** *(mouvement, cabriole)* to do, to execute; **e. une manœuvre compliquée** *(en voiture)* to go through *or* to execute a complicated manoeuvre

2 *(confectionner ▸ maquette, statue)* to make; *(▸ tableau)* to paint; *(▸ décor)* to produce, to execute

3 *(interpréter ▸ symphonie)* to perform, to play; *(▸ chorégraphie)* to perform, to dance

4 *(mener à bien ▸ consigne, ordre, mission, plan)* to carry out, to execute; *(▸ projet)* to carry out

5 *(ordre)* to carry out

6 *(tuer ▸ condamné, otage)* to execute, to put to death

7 *Fam (vaincre ▸ joueur)* to slaughter, to trounce; **elle s'est fait e. en 2 sets 6–1/6–0** she was disposed of in straight sets 6–1/6–0

8 *Jur (testament)* to execute; *(contrat)* to fulfil the terms of, to perform; *(arrêt, jugement, traité)* to enforce; *(débiteur)* to distrain upon

9 *Ordinat (programme)* to run; *(commande)* to execute, to carry out

VPR s'exécuter to comply, to do what one is told; **il faudra bien vous e.** you'll have to bring yourself to do it

exécuteur, -trice [ɛgzekytœr, -tris] **NM,F** *Jur (d'un jugement)* enforcer; **e. testamentaire** executor; **exécutrice testamentaire** executrix

NM *Hist* **e. des hautes œuvres** executioner; *Hum* axeman; **e. des basses œuvres** henchman

exécutif, -ive [ɛgzekytif, -iv] **ADJ** executive; **le pouvoir e.** the executive (branch)

NM l'e. the executive

exécution [ɛgzekysjɔ̃] **NF 1** *(d'une maquette, d'une statue)* execution, making; *(d'un tableau)* execution, painting

2 *(d'une symphonie, d'une chorégraphie)* performance; **un morceau de musique d'une e. difficile** a piece of music which is difficult to play; **droit d'e.** performing rights

3 *(d'une menace, d'un ordre, d'une décision)* carrying out; *(d'un projet)* execution; *(d'une promesse)* fulfilment; **mettre qch à e.** to carry sth out; **mettre un projet à e.** to put a plan into execution *or* operation, to carry out a plan; *Mil* **e.!** at the double!; *Hum* **va ranger ta chambre, e.!** go and tidy up your bedroom, NOW *or* at the double!

4 *(d'une commande)* carrying out

5 *(d'un condamné)* **e. (capitale)** execution; **ordre d'e.** death warrant

6 *Jur (d'un jugement, d'un traité)* enforcement; *(d'un débiteur)* distraint (**de** upon); *(d'un contrat)* fulfilment, performance

7 *Ordinat (d'un programme)* execution, running; *(d'une commande)* execution, carrying out

exécutive [ɛgzekytiv] *voir* **exécutif**

exécutoire [ɛgzekytwar] *Jur* **ADJ** *(jugement)* enforceable; **mesure e.** binding measure; **titre e.** writ of execution

exécutrice [ɛgzekytris] *voir* **exécuteur**

exégèse [ɛgzeʒɛz] **NF** *Littérature* exegesis; **faire l'e. de** to write a critical interpretation of

exégète [ɛgzeʒɛt] **NMF** *Littérature* exegete

exemplaire[1] [ɛgzɑ̃plɛr] **ADJ 1** *(qui donne l'exemple ▸ conduite)* exemplary, perfect; *(▸ personne)* exemplary, model; **d'une correction e.** perfectly correct **2** *(qui sert d'exemple ▸ punition)* exemplary

exemplaire[2] [ɛgzɑ̃plɛr] **NM 1** *(d'un document)* copy; **e. gratuit** presentation copy; **en deux exemplaires** in duplicate; **en trois exemplaires** in triplicate; **photocopier un texte en 20 exemplaires** to make 20 photocopies of a text; **le contrat est fait en quatre exemplaires** there are four copies of the contract; **le livre a été tiré à 10 000 exemplaires** 10,000 copies of the book were published; **le journal tire à 150000 exemplaires** the newspaper has a circulation of 150,000 **2** *(d'un coquillage, d'une plante)* specimen, example

exemplairement [ɛgzɑ̃plɛrmɑ̃] **ADV** exemplarily; **elle a vécu e.** she led an exemplary life; **il a été puni e.** he was punished as an example to others

exemple [ɛgzɑ̃pl] **NM 1** *(d'architecture, d'un défaut, d'une qualité)* example; *(d'une situation)* example, instance; **donner qch en** *ou* **comme e.** to give sth as an example; **un bel e. de poterie égyptienne** a fine example of Egyptian pottery; **c'est un bel e. de coopération** that's a fine example *or* instance of cooperation

2 *(modèle)* example, model; **elle est l'e. de la parfaite secrétaire** she's a model secretary; **il est l'e. type du yuppie** he's a typical yuppie; **il est l'e. même du type qui ne sait pas ce qu'il veut** he's the perfect example of someone who doesn't know what he wants; **c'est l'e. même de la générosité** he's/she's the epitome of generosity; **donner l'e. (à qn)** to set an example (to sb); **donner le bon/mauvais e.** to set a good/bad example; **faire un e. de qn** to make an example of sb; **prendre e. sur qn, prendre qn pour** *ou* **comme e.** to take sb as a model *or* an example, to model oneself on sb; **citer qn en e.** to hold sb up as an example; **servir d'e.** *(personne)* to be taken as an example; **servir d'e. à qn** *(réussite)* to be an example to sb; *(punition)* to be a lesson *or* a warning to sb; **que cela vous serve d'e.** let this be a warning to you; **suivre l'e. de qn** to follow sb's example, to take one's cue from sb

3 *Gram & Ling (illustration d'une règle)* (illustrative) example; **donnez-moi des exemples à l'impératif** give me examples in the imperative; *Fam* **j'en connais plein: e., ma mère** I know lots: my mother, for example *or* for instance

• **à l'exemple de PRÉP à l'e. de son maître** following his master's example

• **par exemple ADV 1** *(comme illustration)* for example *or* instance; **un de ces jours, par e. dimanche** one of these days, say *or* for example *or* for instance on Sunday **2** *(marque la surprise, l'indignation)* **(ça) par e., c'est Pierre!** Pierre! well I never!; **ça par e., le verre a disparu!** well, well, well, the glass has disappeared!; **ah non, par e.!** I should think not!

• **pour l'exemple ADV fusillé pour l'e.** shot as an example (to others)

• **sans exemple ADJ** unprecedented; **être d'une gentillesse/d'un égoïsme sans e.** to be of unparalleled kindness/selfishness

exemplification [ɛgzɑ̃plifikasjɔ̃] **NF** exemplification, exemplifying

exemplifier [9] [ɛgzɑ̃plifje] **VT** to exemplify

exempt, -e [ɛgzɑ̃, -ɑ̃t] **ADJ 1** *(dispensé)* **e. de** *(d'une obligation)* exempt from; **e. d'impôts** tax-exempt, exempt from tax; **produits exempts de taxes** duty-free *or* non dutiable goods; **e. de port** carriage free; **e. de droits (de douane)** free of duty, duty-free; **e. de TVA** zero-rated **2** *(dépourvu)* **e. de danger** danger-free; **e. d'erreur** faultless; **son attitude n'était pas exempte d'un certain mépris** his/her attitude wasn't without contempt, there was a touch of contempt in his/her attitude

NM *Hist* exempt

NM,F *(personne)* **les exempts d'éducation physique** pupils exempted from physical education

exempter [3] [ɛgzɑ̃te] **VT il a été exempté du service militaire** he has been exempted from doing military service; **e. un élève d'éducation physique** to exempt a pupil from physical education; **e. qn d'impôts** to exempt sb from taxes; **cette vie tran-**

quille l'exemptait de tout souci this quiet life freed him/her from all worries

exemption [ɛgzɑ̃psjɔ̃] **NF** exemption (**de** from)

exercé, -e [ɛgzɛrse] **ADJ** *(oreille, œil)* trained, keen; *(main)* practised; *(personne)* trained, experienced

exercer [16] [ɛgzɛrse] **VT 1** *(pratiquer)* **quel métier exercez-vous?** what's your job?; **e. le métier de dentiste/forgeron** to work as a dentist/blacksmith, to be a dentist by profession/a blacksmith by trade; **e. la médecine** to practise medicine; **e. des fonctions** to carry out duties; **il exerce ses talents en tant qu'avocat** he works as a lawyer

2 *(autorité, influence)* to exercise, to exert; *(droit, privilège)* to exercise; *(sanctions)* to carry out; **e. une influence sur** to exercise *or* to exert an influence on; **e. une pression sur qch** to press sth, to exert pressure on sth; **e. une pression sur qn** to put pressure on *or* to pressurize sb; **e. des sanctions contre** to carry out sanctions against; **e. des poursuites contre qn** to bring an action against sb, to take legal action against sb; **e. sa verve contre qn** to make sb the object of one's wit

3 *(entraîner ▸ oreille, esprit, mémoire, corps)* to train, to exercise; **e. qn à faire qch** to train sb to do sth; **e. un chien à attaquer** *ou* **à l'attaque** to train a dog to attack

4 *Littéraire (mettre à l'épreuve ▸ patience)* to try (sorely)

USAGE ABSOLU *(sujet: dentiste, avocat, médecin)* to be in practice, to practise; **elle n'exerce plus** she doesn't practise any more

VPR s'exercer 1 *(s'entraîner)* to practise; **s'e. à qch/à faire qch** to practise sth/doing sth; **s'e. au piano** to practise (playing) the piano **2** *(se manifester ▸ autorité, pouvoir)* to make itself felt; **sa méchanceté s'exerce aussi contre ses enfants** his/her nastiness also affects his/her children **3** *(s'appliquer)* **s'e. sur** *(sujet: force, pression)* to be brought to bear on, to be exerted on

exercice [ɛgzɛrsis] **NM 1** *(mouvement physique)* exercise; **exercices d'assouplissement/d'échauffement** stretching/warm-up exercises; **exercices respiratoires** (deep) breathing exercises; **exercices au sol** floor exercises; **faire des exercices pour les abdominaux** to do exercises for *or* to exercise one's stomach muscles

2 *(sport)* **l'e. (physique)** (physical) exercise; **faire de l'e.** to take exercise, to exercise; **tu devrais faire plus d'e.** you should exercise more *or* take more exercise; **je manque d'e.** I don't take enough exercise

3 *(pour l'apprentissage)* & *Scol* exercise; **faire un e.** to do an exercise; **e. de chimie** chemistry exercise; **faire faire des exercices à qn** to give sb exercises; **faire des exercices au piano** to do (some) piano exercises; *Littérature* **e. de style** stylistic composition; **e. d'évacuation en cas d'incendie** fire drill

4 *Mil* drill, exercise; **exercices de tir** shooting drill *or* practice; **faire l'e.** to drill

5 *(usage)* **l'e. du pouvoir/d'un droit** exercising power/a right; **dans l'e. de ses fonctions** in the exercise of one's duties

6 *(d'une profession)* practice; **il prend sa retraite après 30 ans d'e.** *(dentiste, médecin, avocat)* he is retiring after 30 years in practice; *(fonctionnaire, enseignant)* he's retiring after 30 years in the profession; **être condamné pour e. illégal de la médecine** to be sentenced for practising medicine illegally

7 *Rel* **l'e. du culte** public worship

8 *Fin Br* financial year, *Am* fiscal year; **les impôts pour l'e. 2006** taxes for the 2006 fiscal *or* tax year; **en fin d'e.** at the end of the *Br* financial *or Am* fiscal year; **e. budgétaire** budgetary year; **e. comptable** accounting year; **e. en cours** *Br* current financial year, *Am* current fiscal year; **e. écoulé** last *Br* financial *or Am* fiscal year; **e. financier** *Br* financial *or Am* fiscal year; **e. fiscal** tax year

• **à l'exercice ADV** *Mil* on parade

• **en exercice ADJ** *(député, juge)* sitting; *(membre de comité)* serving; *(avocat, médecin)* practising; **être en e.** *(diplomate, magistrat)* to be in *or* to hold office; **le président en e.** the president in office

exerciseur [ɛgzɛrsizœr] **NM** *(gén)* exercise machine *or* bench; *(pour la poitrine)* chest expander

exergue [ɛgzɛrg] **NM 1** *(au début d'un texte)* epigraph; *(sous une œuvre d'art)* inscription; **mettre une citation en e. à un** *ou* **d'un texte** to head a text with a quotation, to put in a quotation as an epigraph to a text; *Fig* **mettre un argument en e.** to underline *or* to stress an argument **2** *(sur une médaille ▸ espace)* exergue; *(▸ inscription)* epigraph

exfoliant, -e [ɛksfɔljɑ̃, -ɑ̃t] **ADJ** exfoliating, exfoliative

NM exfoliant

exfoliation [ɛksfɔljasjɔ̃] **NF** exfoliation, exfoliating *(UNCOUNT)*

exfolier [9] [ɛksfɔlje] **VT** *(arbre, ardoise, peau)* to exfoliate

VPR s'exfolier *(écorce, os, tendon)* to exfoliate, to scale off

exhalaison [ɛgzalɛzɔ̃] **NF** *(odeur ▸ agréable)* fragrance, *Sout* exhalation; *(▸ désagréable)* unpleasant odour, *Sout* exhalation

exhalation [ɛgzalasjɔ̃] **NF** exhalation

exhaler [3] [ɛgzale] **VT 1** *(dégager ▸ parfum)* to exhale; *(▸ gaz, effluves, vapeur)* to exhale, to give off

2 *(émettre ▸ soupir)* to breathe; *(▸ gémissement)* to utter, *Littéraire* to give forth; *(▸ chaleur)* to give off

3 *Littéraire (être empreint de)* **la maison exhalait la mélancolie/le bonheur** the house exuded melancholy/radiated happiness

4 *(en respirant)* to exhale

VPR s'exhaler *(odeur, vapeur)* to be given off, to waft (**de** from); *Fig (sensualité, autorité, force)* to emanate, to exude (**de** from)

exhaussement [ɛgzosmɑ̃] **NM** *Constr* raising

exhausser [3] [ɛgzose] **VT** *Constr (bâtiment, mur)* to raise; **le bâtiment a été exhaussé de deux étages** two floors were added to the building

exhaustif, -ive [ɛgzostif, -iv] **ADJ** exhaustive

exhaustivement [ɛgzostivmɑ̃] **ADV** exhaustively

exhaustivité [ɛgzostivite] **NF** exhaustiveness

exhiber [3] [ɛgzibe] **VT 1** *Péj (afficher ▸ décorations, muscles)* to display, to show off; *(▸ richesses, savoir)* to show off, to flaunt **2** *(au cirque, à la foire)* to show, to exhibit **3** *(document officiel)* to produce, to show, to present

VPR s'exhiber *(parader)* to parade (around), to flaunt oneself; *(impudiquement)* to expose oneself

exhibition [ɛgzibisjɔ̃] **NF 1** *Péj (comportement)* piece of provocative behaviour; **après cette e. ridicule, tu n'as plus qu'à t'excuser!** apologize for making such an absurd exhibition of yourself!

2 *Péj (étalage)* display; *(de richesses, de savoir)* flaunting, showing off; **une e. de pectoraux sur la plage** a display of muscular chests on the beach; *Jur* **e. sexuelle** indecent exposure

3 *(compétition)* show; *(dans un concours)* showing; **e. de chiens de race** pedigree dog show; **e. de bétail** cattle show

4 *(comme attraction)* exhibiting; **e. d'animaux de cirque** exhibiting circus animals

5 *Sport* exhibition

6 *(présentation ▸ de documents)* presentation

> Il faut noter que le nom anglais **exhibition** est un faux ami. Il signifie le plus souvent **exposition.**

exhibitionnisme [ɛgzibisjɔnism] **NM** exhibitionism

exhibitionniste [ɛgzibisjɔnist] **ADJ** exhibitionistic

NMF exhibitionist

exhibo [ɛgzibo] **NMF** *Fam (abrév* **exhibitionniste)** exhibitionist[□]

exhortation [ɛgzɔrtasjɔ̃] **NF** exhortation; **la foule, excitée par ses exhortations** the crowd, excited by his/her exhortations; **e. à** call for; **exhortations à la modération** calls for moderation

exhorter [3] [ɛgzɔrte] **VT** to urge; **e. qn à la patience** to urge *or* to exhort sb to be patient; **e. qn à la prudence** to urge *or* to exhort sb to be careful; **e. qn à faire qch** to exhort *or* to urge sb to do sth

exhumation [ɛgzymasjɔ̃] **NF 1** *(d'un cadavre)* exhumation; *(d'objets enfouis)* excavation, digging out **2** *Fig (du passé, de vieux sentiments)* resurrection; *(de vieux documents)* unearthing

exhumer [3] [ɛgzyme] **VT 1** *(déterrer ▸ cadavre)* to exhume; *(▸ objets enfouis)* to excavate, to dig out **2** *(passé, vieux sentiments)* to resurrect; *(vieux documents)* to unearth, to rescue from oblivion

exigeant, -e [ɛgziʒɑ̃, -ɑ̃t] **ADJ 1** *(pointilleux ▸ maître, professeur)* demanding, exacting; *(▸ malade)* demanding; *(▸ client)* demanding, particular, hard to please; **je suis très e. sur la qualité** I'm very particular about quality; **tu es trop exigeante avec tes amis** you ask too much of *or* expect too much from your friends; **être e. envers soi-même** to demand a lot of *or* to set high standards for oneself; **ne sois pas trop e., c'est ton premier emploi** don't be too demanding *or* don't expect too much, it's your first job **2** *(ardu ▸ métier, travail)* demanding, exacting

exigence [ɛgziʒɑ̃s] **NF 1** *(demande ▸ d'un client)* requirement; *(▸ d'un ravisseur)* demand; **satisfaire aux exigences de ses clients** to meet one's customers' requirements **2** *(nécessité)* demand, requirement; **répondre aux exigences de qualité/sécurité** to meet quality/safety requirements; **les exigences de ma profession** the demands *or* requirements of my profession **3** *(caractère exigeant ▸ d'un client)* particularity; *(▸ d'un professeur, d'un parent)* strictness; **elle est d'une e. insupportable** she's intolerably demanding

• **exigences NFPL** *(salaire)* expected salary; **quelles sont vos exigences?** what salary do you expect?; **en donnant vos nom, adresse et exigences** stating your name, address and expected salary

exiger [17] [ɛgziʒe] **VT 1** *(compensation, dû)* to demand, to claim; **j'exige réparation** I demand redress; **j'exige d'être payé immédiatement** I demand to be paid *or* I insist on being paid immediately, I demand *or* insist on immediate payment

2 *(excuse, silence)* to require, to demand, to insist on; *(rançon)* to demand; **e. beaucoup/trop de qn** to expect a lot/too much from sb; **j'exige des excuses/que vous vous excusiez** I demand an apology/that you apologize

3 *(déclarer obligatoire)* to require; **la connaissance du russe n'est pas exigée** knowledge of Russian is not a requirement; **le port du casque est exigé** hard hats must be worn; **aucun visa n'est exigé** no visa is needed; **e. qu'une chose soit faite** to insist on a thing being done, to demand that a thing be done

4 *(nécessiter)* to require, to need; **un métier qui exige beaucoup de précision** a job requiring great accuracy; **le poste exige beaucoup de déplacements** the post involves a lot of travelling; **nous interviendrons si la situation l'exige** we'll intervene if it becomes necessary *or* if the situation demands it

exigibilité [ɛgziʒibilite] *Fin* **NF** payability; **date d'e.** due date

• **exigibilités NFPL** current liabilities

exigible [ɛgziʒibl] **ADJ** *(impôt)* due (for payment), payable; **le paiement est e. dès réception de la facture** payment is due upon receipt of the invoice; **e. à vue** payable at sight

exigu, -ë [ɛgzigy] **ADJ** *(appartement, pièce)* very small, tiny; *(couloir)* very narrow

exiguïté [ɛgzigɥite] **NF** *(d'une pièce)* smallness; *(d'un couloir)* narrowness

exil [ɛgzil] **NM** exile; **après plusieurs années d'e.** after several years in exile; **pendant son e. londonien** while he/she was living in exile in London; **terre d'e.** place of exile

• **en exil ADJ** exiled **ADV** *(vivre)* in exile; **envoyer qn en e.** to exile sb

exilé, -e [ɛgzile] **ADJ** exiled

NM,F exile

exiler [3] [ɛgzile] **VT** to exile (**de** from); *(d'une ville, de la cour)* to banish (**de** from); **le dictateur a fait e. tous les opposants au régime** the dictator had all the opponents of the regime sent into exile; *Fig* **on l'a exilé à l'autre bout de la classe** he was banished *or* exiled to the other end of the classroom

VPR s'exiler 1 *(quitter son pays)* to go into self-imposed exile; **s'e. à l'autre bout du monde** to go into self-imposed exile on the other side of the world **2** *(s'isoler)* to cut oneself off; **il s'est exilé à la campagne pour terminer son livre** he withdrew to the country to finish his book

existant, -e [ɛgzistɑ̃, -ɑ̃t] **ADJ** *(modèle, loi, tarif)* existing, current, currently in existence

NM *Com* **e. en caisse/en magasin** cash/stock in hand

existence [ɛgzistɑ̃s] **NF 1** *(vie)* life, existence; **j'aurai travaillé toute mon e. pour rien** I'll have worked all my life *or* days for nothing; **dans l'e.** in life; **j'en ai assez de cette e.** I've had enough of this (kind of) life; **mener une e. tranquille** to lead a quiet existence *or* life

2 *(durée ▸ d'une constitution, d'une civilisation)* lifespan, lifetime

3 *(réalité ▸ d'un complot)* existence (**de** of); *(▸ d'une substance)* presence, existence (**de** of)

4 *(présence ▸ d'une personne)* presence; **manifester** *ou* **signaler son e.** to make one's presence known

5 *Phil (être)* existence, (state of) being

6 *Compta* **existences en caisse** cash in hand

existentialisme [ɛgzistɑ̃sjalism] **NM** *Phil* existentialism

existentialiste [ɛgzistɑ̃sjalist] *Phil* **ADJ** existentialist

NMF existentialist

existentiel, -elle [ɛgzistɑ̃sjɛl] **ADJ** *Phil* existential

exister [3] [ɛgziste] **VI 1** *(être réel)* to exist, to be real; **le père Noël n'existe pas!** Father Christmas doesn't exist!; **les roses noires, ça n'existe pas** there is no such thing as a black rose, black roses don't exist; **pour elle, l'amour/le danger, ça n'existe pas** love/danger doesn't exist for her; **ce personnage a bien existé, il vivait au XVIIème siècle** this character is real *or* did exist, he lived in the 17th century; *Fam* **le savon, ça existe!** there is such a thing as soap, you know!; *Hum* **si elle n'existait pas, il faudrait l'inventer!** if she didn't exist, we'd have to invent her!, what would we do without her!; **l'amour existe, je l'ai rencontré** love really does exist!

2 *(subsister)* to exist; **l'hôtel existe toujours/n'existe plus** the hotel is still there/isn't there anymore; **les vieilles traditions qui existent toujours au village** the old traditions still extant *or* which still exist in the village; **la galanterie, ça n'existe plus** (the age of) chivalry is dead

3 *(être important)* to matter; **seul son métier existe pour lui** his job's the only thing that matters to him

4 *(vivre ▸ personne)* to live; **tant que j'existerai** as long as I live; **fais comme si je n'existais pas** pretend I'm not here

5 *(article)* to be available; **ce modèle existe aussi en cuir/en rouge** this model is also available in leather/red

6 *(tournure impersonnelle)* **il existe** *(suivi d'un singulier)* there is, there's; *(suivi d'un pluriel)* there are; **il n'existe aucune directive à ce sujet** there are no guidelines for that; **il existe des appareils pour dénoyauter les fruits** there are machines for taking stones out of fruit; **la vie existe-t-elle sur Mars?** does life exist on Mars?, is there life on Mars?

exit [ɛgzit] **ADV** *Théât* exit; **e. les gardes** exit *or Sout* exeunt the guards; *Fig* **e. le Président** out goes the President; *Fig Hum* **e. les petits week-ends à Deauville!** no more weekend breaks in Deauville!, that's the end of the weekend breaks in Deauville!

ex-libris [ɛkslibris] **NM INV** ex-libris

ex nihilo [ɛksniilo] **ADV** out of *or* from nothing, ex nihilo

exo [ɛgzo] **NM** *Fam (abrév* **exercice***)* exercise[□]

exocet [ɛgzɔsɛt] **NM** *Ich* flying fish

Exocet® [ɛgzɔsɛt] **NM** *(missile)* Exocet

exocrine [ɛgzɔkrin] **ADJ** *Physiol* exocrine

exode [ɛgzɔd] **NM 1** *(départ)* exodus; **l'e. des Parisiens en août** the annual exodus of Parisians from the capital in August; **l'e. des cerveaux** the brain drain; *Fin* **l'e. des capitaux** the flight of capital; **l'e. rural** = the movement of populations from rural to urban areas; *Hist* **l'e.** = the flight southward and westward of French civilians before the occupying German army in 1940 **2** *Bible* **l'E.** the Exodus; **(le Livre de) l'E.** (the book of) Exodus

exogame [ɛgzɔgam] **ADJ** exogamous, exogamic

NMF exogamous subject

exogamie [ɛgzɔgami] **NF** exogamy

exogène [ɛgzɔʒɛn] **ADJ** *(gén), Biol & Géol* exogenous

exonération [ɛgzɔnerasjɔ̃] **NF** exemption, exempting *(UNCOUNT)* (**de** from); **e. fiscale** *ou* **d'impôt** tax exemption; **e. de TVA** exemption from *Br* VAT *or Am* sales tax

exonérer [18] [ɛgzɔnere] **VT 1** *(contribuable, revenus)* to exempt; **e. qn d'impôts** to exempt sb from income tax; **être exonéré d'impôts** to be exempt from tax; **intérêt: 12 pour cent, exonéré d'impôts** 12 percent interest rate, non-taxable *or* free of tax; **exonéré de TVA** zero-rated, *Br* VAT-exempt **2** *(dégager)* **e. qn de** *(obligation)* to free sb from; *(responsabilité)* to exonerate *or* to free sb from

exophtalmie [ɛgzɔftalmi] **NF** *Méd* exophthalmos, exophthalmus

exoplanète [ɛgsoplanɛt] **NF** *Astron* exoplanet

exorbitant, -e [ɛgzɔrbitɑ̃, -ɑ̃t] **ADJ 1** *(trop cher)* exorbitant, extortionate **2** *(démesuré ▸ requête)* outrageous; *(▸ prétention)* absurd

exorbité, -e [ɛgzɔrbite] **ADJ** bulging; **les yeux exorbités** with bulging eyes, *Hum* with his/her eyes out on stalks

exorciser [3] [ɛgzɔrsize] **VT** to exorcize

exorcisme [ɛgzɔrsism] **NM** exorcism

exorciste [ɛgzɔrsist] **NM** exorcist

exorde [ɛgzɔrd] **NM** *Littérature* exordium

exosmose [ɛgzɔsmoz] **NF** *Phys* exosmosis

exotique [ɛgzɔtik] **ADJ** *(produit, fruit, pays)* exotic; **poisson e.** tropical fish

exotisme [ɛgzɔtism] **NM** exoticism

expansé, -e [ɛkspɑ̃se] **ADJ** *(polystyrène)* expanded

expansibilité [ɛkspɑ̃sibilite] **NF** expansibility

expansible [ɛkspɑ̃sibl] **ADJ** expansible, liable to expand

expansif, -ive [ɛkspɑ̃sif, -iv] **ADJ 1** *(caractère, personne)* expansive, exuberant, effusive; **il n'est pas très e.** he's never very communicative *or* forthcoming **2** *Phys* expansive

expansion [ɛkspɑ̃sjɔ̃] **NF 1** *Écon* **e. (économique)** (economic) growth

2 *(augmentation ▸ d'un territoire, de l'univers)* expansion, expanding *(UNCOUNT)*; **e. coloniale** colonial expansion

3 *(propagation ▸ d'une idéologie, d'une influence)* spread

4 *Chim & Phys* expansion, expanding *(UNCOUNT)*

5 *Littéraire (épanchement)* expansiveness, effusiveness

• **en expansion ADJ** *(univers)* expanding

• **en (pleine) expansion ADJ** *Écon* expanding, booming; **être en pleine e.** *(économie, entreprise)* to be booming

expansionnisme [ɛkspɑ̃sjɔnism] **NM** expansionism

expansionniste [ɛkspɑ̃sjɔnist] **ADJ** expansionist

NMF expansionist

expansive [ɛkspɑ̃siv] *voir* **expansif**

expansivité [ɛkspɑ̃sivite] **NF** expansiveness

expatriation [ɛkspatrijasjɔ̃] **NF** expatriation; *Fin* **e. de capitaux** movement of capital abroad

expatrié, -e [ɛkspatrije] **ADJ** expatriate

NM,F expatriate

expatrier [10] [ɛkspatrije] **VT** *(personne)* to expatriate; *(capitaux)* to move abroad

VPR s'expatrier to become an expatriate, to leave one's country (of origin)

expectative [ɛkspɛktativ] **NF** *(attente ▸ incertaine)* state of uncertainty; *(▸ prudente)* cautious wait; *(▸ pleine d'espoir)* expectancy, expectation

• **dans l'expectative ADV être dans l'e.** *(espérer)* to be in a state of expectation; *(être incertain)* to be in a state of uncertainty; **rester dans l'e.** to wait and see

expectorant [ɛkspɛktɔrɑ̃] **NM** *Méd* expectorant

expectoration [ɛkspɛktɔrasjɔ̃] **NF** *Méd* expectoration

expectorer [3] [ɛkspɛktɔre] *Méd* **VT** to expectorate

VI to expectorate

expédient, -e [ɛkspedjɑ̃, -ɑ̃t] **ADJ** *Littéraire* expedient

NM *(moyen)* expedient; **se tirer d'une difficulté par un e.** to find an expedient for getting out of a difficulty; **vivre d'expédients** to live by one's wits; **user d'expédients** to resort to evasion

expédier [9] [ɛkspedje] **VT 1** *(envoyer ▸ colis, lettre)* to send, to dispatch; **e. par avion** to send by air mail; **e. par bateau** *(marchandises)* to send by sea, to ship; **e. par coursier** to send by courier; **e. par la poste** to send through the mail *or Br* post; **e. par le train** to send by train *or* rail

2 *(se débarrasser de ▸ objet)* to get rid of, to dispose of; *(▸ personne)* to get rid of; **les démarcheurs qui sonnent ici sont vite expédiés!** any door-to-door salesmen ringing my bell soon get sent packing!; **je vais l'e. en colonie de vacances** I'm going to send *or* pack him/her off to a summer camp; **il a tendance à e. ses patients un peu vite** he tends to pack his patients out of the surgery rather quickly; *Fam* **e. qn dans l'autre monde** *ou* **au cimetière** to send sb off to meet their maker

3 *(bâcler, finir sans soin ▸ dissertation, lettre)* to dash off; *(▸ corvée, travail)* to make short work of, to dispatch; *(▸ tâche)* to deal promptly with; **elle a expédié le match en deux sets** she wrapped up the match in two sets

4 *(avaler vite ▸ repas)* to dispatch, to swallow; *(▸ verre de vin)* to knock back; **e. son déjeuner** to make short work of one's lunch

5 *Jur (contrat, acte)* to draw up

6 *(locution)* **e. les affaires courantes** *(employé)* to deal with day-to-day matters (only); *(président)* to be a caretaker president

expéditeur, -trice [ɛkspeditœr, -tris] **ADJ** *(bureau, compagnie, gare)* dispatching, forwarding

NM,F 1 *(d'un colis, d'une lettre)* sender, forwarder **2** *Com (de marchandises)* shipper, consigner; *(par bateau)* shipper

expéditif, -ive [ɛkspeditif, -iv] **ADJ** speedy, expeditious; **il est toujours très e. avec ses patients** he spends very little time with his patients; **je n'aime pas beaucoup ces méthodes expéditives** I don't appreciate this hasty way of doing things; **justice expéditive** summary justice

expédition [ɛkspedisjɔ̃] **NF 1** *(voyage)* expedition; *(équipe)* (members of the) expedition; **e. en Antarctique** expedition to the Antarctic; **partir en e.** to go on an expedition; **pour traverser la capitale, quelle e.!** it's quite an expedition to get across the capital!; **à chaque fois qu'on part en pique-nique, c'est une véritable e.** *ou* **c'est toute une e.** every time we go on a picnic, it's a real expedition

2 *Mil* expedition

3 *(raid)* **e. punitive** punitive raid *or* expedition

4 *(envoi de marchandises)* dispatch; **e. par bateau** *ou* **par mer** shipping, shipment; **e. par avion** air-freighting; **e. par chemin de fer** sending by rail, railfreighting; **e. par courrier** *ou* **par la poste** mailing, *Br* posting; **bulletin d'e.** waybill; *Com* **expéditions** *(service)* dispatch department, shipping department

5 *(cargaison)* consignment, shipment

6 *Admin* **il est chargé de l'e. des affaires courantes** he is in charge of day-to-day matters

7 *Jur (de contrat, d'acte)* copy; **première e.** first authentic copy; **en double e.** in duplicate

expéditionnaire [ɛkspedisjɔnɛr] **ADJ** *Mil* expeditionary

NMF *Com* forwarding agent

expéditive [ɛkspeditiv] *voir* **expéditif**

expéditrice [ɛkspeditris] *voir* **expéditeur**

expérience [ɛksperjɑ̃s] **NF 1** *(connaissance)* experience; **avec l'e., tu sauras que...** you'll find out with experience that...; **avoir de l'e. (en)** to have experience *or* to be experienced (in); **avoir l'e. de qch** to have experience of sth, to be experienced in sth; **il a l'e. des enfants** he is used to children; **manquer d'e.** to be inexperienced, to lack experience; **il nous faut quelqu'un qui a de l'e.** we need someone with experience; **plusieurs années d'e. en gestion seraient souhaitables** several years' experience in management *or* management experience would be desirable **2** *(apprentissage)* experience; **ses premières expériences amoureuses** his/her first sexual experiences; **raconte-nous tes expériences praguoises** tell us about your experiences in Prague; **tenter une e. de vie commune** to try living together; **faire l'e. de la haine/douleur** to experience hatred/pain; **je ne voudrais pas refaire l'e. d'une opération** I wouldn't like to go through an operation again; **j'en ai malheureusement fait l'e.** that has been my experience unfortunately, as I've discovered to my cost **3** *(test)* experiment; **e. de chimie** chemistry experiment; **e. en laboratoire** laboratory experiment; **e. sur le terrain** field experiment; **faire une e.** to carry out *or* do an experiment; **faire des expériences (sur des rats)** to carry out experiments *or* to experiment (on rats); *Fig* **nous avons décidé de tenter l'e.** we've decided to give it a try *or* a go

• **par expérience** ADV from experience

• **sans expérience** ADJ inexperienced; **un petit jeune sans e.** an inexperienced youngster, a youngster still wet behind the ears

> Attention: ne pas confondre **experience** et **experiment** lorsque l'on traduit **expérience**. **Experience** s'applique à la pratique que l'on a d'une chose, alors que **experiment** ne s'utilise que pour l'essai d'une chose nouvelle.

expérimental, -e, -aux, -ales [ɛksperimɑ̃tal, -o] ADJ **1** *(avion, médicament)* trial *(avant n)*, experimental **2** *(méthode, sciences)* experimental; **à titre e.** experimentally, as an experiment

expérimentalement [ɛksperimɑ̃talmɑ̃] ADV experimentally

expérimentateur, -trice [ɛksperimɑ̃tatœr, -tris] NM,F experimenter

expérimentation [ɛksperimɑ̃tasjɔ̃] NF experimentation; **e. animale** *(pratique)* animal experimentation; *(tests)* animal experiments

expérimentatrice [ɛksperimɑ̃tatris] *voir* **expérimentateur**

expérimenté, -e [ɛksperimɑ̃te] ADJ experienced, practised

expérimenter [3] [ɛksperimɑ̃te] VT *(remède, vaccin, machine)* to try out, to test (**sur** on)

USAGE ABSOLU to experiment, to carry out experiments

expert, -e [ɛkspɛr, -ɛrt] ADJ **1** *(agile)* expert; **d'une main experte** with an expert hand; **d'une oreille experte** with a trained ear **2** *(savant)* highly knowledgeable (**en/dans** in); **être e. en la matière** to be an expert on *or* in the subject; **être e. en littérature chinoise** to be an expert on *or* a specialist in Chinese literature

NM **1** *(chargé d'expertise)* expert, specialist; *(en bâtiments)* surveyor; *(en assurances)* assessor; **e. financier/fiscal** financial/tax expert; **e. judiciaire** legal expert; **e. maritime** surveyor **2** *(comme adj; avec ou sans trait d'union)* **chimiste e.** expert in chemistry; **médecin e.** medical expert **3** *(connaisseur)* expert (**de** *ou* **en** on), connoisseur (**de** *ou* **en** of)

expert-comptable [ɛkspɛrkɔ̃tabl] *(pl* **experts-comptables)** NM *Compta Br* ≃ chartered accountant, *Am* ≃ certified public accountant

expert-conseil [ɛkspɛrkɔ̃sɛj] *(pl* **experts-conseils)** NM consultant

expertise [ɛkspɛrtiz] NF **1** *(examen ▸ d'un meuble, d'une voiture)* (expert) appraisal *or* evaluation *or* valuation; *Assur (de dommages)* (expert) assessment; **faire faire une e.** *(pour assurer un bien)* to have a valuation done; *Assur* **rapport d'e.** assessor's report, claims adjuster's report; *Naut* **e. d'avarie** damage survey; *Jur* **e. judiciaire** court-ordered appraisal; *Jur* **e. médicale et psychiatrique** expert opinion *(by a doctor)*; *Jur* **e. médico-légale** forensic examination **2** *Constr (document)* expert's *or* valuer's report **3** *(compétence)* expertise

expertiser [3] [ɛkspɛrtize] VT *(véhicule)* to value; *Assur (dommages, véhicule, meuble, tableau)* to assess; **faire e. une voiture** *(gén)* to have a car valued; *(après un accident)* to have the damage on a car looked at *(for insurance purposes)*

expiable [ɛkspjabl] ADJ expiable, which can be atoned for; **tu as commis une faute, certes, mais elle est e.** yes, you made a mistake but you can make up *or* atone for it

expiation [ɛkspjasjɔ̃] NF **en e. de** in expiation of, in atonement for

expiatoire [ɛkspjatwar] ADJ expiatory

expier [9] [ɛkspje] VT *(crime, péché)* to expiate, to atone for; *(erreur, faute)* to pay *or* to atone for

expirant, -e [ɛkspirɑ̃, -ɑ̃t] ADJ *(personne, entreprise)* dying, expiring, moribund; *(voix)* faint

expiration [ɛkspirasjɔ̃] NF **1** *(d'air)* breathing out; **fléchissez au moment de l'e.** flex your knees when you breathe out **2** *(fin)* expiration, expiry; **venir** *ou* **arriver à e.** to expire, to run out; **le bail arrive à e. le 30 août** the lease expires on 30 August; **date d'e.** expiry date

• **à l'expiration de** PRÉP **à l'e. du bail** when the lease expires; **à l'e. du délai** at the end of the stated period

expirer [3] [ɛkspire] VI **1** *(mourir)* to expire, to breathe one's last **2** *Littéraire (disparaître ▸ lueur, son)* to expire, to die away **3** *(aux avoir ou être) (cesser d'être valide ▸ abonnement, bail, délai)* to expire, to end; *(▸ carte de crédit)* to expire; **mon congé est expiré** my leave is up *or* has expired

VT *(air)* to breathe out

USAGE ABSOLU *(exhaler)* to breathe out; **expirez!** breathe out!

explétif, -ive [ɛkspletif, -iv] ADJ expletive, expletory; **le "ne" e.** "ne" used as an expletive

NM expletive

explicable [ɛksplikabl] ADJ explainable, explicable; **c'est un phénomène difficilement e.** it's a phenomenon which is difficult to explain *or* which is not easily explained

explicatif, -ive [ɛksplikatif, -iv] ADJ **1** *(brochure, lettre)* explanatory; **notice** *ou* **note explicative** *(sur un emballage)* instructions *or* directions for use; *(dans un dossier)* explanatory note **2** *Gram* **proposition relative explicative** non-restrictive relative clause

explication [ɛksplikasjɔ̃] NF **1** *(éclaircissement ▸ d'un fait, d'une situation)* explanation; **demander des explications à qn** to ask sb for some explanations; **il a quitté sa femme sans (aucune) e.** he walked out on his wife without any explanations; **ça se passe d'e.** it's self-explanatory

2 *(motif ▸ d'une attitude, d'un retard)* explanation; **j'exige des explications!** I demand an explanation!

3 *Scol & Univ (d'une œuvre)* commentary, analysis; **e. de texte** critical analysis, appreciation of a text

4 *(discussion)* discussion; *(querelle)* argument; **avoir une e. avec qn sur qch** *(discussion)* to talk sth over with sb; *(querelle)* to have an argument with sb about sth; **je crois qu'il va falloir que nous ayons une petite e. tous les deux** I think we're going to have to have a little talk, you and I

• **explications** NFPL *(mode d'emploi)* instructions *or* directions (for use)

explicative [ɛksplikativ] *voir* **explicatif**

explicite [ɛksplisit] ADJ explicit (**sur** about); **en termes explicites** in explicit terms, plainly; **suis-je assez e.?** do I make myself plain (enough)?; **elle n'a pas été très e. sur ce point** she wasn't very clear on that point

explicitement [ɛksplisitmɑ̃] ADV explicitly; **formuler e. une demande** to make an explicit request

expliciter [3] [ɛksplisite] VT **1** *(intentions)* to make explicit *or* plain **2** *(phrase, clause de contrat)* to clarify, to explain

expliquer [3] [ɛksplike] VT **1** *(faire comprendre ▸ événement, réaction, fonctionnement etc)* to explain; **e. qch à qn** to explain sth to sb; **je te l'ai expliqué mille fois!** I've explained it to *or* told you time and again!; **je me suis fait e. la procédure** I asked someone to explain the procedure to me; **je lui ai expliqué que je ne pouvais pas le faire** I explained to him *or* told him that I couldn't do it; *Fam* **e. le pourquoi du comment** to explain the how and the why of it; *Fam* **on s'est pris un de ces savons, je t'explique pas...** you wouldn't have believed the telling-off we got

2 *(justifier ▸ attitude, retard)* to explain, to account for; **cela explique qu'il se soit présenté en smoking** that explains why he turned up in *or* that accounts for his turning up in a dinner jacket; **ceci n'explique pas cela** that doesn't explain it

3 *Scol & Univ (texte)* to analyse, to make a critical analysis of, to comment on; *(doctrine, théorème, signification)* to explain

4 *(élucider ▸ mystère)* to explain

VPR **s'expliquer 1** *(être intelligible)* to be explained; **cela s'explique facilement** that's easily understandable *or* explainable; **il y a des choses qui ne s'expliquent pas** some things can't be explained; **le mauvais temps s'explique par la présence d'une dépression** the presence of a depression explains the bad weather; **tout s'explique!** that explains it!

2 *(s'exprimer)* to explain oneself, to make oneself clear; **explique-toi mieux** make yourself clearer; **me serais-je mal expliqué?** perhaps I didn't make myself clear *or* wasn't plain enough; **je m'explique** this is what I mean, let me explain

3 *(se justifier)* to justify one's behaviour, to explain oneself; **s'e. sur ses intentions** *(éclaircir)* to make plain *or* to explain one's intentions

4 *(comprendre)* to understand; **je ne m'explique pas pourquoi...** I can't understand why...; **je n'arrive pas à m'e. son silence** I can't understand why he/she is remaining silent

5 s'e. avec *(avoir une discussion avec)* to talk things over with; *(se disputer avec)* to have it out with; **expliquez-vous une bonne fois pour toutes** get it sorted out once and for all; **viens, on va s'e. dehors** come on, we'll settle this outside; **ils se sont expliqués au couteau** they settled it with knives

exploit [ɛksplwa] NM **1** *(acte ▸ héroïque)* exploit; *(▸ remarquable)* feat, achievement; **e. sportif** remarkable sporting achievement; **e. technique** technical feat *or* exploit; **ses exploits amoureux** his/her amorous exploits; **avoir réussi à la convaincre relève de l'e.!** it's no mean achievement to have convinced her!; *Hum* **il est arrivé à l'heure, tu te rends compte d'un e.!** he arrived on time, which was quite an achievement for him! **2** *Jur* **e. (d'huissier)** writ

exploitable [ɛksplwatabl] ADJ *(idée, mine, terre etc)* exploitable, workable; *(énergie)* exploitable; **e. par ordinateur** machine readable

exploitant, -e [ɛksplwatɑ̃, -ɑ̃t] NM,F **1** *(d'une exploitation, d'une carrière ▸ propriétaire)* owner; *(▸ gérant)* operator; **e. (agricole)** farmer; **petit e.** small farmer, *Br* smallholder; **e. forestier** forestry agent **2** *Cin (propriétaire)* owner; *(directeur) Br* manager, *Am* exhibitor

exploitation [ɛksplwatasjɔ̃] NF **1** *(entreprise)* concern; **e. à ciel ouvert** open-cast mine; **e. agricole** farm; **petite e. agricole** small farm, *Br* smallholding; **e. commerciale** business (concern); **e. familiale** family business; **e. forestière** forestry site; **e. industrielle** industrial concern; **e. minière** mine; **e. vinicole** *(vignes)* vineyard; *(société)* wine-producing establishment

2 *(d'un réseau ferroviaire)* running, operating; *(d'un cinéma)* running; *(d'une carrière, d'une forêt, d'une mine, d'un sol)* exploitation, working; *(d'une terre)* farming; *Com (d'un brevet)* commercialization; **l'e. forestière** forestry, lumbering; **mettre en e.** *(carrière, mine)* to exploit, to work; **mettre une terre en e.** to bring a piece of land under cultivation; **faire l'e. industrielle de qch** to produce sth on an industrial scale

3 *(utilisation ▸ d'une idée, d'un talent)* exploitation, exploiting *(UNCOUNT)*, utilizing *(UNCOUNT)*; **elle a confié à une agence de publicité l'e. de son idée** she let an advertising agency make use of her idea

4 *(fait d'abuser)* exploitation, exploiting *(UNCOUNT)*; *(de la main-d'œuvre)* exploitation; **l'e. de l'homme par l'homme** man's exploitation of man; **six euros de l'heure, c'est de l'e.!** six euros per hour, that's sheer exploitation!

• **d'exploitation** ADJ *Fin & Ordinat* operating; **société d'e.** development company

exploiter [3] [ɛksplwate] **VT 1** *(mettre en valeur ▸ forêt, mine etc)* to exploit, to work; *(▸ ressources naturelles)* to exploit; *(▸ brevet)* to commercialize; *(▸ terre)* to farm, to work; *(▸ invention)* to utilize

2 *(faire fonctionner ▸ ferme, tunnel, réseau ferroviaire)* to run, to operate; *(▸ entreprise, cinéma)* to run

3 *(tirer avantage de ▸ talent)* to exploit, to make use of; *(▸ thème)* to exploit; *(▸ situation)* to exploit, to make capital out of, to make the most of

4 *Péj (abuser de)* to exploit, to take (unfair) advantage of; **e. la naïveté de qn** to take advantage of sb's naivety; **e. la gentillesse de qn** to exploit *or* to take advantage of sb's helpfulness

5 *Péj (main-d'œuvre)* to exploit; **se faire e.** to be exploited

exploiteur, -euse [ɛksplwatœr, -øz] **NM,F** exploiter

explorateur, -trice [ɛksplɔratœr, -tris] **NM,F** explorer

exploration [ɛksplɔrasjɔ̃] **NF 1** *Géog & Méd* exploration; **voyage d'e.** voyage of discovery; **partir en e.** to go off exploring *or* on an exploration **2** *(analyse)* exploration, examination

exploratoire [ɛksplɔratwar] **ADJ** exploratory, tentative

exploratrice [ɛksplɔratris] *voir* **explorateur**

explorer [3] [ɛksplɔre] **VT 1** *(contrée, île)* to explore **2** *Méd* to explore **3** *(examiner ▸ possibilité)* to explore, to examine; *(▸ sujet)* to explore

exploser [3] [ɛksploze] **VI 1** *(détoner ▸ grenade, mine, maison, chaudière)* to explode, to blow up; *(▸ bombe)* to explode, to go off; *(▸ dynamite, gaz)* to explode; **faire e. une bombe** to set off *or* to explode *or* to detonate a bomb; **j'avais l'impression que ma tête/jambe allait e.** I felt as if my head/leg was going to explode *or* burst

2 *(augmenter ▸ population)* to explode; *(▸ prix)* to shoot up, to soar, to (sky)rocket

3 *(se révéler soudain ▸ mécontentement, joie)* to explode; *(▸ rage)* to explode, to burst out; *(▸ rires)* to burst out; *Fam (▸ artiste)* to burst onto the scene; **laisser e. sa colère/joie** to give vent to one's anger/joy; **la salle explosa en applaudissements** the audience burst into thunderous applause; *Fam* **ils ont explosé sur la scène rock il y a 20 ans** they burst onto the rock scene 20 years ago

4 *Fam (s'emporter)* to flare up, to lose one's temper *or* cool; **e. de colère** to explode, to blow one's top

VT 1 *très Fam (battre)* **e. qn** *ou* **la gueule à qn** to smash sb's face in; **se faire e. la gueule** to get one's face smashed in

2 *Fam (détruire)* to smash up, *Br* to write off, *Am* to total; **il a explosé sa moto** *Br* he wrote off his motorbike, *Am* he totaled his motorcycle

3 *Fam* **être explosé (de rire)** to be killing oneself (laughing), to be cracking up, to be in stitches

4 *Fam* **l'émission a explosé l'Audimat®** the programme scored record-breaking viewing figures; **elle a explosé le record du monde** she smashed the world record

explosible [ɛksplozibl] **ADJ** explosive

explosif, -ive [ɛksplozif, -iv] **ADJ 1** *(mélange, puissance)* explosive; *(obus)* high-explosive

2 *(dangereux ▸ situation, sujet, dossier)* explosive, highly sensitive; *(▸ atmosphère)* explosive, charged

3 *(fougueux ▸ tempérament)* fiery, explosive

4 *Ling* explosive, plosive

NM explosive

• **explosive NF** *Ling* explosive (consonant), plosive (consonant)

explosion [ɛksplozjɔ̃] **NF 1** *(détonation ▸ d'une bombe, d'une chaudière, d'une mine)* explosion, blowing up; *(▸ d'un gaz)* explosion; **faire e.** *(bombe)* to go off, to explode; *(obus)* to explode; **e. atomique** atomic explosion; **e. volcanique** volcanic explosion *or* eruption **2** *(manifestation)* **e. d'enthousiasme/d'indignation** burst of enthusiasm/indignation; **e. de joie** outburst *or* explosion of joy; **ce fut une e. de rire dans le public** the audience burst out into peals of laughter **3** *(accroissement)* **e. démographique** population boom *or* explosion; **l'e. démographique après la guerre** the post-war baby boom; **e. des naissances** baby boom

explosive [ɛksploziv] *voir* **explosif**

expo [ɛkspo] **NF** *Fam (abrév* **exposition***)* exhibition▫

exponentiel, -elle [ɛkspɔnɑ̃sjɛl] **ADJ** exponential; **de manière exponentielle** exponentially

export [ɛkspɔr] **NM** exportation; **l'e., le service e.** the export branch

exportable [ɛkspɔrtabl] **ADJ** *Com & Écon* exportable, which can be exported

exportateur, -trice [ɛkspɔrtatœr, -tris] **ADJ** *(pays)* exporting *(avant n)*; *(secteur)* export *(avant n)*; **être e. de qch** to be an exporter of sth, to export sth; **les pays exportateurs de pétrole/céréales** oil-/grain-exporting countries

NM,F exporter

exportation [ɛkspɔrtasjɔ̃] **NF 1** *(sortie)* export, exportation; **faire de l'e.** to export; **réservé à l'e.** for export only, reserved for export; **ce produit marche très fort à l'e.** this product is doing very well on the export market; **e. de capitaux** export of capital **2** *Com & Écon* **exportations** *(marchandises)* exports; **exportations visibles/invisibles** visible/invisible exports **3** *Ordinat (d'un fichier)* exporting; *(données exportées)* exported data

• **d'exportation** ADJ export *(avant n)*; **articles d'e.** exports

exportatrice [ɛkspɔrtatris] *voir* **exportateur**

exporter [3] [ɛkspɔrte] **VT 1** *Com & Écon* to export (**vers** to) **2** *(répandre à l'étranger ▸ idées, culture)* to export, to spread abroad **3** *Ordinat* to export (**vers** to)

VPR s'exporter *(marchandises)* to be exported (**vers** to); **ces articles s'exportent mal** these items are difficult to export *or* not good for exporting; *Fig* **cette mode a été** *ou* **s'est exportée dans le monde entier** the fashion has spread throughout the world

exposant, -e [ɛkspozɑ̃, -ɑ̃t] **NM,F 1** *(dans une galerie, dans une foire)* exhibitor **2** *Jur* petitioner

NM 1 *Math* exponent **2** *Typ (chiffre, lettre)* superscript, superior; **3 en e.** superscript 3

exposé, -e [ɛkspoze] **ADJ 1** *(orienté)* **ce balcon est bien/mal e.** the balcony gets a lot of sun/doesn't get much sun; **jardin e. au sud** south-facing garden, garden with a southern aspect; **la chambre est exposée au nord** the room faces north **2** *(non abrité)* exposed, wind-swept; **champ très e.** very exposed field **3** *(montré)* on show, on display; **objet e.** *(dans une galerie, une foire)* item on show, exhibit; **les articles exposés en vitrine** the items on display in the window; **une des voitures exposées** one of the cars on show

NM 1 *(compte rendu)* account, exposition; *(de faits, de situation)* statement, account, report; **faire un e. sur** to give an account of; **après un bref e. de la situation** after outlining the situation briefly; **e. verbal (de mission)** briefing **2** *Scol & Univ (écrit)* (written) paper; *(oral)* talk, presentation; **faire un e. (sur qch)** *(oral)* to give a talk *or* to read a paper (on sth); *(écrit)* to write a paper (on sth) **3** *Jur* **e. des motifs** exposition of motives

exposer [3] [ɛkspoze] **VT 1** *(dans un magasin)* to display, to put on display, to set out; *(dans une galerie, dans une foire)* to exhibit, to show; **e. des marchandises en vitrine** to display goods for sale

2 *(soumettre)* to expose; **e. qch à l'air/lumière** to expose sth to the air/light; **il faut e. cette plante à la lumière le plus possible** the plant must receive *or* get as much light as possible; **e. qch aux radiations** to expose *or* to subject sth to radiation; **e. qn à** *(critiques, ridicule)* to lay sb open to, to expose sb to

3 *(mettre en danger ▸ honneur, vie)* to endanger, to put at risk; **e. qn** to put sb in danger

4 *(faire connaître ▸ arguments, motifs)* to expound, to put forward; *(▸ intentions)* to set forth *or* out, to explain; *(▸ revendications)* to set forth, to put forward, to make known; *(▸ griefs)* to air; **e. son point de vue à qn** to explain one's point of view to sb, to make one's point of view known to sb; **je leur ai exposé ma situation** I explained my situation to them

5 *Hist (nouveau-né)* to expose

6 *Littérature & Mus* to set out; *(thème)* to introduce; **dialogue destiné à e. l'action** expository dialogue

7 *Phot* to expose; **e. un film à la lumière** to expose a film

USAGE ABSOLU nous exposerons à la foire du livre we'll be among the exhibitors at the Book Fair; **ça fait très longtemps qu'il n'a pas exposé** he hasn't exhibited anything for a very long time

VPR s'exposer 1 *(se compromettre)* to leave oneself exposed; **s'e. à des critiques** to lay oneself open *or* to expose oneself to criticism; **s'e. à des poursuites judiciaires** to lay oneself open to *or* to run the risk of prosecution; **s'e. à des représailles** to expose oneself to retaliation **2** *(se placer)* **s'e. au soleil** to expose one's skin to the sun; **si tu t'exposes trop longtemps** if you stay in the sun too long

exposition [ɛkspozisjɔ̃] **NF 1** *(d'œuvres d'art)* show, exhibition; *(de produits manufacturés)* exhibition, exposition; **e. de peinture/photos** painting/photo exhibition; **e. florale** flower show; **l'E. universelle** the World Fair; **salle d'e.** exhibition room

2 *(de marchandises, de fleurs)* display; **l'e. en vitrine a fané les tissus** the fabric has faded from being displayed in the window; *Mktg* **e. sur le lieu de vente** point-of-sale display

3 *(d'un corps)* lying in state

4 *(d'arguments, de motifs)* exposition, expounding *(UNCOUNT)*; *(d'une situation, d'une théorie)* exposition; *Jur* **e. des faits** statement of the facts

5 *Littérature, Théât & Mus* exposition

6 *(soumission)* **e. à** *(danger, radiation, risque, froid)* exposure to; **éviter l'e. au soleil** do not stay in the sun; **il lui faut au minimum une heure d'e. (à la lumière) par jour** it needs at least an hour of light a day

7 *(orientation)* orientation, aspect; **e. au sud** orientation to the south; **l'appartement a une double e. nord-sud** the *Br* flat *or Am* apartment has north-facing and south-facing windows

8 *Phot* exposure

• **d'exposition** ADJ expository, introductory; *Littérature & Théât* **scène d'e.** prologue

exposition-vente [ɛkspozisjɔ̃vɑ̃t] *(pl* **expositions-ventes***)* **NF** *(gén)* display *(where the items are for sale)*; *(d'objets d'artisanat)* craft fair

exprès[1] [ɛksprɛ] **ADV 1** *(délibérément)* on purpose, intentionally, deliberately; **c'est e. que j'ai employé ce mot** I used this word on purpose *or* intentionally *or* deliberately; **je ne l'ai pas fait e.** I didn't mean to do it, I didn't do it on purpose *or* intentionally *or* deliberately; **tu l'as vexé – je ne l'ai pas fait e.** you've offended him – I didn't mean to *or* it wasn't intentional; **elle fait e. de me contredire** she makes a point of contradicting me, she deliberately contradicts me; **j'ai déclenché l'alarme sans le faire e.** I set off the alarm without meaning to; **j'aurais voulu le faire e., je n'y serais pas arrivé** I couldn't have done it if I'd tried *or* if I'd wanted to; **c'est (comme) un** *ou* **on dirait un fait e.** you'd think it was done on purpose *or* was intentional; *Ironique* **comme (par) un fait e., il pleuvait** and of course *or* wouldn't you know it, it was raining; *Ironique* **comme (par) un fait e., il n'avait pas de monnaie** funnily enough, he had no change **2** *(spécialement)* especially, specially; **tu n'aurais pas dû venir e.** you shouldn't have come specially; **elle est sortie e. pour l'acheter** she went out specially *or* expressly to buy it; **c'est fait e. pour ranger des crayons** it's designed *or* meant for holding pencils; **il y a du papier à l'intérieur – c'est fait e.** there's some paper inside – it's meant to be like that

exprès[2]**, expresse** [ɛksprɛ, ɛksprɛs] **ADJ** *(avertissement, autorisation, ordre)* express, explicit; *(recommandation)* express, strict; **défense expresse de fumer** smoking strictly prohibited

exprès[3] [ɛksprɛs] **ADJ INV** *(lettre, paquet)* special delivery *(avant n)*

• **en exprès, par exprès** ADV **envoyer qch en e.** to send sth special delivery

express [ɛksprɛs] **ADJ INV 1** *Rail voir* **train 2** *(café)* espresso

NM 1 *Rail* express *or* fast train **2** *(café)* espresso (coffee)

expressément [ɛkspresemɑ̃] **ADV 1** *(catégoriquement ▸ défendre, ordonner)* expressly, categorically; *(▸ conseiller, prévenir)* expressly **2** *(spécialement)* specially, specifically

expressif, -ive [ɛkspresif, -iv] **ADJ 1** *(suggestif ▸ style)* expressive, vivid; *(▸ regard, visage)* expressive, meaningful; *(▸ ton)* expressive; **sa mimique était expressive** the expression on his/her face said it all **2** *Ling* expressive

expression [ɛkspresjɔ̃] **NF 1** *(mot, tournure)* expression, phrase, turn of phrase; **avoir une e. malheureuse** to use an unfortunate turn of phrase; **passez-moi l'e.** (if you'll) pardon the expression; **veuillez croire à l'e. de ma considération distinguée** *(à quelqu'un dont on connaît le nom) Br* yours sincerely, *Am* sincerely (yours); *(à quelqu'un dont on ne connaît pas le nom) Br* yours faithfully, *Am* sincerely (yours); **e. familière** colloquial expression, colloquialism; **e. figée** set phrase *or* expression, fixed expression, idiom; **e. toute faite** *(figée)* set phrase *or* expression; *(cliché)* hackneyed phrase, cliché

2 *(fait de s'exprimer)* expression, expressing *(UNCOUNT)*, voicing *(UNCOUNT)*; **lutter pour l'e. de ses revendications** to fight for the right to make one's demands heard; **l'e. de nos idées doit se faire par le biais d'un journal** we must express our ideas in a newspaper

3 *(pratique de la langue)* **auteurs d'e. allemande** authors writing in German; **des enfants d'e. française** French-speaking children; **e. écrite/orale** written/oral expression

4 *(extériorisation ▸ d'un besoin, d'un sentiment)* expression; **trouver son e. dans** to find (its) expression in; **au-delà de toute e.** *(employé comme adjectif)* inexpressible; *(employé comme adverbe)* inexpressibly; **e. corporelle** self-expression through movement

5 *(vivacité)* expression; **mets plus d'e. dans le dernier vers** put in more expression *or* feeling when you read the last line; **jouer avec e.** to play expressively; **geste/regard plein d'e.** expressive gesture/look

6 *(du visage)* expression, look; **si tu avais vu ton e.!** if you'd seen the look on your face!

7 *Math* expression; *Fig* **la famille, réduite à sa plus simple e.** the family, reduced to its simplest expression; *Fig* **un meublé dont le mobilier était réduit à sa plus simple e.** a furnished room that hardly merited the term

8 *Ordinat* expression; **e. logique** logical expression; **e. de sélection** selection command; **e. de tri** sort command

9 *Biol (d'un gène)* expression

• **sans expression ADJ** expressionless

expressionnisme [ɛkspresjɔnism] **NM** expressionism

expressionniste [ɛkspresjɔnist] **ADJ** expressionist

NMF expressionist

expressivement [ɛkspresivmɑ̃] **ADV** expressively

expressivité [ɛkspresivite] **NF** expressivity, expressiveness; **avec beaucoup d'e.** very expressively

exprimable [ɛksprimabl] **ADJ** expressible; **ma joie est difficilement e.** my joy is difficult to express

exprimer **[3]** [ɛksprime] **VT 1** *(dire ▸ sentiment)* to express; *(▸ idée, revendication)* to express, to voice; **par là, elle exprime son désespoir** in this way she expresses *or* voices her despair; **comment vous e. toute mon admiration?** how can I tell you how much I admire you?; **je tiens à vous e. mon regret** I want to tell you how sorry I am; **mon émotion est difficile à e.** my emotion is difficult to put into words *or* to express

2 *(manifester ▸ mécontentement, surprise)* to express, to show; **c'est comme ça que j'exprime mes sentiments** that's how I express my feelings

3 *(pour chiffrer une quantité, une somme)* to state, to express; *Math (quantité, valeur)* to express; **e. une quantité en kilos** to state a quantity in kilos; **e. une somme en euros** to state a sum in euros

4 *(extraire ▸ jus, pus)* to express, to squeeze out (**de** from)

5 *Biol (gène)* to express

VPR s'exprimer 1 *(se manifester ▸ talent, sentiment)* to express *or* to show itself; **tant de mélancolie s'exprime dans son poème** his/her poem expresses so much melancholy; **l'étonnement s'exprima sur son visage** his/her astonishment showed on his/her face

2 *(dire sa pensée)* to express oneself; **laissez-le s'e.** let him have his say *or* express himself; **chacun doit s'e.** all opinions must be heard; *Hum* **vas-y, exprime-toi!** come on, out with it!; **je me suis exprimée sur ce sujet** I've expressed myself *or* made my opinions known on the subject; **le président ne s'est pas encore exprimé sur ce sujet** the president has yet to voice an opinion on the matter; **s'e. par gestes/signes** to use sign language

3 *(choisir ses mots)* to express oneself; **exprime-toi clairement** express yourself clearly, make yourself clear; **non, je me suis mal exprimé** no, I've put it badly; **si je peux m'e. ainsi** if I can put it that way

4 *(manifester sa personnalité)* to express oneself; **s'e. par la danse/musique** to express oneself through dancing/music

expropriation [ɛksprɔprijasjɔ̃] **NF 1** *(d'une personne)* expropriation **2** *(d'une propriété)* compulsory purchase

exproprier **[10]** [ɛksprɔprije] **VT 1** *(personne)* to expropriate; **la municipalité a fait e. les occupants de l'immeuble** *Br* the local council placed a compulsory purchase order on the flats; **se faire e.** to be expropriated, *Br* to have a compulsory purchase order placed on one's property **2** *(maison, terre)* to expropriate, *Br* to place a compulsory purchase order on

expulser **[3]** [ɛkspylse] **VT 1** *(renvoyer ▸ locataire)* to evict (**de** from), to throw out (**de** of); *(▸ membre, participant, étudiant)* to expel (**de** from); *(▸ immigrant)* to expel, to deport (**de** from); *(▸ joueur)* to send off; **elle a été expulsée du terrain** she was sent off the field; **la propriétaire a fait e. ses locataires** the owner had the tenants thrown out; **se faire e.** to be thrown out **2** *Méd* to evacuate, to expel

expulsif, -ive [ɛkspylsif, -iv] **ADJ** *Méd* expulsive

expulsion [ɛkspylsjɔ̃] **NF 1** *(d'un locataire)* eviction (**de** from); *(d'un membre de comité, d'un étudiant)* expulsion (**de** from); *(d'un immigrant)* expulsion, deportation (**de** from); *(d'un joueur)* sending off; **décider l'e. d'un élève** *(définitive)* to decide to exclude *or* expel a pupil; *(temporaire)* to decide to suspend a pupil **2** *Méd* expulsion, evacuation

expulsive [ɛkspylsiv] *voir* **expulsif**

expurgation [ɛkspyrgasjɔ̃] **NF** expurgation, bowdlerization

expurger **[17]** [ɛkspyrʒe] **VT** to expurgate, to bowdlerize; **une version très expurgée de cette histoire** an expurgated *or* sanitized version of the matter

exquis, -e [ɛkski, -iz] **ADJ 1** *(saveur, vin, gentillesse etc)* exquisite; *(personne, temps)* delightful **2** *Méd (douleur)* exquisite

exsangue [ɛksɑ̃g, ɛgzɑ̃g] **ADJ 1** *Littéraire (pâle ▸ figure, lèvres)* bloodless, livid **2** *(ayant perdu du sang ▸ corps, victime)* bloodless; *Fig (pays)* bled white; *(œuvre, littérature)* anaemic, bloodless; *Fig* **après la guerre, notre industrie était e.** this country's industry was bled white *or* dry by the war

exsanguino-transfusion [ɛksɑ̃ginotrɑ̃sfyzjɔ̃] *(pl* **exsanguino-transfusions)** **NF** *Méd* exchange transfusion

exsudation [ɛksydasjɔ̃] **NF** *Biol, Bot & Méd* exudation

exsuder **[3]** [ɛksyde] *Biol, Bot & Méd* **VT** to exude

VI to exude

exta [ɛksta] **NF** *Fam Arg drogue* E

extase [ɛkstaz] **NF 1** *(exaltation)* ecstasy, rapture; **être** *ou* **rester en e. devant** to be in raptures *or* ecstasies over; **tomber en e. devant qn/qch** to go into ecstasies at the sight of sb/sth **2** *Rel* ecstasy

extasié, -e [ɛkstazje] **ADJ** enraptured, ecstatic

extasier **[9]** [ɛkstazje] **s'extasier VPR s'e. devant/sur** to go into raptures *or* ecstasies over/about; **elle s'est longuement extasiée sur ses enfants/devant mes géraniums** she went into great raptures about her children/over my geraniums

extatique [ɛkstatik] **ADJ 1** *(de l'extase ▸ vision, transport)* ecstatic; **état e.** ecstasy, trance **2** *(émerveillé)* enraptured

extenseur [ɛkstɑ̃sœr] **ADJ M** *Anat* extensor

NM 1 *Anat* extensor **2** *(machine)* chest expander

extensibilité [ɛkstɑ̃sibilite] **NF** extensibility

extensible [ɛkstɑ̃sibl] **ADJ 1** *(organe)* extensible; *(matière)* tensible, extensible; *(tissu)* stretch; *(liste)* extendable; *Fig (définition)* flexible; *Fig* **mon budget n'est pas e.** I can't stretch my budget any further, I can't make my budget go any further **2** *Ordinat* upgradeable; *(mémoire)* expandable, upgradeable

extensif, -ive [ɛkstɑ̃sif, -iv] **ADJ 1** *Agr* extensive **2** *Phys (paramètre, force)* extensive **3 sens e.** *(d'un mot)* extended meaning

extension [ɛkstɑ̃sjɔ̃] **NF 1** *(étirement ▸ d'un élastique, d'un ressort, d'un muscle)* stretching; *(▸ d'une matière)* extension; *Méd* traction, extension

2 *(agrandissement ▸ d'un territoire)* expansion, enlargement; *(▸ d'une entreprise, d'un marché, d'un réseau)* expansion, extension; *(▸ de pouvoirs, d'un incendie, d'une maladie, d'une infection)* spreading, spread; *(▸ de droits)* extension; **prendre de l'e.** *(territoire)* to get bigger, to expand; *(secteur)* to grow, to develop; *(maladie, infection)* to spread, to extend; **la maladie/l'incendie a pris une e. considérable** the disease/fire has spread considerably

3 *(élargissement)* **on a décidé l'e. des mesures à toute la population** it has been decided to extend the scope of the measures to include the entire population

4 *(partie ajoutée ▸ d'un bâtiment, d'un réseau)* extension

5 *Ordinat (augmentation)* expansion; *(dispositif)* add-on; **carte d'e.** expansion board; **e. de nom de fichier** file name extension; **e. mémoire** memory expansion *or* upgrade

6 *Ling & Math* extension; *(d'un mot)* extended meaning

7 *Belg & Can Tél (poste)* extension

• **en extension ADJ 1** *(secteur)* developing, expanding; *(production)* increasing **2** *Anat (muscle, ressort)* stretched; **être en e.** *(ressort)* to be stretched *or* extended; *(gymnaste etc)* to be stretched out

• **par extension ADV** by extension; **le vocabulaire militaire sert, par e., à décrire les manœuvres électorales** military terminology is used by extension to describe electoral manoeuvring; *Ling & Math* **définir par e.** to define by extension

extensive [ɛkstɑ̃siv] *voir* **extensif**

extenso [ɛkstɛ̃so] *voir* **in extenso**

exténuant, -e [ɛkstenɥɑ̃, -ɑ̃t] **ADJ** exhausting

exténuation [ɛkstenɥasjɔ̃] **NF** exhaustion

exténuer **[7]** [ɛkstenɥe] **VT** to exhaust, to tire out; **être exténué** to be worn out *or* exhausted

VPR s'exténuer to exhaust oneself, to tire *or* to wear oneself out; **s'e. à faire qch** to exhaust oneself doing sth; *Fam* **je m'exténue à lui dire de ne pas y aller** I'm tired of telling him/her not to go

> Il faut noter que le verbe anglais **to extenuate** est un faux ami. Il signifie **atténuer**.

EXTÉRIEUR, -E [ɛksterjœr]

ADJ	
• outside **1, 4, 9**	• outer **1**
• external **1, 3–5, 7**	• outlying **2**
• outward **5**	• superficial **6**
• foreign **7**	• exterior **8**
NM	
• outside **1–3, 5, 7**	• exterior **1, 6**
• abroad **4**	• outward appearance **6**

ADJ 1 *(escalier, bruit, éclairage, intérêts)* outside; *(cour, poche, mur, orbite, bord, boulevards)* outer; *(porte)* external, outer; **les bruits extérieurs la gênent** outside noises *or* noises from outside distract her; **avoir des activités extérieures** *(hors du foyer)* to have interests outside the home; *(hors du travail)* to have interests outside of work; **il habite dans un quartier e. à la ville** he lives outside the city

2 *(excentré ▸ quartier)* outlying, out-of-town
3 *(non subjectif ▸ réalité)* external; **le monde e.** the outside world
4 *(étranger à la personne, la chose considérée ▸ influence, aide)* outside, external; **sans aide extérieure** without outside help; **ce sont des considérations extérieures** these are external considerations; **e. à** outside (of); **personnes extérieures à l'entreprise** persons not belonging to the staff; **une personnalité extérieure au cinéma** a personality outside the world of films; **développement e. au sujet** irrelevant development; **rester e. à une controverse/un débat** to remain aloof from *or* stay out of a controversy/debate
5 *(apparent)* external, surface *(avant n)*, outward; *(calme, joie, assurance)* outward, apparent; *(signe)* outward; **l'aspect e.** *(d'un édifice, d'un objet)* the outward appearance; *(d'une personne)* the exterior; **sa fragilité est toute extérieure** his/her vulnerability is all on the surface
6 *Péj (superficiel)* superficial, surface *(avant n)*, token *(avant n)*; **avec une compassion tout extérieure** with token *or* skin-deep compassion
7 *Écon & Pol (dette, commerce)* foreign, external; *(politique)* foreign
8 *Géom* exterior
9 *Tél* outside
NM 1 *(d'un bâtiment, d'une boîte)* exterior, outside
2 l'e. *(le plein air)* the outside *or* outdoors; **vernis pour l'e.** varnish for exterior use
3 l'e. *(à une personne)* the outside (world); **être tourné vers l'e.** to be outgoing
4 *Écon & Pol* **l'e.** abroad, foreign countries; **les relations avec l'e.** foreign relations
5 *(bord)* **l'e. de la chaussée** the outside (of the road)
6 *(apparence)* outward appearance, exterior; **il a un e. jovial** he's jolly on the outside; **sous un e. rébarbatif** under a forbidding exterior
7 *Sport* **l'e.** *(d'une piste, d'un circuit)* the outside
8 *Cin* location shot; **extérieurs tournés à Montrouge** shot on location in Montrouge; **il tourne en e.** he's on location
• **à l'extérieur** **ADV 1** *(en plein air)* outside, outdoors; **manger à l'e.** *(en plein air)* to eat outside *or* outdoors; *(hors de chez soi)* to eat out
2 *(hors du système, du groupe)* outside; **nous allons d'abord consulter à l'e.** we shall first seek the opinion of outside consultants
3 *Sport (sur une piste)* on the outside; *(dans une autre ville)* away; **jouer à l'e.** to play away; **match (joué) à l'e.** away match
4 *Écon & Pol* abroad
5 *Tél* outside; **téléphoner à l'e.** to make an outside call
• **à l'extérieur de** **PRÉP** *(bâtiment)* outside (of); *(boîte)* on the outside of; **à l'e. de la gare/ville** outside the station/town; **à l'e. du parc** outside of the park; **à l'e. de l'Afrique** outside Africa
• **de l'extérieur** **ADV 1** *(dans l'espace)* from (the) outside; **vue de l'e., la maison paraît petite** seen from (the) outside, the house looks small; **vue de l'e., cette entreprise a l'air de bien marcher** judging by appearances, the company seems to be doing well **2** *(dans un système)* from the outside; **considérer un problème de l'e.** to look at a problem from the outside; **juger de l'e.** to judge by appearances; **des gens venus de l'e.** outsiders

extérieurement [ɛksterjœrmɑ̃] **ADV 1** *(au dehors)* on the outside, externally **2** *(apparemment)* outwardly

extériorisation [ɛksterjɔrizasjɔ̃] **NF 1** *(de sentiments)* expression, show, display **2** *Psy* exteriorization, externalization

extérioriser **[3]** [ɛksterjɔrize] **VT 1** *(montrer ▸ sentiment)* to express, to show **2** *Psy* to exteriorize, to externalize
USAGE ABSOLU **il n'extériorise pas assez** he doesn't show his feelings enough
VPR s'extérioriser *(joie, mécontentement)* to be expressed, to show; *(personne)* to show one's feelings; **il s'extériorise très peu** he shows little of what he's feeling

extériorité [ɛksterjɔrite] **NF** exteriority

exterminateur, -trice [ɛksterminatœr, -tris] **ADJ** *(ange)* exterminating; *(rage)* destructive
NM,F exterminator

extermination [ɛksterminasjɔ̃] **NF** extermination

exterminatrice [ɛksterminatris] *voir* **exterminateur**

exterminer **[3]** [ɛkstermine] **VT 1** *(tuer ▸ peuple, race)* to exterminate; **se faire e.** to be wiped out **2** *Hum (vaincre ▸ adversaire)* to annihilate

externalisation [ɛksternalizasjɔ̃] **NF** *Écon* outsourcing

externaliser **[3]** [ɛksternalize] **VT** *Écon* to outsource

externat [ɛksterna] **NM 1** *Scol (école)* day school; *(élèves)* day pupils; *(statut)* non-residency **2** *(en médecine)* non-resident (medical) studentship; **pendant mon e.** while I was *Br* a non-resident student *or Am* an extern; **faire son e.** to be *Br* a non-resident student *or Am* an extern

externe [ɛkstern] **ADJ 1** *(cause, facteur)* external
2 *(partie, orbite, bord)* outer, external; **angle e.** exterior angle; *Pharm* **à usage e.** for external use only
3 *Scol* **élève e.** day pupil
4 *Ordinat* **dispositif e.** external device
NMF 1 *Scol* day pupil, non-boarder **2** *Méd* **e. (des hôpitaux)** *Br* non-resident (medical) student, *Am* extern

exterritorialité [ɛksteritɔrjalite] **NF** *Jur* exterritoriality, extraterritoriality

extincteur, -trice [ɛkstɛ̃ktœr, -tris] **ADJ** extinguishing *(avant n)*
NM (fire) extinguisher

extinction [ɛkstɛ̃ksjɔ̃] **NF 1** *(arrêt ▸ d'un incendie)* extinction, extinguishment, putting out; **e. des feux** lights out; *Aut* **e. retardée** *(d'une lumière)* delayed cut-off
2 *(suppression ▸ d'une dette)* extinguishment, discharge; **espèce animale menacée** *ou* **en voie d'e.** endangered animal species
3 *(affaiblissement)* **lutter jusqu'à l'e. de ses forces** to struggle until one has no strength left; *Méd* **e. de voix** loss of voice, *Spéc* aphonia; **avoir une e. de voix** to have lost one's voice
4 *Chim (de chaux)* slaking
5 *Jur (d'un droit)* extinguishment; *(d'un contrat)* termination; *(d'une hypothèque)* redemption
6 *Biol & Méd* **e. génique** gene silencing

extinctrice [ɛkstɛ̃ktris] *voir* **extincteur**

extirpateur [ɛkstirpatœr] **NM** *Agr* harrow

extirpation [ɛkstirpasjɔ̃] **NF** *Méd (extraction ▸ d'une tumeur)* removal, removing, *Spéc* extirpation; *(▸ d'une plante)* rooting up, pulling out, uprooting

extirper **[3]** [ɛkstirpe] **VT 1** *(ôter ▸ tumeur)* to remove, *Spéc* to extirpate; *(▸ épine, racine)* to pull out; *(▸ plante)* to root up *or* out, to uproot, to pull up; **e. qn du lit** to drag *or* to haul sb out of bed; **e. qn d'un fauteuil** to drag sb out of an armchair; **e. qn d'une situation impossible/d'un piège** to extricate sb from an impossible situation/from a trap; **je n'ai pas réussi à lui e. un mot** I couldn't drag *or* get a word out of him/her **2** *(détruire ▸ préjugés, vice)* to eradicate, to root out
VPR s'extirper **s'e. du lit** to drag *or* to haul oneself out of bed; **s'e. de dessous la couette** to drag oneself from beneath the quilt; **s'e. de son pull/d'un enchevêtrement de racines** to extricate oneself from one's pullover/a tangle of roots

extorquer **[3]** [ɛkstɔrke] **VT** *(fonds)* to extort; **e. de l'argent à qn** to extort money from sb; **e. des aveux à qn** to wring a confession out of sb; **e. une signature à qn** to force a signature out of sb; **e. une promesse à qn** to extract *or* to extort a promise from sb; **elle s'est fait e. de l'argent par ses enfants** her children extorted money from her

extorqueur, -euse [ɛkstɔrkœr, -øz] **NM,F** extortionist

extorsion [ɛkstɔrsjɔ̃] **NF** extortion; **e. de fonds** extortion of money

extra- [ɛkstra] **PRÉF** extra-

extra [ɛkstra] **ADJ INV 1** *Fam (exceptionnel ▸ journée, personne, spectacle)* great, terrific, super; **tu viens passer le week-end avec nous? c'est e.!** you're spending the weekend with us? (that's) fantastic *or* terrific! **2** *(de qualité supérieure ▸ vin, repas, vêtement)* first-class, first-rate; *Com* **beurre (de qualité) e.** finest quality butter **3** *Can Fam (en supplément)* extra[❑]; **la taxe est e.** the tax is extra *or* on top
NM 1 *(gâterie)* (special) treat; **faire** *ou* **s'offrir un e.** to give oneself a treat, to treat oneself; **on s'est fait un petit e. en achetant du homard** we gave ourselves a bit of a treat by buying lobster
2 *(frais)* extra cost *or* expenditure, incidental expenditure; **avec les extras, la semaine nous est revenue à 400 euros** if you include incidental expenditure *or* with (all) the extras, the week cost us 400 euros
3 *(emploi ponctuel)* **faire des extras chez qn** to do occasional work for sb; **faire des extras comme ouvreuse** to earn extra money by working (occasionally) as an usherette
4 *(serveur)* help; **pour la soirée, on prendra deux extras** we'll take on two extra people for the party
• **extras** **NMPL** *Can Fam (accessoires)* (optional) extras[❑]; **c'est plus cher avec les extras** it's much more expensive with the extras included

extracommunautaire [ɛkstrakɔmynotɛr] **ADJ** non-EU

extraconjugal, -e, -aux, -ales [ɛkstrakɔ̃ʒygal, -o] **ADJ** extramarital

extracteur [ɛkstraktœr] **NM 1** *Mil, Chim & Méd* extractor **2** *Tech (de miel)* extractor, centrifuge **3** *Tech (de fluides)* extractor

extractible [ɛkstraktibl] **ADJ** extractable; *(autoradio, disque)* removable

extractif, -ive [ɛkstraktif, -iv] **ADJ** extractive

extraction [ɛkstraksjɔ̃] **NF 1** *(origine)* extraction, origin; **de basse e.** of humble birth; **de haute e.** highborn; **d'e. bourgeoise** from a bourgeois family
2 *Mines & Pétr* extraction; **e. à ciel ouvert** opencast mining; **l'e. de la pierre** quarrying (for stone); **l'e. du charbon** coal extraction *or* mining
3 *(d'une dent, d'une épine)* pulling out, extraction; *(d'une balle)* removal
4 *Chim & Math* extraction, extracting

extractive [ɛkstraktiv] *voir* **extractif**

extrader **[3]** [ɛkstrade] **VT** to extradite

extradition [ɛkstradisjɔ̃] **NF** extradition

extra-dry [ɛkstradraj] **NM INV** extra-dry champagne

extra-fin, -e, extrafin, -e [ɛkstrafɛ̃, -in] **ADJ** *(haricots, petits pois, papier)* extra-fine; *(collants)* sheer; *(chocolats)* superfine; *(beurre)* finest-quality; **de qualité extra-fine** *ou* **extrafine** extra fine

extrafort, -e [ɛkstrafɔr, -ɔrt] **ADJ** *(carton)* strong, stiff; *(colle)* extra-strong; *(moutarde)* hot
NM bias-binding

extraire **[112]** [ɛkstrɛr] **VT 1** *(charbon)* to extract, to mine; *(pétrole)* to extract; *(pierre)* to extract, to quarry
2 *(ôter ▸ dent, écharde, clou)* to extract, to remove, to pull out; *(▸ balle)* to take out, to remove; *(▸ blessés, corps)* to free (**de** from); **e. une balle d'une jambe** to extract *or* to remove a bullet from a leg; **e. un ticket de sa poche** to take *or* to dig a ticket out of one's pocket; **ils ont eu du mal à l'e. de sa voiture accidentée** they had great difficulty cutting him/her loose from the wreckage of his/her car; **e. un secret/des informations à qn** to worm a secret/information out of sb
3 *Chim, Culin & Pharm* to extract; *(en pressant)* to squeeze out; *(en écrasant)* to crush out; *(en tordant)* to wring out
4 *Math* to extract; **e. la racine carrée/cubique d'un nombre** to extract the square/cube root of a number
5 *(citer ▸ passage, proverbe)* to extract, to excerpt (**de** from); **c'est extrait de la Genèse** it's taken from Genesis
VPR s'extraire **s'e. de qch** to climb *or* to clamber out of sth; **s'e. d'une voiture** *(rescapé d'un accident)* to extricate oneself from (the wreckage of) a car

extrait [ɛkstrɛ] **NM 1** *(morceau choisi)* extract; *(de livre, de discours, d'auteur)* extract, excerpt; *(de film)* extract, clip; **un e. de la conférence** an extract from the lecture; **un petit e. de l'émission d'hier soir** a short sequence from last night's programme; *TV* **extraits pré-enregistrés** recorded highlights; *TV* **extraits d'archives** archive footage

2 *Admin* **e. (d'acte) de naissance** birth certificate; **e. de casier judiciaire** extract from police records *(often used to show that one does not have a criminal record)*; **e. de compte** abstract of accounts; *Compta* statement of account; *Banque* bank statement **3** *Culin & Pharm* extract, essence; **e. de violette** extract *or* essence of violets; **e. de viande** meat extract *or* essence; **e. de café** coffee extract

extrajudiciaire [ɛkstraʒydisjer] **ADJ** *Jur* extrajudicial

extralinguistique [ɛkstralɛ̃gɥistik] **ADJ** *Ling* extralinguistic

extralucide [ɛkstralysid] **ADJ** clairvoyant
NMF clairvoyant

extra-muros [ɛkstramyros] **ADV** outside the town, out of town; **Paris e.** outer Paris

Extranet, extranet [ɛkstranet] **NM** *Ordinat* Extranet

extraordinaire [ɛkstraɔrdinɛr] **ADJ 1** *(inhabituel ▸ histoire)* extraordinary, amazing; *(▸ cas, personnage, intelligence)* extraordinary, exceptional; *(▸ talent, courage)* extraordinary, exceptional, rare; *(▸ circonstances)* extraordinary, special; *(▸ messager, mission)* special; **mais, fait e., il connaissait la réponse** but, amazingly enough *or* would you believe it, he knew the answer; **frais** *ou* **dépenses extraordinaires** *(non prévues)* extras; *(uniques)* non-recurring expenditure

2 *Pol (mesures, impôt)* special; *(pouvoirs)* special, emergency *(avant n)*; **assemblée e.** special session, extraordinary meeting

3 *(remarquable ▸ artiste, joueur, spectacle)* remarkable, outstanding; *(▸ homme, femme, beauté, succès)* extraordinary, outstanding; *(▸ temps)* wonderful; *(▸ chaleur)* extraordinary

4 *Fam (très bon)* really good; **elle a fait un travail e.** she did outstanding work; **le repas n'avait rien d'e.** *ou* **n'était pas e.** there was nothing special about the meal

5 *(étrange)* extraordinary, strange; **cela n'a rien d'e.** that's nothing out of the ordinary; **cela n'a rien d'e. après ce que tu lui as dit** that's not surprising given what you said to him/her; **qu'y-a-t-il d'e. à cela?** what's so strange *or* special about that?; *Fam* **tu es e.!** you're amazing!; *Ironique* you're the limit!

• **par extraordinaire ADV par e., il était chez lui ce soir-là** he was at home that night, which was most unusual; **si par e. tu la voyais** if by some remote chance you should see her; **si par e. il arrivait que...** if by some unlikely chance it happened that...; **quand par e. il me rendait visite** on those rare occasions when he would visit me; **quand par e. nous nous rencontrons** when we meet, which we rarely do; *Fam* **comme par e., il était là** as if by magic, he was there

extraordinairement [ɛkstraɔrdinɛrmɑ̃] **ADV 1** *(très)* extraordinarily, extremely, exceptionally **2** *(bizarrement)* extraordinarily, strangely, bizarrely

extraparlementaire [ɛkstraparləmɑ̃tɛr] **ADJ** extraparliamentary

extraplat, -e [ɛkstrapla, -at] **ADJ** extraflat, very slim, slimline; **une calculatrice extraplate** a slimline calculator

extrapolation [ɛkstrapɔlasjɔ̃] **NF** extrapolation

extrapoler [3] [ɛkstrapɔle] **VT** to extrapolate; **e. qch d'un fait** to extrapolate sth from a fact
VI to extrapolate; **e. à partir de qch** to extrapolate from sth

extrascolaire [ɛkstraskɔlɛr] **ADJ** *(activités)* extra-curricular

extrasensible [ɛkstrasɑ̃sibl] **ADJ** ultrasensitive

extrasensoriel, -elle, extra-sensoriel, -elle [ɛkstrasɑ̃sɔrjɛl] **ADJ** extrasensory

extrasystole [ɛkstrasistɔl] **NF** *Méd* extrasystole

extraterrestre [ɛkstraterɛstr] **ADJ** extraterrestrial
NMF extraterrestrial (being *or* creature)

extraterritorial, -e, -aux, -ales [ɛkstrateritɔrjal, -o] **ADJ** extraterritorial

extraterritorialité [ɛkstrateritɔrjalite] **NF** extraterritoriality

extra-utérin, -e [ɛkstrayterɛ̃, -in] *(mpl* **extra-utérins,** *fpl* **extra-utérines)** **ADJ** *Méd* extra-uterine; **grossesse extra-utérine** ectopic pregnancy

extravagance [ɛkstravagɑ̃s] **NF 1** *(outrance ▸ d'une attitude, d'une personne, d'une réponse, d'une tenue)* extravagance; *(▸ d'une demande)* extravagance, unreasonableness; *(▸ de dépenses)* exorbitance; *(▸ d'une tenue)* extravagance, eccentricity; *(▸ d'un désir)* immoderateness; **des idées d'une telle e.** such extravagant ideas **2** *(acte)* extravagance; *(parole)* foolish thing (to say); **faire des extravagances** to behave extravagantly, to do eccentric things; **dire des extravagances** to talk wildly

> Il faut noter que le nom anglais **extravagance** signifie également **gaspillage, dépense inconsidérée.**

extravagant, -e [ɛkstravagɑ̃, -ɑ̃t] **ADJ 1** *(déraisonnable ▸ attitude, personne, réponse, tenue)* extravagant; *(▸ idée)* extravagant, wild, crazy; **de manière extravagante** extravagantly; **raconter des histoires extravagantes** to tell wild stories **2** *(excessif ▸ demande, exigence, dépenses)* extravagant, unreasonable
NM,F eccentric (person)

> Il faut noter que l'adjectif anglais **extravagant** signifie également **dépensier.**

extraversion [ɛkstravɛrsjɔ̃] **NF** *Psy* extroversion

extraverti, -e [ɛkstravɛrti] **ADJ** extroverted
NM,F extrovert

extrayait *etc voir* **extraire**

extrême [ɛkstrɛm] **ADJ 1** *(intense ▸ confort, importance, soin etc)* extreme, utmost; *(▸ froid)* extreme, intense; **j'ai l'e. regret de vous annoncer que...** to my deepest *or* very great regret, I have to tell you that...; **d'une complexité/maigreur e.** extremely complex/skinny

2 *(radical ▸ idée)* extreme; *(▸ mesures)* extreme, drastic; **être e. dans ses idées** to hold extreme views; **elle est e. en tout** she is extreme in everything; *Pol* **l'e. droite/gauche** the extreme *or* far right/left

3 *(exceptionnel ▸ cas, exemple, situation)* extreme; **ne m'appelle qu'en cas d'e. urgence** only call me in cases of extreme urgency *or* if it's extremely urgent

4 *(le plus éloigné ▸ point, limite)* far, extreme, farthest; **la limite e., l'e. limite** the furthest point; **à l'e. limite, j'accepterai d'attendre une semaine de plus** I'll agree to wait another week at the most *or* at the outside; **la partie e.** the furthest part; **la date e.** the final date

NM 1 *(cas limite)* extreme; **passer d'un e. à l'autre** to go from one extreme to the other *or* to another; **les extrêmes se rejoignent** extremes meet *or* join up **2** *Math* **extrêmes** *(termes)* extremes

• **à l'extrême ADV** extremely, in the extreme; **il est méticuleux à l'e.** he's conscientious in the extreme; **porter** *ou* **pousser les choses à l'e.** to take *or* to carry things to extremes

extrêmement [ɛkstrɛmmɑ̃] **ADV** extremely

extrême-onction [ɛkstrɛmɔ̃ksjɔ̃] *(pl* **extrêmes-onctions)** **NF** *Rel* extreme unction

Extrême-Orient [ɛkstrɛmɔrjɑ̃] **NM l'E.** the Far East

extrême-oriental, -e *(mpl* **extrême-orientaux,** *fpl* **extrême-orientales)** [ɛkstrɛmɔrjɑ̃tal, -o] **ADJ** Far Eastern

• **Extrême-oriental, -e** *(mpl* **Extrême-orientaux,** *fpl* **Extrême-orientales)** **NM,F** Oriental

extremis [ɛkstremis] *voir* **in extremis**

extrémisme [ɛkstremism] **NM** extremism; **l'e. de droite/gauche** right-/left-wing extremism

extrémiste [ɛkstremist] **ADJ** extremist
NMF extremist; **les extrémistes de droite/gauche** right-/left-wing extremists

extrémité [ɛkstremite] **NF 1** *(d'un bâtiment, d'une table, d'une jetée, d'une corde)* end; *(d'un bâton)* end, tip; *(d'un doigt, de la langue, d'une aile)* tip; *(d'un champ)* edge, end; *(d'une aiguille, d'une épée)* point; *(d'un territoire)* (furthest) boundary; **aux extrémités de l'univers** at the outermost limits *or* on the edge of the universe

2 *Anat & Math* extremity; **les extrémités** *(pieds et mains)* the extremities, the hands and feet; **j'ai les extrémités glacées** my hands and feet are frozen

3 *(acte radical)* extreme act; **pousser qn à des extrémités** to drive sb to extremes; **en venir à des extrémités** to resort to extreme measures

4 *(brutalité)* act of violence; **en venir à des extrémités** to resort to violence; **il s'est porté à des extrémités regrettables** unfortunately he resorted to acts of violence

5 *(situation critique)* plight, straits, extremity; **dans cette e.** in this extremity; **être à la dernière e.** to be on the point of death; **être réduit à la dernière e.** to be in dire straits *or* in a dreadful plight

extrinsèque [ɛkstrɛ̃sɛk] **ADJ** extrinsic; **valeur e. d'une monnaie** face value of a currency

extroversion [ɛkstrɔvɛrsjɔ̃] **NF** *Psy* extroversion

extroverti, -e [ɛkstrɔvɛrti] **ADJ** extroverted

extrusion [ɛkstryzjɔ̃] **NF 1** *Ind* extrusion, extruding **2** *Géol* extrusion

exubérance [ɛgzyberɑ̃s] **NF 1** *(entrain)* exuberance, joie de vivre; **avec e.** exuberantly **2** *Littéraire (action)* exuberant behaviour *(UNCOUNT)* **3** *(énergie, vigueur ▸ d'une végétation, d'un style)* luxuriance; *(▸ d'une imagination)* wildness, exuberance; *(▸ de figures, de formes)* abundance, luxuriance

exubérant, -e [ɛgzyberɑ̃, -ɑ̃t] **ADJ 1** *(joyeux ▸ attitude, personne)* exuberant **2** *(vigoureux ▸ végétation, style)* luxuriant; *(▸ imagination)* wild, exuberant

exultation [ɛgzyltasjɔ̃] **NF** *Littéraire* exultation, rejoicing

exulter [3] [ɛgzylte] **VI** to exult, to rejoice; **l'annonce de cette nouvelle la fit e.** when she heard the news she went wild with joy *or* was over the moon

exutoire [ɛgzytwar] **NM 1** *(dérivatif)* **un e. à** an outlet for **2** *(pour liquides)* outlet

ex-voto [ɛksvɔto] **NM INV** *Rel* ex voto

eye-liner [ajlajnœr] *(pl* **eye-liners)** **NM** eyeliner

e-zine, ezine [izin] **NM** *Ordinat* e-zine, ezine

F¹, f [ɛf] **NM INV 1** *(lettre)* F, f; **F comme François** ≃ F for Freddie **2** *Mus (note)* F **3** *(appartement)* **un F3** ≃ a two-bedroomed *Br* flat *or Am* apartment; **un F4** ≃ a three-bedroomed *Br* flat *or Am* apartment

F² [ɛf] **NF** *Sport (abrév* **Formule***)* F; **la F1** F1

F³ 1 *(abrév écrite* **franc***)* F; **500 F** 500 F, F 500 **2** *(abrév écrite* **fahrenheit***)* F **3** *(abrév écrite* **femme***)* F

fa [fa] **NM INV** *(note)* F; *(quand on chante la gamme)* fa, fah; **en fa majeur/mineur** in F major/minor; **un fa bémol/dièse** an F flat/sharp; **en fa bémol/dièse** in F flat/sharp; **chantez-moi un fa** sing me an F; **chantez "ré, mi, fa"** sing "re, mi, fa *or* fah"; **clé de fa** key of F, bass clef

FAB [efabe] **ADJ INV & ADV** *Com (abrév* **franco à bord***)* FOB, fob

fable [fabl] **NF 1** *Littérature* fable; **célèbre dans la f.** famous in fable

2 *Péj (invention)* lie, invention; **c'est une f.!** it's a fairytale!

3 *Littéraire (légende)* legend, tale

4 *Arch (locution)* **être la f. du village** to be the laughing stock of the village

fabliau, -x [fablijo] **NM** *Littérature* fabliau

fablier [fablije] **NM** *Littérature* book *or* collection of fables

fabricant, -e [fabrikɑ̃, -ɑ̃t] **NM,F** manufacturer, maker; **gros/petit f.** large/small manufacturer; **f. de voitures** car manufacturer; **f. de chaussures** shoemaker

fabricateur, -trice [fabrikatœr, -tris] **NM,F f. de fausse monnaie** counterfeiter; **f. de faux papiers** forger of documents; **f. de fausses nouvelles** scandalmonger

fabrication [fabrikasjɔ̃] **NF 1** *(à la main)* making; *Ind* manufacture, production; **f. artisanale** production by craftsmen; **produits de f. artisanale** handmade products; **f. industrielle** industrial manufacture; **f. assistée par ordinateur** computer-aided *or* computer-assisted manufacturing; **f. intégrée par ordinateur** computer-integrated manufacturing; **f. par lots** batch production; **f. en série** mass production

2 *(contrefaçon ▸ de fausses nouvelles)* fabrication; *(▸ document)* counterfeiting, forging; **f. de fausse monnaie** counterfeiting; **f. de faux en écritures** forging of documents

3 *(production)* workmanship; **f. soignée** quality workmanship; **de f. maison** home-made; **article de f. française** article made in France, French-made article; **c'est de ta f.?** did you make it yourself?; **elle a apporté une tarte de sa f.** she brought along a tart she had made herself

4 *Péj* **la f. d'une vedette** the manufacturing of a star; **la f. d'un président** the making of a president

5 *Typ* layout

• **de fabrication ADJ** *(coûts, procédés)* manufacturing *(avant n)*; *(numéro)* serial *(avant n)*; **défaut de f.** manufacturing defect; **secret de f.** trade secret

fabrique [fabrik] **NF 1** *(établissement)* factory, works, mill; **f. de papier** paper mill **2** *(fabrication)* manufacture; **prix de f.** manufacturer's *or* factory price **3** *Rel* **conseil de f.** (parochial) church council

• **de fabrique ADJ** *(prix, secret)* manufacturer's, trade *(avant n)*; *(marque)* trade *(avant n)*

> Il faut noter que le nom anglais **fabric** est un faux ami. Il signifie le plus souvent **tissu**.

fabriquer [3] [fabrike] **VT 1** *Ind* to make, to produce, to manufacture; *(gâteau, pull-over, guirlande)* to make; **f. des véhicules en série** to mass-produce vehicles

2 *(artisanalement)* to make; **nous fabriquons nos produits à la main** we make our products by hand; **cela a contribué à f. son personnage médiatique** that helped to turn him/her into a media figure *or* to make a media figure out of him/her

3 *Fam (faire)* to do▫, to cook up; **je me demande ce qu'il peut f. toute la journée dans sa chambre** I wonder what he gets up to in his room all day (long); **mais qu'est-ce qu'il fabrique?** what's he up to?, what's he doing?; **qu'est-ce que tu fabriques, ces jours-ci?** what are you up to these days?; **ça alors, qu'est-ce que tu fabriques par ici?** what on earth are you doing here?; *Péj* **qu'est-ce que tu as encore fabriqué avec mes clefs?** now what have you gone and done with my keys?; **qu'est-ce qu'il fabrique, ce bus?** what's that bus doing?

4 *Péj (histoire)* to concoct; *(personnalité)* to build up; **f. qch de toutes pièces** to make sth up, to fabricate sth; **c'est une histoire fabriquée de toutes pièces** it's a made-up story, the story is made-up from start to finish **f. de la fausse monnaie** to counterfeit *or* to forge money; **f. des faux papiers** to forge documents

VPR se fabriquer 1 *(être fabriqué)* to be made *or* manufactured; **ils se fabriquent facilement** they are easy to make, they are easily made *or* manufactured **2 se f. qch** to build *or* to make sth for oneself; **il s'était fabriqué une cabane** he had built a hut (for himself) **3 se f. qch** *(s'inventer, se constituer)* to invent sth; **elle s'était fabriqué un passé d'actrice de cinéma** she had invented a past as a film actress for herself

fabulateur, -trice [fabylatœr, -tris] **ADJ** *Psy* confabulatory

NM,F fantasist; *Psy* confabulator

fabulation [fabylasjɔ̃] **NF** fabrication, fantasizing; *Psy* confabulation

fabuler [3] [fabyle] **VI 1** *Psy* to confabulate **2** *Péj (mentir)* to tell tales; **des ours? – je crois qu'il fabule un peu** bears? – I think he's making it up

fabuleusement [fabyløzmɑ̃] **ADV** fabulously, fantastically

fabuleux, -euse [fabylø, -øz] **ADJ 1** *(de légende)* fabulous, legendary; *(caractère, exploits)* mythical, legendary; **des animaux f.** fabulous beasts **2** *(hors du commun)* incredible, fabulous; **un destin f.** an incredible fate **3** *(élevé ▸ prix, somme)* tremendous, astronomical; **elle gagne des sommes fabuleuses** she earns a tremendous amount of money

fabuliste [fabylist] **NMF** *Littérature* fabulist, writer of fables

FAC [ɛfase] **NM** *Admin (abrév* **fonds d'aide et de coopération***)* = French government fund which administers economic and social projects in former colonies

fac [fak] **NF** *Fam* university▫; **f. de droit/de lettres** faculty of law/arts▫; **en f., à la f.** at university▫ *or* college▫, *Br* at uni; **être en f. d'allemand** to be studying *or* doing German at *Br* uni *or Am* college

façade [fasad] **NF 1** *(de bâtiment)* façade; **la f. du château** the front of the palace; **f. latérale** side (aspect); **f. principale** façade, (main) frontage; **hôtel en f. sur la place** hotel facing the square

2 *(paroi)* front wall *or* panel

3 *(apparence)* outward appearance, façade; *Péj (faux-semblant)* cover, pretence; **ce n'est qu'une f.** it's all show *or* a façade

4 *très Fam (visage)* mug, face▫; **se refaire la f.** to touch up one's make-up; **se faire refaire la f.** to have a face-lift; **démolir la f. à qn** to smash sb's face in

5 *Géog* **la f. atlantique** the Atlantic coast

6 *Ordinat (d'un modem etc)* front panel

7 *Tél (d'un téléphone portable)* fascia, cover

8 *Assur* fronting

• **de façade ADJ un optimisme de f.** a show of optimism; **une générosité/un patriotisme de f.** fake *or* sham generosity/patriotism

face [fas] **NF 1** *(visage)* face; **il a reçu le coup en pleine f.** he was hit full in the face; **les muscles de la f.** facial muscles; **f. contre terre** face down; **tomber f. contre terre** to fall flat on one's face; **arborer** *ou* **avoir une f. de carême** to have a long face; **il est arrivé avec une f. de carême** he turned up wearing a long face *or* looking very down in the mouth; *très Fam* **f. de crabe** *ou* **d'œuf** *ou* **de rat** *Br* face-ache, *Am* ratfink; **f. de lune** round face; **perdre/sauver la f.** to lose/to save face; **se voiler la f.** to delude oneself

2 *(aspect)* **la f. des choses** the face of things; **changer la f. de** to alter the face of; **examiner un problème sous toutes ses faces** to consider every aspect of a problem

3 *(côté ▸ d'une médaille)* obverse; *(▸ d'une pièce)* head, headside; *(▸ d'un disque)* side; *(▸ d'une montagne)* face; *(▸ d'une lame d'épée)* flat; **la f. B d'un disque** the B-side *or* flipside of a record; **la f. cachée de la lune** the dark side of the moon; *Fig* **la f. cachée d'un problème** the hidden side *or* aspect of a problem; **à double f.** double-sided; **changer un disque de f.** to turn a record over; **f.!** *(en lançant une pièce)* heads!

4 *Littéraire (surface)* face; **la f. de la terre** the face of the earth

5 *Géom* face, side; **polyèdre à douze faces** twelve-sided polyhedron

6 *Ordinat* **disquette double f.** double-sided disk

7 *Couture* **double f.** double-faced; **tissu double f.** double-faced fabric

8 *(locutions)* **faire f.** to face up to things, to cope; **après l'accident, il lui a fallu faire f.** after the accident, he/she just had to cope; **faire f. à** *(être tourné vers)* to stand opposite to, to face; *(danger, difficultés)* to face up to; *(obligations, dépense)* to meet; **les fenêtres font f. au sud** the windows face south; **les deux maisons se font f.** the two houses face *or* are facing *or* are opposite each other; **faire f. aux critiques** to face one's critics; **faire f. à ses créanciers** to face up to one's creditors

• **à la face de PRÉP** *(devant)* **à la f. de son frère** to his/her brother's face; **jeter des accusations à la f. de qn** to throw accusations in sb's face; **elle lui a jeté à la f. qu'il était hypocrite** she told him straight to his face that he was a hypocrite; **à la f. du monde** *ou* **de tous** *(publiquement)* openly, publicly; **crier sa joie/son désespoir à la f. du monde** to shout out one's joy/despair to the world (at large); **à la f. de Dieu** before God

• **à sa face même** ADV *Can (à l'évidence)* evidently, clearly; **le tribunal a jugé que la demande était, à sa f. même, irrecevable** the court ruled that the claim was clearly inadmissible

• **de face** ADJ face *(avant n)*, facing; *Beaux-Arts & Phot* **photo/portrait de f.** full-face photograph/portrait; *Archit* **vue de f.** front view *or* elevation; *Tech* **clouage de f.** face nailing; *Théât* **loge de f.** box facing the stage; *Transp* **place de f.** seat facing the engine ADV **se présenter de f.** to be face on; **il l'a attaquée de f.** he attacked her from the front; *Fig* he attacked her openly

• **d'en face** ADJ **ceux d'en f.** *(adversaires)* the opposition; *(voisins)* the people opposite; **le garçon d'en f.** the boy from across the road; **la maison d'en f.** the house opposite

• **en face** ADV *(de front)* **avoir le soleil en f.** to have the sun (shining) in one's face; **regarder qn (bien) en f.** to look sb (full *or* straight) in the face; **regarder la mort en f.** to face up to death; **regarder les choses en f.** to face facts; **je lui ai dit la vérité en f.** I told him/her the truth to his/her face

• **en face de** PRÉP **juste en f. de moi** right in front of me; **sa maison est en f. de l'église** his/her house is opposite *or* faces the church; **mettre qn en f. des réalités** to force sb to face reality; **en f. l'un de l'autre, l'un en f. de l'autre** face to face, opposite each other, facing each other; **nous sommes en f. d'un problème difficile** we are faced with a difficult problem

• **face à** PRÉP *(dans l'espace)* facing; **f. au public** in front of *or* facing the audience; **f. à l'ennemi/aux médias** faced with the enemy/the media

• **face à face** ADV face to face; **nous étions enfin f. à f.** at last we had come face to face; **parler à qn f. à f.** to speak to sb face to face *or* in person; **mettre qn f. à f. avec** to bring sb face to face with; **que feras-tu quand tu seras f. à f. avec lui?** what will you do when you're faced with *or* face to face with him?

face-à-face [fasafas] NM INV *(conversation)* (face-to-face) meeting; *(conflit)* (one-to-one) confrontation; **f. télévisé** television debate *(between two politicians)*

face-à-main [fasamɛ̃] *(pl* **faces-à-main)** NM lorgnette

face-texte [fastekst] *(pl* **faces-textes)** NM *Journ* facing matter

facétie [fasesi] NF *Littéraire (plaisanterie)* facetious remark, joke; *(trait d'esprit)* witticism, wisecrack; *(farce)* prank; **dire des facéties** to crack jokes; **se livrer à des facéties** to fool around

facétieux, -euse [fasesjø, -øz] ADJ facetious, humorous

NM,F joker, prankster

facette [faset] NF **1** *Entom, Géol & (en joaillerie)* facet **2** *(aspect)* facet, aspect, side; **sa personnalité présente d'autres facettes** there are other sides to his/her personality; **examiner un problème sous toutes ses facettes** to examine a problem from every angle

• **à facettes** ADJ **1** *Entom, Géol & (en joaillerie)* multifaceted; **taillé à facettes** (cut) in facets, faceted **2** *(personnalité, talent)* multifaceted, many-sided

facetter [4] [fasete] VT *(en joaillerie)* to facet

fâché, -e [faʃe] ADJ **1** *(en colère)* angry, cross, mad; **être f. contre qn** to be angry *or* annoyed with *or Am* mad at sb; **tu n'es pas f., au moins?** you're not angry, are you?; **avoir l'air f.** to look angry *or* cross

2 *(désolé)* sorry; **être f. de qch/pour qn** to be sorry about sth/for sb; **je suis f. de l'avoir manqué** I'm really sorry I missed him; **je ne serais pas f. d'avoir une réponse** I wouldn't mind getting an answer; **ils n'étaient pas fâchés de se retrouver chez eux** they were rather pleased to be home again; **je ne suis pas f. que ce soit terminé** I'm not sorry that it's finished

3 *(brouillé)* **ils sont fâchés** they're not on speaking terms; **être f. avec qn** to have fallen out with sb

4 *Fig Hum (sans goût pour)* **je suis f. avec les langues/les chiffres** languages/figures are not my thing; **il est f. avec le savon** he's allergic to soap; **tu es f. avec ton rasoir?** shaving doesn't come naturally to you, does it?

fâcher [3] [faʃe] VT **1** *(mettre en colère)* to annoy, to make angry, to anger; **un sujet qui fâche** a controversial topic **2** *Vieilli (contrarier)* to annoy, to vex; **acceptez, le contraire les fâcherait** say yes, they'd be offended if you didn't; **ce retard me fâche infiniment** I am extremely annoyed at this delay

VPR **se fâcher 1** *(se brouiller)* to quarrel *or* to fall out (with each other *or* one another); **tes parents se sont fâchés?** did your parents quarrel?; **se f. avec qn** to quarrel *or* to fall out with sb **2** *(se mettre en colère)* to get cross *or* angry, to lose one's temper; **tes parents se sont fâchés?** did your parents get angry?; *Fam* **se f. tout rouge** to blow one's top; **se f. contre qn** to get angry with sb

fâcherie [faʃri] NF quarrel, tiff; **entre eux, ce sont des fâcheries continuelles** they're always quarrelling (with each other *or* one another)

facheuse [faʃøz] *voir* **facheux**

fâcheusement [faʃøzmɑ̃] ADV *(malheureusement)* unfortunately; *(désagréablement)* unpleasantly; **il a été f. impressionné** he was not at all impressed

fâcheux, -euse [faʃø, -øz] ADJ regrettable, unfortunate; **une fâcheuse coïncidence** an unfortunate coincidence; **une formulation fâcheuse** an unfortunate *or* a regrettable choice of words; **c'est f.!** it's rather a pity!; **il est f. qu'il soit parti si tôt** it's a pity (that) he left so early; **il a eu la fâcheuse idée de l'inviter à la soirée** he rather unfortunately invited him/her to the party

NM,F *Littéraire* bore

facho [faʃo] *Fam Péj* ADJ fascist[□]

NMF fascist[□]

facial, -e, -aux, -ales [fasjal, -o] ADJ *(muscle, angle)* facial; **massage f.** facial *or* face massage

faciès [fasjɛs] NM **1** *(traits)* facial aspect, features; *Méd* facies; **le f. caractéristique de Cro-Magnon** Cro-Magnon man's typical features **2** *Péj (visage)* face; **un f. grimaçant derrière le carreau** a grimacing face behind the windowpane **3** *Bot & Géol* facies

facile [fasil] ADJ **1** *(aisé)* easy; **essaie, c'est f. comme tout!** have a go, it's as easy as anything!; **rien de plus f.** nothing easier; **il ne m'est pas f. d'expliquer la situation** it's not easy for me to explain the situation; **f. à faire** easy to do, easily done; **f. à comprendre** easily understood, easy to understand; **f. à lire** (easily) readable, easy to read; **f. à retenir** easy to remember, (easily) memorable; **c'est f. à dire (mais moins f. à faire), c'est plus f. à dire qu'à faire** easier said than done; **f. d'accès** easy to reach, within easy reach; **la gare n'est pas f. d'accès** the station isn't easy to get to; **f. d'emploi** easy to use; **avoir la vie f.** to have an easy life; **c'est f. comme bonjour** *ou* **comme tout** it's as easy as pie; **ça n'est pas si f. que ça** it's not as easy as that, it's not all that easy

2 *(spontané, naturel)* **elle a la parole/plume f.** speaking/writing comes easily to her; **avoir l'argent f.** to be very casual about money; **avoir la larme f.** to be easily moved to tears; **avoir la gâchette f.** to be trigger-happy

3 *Péj (effet, humour)* facile; **avoir l'ironie f.** to be unnecessarily sarcastic

4 *(souple ▸ caractère)* easy-going; **être f. (à vivre)** to be easy-going; **tu n'as pas choisi quelqu'un de f. (à vivre)** you haven't exactly picked someone easy to get on with; **il n'a pas l'air f. en affaires** he doesn't seem an easy man to do business with; **c'est un enfant f.** this child is no trouble

5 *Péj (libertin)* **une femme f.** *ou* **de mœurs faciles** a woman of easy virtue

ADV **1** *Fam (facilement)* **je te fais ça en deux heures f.** I can have it done for you in two hours, no problem; **d'ici à la maison, il reste 30 kilomètres f.** from here to the house, there's still a good 30 kilometres; **on met trois jours f. pour traverser l'île** it takes easily *or* at least three days to cross the island; **en trois jours, j'aurai lu f. deux livres** I'll easily read two books in three days **2** *Belg* **avoir f. à** *ou* **de faire qch** to find it easy to do sth, to have no problem doing sth

facilement [fasilmɑ̃] ADV **1** *(sans difficulté)* easily, readily; **vous trouverez f., c'est à deux pas** you'll find it easily, it's not very far; **pas f. accessible** not readily accessible; **elle est f. déroutée par la critique** she's easily thrown off balance by criticism **2** *(au moins)* at least; **il fait f. trois fautes par page** he makes at least three mistakes per page; **je gagnerais f. le double** I would easily earn twice as much

facilité [fasilite] NF **1** *(simplicité)* easiness; **selon le degré de f. des exercices** depending on how easy the exercises are; **d'une grande f. de lecture** very readable; *Péj* **céder à** *ou* **se laisser aller à** *ou* **choisir la f.** to take the easy way out *or* the easy option; *Péj* **c'est une solution de f.** it's the easy solution *or* way out; **f. d'emploi** *(d'un ordinateur etc)* user-friendliness, ease of use

2 *(possibilité)* opportunity; **avoir toute f.** *ou* **toutes facilités pour faire qch** to have every opportunity of doing sth

3 *(aisance)* ease; **f. de parole** fluency; **avoir beaucoup de f. pour** to have a gift for; **avec f.** easily, with ease; **avec une grande f.** with the greatest of ease; **parler avec f.** *(langue étrangère)* to speak fluently; **écrire avec f.** to write fluently *or* with ease; **il n'a pas la f. de son frère** things don't come as easily to him as they do to his brother; **les enfants comprennent l'informatique avec une f. déconcertante** children understand computers with disconcerting ease

4 *Com* **f. d'écoulement** *(d'un produit)* saleability; **f. de reprise** trade-in facility; **facilités de transport** transport facilities; **f. de vente** saleability

• **facilités** NFPL **1** *(capacités)* ability, aptitude; **avoir des facilités** to have ability *or* aptitude; **avoir des facilités en maths** to have great aptitude for maths; **votre enfant a des facilités** your child shows some aptitude **2** *Fin* facilities; **facilités de caisse** overdraft facilities; **facilités de crédit** credit facilities; **facilités d'endettement** borrowing capacity; **facilités de paiement** payment facilities, easy terms

faciliter [3] [fasilite] VT to ease, to help along, to make easier; **f. qch à qn** to make sth easier for sb; **cela ne va pas f. les choses** it won't make things (any) easier; **tu ne me facilites pas le travail!** you're not making things easy for me!; **le vent ne leur facilite pas la tâche** the wind doesn't make it any easier for them; **sa connaissance de la langue a facilité son insertion** his/her knowledge of the language helped him/her to settle in (more easily)

facob [fakɔb] NM *Assur (abrév* **traité facultatif obligatoire)** open cover

FAÇON [fasɔ̃]

• manner **1**	• way **1, 2**
• making **3**	• cut **4**

NF **1** *(manière)* manner, way; **la phrase peut se comprendre de plusieurs façons** the sentence can be interpreted in several ways; **je l'empêcherai de le faire – et de quelle f.?** I'll stop him/her doing it – how?; **demande-lui de quelle f. il compte payer** ask him how he wishes to pay; **je n'aime pas la f. dont il me parle** I don't like the way he talks to me; **la f. dont l'anglais est enseigné** the way (in which) English is taught; **d'une f. désordonnée** in a disorderly fashion; **d'une** *ou* **de f. générale** generally speaking; **de f. agréable** pleasantly; **de f. définitive** definitively, finally; **de f. systématique** systematically; **d'une f. ou d'une autre** one way or another, somehow or other; **en aucune f.!** not at all!, by no means!; **cela ne me dérange en aucune f.** it doesn't bother me in the slightest; **sa f. d'être** the way he/she is; **je ne tolérerai pas ces façons de parler** I won't tolerate that sort of language; **ce n'est pas une f. de parler à son père** that's no way to speak to one's father; **ce n'est qu'une f. de parler** *ou* **dire** it's just a manner of speaking; *Fam* **généreux, f. de parler, il ne m'a jamais donné un centime!** generous, that's a funny way of putting it, he never gave me a penny!; **tu pars en vacances? – oui, f. de parler, je vais garder mes neveux** are you going on holiday? – yes, I suppose you could say that *or* in a manner of speaking *or* sort of, I'm looking after my nephews; **je vais lui dire ma f. de penser, moi!** I'll give him/her a piece of my mind!; **elle a une curieuse f. de voir les choses** she has a strange way of looking at things; **ils n'ont pas les mêmes façons de voir** they see things differently; **ce n'est pas ma f. de**

faire it's not my way of doing things; **avoir une f. à soi de faire qch** to have one's own way of doing sth

2 *(moyen)* way; **pour obtenir une audience de lui, il n'y a qu'une seule f. de s'y prendre** there's only one way of getting *or* to get an audience with him; **il n'y a pas trente-six façons de le faire** there are no two ways of doing it

3 *(fabrication)* making, fashioning; *(facture)* craftsmanship, workmanship; *(main-d'œuvre)* labour; **f. d'un manteau** making (up) of a coat; **matière et f.** material and labour; **compter 50 euros de f.** to charge 50 euros for labour

4 *Couture* cut; **f. et fournitures** labour and material; **de bonne f.** well-made, (beautifully) tailored

5 *Suisse* **avoir bonne/mauvaise f.** to look good/ bad, to create a good/bad impression; **ne pas avoir de f.** *(être inconvenant)* to be improper; *(manquer de savoir-vivre)* to be lacking in refinement; **il n'a pas de f. avec cette vieille cravate** he doesn't look very presentable in that old tie

6 *Can* **avoir de la f.** *(avoir des manières agréables)* to be pleasant; *(être beau parleur)* to be a smooth talker

7 *Agr* **donner une f. à la terre** to cultivate the soil

8 *(suivi d'un nom) (qui rappelle)* **une nappe f. grand-mère** a tablecloth like grandma used to have; **un dessin f. Dürer** a drawing reminiscent of *or* in the style of Dürer; **f. marbre/bois** imitation marble/wood; **un châle f. cachemire** a paisley-patterned shawl; **sac f. cuir** imitation leather bag

• **façons NFPL** *(manières)* manners, behaviour; **ce ne sont pas des façons!** that's no way to behave!; **avoir des façons engageantes** to be charming; **elle a des façons de petite vieille** she behaves like an old woman; **faire des façons** *(se faire prier)* to make a fuss; *(se pavaner)* to put on airs; *Can (bien recevoir)* to entertain in style; **on est entre nous, on ne va pas faire de façons** we're all friends here, we won't stand on ceremony

• **à façon ADJ** *(artisan)* jobbing; *(travail)* contract *(avant n)*; *Ordinat* **centre de traitement** *ou* **travail à f.** data processing *or* computer *or* service bureau **ADV on travaille à f.** *(dans une annonce)* customers' own materials made up

• **à la façon de PRÉP** like, in the manner of; **à la f. des vieilles gens** like old people; **peindre à la f. des cubistes** to paint in the manner *or* style of the Cubists; **ils vivent encore à la f. de leurs ancêtres** they still live in the manner of their ancestors *or* as their ancestors did

• **à ma façon/à sa façon/** *etc* **ADJ une recette à ma/ta f.** a recipe of mine/yours; **un tour à sa f.** one of his/her tricks; **une invitation à leur f.** their style of invitation **ADV je le ferai à ma f.** I'll do it my way; **chante-le à ta f.** sing it your way *or* any way you like

• **de cette façon ADV 1** *(comme cela)* (in) this way, thus, in this manner; **ouvre la boîte de cette f.** open the box this way **2** *(par conséquent)* that way; **nous irons demain, de cette f. ils ne seront pas déçus** we'll go tomorrow, that way they won't be disappointed

• **de façon à PRÉP** so as to, in order to; **de f. à pouvoir fermer la porte** so as to be able to shut the door; **j'ai fermé la fenêtre de f. à éviter les courants d'air** I shut the window in order to prevent draughts; **parlez de f. à vous faire comprendre** speak so that you can be understood

• **de façon (à ce) que CONJ** so that; **il s'est levé de bonne heure de f. à ce que tout soit prêt** he got up early to make sure everything was ready in time; **elle parle de f. à ce que tout le monde l'entende** she speaks in such a way that everyone can hear her

• **de la belle façon ADV** *Ironique* **il s'est fait recevoir de la belle f.!** he got the sort of reception he deserves!

• **de la même façon ADV** the same (way), identically, in like manner

• **de la même façon que CONJ** like, as, the same (way) as

• **de ma façon/de sa façon/** *etc* **ADJ une recette de ma/ta f.** a recipe of mine/yours; **un tour de sa f.** one of his/her tricks; **un poème de sa f.** a poem of his/her own composition

• **de telle façon ADV** so, like that; **pourquoi criez-vous de telle f.?** why are you shouting like that?

• **de telle façon que CONJ** so that, in such a way that; **écrivez de telle f. que le lecteur comprenne** write in such a way that the reader understands; **il pleuvait de telle f. que je fus obligé de rentrer** it was raining so hard that I had to go home

• **de toute façon, de toutes les façons ADV** anyway, in any case

• **d'une certaine façon ADV** *(en quelque sorte)* in a way, in a manner of speaking, so to speak

• **d'une façon ou d'une autre ADV** somehow

• **sans façon(s) ADJ** *(style)* simple, unadorned; *(cuisine)* plain; *(personne)* simple **ADV 1** *(familièrement)* **elle m'a pris le bras sans f.** *ou* **façons** she took my arm quite naturally; *Péj* **il agit sans f.** *ou* **façons avec ses parents** he's rather off-hand *or* he behaves off-handedly with his parents **2** *(non merci)* no thank you; **encore du fromage? – sans f.** *ou* **façons!** more cheese? – no thank you!

• **sans plus de façons ADV** without further ado

faconde [fakɔ̃d] **NF** *Littéraire Péj* fluency, flow of words; **être doué d'une belle f.** to be a smooth talker; **avoir de la f.** to be fluent *or* voluble, *Péj* to be garrulous; **quelle f.!** he/she's such a chatterbox!

façonnage [fasɔnaʒ] **NM 1** *(mise en forme)* shaping, working; *(sur un tour)* turning; *(de l'argile)* fashioning **2** *(fabrication ▸ à la main)* making, fashioning; *Couture* making (up); *Ind* manufacturing **3** *Typ* forwarding

façonné, -e [fasɔne] *Tex* **ADJ** figured; **étoffe façonnée** figured fabric
NM figured fabric

façonnement [fasɔnmɑ̃] = **façonnage**

façonner [3] [fasɔne] **VT 1** *(modeler ▸ argile)* to shape, to fashion; *(▸ métal, pierre, bois)* to shape, to work; *Agr* **f. la terre** to work the soil **2** *Fig (caractère)* to mould, to shape; **f. qn à son image** to mould sb in one's own image **3** *(fabriquer ▸ à la main)* to make, to fashion; *Couture* to make (up); *Ind* to manufacture, to produce, to make; **façonné à la main** handmade

façonnier, -ère [fasɔnje, -ɛr] **ADJ 1** *(ouvrier)* jobbing **2** *(maniéré)* affected, mannered
NM,F jobbing worker
NM *Ordinat* computer bureau

fac-similé [faksimile] *(pl* **fac-similés) NM 1** *(reproduction)* facsimile, exact copy **2** *Tél (technique)* facsimile; *(document)* facsimile, fax

factage [faktaʒ] **NM 1** *(transport)* parcels cartage, carriage and delivery **2** *(frais)* carriage, transport costs; **payer le f.** to pay the carriage **3** *(distribution)* (postal) delivery

facteur[1] [faktœr] **NM 1** *Math* coefficient, factor; **mettre en facteurs** to factorize; **mise en facteurs** factorization; **f. aléatoire** random factor; **f. commun** common factor; **f. de sécurité** coefficient of safety, safety factor; **f. premier** prime factor

2 *Physiol* **f. VIII** factor 8; **f. Rhésus** rhesus *or* Rh factor; **f. Rhésus négatif/positif** rhesus negative/ positive; *Méd* **f. de risque** risk factor

3 *(élément)* element, factor; **le f. chance** the chance factor; **f. coût** cost factor; **f. de demande** demand factor; **f. économique** economic factor; **le f. humain** the human factor; **f. de situation** situational factor; **le f. temps** the time factor; **f. vent** windchill factor; **la courtoisie peut être un f. de réussite** courtesy may be one of the ways to success

4 *Mktg (manutentionnaire)* (transport) agent; **f. en douane** customs agent

5 *Mus* instrument maker; **f. de pianos** piano maker; **f. d'orgues** organ builder

facteur[2]**, -trice** [faktœr, -tris] **NM,F** *(livreur de courrier) Br* postman, *f* postwoman, *Am* mailman, *f* mailwoman; **est-ce que le f. est passé?** has the *Br* postman *or Am* mailman been yet?

factice [faktis] **ADJ 1** *(imité ▸ diamant)* artificial, false; *(▸ marchandise de présentation)* dummy *(avant n)*; *(▸ moustache, barbe)* false; **les bouteilles de parfum en vitrine sont factices** the bottles of perfume in the window are dummies **2** *(inauthentique ▸ gentillesse, enthousiasme)* artificial, simulated, false; *(▸ sourire)* forced; *(▸ beauté)* artificial

factieux, -euse [faksjø, -øz] **ADJ** seditious
NM,F agitator, troublemaker

faction [faksjɔ̃] **NF 1** *(groupe)* faction **2** *Mil* sentry *or* guard duty; **être en** *ou* **de f.** to be on sentry *or* guard duty; **mettre qn en** *ou* **de f.** to put sb on guard; **mettre une sentinelle de f. devant la porte** to post a sentry in front of the door; **je suis resté en f. plusieurs heures devant sa porte** I kept watch outside his/her door for hours **3** *(dans une entreprise)* (eight-hour) shift

factionnaire [faksjɔnɛr] **NM** *Mil* sentry, guard
NMF *(ouvrier)* shift worker

factitif, -ive [faktitif, -iv] *Gram* **ADJ** factitive, causative
NM causative verb

factoriel, -elle [faktɔrjɛl] *Math* **ADJ** factorial, factor *(avant n)*; **analyse factorielle** factor analysis

• **factorielle NF** factorial

factoring [faktɔriŋ] **NM** factoring

factorisation [faktɔrizasjɔ̃] **NF** *Math* factorization, factorizing

factotum [faktɔtɔm] **NM** factotum, handyman; **je ne suis pas ton f.!** I'm not your servant!

factrice [faktris] *voir* **facteur**[2]

factuel, -elle [faktɥɛl] **ADJ** *(gén) & Phil* factual

facturation [faktyrasjɔ̃] **NF** *Com & Compta* **1** *(action)* invoicing, billing; **la f. interviendra le 10 du mois** you will be invoiced on the 10th of each month; **f. détaillée** itemized invoicing *or* billing; *Ordinat* **f. séparée** unbundling **2** *(service)* invoice department

facture[1] [faktyr] **NF** *Com & Compta* invoice, bill; **f. d'électricité/de gaz** electricity/gas bill; **fausse f.** fake *or* forged invoice; **établir** *ou* **faire** *ou* **dresser une f.** to make out an invoice; **payer** *ou* **régler une f.** to pay a bill, to settle an invoice; **conformément à la f., selon** *ou* **suivant f.** as per invoice; *Écon* **la f. pétrolière de la France** France's oil bill; **affaire des fausses factures** = fraud using fake invoices to disguise illegal cash transfers; *Fig* **c'est moi qui vais payer la f. comme d'habitude** I'm going to have to pay the price as usual; **f. d'achat** purchase invoice; **f. d'avoir** credit note; **f. certifiée** certified invoice; **f. client** guest bill; **f. commerciale** commercial invoice; **f. de confirmation** confirmation invoice; **f. de consignation** consignment invoice; **f. consulaire** consular invoice; **f. de débit** debit note; **f. détaillée** itemized invoice; **f. de doit** debit note; **f. douanière** customs invoice; **f. à l'exportation** export invoice; **f. originale** invoice of origin; **f. pro forma** *ou* **provisoire** pro forma invoice; **f. rectificative** amended invoice; **f. de transitaire** forwarding agent's invoice; **f. de vente** sales invoice

facture[2] [faktyr] **NF 1** *(style ▸ d'un morceau de musique, d'un poème, d'un tableau etc)* construction; *(▸ d'un artiste etc)* style, technique; **d'une belle f.** *(meuble)* beautifully crafted; *(édifice)* beautifully proportioned; *(sculpture)* beautifully carved; *(peinture)* beautifully executed; *Beaux-Arts* **f. picturale** artistic style **2** *Mus (fabrication ▸ gén)* making; *(▸ d'orgues)* building

facturer [3] [faktyre] **VT** *(personne)* to invoice, to bill; *(produit, service)* to charge for; **f. qch à qn** to bill *or* to invoice sb for sth; **ils ne m'ont pas facturé la livraison** they didn't charge me for delivery; **le papier nous a été facturé 50 euros** we were invoiced 50 euros for the paper; *Ordinat* **f. séparément le matériel et le logiciel** to unbundle

facturette [faktyrɛt] **NF** *Com* credit card sales voucher

facturier, -ère [faktyrje, -ɛr] **NM,F** invoice clerk; **f. d'entrée** purchase ledger clerk; **f. de sortie** sales ledger clerk
NM *(registre)* sales book; **f. d'entrée** purchase ledger; **f. de sortie** sales ledger

• **facturière NF** *(machine)* invoicing machine

facultatif, -ive [fakyltatif, -iv] **ADJ 1** *(au choix)* optional; **l'assurance est facultative** insurance is optional; **matière facultative** optional subject **2** *Transp (sur demande)* **arrêt f.** request stop

facultativement [fakyltativmɑ̃] **ADV** optionally, as an option

faculté [fakylte] **NF 1** *(capacité)* ability, capability; **f. d'adaptation** adaptability, ability to adapt; **la f. de comprendre les enfants** the ability to understand children; **ne pas avoir la f. de marcher** to be unable to walk; **les humains possèdent la f. d'abstraction** mankind is capable of abstract thought

2 *(droit)* freedom, right; *(autorité)* power; *(possibilité)* option; **avoir la f. de faire qch** *(droit)* to have the right to do sth; *(autorité)* to be entitled to do sth; *(possibilité)* to have the option of doing sth; **vous avez la f. de refuser le contrat** you have the right to refuse to sign the contract; **il a la f. de rester s'il le désire** he may *or* he's free to stay if he wishes to; *Bourse* **f. de rachat** repurchase option; **avec f. d'achat ou de vente** with the option of purchase or sale

3 *Com* **facultés assurées** insured cargo

4 *Jur* **facultés contributives** ability to pay

5 *Univ (avant 1968)* university, college; *(depuis 1968)* faculty; **la f. des sciences** the science faculty; **on s'est connu à la** *ou* **en f.** we met at university *or* college *or* when we were students; **entrer en f.** to go to university *or* college; **cours/professeur de f.** university *or* college course/teacher; **des souvenirs de f.** memories of one's university *or* college *or* student days

6 *Vieilli* **la F.** the faculty of medicine; *(les médecins)* the medical profession; *Hum* **la F. m'interdit/me recommande de faire du sport** my doctors forbid me/encourage me to do sport *or Am* sports

• **facultés NFPL 1** *(esprit)* faculties, powers; **facultés intellectuelles** intellectual faculties; **facultés mentales** mental faculties; **avoir** *ou* **jouir de toutes ses facultés** to be of sound mind *or* in full possession of one's faculties; **il n'a pas toutes ses facultés** he's not in possession of all his faculties, he's not all there; **homme doué de grandes facultés** man of great abilities **2** *Vieilli (ressources)* resources, means; **dépenser au-dessus de ses facultés** to spend beyond one's means

fada [fada] *Fam (dans le sud de la France)* **ADJ** crazy, nuts, *Am* wacko

NMF nutcase, *Br* nutter, *Am* wacko; **les fadas de la moto** motorbike fanatics

fadaise [fadez] **NF** *(paroles)* piece of nonsense, silly remark; *(chose insignifiante)* trifle; **fadaises** drivel, nonsense; **dire des fadaises** to talk drivel *or* nonsense

fadasse [fadas] **ADJ** *Fam Péj* **1** *(sans goût)* insipid□, bland□ **2** *(sans éclat)* dull□; **des couleurs fadasses** washed-out colours□; **c'est une fille assez f.** she's rather dull

fade [fad] **ADJ 1** *(sans saveur)* insipid, bland; *(couleur)* drab, washed-out; *(beauté)* insipid **2** *(banal)* dull, pointless, vapid; **le compliment est plutôt f.** the compliment is rather flat

fadé, -e [fade] **ADJ** *Fam Ironique* **être f.** *(remarquable)* to beat them all, to take *Br* the biscuit *or Am* the cake

fader [3] [fade] **se fader VPR** *Fam* **se f. qn/qch** to get landed with sb/sth

fadeur [fadœr] **NF 1** *(insipidité)* blandness, lack of flavour; *(d'une couleur)* drabness; *(d'une beauté)* insipidness **2** *(banalité)* blandness, vapidity; *(de compliments)* banality; *(de style)* dullness, dreariness

• **fadeurs NFPL** *Vieilli (compliments)* banal *or* bland compliments; **dire des fadeurs à qn** to pay sb banal *or* bland compliments

fading [fadiŋ] **NM** *Rad* fading

faf [faf] **NMF** *Fam* fascist□

fafiot [fafjo] **NM** *(billet de banque) Br* banknote□, *Am* greenback

• **fafiots NMPL** *(papiers d'identité)* ID

fafouin, -e [fafwɛ̃, -in] *Can Fam* **ADJ** scatterbrained, *Br* scatty

NM,F scatterbrain; **arrête de faire le f., tu vas avoir un accident!** stop acting the fool *or* clowning around, you'll have an accident!

fagot [fago] **NM 1** *(branches)* bundle (of wood); **sentir le f.** *(personne)* to be a suspected heretic; *(opinion)* to smack of heresy **2** *(locution)* **de derrière les fagots** very special; **une bouteille de derrière les fagots** a very special wine

fagotage [fagɔtaʒ] **NM 1** *Péj (habillement)* ridiculous get-up **2** *(du bois)* bundling (up)

fagoter [3] [fagɔte] **VT 1** *(bois, branches)* to bind together, to tie up in bundles **2** *Péj (habiller)* **sa mère le fagote n'importe comment** his mother dresses him in the strangest outfits

VPR se fagoter *Péj* to rig *or* deck oneself out; **t'as vu comme elle se fagote!** have you seen some of the things she wears!

Fahrenheit [farɛnajt] **NPR degré/échelle F.** Fahrenheit degree/scale

FAI [ɛfai] **NM** *Ordinat (abrév* **fournisseur d'accès à l'Internet)** IAP

faiblard, -e [feblar, -ard] **ADJ** *Fam* **1** *(vieillard, convalescent)* weak□, frail□; **se sentir un peu f.** to feel a bit weak **2** *(excuse)* feeble□, lame□; *(argument)* feeble□; *(notes)* poor□; **en chimie, il est un peu f.** he's a bit weak *or* on the slow side in chemistry **3** *(lumière)* weak□, dim□

faible [fɛbl] **ADJ 1** *(malade, vieillard)* weak, frail; **se sentir f.** to feel weak; **avoir la vue f.** to have weak *or* poor eyesight; **avoir le cœur/la poitrine f.** to have a weak heart/chest; **avoir les reins faibles** to have kidney trouble; **être de f. constitution** to have a weak constitution; **une f. femme** a helpless woman

2 *(étai, construction)* weak, flimsy, fragile

3 *(esprit)* weak, deficient; *(intelligence)* low; **il n'a que de faibles moyens intellectuels** his intellectual capacities are rather weak

4 *(médiocre ▸ étudiant, résultat)* weak, poor, mediocre; **une dissertation plutôt f.** a rather weak *or* poor essay; **être f. en qch** *(à l'école)* to be weak at sth; **elle est f. en maths** she's weak *or* not very good at *Br* maths *or Am* math

5 *(trop tempéré ▸ style, argument, réforme)* weak; *(▸ jugement)* mild; *(▸ prétexte)* feeble, flimsy; **le mot est f.!** that's an understatement!; **…et le terme est f.!** …and that's putting it mildly!

6 *(complaisant)* weak, lax; *(sans volonté)* weak, spineless; *(caractère)* weak; **il est f. avec ses enfants** he's lax *or* too lenient with his children; **être f. de caractère** to be weak-willed

7 *(impuissant ▸ nation, candidat)* weak

8 *Com & Écon (demande)* slack; *(marge, revenus)* low; *(monnaie)* weak; *(ressources)* scant, thin

9 *(léger ▸ lumière)* dim, faint; *(▸ bruit)* faint; *(▸ voix)* faint, quiet; *(▸ brise)* light; *(▸ odeur)* faint, slight

10 *(peu important ▸ gén)* low, small; *(▸ avantage, différence, chance, espoir)* slight; *(▸ prix, revenu, loyer)* low; *(▸ récolte, rendement)* poor; *(▸ vitesse)* low, slow; **une f. quantité de sucre** a small quantity of sugar; **à f. débit** low-rate; **aller à f. vitesse** to proceed at low speed; **appareil de f. consommation** low-consumption appliance; **de f. encombrement** compact; **à une f. hauteur/profondeur** not very high up/deep down; **à f. émission** low-emission; **à f. teneur en minerai** of low mineral content, low-grade; **à f. teneur en alcool** low-alcohol; **f. en calories** low-calorie; **une f. différence entre deux ouvrages** a slight difference between two books; **avoir de faibles chances de succès** to have slight *or* slender chances of succeeding; **donner une f. idée de** to give a faint idea of

11 *Ling* weak, unstressed

NMF weak-willed person; **c'est un f.** he's weak-willed; **f. d'esprit** simpleton

NM 1 *(préférence)* **avoir un f. pour qch** to be partial to sth; **avoir un f. pour qn** to have a soft spot for sb **2** *Littéraire (point sensible)* weak spot; **prendre qn par son f.** to find sb's Achilles heel

• **faibles NMPL les faibles** the weak

faiblement [fɛbləmɑ̃] **ADV 1** *(sans force ▸ résister, insister, protester)* weakly, feebly; *(▸ parler)* quietly, faintly; **il protestait assez f.** he was protesting rather feebly **2** *(légèrement ▸ gén)* faintly; *(▸ éclairer)* faintly, dimly; **la cloche résonnait f. dans le lointain** the bell was ringing faintly in the distance

faiblesse [fɛblɛs] **NF 1** *(manque de vigueur physique)* weakness, frailty; *(de la vue, de la poitrine)* weakness; **ressentir une grande f.** to feel very weak; **avoir une f. à l'œil droit** to have a weakness in the right eye; **je tombais de f.** I was ready to drop (with exhaustion); **la f. de sa constitution** his/her weak constitution

2 *(d'une construction)* weakness, flimsiness, fragility; *(d'une économie, d'un système)* weakness, fragility, vulnerability; *(d'un concurrent, d'un produit)* weakness; *(d'une voix, d'un son)* dimness, faintness; *(d'une lumière)* faintness; *(du vent)* lightness; **la f. de la monnaie/des marchés financiers** the weakness of the currency/the financial markets

3 *(médiocrité ▸ d'un élève)* weakness; *(▸ d'une œuvre, d'un argument)* feebleness, weakness; **étant donné la f. de ses notes, il devra redoubler** with such low marks, he will have to repeat a year; **il a des faiblesses à l'oral** his oral skills are weak; **f. d'esprit** feeble-mindedness

4 *(insignifiance ▸ d'une différence, d'un écart)* insignificance; **la f. des effectifs** *(employés)* a shortage of staff; *(élèves)* insufficient numbers; **la f. de leurs revenus** their low income

5 *Littéraire (lâcheté)* weakness, spinelessness; **f. de caractère** weakness of character; **la f. humaine** human weakness *or* frailty; **un homme d'une grande f.** a weak man; **être d'une grande f. envers qn** *(trop indulgent)* to be overlenient with sb; **être d'une f. coupable envers qn** to be inexcusably soft with sb; **avoir la f. de faire qch** to be weak enough to do sth; **avoir la f. de croire/dire** to be foolish enough to believe/to say; **avoir un moment de f.** to have a moment of weakness; **dans un moment de f. je lui ai dit oui** in a moment of weakness I said yes to him/her; **pour lui, l'amour filial est une f.** he considers loving one's parents a weakness

6 *(défaut ▸ d'une personne)* weakness, shortcoming, failing; *(▸ d'une œuvre d'art, d'une théorie)* weakness; **présenter plusieurs faiblesses** to have several weak points *or* weaknesses; **c'est là la grande f. du scénario** this is the major flaw of the script; **à chacun ses petites faiblesses** we all have our little weaknesses *or* shortcomings *or* failings

7 *(préférence)* weakness, partiality; **avoir une f. pour** to have a weakness for, to be partial to

8 *Littéraire (évanouissement)* fainting fit, dizzy spell; **avoir une** *ou* **être pris de f.** to feel faint

faiblir [32] [feblir] **VI 1** *(perdre de sa force ▸ personne, pouls)* to get weaker; *(▸ mémoire, vue, mécanisme)* to fail; *(▸ voix)* to lose its strength, to fail; **ses forces faiblissaient** he/she was getting weaker; **chez elle, c'est la mémoire qui faiblit** her memory is failing; **la batterie faiblit** the battery is failing

2 *(diminuer ▸ vent, orage, bourrasque)* to drop; *(▸ lumière)* to dwindle; *(▸ enthousiasme, colère, intérêt)* to wane, to dwindle; *(▸ courage)* to fail, to flag; **le jour faiblit** it's getting dark; **l'intérêt du public faiblit** public interest is waning; **le succès de la pièce ne faiblit pas** the play continues to be a great success; **l'écart faiblit entre les coureurs** the gap between the runners is narrowing *or* closing

3 *(cesser d'être efficace ▸ athlète, élève)* to get weaker; **son style n'a pas faibli** his/her style is as vigorous as ever; **j'ai faibli en langues à la fin de l'année** my marks in modern languages got weaker towards the end of the year; **le film faiblit vers la fin** the film falls off *or* tails off towards the end

4 *(plier ▸ paroi, tige)* to show signs of weakening; *(▸ résistance)* to weaken; **les premiers rangs de policiers faiblissaient sous l'assaut** the front ranks of the police were weakening under the assault

5 *(perdre de sa valeur ▸ monnaie)* to get weaker

faïence [fajɑ̃s] **NF 1** *(matière)* (glazed) earthenware; **f. fine** china **2** *(objet)* piece of earthenware; **faïences** crockery, earthenware

faïencerie [fajɑ̃sri] **NF 1** *(usine)* pottery works **2** *(articles)* (glazed) earthenware **3** *(commerce)* pottery (trade)

faïencier, -ère [fajɑ̃sje, -ɛr] **NM,F** *(fabricant)* crockery *or* earthenware maker, potter; *(marchand)* crockery *or* earthenware dealer

faignant, -e [fɛɲɑ̃, -ɑ̃t] = **feignant**

faille[1] *voir* **falloir**

faille[2] [faj] **NF 1** *Géol* fault **2** *(faiblesse)* flaw, weakness; *(incohérence)* inconsistency, flaw; *(dans une amitié)* rift, breach; **il y a une f. dans votre démonstration** your demonstration is flawed

• **sans faille** **ADJ** *(logique)* faultless, flawless; *(fidélité, dévouement)* unfailing, unwavering; *(dévotion)* unfailing; **faire preuve d'une volonté sans f.** to be iron-willed, to have a will of iron

failli, -e [faji] *Com* **ADJ** bankrupt

NM,F bankrupt; **f. concordataire** certificated bankrupt; **f. déchargé** discharged bankrupt; **f. non déchargé** undischarged bankrupt; **f. réhabilité** discharged bankrupt

faillibilité [fajibilite] **NF** fallibility

faillible [fajibl] **ADJ** fallible

faillir [46] [fajir] **VI 1** *(être sur le point de)* **j'ai failli rater la marche** I nearly missed the step; **pendant un moment, j'ai failli y croire** I almost believed it for a moment; **il faillit être écrasé** he narrowly missed being run over; **tu l'as attrapé? – non, mais j'ai failli!** did you catch it? – not quite!; *Hum* **j'ai failli attendre** so you decided to come, did you? **2** *Littéraire (manquer à son devoir)* to fail in one's duty **3** *Littéraire (se démentir)* to waver, to falter; **dont la loyauté n'avait jamais failli** whose loyalty had never wavered *or* faltered

• **faillir à** **VT IND** *Littéraire* **f. à une promesse/sa parole** to fail to keep a promise/one's word; **f. à son devoir** to fail in one's duty; **ne pas f. à sa réputation** to live up to one's reputation; **la mémoire me faut** my memory fails me

• **sans faillir** **ADV** unfailingly

faillite [fajit] **NF 1** *Com* bankruptcy, insolvency; **faire f.** to go bankrupt; **f. frauduleuse** fraudulent bankruptcy; **f. personnelle** personal bankruptcy; **f. simple** bankruptcy **2** *(échec)* failure; *Littéraire* **la f. de ses espoirs** the end *or* collapse of his/her hopes; **le spectacle a connu une f. complète** the show was a total failure; **les faits récents montrent la f. de cette politique** recent events demonstrate the failure of this policy; **le projet a fait f.** the project flopped *or* was a failure

• **en faillite** *Com* **ADJ** bankrupt, insolvent; **être en (état de) f.** to be bankrupt; **déclarer qn en f.** to declare sb bankrupt **ADV** **mettre qn en f.** to declare sb bankrupt; **se mettre en f.** to file a petition for bankruptcy

faim [fɛ̃] **NF 1** *(appétit)* hunger; **avoir f.** to be *or* to feel hungry; **avoir très** *ou* **grand f., avoir une grosse f.** to be *or* to feel very hungry; **avoir un peu f.** to be *or* to feel a bit hungry; **j'ai une petite f.** I'm feeling peckish; **avoir une f. de loup** to be ravenous; **j'ai une f. de loup** *ou* **à dévorer les montagnes** I could eat a horse, I'm ravenous; *Fam* **j'ai une de ces faims, je meurs de f., je crève de f.** I'm famished *or* starving; **je n'ai plus f. du tout** I'm not at all hungry any more; **merci, je n'ai plus f.** I've had enough, thank you; **ça me donne f.** it makes me hungry; *Fam* **il fait f.** I'm hungry; **manger à sa f.** to eat one's fill; **mangez à votre f.** eat as much as you like; **rester sur sa f.** to be still hungry; *Fig* to be left unsatisfied *or* frustrated; **tromper sa f.** to stave off hunger; *Prov* **la f. chasse le loup (hors)** *ou* **fait sortir le loup du bois** hunger drives the wolf out of the wood **2** *(famine)* **la f.** hunger, famine; **souffrir de la f.** to be starving *or* a victim of starvation; **mourir de f.** to starve to death, to die of starvation **3** *(envie)* **sa f. de tendresse** his/her yearning for tenderness; **avoir f. de paix** to hunger *or* to yearn for peace; **avoir f. de gloire** to hunger *or* to thirst after glory

fainéant, -e [feneɑ̃, -ɑ̃t] **ADJ** idle, lazy

NM,F layabout, lazybones

fainéanter [3] [feneɑ̃te] **VI** to idle *or* to laze about *or* around; **il passe des heures à f.** he spends hours twiddling his thumbs *or* doing nothing

fainéantise [feneɑ̃tiz] **NF** idleness, laziness

FAIRE [109] [fɛr]

VT	
• to make **A1, 3, B1, 2, D2**	• to build **A1**
• to do **B1–3, 5, 9, C1, 3, H**	• to have **A4**
• to study **B3**	• to carry out **B2**
• to say **B7**	• to write **B6**
• to turn into **D2**	• to clean **B8**
• to be **F2–4, G2**	• to imitate **D6**
• to last **F6**	• to cost **F2**
	• to look (+ adj) **G1**
USAGE ABSOLU	
• to go to the toilet	
VI	**V IMPERSONNEL**
• to do **1**	• to be **1**
V AUXILIAIRE	**NM**
• to make **1, 2**	• doing **2, 3**
• to have **2, 3**	• execution **2**

VT A. *FABRIQUER, RÉALISER* **1** *(confectionner ▸ objet, vêtement, film, vin)* to make; *(▸ construction)* to build; *(▸ tableau)* to paint; *(▸ repas, café)* to make, to prepare; *(▸ gâteau, pain)* to make, to bake; *(▸ bière)* to brew; **il m'a fait une poupée avec de la paille** he's made me a doll out of straw; **qu'as-tu fait (à manger) pour ce soir?** what have you made *or* prepared for dinner?; **je vais f. du café** I'm going to make some coffee; **c'est elle qui fait ses chansons** she writes her own songs; **f. une loi** to make a law; **f. un portrait** *(le peindre)* to paint a portrait; *(le dessiner)* to draw a portrait; **il a fait un portrait fidèle de la situation** he gave a very accurate description of the situation; **il sait tout f.** he can turn his hand to anything; *Fam* **grand-mère est super – oui, on n'en fait plus des comme ça!** grandma's great – yes, they broke the mould when they made her!; **ce pays fait d'excellents athlètes** this country produces excellent athletes; **les deux ou trois créateurs qui font la mode parisienne** the handful of designers who ARE Parisian fashion

2 *(produire, vendre)* **f. de l'élevage de bétail** to breed cattle; **f. du blé/de la vigne** to grow wheat/grapes; **f. une marque/un produit** to stock a make/an article; *Fam* **je vous fais les deux à 40 euros** you can have both for 40 euros, I'll take 40 euros for both

3 *(obtenir, gagner ▸ bénéfices)* to make; **f. de l'argent** to earn *or* to make money

4 *(mettre au monde)* **f. un enfant** to have a child; **il veut que je lui fasse un enfant** he wants me to have his child; **il lui a fait deux enfants** he had two children with her; **la chatte a fait des petits** the cat has had kittens

5 *Euph* **f. ses besoins** to do one's business

B. *ACCOMPLIR, EXÉCUTER* **1** *(effectuer ▸ mouvement, signe)* to make; *(▸ saut périlleux, roue)* to do; **fais-moi un sourire/un bisou** give me a kiss/a smile; **f. des grimaces** to make *or* to pull faces; **f. la grimace** to make a face; **f.** *Fam* **la tête** *ou très Fam* **la gueule** to sulk[□], to be in a huff

2 *(accomplir ▸ choix, erreur, réforme, proposition)* to make; *(▸ discours)* to deliver, to make, to give; *(▸ conférence)* to give; *(▸ inventaire, exercice, thèse, dissertation)* to do; *(▸ recherches)* to do, to carry out; *(▸ enquête)* to carry out; **f. ses études** to study; **il a fait ses études à la Sorbonne** he studied at the Sorbonne; **tu as fait tes maths?** have you done your *Br* maths *or Am* math homework?; **f. son devoir** to do one's duty; **f. une blague à qn** to play a joke on sb; **f. des plaisanteries** to play tricks; **f. la cuisine** to cook; **f. le ménage** to do the housework; **f. son lit** to make one's bed; *Fam* **on ne me la fait pas, à moi!** *(plaisanterie)* you can't fool me!; *Fam* **on me l'a déjà faite, celle-là** I know that one already; *Fam* **les voyages organisés, on me l'a déjà faite une fois et on ne me la fera plus!** one package tour was quite enough for me, thank you very much!; *Fam* **le** *ou* **la f. à l'esbroufe** *ou* **à l'épate** *ou* **au bluff** to bluff one's way through

3 *(étudier ▸ matière, œuvre)* to study, to do; **il veut f. du droit** he wants to do *or* to study law; *Fam* **f. sa médecine** to do *or* to study medicine[□]; **nous faisons 'Richard III' cette année** we're doing *or* studying 'Richard III' this year

4 *(suivre les cours de)* **f. l'ENA** to go to the ENA

5 *(pratiquer)* **f. de la poterie** to do pottery; **f. de la flûte/du violon** to play the flute/the violin; **f. de la danse** *(cours)* to go to dance classes; **il voulait f. de la danse** he wanted to be a dancer; **il a fait un peu de théâtre** he's done some acting; **je veux f. du théâtre** I want to be an actor *or* to go on the stage; **f. de l'équitation/de la natation/de la voile** to go horseriding/swimming/sailing; **f. du basket/du tennis** to play basketball/tennis

6 *(écrire ▸ lettre)* to write; *(▸ contrat, testament)* to write, to make; **fais mieux tes t** write your t's better

7 *(dire)* to say; **il fit oui de la tête** he nodded; **il fit non de la tête** he shook his head; **"non", fit-elle** "no," she said; **la vache fait "meuh!"** cows go "moo!"; **que fait le hibou?** what does an owl say?

8 *(nettoyer ▸ chambre, vitres)* to clean, to do; *(▸ chaussures)* to polish, to clean; *(tapisser, aménager ▸ pièce, maison)* to do, to decorate

9 *(action non précisée)* to do; **que fais-tu dans la vie?** what do you do (for a living)?; **qu'est-ce qu'il t'a fait, ton frère?** what has your brother done to you?; **je ne t'ai jamais rien fait!** I've never done you any harm!; **que pouvais-je f. d'autre?** what else could I do?; **il a fort à f.** he's got lots to do; **tu es libre dimanche? – oui, je ne fais rien de spécial** are you free on Sunday? – yes, I'm not doing anything special; **tu fais quelque chose pour ton anniversaire?** are you doing anything (special) for your birthday?; **elle ne veut jamais rien f. sans lui** she never wants to do anything without him; **je fais ce que je peux!** I do what I can!, I do my best!; **elle ne fait que se plaindre** she does nothing but complain; **ils n'ont fait que chuchoter pendant tout le film** they kept whispering right through the film; **je ne veux rien avoir à f. avec eux!** I don't want anything to do with them!; **qu'ai-je fait de mes clefs?** what have I done with *or* where did I put my keys?; **que fais-tu de mes sentiments dans tout ça?** what about my feelings?, how do you think I feel?; **que vais-je f. de toi?** what am I going to do with you?; **elle fait ce qu'elle veut de lui** she can twist him round her little finger; **donne-le moi! – non, rien à f.!** give it to me! – no way!; **rien à f., le téléphone ne marche plus!** we're stuck, the phone doesn't work!; **tu lui as parlé? – oui, mais rien à f., il ne cédera pas** did you talk to him? – yes, but it's no use, he won't give in; **je vais vous raccompagner – n'en faites rien!** I'll take you back – there's really no need!; *Fam* **f. avec** to make do; **je n'ai que ce stylo – il faudra f. avec!** I've only got this pen – we'll/I'll have to make do with that!; **j'apprécie peu sa façon de travailler mais il faut bien f. avec!** I don't like the way he/she works but I suppose I'll just have to put up with it!; *Fam* **f. sans** to (make) do without; **j'ai oublié le livre chez moi – il faudra f. sans!** I've left the book at home – we'll just have to make do without it!; **autant que f. se peut** if possible, as far as possible; **je n'ai que f. de tes conseils** I can do without your advice; **mais bien sûr, tu n'as que f. de ma carrière!** but of course, my career matters very little to you! *or* you don't care about my career!; **pour ce f.** for that; **ce faisant** in so doing

C. *AVEC IDÉE DE DÉPLACEMENT* **1** *(se déplacer à la vitesse de)* **en marchant vite, tu peux f. dix kilomètres à l'heure** if you walk fast, you can do *or* cover ten kilometres in an hour; **le train peut f. jusqu'à 400 km/h** the train can do 400 km/h; **vous faisiez du 120 km/h** *(en voiture)* you were driving at *or* doing 120 km/h

2 *(couvrir ▸ distance)* **le Concorde a fait Paris-New York en moins de cinq heures** Concorde went *or* flew from Paris to New York in less than five hours; **il y a des cars qui font Londres-Glasgow** there's a coach service between London and Glasgow; **les trains qui font Lyon-Marseille** the trains which run between Lyons and Marseille

3 *(visiter ▸ pays, ville)* to do, to go to, to visit; **nous n'avons jamais fait le sud de l'Italie** we've never been to *or* done the south of Italy

4 *(inspecter, passer au crible)* **j'ai fait tous mes tiroirs, impossible de retrouver la photo** I searched through all my drawers, but I couldn't find the photo; **j'ai fait tous les étages avant de vous trouver** I looked on every floor before I found you; **j'ai fait tous les hôtels de la ville** *(j'y suis allé)* I did *or* went to *or* tried every hotel in town; *(j'ai téléphoné)* I called *or* did *or* tried every hotel in town; **f. les antiquaires** to go round the antique shops; **il fait les bars avant de rentrer chez lui** he goes round the bars before going home

D. *AVEC IDÉE DE TRANSFORMATION* **1** *(nommer)* **elle l'a fait baron** she gave him the title of Baron, she made him a baron; **elle l'a fait chevalier** she knighted him

2 *(transformer en)* **des rats, la fée fit des laquais** the fairy changed the rats into footmen; **ce film en a fait un sex-symbol** this film turned him/her into a sex symbol; **ce feuilleton en a fait une vedette** this series made him/her a star; **et ta robe bleue? – j'en ai fait une jupe** what about your blue dress? – I made it into a skirt; **garde les restes, j'en ferai une soupe** keep the leftovers, I'll make soup with them; **ils ont fait trois appartements de leur grande maison** they converted *or* made their big house into three flats; **c'était mon idée, mais il l'a faite sienne** it was my idea, but he took it from me *or* he made it his own; *Vieilli ou Hum* **quand je te ferai mienne** when I make you mine; **c'était un tyran et votre livre en fait un héros!** he was a tyrant, and your book shows *or* presents him as a hero!

3 *(devenir)* **"cheval" fait "chevaux" au pluriel** the plural of "cheval" is "chevaux"

4 *(servir de)* **une fois plié, le billard fait table** the billiard table, when folded, can be used *or* can serve as a normal table; **un canapé qui fait lit** a convertible settee *or* sofa; **une carotte fera le nez du bonhomme de neige** you can make the snowman's nose with a carrot; **cette peau fera un beau tapis** this animal skin will make a nice rug; **le gymnase fait aussi salle des fêtes** the gymnasium is also used as a community hall; **c'est un hôtel qui fait restaurant** it's a hotel with a restaurant

5 *(remplir le rôle de)* **il fera un bon mari** he'll make *or* be a good husband; **il fait le Père Noël dans les rues** he goes around the streets dressed as Father Christmas; *Théât* **qui fait le comte?** who plays the Count?; **il ferait un parfait Othello** he'd make *or* be a perfect Othello

6 *(imiter ▸ personne)* to imitate, to take off, to impersonate; *(▸ automate, animal)* to imitate; **il fait très bien le hibou** he imitates an owl very well, he does a very good owl imitation; **ne fais pas l'idiot** don't be stupid; **ne fais pas l'innocent** don't play the innocent, *Br* don't come the innocent with me; **elle a fait l'étonnée** she pretended to be surprised *or* feigned surprise; **il faisait son intéressant** he was showing off

E. *INDIQUE UN RÉSULTAT* **1** *(provoquer)* **f. de la poussière** to raise dust; **ce charbon fait beaucoup de fumée** this coal makes a lot of smoke; **ça va f. une marque/une auréole** it will leave a mark/a ring; **l'accident a fait cinq morts** the accident left five dead *or* claimed five lives; **cela fait tout son charme** that's where his/her charm lies; **ce qui fait l'intérêt de son livre** what makes his/her book interesting; **f. de la peine à qn** to upset sb; **f. peur à qn** to frighten sb; **ces propos risquent de vous f. du tort** what you've said may well get you into trouble; **il fera votre malheur** he'll make life very difficult for you; **f. le désespoir de qn** to make sb despair; **f. quelque chose à qn** *(l'émouvoir)* to move sb, to affect sb; **ce n'était qu'un animal, mais ça m'a fait quelque chose quand il est mort** it was only an animal but it really affected me when it died; *Fam* **ça fait comment** *ou* **quoi de voir son nom sur une affiche?** what's it like to see your name on a poster?; **la vue du sang ne me fait rien** I don't mind the sight of blood, the sight of blood doesn't bother me; **si cela ne vous fait rien** if you don't mind; **la gravitation, force qui fait que les objets s'attirent** gravitation, the force which causes objects to be attracted towards each other; **ce qui fait que je suis arrivé en retard** which meant I was late

2 *(pour exprimer un souhait)* **faites qu'il ne lui arrive rien!** please don't let anything happen to him/her!

3 *(importer)* **qu'est-ce que cela peut f.?** what does it matter?, so what?; **qu'est-ce que cela peut te f.?** what's it to (do with) you?; **cela ne fait rien** it doesn't matter, never mind

4 *Fam (locutions)* **ça le fait** it's really cool, it's *Br* wicked *or Am* awesome; **ça le fait pas** it sucks; **ça le fait pas de se pointer avec une heure de retard le premier jour** it's just not on to show up an hour late on your first day; **le rouge sur du rose, ça le fait pas trop** red and pink just don't really work together

F. *INDIQUE UNE QUALITÉ, UNE FORME, UNE MESURE* **1** *(former)* **la route fait un coude** the road bends; **le circuit fait un huit** the circuit is (in the shape of) a figure of eight; **le tas fait une pyramide** the heap looks like a pyramid

2 *(coûter)* to be, to cost; **ça fait combien?** how much is it?; **ça fait trop cher** it's too expensive; **ça vous fait 60 euros en tout** that'll be 60 euros altogether

3 *(valoir, égaler)* to be, to make; **2 et 2 font 4** 2 and 2 are 4; **ça fait 23 en tout** that makes 23 altogether; **on a 15 euros, ça ne fait pas assez** we've got 15 euros, that's not enough

4 *(mesurer)* **le bateau fait 12 m de long/3 m de large** the boat is 12 m long/3 m wide; **il doit bien f. 1 m 90** he must be 1 m 90 tall; **je fais du 38** I take size 38; **je fais 56 kg** I weigh *or* am 56 kg; **cela (vous) fait une bonne livre** it's a bit over the pound

5 *(indique la durée, le temps)* **ça fait deux jours qu'il n'a pas mangé** he hasn't eaten for two days; **elle a téléphoné, cela fait bien une heure** she phoned at least an hour ago; *Fam* **on s'est rencontrés ça fait trois mois** we met three months ago, it's been three months since we met; *Fam* **cela faisait dix ans que je n'avais pas joué** I hadn't played for ten years

6 *Fam (durer ▸ sujet: vêtement, objet)* to last[□]; **ton cartable te fera encore bien cette année** your schoolbag will last *or* do you this year; **une paire de chaussures ne me fait pas plus de six mois** I go through a pair of shoes in six months; **le ragoût m'a bien fait trois repas** I got three meals out of that stew; **il n'a pas fait deux mois dans cette entreprise** he didn't stay in the company more than two months

G. *VERBE ATTRIBUTIF* **1** *(paraître)* **la broche fait bien** *ou* **joli** *ou* **jolie sur ta robe** the brooch looks nice on your dress; **elle parle avec un léger accent, il paraît que ça fait bien!** she talks with a slight accent, it's supposed to be smart!; *Ironique* **j'ai un bleu sur la joue maintenant, ah ça fait bien!** I've got a bruise on my cheek now, that's lovely!; **ça fait bizarre** it looks strange; **il me faudrait un nom qui fasse artiste** I would need a name which sounds typically artistic; **je ne vais pas lui réclamer cinq euros, ça ferait mesquin** I'm not going to ask him/her for five euros, it'd be *or* look petty; **f. son âge** to look one's age; **elle ne fait pas son âge** she doesn't look her age

2 *Fam (devenir)* to be[□]; **je veux f. pompier** I want to be a firefighter *or Br* a fireman

H. *VERBE DE SUBSTITUTION* **range ta chambre – je l'ai déjà fait** go and tidy your room – I've already done it; **vous le lui expliquerez mieux que je ne saurais le f.** you'll explain it to him/her better than I could; **tu lui écriras? – oui, je le ferai** will you write to him/her? – yes I will; **puis-je prendre cette chaise? – (mais) faites donc!** may I take this chair? – please do *or* by all means!

USAGE ABSOLU *(faire ses besoins)* **tu as fait ce matin?** did you go to the toilet this morning?; *Fam* **il a fait dans sa culotte** he messed his pants

VI 1 *(agir)* to do; **fais comme chez toi** *(à l'arrivée de quelqu'un)* make yourself at home; **je peux prendre une douche? – bien sûr, fais comme chez toi** can I have a shower? – of course *or* by all means; *Ironique* **fais comme chez toi, surtout!** you've got a nerve!, don't mind me!; **faites comme vous voulez** do as you please; **fais comme tu veux!** *(ton irrité)* suit *or* please yourself!; **je le lui ai rendu – tu as bien fait!** I gave it back to him/her – you did the right thing *or* you did right!; **pourquoi l'as-tu acheté? – je croyais bien f.!** why did you buy it? – I thought it was a good idea!; **j'ai bien fait de me méfier** I was right to be suspicious; **tu ferais bien d'y réfléchir** you'd do well to *or* you should *or* you'd better think about it!; **pour bien f., il faudrait réserver aujourd'hui** the best thing would be to book today, ideally we should book today; **ça commence à bien f.!** enough is enough!; *Fam* **ça commence à bien f., tes reproches!** I've had quite enough of your criticism!

2 *Can Fam (être seyant)* **f. à qn** *(taille d'un vêtement)* to fit sb; *(style d'un vêtement)* to suit sb

V IMPERSONNEL 1 *(pour exprimer le temps qu'il fait)* **il fait chaud/froid** it's hot/cold; **il faisait nuit** it was dark; **il fait (du) soleil** the sun is shining; **il fait bon au soleil** it's nice and warm in the sun; **il ne faisait pas bon avoir un nom à particule à cette époque** it wasn't a good thing to have an aristocratic-sounding name then

2 *(locutions)* **c'en est fait de vous** you've had it, you're done for; **c'est bien fait pour toi** it serves you right; *Can Fam* **ça va f.!, ça fait!** that's enough!

V AUX 1 *(provoquer une réaction)* **tu l'as fait rougir/pleurer** you made him/her blush/cry; **il sait f. bouger ses oreilles** he can make his ears move, he can move his ears; **le soleil a fait jaunir le papier** the sun has made the paper turn yellow; **les oignons, ça fait pleurer** onions make you cry; **ça me fait dormir** it puts *or* sends me to sleep

2 *(forcer à)* to make, to have; **fais-moi penser à le lui demander** remind me to ask him/her; **faites-le attendre** *(pour qu'il s'impatiente)* let him wait; *(en lui demandant)* ask him to wait; **il faut le f. boire beaucoup** you should give him plenty to drink; **n'essaie pas de me f. croire que...** don't try to make *or* to have me believe that...; **il lui a fait avouer la vérité** he made him/her confess the truth; **ne me fais pas dire ce que je n'ai pas dit** don't put words into my mouth; **il me faisait f. ses dissertations** he had me write his essays for him

3 *(commander de)* **f. faire qch par qn** to have sb do *or* make sth, to have sth done *or* made by sb; **j'ai fait laver/vérifier ma voiture** I had my car washed/checked; **elle fait repasser son linge** she has her ironing done for her; **il fait f. ses costumes sur mesure** he has his suits tailor-made

NM 1 *(fait d'agir)* doing, making; **il y a loin du dire au f.** saying is one thing, doing is another

2 *Littéraire Beaux-Arts* execution; **un tableau d'un f. libre et élégant** a picture of free and elegant execution

• faire dans VT IND *Fam* **il ne fait pas dans le détail** he doesn't bother about details; **son entreprise fait maintenant dans les produits de luxe** his/her company now produces luxury items; **il fait dans le genre tragique** he makes everything sound so serious; **il fait dans le genre comique** he makes light of everything

VPR se faire 1 *(réussir)* **elle s'est faite seule** she's a self-made woman

2 *(se forcer à)* **se f. pleurer/vomir** to make oneself cry/vomit

3 *(emploi réciproque)* **se f. la guerre** to wage war on each other

4 *(être à la mode)* to be fashionable, to be in fashion; **les salopettes ne se font plus** dungarees are out of fashion; **je ne sais pas ce qui se fait en ce moment** I don't know what's in fashion at the moment

5 *(être convenable)* **ça ne se fait pas de demander son âge à une femme** it's rude *or* it's not done to ask a woman her age; **ça ne se fait pas!** it's not done!, you (just) don't do that!; **tu peux dire merci, ça se fait!** you're allowed to say thank you, you know!

6 *(être réalisé)* **sans argent le film ne se fera pas** without money the film will never be made; **le projet ne se fera pas sans elle** the project won't go ahead without her; **finalement ça ne se fera pas** as it turns out, it's not going to happen; **les choses se font petit à petit** things evolve gradually; **la capitale où la mode se fait** the fashion capital; **je dois signer un nouveau contrat, mais je ne sais pas quand cela va se f.** I'm going to sign a new contract, but I don't know when that will be; **tu pourrais me prêter 50 euros? – ça pourrait se f.** could you lend me 50 euros? – that should be possible; **comment se fait-il que...?** how come *or* how is it that...?; **il pourrait se f. que...** it might *or* may be that..., it's possible that...; **c'est ce qui se fait de mieux en papiers peints lavables** it's the best washable wallpaper available

7 *(se former)* **les couples se font et se défont** people get together and separate

8 *(suivi d'un infinitif)* **se f. opérer** to have an operation; **se f. tuer** to get killed; **se f. photographier** *(par quelqu'un)* to get *or* to have one's picture taken; *(dans un Photomaton®)* to have some pictures (of oneself) done; **se f. couper les cheveux** to have one's hair cut; **il se fait f. ses vêtements chez un couturier** he gets his clothes tailor-made

9 *(devenir)* to become; **elle se fit toute douce** she became very gentle; **sa voix se fit plus grave** his/her voice became deeper; **les mesures de sécurité se sont faites plus rigoureuses** security measures have been tightened up *or* have become more stringent; **il s'est fait le porte-parole de toute une génération** he became the mouthpiece for a whole generation; **Dieu s'est fait homme** God took human form; *Fam* **s'il arrive à l'heure, je veux bien me f. nonne!** if he arrives on time, I'll eat my hat!; **il se fait tard** it's getting late

10 *(s'améliorer ▸ fromage)* to ripen; *(▸ vin)* to mature; **mes chaussures me serrent – elles vont se f.** my shoes feel tight – they'll stretch

11 *(fabriquer)* **se f. un gâteau** to make *or* to bake a cake (for oneself); **se f. un thé/un café** to make (oneself) a cup of tea/coffee; **elle se fait ses vêtements** she makes her own clothes

12 *(effectuer sur soi)* **il se fait ses piqûres seul** he gives himself his own injections; **je me suis fait une natte** I've plaited my hair; **se f. les ongles** to do one's nails; **se f. les yeux** to make up one's eyes

13 *Fam (gagner)* to make, to earn; **elle se fait 2000 euros par mois** she makes 2,000 euros per month, she gets 2,000 euros every month; **il ne se fait pas grand-chose** he doesn't earn much

14 *Fam (s'accorder)* **on se fait un film/un petit café?** what about going to see a film/going for a coffee?; **on s'est fait les trois musées dans la journée** we did the three museums in one day; **quand est-ce qu'on se le fait, ce match?** when are we going to have this game?

15 *Fam (supporter)* **il faut se la f.!** she's a real pain!

16 *Fam Arg crime (tuer)* to bump off; *(agresser)* to beat up; **se f. une banque** *(la voler)* to *Br* do over *or Am* boost a bank

17 *Vulg (posséder sexuellement)* to screw, *Br* to shag

18 se f. à *(s'habituer à)* to get used to; **elle ne t'aime plus, il faudra que tu t'y fasses** she doesn't love you anymore, you'll have to get that into your head *or* get used to it; **il s'appelle Odilon – je ne m'y ferai jamais!** his name is Odilon – I'll never get used to it!

19 s'en f. *(s'inquiéter)* to worry; **si je lui en parle, elle va s'en f.** if I tell her about it she'll only worry; **je ne m'en fais pas pour lui** I'm not worried about him; **ne t'en fais pas pour le dîner, je m'en occupe** don't (you) worry about the dinner, I'll see to it; *Fam* **dans la vie faut pas s'en f.** you should take life easy; **elle s'en souviendra, ne t'en fais pas!** she'll remember, don't you worry!; **encore au lit? tu ne t'en fais pas!** still in bed? you're taking it easy, aren't you?; **il roule en Jaguar maintenant – il ne s'en fait pas!** he drives around in a Jaguar now – some people have all the luck!; *Fam* **tu as ouvert mon courrier? faut pas t'en f.!** you've opened my mail? you've got some nerve *or* don't mind me!

faire-part [fɛrpar] **NM INV 1** *(dans la presse)* announcement; **f. de décès** death notice; **f. de mariage** wedding announcement **2** *(carte)* = card sent to family or friends announcing a birth, wedding, death etc; **le présent avis tiendra lieu de f.** friends please accept this intimation

faire-valoir [fɛrvalwar] **NM INV 1** *(personne)* foil; *Théât (de comique)* stooge, straight man; **servir de f. à qn** to serve as a foil to sb, to act as a straight man to sb **2** *Agr* farming; **exploitation** *ou* **terres en f. direct** owner farm

fair-play [fɛrplɛ] **NM INV** fair play, fair-mindedness

ADJ INV fair-minded; **il est f.** *(joueur)* he plays fair; *Fig* he has a sense of fair play

faisabilité [fəzabilite] **NF** *(d'un projet)* feasibility

faisable [fəzabl] **ADJ** *(réalisable)* feasible; *(possible)* possible, practicable; **c'est f.** it can be done; **ce n'est pas f. par un enfant** no child could do it; **tu peux être là à 14 heures? – c'est f.** can you come at 2 o'clock? – I should think so

faisait *etc voir* **faire**

faisan [fəzɑ̃] **NM 1** *(oiseau)* (cock) pheasant **2** *Fam Péj (escroc)* crook, con-man

faisandage [fəzɑ̃daʒ] **NM** hanging (of meat)

faisandé, -e [fəzɑ̃de] **ADJ 1** *Culin* gamy, high **2** *Péj (goût, littérature, personne)* decadent; *(milieu politique)* corrupt

faisandeau, -x [fəzɑ̃do] **NM** young pheasant

faisander [3] [fəzɑ̃de] **VT** *Culin* to hang

VPR se faisander 1 *Culin* to get high **2** *(pourrir)* to rot

faisanderie [fəzɑ̃dri] **NF** pheasant farm

faisane [fəzan] **ADJ F poule f.** (hen) pheasant

NF (hen) pheasant

faisant [fəzɑ̃] *voir* **faire**

faisceau, -x [fɛso] **NM 1** *(rayon)* beam, ray; *Électron* **f. cathodique** cathode ray; *Électron & TV* **f. cathodique explorateur** scanning electron beam; *Électron & Phys* **f. d'électrons** *ou* **électronique** electron beam; *Électron & Phys* **f. hertzien** radio beam; **f. lumineux** *ou* **de lumière** light beam, beam of light, *Spéc* pencil of rays; *Phys* **f. de particules** particle beam; *Électron & Phys* **f. radar** radar beam

2 *(gerbe)* cluster, bundle; *(d'ampoules électriques)* cluster; **f. aimanté** bunch of magnets; **f. de fils** wiring harness; **f. de ressorts** cluster springs; *Fig* **f. de preuves** accumulation of evidence; *Archit* **colonne en f.** clustered column

3 *Mil (pyramide d'armes)* stack of arms; **former/rompre les faisceaux** to stack/to unstack arms

4 *Anat & Bot* fascicle

5 *Rail* **f. de voies** group of sidings

6 *Aut* **f. convergent** converging beam; **f. divergent** diverging beam; **f. parallèle** parallel beam; **f. du radiateur** radiator core

7 *Antiq & Hist* fasces; **les faisceaux consulaires** *ou* **des licteurs** the fasces of the consuls *or* lictors

faiseur, -euse [fəzœr, -øz] **NM,F 1** *(artisan)* maker; **le bon f.** a first-class tailor; **ses costumes sortent de chez le bon f.** his suits are always smart and well-cut; **f. de dentelles** lacemaker; **f. de ponts** bridge builder **2** *(qui se livre à telle activité) Péj* **faiseuse d'anges** back-street abortionist; *Péj* **f. d'embarras** *Br* fusspot, *Am* fussbudget; **faiseuse de mariages** matchmaker; **f. de miracles** miracle worker; **f. de tours** magician; *TV & Rad* **f. d'Audimat®** ratings booster *(personality)* **3** *Vieilli Péj (escroc)* swindler, dishonest businessman; *(hâbleur)* show-off, braggart

faisselle [fɛsɛl] **NF** *Culin* **1** *(récipient)* cheese basket **2** *(fromage)* fromage frais *(packaged in its own draining basket)*

FAIT[1] [fɛ]

• act **1**	• event **2**
• fact **2, 3**	• point **4**

NM 1 *(action)* act, deed; **le f. de boire** (the act of) drinking; **f. d'armes** feat of arms; **faits de guerre** exploits of war; **les faits et gestes de qn** everything sb says and does, sb's every move; **observer** *ou* **épier les (moindres) faits et gestes de qn** to watch sb's every move; **rendre compte de ses faits et gestes** to give an account of oneself; *(à la police)* to give an account of one's movements; **hauts faits** heroic deeds; **prendre qn sur le f.** to catch sb in the act *or* red-handed; **prendre f. et cause pour qn** to side with sb

2 *(événement)* event, fact, occurrence; **f. notoire** piece of common knowledge; **f. nouveau** new development; **les faits lui ont donné raison** he/she was proved right by events; **quels sont les faits?** *(dans un procès)* what are the facts?; **les faits qui lui sont reprochés** the charge laid against him/her; **quels sont les faits reprochés à mon client?** what is my client being accused of *or* charged with?; **où étiez-vous au moment des faits?** where were you at the time in question?; **racontez-nous les faits** tell us what happened; **niez-vous les faits?** do you deny the charge?; **de ce f.** thereby; **le contrat, de ce f., est résilié** the contract is thereby terminated; **il est pénalisé par le seul f. de son divorce** the very fact that he's divorced puts him at a disadvantage; **par le seul f. d'y être** by the mere fact of *or* simply by being there; **par le seul f. que** (solely) because of, due (solely) to the fact that; *Jur* **f. (juridique)** fact; *Jur* **f. concluant** conclusive evidence; *Jur* **faits constitutifs de délit** factors that constitute an offence

3 *(réalité)* fact; **c'est un f.** it's a (matter of) fact; **le f. est là** it's a fact; **le f. est que nous étions en retard** the fact is we were late; **f. accompli** fait accompli; **placer** *ou* **mettre qn devant le f. accompli** to present sb with a fait accompli; **considérer qch comme un f. acquis** to take sth for granted; **c'est loin d'être** *ou* **ce n'est pas un f. acquis** it's not a foregone conclusion; **état de f.** (inescapable) fact; **roi de nom plutôt que de f.** king in name rather than in fact; *Fam* **le f. est!** that's right!, you've said it!; **je n'ai pas eu le temps de le faire, le f. est!** I have to admit that I didn't have enough time to do it!

4 *(sujet, question)* point; **aller (droit) au f.** to get straight to the point; **en venir au f.** to come *or* to get to the point; **au f.!** get to the point!

5 *(locutions)* **dire son f. à qn** to give sb a piece of one's mind; **je vais lui dire son f., à ce goujat!** I'm going to give that lout a piece of my mind!; **être le f. de** to be characteristic of; **c'est le f. de tous les incapables que de se chercher des excuses** incompetents always try to find excuses for themselves; **la renaissance du judo français est le f. de quelques champions** the renaissance of judo in France is entirely due *or* attributable to a few champions; **l'erreur est de son f.** it was his/her mistake; **cela est du f. de Martin** this is Martin's doing; **parler n'était pas son f.** he/she was no talker; **la générosité n'est pas son f.** it's just not his/her way to be generous; *Littéraire* **ce n'est pas le f. d'un chevalier de...** it does not become a knight to...

• **au fait ADV** by the way, incidentally; **au f., je t'ai remboursé?** incidentally *or* by the way, did I pay you back?; **au f., on pourrait peut-être y aller à pied?** by the way, couldn't we walk there?

• **au fait de PRÉP** well aware of, fully informed about; **être au f. de** to know about, to be informed about *or* au fait with; **je ne suis pas très au f. de ce problème** I don't know much about this problem; **il est très au f. de ces questions** he's very well informed about such matters; **mettre qn au f. de la situation** to inform sb about the situation

• **de ce fait ADV** for that reason, on that account

• **de fait ADJ 1** *Jur* actual, de facto; **possession de f.** actual possession **2** *(en affirmation)* **il est de f. que** it is true *or* a fact that; **il est de f. que je n'y avais pas pensé** it is true *or* a fact that it hadn't occurred to me **ADV** in fact, actually, as a matter of fact; **de f., il n'est pas mon père** actually *or* in fact he isn't my father; **de f., je n'ai jamais compris ce qu'il voulait** actually *or* to be honest, I never understood what he wanted; **de f., cela est un refus** that is in effect a refusal

• **du fait de PRÉP** because of, due to, on account of

• **du fait que CONJ** because (of the fact that)

• **en fait** = **de fait ADV**

• **en fait de PRÉP 1** *(en guise de)* by way of; **en f. de nourriture, il n'y a qu'une boîte de sardines** there's only a can of sardines by way of food **2** *(au lieu de)* instead of; **en f. de chien, c'était un loup** it wasn't a dog at all, it was a wolf **3** *(en matière de)* as regards, when it comes to; **expert en f. de vins** expert as regards wine *or* when it comes to wine

fait[2], -e [fɛ, fɛt] **PP** *voir* **faire**

ADJ 1 *(formé)* **être bien f. de sa personne** to be good-looking; **elle a la jambe bien faite** she's got shapely *or* nice legs; **une femme fort bien faite** a very good-looking woman

2 *(adapté)* **être f. pour qn/qch** to be made for sb/sth; **cette voiture est faite pour la ville** this car is made *or* designed for town driving; **ils sont faits l'un pour l'autre** they're made for each other; **il est f. pour faire du cinéma/pour être avocat** he's cut out to act in films/to be a lawyer; *Fam* **on peut mettre un chapeau dans cette boîte – oui, c'est f. pour** you can put a hat in this box – yes, that's what it's for; **sers-toi, c'est f. pour** help yourself, that's what it's there for

3 *(mûr)* mature, ripe; **un fromage f.** a fully ripened cheese; **trop f.** over-ripe

4 *(maquillé)* made-up; **avoir les ongles/yeux faits** to have nail polish on/eye make-up on, to be wearing nail polish/eye make-up

5 *(prêt)* **tout f.** *(vêtement)* ready-made, ready-to-wear; *(tournure)* set, ready-made; **robes toutes faites** ready-to-wear *or Br* off-the-peg dresses; **une expression toute faite** a set phrase, a cliché; **une excuse toute faite** a ready-made excuse

6 *Fam (ivre)* wasted, trashed

faîtage [fɛtaʒ] **NM** *Constr* **1** *(poutre)* ridgepole, ridgepiece **2** *(couverture)* ridge sheathing; *(tuiles)* ridge tiling

fait divers *(pl* **faits divers**), **fait-divers** *(pl* **faits-divers**) [fɛdivɛr] **NM** *Presse* **1** *(événement)* news story, news item **2 faits divers** *(rubrique)* (news) in brief; *(page)* news in brief; **tenir la rubrique des faits divers** = to cover weddings and funerals; *Fam* **ne fréquente pas ces types-là si tu ne veux pas te retrouver dans les faits divers** don't mix with those types if you don't want to end up as a crime statistic

fait-diversier [fɛdivɛrsje] (*pl* **faits-diversiers**) **NM** *Presse* = journalist who covers short news items

faîte [fɛt] **NM 1** *Géog* crest, top; **ligne de f.** watershed, crest line

2 *(sommet)* top, summit; **le f. des arbres était couvert de neige** the tops of the trees were covered with snow

3 *Constr* ridge

4 *(summum)* climax, acme; **le f. de la gloire** the height *or* pinnacle of glory; **atteindre le f. de sa carrière** to reach the climax of one's career

faites *voir* **faire**

faîtière [fɛtjɛr] *Constr* **ADJ** *voir* **lucarne, tuile**

NF crest tile, ridge tile

faitout [fɛtu] **NM** stewpot, cooking pot

faix [fɛ] **NM 1** *Littéraire* burden, load; **le f. des ans** the weight of (advancing) years; **le f. des impôts** the burden of taxation; **ployer sous le f.** to bend beneath the load **2** *Obst* foetus and placenta

fakir [fakir] **NM 1** *Rel* fakir **2** *(magicien)* conjurer

falafel [falafɛl] **NM** *Culin* falafel

falaise [falɛz] **NF** cliff; **f. littorale** *ou* **vive** sea cliff

falbalas [falbala] **NM** *Vieilli (volant de jupe)* flounce, furbelow

• **falbalas NMPL** *Péj* frills (and furbelows); **une architecture sans f.** an unadorned style of architecture

• **à falbalas ADJ** *(robe, rideau)* flouncy, frilly

fallacieuse [falasjøz] *voir* **fallacieux**

fallacieusement [falasjøzmɑ̃] **ADV** deceptively, misleadingly; *(promettre)* misleadingly

fallacieux, -euse [falasjø, -øz] **ADJ 1** *(trompeur)* deceptive, misleading, fallacious; *(apparence)* misleading; **promesses fallacieuses** false *or* deceptive promises; **sous un prétexte f.** on some pretext **2** *(spécieux)* insincere, specious; **des arguments f.** specious arguments

FALLOIR [69] [falwar] **V IMPERSONNEL A.** *EXPRIME LE BESOIN* **1** *(gén)* **il faut deux heures pour y aller** it takes two hours to get there; **faut-il vraiment tout ce matériel?** is all this equipment really necessary?; *Hum* **il est inspecteur des impôts – il en faut!** he's a tax inspector – someone has to do it!; **on a besoin d'un gros marteau – j'ai ce qu'il faut dans la voiture** we need a big hammer – I've got one in the car; **je bois deux litres d'eau par jour – c'est ce qu'il faut** I drink two litres of water a day – that's good; **ajoutez de la moutarde, juste ce qu'il faut** add some mustard, not too much; **je crois que nous avons trouvé l'homme qu'il nous faut** *(pour un poste)* I think we've found the right man for the job; **c'est un homme très tendre qu'il me faut** I need a man who is very loving; **ce n'est pas la femme qu'il te faut** she's not the right woman for you; **pour cette recette, il vous faut...** for this recipe, you need...; **c'est tout ce qu'il vous fallait?** *(dans une boutique)* was there anything else?; **il me faudrait deux filets de cabillaud, s'il vous plaît** I'd like two cod fillets, please; **j'ai plus d'argent qu'il n'en faut** I've got more money than I need; **j'ai plus de temps qu'il ne m'en faut** I've got time on my hands; **il ne lui en faut pas beaucoup pour se mettre en colère** it doesn't take a lot *or* much to make him/her angry; **il te faudrait une voiture** you need a car; *Hum* **j'aime les bonnes choses – oui, mais point trop n'en faut!** I like the good things in life – OK, but you shouldn't overindulge!; *Fam* **je voudrais que tu tapes la lettre en trois exemplaires – et puis qu'est-ce qu'il te faut encore?** I'd like you to type three copies of the letter – is there anything else while I'm at it?; *Fam* **il t'a fait ses excuses, qu'est-ce qu'il te faut de plus?** he apologized, what more do you want?; *Fam* **il n'est pas très beau – qu'est-ce qu'il te faut!** he's not that good-looking – you're hard to please!; *Fam* **je suis satisfait de lui – il t'en faut peu!** I'm satisfied with him – you're not hard to please!; *Fam* **elle a ce qu'il faut où il faut** she's got what it takes; *Fam* **il faut ce qu'il faut!** well, you might as well do things in style!

2 *(suivi d'une complétive au subj)* **il faudrait que nous nous réunissions plus souvent** we should have more regular meetings

B. *EXPRIME L'OBLIGATION* **1** *(gén)* **je ne veux pas me faire opérer – il le faut pourtant** I don't want to have an operation – you have no choice; **je lui ai dit – le fallait-il vraiment?** I told him/her – was it really necessary *or* did you really have to?; *Fam* **il ne fallait pas** *(en recevant un cadeau)* you shouldn't have; **s'il le faut** if I/we/*etc* must, if necessary; **nous irons jusque devant les tribunaux s'il le faut!** we'll take the matter to the courts if we must *or* if necessary!

2 *(suivi de l'infinitif)* **il faut m'excuser** please forgive me, you must forgive me; **il était furieux – il faut le comprendre** he was furious – that's understandable; **j'ai besoin d'aide – d'accord, que faut-il faire?** I need help – all right, what do you want me to do?; **je ne crois pas qu'il faille t'inquiéter** I don't think you should worry; **c'est un film qu'il faut voir (absolument)** this film's a must; **il faut bien se souvenir/se dire que...** it has to be remembered/said that...; **s'il fallait faire attention à tout ce que l'on dit!** if one had to mind one's Ps and Qs all the time!; **il ne fallait pas commencer!** you shouldn't have started!; **j'ai faim – il fallait le dire!** I'm hungry – why didn't you say so?; **qui faut-il croire?** who is to be believed?; **il me fallait lui mentir** I had to lie to him/her

3 *(suivi d'une complétive au subj)* **il faut absolument que je vous parle** I've got to speak to you; **il a fallu que je m'absente** I had to go out for a while; **il a bien fallu que je lui dise!** I had to tell him/her, didn't I?

4 *(au conditionnel, sens affaibli)* **il aurait fallu prévenir la police** the police should have been called; **attention, il ne faudrait pas que tu te trompes!** careful, you'd better not make any mistakes!; **il ne faudrait pas me prendre pour une idiote!** do you think I'm stupid?; **il faudrait pourtant que je m'achète une nouvelle voiture** I ought to buy a new car, really

5 *Fam (en intensif)* **il faut le voir pour le croire!** it has to be seen to be believed!; **c'était dangereux, il fallait y aller** *(ton admiratif)* it was dangerous, it took courage to do it; **il faut le faire!** *(en regardant un acrobate, un magicien)* that's amazing!; **ce qu'il a fait, il fallait le faire!** what he did was quite something!; **trois accidents en une semaine, il faut le faire!** three accidents in a week, that must be a record!; **ne pas fermer sa voiture, faut le faire!** it takes a fool *or* you've got to be completely stupid to leave your car unlocked!; **ça représente un cheval – il fallait le deviner!** it's supposed to be a horse – I'd never have known!; **il fallait l'entendre!** you should have heard him/her!; **il fallait le voir jouer Hamlet!** you should have seen him playing Hamlet!

C. *EXPRIME UNE FATALITÉ* **il a fallu que le téléphone sonne juste à ce moment-là!** the phone had to ring just then!; **je le lui avais défendu, mais non, il a fallu qu'elle le fasse** I'd told her not to, but she would have to do it

D. *POUR JUSTIFIER, EXPLIQUER* **il faut que tu aies fait mal à Rex pour qu'il t'ait mordu!** you must have hurt Rex to make him bite you!; **il fallait que le vase soit** *ou* **fût très fragile pour se casser aussi facilement** the vase must have been very fragile to break that easily

VPR s'en falloir il s'en faut de beaucoup qu'il n'ait fini! he's far from finished!; **elle n'est pas de ton envergure, il s'en faut de beaucoup!** she's not in your league, far from it!; **peu s'en est fallu que je ne manque le train!** I almost *or* very nearly missed the train!; *Fam* **il s'en est fallu de rien** *ou* **d'un cheveu qu'il ne fût décapité** he came within inches of having his head chopped off; **tant s'en faut** far from it, not by a long way; **il n'est pas paresseux, tant s'en faut** he's far from being lazy

Fallope [falɔp] *voir* **trompe**

fallu [faly] **PP** *voir* **falloir**

falot¹ [falo] **NM 1** *(lanterne)* (hand) lantern **2** *Fam Arg mil* court martial

falot², -e [falo, -ɔt] **ADJ** colourless, bland, vapid; **c'est un personnage assez f.** he's rather insipid

falsificateur, -trice [falsifikatœr, -tris] **NM,F** *(de documents, de comptes)* falsifier; *(d'une signature)* forger

falsification [falsifikasjɔ̃] **NF** *(de documents, de comptes)* falsification; *(de la vérité, des propos de quelqu'un)* misrepresentation; *(d'une signature)* forging, forgery; *(d'un vin)* adulteration

falsificatrice [falsifikatris] *voir* **falsificateur**

falsifier [9] [falsifje] **VT** *(document, comptes)* to forge, to falsify; *(vérité, propos de quelqu'un)* to misrepresent; *(signature)* to forge; *(vin)* to adulterate; **les comptes ont été falsifiés** the accounts have been falsified; **il a falsifié les résultats** he tampered with *or* falsified the results; *Fig* **f. la pensée de l'auteur** to misrepresent the author's thinking

falzar [falzar] **NM** *très Fam Br* trousers, keks, *Am* pants

famé, -e [fame] *voir* **mal famé**

famélique [famelik] **ADJ** *(chat)* scrawny; *(prisonnier)* half-starved; **les ventres faméliques de l'Afrique** the starving of Africa

fameuse [famøz] *voir* **fameux**

fameusement [famøzmɑ̃] **ADV** *Fam Br* dead, *Am* real; **il est f. rusé!** he's *Br* dead *or Am* real crafty!; **on s'est f. bien amusé** we had a *Br* good *or Am* real good time

fameux, -euse [famø, -øz] **ADJ 1** *(célèbre)* famous, renowned, well-known; *(ayant bonne réputation)* famous (**par** *ou* **pour** for); *(ayant mauvaise réputation)* notorious (**par** *ou* **pour** for); **f. entre tous** widely recognized

2 *Fam (bon ▸ gén)* excellent, brilliant; *(▸ repas, mets)* excellent, delicious; **ce fut une fameuse journée** it has been a memorable day; **f., ton gâteau** your cake is delicious; **j'ai bien une photo, mais elle n'est pas fameuse** I have got a photograph, but it's not that good; **l'image est bonne, mais la bande-son n'est pas fameuse** the picture is OK, but the soundtrack isn't brilliant

3 *(en intensif)* **c'est un f. mystère** it's quite a mystery; **un f. exemple de courage** an outstanding example of courage; **c'est un f. coquin, celui-là!** he's quite a lad!

4 *(dont on parle)* famous; **et où as-tu acheté ce f. bouquin?** where did you buy this famous book *or* this book you keep going on about?

5 *Ironique (soi-disant)* so-called; **c'est ça, ton f. trésor?** is THAT your famous treasure?; **montre-moi ce f. chef-d'œuvre** show me this so-called masterpiece

familial, -e, -aux, -ales [familjal, -o] **ADJ 1** *(de famille)* domestic, family *(avant n)*; *(usine, hôtel)* family-run, family-owned; **vie/réunion familiale** family life/meeting; **une atmosphère familiale** a friendly atmosphere; **entreprise familiale** family firm; **querelles familiales** domestic quarrels; **cet élève a des problèmes familiaux** this pupil has problems at home; **maladie familiale** hereditary disease *or* condition; **la cuisine familiale** home cooking; **quotient/revenu f.** family quotient/income **2** *Com* family-sized, economy *(avant n)*; **emballage f.** economy-size *or* family pack

• **familiale NF** *Br* estate (car), *Am* station wagon

familiarisation [familjarizasjɔ̃] **NF** familiarization

familiariser [3] [familjarize] **VT f. qn avec** to make sb familiar *or* to familiarize sb with, to get sb used to

VPR se familiariser se f. avec qch *(par la pratique)* to familiarize oneself with sth, to get to know sth; *(par habitude)* to get accustomed *or* used to sth; **se f. avec une technique/langue** to master a technique/language; **se f. avec un lieu** to get to know a place, to get to know one's way around; **peu familiarisé avec** unfamiliar *or* unacquainted with

familiarité [familjarite] **NF 1** *(désinvolture)* familiarity, casualness; **être d'une trop grande f. avec qn** to be too familiar *or* overfamiliar with sb; **je ne tolérerai aucune f. dans mes rapports avec les étudiants** I will not tolerate any familiarity in my relations with the students; **pas de f., je vous prie** please don't be familiar **2** *(connaissance)* **f. avec** familiarity with, knowledge of; **il a une grande f. avec l'œuvre de Proust** he has a close *or* an intimate knowledge of the work of Proust; **sa f. avec les oiseaux d'Europe du Nord** his/her knowledge of the birds of Northern Europe; **acquérir une certaine f. de l'anglais** to gain a certain knowledge of English

• **familiarités NFPL** liberties, undue familiarity; **s'autoriser** *ou* **prendre des familiarités avec qn** to take liberties *or* to be overfamiliar with sb

familier, -ère [familje, -ɛr] **ADJ 1** *(connu)* familiar; *(amical)* friendly; **un visage f.** a familiar face; **le problème m'est f.** I am familiar with the problem; **la maison lui était familière** he/she remembered the house quite clearly; **ce spectacle/bruit lui était f.** it looked/sounded familiar to him/her; **ta voix ne lui est pas familière** he/she doesn't know *or* recognize your voice

2 *(habituel)* usual; **une tâche familière** a routine task; **c'est l'une de ses attitudes familières** it's one of his/her favourite poses; **il est préférable de les voir dans leur décor f.** you should see them in their usual surroundings; **ce genre de travail leur est f.** they are used to this kind of work

3 *(apprivoisé)* **animal f.** pet

4 *Péj (cavalier)* overfamiliar; **je n'aime pas leurs attitudes familières/les gens trop familiers** I don't like their offhand ways/people who are overfamiliar; **il s'est montré trop f.** he was too familiar, he was overfamiliar

5 *Ling* colloquial, informal

6 *(de la maison)* **dieux familiers** household gods

NM 1 *(ami)* familiar, friend; **elle se déplace en tournée avec tous ses familiers** she tours with her regular entourage; **un f. de la maison** a regular visitor to the house, an intimate friend of the household **2** *(client)* habitué, regular; **les familiers de ce café** this café's regulars

familièrement [familjɛrmɑ̃] **ADV 1** *(amicalement)* familiarly, informally, casually; **il lui donna f. une petite tape sur la joue** he gave him/her a friendly little pat on the cheek **2** *(couramment)* colloquially, in conversation; **la saxifrage, f. appelée mignonnette** saxifrage, commonly named London pride

familistère [familistɛr] **NM** *(coopérative)* coop, cooperative

famille [famij] **NF 1** *(foyer)* family; *(ménage)* household; **la f. Laverne** the Laverne family, the Lavernes; **f. étendue/restreinte** extended/nuclear family; **revenu par f.** income per household; **il rentre dans sa f. tous les week-ends** he goes back home every weekend; **f. monoparentale** single-parent family; **f. nombreuse** large family; **réduction f. nombreuse** family reduction *or* discount; **f. nucléaire** nuclear family; **f. patchwork** patchwork family, *Am* blended family *(consisting of children, parents etc of divorced parent's new spouse)*; *Fam* **f. tuyau de poêle** = family whose members have an incestuous relationship

2 *(enfants)* family, children; **comment va la petite f.?** how are the children?; **avec toute sa petite f.** with all his/her brood around him/her; *Can Fam* **être en f.** to be in the family way, to have a bun in the oven; *Can Fam* **partir pour la f.** to get knocked up, to get pregnant[□]

3 *(tous les parents)* family, relatives; **une grande f. de France** one of the noblest families in France; **il n'est pas de ma f.** he's no relation of mine; **ils sont de la même f.** they're related; **prévenir la f.** to inform sb's relatives; *Jur* to inform the next of kin; **il faut que je vous présente à ma f.** *(parents)* I must introduce you to my parents; **c'est une f. de danseurs** they're all dancers in their family, they're a family of dancers; **je souhaite que mes bijoux ne sortent pas de la f.** I'd like my jewels to stay in the family; *Hum* **c'est ça, donne-lui ton rhume pour que ça ne sorte pas de la f.!** that's right, give him/her your cold, let's keep things in the family!

4 *Bot, Ling & Zool (groupe)* family, group; **f. de langues** group of languages; **f. de mots/plantes** family of words/plants; **la f. des instruments à vent** winds, the wind family

5 *Mktg (de produits)* family, line

6 *Typ* **f. de caractères** typeface

7 *(idéologie)* obedience, persuasion; **de la même f. politique** of the same political persuasion; **des gens appartenant à la même f. spirituelle que nous** our brothers in spirit

• **de bonne famille ADJ** well-bred, from a good family

• **de famille ADJ** *(cercle, médecin, biens)* family *(avant n)*; **charges de f.** dependants; **chef de f.** head of the family; *Admin* householder, head of the household; **soutien de f.** (main) wage earner, breadwinner; **fils de f.** young man of good social standing **ADV c'est** *ou* **cela tient de f.** it runs in the family, it's in the blood

• **des familles ADJ** *Fam* cosy, nice (little); **une petite soirée des familles** a cosy little party; **je vais nous faire un petit gigot des familles** I'm going to cook a nice little leg of lamb for us

• **en famille ADV 1** *(en groupe)* **passer Noël/le week-end en f.** to spend Christmas/the weekend with one's family *or* at home; **dîner en f.** to dine at home with one's family; **nous réglons toujours nos problèmes en f.** we always settle our problems within the family **2** *(en confiance)* **se sentir en f.** to feel at home; **ma petite Sylvie, vous êtes (comme) en f. ici!** my dear Sylvie, please consider yourself at home here!

famine [famin] **NF** famine, starvation; **ils souffrent de la f.** they're victims of the famine, they're starving; **crier f.** to plead poverty, to complain of hard times; **salaire de f.** starvation wages

fan [fan] **NMF** fan; **c'est un f. de jazz** he's a jazz fan

fana [fana] *Fam* **ADJ** crazy (**de** about), dead keen (**de** on); **il est f. de sport** he's crazy about sport

NMF fanatic; **f. du football/de la moto** football/motorbike fanatic *or* freak; **c'est une f. de cinéma** she's a real film buff

fanage [fanaʒ] **NM** *Agr (du foin)* tedding, tossing

fanal, -aux [fanal, -o] **NM** lantern, lamp; *Naut (sur les côtes)* beacon, lantern; **f. de locomotive** headlight; *Naut* **f. de bord** ship's lantern, sidelight

fanatique [fanatik] **ADJ 1** *Péj (religieux)* fanatical, bigoted, zealous **2** *(passionné)* enthusiastic; **il est f. des jeux vidéo** he's mad about video games; **je ne suis pas f. de la bière** I'm not (that) keen on beer, I'm not a big fan of beer

NMF 1 *Péj* zealot **2** *(partisan)* fan, fanatic; **des fanatiques de Pavarotti** Pavarotti fans; **je ne suis pas un f. du poisson** I'm not mad *or* crazy about fish, I'm not a big fan of fish

fanatiquement [fanatikmɑ̃] **ADV** fanatically, zealously

fanatisation [fanatizasjɔ̃] **NF** fanaticization; **la f. des foules était due à une propagande très bien menée** extremely skilful propaganda made the crowds fanatical

fanatiser [3] [fanatize] **VT** to fanaticize, to make fanatical; **être fanatisé** to become fanatical; **suivi par une foule fanatisée** followed by a frenzied crowd; **des religieux fanatisés** religious fanatics

fanatisme [fanatism] **NM** fanaticism; *Pol & Rel* fanaticism, zealotry

fanchon [fɑ̃ʃɔ̃] **NF** kerchief, headscarf

fandango [fɑ̃dɑ̃go] **NM** *Mus* fandango

fane [fan] **NF 1** *(de légumes)* top; **fanes de carotte/radis** carrot/radish tops **2** *(feuille morte)* (dead *or* fallen) leaf

faner [3] [fane] **VI 1** *Agr* to make hay **2** *(se flétrir)* to wither

VT 1 *Agr* to ted, to toss **2** *(décolorer)* to fade; **fané par le soleil** faded by the sun, sun-bleached; **des couleurs fanées** faded *or* washed-out colours **3** *(fleur, plante)* to fade, to wither, to wilt

VPR se faner 1 *Bot* to fade, to wither **2** *(perdre son éclat)* to wane, to fade; **sa beauté s'est fanée** her beauty has lost its bloom *or* faded

faneur, -euse [fanœr, -øz] *Agr* **NM,F** haymaker, tedder

• **faneuse NF** *(machine)* tedder, tedding-machine

fanfare [fɑ̃far] **NF** *(air)* fanfare; *(orchestre ▸ civil)* brass band; *(▸ militaire)* military band; **la f. du village** the village band

• **en fanfare ADV** *(réveiller)* noisily, brutally; **réveil en f.** brutal awakening; **annoncer la nouvelle en f.** to trumpet the news

fanfaron, -onne [fɑ̃farɔ̃, -ɔn] **ADJ** boastful, swaggering; **d'un air f.** boastfully

NM,F boaster, braggart, swaggerer; **faire le f.** to crow, to brag and boast; **ah, tu ne fais plus le f., maintenant?** ah, so you're not so pleased with yourself now?

fanfaronnade [fɑ̃farɔnad] **NF 1** *(acte)* bravado *(UNCOUNT)*; **par f.** out of (sheer) bravado **2** *(remarque)* boast **3 fanfaronnades** *(actes, propos)* bragging, boasting

fanfaronner [3] [fɑ̃farɔne] **VI** to boast, to brag, to swagger

fanfic [fanfik], **fanfiction** [fanfiksjɔ̃] **NF** fanfic

fanfreluches [fɑ̃frəlyʃ] **NFPL** *Péj* frills (and furbelows)

fange [fɑ̃ʒ] **NF** *Littéraire* mire; **vivre dans la f.** to live a life of degradation; **sortir de la f.** to climb out of the gutter; **élevé dans la f.** brought up in the gutter; **croupir dans la f.** to be living surrounded by filth

fangeux, -euse [fɑ̃ʒø, -øz] **ADJ** *Littéraire* **1** *(boueux)* miry **2** *(abject)* murky

fanion [fanjɔ̃] **NM** *(de club, bateau, corps d'armée etc)* pennant, pennon; *(balise)* flag; **des fanions** *(guirlandes)* bunting

fanon [fanɔ̃] **NM 1** *Zool (d'une baleine)* whalebone plate

2 *(bajoue ▸ d'un bœuf)* dewlap; *(▸ d'une dinde)* wattle

3 *(d'un cheval)* fetlock

4 *Rel* lappet (of a mitre)

fantaisie [fɑ̃tezi] **NF 1** *(originalité)* imagination; *Péj* fantasy; **avoir beaucoup de f.** to have a lively *or* vivid imagination; **donner libre cours à sa f.** to give free rein to one's imagination; **manquer de f.** *(personne)* to lack imagination; *(vie)* to be monotonous *or* uneventful; **vous interprétez le règlement avec beaucoup de f.** you have a rather imaginative interpretation of the rules; **elle était d'une f. rafraîchissante** she was refreshingly imaginative

2 *(lubie)* whim; **c'est sa dernière f.** it's his/her latest whim; **je ne sais quelle f. lui a pris** I don't know what came over him/her; **et s'il lui prend la f. de partir?** what if he/she should take it into his/her head to leave?; **qu'est-ce que c'est que cette f.?** what's come over you?; **satisfaire une f.** to give in to a whim; **se passer une f.** to indulge a caprice; **il lui passe toutes ses fantaisies** he gives in to his/her every whim; **s'offrir une f.** to give oneself a treat, to treat oneself; **je m'offre une petite f., un week-end à Amsterdam** I'm giving myself a little treat, a weekend in Amsterdam; *Péj* **cette (petite) f. va vous coûter cher** you'll regret this little extravagance; **nous ne pouvons nous permettre aucune f.** we can't afford to indulge ourselves

3 *(bibelot)* fancy; **un magasin de fantaisies** a novelty shop

4 *Beaux-Arts & Littérature* (piece of) fantasy; *Mus* fantasy, fantasia; *(créativité)* imagination, imaginative power; **le récit relève de la plus haute f.** the story is highly imaginative

5 *(comme adj inv) (simulé)* imitation; *(peu classique)* fancy; **kirsch f.** imitation kirsch; **bijou f.** piece of costume jewellery; **des boutons f.** fancy buttons

• **de fantaisie ADJ 1** *(à bon marché)* novelty *(avant n)*; **article de f.** novelty; **pain de f.** fancy bread *(not sold by weight)*; **bijoux de f.** costume jewellery **2** *(imaginaire ▸ œuvre, récit)* fantasy *(avant n)*, imaginative **3** *(non officiel)* **il portait un uniforme de f.** he was wearing a customized uniform

• **à la fantaisie de, selon la fantaisie de PRÉP n'en faire qu'à sa f.** to do exactly as one pleases; **chacun s'amusait à sa f.** everyone amused themselves as the fancy took them *or* as they pleased

> Il faut noter que le nom anglais **fantasy** est un faux ami. Il signifie **rêve, fantasme**.

fantaisiste [fɑ̃tezist] **ADJ 1** *(farfelu)* eccentric, unconventional; *(procédés, mode de vie)* unorthodox; **elle a des horaires fantaisistes** she keeps strange *or* odd hours **2** *(inventé)* fanciful; **c'est une explication f.** that's a fanciful explanation; **les déclarations fantaisistes que vous avez faites à la presse** your extremely fanciful statements to the press

NMF 1 *Théât* variety artist, sketcher **2** *Péj (dilettante)* joker, clown; **méfie-toi, c'est un f.** be careful, he's a bit of a joker

fantasmagorie [fɑ̃tasmagɔri] **NF 1** *(féerie)* phantasmagoria **2** *(effets de style)* gothic effects; **des histoires pleines de fantasmagories** fantasies

fantasmagorique [fɑ̃tasmagɔrik] **ADJ** magical, *Littéraire* phantasmagorical

fantasme [fɑ̃tasm] **NM** fantasy; **tu vis dans tes fantasmes** you're living in a fantasy world

fantasmer [3] [fɑ̃tasme] **VI** to fantasize; **f. sur qn/qch** to fantasize about sb/sth; **faire f. qn** *(sexuellement)* to turn sb on; **tu me fais f. avec tes récits de voyage** you make my imagination run wild talking about your travels

fantasque [fɑ̃task] **ADJ 1** *(capricieux)* capricious, whimsical **2** *Littéraire (bizarre)* odd, weird

fantassin [fɑ̃tasɛ̃] **NM** foot soldier, infantryman

fantastique [fɑ̃tastik] **ADJ 1** *(fabuleux ▸ animal, personnage)* fantastical, fabulous, fantasy *(avant n)*

2 *(surnaturel ▸ lumière, atmosphère)* weird, eerie; **roman f.** Gothic novel; **cinéma f.** science-fiction *or* fantasy films

3 *Fam (formidable)* great, brilliant; **j'ai gagné, n'est-ce pas f.!** I won, isn't it great *or* marvellous?; **c'est un type f.!** he's a great guy!

4 *Fam (étonnant)* extraordinary, unbelievable; **le f. essor des technologies** the extraordinary progress of technology; **une somme f.** a fantastic amount of money; **il a un courage f.** he's incredibly courageous

NM le f. *(l'étrange)* the fantastic, the supernatural; *(genre)* the Gothic (genre); *(littérature)* fantasy literature

fantastiquement [fɑ̃tastikmɑ̃] **ADV** fantastically, terrifically, amazingly

fantoche [fɑ̃tɔʃ] **NM** *Péj* puppet; *(comme adj)* **un gouvernement/souverain f.** a puppet government/king; **une armée f.** a non-existent army

fantomatique [fɑ̃tɔmatik] **ADJ** phantom *(avant n)*, ghostly

fantôme [fɑ̃tom] **NM 1** *(revenant)* ghost, phantom, spirit; **apparaître/disparaître comme un f.** to appear/to disappear as if by magic **2** *Littéraire (apparence)* ghostly image *or* shape, ghost; *Péj* **un f. de chef** a make-believe leader, a leader in name only; *Péj* **un f. de parti politique** a phantom political party; **ce n'est plus qu'un f.** *(très maigre)* he's just a skeleton, he's nothing but skin and bone **3** *(comme adj)* **cabinet f.** shadow cabinet; **membre(-)f.** phantom limb; **société f.** bogus company; **train f.** ghost train; **ville f.** ghost town; **où est ce rapport f.?** where is this supposed report?

fanzine [fɑ̃zin] **NM** fanzine

FAO [ɛfao] **NF 1** *Ind (abrév* **fabrication assistée par ordinateur***)* CAM **2** *(abrév* **Food and Agricultural Organization***)* FAO

faon [fɑ̃] **NM** *Zool (cerf)* fawn, calf; *(daim)* fawn; *(chevreuil)* kid, fawn

FAQ [fak] *Ordinat (abrév* **frequently asked questions, foire aux questions***)* FAQ

faquin [fakɛ̃] **NM** *Arch* knave, varlet

far [far] **NM** *Culin* **f. (breton)** = Breton custard tart with prunes

farad [farad] **NM** *Élec* farad

Faraday [faradɛ] *voir* **cage**

faramineux, -euse [faraminø, -øz] **ADJ** *Fam (somme, fortune)* huge, tremendous; *(prix)* astronomical; **il a un aplomb f.!** he's got an awful nerve!; **c'est f. ce qu'elle a pu dépenser!** the amount of money she spent was incredible!; **il lui a fait des compliments pour le moins f.** his compliments were slightly over the top

farandole [farɑ̃dɔl] **NF 1** *(danse)* farandole **2** *(au restaurant)* **et pour finir, la f. des fromages/desserts** to round off your meal choose from our cheeseboard/dessert trolley

faraud, -e [faro, -od] *Fam Vieilli* **ADJ** boastful; **te voilà bien faraude avec ta robe neuve!** you look very pleased with yourself in your new dress!; **il n'était pas si f. pendant l'orage** he wasn't so cocky during the storm

NM,F swaggerer; **faire le f.** to show off

farce[1] [fars] **NF 1** *(tour)* practical joke, prank, trick; **faire une f. à qn** to play a trick on sb; **quelqu'un t'a fait une f.** somebody has been pulling your leg; **une mauvaise f.** a joke gone wrong; *Can Fam* **f. plate** sick *or* tasteless joke; *Can Fam* **c'est pas des farces!** it's true!, I'm not joking! **2** *Littérature & Théât* farce; *Fig* **la vie n'est qu'une f.** life is nothing but a farce; *Fig* **la situation tournait à la f.** things were becoming farcical

ADJ *Vieilli* comical; **c'était assez f.!** it was hilarious!

• **farces et attrapes NFPL** jokes and novelties; **magasin de farces et attrapes** joke shop

farce[2] [fars] **NF** *Culin* forcemeat, stuffing

farceur, -euse [farsœr, -øz] **ADJ** mischievous; **ils sont farceurs** they like playing tricks

NM,F 1 *(qui fait des farces)* practical joker, prankster; **je me demande qui est le petit f. qui m'a fait ça** I wonder who the joker is that I have to blame for this **2** *(blagueur)* joker, wag; **c'est un f. qui vous aura dit cela** somebody's been pulling your leg

farcir [32] [farsir] **VT 1** *Culin* to stuff **2** *Fam (remplir)* **f. qch avec** *ou* **de** to stuff sth chock-a-block with, to cram sth with; **cesse de lui f. le crâne avec ces sottises!** stop cramming his/her head full of this nonsense!

VPR se farcir se f. qn *Fam (le subir)* to have to put up with sb, to have to take sb; *Vulg (sexuellement)* to screw sb, *Br* to shag sb; *Fam* **se f. qch** *(le subir)* to get stuck *or Br* lumbered *or* landed with sth; *(le boire)* to knock sth back, to down sth; *(le manger)* to stuff oneself with sth; **son beau-frère, faut se le f.!** his/her brother-in-law is a real pain!

fard [far] **NM 1** *(produit)* colour *(for make-up)*; **f. à joues** blusher; **f. à paupières** eyeshadow **2** *Vieilli (maquillage)* **le f.** *(gén)* make-up; *Théât* grease paint

• **sans fard ADJ** straightforward, frank; **la vérité sans f.** the plain unvarnished truth **ADV** straightforwardly, frankly; **parler sans f.** to speak candidly *or* openly

fardage [fardaʒ] **NM** *Com* camouflage

farde [fard] **NF** *Belg* **1** *(cahier)* exercise book **2** *(chemise)* folder **3** *(cartouche)* carton *(of cigarettes)*

fardeau, -x [fardo] **NM 1** *(poids)* burden, load **2** *(contrainte)* burden, millstone; **porter un f. sur les épaules** to carry *or* to bear a burden on one's shoulders; **être un f. pour qn** to be a burden to sb; **le f. des ans** *(la vieillesse)* old age; *Fin* **le f. fiscal** the tax burden

farder [3] [farde] **VT 1** *(maquiller)* to make up; **trop fardé** over-made up **2** *(cacher)* to conceal, to mask; **f. la réalité/ses sentiments** to disguise the truth/one's feelings **3** *Com* to camouflage

VPR se farder to make up one's face, to put one's make-up on; **se f. les yeux** to put eye shadow on

farfadet [farfadɛ] **NM** imp, elf, goblin

farfelu, -e [farfəly] *Fam* **ADJ** crazy, weird

NM,F oddball, weirdo, crackpot

farfouiller [3] [farfuje] *Fam* **VI** to rummage about; **ils ont farfouillé dans tous les tiroirs** they've been rummaging about in all the drawers

VT *(chercher)* **qu'est-ce que tu farfouilles?** what are you after?

faribole [faribɔl] **NF** *Littéraire* piece of nonsense; **dire** *ou* **raconter des fariboles** to talk nonsense; **et autres fariboles** and all that nonsense

farinacé, -e [farinase] **ADJ** farinaceous

farine [farin] **NF 1** *Culin* flour; **f. d'avoine** oatmeal; **f. de blé** wheat flour; **f. complète** wholewheat flour, *Br* wholemeal flour; **f. de froment/seigle** wheat/rye flour; **f. de maïs** cornflour, *Am* cornstarch; **f. de manioc** cassava; **f. de poisson** fish meal **2** *(poudre)* powder; **f. de forage** bore dust; **f. de moutarde** mustard powder **3 farines animales** bone meal

• **de la même farine ADJ** of the same kind; *Littéraire* **ce sont tous gens de la même f.** they're all alike

fariner [3] [farine] **VT** to flour, to sprinkle flour over; **farinez le moule** dredge the tin with flour, flour the tin all over

farineux, -euse [farinø, -øz] **ADJ 1** *(fariné)* floury, flour-covered

2 *(pâteux ▸ poire)* mealy; *(▸ pomme de terre)* floury

3 *(au goût de farine)* chalky, floury

4 *(féculent)* starchy, *Spéc* farinaceous

NM starch, starchy food; **évitez les f. pendant quelque temps** avoid starch *or* starchy foods for a while

farlouse [farluz] **NF** *Orn* meadow pipit

farniente [farnjente, farnjɑ̃t] **NM** idleness, laziness; **amateur de f.** idler

farouche [faruʃ] **ADJ 1** *(caractère)* fierce, unflinching; *(résistance, regard)* fierce; **volonté f.** iron *or* unshakeable will; **elle a une méfiance f. à l'égard des religions** she is fiercely suspicious of all religion **2** *(animal)* wild; *(personne)* shy, coy; **un animal peu f.** a tame animal; **l'enfant est encore un peu f.** the child is still a bit shy; *Euph Hum* **c'est une femme peu f.** she is no model of virtue **3** *(brutal)* cruel, savage; **un combat f.** a savage fight

farouchement [faruʃmɑ̃] **ADV 1** *(ardemment)* definitely, unquestionably; **je suis f. contre!** I am definitely against it!; **il est toujours f. décidé à ne pas bouger** he's still adamant he won't move **2** *(violemment)* fiercely, savagely; **se débattre f.** to kick and struggle

fart [far(t)] **NM** *Ski* ski wax

fartage [fartaʒ] **NM** *Ski* waxing

farter [3] [farte] **VT** *Ski* to wax

fascicule [fasikyl] **NM 1** *(partie d'un ouvrage)* instalment, part, section; **publié par fascicules** published in parts **2** *(livret)* booklet, manual; **le calendrier figure dans un f. séparé** the timetable is given in a separate booklet; *Mil* **f. de mobilisation** mobilization instructions

fasciculé, -e [fasikyle] **ADJ** *Biol & Bot* fasciculate

fascinant, -e [fasinɑ̃, -ɑ̃t] **ADJ** *(personne)* fascinating; *(beauté, yeux, sourire)* captivating

fascinateur, -trice [fasinatœr, -tris] **ADJ** fascinating

NM,F captivator

fascination [fasinasjɔ̃] **NF** fascination; **exercer une f. sur** to be fascinating to

fascinatrice [fasinatris] *voir* **fascinateur**

fascine [fasin] **NF** *Constr* fascine

fasciner[1] **[3]** [fasine] **VT 1** *(sujet: serpent ▸ proie)* to fascinate, to hypnotize **2** *(charmer ▸ sujet: spectacle)* to captivate, to fascinate; **le spectacle les fascine** they're captivated by the show; **elle est fascinée par ce garçon** she has been bewitched by that boy, she is under that boy's spell; **elle se laisse f. par l'argent** she lets herself be blinded *or* dazzled by money

fasciner[2] **[3]** [fasine] **VT** *Constr (rive)* to line with fascines, to fascine, *Am* to corduroy; **route fascinée** corduroy road

fascisant, -e [faʃizɑ̃, -ɑ̃t] **ADJ** *Pol* fascist, fascistic, pro-fascist

fasciser [3] [faʃize] **VT f. un État** to take a state towards fascism; **f. un régime/une politique** to make a regime/policy increasingly fascistic

fascisme [faʃism] **NM 1** *(gén)* fascism **2** *Hist* Fascism

fasciste [faʃist] **ADJ & NMF 1** *(gén)* fascist **2** *Hist* Fascist

fashion [faʃœn] **ADJ INV** *Fam* trendy

fasse *etc voir* **faire**

faste [fast] **ADJ 1** *(favorable ▸ année)* good; *(▸ jour)* good, lucky; **les années fastes, nous mangions de la viande tous les jours** in a good year, we would eat meat every day; **je paie la note, je suis dans une période f.!** I'll pay the bill, I'm in the money *or* I'm flush at the moment! **2** *Antiq* **jour f.** lawful day

NM *(luxe)* sumptuousness, splendour; **avec f.** sumptuously, with pomp (and circumstance), munificently; **sans f.** simply, quietly, plainly; **la cérémonie aura lieu sans f.** the ceremony will be a simple affair

• **fastes NMPL 1** *Littéraire* pomp; **les fastes de l'État** the pomp and circumstance of great state occasions **2** *Antiq* annals

fast-food [fastfud] *(pl* **fast-foods***)* **NM** fast-food restaurant

fastidieuse [fastidjøz] *voir* **fastidieux**

fastidieusement [fastidjøzmɑ̃] **ADV** boringly, tediously

fastidieux, -euse [fastidjø, -øz] **ADJ** boring, tedious

> Il faut noter que l'adjectif anglais **fastidious** est un faux ami. Il signifie **pointilleux, difficile**.

fastoche [fastɔʃ] ADJ easy□; **c'était hyper f.** it was dead easy *or* a walk in the park

fastueuse [fastyøz] *voir* **fastueux**

fastueusement [fastyøzmɑ̃] ADV sumptuously, with pomp (and circumstance), munificently

fastueux, -euse [fastyø, -øz] ADJ magnificent, sumptuous, munificent

Fat [fat] NF *Ordinat* FAT

fat [fa(t)] *Littéraire* ADJ M smug, self-satisfied; **prendre un air f.** to look smug

NM smug person

fatal, -e, -als, -ales [fatal] ADJ **1** *(fixé par le sort)* fateful; **l'instant f.** the fatal moment

2 *(désastreux)* disastrous, terrible; **cette erreur vous a été fatale** this mistake proved disastrous for you; *Ordinat* **erreur fatale** fatal error

3 *(mortel ▸ collision, blessure)* fatal, mortal; **coup f.** deathblow; **porter un coup f. à** *(frapper)* to deliver a deadly *or* mortal blow to; *Fig* to administer the coup de grâce to; **le choc lui a été f.** the shock killed him/her

4 *(inévitable)* inevitable; **c'était f.** it was bound to happen, it was inevitable; **il est revenu, c'était f.** he came back, as was bound to happen

fatalement [fatalmɑ̃] ADV inevitably; **il devait f. perdre** he was bound to lose

> Il faut noter que l'adverbe anglais **fatally** est un faux ami. Il signifie **mortellement** ou **irrémédiablement**.

fatalisme [fatalism] NM fatalism

fataliste [fatalist] ADJ fatalist, fatalistic; **il est f.** he's resigned to his fate

NMF fatalist

fatalité [fatalite] NF **1** *(sort)* destiny, fate; **poursuivi par la f.** pursued by fate; **c'est la f.** it's bad luck; **la f. s'acharne contre eux** they're dogged by misfortune; **il parle de l'analphabétisme comme si c'était une f.** he talks about illiteracy as if it were inevitable **2** *(circonstance fâcheuse)* mischance; **je le vois chaque fois que j'y vais, c'est une f.!** there must be a curse on me! every time I go there, I see him!; **par quelle f. était-il absent ce soir-là?** by what unfortunate coincidence did he happen to be away that evening? **3** *(inévitabilité)* inevitability

> Il faut noter que le nom anglais **fatality** signifie également **victime**.

fatidique [fatidik] ADJ **1** *(marqué par le destin ▸ date, jour)* fated, fateful **2** *(important)* crucial, momentous; **il est arrivé au moment f.** he arrived at the crucial moment; **c'est l'instant f.!** it's now or never!

fatigabilité [fatigabilite] NF fatigability

fatigable [fatigabl] ADJ **facilement f.** easily tired; **difficilement f.** tireless, untiring

fatigant, -e [fatigɑ̃, -ɑ̃t] ADJ **1** *(épuisant)* tiring, wearing; **c'est très f.** it's exhausting; **c'est f. pour le cœur** it strains the heart; **la lumière vive est fatigante pour les yeux** bright light is a strain on the eyes **2** *(agaçant)* tiresome, tedious, annoying; **c'est f., ce bourdonnement incessant** that endless buzzing is very annoying; **ce que tu peux être f.!** you're a real nuisance!; **il est f. avec ses questions** he's tiresome with his questions

> Attention: ne pas confondre **tiring** et **tiresome** lorsqu'on traduit **fatigant**. **Tiring** s'applique à la fatigue physique alors que **tiresome** exprime la lassitude.

fatigue [fatig] NF **1** *(lassitude)* tiredness, weariness; **ressentir une grande/légère f.** to feel very/a bit tired *or* weary; **tomber de f.** to be fit to drop; **je tombe** *ou* **je suis mort de f.** I'm dead on my feet **2** *(tension ▸ physique)* strain; *(▸ nerveuse)* stress; **se remettre de la f.** *ou* **des fatigues de l'examen** to recover from the stress of the exam; **épargner** *ou* **éviter à qn la f. de qch/de faire qch** to save sb the strain *or* effort of sth/of doing sth; **f. intellectuelle** mental strain; **f. musculaire** stiffness; **f. nerveuse** nervous exhaustion; **f. oculaire** eyestrain **3** *Tech* **f. de l'acier** metal fatigue

fatigué, -e [fatige] ADJ **1** *(las ▸ personne)* tired, weary; *(▸ traits, regard, voix)* tired; *(▸ yeux)* strained; **je suis f.** I'm tired; **je suis très f.** I'm exhausted; **je suis si f.!** I'm exhausted *or* so tired!; **f. de rester debout/d'attendre** tired of standing/of waiting; **f. par la promenade** tired from one's walk; **f. par le voyage** travel-worn, travel-weary; *Fig* **f. de qn/qch** tired *or* weary of sb/sth; **être f. de la vie** to be tired *or* weary of life; **f. de faire qch** tired *or* weary of doing sth **2** *(malade ▸ personne)* suffering from fatigue; *(▸ estomac, foie)* upset; *(▸ cœur)* strained **3** *(usé ▸ vêtement)* worn; *(▸ livre)* well-thumbed; **un vieux manteau f.** a shabby old coat

fatiguer [3] [fatige] VT **1** *(épuiser ▸ gén)* to tire *or* to wear out; *(▸ cheval)* to tire; **f. le cœur/les yeux** to strain the heart/the eyes; **les transports en commun me fatiguent beaucoup** using public transport wears me out; *Hum* **si ça ne te fatigue pas trop** if you don't mind

2 *(lasser)* to annoy; **tu me fatigues avec tes critiques!** your constant criticism is getting on my nerves!; **ils nous fatiguent, à la fin, avec leurs publicités!** they're really getting on our nerves with their ads!; **il commence à me f., celui-là!** he's beginning to annoy me!

3 *(user ▸ machine, moteur)* to put a strain on; *(▸ vêtements, chaussures etc)* to wear out; *(▸ champ, sol)* to exhaust, to impoverish; **f. un livre** to give a book a lot of hard wear

4 *Fam (remuer)* **f. la salade** to toss the (green) salad

VI **1** *(peiner)* to grow tired, to flag; **dépêche-toi, je fatigue!** hurry up, I'm getting tired! **2** *Tech (faiblir)* to become weakened; *(forcer)* to bear a heavy strain

VPR **se fatiguer 1** *(s'épuiser ▸ gén)* to get tired; *(▸ en travaillant beaucoup)* to tire oneself out; **les personnes âgées se fatiguent vite** old people tire *or* get tired very easily; **tu ne vas pas te f. à tout nettoyer!** don't tire yourself out cleaning everything!

2 *(faire un effort)* to push oneself; **ils ne se sont pas (trop) fatigués** they didn't exactly kill themselves

3 *(faire des efforts inutiles)* **ne te fatigue pas** don't waste your time; **ne te fatigue pas, je m'en occupe** don't bother, I'll see to it; **c'était bien la peine que je me fatigue!** I don't know why I bothered!; **c'était bien la peine que je me fatigue à préparer le repas** a fat lot of use it was me wearing myself out getting the meal ready; **ne te fatigue pas, je sais tout** don't bother *or* don't waste your breath, I already know everything; **se f. à faire qch** *(s'y appliquer)* to wear oneself out doing sth; **je me fatigue à le lui répéter** I wear myself out telling him/her

4 *(user)* **se f. la vue** *ou* **les yeux** to strain one's eyes

5 se f. de *(se lasser de)* to get tired of; **se f. de qn/qch** to get tired *or* to tire of sb/sth; **se f. de faire qch** to get tired *or* to tire of doing sth; **elle se fatiguera vite de lui** she'll soon get tired of him

fatras [fatra] NM *Péj* **1** *(tas)* clutter, jumble; **tout un f. de vieux papiers** a jumble of old papers **2** *(mélange) Br* hotchpotch, *Am* hodgepodge; **un f. de connaissances** a confused mass of knowledge

fatuité [fatɥite] NF complacency, conceit, smugness

fatwa [fatwa] NF *Rel* fatwa; **prononcer une f. contre qn** to declare *or* issue a fatwa against sb

fauber, faubert [fobɛr] NM *Naut* (deck) swab, mop

faubourg [fobur] NM **1** *(quartier périphérique)* suburb; **accent des faubourgs** (Parisian) working-class accent; **f. industriel/résidentiel** industrial/residential suburb; **les faubourgs de la ville** the outskirts of the city **2** *(quartier de grande ville)* district; **le f. Saint-Antoine** = area in Paris famous for its furniture shops; **le f. Saint-Honoré** = area of Paris well-known for its luxury shops

faubourien, -enne [foburjɛ̃, -ɛn] ADJ suburban; **accent f.** working-class accent

NM,F working-class Parisian

fauchage [foʃaʒ] NM *Agr (du blé, d'un champ de blé)* reaping; *(de l'herbe, d'une prairie)* mowing, cutting; *(avec une faux)* scything

fauchaison [foʃɛzɔ̃] NF *Agr* **1** *(du blé, d'un champ de blé)* reaping; *(de l'herbe, d'une prairie)* mowing, cutting; *(avec une faux)* scything **2** *(saison ▸ gén)* mowing time; *(▸ du blé)* reaping time; *(▸ des prés)* haymaking time

fauchard [foʃar] NM *Agr* double-edged slasher

fauche [foʃ] NF **1** *Fam (vol)* thieving□, (petty) theft□; *(dans un magasin)* shoplifting□; **méfie-toi, il y a de la f. au lycée** watch out, there's a lot of thieving going on at school□ **2** *Vieilli Agr (du blé, d'un champ de blé)* reaping; *(de l'herbe, d'une prairie)* mowing, cutting; *(avec une faux)* scything **3** *Fam (ruine)* **c'est la f.** I'm/he's/*etc* flat broke *or Br* stony broke

fauché, -e [foʃe] ADJ **1** *Fam (sans argent)* broke, *Br* skint, strapped (for cash); **f. comme les blés** flat broke, *Br* stony broke **2** *Agr (blé)* cut; *(herbe)* mown; *(avec une faux)* scythed

NM,F *Fam* penniless individual□; **ce sont tous des fauchés** they haven't got a penny between them

faucher [3] [foʃe] VT **1** *Agr (blé, champ de blé)* to reap; *(herbe, prairie)* to mow, to cut; *(avec une faux)* to scythe

2 *(renverser brutalement ▸ sujet: véhicule)* to knock *or* to mow down; *(▸ sujet: arme)* to mow down; **les cyclistes ont été fauchés par un camion** the cyclists were knocked down by a lorry, a lorry ploughed into the cyclists; **se faire f. par une voiture** to be knocked down by a car; *Sport* **f. son homme** to bring down one's man

3 *(tuer ▸ sujet: guerre, maladie)* to wipe out; **tous ces jeunes artistes fauchés à la fleur de l'âge** all these young artists struck down in the prime of life

4 *Fam (voler)* to pinch, to swipe; **qui a fauché le sel?** who's got the salt?□; **je me suis encore fait f. mon briquet!** my lighter's been pinched again!

VI **1** *(cheval)* to dish **2** *Mil* to sweep the ground (with machine-gun fire)

faucheur, -euse [foʃœr, -øz] NM,F *Agr (personne ▸ qui fauche le blé)* reaper; *(▸ qui fauche les herbes)* mower

NM = **faucheux**

• **faucheuse** NF **1** *Agr* mechanical reaper **2** *Littéraire* **la Faucheuse** the Grim Reaper

faucheux [foʃø] NM *Entom* harvest spider, harvestman, *Am* daddy-long-legs

Fauchon [foʃɔ̃] NM = luxury food shop in Paris

faucille [fosij] NF sickle, reaping hook; **la f. et le marteau** the hammer and sickle

faucon [fokɔ̃] NM **1** *Orn* falcon, hawk; **f. crécerelle** kestrel, *Br* windhover; **f. pèlerin** peregrine falcon; **chasser au f.** to hawk; **chasse au f.** hawking, falconry **2** *Pol* hawk

fauconneau, -x [fokɔno] NM *Orn* young hawk

fauconnerie [fokɔnri] NF **1** *(activité)* hawking **2** *(abri)* hawk-house

fauconnier, -ère [fokɔnje, -ɛr] NM,F falconer

faudra *etc voir* **falloir**

faufil [fofil] NM *Couture* basting *or* tacking thread

faufilage [fofilaʒ] NM *Couture* basting, tacking

faufiler [3] [fofile] VT *Couture* to baste, to tack

VPR **se faufiler** *(se frayer un chemin)* to weave one's way (**dans** *ou* **entre** through); *(s'introduire furtivement)* to slip in (**dans** *ou* **entre** through); **se f. entre les voitures** to weave one's way through the traffic; **le chat s'est faufilé hors du jardin** the cat slipped out of the garden; **les enfants essayaient de se f. au premier rang** the children were trying to sneak up to the front; **il s'était faufilé parmi les invités** he had slipped in *or* sneaked in with the guests

faufilure [fofilyr] NF *Couture* basted *or* tacked seam

faune[1] [fon] NF **1** *Zool* fauna, animal life; **la f. et la flore** flora and fauna, wildlife **2** *Péj (groupe)* mob, bunch, crowd; **la f. prétentieuse des beaux quartiers** the snobbish residents of the fashionable districts; **on rencontre dans ce bar une f. étrange** you meet a strange crowd *or* bunch in this bar

faune[2] [fon] NM *Myth* faun

faunesque [fonesk] ADJ faunlike

faussaire [fosɛr] NMF *(gén)* forger; *(faux-monnayeur)* forger, counterfeiter

fausse [fos] *voir* **faux**[2]

faussement [fosmɑ̃] ADV 1 (à tort) wrongfully 2 (en apparence) falsely, spuriously; d'un air f. ingénu/intéressé with feigned innocence/interest, pretending to look innocent/interested; d'une voix f. inquiète pretending to sound worried; un sourire f. aimable a deceptively pleasant smile; il prit un air f. désinvolte he tried to look casual

fausser [3] [fose] VT 1 (déformer ▸ clef, lame) to bend, to put out of true; (détériorer ▸ serrure) to damage
2 (réalité, résultat, fait) to distort; (comptes) to falsify; f. le sens d'une phrase to distort the meaning of a sentence; faire une présentation qui fausse la réalité to present a distorted vision of reality
3 (jugement, raisonnement) to affect, to distort; (esprit) to warp, to twist
4 (locution) f. compagnie à qn to give sb the slip
VI Can (chanter faux) to sing out of tune or off-key; (jouer faux) to play out of tune or off-key
VPR se fausser 1 (voix d'orateur) to become strained; (voix de chanteur) to lose pitch 2 (clé, serrure, axe etc) to buckle, to bend

fausset[1] [fose] NM Mus falsetto (voice)

fausset[2] [fosɛ] NM Tech (d'un tonneau) spigot, vent peg; trou de f. vent hole

fausseté [foste] NF 1 (inexactitude) falseness, falsity; dénoncer la f. d'une assertion to expose the fallacy of an argument 2 (duplicité) duplicity, treachery; un comportement empreint de f. deceitful behaviour

faustien, -enne [fostjɛ̃, -ɛn] ADJ Faustian

faut voir falloir

faute [fot] NF 1 (erreur) mistake, error; faire une f. to make a mistake; j'ai fait une f. dans ton nom I misspelt your name; cet exercice est rempli de fautes this exercise is full of mistakes; f. d'accord agreement error; f. de conduite driving error; f. de copiste clerical error; f. d'étourderie careless mistake or error; f. de frappe typing error; Ordinat miskey, keying error, typo; commettre une f. de goût to show a lack of taste; f. de français = grammatical mistake or error; f. de grammaire grammatical mistake or error; f. d'impression misprint; f. d'inattention careless mistake or error; f. d'orthographe spelling mistake; f. de prononciation pronunciation mistake; il a fait quelques fautes de prononciation he mispronounced a few words
2 (manquement) misdeed, transgression; f. envers la religion/la morale transgression against religion/morality; commettre une f. to do something wrong, to go wrong; il n'a commis aucune f. he did nothing wrong; il a expié ses fautes he paid dearly for his sins; pour racheter les fautes de l'humanité to redeem mankind; Prov f. avouée est à moitié pardonnée a fault confessed is half redressed
3 (responsabilité) fault; c'est (de) ma/ta/etc f. it's my/your/etc fault; c'est bien sa f. s'il est toujours en retard it's his own fault that he's always late; c'est la f. de ton frère ou Fam à ton frère it's your brother's fault; ce n'est la f. de personne it's nobody's fault, nobody's to blame; Fam à qui la f.?, la f. à qui? (question) who's to blame?, whose fault is it?; (accusation) and whose fault is that?, and who's to blame for that?; Fam ce n'est quand même pas ma f. s'il pleut! it's hardly my fault if it rains!, you can hardly blame me if it rains!; la f. lui en incombe the fault lies with him/her; imputer la f. à qn to lay the blame at sb's door; la f. en revient à l'inflation it's because of inflation, inflation's to blame; Fam c'est la f. à pas de chance it's just bad luck□
4 Admin & Jur offence, misdemeanour; commettre une f. to commit an offence; responsabilité des fautes et négligences du personnel liability for the faults and defaults of the staff; fait ou f. de l'assuré act or fault of the insured; f. par abstention affirmative negligence; f. commise dans l'exercice de fonctions officielles instance of official misconduct; f. contractuelle failure to honour contractual obligations; f. délictuelle technical offence; f. disciplinaire breach of discipline; f. grave serious offence, high misdemeanour; f. intentionnelle deliberate transgression of duty; f. légère minor offence; f. lourde gross negligence; f. partagée contributory negligence; f. professionnelle professional misconduct; f. professionnelle médicale medical malpractice; f. quasi-délictuelle negligence
5 (manque) le courage lui a fait f. his/her courage failed him/her; la main-d'œuvre nous fait f. we're short of labour; et pourtant ce n'est pas l'envie qui lui faisait f. and yet it's not because he/she didn't want to; Littéraire ne pas se faire f. de dire qch to make no bones about saying sth; je ne me suis pas fait f. de lui rappeler sa promesse I didn't fail to remind him/her of his/her promise
6 Vieilli (défaut) faire f. à qn to break one's promise to sb
7 Sport (au tennis) fault; (au football, au baseball etc) foul; commettre une f. sur qn to foul sb; f. de pied foot fault; f. de main handball, handling the ball; faire une f. de main to handle the ball
• **en faute** ADV être en f. to be at fault; prendre qn en f. to catch sb in the act; se sentir en f. to feel that one is at fault or to blame
• **faute de** PRÉP for want of; f. d'argent/de temps for lack or want of money/of time; f. de preuves (relâcher quelqu'un) for lack of evidence; f. d'ordres précis in the absence of definite instructions; Compta f. de provision for lack of funds; il n'a pas réussi, mais ce n'est pas f. d'essayer he failed, but not for want of trying; f. d'un plat plus grand, j'ai posé la tarte sur une assiette I put the pie on a plate because I had no bigger dish; f. de réponse satisfaisante failing a satisfactory reply; f. de paiement sous quinzaine, nous serons dans l'obligation de majorer notre facture de 10 pour cent should payment not be made within fourteen days, we shall be obliged to add a 10 percent surcharge to your bill; f. de mieux for want of anything better; f. de quoi otherwise, failing which; vous devez remplir personnellement l'imprimé, f. de quoi la demande ne sera pas valable you must fill in the form yourself, otherwise or or else the application will be null and void; Prov f. de grives, on mange des merles half a loaf is better than no bread at all, beggars can't be choosers
• **par la faute de** PRÉP because of, owing to; il a été puni par ma f. it's my fault he was punished; j'ai perdu du temps par la f. de cet imbécile I wasted time because of that idiot
• **sans faute** ADJ faultless; un parcours sans f. (dans une course) a perfect race; (dans un concours hippique) a clear round; Fig il a fait ou réussi un parcours sans f. (dans un quiz, à une série d'examens) he got all the answers right; (professionnellement) he has had a remarkable career; (scolairement) he's sailed through school ADV without fail; à demain sans f. see you tomorrow without fail; je le ferai sans f. I'll do it without fail; tu me donneras la clef sans f. be sure and give me the key

> Il faut noter que le nom anglais **fault** signifie également **défaut**.

fauter [3] [fote] VI Euph Hum to sin, to go astray; f. avec qn to be led astray by sb

fauteuil [fotœj] NM 1 (meuble) armchair; f. à bascule rocking chair; f. club club chair; f. de dentiste dentist's chair; f. de jardin garden chair; f. à oreillettes wing chair; f. pivotant swivel chair; f. pliant folding chair; f. roulant wheelchair; f. tournant swivel chair; Fam gagner ou arriver dans un f. to win hands down
2 Théât f. de balcon dress-circle seat; f. d'orchestre seat in Br the stalls or Am the orchestra
3 (présidence) occuper le f. to be in the chair
4 (à l'Académie française) = numbered seat occupied by a member of the "Académie française"

fauteur, -trice [fotœr, -tris] NM,F f. de guerre warmonger; f. de troubles troublemaker

fautif, -ive [fotif, -iv] ADJ 1 (défectueux ▸ liste) incorrect; (▸ citation) inaccurate; mémoire fautive defective memory 2 (coupable) offending, responsible; se sentir f. to feel guilty
NM,F guilty party, culprit; qui est le f.? who's to blame?, who's the culprit?

fautivement [fotivmɑ̃] ADV erroneously, by mistake

fautrice [fotris] voir fauteur

fauve [fov] ADJ 1 (couleur) fawn-coloured, tawny 2 (âpre ▸ odeur) musky 3 Beaux-Arts Fauve, Fauvist
NM 1 Zool big cat; les grands fauves big cats; Fig Hum j'ai envoyé les fauves jouer dans le jardin I sent the monsters out to play in the garden; Fam sentir le f. (personne) to stink; ça sent le f. dans cette pièce this room stinks 2 (couleur) fawn 3 Beaux-Arts Fauve, Fauvist

fauverie [fovri] NF big-cat house

fauvette [fovɛt] NF Orn warbler; f. grisette whitethroat; f. d'hiver hedge sparrow, dunnock; f. des jardins garden warbler; f. des roseaux reed warbler

fauvisme [fovism] NM Beaux-Arts Fauvism

faux[1] [fo] NF 1 Agr scythe; couper de l'herbe à la f. to scythe through grass 2 Anat falx

FAUX[2], FAUSSE [fo, fos]

ADJ
- wrong A1–3
- false A1–3, B1, 2, 5, 6
- faulty A2
- out of tune A4
- imitation B1
- counterfeit B2
- feigned B3
- bogus B4
- deceitful B5

NM
- forgery 1, 2
- falsehood 4

ADV
- out of tune 1

ADJ A. CONTRAIRE À LA VÉRITÉ, À L'EXACTITUDE
1 (mensonger ▸ réponse) wrong; (▸ affirmation) untrue; (▸ prétexte, nouvelle, promesse, témoignage) false; condamné pour f. serment sentenced for perjury; elle m'a donné un f. nom et une fausse adresse she gave me a false name and address; aussi Fig fausse alerte false alarm
2 (inexact ▸ raisonnement) false, faulty; (▸ calcul) wrong; (▸ balance) faulty; Fam t'as tout f. you're completely wrong□; Sport & Fig f. départ false start
3 (non vérifié ▸ argument) false; (▸ impression) mistaken, wrong, false; (▸ espoir) false; tu te fais une fausse idée de lui you've got the wrong idea about him; c'est un f. problème ou débat this is not the issue
4 Mus (piano, voix) out of tune
5 Cin & TV f. raccord jump cut
B. CONTRAIRE AUX APPARENCES 1 (dent, nez, barbe, plafond) false; (bijou, cuir, fourrure, marbre) imitation; f. chignon hairpiece
2 (falsifié ▸ monnaie) false, counterfeit, forged; (▸ carte à jouer) trick (avant n); (▸ papiers, facture) forged, false; (▸ testament) spurious; une fausse pièce (de monnaie) a forged or fake coin; fabriquer de la fausse monnaie to counterfeit money; c'est un f. Renoir it's a fake Renoir; f. bilan fraudulent balance sheet; fausse écriture false entry; fausse facture false bill
3 (feint ▸ candeur, émotion) feigned
4 (pseudo ▸ policier) bogus; (▸ intellectuel) pseudo
5 (hypocrite ▸ caractère, personne) false, deceitful; (▸ regard) deceitful, treacherous; Ling f. ami false friend; f. frère false friend
6 Bot false; f. acacia false acacia
NM 1 Jur (objet, activité) forgery; c'est un f. (document, tableau) it's a fake or a forgery; inculper qn pour f. et usage de f. to prosecute sb for forgery and use of forgeries
2 Compta f. en écritures forgery
3 (imitation) c'est du cuir? – non, c'est du f. is it leather? – no, it's imitation
4 Phil le f. falsehood
ADV 1 Mus (jouer, chanter) out of tune, off-key; sonner f. (excuse) to have a hollow or false ring; il riait d'un rire qui sonnait f. he had a hollow laugh; ça sonne f. it doesn't ring true
2 (locution) porter à f. (cloison) to be out of plumb or true; (objet) to be precariously balanced; (argument, raisonnement) to be unfounded
• **fausse couche** NF Méd miscarriage; faire une fausse couche to have a miscarriage, to miscarry
• **faux jeton** Fam ADJ INV hypocritical□ NMF hypocrite□
• **faux pas** NM 1 (en marchant) faire un f. pas to trip, to stumble 2 (erreur) false move 3 (maladresse) faux pas, gaffe

faux-bourdon [fobuʀdɔ̃] (*pl* **faux-bourdons**) **NM** **1** *Mus* faux-bourdon **2** *Entom* drone

faux-cul [foky] (*pl* **faux-culs**) **ADJ** *très Fam* **il est f.** he's a two-faced bastard

NMF *très Fam* two-faced bastard, *f* two-faced bitch

NM *(vêtement)* bustle

faux-derche [fodɛʀʃ] (*pl* **faux-derches**) **NM** *très Fam* two-faced bastard

faux-facturier [fofaktyʀje] (*pl* **faux-facturiers**) **NM** fake invoice fraudster

faux-filet [fofilɛ] (*pl* **faux-filets**) **NM** *Culin* sirloin

faux-fuyant [fofɥijɑ̃] (*pl* **faux-fuyants**) **NM** **1** *(prétexte)* excuse, subterfuge; **répondre par des faux-fuyants** to give evasive answers; **user de faux-fuyants** to prevaricate; **une réponse claire et nette, sans f.** a straight answer with no hedging *or* without any ifs and buts **2** *Arch (sentier)* bypath

faux-monnayeur [fomɔnɛjœʀ] (*pl* **faux-monnayeurs**) **NM** forger, counterfeiter

faux-semblant [fosɑ̃blɑ̃] (*pl* **faux-semblants**) **NM** pretence, sham; **ne vous laissez pas abuser par des faux-semblants** don't let yourself be taken in by pretence

faux-titre [fotitʀ] (*pl* **faux-titres**) **NM** *Typ* half-title

faveur [favœʀ] **NF** **1** *(plaisir)* favour; **faire une f. à qn** to do sb a favour; **faites-moi une f.** do me a favour; **nous feriez-nous la f. de venir dîner chez nous?** would you do us the honour of coming to have dinner with us?; **nous ferez-vous la f. de votre visite?** will you honour us with a visit?; **elle ne lui fit même pas la f. d'un sourire** she didn't even favour him/her with a smile; **faites-moi la f. de m'écouter quand je parle** would you mind listening when I speak?

2 *(bienveillance)* favour; **par f. spéciale** by special favour; **gagner la f. de qn** to gain sb's favour; **il a la f. du président** he's in the president's good books; **elle a eu la f. de la presse/du public** she found favour with the press/with the public; **être en (grande) f. auprès de qn** to be in (high) favour with sb

3 *(ruban)* ribbon, favour

• **faveurs** **NFPL** favours; *Euph* **accorder/refuser ses faveurs à qn** to give/to refuse sb one's favours; **elle lui a accordé ses faveurs** she obliged him/her with her favours

• **à la faveur de** **PRÉP** owing to, with the help of; **à la f. de la nuit** under cover of darkness

• **de faveur** **ADJ** preferential; **jours de f.** days of grace; **billet de f.** complimentary ticket; **prix de f.** preferential price

• **en faveur** **ADV** **être/ne pas être en f.** to be in/out of favour; **être en f. auprès de qn** to be in favour with sb; **cette mode a été remise en f.** this fashion has come back into vogue

• **en faveur de** **PRÉP** **1** *(à cause de)* on account of **2** *(au profit de)* to the benefit of, in favour of; **en ma/votre f.** in my/your favour; **se décider en f. de qch** to decide in favour of sth; **il a abdiqué en f. de son cousin** he abdicated in favour of his cousin; **quête en f. de qn/qch** collection in aid of sb/sth **3** *(pour)* in favour of; **plaider en f. de qn** to plead in sb's favour

favorable [favɔʀabl] **ADJ** **1** *(propice)* favourable (**à** to), right (**à** for); *(situation, occasion, circonstances)* auspicious; *(vent)* favourable, fair; **arriver au moment f.** to arrive at the right moment; **recevoir un accueil f.** to be given a favourable reception, to be favourably received; **si le temps est f.** weather permitting, if the weather is favourable; **cette île est un lieu f. au repos** this island is an ideal place for resting; **politique f. à la paix** policy that favours peace *or* that is propitious to peace; **peu f.** unfavourable **2** *(bien disposé)* favourable; **se montrer sous un jour f.** to show oneself in a favourable light; **elle a présenté les choses sous un jour f.** she presented things in a favourable light *or* favourably; **préjugé f.** bias; **prêter à qn une oreille f.** to listen favourably to sb; **regarder qch d'un œil f.** to look favourably on sth; **f. à** in favour of; **je suis f. à cette décision/à vos idées** I approve *or* I'm all in favour of this decision/of your ideas; **les taux de change ne vous sont pas favorables** the exchange rates are not in your favour

favorablement [favɔʀabləmɑ̃] **ADV** favourably; **répondre f.** to say yes; **il a répondu f. à mon invitation** he accepted my invitation; **si les choses tournent f.** if things turn out all right

favori, -ite [favɔʀi, -it] **ADJ** *(personne, mélodie, dessert)* favourite; *(idée, projet)* favourite, pet *(avant n)*

NM,F **1** *Sport* favourite; **le grand f.** the odds-on *or* clear favourite **2** *(parmi les enfants)* favourite; **c'est elle la favorite** *(dans la famille)* she's the favourite; *(en classe)* she's the teacher's pet, she's the favourite

NM *Hist* (king's *or* royal) favourite

• **favorite** **NF** *Hist* **la favorite** the King's mistress

• **favoris** **NMPL** **1** *(chez un homme)* sideboards, sideburns **2** *Ordinat (sur l'Internet)* favorites

favorisé, -e [favɔʀize] **ADJ** *(milieu)* fortunate; **les pays les plus favorisés** the most favoured nations; **parmi les classes les plus favorisées de la population** among the most privileged classes of the population

favoriser [3] [favɔʀize] **VT** **1** *(traiter avantageusement)* to favour, to give preferential treatment to; **favorisé par le destin** blessed by fate; *Littéraire* **la nature l'a favorisé de ses dons** nature has favoured him with her gifts; *Littéraire* **f. qn d'un regard** to favour sb with a glance **2** *(être avantageux pour)* to favour, to be to the advantage of; **le partage favorisait traditionnellement l'aîné** traditionally, the distribution of property was to the eldest son's advantage; **le fait qu'elle soit une femme peut la f.** the fact that she's a woman may work in her favour; **les événements l'ont/ne l'ont pas favorisé** events were in his favour *or* on his side/not in his favour *or* against him **3** *(faciliter, encourager)* to further, to promote; **f. les intérêts de la société** to further the interests of the firm; **f. le développement de l'économie** to promote economic development; **f. la fuite de qn** to help sb to escape; **l'obscurité a favorisé sa fuite** the darkness made it easier for him/her to escape; **f. l'élection de qn** to help get sb elected

favorite [favɔʀit] *voir* **favori**

favoritisme [favɔʀitism] **NM** favouritism; **faire du f.** to show favouritism; **on ne fait pas de f. ici** there's no favouritism here

fax [faks] **NM** *Tél* **1** *(machine)* fax (machine); **par f.** by fax; **envoyer qch par f.** to send sth by fax, to fax sth; **numéro de f.** fax number; *Ordinat* **f. modem** fax modem **2** *(message)* fax; **f. sur papier ordinaire** plain paper fax

faxer [3] [fakse] **VT** to fax

fayot [fajo] **NM** *Fam* **1** *(haricot)* bean□ **2** *Péj (personne)* crawler, *Br* creep

fayotage [fajɔtaʒ] **NM** *Fam* crawling, *Br* creeping

fayoter [3] [fajɔte] **VI** *Fam* to crawl, *Br* to creep

FB *Anciennement (abrév écrite* **franc belge**) BF

fco *Com (abrév écrite* **franco**) franco

FCP [ɛfsepe] **NM** *Fin (abrév* **fonds commun de placement**) investment company *or* trust, mutual fund

FCPE [ɛfsepeə] **NM** *Fin (abrév* **fonds commun de placement d'entreprise**) company investment fund

FCPR [ɛfsepeɛʀ] **NM** *Fin (abrév* **fonds commun de placement à risques**) VCT

FDM *(abrév* **fin de mois**) end of month

FDR [ɛfdeɛʀ] **NM** *Fin (abrév* **fonds de roulement**) working capital

féal, -e, -aux, -ales [feal, -o] *Littéraire* **ADJ** faithful, trusty

NM devoted servitor, vassal

fébrifuge [febʀifyʒ] *Pharm* **ADJ** antifebrile, antipyretic, febrifugal

NM antifebrile, antipyretic, febrifuge

fébrile [febʀil] **ADJ** **1** *Méd* febrile; **état f.** feverishness; **un patient f.** a patient who's running a fever **2** *(agité)* feverish, restless; **des préparatifs fébriles** feverish preparations; **le village était f.** the village was in a state of excitement

fébrilement [febʀilmɑ̃] **ADV** **1** *(avec inquiétude)* feverishly **2** *(avec hâte)* hastily

fébrilité [febʀilite] **NF** feverish state, feverishness, *Spéc* febrility, febricity

fécal, -e, -aux, -ales [fekal, -o] **ADJ** faecal; **matières fécales** faeces

fèces [fɛs] **NFPL** **1** *Physiol* faeces **2** *Chim* sediment, precipitate

FECOM [fekɔm] **NM** *Fin & UE (abrév* **Fonds européen de coopération monétaire**) EMCF

fécond, -e [fekɔ̃, -ɔ̃d] **ADJ** **1** *Biol* fecund, fertile **2** *(prolifique ▸ terre)* rich, fertile; *(▸ écrivain, inventeur)* prolific, productive; *(▸ imagination)* lively, powerful; *Littéraire* **une idée féconde** a rich idea; *Littéraire* **puisse votre labeur être f.** may your labour bear much fruit; *Littéraire* **terre féconde en fruits de toute sorte** land rich in every kind of fruit; **une journée féconde en événements** an eventful day

fécondabilité [fekɔ̃dabilite] **NF** *Biol* fertility, *Spéc* fecundability; **taux de f.** fecundability rate

fécondable [fekɔ̃dabl] **ADJ** *Biol* fertilizable

fécondateur, -trice [fekɔ̃datœʀ, -tʀis] *Littéraire* **ADJ** fertilizing

NM fertilizer

fécondation [fekɔ̃dasjɔ̃] **NF** **1** *Biol (d'un mammifère)* impregnation; *(d'un ovipare, d'un ovule)* fertilization; **f. artificielle/in vitro** artificial/in vitro fertilization **2** *Bot* pollination, fertilization; **f. artificielle** artificial pollination

fécondatrice [fekɔ̃datʀis] *voir* **fécondateur**

féconder [3] [fekɔ̃de] **VT** **1** *Biol (mammifère)* to impregnate; *(ovipare, œuf)* to fertilize

2 *Bot* to pollinate, to fertilize

3 *Littéraire (terre, champ)* to make fertile

4 *Littéraire* **f. l'esprit/l'imagination/l'intelligence de qn** to enrich sb's mind/imagination/intelligence

fécondité [fekɔ̃dite] **NF** **1** *Biol* fertility, fecundity **2** *Littéraire (d'une terre, d'un jardin)* fruitfulness **3** *Littéraire (d'un créateur)* fertility

fécule [fekyl] **NF** starch; **f. (de maïs)** *Br* cornflour, *Am* cornstarch; **f. de pomme de terre** potato flour

féculent, -e [fekylɑ̃, -ɑ̃t] **ADJ** *(aliment)* starchy

NM starchy food, starch; **évitez les féculents** avoid starch *or* starchy foods

FED [ɛfəde] **NM** *(abrév* **Fonds européen de développement**) EDF

FEDER [fedɛʀ] **NM** *(abrév* **Fonds européen de développement régional**) ERDF

fédéral, -e, -aux, -ales [federal, -o] **ADJ** **1** *Pol* federal **2** *Suisse* federal *(relative to the Swiss Confederation)*

• **fédéraux** **NMPL** **1** *Hist* Federalist troops **2** **les fédéraux** *(le FBI)* the Feds

fédéraliser [3] [federalize] **VT** to federalize, to turn into a federation

fédéralisme [federalism] **NM** *Pol* federalism

fédéraliste [federalist] **ADJ** federalist, federalistic

NMF federalist, federal

fédérateur, -trice [federatœʀ, -tʀis] **ADJ** federative, federating; **élément/principe f.** unifying element/principle

NM,F unifier

fédératif, -ive [federatif, -iv] **ADJ** federative

fédération [federasjɔ̃] **NF** **1** *Pol (gén)* federation; *(au Canada)* confederation; **F. croato-musulmane** Bosnia-Herzegovina Federation, Muslim-Croat Federation; **la F. de Russie** the Federation of Russia **2** *(groupe)* federation; **F. française de rugby** = French rugby federation; **F. internationale de football association** FIFA; **f. syndicale** trade union; **F. syndicale mondiale** World Federation of Trade Unions; **f. de syndicats (ouvriers)** amalgamated (trade) unions; **f. sportive** sports federation

fédérative [federativ] *voir* **fédératif**

fédératrice [federatʀis] *voir* **fédérateur**

fédéraux [federo] *voir* **fédéral**

fédéré, -e [federe] **ADJ** federated, federate

NM *Hist* federate

fédérer [18] [federe] **VT** to federate, to form into a federation

VPR **se fédérer** to federate

fée [fe] **NF** fairy; **sa bonne f.** his/her good fairy, his/her fairy godmother; **la f. Carabosse** the wicked fairy; **pays des fées** fairyland; *Hum* **c'est une véritable f. du logis** she's a wonderful housewife; *Suisse* **f. verte** absinthe

feed-back [fidbak] NM INV *Tech & Physiol* feedback

feeder [fidœr] NM **1** *Élec* feeder (cable) **2** *(de gaz)* (gas) pipeline

feeling [filiŋ] NM **1** *Mus* feeling **2** *Fam* **y aller** *ou* **faire qch au f.** to do sth by intuition□ *or* by gut feeling; **tout s'est passé** *ou* **s'est fait au f.** I/we/*etc* completely played it by ear; **je crois que ça va marcher, j'ai un bon f.** I think it's going to work, I have a good feeling about it

féerie [fe(e)ri] NF **1** *Théât* spectacular **2** *(merveille)* enchantment; **le feu d'artifice était une f. de lumières** the firework display was pure enchantment; **une f. de couleurs** a riot of colour **3** *Vieilli (pouvoir des fées)* (power of) enchantment; *(monde des fées)* fairyland

féerique [fe(e)rik] ADJ **1** *Myth* fairy *(avant n)*, magic, magical **2** *(beau ▸ vue, spectacle)* enchanting, magical

FEI [ɛfəi] NM *(abrév* **Fonds européen d'investissement***)* EIF

feignait *etc voir* **feindre**

feignant, -e [fɛɲɑ̃, -ɑ̃t] *Fam* ADJ lazy□, idle
NM,F loafer, layabout

feignasse [fɛɲas] NF *Fam* lazy so-and-so, lazybones

feignasser [3] [fɛɲase] VI *Fam* to lounge *or* to laze around

feindre [81] [fɛ̃dr] VT to feign; **sa colère n'était pas feinte** he/she wasn't pretending to be angry, his/her anger wasn't feigned *or* was quite genuine
VI *Littéraire (dissimuler)* to pretend, to dissemble; **inutile de f.** it's no use pretending; **f. de faire qch** to pretend to do sth, to make a pretence of doing sth; **elle feint de s'intéresser à cette histoire** she pretends she's interested in this story

feint, -e [fɛ̃, fɛ̃t] ADJ **1** *(simulé ▸ maladie, joie)* feigned, assumed, sham **2** *Archit (porte, fenêtre)* blind, dummy
• **feinte** NF **1** *(ruse)* ruse **2** *Littéraire (dissimulation)* dissembling *(UNCOUNT)*, dissimulation, pretence; **sans f.** frankly, without pretence **3** *Sport (en boxe, en escrime)* feint; *(au football, au rugby) Br* dummy, *Am* fake; **faire une f. (de passe)** to (sell a) dummy; **il a trompé l'arrière par une f.** *Br* he sold the full back a dummy, *Am* he faked out the full back

feinter [3] [fɛ̃te] VT **1** *Sport* **f. l'adversaire** *(à la boxe, à l'escrime)* to feint at the opponent; **f. la passe** *(au football, au rugby) Br* to sell a dummy, *Am* to fake a pass **2** *Fam (duper)* to fool, to take in; **il t'a bien feinté!** he really took you in!; **feinté!** foiled again!
USAGE ABSOLU **f. du gauche** *(en boxe)* to feint *or* to make a feint with the left
VI *Fam* to fake

feldspath [fɛldspat] NM *Minér* feldspar

fêlé, -e [fele] ADJ **1** *(verre, porcelaine, os)* cracked **2** *(voix, son)* hoarse, cracked **3** *Fam (fou)* nuts, crackers, cracked; **il est complètement f.!, il a le cerveau f.!** he's completely nuts!
NM,F *Fam* nut, loony; **tous des fêlés!** they're all nuts!

fêler [4] [fele] VT to crack; *Fig Littéraire* **une amitié que jamais rien ne fêla** an undying friendship
VPR **se fêler** *(tasse, glace)* to crack; **se f. une côte** to fracture *or* to crack a rib

félicitations [felisitasjɔ̃] NFPL congratulation, congratulations; **(toutes mes) f.!** congratulations!; **adresser** *ou* **faire ses f. à qn (pour qch)** to congratulate sb (on sth); **recevoir les f. de qn pour qch** to be congratulated by sb on sth; *Univ* **avec les f. du jury** with the examining board's utmost praise, summa cum laude

félicité [felisite] NF *Littéraire* bliss, felicity

féliciter [3] [felisite] VT to congratulate; **f. qn de qch** to congratulate sb on sth; **f. qn d'avoir fait qch** to congratulate sb on having done sth; **je l'ai félicité d'avoir réussi son examen** I congratulated him on having passed his exam; **permettez-moi de vous f.!** congratulations!; **je ne vous félicite pas!** you'll get no thanks from me!
VPR **se féliciter 1 se f. de qch/d'avoir fait qch** *(se réjouir de)* to be glad *or* pleased about sth/to have done sth; **tous se félicitaient de sa réussite** they were all pleased about his/her success *or* (that) he/she succeeded **2 se f. de qch/d'avoir fait qch** *(se louer de)* to congratulate oneself on sth/on having done sth; **je me félicite d'être resté calme** I'm pleased to say I remained calm

félidé [felide] NM *Zool* feline **les félidés** the cat family, *Spéc* the Felidae

félidés NMPL cat family, *Spéc* Felidae

félin, -e [felɛ̃, -in] ADJ **1** *Zool* feline **2** *(regard, démarche, souplesse)* feline, catlike
NM **1** *(animal)* cat; **les félins** the cat family; **grand f.** big cat **2** *Bourse* stripped bond

fellah [fela] NM fellah

fellation [felasjɔ̃] NF fellatio, fellation; **faire une f. à qn** to perform fellatio on sb

félon, -onne [felɔ̃, -ɔn] ADJ **1** *Littéraire (perfide)* disloyal, treacherous, felonious **2** *Hist* rebellious
NM **1** *Littéraire (traître)* traitor **2** *Hist* felon

félonie [felɔni] NF **1** *Littéraire (traîtrise)* disloyalty, treachery; *(acte)* act of treachery **2** *Hist* felony

félonne [felɔn] *voir* **félon**

felouque [fəluk] NF *Naut* felucca

fêlure [felyr] NF **1** *(d'un objet)* crack; **la surface de la jarre était couverte de mille petites fêlures** the surface of the jar was covered with a fine network of cracks; *Fig* **il y a une f. dans leur amitié** cracks are beginning to show in their friendship **2** *(de la voix)* crack **3** *Méd* fracture

femelle [fəmɛl] ADJ **1** *Zool* female; *(éléphant, baleine)* cow *(avant n)*; *Orn* hen *(avant n)* **2** *Bot & Élec* female; **une prise f.** a socket
NF **1** *Zool* female **2** *très Fam Péj (femme)* female

féminin, -e [feminɛ̃, -in] ADJ **1** *Biol (hormone)* female; **la morphologie féminine** the female body; **le sexe f.** the female sex
2 *(composé de femmes ▸ population)* female; **notre main-d'œuvre féminine** our female workers; **l'équipe féminine** the women's team; **les conquêtes féminines d'un homme** a man's female conquests
3 *(typique de la femme ▸ personne, charme)* feminine; **une réaction typiquement féminine** a typical female reaction; **elle est très féminine** she's very feminine; **il avait une voix féminine** he had a woman's voice
4 *(qui a rapport à la femme ▸ magazine, presse)* women's; **mode féminine** women's fashions; **revendications féminines** women's demands
5 *Gram & Littérature (nom, rime)* feminine
NM **1** *Gram* feminine (gender); **ce mot est du f.** this word is feminine; **au f.** in the feminine **2** *voir* **éternel**

> Attention: ne pas confondre **female** et **feminine** lorsque l'on traduit **féminin**. On utilise **feminine** pour décrire les qualités que la société associe traditionnellement aux femmes, alors que **female** s'utilise pour qualifier ce qui est propre au sexe féminin.

féminisant, -e [feminizɑ̃, -ɑ̃t] ADJ *Biol* feminizing

féminisation [feminizasjɔ̃] NF **1** *Biol* feminization, feminizing *(UNCOUNT)* **2** *(augmentation du nombre de femmes)* **la f. d'une profession/d'un milieu** increased female participation in a profession/in a group; **depuis la f. de la profession** since women have entered the profession

> **LA FÉMINISATION DES NOMS**
>
> The feminization of nouns for professions, positions, ranks and titles has been official in France since March 1986. It is therefore perfectly correct to add the feminine ending, or use a feminine article, and refer to "une professeure", "une ambassadrice", "madame la ministre" etc. However, despite government recommendations and the publication of a guide by the "Institut national de la langue française", these new feminine forms are not in widespread use although they have been adopted more readily in Quebec, Switzerland and Belgium than in France.

féminiser [3] [feminize] VT **1** *Biol* to feminize **2** *Gram (mot)* to put into the feminine gender **3** *(homme)* to make effeminate **4** *(augmenter le nombre de femmes dans)* **f. une profession** to bring *or* to introduce more women into a profession; **il faut f. ces professions** more women must be encouraged to enter those professions; **profession très féminisée** largely female profession, female-dominated profession
VPR **se féminiser 1** *Biol* to feminize **2** *(femme)* to become more feminine; *(homme)* to become effeminate **3** *(métier, profession)* **notre profession se féminise** more and more women are entering our profession

féminisme [feminism] NM **1** *(mouvement)* feminism **2** *Biol* feminization

féministe [feminist] ADJ feminist
NMF feminist

féminité [feminite] NF femininity

femme [fam] NF **1** *(personne)* woman; **veste de** *ou* **pour f.** lady's jacket; **elle n'est pas f. à se plaindre** she's not the sort (of woman) to complain; *Fam* **une bonne f.** a woman; *Péj* **une vieille bonne f.** a little old woman; **contes/remèdes de bonne f.** old wives' tales/remedies; **f. d'affaires** businesswoman; **f. auteur** woman author, authoress; **f. de chambre** *(dans un hôtel)* chambermaid; *(chez des particuliers)* maid, housemaid; *(attachée au service d'une dame)* (lady's) maid, (personal) maid; **f. de charge** housekeeper; **f. député** *(en France)* (female) deputy; *(en Grande-Bretagne)* (woman) MP; *(aux États-Unis)* Congresswoman; **f. écrivain** woman writer; **f. fatale** femme fatale; **f. ingénieur** woman engineer; **une f. de mauvaise vie** a scarlet *or* loose woman; **f. médecin** woman *or* lady doctor; **f. de ménage** cleaning lady, *Am* maid; **f. ministre** female minister; **f. du monde** socialite; **f. de petite vertu** woman of easy virtue; **f. policier** policewoman, *Br* WPC; **f. politique** (female) politician; **f. de service** cleaner, *Br* charwoman; **f. soldat** woman soldier
2 *(adulte)* **c'est une f. maintenant** she's a woman now; **à treize ans elle fait déjà très f.** at thirteen she already looks very much a woman; **elle devient f.** she's growing up, she's becoming a woman
3 *(ensemble de personnes)* **la f., les femmes** woman, women, womankind; **la libération/les droits de la f.** women's liberation/rights
4 *(épouse)* wife; **prendre qn pour f.** to take sb as one's wife; **prendre f.** to take a wife; *Jur* **la f. Dupont** the wife of Dupont
5 *(comme adj) (féminine)* **être très f.** to be very feminine; **je me sens très f.** I feel very much a woman *or* very womanly; **être très f. du monde** to be a wonderful hostess

femmelette [famlɛt] NF **1** *Péj (homme)* sissy, wimp, drip; **pas de femmelettes chez nous!** we don't want any sissies around here! **2** *(femme)* weak *or* frail woman

femme-objet [famɔbʒɛ] *(pl* **femmes-objets***)* NF = woman seen or treated as an object

fémoral, -e, -aux, -ales [femɔral, -o] ADJ thigh *(avant n)*, *Spéc* femoral

fémur [femyr] NM *Anat* thigh bone, *Spéc* femur

FEN [fɛn] NF *(abrév* **Fédération de l'Éducation nationale***)* = teachers' trade union, *Br* ≃ NUT

fenaison [fənɛzɔ̃] NF **1** *(récolte)* haymaking; *(époque)* haymaking time **2** *(fanage)* tedding, tossing

fendage [fɑ̃daʒ] NM *(du bois)* chopping; *(de l'ardoise)* splitting

fendant[1] [fɑ̃dɑ̃] NM **1** *Escrime* sword thrust **2** *Suisse (raisin)* = chasselas grape variety **3** *Suisse (vin)* = white wine from the Valais canton made from the fendant grape variety

fendant[2]**, -e** [fɑ̃dɑ̃, -ɑ̃t] ADJ *Fam* hilarious, side-splitting

fendard[1] [fɑ̃dar] ADJ *Fam (amusant)* hysterical, side-splitting

fendard[2]**, fendart** [fɑ̃dar] NM *Fam Vieilli (pantalon) Br* trousers□, keks, *Am* pants□

fendeur [fɑ̃dœr] NM = worker specializing in splitting slates or wood

fendillé, -e [fɑ̃dije] ADJ *(miroir, peau, tableau, mur)* cracked; *(poterie, vernis, verre, émail)* crazed, crackled; (bois) split; avoir les lèvres fendillées to have chapped lips

fendillement [fɑ̃dijmɑ̃] NM (d'un miroir, de la peau, d'un mur, d'un tableau) cracking; (du verre, de l'émail, du vernis, de la poterie) crazing, crackling; (du bois) splitting, springing

fendiller [3] [fɑ̃dije] VT (miroir, mur, tableau, peau) to crack; (bois) to split; (émail, verre, vernis, poterie) to craze, to crackle

VPR se fendiller (miroir, mur, tableau, peau) to crack; (bois) to split; (verre, poterie, émail, vernis) to craze, to crackle

fendre [73] [fɑ̃dr] VT 1 (couper ▸ bois, roche, diamant) to split, to cleave; (▸ lèvre) to cut or to split (open); f. une bûche en deux to split or to chop a log down the middle; f. le crâne/la lèvre à qn to split sb's skull/lip (open); ça vous fend ou c'est à vous f. l'âme ou le cœur it breaks your heart, it's heartbreaking, it's heartrending; la vue de cet enfant abandonné lui fendit le cœur the sight of the abandoned child broke his/her heart or made his/her heart bleed

2 (fissurer ▸ terre, sol, mur, plâtre) to crack

3 Couture (veste, jupe, robe) to make a slit in

4 (traverser ▸ foule) to push or to force one's way through; Littéraire ou Hum f. les flots/l'air/le vent to cleave through the seas/the air/the breeze

VPR se fendre 1 (s'ouvrir ▸ bois) to split; (▸ terre, sol, mur) to crack

2 Fam (se ruiner) tu ne t'es pas trop fendu! this really didn't ruin or break you, did it!; se f. de 100 euros to fork out or to shell out 100 euros; il s'est fendu d'une bouteille de vin he forked out or shelled out for a bottle of wine

3 Fam (se fatiguer) to wear or to tire oneself out; tu ne t'es pas fendu! you didn't exactly strain yourself!

4 Escrime to lunge

5 (partie du corps) se f. le crâne to crack one's skull (open); elle s'est fendu la lèvre she cut her lip (open); Fam se f. la pêche ou la pipe ou la poire ou la gueule (rire) to split one's sides; (s'amuser) to have a ball

fendu, -e [fɑ̃dy] ADJ (robe, jupe) slit; (yeux) almond-shaped; (crâne, lèvre) split; (assiette) cracked; (sabot) cloven; une bouche fendue ou un sourire f. jusqu'aux oreilles a broad grin or smile; des yeux fendus en amande almond-shaped eyes; né avec le palais f. born with a cleft palate; vis à tête fendue slotted screw

fenestrage [fənɛstraʒ] NM 1 Archit fenestration 2 Ordinat windowing

fenêtre [fənɛtr] NF 1 Constr window; ouvrir/fermer la f. to open/to close the window; regarder par la f. to look out of the window; sauter par la f. to jump out of the window; Fig ouvrir une f. sur to open a window on; Fig une f. sur le monde/l'actualité a window on the world/on current events; f. croisée ou à battants casement window; f. à coulisse sliding window; f. à guillotine sash window; f. mansardée dormer window; f. en saillie bay window; f. à tabatière skylight; une place côté couloir ou côté f.? an aisle or a window seat?

2 Anat fenestra; f. ovale/ronde fenestra ovalis/rotunda

3 Ordinat window; f. activée active window; f. d'aide help window; f. déroulante pull-down window; f. de dialogue dialog(ue) window; f. d'édition editing or edit window; f. flottante floating window; f. graphique graphics window; f. de lecture-écriture read-write slot; f. de saisie text box

4 TV f. d'observation observation window

5 (espace blanc) space, blank

6 (d'une enveloppe) window

7 Astron f. atmosphérique weather window; f. de lancement (launch) window

fenêtrer [3] [fənetre] VT 1 (bâtiment) to put windows in 2 Méd (bandage) to fenestrate

fenil [fənil] NM hayloft

fennec [fenɛk] NM fennec

fenouil [fənuj] NM fennel

fente [fɑ̃t] NF 1 (fissure ▸ dans du bois) cleft, split; (▸ dans un sol, un mur) crack, fissure; (▸ dans une roche) cleft 2 (ouverture ▸ d'une jupe, d'une poche, des volets) slit; (▸ dans une boîte, sur une vis) slot; (▸ dans une veste) vent; (▸ pour passer les bras) armhole 3 Escrime lunge

fenugrec [fənygrɛk] NM Bot & Culin fenugreek

féodal, -e, -aux, -ales [feɔdal, -o] ADJ feudal

NM (propriétaire) landlord; (seigneur) feudal lord

féodalisme [feɔdalism] NM feudalism

féodalité [feɔdalite] NF 1 (système) feudal system 2 Péj (puissance) feudal power

fer [fɛr] NM 1 Chim iron (UNCOUNT)

2 Métal iron (UNCOUNT); f. doux soft iron; f. forgé wrought iron

3 (dans les aliments) iron (UNCOUNT)

4 (barre) (iron) bar

5 (partie métallique ▸ d'une hache, d'une flèche) head; (▸ d'une pelle) blade; (▸ d'un lacet) tag; (lame) blade; aussi Fig f. de lance spearhead; le f. de lance de l'industrie française the flagship of French industry; tourner ou retourner le f. dans la plaie to twist the knife in the wound

6 (pour repassage) f. à repasser iron; f. à vapeur steam iron; f. électrique (electric) iron; donner un coup de f. à qch to iron or to press sth; passer un coup de f. sur un pantalon to give a pair of trousers a quick iron

7 (instrument) f. à friser curling Br tongs or Am iron; f. à marquer brand, branding iron; f. rouge brand; f. à souder soldering iron

8 (de chaussure) metal tip

9 (pour cheval) (horse) shoe; mettre un f. à un cheval to shoe a horse; perdre un f. to cast a shoe

10 (de golf) iron; grand f. driving iron; f. droit putter; un f. 6 a (number) 6 iron

11 Rail le f. rail, the railway system, the railways; acheminer/transporter par f. to take/to carry by rail

12 Littéraire (épée) blade; par le f. et par le feu by force of arms

• **fers** NMPL (chaînes) irons, shackles; mettre qn aux fers to put sb in irons; Fig briser ses fers to throw off one's chains

• **de fer** ADJ (moral, santé) cast-iron (avant n); (discipline, volonté) iron (avant n); homme de f. man of iron or steel

• **fer à cheval** NM horseshoe; en f. à cheval (escalier, table) horseshoe-shaped, horseshoe (avant n)

fera etc voir faire

fer-blanc [fɛrblɑ̃] (pl fers-blancs) NM tin, tinplate

• **en fer-blanc** ADJ tin (avant n); boîte en f. (tin) can

ferblanterie [fɛrblɑ̃tri] NF 1 (manufacture) tinplate making; (industrie) tinplate industry; (commerce) tinplate trade

2 (objets) tinware

3 (boutique) hardware store, Br ironmonger's (shop)

4 Péj (décorations) medals; ils ont sorti toute leur f. they had all their medals on display

ferblantier [fɛrblɑ̃tje] NM 1 (ouvrier) tinsmith 2 (marchand) hardware dealer, Br ironmonger

feria [ferja] NF fair (yearly, in Spain and southern France)

férié, -e [ferje] ADJ c'est un jour f. it's a (public) holiday; on ne travaille pas les jours fériés we don't work on holidays; demain, c'est f. tomorrow's a (public) holiday

férir [ferir] VT (à l'infinitif seulement) Littéraire sans coup f. without any problem or difficulty; conquérir une région sans coup f. to conquer a region without bloodshed

ferler [3] [fɛrle] VT (voile) to furl

fermage [fɛrmaʒ] NM 1 (location) tenant farming 2 (redevance) farm rent

fermail, -aux [fɛrmaj, -o] NM Arch (ornamental) clasp

ferme¹ [fɛrm] NF 1 (maison) farmhouse; (bâtiments) farm buildings; (exploitation) farm; f. d'élevage cattle farm; produits de la f. farm produce

2 Jur prendre à f. to rent, to farm; donner à f. to let; bail à f. farm lease

3 Archit truss

4 Théât set piece

5 Hist (de taxes) farming (out)

ferme² [fɛrm] ADJ 1 (dur ▸ sol) solid, firm; (▸ corps, chair, fruit, beurre, muscle) firm; (▸ pâte) stiff; une viande un peu trop f. slightly tough meat

2 (stable) être f. sur ses jambes to stand steady on one's legs or firm on one's feet

3 (décidé ▸ ton, pas) firm, steady; ..., dit-elle d'une voix f. ..., she said firmly

4 (inébranlable ▸ volonté, décision) firm; (▸ réponse) definite; des prix fermes et définitifs firm or definite prices; il est resté f. sur le prix he refused to bring the price down; il faut être f. avec elle you must be firm with her

5 Écon steady, firm; le dollar est resté f. the dollar stayed firm

6 Com (achat, vente) firm; prendre un engagement f. to enter into a firm undertaking; vente/offre f. firm sale/offer

ADV 1 (solidement) tenir f. (clou) to hold; (personne, troupe) to stand firm, to hold on

2 (beaucoup ▸ travailler) hard; batailler f. to fight hard; il boit f. he's a heavy or a hard drinker

3 (avec passion ▸ discuter) with passion, passionately

4 Com acheter/vendre f. to buy/to sell firm

fermé, -e [fɛrme] ADJ 1 (passage) closed, blocked; col f. (panneau sur la route) pass closed to traffic

2 (porte, récipient) closed, shut; (à clef) locked; une porte fermée a closed door; j'ai laissé la porte à demi fermée I left the door ajar or half-open; f. à clef locked; f. à double tour double-locked

3 (radiateur, robinet) off; Élec (circuit) closed

4 (bouche, œil) shut, closed (up); dormir la bouche fermée to sleep with one's mouth shut; Fig c'est un très bon vin, tu peux y aller les yeux fermés it's a very good wine, you needn't have any qualms about buying it; je pourrais y aller les yeux fermés I could get there blindfolded or with my eyes closed

5 (magasin, bureau, restaurant) closed; vous restez f. pendant Noël? will you be staying closed over Christmas?; f. le lundi closed on Mondays, closing day Monday

6 (méfiant ▸ visage) inscrutable, impenetrable; (▸ regard) impenetrable; une personnalité fermée a secretive or an uncommunicative personality; être f. à qch to have no feeling for or no appreciation of sth

7 (exclusif ▸ milieu, ambiance) exclusive, select

8 (syllabe, voyelle) closed

fermement [fɛrməmɑ̃] ADV 1 (avec force) firmly, solidly, steadily 2 (résolument) firmly, strongly

ferment [fɛrmɑ̃] NM 1 Chim ferment, leaven (UNCOUNT); ferments lactiques = bacilli used in making yoghurt 2 Littéraire (facteur) leur présence est un f. de haine their presence stirs up hatred

fermentation [fɛrmɑ̃tasjɔ̃] NF 1 Chim fermentation, fermenting 2 Littéraire (agitation) fermentation, commotion, unrest

• **en fermentation** ADJ (raisin) fermenting

fermentative [fɛrmɑ̃tativ] voir fermentatif

fermenter [3] [fɛrmɑ̃te] VI 1 Chim to ferment; (pâte) to rise 2 Littéraire (sentiment) to be stirred; (esprit) to be in a ferment

FERMER [3] [fɛrme]

VT	
• to close 1, 2, 5, 6, 10, 11	• to shut 1, 2
• to block 4	• to turn off 3
	• to close down 6
VI	
• to close 1–3	• to close down 2
VPR	
• to fasten 1	• to close 2, 3

VT 1 (yeux, sac, valise, bocal, livre, parapluie) to shut, to close; (poing, doigts) to close; (enveloppe) to seal, to shut, to close; (éventail) to fold, to close; (col, jupe) to fasten, to do up; fermez vos cahiers close your exercise books; f. les rideaux to draw the curtains (together), to pull the curtains shut; ferme le tiroir shut the drawer; f. les yeux to close or to shut one's eyes; f. les yeux sur qch to turn a blind eye to sth; je n'ai pas fermé l'œil de la nuit I didn't get a wink (of sleep) all night; manger la bouche fermée to eat with one's mouth closed or shut; Fam f. sa bouche ou son bec to shut up, to shut one's trap; très Fam je le savais mais je l'ai fermée I knew it but I didn't let on; très Fam la ferme! shut up!, shut your face!

2 (porte, fenêtre) to close, to shut; f. une porte à

clef to lock a door; **f. une porte au verrou** to bolt a door; **f. une porte à double tour** to double-lock a door; **il a fermé la porte d'un coup de pied** he kicked the door shut; **il a fermé la porte d'un coup d'épaule** *(doucement)* he nudged the door shut with his shoulder; *(durement)* he banged the door shut with his shoulder; **f. violemment la porte** to slam *or* to bang the door (shut); *Fig* **f. la porte à qch** to close the door on sth; **f. ses portes** *(boutique, musée)* to shut, to close; **f. une maison** to shut up a house

3 *(éteindre ▸ électricité, lumière, compteur)* to turn *or* to switch off; *(▸ robinet)* to turn off; *Fam* **f. l'eau dans une maison** to turn the water off (at the mains) in a house; **f. le gaz** to turn off the gas; *Fam* **ferme la télé** switch the TV off[□]; *Élec* **f. un circuit** to close a circuit; *Can* **f. la ligne** *(raccrocher le téléphone)* to hang up

4 *(rendre inaccessible ▸ rue, voie)* to block, to bar, to obstruct; *Rail* **f. la voie** to close (off) the line

5 *(interdire ▸ frontière, port)* to close; **f. l'entrée d'un port** to close a harbour; **f. son pays aux réfugiés politiques** to close one's borders to political refugees; **cette filière vous fermerait toutes les carrières scientifiques** this course would prevent you from following any scientific career

6 *(faire cesser l'activité de)* to close; **f. un restaurant/théâtre** *(pour un congé)* to close a restaurant/theatre; *(définitivement)* to close a restaurant/theatre (down); **ne fermez pas notre école!** don't close our school (down)!; **la police a fait f. l'établissement** the police had the place closed down; **f. boutique** *(pour un congé)* to shut up shop; *(pour cause de faillite)* to stop *or* to cease trading, to close down; *Fig* to give up

7 *(rendre insensible)* **f. son âme à qch** to harden one's heart to sth; **f. son cœur à qn** to harden one's heart to sb; **f. son esprit à qch** to close one's mind to sth; **c'est elle qui m'a fermée aux études** she's the one who turned *or* put me off studying

8 *(être à la fin de)* **f. la marche** to be at the back of the procession; **f. le bal** to be the last to leave the ball

9 *(délimiter)* **les montagnes qui ferment l'horizon/ferment la vue** the mountains which shut off the horizon/block the view

10 *Banque & Fin (compte, portefeuille d'actions)* to close

11 *Ordinat (fichier, fenêtre)* to close; *(commande)* to end

USAGE ABSOLU on ferme! closing now!

VI 1 *(se verrouiller ▸ couvercle, fenêtre, porte)* to close; **le couvercle ferme mal** the lid doesn't shut *or* close properly; **le portail ferme mal** the gate is difficult to close *or* won't close properly; **le radiateur ferme mal** the radiator won't turn off properly

2 *(cesser son activité ▸ temporairement)* to close; *(▸ pour toujours)* to close down; **le musée/parc va f.** the museum/park will soon close; **la banque ferme le samedi** the bank closes Saturdays *or* is closed on Saturdays; **les usines ferment** factories are closing down

3 *Bourse (actions)* to close; **les actions ont fermé à 4,50 euros** shares closed at 4.50 euros

VPR se fermer 1 *(être attaché ▸ col, robe, veste)* to fasten, to do up

2 *(être verrouillé ▸ porte, fenêtre)* to close; *Fig* **les frontières se fermaient devant lui** countries were closing their borders to him; **les sociétés occidentales se ferment à l'immigration** Western societies are closing their doors to immigrants; **son cœur s'est fermé à la pitié** he/she has become impervious to pity

3 *(se serrer, se plier ▸ bras, fleur, huître, main)* to close (up); *(▸ aile)* to fold; *(▸ bouche, œil, paupière, livre, rideau)* to close; *(▸ blessure)* to close (up), to heal; **mes yeux se ferment tout seuls** I can't keep my eyes open

4 *(être impénétrable)* **à cette demande son visage se ferma** at this request his/her face froze; **tu te fermes toujours quand on te parle de tes parents** you always clam up when people talk to you about your parents

5 *TV & Cin* **se f. en fondu** to fade out

---

fermeté [fɛrməte] **NF 1** *(solidité ▸ d'un objet)* solidness, firmness; *(▸ d'une pâte)* stiffness; *(▸ d'un corps)* firmness

2 *(assurance ▸ d'un geste)* assurance, steadiness; *(▸ d'une voix)* firmness

3 *(autorité)* firmness; **faire preuve de f. à l'égard de qn** to be firm with sb; **avec f.** firmly, resolutely, steadfastly; **sans f.** irresolutely, waveringly; **le gouvernement agit sans f. aucune** the government is acting without any determination whatsoever

4 *Bourse* steadiness

fermette [fɛrmɛt] **NF 1** *(habitation)* small farm *or* farmhouse **2** *Constr* small truss

fermeture [fɛrmətyr] **NF 1** *(obstruction ▸ de route, de frontière)* closing; **après la f. du puits/tunnel** once the well/tunnel is blocked off; **la f. du coffre se fera devant témoins** the safe will be locked *or* sealed in the presence of witnesses; *Élec* **f. du circuit** closing of the circuit

2 *(rabattement)* closing; **ne pas gêner la f. des portes** *(dans le métro)* please do not obstruct the doors; **f. automatique des portières** *(dans le train)* doors close *or* shut automatically; *Aut* remote control locking; *Aut* **f. centralisée** central locking

3 *Com (d'un magasin, d'une entreprise ▸ définitive)* closure, closing-down, *Am* closing-out; **les plus belles affaires se font à la f.** you find the best bargains just before closing time *or* before the shop closes; **au moment de la f.** *(du bureau)* at the end of the day's work; *(de la banque, du magasin, du café)* at closing time; **il venait me chercher à la f. du bureau** he came to pick me up after work; **f. annuelle** *(d'un magasin)* closed for annual holiday; **f. définitive** closedown; **jour de f.** *(hebdomadaire)* closing day; *(férié)* public holiday

4 *Fin* closing; **pour faciliter la f. d'un compte courant** to make it easier to close a current account

5 *(fin ▸ d'une session, d'un festival)* close, closing; *Bourse* **à la f.** at the close of trading

6 *(dispositif)* **f. Éclair®** *ou* **à glissière** *Br* zip, *Am* zipper; **f. à rouleau** *(d'un magasin)* revolving shutter

7 *Ordinat (de fichier, de fenêtre)* closing; *(de commande)* ending; *(d'un ordinateur)* shutdown

8 *TV & Cin* fade; **f. en fondu** fade-out; **f. au noir** fade-out, fade-to-black

fermier, -ère [fɛrmje, -ɛr] **ADJ 1** *Écon (compagnie, société)* farm *(avant n)* **2** *Com* **poulet/œuf f.** free-range chicken/egg; **lait/beurre f.** dairy milk/butter

NM 1 *Agr (locataire)* tenant farmer; *(propriétaire, agriculteur)* farmer **2** *Hist* **f. général** farmer general

• **fermière NF 1** *(épouse)* farmer's wife **2** *(cultivatrice)* woman farmer

fermoir [fɛrmwar] **NM** *(de collier, de sac)* clasp, fastener; *Can (fermeture à glissière) Br* zip, *Am* zipper

féroce [ferɔs] **ADJ 1** *(brutal ▸ tyran, soldat)* cruel, bloodthirsty

2 *(acerbe ▸ humour, examinateur)* cruel, harsh, ferocious; *(▸ concurrence)* fierce; **dans une critique f. qui vient de paraître** in a ferocious *or* savage review just out

3 *(qui tue ▸ animal, bête)* ferocious

4 *(extrême ▸ appétit)* voracious; *(▸ désir)* raging, wild

férocement [ferɔsmɑ̃] **ADV 1** *(brutalement)* cruelly **2** *(avec dureté)* harshly, ferociously

férocité [ferɔsite] **NF 1** *(brutalité)* cruelty, bloodlust **2** *(intransigeance)* harshness, ferociousness; **avec f.** ferociously **3** *(d'une bête)* ferocity

Féroé [ferɔe] **NFPL les (îles) F.** the Faroes *or* Faeroes, the Faroe *or* Faeroe Islands

ferrage [feraʒ] **NM 1** *(d'une roue)* rimming; *(d'une canne)* tipping with metal **2** *(d'un cheval, d'un bœuf)* shoeing

ferraillage [ferajaʒ] **NM 1** *(action)* placing of reinforcement **2** *(armatures)* reinforcement

ferraille [feraj] **NF 1** *(débris)* **de la f.** scrap (iron); **un bruit de f.** a clanking noise; **marchand de f.** scrap merchant **2** *(rebut)* scrap; **mettre une machine à la f.** to sell a machine for scrap; **bon pour la** *ou* **à mettre à la f.** ready for the scrapheap, good for scrap **3** *Fam (monnaie)* small change[□], *Br* coppers

ferraillement [ferajmɑ̃] **NM 1** *Péj (combat à l'épée)* sword rattling **2** *(bruit)* rattling, clanking

ferrailler [3] [feraje] **VT** *Constr (béton)* to reinforce

VI 1 *Escrime* to clash swords **2** *Fig (batailler)* to clash, to cross swords; **le gouvernement a ferraillé avec les syndicats** the government clashed with the unions **3** *(faire un bruit de ferraille)* to clank, to rattle

ferrailleur [ferajœr] **NM 1** *Constr* ≃ building worker *(in charge of iron frameworks)* **2** *(commerçant)* scrap merchant **3** *Arch (bretteur)* swashbuckler

ferrate [ferat] **NM** *Chim & Minér* ferrate

ferratisme [feratism] **NM** *Sport* via ferrata climbing

ferré, -e [fere] **ADJ 1** *(muni de fers ▸ cheval)* shod; *(▸ chaussure)* hobnailed; *(▸ roue)* rimmed; *(▸ lacets)* tagged; *(▸ canne)* metal-tipped; **cheval f. à glace** roughshod horse **2** *Fam (locutions)* **être f. sur** *ou* **en qch** to be a genius *or* a whizz at sth; **elle est ferrée en chimie** she's a chemistry whizz

ferrer [4] [fere] **VT 1** *(garnir ▸ roue)* to rim; *(▸ canne)* to tip with metal; *(▸ chaussure)* to nail; *(▸ lacet)* to tag **2** *(cheval, bœuf)* to shoe

ferret [ferɛ] **NM 1** *(de lacet)* aglet **2** *Ordinat* tag

ferreur [ferœr] **NM f. de chevaux** shoeing-smith, *Br* farrier

ferreux, -euse [ferø, -øz] **ADJ** *Chim* ferrous; **alliages f.** iron alloys, ferro-alloys

ferricyanure [ferisjanyr] **NM** *Chim* ferricyanide

ferrimagnétique [ferimaɲetik] **ADJ** ferrimagnetic

ferrique [ferik] **ADJ** *Chim* ferric

ferrite [ferit] **NM** *Chim* ferrite

NF *Métal* ferrite; *Ordinat* **mémoire à f.** ferrite core memory

ferro- [ferɔ] **PRÉF** ferro-

ferrochrome [ferɔkrom] **NM** *Métal* ferrochromium, ferrochrome

ferrocyanure [ferɔsjanyr] **NM** *Chim & Minér* ferrocyanide

ferroélectricité [ferɔelektrisite] **NF** *Phys* ferroelectricity

ferroélectrique [ferɔelektrik] **ADJ** *Phys* ferroelectric

ferromagnétique [ferɔmaɲetik] **ADJ** *Phys* ferromagnetic

ferromagnétisme [ferɔmaɲetism] **NM** *Phys* ferromagnetism

ferronnerie [ferɔnri] **NF 1** *(art)* **f. (d'art)** wrought-iron craft

2 *(ouvrage)* **une belle f. du XVIIIème siècle** a fine piece of 18th-century wrought ironwork *or* wrought-iron work; **des ferronneries, de la f.** wrought ironwork, wrought-iron work

3 *(métier)* ironwork

4 *(atelier)* ironworks *(singulier ou pluriel)*

• **de ferronnerie, en ferronnerie ADJ** wrought-iron *(avant n)*

ferronnier [ferɔnje] **NM 1 f. (d'art)** wrought-iron craftsman **2** *(commerçant)* ironware dealer

ferroutage [ferutaʒ] **NM** *Transp* combined rail and road transport

ferroviaire [ferɔvjer] **ADJ** *(trafic, tunnel, réseau)* rail *(avant n)*, *Br* railway *(avant n)*, *Am* railroad *(avant n)*; *(transports)* rail *(avant n)*

ferrugineux, -euse [feryʒinø, -øz] **ADJ** ferrugineous, ferruginous; **source ferrugineuse** chalybeate spring

ferrure [feryr] **NF 1** *(garniture)* metal hinge; **ferrures de porte** door fittings; **ferrures en cuivre** brass fittings **2** *(fait de ferrer)* shoeing *(UNCOUNT)* **3** *(fers)* horseshoes

ferry [feri] *(pl* **ferries) NM** *(pour voitures)* car-ferry, ferry; *(pour voitures ou trains)* ferry, ferry-boat; **f. roulier** roll-on roll-off ferry; **f. trans-Manche** cross-Channel ferry

ferry-boat [feribot] *(pl* **ferry-boats) NM** ferry, ferry-boat

fertile [fertil] **ADJ 1** *Agr & Géog* fertile, rich; **f. en** rich in; **région f. en agrumes** area rich in citrus fruit **2** *Fig (esprit, imagination)* fertile, inventive; **une année f. en événements** a very eventful year; **un épisode f. en rebondissements** an action-packed episode; **la semaine fut f. en discussions**

the week was packed with discussions 3 *Biol (femelle, femme, couple)* fertile

fertilisable [fɛrtilizabl] ADJ *Agr* fertilizable

fertilisant, -e [fɛrtilizɑ̃, -ɑ̃t] *Agr* ADJ fertilizing
NM fertilizer

fertilisation [fɛrtilizasjɔ̃] NF *Agr & Biol* fertilization, fertilizing

fertiliser [3] [fɛrtilize] VT *Agr* to fertilize

fertilité [fɛrtilite] NF 1 *Agr* fertility, fruitfulness 2 *Biol (d'un couple, d'une femme, d'une femelle)* fertility 3 *(d'un esprit, d'un cerveau)* fertility; connu pour la f. de son imagination famous for his fertile imagination

féru, -e [fery] ADJ être f. de qch to be keen on *or* highly interested in sth; être f. d'une idée to be set on an idea; *Arch* f. de qn smitten with sb

férule [feryl] NF 1 *(fouet)* ferule, ferula; *Fig* être sous la f. de qn to be under sb's strict authority 2 *Bot* ferula

fervent, -e [fɛrvɑ̃, -ɑ̃t] ADJ fervent, ardent; *(amour)* ardent; *(prière)* fervent; *(approbation)* enthusiastic; *(catholique)* devout
NM,F devotee, enthusiast, addict; les fervents du rugby rugby enthusiasts *or* fans; c'est une fervente de romans policiers she's a crime story addict

ferveur [fɛrvœr] NF fervour, ardour, enthusiasm; avec f. *(prier)* fervently, earnestly; *(travailler)* with enthusiasm; *(aimer)* ardently; *(écouter)* eagerly

fesse [fɛs] NF 1 *Anat* buttock; les fesses the buttocks; avoir de belles/grosses fesses to have a nice/fat bottom; cette actrice est toujours en train de montrer ses fesses that actress is always appearing with no clothes on *or* in nude scenes; *Fam* poser ses fesses quelque part to sit down somewhere[□]; *Fam* pose tes fesses! sit yourself down!; *Fam* donner à qn un coup de pied aux fesses to give sb a kick in the pants *or* up the backside; *très Fam* occupe-toi de tes fesses! mind your own damn business! 2 *très Fam* la f. *(le sexe)* sex[□]; *(la pornographie)* pornography[□], the porn industry; *Fam* histoire de fesses dirty story; *(aventure)* purely sexual affair[□]; raconter des histoires de fesses to tell dirty jokes; *Fam* magazine de fesses porn *or* skin mag; *Can Vulg* jouer aux fesses to screw, *Br* to shag 3 *Naut* tuck
• **aux fesses** ADV *Fam* avoir qn aux fesses to have sb on one's back; s'il refuse, je lui mets la police aux fesses! if he refuses, I'll have the law on him *or Am* on his ass!; *très Fam* coller aux fesses à qn to stick to sb like glue; *(camion)* to sit on sb's tail

fessée [fese] NF 1 *(punition)* spanking; avoir *ou* recevoir une f. to get spanked; donner une f. à qn to spank sb 2 *Fig (défaite)* drubbing

fesse-mathieu [fɛsmatjø] *(pl* fesse-mathieux*)* NM *Arch* skinflint, miser

fesser [4] [fese] VT to spank

fessier, -ère [fesje, -ɛr] ADJ buttock *(avant n)*, *Spéc* gluteal; poche fessière *(de pantalon)* hip pocket
NM 1 *Anat* buttocks, *Spéc* gluteus; grand f. gluteus maximus 2 *Fam (postérieur)* behind, bottom, *Br* bum, *Am* butt

festif, -ive [fɛstif, -iv] ADJ festive

festin [fɛstɛ̃] NM feast, banquet; faire un f. to have *or* to hold a feast; quel f.! what a feast!, what a spread!

festival, -als [fɛstival] NM festival; f. du cinéma film festival; un f. de jazz a jazz festival; *Fig* un f. de qch a brilliant display of sth; on a eu droit à un f. de calembours we were treated to pun after pun

festivalier, -ère [fɛstivalje, -ɛr] ADJ festival *(avant n)*
NM,F *(participant)* festival participant; *(visiteur)* festival-goer

festive [fɛstiv] *voir* festif

festivités [fɛstivite] NFPL festivities

fest-noz [fɛstnoz] NM = party with traditional Breton music and dancing

festoie *etc voir* festoyer

feston [fɛstɔ̃] NM 1 *(guirlande) & Archit* festoon 2 *Couture* scallop; à festons scalloped; point de f. blanket stitch, buttonhole stitch

festonner [3] [fɛstɔne] VT 1 *Archit* to festoon 2 *Littéraire (orner)* to adorn, to embellish 3 *Couture* to scallop

festoyer [13] [fɛstwaje] VI to feast

féta, feta [feta] NF feta (cheese)

fêtard, -e [fɛtar, -ard] NM,F party animal

fête [fɛt] NF 1 *(célébration* ► *civile)* holiday; *(*► *religieuse)* feast; demain, c'est f. tomorrow is a special occasion; la f. de l'Assomption (the feast of) the Assumption; f. légale public holiday; la f. des Mères Mother's Day, *Br* Mothering Sunday; f. mobile movable feast; la f. des Morts All Souls' Day; la f. nationale *(gén)* the national holiday; *(en France)* Bastille Day; *(aux États-Unis)* Independence Day; la f. de Noël Christmas; la f. des Pères Father's Day; la f. des Rois Twelfth Night, Epiphany; la f. du Travail Labour Day
2 *(d'un saint)* saint's day, name day; souhaiter sa f. à qn to wish sb a happy saint's *or* name day; *Fam* faire sa f. à qn to give sb a good hiding; *Ironique* on va lui faire sa f.! we're going to teach him/her a lesson he/she won't forget!; ça va être ta f.! you'll *Br* cop it *or Am* catch hell!
3 *(réunion* ► *d'amis)* party; une f. de famille a family celebration *or* gathering; faire une f. to have a party; on donne *ou* organise une petite f. pour son anniversaire we're having *or* giving a party for his/her birthday, we're giving him/her a birthday party; être de la f. to be one of the party; vous serez de la f.? will you be joining us/them?; *Fig* il n'a jamais été à pareille f. he's never had such a good time; *Ironique* il n'était pas à la f. it wasn't much fun for him; le film est une vraie f. pour l'esprit/les sens the film is really uplifting/a real treat for the senses; que la f. commence! let the festivities begin!
4 *(foire)* fair; *(kermesse)* fête, fete; *(festival)* festival, show; f. champêtre *ou* de village village fete *or* fair; c'est la f. au village *(forains de passage)* there's a fair in the village; *(organisée par le village)* the village fete is on; (et) la f. continue! the fun's not over yet!; aujourd'hui, c'est la f.! let's have fun today!; ce n'est pas tous les jours (la) f.! it's not every day you've got something to celebrate!; faire la f. to party; la f. de la bière the beer festival; f. foraine *(attractions) Br* funfair, *Am* carnival; la f. de la Musique = annual music festival organized on June 21st throughout France; f. patronale = town or village festival marking the patron saint's name
5 *(locutions)* faire (la) f. à qn to greet sb warmly; mon chien m'a fait (la) f. quand je suis revenu my dog was all over me when I got back; se faire une f. de to look forward eagerly to; tu ne viens pas? elle qui s'en faisait une telle f.! so you're not coming? she was so looking forward to it!
• **fêtes** NFPL 1 *(gén)* holidays; *(de Noël et du jour de l'an)* Christmas and New Year holidays, *Am* holidays; pendant les fêtes over Christmas and the New Year, over the Christmas period *or Am* the holidays; les fêtes de fin d'année the Christmas and New Year holidays, *Am* the holidays; les fêtes juives/catholiques the Jewish/Catholic holidays 2 *Beaux-Arts* fêtes galantes fêtes galantes
• **de fête** ADJ 1 jour de f. *Rel* feast day; *(jour férié)* public holiday 2 *(air, habits)* festive; donnez un air de f. à votre table give your table a festive appearance
• **en fête** ADJ la ville/les rues en f. the festive town/streets; le village était en f. the village was in a festive mood; regardez la nature en f.! look! what a feast of nature!

FÊTE

The French traditionally wish "bonne fête" to a person who has the same name as the saint commemorated on that particular day.

FÊTE DE LA MUSIQUE

This annual event takes place throughout France on 21 June, the summer solstice. Both amateur and professional musicians take to the streets and there are many impromptu live performances, with bars and restaurants as well as museums and hospitals serving as free venues for all types of music. The festival was originally launched in 1982. Such is its success and popularity in France that the event has now spread to many other European countries.

Fête-Dieu [fɛtdjø] *(pl* Fêtes-Dieu*)* NF la F. Corpus Christi

fêter [4] [fete] VT 1 *(célébrer* ► *anniversaire, événement)* to celebrate; f. ses soixante ans to celebrate one's sixtieth birthday; une promotion? il faut f. ça! a promotion? that calls for a celebration! 2 *(accueillir* ► *personne)* to fête, to fete; ils l'ont fêté à son retour they celebrated his return

fétiche [fetiʃ] NM 1 *(objet de culte)* fetish, fetich 2 *(porte-bonheur)* mascot; *(comme adj)* lucky; mon numéro f. my lucky number 3 *Psy* fetish

fétichisme [fetiʃism] NM 1 *(culte)* fetishism, fetichism 2 *Psy* fetishism, fetichism 3 *(admiration)* worship, cult; le f. des sondages électoraux the obsession with pre-election polls

fétichiste [fetiʃist] ADJ 1 *Rel & Psy* fetishistic 2 *(admiratif)* worshipping
NMF *Rel & Psy* fetishist, fetichist

fétide [fetid] ADJ fetid

fétidité [fetidite] NF fetidness

fétu [fety] NM f. (de paille) (wisp of) straw; comme un f. like a feather

fétuque [fetyk] NF *Bot* fescue (grass)

feu[1]**, -x** [fø] NM 1 *(combustion)* fire; le f. et l'eau fire and water; faire du *ou* un f. to make a fire; allumer un f. *(gén)* to light a fire; *(dehors)* to light a bonfire *or* a fire; faire un bon f. to get a good fire going; assis autour du f./d'un bon f. sitting round the fire/round a roaring fire; au coin du f. by the fire(side); f. de bois (wood) fire; cuire qch au f. de bois to cook sth in a wood-burning oven; f. de braises (glowing) embers; f. de cheminée chimney fire; mettre le f. à une maison to set a house on fire; *Can* passer au f. to burn down; *Fam* flanquer *ou très Fam* foutre le f. à qch to put a match to sth; au f.! fire!; il y a le f. aux rideaux! the curtains are on fire!; f. de camp campfire; f. d'enfer blazing fire; f. de forêt forest fire; f. de joie bonfire; *Belg* f. ouvert hearth; *Méd* le f. Saint-Antoine (St) Anthony's fire; *Fig* f. de paille flash in the pan; f. de pinède forest fire; les feux de la Saint-Jean = bonfires lit to celebrate Midsummer's Day; prendre f. to catch fire; le canapé a pris f. the sofa caught fire; sous un soleil de f. under a blazing *or* fiery sun; *Hum* il n'y a pas le f. (au lac)! there's no need to panic!; faire long f. to hang fire; elle n'a pas fait long f. dans l'entreprise she didn't last long in the company; *Fig* jouer avec le f. to play with fire; jeter *ou* lancer f. et flammes to be raging *or* fuming; il n'y a vu que du f. he never saw a thing, he was completely taken in; il se jetterait dans le f. pour lui/eux he'd do anything for him/them; avoir le f. *Fam* au derrière *ou Vulg* au cul *(être pressé)* to be in a tearing hurry; *(sexuellement)* to be horny, *Br* to be gagging for it; *Can Fam* prendre le f., *Vulg* prendre le f. au cul *(se fâcher)* to blow a fuse, to go ballistic
2 *(brûleur)* ring, burner; cuisinière à trois/quatre feux three-burner/four-burner stove; à f. doux *(plaque)* on a gentle *or* slow heat; *(four)* in a slow oven *or* heat; mijoter *ou* faire cuire à petit f. to cook slowly; *Fig* tuer *ou* faire mourir qn à petit f. to kill sb slowly; à grand f. *ou* f. vif on a fierce heat; avoir qch sur le f. to be (in the middle of) cooking sth; j'ai laissé le lait sur le f.! I've left the milk on!; un plat/ramequin qui va sur le f. a fireproof dish/ramekin
3 *(briquet)* avoir du f. to have a light
4 *(en pyrotechnie)* f. d'artifice *(spectacle)* fireworks display; *Fig* son récital, un vrai f. d'artifice! his/her recital was a virtuoso performance!; des feux d'artifice fireworks; f. de Bengale Bengal light
5 *Mil (tir)* fire, shooting; *(combats)* action; ouvrir le f. (sur) to open fire (on), to start firing (at); cesser le f. to cease fire; faire f. (sur qn/qch) to fire *or* to shoot (at sb/sth); f.! fire!; avoir vu le f. to have seen action; aller au f. to go into battle *or* action; un f. croisé, des feux croisés a crossfire; *Fig* pris dans le f. croisé de leurs questions caught in the crossfire of their questions; f. nourri continuous

or constant stream; *Fig* un f. nourri de plaisanteries a constant stream of jokes; f. roulant constant barrage; *Fig* un f. roulant de commentaires a running commentary; *Fig* être entre deux feux to be caught in the middle, to be in the crossfire; mettre le f. aux poudres to spark off an explosion; *Fig* to spark things off; *Fig* c'est ce qui a mis le f. aux poudres that's what sparked things off

6 *Transp (signal)* f. (tricolore *ou* de signalisation) traffic lights; f. rouge/orange/vert red/amber/green light; à droite au troisième f. (rouge) right at the third set of (traffic) lights; *Fig* donner le f. vert à qn/qch to give sb/sth the green light

7 *Aut, Aviat & Naut* light; f. arrière taillight; f. à éclipses occulting light; f. de gabarit side lamp; f. à occultations occulting light; f. de plaque number plate light; f. de position sidelight; f. de recul reversing light; f. de stop brake light; feux de balisage boundary lights; feux blancs driving lights, headlights and side lights; feux de bord *ou* de navigation navigation lights; feux de brouillard fog lamps; feux de croisement headlights; feux de détresse warning lights; feux de freinage brake lights; feux de mouillage *(d'un navire)* anchor lights; feux de navigation sailing lights; feux de piste runway lights; feux de route headlights on full beam; feux (d'entrée) de port harbour lights; feux de stationnement parking lights; feux stop brake lights; *Aut* rouler tous feux éteints to drive without (any) lights

8 *Rail* f. d'avant *(d'une locomotive)* headlight; f. d'arrière *(d'un train)* tail *or* rear light

9 *Cin & Théât* les feux de la rampe the footlights; être sous le f. des projecteurs to be in front of the spotlights; *Fig* to be in the limelight; il est sous les feux de l'actualité he's very much in the news at the moment

10 *Littéraire (ardeur)* fire, passion, ardour; avoir le f. sacré to burn with enthusiasm; dans le f. de la discussion in the heat of the debate; Vénus et ses feux redoutables Venus and the baleful passions that she kindles

11 *Littéraire (éclat, lumière)* fire, light; le f. de son regard his/her fiery eyes; les feux de la ville the city lights; jeter des feux to sparkle, to glitter; les cristaux brillaient de tous leurs feux the crystals sparkled brightly; le f. d'un diamant the blaze *or* fire of a diamond; une pierre qui brille de mille feux a stone that sparkles brilliantly; faire f. des quatre fers *ou* pieds *(cheval)* to make the sparks fly; *Fig (personne)* to go all out

12 *(sensation de brûlure)* burn; le f. me monta au visage I went *or* turned red, my face *or* I flushed; le f. du rasoir razor burn

13 *Arch (maison)* house, homestead; un hameau de dix feux a hamlet with ten houses *or* homes in it; n'avoir ni f. ni lieu, être sans f. ni lieu to have neither hearth nor home, to have nowhere to lay one's head

14 *Fam (pistolet)* gun, *Am* rod

ADJ INV flame *(avant n)*, tan, flame-coloured; rouge f. flame red; un yorkshire noir et f. a black and tan yorkshire (terrier)

• **à feu et à sang** ADV mettre une ville/un pays à f. et à sang to put a town/country to fire and sword

• **avec feu** ADV passionately

• **dans le feu de** PRÉP in the heat of; dans le f. de l'action in the heat of the moment; dans le f. de la discussion in the heat of the debate

• **en feu** ADJ 1 *(incendié)* blazing, burning; une maison en f. a house on fire, a burning house 2 *(brûlant)* il avait le visage en f. his face was bright red *or* flushed; j'ai la bouche/gorge en f. my mouth/throat is burning

• **tout feu tout flamme** ADJ burning with enthusiasm

• **feu follet** NM will-o'-the-wisp

feu², feue [fø] ADJ *(inv avant l'article ou le possessif)* late; feue la reine the late Queen; ma feue tante, f. ma tante my late aunt; fils de feue Berthe Dupont son of the late Berthe Dupont, son of Berthe Dupont deceased

feudataire [fødatɛr] NM *Hist* feudatory

feuillage [fœjaʒ] NM 1 *(sur l'arbre)* leaves, *Spéc* foliage; là-haut dans le f. *(d'un arbre)* up there amongst the leaves; *(de la forêt)* up in the canopy 2 *(coupé)* greenery, *Spéc* foliage

feuillaison [fœjezɔ̃] NF 1 *(phénomène)* foliation 2 *(époque)* foliation period

feuille [fœj] NF 1 *Bot* leaf; f. morte dead *or* fallen leaf; arbre à feuilles caduques/persistantes deciduous/evergreen tree; f. de chêne *(laitue)* oakleaf; f. de vigne *Bot & Culin* vine leaf; *Beaux-arts* fig leaf

2 *(morceau de papier)* sheet; les feuilles d'un cahier the sheets *or* leaves *or* pages of a notebook; f. intercalaire slip sheet; une f. de papier a sheet (of paper), a piece of paper; f. volante *ou* mobile (loose) sheet of paper

3 *Presse* f. de chou rag; *Fam* il a les oreilles en f. de chou his ears stick out; f. locale local paper; f. à sensations gossip sheet

4 *(imprimé)* form, slip; f. d'accompagnement covering document; f. des arrivées et des départs *(d'un hôtel)* arrival and departure list, A & D list; *Jur* f. d'audience court records; *Compta* f. d'avancement flow sheet; *TV* f. de conducteur cue sheet; f. de déplacement *Mil* travel warrant; *Com* waybill; f. d'émargement pay sheet; *TV & Cin* f. d'exposition exposure sheet; f. d'heures time sheet; f. d'impôts tax form, tax return; *Compta* f. de liquidation settlement note; f. de maladie = claim form for reimbursement of medical expenses; *TV* f. de mixage cue sheet; f. des mouvements *(d'un hôtel)* arrival and departure list, A&D list; f. d'occupation journalière *(d'un hôtel)* daily density chart, daily forecast chart; *TV & Rad* f. d'ordre de passage à l'antenne rundown sheet; f. de paie payslip; f. de présence attendance sheet; *(d'un employé)* time sheet; f. de réservation reservation form, booking form; f. des réveils *(d'un hôtel)* call sheet; *Mil* f. de route travel warrant; *Com* waybill; f. de service (duty) roster; f. de soins = claim form for reimbursement of medical expenses; *Méd* f. de température temperature chart; *Banque* f. de versement paying-in slip

5 *(plaque)* leaf, sheet; f. d'acétate acetate foil; f. de bois thin board f. d'étain tinfoil; f. de métal/d'or metal/gold leaf;

6 *Ordinat* sheet; f. de calcul spreadsheet; f. document data sheet; f. maîtresse master data sheet; f. programme program sheet; f. de style style sheet

feuille-à-feuille [fœjafœj] ADJ INV sheet-fed

feuillée [fœje] NF *Littéraire (abri)* foliage bower; sous la f. under the leafy boughs

• **feuillées** NFPL *Mil* latrine

feuille-morte [fœjmɔrt] ADJ INV russet, yellowish-brown

feuilleret [fœjrɛ] NM *Menuis* rabbet plane

feuillet [fœjɛ] NM 1 *(d'un formulaire)* page, leaf; à feuillets rechargeables loose-leaf 2 *Menuis* thin sheet of wood

feuilletage [fœjtaʒ] NM 1 *Culin (pâte)* puff pastry; le f. de la pâte rolling and folding pastry *(to produce puff pastry)* 2 *Géol* foliation

feuilleté, -e [fœjte] ADJ 1 *Culin* puff *(avant n)*; *(gâteau)* puff-pastry 2 *Géol* foliated 3 *Tech* laminated; pare-brise (en verre) f. laminated windscreen *or Am* windshield

NM 1 *(dessert)* pastry 2 *(hors-d'œuvre)* puff pastry case; f. aux asperges asparagus in puff pastry

feuilleter [27] [fœjte] VT 1 *(album, magazine)* to leaf *or* to flip *or* to flick through, to skim (through) 2 *Culin* f. de la pâte to work the dough (into puff pastry) by rolling and folding it 3 *Ordinat* to scroll through; f. en arrière to page up, to scroll up; f. en avant to page down, to scroll down

feuilleton [fœjtɔ̃] NM 1 *Journ (série)* series *(singulier)*, serial; *(rubrique)* (regular) column; publier un roman en feuilletons to serialize a novel

2 *TV & Rad* serial; *TV* f. (télévisé) *(sur plusieurs semaines)* TV serial; *(sur plusieurs années)* soap opera

3 *Littérature* feuilleton

4 *Fig (histoire à rebondissements)* saga

feuilletoniste [fœjtɔnist] NMF *(auteur de romans-feuilletons)* serial writer; *(chroniqueur)* feature writer

feuillette *etc voir* **feuilleter**

feuillu, -e [fœjy] ADJ leafy, broad-leaved

NM broad-leaved tree

feuillure [fœjyr] NF *Menuis* rabbet, rebate

feulement [følmɑ̃] NM growl

feuler [3] [føle] VI to growl

feutrage [føtraʒ] NM felting; lavez à l'eau froide pour empêcher le f. wash in cold water to prevent felting

feutre [føtr] NM 1 *Tex (étoffe)* felt; de *ou* en f. felt 2 *(chapeau)* felt hat, fedora 3 *(stylo)* (crayon *ou* stylo) f. felt(-tip) pen, felt-tip; couvert de traces de f. covered in felt-tip

feutré, -e [føtre] ADJ 1 *(pull, vêtement)* felted 2 *(garni de feutre ▸ bourrelet)* felt *(avant n)*; porte feutrée baize door 3 *(silencieux ▸ salon, atmosphère)* hushed, quiet; *(▸ voix)* muffled; marcher à pas feutrés to creep stealthily; s'éloigner à pas feutrés to steal away, to slip quietly away; traverser une pièce à pas feutrés to pad across a room

feutrer [3] [føtre] VT 1 *Tex* to felt 2 *(garnir ▸ selle)* to pad *or* to line (with felt) 3 *(son)* to muffle

VI to felt, to become felted *or* matted; l'eau trop chaude fait f. les pulls washing in very hot water makes jumpers lose their finish

VPR se feutrer to felt, to become felted *or* matted

feutrine [føtrin] NF felt; *(sur table de billard)* baize

fève [fɛv] NF 1 *Bot (graine)* bean; *(plante)* broad bean; f. de cacao cocoa bean 2 *Can (haricot)* bean; f. jaune wax bean; f. verte string bean; fèves au lard baked beans with pork, *Am* pork beans 3 *(des Rois)* = lucky charm or token made of porcelain and hidden in a "galette des Rois"

février [fevrije] NM February; *voir aussi* **mars**

fez [fɛz] NM fez

FF *Anciennement (abrév écrite* franc français*)* FF

FFI [ɛfɛfi] NFPL *Hist (abrév* Forces françaises de l'intérieur*)* = French Resistance forces during World War II

FFL [ɛfɛfɛl] NFPL *Hist (abrév* Forces françaises libres*)* = free French Army during World War II

fi [fi] EXCLAM *Hum* pooh!

NM *(locution)* faire fi de *(mépriser)* to turn one's nose up at, to spurn; *(ignorer)* to ignore

fiabilité [fjabilite] NF *(crédibilité)* reliability

fiable [fjabl] ADJ *(crédible)* reliable

fiacre [fjakr] NM fiacre, (horse-drawn) carriage

fiançailles [fijɑ̃saj] NFPL 1 *(promesse)* engagement; à quand tes f.? when are you getting engaged? 2 *(cérémonie)* engagement party 3 *(durée)* engagement (period); pendant leurs f. while they were engaged, during their engagement

fiancé, -e [fijɑ̃se] NM,F fiancé, *f* fiancée; les fiancés the engaged couple, *Littéraire ou Hum* the betrothed

fiancer [16] [fijɑ̃se] VT to betroth; il fiance sa fille his daughter is getting engaged; elle est fiancée à Paul she's engaged to Paul, she and Paul are engaged

VPR se fiancer to get engaged; se f. avec qn to get engaged to sb

FIAS [fjas] NF *(abbr* Force internationale d'assistance et de sécurité*)* ISAF

fiasco [fjasko] NM 1 *(entreprise, tentative)* fiasco, flop; *(film, ouvrage)* flop; faire f. to flop, to be a (total) failure 2 *(échec sexuel)* failure to perform

fiasque [fjask] NF (Italian) wine flask

fibranne [fibran] NF *Tex* staple, bonded fibre

fibre [fibr] NF 1 *(filament)* fibre; *(du bois)* fibre, woodfibre; dans le sens de la f. going with the grain (of the wood); panneau de fibres agglomérées fibreboard; riche en fibres (alimentaires) rich in (dietary) fibre

2 *Opt & Tech* fibre; f. de carbone carbon fibre; f. de verre fibreglass; f. optique fibre optics *(singulier)*; fibres optiques optical fibres; câble en fibres optiques fibre-optic cable

3 *Tex* une f. textile a fibre; les fibres naturelles/synthétiques naturally-occurring/man-made fibres; coton à fibres longues long-staple cotton

4 *(dans un muscle)* muscle fibre; f. nerveuse nerve fibre

5 *(sentiment)* feeling; avoir la f. commerçante to be a born shopkeeper; avoir la f. maternelle/paternelle to have strong maternal/paternal feelings; elle n'a pas la f. maternelle she's not the

maternal sort; *Littéraire* **les fibres du cœur** the heart-strings

fibreux, -euse [fibrø, -øz] **ADJ 1** *(dur ▸ viande)* stringy, tough **2** *(à fibres ▸ tissu, muscle)* fibrous; *Méd* fibroid

fibrillation [fibrijasjɔ̃] **NF** *Méd* fibrillation, fibrillating *(UNCOUNT)*

fibrille [fibrij] **NF 1** *(fibre ▸ courte)* short fibre; *(▸ fine)* thin fibre **2** *Biol & Bot* fibril, fibrilla

fibriller **[3]** [fibrije] **VT** *Méd* to fibrillate

fibrine [fibrin] **NF** *Biol* fibrin

fibrineux, -euse [fibrinø, -øz] **ADJ** *Biol* fibrinous

fibrinogène [fibrinɔʒɛn] **NM** *Biol* fibrinogen

Fibrociment® [fibrɔsimɑ̃] **NM** *Constr* Fibrociment®

fibromateux, -euse [fibrɔmatø, -øz] **ADJ** *Méd* fibromatous

fibrome [fibrom] **NM** *Méd (tumeur)* fibroma; *(dans l'utérus)* fibroid

fibromyalgie [fibromjalʒi] **NF** *Méd* fibromyalgia

fibroscope [fibrɔskɔp] **NM** *Méd* fibrescope

fibroscopie [fibrɔskɔpi] **NF** *Méd* fibre-optic endoscopy

fibule [fibyl] **NF** *Archéol* fibula

ficaire [fikɛr] **NF** *Bot* pilewort, lesser celandine

ficelage [fislaʒ] **NM 1** *(action)* tying up **2** *(liens)* string(s)

ficelé, -e [fisle] **ADJ 1 bien f.** *(dossier)* well put together; *Fig (scénario)* well-crafted; *Fig* **c'est bien/mal f.** *(texte, histoire, film)* it hangs/doesn't hang together well **2** *Fam (habillé)* got up; **être f. comme l'as de pique** to be dressed like a scarecrow

ficeler **[24]** [fisle] **VT** to tie up; *Fig* **ficelé comme un saucisson** trussed up like a chicken

ficelle [fisɛl] **NF 1** *(corde)* piece of string; **de la f.** string; *Fig* **la f. est un peu grosse** it sticks out like a sore thumb; **les ficelles du métier** the tricks of the trade; **connaître toutes les ficelles du métier** to know the ropes; **tirer les ficelles** to pull the strings

2 *(pain)* = very thin baguette

3 *Fam Arg mil* officer's stripe[□]

4 *Vieilli (comme adj) (malin)* cunning

ficellera *etc voir* **ficeler**

fiche¹ **[3]** [fiʃ] *Fam* **VT 1** = **ficher²** **2** *(locutions)* **il n'en a rien à f.** he couldn't care less; **on n'en a rien à f., de leurs états d'âme!** we couldn't care less about their scruples!; **pour ce que j'en ai à f.!** a fat lot I care!; **va te faire f.!** get lost!

• **se fiche** = **se ficher**

• **se fiche de** = **se ficher de**

fiche² [fiʃ] **NF 1** *(carton)* piece of (stiff) card, (index) card; **f. cartonnée** index card; **f. à perforations marginales** edge punched card; **f. perforée** perforated card; **f. en T** T-card; **f. cuisine** recipe card; **mettre qch sur f.** to index *or Br* to card-index sth; **faire des fiches de lecture** to write notes *or* a commentary on a book; **f. de compte** accounts card; **f. de facture** account card; *Com* **f. de pointage** clocking-in card

2 *(papier)* sheet, slip; **f. client** customer record; **f. courrier** mail checklist *or* file; **f. dentaire** dental chart; **f. d'entretien** service record; **f. médicale** medical record (card); **f. explicative** information sheet; **f. fournisseur** supplier file; **f. d'observations** *(questionnaire d'évaluation)* comment card; **f. de paie** pay slip; **f. de poste** *(descriptif des tâches à accomplir)* task sheet; **f. de présence** *(de salarié)* attendance sheet; **f. prospect** potential-customer file; **f. signalétique** identification slip *or* sheet; **f. de stock** stock sheet; *Com* **f. technique** specifications sheet; **f. verticale suspendue** vertical suspension file; **f. à visibilité** visible card record

3 *(formulaire)* form; **remplir une f.** to fill in *or* to fill out a form; **mettre qn en** *ou* **sur f.** to open a file on sb; **lui, on l'a sur f.** we've got a file on him, we've got him on file; **f. d'accueil** registration form; **f. d'appréciation** customer satisfaction questionnaire; **f. d'arrivée** registration form; *Ind* **f. de contrôle** checking form, *Br* docket; *Compta* **f. d'imputation** data entry form; **f. d'inscription** registration form; **f.-message** message form

4 *Admin* **f. anthropométrique** = (criminal) dossier; **f. d'état civil** = record of civil status *(birth details and marital status)*; **f. de police** = registration card to be filled in by hotel guests from non-EU countries; *(au débarquement)* landing card

5 *(d'un hôtel)* **remplir une f. d'hôtel** to register (with a hotel), to fill in a (hotel) registration card; **f. d'hôtel** *(clé)* key card; **f. de blocage** block card, reservation rack card, room rack card; **f. client** room rack card; *(sur ordinateur)* guest folio, guest file; **f. Kardex** guest history card; **f. d'occupation** room rack card; **f. voyageur** = hotel registration card for foreign guests; **f. Whitney** Whitney card

6 *(dans les jeux)* counter

7 *Ordinat* pin; **f. gigogne** dongle; **f. suiveuse** route card; **f. d'état** report form

8 *Constr* hinge; **f. de porte** door hinge

9 *Élec (prise)* plug; *(broche)* pin; **f. multiple** multiple adapter; **f. téléphonique** phone *or* jack plug; *(broche)* telephone jack; *(pour message)* telephone memo

ficher¹ **[3]** [fiʃe] **VT 1** *(enfoncer)* to drive *or* to stick (in); *(lame)* to plunge; *(épingle)* to stick in; **f. un pieu en terre** to drive a stake into the ground; **f. une épingle dans qch** to stick a pin into sth **2** *(information)* to file, to put on file; *(suspect)* to put on file; **il est fiché** the police have got a file on him

VPR se ficher to stick (**dans** in); **la flèche se ficha en plein milieu de la cible** the arrow hit the middle of the target; **la balle se ficha dans le mur** the bullet became embedded in the wall

ficher² **[3]** [fiʃe] *Fam* **VT 1** *(mettre)* to stick, to shove, *Br* to bung; **fiche-le à la porte!** throw *or* kick him out!; **son patron l'a fichu à la porte** his boss fired him *or* threw him out *or Br* sacked him; **fiche ça dans le placard** throw *or* stick it in the cupboard *or Am* closet; **ils l'ont fichu en prison** they threw him in jail; **fiche-moi ça dehors!** get rid of this!; **je lui ai fichu mon poing dans la figure** I punched him/her in the face; **qui a fichu ce rapport ici?** who stuck this report here?; **ce temps me fiche à plat** this weather really wipes me out; **son départ nous a tous fichus à plat** his/her departure took the wind out of our sails; **c'est cette phrase qui m'a fichu dedans** it was that phrase that got me into trouble *or* hot water; **ils ont essayé de nous f. dedans** they tried to land us right in it; **tu l'as fichue en l'air, sa lettre?** did you chuck out his/her letter?; **ce contretemps fiche tout en l'air** this last-minute hitch really messes everything up; **arrête, tu vas le f. en rogne!** stop it, you're going to make him lose his temper!; **c'est le genre de remarque qui me fiche en rogne** that's the kind of remark that drives me mad; **f. qch par terre** to chuck sth on the ground; **t'as tout fichu par terre** *(gâché)* you've messed everything up

2 *(faire)* to do; **qu'est-ce que tu fiches ici?** what on earth *or* the heck are you doing here?; **je n'ai rien fichu aujourd'hui** I haven't done a thing today; **il n'a rien fichu de la journée** he's done damn all *or Br* sod all all day, he hasn't done a thing all day; **bon sang, qu'est-ce qu'il fiche?** *(où est-il?)* for God's sake, where on earth is he?; *(que fait-il?)* what the heck is he doing?

3 *(donner)* **f. une gifle à qn** to give sb a slap in the face; **ça me fiche le cafard** it makes me feel down *or* depressed; **ça m'a fichu la chair de poule/la trouille** it gave me the creeps/the willies; **fiche-moi la paix!** leave me alone!; **je t'en ficherai, moi, du champagne!** champagne? I'll give you champagne!; **je te fiche mon billet que…** I'll bet my bottom dollar that…

4 ça la fiche mal (de ne pas y aller) *(fait mauvais effet)* it looks really bad (not to go)

VPR se ficher 1 *(se mettre)* **de désespoir, elle s'est fichue à la Seine** in despair, she threw herself *or* jumped into the Seine; **ils se sont fichus dans un fossé** *(en voiture)* they drove into a ditch; *(pour passer inaperçus)* they jumped into a ditch; **se f. par terre** *(tomber)* to fall flat; **se f. en l'air** *(se suicider)* to do oneself in; **se f. en colère** to see red, *Br* to lose one's rag; **se f. dedans** to screw up, to get it wrong[□] **2 se f. de** *(railler)* to make fun of[□]; **elle n'arrête pas de se f. de lui** she's forever pulling his leg *or Br* winding him up; **tu te fiches de moi ou quoi?** are you kidding me?; **ils se fichent du monde dans ce restaurant!** *(c'est cher)* this restaurant is an absolute rip-off!; *(le service est mauvais)* they treat the customers like dirt in this restaurant!; **eh bien, tu ne t'es pas fichu de nous!** well, you've really done things in style! **3 se f. de** *(être indifférent à)* not to give a damn about; **je m'en fiche (pas mal)** I don't give a damn, I couldn't care less; **je me fiche de ce que disent les gens** I don't give a damn about what people say; **elle s'en fiche que son père ne soit pas d'accord** she doesn't give a damn *or* couldn't care less if her father doesn't agree; **ils n'ont pas aimé notre spectacle – qu'est-ce qu'on s'en fiche!** they didn't like our show – so what *or* who cares!; **je m'en fiche comme de ma première chemise** *ou* **comme de l'an quarante** *ou* **complètement** I don't give a damn (about it), I couldn't care less

fichet [fiʃɛ] **NM** *(utilisé au trictrac)* peg

fichette [fiʃɛt] **NF f. client** *(d'un hôtel etc)* reservation card; **f. d'arrivée** arrival form

fichier [fiʃje] **NM 1** *(fiches)* (card index) file, catalogue; **pour enrichir mon f.** to add to my files; **f. (des) clients** client *or* customer file; *Ordinat* **f. de commandes** command file; *Journ* **f. de coupures** cuttings file; **f. en cours** current file; **f. des salariés** personnel files

2 *(meuble)* filing cabinet; *(à tiroirs)* card-index filing cabinet; *(boîte)* file; **f. Kardex** *(d'un hôtel)* guest history file; **f. rotatif** rotating card index, rotary (card) file

3 *Ordinat* file; **f. informatique** computer file; **volume du f.** file size; **f. à accès aléatoire** random access file; **f. à accès limité** restricted file; **f. actif** active file; **f. d'adresses** mailing list; *Ordinat* address file; **f. d'application** application file; **f. ASCII** ASCII file; **f. de base de données** database file; **f. BAT** batch file; **f. batch** batch file; **f. binaire** binary file; **f. de commande** command file; **f. compte-rendu** log file; **f. de cookies** command file; **f. en cours** current file; **f. de destination** target file; **f. de détail** detail file; **f. disque** disk file; **f. document** document file; **f. d'entrée** input file; **f. exécutable** executable *or* execute file; **f. FAQ** FAQ file; **f. à imprimer** print job; **f. indexé** indexed file; **f. d'intendance** control file; **f. joint** *(de courrier électronique)* attachment; **f. journal** logging file; **f. en lecture seule** read-only file; **f. lisez-moi** readme file; **f. maître** master file; **f. non structuré** flat file; **f. par points** bitmap file; **f. principal** master file; **f. de sauvegarde** backup file; **f. de secours** backup file; **f. séquentiel** batch *or* sequential file; *Ordinat* **f. son** sound file; **f. de sortie** output file; **f. source** source file; **f. système** system file; *Can* **f. de témoins** cookie file; **f. (de) texte** text file; **f. de travail** scratch file

fichtre [fiʃtr] **EXCLAM** *Fam Vieilli* (my) gosh!, my (my)!; **f. oui!** I should say so!, rather!; **f. non!** not likely!, no fear!

fichtrement [fiʃtrəmɑ̃] **ADV** *Fam Vieilli* darn; **tout cela est f. assommant** this is just too darn boring; **je n'en sais f. rien!** how the heck should I know!

fichu¹ [fiʃy] **NM** (large) scarf; *(couvrant les épaules)* fichu, (small) shawl

fichu², -e [fiʃy] **ADJ** *Fam* **1** *(perdu)* **il est f.** he's had it; **ma robe est fichue** my dress has had it; **ta voiture est fichue** your car's a write-off; **c'est f.!** *(sans espoir)* (we can) forget it!; **pour samedi soir, c'est f.** we can forget Saturday night, Saturday night's down the drain

2 *(avant le nom) (mauvais)* lousy, rotten; **quel f. temps!** what lousy weather!; **quel f. pays!** what a godforsaken country!; **je suis dans un f. état ce matin** I feel lousy this morning; **avoir un f. caractère** to have a lousy *or* filthy temper

3 *(avant le nom) (important)* **ça fait une fichue différence** that makes a heck of a difference; **j'ai un f. mal de dents** I've got one hell of a nasty toothache

4 *(capable)* **il n'est même pas f. de prendre un message correctement** he can't even take a message properly; **elle est fichue de partir!** she's quite capable of leaving!

5 *(habillé)* **être bien/mal f.** to be well/badly turned out *or* dressed

6 *(bâti, conçu)* **elle est vraiment bien fichue, cette fille** that girl's got a great body on her; **il est mal f.** he hasn't got a very nice body; **c'est bien/mal f.** it's well/badly designed□

7 être mal f. *(un peu malade)* to be out of sorts, *Br* to be off colour

8 *Can* **une fichue de belle maison/voiture** a gorgeous house/car□; **un f. de beau garçon** a gorgeous-looking guy

fictif, -ive [fiktif, -iv] **ADJ 1** *(imaginaire)* imaginary, fictitious **2** *(faux ▸ promesse)* false **3** *Fin* fictitious; *(compte)* dead; **valeur fictive** *(de billets)* face value

fiction [fiksjɔ̃] **NF 1** *(domaine de l'imaginaire)* **la f.** fiction; **film de f.** fictional film; **livre de f.** work of fiction; **la réalité dépasse la f.** truth is stranger than fiction; *Péj* **elle vit dans la f.** she's living in a dream world; **la politique-f.** political pie in the sky; **un livre de politique-f.** a political novel **2** *(histoire)* story, (piece of) fiction **3** *Jur* fiction; **f. légale** *ou* **de droit** legal fiction

fictive [fiktiv] *voir* **fictif**

fictivement [fiktivmɑ̃] **ADV** fictitiously; **transposons-nous f. au XVIIIème siècle** let's imagine we're in the 18th century

ficus [fikys] **NM** *Bot* ficus; **f. elastica** rubber plant

fidéicommis [fideikɔmi] **NM** *Jur* trust

fidéicommissaire [fideikɔmisɛr] **NM** *Jur* trustee

fidèle [fidɛl] **ADJ 1** *(constant ▸ ami)* faithful, loyal, true; *(▸ employé, animal)* loyal, faithful; *(▸ conjoint)* faithful; *(▸ client)* loyal; *(▸ lecteur)* regular, loyal; **elle a été f. à sa parole** *ou* **promesse** she kept her word; **il est f. à la promesse qu'il nous a faite** he has kept faith with us, he has kept his promise to us; **rester f. à la mémoire de qn** to remain true *or* faithful to sb's memory; **être f. à ses engagements** to stand by one's commitments; **être f. à une idée** to stand by *or* to be true to an idea; **être f. à un médecin/commerçant** to be a regular patient/customer; **être/rester f. à une marque/un produit** to stick with a particular brand/product; *Mktg* **f. à la marque** brand-loyal; **f. à elle-même** true to herself; *Ironique* **f. à lui-même, il a oublié mon anniversaire** true to character *or* true to form, he forgot my birthday; **comment l'as-tu trouvé? – f. à lui-même** how did you find him? – his usual self; **être f. au poste** to be reliable **2** *(conforme ▸ copie, description)* true, exact; *(▸ traduction)* faithful, close; *(▸ historien, narrateur)* faithful; *(▸ mémoire)* reliable, correct; *(▸ balance)* reliable, accurate; **livre f. à la réalité** book which is true to life; **la traduction n'est pas f. au texte** the translation is not faithful to the original

NMF 1 *Rel* believer; **les fidèles** *(croyants)* the believers; *(pratiquants)* the faithful; *(assemblée)* the congregation **2** *(adepte)* devotee, follower; *(client)* loyal customer; *(lecteur de journal)* regular *or* loyal reader; *TV* regular *or* loyal viewer; **je suis un f. de votre émission** I never miss one of your shows; *Mktg* **f. absolu** hard-core loyal

fidèlement [fidɛlmɑ̃] **ADV 1** *(régulièrement)* regularly; **père venait f. nous voir** father visited us regularly **2** *(loyalement)* faithfully, loyally; **suivre qn f.** to follow sb faithfully **3** *(conformément ▸ copier)* exactly, faithfully; *(▸ traduire, reproduire)* accurately, faithfully

• **fidèlement vôtre ADV** yours

fidélisation [fidelizasjɔ̃] **NF f. des clients** *ou* **d'une clientèle** building up *or* development of customer loyalty; **f. à la marque** creation of brand loyalty

fidéliser [3] [fidelize] **VT f. ses clients** *ou* **la clientèle** to build up *or* to develop customer loyalty; **f. un public** to maintain a regular audience *(by a commercial policy)*; **f. une équipe** to keep a team together

fidélité [fidelite] **NF 1** *(loyauté ▸ d'un ami, d'un employé, d'un animal)* faithfulness, loyalty; *(▸ d'un conjoint)* faithfulness, fidelity; *(▸ d'un client, d'un lecteur)* loyalty; **sa f. à sa parole** *ou* **promesse** his/her faithfulness, his/her keeping faith; **f. à ses engagements** standing by one's commitments; *Mktg* **f. absolue** hard-core loyalty; *Mktg* **f. du client** customer loyalty; *Mktg* **f. du consommateur** consumer loyalty; *Mktg* **f. à la marque** brand loyalty; **f. à** *ou* **de la couleur** colour fidelity **2** *(exactitude ▸ d'un récit, d'une description)* accuracy, faithfulness; *(▸ de la mémoire)* reliability; *(▸ d'un instrument)* accuracy, reliability

Fidji [fidʒi] **NFPL les (îles) F.** Fiji, the Fiji Islands

fidjien, -enne [fidʒjɛ̃, -ɛn] **ADJ** Fijian

• **Fidjien, -enne NM,F** Fijian

fiduciaire [fidysjɛr] **ADJ** fiduciary; **monnaie f.** paper money; **avoirs en monnaie f.** *(d'une banque)* cash holdings; **société f.** trust company; *Jur* **en dépôt f.** in trust

NM *Jur* fiduciary, trustee

fiduciairement [fidysjɛrmɑ̃] **ADV** *Jur* in trust

fief [fjɛf] **NM 1** *Hist* fief **2** *(domaine réservé)* fief, kingdom; **n'entre pas dans la cuisine, c'est son f.!** don't go into the kitchen, it's his/her kingdom *or* domain!; **un f. du parti socialiste** a socialist stronghold

fieffé, -e [fjefe] **ADJ 1** *Hist* enfeoffed **2** *Péj (extrême)* complete, utter; **un f. paresseux** a real old lazybones

fiel [fjɛl] **NM 1** *(bile)* gall, bile **2** *Littéraire (amertume)* rancour, bitterness, gall; *(méchanceté)* venom; **des propos pleins de f.** venomous words; **un sourire plein de f.** a twisted smile

fielleux, -euse [fjelø, -øz] **ADJ** *Littéraire* venomous, spiteful

fiente [fjɑ̃t] **NF de la f.** droppings

fienter [3] [fjɑ̃te] **VI** to leave droppings

fier¹ [9] [fje] **se fier VPR 1 se f. à qn/qch** *(avoir confiance en)* to trust sb/sth; **fiez-vous à moi, je le trouverai** leave it to me *or* trust me, I'll find him; **se f. à la parole de qn** to take sb's word for it, to believe sb; **je ne me fie pas à ce qu'il dit** I don't believe a word he says; **se f. aux apparences** to go by *or* on appearances; **ne vous y fiez pas!** don't be fooled by it/him/her/*etc*! **2 se f. à qn/qch** *(compter sur)* to rely *or* to count on sb/sth; **se f. à sa mémoire** to rely on one's memory

fier², fière [fjɛr] **ADJ 1** *(satisfait)* proud; **l'enfant était tout f.** the child was really proud; **être f. de qch/d'avoir fait qch** to be proud of sth/of having done sth; **j'étais f. d'avoir gagné** I was proud (that) I won; **je n'étais pas f. de moi** I wasn't pleased with *or* proud of myself; **il n'y a pas de quoi être f.** that's nothing to boast about *or* to be proud of

2 *(noble)* noble, proud; *Littéraire* **une âme fière** a noble mind; **ils sont trop fiers pour accepter de l'argent** they're too proud to take money

3 *(arrogant ▸ personnage)* proud, arrogant, haughty; *(▸ regard)* haughty, supercilious; **il est trop f. pour nous serrer la main** he's too proud to shake hands with us; **quand il a fallu sauter, il n'était plus tellement f.** when it came to jumping, he didn't seem so sure of himself; **alors, on est moins f., n'est-ce pas?** not quite so high and mighty now, are we?; *Fam* **c'est une fille pas fière** she's not a stuck-up girl; *Fam* **il n'est pas f. pour deux sous** he's not at all stuck-up; **avoir fière allure** to cut (quite) a dash; **être f. comme Artaban** *ou* **comme un coq** to be as proud as a peacock, to be puffed up with pride

4 *Littéraire (audacieux)* bold

5 *(avant le nom) Fam (extrême)* **tu as un f. culot!** you've got some nerve!; **c'est un f. imbécile!** what an idiot!

NM,F proud person; **faire le f.** to put on airs and graces; **ne joue pas le f. avec moi!** it's no use putting on your airs and graces with me!; **il fait le f. avec sa nouvelle voiture** he's showing off with his new car

fier-à-bras [fjɛrabra] *(pl inv ou* **fiers-à-bras)** **NM** braggart

fièrement [fjɛrmɑ̃] **ADV 1** *(dignement)* proudly **2** *Vieilli (d'une manière hautaine)* haughtily **3** *Vieilli (extrêmement)* famously **4** *Littéraire (avec audace)* boldly

fiérot, -e [fjero, -ɔt] *Fam* **ADJ** proud□ (de of); **il était tout f.** he was as proud as a peacock

NM,F faire le f. to show off

fierté [fjɛrte] **NF 1** *(dignité)* pride; **par f., je ne lui ai pas parlé** my pride wouldn't let me talk to him/her; **ravaler sa f.** to swallow one's pride; **elle n'a pas beaucoup de f.** she hasn't much pride *or* self-respect; **il a trop de f. pour demander de l'aide** he's too proud to ask for help; *Fam* **tu ne le lui as pas réclamé? – on a sa f.!** didn't you ask him/her to give it back? – I do have some pride! **2** *(arrogance)* arrogance, haughtiness, superciliousness **3** *(satisfaction)* (source of) pride; **tirer f.** *ou* **une grande f. de** to take (a) pride in, to pride oneself on; **ma fille/maison est ma f.** my daughter/house is my pride and joy; **la réussite de l'entreprise est notre f.** we pride ourselves on the success of the venture

• **avec fierté ADV** proudly; **c'est avec f. que je vous présente...** I'm proud to present to you..., I proudly present to you...

fiesta [fjɛsta] **NF** *Fam* (wild) party□, *Br* rave-up, *Am* blowout; **faire la f.** to live it up

fièvre [fjɛvr] **NF 1** *Méd* fever, temperature; **avoir de la f.** to have a temperature *or* a fever; **avoir beaucoup de f.** to have a high temperature *or* a fever; **il a 40 de f.** his temperature is up to 40, he has a temperature of 40; **pour faire baisser la f.** (in order) to get the temperature down; *Fig Littéraire* **tomber de la f. en chaud mal** to fall from the frying pan into the fire; **f. amarile** yellow fever; *Vét* **f. aphteuse** foot and mouth disease; **f. jaune** yellow fever; **f. miliaire** prickly heat, *Spéc* miliaria; **f. paludéenne** malaria; **f. typhoïde** typhoid fever **2** *(agitation)* excitement; **elle parlait avec f.** she spoke excitedly; **préparer un examen avec f.** to prepare feverishly for an exam; **la f. des présidentielles** the excitement of the presidential elections; **dans la f. de la campagne électorale** in the heat *or* excitement of the electoral campaign; **sans f.** calmly **3** *(désir)* **avoir la f. de l'or** to have a passion for gold

fiévreuse [fjevrøz] *voir* **fiévreux**

fiévreusement [fjevrøzmɑ̃] **ADV** *Méd & Fig* feverishly; *(attendre)* anxiously

fiévreux, -euse [fjevrø, -øz] **ADJ** *Méd & Fig* feverish, febrile; *(activité, préparations)* feverish, frantic; *(imagination)* feverish; *(attente)* anxious

FIF [ɛfiɛf] **NF** *(abrév* **Fédération internationale du film)** FIF

FIFA [fifa] **NF** *(abrév* **Fédération internationale de football association)** FIFA

fifille [fifij] **NF** *Fam* little girl□

fifre [fifr] **NM 1** *(flûte)* fife **2** *(joueur)* fife player

fifrelin [fifrəlɛ̃] **NM** *Fam (locution)* **ça ne vaut pas un f.** it isn't worth a bean *or Am* a dime

fifty-fifty [fiftififti] **ADV** *Fam* fifty-fifty, half-and-half; **partager qch f.** to share sth fifty-fifty; **faisons f.** let's go halves

figé, -e [fiʒe] **ADJ** set; *(sauce, huile)* congealed; *(sourire)* fixed; *(style)* stilted; *(société)* fossilized; **dans une attitude figée** motionless

figer [17] [fiʒe] **VT 1** *(coaguler ▸ huile)* to congeal; *(▸ sang)* to coagulate, to clot; **des cris à vous f. le sang** bloodcurdling screams; **ce spectacle lui a figé le sang** the sight made his/her blood run cold **2** *(immobiliser ▸ personne)* **la vue du tigre me figea sur place** I froze when I saw the tiger; **sa réponse m'a figé sur place** his/her answer struck me dumb

VI *(huile)* to congeal; *(sang)* to coagulate, to clot

VPR se figer 1 *(être coagulé ▸ huile)* to congeal; *(▸ sang)* to coagulate, to clot; **mon sang s'est figé dans mes veines** my blood froze **2** *(s'immobiliser ▸ attitude, sourire)* to stiffen; *(▸ personne)* to freeze; **elle se figea sous l'effet de la terreur** she was rooted to the spot with fear; **se f. au garde-à-vous** to stand to attention; **se f. dans une attitude/un point de vue** to persist in an attitude/a point of view

fignolage [fiɲɔlaʒ] **NM** perfecting, touching up, polishing (up)

fignoler [3] [fiɲɔle] **VT** *(travail, dessin)* to perfect, to polish *or* to touch up; **un travail fignolé** a polished piece of work

USAGE ABSOLU to be meticulous; **il ne me reste plus qu'à f.** it's just a matter of adding the finishing touches now

fignoleur, -euse [fiɲɔlœr, -øz] **ADJ** meticulous, *Péj* finicky

NM,F meticulous *or Péj* finicky worker

figue [fig] **NF** fig; **f. de Barbarie** prickly pear

figuier [figje] **NM** fig tree; **f. de Barbarie** prickly pear

figurant, -e [figyrɑ̃, -ɑ̃t] NM,F *Cin* extra; *Théât* extra, walk-on actor; *(en danse)* figurant; *Théât* **rôle de f.** walk-on (part), bit part; *Cin* bit part; **être réduit au rôle de f.** *ou* **à jouer les figurants** *(dans une réunion)* to be a mere onlooker; *(auprès d'une personne importante)* to be a stooge

figuratif, -ive [figyratif, -iv] ADJ *(art)* figurative, representational; *(artiste)* representational; *(plan)* figurative
NM representational artist

figuration [figyrasjɔ̃] NF **1** *(figurants)* **la f.** *Cin* extras; *Théât* extras, walk-on actors; *(en danse)* figurants **2** *(métier)* **la f.** *Cin* being an *or* working as an extra; *Théât* doing a walk-on part; *(en danse)* being a *or* dancing as a figurant; **faire de la f.** *Cin* to work as an extra; *Théât* to do walk-on parts; *(en danse)* to dance as a figurant **3** *(fait de représenter)* representation, figuration

figurative [figyrativ] *voir* **figuratif**

figurativement [figyrativmɑ̃] ADV figuratively

figure [figyr] NF **1** *(visage)* face; *(mine)* face, features; **jeter qch à la f. de qn** to throw sth in sb's face; **faire triste** *ou* **piètre f.** to cut a sad figure, to be a sad *or* sorry sight; **faire bonne f.** to make a good impression; **il faisait f. de riche** he was looked on *or* thought of as a rich man; **prendre f.** to take shape; **ne plus avoir f. humaine** to be totally unrecognizable *or* disfigured; *Hum* **le canapé n'avait plus f. humaine** the sofa was totally worn out
2 *(personnage)* figure; **une grande f. de la politique** a great political figure; **c'est une f.!** he's quite a character!
3 *(représentation)* **figures de cire** waxworks, waxwork figures; *Naut & Fig* **f. de proue** figurehead
4 *(illustration)* figure, illustration; *(schéma, diagramme)* diagram, figure; **f. géométrique** geometrical figure
5 *Cartes* picture card, *Am* face card
6 *(en danse, patinage et gymnastique)* figure; **figures libres** freestyle; **figures imposées** compulsory figures
7 *Mus* figure
8 *Ling* **f. de rhétorique** rhetorical figure; **f. de style** stylistic device

> Il faut remarquer que lorsqu'il s'applique à une personne, le nom anglais **figure** signifie **silhouette**.

figuré, -e [figyre] ADJ **1** *(plan)* diagrammatic **2** *Ling (langage, sens)* figurative
• **au figuré** ADV figuratively

figurément [figyremɑ̃] ADV figuratively

figurer [3] [figyre] VT **1** *(représenter)* to represent, to show, to depict; **sur la carte, les villages sont figurés par des points** villages are represented by dots on the map **2** *(symboliser)* to symbolize; **la balance et le glaive figurent la justice** scales and the sword symbolize *or* are the symbols of justice
VI **1** *(apparaître)* to appear; **f. dans un catalogue/une bibliographie** to be listed *or* to appear in a catalogue/a bibliography; **votre nom ne figure pas sur la liste** your name doesn't appear *or* isn't on the list; **f. au nombre des élus** to be among the successful candidates; **voici les chevaux qui figurent à l'arrivée** here are the names of the winning horses; **f. en bonne place** to be well placed, to be up among the winners **2** *Cin* to be an extra; *Théât* to do a walk-on part
VPR **se figurer 1** *(imaginer)* to imagine; **figurez-vous une sorte de grande pièce** imagine *or* picture a huge room **2** *(croire)* to believe; **il se figure qu'il va gagner de l'argent** he believes *or* thinks he's going to make money; **figure-toi qu'il n'a même pas appelé!** he didn't even call, can you believe it!; **eh bien figure-toi que moi non plus, je n'ai pas le temps!** surprising though it may seem, I haven't got the time either!; **je suis à sec, figure-toi** believe it or not, I'm broke

figurine [figyrin] NF figurine, statuette

Fiji [fidʒi] = **Fidji**

fil [fil] NM **1** *Tex (matière ▸ de coton, de soie)* thread; *(▸ de laine)* yarn; *(brin ▸ de coton, de soie)* piece of thread; *(▸ de laine)* strand; **cachemire trois/quatre fils** three-ply/four-ply cashmere **f. à bâtir** basting thread; **f. à coudre** sewing thread; **f. dentaire** dental floss; **f. de coton** cotton thread; **f. d'Écosse** lisle; **f. de Nylon®** nylon thread; *Fig* **de f. en aiguille** one thing leading to another; *Fig* **donner du f. à retordre à qn** to cause sb (no end of) trouble; *Fig* **c'est cousu de f. blanc** you can see right through it, it won't fool anybody
2 *(lin)* linen; **draps de f.** linen sheets
3 *(filament ▸ de haricot)* string; **haricots pleins de/sans fils** stringy/stringless beans
4 *(corde ▸ à linge)* line; *(▸ d'équilibriste)* tightrope, high wire; *(▸ pour marionnette)* string; *Myth* **f. d'Ariane** Ariadne's thread; **f. conducteur** *ou* **d'Ariane** *(d'une enquête)* (vital) lead; *(dans une histoire)* main theme; **il n'y a pas de f. conducteur dans ce roman** there's no unifying thread in this novel; **le f. rouge** the recurrent theme; **débrouiller** *ou* **démêler les fils d'une intrigue** to unravel the threads *or* strands of a plot; *Fig* **sa vie ne tient qu'à un f.** his/her life is hanging by a thread; *Fig* **il ne tenait qu'à un f. qu'il soit renvoyé** it was touch and go whether he would be dismissed; *Fig* **c'est lui qui tient les fils** he's the one who holds (all) the strings; **un f. de la Vierge** a gossamer thread; *Fam* **avoir un f. à la patte** to have one's hands tied
5 *(câble)* wire; **f. (électrique)** (electric) wire; **f. (souple)** lead, cord, *Br* flex; **f. de cuivre/d'acier** copper/steel wire; **f. télégraphique/téléphonique** telegraph/telephone wire; **f. de masse** *ou* **de terre** *Br* earth *or Am* ground wire; **f. à couper le beurre** cheesewire; **f. de fer** wire; **f. de fer barbelé** barbed wire; **clôture en f. de fer** *(gén)* wire fence; *(barbelé)* barbed wire fence; **c'est un f. de fer, ce type!** that guy's as thin as a rake!; **f. à plomb** plumbline; **f. à souder** soldering wire; **f. de bougie** (spark) plug lead
6 *Fam (téléphone)* **au bout du f.** on the phone□, on the line; **à l'autre bout du f.** on the other end of the line; **donner** *ou* **passer un coup de f. à qn** to give sb a call, to call sb (up), *Br* to give sb a ring, to ring sb (up); **avoir** *ou* **recevoir un coup de f. de qn** to get a (phone) call from sb□
7 *(tranchant)* edge; **donner le f. à une lame** to sharpen a blade; *Littéraire* **passer qn au f. de l'épée** to put sb to the sword; **être sur le f. du rasoir** to be on a knife-edge
8 *(sens ▸ du bois, de la viande)* grain; **dans le sens contraire au f., contre le f.** against the grain; **dans le sens du f.** with the grain
9 *(cours ▸ de l'eau)* current, stream; *(▸ de la pensée, d'une discussion)* thread; *Ordinat (▸ d'un groupe de discussion)* thread; **le f. des événements** the chain of events; **perdre/reprendre le f. d'une histoire** to lose/to pick up the thread of a story; **j'ai perdu le f., je ne sais plus où j'en suis** I've lost the thread, I don't know where I am any more; **suivre/interrompre le f. des pensées de qn** to follow/to interrupt sb's train of thought
• **au fil de** PRÉP **1** *(le long de)* **aller au f. de l'eau** to go with the current *or* stream; **se laisser aller au f. de l'eau** to let oneself drift (with the current) **2** *(au fur et à mesure de)* **au f. du temps** as time goes by; **au f. des semaines** as the weeks go by, with the passing weeks; **au f. de la discussion je m'aperçus que...** as the discussion progressed I realized that...
• **sans fil** ADJ *(télégraphie, téléphonie)* wireless *(avant n)*; *(rasoir, téléphone)* cordless

filage [filaʒ] NM **1** *Tex* spinning **2** *Théât* run-through

filaire [filɛr] *Tél* ADJ telegraphic; *(téléphone)* corded, plug-in
NM corded *or* plug-in phone

filament [filamɑ̃] NM **1** *(fibre)* filament **2** *Tex* thread **3** *Élec* filament

filamenteux, -euse [filamɑ̃tø, -øz] ADJ filamentous, filamentary

filandière [filɑ̃djɛr] NF *Arch* spinner; *Littéraire* **les sœurs filandières** the Fates

filandreux, -euse [filɑ̃drø, -øz] ADJ **1** *(fibreux ▸ viande)* stringy **2** *Péj (confus ▸ style, discours)* long-winded

filant, -e [filɑ̃, -ɑ̃t] ADJ **1** *(qui file ▸ liquide)* free-running **2** *Méd (pouls)* (very) weak

filasse [filas] NF tow; **f. de chanvre** hemp
ADJ INV *Péj* **cheveux (blonds) f.** dirty blond hair

filateur [filatœr] NM spinning-factory owner

filature [filatyr] NF **1** *Tex (opérations)* spinning; *(usine)* (spinning) mill; **f. de coton** cotton mill **2** *(surveillance)* shadowing, tailing; **prendre qn en f.** to shadow *or* to tail sb

fil-de-fériste *(pl* **fil-de-féristes)**, **fildefériste** [fildəferist] NMF high wire acrobat

file [fil] NF **1** *(suite ▸ de véhicules)* line, row; *(▸ de personnes)* line; **f. d'attente** *Br* queue, *Am* line; **se mettre en f.** to line up, to stand in line, *Br* to queue up; **prendre la f., se mettre à la f.** to join the queue *or Am* line; **marcher en** *ou* **à la f.** to walk in line; **entrer/sortir en f.** *ou* **à la f.** to file in/out; **en f. indienne** in single file
2 *Transp* lane; **la f. de droite** the right-hand lane; **sur deux files** in two lanes; **stationner en double f.** to double-park; **ne changez pas de f.** keep in lane
3 *Mil* file of soldiers
4 *Ordinat* **f. d'attente** print queue *or* list; **mettre en f. d'attente** to queue, to spool
• **à la file** ADV in a row, one after another *or* the other; **il a bu trois verres à la f.** he drank three glasses in a row *or* one after another

filé [file] ADJ M **1** *(bas, collant)* with a run, *Br* laddered **2 verre f.** spun glass
NM *Tech & Tex* thread; **f. d'or** gold thread

filer [3] [file] VT **1** *Tech & Tex* to spin; *Fam* **f. un mauvais coton** *(être malade)* to be in bad shape; *(se préparer des ennuis)* to be heading for trouble **2** *Entom* to spin
3 *(dérouler ▸ câble)* to pay out; *(▸ amarre)* to pay out, to slip
4 *(développer ▸ image, métaphore)* to draw *or* to spin out; *(tenir ▸ note, son)* to draw out
5 *(carte)* to palm off; **f. les cartes** *(au poker)* to show one's hand
6 *(suivre ▸ sujet: détective)* to tail, to shadow
7 *(déchirer ▸ collant, bas)* to run, *Br* to ladder
8 *Fam (donner)* **f. qch à qn** to give sb sth□; **file-moi cinq euros** give us five euros; **f. une gifle à qn** to give sb a slap, to smack *or* to slap sb in the face; **f. un coup de main à qn** to give sb a hand; **file-moi un coup de main** give us a hand; **f. un coup de pied à qn** to kick sb□; **il m'a filé un coup de poing** he *Br* landed *or Am* beaned me one; **on m'a filé le sale boulot** they *Br* landed *or Am* stuck me with the rotten job; **je te file ma robe, je ne la mets jamais** you can have my dress, I never wear it□; **elle m'a filé la grippe** she's given me the flu□
9 *(locutions)* **f. le parfait amour** to live a great romance; **f. des jours heureux** to live very happily
VI **1** *(liquide)* to run, to flow; *(fromage)* to run
2 *(flamme, lampe)* to smoke
3 *(se dérouler ▸ câble)* to run out; **laisser f. un câble** to pay out a cable
4 *Naut* **f. (à) 20 nœuds** to sail *or* to proceed at 20 knots
5 *(collants, bas)* to run, *Br* to ladder; *(maille)* to run; **j'ai un bas qui file** I've got a run *or Br* ladder
6 *(passer vite ▸ coureur)* to dash; *(▸ véhicule, nuage)* to fly (past); *(▸ temps)* to fly; **f. à toute vitesse** *(voiture)* to bomb along; **il a filé dans sa chambre** *(gén)* he dashed *or* flew into his bedroom; *(après une dispute)* he stormed off to his room; **il faut que je file si je veux avoir mon train** I must dash if I'm going to catch my train; **bon, je file!** right, I'm off!; **sa victime lui a filé entre les doigts** his/her victim slipped through his/her fingers; **l'argent lui file entre les doigts** money just slips through his/her fingers; **les journées filent à une vitesse!** the days are just flying by!
7 *Fam (disparaître ▸ cambrioleur)* to scram, *Br* to scarper, *Am* to skedaddle; **f. (en douce)** to slip away *or* off; **quand je suis entré dans la boutique ils avaient filé!** when I went into the shop I found that they'd taken off!; **je t'ai assez vu, file!** I've had enough of you, scram! *or* clear off!; **f. à l'anglaise** to sneak off, to take French leave; *(pour éviter quelqu'un ou quelque chose)* to make a quick getaway, *Br* to do a runner
8 *Fam (argent)* to go, to disappear, to vanish; **il a eu trois millions à la mort de son père mais tout a filé!** he inherited three million when his father died but now it's all gone!
9 *(locution)* **f. doux** to behave oneself; **avec sa tante, elle file doux!** she's as good as gold with her aunt!; **avec moi, tu as intérêt à f. doux!** just watch your step with me, that's all!

filet [filɛ] NM **1** *Anat* fibre; **f. nerveux** nerve fibre
2 *Bot (d'étamine)* filament
3 *(de reliure) & Archit* fillet
4 *Tech* thread
5 *Typ* rule; **f. maigre** hairline (rule)
6 *(petite quantité)* **un f. d'eau** a trickle of water; **un f. de bave** a dribble of saliva; **un f. de sang** a trickle of blood; **un f. d'air** a (light) stream of air; **un f. de lumière** a (thin) shaft of light; **un f. de fumée** a wisp of smoke; **un f. de citron/vinaigre** a dash of lemon/vinegar; **un (petit) f. de voix** a thin (reedy) voice
7 *Culin (de viande, de poisson)* fillet; **un morceau dans le f.** *(de bœuf)* ≃ a sirloin *or* porterhouse steak; **faire des filets de sole** to fillet a sole; **f. mignon** filet mignon
8 *(ouvrage à mailles)* net; *Mil* **f. de camouflage** camouflage net; **f. à cheveux** hair net; **f. (à bagages)** (luggage) rack; **f. dérivant** *ou* **flottant** drift net; **f. à papillons** butterfly net; **f. (de pêche)** (fishing) net; **f. à provisions** string bag; *Fig* **attirer qn dans ses filets** to entrap *or* to ensnare sb; **tendre un f.** *Chasse* to set a snare; *Fig* to lay a trap; **un beau coup de f. pour la police** a good haul for the police
9 *Sport (au football, au hockey, au tennis)* net; *(d'acrobate)* safety net; **envoyer la balle dans le f.** to hit the ball into the net; **le petit f.** *(au football)* the side netting; **monter au f.** to come up to the net; **balle de f.** let (ball); **travailler sans f.** to perform without a safety net; *Fig* to take risks

filetage [filtaʒ] NM *Tech* **1** *(action)* threading **2** *(filets)* (screw) thread; **f. Acmé** Acme thread; **f. Whitworth** Whitworth thread

fileter [28] [filte] VT **1** *Tech* to thread; *(métal)* to wiredraw; *(fil)* to draw **2** *Culin* to fillet

fileur, -euse [filœr, -øz] NM,F *Tex* spinner

filial, -e, -aux, -ales [filjal, -o] ADJ filial
• **filiale** NF subsidiary (company); **filiale consolidée** consolidated subsidiary; **filiale de distribution** marketing subsidiary; **filiale de vente** sales subsidiary

filialement [filjalmɑ̃] ADV filially

filiation [filjasjɔ̃] NF **1** *(entre individus)* line of descent, filiation; *Jur* filiation; **en f. directe** in direct line; **un descendant en f. directe** a direct descendant **2** *Littéraire (famille)* descendants **3** *(entre des mots, des idées)* relationship; **des théories en f. directe avec ce texte** theories directly related to this text

filière [filjɛr] NF **1** *(procédures)* procedures, channels; **passer par la f. administrative** to go through administrative channels; **passer par** *ou* **suivre la f.** *(pour obtenir quelque chose)* to go through official channels; *(comme employé)* to work one's way up
2 *(réseau ▸ de trafiquants, de criminels)* network, connection; **ils ont démantelé la f. française** they smashed the French connection; **remonter une f.** to trace a network back to its ringleaders
3 *Scol & Univ* **la f. technique/scientifique** technical/scientific subjects; **nous avons suivi la même f. jusqu'à 16 ans** we did the same subjects (as each other) until the age of 16; **il est passé par la f. classique pour devenir éditeur** he had the usual background and training of an editor
4 *Tech (pour fileter une vis)* screw plate; **f. (à machine)** *(pour étirage)* draw, drawing plate; *(pour tréfilage, filage)* die; **travailler un métal à la f.** to draw a metal
5 *Entom* spinneret
6 *Tex* spinneret
7 *Ind* industry; **la f. bois/électronique** the wood/electronics industry

filiforme [filifɔrm] ADJ **1** *(maigre)* lanky, spindly **2** *Méd (pouls)* thready **3** *Entom* filiform, threadlike

filigrane [filigran] NM **1** *(d'un papier)* watermark **2** *(en joaillerie)* filigree; **broche en f.** filigree brooch
• **en filigrane** ADV *(implicitement)* between the lines; **lire en f.** to read between the lines; **le problème du racisme apparaissait en f. dans la discussion** the problem of racism was implicit in the discussion

filigraner [3] [filigrane] VT **1** *(papier)* to watermark; **du papier filigrané** watermarked paper **2** *(en joaillerie)* to filigree

filin [filɛ̃] NM rope

fille [fij] NF **1** *(enfant)* girl; **c'est une belle/gentille f.** she's a good-looking/nice girl; **tu es une grande f. maintenant** you're a big girl now; **c'est encore une petite f.** she's still a little girl; **école de filles** girls' school; **c'est un jeu de filles** that's a girl's game; *Fig* **jouer la f. de l'air** to escape, to get out
2 *(jeune fille)* girl; *(femme)* woman; **c'est une f. que j'ai connue il y a 20 ans** I met that woman 20 years ago; **une f. de la campagne** a country girl; *Vieilli* **rester f.** to remain single *or* unmarried; *Péj* **f. facile** slut; **jeune f.** girl, young woman; *Vieilli Péj* **f. mère** unmarried mother
3 *(descendante)* daughter; **les filles Richard ont toutes fait des études de droit** all the Richard girls *or* daughters studied law; *Fig* **la paresse est la f. de l'oisiveté** laziness is the daughter of idleness; **une f. de bonne famille** a respectable girl; **tu es bien la f. de ton père!** you're just like your father!
4 *(en appellatif)* **ma f.** (my) girl; **ça, ma f., je t'avais prévenue!** don't say I didn't warn you, (my) girl!
5 *Vieilli (employée)* **f. de cuisine** kitchen maid; **f. de ferme** farm girl; **f. de salle** *(dans les hôpitaux)* ward orderly; *(dans un hôtel)* waitress; **f. de service** maidservant
6 *Vieilli (prostituée)* whore; **aller chez les filles** to go to a brothel, to go whoring; *Littéraire* **f. publique** *ou* **de joie** *ou* **des rues** *ou* **perdue** whore, lady of the night; **f. à soldats** camp follower; **f. à matelots** prostitute *(whose customers are primarily sailors)*
7 *Hist* **f. d'honneur** maid of honour
8 *Rel* **les filles du Carmel** the Carmelite nuns; **les filles de Port-Royal** the sisters *or* nuns of Port-Royal

fille-mère [fijmɛr] *(pl* **filles-mères***)* NF *Vieilli Péj* unmarried mother

fillette [fijɛt] NF **1** *(enfant)* little girl **2** *(bouteille)* small bottle *(for wine)*

filleul, -e [fijœl] NM,F godchild, godson, *f* goddaughter; *Mil* **f. de guerre** = soldier taken care of by a woman during a war

film [film] NM **1** *Cin (pellicule)* film; *(œuvre)* movie, *Br* film; **tourner un f.** to shoot a movie *or Br* film; *Fam Fig* **il n'a rien compris au f.** he hasn't taken anything in; *Fam Fig* **se faire un f.** to be living in a dream world; **f. en noir et blanc/en couleur** black and white/colour movie *or Br* film; **f. d'action** action movie *or Br* film; **f. d'actualités** newsreel, news film; **f. d'animation** animated film, cartoon; **f. d'archives** library film; **f. d'art et d'essai** arthouse movie *or Br* film; **f. d'auteur** film d'auteur; **f. d'aventures** adventure movie *or Br* film; **f. biographique** biopic; **f. burlesque** slapstick comedy; **f. de cape et d'épée** swashbuckler; **f. catastrophe** disaster movie *or Br* film; **f. à clef** movie *or Br* film based on real characters *(whose identity is disguised)*; **f. de cow-boys** cowboy movie *or Br* film; **f. culte** cult movie *or Br* film; **f. documentaire** documentary (film); **f. dramatique** drama; **f. d'entreprise** corporate film, corporate video; **f. d'épouvante** horror movie *or Br* film; **f. d'espionnage** spy movie *or Br* film; **f. à faible budget** low-budget movie *or Br* film; **f. fantastique** supernatural thriller; **f. de fiction** fictional movie *or Br* film; **f. de genre** genre movie *or Br* film; **f. à grand spectacle** epic movie *or Br* film; **f. à gros succès** blockbuster; **f. de guerre** war movie *or Br* film; **f. d'horreur** horror movie *or Br* film; **f. institutionnel** corporate film, corporate video; **f. long-métrage** feature-length movie, *Br* feature film; **f. de montage** film montage, compilation movie *or Br* film; **f. muet** silent movie *or Br* film; **f. noir** film noir; **f. parlant** talkie, talking film; **f. plat** two-dimensional movie *or Br* film; **f. policier** detective movie *or Br* film; *Fam* **f. porno** porn film, blue movie, skin flick; **f. pornographique** pornographic movie *or Br* film; **f. de poursuite** chase movie *or Br* film; **f. publicitaire** *(à la télévision)* commercial; *(au cinéma)* cinema advertisement; **f. en relief** 3D movie *or Br* film; **f. de science-fiction** science fiction movie *or Br* film; **f. semi-documentaire** docudrama; **f. de série B** B-movie; **f. sonore** sound film; **f. à succès** box-office hit; **f. à suspense** thriller; **f. télévisé** television movie *or Br* film, TV movie *or Br* film; **f. en 3D** 3D movie *or Br* film; **f. vidéo** video film; **f. de voyage** travelogue; **f. (classé) X** adults-only movie, *Br* X-rated film
2 *Phot* film
3 *(couche)* film; **un f. d'huile** a film of oil; **f. dentaire** (dental) plaque
4 *(pellicule)* **sous f. plastique** shrink-wrapped; **f. transparent** transparency; **recouvert d'un f. protecteur** covered with a protective film; **f. alimentaire** *Br* clingfilm, *Am* Saran® wrap
5 *(déroulement)* sequence; **le f. des événements** the sequence of events; **quand elle retraçait le f. de sa vie** when she looked back on her life

filmage [filmaʒ] NM *Cin* filming

filmer [3] [filme] VT *(scène, événement)* to film, to shoot; *(personnage)* to film; **il a fait f. toute la scène sans le dire** he got somebody to film the whole thing without telling anyone

filmique [filmik] ADJ cinematic

filmographie [filmɔgrafi] NF filmography

filmologie [filmɔlɔʒi] NF cinema *or Br* film studies

filmothèque [filmɔtɛk] NF microfilm collection

filoche [filɔʃ] NF *Fam* shadowing, tailing

filoguidé, -e [filɔgide] ADJ *Mil* wire-guided

filon [filɔ̃] NM **1** *Géol* seam, vein; *Fig* **ils ont déjà exploité ce f.** they have already exploited that gold mine **2** *Fam (locutions)* **il a trouvé le f. pour gagner de l'argent** *(moyen)* he found an easy way to make money[▫]; **trouver le f.** *(situation lucrative)* to strike it rich, *Am* to find the right connection; **j'ai enfin trouvé le f.** I've found a cushy number at last, *Am* I'm on the gravy train at last; **c'est un bon f.** it's a gold mine *or* a money-spinner; **j'ai un bon f. pour avoir des vidéos gratuites** I know where I can get free videos easily[▫]

filou [filu] NM **1** *(voleur)* crook, rogue **2** *(ton affectueux)* rascal, scamp; **oh, le f., il a caché la télécommande!** the little rascal's hidden the TV remote!

filoutage [filutaʒ] NM **1** *Fam* swindling **2** *Ordinat* phishing

filouter [3] [filute] VT *Fam* **1** *(dérober)* to pinch, to swipe **2** *(escroquer)* to cheat[▫], to swindle

filouterie [filutri] NF *Jur* fraud, swindle

fils [fis] NM **1** *(enfant)* son, boy; **viens là, mon f.** come here my son *or* boy; *Fam* **tous les f. Fouillat ont mal tourné** all the Fouillat boys *or* sons went off the straight and narrow; **le f. de la maison** the son of the house; *Fam* **un f. à papa** a daddy's boy; **il est bien le f. de son père!** he's just like his father!; **un f. de famille** a wealthy young man; *Vulg* **f. de pute** son of a bitch; *Bible* **le f. prodigue** the prodigal son; **f. spirituel** spiritual son
2 *Com* **Brunet & F.** Brunet & Son *or* Sons; **je voudrais parler à M. Picard f.** I'd like to talk to Mr Picard junior
3 *Littéraire (descendant)* descendant; *(natif)* son; **la patrie reconnaissante à ses f. sacrifiés** *(sur monument aux morts)* lest we forget; **un f. du terroir** a son of the land
4 *Rel* **le F. de l'homme** *ou* **de Dieu** the son of man *or* of God; **mon f.** my son
5 *(locution)* **être f. de ses œuvres** to be a self-made man

filtrage [filtraʒ] NM **1** *(d'un liquide)* filtering; *Chim* filtration **2** *(de l'information, de personnes)* screening **3** *Opt & Phot* filtering; **f. des images** image filtering

filtrant, -e [filtrɑ̃, -ɑ̃t] ADJ *(matériau, dispositif)* filtering *(avant n)*; *(verre)* filter *(avant n)*; *Méd* filterable, filtrable; **lunettes à verres filtrants** glasses with filter lenses; **une crème filtrante** a sunscreen

filtration [filtrasjɔ̃] NF filtration, filtering

filtre [filtr] ADJ *(papier, cigarette, café)* filter *(avant n)*
NM filter; **f. à air** air filter; *Rad & TV* **f. antiparasites** interference filter *or* suppressor; *Ordinat* **f. antireflet** glare screen; **f. audio** audio filter; **f. à brouillard** *(pour une caméra)* fog filter; **f. à café** coffee filter; **f. à carburant** fuel filter; **f. au charbon** carbon filter; **f. à combustible** fuel filter; **f. correcteur** corrective filter; *Phot* **f. couleur** *ou* **de couleur** *ou* **coloré** colour filter; *Ordinat* **f. écran** screen filter; **f. à essence** petrol filter; *Ordinat* **f. d'exportation** export filter; **f. à huile** oil filter; *Ordinat* **f. d'importation** import filter; *TV & Cin* **f. pour objectif de caméra** camera lens filter; **f. à particules**

dust filter; *Cin & TV* **f. polarisant** polarizing filter; **f. à pollen** pollen filter; *Rad* **f. séparateur** crossover; **f. solaire** sunscreen

filtrer [3] [filtre] VT **1** *(liquide, air, lumière)* to filter **2** *(visiteurs, informations)* to screen

VI **1** *(liquide)* to seep, to filter (**à travers** through); *(lumière, bruit)* to filter (**à travers** through) **2** *(nouvelles)* to filter through; *(par accident)* to leak out; **ils n'ont rien laissé f. de ses déclarations** they have said nothing about his/her statement

FIN[1] [fɛ̃]

- end **1–4, 6, 7**
- death **3**
- purpose **4**

NF **1** *(terme ▸ d'une période, d'un mandat)* end; *(▸ d'une journée, d'un match)* end, close; *(▸ d'une course)* end, finish; *(▸ d'un film, d'un roman)* end, ending; *(▸ d'un contrat, d'un bail)* expiry, expiration; **la f. de l'année/de sa vie/d'un concert** the end of the year/his/her life/a concert; **la f. de la journée** the end of the day; **à la f. de la journée** at the end of the day; **jusqu'à la f. des temps** *ou* **des siècles** until the end of time; **par une f. d'après-midi de juin** late on a June afternoon; **f. mai/2006** (at the) end of May/2006; **on se reverra f. mars** *ou* **à la f. de mars** we'll meet again at the end of March; **se battre/rester jusqu'à la f.** to fight/to stay to the very end; **mener qch à bonne f.** to carry sth off (successfully), to bring sth to a successful conclusion, to deal successfully with sth; **mettre f. à qch** to put an end to sth; **mettre f. à ses jours** to put an end to one's life, to take one's own life; **prendre f.** to come to an end; **tirer** *ou* **toucher à sa f.** to come to an end, to draw to a close; **nos vacances touchent à leur f.** our holidays are coming to an end *or* will soon be over; **le contrat touche à sa f.** the contract will expire soon; **f. de semaine** end of the week; *(week-end)* weekend; **la f. du mois** the end of the month; *Com* **f. de mois** monthly statement; **de f. de mois** end-of-month; **assurer ses fins de mois** to make sure one has enough money at the end of the month; **avoir des fins de mois difficiles** to find it hard to make ends meet (at the end of the month); **faire une f.** to settle down, to get married; **on n'en voit pas la f.** there doesn't seem to be any end to it; **ça y est, j'en vois la f.!** at last, I can see the light at the end of the tunnel!; **f.** *(d'un film)* The End

2 *(disparition)* end; **la f. de la civilisation inca** the end *or* death of Inca civilization; **la f. du monde** the end of the world; **ce n'est quand même pas la f. du monde!** it's not the end of the world, is it!; *Fam Hum* **c'est la f. de tout** *ou* **des haricots!** our goose is cooked!

3 *(mort)* death, end; **avoir une f. tragique/lente** to die a tragic/slow death; **connaître une f. prématurée** to come to *or* to meet an untimely end; **avoir une belle f.** to have a fine end; **il a eu une f. affreuse** he had *or* came to a terrible end *or* death; **la f. approche** the end is near; **vers la f., il n'était plus le même** he wasn't the same towards the end; **le lave-vaisselle est sur sa f.** the dishwasher is on its last legs

4 *(objectif)* end, purpose; **à cette f.** to this end, for this purpose, with that aim in mind; **à quelle f.?** for what purpose?, to what end?, with what end in view?; **à seule f. de faire** with the sole aim of doing, (simply) for the sake of doing, purely in order to do; *Jur* **aux fins de débauche** for immoral purposes; **aux fins de faire qch** with a view to doing sth; **arriver** *ou* **parvenir à ses fins** to achieve one's aim; **à des fins personnelles** for personal *or* private use; **à des fins politiques/religieuses** to political/religious ends; **f. en soi** end in itself; *Prov* **la f. justifie les moyens, qui veut la f. veut les moyens** the end justifies the means

5 *Jur* **f. de non-recevoir** demurrer; *Fig* **opposer une f. de non-recevoir à qn** to turn down sb's request bluntly; **renvoyé des fins de la plainte** discharged, acquitted

6 *Com* **f. courant** at the end of the current month; **payable f. courant/prochain** payable at the end of this/next month; **f. de série** *(d'articles)* discontinued line

7 *Compta* **f. d'exercice** year end, end of the financial year

8 *Ordinat* **f. de ligne** line end; **f. de page** page-break; **f. de page obligatoire** hard page break; **f. de paragraphe** paragraph break; **f. de session** log-off

• **à la fin** ADV **1** *(finalement)* in the end, eventually **2** *Fam (ton irrité)* **mais à la f., où est-il?** where on earth is it?; **tu es stupide à la f.** you really are very stupid; **tu m'ennuies à la f.!** you're really annoying me!

• **à la fin de** PRÉP at the end *or* close of; **le glossaire est à la f. du livre** the glossary is at the back of the book

• **à toutes fins utiles** ADV **1** *(pour information)* **je vous signale à toutes fins utiles que...** for your information, let me point out that... **2** *(le cas échéant)* just in case; **dans la boîte à gants, j'avais mis à toutes fins utiles une carte de France** I had put a map of France in the glove compartment, just in case

• **en fin de** PRÉP **en f. de soirée/match** towards the end of the evening/match; **en f. d'année** at the end of the year; **il a faibli en f. de trimestre** his work fell off towards the end of the term; **être en f. de liste** to be *or* to come at the end of the list; *Fig* **être en f. de course** *(athlète, président)* to be at the end of the road; *(vis)* to be screwed fully home; *(piston)* to have reached the end of its stroke; **être en f. de droits** to come to the end of one's entitlement *(to an allowance)*

• **en fin de compte** ADV *(après tout)* in the end, after all; *(tout bien considéré)* all things considered, taking everything into account; *(pour conclure)* finally, to conclude

• **fin de race** ADJ degenerate

• **fin de siècle** ADJ decadent, fin de siècle

• **sans fin** ADJ **1** *(interminable)* endless, interminable, never-ending **2** *Tech* endless ADV endlessly, interminably

FIN[2], -E[1] [fɛ̃, fin]

ADJ
- fine **1**
- sharp **3, 6**
- subtle **5**
- delicate **2, 4**
- high-quality **4**

ADV
- finely **1**
- sharply **1**

ADJ **1** *(mince ▸ sable, pinceau, aiguille, pointe, cheveu, fil)* fine; *(▸ étoffe)* fine, thin; *(▸ écriture)* fine, small; *(▸ doigt, jambe, taille, main)* slim, slender; *(▸ papier, tranche)* thin; *(▸ collant, bas)* sheer; **pluie fine** drizzle; **haricots verts fins** dwarf beans

2 *(délicat ▸ visage, traits)* delicate

3 *(aiguisé ▸ pointe)* sharp

4 *(de qualité ▸ aliments, produit)* high-quality, top-quality; *(▸ mets, repas)* delicate, exquisite, refined; *(▸ dentelle, lingerie)* delicate, fine; *(▸ or, pierre, vin)* fine

5 *(subtil ▸ observation, description)* subtle, clever; *(▸ personne)* perceptive, subtle; *(▸ esprit)* sharp, keen, shrewd; *(▸ plaisanterie)* witty; **ce n'était pas très f. de ta part** it wasn't very smart *or* clever of you; **bien f. qui le prendra** it would take a smart man to catch him; *Ironique* **c'est f.!** very clever!; **tu as l'air f. avec ce chapeau!** you look *Br* a right wally *or Am* a total jerk in that hat!

6 *(sensible ▸ ouïe, vue)* sharp, keen, acute; *(▸ odorat)* discriminating, sensitive; **avoir le nez f.** to have a keen sense of smell; *Fig* **elle a le nez f.** she's sharp

7 *Can (gentil)* nice, kind, sweet(-natured); **avoir l'air f.** *(beau)* to be good-looking

8 *(avant le nom) (extrême)* **dans le** *ou* **au f. fond du placard** at the very back of the cupboard *or Am* closet; **au f. fond de la campagne** in the depths of the countryside, *Péj* in the middle of nowhere; **au f. fond de la Sibérie** in deepest Siberia; **le f. mot de l'histoire** the truth of the matter

9 *(avant le nom) (excellent)* **un f. connaisseur** a (great) connoisseur; **un f. connaisseur en vins** an expert on *or* a (great) connoisseur of wines; **une fine cuisinière** a gourmet cook; **un f. gourmet** a gourmet; **c'est une fine mouche** he's/she's a sharp customer; **un f. stratège** a fine *or* an expert strategist; **un f. tireur** a crack shot; **une fine lame** a fine swordsman, *f* swordswoman; **la fine équipe!** what a team!

NM **1 le f. du f.** the ultimate

2 jouer au (plus) f. to have a battle of wits; **ne joue pas au plus f. avec moi** don't try to outwit *or* to outsmart me

NM,F *Can Fam Ironique* **beau f./belle fine!** you fool!; **tu n'aurais pas dû mettre ton nez dans cette affaire, espèce de beau f.!** you should never have got mixed up in that business, you fool!

ADV **1** *(finement ▸ moulu)* fine, finely; *(▸ taillé)* sharp, sharply; **des crayons taillés f.** sharp-pointed pencils; **c'est écrit trop f.** it's written too small; **haché f.** *(herbes)* finely chopped

2 *(tout à fait)* **être f. prêt** to be ready; **être f. saoul** to be blind drunk

• **fine bouche** NF **1** *(gourmet)* **c'est une fine bouche** he's/she's a gourmet **2** *(locution)* **tu ne vas pas faire la fine bouche!** don't be so choosy!

• **fine gueule** NF *Fam* gourmet□

final, -e, -als *ou* **-aux, -ales** [final, -o] ADJ **1** *(qui termine)* final, end *(avant n)* **2** *Ling & Phil* final **3** *(règlement, solde)* final

NM *Mus & (en danse)* finale

• **finale** NM *Mus & (en danse)* finale NF **1** *Ling (syllabe)* final syllable; *(voyelle)* final vowel **2** *Sport* final; **la finale de la coupe** the cup final; **aller/être en finale** to go *or* to get through to/to be in the finals

• **au final** ADV *Fam* in the end

finalement [finalmɑ̃] ADV **1** *(à la fin)* finally, eventually, in the end **2** *(tout compte fait)* after all, when all is said and done

finaliser [3] [finalize] VT to finalize

finaliste [finalist] ADJ **1** *Sport* **l'équipe f.** the team of finalists; **candidat f.** *(dans un concours)* finalist **2** *Phil* finalistic

NMF *Phil, Sport & (dans un concours)* finalist

finalité [finalite] NF **1** *(but)* aim, purpose, end **2** *Phil* finality **3** *Biol* adaptation

finance [finɑ̃s] NF *(profession)* **la f., le monde de la f.** (the world of) finance; **entrer dans la f.** to enter the world of finance; **la haute f.** *(milieu)* high finance; *(personnes)* the financiers, the bankers; **f. d'entreprise** corporate finance; **f. internationale** global finance

• **finances** NFPL **1** *Pol* **les Finances** *Br* ≃ the Exchequer, *Am* ≃ the Treasury Department; **finances publiques** public funds **2** *Fam (argent)* finances; **les finances de la société vont mal** the company's finances are in a bad way; **ça dépendra de mes finances** it will depend on whether I can afford it or not; **mes finances sont à zéro** my finances have hit rock bottom

financement [finɑ̃smɑ̃] NM financing *(UNCOUNT)*, finance; *(surtout d'un mécène)* (financial) backing; **le f. du projet sera assuré par la compagnie** the company will finance *or* fund the project; **f. à court terme** short-term financing; **f. de départ** start-up capital; **f. par emprunt** debt financing; **f. par endettement** debt financing; **f. d'entreprise** corporate financing; **f. initial** start-up capital; **f. à long terme** long-term financing; **f. à moyen terme** medium-term financing; **f. à taux fixe** fixed-rate financing

financement-relais [finɑ̃smɑ̃rəlɛ] *(pl* **financements-relais)** NM *Fin* bridge financing

financer [16] [finɑ̃se] VT *(journal, projet)* to finance, to back (financially), to put up the finance for; *(sujet: mécène)* to back, to put up the money for; **l'opération a été entièrement financée par emprunt** the transaction was financed entirely through borrowing; **BP financera le projet à 50 pour cent** BP will put up half of the funding for the project

USAGE ABSOLU *Fam* **une fois de plus, ce sont ses parents qui vont f.** once again, his/her parents will fork out

financier, -ère [finɑ̃sje, -ɛr] ADJ *(crise, politique)* financial; **problèmes financiers** *(d'un État)* financial problems; *(d'une personne)* money problems

NM **1** *Fin* financier; **f. d'entreprise** corporate finance manager **2** *Culin* financier *(rectangular sponge finger made with almonds)*

• **financière** NF *Culin* sauce financière, financière sauce *(made with sweetbreads, mushrooms etc)*

• **à la financière** ADJ *Culin* à la financière, with financière sauce

financièrement [finɑ̃sjɛrmɑ̃] ADV financially

finasser [3] [finase] VI *Fam* to scheme

finasserie [finasri] NF *Fam* scheming

finasseur, -euse [finasœr, -øz], **finassier, -ère** [finasje, -ɛr] NM,F *Fam Vieilli* trickster

finaud, -e [fino, -od] ADJ cunning, shrewd, wily
NM,F **1** *(malin)* **c'est un (petit) f.** he's a crafty *or* sly one **2** *Ordinat* hacker

finauderie [finodri] NF shrewdness, wiliness

fine[2] [fin] ADJ *voir* **fin**[2]
NF **1** *(eau-de-vie)* ≃ brandy; **f. champagne** = variety of Cognac; **une f. à l'eau** = a brandy and soda **2** *(huître)* **fines de claire** = specially fattened greenish oysters

finement [finmɑ̃] ADV **1** *(de façon fine ▸ hacher, dessiner)* finely **2** *(subtilement)* subtly, with finesse

finesse [finɛs] NF **1** *(délicatesse ▸ d'un mets, d'un vin)* delicacy; *(▸ d'une étoffe)* delicacy, fineness; *(▸ du sable)* fineness; **la f. du trait dans les dessins de Dürer** the delicate lines of *or* the finesse of Dürer's drawings; **jouer Chopin avec beaucoup de f.** to give a sensitive interpretation of Chopin
2 *(perspicacité)* flair, finesse, shrewdness
3 *(subtilité)* subtlety *(UNCOUNT)*; **une remarque pleine de f.** a very subtle remark; **f. d'esprit** shrewdness; **f. de goût** refined taste
4 *(acuité)* sharpness, keenness; **f. d'ouïe/de l'odorat** keenness *or* acuteness of hearing/of smell
5 *(minceur ▸ de la taille)* slenderness, slimness; *(▸ des cheveux, d'une poudre)* fineness; *(▸ du papier, d'un fil)* thinness; **la f. de ses traits** the fineness of his/her features; **des draps d'une grande f.** sheets of the finest cloth
6 *(d'une pointe, d'une image optique)* sharpness; *(d'une lame)* keenness
• **finesses** NFPL *(subtilités)* subtleties, niceties; **les finesses du français** the subtleties of the French language; **les finesses de la diplomatie** diplomatic niceties; **il connaît toutes les finesses du métier** he knows all the tricks of the trade

finette [finɛt] NF *Tex* brushed cotton

fini, -e [fini] ADJ **1** *(perdu)* finished; **c'est un homme f.** he's finished; **en tant que banquier, je suis f.** my banking career is finished
2 *Péj (en intensif)* complete, utter; **un imbécile f.** a complete *or* an utter fool; **un voleur f.** an out-and-out thief
3 *Math & Phil* finite
4 *(accompli, terminé)* finished; **c'est f. (tout cela), tout est f.** that's all over (and done with); **c'est f. entre nous** we're finished, it's all over between us; **(c'est) f. de rire** the fun's over
5 *(ouvrage ▸ parfait)* well finished; **cette robe est mal finie** this dress is badly finished
NM **1** *(perfection)* finish **2** *Phil* **le f.** that which is finite

finir [32] [finir] VT **1** *(achever ▸ tâche, ouvrage)* to finish (off); *(▸ guerre, liaison, vie)* to end; *(▸ études)* to complete; *(▸ période, séjour)* to finish, to complete; **f. un tableau/une sculpture** to finish (off) a picture/sculpture; **il a fini ses jours à Cannes** he ended his days in Cannes; **il a fini la soirée au poste** he wound up in a police cell (at the end of the evening); **finissez la vaisselle d'abord** first finish the dishes, get the dishes finished first; **mon travail est fini maintenant** my work's done now; *Littéraire* **finissez mes craintes** put an end to my fears; **f. de faire qch** to finish doing sth; **il avait fini de travailler** he had finished working *or* work
2 *(plat, boisson)* to finish (off *or* up); **qui a fini le shampooing?** who's used up all *or* finished off the shampoo?; *Fam* **finis ton assiette** eat up *or* finish off what's on your plate; **il a fini le gâteau/la bouteille** he finished off the cake/the bottle; **je finissais toujours les vêtements de mes aînés** I was always dressed in my elder brothers' hand-me-downs; **je vais f. ces chaussures** I'll wear these shoes out
3 *(en réprimande)* **vous n'avez pas fini de vous plaindre?** haven't you done enough moaning?, can't you stop moaning?; *Fam* **c'est pas bientôt fini, ce bazar?** is this racket going to stop soon?; **c'est fini, ce boucan?** stop that racket, will you!
USAGE ABSOLU **1** *(achever)* **laisse-moi seulement f.** just let me finish; **je n'ai pas fini!** I haven't finished (what I have to say)!; **tu n'as pas bientôt fini!** will you stop it!; **tu as fini, oui, ou c'est une claque!** stop it now or you'll get a smack!; **c'en est bien fini de mes rêves!** that's the end of all my dreams!; **finissons-en** let's get it over with; **elle a voulu en f.** *(se suicider)* she tried to end it all; **il faut en f., cette situation ne peut plus durer** it can't continue, we must do something to put an end to this state of affairs
2 en f. avec qn/qch to be *or* to have done with sb/sth; **il faut en f. avec ces idées reçues** we must break with *or* shake off these preconceived ideas; **il veut en f. avec la vie** he's had enough of life; **j'en aurai bientôt fini avec lui** I'll be done with him soon
VI **1** *(arriver à son terme)* to finish, to end; **f. en pointe** to end in a point; **la route finit au pont** the road stops at the bridge; **la réunion a fini dans les hurlements** the meeting ended in uproar; **ça a fini par des embrassades** it ended in a lot of hugging and kissing; **la leçon finit à quatre heures** the lesson finishes at four; **l'école finit en juin** school ends in June; **quand est-ce que ça finit?** when does it end *or* finish?; **quand finit ton stage?** when's the end of your placement?; **comment est-ce que ça a fini?** how did it end?; **à quelle heure tu finis?** what time do you finish?; **je finirai sur ce vers de Villon** let me end with this line from Villon; **pour f.** in the end, finally; **et pour f., voici le dessert** and to finish (with), here's the dessert; **elle a marchandé mais pour f. elle n'a pas acheté le tapis** she haggled over the price of the carpet but in the end she didn't buy it; **f. par faire qch** to end up (by) doing sth; **il a fini par renoncer/réussir** he finally gave up/succeeded; **la justice finit par triompher** justice triumphs in the end *or* in the long run *or* eventually; **ça finit par coûter cher** it costs a lot of money in the end; **tu finis par m'agacer** you're beginning to annoy me; **tu vas f. par le faire pleurer** you'll end up (by) making him cry; *Fam* **et maintenant, fini de se croiser les bras!** and now let's see some action!; **en janvier, fini de rigoler, tu te remets au travail** come January there'll be no more messing around, you're going to have to get down to some work; **son discours n'en finit pas** his/her speech is never-ending; **cette journée n'en finit pas** there's no end to this day; **cela n'en finit pas** there's no end to it; **il n'en finit plus de se préparer dans la salle de bain** he's taking ages in the bathroom getting ready; **si on tient compte des exceptions, on ne va plus en f.!** we'll never see the end of this if we take exceptions into account!; *Hum* **un grand adolescent qui n'en finit pas** a big kid; **à n'en plus f.** endless, never-ending, interminable; **elle a des jambes à n'en plus f.** she has incredibly long legs; **des plaintes à n'en plus f.** endless *or* never-ending complaints; *Fam* **f. en queue de poisson** to fizzle out
2 *(avoir telle issue)* **elle a fini juge** she ended up a judge; **il a mal fini** *(délinquant)* he came to a bad end; **une histoire qui finit bien/mal** a story with a happy/sad ending; **l'histoire ne finit pas là** that's not the end of the story; **comment tout cela va-t-il f.?** where *or* how will it all end?; **ça va mal f.** no good will come of it, it will all end in disaster; *Prov* **tout est bien qui finit bien** all's well that ends well
3 *(mourir)* to die; **f. à l'hôpital** to end one's days *or* to die in hospital; **f. sous un autobus** to end up under a bus

finish [finiʃ] NM INV *Sport* finish; **jouer un match/une partie au f.** to play a match/game to the finish; *Fam Fig* **je l'ai eu au f.** I got him in the end

finissage [finisaʒ] NM *Tech* finishing

finissant, -e [finisɑ̃, -ɑ̃t] ADJ **1** *Littéraire* finishing; *(société)* in decline; **au jour f.** at dusk **2** *Can (élève)* in his/her last year at school
NM,F *Can* final-year student

finisseur, -euse [finisœr, -øz] NM,F *(gén) & Sport* finisher; **on peut lui faire confiance pour le marathon, c'est un f.!** we can count on him in the marathon, he's a finisher!
NM *(dans les travaux publics)* finisher

finition [finisjɔ̃] NF **1** *(détail)* **la f. du manteau est très bien faite** the coat's nicely finished; **les finitions** the finishing touches; *Couture* **je déteste faire les finitions** I hate the sewing up **2** *(perfectionnement)* finishing off *(UNCOUNT)*; **les travaux de f. prendront plusieurs jours** it will take several days to finish off the work

finlandais, -e [fɛ̃lɑ̃dɛ, -ɛz] ADJ Finnish
• **Finlandais, -e** NM,F Finn

Finlande [fɛ̃lɑ̃d] NF **la F.** Finland

finnois, -e [finwa, -az] ADJ Finnish
NM *(langue)* Finnish
• **Finnois, -e** NM,F Finn

finno-ougrien, -enne [finougrijɛ̃, -ɛn] *(mpl* **finno-ougriens**, *fpl* **finno-ougriennes)** *Ling* ADJ Finno-Ugric, Finno-Ugrian
NM Finno-Ugric, Finno-Ugrian

fiole [fjɔl] NF **1** *(bouteille)* phial, vial **2** *très Fam (tête)* nut, *Br* bonce; *(visage)* mug; **se payer la f. de qn** to make a fool of sb

fion [fjɔ̃] NM **1** *Vulg (postérieur) Br* arse, *Am* ass; **se casser le f. (pour faire qch)** to bust a gut *or Am* one's ass (doing sth)
2 *Vulg (anus) Br* arsehole, *Am* asshole
3 *Vulg (chance)* luck[□]; **avoir du f.** to be lucky[□] *or Br* jammy; **ne pas avoir de f.** to be unlucky[□]
4 *très Fam* **donner le coup de f. à** to put the finishing touch to
5 *(pique)* taunt; **lancer des fions à qn** to taunt sb

Fionie [fjɔni] NF *Géog* Fyn

fioritures [fjɔrityr] NFPL **1** *(décorations)* embellishments; *(d'une écriture)* flourishes; **une lettre pleine de f.** a flowery letter **2** *Mus* fioritura
• **sans fioritures** ADJ plain, unadorned

fiotte [fjɔt] NF *Vulg* queer, *Br* poof, *Am* fag

fioul [fjul] NM fuel oil, heating oil

FIP [fip] NF *(abrév* **France Inter Paris)** = Paris radio station broadcasting continuous music and traffic information

firewall [fajœrwol] NM *Ordinat* firewall

FireWire® [fajœrwajœr] NM INV *Ordinat* FireWire®

firmament [firmamɑ̃] NM *Littéraire* firmament, heavens; *Fig* **au f. de sa gloire** at the zenith *or* height of his fame

firme [firm] NF firm, company; **f. multinationale** multinational company

firmware [fœrmwer] NM *Ordinat* firmware

FIS [fis] NM *(abrév* **Front islamique du salut) le F.** the FIS, the Islamic Salvation Front

fisc [fisk] NM *Br* ≃ Inland Revenue, *Am* ≃ Internal Revenue, IRS; **avoir des ennuis avec le f.** to have problems with the *Br* taxman *or Am* IRS; **les employés du f.** tax officials; **frauder le f.** to evade tax

fiscal, -e, -aux, -ales [fiskal, -o] ADJ *Fin* fiscal, tax *(avant n)*; **dans un but f.** for tax purposes; **pression** *ou* **charge fiscale** tax burden; **l'administration fiscale** the tax authorities; **conseiller f.** tax adviser; **abri f.** tax shelter

fiscalement [fiskalmɑ̃] ADV fiscally, from the point of view of taxation; **dans quel pays êtes-vous f. domicilié?** in which country do you pay tax?

fiscalisation [fiskalizasjɔ̃] NF *Fin* taxing, taxation

fiscaliser [3] [fiskalize] VT *Fin* to tax

fiscaliste [fiskalist] NMF *Fin* tax specialist, tax consultant

fiscalité [fiskalite] NF *Fin (système, législation)* tax system; **f. écologique** green taxation; **f. des entreprises** corporate taxation; **f. directe** direct taxation; **f. indirecte** indirect taxation; **f. locale** local taxation; **optimiser la f. de qch** to improve the tax efficiency of sth, to make sth more tax efficient

fissa [fisa] ADV *Fam* **faire f.** to get a move on, to get one's skates on

fissible [fisibl], **fissile** [fisil] ADJ *Minér & Nucl* fissile

fission [fisjɔ̃] NF fission; **f. nucléaire** nuclear fission; **f. de l'atome** atomic fission, splitting of the atom

fissuration [fisyrasjɔ̃] NF cracking, *Spéc* fissuring

fissure [fisyr] NF **1** *(fente)* crack, *Spéc* fissure; **les fissures du mur** the cracks in the wall **2** *Méd* fissure **3** *Fig (défaut)* fissure, crack, chink; **il y a des fissures dans son raisonnement** his/her argument doesn't hold water

fissurer [3] [fisyre] VT *(mur, paroi)* to crack, *Spéc* to fissure
VPR **se fissurer** to crack

fiston [fistõ] NM *Fam* sonny; **allez f.!** now then, young fellow *or* my lad *or* sonny!

fistule [fistyl] NF *Méd* fistula

fistuleux, -euse [fistylø, -øz] ADJ *Méd* fistulous

fit *etc voir* **faire**

FIV [ɛfive] NF *(abrév* **fécondation in vitro)** IVF

FIVETE, fivete [fivɛt] NF *(abrév* **fécondation in vitro et transfert d'embryon)** GIFT; **une F.** a test-tube baby

fixage [fiksaʒ] NM **1** *Phot* fixing; **bain de f.** fixing bath **2** *Bourse* fixing

fixateur, -trice [fiksatœr, -tris] ADJ fixative; **bactéries fixatrices d'azote** nitrogen-fixing bacteria
NM **1** *Phot* fixer
2 *(pour les cheveux)* setting lotion
3 *Biol* fixative
4 *Beaux-Arts* fixative

fixatif, -ive [fiksatif, -iv] ADJ fixative *(avant n)*
NM fixative

fixation [fiksasjõ] NF **1** *(accrochage)* fixing, fastening; **quel est le système de f. des étagères?** how are the shelves fixed to the wall?; **f. par bride** *ou* **par collier** clamping
2 *(établissement ▸ d'un prix, d'un salaire)* setting; *(▸ d'un rendez-vous)* making, fixing; **être chargé de la f. de l'impôt** to be responsible for setting tax levels; **f. de prix** *ou* **des prix** price fixing, pricing; **f. concertée des prix** common pricing, common price fixing; **f. du prix unitaire** unit pricing; **f. d'un prix d'appel** loss-leader pricing; **f. d'un prix de soumission** sealed-bid pricing; **f. de l'impôt** tax assessment; **f. du prix en fonction du coût** cost-plus pricing; **f. du prix en fonction du taux de rentabilité souhaité** target-return pricing; **f. du prix optimal** optimal pricing
3 *Chim & Biol* fixation
4 *Beaux-Arts & Phot* fixing
5 *Psy* fixation, obsession; **la f. au père/à la mère** father/mother fixation; **faire une f. sur qch** to be obsessed with *or* by sth; *Fam* **il fait une f. sur les examens** he's obsessed by exams
6 *(de ski)* binding

fixative [fiksativ] *voir* **fixatif**

fixatrice [fiksatris] *voir* **fixateur**

fixe [fiks] ADJ **1** *(invariable ▸ repère)* fixed; **prendre ses repas à heure f.** to eat at fixed *or* set times; *Ordinat* **virgule f.** fixed point
2 *Mil* **(à vos rangs,) f.!** attention!
3 *(immobile ▸ œil, regard)* fixed, staring
4 *(durable ▸ emploi)* permanent, steady
5 *Écon, Fin & Jur (droit)* fixed duty *(avant n)*; *(prix)* set; *(revenu, salaire)* fixed; **à prix f.** at fixed prices; **assignation à jour f.** fixed summons
6 *Tél (ligne)* fixed; *(poste)* landline *(avant n)*
NM **1** *(salaire)* (fixed *or* regular) salary; **toucher un f.** to be on a fixed salary **2** *Tél (poste fixe)* fixed phone, landline phone **3** *Fam (de drogue)* fix *(of drug)*

fixé, -e [fikse] ADJ **1** *(date, heure, jour)* agreed, appointed; **à la date fixée** on the agreed *or* appointed day **2 être f. sur qch** *(décidé)* to have made up one's mind about sth; **je ne suis pas f.** I haven't made my mind up yet; **te voilà f.!** now you know!

fixement [fiksəmɑ̃] ADV fixedly; **elle le regarde f.** she's staring at him

fixer [3] [fikse] VT **1** *(accrocher ▸ gén)* to fix; *(▸ par des épingles, des punaises)* to pin (on); *(▸ avec de l'adhésif)* to tape (on); *(▸ avec un fermoir, un nœud)* to fasten; **f. un tableau au mur** to put up a painting on a wall; **f. un badge sur un vêtement** *(avec une épingle)* to pin a badge on (to) a garment; *(en le cousant)* to sew a badge on (to) a garment; **les vis qui fixent la serrure** the screws that hold the lock
2 *(en regardant)* to stare; **f. qn du regard** to stare at sb; **f. les yeux** *ou* **son regard sur qn/qch** to stare at sb/sth; *(scruter)* to look hard *or* intently at sb/sth; **il la fixe droit dans les yeux** he's staring straight into her eyes
3 *(concentrer)* **f. son attention/esprit sur qch** to fix one's attention/mind on sth; **f. son choix sur qch** to decide *or* to settle on sth; **f. qch dans sa mémoire** to implant sth in one's memory
4 *(définir ▸ date, lieu)* to fix, to set, to decide on; *(▸ conditions)* to fix, to lay down; *(▸ prix, impôt)* to fix, to set; *(▸ délai)* to set; **f. le prix des matières premières** to fix a price for *or* the price of raw materials; **f. le prix de** to price; **f. le prix d'une réparation** to cost a repair job; **f. un rendez-vous à qn** to arrange a meeting with sb; **vous fixerez votre heure** you decide on the time that suits you (best)
5 *(informer)* **f. qn sur qch** to put sb in the picture about sth; **cette conversation m'a fixé sur son compte** that conversation set me straight about him/her
6 *(établir)* **f. son domicile à Paris** to take up (permanent) residence *or* to settle (down) in Paris
7 *(stabiliser)* to fix; **f. la langue/l'orthographe** to standardize the language/the spelling
8 *Beaux-Arts, Chim & Phot* to fix
9 *Bourse* **f. un cours** to make a price
VPR **se fixer 1** *(s'accrocher)* to be fixed *or* fastened; **ça se fixe facilement sur le ski** it fastens easily onto the ski; **ça se fixe avec une courroie** you attach it with a strap, you strap it on
2 *(s'installer)* to settle; **elle s'est fixée en Irlande** she settled (permanently) in Ireland
3 *(se stabiliser)* to settle down; **il s'est fixé après son mariage** he settled down after he got married; **l'orthographe du mot se fixe au XVIIIème siècle** the spelling of the word became fixed in the 18th century
4 *très Fam Arg drogue (s'injecter de la drogue)* to shoot up
5 *(se donner)* **il s'est fixé un objectif dans la vie, réussir** he has (set himself) one aim in life, to succeed; **fixons-nous trois tâches** let's set ourselves three tasks
6 se f. sur *(choisir)* to decide on; **il s'est fixé sur une cravate bleue** he decided on a blue tie; **elle s'est fixée sur cette idée** she's got the idea in her head (and nothing will shift it)

fixette [fiksɛt] NF *Fam* **faire une f. sur qn/qch** to be obsessed with sb/sth❑, *Br* to have sb/sth on the brain

fixeur [fiksœr] NM *Bourse* **f. de prix** price maker

fixisme [fiksism] NM creationism

fixité [fiksite] NF *(d'une disposition)* fixity, unchangeableness; *(du regard)* fixedness, steadiness

fjord [fjɔrd] NM *Géog* fjord

flac [flak] ONOMAT splash!; **faire f.** to splash, to go splash

flaccidité [flaksidite] NF flaccidity, flaccidness

flacon [flakõ] NM *(de parfum, de solvant)* (small) bottle; *(de spiritueux, de laboratoire)* flask; **f. à parfum** perfume bottle; **f. à liqueur** liqueur decanter

fla-fla [flafla] *(pl* **fla-flas)** *Fam* NM *Vieilli* **faire du f.** to make a huge fuss
• **sans fla-flas** ADV simply❑, without fuss❑

flagada [flagada] ADJ INV *Fam* washed-out, dead beat

flagellation [flaʒɛlasjõ] NF flogging, whipping; *(sur soi-même)* flagellation

flagelle [flaʒɛl] NM *Biol* flagellum

flagellé, -e [flaʒele] *Biol* ADJ flagellate, flagellated
NM flagellate

flageller [4] [flaʒele] VT *(battre)* to whip
VPR **se flageller** to scourge oneself

flageolant, -e [flaʒɔlɑ̃, -ɑ̃t] ADJ *(jambe)* shaking, trembling, wobbly

flageoler [3] [flaʒɔle] VI *(jambes)* to shake, to tremble, to wobble; **il flageolait sur ses jambes** *(de peur)* he was shaking *or* quaking at the knees; *(de fatigue)* he was dead on his feet, his legs were trembling *or* shaking

flageolet[1] [flaʒɔlɛ] NM *Mus* flageolet

flageolet[2] [flaʒɔlɛ] NM *Bot & Culin* flageolet (bean)

flagorner [3] [flagɔrne] VT *Littéraire* to fawn on

flagornerie [flagɔrnəri] NF *Littéraire* fawning, toadying

flagorneur, -euse [flagɔrnœr, -øz] NM,F *Littéraire* flatterer, toady

flagrant, -e [flagrɑ̃, -ɑ̃t] ADJ **1** *(évident)* blatant, obvious, flagrant; **de façon flagrante** blatantly; **il apparaît de façon flagrante que...** it is blatantly obvious that... **2** *Jur* **f. délit** flagrante delicto; **pris en f. délit** caught in the act, caught red-handed; **pris en f. délit d'adultère** caught in flagrante; **pris en f. délit de mensonge** caught lying

flair [flɛr] NM **1** *(odorat)* scent, (sense of) smell, nose; **avoir du f.** to have a good sense of smell **2** *Fig (perspicacité)* intuition, sixth sense; **avoir du f.** to have intuition *or* a sixth sense

flairer [4] [flɛre] VT **1** *(humer ▸ sujet: chien)* to scent, to sniff at; *(▸ sujet: personne)* to smell; **le chien flairait sa pâtée/le gibier** the dog sniffed (at) its food/scented the game **2** *(deviner)* to sense; **f. le danger** to have a sense of impending danger; **f. le mensonge** to detect a lie; **f. le vent** to see which way *or* how the wind blows

flamand, -e [flamɑ̃, -ɑ̃d] ADJ Flemish
NM *(langue)* Flemish
• **Flamand, -e** NM,F Fleming; **les Flamands** the Flemish

flamant [flamɑ̃] NM flamingo; **f. rose** (pink) flamingo

flambage [flɑ̃baʒ] NM **1** *Culin (d'une omelette, d'une crêpe)* flambéing; *(d'un poulet)* singeing **2** *(d'un instrument)* sterilization **3** *Tech (déformation)* buckling

flambant, -e [flɑ̃bɑ̃, -ɑ̃t] ADJ *Littéraire (bois, fagot)* burning, blazing; *Mines (houille)* bituminous
ADV **1** *(locution)* **f. neuf** brand new **2** *Can Fam (complètement)* completely❑, totally❑; **f. nu** stark naked❑, *Br* starkers
NM *Mines* bituminous coal

flambard, flambart [flɑ̃bar] NM *Fam Vieilli* braggart❑; **faire le f.** to show off❑

flambé, -e [flɑ̃be] ADJ **1** *Culin* flambéed **2** *Fam (personne)* ruined❑; **il est f.** *(ruiné)* he's all washed up; *(dans une situation sans issue)* he's had it, his goose is cooked
• **flambée** NF **1** *(feu)* blaze, fire; **faire une petite flambée** to light a small fire; **faire une bonne flambée** to get a roaring fire going **2** *Fig (poussée)* **une flambée de colère** an outburst of rage; **la flambée des prix** the leap in prices

flambeau, -x [flɑ̃bo] NM *(torche)* torch; *(chandelier)* candlestick; *Fig* torch; **à la lumière** *ou* **à la lueur des flambeaux** by torchlight; **marche** *ou* **retraite aux flambeaux** torchlit procession; *Fig* **passer** *ou* **transmettre le f.** to pass on the torch; *Fig* **reprendre le f.** to take up the torch

flambement [flɑ̃bmɑ̃] NM *Tech* buckling

flamber [3] [flɑ̃be] VT **1** *Culin (poulet)* to singe; *(omelette, crêpe)* to flambé **2** *(stériliser)* **f. une aiguille** to sterilize a needle (in a flame) **3** *Fam (dilapider)* to blow, to throw away; **il a de l'argent à f.** he has money to burn
VI **1** *(se consumer)* to burn (brightly); **f. comme une allumette** to burn like matchwood
2 *(briller)* to flash
3 *Fam (augmenter)* to rocket
4 *Fam (jouer)* to gamble (for big stakes)❑
5 *Tech (se déformer)* to buckle

flambeur, -euse [flɑ̃bœr, -øz] NM,F *Fam* big-time gambler

flamboie *etc voir* **flamboyer**

flamboiement [flɑ̃bwamɑ̃] NM *(d'un incendie)* blaze; *(du regard)* flashing

flamboyant, -e [flɑ̃bwajɑ̃, -ɑ̃t] ADJ **1** *(brillant ▸ foyer)* blazing, flaming; *(▸ regard)* flashing **2** *Archit* flamboyant

flamboyer [13] [flɑ̃bwaje] VI **1** *(être en flammes)* to blaze *or* to flare (up); **dans l'âtre qui flamboie** in the blazing hearth **2** *(briller ▸ œil, regard)* to flash; **f. de colère** *(yeux)* to blaze *or* to flash with anger

flamingant, -e [flamɛ̃gɑ̃, -ɑ̃t] ADJ Flemish-speaking
NM,F **1** *Ling* Flemish speaker **2** *Pol* Flemish nationalist

flamme [flam] NF **1** *(feu)* flame; **faire une f.** to flare *or* to blaze up; **cracher** *ou* **jeter** *ou* **lancer des flammes** *(dragon)* to breathe fire; *(canon)* to flare; **passer qch à la f.** to singe sth; **la f. du tombeau du Soldat inconnu** the Eternal Flame
2 *Littéraire (éclat)* fire; **dans la f. de son regard** in his/her fiery eyes; **la f. de son intelligence** the bril-

liance of his/her intellect
3 *(ferveur)* fire; **discours plein de f.** impassioned speech
4 *Arch & Littéraire (amour)* ardour; **déclarer sa f. à une femme** to declare one's love for a woman
5 *(drapeau)* pennant, streamer
6 *(sur une lettre)* slogan
7 *Élec* **(ampoule) f.** candle bulb
• **flammes** NFPL **les flammes** fire; **périr dans les flammes** to burn to death, to be burnt alive; *Fig* **les flammes éternelles** *ou* **de l'enfer** hellfire
• **à la flamme de** PRÉP by the light of
• **avec flamme** ADV passionately
• **en flammes** ADJ burning, blazing ADV **l'avion est tombé en flammes** the plane went down in flames; *Fam* **descendre un auteur/une pièce en flammes** to shoot an author/a play down in flames

flammèche [flamɛʃ] NF (flying) spark

flan [flɑ̃] NM **1** *Culin* custard tart; **f. à la vanille** vanilla(-flavoured) custard tart
2 *Typ* flong
3 *Métal (d'une pièce, d'un disque)* flan
4 *Fam (locutions)* **c'est du f.!** it's a load of bunkum *or* bunk!; **en rester comme deux ronds de f.** to be flabbergasted; **y aller au f.** to try it on, to bluff; **j'ai dit ça au f.** I said it just for the sake of it *or* just for something to say
• **à la flan** ADJ *Fam* **des arguments à la f.** *Br* waffle, *Am* hooey

flanc [flɑ̃] NM **1** *Anat (entre les côtes et le bassin)* flank; *(côté du corps)* side
2 *Zool* flank, side; **battre des flancs** *(cheval)* to heave, to pant
3 *(côté ▸ d'un navire)* side; *(▸ d'une colline)* side, slope; **le navire se présentait de f.** the ship was broadside on
4 *Mil* flank; **par le f. droit!** by the right!; **attaquer de f.** to attack on the flank
5 *Littéraire (ventre maternel)* womb
6 *(locution)* **tirer au f.** to be bone idle
• **à flanc de** PRÉP **à f. de coteau** on the hillside
• **sur le flanc** ADJ **être sur le f.** *(épuisé)* to be exhausted; *(malade)* to be laid up ADV *(sur le côté)* on one's side; **il s'est retourné et s'est mis sur le f.** he rolled over on to his side; **mettre qn sur le f.** to exhaust sb

flancher [3] [flɑ̃ʃe] VI **1** *(faiblir)* to give out, to fail; **son cœur a flanché** his/her heart gave out on him/her **2** *(manquer de courage)* to waver; **ce n'est pas le moment de f.** this is no time for weakness

flanchet [flɑ̃ʃe] NM flank

Flandre [flɑ̃dr] NF **(la) F., (les) Flandres** Flanders

flandrin [flɑ̃drɛ̃] NM *Arch* **grand f.** lanky fellow, beanpole

flanelle [flanel] NF *Tex* flannel; **f. (de) coton** flannelette; **pantalon de f. grise** grey flannels

flâner [3] [flane] VI **1** *(se promener)* to stroll *or* to amble (along) **2** *Péj (perdre son temps)* to hang about, to lounge around, to idle; **on n'a pas le temps de f. avant les examens** there's no time for hanging about before the exams

flânerie [flanri] NF stroll, wander

flâneur, -euse [flanœr, -øz] NM,F **1** *(promeneur)* stroller **2** *(oisif)* idler, loafer

flanquer¹ [3] [flɑ̃ke] VT **1** *(être à côté de)* to flank
2 *Fam Péj (accompagner)* **elle est arrivée, flanquée de ses deux frères** she came in with her two brothers at her side□ *or* flanked by her two brothers **3** *Mil* to flank

flanquer² [3] [flɑ̃ke] *Fam* VT **1** *(lancer)* to fling, to chuck; **il lui a flanqué son verre d'eau à la figure** he threw *or* chucked his glass of water in his/her face; **f. qn dehors** *ou* **à la porte** *(l'expulser)* to kick sb out; *(le licencier)* *Br* to sack *or Am* to can sb; **il a flanqué les bouquins par terre** *(volontairement)* he chucked the books on the floor; *(par maladresse)* he knocked the books onto the floor **2** *(donner)* **f. un P-V à qn** to give sb a ticket□; **f. une gifle à qn** to smack *or* to slap sb□; **f. un coup de poing à qn** to punch sb□; **f. un coup de pied à qn** to kick sb□; **f. la trouille** *ou* **la frousse** *ou* **les jetons à qn** to scare the pants off sb; **ça m'a flanqué le cafard** it really got me down
VPR **se flanquer 1** *(tomber)* **se f. par terre** to take a tumble, *Br* to come a cropper; **se f. la figure** *ou* **la gueule par terre** to fall flat on one's face **2** *(se jeter)* **se f. par la fenêtre** to throw oneself out of the window; **elle s'est flanquée dans le ravin** she plunged into the ravine **3** *(se donner)* **ils se sont flanqué des coups** they exchanged blows□, they had a fistfight *or Br* a punch-up; **je me suis flanqué une bonne indigestion** I gave myself a real dose of indigestion

flapi, -e [flapi] ADJ *Fam* dead beat, bushed, *Br* knackered

flaque [flak] NF puddle; **une large f. d'huile** a pool of oil

flash [flaʃ] *(pl* **flashs** *ou* **flashes)** NM **1** *Phot (éclair)* flash; *(ampoule)* flash bulb; **prendre une photo au f.** to take a picture using a flash; *Fam* **avoir un f.** to have a brainwave
2 *Rad & TV* **f. (d'informations)** newsflash; **f. spécial** (special) newsflash
3 *Cin & TV (plan)* flash; **f. publicitaire** commercial
4 *Fam Arg drogue* rush *(after taking drugs)*

flashant [flaʃɑ̃] ADJ *Fam* flashy

flash-back [flaʃbak] NM INV flashback

flash-ball [flaʃbol] *(pl* **flash-balls)** NM riot gun

flasher [3] [flaʃe] VI **1** *(clignoter)* to flash (on and off) **2** *Fam (craquer)* **elle me fait f., cette nana!** I've really got the hots for that girl! **3** *Fam Arg drogue* to get a rush
• **flasher sur** VT IND *Fam* to go crazy over, to fall for in a big way; **elle a vraiment flashé sur cette robe** she fell in love with *or* just went crazy over this dress

flashy [flaʃi] ADJ loud, gaudy

flasque¹ [flask] ADJ **1** *(muscle, peau)* flaccid, flabby **2** *(veule)* spineless; **c'est un être f.** he has no backbone

flasque² [flask] NM **1** *Tech (d'une machine)* flange, end-plate; *Aut* hubcap, wheel disc; *(d'une roue)* flange **2** *Mil* cheek *(of gun carriage)*

flasque³ [flask] NF *(pour whisky)* (hip) flask; *(à mercure)* flask

flatter [3] [flate] VT **1** *(encenser)* to flatter; **f. qn sur son bel esprit** to flatter sb on his/her wit; **n'essaie pas de me f.** flattery will get you nowhere!; **tu me flattes, je ne pense pas avoir si bien réussi** you flatter me, I don't think I did that well; **f. bassement qn** to fawn upon sb
2 *(embellir)* to be flattering to; **cette coupe ne la flatte pas** that style doesn't flatter her; **ce portrait la flatte plutôt** this portrait of her is rather flattering
3 *(toucher)* to touch, to flatter; **je suis flatté de votre proposition** I am flattered by your proposal; **j'ai été flatté qu'on me confie cette responsabilité** I was very touched *or* flattered to be entrusted with this responsibility
4 *Littéraire (encourager)* to encourage; **f. les caprices de qn** to pander to sb's whims; **f. la vanité de qn** to indulge sb's vanity
5 *Littéraire (tromper)* to delude; **f. qn de l'espoir de qch** to hold out false hopes of sth to sb
6 *(caresser ▸ animal)* to stroke; *(▸ cheval)* to pat
7 *(être agréable à ▸ vue, odorat)* to delight, to be pleasing to; **un vin qui flatte le palais** a (wonderfully) smooth wine
VPR **se flatter** to flatter oneself; **sans vouloir me f., je crois que j'ai raison** though I say it myself, I think I'm right; **elle se flatte de savoir recevoir** she prides herself on knowing how to entertain *or* on her skills as a hostess

flatterie [flatri] NF **1** *(adulation)* flattery **2** *(propos)* flattering remark; **flatteries** sweet talk; **ce ne sont que de viles flatteries** it's just base flattery

flatteur, -euse [flatœr, -øz] ADJ *(remarque, portrait, couleur)* flattering; *(personne)* full of flattery; **peu f.** unflattering; **il a fait un tableau f. de la situation** he painted a rosy picture of the situation
NM,F flatterer

flatulence [flatylɑ̃s] NF flatulence; **avoir des flatulences** to suffer from flatulence

flatulent, -e [flatylɑ̃, -ɑ̃t] ADJ flatulent

flatuosité [flatɥozite] NF *Méd* flatus

FLE [flə] NM *(abrév* **français langue étrangère)** French as a foreign language

fléau, -x [fleo] NM **1** *(désastre)* curse, plague
2 *Fam (cause de désagréments)* pain; **sa fille est un véritable f.** his/her daughter is a real pain *or* pest
3 *(d'une balance)* beam
4 *Agr* flail
5 *Mil* **f. d'armes** flail

fléchage [fleʃaʒ] NM signposting *(with arrows)*

flèche¹ [flɛʃ] NF **1** *(projectile)* arrow, *Littéraire* shaft; *(d'un canon)* trail; **partir comme une f.** to shoot off; *Fig* **faire f. de tout bois** to use all available means, to use all means at one's disposal
2 *(en balistique)* **f. d'une trajectoire** highest point of a trajectory
3 *(signe)* arrow; **f. lumineuse** *(pour projection)* pointer
4 *Archit (d'un arc)* broach; *(d'un clocher)* spire
5 *(d'une balance)* pointer
6 *Tech (d'une grue)* boom
7 *(d'un câble)* sag, dip
8 *Ordinat* pointer, arrow; **f. de défilement** scroll arrow; **f. vers la droite** right arrow; **f. vers la gauche** left arrow; **f. vers le bas** down arrow; **f. vers le haut** up arrow; **flèches verticales** up and down arrow keys
9 *Aviat* sweep-back
10 *Bot* **f. d'eau** arrowhead
11 *Littéraire (raillerie)* jibe; **ses flèches ne m'atteignent pas** I pay no heed to his/her jibes
• **en flèche** ADJ rising; **des cinéastes en f.** rising film-makers, film-makers on the way up ADV **1** *(spectaculairement)* **monter** *ou* **grimper en f.** to go straight up (like an arrow), to shoot up; *Fig* to shoot up; **les tarifs montent en f.** prices are rocketing; **partir en f.** to go off like an arrow, to shoot off; *Fig* to shoot off **2** *(atteler)* **bœufs/chevaux attelés en f.** oxen/horses harnessed in tandem

flèche² [flɛʃ] NF *(de lard)* flitch

flèche³ [flɛʃ] NM *Fam* **j'ai pas un f.** I'm totally broke *or Br* skint

flécher [18] [fleʃe] VT to mark with arrows, to signpost

fléchette [fleʃɛt] NF dart; **jouer aux fléchettes** to play darts

fléchi, -e [fleʃi] ADJ *Ling* inflected

fléchir [32] [fleʃir] VT **1** *(ployer)* to bend, to flex; **fléchissez l'avant-bras** flex your forearm; **f. le genou devant qn** to bow the knee to sb **2** *(apitoyer ▸ juge, tribunal)* to move to pity; **se laisser f.** to relent, to let oneself be swayed
VI **1** *(se ployer)* to bend; *(jambes)* to give way; *(câble, poutre)* to sag; **elle sentait ses genoux f. sous elle** she could feel her knees giving way **2** *(baisser)* to fall; *(marché, devises)* to weaken; *(prix, cours, demande)* to fall, to drop; **le dollar a de nouveau fléchi** the dollar has fallen again **3** *(céder)* to weaken; **nous ne fléchirons pas devant la menace** we will not give in to threats

fléchissement [fleʃismɑ̃] NM **1** *(flexion ▸ d'une partie du corps)* flexing, bending; *(▸ d'une poutre)* yielding, bending; *(▸ d'un câble)* sagging
2 *(affaiblissement ▸ des genoux)* sagging; *(▸ de la nuque)* drooping
3 *(baisse)* fall; *(du marché, d'une devise)* weakening; *(des prix, des cours, de la demande)* fall, drop; **un f. de la production/de la natalité** a fall in production/in the birthrate
4 *(de la volonté)* failing

fléchisseur [fleʃisœr] *Anat* ADJ M **muscle f.** flexor
NM flexor

flegmatique [flɛgmatik] ADJ phlegmatic
NMF phlegmatic person

flegmatiquement [flɛgmatikmɑ̃] ADV phlegmatically

flegme [flɛgm] NM **1** phlegm, composure; **perdre son f.** to lose one's composure **2** *Méd* phlegm
• **avec flegme** ADV coolly, phlegmatically

flémingite [flemɛ̃ʒit] NF *Fam Hum* laziness□, lazyitis

flemmard, -e [flemar, -ard] *Fam* ADJ idle□, lazy□
NM,F loafer, lazy so-and-so

flemmarder [3] [flemarde] VI *Fam* to loaf about; **f. au lit** to laze in bed□

flemmardise [flemardiz] NF *Fam* idleness□, laziness□

flemme [flɛm] **NF** *Fam* laziness☐; **j'ai vraiment la f. d'y aller** I just can't be bothered to go; **tirer sa f.** to be bone idle; **il tire une de ces flemmes aujourd'hui!** he's been loafing around all day!

flet [flɛ] **NM** *Ich* flounder

flétan [fletɑ̃] **NM** *Ich* halibut

flétri, -e [fletri] **ADJ 1** *(plante, feuille)* withered **2** *Littéraire (peau, visage)* wrinkled, withered; *(beauté)* faded

flétrir[1] **[32]** [fletrir] **VT 1** *Bot* to wither, to wilt **2** *Littéraire (ôter l'éclat de ▸ couleur)* to fade; *(▸ teint, peau)* to wither **3** *Littéraire (avilir ▸ ambition, espoir)* to sully, to corrupt, to debase

VPR se flétrir 1 *Bot* to wither, to wilt **2** *Littéraire (peau)* to wither; *(couleur, beauté)* to fade

flétrir[2] **[32]** [fletrir] **VT 1** *Hist (criminel)* to brand **2** *Littéraire (condamner)* to condemn, to denounce **3** *(la réputation de quelqu'un)* to blacken, to sully, to stain

flétrissure[1] [fletrisyr] **NF 1** *Bot* wilting **2** *Littéraire (de la peau)* withering *(UNCOUNT)*; *(de la couleur, de la beauté)* fading *(UNCOUNT)*

flétrissure[2] [fletrisyr] **NF** *Littéraire (déshonneur)* stain; **l'ignoble f. dont vous l'avez marquée** the foul stain you placed upon her honour

fleur [flœr] **NF 1** *Bot* flower; *(d'un arbre)* blossom; **les fleurs du cerisier** the cherry blossom; **le langage des fleurs** the language of flowers; **fleurs des champs** wild flowers; **fraîche comme une f.** as fresh as a daisy; **jolie comme une f.** as pretty as a picture; **ni fleurs, ni couronnes** *(dans une annonce nécrologique)* no flowers by request

2 *Fig (le meilleur de)* **la f. de l'âge** the prime of life; **f. de farine** fine wheat flour; **la f. de la jeunesse** the full bloom of youth; **dans la première f. de la jeunesse** in the first flush *or* flower of youth; **c'est la fine f. de l'école** he's/she's the pride of his/her school; **la fine f. de la canaille** a prize swine

3 *Hér* **f. de lis** *ou* **lys** fleur-de-lis

4 *Vieilli (virginité)* virginity; **perdre sa f.** to lose one's virtue

5 *Can (farine)* flour

6 *Fam (locutions)* **faire une f. à qn** to do sb an unexpected favour *or* a favour; **arriver comme une f.** to turn up out of the blue; **faire qch comme une f.** to do sth almost without trying; **c'est passé comme une f.** it was as easy as pie

• **fleurs NFPL 1** *Littérature* **fleurs de rhétorique** flowers of rhetoric, rhetorical flourishes; **sans fleurs de rhétorique** in plain language **2** *(louanges)* **couvrir qn de fleurs** to praise sb highly; *Fam* **s'envoyer** *ou* **se jeter des fleurs** *(mutuellement)* to sing one another's praises, to pat one another on the back; *(à soi-même)* to pat oneself on the back

• **à fleur de PRÉP** on the surface of; **à f. d'eau** just above the surface (of the water); **des yeux à f. de tête** prominent eyes; **une sensibilité à f. de peau** hypersensitivity; **avoir les nerfs à f. de peau** to be all on edge

• **à fleurs ADJ** *(papier, tapisserie, nappe)* floral, flowery; **tissu à fleurs** floral *or* flowery material; **une robe à fleurs** a floral *or* flowery dress, a dress with a flower motif

• **en fleur, en fleurs ADJ** *(rose, pivoine)* in flower *or* bloom, blooming; *(arbre, arbuste)* blossoming, in blossom

• **fleur bleue ADJ INV** sentimental, romantic; **un roman f. bleue** a sentimental novel; **il adore tout ce qui est f. bleue** he's an incurable romantic

fleurage [flœraʒ] **NM** *(sur un tissu, sur un tapis)* floral pattern

fleurdelisé, -e [flœrdəlize] **ADJ** decorated with fleurs-de-lis

NM *Can* flag of Quebec

fleurer **[5]** [flœre] **VT** *Littéraire* to smell of; **la chambre fleure le bois de pin** the bedroom smells of pinewood; *Fig* **son histoire fleure le scandale** his/her story smacks of scandal

VI f. bon to smell nice

fleuret [flœrɛ] **NM 1** *Escrime* foil **2** *Mines* borer, drill (bit)

fleurette [flœrɛt] **NF** small flower, floweret, floret

fleuri, -e [flœri] **ADJ 1** *(arbre, arbuste)* in bloom *or* blossom

2 *(orné de fleurs)* flowered, flowery; *(papier peint, tapis, vêtement)* floral; *(vaisselle)* flower-patterned; **une nappe fleurie** a flowered *or* flowery tablecloth; **un balcon f.** a balcony decorated with flowers; **village f.** = village taking part in a flower competition; **avoir la boutonnière fleurie** to have a flower in one's buttonhole; *(décoré)* to wear a decoration

3 *Littéraire (teint)* florid

4 *(conversation, style)* flowery

fleurir **[32]** [flœrir] **VI 1** *Bot (fleur)* to flower, to bloom; *(arbre, arbuste)* to flower, to blossom; **les arbres ont entièrement fleuri** the trees are in full bloom **2** *(apparaître)* to burgeon; **les antennes paraboliques qui fleurissent sur tous les toits** the satellite dishes mushrooming *or* burgeoning over every roof **3** *(se développer ▸ affaire, commerce)* to flourish, to thrive

VT to decorate with flowers; *(boutonnière)* to put a flower in; **les villageois ont fleuri leurs maisons** the villagers have decorated their houses with flowers; **f. la tombe de qn** to put flowers on sb's grave; **f. qn** to pin a flower on sb's lapel

fleurissement [flœrismɑ̃] **NM** = decorating with flowers (particularly a public place)

fleuriste [flœrist] **NMF 1** *(vendeur)* florist **2** *(cultivateur)* flower grower

fleuron [flœrɔ̃] **NM 1** *(ornement ▸ de reliure)* flower, fleuron; *Archit* finial; *Fig* **le (plus beau) f. de...** the jewel of...; **cette bouteille est le plus beau f. de ma cave** this is the finest bottle in my cellar **2** *Bot* floret

fleuve [flœv] **NM 1** *(rivière)* river *(flowing into the sea)*; **f. côtier** coastal river **2** *(écoulement)* **un f. de boue** a river of mud, a mudslide; **un f. de larmes** a flood of tears **3** *(comme adj; avec ou sans trait d'union)* **roman-f.** saga; **discours-f.** lengthy speech

flexibilité [flɛksibilite] **NF 1** *(d'un matériau)* pliability; *(du corps)* flexibility, suppleness **2** *Psy* flexible *or* adaptable nature **3** *(d'un arrangement, d'un horaire)* flexibility, adaptability; *(d'un dispositif)* versatility; *(d'une entreprise, de la main-d'œuvre)* flexibility

flexible [flɛksibl] **ADJ 1** *(pliable)* pliable, flexible **2** *Psy* flexible, adaptable; *(accommodant)* accommodating **3** *(variable ▸ arrangement, horaire)* flexible; *(▸ dispositif)* versatile; **avoir des horaires flexibles** to work flexible hours

NM 1 *(tuyau)* flexible tube **2** *Tech* flexible shaft; *Aut* **f. de frein** brake hose

flexion [flɛksjɔ̃] **NF 1** *(d'un arc, d'un ressort)* bending *(UNCOUNT)*, flexion; *Tech* **effort de f.** bending stress **2** *(des membres)* flexing *(UNCOUNT)*; *Gym* **f. du corps** trunk exercise **3** *Ling* inflection; **langue à flexions** inflected language; **f. nominale** noun inflection

flexionnel, -elle [flɛksjɔnɛl] **ADJ** *Ling (langue, langage)* inflected

flexisécurité [flɛksisekyrite] **NF** flexicurity

flibuste [flibyst] **NF la f.** *(piraterie)* freebooting; *(pirates)* freebooters

flibustier [flibystje] **NM 1** *Hist* freebooter, buccaneer **2** *Fam & Arch (escroc)* cheat☐, crook☐

flic [flik] **NM** *Fam* cop, policeman☐

flicage [flikaʒ] **NM** *Fam Péj (par la police)* heavy policing☐; *Fig* **ils craignent le f. du courrier électronique par la direction** they're afraid that the management are checking their e-mails☐

flicaille [flikaj] **NF** *très Fam Péj* **la f.** the pigs, the cops, *Br* the filth

flic flac [flikflak] **ONOMAT** splish splash, splish splosh; *(d'un fouet)* crack

flingot [flɛ̃go], **flingue** [flɛ̃g] **NM** *très Fam* shooter, *Am* piece

flinguer **[3]** [flɛ̃ge] *très Fam* **VT 1** *(tuer)* to blow away, to waste **2** *(abîmer)* to wreck, to bust, *Br* to knacker **3** *(critiquer sévèrement)* to shoot down, to savage

VPR se flinguer to blow one's brains out; **c'est à se f.! il y a de quoi se f.!** it's enough to drive you to suicide!

flip [flip] **NM** *Fam* **1** *(déprime)* **être en plein f.** to be on a real downer; **c'est le f.!** what a downer! **2** *(après absorption de drogue)* downer, comedown *(as the after-effect of taking cocaine or amphetamines)*

flip-flap [flipflap] *(pl* **flips-flaps)** **NM** *Gym* back(-ward) flip

flippant, -e [flipɑ̃, -ɑ̃t] **ADJ** *très Fam (déprimant)* depressing☐; *(inquiétant)* worrying☐; *(effrayant)* creepy; **c'était f.** it was a real downer

flipper[1] [flipœr] **NM** *(appareil)* pinball (machine); *(jeu)* pinball; **jouer au f.** to play pinball

flipper[2] **[3]** [flipe] **VI** *très Fam* **1** *(être déprimé)* to feel down **2** *(paniquer)* to flip, to freak out; **ça me fait f.** that freaks me out; **elle flippe à cause de son travail** she's cracking up under her workload **3** *(après absorption de drogue)* to come down *(as the after-effect of taking cocaine or amphetamines)*

fliquer **[3]** [flike] **VT** *Fam* to police heavily☐; **fliqué** *(endroit)* overrun with cops; *Fig* **au bureau, on a vraiment l'impression d'être fliqués** in the office we really feel we're being watched like criminals☐; *Fig* **il flique complètement sa femme** he watches his wife like a hawk

flirt [flœrt] **NM** *Vieilli* **1** *(relation)* fling; **ce n'est qu'un petit f. entre eux** they're just having a fling **2** *(ami)* boyfriend; *(amie)* girlfriend; **un de ses anciens flirts** an old flame

flirter **[3]** [flœrte] **VI** *(badiner)* to flirt; **elle aime f.** she's a flirt, she loves flirting; **f. avec qn** to have a fling with sb; *Fig* **f. avec qn/qch** to flirt with sb/sth; **il a longtemps flirté avec le socialisme** he had a long flirtation with socialism

FLN [ɛfɛlɛn] **NM** *Hist (abrév* **Front de libération nationale)** = one of the main political parties in Algeria, established as a resistance movement in 1954 at the start of the war for independence

FLNC [ɛfɛlɛnse] **NM** *(abrév* **Front de libération nationale corse)** = Corsican liberation front

flo [flo] **NMF** *Can Fam* teenager☐, teen

floc [flɔk] **ONOMAT** splash!

flocage [flɔkaʒ] **NM 1** *Tex* flocking **2** *Constr* insulation, lining

floche [flɔʃ] **ADJ** flossy; **fil/soie f.** floss thread/silk

flocon [flɔkɔ̃] **NM** *(parcelle ▸ de laine, de coton)* flock; *(▸ de neige)* snowflake, flake; **flocons d'avoine** oatmeal; **flocons de maïs** cornflakes; **purée en flocons** instant mashed potato

floconneux, -euse [flɔkɔnø, -øz] **ADJ** fluffy

floculation [flɔkylasjɔ̃] **NF** *Chim* flocculation, flocculating

flop [flɔp] **NM** *Fam* flop; **faire un f.** to be a flop

flopée [flɔpe] **NF** *Fam* **une f.** *ou* **des flopées (de qch)** loads *or* masses (of sth)

floquer **[3]** [flɔke] **VT** *Tex* to flock; *Constr* to insulate, to line

floraison [flɔrɛzɔ̃] **NF 1** *Bot (éclosion)* blooming, blossoming, flowering; *(saison)* flowering time; **quand les arbres sont en pleine f.** when the trees are in full bloom **2** *(apparition ▸ d'artistes, d'œuvres)* **une f. de** a boom in; **il y a actuellement une f. de publicités pour des banques** at present there is something of a rash of advertisements for banks

floral, -e, -aux, -ales [flɔral, -o] **ADJ** *(décor)* floral; **composition florale** flower arrangement; **exposition florale** flower show

floralies [flɔrali] **NFPL** flower show

flore [flɔr] **NF 1** *(végétation)* flora **2** *(ouvrage)* flora **3** *Biol & Méd* **f. bactérienne** bacterial flora; **f. intestinale** intestinal flora

floréal [flɔreal] **NM** = 8th month of the French Revolutionary calendar (from 21 April to 20 May)

florès [flɔrɛs] **NM** *Littéraire* **faire f.** to enjoy great success, to be a huge success

Floride [flɔrid] **NF la F.** Florida

florifère [flɔrifɛr] **ADJ** flowering; **plante très f.** prolific flowerer

florilège [flɔrilɛʒ] **NM** anthology

florin [flɔrɛ̃] **NM** florin

florissait *etc voir* **fleurir**

florissant, -e [flɔrisɑ̃, -ɑ̃t] *voir* **fleurir**

ADJ *(affaire, plante)* thriving, flourishing; *(santé, mine)* blooming; **être d'une santé florissante** to be in the best of health

flot [flo] NM **1** *(de larmes, de paroles)* flood; *(de sang, d'injures)* torrent, stream; *(de boue, de voitures)* stream; **un f. de gens** a stream of people; *Littéraire* **un f. de cheveux blonds** flowing blond hair; **faire couler des flots d'encre** to cause much ink to flow **2** *(marée)* **le f.** the incoming *or* rising tide
• **flots** NMPL *Littéraire* **les flots** the waves; **les flots bleus** the ocean blue
• **à flot** ADV **1** *Naut* **être à f.** to be afloat; **mettre un navire à f.** to launch a ship; **remettre un bateau à f.** to refloat a boat **2** *(sorti de difficultés financières)* **être à f.** *(personne)* to keep one's head above water; **je suis à f. maintenant** I'm back on an even keel now; **remettre à f.** *(personne, entreprise)* to get back on an even keel
• **à flots** ADV in floods *or* torrents; **la pluie ruisselle à flots sur les toits** the rain is running down the rooftops in torrents; **la lumière du soleil entre à flots dans la chambre** sunlight is flooding *or* streaming into the bedroom; **le champagne coulait à flots** champagne flowed freely

flottabilité [flɔtabilite] NF buoyancy; **caisson** *ou* **réservoir de f.** buoyancy tank

flottable [flɔtabl] ADJ **1** *(bois)* buoyant **2** *(fleuve)* floatable

flottage [flɔtaʒ] NM *(du bois, du verre)* floating; **bois de f.** raft wood; **train de f.** timber raft

flottaison [flɔtɛzɔ̃] NF **1** *(sur l'eau)* buoyancy; **f. en charge** load line; **f. lège** light waterline **2** *Fin* floating

flottant, -e [flɔtɑ̃, -ɑ̃t] ADJ **1** *(sur l'eau ▸ épave, mine)* floating
2 *(ondoyant ▸ chevelure)* flowing; *(▸ drapeau)* billowing
3 *(hésitant ▸ caractère, pensée)* irresolute; **électeur f.** floating voter; **le raisonnement est un peu f. dans le dernier chapitre** the line of argument loses its way slightly in the final chapter
4 *(variable)* fluctuating, variable; **les effectifs sont flottants** the numbers fluctuate *or* go up and down
5 *Fin (dette, capitaux, taux de change, police d'assurance)* floating
6 *Anat (côte, rein)* floating
NM **1** *(short)* pair of baggy shorts **2** *Bourse* float

flotte [flɔt] NF **1** *Aviat & Naut* fleet; **f. aérienne** air fleet; **f. de commerce** merchant fleet; **f. de ligne** *ou* **de combat** battle fleet; **f. marchande** merchant marine **2** *Fam (pluie)* rain□; *(eau)* water□; **on a eu de la f. pendant une semaine** it poured (down) for a week; **c'est de la f., ce café!** this coffee's like water!

flottement [flɔtmɑ̃] NM **1** *(incertitude)* indecisiveness, wavering *(UNCOUNT)*; **il y eut un moment de f.** there was a moment's hesitation
2 *(imprécision)* looseness, imprecision; **il y a du f. dans la boîte de vitesses** the gears are a bit loose
3 *(ondoiement)* flapping, fluttering
4 *(d'une chaîne, d'une roue)* wobble
5 *(fluctuation ▸ d'une monnaie)* floating; *(▸ de chiffres)* fluctuation; **il y a du f. dans les effectifs** numbers keep fluctuating *or* going up and down

flotter [3] [flɔte] VI **1** *(surnager)* to float; **réussir à faire f. un modèle réduit de bateau** to keep a model boat afloat, to get a model boat to float
2 *(être en suspension)* to hang; **une bonne odeur de soupe flottait dans la cuisine** the kitchen was filled with a delicious smell of soup; **f. dans l'air** *(idée, rumeur)* to be going around
3 *(ondoyer ▸ banderole)* to flap, to flutter; **ses cheveux flottent au vent/sur ses épaules** his/her hair is streaming in the wind/hangs loose over his/her shoulders
4 *(être trop large)* to flap (around); **un short qui flottait autour de ses cuisses** a pair of shorts flapping around his/her thighs
5 *(être au large)* **elle flotte dans sa robe** she's lost in that dress, her dress is too big for her
6 *Littéraire (errer)* to wander, to roam; **un vague sourire flottait sur ses lèvres** a faint smile crossed his/her lips
7 *Fin (monnaie)* to float; **faire f. la livre** to float the pound
VT **f. du bois** to float timber *(down a stream)*; **bois flotté** driftwood
V IMPERSONNEL *Fam (pleuvoir)* to rain□; **il a flotté toute la nuit** it poured *or Br* it bucketed down all night long

flotteur [flɔtœr] NM **1** *(ouvrier)* raftsman *(in charge of timber raft)* **2** *(d'une canne à pêche, d'un hydravion, d'un carburateur)* float **3** *(d'un robinet)* ball; **robinet à f.** ballcock

flottille [flɔtij] NF **1** *Naut* flotilla; **f. de pêche** fishing fleet **2** *Aviat* squadron

flou, -e [flu] ADJ **1** *(imprécis ▸ souvenir)* blurred, hazy; *(▸ renseignements, argumentation)* vague; *(▸ horizon)* hazy; *(▸ idée)* hazy, vague **2** *Cin & Phot* out of focus **3** *(souple ▸ vêtement)* flowing, loose-fitting; *(▸ coiffure)* soft
NM **1** *Cin & Phot* blurredness, fuzziness; **f. artistique** soft-focus effect; *Fig* **c'est un peu le f. artistique en ce moment** things are very much up in the air at the moment; *Fig* **il entretient un certain f. artistique** he's being fairly vague about it **2** *(imprécision)* vagueness; *(▸ de l'horizon)* haziness; *(▸ d'une idée)* haziness, vagueness; **rester dans le f.** to remain vague **3** *(des cheveux)* softness, fluffiness; *(d'une robe)* looseness
ADV **je vois f.** I can't focus properly

flouche [fluʃ] NM,F *Can Fam* teenager□, teen

flouer [6] [flue] VT *Fam* to con, to swindle; **il s'est fait f.** he was conned

flouse [fluz] NM *Fam* cash, dough

flouter [3] [flute] VT *Phot & TV (image)* to blur

flouze [fluz] = **flouse**

FLQ[1] [ɛfɛlky] *Com (abrév* **franco long du quai***)* ADJ INV FAQ
ADV FAQ

FLQ[2] [ɛfɛlky] NM *(abrév* **Front de Libération Québécois***)* = militant political movement in favour of Quebec's independence in the 1960s

fluctuant, -e [flyktɥɑ̃, -ɑ̃t] ADJ fluctuating

fluctuation [flyktɥasjɔ̃] NF fluctuation; **f. des prix** price fluctuation; **f. saisonnière** seasonal fluctuation; *Écon* **bande** *ou* **marge de f.** fluctuation band *or* margin; *Élec* **fluctuations de tension** voltage fluctuations

fluctuer [7] [flyktɥe] VI to fluctuate

fluent, -e [flyɑ̃, -ɑ̃t] ADJ **1** *Méd* bleeding **2** *Littéraire (mouvant)* flowing

fluet, -ette [flyɛ, -ɛt] ADJ *(personne)* slender, slim; *(voix)* reedy

fluide [flɥid] ADJ **1** *(liquide)* fluid
2 *(qui coule facilement)* fluid, smooth; *Fig* **la circulation est f.** there are no hold-ups (in the traffic); *Fig* **en un style f.** in a flowing style; *Fig* **en une langue f.** fluently
3 *(fluctuant ▸ situation)* fluctuating, changeable; *(▸ pensée)* elusive
4 *(flou ▸ forme, blouse, robe)* flowing
NM **1** *(liquide)* fluid; *Chim* **f. aéré** aerated fluid; *Aut* **f. d'embrayage** clutch fluid; *Aut* **f. de frein** brake fluid; **f. glacial** = ice-cold liquid used by children for pranks; **f. moteur** engine fluid **f. de nettoyage** cleaning fluid; **f. de refroidissement** coolant **2** *(d'un médium)* aura; **il a du f.** he has occult powers

fluidifier [9] [flɥidifje] VT to fluidize

fluidité [flɥidite] NF **1** *(qualité ▸ d'une crème, d'une sauce)* smoothness, fluidity; **grâce à la f. de la circulation** because there were no hold-ups in the traffic, because the traffic was flowing smoothly **2** *(flou ▸ d'une forme, d'un vêtement)* fluid *or* flowing contours **3** *Écon (de la main-d'œuvre)* flexibility

fluo [flyo] ADJ INV *Fam* fluorescent□, Day-Glo®□

fluor [flyɔr] NM fluorine; **dentifrice au f.** fluoride toothpaste

fluoration [flyɔrasjɔ̃] NF *(de l'eau)* fluoridation

fluoré, -e [flyɔre] ADJ fluoridated

fluorescence [flyɔresɑ̃s] NF fluorescence

fluorescent, -e [flyɔresɑ̃, -ɑ̃t] ADJ fluorescent; **rose/vert f.** fluorescent pink/green

fluorine [flyɔrin], **fluorite** [flyɔrit] NF fluor, fluorspar, *Am* fluorite

fluorure [flyɔryr] NM *Chim* fluoride

flusher [3] [flœʃe] VT *Can Joual* **1 f. la toilette** to flush the toilet□
2 *(se séparer de ▸ employé)* to fire; *(▸ petit ami)* to dump, *Br* to chuck
3 *Ordinat* to flush
4 *(supprimer)* **ils ont décidé de f. l'émission** they decided to pull the plug on the programme

flûte [flyt] NF **1** *(instrument)* flute; **f. à bec** recorder; **f. de Pan** panpipe; **f. traversière, grande f.** flute; **petite f.** piccolo
2 *(verre)* flute (glass); **f. à champagne** champagne flute
3 *(pain)* = thin loaf of French bread
4 *Suisse (biscuit salé)* breadstick
EXCLAM *Fam* drat!, bother!
• **flûtes** NFPL *Fam (jambes) Br* pins, *Am* gams; **jouer** *ou* **se tirer des flûtes** to take to one's heels

flûté, -e [flyte] ADJ *(rire, voix)* reedy

flûtiau, -x [flytjo] NM tin *or* penny whistle

flûtiste [flytist] NMF flautist

fluvial, -e, -aux, -ales [flyvjal, -o] ADJ *(érosion)* fluvial; *(navigation)* river *(avant n)*; **alluvions fluviales** fluvial deposits

fluviatile [flyvjatil] ADJ fluviatile; **mollusques fluviatiles** river *or* freshwater molluscs

flux [fly] NM **1** *(marée)* incoming tide, floodtide; **le f. et le reflux** the ebb and flow; **le f. et le reflux des visiteurs** the coming and going of visitors
2 *(écoulement ▸ d'un liquide)* flow; *(▸ du sang menstruel)* (menstrual) flow; **un f. menstruel abondant/léger** a heavy/light flow; *Can* **avoir le f.** to have diarrhoea
3 *(abondance)* **noyé dans un f. de paroles** carried away by a torrent of words; **devant ce f. de recommandations** faced with this string of recommendations
4 *Phys* flux; **f. de courant** current flow; **f. électrique** electric flux; **f. électronique** electron flow *or* stream; **f. lumineux** luminous flux; **f. magnétique** magnetic flux
5 *Com* **distribution à f. tendus** just-in-time distribution; **méthode des f. tendus** just-in-time method
6 *Métal* flux
7 *Fin* **f. circulaire des revenus** circular flow of income; **f. monétaire** flow of money, cash flow; **f. de fonds** flow of funds; **f. de trésorerie** cashflow

fluxion [flyksjɔ̃] NF *Méd* inflammation; **f. dentaire** gumboil; *Vieilli* **f. de poitrine** pneumonia

flyer [flajœr] NM *Fam (prospectus de club)* flier□, flyer□

FM [ɛfɛm] NF *(abrév* **frequency modulation***)* FM

FME [ɛfɛmə] NM *(abrév* **Fonds monétaire européen***)* EMF

FMI [ɛfɛmi] NM *(abrév* **Fonds monétaire international***)* IMF

FN [ɛfɛn] NM *(abrév* **Front national***)* Front National *(French extreme right-wing political party)*

FNAC, Fnac [fnak] NF *(abrév* **Fédération nationale des achats des cadres***)* = chain of large stores selling hi-fi, books, CDs etc

FNE [ɛfɛnə] NM *(abrév* **Fonds national de l'emploi***)* = state fund providing aid to jobseekers and workers who accept lower-paid work to avoid redundancy

FNGS [ɛfɛnʒeɛs] NM *(abrév* **Fonds national de garantie des salaires***)* national guarantee fund for the payment of salaries

FNI [ɛfɛni] NFPL *Mil (abrév* **Forces nucléaires intermédiaires***)* INF

FNSEA [ɛfɛnesəa] NF *(abrév* **Fédération nationale des syndicats d'exploitants agricoles***)* = farmers' union, *Br* ≃ NFU

FO [ɛfo] NF *(abrév* **Force ouvrière***)* = moderate workers' union (formed out of the split with Communist CGT in 1948)

FOB [fɔb, ɛfobe] ADJ INV *Com (abrév* **free on board***)* FOB; **vente F.** FOB sale

foc [fɔk] NM *Naut* jib

focal, -e, -aux, -ales [fɔkal, -o] ADJ **1** *(central)* **point f. d'un raisonnement** main *or* central point in an argument **2** *Math, Opt & Phot* focal
• **focale** NF *Opt & Phot* focal distance *or* length

focalisation [fɔkalizasjɔ̃] NF **1** *Opt & Phys* focalization, focussing **2** *(concentration)* focussing **3** *Mktg* targeting; **f. stratégique** strategic targeting

focaliser [3] [fɔkalize] VT **1** *Opt & Phys* to focus **2** *(concentrer)* to focus (**sur** on) **3** *Mktg* to target

VPR se focaliser se f. sur to be focussed *or* to focus on

focus [fɔkys] **NM 1** *Phot* focus **2** *(dans un titre)* **f. sur la Bretagne/sur le dernier modèle** spotlight on Brittany/on the latest model; **f. sur le trafic de drogue international** exposed: international drug trafficking **3** *Ordinat* activation

fœhn [føn] **NM 1** *(vent)* foehn, föhn **2** *Suisse* hairdryer

fœtal, -e, -aux, -ales [fetal, -o] **ADJ** foetal

fœtus [fetys] **NM** foetus

fofolle [fɔfɔl] *voir* **foufou**

foi [fwa] **NF 1** *Rel* faith; **avoir la f.** to have faith; *Hum* **il faut avoir la f. pour travailler avec elle** you have to be really dedicated to work with her; **acte/article de f.** act/article of faith; *Fig* **faire sa profession de f.** to set out one's ideas and beliefs; *Rel* **avoir la f. du charbonnier** to have a naive belief in God; *Fig* to be naively trusting; **n'avoir ni f. ni loi, être sans f. ni loi** to fear neither God nor man; *Hum* **il n'y a que la f. qui sauve!** faith is a wonderful thing!

2 *(confiance)* faith, trust; **ajouter** *ou* **accorder f. à des rumeurs** to give credence to rumours; **il faut toujours garder f. en soi-même** you must always trust (in) yourself; **avoir f. en** *ou* **dans qn** to have faith in *or* to trust (in) sb; **elle a une f. aveugle en lui** she trusts him blindly; **avoir f. en l'avenir** to have confidence in the future

3 *Littéraire (parole)* pledged word; **elle n'a pas respecté la f. conjugale** she has broken her marital vows; **f. d'honnête homme!** on my word of honour!

4 *(preuve)* **faire f.** to be valid; **il n'y a qu'une pièce officielle qui fasse f.** only an official paper is valid; **les coupons doivent être envoyés avant le 1er septembre, le cachet de la poste faisant f.** the coupons must be postmarked no later than 1 September

5 *(locutions) Jur* **en f. de quoi** in witness whereof; **ma f.!** well!; **viendrez-vous? – ma f. oui!** will you come? – why, certainly!; **c'est ma f. possible, qui sait?** it might be possible, who knows?

• **sous la foi de PRÉP sous la f. du serment** on *or* under oath

• **sur la foi de PRÉP sur la f. de leur déclaration/réputation** on the strength of their statement/reputation

• **bonne foi NF être de bonne f.** to be sincere; **les gens de bonne f.** honest people, decent folk; **témoin de bonne f.** truthful witness; **il a agi en toute bonne f.** he acted in good faith

• **mauvaise foi NF être de mauvaise f.** to be insincere; **témoin de mauvaise f.** untruthful witness

foie [fwa] **NM 1** *Anat* liver **2** *Culin* liver; **f. de génisse** cow's liver; **f. gras** foie gras; **f. de veau** calf's liver *(from a milk-fed animal)*; **f. de volaille** chicken liver

• **foies NMPL** *Fam* **se ronger** *ou* **se manger les foies** to be climbing the walls, to go berserk; *très Fam* **avoir les foies** to be scared stiff; *très Fam* **il m'a foutu les foies** he scared the pants off me

foie-de-bœuf [fwadəbœf] *(pl* **foies-de-bœuf***)* **NM** beefsteak fungus

foin [fwɛ̃] **NM 1** *Agr* hay; **tas de f.** haycock; **meule de f.** haystack; **rentrer le f.** to bring in the hay; **c'est la saison des foins** it's haymaking season; **faire les foins** to make hay; **avoir du f. dans ses bottes** to have a fair bit (of money) tucked away; *Fig* **chercher une aiguille** *ou* **une épingle dans une botte** *ou* **une meule de f.** to look for a needle in a haystack; *Can Fam* **avoir du f.** to be loaded; *Can Fam* **il a du f. à vendre** he's flying low, his flies are undone□ **2** *(d'un artichaut)* choke **3** *Fam (locution)* **faire du f.** *(être bruyant)* to make a racket; *(faire un scandale)* to kick up a fuss

• **foin de EXCLAM** *Littéraire* **f. de l'argent et de la gloire!** the Devil take money and glory!

foire [fwar] **NF 1** *(marché)* fair; **f. agricole** agricultural show; **f. aux bestiaux** cattle fair *or* market; **champ de f.** fairground; *Ordinat* **f. aux questions** frequently asked questions

2 *(exposition)* trade fair; **f. commerciale** trade show; **f. internationale** international (trade) fair; **f. professionnelle** trade fair

3 *(fête foraine)* funfair

4 *Fam (désordre)* mess; **c'est la f. dans cette maison!** this house is a real dump!; *(bruit)* it's a madhouse *or Br* it's bedlam in here!; **faire la f.** to live it up

5 *(locutions)* **f. d'empoigne** free-for-all; *Vulg Vieilli* **avoir la f.** to have the runs

foire-exposition [fwarɛkspozisjɔ̃] *(pl* **foires-expositions***)* **NF** trade fair

foirer [3] [fware] **VI 1** *très Fam (rater)* to be a *Br* cock-up *or* balls-up *or Am* ball-up; **il a tout fait f.** he *Br* cocked *or* ballsed *or Am* balled everything up **2** *(fusée, obus)* to fail **3** *(vis)* to slip

VT *très Fam (rater)* to make a *Br* cock-up *or* balls-up *or Am* ball-up of

foireux, -euse [fwarø, -øz] **ADJ 1** *Fam Péj (mal fait)* hopeless, useless; **leur espèce de festival f.** their washout of a festival; **c'est un plan f.** that plan is going to be a *Br* cock-up *or* balls-up *or Am* ball-up **2** *Fam (poltron)* yellow-bellied, chicken; **quel mec f.!** what a chicken! **3** *Vulg (diarrhéique)* shitty

fois [fwa] **NF 1** *(exprime la fréquence)* **une f.** once; **deux f.** twice; **trois f.** three times, *Littéraire* thrice; **payez en six f.** pay in six instalments; **ça a raté tellement de f. que je n'essaie même plus** it went wrong so many times I don't even try any more; **une autre f., il avait oublié ses gants** another time he'd left his gloves behind; **une autre f. peut-être** *(pour refuser une invitation)* some other *or* another time maybe; **une f. et une seule** just the once, once and once only; **c'est la seule f. où j'ai regretté** that's the only time when *or* that I had regrets; **il faut le boire en une f.** you must drink it at *or* in one go; **d'autres f.** at other times; **bien des f.** many times, often; **encore une f.** once more, once again; **que de f. te l'ai-je dit!** how many times have I told you!; **combien de f.?** how many times?, how often?; **neuf f. sur dix** nine times out of ten; **quatre-vingt-dix-neuf f. sur cent** ninety-nine times out of a hundred; *Littéraire* **par deux f.** twice, not once but twice; *Littéraire* **par trois f.** three times, thrice; **pour la énième f.** for the umpteenth time; **pour une f.** for once; **pour une f. que je peux y aller, il faut qu'il vienne aussi!** it's the one time I can go *or* for once I can go and he has to come as well!; **allez, viens en boîte, pour une f.!** come to a club for once!; **une (bonne) f. pour toutes** once and for all; **la première/deuxième f.** the first/second time; **c'est la première f. que j'en fais** it's my first time, it's the first time I've done it; **une dernière f., arrête!** for the last time, stop it!; **cette f.** this time; **cette f., je gagnerai** this time, I'll win; **pour cette f.** (just) this once; **ça ira pour cette f., mais ne recommencez pas** it's all right this once, but don't do it again; **(à) chaque f. que, toutes les f. que** every *or* each time; **chaque f. que j'essaie, je rate** every time I try, I fail; **la f. suivante** *ou* **d'après** the time after that; **il y a des f. où je me demande à quoi tu penses** there are times when I wonder what you're thinking about; **cent euros une f., deux f., trois f., adjugé, vendu!** a hundred euros, going, going, gone!; **une f. n'est pas coutume** just the once won't hurt; **il était une f. un roi** once upon a time there was a king

2 *(dans les comparaisons)* time; **c'est trois f. plus grand** it's three times as big; **il y a dix f. moins de spectateurs que l'année dernière** there are ten times fewer spectators than last year

3 *(comme distributif)* **deux f. par jour** twice daily *or* a day; **deux f. par mois** twice a month; **une f. par semaine** once a week; **trois f. par an, trois f. l'an** three times a year

4 *Math* times; **trois f. quatre font douze** three times four is twelve; **deux** *ou* **trois f. rien** virtually nothing, hardly anything; **il faut du beurre? – oui, mais trois f. rien** do you need some butter? – yes, but only the smallest amount *or* but hardly any; **je l'ai acheté pour trois f. rien** I bought it for next to nothing

5 *(locutions)* **une f. nettoyé, il sera comme neuf** once *or* after it's been cleaned, it'll be as good as new; **tu n'as qu'à venir une f. ton travail terminé** just come as soon as your work is finished; **nous aurons plus de temps une f. installés** we'll have more time when we've settled in; *Fam* **des f.** *(parfois)* sometimes; **des f., elle est plutôt bizarre** she's a bit strange sometimes; **non mais des f.!** honestly!; *Fam* **des f. que** (just) in case; **tu n'aurais pas vu mon livre, des f.?** you wouldn't happen to have seen my book anywhere, would you?; **je préfère l'appeler, des f. qu'elle aurait oublié** I'd rather call her in case she's forgotten

• **à la fois ADV** together, at a time, at the same time; **versez la farine et le sucre à la f.** add the flour and (the) sugar at the same time; **à la f. utile et pas cher** both useful and inexpensive; **pas tous à la f.!** one at a time!, not all at once!; **pas trop vite, une chose à la f.** slow down, one thing at a time

• **(tout) à la fois ADV** both; **il rit et pleure (tout) à la f.** he's laughing and crying at (one and) the same time; **elle est (tout) à la f. auteur et traductrice** she's both an author and a translator

• **une fois ADV** *Belg* indeed; **venez une f. voir** *(donc)* just come and see

foison [fwazɔ̃] **NF** *Arch* abundance, plenty

• **à foison ADV** *Littéraire* galore, plenty; **des pommes à f.** apples in abundance, apples galore; **il y en a à f.** there are plenty of them, they are abundant

foisonnant, -e [fwazɔnɑ̃, -ɑ̃t] **ADJ** abundant

foisonnement [fwazɔnmɑ̃] **NM 1** *(abondance)* abundance, proliferation **2** *Chim & Tech* expansion

foisonner [3] [fwazɔne] **VI 1** *(abonder)* to abound; **une œuvre où les idées foisonnent** a work rich in ideas; **le gibier foisonne ici** game is plentiful here; **f. de** *ou* **en qch** to abound in sth, to be full of sth **2** *Chim & Tech* to expand

fol [fɔl] *voir* **fou**

folâtre [fɔlatr] **ADJ** *(enjoué)* frisky, frolicsome; **être d'humeur f.** to be in a playful mood

folâtrer [3] [fɔlatre] **VI** *(personne)* to romp, to frolic; *(animal)* to gambol, to frolic, to frisk about

folâtrerie [fɔlatrəri] **NF** *Littéraire* **1** *(de tempérament ▸ d'un agneau)* friskiness; *(▸ d'un chaton, d'un enfant)* playfulness **2** *(action)* frolicking

foldingue [fɔldɛ̃g] **ADJ** *Fam* crazy, batty

folerie [fɔləri] **NF** *Can Fam* **elle a fait une f. en épousant cet homme** she was crazy *or* mad□ to marry that man; **faire des foleries** *(faire le clown)* to clown about; *(dépenser beaucoup)* to be extravagant□

foliacé, -e [fɔljase] **ADJ** foliaceous, foliate

foliaire [fɔljɛr] **ADJ** foliar

foliation [fɔljasjɔ̃] **NF** *Bot & Géol* foliation

folichon, -onne [fɔliʃɔ̃, -ɔn] **ADJ** *Fam* playful□, lighthearted□; **pas f.** not much fun; **un après-midi pas bien f.** a pretty dull afternoon; **elle n'est pas du genre f.** she's a bit strait-laced

folie [fɔli] **NF 1** *Psy (démence)* madness; **un accès** *ou* **une crise de f.** a fit of madness

2 *(déraison)* madness, lunacy; **c'est pure f.** it's utter madness *or* sheer folly; **elle a la f. du ski** she's mad about skiing; **elle a la f. du jeu** she's got the gambling bug; **c'est de la f. douce que de vouloir la raisonner** it's sheer lunacy to try to reason with her; **sortir par ce temps, c'est de la f. furieuse!** it's (sheer) madness to go out in weather like this!; **avoir la f. des grandeurs** to suffer from *or* to have delusions of grandeur

3 *(acte déraisonnable)* crazy thing to do, *Littéraire* folly; **il a eu la f. de céder** he was mad enough to give in; **ce sont des folies de jeunesse** those are just the crazy things you get up to when you're young; **j'ai fait une f. en achetant ce manteau** I was crazy *or* mad to buy that coat; **faire des folies** *(dépenser)* to be extravagant; *Hum* **faire des folies de son corps** to put oneself about; **dire des folies** to talk wildly, to say crazy things

4 *Hist (maison)* folly

• **à la folie ADV** passionately, to distraction; **aimer qn à la f.** to be madly in love with sb, to love sb to distraction

folio [fɔljo] **NM** folio

foliole [fɔljɔl] **NF** *Bot* leaflet

folioter [3] [fɔljɔte] **VT** to folio, to foliate; *(par page)* to paginate

folk [fɔlk] **ADJ** folk *(avant n)*

NM folk music

folkeux, -euse [fɔlkø, -øz] **NM,F** *Fam* folk music fan□, folkie

folklo [fɔlklo] ADJ INV *Fam* bizarre, weird and wonderful; *(personne)* eccentric[○], wacky, off-the-wall, *Am* kooky

folklore [fɔlklɔr] NM **1** *Mus & (en danse)* **le f.** folklore **2** *Fam Péj* **c'est du f.** it's a load of nonsense

folklorique [fɔlklɔrik] ADJ **1** *Mus & (en danse)* folk *(avant n)*; *(costume)* traditional **2** *Fam (insolite, ridicule)* bizarre, weird

folkloriste [fɔlklɔrist] NMF folklorist, specialist in folklore

folle [fɔl] *voir* **fou**

follement [fɔlmɑ̃] ADV **1** *(excessivement)* madly; **il l'aime f.** he's madly in love with him/her; **s'amuser f.** to have a great time; **le prix en est f. élevé** the price is ridiculously high; **ce n'est pas f. gai** it's not that much fun **2** *(déraisonnablement)* madly, wildly

follet [fɔlɛ] *voir* **feu, poil**

folliculaire [fɔlikylɛr] ADJ follicular
NM *Vieilli Péj* hack writer

follicule [fɔlikyl] NM *Anat & Bot* follicle

folliculine [fɔlikylin] NF *Biol* folliculin, oestrone

fomentateur, -trice [fɔmɑ̃tatœr, -tris] N *Littéraire* agitator, troublemaker

fomentation [fɔmɑ̃tasjɔ̃] NF *Méd & Littéraire* fomenting, fomentation

fomentatrice [fɔmɑ̃tatris] *voir* **fomentateur**

fomenter [3] [fɔmɑ̃te] VT *Méd & Littéraire* to foment

fonçage [fɔ̃saʒ] NM **1** *(de tonneau)* bottoming, heading **2** *Mines (de puits)* boring, sinking

foncé, -e [fɔ̃se] ADJ dark, deep

foncer [16] [fɔ̃se] VI **1** *(s'élancer)* to charge; **f. contre** *ou* **sur son adversaire** to rush at one's adversary; **f. droit devant soi** to go straight ahead; *Fam* **f. dans le tas** to charge in, to pile in

2 *Fam (se déplacer très vite)* to speed along; **les coureurs foncent vers la victoire** the runners are sprinting on to victory; **il a foncé à l'hôpital** he rushed straight to the hospital

3 *Fam (se hâter)* **il a fallu f. pour boucler le journal** we had to work flat out to get the newspaper out on time; *Fig* **il a toujours su f.** he has always been the dynamic type; **f. dans le brouillard** to forge ahead (without worrying about the consequences)

4 *Fam (s'y mettre)* to get one's head down; **ne te pose pas de questions, fonce!** don't ask any questions, just do it!

5 *(s'assombrir* ▸ *cheveux)* to go darker

VT **1** *(teinte)* to make darker, to darken

2 *(mettre un fond à)* to (fit with a) bottom

3 *Culin (au lard)* to line with bacon fat; *(avec de la pâte)* to line with pastry

4 *Mines (pieu)* to sink, to drive (in); *(puits)* to bore, to sink

fonceur, -euse [fɔ̃sœr, -øz] *Fam* ADJ dynamic[○], go-getting
NM,F dynamic type, go-getter

foncier, -ère [fɔ̃sje, -ɛr] ADJ **1** *Admin & Fin (impôt, politique, problème)* land *(avant n)*; **biens fonciers** (real) property, real estate; **crédit f.** land bank; **droit f.** ground law; **propriétaire f.** landowner; **propriété foncière** land ownership, ownership of land **2** *(fondamental)* fundamental, basic
NM land *or* property tax; **f. bâti** landed property; **f. non bâti** land for development

foncièrement [fɔ̃sjɛrmɑ̃] ADV **1** *(fondamentalement)* fundamentally, basically; **l'argument est f. vicieux** the argument is fundamentally flawed **2** *(totalement)* deeply, profoundly; **il est f. ignorant** he's profoundly ignorant

fonction [fɔ̃ksjɔ̃] NF **1** *(emploi)* office; **entrer en f.** *ou* **fonctions, prendre ses fonctions** to take up one's post *or* one's duties; *(président, ministre)* to take up office; **être en f.** to be in office; **faire f. de** to act as; **ce couteau fera f. de tournevis** this knife will do instead of a screwdriver; **il a pour f. d'écrire les discours du président** his job is to write the president's speeches; **il occupe de hautes fonctions** he has important responsibilities; **est-ce que cela entre dans tes fonctions?** is this part of your duties?; **remplir ses fonctions** to carry out one's job *or* functions; **elle remplit les fonctions d'interprète** she acts as interpreter; **se démettre de ses fonctions** to resign one's post *or* from one's duties; **démettre qn de ses fonctions** to dismiss sb (from his/her duties)

2 *(rôle)* function; **c'est la première f. de l'estomac** it's the main function of the stomach; **faire f. de gérant** to act as manager; **les fonctions de directeur** the functions of a director; **fonctions d'encadrement** executive functions; **cette table fait f. de table à café** this table acts *or* serves as a coffee table; **adjectif qui fait f. d'adverbe** adjective that is used *or* functions as an adverb; **la f. crée l'organe** necessity is the mother of invention

3 être f. de *(dépendre de)* **sa venue est f. de son travail** whether he/she comes or not depends on his/her work

4 *Chim, Ling & Math* function; **en f. inverse de** in inverse ratio to; **être f. de** to be a function of; *Écon & Mktg* **f. de la demande** demand function, market demand function

5 *Ordinat* function, facility; **f. booléenne** Boolean function; **f. de comptage de mots** word count facility; **f. de contrôle** control function; **f. couper-coller** cut-and-paste function *or* facility; **f. multimédia** multimedia facility; **f. recherche et remplacement** search and replace function *or* facility; **f. de recopie** copy function *or* facility; **f. de répétition** repeat function; **f. de sauvegarde** save function *or* facility

• **de fonction** ADJ **appartement** *ou* **logement de f.** accommodation that goes with the job, *Br* tied accommodation; **voiture de f.** company car

• **en fonction de** PRÉP according to; **payé en f. de sa contribution au projet** paid according to one's contribution to the project; **exprimer une quantité en f. d'une autre** to express one quantity in terms of *or* as a function of another; **les prix varient en f. de la demande** prices vary in accordance with *or* according to demand

• **fonction publique** NF **la f. publique** ≃ the civil *or* public service

fonctionnaire [fɔ̃ksjɔnɛr] NMF ≃ civil servant; **f. détaché** ≃ civil servant *Br* on secondment *or Am* on a temporary assignment; **f. municipal** local government official; **haut f.** senior civil servant, senior official; **petit f.** minor official; *Péj* **avoir une mentalité de petit f.** to have a petty bureaucratic mentality, *Br* to be a jobsworth

> **FONCTIONNAIRE**
>
> This term covers a broader range of public service employees than the term "civil servant", from high-ranking members of the state administration to public-sector teachers and post office workers. "Fonctionnaires", of whom there are more than four and a half million in France, are normally recruited through competitive state examination and enjoy greater job security and other privileges to which private sector employees are not automatically entitled.

fonctionnalisme [fɔ̃ksjɔnalism] NM functionalism

fonctionnaliste [fɔ̃ksjɔnalist] ADJ functionalist, functionalistic
NMF functionalist

fonctionnalité [fɔ̃ksjɔnalite] NF practicality, functionality

• **fonctionnalités** NFPL *Ordinat* functions, features

fonctionnariat [fɔ̃ksjɔnarja] NM employment by the state

fonctionnariser [3] [fɔ̃ksjɔnarize] VT to make part of the civil service

fonctionnarisme [fɔ̃ksjɔnarism] NM *Péj* officialdom, bureaucracy

fonctionnel, -elle [fɔ̃ksjɔnɛl] ADJ **1** *Math, Méd & Psy* functional **2** *(adapté)* practical, functional

fonctionnellement [fɔ̃ksjɔnɛlmɑ̃] ADV functionally

fonctionnement [fɔ̃ksjɔnmɑ̃] NM *(d'un mécanisme, d'un engin)* running, working; *(du métro, d'un véhicule)* running; *(d'une entreprise)* running, functioning; **en (bon) état de f.** in (good) working order; **pour assurer le bon f. de votre machine à laver** to keep your washing machine in good working order; **ça vient d'un mauvais f. de la prise** it's due to a fault in the plug; *Ordinat* **f. en réseau** networking

fonctionner [3] [fɔ̃ksjɔne] VI *(mécanisme, engin)* to run, to work; *(métro, véhicule)* to run; *(personne)* to function, to operate; *(entreprise)* to run, to function; *Ordinat* to run; **le moteur fonctionne mal/bien** the engine isn't/is working properly; **les freins n'ont pas fonctionné** the brakes failed, the brakes didn't work; **mon cœur fonctionne encore bien!** my heart is still going strong!; **faire f. une machine** to operate a machine; **je n'arrive pas à faire f. la machine à laver** I can't get the washing machine to work; **ça fonctionne avec des pièces de deux euros** it works with two-euro coins, you need two-euro coins to work it; *Élec* **f. sur courant continu** to operate *or* to run on direct current; **f. sur piles** to run on batteries, to be battery-operated; **f. au gaz** to be gas-powered, to run on gas

FOND [fɔ̃]

• bottom **1**	• back **1**
• depths **2**	• heart **3**
• core **3**	• background **5**
• drop **7**	• long-distance running **10**

NM **1** *(d'un récipient)* bottom; *(d'un placard)* back; *(extrémité)* bottom, far end; *(de la gorge)* back; *(d'une pièce)* far end, back; *(d'un jardin)* far end, bottom; *(d'un océan)* bottom, bed; *(d'un chapeau)* crown; *(d'une chaise)* seat; *(d'un tonneau)* bottom, head; **sans f.** bottomless; **bateau à f. plat** flat-bottomed boat; **le f. d'un puits** the bottom of a well; **regarde bien dans le f. du placard** take a good look at the back of the cupboard; **le f. de sa gorge est un peu rouge** the back of his/her throat is a bit red; **la salle du f.** the room at the end, the far room; **au fin f. du désert** in the middle of the desert; **au fin f. de la campagne irlandaise** in the depths of the Irish countryside; **il y a cinq mètres de f.** *(de profondeur)* the water is five metres deep *or* in depth; **aller par le f.** to sink; **envoyer par le f.** to send to the bottom, to sink; **couler par 100 mètres de f.** to sink to a depth of 100 metres; **prendre f.** *(d'une ancre)* to bite, to grip; **il n'y a pas assez de f. pour plonger** the water isn't deep enough for diving; **f. de cylindre/chaudière** cylinder/boiler head; **f. de culotte** *ou* **de pantalon** seat (of one's pants); **les grands fonds marins** the depths of the ocean; **à f. de cale** at rock bottom; *Fam Fig* **gratter** *ou* **vider** *ou* **racler les fonds de tiroir** to scrape around *(for money, food etc)*

2 *Fig* depths; **atteindre le f. de la misère** to reach the depths of poverty; **toucher le f. (du désespoir)** to reach the depths of despair, to hit rock bottom; **il connaît le f. de mon cœur/âme** he knows what's in my heart/soul; **je vous remercie du f. du cœur** I thank you from the bottom of my heart; **il faut aller jusqu'au f. de ce mystère** we must get to the bottom of this mystery

3 *(cœur, substance)* heart, core, nub; **voilà le f. du problème** here is the core *or* the root of the problem; **le f. de notre politique** the essential features of our policy; **puis-je te dire le f. de ma pensée?** can I tell you what I really think?; *Littérature* **le f. et la forme** substance and form; **sur le f., vous avez raison** you're basically right

4 *(tempérament)* **il a un bon f.** he's basically a good *or* kind person; **elle n'a pas vraiment un mauvais f.** she's not a bad person really

5 *(arrière-plan)* background; **des fleurs sur f. blanc** flowers on a white background; **sur un f. de violons** with violins in the background; **il y a un f. de vérité dans ce que vous dites** there's some truth in what you're saying; **f. sonore** *ou* **musical** background music; **bruit de f.** background noise; **il y avait du jazz en f. sonore** there was jazz playing in the background; **le f. de l'air est frais** there's a chill *or* nip in the air

6 *Typ* **f. perdu** bleed; **à f. perdu** bleeding; **(blanc de) petit f.** back margin, gutter; **(blanc de) grand f.** fore-edge, gutter

7 *(reste)* drop; **il reste un f. de café** there's a drop of coffee left; **boire** *ou* **vider le f. d'une coupe de champagne** to empty one's champagne glass; **boire** *ou* **vider les fonds de bouteilles** to drink up the dregs; **le f. du panier** the leftovers

8 *Culin* **f. de sauce/soupe** base for a sauce/soup;

f. d'artichaut artichoke heart; **f. de tarte** pastry case

9 *Mines* **travailler au f.** to work at the coal face; **descendre au f. de la mine** to go down the pit

10 *Sport* **le f.** long-distance running; **course de (grand) f.** long-distance race; *Ski* cross-country race; **cheval qui a du f.** horse with staying power

11 *(locution)* **faire f. sur** to put one's trust in

• **à fond** ADV in depth; **enfoncer un clou à f.** to hammer a nail home, to drive a nail all the way in; **respirer à f.** to breathe deeply; *Fam* **faire le ménage à f. dans la maison** to clean the house thoroughly, to spring-clean; *Fam* **se consacrer** *ou* **se donner à f. à qch** to give one's all to sth, to devote all one's energy to sth; **il s'est donné à f. dans son travail** he threw himself completely into his work; *Fam* **s'engager à f. dans une aventure** to get deeply involved in an adventure; **il s'est engagé à f. dans le combat écologique** he committed himself wholeheartedly *or* body and soul to the struggle for the environment; *Fam* **apprendre** *ou* **connaître une langue à f.** to acquire *or* to have a thorough knowledge of a language

• **à fond de train** ADV *Fam* (at) full tilt

• **à fond la caisse, à fond les manettes** ADV *Fam* (at) full tilt

• **au fond** ADV basically; **au f., c'est mieux comme ça** it's better that way, really; **au f., on pourrait y aller en janvier** in fact, we could go in January; **au f. elle n'est pas méchante** she's not a bad sort at heart *or* deep down, she's basically not a bad sort; **au f., c'est ce qu'il voulait** (deep down) that's what he really wanted

• **au fond de** PRÉP **au f. de soi-même** deep down; **c'est au f. du couloir/de la salle** it's at the (far) end of the corridor/of the hall; **au f. de la rivière** at the bottom of the river; **regarder qn au f. des yeux** to look deeply into sb's eyes

• **dans le fond** PRÉP = au fond

• **de fond** ADJ **1** *Sport (épreuve, coureur, course)* long-distance *(avant n)*; **ski de f.** cross-country skiing **2** *(analyse, remarque, texte, question)* basic, fundamental; **article de f.** feature (article)

• **de fond en comble** ADV *(nettoyer, fouiller)* from top to bottom; *Fig* **revoir un texte de f. en comble** to revise a text thoroughly

• **fond de robe** NM slip

• **fond de teint** NM foundation (cream)

fondamental, -e, -aux, -ales [fɔ̃damɑ̃tal, -o] ADJ **1** *(théorique ▸ science)* fundamental, basic; **la recherche fondamentale** basic *or* fundamental research

2 *(de base)* elementary, basic; **couleurs fondamentales** primary colours; **ce sont des choses fondamentales que vous devriez connaître** these are fundamental *or* basic things you should know

3 *(important)* fundamental, essential, crucial; **il est f. que nous réparions notre erreur** it's crucial *or* fundamental that we should correct our mistake

4 *Mus* fundamental; **son f.** *(d'une corde)* root, generator

• **fondamentale** NF *Mus* fundamental

• **fondamentaux** NMPL **les fondamentaux de qch** the basics *or* fundamentals of sth

fondamentalement [fɔ̃damɑ̃talmɑ̃] ADV fundamentally; **c'est f. la même chose** it's basically the same thing

fondamentalisme [fɔ̃damɑ̃talism] NM (religious) fundamentalism

fondamentaliste [fɔ̃damɑ̃talist] ADJ fundamentalist, fundamentalistic

NMF **1** *(scientifique)* scientist engaged in basic research **2** *Rel* fundamentalist

fondant, -e [fɔ̃dɑ̃, -ɑ̃t] ADJ **1** *(glace, neige)* melting, thawing **2** *(aliment)* **un rôti f.** a tender roast; **un bonbon/chocolat f.** a sweet/chocolate that melts in the mouth

NM **1** *Culin (bonbon, gâteau)* fondant; **un f. au chocolat** a chocolate fondant **2** *Métal* flux

fondateur, -trice [fɔ̃datœr, -tris] NM,F **1** *(gén)* founder **2** *Jur* incorporator

fondation [fɔ̃dasjɔ̃] NF **1** *(création ▸ d'une ville, d'une société)* foundation; *(▸ d'une bourse, d'un prix)* establishment, creation; **f. d'une entreprise** setting up of a business **2** *(fonds)* endowment (fund), foundation **3** *(institution)* foundation

• **fondations** NFPL *Constr* foundations

fondatrice [fɔ̃datris] *voir* **fondateur**

fondé, -e [fɔ̃de] ADJ **1** *(argument, peur)* justified; **mes craintes ne sont que trop fondées** my fears are only too justified; **vos craintes ne sont pas fondées** your fears are groundless *or* unfounded *or* unjustified; **qu'est-ce qu'il y a de f. dans ces bruits?** is there any truth in these reports? **un reproche non f.** an unjustified reproach; **mal f.** ill-founded **2** *(créé)* founded; **établissement f. en 1850** established 1850 **3** *(locution)* **je serais f. à croire qu'il y a eu malversation** I would be justified in thinking *or* I would have grounds for believing that embezzlement has taken place

• **fondé de pouvoir** NM agent *(holding power of attorney)*; *(mandant)* proxy; *(directeur de banque)* manager with signing authority; **il est le f. de pouvoir (de)** he holds power of attorney (for)

fondement [fɔ̃dmɑ̃] NM **1** *(base)* foundation; **jeter les fondements d'une nouvelle politique** to lay the foundations of a new policy **2** *Hum (derrière)* behind, backside; *(anus)* back passage **3** *Phil* fundament

• **sans fondement** ADJ *(crainte, rumeur)* groundless, unfounded

fonder [3] [fɔ̃de] VT **1** *(construire ▸ ville, empire, parti)* to found; **f. un foyer** *ou* **une famille** to start a family; **f. un hôpital** *(en donnant un legs)* to found a hospital

2 *Com (société, journal)* to found, to set up; **fondé en 1928** established in 1928

3 *(appuyer)* **f. qch sur** to base *or* to found *or* to pin sth on; **f. ses espérances sur qch** to base *or* to build one's hopes on sth; **elle fondait tous ses espoirs sur son fils** she pinned all her hopes on her son

4 *(légitimer ▸ réclamation, plainte)* to justify

VPR **se fonder 1 se f. sur qn/qch** *(se prévaloir de)* to base oneself on sb/sth; **sur quoi te fondes-tu pour affirmer pareille chose?** what grounds do you have for such a claim? **2 se f. sur** *(remarque, théorie)* to be based on

fonderie [fɔ̃dri] NF **1** *(extraction ▸ de minerai)* smelting; *(fusion ▸ de métaux)* founding, casting **2** *(usine)* smelting works **3** *(atelier)* foundry

fondeur[1], -euse[1] [fɔ̃dœr, -øz] NM,F *Sport* cross-country skier

fondeur[2], -euse[2] [fɔ̃dœr, -øz] NM,F **1** *(maître de forges)* ironmaster **2** *(ouvrier ▸ de bronze)* caster; *(▸ de l'or, de l'argent)* smelter; *(▸ de fusion)* (metal) founder; **f. en cuivre** brass founder; **f. en caractères, f. typographe** type founder

• **fondeuse** NF *(machine)* smelter

fondre [75] [fɔ̃dr] VT **1** *(rendre liquide ▸ minerai)* to smelt; *(▸ métal)* to melt down; *(▸ sucre)* to dissolve; *(▸ neige, cire)* to melt; **f. de l'or/de l'argent** to smelt gold/silver; **f. des pièces** to melt coins down

2 *(fabriquer ▸ statue, canon, cloche)* to cast, to found

3 *(dissoudre)* to dissolve

4 *(combiner ▸ couleurs)* to blend, to merge; *(▸ sociétés)* to merge, to amalgamate, to combine; **f. deux livres en un seul** to combine two books in one *or* in a single volume

5 *TV* to fade; **f. des teintes** to blend colours

VI **1** *(se liquéfier)* to melt; *(de la neige)* to melt, to thaw; **la glace fond au-dessus de 0°C** ice melts at 0°C; **faites f. le chocolat** melt the chocolate; **f. comme cire** *ou* **comme neige au soleil** to vanish into thin air; *Élec* **faire f. un fusible** to blow a fuse

2 *(se dissoudre)* to dissolve; **faire f. du sucre** to dissolve sugar; **f. dans la bouche** to melt in the mouth

3 *(s'affaiblir ▸ animosité, rage)* to melt away, to disappear; **mon cœur fondit (de pitié)** my heart melted (with pity); **je fonds** my heart melts; **le général a vu sa division f. en quelques heures** the general saw his entire division vanish in a few hours; **f. en larmes** to dissolve into tears

4 *Fam (maigrir)* to get thin; **il fond à vue d'œil** the weight's dropping off him; **j'ai fondu de trois kilos** I've lost three kilos

5 f. sur *(se jeter sur ▸ sujet: personne, avion, rapace)* to swoop down on

VPR **se fondre 1** *(se liquéfier)* to melt **2** *(se mêler)* to merge, to mix; **les couleurs se fondent à l'arrière-plan du tableau** the colours merge into the background of the painting; **se f. dans la nuit/le brouillard** to disappear into the night/mist; **se f. dans la foule** to merge *or* to blend into the crowd; **se f. dans l'anonymat** to hide under the cloak of anonymity

fondrière [fɔ̃drijɛr] NF **1** *(sur une route)* pothole **2** *(marécage)* bog, quagmire; *Can* **f. de mousse** muskeg

fonds [fɔ̃] NM **1** *(propriété)* business; **un f. de commerce** a business; **f. de commerce à vendre** business for sale (as a going concern); **un f. de boulangerie** a bakery business; **f. de clientèle** customer base

2 *Fin* fund; **f. d'amortissement** sinking fund; **f. de caisse** cash in hand, float; **f. de capital-risque maison** captive fund; **f. commun de placement** investment company *or* trust, *Am* mutual fund; **f. commun de placement d'entreprise** company investment fund; **f. commun de placement à risques** venture capital trust; **f. dédié** captive fund; **f. de dotation** endowment fund; **f. d'entreprise** occupational pension scheme; **f. d'épargne-retraite** retirement savings fund; **F. européen de coopération monétaire** European Monetary Cooperation Fund; **F. européen de développement** European Development Fund; **F. européen de développement régional** European Regional Development Fund; **f. à faible frais d'entrée** low-load fund; **f. de garantie** guarantee fund; **f. de garantie automobile** = emergency fund to compensate victims of accidents caused by uninsured drivers; **f. géré** managed fund; **f. à gestion indicielle, f. indiciel** index *or* tracker fund; **f. indiciel négociable en bourse** exchange-traded fund; **f. d'investissement** investment fund; **f. monétaire** money market fund; **F. monétaire européen** European Monetary Fund; **F. monétaire international** International Monetary Fund; **F. national de l'emploi** = French national employment fund; **F. national de garantie des salaires** = national guarantee fund for the payment of salaries; **F. national de solidarité** = support scheme for the old and needy; **f. obligatoire** bond fund; **f. off shore** offshore funds; *Can* **f. de parité** equalization fund; **f. de pension** pension fund; **f. perdus** annuity; **placer son argent à f. perdus** to purchase an annuity; **f. de placements spéculatifs** dynamic fund; **f. de placement sur le marché monétaire** money market fund; **f. de prévoyance** contingency fund; **f. de réserve** reserve fund; **f. de retraite maison** occupational pension scheme; **f. de roulement** working capital; **f. social** company funds; **F. social européen** European Social Fund; **f. de solidarité** fighting fund; **f. de stabilisation des changes** exchange equalization account; **f. structurel** structural fund

3 *(ressources)* collection; **notre bibliothèque a un f. très riche d'ouvrages du XVIIIème siècle** our library has a very rich collection of 18th-century books; **c'est un f. inestimable pour les chercheurs** it is an invaluable resource for researchers; **le f. commun de toutes les langues indo-européennes** the common stock of all Indo-European languages

NMPL **1** *Fin* funds; **réunir des f.** to raise funds; **des f. ont été détournés** funds were embezzled; **être en f.** to be in funds; **rentrer dans ses f.** to recoup one's costs; **je n'ai pas les f. suffisants pour ouvrir un magasin** I don't have the (necessary) funds *or* capital to open a shop; *Hum* **mes f. sont au plus bas** funds are low; **prêter de l'argent à f. perdus** to loan money without security; **collecte de f.** financial appeal, fund-raising *(UNCOUNT)*; **organiser un dîner pour une collecte de f.** to organize a fund-raising dinner; **la mise de f. initiale a été de 10 millions de livres** the venture capital was 10 million pounds; **f. communs** pool; **f. disponibles** liquid assets, available funds; **f. fédéraux** federal funds; **f. liquides** available funds; **f. propres** shareholders' *or* stockholders' equity; **les f. publics** public funds; **f. secrets** secret funds

2 *(argent)* money; **je n'ai pas les f. sur moi** I don't have the ready cash with *or* on me

3 *Bourse* stocks, securities; **f. consolidés** consolidated stock, *Br* consols; **f. d'État, f. publics** government stock(s)

fondu, -e [fɔ̃dy] PP *voir* **fondre**

ADJ **1** *(liquéfié)* melted; *Métal* molten; **de la neige**

fondue *(qui tombe)* sleet; *(par terre)* slush
2 *(ramolli)* melted
3 *Beaux-Arts (teinte)* blending
4 *Fam (fou)* round the bend, out to lunch
NM 1 *Cin* dissolve; **faire un f.** to fade; **faire un f. au noir** to fade to black; **s'ouvrir en f.** to fade in; **ouverture en f.** fade-in; **fermeture en f.** fade-out; **les personnages apparaissent/disparaissent en f.** the characters fade in/out; **f. enchaîné** (lap-)dissolve, fade-in fade-out; **faire un f. enchaîné** to (lap-)dissolve, to fade in-fade out; **f. en ouverture** fade-in; **f. en fermeture** fade-out; **f. sonore** *(au début)* fade-in; *(à la fin)* fade-out; **f. par ondulation** ripple dissolve; **f. par passage au flou** defocus dissolve **2** *Beaux-Arts* blend **3** *Fam (passionné)* fanatic, freak; **un f. d'informatique/de skateboard** he's a computer/skateboard freak
• **fondue** **NF** *Culin* fondue; **fondue bourguignonne** fondue bourguignonne, = fondue consisting of cubes of raw beef cooked in hot oil; **fondue de légumes** vegetable fondue; **fondue savoyarde** cheese fondue

fongible [fɔ̃ʒibl] **ADJ** fungible

fongicide [fɔ̃ʒisid] **ADJ** fungicidal
NM fungicide

fongueux, -euse [fɔ̃gø, -øz] **ADJ** fungous

font *voir* **faire**

fontaine [fɔ̃tɛn] **NF 1** *(édifice)* fountain **2** *(petit réservoir)* cistern; **f. filtrante** *ou* **de ménage** (household) filter **3** *(source)* spring; **la F. de Jouvence** the Fountain of Youth; *Prov* **il ne faut pas dire: f. je ne boirai pas de ton eau** never say never

fontainier [fɔ̃tenje] **NM** hydraulic engineer

fontanelle [fɔ̃tanɛl] **NF** fontanelle

fonte[1] [fɔ̃t] **NF 1** *Métal* cast iron; **(fer de) f., f. de fer** cast iron; **f. d'acier** cast steel; **poêle en f.** cast-iron stove
2 *(fusion ▸ gén)* melting; *(▸ des neiges, de glace)* thawing, melting; *(▸ d'objet en or ou argent)* melting down; *(▸ du métal, de minerai)* smelting; *(▸ de cloche, de statue)* casting, founding; **pièces de f.** castings; **à la f. des neiges/glaces** when the snow/ice thaws
3 *Typ & Ordinat* font; **f. bitmap** bitmap font; **f. de caractère** character font; **f. écran** screen font; **f. imprimante** printer font; **f. reconnue optiquement** OCR-font; **f. vectorielle** outline font
4 *Méd* **f. musculaire** wasting of muscle

fonte[2] [fɔ̃t] **NF** *(d'une selle)* holster

fonts [fɔ̃] **NMPL f. (baptismaux)** (baptismal) font; **tenir un enfant sur les f. baptismaux** to be godfather/godmother to a child

foot [fut] **NM** *Fam* soccer◻, *Br* football◻, footie; **jouer au f.** to play soccer *or Br* football

football [futbol] **NM** soccer, *Br* football; **jouer au f.** to play soccer *or Br* football; **f. américain** *Br* American football, *Am* football

footballeur, -euse [futbolœr, -øz] **NM,F** soccer *or Br* football player, *Br* footballer

footballistique [futbolistik] **ADJ** soccer *(avant n)*, *Br* football *(avant n)*

footeux [futø] **NM** *Fam (joueur)* soccer *or Br* football player◻, *Br* footballer◻; *(supporter)* soccer *or Br* football fan◻

footing [futiŋ] **NM le f.** jogging; **faire un f.** to go jogging, to go for a jog

for [fɔr] **NM en** *ou* **dans son f. intérieur** in one's heart of hearts; **en mon f. intérieur** deep down, in my heart of hearts

forage [fɔraʒ] **NM** *Tech* **1** *(creusement ▸ d'un puits de pétrole)* boring, drilling; *(▸ d'un puits, d'une mine)* sinking; **f. pétrolier** drilling oil wells; **effectuer un f.** *(de puits de pétrole)* to drill an oil well; *(de puits)* to sink a well **2** *(diamètre d'un cylindre, du canon d'un fusil)* bore

forain, -e [fɔrɛ̃, -ɛn] **ADJ 1** *(boutique)* fairground *(avant n)*; **marchand f.** stallholder; **spectacle f.** travelling show; **hercule f.** strongman *(at a fair)*; **baraque foraine** fairground stall **2** *Naut* **mouillage f.** open berth
NM,F stallholder

forban [fɔrbɑ̃] **NM 1** *(pirate)* freebooter **2** *Péj (escroc)* crook

forçage [fɔrsaʒ] **NM 1** *Archit & Hort* forcing **2** *Aut* **introduction d'air par f.** ram air induction

forçat [fɔrsa] **NM** *Hist (sur une galère)* galley slave; *(dans un bagne)* convict; **travailler comme un f.** to work like a slave; **mener une vie de f.** to have a hard life; **la maçonnerie est un métier de f.** building work is really backbreaking

FORCE [fɔrs]

> **NF**
> • strength **1, 2, 4, 7, 13** • force **1, 3, 8**
> **ADV**
> • many

NF 1 *(puissance ▸ d'une tempête, d'un coup)* strength, force; *(▸ d'un sentiment)* strength; *(▸ d'une idée, d'un argument)* strength, power; **avec f.** forcefully; **ce qui fait votre f., c'est...** your strength is...; **dans toute la f. du mot** *ou* **terme** in the strongest sense of the word *or* term; *Météo* **un vent (de) f. 7** a force 7 wind; **la f. de l'habitude** force of habit; **les forces de la nature** the forces of nature; **les forces du mal** the forces of evil; **f. vitale** life force
2 *(vigueur physique)* strength; **avoir beaucoup de f.** to be very strong; **être d'une f. herculéenne** to be as strong as an ox; **avoir la f. de** to have the strength to; **il sent sa f. l'abandonner avec l'âge** he feels himself growing weaker with age; **elle était sans f.** she had no strength, she was bereft of strength; **la maladie le laissa sans f.** the illness left him (feeling) weak, the illness sapped his strength; **sentir ses forces décliner** to feel one's strength ebbing (away); **elle n'avait plus la f. de répondre** she didn't have the strength (left) to answer, she had no strength left to answer; **je ne me sens pas/ne suis pas de f. à faire cela** I don't feel/I'm not up to *or* equal to doing it; **donner des forces à qn** to give sb strength; **reprendre des forces** to regain one's strength; **de f. égale, de même f.** equally matched, well matched; **c'est au-dessus de mes forces** it's beyond me; **de toutes mes/ses forces** with all my/his/her/her strength, with all my/his/her might; **j'ai poussé la porte de toutes mes forces** I pushed the door with all my might; **je le veux de toutes mes forces** I want it with all my heart; **j'essaie de toutes mes forces de le convaincre** I'm trying as hard as I can to convince him; **ne pas sentir** *ou* **connaître sa f.** not to know one's own strength; **être bâti en f.** to be stocky, to be strongly built; **f. motrice** *(personne)* prime mover; **être une f. de la nature** to be a mighty force; **être dans la f. de l'âge** to be in the prime of life; **les forces vives de la nation** the nation's resources
3 *(contrainte, autorité)* force; **vaincre par la f.** to win by (using) force; **avoir recours à la f.** to resort to force; **nous ne céderons pas à la f.** we will not yield to force; *Jur* **f. exécutoire** legal force; **avoir f. exécutoire** to be enforceable; **avoir f. de loi** to have the force of law; *Jur* **f. majeure** force majeure; **c'est un cas de f. majeure** it's completely unavoidable; *Pol & Écon* **un coup de f.** a takeover by force; **la f. prime le droit** might is right
4 *(puissance morale)* strength; **ce qui fait sa f., c'est sa conviction politique** his/her political commitment is his/her strength; **f. d'âme** spiritual strength; **f. de caractère** strength of character; **elle a une sacrée f. de caractère** she has incredible strength of character
5 *(niveau)* **c'est un orateur de première f.** he's a first-class speaker; **elles sont de la même f. en sciences** they're well matched in science; **je ne suis pas de f. à lui faire concurrence** I'm no match for him/her
6 *Admin & Mil* **F. d'action rapide** = section of the French armed forces responding immediately in emergencies; **la f. nucléaire stratégique** *ou* **la f. de frappe** *ou* **la f. de dissuasion de la France** France's nuclear strike capacity; **les forces armées** the (armed) forces; **Forces françaises en Allemagne** = French forces in Germany; *Hist* **Forces françaises de l'intérieur** = French Resistance forces during World War II; *Hist* **Forces françaises libres** = free French Army during World War II; **les forces navales/aériennes** the naval/air forces; **la f. publique, les forces de l'ordre** *ou* **de police** the police; **f. tactique** *ou* **d'intervention** task force
7 *(suprématie)* strength, might; **occuper une position de f.** to be in a position of strength; **f. est restée à la loi** the law prevailed
8 *Phys* force; **f. centrifuge/centripète** centrifugal/centripetal force; **f. électromotrice** electromotive force; **f. d'inertie** force of inertia; **f. motrice** motive power; *Fig* driving force; **f. de traction** traction *or* tractive force; **f. vive** kinetic energy, momentum; **forces de cisaillement** shear forces; *Aut* **forces en virage** cornering force
9 *Pol* **F. ouvrière** = trade union
10 *Typ* **f. de corps** body size
11 *Naut* **faire f. de rames** to ply the oars; **faire f. de voiles** to cram on sail
12 *Constr* **(jambe de) f.** force piece, strut; **f. de résistance à la tension** tensile strength
13 *(d'un produit, d'un concurrent)* strength; *Com* **f. de vente** sales force; *Écon* **les forces du marché** market forces; *Mktg* **forces, faiblesses, opportunités et menaces** strengths, weaknesses, opportunities and threats, SWOT
14 *(locutions)* **f. est de constater que...** there is no choice but to accept that...; **f. lui fut d'obéir** he/she was obliged to obey, he/she had no option but to obey; **par la f. des choses/de l'habitude** by force of circumstance/of habit
ADV *Littéraire ou Hum* many; **nous avons bu f. bière** we drank copious amounts of beer; **je le lui ai expliqué avec f. exemples** I explained it to him/her by giving numerous examples
• **à force** **ADV** *Fam* **tu vas le casser, à f.!** you'll break it if you go on like that!; **il va se lasser, à f.** he'll get tired of it eventually; **à f., je suis fatigué** I'm getting tired
• **à force de** **PRÉP** by dint of; **à f. de parler** by dint of talking; **à f. de travailler** by (dint of) hard work; **à f. de répéter** by constant repetition; **à f. de volonté** by sheer will power; **il s'est enroué à f. de crier** he shouted himself hoarse
• **à la force de** **PRÉP** by the strength of; **grimper à la f. des bras** to climb by the strength of one's arms; *Fig* **s'élever à la f. du poignet** to go up in the world by the sweat of one's brow
• **à toute force** **ADV** at all costs
• **de force** **ADV** by force; **il est entré de f.** he forced his way in; **entrer** *ou* **pénétrer de f. dans une maison** to force one's way into a house; **faire entrer qch de f. dans qch** to force sth into sth; **on les a fait sortir de f.** they were made to leave
• **en force** **ADV 1** *(en nombre)* in force, in large numbers; **ils sont arrivés en f.** they arrived in force *or* in great numbers **2** *(sans souplesse)* **faire qch en f.** to do sth by brute force
• **par force** **ADV par f. nous nous sommes résignés à son départ** we were forced to accept *or* we had to resign ourselves to his/her departure

forcé, -e [fɔrse] **ADJ 1** *(obligé)* forced; *(emprunt)* forced, compulsory; *(cours, vente)* forced; **consentement/mariage f.** forced consent/marriage; **atterrissage f.** emergency *or* forced landing; **contraint et f.** under duress
2 *(inévitable)* inevitable; **ça n'a pas marché, c'est f., il était mal préparé** it didn't work out, which isn't surprising because he wasn't properly prepared
3 *(involontaire)* **prendre un bain f.** to fall in (the water)
4 *(sans spontanéité)* strained; **un rire/un sourire f.** a forced laugh/smile; **comparaison forcée** artificial comparison

forcement [fɔrsəmɑ̃] **NM** forcing; **f. de blocus** blockade running

forcément [fɔrsemɑ̃] **ADV** inevitably, necessarily; **pas f.** not necessarily; **ça devait f. arriver** it was bound to happen; **elle sera f. déçue** she's bound to be disappointed; **f.! of course!**; **elle est très mince – f., elle ne mange rien!** she's very slim – that's hardly surprising, she never eats a thing!

forcené, -e [fɔrsəne] **ADJ 1** *(passionné)* fanatical, frenzied; **un goût f. du travail** a fanatical liking for work; **c'est un admirateur f. de Mozart** he's an ardent fan of Mozart **2** *(violent)* frenzied; **frapper des coups forcenés à la porte** to knock frenziedly at the door; **une haine forcenée** a fanatical hatred
NM,F 1 *(fou)* maniac **2** *(passionné)* **un f. du karaté** a karate fanatic *or* maniac; **crier comme un f.** to scream like a madman/madwoman

forceps [fɔrseps] **NM** forceps; **accouchement au f.** forceps delivery

forcer **[16]** [fɔrse] **VT** **1** *(obliger)* to compel, to force; **f. qn à faire qch** to force *or* to compel sb to do sth, to make sb do sth; **l'ennemi a forcé l'avion à atterrir** the enemy forced the plane down; **il l'a forcée à quitter la société** he forced her out of the firm; **sans vouloir te f. il faudrait faire la vaisselle** I don't want to force you, but the washing-up has to be done; **être forcé de faire qch** to be forced to do sth; **écoute, personne ne te** *ou* **ne t'y force!** listen, nobody's forcing you!; **f. la main à qn** to force sb's hand; **on lui a forcé la main** he/she was made to do it, his/her hand was forced

2 *(ouvrir de force ▸ tiroir, valise)* to force (open); *(▸serrure, mécanisme)* to force; **f. un coffre-fort** to force a safe open; **f. la caisse** to force open the till, to break into the till; **f. une porte** to force (open) *or* to break open a door; *Fig* **f. la porte de qn** to barge *or* to force one's way into sb's house; **f. le passage** to push (one's way) through

3 *(outrepasser)* **f. la dose** *Pharm* to prescribe too large a dose; *Fig* to go too far; **f. la note** to overdo it

4 *Arch (violer ▸ personne)* to violate

5 *(susciter)* **f. le respect/l'admiration (de qn)** to command (sb's) respect/admiration

6 *(influencer ▸ événements)* to influence; **f. le destin** to force the hand of destiny

7 *(presser)* **f. le pas** *ou* **l'allure** to force the pace; *Équitation* **f. son cheval** to overtax *or* to override one's horse

8 *Agr & Hort* to force

9 *(pousser trop loin)* **f. sa voix** to strain one's voice; **f. sa nature** to go against one's true nature; **f. le sens d'un texte** to distort the meaning of a text

10 *Ordinat (justification, coupure de page)* to force

VI *(en faire trop)* to strain oneself, to overdo it; *(pousser, tirer)* to force it; **ne force pas, tu vas casser le mécanisme** don't force it, you'll break the mechanism; **pliez la jambe sans f.** bend your leg very gently *or* without straining; **il y est arrivé sans f.** he managed without straining himself *or* without too much effort; **le vent force** the wind is rising

• **forcer sur** **VT IND** to overdo; **ne forcez pas sur les abdominaux** don't do too many stomach exercises; **je crains d'avoir forcé sur le poivre** I'm afraid I've overdone (it with) the pepper; *Fam Hum* **f. sur la bouteille** to be fond of the bottle; **f. sur les avirons** to strain at the oars; *Cartes* **f. sur l'annonce de qn** to overcall *or* to overbid sb

VPR se forcer *(gén)* to make an effort; *(en mangeant)* to force oneself; **se f. à lire/à travailler** to force oneself to read/to work

forcing [fɔrsiŋ] **NM** *Sport* pressure; **faire le f.** to put the pressure on; **avoir qn au f.** to pressurize sb, to put pressure on sb

forcir **[32]** [fɔrsir] **VI** **1** *(personne)* to get bigger **2** *(tempête, vent)* to pick up, to get stronger

forclore **[113]** [fɔrklɔr] **VT** *(à l'infinitif et au participe passé seulement) Jur* to debar

forclusion [fɔrklyzjɔ̃] **NF** *Jur* debarment

forer **[3]** [fɔre] **VT** *(roche, puits de pétrole)* to bore, to drill; *(puits, mine)* to sink

forestier, -ère [fɔrestje, -ɛr] **ADJ** *(chemin, code)* forest *(avant n)*; **chemin f.** forest road; **essences forestières** forest trees; **une exploitation forestière** a forestry development

NM,F forester

• **forestière** **NF** *Culin* **poulet/champignons à la forestière** chicken/mushrooms forestière

foret [fɔrɛ] **NM** **1** *(vrille)* drill **2** **f. à bois** gimlet; **f. de charpentier** auger **3** *(vilebrequin)* (brace) bit

forêt [fɔrɛ] **NF** **1** *(arbres)* forest; **f. vierge** virgin forest; **région couverte de forêts** forest(ed) region **2** *(multitude)* **une f. de** a forest of

Forêt-Noire [fɔrɛnwar] **NF** *Géog* **la F.** the Black Forest

forêt-noire [fɔrɛnwar] *(pl* **forêts-noires)** **NF** *(gâteau)* Black Forest gateau

foreur [fɔrœr] **ADJ M** *(ingénieur, ouvrier)* drilling *(avant n)*

NM *Tech* driller; *Pétr* **f. d'exploration** oil prospector, *Am Fam* wildcatter

foreuse [fɔrøz] **NF** drill; *Mines* rock drill; **f. à main** hand drill

forfaire **[109]** [fɔrfɛr] **forfaire à** **VT IND** *Littéraire* to be false to; **f. à son devoir** to fail in one's duty; **f. à l'honneur** to forfeit one's honour; **f. à sa parole** to break one's word

forfait[1] [fɔrfɛ] **NM** **1** *(abonnement ▸ de transport, à l'opéra)* season ticket; *(▸au ski)* pass, ski-pass; **le f. comprend les frais de location et d'entretien du matériel** the package *or* the price includes the cost of hire and maintenance of the equipment; **et pour un f. de 70 euros...** and for an all-in *or* all-inclusive price of 70 euros..., and for 70 euros all in...; **f. train + hôtel** package deal including train ticket and hotel reservation; **f. avion + location de voiture** fly drive; **f. week-end** weekend package; **f.(-voyage)** package (deal) **2** *Com* flat rate *or* fee, fixed rate; **payer qn au f.** to pay sb a flat *or* fixed rate; **travailler au f.** to work for a flat rate *or* fee; **vente à f.** outright sale; **f. de port** carriage forward **3** *Fin* **être au f.** to be taxed on estimated income

forfait[2] [fɔrfɛ] **NM** *Littéraire (crime)* infamy, (heinous) crime

forfait[3] [fɔrfɛ] **NM** *Sport (somme)* forfeit, fine; *(renoncement à participer)* withdrawal; **gagner par f.** to win by default; **déclarer f. pour un cheval** to scratch a horse; **déclarer f.** *(athlète, concurrent)* to scratch; *Fig* to throw in the towel; **l'équipe a déclaré f.** the team withdrew

forfaitage [fɔrfɛtaʒ] **NM** forfaiting

forfaitaire [fɔrfɛtɛr] **ADJ** inclusive; **marché f.** fixed-price contract; **paiement f.** lump sum; **somme** *ou* **montant f.** lump sum; **indemnités forfaitaires** basic allowance; **prix f.** all-inclusive *or* all-in price; **voyage à prix f.** package tour

forfaitairement [fɔrfɛtɛrmɑ̃] **ADV** *Fin* in a lump sum; *(facturer)* in a lump sum, in one amount

forfaiture [fɔrfɛtyr] **NF** **1** *Jur* abuse of authority; **f. au devoir** failure in duty; **f. à l'honneur** breach of honour **2** *Hist* forfeiture

forfait-vacances [fɔrfɛvakɑ̃s] *(pl* **forfaits-vacances)** **NM** package holiday

forfanterie [fɔrfɑ̃tri] **NF** *Littéraire* boastfulness

forge [fɔrʒ] **NF** **1** *(atelier)* forge, smithy; **f. (de maréchal-ferrant)** smithy; **mener un cheval à la f.** to take a horse to the blacksmith's; **f. de serrurier** locksmith's workshop; **pièce de f.** forging **2** *(fourneau)* forge

forgeable [fɔrʒabl] **ADJ** *Tech* forgeable

forgeage [fɔrʒaʒ] **NM** *Tech* forging

forger **[17]** [fɔrʒe] **VT** **1** *Tech* to forge; **f. à chaud** to hot-forge; *Fig Littéraire* **f. les chaînes de qn** to forge bonds for sb; *Prov* **c'est en forgeant qu'on devient forgeron** practice makes perfect

2 *(inventer ▸ alibi)* to make up; *(▸phrase, mot)* to coin; *(▸ accusation)* to trump up; *(▸ vision)* to conjure up; **une histoire forgée de toutes pièces** a fabricated *or* a cock-and-bull story

3 *(fabriquer ▸ document, preuve)* to forge

4 *(aguerrir ▸ personnalité)* to form, to forge; *(▸ caractère)* to build, to form; **f. un homme** to build *or* to form a man's character

VPR se forger **se f. une réputation** to earn oneself a reputation; **se f. un idéal de vie** to create an ideal lifestyle for oneself; **se f. le caractère** to build up one's character

> Il faut noter que le verbe anglais **to forge** signifie également **contrefaire**.

forgeron [fɔrʒərɔ̃] **NM** blacksmith

forgeur[1], **-euse** [fɔrʒœr, -øz] **NM,F** *Littéraire (de mots, de phrases)* coiner; *(de documents)* forger

forgeur[2] [fɔrʒœr] **NM** *Littéraire (forgeron)* metal worker

forgeuse [fɔrʒøz] *voir* **forgeur**[1]

formage [fɔrmaʒ] **NM** **1** *Métal* forming **2** *(de plastique)* moulding

formaldéhyde [fɔrmaldeid] **NM** formaldehyde

formalisation [fɔrmalizasjɔ̃] **NF** formalization

formaliser **[3]** [fɔrmalize] **VT** *(idée, théorie)* to formalize; **logique formalisée** formal logic

VPR se formaliser **se f. de** to take offence at

formalisme [fɔrmalism] **NM** **1** *(attitude)* respect for etiquette; **faire preuve de f.** to be a stickler for etiquette *or* form **2** *Beaux-Arts, Phil & Littérature* formalism

formaliste [fɔrmalist] **ADJ** **1** *(guindé)* strict about etiquette **2** *Beaux-Arts, Littérature & Phil* formalistic

NMF **1** *(personne guindée)* stickler for etiquette *or* form **2** *Beaux-Arts, Littérature & Phil* formalist

formalité [fɔrmalite] **NF** **1** *Admin* formality; **formalités administratives/douanières** administrative/customs formalities **2** *(acte sans importance)* formality; **cet examen n'est qu'une f.** this medical test is a mere formality; **notre enquête n'est qu'une simple** *ou* **pure f.** we're just making routine enquiries; **les formalités d'usage** the usual formalities **3** *(cérémonial)* formality; **sans autre f., sans plus de formalités** without further ado

format [fɔrma] **NM** **1** *(dimension)* size; *Phot* size, format; **photo petit f.** small (format) print; *Phot* **f. normal** enprint; **f. de poche** pocket size

2 *Typ* format; **livre en f. de poche** paperback (book); **f. d'impression** print format; **f. de papier** paper format; **f. tabloïd** tabloid; **papier f. A4/A3** A4/A3 paper

3 *Ordinat* format; **f. ASCII** ASCII format; **f. d'écran** screen format; **f. de fichier** file format; **f. graphique** image format; **f. d'impression** print format; **f. de page** page format *or* setup; **f. de paragraphe** paragraph format; **f. TIFF** TIFF

4 *TV & Cin* **f. de l'image** aspect ratio; **f. de présentation** show format

formatage [fɔrmataʒ] **NM** *Ordinat* formatting; **f. de bas niveau** low-level formatting; **f. de haut niveau** high-level formatting; **f. logiciel** soft sectoring

formater **[3]** [fɔrmate] **VT** *Ordinat* to format

formateur, -trice [fɔrmatœr, -tris] **ADJ** *(rôle, influence, expérience)* formative; **ce stage en entreprise a été très f.** this placement was very instructive

NM,F trainer

formation [fɔrmasjɔ̃] **NF** **1** *(naissance)* development, formation, forming; **la f. du goût/de la personnalité** the development of taste/of the personality; **volcan en voie** *ou* **en cours de f.** volcano in the process of formation

2 *(groupe)* group; **f. musicale** *(classique)* orchestra; *(moderne)* band; **f. paramilitaire** paramilitary group; **f. politique** political group; **f. syndicale** (trade) union

3 *(apprentissage)* training *(UNCOUNT)*; *(connaissances)* cultural background; **il faut que nous leur donnions une f.** we must train them; **suivre une f.** to do *or* to take a training course; **elle a une bonne f. littéraire/scientifique** she has a good literary/scientific background; **il n'a aucune f. musicale** he has no musical training; **il est technicien de f.** he trained as a technician; **être en f.** to be undergoing training; **f. en alternance** *ou* **alternée** = training given partly in an educational institution and partly in the workplace; **f. continue** *ou* **permanente** continuing education; **f. des maîtres** *ou* **pédagogique** *Br* teacher training, *Am* teacher education; **f. courte** *ou* **accélérée** intensive training; **f. dans l'entreprise** *ou* **interne** in-house training; **f. professionnelle** vocational training; **f. professionnelle pour adultes** adult education; **f. sur le tas** *ou* **par la pratique** on-the-job training

4 *Mil (détachement)* unit; *(disposition)* formation; **f. serrée** close formation

5 *Sport & (en danse)* formation

6 *Physiol* puberty

7 *Géol* formation

8 *Ling* **la f. du vocabulaire** vocabulary formation; **la f. du féminin/pluriel** the formation of the feminine/plural; **mot de f. savante** word of learned origin

formatrice [fɔrmatris] *voir* **formateur**

forme [fɔrm] **NF** **1** *(configuration)* shape, form; **donner une f. courbe à un vase** to give a curved shape to a vase; **un dessin de f. géométrique** a geometrical pattern; **la Terre a la f. d'une sphère** the Earth is spherical; **sans f.** shapeless; **ne plus avoir f. humaine** to be unrecognizable; **mettre en f.** *(texte)* to format; **mettez vos idées en f.** give your ideas some shape; **mettre un écrit en f.** to structure a piece of writing; **prendre la f. de** to take (on) the form of, to assume the shape of; **prendre f.** to take shape, to shape up

2 *(état)* form; **se présenter sous f. gazeuse** to

come in gaseous form *or* in the form of a gas; **c'est le même sentiment sous plusieurs formes** it's the same feeling expressed in several different ways; **nous voulons combattre la misère sous toutes ses formes** we want to fight poverty in all its forms; **présenter les choses sous une autre f.** to present things in a different *or* in another way
3 *(silhouette)* figure, shape; **une vague f. apparut dans le brouillard** a hazy figure appeared in the fog
4 *(type)* form; **la f. de gouvernement qui convient au pays** the form *or* type of government (best) suited to the country; **la f. monarchique/républicaine** the monarchical/republican form of government; **des formes de vie différentes sur d'autres planètes** different forms of life on other planets
5 *(style)* form; **sacrifier à la f.** to put form above content; **une f. plus concise serait préférable** a more concise form would be preferable
6 *Mus* form; **f. sonate** sonata form
7 *Ling* form; **mettre un verbe à la f. interrogative/négative** to put a verb into the interrogative/in the negative (form); **la f. progressive** the progressive; **les formes du futur** future tense forms
8 *Jur* form; **respecter la f. légale** to respect legal procedures; **arrêt cassé pour vice de f.** judgment quashed on a technical point
9 *(condition physique)* form; **f. physique** physical fitness; **être en bonne f. physique** to be fit; *Fam* **avoir** *ou* **tenir la f.** to be in great shape; **je n'ai** *ou* **ne tiens pas la f.** I'm in poor shape; **il tient la grande f. en ce moment** he's in great form at the moment; **être en f.** to be on form; **être au mieux** *ou* **sommet de sa f., être en pleine f.** to be on top form; **c'est bon pour la f.** it's good for you, it'll do you good; *Fam* **alors, c'est la f.?** how are you doing?
10 *(moule ▸ gén)* former, forming block; *(▸ pour chapeau)* block; *(▸ pour chaussure)* last; *(▸ pour élargir)* shoe tree; *(▸ pour fromage)* mould
11 *Typ* forme
12 *Naut* dock
13 *Com* **f. sociale** type of company
• **formes** NFPL **1** *(physique ▸ d'un bateau)* lines; *(▸ d'une personne)* figure; *(▸ d'une femme)* curves; **avoir des formes** to have a shapely figure; **avoir des formes généreuses** to be curvaceous; **vêtement qui épouse les formes** close-fitting *or* figure-hugging garment; **les formes d'un tableau/paysage** the lines of a picture/shapes of a landscape **2** *(convention)* **les formes** the conventions *or* proprieties; **y mettre les formes** to be tactful; **elle a toujours respecté les formes** she has always respected convention
• **dans les formes** ADV according to form; **faire qch dans les formes** to do sth in the accepted way; **avertir qn dans les formes** to give sb formal *or* due warning
• **de pure forme** ADJ purely formal; **vérification de pure f.** routine check
• **en bonne (et due) forme** ADJ *(contrat)* bona fide ADV *(établir un document)* in due form, according to the proper form; **faire une réclamation en bonne et due f.** to use the correct procedure in making a complaint
• **en forme de** PRÉP *(ressemblant à)* **en f. de poisson** shaped like a fish, fish-shaped; **en f. d'œuf** egg-shaped; **en f. de croix** in the shape of a cross; **yeux en f. de billes** eyes like marbles
• **pour la forme** ADV for the sake of form, as a matter of form
• **sans autre forme de procès** ADV without further ado
• **sans forme** ADJ shapeless
• **sous forme de, sous la forme de** PRÉP in the form of, as; **un médicament qui existe sous f. de comprimés** a drug available in tablet form; **sous la f. d'une nymphe** in the form *or* shape of a nymph; **statistiques sous f. de tableau** statistics in tabular form; **sous toutes ses formes** in all its forms *or* guises

formé, -e [fɔrme] ADJ **1** *Physiol* fully formed, fully developed **2 un personnel bien f.** well-trained staff
• **formée** ADJ F *(jeune fille)* pubescent

formel, -elle [fɔrmɛl] ADJ **1** *(net ▸ ordre, refus)* definite; *(▸ démenti)* flat, categorical; *(▸ interdiction)* strict; *(▸ identification, preuve)* positive; **je suis f., il ne viendra pas** I'm positive he won't come; **le médecin a été f., pas de laitages!** no dairy products, the doctor was quite clear about that!; **il a été tout à fait f. sur ce point** he was quite adamant *or* definite on this point
2 *(de la forme)* formal; **la beauté formelle d'une nouvelle** the formal beauty of a short story
3 *(superficiel)* **leur protestation était purement formelle** their protest was purely for the sake of form
4 *Phil* formal

formellement [fɔrmɛlmɑ̃] ADV **1** *(nettement)* categorically; **s'engager f. à régler ses dettes** to vow to pay off one's debts; **accuser f. qn** to specifically accuse sb; **il m'a f. interdit de fumer** he strictly forbade me to smoke; **l'homme a été f. reconnu** the man was positively identified **2** *(stylistiquement)* formally; **une argumentation f. inattaquable** an argument that cannot be attacked on formal grounds **3** *Phil* formally

> Il faut noter que l'adverbe anglais **formally** signifie le plus souvent **officiellement** ou **de façon cérémonieuse**, selon le contexte.

former [3] [fɔrme] VT **1** *(donner un contour à ▸ lettre)* to shape, to form; *(▸ phrase)* to put together, to shape; *Bible* **Dieu forma l'homme à son image** God made man in his own image
2 *(créer ▸ gouvernement, association)* to form; **f. une unité de combat** to form a combat unit; **f. un train** to make up a train
3 *(se constituer en)* to form; **ils ont formé un cortège/attroupement** they formed a procession/a mob
4 *(dessiner)* to form; **le nuage forme un cœur** the cloud is shaped like a heart *or* is heart-shaped; **les collines alentour forment une vaste cuvette** the surrounding hills form a vast basin
5 *(constituer)* to form; **nous ne formions qu'un seul être** we were as one; **ils forment un couple uni** they're a united couple; **ils forment un couple étrange** they make a strange couple
6 *(faire apparaître)* to make, to form; **le froid forme du givre sur les vitres** the cold makes frost form on the windowpanes
7 *(créer, faire par la pensée)* **f. un projet** to think up a plan; **nous avons formé le dessein de nous marier** we are planning to marry; **f. des vœux pour le succès de qn/qch** to wish sb/sth success
8 *Ling* to form; **formez le pluriel de "marteau-piqueur"** form *or* give the plural of "marteau-piqueur"; **formez le conditionnel sur le futur** form the conditional tense using the future tense as a model
9 *Ind & Scol* to train; **f. les jeunes en entreprise** to give young people industrial training; **cette université a formé des hommes remarquables** this university has turned out *or* produced some remarkable men; **f. qn à qch** to train sb in sth; **f. son personnel à l'informatique** to train one's staff to use computers; **formé à la gestion** trained in management (techniques)
10 *(développer ▸ caractère, goût)* to develop; **un exercice qui forme l'oreille** an exercise which trains *or* develops the ear; **f. l'esprit de qn** to develop sb's mind; **cela forme le caractère** it's character-forming *or* character-building
11 *Tech* **f. par roulage** to roll
VPR **se former 1** *(apparaître ▸ croûte, pellicule, peau)* to form; *(▸ couche, dépôt)* to form, to build up; **ces montagnes se sont formées à l'ère tertiaire** these mountains were formed during the Tertiary period
2 *(se perfectionner)* to train oneself; *(s'instruire)* to educate oneself; **elle s'est surtout formée au contact du public** she has learnt most of what she knows through dealing with the public; **se f. sur le tas** to learn on the job *or* as one goes along; **se f. aux affaires** to acquire a business training
3 une jeune fille qui se forme a girl who is developing
4 se f. en *(se placer en)* to form, to make; **se f. en cortège** to form a procession; **se f. en carré** to form a square
5 *(se constituer)* **se f. une opinion** to form an opinion

Formica® [fɔrmika] NM Formica®; **en F.** Formica®

formidable [fɔrmidabl] ADJ **1** *(imposant)* tremendous, *Littéraire* formidable; **elle a une volonté f., elle réussira!** she has tremendous willpower, she'll succeed!
2 *Fam (invraisemblable)* incredible, unbelievable[□]; **tu n'en as jamais entendu parler, c'est f., ça!** it's incredible, you've never heard of it!
3 *Fam (admirable)* great, wonderful; **c'est un type f.** he's a great guy
4 *Littéraire (effrayant)* fearsome, formidable

> Il faut noter que l'adjectif anglais **formidable** est un faux ami. Il signifie le plus souvent **redoutable**.

formidablement [fɔrmidabləmɑ̃] ADV **1** *Fam (admirablement)* tremendously; **nous avons été f. accueillis** we were given a tremendous *or* fantastic welcome **2** *Littéraire (de manière effrayante)* formidably, fearsomely

formique [fɔrmik] ADJ *Chim* formic

formol [fɔrmɔl] NM *Chim* formalin

formulable [fɔrmylabl] ADJ **la proposition n'est pas encore f.** the proposal can't yet be formulated; **une théorie f. en termes clairs** a theory that can be clearly formulated; **une opinion difficilement f.** an opinion that is difficult to formulate

formulaire [fɔrmylɛr] NM **1** *(document)* form; **f. E111** form E111; **f. d'appréciation** customer satisfaction questionnaire; **f. d'assurance** insurance form; **f. de candidature** (job) application form; **f. de détaxe** tax-free shopping form; **f. de recensement** census return; *Ordinat* **f. de saisie** input form **2** *(recueil)* formulary; *(de pharmaciens)* formulary, pharmacopoeia

formulation [fɔrmylasjɔ̃] NF formulation, wording; **la f. de votre problème est incorrecte** you formulated your problem incorrectly, the way you formulated your problem is incorrect

formule [fɔrmyl] NF **1** *(tournure)* expression, (turn of) phrase; **trouver la f. qui convient** to find the right expression; **f. consacrée** accepted expression; **selon la f. consacrée** as the expression goes; **la f. magique** the magic words; *Suisse Pol* = name given to the coalition that forms the executive body of the Swiss government; **f. de politesse** *(dans une lettre)* standard letter ending
2 *(imprimé)* form; **f. de chèque** *Br* cheque form, *Am* blank check; **f. de demande de crédit** credit application form; **f. de réponse** reply form; *Com* **f. de soumission** tender form; **f. de télégramme** telegram form
3 *Chim & Math* formula; **f. empirique** empirical formula
4 *Pharm* formula, composition
5 *(solution)* formula, trick; **ils ont (trouvé) la f. pour ne pas avoir d'ennuis** they've found a way of avoiding problems
6 *(méthode)* way; **une f. économique pour vos vacances** an economical way to spend your holidays; **nous vous proposons plusieurs formules de crédit** we offer you several credit options; **formules de paiement** methods of payment, payment options; **formules de remboursement** repayment options; **nouvelle f.** *(menu, abonnement)* new-style; **une nouvelle f. de spectacle** a new kind of show; **notre restaurant vous propose sa f. à 20 euros ou sa carte** our restaurant offers you a set menu at 20 euros or an à la carte menu
7 *Aut* formula; **f. 1/2/3** formula 1/2/3; **courir en f. 3** to compete in formula 3 races
8 *Méd* **f. dentaire** dental formula

formule-hôtel *(pl* **formules-hôtel)** NF hotel package

formuler [3] [fɔrmyle] VT **1** *(exprimer ▸ doctrine, revendication)* to formulate, to express; *(▸ souhait)* to express; *(▸ proposition)* to formulate, to put into words; *(▸ plainte)* to lodge; **elle m'a regardé sans oser f. sa question** she looked at me without daring to ask her question **2** *(rédiger ▸ théorème)* to formulate; *(▸ décret, acte)* to draw up

fornication [fɔrnikasjɔ̃] NF *Littéraire ou Hum* fornication

forniquer [3] [fɔrnike] VI *Littéraire ou Hum* to fornicate

FORPRONU [fɔrprɔny] NF *(abrév* **Forces de protection des Nations unies)** UNPROFOR

fors [fɔr] PRÉP *Arch* except, save; **tout est perdu, f. l'honneur** all is lost save honour

forsythia [fɔrsisja] NM forsythia

FORT, -E [fɔr, fɔrt]

ADJ
- strong **A1, 4, 6, B3, 4**
- hard **A1, 6**
- powerful **A4, 5**
- big **B1**
- thick **B1**
- broad **B1**
- pronounced **B2**
- loud **B2**
- intense **B3**

ADV
- hard **1**
- loud **3**
- loudly **3**
- very **4**

NM
- forte **2**
- fort **3**

ADJ **A.** *QUI A DE LA PUISSANCE, DE L'EFFET* **1** *(vigoureux ▸ personne, bras)* strong, sturdy; *(▸ vent)* strong, high; *(▸ courant, jet)* strong; *(▸ secousse)* hard; *(▸ pluies)* heavy; *Météo* **mer forte** rough sea; **f. comme un Turc** *ou* **un bœuf** as strong as an ox

2 *(d'une grande résistance morale)* **une âme forte** a steadfast soul; **rester f. dans l'adversité** to remain strong *or* to stand firm in the face of adversity

3 *(autoritaire, contraignant ▸ régime)* strong-arm *(avant n)*

4 *(puissant ▸ syndicat, parti, économie)* strong, powerful; *(▸ monnaie)* strong, hard; *(▸ carton, loupe, tranquillisant)* strong; **l'as est plus f. que le roi** the ace is higher than the king; **colle (très) forte** (super *or* extra) strong glue; **tes lunettes sont trop fortes pour moi** your glasses are too strong for me; **c'est plus f. que moi** I can't help it; **f. de son expérience** with a wealth of experience behind him; **f. de leur protection** reassured by their protection; **une équipe forte de 40 hommes** a 40-strong team; **l'homme f. du parti** the strong man of the party

5 *(de grand impact ▸ œuvre, film)* powerful; *(▸ argument)* weighty, powerful; **le moment le plus f. de la pièce** the most powerful moment in the play

6 *Ling (formation, verbe)* strong; *(consonne)* hard

B. *MARQUÉ* **1** *(épais, corpulent ▸ jambes)* big, thick; *(▸ personne)* stout, large; *(▸ hanches)* broad, large, wide; **avoir la taille forte** to be big around the waist; **ils ont de jolis modèles pour les femmes fortes** they've got some nice outsize designs

2 *(important quantitativement ▸ dénivellation)* steep, pronounced; *(▸ accent)* strong, pronounced, marked; *(▸ fièvre, taux)* high; *(▸ hausse)* large; *(▸ somme)* large, big; *(▸ concentration)* high; *(▸ bruit)* loud; *(▸ différence)* great, big; **il est prêt à payer le prix f.** he's willing to pay the full price; **au prix f., le lave-linge vous coûterait 800 euros** if you had to pay the full price, the washing machine would cost you 800 euros; **baisse le son, c'est trop f.** turn the sound down, it's too loud

3 *(grand, intense ▸ amour, haine)* strong, intense; *(▸ douleur)* intense, great; *(▸ influence)* strong, big, great; *(▸ propension)* marked; **il recherche les sensations fortes** he's after big thrills; **avoir une forte volonté** to be strong-willed, to have a strong will; **elle a une forte personnalité** she's got a strong personality

4 *(café, thé, moutarde, tabac)* strong; *(sauce)* hot, spicy; *(odeur)* strong

5 *Fam (locutions)* **c'est un peu f. (de café)** that's a bit rich; **et c'est moi qui devrais payer? alors ça c'est trop f.!** and I should pay? that's a bit much!; **le plus f., c'est qu'il avait raison!** the best of it is that he was right!; **trop f.!** cool!, *Br* wicked!, *Am* awesome!

C. *HABILE* **son frère est magicien/acrobate, il est très f.** his/her brother's a magician/an acrobat, and a very good one; **le marketing, c'est là qu'il est f./que sa société est forte** marketing is his/his company's strong point; **trouver plus f. que soi** to meet one's match; **pour faire des gaffes, tu es forte!** when it comes to putting your foot in it, you take some beating!; **f. en** very good at; **f. en gymnastique/en langues** very good at gymnastics/at languages; **il est très f. à la volée** he volleys very well; **encore plus f., il va vous dire le numéro de votre passeport!** better still, he's going to tell you what your passport number is!

ADV **1** *(avec vigueur ▸ taper, tirer)* hard; **pousse plus f.** push harder

2 *Fam (avec intensité)* **il pleut f.** it's pelting down; **sentir f.** to smell; **mets le gaz plus/moins f.** turn the gas up/down; **le gaz est trop f.** the gas is too high; **tu y vas un peu f.!** you're going a bit far!

3 *(bruyamment ▸ parler)* loudly, loud; **parle plus f., on ne t'entend pas** speak up, we can't hear you; **parle moins f.** lower your voice; **ne chante pas si f.** don't sing so loud; **mets le son plus/moins f.** turn the sound up/down

4 *(très)* very; **f. joli** very pretty; **c'est f. bien dit!** well said!; **f. bien, partons à midi!** very well, let's leave at noon!; *Hum* **j'en suis f. aise!** I'm very pleased to hear it!

5 *(locution)* **faire f.** to do really well[□], to excel oneself[□]; **là, tu as fait très f.!** you've really excelled yourself!

NM **1** *(physiquement, moralement)* **les forts et les faibles** the strong and the weak; **un f. en thème** *(intellectuellement)* *Br* a swot, *Am* a grind

2 *(spécialité)* forte; **la cuisine, ce n'est pas ton f.!** cooking isn't your forte!; **la politesse n'est pas son f.!** politeness isn't his/her strongest point!

3 *(forteresse)* fort

• **au (plus) fort de** PRÉP **au (plus) f. de l'hiver** in the depths of winter; **au (plus) f. de l'été** in the height of summer

fortement [fɔrtəmɑ̃] ADV **1** *(avec force)* hard; **appuyer f. sur les deux bords pour les coller** press both ends tight to glue them together; **f. salé** heavily salted; **f. épicé** highly spiced; **f. charpenté** solidly built **2** *(avec netteté)* strongly; **des traits f. marqués** strongly marked features **3** *(beaucoup ▸ souhaiter, influencer)* strongly; **il désire f. vous rencontrer** he very much wishes to meet you; **être f. tenté** to be sorely tempted; **être f. intéressé par qch** to be most interested in sth; **être f. impressionné (par qn/qch)** to be most impressed (by sb/sth); **insister f. sur qch** to insist firmly *or* strongly on sth; **f. critiqué** strongly *or* highly criticized; **f. irrité** greatly *or* extremely irritated; **c'est f. conseillé** it's strongly advised

forteresse [fɔrtərɛs] NF **1** *(citadelle)* fortress

2 *(prison)* fortress

3 *Aviat* **f. volante** flying fortress

4 *Fig* wall, barrier; **f. de préjugés** wall of prejudice

fortiche [fɔrtiʃ] ADJ *Fam* clever[□], smart[□]; **elle est f. en anglais!** she's *Br* dead *or Am* real good at English!

fortifiant, -e [fɔrtifjɑ̃, -ɑ̃t] ADJ **1** *(nourriture)* fortifying; *(climat)* bracing, invigorating **2** *Littéraire (édifiant)* uplifting

NM tonic

fortification [fɔrtifikasjɔ̃] NF **1** *(mur)* fortification, wall **2** *(action)* fortification

fortifier **[9]** [fɔrtifje] VT **1** *(affermir ▸ muscle, santé)* to fortify, to strengthen; *(▸ volonté, opinion, impression)* to strengthen; *(▸ mur)* to fortify, to strengthen; **il m'a fortifié dans ma décision** he strengthened me in my decision **2** *(protéger)* to fortify; **une ville fortifiée** a walled *or* fortified town

VPR **se fortifier 1** *(emploi passif)* **la ville s'est fortifiée au XIIème siècle** the town was fortified *or* walls were built around the town in the 12th century

2 *Mil* to raise a line of defences; *(en creusant des tranchées)* to dig oneself in

3 *(devenir plus fort)* to get *or* to become stronger; *(▸ muscle)* to firm up, to grow stronger; *(▸ amitié, amour)* to grow stronger

4 se f. le dos/les chevilles to strengthen one's back/ankles

fortin [fɔrtɛ̃] NM small fort

fortiori [fɔrsjɔri] *voir* **a fortiori**

Fortran [fɔrtrɑ̃] NM *Ordinat* FORTRAN, Fortran

fortuit, -e [fɔrtɥi, -it] ADJ *(événement)* fortuitous; **faire une rencontre fortuite** to meet somebody by chance, to have a chance encounter *or* meeting; **dans cette affaire, rien n'est f.** nothing is fortuitous *or* nothing can be put down to chance in this matter; *Jur* **cas f.** act of God

fortuitement [fɔrtɥitmɑ̃] ADV by chance, fortuitously

fortune [fɔrtyn] NF **1** *(biens)* wealth, fortune; **une f. personnelle** private wealth, a private fortune; **sa f. est importante** he/she has a considerable fortune, he/she has considerable wealth; **toute sa f. est en biens immobiliers** his/her entire fortune is in property *or* real estate; *Fam* **ça lui a rapporté une (petite) f.** it brought him/her a nice little sum; **c'était une f. à l'époque** it was a lot of money at the time; *Hum* **voici 20 euros, c'est toute ma f.!** here's 20 euros, it's all my worldly wealth!; **son père est une grosse f.** his father is a very wealthy man; **avoir de la f.** to be wealthy; **faire f.** to make one's fortune; **valoir une f.** to be worth a fortune

2 *Littéraire (hasard)* good fortune, luck; **il a eu la bonne** *ou* **l'heureuse f. de la connaître** he was fortunate enough to know her; **il a eu la mauvaise f. de tomber malade** he was unlucky enough *or* he had the misfortune to fall ill; **être en bonne f.** to be successful *(with women)*; **faire contre mauvaise f. bon cœur** to make the best of a bad job; *Prov* **la f. sourit aux audacieux** fortune favours the bold; **la f. vient en dormant** good luck comes when you least expect it; **dîner à la f. du pot** to take pot luck

3 *Littéraire (sort)* fortune; **leurs livres ont connu des fortunes très diverses** their books had varying success

4 *Naut* **f. de mer** *(biens)* property at sea; *(risques)* perils of the sea; **voile de f.** crossjack; **mât de f.** jury mast

• **de fortune** ADJ *(lit, moyens)* makeshift; *(installation, réparation)* temporary

• **sans fortune** ADJ with no hope of an inheritance

fortuné, -e [fɔrtyne] ADJ **1** *(riche)* rich, wealthy **2** *Littéraire (heureux)* fortunate, blessed

> Il faut noter que l'adjectif anglais **fortunate** signifie uniquement **qui a de la chance**.

forum [fɔrɔm] NM *Antiq & Archit* forum; *(débat)* forum; *Ordinat* **f. de discussion** forum; **F. économique mondial** World Economic Forum; **f. sur l'éducation** forum *or* symposium on education; **le F. des Halles** = shopping complex at Les Halles in Paris; *Rad* **f. populaire** vox pop; **F. social mondial** World Social Forum

fosse [fos] NF **1** *(cavité)* pit; **f. à fumier/à purin** manure/slurry pit; **f. (d'aisances)** cesspool; **f. aux lions** lions' den; *Fig* **descendre dans la f. aux lions** to enter the lions' den; **f. aux ours** bear pit; **f. septique** septic tank

2 *Aut & Sport* pit; *Aut* **f. (de réparation)** inspection pit

3 *Mus* **f. d'orchestre** orchestra pit

4 *(tombe)* grave; **f. commune** common grave; **creuser sa f. avec ses dents** to eat oneself into an early grave; **avoir un pied dans la f.** to have one foot in the grave

5 *Anat* fossa

6 *Géol* trough; *(abyssale)* trench; **f. sous-marine** deep-sea *or* ocean trench; **les animaux des grandes fosses** animals living on the ocean bed

7 *Mines* pit

8 *Golf* **f. de sable** sand trap, bunker

> Do not confuse with **fossé**.

fossé [fose] NM **1** *(tranchée)* ditch; *(douve)* moat; **finir** *ou* **se retrouver dans le f.** to end up in a ditch; *Mil* **f. antichar** antitank ditch; *Aut* **f. d'inspection** inspection pit **2** *Fig* gulf, gap; **f. culturel** culture gap; **le f. qui nous sépare** the gulf between us; **le f. ne cesse de se creuser entre eux** there is an ever-widening gulf between them; **le f. des générations** the generation gap **3** *Géol* trough

> Do not confuse with **fosse**.

fossette [foset] NF dimple

fossile [fosil] ADJ fossil *(avant n)*; *Fig* fossil-like, fossilized

NM *aussi Fig* fossil; *Fam* **un vieux f.** an old fossil

fossilifère [fosilifɛr] ADJ fossiliferous

fossilisation [fosilizasjɔ̃] NF fossilization

fossiliser **[3]** [fosilize] VT to fossilize

VPR **se fossiliser** to become fossilized

fossoyeur [foswajœr] NM gravedigger; *Fig Littéraire* **les fossoyeurs de la révolution** the destroyers *or* gravediggers of the revolution

fou, folle [fu, fɔl]

> **Fol** is used before masculine singular nouns beginning with a vowel or h mute.

ADJ **1** *(dément)* insane, mad; **devenir f.** to go mad *or* insane; **il y a de quoi devenir f.!** it's enough to drive you mad!; **un regard un peu f.** a somewhat crazed look; **être f. de joie/douleur** to be beside oneself with joy/grief; **être f. d'inquiétude** to be mad with worry; **être f. d'amour pour qn, être f. amoureux de qn** to be madly in love with sb; **être f. furieux** *ou* **à lier** to be (stark) raving mad

2 *(déraisonnable)* mad; **tu serais f. de ne pas accepter** you'd be mad *or* crazy not to accept; **je ne suis pas assez f. pour y aller tout seul** I'm not mad *or* crazy enough to go by myself; **ton projet est complètement f.** your plan is completely crazy *or* mad; **un fol espoir** a foolish *or* mad hope; **avoir de folles pensées** to have wild thoughts; **il n'est pas f.** he's no fool; *Fam* **pas folle, la guêpe!** he's/she's not stupid!

3 *(hors de soi)* wild, mad; **des diamants? mais tu es f.!** diamonds? you're mad *or* crazy!; **rendre qn f.** to drive *or* to send sb mad; **il est encore en retard, ça me rend folle!** he's late again, it drives me wild *or* mad!; **cette musique/situation me rend f.** the music/situation is driving me mad

4 *(passionné)* **être f. de qn/qch** to be mad *or* wild about sb/sth; **elle est folle de football** she's crazy about soccer *or Br* football

5 *(intense)* mad, wild; **nous avons passé une folle soirée** we had a wild evening; **entre eux, c'est l'amour f.** they're crazy about each other, they're madly in love

6 *(incontrôlé)* wild; **se lancer dans une course folle** to embark on a headlong chase; **camion/train f.** runaway truck/train; **folle avoine** wild oats; **folles illusions** wild delusions; **avoir des mèches folles** to have wild *or* straggly hair; **f. rire** (uncontrollable) giggle *or* giggles; **avoir** *ou* **être pris d'un f. rire** to have a fit of the giggles; *Bible* **les vierges folles** the foolish virgins; *Littéraire* **les tourbillonnements fols des feuilles** the wild whirlings of the leaves

7 *Fam (très important)* tremendous; **il y avait un monde f.** there was a huge crowd☐; **un prix f.** an extortionate price☐; **un succès f.** a tremendous *or* wild success; **mettre un temps f. à faire qch** to take absolutely ages to do sth; **ça dure un temps f.** it goes on for ages; **gagner un argent f.** to make piles *or* a lot of money; **à une allure folle** at breakneck speed; **d'une gaieté folle** wildly happy; *Fam* **c'est f. ce que c'est grand!** it's incredible how big it is!

8 *(incroyable)* incredible; **c'est une histoire complètement folle!** it's the most incredible story!

NM,F **1** *(dément)* madman, *f* madwoman; *Vieilli* **envoyer qn chez les fous** to have sb locked up *or* put away; **tais-toi, vieille folle!** shut up, you crazy old woman!; **comme un f.** dementedly; *(intensément)* like mad *or* crazy; **c'est une histoire de fous** I can't make head (n)or tail of it; **c'est un f.** **fou** he's a raving lunatic **2** *(excité)* lunatic, fool; **ce jeune f. va nous entraîner dans une catastrophe** that young fool will ruin us; **faire le f.** to act the fool *or* idiot **3** *(passionné)* **c'est un f. de moto** he's mad on *or* crazy about bikes; **f. du volant** reckless driver

NM **1** *Échecs* bishop

2 *Hist* **f. (du roi)** (court) jester

3 *Orn* booby; **f. de Bassan** gannet

4 *(locution)* **plus on est de fous plus on rit** the more the merrier

• **folle** NF **1** *Fam Péj (homosexuel)* queen; **grande folle** raving *or* screaming queen **2** *Littéraire (locution)* **la folle du logis** a vivid imagination

fouace [fwas] = **fougasse**

foucade [fukad] NF *Littéraire* whim, passing fancy

foudre¹ [fudr] NM **1** *(tonneau)* tun **2** *Myth* thunderbolt

• **foudre de guerre** NM **1** *(guerrier)* great warrior **2** *Fig Hum* **ce n'est pas un f. de guerre** he wouldn't say boo to a goose; *Fig* **f. d'éloquence** powerful orator

foudre² [fudr] NF *Météo* lightning; *Bible* thunderbolt; **être frappé par la f.** to be struck by lightning; **prompt** *ou* **rapide comme la f.** (as) quick as lightning

• **foudres** NFPL *Littéraire* wrath, ire; **il a tout fait pour s'attirer les foudres du public** he did everything to bring down the public's wrath upon him *or* to incur the public's wrath

foudroyant, -e [fudrwajɑ̃, -ɑ̃t] ADJ **1** *(soudain)* violent; *(attaque, nouvelles)* devastating; **une crise cardiaque foudroyante** a massive coronary; **une mort foudroyante** (an) instant death; **un poison f.** a devastatingly lethal poison **2** *(extraordinaire)* striking, lightning *(avant n)*; **faire des progrès foudroyants** to make lightning progress; **la pièce a connu un succès f.** the play was a massive success; **à une vitesse foudroyante** with lightning speed **3** *(furieux ▸ regard)* thunderous; **jeter des regards foudroyants à qn** to look daggers at sb

foudroyer [13] [fudrwaje] VT **1** *Météo* to strike; **être foudroyé** to be struck by lightning **2** *(tuer)* to strike down; **la sentinelle a été foudroyée par une balle perdue** the sentry was struck by a stray bullet; **foudroyé par une décharge électrique** killed by an electric shock, electrocuted; *Fig* **f. qn du regard** *ou* **des yeux** to look daggers at sb **3** *(anéantir)* to strike down; **la mort de ses parents l'a foudroyé** he was crushed by his parents' death; **la division fut foudroyée par la puissance de feu de l'ennemi** the division was decimated by enemy fire power

fouet [fwɛ] NM **1** *(instrument)* whip; **donner le f. à qn** to whip *or* to flog sb; **coup de f.** lash, stroke; *Fig* fillip, stimulus; **l'air de la mer lui a donné un coup de f.** the sea air has perked him/her up *or* given him/her a lift; **donner un coup de f. à l'économie** to stimulate *or* to boost the economy, to give a fillip to the economy

2 *Culin* whisk

3 *Orn* **f. de l'aile** wing tip

4 *Naut (d'une poulie)* tail

fouettard [fwetar] *voir* **père**

fouettement [fwɛtmɑ̃] NM *(de la pluie, de la grêle)* lashing; *(d'une voile)* flapping

fouetter [4] [fwete] VT **1** *(frapper)* to whip, to flog; **f. son cheval** to whip one's horse; **il n'y a pas de quoi f. un chat** there's nothing to get excited about; **avoir d'autres chats à f.** to have other fish to fry

2 *Culin (crème)* to whip; *(blanc d'œuf)* to beat, to whisk

3 *(cingler ▸ sujet: pluie)* to lash

4 *Fig (exciter)* to excite, to stimulate; **vent qui fouette le sang** wind that makes the blood tingle; **le sang fouetté par le désir** spurred on *or* stimulated by desire; **l'air glacé lui fouettait le sang** the icy air got his/her circulation going

VI **1** *(câble)* to lash, to whip; *(voile)* to flap; **la pluie fouette contre les vitres** the rain is lashing (against) the panes **2** *très Fam (empester)* to stink☐, *Br* to pong; **ça fouette par ici!** there's a hell of a stink *or Br* a pong in here! **3** *très Fam (avoir peur)* to piss oneself

foufou, fofolle [fufu, fɔfɔl] ADJ *Fam* crazy, loopy

foufoune [fufun], **foufounette** [fufunɛt] NF *Vulg (sexe de femme)* pussy, *Br* fanny

• **foufounes** NFPL *Can Fam (en langage enfantin)* bum, botty

fougasse [fugas] NF = flat loaf traditionally cooked in wood-ash and sometimes flavoured with olives or anchovies

fougeraie [fuʒrɛ] NF patch of ferns

fougère [fuʒɛr] NF fern; **f. aigle** bracken; **f. arborescente** tree fern

fougue [fug] NF *(ardeur)* passion, spirit, ardour; **la f. de la jeunesse** youthful high spirits; **cheval plein de f.** spirited horse; **un discours rempli** *ou* **plein de f.** a fiery speech; **se battre avec f.** to fight with spirit, to put up a spirited fight; **répondre avec f.** to answer with brio

fougueuse [fugøz] *voir* **fougueux**

fougueusement [fugøzmɑ̃] ADV ardently, with brio, with passion; *(s'élancer)* impetuously; *(s'embrasser)* passionately

fougueux, -euse [fugø, -øz] ADJ *(personne)* ardent, fiery, impetuous; *(cheval)* spirited; *(réponse, résistance)* spirited, lively; **tempérament f.** fiery temperament

fouille [fuj] NF **1** *(d'un lieu)* search; **passer à la f.** to be searched; **f. corporelle** *(rapide)* frisking; *(approfondie)* body search

2 *Agr* digging (up)

3 *Mines* exploration, search; **travail en f.** earth digging; **f. à ciel ouvert** open pit

4 *très Fam (poche)* pocket☐; *Fig* **se remplir les fouilles, s'en mettre plein les fouilles** to line one's pockets

5 *Can (chute)* fall; **prendre une f.** to fall, to have a fall

• **fouilles** NFPL *Archéol* dig, excavations; **faire des fouilles** to carry out excavations *or* a dig; **participer à des fouilles** to take part in a dig

fouillé, -e [fuje] ADJ *(enquête)* thorough, wide-ranging; *(étude)* detailed; *(détails)* elaborate

fouille-merde [fujmɛrd] NMF INV *très Fam* nosey parker

fouiller [3] [fuje] VT **1** *(explorer ▸ tiroir)* to search (through); *(▸ valise)* to go through; *(▸ au cours d'une vérification)* to search, to go through; **nous avons fouillé toute la maison/région** we searched the entire house/area; **fouille un peu tes poches, tu vas sûrement le retrouver!** have a look in your pockets, you're sure to find it!; **la police a fouillé tous les bagages** the police went through all the luggage; **f. qn** *(rapidement)* to frisk sb; *(de façon approfondie)* to search sb; **ses yeux fouillaient la salle** his/her eyes *or* he/she scanned the room

2 *(creuser ▸ sujet: cochon, taupe)* to dig; **f. la terre** to root in *or* to burrow in *or* to dig the earth; *Archéol* **f. un site** to excavate a site

3 *(approfondir)* to go deeply *or* thoroughly into; **il aurait fallu f. la question** the question should have been researched more thoroughly

VI **1** *(creuser ▸ gén)* to dig; *(▸ lapin)* to burrow; *(▸ cochon)* to root

2 *(faire une recherche)* **f. dans qch** *(légitimement)* to go through sth, to search sth; *(par indiscrétion)* to go through sth, *Péj* to rifle through sth; **f. dans une armoire/sa poche** to search *or* to rummage in a cupboard/in one's pocket; **f. dans les papiers de qn** to search through *or* to go through sb's papers; **f. dans les librairies pour trouver un livre** to search around in bookshops for a book; **f. dans sa mémoire** to search one's memory; **f. dans son esprit** to rack one's brains; **f. dans le passé de qn** to delve into sb's past

3 *Can (tomber)* to fall, to tumble (over)

VPR **se fouiller 1** *(emploi réfléchi)* **se f. les poches** to go through one's pockets **2** *Fam* **tu peux toujours te f.!** dream on!; **une participation? il peut se f.!** let him have a share in the profits? he can whistle for it *or* not likely!

fouilleur, -euse [fujœr, -øz] NM,F **1** *Archéol* excavator **2** *(policier)* searcher; *(à la douane)* officer who carries out body-searches **3** *(fouineur)* rummager, searcher; **un f. de brocantes/bibliothèques** an avid frequenter of second-hand shops/libraries

• **fouilleuse** NF *Agr* subsoil plough

fouillis [fuji] NM jumble; **faire du f.** *(personne)* to make a mess; **range ton f.** put away your mess; **quel f. dans ta chambre!** what a mess *or* shambles your room is!; **un f. de** a mass *or* a jumble of; **le jardin n'est qu'un f. de ronces** the garden's nothing but a mass of brambles; **se perdre dans un f. de détails** to get bogged down in (a mass of) details

ADJ messy, untidy; **ce que tu peux être f.!** you're so messy!; *Fam* **faire f.** to look messy *or* a mess

• **en fouillis** *Fam* ADJ in a mess; **une chambre en f.** a messy room ADV **laisser un lieu en f.** to leave a place in a mess

fouinard, -e [fwinar, -ard] *Fam* ADJ nosey

NM busybody, *Br* nosey parker

fouine [fwin] NF **1** *Zool* stone *or* beech marten; **avoir un visage de f.** to be weasel-faced **2** *Fam (fouineur)* busybody, *Br* nosy parker

fouiner [3] [fwine] VI *Fam* **1** *(explorer)* **f. au marché aux puces** to go hunting for bargains at the flea market **2** *Péj (être indiscret)* to nose about *or* around; **il est toujours à f. dans les affaires des autres** he's always poking his nose into other people's business

fouineur, -euse [fwinœr, -øz] *Fam* ADJ nosy, prying
NM,F **1** *(indiscret)* busybody, *Br* nosey parker **2** *(chez les brocanteurs)* bargain hunter **3** *Offic Ordinat (pirate informatique)* hacker

fouir [32] [fwir] VT to burrow, to dig

fouisseur, -euse [fwisœr, -øz] ADJ burrowing *(avant n)*
NM burrower

foulage [fulaʒ] NM **1** *(du raisin)* pressing, treading; *(d'une peau)* tanning; *(d'un tissu)* fulling **2** *Typ* impression

foulant, -e [fulɑ̃, -ɑ̃t] ADJ **1** *Fam (fatigant)* backbreaking, *Br* knackering; **c'est pas f.!** it's not exactly backbreaking work! **2** *voir* **pompe**

foulard [fular] NM **1** *(pièce d'étoffe)* scarf; **le F. islamique** Muslim headscarf **2** *Tex* foulard

LE FOULARD ISLAMIQUE

The issue of the wearing of the Muslim headscarf in state schools and other public buildings has been a source of huge controversy and debate in France for a number of years. The principle of secularism has long been a cornerstone of the French educational system, but the question of deciding whether it was acceptable for female Muslim pupils to wear the headscarf at school had been left to the discretion of school heads. Given the growing number of incidents involving girls being banned from school for insisting on wearing the headscarf and refusing to take part in activities such as physical education on religious grounds, the government passed a law in 2004 prohibiting the display of any obvious religious signs at school (as well as in state jobs that involve contact with the public). This measure was described as an attempt to safeguard the principle of secularism and to keep issues of ethnicity and religion from being a divisive factor among children.

foule [ful] NF **1** *(gens)* crowd, *Péj* mob, *Littéraire* throng; *Fam* **il y a f.** there are crowds *or* masses of people; *Fam* **il n'y a pas f.** there's hardly anyone around; **fuir la f.** to flee the crowds; **mouvement de f.** *ou* **de foules** movement in the crowd; **quelle f. dans les rues!** the streets are so crowded! **2** *(masses populaires)* **la f., les foules** the masses; **un président qui plaît aux foules** a popular president **3** *(grand nombre)* **une f. de gens** a crowd of people; **une f. d'amis** a host of friends; **j'ai une f. de choses à te raconter** I've got lots of things to tell you
• **en foule** ADV *(venir, se présenter)* in huge numbers; **entrer en f.** to crowd in

foulée [fule] NF **1** *(enjambée)* stride; **avancer à longues foulées** to stride along; **courir à petites foulées** to trot along **2 foulées** *(d'animaux sauvages)* track(s), spoor
• **dans la foulée** ADV *Fam* **dans la f., j'ai fait aussi le repassage** I did the ironing while I was at it
• **dans la foulée de** PRÉP *Sport* **rester dans la f. de qn** to stay close on sb's heels

fouler [3] [fule] VT **1** *(écraser* ▸ *raisin)* to press, to tread; *(*▸ *céréale)* to tread
2 *(marcher sur)* to tread *or* to walk on; *Littéraire* **f. le sol natal** to tread the native soil; **nous foulions pour la première fois le sol de Grèce** we were setting foot for the first time on Greek soil; **f. qch aux pieds** to trample on sth
3 *(cuir, peau)* to tan
4 *Tex* to full
VPR **se fouler 1** *Fam* **se f. (la rate)** *(se fatiguer)* to strain oneself, to overexert oneself; **tu ne t'es pas beaucoup foulé** you didn't exactly strain *or* overexert yourself, did you? **2** *(se faire mal)* **se f. le poignet** to sprain one's wrist

fouleur, -euse [fulœr, -øz] NM,F **1** *(de raisins) (personne)* winepresser **2** *(de tissu)* fuller **3** *(de cuir)* tanner

fouloir [fulwar] NM **1** *(pour le raisin)* wine press **2** *Tex* fulling mill **3** *(de tanneur)* tanning drum

foulon [fulɔ̃] NM **1** *Tex (machine)* **(moulin à) f.** fulling mill; *(ouvrier)* fuller **2 terre à f.** fuller's earth **3** *(de tanneur)* tanning drum

foulque [fulk] NF *Orn* **f. (macroule)** coot

foultitude [fultityd] NF *Fam* **une f. de** loads *or* masses of; **avoir une f. de choses à faire** to have loads of things to do

foulure [fulyr] NF sprain; **f. du poignet/de la cheville** sprained wrist/ankle

four [fur] NM **1** *Culin* oven; **un plat allant au f.** an ovenproof dish; **de la vaisselle allant au f.** ovenware; **faire cuire au f.** *(pain)* to bake; *(viande)* to roast; **avoir qch au f.** to have sth cooking (in the oven); *Fig* to have sth in the pipeline *or Br* on the go; **f. électrique/à gaz** electric/gas oven; **f. à chaleur tournante** fan-assisted oven; **f. combiné** *ou* **multifonctions** combi-oven; **f. à micro-ondes** microwave oven; **f. à pain** *ou* **de boulanger** baker's oven; **ouvrir la bouche comme un f.** to open one's mouth wide; **il fait chaud comme dans un f.** it's like an oven (in here); **on ne peut pas être à la fois au f. et au moulin** you can't be in two places at the same time
2 *Tech* furnace, kiln; **f. à briques** brick kiln; **f. à céramique** pottery kiln; **f. à chaux** lime kiln; **f. à émaux** enamelling kiln; **f. solaire** solar furnace
3 *Hist* **f. crématoire** gas oven *(in the Nazi concentration camps)*
4 *Fam (fiasco)* flop; **sa pièce a été** *ou* **a fait un f.** his/her play was a flop

fourbe [furb] *Littéraire* ADJ deceitful, treacherous
NMF cheat, treacherous *or* false-hearted person

fourberie [furbəri] NF *Littéraire* **1** *(duplicité)* treacherousness **2** *(acte)* treachery

fourbi [furbi] NM *Fam* **1** *(désordre)* shambles *(singulier)*, mess; **quel f., je ne retrouve rien!** what a muddle *or* mess, I can't find anything! **2** *(affaires)* stuff, *Br* gear; *(de soldat)* kit; **et tout le f.** the whole (kit and) caboodle **3** *(truc)* thingummy, thingy

fourbir [32] [furbir] VT **1** *(nettoyer)* to polish (up) **2** *Fig Littéraire* **f. ses armes** to prepare for war; **f. ses arguments** to line up one's arguments

fourbissage [furbisaʒ] NM polishing (up)

fourbu, -e [furby] ADJ **1** *(personne)* exhausted; **je suis f.** I'm tired out *or* exhausted **2** *(cheval)* foundered

fourche [furʃ] NF **1** *Agr* fork; **f. à foin** pitchfork, hayfork; **remuer le sol à la f.** to fork the ground
2 *(embranchement)* fork; *Aut* Y-junction; **la route fait une f.** the road forks
3 *(d'une bicyclette, d'un arbre)* fork
4 *Aut* **f. d'attelage** trailer hitch
5 *(de cheveux)* split end; **j'ai des fourches** I've got split ends
6 *Antiq* **les fourches Caudines** the Caudine Forks; *Fig* **passer sous les fourches Caudines** to be humiliated
7 *Hist* **les fourches patibulaires** the gallows

fourchée [furʃe] NF *Vieilli (de foin)* pitchforkful

fourcher [3] [furʃe] VI **1** *Arch* to fork, to divide; **j'ai les cheveux qui fourchent** I've got split ends **2** *(locutions)* **sa langue a fourché** he/she made a slip (of the tongue); **excusez-moi, ma langue a fourché** sorry, it was a slip of the tongue
VT *(sol)* to fork

fourchet [furʃɛ] NM *Vét* foot rot

fourchette [furʃɛt] NF **1** *(pour manger)* fork; **f. à dessert** dessert fork; **f. à escargots** snail fork; **f. à huîtres** oyster fork; **f. à poisson** fish fork; **être une bonne f.** to be a hearty eater; **elle a un bon coup de f.** she's a hearty eater; *Hum* **la f. du père Adam** the fingers
2 *(écart)* bracket; **une f. comprise entre 1000 et 1500 euros** prices ranging from 1,000 to 1,500 euros; *Bourse* **f. de cotation** trading range; *Bourse* **f. de cours de clôture** closing range; *Bourse* **f. de cours d'ouverture** opening range; **f. d'imposition** tax bracket; **f. de prix** price bracket *or* range; **f. de salaire** wage bracket; **f. de taux** rate band
3 *Mil* bracket; **prendre une cible en f.** *ou* **à la f.** to bracket a target
4 *Zool (du cheval)* frog; *(de l'oiseau)* wishbone, *Spéc* furcula
5 *Cartes* tenace; *Échecs* fork
6 *(de balance)* beam support
7 *Tech* belt guide, shifter; **f. de débrayage** clutch throw-out fork; **f. d'embrayage** clutch fork

fourchu, -e [furʃy] ADJ **1** *(cheveux)* **avoir les cheveux fourchus** to have split ends **2** *(tronc, route)* forked; *(bâton)* cleft **3** *(pied)* cloven; *(sabot)* cloven, cleft; *(menton)* cleft; *(langue)* forked; **aux pieds fourchus** cloven-hoofed; **avoir la langue fourchue** to speak with a forked tongue

fourgon [furgɔ̃] NM **1** *(voiture)* van; *Br* **f. cellulaire** police van, *Am* patrol *or* police wagon; *Br* **f. de déménagement** removal *or Am* moving van; **f. funèbre** *ou* **funéraire** *ou* **mortuaire** hearse; **f. postal** mail van **2** *Rail* coach, *Br* wagon; *Br* **f. à bagages** luggage van, *Am* baggage car; **f. à bestiaux** *ou* **à bétail** cattle truck; **f. de queue** rear (brake) van, guard's van, *Am* caboose **3** *(tige de métal)* poker

fourgonner [3] [furgɔne] VT *(feu, poêle)* to poke, to rake
VI *Fam (fouiller)* to poke *or* to rummage about

fourgonnette [furgɔnɛt] NF (small) van

fourguer [3] [furge] VT **1** *Fam Arg crime (vendre)* to fence, to flog; **f. qch à qn** to flog sth to sb; **2** *Fam Péj (donner)* to unload; **f. qch à qn** to unload sth on sb, to palm sth off on sb **3** *Fam (dénoncer)* to squeal on, *Br* to grass on

fourmi [furmi] NF **1** *Entom* ant; **f. blanche** termite; **f. rouge** red ant
2 *(personne)* busy bee; **ma tante a toujours été une (vraie) f.** my aunt has always been a busy bee
3 *Fam Arg crime (passeur)* (small-time) pusher
4 *(locution)* **avoir des fourmis dans les jambes** to have pins and needles in one's legs
• **de fourmi** ADJ *(travail)* meticulous, painstaking

fourmilier [furmilje] NM *Zool* anteater

fourmilière [furmiljɛr] NF **1** *Entom* anthill, antheap; *Fig* **donner des coups de pied dans la f.** to stir things up **2** *Fig (lieu animé)* hive of activity; **l'aéroport s'est transformé en une véritable f.** the airport was bustling with activity; **cette banlieue est une véritable f. (humaine)** this suburb is swarming *or* teeming with people

fourmillement [furmijmɑ̃] NM **1** *(picotement)* tingle; *Méd* formication; **j'ai des fourmillements dans les doigts** I've got pins and needles in my fingers **2** *(foisonnement* ▸ *d'insectes, de promeneurs)* swarm; *(*▸ *d'idées)* welter; **il fut pris de panique devant ce f. d'insectes** he panicked when he saw the swarm of insects *or* the swarming insects; **un f. de détails** a mass *or* wealth of detail

fourmiller [3] [furmije] VI **1** *(s'agiter)* to swarm; **les vers fourmillaient dans ce fromage** the cheese was alive with maggots **2** *(être abondant)* to abound; **un documentaire où fourmillent les révélations intéressantes** a documentary full of *or* teeming with interesting revelations; **f. de** *(insectes, personnes)* to swarm with; *(fautes)* to be full of, to be riddled with; *(idées)* to be bursting with, to be full of **3** *(picoter)* to tingle; **j'ai les doigts qui fourmillent** I have pins and needles in my fingers, my fingers are tingling

fournaise [furnɛz] NF **1** *Littéraire (feu)* blaze **2** *Can (poêle à bois)* (wood-burning) stove; *(poêle au charbon)* (coal-burning) stove; *(chaudière de chauffage central) Br* boiler, *Am* (central heating) furnace; **f. à l'huile** oil boiler **3** *(lieu caniculaire)* **la ville/cette chambre est une (vraie) f. en été** the city/this room is like an oven in the summer

fourneau, -x [furno] NM **1** *(cuisinière)* stove; **f. de cuisine** (kitchen) range; **f. à gaz** gas stove *or Br* cooker; **être aux** *ou* **derrière les fourneaux** to be cooking; **toujours à ses fourneaux!** always slaving over a hot stove!
2 *Métal* furnace; **haut f.** blast furnace
3 *(d'une pipe)* bowl
4 *(pour explosif)* mine chamber

fournée [furne] NF **1** *(du boulanger)* batch **2** *Fam Fig (ensemble de choses)* batch; *(ensemble de personnes)* lot; **le métro dégorge sa dernière f.** the last lot of passengers are leaving the metro

fourni, -e [furni] ADJ **1** *(touffu* ▸ *cheveux)* thick; *(*▸ *barbe)* heavy, thick; *(*▸ *sourcils)* bushy; *(*▸ *haie)* luxuriant; **barbe peu fournie** sparse *or* thin beard **2** *(approvisionné)* **abondamment** *ou* **bien f.** well-stocked; **mal f.** poorly stocked

fournil [furni] NM bakehouse, bakery

fourniment [furnimɑ̃] **NM 1** *Mil* pack, equipment **2** *Fam (attirail)* gear, paraphernalia

fournir [32] [furnir] **VT 1** *(approvisionner)* to supply; **f. qch à qn** to supply sb with sth; **il n'y a plus de quoi f. les troupes** there's nothing left to feed the army; **f. qn en** to supply sb with; **f. une entreprise en matières premières** to supply a firm with raw materials; **c'est eux qui me fournissent en pain** I buy (my) bread from them
2 *(procurer)* to provide; **f. qch à qn** to provide sb with sth; **c'est la France qui leur fournit des armes** it's France who is providing *or* supplying them with weapons; **il pourra peut-être te f. du travail** he might be able to give you some work; **vous devez nous f. un devis/une pièce d'identité** you must provide us with an estimate/some form of identification; **voici la liste des pièces à f.** here is a list of required documents; **f. un alibi à qn** to provide sb with an alibi; **f. des renseignements à qn** to supply *or* to provide *or* to furnish sb with information; **fournissez-moi l'argent demain** let me have the money tomorrow
3 *(produire)* to produce; **ces vignes fournissent un vin de qualité moyenne** this vineyard produces a wine of average quality
4 *(accomplir)* **f. un effort** to make an effort
5 *Cartes* **f. la couleur demandée** to follow suit; **f. à trèfle** to follow suit in clubs
USAGE ABSOLU 1 *(approvisionner)* **qui fournit la famille royale?** who is the Royal Family's supplier?, who supplies the Royal Family? **2** *Hum (produire)* **je ne peux plus f., moi!** I can't cope any more!
• **fournir à VT IND** *Vieilli* **f. aux besoins de qn** to provide for sb's needs; **f. à la dépense** to defray the cost; **f. aux frais** to defray expenses
VPR se fournir se f. chez qn to get one's supplies from sb; **je me fournis toujours chez le même boucher** I always shop at the same butcher's, I get all my meat from the same place; **se f. en qch** to get in supplies of sth; **ils se fournissent (en vin) chez ce négociant** they get their supplies (of wine) from this merchant; **il se fournit chez nous** he is a customer of ours, he's one of our customers

fournissement [furnismɑ̃] **NM** *Fin* contribution *(in shares)*

fournisseur, -euse [furnisœr, -øz] **NMF 1** *(établissement, marchand)* supplier; **fournisseurs de l'armée** army contractors; **f. de navires** *ou* **de la marine** ship's chandler; *Fin* **f. en capitaux** funder, supplier of capital; **f. exclusif** sole supplier; **f. principal** main supplier; **f. secondaire** secondary supplier; **c'est le plus gros f. de papier de tout le pays** he's the biggest supplier of paper in the whole country **2** *Ordinat* **f. d'accès (à Internet)** (Internet) access provider; **f. de contenu** content provider
ADJ les pays fournisseurs de la France the countries that supply France (with goods), France's suppliers

fourniture [furnityr] **NF** *(action)* supplying, providing
• **fournitures NFPL** *(objets)* materials; **fournitures de bureau** office supplies; **fournitures de navires** ship's chandlery; **fournitures scolaires** school stationery

> Il faut noter que le mot anglais **furniture** est un faux ami. Il signifie **meubles**.

fourrage [furaʒ] **NM 1** *Agr* fodder; **f. sec/vert** hay/silage; **rentrer du f.** to harvest forage **2** *(d'un vêtement ▸ action)* lining; *(▸ peau)* lining fur

fourrager¹ [17] [furaʒe] **VI** *(faire du fourrage)* to make fodder; *(se nourrir de fourrage)* to feed
VT 1 *Fam (papiers)* to rummage through **2** *Arch (pays)* to pillage, to ravage
• **fourrager dans VT IND** to rummage through

fourrager², -ère [furaʒe, -ɛr] **ADJ** fodder *(avant n)*; **plantes fourragères** fodder crops
• **fourragère NF 1** *Mil (décoration)* fourragère **2** *(champ)* field *(in which a fodder crop is grown)* **3** *(charrette)* cart *(for fodder)*

fourre [fur] **NF** *Suisse (d'un oreiller)* pillowcase; *(pour un édredon)* quilt cover; *(d'un disque)* sleeve; *(d'un livre)* jacket

fourré¹ [fure] **NM** *(bois)* thicket; *(à la chasse)* cover; **il disparut dans les fourrés** he disappeared into the undergrowth *or* bushes

fourré², -e [fure] **ADJ 1** *(doublé de fourrure)* fur-lined; **des chaussons/gants fourrés** lined slippers/gloves **2** *Culin* filled, stuffed; **bonbons fourrés à la fraise** *Br* sweets *or Am* candy with strawberry-flavoured centres; **chocolats fourrés** soft-centred chocolates **3** *Fig Vieilli* **paix fourrée** hollow *or* mock peace

fourreau, -x [furo] **NM 1** *(d'une arme)* sheath; *(d'un parapluie)* cover; **remettre son épée au f.** to sheathe one's sword **2** *(robe)* sheath dress **3** *Élec* sleeve
ADJ jupe/robe f. pencil skirt/sheath dress

fourrer [3] [fure] **VT 1** *(doubler de fourrure)* to line with fur
2 *Culin (fruit, gâteau)* to fill; **f. un chocolat/une crêpe de qch** to fill a chocolate/a pancake with sth; **f. une dinde de marrons** to stuff a turkey with chestnuts
3 *Fam (mettre)* to stick, to shove; **f. qch dans qch** to stuff sth in *or* into sth; **je les ai fourrés dans le coin** I stuck them in the corner; **ne fourre pas tes affaires dans le sac, range-les** don't just shove your things into the bag, put them in neatly; *Fig* **f. qch dans la tête à qn** to get sth into sb's head; **ils lui ont fourré dans la tête que...** they managed to get it into his/her head that...; **mais où ai-je bien pu f. ça?** where on earth have I stuck it?; **f. ses mains dans ses poches** to stick *or* to shove one's hands into one's pockets; **avoir les mains fourrées dans les poches** to have one's hands (deep) in one's pockets; **f. son doigt dans son nez** to stick one's finger up one's nose; *Fig* **f. son nez partout** to poke *or* to stick one's nose into everything; *Can Joual Vulg* **f. le chien** to screw around, to waste time mucking about
4 *Fam (laisser ▸ papier, vêtement)* to stick, to put□; **f. qch quelque part** to stick *or* to leave□ sth somewhere; **où as-tu fourré ce dossier?** where have you put *or* left that file?□
5 *Fam (placer ▸ personne, animal)* to stick, to put□; **on l'a fourré en prison** *ou* **au trou** they stuck him in jail; **il est toujours fourré chez ses parents/à l'église** he's always at his parents'/in church□; **ce chat/gosse, toujours fourré dans mes jambes** *ou* **pattes!** that child/cat is always under my feet!
6 *Vulg (posséder sexuellement)* to screw, *Br* to shag
7 *Can Joual Vulg (tromper)* to screw, to shaft; **se faire f.** to get screwed *or* shafted
8 *Tech (jointure)* to pack
VPR se fourrer *Fam* **1** *(se mettre)* **se f. au lit/sous les couvertures** to snuggle down in bed/under the blankets; **il s'est fourré dans le coin/sous le lit** he got into the corner/under the bed; **où est-il allé se f.?** wherever has he got to?, wherever has he hidden himself?; **il ne savait plus où se f.** he didn't know where to put himself **2** *(s'engager)* **se f. dans une sale affaire** to get mixed up in a nasty business; **se f. dans un (vrai) guêpier** to land oneself in real trouble **3** *(se mettre)* **se f. un doigt dans le nez** to stick one's finger up one's nose; **se f. une idée dans la tête** to get an idea into one's head; *Fig* **il s'est fourré dans le crâne que...** he's got it into his head that...; *Fig* **si tu crois que je vais l'attendre, tu te fourres le doigt dans l'œil (jusqu'à la clavicule)** if you think I'm going to wait for him/her, you've got another think coming

fourre-tout [furtu] **NM INV 1** *(pièce)* junk room; *(placard)* junk cupboard **2** *(sac léger)* *Br* holdall, *Am* carryall; *(trousse)* pencil case **3** *Fig* jumble, ragbag; **cette loi est un (vrai) f.** this law is a real mess
ADJ INV sac f. *Br* holdall, *Am* carryall; **placard f.** junk cupboard; *Péj* **une loi f.** a mishmash *or* ragbag of a law

fourreur [furœr] **NM** furrier

fourrier [furje] **NM 1** *Mil & Naut* quartermaster **2** *Littéraire* **être le f. de** to be a harbinger of **3** *Hist & Mil (responsable de la nourriture)* quartermaster sergeant; *(responsable du logement)* billeting officer

fourrière [furjɛr] **NF** *(pour chiens, pour voitures)* pound; **mettre une voiture en** *ou* **à la f.** to impound a car

fourrure [furyr] **NF 1** *(vêtement)* fur; **un manteau/une veste de f.** a fur coat/jacket; **f. polaire** fleece
2 *(peau préparée)* fur
3 *Zool* fur, coat
4 *(commerce)* **la f.** the fur trade
5 *Tech* packing; *Aut* **f. de frein** brake lining

fourvoiement [furvwamɑ̃] **NM** *Littéraire* going astray

fourvoyer [13] [furvwaje] **VT** *Littéraire* to lead astray, to mislead
VPR se fourvoyer *(s'égarer)* to lose one's way, to go astray; *Fig (se tromper)* to be mistaken, to be in error; **tu te fourvoies si tu crois qu'il va y renoncer** you're mistaken *or* you're making a mistake if you think he'll give it up; **se f. dans qch** to get oneself involved in sth; **où donc est-elle allée se f.?** where on earth has she got to?

fous *etc voir* **foutre¹**

foutage [futaʒ] **NM** *très Fam* **c'est du f. de gueule!** you/they/*etc* gotta be kidding!, *Br* that's just taking the piss!

foutaise [futɛz] **NF** *très Fam* crap, *Am* bull; **tout ça, c'est de la f.!** that's just a load of crap *or Am* bull!

fouteur, -euse [futœr, -øz] **NM,F** *très Fam* **f. de merde** shit-stirrer

foutimasser [3] [futimase] **VI** *Suisse Fam (perdre son temps)* to mess about; *(faire quelque chose de douteux)* to be up to something

foutoir [futwar] **NM** *très Fam* dump, *Br* tip; **sa chambre est un vrai f.** his/her room is a complete tip

foutraque [futrak] **ADJ** *Fam* nuts, *Br* crackers

foutre¹ [116] [futr] *très Fam* **ADV je n'en sais f. rien** *Br* I'm buggered if I know, *Am* the hell if I know; **personne n'en sait f. rien** fuck knows
VT 1 *(envoyer, mettre)* **fous-le dans la valise** bung it in the case; **je me demande où elle a pu le f.** where the hell has she put it?; **f. qch par la fenêtre** to chuck sth out of the window; **f. qn par terre** to throw sb to the ground□; **f. une pile de livres par terre** to knock a pile of books to the ground□; *Fig* **f. un rêve/un projet par terre** to wreck a dream/a project; **f. qn dehors** to kick sb out; **f. qn à la porte** to throw *or* to chuck sb out; **f. qch en l'air** to screw sth up; **f. sur la gueule à qn** to bash *or* to smash sb's face in; **ils ont foutu le feu à l'église** they set fire to the church□; *Suisse* **f. qch bas** *(démolir)* to knock sth down□; *Suisse* **f. qn bas** *(tuer)* to kill sb□, *Br* to do sb in
2 *(donner)* to give; **f. une claque à qn** to give sb a thump; **f. la trouille à qn** to put the wind up sb, to scare sb stiff; **f. le cafard à qn** to get sb down; **f. la paix à qn** to leave sb alone, to get out of sb's hair; **f. une (bonne) raclée à qn** to thump sb; **il m'a foutu une raclée au tennis** he thrashed me at tennis; **elle m'a foutu la honte** *(d'elle)* I was ashamed of her; *(de moi)* she made me ashamed of myself; **ça nous a foutu un coup** it gave us a nasty shock; **qu'est-ce qui m'a foutu un empoté pareil!** you're such a *Br* bloody oaf *or Am* goddamn klutz!
3 *(faire)* to do; **il ne fout rien de la journée** he doesn't do a damn *or Br* bloody thing all day; **qu'est-ce que tu fous là?** what the hell are you doing here?; **qu'est-ce que ça peut f.?** what the hell difference does that make?; **qu'est-ce que ça peut f. qu'on soit en retard?** so what if we're late, what the hell does it matter if we're late?; **qu'est-ce que ça peut te/lui f.?** what the hell does it matter to you/him/her?; **je ne sais pas quoi f. de lui/de cette vieille table** I don't know what the hell to do with him/with this old table; **il en a rien à f.** he couldn't give a damn *or Br* a toss *or* a monkey's; **rien à f., de leur bagnole!** who cares about their damn car?
4 *Vulg Vieilli (posséder sexuellement)* to fuck
5 *(locutions)* **ça la fout mal** it looks pretty bad; **il va falloir en f. un coup si on veut avoir fini demain** we'll have to get a move on if we want to be finished by tomorrow!; **mon mec a foutu le camp** my man's *Br* buggered off (and left me) *or Am* run out on me; **fous le camp de chez moi!** get the hell out of my house!; **y'a ta barrette qui fout le camp** your *Br* hair slide's *or Am* barrette's falling out□; **tout fout le camp!** this place is going to the dogs!; **je te fous mon billet qu'ils sont déjà partis** I'll bet you

anything you like they've already left; **rembourser? je t'en fous, il ne remboursera jamais!** you think he's going to pay you back? you'll be lucky!; **je t'en foutrai, moi, du caviar!** caviar? I'll give you bloody caviar!; *Vulg* **va te faire f.!** fuck off!; **qu'il aille se faire f.!** he can fuck off!

VPR se foutre 1 se f. entre les pattes de qn to fall into sb's clutches; **il s'est foutu par terre** he fell flat on his face; **se f. dedans** to blow it; **il s'est encore foutu dedans** he blew it yet again; **il s'est encore foutu dans une affaire louche** he's got (himself) mixed up in some shady business again; **se f. en colère** to lose one's rag, to go spare; **se f. à crier/rire** to start shouting/laughing; **se f. sur la gueule** to beat the living daylights out of each other; **se f. en l'air** to top oneself

2 il s'est foutu de la peinture sur son pantalon he spilt paint all over his trousers; **s'en f. plein la lampe** to make a pig of oneself; **s'en f. plein les poches** to line one's pockets

3 se f. de *(se moquer de)* to laugh at, to make fun of; **se f. de la gueule de qn** to take the piss out of sb; **tu te fous de moi ou quoi!** are you taking the piss?; **ils se foutent du monde!** they really take people for idiots!

4 se f. de *(être indifférent à)* not to give a damn *or Br* a toss about; **je me fous de ce qu'il fera** I don't give a damn *or Br* a toss about what he'll do; **il se fout de l'argent** he doesn't give a damn about money; **je m'en fous** I don't give a damn

5 *Suisse (se suicider)* to commit suicide❑, *Br* to top oneself

foutre² [futr] **NM** *Vulg (sperme)* cum, *Br* spunk

foutrement [futrəmɑ̃] **ADV** *très Fam* extremely❑, damn, *Br* bloody; **c'est f. bon** it's damn *or Br* bloody good; **elle sait f. bien qu'il ne l'épousera jamais** she knows damn well he'll never marry her; **je n'en sais f. rien** I know damn all *or Br* bugger all about it

foutriquet [futrikɛ] **NM** *Vieilli Fam Péj* little runt *or* squirt

foutu, -e [futy] *très Fam* **PP** *voir* **foutre¹**

ADJ 1 *(abîmé) Br* buggered, *Am* screwed-up; *(gâché)* ruined❑; **une voiture foutue** a write-off; **encore un collant (de) f.!** another pair of tights ruined!; **ma bagnole/robe est foutue** my car/dress has had it; **il est f.** he's had it, he's done for; **c'est f.!** forget it!; **pour la fête de demain, c'est f.** you can forget the party tomorrow; **c'est f. pour mon augmentation** I can forget *or* it's goodbye to my pay rise

2 *(avant le nom) (considérable)* damn(ed), *Br* bloody; **tu as eu une foutue chance** you were damn(ed) *or Br* bloody lucky; **il lui a fallu une foutue volonté pour rester** he/she needed a hell of a lot of willpower to stay

3 *(avant le nom) (détestable)* god awful, *Br* bloody; **elle a un f. caractère** she's so damn(ed) *or Br* bloody difficult; **quel f. temps!** what shitty *or Br* bloody awful weather!

4 *(locutions)* **c'est bien/mal f.** *(bien conçu)* it's well/badly designed❑; **cette machine est bien foutue** what a clever machine; **elle est plutôt bien foutue, sa pièce** his/her play is pretty good; **une fille très bien foutue** a girl with a great body; **il est mal f.** *(de corps)* he's not well-built❑, he doesn't have a good body❑; *(malade)* he feels rotten; **f. de** *(en mesure de)* **il est f. de réussir** he just might succeed; **elle serait foutue de le lui dire** she's quite likely to tell him/her; **ne pas être f. de faire qch** to be incapable of doing sth❑; **elle est pas foutue d'être à l'heure!** she can't even be bothered *or Br* arsed to be on time!, *Br* she can't even be on bloody time!

fox-hound [fɔksaund] *(pl* **fox-hounds)** **NM** foxhound

fox-terrier [fɔksterje] *(pl* **fox-terriers)** **NM** fox terrier

fox-trot [fɔkstrɔt] **NM INV** fox-trot

foyer [fwaje] **NM 1** *(chez soi)* home; *(domicile)* household; *Fin & Mktg* household unit; **rentrer dans** *ou* **regagner ses foyers** *(pays natal)* to go back to one's own country; *(domicile)* to return home; **renvoyer qn dans ses foyers** to send sb home; **f. conjugal** marital home; **femme** *ou* **mère au f.** housewife; **être mère au f.** to be a housewife and mother, to be a stay-at-home mother; **père au f.** house husband

2 *(résidence collective)* hall; **f. pour le troisième âge** retirement home; **f. d'accueil et d'hébergement** *(pour les gens à la rue)* hostel for the homeless; **f. d'étudiants** student hostel; **f. d'immigrés** immigrant workers' hostel; **f. des jeunes travailleurs** = hostel for young workers

3 *(lieu de réunion ▸ gén)* hall; *(▸ pour le public d'un théâtre)* foyer; *(▸ de lycée)* common room; **f. des artistes** greenroom; **f. socio-éducatif** ≃ community centre

4 *(âtre)* hearth

5 *(dans une machine)* firebox; **f. de chaudière** boiler furnace

6 *(centre)* seat, centre; *(de chaleur)* source; **le f. d'agitation** the centre of the disturbance; **un f. d'incendie** the source of a fire; **f. d'intrigue** hotbed of intrigue; **le f. de la rébellion** the centre of the rebellion

7 *Méd* **f. infectieux** *ou* **d'infection** source of infection; **f. tuberculeux** tubercle

8 *Opt & Phys* focus, focal point; **des lunettes à double f.** bifocals; **des verres à double f.** bifocal lenses, bifocals; **lentilles à f. variable** variable focus lenses

9 *Admin* **f. fiscal** household *(as a tax unit)*

foyer-logement [fwajelɔʒmɑ̃] *(pl* **foyers-logements)** **NM** assisted living facility

frac [frak] **NM** tailcoat; **en f.** wearing tails

fracas [fraka] **NM** *(bruit)* crash, roar; *(de l'orage)* din; *(des armes)* clash; *(vacarme)* racket, din; **le f. des vagues contre la falaise** the crashing of the waves against the cliff; **faire du f.** *(d'un événement)* to create a sensation; **elle sortit avec f.** she stormed out

• **à grand fracas ADV 1** *(bruyamment)* with a great deal of crashing and banging **2** *(spectaculairement)* with a lot of fuss

fracassant, -e [frakasɑ̃, -ɑ̃t] **ADJ 1** *(assourdissant)* deafening, thunderous; **la porte s'ouvrit avec un bruit f.** the door opened with a deafening crash **2** *(qui fait de l'effet)* sensational, staggering; *(succès)* resounding; **faire une déclaration fracassante** to make a sensational statement

fracasser [3] [frakase] **VT** to smash; **f. qch en mille morceaux** to smash sth into pieces; **f. une porte** *(volontairement)* to smash a door in, to break a door down; **il aurait pu avoir la tête fracassée** *(lors d'une agression)* he could have had *or* got his head smashed in; *(dans un accident)* he could have smashed his head in

VPR se fracasser 1 *(s'écraser)* to smash; **se f. contre** *ou* **sur** to smash into; **aller se f. contre qch** *(voiture, personne)* to smash *or* to slam into sth; **le bateau est allé se f. contre les rochers** the boat was smashed to pieces on the rocks **2 se f. le crâne** to crack one's head

fractal, -e, -als, -ales [fraktal] **ADJ** fractal

• **fractale NF** fractal

fraction [fraksjɔ̃] **NF 1** *Math* fraction; **f. ordinaire** vulgar fraction; **f. décimale** decimal fraction; **f. périodique** recurring decimal **2** *(partie)* fraction, part; *Pol* splinter group; **une large f. de la population** a large proportion of the population; **une f. de seconde** a fraction of a second; *Compta* **f. imposable** part subject to tax; **f. d'intérêt** interest accrued **3** *Rel* breaking of the bread

fractionnaire [fraksjɔnɛr] **ADJ** *Math* fractional; **nombre f.** improper fraction

fractionnel, -elle [fraksjɔnɛl] **ADJ** divisive

fractionnement [fraksjɔnmɑ̃] **NM 1** *Chim* fractionation; *(d'huiles minérales)* cracking

2 *(morcellement)* splitting *or* dividing up; *(des paiements)* spreading (out)

3 *Com* breaking bulk

4 *Bourse (des actions)* splitting

fractionner [3] [fraksjɔne] **VT 1** *(diviser)* to divide, to split up; **vous pouvez f. le remboursement** you may pay in instalments; **la propriété a été fractionnée entre les héritiers** the estate was divided up between the heirs **2** *Chim* to fractionate; *(huiles minérales)* to crack **3** *Bourse (actions)* to split

VPR se fractionner to split (up); **le groupe se fractionne en deux** the group splits *or* divides in two

fractionnisme [fraksjɔnism] **NM** *(tactique)* divisive tactics; *(caractère)* factionalism

fractionniste [fraksjɔnist] **ADJ** factionalist

NMF factionalist

fracture [fraktyr] **NF 1** *Méd* fracture; **f. du crâne** fractured skull; **il a eu une f. du crâne** his skull was fractured; **f. fermée** closed *or* simple fracture; **f. multiple** compound fracture; **f. ouverte** open fracture; **f. simple** simple *or* closed fracture

2 *Vieilli (effraction)* breaking open *(UNCOUNT)*; **y a-t-il eu f. du coffre?** was the safe broken open *or* into?

3 *Géol* fracture

4 *Fig (écart)* split; **f. Nord-Sud** North-South divide; **f. numérique** digital divide; **la f. sociale** the social divide

fracturer [3] [fraktyre] **VT 1** *(briser)* to break open; **f. un coffre-fort à l'explosif** to blow a safe **2** *(os)* to fracture

VPR se fracturer se f. le bras/poignet to fracture one's arm/wrist

fragile [fraʒil] **ADJ 1** *(peu solide)* fragile; **attention, f.** *(sur un colis)* fragile, handle with care; **avoir les cheveux fragiles** to have brittle hair

2 *(constitution)* frail; **un enfant f.** a frail child; **avoir l'estomac f.** to have a delicate stomach; **avoir les yeux fragiles** to have sensitive eyes; **être f. des poumons/de la gorge** to have delicate lungs/a delicate throat; **il est de santé f.** his health is rather delicate

3 *(personnalité)* delicate; **une adolescente f. qui est souvent déprimée** a sensitive teenager who is often depressed; **ne la brutalise pas, elle est encore f.** don't be rough with her, she's still (feeling) fragile

4 *(équilibre)* fragile, frail; **un bonheur f.** a fragile *or* precarious happiness; **un pays à l'économie f.** a country with a shaky *or* precarious economy; **une hypothèse/argumentation f.** a flimsy hypothesis/argument

fragilisation [fraʒilizasjɔ̃] **NF** *(affaiblissement)* weakening

fragiliser [3] [fraʒilize] **VT** *(affaiblir)* to weaken; **la mort de son père l'a beaucoup fragilisé** his father's death affected him deeply; **le régime a été fragilisé par une série de scandales** the regime has been weakened *or* damaged *or* undermined by a series of scandals

fragilité [fraʒilite] **NF 1** *(d'une horloge, d'une construction)* fragility, weakness; *(du verre)* fragility; *(des cheveux)* brittleness; **l'effondrement de l'immeuble est dû à la f. des fondations** the building collapsed because of its weak foundations **2** *(d'un organe, d'un malade)* weakness **3** *(d'un sentiment, d'une conviction, d'une victoire)* fragility; *(d'une hypothèse, d'une argumentation)* shakiness, flimsiness; *(d'un équilibre)* delicacy; *(d'un bonheur)* precariousness, fragility; *(d'une économie)* weakness, shakiness

fragment [fragmɑ̃] **NM 1** *(débris)* chip, fragment, piece; *(d'os)* fragment, splinter; **des fragments de verre** bits of shattered glass, shards of glass **2** *(morceau ▸ d'une œuvre en partie perdue)* fragment; *(▸ d'un air, d'une conversation)* snatch; **il nous a lu quelques fragments de son dernier roman** he read a few extracts of his last novel for us; **f. de vérité** shred of truth

fragmentaire [fragmɑ̃tɛr] **ADJ** fragmentary, sketchy, incomplete

fragmentation [fragmɑ̃tasjɔ̃] **NF** *(fractionnement)* division, splitting up; *Ordinat* fragmentation

fragmenter [3] [fragmɑ̃te] **VT** to divide, to split (up); **avoir une vision fragmentée des choses** to have a fragmented view of things

VPR se fragmenter to fragment, to split

frai¹ [frɛ] **NM 1** *(œufs)* spawn **2** *(poissons)* fry **3** *(période)* spawning season

frai² [frɛ] **NM** *(de pièces de monnaie)* abrasion, wear

fraîche [frɛʃ] *voir* **frais²**

fraîchement [frɛʃmɑ̃] **ADV 1** *(nouvellement)* freshly, newly; **f. repeint** freshly *or* newly painted; **f. coupé** *(herbe)* new-mown; **fleurs f. cueillies** freshly picked flowers; **f. marié/divorcé/arrivé** newly *or* recently married/divorced/arrived **2** *(froidement)* coolly; **il nous a reçus plutôt f.** he greeted us rather coolly **3** *Fam (locution)* **ça va plutôt f. aujourd'hui** it's a bit chilly today❑

fraîcheur [frɛʃœr] **NF 1** *(température)* coolness; **dans la f. du petit jour/du soir** in the cool of early dawn/of the evening; **une sensation de f.** a feeling of freshness; **rechercher un peu de f.** to seek out a cool spot

2 *(bonne qualité)* freshness; **pour conserver la f. de vos légumes** to keep your vegetables fresh

3 *(intensité ▸ des couleurs)* freshness, brightness; **les coloris des rideaux ont gardé toute leur f.** the curtains have retained their fresh *or* crisp colours; *Fam* **la robe n'est plus de la première f.** the dress isn't exactly brand new

4 *(éclat)* freshness; **dans toute la f. de ses vingt ans** with all the freshness of his/her youth

5 *(indifférence)* coolness; **la f. de son accueil nous a surpris** his/her cool reception was a surprise to us

fraîchir [32] [freʃir] **VI 1** *(se refroidir)* to get cooler; **les jours fraîchissent** the weather is getting cooler **2** *Naut (vent)* to freshen, to get stronger

fraie *etc voir* **frayer**

frais¹ [frɛ] **NMPL 1** *(dépenses)* expenses, costs; **j'ai eu beaucoup de f. ce mois-ci** I've had a lot of expense(s) this month; **cela lui a occasionné des f.** it cost him/her a certain amount (of money); **les f. du ménage** a family's everyday expenses *or* expenditure; **faire des f.** to go to great expense; **faire des f. de toilette** to spend money on clothes; **à f. communs** sharing the expense; **à grands f.** at great expense; **à moindre f.** less expensively, at a cheaper price; **à peu de f.** cheaply; *Fam* **aux f. de la princesse** at the firm's/government's/*etc* expense□; **exempt de f., sans f.** free of charge; *(sur une lettre de change)* no expenses; **tous f. payés** all expenses paid; **rentrer dans** *ou* **faire ses f.** to break even, to recoup one's expenses; **se mettre en f.** to spend money; **tu ne t'es pas mis en f.** you didn't exactly *Br* splash out *or Am* put yourself out of pocket; **se mettre en f. de politesse** to go out of one's way to be polite; **faire qch à ses f.** to do sth at one's own expense; **en être pour ses f.** to be out of pocket; *Fig* to waste one's time; **il en a été pour ses f.** he didn't even break even; *Fig* he was let down; *Fig* **j'en suis pour mes f.** it's been a lot of trouble for nothing, I've been wasting my time; *Fig* **faire les f. de qch** to pay the price for sth; **faire les f. de la conversation** to be the main topic of conversation; **j'ai fait les f. de la plaisanterie** the joke was at my expense; **faire les f. d'une politique** to pay the price for a policy; **f. accessoires** incidental costs *or* expenses; **f. d'achat** purchase costs; **f. de camionnage** haulage; **f. de commercialisation** marketing costs; **f. commerciaux** selling costs; **f. de constitution** *(de société)* start-up costs; *(de compte)* set-up fee; *Bourse* **f. de courtage** brokerage, commission; **f. de déplacement** travel *or* travelling expenses; **f. directs** direct costs; **f. de distribution** distribution costs; **f. de douane** customs duties; **f. d'entretien** maintenance costs; **f. d'envoi** carriage costs; *(par courrier)* postage; **f. d'établissement** start-up costs; **f. d'expédition** carriage costs; *(par courrier)* postage; **f. d'exploitation** operating costs; **f. extraordinaires** extraordinary expenses; **f. fixes** fixed costs; **f. de fonctionnement** operating costs; **f. de gestion** running costs; **f. inclus** inclusive of costs; **f. d'installation** initial expenses; **f. de lancement** set-up *or* start-up costs; **f. de liquidation** closing-down costs; **f. de livraison** delivery charges; **f. de main-d'œuvre** labour costs; **f. de manutention** handling charges; **f. de mission** travelling expenses; **f. de port** *(de marchandises)* carriage; *(de lettres, de colis)* postage; **f. de port et d'emballage** postage and packing; **f. de portage** porterage; **f. de production** production costs; **f. professionnels** professional expenses; **f. de publicité** advertising costs; **f. de recouvrement** collection fees; **f. de représentation** entertainment allowance; **f. de sortie** exit charges, back-end load; **f. de transport** carriage; **f. de trésorerie** finance costs; *Can Tél* **appeler qn à f. virés** *Br* to make a reverse-charge call to sb, *Am* to call sb collect

2 *Compta* outgoings; **f. accumulés** accrued expenses; **f. d'amortissement** amortization *or* depreciation charges; **f. bancaires** *ou* **de banque** bank charges; **f. différés** deferred charges; **f. divers** miscellaneous costs; **f. facturables** chargeable expenses; **f. financiers** interest charges; **f. fixes** fixed charges; **f. généraux** *Br* overheads, *Am* overhead; **f. variables** variable costs; **f. de tenue de compte** account charges; *(de compte bancaire)* bank charges; **faux f.** incidental costs

3 *Jur* **f. (de justice)** (legal) costs; **être condamné aux f.** to be ordered to pay costs; **devoir payer les f. d'un procès** to have to pay (legal) costs

4 *Admin* fees; **f. d'abonnement** standing charges; **f. d'adhésion** membership fee; **f. d'administration** administrative costs; *(en échange d'un service)* handling charge; **f. d'administration générale** *Br* general overheads, *Am* general overhead; **f. d'agence** agency fee; **f. d'annulation** cancellation charge; **f. de Bourse** transaction costs; **f. consulaires** consular fees; **f. de dossier** administration charges; **f. d'encaissement** collection charges *or* fees; **f. d'entrée** *(d'une sicav)* front-end *or* front-load fees; *Bourse* commission on purchase of shares; **f. d'inscription** registration fee, membership fee; *Ordinat* set-up charge, set-up fee; **f. de réservation** booking fee, reservation charge; **f. de scolarité** school fees; **f. de tenue de compte** account charges; *(de compte bancaire)* bank charges

frais², fraîche [frɛ, frɛʃ] **ADJ 1** *(un peu froid)* cool, fresh; **l'air est f. ce soir** it's chilly tonight

2 *(rafraîchissant)* cooled, chilled; **des boissons fraîches** cold drinks

3 *(récent ▸ œuf, huître)* fresh; *(▸ encre, peinture)* wet; *(▸ souvenir)* recent, fresh; **œufs f. de ce matin** eggs newly laid this morning; **les croissants sont tout f. de ce matin** the croissants are fresh this morning; **peinture fraîche** *(sur panneau)* wet paint; **il y avait des fleurs fraîches sur la table** there were freshly cut flowers on the table; **j'ai reçu des nouvelles fraîches** I've got some recent news; **la blessure** *ou* **la plaie est encore fraîche** the wound is still fresh; **cette robe n'est plus très fraîche, mais elle fera l'affaire** this dress isn't very fresh any more, but it will do; **de fraîche date** recent, new; **des amis de fraîche date** recent friends

4 *(agréable)* fresh, sweet; **un f. parfum de lavande** a sweet smell of lavender; **avoir la bouche** *ou* **l'haleine fraîche** to have fresh breath

5 *(reposé)* fresh; **envoyer des troupes fraîches sur le front** to send fresh troops to the front; *Fam* **je ne me sens pas trop f. ce matin** I don't feel too good *or* well this morning; **être f. comme un gardon** to be on top form; **f. et dispos, f. comme une rose** as fresh as a daisy

6 *(éclatant)* fresh; **avoir une peau jeune et fraîche** to have young and fresh looking skin; **avoir le teint f.** to have a fresh complexion

7 *Fig (indifférent ▸ accueil, réception)* cool

8 *Fam (en mauvais état)* **être f.** to be in the soup; **me voilà f.!** I'm in a mess!

9 *Can Fam Péj (vaniteux, arrogant)* stuck up, snooty

10 *Écon* **argent f.** ready cash; **avoir de l'argent f.** to have new money

ADV 1 *(nouvellement)* newly; **il est f. débarqué de sa province** he is fresh from the country; **f. émoulu de la faculté de droit** newly graduated from law school **2** *(froid)* **il fait f.** it's cool *or* fresh; **il fait f. dans la maison** it's chilly in the house; **boire f.** *(sur brick, bouteille)* drink chilled; **servir f.** *(sur étiquette)* serve cold *or* chilled

NM 1 *(air frais)* **le f.** the fresh air; **prendre le f.** to take some *or* a breath of (fresh) air; **si on allait prendre un peu le f. à la campagne?** how about going to the countryside for a breath of (fresh) air? **2** *Météo & Naut* **grand f.** gale; **avis de grand f.** gale warning **3** *Can Fam Péj* **faire le f.** to show off□, to be full of oneself□

• **fraîche NF 1** *(heure)* cool (of evening); **attendre la fraîche pour sortir** to wait for it to cool down before going out; **à la fraîche** in the cool evening air; *Can* **prendre la fraîche** *(sortir prendre l'air)* to go for a stroll; *(prendre froid)* to catch a chill **2** *Fam Arg crime* cash

• **au frais ADV 1** *(dans un lieu froid)* in a cool place; **à conserver au f.** *(sur étiquette)* to be kept cool *or* in a cool place, store in a cool place; **mettre le vin au f.** to put the wine to cool **2** *Fam Arg crime (en prison)* in the cooler; **mettre qn au f.** to throw sb in the cooler

• **de frais ADV habillé de f.** wearing a fresh set of clothes *or* clean clothes; **rasé de f.** having recently had a shave

fraisage [frɛzaʒ] **NM 1** *(usinage)* milling **2** *(élargissement ▸ d'un trou)* reaming; *(▸ pour vis)* countersinking **3** *(par le dentiste)* drilling

fraise [frɛz] **NF 1** *(fruit)* strawberry; **f. des bois** wild strawberry; *Fig* **aller aux fraises** to go (off) for a roll in the hay

2 *Fam (visage)* mug; **un coup en pleine f.** a punch in the kisser; **amène ta f.!** get yourself *or très Fam Br* your arse *or Am* your ass over here!; **il est tout le temps à ramener sa f.** he's always sticking his oar in

3 *(pour couper)* mill, cutter; **f. (conique)** countersink

4 *(pour faire ▸ un trou)* reamer; *(▸ un trou de vis)* countersink (bit)

5 *(en odontologie)* drill

6 *Orn* wattle

7 *Culin (de veau)* caul

8 *Hist (collerette)* ruff

9 *Méd* strawberry (mark)

ADJ INV strawberry (pink), strawberry-coloured; **f. écrasée** crushed strawberry

• **à la fraise, aux fraises ADJ** strawberry *(avant n)*, strawberry-flavoured; **tarte aux fraises** strawberry tart

fraiser [4] [freze] **VT 1** *(usiner)* to mill; *(évaser ▸ trou)* to ream; *(▸ trou de vis)* to countersink, to knead **2** *(dent)* to drill

fraiseraie [frɛzrɛ] **NF** strawberry field

fraisier [frezje] **NM 1** *Bot* strawberry plant **2** *Culin* strawberry cream cake

fraisil [frezi(l)] **NM** coal cinders

fraisure [frezyr] **NF** countersink (hole)

framboise [frɑ̃bwaz] **NF 1** *(fruit)* raspberry **2** *(alcool)* raspberry liqueur

ADJ INV raspberry *(avant n)*

framboisier [frɑ̃bwazje] **NM 1** *Bot* raspberry cane **2** *Culin* raspberry cream cake

franc¹ [frɑ̃] **NM** *(monnaie)* franc; *Anciennement* **ancien/nouveau f.** old/new franc; *Anciennement* **f. belge** Belgian franc; *Anciennement* **f. français** French franc; *Anciennement* **f. luxembourgeois** Luxembourg franc; **f. suisse** Swiss franc; **f. CFA** = currency used in former French colonies in Africa; **f. CFP** = currency used in former French colonies in the Pacific area; **f. constant** constant *or* inflation-adjusted francs; **exprimé en francs courants** in real terms; **f. or** gold value of the franc; **f. pacifique** = currency used in former French colonies in the Pacific area; *Anciennement* **f. symbolique** nominal sum; *Anciennement* **un f. symbolique de dommages et intérêts** token damages; *Anciennement* **f. vert** green franc; **je l'ai eu pour trois francs six sous** I got it for next to nothing; *Anciennement* **le f. fort** = the policy of the French government of not devaluing the franc, whatever the pressure

> **LE FRANC**
>
> On 17 February 2002, the French franc ceased to be legal tender in France as it was replaced by the euro – one euro being worth exactly 6.55957 French francs. When referring to the value of very expensive things, such as property, it is common for people still to talk in francs. The situation is further complicated by the fact that some older people still think in terms of "anciens francs" (old francs), which were replaced by the "nouveau franc" (new franc) in 1960, one new franc being worth 100 old francs.

franc², franche [frɑ̃, frɑ̃ʃ] **ADJ 1** *(honnête ▸ réponse)* frank, honest; *(▸ conversation)* frank, candid; **un rire f.** an open laugh; **un regard f.** an open look; **sois f. avec moi** be honest *or* frank with me; **il a l'air f.** he looks like an honest person, he has an honest look (about him); **être f. comme l'or** to be as honest as the day is long; **être f. du collier** to be straightforward; **sa réponse a au moins le mérite d'être franche** at least he/she answered frankly *or* candidly; **jouer f. jeu (avec qn)** to play fair (with sb); **il n'a pas joué f. jeu** he didn't play fair, he played dirty

2 *(pur)* strong; *(rupture)* clean; **un rouge f.** a strong red

3 *(avant le nom) (parfait, extrême)* utter; **un f. scélérat, une franche canaille** a downright scoundrel;

l'ambiance n'était pas à la franche gaieté the atmosphere wasn't exactly a happy one; **rencontrer une franche hostilité** to encounter outright hostility; **huit jours francs** eight clear days

4 *Agr* **terre franche** loam

5 *Jur* **le jugement est exécutable au bout de trois jours francs** the decision of the court to be carried out within three clear days

6 *Com & Fin (gratuit)* free; **port f.** free port; **f. de tout droit** duty-free, free of duty; **f. d'avarie commune** free of general average, FGA; **f. d'avarie particulière** free of particular average, FPA; **f. de casse** free of breakage; **f. de douane** duty paid; **f. d'impôts** tax free, free of tax; **f. de port** carriage paid, carriage free; **f. de port (et d'emballage)** postage paid; **f. de toute avarie** free of average; *Hist* **ville franche** free city; **zone franche** free zone

ADV parlons f. let's be frank (with each other); **je préfère te parler f.** I prefer to be frank with you

franc[3], franque [frɑ̃, frɑ̃k] *Hist* **ADJ** Frankish
• **Franc, Franque NM,F** Frank

français, -e [frɑ̃sɛ, -ez] **ADJ** French; **c'est une attitude bien française** that's a typically French attitude

ADV acheter f. to buy French; **rouler/boire/manger f.** to drive French cars/drink French wine/eat French food

NM *(langue)* French; **en bon f.** in proper French; **parler f.** to speak French; *(correctement)* to speak properly; **f. langue étrangère** French as a foreign language; *Fam* **tu ne comprends pas le f.?** ≃ don't you understand (plain) English?
• **Français, -e NM,F** Frenchman, *f* Frenchwoman; **les F.** *(la population)* French people, the French; *(les hommes)* Frenchmen; **les Françaises** French women; **le F. n'aime pas...** the average Frenchman *or* French person doesn't like...
• **à la française ADJ** *(jardin, parquet)* French, French-style **ADV** (in) the French way; **imprimer à la française** to print portrait

franc-bord [frɑ̃bɔr] *(pl* **francs-bords)** **NM** *Naut* freeboard

franc-bourgeois [frɑ̃burʒwa] *(pl* **francs-bourgeois)** **NM** *Hist* freeman

France [frɑ̃s] **NF la F.** France; **les vins de F.** French wines; **l'histoire de F.** French history, the history of France; *Fig* **la F. d'en bas** the French underclass; *TV* **F. 2** = French state-owned television channel; *TV* **F. 3** = French state-owned television channel; *Télécom* **F. Télécom** = state-owned company which runs all telecommunications services, until 1991 part of the PTT; *TV* **F. Télévision** = the state-owned television channels France 2, France 3 and La Cinquième
• **vieille France ADJ INV être** *ou* **faire (très) vieille F.** to be rather old-fashioned

France-Infos [frɑ̃sɛ̃fo] **NF** = 24-hour radio news station

France-Inter [frɑ̃sɛ̃tɛr] **NF** = radio station broadcasting mainly current affairs programmes, interviews and debates

Francfort [frɑ̃kfɔr] **NM F. (sur-le-Main)** Frankfurt (am Main)

franche [frɑ̃ʃ] *voir* **franc[2]**

franchement [frɑ̃ʃmɑ̃] **ADV 1** *(sincèrement)* frankly; **parlons f.** let's be frank; **je vais te parler f.** I'll be frank with you; **pour vous parler f., je ne sais pas de quoi il s'agit** to be honest with you, I don't know what it's all about; **f., je ne sais que faire** I honestly don't know what to do; **écoute, f., tu crois vraiment qu'il le fera?** listen, do you honestly think he'll do it?; **il me l'a dit f.** he told me openly

2 *(sans équivoque)* clearly, definitely; **il a pris f. parti pour son Premier ministre** he came down unequivocally on the side of his Prime Minister

3 *(résolument)* boldly; **appuie f. sur le bouton** press firmly on the button; **ils y sont allés f.** *(dans un projet)* they got right down to it; *(dans une conversation, dans une négociation)* they didn't mince words

4 *(vraiment)* really; **elle est devenue f. jolie** she became really pretty; **il est f. insupportable** he's downright unbearable; **j'en suis f. dégoûté** I'm absolutely sick of it; **non, mais f.!** no, honestly *or* really!; **tu as de ces idées, f.!** the ideas you have, honestly *or* really!

franchir [32] [frɑ̃ʃir] **VT 1** *(passer par-dessus* ▸ *barrière, mur)* to get over; *(*▸ *rapides)* to shoot, to cross; **la panthère franchit le mur d'un seul bond** the panther cleared *or* jumped over the wall in one bound; *Fig* **f. un obstacle** to get over an obstacle; **f. une difficulté** to overcome a difficulty **2** *(outrepasser* ▸ *ligne, limite, frontière, date)* to cross; *(*▸ *porte)* to pass *or* to walk through; **au moment de f. le seuil, je m'arrêtai** I halted just as I was stepping across the threshold; **f. la ligne d'arrivée** to cross the finishing line; **f. le mur du son** to break the sound barrier; **il y a certaines limites à ne pas f.** there are certain limits which should not be overstepped; *Fig* **f. un cap** to reach a milestone *or* turning point; **f. le cap de la trentaine/cinquantaine** to turn thirty/fifty; **f. la barre des 3 millions** to pass the 3 million mark **3** *(dans le temps)* to last through; **sa renommée a franchi les siècles** his/her reputation has lasted *or* come down intact through the centuries

franchisage [frɑ̃ʃizaʒ] **NM** franchising

franchise [frɑ̃ʃiz] **NF 1** *Com & Fin (exploitation)* franchise agreement; *(exonération)* exemption; **f. de bagages** baggage allowance; **f. douanière** exemption from customs duties; **f. fiscale** tax exemption; **f. de TVA** VAT exemption, zero-rating; **importer/faire entrer qch en f.** to import sth duty-free; **en f. d'impôt** exempt from tax, tax-free; **en f. postale** official paid; **bagages en f.** baggage allowance; **en f. de TVA** VAT-exempt, zero-rated

2 *Com (de commerce)* franchise; **ouvrir un magasin en f.** to open a franchise

3 *(d'une assurance)* *Br* excess, *Am* deductible

4 *(honnêteté)* frankness, straightforwardness; *(franc-parler)* plain speaking, outspokenness; **avec f.** frankly, straightforwardly; **en toute f.** quite frankly, to be honest with you

> Il faut noter que le nom anglais **franchise** ne signifie jamais **sincérité**.

franchisé [frɑ̃ʃize] **ADJ magasin f.** franchise
NM franchisee

franchiser [3] [frɑ̃ʃize] **VT** to franchise

franchiseur, -euse [frɑ̃ʃizœr, -øz] **NM,F** franchiser

franchissable [frɑ̃ʃisabl] **ADJ** *(route)* passable; *(col de montagne)* negotiable; *(obstacle)* surmountable; **un mur difficilement f.** a wall which is difficult to climb

franchissement [frɑ̃ʃismɑ̃] **NM** *(d'une barrière, d'un mur)* getting over; *(d'une rivière)* crossing; *(de fossé)* jumping; *(d'un obstacle, d'une difficulté)* getting over, overcoming

franchouillard, -e [frɑ̃ʃujar, -ard] *Fam Péj* **ADJ** typically French[□]
NM,F typical Frenchman, *f* Frenchwoman[□]

francilien, -enne [fresiljɛ̃, -ɛn] **ADJ** of/from the Île-de-France *(region around Paris)*
• **Francilien, -enne NM,F** = inhabitant of or person from the Île-de-France

francisant, -e [frɑ̃sizɑ̃, -ɑ̃t] **NM,F** French specialist, specialist in French language and literature

francisation [frɑ̃sizasjɔ̃] **NF 1** *Ling (d'un mot)* gallicizing, gallicization **2** *Naut* registering as French

franciscain, -e [frɑ̃siskɛ̃, -ɛn] **ADJ & NM,F** *Rel* Franciscan

franciser [3] [frɑ̃size] **VT 1** *Ling (mot, terme)* to gallicize **2** *Naut (navire)* to register as French

francisque [frɑ̃sisk] **NF** francisc, francesque; **f. gallique** = double-headed battleaxe (symbol of the Vichy government)

francité [frɑ̃site] **NF** Frenchness

franc-maçon, -onne [frɑ̃masɔ̃, -ɔn] *(mpl* **francs-maçons,** *fpl* **franc-maçonnes)** **NM,F** Freemason

franc-maçonnerie [frɑ̃masɔnri] *(pl* **franc-maçonneries)** **NF** *(société secrète)* **la f.** Freemasonry

franc-maçonnique [frɑ̃masɔnik] **ADJ** Masonic

franco [frɑ̃ko] **ADV 1** *Com (dans un envoi)* **f. (de port)** carriage paid; **livraison f. frontière française** delivered free as far as the French border; **livré f.** delivered free; **échantillons f. sur demande** free samples available on request; **f. allège** free over side; **f. à bord** FOB, fob; **f. (à) domicile** delivery free, carriage paid; **f. d'emballage** free of packing charges; **f. de douane** free of customs duty; **f. frontière** free at frontier; **f. gare** free on rail; **f. gare de réception** free on rail; **f. le long du navire** free alongside ship; **f. long du bord** free alongside ship; **f. long du quai** free alongside quay; **f. de port et d'emballage** postage and packing paid; **f. rendu** free at; **f. de tous frais** free of all charges; **f. transporteur** free carrier; **f. wagon** free on rail, FOR **2** *Fam (franchement)* **y aller f.** to go straight *or* right ahead; **elle lui a dit ce qu'elle pensait de lui et elle y est allée f.** she told him what she thought of him and she didn't mince her words

franco-allemand [frɑ̃koalmɑ̃] *(pl* **franco-allemands)** **ADJ** Franco-German

franco-britannique [frɑ̃kobritanik] *(pl* **franco-britanniques)** **ADJ** Anglo-French

franco-canadien, -enne [frɑ̃kokanadjɛ̃, -ɛn] *(mpl* **franco-canadiens,** *fpl* **franco-canadiennes)** **ADJ** French Canadian
NM *Ling* Canadian French

franco-français, -e [frɑ̃kofrɑ̃sɛ, -ɛz] *(mpl* **franco-français,** *fpl* **franco-françaises)** **ADJ** pure French; **une entreprise franco-française** a hundred per cent French-owned company

francophile [frɑ̃kɔfil] **ADJ** Francophil, Francophile
NMF Francophile

francophilie [frɑ̃kɔfili] **NF** love of (all) things French

francophobe [frɑ̃kɔfɔb] **ADJ** Francophobe
NMF Francophobe

francophobie [frɑ̃kɔfɔbi] **NF** Francophobia, dislike of (all) things French

francophone [frɑ̃kɔfɔn] **ADJ** Francophone, French-speaking
NMF Francophone, French speaker

francophonie [frɑ̃kɔfɔni] **NF la f.** = the speaking and promotion of French around the world

franc-parler [frɑ̃parle] *(pl* **francs-parlers)** **NM** outspokenness; **il a son f.** he doesn't mince (his) words

franc-tireur [frɑ̃tirœr] *(pl* **francs-tireurs)** **NM 1** *Mil* franc-tireur, irregular (soldier) **2** *(indépendant)* maverick

frange [frɑ̃ʒ] **NF 1** *(de cheveux)* *Br* fringe, *Am* bangs

2 *(de tissu)* fringe

3 *(minorité)* fringe; **la f. des indécis** the waverers

4 *(bordure)* (fringed) edge
• **à franges ADJ** fringed

frangeant [frɑ̃ʒɑ̃] *voir* **récif**

franger [17] [frɑ̃ʒe] **VT** *(vêtement, tissu)* to (edge with a) fringe

frangin [frɑ̃ʒɛ̃] **NM** *Fam* bro, brother[□]

frangine [frɑ̃ʒin] **NF** *Fam* **1** *(sœur)* sis, sister[□] **2** *(femme)* chick

frangipane [frɑ̃ʒipan] **NF 1** *Culin (crème, gâteau)* frangipane **2** *(fruit)* frangipani

frangipanier [frɑ̃ʒipanje] **NM** *Bot* frangipani (tree)

franglais [frɑ̃glɛ] **NM** Franglais

franque [frɑ̃k] *voir* **franc[3]**

franquette [frɑ̃kɛt] **NF** *Fam* **à la bonne f.** simply[□], informally[□]; **recevoir qn à la bonne f.** to have sb round for a simple meal (among friends)[□]; **on mangera à la bonne f.** we'll have a simple meal[□]

franquisme [frɑ̃kism] **NM** Francoism

franquiste [frɑ̃kist] **ADJ** pro-Franco
NMF Franco supporter

frappadingue [frapadɛ̃g] **ADJ** *Fam* crazy, *Br* bonkers, crackers

frappant, -e [frapɑ̃, -ɑ̃t] **ADJ** *(ressemblance, exemple)* striking

frappe [frap] **NF 1** *(d'une secrétaire, d'un pianiste)* touch; *(sur une machine à écrire)* typing; *(sur un ordinateur)* keying; **donner son texte à la f.** to give one's text (in) to be typed; **vitesse de f.** typing/keying speed; *Ordinat* **f. au kilomètre** continuous input; *Ordinat* **f. en continu** type-ahead; **f. de touche** keystroke

2 *(copie)* typed copy, typescript; **lire la première f.** to read the top copy

3 *(d'une monnaie)* minting
4 *Sport (d'un footballeur)* shot; *(d'un boxeur)* punch
5 *très Fam (voyou)* hooligan, hoodlum; **une petite f.** a young hooligan
• **frappes** NFPL *(bombardements)* strikes; **frappes aériennes** air-strikes; **frappes militaires** military strikes; **frappes de précision** precision strikes

frappé, -e [frape] ADJ **1** *(boisson)* iced; **café f.** iced coffee; **champagne f.** chilled champagne; **servir bien f.** *(sur étiquette)* serve chilled **2** *Fam (fou)* crazy, *Br* bonkers, crackers **3** *(bien exprimé)* **parole bien frappée** well-chosen word

frappement [frapmɑ̃] NM knock, knocking *(UNCOUNT)*

frapper [3] [frape] VT **1** *(battre ▸ adversaire)* to hit, to strike; **je ne frappe jamais un enfant** I never hit *or* smack a child; **f. qn à la tête** to hit sb on the head; **frappé à mort** mortally wounded
2 *(donner)* to hit, to strike; *Fig* **f. un grand coup** *ou* **un coup décisif** to strike a decisive blow; *Théât* **f. les trois coups** = to give three knocks to announce the start of a theatrical performance
3 *(percuter)* to hit; **f. les touches d'un clavier** to strike the keys on a keyboard; **f. la terre** *ou* **le sol du pied** to stamp (one's foot); **les grêlons frappaient durement la fenêtre** hailstones were lashing the windowpane; **f. légèrement** to tap; **être frappé d'une balle au front** to be hit *or* struck by a bullet in the forehead; *Can Fam Fig* **f. un nœud** to hit a snag
4 *(affecter)* to strike *or* to bring down, to hit; **être frappé par une maladie** to be struck down by a disease; **être frappé par le malheur** to be struck by misfortune; **être frappé de mutisme** to be struck dumb; **f. qn d'étonnement** to strike sb with amazement; **le deuil/mal qui nous frappe** the bereavement/pain we are suffering
5 *(s'appliquer à ▸ sujet: loi, sanction, taxe)* to hit; **un châtiment qui frappe les coupables** a punishment which falls on the guilty
6 *(surprendre)* to strike; *(impressionner)* to upset, to shock; **un style qui frappe l'œil/l'oreille** a striking visual/musical style; **ce qui me frappe chez lui, c'est sa désinvolture** what strikes me about him is his offhandedness; **ce qui m'a frappé le plus, c'était son sang-froid** what struck *or* impressed me most was his/her coolness; **j'ai été frappé de sa pâleur** I was shocked by his/her pallor; **être frappé de stupeur** to be stupefied *or* struck dumb
7 f. qn/qch de *(le soumettre à)* **f. qn d'une interdiction de séjour** to ban sb; **f. l'alcool d'un impôt spécial** to put a special tax on alcohol
8 *Can (entrer en collision avec)* to hit
9 *Can Fam (trouver ▸ emploi, affaire)* to land
10 *(refroidir)* to ice; *(boisson)* to chill; **f. le champagne** to put the champagne on ice; **faut-il ou non f. le champagne?** should champagne be chilled or not?
11 *Métal* to stamp; *(médaille)* to strike; *(pièces de monnaie)* to strike, to mint; *Fig* **frappé au coin de** bearing the mark *or* hallmark of; **une remarque frappée au coin du bon sens** a remark showing common sense
12 *(lettre)* to type; *Ordinat* to key; *Ordinat* **f. au kilomètre** to input continuously
USAGE ABSOLU *Hum* **le voleur de parapluies a encore frappé!** the umbrella thief strikes again!
VI **1** *(pour entrer)* to knock; **f. à la porte/fenêtre** to knock on the door/window; **on a frappé** someone knocked at the door; **f. doucement** *ou* **légèrement à la porte** to tap on *or* at the door; **la prochaine fois vous pourrez entrer sans f.** next time you can come in without knocking; *Fig* **f. à toutes les portes** to try every avenue; *Fig* **f. à la bonne/mauvaise porte** to go to the right/wrong place
2 *(pour exprimer un sentiment)* **f. des mains** *ou* **dans ses mains** to clap one's hands; **f. du poing sur la table** to bang one's fist on the table; **f. du pied** to stamp one's foot
3 *(cogner)* to strike; **les branches frappent contre la vitre** the branches are tapping against the windowpane; **f. dur** *ou* **sec** to strike hard; **f. fort** to hit hard; *Fig* to hit hard, to act decisively; *Fig* **f. à la tête** to aim for the top
4 *Fam (agir)* to strike; **le gang a encore frappé** the gang has struck again; **la grippe va f. durement** the flu will hit everyone hard
5 *(footballeur)* to shoot, to take a shot; **il frappe du pied gauche** he kicks with his left foot
VPR **se frapper 1** *(emploi réfléchi)* to hit oneself; **se f. la poitrine** to beat one's chest; **se f. le front** to slap one's forehead
2 *(emploi réciproque)* to hit one another *or* each other
3 *Fam (s'inquiéter)* to get (oneself) worked up, to panic□; **ne te frappe pas pour si peu!** don't get all worked up about such a little thing!
4 *Can (entrer en collision)* to collide

frappeur [frapœr] ADJ M *voir* **esprit**
NM *Métal* striker; *(de papier peint)* embosser

fraser [3] [fraze] = **fraiser**

frasque [frask] NF escapade, prank; **des frasques de jeunesse** youthful indiscretions; **faire des frasques** to get up to mischief *or* to no good

fraternel, -elle [fratɛrnɛl] ADJ brotherly, fraternal; **amour f.** brotherly love; **geste f.** friendly gesture; **ils sont unis par des liens quasi fraternels** they're almost as close as brothers

fraternellement [fratɛrnɛlmɑ̃] ADV fraternally; **agir f. envers qn** to act in a brotherly way towards sb

fraternisation [fratɛrnizasjɔ̃] NF fraternizing; **la f. entre les peuples** fraternization between peoples

fraterniser [3] [fratɛrnize] VI to fraternize

fraternité [fratɛrnite] NF *(lien)* brotherhood, fraternity; **f. d'armes** brotherhood of arms; **on constate une certaine f. d'esprit entre eux** you can see a certain kinship of spirit between them

fratricide [fratrisid] ADJ *(guerre, haine)* fratricidal
NMF *(meurtrier)* fratricide
NM *(meurtre)* fratricide

fraude [frod] NF **1** *(tromperie)* fraud; **la f. aux examens** cheating at exams **2** *Jur* **f. électorale** electoral fraud, vote *or* ballot rigging; **f. fiscale** tax evasion *or* fraud; **f. sur les produits** fraudulent trading
• **en fraude** ADV *(vendre)* fraudulently; **entrer/sortir en f.** to sneak in/out; **passer qch en f.** to smuggle sth in; **il entra en f. dans le pays** he entered the country illegally *or* unlawfully

frauder [3] [frode] VT *(état)* to defraud; **f. le fisc** to evade taxation; **f. la douane** to defraud customs, to smuggle
VI to cheat; **f. à** *ou* **dans un examen** to cheat at an exam; **f. sur le poids** to cheat on the weight, to give short measure; **il a l'habitude de f. dans le métro** he always avoids buying a ticket for the *Br* underground *or Am* subway

fraudeur, -euse [frodœr, -øz] ADJ *(attitude, tempérament)* cheating
NM,F *(envers le fisc)* tax evader; *(à la douane)* smuggler; *(à un examen)* cheat; *(dans le métro, dans le bus)* fare-dodger

frauduleuse [frodyløz] *voir* **frauduleux**

frauduleusement [frodyløzmɑ̃] ADV fraudulently; **faire entrer/sortir qch f.** to smuggle sth in/out

frauduleux, -euse [frodylø, -øz] ADJ fraudulent; **édition frauduleuse** pirate edition

frayer [11] [frɛje] VT **1** *(route, voie)* to clear; **f. un chemin en abattant les arbres** to clear a path by felling the trees; *Fig* **f. la voie à qn/qch** to pave the way for sb/sth **2** *(sujet: cerf ▸ tête)* to scrape, to rub, to fray; *Vét (sujet: cheval)* to gall
VI *Ich* to spawn
• **frayer avec** VT IND to associate with; **je ne fraye pas avec des gens de cette espèce** I don't mix with that sort of people
VPR **se frayer se f. un passage** to clear a way (for oneself); **se f. un chemin** *ou* **un passage dans la foule** to force *or* to push one's way through the crowd; *Fig* **se f. un chemin** *ou* **une route vers la gloire** to work one's way towards fame

frayère [frɛjɛr] NF spawning ground *(of fish)*

frayeur [frɛjœr] NF fright; **avoir des frayeurs nocturnes** to suffer from night terrors; **faire une f. à qn** to give sb a fright; **vous me donnez des frayeurs** you're getting me worried; **j'ai eu une f., j'ai cru que j'avais oublié mes clés** I had *or* got a fright, I thought I had forgotten my keys; **se remettre de ses frayeurs** to recover from one's fright

FRBG [ɛfɛrbeʒe] NM *(abrév* **fonds pour risques bancaires généraux***)* FGBR

fredaine [frədɛn] NF escapade, prank; **faire des fredaines** to get into *or* up to mischief; *(amoureuses)* to carry on

fredonnement [frədɔnmɑ̃] NM humming

fredonner [3] [frədɔne] VT *(air, chanson)* to hum
VI to hum

free-jazz [fridʒaz] NM INV *Mus* free jazz

free-lance [frilɑ̃s] *(pl* **free-lances***)* ADJ INV freelance
NMF freelance, freelancer
NM freelancing, freelance work; **travailler** *ou* **être en f., faire du f.** to work on a freelance basis *or* as a freelancer, to freelance

freesia [frezja] NM freesia

freestyle [fristajl] NM *(au ski, snowboard, skateboard)* freestyle

freeware [friwer] NM *Ordinat* freeware; **freewares** freeware programs

freezer [frizœr] NM freezer compartment

frégate [fregat] NF **1** *Orn* frigate bird **2** *Naut* frigate

frein [frɛ̃] NM **1** *Aut* brake; **actionner les freins** to brake; *Fam* **mettre le f.** to pull on the handbrake; *Fig* **mettre un f. à qch** to curb sth; **mettre un f. à la montée de la colère/du chômage** to stem *or* to check *or* to curb the rising tide of anger/rising unemployment; *Fig* **f. à l'expansion** brake on growth; **donner un brusque coup de f.** to brake sharply *or* suddenly; *Fig* **un coup de f. à la création d'entreprises** a check *or* curb on the creation of new companies; *Fig* **c'est un coup de f. à l'économie** this will act as a brake on the economy; **f. à air comprimé** airbrake; **freins arrière** rear brakes; **freins assistés** power brakes; **freins avant** front brakes; **freins à bande** band brakes; *Can* **f. à bras** handbrake, *Am* parking brake; **f. à disque** disc brake; **f. sur échappement** exhaust brake; **f. d'embrayage** clutch stop; *Écon* **f. fiscal** fiscal drag; **f. hydraulique** hydraulic brake; **f. à main** handbrake; **f. moteur** engine brake; **utilisez votre f. moteur** *(sur panneau)* engage low gear; **f. à pédale** footbrake; **f. au pied** footbrake; **f. secondaire** emergency brake; **f. de stationnement** handbrake, *Am* parking brake; **f. à tambour** drum brake; **f. sur transmission** transmission brake; **f. à vide** vacuum brake **2** *Anat* frenum **3** *(mors)* bit; **ronger son f.** *(cheval) & Fig(personne)* to champ at the bit
• **sans frein** ADJ unbridled

freinage [frenaʒ] NM **1** *(action)* braking; **distance de f.** braking distance; **traces de f.** skid marks; *Aviat* **parachute de f.** brake parachute **2** *(système)* brake system, brakes **3** *(de l'inflation)* curbing; *(de production)* cutting back; *(des importations, des salaires)* reduction

freiner [4] [frene] VT **1** *(ralentir ▸ véhicule)* to slow down; *(▸ évolution)* to check; **des arbres ont freiné sa chute** trees broke his/her fall **2** *(amoindrir ▸ impatience)* to curb; *(▸ enthousiasme)* to dampen; *(▸ inflation, production)* to curb, to check; *(▸ importations, salaires)* to reduce **3** *(personne)* to restrain
VI *(conducteur, auto)* to brake; **ta voiture freine bien/mal** your car brakes are good/bad; *Fig* **il voudrait moderniser l'usine mais son père freine des quatre fers** he'd like to modernize the factory, but his father's holding him back
VPR **se freiner** *Fig* to keep oneself in check, to restrain oneself

freinte [frɛ̃t] NF *Com* = loss in volume or weight *(during transit or manufacture)*

frelatage [frəlataʒ] NM adulteration

frelater [3] [frəlate] VT *(lait, vin, huile)* to adulterate

frêle [frɛl] ADJ **1** *(fragile ▸ corps, santé)* frail, fragile; *(▸ voix)* thin, reedy; *(▸ embarcation, cabane)* flimsy, frail **2** *(ténu ▸ espoir)* frail, flimsy

frelon [frəlɔ̃] NM hornet

freluquet [frəlykɛ] NM **1** *Fam (homme chétif)* pipsqueak, (little) runt **2** *Littéraire (prétentieux)* (young) whippersnapper

frémir [32] [fremir] VI 1 *(trembler ▸ de froid)* to shiver, to shudder; *(▸ de peur)* to shake, to tremble, to shudder, to quake; **je frémis encore en y pensant** thinking about it still sends shivers down my spine; **f. de colère** to shake *or* to tremble *or* to quiver with anger; **f. de plaisir/de joie** to quiver with pleasure/happiness 2 *Littéraire (vibrer ▸ tige, herbe)* to quiver, to tremble; *(▸ surface d'un lac)* to ripple; *(▸ vitres)* to shake, to rattle; *(▸ feuilles)* to rustle; *(▸ vent)* to sigh; **l'air frémissait encore des échos d'une flûte lointaine** the air was still vibrating to the echoes of a distant flute 3 *(avant l'ébullition)* to simmer

frémissant, -e [fremisã, -ãt] ADJ 1 *(avant l'ébullition)* simmering 2 *Littéraire (feuilles)* quivering, rustling; *(surface d'un lac)* quivering; *(chair)* quivering, trembling 3 *(en émoi)* quivering, trembling; **une sensibilité frémissante** a trembling sensitivity; **être f. de colère** to be shaking *or* trembling *or* quivering with anger; **être f. de plaisir/joie** to be quivering with pleasure/happiness

frémissement [fremismã] NM 1 *(d'indignation, de colère)* quiver, shiver, shudder; *(de peur)* shudder; **un f. de colère** a quiver of anger; **un f. parcourut le public** a shudder ran through the audience; **avec un f. de crainte** shaking *or* quaking with fear; **avec un f. dans la voix** with a trembling *or* shaky voice 2 *Littéraire (des feuilles)* rustling; *(de la surface d'un lac)* rippling; *(du vent)* sighing; **le f. des champs de blé sous la brise** the wheatfields quivering in the breeze 3 *(avant l'ébullition)* simmer, simmering

frênaie [frene] NF ash plantation

french cancan [frenʃkãkã] *(pl* **french cancans***)* NM (French) cancan

frêne [fren] NM 1 *(arbre)* ash (tree) 2 *(bois)* ash

frénésie [frenezi] NF frenzy; **f. d'achat** shopping *or* buying spree; **être pris d'une f. de voyages** to have a strong urge to travel, to have the travel bug; **avec f.** frantically, frenetically, wildly; **travailler/parler avec f.** to work/talk frenziedly

frénétique [frenetik] ADJ *(agitation, hurlement)* frantic; *(activité)* frenzied, frantic; *(joie, passion)* frenzied; *(rythme)* frenetic, frenzied

frénétiquement [frenetikmã] ADV frantically, frenetically, wildly

Fréon® [freɔ̃] NM Freon®

fréquemment [frekamã] ADV frequently, often

fréquence [frekãs] NF 1 *(périodicité)* frequency; **quelle est la f. des trains sur cette ligne?** how many trains a day run on this line?; *Mktg* **f. d'achat** purchase frequency; **f. d'utilisation** usage frequency

2 *Méd* **f. du pouls** *ou* **cardiaque** fast pulse rate

3 *(en acoustique)* frequency; *(de son)* tone; *Tél* wavelength, (wave) band, frequency; **basse/moyenne/haute f.** low/middle/high frequency; **f. cumulée** cumulative frequency; **f. porteuse** carrier; **f. radio** radio frequency; **f. réglée** adjusted frequency; **f. relative** relative frequency; **f. du signal** signal frequency; **f. sonore** audio frequency; **f. vocale** vocal frequency

4 *(en statistique)* frequency; **f. absolue** absolute frequency; **f. cumulée** cumulative frequency

5 *Ordinat* **f. d'horloge** clock speed *or* frequency; **f. de rafraîchissement** refresh rate

fréquent, -e [frekã, -ãt] ADJ 1 *(répété)* frequent; **peu f.** infrequent; **il est f. de voir des jeunes couples divorcer** you frequently *or* often see young couples getting divorced; **il est peu f. que...** it is not very often that... 2 *Méd* **pouls f.** fast pulse

fréquentable [frekãtabl] ADJ **sa famille n'est guère f.** his/her family isn't exactly the kind you'd care to associate with; **c'est un endroit bien peu f.** it's not the sort of place you'd like to be seen in

fréquentatif, -ive [frekãtatif, -iv] ADJ *Ling* frequentative

fréquentation [frekãtasjɔ̃] NF 1 *(d'un lieu)* frequenting (**de** of); **f. des théâtres** theatre-going; **la f. des cinémas a baissé** cinema-going has decreased 2 *(relation)* acquaintance; **quelles sont ses fréquentations?** who does he/she associate with?; **avoir de mauvaises fréquentations** to keep bad company; **surveillez ses fréquentations** keep a watch on the company he/she keeps; **ce ne sont pas des fréquentations pour une jeune fille** these are not the sort of people a young girl should be associating with 3 *Littéraire (lecture)* **la f. des bons auteurs/de la littérature italienne** acquaintance with the great authors/Italian literature, reading good books/Italian literature

fréquentative [frekãtativ] *voir* **fréquentatif**

fréquenté, -e [frekãte] ADJ busy; **un endroit bien/mal f.** a place with a good/bad reputation; **c'est un café très f. par les jeunes** it's a café that's very popular with young people; **un endroit peu f.** a place hardly anyone ever goes to

fréquenter [3] [frekãte] VT 1 *(lieu)* to frequent

2 *(voir régulièrement)* to see frequently, to associate with; **nous ne nous fréquentons plus beaucoup** we don't see much of each other any more; **je fréquente peu ce genre de personnes** I don't associate much with that type of person; **qui fréquente-t-il?** who does he go around with?, what company does he keep?; **je t'interdis de f. les voisins** I forbid you to speak to the neighbours; **parmi tous ceux que je fréquente** amongst all my acquaintances

3 *Vieilli (courtiser)* **elle fréquente mon frère depuis un an** she's been going out with my brother for a year

4 *Littéraire (lire)* **f. les bons écrivains/la littérature italienne** to read good books/Italian literature

USAGE ABSOLU *Fam Vieilli* **il paraît qu'elle fréquente** there are rumours she's courting

VI *Arch ou Littéraire* **f. chez qn/dans des familles riches** to be on visiting terms with sb/with wealthy people

VPR **se fréquenter** *Vieilli* **ils se fréquentent depuis deux ans** they've been going out for two years; **ils se fréquentent assez peu** they don't see much of each other

frère [frer] NM 1 *(dans une famille)* brother; **tu es un (vrai) f. pour moi** you're like a brother to me; **mon grand/petit f.** *(de deux)* my older/younger brother; *(de plusieurs)* my oldest/youngest brother; **tu vas avoir un petit f.** you're going to have a little *or* baby brother; **se ressembler comme des frères** to be like two peas (in a pod); **s'aimer comme des frères** to love each other like brothers; **en frères** as brothers; **partager en frères** to share fairly; **ce sont des frères ennemis** a friendly rivalry exists between them; **f. aîné/cadet** older/younger brother; **f. jumeau** twin brother; **f. de lait** foster brother; **f. de sang** blood brother; *Fam* **f. Trois-points** freemason

2 *(compagnon)* brother; *Fam* **salut, vieux f.!** hello, old pal!; *Fam Hum* **j'ai un bougeoir qui a perdu son f.** I've got one candle-holder but I've lost its companion; **frères d'armes** brothers in arms; **frères de race** brothers

3 *Rel* brother, friar; **aller à l'école chez les frères** to go to a Catholic boys' school; **mes bien chers frères** dearly beloved brethren; **f. lai** lay brother; **le f. Dominique** Brother Dominic

4 *(au sein d'une communauté)* brother

5 *(comme adj) (groupe, parti, pays)* sister *(avant n)*

frérot [frero] NM *Fam* kid brother, little brother▫

fresque [fresk] NF 1 *Beaux-Arts* fresco; **peindre à f.** to paint in fresco 2 *(description)* panorama, detailed picture; **ce roman est une f. historique** this novel is a historical epic; **le film est une f. sociale sur l'Italie des années 50** the film is a social portrait of Italy in the 50s

fresquiste [freskist] NMF fresco painter

fressure [fresyr] NF *(d'un veau, mouton etc)* pluck; *Culin* fry

fret[1] [frɛ] NM 1 *(chargement ▸ d'un avion, d'un navire)* cargo, freight; *(▸ d'un camion)* load; **avion de f.** charter aircraft; **donner à f.** to freight; **prendre à f.** to charter; **f. aérien** airfreight; **expédier par f. aérien** to airfreight; **f. d'aller** outward freight; **f. express** express freight; **f. à forfait** through freight; **f. intérieur** inland freight; **f. maritime** sea *or* ocean freight; **f. par conteneur** containerized freight; **f. payé** freight paid; **f. au poids** freight by weight; **f. de retour** home freight 2 *(prix ▸ par air, mer)* freight (charges), freightage; *(▸ par route)* carriage; **payer le f.** to pay the freight charges *or* freightage

fret[2], **frette** [frɛt] *Can Fam* ADJ freezing

ADV **il fait f.** it's freezing cold

NM **le f.** the cold▫; **il fait un f. noir** it's freezing cold *or Br* baltic

fréter [18] [frete] VT *(avion)* to charter; *(navire)* to freight; *(camionnette)* to hire

fréteur [fretœr] NM freighter; *(armateur)* shipowner; **f. et affréteur** owner and charterer

frétillant, -e [fretijã, -ãt] ADJ *(ver, poisson)* wriggling; *(queue)* wagging; *Fig (personne)* lively; *Fig* **tout f. d'impatience** quivering with impatience

frétillement [fretijmã] NM *(de la queue)* wagging; *(de vers, de poissons)* wriggling; *Fig* fidgeting

frétiller [3] [fretije] VI *(ver, poisson)* to wriggle; *(queue)* to wag; **le chien frétille de la queue** the dog is wagging its tail; *Fig* **il frétille d'impatience/de joie** he's quivering with impatience/joy

fretin [frətɛ̃] NM fry; *Fig* **(menu) f.** small fry

frette[1] [fret] NF 1 *Tech* hoop, collar; **f. de moyeu** nave ring 2 *Mus* fret

frette[2] [fret] NF *Archit & Hér* fret

frette[3] [fret] ADJ *voir* **fret**[2]

freudien, -enne [frødjɛ̃, -en] ADJ & NM,F Freudian

freudisme [frødism] NM Freudianism

freux [frø] NM *Orn* rook; **colonie de f.** rookery

friabilité [frijabilite] NF *(d'une roche)* friableness, friability; *(d'un biscuit)* crumbliness

friable [frijabl] ADJ *(roche)* crumbly, friable; *(biscuit)* crumbly

friand, -e [frijã, -ãd] ADJ 1 *Vieilli (gourmand)* fond of delicacies 2 **f. de** *(sucreries)* fond of; *Fig* **être f. de compliments** to enjoy receiving compliments

NM 1 *(salé)* ≃ meat pie (made with puff pastry); **f. au fromage** ≃ cheese pie (made with puff pastry) 2 *(sucré)* ≃ almond *Br* biscuit *or Am* cookie

friandise [frijãdiz] NF sweetmeat, (sweet) delicacy, titbit; **aimer les friandises** to have a sweet tooth

Fribourg [fribur] NF *(en Allemagne)* Freiburg; *(en Suisse)* Fribourg

fric [frik] NM *Fam* cash, dough; **gagner plein de f.** to make loads of money; **il est bourré de f.** he's loaded; **j'ai plus de f.!** I'm broke *or Br* skint!

fricassée [frikase] NF 1 *(ragoût)* fricassee; *Fam Hum* **f. de museaux** exchange of kisses▫ 2 *Belg* ≃ eggs and bacon

fricasser [3] [frikase] VT to fricassee; **faire f. des champignons** to fricassee mushrooms

fricatif, -ive [frikatif, -iv] *Ling* ADJ fricative

• **fricative** NF fricative

fric-frac [frikfrak] NM INV *très Fam* burglary▫, break-in▫

friche [friʃ] NF 1 *Agr* piece of fallow land, fallow; *Fig* **une idée/un projet qui est** *ou* **reste en f.** an idea/a plan which has not yet been taken up 2 *Ind* **f. industrielle** industrial wasteland

• **en friche** ADJ 1 *Agr* **terre en f.** plot of fallow land; **rester** *ou* **être en f.** to lie fallow, to remain uncultivated 2 *(inactif)* unused; **avoir l'esprit en f.** to have intellectual capacities which go unused; **avoir des dons en f.** to have hidden talents; **une idée/un projet qui est** *ou* **reste en f.** an idea/a plan which has not yet been taken up

frichti [friʃti] NM *Fam* 1 *(nourriture) Br* grub, *Am* chow 2 *(repas)* cooked meal▫

fricot [friko] NM *Fam* 1 *(ragoût)* stew▫ 2 *(cuisine) Br* grub, *Am* chow; **faire le f.** to cook▫

fricotage [frikɔtaʒ] NM *Fam Péj* scheming▫

fricoter [3] [frikɔte] *Fam* VT 1 *(cuisiner)* to stew▫ 2 *(manigancer)* to cook up; **je me demande ce qu'il fricote** I wonder what he's up to *or* what he's cooking up

VI 1 *(trafiquer)* to be on the fiddle 2 *(avoir des relations sexuelles)* **ils fricotent ensemble** they're sleeping together

• **fricoter avec** VT IND 1 *(sexuellement)* to knock around with 2 *(être complice de)* to cook something up with

fricoteur, -euse [frikɔtœr, -øz] NM,F *Fam (trafiquant)* fiddler

friction [friksjɔ̃] **NF 1** *(frottement)* chafing **2** *(massage ▸ gén)* rub (down); *(▸ du cuir chevelu)* scalp massage **3** *(désaccord)* friction; **il y a des frictions entre eux** they don't see eye to eye; **cela reste un point de f.** that remains a bone of contention **4** *Géol & Tech* friction; **embrayage à f.** friction clutch; **entraînement par f.** *(d'une imprimante)* friction feed; **réduire les frictions** to reduce friction

frictionnel, -elle [friksjɔnɛl] **ADJ** *Tech* frictional; *(chômage)* temporary

frictionner [3] [friksjɔne] **VT** to rub (down); **f. qn** to rub sb down, to give sb a rubdown; **f. la tête de qn** to massage sb's scalp, to give sb a scalp massage

VPR se frictionner to rub oneself; **frictionne-toi bien** give yourself a good rub down; **se f. le bras/la jambe** to rub one's arm/leg

fridolin [fridɔlɛ̃] **NM** *très Fam* Kraut, Fritz, = offensive term used to refer to a German person; **les fridolins** Jerry

Frigidaire® [friʒidɛr] **NM 1** *(portant la marque)* Frigidaire® (refrigerator) **2** *(appareil quelconque)* refrigerator, fridge; *Fig* **mettre qch au F.** to put sth on the back burner, to shelve sth

frigide [friʒid] **ADJ** frigid; *Littéraire (cœur, caractère)* cold, icy

frigidité [friʒidite] **NF** frigidity

frigo [frigo] **NM** *Fam* **1** *(réfrigérateur)* fridge□ **2** *(chambre froide)* cold room□

frigorification [frigɔrifikasjɔ̃] **NF** refrigerating, refrigeration

frigorifié, -e [frigɔrifje] **ADJ** frozen; *Fam Fig* frozen stiff

frigorifier [9] [frigɔrifje] **VT** to refrigerate; *Fam Fig* **la promenade m'a complètement frigorifié** I'm frozen stiff after that walk

frigorifique [frigɔrifik] **ADJ** refrigerated; **appareil f.** refrigerator; **mélange f.** freezing mixture; **camion f.** refrigerated lorry; **wagon f.** refrigerator van; **entrepôt f.** cold store

NM 1 *(établissement)* cold store **2** *(appareil)* refrigerator

frigoriste [frigɔrist] **NMF** refrigerating engineer

frileuse [friløz] *voir* **frileux**

frileusement [friløzmɑ̃] **ADV s'envelopper f. dans des couvertures** to wrap oneself in blankets

frileux, -euse [frilø, -øz] **ADJ 1** *(qui a froid)* sensitive to (the) cold; **je suis très f.** I really feel the cold **2** *(prudent)* timid, unadventurous **3** *Arch & Littéraire (temps, jour)* cold

NM,F = person who feels the cold

frilosité [frilozite] **NF** *Littéraire* sensitivity to the cold; *Fig* nervousness, hesitancy; **la f. des marchés financiers** the nervousness of the financial markets

frimaire [frimɛr] **NM** = 3rd month of the French Revolutionary calendar (from 22 November to 21 December)

frimas [frima] **NM** *Littéraire* hoar frost

frime [frim] **NF** *Fam* **1** *(fanfaronnade)* **les lunettes noires, c'est pour la f.** sunglasses are just for posing in; **bon, t'arrêtes ta f.?** will you stop showing off!; **tu l'aurais vu avec son nouveau cuir, la f.!** you should have seen him in his new leather jacket, what a poser! **2** *(comportement trompeur)* **c'est de la f.** it's all an act, it's all put on

frimer [3] [frime] **VI** *Fam* to show off, to put on an act

frimeur, -euse [frimœr, -øz] *Fam* **ADJ** *(attitude, ton)* showy

NM,F show-off

frimousse [frimus] **NF 1** *Fam* (sweet) little face□ **2** *Ordinat (smiley)* smiley

fringale [frɛ̃gal] **NF** *Fam* **1** *(faim)* hunger□; **avoir la f.** to be ravenous *or* starving *or* famished; **j'ai une de ces fringales!** I'm starving! **2** *(désir)* **une f. de** a craving for

fringant, -e [frɛ̃gɑ̃, -ɑ̃t] **ADJ 1** *(personne)* dashing; **encore f.** (still) spry; **je ne me sens pas trop f. aujourd'hui** I don't feel too good *or* well today **2** *(cheval)* frisky, spirited

fringue [frɛ̃g] **NF** *Fam* piece of clothing□; **j'ai plus une f. à me mettre** I haven't a thing to wear; **des fringues** clothes□, threads, *Br* gear

fringuer [3] [frɛ̃ge] **VT** *Fam* to dress□; **être bien/mal fringué** to be well/badly dressed□; **elle est fringuée n'importe comment!** she's got no dress sense!

VI *Arch ou Can Fam* to prance about, to skip about

VPR se fringuer *Fam* **1** *(s'habiller)* to get dressed□ **2** *(s'habiller bien)* to do *or* to get oneself up

fripe [frip] **NF la f., les fripes** second-hand clothes

fripé, -e [fripe] **ADJ** *Can Fam* dead beat, *Br* knackered

friper [3] [fripe] **VT 1** *(chiffonner)* to crumple *or* to crease (up); **son pantalon était tout fripé aux genoux** his/her trousers were all creased around the knee **2** *(rider)* **avoir un visage tout fripé** to have crease-marks all over one's face

VPR se friper to crumple, to get crumpled

friperie [fripri] **NF 1** *(boutique)* second-hand clothes *Br* shop *or Am* store **2** *(vêtements)* second-hand clothes

fripier, -ère [fripje, -ɛr] **NM,F** second-hand clothes dealer

fripon, -onne [fripɔ̃, -ɔn] **ADJ** *(enfant)* mischievous, roguish; *(sourire)* roguish

NM,F rogue; **tu n'es qu'un petit f.!** you little rogue!

friponnerie [fripɔnri] **NF** *Vieilli (caractère)* roguery, knavery; *(action)* mischievous prank

fripouille [fripuj] **NF 1** *Péj (scélérat)* rascal, rogue **2** *(ton affectueux)* **(petite) f.!** you little rogue! **3** *Arch (racaille)* rabble, riff-raff

friqué, -e [frike] **ADJ** *Fam (person)* loaded; *(quartier)* rich□, *Br* posh; **c'est un mec vachement f.** the guy's loaded

friquet [frikɛ] **NM** *Orn* tree sparrow

frire [115] [frir] **VT** *Culin* to fry; *(en friteuse, dans un bain d'huile)* to deep-fry; **poisson frit** fried fish

VI to fry; **faire f. des poissons** to fry fish

frisant, -e [frizɑ̃, -ɑ̃t] **ADJ** *(lumière)* oblique

Frisbee® [frizbi] **NM** Frisbee®

Frise [friz] **NF la F.** Friesland

frise [friz] **NF 1** *Archit & Beaux-Arts* frieze **2** *Théât* border **3 f. chronologique** timeline

frisé, -e [frize] **ADJ 1** *(barbe, cheveux)* curly; *(personne)* curly-haired; **être f. comme un mouton** to have curly *or* frizzy hair **2** *(chicorée)* curly

NM,F *Fam* **1** *(personne)* curly-haired person□; *(enfant)* curly-haired child□ **2** *Fam* Kraut, Fritz, *Br* Jerry, = offensive term used to refer to German people

• **frisée NF** *(chicorée)* curly endive

friselis [frizli] **NM** *Littéraire (des feuilles)* rustling; *(de l'eau)* quivering

friser [3] [frize] **VT 1** *(barbe, cheveux)* to curl; **se faire f. (les cheveux)** to have one's hair curled **2** *(effleurer)* to graze, to skim; **le ballon a frisé la vitre** the ball skimmed past the window **3** *(être proche de)* **elle doit f. la quarantaine** she must be getting on for *or* pushing forty; **nous avons frisé la catastrophe** we came within an inch of disaster; **cela frise l'impertinence** it's verging on the impertinent **4** *Métal* to crimp

VI to have curly hair; **f. naturellement** to have naturally curly hair

frisette [frizɛt] **NF** *(de cheveux)* small curl; **avoir des frisettes** to have curly hair

frison¹ [frizɔ̃] **NM** *(de cheveux)* curl; *(de bois, de papier etc)* shaving

frison², -onne [frizɔ̃, -ɔn] **ADJ** Friesian, Frisian; **vache frisonne** Friesian cow

NM *(langue)* Friesian, Frisian

• **Frison, -onne NM,F** Frisian

• **frisonne NF** *(vache)* **frisonne (pie-noire)** *Br* Friesian, *Am* Holstein

frisotter [3] [frizɔte] **VT** to frizz

VI to be frizzy; **la pluie fait f. mes cheveux** the rain makes my hair go all frizzy

frisquet, -ette [friskɛ, -ɛt] **ADJ** *Fam (temps, vent)* chilly; **il fait plutôt f. aujourd'hui** it's quite chilly *or* there's a nip in the air today

frisson [frisɔ̃] **NM 1** *(de froid, de fièvre)* shiver; *(de peur)* shudder; *(de plaisir)* thrill; **avoir des frissons** to shiver, *Fam* to have the shivers; **être pris** *ou* **saisi de frissons** to get the shivers; **j'en ai des frissons** it makes me shudder; **ça me donne des frissons rien que d'y penser** it makes me shudder just thinking of it; **ça a été le grand f.** it was a big thrill **2** *Littéraire (bruissement ▸ de l'eau, des feuilles)* ripple; *(▸ des feuilles)* rustle

frissonnement [frisɔnmɑ̃] **NM 1** *(de froid, de fièvre)* shiver; *(de peur)* shudder; **un f. de plaisir** a thrill of pleasure; **un f. lui parcourut le corps** a shiver ran through his/her body **2** *Littéraire (de la surface d'un étang)* ripple, rippling *(UNCOUNT)*; *(des feuilles)* rustling *(UNCOUNT)*

frissonner [3] [frisɔne] **VI 1** *(de froid, de fièvre)* to shiver; *(de peur)* to shudder; *(de joie)* to quiver; **elle frissonnait de bonheur** she was trembling with happiness; **ça me fait f. rien que d'y penser** the very thought of it makes me shudder **2** *Littéraire (feuilles)* to rustle; *(surface d'un étang)* to ripple

frisure [frizyr] **NF** curls; **elle a une f. légère** her hair is slightly curly

frit, frite¹ [fri, frit] **PP** *voir* **frire**

ADJ 1 *Culin* fried **2** *Fam* **il est f.** he's had it, his goose is cooked

frite² [frit] **NF 1** *Culin Br* chip, *Am* (French) fry **2** *Fam (sur les fesses)* **faire une f. à qn** to flick sb on the bottom **3** *Fam (locutions)* **avoir la f.** to be on top form, to have bags of energy

friter [3] [frite] *Fam* **VT** *(battre)* **f. qn** to beat sb up, to kick sb's head in

VPR se friter to have a fistfight *or Br* punch-up

friterie [fritri] **NF** *(restaurant)* ≃ fast-food restaurant; *(ambulante) Br* ≃ chip van, *Am* ≃ French fry vendor

friteuse [fritøz] **NF** deep fryer, *Br* chip pan; **f. électrique** electric fryer

fritillaire [fritilɛr] **NF 1** *Entom (papillon)* fritillary **2** *Bot* fritillary

fritter [3] [frite] **VT 1** *Métal* to sinter **2** *(verre)* to frit

friture [frityr] **NF 1** *(aliments frits)* fried food; *(poissons)* fried fish; **acheter de la f.** to buy (small) fish for frying; **petite f.** small fry **2** *Culin (cuisson)* frying; *(matière grasse)* deep fat **3** *(en acoustique)* static; **(bruits de) f.** crackling (noise), interference **4** *Belg (friterie) Br* ≃ chip van, *Am* ≃ French fry vendor

frivole [frivɔl] **ADJ** *(personne, sujet)* frivolous

frivolement [frivɔlmɑ̃] **ADV** frivolously

frivolité [frivɔlite] **NF 1** *(légèreté)* frivolity, frivolousness; *(manque de sérieux ▸ d'un projet, d'une œuvre)* triviality **2** *(vétille)* trifle; **perdre son temps à des frivolités** to waste time in frivolous pursuits *or* frivolities

• **frivolités NFPL** *Vieilli* fancy goods, novelties

froc [frɔk] **NM 1** *Fam (pantalon) Br* trousers□, keks, *Am* pants□; *aussi Fig* **faire dans son f.** to crap *or très Fam* to shit oneself; **baisser son f.** to demean oneself□ **2** *Rel (habit)* habit, frock; **prendre le f.** to become a monk; **porter le f.** to be a monk; **jeter son f. aux orties** to leave holy orders

froid, -e [frwa, frwad] **ADJ 1** *(boisson, temps, moteur, bain)* cold; **un vent f.** a cold wind; **un jour d'hiver f. et sec** a crisp winter's day; **par un matin très f.** on a raw morning; **mange donc!, ça va être f.!** eat up or it'll be cold! **2** *(indifférent ▸ personne)* cold, insensitive, unfeeling; *(▸ tempérament)* cold; *(▸ accueil)* cold, chilly; *(▸ réponse)* cold, cool; *(▸ attitude)* cold, unfriendly; *(▸ style)* cold, unemotional; **ton/regard f.** hostile tone/stare; **se montrer** *ou* **être f. avec** *ou* **envers qn** to be cold towards sb, to treat sb coldly *or* coolly; **devant ce spectacle, il est resté f.** he was unmoved by the sight; **ça me laisse f.** it leaves me cold; **style f.** bloodless *or* cold style; **colère froide** cold fury; **f. comme le marbre** as cold as marble **3** *(triste)* cold, bleak; **des murs froids et nus** cold bare walls **4** *(couleur)* cold, cool **5** *(ancien)* cold, dead; **la piste est froide** the scent is cold, the trail's gone dead

NM 1 *(température)* **le f.** *(climat)* cold weather, the cold; *(air)* the cold (air); **les grands froids** the coldest part of the winter; **par ce f.** in this cold; **conserver qch au f.** to store sth in a cold place; **coup de f.** cold spell *or* snap; **il fait un f. de canard** *ou* **de loup** *ou* **sibérien** it's freezing *or* bitterly cold

2 *(sensation)* **avoir f.** to be *or* to feel cold; **j'ai f. aux mains** my hands are cold; **attraper** *ou* **prendre f.** to get *or* to catch a cold; **je meurs de f.** I'm freezing (cold); *Fig* **avoir f. dans le dos** to feel one's blood run cold; **ça me donne f. dans le dos** it makes my blood run cold, it sends shivers down my spine; **une histoire qui fait f. dans le dos** a chilling *or* creepy story; *Fig* **il n'a pas f. aux yeux** he's bold *or* plucky

3 *(malaise)* **il y a un f. entre eux** things have gone cool between them; **cela a jeté un f.** it cast a chill over the proceedings; **être en f. avec qn** to be on bad terms with sb; **ils sont en f.** they've fallen out, things are a bit strained between them

4 l'industrie du f. the refrigerating industry; **le f. industriel** refrigeration; **la chaîne du f.** the refrigeration chain

ADV il fait f. dehors it's cold out; **en janvier, il fait f.** the weather's cold in January; **boire f.** *(habituellement)* to drink cold drinks; **remuez et buvez f.** stir and chill before drinking; **manger f.** *(habituellement)* to have one's food cold; **assaisonnez et mangez f.** season and leave to cool before eating

• **à froid ADJ** *voir* **opération ADV 1** *(sans émotion)* calmly, dispassionately

2 *(sans préparation)* **je ne peux pas répondre à f.** I can't answer off the top of my head; **prendre qn à f.** to catch sb unawares *or* off guard

3 *Tech & Métal* cold; **démarrer à f.** to start from cold; **soluble à f.** soluble when cold; **lavage à f.** cold water rinse

4 *Méd* **intervenir** *ou* **opérer à f.** to operate between attacks

froidement [frwadmɑ̃] **ADV 1** *(avec réserve)* coldly, coolly; *(répondre)* coolly; **recevoir qn f.** to give sb a cool reception

2 *(lucidement)* dispassionately; **raisonner f.** to use cold logic

3 *(avec indifférence)* cold-bloodedly; **abattre qn f.** to shoot down sb in cold blood

4 *Fam (locution)* **ça va f.!** I'm fine but a bit chilly!

froideur [frwadœr] **NF 1** *(indifférence méprisante)* coldness, cold indifference; **il est toujours d'une très grande f. avec moi** he is always very cold towards me **2** *(manque de sensualité)* coldness **3** *Littéraire (au toucher)* feel; **son front avait la f. du marbre** his/her forehead was cold as marble

• **avec froideur ADV** coldly, indifferently; **accueillir qn avec f.** to give sb a frosty reception

froidure [frwadyr] **NF 1** *Littéraire (temps)* intense cold; *(saison)* cold season *or* weather; **par ces temps de f.** in this cold weather **2** *Méd* frostbite

froissant, -e [frwasɑ̃, -ɑ̃t] **ADJ** hurtful, wounding

froissement [frwasmɑ̃] **NM 1** *(plis ▸ d'un papier, d'une étoffe)* crumpling, creasing

2 *(bruit)* rustling, rustle

3 *Littéraire (vexation)* hurt feelings; **un f. d'amour-propre** a blow to one's pride

4 *Méd* straining *(UNCOUNT)*

froisser [3] [frwase] **VT 1** *(friper ▸ tissu)* to crease, to crumple; *(▸ papier)* to crumple, to crease

2 *(carrosserie)* to dent

3 *(blesser ▸ orgueil)* to ruffle, to bruise; *(▸ personne)* to offend

4 *Méd* to strain

VPR se froisser 1 *(vêtement)* to crush, to crease **2** *(personne)* to take offence (**de** at), to be offended (**de** by) **3 se f. un muscle** to strain a muscle

frôlement [frolmɑ̃] **NM 1** *(frottement)* brush, light touch; **j'ai senti le f. du chat contre ma jambe** I felt the cat brushing *or* rubbing against my leg **2** *(bruit)* rustle, swish, rustling sound

frôler [3] [frole] **VT 1** *(effleurer)* to brush, to touch lightly, to graze; **l'avion a frôlé les arbres** the plane skimmed *or* grazed the treetops; **il m'a frôlé la joue du doigt** he stroked my cheek lightly; **la branche lui a frôlé les cheveux** the branch brushed against his/her hair **2** *(passer très près de)* to come close to touching; **f. les murs** to hug the walls; **la livre a frôlé la barre des 1,50 euros** the pound was hovering just short of the 1.50 euro mark **3** *(échapper à)* to come within a hair's breadth *or* an ace of, to escape narrowly; **f. la mort** to have a brush with death; **mon métier m'a fait f. la mort plusieurs fois** I've diced with death more than once in my job; **f. la catastrophe** to come within a hair's breadth of disaster; **f. la rupture** to come close to splitting up; **ton attitude frôle le ridicule** your attitude verges on *or* borders on the ridiculous

VPR se frôler to brush against each other; **les deux voitures se sont frôlées** the two cars brushed past each other

fromage [frɔmaʒ] **NM 1** *(laitage)* cheese; **un f.** a cheese; **du f.** cheese; **prenez du f.** have some cheese; **plusieurs sortes de fromages** several kinds of cheese; **f. de vache/brebis/chèvre** cow's/sheep's/goat's milk cheese; **f. blanc** fromage frais; **f. blanc battu** smooth fromage frais; **f. fondu** cheese spread; **f. frais** fromage frais; **f. à pâte molle/dur** soft/hard cheese; **f. à pâte persillée** blue(-veined) cheese; **f. à pâte pressée** hard cheese; **f. à tartiner** cheese spread; *Fam* **en faire tout un f.** to kick up a (huge) fuss, to make a mountain out of a molehill; **pas la peine d'en faire un f.** it's not worth making a fuss about **2** *Fam* **un (gentil petit) f.** *(sinécure)* a cushy job *or* number, a nice little earner **3** *Fam Fig* **f. blanc** *(Français de souche)* = French person of native stock as opposed to immigrants or their descendants

• **au fromage ADJ** *(omelette, soufflé, sandwich)* cheese *(avant n)*; **des pâtes au f.** pasta with cheese

• **fromage de tête NM** *Br* brawn, *Am* headcheese

fromager, -ère [frɔmaʒe, -ɛr] **ADJ** cheese *(avant n)*

NM,F 1 *(commerçant) Br* cheesemonger, *Am* cheese seller **2** *(fabricant)* cheese maker, dairyman, *f* dairywoman

NM 1 *(récipient)* cheese mould

fromagerie [frɔmaʒri] **NF 1** *(boutique)* cheese *Br* shop *or Am* store **2** *(fabrique)* dairy

froment [frɔmɑ̃] **NM** wheat

fronce [frɔ̃s] *Couture* **NF** *(de tissu)* gather; **faire des fronces à un tissu** to gather a piece of material

• **à fronces ADJ** gathered

froncement [frɔ̃smɑ̃] **NM f. de sourcils** frown

froncer [16] [frɔ̃se] **VT 1** *Couture* to gather **2** *(rider)* **f. le nez** to wrinkle one's nose; **f. les sourcils** to knit one's brow, to frown

frondaison [frɔ̃dɛzɔ̃] **NF 1** *(feuillage)* foliage, leaves **2** *(époque)* foliation

fronde[1] [frɔ̃d] **NF 1** *(arme)* sling **2** *(lance-pierres) Br* catapult, *Am* slingshot **3** *Littéraire (révolte)* rebellion, revolt; *Hist* **la F.** the Fronde rebellion

fronde[2] [frɔ̃d] **NF** *Bot* frond

fronder [3] [frɔ̃de] **VT** *Littéraire* to revolt against; *(critiquer)* to lampoon

VI 1 *Hist* to belong to the Fronde; *Fig* to rebel **2** *Arch* to use one's sling

frondeur, -euse [frɔ̃dœr, -øz] **ADJ** insubordinate, rebellious; **elle est d'un tempérament f.** she has a rebellious nature

NM,F 1 *Hist* member of the Fronde, Frondeur **2** *(rebelle)* rebel, troublemaker

front [frɔ̃] **NM 1** *Anat* forehead, brow; **baisser le f.** to lower one's head; *Fig* **baisser** *ou* **courber le f.** to submit; **relever le f.** to regain confidence; **le f. haut** proudly, with one's head held high; *Littéraire* **avoir le f. d'airain** to be cruel

2 *(d'une montagne)* face; *(de colline)* brow; *(d'un monument)* frontage, façade; **f. de mer** seafront; **villa sur le f. de mer** villa on the seafront *or* facing the sea

3 *(audace)* **avoir le f. de faire qch** to have the audacity *or* impudence to do sth

4 *Pol* front; **F. de libération nationale** = one of the main political parties in Algeria, established as a resistance movement in 1954, at the start of the war for independence; **F. de libération nationale corse** = Corsican liberation front; **le F. national** the National Front *(extreme right-wing French political party)*; **le F. populaire** the Popular Front; **f. uni** united front; **faire f.** to form a united front, to close ranks; **faire f. devant l'adversaire** to present a united front to the enemy; **faire f. commun contre qn/qch** to make common cause against sb/sth; **faire f. à qn/qch** to face up to *or* to stand up to sb/sth; **je ne suis pas sûr qu'il puisse faire f. seul** I'm not sure he'll be able to cope alone; **tu vas devoir faire f.** you'll have to face up to it

5 *Mil (zone)* front; *(ligne)* front line; **partir sur le** *ou* **au f.** to go (up) to the front; **des nouvelles du f.** news from the front

6 *Mines (gén)* face; *(dans une houillère)* coalface; **f. de taille** working face

7 *Météo* front; **f. froid/chaud** cold/warm front

8 *Can (impudence)* **avoir du f. (tout le tour de la tête)** to be very rude

• **de front ADV 1** *(attaquer)* head-on; **attaquer qn de f.** to attack sb from the front; *Fig* to attack sb head-on; **aborder une difficulté de f.** to tackle a problem head-on

2 *(en vis-à-vis)* head-on; **heurter qn/qch de f.** to run head-on into sb/sth; **se heurter de f.** *(véhicules)* to collide head-on; *(adversaires)* to come into direct confrontation

3 *(côte à côte)* abreast; **on ne peut pas passer de f.** you can't get through side by side; **nous marchions de f.** we were walking next to one another; **rouler à trois voitures de f.** to drive three (cars) abreast; *Mil* **marche de f.** march in line; *Naut* **en ligne de f.** line abreast

4 *(en même temps)* at the same time, at a time; **faire marcher deux affaires de f.** to run two businesses at once *or* at a time; **mener plusieurs choses de f.** to have several things on the go at once

frontal, -e, -aux, -ales [frɔ̃tal, -o] **ADJ 1** *Anat & Géom* frontal; *Mines* **lampe frontale** cap lamp **2** *(conflit, attaque, collision)* head-on; *(concurrence)* direct **3** *Ordinat* front-end; **ordinateur f.** front end

NM 1 *Anat* frontal bone **2** *Com* facing; **f. de rayonnage** shelf facing

• **frontale NF** *Com* shelf facing

frontalier, -ère [frɔ̃talje, -ɛr] **ADJ** border *(avant n)*

NM,F *(habitant)* inhabitant of the frontier zone; *(travailleur)* cross-border commuter

fronteau, -x [frɔ̃to] **NM 1** *Archit* small pediment **2** *Rel (de nonne)* frontlet

frontière [frɔ̃tjɛr] **NF 1** *Pol* border; **incident de f.** border incident; **au-delà de la f.** over the border; **dans nos frontières** within our borders; **poste/ville/zone f.** border post/town/area

2 *Fig (démarcation)* boundary; **la f. entre la veille et le sommeil** the borderline between sleeping and waking; **aux frontières de la vie et de la mort** between life and death; **f. naturelle/linguistique** natural/linguistic boundary

3 *Fig (limite)* frontier; **reculer les frontières de l'inconnu** to roll back the frontiers of the unknown; **faire reculer les frontières du savoir** to roll back the frontiers of knowledge; **dépasser les frontières du possible** to go beyond the bounds of what is possible; **son imagination n'a pas de f.** he/she has a boundless imagination; **ma liberté ne connaît pas de f.** my freedom knows no bounds

4 *Math* **(point) f.** frontier

> Attention: ne pas confondre **frontier** et **border** lorsque l'on traduit **frontière**. On ne peut utiliser que **border** pour décrire la limite qui sépare deux États.

frontispice [frɔ̃tispis] **NM** *(titre, illustration)* frontispiece

frontiste [frɔ̃tist] *Pol* **ADJ** of the (French) National Front

NMF member of the (French) National Front

front-office [frɔ̃tɔfis] *(pl* **front-offices)** **NM** *Banque* front office

fronton [frɔ̃tɔ̃] **NM 1** *Archit* pediment **2** *Sport (mur)* fronton; *(court)* pelota court

frottage [frɔtaʒ] **NM 1** *(frottement)* rubbing, scrubbing; *(des sols)* polishing **2** *Beaux-Arts* frottage

frottée [frɔte] **NF 1** *Fam Vieilli (volée)* beating, thrashing **2** *Culin* **f. (d'ail)** = bread which has been toasted and then rubbed with a clove of garlic

frotte-manche [frɔtmɑ̃ʃ] (*pl* **frotte-manches**) NMF *Belg Fam* bootlicker, toady

frottement [frɔtmɑ̃] NM **1** *(friction)* rubbing *(UNCOUNT)*, friction; **le f. a fait un trou à ma chaussette** I've worn a hole in my sock; *Phot* **marques de f.** stress marks

2 *(bruit)* rubbing *or* scraping noise

3 *Méd* friction murmur; **f. à deux temps** to and fro sound; **f. pleural** pleural rub

4 *Tech* friction; *(de freins)* binding; **f. de glissement** sliding friction; **usure par f.** abrasion

• **frottements** NMPL *(mésentente)* dispute, disagreement; **il y a des frottements entre eux** there is some friction between them

frotter [3] [frɔte] VT **1** *(pour nettoyer)* to rub, to scrub; *(avec une brosse)* to brush; *(cuivre)* to polish; **f. une tache avec une brosse/avec du savon** to scrub a stain with a brush/with soap; **f. une casserole** to scour a saucepan; **f. ses chaussures pour enlever la boue** to scrape the mud off one's shoes

2 *(pour enduire)* to rub; **f. une table** to polish a table; **f. d'ail des croûtons** to rub croûtons with garlic; *Belg Fam* **f. la manche à** *ou* **de qn** to softsoap sb

3 *(mettre en contact)* **f. deux pierres l'une contre l'autre** to rub *or* to scrape two stones together; **f. une allumette** to strike a match; **f. un mur avec sa main** to rub one's hand against a wall; *Fam Vieilli* **être frotté de latin** to have a smattering of Latin

4 *(frictionner)* to rub; **f. le dos à qn** to give sb's back a rub, to rub sb's back

VI to scrape, to rub; **le frein de mon vélo frotte** the brakes on my bike keep sticking

VPR **se frotter 1** *(se frictionner)* to rub oneself (down); **se f. avec une serviette** to rub oneself (down) *or* to give oneself a rub-down with a towel; **se f. contre qn/qch** to rub (up) against sb/sth; **se f. les yeux** to rub one's eyes; **se f. les mains** to rub one's hands (together); *Fig* to rub one's hands **2 se f. à qn/qch** *(effleurer)* to rub (up) against sb/sth; *Fam Fig* **se f. à qn** *(fréquenter)* to rub shoulders with sb; **le chat se frotte à ma jambe** the cat rubs (up) against my leg; *Fig* **ne te frotte pas à lui quand il est en colère** steer clear of him when he's angry; **ne vous y frottez pas, c'est trop dangereux** don't interfere *or* meddle, it's too dangerous; **qui s'y frotte s'y pique** if you meddle you'll get your fingers burnt; *Fam Fig* **depuis le temps que je me frotte aux artistes, je les connais!** I've been around artists for long enough to know what they're like! **3 se f. à qch** *(se confronter à)* to face sth; **elle a dû très vite se f. au monde des affaires** she soon had to face the business world

frotteur, -euse [frɔtœr, -øz] ADJ rubbing

NM **1** *Élec* brush spring, wiper; **f. de contact** contact finger

2 *Rail* carbon sliding, slip contact; *Aut* slipper

3 *(personne)* floor polisher

4 *Fam (frôleur)* pervert[□] *(who likes to rub up against women in crowds)*

frotti-frotta [frɔtifrɔta] NM *Fam* **faire du f.** to rub up against each other

frottis [frɔti] NM **1** *Méd* smear; **f. vaginal** cervical smear, smear test; **se faire faire un f. (vaginal)** to have a smear test *or* a cervical smear **2** *Beaux-Arts* scumbling

frottoir [frɔtwar] NM *(sur une boîte d'allumettes)* striking surface; *(ustensile)* rubber; *(brosse)* scrubbing brush; *(de dynamo)* brush

froufrou, frou-frou [frufru] (*pl* **frous-frous**) NM *(bruit)* swish, rustle, frou-frou

• **froufrous, frous-frous** NMPL *(ornement de vêtement)* frills (and furbelows)

froufroutant, -e [frufrutɑ̃, -ɑ̃t] ADJ **1** *(bruissant)* rustling, swishing **2** *(à volants ▸ robe, jupe)* frilly, flouncy

froufrouter [3] [frufrute] VI to rustle, to swish

froussard, -e [frusar, -ard] *Fam* ADJ cowardly[□], chicken, yellow-bellied

NM,F coward[□], chicken, yellow-belly

frousse [frus] NF *Fam* fright[□]; **avoir la f.** to be scared[□]; **elle ne veut plus se présenter à l'examen, elle a la f.** she won't take the exam, she's got cold feet; **avoir la f. de faire qch** to be scared to do *or* of doing sth[□]; **donner** *ou* **flanquer la f. à qn** to scare the pants off sb

fructidor [fryktidɔr] NM = 12th month of the French Revolutionary calendar (from 18/19 August to 17/18 September)

fructifère [fryktifɛr] ADJ *Bot* fruit-bearing

fructification [fryktifikasjɔ̃] NF **1** *(processus)* fructification **2** *(période)* fruitage

fructifier [9] [fryktifje] VI **1** *Agr* to be productive; *Bot* to bear fruit, to fructify **2** *Écon* to yield a profit; **faire f. son capital** to make one's capital yield a profit; **il sait faire f. son argent** he knows how to get a return on his money **3** *(produire des résultats)* to bear fruit, to be productive *or* fruitful; **une idée qui fructifie** an idea that bears fruit

fructose [fryktoz] NM fructose

fructueuse [fryktyøz] *voir* **fructueux**

fructueusement [fryktɥøzmɑ̃] ADV *(avantageusement)* fruitfully, productively

fructueux, -euse [fryktɥø, -øz] ADJ **1** *(fécond)* fruitful, productive **2** *(profitable)* profitable; **une opération fructueuse** a profitable deal

frugal, -e, -aux, -ales [frygal, -o] ADJ **1** *(simple)* frugal, simple **2** *(qui mange peu)* frugal

frugalement [frygalmɑ̃] ADV frugally

frugalité [frygalite] NF frugality

frugivore [fryʒivɔr] ADJ fruit-eating

NM fruit-eater

fruit[1] [frɥi] NM **1** *Bot* **manger un f.** to eat some fruit *or* a piece of fruit; **des fruits** fruit; **manger des fruits** to eat (some) fruit; **porter des fruits** *(d'un arbre)* to bear fruit; *Fig* **porter ses fruits** *(d'une action, d'un investissement)* to bear fruit; **la tomate est un f.** the tomato is a (type of) fruit; **fruits des bois,** *Suisse* **petits fruits** fruits of the forest; **fruits confits** candied *or* crystallized fruit; **f. défendu** forbidden fruit; **fruits déguisés** = prunes, dates etc stuffed with almond paste; **f. du dragon** dragon fruit, pitahaya; **fruits jumeaux** double fruits; **f. de la passion** passion fruit; **fruits rafraîchis** (chilled) fruit salad; **fruits rouges** red berries, red fruits; **un f. sec** a piece of dried fruit; *Fig* a failure; *Fig* **un f. vert** an immature young girl; *Prov* **c'est au f. qu'on connaît l'arbre** = the tree is known by its fruit

2 *Culin* **fruits de mer** seafood

3 *(résultat)* fruit; **le f. de son travail** the fruit *or* result of his/her labours; **le f. d'un mariage** the offspring of a marriage; **le f. de leur amour** the fruit of their love; *Littéraire* **le f. de ses entrailles** the fruit of her womb; **cela a porté ses fruits** it bore fruit; **les fruits de la Terre** the fruits *or* bounty of the Earth; *Littéraire* **avec f.** fruitfully, profitably

fruit[2] [frɥi] NM *Constr* batter; **avoir du f.** to batter

fruité, -e [frɥite] ADJ fruity

fruiterie [frɥitri] NF **1** *(boutique) Br* fruit shop, *Am* fruit store **2** *(dépôt)* storeroom (for fruit)

fruiticulteur, -trice [frɥitikyltœr, -tris] NM,F fruit grower

fruitier, -ère [frɥitje, -ɛr] ADJ fruit *(avant n)*

NM,F fruiterer, *Br* greengrocer, *Am* fruit seller

NM **1** *(verger)* orchard **2** *(arbre)* fruit tree **3** *(local)* storeroom (for fruit)

frusques [frysk] NFPL *Fam* threads, *Br* gear

fruste [fryst] ADJ **1** *(grossier ▸ personne)* uncouth, rough

2 *(sans élégance ▸ style)* unpolished, crude, rough

3 *(pièce, statue)* worn

4 *Méd* mild

frustrant, -e [frystrɑ̃, -ɑ̃t] ADJ frustrating

frustration [frystrasjɔ̃] NF **1** *Psy* frustration **2** *(d'un légataire)* cheating, defrauding

frustré, -e [frystre] ADJ frustrated

NM,F frustrated person; **c'est un f.** he's so frustrated

frustrer [3] [frystre] VT **1** *(décevoir)* to frustrate, to thwart; **être frustré dans ses espoirs** to be thwarted in one's hopes

2 *(priver)* **f. qn de qch** to rob *or* to deprive sb of sth; **ils ont été frustrés de la victoire** they were robbed of their victory

3 *Psy* to frustrate

4 *Jur* **f. qn de** to defraud sb of

FS *(abrév écrite* **franc suisse**) SFr

FSE [ɛfɛsə] NM **1** *(abrév* **foyer socio-éducatif**) ≃ community centre **2** *(abrév* **Fonds social européen**) ESF

FSM [ɛfɛsɛm] NF *(abrév* **Fédération syndicale mondiale**) WFTU

NM *(abrév* **Forum social mondial**) WSF

FTP [ɛftepe] NM *Ordinat (abrév* **File Transfer Protocol**) FTP

NMPL *Hist (abrév* **Francs-tireurs et partisans**) = Communist resistance during World War II

fuchsia [fyʃja] ADJ INV fuchsia

NM fuchsia

fucus [fykys] NM wrack; **f. vésiculeux** bladderwrack

fuel [fjul], **fuel-oil** [fjulɔjl] (*pl* **fuel-oils**) NM (fuel *or* heating) oil; **f. domestique** domestic heating oil

fufute [fyfyt] ADJ *Fam* **il n'est pas très f.** he's a bit thick, he's not the sharpest knife in the drawer

fugace [fygas] ADJ *(beauté)* transient, evanescent, ephemeral; *(impression, souvenir, pensée)* transient, fleeting; *(parfum)* elusive, fleeting

fugacité [fygasite] NF *Littéraire* transience, fleetingness

fugitif, -ive [fyʒitif, -iv] ADJ **1** *(en fuite)* runaway *(avant n)*, fugitive *(avant n)* **2** *(fugace ▸ vision, idée)* fleeting, transient; *(▸ bonheur)* short-lived; *(▸ souvenir)* elusive; *(▸ ombre)* fleeting

NM,F runaway, fugitive

fugitivement [fyʒitivmɑ̃] ADV fleetingly, briefly

fugue [fyg] NF **1** *Mus* fugue **2** *(fuite)* **faire une f.** *(de chez soi)* to run away from home; *(pour se marier)* to elope

fuguer [1] [fyge] VI *Fam* to clear off, *Br* to do a bunk, *Am* to split

fugueur, -euse [fygœr, -øz] ADJ **être f.** to keep running away; **c'était un enfant f.** as a child, he used to run away repeatedly

NM,F runaway

fuir [35] [fɥir] VI **1** *(s'enfuir)* to run away, to flee (**devant** from); **les animaux fuyaient à notre approche** the animals fled *or* ran away as we came near; **f. de son pays** to flee the country; **faire f. qn** to frighten sb away, to put sb to flight; **f. à toutes jambes** to run for dear *or* one's life; **f. devant le danger** to flee in the face of danger; **laid à faire f.** as ugly as sin; **bête à faire f.** as stupid as can be; **son agressivité fait f. tout le monde** he puts everyone off by being so aggressive

2 *(s'éloigner)* to vanish, to recede; **des lignes qui fuient vers l'horizon** lines that converge towards the horizon; **le paysage fuyait par la vitre du train** the landscape flashed past the window of the train

3 *Littéraire (passer)* to fly, to slip away; **le temps fuit** time flies

4 *(se dérober)* to run away; **f. devant ses responsabilités** to shirk *or* to evade one's responsibilities; *Naut* **f. devant le vent** to scud *or* to run before the wind; **il a le regard qui fuit** he has shifty eyes

5 *(se répandre ▸ eau)* to leak; *(▸ gaz)* to leak, to escape; **f. à petites gouttes** to seep *or* to ooze (through)

6 *(perdre son contenu ▸ tonneau, stylo)* to leak, to be leaky; **un tuyau qui fuit** a leaky pipe

VT **1** *(abandonner)* to flee (from); **elle a fui le pays** she fled the country

2 *(éviter)* to avoid, to shun; **il me fuit** he's avoiding me; **f. les gens** to avoid contact with other people; **f. sa famille** to shun one's family; **f. le monde** to flee society; **f. le regard de qn** to avoid looking sb in the eye; **f. le danger** to keep away from *or* to avoid danger

3 *(se soustraire à, s'éloigner de)* to shirk, to evade; **f. la tentation** to flee from *or* to avoid temptation

4 *(résister à)* to elude; **le sommeil le fuyait** he couldn't sleep, sleep eluded him

fuite [fɥit] NF **1** *(départ)* escape, flight (**devant** from); **prendre la f.** *(prisonnier)* to run away, to (make one's) escape; **le chauffard a pris la f.** it was a hit-and-run accident; **être en f.** to be on the run; **mettre qn/un animal en f.** to put sb/an animal to flight; **l'action du gouvernement est considérée par certains comme une f. en avant** some people accuse the government of blindly refusing to come to terms with the problem; **la f. des cerveaux** the brain drain

2 *Fig (devant des difficultés, des problèmes)* evasion, avoidance
3 *Fin* **f. de capitaux** flight of capital (abroad); **f. devant l'impôt** tax evasion
4 *(écoulement ▸ de liquide)* leak, leakage; *(▸ de gaz)* leak; *(▸ de courant)* escape; **f. de gaz** gas leak; *Littéraire* **la f. du temps** the passage *or* passing of time
5 *(d'un pneu)* puncture; *(d'une canalisation, d'un récipient)* leak; **as-tu trouvé la f.?** did you find the leak?
6 *(indiscrétion)* leak; **il y a eu des fuites en histoire** some of the history questions leaked out
7 *Beaux-Arts* **point de f.** vanishing point

fulgurant, -e [fylgyrɑ̃, -ɑ̃t] **ADJ 1** *(rapide ▸ réponse, attaque)* lightning *(avant n)*; *(▸ idée)* sudden; *(▸ carrière)* dazzling; **j'ai eu une idée fulgurante** an idea flashed *or* shot through my mind; **elle a connu un succès f.** she was brilliantly successful **2** *(intense ▸ douleur)* shooting, *Spéc* fulgurating; *(▸ lumière)* blinding, dazzling, fulgurant **3** *Littéraire (éclatant ▸ éclair)* flashing; *(▸ regard)* blazing, flashing; *(▸ beauté)* dazzling; **lancer un regard f. à qn** to look daggers at sb

fulguration [fylgyrasjɔ̃] **NF 1** *Météo* heat lightning **2** *Méd* fulguration

fulgurer [3] [fylgyre] **VI** *Littéraire* to flash, to blaze

fuligineux, -euse [fyliʒinø, -øz] **ADJ 1** *(qui produit de la suie)* sooty, smoky **2** *Fig Littéraire* fuliginous

fulmicoton [fylmikɔtɔ̃] **NM** guncotton

fulminant, -e [fylminɑ̃, -ɑ̃t] **ADJ 1** *Littéraire (menaçant ▸ regard)* furious, enraged, irate; *(▸ lettre)* venomous, vituperative **2** *(soudain ▸ douleur)* fulminant **3** *Chim* fulminating

fulminer [3] [fylmine] **VI** *Littéraire* to fulminate, to rail; **f. contre le gouvernement** to rail against the government
VT 1 *Littéraire (proférer)* to thunder, to roar, to utter; **f. des menaces à l'égard de qn** to thunder *or* to roar threats at sb **2** *Rel* to fulminate

fumage[1] [fymaʒ] **NM** *Culin* smoking, curing

fumage[2] [fymaʒ] **NM** *Agr* manuring, dunging

fumant, -e [fymɑ̃, -ɑ̃t] **ADJ 1** *(cheminée, feu)* smoking, smoky; *(cendres, décombres)* smouldering
2 *(liquide, nourriture)* steaming; **assis autour de la soupe fumante** sitting around a steaming bowl of soup
3 *(furieux)* fuming; **être f. de colère** to flare up with anger
4 *Fam (remarquable)* amazing, incredible; **coup f.** a masterstroke□; **faire un coup f. (à qn)** to play a dirty trick (on sb)
5 *Chim* fuming
• **fumantes NFPL** *très Fam (chaussettes)* socks□

fumasse [fymas] **ADJ** *Fam* furious□, fuming

fumé, -e[1] [fyme] **ADJ 1** *(poisson, viande etc)* smoked, smoke-cured **2 verre f.** smoked glass; **verres fumés** dark lenses; *(lunettes)* dark glasses, sunglasses
NM *(aliment)* smoked food; **évitez de consommer du f.** avoid smoked foods

fume-cigare [fymsigar] **NM INV** cigar holder

fume-cigarette [fymsigarɛt] **NM INV** cigarette holder

fumée[2] [fyme] **NF 1** *(de combustion)* smoke; **partir** *ou* **s'en aller en f.** to go up in smoke; *Prov* **il n'y a pas de f. sans feu** there's no smoke without fire; **la f. (du tabac) vous gêne-t-elle?** do you mind my smoking? **2** *(vapeur)* steam; *(du charbon de bois)* fumes
• **fumées NFPL** *Littéraire* stupor; **dans les fumées de l'ivresse** *ou* **du vin** in a drunken stupor

fumer[1] [3] [fyme] **VT 1** *(tabac)* to smoke; **f. la pipe** to smoke a pipe; **f. cigarette sur cigarette** to chain-smoke; *Fam* **en f. une** to have a smoke□ **2** *Culin* to smoke **3** *très Fam Arg crime (battre)* to clobber, to thump; *(tuer)* to kill□, *Br* to do in
USAGE ABSOLU *(personne)* to smoke; **je ne fume plus** I don't smoke any more, I've given up smoking; **f. comme un pompier** *ou* **un sapeur** to smoke like a chimney
VI 1 *(feu, cheminée)* to smoke, to give off smoke; *(cendres, décombres)* to smoke, to smoulder
2 *(liquide, nourriture)* to steam, to give off steam; **vois la bonne soupe qui fume** look at the lovely steaming bowl of soup
3 *Chim* to fume, to give off fumes
4 *Fam (être furieux)* to fume, *Am* to be mad

> Il faut noter que le verbe anglais **to fume** est un faux ami. Il signifie **fulminer**.

fumer[2] [3] [fyme] **VT** *(terre)* to manure, to dress, to dung

fumerie [fymri] **NF** opium den

fumerolle [fymrɔl] **NF** fumarole

fumet [fymɛ] **NM 1** *(odeur ▸ d'un plat)* (pleasant) smell, aroma; *(▸ d'un vin)* bouquet **2** *Culin* stock, fumet **3** *Chasse* scent

fumeterre [fymtɛr] **NF** *Bot* fumitory

fumette [fymɛt] **NF** *Fam* getting stoned; **c'est un habitué de la f.** he gets stoned regularly, he's a real stoner; **il y a que la f. qui l'intéresse** all he's/she's interested in is getting stoned

fumeur, -euse[1] [fymœr, -øz] **NM,F** *(adepte du tabac)* smoker; **un gros f.** a heavy smoker; **f. de pipe/cigares** pipe/cigar smoker; **f. d'opium** opium smoker; **compartiment fumeurs** smoking compartment *or Am* car

fumeux, -euse[2] [fymø, -øz] **ADJ 1** *(confus)* hazy; **idée fumeuse** vague *or* nebulous idea; **il a l'esprit f.** his ideas are a bit woolly, he's woolly-minded **2** *(bougie, lampe)* smoky

fumier [fymje] **NM 1** *(engrais)* manure, dung; **fosse à f.** slurry pit **2** *(tas)* dunghill, manure **3** *très Fam (personne)* bastard; **espèce de f.!** you bastard!; **le f.!, il m'a menti!** he lied to me, the bastard!

fumigation [fymigasjɔ̃] **NF 1** *(pour un local)* fumigation; **faire des fumigations** to fumigate **2** *Agr & Méd* fumigation

fumigène [fymiʒɛn] **ADJ** smoke *(avant n)*; *Mil* **grenade f.** smoke grenade
NM smoke generator

fumiger [17] [fymiʒe] **VT** to fumigate

fumiste [fymist] **NM 1** *(installateur)* heating specialist **2** *(ramoneur)* chimney sweep
ADJ *Fam Péj (attitude, personne)* lazy□; **il est un peu f.** he's a bit of a shirker
NMF *Fam Péj* shirker, *Br* layabout; **c'est un f.** he doesn't exactly kill himself working

fumisterie [fymistəri] **NF 1** *Fam Péj* humbug, sham, farce; **une vaste f.** an absolute farce **2** *(métier ▸ d'installateur)* boiler installation *or* fitting; *(▸ de ramoneur)* chimney sweeping

fumivore [fymivɔr] **ADJ** *(appareil)* smoke extracting; *(combustion)* smokeless
NM smoke extractor

fumoir [fymwar] **NM 1** *(pour fumeurs)* smoking room **2** *(pour aliments)* smokehouse

fumure [fymyr] **NF 1** *(engrais)* manure, fertilizer **2** *(fertilisation)* manuring, fertilizing

fun [fœn] **ADJ INV** *Fam* funny
NM 1 *Fam* **le f.** entertainment□; **faire qch pour le f.** to do sth for fun **2** *Sport* funboard

funambule [fynɑ̃byl] **NMF** tightrope walker, funambulist

funambulesque [fynɑ̃bylɛsk] **ADJ 1 l'art f.** the art of tightrope walking; **acrobatie f.** high-wire acrobatics **2** *Fig (idées, projet etc)* fantastic, bizarre

funboard [fœnbɔrd] **NM** funboard

funèbre [fynɛbr] **ADJ 1** *(relatif aux funérailles)* funeral *(avant n)*; **cérémonie f.** funeral service; **chant f.** dirge; **veillée f.** deathwatch, wake **2** *(lugubre)* gloomy, lugubrious, funereal

funérailles [fyneraj] **NFPL** funeral; **f. nationales** state funeral
EXCLAM *Fam* heavens!, *Br* blimey!

funéraire [fynerɛr] **ADJ** funeral *(avant n)*, *Spéc* funerary; **urne/chambre f.** funeral *or* funerary urn/chamber; **site f.** burial site

funérarium [fynerarjɔm] **NM** funeral parlour, *Am* funeral home

funeste [fynɛst] **ADJ 1** *(désastreux)* disastrous, catastrophic; **l'ignorance est souvent f.** ignorance is often dangerous *or* harmful; **être f. à qn** to have terrible consequences for sb; **être f. à qch** to be fatal to sth **2** *Littéraire (triste)* lugubrious, sad **3** *Littéraire (mortel)* fatal, lethal

funiculaire [fynikylɛr] **ADJ** funicular
NM funicular (railway)

funk [fœnk] *Mus* **ADJ INV** funk
NM INV le f. funk

funky [fœnki] **ADJ INV** funky
NM *Mus* jazz funk

fur [fyr] **au fur et à mesure ADV** gradually; **donnez-les-moi au f. et à mesure** give them to me gradually *or* as we go along; **je préfère faire mon travail au f. et à mesure plutôt que de le laisser s'accumuler** I prefer to do my work as and when it comes rather than letting it pile up; **au f. et à mesure, j'ai compris comment ça fonctionnait** I understood how it worked as I went along *or* bit by bit
• **au fur et à mesure de PRÉP** as; **au f. et à mesure de l'avance des travaux** as work proceeds; **au f. et à mesure des besoins** as needed; **au f. et à mesure de ses recherches** as he progressed with his/her research; **je vous les enverrai au f. et à mesure de leur disponibilité** I'll send them to you as and when they are available
• **au fur et à mesure que CONJ** as; **au f. et à mesure que le temps passe, l'angoisse augmente** as time goes by, anxiety grows; **l'eau s'écoule au f. et à mesure que je remplis l'évier** the water drains away as (soon as) I fill up the sink

furax [fyraks] **ADJ INV** *Fam* fuming, hopping mad

furet [fyrɛ] **NM 1** *Zool* ferret; **aller à la chasse au f.** to go ferreting **2** *Vieilli (curieux)* snoop **3** *(jeu)* pass the slipper

furetage [fyrtaʒ] **NM 1** *(recherche)* ferreting (around *or* about), nosing (around *or* about) **2** *Chasse* ferreting

fureter [28] [fyrte] **VI 1** *(fouiller)* to ferret (around *or* about), to snoop (around *or* about); **f. dans le sac de qn** to ferret around in sb's bag; **je suis allé f. dans sa chambre** I had a snoop around his/her room; **les journalistes ont fureté dans mon passé** journalists pried into my past **2** *Chasse* to ferret

fureteur, -euse [fyrtœr, -øz] **ADJ** *Péj* prying; **regard f.** inquisitive look
NM,F 1 *Péj (indiscret)* snooper **2** *(fouilleur)* **elle a trouvé des merveilles à la brocante, c'est une fureteuse** she found some real treasures in the junkshop, she loves poking around **3** *(chasseur)* ferreter
NM *Can Ordinat* browser

fureur [fyrœr] **NF 1** *(colère)* rage, fury; **accès de f.** fit of anger *or* rage; **f. noire** blind anger *or* rage; **se mettre dans une f. noire** to fly into a rage; **quand sa f. s'est calmée** when his/her anger had died down **2** *(passion)* passion; **la f. du jeu** a mania *or* passion for gambling; **la f. de vivre** a lust for life; **faire f.** to be all the rage **3** *Littéraire (violence)* rage, fury, wrath; **la f. des flots** the wrath of the sea
• **avec fureur ADV 1** *(colériquement)* furiously **2** *(passionnément)* passionately
• **en fureur ADJ** furious, enraged **ADV entrer en f.** to fly into a rage *or* fury; **mettre qn en f.** to send sb wild with rage, to enrage sb

furia [fyrja] **NF** *(d'une foule)* frenzy; **ils n'ont pas pu résister à la f. bordelaise** they were overwhelmed by the Bordeaux team's furious onslaught

furibard, -e [fyribar, -ard] **ADJ** *Fam* fuming, hopping mad

furibond, -e [fyribɔ̃, -ɔ̃d] **ADJ** furious; **être f. contre qn** to be furious with sb; **elle lui a lancé un regard f.** she glared at him/her

furie [fyri] **NF 1** *(colère)* fury, rage **2** *(mégère)* fury; **elle s'est jetée sur lui comme une f.** she flew at him like a fury
• **avec furie ADV 1** *(avec colère)* furiously, angrily **2** *(ardemment)* ardently, passionately, furiously; **elle écrivait avec f.** she was writing furiously **3** *(violemment)* furiously, wildly, savagely
• **en furie ADJ** furious, enraged; *Littéraire* **les éléments en f.** the raging elements

furieuse [fyrjøz] *voir* **furieux**

furieusement [fyrjøzmɑ̃] **ADV 1** *(avec colère)* furiously, angrily **2** *(violemment)* furiously, wildly, savagely **3** *(extrêmement)* hugely, tremendously, extremely; **avoir f. envie de** to have a tremendous urge to

furieux, -euse [fyrjø, -øz] **ADJ 1** *(enragé ▸ personne)* furious, (very) angry; *(▸ geste, cri)* furious; *(▸ taureau)* mad, raging; **cela me rend f.** it makes me furious; **d'un air f.** looking like thunder; **être f. contre qn** to be furious with sb; **être f. de son échec** to be enraged *or* infuriated at one's failure; **il est f. d'apprendre que tout a été fait sans lui** he's furious to hear that it's all been done without him; **il est f. d'avoir attendu** he's furious at having been kept waiting; **elle est furieuse qu'on ne l'ait pas prévenue** she's furious that nobody told her

2 *Littéraire (violent)* raging, wild; **tempête furieuse** raging storm; **les flots f.** the raging seas

3 *Littéraire (passionné)* furious; **une haine furieuse** a furious *or* wild hatred

4 *(extrême)* tremendous; **avoir une furieuse envie de dormir** to have an overwhelming desire to go to sleep

NM,F maniac, madman, *f* madwoman

furoncle [fyrɔ̃kl] **NM** boil, *Spéc* furuncle

furonculose [fyrɔ̃kyloz] **NF** furunculosis

furtif, -ive [fyrtif, -iv] **ADJ 1** *(comportement)* furtive; *(geste, action)* furtive, surreptitious, stealthy; *(regard)* furtive, sly; *(sourire)* quiet, secret; *(larme)* hidden **2** *Mil (avion)* stealth *(avant n)*

furtivement [fyrtivmɑ̃] **ADV** stealthily, surreptitiously, furtively; **entrer/sortir f.** to steal in/out, to enter/leave furtively

fusain [fyzɛ̃] **NM 1** *Bot* spindle (tree) **2** *Beaux-Arts (crayon)* piece of charcoal; *(dessin)* charcoal

• **au fusain ADJ** charcoal *(avant n)* **ADV** *(dessiner, illustrer)* in charcoal

fusant, -e [fyzɑ̃, -ɑ̃t] **ADJ** *(qui ne détonne pas)* fusing; **obus f.** time shell

NM time shell

fuseau, -x [fyzo] **NM 1** *(bobine)* spindle; *(pour la dentelle)* bobbin; **dentelle/ouvrage aux fuseaux** bobbin lace/needlework **2** *(pantalon)* stirrup pants, ski pants **3** *Biol* spindle

• **en fuseau ADJ** tapered, spindle-shaped; **jambes en f.** slender legs **ADV tailler qch en f.** to taper sth

• **fuseau horaire NM** time zone

fusée [fyze] **NF 1** *Astron* rocket; **f. à étages multiples, fusées gigognes** multiple-stage rocket; **f. à trois étages** three-stage rocket; **f. d'appoint** booster; **f. interplanétaire** space rocket; **f. orbitale** orbital rocket; **lancer une f.** to launch a rocket; **partir comme une f.** to be off like a shot, to shoot off

2 *(signal)* rocket; **f. de détresse** flare; **f. éclairante** flare; **f. à pétard** maroon; *Naut* **f. porte-amarre** life (-saving) rocket; **f. de signalisation** signal (sky) rocket

3 *(projectile)* rocket, missile; *(détonateur)* fuse; **f. air-air** air-to-air missile; **f. anti-engin** antimissile missile; **f.-engin** missile; **f. percutante** percussion fuse; **f. porteuse** carrier rocket; **f. à temps** time fuse

4 *(d'arbre, d'axe)* spindle; *(de roue)* stub axle; **f. de direction** stub axle

fusée-sonde [fyzesɔ̃d] *(pl* **fusées-sondes***)* **NF** probe, sounding rocket

fuselage [fyzlaʒ] **NM** fuselage

fuselé, -e [fyzle] **ADJ** *(doigt)* slender, tapered, tapering; *(jambe)* slender; *(muscle)* well-shaped; *(colonne)* tapered, tapering, spindle-shaped; *Aut* streamlined

fuseler [24] [fyzle] **VT 1** *(former en fuseau)* to taper **2** *Aviat, Aut & Naut* to streamline

fuser [3] [fyze] **VI 1** *(jaillir ▸ vapeur)* to gush *or* to spurt (out); *(▸ liquide)* to jet *or* to gush *or* to spurt (out); *(▸ lumière)* to stream out; *(▸ étincelle)* to fly; **un projectile a fusé dans l'espace** a missile shot through the air **2** *(retentir ▸ rire, voix)* to burst out; **des rires fusèrent de toutes parts** there were bursts of laughter from all sides, laughter erupted from all sides; **des cris/des remarques fusèrent de toutes parts** cries/comments were suddenly heard from all sides **3** *(bougie)* to melt; *(poudre)* to burn slowly; *(sels)* to crackle

fusibilité [fyzibilite] **NF** fusibility

fusible [fyzibl] **ADJ 1** *(qui peut fondre)* fusible, meltable **2** *(à point de fusion bas)* fusible

NM fuse; *(fil métallique)* fuse wire; **un f. a grillé** a fuse blew; **où sont les fusibles?** where is the fuse box?; **f. de sûreté** safety fuse, cut-out

fusiforme [fyzifɔrm] **ADJ** spindle-shaped

fusil [fyzi] **NM 1** *(arme)* gun, rifle; **f. à air comprimé** air gun; **f. d'assaut** assault rifle; **f. automatique** automatic rifle; **f. à canon scié** sawn-off shotgun; **f. à chargeur** magazine rifle; **f. de chasse** shotgun; **f. à deux coups** double-barrelled *or* double barrel shotgun; **f. harpon** harpoon gun; **f. à lunette** rifle with telescopic sight; **f. à pompe** pump-action rifle; **f. rayé** rifle; **f. à répétition** repeating rifle; **f. semi-automatique** semi-automatic rifle; **f. sous-marin** speargun; *Fig* **changer son f. d'épaule** to change (one's) tack; *Can* **partir/entrer en coup de f.** to storm out/in **2** *(tireur)* **un bon f.** a good shot **3** *(affiloir)* **f. (à aiguiser)** steel

fusilier [fyzilje] **NM** rifleman, *Br* fusilier; **f. marin** marine

fusillade [fyzijad] **NF 1** *(bruit)* shooting *(UNCOUNT)*, gunfire **2** *(combat)* gunfight, gun battle **3** *(exécution)* shooting

fusiller [3] [fyzije] **VT 1** *(exécuter)* to shoot; *Fig* **f. qn du regard** to look daggers *or* to glare at sb **2** *Fam (détruire)* to wreck, to bust, *Br* to knacker; **il a loupé le virage et fusillé sa bagnole** he missed the turn and *Br* wrote his car off *or Am* totaled his car **3** *Fam (dépenser)* to blow

fusil-mitrailleur [fyzimitrajœr] *(pl* **fusils-mitrailleurs***)* **NM** light machinegun

fusion [fyzjɔ̃] **NF 1** *Métal* fusion, melting; **f. froide, f. à froid** cold fusion

2 *Mines* smelting

3 *(dissolution ▸ du sucre, de la glace)* melting

4 *Nucl* **f. (nucléaire)** fusion

5 *Fig (union ▸ d'idées, de sentiments)* fusion; *(▸ de groupes, de peuples, de cultures)* fusion, merging

6 *Écon* merger, merging, amalgamation; **f. horizontale** horizontal merger; **f. verticale** vertical merger; **fusions-rachats** *ou* **fusions-acquisitions** mergers and acquisitions

7 *Ordinat* merge, merging; **f. de fichiers** file merge

• **en fusion ADJ** *Métal* molten **ADV mettre deux éléments en f.** to fuse two elements (together)

fusionnement [fyzjɔnmɑ̃] **NM 1** *Écon* amalgamation, merger **2** *(rassemblement ▸ de groupes, de cultures)* merging, fusion

fusionner [3] [fyzjɔne] **VT 1** *(sociétés)* to merge, to amalgamate **2** *Ordinat (fichiers)* to merge

VI 1 *Écon* to merge, to amalgamate **2** *Ordinat* to merge

fusse *etc voir* **être**[1]

fustigation [fystigasjɔ̃] **NF** *Littéraire* **1** *(correction)* thrashing, beating **2** *(critique ▸ d'une personne)* censure; *(▸ d'un vice)* castigation, censure

fustiger [17] [fystiʒe] **VT** *Littéraire* **1** *(battre)* to thrash **2** *(critiquer ▸ personne, attitude)* to censure, to criticize harshly; *(▸ vice)* to castigate

fut *etc voir* **être**[1]

fût [fy] **NM 1** *(d'un arbre)* bole

2 *(tonneau)* cask; *(pour l'huile)* drum; **tirer de la bière du f.** to draw beer from the wood *or* cask *or* barrel

3 *(partie ▸ d'une vis, d'un poteau)* shaft; *(▸ d'une colonne)* shaft, body; *(▸ de candélabre)* stem; *(▸ de rivet)* shank

4 *(d'un canon)* stock

5 *(d'un tambour)* barrel, body

6 *(de scie, de raquette)* handle

futaie [fytɛ] **NF** forest, *Am* (piece of) timberland; **haute** *ou* **vieille f.** established *or* mature forest; **arbre de haute f.** full-grown tree

futaille [fytaj] **NF** cask, barrel

futaine [fytɛn] **NF** *Tex* fustian

futal, -als [fytal], **fute** [fyt] **NM** *Fam Br* trousers[□], keks, *Am* pants[□]

futé, -e [fyte] **ADJ** sharp, smart, clever; *aussi Ironique* **ça, c'est f.!** that was clever!; **il n'est pas très f.** he's not very bright

NM,F sharp *or* smart person; **c'est une futée** she's very sharp *or* shrewd; **hé, petit f., comment tu l'enlèves maintenant?** hey, smarty-pants, now how are you going to get it off again?

fute-fute [fytfyt] = **fufute**

futile [fytil] **ADJ 1** *(frivole ▸ raison)* frivolous, trifling; *(▸ occupation, lecture, personne)* frivolous; *(▸ prétexte)* idle **2** *(sans valeur ▸ vie)* pointless, futile

futilement [fytilmɑ̃] **ADV** pointlessly

futilité [fytilite] **NF** *(caractère futile)* triviality; **il perd son temps à des futilités** he wastes his time in trivial pursuits; **ils ne se racontaient que des futilités** their conversation consisted of nothing but trivialities; **s'occuper à des futilités** to fritter away one's time

futon [fytɔ̃] **NM** futon

futur, -e [fytyr] **ADJ 1** *(à venir ▸ difficulté, joie)* future *(avant n)*; **les générations futures** future *or* coming generations; *Rel* **la vie future** the afterlife **2** *(avant le nom)* **une future mère** a mother-to-be; **mon f. mari** my future husband, my husband-to-be; **les futurs époux** the engaged couple, the bride-and-groom-to-be; **mes futurs collègues** my future colleagues; **un f. client** a prospective client; **un f. acheteur** a prospective buyer; **un f. mathématicien** a future *or* budding mathematician; **un f. artiste** a budding artist; **mon f. emploi/appartement** my next job/flat

NM,F *Hum* intended, husband-to-be, *f* wife-to-be

NM 1 *(avenir)* **le f.** the future; **quel f. pour l'Europe?** what will Europe's future be? **2** *Gram* **le f.** the future (tense); **au f.** in the future; **f. antérieur** future perfect; **le f. proche** the immediate future

futurisme [fytyrism] **NM** futurism

futuriste [fytyrist] **ADJ 1** *(d'anticipation)* futuristic **2** *Beaux-Arts & Littérature* futurist

NMF futurist

fuyait *etc voir* **fuir**

fuyant, -e [fɥijɑ̃, -ɑ̃t] **ADJ 1** *(insaisissable ▸ caractère)* elusive; *(▸ regard)* shifty, elusive; **avoir le regard f.** to have shifty eyes, to be shifty-eyed

2 *(menton, front)* receding; **un homme au menton f.** a weak-chinned man

3 *Beaux-Arts* vanishing; **ligne fuyante** receding line

4 *Littéraire (fugitif)* fleeting, transient

NM vanishing perspective

fuyard, -e [fɥijar, -ard] **ADJ** *Arch* shy, timid

NM,F runaway, fugitive

NM *Mil* retreating soldier

FV *(abrév écrite* **fréquence vocale***)* VF

g

G¹, g [ʒe] **NM INV 1** *(lettre)* G, g; **G comme Gaston** ≃ G for George **2** *Mus (note)* G **3** *Phys (accélération de l'apesanteur)* g

G² [ʒe] **NM** *Belg Fam (abrév* **GSM***)* mobile

G7 [ʒesɛt] **NM** *(abrév* **Groupe des Sept***)* **le G7** G7

G8 [ʒeɥit] **NM** *(abrév* **Groupe des Huit***)* **le G8** G8

gabardine [gabardin] **NF 1** *(tissu)* gabardine, gaberdine **2** *(vêtement)* gabardine (coat)

gabare [gabar] **NF 1** *Naut* (sailing) barge; *(pour charger, décharger un navire)* lighter; *(chaland)* scow, store ship **2** *Pêche* dragnet

gabarit [gabari] **NM 1** *(dimension)* size; **de g. réglementaire** regulation size

2 *Fam (carrure)* size□, build□; **c'est un tout petit g.** he/she is very slightly built□; *(stature)* he's/she's a bit on the short side

3 *Fam Fig* calibre; **elle a/n'a pas le g.** she is/isn't up to it

4 *Tech (pour mesure)* gauge; *(maquette) & Ordinat* template; *(d'un bateau)* model; *(d'une pièce de bateau)* mould; *Constr (d'un bâtiment)* outline; **g. d'assemblage** assembly jig, assembling gauge; *Rail* **g. de chargement** loading gauge; **g. d'écartement (des voies)** rail *or* track gauge; *Typ* **g. de mise en page** (typesetting) grid

gabarre [gabar] = **gabare**

gabegie [gabʒi] **NF** *(mauvaise gestion)* mismanagement; *(désordre)* muddle, chaos

gabelle [gabɛl] **NF** *Hist* salt tax

gabelou [gablu] **NM 1** *Péj Hum* customs officer **2** *Hist* salt-tax collector

gabier [gabje] **NM 1** *Naut* deckhand; **g. breveté** able(-bodied) seaman **2** *Hist* topman

gâble, gable [gabl] **NM** *(pignon)* (Gothic) gable; *(charpente)* (triangular) window canopy

Gabon [gabɔ̃] **NM le G.** Gabon

gabonais, -e [gabɔnɛ, -ɛz] **ADJ** Gabonese

• **Gabonais, -e NM,F** Gabonese; **les G.** the Gabonese

gâchage [gɑʃaʒ] **NM 1** *Constr* mixing **2** *(gaspillage)* waste **3 g. des prix** price undercutting

gâche¹ [gɑʃ] **NF 1** *(pour le plâtre)* trowel **2** *(de pâtissier)* spatula

gâche² [gɑʃ] **NF 1** *(d'une serrure)* (box) staple, keeper; *(d'une fenêtre)* (latch) catch; *(d'un pêne)* striking box *or* plate, strike box; *Aut* **g. de porte** striker plate **2** *Tech (pour cliquet)* notch

3 *(de serrure)* spring catch

4 *Tech* pawl

gâcher [3] [gɑʃe] **VT 1** *(gaspiller ▸ argent, talent, temps)* to waste; **c'est de la nourriture gâchée** it's a waste of food; **g. sa vie** to waste one's life **2** *(abîmer)* to spoil, to ruin; **ne dis rien, tu risques de tout g.!** keep quiet or you might spoil *or* ruin everything!; *Fam* **ne va pas me g. le plaisir** don't go spoiling *or* ruining it for me; **il a gâché la soirée** he spoiled the evening; **g. le métier** to spoil it for the others *(by undercutting prices or working for lower wages)* **3** *Constr (plâtre, ciment)* to mix; **g. la chaux** to slack lime

gâchette [gɑʃɛt] **NF 1** *(d'arme à feu)* trigger; **appuyez sur la g.** pull the trigger; **avoir la g. facile/rapide** to be trigger-happy/quick on the draw

2 *Électron (de semi-conducteur)* gate; *(de tube)* grid (electrode)

gâcheur, -euse [gɑʃœr, -øz] **ADJ** wasteful

NM,F *(gaspilleur)* wasteful person, wastrel; *(bâcleur)* bungler, botcher

NM *Constr Br* plasterer's mate, *Am* plasterer's helper

gâchis [gɑʃi] **NM 1** *(gaspillage)* waste; **je ne supporte pas le g.** I can't stand waste *or* wastefulness; **vous avez fait un beau g. dans la cuisine!** you've made a right mess in the kitchen!; **sa vie est un véritable g.** his/her life has been completely wasted **2** *(désordre)* mess; **faire du g.** to make a mess **3** *(mortier)* wet mortar

gadelle [gadɛl] **NF** *Can Bot* currant; **g. blanche** white currant; **g. noire** blackcurrant; **g. rouge** redcurrant

gadget [gadʒɛt] **NM 1** *(appareil)* gadget; **une cuisine pleine de gadgets** a kitchen full of gadgets **2** *(idée, projet)* gimmick; **g. publicitaire** advertising gimmick **3** *(comme adj; avec ou sans trait d'union)* **une mesure g.** a gimmicky measure

gadgétisation [gadʒetizasjɔ̃] **NF la g. croissante de la vie moderne** the increasing use of gadgetry in modern life

gadgétiser [3] [gadʒetize] **VT** to add gadgets to; **g. une voiture** to customize a car (with gadgets)

gadin [gadɛ̃] **NM** *très Fam* **prendre** *ou* **ramasser un g.** to fall flat on one's face, *Br* to come a cropper

gaditan, -ane [gaditɑ̃, -an] **ADJ** of/from Cadiz

• **Gaditan, -e NM,F** = native or inhabitant of Cadiz

gadoue [gadu] **NF** *(boue)* mud, muck

• **gadoues NFPL** *Agr* treated sewage

Gaël [gaɛl] **NM** Gael

gaélique [gaelik] **ADJ** Gaelic

NM *Ling* Gaelic

gaffe [gaf] **NF 1** *Fam (bêtise ▸ en paroles)* gaffe; *(▸ en actions)* blunder, *Br* boob, *Am* goof; **faire une g.** to put one's foot in it

2 *Naut* boathook, hook

3 *Pêche* gaff; *Fam* **avaler sa g.** to die□, to kick the bucket

4 *Fam Arg crime* screw, prison warder□

5 *Fam (locution)* **faire g.** *(faire attention)* to be careful□; **fais g. à toi!** *(prends soin de toi)* take care of yourself!; *(menace)* be careful!, watch it!

gaffer¹ [gafœr] **NM** *TV & Cin* gaffer

gaffer² [3] [gafe] **VI 1** *Fam (commettre une bévue ▸ en parlant)* to make a gaffe, *Br* to drop a clanger; *(▸ en agissant)* to put one's foot in it, *Br* to boob, *Am* to goof **2** *très Fam (surveiller)* **va g. au coin de la rue** go and keep a lookout at the corner of the street

VT 1 *très Fam (regarder)* **gaffe un peu ça!** get a load of this!; **gaffez si les flics s'amènent pas** keep an eye open for the cops **2** *(objet flottant)* to hook; *Pêche (poisson)* to gaff

VPR se gaffer *Suisse Fam* to watch out□

gaffeur¹ [gafœr] **NM** *TV & Cin* **g. grip** gator clip

gaffeur², -euse [gafœr, -øz] *Fam* **ADJ être g.** to be always putting one's foot in it

NM,F blunderer; **son g. de frère** his/her blundering idiot of a brother

gag [gag] **NM** gag, joke; **du coup, j'ai laissé mes clefs à l'intérieur, c'est le g.!** now I've gone and locked myself out, what a farce this is!; **tu es renvoyé – c'est un g.?** you're fired – you're kidding *or* joking!; **son pantalon a craqué au milieu de la réunion, le g.!** his/her trousers split during the meeting, what a scream!

gaga [gaga] *Fam* **ADJ** senile□, gaga; **il est complètement g., le vieux** he's a senile old fool

NMF un vieux g. a doddering old fool

gage [gaʒ] **NM 1** *(caution)* security, collateral *(UNCOUNT)*; *(au mont-de-piété)* pledge; **laisser qch en g.** to leave sth as security; **mettre qch en g.** to pawn *or Am* to hock sth; **mise en g.** pawning; **ma montre est en g.** my watch is in pawn; **rester en g.** to remain as surety; **lettre de g.** debenture bond; *(pour hypothèque)* mortgage bond; *Jur* **g. mobilier** mortgage over assets, mortgage over property

2 *Fig (garantie)* guarantee; **sa compétence sera le g. d'une bonne gestion** his/her competence will guarantee *or* secure good management; **votre parole sera le meilleur des gages** your word will be the best guarantee

3 *(témoignage)* proof, token; **g. d'amour** token of love, love token; **en g. de mon amour** as proof *or* a pledge of my love; **en g. de ma bonne volonté** as a token of my goodwill; **je t'offre ce livre en g. de notre amitié** I offer you this book as a token of our friendship

4 *(dans un jeu)* forfeit

• **gages NMPL** *Vieilli (salaire)* wages, pay; **être aux gages de qn** to be in sb's employ (as a servant)

gagé, -e [gaʒe] **ADJ 1** *(objet)* pledged, pawned; **meubles gagés** furniture under distraint; **recettes non gagées** unassigned *or* unpledged revenue **2** *(emprunt)* secured; **g. sur l'or** backed by gold

gager [17] [gaʒe] **VT 1** *Fin (emprunt)* to secure, to guarantee **2** *Littéraire (parier)* to wager; **gageons qu'il l'épousera** I wager he'll marry her

gageur, -euse [gaʒœr, -øz] **NM,F** *Com & Jur* pledger, pawner

gageure [gaʒyr] **NF 1** *(action difficile)* challenge; **c'est une g. de vouloir la raisonner** trying to reason with her is quite a challenge; **réussir la g. de faire qch** to succeed in the difficult task of doing sth **2** *Littéraire (pari)* wager, *Can* bet

gageuse [gaʒøz] *voir* **gageur**

gagiste [gaʒist] **NMF** *Jur* pledgee, secured creditor

gagnant, -e [gaɲɑ̃, -ɑ̃t] **ADJ** *(ticket, coupon)* winning *(avant n)*; **il est donné g.** he is favourite *or* has been tipped to win; **coup g.** *(au tennis)* winner *(shot)*; *Fig* **elle part gagnante** all the odds are in her favour; *Fig* **jouer g.** to hold all the trump cards

NM,F winner; *Fig* **c'est toi le grand g. de l'histoire** you've come out on top, you've got the best of the bargain

gagne-pain [gaɲpɛ̃] **NM INV** livelihood; **ces traductions sont son g.** these translations are his/her livelihood; **c'est mon seul g.** it's my only means of existence

gagne-petit [gaɲpəti] **NMF INV** *Péj* **1** *(qui gagne peu)* **les g.** the low-paid **2** *(qui manque d'ambition)* small-time operator, small-timer

GAGNER **[3]** [gaɲe]

VT	
• to win **1, 6**	• to earn **2**
• to make **2**	• to gain **3, 5**
• to save **4**	• to win over **6**
• to overcome **7**	• to reach **9**
VI	
• to win **1**	• to gain ground **2**
VPR	
• to win **2**	• to earn **2**

VT 1 *(partie, match, élection, prix)* to win; *aussi Fig* **g. le gros lot** to win *or* to hit the jackpot; **g. un procès** to win a (court) case; *Fig* **la partie n'est pas gagnée** we haven't won yet; **ce n'est pas gagné d'avance** it's a bit early to start talking about success; *Ironique* **c'est gagné!** now you've got what you asked for!

2 *(argent ▸ comme rémunération)* to earn, to make; *(▸ comme récompense)* to earn; *(▸ dans une transaction)* to make a profit of, to make; **combien gagne-t-elle par mois?** how much does she earn a month?; *Fam* **g. gros** to earn *or* to make big money; *(société)* to make large profits; **il ne gagne presque rien** he earns next to nothing; **elle a gagné 500 euros sur la vente du tableau** she made 500 euros on the sale of the painting; **g. une fortune à la loterie** to win a fortune on the lottery; *aussi Fig* **allez, prends, tu l'as bien gagné!** go on, take it, you've earned it!; **g. des mille et des cents** to earn a fortune; *Fam* **g. sa vie** *ou* **son pain** *ou* **son bifteck** *ou* **sa croûte** to earn a living *or* one's daily bread; **g. qch à la sueur de son front** to earn sth with the sweat of one's brow; **g. de quoi vivre** to earn a living, to earn enough to live on; *Fam Ironique* **eh bien, j'ai gagné ma journée!** I should have stayed in bed today!

3 *(obtenir ▸ avantage)* to gain; *(▸ part de marché)* to capture; **il y a tout à g. à faire cette démarche** there's everything to gain *or* to be gained from making this move; **nous ne gagnerons rien à attendre** there is nothing to be gained *or* we'll gain nothing by waiting; **et si j'accepte, qu'est-ce que j'y gagne?** and if I accept, what do I get out of it?; **qu'est-ce que tu gagnes à tout changer?** what's the point of changing everything?; **il y a gagné un bras cassé/une réputation de menteur** all he got out of it was a broken arm/a reputation for being a liar; **c'est toujours ça de gagné!, c'est autant de gagné!** that's something, anyway!

4 *(économiser)* to save; **g. de la place** to save space; **en enlevant la porte on gagne 10 cm** if you take the door off you gain an extra 10 cm; **g. du temps** *(en allant très vite)* to save time; *(en atermoyant)* to play for time; **chercher à g. du temps** to play for time

5 *Bourse* to gain; **l'indice a gagné deux points** the index has gone up by *or* has gained two points

6 *(conquérir ▸ ami)* to win; *(▸ partisan)* to win over; **g. l'appui de qn** to win sb's support; **g. la confiance/l'estime/l'amitié de qn** to win *or* to gain sb's confidence/respect/friendship; **g. qn à une cause** to win sb over (to a cause)

7 *(sujet: sentiment, sensation)* to overcome; *(sujet: épidémie, infection, feu, nuages)* to spread to; **je sentais la panique me g.** I could feel panic creeping over me; **la faim nous gagnait** we were getting hungry; **le cancer gagne l'autre poumon** the cancer is spreading to the other lung; **s'ils se laissent g. par le froid, ils sont perdus** if they allow the cold to take a grip of *or* to get to them, they are finished; **le rire gagna l'assemblée tout entière** the laughter spread through the whole audience

8 *(avancer)* **g. du terrain** *Naut & Fig* to gain ground; *Naut (sur la mer)* to reclaim land; **la mer gagne du terrain** the sea is encroaching on the land; **nos concurrents gagnent du terrain** our competitors are gaining ground

9 *(rejoindre)* to reach, to get to; **nous gagnerons Paris/le refuge avant la nuit** we will reach Paris/the refuge before nightfall; **il gagna la sortie** he made his way to the exit; *Naut* **g. le port** to reach port, *Spéc* to fetch into port; **le ferry gagna le large** the ferry got out into the open sea

10 *Naut (rattraper)* **g. un navire** to gain on *or* overhaul a ship; **g. le devant** to forge ahead, to take the lead; **g. le vent** to make *or* to fetch to windward; **g. le vent d'une pointe** to weather a headland; **g. de l'avant** to forge ahead

VI 1 *(l'emporter)* to win; **on a gagné (par) 3 buts à 2** we won (by) 3 goals to 2, we won 3–2; **g. aux points** to win on points; **g. aux courses** to win at the races; **g. aux échecs** to win at chess; **g. aux élections** to win the election; **tu as gagné, on fera ce que tu demandes** you win, we'll do as you say; **à tous les coups l'on** *ou* **on gagne!** everyone's a winner!

2 *(avancer ▸ incendie, érosion)* to gain ground; **g. sur** to gain *or* to advance on; **ses concurrents gagnent sur lui** his competitors are gaining on him; **la mer gagne sur la côte** the sea is eating away at the coastline; **g. en** to increase *or* to gain in; **g. en longueur** to increase in length, to grow longer; **g. en vigueur** to become stronger

3 *Naut* **g. au vent** to make *or* to fetch to windward

• gagner à **VT IND g. à qch/à faire qch** to benefit from sth/from doing sth; **elle gagne à être connue** once you get to know her a bit she grows on you; **ils gagneraient à ce que nul ne l'apprenne** it would be to their advantage if nobody found out; **accepte, tu y gagnes** *ou* **tu gagnes au change** say yes, it's to your advantage *or* you get the best of the deal

VPR se gagner 1 *(emploi passif)* **l'argent ne se gagne pas si facilement** it isn't so easy to make money **2 se g. qch** to win *or* to earn sth; **se g. l'estime de qn** to win sb's esteem; **se g. le respect de qn** to earn sb's respect; **se g. un adepte** to win over a follower

gagneur, -euse [gaɲœr, -øz] **NM,F** winner; **c'est un g. né** he's a born winner

• gagneuse NF *très Fam (prostituée)* pro

gai, -e [ge] **ADJ 1** *(personne)* cheerful, merry, lively, in good spirits; *(mine, décor, personnalité)* cheerful, happy; *(musique)* cheerful, jolly; *(voix)* cheerful, cheery; *(couleur)* bright, cheerful; **g. comme un pinson** happy as a lark *or Br* a sandboy; **sa vie n'a pas toujours été très gaie** his/her life hasn't always been much fun *or* a happy one; **cette couleur rend la pièce plus gaie** this colour makes the room look more cheerful; **encore une panne! ça n'est vraiment pas g.!** another breakdown! that's (just) great!; **tout cela n'est pas très g.** it's all a bit depressing; *Ironique* **il vérifie en permanence ce que je fais, c'est g.** he's constantly checking what I'm doing, it's charming *or* really nice; *Ironique* **il pleut encore, c'est g.!** great, it's raining again!

2 *(un peu ivre)* merry, tipsy

3 *Belg (agréable)* nice, pleasant

4 *(homosexuel)* = **gay**

NM,F = **gay**

gaiement [gemɑ̃] **ADV** *(avec joie)* cheerfully, cheerily; **allons-y g.!** let's get on with it!

gaieté [gete] **NF 1** *(bonne humeur)* cheerfulness, gaiety; **elle a retrouvé sa g.** she's cheered up again; **tu n'es pas d'une g. folle ce matin** you're not exactly a bundle of fun this morning **2** *(d'une couleur)* brightness, cheerfulness

• gaietés NFPL *Ironique* **les gaietés du métro aux heures de pointe** the delights of the underground in the rush hour

• de gaieté de cœur ADV willingly, gladly; **je ne l'ai pas fait de g. de cœur!** it's not something I enjoyed doing!

gaillard, -e [gajar, -ard] **ADJ 1** *(grivois)* bawdy, lewd, ribald **2** *(vigoureux)* lusty; **se sentir g.** to feel in good form, *Br* to be full of beans; **il est encore g.** he is still sprightly *or* lively; **un petit vent g.** a good stiff breeze, a lively breeze

NM,F *(personne forte)* fellow; **un grand et solide g.** a great strapping man; **tu ne vas pas pleurer, un grand g. comme toi!** you're not going to cry, a big guy like you!; **c'est un sacré g.!** *(homme viril)* he's a lusty *or* red-blooded fellow!; *(costaud)* he's a great strapping lad!; **c'est une grande gaillarde** she's a big strapping girl *or Br* lass

NM 1 *Fam* **toi, mon g., tu n'as pas intérêt à bouger!** *(avec menace)* you'd better not move, *Br* mate *or Am* buddy! **2** *Naut* **g. d'avant** forecastle, fo'c'sle; **g. d'arrière** poop; **haut de g.** deep-waisted

• gaillarde NF *Mus & (danse)* galliard

gaillardement [gajardəmɑ̃] **ADV 1** *(gaiement)* cheerfully, good-humouredly; **elle accepte/supporte tout ça g.** she accepts/bears it all cheerfully **2** *(vaillamment)* valiantly, gamely; **on se mit en marche g.** we set off boldly *or* in good spirits

gaillardise [gajardiz] **NF** *Vieilli* **1** *(bonne humeur)* cheerfulness, good humour **2** *(grivoiserie)* ribald *or* risqué remark; **conter des gaillardises** to tell risqué *or Am* off-colour stories

gaîment [gemɑ̃] *Arch* = **gaiement**

gain [gɛ̃] **NM 1** *(succès)* winning; **elle a eu** *ou* **obtenu g. de cause** *(dans un procès)* she won the case; *Fig* it was agreed that she was in the right; **donner g. de cause à qn** to decide in favour of sb

2 *(économie)* saving; **un g. de place/temps** a saving of space/time; **cela permet un (énorme) g. de place/temps** it saves (a lot of) space/time; **gains de productivité** productivity gains

3 *(progrès)* benefit; **un g. de 30 sièges aux élections** a gain of 30 seats in the elections

4 *(bénéfice financier)* profit, gain; *(rémunération)* earnings; *(au jeu)* winnings; **faire des gains importants à la Bourse** to make a big profit on the stock exchange; **avoir l'amour du g.** to love making money; **gains illicites** illicit earnings; **gains invisibles** invisible earnings; *Compta* **g. latent** unrealized gain

5 *Électron* gain; **commande automatique de g.** automatic gain control; **g. en courant** current gain; **g. en tension** voltage magnification; **g. d'étage** stage gain; *Nucl* **g. de régénération** breeding gain

gainage [gɛnaʒ] **NM** *(de câble)* sheathing; *(de cylindre, de tuyau)* lagging, cladding

gaine [gɛn] **NF 1** *(étui ▸ de poignard)* sheath; *(▸ de parapluie)* cover; **g. métallique** metallic sheath *or* sleeve; **câble sous g.** sheathed cable

2 *Anat & Bot* sheath

3 *(d'amorce)* priming tube

4 *Constr (conduit vertical)* shaft, duct; *(de climatisation)* duct; **g. d'aération** ventilation shaft; **g. d'ascenseur** *Br* lift shaft, *Am* elevator shaft; **g. de ventilation** ventilation shaft

5 *Nucl* can; **g. d'électrons/d'ions** electron/ion sheath

6 *(sous-vêtement)* girdle

gaine-combinaison [gɛnkɔ̃binɛzɔ̃] *(pl* **gaines-combinaisons) NF** corselet

gaine-culotte [gɛnkylɔt] *(pl* **gaines-culottes) NF** panty girdle

gainer **[4]** [gene] **VT** *(câble)* to sheathe, to encase (**de** in); *(cylindre, tuyau)* to lag, to clad; **le corps gainé de vinyle bleu** his/her body sheathed in blue vinyl

gaîté [gete] *Arch* = **gaieté**

Gal *(abrév écrite* **Général)** Gen

gal, -als [gal] **NM** *Phys* gal

gala [gala] **NM** gala; **dîner en grand g.** to dine in state, to dine with great ceremony; **g. de charité** charity gala

• de gala ADJ gala *(avant n)*; **en habit** *ou* **tenue de g.** in gala dress, in full dress

Galaad [galaad] **NM** *Géog, Bible & Myth* Galahad

galactique [galaktik] **ADJ** galactic

galactogène [galaktɔʒɛn] **ADJ** galactagogue, galactogenetic

NM galactagogue, galactogenetic

galamment [galamɑ̃] **ADV** gallantly; *Littéraire (noblement)* honourably; **que c'est g. dit!** there speaks a *or* spoken like a true gentleman!

galandage [galɑ̃daʒ] **NM** *Constr* brick-on-edge partition

galant, -e [galɑ̃, -ɑ̃t] **ADJ 1** *(courtois)* gallant, gentlemanly; **un homme g.** a gentleman; **sois g., porte-lui son paquet** be a gentleman and carry her parcel for her; **un g. homme** an honourable man, a gentleman; **se conduire en g. homme** to behave like a gentleman **2** *Littéraire (amoureux)* **un rendez-vous g.** a date, a rendezvous, *Vieilli* a lover's tryst; **une femme galante** a woman of easy virtue

NM *Vieilli* suitor, admirer; *Littéraire* **un vert g.** an ageing beau; **faire le g. auprès d'une dame** to court *or* to pay court to a lady; *(flirter)* to flirt with a lady

galanterie [galɑ̃tri] **NF 1** *(courtoisie)* courteousness, gallantry, chivalry; **la g. se perd!** the age of chivalry is dead! **2** *(compliment)* gallant remark, gallantry; **dire des galanteries à qn** to pay sb compliments **3** *(intrigue)* love affair, intrigue

galantine [galɑ̃tin] **NF** *Culin* galantine

Galapagos [galapagos] **NFPL les (îles) G.** the Galapagos Islands

Galatée [galate] **NF** *Myth* Galatea

galaxie [galaksi] **NF** galaxy; *Astron* **la G.** the Galaxy

galbe [galb] **NM** curve; **des jambes d'un g. parfait** shapely legs

galbé, -e [galbe] **ADJ 1** *(commode, poterie)* curved, with a curved outline; **les pieds galbés d'une commode** the curved legs of a chest of drawers **2** *(mollet ▸ de femme)* shapely; *(▸ de sportif)* muscular

galber **[3]** [galbe] **VT** *(vase, commode)* to give curves to

gale [gal] **NF 1** *Méd* scabies; **g. bédouine** prickly heat; *Fam* **embrasse-le, il n'a pas la g.!** give him a kiss, you won't catch anything!; **mauvais** *ou* **méchant comme la g.** wicked as sin

2 *Fam (personne odieuse)* rat, *Br* nasty piece of work

3 *Vét (du chien, du chat)* mange; *(du mouton)* scab

4 *Bot* scab

galée [gale] **NF** *(en imprimerie)* galley

galéjer **[18]** [galeʒe] **VI** *Fam* to spin a yarn; **tu galèjes!** a likely story!

galène [galɛn] **NF** *Minér* galena, galenite

galéopithèque [galeɔpitɛk] **NM** *Zool* flying lemur

galère [galɛr] **NF 1** *(navire)* galley; **condamné** *ou* **envoyé aux galères** sent to the galleys; *Naut* **avirons en g.!** rest on your oars! **2** *Fam (situation pénible)* hassle, mess; **après des années de g.** after years of hardship[□]; **c'est la g. pour obtenir des places de théâtre** it's a real hassle getting theatre tickets; **vivre à Los Angeles sans voiture, c'est une vraie g.** life in Los Angeles without a car is the pits *or* is a real hassle; **c'est la g.!, quelle g.!** what a pain *or* drag *or* hassle!; *très Fam* **se foutre dans une g.** to get oneself into a mess

ADJ *Fam* **il est vraiment g., ce mec** he's nothing but trouble; **c'est un peu g.** it's a bit of a hassle; **c'est g. de trouver une cabine téléphonique dans cette ville** it's a (real) hassle to find a phone box in this town

galérer **[18]** [galere] **VI** *Fam (avoir du mal)* to have a hard time (of it); **on a galéré deux heures en banlieue** we wasted two whole hours driving around the suburbs; **elle a vraiment galéré avant d'être connue** she had a hard time of it before she made it

galerie [galri] **NF 1** *(local ▸ d'expositions, de ventes)* (art) gallery, private gallery; **g. d'art** *ou* **de peinture** *ou* **de tableaux** art gallery; **g. de portraits** portrait gallery; *Fig* rogue's gallery

2 *(salle d'apparat)* hall, gallery

3 *(passage couvert)* gallery; *(arcade)* arcade; **g. marchande** *(passage couvert)* shopping arcade; *(centre commercial) Br* shopping centre, *Am* shopping mall

4 *Can (véranda)* porch

5 *Théât* **la g.** the gallery, the balcony; **les deuxièmes galeries** *(qui ne sont pas les plus hautes)* the dress circle; *(les plus hautes)* the upper circle; **la troisième g.** the gallery, *Fam* the gods; *Fig* **jouer pour la g.** to play to the gallery; *Fig* **tout ce qu'il fait, c'est pour la g.** everything he does is to show off *or* to play to the gallery; *Fig* **amuser la g.** to play for laughs

6 *Mines* gallery, level; **g. d'avancement** heading

7 *Aut* roof rack

8 *(sur meuble)* cornice

9 *Élec* **g. des câbles** cable tunnel

galérien [galerjɛ̃] **NM** galley slave; **travailler comme un g.** to work like a (galley) slave *or* a horse *or* a Trojan; **mener une vie de g.** to lead a dog's life

galeriste [galrist] **NMF** gallery owner

galet [galɛ] **NM 1** *(caillou)* pebble; **sur les galets** on the shingle *or* the pebble beach **2** *(roue)* roller; *Tech* roller; *Ordinat (de souris)* roller, wheel; *Aut* **g. de direction** roller; **g. de roulement** travelling *or* running wheel

galetas [galta] **NM 1** *Littéraire (logement)* hovel **2** *Suisse & (en français régional) (grenier)* attic, garret

galetouse [galtuz] **NF** *très Fam* mess tin, dixie

galette [galɛt] **NF 1** *(crêpe ▸ épaisse)* pancake, griddle cake; *(▸ de froment, de sarrasin, de blé noir)* buckwheat pancake; *(pain azyme)* matzo bread; *(biscuit)* butter biscuit; **g. de maïs** corn bread *(UNCOUNT)*; **g. de pommes de terre** potato pancake; **la g. des Rois** = pastry traditionally eaten on Twelfth Night (in France)

2 *très Fam (argent)* dough, *Br* dosh; **elle a de la g.** she's rolling in it

3 *Belg (gaufrette)* wafer

4 *Fam (disque, CD)* disc[□]

galetteux, -euse [galɛtø, -øz] **ADJ** *Fam Vieilli* loaded, rolling in it

galeux, -euse [galø, -øz] **ADJ 1** *(qui a la gale)* mangy; *(arbre)* scabby; *Méd* **plaie galeuse** sore caused by scabies **2** *(dégoûtant ▸ façade, bâtisse)* scruffy, dingy; *(▸ quartier)* squalid, seedy

NM,F *Péj* **on y trouve réunis tous les g. de la terre** all the scum of the earth is there

galgal, -als [galgal] **NM** *Archéol* cairn, barrow

galibot [galibo] **NM** *Mines* pit boy

Galice [galis] **NF la G.** Galicia

Galicie [galisi] **NF la G.** Galicia

galicien, -enne [galisjɛ̃, -ɛn] **ADJ** *(de Galice, de Galicie)* Galician

NM *(langue de Galice)* Galician

• **Galicien, -enne** **NM,F** *(de Galice, de Galicie)* Galician

Galilée[1] [galile] **NF** *Géog* **la G.** Galilee

Galilée[2] [galile] **NPR** Galileo

galiléen, -enne [galileɛ̃, -ɛn] **ADJ** Galilean

• **Galiléen, -enne** **NM,F** Galilean

• **Galiléen** **NM le G.** the Galilean

galimatias [galimatja] **NM** gibberish *(UNCOUNT)*, gobbledegook *(UNCOUNT)*

galion [galjɔ̃] **NM** *Naut* galleon

galipette [galipɛt] **NF** *Fam* somersault[□]; **faire des galipettes** *(faire des sauts)* to do somersaults[□]; *(gambader)* to romp about[□]; *Hum (ébats amoureux)* to have a roll around

galipot [galipo] **NM 1** *(résine)* galipot, white resin **2** *Naut* blacking

galipote [galipɔt] **NF** *Can Fam* **courir la g.** to chase women

galle [gal] **NF** *Bot* gall; **g. de chêne** oak apple

Galles [gal] **NM le pays de G.** Wales

gallican, -e [galikɑ̃, -an] *Rel* **ADJ** Gallican

• **Gallican, -e** **NM,F** Gallican

gallicanisme [galikanism] **NM** *Rel* Gallicanism

gallicisme [galisism] **NM** *Ling (calque du français)* Gallicism; *(emprunt au français)* French idiom, Gallicism

gallinacé, -e [galinase] *Orn* **ADJ** gallinaceous, gallinacean

NM gallinacean

• **gallinacés** **NMPL** chicken family, *Spéc* Gallinaceae

Gallipoli [galipɔli] **N** *Géog* Gallipoli

gallique[1] [galik] **ADJ** *Chim & Minér* gallic; **acide g.** gallic acid

gallique[2] [galik] **ADJ** *Hist* Gallic

gallium [galjɔm] **NM** *Chim* gallium

gallois, -e [galwa, -az] **ADJ** Welsh

NM *(langue)* Welsh

• **Gallois, -e** **NM,F** Welshman, *f* Welshwoman; **les G.** the Welsh

gallomanie [galɔmani] **NF** Gallomania

gallon [galɔ̃] **NM** gallon

gallo-romain, -e [galɔrɔmɛ̃, -ɛn] *(mpl* **gallo-romains,** *fpl* **gallo-romaines)** **ADJ** Gallo-Roman

• **Gallo-Romain, -e** **NM,F** Gallo-Roman

galoche [galɔʃ] **NF 1** *(chaussure)* wooden-soled shoe, clog *(with leather uppers)* **2** *très Fam* French kiss; **rouler une g. à qn** to French-kiss sb, *Br* to snog sb

galon [galɔ̃] **NM 1** *Tex (ruban)* braid *(UNCOUNT)*, trimming *(UNCOUNT)*; **un g. doré** a piece of gold braid; **g. de finition** *(d'ameublement)* upholstery binding **2** *Mil (insigne)* stripe; **il a mis du temps pour gagner ses galons d'officier** it took him a long time to earn his stripes; *Fig* **prendre du g.** to take a step up the ladder, to get a promotion **3** *Can* **g. (à mesurer)** tape measure, *Br* measuring tape

galonné [galɔne] **NM** *Fam Arg mil (officier)* officer[□], *Br* brass hat; *(sous-officier)* non-commissioned officer[□], NCO[□]; **les galonnés** the top brass

galonner **[3]** [galɔne] **VT** *Couture* to braid, to trim (with braid); **col galonné de velours** velvet-trimmed collar

galop [galo] **NM** *Équitation* gallop; **prendre le g.** to break into a gallop; **petit g.** canter; **grand g., triple g.** full gallop; **g. de manège** hand gallop; **g. d'essai** warm-up gallop; *Fig* dry run; *(examen blanc)* mock exam

• **au galop** **ADV** at a gallop; **mettre sa monture au g.** to put one's horse into a gallop; **partir au (grand** *ou* **triple) g.** to gallop away; **il a descendu la colline au g.** he galloped down the hill; **va m'acheter le journal, et au g.!** go and buy me the newspaper, and be quick about it!; *Fig* **au triple g.** at top speed; **arriver au (grand** *ou* **triple) g.** to come like a shot

galopade [galɔpad] **NF 1** *(course)* (mad) rush; **on est arrivés à l'heure, mais après quelle g.!** we got there on time, but it was a real scramble *or* dash! **2** *(bruit)* stampede **3** *Équitation* lope

galopant, -e [galɔpɑ̃, -ɑ̃t] **ADJ** *(consommation, inflation)* galloping; *(urbanisation)* uncontrolled, unplanned; **démographie galopante** rapid population growth; **le flot g. des vagues** the rushing waves

galoper **[3]** [galɔpe] **VI 1** *Équitation* to gallop; **se mettre à g.** to break into a gallop **2** *(aller trop vite ▸ idées, images)* to race; *(▸ enfants)* to charge; *(çà et là)* to gallop *or* rush around; **ne galopez pas dans les escaliers!** don't charge up and down the stairs!; *Fam* **g. après qn/qch** to chase (around) after sb/sth

VT *(cheval)* to gallop

galopeur [galɔpœr] **NM** *Équitation* galloper

galopin [galɔpɛ̃] **NM** *Fam* (street) urchin, scamp; **espèce de petit g.!** you little devil!, you little brat!

galure [galyr], **galurin** [galyrɛ̃] **NM** *Fam* hat[□]

galvanique [galvanik] **ADJ 1** *Méd* galvanic; **courant g.** galvanic current **2** *Métal* electroplating *(avant n)*; **plaqué g.** electroplate; **dorure g.** electrogilding

galvanisation [galvanizasjɔ̃] **NF 1** *Méd* galvanization **2** *Métal* galvanization

galvaniser **[3]** [galvanize] **VT 1** *Méd* to galvanize **2** *Métal* to electroplate, to galvanize, to zinc-plate **3** *Fig (stimuler)* to galvanize *or* to spur into action; **ça l'a galvanisé** *(après une catastrophe)* it galvanized *or* spurred him into action; *(après une bonne nouvelle)* it lifted his spirits

galvanisme [galvanism] **NM** *Méd* galvanism

galvano [galvano] **NM** *Fam Typ* electro

galvanomètre [galvanɔmɛtr] **NM** galvanometer

galvanoplastie [galvanɔplasti] **NF** electroplating, electrodeposition; *Typ* electrotyping

galvanoplastique [galvanɔplastik] **ADJ** electroplating *(avant n)*, *Spéc* galvanoplastic

galvanoscope [galvanɔskɔp] **NM** galvanoscope

galvanotype [galvanotip] **NM** *Typ* electrotype

galvanotypie [galvanotipi] **NF** *Typ* electrotyping

galvaudage [galvodaʒ] **NM** *(de dons, de qualités)* prostituting

galvauder **[3]** [galvode] **VT 1** *(réputation, nom)* to sully, to tarnish **2** *(don, qualité)* to prostitute **3** *(mot, sens)* to debase; **le mot a été galvaudé** the word has become clichéd *or* hackneyed through overuse

VPR se galvauder to demean *or* to lower oneself

gamba [gɑ̃ba, gɑ̃mba, *pl* gɑ̃bas, gɑ̃mbas] **NF** gamba, = type of large Mediterranean prawn

gambade [gɑ̃bad] **NF** *(cabriole)* leap, caper; **faire des gambades** *(chien)* to frisk about; *(enfant)* to skip about

gambader [3] [gɑ̃bade] **VI** to gambol, to leap *or* to caper about; **les enfants gambadaient de joie autour de l'arbre de Noël** the children were gleefully capering around the Christmas tree

gambe [gɑ̃b] *voir* **viole**

gamberge [gɑ̃bɛrʒ] **NF** *Fam* **il est en pleine g.** *(il combine quelque chose)* he's plotting something; *(il rêvasse)* he's daydreaming

gamberger [17] [gɑ̃bɛrʒe] *Fam* **VI** *(penser)* to think hard; **j'ai gambergé** *(j'ai réfléchi)* I've been mulling things over; *(je me suis inquiété)* I've been brooding

VT *(combiner)* **je me demande ce qu'il gamberge** I wonder what he's up to; **c'est lui qui a gambergé le coup de la banque** he's the one who masterminded the bank job

gambette¹ [gɑ̃bɛt] **NM** *(oiseau)* redshank

gambette² [gɑ̃bɛt] **NF** *Fam (jambe)* leg, *Br* pin, *Am* gam; **jouer** *ou* **tricoter des gambettes** to go off like a shot, to leg it

Gambie [gɑ̃bi] **NF 1** *(pays)* **la G.** the Gambia **2** *(fleuve)* **la G., le fleuve G.** the Gambia (River)

gambiller [3] [gɑ̃bije] **VI** *Fam Vieilli* to jig about, to dance

gambit [gɑ̃bi] **NM** *Échecs* gambit; **g. du roi/de la reine** king's/queen's gambit

gamelle [gamɛl] **NF 1** *(récipient ▸ d'un soldat)* mess tin; *(▸ d'un ouvrier)* lunch *Br* box *or Am* pail; *(▸ d'animal)* bowl; *Fam* **passe-moi ta g.** *(assiette)* give me your plate

2 *Mil & Naut* mess; **la g. des officiers** the officers' mess

3 *très Fam (baiser)* French kiss; **rouler une g. à qn** to French-kiss sb, *Br* to snog sb

4 *très Fam (locutions)* **ramasser** *ou* **(se) prendre une g.** to fall flat on one's face, *Br* to come a cropper

gamète [gamɛt] **NM** *Biol* gamete

gamétique [gametik] **ADJ** *Biol* gametic

gamétogenèse [gametɔʒənɛz] **NF** *Biol* gametogenesis

gamin, -e [gamɛ̃, -in] **NM,F** *Fam* kid; **une gamine de dix ans** a girl of ten

ADJ *(puéril)* childish; *(espiègle)* childlike, impish, playful; **elle est encore gamine** she's still just a child

gaminerie [gaminri] **NF** *(acte)* childish *or* silly prank; *(comportement)* childishness *(UNCOUNT)*, infantile behaviour *(UNCOUNT)*; **ses gamineries m'exaspéraient** his/her childish ways were driving me mad; **il a passé l'âge de ces gamineries** he's too old to behave so childishly *or* in such a childish way

gamma [gama] **NM INV** gamma

gammaglobuline [gamaglɔbylin] **NF** *Biol* gamma globulin

gammathérapie [gamaterapi] **NF** *Méd* gamma-ray therapy

gamme [gam] **NF 1** *Mus* scale, *Spéc* gamut; **gammes chromatiques** chromatic scales; **g. montante/descendante** rising/falling scale; **faire des gammes** to do *or* practise scales; **faire ses gammes** to play one's scales; *Fig* to go through the basics, to learn the ropes

2 *(de produits)* range, series; *(de prix, de couleurs)* range; *(de sentiments)* gamut; **étendre sa g. de produits** to widen one's product range; **une nouvelle g. de produits de beauté** a new range of beauty products; **le film joue sur toute la g. des sentiments humains** the film runs the (whole) gamut of human feelings; **g. de prix** price range

3 *Com* **bas de g.** *(de qualité inférieure)* bottom-of-the-range; *(peu prestigieux)* downmarket; **haut de g.** *(de qualité supérieure)* top-of-the-range; *(prestigieux)* upmarket; **milieu de g.** middle-of-the-range; **un ordinateur d'entrée de g.** an entry-level computer

4 *Aut* **g. moyenne** mid-range; *Aut* **g. de transmission** driving range

gammée [game] *voir* **croix**

gamopétale [gamɔpetal] *Bot* **ADJ** gamopetalous

• **gamopétales NFPL** Gamopetalae

ganache [ganaʃ] **NF 1** *Péj* **une (vieille) g.** an old codger **2** *(du cheval)* lower jaw, cheek **3** *Culin* ganache, = cake filling made from chocolate, butter and cream

Gand [gɑ̃] **NF** Ghent

gang¹ [gɑ̃g] **NM** *(bande)* gang; **guerre des gangs** gang warfare

gang² [gaŋ] **NF** *Can (bande)* band, group; **une g. de bandits** a gang

ganga [gɑ̃ga] **NM** *Orn* sand grouse

Gange [gɑ̃ʒ] **NM le G.** the (River) Ganges

ganglion [gɑ̃glijɔ̃] **NM** *Méd* ganglion; **g. lymphatique** lymph gland; **g. nerveux** ganglion cell; *Fam* **avoir des ganglions** to have swollen glands

ganglionnaire [gɑ̃glijɔnɛr] **ADJ** *Méd* ganglionic, ganglial

gangrène [gɑ̃grɛn] **NF 1** *Méd* gangrene; **g. sèche/humide/gazeuse** dry/moist/gas gangrene; **avoir la g.** to have gangrene **2** *Fig (corruption)* scourge, canker; **la g. du terrorisme** the scourge of terrorism

gangrené, -e [gɑ̃grəne] **ADJ 1** *Méd* gangrenous, gangrened **2** *Fig* corrupt

gangrener [19] [gɑ̃grəne] **VT 1** *Méd* to cause to become gangrenous, to gangrene **2** *Fig (corrompre)* to corrupt, to rot

VPR se gangrener 1 *Méd* to become gangrenous **2** *Fig* to become corrupt

gangreneux, -euse [gɑ̃grənø, -øz] **ADJ** *Méd* gangrenous

gangster [gɑ̃gstɛr] **NM 1** *(bandit)* gangster; **un film de gangsters** a gangster movie *or Br* film **2** *(escroc)* cheat, swindler

gangstérisme [gɑ̃gsterism] **NM** gangsterism

gangue [gɑ̃g] **NF 1** *Mines (d'une pierre précieuse, d'un minerai)* gangue **2** *(couche)* coating; **recouvert d'une g. de glace** coated with ice **3** *Fig* **il n'a jamais pu sortir de la g. de son éducation/de la religion** he was never able to free himself from the straitjacket of his education/of religion

ganse [gɑ̃s] **NF 1** *Couture* braid *or* twine binding **2** *Can (passant)* belt loop; *Fig* **tenir qn par la g.** to have a hold on sb

gansé, -e [gɑ̃se] **ADJ** *(vêtement)* braided

ganser [3] [gɑ̃se] **VT** *(robe, tissu)* to braid, to trim; *(chapeau)* to trim; **des canotiers gansés de velours** velvet-trimmed boaters

gant [gɑ̃] **NM** *(accessoire)* glove; **mettre ses gants** to put one's gloves on; **g. de boxe** boxing glove; **g. de crin** massage glove; **g. d'escrime** fencing glove; **g. de Neptune** glove sponge; **g. de toilette** *Br* flannel, facecloth, *Am* washcloth; **gants de ménage** rubber gloves; **ça te va comme un g.** it fits you like a glove; *Fig* **se donner les gants de qch** to claim credit for sth; *Fig* **mettre** *ou* **prendre des gants avec qn** to handle sb with kid gloves; **tu as intérêt à prendre** *ou* **mettre des gants pour le lui dire** you'd do well to tell him/her gently; *Fig* **jeter le g. (à qn)** to throw down the gauntlet (to sb); *Fig* **relever** *ou* **ramasser le g.** to take up the gauntlet, to accept the challenge

gantelée [gɑ̃tle] **NF** *Bot (digitale pourprée)* foxglove

gantelet [gɑ̃tlɛ] **NM 1** *Hist & Sport* gauntlet **2** *Ind* gauntlet, hand leather

ganter [3] [gɑ̃te] **VT** *Littéraire* to glove; **ses mains étaient gantées de dentelle noire** her hands were gloved in black lace, she was wearing black lace gloves

VI vous gantez du combien? what size gloves do you take?

VPR se ganter to put on one's gloves

ganterie [gɑ̃tri] **NF 1** *(industrie)* glove-making industry; *(fabrique)* glove factory **2** *(négoce)* **la g.** the glove trade **3** *(boutique)* glove *Br* shop *or Am* store; *(rayon)* glove counter *or* department

gantier, -ère [gɑ̃tje, -ɛr] **NM,F** glover

gantois, -e [gɑ̃twa, -az] **ADJ** of/from Ghent

• **Gantois, -e NM,F** = inhabitant of or person from Ghent

gapette [gapɛt] **NF** *Fam* (flat) cap

garage [garaʒ] **NM 1** *(de voitures)* garage; *(de bateaux)* boathouse; *(de vélos)* shed; *(d'avions)* shed, hangar; *(de bus)* garage, depot; **la voiture est au g.** the car is in the garage; **j'ai mis la voiture au g.** I've put the car in the garage **2** *(atelier) Br* garage, *Am* car repair shop; **ma voiture est au g.** my car is at the garage **3** *Rail* siding; **g. de machines** engine shed

garagiste [garaʒist] **NMF** *(propriétaire)* garage owner; *(gérant)* garage manager; *(mécanicien)* (garage) mechanic; *Fam* **j'emmène la voiture chez le g.** I'm taking the car to the garage

garance [garɑ̃s] **NF 1** *Bot* madder **2** *(teinture)* madder (dye)

ADJ INV *(rouge)* ruby red

garant, -e [garɑ̃, -ɑ̃t] **ADJ 1** *Jur* **être g. d'une dette** to stand guarantor *or* surety for a debt **2** *(responsable)* **être/se porter g. de qn** to vouch *or* to answer for sb; *(devant la justice)* to go bail for sb; *(à la banque)* to stand guarantor for sb; **elle viendra, je m'en porte g.** she'll come, I can vouch for that; **désormais, vous serez g. de ses faits et gestes** from now on, you'll be answerable *or* responsible for his/her conduct

NM,F 1 *(personne)* **tu es la garante de notre réussite** thanks to you, we are assured of success **2** *(responsable)* guarantor; **les membres du GATT sont les garants de la liberté des échanges** the members of GATT are the guarantors of free trade

NM 1 *Jur (personne)* guarantor; *(somme, bien, document)* surety, security; **être le g. de qn** to stand surety for sb; **g. solidaire** joint and several guarantor **2** *(garantie)* guarantee, warranty

garantie [garɑ̃ti] **NF 1** *Com (assurance)* guarantee, warranty (**contre** against); **j'ai acheté une voiture d'occasion avec six mois de g.** I've bought a second-hand car with a six-month guarantee *or* warranty; **contrat de g.** guarantee; **rupture de g.** breach of warranty; **lettre de g. d'indemnité** letter of indemnity; **g. accessoire** collateral security; **g. de bonne exécution** *ou* **de bonne fin** performance bond; **g. contractuelle** contractual guarantee; **g. conventionnelle** contractual cover; **g. de crédit acheteur** buyer credit guarantee; **g. de crédit à l'exportation** export credit guarantee; **g. décennale** = ten-year guarantee on newly built property; **g. illimitée** unlimited warranty; **g. légale** legal guarantee; **g. limitée** limited warranty; **g. pièces et main-d'œuvre** parts and labour warranty; **g. prolongée** extended warranty; **g. de remboursement** money-back guarantee; **g. retour atelier** return-to-base warranty *or* guarantee; **g. sur site** on-site warranty *or* guarantee; **g. totale** full warranty; **g. des vices** guarantee against hidden defects *or* faults

2 *Jur (obligation)* guarantee; **g. bancaire** bank guarantee; *Bourse* **g. de cours** hedging; **g. d'exécution** contract bond; **g. de paiement** guarantee of payment

3 *(gage)* guarantee; **demander des garanties à qn** to ask sb for guarantees; **il me faut des garanties sérieuses** I need some reliable guarantees; **c'est sans g.!** I'm not promising *or* guaranteeing anything!; **elle m'a donné toutes les garanties que...** she gave me every guarantee that...; **fonds déposés** *ou* **détenus en g.** funds lodged *or* held as security

• **sous garantie ADJ** under guarantee; **un appareil sous g.** an appliance under guarantee

garantir [32] [garɑ̃tir] **VT 1** *(veiller sur)* to guarantee, to safeguard

2 *(assurer ▸ produit, service)* to guarantee; **cet appareil est garanti deux ans** this appliance is guaranteed for two years *or* has a two-year guarantee; **l'antiquaire me l'a garanti d'époque** the antique dealer assured me *or* guaranteed me it's a period piece; **nous garantissons un délai de livraison d'une semaine** we guarantee delivery within seven days

3 *(promettre)* to guarantee, to assure; **suis mes conseils et je te garantis le succès** take my advice and I guarantee you'll succeed *or* I guarantee you success; **il m'a garanti que ça serait livré demain, il m'a garanti la livraison pour demain** he assured me that it would be delivered tomorrow, he guaranteed delivery for tomorrow; **je te garantis que tu le regretteras!** I can assure you

you'll regret it!; **je peux te g. qu'il ne reviendra pas** I can guarantee you he won't come back, he won't come back, I warrant you; **elle m'a garanti qu'elle serait à l'heure** she gave me a guarantee that she'd be on time; **je te le garantis** I can vouch for it

4 *(protéger)* **g. qn de qch** to protect sb from sth; **ce double vitrage va vous g. du froid** this double-glazing will protect *or* shield you from the cold

5 *Jur* **g. qn contre qch** to cover sb against sth; **mon assurance me garantit contre l'incendie** my insurance covers me against fire, I'm covered against fire

6 *Fin (paiement, dette)* to guarantee; *(emprunt)* to guarantee, to secure; *(créance)* to secure; *(émission d'actions)* to underwrite

7 *Assur* to cover; **son assurance le garantit contre le vol** his insurance covers him against theft

VPR se garantir se g. contre le froid/le vent to protect oneself from the cold/the wind

garce [gars] **NF** *très Fam* **1** *Péj* bitch, *Br* cow; **sale g.!** you rotten bitch!; **j'en ai marre de cette g. de vie!** I'm fed up with this shitty life! **2** *Vieilli (prostituée)* whore, hooker

garçon [garsɔ̃] **NM 1** *(enfant)* boy; **école de/vestiaire des garçons** boys' school/cloakroom; **nous avons un g. et une fille** we've got a boy and a girl; **tu es un grand g. maintenant** you're a big boy now; **petit g.** little boy; **g. manqué** tomboy

2 *(homme)* boy, young man; **c'est un g. qui connaît très bien l'entreprise** that fellow knows the company very well; **g. d'honneur** best man; **il est plutôt beau** *ou* **joli g.** he's quite good-looking; **c'est un bon** *ou* **brave g.** he's a good sort; **c'est un mauvais g.** he's bad news, *Br* he's a bad lot

3 *(fils)* boy, son

4 *(célibataire)* bachelor

5 *(employé)* **g. d'ascenseur** *Br* liftboy, lift attendant, *Am* elevator operator; **g. boucher** butcher's boy *or* assistant; **g. de bureau** office boy; *Naut* **g. de cabine** (cabin) steward; **g. coiffeur** *Br* junior *(in a hairdressing salon)*, *Am* hairdresser's assistant; **g. de courses** errand boy; **g. d'écurie** stableboy; **g. d'étage** floor waiter; **g. de ferme** farm hand; *Naut* **g. de pont** deck steward; **g. de recette** bank messenger

6 *(serveur)* waiter; **g. (de café** *ou* **de salle)** waiter; **g., une bière, s'il vous plaît!** waiter, one beer please!

7 *Fam (en appellatif)* **attention, mon g.!** watch it, sonny!

ADJ M 1 *(célibataire)* unmarried; **il est resté g.** he remained unmarried *or* single *or* a bachelor **2** *(qui a une apparence masculine)* boyish; **ça fait très g., cette coiffure** that haircut looks very boyish

garçonne [garsɔn] **NF** *Hist* **les garçonnes des années vingt** the flappers

• **à la garçonne ADV coiffée à la g.** with an Eton crop; **habillée à la g.** dressed like a (twenties) flapper

garçonnet [garsɔnɛ] **NM 1** *(petit garçon)* (little) boy **2** *(comme adj)* **rayon g.** boyswear (department); **taille g.** boy's size

garçonnier, -ère [garsɔnje, -ɛr] **ADJ** boyish

• **garçonnière NF** bachelor pad

Garde [gard] *voir* **lac**

GARDE[1] [gard]

- guarding **A1**
- care **A2**
- duty **A3**
- custody **A4**
- guard **B, C**
- hilt **D**

NF A. 1 *(surveillance ▸ d'un bien, d'un lieu)* guarding; **je te confie la g. du manuscrit** I am entrusting you with the manuscript, I am leaving the manuscript in your safekeeping *or* care; **assurer la g. d'un immeuble** *(police)* to guard a building; *(concierge)* to look after a building, to be caretaker of a building; **ils dressent des chiens pour la g.** they train guard dogs; **on te prête la maison pour le week-end, mais fais bonne g.** we'll let you use our house for the weekend, but look after it carefully; **affecté à la g. du palais présidentiel** on guard duty at the presidential palace; **monter la g.** to stand guard

2 *(protection ▸ d'un enfant, d'un animal)* care; **je confierai la g. des enfants à ma tante** I will leave the children in the care of my aunt; **puis-je te confier la g. de mon chien pendant deux jours?** would you take care of *or* look after my dog for two days?

3 *Méd (service de surveillance)* **interne qui fait des gardes** *Br* locum, locum tenens, *Am* intern on duty; **g. de nuit** night duty

4 *Jur* custody; **la g. des enfants fut confiée à la mère** the mother was given custody of the children, the children were left in the custody of their mother; **g. à vue** police custody; **placé en g. à vue** put into police custody; **droit de g.** (right of) custody; **g. alternée** *(d'enfant)* alternating custody

B. *Sport* guard; **tenir la g. haute** to keep one's guard up; **fermer/ouvrir sa g.** to close/to open one's guard; **baisser sa g.** to drop one's guard; **ne pas baisser sa g. (devant qn)** to remain on one's guard (with sb)

C. 1 *(escorte, milice)* guard; **g. (d'honneur)** guard of honour; **g. mobile** (State) security police; *Hist* **G. nationale** national guard *(civil militia, 1789–1871)*; **la G. républicaine** the Republican Guard *(on duty at French state occasions)*; **la vieille g.** the old guard *(of a political party)*

2 *(soldats en faction)* guard; **g. montante/descendante** relief/old guard

D. *(d'une arme blanche)* hilt; *Fig* **jusqu'à la g.** up to the hilt; **il s'est enferré dans ses mensonges jusqu'à la g.** he got completely tangled up in his own lies

E. *(locutions) Arch & Littéraire* **n'avoir g. de faire qch** to take good care not to do sth; **prends g.!** watch out!; **prenez g. à la marche** *Br* mind *or Am* watch the step; **prenez g. de ne rien oublier** make sure *or* take care you don't leave anything behind; **je prendrai g. à ce qu'il ne parle pas** I shall ensure *or* make sure he doesn't talk; **prends g. qu'on ne te voie pas** make sure nobody sees you

• **gardes NFPL** guard *(civil militia, 1789–1871)*; **être/se tenir sur ses gardes** to be/to stay on one's guard

• **de garde ADJ 1** *voir* **chien 2** *(qui se conserve)* **fromage de (bonne) g.** cheese that keeps well; **vin de g.** wine for keeping *or* laying down **3** *Méd* duty *(avant n)*; **médecin de g.** duty doctor, doctor on duty; **elle est de g. trois nuits par semaine** she's on duty three nights a week; **je suis de g. demain soir** I'm on night duty tomorrow

• **en garde ADV 1** *Mil & Sport* **en g.!** on (your) guard!; **mettez-vous en g.** take your guard

2 *(sous surveillance)* **ils prennent des animaux en g. l'été** they board pets during the summer

3 *Jur Br* in care, *Am* in custody; **le juge a placé les enfants en g.** the judge made the children wards of court, *Br* the judge had the children put into care

4 *(locution)* **mettre qn en g.** to warn sb; **je l'avais mise en g. contre les dangers du tabac** I had warned her against the dangers of smoking

• **sous bonne garde ADV le stade est sous bonne g.** the stadium is under (heavy) guard; **ton argent est sous bonne g.** your money is in safe hands

garde[2] [gard] **NMF 1** *(personne)* **une g. d'enfants** a babysitter **2 g. des Sceaux** (French) Minister of Justice, *Br* ≃ Lord Chancellor, *Am* ≃ Attorney General

NM 1 *(surveillant)* warden; **g. champêtre** = council employee with various minor duties including, traditionally, informing townspeople of news and events; **g. du corps** bodyguard; **g. forestier** *Br* forest warden, *Am* forest ranger; **g. maritime** coastguard; **g. mobile** member of the (State) security police; **g. de nuit** *(pour un malade)* night nurse *(privately employed)*; *Mil* night watchman; **g. républicain** Republican guardsman *(on duty at French state occasions)* **2** *(soldat ▸ en faction)* guard; *(▸ en service d'honneur)* guardsman; *Hist* **g. rouge** Red Guard

NF *Méd* nurse

garde-à-vous [gardavu] **NM INV** *Mil* (position of) attention; **des soldats au g.** soldiers standing at *or* to attention; **g., fixe!** attention!, 'shun!; **se mettre au g.** to stand to attention

garde-barrière [gardəbarjɛr] *(pl* **gardes-barrière** *ou* **gardes-barrières)** **NMF** *Br* level-crossing keeper, *Am* grade-crossing keeper

NF *Ordinat* firewall

garde-boue [gardəbu] **NM INV** mudguard

garde-chasse [gardəʃas] *(pl* **gardes-chasse** *ou* **gardes-chasses)** **NM** gamekeeper

garde-chiourme [gardəʃjurm] *(pl* **gardes-chiourme** *ou* **gardes-chiourmes)** **NM 1** *Hist* warder *(in charge of a gang of convicts)* **2** *Péj (surveillant brutal)* martinet, disciplinarian

garde-corps [gardəkɔr] **NM INV 1** *(balustrade)* railing, handrail; *(parapet)* parapet **2** *Naut (le long d'une vergue)* lifeline; *(sur le pont)* manrope; **g. arrière** stern rail

garde-côte[1] [gardəkot] *(pl* **garde-côtes)** **NM** *(bateau)* coastguard vessel

garde-côte[2] [gardəkot] *(pl* **gardes-côtes)** **NM** *Vieilli (soldat)* coastguard

garde-feu [gardəfø] *(pl* **inv** *ou* **garde-feux)** **NM 1** *(grille)* fireguard, firescreen **2** *Can (personne)* fire ranger

garde-fou [gardəfu] *(pl* **garde-fous)** **NM 1** *(barrière)* railing, guardrail; *(talus)* (raised) bank; *(mur)* parapet, balustrade **2** *Fig (défense)* **servir de g. (contre)** to safeguard (against)

garde-frein [gardəfrɛ̃] *(pl* **gardes-frein(s))** **NM** *Rail Br* brakesman, *Am* brakeman

garde-frontière, garde-frontières [gardəfrɔ̃tjɛr] *(pl* **gardes-frontières)** **NM** border guard

garde-ligne [gard(ə)liɲ] *(pl* **gardes-ligne(s))** **NM** *Rail* track watchman

garde-magasin [gardmagazɛ̃] *(pl* **gardes-magasin** *ou* **gardes-magasins)** **NM** warehouseman; *Mil* storekeeper, quartermaster

garde-malade [gardəmalad] *(pl* **gardes-malade** *ou* **gardes-malades)** **NMF** nurse

garde-manger [gardəmɑ̃ʒe] **NM INV** *(placard)* food *or* meat safe; *(réserve)* pantry, larder

garde-meuble, garde-meubles [gardəmœbl] *(pl* **garde-meubles)** **NM** storehouse *or Br* furniture depository; **mettre qch au g.** to put sth in storage

Gardénal® [gardenal] **NM** *Pharm Br* phenobarbitone, *Am* phenobarbital

gardénia [gardenja] **NM** *Bot* gardenia

garde-pêche [gardəpɛʃ] **NM** *(pl* **gardes-pêche)** *(personne) Br* water bailiff, *Am* fish warden

NM INV *(bateau ▸ en mer)* fisheries protection vessel; *(▸ sur rivière) Br* bailiff's boat, *Am* fish warden's boat

garde-place [gardəplas] *(pl* **garde-places)** **NM** *Rail* reservation holder; *(ticket)* reservation ticket

garde-port [gardəpɔr] *(pl* **gardes-port** *ou* **gardes-ports)** **NM** wharfmaster *(on river)*

GARDER [3] [garde]

VT
- to look after **A1**
- to guard **A2**
- to save **A3, C5**
- to keep **C1, 2, 4–7, 9, 11**
- to keep on **C3**

VPR
- to keep **1**
- to be careful not to **3**
- to beware of **4**

VT A. 1 *(veiller sur ▸ personne, animal)* to look after; *(▸ boutique)* to keep an eye on, to mind; **il a fallu trouver quelqu'un pour g. le bébé** we had to find someone to look after the baby; **elle garde des enfants** she does some babysitting *or Br* childminding; **les moutons sont gardés par des chiens** the sheep are guarded by dogs; **pourriez-vous g. mes affaires un instant?** would you mind keeping an eye on my things for a minute?; **il doit faire g. les enfants le soir** he has to get somebody to look after the children in the evening; *Fam* **on n'a pas gardé les cochons ensemble!** don't be so familiar!

2 *(surveiller ▸ personne, lieu)* to guard; **le stade était gardé par des hommes en armes** the stadium was guarded by armed men; **un cyprès garde l'entrée du cimetière** a cypress stands guard at the entrance to the cemetery

3 *Littéraire (prémunir)* **g. qn de qch** to protect *or* to save sb from sth; **cette sage parole m'a gardé de bien des erreurs** this sound advice has kept *or* saved me from many a mistake

4 *Jur* **g. qn à vue** to keep *or* to hold sb in custody

B. 1 *(sujet: malade)* **g. le lit** to be confined to bed, to be laid up; **elle garde la chambre** she is confined to her room *or* staying in her room

2 *Mil* **g. les arrêts** to remain under arrest

C. 1 *(conserver ▸ aliment)* to keep; **on peut g. ce gâteau plusieurs mois** you can keep this cake *or* this cake will keep for several months; **g. à l'abri de la chaleur et de la lumière** *(sur emballage)* store in a cool dark place

2 *(ne pas se dessaisir de)* to keep; **j'ai gardé toutes ses lettres** I kept all his/her letters; **garde-le, un jour il aura de la valeur** hold on to it, one day it will be valuable

3 *(conserver sur soi)* to keep on; **puis-je g. mon chapeau/manteau?** may I keep my hat/coat on?

4 *(conserver en dépôt)* to keep; **la voisine garde mon courrier pendant mon absence** my neighbour keeps my mail for me when I'm away

5 *(réserver)* to save, to keep; **je t'ai gardé du poulet** I've saved you some chicken, I've kept some chicken for you; **ne te fatigue pas trop, il faut g. des forces pour ce soir** don't overtire yourself, save some of your energy for tonight; **garde-moi une place pour le cas où j'arriverais en retard** keep a seat for me in case I'm late; *Fig* **g. une poire pour la soif** to keep something for a rainy day

6 *(retenir ▸ personne)* to keep; **tu es pressé, je ne te garderai pas longtemps** as you're in a hurry, I won't keep you long; **g. qn à dîner** to have sb stay for dinner; **il a gardé sa secrétaire** he kept his secretary on; **on les a gardés au commissariat** they were held at the police station; **va-t-elle g. le bébé?** is she going to keep the baby?

7 *(ne pas révéler)* to keep; **g. un secret** to keep a secret; **g. le secret sur qch** to keep sth secret; **tu ferais bien de g. ça pour toi** you'd better keep that to yourself

8 *(avoir à l'esprit)* **elle garde de son enfance une image heureuse** she has happy memories of her childhood; **je n'ai pas gardé de très bons souvenirs de cette époque** my memories of that time are not very happy ones; **g. qch présent à l'esprit** to bear *or* to keep sth in mind

9 *(maintenir ▸ attitude, sentiment)* to keep; **g. l'anonymat** to remain anonymous; **g. son calme** to keep calm *or* cool; **g. son sérieux** to keep a straight face; **g. le silence** to keep silent; **g. rancune à qn de qch** to bear *or* to harbour a grudge against sb for sth; **g. la tête froide** to keep one's head *or* a cool head; **g. les yeux baissés** to keep one's eyes lowered

10 *(observer, respecter ▸ règle, loi)* **g. le jeûne** to observe a fast; **g. ses distances** to keep one's distance

11 *(ne pas perdre ▸ qualité)* to keep; **le mot garde encore toute sa valeur** the word still retains its full meaning

VPR se garder 1 *(emploi passif) (aliment)* to keep; **les framboises ne se gardent pas (longtemps)** raspberries do not keep (long); **ça se garde une semaine au congélateur** it will keep for a week in the freezer

2 *(emploi réfléchi)* **les enfants sont grands, ils se gardent tout seuls maintenant** the children are old enough to be left on their own now

3 se g. de faire qch *(éviter de)* to be careful not to do sth; **je me garderai bien de lui en parler** I'll be very careful not to talk to him/her about it; **garde-toi bien de le vexer** be very careful not to offend him

4 se g. de *(se méfier de)* to beware of *or* be wary of; **il faut se g. des gens trop expansifs** one should beware *or* be wary of over-effusive people; **gardons-nous de nos tendances égoïstes** let us try to curb our selfish tendencies

---

garderie [gardəri] **NF 1** *(de quartier) Br* day nursery, *Am* day-care center; *(liée à une entreprise) Br* crèche, *Am* baby-sitting service; *(le soir, après l'école)* childminding service **2** *(étendue de bois)* (forest ranger's) beat

garde-rivière [gardərivjɛr] *(pl* **gardes-rivière** *ou* **gardes-rivières) NM** riverkeeper, river patrolman, *Br* waterways board official

garde-robe [gardərɔb] *(pl* **garde-robes) NF 1** *(vêtements)* wardrobe; **g. d'hiver** winter wardrobe; **il serait temps que je renouvelle ma g.** it's high time I bought myself some new clothes *or* a new wardrobe **2** *(penderie)* wardrobe

gardeur, -euse [gardœr, -øz] **NM,F** *Littéraire (d'animaux)* keeper; **g. d'oies** gooseherd; **g. de vaches** cowherd; **g. de cochons** pig keeper, *Fam Vieilli* swineherd

garde-voie [gardəvwa] *(pl* **gardes-voie** *ou* **gardes-voies) NM** *Rail* track watchman, lineman, line guard

gardian [gardjɑ̃] **NM** herdsman *(in the Camargue)*

gardien, -enne [gardjɛ̃, -ɛn] **NM,F 1** *(surveillant ▸ d'une usine, d'une société)* (security) guard; *(▸ d'un immeuble, d'un cimetière)* caretaker; *(▸ d'un domaine)* warden; *(▸ d'un zoo)* keeper; *(▸ d'un musée, d'un parking)* attendant; **g. d'immeuble** *Br* caretaker, porter, *Am* janitor; **g. de musée** museum attendant; **g. de nuit** night watchman; **g. de parking** *Br* car park *or Am* parking lot attendant; **g. de phare** lighthouse keeper; **g. de prison** prison officer *or Br* warder, *Am* prison guard **2** *Fig (protecteur)* guardian, custodian; **le g. de nos libertés/de la tradition/du patrimoine** the guardian of our freedom/of tradition/of our heritage **3** *Can* childminder

NM g. de but goalkeeper; **g. de la paix** = low-ranking police officer; *Fig* **g. du temple** *(défenseur)* gatekeeper

• **gardienne NF 1 gardienne d'enfants** nursery help *or Br* helper, *Am* day-care assistant **2** *Belg (école)* nursery school, kindergarten, *Br* infant school

gardiennage [gardjenaʒ] **NM** *(d'un bâtiment)* caretaking; **assurer le g. d'un entrepôt** to be in charge of security in a warehouse; **assurer le g. d'une résidence** *Br* to be the caretaker *or* porter in a block of flats, *Am* to be the doorman *or* janitor in an apartment block; **société de g.** security firm

gardienne [gardjɛn] *voir* **gardien**

gardon [gardɔ̃] **NM** *Ich* roach

gare[1] [gar] **NF 1** *Rail (installations et voies)* station; *(hall)* (station) concourse; *(bâtiments)* station building *or* buildings; **de quelle g. part le train pour Calais?** which station does the train to Calais leave from?; **entrer** *ou* **arriver en g.** *(d'un train)* to arrive in *or* come into the station; **le train de 14h 30 à destination de Paris va entrer en g. voie 10** the train now arriving at platform 10 is the two-thirty to Paris; **g. frontière/maritime** border/harbour station; **g. de voyageurs/marchandises** passenger/goods station; **g. de triage** *Br* marshalling yard, *Am* switchyard; **g. d'arrivée** *(pour passagers)* arrival station; *(pour marchandises)* receiving station; **g. de départ** *(pour passagers)* departure station; **g. expéditrice, g. d'expédition** forwarding station, dispatch station; **romans de g.** cheap *or* trashy novels; **café/hôtel de la g.** station café/hotel **2** *(garage à bateaux)* (river) basin; *(d'un canal)* passing place; **g. fluviale** dock **3** *Transp* **g. routière** *(de poids lourds)* haulage depot; *(de cars)* bus station, *Br* coach station; **g. routière de marchandises** road haulage depot; **g. de péage** (motorway) toll station

gare[2] [gar] **EXCLAM** *Fam* **g. à toi!, g. à tes fesses!** you just watch it!; **si je te reprends à voler du gâteau, g. à tes fesses!** if I catch you stealing cake again, you've had it *or Br* you're for it!; **g. à vous si vous rentrez après minuit!** if you come home after midnight, there'll be trouble!, you'd better be in by midnight, or else!; **g. à toi si on l'apprend** woe betide you if anyone finds out; **g. à tes doigts avec ce couteau** watch your fingers with that knife; **g. dessous!** look out *or* watch out down below!

garenne [garɛn] **NF 1** *(lieu boisé)* (rabbit) warren **2** *(de pêche)* fishing preserve

NM *Zool* wild rabbit

garer [3] [gare] **VT 1** *(véhicule)* to park; **bien/mal garé** parked legally/illegally; **garé en double file** double-parked **2** *Transp (canot)* to dock, to berth; *(avion léger ▸ dans un hangar)* to put away; *(▸ sur la piste)* to park **3** *Rail* to shunt, to move into a siding, *Am* to switch

VPR se garer 1 *(en voiture)* to park; **se g. facilement** to have no trouble parking; **trouver à se g.** to find a parking place *or* space; **tu trouveras à te g. dans le quartier** you'll find somewhere to park in the area; **j'ai eu de la peine à me g.** I had trouble parking **2** *Fam (s'écarter)* **gare-toi!** get out of the way! **3 se g. de** *(éviter)* to steer clear of; **garez-vous de ces gens-là** give those people a wide berth, steer clear of those people

Gargantua [gargɑ̃tɥa] **NPR** = the giant in Rabelais' novel of the same name (1534)

gargantuesque [gargɑ̃tɥɛsk] **ADJ** gargantuan

gargariser [3] [gargarize] **se gargariser VPR 1** *(se rincer la gorge)* to gargle **2 se g. de** to delight in; **il se gargarise volontiers de noms célèbres** he delights in name-dropping

gargarisme [gargarism] **NM** *(rinçage)* gargling; *(produit)* mouthwash; **faire des gargarismes** to gargle

gargote [gargɔt] **NF** *Péj* cheap restaurant

gargotier, -ère [gargɔtje, -ɛr] **NM,F** *Péj* **1** *(propriétaire)* **demande au g.** ask the guy who runs this cheap joint **2** *(mauvais cuisinier)* bad cook

gargouille [garguj] **NF 1** *(de gouttière)* waterspout **2** *Archit* gargoyle

gargouillement [gargujmɑ̃] **NM 1** *(d'une fontaine)* gurgling *(UNCOUNT)* **2** *(de l'estomac)* rumbling *(UNCOUNT)*; **j'ai des gargouillements (dans le ventre)** my stomach's rumbling

gargouiller [3] [garguje] **VI 1** *(liquide)* to gurgle **2** *(estomac)* to rumble

gargouillis [garguji] = **gargouillement**

garnement [garnəmɑ̃] **NM** scamp, rascal

garni, -e [garni] **ADJ 1** *Culin (plat du jour, viande)* with vegetables; **panier g.** food hamper, hamper of food **2 bien g.** *(bourse)* well-lined; *(compte en banque)* healthy; *(magasin)* well-stocked; *(maison)* well-appointed; **il est bien g., ton frigo!** your fridge is very well stocked! **3** *Vieilli (chambre, logement, hôtel)* furnished

NM *Vieilli* furnished rooms *or* accommodation

garnir [32] [garnir] **VT 1** *(décorer)* to trim (**de** with); **ils ont garni la table de fleurs et de bougies** they decorated the table with flowers and candles; **l'arbre sera garni de cheveux d'anges** the tree will be hung *or* decorated with Christmas floss; **une robe garnie de dentelle** a dress trimmed with lace, a lace-trimmed dress; **la passementerie qui garnit cette veste est très colorée** the braid trimming on that jacket is very colourful

2 *(remplir)* to fill (**de** with); *(cave)* to stock; **nous vendons la corbeille garnie de fruits** the basket is sold (complete) with an assortment of fruit; **la trousse de toilette est vendue entièrement garnie** the *Br* sponge bag *or Am* toilet case comes complete with toiletries

3 *(munir de ce qui protège, renforce etc)* to fit out (**de** with); **les semelles sont garnies de pointes d'acier** the soles are steel-tipped

4 *(de tissu ▸ siège) (rembourrer)* to stuff; *(couvrir)* to cover, to upholster; *(▸ vêtement, coffret, tiroir)* to line; **elle a garni la robe d'une doublure en satin** she lined the dress with satin; **je vais g. les tiroirs de papier de soie** I'll line the drawers with tissue paper

5 *Culin (plat)* to garnish; *(remplir)* to fill; **toutes nos viandes sont garnies de pommes sautées** all our meat dishes come with *or* are served with sautéed potatoes

6 *(remplir du nécessaire)* to fill (up); **g. la chaudière pour la nuit** to stoke *or* to fill (up) the boiler for the night

VPR se garnir 1 *(se remplir)* to fill up; **le théâtre se garnissait de personnalités connues** the theatre was filling up with celebrities **2** *(se couvrir)* **les murs du nouveau musée se garnissent peu à peu** the walls of the new museum are gradually becoming lined with exhibits

garnison [garnizɔ̃] **NF** garrison; **le régiment est en g. à Nancy** the regiment is garrisoned *or* stationed in Nancy

• **de garnison ADJ** garrison *(avant n)*

garnissage [garnisaʒ] **NM 1** *(remplissage ▸ d'un coussin, d'une couette)* stuffing; *(décoration ▸ d'un manteau)* trimming; *(▸ d'un chapeau)* trim

2 *Aut (intérieur d'un véhicule)* (interior) trim; **g. de plafond** headliner, headlining; **g. de siège** seat trim

3 *(matériau)* packing, stuffing; *Métal* lining

4 *Tech (d'un piston)* packing; *(d'une chaudière)* lagging

garniture [garnityr] **NF 1** *(ensemble)* (matching) set; **une g. de boutons** a set of buttons; **une g. de bureau** a set of desk accessories; **g. de cheminée** (set of) mantelpiece ornaments; **une g. de lit** a matching set of sheets and pillowcases; **g. de toilette** toilet set
2 *(ornementation ▸ d'un chapeau, d'une robe)* trimming, decoration; **avec une g. de dentelle** trimmed with lace; **la g. d'une automobile** the interior trim *or* the upholstery of a car
3 *(protection ▸ de joint)* packing; *(▸ de piston)* stuffing (piece); *(▸ de chaudière)* lagging; *Typ* furniture; *Aut* **g. d'embrayage** clutch lining; *Aut* **g. de frein** brake lining; *(de disque de frein)* brake pad; **g. de porte** door liner
4 *Culin (d'un feuilleté)* filling; *(accompagnement ▸ décoratif)* garnish; *(▸ légumes)* vegetables; **que servez-vous comme g. avec le poisson?** what does the fish come with?, what is the fish served with?; **c'est servi sans g.** it's served without vegetables *or* on its own
• **garnitures NFPL** *(d'une serrure)* wards

Garonne [garɔn] **NF la G.** the (River) Garonne

garrigue [garig] **NF** scrubland, garigue

garrocher [3] [garɔʃe] *Can* **VT** to throw
VPR se garrocher to rush, to hurry; **se g. sur qn** *(attaquer)* to throw oneself on sb

garrot¹ [garo] **NM 1** *Méd* tourniquet; **mettre** *ou* **poser un g.** to apply a tourniquet **2** *Hist (supplice)* garrotte

garrot² [garo] **NM** *Zool (d'animal)* withers; **mesurer 1,20 m au g.** to be 12 hands high

garrottage [garɔtaʒ] **NM 1** *Méd (d'une blessure)* putting a tourniquet on **2** *(supplice)* garrotting

garrotte [garɔt] **NF** *Hist* gar(r)otte, gar(r)otting

garrotter [3] [garɔte] **VT 1** *(attacher)* to tie up, to bind; *Méd* to put a tourniquet on **2** *Fig (priver de liberté)* to stifle, to muzzle; **tous les partis d'opposition ont été garrottés** the opposition parties have all been stifled *or* muzzled **3** *(supplicier)* to garrotte

gars [ga] **NM** *Fam* **1** *(garçon, fils)* boy□, *Br* lad; **qu'est-ce qui ne va pas, mon petit g.?** what's the matter, kid *or* sonny? **2** *(jeune homme)* boy□, guy, *Br* lad; **allons-y, les g.** let's go, boys; **c'est un g. bizarre** he's a weird guy *or Br* bloke; **salut, les g.!** hi, guys!, *Br* hi, lads!

Gascogne [gaskɔɲ] **NF la G.** Gascony; **le golfe de G.** the Bay of Biscay

gascon, -onne [gaskɔ̃, -ɔn] **ADJ** Gascon
NM *(dialecte)* Gascon (dialect)
• **Gascon, -onne NM,F** Gascon; **une offre** *ou* **une promesse de G.** an empty promise

gasconnade [gaskɔnad] **NF** *Littéraire (vantardise)* **des gasconnades** bragging *(UNCOUNT)*; **raconter des gasconnades** to brag

gasconne [gaskɔn] *voir* **gascon**

gas-oil *(pl* **gas-oils**), **gasoil** [gazɔjl, gazwal] = **gazole**

gaspacho [gaspatʃo] = **gazpacho**

gaspard [gaspar] **NM** *Fam* rat□

gaspillage [gaspijaʒ] **NM** *(action ▸ de nourriture, temps)* wasting; *(▸ d'argent)* wasting, squandering; *(résultat)* waste; **un g. de temps et d'argent** a waste of time and money; **évitez le g. de nourriture/d'électricité** don't waste food/electricity; **j'ai horreur du g.** I hate waste, I hate wasting things; **c'est du g.** it's a waste, it's wasteful; **pas de g.!** don't be wasteful!

gaspiller [3] [gaspije] **VT** *(denrée, temps, talent, énergie)* to waste; *(économies)* to squander; **il a gaspillé son talent** he has wasted his talent; **elle me fait g. mon temps et mon argent** she wastes both my time and my money; **arrête de me faire g. mon temps** stop wasting my time

gaspilleur, -euse [gaspijœr, -øz] **ADJ** wasteful
NM,F squanderer, spendthrift

gastéropode [gasterɔpɔd] *Zool* **NM** gastropod, gasteropod, *Spéc* member of the Gastropoda
• **gastéropodes NMPL** the snail family, *Spéc* Gastropoda

gastralgie [gastralʒi] **NF** *Méd* stomach pains, *Spéc* gastralgia

gastralgique [gastralʒik] **ADJ** *Méd* gastralgic

gastrectomie [gastrɛktɔmi] **NF** *Méd* gastrectomy

gastrique [gastrik] **ADJ** gastric, stomach *(avant n)*; **embarras/lésion g.** stomach trouble/lesion

gastrite [gastrit] **NF** *Méd* gastritis

gastro [gastro] **NF** *Fam* gastroenteritis□ *(UNCOUNT)*

gastro-duodénal, -e [gastrɔdɥɔdenal, -o] *(mpl* **gastro-duodénaux**, *fpl* **gastro-duodénales**) **ADJ** *Anat* gastroduodenal; **ulcère g.** gastroduodenal ulcer

gastro-entérite [gastrɔɑ̃terit] *(pl* **gastro-entérites**) **NF** *Méd* gastroenteritis *(UNCOUNT)*

gastro-entérologie [gastrɔɑ̃terɔlɔʒi] **NF** *Méd* gastroenterology

gastro-entérologue [gastroɑ̃terɔlɔg] *(pl* **gastro-entérologues**) **NMF** *Méd* gastroenterologist

gastro-hépatite [gastrɔepatit] *(pl* **gastro-hépatites**) **NF** *Méd* gastrohepatitis *(UNCOUNT)*

gastro-intestinal, -e [gastrɔɛ̃testinal,-o] *(mpl* **gastro-intestinaux**, *fpl* **gastro-intestinales**) **ADJ** *Anat* gastrointestinal

gastronome [gastrɔnɔm] **NMF** gastronome, gourmet

gastronomie [gastrɔnɔmi] **NF** gastronomy

gastronomique [gastrɔnɔmik] **ADJ** gastronomic, gastronomical; **buffet g.** gourmet buffet

gastropode [gastrɔpɔd] = **gastéropode**

gâté, -e [gɑte] **ADJ 1** *(pourri ▸ fruit)* damaged, spoilt; *(▸ dents)* rotten, decayed; **viande gâtée** meat that has gone off *or* is bad, bad meat **2** *Fig* **enfant g.** spoilt *or* pampered child; **l'enfant g. de la famille/de la littérature russe** the blue-eyed boy of the family/of Russian literature

gâteau, -x [gato] **NM 1** *Culin (pâtisserie)* cake; *(biscuit) Br* biscuit, *Am* cookie; **faire un g.** to make *or* to bake a cake; *Fam* **avoir sa part du g.** to have one's slice *or* share of the cake; **g. d'anniversaire** birthday cake; **g. apéritif** cracker, *Br* savoury biscuit *(to eat with drinks)*; **g. éponge** sponge cake; **g. marbré** marble cake; **g. de riz** rice pudding; **g. de Savoie** sponge cake; **g. sec** *Br* (sweet) biscuit, *Am* cookie; **g. de semoule** ≃ semolina pudding; *Fam* **ça n'est pas du g.** it isn't as easy as it looks; *Fam* **c'est du g.** it's a piece of cake *or* a walkover **2** *Suisse Culin* tart **3** *(masse pressée)* cake; *(de fulmicoton)* disc; **g. de miel** *ou* **de cire** honeycomb
ADJ INV *Fam* **c'est un papa g.** he's a soft touch with his children; **j'ai eu un tonton g.** I had an uncle who spoilt me rotten; **marraine g.** fairy godmother

gâter [3] [gɑte] **VT 1** *(combler ▸ ami, enfant)* to spoil; **j'aime bien les g. à Noël** I like to spoil them at Christmas; **j'ai été gâté aujourd'hui, j'ai eu trois offres d'emploi** today was my lucky day, I had three job offers; **quel beau temps, nous sommes vraiment gâtés** we're really lucky with the weather; **tu as vu ce qu'il y a à la télé ce soir, on n'est pas gâtés!** have you seen what's on TV tonight, great, isn't it?; **la vie ne les avait pas gâtés** life hadn't treated them kindly; **il n'est pas gâté par la nature** nature wasn't very kind to him **2** *(abîmer)* to spoil; **l'humidité gâte les fruits** moisture makes fruit go bad *or* spoils fruit; **la sauce a bouilli, ça l'a gâtée** the sauce boiled, that's what spoiled it; **elle a beaucoup de dents gâtées** she's got a lot of bad teeth **3** *(gâcher)* to spoil; **ce qui ne gâte rien** which is no bad thing; **il est beau et riche, ce qui ne gâte rien** he's good-looking and he's wealthy to boot, he's good-looking and wealthy into the bargain
VPR se gâter 1 *(pourrir ▸ viande, poisson, lait)* to go bad *or Br* off; *(▸ fruit)* to go bad **2** *(se carier ▸ dent)* to decay, to go rotten **3** *(se détériorer ▸ situation)* to take a turn for the worse, to deteriorate; **voilà ses potes, attention, ça va se g.** here come his/her mates, things are going to get nasty; **regarde le ciel, le temps se gâte** look at the sky, it's starting to cloud over *or* the weather's changing for the worse

gâterie [gɑtri] **NF 1** *(cadeau)* treat, present; **laisse-moi t'offrir une petite g.** let me treat you to a little something, let me buy you a little treat **2** *(friandise)* treat, titbit **3** *très Fam Hum* **faire une petite g. à qn** to go down on sb

gâte-sauce [gɑtsos] *(pl inv ou* **gâte-sauces**) **NM** kitchen help; *Péj* bad cook

gâteux, -euse [gɑtø, -øz] **ADJ 1** *(sénile)* doddering, doddery; **un vieillard g.** an old dodderer **2** *Fam (stupide)* gaga; **le bébé les rend tous g.** they are all completely besotted by the baby, they all go gaga over the baby
NM,F *Péj* **un vieux g.** a silly *or* doddering old fool

gâtifier [9] [gɑtifje] **VI** *Fam* **1** *(devenir gâteux)* to go soft in the head **2** *(bêtifier)* **autour du bébé, tout le monde gâtifie** everyone goes gaga over the baby

gâtisme [gɑtism] **NM** *Méd* senility; *Péj* **il se répète, c'est du g.!** he's repeating himself, he must be going senile!

GATT, Gatt [gat] **NM** *(abrév* **General Agreement on Tariffs and Trade**) GATT

gatter [3] [gate] **VT** *Suisse Fam Arg scol (cours)* to skip, to cut; **g. l'école** to play *Br* truant *or Am* hooky

gauche [goʃ] **ADJ 1** *(dans l'espace)* left; **la partie g. du tableau est endommagée** the left *or* left-hand side of the painting is damaged
2 *(maladroit ▸ adolescent)* awkward, gawky; *(▸ démarche)* ungainly; *(▸ manières)* awkward, gauche; *(▸ geste, mouvement)* awkward, clumsy; **qu'il est g.!** *Br* he's all fingers and thumbs!, *Am* he's all thumbs!; **ses excuses étaient encore plus gauches que sa gaffe** his/her apologies were even clumsier *or* more awkward than his/her mistake
3 *Constr* warped
NM 1 *Sport (pied gauche)* **marquer un but du g.** to score a goal with one's left (foot)
2 *Sport (poing gauche)* left; **il a un g. imparable** he has an unstoppable left
3 *Constr* warping
NF 1 *(côté gauche)* **la g.** the left *or* left-hand side; **la page de g.** the left-hand page; **le tiroir de g.** the left-hand drawer; **le magasin de g.** the shop on the left; **mon voisin de g.** my left-hand neighbour; **l'homme assis à ma g.** the man seated on my left; **il y a deux ascenseurs, prenez celui de g.** there are two lifts, take the one on your *or* on the left; **l'église est à g. de l'hôtel** the church is to the left of the hotel; **la deuxième rue sur votre g.** the second street on your left; **sur votre g., vous pouvez voir la tour Eiffel** on your left(-hand side) you can see the Eiffel Tower; **l'arabe s'écrit de droite à g.** Arabic is written from right to left
2 *Pol* **la g.** the left; **quand la g. est arrivée au pouvoir** when the left came to power; **voter à g.** to vote (for the) left; **être très à g.** to be very left-wing; **à droite comme à g., on condamne les essais nucléaires** right and left both condemn nuclear testing; *Fam* **la g. caviar** champagne socialism; **la g. dure** the hard left; **la g. modérée** the soft left; **la g. plurielle** = the rainbow coalition of socialists, communists and ecologists in the government of Lionel Jospin *(1997–2002)*
• **à gauche EXCLAM 1** *Mil* **à g., g.!** left (turn)! **2** *Naut* **à g.!** left! **ADV 1** *(sur le côté gauche)* on the left; **conduire à g.** to drive on the left; **tournez à g.** turn left; **la première rue à g.** the first street on the left **2** *Fam (locutions)* **mettre de l'argent à g.** to put *or* to tuck some money away
• **à gauche de ADV à g. de la porte d'entrée/de Marie** on *or* to the left of the entrance/of Marie
• **de gauche ADJ** *Pol* left-wing; **idées/parti de g.** left-wing ideas/party; **homme de g.** man of the left; **être de g.** to be left-wing *or* a left-winger
• **jusqu'à la gauche ADV** *Fam* to the end, to the last; **on s'est fait arnaquer jusqu'à la g.** we got completely ripped off, they cheated us good and proper; **il est compromis jusqu'à la g. dans cette affaire** he's involved right up to the hilt in this business

gauchement [goʃmɑ̃] **ADV** clumsily

gaucher, -ère [goʃe, -ɛr] **ADJ** left-handed; **il n'est pas g.!** he is (rather) good with his hands!
NM,F *(gén)* left-hander; *(boxeur)* southpaw; **g. contrarié** = natural left-hander brought up to be right-handed

gaucherie [goʃri] **NF 1** *(attitude)* clumsiness *(UNCOUNT)*; **ils ont fait preuve d'une g. inhabituelle dans cette affaire** they have handled this case with unusual clumsiness **2** *(acte, geste)* awkwardness *(UNCOUNT)*; *(expression)* tactless *or* insensitive statement; **bon exposé, malgré quelques gaucheries** a good essay, despite some clumsy turns of phrase

gauchir [32] [goʃir] **VT 1** *Constr* to warp **2** *Aviat* **g. l'aileron** to bank **3** *Fig (altérer)* to distort; **il accuse les journalistes d'avoir gauchi ses propos** he's accusing the journalists of distorting *or* misrepresenting his words

VI to warp

VPR se gauchir to warp

gauchisant, -e [goʃizɑ̃, -ɑ̃t] *Pol* **ADJ être g.** to have left-wing tendencies, to be a left-winger

NM,F c'est un g. he's a left-winger, he's got left-wing tendencies

gauchisme [goʃism] **NM** *Pol (gén)* leftism; *(depuis 1968)* New Leftism

gauchissement [goʃismɑ̃] **NM 1** *Constr* warping **2** *Aviat* banking **3** *Fig* distortion, misrepresentation

gauchiste [goʃist] *Pol* **ADJ** *(gén)* left; *(depuis 1968)* (New) Leftist

NMF *(gén)* leftist; *(depuis 1968)* (New) Leftist

gaucho[1] [goʃo] **NM** *(gardien de troupeaux)* gaucho

gaucho[2] [goʃo, gawtʃo] *Fam Péj Pol* **ADJ INV** lefty, pinko

NMF lefty, pinko

gaudriole [godrijɔl] **NF** *Fam* **1** *(plaisanterie)* bawdy joke **2** *(sexe)* **il ne pense qu'à la g.** he's got a one-track mind

gaufrage [gofraʒ] **NM 1** *(relief ▸ sur du cuir, du métal)* embossing; *(▸ sur une étoffe)* diapering; **g. à froid** blind embossing **2** *(plissage d'un tissu)* goffering **3** *Typ* goffering

gaufre[1] [gofr] **NF 1** *Culin* waffle **2** *(de cire)* honeycomb

gaufre[2] [gofr] **NM** *Zool* (pocket) gopher

gaufrer [3] [gofre] **VT 1** *(imprimer un relief sur ▸ cuir, métal)* to emboss, to boss; *(▸ papier, étoffe)* to emboss **2** *(plisser ▸ tissu)* to goffer; *(▸ cheveux)* to crimp; **elle s'est fait g. les cheveux** she had her hair crimped

gaufrette [gofrɛt] **NF** *Culin* wafer (biscuit)

gaufrier [gofrije] **NM** waffle iron

gaufrure [gofryr] **NF 1** *(sur du métal, du cuir, du papier, de l'étoffe)* embossed design **2** *(plissure ▸ du tissu)* goffering

Gaule [gol] **NF** *Hist* **la G.** Gaul

gaule [gol] **NF 1** *(perche)* pole; *Vulg* **avoir la g.** to have a hard-on **2** *Pêche* fishing rod

gaulé, -e [gole] **ADJ** *très Fam* **être bien/mal g.** to have/not to have a great bod

gauler [3] [gole] **VT 1** *(arbre)* to beat; *(fruit)* to beat down (from the tree) **2** *Fam (locution)* **se faire g.** to get *Br* nicked *or Am* busted

gaullien, -enne [goljɛ̃, -ɛn] **ADJ** of de Gaulle, de Gaulle's; **l'éloquence gaullienne** de Gaulle's eloquence

gaullisme [golism] **NM** Gaullism

> **GAULLISME**
>
> The political ideology inspired by the ideas of General de Gaulle includes nationalism, independence from foreign powers, and a strong executive. Gaullists are strongly committed to the defence of France's prestige on the international scene.

gaulliste [golist] **ADJ** Gaullist

NMF Gaullist

gaulois, -e [golwa, -az] **ADJ 1** *Hist* Gallic, Gaulish **2** *(grivois)* bawdy; **plaisanterie gauloise** bawdy joke; **l'humour g.** bawdy humour

NM *(langue)* Gaulish

• **Gaulois, -e NM,F** Gaul

• **gauloise®** **NF** *(cigarette)* Gauloise®

gauloiserie [golwazri] **NF 1** *(plaisanterie)* bawdy joke; *(remarque)* bawdy remark **2** *(attitude)* bawdiness

gauphre [gofr] = **gaufre[2]**

gausser [3] [gose] **se gausser VPR** *Littéraire* to mock; **gaussez-vous donc, braves gens!** well may you mock, good people!

gavage [gavaʒ] **NM 1** *Agr* force-feeding, gavage **2** *Méd* tube-feeding

gave [gav] **NM** (mountain) stream *(in south-west France)*

gaver [3] [gave] **VT 1** *Agr* to force-feed **2** *(bourrer ▸ personne) (de nourriture)* to fill up, to stuff (**de** with); **on l'a gavé d'antibiotiques** he has been stuffed with antibiotics; **j'ai été gavé de littérature classique** I had classical literature crammed into me; **la télévision nous gave de publicités** we get an overdose of commercials on television

VPR se gaver to stuff oneself (**de** with); **ils se sont gavés de fraises** they stuffed themselves with strawberries; *Fig* **cet été, je me suis gavé de romans policiers** this summer I indulged myself with detective stories

gavotte [gavɔt] **NF** *Mus & (danse)* gavotte

gay [gɛ] **ADJ** gay *(homosexual)*; **il/elle est g.** he's/she's gay

NMF gay *(homosexual)*

gaz [gaz] **NM INV 1** *(pour le chauffage, l'éclairage)* gas *(UNCOUNT)*; **cuisiner au g.** to cook with gas, to use a gas cooker; **se chauffer au g.** to have gas-powered heating; **allumer/couper le g.** to light/turn off the gas; **l'employé du g.** the gasman; **g. d'éclairage** town gas; **G. de France** = the French gas board; **g. de ville** town gas; **la cuisinière est-elle branchée sur le g. de ville?** is the stove connected to the mains gas?

2 *Chim* gas; **g. ammoniac** ammonia gas; **g. asphyxiant** asphyxiant gas; **g. carbonique** carbon dioxide; *Mil* **g. de combat** poison gas; **g. CS** CS gas; *Chim* **g. délétères** after-damp; **des g. à effet de serre** greenhouse gases; **g. hilarant** laughing gas; **g. inerte** inert gas; **g. innervant** nerve gas; **g. lacrymogène** tear gas; **g. des marais** marsh gas; **g. naturel** natural gas; **g. neurotoxique** nerve gas; **g. parfait** ideal gas; **g. de pétrole liquéfié** liquefied petroleum gas; **g. propulseur** propellant; **g. rare** rare gas; **g. toxique** poison *or* toxic gas

3 *Méd* **g. (anesthésique** *ou* **anesthésiant)** *(pour anesthésie)* gas

4 *Fam (locution)* **être dans le g.** to be out of it

NMPL 1 *Physiol* **avoir des g.** to have *Br* wind *or Am* gas **2** *(carburant)* **g. d'admission** air-fuel mixture; **g. brûlés** *ou* **d'échappement** exhaust fumes; *Fam* **mettre les g.** *(en voiture) Br* to put one's foot down, *Am* to step on the gas; *(en avion)* to open up the throttle□; *Fam* **on roulait (à) pleins g.** we were going flat out *or* at full speed□

• **à gaz ADJ** gas *(avant n)*; **réchaud à g.** (portable) gas stove; **usine à g.** gasworks

Gaza [gaza] **NM** Gaza; **la bande de G.** the Gaza Strip

gazage [gazaʒ] **NM 1** *Tex* singeing **2** *Mil* gassing

gaze [gaz] **NF 1** *Tex* gauze; **g. métallique** wire gauze **2** *Méd* gauze; **g. stérilisée** aseptic gauze

gazé, -e [gaze] **ADJ** gassed; **soldats gazés** soldiers killed by (poison) gas

NM,F (poison) gas victim

gazéification [gazeifikasjɔ̃] **NF 1** *Chim* gasification **2** *Mines* **g. souterraine** underground gasification **3** *(de l'eau)* aeration; *(avec du gaz carbonique)* carbonation

gazéifier [9] [gazeifje] **VT 1** *Chim* to gasify **2** *(eau)* to aerate; *(avec du gaz carbonique)* to carbonate

gazelle [gazɛl] **NF** *Zool* gazelle; *Fig* **avoir des yeux de gazelle** to be doe-eyed

gazer [3] [gaze] **VT 1** *(asphyxier)* to gas **2** *Tex* to singe

VI *Fam* **1** *(aller bien)* **alors, ça gaze? – ça gaze!** how's things *or* how's it going? – great!; **ça ne gaze pas du tout en ce moment** things aren't too great at the moment **2** *(foncer)* **allez, gaze!** step on it!, get a move on!

gazetier, -ère [gaztje, -ɛr] **NM,F 1** *Arch* gazette proprietor, gazetteer **2** *Péj* hack

gazette [gazɛt] **NF 1** *Arch (journal)* gazette, newspaper **2** *Fam Vieilli (bavard)* **son mari est une vraie g.!** her husband knows everybody's business *or* all the latest gossip!

gazeux, -euse [gazø, -øz] **ADJ 1** *Chim* gaseous **2** *(boisson)* fizzy, carbonated; *(eau)* sparkling, fizzy; **eau gazeuse naturelle** naturally carbonated water **3** *Méd* gas *(avant n)*

gazier, -ère [gazje, -ɛr] **ADJ** gas *(avant n)*

NM 1 *(employé du gaz)* gasman; *(dans une usine à gaz)* gasworks employee **2** *très Fam (individu)* guy, *Br* bloke, *Am* dude

gazinière [gazinjɛr] **NF** gas stove, *Br* gas cooker

gazoduc [gazɔdyk] **NM** gas pipeline

gazogène [gazɔʒɛn] **NM** *(appareil)* gas producer; **gaz de g.** producer gas

gazole [gazɔl] **NM 1** *(pour moteur Diesel)* diesel (oil), *Br* derv **2** *(combustible)* **g. de chauffe** (domestic) fuel oil

gazoline [gazɔlin] **NF** gasoline, gasolene

gazomètre [gazɔmɛtr] **NM** gasholder, gasometer

gazon [gazɔ̃] **NM 1** *(herbe)* **du g.** turf

2 *(pelouse)* lawn; **g. anglais** well-kept lawn, smooth lawn; **défense de marcher sur le g.** *(sur panneau)* keep off the grass

3 *(motte de terre)* turf, sod

4 *Bot* **g. mousse** mossy saxifrage

gazonnage [gazɔnaʒ] **NM** turfing, grassing (over)

gazonné, -e [gazɔne] **ADJ** grass-covered, turfed

gazonnement [gazɔnmɑ̃] **NM** turfing, planting with turf

gazonner [3] [gazɔne] **VT** to turf, to grass (over)

VI *(terrain)* to become covered with grass

gazouillant, -e [gazujɑ̃, -ɑ̃t] **ADJ 1** *(oiseau)* chirping, warbling **2** *(bébé)* babbling, gurgling **3** *Littéraire (eau)* babbling; **ruisseau g.** babbling brook

gazouillement [gazujmɑ̃] **NM 1** *(d'oiseau)* chirping *(UNCOUNT)*, warbling *(UNCOUNT)* **2** *(d'un bébé)* babbling *(UNCOUNT)*, gurgling *(UNCOUNT)* **3** *Littéraire (de l'eau)* babbling *(UNCOUNT)*; **on n'entendait que le g. d'une fontaine** all that could be heard was the gurgling *or* babbling of a fountain

gazouiller [3] [gazuje] **VI 1** *(oiseau)* to chirp, to warble **2** *(bébé)* to babble, to gurgle **3** *Littéraire (ruisseau, eau)* to babble, to murmur, to gurgle

gazouilleur, -euse [gazujœr, -øz] **ADJ 1** *(oiseau)* chirping, warbling **2** *(bébé)* babbling, gurgling; **ruisseau g.** babbling brook

gazouillis [gazuji] = **gazouillement**

GB, G-B *(abrév écrite* **Grande-Bretagne)** GB

GDB [ʒedebe] **NF** *Fam (abrév* **gueule de bois)** hangover□

GDF [ʒedeɛf] **NM** *(abrév* **Gaz de France)** = the French gas board

GDN [ʒedeɛn] **NF** *(abrév* **gestion des droits numériques)** DRM

geai [ʒɛ] **NM** *Orn* jay; **g. bleu** blue jay

géant, -e [ʒeɑ̃, -ɑ̃t] **ADJ 1** *(énorme)* giant *(avant n)*; *(carton, paquet)* giant-sized; **un écran g.** a giant screen; **une clameur géante** an almighty clamour **2** *Astron* giant *(avant n)* **3** *Fam (formidable)* **c'est g.!** it's wicked!

NM,F 1 *(personne, chose de grande taille)* giant; *Littéraire* **le chêne, g. de la forêt** the oak, giant of the forest; **le projet avance à pas de g.** the project is *Br* coming on *or Am* moving along in leaps and bounds **2** *Fig* **les géants de la littérature classique** the giants *or* great names of classical literature; **ils ont couronné un g.** they have given the award to one of the all-time greats; *Écon* **c'est un des géants de l'électronique** it's one of the giants of the electronics industry **3** *Myth* giant, *f* giantess

• **géante NF** *Astron* giant; **géante rouge** red giant

gecko [ʒeko] **NM** *Zool* gecko

gégène [ʒeʒɛn] *Fam* **ADJ** brilliant, wicked

NF = torture by electric shock

Géhenne [ʒeɛn] **NF** *Bible* **la G.** Gehenna

geignait *etc voir* **geindre**

geignard, -e [ʒɛɲar, -ard] *Fam* **ADJ** *(personne, voix)* whining, *Br* whingeing; **"et moi?" dit-il d'une voix geignarde** "what about me?" he whined

NM,F *(enfant)* crybaby; *(adulte)* moaner, *Br* whinger, *Am* bellyacher

geignement [ʒɛɲəmɑ̃] **NM** moaning *(UNCOUNT)*, groaning *(UNCOUNT)*

geindre [81] [ʒɛ̃dr] **VI 1** *(gémir)* to groan, to moan; **g. de douleur** to moan *or* to groan with pain **2** *Fam (pour des riens)* to whine, to gripe **3** *Littéraire (vent)* to moan

geisha [geʃa] **NF** geisha (girl)

gel [ʒɛl] **NM 1** *Météo* frost

2 *(suspension)* **le g. des opérations militaires** the suspension of military operations; **g. des négociations** suspension of negotiations; *UE* **g. des terres** set-aside

3 *Écon* freeze; **g. des crédits** credit freeze; **g. des prix** price freeze; **g. des salaires** wage freeze

4 *Chim* gel; **g. coiffant** hair gel; **se mettre du g.** to put gel on one's hair; **g. douche** shower gel; **dentifrice en g.** gel toothpaste

gélatine [ʒelatin] **NF** *Culin* gelatine; **g. de poisson** isinglass, fish glue; **feuille de g.** sheet of gelatine

gélatiné, -e [ʒelatine] **ADJ** *Phot* **papier g.** gelatine paper; **plaque gélatinée** gelatinized plate

gélatineux, -euse [ʒelatinø, -øz] **ADJ 1** *(contenant de la gélatine)* gelatinous; **substance gélatineuse** gelatinous substance; **solution gélatineuse** gelatine solution **2** *(flasque)* gelatinous, jellylike, flaccid

gelé, -e [ʒəle] **ADJ 1** *Agr & Météo (sol)* frozen; *(pousse, bourgeon)* frostbitten, frozen; *(arbre)* frozen

2 *Fig (glacé)* frozen; **être g. jusqu'aux os** to be frozen to the bone, to be frozen stiff; **je suis complètement g.** I'm absolutely frozen *or* freezing

3 *Méd* frostbitten; **il a eu les orteils gelés** his toes were frostbitten, he got frostbite in his toes; **mourir g.** to freeze to death

4 *Écon & Fin* frozen

5 *(hostile)* icy, stone-cold

• **gelée NF 1** *Météo* frost; **gelée blanche** white frost, hoarfrost; **forte gelée** hard frost **2** *Culin* jelly; **gelée de groseilles** redcurrant jelly *or* preserve

• **en gelée ADJ** *Culin* in jelly; **volaille en gelée** chicken in aspic *or* jelly

• **gelée royale NF** royal jelly

geler [25] [ʒəle] **VT 1** *(transformer en glace ▸ eau, sol)* to freeze; *(▸ route)* to make icy; **le froid a gelé la rivière** the cold has frozen the river (over)

2 *(bloquer ▸ tuyau, serrure)* to freeze up

3 *(détruire ▸ plante, tissu organique)* to freeze; **le froid a gelé les premières fleurs** the cold has frozen *or* nipped the first flowers

4 *(transir ▸ visage)* to chill, to numb; *(▸ membres)* to freeze

5 *(paralyser ▸ négociations)* to halt; *(▸ projet)* to halt, to block; *Fin (▸ capitaux, salaires, prix)* to freeze; **tous les crédits sont gelés jusqu'à nouvel ordre** all funding has been frozen until further notice

VI 1 *(eau, liquide)* to freeze; *(lac, rivière)* to freeze over

2 *(tuyau, serrure)* to freeze up

3 *(pousses, légumes)* to freeze, to be nipped by the frost

4 *Fig (personne)* to freeze; **je gèle** I'm frozen (stiff); **on gèle dans cette salle** it's freezing in this room; **ferme la porte, on gèle ici** shut the door, it's freezing in here

V IMPERSONNEL il gèle it's freezing; **il a gelé blanc** there's been a frost; **il gèle à pierre fendre** it is freezing hard

VPR se geler 1 *(personne)* **je me suis gelé là-bas** I got (absolutely) frozen down there **2** *très Fam* **on se les gèle** it's damned cold, *Br* it's brass monkey weather *or* brass monkeys

gélifiant, -e [ʒelifjɑ̃, -ɑ̃t] **ADJ** gelling *(avant n)*

NM gelling agent

gélifier [9] [ʒelifje] **VT 1** *Chim* to gel **2** *Culin* to make into a jelly, to jellify

VPR se gélifier to gel

gélignite [ʒeliɲit] **NF** gelignite

gélinotte [ʒelinɔt], **gelinotte** [ʒəlinɔt] **NF** *Orn* **g. (des bois)** hazel grouse, hazel hen; **g. des prairies** prairie chicken

gélose [ʒeloz] **NF** agar-agar

gélule [ʒelyl] **NF** *Pharm* capsule

gelure [ʒəlyr] **NF** *Méd* frostbite *(UNCOUNT)*

gémeau, -elle, -aux, -elles [ʒemo, -ɛl] **ADJ** *Vieilli* twin

NM,F *Vieilli* twin

• **Gémeaux NMPL 1** *Astron* Gemini **2** *Astrol* Gemini; **être G.** to be Gemini *or* a Geminian

gémellaire [ʒemelɛr] **ADJ** twin *(avant n)*, *Spéc* gemellary; **grossesse g.** twin pregnancy

gémellité [ʒemelite] **NF le taux de g. varie selon les pays** the number of twin births varies from country to country

gémination [ʒeminasjɔ̃] **NF** *Ling & Méd* gemination

géminé, -e [ʒemine] **ADJ 1** *(double)* twin *(avant n)*, *Spéc* geminate; *Archit* **arcades géminées** twin *or* dual arcades **2** *Ling* **consonne géminée** geminate consonant

• **géminée NF** *Ling* geminate

gémir [32] [ʒemir] **VI 1** *(blessé, malade)* to moan, to groan; **g. de douleur** to groan *or* to moan with pain

2 *(vent)* to moan, to wail; *(parquet, gonds)* to creak

3 *(se plaindre)* to moan, to whine

4 *Littéraire (souffrir)* **g. sous le joug de la tyrannie** to groan under the yoke of tyranny

5 *(colombe, tourterelle)* to coo

gémissant, -e [ʒemisɑ̃, -ɑ̃t] **ADJ** *(blessé, malade)* moaning, groaning; *(voix)* wailing; *Fig* **les accents gémissants de la bise** the moaning of the north wind

gémissement [ʒemismɑ̃] **NM 1** *(gén)* moan, groan; **pousser un g.** to (utter a) groan; **le g. du vent** the moaning *or* wailing of the wind; **gémissements** *(plaintes)* whimpering *(UNCOUNT)*, whining *(UNCOUNT)* **2** *(de la colombe, de la tourterelle)* cooing *(UNCOUNT)*

gemmage [ʒɛmaʒ] **NM** tapping *(of a pine tree)*

gemme [ʒɛm] **NF 1** *(pierre précieuse)* gem **2** *(résine)* (pine) resin **3** *Arch Bot* (leaf) bud

ADJ *voir* **sel**

gemmé, -e [ʒeme] **ADJ** *Littéraire* gemmed, jewelled

gemmer [4] [ʒeme] **VT** *(arbre)* to tap *(pine trees)*

gemmeur, -euse [ʒɛmœr, -øz] **NM,F** tapper *(of pine trees)*

gémonies [ʒemɔni] **NFPL** *Littéraire (locutions)* **traîner** *ou* **vouer qn aux g.** to pillory sb; **traîner** *ou* **vouer qch aux g.** to hold sth up to public ridicule

gênant, -e [ʒenɑ̃, -ɑ̃t] **ADJ 1** *(qui bloque le passage)* in the way; *(qui est encombrant)* cumbersome; **enlève ce fauteuil, il est g.** move that armchair, it's in the way **2** *(ennuyeux ▸ situation, lumière, bruit)* annoying, irritating; **les bus sont en grève? c'est g., ça** so the buses are on strike? what a nuisance *or* how annoying **3** *(embarrassant ▸ situation, silence)* awkward, embarrassing; *(▸ témoin)* awkward; **j'ai trouvé extrêmement g. que tu abordes ce sujet** it was extremely embarrassing of you to mention the subject

gencive [ʒɑ̃siv] **NF** *Anat* gum; *Fam* **prendre un coup dans les gencives** to get socked in the jaw, to get a kick in the teeth; **prends ça dans les gencives!** take that!; **elle lui a envoyé dans les gencives que...** she told him/her straight to his/her face that...

gendarme [ʒɑ̃darm] **NM 1** *(policier)* gendarme, policeman; **gendarmes à cheval** mounted police; **gendarmes mobiles** riot police; **gendarmes motocyclistes** motorcycle police; **jouer au g. et au voleur** *ou* **aux gendarmes et aux voleurs** to play cops and robbers; *Fam Aut* **g. couché** sleeping policeman

2 *Fam (personne autoritaire)* **faire le g.** to lay down the law; **leur mère est un vrai g.** their mother's a real *or Br* right battle-axe

3 *Fam (hareng)* smoked herring▫

4 *(saucisse)* = dry, flat sausage

5 *(pointe rocheuse)* gendarme

6 *(d'une pierre précieuse)* flaw

gendarmer [3] [ʒɑ̃darme] **se gendarmer VPR se g. (contre)** *(protester)* to kick up a fuss (about); *(s'indigner)* to get on one's high horse (about); **il n'y a pas de quoi se g.** there's nothing to get worked up about

gendarmerie [ʒɑ̃darməri] **NF 1** *(corporation)* gendarmerie, police force; **g. mobile** riot police; **g. nationale** = national police force, gendarmerie; **la G. royale du Canada** the Royal Canadian Mounted Police **2** *(bureaux)* gendarmerie, police station; *(caserne)* police *or* gendarmerie barracks

gendre [ʒɑ̃dr] **NM** son-in-law

gène [ʒɛn] **NM** gene; **structure du g.** gene structure; **banque/famille de gènes** gene bank/family; **g. aberrant** rogue gene

gêne [ʒɛn] **NF 1** *(matérielle)* inconvenience; **je resterais bien un jour de plus si ça ne vous cause aucune g.** I would like to stay for another day if it doesn't put you to any trouble *or* if that's no bother; **sa présence parmi nous est une g.** his/her being here with us is a bit awkward; **nous prions nos clients de bien vouloir excuser la g. occasionnée par les travaux** we apologize to customers for the inconvenience caused by the work

2 *(morale)* embarrassment; **ressentir ou éprouver de la g.** to feel embarrassed; **j'éprouvais une grande g. à lui annoncer qu'il était renvoyé** I felt deeply embarrassed having to tell him that he was dismissed; **il a accepté l'argent avec une certaine g.** he was uncomfortable about taking the money; **un moment de g.** an awkward moment; **il y a une certaine g. dans leurs relations** relations between them are rather strained; **où (il) y a de la g., (il n')y a pas de plaisir** there's no need to stand on ceremony; *Ironique (ton indigné)* don't mind me

3 *(physique)* difficulty, discomfort; **éprouver** *ou* **avoir de la g. à faire qch** to find it difficult to do sth; **sentir une g. respiratoire** *ou* **pour respirer** to have difficulty (in) breathing

4 *(pauvreté)* **être dans la g.** to be in need

5 *Arch (physique, morale)* torture

• **sans gêne ADJ** inconsiderate

gêné, -e [ʒene] **ADJ 1** *(personne, sourire)* embarrassed; **silence g.** embarrassed *or* awkward *or* uneasy silence; *Fam* **il n'est pas g., lui!** he's got a nerve *or Br* a cheek! **2** *(serré)* ill at ease, uncomfortable; **il se sentait g. dans son nouvel uniforme** he felt uncomfortable in his new uniform; *Fig* **être g. aux entournures** *(mal à l'aise)* to feel ill at ease *or* self-conscious **3** *(financièrement)* in financial difficultes; **les personnes momentanément gênées peuvent demander une avance** people with temporary financial difficulties can ask for an advance

généalogie [ʒenealɔʒi] **NF 1** *(ascendance)* ancestry; *(d'un cheval, d'un chien)* pedigree; **faire** *ou* **dresser sa g.** to trace one's ancestry *or* family tree **2** *(science)* genealogy

généalogique [ʒenealɔʒik] **ADJ** genealogical; **livre g.** *(de chevaux)* stud book; *(du bétail)* herd book

généalogiste [ʒenealɔʒist] **NMF** genealogist

gêner [4] [ʒene] **VT 1** *(incommoder ▸ sujet: chose)* to bother; **est-ce que la fumée vous gêne?** does the smoke bother you?; **la lanière de mes sandales me gêne quand je marche** the straps on my sandals are uncomfortable when I walk; **mes lunettes me gênent pour mettre mon casque** my glasses get in the way when I put my helmet on; **j'ai oublié mes lunettes, ça me gêne pour lire** I've left my glasses behind and I'm finding it difficult to read; **ça me gêne dans mon travail** it disturbs me when I'm trying to work; **j'ai été gêné par le manque de temps/ma méconnaissance du milieu** I was hindered *or* hampered by the lack of time/my ignorance of the milieu; **j'ai été gêné par le bruit/la lumière/le monde** I was disturbed by the noise/the light/the people; **ce qui me gêne, c'est que...** what bothers me is that...; **le froid ne me gêne pas** I don't mind the cold

2 *(encombrer)* to be in the way of; **g. le passage** to be in the way; **ma valise vous gêne-t-elle?** is my case in your way?; **ne bougez pas, vous ne me gênez pas du tout** don't move, you're not in my *or* the way at all; **recule-toi, tu me gênes pour passer** move back, you're in my way *or* you're stopping me from getting past; **si tu pouvais te pousser, tu me gênes pour passer les vitesses** could you move over, I can't change gear with you there

3 *(empêcher ▸ activité)* to interfere with; **ce camion gêne la circulation** that lorry is holding up the traffic; **la neige gênait la visibilité** visibility was hindered *or* impaired by the snow; **je suis gêné dans mon métier par mes lacunes en mathématiques** the gaps in my knowledge of mathematics are a handicap *or* a drawback in my line of business

4 *(importuner ▸ sujet: personne)* to put out, to

bother, to inconvenience; **ça ne le gênerait pas que j'arrive après minuit?** would it bother him if I arrived after midnight?; **ça vous gêne si j'ouvre la fenêtre?** do you mind if I open the window?; **ça ne me gêne pas de le lui dire** I don't mind telling him/her (about it); **cela ne te gênerait pas de me prêter ta voiture?** would you mind lending me your car?; **cela vous gênerait-il que je revienne demain?** would it disturb you *or* bother you if I came back tomorrow?; *Fam* **oui, pourquoi, ça te gêne?** yes, why, what's it to you *or* got any objections?

5 *(intimider)* to embarrass; **les plaisanteries de son ami la gênaient** her friend's jokes embarrassed her *or* made her feel uncomfortable; **cela me gênerait de le rencontrer** it would be awkward for me to meet him, I would feel uncomfortable meeting him; **sa présence me gêne** I feel awkward *or* embarrassed in his/her presence, his/her presence makes me feel ill at ease; **ça me gêne qu'il écoute** I feel uneasy with him listening; *Can* **être gêné** to be shy

6 *(serrer)* **mes souliers me gênent** my shoes pinch *or* are too tight; **cette ceinture/ce col me gêne** this belt/this collar is too tight

7 *(mettre en difficulté financière)* **en ce moment, cela me gênerait un peu de vous prêter cet argent** I can't really afford to lend you the money at the moment

USAGE ABSOLU **1** *(encombrer)* **c'est le placard qui gêne pour ouvrir la porte** the door won't open because of the cupboard; **pousse-toi, tu vois bien que tu gênes!** move along, you can see you're in the way! **2** *(importuner)* **ça ne gêne pas que tu viennes, il y a de la place** it'll be no bother *or* trouble at all if you come, there's enough room

VPR **se gêner 1** *(emploi réciproque)* **la chambre est trop petite, on se gêne les uns les autres** the room is too small, we're in each other's way; **il y a beaucoup de place, nous ne nous gênerons pas** there's a lot of room, we won't be in each other's way **2** *Fam* **je vais me g., tiens!** just watch me!; **tu aurais tort de te g.!** why should you worry *or* care?□; **il ne se gêne pas avec nous** he doesn't stand on ceremony with us; **continuez votre repas, ne vous gênez pas pour moi** go on with your meal, don't mind me; **je ne me suis pas gêné pour le lui dire** I didn't hesitate to tell him/her so□, I made no bones about telling him/her so; *Ironique* **vous avez pris ma place, surtout ne vous gênez pas!** go on, take my seat, don't mind me!; **il y en a qui ne se gênent pas!** some people have got a nerve! **3** *Suisse (être intimidé)* to be shy

général, -e, -aux, -ales [ʒeneral, -o] ADJ **1** *(d'ensemble)* general; **la situation générale** the general *or* overall situation; **le phénomène est g.** the phenomenon is widespread, it's a general phenomenon; **le sens g. d'un mot** the general *or* broad meaning of a word; **état g.** general *or* overall condition; **l'état g. du malade est bon** the patient's overall condition is good

2 *(imprécis)* general; **il s'en est tenu à des remarques générales** he confined himself to generalities *or* to some general remarks

3 *(collectif)* general, common; **le bien g.** the common good; **à la surprise/l'indignation générale** to everybody's surprise/indignation

4 *(total)* general; **amnistie générale** general amnesty

5 *Admin & Pol (assemblée, direction)* general; **il a été nommé directeur g.** he's been appointed managing director

NM **1** *Mil* general; **g. d'armée** general; **g. d'armée aérienne** *Br* air chief marshal, *Am* general **g. de brigade** *Br* brigadier, *Am* brigadier general; **g. de brigade aérienne** *Br* air commodore, *Am* brigadier general; **g. en chef** commander in chief; **g. de corps d'armée** lieutenant general; **g. de corps aérien** *ou* **de corps d'armée aérienne** *Br* air marshal, *Am* lieutenant general; **g. de division** major general; **g. de division aérienne** *Br* air vice-marshal, *Am* major general **2** *Rel* general **3** *(toujours au singulier)* general; **aller du g. au particulier** to move from the general to the particular

• **Général** NPR **le G.** General de Gaulle

• **générale** NF **1** *Théât* (final) dress rehearsal **2** *Mil* alarm call; **battre** *ou* **sonner la générale** *Mil* to sound the alarm; *Naut* to beat to quarters **3** *(épouse du général)* general's wife; **bonjour, madame la générale** *(qui s'appelle Leclerc)* hello, Mrs Leclerc

• **Générale** NF **la Générale des Eaux** = water utility

• **en général** ADV **1** *(habituellement)* generally, as a rule; **en g. elle se couche tôt** she goes to bed early as a rule, she generally goes to bed early; **en g., il me prévient quand il rentre tard** he generally *or* usually lets me know if he's going to be late (home) **2** *(globalement)* in general; **le genre humain en g.** mankind in general; **tu parles en g. ou (tu parles) de nous?** are you talking generally *or* in general terms or (are you talking) about us?; **est-ce que vous êtes d'accord avec ses propos? – en g., non** do you agree with what he says? – generally speaking, no

généralement [ʒeneralmɑ̃] ADV **1** *(habituellement)* generally, usually; **les magasins sont g. fermés le dimanche** (the) shops are generally closed on Sundays **2** *(globalement)* generally; **g. parlant** generally speaking

généralisable [ʒeneralizabl] ADJ that can be generalized; **l'expérience/la théorie est intéressante, mais est-elle g.?** it's an interesting experiment/theory, but can it be applied more generally?

généralisateur, -trice [ʒeneralizatœr,-tris] ADJ *(esprit, méthode)* generalizing; **c'est un livre trop g.** the book generalizes too much

généralisation [ʒeneralizasjɔ̃] NF **1** *(propos, idée)* generalization; **faire des généralisations** to make generalizations, to generalize; **avoir tendance à la g.** to tend to make generalizations *or* to generalize; **une g. hâtive** a sweeping generalization **2** *(extension)* generalization; **nous assistons à la g. du conflit/de la maladie** the conflict/the disease is spreading

généralisatrice [ʒeneralizatris] *voir* **généralisateur**

généraliser [3] [ʒeneralize] VT **1** *(répandre)* **cette méthode/interdiction a été généralisée** this method/ban now applies to everybody; **cette mesure a été généralisée en 1969** this measure was extended across the board in 1969 **2** *(globaliser)* to generalize; **il a tendance à tout g.** he tends to generalize; **ne généralise pas ton cas personnel** don't generalize from your own experience

USAGE ABSOLU to generalize; **on ne peut pas g.** you can't generalize

VPR **se généraliser** *(crise, famine)* to become widespread; *(usage, conflit, grève)* to spread; **la crise économique s'est généralisée à tous les pays occidentaux** the economic crisis has spread to all countries in the West

généralissime [ʒeneralisim] NM generalissimo

généraliste [ʒeneralist] ADJ **une chaîne de télévision g.** a general-interest TV channel; **le caractère g. de l'entreprise** the diversity of the company's activities

NMF *Méd Br* general practitioner, GP, *Am* family practitioner

généralité [ʒeneralite] NF **1** *(universalité)* generality **2** *(majorité)* **dans la g. des cas** in most cases

• **généralités** NFPL *(points généraux)* general remarks; *(banalités)* generalities; **s'en tenir à des généralités** to confine oneself to generalities *or* to general remarks; **exposer quelques généralités dans un cours d'introduction** to present some general ideas in an introductory course

générateur, -trice [ʒeneratœr, -tris] ADJ **1** *(machine)* generating; *(force, organe)* generative; *Élec* **station** *ou* **usine génératrice** generating station *or* plant; **chaudière génératrice** steam boiler **2** *(créateur)* **être g. de** to generate; **une industrie génératrice d'emplois** a job-creating industry; **un fanatisme g. de violence** a fanaticism that breeds violence; **un colorant alimentaire g. de troubles gastriques** a food colouring which causes gastric problems **3** *Math* **ligne génératrice d'une surface** line which generates a surface

NM **1** *Élec* generator; **g. d'électricité** electricity generator; *Électron* **g. d'impulsions** pulse generator; *Électron* **g. de signaux** signal *or* signalling generator; **g. de vapeur** steam generator

2 *Nucl* **g. isotopique** radioisotopic (power) generator

3 *Ordinat* generator; **g. de caractères** character generator; **g. d'effets numériques** digital effects generator; **g. d'états** report generator; **g. graphique** graphics generator; **g. de menus** menu builder; **g. de programmes** (program) generator; **g. de système expert** generic expert system tool

4 *TV & Cin* **g. de couleur** colour synthesizer; **g. d'effets spéciaux** (special) effects generator, SEG; **g. de signaux** colour coder; **g. de titres graphiques** graphic titler

• **génératrice** NF **1** *Élec* generator; *Nucl* **génératrice nucléaire** nuclear power reactor **2** *Math* generatrix

génératif, -ive [ʒeneratif, -iv] ADJ generative

génération [ʒenerasjɔ̃] NF **1** *Biol* generation; **les organes de la g.** the reproductive organs; **g. spontanée** spontaneous generation

2 *(action de générer)* generation; *(de vapeur)* generation, production; *(de métaux)* formation

3 *(groupe d'âge)* generation; **la g. actuelle** the present generation; **la jeune g.** the younger generation; **la g. montante** the new generation; **les jeunes de ma g.** young people my age *or* of my generation; **de g. en g.** from generation to generation, through the generations; **des immigrés de la seconde g.** second-generation immigrants; *Fig* **la g. perdue** the lost generation; **g. sandwich** sandwich generation; **g. X** generation X

4 *(durée)* generation; **il y a environ trois générations par siècle** there are approximately three generations per century

5 *(d'une technique)* **la nouvelle g. de machines à laver** the new generation of washing machines; **les lecteurs MP3 de la quatrième g.** fourth-generation MP3 players

6 *Ordinat* generation; **g. automatique de textes** automatic generation of texts; **g. d'écrans** screen generation; **g. de langage/machine/système** language/computer/system generation

générative [ʒenerativ] *voir* **génératif**

génératrice [ʒeneratris] *voir* **générateur**

générer [18] [ʒenere] VT **1** *(faire naître ▸ idées, images, profits)* to generate; *Ordinat* **généré par ordinateur** computer-generated **2** *(produire ▸ électricité, vapeur)* to generate, to produce

généreuse [ʒenerøz] *voir* **généreux**

généreusement [ʒenerøzmɑ̃] ADV **1** *(avec libéralité)* generously; **g. rétribué** generously rewarded **2** *(avec noblesse)* generously; **il a g. offert de nous aider** he generously offered to help us **3** *(en grande quantité)* **se servir à manger g.** to help oneself to a generous portion; **se verser g. à boire** to pour oneself a good measure

généreux, -euse [ʒenerø, -øz] ADJ **1** *(prodigue)* generous; **être** *ou* **se montrer g. (avec** *ou* **envers qn)** to be generous (with sb); **laisser un pourboire g.** to leave a generous *or* handsome tip

2 *(noble ▸ geste, tempérament, âme)* noble; **des sentiments g.** unselfish *or* noble sentiments

3 *(fertile ▸ terre)* generous, fertile

4 *(abondant ▸ portion)* generous; *(▸ repas)* lavish

5 *(plantureux)* **aux formes généreuses** curvaceous

6 *(vin ▸ riche en alcool)* high in alcohol; *(▸ riche en saveur)* full-bodied

générique [ʒenerik] ADJ *(publicité, marché, produit)* generic; **produit g.** no-name *or* generic product; **médicament g.** generic drug

NM **1** *Cin & TV* credits; **figurer au g.** to appear in the credits, to get a credit; **g. de début** opening credits; **g. de fin** closing credits, end titles **2** *(indicatif musical)* signature tune

générosité [ʒenerɔzite] NF **1** *(largesse)* generosity

2 *(bonté)* generosity, kindness; **avec g.** generously; **je l'ai fait dans un élan de g.** I did it in a sudden fit of kindness; **tu fais ça par (pure) g.?** are you doing this out of the kindness of your heart?

3 *(d'un vin)* full body

4 *(des formes)* opulence

• **générosités** NFPL *(cadeaux)* gifts, liberalities

Gênes [ʒɛn] NF Genoa

genèse [ʒənɛz] NF **1** *(élaboration)* genesis; **faire la g. de qch** to trace the evolution of sth **2** *Bible* **la G.** (the Book of) Genesis

genet [ʒənɛ] NM *Zool* jennet *(horse)*

genêt [ʒənɛ] NM *Bot* broom *(UNCOUNT)*

généticien, -enne [ʒenetisjɛ̃, -ɛn] **NM,F** geneticist

génétique [ʒenetik] **ADJ** genetic; **fond g. commun** gene pool
NF genetics *(singulier)*

génétiquement [ʒenetikmɑ̃] **ADV** genetically; **g. modifié** genetically modified

genette [ʒənɛt] **NF** *Zool* genet

gêneur, -euse [ʒɛnœr, -øz] **NM,F** nuisance

Genève [ʒənɛv] **NF** Geneva; **le lac de G.** Lake Geneva; **le canton de G.** Geneva

genevois, -e [ʒənvwa, -az] **ADJ** Genevan, Genevese
• **Genevois, -e NM,F** Genevan, Genevese; **les G.** the Genevans, the Genevese

genévrier [ʒənevrije] **NM** *Bot* juniper

génial, -e, -aux, -ales [ʒenjal, -o] **ADJ 1** *(qui a du génie)* of genius; **Mozart était un compositeur g.** Mozart was a composer of genius **2** *(ingénieux)* brilliant; **ce fut une invention géniale** it was a brilliant invention **3** *Fam (extraordinaire)* brilliant, great, fantastic; **un mec g.** a great guy; **je n'ai pas trouvé cette exposition géniale** I didn't think much of that exhibition; **tu as vu le film hier soir? pas g., hein?** did you see the film last night? no great shakes *or* not up to much, was it?
EXCLAM brilliant!, great!

> Il faut noter que l'adjectif anglais **genial** est un faux ami. Il signifie **cordial**.

génialement [ʒenjalmɑ̃] **ADV** with genius, masterfully, brilliantly

génie [ʒeni] **NM 1** *(don)* genius; **avoir du g.** to be a genius; **avoir le g. de qch/pour faire qch** to have a genius *or* gift for sth/for doing sth; **elle a le g. des affaires** she has a genius for business; *Ironique* **tu as vraiment le g. pour te mettre dans des situations impossibles!** you have a real gift for *or* the knack of always getting into difficult situations!
2 *(personne)* genius; **c'est loin d'être un g.** he's/she's no genius
3 *(essence)* genius; **le g. de la langue française** the genius *or* spirit of the French language; **le g. d'un peuple** the genius of a people
4 *Littérature & Myth (magicien)* genie; *(esprit)* spirit; **g. des airs** spirit of the air; **être le bon/mauvais g. de qn** to be a good/bad influence on sb; **le petit g. de la forêt** the forest sprite
5 *Tech* **le G.** engineering; **les officiers du g.** *Br* ≃ the Royal Engineers, *Am* ≃ the (Army) Corps of Engineers; **soldat du g.** engineer, *Br* sapper; **g. aéroporté** airborne engineers; **g. de l'air** aviation engineers; **g. atomique** nuclear engineering; **g. biologique** bioengineering; **g. chimique** chemical engineering; **g. civil** civil engineering; **g. électronique** electronic engineering; **g. génétique** genetic engineering; **g. industriel** industrial engineering; **g. logiciel** systems engineering; **g. maritime** marine engineering; **g. militaire** military engineering; **g. rural** agricultural engineering
• **de génie ADJ** *(musicien, inventeur)* of genius; *(idée)* brilliant

genièvre [ʒənjɛvr] **NM 1** *Bot (arbre)* juniper; *(fruit)* juniper berry; **grain de g.** juniper berry **2** *(eau-de-vie)* geneva

génique [ʒenik] **ADJ** genic; **thérapie g.** gene therapy

génisse [ʒenis] **NF** *Zool* heifer

génital, -e, -aux, -ales [ʒenital, -o] **ADJ** *Anat* genital; **appareil g.** genitalia

géniteur, -trice [ʒenitœr, -tris] **NM,F** *Hum* progenitor, parent
NM *Zool* sire

génitif [ʒenitif] **NM** *Gram* genitive (case); **au g.** in the genitive

génito-urinaire [ʒenitoyrinɛr] *(pl* **génito-urinaires)** **ADJ** genito-urinary

génitrice [ʒenitris] *voir* **géniteur**

génocide [ʒenɔsid] **NM** genocide

génois, -e [ʒenwa, -az] **ADJ** Genoese, Genovese
NM *(dialecte)* Genoese *or* Genovese (dialect)
• **Génois, -e NM,F** Genoese, Genovese; **les G.** the Genoese, the Genovese
• **génoise NF** *Culin* sponge cake

génome [ʒenom] **NM** *Biol* genome

génomique [ʒenɔmik] *Biol* **ADJ** genomic, genome *(avant n)*
NF genomics *(singulier)*

génothérapie [ʒenɔterapi] **NF** *Biol* genotherapy, gene therapy

génotype [ʒenɔtip] **NM** *Biol* genotype

genou, -x [ʒənu] **NM 1** *Anat* knee; **on était dans la neige jusqu'aux genoux** we were knee-deep *or* up to our knees in snow; **sa robe lui arrivait au-dessus du g./aux genoux** her dress came down to just above the knee/to her knees; **cette année les jupes s'arrêtent au g.** knee-length skirts are the fashion this year; **mon jean est troué aux genoux** my jeans have got holes at *or* in the knees; **avoir les genoux en dedans** to be knock-kneed; **mettre un g. à terre** to go down on one knee; **assis sur les genoux de sa mère** sitting on his mother's lap *or* knee; **plier** *ou* **fléchir** *ou* **ployer le g. devant qn** to bow down *or* to kneel before sb; **faire du g. à qn** to play footsie with sb; **être sur les genoux** to be exhausted; **être aux genoux de qn** to be at sb's feet **2** *Tech (joint)* ball-and-socket joint
• **à genoux ADV 1** *(sur le sol)* **se mettre à genoux** to kneel (down), to go down on one's knees; **se mettre à genoux devant qn** to go down on one's knees to sb; **elle lavait le sol à genoux** she was cleaning the floor on her hands and knees **2** *Fig* **être à genoux devant qn** *(lui être soumis)* to be on one's knees before sb; *(être en adoration devant lui)* to worship sb; **le public français est à genoux devant lui** French audiences worship him; **je ne vais pas me mettre à genoux devant lui** *(le supplier)* I'm not going to go down on my knees to him; **demander qch à genoux** to ask for sth on bended knee; **je te le demande à genoux** I beg of you

genouillère [ʒənujɛr] **NF 1** *(protection)* knee pad
2 *(bandage)* knee bandage *or* support
3 *(pièce d'armure)* knee piece, genouillère
4 *Tech* **articulation à g.** toggle joint

genre [ʒɑ̃r] **NM 1** *(sorte, espèce)* kind, sort, type; **on y trouve des livres de tous les genres** all sorts *or* kinds *or* types of books are found there; **quel g. de femme est-elle?** what kind of woman is she?; **quel g. de vie mène-t-il?** what kind *or* sort of (a) life does he lead?; **ce n'est pas le g. à renoncer** he's/she's not the sort to give up *or* who gives up; **partir sans payer, ce n'est pas son g.** it's not like him/her to leave without paying; **c'est ce qu'on fait de mieux dans le g.** it's the best of its kind; **un g. de** *(une sorte de)* a kind *or* sort of; **un peu dans le g. de...** rather *or* a bit like...; **elle m'a répondu quelque chose du g. "je ne suis pas ta bonne"** she answered something along the lines of "I'm not here to wait on you"; **un vin blanc g. sauternes** a Sauternes-type white wine; **étui g. maroquin** case in imitation morocco
2 *(comportement, manières)* type, style; **le g. intellectuel** the intellectual type; **c'est le g. star** he's/she's the film star type; **avoir un drôle de g.** to be an odd sort; **leurs enfants ont vraiment bon g.** their children really know how to behave; **elle a mauvais g.** she's a bit vulgar; **dans le g. vulgaire, on ne fait pas mieux!** beat that for vulgarity!; **il a exigé qu'on lui rembourse le dessert, tu vois le g.!** he had the dessert deducted from the bill, you know the sort!; **il est romantique, tout à fait mon g.!** he's a romantic, just my type!; **faire du g., se donner un g.** to put on airs, to give oneself airs; **g. de vie** lifestyle
3 *Biol* genus; **le g. humain** mankind, the human race
4 *Beaux-Arts* genre; **le grand g.** historical painting; **peinture de g.** genre painting
5 *Gram* gender; **s'accorder en g. et en nombre** to agree in gender and number
6 *Littérature* genre; **le g. policier** the detective genre, detective stories; **le g. romanesque** the novel; **le g. comique** comedy; **le g. tragique** tragedy
• **dans son genre ADV** *(à sa façon)* in his/her (own) way; **c'est un artiste dans son g.** he's/she's an artist in his/her (own) way
• **en son genre ADV** *(dans sa catégorie)* **un voyage vraiment unique en son g.** a journey unique of its kind; **elle est unique en son g.** she's in a class of her own
• **en tout genre, en tous genres ADV** of all kinds; **fournitures de bureau en tout g.** office equipment of all kinds

gens[1] [ʒɛ̃s] *(pl* **gentes** [ʒɛ̃tes]) **NF** *Antiq (groupe de familles)* gens; **la g. Cornelia** the gens Cornelia

gens[2] [ʒɑ̃]

> Any adjective before **gens** will be in the feminine; any adjective coming after will be in the masculine.

NMPL OU NFPL 1 *(personnes)* people; **les vieilles g.** old people, old folk; **que vont dire les g.?** what will people say?; **beaucoup de g., bien des g.** many people, a lot of people; **il y avait peu de g. dans la salle** there were not many people in the hall; **il y a des g. qui demandent à vous voir** there are some people who want to see you; **des g. de la campagne** country folk *or* people; **les g. d'ici, les g. du pays** people from around here, the locals; **les g. du monde** society people; **des g. simples** ordinary folk *or* people; **les g. de la ville** townspeople, townsfolk; **petites g.** people of limited means; **les bonnes g. murmurent que...** people are saying *or* whispering that...
2 *(corporation)* **comme disent les g. du métier** as the experts *or* the professionals say; **les g. d'Église** clergymen, the clergy, the cloth; **g. de lettres** men and women of letters; **g. de maison** servants, domestic staff; **g. de mer** seafarers; *Littéraire* **les g. de robe** the legal profession; **g. du spectacle** stage *or* showbusiness people; **g. de théâtre** theatre *or* theatrical people; **les g. du voyage** *(artistes)* travelling players *or* performers; *(gitans)* travellers
3 *(nation)* **le droit des g.** the law of nations
4 *Vieilli (domestiques)* servants, domestics; *(de roi)* retinue

gent [ʒɑ̃] **NF** *Hum (espèce)* race, tribe; **la g. ailée** our feathered friends; **la g. masculine/féminine** the male/female sex

gentes [ʒɛ̃tes] *voir* **gens**[1]

gentiane [ʒɑ̃sjan] **NF 1** *Bot* gentian **2** *(liqueur)* gentian bitters

gentil, -ille [ʒɑ̃ti, -ij] **ADJ 1** *(serviable)* kind; **ils sont gentils avec moi** they're kind *or* nice to me; **sois g., apporte-moi mes lunettes** do me a favour and get my glasses for me; **merci, c'est g.** thanks, that's very kind of you
2 *(aimable)* nice, sweet; **tu es bien g. de m'aider** it's very nice *or* kind *or* good of you to help me; **c'est g. de votre part (de m'écrire)** it is kind *or* good of you (to write to me); **je l'aime bien, il est g.** I like him, he's nice; **ils ont écrit sur moi des choses gentilles** they wrote some very nice things about me; **elle a pris mon idée sans me le dire, ce n'est pas très g.** she stole my idea without telling me, that's not very nice (of her); **il est g. comme un cœur** he's an absolute angel; **g. membre** holidaymaker *(at Club Méditerranée)*; **g. organisateur** group leader *(at Club Méditerranée)*
3 *(joli)* nice, pretty, cute; **un g. petit village** a nice *or* pretty little village; **c'est g. par ici** it's nice *or* pleasant around here
4 *(exprimant l'impatience)* **c'est bien g. mais...** that's all very well but...; **tu es bien g. mais quand est-ce que je vais récupérer mon argent?** that's all very well but when do I get my money back?; **elle est bien gentille mais elle n'y comprend rien** she's means well but she hasn't got a clue
5 *(obéissant)* good; **il a été g.?** was he good?; **si tu es g./gentille** if you're a good boy/girl
6 *(avant le nom) (considérable)* **une gentille somme** a tidy *or* fair sum
NM *(non-juif)* Gentile; **les gentils** the Gentiles

> Il faut noter que les adjectifs anglais **genteel** et **gentle** sont des faux amis. **Genteel** signifie **respectable** ou **affecté**, selon le contexte, et **gentle** signifie **doux**.

gentilhomme [ʒɑ̃tijɔm] *(pl* **gentilshommes** [ʒɑ̃tizɔm]) **NM 1** *Hist* nobleman, gentleman; **g. campagnard** (country) squire, country gentleman; **g. de la Chambre du Roi** gentleman of the Privy Chamber; **2** *Littéraire (gentleman)* gentleman

gentilhommière [ʒɑ̃tijɔmjɛr] **NF 1** *(demeure)* country seat, manor house **2** *(en Belgique)* boarding house for men

gentilité [ʒɑ̃tilite] **NF** *Hist & Rel* Gentiles

gentille [ʒɑ̃tij] *voir* **gentil**

gentillesse [ʒɑ̃tijɛs] **NF 1** *(d'une personne)* kindness *(UNCOUNT)*; **elle a fait cela par g.** she did that out of kindness; **elle a eu la g. de venir elle-même** she was kind enough to come herself

2 *(dans des formules de politesse)* **auriez-vous la g. de me prévenir à l'avance?** would you be so kind as to let me know beforehand?

3 *(parole)* kind word; **il lui chuchotait des gentillesses à l'oreille** he whispered kind words *or* sweet nothings in her ear

4 *(acte)* act of kindness; **elle est toujours prête à toutes les gentillesses** she's always ready to help people out

gentillet, -ette [ʒɑ̃tijɛ, -ɛt] **ADJ 1** *(mignon)* rather *or* quite nice; **il est g., leur appartement** they've got a lovely little *Br* flat *orAm* apartment **2** *Péj* **c'est un film g., sans plus** it's a pleasant enough film, but that's about it

gentiment [ʒɑ̃timɑ̃] **ADV 1** *(aimablement)* kindly; **ils nous ont g. proposé de nous raccompagner** they kindly offered to drive us home; **elle m'a g. tenu compagnie** she was kind enough to keep me company, she kindly kept me company **2** *(sagement)* nicely; **on discutait g. quand...** we were quietly chatting away when... **3** *Suisse (sans précipitation)* **fais-le g., tu as tout le temps** take your time, there's no hurry

gentleman [dʒɛntləman] *(pl* **gentlemen** [-mɛn]) **NM 1** *(homme distingué)* gentleman; **en parfait g.** like a true gentleman **2** *Courses de chevaux* amateur jockey

gentleman-farmer [dʒɛntləmanfarmœr] *(pl* **gentlemen-farmers** [-mɛn-]) **NM** gentleman farmer

gentlemen [dʒɛntləmɛn] *voir* **gentleman**

génuflexion [ʒenyflɛksjɔ̃] **NF** genuflection; **faire une g.** to genuflect

géo [ʒeo] **NF** *Fam Arg scol* geog, geography[□]

géocentrique [ʒeosɑ̃trik] **ADJ** geocentric

géocentrisme [ʒeosɑ̃trism] **NM** geocentrism

géochimie [ʒeoʃimi] **NF** geochemistry

géocroiseur [ʒeokrwazœr] **NM** *Astron* near-earth asteroid

géode [ʒeɔd] **NF 1** *Géol & Méd* geode **2** *(à Paris)* **la G.** the Géode *(the spherical building housing a cinema at the Cité des Sciences in Paris)*

géodésie [ʒeɔdezi] **NF** geodesy, geodetics *(singulier)*

géodésique [ʒeɔdezik] **ADJ 1** *Math* geodesic; **point g.** triangulation point **2** *Géog* geodetic

NF *Math & Géog* geodesic (line)

géodiversité [ʒeɔdiversite] **NF** geodiversity

géodynamique [ʒeɔdinamik] **ADJ** geodynamic

NF geodynamics *(singulier)*

géographe [ʒeɔgraf] **NMF** geographer

géographie [ʒeɔgrafi] **NF 1** *(science)* geography; **g. humaine/physique/politique** human/physical/political geography **2** *(livre)* geography book

géographique [ʒeɔgrafik] **ADJ** geographic, geographical; **carte g.** map; **dictionnaire g.** gazetteer

géographiquement [ʒeɔgrafikmɑ̃] **ADV** geographically

geôle [ʒol] **NF** *Arch ou Littéraire* jail, *Br* gaol

geôlier, -ère [ʒolje, -ɛr] **NM,F** *Arch ou Littéraire* jailer, *Br* gaoler

géolocalisation [ʒeɔlɔkalizasjɔ̃] **NF** geolocation

géologie [ʒeɔlɔʒi] **NF** geology

géologique [ʒeɔlɔʒik] **ADJ** geologic, geological

géologiquement [ʒeɔlɔʒikmɑ̃] **ADV** geologically

géologue [ʒeɔlɔg] **NMF** geologist

géomagnétique [ʒeɔmaɲetik] **ADJ** geomagnetic

géomagnétisme [ʒeɔmaɲetism] **NM** geomagnetism

géomancie [ʒeɔmɑ̃si] **NF** geomancy

géométral, -e, -aux, -ales [ʒeɔmetral, -o] **ADJ** flat, plane

NM flat projection

géomètre [ʒeɔmɛtr] **NMF 1** *Math* geometer, geometrician **2** *(arpenteur)* land surveyor

NM *Entom (chenille)* measuring worm, looper; *(papillon)* geometer moth

géométrie [ʒeɔmetri] **NF 1** *Math* geometry; **g. analytique** analytical *or* co-ordinate geometry; **g. plane/dans l'espace** plane/solid geometry **2** *(livre)* geometry book

• **à géométrie variable ADJ 1** *(avion)* swing-wing *(avant n)* **2** *Fig (susceptible d'évoluer)* flexible, adaptable

géométrique [ʒeɔmetrik] **ADJ 1** *Math* geometric, geometrical; **progression/suite g.** geometric progression/series **2** *Beaux-Arts* geometric **3** *Fig (précision)* mathematical; **être d'une rigueur toute g.** to be extremely rigorous

géométriquement [ʒeɔmetrikmɑ̃] **ADV** geometrically

géomorphologie [ʒeɔmɔrfɔlɔʒi] **NF** geomorphology

géophone [ʒeɔfɔn] **NM** geophone

géophysicien, -enne [ʒeɔfizisjɛ̃, -ɛn] **NM,F** geophysicist

géophysique [ʒeɔfizik] **ADJ** geophysical

NF geophysics *(singulier)*

géopolitique [ʒeɔpɔlitik] **ADJ** geopolitical

NF geopolitics *(singulier)*

Georgetown [dʒɔrʒtaun] **N** Georgetown

georgette [ʒɔrʒɛt] **NF** *Tex* **crêpe g.** georgette (crepe)

Géorgie [ʒeɔrʒi] **NF la G.** Georgia

géorgien, -enne [ʒeɔrʒjɛ̃, -ɛn] **ADJ** *Géog* Georgian

NM *(langue)* Georgian

• **Géorgien, -enne NM,F** Georgian

géostationnaire [ʒeɔstasjɔnɛr] **ADJ** *Astron* **satellite g.** geostationary satellite

géostratégique [ʒeɔstrateʒik] **ADJ** geostrategic

géosynchrone [ʒeɔsɛ̃kron] **ADJ** geosynchronous

géosynclinal, -aux [ʒeɔsɛ̃klinal, -o] **NM** geosyncline

géothermie [ʒeɔtɛrmi] **NF** geothermal science, geothermics *(singulier)*

géothermique [ʒeɔtɛrmik] **ADJ** geothermic, geothermal

gérance [ʒerɑ̃s] **NF 1** *(fonction)* management; **assurer la g. de** to be (the) manager of, to manage; **prendre/reprendre un fonds en g.** to take on/to take over the management of a business; **donner la g. d'un commerce à qn** to appoint sb manager of a business; **une g. de cinq ans** a five-year managership; **g. libre** lease management; **g. de portefeuille** portfolio management **2** *(période)* managership; **pendant sa g.** during his/her time as manager

géranium [ʒeranjɔm] **NM** *Bot* geranium; *(sauvage)* crane's bill

gérant, -e [ʒerɑ̃, -ɑ̃t] **NM,F** manager; *(d'un journal)* managing editor; **g. d'affaires** business manager; **g. de fonds** fund manager; **g. d'hôtel** hotel manager; **g. de magasin** store manager; **g. majoritaire** manager with a controlling interest; **g. minoritaire** manager with a minority interest; **g. non associé** salaried manager, manager with no holding in a business; **g. de portefeuille** portfolio manager; **g. de société** managing director *(of a company)*

gerbage [ʒɛrbaʒ] **NM 1** *(du blé)* binding, sheaving **2** *(de fûts, de paquets)* stacking, piling

gerbe [ʒɛrb] **NF 1** *(de blé)* sheaf; *(de fleurs)* spray; **lier le blé en gerbes** to sheave the corn, to bind the corn into sheaves; **g. de fleurs** spray of flowers;

2 *(de feu d'artifice)* spray, *Spéc* gerbe

3 *(jaillissement* ▸ *d'eau)* spray; *(*▸ *d'étincelles)* shower; **une g. de flammes** a blaze, a burst of flame; **la voiture faisait jaillir des gerbes d'eau sur son passage** the car sent up a spray of water as it went by

4 *Astron & Phys* shower

5 *Mil* cone of fire

6 *Vulg* **avoir la g.** *(avoir envie de vomir)* to feel like throwing up *or* puking; *(vomir)* to throw up, to puke

gerber [3] [ʒɛrbe] **VT 1** *(blé)* to bind, to sheave, to bind into sheaves **2** *(fûts, paquets)* to pile (up), to stack (up)

VI 1 *Vulg (vomir)* to throw up, to puke; **ça me fait g.** it makes me want to throw up *or* puke **2** *(feu d'artifice)* to shower, to fan out

gerbera [ʒɛrbera] **NM** *Bot* gerbera

gerbeuse [ʒɛrbøz] **NF** stacker, stacking machine

gerbier [ʒɛrbje] **NM** stack, rick

gerbille [ʒɛrbil] **NF** *Zool* gerbil

gerboise [ʒɛrbwaz] **NF** *Zool* jerboa

gerce [ʒɛrs] **NF 1** *Métal* crack **2** *(dans le bois)* crack, flaw

gercé, -e [ʒɛrse] **ADJ** cracked; *(mains, lèvres)* chapped

gercer [16] [ʒɛrse] **VI 1** *(peau, mains, lèvres)* to chap, to crack; **chaque hiver, j'ai les mains qui gercent** every winter I get chapped hands **2** *(bois, métal, enduit)* to crack

VT to chap, to crack

VPR se gercer *(peau, mains, lèvres)* to chap, to get chapped, to crack; *(terre)* to crack

gerçure [ʒɛrsyr] **NF 1** *(des mains, des lèvres)* crack, chapping *(UNCOUNT)*; **j'ai des gerçures aux mains/lèvres** I've got chapped hands/lips **2** *Tech (d'un métal, d'un enduit)* hairline crack; *(d'un diamant, du bois)* flaw; *(d'un tronc)* heart shake

gérer [18] [ʒere] **VT 1** *(budget, fortune, ville)* to administer, to manage; *(finances, conflit, situation difficile)* to manage; **elle a bien géré ses comptes** she managed her accounts well; **mal g. qch** to mismanage sth; *Fig* **ils se contentent de g. la crise** they're (quite) happy to sit out the crisis **2** *(entreprise, hôtel, magasin)* to manage, to run; *(stock, production)* to control **3** *(ménage)* to administer; *(temps)* to organize

gerfaut [ʒɛrfo] **NM** *Orn* gyrfalcon

gériatre [ʒerjatr] **NMF** geriatrician, geriatrist

gériatrie [ʒerjatri] **NF** geriatrics *(singulier)*

gériatrique [ʒerjatrik] **ADJ** geriatric

germain, -e [ʒɛrmɛ̃, -ɛn] **ADJ 1** *(ayant un grand-parent commun)* **cousine germaine** first cousin **2** *(du même père et de la même mère)* **frère g.** full brother; **sœur germaine** full sister **3** *(d'Allemagne)* Germanic, German

NM,F cousin issu de g. second cousin

• **Germain, -e NM,F** German, Teuton

germandrée [ʒɛrmɑ̃dre] **NF** *Bot* germander

germanique [ʒɛrmanik] **ADJ 1** *Hist* Germanic **2** *(allemand)* Germanic, German; **à consonance g.** German-sounding

NM *Ling* Germanic; *Hist & Ling* Germanic, Proto-Germanic

germanisant, -e [ʒɛrmanizɑ̃, -ɑ̃t] **NM,F** Germanist

germanisation [ʒɛrmanizasjɔ̃] **NF** Germanization

germaniser [3] [ʒɛrmanize] **VT** to Germanize

germanisme [ʒɛrmanism] **NM** Germanism

germaniste [ʒɛrmanist] **NMF** Germanist

germanium [ʒɛrmanjɔm] **NM** *Chim* germanium

germanophile [ʒɛrmanɔfil] **ADJ** German-loving, Germanophile

NMF Germanophile

germanophobe [ʒɛrmanɔfɔb] **ADJ** German-hating, Germanophobic

NMF Germanophobe

germanophobie [ʒɛrmanɔfɔbi] **NF** hatred towards Germany, Germanophobia

germanophone [ʒɛrmanɔfɔn] **ADJ** German-speaking

NMF German speaker

germanopratin, -e [ʒɛrmanɔpratɛ̃, -in] **ADJ** of/from Saint-Germain-des-Prés; **les bars germanopratins** the bars in Saint-Germain-des-Prés

NM,F = resident of Saint-Germain-des-Prés

germe [ʒɛrm] **NM 1** *Anat, Biol & Méd* germ; **g. dentaire** tooth bud; **germes pathogènes** pathogenic bacteria **2** *(pousse ▸ de pomme de terre)* eye; **g. de blé** wheat germ; **germes de soja** bean sprouts **3** *(origine)* **le g. d'une idée** the germ of an idea; **les germes de la révolution/corruption** the seeds of revolution/corruption

• **en germe ADV contenir qch en g.** to contain the seeds of sth

germer [3] [ʒɛrme] **VI 1** *Agr & Hort (graine)* to germinate; *(bulbe, tubercule)* to shoot, to sprout; **faire g. du blé** to germinate corn **2** *Fig (idées)* to germinate; **l'idée de révolte a mis du temps à g.** the idea of revolt took some time to germinate *or* to develop

germicide [ʒɛrmisid] **ADJ** germicidal

NM germicide

germinal, -e, -aux, -ales [ʒɛrminal, -o] **ADJ** *Biol* germinal

NM = 7th month of the French revolutionary calendar (from 22 March to 20 April)

germinateur, -trice [ʒɛrminatœr, -tris] **ADJ** germinative

germinatif, -ive [ʒɛrminatif, -iv] **ADJ** *Biol* **1** *(du germe)* germinative **2** *(du germen ▸ pouvoir)* germinal; *(▸ cellule, plasma)* germ *(avant n)*

germination [ʒɛrminasjɔ̃] **NF** *Biol* germination

germinative [ʒɛrminativ] *voir* **germinatif**

germinatrice [ʒɛrminatris] *voir* **germinateur**

germoir [ʒɛrmwar] **NM** *Biol* **1** *(pot)* seed tray **2** *(bâtiment)* germination area **3** *(d'une brasserie)* malt house, malting

gérondif [ʒerɔ̃dif] **NM** *Ling* **1** *(en latin)* gerundive; **au g.** in the gerundive **2** *(dans d'autres langues)* gerund

gérontocratie [ʒerɔ̃tɔkrasi] **NF** gerontocracy

gérontologie [ʒerɔ̃tɔlɔʒi] **NF** gerontology

gérontologue [ʒerɔ̃tɔlɔg] **NMF** gerontologist

gérontophile [ʒerɔ̃tɔfil] **ADJ** gerontophile

NMF gerontophile

gérontophilie [ʒerɔ̃tɔfili] **NF** gerontophilia

gésier [ʒezje] **NM** gizzard

gésir [49] [ʒezir] **VI 1** *(être étendu)* to lie, to be lying; **elle gisait là, comme endormie** there she lay (dead), as if asleep; **il gisait dans son sang** he was lying *or* weltering in his blood **2** *(être épars)* to lie; **ce qui restait de la statue gisait sur le sol** what was left of the statue was lying on the ground **3** *Littéraire (résider)* **c'est là que gît la difficulté** therein lies the difficulty; *Fig* **c'est là que gît le lièvre** that's the crux of the matter, there's the rub

gesse [ʒɛs] **NF** *Bot* vetch; **g. odorante** sweet pea

gestaltisme [geʃtaltism] **NM** *Psy* Gestalt (psychology)

Gestapo [gestapo] **NF la G.** the Gestapo; **un officier de la G.** a Gestapo officer

gestation [ʒɛstasjɔ̃] **NF 1** *Biol* gestation; **la g. n'est que de 21 jours** gestation takes only 21 days; **période de g.** gestation period **2** *Fig (d'une œuvre)* gestation (period)

• **en gestation ADJ 1** *Biol (fœtus)* gestating **2** *Fig* **un roman en g.** a novel in preparation

geste [ʒɛst] **NM 1** *(mouvement)* movement; *(signe)* gesture; **ses gestes étaient d'une grande précision** his/her movements were very precise; **faire un g.** to make a gesture; **faire un g. de la main** to gesture (with one's hand); *(pour saluer)* to wave; **faire des gestes en parlant** to speak with one's hands; **faire un g. approbateur** to nod one's assent *or* approval; **d'un g. de la main, il refusa le whisky** he waved aside the glass of whisky; **d'un g., il nous a fait sortir/entrer** he motioned *or* gestured to us to go out/come in; **il lui montra la porte d'un g.** he gestured him/her towards the door; **d'un g., elle m'indiqua où se trouvait le coffre-fort** she gestured to where the safe was; **il me le fit comprendre d'un g.** he indicated it to me with a gesture; **d'un g. de la main** with a wave of the hand; **je te l'indiquerai d'un g. de la main** I'll indicate it to you; **à grand renfort de gestes, elle appela le maître d'hôtel** she waved the head waiter over; **saluer qn d'un g.** to wave to sb; **avoir un g. de surprise** to start, to look startled; **avoir un g. malheureux** to make a clumsy gesture *or* movement; **il eut un g. de résignation** he gave a shrug of resignation, he shrugged in resignation; **congédier qn d'un g.** to dismiss sb with a wave of the hand; **encourager qn de la voix et du g.** to cheer sb on; **sans un g.** without moving; **pas un g. ou je tire!** don't move or I'll shoot!; **faites** *ou* **ayez le g. qui sauve** learn how to give first aid; **il épie mes moindres gestes** *ou* **tous mes gestes** he watches my every move

2 *(action)* gesture; **un g. politique/diplomatique** a political/diplomatic gesture; **faire un beau g.** to make a noble gesture; **un g. lâche** a cowardly act *or* deed; **allez, fais un g.!** come on, do something!; **vous n'avez qu'un g. à faire** you only have to say the word; **elle n'a pas fait un g. (pour l'aider)** she didn't do a thing *or* lift a finger (to help him); **il a eu un g. touchant, il m'a apporté des fleurs** a rather touching thing he did was to bring me some flowers; **joindre le g. à la parole** to suit the action to the word

NF *Littérature* gest, geste

gesticulation [ʒɛstikylasjɔ̃] **NF** gesticulation; **cesse tes gesticulations!** stop gesticulating!, stop waving your arms about!

gesticuler [3] [ʒɛstikyle] **VI** to gesticulate, to wave one's arms about

gestion [ʒɛstjɔ̃] **NF 1** *Com & Ind* management; **chargé de la g. de l'hôtel** in charge of running *or* managing the hotel; **par une mauvaise g.** through bad management, through mismanagement; **techniques de g.** management techniques *or* methods; **g. actif-passif** assets and liabilities management; **g. administrative** administration, administrative management; **g. d'affaires** (day-to-day) running of affairs *or* business; **g. assistée par ordinateur** computer-aided management; **g. budgétaire** budgetary control; **g. de capital** asset management; **g. du changement** change management; **g. de comptes-clés** key-account management; **g. des connaissances** knowledge management; **g. par consensus** consensus management; **g. des coûts** cost management; **g. de la distribution** distribution management; **g. de la distribution physique** physical distribution management; **g. de division** divisional management; **g. des droits numériques** digital rights management; **g. des effectifs** manpower management; **g. d'entreprise** business management; **g. financière** financial management; **g. de fonds** fund management; **g. hôtelière** hotel administration *or* management, hospitality management; **g. indicielle** indexed portfolio; **g. des investissements** investment management; **g. logistique** logistics management; **g. marketing** marketing management; **g. de marque** brand management; **g. des matières** materials management; **g. par objectifs** management by objective; **g. passive** passive management; **g. de portefeuille** portfolio management; **g. prévisionnelle** forward planning; **g. de la production** production management; **g. de produits** product management; **g. (de** *ou* **de la) qualité** quality control, quality management; **g. de la qualité totale** total quality management, TQM; **g. des ressources humaines** human resources management; **g. des risques** risk management; **g. des sociétés** business management; **g. sonore** sound handling, sound management; **g. de stock** *ou* **des stocks** *Br* stock *or* *Am* inventory control; **g. stratégique** strategic management; **g. de trésorerie** cash management

2 *Ordinat* management; **g. de bases de données** database management; **système de g. de base de données** database management system; **g. des césures** hyphenation control; **g. des couleurs** colour management; **g. des disquettes** disk management; **g. de données** data management; **g. de fichiers** file management; **g. intégrée** integrated management; **g. de mémoire** memory management; **g. multifeuille** *(de tableur)* multispreadsheet handling; **g. de parc réseau** network management; **g. des performances** performance monitoring *or* tuning; **g. des projets** project scheduling; **g. des systèmes d'information** informations systems management; **g. des travaux** job scheduling

gestionnaire [ʒɛstjɔnɛr] **ADJ** administrative, managing, management *(avant n)*

NMF 1 *Admin* administrator **2** *Com & Ind* manager, administrator; **g. de fonds** fund manager; **g. de fonds obligatoire** bond fund manager; **g. de portefeuille** portfolio manager; **g. de risques** risk manager; **g. de stock** *ou* **des stocks** *Br* stock controller, *Am* inventory controller

NM *Ordinat* manager; **g. de base de données** database administrator; **g. de fichiers** file manager; **g. de fichiers et de répertoires** filer; **g. de mémoire** memory manager; **g. de périphérique** device driver; **g. de projets** project management package; **g. de réseau** network manager; **g. de la souris** mouse driver; **g. de tâches** task scheduler

gestuel, -elle [ʒɛstɥɛl] **ADJ** gestural; **langage g.** gestural language

• **gestuelle NF 1** *(gén)* non-verbal behaviour *or* communication, body language **2** *Théât & (en danse)* gesture

Gethsémani [ʒɛtsemani] **NM** *Bible* Gethsemane

geyser [ʒezɛr] **NM** geyser

Ghana [gana] **NM le G.** Ghana

ghanéen, -enne [ganeɛ̃, -ɛn] **ADJ** Ghanaian, Ghanian

• **Ghanéen, -enne NM,F** Ghanaian, Ghanian

ghetto [geto] **NM** ghetto

ghettoïsation [getoizasjɔ̃] **NF** ghettoization

ghilde [gild] = **gilde**

GIA [ʒeia] **NM** *(abrév* **Groupes islamiques armés***)* GIA

gibbeux, -euse [ʒibø, -øz] **ADJ 1** *Astron* gibbous **2** *(animal)* humpbacked, *Spéc* gibbous

gibbon [ʒibɔ̃] **NM** *Zool* gibbon

gibbosité [ʒibozite] **NF** *Anat* hump, *Spéc* gibbosity

gibecière [ʒibsjɛr] **NF** *Chasse* game bag, gamekeeper's pouch

gibelotte [ʒiblɔt] *Culin* **NF** *(ragoût de lapin)* rabbit stew *(made with white wine)*

• **en gibelotte ADJ** stewed in white wine

giberne [ʒibɛrn] **NF** cartridge pouch; *Prov* **tout soldat a un bâton de maréchal dans sa g.** = every private has the makings of a general

gibet [ʒibɛ] **NM** *(potence)* gibbet, gallows *(singulier)*

gibier [ʒibje] **NM 1** *(animaux)* game *(UNCOUNT)*; **gros/petit g.** big/small game; **g. d'eau** waterfowl; **g. à plumes** game birds *or* fowl *(UNCOUNT)*; **g. à poils** game animals **2** *Culin (viande)* game; **manger du g.** to eat game; **pâté de g.** game pâté **3** *Fam (personne)* quarry, prey; **ces types-là, c'est du gros g.** these guys are in the big-time; **un g. de potence** a gallows bird

giboulée [ʒibule] **NF** shower; **giboulées de mars** ≃ April showers

giboyeux, -euse [ʒibwajø, -øz] **ADJ** abounding *or* rich in game, well stocked with game

Gibraltar [ʒibraltar] **NM** Gibraltar; **à G.** in Gibraltar; **le détroit de G.** the strait of Gibraltar

gibus [ʒibys] **NM** opera *or* crush hat

giclée [ʒikle] **NF 1** *(de liquide)* jet, spurt, squirt **2** *très Fam (coup de feu)* burst (of machine-gun fire)▫

giclement [ʒikləmɑ̃] **NM** *(gén ▸ d'un liquide)* spurting *(UNCOUNT)*, squirting *(UNCOUNT)*; *(▸ du sang)* spurting *(UNCOUNT)*

gicler [3] [ʒikle] **VI 1** *(liquide ▸ gén)* to spurt, to squirt; *(▸ sang)* to spurt; **faire g. de l'eau avec un pistolet à eau** to squirt water out of a water pistol; **et ça m'a giclé à la figure** and it splashed into my face

2 *Fam (partir)* to be off, to push off, *Am* to split

3 *Suisse (être projeté)* **g. en l'air** to be thrown into the air

4 *Suisse (précipiter)* to rush; *(être mis à la porte)* to get fired, *Br* to get the sack

gicleur [ʒiklœr] **NM** *Aut* (carburettor) jet; **g. de pompe** pump nozzle; **g. de ralenti** idling jet

GIE, G.I.E. [ʒeiə] **NM** *(abrév* **groupement d'intérêt économique***)* economic interest group

GIF [ʒeiɛf] **NM** *Ordinat (abrév* **Graphics Interchange Format***)* GIF

gifle [ʒifl] **NF 1** *(coup)* slap (in the face); **donner une g. à qn** to slap sb's face, to box sb's ears; **prendre** *ou* **recevoir une g.** to get a slap (in the face) **2** *Fig (humiliation)* (burning) insult, slap in the face

gifler **[3]** [ʒifle] **VT 1** *(sujet: personne)* **g. qn** to slap sb's face *or* sb in the face; **tu vas te faire g. si tu continues!** you'll get a slap in the face if you carry on like that! **2** *(sujet: pluie, vent)* to lash; **la bourrasque lui giflait le visage** the wind lashed his/her face **3** *Fig (humilier)* to humiliate; **ses paroles m'avaient giflé** his/her words were like a slap in the face

GIG, G.I.G. [ʒeiʒe] **NM** *(abrév* **grand invalide de guerre***)* = war invalid

giga [ʒiga] **ADJ INV** *Fam* wicked, mega

> **PREFIX**
> **GIGA-**
> This prefix of scientific origin has come to prominence with the advent of mass computing and its gigabytes (**gigaoctets**) of memory. It has since passed into colloquial language as an INTENSIFIER, used as a prefix but also on its own, as a term of appreciation:
> **on a fait une giga-teuf** we had a massive party; **il a poussé un giga coup de gueule** he yelled really loud; **c'est giga marrant** it's well funny, it's hysterical; **c'est giga (cool)!** wicked!
> It is worth noting that, in colloquial computing speak, **gigaoctet** is often abbreviated to just **giga** (translated in English as *gig*), as in **un disque dur de 120 gigas** a 120 gig hard disk

gigahertz [ʒigaɛrts] **NM** gigahertz

gigantesque [ʒigɑ̃tɛsk] **ADJ 1** *(animal, plante, ville)* gigantic, giant *(avant n)*; **d'une taille g.** gigantic, of a gigantic size **2** *(projet, erreur)* gigantic, giant *(avant n)*

gigantisme [ʒigɑ̃tism] **NM 1** *Méd, Bot & Zool* gigantism, giantism **2** *Fig* gigantic size; **une ville atteinte de g.** a city that has grown to enormous proportions

gigaoctet [ʒigaɔktɛ] **NM** *Ordinat* gigabyte

GIGN [ʒeiʒeɛn] **NM** *(abrév* **Groupe d'intervention de la gendarmerie nationale***)* = special crack force of the gendarmerie, *Br* ≃ SAS, *Am* ≃ SWAT

gigogne [ʒigɔɲ] *voir* **lit, poupée, table**

gigolette [ʒigɔlɛt] **NF 1** *Fam Vieilli (fille délurée)* floozy **2** *Culin* leg of turkey

gigolo [ʒigɔlo] **NM** *Fam* gigolo

gigot [ʒigo] **NM 1** *Culin* leg; **g. (d'agneau)** leg of lamb **2** *(d'un cheval)* hind leg **3** *Hum (d'une personne)* leg, thigh

gigoter **[3]** [ʒigɔte] **VI 1** *(bébé)* to wriggle (about); *(enfant)* to fidget **2** *(animal à l'agonie)* to give a convulsive jerk

gigoteuse [ʒigɔtøz] **NF** Grobag®, baby sleeping bag

gigue[1] [ʒig] **NF** *(danse)* gigue, jig; **danser la g.** to jig; *Fig* to wriggle about, to jig up and down

gigue[2] [ʒig] **NF 1** *Culin* **g. de chevreuil** haunch of venison **2** *Fam (jambe)* leg[□]; **les gigues** legs[□], *Br* pins **3** *Fam (personne)* **une grande g.** a beanpole

gilde [gild] **NF** *Hist* guild

gilet [ʒilɛ] **NM 1** *(vêtement ▸ taillé) Br* waistcoat, *Am* vest; *(▸ tricoté) Br* cardigan, *Am* cardigan sweater **2** *(sous-vêtement) Br* vest, *Am* undershirt **3** *(protection)* **g. d'armes** fencing jacket; **g. pare-balles** bulletproof vest; **g. de sauvetage** life jacket

gin [dʒin] **NM** gin

gindre [ʒɛ̃dr] **NM** baker's assistant

gingembre [ʒɛ̃ʒɑ̃br] **NM** ginger; **racine de g.** root ginger, fresh ginger; **biscuits au g.** ginger biscuits

gingival, -e, -aux, -ales [ʒɛ̃ʒival, -o] **ADJ** *Anat* gum *(avant n)*, *Spéc* gingival

gingivite [ʒɛ̃ʒivit] **NF** *Méd* gum disease, *Spéc* gingivitis

gingko [ʒinko] **NM** *Bot* gingko

ginseng [ʒinsɛŋ] **NM** *Bot* ginseng

gin-tonic [dʒintɔnik] *(pl* **gin-tonics***)* **NM** gin and tonic

girafe [ʒiraf] **NF 1** *Zool* giraffe; *Fig* **avoir un cou de g.** to have a long neck **2** *Fam (personne)* beanpole **3** *Fam Rad & TV* boom[□]

girafeau, -x [ʒirafo], **girafon** [ʒirafɔ̃] **NM** *Zool* baby giraffe

girandole [ʒirɑ̃dɔl] **NF 1** *(chandelier)* girandole, candelabra; *(feux d'artifice)* girandole **2** *(grappe ▸ de fleurs)* cluster; *(▸ de bijoux)* girandole

girasol [ʒirasɔl] **NM** girasol, girasole

giration [ʒirasjɔ̃] **NF** gyration; *Naut* **cercle de g.** turning circle

giratoire [ʒiratwar] **ADJ** gyrating, gyratory
NM *Suisse (rond-point) Br* roundabout, *Am* traffic circle

giravion [ʒiravjɔ̃] **NM** *Aviat* gyroplane, rotorcraft

girelle [ʒirɛl] **NF** *Ich* rainbow wrasse

girl [gœrl] **NF** chorus *or* show girl

girofle [ʒirɔfl] **NM** clove; **huile de g.** oil of cloves

giroflée [ʒirɔfle] **NF 1** *Bot* stock, gillyflower; **g. des murailles** wallflower, gillyflower **2** *Fam Fig* **une g. à cinq feuilles** *(une gifle)* a stinging slap

giroflier [ʒirɔflije] **NM** clove (tree)

girolle [ʒirɔl] **NF** chanterelle

giron [ʒirɔ̃] **NM 1** *(d'une personne)* lap; **dans le g. de sa mère** in his/her mother's lap **2** *Littéraire (communauté)* bosom; **le g. familial** the family fold; **accepté dans le g. de l'Église** accepted into the fold *or* the bosom of the Church **3** *(d'une marche)* tread

girond, -e [ʒirɔ̃, -ɔ̃d] **ADJ** *Fam Vieilli* plump[□], buxom[□], well-padded; **une femme plutôt gironde** a buxom *or* plump woman

girondin, -e [ʒirɔ̃dɛ̃, -in] **ADJ 1** *(gén)* of/from the Gironde **2** *Hist* Girondist
• **Girondin, -e NM,F 1** *(personne)* = inhabitant of or person from the Gironde **2** *Hist* Girondist

girouette [ʒirwɛt] **NF 1** *(sur un toit)* weathercock, weather vane **2** *Fam (personne)* weathercock; **c'est une vraie g.!** he keeps changing his mind!, he's a real weathercock!

gis *etc voir* **gésir**

gisait *etc voir* **gésir**

gisant, -e [ʒizɑ̃, -ɑ̃t] **ADJ** *Littéraire (corps)* lifeless, motionless
NM *Beaux-Arts* recumbent figure *or* statue

gisement [ʒizmɑ̃] **NM 1** *Géol & Mines* deposit; **g. houiller** *(filon)* coal deposit *or* measures; *(bassin)* coalfield; **g. de pétrole, g. pétrolifère** oilfield
2 *Aviat & Naut* bearing; **relever/tracer un g.** to take/to plot a bearing; **g. à la boussole** compass bearing
3 *Com* **g. de clientèle** pool of customers, potential customers
4 *Archéol* **g. préhistorique** prehistoric site

gît *voir* **gésir**

gitan, -e [ʒitɑ̃, -an] **ADJ** Gypsy *(avant n)*
• **Gitan, -e NM,F** Gypsy
• **Gitane**® **NF** *(cigarette)* Gitane®

gîte[1] [ʒit] **NM 1** *(logement)* lodging, resting place; *(foyer)* home; **retrouver son g.** to get back home; **ne pas avoir de g.** to be homeless; **le g. et le couvert** room and board; **g. camping-caravaning à la ferme** campsite in close proximity to a farm; **g. chambre d'hôte** bed and breakfast; **g. d'enfants** holiday placements for children with a rural family; **g. équestre** rural gîte with horses for hire; **g. d'étape** *(pour randonneurs)* halt; **g. rural** gîte; **g. rural communal** = gîte communally owned by a village or group of villages
2 *Chasse (de gibier)* lair; *(de lièvre)* form
3 *(viande) Br* shin *or Am* shank (of beef); **g. à la noix** *Br* topside, *Am* round
4 *Mines* bed, deposit

gîte[2] [ʒit] **NF** *Naut* list; **avoir** *ou* **prendre de la g.** to list, to heel; **donner de la g. sur tribord** to list to starboard

gîter **[3]** [ʒite] **VI 1** *Vieilli ou Littéraire (loger)* to lodge; *(voyageur)* to stay **2** *(animal)* to find shelter; *(lapin)* to couch; *(oiseau)* to perch **3** *Naut* to list

giton [ʒitɔ̃] **NM** *Littéraire* catamite

givrage [ʒivraʒ] **NM 1** *Aviat* icing **2** *(sur un verre)* frosting

givrant, -e [ʒivrɑ̃, -ɑ̃t] **ADJ** **brouillard g.** freezing fog

givre [ʒivr] **NM** *(glace)* frost; **couvert de g.** frosted over

givré, -e [ʒivre] **ADJ 1** *(arbre)* covered with frost; *(serrure)* iced up
2 *(verre)* frosted *(with sugar)*
3 *Culin* **orange givrée** orange *Br* sorbet *or Am* sherbet *(served inside an orange skin)*
4 *Fam (fou)* crackers, nuts; **il est complètement g.!** he's completely nuts *or* off his head!

givrer **[3]** [ʒivre] **VT 1** *(avec du sucre)* to frost **2** *(couvrir de givre)* to cover with frost
VI *Aviat* to ice up
VPR se givrer *(se couvrir de givre)* to frost *or* to ice up

givreux, -euse [ʒivrø, -øz] **ADJ** *(en joaillerie)* with icy flecks, flawed

givrure [ʒivryr] **NF** white fleck *(in a gem)*

glabre [glabr] **ADJ 1** *(imberbe)* smooth-chinned; *(rasé)* clean-shaven; **le visage g.** with a smooth face **2** *Bot* glabrous, hairless

glaçage [glasaʒ] **NM 1** *(d'un tissu, du papier)* glazing; *Ind (polissage)* surfacing, burnishing **2** *Culin (d'un gâteau) Br* icing, *Am* frosting; *(de bonbons)* sugar coating; *(de légumes, d'une viande)* glazing

glaçant, -e [glasɑ̃, -ɑ̃t] **ADJ** *(regard, attitude)* cold, frosty; *Vieilli (vent)* icy

glace [glas] **NF 1** *(eau gelée)* ice; **g. flottante** floating ice, drift ice; **g. de fond** bottom ice; *Can* **g. noire** black ice; **g. pilée** crushed ice; *Fig* **rompre** *ou* **briser la g.** to break the ice; **sur g.** *(boisson)* on the rocks
2 *(crème glacée)* ice cream; *(sucette) Br* ice lolly, *Am* Popsicle®; *(cône)* ice cream (cone); **g. à la vanille/à l'abricot** vanilla/apricot ice cream; **g. à l'eau** *Br* water ice, *Am* sherbet
3 *Culin Br* icing, *Am* frosting; *(de viande)* glaze; **g. royale** royal icing
4 *(miroir)* mirror; **se regarder dans la g.** to look at oneself in the mirror; **une g. sans tain** a two-way mirror
5 *(vitre ▸ d'un véhicule, d'une boutique)* window
6 *Tech* sheet of plate glass
7 *(en joaillerie)* (white) fleck *or* flaw
8 *Ind* **g. sèche** *ou* **carbonique** dry ice
• **glaces NFPL** *(du pôle)* ice fields; *(sur un fleuve)* ice sheets; *(en mer)* ice floes, drift ice; **le navire est pris dans les glaces** the ship is icebound
• **de glace ADJ** *(accueil, visage, regard)* icy, frosty; **être** *ou* **rester de g.** to remain unmoved; **tu as un cœur de g.** you've got a heart of stone

glacé, -e [glase] **ADJ 1** *(transformé en glace)* frozen
2 *(lieu)* freezing *or* icy (cold); **les plages glacées du nord** the icy cold beaches of the north
3 *(personne)* frozen, freezing cold; **j'ai les pieds glacés** my feet are frozen
4 *(hostile)* frosty, icy; **d'une politesse glacée** with icy politeness; **regard g.** cold stare
5 *Culin (dessert, soufflé, café)* iced; *(petit four)* glacé; *(oignon, viande)* glazed; **cerises glacées** glacé cherries
6 *(brillant ▸ photo)* glossy; *(▸ papier)* glazed; *(▸ cuir)* glazed, glacé; **soie glacée** watered silk, glazed thread
NM glaze, gloss

glacer **[16]** [glase] **VT 1** *(transformer en glace)* to freeze
2 *(refroidir ▸ bouteille)* to chill
3 *(transir)* **le vent me glace** the wind is icy; **un froid qui vous glace jusqu'aux os** weather that chills you to the bone
4 *Fig (pétrifier)* **ça m'a glacé le sang (dans les veines)** it made my blood run cold; **un hurlement à vous g. le sang** a bloodcurdling scream; **ce souvenir me glace encore le cœur** the memory still sends shivers down my spine; **g. qn de terreur** to paralyse sb with terror
5 *Culin (petit four, oignon etc)* to glaze; *(gâteau) Br* to ice, *Am* to frost
6 *Ind & Tech* to glaze, to glacé
VPR se glacer leur sang se glaça dans leurs veines their blood ran cold

glacerie [glasri] **NF 1** *(fabrication de glaces)* ice-cream making; *(commerce)* ice-cream trade **2** *(fabrique de verre)* glassworks *(singulier)*; *(commerce)* glass trade

glaceur [glasœr] **NM** glazer

glaceux, -euse [glasø, -øz] **ADJ** *(diamant)* with icy flecks, flawed

glaciaire [glasjɛr] **ADJ** glacial

NM le g. the Ice Age, the Glacial Period *or* Epoch

glacial, -e, -als *ou* **-aux, -ales** [glasjal, -o] **ADJ 1** *(climat)* icy, freezing; *(vent)* bitter, freezing; *(pluie)* freezing (cold) **2** *(accueil, ambiance)* frosty, icy; *(sourire)* frosty; *(abord, personne)* cold; **elle est vraiment glaciale** she's really cold *or* a real iceberg

ADV il fait g. it's freezing cold

glacialement [glasjalmɑ̃] **ADV** frostily, icily

glaciation [glasjasjɔ̃] **NF** glaciation; **pendant la g.** during the Ice Age

glacier [glasje] **NM 1** *Géol* glacier **2** *(confiseur)* ice-cream man *or* salesman; *(fabricant)* ice-cream maker; **g.-confiseur** confectioner and ice-cream seller

glacière [glasjɛr] **NF 1** *(local)* cold-room **2** *(armoire)* refrigerated cabinet; *(récipient)* cool box; *(de réfrigérateur)* freezer compartment, icebox; *Fig* **mon bureau est une vraie g.!** my office is like a fridge *or* an icebox!

glaciérisme [glasjerism] **NM** glacier climbing

glaciériste [glasjerist] **NMF** glacier climber

glaciologue [glasjɔlɔg] **NMF** glaciologist

glacis [glasi] **NM 1** *Hist* **le g. soviétique** the Soviet buffer zone

2 *Constr* ramp; **g. d'écoulement** weathering

3 *Beaux-Arts* glaze, scumble

4 *Mil & Géog* glacis

glaçon [glasɔ̃] **NM 1** *Géog & Météo (sur un fleuve)* block of ice, ice floe; *(sur un étang)* patch of ice; *(en mer)* ice floe; *(pendant)* icicle; **glaçons** *(sur une rivière)* drift *or* broken ice; *Fam* **j'ai le nez comme un g.** my nose is like a block of ice *or* is frozen **2** *(pour boisson)* ice cube; **voulez-vous un g.?** would you like (some) ice?; **servi avec des glaçons** served with ice *or* on the rocks **3** *Fig* **cette fille est un g.** that girl's a real ice queen

glaçure [glasyr] **NF** *Cér* glaze

gladiateur [gladjatœr] **NM** *Antiq* gladiator; **combat de gladiateurs** gladiatorial combat

glaïeul [glajœl] **NM** *Bot* gladiolus; **des glaïeuls** gladioli; **g. des marais** (sword) flag

glaire [glɛr] **NF 1** *Physiol* mucus; **g. cervicale** cervical mucus **2** *(d'œuf)* white

glaireux, -euse [glɛrø, -øz] **ADJ** glairy, glaireous

glaise [glɛz] **NF** clay

ADJ F terre g. (potter's) clay

glaiser [3] [glɛze] **VT 1** *(amender avec de la glaise)* to clay, to dress with clay **2** *(enduire de glaise)* to line with clay

glaiseux, -euse [glɛzø, -øz] **ADJ** clayey, clay *(avant n)*

glaisière [glɛzjɛr] **NF** clay pit

glaive [glɛv] **NM** broadsword, *Arch* glaive; *Littéraire* **le g. de la Justice** the sword of justice

glam [glam] **ADJ INV** *Fam* glam

glamour [glamur] *Fam* **ADJ INV** *(personne, allure)* glam

NM le g. glamour□

glanage [glanaʒ] **NM le g.** gleaning, gathering

gland [glɑ̃] **NM 1** *Bot (du chêne)* acorn; **glands** *(pour les cochons)* mast

2 *Couture* tassel

3 *Anat* glans

4 *très Fam (imbécile) Br* prat, *Am* jerk

glande [glɑ̃d] **NF 1** *Anat* gland; **glandes de Bartholin** Bartholin's glands; **g. lacrymale** tear gland; **g. salivaire** salivary gland; **g. sébacée** sebaceous gland; **g. uporygienne** oil gland **2** *Anat (ganglion)* (neck) gland **3** *Vulg* **avoir les glandes** *(être énervé)* to be hacked off *or* cheesed off; *(être triste)* to be upset□; **foutre les glandes à qn** *(énerver)* to hack *or* cheese sb off; *(attrister)* to upset sb□

glander [3] [glɑ̃de] **VI** *très Fam* **1** *(ne rien faire)* to loaf about; **mais qu'est-ce qu'il glande, il devait arriver à trois heures!** where the hell is he, he was supposed to be here at three; **il a glandé toute l'année** he's done nothing but loaf about all year; **arrête de g. et fais quelque chose d'utile** *(ne rien faire)* get off your backside and do something useful; *(ne rien faire d'utile)* stop mucking around and do something useful **2** *(attendre)* to hang around; **ça fait trois heures que je glande** I've been hanging around for three hours **3** *(locution)* **j'en ai rien à g.** I don't give a shit

glandeur, -euse [glɑ̃dœr, -øz] **NM,F** *très Fam* layabout, *Am* goldbrick

glandouiller [glɑ̃duje] = **glander**

glandu [glɑ̃dy] **NM** *très Fam* halfwit, dope

glandulaire [glɑ̃dylɛr], **glanduleux, -euse** [glɑ̃dylø, -øz] **ADJ** glandular; **infection glanduleuse** glandular infection

glane [glan] **NF 1** *(ramassage)* **la g.** gleaning; **faire la g.** to glean **2** *(tresse)* **g. d'oignons** string of onions

glaner [3] [glane] **VT 1** *(ramasser ▸ épis)* to glean; *(▸ bois)* to gather; *(▸ fruits)* to gather, to pick up; **g. du petit bois** to gather sticks **2** *Fig (renseignements, détails)* to glean, to gather

glaneur, -euse [glanœr, -øz] **NM,F** gleaner

glaouis [glawi] **NMPL** *très Fam* balls, nuts, *Br* bollocks

glapir [32] [glapir] **VI 1** *(renard)* to bark; *(chiot)* to yelp, to yap **2** *(personne)* to yelp, to squeal

VT to shriek

glapissant, -e [glapisɑ̃, -ɑ̃t] **ADJ** *(chien)* yapping, yelping; *(voix)* shrill

glapissement [glapismɑ̃] **NM 1** *(du chien)* yelp; *(du renard)* bark **2** *(de personne, de tempête, du vent)* shrieking *(UNCOUNT)*; **les enfants surexcités poussaient des glapissements** the children were squealing *or* shrieking with excitement

glas [gla] **NM** knell; **on sonne le g. pour notre cousin** the bell is tolling *or* they are tolling the knell for our cousin; *Fig* **cette nouvelle sonne le g. de toutes ses espérances** this news sounds the death knell for all his/her hopes

glasnost [glasnɔst] **NF** *Hist* glasnost

glaucome [glokom] **NM** *Méd* glaucoma

glauque [glok] **ADJ 1** *(verdâtre)* bluish-green, *Littéraire* glaucous **2** *(trouble ▸ eau)* murky **3** *Fam (lugubre ▸ pièce)* dreary; *(▸ film, plaisanteries)* tasteless□, in bad taste□; **je suis partie très vite, l'ambiance était g.** I left very quickly since the atmosphere was pretty heavy; **il est un peu g., son copain** his/her friend's a bit creepy

glauquerie [glokri] **NF** *Fam (d'une pièce, d'une maison)* dreariness; *(d'un film, d'une plaisanterie)* bad taste□

glaviot [glavjo] **NM** *très Fam* gob of spit

glavioter [3] [glavjɔte] **VI** *très Fam* to spit□, *Br* to gob

glèbe [glɛb] **NF 1** *Littéraire (sol cultivé)* soil, glebe

2 *Hist (domaine)* feudal land, glebe

glène[1] [glɛn] **NF** *Anat* socket

glène[2] [glɛn] **NF** *Naut* coil (of rope)

glissade [glisad] **NF 1** *(jeu)* sliding *(UNCOUNT)*; **faire une g./des glissades** to slide

2 *(en danse)* glissade

3 *Aviat* **g. sur l'aile** sideslip; **g. sur la queue** tail slide

4 *(glissoire)* slide

glissage [glisaʒ] **NM le g. du bois** = sliding timber down a mountainside

glissant, -e [glisɑ̃, -ɑ̃t] **ADJ 1** *(sol)* slippery; *Fig* **être sur une pente glissante/sur un terrain g.** to be on a slippery slope/on slippery ground **2** *(coulissant)* sliding; **joint g.** sliding joint, slip joint

glisse [glis] **NF** *(d'un ski)* friction coefficient; **sports de g.** = generic term referring to sports such as skiing, snowboarding, surfing, windsurfing etc

glissé [glise] **ADJ M pas g.** glissé

NM glissé

glissement [glismɑ̃] **NM 1** *(déplacement)* sliding *(UNCOUNT)*

2 *(évolution)* shift; **la politique du gouvernement a connu un net g. à droite** there's been a marked shift to the right in government policy

3 *Ling* **g. de sens** shift in meaning

4 *Géol* **g. de terrain** landslide; *(moins important)* landslip

5 *Écon (d'une monnaie, des salaires)* slide; **une progression annuelle de 4 pour cent en g.** a yearly 4 percent slide

6 *Aviat* sideslipping

7 *Électron* **g. de fréquence** frequency variation

glisser[1] [3] [glise] **VI 1** *(déraper ▸ personne)* to slip; *(▸ voiture)* to skid; **mon pied a glissé** my foot slipped

2 *(s'échapper accidentellement)* to slip; **ça m'a glissé des mains** it slipped out of my hands; *aussi Fig* **g. entre les mains** *ou* **les doigts de qn** to slip through sb's fingers

3 *(tomber)* to slide; **faire g.** *(pièce de machine)* to slide; **il se laissa g. à terre** he slid to the ground; **se laisser g. le long d'une corde** to slide down a rope

4 *(avancer sans heurt ▸ skieur, patineur)* to glide along; *(▸ péniche, ski)* to glide; *Aviat* **g. sur l'aile** to sideslip

5 *(passer)* **son regard glissa de la fenêtre à mon fauteuil** his/her eyes drifted from the window to my chair; **un sourire ironique glissa sur ses lèvres** an ironic smile stole over his/her face; **g. sur** *(sujet)* to touch lightly on, to skip over; **glissons (sur ce sujet)!** let's say no more about it!; **sur toi, tout glisse comme sur les plumes d'un canard** it's like water off a duck's back with you; **une larme glissa sur sa joue** a tear slid *or* ran down his/her cheek

6 *(avoir une surface glissante)* to be slippery; **la chaussée glisse beaucoup** the road is very slippery

7 *Fig (s'orienter)* **g. à** *ou* **vers** to shift to *or* towards; **g. dans le sommeil** to fall asleep; **g. vers le désespoir** to slide *or* to slip into despair; **une partie de l'électorat a glissé à gauche** part of the electorate has shifted *or* moved to the left; **le sens du mot a glissé vers autre chose** the meaning of the word has shifted towards something else

8 *Écon (salaires, monnaie)* to slip, to slide

9 *Ordinat* **faire g.** *(pointeur)* to drag

VT 1 *(introduire)* to slip; **g. une lettre sous la porte** to slip a letter under the door; **g. qch dans la poche de qn** to slip sth into sb's pocket

2 *(confier)* **g. un petit mot/une lettre à qn** to slip sb a note/a letter; **g. un mot à qn** to have a quick word with sb; **g. à qn que...** to whisper to sb that...; **g. qch à l'oreille de qn** to whisper sth in sb's ear

3 *(mentionner)* **j'ai glissé ton nom dans la conversation** I managed to slip *or* to drop your name into the conversation; **essaie de g. quelques citations dans ta dissertation** try to slip a few quotations into your essay

4 *(locution)* **g. un œil dans une pièce** to peep *or* to peek into a room

VPR se glisser 1 *(se faufiler)* to slip (**dans** into); **se g. au premier rang** *(rapidement)* to slip into the front row; **se g. dans son lit** to slip *or* to creep into bed **2** *(erreur)* **des fautes ont pu se g. dans l'article** some mistakes may have slipped *or* crept into the article **3** *(sentiment)* **le doute s'est peu à peu glissé en lui** little by little, doubt crept into his mind; **la haine s'était glissée dans son cœur** hatred had crept into his/her heart

glisser[2] [glise] **NM** *Ordinat* **g. d'icônes** icon drag

glisser-lâcher [gliselaʃe] **NM INV** *Ordinat* drag and drop; **g. d'icônes** icon drag and drop

glissière [glisjɛr] **NF 1** *Tech* slide, runner; **à g.** sliding; **porte à g.** sliding door; **banc à glissières** *(en aviron)* sliding seat **2** *(en travaux publics)* **g. de sécurité** crash barrier **3** *Ind (pour le charbon)* chute

glissoir [gliswar] **NM 1** *(d'une machine)* slide, sliding block **2** *(pour le bois)* timber chute

glissoire [gliswar] **NF** slide *(on ice)*

global, -e, -aux, -ales [glɔbal, -o] **ADJ** *(résultat, vision)* overall, global; *(somme, budget, demande)* total; *(paiement)* lump; *(production)* aggregate; *(revenu)* gross; **as-tu une idée globale du coût?** have you got a rough idea of the cost?; **avoir une vue** *ou* **vision globale d'une situation** to have an overview *or* an overall view

globalement [glɔbalmɑ̃] **ADV** all in all, overall; **g., l'entreprise se porte bien** all in all *or* by and large, the company is doing well

globalisation [glɔbalizasjɔ̃] **NF** *(d'un marché, d'un conflit)* globalization

globaliser [3] [glɔbalize] **VT 1** *(réunir)* **le syndicat a globalisé ses revendications** the union is putting forward its demands en bloc **2** *(mondialiser)* to globalize

globalité [glɔbalite] **NF** *(ensemble)* **prendre un problème dans sa g.** to tackle a problem as a whole; **envisageons le processus dans sa g.** let's view the process as a whole

globe [glɔb] **NM 1** *(sphère)* globe; **le g.** *(la Terre)* the globe, the world; **sur toute la surface du g.** all over the globe; **une région déshéritée du g.** a poor part of the world; **faire le tour du g.** to go round the world; **le g. terrestre** the terrestrial globe

2 *(d'une lampe)* (glass) globe; *(d'une pendule)* glass dome *or* cover

3 *(pour protéger)* glass dome; **conserver qch sous g.** to keep sth under glass; *Fig* **c'est une idée géniale, il faut la mettre sous g.!** that's a brilliant idea, we must keep it under wraps!

4 *Anat* globe; **g. oculaire** eye

globe-trotter [glɔbtrɔtœr] *(pl* **globe-trotters)** **NM** globe-trotter

globine [glɔbin] **NF** *Biol & Chim* globin

globulaire [glɔbylɛr] **ADJ 1** *(sphérique)* globular, globe-shaped **2** *Biol & Physiol* corpuscular

globule [glɔbyl] **NM 1** *Biol & Physiol* corpuscle; **g. blanc** white corpuscle; **g. rouge** red corpuscle, red blood cell **2** *Pharm* (spherical) capsule **3** *Vieilli (d'air, d'eau)* globule

globuleux, -euse [glɔbylø, -øz] **ADJ 1** *(forme)* globular, globulous **2** *(œil)* protruding, bulging

globuline [glɔbylin] **NF** globulin

glockenspiel [glɔkənʃpil] **NM** *Mus* glockenspiel

gloire [glwar] **NF 1** *(renom)* fame; **connaître la g.** to find fame; **au faîte** *ou* **sommet de sa g.** at the height *or* pinnacle of his/her fame; **cette salle est la g. du musée du Louvre** this gallery is the (crowning) glory of the Louvre museum; **elle a eu son heure de g.** she has had her hour of glory

2 *(mérite)* glory, credit; **toute la g. vous en revient** the credit is all yours; **tirer g. de qch** to glory in sth, to pride oneself on sth; **se faire g. de** to boast about; *Fam* **c'est pas la g.** it's not exactly brilliant

3 *(éloge)* praise; **écrit à la g. de...** written in praise of...; **rendre g. au courage de qn** to praise sb's courage; **g. à Dieu** praise be to *or* glory to God; **g. aux soldats morts pour la France!** glory to the soldiers who died for France!

4 *(personne)* celebrity; **il est la g. de notre école** he is the pride of our school

5 *Beaux-Arts (auréole)* aureole; *(ciel décoré)* glory

6 *(splendeur) & Rel* glory; **la famille royale dans toute sa g.** the royal family in all its splendour; **la g. éternelle** eternal glory

glomérule [glɔmeryl] **NM** *Anat* glomerulus; *Bot* glomerule

gloria[1] [glɔrja] **NM INV** *Rel* Gloria

gloria[2] [glɔrja] **NM** *Fam Vieilli (café)* = coffee served with spirits

glorieuse [glɔrjøz] *voir* **glorieux**

glorieusement [glɔrjøzmɑ̃] **ADV** gloriously

glorieux, -euse [glɔrjø, -øz] **ADJ 1** *(remarquable)* glorious; **il a eu une mort glorieuse** he died a glorious death; **porter un nom g.** to have an illustrious name; **un g. général** a glorious *or* triumphant general

2 *Littéraire (fier)* **g. de sa victoire** priding himself on his victory

3 *Rel* glorious

4 *Fam Fig* **ce n'est pas g.** it's not exactly brilliant

• **Glorieuse NF** *Hist* **les Trente Glorieuses** = the thirty years following the Second World War, a period of rapid economic growth in France; **les Trois Glorieuses** = the three-day Revolution in 1830 (27, 28 and 29 July)

glorification [glɔrifikasjɔ̃] **NF** glorification

glorifier [9] [glɔrifje] **VT** *(exploit, qualité, héros)* to glorify, to praise; *(Dieu)* to glorify

VPR se glorifier se g. de qch to glory in sth; **se g. d'avoir fait qch** to boast of having done sth

gloriole [glɔrjɔl] **NF** vainglory; **faire qch par g.** to do sth to show off *or* for show; **pour la g.** for the kudos of it

glose [gloz] **NF** *Ling* gloss; **g. marginale** marginal note

• **gloses NFPL** *Vieilli (commérages)* gossip *(UNCOUNT)*; **faire des gloses sur qn** to gossip about sb

gloser [3] [gloze] **VT** *(annoter)* to annotate, to gloss

• **gloser sur VT IND 1** *(discourir sur)* **g. sur qch** to ramble on about sth **2** *(jaser sur)* **g. sur qn/qch** to gossip about sb/sth

gloss [glɔs] **NM** *(pour les lèvres)* lip gloss; *(pour les joues)* highlighter

glossaire [glɔsɛr] **NM** glossary, vocabulary

glossine [glɔsin] **NF** *Entom* glossina

glossolalie [glɔsɔlali] **NF** glossolalia

glottal, -e, -aux, -ales [glɔtal, -o] **ADJ** glottal

glotte [glɔt] **NF** *Anat* glottis; *Ling* **coup de g.** glottal stop

glouglou [gluglu] **NM 1** *Fam (d'une fontaine)* gurgle, gurgling *(UNCOUNT)*; *(d'une bouteille)* glug-glug; **faire g.** *(fontaine)* to gurgle; *(bouteille)* to go glug-glug **2** *(du dindon)* gobbling *(UNCOUNT)*

glouglouter [3] [gluglute] **VI 1** *Fam (fontaine)* to gurgle; *(bouteille)* to go glug-glug **2** *(dindon)* to gobble

gloussement [glusmɑ̃] **NM 1** *(d'une personne)* chuckle; **gloussements** chuckling *(UNCOUNT)*; **pousser un g. de satisfaction** to chuckle with satisfaction **2** *(d'une poule)* clucking *(UNCOUNT)*

glousser [3] [gluse] **VI 1** *(personne)* to chuckle **2** *(poule)* to cluck

glouteron [glutrɔ̃] **NM** *Bot* burdock

glouton, -onne [glutɔ̃, -ɔn] **ADJ** greedy, gluttonous; **que ce bébé est g.!** what a greedy baby!

NM,F glutton

NM *Zool* wolverine, glutton

gloutonnement [glutɔnmɑ̃] **ADV** greedily, gluttonously; **il dévora g. son déjeuner** he devoured his lunch greedily

gloutonnerie [glutɔnri] **NF** gluttony

glu [gly] **NF 1** *(substance visqueuse)* birdlime; **prendre des oiseaux à la g.** to lime birds **2** *(colle)* glue **3** *Fam (personne)* **c'est une vraie g.** she sticks to you like glue

gluant, -e [glyɑ̃, -ɑ̃t] **ADJ** *(collant)* sticky; *(boue, limace, paroi, poisson)* slimy; **riz g.** sticky rice

gluau, -x [glyo] **NM** lime twig

glucide [glysid] **NM** carbohydrate

glucosamine [glykozamin] **NF** *Pharm* glucosamine

glucose [glykoz] **NM** glucose; **g. sanguin** blood sugar

glucosé, -e [glykoze] **ADJ** containing glucose; **une solution glucosée** a glucose solution

glutamate [glytamat] **NM** glutamate; **g. de sodium** monosodium glutamate

gluten [glyten] **NM** gluten; **sans g.** gluten-free

glutineux, -euse [glytinø, -øz] **ADJ** glutinous

glycémie [glisemi] **NF** blood-sugar level, *Spéc* glycaemia

glycérine [gliserin] **NF** glycerin, glycerine

glycériner [3] [gliserine] **VT** to treat with glycerine

glycérol [gliserɔl] **NM** *Chim* glycerol

glycine [glisin] **NF 1** *Bot* wisteria **2** *Biol & Chim* glycine, glycocoll

glycogène [glikɔʒɛn] **NM** glycogen

glycol [glikɔl] **NM** glycol

glyphe [glif] **NM** *Archit* glyph

glyptique [gliptik] **NF** glyptics *(singulier)*

GM [ʒeɛm] **NM 1** *(abrév* **gentil membre)** holidaymaker *(at Club Méditerranée)* **2** *Com (abrév* **grand magasin)** department store

GMS [ʒeɛmɛs] **NFPL** *Com (abrév* **grandes et moyennes surfaces)** large and medium-sized commercial outlets

gnangnan [ɲɑ̃ɲɑ̃] *Fam Péj* **ADJ INV 1** *(personne)* drippy **2** *(œuvre, style)* **j'ai vu le film, que c'était g.!** I saw the film, it was so soppy!

NMF drip, wimp

gnaque [ɲak] = **gniac**

gnaule [ɲol] = **gnôle**

gneiss [gnɛs] **NM** gneiss

gniac [ɲjak] **NF** *Fam* fighting spirit◻, drive◻; **avoir la g., être plein de g.** to have plenty of drive

gniole [ɲol] = **gnôle**

gnocchi [ɲɔki] *(pl* **inv** *ou* **gnocchis) NM** piece of gnocchi; **des g.** *ou* **gnocchis** gnocchi

gnognote, gnognotte [ɲɔɲɔt] **NF** *Fam* **c'est de la g.** *(c'est facile)* it's a cinch; *(c'est sans valeur)* it's *Br* rubbish *or Am* garbage; **c'est pas de la g., cette voiture** that car is quite something

gnôle, gnole [ɲol] **NF** *très Fam* firewater

gnome [gnom] **NM 1** *(génie)* gnome **2** *(nabot)* dwarf, gnome

gnomique [gnɔmik] **ADJ** gnomic

gnon [ɲɔ̃] **NM** *Fam (coup)* thump; **se prendre un g.** to get thumped *or* walloped; **elle lui a flanqué un sacré g.** she gave him/her a real thump

gnose [gnoz] **NF 1** *Rel (mouvement)* gnosticism **2** *Vieilli (mode de connaissance)* gnosis

gnosticisme [gnɔstisism] **NM** Gnosticism

gnostique [gnɔstik] **ADJ** Gnostic

NMF Gnostic

gnou [gnu] **NM** *Zool* wildebeest, gnu

gnouf [ɲuf] **NM 1** *Fam Arg mil (prison)* glasshouse; **au g.** in the glasshouse **2** *Fam Arg crime (poste de police)* police station◻, cop shop; *(cellule)* police cell◻

GO [ʒeo] **NFPL** *Rad (abrév* **grandes ondes)** LW

NM *(abrév* **gentil organisateur)** group leader *(at Club Méditerranée)*

Go NM *Ordinat (abrév écrite* **gigaoctet)** GB

go [go] **NM INV** go; **le jeu de go** go

• **tout de go ADV** *Fam (dire, annoncer etc)* straight out; **répondre tout de go** to answer straight off *or* straight out; **il est entré tout de go** he went straight in

Goa [goa] **N** Goa

goal [gol] **NM** *(gardien)* goalkeeper

gobelet [gɔblɛ] **NM 1** *(timbale)* tumbler, beaker; **g. jetable** *(en carton)* paper cup; *(en plastique)* plastic cup **2** *(au jeu)* shaker

gobe-mouches [gɔbmuʃ] **NM INV 1** *Orn* flycatcher **2** *Fam Vieilli (naïf)* gull

gober [3] [gɔbe] **VT 1** *(avaler* ▸ *nourriture)* to gulp down; *(*▸ *huître)* to swallow; *(*▸ *œuf)* to suck; *(*▸ *insecte)* to catch (and eat)

2 *Fam (croire)* to swallow; **alors, elle a gobé ton histoire?** so, did she swallow *or* buy it?; **il gobe tout ce qu'on lui dit** he believes everything he's told◻, he'll swallow anything

3 *Fam (supporter)* **je n'ai jamais pu la g.!** I never could stand *or Br* stick her!

4 *Fam (locution)* **ne reste pas là à g. les mouches!** don't just stand there gaping!

VPR se gober *Fam* to fancy oneself

goberger [17] [gɔbɛrʒe] **se goberger VPR** *Fam* **1** *(se prélasser)* to laze (about), to take it easy **2** *(faire bonne chère)* to indulge oneself◻

gobeur, -euse [gɔbœr, -øz] **NM,F** *(de nourriture)* gulper, swallower; *Fam Fig* **c'est un g.** he's very gullible◻, he'll swallow anything

gobie [gɔbi] **NM** *Ich* goby

godailler [3] [gɔdaje] **VI** *Couture* to pucker, to be puckered; **g. aux genoux** to bag at the knees

godasse [gɔdas] **NF** *Fam* shoe◻

godelureau, -x [gɔdlyro] **NM** *Hum* ladies' man

godemiché [gɔdmiʃe] **NM** dildo

goder [3] [gɔde] = **godailler**

godet [gɔdɛ] **NM 1** *(petit récipient)* jar; *(verre)* tumbler; **un g. en étain** a pewter mug; **g. à huile** *(d'une machine)* waste oil cup; *Fam* **on va boire un g.?** let's have a drink◻

2 *(pour peinture)* pot

3 *(d'une pipe)* bowl

4 *(nacelle* ▸ *d'une noria)* scoop; *(*▸ *d'une roue à eau, en manutention)* bucket; *Tech (au pied d'une machine)* socket; *Mines* skip

5 *Couture (à ondulation)* flare; *(à découpe)* gore; *(défaut)* pucker, ruck

• **à godets ADJ** *Couture* flared; *(à lés)* gored

godiche [gɔdiʃ] *Fam* **ADJ** *(maladroit)* oafish; *(niais)* silly, *Am* dumb; **ce qu'il peut être g.!** he's such an oaf!

NF *(maladroite)* clumsy thing; *(niaise)* silly thing

godille [gɔdij] **NF 1** *Naut (rame)* (stern-mounted) scull; **avancer à la g.** to scull **2** *(en ski)* wedeln; **descendre en g., faire la g.** to wedeln

godiller [3] [gɔdije] VI **1** *Naut* to scull **2** *(au ski)* to wedeln

godilleur [gɔdijœr] NM *Naut* sculler

godillot [gɔdijo] NM *(chaussure ▸ de soldat)* boot; *Fam (chaussure de marche)* clodhopper

goéland [gɔelɑ̃] NM *Orn* seagull; **g. argenté** herring gull; **g. cendré** common gull

goélette [gɔelɛt] NF schooner; **(voile) g.** trysail

goémon [gɔemɔ̃] NM wrack

goglu [gɔgly] NM *Can Orn* bobolink

gogo [gogo] *Fam* NM sucker, *Br* mug, *Am* patsy; **c'est pour les gogos, leur publicité** you'd have to be a real sucker to fall for their advert

• **à gogo** ADV galore; **il y avait du vin à g.** there was wine galore

goguenard, -e [gɔgnar, -ard] ADJ mocking, jeering

goguenardise [gɔgnardiz] NF mocking, jeering; **avec g.** mockingly

goguenots [gɔgno], **gogues** [gɔg] NMPL *très Fam Br* loo, *Am* john

goguette [gɔgɛt] **en goguette** ADJ tipsy, *Br* merry; **être en g.** to be (a bit) tight *or Br* merry; *(faire la noce)* to be out for a good time

goï [gɔj] = **goy**

goïm [gɔjim] *voir* **goy**

goinfre [gwɛ̃fr] *Fam* NMF pig, *Br* gannet **manger comme un g.** to eat like a pig

ADJ greedy[□], piggish

goinfrer [3] [gwɛ̃fre] **se goinfrer** VPR *Fam* to pig *or* to stuff oneself; **se g. de qch** to stuff oneself with sth

goinfrerie [gwɛ̃frəri] NF *Fam* piggishness; **arrête de manger, c'est de la g.** stop eating, you're just being a pig *or* making a pig of yourself

goitre [gwatr] NM *Méd* goitre

goitreux, -euse [gwatrø, -øz] *Méd* ADJ goitrous

NM,F = person with a goitre

gol [gɔl] NMF *Fam* spaz, *Br* mong

golden [gɔldɛn] NF Golden Delicious

goldo [gɔldo] NF *Fam* = Gauloise® cigarette

golem [gɔlɛm] NM golem

golf [gɔlf] NM **1** *Sport* **le g.** golf; **jouer au g.** to play golf **2** *(terrain)* golf course; **g. miniature** miniature golf, mini-golf

golfe [gɔlf] NM gulf; **le g. d'Alaska** *ou* **de l'Alaska** the Gulf of Alaska; **le g. du Bengale** the Bay of Bengal; **le g. de Cadix** the Gulf of Cadiz; **le g. de Gascogne** the Bay of Biscay; **le g. de Gênes** the Gulf of Genoa; **le g. du Mexique** the Gulf of Mexico; **le g. d'Oman** the Gulf of Oman; **le g. Persique** the Persian Gulf; **le g. de Suez** the Gulf of Suez

golfer [3] [gɔlfe] VI *Can* to play golf

golfeur, -euse [gɔlfœr, -øz] NM,F golfer

Gomina® [gɔmina] NF brilliantine, ≃ Brylcreem®

gominer [3] [gɔmine] **se gominer** VPR to put Brylcreem® *or* hair cream on

gommage [gɔmaʒ] NM **1** *(effacement)* erasing **2** *(de la peau)* exfoliation; **se faire faire un g.** to have one's skin deep-cleansed; **g. pour le corps** body scrub **3** *(encollage)* gumming; *Tech (des valves, des pistons)* sticking, gumming

gommant, -e [gɔmɑ̃, -ɑ̃t] ADJ **crème gommante, soin g.** face scrub

gomme [gɔm] NF **1** *(pour effacer)* eraser, *Br* rubber; **g. à crayon** eraser, *Br* rubber; **g. à encre** ink eraser *or Br* rubber

2 *(substance)* gum; **g. arabique** gum arabic

3 *(friandise)* gum; **g. à mâcher** chewing-gum

4 *Fam (locutions)* **à la g.** lousy; **des conseils à la g.** lousy advice; **mettre (toute) la g.** *(en voiture)* to put one's foot down; *(au travail)* to pull out all the stops

gomme-gutte [gɔmgyt] *(pl* **gommes-guttes***)* NF gamboge

gomme-laque [gɔmlak] *(pl* **gommes-laques***)* NF lac

gommer [3] [gɔme] VT **1** *(avec une gomme)* to erase, *Br* to rub out

2 *(faire disparaître)* to chase away, to erase; **g. les cellules mortes de la peau** to scrub off dead skin

3 *(estomper)* **g. une partie de son passé/un souvenir pénible** to erase part of one's past/a painful memory; *Fig* **le reportage a gommé les moments les plus pénibles** the report played down *or* glossed over the toughest moments

4 *(encoller)* to gum; *Tech* to stick, to gum; **piston gommé** gummed piston

gomme-résine [gɔmrezin] *(pl* **gommes-résines***)* NF gum resin

gommette [gɔmɛt] NF (small) sticker

gommeux, -euse [gɔmø, -øz] ADJ **1** *Bot* gumyielding, *Spéc* gummiferous **2** *(collant)* gummy, sticky

NM *Vieilli* young fop

• **gommeuse** NF gumming machine

gommier [gɔmje] NM *Bot* gum tree, *Spéc* gummiferous tree

Gomorrhe [gɔmɔr] *voir* **Sodome**

gonade [gɔnad] NF gonad

gond [gɔ̃] NM hinge; **mettre une porte sur ses gonds** to hang a door; *Fig* **sortir de ses gonds** to blow one's top, to fly off the handle

gondolage [gɔ̃dɔlaʒ] NM *(du bois)* warping; *(d'une tôle)* buckling; *(du papier)* cockling, curling

gondolant, -e [gɔ̃dɔlɑ̃, -ɑ̃t] ADJ *Fam Vieilli* hysterical, side-splitting

gondole [gɔ̃dɔl] NF **1** *Naut* gondola **2** *Mktg (présentoir)* gondola; **tête de g.** gondola end

gondolement [gɔ̃dɔlmɑ̃] = **gondolage**

gondoler [3] [gɔ̃dɔle] VI *(bois)* to warp, to get warped; *(tôle)* to buckle; *(papier)* to crinkle, to curl, to cockle

VT *(papier)* to crinkle, to curl, to cockle; *(disque)* to warp

VPR **se gondoler 1** *(se déformer ▸ bois)* to warp; *(▸ papier)* to crinkle, to curl, to cockle; *(▸ tôle)* to buckle; **mon disque s'est gondolé à la chaleur** the heat has warped my record **2** *très Fam (rire)* to fall about (laughing)

gondolier, -ère [gɔ̃dɔlje, -ɛr] NM,F *Com* merchandise assistant

NM *(batelier)* gondolier

gonfalon [gɔ̃falɔ̃] NM *Hist* gonfalon, gonfanon

gonflable [gɔ̃flabl] ADJ *(canot)* inflatable; *(ballon, poupée)* blow-up, inflatable

gonflage [gɔ̃flaʒ] NM *(d'un pneu)* inflating; *(d'un ballon)* blowing up; **vérifie le g. des pneus** check the tyre pressure

gonflant, -e [gɔ̃flɑ̃, -ɑ̃t] ADJ **1** *(bouffant ▸ jupon)* full; *(▸ manche)* puffed **2** *très Fam (irritant)* maddening[□], irritating[□]; **c'est g.!** what a drag!

NM *(d'un tissu)* volume; *(d'une chevelure)* volume, body; **donner du g. à ses cheveux** to give body *or* volume to one's hair

gonfle [gɔ̃fl] NF *Suisse (congère)* snowdrift

gonflé, -e [gɔ̃fle] ADJ **1** *(enflé)* swollen, puffed up; *(yeux)* swollen, puffy; *(visage)* bloated, swollen, puffy; *(estomac)* bloated, swollen; *(pieds, chevilles)* swollen; **elle avait les yeux gonflés de larmes** her eyes were swollen with tears; **g. comme une outre** full to bursting (point); *Fig* **être g. d'orgueil** to be puffed up with pride; **2** *Naut (voile)* full **3** *Fam (locutions)* **t'es g.!** *(effronté)* you've got a nerve *or* some cheek!; *(courageux)* you've got guts!; **c'est g. ce qu'il a fait là** what he did took some nerve; **être g. à bloc** to be raring to go

gonflement [gɔ̃fləmɑ̃] NM **1** *(de pneu, de ballon)* inflating, inflation **2** *(grosseur)* swelling **3** *(augmentation ▸ des prix)* inflation; *(▸ des statistiques)* exaggeration; *(▸ des impôts)* excessive increase (**de** in)

gonfler [3] [gɔ̃fle] VT **1** *(remplir d'un gaz ▸ bouée, pneu)* to inflate, to blow up; *(▸ poumons)* to fill; **g. les joues** to puff out one's cheeks; **avoir le cœur gonflé de peine/de chagrin/de joie** to be heartbroken/grief-stricken/overjoyed

2 *(faire grossir)* **gonfle tes muscles** flex your muscles; **un abcès lui gonflait la joue** his/her cheek was swollen with an abscess; **la brise gonflait sa jupe** her skirt was billowing in the breeze; **le vent gonfle les voiles** the wind is filling the sails

3 *(faire augmenter de volume)* to swell; *(prix, devis)* to inflate, to push up; *(frais, statistiques)* to exaggerate, to inflate; *(impact, conséquences)* to exaggerate, to blow out of all proportion; **g. l'importance de qn/qch** to exaggerate *or* to overstress the importance of sb/sth; **le prof a gonflé les notes** the teacher bumped up the marks

4 *Fam Aut (moteur)* to hot up, to soup up

5 *Cin* to blow up, to enlarge

6 *très Fam (irriter)* **g. qn** to get on sb's nerves *or Br* wick; **il nous les gonfle avec ses matchs de foot** he really gets on our nerves *or* he's a real pain in the neck with his football matches

VI **1** *Culin (pâte)* to rise; *(riz)* to swell (up) **2** *(enfler)* to be puffed up *or* bloated; **le bois a gonflé** the wood has warped; **la bière fait g. l'estomac** beer bloats the stomach

VPR **se gonfler 1** *(d'air, de gaz)* to inflate; **les poumons se gonflent** the lungs fill; **ce matelas se gonfle à l'aide d'une pompe** this air bed can be blown up *or* inflated with a pump **2** *(voile)* to swell; *(éponge)* to swell up **3** *Fig* **se g. de colère** to be bursting with rage; **son cœur se gonfle d'allégresse** his/her heart is bursting with joy

gonflette [gɔ̃flɛt] NF *Fam Péj* pumping iron; **faire de la g.** to pump iron

gonfleur [gɔ̃flœr] NM (air) pump

gong [gɔ̃g] NM **1** *Mus* gong **2** *Sport* bell; *Fig* **sauvé par le g.** saved by the bell

goniomètre [gɔnjɔmɛtr] NM goniometer

goniométrie [gɔnjɔmetri] NF goniometry

gonococcie [gɔnɔkɔksi] NF *Méd* gonococcal infection

gonocoque [gɔnɔkɔk] NM *Méd* gonococcus; **des gonocoques** gonococci

gonze [gɔ̃z] NM *très Fam* guy, *Br* bloke

gonzesse [gɔ̃zɛs] NF *très Fam (femme) Br* bird, *Am* chick

gordien [gɔrdjɛ̃] *voir* **nœud**

gore [gɔr] *Fam* ADJ INV *(film)* gory

NM *(genre)* gore (cinema); *(film)* gore film

goret [gɔrɛ] NM **1** *(porcelet)* piglet **2** *Fam (personne)* **petit g.!** you grubby little pig!; **manger comme un g.** to eat like a pig

Gore-Tex® [gɔrtɛks] NM *Tex* Gore-Tex®

gorge [gɔrʒ] NF **1** *(gosier)* throat; **avoir mal à la g., avoir un mal de g.** to have a sore throat; **j'ai la g. sèche** my throat is dry *or* parched; **l'arête m'est restée en travers de la g.** the bone got stuck in my throat; *Fig* **son refus m'est resté en travers de la g.** his/her refusal stuck in my throat; **avoir la g. nouée** *ou* **serrée** to have a lump in one's throat; **parler avec la g. serrée par la peine/l'angoisse** to speak in a voice trembling with sorrow/anguish; **l'odeur/la fumée vous prenait à la g.** the smell/smoke made you gag; **crier à pleine g.** *ou* **à g. déployée** to shout at the top of one's voice; **rire à g. déployée** to roar with laughter; **on lui enfoncera** *ou* **lui fera rentrer ses mots dans la g.** we'll make him/her eat his/her words; **prendre qn à la g.** to grab *or* to take sb by the throat; *Fig* **pris à la g., ils ont dû emprunter** they had a gun to their heads, so they had to borrow money; **tenir qn à la g.** to hold sb by the throat; *Fig* to have a stranglehold on sb; **faire rendre g. à qn** to force sb to pay *or* to cough up; **faire des gorges chaudes de qn/qch** to have a good laugh about sb/sth; **quand ils sauront, ils vont en faire des gorges chaudes** when they find out, they'll have a good laugh about it

2 *Littéraire (poitrine ▸ d'une femme)* bosom, breast; *(▸ d'un pigeon)* breast

3 *Géog* gorge

4 *Archit* groove, glyph, quirk; **moulure à g.** grooved moulding

5 *Constr (d'une cheminée)* throat; *(d'une fenêtre)* groove

6 *Tech (d'une poulie)* groove, score; *(d'une serrure)* tumbler; *(d'un écrou)* furrow; *(d'un pistolet, d'un étui à cartouches)* neck

gorgé, -e[1] [gɔrʒe] ADJ **une éponge gorgée d'eau** a sponge full of water; **sol g. d'eau** sodden soil; **champs gorgés d'eau** waterlogged fields; **des fruits gorgés de soleil** sun-kissed fruit; **g. de sang** gorged with blood

gorge-de-pigeon [gɔrʒdəpiʒɔ̃] ADJ INV dovecoloured

gorgée[2] [gɔrʒe] **NF** mouthful; **à petites gorgées** in little sips; **boire qch à petites gorgées** to sip sth; **à grandes gorgées** in great gulps; **d'une seule g.** in one gulp

gorgeon [gɔrʒɔ̃] **NM** *Fam* drink

gorger [17] [gɔrʒe] **VT** *(oies)* to cram; **g. un enfant de sucreries** to stuff a child full of sweets

VPR se gorger se g. (de qch) *(se remplir de)* to stuff oneself (with sth); **se g. d'eau** *(terre, rizière)* to become waterlogged; *Fig* **elle semblait se g. de sa présence** it seemed as if she couldn't see enough of him/her

gorgonzola [gɔrgɔ̃zɔla] **NM** Gorgonzola (cheese)

gorille [gɔrij] **NM 1** *Zool* gorilla **2** *Fam (garde)* gorilla, bodyguard

gosier [gozje] **NM** *(gorge)* throat, gullet; **rire à plein g.** to laugh loudly *or* heartily; *Fam* **j'ai le g. sec** I could do with a drink, I'm parched; *Fam* **ça m'est resté en travers du g.** it really stuck in my throat; *Fam* **avoir le g. en pente** to have a permanent thirst, to like one's drink

gospel [gɔspɛl] **NM** gospel (music)

gosse [gɔs] **NMF** *Fam* **1** *(enfant)* kid; **ses trois gosses** his/her three kids; **sale g.!** you brat!; **c'est un/une brave g.** he's/she's a nice kid; **c'est une g. de la rue** she grew up in the street **2** *(jeune)* **il est beau g.** he's a good-looking guy; **une belle g.** a good-looking girl **3** *Can Vulg* **gosses** balls, nuts, *Br* bollocks

gotha [gɔta] **NM** *(aristocratie)* aristocracy; *(élite)* élite; **le g. de l'édition** the leading lights of the publishing world; **tout le g. de la mode était là** (all) the big names in fashion were there; **le g.** *(almanach)* ≃ Burke's Peerage

gothique [gɔtik] **ADJ 1** *Beaux-Arts & Hist* Gothic; **écriture g.** Gothic script **2** *Littérature* Gothic

NM 1 *Beaux-Arts* **le g.** the Gothic style **2** *Littérature* **le g.** Gothic

NF Gothic (type); **écrire en g.** to write in Gothic script

Goths [go] **NMPL les G.** the Goths

gotique [gɔtik] **NM** *Ling* Gothic

Gotland [gɔtlɑ̃d] **NM** *Géog* Gothland, Gotland

gouache [gwaʃ] **NF** gouache; **peindre à la g.** to paint in *or* with gouache

gouailler [3] [gwaje] **VI** *Vieilli* to joke

gouailleur, -euse [gwajœr, -øz] **ADJ** *Vieilli* mocking, cheeky

goualante [gwalɑ̃t] **NF** *Fam Vieilli* popular song

gouape [gwap] **NF** *Fam Vieilli* hoodlum, hood

gouda [guda] **NM** Gouda (cheese)

goudron [gudrɔ̃] **NM** tar; **g. bitumineux** bitumen; **g. de bois/houille** wood/coal tar; **g. minéral** asphalt, bitumen

• **goudrons NMPL** (cigarette) tar

goudronnage [gudrɔnaʒ] **NM** tarring, surfacing

goudronner [3] [gudrɔne] **VT** *(route)* to tar, to surface (with tar)

goudronneur [gudrɔnœr] **NM** *(ouvrier)* tar sprayer *or* spreader

goudronneux, -euse [gudrɔnø, -øz] **ADJ** tarry

• **goudronneuse NF** *(machine)* tar tank *or* spreader

gouffre [gufr] **NM** *Géol (dû à l'effondrement)* trough fault (valley); *(dû à un fleuve)* swallow hole; *(abîme)* chasm, abyss, pit; **un g. béant** a yawning *or* gaping chasm; **g. sous-marin** oceanic abyss; *Fig* **être au bord du g.** to be on the edge of the abyss; *Littéraire* **tombé dans le g. de l'oubli/du désespoir** fallen into the depths of oblivion/despair; *Fig* **c'est un g. d'ignorance** the depths of his/her ignorance are unfathomable; *Fig* **cette voiture est un g.** this car just swallows up money, with this car it's like pouring money into a bottomless pit; **g. financier** *(produit)* financial disaster, dog

gouge [guʒ] **NF** *(ciseau à bois)* gouge; *(pour évider)* hollow chisel

gougère [guʒɛr] **NF** gougère *(choux pastry made from dough containing Gruyère cheese)*

gougnafier [guɲafje] **NM** *Fam Vieilli (individu grossier)* peasant, *Am* hick; *(bon à rien)* good-for-nothing, *Br* waster, *Am* slacker; *(mauvais ouvrier)* careless workman, *Br* cowboy

gouille [guj] **NF** *Suisse (flaque d'eau)* puddle; *(étang, mare)* pond

gouine [gwin] **NF** *très Fam* dyke, = offensive term used to refer to a lesbian

goujat [guʒa] **NM** boor

goujaterie [guʒatri] **NF** boorishness, uncouthness; **quelle g.!** how uncouth!

goujon[1] [guʒɔ̃] **NM 1** *Ich* gudgeon **2** *Culin* **g. de sole** sole goujon

goujon[2] [guʒɔ̃] **NM 1** *Constr (gén)* pin; *(de bois)* dowel; *(de métal)* gudgeon; *Menuis* **g. perdu, g. prisonnier** dowel (pin) **2** *Tech (de poulie)* pin; **g. de jonction** assembling pin, bolt; **g. de charnière** hinge pin; **g. d'arbre** shaft gudgeon

goujonner [3] [guʒɔne] **VT 1** *Constr* to joggle; *(bois)* to dowel; *(métal)* to bolt **2** *Tech* to bolt (with gudgeons)

goulache [gulaʃ] **NM** goulash

goulafre [gulafr] *Belg* **ADJ** greedy

NMF greedy person

goulag [gulag] **NM** Gulag

goulasch [gulaʃ] = **goulache**

goulée [gule] **NF** *Fam* **1** *(de liquide)* gulp; **vider son verre à grandes goulées** to gulp down one's drink **2** *(d'air)* **prendre une g. d'air** to take in a lungful of air; **il tira sur son havane, et aspira une grosse g.** he drew deeply on his cigar

goulet [gulɛ] **NM 1** *(rétrécissement)* narrowing; **la rue fait un g.** the road narrows; **g. d'étranglement** bottleneck **2** *Géol* gully, (narrow) gorge **3** *(chenal)* channel; **le G. de Brest** the Brest Channel

gouleyant, -e [gulejɑ̃, -ɑ̃t] **ADJ** *(vin)* lively

goulot [gulo] **NM 1** *(de bouteille)* neck; **boire au g.** to drink straight from the bottle **2** *Fig* **g. d'étranglement** bottleneck **3** *Vulg* **refouler du g.** to have foul breath

goulotte [gulɔt] **NF** *(conduit)* conduit; *(rigole)* channel; *(d'un wagonnet à charbon)* spout

goulu, -e [guly] **ADJ** greedy, gluttonous; *(regards)* hungry, greedy

NM,F *(glouton)* glutton

goulûment [gulymɑ̃] **ADV** greedily; *(regarder)* hungrily, greedily

goupil [gupi] **NM** *Arch* fox

goupille [gupij] **NF** (joining) pin, cotter (pin); **g. fendue** split pin; **g. d'arrêt** stop bolt

goupiller [3] [gupije] **VT 1** *Tech* to pin, to (fix with a) cotter **2** *Fam (combiner)* to set up; **bien/mal goupillé** well/badly organized; **ils avaient tout goupillé d'avance!** they had it all set up *or* worked out!

VPR se goupiller *Fam (se dérouler)* to turn out; **ça dépend comment les choses vont se g.** it depends how things turn *or* work out; **ça s'est bien/mal goupillé** things turned out well/badly

goupillon [gupijɔ̃] **NM 1** *(brosse)* bottle-brush **2** *Rel* aspersorium

gourance [gurɑ̃s], **gourante** [gurɑ̃t] **NF** *très Fam Br* boob, bloomer, *Am* goof; **faire une g.** *Br* to (make a) boob, to make a bloomer, *Am* to goof

gourbi [gurbi] **NM 1** *Fam (taudis)* dump, hovel **2** *(en Afrique du Nord)* gourbi, shack

gourd, -e[1] [gur, gurd] **ADJ** *(engourdi)* numb, stiff; **j'ai les doigts gourds** my fingers are numb *or* stiff (with cold)

gourdasse [gurdas] **NF** *Fam* fool, twit

gourde[2] [gurd] **NF 1** *(récipient ▸ en peau)* leather flask, wineskin; *(▸ en métal ou plastique)* bottle, flask **2** *(courge)* gourd **3** *Fam (personne)* blockhead, twit

ADJ *Fam* dopey, dimwitted

gourde[3] [gurd] **NF** *(monnaie de Haïti)* gourde

gourdin [gurdɛ̃] **NM 1** *(arme)* cudgel **2** *Vulg (pénis)* dick, prick; **avoir le g.** to have a hard-on

gourer [3] [gure] **se gourer VPR** *Fam* **1** *(se tromper) Br* to boob, to make a boob *or* bloomer, *Am* to goof; **se g. d'adresse** to get the address wrong; **tu t'es complètement gouré!** you've got it all mixed up *or* all wrong! **2** *(se douter)* **je m'en gourais!** I thought as much!

gourgandine [gurgɑ̃din] **NF** *Vieilli Péj* hussy

gourgane [gurgan] **NF** *Can* broad bean

gourmand, -e [gurmɑ̃, -ɑ̃d] **ADJ 1** *(personne ▸ gén)* who likes his/her food; *(▸ à l'excès)* greedy; **g. de chocolat** fond of chocolate **2** *(gastronomique)* **notre page gourmande** our food page; **pause gourmande** snack **3** *(bouche)* greedy; *(lèvres)* eager; *(regard)* greedy, eager

NM,F person who loves his/her food, *Sout* gourmand

NM *Bot* sucker

gourmander [3] [gurmɑ̃de] **VT** to rebuke, to castigate, to upbraid

gourmandise [gurmɑ̃diz] **NF 1** *(caractère)* greediness, greed **2** *(sucrerie)* delicacy

gourme [gurm] **NF 1** *(du cheval)* strangles *(singulier)*, equine distemper **2** *Vieilli Méd* impetigo **3** *Fam Vieilli (locution)* **jeter sa g.** to sow one's wild oats

gourmé, -e [gurme] **ADJ** *Littéraire* stiff, starched

gourmet [gurmɛ] **NM** gourmet, epicure

gourmette [gurmɛt] **NF 1** *(chaînette)* (chain) bracelet; *(d'une montre)* chain **2** *(pour cheval)* curb (chain)

gourou [guru] **NM 1** *Rel* guru **2** *Fig* guru, mentor

gousse [gus] **NF 1** *(de haricot)* pod, husk; *(de petit pois)* pod; **g. d'ail** clove of garlic; **g. de cardamome** cardamom pod; **g. de vanille** vanilla pod **2** *Vulg (lesbienne)* dyke, = offensive term used to refer to a lesbian

gousset [gusɛ] **NM 1** *Couture (de gilet)* waistcoat pocket; *(de pantalon)* fob pocket; *Fig* **il a le g. bien garni** his pockets are well lined **2** *Constr (traverse)* support; *(plaque)* gusset, plate

GOÛT [gu] **NM 1** *(sens)* taste; **perdre le g.** to lose one's sense of taste

2 *(saveur)* taste; **avoir un drôle de g.** to taste funny; **ne pas avoir de g.** to be tasteless, to have no taste; **ça a un g. très épicé** it tastes very hot; **ça a un g. de miel/moutarde** it tastes of honey/mustard; **avec ce rhume, je ne trouve aucun g. à la nourriture** I can't taste my food (properly) because of this cold; **donner du g. à un mets** to give a dish flavour

3 *(préférence)* taste; **sucrez selon votre g.** add sugar to taste; **tu choisiras selon ton g.** you'll choose what you like *or* whatever appeals to you; **un g. marqué** *ou* **particulier pour...** a great liking *or* fondness for...; **avoir des goûts de luxe** to have expensive tastes; **c'est (une) affaire** *ou* **question de g.** it's a matter of taste; **à chacun son g., chacun ses goûts** each to his own; **tous les goûts sont dans la nature** it takes all sorts (to make a world); *Prov* **des goûts et des couleurs, on ne discute pas** there's no accounting for taste

4 *(intérêt)* taste, liking; **avoir du g. pour** *ou* **le g. de qch** to have a taste *or* liking for sth; **il faut leur donner le g. des maths** we've got to give them a taste *or* a liking for maths; **prendre g. à qch** to develop a taste for sth; **avec le temps, elle y a pris g.** it grew on her, she developed a liking for it; **ne plus avoir g. à qch** to have lost one's taste for sth; **elle n'a plus (de) g. à rien** she no longer wants to do anything; **reprendre g. à la lecture/à la musique** to regain one's taste for reading/music; **reprendre g. à la vie** to regain one's zest for living, to find life worth living again; **faire qch par g.** to do sth out of *or* by inclination; **je ne le fais pas par g.** I don't do it from choice; **je le fais par g. du travail bien fait** I do it because I like to see work well done; *Fig* **je vais lui faire passer le g. du pain** *(tuer)* I'm going to do away with him/her; *(dissuader)* I'm going to cure him/her (of that) once and for all; **je vais lui faire passer le g. du mensonge** I'm going to put a stop to his/her lying once and for all

5 *(jugement esthétique)* taste; **les gens de g.** people of taste; **avoir du g.** to have (good) taste; **elle a bon/mauvais g.** she has good/bad taste; **elle n'a aucun g.** she has no taste; **s'habiller avec g.** to have good dress sense, to have good taste in clothes; **une décoration de bon g.** a tasteful decoration; **il a eu le (bon) g. de se taire** he had the sense to remain silent; **cette plaisanterie est**

d'un g. douteux that joke is in poor *or* doubtful taste; **une remarque de mauvais g.** a remark in poor *or* bad taste; **une robe de mauvais g.** a tasteless dress

6 *(mode)* **c'était le g. de l'époque** it was the style of the time; **c'est le g. du jour** it's the current fashion; **être au g. du jour** to be in line with current tastes; **remettre qch au g. du jour** to update sth; *Littéraire* **un opéra dans le g. de Verdi** an opera in the style of Verdi; **c'était une fourrure en renard, ou quelque chose dans ce g.-là** it was a fox fur, or something of the sort

• **à mon/son/***etc* **goût** ADJ & ADV to my/his/*etc* liking; **trouver qn/qch à son g.** to find sb/sth to one's taste *or* liking; **le décor est tout à fait à mon g.** the decor is exactly to my liking; **à mon/son g., on est trop lents** we're not going fast enough for my/his liking

---

goûter[1] [3] [gute] VT **1** *(aliment, boisson)* to taste, to try; **voulez-vous g. ma sauce?** would you like to taste *or* try my sauce?; **fais-moi g.** let me have a taste, give me a taste **2** *(apprécier)* to savour, to enjoy; **goûtons ensemble le calme du soir** let's savour *or* enjoy the peace of the evening together; **elle n'a pas goûté l'humour de leurs commentaires** she didn't appreciate their witticisms **3** *Belg & Can (avoir un goût de)* to taste of; **ce fruit goûte le pourri** this fruit tastes rotten

VI **1** *(prendre une collation)* to have an afternoon snack, *Br* to have tea; **venez g., les enfants!** come and have your snack, children!; **il goûte toujours d'une pomme et d'un verre de lait** he always has an apple and a glass of milk for his afternoon snack **2** *Belg (avoir bon goût)* to taste nice

• **goûter à** VT IND **1** *(manger)* to taste, to try; **goûtez donc à ces biscuits** do try some of these biscuits **2** *(faire l'expérience de)* to have a taste of; **maintenant qu'elle a goûté à la célébrité** now that she's tasted *or* had a taste of fame **3** *Belg (plaire à)* **ça ne me goûte pas** I don't like it

• **goûter de** VT IND **1** *(plat)* to taste, to try; **puis-je g. un peu de ce fromage?** may I taste *or* try some of this cheese? **2** *(faire l'expérience de)* to have a taste of; **depuis qu'elle a goûté du piano, c'est une passionnée** since she's had a taste of piano playing, she's become an enthusiast

goûter[2] [gute] NM *(collation)* = afternoon snack for children, typically consisting of bread, butter, chocolate, and a drink; *(fête)* children's party; **g. d'anniversaire** (children's) birthday party; **l'heure du g.** = time for the children's afternoon snack

goûteur, -euse [gutœr, -øz] NM,F taster

goutte [gut] NF **1** *(d'eau, de lait, de sang)* drop; *(de sueur)* drop, bead; *(de pluie)* drop (of rain), raindrop; **il est tombé une g. (ou deux)** there was a drop (or two) of rain; **il tombait quelques gouttes** it was spitting with rain; **g. d'eau** drop of water; *(bijou)* drop; **g. de rosée** dewdrop; **boire qch jusqu'à la dernière g.** to drink every last drop of sth; **avoir la g. au nez** to have a runny nose; **c'est une g. d'eau dans la mer** it's a drop in the ocean; **c'est la g. d'eau qui fait déborder le vase** it's the straw that broke the camel's back

2 *(petite quantité)* **une g. de** a (tiny) drop of; **une g. de vin?** a drop of wine?; **boire une g. de cognac après le repas** to have a drop *or* nip of brandy after one's meal; *Fam* **boire la g.** to have a nip

3 *Méd (maladie)* gout; **avoir la g.** to suffer from *or* have gout, to be gouty

4 *Fam (eau-de-vie)* **la g.** the hard stuff

• **gouttes** NFPL *Pharm* **gouttes pour le nez/les oreilles/les yeux** nose/ear/eye drops; **prendre des gouttes** to take drops

• **goutte à goutte** ADV drop by drop; **tomber g. à g.** to drip; *Fig* **ils laissent filtrer les informations g. à g.** they are letting the news filter out bit by bit

• **ne... goutte** ADV *Arch* **je n'y comprends** *ou* **entends g.** I can't understand a thing; **je n'y vois g.** I can't see a thing

goutte-à-goutte [gutagut] NM INV *Méd Br* drip, *Am* IV; **ils lui ont mis un g.** they've put him/her on *Br* a drip *or Am* an IV

gouttelette [gutlɛt] NF droplet

goutter [3] [gute] VI to drip

goutteux, -euse [gutø, -øz] ADJ gouty

NM,F gout-sufferer

gouttière [gutjɛr] NF **1** *Constr* gutter; **g. verticale** drainpipe

2 *Méd* splint

3 *Anat (d'un os)* groove

4 *Typ (de page)* gutter

gouvernable [guvɛrnabl] ADJ governable; **ce pays n'est pas g.** it's impossible to govern this country, this country is ungovernable

gouvernail [guvɛrnaj] NM **1** *Naut* rudder; **g. automatique/compensé** automatic/balanced rudder; *Aviat* **g. de direction** rudder; *Naut* **g. de plongée** *(d'un sous-marin)* horizontal rudder; **g. de profondeur** *(d'un sous-marin)* hydroplane; **roue du g.** (steering) wheel **2** *Fig* **être au** *ou* **tenir le g.** to call the tune; **tenir le g. de l'État/d'une affaire** to be at the helm of the state/a business

gouvernance [guvɛrnɑ̃s] NF **1** *(action de gouverner)* government **2** *(manière de gérer)* governance, government; **g. mondiale** global governance

gouvernant, -e [guvɛrnɑ̃, -ɑ̃t] ADJ ruling *(avant n)*; **les classes gouvernantes** the ruling classes

NM,F man, *f* woman in power; **les gouvernants** the people in power, the Government

• **gouvernante** NF **1** *(préceptrice)* governess **2** *Vieilli (domestique)* housekeeper **3** *(d'un hôtel)* **gouvernante d'étage** floor housekeeper; **gouvernante générale** executive *or* head housekeeper

gouverne [guvɛrn] NF **1** *(instruction)* **pour ma/ta g.** for my/your information **2** *Naut* steering; **aviron de g.** stern *or* steering oar **3** *Aviat* control surface; **gouvernes** control surfaces; **g. compensée** balanced surface; **g. de direction** (tail) rudder; **g. de profondeur** elevator

gouvernement [guvɛrnəmɑ̃] NM **1** *(régime)* government; **sous le g. socialiste** under the socialist government; **g. central** central government; **g. de coalition** coalition government; **g. démocratique** democratic government; **g. d'État** state government; **g. fantoche** puppet government; **g. fédéral** federal government; **g. majoritaire** majority government; **g. minoritaire** minority government; **g. provisoire** provisional government; **g. représentatif** representative government; **g. de transition** interim government **2** *(ensemble des ministres)* Government; **le Premier ministre a formé son g.** the Prime Minister has formed his government *or* cabinet; **le g. a démissionné** the Government has resigned; **sous le g. Raffarin** during Raffarin's term of office, during Raffarin's administration; **g. de cohabitation** = government in which the President and the parliamentary majority are from different parties **3 g. d'entreprise** corporate governance

gouvernemental, -e, -aux, -ales [guvɛrnəmɑ̃tal, -o] ADJ *(parti)* ruling *(avant n)*, governing *(avant n)*; *(presse)* pro-government; *(politique, décision, crise)* government *(avant n)*; **des dispositions gouvernementales** measures taken by the government; **l'équipe gouvernementale** the Government *or Br* Cabinet *or Am* Administration

gouverner [3] [guvɛrne] VT **1** *Pol* to rule, to govern; **le pays n'était plus gouverné** the country no longer had a government

2 *Littéraire (maîtriser)* to govern, to control; **g. ses passions** to control one's passions; **ne nous laissons pas g. par la haine** let us not be governed *or* ruled by hatred

3 *Naut* to steer; **faire g.** to con; **g. sur un port** to steer *or* stand *or* head for a port, to bear in with a port; **g. à la lame** to steer by the sea

4 *Gram* to govern

5 *Tech* **mouvement gouverné par un pendule** movement regulated *or* governed *or* controlled by a pendulum

6 *Vieilli (régir)* to manage, to administer; **bien g. ses ressources** to husband one's resources

USAGE ABSOLU *Pol* to govern; **un parti qui gouverne depuis des années** a party which has governed *or* has been in government for years

VI *Naut* to steer; **g. à la lame/à tribord** to steer by the sea/to starboard; **g. de l'arrière** to steer aft; **navire qui ne gouverne plus** ship that no longer answers to her helm; **bateau qui gouverne bien** boat that steers well

VPR **se gouverner 1** *Pol* to govern oneself; **le droit des peuples à se g. eux-mêmes** the right of peoples to self-government **2** *(se maîtriser)* to control oneself

gouverneur, -e [guvɛrnœr] NM,F *Admin & Pol* governor; *Mil (d'une position fortifiée)* commanding officer; **le G. de la Banque de France** the Governor of the Bank of France; *Can* **G. général** Governor General

goy [gɔj] (*pl* **goyim** *ou* **goïm** [gɔjim]) ADJ goyish

NMF goy; **les goyim** goyim, goys

goyave [gɔjav] NF guava

goyavier [gɔjavje] NM guava (tree)

goyim [gɔjim] *voir* **goy**

Gozo [gozo] NM Gozo

GPAO [ʒepeao] NF *Ordinat (abrév* **gestion de production assistée par ordinateur***)* computer-aided production management

GPL [ʒepeɛl] NM *(abrév* **gaz de pétrole liquéfié***)* LPG

GPO [ʒepeo] NF *(abrév* **gestion par objectifs***)* MBO

GPS [ʒepeɛs] NM *Tél (abrév* **global positioning system***)* GPS

GQG [ʒekyʒe] NM *(abrév* **grand quartier général***)* GHQ

GR® [ʒeɛr] NM *(abrév* **sentier de grande randonnée***)* long-distance hiking path

Graal [gral] NM **le G.** the (Holy) Grail

grabat [graba] NM pallet, litter

grabataire [grabatɛr] ADJ bedridden

NMF (bedridden) invalid

grabuge [grabyʒ] NM *Fam* **il y avait du g.** there was a bit of a rumpus; **ça va faire du g.** that's going to cause havoc; **il y a eu du g.?** was there any trouble?

grâce [gras] NF **1** *(beauté ▸ d'un paysage)* charm; *(▸ d'une personne)* grace; **avoir de la g.** to be graceful; **avec g.** gracefully; **plein de g.** graceful; **sans g.** graceless; **la vue n'est pas sans g.** the view is not without charm

2 *(volonté)* **de bonne g.** with good grace, willingly; **avoir la bonne g. de dire/faire** to have the grace to say/to do; **de mauvaise g.** grudgingly, with bad grace; **vous auriez mauvaise g. à** *ou* **de vous plaindre** it would be ungracious of you to complain

3 *(faveur)* favour; **je te le demande comme une g.** I'm asking you this as a favour; **être en g. auprès de qn** to be in favour with sb; **rentrer en g. auprès de qn** to come back into sb's favour; **fais-moi la g. de m'écouter** do me the favour of listening to me; **nous ferez-vous la g. de signer votre dessin?** would you do us the honour of signing your drawing?; **trouver g. aux yeux de qn** to find favour with sb; **c'est (toute) la g. que je vous souhaite** that is what I would wish for you

4 *(sursis ▸ de peine)* pardon; *(▸ dans un délai)* grace; **lettre(s) de g.** reprieve; **accorder sa g. à qn** to pardon sb; **crier** *ou* **demander g.** to beg for mercy; **je te fais g. des centimes** I'll let you off the cents; **je te fais g. du reste** I'll spare you the rest; *(ne m'en dites ou n'en faites pas plus)* you needn't do/say any more; **je vous fais g. des détails** I'll spare you the details; **je vous fais g. cette fois-ci** I'll let you off this time; **une semaine/un mois de g.** one week's/month's grace; **g. amnistiante** free pardon; **g. présidentielle** presidential pardon; *Com* **jours** *ou* **terme de g.** days of grace

5 *Rel* grace; **la g. divine** divine grace; **avoir la g.** to be inspired; **en état de g.** in a state of grace; **par la g. de Dieu** by the grace of God; **à la g. de Dieu** *(advienne que pourra)* come what may; *(n'importe comment)* any old way

6 *(pour exprimer la reconnaissance)* **rendre g.** *ou* **grâces à Dieu** to give thanks to God; **(rendons) g. à Dieu!** thanks be to God!

7 *(titre)* **Sa G.** His/Her Grace; **Votre G.** Your Grace

EXCLAM *Arch* mercy!; **ah, g.!** have mercy!; **de g.!** for God's *or* pity's sake!

• **grâces** NFPL **1** *(faveurs)* **rechercher les bonnes grâces de qn** to curry favour with sb, to seek sb's favour; **être/entrer dans les bonnes grâces de qn** to be/to get in favour with sb **2** *(manières)* **faire des grâces à qn** to make up to sb; **faire des grâces** to put on airs (and graces) **3** *Rel* **dire les grâces** to give thanks (after eating)

• **grâce à** PRÉP *(avec l'aide de)* **g. à qn/qch** thanks to sb/sth; **g. à votre aide** thanks to your help; **g. à Dieu** with God's help, by God's grace

gracier [9] [grasje] **VT** to reprieve

gracieuse [grasjøz] *voir* **gracieux**

gracieusement [grasjøzmɑ̃] **ADV 1** *(joliment)* gracefully **2** *(aimablement)* graciously, kindly **3** *(gratuitement)* free (of charge), gratis; **un repas vous sera servi g.** you will be served a free *or* complimentary meal

gracieuseté [grasjøzte] **NF 1** *(parole aimable)* pleasantry **2** *Vieilli (cadeau)* gratuity

gracieux, -euse [grasjø, -øz] **ADJ 1** *(joli)* charming, graceful; **qu'il est g., ce bébé!** what a charming baby!

2 *(aimable)* affable, amiable, gracious; **sa lettre était écrite sur le ton le plus g.** his/her letter was most amiable

3 *(gratuit)* free (of charge); **à titre g.** gratis, free of charge; **exemplaire envoyé à titre g.** complimentary *or* presentation copy

4 *(pour exprimer le respect)* **notre g. souverain** our gracious Sovereign

gracile [grasil] **ADJ** *Littéraire* slender

gracilité [grasilite] **NF** *Littéraire* slenderness, slimness

Gracques [grak] **NPR les G.** the Gracchi

gradation [gradasjɔ̃] **NF 1** *(progression)* gradation; **avec une g. lente** gradually, by degrees; **g. ascendante/descendante** gradual increase/decrease **2** *(étape)* stage; **procédons par gradations** let's proceed step by step *or* gradually

grade [grad] **NM 1** *(rang)* rank; **il a le g. de capitaine** his rank is captain; **avancer** *ou* **monter en g.** to be promoted; *Fam* **en prendre pour son g.** to get hauled over the coals, *esp Br* to get it in the neck

2 *(niveau)* **g. universitaire** degree

3 *Géom* (centesimal) grade

4 *Chim* grade

gradé, -e [grade] **ADJ militaire g.** non-commissioned officer, NCO

NM,F 1 *Mil* non-commissioned officer, NCO; **tous les gradés** all ranks **2** *Naut* **les gradés** the petty officers

grader [3] [grade] **VI** *Suisse* to be promoted

gradient [gradjɑ̃] **NM 1** *Météo* gradient; **g. thermique** temperature gradient **2** *Math* **g. d'une fonction** gradient of a function **3** *Élec* **g. de potentiel** voltage gradient

gradin [gradɛ̃] **NM 1** *(dans un amphithéâtre)* tier, (stepped) row of seats; **les gradins** *(dans un stade) Br* the terraces, *Am* the bleachers **2** *Géog* step, terrace; **à gradins** stepped **3** *Agr* terrace; **à gradins** terraced

graduation [gradɥasjɔ̃] **NF 1** *(repère)* mark; **verser le liquide jusqu'à la deuxième g.** pour the liquid up to the second mark **2** *(échelle de mesure)* scale; **la g. va jusqu'à 20** the scale goes up to 20

gradué, -e [gradɥe] **ADJ 1** *(à graduations)* graduated **2** *(progressif)* graded

graduel, -elle [gradɥɛl] **ADJ** gradual, progressive

NM gradual

graduellement [gradɥɛlmɑ̃] **ADV** gradually

graduer [7] [gradɥe] **VT 1** *(augmenter)* to increase gradually; **il faut g. la difficulté des tests** the tests should become gradually more difficult **2** *(diviser)* to graduate

graffiter [3] [grafite] **VT** to cover with graffiti

graffiteur, -euse [grafitœr, -øz] **NM,F** graffiti artist

graffiti [grafiti] *(pl* **inv** *ou* **graffitis)** **NM** *(inscription)* graffiti *(UNCOUNT)*; **un g.** a piece of graffiti; **des graffitis** *ou* **graffiti** graffiti

graille [graj] **NF** *très Fam (aliments)* food□, grub, nosh

graillé, -e [graje] **ADJ** *Can (pour faire quelque chose)* well-equipped; *Fam (bien monté)* well-hung

grailler [3] [graje] **VI 1** *(corneille)* to caw **2** *(personne)* to speak hoarsely *or* throatily **3** *très Fam (manger)* to eat□

VT *très Fam* to eat□; **il n'y a plus rien à g.** there's no grub left

graillon [grajɔ̃] **NM 1** *Fam (friture)* **une odeur de g.** a smell of burnt fat□; **sentir le g.** to smell of burnt fat; **avoir un goût de g.** to taste greasy□ **2** *très Fam (crachat)* gob (of spit)

graillonner [3] [grajɔne] **VI 1** *(sentir la friture)* to smell of greasy food **2** *Fam (cracher en toussant)* to hawk (up), *Br* to gob; *(parler)* to speak hoarsely□ *or* huskily□

grain¹ [grɛ̃] **NM 1** *(de sel, de sable)* grain, particle; *(de riz, de poudre)* grain; *(de poussière)* speck; *Fig* **un g. de cruauté** a touch of cruelty; *Fig* **un g. de lucidité** a grain *or* flicker of understanding; *Fig* **un g. de folie** a touch of madness; *Fig* **un g. de coquetterie/d'originalité** a touch *or* hint of coquetry/originality; *Fig* **il n'a pas un g. de bon sens** he hasn't got an ounce *or* a grain of common sense; *Fig* **donner du g. à moudre à qn** to give sb food for thought; *Fam* **mettre son g. de sel** to stick one's oar in; *Fam* **elle a un g.** she's got a screw loose

2 *(céréales)* **le g., les grains** (cereal) grain; **alcool** *ou* **eau-de-vie de g.** grain alcohol

3 *(d'un fruit, d'une plante)* **g. de blé** grain of wheat; **g. de café** *(après torréfaction)* coffee bean; **g. de cassis** blackcurrant (berry); **g. de grenade** pomegranate seed; **g. de groseille** redcurrant (berry); **g. de moutarde** mustard seed; **g. d'orge** barleycorn, grain of barley; **g. de poivre** peppercorn; **g. de raisin** grape

4 *(perle)* bead; **g. de chapelet** rosary bead

5 *(aspect ▸ de la peau)* grain, texture; *(▸ du bois, du papier)* grain; *(▸ de la peau, d'un animal)* rough side; **à gros g.** coarse-grained; **ruban gros g.** petersham; **à petit g.** close-grained, fine-grained; **à grains fins/serrés** fine-/close-grained; **aller/travailler dans le sens du g.** to go/to work with the grain; **contre le g.** against the grain

6 *Phot* grain; **la photo a du g.** the photo is *or* looks grainy

7 *Pharm* pellet

• **en grains ADJ** *(café)* unground, whole; **moulu ou en grains?** ground or not?, ground or whole?; **poivre en grains** whole peppercorns

• **grain de beauté NM** beauty spot, mole

> Do not confuse with **graine**.

grain² [grɛ̃] **NM** *Météo* squall; **essuyer un g.** to meet with a squall; **g. en ligne** line squall

graine [grɛn] **NF** *(semence)* seed; **g. d'anis** aniseed; **g. de lin** linseed; **graines (pour oiseaux)** birdseed; **monter en g.** to go to seed; *Fig (personne ▸ grandir)* to shoot up; *(femme ▸ rester célibataire)* to be (left) on the shelf; **casser la g.** to have a bite to eat; **c'est de la mauvaise g., ce garçon-là!** that boy is bad news!; **son frère, c'est de la g. de voyou!** his brother has the makings of a hooligan!; *Fam* **ton frère a réussi tous ses examens, prends-en de la g.** your brother has passed all his exams, take a leaf out of his book

> Do not confuse with **grain**.

grainer [4] [grene] **VI** *Agr* to seed

VT 1 *(réduire en grains ▸ poudre à canon)* to granulate; *(▸ cire)* to shred; *(▸ sel)* to grain **2** *(donner un aspect grené à ▸ papier, cuir)* to grain

graineterie [grɛntri] **NF 1** *(commerce)* seed trade **2** *(magasin)* seed merchant's

grainetier, -ère [grɛntje, -ɛr] **ADJ le commerce g.** the seed trade

NM,F *(marchand ▸ de graines)* seed merchant; *(▸ de grain)* corn chandler

graissage [grɛsaʒ] **NM 1** *Aut & Tech (avec de l'huile)* oiling, lubrication; *(avec de la graisse)* greasing, lubrication; **faire faire un g.** to have one's car lubricated; **circuit de g.** lubrication system **2** *Typ* emboldening

graisse [grɛs] **NF 1** *(corps gras)* fat; **régime pauvre en graisses** low-fat diet; *Fam* **prendre de la g.** to pile on the pounds; **g. animale/végétale** animal/vegetable fat; **g. de baleine/phoque** whale/seal blubber; **g. de porc** lard; **g. de rognon** suet

2 *Tech* grease; **pistolet** *ou* **pompe** *ou* **injecteur à g.** grease gun; **g. pour engrenages** gear lubricant; **g. pour essieux** axle grease; **g. lubrifiante** lubricant; **g. minérale** crude paraffin, mineral jelly; **g. au silicone** silicone grease

3 *(en œnologie)* ropiness; **tourner à la g.** to become ropy

4 *Typ* thickness, boldness; *(de caractère)* weight

graisser [4] [grese] **VT 1** *(enduire ▸ moteur)* to lubricate; *(▸ pièce, mécanisme)* to grease, to oil; *(▸ fusil)* to grease; *(▸ chaussures)* to dub; *(▸ moule)* to grease; **g. la patte à qn** to grease sb's palm **2** *(tacher)* to grease, to soil with grease **3** *Typ* to embolden

VI 1 *(devenir gras)* **ses cheveux graissent très vite** his/her hair gets greasy very quickly **2** *(rendre quelque chose gras)* **onguent qui ne graisse pas** non-greasy ointment **3** *(en œnologie)* to become ropy

VPR se graisser se g. les mains avec une crème to rub cream into one's hands

graisseur, -euse¹ [grɛsœr, -øz] **ADJ** greasing, lubricating; **godet g.** grease box; **pistolet g.** grease gun

NM 1 *(appareil)* lubricator, oiler **2** *Aut* grease nipple **3** *(ouvrier)* greaser, oiler

graisseux, -euse² [grɛsø, -øz] **ADJ 1** *(cheveux, col)* greasy **2** *(tumeur, tissu)* fatty; **bourrelet g.** roll of fat

grammage [gramaʒ] **NM** grammage

grammaire [gramɛr] **NF 1** *(règles)* grammar; **la g.** grammar; **règle de g.** grammatical rule **2** *(livre)* grammar (book)

grammairien, -enne [gramɛrjɛ̃, -ɛn] **NM,F** grammarian

grammatical, -e, -aux, -ales [gramatikal, -o] **ADJ 1** *(de grammaire)* grammatical; **exercice g.** grammar exercise; **catégorie grammaticale** part of speech **2** *(correct)* grammatical; **non g.** ungrammatical

grammaticalement [gramatikalmɑ̃] **ADV** grammatically

gramme [gram] **NM** gram(me); **elle n'a pas un g. de graisse** she hasn't got an ounce of fat (on her); *Fig* **pas un g. de bon sens/de compassion** not an ounce of common sense/of compassion

gramophone [gramɔfɔn] **NM** gramophone

GRAND, -E [grɑ̃, grɑ̃d]

ADJ	
• tall **A1**	• big **A1–4, B7**
• large **A2, 7**	• long **A2, 5**
• grown-up **A4**	• great **A6, 7, 10, B1, 2, 8, 10, C**
• major **B1**	
• top **B3**	
NM,F	
• grown-up **2**	• tall person **3**

ADJ A. *ASPECT QUANTITATIF* **1** *(de taille élevée ▸ adulte)* tall; *(▸ enfant)* tall, big; **une grande femme maigre** a tall thin woman; **il est maintenant aussi g. que son frère** he's now as big as his brother

2 *(de grandes dimensions ▸ objet, salle, ville)* big, large; *(▸ distance)* long; **une grande pendule** a big clock; **il te faudrait un g. couteau** you'll need a big *or* long knife; **g. A** capital A; **une grande tour** a high *or* tall tower; **la grande pyramide de Kheops** the Great Pyramid of Cheops; **un g. désert** a big desert; **dans toutes les grandes villes** in all the big *or* major towns; **de grandes forêts** large areas of forest; **un g. fleuve** a long *or* big river; **c'est un instrument plus g. que le violon** it's a bigger *or* larger instrument than the violin; **une statue plus grande que nature** a large-scale statue; **de grandes jambes** long legs; **un g. front** a prominent forehead; **avoir de grands pieds** to have big *or* large feet; **ses grands yeux bleus** his/her big blue eyes; **marcher à grands pas** to walk with great *or* long strides; **ouvrir la bouche toute grande** to open one's mouth wide; **g. ensemble** *Br* housing scheme, *Am* housing project; **g. magasin** department store; **grande surface** superstore, hypermarket; **grandes et moyennes surfaces** large and medium commercial outlets; **grande surface spécialisée** specialist superstore; *Cin & TV* **g. écran** widescreen; *Rad* **grandes ondes** long wave; **sur grandes ondes** on long wave

3 *(d'un certain âge ▸ être humain)* big; **tu es un g. garçon maintenant** you're a big boy now; **être assez g. pour faire qch** to be old *or* big enough to do sth

4 *(aîné ▸ frère, sœur)* big; *(au terme de sa croissance ▸ personne)* grown-up; *(▸ animal)* fully grown, adult; **quand je serai g.** when I'm grown-up *or* big; **elle a de grands enfants** she has grown-up children

5 *(qui dure longtemps)* long; **pendant un g. moment** for quite some time; **une grande explication** a long explanation; **une grande période de beau temps** a long *or* lengthy spell of good weather

6 *(intense, considérable)* great; **un g. cri** a loud cry; **un g. remue-ménage/vacarme** a great commotion/noise; **les risques sont grands** there are considerable risks; **un g. mouvement de protestation** a great *or* big *or* widespread protest movement; **de grande diffusion** widely distributed; *Com* **grande distribution** mass distribution; **une grande fortune** great wealth, a large fortune; **faire de grands frais** to go to great expense; **il y avait une grande affluence à la poste** there was a great *or* an enormous crush at the post office; **rincer à grande eau** to rinse thoroughly; **les grands froids** intense cold; **pendant les grandes chaleurs** in high summer, in *or* at the height of summer; **un g. vent soufflait du nord** a strong wind was blowing from the north; **nous avons fait un g. feu** we made a big fire; **un g. incendie** a major *or* great fire; **ce sont des articles de grande consommation** they are everyday consumer articles; **(à l'époque des) grandes marées** (at) spring tide; **au g. jour** in broad daylight; **le g. public** the general public, the public at large; **une émission g. public** a programme designed to appeal to a wide audience; **un livre g. public** a mass-market book; **un film g. public** a mainstream movie *or Br* film; **musique g. public** middle-of-the-road music

7 *(pour qualifier une mesure)* large, great; **la grande majorité de** the great *or* vast majority of; **son g. âge explique cette erreur** this mistake can be put down to his/her being so old; **des arbres d'une grande hauteur** very tall trees; **ils plongent à une grande profondeur** they dive very deep *or* to a great depth

8 *(entier)* **une grande cuillerée de sucre** a heaped spoonful of sugar; **elle m'a fait attendre une grande heure/semaine** she made me wait a good hour/a good week

9 *Géog* **la Grande Baie Australienne** the Great Australian Bight; **Grande Canarie** Gran Canaria; **le G. Canyon** the Grand Canyon; **le G. Désert de Sable** the Great Sandy Desert; **le G. Lac de l'Ours** Great Bear Lake; **le G. Lac Salé** the Great Salt Lake; **les Grands Lacs** the Great Lakes; **les Grandes Plaines** the Great Plains

10 *Géom* **g. axe** major axis; **g. cercle** great circle

11 *Zool* **les grands animaux** (the) larger animals; **grands chiens** big dogs

B. *ASPECT QUALITATIF* **1** *(important)* great, major; **de grands progrès** great progress *or* strides; **les grands thèmes de son œuvre** the major themes in his/her work

2 *(acharné, invétéré)* great, keen; **un g. amateur de livres rares** a great *or* keen collector of rare books; **c'est un g. travailleur** he's a hard worker, he's hard-working; **tu n'es qu'une grande menteuse** you're just a big liar; **c'est une grande timide** she's really shy; **ce sont de grands amis** they're great *or* very good friends; **un g. buveur** a heavy drinker; **grands fumeurs** heavy smokers; **g. invalide civil** severely disabled person; **les grands blessés/brûlés/invalides** the seriously wounded/burned/disabled; **les grands handicapés** the severely handicapped

3 *(puissant, influent ▸ banque)* top; *(▸ industriel)* top, leading, major; *(▸ propriétaire, famille)* important; *(▸ personnage)* great

4 *(dans une hiérarchie)* **les grands dignitaires du régime** the leading *or* important dignitaries of the regime; *Pol* **grands électeurs** *(en France)* = body electing members of the (French) Senate; *(aux États-Unis)* presidential electors; *Écon* **le G. Marché (européen)** the European Market; **le G. rabbin (de France)** the Chief Rabbi (of France); **les grands corps de l'État** the major public bodies

5 *(noble)* **de grande naissance** of high *or* noble birth; **avoir g. air** *ou* **grande allure** to carry oneself well, to be imposing

6 *(généreux)* **c'est un g. cœur** his/her heart is in the right place; **il a un g. cœur** he's big-hearted, he has a big heart; **une grande âme** a noble soul

7 *(exagéré)* big; **de grands gestes** extravagant gestures; **de grandes promesses** big promises; **grands mots** high-sounding words, high-flown language; **grandes phrases** high-flown phrases

8 *(fameux, reconnu)* great; **un g. homme** a great man; **un g. journaliste** a great *or* top journalist; **un des plus grands spécialistes** one of the greatest *or* top experts; **un g. esprit/talent** a great mind/talent; **il a accompli de grandes choses** he has accomplished great things; **une grande œuvre d'art** a great work of art; **son dernier essai est un g. texte** his/her latest essay is a brilliant piece of writing; **les grands textes classiques** the classics; **il ne descend que dans les grands hôtels** he only stays in the best hotels *or* the most luxurious hotels; **le g. jour** the big day; **les grandes dates de l'histoire de France** the great *or* most significant dates in French history; **un g. nom** a great name; **un g. nom de la peinture contemporaine** one of today's great painters; **les grands couturiers** the top fashion designers

9 *Hist* **la Grande Armée** the Grande Armée; **la Grande Catherine** Catherine the Great; **le G. Turc** the Grand Turk

10 *(omnipotent, suprême)* great; **Dieu est g.** God is great

C. *EN INTENSIF* great; **avec une (très) grande facilité** with (the greatest of) ease; **sans g. enthousiasme/intérêt** without much enthusiasm/interest; **sa grande fierté, c'est son jardin** he's/she's very proud of *or* he/she takes great pride in his/her garden; **quel g. bonheur de t'avoir parmi nous!** how happy we all are to have you with us!; **c'était un g. moment** it was a great moment; **il était dans un g. état de fatigue** he was extremely tired; **un g. merci à ta sœur** *or* a big thank you to your sister; **c'est le g. amour!** it's true love!; **Robert fut son g. amour** Robert was the love of her life; **tu aurais g. avantage à la prévenir** you'd be well advised to warn her; **cette cuisine a g. besoin d'être nettoyée** this kitchen really needs *or* is in dire need of a clean; **ça m'a fait le plus g. bien** it did me a power of *or* the world of good; **il en a pensé le plus g. bien** he thought most highly of it; **g. bien lui fasse!** much good may it do him/her!; **faire g. cas de** to set great store by; **toute la famille au g. complet** the whole family, every single member of the family; **à sa grande honte** to his/her great shame; **jamais, au g. jamais je n'accepterai** never in a million years will I accept; **il n'y a pas g. mal à demander des précisions** there's no harm in asking for further details; **il est parti de g. matin** he left at the crack of dawn; **il n'y avait pas g. monde à son concert** there weren't many people at his/her concert; **pour notre plus g. plaisir** to our (great) delight; **prendre g. soin de** to take great care of; **à sa grande surprise** much to his/her surprise, to his/her great surprise; **il est g. temps que tu le lises** it's high time you read it

NM,F 1 *(enfant d'un certain âge)* **l'école des grands** primary school; **merci, mon g.!** *(en appellatif)* thanks, son!; **allons, ma grande, ne pleure pas!** come on now, love, don't cry!

2 *(adulte)* grown-up, adult; **un jeu pour petits et grands** a game for young and old (alike); **alors, ma grande, tu as pu te reposer un peu?** well dear, did you manage to get some rest?

3 *(personne de grande taille)* **pour la photo, les grands se mettront derrière** for the photo, tall people *or* the taller people will stand at the back

NM 1 *voir* **infiniment**

2 *(entrepreneur, industriel)* **un g. de la mode** a leading light in the fashion business; **les grands de l'automobile** the major *or* leading car manufacturers

ADV 1 *(dans l'habillement)* **c'est un modèle qui chausse g.** this is a large-fitting shoe; **ça devrait vous aller, ça taille g.** it should fit you, it's cut large

2 *(largement)* **g. ouvert** wide-open; **elle dort la fenêtre g.** *ou* **grande ouverte** she sleeps with the window wide open *or* open wide; **il avait maintenant les yeux g.** *ou* **grands ouverts** now he had his eyes wide open

3 *Beaux-Arts* **représenter qch plus g. que nature** to enlarge sth

4 *(locution)* **voir g.** *(avoir de vastes projets)* to think big; **ils ont vu trop g.** they bit off more than they could chew; **elle voit g. pour son fils** she's got great hopes for her son

• **grande NF** *Can Aut* top (gear); *Fig* **en grande** at top speed, in a rush

• **grands NMPL** *Écon & Pol* **les grands** *(les puissants)* the rich (and powerful); **les grands de ce monde** the people in (positions of) power *or* in high places; *Pol* **les deux Grands** the two superpowers

• **en grand ADV 1** *(complètement)* on a large scale; **il faut aérer la maison en g.** the house needs a thorough *or* good airing; *Fig* **il a fait les choses en g.** he really did things properly **2** *Naut* **gouverner en g.** to make a heading; **navire en g. sur un bord** ship listing heavily to one side **3** *Can (beaucoup)* a lot; *(très)* very; **il est laid en g.** he's very *or* really ugly

grand-angle [grɑ̃tɑ̃gl] *(pl* **grands-angles** [grɑ̃zɑ̃gl]*)*, **grand-angulaire** [grɑ̃tɑ̃gylɛr] *(pl* **grands-angulaires** [grɑ̃zɑ̃gylɛr]*)* **NM** *Phot* wide-angle lens

grand-chose [grɑ̃ʃoz] **PRON INDÉFINI pas g.** not much; **ce ne sont que quelques fleurs, ce n'est pas g.** it's just a few flowers, nothing much; **ce que je te demande, ce n'est pas g.** I'm not asking you for much; **je n'y comprends pas g.** I don't understand much of it; **plus g.** not much (left); **il ne me reste plus g. à dire** there's not much more (left) to say; **il n'y a plus g. à manger** there's not much left to eat

grand-croix [grɑ̃krwa] *(pl* **grands-croix)** **NF** Grand Cross *(in various orders, including the "Légion d'honneur")*

NMF holder *or* Knight of the Grand Cross

grand-duc [grɑ̃dyk] *(pl* **grands-ducs)** **NM 1** *(titre)* grand duke **2** *Orn* eagle owl

grand-ducal [grɑ̃dykal] *(mpl* **grand-ducaux** [-o], *fpl* **grand-ducales)** **ADJ 1** *(du grand-duc)* grand-ducal **2** *(du grand-duché)* of the grand duchy

grand-duché [grɑ̃dyʃe] *(pl* **grands-duchés)** **NM** grand duchy

Grande-Bretagne [grɑ̃dbrətaɲ] **NF la G.** (Great) Britain

grande-duchesse [grɑ̃ddyʃɛs] *(pl* **grandes-duchesses)** **NF** grand duchess

grandelet, -ette [grɑ̃dlɛ, -ɛt] **ADJ** *Fam Vieilli* tallish

grandement [grɑ̃dmɑ̃] **ADV 1** *(largement)* absolutely; **si c'est là votre opinion, vous vous trompez g.!** if that is what you believe, you are very much mistaken!; **vous avez g. raison/tort** you are quite right/wrong; **nous avons g. le temps** we have ample time; **avoir g. de quoi vivre** to have plenty to live on

2 *(beaucoup)* a great deal, greatly; **il m'a g. aidée** he helped me a great deal, he's been a great help to me; **être g. reconnaissant à qn de qch** to be truly grateful to sb for sth

3 *(généreusement)* **vous avez fait les choses g.!** you've done things in great style!; **ils ne seront pas g. logés** their accommodation will be nothing grand *or* special

4 *(noblement)* grandly, nobly

grandeur [grɑ̃dœr] **NF 1** *(taille)* size; *(d'un arbre)* height, size; **deux vases de la même g.** two vases (of) the same size; **dimensions données en vraie g.** full-size measurement; **(en) g. nature** life-size

2 *(importance)* importance; *(d'un amour, d'une folie)* greatness; **se donner des airs de g.** to give oneself airs (and graces)

3 *(noblesse)* greatness; **avec g.** nobly; **la g. de son sacrifice** the greatness *or* the beauty of his/her sacrifice; **la g. humaine** the greatness of man; **g. d'âme** generosity of spirit, magnanimity

4 *(splendeur)* grandeur, splendour; **la g. de Rome** the grandeur *or* greatness of Rome; **g. et décadence de Byzance** rise and fall of Byzantium

5 *Arch* **Votre G.** Your Grace; **Sa G. l'archevêque** His Grace the Archbishop

6 *Astron* magnitude; **étoile de première g.** star of the first magnitude

7 *Math & Phys* **chiffres de la même g.** figures of the same magnitude; **g. de sortie** output; **grandeurs énergétiques** energy consumption and supply

grand-guignol [grɑ̃giɲɔl] **NM** *Fam* **c'est du g.** it's all blood and thunder

grand-guignolesque [grɑ̃giɲɔlɛsk] *(pl* **grand-guignolesques)** **ADJ** *(personne)* blood-and-thunder; *(pièce de théâtre, film)* gruesome

grandiloquence [grɑ̃dilɔkɑ̃s] **NF** grandiloquence, *Péj* pomposity

grandiloquent, -e [grɑ̃dilɔkɑ̃, -ɑ̃t] **ADJ** grandiloquent, *Péj* pompous

grandiose [grɑ̃djoz] ADJ *(cérémonie, proportions)* imposing, grandiose; *(spectacle, vue)* imposing, awe-inspiring; **la gaffe était g.** it was an incredible blunder

grandir [32] [grɑ̃dir] VI **1** *(devenir grand)* to grow; **elle a grandi** she has grown, she is taller; **sa fille a grandi de cinq centimètres** her daughter is five centimetres taller (than when I last saw her); **je te trouve grandie** you've grown *or* you look taller since I last saw you; **un enfant qui aurait grandi trop vite** a lanky child; **un arbre qui grandit vite** a tree which grows quickly, a fast-growing tree; **le lait, ça fait g.** milk makes you big and strong
2 *(mûrir)* to grow up; **j'ai compris en grandissant** I understood as I grew up *or* older
3 *(s'intensifier ▸ bruit)* to increase, to grow louder; *(▸ influence, importance)* to increase; **une inquiétude qui grandit** a growing *or* an increasing feeling of unease; **sa faim allait grandissant** he/she grew more and more hungry
4 *(s'étendre ▸ ville)* to spread
5 *Fig* **g. en force/sagesse/beauté** to get stronger/wiser/more beautiful, to grow in strength/wisdom/beauty; **il a grandi dans mon estime** he has gone up in my esteem
VT **1** *(faire paraître plus grand)* **ces talons hauts la grandissent encore** these high-heeled shoes make her (look) even taller **2** *(surestimer)* **g. l'importance de qch** to exaggerate *or* overstate the importance of sth **3** *(ennoblir)* **notre profession sort grandie de cette longue lutte** our profession emerges from this long struggle with greater prestige; **il est sorti grandi de ce conflit/de cette épreuve** he came out of this conflict/the ordeal a stronger person; **cela ne la grandit pas à mes yeux** that does not improve her standing in my eyes
VPR **se grandir 1** *(vouloir paraître plus grand)* to make oneself (look) taller; *(vouloir paraître plus important)* to show oneself in the best possible light; **se g. en se haussant sur la pointe des pieds** to make oneself taller by standing on tiptoe **2** *(s'élever en dignité)* **elle s'est grandie en ne révélant rien** she has improved her reputation *or* people's opinion of her by disclosing nothing

grandissant, -e [grɑ̃disɑ̃, -ɑ̃t] ADJ *(effectifs, douleur, renommée)* growing, increasing; *(vacarme)* growing; *(pénombre)* deepening

grandissement [grɑ̃dismɑ̃] NM **1** *Opt* magnification **2** *Vieilli (fait d'agrandir)* growth, increase

grandissime [grɑ̃disim] ADJ *Hum* extraordinary, marvellous; **le g. favori** the firm favourite

grand-livre [grɑ̃livr] *(pl* **grands-livres**) NM ledger; **porter qch au g.** to enter sth in the ledger; **g. d'achats** purchase ledger; **le g. (de la dette publique)** the National Debt register; **g. général** nominal ledger; **g. de ventes** sales ledger

grand-maman [grɑ̃mamɑ̃] *(pl* **grand-mamans** *ou* **grands-mamans**) NF *Suisse & Can (en langage enfantin)* granny, grandma

grand-mère [grɑ̃mɛr] *(pl* **grand-mères** *ou* **grands-mères**) NF **1** *(aïeule)* grandmother **2** *Fam (vieille femme)* little old lady, old granny, *Péj* old biddy

grand-messe [grɑ̃mɛs] *(pl* **grand-messes** *ou* **grands-messes**) NF **1** *Rel* High Mass **2** *Fig* **la g. du parti** the party jamboree

grand-monde [grɑ̃mɔ̃d] NM *Can (adultes)* grown-ups

grand-oncle [grɑ̃tɔ̃kl] *(pl* **grands-oncles** [grɑ̃zɔ̃kl]) NM great-uncle

grand-papa [grɑ̃papa] *(pl* **grands-papas**) NM *Suisse & Can (en langage enfantin)* grandpa, grandad

grand-peine [grɑ̃pɛn] **à grand-peine** ADV with great difficulty

grand-père [grɑ̃pɛr] *(pl* **grands-pères**) NM **1** *(parent)* grandfather **2** *Fam (vieil homme) Br* grandad, *Am* old-timer

grand-prêtre [grɑ̃prɛtr] *(pl* **grands-prêtres**) NM high priest

grand-route [grɑ̃rut] *(pl* **grand-routes**) NF main road

grand-rue [grɑ̃ry] *(pl* **grand-rues**) NF high *or Br* main street, *Am* mainstreet

grands-parents [grɑ̃parɑ̃] NMPL grandparents

grand-tante [grɑ̃tɑ̃t] *(pl* **grand-tantes** *ou* **grands-tantes**) NF great-aunt

grand-vergue [grɑ̃vɛrg] *(pl* **grand-vergues** *ou* **grands-vergues**) NF *Naut* main yard

grand-voile [grɑ̃vwal] *(pl* **grand-voiles** *ou* **grands-voiles**) NF mainsail

grange [grɑ̃ʒ] NF barn

granit, granite [granit] NM *Géol* granite; **de g.** *(indestructible)* granite-like, made of granite; *(insensible)* of stone

granité, -e [granite] ADJ granite-like
NM **1** *(sorbet)* granita **2** *Tex* pebble-weave fabric *or* cloth

graniteux, -euse [granitø, -øz] ADJ granitic

granitique [granitik] ADJ granitic, granite *(avant n)*

granivore [granivɔr] ADJ seed-eating, *Spéc* granivorous
NM seedeater, *Spéc* granivore

granulaire [granylɛr] ADJ granular, granulous

granulation [granylasjɔ̃] NF **1** *(d'une substance)* graining, granulation **2** *Méd* granulation

granule [granyl] NM **1** *(particule)* (small) grain, granule; *(pour animaux)* pellet **2** *Pharm* (small) tablet, pill

granulé, -e [granyle] ADJ *(surface)* granular; *(présentation)* granulated
NM granule

granuler [3] [granyle] VT to granulate

granuleux, -euse [granylø, -øz] ADJ **1** *(aspect)* granular, grainy **2** *Méd* granular; *Biol* **cellule granuleuse** granule cell

grape-fruit *(pl* **grape-fruits**), **grapefruit** [grɛpfrut] NM grapefruit

graphe [graf] NM **1** *Math* graph **2** *Ordinat* graph; **g. complet/non orienté** complete/indirected graph **3** *Mktg* graph, chart; **g. en ligne** line chart

grapheur [grafœr] NM *Ordinat* graphics package

graphie [grafi] NF *Ling* written form

graphique [grafik] ADJ **1** *(relatif au dessin)* graphic
2 *(relatif à l'écriture)* written
3 *Ordinat* **informatique g.** computer graphics *(singulier)*
4 *Math* graphical
NM **1** *(schéma)* graph, chart; **tracer un g.** to plot a graph; **faire le g. de qch** to chart sth; **g. des activités** activity chart; **g. à** *ou* **en barres** bar chart; **g. circulaire** pie chart; **g. en colonnes** bar chart; **g. d'évolution** flow chart; **g. à secteurs** pie chart; **g. de type camembert** pie chart; **g. de type lignes** line chart **2** *(de température)* chart **3** *Ordinat* graphic
NF graphics *(singulier)*

> Il faut noter que l'adjectif anglais **graphic** signifie également **détaillé** ou **cru**, selon le contexte.

graphiquement [grafikmɑ̃] ADV graphically

graphisme [grafism] NM **1** *(écriture)* handwriting **2** *(dessin)* **un g. vigoureux** a vigorously executed drawing; **le g. de Dürer** Dürer's draughtsmanship **3** *Ordinat* **graphismes** graphics

graphiste [grafist] NMF graphic artist

graphitage [grafitaʒ] NM *Tech* graphitization

graphite [grafit] NM graphite; **lubrifiant au g.** graphite lubricant

graphiteux, -euse [grafitø, -øz], **graphitique** [grafitik] ADJ graphitic

graphologie [grafɔlɔʒi] NF graphology

graphologique [grafɔlɔʒik] ADJ graphological

graphologue [grafɔlɔg] NMF graphologist

grappe [grap] NF **1** *(de fruits)* bunch; *(de fleurs)* cluster; **g. de raisins** bunch of grapes; *Fig* **grappes humaines** clusters of people
2 *Bot* raceme
3 *Ordinat (de terminaux)* cluster
4 *Vulg* **lâche-moi la g.!** piss off!
• **en grappe(s)** ADV *(tomber ▸ fleurs)* in bunches

> Il faut noter que le nom anglais **grape** est un faux ami. Il signifie **grain de raisin**.

grappillage [grapijaʒ] NM **1** *(de raisin)* gleaning **2** *(d'argent) Br* fiddling, *Am* chiseling

grappiller [3] [grapije] VI **1** *Littéraire (après la vendange)* to glean, to gather grapes left after the harvest **2** *(faire de petits profits)* to be on the take *or Br* the fiddle
VT **1** *Littéraire (cerises, prunes)* to pick; *(brindilles)* to gather; *(fleurs)* to pick, to gather
2 *(argent) Br* to fiddle, *Am* to chisel
3 *(temps)* **elle grappille tous les jours une demi-heure sur l'horaire** she sneaks off half an hour early every day
4 *(renseignements)* to pick up; **on n'a pu g. que quelques détails insignifiants** we could only pick up a few minor clues

grappin [grapɛ̃] NM **1** *Naut (ancre)* grapnel; *(d'abordage)* grappling iron
2 *(de levage)* grab; *(d'une grue)* clutch
3 *(pour grimper)* grappler, climbing iron
4 *Fam (locution)* **mettre le g. sur qn/qch** to get one's hands on *or* get hold of sb/sth

GRAS, GRASSE [gra, gras]

ADJ	
• fatty **A1, 6**	• fat **A2**
• greasy **A3, 4**	• crude **A5**
• sticky **B1**	• slippery **B2**
• throaty **B3**	• thick **B5**
NM	
• fat **1**	• fleshy part **2**
• grease **3**	

ADJ **A. 1** *Culin* fatty; **ne mettez pas trop de matière grasse** don't add too much fat; **fromage g.** full-fat cheese; **évitez la cuisine grasse** avoid fatty foods
2 *(dodu)* fat, plump; **il est très g.** he's very fat; **être g. comme un chanoine** *ou* **un cochon, être g. à lard** to be as round as a barrel
3 *(huileux)* greasy, oily; *(taché)* greasy
4 *(peau, cheveux)* greasy
5 *(vulgaire)* crude, coarse
6 *Chim* fatty; **série grasse** acyl group
7 *Rel* **jours g.** meat days
B. 1 *(terre, boue)* sticky, slimy
2 *(pavé)* slippery
3 *(voix, rire)* throaty
4 *Littéraire (abondant ▸ récompense)* generous; *(▸ pâturage)* rich; *Fam* **ce n'est pas g.** *(peu de chose)* that's not much; *(profit médiocre)* it's not a fortune; **l'herbe grasse était douce sous le pied** the thick grass was soft underfoot
5 *(épais ▸ gén)* thick; *(▸ trait)* bold; *(▸ caractère)* bold, bold-faced; *Typ* **en g.** in bold (type)
6 *Méd (toux)* phlegmy
7 *(vin, bierre etc)* ropy
8 *(locution)* **faire la grasse matinée** to stay in bed (very) late, *Br* to have a long lie-in
NM **1** *(d'une viande)* fat; *Culin* **au g.** cooked with meat stock
2 *(du corps)* fleshy part; **le g. de la jambe** the calf
3 *(substance)* grease; **j'ai les doigts pleins de g.** my fingers are covered in grease; **des taches de g.** greasy stains
ADV **1** *(dans l'alimentation)* **il mange trop g.** he eats too much fatty food
2 *Rel* **faire g.** to eat meat
3 *(en grasseyant)* **parler g.** to pronounce one's Rs in the back of the throat
4 *Fam (beaucoup)* **il n'y a pas g. à manger** there's not much to eat; **il y a pas g. de monde dans les rues aujourd'hui** there's not many people out today

gras-double [gradubl] *(pl* **gras-doubles**) NM *Culin* (ox) tripe

grasse [gras] *voir* **gras**

grassement [grasmɑ̃] ADV **1** *(largement)* handsomely; **g. payé** *ou* **rémunéré** generously *or* handsomely paid; *Littéraire* **vivre g.** to live off the fat of the land **2** *(vulgairement)* coarsely, crudely; **plaisanter g.** to make coarse *or* crude jokes

grasseyement [grasɛjmɑ̃] NM **le g. des Parisiens** = the Parisian way of pronouncing Rs from the back of the throat

grasseyer [12] [graseje] **VI** to pronounce one's Rs from the back of the throat

VT *Ling* **un R grasseyé** a uvular R

grassouillet, -ette [grasujɛ, -ɛt] **ADJ** *Br* podgy, *Am* pudgy

grateron [gratrɔ̃] **NM** *Bot* goose-grass, cleavers *(singulier)*

graticiel [gratisjel] **NM** *Ordinat* freeware

gratifiant, -e [gratifjɑ̃, -ɑ̃t] **ADJ** gratifying, rewarding

gratification [gratifikasjɔ̃] **NF 1** *(pourboire)* tip; *(prime)* bonus; **g. de fin d'année** Christmas *or* end-of-year bonus **2** *(satisfaction)* gratification *(UNCOUNT)*

> Il faut noter que le nom anglais **gratification** ne signifie jamais **prime**.

gratifier [9] [gratifje] **VT 1** *(satisfaire)* to gratify; **sa réussite a beaucoup gratifié ses parents** his/her success was very gratifying for his/her parents **2 g. qn d'une récompense** to present sb with a reward; *Ironique* **être gratifié d'une amende** to be landed with a fine; **elle m'a gratifié d'un sourire** she favoured me with a smile; **et je fus gratifié d'une paire de gifles** and my reward was a slap in the face

gratin [gratɛ̃] **NM 1** *Culin (plat ▸ recouvert de fromage)* gratin *(dish with a topping of toasted cheese)*; *(▸ recouvert de chapelure)* = dish with a crispy topping; **un g. de poisson** a fish gratin; **g. dauphinois** gratin dauphinois, = sliced potatoes baked with cream and browned on top; **g. de macaronis** *Br* macaroni cheese, *Am* macaroni and cheese **2** *(croûte ▸ de fromage)* cheese topping; *(▸ de chapelure)* crispy topping **3** *Fam (élite)* **le g.** the upper crust

• **au gratin ADJ** au gratin, (cooked) with (breadcrumbs and) grated cheese; **chou-fleur au g.** ≃ cauliflower cheese

gratiné, -e [gratine] **ADJ 1** *Culin (doré)* browned; *(cuit au gratin)* (cooked) au gratin **2** *Fam (addition)* huge; *(examen, problème)* tough; **elle va avoir droit à un savon g.!** she's in for a real telling-off!; **dans le genre paresseux, il est g.!** he's as lazy as can be!

• **gratinée NF** French onion soup

gratiner [3] [gratine] **VT** *(cuire en gratin)* to cook au gratin; *(dorer)* to brown

VI to brown; **faire g. qch, mettre qch à g.** to brown sth; **faire g. avant de servir** brown under the grill before serving

gratis [gratis] *Fam* **ADV** free (of charge)❑; **il a fait la réparation g.** he repaired it for nothing❑

ADJ free❑

gratitude [gratityd] **NF** gratitude, gratefulness

gratos [gratɔs] **ADJ** *Fam* free (of charge)❑

gratouiller [3] [gratuje] = **grattouiller**

grattage [grataʒ] **NM** *(avec des griffes, des ongles, une plume)* scratching; *(avec quelque chose de dur)* scraping; **effacer qch par g.** to scratch sth out; **gagner au g.** *(à la loterie)* to win on the scratchcards

gratte [grat] **NF 1** *Fam (profit)* **faire de la g.** to make a bit on the side

2 *Fam (guitare)* guitar❑

3 *Can (outil)* scraper; *(machine) Br* snowplough, *Am* snow-pusher

4 *Belg (griffure)* scratch; *(éraflure)* scratch, scrape

gratte-ciel [gratsjel] **NM INV** skyscraper

gratte-cul [gratky] **NM INV** *Fam* rosehip❑

gratte-dos [gratdo] **NM INV** backscratcher

grattement [gratmɑ̃] **NM** scratching; **elle entendit un léger g. à la porte** she heard a gentle scratching at the door

gratte-papier [gratpapje] **NM INV** *Fam Péj* penpusher

gratte-pieds [gratpje] **NM INV** shoe scraper, metal doormat

gratter [3] [grate] **VT 1** *(avec des griffes, des ongles, une plume)* to scratch; *(avec quelque chose de dur)* to scrape; **g. la terre du pied** *(cheval)* to paw the ground; **g. le dos à qn** to scratch sb's back

2 *(frotter ▸ allumette)* to strike; *(▸ métal oxydé)* to scrape, to rub; *(▸ couche de saleté)* to scrape *or* to rub off; **g. une vieille peinture/du vieux papier peint** to scrape off old paint/old wallpaper

3 *(effacer)* to scratch out; *(tache)* to scrape off

4 *(irriter)* **une chemise/un pull-over qui gratte la peau** a shirt/sweater which makes you itch, an itchy shirt/sweater; *Fam* **ça me gratte** it's itchy; *Fam* **un gros rouge qui gratte la gorge** a rough red wine which catches in the throat

5 *Fam (grappiller) Br* to fiddle, *Am* to chisel; **il n'y a pas grand-chose à g.** there's not much to be made out of that, there isn't much money in that

6 *Fam (devancer)* to overtake❑; **on s'est fait g. par la concurrence** we were overtaken by our competitors

VI 1 *(plume)* to scratch; **prête-moi une plume, la mienne gratte** lend me a pen, mine keeps scratching (the paper)

2 *(faire du bruit)* **g. à la porte** to tap lightly at the door; **ces vieux disques grattent beaucoup** these old records are very scratchy *or* crackly

3 *(tissu, laine, pull)* to itch, to be itchy

4 *Fam (jouer de)* **g. du violon** to scrape away at the violin

5 *Fam (approfondir)* **il a l'air très cultivé, mais si tu grattes un peu...** he has a very cultured air, but if you scratch away his veneer a bit...

6 *Fam (travailler)* to work❑, to do odd jobs; *(écrire)* to scribble; **il gratte quelques heures par semaine chez un avocat** he does a few hours a week in a lawyer's office

VPR se gratter to scratch (oneself), to have a scratch; **se g. la tête/le bras** to scratch one's head/arm; *très Fam* **tu peux toujours te g.!** you'll be lucky!

gratteron [gratrɔ̃] = **grateron**

gratteux, -euse [gratø, -øz] *Fam* **ADJ** *Can* stingy, mean

NM,F 1 *Can (avare)* miser **2** *(joueur de guitare)* guitarist❑

grattoir [gratwar] **NM 1** *(de bureau)* erasing-knife **2** *(de graveur)* scraper; *Typ* slice **3** *(de boîte d'allumettes)* striking surface

grattons [gratɔ̃] **NMPL** crackling *(UNCOUNT)*

grattouiller [3] [gratuje] **VT** *Fam* **1** *(démanger)* **ça me grattouille** it makes me itch❑, it's itchy **2** *(guitare)* to strum away on

gratuiciel [gratyisjel] = **graticiel**

gratuit, -e [gratɥi, -it] **ADJ 1** *(en cadeau)* free; **entrée gratuite** *(concert, musée)* admission free; **c'est g.** it's free, there's no charge; **à titre g.** gratis, free of charge **2** *(sans fondement)* unwarranted, unfounded; **tu fais là une supposition tout à fait gratuite** your assumption is absolutely unwarranted *or* unfounded **3** *(absurde ▸ acte, violence)* gratuitous

NM *(magazine)* free magazine

gratuité [gratɥite] **NF 1** *(accès non payant)* **nous voulons la g. de l'enseignement/des livres scolaires** we want free education/schoolbooks **2** *(absence de motif ▸ d'une accusation, d'un acte violent)* gratuitousness; *(▸ d'une supposition)* unwarranted *or* unfounded nature; **la g. d'un tel acte** the gratuitousness of such an act

> Il faut noter que le nom anglais **gratuity** est un faux ami. Il signifie **pourboire**.

gratuitement [gratɥitmɑ̃] **ADV 1** *(sans payer)* free (of charge); **pour deux livres achetés, ils en donnent un g.** if you buy two books, they give you one free **2** *(sans motif)* gratuitously, for no reason; **vous l'agressez g., elle ne vous a rien fait!** you're attacking her for no reason, she hasn't done you any harm!

gravats [grava] **NMPL 1** *(décombres)* rubble *(UNCOUNT)* **2** *(de plâtre)* screenings

grave [grav] **ADJ 1** *(après le nom) (solennel)* grave, solemn; **il la dévisageait, l'air g.** he stared at her solemnly

2 *(sérieux ▸ motif, problème, blessure, maladie)* serious; *(▸ opération)* serious, major; **une faute g.** a grave error; **ce n'est pas g.!** never mind!, it doesn't matter!; **c'est g.!** it's serious!; **elle a eu une g. maladie** she's been seriously ill; **hélas!, il y avait plus g.** alas! there was worse to come

3 *Mus & (en acoustique ▸ note)* low; *(▸ voix)* deep; **un son g.** a bass *or* low note

4 *(accent)* grave

5 *Fam (dérangé)* **il est g.** he's not all there, he's off his rocker *or Br* head

6 *Arch (lourd)* heavy; *Phys* **corps g.** heavy body

NM *Mus* **le g.** the low register; **les graves et les aigus** low and high notes, the low and high registers

NF *(en travaux publics)* aggregate

ADV *Fam* in a bad way; **il me prend la tête g.** he really *or Br* seriously bugs me

gravé, -e [grave] **ADJ pierre gravée** engraved stone; **image gravée** graven image

graveleux, -euse [gravlø, -øz] **ADJ 1** *(grivois)* smutty **2** *Géog* gravelly **3** *(fruit)* gritty

gravelle [gravel] **NF** *Arch Méd* gravel

gravement [gravmɑ̃] **ADV 1** *(solennellement)* gravely, solemnly **2** *(en intensif)* **g. handicapé** severely disabled; **g. malade/blessé** seriously ill/injured; **être g. menacé** to face a serious threat; **tu t'es g. trompé** you've made a serious *or* big mistake

graver [3] [grave] **VT 1** *(tracer ▸ sur métal, sur pierre)* to carve, to engrave; *(▸ sur bois)* to carve

2 *Fig* **cela reste gravé dans ma mémoire** *ou* **en moi** it is engraved on my memory; **la souffrance était gravée sur son visage** suffering was written on his/her face; *Hum* **ce n'est pas gravé sur son front** you can't tell from looking at him/her

3 *Typ (imprimer)* to print

4 *Beaux-Arts* to engrave; **g. à l'eau-forte** to etch

5 *(disque, CD)* to cut; **le dernier album qu'ils ont gravé n'a pas marché** the last album they made wasn't a success

6 *Ordinat (CD-ROM)* to write, to burn

graveur, -euse [gravœr, -øz] **NM,F** *(personne)* engraver, carver; **g. sur bois** wood engraver *or* cutter; **g. à l'eau-forte** etcher

NM 1 *(pour disques)* cutter **2** *Ordinat (de CD-ROM)* writer, burner

gravide [gravid] **ADJ** *Méd* pregnant, *Spéc* gravid; **truie g.** sow in pig

gravier [gravje] **NM 1** *Géol* grit, gravel **2** *(petits cailloux)* gravel; **couvrir une allée de g.** to gravel a path; **allée de g.** gravel path

gravillon [gravijɔ̃] **NM 1** *(caillou)* piece of gravel *or* grit **2** *(revêtement)* grit *(UNCOUNT)*, fine gravel; *(UNCOUNT)* **gravillons** *(panneau sur la route) Br* loose chippings, *Am* gravel

gravillonnage [gravijɔnaʒ] **NM** gritting

gravillonner [3] [gravijɔne] **VT** to grit

gravimétrie [gravimetri] **NF** gravimetry

gravimétrique [gravimetrik] **ADJ** gravimetric, gravimetrical

gravir [32] [gravir] **VT 1** *(montagne, escalier, échelle)* to climb; **il gravit les marches d'un pas lourd** he trudged up the steps **2** *Fig (dans une hiérarchie)* **g. les échelons** to climb the ladder; **il faut g. (tous) les échelons** you must go up through the ranks; **quand elle aura gravi tous les échelons** once she's got to the top

gravissime [gravisim] **ADJ** extremely serious

gravitation [gravitasjɔ̃] **NF** *Phys* gravitation

gravitationnel, -elle [gravitasjɔnel] **ADJ** gravitational; **force gravitationnelle** force of gravity

gravité [gravite] **NF 1** *(sérieux, dignité)* seriousness, solemnity; **son visage exprimait une profonde g.** he/she looked very solemn *or* serious; **l'enfant la dévisagea avec g.** the child stared at her solemnly

2 *(importance)* seriousness, gravity; **tu ne perçois pas la g. du problème** you don't realize the seriousness *or* gravity of the problem

3 *(caractère alarmant)* seriousness; *(d'une blessure)* severity; **une blessure sans g.** a slight *or* minor wound; **une chute/maladie sans g.** a minor fall/ailment

4 *(pesanteur)* gravity; **g. spécifique** specific gravity; **alimentation par g.** gravity feed

graviter [3] [gravite] **VI 1** *Astron* **g. autour de** to revolve *or* to orbit around; **g. autour de la terre** to orbit the earth **2** *Fig (évoluer)* **g. autour de qn** to hover around sb; **il a toujours gravité dans les sphères gouvernementales** he has always moved in government circles **3** *Vieilli (tendre)* to gravitate (**vers** towards)

gravois [gravwa] = **gravats**

gravure [gravyr] **NF 1** *(tracé en creux)* engraving; **g. en creux** intaglio engraving; **g. sur bois** *(procédé)* woodcutting; *(objet)* woodcut; **g. sur pierre** stone carving; **g. sur verre** glass engraving **2** *Typ (processus)* engraving, imprinting; **g. sur cuivre** *(procédé)* copperplating; *(plaque)* copperplate; **g. à l'eau-forte** etching; *(image)* engraving, etching; **g. en taille-douce** copperplate engraving; **une g. de Dürer** an engraving by Dürer; **g. de mode** fashion plate; **habillé** *ou* **vêtu comme une g. de mode** dressed like a fashion model; **g. en couleurs** colour print; **g. hors texte** full-page plate; **g. avant la lettre** proof before letters

grayé, -e [greje] **ADJ** *Can (pour faire quelque chose)* well-equipped; *Fam (bien monté)* well-hung

gré [gre] **NM 1** *(goût, convenance)* **à mon g., selon mon g.** to my liking, to my taste; **prenez n'importe quelle chaise, à votre g.** sit down wherever you wish *or* please; **la chambre est-elle à votre g.?** is the room to your liking?; **il est trop jeune à mon g.** he's too young for my liking; **trouver qch à son g.** to find sth to one's liking **2** *(volonté, accord)* **à mon g., selon mon g.** as I please *or* like; **de mon propre g., de mon plein g.** of my own free will, of my own accord; **elle a toujours agi à son g.** she has always done as she pleases; **je m'habille à mon g.** I dress to please myself; **de bon g.** willingly, gladly; **de mauvais g.** reluctantly; **il la suivit de bon g.** he followed her willingly *or* of his own accord; **on l'a fait signer contre son g.** they made him/her sign against his/her will; **bon g. mal g. il faudra que tu m'écoutes** whether you like it or not you'll have to listen to me; **il le fera, de g. ou de force** he'll do it whether he likes it or not, he'll have to do it willy-nilly **3** *Sout (gratitude)* **savoir g. à qn de qch** to be grateful to sb for sth; **je vous saurais g. de bien vouloir me faire parvenir...** I should be grateful if you would kindly send me...; *Vieilli* **savoir mauvais g. à qn de qch** to be annoyed with sb about sth

• **au gré de** **PRÉP** **le bail est renouvelable au g. du locataire** the lease is renewable at the tenant's request; **au g. des flots** at the mercy of the waves; **se laisser aller au g. du courant** to let oneself drift along with the current

• **de gré à gré** **ADV** *Jur* by mutual agreement; **vendre de g. à g.** to sell by private contract, to sell privately

grèbe [grɛb] **NM** *Orn* grebe

grébiche [grebiʃ], **grébige** [grebiʒ] **NF** *Typ* **1** *(numéro d'ordre)* file number **2** *(classeur)* loose-leaf binder

grec, grecque [grɛk] **ADJ** Greek; **profil g.** Grecian profile

NM *(langue)* Greek; **le g. ancien** ancient Greek; **le g. moderne** modern *or* demotic Greek

• **Grec, Grecque** **NM,F** Greek

• **grecque** **NF 1** *Archit & Beaux-Arts* (Greek) fret, Greek key pattern **2** *Typ (scie)* bookbinder's saw

• **à la grecque** **ADJ** *Culin* (cooked) à la grecque *(in olive oil and spices)*

Grèce [grɛs] **NF la G.** Greece

gréciser [3] [gresize] **VT** *(mot)* to give a Greek form to

gréco-latin, -e [grekɔlatɛ̃, -in] *(mpl* **gréco-latins,** *fpl* **gréco-latines)** **ADJ** Graeco-Latin

gréco-romain, -e [grekɔrɔmɛ̃, -ɛn] *(mpl* **gréco-romains,** *fpl* **gréco-romaines)** **ADJ** Graeco-Roman

grecque [grɛk] *voir* **grec**

gredin, -e [grədɛ̃, -in] **NM,F** rascal, rogue

gredinerie [grədinri] **NF** *Littéraire* **1** *(caractère)* roguishness **2** *(acte)* roguish act

gréement [gremɑ̃] **NM 1** *(voilure)* rigging *(UNCOUNT)*, rig; *(équipement)* gear *(UNCOUNT)*; *(processus)* rigging **2** *(disposition des mâts et des voiles)* rig; **g. marconi** Marconi rig

gréer [15] [gree] **VT** *(navire)* to rig; *(hamac, filets)* to sling; **gréé en carré** square-rigged; **g. une vergue** to send up a yard

gréeur [greœr] **NM** *Naut* rigger

greffage [grefaʒ] **NM** *Hort* grafting

greffe[1] [grɛf] **NM 1** *Jur* clerk's office, clerk of the court's office; **g. du tribunal de commerce** commercial court **2** *Fin (de société par actions)* registry **3** *Suisse (secrétariat)* town hall secretary's office; *(secrétaire)* town hall secretary

greffe[2] [grɛf] **NF 1** *Hort (processus)* grafting; *(pousse)* graft; **g. par œil détaché** budding **2** *Méd (d'un organe, de moelle osseuse)* transplant; *(d'un os)* graft; **g. du cœur** heart transplant; **g. cœur-poumon** heart-lung transplant; **g. de la cornée** corneal graft; **g. de peau** skin graft; **g. du rein** kidney transplant

greffé, -e [grefe] **NM,F** transplant patient; **les greffés du cœur** heart-transplant patients

greffer [4] [grefe] **VT 1** *Hort* to graft; **g. sur franc/sauvageon** to graft onto a hybrid/stock **2** *Méd (os, peau)* to graft; *(organe, moelle osseuse)* to transplant; **se faire g. un rein** to have a kidney transplant

VPR se greffer puis d'autres problèmes sont venus se g. là-dessus then additional problems came along *or* arose

greffeur [grefœr] **NM** *Hort* grafter

greffier [grefje] **NM 1** *Jur* clerk (of the court), registrar; **g. en chef** registrar **2** *Fam (chat)* puss, moggy

greffoir [grefwar] **NM** grafting knife

greffon [grefɔ̃] **NM 1** *Hort* graft, *Spéc* scion **2** *Méd (tissu)* graft; *(organe)* transplant

grégaire [gregɛr] **ADJ** gregarious; **l'instinct g.** the herd instinct

> Il faut noter que lorsque l'adjectif anglais **gregarious** s'emploie à propos de personnes, il signifie **sociable**.

grégarisme [gregarism] **NM** gregariousness, herd instinct

grège [grɛʒ] **ADJ** *(soie)* raw, unbleached, undyed

ADJ INV *(couleur)* greyish-beige, beigey-grey

NM greyish-beige, beigey-grey

grégeois [greʒwa] **ADJ M** *Hist & Mil* **feu g.** Greek fire

grégorien, -enne [gregɔrjɛ̃, -ɛn] **ADJ** Gregorian

NM Gregorian chant

grêle[1] [grɛl] **ADJ 1** *(mince et long ▸ jambes)* spindly, thin; *(▸ personne)* skinny; *(▸ tige, silhouette)* slender **2** *(aigu ▸ voix)* reedy

grêle[2] [grɛl] **NF 1** *Météo* hail; **une averse de g.** a hailstorm **2** *Fig* **une g. de coups** a shower of blows; **une g. de flèches** a hail *or* shower of arrows; **une g. d'insultes** a volley of insults

grêlé, -e [grele] **ADJ** *(peau, visage)* pockmarked, pitted

grêler [4] [grele] **V IMPERSONNEL il grêle** it's hailing

VT *(cultures)* to damage by hail; **l'orage a grêlé les vignes** the vines suffered hail damage in the storm

grelin [grəlɛ̃] **NM** hawser

grêlon [grɛlɔ̃] **NM** hailstone

grelot [grəlo] **NM 1** *(clochette)* (small sleigh *or* jingle) bell; *(de traîneau)* sleigh bell **2** *Fam (téléphone)* **passe-moi un coup de g.** give me a buzz

• **grelots** **NMPL** *très Fam* **1** *(testicules)* balls, nuts, *Br* bollocks **2** *(locution)* **avoir les grelots** to have the heebie-jeebies

grelottement [grəlɔtmɑ̃] **NM 1** *(tremblement)* shivering **2** *(sonnerie)* jingling

grelotter [3] [grəlɔte] **VI 1** *(avoir froid)* **ferme la fenêtre, on grelotte** shut the window, it's freezing in here **2** *(trembler)* **g. de froid** to shiver *or* to tremble with cold; **g. de peur** to shake with fear; **g. de fièvre** to shiver with fever **3** *(cloche)* to jingle

greluche [grəlyʃ] **NF** *très Fam Péj* chick, *Br* bird

Grenade [grənad] **NF 1** *(île)* **la G.** Grenada **2** *(ville d'Espagne)* Granada

grenade [grənad] **NF 1** *(projectile)* grenade; **g. d'exercice** training grenade; **g. fumigène/incendiaire/lacrymogène** smoke/incendiary/tear-gas grenade; **g. à fusil/à main** rifle/hand grenade; **g. sous-marine** depth charge **2** *(écusson militaire)* grenade ornament **3** *Bot* pomegranate

grenadier [grənadje] **NM 1** *Mil* grenadier; *(femme)* tall and masculine woman; **boire comme un g.** to drink like a fish **2** *Bot* pomegranate tree

grenadière [grənadjɛr] **NF** *(de fusil)* band

grenadine [grənadin] **NF 1** *(sirop)* grenadine *(bright red fruit syrup used in making drinks)*; **une g.** *(boisson)* a (glass of) grenadine **2** *Tex* grenadine

grenaillage [grənajaʒ] **NM** shot-blasting, steel grit blasting

grenaille [grənaj] **NF 1** *Métal* shot *(UNCOUNT)*, steel grit *(UNCOUNT)*

2 *(plomb de chasse)* shot; **g. de plomb** lead shot

3 *(pour la volaille)* refuse grain *(UNCOUNT)*, tailings

4 *Belg (revêtement)* grit *(UNCOUNT)*, fine gravel *(UNCOUNT)*; **grenailles errantes** *(sur panneau)* loose chippings, *Am* gravel

grenailler [3] [grənaje] **VT** to granulate

grenat [grəna] **NM** *(pierre, couleur)* garnet

ADJ INV garnet, garnet-coloured

grené, -e [grəne] **ADJ** *(dessin)* stippled; *(cuir)* grainy

NM *(de dessin)* stipple; *(de cuir)* grain

greneler [24] [grenle] **VT** to grain

Grenelle [grənɛl] **NM** = summit for discussing an important political issue; **G. de l'environnement** environmental summit; **les accords de G.** = an agreement between the government and trade unions (27 May 1968) improving wages and working conditions and aimed at ending workers' support for student disturbances

grener [19] [grəne] **VI** *(céréales)* to seed

VT 1 *(réduire en grains ▸ poudre à canon)* to granulate; *(▸ cire)* to shred; *(▸ sel)* to grain **2** *(donner un aspect grené à ▸ papier, cuir)* to grain

grènetis [grenti] **NM** milled edge

grenier [grənje] **NM 1** *(combles)* attic; **g. aménagé** converted loft **2** *(à grain)* loft; *(pour grain, fourrage)* granary; **g. à foin** hayloft; **g. à blé** granary; *Fig* **le g. à blé de la France** the granary of France

grenouillage [grənujaʒ] **NM** *Fam* jiggery-pokery *(UNCOUNT)*, skullduggery *(UNCOUNT)*

grenouille [grənuj] **NF 1** *Zool* frog; **g. taureau** *ou* **mugissante** bullfrog; *Fam Fig Péj* **g. de bénitier** *(homme)* Holy Joe; *(femme)* Holy Mary **2** *Fam (cagnotte)* kitty, cash-box[□]; **manger** *ou* **faire sauter la g.** to make off with the kitty

grenouiller [3] [grənuje] **VI** *Fam* to scheme, to connive

grenouillère [grənujɛr] **NF 1** *(pyjama)* sleep-suit, sleeping-suit **2** *(lieu)* frog pond

grenu, -e [grəny] **ADJ 1** *(blé etc)* grainy, full of grain **2** *(surface)* grainy, grained; *(cuir, peau)* grained

grenure [grənyr] **NF** *(du cuir)* grain

grès [grɛ] **NM 1** *Géol* sandstone **2** *(vaisselle)* **g. (cérame)** stoneware; **des assiettes en g.** stoneware plates

gréseux, -euse [grezø, -øz] **ADJ** sandstone *(avant n)*

grésil [grezil] **NM** fine hail

grésillement [grezijmɑ̃] **NM 1** *(de l'huile)* sizzling *(UNCOUNT)*; *(de la flamme)* sputtering *(UNCOUNT)*; *(de téléphone, de radio)* crackling *(UNCOUNT)*; **il y a des grésillements sur la ligne** there's some interference on the line, the line's crackling **2** *(cri du grillon)* chirping *(UNCOUNT)*

grésiller [3] [grezije] **V IMPERSONNEL il grésille** it's hailing

VI 1 *(huile)* to sizzle; *(flamme)* to sputter; *(feu, téléphone, radio)* to crackle; **ça grésille** *(téléphone, radio)* it's all crackly **2** *(grillon)* to chirp

gressin [gresɛ̃] **NM** breadstick

greubons [grøbɔ̃] **NMPL** *Suisse* = leftover fat from cooked pork, fried and used as an ingredient in certain Swiss dishes

grève [grɛv] **NF 1** *(cessation d'une activité)* strike; **g. des cheminots** train strike; **être en g., faire g.** to be on strike, to strike; **se mettre en g.** to go on strike; **g. bouchon** disruptive strike; **g. de la faim** hunger strike; **commencer une g. de la faim** to go on hunger strike; **g. générale** general strike; **g. illégale** wildcat strike; **g. partielle** partial *or* localized strike; **g. perlée** *Br* go-slow, *Am* slowdown; **g. avec préavis** official strike; **g. de protestation** protest strike; **g. sauvage** wildcat strike; **g. de solidarité** sympathy strike; **ils font une g. de solidarité**

they've come out in sympathy; **g. surprise** lightning strike; **g. sur le tas** sit-down strike; **g. tournante** staggered strike; **g. du zèle** work-to-rule; **faire la g. du zèle** to work to rule **2** *Littéraire (plage)* shore, strand; *(rive)* bank, strand; **les grèves de la Loire** the sandbanks of the Loire; *Hist* **la (place de) G.** = open space on the banks of the Seine where dissatisfied workmen used to assemble

grever [19] [grəve] **VT 1** *(économie)* to put a strain on; *(succession)* to burden, to encumber; **l'inflation a grevé le pouvoir d'achat** inflation has restricted *or* put a squeeze on purchasing power; **les vacances ont grevé mon budget** the holidays have put a severe strain on my finances; **grevé d'impôts** weighed down *or* burdened with tax **2** *Jur* to mortgage

gréviste [grevist] **NMF** striker, striking worker; **g. de la faim** hunger striker

ADJ striking; **les étudiants grévistes** the striking students

GRH [ʒeɛraʃ] **NF** *(abrév* **gestion des ressources humaines***)* HRM

gribiche [gribiʃ] **ADJ sauce g.** = flavoured mayonnaise with chopped hard-boiled egg and capers

NF 1 *Suisse & Can Fam (femme acariâtre)* shrew **2** *Typ (de manuscrit)* file number

gribouillage [gribujaʒ] **NM 1** *(dessin)* doodle; **faire des gribouillages** to doodle **2** *(écriture illisible)* scrawl, scribble

gribouille [gribuj] **NM 1** *Fam Vieilli (personne)* simpleton, nitwit **2** *Can (dispute)* quarrel, fight

gribouiller [3] [gribuje] **VT** to scribble

VI to doodle, to scribble

gribouilleur, -euse [gribujœr, -øz] **NM,F** scribbler

gribouillis [gribuji] **NM 1** *(dessin)* doodle; **faire des g.** to doodle **2** *(écriture illisible)* scrawl, scribble

grief [grijɛf] **NM** *Littéraire* grievance; **faire** *ou* **tenir g. à qn de qch** to hold sth against sb; **on lui a fait g. d'avoir épousé un banquier** they resented her marrying a banker

> Il faut noter que le nom anglais **grief** est un faux ami. Il signifie **chagrin**.

grièvement [grijɛvmɑ̃] **ADV** *(blessé)* severely, seriously; **g. brûlé/touché** severely burnt/wounded

griffe [grif] **NF 1** *(d'un animal)* claw; *(d'un faucon)* claw, talon; **faire ses griffes** *(chat)* to sharpen its claws; *Fig* to cut one's teeth; **rentrer/sortir ses griffes** to draw in/to show one's claws; *Fig* **le voilà qui montre ses griffes** now he's showing his claws; **tomber dans les griffes de qn** to fall into sb's clutches; *Fig* **arracher qn des griffes de qn** to snatch sb out of sb's clutches; **coup de g.** scratch; **donner un coup de g. à qn** to scratch *or* to claw sb

2 *(de vêtement)* label; **une grande g.** a famous (designer) label

3 *(empreinte)* stamped signature; *(ce qui sert à faire cette empreinte)* (signature) stamp; *Fig (d'un auteur, d'un artiste)* stamp; **on reconnaît la g. de Zola dans ce roman** the novel bears Zola's stamp; **on reconnaît la g. de Saint Laurent** you can recognize the Saint Laurent style

4 *Bot (de l'asperge)* crown; *(du lierre, de la vigne)* tendril

5 *(en joaillerie)* claw

6 *Tech* claw, clip, clamp; *(outil)* dog; **accouplement/embrayage à griffes** claw coupling/clutch; **griffes de monteur** climbing irons

griffé, -e [grife] **ADJ** *(vêtement)* designer *(avant n)*

griffer [3] [grife] **VT 1** *(sujet: personne, animal)* to scratch; **Marie m'a griffé** Marie scratched me; **g. la joue à qn** to scratch sb's cheek, to scratch sb on the cheek **2** *(sujet: couturier)* to put one's label on; **Chanel a griffé cette veste** this jacket bears the Chanel label

VPR se griffer to scratch oneself; **je me suis griffé au rosier** I scratched myself on the rosebush

griffon [grifɔ̃] **NM 1** *Myth* griffin **2** *Zool (chien)* griffon **3** *Orn* griffon (vulture)

griffonnage [grifɔnaʒ] **NM 1** *(écrit)* scribble; **griffonnages** scribbling **2** *(dessin)* rough sketch

griffonnement [grifɔnmɑ̃] **NM** *Beaux-Arts (en cire)* wax model; *(en terre)* clay model

griffonner [3] [grifɔne] **VT 1** *(noter ▸ adresse)* to scribble (down); *(▸ plan)* to sketch roughly, to do a quick sketch of; *Beaux-Arts (dessiner)* to sketch quickly **2** *(mal écrire)* to scribble; **les pages étaient toutes griffonnées au crayon noir** the pages were all scribbled over in black pencil

USAGE ABSOLU *(gribouiller)* to scribble

griffton [griftɔ̃] = **griveton**

griffu, -e [grify] **ADJ** clawed; **main griffue** claw-like hand

griffure [grifyr] **NF** *(d'une personne, d'une ronce)* scratch; *(d'un animal)* scratch, claw mark

grifton [griftɔ̃] = **griveton**

grigner [3] [griɲe] **VI** to crease, to wrinkle

grignotage [griɲɔtaʒ] **NM** nibbling; *Fig* wearing away, erosion; **le g. des voix par l'opposition** the gradual loss of votes to the opposition; **le g. de nos droits** the gradual whittling away of our rights

grignotement [griɲɔtmɑ̃] **NM** nibbling

grignoter [3] [griɲɔte] **VT 1** *(ronger)* to nibble (at *or* on) **2** *Fig (amoindrir)* to erode; **g. son capital/ses économies** to eat into one's capital/one's savings **3** *(acquérir)* to acquire gradually; **ils ont réussi à g. pas mal d'avantages** they gradually managed to win quite a few advantages

VI to nibble

grigou [grigu] **NM** *Fam* skinflint

gri-gri [grigri] *(pl* **gris-gris***)*, **grigri** [grigri] **NM** grigri, grisgris

gril [gril] **NM 1** *Culin* grill, *Am* broiler; **faire cuire qch sur le g.** to grill sth, *Am* to broil sth; *Fam Fig* **être sur le g.** to be on tenterhooks **2** *Tech* grating *(protecting sluice gate)*; *Rail & Naut* gridiron; *Théât* grid, gridiron **3** *Anat* **g. costal** rib cage

grill [gril] **NM 1** *(restaurant)* grill-room, grill **2** *TV (pour l'éclairage)* pipe grid

grillade [grijad] **NF** grill, grilled meat; **faire des grillades** to have a barbecue

grillage[1] [grijaʒ] **NM 1** *(matériau)* wire netting *or* mesh **2** *(clôture)* wire fence *or* fencing; **poser un g. électrifié** to put up an electrified fence **3** *Élec (de plaque d'accumulateur)* grid, frame

grillage[2] [grijaʒ] **NM 1** *Culin* roasting **2** *Métal (de minerai)* calcining, roasting **3** *Tex* singeing

grillager [17] [grijaʒe] **VT 1** *(fenêtre)* to put wire mesh on **2** *(terrain, jardin)* to put a wire fence *or* wire fencing around

grille [grij] **NF 1** *(porte)* (iron) gate; *(barrière)* railing; *(clôture basse)* railings; *(d'une fenêtre)* bars

2 *(d'un égout, d'un foyer)* grate; *(d'un parloir, d'un comptoir)* grill, grille; **g. d'entrée d'air** air vent; **g. de réchauffeur** heater matrix

3 *Can Aut (calandre)* grille

4 *Élec (d'un accumulateur, d'un tube à électrons)* grid; **courant de g.** grid current

5 *(programme)* schedule; **voici notre nouvelle g. pour l'été** here's our new summer schedule; *Rad & TV* **g. des programmes** programme schedule *or* grid

6 *(au jeu)* **une g. de mots croisés** a crossword grid *or* puzzle; **la g. du Loto** Loto card

7 *(en travaux publics)* (frame) grate

8 *Jur & Écon* **g. des salaires** pay *or* salary scale; **g. indiciaire** salary structure *or* scale; *(de la fonction publique)* wage index; **g. d'avancement** career structure; **g. de gestion** managerial grid; *Compta* **g. d'imputation** table of account codes; **g. produit/marché** product/market grid; **g. de rémunération** salary scale

9 *Ordinat* **g. de saisie** input grid

grille-calandres [grijkalɑ̃dr] *(pl* **grilles-calandres***)* **NF** *Aut* grille

grille-pain [grijpɛ̃] **NM INV** toaster

griller[1] **[3]** [grije] **VT 1** *Culin (pain)* to toast; *(cacahuètes, café)* to roast; *(poisson, viande)* to grill, *Am* to broil

2 *(brûler)* to scorch, to burn; **grillé par la chaleur** scorched by the heat; **grillé par le froid** killed by the cold

3 *Fam (ampoule, fusible)* to blow; *(moteur)* to burn out

4 *Métal (minerai)* to roast, to calcine

5 *Tex* to singe

6 *Fam (dépasser)* **le bus a grillé mon arrêt** the bus went right past my stop; **g. un feu rouge** to jump the lights, to jump *or* go through a red light; **g. les étapes** *(dans sa carrière)* to shoot up the ladder; *(dans un travail)* to cut corners; **g. quelques étapes** to jump a few stages; **g. qn (à l'arrivée)** *Br* to pip sb at the post, *Am* to beat sb out; **g. un concurrent** to leave a competitor standing

7 *Fam (fumer)* **g. une cigarette, en g. une** to have a smoke

8 *Fam (compromettre)* **il est grillé** *(dévoilé)* his game's up; *(fini)* he's had it; **il nous a grillés auprès du patron** he's really landed us in it with the boss

VI 1 *Culin* **faire g. du pain** to toast some bread; **faire g. du café** to roast coffee beans

2 *Élec (sauter ▸ fusible)* to blow

3 *Fam (avoir trop chaud)* to roast, to boil; **ouvre la fenêtre, on grille ici** open the window, it's boiling in here

4 *Fam (brûler)* **la ferme a entièrement grillé** the farmhouse was burnt to the ground[□]

5 *Fig* **g. de curiosité** to be consumed with curiosity; **je grille (d'envie** *ou* **d'impatience) de la rencontrer** I'm itching *or* dying to meet her

VPR se griller *Fam* **1** *(se démasquer)* **il s'est grillé en disant cela** he gave himself away by saying that; **se g. auprès de qn** to blot one's copybook with sb **2 se g. au soleil** to roast in the sun **3 on s'en grille une?** how about a (quick) smoke?

griller[2] **[3]** [grije] **VT** *(fermer d'une grille)* to put bars on; **les fenêtres de la chapelle ont été grillées** they have put bars on the chapel windows

grilloir [grijwar] **NM** grill, *Am* broiler

grillon [grijɔ̃] **NM** *Entom* cricket

grill-room [grilrum] *(pl* **grill-rooms***)* **NM** grill-room, grill

grimaçant, -e [grimasɑ̃, -ɑ̃t] **ADJ** *(sourire)* painful; *(bouche)* twisted; *(visage)* contorted; *(clown, gargouille)* grimacing

grimace [grimas] **NF 1** *(expression ▸ amusante)* funny face; *(▸ douloureuse)* grimace; **faire une g.** *(pour faire rire)* to make a funny face; *(de douleur)* to wince; *(de peur)* to grimace; **une g. de dégoût** a disgusted look; **faire la g.** to make a face **2** *(faux-pli)* pucker; **faire une g.** to pucker

• **grimaces NFPL** *Littéraire (manières)* airs

grimacer [16] [grimase] **VI 1** *(de douleur)* to grimace, to wince; *(de dégoût)* to make a face; **g. de douleur** to grimace *or* to wince with pain **2** *(pour faire rire)* to make a funny face **3** *(robe)* to pucker

VT malgré la douleur, elle grimaça un sourire she forced a smile in spite of the pain

grimacier, -ère [grimasje, -ɛr] **ADJ 1** *(grotesque)* grimacing **2** *Littéraire (maniéré)* affected

grimage [grimaʒ] **NM** *(action)* making up; *(résultat)* make-up

grimer [3] [grime] **VT** to make up

VPR se grimer to put one's make-up on; **se g. en...** to make oneself up as...

grimoire [grimwar] **NM 1** *(livre de sorcellerie)* book of magic spells **2** *(écrit illisible)* illegible scrawl *or* scribble; *(ouvrage confus)* piece of gibberish *or* mumbo-jumbo

grimpant, -e [grɛ̃pɑ̃, -ɑ̃t] **ADJ** *(arbuste)* climbing; *(fraisier)* creeping

NM *Fam Arg crime Br* trousers[□], keks, *Am* pants[□]

grimpe [grɛ̃p] **NF** rock-climbing; **faire de la g.** to go rock-climbing

grimpée [grɛ̃pe] **NF** *(pente, montée)* stiff *or* steep climb

grimper [3] [grɛ̃pe] **VI 1** *(personne, animal, plante)* to climb; **g. à une échelle/un mur** to climb up a ladder/wall; **g. à un arbre** to climb (up) a tree; **g. sur une table** to climb on (to) a table; **grimpe dans la voiture** get into the car; **le lierre grimpe le long du mur** the ivy climbs up the wall; *Fam* **g. aux rideaux** to hit the roof **2** *(s'élever en pente raide)* to climb; **la route grimpe beaucoup à cet endroit** the road climbs steeply here; **ça grimpe!** it's steep! **3** *(température, inflation)* to soar; **la température a grimpé à 35°** the temperature rocketed *or* soared to 35°

VT 1 *(escalier, pente)* to climb (up) **2** *très Fam (posséder sexuellement)* to ride, *Br* to shag

NM *Sport* rope-climbing

grimpette [grẽpɛt] **NF** *Fam* steep *or* stiff climb▫

grimpeur, -euse [grẽpœr, -øz] **ADJ** *Orn* scansorial

NM,F 1 *Sport* climber; *(de rocher)* rock-climber; *(en cyclisme)* hill climber **2** *Orn* **les grimpeurs** scansorial birds

grinçant, -e [grẽsɑ̃, -ɑ̃t] **ADJ 1** *(porte, parquet)* squeaking, creaking **2** *(voix, musique)* grating **3** *(humour)* sardonic

grincement [grẽsmɑ̃] **NM** *(bruit)* grating, creaking; **dans un g. de freins** with a squeal of brakes; *Fig* **il y a eu des grincements de dents** there was much gnashing of teeth

grincer [16] [grẽse] **VI 1** *(bois)* to creak; *(frein)* to squeal; *(métal)* to grate; *(ressort)* to squeak **2** *(personne)* **g. des dents** to gnash one's teeth; *Fig* **cela fait g. des dents** it sets your teeth on edge

grinche [grẽʃ] **ADJ** *Suisse* grumpy, grouchy

grincheux, -euse [grẽʃø, -øz] **ADJ** grumpy, grouchy

NM,F grumbler, grouch

gringalet [grẽgalɛ] **NM** shrimp, weakling

ADJ M puny

gringue [grẽg] **NM** *très Fam* **faire du g. à qn** to come on to sb, *Br* to chat sb up, *Am* to hit on sb

griotte [grijɔt] **NF 1** *Bot* morello (cherry) **2** *(marbre)* (griotte) marble

grip [grip] **NM** *Sport (position de la main, revêtement)* grip

grippage [gripaʒ] **NM** *Tech* jamming, seizing (up)

grippal, -e, -aux, -ales [gripal, -o] **ADJ** flu *(avant n)*, *Spéc* influenzal; **soulage les états grippaux** *(sur médicament)* relieves flu symptoms

grippe [grip] **NF 1** *Méd* flu, *Spéc* influenza; **attraper/avoir la g.** to catch/to have (the) flu; **g. asiatique** Asian flu; **g. aviaire** bird flu, *Spéc* avian flu; **g. intestinale** gastric flu **2 prendre qn/qch en g.** to take a (strong) dislike to sb/sth

grippé, -e [gripe] **ADJ 1** *Méd* **être g.** to have (the) flu **2** *Tech* seized (up), jammed **3** *Méd (visage)* pinched, drawn

gripper [3] [gripe] **VT** to block, to jam

VI 1 *(se coincer)* to jam, to seize up **2** *(se froisser)* to crinkle (up), to wrinkle, to pucker

VPR se gripper to jam, to seize up

grippe-sou [gripsu] *(pl* **grippe-sous***)* *Fam* **NM** skinflint; **un vieux g.** an old Scrooge

ADJ INV money-grabbing

gris, -e [gri, griz] **ADJ 1** *(couleur)* grey; **g. acier/anthracite/ardoise/argent/fer/perle** steel/charcoal/slate/silver/iron/pearl grey; **g. clair** light grey; **g. pommelé** dapple-grey; **g. souris** mouse-coloured; **g. bleu/vert** bluish/greenish grey; **une robe g. foncé** a dark grey dress; **avoir les cheveux g.** to be grey-haired

2 *Météo* overcast; **il fait g. ce matin** it's cloudy *or* dull *or* overcast this morning, it's a grey *or* dull morning

3 *(terne)* dull, grey; **son existence a été plutôt grise et monotone** his/her life was dull and dreary; **en apprenant la nouvelle, il a fait grise mine** his face fell when he heard the news

4 *Fam (ivre)* tipsy

5 *(en œnologie)* **vin g.** rosé (wine)

NM 1 *(couleur)* grey; **porter du g.** to wear grey **2** *(tabac)* = French caporal tobacco in grey packet, ≃ shag **3** *(cheval)* grey (horse)

ADV il a fait g. toute la journée it's been grey *or* dull all day

grisaille [grizaj] **NF 1** *(morosité)* dullness, greyness **2** *Météo* dull weather **3** *Beaux-Arts* grisaille; **une marine en g.** a seascape in shades of grey

grisailler [3] [grizaje] **VT** *Beaux-Arts* to paint in grisaille

VI to turn *or* to become grey

grisant, -e [grizɑ̃, -ɑ̃t] **ADJ 1** *(enivrant)* intoxicating, heady **2** *(excitant)* exhilarating

grisâtre [grizatr] **ADJ 1** *(couleur)* greyish **2** *(monotone)* **une vie g.** a dull life

grisbi [grizbi] **NM** *Fam Arg crime* dough, cash

grise [griz] *voir* **gris**

grisé [grize] **NM** grey tint; *Ordinat* grey tone; **en g.** *(article)* dimmed

griser [3] [grize] **VT 1** *(colorer)* to tint; *(rendre gris)* to make grey

2 *(enivrer)* to intoxicate

3 *Fig (étourdir, exciter)* to intoxicate, to fascinate; **grisé par le succès** carried away *or* intoxicated by *or* with success

4 *Ordinat* to shade

VPR se griser to get drunk; **se g. de qch** to get drunk on sth; **se g. des paroles de qn/de musique** to get carried away by sb's words/by music

griserie [grizri] **NF 1** *(ivresse)* intoxication **2** *Fig (exaltation)* exhilaration, excitement; **se laisser porter par la g. du succès** to let success go to one's head

grisette [grizɛt] **NF** *Vieilli* grisette

gris-gris [grigri] = **gri-gri**

grisonnant, -e [grizɔnɑ̃, -ɑ̃t] **ADJ** greying; **elle est grisonnante, elle a les cheveux grisonnants** she's going grey; **avoir les tempes grisonnantes** to be greying at the temples

grisonner [3] [grizɔne] **VI** *(barbe, cheveux, personne)* to be going grey

grisou [grizu] **NM** firedamp; **coup de g.** firedamp explosion

grive [griv] **NF** *Orn* thrush

grivelé, -e [grivle] **ADJ** speckled with grey

grivèlerie [grivɛlri] **NF** = offence of leaving a restaurant or a hotel without having paid

griveton [grivtɔ̃] **NM** *Fam Arg mil Br* ≃ squaddy, *Am* ≃ grunt

grivois, -e [grivwa, -az] **ADJ** risqué, bawdy

grivoiserie [grivwazri] **NF 1** *(caractère)* bawdiness **2** *(histoire)* bawdy story; *(plaisanterie)* risqué *or* saucy joke; *(acte)* rude gesture

grizzli, grizzly [grizli] **NM** grizzly (bear)

Groenland [grɔenlɑ̃d] **NM le G.** Greenland

groenlandais, -e [grɔenlɑ̃dɛ, -ɛz] **ADJ** of/from Greenland, Greenland *(avant n)*

• **Groenlandais, -e NM,F** Greenlander

grog [grɔg] **NM** hot toddy; **g. au rhum** rum toddy

groggy [grɔgi] **ADJ INV 1** *(boxeur)* groggy **2** *Fam (abruti)* stunned, dazed

grognard [grɔɲar] **NM 1** *Hist* = soldier of Napoleon's Old Guard **2** *(militant traditionnaliste)* member of the old guard **3** *Vieilli (grincheux)* grouch, curmudgeon

grognasse [grɔɲas] **NF** *très Fam* old bag, old bat

grognasser [3] [grɔɲase] **VI** *Fam* to grumble, *Br* to whinge

grogne [grɔɲ] **NF** dissatisfaction, discontent; **c'est la g. chez les ouvriers/dans le milieu étudiant** the workers/the students are grumbling

grognement [grɔɲmɑ̃] **NM 1** *(d'une personne)* grunt, growl; **pousser des grognements** to grunt, to growl **2** *(d'un cochon)* grunt, grunting *(UNCOUNT)*; *(d'un chien)* growl, growling *(UNCOUNT)*; **pousser des grognements** *(cochon)* to grunt; *(chien)* to growl

grogner [3] [grɔɲe] **VI 1** *(personne)* to grumble, to grouse; **g. après** *ou* **contre qn** to grumble *or* moan about sb **2** *(cochon)* to grunt; *(chien)* to growl

VT *(réponse, phrase)* to grunt (out)

grognon, -onne [grɔɲɔ̃, -ɔn] *Fam* **ADJ** grumpy, crotchety; **un air g.** a surly look

NM,F grumbler, moaner; **c'est une vraie grognonne** she's such a moaner

grognonner [3] [grɔɲɔne] **VI** *Fam* to grumble, *Br* to whinge

groin [grwẽ] **NM 1** *(d'un porc)* snout **2** *Fam (visage laid)* mug

grole, grolle [grɔl] **NF** *très Fam* shoe▫; **mets des groles** put something on your feet

grommeler [24] [grɔmle] **VI 1** *(personne)* to grumble, to mutter **2** *(sanglier)* to snort

VT to mutter

grommellement [grɔmɛlmɑ̃] **NM 1** *(du sanglier)* snorting **2** *(d'une personne)* grumbling, muttering

grommellera *etc voir* **grommeler**

grondement [grɔ̃dmɑ̃] **NM 1** *(du tonnerre, du métro)* rumbling; *(d'un torrent de montagne, des vagues, d'un moteur)* roar(ing); *(de canons)* booming **2** *(d'un chien)* growling

gronder [3] [grɔ̃de] **VI 1** *(rivière, tonnerre, métro)* to rumble; *(canons)* to boom; *(vagues)* to roar **2** *(chien)* to growl **3** *Littéraire (révolte)* to be brewing; **la colère gronde chez les étudiants** students are becoming increasingly discontented, there are rumblings of discontent among students

VT *(réprimander)* to scold, to tell off; **se faire g.** to get told off

gronderie [grɔ̃dri] **NF** scolding, telling-off

grondeur, -euse [grɔ̃dœr, -øz] **ADJ 1** *(personne, voix)* scolding, grumbling; **d'un ton g.** in a tone of reproof **2** *(orage, torrent)* rumbling

grondin [grɔ̃dẽ] **NM** *Ich* gurnard

groom [grum] **NM 1** *(employé d'hôtel)* bellboy **2** *Arch Équitation* groom

GROS, GROSSE [gro, gros]

ADJ	
• large **1**	• big **1–3, 5, 6**
• fat **2**	• heavy **3, 4**
• hearty **3**	
NM,F	
• fat person	
NM	
• most part **1**	• bulk **1**
• wholesale **2**	• rich person **3**
NF	
• engrossment **1**	• gross **2**

ADJ 1 *(grand)* large, big; *(épais, solide)* big, thick; **une grosse boîte de haricots** a large *or* big can of beans; **une orange grosse comme le poing** an orange the size of *or* as big as your fist; **prends-le par le g. bout** pick it up by the thick *or* thicker end; **écrire qch en g. caractères** to write sth in big *or* large letters; **un g. crayon** a (big) thick pencil; **de grosses chaussures** heavy shoes; **de grosses chaussettes** thick *or* heavy socks; **un g. pull** a thick *or* heavy jumper; **g. drap** coarse linen; **de grosses lèvres** thick lips; **g. trait de crayon** thick pencil mark; **une grosse tranche** a thick slice; *Fam* **un bon g. sandwich** a nice big sandwich; **g. morceau** big *or* large piece, lump; *Fig* **l'examen de statistiques, voilà le g. morceau** the statistics exam is the big one; *Ordinat* **g. système** mainframe; *Typ* **g. corps** headings type, headline type; *Journ* **g. titre** banner headline; **en g. titres** in banner headlines

2 *(corpulent)* big, fat; **un g. bébé** a big *or* fat baby; **un homme grand et g.** a tall fat man; **une grosse dame** a big *or* fat lady; **de grosses jambes** fat *or* stout legs

3 *(en intensif)* **un g. appétit** a big *or* hearty appetite; **les grosses chaleurs** the hot season, the height of summer; *Fam* **un g. bisou** a big kiss; **un g. bruit** a loud *or* big noise; **un g. kilo** a good kilo; **une grosse récolte** a bumper harvest; **un g. sanglot** a big *or* heavy sob; **un g. soupir** a big *or* heavy sigh; **un g. mangeur** a big *or* hearty eater; **un g. buveur** a heavy drinker; **un g. utilisateur** a heavy user; **g. bêta!** you silly fool!; *Fam* **le plus g. buteur du championnat** the highest scorer in the championship

4 *(abondant)* heavy; **une grosse averse** a heavy shower; **de grosses pluies/chutes de neige** heavy rainfall/snowfall; **son usine a de g. effectifs** his/her factory employs large numbers of people *or* has a large workforce

5 *(important)* big; **un g. consommateur de pétrole** a major oil consumer; **de g. dégâts** extensive *or* widespread damage; **une grosse entreprise** a large *or* big company; **une grosse erreur** a big *or* serious mistake; **une grosse commande** a bulk order; **une grosse somme** a large sum of money; **de g. frais** heavy expenses; **de g. progrès** considerable progress, a lot of progress; **de g. profits** big *or* fat profits; **il y a de g. travaux à faire dans cette maison** that house needs a lot (of work) done to it; **la plus grosse partie de nos affaires/notre personnel** the bulk of our business/our staff; **une grosse angine** a (very) sore throat; **un g. rhume** a bad *or* heavy cold; **une grosse fièvre** a high fever; **de g. ennuis** serious trouble, lots of trouble; **une grosse journée (de travail)** a hard day's work; **de grosses pertes** heavy losses

6 *(prospère)* big; **un g. commerçant** a major retailer; **un g. producteur d'Hollywood** a big Hollywood producer; **un g. propriétaire (terrien)** a big landowner; **une grosse héritière** a wealthy heiress; **les g. actionnaires** the major shareholders

7 *(rude)* **une grosse voix** a rough *or* gruff voice; **un g. rire** coarse laughter; **l'astuce/la supercherie était un peu grosse** the trick/the hoax was a bit obvious; **grosse blague** crude joke

8 *(exagéré)* **j'ai trouvé ça un peu g.!** I thought it was a bit much!; **un g. drame** a big tragedy *or* catastrophe; **ne lui dis pas, sinon ça va faire une grosse histoire** don't tell him/her or you'll never hear the end of it; **ce n'est pas une grosse affaire** it's no big deal; *Fam* **tout de suite, les grosses menaces!** so it's threats already, is it?

9 *Météo* **par g. temps/grosse mer** in heavy weather/seas; **g. vent** gale

10 *(rempli)* **un ciel g. d'orage** stormy skies; **yeux g. de larmes** eyes moist with tears; **un cœur g. de tendresse** a heart full of tenderness; **un regard g. de menaces** a threatening look; **un choix g. de conséquences** a choice fraught with implications

11 *Cin & TV* **g. plan** close-up, close-shot; **g. plan de tête** head shot

NM,F fat person; **les g.** fat people; **un petit g.** a fat little man; *Fam* **ça va, mon g.?** all right, old boy *or Br* chap?

NM 1 *(la plus grande partie)* **le g. de la classe a du mal à suivre** most of the class has trouble keeping up; **le g. du débat sera télévisé** the main part of the debate will be televised; **le g. de l'hiver est passé** the worst of the winter is over; **le g. du chargement/personnel** the bulk of the cargo/staff; **le plus g. est fait** the biggest part of the job is done

2 *Com* wholesale (trade); **ils ne vendent/font que du g.** they only sell/deal wholesale

3 *Fam (riche)* rich person❑; **les g.** the rich

ADV couper g. to cut in large slices; **écrire g.** to write big; **coûter/gagner g.** to cost/to win a lot (of money); *aussi Fig* **ça va vous coûter g.** it'll cost you dear; **ça peut rapporter g.** it can bring in a lot; **il y a g. à parier qu'il ne viendra pas!** a hundred to one he won't come!; **jouer g.** to play for high stakes; *Fig* **jouer** *ou* **miser** *ou* **risquer g.** to take *or* to run a big risk, to stick one's neck out; **elle donnerait g. pour savoir qui a fait ça** she'd give her right arm *or* anything to know who did it

• **grosse NF 1** *Jur* engrossment **2** *Com* gross

ADJ F *Vieilli (enceinte)* pregnant

• **de gros ADJ** *Com* wholesale *(avant n)*

• **en gros ADJ** bulk *(avant n)* **ADV 1** *(approximativement)* roughly; **il y avait en g. quinze personnes** there were roughly *or* about fifteen people there; **je sais en g. de quoi il s'agit** I know roughly what it's about **2** *(en lettres capitales)* **c'est imprimé en g.** it's printed in big letters **3** *Com* wholesale; **acheter en g.** to buy wholesale; *(en grosse quantité)* to buy in bulk; **vendre en g.** to sell wholesale

• **gros bonnet NM** *Fam* bigwig, big shot; **tous les g. bonnets de la finance** all the financial bigwigs

• **grosse légume NF** *Fam (personne influente)* bigwig, big shot; *(officier)* brass hat; **les grosses légumes du régiment** the top brass (of the regiment)

gros-bec [grobɛk] *(pl* **gros-becs)** **NM** *Orn* hawfinch, grosbeak

gros-cul [groky] *(pl* **gros-culs)** **NM** *Fam* truck❑, *Br* lorry❑

groseille [grozej] **NF g. (blanche)** white currant; **g. rouge** redcurrant; **sirop de g.** redcurrant syrup; **g. à maquereau** gooseberry

ADJ INV light red

groseillier [grozeje] **NM** currant bush; **g. rouge** redcurrant bush; **g. blanc** white currant bush; **g. à maquereau** gooseberry bush

gros-grain [grogrɛ̃] *(pl* **gros-grains)** **NM** *Tex* grosgrain

Gros-Jean [groʒɑ̃] **NM INV se retrouver** *ou* **être G. comme devant** to feel deflated *(by failure)*

gros-porteur [grop ɔrtœr] *(pl* **gros-porteurs)** **NM** jumbo, jumbo jet

grosse [gros] *voir* **gros**

grossesse [grosɛs] **NF** pregnancy; **pendant ma g.** when I was pregnant; **g. extra-utérine** ectopic pregnancy; **g. gémellaire** twin pregnancy; **g. môlaire** molar pregnancy; **g. nerveuse** phantom pregnancy; **g. à risque** high-risk pregnancy

grosseur [grosœr] **NF 1** *(taille)* size; **de la g. d'une noix** the size of a walnut **2** *(obésité)* weight, fatness **3** *Méd* lump

grossier, -ère [grosje, -ɛr] **ADJ 1** *(approximatif)* rough, *Péj* crude; **c'est du travail g.** it's shoddy work; **un dessin g.** a rough sketch; **je n'ai qu'une idée grossière de l'endroit où il se trouve** I've only got a rough idea (of) where he is

2 *(peu raffiné)* coarse, rough; **des traits grossiers** coarse features

3 *(impoli)* rude, crude (**envers** to); **il est vraiment g.** he's so rude *or* impolite

4 *(vulgaire)* vulgar, uncouth; *(langage, plaisanterie)* coarse, crude; *(plaisirs)* base; **(quel) g. personnage!** what a vulgar individual!; **c'est un esprit g.** he's/she's ignorant, he's/she's a Philistine

5 *(erreur)* gross, stupid; *(ignorance)* gross, crass; **une ruse grossière** a very obvious trick; **les ficelles de l'intrigue sont vraiment grossières** the plot is really obvious

grossièrement [grosjɛrmɑ̃] **ADV 1** *(approximativement)* roughly (speaking); **j'ai évalué g. les frais** I made a rough estimate of the costs; **voilà, g., comment je vois les choses** roughly (speaking), that's how I see things

2 *(sans délicatesse)* roughly; **un visage g. dessiné** a face that has been roughly sketched

3 *(injurieusement)* rudely; **elle m'a parlé g.** she was rude to me

4 *(beaucoup)* **tu te méprends g.** you're grossly *or* wildly mistaken

grossièreté [grosjɛrte] **NF 1** *(impolitesse)* rudeness; **il est d'une incroyable g.** he is incredibly rude

2 *(manque de finesse ▸ d'une personne)* coarseness; *(▸ d'une chose)* crudeness, coarseness

3 *(gros mot)* coarse remark; **je me suis retenu pour ne pas lui dire des grossièretés** I had to bite my tongue to avoid swearing at him/her

4 *(obscénité)* rude joke; **il aime raconter des grossièretés** he likes telling rude jokes

grossir **[32]** [grosir] **VI 1** *(prendre du poids ▸ personne)* to put on weight, to get fatter; *(▸ animaux, fruits)* to get bigger *or* larger; **elle a beaucoup grossi** she's put on a lot of weight; **j'ai grossi d'un kilo** I've put on a kilo **2** *(augmenter)* to grow; *(mer)* to get rough, to rise; *(rivière)* to swell; **la foule grossissait sans cesse** the crowd was constantly getting bigger *or* growing; **le bruit grossit** the noise is getting louder

VT 1 *(faire paraître gros)* **ta robe te grossit** your dress makes you look fatter

2 *(augmenter)* to raise, to swell; **torrent grossi par les pluies** torrent swollen by the rain; **g. le nombre/les rangs des manifestants** to join the growing numbers of demonstrators/swell the ranks of the demonstrators; **g. sa voix** to raise one's voice

3 *(exagérer)* to exaggerate, to overexaggerate; **les journaux ont grossi les conséquences de la grève** the newspapers exaggerated *or* magnified the consequences of the strike; **on a grossi l'affaire** the affair was blown up out of all proportion

4 *(à la loupe)* to magnify, to enlarge; **objet grossi trois fois** object magnified three times

grossissant, -e [grosisɑ̃, -ɑ̃t] **ADJ 1** *(verre)* magnifying **2** *Littéraire (qui s'accroît)* growing, swelling

grossissement [grosismɑ̃] **NM 1** *(augmentation de taille)* increase in size

2 *(d'une tumeur)* swelling, growth

3 *(avec une loupe)* magnifying

4 *(capacité d'un instrument d'optique)* magnification, magnifying power

grossiste [grosist] **NMF** wholesaler; **g. généraliste** general wholesaler; **g. importateur** import wholesaler

grosso modo [grosomodo] **ADV** roughly, more or less; **g., c'est une comédie** roughly speaking *or* broadly speaking, it's a comedy; **laisse-moi t'expliquer l'histoire g.** let me give you a rough idea of the story

grossoyer **[13]** [groswaje] **VT** *Jur (document)* to engross

grotesque [grɔtɛsk] **ADJ 1** *(burlesque)* ridiculous **2** *(absurde)* ridiculous, ludicrous; **ne sois pas g.!** don't be absurd *or* ridiculous! **3** *Beaux-Arts (personnage)* grotesque

NM 1 *Beaux-Arts & Littérature* **le g.** the grotesque **2** *(absurdité)* ludicrousness, preposterousness; **cet homme/cette situation est d'un g.!** the man's/the situation's ludicrous *or* ridiculous!

• **grotesques NFPL** *Beaux-Arts* grotesques

grotte [grɔt] **NF 1** *Géol* cave; **g. naturelle/préhistorique** natural/prehistoric cave; **les grottes de Lascaux** the Lascaux Caves **2** *Archit* grotto

grouillant, -e [grujɑ̃, -ɑ̃t] **ADJ** swarming, teeming; **les rues grouillantes de monde** the streets swarming *or* teeming with people; **il y avait une foule grouillante sur la place** the square was teeming with people

grouillement [grujmɑ̃] **NM** swarming; **un g. d'insectes** a swarm of insects; **un g. de vers** a wriggling mass of worms; **le g. de la foule** the bustling *or* milling *or* seething crowd

grouiller **[3]** [gruje] **VI 1** *(clients, touristes)* to mill *or* to swarm about; **la foule grouille sur les boulevards** the boulevards are bustling with people; **les vers grouillent sur la viande** the meat is crawling with maggots

2 g. de *(être plein de)* to be swarming *or* crawling with; **les rues grouillent de monde** the streets are swarming with people; **ce bouquin grouille de bonnes idées** this book is teeming with good ideas

3 *très Fam (se dépêcher)* **allez, grouillez, ça commence dans cinq minutes** come on, get cracking *or* get a move on, it starts in five minutes

4 *Fam Vieilli (bouger)* to move❑

VPR se grouiller *Fam* to get a move on; **grouille-toi, on est en retard** get a move on, we're late

grouillot [grujo] **NM 1** *Fam (employé qui fait les courses)* errand boy **2** *Bourse* messenger (boy), runner **3** *TV & Cin* best boy, runner

groupage [grupaʒ] **NM 1** *Com (de paquets)* bulking; *(de commandes, d'envois, de livraisons)* bundling **2** *Méd* (blood) grouping

groupe [grup] **NM 1** *(de gens, d'objets)* group; **ils sont venus par groupes de quatre ou cinq** they came in groups of four or five *or* in fours and fives; **g. d'âge** age group; *Pol* **g. de contact** contact group; **g. dissident** splinter *or* dissident group; **g. familial** family group; **g. hospitalier** hospital complex; **g. d'intérêt** interest group; *Pol* **g. marginal** fringe group; *Scol* **g. de niveau** stream; **g. parlementaire** parliamentary group; *Scol* **g. de pression** pressure group; **g. de réflexion** think tank; **g. de rock** rock band *or* group; **g. scolaire** *(bâtiments)* school complex; *(élèves)* school party; **g. socio-économique** socio-economic group; **g. de travail** working group *or* party

2 *Écon* group; **les grands groupes de l'édition** the big publishing groups; **g. de détaillants** retailer co-operative; **g. industriel** industrial group; **g. de presse** press consortium *or* group; **g. multimédia** multimedia group, communications conglomerate; *Pol & Écon* **le G. des Sept** the Group of Seven; **le G. des Huit** the Group of Eight

3 *Mktg* **g. de consommateurs** consumer group; **g. de prospects** prospect pool; **g. de référence** reference group; **g. suivi** control group; **g. témoin** focus group

4 *Beaux-Arts* group

5 *Élec* set; **g. électrogène** generator; *Aut* **g. motopropulseur** powerplant

6 *Ling* **g. consonantique** consonant cluster; **g. de mots** word group; **g. du nom** *ou* **nominal** nominal group; **g. du verbe** *ou* **verbal** verbal group

7 *Math* group

8 *Méd* **g. sanguin** blood group; **quel est votre g. sanguin?** what's your blood group?, what blood group are you?; **g. à risque** risk group

9 *Mil* group; **g. d'artillerie** battery, *Am* battalion; **g. de combat** squad; **g. d'intervention** task force; **g. d'aviation** squadron *(of transport aircraft)*

10 *Bot & Zool (classification)* group

11 *Ordinat* **g. de discussion** discussion group; **g. de nouvelles** newsgroup

• **de groupe ADJ** group *(avant n)*; **billet de g.** group ticket; **psychologie/psychothérapie de g.** group psychology/therapy

• **en groupe ADV** in a group

groupé, -e [grupe] **ADJ 1** *(commandes, envois, livraisons)* grouped, consolidated **2** *Ordinat* blocked **3** *Sport voir* **saut**

groupement [grupmɑ̃] **NM 1** *(association)* group; **g. d'achat (commercial)** bulk-buying group, purchasing group; **g. de défense des consommateurs** consumers' association; *Écon* **G. européen d'intérêt économique** European Economic Interest Group; **g. d'intérêt économique** economic interest group; **g. de détaillants** retailers' group **2** *(rassemblement)* grouping; *Com & Ind (d'intérêts)* pooling; **g. des enfants d'après l'âge** classification of children by age groups **3** *Mil* group, formation; **g. d'infanterie** brigade group, *Am* battle group; **g. tactique** task force

grouper [3] [grupe] **VT 1** *(réunir ▸ personnes)* to group together; *(▸ ressources)* to pool; **groupons nos forces** let's pool our resources
2 *(classer)* to put *or* to group together; **on peut g. ces articles sous la même rubrique** we can put all these articles together under the same heading
3 *Com (commandes, envois, livraisons)* to consolidate, to group; *(paquets)* to bulk
4 *Méd* to determine the blood group of
VPR se grouper 1 *(dans un lieu)* to gather; **la foule s'est groupée sous le balcon** the crowd gathered under the balcony **2** *(dans une association)* to join together; **nous devons nous g. pour mieux défendre nos droits** we must band together *or* join together to protect our rights; **se g. autour d'un chef** to join forces under one leader

groupeur [grupœr] **NM** *Com* consolidator; **g. de fret aérien** air freight consolidator; **g. maritime** maritime freight consolidator; **g. routier** road haulage consolidator

groupie [grupi] **NMF** *Fam* **1** *(d'un chanteur)* groupie **2** *(inconditionnel)* avid follower□, groupie

groupusculaire [grupyskylɛr] **ADJ** *(qui tient du groupuscule)* small-scale; **la gauche g.** *(formée de groupuscules)* the small (splinter) groups of the left

groupuscule [grupyskyl] **NM** *Péj Pol* small group; **les groupuscules gauchistes** small leftwing (splinter) groups

grouse [gruz] **NF** *Orn* (red) grouse

Groznyï [grɔzni] **NM** Grozny

gruau [gryo] **NM 1 g. (d'avoine)** groats; **farine de g.** fine wheat flour; **pain de g.** fine wheaten bread **2** *Can Culin* porridge

grue [gry] **NF 1** *Tech* crane; *Rail* **g. d'alimentation** (water) crane **g. flottante** floating crane; **g. à flotteur** pontoon crane; **g. de levage** wrecking crane; **g. à pivot** revolving crane; **g. à volée** *ou* **à flèche** jib crane
2 *Cin & TV* crane; **g. de prise de vue** camera crane; **g. hydraulique** simon crane
3 *Orn* crane
4 *très Fam Vieilli (prostituée) Br* tart, *Am* hooker

gruger [17] [gryʒe] **VT 1** *Littéraire (tromper)* to deceive, to swindle; **se faire g.** to get swindled **2** *Fam* **g. la place de qn** *(dans une file d'attente)* to push in in front of sb□; *Can* **g. l'avance de qn** *(dans un sondage)* to eat into sb's lead

grume [grym] **NF** trunk, log; **bois en g.** unhewn *or* undressed wood

grumeau, -x [grymo] **NM 1** *(boule)* lump; **plein de grumeaux** lumpy; **faire des grumeaux** to go lumpy, to form lumps **2 grumeaux de sel** specks of salt

grumeler [24] [grymle] **se grumeler VPR 1** *(sauce)* to go lumpy **2** *(lait)* to curdle, to clot

grumeleux, -euse [grymlø, -øz] **ADJ 1** *(sauce)* lumpy **2** *(lait)* curdled **3** *(fruit)* gritty

grumelle *etc voir* **grumeler**

grumier [grymje] **NM** timber lorry

grunge [grœnʒ] **NM** *Mus* grunge
ADJ INV *(vêtements, bar, mode)* grungy

grutier [grytje] **NM** crane driver *or* operator

gruyère [gryjɛr] **NM (fromage de) g.** Gruyère (cheese); **crème de g.** = processed Gruyère (cheese)

GSM [ʒeesem] **NM** *Tél (abrév* **global system for mobile communications) 1** *(système)* GSM; **réseau G.** GSM network **2** *Belg (téléphone portable) Br* mobile phone, *Am* cellphone

GSS [ʒeeses] **NF** *Com (abrév* **grande surface spécialisée)** specialist superstore

guacamole [gwakamɔl] **NM** guacamole

Guadeloupe [gwadlup] **NF la G.** Guadeloupe

guadeloupéen, -enne [gwadlupeɛ̃, -ɛn] **ADJ** Guadeloupean
• **Guadeloupéen, -enne NM,F** Guadeloupean

guano [gwano] **NM** guano

Guatemala [gwatemala] **NM le G.** Guatemala

guatémaltèque [gwatemaltɛk] **ADJ** Guatemalan
• **Guatémaltèque NMF** Guatemalan

gué [ge] **NM** *(passage)* ford; **passer un ruisseau à g.** to ford a stream

guéable [geabl] **ADJ** fordable

guède [gɛd] **NF** *Bot* woad, pastel

guéer [15] [gee] **VT** to ford

guéguerre [gegɛr] **NF** *Fam* (little) war, squabble; **se faire la g.** to squabble, to bicker

guelfe [gɛlf] **ADJ** Guelphic, Guelfic
NMF Guelph, Guelf

guelte [gɛlt] **NF** *Vieilli Com* commission, percentage *(on sales)*

guenille [gənij] **NF 1** *(vêtements)* **(en) guenilles** (in) rags (and tatters) **2** *Can (chiffon)* cloth; *(serpillière)* floor cloth; *Fig* **c'est de la g.** it's rubbish

guenon [gənɔ̃] **NF 1** *Zool* female monkey, shemonkey **2** *très Fam Péj (femme)* dog, *Br* boot, *Am* beast

guépard [gepar] **NM** cheetah

guêpe [gɛp] **NF 1** *Entom* wasp **2** *Vieilli (femme rusée)* **c'est une fine g.** she's very sharp

guêpier [gepje] **NM 1** *(nid de guêpes)* wasp's nest **2** *Fig (situation périlleuse)* sticky situation; **il s'est fourré** *ou* **mis dans un beau g.** he got himself into a sticky situation **3** *Orn* bee-eater

guêpière [gepjɛr] **NF** basque

guère [gɛr] **ADV 1** *(employé avec "ne")* **ne... g.** *(pas beaucoup)* not much; *(pas longtemps)* hardly, scarcely; **il n'est g. aimable** he's not very nice; **je ne suis g. contente de vous** I'm not terribly pleased with you; **je ne l'aime g.** I don't care much for him/her; **je n'aime g. cela** I don't much like that, I don't like that much; **elle n'y voit plus g.** she can hardly see any more; **je n'ai g. dormi** I didn't get much sleep, I hardly slept, I didn't sleep much; **il n'a g. apprécié votre remarque** he didn't appreciate your remark much; **il ne nous en parle g.** he hardly *or* scarcely talks to us about it; **il n'est g. plus aimable qu'elle** he's not much nicer than she is; **il n'y a g. de monde** there's hardly anyone; **il n'a g. d'argent/d'amis** he hasn't much money/many friends; **je n'en sais g. plus** I hardly know anything more about it, I don't know much more about it; **ça ne durera g. longtemps** it won't last very long; **cela ne se dit plus g.** you don't hear that much now, hardly anybody says that now; **il n'en reste plus g.** *(non comptable)* there's hardly any left; *(comptable)* there are hardly any left; **il ne vient g. nous voir** he hardly ever comes to see us; **on ne tarda g. à entendre parler de lui dans les journaux** it wasn't long before he was mentioned in the newspapers; **il n'a g. plus de vingt ans** he is barely *or* scarcely twenty years old; **il ne nous reste g. que deux heures à attendre** we have barely two hours left to wait; **je ne suis plus g. qu'à une heure de Paris** I'm only an hour away from Paris; **il n'y a g. que moi qui m'en soucie** I'm practically the only one who cares about it; **il ne se déplace plus g. qu'avec une canne** he can hardly walk without a stick any more
2 *(dans une réponse)* **aimez-vous l'art abstrait? – g.** do you like abstract art? – not really; **la voyez-vous? – g.!** do you see her? – hardly ever!; **comment allez-vous? – g. mieux** how are you? – not much better *or* hardly any better; **tu as mieux dormi qu'hier? – oh, g. mieux!** did you sleep better than yesterday? – hardly!

guéret [gerɛ] **NM** *(non ensemencé)* fallow land; *(non labouré)* balk

guéri, -e [geri] **ADJ** cured (**de** of); *(rétabli)* better, recovered; **elle est guérie de sa rougeole** she's cured of *or* recovered from her measles; *Fig* **être g. d'une peur/d'un préjugé** to be cured of a fear/a prejudice; **il est g. de sa timidité** he is cured of *or* he has got over his shyness; **je ne pense plus à lui, je suis guérie** I don't think of him any more, I've got over him

guéridon [geridɔ̃] **NM** *(table)* occasional table

guérilla [gerija] **NF 1** *(guerre)* guerrilla warfare; *Com* guerrilla attack; **g. urbaine** urban guerrilla warfare; **la g. parlementaire de l'opposition** the guerrilla tactics employed by the opposition in parliament **2** *(soldats)* group of guerrillas, guerrilla unit

guérillero [gerijero] **NM** guerrilla

> Il faut noter que le nom anglais **guerrilla** est un faux ami. Il signifie **guérillero**.

guérir [32] [gerir] **VT 1** *Méd (malade, maladie)* to cure; *(blessure)* to heal; **g. un malade de son cancer** to cure a patient of his/her cancer **2** *Fig* **g. qn d'une habitude** to cure *or* break sb of a habit
VI 1 *Méd (convalescent)* to recover, to be cured; **il n'en guérira pas** he won't recover from it **2** *(blessure)* to heal, to mend; **son épaule guérit lentement** his/her shoulder is healing *or* mending slowly; **un chagrin qui ne guérit pas** an incurable grief, a grief that cannot be cured **3** *Fig* **il n'en guérira pas** he won't get over it
VPR se guérir 1 *(malade)* to cure oneself; **il s'est guéri grâce à l'homéopathie** he cured himself thanks to homeopathy **2** *(maladie)* **est-ce que ça se guérit facilement?** is it easy to cure? **3 se g. de qch** *(timidité, habitude)* to cure oneself of sth; **il ne s'est jamais guéri de sa jalousie** he never got over his jealousy

guérison [gerizɔ̃] **NF 1** *Méd (d'un patient)* recovery; *(d'une blessure)* healing; **il est maintenant en voie de g.** he's now on the road to recovery **2** *Fig* **la g. sera lente après une telle déception** it'll take a long time to get over such a disappointment

guérissable [gerisabl] **ADJ 1** *Méd (patient, mal)* curable; *(blessure)* that can be healed **2** *Fig* **son chagrin n'est pas g.** there is no cure for his/her sorrow

guérisseur, -euse [gerisœr, -øz] **NM,F** healer, *Péj* quack
NM *(d'une tribu)* medicine man

guérite [gerit] **NF 1** *(sur un chantier)* site office **2** *Mil* sentry box

Guernica [gɛrnika] **N** *Beaux-Arts & Géog* Guernica

guerre [gɛr] **NF 1** *(conflit)* war; **en temps de g.** in wartime; **être en g. (contre)** to be at war (with); **pays en g.** country at war; **faire la g. (à)** to wage war (against); *Fig* to battle (with); **il a fait la g. en Europe** he was in the war in Europe; **faire la g. aux inégalités** to wage war on inequality; **je fais la g. aux moustiques/fumeurs** I've declared war on mosquitoes/smokers; **elle lui fait la g. pour qu'il mange plus lentement** she's always (nagging) on at him to eat more slowly; *Fam* **mes chaussures/gants ont fait la g.** my shoes/gloves have been in the wars; **partir en g. (contre)** to go to war (against); *Fig* to launch an attack (on); *Fig* **entrer** *ou* **se mettre en g. (contre)** to go to war (with); **déclarer la g. (à)** to declare war (against *or* on); **la g. a éclaté entre...** war has broken out between...; **on entre dans une logique de g.** war is the only logical outcome; **maintenant, entre Jeanne et moi, c'est la g.** Jeanne and I are at each other's throats all the time now; *Fam* **à la g. comme à la g.** well, you just have to make the best of things; *Prov* **c'est de bonne g.** all's fair in love and war; **de g. lasse, je l'ai laissé sortir** in the end I let him go out just to have some peace (and quiet); **crime de g.** war crime; **g. aérienne** air war; **g. atomique** atomic war; **la g. de Cent Ans** the Hundred Years' War; **g. civile** civil war; *Écon* **g. commerciale** trade war; **la g. de Corée** the Korean War; **la g. de Crimée** the Crimean War; **g. des Deux-Roses** War of the Roses; **g. d'embuscade** guerrilla war; **la g. des étoiles** Star Wars; **la g. franco-allemande** the Franco-Prussian War; **la g. froide** the cold war; **g. des gangs** gang warfare; **la g. du Golfe** the Gulf War; **la g. d'Indochine** the first Indo-Chinese War

(1946–54); **la g. du Kippour** the Yom Kippur War; **g. mondiale** world war; *Fig* **g. des nerfs** war of nerves; **g. nucléaire** nuclear war; **g. à outrance** all-out war; **g. ouverte** open war; **g. préventive** preemptive *or* preventive war; **g. des prix** price war; **g. de religion** war of religion; **g. sainte** Holy War; **la g. de Sécession** the American Civil War; **la g. des sexes** the battle of the sexes; **la g. des Six Jours** the Six-Day War; **la g. de 70** the Franco-Prussian War; **g. des tarifs** price war; **g. totale** total war; **g. de Trente Ans** Thirty Years' War; **la g. de Troie** the Trojan War; **g. d'usure** war of attrition; **g. zéro-mort** casualty-free war; **la Grande G., la Première G. (mondiale), la g. de 14** the Great War, the First World War, World War I; **la Seconde G. mondiale, la g. de 40** World War II, the Second World War

2 *(technique)* warfare; **g. atomique** atomic warfare; **g. bactériologique** germ warfare; **g. biologique** biological warfare; **g. chimique** chemical warfare; **g. conventionnelle** conventional warfare; **g. éclair** blitzkrieg; **g. économique** economic warfare; **g. électronique** electronic warfare; **g. de positions** static warfare; **g. psychologique** psychological warfare; **g. de tranchées** trench warfare

guerrier, -ère [gɛrje, -ɛr] **ADJ** *(peuple)* warlike; **un chant g.** a battle song *or* chant; **une danse guerrière** a war dance; **être d'humeur guerrière** to be in a belligerent mood

NM warrior

guerroyer [13] [gɛrwaje] **VI** to (wage) war (**contre** against); *Fig* **g. contre l'inégalité/l'hypocrisie** to struggle against *or* to wage war on inequality/hypocrisy

guet [gɛ] **NM 1** *(action)* watch; **faire le g.** to be on the lookout; **poste de g.** lookout post **2** *Hist (patrouille)* watch

guet-apens [gɛtapɑ̃] *(pl* **guets-apens** [gɛtapɑ̃]) **NM** ambush, trap; **tendre un g. à qn** to set a trap *or* an ambush for sb; **tomber dans un g.** to fall into a trap, to be ambushed

guêtre [gɛtr] **NF 1** *(bande de cuir)* gaiter; *Fam* **traîner ses guêtres** to wander about *or* around□ **2** *(en tricot)* leggings

guetter [4] [gete] **VT 1** *(surveiller)* to watch; **il guette chacun de ses mouvements** he studies his/her every move **2** *Fig (menacer)* **la mort le guette** death is lying in wait for him; **l'infarctus la guette** she's liable to have a heart attack; **les ennuis la guettent** there's trouble in store for her; **le surmenage/la dépression le guette** overwork/depression will get him in the end **3** *(attendre)* to watch out for; **le chat guette la souris** the cat is watching for the mouse; **le guépard guettait sa proie** the cheetah was lying in wait for its prey; **il guette le facteur** he is on the lookout for the postman

USAGE ABSOLU *(surveiller)* **tu vas g. pendant qu'on entre** you keep watch while we go in

guetteur, -euse [gɛtœr, -øz] **NM,F 1** *(gén)* lookout **2** *Mil* lookout; *Hist* watch, watchman

gueulante [gœlɑ̃t] **NF** *très Fam* **pousser une g.** to kick up a stink, to hit the *Br* roof *or Am* ceiling

gueulard, -e [gœlar, -ard] **ADJ 1** *très Fam (personne)* loud, loudmouthed **2** *Fam (gourmand)* greedy□ **3** *très Fam (couleur)* loud

NM,F 1 *très Fam (adulte)* loudmouth; *(bébé)* bawler **2** *Fam (gourmand)* greedy guts

NM 1 *Métal* (blast furnace) throat *or* shaft **2** *Naut* loudhailer

gueule [gœl] **NF 1** *très Fam (bouche)* mouth□, *Br* gob, *Am* yap; **un whisky/curry qui emporte** *ou* **arrache la g.** a whisky/curry that takes the roof off your mouth; **s'en mettre plein la g.** to make a pig of oneself; **se soûler** *ou* **se bourrer la g.** to get *Br* pissed *or Am* juiced; **pousser un coup de g.** to yell out□; **c'est une grande g.** *ou* **un fort en g.** he's a big mouth *or* a loudmouth, he's always shooting his mouth off; **il faut toujours qu'il ouvre sa grande g.!** he always has to open his big mouth!; **(ferme) ta g.!** shut your mouth *or* trap!; **vos gueules!** shut up (, you lot)!

2 *très Fam (visage)* mug, face□; **avoir une sale g.** *(être moche)* to have an ugly mug; *(avoir mauvaise mine)* to look rotten; *(avoir l'air déprimé)* to look down in the mouth; **il va faire une sale g. quand il saura la vérité** he's going to be mad *or* livid when he finds out the truth; **je te pète la g.!** I'll smash your face in!; **sa g. ne me revient pas** I don't like the look of him/her; **t'aurais vu sa g.!** you should have seen his/her face!; **avoir** *ou* **faire une drôle de g.** to look funny *or* weird; **avoir une belle g.** to have a pretty face; **faire la g.** to sulk; **faire la g. à qn** to be in a huff *or* a bad mood with sb; **faire une g. d'enterrement** to look thoroughly depressed; **elle a fait une de ces gueules en trouvant la porte fermée!** you should have seen her face when she saw the door was shut!; **se foutre de** *ou* **se payer la g. de qn** to take the piss out of sb; **(s')en prendre plein la g.** *(se faire insulter)* to get a right mouthful (of abuse); *(se faire frapper)* to get one's face smashed in; *(se faire critiquer)* to get torn to pieces; **g. noire** miner□; **g. de raie** fish face

3 *Fam (apparence)* **ce fromage a une bonne g.** I like the look of this cheese□; **cette pizza a une sale g.** that pizza looks gross *or Br* minging

4 *très Fam (charme)* **elle n'est pas belle, mais elle a de la g.** she's not beautiful but she's got something about her; **il a de la g., ce type** that guy's really got something; **ce tableau a de la g.** that's some picture

5 *(d'un animal)* mouth; **se jeter dans la g. du loup** to throw oneself into the lion's mouth *or* jaws

6 *(d'un canon, d'un fusil)* muzzle; *(d'un four)* mouth

• **gueule de bois NF** *Fam* hangover; **se réveiller avec/avoir la g. de bois** to wake up with/to have a hangover

gueule-de-loup [gœldəlu] *(pl* **gueules-de-loup) NF 1** *Bot* snapdragon **2** *Constr* (chimney) cowl, chimney jack **3** *(de machine)* (exhaust) muffler

gueulement [gœlmɑ̃] **NM** *Fam* bawl, yell; **pousser des gueulements** to yell, to bawl

gueuler [5] [gœle] *Fam* **VI 1** *(personne ▸ de colère)* to shout□; *(▸ de douleur)* to yell out; *(protester)* to kick up a fuss; **arrête de g., on va t'aider** stop shouting, we're going to help you□; **quand il a su ça, il a gueulé** when he found out he blew his top *or* he hit the *Br* roof *or Am* ceiling; **g. sur qn** to shout at sb **2** *(radio, haut-parleur)* to blare out; **faire g. sa radio** to turn one's radio up full blast

VT *(chanson, ordres)* to bellow out, to bawl out; **g. qn** to bawl sb out, to roar at sb

gueules [gœl] **NM** *Hér* gules

gueuleton [gœltɔ̃] **NM** *Fam (repas)* blowout; **faire un bon petit g. entre amis** to have a good blowout with some friends

gueuletonner [3] [gœltɔne] **VI** *Fam* to have a blowout

gueuse [gøz] **NF 1** *voir* **gueux 2** *(bière)* = **gueuze**

gueuserie [gøzri] **NF** *Arch ou Littéraire* **1** *(état)* beggary *(UNCOUNT)* **2** *(action)* foul deed

gueux, -euse [gø, gøz] **NM,F** *Arch ou Littéraire* **1** *(mendiant)* beggar; **les g.** the wretched **2** *(fripon)* rascal, rogue

• **gueuse NF** *Arch ou Littéraire (femme de mauvaise vie)* harlot, strumpet

gueuze [gøz] **NF** gueuze *(variety of strong Belgian beer)*

gugusse [gygys] **NM** *Fam* clown; **faire le g.** to fool around

gui [gi] **NM 1** *Bot* mistletoe; **boules de g.** clumps of mistletoe **2** *Naut* boom

guibolle, guibole [gibɔl] **NF** *très Fam Br* pin, *Am* gam; **j'en ai plein les guibolles** my legs have had it

guiche [giʃ] **NF** *(mèche de cheveux) Br* kiss curl, *Am* spit curl

guichet [giʃɛ] **NM 1** *(d'une banque)* counter; *(d'un théâtre)* ticket office; *(d'une poste)* counter, window; **allez au g. numéro 2 pour les renseignements** go to window *or* position number 2 for information; **g. fermé** *(dans une banque, à la poste)* position closed; **g. automatique (de banque)** *Br* cashpoint, *Am* ATM; **jouer à guichets fermés** to play to packed houses; **on joue à guichets fermés** the performance is sold out

2 *(porte)* hatch, wicket

3 *(judas)* judas; *(d'un confessionnal)* shutter

4 *Sport (en cricket)* wicket; **gardien de g.** wicket-keeper

guichetier, -ère [giʃtje, -ɛr] **NM,F** *(de gare)* ticket clerk; *(de poste, de banque)* counter clerk, teller

guidage [gidaʒ] **NM 1** *Tech (d'une pièce mobile)* guiding; *(sur un tour de forage)* centring; *Aut* steering; **système de g.** guiding system **2** *Électron (d'un avion)* guidance; **tête de g.** homing head; **g. de missile** missile guidance *or* tracking

guide [gid] **NMF** *(personne)* guide, leader; *(pour touristes)* (tour) guide; *Sport* **g. (de haute montagne)** mountain guide

NM 1 *(principe)* guiding principle

2 *(livre)* guidebook; **g. de conversation** phrasebook; **g. gastronomique** restaurant guide, good food guide; **g. touristique** guidebook; *Ordinat* **g. de l'utilisateur** instruction manual; **G. Vert** Michelin guide

3 *Tél* **g. d'ondes** (wave) guide

4 *Aut* **g. chaîne** chain guide; *Tech* **g. de courroie** belt guide

5 *Typ* **g. de caractères** type book; **g. du style maison** stylebook, style guide

7 *Belg (indicateur de chemin de fer)* railway timetable; *(annuaire)* telephone book

NF 1 *(scout) Br* girl guide, *Am* girl scout; **g. aînée** ranger **2** *(rêne)* rein

guide-âne [gidan] *(pl* **guide-ânes) NM** *Vieilli* (basic) handbook

guide-classement [gidklasmɑ̃] *(pl* **guide-classements) NM** file divider

guide-fil [gidfil] *(pl* **guide-fils) NM** *Tex* thread guide

guide-papier [gidpapje] *(pl* **guide-papiers) NM** *(d'une imprimante)* paper guide

guider [3] [gide] **VT 1** *(diriger)* to guide; **le chien guide l'aveugle** the dog is guiding the blind man; **guidé par radio** radio-controlled **2** *(conseiller)* to guide; **guidée par son expérience** guided by his/her experience; **se laisser g. par son intuition** to be guided by one's intuition; **j'ai besoin d'être guidé** I need some guidance

VPR se guider il s'est guidé sur le soleil he used the sun as a guide

guidon [gidɔ̃] **NM 1** *(d'un vélo)* handlebars; *Fig* **avoir la tête** *ou* **le nez dans le g.** to have one's nose to the ground; **moustaches en g. de bicyclette** handlebar moustache **2** *Mil & Naut (pavillon)* guidon **3** *(d'une arme à feu)* foresight

guignard, -e [giɲar, -ard] **ADJ** *Fam (malchanceux)* jinxed, unlucky□

guigne[1] [giɲ] **NF** *Bot* sweet cherry; **se soucier de qn/qch comme d'une g.** not to give a fig about sb/sth

guigne[2] [giɲ] **NF** *Fam (malchance)* bad luck□; **porter la g. à qn** to bring sb bad luck; **avoir la g.** to be jinxed, to have rotten luck

guigner [3] [giɲe] **VT** to sneak a look at; *Fig (avoir des vues sur)* to have one's eye on; *Cartes* **g. le jeu du voisin** to sneak a look at one's opponent's hand

guignol [giɲɔl] **NM 1** *(pantin)* (glove) puppet; *(théâtre)* puppet theatre; *(spectacle)* ≃ Punch and Judy show **2** *Fam Fig* clown, joker; **faire le g.** to clown around, to play the fool

• **Guignol NPR** (Mister) Punch

guignolade [giɲɔlad] **NF** *(situation grotesque)* farcical situation, farce; *(farce)* trick; **il faudrait qu'ils arrêtent leurs guignolades** they should stop their nonsense *or* stop fooling around

guignolet [giɲɔlɛ] **NM** = liqueur made from cherries

guignon [giɲɔ̃] **NM** *Fam Vieilli* bad luck□

guilde [gild] **NF 1** *(club)* club **2** *Hist* guild

guili-guili [giligili] **NM INV** *(en langage enfantin)* tickle; **faire g. à qn** to tickle sb

Guillaume [gijom] **NPR G. le Conquérant** William the Conqueror; **G. d'Orange** William of Orange; **G. Tell** William Tell

guillaume [gijom] **NM** *Menuis* rabbet plane; **g. à onglet** mitre plane

guilledou [gijdu] *voir* **courir**

guillemet [gijmɛ] **NM** quotation mark, *Br* inverted comma; **ouvrir/fermer les guillemets** to open/to close (the) quotation marks *or Br* inverted commas; **entre guillemets** in quotation marks, in quotes, *Br* in inverted commas; **tu connais son sens de la "justice", entre guillemets** you know his/her so-called sense of justice; *Typ* **guillemets fermants** closing quotation marks; *Typ* **guillemets ouvrants** opening quotation marks; *Typ* **guillemets simples** single quotes

guillemot [gijmo] **NM** *Orn* guillemot

guilleret, -ette [gijrɛ, -ɛt] **ADJ 1** *(gai)* jolly, cheerful; **d'un air g.** jauntily **2** *(léger* ► *plaisanterie)* risqué

guillotine [gijɔtin] **NF** guillotine; **aller à la g.** to go to the guillotine

guillotiner [3] [gijɔtine] **VT** to guillotine

guimauve [gimov] **NF 1** *Bot & Culin* marshmallow; **g. rose** hollyhock **2** *Fig Péj* **ses chansons, c'est de la g.** his/her songs are all soppy *or* schmaltzy

guimbarde [gɛ̃bard] **NF 1** *Fam (voiture)* jalopy, *Br* (old) banger **2** *Mus* Jew's-harp **3** *(outil)* router plane, grooving plane

guimpe [gɛ̃p] **NF 1** *(chemisier)* chemisette **2** *(d'une religieuse)* wimple

guincher [3] [gɛ̃ʃe] **VI** *Fam Vieilli* to bop, to dance□

guindage [gɛ̃daʒ] **NM** lifting, hoisting

guindaille [gɛ̃daj] **NF** *Belg Fam* student party□

guindé, -e [gɛ̃de] **ADJ** *(personne)* stiff, starchy; *(discours)* stilted; *(atmosphère)* strained; *(langage)* affected; *(style)* stilted, stiff; *(réception)* posh; **d'un air g.** starchily, stiffly

guindeau, -x [gɛ̃do] **NM** *Naut* windlass

guinder [3] [gɛ̃de] **VT 1** *(personne)* **son costume le guinde** he looks very stiff and starchy in that suit **2** *Tech* to hoist; *Naut (mât)* to send up, to sway up **VPR se guinder** *(personne, ambiance)* to become stiff; *(style)* to become stilted *or* stiff

Guinée [gine] **NF la G.** Guinea; **la G.-Bissau** Guinea-Bissau; **la G.-Équatoriale** Equatorial Guinea

guinée [gine] **NF** *(monnaie)* guinea

guinéen, -enne [gineɛ̃, -ɛn] **ADJ** Guinean
• **Guinéen, -enne NM,F** Guinean

guingois [gɛ̃gwa] **de guingois ADJ l'affiche est de g.** the poster is lopsided
ADV marcher de g. to walk lopsidedly; *Fig* **aller de g.** to go haywire

guinguette [gɛ̃gɛt] **NF** = open-air café or restaurant with dance floor

guipure [gipyr] **NF 1** *Tex* guipure (lace) **2** *Littéraire (givre)* tracery

guirlande [girlɑ̃d] **NF 1** *(de fleurs)* garland **2** *(de papier)* paper chain *or* garland; **g. de Noël** (piece of) tinsel *(UNCOUNT)* **3** *(de lumières)* **g. électrique** *(de Noël)* Christmas tree lights, fairy lights; *(pour une fête)* fairy lights; **g. lumineuse** string of lights **4** *Ordinat* **connecté en g.** in a token ring configuration

guise [giz] **à ma/ta/***etc* **guise ADV** as I/you/*etc* please; **il n'en fait qu'à sa g.** he just does as he pleases *or* likes
• **en guise de PRÉP** by way of; **en g. de dîner, nous n'avons eu qu'un peu de soupe** for dinner, we just had a little soup

guitare [gitar] **NF** guitar; **avec Christophe Banti à la g.** with Christophe Banti on guitar; **g. basse** bass/electric guitar; **g. classique** classical guitar; **g. électrique** electric guitar; **g. hawaïenne** Hawaiian/acoustic guitar; **g. sèche** acoustic guitar

guitariste [gitarist] **NMF** guitar player, guitarist

guitoune [gitun] **NF 1** *Fam (tente)* tent□ **2** *Fam Arg mil* dugout□, shelter□

gulden [guldɛn] **NM** guilder

guppy [gypi] **NM** *Ich* guppy

guru [guru] = **gourou**

gus, gusse [gys] **NM** *Fam* guy, *Br* bloke

gustatif, -ive [gystatif, -iv] **ADJ** gustatory, gustative

gustation [gystasjɔ̃] **NF** tasting, *Spéc* gustation

gustative [gystativ] *voir* **gustatif**

gutta-percha [gytapɛrka] *(pl* **guttas-perchas)** **NF** gutta-percha

guttural, -e, -aux, -ales [gytyral, -o] **ADJ 1** *(ton)* guttural; *(voix)* guttural, throaty; *Anat* **artère gutturale** carotid artery **2** *Ling* guttural
• **gutturale NF** *Ling* guttural

Guyana [gɥijana] **NF OU NM la** *ou* **le G.** Guyana

guyanais, -e [gɥijanɛ, -ɛz] **ADJ 1** *(région, département)* Guianese, Guianian **2** *(république)* Guyanan, Guyanese
• **Guyanais, -e NM,F 1** *(région, département)* Guianese, Guianian; **les G.** the Guianese, the Guianians **2** *(république)* Guyanan, Guyanese; **les G.** the Guyanans, the Guyanese

Guyane [gɥijan] **NF la G., les Guyanes** Guiana, the Guianas; **la G. française** French Guiana; **la G. hollandaise** Dutch Guiana; *Hist* **la G. britannique** British Guiana

guyot[1] [gɥijo] **NM** *Géog* guyot

guyot[2] [gɥijo] **NF** *Bot* guyot pear

gym [ʒim] **NF** *(à l'école)* PE; *(pour adultes)* gym; **faire de la g.** to do exercises; **un cours de g.** a gym class

gymkhana [ʒimkana] **NM 1** *Sport* rally **2** *Fam Fig* obstacle course□

gymnase [ʒimnaz] **NM 1** *(salle)* gym, gymnasium **2** *Suisse (lycée)* = state school attended by pupils between ages of 15 and 19, *Br* ≃ secondary school, *Am* ≃ high school

gymnaste [ʒimnast] **NMF** gymnast

gymnastique [ʒimnastik] **NF 1** *Sport* physical education, gymnastics *(singulier)*; **faire de la g.** to do exercises; **faire sa g. matinale** to do one's morning exercises; **g. corrective** remedial gymnastics; **g. respiratoire** breathing exercises; **g. rythmique** eurhythmics *(singulier)*; **au pas (de) g.** at a jog trot **2** *Fig* gymnastics *(singulier)*; **g. mentale** *ou* **intellectuelle** mental gymnastics; **il faut faire toute une g. pour sortir de cette auto** you have to be a contortionist to get out of this car

gymnote [ʒimnɔt] **NM** *Ich* electric eel, *Spéc* gymnotus

gynécée [ʒinese] **NM 1** *Antiq* gynaeceum **2** *Bot* gynoecium

gynécologie [ʒinekɔlɔʒi] **NF** gynaecology

gynécologique [ʒinekɔlɔʒik] **ADJ** gynaecological

gynécologue [ʒinekɔlɔg] **NMF** gynaecologist

gypaète [ʒipaɛt] **NM** *Orn* **g. barbu** lammergeier, bearded vulture

gypse [ʒips] **NM** gypsum

gypseux, -euse [ʒipsø, -øz] **ADJ** gypseous

gypsophile [ʒipsɔfil] **NF** *Bot* gypsophila

gyrocompas [ʒirɔkɔ̃pa] **NM** gyrocompass

gyromètre [ʒirɔmɛtr] **NM** gyrometer

gyrophare [ʒirɔfar] **NM** rotating light *or* beacon

gyropilote [ʒiropilɔt] **NM** *Aviat* gyropilot, automatic pilot

gyroscope [ʒirɔskɔp] **NM** gyroscope; *Aviat* **g. directionnel** directional gyroscope

gyrostat [ʒirɔsta] **NM** gyrostat

H[1], h [aʃ] NM INV *(lettre)* H, h; **H comme Henri** ≃ H for Harry

H[2] [aʃ] NM INV *Fam (abrév* **haschisch***)* hash, *Br* blow

H[3] *(abrév écrite* **homme***)* M

***ha** [a] EXCLAM **1** *(surprise)* **h., vous partez déjà?** what, (are you) leaving already?; *(ironie, suspicion)* **ha, ha, je t'y prends!** aha! caught you! **2** *(rire)* **ha, ha, que c'est drôle!** ha ha, very funny!

***habanera** [abanera] NF habanera

habeas corpus [abeaskɔrpys] NM INV **l'h.** habeas corpus

habile [abil] ADJ **1** *(adroit)* skilful; **il est très h. aux échecs** he's very good at chess; **il est h. en affaires** he's got good business sense; **être h. de ses mains** to be good *or* clever with one's hands; **il n'est pas encore bien h. de ses mains** *(bébé)* his manual skills are still not fully developed; *(accidenté)* he still hasn't fully recovered his manual skills; **h. dans son travail** good at one's work

2 *(intelligent, fin* ▸ *personne)* clever, bright; *(*▸ *film, roman)* clever; **sa présentation des faits est très h.** his/her presentation of the facts is very clever

3 *(rusé)* clever, cunning; **une manœuvre h.** a clever move; **il est h. à se décharger de ses responsabilités** he is good *or* very clever at offloading his responsibilities

4 *Jur* **h. à tester** fit to make out one's will; **h. à succéder** entitled to inherit

habilement [abilmɑ̃] ADV *(travailler)* cleverly, skilfully; *(répondre)* cleverly; **elle a négocié h.** she negotiated skilfully; **les négociations ont été h. menées** the negotiations were conducted with skill; **elle a h. tiré son épingle du jeu** she cleverly *or* skilfully managed to wriggle out of it

habileté [abilte] NF **1** *(dextérité)* skill, dexterity *(UNCOUNT)*; **un orfèvre d'une grande h.** a very skilful goldsmith, a goldsmith of great skill **2** *(ingéniosité)* cleverness, smartness; **il lui fallut mettre toute son h. au service de cette démarche** he/she had to use all his/her artfulness to do this; **h. en affaires** business sense *or* flair

habilitation [abilitasjɔ̃] NF **1** *Jur* capacitation **2** *Univ* accreditation, habilitation

habilité, -e [abilite] ADJ *Jur* **h. à** fit to; **toute personne habilitée à signer** any person who is entitled to sign; **je suis h. à parler en son nom** I'm legally entitled *or* empowered to speak in his/her name

• **habilité** NF *Jur* capacity, entitlement

habiliter [3] [abilite] VT **1** *Jur* to entitle, to empower (**à faire qch** to do sth) **2** *Univ* to accredit, to habilitate

habillage [abijaʒ] NM **1** *(revêtement* ▸ *d'une machine)* casing; *(*▸ *d'un produit)* packaging; *(*▸ *d'un ordinateur)* cabinetry; *(*▸ *d'un intérieur)* trim; **h. transparent** *(emballage)* blister pack

2 *Culin (de la viande, du gibier à plumes)* dressing; *(d'un poisson)* cleaning; **l'h. d'un poulet** cleaning and trussing a chicken

3 *(d'un acteur, d'un enfant)* dressing

4 *(montage* ▸ *d'une montre, d'une horloge)* assembly, putting together

5 *Hort (des arbres)* pruning, trimming

6 *TV & Rad* **h. chaîne** station identification *(including on-air promos, transitions and titles)*

7 *Compta (d'un bilan)* window-dressing

• **en habillage** ADJ *Typ* **texte en h.** text wrap

habillé, -e [abije] ADJ *(vêtements)* smart, dressy; **dîner h.** dinner in evening dress

habillement [abijmɑ̃] NM **1** *(vêtements)* clothes, clothing; *(action d'habiller)* dressing, clothing; **magasin d'h.** *Br* clothes shop, *Am* clothing store; **il a de grosses dépenses d'h.** he spends a lot on clothes **2** *(industrie) Br* clothing trade, *Am* garment industry

habiller [3] [abije] VT **1** *(vêtir)* to dress; **elle a habillé sa fille d'une salopette rouge** she dressed her daughter in a pair of red *Br* dungarees *or Am* overalls; **habillé de** *ou* **en vert** dressed in green; **il est mal habillé** *(sans goût)* he's badly dressed; *Fam Fig* **h. qn pour l'hiver** to badmouth sb, *Br* to slag sb off

2 *(équiper* ▸ *famille, groupe)* to clothe; *(*▸ *skieur, écolier)* to kit out; **j'habille toute la famille** I make clothes for all the family; **la somme devrait suffire à h. toute la famille** the money should be enough to clothe the entire family

3 *(sujet: couturier, tailleur)* to design clothes for; **elle se fait h. par un grand couturier** she gets her clothes from a top designer

4 *(déguiser)* **h. qn en** to dress sb up as; **elle a habillé sa fille en Zorro** she dressed her daughter up as Zorro

5 *(décorer, recouvrir)* to cover; **h. un mur de toile de jute** to cover a wall with hessian; **h. des meubles de housses** to put loose covers on furniture; **tableau de bord habillé de cuir** leather-padded dashboard

6 *Mktg* to package (and present)

7 *Compta (bilan)* to window-dress

8 *Culin (viande, gibier à plumes)* to dress; *(volaille)* to clean and truss; *(poisson)* to clean

9 *(monter* ▸ *montre, horloge)* to assemble, to put together

VPR **s'habiller 1** *(se vêtir)* to get dressed, to dress; **habille-toi vite!** hurry up and get dressed!; **il s'habille tout seul maintenant** he's able to dress himself now; **tu devrais t'h. plus jeune** you should wear younger clothes; **tu t'habilles mal** you have no dress sense; **comment vous habillez-vous pour la soirée?** what are you wearing to the party?; **habille-toi chaudement** wrap up well *or* warm; **il s'habille chez un jeune couturier** he buys his clothes from a young fashion designer; **s'h. sur mesure** to have one's clothes made *or* tailor-made; **s'h. en** *(se déguiser en)* to dress up as; **s'h. en page** to dress up as a pageboy **2** *(se parer)* to dress up; **j'aime m'h. pour sortir le soir** I like dressing up to go out in the evening; **s'h. pour le dîner** to dress for dinner

habilleur, -euse [abijœr, -øz] NM,F *Cin, Théât & TV* dresser

habit [abi] NM **1** *(déguisement)* costume, outfit; **un h. de fée/sorcière** a fairy/witch outfit; **h. d'arlequin** Harlequin suit *or* costume **2** *(vêtement de cérémonie)* **h. (de soirée)** tails; **en h.** wearing tails; **se mettre en h.** to wear tails; **h. de cour** court dress; **l'h. vert** = regalia (hat, jacket and sword) worn by members of the Académie française; **porter l'h. vert** to be a member of the Académie française **3** *Rel* habit; **l'h. ecclésiastique** ecclesiastical dress; **prendre l'h.** *(femme)* to take the veil; *(homme)* to go into holy orders; **quitter l'h.** to leave orders; *Prov* **l'h. ne fait pas le moine** you can't judge a book by its cover

NM OU NF *Can* suit; **h. de neige** snowsuit

• **habits** NMPL clothes; **mettre ses habits du dimanche** to put on one's Sunday best

habitabilité [abitabilite] NF **1** *(d'un véhicule)* capacity **2** *(d'un lieu)* habitability

habitable [abitabl] ADJ habitable; **la maison est tout à fait h.** the house is perfectly habitable

habitacle [abitakl] NM **1** *Aviat* cockpit

2 *Aut* passenger compartment

3 *Littéraire (demeure)* abode, dwelling

4 *Naut* binnacle

habitant, -e [abitɑ̃, -ɑ̃t] NM,F **1** *(d'une ville, d'un pays)* inhabitant; *(d'un immeuble)* occupant; *(d'un quartier)* inhabitant, resident; **une ville de 30 000 habitants** a town of 30,000 inhabitants; **nous avons logé chez l'h.** we stayed with a family; **par h.** per person, per capita

2 *(gén pl) Littéraire (animal)* denizen; **les habitants des bois/des airs** the denizens of the forest/of the air

3 *(gén pl) (être humain)* dweller; **les habitants des cavernes** cave-dwellers

4 *Can (cultivateur)* farmer; *Péj Br* country bumpkin, *Am* hick

ADJ *Can* **1** *(nourriture, objets)* rustic **2** *Péj (personne)* uneducated; **il est un peu h. sur les bords** he's a bit of a *Br* country bumpkin *or Am* hick

habitat [abita] NM **1** *Bot & Zool* habitat **2** *(en anthropologie et sociologie)* settlement; **h. dispersé** open settlement **3** *(conditions de logement)* housing; **h. rural/urbain** rural/urban housing; **amélioration de l'h.** better housing (conditions)

habitation [abitasjɔ̃] NF **1** *(immeuble)* house, building; **groupe d'habitations** housing *Br* estate *or Am* development; **h. à loyer modéré** *(immeuble) Br* ≃ block of council flats, *Am* ≃ public housing unit; *(appartement) Br* ≃ council flat, *Am* ≃ (apartment in a) public housing unit; *(maison) Br* ≃ council house, *Am* ≃ low-rent house **2** *(domicile)* residence; **h. principale** main residence **3** *(action d'habiter)* living, *Sout* habitation; **les conditions d'h. sont très difficiles** living *or* housing conditions are very hard; **locaux à usage d'h.** premises for residential use; **impropre à l'h.** unsuitable *or* unfit for human habitation

habiter [3] [abite] VT **1** *(maison, ville, quartier)* to live in; *(ferme)* to live on; **qui habite au** *ou* **le numéro 22?** who lives at number 22? **2** *Fig* to inhabit, to be *or* to dwell in; **les craintes/démons qui l'habitent** the fears/demons within him/her; **elle est habitée par la haine** she is full of hatred **3** *(sujet: animaux)* to inhabit; **les oiseaux qui habitent nos forêts** the birds which inhabit our forests

VI to live; **h. Paris** *ou* **à Paris** to live in Paris; **h. en Italie** to live in Italy; **j'habite au 3, place des Cardeurs** I live at number 3, place des Cardeurs; **h. à l'hôtel** to live *or* to stay in a hotel; **h. chez des amis** to be staying with friends; **vous habitez chez vos parents?** do you live at home?; *Hum* ≃ do you come here often?

habitude [abityd] NF **1** *(manière d'agir)* habit; **j'ai l'h. de me coucher tôt** I normally *or* usually go to bed early; **je n'ai pas l'h. d'attendre!** I am not in the habit of being kept waiting!; **ça ne la gênera pas, elle a l'h.** that won't bother her *or* she won't

The symbol * indicates that the initial **h** is aspirate and that hence there is no liaison, eg **les haricots** [leariko] and not [lezariko], or contraction in spelling, eg **la haine** and not **l'haine**.

mind, she's used to it; **avoir pour h. de faire qch** to be in the habit of doing sth; **prendre l'h. de faire qch** to get into the habit of doing sth; **ce sont de bonnes/mauvaises habitudes** those are good/bad habits; **prendre de mauvaises habitudes** to get into *or* to pick up bad habits; **elle a ses petites habitudes** she's got her own (little) ways *or* habits; **ce n'est pas dans mes habitudes d'insister ainsi** I don't usually insist on things like that; **à** *ou* **selon** *ou* **suivant son h.** as is his/her wont, as usual; **tu n'as rien préparé, comme à ton h.!** you didn't get a thing ready, as usual *or* as always!; *Prov* **l'h. est une seconde nature** = habits are just like instincts; *Com* **habitudes d'achat** buying *or* purchasing habits **2** *(pratique)* experience; **avoir une longue h. du travail en commun** to have long experience of working together **3** *(usage)* custom; **c'est l'h. chez nous** it's a custom with us, it's our custom

• **d'habitude** ADV usually; **d'h., je suis d'accord avec elle** I usually *or* generally agree with her; **comme d'h.** as usual; **plus tôt que d'h.** earlier than usual

• **par habitude** ADV out of habit; **oh pardon, j'ai fait ça par h.!** sorry, I did it automatically *or* out of sheer habit!

habitué, -e [abitɥe] NM,F regular; **ça va déplaire aux habitués** the regulars won't like it

habituel, -elle [abitɥɛl] ADJ **1** *(traditionnel)* usual, regular; **le public h. des concerts de jazz était là** the usual *or* regular jazz audience was there; **il nous reçut avec sa ponctualité habituelle** he received us with his usual punctuality; **cette attitude ne lui est pas habituelle** this is not his/her usual attitude, he/she doesn't usually take this attitude; *Fam* **c'est le coup h.** it's the same old story, it's par for the course **2** *(ordinaire, courant)* usual; **au sens h. du terme** in the everyday sense of the term

habituellement [abitɥɛlmɑ̃] ADV usually, normally

habituer [7] [abitɥe] VT to accustom; **h. qn à qch** to get sb used to sth, to accustom sb to sth; **il faut h. les enfants à manger un peu de tout** one should get children used to eating a little bit of everything; **on l'a habitué à se taire** he's/she's been taught to keep quiet; **il est habitué** *(il a l'habitude)* he's used to it; **c'est facile quand on est habitué** it's easy once you're used to it *or* once you get used to it; **elle est habituée à rester seule** she's used to being alone

VPR **s'habituer s'h. à** to get *or* to grow *or* to become used to; **elle a fini par s'h. à notre petite ville** she eventually got used to our little town; **je ne pourrai jamais m'y h.** I'll never get used to it

***hâblerie** [ɑbləri] NF *Littéraire (parole)* boast; **ce n'était qu'une h. de sa part** he/she was only bragging

***hâbleur, -euse** [ɑblœr, -øz] *Littéraire* ADJ boastful

NM,F boaster, braggart

***Habsbourg** [abzbur] NPR Hapsburg, Habsburg

***hachage** [aʃaʒ] NM *(gén)* chopping (up); *Culin (de la viande) Br* mincing, *Am* grinding

***hache** [aʃ] NF **1** *(instrument tranchant)* axe; **abattre un arbre à la h.** to chop a tree down; **h. d'armes** battleaxe; **h. à main** hatchet; **la h. du bourreau** the executioner's axe; **h. de guerre** tomahawk; *Fig* **enterrer la h. de guerre** to bury the hatchet; *Fig* **déterrer la h. de guerre** to be on the warpath (again) **2** *Fig* **fait** *ou* **taillé à coups de h.** *(ouvrage)* rough-hewn, crudely worked; *(visage)* rough-hewn, rugged

***haché, -e** [aʃe] ADJ **1** *Culin (légume, amandes)* chopped; *(viande) Br* minced, *Am* ground; *Fig* **un film h. par des publicités** a film interspersed with adverts **2** *(style, tirade)* jerky

NM *Culin Br* mince, *Am* ground meat

***hache-légumes** [aʃlegym] NM INV vegetable chopper

***hachement** [aʃmɑ̃] = **hachage**

***hache-paille** [aʃpaj] NM INV *Agr* chaffcutter

***hacher** [3] [aʃe] VT **1** *Culin (légumes, fines herbes)* to chop (up); *(viande) Br* to mince, *Am* to grind; **le persil doit être haché menu** the parsley should be chopped finely; **je vais le h. menu comme chair à pâté** I'll make mincemeat (out) of him; **elle se ferait h. (menu** *ou* **en morceaux) pour ses enfants** she would go through hell and high water for her children

2 *(mettre en pièces, lacérer)* to cut to pieces; **la grêle a haché la vigne** the hail ripped the vines to pieces; **les mitraillettes ennemies ont haché le bataillon** the enemy submachine guns mowed down *or* cut down the battalion

3 *(saccader)* to break up; **il hachait toutes ses phrases, je n'y comprenais rien** all his sentences were so broken up *or* jerky that I didn't understand a thing

4 *(hachurer)* to hatch

***hachette** [aʃɛt] NF *(outil)* hatchet

***hache-viande** [aʃvjɑ̃d] NM INV *Br* mincer, *Am* grinder

***hachis** [aʃi] NM *Culin (de viande) Br* mince, *Am* ground meat; *(pour farce)* (meat) stuffing, forcemeat; *(de légumes)* chopped vegetables; **h. de veau** minced veal; **h. d'herbes** chopped herbs; **h. Parmentier** hachis Parmentier *(dish similar to shepherd's pie)*

***hachisch** [aʃiʃ] = **haschisch**

***hachoir** [aʃwar] NM **1** *(couteau)* chopping knife, chopper **2** *(planche)* chopping board; *(machine) Br* mincer, *Am* grinder

***hachure** [aʃyr] NF **1** *(en cartographie et dessin industriel)* hachure **2** *(sur un dessin, une gravure)* hatching *(UNCOUNT)*

***hachurer** [3] [aʃyre] VT **1** *(carte)* to hachure **2** *(dessin, gravure)* to hatch

hacienda [asjɛnda] NF hacienda

hacker [akœr] NM *Ordinat* hacker

***haddock** [adɔk] NM *Culin* smoked haddock

Hadrien [adrijɛ̃] NPR Hadrian

***Haendel** [ɛndel] NPR Handel

***hagard, -e** [agar, -ard] ADJ wild, crazed; **il me regardait avec des yeux hagards** he was looking at me with wild *or* staring eyes; **avoir l'air h.** to look crazed, to have a wild look in one's eyes

hagiographe [aʒjɔgraf] NMF hagiographer

hagiographie [aʒjɔgrafi] NF hagiography

hagiographique [aʒjɔgrafik] ADJ hagiographic, hagiographical

***haï, -e** [ai] PP *voir* **haïr**

***haie** [ɛ] NF **1** *Hort* hedge

2 *Sport* hurdle; **course de haies** hurdles race **courir le 400 mètres haies** to run the 400 metres hurdles

3 *Équitation* fence; **cheval de haies** hurdler

4 *(file de gens)* line, row; **les spectateurs ont fait une h. pour laisser passer les coureurs** the spectators all drew back to let the runners go through; **h. d'honneur** guard of honour

***haïe** [ai] *voir* **haïr**

***haïku** [ajku] NM *Littérature* haiku

***haillons** [ajɔ̃] NMPL rags, torn and tattered clothes; **être vêtu de h.** to be dressed in rags; **être en h.** to be in rags

***haine** [ɛn] NF hatred, hate; **sa h. de la guerre** his/her hatred of war; **avoir de la h. pour qn/qch** to hate *or* to detest sb/sth; **être plein de h. envers qn** to be full of hatred *or* filled with hatred for sb; **prendre qn/qch en h.** to take an immense dislike to sb/sth; **sans h.** without hatred, with no hatred; *Fam* **avoir la h.** to be fuming

• **par haine de** PRÉP out of hatred for

***haineuse** [ɛnøz] *voir* **haineux**

***haineusement** [ɛnøzmɑ̃] ADV with hatred

***haineux, -euse** [ɛnø, -øz] ADJ full of hatred *or* hate; **d'un ton h.** with a voice full of hate

> Il faut noter que l'adjectif anglais **heinous** est un faux ami. Il signifie **atroce, abominable.**

***haïr** [33] [air] VT **1** *(personne)* to hate; **il me hait de lui avoir menti** he hates me for having lied to him **2** *(attitude, comportement)* to hate, to detest; **h. l'hypocrisie** to hate *or* to detest hypocrisy

VPR **se haïr** *(soi-même)* to hate oneself; *(mutuellement)* to hate each other; **je me hais de lui mentir** I hate myself for lying to him/her

***haire** [ɛr] NF *Hist* hair shirt

***haïssable** [aisabl] ADJ *(préjugé, attitude, personne)* hateful, detestable

***haïssait** *etc voir* **haïr**

Haïti [aiti] NM Haiti

haïtien, -enne [aisjɛ̃, -ɛn] ADJ Haitian

• **Haïtien, -enne** NM,F Haitian

***halage** [alaʒ] NM *Naut (traction)* hauling; *(remorquage)* warping, towing

***halal** [alal] ADJ INV *Rel (viande)* halal

***hâle** [al] NM suntan, tan

***hâlé, -e** [ɑle] ADJ suntanned, tanned

haleine [alɛn] NF **1** *(mouvement de respiration)* breath, breathing; **hors d'h.** out of breath; **reprendre h.** to get one's breath back; **tenir qn en h.** to keep sb in suspense *or* on tenterhooks; **courir à perdre h.** to run until one is out of breath **2** *(air expiré)* breath; **avoir mauvaise h.** to have bad breath; **avoir l'h. fraîche** to have fresh breath

• **de longue haleine** ADJ long-term

***haler** [3] [ale] VT *Naut* **1** *(tirer ▸ bateau)* to haul; *(remorquer ▸ bateau)* to warp, to tow **2** *(tirer sur ▸ cordage)* to haul in, to heave

***hâler** [3] [ɑle] VT *(peau, corps)* to tan

***haletant, -e** [altɑ̃, -ɑ̃t] ADJ *(personne)* out of breath, panting; *(chien)* panting; **sa respiration haletante l'empêche de parler** he's/she's so out of breath he can't talk; **son père était h. de fureur** his/her father was choking with anger

***halètement** [alɛtmɑ̃] NM **1** *(respiration saccadée)* panting *(UNCOUNT)* **2** *(rythme saccadé)* **le h. de la locomotive** the puffing of the locomotive

***haleter** [28] [alte] VI **1** *(coureur)* to gasp for breath, to pant; *(pendant l'accouchement)* to breathe hard, to pant; *(chien)* to pant; **h. d'émotion** to be breathless with emotion; **h. de colère** to choke with anger **2** *(faire un bruit saccadé)* to sputter; **la locomotive haletait** the locomotive was puffing

***haleur, -euse** [alœr, -øz] NM,F *Naut (personne)* tower, hauler

NM *(remorqueur)* tug

***half-track** [alftrak] *(pl* **half-tracks)** NM half-track (vehicle)

***hall** [ol] NM *(d'un hôtel)* hall, lobby, foyer; *(d'une banque)* lobby, hall; **h. d'accueil** reception, lobby; **h. d'entrée** entrance hall; **h. de gare** concourse; **je t'attendrai dans le h. de la gare** I'll wait for you inside the station; **roman de h. de gare** trashy novel; **c'est un vrai h. de gare ici!** it's like Piccadilly Circus here!; **h. d'exposition** exhibition hall

***hallage** [alaʒ] NM *Com* market trader's dues

hallali [alali] NM **1** *Chasse* **l'h.** *(sonnerie)* the mort; **sonner l'h.** to sound the mort **2** *Fig (défaite)* (death) knell; **sonner l'h. de qn/qch** to sound the death knell for sb/sth

***halle** [al] NF **1** *(marché)* (covered) market; **h. au blé** corn exchange; **h. aux poissons** fish market; **le marché sous la h.** the covered market; **elle fait ses courses aux halles** she goes to the central food market to do her shopping **2 les Halles** = the Paris wholesale food market until 1968 (now a shopping centre) **3** *Suisse (bâtiment)* hall; **h. d'exposition** exhibition centre; **h. de fête** community centre; **h. de gymnastique** sports centre, sports hall; **h. polyvalente** community centre; **h. de sport** sports centre, sports hall

***hallebarde** [albard] NF **1** *(arme)* halberd, halbert **2** *Fam (locution)* **il pleut** *ou* **il tombe des hallebardes** it's raining cats and dogs

***hallebardier** [albardje] NM halberdier

***hallier** [alje] NM *Chasse* thicket, (brush) covert

***Halloween** [alɔwin] NF Hallowe'en

hallu [aly] NF *Fam (abrév* **hallucination)** hallucination▫; **je dois avoir des hallus!** I must be seeing things!

hallucinant, -e [alysinɑ̃, -ɑ̃t] ADJ **1** *(frappant)* unbelievable, incredible; **un paysage d'une beauté hallucinante** strikingly beautiful scenery **2** *(hallucinogène)* hallucinatory

hallucination [alysinasjɔ̃] NF hallucination; **avoir des hallucinations** to hallucinate; *Fam* **j'ai des hallucinations (ou quoi)!** I must be seeing things!; **une h. collective** a collective hallucination

hallucinatoire [alysinatwar] ADJ hallucinatory

halluciné, -e [alysine] ADJ *(regard)* wild-eyed, crazed

NM,F visionary, *Péj* lunatic; **comme un h.** like a madman

halluciner [3] [alysine] VI **1** *Psy* to hallucinate, to suffer from *or* to have hallucinations **2** *Fam Fig* **mais j'hallucine ou quoi?** I don't believe this!

VT *Littéraire* **h. qn** to make sb hallucinate; **halluciné par le manque de sommeil** seeing double through lack of sleep

hallucinogène [alysinɔʒɛn] ADJ hallucinogenic

NM hallucinogen

***halo** [alo] NM **1** *Astron* halo, corona **2** *Phot* halo, halation **3** *Littéraire* halo; **un h. de lumière/de gloire** a halo of light/of glory; **entouré d'un h. de mystère** shrouded in mystery

halogène [alɔʒɛn] ADJ halogenous

NM **1** *Chim* halogen **2** *(éclairage)* **(lampe à) h.** halogen lamp

***halte** [alt] NF **1** *(arrêt)* stop, break; **faire h.** to halt, to stop; **faire une h.** to have a break, to pause; **nous disons h. à la guerre** we are calling for a halt *or* an end to the war **2** *(répit)* pause, break; **le gouvernement a décidé une h. dans le programme spatial** the government decided to call a temporary halt to the space programme **3** *(lieu)* stopping *or* resting place; *Rail* halt; *Can (aire de repos ▸ côtière)* viewpoint, *Am* scenic overlook; *(▸ routière) Br* service area, *Am* rest area

EXCLAM stop!; *Mil* halt!; **h. à la pollution!** no more pollution!; **h., qui va là?** halt, who goes there?; **h.-là, ne t'emballe pas trop** hold on, don't get carried away

***halte-garderie** [altəgardəri] *(pl* **haltes-garderies)** NF ≃ day nursery

haltère [alter] NM *(avec des sphères)* dumbbell; *(avec des disques)* barbell; **faire des haltères** to do weight-lifting

haltérophile [alterɔfil] NMF weight-lifter

haltérophilie [alterɔfili] NF weight-lifting

***halva** [alva] NM *Culin* halva

***hamac** [amak] NM hammock

hamadryade [amadrijad] NF **1** *Myth* hamadryad, dryad, wood nymph **2** *Zool* king cobra

hamamélis [amamelis] NM *Bot* witch hazel *(UNCOUNT)*

***Hambourg** [ɑ̃bur] NF Hamburg

***hambourgeois, -e** [ɑ̃burʒwa, -az] ADJ of/from Hamburg

• **Hambourgeois, -e** NM,F = inhabitant of or person from Hamburg

***hamburger** [ɑ̃bœrgœr] NM hamburger

***hameau, -x** [amo] NM hamlet

hameçon [amsɔ̃] NM (fish) hook

***hammam** [amam] NM Turkish *or* steam bath, hammam

***hammerless** [amerles] NM INV *(fusil)* hammerless shotgun

***hampe** [ɑ̃p] NF **1** *(d'un drapeau)* pole

2 *Pêche & (d'une arme)* shaft

3 *Typ (d'une lettre)* stem; **h. montante** ascender

4 *(d'un pinceau)* handle

5 *(du bœuf)* flank; *(du cerf)* breast

***hamster** [amster] NM hamster

***han** [ɑ̃] NM INV oof; **pousser des h.** to grunt (with effort)

***hanap** [anap] NM hanap, goblet

***hanche** [ɑ̃ʃ] NF **1** *Anat* hip; **avoir les hanches larges/étroites** to have broad/narrow hips; **être large des hanches** to have broad hips **2** *Zool* haunch, hindquarter **3** *Naut (d'un navire)* quarter; **par la h.** on the quarter

***hand** [ɑ̃d] NM *Fam Sport* handball

***handball** [ɑ̃dbal] NM handball

***handballeur, -euse** [ɑ̃dbalœr, -øz] NM,F handball player

***handicap** [ɑ̃dikap] NM **1** *(gén) & Sport* handicap; **son poids est un grand h.** his/her weight is a great handicap **2** *(comme adj; avec ou sans trait d'union)* handicap *(avant n)*

***handicapant, -e** [ɑ̃dikapɑ̃, -ɑ̃t] ADJ **c'est (très) h.** it's a (great) handicap

***handicapé, -e** [ɑ̃dikape] ADJ *(physique)* handicapped, disabled; **h. mental** mentally handicapped; **h. physique** disabled

NM,F *(physique)* handicapped *or* disabled person; **les handicapés (physiques)** the disabled; **h. mental** mentally handicapped person

***handicaper** [3] [ɑ̃dikape] VT to handicap; **il sera handicapé par son poids** his weight will be a handicap; **ça l'a handicapé dans sa carrière** it was a handicap to his career

***handicapeur** [ɑ̃dikapœr] NM *(aux courses de chevaux)* (official) handicapper

***handisport** [ɑ̃dispɔr] ADJ INV **activité/jeux h.** sport/games for the disabled

***hangar** [ɑ̃gar] NM *(gén)* shed; *(pour avions)* (aircraft) hangar; *(pour locomotives, bus)* depot; **h. à bateaux** boathouse

***hanneton** [antɔ̃] NM *Entom* cockchafer, May bug, June bug

***Hanoi** [anɔj] NF Hanoi

***Hanoukka** [anuka] NF *Rel* Hanukkah

***Hanovre** [anɔvr] NF Hanover

***hanovrien, -enne** [anɔvrijɛ̃, -ɛn] ADJ Hanoverian

• **Hanovrien, -enne** NM,F Hanoverian

***hanse** [ɑ̃s] *Hist* NF Hanse, Hansa; **la H.** the Hanseatic League

***hanséatique** [ɑ̃seatik] ADJ Hanseatic

***hanté, -e** [ɑ̃te] ADJ *(maison, forêt)* haunted

***hanter** [3] [ɑ̃te] VT **1** *(sujet: fantôme, esprit)* to haunt; **ce souvenir le hante** he's haunted by the memory; **hanté par de vieux souvenirs** haunted *or* obsessed by old memories **2** *Littéraire (fréquenter)* to haunt; *Prov* **dis-moi qui tu hantes et je te dirai qui tu es** a man is known by the company he keeps

USAGE ABSOLU *Belg (couple ▸ sortir ensemble)* to go out together; *(▸ flirter)* to flirt with each other

• **hanter avec** VT IND *Belg* to go out with

***hantise** [ɑ̃tiz] NF obsession, obsessive fear; **avoir la h. de la mort** to be haunted *or* obsessed by the fear of death; **j'ai la h. de ce genre de réunion** I dread this kind of meeting; **chez lui, c'est une h.** he's obsessed by it, it's an obsession with him

haplodiploïde [aplɔdiplɔid] ADJ *Biol* haplodiploid

***happe** [ap] NF *Menuis* cramp *or* clamp iron

***happement** [apmɑ̃] NM snapping *(with the mouth)*

***happening** [apəniŋ] NM *(spectacle)* happening

***happer** [3] [ape] VT **1** *(avec le bec ou la bouche)* to snap up; *(avec la main ou la patte)* to snatch, to grab; **la machine a happé sa main** his/her hand got caught in the machine **2** *(accrocher violemment)* to strike *or* to hit violently; **être happé par un train/une voiture** to be mown down *or* hit by a train/a car

***happy end** [apiɛnd] *(pl* **happy ends)** NM happy ending

***happy few** [apifju] NMPL happy few; **une soirée réservée à quelques h.** a reception for a few selected guests

***haquenée** [akne] NF *Arch* palfrey

***hara-kiri** [arakiri] *(pl* **hara-kiris)** NM hara-kiri; **(se) faire h.** to commit hara-kiri

***harangue** [arɑ̃g] NF **1** *(discours solennel)* harangue **2** *Péj (sermon)* sermon

***haranguer** [3] [arɑ̃ge] VT to harangue

***haras** [ara] NM stud farm

***harassant, -e** [arasɑ̃, -ɑ̃t] ADJ exhausting, wearing

***harassé, -e** [arase] ADJ exhausted, worn out; **avoir l'air h.** to look exhausted

***harassement** [arasmɑ̃] NM *Littéraire* exhaustion, fatigue

***harasser** [3] [arase] VT to exhaust, to wear out

> Il faut noter que le verbe anglais **to harass** est un faux ami. Il signifie **harceler**.

***harcelant, -e** [arsəlɑ̃, -ɑ̃t] ADJ **1** *(obsédant)* haunting **2** *(importun)* harassing, pestering

***harcèlement** [arsɛlmɑ̃] NM harassment; **h. électronique** cyberbullying; **h. moral** moral harassment; **h. sexuel** sexual harassment

***harceler** [25] [arsəle] VT *(personne)* to harass; *(animal)* to bait; **h. qn de questions** to plague *or* to pester sb with questions; **cesse de me h.!** stop pestering *or* bothering me!; **les remords le harcèlent** he's tormented *or* plagued by remorse; **h. qn sexuellement** to sexually harass sb

***harceleur, -euse** [arsəlœr, -øz] NM,F pest; **h. téléphonique** phone pest

***hard** [ard] *Fam* = **hardware**

***harde** [ard] NF **1** *(d'animaux sauvages)* herd **2** *Chasse (lien)* leash; *(chiens liés)* set (of coupled hounds)

***hardes** [ard] NFPL *Littéraire Péj* rags, tatters

***hardeur, -euse** [ardœr, -øz] NM,F hardcore porn star

***hardi, -e** [ardi] ADJ **1** *(intrépide)* bold, daring; *(original)* bold; **nos hardis explorateurs** our bold *or* intrepid explorers **2** *(téméraire)* rash; *Fig* **l'hypothèse est un peu hardie** the supposition is a bit rash *or* hasty **3** *(licencieux)* daring, bold; **on a censuré les passages les plus hardis** the most risqué *or* the raciest parts were cut out

• **hardi** EXCLAM *Arch* **h., les gars!** go to it, boys!

***hardiesse** [ardjɛs] NF **1** *(intrépidité)* boldness, daring, audacity; *(originalité ▸ du style, d'une figure)* boldness

2 *(témérité)* **avoir la h. de faire qch** to be forward *or* daring enough to do sth; **auriez-vous la h. de réclamer un pourcentage?** would you have the audacity to ask for a commission?

3 *(acte, parole)* **h. de langage** bold turn of phrase; **des hardiesses de langage** *(propos crus)* bold language; *(effets de style)* daring stylistic effects; **se permettre des hardiesses avec qn** to take liberties with sb

4 *(indécence)* boldness, raciness; **la h. de certaines scènes peut choquer** you may find the explicitness of some of the scenes offensive

***hardiment** [ardimɑ̃] ADV **1** *(avec audace)* boldly, daringly **2** *(avec effronterie)* impudently; *(à la légère)* rashly

***hardos** [ardos] NM *Fam (musicien de hard-rock)* hard rocker; *(amateur de hard-rock)* hard rocker, metalhead

***hard-top** [ardtɔp] *(pl* **hard-tops)** NM hardtop (roof)

***hardware** [ardwɛr] NM *Ordinat* hardware

***harem** [arem] NM harem

***hareng** [arɑ̃] NM **1** *(poisson)* herring; **h. fumé** kipper; **h. saur** smoked herring, kipper; *Fam* **on était serrés comme des harengs dans le bus** we were packed together like sardines in the bus **2** *très Fam (souteneur)* pimp

***harengère** [arɑ̃ʒɛr] NF **1** *(marchande)* fishwife, fishwoman **2** *Fam Vieilli (femme querelleuse et grossière)* fishwife, harridan

***harenguier** [arɑ̃gje] NM *Pêche* **1** *(bateau)* herring boat **2** *(personne)* herring fisherman

***harfang** [arfɑ̃] NM *Orn* great white owl; **h. des neiges** snowy owl

***hargne** [arɲ] NF aggressiveness; **avec h.** aggressively, cantankerously; **des propos pleins de h.** aggressive remarks

***hargneuse** [arɲøz] *voir* **hargneux**

***hargneusement** [arɲøzmɑ̃] ADV aggressively, cantankerously

***hargneux, -euse** [arɲø, -øz] ADJ **1** *(caractère, ton)* aggressive, quarrelsome; **une femme hargneuse** a shrew, an ill-tempered woman; **un vieil homme h.** a cantankerous old man **2** *(combatif)* aggressive; **il est h. dans les sprints** he's an aggressive sprinter **3** *(animal)* vicious

***haricot** [ariko] NM **1** *(légume)* bean; **h. beurre** = yellow variety of string bean; **h. blanc** white (haricot) bean; **h. d'Espagne** scarlet runner; **h. flageolet** flageolet bean; **h. de Lima** Lima bean; **h. mange-tout** runner *or* string bean; **h. noir** black bean; **h. rouge** red *or* kidney bean; **h. vert** string *or* green *or Br* French bean; **haricots fins/extra-fins** high-quality/superfine string *or* green *or Br*

French beans; **haricots à écosser** shell beans; **haricots en grains** dried beans **2** *Culin (ragoût)* **h. de mouton** mutton haricot *or* stew **3** *Méd (cuvette)* kidney tray *or* dish

• **haricots** NMPL *Fam* **des haricots** not a thing, *Am* zilch; **travailler pour des haricots** to work for peanuts

***haridelle** [aridɛl] NF **1** *(cheval)* jade, nag **2** *(femme)* beanpole

***harissa** [arisa] NF harissa (sauce)

***harki** [arki] NM = Algerian who fought for the French during the Franco-Algerian War and who was subsequently given French nationality

***harle** [arl] NM *Orn* merganser

harmonica [armɔnika] NM harmonica, mouth organ

harmonie [armɔni] NF **1** *(élégance)* harmony; **l'h. du corps humain** the beauty of the human body

2 *(entente)* harmony; **il régnait dans leur couple une grande h.** the couple lived together in great harmony

3 *Mus (accord)* harmony; *(instruments à vent et percussions)* wind section with percussion; *(fanfare)* brass band

4 *Littérature* **h. imitative** onomatopoeia

• **en harmonie** ADV in harmony, harmoniously; **en parfaite h.** in perfect harmony ADJ in harmony; **le tapis n'est pas en h. avec les meubles** the carpet doesn't go with *or* match the furniture; **quand les sentiments de l'un sont en h. avec ceux de l'autre** when two people feel the same way

harmonieuse [armɔnjøz] *voir* **harmonieux**

harmonieusement [armɔnjøzmɑ̃] ADV harmoniously, in harmony

harmonieux, -euse [armɔnjø, -øz] ADJ **1** *(mélodieux ▸ son, instrument)* harmonious; *(▸ voix)* harmonious, tuneful, melodious **2** *(équilibré)* harmonious, balanced; **des teintes harmonieuses** well-matched colours; **un visage h.** well-balanced features; **un couple h.** a well-matched *or* happy couple

harmonique [armɔnik] ADJ *Math & Mus & (en acoustique)* harmonic; **son h.** harmonic

NM **1** *Mus & (en acoustique)* harmonic **2** *Phys* harmonic, overtone

harmoniquement [armɔnikmɑ̃] ADV *Mus* harmonically

harmonisation [armɔnizasjɔ̃] NF **1** *(mise en accord)* harmonization; **réclamer l'h. des salaires du public et du privé** to demand that public sector salaries be brought into line with those in the private sector; **h. fiscale** tax harmonization **2** *Mus* harmonizing **3** *Ling* **h. vocalique** vowel harmony

harmoniser [3] [armɔnize] VT *Mus* to harmonize; *(styles, couleurs)* to match; **h. les théories en présence** to reconcile the various opposing theories; **h. les salaires du public et du privé** to bring public and private sector salaries into line; **h. les rideaux avec la moquette** to match the curtains with the carpet, to match up the curtains and the carpet

VPR **s'harmoniser s'h. avec** to harmonize with; **ces couleurs s'harmonisent bien entre elles** these colours go together well

harmonium [armɔnjɔm] NM *Mus* harmonium

***harnachement** [arnaʃmɑ̃] NM **1** *(d'un cheval ▸ équipement)* harness; *(▸ action)* harnessing **2** *Hum (accoutrement)* outfit, get-up; *(attirail)* paraphernalia

***harnacher** [3] [arnaʃe] VT **1** *(cheval)* to harness **2** *Hum (accoutrer)* to deck *or* to rig out; *(équiper)* to kit out; **il fallait voir comment elle était harnachée** you should have seen the ridiculous get-up she was wearing

VPR **se harnacher** *(s'équiper)* to get kitted out; **ils s'étaient harnachés de cordes et de piolets pour l'ascension** they were kitted out with ropes and ice axes for the climb

***harnais** [arnɛ] NM **1** *(d'un cheval)* harness

2 *(sangles)* **h. (de sécurité)** (safety) harness; **mettre le h. (de sécurité) à qn** to strap sb in

3 *Tech* backgear; **h. d'engrenage** (back) gear train

4 *Arch (armure)* armour

***harnois** [arnwa] NM *Littéraire* **blanchi sous le h.** gone grey in the saddle

***haro** [aro] NM **crier h. sur qn** to raise a hue and cry against sb; **on a crié h. sur le baudet** there was a hue and cry

Harpagon [arpagɔ̃] NM *Littéraire* Scrooge, skinflint

***harpe** [arp] NF **1** *Mus* harp; **h. celtique** Celtic harp; **h. éolienne** wind *or* aeolian harp **2** *Zool (mollusque)* harp (shell)

***harpie** [arpi] NF **1** *(mégère)* shrew, harpy **2** *Orn (aigle)* harpy eagle; *(chauve-souris)* harpy bat

***harpiste** [arpist] NMF harpist

***harpon** [arpɔ̃] NM *Pêche* harpoon

***harponnage** [arpɔnaʒ], ***harponnement** [arpɔnmɑ̃] NM *Pêche* harpooning

***harponner** [3] [arpɔne] VT **1** *Pêche* to harpoon **2** *Fam (accaparer)* to grab, to collar; **harponne-le à la sortie de la réunion** grab him when he comes out of the meeting; **je me suis fait h. par un collègue juste avant de partir** I got collared by a colleague just as I was about to leave **3** *Fam (arrêter)* to pick up, to nab; **les flics l'ont harponné à la sortie du club** the cops nabbed him outside the club

***harponneur** [arpɔnœr] NM *Pêche* harpooner

***hasard** [azar] NM **1** *(providence)* chance, fate; **s'il gagne, c'est le h.** if he wins it's by sheer luck *or* chance; **s'en remettre au h.** to leave it to chance, to trust to luck; **ne rien laisser au h.** to leave nothing to chance; **le h. a voulu que je sois à l'étranger** as it happened, I was abroad; **le h. fait bien les choses** there are some lucky coincidences; **le h. faisant bien les choses, ils se retrouvèrent quelques années plus tard** as chance would have it, they met again some years later

2 *(incident imprévu)* **quel heureux h.!** what a stroke of luck *or* piece of good fortune!; **un h. malheureux** a piece of bad luck

3 *(coïncidence)* **quel heureux h.!** what a fantastic coincidence!; **un heureux h. a fait qu'il a été muté dans la même région que moi** by a stroke of luck he was transferred to the same area as me; **c'est un (pur) h. que vous m'ayez trouvé chez moi à cette heure-ci** it's sheer luck that you've found me in at this time of day; **par un curieux h., il était né le même jour** by a strange coincidence he was born on the same day; **par quel h. étiez-vous là ce jour-là?** how come you happened to be there that day?; **par le plus grand des hasards** by the most extraordinary *or* incredible coincidence; **tu n'aurais pas, par le plus grand des hasards, vu mes lunettes?** you wouldn't by any chance have happened to see my glasses, would you?

4 *(jeu)* **jeu de h.** game of chance; *Fig* **l'amour est un jeu de h.** love is like a game of chance

5 *(en statistique)* chance; **échantillonnage/nombres au h.** random sampling/numbers

• **hasards** NMPL **1** *(aléas)* **les hasards de la vie** life's ups and downs **2** *Littéraire (périls)* hazards, dangers; **les hasards de la guerre** the hazards *or* dangers of war

• **à tout hasard** ADV on the off chance, just in case

• **au hasard** ADV at random; **j'ai ouvert le livre au h.** I opened the book at random; **aller** *ou* **marcher au h.** *(par indifférence)* to walk aimlessly; *(par plaisir)* to go where one's fancy takes one; **tirez** *ou* **piochez une carte au h.** pick a card(, any card)

• **au hasard de** PRÉP **toute sa vie, elle a pris des notes au h. de ses lectures** throughout her life, she took notes of things she happened to come across in her reading

• **de hasard** ADJ chance *(avant n)*; **une rencontre de h.** a chance meeting; **des amours de h.** brief encounters

• **par hasard** ADV by chance *or* accident; **je l'ai appris par h.** I heard about it completely by chance; **si par h. vous la voyez** if by any chance you should see her, should you happen to see her; **je suis entré par h. et je l'ai pris la main dans le sac** I went in quite by chance and caught him red-handed; *Ironique* **comme par h.!** that's a surprise!, surprise, surprise!; **comme par h., elle n'a rien entendu!** surprisingly enough, she didn't hear a thing!

> Il faut noter que le nom anglais **hazard** signifie uniquement **danger**.

***hasardé, -e** [azarde] = **hasardeux**

***hasarder** [3] [azarde] VT *(opinion, démarche)* to hazard, to venture, to risk; **h. un orteil dans l'eau glacée** to cautiously dip one toe into the icy water; **je me permettrai de h. une question** I'll venture a question, I'll take the liberty of asking a question

VPR **se hasarder 1** *Arch (s'exposer au danger)* to venture forth **2** *(s'aventurer)* to venture; **il se hasarda dans l'obscurité** he ventured into the darkness; **la nouvelle élève se hasarda à répondre** the new student plucked up courage to answer; **je ne m'y hasarderais pas** I wouldn't risk it *or* chance it

***hasardeux, -euse** [azardø, -øz] ADJ **1** *(douteux)* dubious; **l'issue en est hasardeuse** the outcome of all this is uncertain **2** *(dangereux)* hazardous, dangerous; **une affaire hasardeuse** a risky business

***hasch** [aʃ] NM *Fam* hash

***haschisch, *haschich** [aʃiʃ] NM hashish

***hase** [ɑz] NF *Zool* doe

***hassidisme** [asidism] NM *Rel* Hasidism

hast [ast] NM *Arch* shaft; **arme d'h.** shafted weapon

***hâte** [ɑt] NF **1** *(précipitation)* haste, hurry, rush; **dans sa h., il a oublié ses clés** he was in such a hurry *or* rush (that) he left his keys behind; **mettre trop de h. à faire qch** to be in too great a hurry *or* too much of a hurry to do sth; **avec h.** hastily, hurriedly; **sans h.** at a leisurely pace, without hurrying **2** *(être impatient)* **avoir h. de faire qch** to be looking forward to doing sth; **j'ai h. que vous veniez** I can't wait for you to come; **pourquoi avez-vous h. de partir?** why are you in (such) a hurry *or* rush to leave?; **il n'a qu'une h., c'est d'avoir un petit-fils** he's dying to have a grandson

• **à la hâte** ADV hurriedly, hastily, in a rush

• **en hâte, en grande hâte, en toute hâte** ADV hurriedly, in (great) haste; **envoyez votre réponse en toute h. à l'adresse suivante** send your reply without delay to the following address

***hâter** [3] [ɑte] VT **1** *(accélérer)* to speed up, to hasten; **h. le pas** to quicken one's pace, to walk quicker **2** *(avancer ▸ date)* to bring forward; *(▸ naissance, mort, mariage)* to precipitate; **je dois h. mon départ** I must go sooner than I thought

VPR **se hâter** to hurry (up), to hasten, to make haste; **les travailleurs se hâtaient vers les gares** the workers were hurrying towards the stations; **hâtez-vous de me répondre** answer me posthaste; **hâte-toi lentement** more haste, less speed

***hâtif, -ive** [ɑtif, -iv] ADJ **1** *(rapide ▸ travail, repas)* hurried, rushed; *(▸ décision)* hasty, rash **2** *(précoce ▸ croissance, fruit)* early

***hâtivement** [ɑtivmɑ̃] ADV hastily, hurriedly, in a rush; **le livre a été écrit un peu h.** the book was written in somewhat of a rush

***hauban** [obɑ̃] NM **1** *Aviat & Naut* shroud **2** *Tech* stay

***haubaner** [3] [obane] VT *Naut (mât)* to stay (with shrouds)

***haubert** [obɛr] NM *Hist* hauberk, shirt of mail

***hausse** [os] NF **1** *(augmentation)* rise, increase (**de** in); **la h. du coût de la vie** the rise in the cost of living; **une h. de 4 pour cent** a 4 percent rise; **une h. des prix** a price increase; *Bourse* **h. des cours** stock market rise **2** *(élévation)* rise **3** *(d'une arme)* back-sight

• **à la hausse** ADV **1** *(au maximum)* **réviser le budget à la h.** to increase the budget, to revise the budget upwards **2** *Bourse* **à la h.** *(tendance, marché, position)* bullish; **être à la h.** to go up; **le marché évolue** *ou* **est à la h.** there is an upward trend in the market; **jouer à la h.** to speculate on the rising market *or* on the bull market; **pousser à la h.** to bull; **pousser les actions à la h.** to bull the market; **les cours sont orientés à la h.** there is an upward trend in share prices; **vendre à la h.** to sell in a rising market, *Spéc* to contrary sell

• **en hausse** **ADJ** increasing, rising; **être en h.** to be on the increase, to be rising; **des prix en h.** rising prices; **les vols de voitures sont en h. de 30 pour cent sur l'année dernière** car thefts are up 30 percent on last year

***haussement** [osmɑ̃] **NM avec un h. d'épaules** with a shrug (of one's shoulders); **avec un h. de sourcils** with raised eyebrows

***hausser** **[3]** [ose] **VT 1** *Écon* to raise, to increase, to put up; **le prix a été haussé de 10 pour cent** the price has been increased *or* has gone up by 10 percent; **h. ses prétentions** to aim higher

2 *Constr* to raise; **l'immeuble a été haussé d'un étage** the building was made higher by adding another floor; *Fig* **h. qn au niveau de** to raise sb up to the level of

3 *(partie du corps)* **h. les épaules** to shrug (one's shoulders); **h. les sourcils** to raise one's eyebrows

4 *(intensifier)* **h. la voix** *ou* **le ton** to raise one's voice

VI to rise; **faire h. les prix** to force up prices

VPR se hausser 1 *(se hisser)* **se h. sur la pointe des pieds** to stand on tiptoe; **je me suis haussé jusqu'à la fenêtre** I stretched up to the window; *Fig* **se h. du col** to show off **2** *(atteindre un degré supérieur)* **se h. à** to attain, to reach; **elle est parvenue à se h. au niveau de la classe** she managed to reach the level of the other students in her class

***haussier, -ère** [osje, ɛr] *Bourse* **ADJ un marché h.** a rising *or* bull market

NM,F bull

***haussmannien, -enne** [osmanjɛ̃, -ɛn] **ADJ** *(immeuble, architecture etc)* Haussmann *(avant n)*, Haussmann-style *(avant n)*

***HAUT, -E** [o, ot]

> **ADJ**
> • high **1–8** • tall **1**
> • top **5**
> **NM**
> • top **1, 2** • top end **5**
> **ADV**
> • high **1, 4–6** • far (back) **2**
> • above **2** • aloud **3**

ADJ 1 *(de grande dimension* ▸ *bâtiment)* high, tall; *(*▸ *tige, tronc)* tall; *(*▸ *qui a poussé)* high; **les hautes colonnes du temple** the lofty *or* towering columns of the temple; **un homme de haute taille** a tall man; **les pièces sont hautes de plafond** the rooms have high ceilings; **j'aime les fleurs hautes** I like long-stemmed *or* tall flowers

2 *(d'une certaine dimension)* high; **la maison est haute de trois mètres** the house is three metres high

3 *(situé en hauteur)* high; **le soleil est h. dans le ciel** the sun is high (up) in the sky; **la mer était haute** the tide was in *or* high; **une robe à taille haute** a high-waisted dress; **sur les hautes branches** on the top *or* topmost branches; **en haute montagne** high in the mountains; **la partie haute de l'arbre** the top of the tree; **le H. Nil** the upper (reaches of the) Nile

4 *(extrême, intense)* high; **c'est de la plus haute importance** it's of the utmost *or* greatest importance; **à h. risque** high-risk; **à haute température** high-temperature; **c'était du plus h. comique** it was high farce; *Ordinat & Tél* **h. débit** broadband; *TV* **haute définition** high definition; *Ordinat* **haute densité** high density; **haute fréquence** high frequency; **de haute précision** high-precision; **haute pression** high pressure; **haute technologie** high technology; **haute tension** high tension

5 *(dans une hiérarchie)* high, top *(avant n)*; **de h. niveau** top-level, high-level; **des officiers de h. niveau** high-ranking officers; **de hauts dignitaires** eminent *or* leading dignitaries; **la haute cuisine** haute cuisine; *Suisse* **haute école** = higher education establishment (university, technical college or "grande école"); **de hautes études commerciales/militaires** advanced business/military studies; **Hautes études commerciales** = prestigious business school in Paris; **les hauts fonctionnaires** top *or* top-ranking civil servants; **les hauts salaires** the highest *or* top salaries; **politique des hauts salaires** high income policy

6 *(dans une échelle de valeurs)* high; **d'une haute intelligence** highly intelligent; **avoir une haute idée de soi-même** to have a high opinion of oneself; **tenir qch en haute estime** to hold sb/sth in high esteem

7 *Bourse & Com* high; **la livre est à son niveau le plus h.** the pound is at its highest level *or* has reached a high

8 *Mus & Ling* high; **une note/voyelle haute** a high note/vowel

9 *Ling* **le h. allemand** (Old) High German; *Hist* **le h. Moyen Âge** the Early Middle Ages; *Art & Hist* **la haute Renaissance** the High Renaissance

10 *Littéraire (noble)* lofty, high-minded; **cette haute pensée/âme** this exalted thought/soul

NM 1 *(partie supérieure* ▸ *gén)* top; *(*▸ *de robe)* bodice; **vers le h.** upwards; **h.** *(sur une caisse)* (this way *or* side) up; *Compta* **h. de bilan** *(fonds propres)* shareholders' funds

2 *(vêtement)* top

3 *(hauteur)* **un mur d'un mètre de h.** a one-metre (high) wall; **le mur fait six mètres de h.** the wall is six metres high; **regarder qn de (tout) son h.** to look down on sb; **tomber de tout son h.** *(chuter)* to fall headlong; *(être déçu)* to come down (to earth) with a bump; *(être surpris)* to be flabbergasted

4 *Can (d'un immeuble)* top floor

5 *Mktg (du marché)* high end, top end

ADV 1 *(dans l'espace)* high; **h. dans les airs** high (up) in the air; **levez h. la jambe** raise your leg (up) high; **l'aigle monte h. dans le ciel** the eagle soars (high up) in the sky

2 *(dans le temps)* far (back); *(dans un livre, un article)* above; **remonter plus h. (dans le temps)** to go further back; **voir plus h.** see above; **l'exemple cité plus h.** the example given above

3 *(fort, avec puissance)* **(tout) h.** aloud; **dire tout h. ce que tout le monde pense tout bas** to say out loud what everyone else is thinking; **penser tout h.** to think aloud *or* out loud; **parlez plus h.** speak up, speak louder; **dites-le h. et clair** *ou* **bien h.** tell (it to) everyone, say it out loud; **parler h. et clair** to speak one's mind

4 *Mus* high; **elle monte très h. dans les aigus** she gets up to the really high notes; **tu prends la deuxième mesure un peu trop h.** *(chanteur)* you're singing the second bar a bit sharp *or* high; *(musicien)* you're playing the second bar a bit sharp *or* high

5 *(dans une hiérarchie)* high; **être h. placé** to be highly placed, to hold high office; **des amis h. placés** friends in high places; **nous l'avons toujours placé très h. dans notre estime** we've always held him in high regard

6 *Bourse & Com* high; **les enchères sont montées très h.** the bidding went sky high *or* hit the roof

• **hauts NMPL 1** *(dans des noms de lieux)* heights **2** *Naut (partie émergée)* topsider; *(du gréement)* top *or* higher rigging **3** *(locution)* **avoir** *ou* **connaître des hauts et des bas** to have one's ups and downs

• **haute NF** *Fam* **la haute** high society[□], the upper crust; **les gens de la haute** upper crust people

• **de haut ADV 1** *(d'un lieu élevé)* from a great height; **regarder qch de h.** to look down on sth; **tomber de h.** to fall from a great height; *Fig (être surpris)* to be flabbergasted; *(être déçu)* to come down (to earth) with a bump **2** *(avec détachement)* casually, unconcernedly; **prendre** *ou* **regarder** *ou* **voir les choses de h.** to look at things with an air of detachment **3** *(avec mépris)* **prendre qch de h.** to be high and mighty about sth; **regarder qn de h.** to look down on sb; **traiter qn de h.** to treat sb high-handedly

• **de haut en bas ADV 1** *(sans mouvement)* from top to bottom; **nettoyer la maison de h. en bas** to clean the house from top to bottom **2** *(avec mouvement, vers le bas)* from top to bottom, downwards; **il faut toujours se raser de h. en bas** you should always shave with a downward movement **3** *(avec mépris)* **regarder** *ou* **considérer qn de h. en bas** to look sb up and down

• **d'en haut ADV 1** *(depuis la partie élevée)* from above; **d'en h. on voit la mer** you can see the sea from up there **2** *Fig (dans la hiérarchie)* from on high; **le bon exemple doit venir d'en h.** people in positions of authority must set an example; **la directive est venue d'en h.** the directive came from the top *or* from on high

• **du haut ADJ** *(de l'étage supérieur)* upstairs; **les gens du h.** the people upstairs; **les chambres du h.** the upstairs bedrooms; **l'étage du h.** the top floor

• **du haut de PRÉP** *(échelle, colline)* from the top of; **du h. de la colline, on voit toute la ville** you can see the whole town from the top of the hill; *Fig* **il nous regarde du h. de sa grandeur** he looks down his nose at us

• **en haut ADV 1** *(à l'étage supérieur)* upstairs **2** *(dans la partie élevée)* at the top; **regarde dans le placard, les verres sont en h.** look in the cupboard, the glasses are at the top; **nous sommes passés par en h.** *(par la route du haut)* we came along the high road; **tout en h.** at the very top, right at the top **3** *(en l'air)* up in the air; **lancer qch en h.** to throw sth (up) in the air

• **en haut de PRÉP** at the top of; **regarde en h. de l'armoire** look at the top of the wardrobe; **grimper en h. d'un arbre** to climb (up) to the top of a tree; **tout en h. d'une colline** high up on a hill

• **haut lieu NM le h. lieu de…** the Mecca of…, a Mecca for…; **en août, la ville devient un h. lieu de la musique** in August, the town is THE place *or* a major centre for music

***hautain, -e** [otɛ̃, -ɛn] **ADJ** haughty; **d'une façon hautaine** haughtily

***hautbois** [obwa] **NM 1** *(instrument)* oboe; **h. alto** cor anglais, English horn **2** *(instrumentiste)* oboe (player)

***hautboïste** [obɔist] **NMF** *Mus* oboist, oboe (player)

***haut-commissaire** [okɔmisɛr] *(pl* **hauts-commissaires)** **NM** high commissioner

***haut-commissariat** [okɔmisarja] *(pl* **hauts-commissariats)** **NM 1** *(fonction)* high commissionership **2** *(bureaux)* high commission

***haut-de-forme** [odfɔrm] *(pl* **hauts-de-forme)** **NM** top hat

***haute** [ot] *voir* **haut**

***haute-contre** [otkɔ̃tr] *(pl* **hautes-contre)** **NF** *(voix)* countertenor (voice)

NM *(chanteur)* countertenor

***haute-fidélité** [otfidelite] *(pl* **hautes-fidélités)** **NF 1** *(technique)* high fidelity, hi-fi **2** *(comme adj)* high-fidelity *(avant n)*, hi-fi

***hautement** [otmɑ̃] **ADV 1** *(fortement)* highly, extremely; **c'est h. improbable** it's highly unlikely **2** *Vieilli (ouvertement)* openly

***hauteur** [otœr] **NF 1** *(mesure verticale)* height; **quelle est la h. du mur?** how high is the wall?; **l'immeuble a une h. de 40 mètres** the building is 40 metres high; **il est tombé de toute sa h.** he fell headlong; **de faible h.** low; **h. libre** *Constr* headroom, *Rail* overhead clearance; *Ordinat* **h. de ligne** line height; *Typ* **h. de page** page depth; *Constr* **h. de passage** headroom; **h. sous plafond** ceiling height; **quelle est la h. sous plafond?** what is the height of *or* how high is the ceiling?

2 *(altitude)* height, altitude; **prendre de la h.** to gain altitude *or* height; **une occupation qui sied à la h. de son rang** a post in keeping with his/her high rank; **n'étant plus mandaté, je me permets de voir les choses avec (une certaine) h.** as I'm no longer in office, I can afford to look upon things with a certain detachment

3 *Mus & Ling* height, pitch; **deux notes/voyelles de la même h.** two equally pitched notes/vowels

4 *(noblesse)* loftiness; **rien n'égala la h. de vues** *ou* **de pensées de ce monarque** nothing could equal the loftiness of this monarch's ideas

5 *(arrogance)* haughtiness, arrogance; **un refus plein de h.** a haughty refusal

6 *Sport* **la h.** the high jump; **recordman du monde de h.** world record holder for the men's high jump

7 *Géom (d'un triangle)* altitude

8 *Couture* length

• **hauteurs NFPL** heights; **il y a de la neige sur les hauteurs** there's snow on the higher slopes; **l'aigle s'envola vers les hauteurs** the eagle soared high up (into the sky *or* air); **les hauteurs de Montmartre** the top of Montmartre

• **à hauteur de PRÉP à h. des yeux** at eye level; **à h. d'homme** about six feet off the ground; **à h. d'appui** at elbow height; **vous serez remboursé à h. de 1000 euros** you'll be reimbursed up to 1,000 euros; **un actionnaire à h. de 5 pour cent** a shareholder with 5 percent of the shares

• **à la hauteur** ADJ *Fam* **tu ne t'es pas montré à la h.** you weren't up to it *or* equal to the task; **elle a été tout à fait à la h.** she coped beautifully
• **à la hauteur de** PRÉP **1** *(au niveau de)* up to; **l'eau nous arrivait à la h. des épaules** the water came up to our shoulders **2** *(à côté de)* **arrivé à sa h., je m'aperçus qu'il parlait tout seul** when I was *or* drew level with him, I noticed he was talking to himself; **elle habite à la h. de l'église** she lives near the church *or* up by the church; **à la h. de Grenoble, il faudra commencer à penser à mettre les chaînes** when you get (up) to Grenoble, you will have to start thinking about putting the snow chains on; **il y a des embouteillages à la h. de l'échangeur de Rocquencourt** there are traffic jams at the Rocquencourt interchange **3** *(digne de)* worthy of; **une carrière à la h. de ses ambitions** a career commensurate with his/her ambitions; **être** *ou* **se montrer à la h. d'une tâche** to be *or* to prove equal to *or* up to a task
• **en hauteur** ADV **1** *(debout)* upright; **mettez-le en h.** stand it upright *or* on its end **2** *(dans un endroit élevé)* **nous avons installé les étagères en h.** we put the shelves high up on the wall; **ça ne vous ennuie pas d'habiter en h.?** doesn't living high up bother you?

***haut-fond** [ofɔ̃] *(pl* **hauts-fonds)** NM shallow, shoal

***haut-fourneau** [ofurno] *(pl* **hauts-fourneaux)** NM blast furnace

***haut-le-cœur** [olkœr] NM INV **1** *(nausée)* **avoir un/des h.** to retch **2** *Fig* **une attitude aussi lâche me donne des h.** such cowardly behaviour makes me (feel) sick

***haut-le-corps** [olkɔr] NM INV start, jump; **avoir un h.** to start, to jump

***haut-parleur** [oparlœr] *(pl* **haut-parleurs)** NM loudspeaker, speaker; **h. d'aigus** tweeter; **h. de graves** woofer

***haut-relief** [orəljef] *(pl* **hauts-reliefs)** NM *Beaux-Arts* high relief

***Haut-Rhin** [orɛ̃] NM **le H.** Haut-Rhin

***hauturier, -ère** [otyrje, -ɛr] ADJ deep-sea *(avant n)*; **navigation hauturière** ocean navigation; **pêche hauturière** deep-sea fishing

***havage** [avaʒ] NM *Mines* cutting, hewing

***havanais, -e** [avanɛ, -ɛz] ADJ of/from Havana
• **havanaise** NF habanera
• **Havanais, -e** NM,F = inhabitant of or person from Havana

***Havane** [avan] NF **La H.** Havana

***hâve** [ɑv] ADJ haggard; *(joues)* sunken

***haveuse** [avøz] NF *Mines* cutting machine, cutter

***havrais, -e** [avrɛ, -ɛz] ADJ of/from Le Havre
• **Havrais, -e** NM,F = inhabitant of or person from Le Havre

***Havre** [avr] NM **Le H.** Le Havre

***havre** [avr] NM *Littéraire* haven, harbour; **un h. de paix** a haven of peace

***havresac** [avrəsak] NM *(de campeur)* haversack, knapsack; *(de militaire)* haversack, kitbag

hawaïen, -enne [awajɛ̃, -ɛn] = **hawaiien**

Hawaii [awaj] NM Hawaii

hawaiien, -enne [awajɛ̃, -ɛn] ADJ Hawaiian
NM *(langue)* Hawaiian
• **Hawaiien, -enne** NM,F Hawaiian

***Haye** [ɛ] NF **La H.** The Hague

***hayon** [ajɔ̃] NM **1** *(de voiture)* hatchback, tailgate; *(d'une charrette)* tailboard **2** *Tech* **h. élévateur** (fork) lift

***HCR** [aʃseɛr] NM *(abrév* **Haut-Commissariat des Nations unies pour les réfugiés)** UNHCR

HD *Ordinat (abrév écrite* **haute densité)** HD

***HDL-cholestérol** [aʃdeɛlkɔlesterɔl] NM *Méd* HDL cholesterol, high-density lipoproteins

***hé** [e] EXCLAM **1** *(pour interpeller quelqu'un)* hey!; **h., vous, là!** hey, you!; **hé! arrêtez!** hey *or* oi! stop it! **2** *(d'étonnement)* hey!, well (well, well)!; **hé hé, quelle surprise!** well (well, well), what a surprise!; **hé, la voilà qui arrive!** hey, here she comes!

***heaume** [om] NM *Hér & Hist* helm, helmet

***heavy metal** [ɛvimetal] NM *Mus* heavy metal

hebdo [ɛbdo] NM *Fam Journ* weekly; **h. télé** TV magazine

hebdomadaire [ɛbdɔmadɛr] ADJ weekly
NM weekly

hebdomadairement [ɛbdɔmadɛrmɑ̃] ADV weekly, once a week

hébergement [ebɛrʒəmɑ̃] NM **1** *(lieu)* lodgings, accommodation **2** *(action)* lodging; **l'h. est en chalet** chalet accommodation is provided **3** *Ordinat (de site Web)* hosting

héberger [17] [ebɛrʒe] VT **1** *(loger ▸ pour une certaine durée)* to lodge, to accommodate; *(▸ à l'improviste)* to put up; *(▸ réfugié, vagabond)* to take in, to shelter; *(▸ criminel)* to harbour, to shelter; **notre bâtiment hébergera le secrétariat pendant les travaux** the secretarial department will be housed in our building during the alterations **2** *Ordinat (site Web)* to host

hébergeur [ebɛrʒœr] NM *Ordinat (de site Web)* host

hébété, -e [ebete] ADJ dazed, in a daze; **il avait un air h.** he looked dazed
NM,F **il était là comme un h.** he stood there looking stunned

hébétement [ebetmɑ̃] NM stupor; **son h. est dû à l'alcool** he's in a drunken stupor

hébéter [18] [ebete] VT to daze; **hébété par l'alcool/la drogue** in a drunken/drug-induced stupor; **hébété de douleur** numb with grief

hébétude [ebetyd] NF **1** *Littéraire* stupor, stupefaction **2** *Psy* hebetude

hébraïque [ebraik] ADJ Hebraic, Hebrew *(avant n)*

hébraïsant, -e [ebraizɑ̃, -ɑ̃t] NM,F Hebraist, Hebrew scholar

hébraïser [3] [ebraize] VT to Hebraize

hébraïsme [ebraism] NM *Ling* Hebraism

hébraïste [ebraist] NMF Hebraist, Hebrew scholar

hébreu, -x [ebrø] ADJ M Hebrew; **l'État h.** the Hebrew State, Israel
NM **1** *(langue)* Hebrew **2** *Fam (locution)* **pour moi, c'est de l'h.** it's all Greek to me
• **Hébreux** NMPL **les Hébreux** the Hebrews

Hébrides [ebrid] NFPL **les (îles) H.** the Hebrides; **les H. extérieures** the Outer Hebrides; **les H. intérieures** the Inner Hebrides

HEC [aʃse] NF *(abrév* **Hautes études commerciales)** = prestigious business school in Paris

hécatombe [ekatɔ̃b] NF **1** *(carnage)* slaughter, massacre; **l'h. annuelle des blessés de la route** the carnage that occurs every year on the roads **2** *Fig* **ça a été une h. cette année aux examens!** the exam results were disastrous this year! **3** *Antiq* hecatomb

hectare [ɛktar] NM hectare

hectique [ɛktik] ADJ *Méd* **fièvre h.** hectic fever

hecto [ɛkto] NM *Fam* **1** *(abrév* **hectogramme)** hectogram▫, hectogramme▫ **2** *(abrév* **hectolitre)** hectolitre▫

hectogramme [ɛktɔgram] NM hectogram, hectogramme; **un h.** a hundred grams, a hectogram

hectolitre [ɛktɔlitr] NM hectolitre; **un h.** a hundred litres, a hectolitre

hectomètre [ɛktɔmɛtr] NM hectometre; **un h.** a hundred metres, a hectometre

hectométrique [ɛktɔmetrik] ADJ hectometre *(avant n)*

hectopascal, -als [ɛktɔpaskal] NM millibar

hectowatt [ɛktɔwat] NM hectowatt; **un h.** a hundred watts, a hectowatt

hédonisme [edɔnism] NM hedonism

hédoniste [edɔnist] ADJ hedonist, hedonistic
NMF hedonist

hégélianisme [egeljanism] NM *Phil* Hegelianism

hégélien, -enne [egeljɛ̃, -ɛn] *Phil* ADJ Hegelian
NM,F Hegelian

hégémonie [eʒemɔni] NF hegemony; **l'h. des USA sur le monde** the USA's position of hegemony in the world

hégire [eʒir] NF *Rel* **l'h.** the hegira, the hejira

***hein** [ɛ̃] EXCLAM *Fam* **1** *(quoi)* **h.?** eh?, what? **2** *(n'est-ce pas)* eh; **c'est drôle, h.!** funny, eh *or* isn't it!▫; **tu ne vas pas le répéter, h.?** you won't say anything, will you?▫, you won't tell anyone, will you?▫; **h. qu'il fait bien la cuisine!** he's a good cook, isn't he?▫ **3** *(exprimant la colère)* OK!, right!; **on se calme, h.!** cool it, will you!, that's enough, OK?

***hélas** [elas] EXCLAM unfortunately, unhappily, *Littéraire* alas; **h., je ne pourrai pas venir** unfortunately *or* I'm afraid I won't be able to come; **h., trois fois h.!** alas and alack!

Hélène [elɛn] NPR Helen; *Myth* **H. de Troie** Helen of Troy

***héler [18]** [ele] VT *(personne)* to call out to, to hail; *(taxi, porteur)* to hail

hélianthe [eljɑ̃t] NM *Bot* sunflower, *Spéc* helianthus

hélianthine [eljɑ̃tin] NF *Chim* methyl orange

héliaque [eljak] ADJ *Astron* heliacal

hélice [elis] NF **1** *Tech & Naut* propeller, screw, screwpropeller; **h. d'avion** air screw, aircraft propeller **2** *Archit & Math* helix; **escalier en h.** spiral staircase

hélico [eliko] NM *Fam (abrév* **hélicoptère)** chopper

hélicoïdal, -e, -aux, -ales [elikɔidal, -o] ADJ **1** *(en forme de vrille)* helical, spiral; **escalier h.** spiral staircase **2** *Math & Tech* helicoid, helicoidal

hélicoïde [elikɔid] *Math* ADJ helicoid
NM helicoid

hélicon [elikɔ̃] NM helicon

hélicoptère [elikɔptɛr] NM helicopter; **h. d'attaque** attack helicopter; **h. de combat** helicopter gunship

héligare [eligar] NF heliport

héliocentrique [eljɔsɑ̃trik] ADJ heliocentric

héliographe [eljɔgraf] NM *Météo* heliograph

héliographie [eljɔgrafi] NF *Typ* heliography

héliograveur, -euse [eljɔgravœr, -øz] NM,F photoengraver

héliogravure [eljɔgravyr] NF heliogravure

héliomarin, -e [eljɔmarɛ̃, -in] ADJ *(cure)* involving sunshine and sea air therapy; *(établissement)* offering sunshine and sea air therapy

héliothérapie [eljɔterapi] NF *Méd* heliotherapy; **h. artificielle** sunray treatment

héliotrope [eljɔtrɔp] NM *Bot & Minér* heliotrope

héliport [elipɔr] NM heliport

héliportage [elipɔrtaʒ] NM helicopter transportation

héliporté, -e [elipɔrte] ADJ **1** *(transporté par hélicoptère)* helicoptered; **troupes héliportées** airborne troops *(brought in by helicopter)* **2** *(exécuté par hélicoptère)* **une opération héliportée** a helicopter mission

héliski [eliski] NM heliskiing

hélisurface [elisyrfas] NF *Naut* helideck; *(sur un immeuble)* helipad

hélitreuiller [5] [elitrœje] VT to winch up (into a helicopter)

hélium [eljɔm] NM *Chim* helium

hélix [eliks] NM *Anat & Zool* helix

hellébore [elebɔr] NM *Bot* hellebore

hellène [elɛn] ADJ Hellenic
• **Hellène** NMF Hellene

hellénique [elenik] ADJ *Antiq (des Hellènes)* Hellenic; *(de la Grèce moderne)* Greek

hellénisant, -e [elenizɑ̃, -ɑ̃t] NM,F Hellenist

hellénisation [elenizasjɔ̃] NF Hellenization

helléniser [3] [elenize] VT to Hellenize

hellénisme [elenism] NM **1** *(civilisation)* Hellenism **2** *Ling* Hellenism, Graecism

helléniste [elenist] NMF Hellenist

hellénistique [elenistik] ADJ Hellenistic

***hello** [ɛlo] EXCLAM hello!

***Helsinki** [ɛlsiŋki] NF Helsinki

helvète [ɛlvɛt] ADJ Helvetian
• **Helvète** NMF Helvetian

Helvétie [ɛlvesi] NF *Hist* **l'H.** Helvetia

helvétique [ɛlvetik] ADJ Swiss

helvétisme [ɛlvetism] **NM** = characteristic word or expression used by French-speaking Swiss

***hem** [ɛm] **EXCLAM 1** *(exprimant le doute)* hum, ahem, mmm; *(exprimant une hésitation)* um, er **2** *(pour attirer l'attention)* ahem!

hématie [emasi] **NF** *Biol* erythrocyte

hématologie [ematɔlɔʒi] **NF** *Méd* haematology

hématologique [ematɔlɔʒik] **ADJ** *Méd* haematological, haematologic

hématologiste [ematɔlɔʒist], **hématologue** [ematɔlɔg] **NMF** *Méd* haematologist

hématome [ematom] **NM** bruise, *Spéc* haematoma; **se faire un h.** to bruise oneself

héméralopie [emeralɔpi] **NF** *Méd* night blindness, *Spéc* nyctalopia

hémicycle [emisikl] **NM 1** *(espace en demi-cercle)* semicircle; **l'abside de l'église est un h.** the apse of the church is semicircular **2** *(salle garnie de gradins)* semicircular amphitheatre; *Pol* **l'H.** *(salle)* = the benches chamber of the French National Assembly; *(Assemblée)* the French National Assembly

hémiplégie [emipleʒi] **NF** *Méd* hemiplegia

hémiplégique [emipleʒik] *Méd* **ADJ** hemiplegic

NMF hemiplegic

hémisphère [emisfɛr] **NM** hemisphere; **l'h. Nord/Sud** the Northern/Southern hemisphere; **h. cérébral** cerebral hemisphere

hémisphérique [emisferik] **ADJ** hemispheric, hemispherical

hémistiche [emistiʃ] **NM** *Littérature* hemistich

hémoculture [emɔkyltyr] **NF** *Méd* blood culture

hémodialyse [emɔdjaliz] **NF** *Méd* haemodialysis

hémoglobine [emɔglɔbin] **NF 1** *Physiol* haemoglobin **2** *Fam (sang)* gore, blood and guts

hémophile [emɔfil] *Méd* **ADJ** haemophiliac

NM haemophiliac

hémophilie [emɔfili] **NF** *Méd* haemophilia; **être atteint d'h.** to suffer from haemophilia, to be a haemophiliac

hémoptysie [emɔptizi] **NF** *Méd* haemoptysis

hémorragie [emɔraʒi] **NF 1** *Méd* haemorrhage, bleeding *(UNCOUNT)*; **h. cérébrale** cerebral haemorrhage; **h. interne/externe** internal/external haemorrhage; **faire une h.** to haemorrhage **2** *Fig (perte)* drain; **les universités connaissent une véritable h. depuis la crise** the universities have been drained of their manpower since the beginning of the crisis; **l'h. des cerveaux** the brain drain; **l'h. des capitaux** the drain *or* haemorrhage of capital

hémorragique [emɔraʒik] **ADJ** *Méd* haemorrhagic

hémorroïdaire [emɔrɔidɛr] *Méd* **ADJ** *(gén)* haemorrhoidal; *(malade)* suffering from haemorrhoids

NMF haemorrhoids sufferer

hémorroïdal, -e, -aux, -ales [emɔrɔidal, -o] **ADJ** *Méd* haemorrhoidal

hémorroïdes [emɔrɔid] **NFPL** *Méd* haemorrhoids, piles; **avoir des h.** to suffer from haemorrhoids, to have piles

hémostatique [emɔstatik] *Physiol* **ADJ** haemostatic

NM haemostatic

hendécagone [ɛ̃dekagɔn] **NM** *Géom* hendecagon

hendécasyllabe [ɛ̃dekasilab] *Littérature* **ADJ** hendecasyllabic

NM hendecasyllable

***henné** [ene] **NM** henna; **se faire un h.** to henna one's hair, to give one's hair a henna rinse; **les cheveux teints au h.** hennaed hair

***hennir [32]** [enir] **VI 1** *(cheval)* to neigh, to whinny **2** *(personne)* to bray

***hennissement** [enismɑ̃] **NM 1** *(d'un cheval)* neigh, whinny **2** *(d'une personne)* braying *(UNCOUNT)*

henry [ɑ̃ri] **NM** *Élec* henry

***hep** [ɛp] **EXCLAM** hey!

héparine [eparin] **NF** *Pharm* heparin

hépatique [epatik] **ADJ** *Physiol & Méd* hepatic, liver *(avant n)*

NMF *Méd* = person suffering from a liver ailment

NF *Bot* liverwort, hepatic

hépatisme [epatism] **NM** *Méd* liver ailments

hépatite [epatit] **NF** *Méd* hepatitis; **h. infectieuse** infectious hepatitis; **h. virale** viral hepatitis; **h. A/B/C** hepatitis A/B/C

hépatologie [epatɔlɔʒi] **NF** *Méd* hepatology

heptaèdre [ɛptaɛdr] **NM** *Géom* heptahedron

heptagonal, -e, -aux, -ales [ɛptagɔnal, -o] **ADJ** *Géom* heptagonal

heptagone [ɛptagɔn] **NM** *Géom* heptagon

heptasyllabe [ɛptasilab] *Littérature* **ADJ** heptasyllabic

NM heptasyllabic verse

heptathlète [ɛptatlɛt] **NMF** heptathlete

heptathlon [ɛptatlɔ̃] **NM** heptathlon

héraldique [eraldik] **ADJ** heraldic

NF heraldry

héraldiste [eraldist] **NMF** heraldry specialist, heraldist

***héraut** [ero] **NM 1** *Hist* herald; **h. d'armes** officer *or* herald of arms **2** *Fig Littéraire* herald, messenger

herbacé, -e [ɛrbase] **ADJ** *Bot* herbaceous

herbage [ɛrbaʒ] **NM** *(prairie)* grazing land, pasture (land); *(herbe)* grass, pasture

• **herbages** **NMPL** *Pêche* coral fishing nets

herbager¹ [17] [ɛrbaʒe] **VT** *Vieilli* to graze, to put out to grass

herbager², -ère [ɛrbaʒe, ɛr] **NM,F** grazier

herbe [ɛrb] **NF 1** *(plante, gazon)* grass; **faire de l'h.** *(pour les lapins)* to cut grass; *Bot* **h. de blé** wheatgrass; *Bot* **h. à chats** catmint, catnip; *Bot* **herbes folles** wild grass; **herbes marines** seaweed; *Bot* **h. à puces** poison ivy; *Bot* **h. sacrée, h. à tous les maux** wild vervain; **hautes herbes** tall grass; **une mauvaise h.** a weed; **de la mauvaise h.** weeds; *Fam Fig* **je connais ce type, c'est de la mauvaise h.** I know this guy, he's no good *or* bad news; **comme de la mauvaise h.** like wildfire; **couper** *ou* **faucher l'h. sous le pied à qn** to cut the ground *or* to pull the rug from under sb's feet; *Prov* **l'h. du voisin est toujours plus verte** the grass is always greener on the other side (of the fence) **2** *Bot & Culin (aromatique, médicinale)* herb; **fines herbes** herbs, fines herbes; **herbes de Provence** mixed herbs, herbes de Provence **3** *Fam (marijuana)* grass, weed

• **en herbe** **ADJ** *Bot* green; *Fig* in the making; **c'est un musicien en h.** he has the makings of a musician, he's a budding musician

> Il faut noter que le nom anglais **herb** s'applique uniquement à des herbes aromatiques ou à des plantes médicinales.

herbe-aux-chats [ɛrboʃa] *(pl* **herbes-aux-chats)** **NF 1** *(cataire)* catnip, catmint **2** *(valériane)* valerian

herbeux, -euse [ɛrbø, -øz] **ADJ** grassy

herbicide [ɛrbisid] **ADJ** herbicidal

NM weedkiller, *Spéc* herbicide

herbier [ɛrbje] **NM** *(collection)* dried flower collection, *Spéc* herbarium; *(lieu)* herbarium; **faire un h.** to build up a collection of dried plants

herbivore [ɛrbivɔr] **ADJ** herbivorous

NM herbivore

herborisation [ɛrbɔrizasjɔ̃] **NF** botanizing, plant-collecting

herboriser [3] [ɛrbɔrize] **VI** to botanize, to collect plants

herboriste [ɛrbɔrist] **NMF** *Méd & Pharm* herbalist, herb doctor

herboristerie [ɛrbɔristəri] **NF** herbalist's (shop)

herbu, -e [ɛrby] **ADJ** grassy

***hercher [3]** [ɛrʃe] **VI** *Mines* to haul coal

Herculanum [ɛrkylanɔm] **N** *Géog* Herculaneum

Hercule [ɛrkyl] **NPR** *Myth* Hercules

herculéen, -enne [ɛrkyleɛ̃, -ɛn] **ADJ** *(tâche)* Herculean; *(force)* Herculean, superhuman

hercynien, -enne [ɛrsinjɛ̃, -ɛn] **ADJ** *Géol* Hercynian

***hère** [ɛr] **NM** *Littéraire* **pauvre h.** poor wretch

héréditaire [ereditɛr] **ADJ 1** *Jur* hereditary **2** *Biol* inherited, hereditary; *Hum* **il est toujours grincheux, c'est h.!** he's always moaning, he was born like that!

héréditairement [ereditɛrmɑ̃] **ADV** hereditarily, through heredity

hérédité [eredite] **NF 1** *Biol* heredity; **h. liée au sexe** sex-linkage; **elle a une h. chargée** *ou* **une lourde h.** her family history has a lot to answer for; *Hum* **c'est l'h. qui veut ça!** it's in the blood! **2** *Jur* **action en pétition d'h.** = claim to succeed to an estate held by a third party

hérésiarque [erezjark] **NMF** heresiarch

hérésie [erezi] **NF** *Rel* sacrilege, heresy; *Fig* **une table Régence dans la cuisine, c'est de l'h.!** a Regency table in the kitchen, that's (a) sacrilege!

hérétique [eretik] **ADJ** heretical

NMF heretic

***hérissé, -e** [erise] **ADJ 1** *(cheveux, poils ▸ naturellement raides)* bristly; *(▸ dressés de peur)* bristling, standing on end; **un chien à l'échine hérissée** a dog with its hackles up **2** *(parsemé)* **h. de** *(clous, pointes)* covered in, bristling with; *(citations, fautes)* full of; **un texte h. de difficultés** a text full of difficult points **3** *Bot* spiny

***hérissement** [erismɑ̃] **NM** *(du pelage)* bristling

***hérisser [3]** [erise] **VT 1** *(dresser)* **le chat hérissait ses poils** the cat's fur was bristling; **le chien hérissait ses poils** the dog's hackles were rising *or* up; **le perroquet hérissait ses plumes** the parrot was ruffling its feathers; **les cheveux hérissés par le vent** his/her hair sticking up with the wind **2** *(irriter)* **cette question le hérisse** *ou* **lui hérisse le poil** that question gets his back up *or* makes his hackles rise **3** *(remplir)* **h. un texte de citations/de jeux de mots** to fill a text with quotations/puns

VPR se hérisser 1 *(se dresser ▸ pelage)* to bristle; *(▸ cheveux)* to stand on end **2** *(dresser son pelage)* **le chat se hérisse** the cat's coat is bristling; **le chien se hérisse** the dog's hackles are up **3** *(s'irriter)* to bristle; **elle se hérisse facilement** she's easily ruffled

***hérisson** [erisɔ̃] **NM 1** *Zool* hedgehog; **h. de mer** sea urchin

2 *Fam (personne)* **c'est un vrai h.** he's really prickly

3 *Mil* cheval-de-frise

4 *Constr (pointes)* spiked wall strip

5 *(égouttoir)* bottle drainer

6 *(brosse)* flue brush, chimney sweep's brush

héritage [eritaʒ] **NM 1** *Jur (destiné à une personne)* inheritance; *(destiné à une institution)* bequest; **faire un h.** to inherit; **faire un gros h.** to come into a fortune; **elle m'a laissé ses bijoux en h.** she left me her jewels; **avoir eu qch en h.** to have inherited sth; **sa part de l'h.** his/her part of the inheritance; **mon oncle à h.** my rich uncle **2** *Fig* heritage, legacy; **notre h. culturel** our cultural heritage; **nos problèmes sont l'h. de la décennie précédente** our problems are the legacy of the previous decade

hériter [3] [erite] **VI** to inherit; **h. de qch** *(recevoir en legs)* to inherit sth; *Fig* **nous héritons d'une longue tradition humaniste** we are the inheritors of a long-standing tradition of humanism; **comment as-tu hérité de cette toile?** how did you come by *or* acquire this canvas?; **j'ai hérité de son vieux pantalon** his/her old trousers were handed down to me; **j'espère que le bébé n'héritera pas de ton sale caractère!** I hope the baby won't inherit your foul temper!

VT 1 *Jur (bien matériel)* to inherit; **h. qch de qn** to inherit sth from sb **2** *(trait physique ou moral)* **elle a hérité sa bonne humeur de sa famille paternelle** she inherited her even temper from her father's side of the family

USAGE ABSOLU *Jur* **h. de qn** to inherit from sb; **elle a hérité de sa mère** she received an inheritance *or* a legacy from her mother

The symbol * indicates that the initial **h** is aspirate and that hence there is no liaison, eg **les haricots** [leariko] and not [lezariko], or contraction in spelling, eg **la haine** and not **l'haine**.

héritier, -ère [eritje, -ɛr] NM,F **1** *Jur* heir, *f* heiress; l'h. d'une fortune/d'une grosse entreprise the heir to a fortune/to a big firm; l'unique *ou* le seul h. the sole heir; l'h. apparent/présomptif the heir apparent/presumptive; h. indirect collateral heir; h. légitime rightful heir; l'h. naturel the heir-at-law; h. testamentaire devisee, legatee **2** *Hum (enfant)* heir; *(fils)* son and heir; *(fille)* daughter **3** *(disciple)* heir, follower

hermaphrodisme [ɛrmafrɔdism] NM *Biol* hermaphroditism

Hermaphrodite [ɛrmafrɔdit] NPR *Myth* Hermaphroditus

hermaphrodite [ɛrmafrɔdit] *Biol* ADJ hermaphrodite, hermaphroditic
NMF hermaphrodite

herméneutique [ɛrmenøtik] *Rel & Phil* ADJ hermeneutic, hermeneutical
NF hermeneutics *(singulier)*

Hermès [ɛrmɛs] NPR *Myth* Hermes

hermès [ɛrmɛs] NM INV *Beaux-Arts* herm, herma; buste en h. herm bust

hermétique [ɛrmetik] ADJ **1** *(étanche ▸ gén)* hermetically sealed, hermetic; *(▸ à l'eau)* watertight; *(▸ à l'air)* airtight
2 *(incompréhensible)* abstruse
3 *(impénétrable ▸ visage)* inscrutable, impenetrable; son expression était parfaitement h. his/her face was totally expressionless
4 *(insensible)* être h. à to be unreceptive *or* impervious to; je suis complètement h. à l'art moderne modern art is a closed book to me

hermétiquement [ɛrmetikmɑ̃] ADV hermetically

hermétisme [ɛrmetism] NM **1** *(doctrine)* alchemy **2** *(caractère incompréhensible)* abstruseness, reconditeness

hermine [ɛrmin] NF **1** *Zool (brune)* stoat; *(blanche)* ermine **2** *(fourrure)* ermine *(UNCOUNT)*; manteau d'h. ermine coat

***herniaire** [ɛrnjɛr] ADJ hernial

***hernie** [ɛrni] NF **1** *Méd* hernia, rupture; h. discale slipped disc; h. étranglée/hiatale strangulated/hiatus hernia **2** *(d'un pneu)* bulge

***hernié, -e** [ɛrnje] ADJ *Méd* herniated, ruptured

héro [ero] NF *Fam Arg drogue (abrév* héroïne*)* smack, scag, skag

Hérode [erɔd] NPR *Bible* Herod; vieux comme H. as old as Methuselah *or* the hills

Hérodote [erɔdɔt] NPR Herodotus

héroï-comique [erɔikɔmik] *(pl* héroï-comiques*)* ADJ mock-heroic

héroïne [erɔin] NF **1** *(drogue)* heroin **2** *(femme)* voir héros

héroïnomane [erɔinɔman] NMF heroin addict

héroïnomanie [erɔinɔmani] NF heroin addiction

héroïque [erɔik] ADJ **1** *(courageux)* heroic; *Hum* je lui ai opposé un refus h. I heroically refused his/her offer **2** *Littérature* heroic **3** *(mémorable)* l'époque h. des machines volantes the pioneering *or* great days of the flying machines

héroïquement [erɔikmɑ̃] ADV heroically

héroïsme [erɔism] NM heroism; *Hum* épouser un homme comme ça, mais c'est de l'h.! marrying a man like that is nothing short of heroic!

***héron** [erɔ̃] NM *Orn* heron

***héros, héroïne** [ero, erɔin] NM,F hero, *f* heroine; les h. de Dickens Dickens' heroes (and heroines); il est mort en h. he died a hero's death *or* like a hero; tu ne t'es pas comporté en h. you weren't exactly heroic

herpès [ɛrpɛs] NM *Méd* herpes *(UNCOUNT)*; avoir de l'h. à la bouche to have a cold sore (on one's mouth)

herpétique [ɛrpetik] ADJ *Méd* herpes *(avant n)*, *Spéc* herpetic

***hersage** [ɛrsaʒ] NM *Agr* harrowing

***herscher** [ɛrʃe] = hercher

***herse** [ɛrs] NF **1** *Agr* harrow **2** *(d'un château)* portcullis; *(pour barrer la route)* cheval-de-frise **3** *Théât* batten

***herser** [3] [ɛrse] VT *Agr* to harrow

***herseuse** [ɛrsøz] NF *Agr* harrow

***hertz** [ɛrts] NM hertz

***hertzien, -enne** [ɛrtsjɛ̃, -ɛn] ADJ *TV* terrestrial; *Rad* hertzian; *TV* par voie hertzienne terrestrially; *Rad* réseau h. radio relay system
NM *TV* le h. terrestrial (broadcasting)

hésitant, -e [ezitɑ̃, -ɑ̃t] ADJ **1** *(indécis)* hesitant; je suis encore un peu h. I haven't quite made up my mind yet; les réponses sont encore un peu hésitantes the answers are still rather hesitant **2** *(peu assuré)* hesitant, faltering; une voix hésitante a faltering voice

hésitation [ezitasjɔ̃] NF **1** *(atermoiement)* hesitation; après quelques minutes d'h. after hesitating for a few minutes, after a few minutes' hesitation; après bien des hésitations after much hesitation; pas d'h., vas-y! no dithering, off you go! **2** *(arrêt)* pause; marquer *ou* avoir une h. to pause, to hesitate **3** *(doute)* doubt; pas d'h., c'est lui! it's him, no doubt about it *or* without a doubt!; il lui confia ses hésitations he confided his doubts *or* misgivings to him/her
• **sans hésitation** ADV unhesitatingly, without hesitation; c'est sans h. que je lui ai menti I had no hesitation in lying to him/her; je préfère le ciné à la télé, sans h. I prefer cinema to television any day

hésiter [3] [ezite] VI **1** *(être dans l'incertitude)* to hesitate; je ne sais pas, j'hésite I don't know, I can't make up my mind; sans h. without hesitating *or* hesitation; il n'y a pas à h. why wait?; elle hésite encore sur la pointure she's still not sure about the size; l'enfant hésitait entre le rire et les larmes the child didn't know whether to laugh or cry **2** *(être réticent)* h. à faire qch to hesitate to do sth; n'hésitez pas à m'appeler don't hesitate to call me; j'hésite à le lui dire I'm not sure whether to tell him/her **3** *(marquer un temps d'arrêt)* to pause, to falter; son pas hésita un instant dans l'escalier his/her footsteps paused for a moment on the stairs; il a hésité en prononçant le nom he faltered *or* stumbled over the name; h. devant l'obstacle *(cheval)* to refuse a fence

Hespérides [ɛsperid] NFPL *Myth* **1** *(nymphes)* les H. the Hesperides **2** *(îles)* les H. the Hesperides, the Islands of the Blessed

hétaïre [etair] NF *Littéraire & Antiq* hetaera, hetaira

hétéro [etero] *Fam (abrév* hétérosexuel*)* ADJ hetero, straight
NMF hetero, straight

hétéroclite [eterɔklit] ADJ disparate; il y avait là toutes sortes d'objets hétéroclites there was a strange collection *or* assortment of disparate objects; tout le mobilier est h. none of the furniture matches

hétérodoxe [eterɔdɔks] ADJ **1** *Rel* heterodox **2** *(non conformiste)* heterodox, unorthodox
NMF les hétérodoxes ne sont pas très bien vus dans ce pays unorthodox believers are frowned upon in this country

hétérodoxie [eterɔdɔksi] NF heterodoxy

hétérodyne [eterɔdin] NF *Rad* heterodyne (generator)

hétérogène [eterɔʒɛn] ADJ **1** *(mêlé)* heterogeneous, mixed **2** *Chim* heterogeneous

hétérogénéité [eterɔʒeneite] NF heterogeneousness, heterogeneity

hétéroplastie [eterɔplasti] NF *Méd* heteroplasty

hétérosexualité [eterɔseksyalite] NF heterosexuality

hétérosexuel, -elle [eterɔseksyɛl] ADJ heterosexual
NM,F heterosexual

***hêtraie** [etrɛ] NF beech grove

***hêtre** [ɛtr] NM **1** *(arbre)* beech (tree) **2** *(bois)* beech (wood)

***heu** [ø] EXCLAM **1** *(exprime le doute)* hmm, um, er **2** *(exprime l'hésitation)* um, er; h., h., je ne sais pas um, er, I don't know

heur [œr] NM *Littéraire* good fortune; je n'ai pas eu l'h. de lui plaire I did not have the good fortune to please him/her; je n'ai pas l'h. de la connaître I have not the pleasure of her acquaintance

HEURE [œr]

• hour **1–3, 6**	• time **4, 5**

NF **1** *(unité de temps)* hour; une h. d'horloge a whole hour; j'attends depuis une bonne h. I've been waiting for a good *or* full hour; il faut deux bonnes heures it takes a good two hours; revenez dans une petite h. be *or* come back in less than *or* in under an hour; les heures passent vite/sont longues the hours fly past/drag by; à 45 km à l'h. at 45 km an *or* per hour; faire du 100 kilomètres h. to do 100 kilometres an hour; 24 heures sur 24 round-the-clock, 24 hours a day; pharmacie ouverte 24 heures sur 24 all-night *or* 24-hour chemist; d'h. en h. by the hour; la situation s'aggrave d'h. en h. the situation is getting worse by the hour

2 *(durée d'un trajet)* hour; à deux heures (de voiture *ou* de route) de chez moi two hours('drive) from my home; il y a trois heures de marche/vol it's a three-hour walk/flight

3 *(unité de travail ou de salaire)* hour; un travail payé à l'h. a job paid by the hour; dix euros de l'h. ten euros an *or* per hour; une h. de travail an hour's work, an hour of work; sans compter les heures de main-d'œuvre excluding labour (costs); la semaine de 35 heures, les 35 heures the 35-hour week; *Scol* une h. de chimie a chemistry period *or* class; elle a dix heures de cours par semaine she has ten hours of lessons a week; une h. supplémentaire an *or* one hour's overtime; des heures supplémentaires overtime; faire des heures supplémentaires to do *or* to work overtime

4 *(point précis de la journée)* time; il n'est pas la même h. à Rome qu'à Tokyo it's not the same time *or* the time's not the same in Rome as it is in Tokyo; 15 h h. locale 3 p.m. local time; il est deux heures it's two o'clock; cinq heures moins dix ten (minutes) to *or Am* of five; vingt heures quarante eight forty p.m.; le train de neuf heures the nine o'clock train; *Fam* elle est passée sur le coup de huit heures she dropped in at about eight; à la même h. at the same time; que fais-tu debout à cette h.-ci? what are you doing up at this time?; à cette h.-ci je devrais déjà être parti I should have left by now; c'est l'h.! *(de partir)* it's time (to go)!; *(de rendre sa copie)* time's up!; c'est l'h. de partir it's time to go; l'h., c'est l'h. on time is on time; *Fam* quand c'est l'h., c'est l'h.! when you've got to go, you've got to go!; avant l'h. before time; *Fam* avant l'h., c'est pas l'h., après l'h. c'est plus l'h. there's a right time for everything; quelle h. est-il? what time is it?, what's the time?; vous avez l'h.? do you have the time?; quelle h. avez-vous? what time do you make it?; est-ce que vous avez l'h. exacte *ou* juste? do you have the right time?; tu as vu l'h. (qu'il est)? have you any idea what time it is?; il ne sait pas encore lire l'h. he can't tell the time yet; il y a une h. pour tout, chaque chose à son h. there's a time (and a place) for everything; il n'y a pas d'h. pour les braves! when a man's got to go, a man's got to go!; il n'a pas d'h., avec lui il n'y a pas d'h. *(il n'est pas ponctuel)* he just turns up when it suits him; *Fam* jusqu'à pas d'h. until some ungodly hour; *Fam* se coucher à pas d'h. to go to bed at all hours; *Fam* elle est rentrée à pas d'h. she didn't get home until some ungodly hour; h. d'arrivée arrival time; h. probable d'arrivée expected time of arrival; h. probable de départ expected time of departure; l'h. d'été *Br* British Summer Time, *Am* daylight (saving) time; passer à l'h. d'été/d'hiver to put the clocks forward/back; l'h. de Greenwich Greenwich Mean Time, GMT; l'h. H zero hour

5 *(moment)* time; à une h. avancée at a late hour; à une h. indue at some ungodly hour; ce doit être ma tante qui appelle, c'est son h. that must be my aunt, she usually calls about now; ton h. sera la mienne (you) choose *or* name a time; elle est romancière à ses heures she writes the odd novel (now and again); *Journ* nouvelles de dernière h. latest news, stop-press (news); un partisan de la dernière h. a late convert to the cause, *Fam* a Johnny-come-lately; un partisan de la première h. a supporter from the word go; *Fam* ils ont dû atterrir à l'h. qu'il est they must have landed by now; à l'h. qu'il est *ou* à l'h. actuelle, je ne sais pas si les otages ont été libérés at this (point in) time I don't know whether the hostages have been freed; **l'h. d'aller au lit** bedtime; **l'h. du déjeuner** lunchtime; **l'h. du dîner** dinnertime; **l'h. du thé** teatime; **les heures d'affluence** the rush hour; **heures de bureau** office hours; *Bourse* **heures de cotation** trading time; **les heures creuses** *(sans foule)* off-peak period; *(sans clients)* slack period; *Transp, Élec & Tél* off-peak hours; **heures d'écoute** *Rad* listening time; *TV* viewing hours; **heures de grande écoute** *Rad* peak listening time; *TV* peak viewing time, prime time; **heures de fermeture** closing times; **h. limite** deadline; **les heures de pointe** *(où il y a foule)* peak time, the rush hour; **heures d'ouverture** opening hours; **pendant les heures d'ouverture** *Com* when the shops are open, during (normal) opening hours; *Admin* during (normal) office *or* working hours; **h. de table** lunch hour

6 *(période d'une vie)* hour; **l'h. est grave** things are serious; **l'h. est à l'action** now is the time for action; **c'est sa dernière h.** his/her time is near; **dis-toi que ce n'était pas ton h.** don't worry, your time will come; **son h. est venue** his/her time has come; **son h. de gloire** his/her moment of glory; **l'h. de vérité** the moment of truth

• **heures** NFPL *Rel* hours; **livre d'heures** Book of Hours

• **à la bonne heure** ADV good; **elle est reçue, à la bonne h.!** so she passed, good *or* marvellous!; *Ironique* **tu as perdu tes clés, à la bonne h.!** you've lost your keys!, marvellous!

• **à l'heure** ADJ **1** *(personne)* on time; **être à l'h.** to be on time **2** *(montre)* **la montre est à l'h.** the watch is keeping good time; **ma montre n'est pas à l'h.** my watch is wrong ADV **mettre sa montre/une pendule à l'h.** to set one's watch/a clock right; **les trains partent à l'h.** the trains leave on time; **le Japon à l'h. anglaise** the Japanese go British

• **à l'heure de** PRÉP in the era *or* age of; **nous vivons à l'h. de la robotique** we're living in the age of robots

• **de bonne heure** ADV *(tôt)* early; *(en avance)* in good time

• **pour l'heure** ADV for now *or* the time being *or* the moment

• **sur l'heure** ADV *Littéraire* straightaway, at once

• **tout à l'heure** ADV **1** *(dans un moment)* later, in a (short *or* little) while; **je passerai la voir tout à l'h.** I'll go and see her a bit later on *or* in a little while; **à tout à l'h.!** see you later! **2** *(il y a un moment)* a little while ago; **je l'ai vu tout à l'h.** I saw him a little while ago

• **à toute heure** ADV at any time, at all hours of the day, round the clock; **ouvert à toute h.** open 24 hours (a day); **repas chauds à toute h.** hot meals 24 hours a day; **à toute h. du jour ou de la nuit** round the clock

---

heure-homme [œrɔm] (*pl* **heures-hommes**) NF man-hour

heureuse [œrøz] *voir* **heureux**

heureusement [œrøzmɑ̃] ADV **1** *(par chance)* fortunately, luckily; **il les a invités à l'improviste, h. j'avais fait des courses** he asked them to dinner without warning me, fortunately I'd done some shopping; **il a freiné à temps – oh, h.!** he braked in time – thank God *or* goodness for that!; **il m'a remboursé et s'est même excusé – eh bien, h.!** he paid me back and even apologized – I should hope *or* think so too!; **la soirée fut une catastrophe, h. que tu n'es pas venu** the party was a total flop, (it's a) good thing you didn't come

2 *(avec succès)* successfully; **le débat fut h. mené** the debate went off smoothly

3 *(favorablement)* well; **le procès s'est terminé h.** the trial ended satisfactorily

4 *(dans le bonheur)* happily; **vivre h.** to live happily

heureux, -euse [œrø, -øz] ADJ **1** *(qui éprouve du bonheur)* happy; **rendre qn h.** to make sb happy; **elle a tout pour être heureuse** she has everything going for her; **h. en ménage** happily married; **ils vécurent h. et eurent beaucoup d'enfants** they lived happily ever after

2 *(satisfait)* happy, glad; **être h. de** to be happy with; **je suis heureuse de cette conclusion** I'm happy *or* pleased it ended like this; **h. de te revoir** glad *or* pleased to see you again; **(très) h. de faire votre connaissance** pleased *or* nice to meet you

3 *(chanceux)* lucky, fortunate; **il est h. que...** it's fortunate *or* it's a good thing that...; **l'h. élu** the lucky man *(to be married or recently married)*; **l'heureuse élue** the lucky girl *(to be married or recently married)*; *Prov* **h. au jeu, malheureux en amour** lucky at cards, unlucky in love

4 *(bon)* good; *Euph* **un h. événement** a happy event; **h. anniversaire!** happy birthday!; **bonne et heureuse année!** happy New Year!

5 *(réussi)* good, happy, *Sout ou Hum* felicitous; **c'est un choix h.** it's well-chosen; **ce n'est pas très h. comme prénom pour une fille** it's a rather unfortunate name for a girl; **la formulation n'est pas toujours très heureuse dans ce texte** this text is not always very well worded

NM,F happy man, *f* woman; **faire des h.** to make some people happy; **le changement ne fera pas que des h.** the change won't suit everybody *or* be to everybody's liking

heuristique [øristik] ADJ heuristic

NF heuristics *(singulier)*

***heurt** [œr] NM **1** *(choc ▸ léger)* bump, knock, collision; *(▸ violent)* crash, collision **2** *(contraste)* clash; **le h. de deux caractères** the clash of two personalities **3** *(conflit)* clash, conflict; **le concert/débat s'est déroulé sans heurts** the concert/debate went off smoothly; **leur collaboration ne va pas sans heurts** their collaboration has its ups and downs *or* its rough patches

***heurté, -e** [œrte] ADJ **1** *(couleurs, sons)* clashing **2** *Littéraire (style)* jerky, abrupt **3** *(mouvement)* halting, jerky

***heurter** [3] [œrte] VT **1** *(cogner)* to strike, to hit, to knock; **en descendant du train, je l'ai heurté avec mon sac** I caught him with my bag *or* I bumped into him with my bag as I got off the train; **l'hélice l'a heurté de plein fouet** he was hit with the full force of the propeller; **h. qn du coude** to jostle sb with one's elbow; **h. qch du coude** to bump sth with one's elbow **2** *(aller à l'encontre de)* to run counter to, to go against; **son discours risque de h. l'opinion publique** his/her speech is likely to go against public opinion; **ce sont des idées qui heurtent ma conception de la justice** those are ideas which offend my sense of justice **3** *(choquer)* to shock, to offend; **sa grossièreté m'a toujours heurtée** I've always been shocked by his/her rudeness; **h. la sensibilité de qn** to hurt sb's feelings

VI *Suisse ou Littéraire* to knock; **h. à la porte** to knock at the door

• **heurter contre** VT IND to bang *or* to bump into; **dans le noir j'ai heurté contre le mur de la cave** in the dark I bumped into the cellar wall; **le voilier a heurté contre un récif** the sailing boat struck a reef

VPR **se heurter 1** *(passants, véhicules)* to collide, to bump *or* to run into each other; **les deux voitures se sont heurtées** the two cars collided (with each other)

2 *(être en désaccord)* to clash (with each other); **nous nous sommes heurtés à la dernière réunion** we crossed swords *or* clashed at the last meeting

3 se h. à *ou* **contre qch** *(se cogner)* to bang *or* to bump into sth

4 *Fig* **se h. à qch** *(rencontrer)* to come up against sth; **l'entreprise va se h. à de gros problèmes économiques** the company is going to come up against severe economic difficulties; **il s'est heurté à un refus catégorique** he met with a categorical refusal

***heurtoir** [œrtwar] NM **1** *(de porte)* (door) knocker **2** *Tech* stop, stopper **3** *Rail* buffer

hévéa [evea] NM hevea

hexacorde [ɛgzakɔrd] NM *Mus* hexachord

hexadécimal, -e, -aux, -ales [ɛgzadesimal, -o] ADJ hexadecimal

hexaèdre [ɛgzaɛdr] *Géom* ADJ hexahedral

NM hexahedron

hexagonal, -e, -aux, -ales [ɛgzagɔnal, -o] ADJ **1** *Géom* hexagonal **2** *Fig (français)* French; *Péj* chauvinistically French

hexagone [ɛgzagɔn] NM **1** *Géom* hexagon **2** *Fig* **l'H.** *(la France)* France

hexamètre [ɛgzamɛtr] ADJ hexametric, hexametrical

NM hexameter

HF *Tél (abrév écrite* **hautes fréquences***)* HF

***hi** [i] EXCLAM **hi hi** ha ha!

hiatal, -e, -aux, -ales [jatal, -o] ADJ *Méd* hiatal

hiatus [jatys] NM **1** *(interruption)* break, hiatus, gap **2** *Ling* hiatus **3** *Méd* hiatus; **h. œsophagien** hiatus oesophageus

hibernal, -e, -aux, -ales [ibɛrnal, -o] ADJ **1** *Bot* hibernal; **germination hibernale** hibernal germination **2** *Zool* winter *(avant n)*; **pendant leur sommeil h.** during their hibernation

hibernant, -e [ibɛrnɑ̃, -ɑ̃t] ADJ *Zool* hibernating

hibernation [ibɛrnasjɔ̃] NF **1** *Zool* hibernation; *Fig* **l'industrie textile est en état d'h.** the textile industry is in the doldrums **2** *Méd* **h. artificielle** induced hypothermia

• **en hibernation** ADJ *Fig* in mothballs; **mettre un projet en h.** to shelve *or* to mothball a project

hiberner [3] [ibɛrne] VI *Zool* to hibernate

hibiscus [ibiskys] NM *Bot* hibiscus

***hibou, -x** [ibu] NM owl; *Fig* **un vieux h.** a grumpy old recluse

***hic** [ik] NM INV *Fam* snag; **c'est bien là** *ou* **voilà le h.** there's the rub, that's the trouble; **il y a un h. quelque part** there's a snag *or* catch somewhere

***hickory** [ikɔri] NM *Bot* hickory

hidalgo [idalgo] NM hidalgo; **un bel h.** a dark handsome man *(with Latin looks)*

***hideur** [idœr] NF *Littéraire* hideousness

***hideuse** [idøz] *voir* **hideux**

***hideusement** [idøzmɑ̃] ADV hideously

***hideux, -euse** [idø, -øz] ADJ hideous

***hidjab** [idʒab] NM hijab

hiémal, -e, -aux, -ales [jemal, -o] ADJ *Littéraire* winter *(avant n)*

hier [ijɛr] ADV **1** *(désignant le jour précédent)* yesterday; **h. matin** yesterday morning; **h. (au) soir** yesterday evening; **le journal d'h.** yesterday's paper; **j'y ai consacré la journée/l'après-midi d'h.** I spent all (day) yesterday/all yesterday afternoon doing it; **je m'en souviens comme si c'était h.** I remember it as if it were yesterday **2** *(désignant un passé récent)* **la technologie d'h.** outdated *or* outmoded technology; **h. encore on ignorait tout de cette maladie** until very recently, this disease was totally unknown; **ça ne date pas d'h.** that's nothing new

NM **tu avais tout h. pour te décider** you had all (day) yesterday to make up your mind

***hiérarchie** [jerarʃi] NF **1** *Admin (structure)* hierarchy; **la h. des salaires** the wage ladder; **la h. des valeurs sociales** the scale of social values **2** *Fam (supérieurs)* **la h.** the top brass **3** *Ordinat* **h. de mémoire** memory hierarchy, hierarchical memory structure

***hiérarchique** [jerarʃik] ADJ hierarchic, hierarchical; **passer par la voie h.** to go through official channels; **c'est mon supérieur h.** he's my immediate superior

***hiérarchiquement** [jerarʃikmɑ̃] ADV hierarchically; **dépendre h. de qn** to report to sb

***hiérarchisation** [jerarʃizasjɔ̃] NF **1** *(action)* establishment of a hierarchy; *(structure)* hierarchical structure; **la h. des fonctions** the grading of jobs **2** *(de tâches)* prioritization

***hiérarchisé, -e** [jerarʃize] ADJ *(gén) & Ordinat* hierarchical

***hiérarchiser** [3] [jerarʃize] VT **1** *Admin* to organize along hierarchical lines; **h. les salaires** to introduce wage differentials **2** *(classer ▸ données)* to structure, to classify; *(▸ besoins)* to grade *or* to assess according to importance; *(▸ tâches)* to prioritize

hiératique [jeratik] ADJ **1** *(sacré)* hieratic **2** *(geste)* solemn

***hiéroglyphe** [jerɔglif] NM *Archéol* hieroglyph

• **hiéroglyphes** NMPL *Hum (écriture illisible)* hieroglyphics

***hiéroglyphique** [jerɔglifik] ADJ **1** *Archéol* hieroglyphic, hieroglyphical **2** *(illisible)* scrawled, illegible

***hi-fi** [ifi] NF INV hi-fi

***hi-han** [iɑ̃] **EXCLAM** hee-haw!
NM INV hee-haw

***hijab** [idʒab] **NM** hijab

hilarant, -e [ilarɑ̃, -ɑ̃t] **ADJ** *(drôle)* hilarious

hilare [ilar] **ADJ** laughing, smiling, joyful; **un visage h.** a laughing *or* merry face

hilarité [ilarite] **NF** hilarity, mirth, gaiety; **provoquer l'h. générale** to cause general hilarity

***hile** [il] **NM** *Anat & Bot* hilum

Himalaya [imalaja] **NM l'H.** the Himalayas

himalayen, -enne [imalajɛ̃, -ɛn] **ADJ** Himalayan

***hindi** [indi] **NM** *(langue)* Hindi

hindou, -e [ɛ̃du] **ADJ** hindu
• **Hindou, -e NM,F** Hindu

hindouisme [ɛ̃duism] **NM** Hinduism

hindouiste [ɛ̃duist] **ADJ** Hindu
NMF Hindu

Hindoustan [ɛ̃dustɑ̃] **NM l'H.** Hindustan

hindoustani [ɛ̃dustani] **NM** *Ling* Hindustani

hinterland [intɛrlɑ̃d] **NM** *Géog* hinterland

***hippie** [ipi] **ADJ** hippie, hippy
NMF hippie, hippy

hippique [ipik] **ADJ** horse *(avant n)*; **concours h.** horse trials *or* show; **course h.** *(activité)* horse racing; *(épreuve)* horse race; **sport h.** equestrian sports

hippisme [ipism] **NM** equestrian sports, equestrianism

hippocampe [ipɔkɑ̃p] **NM 1** *Zool* seahorse **2** *Myth (animal mythologique)* hippocampus **3** *Anat* hippocampus (major)

Hippocrate [ipɔkrat] **NPR** Hippocrates; **le serment d'H.** the Hippocratic oath

hippocratique [ipɔkratik] **ADJ** Hippocratic

hippodrome [ipɔdrom] **NM 1** *(champ de courses)* racecourse **2** *Antiq* hippodrome

hippomobile [ipɔmɔbil] **ADJ** horsedrawn

hippophagique [ipɔfaʒik] **ADJ boucherie h.** horsemeat butcher's

hippopotame [ipɔpɔtam] **NM 1** *Zool* hippopotamus, *Fam* hippo **2** *Fam (personne)* elephant; **c'est un vrai h.!** what an elephant!

hippopotamesque [ipɔpɔtamɛsk] **ADJ** *Fam* hippo-like; **une grâce h.** the grace of a hippo

hippotechnie [ipɔtekni] **NF** horse breeding and training

***hippy** [ipi] = **hippie**

hirondelle [irɔ̃dɛl] **NF 1** *Orn* swallow; **h. de cheminée** swallow, *Am* barn swallow; **h. de fenêtre** house martin; **h. de mer** tern; **h. de rivage** sand martin; *Prov* **une h. ne fait pas le printemps** one swallow doesn't make a summer **2** *Fam Vieilli (policier) Br* bobby, *Am* cop

hirsute [irsyt] **ADJ 1** *(échevelé)* bushy-haired; *(touffu ▸ sourcils)* bushy; *(▸ barbe, cheveux)* unkempt **2** *Biol* hirsute, hairy

hispanique [ispanik] **ADJ 1** *(gén)* Hispanic **2** *(aux États-Unis)* Spanish-American
• **Hispanique NMF** *(aux États-Unis)* Spanish American

hispanisant, -e [ispanizɑ̃, -ɑ̃t] **NM,F** Hispanicist

hispaniser [3] [ispanize] **VT** to Hispanicize

hispanisme [ispanism] **NM** *Ling* Hispanicism

hispano-américain, -e [ispanoamerikɛ̃, -ɛn] *(mpl* **hispano-américains**, *fpl* **hispano-américaines)** **ADJ** Spanish-American
• **Hispano-Américain, -e NM,F** Spanish American

hispano-arabe [ispanoarab] *(pl* **hispano-arabes)** **ADJ** Hispano-Moorish

hispanophone [ispanofɔn] **ADJ** Spanish-speaking
NMF Spanish speaker

hispide [ispid] **ADJ** *Bot* hispid

***hisser [3]** [ise] **VT 1** *(lever ▸ drapeau)* to run up; *(▸ voile)* to hoist; *(▸ ancre)* to raise; *(▸ épave)* to raise, to haul up; *(soulever ▸ personne)* to lift up; **h. qn sur ses épaules** to lift sb onto one's shoulders **2** *Fig* **h. qn au poste de directeur** to raise sb to the position of manager; **h. une petite entreprise au rang des meilleures** to push a small company to the top
VPR se hisser 1 *(s'élever)* to hoist oneself; **se h. sur la pointe des pieds** to stand up on tiptoe; **se h. sur une balançoire** to heave *or* to hoist oneself (up) onto a swing **2** *Fig* **elle s'est hissée au poste d'adjointe de direction** she worked her way up to the position of assistant manager; **l'équipe s'est hissée en deuxième division** the team clawed its way into the second division

histogramme [istɔgram] **NM** histogram, column graph

HISTOIRE [istwar]

• history **1–4**	• story **5, 6, 8**
• plot **6**	• history book **7**
• fib **8**	• trouble **9, 10**

NF 1 *(passé)* history; **un lieu chargé d'h.** a place steeped in history; **les hommes et les femmes qui ont fait l'h.** the men and women who have made history; **l'h. d'une croyance** the history of a belief
2 *(mémoire, postérité)* history; **ces faits appartiennent à l'h.** these facts are history; **rester dans l'h.** to go down in history *or* in the history books; **l'h. dira si nous avons eu raison** only time will tell whether we were right
3 *(période précise)* history; **l'h. et la préhistoire** history and prehistory
4 *(discipline)* history; **l'h. de l'art/la littérature** art/literary history; **l'h. de France** the history of France, French history; **l'h. ancienne/contemporaine/du Moyen Âge** ancient/contemporary/medieval history; *Fig* **tout ça, c'est de l'h. ancienne** that's all ancient history; *Vieilli & Biol* **h. naturelle** natural history; **licence d'h.** ≃ BA in History, *Br* ≃ History degree; **pour la petite h.** for the record; **je te le dis pour la petite h.** I'm (only) telling you so you'll know; **sais-tu, pour la petite h., qu'il est né au Pérou?** do you know that he was born in Peru, by the way?
5 *(récit, écrit)* story; **je leur raconte une h. tous les soirs** every night I tell them a story; **écrire des histoires pour enfants** to write children's stories; **c'est une h. vraie** it's a true story; **c'est une longue h.** it's a long story; **nous avons vécu ensemble une belle h. d'amour** we had a wonderful romance; **attends, je ne t'ai pas encore dit le plus beau** *ou* **le meilleur de l'h.!** wait, the best part *or* bit is still to come!; **une h. drôle** a joke, a funny story; *Fam* **h. à dormir debout** cock and bull story, tall story
6 *(intrigue ▸ d'une pièce, d'un film)* plot, story; *(▸ d'une chanson)* story
7 *(livre)* history book; **elle a écrit une h. du village** she wrote a history of the village
8 *Fam (mensonge)* fib, (tall) story; **tout ça, c'est des histoires** that's a load of (stuff and) nonsense *or Am* baloney; **raconter des histoires** to tell tall stories; **allez, tu me racontes des histoires!** come on, you're pulling my leg!; **je t'assure, je ne te raconte pas d'histoires!** I assure you, I'm not making it up!
9 *Fam (complications)* trouble, fuss; **faire des histoires** to make a fuss; **il n'a pas fait d'histoires pour accepter le chèque?** did he make any fuss about accepting the cheque?; **ça va faire toute une h.** there'll be hell to pay; **ç'a été toute une h.** it was quite a business *or Br* a to-do; **pour faire venir l'électricien, ç'a été toute une h.** we had a hell of a time getting the electrician to come; **elle en a fait toute une h.** she kicked up a (huge) fuss about it; **sans faire d'h.** *ou* **d'histoires** without (making) a fuss; **vous allez me suivre au poste et pas d'h.** *ou* **d'histoires!** you're coming with me to the station and I don't want any trouble (from you)!
10 *(ennuis)* trouble; **faire des histoires (à qn)** to cause *or* to make trouble (for sb); **si tu ne veux pas avoir d'histoires** if you want to keep *or* to stay out of trouble; **tu vas nous attirer** *ou* **nous faire avoir des histoires** you'll get us into trouble; **taisez-vous toutes les trois, j'en ai assez de vos histoires!** shut up you three, I've had enough of you going on like that!
11 *(question, problème)* **pourquoi démissionne-t-elle? – oh, une h. de contrat** why is she resigning? – oh, something to do with her contract; **c'est une h. de fous!** it's crazy!; **il m'arrive une sale h.** something terrible's happened (to me); **ne pensons plus à cette h.** let's forget the whole thing *or* business; **qu'est-ce que c'est que cette h.?** what's this I hear?, what's all this about?; **c'est toujours la même h.** it's always the same (old) story; **c'est une (toute) autre h.** that's quite a different matter
12 *Fam (locution)* **h. de** *(afin de)* just to; **faire qch h. de rigoler** to do sth just for a laugh; **h. de dire quelque chose** just for something to say
• **à histoires ADJ c'est une femme à histoires** she's nothing but trouble
• **sans histoires ADJ** *(gens)* ordinary; *(voyage)* uneventful, trouble-free

> Attention: ne pas confondre **history** et **story** lorsque l'on traduit **histoire**. Le terme **history** désigne la discipline, alors que **story** signifie **récit**.

histologie [istɔlɔʒi] **NF** *Biol* histology

histologique [istɔlɔʒik] **ADJ** *Biol* histologic, histological

historicité [istɔrisite] **NF** historicity

historié, -e [istɔrje] **ADJ** *(manuscrit)* storiated, historiated

historien, -enne [istɔrjɛ̃, -ɛn] **NM,F 1** *(spécialiste)* historian; **se faire l'h. d'un village/d'une institution** to tell the story of a village/an institution; **h. d'art** art historian **2** *(étudiant)* history student

historiette [istɔrjɛt] **NF** anecdote

historiographe [istɔrjɔgraf] **NM** historiographer

historiographie [istɔrjɔgrafi] **NF** historiography

historique [istɔrik] **ADJ 1** *(relatif à l'histoire ▸ méthode, roman)* historical; *(▸ fait, personnage)* historical **2** *(célèbre)* historic; **une émission/poignée de main h.** a historic programme/handshake; **la parole** *ou* **le mot h. de Pu Yi** Pu Yi's famous remark **3** *(mémorable)* historic; **c'est un moment/match h.** this is a historic moment/match; **nous avons atteint le cours h. de 42 dollars l'once** we've reached the record *or* unprecedented level of 42 dollars an ounce
NM 1 *(chronologie)* background history, (historical) review; **faire l'h. des événements** to give a chronological account of events; **faire l'h. des jeux Olympiques** to trace the (past) history of the Olympic Games **2** *Ordinat (d'un document)* log; *(dans un logiciel de navigation)* history list

> Attention: ne pas confondre **historic** et **historical** lorsque l'on traduit **historique**. **Historic** signifie **important d'un point de vue historique**, alors que **historical** signifie **qui se rapporte à l'histoire**.

historiquement [istɔrikmɑ̃] **ADV** historically; **le fait n'est pas h. prouvé** it's not a historically proven fact

histrion [istrijɔ̃] **NM 1** *Hist (jongleur)* wandering minstrel, troubadour **2** *Fig Péj* exhibitionist; **un h. politique** a politician who likes to play to the crowd

hi-tech [aitek] **ADJ INV** hi-tech

hitlérien, -enne [itlerjɛ̃, -ɛn] **ADJ** Hitlerian, Hitlerite
NM,F Hitlerite

hitlérisme [itlerism] **NM** Hitlerism

***hit-parade** [itparad] *(pl* **hit-parades)** **NM 1** *Mus* charts; **ils sont premiers** *ou* **numéro un au h.** they're (at the) top of *or* they're number one in the charts **2** *Fig (classement)* **placé au h. des hommes politiques** among the top *or* leading politicians

***hittite** [itit] **ADJ** Hittite
NM *(langue)* Hittite
• **Hittite NMF les Hittites** the Hittites

HIV [aʃive] **NM** *Méd (abrév* **human immunodeficiency virus)** HIV; **être atteint du H.** to be HIV-positive

hiver [ivɛr] **NM 1** *(saison)* winter; **en h.** *ou* **l'h., on rentre les géraniums** we bring in the geraniums in (the) winter; **l'h. dernier** last winter; **l'h. prochain** next winter; **l'h. fut précoce/tardif** winter came early/late; **tout l'h.** all winter long, all through the winter; **au cœur de l'h.** in the middle of winter, in midwinter; *Fam* **elle ne passera pas l'h.** she won't make it through the winter; **h. nucléaire** nuclear winter **2** *Fig Littéraire* **à l'h. de sa vie** in the twilight *or* evening of his/her life

• **d'hiver ADJ** *(ciel, paysage, temps)* wintry; *(quartiers, vêtements, fruits)* winter *(avant n)*

hivernage [ivɛrnaʒ] **NM 1** *Agr (activité)* wintering, winter feeding; *Vieilli (fourrage)* winter fodder

2 *Météo* winter season *(in tropical regions)*

3 *Naut (activité)* wintering; *(port)* winter harbour

4 *(d'oiseaux, d'animaux)* (over)wintering

hivernal, -e, -aux, -ales [ivɛrnal, -o] **ADJ** *(propre à l'hiver)* winter *(avant n)*; *(qui rappelle l'hiver)* wintry; **journées/températures hivernales** winter days/temperatures; **un temps h.** wintry weather; **un ciel h.** a wintry sky

hivernant, -e [ivɛrnɑ̃, -ɑ̃t] **ADJ** wintering

NM,F winter tourist

hiverner [3] [ivɛrne] **VI** *(passer l'hiver)* to (over) winter

VT *Agr* to winter

HLM** [aʃɛlɛm] **NM OU NF** *(abrév* **habitation à loyer modéré)* *(immeuble) Br* ≃ block of council flats, *Am* ≃ public housing unit; *(appartement) Br* ≃ council flat, *Am* ≃ (apartment in a) public housing unit; *(maison) Br* ≃ council house, *Am* ≃ low-rent house

***ho** [o] **EXCLAM 1** *(de surprise)* oh! **2** *(pour interpeller)* hey!

hobby** [ɔbi] *(pl* **hobbys** *ou* **hobbies)* **NM** hobby

***hobereau, -x** [ɔbro] **NM 1** *Péj (gentilhomme)* country squire **2** *Orn* hobby

***hochement** [ɔʃmɑ̃] **NM h. de tête** *(approbateur)* nod; *(désapprobateur)* shake of the head; **accepter d'un h. de tête** to accept with a nod; **refuser d'un h. de tête** to refuse with a shake of the head

***hochepot** [ɔʃpo] **NM** *Culin* **h. (à la flamande)** (Flemish) hotchpotch *(stew of meat and vegetables)*

***hocher [3]** [ɔʃe] **VT h. la tête** *(pour accepter)* to nod; *(pour refuser)* to shake one's head; **elle hocha la tête en signe d'acquiescement** she nodded in agreement; **elle hocha la tête en signe de refus** she refused with a shake of the head

***hochet** [ɔʃɛ] **NM 1** *(jouet)* rattle **2** *Fig Littéraire* gewgaw

***hockey** [ɔkɛ] **NM** hockey; **h. sur glace** ice hockey; **h. sur gazon** *Br* hockey, *Am* field hockey

***hockeyeur, -euse** [ɔkejœr, -øz] **NM,F** hockey player

hoirie [wari] **NF** *Jur* **avancement d'h.** advancement *(of an inheritance)*

***holà** [ɔla] **EXCLAM** hey!, whoa!; **h.! attention!** hey *or* whoa, be careful!

NM mettre le h. à qch to put a stop to sth; **il se remet à boire trop, il faut que j'y mette le h.** he's drinking too much again, I must put a stop to it *or* put my foot down

***holding** [ɔldiŋ] **NM OU NF** *Fin* holding company

***hold-up** [ɔldœp] **NM INV** raid, hold-up; **un h. à la banque/poste** a bank/post office raid

***hollandais, -e** [ɔlɑ̃dɛ, -ɛz] **ADJ** Dutch

NM *(langue)* Dutch

• **Hollandais, -e NM,F** Dutchman, *f* Dutchwoman; **les H.** the Dutch

• **hollandaise NF** *Culin* hollandaise (sauce)

***Hollande** [ɔlɑ̃d] **NF la H.** Holland

***hollande** [ɔlɑ̃d] **NM** *Culin* Dutch cheese *(Edam or Gouda)*

NF 1 *Culin* Dutch potato **2** *Tex* holland **3** *(porcelaine)* Dutch porcelain

***hollywoodien, -enne** [ɔliwudjɛ̃, -ɛn] **ADJ** *(de Hollywood)* Hollywood *(avant n)*; *(évoquant Hollywood)* Hollywood-style, Hollywood-like

holmium [ɔlmjɔm] **NM** *Chim* holmium

holocauste [ɔlɔkost] **NM 1** *Hist* **l'h., l'H.** the Holocaust

2 *(massacre)* holocaust, mass murder

3 *Rel* burnt offering; **offrir un animal en h.** to offer an animal in sacrifice

4 *(victime)* sacrifice

hologramme [ɔlɔgram] **NM** *Phot* hologram

holographe [ɔlɔgraf] **NM** *Jur* holograph

holographie [ɔlɔgrafi] **NF** *Phot* holography

holothurie [ɔlɔtyri] **NF** *Zool* sea cucumber, sea slug, *Spéc* holothurian

***homard** [ɔmar] **NM** lobster; *Fam* **rouge comme un h.** *(de honte, de gêne)* as red as a beetroot; *(après un coup de soleil)* as red as a lobster

***home** [om] **NM 1** *(centre d'accueil)* **h. d'enfants** residential leisure centre (for children); *Belg* **h. d'étudiants** student hall of residence *or Am* dormitory, student hostel; *Belg* **h. pour personnes âgées** old people's home, retirement home **2** *Vieilli (chez-soi)* home; **ici c'est mon h.** I feel at home here

***HomeCam®** [omkam] **NF** HomeCam®

home cinéma** [omsinema] *(pl* **home cinémas)* **NM** home cinema

homélie [ɔmeli] **NF** homily, lecture; **suivit une longue h. sur les dangers du tabac** there then followed a long lecture on the dangers of smoking

homéopathe [ɔmeɔpat] *Méd* **NMF** homeopath, homeopathist

ADJ médecin h. homeopathic doctor

homéopathie [ɔmeɔpati] **NF** *Méd* homeopathy

homéopathique [ɔmeɔpatik] **ADJ** *Méd* homeopathic

Homère [ɔmɛr] **NPR** Homer

homérique [ɔmerik] **ADJ** Homeric

homicide [ɔmisid] **ADJ** *Littéraire* homicidal

NMF *Littéraire (personne)* homicide

NM 1 *(acte)* killing *(UNCOUNT)* **2** *Jur* homicide; **commettre un h.** to commit homicide; **h. involontaire** *Br* ≃ manslaughter, *Am* ≃ second-degree murder, *Scot* ≃ culpable homicide; **h. par imprudence** *Br* ≃ reckless manslaughter, *Am* ≃ second-degree murder, *Scot* ≃ culpable homicide; **h. volontaire** murder

hominidé [ɔminide] *Zool* **NM** hominid

• **hominidés NMPL** Hominidae

hominoïde [ɔminɔid] *Zool* **ADJ** hominoid

NM hominoid

hommage [ɔmaʒ] **NM 1** *(marque de respect)* tribute, homage; **recevoir l'h. de qn** to receive sb's tribute; **rendre h. à** to pay homage *or* (a) tribute to; **ce soir nous rendons h. à Édith Piaf** tonight we pay tribute to Edith Piaf; **il faut rendre h. à sa perspicacité** you have to admire his/her clear-sightedness **2** *(don)* **h. de l'éditeur** complimentary copy **3** *Hist* homage

• **hommages NMPL être sensible aux hommages** to appreciate receiving compliments; **mes hommages à votre épouse** please give my regards to your wife; **veuillez agréer, Madame, mes hommages respectueux** *ou* **mes respectueux hommages** *(à quelqu'un dont on connaît le nom) Br* yours sincerely, *Am* sincerely (yours); *(à quelqu'un dont on ne connaît pas le nom) Br* yours sincerely, *Am* sincerely (yours)

• **en hommage à PRÉP** in tribute *or* homage to

hommasse [ɔmas] **ADJ** *Péj* mannish, masculine; **elle a des manières hommasses** she has very masculine ways

homme [ɔm] **NM 1** *(individu de sexe masculin)* man; **l'h. a une espérance de vie plus courte que celle de la femme** men have a shorter life expectancy than women; **alors, t'es un h. (ou un lâche)?** what are you, a man or a mouse?; **sors si t'es un h.!** step outside if you're a man!; **le service militaire en a fait un h.** national service made a man of him; *Com* **rayon hommes** men's department, menswear; **je ne suis pas h. à croire les gens sur parole** I'm not the sort of man who blindly believes what I'm told; **trouver son h.** *(pour un travail)* to find one's man; **si vous voulez quelqu'un de tenace, Lambert est votre h.** if you want somebody who'll stick at it, then Lambert's your man; **une double page sur l'h. du jour** a two-page spread on the man of the moment; **c'est l'h. fort du parti** he is the kingpin of the party; **une discussion d'h. à h.** a man-to-man talk; **je n'ai que des professeurs hommes** all my teachers are male *or* men; **h. d'action** man of action; **h. d'affaires** businessman; **h. d'Église** man of the Church *or* cloth; **h. d'État** statesman; **h. à femmes** lady's *or* ladies' man, *Péj* womanizer; *Can* **être un h. aux hommes** to be a homosexual; *Suisse* **h. du feu** *Br* fireman, *Am* fire fighter; **h. de loi** lawyer, man of law; **h. de main** henchman; **c'est un parfait h. du monde** he's a real gentleman; **h. de paille** man of straw, figurehead; **h. de peine** labourer; **h. politique** politician; **h. de science** scientist, man of science; **h. à tout faire** odd-job man, handyman; **les hommes du Président** the President's men; **comme un seul h.** as one man; *Prov* **un h. averti en vaut deux** forewarned is forearmed; **les hommes naissent libres et égaux en droit** ≃ all men are born equal

2 *(être humain)* man; **un h. sur la Lune** a man on the Moon; **l'h.** man, mankind, humankind; **les hommes** man, mankind, human beings; **l'h. descend du singe** human beings are *or* man is descended from the apes; **h. des cavernes** caveman; **l'h. de Cro-Magnon/de Neandertal** Cro-Magnon/Neanderthal Man; **l'h. de la rue** the man in the street; *Prov* **l'h. propose, Dieu dispose** man proposes, God disposes

3 *Fam (amant, époux)* **mon/son h.** my/her man; **elles laissent leurs hommes à la maison** they leave their men at home; **où est mon petit h.?** *(fils)* where's my little man?; **l'h. idéal** Mr Right; **elle a rencontré l'h. de sa vie** she's met the love of her life

4 *Naut (marin)* **h. de barre** helmsman; **h. d'équipage** crew member, crewman; **h. de vigie** lookout; **un h. à la mer!** man overboard!

5 *Mil* **les officiers et leurs hommes** the officers and their men; **h. de troupe** private, ordinary soldier

6 *Aviat* crewman, crew member

> Il faut noter que le terme anglais **man of the world** ne signifie pas **homme du monde** mais **homme d'expérience.**

homo[1] [ɔmo] **NM INV** *Zool* Homo

homo[2] [ɔmo] *Fam (abrév* **homosexuel***)* **ADJ** gay

NMF gay

homocentrique [ɔmɔsɑ̃trik] **ADJ** *Géom* homocentric

homogène [ɔmɔʒɛn] **ADJ 1** *(substance, liquide, marché, produits)* homogeneous; **jusqu'à obtention d'une pâte bien h.** until you have a nice smooth mixture

2 *(gouvernement, classe)* uniform, consistent, coherent

3 *Chim & Math* homogeneous

4 *Mktg (marché, produits)* homogeneous

homogénéisation [ɔmɔʒeneizasjɔ̃] **NF 1** *(d'une substance)* homogenization **2** *Fig (uniformisation)* standardization; **on constate une h. des modes de paiement** payment methods are being standardized

homogénéiser [3] [ɔmɔʒeneize] **VT** to make homogeneous; *(lait)* to homogenize

homogénéité [ɔmɔʒeneite] **NF 1** *(d'une substance)* homogeneity, homogeneousness **2** *(d'une œuvre, d'une équipe)* coherence, unity

homographe [ɔmɔgraf] **ADJ** homographic

NM homograph

homologation [ɔmɔlɔgasjɔ̃] **NF 1** *(déclaration de conformité)* accreditation **2** *Jur (entérinement)* ratification, approval; *(d'un testament)* probate **3** *Sport (d'un record)* ratification

homologie [ɔmɔlɔʒi] **NF** *Math, Biol & Chim* homology

homologue [ɔmɔlɔg] **ADJ 1** *(équivalent) & Math* homologous, homologic, homological; **amiral est le grade h. de général** an admiral is equal in rank to a general **2** *Biol & Chim* homologous

NMF *(personne)* counterpart, opposite number

NM *Biol & Chim* homologue

homologuer [3] [ɔmɔlɔge] **VT 1** *(déclarer conforme)* to approve, to accredit; **prix homologué** authorized price **2** *Jur (entériner)* to sanction, to ratify; *(testament)* to probate **3** *Sport (record)* to ratify

homoncule [ɔmɔ̃kyl] = **homuncule**

homonyme [ɔmɔnim] **ADJ** homonymous

NMF *(personne, ville)* namesake

NM homonym

homonymie [ɔmɔnimi] **NF** homonymy

homoparental, -e, -aux, -ales [ɔmɔparɑ̃tal, -o] **ADJ** relating to gay parenting, *Spéc* homoparental

homoparentalité [ɔmɔparɑ̃talite] **NF** gay parenting

homophobe [ɔmɔfɔb] **ADJ** homophobic
NMF homophobe

homophobie [ɔmɔfɔbi] **NF** homophobia

homophone [ɔmɔfɔn] **ADJ 1** *Ling* homophonous **2** *Mus* homophonic
NM *Ling* homophone

homophonie [ɔmɔfɔni] **NF** *Ling & Mus* homophony

homosexualité [ɔmɔsɛksɥalite] **NF** homosexuality

homosexuel, -elle [ɔmɔsɛksɥɛl] **ADJ** homosexual, gay
NM,F homosexual, gay

homuncule [ɔmɔ̃kyl] **NM 1** *(en alchimie)* homunculus **2** *Fam Vieilli (petit homme)* squirt

***Honduras** [ɔ̃dyras] **NM le H.** Honduras; **le H. britannique** British Honduras

***hondurien, -enne** [ɔ̃dyrjɛ̃, -ɛn] **ADJ** Honduran
• **Hondurien, -enne NM,F** Honduran

***Hongkong, *Hong Kong** [ɔ̃gkɔ̃g] **NM** Hong Kong

***hongre** [ɔ̃gr] **ADJ M** gelded
NM gelding

***hongrer [3]** [ɔ̃gre] **VT** *Vét* to geld, to castrate

***Hongrie** [ɔ̃gri] **NF la H.** Hungary

***hongrois, -e** [ɔ̃grwa, -az] **ADJ** Hungarian
NM *(langue)* Hungarian, Magyar
• **Hongrois, -e NM,F** Hungarian

honnête [ɔnɛt] **ADJ 1** *(scrupuleux ▸ vendeur, associé)* honest; **le procédé n'est pas très h. mais j'ai besoin d'argent** it's a rather unscrupulous *or* dishonest thing to do but I need the money
2 *(franc)* honest; **soyons honnêtes** let's be honest; **il faut être h., elle n'a aucune chance de réussir** let's be honest *or* let's face it, she hasn't got a hope of succeeding
3 *(acceptable ▸ prix)* fair, reasonable; *(▸ résultat)* decent, reasonable; *(▸ repas)* decent; **12 sur 20, c'est h.** 12 out of 20, that's not bad; **une note plus qu'h.** a perfectly respectable mark
4 *(respectable)* honest, respectable, decent; **des gens honnêtes** respectable people; *Littéraire* **un h. homme** ≃ a gentleman
5 *Arch (poli)* courteous, polite, well-bred

honnêtement [ɔnɛtmɑ̃] **ADV 1** *(sincèrement)* honestly, frankly, sincerely; **répondez h.** answer honestly, give an honest answer; **h., je ne la connais pas!** honestly, I don't know her!; **non mais, h., tu la crois?** come on now, be honest, do you believe her?
2 *(décemment)* fairly, decently; **je connais cet endroit, on y mange h.** I know that place, their food is quite decent; **elle a terminé h. son année scolaire** she finished the year with reasonable marks
3 *(de façon morale)* honestly; **vivre h.** to live *or* to lead an honest life; **c'est de l'argent h. gagné** it's money honestly earned; **il a relaté les faits h.** he told the story honestly *or* candidly
4 *Arch (avec courtoisie)* courteously, politely

honnêteté [ɔnɛtte] **NF 1** *(franchise)* honesty, candour; **avec h.** honestly, candidly; **il a reconnu son erreur avec h.** he admitted honestly that he was wrong
2 *(intégrité ▸ d'une conduite)* honesty, decency; *(▸ d'une personne)* integrity, decency
3 *Arch (décence)* decency, propriety, decorum
4 *Arch (courtoisie)* courtesy, politeness
• **en toute honnêteté ADV 1** *(avec sincérité)* in all honesty, frankly; **répondez en toute h.** give an honest answer **2** *(pour être honnête)* to tell the truth, to be perfectly honest

honneur [ɔnœr] **NM 1** *(dignité)* honour; **homme d'h.** man of honour, honourable man; **mon h. est en jeu** my honour is at stake; **l'h. est sauf** my/his/*etc* honour is saved *or* intact; **c'est une question d'h.** it's a matter of honour; **mettre un point d'h. à** *ou* **se faire un point d'h. de faire qch** to make a point of honour of doing sth; **venger l'h. de qn** to avenge sb's honour; **rendre l'h. à une femme** to restore a woman's honour; **je finirai la partie pour l'h.** I'll play to the end (even though I've lost); **se faire h. de** to pride oneself on *or* upon
2 *(mérite)* **c'est tout à son h.** it's entirely to his/her credit; **l'h. vous en revient** the credit is yours; **être l'h. de sa nation** to be a credit *or* an honour to one's country; **faire h. à qn** to do sb credit; **ces sentiments ne lui font pas h.** these feelings do him/her no credit
3 *(marque de respect)* honour; *(dans des formules de politesse)* privilege, honour; **vous me faites trop d'h.** you're being too kind (to me); **c'est lui faire trop d'h.** he/she doesn't deserve such respect; **à vous l'h.!** after you!; **h. aux dames!** ladies first!; **c'est un h. pour moi de vous présenter…** it's a great privilege for me to introduce to you…; **nous avons l'h. de vous informer que…** we have the pleasure of informing you that…; **faites-nous l'h. de venir nous voir** would you honour us with a visit?; **à qui ai-je l'h.?** to whom do I have the honour (of speaking)?
4 *(titre)* **votre/son H.** Your/His/Her Honour
5 *(locutions)* **faire h. à qch** *(signature, chèque, facture, traite)* to honour; **faire h. à ses engagements** to honour one's commitments; **ils ont fait h. à ma cuisine** they did justice to my cooking
• **honneurs NMPL 1** *(cérémonie)* honours; **les honneurs dus à son rang** the honours due to his/her rank; **honneurs funèbres** last honours; **enterré avec les honneurs militaires** buried with (full) military honours; **rendre les honneurs à qn** *Mil (saluer)* to present arms to sb, to give *or* pay (military) honours to sb; *(funèbres)* to pay sb one's last respects; *Mil* **les honneurs de la guerre** the honours of war; *Fig* **avec les honneurs de la guerre** honourably **2** *(distinction)* **briguer** *ou* **rechercher les honneurs** to seek public recognition; **avoir les honneurs de la première page** to make the front page; **faire à qn les honneurs de qch** to show sb round sth; **permettez que je vous fasse les honneurs de la cave** do let me show you round the cellar **3** *Cartes* honours
• **à l'honneur ADJ être à l'h.** to have the place of honour; **ce soir, c'est vous qui êtes à l'h.** tonight is in your honour; **les organisateurs de l'exposition ont voulu que la sculpture soit à l'h.** the exhibition organizers wanted the sculpture to take pride of place
• **d'honneur ADJ** *(invité, place, tour)* of honour; *(membre, président)* honorary; *(cour, escalier)* main
• **en honneur ADJ** in favour; **mettre qch en h.** to bring sth into favour
• **en l'honneur de PRÉP** in honour of; **en l'h. de notre ami Maurice** in honour of our friend Maurice; **une fête en mon/son h.** a party for me/him/her
• **en quel honneur ADV** *Fam* **il faut que tu m'aides – ah bon, et en quel h.?** you've got to help me – give me one good reason why I should!; *Fam Hum* **ce regard noir, c'est en quel h.?** what's that scowl in aid of?, what's that scowl for?
• **sur l'honneur ADV** upon *or* on one's honour; **jurer sur l'h.** to swear on one's honour

***honnir [32]** [ɔnir] **VT** *Littéraire* to despise; **un dictateur honni** a hated dictator; **honni soit qui mal y pense** honi soit qui mal y pense, shame be to him who thinks evil of it

honorabilité [ɔnɔrabilite] **NF** respectability

honorable [ɔnɔrabl] **ADJ 1** *(digne de respect)* respectable, honourable; **les citoyens honorables** respectable *or* upright citizens; **ses motifs ne sont pas des plus honorables** his/her intentions are less than honourable **2** *(avant le nom) Hum* **mon h. collègue** my esteemed colleague; **j'en appelle à l'h. compagnie** I appeal to this honourable company **3** *(satisfaisant)* fair, decent; **son bulletin scolaire est tout à fait h./est h. sans plus** his/her school report is quite satisfactory/is just satisfactory

honorablement [ɔnɔrabləmɑ̃] **ADV 1** *(de façon respectable)* decently, honourably; **h. connu** known and respected; **vivre h.** to lead a respectable life **2** *(de façon satisfaisante)* creditably, honourably; **gagner h. sa vie** to earn a decent living

honoraire [ɔnɔrɛr] **ADJ 1** *(conservant son ancien titre)* **professeur h.** professor emeritus **2** *(ayant le titre mais non les fonctions)* honorary

honoraires [ɔnɔrɛr] **NMPL** fee, fees; **il demande des h. raisonnables** he charges reasonable fees *or* a reasonable fee

honorariat [ɔnɔrarja] **NM** *(titre)* honorary title; **obtenir** *ou* **recevoir l'h.** to become an honorary member

honoré, -e [ɔnɔre] **ADJ 1** *(honorable)* **mes chers et honorés confrères** most honourable and esteemed colleagues **2** *(lors de présentations)* **très h.!** I'm (greatly) honoured!
• **honorée NF** *Vieilli Com* **par votre honorée du 20 avril** by your letter of 20 April

honorer [3] [ɔnɔre] **VT 1** *(rendre hommage à)* to honour; **honorons nos héros disparus** let us pay tribute to our dead heroes; **h. qn de sa confiance** to honour sb with one's confidence; *Hum* **elle ne nous a même pas honorés d'un regard** she never even honoured us with a glance
2 *(respecter, estimer)* to honour; **nous honorons tous l'homme qui a pris cette décision** the man who made that decision is held in great esteem by us all; **tu honoreras ta famille** you will respect your family
3 *(contribuer à la réputation de)* to honour, to be a credit *or* an honour to; **votre sincérité vous honore** your sincerity does you credit
4 *(gratifier)* to honour; **votre présence m'honore** you honour me with your presence
5 *(s'acquitter de ▸ facture, chèque, traite, engagements)* to honour
6 *Hum (sexuellement)* to make love to
VPR s'honorer s'h. de to be proud of, to take pride in, to pride oneself upon; **je m'honore de votre amitié** *ou* **d'être votre ami** I'm honoured *or* proud to be your friend

honorifique [ɔnɔrifik] **ADJ** *(titre, poste)* honorary; **président à titre h.** honorary president

***honte** [ɔ̃t] **NF 1** *(sentiment d'humiliation)* shame; **avoir h. (de qn/qch)** to be *or* to feel ashamed (of sb/sth); **vous devriez avoir h.!** you should be ashamed!; **j'ai h. d'arriver les mains vides** I feel *or* I'm ashamed at arriving empty-handed; **faire h. à qn** to make sb (feel) ashamed, to shame sb; **il fait h. à son père** *(il lui est un sujet de mécontentement)* his father is ashamed of him; *(il lui donne un sentiment d'infériorité)* he puts his father to shame; **ne me fais pas h. devant nos invités** don't show me up in front of our guests; **trois ans plus tard, toute h. bue, il recommençait son trafic** three years later, totally lacking in any sense of shame, he started up his little racket again; *Fam* **(c'est) la h.!** the shame of it!; *Fam* **avoir la h.** to be embarrassed *or* mortified
2 *(indignité, scandale)* disgrace, (object of) shame; **être la h. de sa famille** to be a disgrace to one's family; **la société laisse faire, c'est une h.!** it's outrageous *or* it's a crying shame that society just lets it happen!
3 *(déshonneur)* shame, shamefulness; **à ma grande h.** to my shame; **h. à celui/celle qui…** shame on him/her who…; **h. à toi!** shame on you!; **il n'y a pas de h. à être au chômage** being unemployed is nothing to be ashamed of
4 *(peur)* fear; **tu as h. de venir me dire bonjour?** are you afraid to come and say hello?
5 *(pudeur)* **fausse h.** bashfulness; **n'ayez pas de fausse h. à parler au médecin** don't feel bashful *or* self-conscious about talking to the doctor
• **sans honte ADV** shamelessly, without shame, unashamedly; **vous pouvez parler sans h.** you may talk quite openly

***honteuse** [ɔ̃tøz] *voir* **honteux**

***honteusement** [ɔ̃tøzmɑ̃] **ADV 1** *(avec gêne)* shamefully, ashamedly; **elle cacha h. son visage dans ses mains** she hid her face in shame **2** *(scandaleusement)* shamefully, disgracefully; **on les exploite h.** they are disgracefully *or* scandalously exploited

***honteux, -euse** [ɔ̃tø, -øz] **ADJ 1** *(déshonorant)* shameful, disgraceful; **de h. secrets** shameful secrets; **un passé h.** a shameful past, an inglorious past; **maladie honteuse** venereal disease
2 *(scandaleux ▸ exploitation, politique)* disgraceful, outrageous, shocking; **c'est h. de lui prendre le peu qu'elle a** it's disgraceful *or* a disgrace to take from her the little she has; **ils continuent leur h. trafic de stupéfiants** they keep up their vile drug trafficking
3 *(qui a des remords)* ashamed; **être h. de qch/d'avoir fait qch** to be ashamed of sth/of having done sth
4 *(qui cache ses opinions)* closet *(avant n)*

***hooligan** [uligan] NM (football) hooligan

***hooliganisme** [uliganism] NM (football) hooliganism

***hop** [ɔp] EXCLAM **allez, h.!** *(à un enfant)* come on then!; **allez h., on s'en va!** (right,) off we go!; **h.-là!** oops(-a-daisy)!

hôpital, -aux [ɔpital, -o] NM **1** *(établissement)* hospital; **il est bien soigné à l'h.** he is being well cared for *Br* in hospital *or Am* in the hospital; **h. de campagne** field hospital; **h. de jour** outpatient clinic; **h. naval** naval hospital; **h. psychiatrique** psychiatric hospital; **c'est l'h. qui se moque de la Charité** it's the pot calling the kettle black **2** *(comme adj; avec ou sans trait d'union)* hospital *(avant n)*; **navire h.** hospital ship

***hoquet** [ɔkɛ] NM **1** *(spasme)* hiccup, hiccough; **avoir le h.** to have (the) hiccups; **dans un h. de dégoût** with a gasp of disgust **2** *(d'un appareil)* chug, gasp; **le moteur eut un dernier h. et rendit l'âme** the engine gave a final splutter and died

***hoqueter [27]** [ɔkte] VI **1** *(personne)* to hiccup, to have (the) hiccups **2** *(appareil)* to judder; **le moteur hoqueta puis s'arrêta** the engine spluttered to a halt

horaire [ɔrɛr] ADJ hourly

NM **1** *(de travail)* schedule, timetable; *(d'un magasin)* opening hours; **j'ai un h. réduit** I work shorter hours; **nos horaires sont chargés** we work a busy *or* heavy schedule *or* a lot of hours; **nous n'avons pas les mêmes horaires** we don't work the same hours; **je n'ai pas d'h.** I don't have any particular schedule; **h. individualisé** *ou* **souple** *ou* **à la carte** flexible working hours, *Br* flexitime; **horaires de bureau/de travail** office/working hours **2** *(de train, d'avion)* schedule, timetable; **horaires d'avion** flight timetable; **je ne connais pas l'h. des trains** I don't know the train times; **être en retard sur l'h.** to be running late

***horde** [ɔrd] NF horde; **des hordes de gens** hordes of people

***horion** [ɔrjɔ̃] NM *Littéraire* blow, punch; **les horions pleuvaient de partout** fists were flying

horizon [ɔrizɔ̃] NM **1** *(ligne)* horizon; *aussi Fig* **à l'h.** on the horizon; **le soleil disparaît à l'h.** the sun is disappearing below the horizon; **on voit encore le bateau à l'h.** the ship is still visible on the horizon; *aussi Fig* **rien à l'h.** nothing in sight *or* view; *Fam* **pas le moindre petit boulot à l'h.** no job anywhere to be had

2 *(paysage)* horizon, view, vista; **un h. de toits et de coupoles** a skyline of rooftops and domes; **changer d'h.** to have a change of scene *or* scenery

3 *(domaine d'activité)* horizon; **élargir ses horizons** to broaden one's horizons; **h. intellectuel** intellectual horizons *or* boundaries

4 *(perspectives d'avenir)* **notre h. est janvier 2010** our objective is *or* we are working towards January 2010; **les prévisions à l'h. 2010** the forecast for 2010; **ouvrir des horizons** to open up new horizons *or* prospects; **h. économique/politique** economic/political prospects

5 *Géol* horizon; **h. A/B/C** A/B/C horizon

6 *Aviat* **h. artificiel** artificial horizon

horizontal, -e, -aux, -ales [ɔrizɔ̃tal, -o] ADJ **1** *(position)* horizontal; **mettez-vous en position horizontale** lie down (flat); **le un h.** *(aux mots croisés)* one across **2** *Écon (concentration, intégration)* horizontal

• **horizontale** NF horizontal

• **à l'horizontale** ADV horizontally, in a horizontal position; **placer qch à l'horizontale** to lay sth down (flat)

horizontalement [ɔrizɔ̃talmɑ̃] ADV horizontally; **pose l'échelle h.** lay the ladder down flat; **h.: un, en six lettres, oiseau** *(aux mots croisés)* one across: six letters, bird

horizontalité [ɔrizɔ̃talite] NF horizontalness, horizontality

horloge [ɔrlɔʒ] NF *(pendule)* clock; **il est deux heures à l'h.** it's two by the clock; **j'ai attendu une bonne heure d'h.** I waited a full *or* solid hour by the clock; **h. atomique** atomic clock; *Can* **h. grand-père** grandfather *or* longcase clock; **h. horodatrice** time clock; **h. interne** *ou* **biologique** body *or* biological clock; **h. mystérieuse** mystery clock; **h. normande** grandfather *or* longcase clock; **h. parlante** *Br* speaking clock, *Am* time (telephone) service; **h. de parquet** grandfather *or* longcase clock; **h. pointeuse** time clock; *Ordinat* **h. du système** system clock; *Ordinat* **h. en temps réel** real-time clock

horloger, -ère [ɔrlɔʒe, -ɛr] ADJ clock-making; **la production horlogère** clock and watch making

NM,F watchmaker, clockmaker; **h. bijoutier** jeweller

horlogerie [ɔrlɔʒri] NF **1** *(technique, métier)* clock (and watch) *or* timepiece making; **pièce d'h.** *(interne)* clock component; *(horloge)* timepiece **2** *(boutique)* watchmaker's, clockmaker's; **h. (bijouterie)** *Br* jewellery shop, *Am* jewelry store **3** *(articles)* clocks and watches

***hormis** [ɔrmi] *Littéraire* PRÉP save (for); **le stade était vide, h. quelques rares spectateurs** the stadium was empty, save for *or* apart from a handful of spectators

• **hormis que** CONJ *(à part que)* except *or* save that; *Can (à moins que)* unless

hormonal, -e, -aux, -ales [ɔrmɔnal, -o] ADJ *(gén)* hormonal; *(traitement, crème)* hormone *(avant n)*

hormone [ɔrmɔn] NF *Biol* hormone; **h. de croissance** growth hormone; **h. folliculo-stimulante** follicle-stimulating hormone, FSH; **h. lutéinisante** luteinizing hormone; **aux hormones** *(animaux)* hormone-fed

hormonothérapie [ɔrmɔnɔterapi] NF *Méd* hormone therapy, *Spéc* hormonotherapy

***hornblende** [ɔrnblɛ̃d] NF *Minér* hornblende

horodatage [ɔrɔdataʒ] NM *(de ticket)* time and date stamping

horodaté, -e [ɔrɔdate] ADJ *(ticket)* stamped *(with the date and time)*; **stationnement h.** pay-and-display parking zone

horodateur, -trice [ɔrɔdatœr, -tris] ADJ time-stamping

NM *(administratif)* time-stamp; *(de parking)* ticket machine

horoscope [ɔrɔskɔp] NM horoscope

horreur [ɔrœr] NF **1** *(effroi)* horror; **saisi** *ou* **rempli d'h.** horror-stricken, filled with horror; **hurler/reculer d'h.** to cry out/to shrink away in horror; **avoir qch en h.** *(dégoût)* to have a horror of *or* to loathe sth; **avoir qn en h.** to loathe sb; **avoir h. de** to loathe, to hate; **j'ai h. des araignées** I hate *or* I'm terrified of spiders; **j'ai h. qu'on me dérange** I hate *or* I can't stand being disturbed; **faire h. à qn** to horrify *or* to terrify sb, to fill sb with horror; **rien que l'idée de manger des escargots me fait h.** the very idea of eating snails fills me with horror *or* disgust; *Fam* **c'est l'h.** it's the pits, it sucks; **film d'h.** horror movie *or Br* film

2 *(cruauté)* horror, ghastliness; **l'h. des images était insoutenable** the pictures were unbearably horrific; **il décrit la guerre des tranchées dans toute son h.** he describes trench warfare in all its horror

3 *Fam (chose ou personne laide)* **c'est une h.** *(personne)* he's/she's repulsive; *(objet)* it's hideous; **jette-moi toutes ces vieilles horreurs** throw away all these horrible old things

4 *(dans des exclamations)* **oh, quelle h.!** that's awful *or* terrible!; *Hum* **une goutte de bière sur mon tapis neuf, l'h.!** a drop of beer on my new carpet, oh, no!

• **horreurs** NFPL **1** *(crimes)* horrors; **les horreurs de la guerre** the horrors of war **2** *(calomnies)* **on m'a raconté des horreurs sur lui** I've heard horrible *or* dreadful things about him

horrible [ɔribl] ADJ **1** *(effroyable ▸ cauchemar)* horrible, dreadful; *(▸ mutilation, accident)* horrible, horrific; *(▸ crime)* horrible, ghastly; **ce fut une guerre particulièrement h.** it was a particularly horrific war

2 *(laid ▸ personne)* horrible, hideous, repulsive; *(▸ décor, style, vêtement)* horrible, hideous, ghastly; **une espèce d'h. chapeau** a really ghastly hat

3 *(méchant)* horrible, nasty, horrid; **être h. avec qn** to be nasty *or* horrible to sb; **raconter des histoires horribles sur qn** to say horrible *or* nasty things about sb

4 *(infect)* horrible, disgusting; **la nourriture était h.** the food was disgusting

5 *(très désagréable ▸ temps, douleur)* terrible, awful; **un vacarme h.** a horrible noise; **des douleurs horribles** excruciating pain

horriblement [ɔribləmɑ̃] ADV **1** *(en intensif)* horribly, terribly, awfully; **nous étions h. déçus** we were terribly disappointed; **h. mal habillé** appallingly dressed; **ça fait h. mal** it's horribly painful **2** *(atrocement)* horribly

horrifiant, -e [ɔrifjɑ̃, -ɑ̃t] ADJ horrifying, terrifying

horrifier [9] [ɔrifje] VT **h. qn** to horrify sb, to fill sb with horror; **être horrifié par** to be horrified at; **elle recula, horrifiée** she shrank back in horror

horrifique [ɔrifik] ADJ *Littéraire* horrific, horrendous, horrifying

horripilant, -e [ɔripilɑ̃, -ɑ̃t] ADJ *Fam* infuriating, exasperating, irritating; **ne fais pas grincer ta craie, c'est h.** don't grate your chalk on the board, it sets my teeth on edge; **il est h., avec sa manie de jeter les journaux!** he gets on my nerves, always throwing out the papers!

horripilation [ɔripilasjɔ̃] NF **1** *Fam (exaspération)* exasperation, irritation **2** *Physiol* gooseflesh, goose pimples *or* bumps, *Spéc* horripilation

horripiler [3] [ɔripile] VT *Fam (exaspérer)* to exasperate; **ses petites manies m'horripilaient** his/her annoying little habits were getting on my nerves

***HORS** [ɔr] PRÉP **1** *Littéraire (hormis)* except (for), save (for); **personne h. les initiés** no one save *or* but the initiated

2 *(locutions) Rad & TV* **h. antenne** off the air, off-air; *Compta* **h. bilan** off-balance sheet; **h. Bourse** after hours; **h. budget** not included in the budget; *Admin* **h. cadre** seconded, on secondment; **h. catégorie** outstanding, exceptional; *TV & Cin* **h. champ** out of vision, out of shot; **mettre une lampe h. circuit** to disconnect a lamp; *Fig* **être h. circuit** to be out of circulation; **h. commerce** not for sale to the general public; **il est h. concours** *(exclu)* he's been disqualified; *Fig* he is in a class of his own; **le film a été présenté h. concours** the movie *or Br* film was exempted from the competition; **être h. course** to be out of touch; *Sport* **il est h. jeu** he's offside; **h. ligne** *(exceptionnel)* exceptional, outstanding; **mettre qn h. la loi** to declare sb an outlaw, to outlaw sb; **se mettre h. la loi** to place oneself outside the law; **h. les murs** *(festival)* out of town; **h. normes** non-standard; *Archit* **h. œuvre** out of alignment, projecting; **h. pair** exceptional, outstanding; **une cuisinière h. pair** an exceptional *or* outstanding cook; **skier h. piste** to ski off piste; **h. saison** off-season; **louer h. saison** to rent in the off-season; **h. série** *(remarquable)* outstanding, exceptional; *(personnalisé)* custom-built, customized; **numéro h. série** *(publication)* special issue; **h. service** out of order; **mettre qch h. service** to decommission sth; *Fam* **mettre qn h. service** to knock sb out; **h. sujet** irrelevant, off the subject; **h. taxe** *ou* **taxes** excluding tax; *(à la douane)* duty-free; **h. tout** overall; **h. TVA** net of *Br* VAT *or Am* sales tax

• **hors de** PRÉP **1** *(dans l'espace ▸ à l'extérieur de)* out of, outside; *(▸ loin de)* away from; **h. de la ville** out of town, outside the town; **h. de son monde** away from his/her surroundings; **h. de ma vue** out of my sight; **h. d'ici!** get out of here!

2 *(dans le temps)* **h. de saison** out of season; **h. du temps** timeless; **elle est** *ou* **elle vit h. de son temps** she lives in a different age

3 *(locutions)* **il était h. de lui** he was beside himself; **elle m'a mis h. de moi** she infuriated me, she made me furious *or* mad; **mettre qch h. d'action** to disable sth; **être h. d'affaire** to have come *or* pulled through; **te voilà h. d'affaire!** that's you over the worst!; **être h. de combat** *Sport* to be knocked out *or* hors de combat; *Fig* to be out of the game *or* running; **mettre qn h. de combat** to disable sb; **mettre qn h. de cause** to exonerate sb; **h. du commun** outstanding, exceptional; **ici, vous êtes h. de danger** you're safe *or* out of harm's reach here; **la victime n'est pas encore h. de danger** the victim isn't out of danger yet; **il est h. de doute que…** it's beyond doubt that…; **il est h. d'état de nuire** he's been rendered harmless; *Euph (tué)* he's been taken care of; *Archit* **h. d'œuvre** out of alignment, projecting; **h. de por-**

The symbol * indicates that the initial **h** is aspirate and that hence there is no liaison, eg **les haricots** [leariko] and not [lezariko], or contraction in spelling, eg **la haine** and not **l'haine**.

tée (de) *(trop loin)* out of reach *or* range (of); *Fig* out of reach (of); **h. de prix** prohibitively *or* ruinously expensive; **h. de propos** inopportune, untimely; **c'est h. de question** it's out of the question; **h. d'usage** out of service

***hors-bord** [ɔrbɔr] **NM INV 1 (moteur) h.** outboard motor **2** *(bateau)* speedboat, outboard

***hors-concours NM INV** = person/exhibit ineligible for competition (because of superiority)

***hors-cote** [ɔrkɔt] *Bourse* **ADJ INV** unlisted

NM INV *(marché)* unlisted securities market

***hors-d'œuvre** [ɔrdœvr] **NM INV 1** *Culin* starter, hors d'œuvre; **h. variés** (assorted) cold meats and salads **2** *Fig* **et ce n'était qu'un h.** and that was just the beginning **3** *Archit* annexe, outwork

***horse power** [ɔrspɔwœr] **NM INV** horsepower

***hors-jeu** [ɔrʒø] **ADJ INV** offside; **le joueur est h.** the player is offside

NM INV offside; **h. de position** offside *(where the player is not interfering with play)*

***hors-la-loi** [ɔrlalwa] **NM INV** outlaw

***hors-média** [ɔrmedja] *Mktg* **ADJ INV** *(publicité, promotion, coûts)* below-the-line

NM INV below-the-line advertising

***hors-micro** [ɔrmikro] **ADJ INV** *Rad* off-mike

***hors-piste, *hors-pistes** [ɔrpist] **NM INV faire du h.** to ski off piste

ADJ INV le ski h. off-piste skiing

***hors-route** [ɔrrut] **ADJ INV** off-highway

hors-série** [ɔrseri] *(pl* **hors-séries)* *Presse* **ADJ INV** special

NM special edition

***hors-texte** [ɔrtekst] **NM INV** *Typ* (inset) plate, tip-in

hortensia [ɔrtɑ̃sja] **NM** *Bot* hydrangea

horticole [ɔrtikɔl] **ADJ** horticultural; **exposition h.** flower show

horticulteur, -trice [ɔrtikyltœr, -tris] **NM,F** horticulturist

horticulture [ɔrtikyltyr] **NF** horticulture

hosanna [ozana] **NM** *Littéraire Rel* hosanna

hospice [ɔspis] **NM 1** *(asile)* **h. (de vieillards)** (old people's) home; **finir à l'h.** to end up in the poorhouse **2** *(hôpital)* hospice

hospitalier, -ère [ɔspitalje, ɛr] **ADJ 1** *Admin (frais, service, personnel)* hospital *(avant n)*; **en milieu h.** in a hospital environment; **établissement h.** hospital **2** *(accueillant ▸ personne, peuple, demeure)* hospitable, welcoming; *(▸ rivage, île)* inviting **3** *Rel* **frère h.** Hospitaller; **sœur hospitalière** Hospitaller

NM,F hospital worker; **les hospitaliers** hospital staff *or* workers

NM *Rel* Hospitaller

hospitalisation [ɔspitalizasjɔ̃] **NF** hospitalization; **son état nécessite une h. immédiate** in his/her state, he/she should be admitted *Br* to hospital *or Am* to the hospitalimmediately; **pendant mon h.** while I was *Br* in hospital *or Am* in the hospital; **h. à domicile** home care

hospitalisé, -e [ɔspitalize] **NM,F** hospital patient

hospitaliser [3] [ɔspitalize] **VT** to hospitalize; **se faire h.** to be admitted *or* taken *Br* to hospital *or Am* to the hospital; **le médecin veut le faire h.** the doctor wants to hospitalize him *or* to send him *Br* to hospital *or Am* to the hospital; **elle est hospitalisée à La Salpêtrière** she's *Br* in hospital *or Am* in the hospital at La Salpêtrière

hospitalité [ɔspitalite] **NF 1** *(hébergement)* hospitality; **offrir/donner l'h. à qn** to offer/to give sb hospitality **2** *(cordialité)* **nous vous remercions de votre h.** *(après un séjour, un repas)* thank you for making us (feel) welcome; **avoir le sens de l'h.** to be hospitable **3** *(asile)* **donner l'h. à des réfugiés politiques** to give shelter to *or* to take in political refugees

hospitalo-universitaire [ɔspitaloyniversitɛr] *(pl* **hospitalo-universitaires***)* **ADJ centre h.** teaching *or* university hospital; **enseignement h.** clinical teaching

hostellerie [ɔstelri] **NF** country inn

hostie [ɔsti] **NF 1** *Rel* host **2** *Vieilli & Littéraire (victime)* victim, offering *(for sacrifice)*

EXCLAM *Can très Fam Br* bloody hell!, *Am* goddammit!

hostile [ɔstil] **ADJ 1** *(inamical)* hostile, unfriendly; **un regard h.** a hostile look; *Littéraire* **cette nature h.** this hostile *or* unfriendly environment **2** *(opposé)* hostile; **être h. à** to be hostile to *or* opposed to *or* against

hostilement [ɔstilmɑ̃] **ADV** hostilely, with hostility

hostilité [ɔstilite] **NF** hostility; **manifester de l'h. envers** to show hostility to *or* towards

• **hostilités NFPL** *Mil* **les hostilités** hostilities; **reprendre les hostilités** to reopen *or* to resume hostilities

hosto [ɔsto] **NM** *Fam (hôpital)* hospital[□]

hot dog** [ɔtdɔg] *(pl* **hot dogs)* **NM** hot dog

hôte, hôtesse [ot, otɛs] **NM,F** *(personne qui reçoit)* host, *f* hostess; **notre h.** our host

NM 1 *(invité)* guest; *(client dans un hôtel)* patron, guest; **un h. de marque** an important guest; **h. payant** paying guest

2 *Littéraire (habitant)* **les hôtes des bois/lacs** the denizens of the woodlands/lakes

3 *Biol* host

4 *Ordinat* host (computer)

• **hôtesse NF** *(responsable de l'accueil ▸ dans un hôtel)* receptionist; *(▸ dans une exposition)* hostess; **hôtesse d'accueil** receptionist; **hôtesse de l'air** stewardess, *Br* air hostess

hôtel [otɛl] **NM 1** *(établissement commercial)* hotel; **h. de charme** country house hotel; *(en ville)* = hotel of distinctive character; **h. tout confort** hotel with all *Br* mod cons *or Am* modern conveniences; **h. social** hostel *(for people who are homeless or in difficulty)*; **h. de tourisme** basic hotel; *Fam* **on n'est pas dans un h. ici!** stop treating this place like a hotel!; **h. de passe** = hotel used for prostitution **2** *(bâtiments administratifs)* **l'h. de Brienne** = building in Paris where the French Ministry of Defence is situated; **h. des impôts** tax office; **l'h. de la Monnaie** = the French Mint, in Paris; **h. des ventes** saleroom, salerooms, auction room *or* rooms; **h. de ville** town *or* city hall

• **hôtel particulier NM** (private) mansion, town house

hôtel-Dieu [otɛldjø] *(pl* **hôtels-Dieu***)* **NM** *Arch* general hospital

hôtelier, -ère [otəlje, -ɛr] **ADJ** *(relatif à l'hôtellerie)* hotel *(avant n)*; **le personnel h.** hotel staff; **gestion hôtelière** hotel management; **la qualité de l'accueil h.** the standards of hotel accommodation; **l'infrastructure hôtelière** hotel facilities; **l'industrie hôtelière** the hotel industry *or* trade

NM,F hotelier, hotel manager

hôtellerie [otɛlri] **NF 1** *Com* hotel trade *or* business *or* industry; **l'h. de plein air** the camping and caravanning business **2** *(hôtel)* country inn

hôtel-restaurant [otɛlrestɔrɑ̃] *(pl* **hôtels-restaurants***)* **NM** hotel and restaurant

hôtesse [otɛs] *voir* **hôte**

hot line** [ɔtlajn] *(pl* **hot lines)* **NF** hot line

***hotspot** [ɔtspɔt] **NM** *Ordinat* hot spot

***hotte** [ɔt] **NF 1** *(de cheminée, de laboratoire)* hood; **h. aspirante** *ou* **filtrante** *(de cuisine)* extractor hood **2** *(de vendangeur)* basket; **la h. du Père Noël** Santa's *or* Father Christmas's sack; *Fam* **en avoir plein la h.** to be bushed *or Br* knackered *or Am* beat

***hottentot, -e** [ɔtɑ̃to, -ɔt] **ADJ** Hottentot

• **Hottentot, -e NM,F** Hottentot; **les Hottentots** the Hottentots, the Hottentot

***hou** [u] **EXCLAM** *(pour effrayer)* boo!; *(pour faire honte)* shame!

***houblon** [ublɔ̃] **NM** *Bot* hop (plant); *(de bière)* hops

***houblonnier, -ère** [ublɔnje, ɛr] *Agr* **ADJ** *(région)* hopgrowing; *(industrie)* hop *(avant n)*

NM,F hop grower

• **houblonnière NF** *(champ de houblon)* hop field *or* garden

***houe** [u] **NF 1** *Hort & Agr* hoe **2** *Constr* pestle

***houille** [uj] **NF 1** *Mines* coal **2** *(énergie)* **h. rouge/d'or** geothermal/solar energy; **h. blanche** hydroelectric power; **h. bleue** wave and tidal power; **h. incolore** wind power; **h. verte** hydroelectric power *(from rivers)*

***houiller, -ère** [uje, ɛr] **ADJ** *Mines (bassin, production)* coal *(avant n)*; *(sol, roche)* coal-bearing, *Spéc* carboniferous

NM *(en Europe)* Upper Carboniferous; *(aux États-Unis)* Pennsylvanian

• **houillère NF** coalmine

***houle** [ul] **NF** *(mouvement de la mer)* swell; **grosse** *ou* **grande h.** heavy swell; **il y a de la h.** the sea's rough

***houlette** [ulɛt] **NF 1** *Arch (d'un berger)* crook **2** *Hort* trowel

• **sous la houlette de PRÉP** under the leadership *or* direction *or* aegis of

***houleux, -euse** [ulø, -øz] **ADJ 1** *(mer)* rough, choppy **2** *(débat, réunion)* stormy

***houligan** [uligan] = **hooligan**

***houliganisme** [uliganism] = **hooliganisme**

***houmous** [umus] **NM** houmous, hummus

***houp** [up] = **hop**

***houppe** [up] **NF 1** *(à maquillage)* powder puff **2** *(de cheveux)* tuft (of hair) **3** *(décorative)* tassel

***houppelande** [uplɑ̃d] **NF** *Arch* mantle

***houppette** [upɛt] **NF** powder puff

***hourdage** [urdaʒ] **NM** *Constr* roughcasting

***hourder [3]** [urde] **VT** *Constr* to roughcast

***houri** [uri] **NF** *Littéraire Rel* houri

***hourra** [ura] **EXCLAM** hurrah!, hooray!

NM cheer (of joy); **pousser des hourras** to cheer

***hourvari** [urvari] **NM 1** *Chasse (ruse)* doubling back **2** *Littéraire (tumulte)* uproar, tumult

***house** [aus] **NF** *Mus* **la h. (music)** house music

***houspiller [3]** [uspije] **VT** to tell off, to scold

***housse** [us] **NF** *(de machine à écrire)* dust cover; *(de meubles ▸ pour protéger)* dustsheet; *(▸ pour décorer) Br* cover, *Am* slipcover; *(de vêtements)* suit carrier; *(de voiture)* seat cover; **h. de couette** duvet *or* quilt cover

***houx** [u] **NM** holly

hovercraft [ɔvœrkraft] **NM** hovercraft

HP[1] [aʃpe] **NM** *Fam (abrév* **hôpital psychiatrique***)* psychiatric hospital[□]

HP[2] **NM** *(abrév écrite* **haut-parleur***)* loudspeaker

HS** [aʃɛs] **ADJ** *Fam (abrév* **hors service)* *(appareil)* bust, *Br* clapped-out, knackered; *(personne)* bushed, *Br* knackered, *Am* beat

HT ADJ *Com (abrév écrite* **hors taxe***)* not including tax, exclusive of tax; **200 euros HT** 200 euros plus VAT

NF *(abrév écrite* **haute tension***)* HT

HTML [aʃteɛmɛl] **NM** *Ordinat (abrév* **Hyper Text Markup Language***)* HTML

HTTP [aʃtetepe] **NM** *Ordinat (abrév* **Hyper Text Transfer Protocol***)* HTTP

***huard, *huart** [ɥar] **NM 1** *Orn (rapace)* osprey, *Am* fish hawk **2** *Can Orn (plongeon) Br* black-throated diver, *Am* loon **3** *Can Fam Hum (pièce de monnaie)* = humorous name for a Canadian one-dollar coin, *Can* loonie

***hub** [œb] **NM** *Ordinat & Transp* hub

***hublot** [yblo] **NM** *(de bateau)* porthole; *(d'avion)* window; *(de machine à laver)* (glass) door

• **hublots NMPL** *Fam (lunettes)* specs

***huche** [yʃ] **NF** chest; **h. à pain** bread bin

***hue** [y] **EXCLAM** *(à un cheval)* gee up!, giddy up!

• **à hue et à dia ADV tirer à h. et à dia** to pull *or* to tug in opposite directions (at once)

***huée** [ɥe] **NF** *Chasse* hallooing, halloos

• **huées NFPL** boos, booing; **il quitta la scène sous les huées** he was booed *or* hissed off stage

***huer [7]** [ɥe] **VT 1** *(par dérision)* to boo **2** *Chasse* to halloo

VI *(hibou)* to hoot; *(héron)* to croak

***huerta** [wɛrta] **NF** = irrigated plain in Spain

***huguenot, -e** [ygno, -ɔt] **ADJ** Huguenot

NM,F Huguenot

huilage [ɥilaʒ] **NM** oiling, lubrication

huile [ɥil] **NF 1** *Culin* oil; **faire frire qch à l'h.** to fry sth in oil; **h. d'arachide/de coco/de colza/d'olive/de**

The symbol * indicates that the initial **h** is aspirate and that hence there is no liaison, eg **les haricots** [leariko] and not [lezariko], or contraction in spelling, eg **la haine** and not **l'haine**.

maïs/de noix/de tournesol groundnut/coconut/rapeseed *or* colza/olive/corn/walnut/sunflower oil; **h. pour assaisonnement** salad oil; **h. de cuisson** cooking oil; **h. de table** (salad) oil; **h. végétale** vegetable oil; **h. vierge** unrefined *or* virgin oil; *Fig* **jeter** *ou* **mettre** *ou* **verser de l'h. sur le feu** to add fuel to the fire *or* flames

2 *(pour chauffer, pour lubrifier)* oil; *Can* **h. (de) chauffage** domestic fuel, heating oil; *Fam* **h. de coude,** *Can* **h. de bras** elbow grease; **h. de graissage** lubricating *or* lubrication oil; **h. minérale** mineral oil; **h. (pour) moteur** engine oil; **h. de vidange** waste (lubricating) oil; *Fig* **mettre de l'h. dans les rouages de** to oil the wheels of

3 *Pharm* **h. d'amandes douces/amères** sweet/bitter almond oil; **h. de bain** bath oil; **h. pour bébés** baby oil; **h. pour le corps** body oil; **h. essentielle** essential oil; **h. de foie de morue** cod-liver oil; **h. de lin** linseed oil; **h. de paraffine** paraffin oil; **h. de ricin** castor oil; **h. solaire** suntan oil; **h. de vaseline** paraffin oil; **h. volatile** essential oil

4 *Beaux-Arts (œuvre)* oil (painting); **un portrait à l'h.** a portrait in oils

5 *Fam (personne importante)* bigwig, big shot

• **d'huile** ADJ *(mer)* glassy; **la mer était d'h.** the sea was like glass *or* a mill pond

huiler [3] [ɥile] VT to oil, to lubricate

huilerie [ɥilri] NF *(fabrique)* oil works *or* factory; *(commerce)* oil trade

huileux, -euse [ɥilø, -øz] ADJ **1** *(substance)* oily **2** *(cheveux, doigts)* oily, greasy

huilier, -ère [ɥilje, ɛr] ADJ oil *(avant n)*

NM **1** *(ustensile de table)* oil and vinegar set; *(avec moutardier)* cruet (stand) **2** *(fabricant)* oil manufacturer

***huis** [ɥi] NM *Littéraire* door

• **huis clos** NM *Jur* **demander le h. clos** to ask for proceedings to be held in camera; *Jur* **le procès se déroulera à h. clos** the trial will be held in camera; **avoir une discussion à h. clos** to have a discussion behind closed doors

huisserie [ɥisri] NF *Constr (de porte)* (door) frame; *(de fenêtre)* (window) frame

huissier [ɥisje] NM **1** *(gardien, appariteur)* usher **2** *Jur* **h. (de justice)** ≃ court bailiff; **h. d'audience** court crier, usher

***huit** [ɥit, *before consonant* ɥi] ADJ eight; **h. jours** *(une semaine)* a week; **donner ses h. jours à qn** to give sb their notice; **page/numéro h.** page/number eight

PRON eight

NM INV **1** *(gén)* eight; **aujourd'hui en h.** this time next week; **jeudi en h.** a week from *or Br* on Thursday

2 *(numéro d'ordre)* number eight

3 *(chiffre écrit)* eight

4 *Cartes* eight; **le h. de carreau** the eight of diamonds

5 *(en patinage)* figure of eight; **l'ivrogne avançait en faisant des h.** the drunk was reeling *or* staggering along

6 *(attraction)* **le grand h.** rollercoaster *(in figure of eight)*; *voir aussi* **cinq**

***huitain** [ɥitɛ̃] NM *Littérature* octave

***huitaine** [ɥitɛn] NF **une h.** around *or* about eight, eight or so; **une h. (de jours)** about a week, a week or so; **sous h.** within a week

***huitante** [ɥitɑ̃t] *Suisse (dans les cantons de Vaud, du Valais et de Fribourg)* ADJ **1** *(gén)* eighty **2** *(dans des séries)* eightieth; **page/numéro h.** page/number eighty

PRON eighty

NM INV **1** *(gén)* eighty **2** *(numéro d'ordre)* number eighty **3** *(chiffre écrit)* eighty; *voir aussi* **cinquante**

***huitantième** [ɥitɑ̃tjɛm] *Suisse (dans les cantons de Vaud, du Valais et de Fribourg)* ADJ eightieth

NMF **1** *(personne)* eightieth **2** *(objet)* eightieth (one)

NM **1** *(partie)* eightieth **2** *(étage) Br* eightieth floor, *Am* eighty-first floor; *voir aussi* **cinquième**

***huitième** [ɥitjɛm] ADJ eighth; **le h. art** television

NMF **1** *(personne)* eighth **2** *(objet)* eighth (one)

NM **1** *(partie)* eighth **2** *(étage) Br* eighth floor, *Am* ninth floor **3** *(arrondissement de Paris)* eighth (arrondissement)

NF *Anciennement Scol Br* = fourth year of primary school, *Am* ≃ fourth grade; *voir aussi* **cinquième**

• **huitièmes** NMPL *Sport* **les huitièmes de finale** the round before the quarterfinals, the last sixteen

***huitièmement** [ɥitjɛmmɑ̃] ADV in eighth place

huître [ɥitr] NF **1** *Zool & Culin* oyster; **h. perlière** pearl oyster **2** *Fam Vieilli (personne stupide)* twit, fool

***huit-reflets** [ɥirəflɛ] NM INV *Vieilli* top hat

huîtrier, -ère [ɥitrije, ɛr] ADJ oyster *(avant n)*

NM *Orn* oystercatcher

• **huîtrière** NF oyster bed

***hulotte** [ylɔt] NF *Orn* brown owl

***hululement** [ylylmɑ̃] NM hooting *(UNCOUNT)*; **des hululements** hooting

***hululer** [3] [ylyle] VI to hoot

***hum** [œm] EXCLAM **1** *(marquant le doute)* hmm, er, um **2** *(pour signaler sa présence)* ahem

humain, -e [ymɛ̃, -ɛn] ADJ **1** *(propre à l'homme ▸ corps, race, condition)* human; **il cherche à se venger, c'est h.** he's looking for revenge, it's only human; **nous faire travailler par cette chaleur, ce n'est pas h.** forcing us to work in this heat is inhuman; **une ville nouvelle aux dimensions humaines** a new town planned with people in mind *or* on a human scale **2** *(bienveillant)* humane; **il est très h.** he's very understanding; **être h. avec qn** to act humanely towards sb, to treat sb humanely

NM **1** *(être)* **un h.** a human (being); **les humains** mankind, humans, human beings **2** *Littéraire* **l'h.** *(nature)* human nature; *(facteur)* the human element *or* factor

> Attention: ne pas confondre **human** et **humane** lorsque l'on traduit **humain. Human** signifie **qui se rapporte à l'être humain** alors que **humane** signifie **bienveillant**.

humainement [ymɛnmɑ̃] ADV **1** *(avec bienveillance)* humanely; **traiter qn h.** to treat sb humanely **2** *(par l'homme)* humanly; **faire tout ce qui est h. possible** to do everything that is humanly possible

humanisation [ymanizasjɔ̃] NF humanization; **aujourd'hui, on vise à une h. des rapports dans l'entreprise** today, the aim is to make relationships in the company more human

humaniser [3] [ymanize] VT *(environnement)* to humanize, to adapt to human needs; *(personne)* to make more human

VPR **s'humaniser** to become more human; **l'environnement industriel s'est humanisé** the industrial environment has a more human face

humanisme [ymanism] NM humanism

humaniste [ymanist] ADJ humanist, humanistic

NMF humanist

humanitaire [ymanitɛr] ADJ humanitarian; **organisation h.** humanitarian *or* relief *or* aid organization

NMF *(personne)* humanitarian (aid) worker

NM **l'humanitaire** the humanitarian sector

humanitarisme [ymanitarism] NM *Péj* humanitarianism

humanité [ymanite] NF **1** *(êtres)* **l'h.** humanity, mankind, humankind **2** *(compassion)* humanity, humaneness; **traiter qn avec h.** to treat sb humanely

• **humanités** NFPL **1** *Belg Scol* = the three years leading to the baccalauréat examination in Belgium **2** *Vieilli Univ* **les humanités** the classics

humanoïde [ymanɔid] ADJ humanoid

NMF humanoid

humble [œbl] ADJ **1** *(effacé ▸ personne)* humble, meek; **d'un ton h.** humbly, meekly **2** *(par déférence)* humble; **veuillez accepter mes humbles excuses** please accept my most humble apologies; **à mon h. avis** in my humble opinion **3** *(pauvre, simple ▸ demeure, origine)* humble; *(▸ employé)* humble, lowly

humblement [œbləmɑ̃] ADV **1** *(sans prétention)* humbly; **je vous ferai h. remarquer que...** may I humbly point out that...? **2** *(sans richesse)* humbly; **vivre h.** to live modestly *or* humbly

humectage [ymɛktaʒ] NM dampening, moistening

humecter [4] [ymɛkte] VT to dampen, to moisten; **la sueur humectait son front** his/her forehead was damp with perspiration

VPR **s'humecter s'h. les lèvres** to moisten one's lips; *Fam* **s'h. le gosier** to wet one's whistle

***humer** [3] [yme] VT *(sentir)* to smell; *(inspirer)* to inhale, to breathe in

huméral, -e, -aux, -ales [ymeral, -o] ADJ *Anat* humeral

humérus [ymerys] NM *Anat* humerus

humeur [ymœr] NF **1** *(état d'esprit)* mood; **être d'h. à faire qch** to be in the mood to do sth *or* for doing sth; **je ne suis pas d'h. à écouter ses commérages** I am not in the mood to listen to *or* I am in no mood for listening to his/her gossip; **selon l'h. du jour** it depends (on) how the mood takes me/him/her/*etc*; **être d'h. changeante** to be moody; **être de bonne/mauvaise h.** to be in a good/bad mood; **la bonne h. régnait dans la maison** the whole household was in a good mood; **un livre/film plein de bonne h.** a good-humoured book/film; **passer sa mauvaise h. sur** to take one's bad mood out on; **être d'une h. de dogue** to be like a bear with a sore head; **être d'une h. noire** to be in a foul mood

2 *(caractère)* temper; **être d'h. chagrine** to be bad-tempered *or* sullen; **être d'h. égale/inégale** to be even-tempered/moody

3 *Littéraire (acrimonie)* bad temper, ill humour; **montrer de l'h.** to show ill temper; **répondre avec h.** to answer testily *or* moodily; **accès/mouvement d'h.** outburst/fit of temper

4 *(caprice)* **il a ses humeurs** he has his whims

5 *Méd* **h. aqueuse/vitrée** aqueous/vitreous humour

• **humeurs** NFPL *Arch* humours

> Do not confuse with **humour**.

humide [ymid] ADJ *(linge, mur)* damp; *(éponge)* damp, moist; *(cave)* damp, dank; *(chaussée)* wet; *(chaleur, air, climat)* humid; *(terre)* moist; **j'ai les mains humides** my hands are damp; **temps chaud et h.** muggy weather; **il fait h.** it *or* the weather is humid; **les yeux humides de larmes** eyes moist with tears

humidificateur [ymidifikatœr] NM *(gén)* humidifier; *(pour les cigares)* humidor

humidification [ymidifikasjɔ̃] NF **1** *(de l'air)* humidifying, moisturizing, *Spéc* humidification **2** *(du linge)* dampening, moistening

humidifier [9] [ymidifje] VT **1** *(air)* to humidify, to moisturize **2** *(linge)* to dampen, to moisten

humidité [ymidite] NF *(de l'air chaud)* humidity, moisture; *(de l'air froid, d'une terre)* dampness; *(d'une cave)* dampness, dankness; **il faut beaucoup d'h. à cette plante** this plant needs a lot of moisture; **il y a des taches d'h. au plafond** there are damp patches on the ceiling; **la pièce sent l'h.** the room smells (of) damp; **craint l'h.** *(sur un paquet)* keep dry, store in a dry place

humiliant, -e [ymiljɑ̃, -ɑ̃t] ADJ humiliating; **critique humiliante** galling *or* mortifying criticism

humiliation [ymiljasjɔ̃] NF humiliation; **infliger une h. à qn** to humiliate sb; **subir les pires humiliations** to suffer the deepest humiliation

humilier [9] [ymilje] VT **1** *(abaisser)* to humiliate, to shame **2** *Vieilli (rendre humble)* to humble

VPR **s'humilier 1** *(s'abaisser)* to humiliate oneself **2** *Vieilli* **s'h. devant** *(être humble)* to humble oneself before

humilité [ymilite] NF **1** *(d'une personne)* humility, humbleness, modesty; **avec h.** humbly; **une leçon d'h.** a lesson in humility **2** *Littéraire (d'une tâche)* humbleness, lowliness

• **en toute humilité** ADV in all humility

humoral, -e, -aux, -ales [ymɔral, -o] ADJ *Méd* humoral

humoriste [ymɔrist] ADJ humorous

NMF humorist

The symbol * indicates that the initial **h** is aspirate and that hence there is no liaison, eg **les haricots** [leariko] and not [lezariko], or contraction in spelling, eg **la haine** and not **l'haine**.

humoristique [ymɔristik] ADJ *(récit, ton)* humorous

humour [ymur] NM humour; **avec h.** humorously; **il a pris ça avec (beaucoup d')h.** he took it in (very) good part; **plein d'h.** humorous; **il n'y a aucun h. dans le scénario** the script is totally humourless; **avoir de** *ou* **le sens de l'h.** to have a sense of humour; **faire de l'h.** to make jokes; **h. noir** black humour

> Do not confuse with **humeur**.

humus [ymys] NM humus

***Hun** [œ̃] NMF Hun; **les Huns** (the) Hun

***hune** [yn] NF *Arch Naut* top

***hunier** [ynje] NM *Arch Naut* topsail

***huppe** [yp] NF *Orn* **1** *(oiseau)* hoopoe **2** *(plumes)* crest; *(chez certains pigeons)* tuft, tufts

***huppé, -e** [ype] ADJ **1** *Fam (personne, restaurant, soirée)* smart[□], *Br* posh; **les gens huppés** the upper crust, the smart set **2** *Orn* crested

***hure** [yr] NF **1** *Zool* head *(of wild boar, fish etc)* **2** *Culin* brawn, *Am* headcheese

***hurlement** [yrləmɑ̃] NM **1** *(humain)* yell, roar; **des hurlements de joie** whoops of joy; **des hurlements d'indignation** howls of indignation; **pourquoi tous ces hurlements?** what's all this shouting *or* yelling about? **2** *(d'un chien, d'un loup)* howl; **des hurlements** howling *(UNCOUNT)* **3** *Littéraire (de la tempête)* roar; *(du vent)* howling *(UNCOUNT)*; *(d'une sirène)* howl

***hurler [3]** [yrle] VI **1** *(crier)* to yell, to scream; **h. de douleur/de rage** to howl with pain/rage; **h. de joie** to whoop *or* to shout with joy; **h. de rire** to scream with laughter; **c'était à h. de rire** it was screamingly funny, it was a scream; **ça me fait h. d'entendre ça!** it makes me so mad to hear things like that!

2 *(parler fort ▸ personne)* to shout, to bellow; *(avoir un niveau sonore élevé ▸ radio)* to blare

3 *(singe)* to howl, to shriek; *(chien, loup)* to howl; **h. à la mort** *ou* **à la lune** to bay at the moon; *Fig* **h. avec les loups** to follow the pack

4 *Littéraire (tempête)* to roar; *(vent)* to howl; *(sirène)* to shriek, to wail

5 *(jurer ▸ couleur)* to clash

VT **1** *(ordre, réponse, chanson)* to bawl out, to bellow out **2** *(douleur, indignation)* to howl out

***hurleur, -euse** [yrlœr, -øz] ADJ **1** *(personne)* howling, bawling, yelling **2** *Zool* **singe h.** howler monkey

NM,F howler, bawler

NM *(singe)* howler (monkey)

hurluberlu, -e [yrlybɛrly] NM,F *Fam* crank, weirdo

***huron, -onne** [yrɔ̃, ɔn] ADJ Huron

NM *(langue)* Huron

• **Huron, -onne** NM,F Huron

• **Huron** NM **le lac H.** Lake Huron

***hurrah** [ura] = **hourra**

***husky** [œski] NM *(chien)* husky

***hussard** [ysar] NM hussar

***hussarde** [ysard] **à la hussarde** ADV *Fam* roughly, brutally

***hussite** [ysit] NM *Hist & Rel* Hussite

***hutte** [yt] NF **1** *(abri)* hut, cabin **2** *Chasse Br* hide, *Am* blind

hyacinthe [jasɛ̃t] NF **1** *Vieilli Bot* hyacinth **2** *Minér* hyacinth, jacinth

hyalin, -e [jalɛ̃, -in] ADJ *Minér* transparent, glassy; **quartz h.** rock crystal

hybridation [ibridasjɔ̃] NF *Biol* hybridization

hybride [ibrid] ADJ **1** *Bot, Zool & Ling* hybrid **2** *(mêlé)* hybrid, mixed; **une architecture h.** a patchwork of architectural styles; **un album h.** a crossover album

NM hybrid

hybrider [3] [ibride] VT *Biol* to hybridize

hybridité [ibridite] NF *Biol* hybridity

hydracide [idrasid] NM *Chim* hydracid

hydratant, -e [idratɑ̃, -ɑ̃t] ADJ **1** *(crème, lotion)* moisturizing **2** *Chim* hydrating

NM moisturizer

hydratation [idratasjɔ̃] NF **1** *(de la peau)* moisturizing **2** *Chim* hydration

hydrate [idrat] NM *Chim* hydrate; *Vieilli* **h. de carbone** carbohydrate

hydrater [3] [idrate] VT **1** *(peau)* to moisturize **2** *Chim* to hydrate

VPR **s'hydrater 1** *(peau)* to become moisturized **2** *Chim* to become hydrated, to hydrate

hydraulicien, -enne [idrolisjɛ̃, -ɛn] NM,F hydraulic engineer

hydraulique [idrolik] ADJ hydraulic

NF hydraulics *(singulier)*

hydravion [idravjɔ̃] NM seaplane, hydroplane, *Am* float plane

hydre [idr] NF **1** *Zool* hydra **2** *Littéraire* **l'h. de l'anarchie** the hydra of anarchy

hydrique [idrik] ADJ *Chim* hydric

hydrocarbure [idrɔkarbyr] NM *Chim* hydrocarbon

hydrocéphale [idrɔsefal] *Méd* ADJ hydrocephalic, hydrocephalous

NMF hydrocephalic

hydrocortisone [idrɔkɔrtizɔn] NF *Méd* hydrocortisone

hydrocracking [idrɔkrakiŋ], **hydrocraquage** [idrɔkrakaʒ] NM *Pétr* hydrocracking

hydrocution [idrɔkysjɔ̃] NF immersion syncope

hydrodynamique [idrɔdinamik] ADJ hydrodynamic

NF hydrodynamics *(singulier)*

hydroélectricité [idrɔelɛktrisite] NF hydroelectricity

hydroélectrique [idrɔelɛktrik] ADJ hydroelectric

hydrofoil [idrɔfɔjl] NM *Naut* hydrofoil

hydrofuge [idrɔfyʒ] ADJ waterproof, water-repellent

NM water-repellent

hydrofuger [17] [idrɔfyʒe] VT to waterproof

hydrogénation [idrɔʒenasjɔ̃] NF *Chim* hydrogenation, hydrogenization

hydrogène [idrɔʒɛn] NM *Chim & Phys* **1** *(élément)* hydrogen; **h. lourd** heavy hydrogen, deuterium **2** *(comme adj)* hydrogen *(avant n)*

hydrogéné, -e [idrɔʒene] ADJ *Chim* hydrogenated

hydrogéner [8] [idrɔʒene] VT *Chim* to hydrogenate

hydroglisseur [idrɔglisœr] NM hydroplane (boat)

hydrographe [idrɔgraf] NMF hydrographer

hydrographie [idrɔgrafi] NF hydrography

hydrographique [idrɔgrafik] ADJ hydrographic, hydrographical

hydrologie [idrɔlɔʒi] NF hydrology

hydrologique [idrɔlɔʒik] ADJ hydrologic, hydrological

hydrologiste [idrɔlɔʒist], **hydrologue** [idrɔlɔg] NMF hydrologist

hydrolyse [idrɔliz] NF *Chim* hydrolysis

hydrolyser [3] [idrɔlize] VT *Chim* to hydrolyse

hydromassage [idrɔmasaʒ] NM hydromassage

hydromel [idrɔmɛl] NM *(non fermenté)* hydromel; *(fermenté)* mead

hydromètre [idrɔmɛtr] NM *Phys (pour densité)* hydrometer; *(de réservoir)* depth gauge

NF *Entom* water measurer

hydrométrie [idrɔmetri] NF *Phys* hydrometry

hydrophile [idrɔfil] ADJ *Chim* hydrophilic

NM *Entom* scavenger beetle

hydrophobe [idrɔfɔb] ADJ *Chim & Méd* hydrophobic

hydrophobie [idrɔfɔbi] NF **1** *Méd* hydrophobia, rabies **2** *Chim* hydrophobic property

hydropique [idrɔpik] *Méd* ADJ dropsical

NMF dropsical patient

hydropisie [idrɔpizi] NF *Méd* dropsy

hydroponique [idrɔpɔnik] ADJ *Agr* hydroponic

hydropropulseur [idrɔprɔpylsœr] NM water jet attachment *(for electric toothbrush)*

hydroptère [idrɔptɛr] NM *Naut* hydrofoil

hydroquinone [idrɔkinɔn] NF *Chim & Phot* hydroquinone

hydrosol [idrɔsɔl] NM *Chim* hydrosol

hydrosoluble [idrɔsɔlybl] ADJ *Chim* water-soluble

hydrospeed [idrɔspid] NM *Sport* = type of water sport consisting of shooting the rapids on a board

hydrosphère [idrɔsfɛr] NF hydrosphere

hydrostatique [idrɔstatik] *Phys* ADJ hydrostatic

NF hydrostatics *(singulier)*

hydrothérapie [idrɔterapi] NF *Méd* **1** *(cure)* hydrotherapy **2** *(science)* hydrotherapeutics *(singulier)*

hydrothérapique [idrɔterapik] ADJ *Méd* hydrotherapeutic, hydrotherapy *(avant n)*

hydrothermal, -e, -aux, -ales [idrɔtɛrmal, -o] ADJ hydrothermal

hydroxyde [idrɔksid] NM *Chim* hydroxide

hydrure [idryr] NM *Chim* hydride; **h. lourd** deuteride

***hyène** [jɛn] NF *Zool* hyena

Hygiaphone® [iʒjafɔn] NM speaking grille

hygiène [iʒjɛn] NF **1** *(principes)* hygiene; **pour l'h. des pieds/du cuir chevelu** to keep feet/the scalp clean *or* in good condition; **il n'a aucune h.** he doesn't bother about personal hygiene; **h. alimentaire/corporelle** food/personal hygiene; **avoir une mauvaise h. alimentaire** to have bad eating habits *or* a poor diet; **h. mentale/publique** mental/public health; **avoir une bonne h. de vie** to live healthily **2** *(science)* hygienics *(singulier)*, hygiene

hygiénique [iʒjenik] ADJ hygienic; **ce n'est pas h.** it's unhygienic; **un mode de vie h.** a healthy lifestyle; **une promenade h.** a constitutional

hygiéniquement [iʒjenikmɑ̃] ADV hygienically

hygrométrie [igrɔmetri] NF *Météo* hygrometry

hygroscope [igrɔskɔp] NM *Phys* hygroscope

hygroscopique [igrɔskɔpik] ADJ *Phys* hygroscopic

hymen [imɛn] NM **1** *Anat* hymen **2** *Littéraire* (bonds of) marriage

hyménée [imene] NM *Littéraire* (ties *or* bonds of) marriage

hyménoptère [imenɔptɛr] *Entom* ADJ hymenopterous

NM hymenopteran, hymenopteron

hymne [imn] NM **1** *Littérature & Rel* hymn; **h. national** national anthem **2** *Littéraire (glorification)* hymn; **un h. à l'amour** a hymn *or* paean to love

hyoïde [jɔid] *Anat* ADJ *(os)* hyoid

NM hyoid (bone)

hype [ip] ADJ INV *Fam* hip, cool, trendy

hyper [ipɛr] NM *Fam (abrév* **hypermarché***)* hypermarket[□], superstore[□]

> PREFIX
>
> **HYPER-**
>
> This very productive prefix acts as an INTENSIFIER.
>
> • It appears in nouns and adjectives belonging to science and in particular medicine:
>
> **hypermétrope** farsighted, longsighted; **hyperglicémie** hyperglycaemia; **hypertension** high blood pressure; **hyperactif** hyperactive; **hyperbole** hyperbole/hyperbola; **hypermarché** (sometimes abbreviated colloquially to **hyper**) superstore
>
> • It is widely used in colloquial French as an adverb, to intensify an adjective with positive connotations. It can be translated by *really, dead, well*, etc, eg:
>
> **il est hyper-sympa** he's dead nice; **un bar hyper-branché** a really trendy bar; **un film hyper-marrant** a hysterical film; **c'est hyper-grand chez elle** her place is massive

hyperacidité [iperasidite] NF *Méd* hyperacidity

hyperactif, -ive [iperaktif, -iv] ADJ hyperactive

hyperactivité [iperaktivite] NF hyperactivity

hyperbare [iperbar] ADJ *Tech* hyperbaric

hyperbole [ipɛrbɔl] NF **1** *(figure de style)* hyperbole **2** *Géom* hyperbola

hyperbolique [ipɛrbɔlik] ADJ *Ling & Géom* hyperbolic

hyperboloïde [ipɛrbɔlɔid] *Math* ADJ hyperboloidal
NM hyperboloid

hyperboréen, -enne [ipɛrbɔreɛ̃, -ɛn] ADJ *Littéraire* hyperborean

hypercalorique [ipɛrkalɔrik] ADJ hypercaloric

hypercritique [ipɛrkritik] ADJ *Fam* hypercritical

hyperémotivité [ipɛremɔtivite] NF hyperemotivity, hyperemotionality

hyperfréquence [ipɛrfrekɑ̃s] NF ultra-high frequency

hyperglycémie [ipɛrglisemi] NF *Méd* hyperglycaemia

hyperinflation [ipɛrɛ̃flasjɔ̃] NF *Écon* hyperinflation

hyperlien [ipɛrljɛ̃] NM *Ordinat* hyperlink

hypermarché [ipɛrmarʃe] NM hypermarket, superstore

hypermédia [ipɛrmedja] NM *Ordinat* hypermedia

hypermétrope [ipɛrmetrɔp] *Opt* ADJ farsighted, longsighted, *Spéc* hypermetropic
NMF farsighted *or* longsighted person, *Spéc* hypermetropic person

hypermétropie [ipɛrmetrɔpi] NF *Opt* farsightedness, longsightedness, *Spéc* hypermetropia

hypernerveux, -euse [ipɛrnɛrvø, -øz] ADJ overexcitable
NM,F overexcitable person

hypernova [ipɛrnova] *(pl* **-ae**) NM *Astron* hypernova

hyperonyme [ipɛrɔnim] NM *Ling* hypernym, superordinate (term)

hyperpuissance [ipɛrpɥisɑ̃s] NF *Pol* hyperpower

hyperréalisme [ipɛrrealism] NM *Beaux-Arts* hyperrealism

hyperréaliste [ipɛrrealist] *Beaux-Arts* ADJ hyperrealistic
NMF hyperrealist

hypersensibilité [ipɛrsɑ̃sibilite] NF hypersensitivity, hypersensitiveness

hypersensible [ipɛrsɑ̃sibl] ADJ hypersensitive
NMF hypersensitive (person)

hypertendu, -e [ipɛrtɑ̃dy] *Méd* ADJ suffering from high blood pressure, *Spéc* hypertensive
NM,F person suffering from high blood pressure, *Spéc* hypertensive

hypertensif, -ive [ipɛrtɑ̃sif, -iv] ADJ *Méd* = relating to high blood pressure, *Spéc* hypertensive

hypertension [ipɛrtɑ̃sjɔ̃] NF *Méd* high blood pressure, *Spéc* hypertension

hypertensive [ipɛrtɑ̃siv] *voir* **hypertensif**

hypertexte [ipɛrtɛkst] NM *Ordinat* hypertext

hyperthyroïdie [ipɛrtirɔidi] NF *Méd* hyperthyroidism; **faire de l'h.** to have an overactive thyroid

hypertoile [ipɛrtwal] NF *Ordinat* World Wide Web

hypertrophie [ipɛrtrɔfi] NF **1** *Méd* hypertrophia, hypertrophy **2** *Fig* exaggeration; **une h. de l'amour-propre** an inflated sense of self-importance

hypertrophié, -e [ipɛrtrɔfje] ADJ *Méd* abnormally enlarged, *Spéc* hypertrophied

hypertrophier [9] [ipɛrtrɔfje] VT *Méd* to enlarge abnormally, *Spéc* to hypertrophy
VPR **s'hypertrophier** *Méd* to become abnormally large, *Spéc* to hypertrophy

hypertrophique [ipɛrtrɔfik] ADJ *Méd* abnormally enlarged, *Spéc* hypertrophic

hyperventilation [ipɛrvɑ̃tilasjɔ̃] NF *Méd* hyperventilation

hypervitaminose [ipɛrvitaminoz] NF *Méd* hypervitaminosis

hypnose [ipnoz] NF *Psy* hypnosis; **sous h.** under hypnosis; **être en état d'h.** to be under hypnosis, to be in a hypnotic trance

hypnothérapeute [ipnɔterapøt] NMF *Psy* hypnotherapist

hypnothérapie [ipnɔterapi] NF *Psy* hypnotherapy

hypnotique [ipnɔtik] ADJ *Psy* hypnotic
NM hypnotic (drug)

hypnotiser [3] [ipnɔtize] VT **1** *Psy* to hypnotize **2** *(fasciner)* to fascinate
VPR **s'hypnotiser s'h. sur** to become obsessed with

hypnotiseur, -euse [ipnɔtizœr, -øz] NM,F *Psy* hypnotist

hypnotisme [ipnɔtism] NM *Psy* hypnotism

hypoallergénique [ipɔalɛrʒenik] ADJ = **hypoallergique**

hypoallergique [ipɔalɛrʒik] ADJ hypoallergenic
NM hypoallergenic

hypocalcémie [ipɔkalsemi] NF *Méd* hypocalcaemia

hypocalorique [ipɔkalɔrik] ADJ *(régime)* low-calorie

hypocentre [ipɔsɑ̃tr] NM hypocentre

hypocondre [ipɔkɔ̃dr] NM *Anat* hypochondrium
NMF *Vieilli* hypochondriac

hypocondriaque [ipɔkɔ̃drijak] *Méd* ADJ hypochondriac, hypochondriacal
NMF hypochondriac

hypocondrie [ipɔkɔ̃dri] NF *Méd* hypochondria; **être atteint d'h.** to be a hypochondriac, to suffer from hypochondria

hypocras [ipɔkras] NM *Arch (alcool)* hippocras

hypocrisie [ipɔkrizi] NF **1** *(attitude)* hypocrisy **2** *(action)* hypocritical act; **assez d'hypocrisies** let's stop this pretence

hypocrite [ipɔkrit] ADJ **1** *(sournois ▸ personne)* hypocritical, insincere **2** *(mensonger ▸ attitude, regard)* hypocritical; *(▸ promesse)* hollow
NMF hypocrite; **faire l'h.** to be a hypocrite

hypocritement [ipɔkritmɑ̃] ADV hypocritically

hypodermique [ipɔdɛrmik] ADJ *Anat* hypodermic

hypogastrique [ipɔgastrik] ADJ *Anat* hypogastric

hypogée [ipɔʒe] NM *Archéol* underground (burial) vault, *Spéc* hypogeum

hypoglycémiant, -e [ipɔglisemjɑ̃, -ɑ̃t] *Méd* ADJ hypoglycaemic
NM hypoglycaemic

hypoglycémie [ipɔglisemi] NF *Méd* hypoglycaemia; **je suis en h.** my blood sugar's low

hypoïde [ipɔid] ADJ *Tech* **engrenage h.** crownwheel and pinion, hypoid (gear)

hypokhâgne [ipɔkaɲ] NF *Fam Arg scol* = first year of a two-year arts course, preparing for entrance to the "École normale supérieure"

hyponyme [ipɔnim] NM hyponym

hypophosphite [ipɔfɔsfit] NM *Chim* hypophosphite

hypophyse [ipɔfiz] NF *Physiol* hypophysis, pituitary gland

hypostase [ipɔstaz] NF *Phil, Rel & Méd* hypostasis

hypostatique [ipɔstatik] ADJ *Rel* hypostatic

hypostyle [ipɔstil] ADJ *Archit* hypostyle, pillared

hypotendu, -e [ipɔtɑ̃dy] *Méd* ADJ suffering from low blood pressure, *Spéc* hypotensive
NM,F person suffering from low blood pressure, *Spéc* hypotensive

hypotenseur [ipɔtɑ̃sœr] *Méd* ADJ M hypotensive
NM hypotensive (drug)

hypotension [ipɔtɑ̃sjɔ̃] NF low blood pressure, *Spéc* hypotension

hypoténuse [ipɔtenyz] NF hypotenuse

hypothalamus [ipɔtalamys] NM hypothalamus

hypothécable [ipɔtekabl] ADJ *Jur* mortgageable

hypothécaire [ipɔtekɛr] ADJ *Jur* mortgage *(avant n)*

hypothécairement [ipɔtekɛrmɑ̃] ADV *Jur* by *or* on mortgage

hypothèque [ipɔtɛk] NF **1** *Jur* mortgage; **franc** *ou* **libre d'hypothèques** unmortgaged; **prendre une h.** to take out a mortgage; **emprunter sur h.** to borrow on mortgage; **lever une h.** to raise a mortgage; **purger une h.** to pay off *or* to clear *or* to redeem a mortgage; **h. générale** blanket mortgage; **h. de premier rang** first legal mortgage; **propriété grevée d'hypothèques** encumbered estate **2** *Fig* **prendre une h. sur l'avenir** to count one's chickens before they're hatched; **lever l'h.** to remove the stumbling block *or* the obstacle

hypothéquer [18] [ipɔteke] VT **1** *Jur (propriété)* to mortgage; *(dette)* to secure by mortgage **2** *Fig* **h. son avenir** to mortgage one's future

hypothermie [ipɔtɛrmi] NF *Méd* hypothermia

hypothèse [ipɔtɛz] NF **1** *(supposition)* hypothesis, assumption; **dans la meilleure des hypothèses** at best; **dans l'h. où il refuserait, que feriez-vous?** supposing he refuses, what would you do?; **dans l'h. d'un tremblement de terre** in the event of an earthquake; **selon cette h.** on this assumption; **h. de travail** working hypothesis; *Écon* **h. du cycle de vie** life-cycle hypothesis **2** *Ling* hypothesis
• **en toute hypothèse** ADV in any event, whatever the case

hypothétique [ipɔtetik] ADJ **1** *(supposé)* hypothetical, assumed **2** *(peu probable)* hypothetical, unlikely, dubious; **c'est très h.** it's extremely doubtful **3** *Ling* hypothetical

hypothétiquement [ipɔtetikmɑ̃] ADV hypothetically

hypothyroïdie [ipɔtirɔidi] NF *Méd* hypothyroidism; **faire de l'h.** to have an underactive thyroid

hypotrophie [ipɔtrɔfi] NF *Méd* underdevelopment, hypotrophy

hypovitaminose [ipɔvitaminoz] NF *Méd* hypovitaminosis

hypsomètre [ipsɔmɛtr] NM *Phys* hypsometer

hypsométrie [ipsɔmetri] NF hypsometry; *(représentation des altitudes)* hypsography

hypsométrique [ipsɔmetrik] ADJ hypsometric, hypsometrical; **carte h.** contour map

hysope [izɔp] NF *Bot* hyssop

hystérectomie [isterɛktɔmi] NF *Méd* hysterectomy

hystérésis [isterezis] NF *Phys* hysteresis

hystérie [isteri] NF hysteria; **je ne veux pas de crise d'h.** I don't want any hysterics; **h. collective** mass hysteria

hystérique [isterik] *Psy* ADJ hysterical
NMF hysteric

hystérotomie [isterɔtɔmi] NF *Obst* hysterotomy

I

I, i [i] **NM INV** *(lettre)* I, i; **I comme Irma** ≃ I for Ivor; *Fig* **mettre les points sur les i** to dot the i's and cross the t's

IA [ia] **NF** *Ordinat (abrév* **intelligence artificielle**) AI

iambe [jɑ̃b] **NM** *(pied)* iamb, iambus; *(vers)* iambic

• **iambes NMPL** *(pièce satirique)* iambic

iambique [jɑ̃bik] **ADJ** iambic

IAO [iao] **NF** *(abrév* **ingénierie assistée par ordinateur**) CAE

IATA [jata] **NF** *(abrév* **Association internationale des transporteurs aériens**) IATA

ibère [ibɛr] **ADJ** Iberian

• **Ibère NMF** Iberian

ibérique [iberik] **ADJ** Iberian

ibis [ibis] **NM** *Orn* ibis

> **-IBLE** — SUFFIX
>
> • This suffix expresses the idea of POSSIBILITY and is used to create adjectives, mainly from transitive verbs but also sometimes intransitive verbs or nouns. Its equivalent in English is, in a lot of cases, *-ible* or *-able*. When there isn't an equivalent suffix form, the translation often includes an expression like "which can be..." or "easy to...", eg: **accessible** accessible/affordable; **audible** audible; **convertible** convertible; **flexible** flexible; **lisible** legible/readable; **9 est divisible par 3** 9 can be divided by 3
>
> • The suffix **-ible** is often found in conjunction with a base and the prefix **in-** (or **im-**), with the idea of IMPOSSIBILITY, even if there is no equivalent positive form: **incompréhensible** incomprehensible; **incorrigible** incorrigible; **invincible** invincible; **impassible** impassive; **indéfectible** staunch, unfailing

ibuprofène [ibyprɔfɛn] **NM** *Pharm* ibuprofen

Icare [ikar] **NPR** *Myth* Icarus

iceberg [ajsbɛrg] **NM 1** *(glace)* iceberg **2** *Fig* **la partie cachée** *ou* **immergée de l'i.** the hidden aspects of the problem; **la partie visible de l'i.** the tip of the iceberg

icelui [isəlɥi] *(pl* **iceux** [isø]) *Arch* **PRON DÉMONSTRATIF** *(personne)* he; *(objet)* it

ADJ DÉMONSTRATIF this

ichtyocolle [iktjɔkɔl] **NF** isinglass, fish glue

ichtyologie [iktjɔlɔʒi] **NF** ichthyology

ichtyologique [iktjɔlɔʒik] **ADJ** *(science)* ichthyological; *(traité)* ichthyology *(avant n)*; **étude i. du Saint-Laurent** study of the fish life of the Saint Lawrence River

ichtyologiste [iktjɔlɔʒist] **NMF** ichthyologist

ichtyophage [iktjɔfaʒ] **ADJ** ichthyophagous

ICI [isi] **ADV 1** *(dans ce lieu, à cet endroit)* here; *(dans un écrit, un discours)* here, at this point; **posez-le i.** put it here; **i. même** on this very spot, in this very place; **il fait beau i.** the weather's nice here; **vous i.!** what are you doing here?; **i. et là** here and there; **vous êtes i. chez vous** make yourself at home; **pour toute demande, s'adresser i.** please enquire within; **c'est i. que ça s'est passé** this is (the place) where it happened; **viens, d'i. on voit mieux** come on, you can see better from here; **il y a 11 km d'i. au village** it's 11 km from here to the village; **c'est à cinq minutes/15 km d'i.** it's five minutes/15 km from here; **c'est loin/près d'i.** it's a long way from here/near here; **les gens d'i.** the locals, the people from around here; **je ne suis pas d'i.** I'm a stranger here, I'm not from around here; **le car vient jusqu'i.** the bus comes as far as here *or* as far as this; **Descartes écrit i. que...** Descartes writes here that...; **je voudrais souligner i. l'importance de cette décision** here *or* at this point I would like to emphasize the importance of this decision

2 *(dans le temps)* **d'i. (à) lundi, on a le temps** we've got time between now and Monday; **d'i. demain ce sera terminé** it will be finished by tomorrow; **d'i. peu** before (very) long; **d'i. là, tout peut arriver!** in the meantime *or* until then *or* between now and then anything can happen!; **d'i. à ce que vous ayez fini, je serai parti** by the time you've finished, I'll have gone; *Fam* **d'i. à ce qu'il rechange d'avis, il n'y a pas loin** *ou* **il n'y a qu'un pas!** it won't be long before he changes his mind again!; **je vois ça d'i.!** I can just see that!; *Fam* **tu vois d'i. la pagaille!** you can (just) imagine the mess!

3 *(au téléphone, à la radio)* **allô, i. Paul** hello, (it's) Paul here *or* Paul speaking; **i. France Culture** this is *or* you are listening to France Culture

• **par ici ADV 1** *(dans cette direction)* this way; **venez par i.** come this way; **regarde par i.** look over here; **par i. la visite guidée** this way for the guided tour; **par i. la sortie** this way out, the exit is this way; **elle est passée par i. avant d'aller à la gare** she stopped off here on her way to the station; *Hum* **c'est par i. que ça se passe** pay attention; *Fam Hum* **par i. la monnaie!** come on now, cough up!

2 *(dans les environs)* around here; **j'habitais par i. autrefois** I used to live around here

ici-bas [isiba] **ADV** here below, on earth

ici-dans [isidɑ̃], **ici-dedans** [isidədɑ̃] **ADV** *Can* here; **qu'est-ce qu'il fait froid i.!** it's freezing in here!

icône [ikon] **NF 1** *Rel* icon **2** *(image, symbole)* icon; *Ordinat* **i. contrastée** highlighted icon; *Ordinat* **i. de la corbeille** wastebasket icon, *Am* trash icon

iconoclasme [ikɔnɔklasm] **NM** iconoclasm

iconoclaste [ikɔnɔklast] **ADJ** iconoclastic

NMF iconoclast

iconographe [ikɔnɔgraf] **NMF** *(spécialiste)* iconographer; *(dans l'édition)* art *or* picture editor

iconographie [ikɔnɔgrafi] **NF 1** *(étude théorique)* iconography **2** *(illustrations)* artwork

iconographique [ikɔnɔgrafik] **ADJ** iconographical

iconoscope [ikɔnɔskɔp] **NM** *TV* iconoscope

ictère [iktɛr] **NM** *Méd* jaundice, *Spéc* icterus

ictérique [ikterik] *Méd* **ADJ** jaundice *(avant n)*, *Spéc* icteric

NMF jaundice *or Spéc* icterus sufferer

idéal, -e, -als *ou* **-aux, -ales** [ideal, -o] **ADJ 1** *(demeure, société, solution)* ideal, best, perfect; **ce n'est pas le comédien i. pour le rôle de Falstaff** he's not the ideal actor for playing Falstaff **2** *(pureté, bonheur)* absolute

NM 1 *(modèle parfait)* ideal; **l'i. de la beauté chez les Grecs** the Greek ideal of beauty **2** *(valeurs)* ideal, ideals; **tous ces jeunes sans i.** *ou* **qui n'ont pas d'i.!** all these young people with no ideal in life! **3** *(solution parfaite)* **c'est l'i. pour se remettre en forme** it's the ideal thing for getting back into shape; **l'i. serait de/que...** the ideal *or* best solution would be to/if...; **dans l'i.** ideally; **camper quand il pleut, ce n'est pas l'i.!** when it's raining, camping isn't exactly ideal!

idéalement [idealmɑ̃] **ADV** ideally; **i. situé à proximité de la plage** ideally situated *or* situated in an ideal position close to the beach; **les Vierges de Raphaël sont i. belles** Raphael's Madonnas are the very embodiment of beauty

idéalisation [idealizasjɔ̃] **NF** idealization

idéaliser [3] [idealize] **VT** to idealize

idéalisme [idealism] **NM** idealism

idéaliste [idealist] **ADJ** idealistic

NMF idealist

idée [ide] **NF 1** *(pensée)* idea; **j'ai jeté quelques idées sur le papier** I've jotted down a few ideas; **c'est une i. de génie!** that's a brilliant idea!; **bonne i.!** good idea!; **c'était une bonne i. de l'emmener au restaurant** it was a good idea to take him/her out to eat; **je ne peux pas supporter l'i. qu'il est malheureux** I can't bear the idea *or* thought of him being unhappy; **se faire à l'i. (de/que...)** to get used to the idea (of/that...); *Fam* **j'ai i. que...** I've got the feeling that...; *Fam* **on n'a pas i. de faire des choses pareilles!** whoever heard of doing things like that!; **heureusement qu'il a eu l'i. d'éteindre le gaz** luckily he thought of turning the gas off *or* it occurred to him to turn the gas off; **avoir la bonne i. de faire qch** to have the bright idea of doing sth; *Hum* **il a eu la bonne i. de ne pas venir** he was quite right not to come; **qu'est-ce qui vous a donné l'i. de venir?** what gave you the idea *or* made you think of coming?; **rien qu'à l'i. de la revoir, je tremble** the mere thought *or* the very idea of seeing her again makes me nervous; **je me faisais une autre i. de sa femme** I had imagined his wife to be different; **moi, t'en vouloir? en voilà une i.** *ou* **quelle drôle d'i.!** me, hold it against you? where did you get that idea (from)?; **se faire des idées** to imagine things; **s'il croit obtenir le rôle, il se fait des idées** if he thinks he's going to get the part, he's deceiving himself; **se faire des idées sur qn** to have the wrong idea about sb; **donner des idées à qn** to give sb ideas *or* to put ideas in *or* into sb's head; **l'i., c'est de se débarrasser de ses cartes le plus vite possible** the idea *or* aim (of the game) is to get rid of one's cards as quickly as possible; **avoir une i. derrière la tête** to be up to sth; **avoir des idées noires** to be down in the dumps, to have the blues

2 *(inspiration, création)* idea; **qui a eu l'i. du barbecue?** whose idea was it to have *or* who suggested having a barbecue?; **d'après une i. originale de** *(dans un film)* based on an (original) idea by; **je tiens l'i. d'un spectacle** I've got an idea for a show

3 *(imagination)* ideas, imagination; **avoir de l'i.** to be quite inventive; *Fam* **aie un peu d'i.!** try and use your head *or* imagination a bit!; **il y a de l'i. mais le plan du devoir laisse à désirer** the idea is good but your presentation leaves something to be desired

4 *(gré, convenance)* **fais à ton i.** do as you see fit *or* as you please; **elle n'en fait toujours qu'à son i.** she always does just what she wants

5 *(esprit)* **avoir dans l'i. que...** to have an idea that..., to think that...; **avais-tu dans l'i. d'acheter des actions?** were you thinking of buying shares?; **tu la connais, quand elle a dans l'i. de faire quelque chose!** you know her, when she's got it into her head to do something *or* when she's set her mind on doing something!; **se mettre dans l'i. de/que...** to get it into one's head to/that...; **t'est-il jamais venu à l'i. que...?** has it never occurred to you *or* entered your head that...?; **il ne me viendrait jamais à l'i. de le frapper** it would never cross my mind *or* occur to me to hit him; *Fam* **ça m'était complètement sorti de l'i.** it had gone clean *or* right out of my mind

6 *(point de vue, opinion)* **il a une i. un peu étrange de l'amour** he has rather a strange idea of love; **on a tous une i. différente sur la question** we all have a different opinion *or* view on the matter; **avoir des idées bien arrêtées sur** to have set ideas *or* definite views about; **je préfère me faire une i. (par) moi-même** I prefer to make up my own mind; **à ton i., je raccourcis la robe?** what do you think *or* reckon, should I shorten the dress?; **changer d'i.** to change one's mind; **i. fixe** idée fixe, obsession; **c'est une i. fixe chez toi!** it's an obsession with you!; **elle a une i. fixe** she's got a fixed idea *or* an idée fixe; **i. reçue** commonplace, received idea, idée reçue; **idées préconçues** preconceived ideas, preconceptions; **avoir les idées larges/étroites** to be broad-/narrow-minded; **avoir une haute i. de qn/qch** to have a high opinion of sb/sth, to think highly of sb/sth; **avoir sa petite i. sur qch** to have one's own little ideas about sth

7 *(aperçu, impression)* idea; **une vague** *ou* **petite i.** an inkling; **donnez-moi une i. du temps que ça va prendre** give me a rough idea *or* some idea of the time it will take; **as-tu (une) i.** *ou* **la moindre i. du prix que ça coûte?** have you any idea how much it costs?; **tu n'as pas i. de son entêtement!** you have no idea *or* you can't imagine how stubborn he is!; *Fam* **elle est belle, t'as pas i.!** you wouldn't believe how beautiful she is; **je n'en ai pas la moindre i.** I haven't the slightest *or* faintest idea; **aucune i.!** I haven't a clue!, no idea!

8 *(en composition; avec ou sans trait d'union)* idea; **une i.-cadeau** a gift idea; **une i.-repas** an idea for a meal

idée-force [idefɔrs] *(pl* **idées-forces***)* **NF** *(point principal)* crux, nub, mainstay; *(point fort)* strong point

idem [idɛm] **ADV** idem, ditto; *Fam* **je suis venu en voiture et lui i.** I came by car and so did he *or* and he did too

identifiable [idɑ̃tifjabl] **ADJ** identifiable; **difficilement i.** difficult to identify

identifiant [idɑ̃tifjɑ̃] **NM** *Ordinat* identifier; **i. biométrique** biometric identifier

identificateur [idɑ̃tifikatœr] **NM 1** *Ordinat* identifier **2** *Mktg* **i. de marque** brand identifier

identification [idɑ̃tifikasjɔ̃] **NF 1** *(assimilation)* identification (à with); **son i. à son père est complète** he/she completely identifies with his/her father

2 *(d'un cadavre)* identification; *(d'un tableau)* identification, attribution

3 *Tél* **i. d'appel** caller identification, *Fam* caller ID; *Ordinat* **i. de l'utilisateur** user identification

4 *Mktg* **i. de la marque** brand recognition

identifier [9] [idɑ̃tifje] **VT 1** *(reconnaître)* to identify; **il a été identifié comme étant le voleur** he was identified as the robber; **le tableau n'a jamais été identifié** the painting was never attributed *or* identified; **se faire i.** to give one's identity, to identify oneself **2** *(assimiler)* **i. qn/qch à** *ou* **avec** to identify sb/sth with

VPR s'identifier s'i. à qn/qch to identify oneself with sb/sth; **elle s'est complètement identifiée à son personnage** she's got right into the part; **je ne m'identifie à aucun parti** I don't identify myself with any particular party

identifieur [idɑ̃tifjœr] = **identificateur**

identique [idɑ̃tik] **ADJ** identical; **i. à qn/qch** identical to sb/sth; **le village est resté i.** the village has stayed much the same; **elle reste i. à elle-même** she's still the same as she always *or* ever was

• **à l'identique ADV** identically; **j'en ai fait un à l'i.** I made an identical one

identiquement [idɑ̃tikmɑ̃] **ADV** identically

identitaire [idɑ̃titɛr] **ADJ obsession i.** obsession with issues of identity; **les revendications identitaires des minorités ethniques** ethnic minorities' demands for recognition; **l'afflux d'immigrants a donné lieu à un phénomène de repli i.** the large influx of immigrants has caused people to cling to their idea of cultural identity

identité [idɑ̃tite] **NF 1** *(personnalité, état civil)* identity; **sous une fausse i.** under an assumed name; **établir son i.** to prove one's identity; **l'i. des victimes n'a pas été révélée** the names of the victims haven't been released; **contrôle** *ou* **vérification d'i.** (police) identity check

2 *(similitude)* identity, similarity; **l'i. d'humeur entre eux** the similarity in their characters

3 *Jur* **I. judiciaire** ≃ Criminal Record Office

4 *Mktg* **i. graphique** logo; **i. de marque** brand identity

idéogramme [ideɔgram] **NM** ideogram

idéographie [ideɔgrafi] **NF** ideography

idéographique [ideɔgrafik] **ADJ** ideographic, ideographical

idéologie [ideɔlɔʒi] **NF** ideology

idéologique [ideɔlɔʒik] **ADJ** ideological

idéologue [ideɔlɔg] **NMF** ideologist

IDH [ideaʃ] **NM** *Écon (abrév* **indicateur de développement humain***)* HDI

idiolecte [idjɔlɛkt] **NM** *Ling* idiolect

idiomatique [idjɔmatik] **ADJ** idiomatic; **une expression** *ou* **une tournure i.** an idiom, an idiomatic expression

idiome [idjom] **NM** idiom

idiosyncrasie [idjɔsɛ̃krazi] **NF** idiosyncrasy

idiot, -e [idjo, -ɔt] **ADJ 1** *(stupide ▸ individu, réponse, sourire)* idiotic, stupid; *(▸ accident, mort)* stupid; **un ricanement i.** a stupid *or* foolish snigger; **ça n'est pas i. du tout, ton système** that's quite a smart system you've got; **ce serait vraiment i. de ne pas en profiter** it would be foolish *or* stupid not to take advantage of it; *Hum* **dis-moi comment faire, je ne veux pas mourir i.** tell me how to do it, I don't want to be a complete ignoramus **2** *Vieilli Méd* idiotic

NM,F 1 *(imbécile)* idiot; **arrête de faire l'i.!** *(de faire le pitre)* stop fooling around *or* about!; *(à un enfant)* stop being silly!; *(à un simulateur)* stop acting stupid!; **tu me prends pour un i.?** what kind of idiot do you take me for?, do you take me for a complete idiot? **2** *Vieilli Méd* idiot; **l'i. du village** the village idiot

idiotement [idjɔtmɑ̃] **ADV** idiotically, stupidly; **ricaner i.** to snigger like an idiot

idiotie [idjɔsi] **NF 1** *(caractère)* idiocy, stupidity **2** *(acte, parole)* stupid thing; **arrête de dire des idioties** stop talking nonsense; **aïe! j'ai fait une i.!** oh dear, I've done something stupid! **3** *Vieilli Méd* idiocy

idiotisme [idjɔtism] **NM** idiom, idiomatic phrase, idiomatic expression

idoine [idwan] **ADJ** *Littéraire* appropriate

idolâtre [idɔlatr] **ADJ 1** *Rel* idolatrous **2** *(fanatique)* adulatory; **un public i.** an idolizing *or* adulatory public

NMF 1 *Rel* idolater, *f* idolatress **2** *(fanatique)* devotee

idolâtrer [3] [idɔlatre] **VT 1** *Rel* to idolize **2** *(adorer)* to idolize

idolâtrie [idɔlatri] **NF 1** *Rel* idolatry, idol worshipping **2** *(fanatisme)* **il l'aime jusqu'à l'i.** he idolizes her

idolâtrique [idɔlatrik] **ADJ** idolatrous

idole [idɔl] **NF 1** *Rel* idol **2** *(personne)* idol; **mon frère était mon i.** I used to idolize my brother; **c'est l'i. des jeunes** he's/she's a teen idol

IDS [idees] **NF** *Mil (abrév* **initiative de défense stratégique***)* SDI

idylle [idil] **NF 1** *(poème)* idyll **2** *(amourette)* romantic idyll

Il faut noter que le terme anglais **idyll** employé seul ne s'applique jamais à une liaison entre deux personnes.

idyllique [idilik] **ADJ 1** *Littérature* idyllic **2** *(amour, couple, paysage)* idyllic, perfect; **se faire une idée i. de qch** to have an idealized view of sth

-IE SUFFIX

• Among its various uses, the suffix **-ie** can be found at the end of names of countries or regions (**la Normandie, l'Andalousie, la Roumanie** etc.). It also appears in words referring to types of government, eg **monarchie** (monarchy), **tyrannie** (tyranny).

• It is a combination of these two features that has given rise in recent years to a humorous use of the suffix **-ie**, mostly in combination with names of political leaders. This type of neologism is mostly used in newspaper headlines, eg:

bienvenue en Chiraquie welcome to Chirac's world; **ouragan sur la Chiraquie** storm hits the Chirac camp; **les déçus de la Mitterrandie** the people disappointed by the Mitterrand era

• The word **ovalie** follows the same pattern, but is derived from the word "ovale" (as in the shape of a rugby ball) as opposed to a proper noun. Again, it refers to the world of rugby in general, to rugby players as a whole or even to the sport itself, eg:

votre voyage en Ovalie va durer six semaines [about the rugby World Cup] welcome to six weeks of rugby; **il a quitté l'ovalie** he left rugby

• Note that, like a lot of recent coinages, the spelling for **ovalie, chiraquie, jospinie** etc can fluctuate between the capitalized and uncapitalized forms.

-IEN, -IENNE SUFFIX

This suffix has a wide variety of uses, some of which are particularly productive.

• **-ien, -ienne** appears in names of INHABITANTS of countries, regions, cities or even planets. It is often translated by the English suffix *-ian*, eg:

parisien(ne)/Parisien(ne) Parisian; **italien(ne)/Italien(ne)** Italian; **la banlieue londonienne** the London suburbs; **les Londoniens** Londoners; **les Terriens** inhabitants of the Earth, Earthlings; **un martien** a Martian

• The same word can be used to refer to the language spoken by such inhabitants, eg:

elle parle bien italien she speaks good Italian

• When added to a noun referring to a particular field, it takes on the meaning of PERSON WHO SPECIALIZES IN..., eg:

un(e) chirurgien(ne) a surgeon; **un(e) comédien(ne)** an actor; **un(e) généticien(ne)** a geneticist; **un(e) électricien(ne)** an electrician

• In the medical world, **-ien, -ienne** is used to form adjectives with the meaning of RELATING TO. Their English equivalents are often *-ian* or *-ial*, eg:

coronarien(ne) coronary; **microbien(ne)** microbial/bacterial; **rachidien(ne)** rachidian, rachidial

• A similar meaning is contained in adjectives and nouns derived from people's names, and it is in this area that the suffix **-ien, -ienne** becomes most productive as it can be added to the name of virtually any politician, writer etc, eg:

l'inconscient freudien the Freudian unconscious; **l'école platonicienne** the Platonic school; **l'univers faulknérien** the world of Faulkner; **la période mitterrandienne** the Mitterand period; **les jospiniens** Jospin supporters; **un fervent chiraquien** a die-hard Chirac supporter

IEP [iəpe] **NM** *(abrév* **Institut d'études politiques***)* = "grande école" for political science

-IER, -IÈRE SUFFIX

Among the many uses of this suffix, three are particularly productive.

• A lot of nouns describing a person's JOB, TRADE OR STATUS end in **-ier**, **-ière**. The most common English equivalent is probably the suffix *-er*, eg:

un(e) jardinier(ère) a gardener; **un plombier (ère)** a plumber; **un(e) ouvrier(ère)** a worker; **un(e) prisonnier(ère)** a prisoner; **un(e) cuisinier(ère)** a cook; **un(e) écolier(ère)** a schoolboy/schoolgirl

• The idea of PRODUCTION is an important one with this suffix. It appears in masculine names of trees or plants bearing a particular fruit (**prunier** plumtree; **poirier** pear tree; **fraisier** strawberry plant; **olivier** olive tree), as well as in feminine names of places where a particular plant or tree grows or where a mineral is produced (**sapinière** fir plantation; **rizière** rice field).

• When added to nouns describing a food item or cosmetic, **-ier** or **-ière** carry the idea of CONTAINER, eg:

poudrier powder compact; **cendrier** ashtray; **soupière** soup tureen; **cafetière** coffee pot; **salière** saltcellar

-ieux, -ieuse [jø, jøz] *voir* **-eux, -euse**

if [if] **NM 1** *(arbre)* yew (tree) **2** *(bois)* yew **3** *(égouttoir)* **if (à bouteilles)** (bottle draining) rack

-IF SUFFIX

In French "traditional" argot, this suffix is added to nouns, sometimes along with an extra consonant and sometimes also with the base noun truncated, eg:

calcif (from *caleçon*) underpants; **porcif** (from *portion*) portion; **soutif** (from *soutien-gorge*) bra; **beaujolpif** Beaujolais

IFOP, Ifop [ifɔp] **NM** *Mktg* (*abrév* **Institut français d'opinion publique**) = French market research institute

IG [iʒe] **NM** *Méd* (*abrév* **index glycémique**) GI

IGF [iʒeɛf] **NM INV** *Anciennement Fin* (*abrév* **impôt sur les grandes fortunes**) wealth tax

igloo, iglou [iglu] **NM** igloo

IGN [iʒeɛn] **NM** (*abrév* **Institut géographique national**) = French national geographical institute, *Br* ≃ Ordnance Survey, *Am* ≃ United States Geological Survey

IGN

Created in 1940, this state agency is responsible for the official map of France and for keeping a geographical database. It is organized into regional offices and sponsors a school which trains 200 students a year.

igname [iɲam] **NF** *Bot* yam

ignare [iɲar] **ADJ** ignorant, uncultivated
NMF ignoramus

ignifugation [ignifygasjɔ̃, iɲifygasjɔ̃] **NF** fireproofing

ignifuge [ignifyʒ, iɲifyʒ] **ADJ** *(qui ne brûle pas)* fireproof; *(qui brûle difficilement)* fire-retardant
NM *(pour protéger du feu)* fireproof substance; *(pour ralentir la propagation)* fire-retardant substance

ignifugé, -e [ignifyʒe] **ADJ** *(matériau)* fireproofed

ignifugeant, -e [ignifyʒɑ̃, -ɑ̃t, iɲifyʒɑ̃, -ɑ̃t] **ADJ** *(qui ne brûle pas)* fireproof; *(qui brûle difficilement)* fire-retardant

ignifuger [17] [ignifyʒe, iɲifyʒe] **VT** to fireproof

ignoble [iɲɔbl] **ADJ 1** *(vil ▸ individu)* low, base; *(▸ crime)* infamous, heinous; *(▸ accusation)* shameful; *(▸ conduite)* unspeakable, disgraceful; **tu as vraiment été i. avec elle** you were really vile to her **2** *Fam (bâtisse)* hideous; *(nourriture)* revolting, vile; *(logement)* squalid

ignoblement [iɲɔbləmɑ̃] **ADV** vilely, disgracefully

ignominie [iɲɔmini] **NF 1** *(caractère vil)* ignominy, infamy; *(déshonneur)* ignominy, (public) disgrace *or* dishonour; **se couvrir d'i.** to disgrace oneself **2** *(action)* disgraceful act; *(parole)* disgraceful remark; **commettre une i.** to behave ignominiously *or* disgracefully; **dire des ignominies** to say disgraceful *or* hateful things; **c'est une i.!** it's a disgrace!, it's shameful!

ignominieuse [iɲɔminjøz] *voir* **ignominieux**

ignominieusement [iɲɔminjøzmɑ̃] **ADV** *Littéraire* ignominiously, disgracefully

ignominieux, -euse [iɲɔminjø, -øz] **ADJ** *Littéraire* ignominious

ignorance [iɲɔrɑ̃s] **NF** ignorance; **être dans l'i. de qch** to be unaware of sth; **tenir qn dans l'i. de qch** to keep sb in ignorance of sth; **j'avoue mon i. en géologie** I must confess my ignorance of geology

ignorant, -e [iɲɔrɑ̃, -ɑ̃t] **ADJ 1** *(inculte)* ignorant, uncultivated **2** *(incompétent)* **i. en** ignorant about; **il est i. en informatique** he doesn't know anything about computers **3** *(pas au courant)* **i. de** ignorant *or* unaware of
NM,F ignoramus; **ne fais pas l'i.** don't pretend you don't know

Il faut noter qu'en anglais l'adjectif **ignorant** signifie également **mal élevé**.

ignoré, -e [iɲɔre] **ADJ 1** *(cause, événement)* unknown; **être i. de qn** to be unknown to sb **2** *(artiste)* unrecognized

ignorer [3] [iɲɔre] **VT 1** *(cause, événement etc)* to be unaware of; **j'ignore ton adresse/où il est/quand elle revient** I don't know your address/where he is/when she's coming back; **il ignorait tout de mon passé** he knew nothing about my past; **j'ignorais qu'il était malade** I was unaware *or* I didn't know that he was ill; **personne n'ignore que...** everybody knows that...; **nous n'ignorons pas les difficultés qu'elle rencontre** we are not unaware of her difficulties **2** *(personne, regard)* to ignore, to take no notice of; *(avertissement, panneau, ordre)* to ignore, to take no heed of; **ignore-le** ignore him **3** *(faim, pauvreté)* to have had no experience of; **nous ignorons la faim** we don't know what it is to be hungry
VPR s'ignorer 1 *(mutuellement)* to ignore each other **2** *(soi-même)* **c'est un comédien qui s'ignore** he is unaware of his talent as an actor, he's an actor without knowing it

Il faut noter que le verbe anglais **to ignore** ne signifie jamais **ne pas savoir**.

IGP [iʒepe] **NF** *Com* (*abrév* **indication géographique protégée**) = designation of a product which guarantees its authentic place of origin and gives the name protected status

IGPN [iʒepeɛn] **NF** (*abrév* **Inspection générale de la police nationale**) = police disciplinary body, *Br* ≃ Police Committee

IGS [iʒeɛs] **NF** (*abrév* **Inspection générale des services**) = police disciplinary body for Paris, *Br* ≃ Metropolitan Police Commission

iguane [igwan] **NM** *Zool* iguana

il [il] (*pl* **ils**) **PRON 1** *(sujet d'un verbe ▸ homme)* he; *(▸ animal, chose)* it; *(▸ animal de compagnie)* he; **ils** they; **ils ont augmenté l'essence/les impôts** they've put petrol/taxes up; **viendra-t-il?** will he come? **2** *(dans des tournures impersonnelles)* **il pleut** it's raining; **il faut que tu viennes** you must come; **il me faut du pain** I need some bread; **il faut patienter** you/we have to wait; **il commence à se faire tard** it's getting late; **il manque deux élèves** two pupils are missing; **il suffit de patienter** all you/we have to do is wait; **il est facile de s'en assurer** it's easy to make sure **3** *(emphatique)* **ton père est-il rentré?** has your father come back?; **qu'il est joli, ce foulard!** what a pretty scarf (that is)!

île [il] **NF 1** *Géog* island, isle; **une petite î.** an islet; **les habitants de l'î.** the islanders; **vivre sur** *ou* **dans une î.** to live on an island; **aller sur une î.** to go to an island; **î. déserte** desert island; **les îles Anglo-Normandes** the Channel Islands; **les îles Baléares** the Balearic Islands; **l'î. de Beauté** Corsica; **les îles Britanniques** the British Isles; **les îles Canaries** the Canary Islands; **les îles Cayman** the Cayman Islands; **l'î. Christmas** Christmas Island; **l'î. de la Cité** = island on the Seine in Paris where Notre-Dame stands; **l'î. d'Elbe** Elba; **les îles Falkland** the Falkland Islands, the Falklands; **les îles Féroé** the Faeroes; **les îles Fidji** the Fiji Islands; **les îles Galapagos** the Galapagos Islands; **l'î. Krakatoa** Krakatau, Krakatoa; **les îles Maldives** the Maldives; **l'î. de Man** the Isle of Man; **l'î. Maurice** Mauritius; **les îles de la mer Égée** the Aegean *or* Greek Islands; **l'î. de Pâques** Easter Island; **l'î. du Prince-Édouard** Prince Edward Island; **les îles Shetland** the Shetland Islands, the Shetlands; **les îles Sorlingues** the Scilly Isles; **l'î. de la Trinité** Trinidad; **les îles Vierges** the Virgin Islands; **l'î. de Wight** the Isle of Wight **2** *Littéraire ou Vieilli (colonie)* **les îles** the Caribbean (Islands), the West Indies **3** *Culin* **î. flottante** floating island

Île-de-France [ildəfrɑ̃s] **NF l'Î.** the Île-de-France; **en Î.** in the Île-de-France region

iléon [ileɔ̃] **NM** *Anat* ileum

iliaque [iljak] **ADJ** *Anat* iliac

illégal, -e, -aux, -ales [ilegal, -o] **ADJ** *(contre la loi)* illegal, unlawful; *(sans autorisation)* illicit; **de façon illégale** illegally; **c'est maintenant i.** it's now illegal, it's now against the law; **détention illégale** unlawful detention

illégalement [ilegalmɑ̃] **ADV** illegally, unlawfully

illégalité [ilegalite] **NF 1** *(caractère)* illegality, unlawfulness; **être dans l'i.** to be in breach of the law; **vivre dans l'i.** to live outside the law, to be an outlaw **2** *(délit)* illegal *or* unlawful act; **commettre une i.** to break the law

illégitime [ileʒitim] **ADJ 1** *Jur (enfant, acte)* illegitimate; *(mariage)* unlawful **2** *(requête, prétention)* illegitimate; *(frayeur, soupçons)* groundless

illégitimement [ileʒitimmɑ̃] **ADV 1** *Jur* illegitimately, unlawfully **2** *(injustement)* unwarrantedly, unjustifiably

illégitimité [ileʒitimite] **NF 1** *Jur (d'un enfant, d'un acte)* illegitimacy; *(d'un mariage)* unlawfulness **2** *(injustice)* unwarrantedness, unfoundedness

illettré, -e [iletre] **ADJ 1** *(qui ne peut ni lire ni écrire)* functionally illiterate **2** *(ignorant)* uncultivated, uneducated
NM,F 1 *(personne qui ne peut ni lire ni écrire)* functionally illiterate person, functional illiterate **2** *(ignorant)* uncultivated *or* uneducated person

illettrisme [iletrism] **NM** functional illiteracy

illicite [ilisit] **ADJ** illicit, unlawful

illicitement [ilisitmɑ̃] **ADV** illicitly, unlawfully

illico [iliko] **ADV i. (presto)** right away, pronto

illimité, -e [ilimite] **ADJ 1** *(en abondance ▸ ressources, espace)* unlimited; *(▸ patience, bonté)* boundless, limitless **2** *(non défini ▸ durée)* unlimited, indefinite; **en congé i.** on indefinite leave **3** *Ordinat* **accès i.** unrestricted access

illisibilité [ilizibilite] **NF** illegibility

illisible [ilizibl] **ADJ 1** *(écriture)* illegible, unreadable **2** *(écrivain, roman)* unreadable **3** *Ordinat (fichier, disquette)* unreadable

illisiblement [iliziblәmɑ̃] **ADV** illegibly

illogique [ilɔʒik] **ADJ** illogical; **de façon i.** illogically

illogiquement [ilɔʒikmɑ̃] **ADV** illogically

illogisme [ilɔʒism] **NM** illogicality, absurdity

illumination [ilyminasjɔ̃] **NF 1** *(d'un monument)* floodlighting **2** *(lumière)* illumination, lighting (up) **3** *(idée)* flash of inspiration *or* understanding; *(révélation)* illumination
• **illuminations NFPL** illuminations, lights; **les illuminations de Noël** the Christmas lights

illuminé, -e [ilymine] **ADJ** *(monument)* lit up, floodlit, illuminated; *(rue)* lit up, illuminated
NM,F 1 *(visionnaire)* visionary, *Arch* illuminate **2** *Péj (fou)* lunatic

illuminer [3] [ilymine] **VT 1** *(ciel ▸ sujet: étoiles, éclairs)* to light up; *(monument)* to floodlight; *(pièce)* to light; *Fig* **cet événement a illuminé sa vie** this event has lit up his/her life **2** *(visage, regard)* to light up; **un sourire illumina son visage** a smile lit up his/her face **3** *Rel* to enlighten
VPR s'illuminer 1 *(ciel, regard, visage)* to light up;

s'i. de to light up with **2** *(vitrine)* to be lit up; *(guirlande)* to light up

illusion [ilyzjɔ̃] **NF 1** *(idée fausse)* illusion; **ne lui donne pas d'illusions** don't give him/her (any) false ideas; **perdre ses illusions** to lose one's illusions; **faire perdre ses illusions à qn** to disillusion sb; **se faire des illusions** to delude oneself; **je ne me fais pas d'illusions là-dessus** I have no illusions *or* I'm not deluding myself about it; **se bercer d'illusions** to delude oneself **2** *(erreur de perception)* illusion, trick; **c'est une i. due à la lumière** it's a trick of the light; **le miroir donne une i. de profondeur** the mirror gives an illusion of depth; **en donnant** *ou* **créant une i. de stabilité** with an outward show of stability; **Mirax, le roi de l'i.!** Mirax, the great illusionist!; **faire i.** to fool people; **c'est un vieux manteau mais il fait i.** it's an old coat but you wouldn't think so to look at it; **son aisance fait i.** his/her apparent ease is deceptive; **i. d'optique** optical illusion

illusionner [3] [ilyzjɔne] **VT** to delude

VPR s'illusionner to delude *or* to deceive oneself; **tu t'illusionnes sur ses intentions** you're deluding yourself about his/her intentions; **ne t'illusionne pas sur sa détermination** make no mistake about his/her determination

illusionnisme [ilyzjɔnism] **NM** *(prestidigitation)* conjuring tricks; *(truquage)* illusionism

illusionniste [ilyzjɔnist] **NMF** conjurer, illusionist

illusoire [ilyzwar] **ADJ** *(promesse)* deceptive, illusory; *(bonheur, victoire)* illusory, fanciful; **il serait i. de croire que…** it would be wrong *or* mistaken to believe that…

illusoirement [ilyzwarmɑ̃] **ADV** *Littéraire* illusorily, deceptively

illustrateur, -trice [ilystratœr, -tris] **NM,F** illustrator

illustration [ilystrasjɔ̃] **NF 1** *(image, activité)* illustration; *(ensemble d'images)* illustrations; **l'i. de cette édition est somptueuse** this book is lavishly illustrated **2** *Fig (démonstration)* illustration; *(exemple)* illustration, example

illustratrice [ilystratris] *voir* **illustrateur**

illustre [ilystr] **ADJ** illustrious; **une ville au passé i.** a town with an illustrious *or* a glorious past; **l'i. compagnie** the Académie française; *Hum* **qui est cet i. inconnu?** who is this famous person I've never heard of?

illustré, -e [ilystre] **ADJ** illustrated

NM pictorial, illustrated magazine; *(pour enfants)* comic

illustrer [3] [ilystre] **VT 1** *(livre)* to illustrate **2** *(définition, théorie)* to illustrate (**de** *ou* **par** with) **3** *Littéraire (rendre prestigieux)* to lend distinction to; **Molière a illustré la langue française** Molière contributed to the greatness of the French language

VPR s'illustrer to become renowned *or* famous; **elle s'est illustrée par son interprétation de Carmen** she won fame through her performance of Carmen; **les Français se sont illustrés en natation** the French distinguished themselves at swimming

ILM [iɛlɛm] **NM** *(abrév* **immeuble à loyer moyen**) = apartment building with low-rent accommodation (more expensive than an HLM)

ILN [iɛlɛn] **NM** *(abrév* **immeuble à loyer normal**) = apartment building with low-rent accommodation

îlot [ilo] **NM 1** *Géog* small island, islet

2 *(espace)* island; **dans l'î. de calme où je travaille** in the island *or* oasis of peace where I work; **î. de résistance** pocket of resistance

3 *(pâté de maisons)* block; *(pour surveillance policière)* patrol area, beat

4 *(sur une route)* **î. directionnel** traffic *or* lane divider

5 *(dans un magasin)* gondola; **î. de vente** (display) stand, island

îlotage [ilɔtaʒ] **NM** *(d'un quartier)* community policing

ilote [ilɔt] **NM 1** *Antiq* Helot **2** *Fig Littéraire* helot

îlotier [ilɔtje] **NM** community policeman, policeman on the beat

ils [il] *voir* **il**

ILV [iɛlve] **NF** *Mktg (abrév* **information sur le lieu de vente**) point-of-sale information

image [imaʒ] **NF 1** *(illustration ▸ gén)* picture; (▸ *comme récompense scolaire)* ≃ gold star; *Fig* **l'i. de** the picture of; **elle était l'i. de la bonne santé** she was the very picture of health; **i. de la mère/du père** mother/father figure; *Fig* **c'est une véritable i. d'Épinal** it's a very stereotyped image; **i. pieuse** holy image; **livre d'images** picture book

2 *(reflet)* image, reflection; *Phys* image; **i. réelle/virtuelle** real/virtual image

3 *(au cinéma ▸ plan)* frame; *(à la télévision ▸ réception)* picture; **25 images par seconde** 25 frames per second; **l'i. est floue** *(télévision)* the picture is fuzzy; **il n'y a plus d'i.** the picture's gone; **certaines scènes du roman sont difficiles à mettre en images** some scenes from the novel are difficult to adapt for the screen; **i. d'archive** library picture; *Cin, TV* library shot; *TV* **i. fantôme** ghosting; **i. multiple** multiple image; *Phot* **i. de solarisation** solarized image; **images de synthèse** computer-generated images, CGI; **i. de télévision** television picture; **i. tramée** raster image; **i. virtuelle** virtual image

4 *Littérature* image; **les images de Hugo** Hugo's imagery

5 *(idée)* image, picture; **quelle i. te fais-tu de lui?** how do you picture him?; **donner une fausse i. de qch** to misrepresent sth, to give a false impression of sth; **soigner son i.** to cultivate one's image; *Littéraire* **son i. me hante** his/her face haunts me; *Compta* **i. fidèle** true and fair view; **i. mentale** mental image

6 *Math* image

7 *Ordinat (imprimée)* hard copy; *(sur l'écran)* image; **i. bitmap** bitmap image; **i. cliquable** clickable image; **i. digitalisée** digitized image; **i. intégrée** inline image; **i. mémoire** dump; **prendre une i. mémoire** to take a hard copy, to dump; **images de synthèse** computer-generated images, CGI; **i. vectorielle** outline image

8 *Mktg* **i. de l'entreprise** *ou* **institutionnelle** corporate image; **i. de marque** *(d'un produit)* brand image; *(d'une entreprise)* corporate image; *(d'une personnalité, d'une institution)* (public) image; **i. de produit** product image; **images à compléter** picture completion

• **à l'image de PRÉP Dieu créa l'homme à son i.** God created man in his own image; **cet enfant est tout à fait à l'i. de sa mère** this child is the very image of his mother; **ce jardin est à l'i. de son propriétaire** this garden is the reflection of its owner

imagé, -e [imaʒe] **ADJ** full of imagery; **elle a un langage très i.** she uses colourful imagery

imager [17] [imaʒe] **VT** *Littéraire (style, discours)* to colour

imagerie [imaʒri] **NF 1** *(ensemble d'images)* prints, pictures; **l'i. napoléonienne** the imagery of the Napoleonic era

2 *(commerce)* coloured print trade; *(fabrication)* printing

3 *Météo* satellite photography

4 *Méd* **i. cérébrale** brain imaging *or* scanning; **i. médicale** medical imaging; **i. par résonance magnétique** magnetic resonance imaging; **i. par résonance magnétique fonctionnelle** functional magnetic resonance imaging; **i. par résonance magnétique nucléaire** nuclear magnetic resonance imaging

5 *Ordinat* imagery

6 *Tech* imaging; **i. infrarouge** infrared imaging; **i. radar** radar imagery

imageur, -euse [imaʒœr, -øz] **ADJ** *(radar, radiomètre)* imaging

NM *Ordinat* imager; **i. documentaire** document imager

imagier, -ère [imaʒje, -ɛr] **NM,F 1** *(dessinateur)* drawer *or* painter *(of popular pictures)*; *Vieilli (imprimeur)* printer *(of popular pictures)*; *Vieilli (vendeur)* print seller **2** *(sculpteur)* sculptor *(of human figures or animals)*

imaginable [imaʒinabl] **ADJ** imaginable, conceivable; **ce n'est pas i. d'être aussi têtu!** it's unbelievable how stubborn you can be!; **c'est difficilement i.** it's hard to imagine; **ce n'est plus i. à notre époque** it's just unthinkable nowadays

imaginaire [imaʒinɛr] **ADJ 1** *(fictif)* imaginary

NM imagination; **le domaine de l'i.** the realm of fancy; *Psy* **l'i. collectif** the collective imagination

imaginatif, -ive [imaʒinatif, -iv] **ADJ** imaginative, fanciful

imagination [imaʒinasjɔ̃] **NF 1** *(faculté)* imagination; **essaie d'avoir un peu d'i.** try using your imagination; **avoir beaucoup d'i.** to have a lot of imagination, to be very imaginative; **tu as vraiment trop d'i.!** you imagine things!; **tu manques d'i.!** you have no imagination!; **tu as l'i. fertile** you have a fertile *or* good imagination; **son récit frappe l'i.** his/her story strikes the imagination; **les derniers événements dépassent l'i.** the latest incidents defy the imagination *or* beggar belief; **elle lui parlait en i.** she imagined herself talking to him/her; **c'est de l'i. pure et simple** it's sheer *or* pure imagination **2** *(chimère)* **ce sont de pures imaginations** that's pure fancy; **imaginations que tout cela!** those are just imaginings!

imaginative [imaʒinativ] *voir* **imaginatif**

imaginer [3] [imaʒine] **VT 1** *(concevoir)* to imagine; **c'est l'homme le plus gentil qu'on puisse i.** he is the kindest man imaginable; **je n'imaginais pas que cela soit faisable** I didn't think it could be done; **la maison est plus grande que je l'imaginais** the house is bigger than I imagined it (to be); **tu imagines sa tête quand je lui ai dit ça!** you can imagine *or* picture his/her face when I told him/her that!; **on imagine facilement qu'elle n'était pas ravie** as you can imagine, she wasn't very pleased; **on imagine mal la suite** it's hard to imagine what happened next; **tu n'imagines tout de même pas que je vais céder?** you don't really think *or* imagine I'm going to give in, do you?; **que vas-tu i. là?** how can you think such a thing? **2** *(supposer)* to imagine, to suppose; **imaginons qu'il refuse** supposing he refuses; **tu veux de l'argent, j'imagine!** you want some money, I suppose! **3** *(inventer ▸ personnage)* to create, to imagine; (▸ *gadget, mécanisme)* to devise, to think up

VPR s'imaginer 1 *(soi-même)* to imagine oneself; **elle s'imagine déjà danseuse étoile!** she already imagines *or* pictures herself as a prima ballerina! **2** *(se représenter)* to imagine, to picture; **imaginez-vous un petit chalet blotti dans la montagne** picture, if you will, a little chalet nestling in the mountains; **je me l'imaginais bien plus grand** I imagined him much taller; **comme vous pouvez vous l'i.** as you can (well) imagine; **s'i. que…** to imagine *or* to think that…; **si tu t'imagines que je vais démissionner, tu te trompes** if you think that I'm going to resign, you're mistaken; **tu t'imagines bien que je n'ai pas vraiment apprécié** as you can imagine, I wasn't too pleased; **il s'imagine tout savoir** he thinks he knows everything; **si je m'imaginais te rencontrer ici!** fancy meeting you here!

imago [imago] **NM** *Entom* imago

NF *Psy* imago

imam [imam] **NM** *Rel* imam

Imax [imaks] **NM** *Cin* IMAX

imbattable [ɛ̃batabl] **ADJ** unbeatable

imbécile [ɛ̃besil] **ADJ 1** *(niais)* stupid **2** *Vieilli Méd* imbecilic

NMF 1 *(niais)* idiot, fool; **ne fais pas l'i.** *(ne fais pas le pitre)* stop fooling about *or* around; *(ne simule pas)* stop acting stupid; *Fam* **le premier i. venu peut comprendre ça** any (old) fool can understand that; *Fam* **espèce d'i. heureux!** you stupid idiot! **2** *Vieilli Méd* imbecile

imbécilement [ɛ̃besilmɑ̃] **ADV** idiotically, stupidly

imbécillité [ɛ̃besilite] **NF 1** *(caractère)* stupidity, idiocy **2** *(parole)* nonsense *(UNCOUNT)*; *(acte)* stupid behaviour *(UNCOUNT)*; **n'écoute pas ces imbécillités!** don't listen to this nonsense!; **avec ses imbécillités il va finir par se faire prendre** his foolish behaviour is going to land him in trouble one of these days **3** *Vieilli Méd* imbecility

imberbe [ɛ̃bɛrb] **ADJ** beardless

imbibé, -e [ɛ̃bibe] **ADJ** *Fam* tanked up, *Br* sozzled, *Am* soused

imbiber [3] [ɛ̃bibe] **VT** to soak; **imbibez les biscuits de kirsch** soak the biscuits in kirsch; **la**

terre est imbibée d'eau the earth is completely waterlogged

VPR s'imbiber 1 *(s'imprégner)* to become soaked; **s'i. de** *(sujet: gâteau)* to become soaked with *or* in; *(sujet: terre)* to become saturated with **2** *Fam (boire)* to booze

imbitable, imbittable [ɛ̃bitabl] **ADJ** *très Fam Br* bloody *or Am* goddamn incomprehensible

imbrication [ɛ̃brikasjɔ̃] **NF 1** *(d'écailles, de pièces, de tuiles)* overlapping, *Spéc* imbrication **2** *(de considérations, d'hypothèses)* interweaving, overlapping; *(de questions)* overlapping, interlinking **3** *Ordinat* embedding; *(de commandes)* nesting

imbriqué, -e [ɛ̃brike] **ADJ 1** *(écailles, pièces, tuiles)* overlapping, *Spéc* imbricated **2** *(considérations, hypothèses)* interwoven, overlapping; *(questions)* overlapping, interlinked **3** *Ordinat* embedded; *(commandes)* nested

imbriquer [3] [ɛ̃brike] **VT 1** *(pièces)* to fit into *or* over each other; *(tuiles)* to overlap; **il faut i. les différents morceaux les uns dans les autres** the different pieces have to be fitted into each other **2** *Ordinat* to embed; *(commandes)* to nest

VPR s'imbriquer 1 *(pièces)* to fit into *or* over each other; *(tuiles, feuilles, écailles)* to overlap, *Spéc* to imbricate **2** *(être lié)* to be interlinked *or* closely linked; **le scénariste a fait s'i. les vies de tous les personnages** the screenwriter linked the lives of all his characters together

imbroglio [ɛ̃brɔljo] **NM** *(gén)* & *Théât* imbroglio

imbu, -e [ɛ̃by] **ADJ être i. de sa personne** *ou* **de soi-même** to be full of oneself, to be full of a sense of one's own importance; **être i. de préjugés** to be imbued with prejudices

imbuvable [ɛ̃byvabl] **ADJ 1** *(boisson)* undrinkable **2** *Fam (individu)* unbearable[□]; **je le trouve i., ce mec** I can't stand (the sight of) that guy

IMC [iɛmse] *Méd* **NM 1** *(abrév* **indice de masse corporelle)** BMI **2** *(abrév* **infirme moteur cérébral)** person suffering from cerebral palsy

NF *(abrév* **infirmité motrice cérébrale)** cerebral palsy

IME [iɛmə] **NM 1** *Écon (abrév* **Institut monétaire européen)** EMI **2** *(abrév* **Institut médico-éducatif)** special needs school

imitable [imitabl] **ADJ** imitable; **difficilement i.** hard to imitate

imitateur, -trice [imitatœr, -tris] **NM,F** imitator; *(de personnalités connues)* impersonator, mimic

ADJ *(moutonnier)* imitating, mimicking

imitatif, -ive [imitatif, -iv] **ADJ** imitative, mimicking

imitation [imitasjɔ̃] **NF 1** *(parodie)* imitation, impression; **elle fait d'excellentes imitations** she does excellent imitations, she's an excellent mimic

2 *Beaux-Arts* imitation, copy; *Littérature* imitation

3 *(matière artificielle)* imitation; **ce n'est pas du liège, c'est de l'i.** it's not genuine cork, it's only imitation; **des bijoux en i. or** imitation gold jewels

4 *(contrefaçon* ▸ *d'un produit)* imitation; *(*▸ *d'une signature, d'un billet)* forgery

• **à l'imitation de PRÉP** in imitation of

imitative [imitativ] *voir* **imitatif**

imitatrice [imitatris] *voir* **imitateur**

imiter [3] [imite] **VT 1** *(copier* ▸ *bruit, personne)* to imitate; *(*▸ *mouvements, façon de parler)* to imitate, to mimic; *(*▸ *produit)* to imitate; **Jacques imite très bien ses collègues** Jacques does good impressions of his colleagues; **i. la signature de qn** to imitate sb's signature; *(à des fins criminelles)* to forge sb's signature; **le peintre imite les couleurs de la nature** the painter reproduces the colours of nature **2** *(suivre l'exemple de)* to imitate, to copy; **si elle démissionne, d'autres l'imiteront** if she resigns, others will do the same *or* follow suit *or* do likewise **3** *(ressembler à)* to look like; **c'est une matière qui imite le liège** it's imitation cork; **un style imité du Berlin des années 30** a style modelled on Berlin in the thirties

immaculé, -e [imakyle] **ADJ** *(blanc, nappe, draps)* immaculate; *(réputation)* immaculate, unsullied, spotless; *Rel* **l'Immaculée Conception** the Immaculate Conception

immanence [imanɑ̃s] **NF** *Phil* immanence

immanent, -e [imanɑ̃, -ɑ̃t] **ADJ** *Phil* immanent

immangeable [ɛ̃mɑ̃ʒabl] **ADJ** uneatable, inedible

immanquable [ɛ̃mɑ̃kabl] **ADJ 1** *(inévitable)* inevitable **2** *(infaillible)* reliable, infallible

immanquablement [ɛ̃mɑ̃kabləmɑ̃] **ADV** without fail

immatérialité [imaterjalite] **NF** immateriality

immatériel, -elle [imaterjɛl] **ADJ 1** *Phil* immaterial **2** *Littéraire (léger)* ethereal **3** *Fin (actif, valeurs)* intangible

immatriculation [imatrikylasjɔ̃] **NF** registration; **numéro d'i.** *(d'une voiture) Br* registration number, *Am* license number; **numéro d'i. à la Sécurité sociale** *Br* ≃ National Insurance number, *Am* ≃ Social Security number

> **IMMATRICULATION**
>
> The last two numbers on French number plates refer to the "département" where the vehicle was registered. Vehicles from the Val-de-Marne, for example, bear the number 94.

immatriculer [3] [imatrikyle] **VT (faire) i. qch** to register sth; **car immatriculé 75** coach with the *Br* registration *or Am* license number ending in 75; **car immatriculé à Paris** coach with a Paris *Br* registration *or Am* license number; **elle n'est pas immatriculée à la Sécurité sociale** ≃ she has no *Br* National Insurance number *or Am* Social Security number

immature [imatyr] **ADJ** immature

immaturité [imatyrite] **NF 1** *(d'une personne, d'une attitude)* immaturity **2** *(d'un fruit)* unripeness

immédiat, -e [imedja, -at] **ADJ 1** *(avenir)* immediate; *(réponse)* immediate, instantaneous; *(effet)* immediate, direct; *(soulagement)* immediate, instant; **sa mort fut immédiate** he/she died instantly **2** *(voisins)* immediate, next-door *(avant n)*; *(environs)* immediate; **dans mon voisinage i.** in close proximity to *or* very near where I live; **supérieur i.** direct superior

• **dans l'immédiat ADV** for the time being, for the moment, for now

immédiatement [imedjatmɑ̃] **ADV 1** *(dans le temps)* immediately, at once, *Sout ou Hum* forthwith; **viens ici i.!** come here at once!; **la nouvelle disposition prend effet i.** the new measure comes into immediate effect *or* into effect immediately **2** *(dans l'espace)* directly, immediately; **tournez à gauche i. après le prochain feu** turn left immediately *or Br* straight after the next traffic lights

immédiateté [imedjatte] **NF 1** *(instantanéité)* immediacy, immediateness **2** *Phil* immediacy

immémorial, -e, -aux, -ales [imemɔrjal, -o] **ADJ** *Littéraire* age-old, immemorial; **de temps i.** from time immemorial

immense [imɑ̃s] **ADJ** *(forêt, bâtiment, plaine)* vast, huge; *(talent)* immense, towering; *(acteur, écrivain)* great, tremendous; *(soulagement, impact)* immense, great, tremendous; *(sacrifice, dévotion)* immense, boundless; *(succès)* huge, great

immensément [imɑ̃semɑ̃] **ADV** immensely, hugely; **ce cadeau me fait i. plaisir** this gift gives me tremendous *or* great pleasure, this gift pleases me greatly

immensité [imɑ̃site] **NF 1** *(d'un lieu)* immensity, vastness; *(de la mer)* immensity; *Littéraire* **dans l'i.** in infinity, in infinite space **2** *(d'une tâche, d'un problème)* enormity; *(d'un talent, d'un chagrin)* immensity

immergé, -e [imɛrʒe] **ADJ 1** *(au-dessous de l'eau)* submerged; **la majeure partie d'un iceberg est immergée** the bulk of an iceberg is underwater; **l'épave est immergée par 500 m de fond** the wreck is lying 500 m underwater *or* under 500 m of water; **plante immergée** aquatic plant **2** *Fig* **l'économie immergée** the underground economy

immerger [17] [imɛrʒe] **VT** *(oléoduc, bombes)* to lay under water, to submerge; *(produits radioactifs)* to dump *or* to deposit at sea; *(cadavre)* to bury at sea

VPR s'immerger *(sous-marin)* to dive, to submerge

immérité, -e [imerite] **ADJ** undeserved, unmerited

immersion [imɛrsjɔ̃] **NF** *(gén)* immersion; *(d'un sous-marin)* diving, submersion; *(d'un oléoduc, de bombes)* underwater laying, submersion; *(de déchets)* dumping at sea; *(d'un cadavre)* burying at sea

immettable [ɛ̃metabl] **ADJ** *(vêtement* ▸ *abîmé)* no longer fit to wear; *(*▸ *indécent)* unwearable

immeuble [imœbl] **ADJ** *Jur* immovable, real; **biens immeubles** immovables, real estate

NM 1 *Archit (gén)* building; **i. de bureaux** office building *or Br* block; **i. de grande hauteur** = very high building; **i. d'habitation** residential building, *Br* block of flats, *Am* apartment building; **i. à loyer moyen** = apartment building with low-rent accommodation (more expensive than an HLM); **i. à loyer normal** = apartment building with low-rent accommodation; **i. miroir** building glazed with reflective glass; **i. de rapport** investment property, rental property; **i. à usage locatif** *(résidentiel) Br* block of rented flats, *Am* rental apartment building **2** *Jur* real estate, landed property, *Am* realty; **placer son argent en immeubles** to invest in property

immigrant, -e [imigrɑ̃, -ɑ̃t] **ADJ** immigrant

NM,F immigrant

immigration [imigrasjɔ̃] **NF** immigration; **les populations issues de l'i.** immigrant populations; **les Français issus de l'i.** = French citizens from ethnic minorities

immigré, -e [imigre] **ADJ** immigrant; **travailleur i.** immigrant worker, guest worker

NM,F immigrant; **i. clandestin** illegal immigrant

immigrer [3] [imigre] **VI** to immigrate; **i. en France/aux États-Unis** to immigrate to France/to the (United) States

imminence [iminɑ̃s] **NF** imminence

imminent, -e [iminɑ̃, -ɑ̃t] **ADJ** imminent, impending; **c'est i.** it's imminent, it won't be long (now); **sa décision est imminente** he's/she's about to make a decision

immiscer [16] [imise] **s'immiscer VPR 1** *(intervenir)* to interfere; **s'i. dans une affaire** to interfere with *or* in a matter; **elle s'immisce toujours dans la conversation** she's always interrupting **2** *Jur* **s'i. dans une succession** to enter into *or* to assume a succession

immixtion [imiksjɔ̃] **NF 1** *Littéraire* interference, interfering **2** *Jur* assumption

immobile [imɔbil] **ADJ 1** *(mer, surface)* still, calm; *(nuit, air)* still; *(feuillage, animal, personne)* still, motionless; *(visage)* immobile; **gardez votre bras i.** keep your arm still **2** *Littéraire (temps)* immobile; *(institution, dogme)* unchanging, changeless

immobilier, -ère [imɔbilje, -ɛr] **ADJ** *Com* & *Jur Br* property *(avant n)*, *Am* real-estate *(avant n)*

NM *Com* **l'i.** the *Br* property *or Am* real-estate business; **l'i. de loisir** the holiday rentals business; **l'i. d'entreprise** the commercial *Br* property *or Am* real-estate business; **l'i. locatif** the *Br* property *or Am* real-estate rental business

immobilisation [imɔbilizasjɔ̃] **NF 1** *(arrêt* ▸ *d'un adversaire, de forces armées)* immobilization; **le manque à gagner dû à l'i. des machines** losses through downtime; **attendre l'i. complète du train** wait until the train comes to a complete stop *or* standstill

2 *Fin (de capital)* locking up, tying up, immobilization; *(d'actif, de valeurs)* freezing

3 *Jur* conversion *(of personalty into realty)*

4 *Sport* hold

5 *Méd* immobilization

• **immobilisations NFPL** fixed *or* capital assets; **faire de grosses immobilisations** to carry heavy stocks; **immobilisations capitaux** tied-up capital, capital assets; **immobilisations corporelles** tangible (fixed) assets; **immobilisations financières** long-term investments; **immobilisations incorporelles** intangible (fixed) assets; **immobilisations non financières** physical fixed assets

immobiliser [3] [imɔbilize] **VT 1** *(membre)* to strap up, to immobilize; *(adversaire, forces* *armées)* to immobilize; *(balancier)* to stop; *(circulation)* to bring to a standstill *or* to a halt; **les véhicules sont immobilisés à la sortie du tunnel** the vehicles have been brought to a standstill at the tunnel exit; *Méd* **être immobilisé** *(personne)* to be laid up **2** *Fin (capitaux)* to tie up, to immobilize; *(actifs, valeurs)* to freeze **3** *Jur* to convert *(personalty into realty)*

VPR s'immobiliser *(personne)* to stand still; *(véhicule)* to come to a halt, to pull up; **la libellule s'immobilisa sur la fleur** the dragonfly came to rest *or* settled on the flower

immobilisme [imɔbilism] **NM 1** *(gén)* opposition to change **2** *Pol* immobilism

immobiliste [imɔbilist] **ADJ** conservative, *Spéc* immobilist; **la politique i. du gouvernement** the government's conservative policies

NMF conservative, upholder of the status quo

immobilité [imɔbilite] **NF** *(d'un lac, d'une personne)* stillness, motionlessness; *(d'un regard)* immobility, steadiness; **je suis contraint à l'i. totale** I've been told not to move at all

immodération [imɔderasjɔ̃] **NF** immoderation

immodéré, -e [imɔdere] **ADJ** immoderate, inordinate

immodérément [imɔderemɑ̃] **ADV** immoderately, excessively

immodeste [imɔdɛst] **ADJ** *Littéraire* immodest

immodestie [imɔdɛsti] **NF** *Littéraire* immodesty

immolateur [imɔlatœr] **NM** *Littéraire* immolator

immolation [imɔlasjɔ̃] **NF** immolation

immoler **[3]** [imɔle] **VT 1** *Rel (sacrifier)* to immolate; **i. qn à** to sacrifice sb to **2** *Littéraire (exterminer)* to kill **3** *Fig Littéraire (renoncer à)* to sacrifice

VPR s'immoler *Littéraire* to sacrifice oneself; **s'i. par le feu** to set fire to oneself

immonde [imɔ̃d] **ADJ 1** *Rel (impur)* unclean, impure

2 *(sale)* foul, filthy, obnoxious

3 *(ignoble ▸ crime, pensées, propos)* sordid, vile, base; *(▸ individu)* vile, base, obnoxious

4 *(laid)* vile, hideous

immondice [imɔ̃dis] **NF** *Vieilli (chose sale ou impure)* unclean thing

• **immondices NFPL** refuse, *Br* rubbish, *Am* trash

immoral, -e, -aux, -ales [imɔral, -o] **ADJ** immoral

immoralement [imɔralmɑ̃] **ADV** immorally

immoralisme [imɔralism] **NM** immoralism

immoraliste [imɔralist] **ADJ** immoralist

NMF immoralist

immoralité [imɔralite] **NF** immorality

immortaliser **[3]** [imɔrtalize] **VT** to immortalize

VPR s'immortaliser to gain immortality, to win everlasting fame (**par** through *or* with)

immortalité [imɔrtalite] **NF** immortality; **son œuvre lui a assuré l'i.** his/her work won him/her everlasting fame *or* immortality; **entrer dans l'i.** to gain immortality, to win everlasting fame

immortel, -elle [imɔrtɛl] **ADJ** *(dieu)* immortal; *(bonheur, gloire)* immortal, everlasting, eternal

NM,F les Immortels = the members of the Académie française

• **immortelle NF** *Bot* everlasting (flower), immortelle

immotivé, -e [imɔtive] **ADJ** *(attaque, décision, demande)* unmotivated; *(peur, allégation)* groundless

immuabilité [imɥabilite] **NF** *Jur* immutability

immuable [imɥabl] **ADJ** *(vérité, amour)* immutable, unchanging; *(sourire)* unchanging, fixed; *(politesse)* eternal, unfailing; *(opinion)* unwavering, unchanging

immuablement [imɥabləmɑ̃] **ADV** eternally, perpetually, immutably

immun, -e [imœ̃, -yn] **ADJ** *Méd* immune

immunisant, -e [imynizɑ̃, -ɑ̃t] **ADJ** *Méd* immunizing

immunisation [imynizasjɔ̃] **NF** *Méd* immunization

immuniser **[3]** [imynize] **VT** *Méd* to immunize; *aussi Fig* **i. qn contre qch** to immunize sb against sth; **depuis le temps qu'elle me critique, je suis immunisé!** she's been criticizing me for so long, I'm immune to it now!; **son échec l'a immunisé contre l'aventurisme politique** his failure has cured him of political adventurism

immunitaire [imynitɛr] **ADJ** *Biol* immune; **réaction i.** immune reaction; **système i.** immune system

immunité [imynite] **NF 1** *Jur* immunity; **i. diplomatique** diplomatic immunity; **i. d'exécution** immunity from execution; **i. fiscale** immunity from taxation; **i. de juridiction** immunity from jurisdiction; **i. parlementaire** *Br* parliamentary privilege, *Am* congressional immunity; **i. souveraine** sovereign immunity **2** *Biol* immunity; **acquérir une i. (à)** to become immune (to) *or* immunized (against); **i. acquise** acquired immunity; **i. naturelle** natural immunity; **i. passive** passive immunity

immunodéficience [imynɔdefisjɑ̃s] **NF** *Méd* immunodeficiency

immunodéficitaire [imynɔdefisitɛr] **ADJ** *Méd* immunodeficient

immunodépresseur [imynɔdeprɛsœr] **NM** *Méd* immunodepressant, immunosuppressive

immunodépressif, -ive [imynɔdepresif,-iv] **ADJ** *Méd* immunodepressive, immunosuppressive

immunodéprimé, -e [imynɔdeprime] *Méd* **ADJ** immunodepressed

NM,F person with immunodepression

immunogène [imynɔʒɛn] **ADJ** *Biol & Med* immunogenic

immunoglobuline [imynɔglɔbylin] **NF** *Biol* immunoglobulin

immunologie [imynɔlɔʒi] **NF** immunology

immunologique [imynɔlɔʒik] **ADJ** immunological

immunologiste [imynɔlɔʒist] **NMF** immunologist

immunopathologie [imynɔpatɔlɔʒi] **NF** *Méd* immunopathology

immunosuppresseur [imynɔsyprɛsœr] **NM** *Méd* immunosuppressive

immunothérapie [imynɔterapi] **NF** immunotherapy

immunsérum [imynserɔm] **NM** *Méd* immune serum

immutabilité [imytabilite] **NF** *Jur* immutability

impact [ɛ̃pakt] **NM 1** *(choc ▸ de corps)* impact, collision; *(▸ de projectiles)* impact; **au moment de l'i.** on impact; **point d'i.** point of impact **2** *(influence, effet ▸ de mesures)* impact, effect; *(▸ d'une publicité, d'une campagne)* impact; *(▸ d'un mouvement, d'un artiste)* impact, influence; **les sondages ont-ils un grand i. sur le résultat des élections?** do opinion polls have a major impact on election results?; *Écol* **étude d'i. (sur l'environnement)** environmental impact assessment; **i. à long terme** long-term impact

impacter **[3]** [ɛ̃pakte] **VT** to impact on, to have an impact on

impair, -e [ɛ̃pɛr] **ADJ 1** *(chiffre)* odd, uneven; **les jours impairs** odd *or* odd-numbered days; **les années impaires** odd *or* odd-numbered years; **le côté i.** *(dans la rue)* the uneven numbers **2** *Littérature (vers)* irregular *(having an odd number of syllables)* **3** *Anat* single

NM 1 *(bévue)* blunder; **faire** *ou* **commettre un i.** to (make a) blunder **2** *(au jeu)* **l'i.** odd numbers; *(à la roulette)* impair

impala [impala] **NM** *Zool* impala

impalpable [ɛ̃palpabl] **ADJ** impalpable, intangible

impaludation [ɛ̃palydasjɔ̃] **NF** *Méd* malarial infection; **i. thérapeutique** malaria therapy

impaludé, -e [ɛ̃palyde] **ADJ** *(région)* malaria-infested, malarious

imparable [ɛ̃parabl] **ADJ 1** *(coup, ballon)* unstoppable **2** *(argument)* unanswerable; *(logique)* irrefutable

impardonnable [ɛ̃pardɔnabl] **ADJ** *(erreur, oubli)* unforgivable, inexcusable; **tu es i. d'avoir oublié son anniversaire** it's unforgivable of *or* inexcusable for you to have forgotten his/her birthday

imparfait, -e [ɛ̃parfɛ, -ɛt] **ADJ 1** *(incomplet)* imperfect, partial; **une connaissance imparfaite du problème** imperfect *or* insufficient knowledge of the problem; **guérison imparfaite** incomplete recovery **2** *(personne)* imperfect; **l'homme est une créature imparfaite** Man is an imperfect creature **3** *(inexact)* inaccurate; **une image imparfaite de la réalité** an inaccurate picture of reality

NM *Ling* **l'i.** the imperfect (tense); **l'i. du subjonctif** the imperfect subjunctive; **à l'i.** in the imperfect

imparfaitement [ɛ̃parfɛtmɑ̃] **ADV** imperfectly

impartial, -e, -aux, -ales [ɛ̃parsjal, -o] **ADJ** impartial, unprejudiced, unbiased

impartialement [ɛ̃parsjalmɑ̃] **ADV** impartially, without prejudice *or* bias

impartialité [ɛ̃parsjalite] **NF** impartiality, fairness; **juger avec i.** to judge impartially

impartir **[32]** [ɛ̃partir] **VT 1** *(temps)* **i. un délai à qn** to grant sb an extension; **le temps qui vous était imparti est écoulé** you have used up the time allotted to you **2** *Littéraire (don)* to bestow (**à** on); **en vertu des pouvoirs qui me sont impartis** by virtue of the powers (that are) vested in me **3** *Jur (droit, faveur)* to grant (**à** to)

impartition [ɛ̃partisjɔ̃] **NF** *Écon* subcontracting

impasse [ɛ̃pas] **NF 1** *(rue)* dead end, cul-de-sac; **i.** *(sur panneau)* no through road

2 *(situation)* impasse, blind alley; **nous sommes dans l'i.** we have reached an impasse *or* a stalemate; **il faut absolument faire sortir les négociations de l'i.** we must break the deadlock in the negotiations; *Fin* **i. budgétaire** budget deficit

3 *Fam Arg scol* **j'ai fait une i. sur la Seconde Guerre mondiale** I skipped (over) World War II in my revision

4 *Cartes* finesse; **faire une i.** to (make a) finesse; **j'ai fait l'i. au roi** I finessed against the king

impassibilité [ɛ̃pasibilite] **NF** impassiveness, impassivity, composure; **être d'une grande i.** to show great composure

impassible [ɛ̃pasibl] **ADJ** impassive, imperturbable

impassiblement [ɛ̃pasibləmɑ̃] **ADV** impassively, imperturbably

impatiemment [ɛ̃pasjamɑ̃] **ADV** impatiently; **nous attendons i. le résultat** we eagerly await the result

impatience [ɛ̃pasjɑ̃s] **NF** impatience; **avec i.** impatiently, with impatience; **sans i.** patiently; **donner des signes d'i.** to show signs of impatience

impatient, -e [ɛ̃pasjɑ̃, -ɑ̃t] **ADJ** *(personne, geste)* impatient; **d'un air i.** impatiently; **êtes-vous i. de rentrer?** are you anxious *or* eager to get home?

• **impatiente NF** *Bot* balsam, *Br* busy lizzie, *Spéc* impatiens

impatienter **[3]** [ɛ̃pasjɑ̃te] **VT** to annoy, to irritate; **son entêtement a fini par m'i.** his/her stubbornness made me lose my patience in the end

VPR s'impatienter *(dans une attente)* to grow *or* to become impatient; *(dans une discussion)* to lose (one's) patience; **j'ai fini par m'i.** I lost (my) patience in the end; **s'i. de qch** to get impatient with sth; **s'i. contre qn** to get impatient with sb

impavide [ɛ̃pavid] **ADJ** *Littéraire* impassive, unruffled, composed

impayable [ɛ̃pɛjabl] **ADJ** *Fam* priceless; **il est vraiment i.!** he's priceless *or* a scream!

impayé, -e [ɛ̃peje] **ADJ** *(facture)* unpaid; *(dette)* outstanding; *(comptes)* unsettled; *(effet)* dishonoured; **tous les effets impayés le 8 mai** all bills not settled by 8 May

NM *(somme)* outstanding payment

impeachment [impitʃmɛnt] **NM** impeachment

impec [ɛ̃pɛk] *Fam* **ADJ** *(très propre)* spotless; *(parfait)* perfect[□]

ADV perfectly[□]; **tout s'est passé i.** everything went off like a dream; **c'est du travail de pro, il a fait ça i.** it's a really professional job, his work was faultless[□]

impeccable [ɛ̃pekabl] **ADJ 1** *(propre et net ▸ intérieur, vêtement)* spotless, impeccable; *(▸ coiffure, ongles)* impeccable; **et que les escaliers soient**

impeccables! and I don't want to see a speck of dirt on the stairs! **2** *(parfait ▸ manières, travail)* impeccable, flawless, perfect; **il parle un espagnol i.** he speaks impeccable *or* perfect Spanish; **d'une propreté i.** impeccably clean; *Fam* **10 heures, ça te va? – oui, i.!** would 10 o'clock suit you? – yes, great *or* perfect!

impeccablement [ɛ̃pekabləmɑ̃] **ADV** impeccably; **elle parle i. russe** she speaks impeccable *or* perfect Russian

impécunieux, -euse [ɛ̃pekynjø, -øz] **ADJ** *Littéraire* impecunious, penurious

impédance [ɛ̃pedɑ̃s] **NF** *Phys* impedance; **i. acoustique** sound *or* acoustic impedance; **i. du vide** *ou* **de l'espace** (intrinsic) impedance in the vacuum

impedimenta [ɛ̃pedimɛ̃ta] **NMPL** *Mil & Littéraire* impedimenta

impénétrabilité [ɛ̃penetrabilite] **NF** *(d'une forêt, d'une citadelle, d'un texte, d'un mystère)* impenetrability; *(d'une personne, d'un air, d'un visage)* inscrutability

impénétrable [ɛ̃penetrabl] **ADJ** *(forêt, citadelle, texte, mystère)* impenetrable; *(personne, air, visage)* inscrutable

impénitence [ɛ̃penitɑ̃s] **NF** *Rel* impenitence, impenitent state

impénitent, -e [ɛ̃penitɑ̃, -ɑ̃t] **ADJ 1** *Rel* impenitent, unrepentant **2** *(buveur, fumeur)* inveterate

impensable [ɛ̃pɑ̃sabl] **ADJ** *(inconcevable)* unthinkable, inconceivable; *(incroyable)* unbelievable

impenses [ɛ̃pɑ̃s] **NFPL** *Jur* expenses

imper [ɛ̃pɛr] **NM** *Fam* raincoat◻, *Br* mac

impératif, -ive [ɛ̃peratif, -iv] **ADJ 1** *(qui s'impose ▸ mesure, intervention)* imperative, urgent, vital; *(▸ besoin, date)* imperative; **il est i. de...** it is imperative *or* essential to... **2** *(de commandement ▸ appel, geste, voix)* imperative, peremptory **3** *Ling* imperative

NM 1 *(souvent pl) (exigence)* requirement, necessity; **savoir nager est un i.** it is essential to be able to swim; **les impératifs de la mode** the dictates of fashion; **les impératifs du direct** the constraints of live broadcasting; *Phil* **l'i. catégorique** the (categorical) imperative **2** *Ling* **l'i.** the imperative (mood); **à l'i.** in the imperative

impérativement [ɛ̃perativmɑ̃] **ADV il faut que je termine i. pour ce soir** it's essential that I should finish tonight

impératrice [ɛ̃peratris] **NF** empress

imperceptibilité [ɛ̃pɛrseptibilite] **NF** imperceptibility

imperceptible [ɛ̃pɛrseptibl] **ADJ** imperceptible (**à** to); **de manière i.** imperceptibly; **elle eut un sourire i.** she gave a barely perceptible smile; **i. à l'œil nu** imperceptible to the naked eye

imperceptiblement [ɛ̃pɛrseptibləmɑ̃] **ADV** imperceptibly; **sourire i.** to give a barely perceptible smile

imperdable [ɛ̃pɛrdabl] **ADJ ce match est i.!** this is a match you can't lose!

NF *Suisse* safety pin

imperfectible [ɛ̃pɛrfɛktibl] **ADJ** non-perfectible

imperfectif, -ive [ɛ̃pɛrfɛktif, -iv] *Ling* **ADJ** imperfective

NM l'i. the imperfective; **à l'i.** in the imperfective

imperfection [ɛ̃pɛrfɛksjɔ̃] **NF 1** *(défaut ▸ d'un tissu, d'un cuir)* imperfection, defect; *(▸ d'une personne)* imperfection, shortcoming; *(▸ d'un style, d'une œuvre)* imperfection, weakness; *(▸ d'un système)* shortcoming; **toutes les petites imperfections de la peau** all the small blemishes on the skin **2** *(état)* imperfection

imperfective [ɛ̃pɛrfɛktiv] *voir* **imperfectif**

impérial, -e, -aux, -ales [ɛ̃perjal, -o] **ADJ 1** *Hist & Pol* imperial **2** *Fig (allure, manières)* imperial, majestic **3** *Com* imperial, of superior quality

• **impériale NF 1** *(étage)* top deck; **bus/rame à impériale** double-decker bus/train

2 *(dais)* crown; *(de lit)* (domed) tester

3 *Cartes* royal flush

4 *(barbe)* imperial

impérialement [ɛ̃perjalmɑ̃] **ADV** imperially, majestically

impérialisme [ɛ̃perjalism] **NM** imperialism

impérialiste [ɛ̃perjalist] **ADJ** imperialist

NMF imperialist

impérieuse [ɛperjøz] *voir* **impérieux**

impérieusement [ɛ̃perjøzmɑ̃] **ADV 1** *(de façon pressante)* urgently **2** *(autoritairement)* imperiously, peremptorily

impérieux, -euse [ɛ̃perjø, -øz] **ADJ 1** *(irrésistible ▸ désir)* urgent, compelling, pressing; **un besoin i.** a pressing need **2** *(de commandement ▸ appel, personne, voix)* imperious, peremptory; **d'un ton i.** in a commanding tone

impérissable [ɛ̃perisabl] **ADJ** *(vérité)* eternal, *Sout* imperishable; *(splendeur)* undying; *(gloire)* everlasting, eternal; *(souvenir)* enduring; **ce film ne me laissera pas un souvenir i.** that film's pretty forgettable

imperméabilisant, -e [ɛ̃pɛrmeabilizɑ̃, -ɑ̃t] **ADJ** waterproofing

NM waterproofing (substance)

imperméabilisation [ɛ̃pɛrmeabilizasjɔ̃] **NF** waterproofing

imperméabiliser [3] [ɛ̃pɛrmeabilize] **VT** to (make) waterproof *or* rainproof

imperméabilité [ɛ̃pɛrmeabilite] **NF 1** *(gén) & Géol* impermeability **2** *(incompréhension)* imperviousness (**à** to)

imperméable [ɛ̃pɛrmeabl] **ADJ 1** *Géol* impermeable **2** *(combinaison de plongée)* waterproof; *(enduit intérieur)* waterproof, *Spéc* water-resistant; *(vêtement, chaussure, enduit extérieur)* waterproof, rainproof **3** *(insensible)* **être i. à** to be impervious to

NM *(vêtement)* raincoat

impersonnalité [ɛ̃pɛrsɔnalite] **NF** impersonality

impersonnel, -elle [ɛ̃pɛrsɔnɛl] **ADJ 1** *(atmosphère, décor, ton)* impersonal, cold; **de manière impersonnelle** impersonally **2** *(approche, texte)* impersonal

impersonnellement [ɛ̃pɛrsɔnɛlmɑ̃] **ADV** impersonally

impertinence [ɛ̃pɛrtinɑ̃s] **NF 1** *(caractère)* impertinence, impudence, effrontery; **avec i.** impertinently; **quelle i.!** how impertinent *or* impudent! **2** *(parole)* impertinence, impertinent remark; **dire des impertinences à qn** to speak impertinently to sb **3** *(manque d'à-propos)* irrelevance, inappropriateness

impertinent, -e [ɛ̃pɛrtinɑ̃, -ɑ̃t] **ADJ 1** *(impudent)* impertinent, impudent **2** *(question, remarque)* irrelevant

NM,F impertinent person; **un petit i.** an impertinent little boy

imperturbabilité [ɛ̃pɛrtyrbabilite] **NF** imperturbability

imperturbable [ɛ̃pɛrtyrbabl] **ADJ** *(personne)* imperturbable; *(optimisme)* unshakeable; **il restait i.** he remained impassive *or* unruffled

imperturbablement [ɛ̃pɛrtyrbabləmɑ̃] **ADV** imperturbably

impétigo [ɛ̃petigo] **NM** *Méd* impetigo

impétueuse [ɛ̃petɥøz] *voir* **impétueux**

impétueusement [ɛ̃petɥøzmɑ̃] **ADV** *Littéraire* impetuously, impulsively

impétueux, -euse [ɛ̃petɥø, -øz] **ADJ 1** *(personne)* impetuous, impulsive; *(tempérament)* fiery, impetuous; *(amour)* impetuous **2** *Littéraire (flot, rythme)* impetuous, wild; *(torrent)* raging

impétuosité [ɛ̃petɥozite] **NF 1** *(d'une personne, d'un tempérament)* impetuousness, impetuosity, foolhardiness **2** *Littéraire (des flots, d'un rythme)* impetuosity, impetuousness

impie [ɛ̃pi] *Littéraire* **ADJ** impious; **des paroles impies** blasphemy

NMF impious *or* ungodly person

impiété [ɛ̃pjete] **NF** *Littéraire* **1** *(caractère)* impiety, ungodliness **2** *(parole, acte)* impiety

impitoyable [ɛ̃pitwajabl] **ADJ** *(juge, adversaire)* merciless, pitiless; *(haine, combat)* merciless, relentless

impitoyablement [ɛ̃pitwajabləmɑ̃] **ADV** mercilessly, ruthlessly, pitilessly

implacable [ɛ̃plakabl] **ADJ 1** *(acharné, inflexible)* implacable; **une haine i.** implacable hatred **2** *Littéraire (inéluctable)* relentless, implacable; **avec une logique i.** with relentless logic

implacablement [ɛ̃plakabləmɑ̃] **ADV** implacably, mercilessly, relentlessly

implant [ɛ̃plɑ̃] **NM** *Méd* implant; **i. dentaire** (dental) implant; **implants capillaires** hair graft; **il s'est fait faire des implants** he had a hair graft; **implants mammaires** breast implants

implantation [ɛ̃plɑ̃tasjɔ̃] **NF 1** *(établissement ▸ d'une entreprise)* establishment, setting up; *(▸ d'un parti politique)* establishment; *(▸ d'une mode, d'une coutume)* introduction; **l'i. d'une usine a permis la création de cent emplois** the setting up of a factory has led to the creation of one hundred jobs

2 *(d'un magasin, d'un rayon)* location

3 *(des cheveux)* hairline

4 *Méd* (lateral) implantation; *(en odontologie)* implant

implanter [3] [ɛ̃plɑ̃te] **VT 1** *(bâtiment, magasin, rayon)* to locate; *(entreprise)* to set up, to establish, to locate; *(idées)* to implant; *(coutumes, mode)* to introduce; *(parti politique)* to establish **2** *Méd* to implant **3** *Constr (tracer)* to stake out

VPR s'implanter *(entreprise, ville, rayon)* to be set up *or* located *or* established; *(peuple)* to settle; *(coutumes, mode)* to become established; **s'i. sur un marché** to establish oneself in a market

implémentation [ɛ̃plemɑ̃tasjɔ̃] **NF** *Ordinat* implementation

implémenter [ɛ̃plemɑ̃te] **VT** *Ordinat* to implement

implication [ɛ̃plikasjɔ̃] **NF 1** *(participation)* involvement, implication **2** *Phil & Math* implication

• **implications NFPL** implications, consequences

implicite [ɛ̃plisit] **ADJ 1** *(tacite)* implicit **2** *Ordinat (option, valeur)* default *(avant n)*

implicitement [ɛ̃plisitmɑ̃] **ADV 1** *(tacitement)* implicitly **2** *Ordinat* **toutes les variables prennent i. la valeur 0** all the variables have the default value 0

impliquer [3] [ɛ̃plike] **VT 1** *(compromettre)* to implicate, to involve; **i. qn dans qch** to implicate sb in sth; **elle ne se sent pas très impliquée dans son travail** she's not very involved in her work

2 *(supposer ▸ sujet: terme, phrase)* to imply

3 *(entraîner ▸ dépenses, remaniements)* to imply, to involve, to entail; **ce poste implique d'être souvent en déplacement** the job involves a lot of travelling

4 *Math* **p implique q** if p then q

VPR s'impliquer s'i. dans qch to get (oneself) involved in sth

implorant, -e [ɛ̃plɔrɑ̃, -ɑ̃t] **ADJ** *Littéraire (voix, regard, geste)* imploring, beseeching; **d'un ton i.** imploringly, beseechingly

imploration [ɛ̃plɔrasjɔ̃] **NF** *Littéraire* entreaty

implorer [3] [ɛ̃plɔre] **VT 1** *(solliciter)* to implore, to beseech; **i. le pardon de qn** to beg sb's forgiveness **2** *(supplier)* **i. qn de faire qch** to implore *or* to beg sb to do sth; **i. qn du regard** to give sb an imploring look

imploser [3] [ɛ̃ploze] **VI** to implode

implosion [ɛ̃plozjɔ̃] **NF** *Ling & Phys* implosion

impoli, -e [ɛ̃pɔli] **ADJ** impolite, rude; **être i. envers qn** to be impolite *or* rude to sb

NM,F impolite *or* ill-mannered person

impoliment [ɛ̃pɔlimɑ̃] **ADV** impolitely, rudely

impolitesse [ɛ̃pɔlitɛs] **NF 1** *(caractère)* impoliteness, rudeness; **avec i.** impolitely, rudely; **quelle i.!** how rude!; **il est d'une i.!** he's so rude! **2** *(acte, parole)* impolite thing; **commettre une i.** to do something rude *or* impolite; **dire des impolitesses** to be impolite *or* rude, to say impolite things

impolitique [ɛ̃pɔlitik] **ADJ** impolitic, unwise

impondérabilité [ɛ̃pɔ̃derabilite] **NF** imponderability

impondérable [ɛ̃pɔ̃derabl] **ADJ** imponderable
NM *(gén pl)* imponderable; **les impondérables** the imponderables

impopulaire [ɛ̃pɔpylɛr] **ADJ** *(mesure, dirigeant)* unpopular

impopularité [ɛ̃pɔpylarite] **NF** unpopularity

import [ɛ̃pɔr] **NM 1** *Com* importation **2** *Belg (montant)* amount; **une facture d'un i. de 300 euros** a bill for 300 euros **3** *Ordinat* **i. de données** data import

importable [ɛ̃pɔrtabl] **ADJ 1** *Écon* importable **2** *(habit)* unwearable

importance [ɛ̃pɔrtɑ̃s] **NF 1** *(qualitative ▸ d'une décision, d'un discours, d'une personne)* importance, significance; **de peu d'i.** of little importance, of no great significance; **avoir de l'i.** to be of importance, to matter; **tout ceci n'a plus d'i.** none of this matters any longer; **cela a beaucoup d'i. pour moi** it's very important to me, it matters a lot to me; **sans i.** *(personne)* unimportant, insignificant; *(fait)* of no importance, irrelevant; *(somme)* insignificant, trifling; **que disais-tu? – c'est sans i.** what were you saying? – it's of no importance *or* it doesn't matter; **accorder** *ou* **attacher trop d'i. à qch** to attach too much importance *or* significance to sth; **et alors, quelle i.?** so, what does it matter?; **se donner de l'i.** to act important **2** *(quantitative ▸ d'une somme, d'une agglomération)* size; *(▸ de dégâts, de pertes)* extent; **prendre de l'i.** *(entreprise)* to expand; *(mouvement)* to gain ground; **notre coopérative prend de plus en plus d'i.** our cooperative is expanding *or* is getting bigger and bigger; **une entreprise d'i. moyenne** a medium-sized business
• **d'importance ADJ** important **ADV** *Littéraire* soundly, thoroughly; **il s'est fait rosser d'i.** he was soundly thrashed

important, -e [ɛ̃pɔrtɑ̃, -ɑ̃t] **ADJ 1** *(qualitativement ▸ découverte, témoignage, rencontre, personnalité)* important; *(▸ date, changement)* important, significant; *(▸ conséquence)* important, serious, far-reaching; *(▸ position)* important, high; **peu i.** unimportant; **j'ai quelque chose de très i. à te dire** I've got something very important to tell you; **il est i. que tu viennes** it's important (that) you come; **ta carrière n'est-elle pas importante pour toi?** isn't your career important to you?; **c'est i. pour moi de connaître la vérité** finding out the truth matters *or* is important to me **2** *(quantitativement ▸ collection, effectif)* sizeable, large; *(▸ ville)* large, major; *(▸ augmentation, proportion)* substantial, significant, large; *(▸ somme)* substantial, considerable, sizeable; *(▸ retard)* considerable; *(▸ dégâts)* considerable, extensive; **peu i.** small **3** *(présomptueux)* **prendre** *ou* **se donner des airs importants** to act important, to give oneself airs
NM,F *(personne)* **faire l'i.** to act important
NM l'i., c'est de... the important thing is to..., the main thing is to...; **l'i., c'est que tu sois satisfait** the important *or* main thing is for you to be satisfied

> Il faut noter que l'adjectif anglais **important** ne signifie jamais **considérable** et ne se rapporte donc jamais à des proportions ou à une quantité.

importateur, -trice [ɛ̃pɔrtatœr, -tris] **ADJ** importing; **les pays importateurs de pétrole** oil-importing countries
NM,F importer

importation [ɛ̃pɔrtasjɔ̃] **NF 1** *Écon (action)* importing; *(produit)* import, importation; **produit d'i.** imported product, import; **droits/licence d'i.** import duties/licence; **i. en franchise** duty-free import **2** *(d'un mouvement, d'une invention)* introduction, importation; *(d'un animal)* importing
• **importations NFPL** *Com* imports; **nos importations dépassent nos exportations** we import more than we export; **importations invisibles** invisible imports; **importations parallèles** parallel imports; **importations visibles** visible imports

importatrice [ɛ̃pɔrtatris] *voir* **importateur**

importer [3] [ɛ̃pɔrte] **VT 1** *(marchandises, main-d'œuvre)* to import; *(animal, végétal)* to import, to introduce into the country; *(idée)* to import, to bring in; **musique importée des États-Unis** music imported from the United States **2** *Ordinat* to import (**depuis** from)
VI *(avoir de l'importance)* to matter (**à** to); **son âge importe peu** his/her age is of little importance *or* doesn't matter much; **ton opinion m'importe beaucoup** your opinion is very important *or* matters a lot to me; **peu importe** *(ce n'est pas grave)* it doesn't matter; *(ça m'est égal)* I don't mind; **peu importe le prix** the price isn't important *or* doesn't matter; **peu importe que le voile soit blanc ou écru** it doesn't matter much whether the veil is white or beige; **qu'importe!** what does it matter!; **qu'importe qu'il vienne ou non?** what does it matter whether he comes or not?; **ce qui importe avant tout c'est que tu sois heureuse** the most important thing *or* what matters most is your happiness; **peu m'importe!** it doesn't matter to me!
V IMPERSONNEL il importe de ne pas faire d'erreurs it's important not to make mistakes; **il importe qu'elle soit consciente de ses responsabilités** it's important that she should be aware of her responsibilities

import-export [ɛ̃pɔrɛkspɔr] *(pl* **imports-exports) NM** import-export; **il travaille dans l'i.** he works in the import-export business

importun, -e [ɛ̃pɔrtœ̃, -yn] **ADJ** *(personne, visiteur, question)* importunate; *(arrivée, remarque)* ill-timed; **je crains d'être i. en restant** I would not wish to outstay my welcome; **les insectes importuns l'agaçaient** the troublesome insects irritated him/her
NM,F pest, nuisance

importunément [ɛ̃pɔrtynemɑ̃] **ADV** *Littéraire* **1** *(fâcheusement)* irritatingly, importunately **2** *(mal à propos)* inopportunely

importuner [3] [ɛ̃pɔrtyne] **VT** *(sujet: musique, insecte)* to bother, to disturb, to annoy; *(sujet: personne ▸ ennuyer)* to importune, to bother; *(▸ déranger)* to disturb; **j'espère que je ne vous importune pas** I hope I'm not disturbing you; **de crainte de les i. avec mes problèmes** for fear of bothering them with my problems

importunité [ɛ̃pɔrtynite] **NF** *Littéraire (d'une question, d'une arrivée)* untimeliness, importunity

imposable [ɛ̃pozabl] **ADJ** *(revenu)* taxable; *(personne)* liable for tax; *(propriété)* rateable; **non i.** *(revenu, personne)* not liable for tax

imposant, -e [ɛ̃pozɑ̃, -ɑ̃t] **ADJ** imposing, impressive; **une imposante majorité** an impressive majority

imposé, -e [ɛ̃poze] **ADJ 1** *Sport voir* **figure 2** *Com voir* **prix 3** *(soumis à l'impôt)* taxed; **être lourdement i.** to be heavily taxed
NM,F *(contribuable)* taxpayer
• **imposée NF** *Sport (figure)* compulsory figure

imposer [3] [ɛ̃poze] **VT 1** *(fixer ▸ règlement, discipline)* to impose, to enforce; *(▸ méthode, délai, corvée)* to impose; **i. qch à qn** to force sth on sb; **i. le silence à qn** to impose silence on sb; **i. un effort à qn** to force sb to make an effort; **i. sa volonté/son point de vue** to impose one's will/one's ideas; **i. sa loi (à qn)** to lay down the law (to sb); **il a imposé son fils dans l'entreprise** he foisted his son on the company
2 *(provoquer)* **i. l'admiration/le respect** to command admiration/respect; **cette affaire impose la prudence/la discrétion** this matter requires prudence/discretion
3 *(rendre célèbre)* **i. son nom** *(personne)* to make oneself known; *(entreprise)* to become established
4 *Fin (personne, revenu)* to tax; *(propriété)* to levy a rate on; **i. qn/qch** to tax sb/sth; **imposé à 33 pour cent** taxed at 33 percent; **i. des droits sur qch** to impose *or* to put a tax on sth, to tax sth
5 *Typ* to impose
6 *(locutions)* **en i.** to be impressive; **elle en impose par son savoir-faire** her know-how is impressive; **en i. à qn** to impress sb; **s'en laisser i.** to let oneself be intimidated
VPR s'imposer 1 *(se faire accepter de force)* to impose oneself; **de peur de s'i.** for fear of being in the way *or* of imposing
2 *(se faire reconnaître)* to stand out; **elle s'impose actuellement comme la meilleure cycliste** she has established herself as today's top cyclist; **Bordeaux s'est imposé (par) 5 à 2** Bordeaux won 5–2; **s'i. dans un domaine** to make a name for oneself in a field; **elle s'est imposée par sa compétence** she made a name for herself through sheer ability; **la solution s'impose comme la seule viable** this stands out as the only viable solution
3 *(être inévitable)* to be necessary; **les modifications qui s'imposent** the adjustments that have to be made; **cette dernière remarque ne s'imposait pas** that last remark was unnecessary *or* uncalled for; **une coupe de champagne s'impose!** this calls for champagne!
4 s'i. qch *(se fixer)* to impose sth on oneself; **s'i. un effort/un sacrifice** to force oneself to make an effort/a sacrifice; **s'i. la discrétion** to make it a rule to be discreet; **s'i. un régime sévère** to follow a strict diet; **s'i. de faire qch** to make it a rule to do sth

imposition [ɛ̃pozisjɔ̃] **NF 1** *Fin (procédé)* taxation; *(impôt)* tax; **i. en cascade** cascade taxation; **i. des entreprises** business taxation; **i. forfaitaire** basic-rate taxation; **i. progressive** progressive taxation; **i. régressive** regressive taxation; **i. à la source** taxation at source **2** *Typ* imposition

impossibilité [ɛ̃pɔsibilite] **NF** impossibility; **se heurter à une i.** to come up against an insurmountable problem; **être** *ou* **se trouver dans l'i. de faire qch** to be unable to do sth; **je suis dans l'i. de me déplacer** I'm unable to travel, it's impossible for me to travel

impossible [ɛ̃pɔsibl] **ADJ 1** *(infaisable)* impossible; **i. à déchiffrer** impossible to decipher; **ton problème est i. à résoudre** there is no answer to your problem; **il est i. de...** it's impossible *or* not possible to...; **il est i. qu'il revienne avant lundi** he can't possibly be back before Monday; **il m'est i. de te répondre** it's impossible for me to give you an answer, I can't possibly answer you; **désolé, cela m'est i.** I'm sorry but I can't (possibly); **il n'est pas i. que je vienne aussi** I might (just) *or* there's a chance I might come too; **est-ce que tu vas venir? – ce n'est pas i.** are you going to come? – it's not impossible *or* I might; **i. n'est pas français** there's no such word as "can't" **2** *(insupportable ▸ personne)* impossible, unbearable; *(▸ situation)* impossible, intolerable; **vous lui rendez la vie i.** you're making life impossible for him/her, you're making his/her life a misery **3** *Fam (extravagant)* impossible, ridiculous, incredible; **il t'arrive toujours des trucs impossibles** the weirdest *or* wildest things are always happening to you; **à des heures impossibles** at the most ungodly hours
NM l'i. *(l'irréalisable)* the impossible; **tenter l'i.** to attempt the impossible; **ne me demande pas l'i.** don't ask me to do the impossible *or* to perform miracles; **nous ferons l'i.** we will do our utmost, we will move heaven and earth; *Prov* **à l'i. nul n'est tenu** = nobody is expected to do the impossible
• **par impossible ADV si par i.** if by any (remote) chance *or* by some miracle

imposte [ɛ̃pɔst] **NF 1** *Archit (pierre en saillie)* impost **2** *Menuis (d'une porte, d'une fenêtre) Br* fanlight, *Am* transom

imposteur [ɛ̃pɔstœr] **NM** impostor

imposture [ɛ̃pɔstyr] **NF** *Littéraire* fraud, (piece of) trickery, deception

impôt [ɛ̃po] **NM 1** *(prélèvement)* tax; **l'i.** taxation, taxes; **les impôts** *(sur le revenu)* income tax; **payer des impôts** to pay (income) tax; **payer 200 euros d'i.** to pay 200 euros in taxes *or* (in) tax; **c'est déductible des impôts** it's tax-deductible; *Fam* **écrire/aller aux impôts** *(à l'hôtel des impôts)* to write to/to go and see the tax people; **financé par l'i.** paid for out of taxes *or* with the taxpayers' money; **après/avant impôts** after/before tax; **i. sur les bénéfices** profit tax; **i. de Bourse** transaction tax; **i. sur le capital** capital tax; **i. sur le chiffre d'affaires** turnover *or Br* cascade tax; **i. à la consommation** output tax; **i. dégressif** sliding scale taxation, degressive taxation; **i. déguisé** hidden tax; **i. différé** deferred taxation; **i. direct** direct tax; **i. sur les dividendes** dividend tax; **i. sur les donations et les successions** gift and inheritance tax; **i. extraordinaire** emergency tax; **i. foncier** property tax; **i. forfaitaire** basic-rate tax; **i. sur la fortune** wealth tax; **i. sur les gains exception-**

nels windfall tax; *Anciennement* **i. sur les grandes fortunes** wealth tax; **i. indiciaire** wealth tax; **i. indirect** indirect tax; **impôts locaux** *Br* ≃ council tax, *Am* ≃ local property tax; **i. de luxe** tax on luxury goods; **i. sur la masse salariale** payroll tax; **i. négatif sur le revenu** negative income tax; **i. sur les plus-values** capital gains tax; **i. à la production** input tax; **i. progressif** progressive tax; *(sur le revenu)* graduated income tax; **i. proportionnel** proportional tax; **i. de quotité** coefficient tax; **i. retenu à la source** withholding tax; **i. sur le revenu** income tax; **i. sur le revenu des personnes physiques** income tax; **i. sur les sociétés** *Br* corporation tax, *Am* corporate income tax; **i. sur le transfert des capitaux** capital transfer tax; **i. sur le travail** payroll tax **2** *Fig Littéraire* **l'i. du sang** the duty to serve one's country

IMPÔTS LOCAUX

These are taxes levied to finance local, departmental or regional government. The best-known are the "taxe d'habitation" (paid by rent-paying tenants), the "taxe foncière" (paid by homeowners) and the "taxe professionnelle" (paid by the self-employed). The rate of each tax is decided at local level.

impotence [ɛ̃pɔtɑ̃s] **NF** loss of mobility *(through old age)*, infirmity

impotent, -e [ɛpɔtɑ̃, -ɑ̃t] **ADJ** *(personne)* infirm; *(membre)* withered

NM,F *(personne)* cripple

Il faut noter que l'adjectif anglais **impotent** est un faux ami. Il signifie **impuissant**.

impraticabilité [ɛ̃pratikabilite] **NF 1** *(d'un col)* impassability; *(d'un terrain de sport)* unplayable condition; *(d'une route)* impracticability **2** *Littéraire (d'une méthode, d'une idée)* impracticability

impraticable [ɛ̃pratikabl] **ADJ 1** *(col)* inaccessible, impassable; *(fleuve)* unnavigable; *(route)* impassable; *(terrain de sport)* unfit for play; **un chemin i. pour les voitures** a road unfit for cars **2** *Littéraire (méthode, idée)* unfeasible, unworkable, impracticable

imprécateur, -trice [ɛ̃prekatœr, -tris] **NM,F** *Littéraire* imprecator

imprécation [ɛ̃prekasjɔ̃] **NF** *Littéraire* imprecation, curse; **proférer des imprécations à l'encontre de qn** to call down curses upon sb's head, to inveigh against sb

imprécatoire [ɛ̃prekatwar] **ADJ** *Littéraire* imprecatory, damning

imprécatrice [ɛ̃prekatris] *voir* **imprécateur**

imprécis, -e [ɛ̃presi, -iz] **ADJ 1** *(témoignage, souvenir, contours)* vague, imprecise **2** *(appareil, instrument)* imprecise, inaccurate

imprécision [ɛ̃presizjɔ̃] **NF 1** *(d'un souvenir, d'un témoignage)* vagueness, imprecision; *(de contours)* lack of definition **2** *(d'un appareil, d'un instrument)* inaccuracy, lack of precision

imprégnation [ɛ̃preɲasjɔ̃] **NF 1** *(d'une matière)* impregnation, saturation; *(d'un esprit)* impregnation, inculcation, imbuing; **i. alcoolique** blood alcohol level **2** *Zool* imprinting

imprégner [18] [ɛ̃preɲe] **VT 1** *(imbiber)* to soak (**de** in), to impregnate (**de** with); **un coton imprégné d'alcool** a piece of *Br* cotton wool *or Am* absorbent cotton impregnated with alcohol; *Fig* **il est encore imprégné du souvenir de la guerre** his mind is still filled with memories of the war **2** *(être présent dans)* to permeate, to pervade, to fill; **cette odeur imprègne toute la maison** the smell permeates *or* pervades *or* fills the whole house; **l'odeur du tabac imprègne ses vêtements** his/her clothes reek of tobacco

VPR s'imprégner s'i. de *(éponge, bois)* to become soaked *or* impregnated with; *(air)* to become permeated *or* filled with; *(personne, esprit)* to become immersed in *or* imbued with; **ils se sont imprégnés de culture orientale** they immersed themselves in Eastern culture

imprenable [ɛ̃prənabl] **ADJ 1** *Mil (ville)* impregnable; *(position)* unassailable **2** *(vue)* unobstructed; **avec vue i. sur la baie** with an unobstructed view of the bay

impréparation [ɛ̃preparasjɔ̃] **NF** unpreparedness, lack of preparation

imprésario, impresario [ɛ̃presarjo] *(pl* **impresarii** [-rji]) **NM** impresario

imprescriptibilité [ɛ̃preskriptibilite] **NF** *Jur* imprescriptibility, indefeasibility

imprescriptible [ɛ̃preskriptibl] **ADJ 1** *Jur* imprescriptible, indefeasible **2** *(éternel)* eternal

impression [ɛ̃presjɔ̃] **NF 1** *(effet, réaction)* impression; **premières impressions** first impressions; **faire bonne/mauvaise i. (sur qn)** to make a good/a bad impression (on sb); **faire une forte** *ou* **grosse i.** to make a strong impression; **il ne m'a pas fait une grande i.** he did not make a great impression on me; **faire i.** to make an impression, to be impressive; **il me fait l'i. de savoir ce qu'il veut** he strikes me as someone who knows what he wants; **il donne l'i. de s'ennuyer** he seems to be bored

2 *(sensation)* feeling; **une i. de bien-être** an impression *or* a feeling of well-being; **ça fait une drôle d'i. de s'entendre parler** it's a funny feeling, hearing yourself speak; **cela m'a fait une drôle d'i.** it really had a funny effect on me; **avoir l'i. que** *(croire)* to have a feeling that; **j'ai l'i. qu'elle ne viendra plus** I have a feeling (that) she won't come; **j'ai l'i. qu'elle est assez timide** I have the impression that *or* my impression of her is that she's rather shy; *Fam* **j'ai comme l'i. qu'il mentait** I have a hunch he was lying; **j'ai l'i. de l'avoir déjà vue** I've a feeling that I've seen her before

3 *Vieilli (empreinte)* impression, mark; **l'i. d'un cachet dans la cire** the impression *or* imprint of a seal on wax

4 *(motif, dessin)* pattern; **tissu à impressions géométriques** cloth with a geometrical pattern *or* print

5 *Typ* printing; **envoyer un manuscrit à l'i.** to send a manuscript off to press *or* the printer's; **le livre est à l'i.** the book is with the printer's *or* in (the) press; **la troisième i. d'un livre** the third impression *or* printing of a book; **i. continue** web-offset printing; **i. couleur** colour printing; **i. en deux couleurs** two-tone printing; **i. polychrome** chromatic printing; **i. sans presse** plateless printing; **i. en quadrichromie** process colours *or* four-colour printing; **i. en relief** relief printing; **i. en retiration** backing up; **i. en surcharge** overprinting; **i. en taille-douce** intaglio printing; **i. tête à queue** work and tumble; **i. tremblée** slurring; **i. au verso** backing up

6 *Ordinat* printing; **i. en arrière-plan** background (mode) printing; **i. bidirectionnelle** bidirectional printing; **i. en colonnes** column printing; **i. à la demande** print on demand; **i. écran** screen dump; **i. numérique** digital printing; **i. ombrée** shadow printing **i. en qualité brouillon** draft quality printing

7 *Phot* exposure

impressionnabilité [ɛ̃presjɔnabilite] **NF 1** *Littéraire (émotivité)* impressionability **2** *Phot* (photo)sensitivity

impressionnable [ɛ̃presjɔnabl] **ADJ 1** *(émotif)* easily upset; **c'est quelqu'un de facilement i.** he's/she's very easily upset **2** *Phot* (photo)sensitive

Il faut noter que l'adjectif anglais **impressionable** est un faux ami. Il signifie **influençable**.

impressionnant, -e [ɛ̃presjɔnɑ̃, -ɑ̃t] **ADJ 1** *(imposant* ► *œuvre, personnalité)* impressive; *(*► *portail, temple)* awe-inspiring; *(*► *exploit)* impressive, stunning, sensational; *(*► *somme)* considerable **2** *(bouleversant)* disturbing, upsetting

impressionner [3] [ɛ̃presjɔne] **VT 1** *(frapper)* to impress; **être impressionné par qch** to be impressed by sth; **si tu crois que tu m'impressionnes!** don't think you impress me!; **se laisser i.** to let oneself be impressed **2** *(bouleverser)* to distress, to upset; **la vue du sang m'impressionne toujours** the sight of blood always upsets *or* distresses me **3** *Phot* to expose

impressionnisme [ɛ̃presjɔnism] **NM** impressionism

impressionniste [ɛ̃presjɔnist] **ADJ 1** *Beaux-Arts* impressionist **2** *(subjectif)* impressionistic

NMF impressionist

imprévisibilité [ɛ̃previzibilite] **NF** unpredictability

imprévisible [ɛ̃previzibl] **ADJ** *(temps, réaction, personne)* unpredictable; *(événement)* unforeseeable

imprévoyance [ɛ̃prevwajɑ̃s] **NF** *(gén)* lack of foresight; *(financière)* improvidence

imprévoyant, -e [ɛ̃prevwajɑ̃, -ɑ̃t] **ADJ** *(gén)* lacking (in) foresight; *(financièrement)* improvident

NM,F improvident person

imprévu, -e [ɛ̃prevy] **ADJ** *(inattendu)* unexpected, unforeseen; **des dépenses imprévues** unforeseen expenses; **un dénouement i.** an unexpected *or* a surprise ending; **de manière imprévue** unexpectedly

NM 1 l'i. *(les surprises)* the unexpected; **un séjour plein d'i.** a stay full of surprises **2** *(événement)* unexpected event; **sauf i.** *ou* **à moins d'un i., je serai à l'heure** unless anything unforeseen happens, I'll be on time; **prévenez-moi en cas d'i.** let me know if anything crops up; **les imprévus de la vie** life's little surprises **3** *(dépense)* unforeseen *or* hidden expense

imprimable [ɛ̃primabl] **ADJ** printable

imprimante [ɛ̃primɑ̃t] **NF** *Ordinat* printer; **i. à barre** bar printer; **i. à bulles (d'encre)** bubble-jet printer; **i. à chaîne** chain printer; **i. couleur** colour printer; **i. feuille à feuille** sheet-fed printer; **i. graphique** graphics printer; **i. à impact** impact printer; **i. à jet d'encre** ink-jet printer; **i. (à) laser** laser printer; **i. (ligne) par ligne** line printer; **i. à marguerite** daisy-wheel printer; **i. matricielle** dot matrix printer; **i. parallèle** parallel printer; **i. par points** dot matrix printer; **i. photo** photo printer; **i. PostScript®** Postscript® printer; **i. à roues** wheel printer; **i. série** serial printer; **i. thermique, i. thermoélectrique** thermal printer

imprimatur [ɛ̃primatyr] **NM INV** imprimatur

imprimé [ɛ̃prime] **NM 1** *(brochure, livre)* printed book *or* booklet; **imprimés** *(sur une enveloppe)* printed matter; **i. publicitaire** advertising leaflet, publicity handout **2** *(formulaire)* (printed) form **3** *(étoffe)* printed fabric *or* material; **un i. à fleurs/à motifs géométriques** a flower/geometric print

imprimer [3] [ɛ̃prime] **VT 1** *Typ (fabriquer)* to print (out); *(publier)* to print, to publish; **i. en offset** to offset

2 *Tex* to print

3 *Ordinat* to print (out); **i. un écran** to do a print screen

4 *(transmettre)* to transmit, to impart, to give; **i. un mouvement à qch** to impart *or* to transmit a movement to sth

5 *Littéraire (marquer)* to imprint; **des traces de pas imprimées dans la neige** footprints in the snow; **il voulait i. tous ces détails dans sa mémoire** he wanted to impress all these details on his memory

VPR s'imprimer to be printed; *Ordinat (document)* to print

imprimerie [ɛ̃primri] **NF 1** *(technique)* printing **2** *(établissement)* printing works *(singulier)*, printer's; *(atelier)* printing office *or* house; *Presse* print room; **le livre est parti à l'i.** the book's gone to the printer's; **i. intégrée** in-house printing office; **l'I. Nationale** = the French government stationery office, *Br* ≃ HMSO, *Am* ≃ the Government Printing Office

3 *(matériel)* printing press *or* machines; *(jouet)* printing set

4 *(industrie)* **l'i.** the printing industry

imprimeur [ɛ̃primœr] **NM** *(industriel)* printer; *(ouvrier)* printer, print worker

impro [ɛ̃pro] **NF** *Fam Mus & Théât (abrév* **improvisation)** improvisation[□], improv

improbabilité [ɛ̃prɔbabilite] **NF** unlikelihood, improbability

improbable [ɛ̃prɔbabl] **ADJ** unlikely, improbable; **dans le cas très i. où...** in the very unlikely event that...

improbité [ɛ̃prɔbite] **NF** *Littéraire* **1** *(manque de probité)* dishonesty, improbity **2** *(acte)* dishonest act

improductif, -ive [ɛ̃prɔdyktif, -iv] **ADJ** unproductive; *(capital)* unproductive, idle

NM,F unproductive person; **les improductifs** the nonproductive members of society

improductivité [ɛ̃prɔdyktivite] **NF** unproductiveness, nonproductiveness

impromptu, -e [ɛ̃prɔ̃pty] **ADJ** *(improvisé ▸ gén)* impromptu, unexpected, surprise *(avant n)*; *(▸ repas)* impromptu; *(▸ discours)* impromptu, off-the-cuff; **une visite impromptue** a surprise *or* an unexpected visit

ADV *(faire un discours)* off the cuff, impromptu; *(répondre)* off the cuff

NM *Littérature, Mus & Théât* impromptu

imprononçable [ɛ̃prɔnɔ̃sabl] **ADJ** unpronounceable

impropre [ɛ̃prɔpr] **ADJ 1** *(personne, produit)* unsuitable, unsuited, unfit; **il est i. à ce type de travail** he's unsuited to *or* unsuitable for this kind of work; **produits impropres à la consommation** products not fit *or* unfit for human consumption **2** *(terme)* inappropriate

improprement [ɛ̃prɔprəmɑ̃] **ADV** incorrectly, improperly

impropriété [ɛ̃prɔprijete] **NF 1** *(caractère)* incorrectness, *Sout* impropriety **2** *(terme)* mistake, *Sout* impropriety

improuvable [ɛ̃pruvabl] **ADJ** unprovable

improvisateur, -trice [ɛ̃prɔvizatœr, -tris] **ADJ** improvisational, improvising

NM,F improviser, improvisor; **avoir un talent d'i.** to have a talent for improvising

improvisation [ɛ̃prɔvizasjɔ̃] **NF 1** *(gén)* improvisation, improvising **2** *Mus & Théât* improvisation; *(d'un comique)* ad-libbing; **faire de l'i.** to improvise; *(comique)* to ad-lib

improvisatrice [ɛ̃prɔvizatris] *voir* **improvisateur**

improvisé, -e [ɛ̃prɔvize] **ADJ** *(discours)* improvised, *Sout* extempore; *(explication)* off-the-cuff, ad hoc; *(mesure, réforme)* hurried, makeshift, improvised; *(décision)* snap

improviser [3] [ɛ̃prɔvize] **VT** to improvise; **i. un repas** to improvise a meal, to throw a meal together; **i. un discours** to improvise a speech, to make an extempore speech; **i. une explication** to give an off-the-cuff explanation; **on l'a improvisé trésorier** they set him up as treasurer ad hoc

VI 1 *(parler spontanément)* to improvise; *(comique)* to ad-lib; **i. autour d'un** *ou* **sur un thème** to improvise on a theme **2** *Mus* to improvise; **i. au piano** to improvise on the piano

VPR s'improviser 1 *(s'inventer)* to be improvised; **un départ en vacances, ça ne s'improvise pas** going on holiday isn't something you can do just like that **2** *(devenir)* **s'i. journaliste/photographe** to act as a journalist/photographer; **on ne s'improvise pas peintre** you don't become a painter overnight *or* just like that

improviste [ɛ̃prɔvist] **à l'improviste ADV** unexpectedly, without warning; **arriver à l'i.** to turn up unexpectedly *or* without warning; **prendre qn à l'i.** to take *or* to catch sb unawares *or* by surprise

imprudemment [ɛ̃prydamɑ̃] **ADV** *(gén)* recklessly, carelessly, imprudently; *(conduire)* recklessly, carelessly

imprudence [ɛ̃prydɑ̃s] **NF 1** *(caractère)* imprudence, carelessness, foolhardiness; **i. au volant** careless driving **2** *(acte)* careless act *or* action; **commettre une i.** to do something stupid *or* thoughtless *or* careless; **il a commis l'i. d'en parler aux journalistes** he was stupid enough to talk to the press about it; **pas d'imprudences!** be careful!, don't do anything silly!

imprudent, -e [ɛ̃prydɑ̃, -ɑ̃t] **ADJ 1** *(conducteur)* careless; *(joueur)* reckless **2** *(acte, comportement)* unwise, imprudent; *(remarque)* foolish, careless, unwise; *(projet)* foolish, ill-considered; *(décision)* rash, unwise, ill-advised

NM,F *(personne)* careless *or* reckless person

impubère [ɛ̃pybɛr] **ADJ** prepubescent

NMF prepubescent; *Jur* minor

impubliable [ɛ̃pyblijabl] **ADJ** unpublishable, unprintable

impudemment [ɛ̃pydamɑ̃] **ADV** impudently, insolently, brazenly; **il ment i.** he's a brazen *or* shameless liar

impudence [ɛ̃pydɑ̃s] **NF 1** *(caractère)* impudence, insolence, brazenness; **il est d'une i.!** he is so impudent!; **il n'aura pas l'i. de revenir** he won't have the impudence *or* be impudent enough to come back **2** *(action)* impudent act; *(remarque)* impudent remark

impudent, -e [ɛ̃pydɑ̃, -ɑ̃t] **ADJ** impudent, insolent, brazen

NM,F impudent person

impudeur [ɛ̃pydœr] **NF 1** *(immodestie)* immodesty, shamelessness **2** *(impudence)* brazenness, shamelessness

impudicité [ɛ̃pydisite] **NF** *Littéraire* **1** *(immodestie)* immodesty, shamelessness, impudicity **2** *(caractère, acte, parole)* indecency

impudique [ɛ̃pydik] **ADJ 1** *(immodeste)* immodest, shameless **2** *(indécent)* shameless, indecent

impudiquement [ɛ̃pydikmɑ̃] **ADV 1** *(sans modestie)* immodestly, shamelessly **2** *(de façon indécente)* shamelessly, indecently

impuissance [ɛ̃pɥisɑ̃s] **NF 1** *(faiblesse)* powerlessness, helplessness; **un sentiment d'i.** a feeling of helplessness; **réduire qn à l'i.** to render sb helpless *or* powerless **2** *(incapacité)* inability, powerlessness; **i. à faire qch** inability to do sth **3** *Méd & Physiol* impotence

impuissant, -e [ɛ̃pɥisɑ̃, -ɑ̃t] **ADJ 1** *(inutile)* powerless, helpless; **on est i. devant un tel malheur!** one is powerless in the face of such a misfortune!; **être i. à faire qch** to be powerless to do sth; **des efforts impuissants** unsuccessful *or* ineffectual *or* futile efforts **2** *Méd & Physiol* impotent

NM *Méd & Physiol* impotent (man)

impulsif, -ive [ɛ̃pylsif, -iv] **ADJ** impulsive

NM,F impulsive person

impulsion [ɛ̃pylsjɔ̃] **NF 1** *Tech & Phys* impulse; *Électron* pulse, impulse; **radar à impulsions** pulse radar; *TV* **i. de synchro** sync pulse **2** *Fig (dynamisme)* impetus, impulse; **donner une i. au commerce** to give an impetus to *or* to boost trade; **sous l'i. des dirigeants syndicaux** spurred on by the union leaders **3** *(élan)* impulse; **céder à une i.** to give in to an impulse; **sous l'i. de la haine** spurred on *or* driven by hatred; **sur** *ou* **sous l'i. du moment** on the spur of the moment

impulsive [ɛ̃pylsiv] *voir* **impulsif**

impulsivité [ɛ̃pylsivite] **NF** impulsiveness

impunément [ɛ̃pynemɑ̃] **ADV** with impunity; **je vais vous prouver qu'on ne se moque pas i. de moi!** I'll show you that you can't laugh at me and get away with it!

impuni, -e [ɛ̃pyni] **ADJ** unpunished

impunité [ɛ̃pynite] **NF** impunity; **en toute i.** with impunity

impur, -e [ɛ̃pyr] **ADJ 1** *(pensée, sentiment)* impure, unclean; *(air, eau)* impure, foul; *(style)* impure; *(race)* mixed, mongrel; **les esprits impurs** the demons **2** *Rel (viande, personne)* unclean

impureté [ɛ̃pyrte] **NF 1** *(caractère)* impurity, foulness; **l'i. de l'air** the impurity of the air

2 *(élément)* impurity; **l'eau contient de nombreuses impuretés** the water contains numerous impurities

3 *Littéraire (impudicité)* lewdness

4 *Rel (souillure)* uncleanness

imputabilité [ɛ̃pytabilite] **NF** imputability

imputable [ɛ̃pytabl] **ADJ 1** *(attribuable)* **i. à** imputable *or* ascribable *or* attributable to **2** *Fin (crédit)* chargeable (**sur** to); *(débit)* to be debited (**sur** from)

imputation [ɛ̃pytasjɔ̃] **NF 1** *(accusation)* charge, *Sout* imputation **2** *Fin* charging (**à** to); **l'i. d'une somme au crédit/débit d'un compte** crediting an amount to/debiting an amount from an account; **imputations budgétaires** budget allocations; **i. des charges** cost allocation

imputer [3] [ɛ̃pyte] **VT 1** *(attribuer)* **i. un crime à qn** to impute a crime to sb; **i. ses échecs à la malchance** to put one's failures down to bad luck **2** *Fin* **i. des frais à un budget** to deduct expenses from a budget; **i. une somme à un budget** to allocate a sum to a budget; **i. des frais à un compte** to charge expenses to an account

imputrescibilité [ɛ̃pytresibilite] **NF** rot-resistance

imputrescible [ɛ̃pytresibl] **ADJ** rot-resistant, antirot

in [in] **ADJ INV** *Fam* in, hip, trendy; **l'endroit le plus in de Paris** the trendiest *or* hippest spot in Paris

NM *(au Festival d'Avignon)* **le in** the official festival; **au programme du in** on the official festival programme

INA [ina] **NM 1** *(abrév* **Institut national de l'audiovisuel)** = national television archive **2** *(abrév* **Institut national d'agronomie)** = "grande école" for agricultural studies

inabordable [inabɔrdabl] **ADJ 1** *(lieu)* inaccessible; **l'île est i. par mauvais temps** the island is inaccessible in bad weather **2** *(personne)* unapproachable, inaccessible; **sa fonction le rendait i.** his position made him inaccessible *or* unapproachable **3** *(prix)* prohibitive; *(produit, service)* prohibitively expensive

inabrogeable [inabrɔʒabl] **ADJ** *Jur* unrepealable

inaccentué, -e [inaksɑ̃tɥe] **ADJ** *(voyelle)* unstressed; *(syllabe)* unstressed, unaccentuated

inacceptable [inakseptabl] **ADJ** *(mesure, proposition)* unacceptable; *(propos, comportement)* unacceptable, intolerable, inadmissible

inaccessibilité [inaksesibilite] **NF** inaccessibility

inaccessible [inaksesibl] **ADJ 1** *(hors d'atteinte ▸ sommet)* inaccessible, out-of-reach, unreachable

2 *(irréalisable ▸ objectif, rêve)* unfeasible, unrealizable

3 *(inabordable ▸ personne)* unapproachable, inaccessible

4 *(obscur ▸ ouvrage)* inaccessible, opaque

5 *(indifférent)* **être i. à la pitié** to be incapable of feeling pity

inaccompli, -e [inakɔ̃pli] **ADJ 1** *(inachevé)* unaccomplished **2** *(non réalisé ▸ rêve, vœu)* unfulfilled

inaccoutumé, -e [inakutyme] **ADJ 1** *(inhabituel)* unusual, unaccustomed **2** *Littéraire (non habitué)* **i. à obéir** unused *or* unaccustomed to obeying

inachevé, -e [inaʃve] **ADJ** *(non terminé)* unfinished, uncompleted; *(incomplet)* incomplete

inachèvement [inaʃɛvmɑ̃] **NM** incompletion

inacquitté, -e [inakite] **ADJ** *Fin (effet)* unreceipted

inactif, -ive [inaktif, -iv] **ADJ 1** *(personne ▸ oisive)* inactive, idle; *(▸ sans travail)* non-working; **rester i.** to be idle

2 *(traitement, produit)* ineffective

3 *Bourse & Com (marché)* slack, slow, sluggish

4 *Fin (fonds)* unemployed, idle

5 *Géol* **volcan i.** dormant volcano

6 *Chim* inert

NM,F les inactifs the non-working population, those not in active employment

inaction [inaksjɔ̃] **NF** *(absence d'activité)* inaction; *(oisiveté)* idleness, lethargy; **je ne supporte pas l'i.** I can't bear being idle *or* having nothing to do; **sa maladie l'a réduit à l'i. pendant plusieurs mois** his illness put him out of action for several months

inactive [inaktiv] *voir* **inactif**

inactivité [inaktivite] **NF 1** *(oisiveté)* inactivity; **une période d'i.** a slack period; *Admin & Mil* **en i.** not in active service **2** *Bourse & Com (du marché)* slackness, slowness, sluggishness **3** *Chim* inertness

inadaptation [inadaptasjɔ̃] **NF** maladjustment; **i. à la vie scolaire** failure to adapt to school life; **l'i. du réseau routier aux besoins actuels** the inadequacy of the road system to cope with present-day traffic

inadapté, -e [inadapte] **ADJ 1** *(enfant)* with special needs; **enfants inadaptés au système scolaire** children who fail to adapt to the educational system; *Psy* **enfance inadaptée** children with special needs **2** *(outil, méthode)* **i. à** unsuited *or* not adapted to; **du matériel i. aux besoins actuels** equipment unsuited to *or* unsuitable for today's needs

NM,F *(adulte)* person with social difficulties, *Péj* social misfit; *(enfant)* child with special needs

inadéquat, -e [inadekwa, -at] ADJ *(insuffisant)* inadequate (**à** for); *(mal adapté)* unsuitable, inappropriate (**à** for)

inadéquation [inadekwasjɔ̃] NF *(insuffisance)* inadequacy; *(inadaptation)* unsuitability, inappropriateness; **étant donné l'i. des moyens au problème** given the unsuitability of the means used to deal with the problem; **il y a i. entre développement économique et progrès social** there is a contradiction between economic development and social progress

inadmissibilité [inadmisibilite] NF inadmissibility

inadmissible [inadmisibl] ADJ *(intolérable ▸ attitude, erreur)* inadmissible, intolerable, unacceptable; *(irrecevable ▸ demande, proposition)* unacceptable

inadvertance [inadvɛrtɑ̃s] NF *Littéraire* oversight, inadvertence

• **par inadvertance** ADV inadvertently, by mistake

inaliénabilité [inaljenabilite] NF *Jur* inalienability

inaliénable [inaljenabl] ADJ *Jur* inalienable

inalliable [inaljabl] ADJ *Métal* that cannot be alloyed, non-alloyable

inaltérabilité [inalterabilite] NF **1** *(à la lumière)* fade-resistance; *(au lavage)* fastness; *(d'une couleur)* permanence **2** *Métal* stability

inaltérable [inalterabl] ADJ **1** *(couleur)* permanent, fast; *(peinture)* non-fade; **i. à l'air** air-resistant **2** *Métal* stable **3** *(amitié, espoir)* unfailing, steadfast; *(haine)* eternal; *(bonne humeur, courage)* unfailing; *(calme)* unwavering

inaltéré, -e [inaltere] ADJ **1** *(bois, pierre)* unweathered **2** *(sentiment)* unchanged

inamical, -e, -aux, -ales [inamikal, -o] ADJ unfriendly, inimical

inamovibilité [inamɔvibilite] NF *Admin (d'une personne)* irremovability, security of tenure *or* office

inamovible [inamɔvibl] ADJ **1** *Admin (fonctionnaire)* permanent, irremovable; *Hum* **il est i.** he's a permanent fixture **2** *(fixé)* fixed

inanimé, -e [inanime] ADJ **1** *(mort)* lifeless; *(évanoui)* unconscious; **tomber i.** to faint; *Littéraire* **style i.** lifeless *or* flat style **2** *Ling* inanimate; **objets inanimés** inanimate objects

inanité [inanite] NF *Littéraire (manque d'intérêt ▸ d'une conversation)* inanity; *(inutilité)* futility, pointlessness; **des conversations d'une i. terrifiante** incredibly inane conversations

inanition [inanisjɔ̃] NF *(faim)* starvation; *(épuisement)* total exhaustion; **tomber/mourir d'i.** to faint with/to die of hunger; *Fig Hum* to be starving

inapaisable [inapezabl] ADJ *Littéraire (soif)* unquenchable; *(faim)* voracious, insatiable; *(chagrin, souffrance)* unappeasable

inapaisé, -e [inapeze] ADJ *Littéraire (soif)* unquenched; *(faim)* unsatiated; *(chagrin, souffrance)* unappeased

inaperçu, -e [inapɛrsy] ADJ unnoticed; **passer i.** to go unnoticed

inappétence [inapetɑ̃s] NF **1** *Méd (perte d'appétit)* loss of appetite, *Spéc* inappetence **2** *Littéraire (perte du désir)* diminishing desire

inapplicable [inaplikabl] ADJ inapplicable, not applicable; *(loi, décret)* unenforceable

inapplication [inaplikasjɔ̃] NF **1** *(d'une loi, d'un décret)* non-enforcement **2** *(d'une personne)* lack of application *or* concentration

inappliqué, -e [inaplike] ADJ **1** *(loi, décret)* not enforced **2** *(personne)* lacking in application

inappréciable [inapresjabl] ADJ **1** *(précieux)* invaluable, priceless **2** *(difficile à évaluer)* inappreciable, imperceptible

inapprécié, -e [inapresje] ADJ unappreciated, not appreciated

inapprivoisable [inaprivwazabl] ADJ untameable

inapproprié, -e [inaprɔprije] ADJ inappropriate; **i. à qch** inappropriate to *or* unsuitable for sth

inapte [inapt] ADJ **1** *(incapable ▸ intellectuellement)* unsuitable; *(▸ pour raisons médicales)* unfit; **être i. à qch** to be unsuitable/unfit for sth; **être i. à faire qch** to be unfit to do sth; **il est i. à occuper ce poste** he's ill-suited to the job **2** *Mil* **i. (au service militaire)** unfit (for military service)

NMF *Mil* army reject

inaptitude [inaptityd] NF **1** *(incapacité ▸ physique)* incapacity, unfitness; *(▸ intellectuelle)* (mental) inaptitude; **i. à qch** unfitness for sth; **i. à faire qch** unfitness for doing *or* to do sth **2** *Mil* unfitness (for military service)

inarticulé, -e [inartikyle] ADJ inarticulate

inassimilable [inasimilabl] ADJ *(substance)* indigestible, *Spéc* unassimilable; *(connaissances)* impossible to take in; *(population)* which cannot become integrated

inassouvi, -e [inasuvi] ADJ **1** *(soif)* unquenched; *(faim)* unappeased, unsatiated **2** *(passion)* unappeased, unsatiated; *(désir)* unfulfilled; *(vengeance)* unsatisfied, unassuaged

inattaquable [inatakabl] ADJ *(personne)* beyond reproach *or* criticism; *(conduite)* unimpeachable, irreproachable; *(argument, preuve)* unassailable, irrefutable, unquestionable; *(forteresse, lieu)* impregnable

inatteignable [inateɲabl] ADJ unreachable

inattendu, -e [inatɑ̃dy] ADJ *(personne)* unexpected; *(réflexion, événement)* unexpected, unforeseen; **c'est assez i. de votre part** I didn't quite expect this from you

inattentif, -ive [inatɑ̃tif, -iv] ADJ inattentive; **vous êtes trop i. (à)** you don't pay enough attention (to)

inattention [inatɑ̃sjɔ̃] NF lack of attention *or* concentration, inattentiveness; **un moment** *ou* **une minute d'i.** a momentary lapse of concentration; **faute** *ou* **erreur d'i.** careless mistake

inattentive [inatɑ̃tiv] *voir* **inattentif**

inaudible [inodibl] ADJ **1** *(imperceptible)* inaudible **2** *(insupportable)* unbearable

inaugural, -e, -aux, -ales [inogyral, -o] ADJ *(discours, cérémonie)* opening *(avant n)*, inaugural; *(voyage)* maiden *(avant n)*

inauguration [inogyrasjɔ̃] NF **1** *(d'une route, d'une exposition)* inauguration; *(d'une statue, d'un monument)* unveiling **2** *(commencement)* beginning, inauguration, initiation

inaugurer [3] [inogyre] VT **1** *(route, exposition)* to inaugurate; *(statue, monument)* to unveil; *Fig (système, méthode)* to initiate, to launch **2** *(marquer le début de)* to usher in; **le changement de gouvernement inaugurait une ère de liberté** the change of government ushered in an era of freedom

inauthenticité [inotɑ̃tisite] NF inauthenticity

inauthentique [inotɑ̃tik] ADJ inauthentic

inavouable [inavwabl] ADJ unmentionable, shameful

inavoué, -e [inavwe] ADJ secret, unconfessed

INC [iɛnse] NM *(abrév* **Institut national de la consommation**) = national institute for consumer advice, *Br* ≃ National Consumer Council

inca [ɛ̃ka] ADJ Inca

• **Inca** NMF Inca; **les Incas** the Inca, the Incas

• **Inca** NM *(souverain)* Inca

incalculable [ɛ̃kalkylabl] ADJ **1** *(considérable)* incalculable, countless; **des fortunes incalculables** incalculable *or* untold wealth; **un nombre i. de fois/d'erreurs** countless times/mistakes **2** *(imprévisible)* incalculable; **des conséquences incalculables** incalculable *or* far-reaching consequences

incandescence [ɛ̃kɑ̃desɑ̃s] NF incandescence; **être en i.** to be incandescent; **porté à i.** heated until glowing, incandescent

incandescent, -e [ɛ̃kɑ̃desɑ̃, -ɑ̃t] ADJ incandescent; *Fig (imagination)* ardent

incantation [ɛ̃kɑ̃tasjɔ̃] NF incantation

incantatoire [ɛ̃kɑ̃tatwar] ADJ incantatory; **formule i., paroles incantatoires** incantation

incapable [ɛ̃kapabl] ADJ **1** *(par incompétence)* incapable, incompetent, inefficient; **être i. de faire qch** to be incapable of doing sth; **elle était i. de répondre** she was unable to answer, she couldn't answer; **je serais bien i. de le dire** I really wouldn't know, I really couldn't tell you **2** *(par nature)* **être i. de qch** to be incapable of sth; **il est i. d'un effort** he's incapable of making an effort; **elle est i. d'amour** she's incapable of loving *or* love; **elle est i. de méchanceté** there's no malice in her; **être i. de faire** to be incapable of doing; **elle est i. de tricher** she's incapable of cheating **3** *Jur* incompetent

NMF **1** *(incompétent)* incompetent; **ce sont des incapables** they're all incapable *or* incompetent **2** *Jur* person who is legally incompetent

incapacité [ɛ̃kapasite] NF **1** *(impossibilité)* incapacity, inability; **être dans l'i. de faire qch** to be unable to do sth; **son i. à se décider** his/her incapacity *or* inability to make up his/her mind

2 *(incompétence)* incapacity, incompetence, inefficiency

3 *Méd* disablement, disability; **i. permanente** permanent disablement *or* disability

4 *Jur* (legal) incapacity; **i. de travail** industrial disablement; **i. temporaire de travail** temporary disability; **i. électorale** legal incapacity to vote

incarcération [ɛ̃karserasjɔ̃] NF imprisonment, jailing, *Sout* incarceration; **i. provisoire** remand

incarcérer [18] [ɛ̃karsere] VT to imprison, to jail; **il est incarcéré à la prison des Baumettes** he is (being held) in Baumettes prison

incarnat, -e [ɛ̃karna, -at] ADJ incarnadine

NM incarnadine; *(du teint)* rosiness

incarnation [ɛ̃karnasjɔ̃] NF **1** *Myth & Rel* incarnation **2** *(manifestation)* embodiment; **elle est l'i. de la bonté** she's the embodiment *or* personification of goodness

incarné, -e [ɛ̃karne] ADJ **1** *(personnifié)* incarnate, personified; **le diable i.** the devil incarnate **2** *Méd (ongle)* ingrowing, ingrown

incarner [3] [ɛ̃karne] VT **1** *(symboliser)* to embody, to personify **2** *(interpréter ▸ personnage)* to play

VPR **s'incarner 1** *Rel* to become incarnate **2** *(se matérialiser)* to be embodied; **en toi s'incarne la beauté idéale** you are the embodiment of ideal beauty **3** *Méd* **un ongle qui s'incarne** an ingrowing toenail

incartade [ɛ̃kartad] NF **1** *(écart de conduite)* misdemeanour, escapade; **à la moindre i., vous serez puni** put one foot wrong and you'll be punished **2** *(d'un cheval)* swerve

incassable [ɛ̃kasabl] ADJ unbreakable

incendiaire [ɛ̃sɑ̃djɛr] ADJ **1** *(balle, bombe)* incendiary **2** *(propos)* incendiary, inflammatory

NMF arsonist, *Br* fire-raiser

incendie [ɛ̃sɑ̃di] NM **1** *(feu)* fire; **maîtriser un i.** to bring a fire *or* blaze under control; **i. criminel** (act of deliberate) arson; **i. de forêt** forest fire; **i. volontaire** arson **2** *Littéraire (lumière)* blaze, glow **3** *Fig (violence)* fire; **l'i. de la révolte** the frenzy of revolt

incendié, -e [ɛ̃sɑ̃dje] ADJ **1** *(ville, maison)* burnt (down), destroyed by fire; **les familles incendiées seront dédommagées** the families affected by the fire will be given compensation; **les bâtiments incendiés** the buildings gutted by fire **2** *Littéraire (éclairé)* ablaze, aglow

NM,F fire victim

incendier [9] [ɛ̃sɑ̃dje] VT **1** *(mettre le feu à)* to set fire to, to set on fire; **la forêt a été incendiée** the forest was set on fire

2 *Fam (invectiver)* **i. qn** to give sb hell; **tu vas te faire i.!** you'll be in for it!

3 *Fig (brûler)* to burn; **une vodka qui incendie la gorge** a vodka that burns one's throat

4 *(esprit, imagination)* to stir; **des discours destinés à i. les esprits** inflammatory speeches

5 *Littéraire (illuminer)* to light up; **le soleil couchant incendiait les champs** the setting sun gave the fields a fiery glow

incertain, -e [ɛ̃sɛrtɛ̃, -ɛn] ADJ **1** *(peu sûr ▸ personne)* uncertain, unsure; **être i. de qch** to be uncertain *or* unsure of sth

2 *(indéterminé ▸ durée, date, quantité)* uncertain, undetermined; *(▸ résultat, fait)* uncertain, doubtful

3 *(aléatoire ▸ gén)* uncertain; *(▸ temps)* unsettled

4 *(vague ▸ contour)* indistinct, vague, blurred; *(▸ couleur)* indeterminate
5 *(mal équilibré ▸ démarche, appui)* unsteady, uncertain, hesitant; **il avançait vers sa mère d'un pas i.** he walked unsteadily *or* tottered towards his mother
NM *Bourse & Fin* variable exchange; **coter l'i.** to quote on the exchange rate

incertitude [ɛ̃sɛrtityd] **NF 1** *(doute, précarité)* uncertainty; **nous sommes dans l'i.** we're uncertain, we're not sure; **vivre dans l'i.** to live in a state of uncertainty; **il est seul face à ses incertitudes** he's left alone with his doubts; **il reste encore bien des incertitudes dans cette affaire** there are still a great many uncertainties *or* unresolved questions in the matter **2** *Math & Phys* uncertainty

incessamment [ɛ̃sesamɑ̃] **ADV 1** *(bientôt)* very soon; **il doit arriver i.** he'll be here any minute now; *Hum* **i. sous peu** very soon **2** *Arch (sans cesse)* unceasingly, incessantly

> Il faut noter que l'adverbe anglais **incessantly** est un faux ami. Il signifie uniquement **sans cesse**.

incessant, -e [ɛ̃sesɑ̃, -ɑ̃t] **ADJ** *(effort)* ceaseless, continual; *(bruit, bavardage)* incessant, ceaseless, continual; *(douleur, pluie)* unremitting, constant

incessibilité [ɛ̃sesibilite] **NF** *Jur (d'un privilège)* non-transferability; *(d'un droit)* inalienability, indefeasibility

incessible [ɛ̃sesibl] **ADJ** *Jur (privilège)* non-transferable; *(droit)* inalienable, indefeasible

inceste [ɛ̃sɛst] **NM** incest

incestueux, -euse [ɛ̃sɛstɥø, -øz] **ADJ 1** *(personne, relation)* incestuous **2** *(né d'un inceste)* **enfant i.** child born of an incestuous relationship

inchangé, -e [ɛ̃ʃɑ̃ʒe] **ADJ** unchanged, unaltered

inchangeable [ɛ̃ʃɑ̃ʒabl] **ADJ** unchangeable

inchantable [ɛ̃ʃɑ̃tabl] **ADJ** unsingable

inchauffable [ɛ̃ʃofabl] **ADJ** impossible to heat

inchavirable [ɛ̃ʃavirabl] **ADJ** non-capsizing, self-righting

inchoatif, -ive [ɛ̃kɔatif, -iv] *Ling* **ADJ** inchoative, ingressive
NM inchoative, ingressive

incidemment [ɛ̃sidamɑ̃] **ADV** *(accessoirement)* incidentally, in passing; *(par hasard)* by chance; **il a été i. question du problème des retards** the problem of lateness came up in passing *or* incidentally

> Il faut noter que l'adverbe anglais **incidentally** signifie le plus souvent **à propos** ou **soit dit en passant**.

incidence [ɛ̃sidɑ̃s] **NF 1** *(répercussion)* effect, repercussion, impact; **avoir une i. sur** to affect **2** *Méd (d'une maladie)* incidence **3** *Aviat & Phys* incidence

incident[1] [ɛ̃sidɑ̃] **NM 1** *(événement)* incident, event; *(accrochage)* incident; **sans i.** without a hitch, without incident, smoothly; **i. diplomatique/de frontière** diplomatic/border incident; **i. technique** technical hitch *or* incident; **avoir un i. de parcours** to come across a hitch (on the way); **sa démission n'est qu'un i. de parcours** his/her resignation is only a minor incident; **l'i. est clos** the matter is (now) closed **2** *Jur* **i. (de procédure)** objection (on a point of law); **soulever un i.** to raise an objection

incident[2]**, -e** [ɛ̃sidɑ̃, -ɑ̃t] **ADJ 1** *(accessoire ▸ remarque)* incidental **2** *Phys* incident **3** *Jur* incidental; **demande incidente** accessory claim

incinérateur [ɛ̃sineratœr] **NM** incinerator

incinération [ɛ̃sinerasjɔ̃] **NF** *(de linge, de papiers)* incineration; *(de cadavres)* cremation

incinérer [18] [ɛ̃sinere] **VT** *(linge, papiers)* to incinerate; *(cadavres)* to cremate

incise [ɛ̃siz] **NF 1** *Ling* interpolated clause **2** *Mus* phrase

inciser [3] [ɛ̃size] **VT 1** *Méd* to incise, to make an incision in; *(furoncle, abcès)* to lance **2** *Bot & Hort* to incise, to cut (a notch into); *(pour extraire la résine)* to tap

incisif, -ive[1] [ɛ̃sizif, -iv] **ADJ** *(ironie, remarque, ton)* cutting, biting; *(personne, style)* incisive; *(regard)* piercing

incision [ɛ̃sizjɔ̃] **NF 1** *Méd (action, coupure ▸ de gencive)* incision; *(▸ d'un furoncle, d'un abcès)* lancing **2** *Bot & Hort* incision; *(pour extraire la résine)* tapping

incisive[2] [ɛ̃siziv] **ADJ** *voir* **incisif**
NF incisor

incitation [ɛ̃sitasjɔ̃] **NF 1** *(encouragement)* incitement, encouragement; **c'est une i. à la violence** it's incitement to *or* it encourages violence; **i. au crime** abetting, abetment; *Jur* **i. à la haine raciale** incitement to racial hatred; *Jur* **i. de mineurs à la débauche** corruption of minors **2** *Mktg* incentive; **i. à l'achat** buying incentive; **i. à la vente** sales incentive; *Fin* **i. fiscale** tax incentive

inciter [3] [ɛ̃site] **VT 1** *(encourager)* **i. qn à faire qch** to prompt *or* to encourage sb to do sth; **son succès l'incita à continuer** his/her success encouraged *or* prompted him/her to continue; **cela m'incite à penser qu'une réforme est nécessaire** that leads me to think that a reform is needed; **cela incite à la réflexion/prudence** it makes you stop and think/makes you cautious **2** *Jur* to incite

incivil, -e [ɛ̃sivil] **ADJ** discourteous

incivilisable [ɛ̃sivilizabl] **ADJ** which cannot be civilized

incivilité [ɛ̃sivilite] **NF 1** *(manque de courtoisie)* discourteousness **2** *(acte, comportement)* discourtesy

incivique [ɛ̃sivik] **ADJ** *Vieilli* lacking in civic *or* public spirit, lacking in public-mindedness; **il tient des propos inciviques** what he says isn't very public-spirited

inclassable [ɛ̃klasabl] **ADJ** unclassifiable; **un film/peintre i.** a film that/painter who cannot be pigeonholed

inclassifiable [ɛ̃klasifjabl] **ADJ** *Méd* untypable

inclémence [ɛ̃klemɑ̃s] **NF** *Littéraire* **1** *(manque d'indulgence)* mercilessness, pitilessness **2** *(rigueur ▸ du climat)* inclemency

inclément, -e [ɛ̃klemɑ̃, -ɑ̃t] **ADJ** *Littéraire* **1** *(qui manque d'indulgence)* merciless, pitiless **2** *(rigoureux ▸ climat)* inclement

inclinable [ɛ̃klinabl] **ADJ** *(siège, dossier)* reclining; *(table, plan)* tilting

inclinaison [ɛ̃klinɛzɔ̃] **NF 1** *(d'un plan)* incline, slant; *(d'un avion)* tilt, tilting; *(d'un toit, d'un pignon)* pitch, slope; *(d'un navire)* list, listing; **la faible/forte i. du jardin** the gentle slope/the steepness of the garden; **l'i. de la voie** *(route, chemin de fer)* the gradient, the incline
2 *(d'une partie du corps)* **l'i. de la tête** the tilt of the head
3 *Géom* inclination, angle
4 *Astron* declination; **i. magnétique** inclination, magnetic dip

inclination [ɛ̃klinasjɔ̃] **NF 1** *(tendance)* inclination, tendency; *(goût)* inclination, liking; **avoir une i. pour la musique** to have a liking for music, to be musically inclined; **une i. à douter** a tendency to doubt things; **suivre son i.** to follow one's (natural) inclination **2** *(mouvement ▸ de la tête)* bow, inclination; *(▸ du corps)* bow; *(signe d'acquiescement)* nod **3** *Littéraire (attirance)* **avoir de l'i. pour qn** to have a liking for sb; **un mariage d'i.** a love match

incliné, -e [ɛ̃kline] **ADJ 1** *(en pente)* sloping; *(penché ▸ mur)* leaning; *(▸ dossier, siège)* reclining; **le poteau est légèrement i.** the stake is at a bit of an angle; **la tête inclinée** *(sur le côté)* with one's head (tilted) to one side; *(en avant)* with bowed head **2** *(enclin)* **une nature inclinée au mal** a character inclined *or* disposed to evil

incliner [3] [ɛ̃kline] **VT 1** *(courber)* to bend; **i. la tête** *ou* **le front** *(en avant)* to bow *or Littéraire* to incline one's head; *(pour acquiescer ou saluer)* to nod (one's head); *(sur le côté)* to tilt one's head to one side; **i. le corps (en avant)** to bend forward; *(pour saluer)* to bow **2** *(pencher ▸ dossier, siège)* to tilt; **être incliné** *(avion)* to tilt; *(bateau)* to list **3** *(inciter)* **i. qn à faire** to encourage *or* to prompt sb to do; **cette information m'incline à revoir mon point de vue** this news leads me *or* makes me inclined to reconsider my position; **ceci ne les incline pas à la clémence/au travail** this makes them disinclined to be lenient/to work
• **incliner à VT IND** to tend to *or* towards, to incline towards; **j'incline à penser qu'elle a tort** I'm inclined to think she's wrong
VPR s'incliner 1 *(se courber ▸ personne)* to bend forward; *(▸ personne qui salue)* to bow; *(▸ cime d'arbre)* to bend (over)
2 *(pencher ▸ mur)* to lean (over); *(▸ toit, route)* to slope; *(▸ avion)* to tilt, to bank; *(▸ navire)* to list; *(▸ siège)* to tilt
3 *Fig (se soumettre)* **s'i. devant le talent** to bow before talent; **s'i. devant les faits** to submit to *or* to accept the facts; **s'i. devant la supériorité de qn** to yield to sb's superiority; *Sport* **leur équipe a finalement dû s'i.** their team had to give in *or* had to admit defeat eventually
4 *(se recueillir)* **s'i. devant la dépouille mortelle de qn** to pay one's last respects to sb

inclinomètre [ɛ̃klinɔmɛtr] **NM** *Tech* inclinometer

inclure [96] [ɛ̃klyr] **VT 1** *(ajouter)* to include, to add, to insert; **i. de nouvelles données dans une liste** to include new data in a list
2 *(joindre)* to enclose
3 *(comporter)* to include; **le contrat inclut une nouvelle clause importante** the contract includes *or* comprises an important new clause
4 *Jur (introduire ▸ clause)* to insert

inclus, -e [ɛ̃kly, -yz] **ADJ 1** *(contenu)* enclosed; **le reçu i. dans ce courrier** the receipt enclosed with this letter
2 *(compris)* included; **le service est i.** service is included; **20, les enfants i.** 20, including the children; **du 1**[er] **au 12 juin i.** from June 1 to June 12 inclusive, *Am* from June 1 through June 12; **jusqu'à la page 32 incluse** up to and including page 32
3 *Math* **l'ensemble X est i. dans l'ensemble Z** the set X is included in the set Z *or* is a subset of Z
4 *Méd* **dent incluse** impacted tooth

inclusif, -ive [ɛ̃klyzif, -iv] **ADJ** inclusive; **prix i.** all-inclusive price

inclusion [ɛ̃klyzjɔ̃] **NF 1** *(action)* inclusion; *(dans un courrier)* enclosure (**dans** with)
2 *(objet décoratif)* = flower, shell etc set into plastic and used as paperweight, ornament, jewellery etc
3 *Méd (d'une dent)* impaction
4 *Math & Métal* inclusion
5 *Ordinat (de fichier)* insertion

inclusive [ɛ̃klyziv] *voir* **inclusif**

inclusivement [ɛ̃klyzivmɑ̃] **ADV** up to and including, *Am* through; **jusqu'au 14 mars i.** up to and including 14 March, *Am* through March 14

incoercible [ɛ̃kɔɛrsibl] **ADJ** irrepressible, *Sout* incoercible

incognito [ɛ̃kɔɲito] **ADV** incognito
NM incognito; **garder l'i.** to remain anonymous *or* incognito

incohérence [ɛ̃kɔerɑ̃s] **NF 1** *(manque d'unité ▸ d'une attitude, d'une personne)* inconsistency, incoherence; *(▸ d'un discours, d'idées)* incoherence **2** *(contradiction)* inconsistency, contradiction, discrepancy

incohérent, -e [ɛ̃kɔerɑ̃, -ɑ̃t] **ADJ 1** *(d'une attitude, d'une personne)* incoherent, inconsistent; *(d'un discours, d'idées)* incoherent; **de manière incohérente** incoherently; **tenir des propos incohérents** to speak incoherently **2** *(disparate)* divided

incollable [ɛ̃kɔlabl] **ADJ 1** *Culin* **riz i.** non-stick rice **2** *Fam (connaisseur)* unbeatable[□]; **elle est i. en géographie** you can't catch her out in geography

incolore [ɛ̃kɔlɔr] **ADJ 1** *(transparent ▸ liquide)* colourless; *(▸ vernis, verre)* clear; *(▸ cirage)* neutral **2** *Fig (terne ▸ sourire)* wan; *(▸ style)* colourless, bland, nondescript; **i., inodore et sans saveur** deadly dull

incomber [3] [ɛ̃kɔ̃be] **incomber à VT IND 1** *(revenir à)* **les frais de déplacement incombent à l'entreprise** travelling expenses are to be paid by the company; **à qui en incombe la responsabilité?** who is responsible for it?; **cette tâche vous incombe** this task is your responsibility **2** *(tournure* *impersonnelle)* **il vous incombe de la recevoir** it's your duty *or Sout* it's incumbent upon you to see her; **il vous incombe de le faire** the onus is on you to do it **3** *Jur (être rattaché)* **cette pièce incombe au dossier Falon** this document belongs in the Falon file

incombustibilité [ɛ̃kɔ̃bystibilite] **NF** incombustibility

incombustible [ɛ̃kɔ̃bystibl] **ADJ** non-combustible

incommensurable [ɛ̃kɔmɑ̃syrabl] **ADJ 1** *(énorme)* immeasurable; **il est d'une bêtise i.** he's immensely *or* inordinately stupid **2** *Math* incommensurable

incommensurablement [ɛ̃kɔmɑ̃syrabləmɑ̃] **ADV 1** *(très)* immeasurably; **il est i. stupide** he's immensely *or* inordinately stupid **2** *Math* incommensurably

incommodant, -e [ɛ̃kɔmɔdɑ̃, -ɑ̃t] **ADJ** *(chaleur)* unpleasant, uncomfortable; *(bruit)* irritating, irksome; *(odeur)* offensive, nauseating

incommode [ɛ̃kɔmɔd] **ADJ 1** *(peu pratique ▸ outil)* impractical, awkward, unwieldy; *(▸ maison)* inconvenient; *(▸ horaire, arrangement)* inconvenient, awkward **2** *(inconfortable ▸ position)* uncomfortable, awkward; *(▸ fauteuil)* uncomfortable

incommoder [3] [ɛ̃kɔmɔde] **VT** to bother; **la chaleur commence à m'i.** the heat is beginning to bother me *or* to make me feel uncomfortable; *Vieilli* **être incommodé** *(souffrant)* to feel unwell *or* off colour

incommodité [ɛ̃kɔmɔdite] **NF** *(d'un outil)* inconvenience, impracticability; *(d'un meuble, d'une posture, d'un trajet)* uncomfortableness, discomfort; *(d'un horaire, d'un arrangement)* inconvenience, awkwardness

incommunicabilité [ɛ̃kɔmynikabilite] **NF** incommunicability

incommunicable [ɛ̃kɔmynikabl] **ADJ** incommunicable

incommutable [ɛ̃kɔmytabl] **ADJ** *Jur* non-transferable

incomparable [ɛ̃kɔ̃parabl] **ADJ 1** *(très différent)* not comparable, unique, singular; **nos deux situations sont incomparables** you can't compare our two situations; **vous sentez la différence? c'est i.!** do you feel the difference? there's just no comparison! **2** *(inégalable)* incomparable, matchless, peerless

incomparablement [ɛ̃kɔ̃parabləmɑ̃] **ADV** incomparably; **il est i. plus beau que moi** he's incomparably *or* infinitely more handsome than me

incompatibilité [ɛ̃kɔ̃patibilite] **NF 1** *(opposition)* incompatibility; **i. d'humeur** mutual incompatibility; **il y a une totale i. entre eux** they are totally incompatible **2** *Bot, Méd & Ordinat* incompatibility

incompatible [ɛ̃kɔ̃patibl] **ADJ** incompatible; **ces deux solutions sont incompatibles** these two solutions are mutually exclusive

incompétence [ɛ̃kɔ̃petɑ̃s] **NF 1** *(incapacité)* incompetence **2** *(ignorance)* ignorance, lack of knowledge; **son i. en informatique** his/her ignorance about *or* lack of knowledge of computers **3** *Jur* incompetence, incompetency, (legal) incapacity

incompétent, -e [ɛ̃kɔ̃petɑ̃, -ɑ̃t] **ADJ 1** *(incapable)* incompetent, inefficient **2** *(ignorant)* ignorant; **je suis i. en la matière** I'm not qualified *or* competent to speak about this; **je suis i. en informatique** I know nothing *or* I am ignorant about computers **3** *Jur & Pol* incompetent

NM,F incompetent

incomplet, -ète [ɛ̃kɔ̃plɛ, -ɛt] **ADJ** *(fragmentaire)* incomplete; *(inachevé)* unfinished

incomplètement [ɛ̃kɔ̃plɛtmɑ̃] **ADV** incompletely, not completely

incomplétude [ɛ̃kɔ̃pletyd] **NF** *Littéraire (inassouvissement)* nonfulfilment

incompréhensibilité [ɛ̃kɔ̃preɑ̃sibilite] **NF** incomprehensibility

incompréhensible [ɛ̃kɔ̃preɑ̃sibl] **ADJ** incomprehensible, impossible to understand; **de manière i.** incomprehensibly; **c'est i., je les avais posées là!** I don't understand it, I put them right there!

incompréhensif, -ive [ɛ̃kɔ̃preɑ̃sif, -iv] **ADJ** unsympathetic, unfeeling

incompréhension [ɛ̃kɔ̃preɑ̃sjɔ̃] **NF** lack of understanding *or* comprehension; **leur i. était totale** they found it totally impossible to understand

incompréhensive [ɛ̃kɔ̃preɑ̃siv] *voir* **incompréhensif**

incompressible [ɛ̃kɔ̃presibl] **ADJ 1** *Phys* incompressible **2** *(dépenses)* which cannot be reduced; **notre budget est i.** we can't cut down on our budget **3** *Jur (peine)* irreducible

incompris, -e [ɛ̃kɔ̃pri, -iz] **ADJ 1** *(méconnu)* misunderstood **2** *(énigmatique)* impenetrable; **un texte qui jusqu'à ce jour était resté i.** a text which had not been understood until today

NM,F *Hum* **je suis un éternel i.** nobody ever understands me

inconcevable [ɛ̃kɔ̃svabl] **ADJ** inconceivable, unthinkable, unimaginable; **avec un aplomb i.** with an incredible *or* amazing nerve

inconcevablement [ɛ̃kɔ̃svabləmɑ̃] **ADV** incredibly, inconceivably

inconciliable [ɛ̃kɔ̃siljabl] **ADJ** *(incompatible)* incompatible, irreconcilable; **des intérêts inconciliables** incompatible interests; **des points de vue inconciliables** irreconcilable points of view; **i. avec qch** incompatible with sth

inconditionnalité [ɛ̃kɔ̃disjɔnalite] **NF** *(d'un partisan)* unreservedness, wholeheartedness; **l'i. de notre soutien** our unwavering *or* unconditional support

inconditionné, -e [ɛ̃kɔ̃disjɔne] **ADJ** *Phil* unconditioned

inconditionnel, -elle [ɛ̃kɔ̃disjɔnɛl] **ADJ 1** *(partisan)* staunch, unwavering; *(appui)* unconditional, unreserved, wholehearted; *(reddition)* unconditional

NM,F un i. de a fan of; **je suis une inconditionnelle de l'Espagne** I am mad about *or* I adore Spain; **pour les inconditionnels de l'informatique** for computer buffs *or* enthusiasts

inconditionnellement [ɛ̃kɔ̃disjɔnɛlmɑ̃] **ADV** unconditionally, unreservedly, wholeheartedly

inconduite [ɛ̃kɔ̃dɥit] **NF** *(dévergondage)* loose living; *(mauvaise conduite)* misconduct

inconfort [ɛ̃kɔ̃fɔr] **NM** *(d'une maison)* lack of comfort; *(d'une posture)* discomfort; *(d'une situation)* awkwardness

inconfortable [ɛ̃kɔ̃fɔrtabl] **ADJ 1** *(maison, siège)* uncomfortable **2** *(situation, posture)* uncomfortable, awkward

inconfortablement [ɛ̃kɔ̃fɔrtabləmɑ̃] **ADV** uncomfortably

incongru, -e [ɛ̃kɔ̃gry] **ADJ** *(remarque, réponse)* inappropriate, out of place; *(bruit)* rude; *(tenue)* extravagant; *Vieilli (personne)* uncouth

incongruité [ɛ̃kɔ̃gryite] **NF 1** *(d'une remarque, d'une réponse)* inappropriateness; *(d'une tenue)* extravagance **2** *(parole)* inappropriate remark; *(action)* inappropriate action

incongrûment [ɛ̃kɔ̃grymɑ̃] **ADV** inappropriately

inconnaissable [ɛ̃kɔnɛsabl] **ADJ** unknowable

NM l'i. the unknowable

inconnu, -e [ɛ̃kɔny] **ADJ 1** *(personne ▸ dont on ignore l'existence)* unknown; **il est né de père i.** the name of his father is not known; **i. à cette adresse** *(sur une enveloppe ou un colis)* not known at this address **2** *(destination)* unknown **3** *(étranger)* unknown; **il m'était i.** I didn't know him, he was a stranger to me; **ce visage ne m'est pas i.** I've seen that face before; **c'est un problème qui lui est totalement i.** the problem is totally foreign to him/her, it's a problem he/she knows absolutely nothing about; *Fam* **i. au bataillon** never heard of him

NM,F 1 *(étranger)* unknown person, stranger; **ne parle pas aux inconnus** don't talk to strangers **2** *(personne sans notoriété)* unknown person; **une pièce jouée par des inconnus** a play with a cast of unknowns; **c'est un i. qui a remporté le prix Nobel** someone no one has ever heard of has won the Nobel prize

NM l'i. the unknown; **un saut dans l'i.** a leap in the dark

• **inconnue NF 1** *(élément ignoré)* unknown quantity *or* factor; **il y a trop d'inconnues pour que je prenne une décision** there are too many unknown factors for me to decide **2** *Math* unknown

inconsciemment [ɛ̃kɔ̃sjamɑ̃] **ADV** *(machinalement)* unconsciously, unwittingly; *(dans l'inconscient)* unconsciously

inconscience [ɛ̃kɔ̃sjɑ̃s] **NF 1** *(insouciance)* recklessness, irresponsibility; *(folie)* madness, craziness; **faire preuve d'i.** to be reckless *or* irresponsible; **c'est de l'i.!** it's sheer madness! **2** *(perte de connaissance)* unconsciousness; **sombrer** *ou* **tomber dans l'i.** to lose consciousness

inconscient, -e [ɛ̃kɔ̃sjɑ̃, -ɑ̃t] **ADJ 1 être i. de qch** *(ne pas s'en rendre compte)* to be unaware of sth **2** *(insouciant)* reckless, rash; *(fou)* mad, crazy **3** *(automatique)* mechanical, unconscious; *Psy* unconscious **4** *(évanoui)* unconscious

NM,F *(personne insouciante)* reckless *or* irresponsible person; *(personne folle)* mad person, crazy person

NM *Psy* **l'i.** the unconscious; **l'i. collectif** the collective unconscious

inconséquence [ɛ̃kɔ̃sekɑ̃s] **NF 1** *(manque de cohérence)* incoherence, inconsistency; *(manque de prudence)* thoughtlessness, carelessness, recklessness **2** *(action imprudente)* reckless *or* irresponsible act; *(parole illogique)* non sequitur

inconséquent, -e [ɛ̃kɔ̃sekɑ̃, -ɑ̃t] **ADJ 1** *(incohérent)* incoherent, inconsistent; **être i. dans ses propos** to contradict oneself, to speak illogically **2** *(imprudent)* thoughtless, unthinking, reckless

inconsidéré, -e [ɛ̃kɔ̃sidere] **ADJ** *(acte, remarque)* thoughtless, rash, foolhardy; *(dépenses)* reckless

inconsidérément [ɛ̃kɔ̃sideremɑ̃] **ADV** *(agir, parler)* rashly, thoughtlessly, unwisely; *(dépenser)* recklessly

inconsistance [ɛ̃kɔ̃sistɑ̃s] **NF 1** *(d'un roman, d'un argument)* flimsiness, shallowness; *(d'une personne, du caractère)* shallowness, superficiality; **le film/roman était d'une i. telle que...** the film/novel was so lacking in substance that... **2** *(de la boue, de la vase)* softness; *(d'une crème, d'un enduit)* thinness, runniness; *(d'une soupe)* wateriness

inconsistant, -e [ɛ̃kɔ̃sistɑ̃, -ɑ̃t] **ADJ 1** *(roman, argument)* flimsy, weak, shallow; *(personne, caractère)* shallow, superficial **2** *(boue, vase)* soft; *(crème, enduit)* thin, runny; *(soupe)* watery

> Il faut noter que l'adjectif anglais **inconsistent** est un faux ami. Il signifie **incohérent**.

inconsolable [ɛ̃kɔ̃sɔlabl] **ADJ** inconsolable

inconsolé, -e [ɛ̃kɔ̃sɔle] **ADJ** *(peine, chagrin)* unconsoled; *(personne)* disconsolate

inconsommable [ɛ̃kɔ̃sɔmabl] **ADJ** unfit for consumption

inconstance [ɛ̃kɔ̃stɑ̃s] **NF 1** *(infidélité, variabilité)* inconstancy, fickleness **2** *Littéraire* **l'i. du succès** the fickleness of fortune

inconstant, -e [ɛ̃kɔ̃stɑ̃, -ɑ̃t] **ADJ 1** *(infidèle, d'humeur changeante)* inconstant, fickle; **être i. en amour** to be fickle **2** *Littéraire (changeant ▸ temps)* changeable, unsettled

NM,F fickle person

inconstatable [ɛ̃kɔ̃statabl] **ADJ** impossible to ascertain, unascertainable

inconstitutionnalité [ɛ̃kɔ̃stitysjɔnalite] **NF** *Jur* unconstitutionality

inconstitutionnel, -elle [ɛ̃kɔ̃stitysjɔnɛl] **ADJ** *Jur* unconstitutional

inconstitutionnellement [ɛ̃kɔ̃stitysjɔnɛlmɑ̃] **ADV** *Jur* unconstitutionally

inconstructible [ɛ̃kɔ̃stryktibl] **ADJ zone i.** site without development approval, *Am* permanently restricted zone

incontestabilité [ɛ̃kɔ̃tɛstabilite] **NF** *(d'une preuve, d'un argument)* indisputability

incontestable [ɛ̃kɔ̃testabl] ADJ incontestable, indisputable, undeniable; **sa compétence est i.** his/her competence is indisputable *or* beyond question; **il a fait un gros effort, c'est i.** there's no denying the fact that he put in a lot of effort

incontestablement [ɛ̃kɔ̃tɛstabləmɑ̃] ADV indisputably, undeniably, beyond any shadow of (a) doubt; **i. coupable** unquestionably guilty

incontesté, -e [ɛ̃kɔ̃tɛste] ADJ uncontested, undisputed; **c'est un expert i.** he's an unchallenged *or* undisputed expert

incontinence [ɛ̃kɔ̃tinɑ̃s] NF **1** *Méd* incontinence; **i. nocturne** bed-wetting **2** *Littéraire (débauche)* debauchery **3** *(dans le discours)* **i. verbale** logorrhoea, *Hum* verbal diarrhoea

incontinent, -e [ɛ̃kɔ̃tinɑ̃, -ɑ̃t] ADJ **1** *Méd* incontinent **2** *Littéraire (débauché)* debauched **3** *Littéraire (dans ses propos)* unrestrained (in one's speech)

ADV *Arch* forthwith, straightaway, directly

incontournable [ɛ̃kɔ̃turnabl] ADJ **c'est un problème i.** this problem can't be ignored; **son argument était i.** there was no getting away from his/her argument; **son œuvre est i.** his/her work cannot be overlooked *or* has exercised a major influence; **son dernier film est absolument i.** his latest film is an absolute must

incontrôlable [ɛ̃kɔ̃trolabl] ADJ **1** *(sentiment, colère)* uncontrollable, ungovernable, wild; *(personne)* out of control; **l'incendie/la foule était i.** the fire/crowd was out of control; **des éléments incontrôlables** rowdy elements **2** *(non vérifiable ▸ affirmation)* unverifiable, unconfirmable

incontrôlé, -e [ɛ̃kɔ̃trole] ADJ **1** *(bande, groupe)* unrestrained, unruly, out of control; **des éléments incontrôlés** unruly elements **2** *(non vérifié ▸ nouvelle)* unverified, unconfirmed

inconvenance [ɛ̃kɔ̃vnɑ̃s] NF **1** *(caractère)* impropriety, indecency; **vous avez été d'une i. choquante** you behaved in a most unseemly manner **2** *(parole)* impropriety, rude remark; *(acte)* impropriety, rude gesture; **dire/commettre une i.** to say/to do something improper

inconvenant, -e [ɛ̃kɔ̃vnɑ̃, -ɑ̃t] ADJ *(déplacé)* improper, indecorous, unseemly; *(indécent)* indecent, improper; **rien d'i. ne s'est passé entre eux** nothing improper *or* untoward passed between them

inconvénient [ɛ̃kɔ̃venjɑ̃] NM *(désagrément)* disadvantage, drawback, inconvenience; *(danger)* risk; **les avantages et les inconvénients** the advantages and disadvantages, the pros and cons; **les inconvénients qu'il y a à vivre si loin de la ville** the disadvantages *or* drawbacks *or* inconvenience of living so far from town; **je ne vois pas d'i. à ce que tu y ailles** I can see nothing against your going; **y voyez-vous un i.?** *(désagrément)* can you see any difficulties *or* drawbacks in this?; *(objection)* do you have any objection to this?, do you mind?; **l'i., c'est que...** the problem is that...

inconvertible [ɛ̃kɔ̃vɛrtibl] ADJ **1** *Fin* inconvertible **2** *Rel* unconvertible

incoordination [ɛ̃kɔɔrdinasjɔ̃] NF **1** *(incohérence ▸ de la pensée, d'un discours)* lack of coordination **2** *(des mouvements)* uncoordination, lack of coordination, *Spéc* ataxia

incorporable [ɛ̃kɔrpɔrabl] ADJ **1** *Mil Br* recruitable, *Am* draftable **2** *(parcelle, matériau)* incorporable

incorporation [ɛ̃kɔrpɔrasjɔ̃] NF **1** *Mil* recruitment, *Br* conscription, *Am* induction; **j'attends mon i.** I'm waiting to be called up

2 *Psy* incorporation

3 *(d'un produit)* blending, mixing (**dans** into *or* with); *(d'un territoire)* incorporation

4 *Fin* **i. des réserves au capital** capitalization of reserves

incorporéité [ɛ̃kɔrpɔreite] NF incorporeity

incorporel, -elle [ɛ̃kɔrpɔrɛl] ADJ **1** *(intangible)* insubstantial, incorporeal **2** *Jur (actif, valeurs)* intangible; **bien i.** intangible property

incorporer [3] [ɛ̃kɔrpɔre] VT **1** *Culin (mêler)* to blend, to mix; **incorporez le sucre peu à peu** gradually mix in the sugar; **incorporez le fromage râpé aux jaunes d'œufs** blend *or* mix the grated cheese with the egg yolks **2** *Mil Br* to recruit, *Am* to draft, to induct **3** *(intégrer)* to incorporate, to integrate; **quand la Savoie a été incorporée à la France** when Savoy became part of France; **incorporez quelques citations dans le texte** add a few quotations to the text

VPR **s'incorporer s'i. à** *(groupe)* to join

incorrect, -e [ɛ̃kɔrɛkt] ADJ **1** *(erroné)* incorrect, wrong

2 *(indécent)* improper, impolite, indecent; **dans une tenue incorrecte** improperly dressed

3 *(impoli)* rude, impolite

4 *(irrégulier)* underhand, irregular, unscrupulous; **c'était i. de leur part de ne pas nous prévenir** it was wrong of them not to warn us; **il a été très i. avec ses concurrents** he behaved quite unscrupulously towards his competitors

incorrectement [ɛ̃kɔrɛktəmɑ̃] ADV **1** *(de façon erronée)* wrongly, incorrectly; **mots orthographiés i.** wrongly spelt words, misspelt words

2 *(indécemment)* improperly, impolitely, indecently

3 *(impoliment)* rudely, impolitely

4 *(irrégulièrement)* underhand, irregularly, unscrupulously

incorrection [ɛ̃kɔrɛksjɔ̃] NF **1** *(caractère ▸ indécent)* impropriety, indecency; *(▸ impoli)* rudeness, impoliteness; **elle est d'une i.!** she's incredibly rude! **2** *(propos)* impropriety, improper remark; *(acte)* improper act; **à la suite d'une grave i. envers un professeur** after being extremely rude to a teacher **3** *(emploi fautif)* impropriety

incorrigibilité [ɛ̃kɔriʒibilite] NF incorrigibility

incorrigible [ɛ̃kɔriʒibl] ADJ **1** *(personne)* incorrigible; **c'est un i. paresseux** he's incorrigibly lazy **2** *(défaut)* incorrigible

incorrigiblement [ɛ̃kɔriʒibləmɑ̃] ADV incorrigibly

incorruptibilité [ɛ̃kɔryptibilite] NF *(honnêteté)* incorruptibility

incorruptible [ɛ̃kɔryptibl] ADJ *(honnête)* incorruptible; **on la sait i.** everybody knows she wouldn't take a bribe

NMF incorruptible; **c'est un i.** he's incorruptible

incoté, -e [ɛ̃kɔte] ADJ *Bourse* unquoted

incoterms [ɛ̃kɔtɛrm] NMPL *Com* incoterms

incrédibilité [ɛ̃kredibilite] NF incredibleness, incredibility

incrédule [ɛ̃kredyl] ADJ **1** *(sceptique)* incredulous, disbelieving; **d'un air i.** incredulously, in disbelief **2** *Rel (incroyant)* unbelieving

NMF *Rel (incroyant)* nonbeliever, unbeliever

incrédulité [ɛ̃kredylite] NF **1** *(doute)* incredulity, disbelief, unbelief; **avec i.** incredulously, in disbelief **2** *Rel (incroyance)* lack of belief, unbelief

incrémenter [3] [ɛ̃kremɑ̃te] VT *Ordinat* to increment

increvable [ɛ̃krəvabl] ADJ **1** *(pneu, ballon)* puncture-proof **2** *Fam (personne)* tireless[□]; **les gosses sont increvables** kids never seem to get tired; **cette voiture est i.** this car will last for ever

incriminer [3] [ɛ̃krimine] VT **1** *(rejeter la faute sur)* to put the blame on, to incriminate **2** *(accuser ▸ décision, négligence)* to (call into) question; *(▸ personne)* to accuse; **il avait déjà été incriminé dans une affaire de drogue** he'd previously been implicated in a drugs case

incrochetable [ɛ̃krɔʃtabl] ADJ *(serrure)* unpickable; *(coffre)* burglar-proof

incroyable [ɛ̃krwajabl] ADJ **1** *(peu vraisemblable)* incredible, unbelievable; **quelle histoire i.!** what an incredible story!; **il est i. que...** it's incredible *or* hard to believe that... **2** *(étonnant)* incredible, amazing; **tu es vraiment i., pourquoi ne veux-tu pas venir?** you're unbelievable, why don't you want to come?; **j'ai eu une chance i.** I was incredibly lucky, I had incredible luck; **d'une bêtise i.** incredibly stupid; **c'est quand même i., ce retard!** this delay is getting ridiculous!; **c'est i., ça!** I don't believe it!; **ils sont incroyables de suffisance** they're unbelievably self-important

incroyablement [ɛ̃krwajabləmɑ̃] ADV incredibly, unbelievably, amazingly

incroyance [ɛ̃krwajɑ̃s] NF unbelief

incroyant, -e [ɛ̃krwajɑ̃, -ɑ̃t] ADJ unbelieving

NM,F unbeliever

incrustation [ɛ̃krystasjɔ̃] NF **1** *(décoration)* inlay; *(procédé)* inlaying; **avec incrustations de nacre** inlaid with mother-of-pearl

2 *Géol (action)* encrusting; *(résultat)* incrustation

3 *Couture* insertion

4 *TV* (image) inlay, cut-in; **i. couleur** chroma key

5 *(dépôt ▸ sur une chaudière)* fur, scale

incruste [ɛ̃kryst] NF *Fam* **si on l'invite, il va encore taper l'i.** if we invite him, we'll never get rid of him; **il a tapé l'i. à ma soirée** he gatecrashed my party

incruster [3] [ɛ̃kryste] VT **1** *(orner)* to inlay; **i. qch de** to inlay sth with; **un bracelet incrusté d'émeraudes** a bracelet inlaid with emeralds

2 *(recouvrir ▸ gén)* to incrust, to coat; *(▸ de calcaire)* to fur up

3 *Constr (pierre)* to insert

4 *TV* to inlay

VPR **s'incruster 1** *(se couvrir de calcaire)* to become incrusted, to become covered in scale, to fur up **2** *(adhérer)* to build up; **enlever le calcaire qui s'est incrusté** to remove the build-up of scale **3** *Fam (personne)* **l'ennui, c'est que si on l'invite, il s'incruste** the problem is that if we invite him over, he'll overstay his welcome; **ils font une fête, on s'incruste?** they're having a party, let's gatecrash

incubateur, -trice [ɛ̃kybatœr, -tris] ADJ *Biol* incubating

NM *Méd & Écon* incubator

incubation [ɛ̃kybasjɔ̃] NF **1** *(d'œufs)* incubation **2** *(d'une maladie)* incubation; **l'i. dure trois jours, il y a une période d'i. de trois jours** the incubation period is three days

incubatrice [ɛ̃kybatris] *voir* **incubateur**

incube [ɛ̃kyb] NM *(démon)* incubus

incuber [3] [ɛ̃kybe] VT *(œuf)* to incubate

inculcation [ɛ̃kylkasjɔ̃] NF *Littéraire* inculcation, instilling

inculpation [ɛ̃kylpasjɔ̃] NF indictment, charge; **le juge lui a notifié son i.** the judge informed him/her that he/she was being charged; **sous l'i. d'assassinat** charged with murder; **être sous le coup d'une i. (pour)** to be indicted (for) *or* on a charge (of)

inculpé, -e [ɛ̃kylpe] NM,F **l'i.** the accused

inculper [3] [ɛ̃kylpe] VT to charge (**de** *ou* **pour** with)

inculquer [3] [ɛ̃kylke] VT to inculcate; **i. qch à qn** to inculcate sth in sb

inculte [ɛ̃kylt] ADJ **1** *(campagne, pays)* uncultivated **2** *(esprit, intelligence, personne)* uneducated, uncultured, uncultivated; **ils sont complètement incultes** they're totally ignorant **3** *(cheveux)* unkempt, dishevelled; *(barbe)* untidy

incultivable [ɛ̃kyltivabl] ADJ unworkable, uncultivable; **des terres incultivables** wasteland; **ces landes sont incultivables** these moors are no use for farming *or* as farmland

incultivé, -e [ɛ̃kyltive] ADJ *Littéraire (région, terre)* uncultivated

inculture [ɛ̃kyltyr] NF *(d'une personne)* lack of culture *or* education

incunable [ɛ̃kynabl] ADJ *(édition)* incunabular

NM incunabulum, incunable; **les incunables** the incunabula

incurable [ɛ̃kyrabl] ADJ **1** *Méd* incurable **2** *(incorrigible ▸ personne, défaut)* incurable, inveterate; **d'une paresse/bêtise i.** incurably lazy/stupid

NMF *Méd* incurable

incurablement [ɛ̃kyrabləmɑ̃] ADV **1** *Méd* incurably **2** *(irrémédiablement)* incurably, desperately, hopelessly

incurie [ɛ̃kyri] NF *Sout* negligence; **faire preuve d'i.** to be negligent, to be guilty of negligence

incursion [ɛ̃kyrsjɔ̃] NF **1** *Mil* foray, raid **2** *(exploration ▸ d'un domaine)* foray, incursion **3** *(entrée soudaine)* intrusion; **faire une i. dans une réunion** to burst into a meeting

incurvation [ɛ̃kyrvasjɔ̃] NF bending, curving, incurvation

incurvé, -e [ɛ̃kyrve] ADJ curved, bent, incurved

incurver [3] [ɛ̃kyrve] VT to curve (inwards), to make into a curve

VPR **s'incurver 1** *(trajectoire)* to curve (inwards *or* in), to bend **2** *(étagère)* to sag

indatable [ɛ̃databl] ADJ *(manuscrit, ruines)* undatable, undateable

Inde [ɛ̃d] NF **l'I.** India

indé, -e [ɛ̃de] ADJ *Fam (abrév* **indépendant***)* indie; **le rock i.** indie (rock)

indéboulonnable [ɛ̃debulɔnabl] ADJ *Hum* **il est i.!** they'll never be able to sack him!

indébrouillable [ɛ̃debrujabl] ADJ *(écheveau, procès)* hopelessly entangled, inextricable

indécemment [ɛ̃desamɑ̃] ADV indecently

indécence [ɛ̃desɑ̃s] NF **1** *(manque de pudeur)* indecency **2** *(propos, acte)* indecency, impropriety

indécent, -e [ɛ̃desɑ̃, -ɑ̃t] ADJ **1** *(honteux)* indecent **2** *(licencieux)* indecent, obscene

indéchiffrable [ɛ̃deʃifrabl] ADJ **1** *(code)* undecipherable, indecipherable; **aucun code n'est i.** there's no code that can't be broken *or* cracked **2** *(écriture)* illegible, unreadable **3** *(visage, mystère, pensée)* inscrutable, impenetrable

indéchirable [ɛ̃deʃirabl] ADJ tear-resistant

indécis, -e [ɛ̃desi, -iz] ADJ **1** *(flou)* vague, indistinct; **on apercevait quelques formes indécises dans le brouillard** a few blurred shapes could be made out in the fog **2** *(incertain)* undecided, unsettled; **la victoire est restée indécise jusqu'à la fin** victory was uncertain until the very end; **le temps est i.** the weather is unsettled **3** *(hésitant* ▸ *momentanément)* undecided, unsure, uncertain; *(*▸ *de nature)* indecisive, irresolute; **je suis i. (sur la solution à choisir)** I'm undecided (as to the best solution), I can't make up my mind (which solution is the best); **il a toujours été i.** he's always been indecisive, he never has been able to make up his mind

NM,F indecisive person; *(électeur)* floating voter, don't-know; **c'est un i.** he can never make his mind up; **le vote des i.** the floating vote

indécision [ɛ̃desizjɔ̃] NF *(caractère irrésolu)* indecisiveness; *(hésitation)* indecision; **être dans l'i. (quant à)** to be undecided *or* unsure (about)

indécollable [ɛ̃dekɔlabl] ADJ non-removable; *(revêtement)* permanent

indécomposable [ɛ̃dekɔ̃pozabl] ADJ *(corps, ensemble)* indecomposable

indécrottable [ɛ̃dekrɔtabl] ADJ *Fam* hopeless; **c'est un i. imbécile!** he's hopelessly stupid!; **un i. réactionnaire** an out-and-out reactionary

indéfectibilité [ɛ̃defɛktibilite] NF **1** *(d'une amitié, du soutien)* staunchness, unfailingness **2** *Rel* indefectibility

indéfectible [ɛ̃defɛktibl] ADJ **1** *(amitié, soutien)* staunch, unfailing, unshakeable; *(confiance)* unshakeable; *(mémoire)* unfailing; **une i. volonté** staunch determination; **une foi i. en l'informatique** an unshakeable faith in computers; **avec une ambition i.** with unflagging *or* unfailing ambition **2** *Rel* indefectible

indéfendable [ɛ̃defɑ̃dabl] ADJ **1** *(condamnable* ▸ *personne, comportement)* indefensible **2** *(insoutenable* ▸ *théorie, opinion)* indefensible, untenable

indéfini, -e [ɛ̃defini] ADJ **1** *(sans limites)* indefinite, unlimited; **un temps i.** an undetermined length of time **2** *(confus)* ill-defined, vague; **un trouble i. l'envahit** a vague feeling of uneasiness crept over him/her **3** *Ling* indefinite

NM *Ling* indefinite

indéfiniment [ɛ̃definimɑ̃] ADV indefinitely, for ever; **répéter qch i.** to say sth over and over again, to keep repeating sth

indéfinissable [ɛ̃definisabl] ADJ indefinable

indéformable [ɛ̃defɔrmabl] ADJ *(chapeau, vêtement)* which cannot be pulled out of shape; *(semelle)* rigid; *(acier)* that does not buckle

indéfrisable [ɛ̃defrizabl] NF *Vieilli* perm, permanent wave

indélébile [ɛ̃delebil] ADJ **1** *(ineffaçable* ▸ *encre)* indelible, permanent; *(*▸ *tache)* indelible **2** *(indestructible* ▸ *souvenir)* indelible

indélicat, -e [ɛ̃delika, -at] ADJ **1** *(grossier)* coarse, indelicate, rude **2** *(véreux)* dishonest, unscrupulous

indélicatement [ɛ̃delikatmɑ̃] ADV **1** *(grossièrement)* coarsely, indelicately **2** *(malhonnêtement)* dishonestly, unscrupulously

indélicatesse [ɛ̃delikatɛs] NF **1** *(des manières)* coarseness, indelicacy **2** *(caractère malhonnête)* dishonesty, unscrupulousness **3** *(acte malhonnête)* dishonest *or* unscrupulous act; **commettre une i.** to behave dishonestly

indémaillable [ɛ̃demajabl] ADJ *(bas, collant)* runproof, *Br* ladderproof; *(pull, tissu)* run-resistant, runproof

NM non-run *or* runproof fabric

indemne [ɛ̃dɛmn] ADJ **1** *(physiquement)* unhurt, unharmed; **ma sœur est sortie i. de la collision** my sister was unhurt in the collision **2** *(moralement)* unscathed; **il est sorti i. du scandale** he emerged unscathed from the scandal

indemnisable [ɛ̃dɛmnizabl] ADJ *(propriétaire, réfugié)* entitled to compensation, *Am* compensable

indemnisation [ɛ̃dɛmnizasjɔ̃] NF **1** *(argent)* compensation, indemnity; **il a reçu 5000 euros d'i.** he received 5,000 euros compensation **2** *(procédé)* compensating; **l'i. des sinistrés prendra plusieurs mois** it will take several months to compensate the disaster victims

indemniser [3] [ɛ̃dɛmnize] VT **1** *(après un sinistre)* to compensate, to indemnify; **ils seront tous indemnisés** they will all receive compensation; **se faire i.** to receive compensation **2** *(après une dépense)* **être indemnisé de ses frais** to have one's expenses paid for *or* reimbursed; **quand je voyage, je suis indemnisé (de mes frais)** when I travel, it all goes on expenses

indemnitaire [ɛ̃dɛmnitɛr] ADJ compensative, compensatory

NMF **1** *(recevant une allocation)* recipient of an allowance **2** *(après un sinistre)* person awarded compensation

indemnité [ɛ̃dɛmnite] NF **1** *(après un sinistre)* compensation; *(dommages et intérêts)* damages; **i. en argent** cash compensation; **i. de clientèle** compensation for loss of custom; **i. compensatrice** compensation; **i. compensatrice de congés payés** pay in lieu of holidays; **i. d'éviction** compensation for eviction; **i. de retard** late payment penalty; **i. de rupture** severance pay; **i. de rupture abusive** compensation for breach of contract **2** *(allocation)* allowance; **i. de cherté de vie** cost of living allowance, *Br* weighting; **i. de chômage** unemployment benefit; **i. complémentaire** additional allowance; **i. conventionnelle** contractual allowance; **i. de déménagement** relocation grant *or* allowance; **i. de départ** severance pay; **i. de déplacement** travel *or* transport allowance; **i. journalière** daily allowance; **i. kilométrique** = mileage allowance; **i. de licenciement** redundancy payment; **i. de logement** accommodation allowance; **i. de maladie** sickness benefit; **i. parlementaire** *Br* ≃ member of parliament's salary; **i. de représentation** entertainment allowance; **i. de résidence** housing allowance; **i. de retard** late payment penalty; **i. de séjour** living expenses; **i. de transport** travel allowance *or* expenses; **i. de vie chère** cost of living allowance

indémodable [ɛ̃demɔdabl] ADJ perennially fashionable; **un tailleur i.** a classic suit, a suit that will never go out of fashion

indémontable [ɛ̃demɔ̃tabl] ADJ *(jouet, serrure)* which cannot be taken apart *or* dismantled; *(étagère)* fixed

indémontrable [ɛ̃demɔ̃trabl] ADJ **1** *Ling & Math* indemonstrable **2** *(non prouvable)* unprovable

indéniable [ɛ̃denjabl] ADJ undeniable; **il est i. que...** it cannot be denied that..., there's no denying that...

indéniablement [ɛ̃denjabləmɑ̃] ADV undeniably

indénombrable [ɛ̃denɔ̃brabl] ADJ innumerable, uncountable

indentation [ɛ̃dɑ̃tasjɔ̃] NF **1** *(échancrure)* indentation; **les indentations du littoral** the ragged coastline **2** *Typ* indent; **i. à droite/gauche** right/left indent

indenter [ɛ̃dɑ̃te] VT *Typ* to indent

indépassable [ɛ̃depasabl] ADJ *(crédit, limite)* unextendable, fixed; *(coureur)* unbeatable

indépendamment [ɛ̃depɑ̃damɑ̃] ADV *(séparément)* independently

• **indépendamment de** PRÉP *(outre, mis à part)* apart from; *(en faisant abstraction de)* regardless of; **i. de son salaire, il a des rentes** apart from his salary he has a private income; **i. l'un de l'autre** independently of one another; **i. du résultat** regardless of the result

indépendance [ɛ̃depɑ̃dɑ̃s] NF **1** *(d'un pays, d'une personne)* independence; **prendre son i.** to assume one's independence; **le jour de l'I.** Independence Day; **il a une grande i. d'esprit** he's very independently minded, he's good at thinking for himself **2** *(absence de relation)* independence

indépendant, -e [ɛ̃depɑ̃dɑ̃, -ɑ̃t] ADJ **1** *(gén) & Pol* independent; **pour des raisons indépendantes de notre volonté** for reasons beyond our control

2 *(distinct)* **ces deux problèmes sont indépendants l'un de l'autre** these two problems are separate *or* distinct from each other; **une chambre indépendante** a self-contained room; **avec salle de bains indépendante** with own *or* separate bathroom

3 *(traducteur, photographe)* freelance; *(député)* independent

4 *Gram* **proposition indépendante** independent clause

NM,F **1** *Pol* independent **2** *(travailleur)* self-employed worker; *(traducteur, journaliste, photographe)* freelancer

• **indépendante** NF *Gram* independent clause

• **en indépendant** ADV **travailler en i.** to work freelance *or* on a freelance basis

indépendantisme [ɛ̃depɑ̃dɑ̃tism] NM **l'i.** the independence *or* separatist movement

indépendantiste [ɛ̃depɑ̃dɑ̃tist] ADJ **mouvement i.** independence *or* separatist movement

NMF separatist

indépensé, -e [ɛ̃depɑ̃se] ADJ *Fin* unspent

indéracinable [ɛ̃derasinabl] ADJ **1** *(préjugé, habitude)* entrenched, ineradicable **2** *Fam (personne)* **deux ou trois poivrots indéracinables** two or three drunks who couldn't be shifted

indéréglable [ɛ̃dereglabl] ADJ *(mécanisme, montre)* extremely reliable

Indes [ɛ̃d] NFPL Indies; *Hist* **les I. occidentales/orientales** the West/East Indies; *Hist* **la Compagnie des I. orientales** the East India Company; **aux I.** *(en Inde)* in India

indescriptible [ɛ̃dɛskriptibl] ADJ indescribable

indésirable [ɛ̃dezirabl] ADJ undesirable, unwanted; **une présence i.** an undesirable *or* unwanted presence; **effets indésirables: assoupissements, nausées** may cause drowsiness or nausea

NMF undesirable; **on nous traite comme des indésirables** we are treated as though we were not wanted

Indes-Occidentales [ɛ̃dɔksidɑ̃tal] NFPL the (British) West Indies

indestructibilité [ɛ̃dɛstryktibilite] NF indestructibility, indestructibleness

indestructible [ɛ̃dɛstryktibl] ADJ *(bâtiment, canon)* indestructible, built to last; *(amour, lien)* indestructible

indétectable [ɛ̃detɛktabl] ADJ undetectable

indéterminable [ɛ̃determinabl] ADJ indeterminable; **sa date de naissance est i.** his/her date of birth cannot be determined (with any certainty)

indétermination [ɛ̃determinasjɔ̃] NF **1** *(approximation)* vagueness **2** *(indécision* ▸ *momentanée)* indecision; *(*▸ *de nature)* indecisiveness

indéterminé, -e [ɛ̃determine] ADJ **1** *(non défini)* indeterminate, unspecified; **à une date indéterminée** at an unspecified date; **pour une raison indéterminée** for some unknown reason; **l'origine du mot est indéterminée** the origin of the word is uncertain *or* not known **2** *Phil* indeterminate

indétrônable [ɛ̃detronabl] **ADJ il est i.** his position is uncontested; **c'est le leader i. du téléphone portable** it's the uncontested leader of the mobile phone market; **leur chanson est i. au sommet des charts** their song refuses to budge from the top of the charts; **après le succès remporté en Coupe du Monde, l'entraîneur de l'équipe nationale est i.** following his World Cup success, the national team's coach isn't going anywhere

index [ɛ̃dɛks] **NM 1** *(doigt)* index finger, forefinger
2 *(repère)* pointer
3 *(liste)* index
4 *Hist* **l'I.** the Index; **mettre qn/qch à l'i.** to blacklist sb/sth
5 *Ordinat* (fixed) index
6 *Méd* **i. glycémique** glycaemic index

indexage [ɛ̃dɛksaʒ] **NM** indexing, indexation

indexation [ɛ̃dɛksasjɔ̃] **NF 1** *(classement)* indexation, indexing **2** *Écon (des prix, des salaires)* indexation, index-linking (**sur** to)

indexé, -e [ɛ̃dɛkse] **ADJ** *Écon (prix, salaires)* indexed, index-linked (**sur** to); *Ordinat (valeur)* indexed

indexer [4] [ɛ̃dɛkse] **VT 1** *(ouvrage)* to index **2** *Écon* to index, to index-link (**sur** to) **3** *Ordinat* to index

indic [ɛ̃dik] **NM** *Fam* squealer, *Br* grass, *Am* rat

indicateur, -trice [ɛ̃dikatœr, -tris] **ADJ** indicative

NM,F *(informateur)* (police) informer *or* spy

NM 1 *(plan, liste)* **i. des rues** street guide *or* directory; **i. des chemins de fer** *Br* railway *or Am* railroad timetable
2 *(appareil)* indicator, gauge; **i. d'altitude** altimeter; **i. de changement de direction** (directional *or* direction) indicator; **i. de niveau de carburant** fuel gauge; **i. de pression** pressure gauge; **i. de vitesse** speedometer
3 *(indice)* indicator, pointer; **indicateurs d'alerte** economic indicators, business indicators; **i. de développement humain** Human Development Index; **i. (d'activité) économique** economic indicator; **i. de marché** market indicator; **i. statistique** statistical indicator; *Bourse* **i. de tendance** market indicator
4 *Chim & Ling* indicator

indicatif, -ive [ɛ̃dikatif, -iv] **ADJ** *(état, signe)* indicative; *Gram (mode)* indicative

NM 1 *Gram* indicative
2 *Rad & TV* **i. (musical)** signature *or Br* theme tune
3 *Tél (de zone)* (dialling) code; **i. du pays** international dialling code; **i. de zone** area code
4 *Ordinat* **i. d'appel** ident; **i. de fichier** filename; **i. de tri** sort key; **i. (du) DOS** DOS prompt

indication [ɛ̃dikasjɔ̃] **NF 1** *(action d'indiquer)* indication, indicating, pointing out; **l'i. de la date de péremption est obligatoire** the use-by date must be shown *or* indicated
2 *(recommandation)* instruction; **j'ai suivi toutes vos indications** I followed all your instructions; **sauf i. contraire** unless otherwise specified; **les indications du mode d'emploi** the directions for use; **les indications de montage** the assembly instructions; **indications scéniques** stage directions
3 *(information, renseignement)* information *(UNCOUNT)*, piece of information
4 *(signe)* sign, indication
5 *(aperçu)* indication; **c'est une excellente i. sur l'état de l'économie** it's an excellent indication of the state of the economy
6 *Méd & Pharm* **sauf i. contraire du médecin** unless otherwise stated by the doctor; **indications (thérapeutiques)** indications; **indications:...** *(sur notice)* suitable for...
7 *Com* **i. d'origine** label of origin

indicative [ɛ̃dikativ] *voir* **indicatif**

indicatrice [ɛ̃dikatris] *voir* **indicateur**

indice [ɛ̃dis] **NM 1** *(symptôme ▸ d'un changement, d'un phénomène)* indication, sign; *(▸ d'une maladie)* sign, symptom; **aucun i. ne laissait présager le drame** there was no sign of the impending tragedy
2 *(d'une enquête policière)* clue; *(d'une énigme)* clue, hint
3 *(chiffre indicateur) Écon & Bourse* index, average; *Mktg* **i. ad hoc** specific indicator; **i. boursier** share index; **l'i. CAC 40** the CAC 40 index; *Pétr* **i. de cétane** cetane number; **i. de confiance** consumer confidence index; *Bourse* **i. composé, i. composite** composite index; *Écon* **i. corrigé des variations saisonnières** seasonally adjusted index; *Bourse* **i. non-corrigé des variations saisonnières** non-seasonally adjusted index; *Écon* **i. des cours d'actions** share price index; **i. du coût de la vie** cost of living index; *Écon* **i. de croissance** index of growth; *Bourse* **l'i. DAX** the Dax index; *Écon* **i. de développement humain** Human Development Index; *Bourse* **l'i. Dow Jones** the Dow Jones index; *Bourse* **l'i. FTSE des 100 valeurs** the FTSE 100 share index; *Bourse* **l'i. Hang Seng** the Hang Seng index; **l'i. de l'INSEE** ≃ the retail price index; *Phot* **i. de lumination** exposure value *or* index; *Méd* **i. de masse corporelle** body mass index; *Bourse* **l'i. MidCAC** = Paris stock exchange index of 100 medium range shares, *Am* ≃ MidCap index; *Bourse* **l'i. Nikkei** the Nikkei index; *Pétr* **i. d'octane** octane rating; *Aut* **i. d'octane moteur** motor octane numbers; *Pétr* **i. d'octane recherche** research octane number; **i. pollinique (de l'air)** pollen count; **i. pondéré** weighted index; **i. pondéré par le commerce extérieur** trade-weighted index; **i. des prix (à la consommation)** (consumer) price index; **i. des prix de détail** retail price index; **i. des prix de gros** wholesale price index; *Écon* **i. des prix et des salaires** wage and price index; **i. des prix à la production** producer price index; **i. de profit** profit indicator; *Météo* **i. de refroidissement (au vent)** windchill factor; *Admin* **i. de rémunération** salary grading; **i. de rentabilité** profitability index; *Écon* **i. de richesse vive** consumer purchasing power index; *Bourse* **l'i. SBF** the SBF index *(broad-based French Stock Exchange index)*; *Bourse* **i. des titres** stock average; *Admin* **i. de traitement** salary grading; **i. des valeurs boursières** share index; **l'i. Xetra-Dax** the Xetra-Dax index
4 *Rad & TV* **l'i. d'écoute** the audience rating, the ratings; **avoir un mauvais i. d'écoute** to have a low (audience) rating, to get bad ratings
5 i. de protection *(d'une crème solaire)* sun protection factor
6 *Math* index; *Typ* subscript; **b i. 3** b subscript *or* index 3; **3 en i.** subscript 3

indiciaire [ɛ̃disjɛr] **ADJ 1** *Écon* index-based; **impôt i.** wealth-related tax **2** *Admin* grade-related

indicible [ɛ̃disibl] **ADJ** indescribable, unutterable

indiciblement [ɛ̃disibləmɑ̃] **ADV** ineffably

indiciel, -elle [ɛ̃disjɛl] **ADJ** *Écon & Math* index *(épith)*

indien, -enne [ɛ̃djɛ̃, -ɛn] **ADJ 1** *(de l'Inde)* Indian **2** *(d'Amérique)* American Indian, Native American

• **Indien, -enne NM,F 1** *(de l'Inde)* Indian **2 I. (d'Amérique)** American Indian, Native American
• **indienne NF 1** *Tex Br* printed (Indian) cotton, *Am* printed calico **2** *(nage)* overarm stroke

indifféremment [ɛ̃diferamɑ̃] **ADV 1** *(aussi bien)* **elle joue i. de la main droite ou de la main gauche** she plays equally well with her right or left hand; **la radio marche i. sur piles ou sur secteur** the radio can run on batteries or be plugged into the mains **2** *(sans discrimination)* indiscriminately; **il regarde toutes les émissions i.** he watches television whatever is on

indifférence [ɛ̃diferɑ̃s] **NF** *(détachement ▸ envers une situation, un sujet)* indifference, lack of interest; *(▸ envers quelqu'un)* indifference; **son roman est paru dans la plus grande i.** the publication of his/her novel went completely unnoticed; **faire qch avec i.** to do sth indifferently *or* with indifference; *Fam* **il me fait le coup de l'i.** he's pretending not to notice me; **i. pour qch** lack of concern for sth; **son i. totale pour la politique** his/her total lack of interest in *or* complete indifference to politics

indifférenciable [ɛ̃diferɑ̃sjabl] **ADJ** indistinguishable; **ces jumeaux sont absolument indifférenciables** it's impossible to tell the twins apart

indifférenciation [ɛ̃diferɑ̃sjasjɔ̃] **NF** *Physiol* absence of differentiation; **pendant l'i. sexuelle de l'embryon** while the embryo is still sexually undifferentiated

indifférencié, -e [ɛ̃diferɑ̃sje] **ADJ** *Physiol (organisme)* undifferentiated; *(cellule)* unspecialized

indifférent, -e [ɛ̃diferɑ̃, -ɑ̃t] **ADJ 1** *(insensible, détaché)* indifferent; **leur divorce me laisse i.** their divorce is of no interest to me *or* is a matter of indifference to me; **sa mort ne laissera personne i.** his/her death will leave no one indifferent; **elle me laisse i.** she leaves me cold; **elle ne le laisse pas i.** he's not blind *or* indifferent to her charms; **être i. à la politique** to be indifferent towards politics; **il a été i. à tous mes arguments** he was unmoved by my arguments **2** *(d'intérêt égal)* indifferent, immaterial; **âge i.** *(dans les petites annonces)* age unimportant *or* immaterial; **religion/race indifférente** *(dans les petites annonces)* religion/race no barrier **3** *(insignifiant)* indifferent, uninteresting, of no interest; **parler de choses indifférentes** to talk about this and that; **ça m'est i.** it's (all) the same to me, I don't care either way; **la mort ne m'est pas/m'est complètement indifférente** I do care/don't care if I live or die; **il lui était i. de partir (ou non)** it didn't matter *or* it was immaterial to him/her whether he/she left or not

NM,F indifferent *or* apathetic person; **il fait l'i.** *ou* **joue les indifférents** he's feigning indifference

indifférer [18] [ɛ̃difere] **indifférer à VT IND 1** *(n'inspirer aucun intérêt à)* **il m'indiffère complètement** I'm totally indifferent to him, I couldn't care less about him; **tout l'indiffère** he/she takes no interest in anything **2** *(être égal à)* to be of no importance to; **le prix m'indiffère** the price is of no importance (to me); **ça m'indiffère** I don't mind, it's all the same to me

indigence [ɛ̃diʒɑ̃s] **NF 1** *(matérielle)* poverty, *Sout* indigence; **vivre dans l'i.** to be destitute **2** *(intellectuelle)* paucity, poverty

indigène [ɛ̃diʒɛn] **ADJ 1** *(d'avant la colonisation ▸ droits, pratique)* native, indigenous; *(▸ coutumes)* native **2** *(autochtone ▸ population)* native, indigenous **3** *Bot & Zool* indigenous, native (**de** to); **la faune i. de ces régions** the fauna indigenous to these regions

NMF 1 *(colonisé)* native **2** *(autochtone)* native **3** *Bot & Zool* indigen, indigene, native

indigent, -e [ɛ̃diʒɑ̃, -ɑ̃t] **ADJ 1** *(pauvre)* destitute, poor **2** *(insuffisant)* poor; **un esprit i.** an impoverished mind; **avoir une imagination indigente** to be totally lacking in imagination

NM,F pauper; **les indigents** the destitute, the poor

indigeste [ɛ̃diʒɛst] **ADJ 1** *(nourriture)* indigestible, heavy; **je trouve la choucroute très i.** I find sauerkraut very heavy on the stomach **2** *(livre, compte-rendu)* indigestible; **je trouve ce livre i.** this book is heavy going

indigestion [ɛ̃diʒɛstjɔ̃] **NF 1** *Méd* indigestion *(UNCOUNT)*; **avoir une i.** to have indigestion; **se donner une i.** to give onself indigestion; **j'ai mangé tellement de chocolat que je m'en suis donné une i.** I ate so much chocolate that I made myself ill **2** *Fig* **avoir une i. de qch** to be sick of sth

indignation [ɛ̃diɲasjɔ̃] **NF** indignation; **protester avec i.** to protest indignantly; **un regard d'i.** an indignant look; **à l'i. de tous** to the indignation of everyone present

indigne [ɛ̃diɲ] **ADJ 1 i. de** *(honneur, confiance)* unworthy of; **i. d'un tel honneur** unworthy *or* undeserving of such an honour; **un mensonge i. de lui** a lie unworthy of him; **ce travail est i. de lui** this work is not good enough for him *or* is beneath him; **des médisances indignes d'une sœur** malicious gossip one doesn't expect from a sister; **il est i. de succéder à son père** he's not fit to take his father's place **2** *(choquant ▸ action, propos)* disgraceful, outrageous, shameful; **avoir une attitude i.** to behave shamefully *or* disgracefully **3** *(méprisable ▸ personne)* unworthy; **c'est une mère i.** she's not fit to be a mother; **un fils i.** an unworthy son

indigné, -e [ɛ̃diɲe] **ADJ** indignant, shocked, outraged; **d'un air/ton i.** indignantly

indignement [ɛ̃diɲəmɑ̃] **ADV** disgracefully, shamefully

indigner [3] [ɛ̃diɲe] **VT** to make indignant, to incense, to gall

VPR s'indigner *(se révolter)* to be indignant; **il y a de quoi s'i.!** there's good reason to be indignant!;

s'i. de qch to be indignant about sth; **je m'indigne de voir ce crime impuni** it makes me indignant to see this crime go unpunished; **s'i. contre l'injustice** to cry out *or* to inveigh against injustice

indignité [ɛ̃diɲite] **NF 1** *(caractère indigne)* unworthiness, disgracefulness **2** *(acte)* shameful *or* disgraceful act **3** *Hist* **i. nationale** loss of citizenship rights *(for having collaborated with Germany during WWII)*

indigo [ɛ̃digo] **ADJ INV** indigo (blue)
NM indigo

indiqué, -e [ɛ̃dike] **ADJ 1** *(recommandé ▸ conduite)* advisable; **dans ton état, ce n'est pas très i. de fumer!** in your condition, smoking isn't really advisable *or* isn't really a sensible thing to do!; **dans votre cas, un séjour à la montagne me paraît tout à fait i.** a stay in the mountains seems to me to be just the thing you need **2** *(approprié ▸ personne, objet)* **un vérin serait tout i.** what we need is a jack; **voilà une carrière tout indiquée pour un homme ambitieux** that's the obvious *or* very career for an ambitious man; **ce médicament est/n'est pas i. dans ce cas** this drug is appropriate/inappropriate in this case **3** *(date, jour)* agreed; *(endroit)* agreed, appointed; *(heure)* appointed

INDIQUER [3] [ɛ̃dike]

• to show **1–3, 8**	• to point out **1**
• to show the way to **2**	• to indicate **3, 8**
• to note down **4**	• to mark **4**
• to suggest **5**	• to prescribe **5**
• to tell **6**	• to name **7**

VT 1 *(montrer d'un geste ▸ chose, personne, lieu)* to show, to point out; **i. qch de la tête** to nod towards sth, to indicate sth with a nod; **i. qch de la main** to point out *or* to indicate sth with one's hand; **i. qn/qch du doigt** to point at sb/sth; **elle m'avait indiqué le suspect du regard** she'd shown me the suspect by looking at him; **il indiqua la porte avec son revolver** he pointed to the door with his gun; **je ne pourrais pas t'i. la ville avec précision sur la carte** I couldn't pinpoint the town on the map for you; **i. une fuite à qn** to show sb where a leak is

2 *(musée, autoroute, plage)* to show the way to; *(chemin)* to indicate, to show; **pouvez-vous m'i. (le chemin de) la gare?** could you show me the way to *or* direct me to the station?; **il ne s'est trouvé personne pour m'i. où se trouvait la galerie** nobody could tell me where the gallery was *or* show me the way to the gallery; **je me suis fait i. la station de métro la plus proche** I asked someone to tell me where the nearest *Br* tube station *or Am* subway was

3 *(sujet: carte, enseigne, statistiques)* to show, to say, to indicate; *(sujet: flèche, graphique)* to show; *(sujet: horaire)* to show, to say, to give; *(sujet: dictionnaire)* to say, to give; **l'aiguille de la boussole indique toujours le nord** the compass needle always points North; **le cadran indique la vitesse** the speed is shown on the dial; **l'horloge indique 6 heures** the clock says 6 o'clock; **qu'indique le devis?** what does the estimate say?, how much does it say in the estimate?

4 *(noter ▸ date, prix)* to note *or* to write (down); *(▸ repère)* to mark, to draw; **indiquez votre adresse ici** write your address here; **ce n'est pas indiqué dans le contrat** it's not written down *or* mentioned in the contract; **il indiqua la cache d'une croix sur la carte** he marked the hiding place with a cross on the map; **indique sur la liste les achats qui sont déjà faits** tick off on *or* mark on the list the items that have already been bought

5 *(conseiller ▸ ouvrage, professionnel, restaurant)* to suggest, to recommend; *(▸ traitement)* to prescribe, to give; **tu peux m'i. un bon coiffeur?** can you recommend a good hairdresser?; **une auberge qu'elle m'avait indiquée** a hostel she'd told me about

6 *(dire ▸ marche à suivre, heure)* to tell; **je t'indiquerai comment faire** I'll tell you how to do it; **pourriez-vous m'i. le prix de ce vase?** could you tell me how much the vase is?

7 *(fixer ▸ lieu de rendez-vous, jour)* to give, to name; **indique-moi où et quand, j'y serai** tell me where and when *or* name the place and the time and I'll be there; **à l'heure indiquée** at the appointed *or* agreed time

8 *(être le signe de ▸ phénomène)* to point to, to indicate; *(▸ crainte, joie)* to show, to betray; **tout indique que nous allons vers une crise** everything suggests that we are heading towards a crisis; **ce cri indique que l'animal va attaquer** this cry indicates *or* means that the animal is going to attack

indirect, -e [ɛ̃dirɛkt] **ADJ 1** *(itinéraire, critique)* indirect; *(approche)* indirect, roundabout; *(influence)* indirect; **j'ai appris la nouvelle de façon indirecte** I heard the news in an indirect way; **faire allusion à qch de façon indirecte** to refer obliquely *or* indirectly to sth; **elle m'a fait des reproches indirects** she told me off in a roundabout way
2 *Jur* **héritier i.** collateral heir
3 *Com (coûts, vente)* indirect
4 *Gram* **complément i.** *(d'un verbe transitif)* indirect complement; *(d'un verbe intransitif)* prepositional complement; **discours** *ou* **style i.** indirect *or* reported speech

indirectement [ɛ̃dirɛktəmɑ̃] **ADV** indirectly; **je suis i. responsable** I'm indirectly responsible; **dire les choses i.** to say things in an indirect *or* a roundabout way

indiscernable [ɛ̃discrnabl] **ADJ** indiscernible

indiscipline [ɛ̃disiplin] **NF** *(dans un groupe)* lack of discipline, indiscipline; *(d'un enfant)* disobedience; *(d'un soldat)* insubordination; **faire preuve d'i.** *(écoliers)* to be undisciplined; *(militaires)* to defy orders

indiscipliné, -e [ɛ̃disipline] **ADJ** *(dans un groupe)* undisciplined, unruly; *(enfant)* unruly, disobedient; *(soldat)* insubordinate; *Fig (cheveux)* unmanageable, unruly

indiscret, -ète [ɛ̃diskrɛ, -ɛt] **ADJ 1** *(curieux ▸ personne)* inquisitive; *(▸ demande, question)* indiscreet; *(▸ regard)* inquisitive, prying; **sans (vouloir) être i., combien est-ce que ça vous a coûté?** could I possibly ask you how much you paid for it?; **comment le lui demander sans avoir l'air i.?** how could I ask him/her without seeming indiscreet *or* as though I'm prying?; **à l'abri des regards indiscrets** safe from prying eyes **2** *(révélateur ▸ propos, geste)* indiscreet, telltale; *(▸ personne)* indiscreet, garrulous; **trahi par des langues indiscrètes** given away by wagging tongues; **des témoins indiscrets en ont parlé aux journalistes** witnesses have leaked it to the press
NM,F 1 *(personne curieuse)* inquisitive person **2** *(personne bavarde)* indiscreet person

indiscrètement [ɛ̃diskrɛtmɑ̃] **ADV 1** *(sans tact)* indiscreetly **2** *(avec curiosité)* inquisitively

indiscrétion [ɛ̃diskresjɔ̃] **NF 1** *(d'une personne)* inquisitiveness, curiosity; *(d'une question)* indiscreetness, tactlessness; **pardonnez mon i.** forgive me for asking; **il a poussé l'i. jusqu'à demander des détails** he was so indiscreet as to ask for details; **sans i., avez-vous des enfants?** do you mind if I ask you if you've got any children? **2** *(révélation)* indiscretion; **nous savons par des indiscrétions que…** we know unofficially that…, it's been leaked that…; **commettre une i.** to commit an indiscretion, to say something one shouldn't

indiscutable [ɛ̃diskytabl] **ADJ** indisputable, unquestionable; **vous avez raison, c'est i.** you're indisputably *or* unquestionably right

indiscutablement [ɛ̃diskytabləmɑ̃] **ADV** indisputably, unquestionably

indiscuté, -e [ɛ̃diskyte] **ADJ** undisputed; **le maître i. de la cuisine japonaise** the undisputed *or* uncontested master of Japanese cooking; **ses vertus curatives sont indiscutées** its curative powers are unquestioned

indispensable [ɛ̃dispɑ̃sabl] **ADJ** *(fournitures, machine)* essential, indispensable; *(mesures)* essential, vital, indispensable; *(précautions)* essential, required, necessary; *(personne)* indispensable; **cette entrevue est-elle vraiment i.?** is this interview really necessary?; **tu te crois i.?** so you think you're indispensable?; **tes réflexions n'étaient pas indispensables!** we could have done without your remarks!; **des connaissances en électricité sont indispensables** some knowledge of electricity is essential; **anglais i.** *(dans une offre d'emploi)* English indispensable *or* essential; **il est i. de/que…** it's essential to/that…; **son fils lui est i.** he/she can't do without his/her son; **tu ne m'es pas i., tu sais!** I can do without you, you know!; **i. à tous les sportifs!** essential *or* a must for all sportsmen!; **ce document m'est i. pour continuer mes recherches** this document is absolutely vital *or* essential if I am to carry on my research; **tu n'es pas/tu es i. au projet** the project can/can't proceed without you
NM l'i. *(le nécessaire)* the essentials; **n'emporte que l'i.** only take what you really need

indisponibilité [ɛ̃disponibilite] **NF 1** *(d'une machine)* downtime; *(d'une marchandise, d'une personne, de fonds)* non-availability, unavailability
2 *Jur* inalienability

indisponible [ɛ̃disponibl] **ADJ 1** *(marchandise, personne, fonds)* not available, unavailable; **elle est i. actuellement, rappelez plus tard** she's not available at the moment, please call back later; **je suis i. jusqu'à 19 heures** I'm not free until 7 o'clock **2** *Jur* inalienable

indisposé, -e [ɛ̃dispoze] **ADJ** *(légèrement souffrant)* unwell, *Sout* indisposed
• **indisposée ADJ F** *Euph* **je suis indisposée** it's my *or* that time of the month

indisposer [3] [ɛ̃dispoze] **VT 1** *(irriter)* to annoy; **elle a l'art d'i. les gens** she's got a talent for rubbing people up the wrong way *or* putting people's backs up; **je ne sais pas pourquoi je l'indispose** I don't know why he/she finds me irritating; **i. qn contre qn** to set sb against sb **2** *(rendre malade)* to upset, to make (slightly) ill, *Sout* to indispose

indisposition [ɛ̃dispozisjɔ̃] **NF 1** *(malaise)* discomfort, ailment, *Sout* indisposition; **j'ai eu une i. passagère** I felt slightly off colour for a little while **2** *Euph (menstruation)* period

indissociable [ɛ̃disɔsjabl] **ADJ** indissociable, inseparable (**de** from)

indissolubilité [ɛ̃disɔlybilite] **NF** indissolubility

indissoluble [ɛ̃disɔlybl] **ADJ** *(lien, union)* indissoluble

indissolublement [ɛ̃disɔlybləmɑ̃] **ADV** *(allier, unir)* indissolubly

indistinct, -e [ɛ̃distɛ̃(kt), -ɛ̃kt] **ADJ** *(chuchotement)* indistinct, faint; *(forme)* indistinct, unclear, vague; **prononcer des paroles indistinctes** to mumble inaudibly

indistinctement [ɛ̃distɛ̃ktəmɑ̃] **ADV 1** *(confusément ▸ parler)* indistinctly, unclearly; *(▸ se souvenir)* indistinctly, vaguely; **les sommets m'apparaissaient i.** I could just make out the mountain tops **2** *(sans distinction)* indiscriminately; **recruter i. hommes et femmes** to recruit people regardless of sex

individu [ɛ̃dividy] **NM 1** *(personne humaine)* individual **2** *(quidam)* individual, person; **deux individus ont été aperçus par le concierge** the porter saw two men *or* individuals; **un drôle d'i.** a strange character **3** *Biol, Bot & Phil* individual

individualisation [ɛ̃dividɥalizasjɔ̃] **NF 1** *(d'une espèce animale, d'une langue)* individualization; *(d'un système)* adapting to individual requirements **2** *Jur* **i. de la peine** = sentencing depending upon the individual requirements or characteristics of the defendant

individualiser [3] [ɛ̃dividɥalize] **VT 1** *(système)* to adapt to individual needs, to tailor **2** *Jur* **i. les peines** to tailor sentencing to fit offenders' needs
VPR s'individualiser to acquire individual characteristics

individualisme [ɛ̃dividɥalism] **NM** individualism

individualiste [ɛ̃dividɥalist] **ADJ** individualistic
NMF individualist

individualité [ɛ̃dividɥalite] **NF 1** *(caractère ▸ unique)* individuality; *(▸ original)* originality **2** *(style)* **une forte i.** a strong personal *or* individual style

individuel, -elle [ɛ̃dividɥɛl] **ADJ 1** *(personnel)* individual, personal; **c'est votre responsabilité individuelle** it's your personal responsibility; **faire**

qch à titre i. to do sth independently **2** *(particulier)* individual, private; **chambre individuelle** (private) single room; **compartiment i.** private compartment; **cas i.** individual case; *Tél* **ligne individuelle** private line **3** *Sport* **épreuve individuelle** individual event

NM,F *Sport (gén)* individual sportsman, *f* sportswoman; *(athlète)* individual athlete

individuellement [ɛ̃dividɥɛlmɑ̃] **ADV 1** *(séparément)* individually, separately, one by one; **chaque cas sera examiné i.** each case will be examined individually **2** *(de façon personnelle)* individually, personally; **vous êtes tous i. responsables** you are all personally responsible **3** *Jur* severally; **responsables i.** severally liable

indivis, -e [ɛ̃divi, -iz] *Jur* **ADJ** *(domaine, succession)* joint, undivided; *(propriétaires)* joint

• **en indivis, par indivis ADV** in common; **posséder une propriété en i.** to own a property jointly

indivisaire [ɛ̃divizɛr] **NMF** *Jur (propriétaire)* joint owner

indivisément [ɛ̃divizemɑ̃] **ADV** *Jur* jointly

indivisibilité [ɛ̃divizibilite] **NF** indivisibility

indivisible [ɛ̃divizibl] **ADJ** indivisible

indivision [ɛ̃divizjɔ̃] **NF** *Jur* joint ownership; **propriété/biens en i.** jointly-owned property/goods

Indochine [ɛ̃dɔʃin] **NF l'I.** Indochina; **la guerre d'I.** the Indo-Chinese War

LA GUERRE D'INDOCHINE

French military operations in Indochina from 1940 to 1954 were first directed against Japan and Thailand, and then against the Vietminh revolutionary movement (from 1946 onwards). After the defeat of the French forces at Dien Bien Phu in 1954, a conference in Geneva of countries with interests in the region ended the war by dividing Vietnam into two independent northern and southern states. This war, together with the Algerian war, was a landmark in the French decolonization process.

indochinois, -e [ɛ̃dɔʃinwa, -az] **ADJ** Indo-Chinese

• **Indochinois, -e NM,F** Indo-Chinese

indocile [ɛ̃dɔsil] **ADJ** disobedient, recalcitrant, *Sout* indocile

NMF rebel

indocilité [ɛ̃dɔsilite] **NF** disobedience, recalcitrance

indo-européen, -enne [ɛ̃doœrɔpeɛ̃, -ɛn] *(mpl* **indo-européens,** *fpl* **indo-européennes) ADJ** Indo-European

NM *Ling* Indo-European

• **Indo-Européen, -enne NM,F** Indo-European

indolemment [ɛ̃dɔlamɑ̃] **ADV** indolently, lazily

indolence [ɛ̃dɔlɑ̃s] **NF 1** *(mollesse ▸ dans le travail)* indolence, apathy, lethargy; *(▸ dans l'attitude)* indolence, languidness; **une pose pleine d'i.** a languid posture **2** *Méd* indolence, benignancy

indolent, -e [ɛ̃dɔlɑ̃, -ɑ̃t] **ADJ 1** *(apathique)* indolent, apathetic, lethargic **2** *(languissant)* indolent, languid **3** *Vieilli Méd* indolent, benign

indolore [ɛ̃dɔlɔr] **ADJ** painless

indomptable [ɛ̃dɔ̃tabl] **ADJ 1** *(animal)* untamable, untameable **2** *Fig (nation)* indomitable; *(volonté)* indomitable, invincible; *(passion)* ungovernable, uncontrollable

indompté, -e [ɛ̃dɔ̃te] **ADJ 1** *(sauvage)* untamed, wild; **cheval i.** unbroken horse **2** *Fig (nation)* unvanquished; *(volonté)* unbroken; *(passion)* ungoverned, uncontrolled

Indonésie [ɛ̃dɔnezi] **NF l'I.** Indonesia

indonésien, -enne [ɛ̃dɔnezjɛ̃, -ɛn] **ADJ** Indonesian

NM *(langue)* Indonesian

• **Indonésien, -enne NM,F** Indonesian

in-douze [induz] *Typ* **ADJ INV** duodecimo, twelvemo

NM INV duodecimo, twelvemo

indu, -e [ɛ̃dy] **ADJ 1** *(inconvenant)* undue, excessive; **à une heure indue** at an ungodly hour; **il rentre à des heures indues** he comes home at all hours of the night **2** *Jur (non fondé ▸ réclamation)* unjustified, unfounded

indubitable [ɛ̃dybitabl] **ADJ** undoubted, indubitable, undisputed; **c'est i.** it's beyond doubt *or* dispute; **il est i. que...** there's no doubt that...

indubitablement [ɛ̃dybitabləmɑ̃] **ADV** undoubtedly, indubitably

inductance [ɛ̃dyktɑ̃s] **NF** *Phys* inductance; *Aut* induction

inducteur, -trice [ɛ̃dyktœr, -tris] **ADJ** *Phys (capacité, champ)* inductive; *(courant)* inducing

NM 1 *Phys* inductor **2** *Biol & Chim* inducer

inductif, -ive [ɛ̃dyktif, -iv] **ADJ** *Phil & Phys* inductive

induction [ɛ̃dyksjɔ̃] **NF** *Phil & Phys* induction; **procéder** *ou* **raisonner par i.** to employ inductive reasoning, to induce; **par i., nous pouvons conclure que...** by induction we may conclude that...; **courant d'i.** induced current

inductive [ɛ̃dyktiv] *voir* **inductif**

inductrice [ɛ̃dyktris] *voir* **inducteur**

induire [98] [ɛ̃dɥir] **VT 1** *(inciter)* **i. qn en erreur** to mislead sb; **i. qn en tentation** to lead sb into temptation; *Littéraire* **i. qn à faire qch** to induce sb to do sth

2 *(avoir pour conséquence)* to lead to

3 *(conclure)* to infer, to induce; **que pouvez-vous en i.?** what can you infer from that?

4 *Phys & Phil* to induce

induit, -e [ɛ̃dɥi, -it] **ADJ 1** *Élec (circuit)* induced, secondary; *(courant)* induction *(avant n)* **2** *(demande, investissement)* induced

NM *(circuit)* induced circuit; *(rotor)* rotor

indulgence [ɛ̃dylʒɑ̃s] **NF 1** *(clémence)* indulgence, leniency; **avec i.** indulgently, leniently; **un regard plein d'i.** an indulgent look; **je fais appel à votre i.** I'm asking you to make allowances; **faire preuve d'i. envers qn** to be indulgent with sb, to make allowances for sb; **elle a été d'une i. coupable avec ses enfants** she was far too over-indulgent with her children **2** *Rel* indulgence

• **sans indulgence ADJ** *(traitement, critique)* severe, harsh; *(regard)* stern, merciless **ADV** *(traiter, critiquer)* severely, harshly; *(regarder)* sternly, mercilessly

indulgent, -e [ɛ̃dylʒɑ̃, -ɑ̃t] **ADJ 1** *(qui pardonne)* lenient, forgiving; **soyons indulgents** let's forgive and forget **2** *(sans sévérité ▸ personne)* indulgent, lenient; *(▸ verdict)* lenient; **tu es trop i. avec eux** you're not strict enough with them; **sois i. avec elle** go easy on her

indûment [ɛ̃dymɑ̃] **ADV** unjustifiably, without due *or* just cause; **tu te l'es i. approprié** you had no right to take it; **il réclame i. une somme colossale** he's claiming a huge sum of money to which he is not entitled

industrialisation [ɛ̃dystrijalizasjɔ̃] **NF** industrialization; **économie en voie d'i.** industrializing economy

industrialisé, -e [ɛ̃dystrijalize] **ADJ** *(pays)* industrialized; *(agriculture)* industrial

industrialiser [3] [ɛ̃dystrijalize] **VT 1** *(doter d'industries)* to industrialize **2** *(mécaniser)* to mechanize, to industrialize

VPR s'industrialiser 1 *(se doter d'industries)* to industrialize, to become industrialized **2** *(se mécaniser)* to become mechanized *or* industrialized

industrialisme [ɛ̃dystrijalism] **NM** *Écon* industrialism

industrie [ɛ̃dystri] **NF 1** *(secteur de production)* industry; **travailler dans l'i.** to work in industry *or* in manufacturing; **i. alimentaire** food (processing) industry; **i. automobile** *Br* car *or Am* automobile industry; **i. de base** basic industry; **i. chimique** chemical industry; **i. de consommation** consumer goods industry; **i. en croissance rapide** growth industry; **i. clé** key industry; **i. de l'énergie** power industry; **i. extractive** mining industry; **i. laitière** dairying; **i. légère** light industry; **i. lourde** heavy industry; **i. de luxe** luxury goods industry; **i. manufacturière** manufacturing industry; **i. minière** mining industry; **i. nationalisée** nationalized *or* state-owned industry; **i. pétrolière** oil industry; **i. de pointe** high-tech industry; **i. de précision** precision tool industry; **i. primaire** primary industry; **i. secondaire** secondary industry; **i. de services** service industry; **i. sidérurgique** iron and steel industry; **i. subventionnée** subsidized industry; **i. textile** textile industry; **i. de transformation** processing industry

2 *(secteur commercial)* industry, trade, business; **l'i. hôtelière** the hotel industry *or* trade *or* business; **l'i. du livre** publishing; **l'i. du spectacle** the entertainment business; **l'i. des loisirs** the leisure industry; **les industries de la langue** the language professions; **l'i. du crime** organized crime

3 *(équipements)* plant, industry

4 *(entreprise)* industrial concern

5 *Hum (profession)* **elle exerçait** *ou* **pratiquait de nuit sa douteuse i.** at night, she plied her dubious trade

6 *Arch (ingéniosité)* ingenuity, cleverness

industriel, -elle [ɛ̃dystrijɛl] **ADJ 1** *(procédé, secteur, zone, révolution, société)* industrial; *(pays)* industrial, industrialized **2** *(destiné à l'industrie ▸ véhicule, équipement, rayonnages)* industrial, heavy, heavy-duty **3** *(non artisanal)* mass-produced, factory-made; **des crêpes industrielles** ready-made *or* factory-made pancakes

NM industrialist, manufacturer

Il faut noter que l'adjectif anglais **industrial** ne signifie pas toujours **industriel**. Il s'emploie également à propos des relations entre employeurs et employés dans des expressions du type **industrial relations** ou **industrial unrest**.

industriellement [ɛ̃dystrijɛlmɑ̃] **ADV** industrially; **fabriqué i.** factory-made, mass-produced

industrieux, -euse [ɛ̃dystrijø, -øz] **ADJ** *Littéraire* industrious

inébranlable [inebrɑ̃labl] **ADJ 1** *(ferme)* steadfast, unshakeable, unwavering; **ma décision est i.** my decision is final; **elle a été i.** there was no moving her, she was adamant **2** *(solide ▸ mur)* immovable, (rock) solid

inébranlablement [inebrɑ̃labləmɑ̃] **ADV** steadfastly, unshakeably, unwaveringly

inéchangeable [ineʃɑ̃ʒabl] **ADJ** non-exchangeable

inécoutable [inekutabl] **ADJ** unbearable, impossible to listen to

inécouté, -e [inekute] **ADJ rester i.** to remain unheeded *or* ignored

inédit, -e [inedi, -it] **ADJ 1** *(correspondance, auteur)* (hitherto) unpublished; **ce film est i. en France** this film has never been released in France **2** *(jamais vu)* new, original

NM 1 *(œuvre)* unpublished work; **un i. de Gide** an unpublished work by Gide **2** *(nouveauté)* **c'est de l'i. pour nos trois alpinistes** it's a first for our three climbers

ineffable [inefabl] **ADJ** *Littéraire* **1** *(indicible)* ineffable, indescribable **2** *(amusant)* hilarious

ineffablement [inefabləmɑ̃] **ADV** *Littéraire (indiciblement)* ineffably, indescribably

ineffaçable [inefasabl] **ADJ** *(marque)* indelible; *(souvenir, traumatisme)* unforgettable, enduring

inefficace [inefikas] **ADJ** *(méthode, médicament)* ineffective; *(personne)* ineffective, ineffectual; *(dans son travail)* inefficient

inefficacement [inefikasmɑ̃] **ADV** ineffectively, ineffectually; *(travailler)* inefficiently

inefficacité [inefikasite] **NF** *(d'une méthode, d'un médicament)* inefficacy, ineffectiveness; *(d'une personne)* ineffectuality; *(dans son travail)* inefficiency; **d'une totale i.** totally ineffective

inégal, -e, -aux, -ales [inegal, -o] **ADJ 1** *(varié ▸ longueurs, salaires)* unequal, different; *(mal équilibré)* uneven, unequal; **leurs chances sont inégales** their chances are not equal, they haven't got equal chances; **le combat était i.** the fight was one-sided **2** *(changeant ▸ écrivain, élève, pouls)* uneven, erratic; *(▸ humeur)* changeable, uneven; **la qualité est inégale** it varies in quality **3** *(rugueux)* rough, uneven, bumpy

inégalable [inegalabl] **ADJ** incomparable, matchless, peerless

inégalé, -e [inegale] ADJ *(personne, qualité)* unequalled, unmatched, unrivalled; *(record)* unbeaten

inégalement [inegalmɑ̃] ADV **1** *(différemment)* unequally; **le film a été i. apprécié par les critiques** the film received mixed reviews from the critics **2** *(irrégulièrement)* unevenly

inégalitaire [inegalitɛr] ADJ non-egalitarian, elitist

inégalité [inegalite] NF **1** *(disparité)* difference, disparity; **i. entre deux variables/nombres** difference between two variables/numbers; **i. de l'offre et de la demande** imbalance between supply and demand
2 *(injustice)* inequality (**entre** between); **l'i. des salaires** the difference *or* disparity in wages; **l'i. des chances** the lack of equal opportunities; **les inégalités sociales** social inequalities
3 *(qualité variable ▸ d'une surface)* roughness, unevenness; *(▸ d'un travail, d'une œuvre)* uneven quality, unevenness; *(▸ du caractère)* changeability; **elle a des inégalités d'humeur** she's moody
4 *Math* inequality

inélastique [inelastik] ADJ *Phys* inelastic

inélégamment [inelegamɑ̃] ADV inelegantly

inélégance [inelegɑ̃s] NF **1** *(d'allure)* inelegance, ungainliness; *(d'une méthode, de manières)* inelegance; **le procédé était d'une grande i.** his/her behaviour was most ungracious **2** *(acte, tournure)* impropriety

inélégant, -e [inelegɑ̃, -ɑ̃t] ADJ **1** *(qui manque d'élégance ▸ allure)* inelegant, ungainly; *(▸ méthode, manières)* inelegant **2** *(indélicat)* indelicate, inelegant

inéligibilité [inelizibilite] NF *Jur* ineligibility

inéligible [inelizibl] ADJ *Jur* ineligible

inéluctabilité [inelyktabilite] NF *Sout* ineluctability

inéluctable [inelyktabl] ADJ inevitable, unavoidable, *Littéraire* ineluctable

inéluctablement [inelyktabləmɑ̃] ADV inevitably, inescapably, unavoidably

inemployable [inɑ̃plwajabl] ADJ **1** *(ressources, matériaux)* unusable; *(méthode)* useless, unserviceable **2** *(travailleur)* unemployable

inemployé, -e [inɑ̃plwaje] ADJ *(ressources, talent)* dormant, untapped; *(énergie)* untapped, unused

inénarrable [inenarabl] ADJ hilarious; **si tu avais vu le tableau, c'était i.!** I wish you'd seen it, I can't tell you how funny it was!

inentamé, -e [inɑ̃tame] ADJ *(économies)* intact, untouched; *(bouteille, boîte)* unopened; *(pain, camembert, gâteau)* uncut

inéprouvé, -e [inepruve] ADJ **1** *(non mis à l'épreuve)* untried, untested **2** *(non ressenti)* unknown

inepte [inept] ADJ *(personne)* inept, incompetent; *(réponse, raisonnement)* inept, foolish; *(plan)* inept, ill-considered

ineptie [inepsi] NF **1** *(caractère d'absurdité)* ineptitude, stupidity **2** *(acte, parole)* piece of nonsense; **dire des inepties** to talk nonsense; **c'est une i. de dire que...** it's idiotic *or* absurd to say that...

inépuisable [inepɥizabl] ADJ **1** *(réserves)* inexhaustible, unlimited; *(courage)* endless, unlimited; *(imagination)* limitless, boundless **2** *(bavard)* inexhaustible; **elle est i. sur mes imperfections** once she gets going about my faults, there's no stopping her

inéquation [inekwasjɔ̃] NF *Math* inequality, *Spéc* inequation

inéquitable [inekitabl] ADJ unjust, unfair, *Littéraire* inequitable

inerte [inɛrt] ADJ **1** *(léthargique ▸ personne)* inert, apathetic, lethargic; *(▸ visage)* expressionless **2** *(semblant mort)* inert, lifeless **3** *Chim & Phys* inert

inertie [inɛrsi] NF **1** *(passivité)* lethargy, inertia, passivity **2** *Chim & Phys* inertia

inescomptable [inɛskɔ̃tabl] ADJ *Fin* undiscountable

inespéré, -e [inɛspere] ADJ unhoped-for; **c'est pour moi un bonheur i.** it's a pleasure I hadn't dared hope for

inesthétique [inɛstetik] ADJ unsightly, unattractive

inestimable [inɛstimabl] ADJ **1** *(impossible à évaluer)* incalculable, inestimable; **les dégâts sont inestimables** it's impossible to work out the extent of the damage; **des bijoux d'une valeur i.** priceless jewels **2** *(précieux)* inestimable, invaluable, priceless

inévitable [inevitabl] ADJ **1** *(auquel on ne peut échapper)* unavoidable, inevitable; **et ce fut l'i. catastrophe** and then came the inevitable catastrophe; **c'était i.!** it was bound to happen *or* inevitable! **2** *(avant le nom) (habituel)* inevitable; **l'i. pilier de bar** the inevitable figure propping up the bar; **l'i. Lulu était là** Lulu was there as per usual
NM **l'i.** the inevitable

inévitablement [inevitabləmɑ̃] ADV inevitably, predictably; **et i., elle se décommanda à la dernière minute** and predictably *or* sure enough, she cancelled at the last minute; **si on passe par là, il va i. nous voir** if we go that way he's bound to see us

inexact, -e [inɛgza(kt), -akt] ADJ **1** *(erroné)* inexact, incorrect, inaccurate; **le calcul est i.** there's a mistake in the calculations; **une version inexacte des faits** an inaccurate version of the facts; **il serait i. de dire...** it would be wrong *or* incorrect to say...; **non, c'est i.** no, that's wrong *or* incorrect **2** *(en retard)* unpunctual, late; **il est très i.** he's always late

inexactement [inɛgzaktəmɑ̃] ADV inaccurately, incorrectly

inexactitude [inɛgzaktityd] NF **1** *(d'un raisonnement)* inaccuracy, imprecision; *(d'un récit)* inaccuracy, inexactness; *(d'un calcul)* inaccuracy, inexactitude **2** *(erreur)* inaccuracy, error **3** *(manque de ponctualité)* unpunctuality, lateness

inexaucé, -e [inɛgzose] ADJ *(demande)* unanswered; *(vœu)* unfulfilled

inexcusable [inɛkskyzabl] ADJ *(action)* inexcusable, unforgivable; *(personne)* unforgivable

inexécutable [inɛgzekytabl] ADJ *(plan, programme)* unworkable, impractical; *(tâche)* unfeasible, impossible; *(ordre)* impossible to carry out *or* to execute

inexécuté, -e [inɛgzekyte] ADJ *(ordre, travaux)* not (yet) carried out *or* executed; *(contrat)* unfulfilled; **l'ordre de tirer sur les civils resta i.** the order to shoot civilians was not carried out *or* executed; **le projet resta i.** the project did not go ahead

inexécution [inɛgzekysjɔ̃] NF *(d'un contrat)* nonfulfilment; **i. des travaux** failure to carry out work

inexercé, -e [inɛgzɛrse] ADJ *(recrue, novice)* untrained, inexperienced; *(oreille, main)* unpractised, untrained, untutored

inexigible [inɛgzizibl] ADJ *Jur (dette, impôt)* irrecoverable, *Sout* inexigible

inexistant, -e [inɛgzistɑ̃, -ɑ̃t] ADJ **1** *(très insuffisant)* nonexistent, inadequate; **devant un public i.** in front of a nearly empty house; **ce bonhomme est totalement i.** this guy's a complete nonentity; **lors de la réunion, il a été i.** at the meeting he didn't utter a word; **les structures de base sont inexistantes** the basic structures are lacking, there are hardly any basic structures **2** *(irréel ▸ monstre, peur)* imaginary

inexistence [inɛgzistɑ̃s] NF **1** *(de Dieu)* nonexistence; *(de preuves, de structures)* lack, absence **2** *(manque de valeur)* uselessness

inexorabilité [inɛgzɔrabilite] NF *Littéraire* inexorability

inexorable [inɛgzɔrabl] ADJ **1** *(inévitable)* inexorable, inevitable **2** *(impitoyable)* inexorable

inexorablement [inɛgzɔrabləmɑ̃] ADV **1** *(inévitablement)* inexorably, inevitably **2** *(impitoyablement)* inexorably

inexpérience [inɛksperjɑ̃s] NF lack of experience

inexpérimenté, -e [inɛksperimɑ̃te] ADJ **1** *(sans expérience ▸ personne)* inexperienced; **avec des gestes inexpérimentés** with unpractised hands **2** *(non testé)* (as yet) untested

inexpert, -e [inɛkspɛr, -ɛrt] ADJ inexpert, untrained, untutored; **confié à des mains inexpertes** placed in the hands of a novice

inexpiable [inɛkspjabl] ADJ **1** *(inexcusable)* inexpiable; **un crime i.** an unpardonable crime **2** *Littéraire (impitoyable)* **une lutte i.** a merciless struggle

inexpié, -e [inɛkspje] ADJ unexpiated

inexplicable [inɛksplikabl] ADJ *(comportement)* inexplicable; *(raison, crainte)* inexplicable, unaccountable
NM **l'i.** the inexplicable

inexplicablement [inɛksplikabləmɑ̃] ADV inexplicably, unaccountably

inexpliqué, -e [inɛksplike] ADJ *(décision)* unexplained; *(phénomène)* unexplained, unsolved; *(agissements, départ)* unexplained, mysterious; **une disparition restée inexpliquée jusqu'à ce jour** a disappearance that remains a mystery to this day

inexploitable [inɛksplwatabl] ADJ *(ressources)* unexploitable; *(mine, terres)* unworkable; *(idée)* impractical, unfeasible

inexploité, -e [inɛksplwate] ADJ *(richesses)* undeveloped, untapped; *(mine, terres)* unworked; *(idée, talent)* untapped, untried; *(technique)* unexploited, untried; **laisser un don i.** to fail to exploit a latent talent

inexplorable [inɛksplɔrabl] ADJ unexplorable

inexploré, -e [inɛksplɔre] ADJ unexplored

inexplosible [inɛksplozibl] ADJ nonexplosive

inexpressif, -ive [inɛkspresif, -iv] ADJ *(visage, regard)* inexpressive, expressionless, blank

inexprimable [inɛksprimabl] ADJ inexpressible, ineffable, indescribable

inexprimé, -e [inɛksprime] ADJ unspoken; **une rancœur inexprimée** unspoken resentment

inexpugnable [inɛkspygnabl] ADJ *Littéraire (forteresse)* unassailable, impregnable; *(vertu)* inexpugnable

inextensible [inɛkstɑ̃sibl] ADJ *Tech (appareil, câble)* non-stretchable, inextensible; *(tissu)* non-stretch

in extenso [inɛkstɛ̃so] ADV in full, *Sout* in extenso; **recopie le paragraphe i.** copy out the paragraph in full *or* the whole paragraph

inextinguible [inɛkstɛ̃gibl] ADJ **1** *Littéraire (feu)* inextinguishable **2** *(soif, désir)* inextinguishable, unquenchable; *(amour)* undying **3** *(rire)* uncontrollable

in extremis [inɛkstremis] ADV **1** *(de justesse)* at the last minute, in the nick of time, at the eleventh hour; **réussir qch i.** to (only) just manage to do sth; **vous avez réussi? – oui, mais i.!** did you manage? – yes, but it was a close call! **2** *(avant la mort)* in extremis; **baptiser un enfant/un adulte i.** to christen a child before he dies/an adult on his deathbed

inextricable [inɛkstrikabl] ADJ *(situation, problème, conflit)* inextricable; *(labyrinthe)* inescapable; **cette affaire est i.** this matter is a real tangle; **tu t'es mise dans une situation i.** you've got yourself into an impossible position

inextricablement [inɛkstrikabləmɑ̃] ADV inextricably

infaillibilité [ɛ̃fajibilite] NF infallibility

infaillible [ɛ̃fajibl] ADJ **1** *(efficace à coup sûr)* infallible; **c'est un remède i. contre la toux** it's an infallible cure for coughs **2** *(certain)* infallible, reliable, guaranteed; **c'est la marque i. d'une forte personnalité** it's a sure sign of a strong personality **3** *(qui ne peut se tromper)* infallible; **nul n'est i.** no one is infallible, everyone makes mistakes

infailliblement [ɛ̃fajibləmɑ̃] ADV **1** *(inévitablement)* inevitably, without fail **2** *Littéraire (sans se tromper)* infallibly

infaisable [ɛ̃fəzabl] ADJ *(choix)* impossible; **c'est i.** *(projet, mots croisés)* it can't be done

infalsifiable [ɛ̃falsifjabl] ADJ *(carte d'identité)* forgery-proof

infamant, -e [ɛ̃famɑ̃, -ɑ̃t] ADJ **1** *(déshonorant ▸ acte, crime)* heinous, infamous, abominable; *(▸ propos, accusation)* defamatory, slanderous; **tu peux réclamer ton argent, ce n'est pas i.** you can go and ask for your money, there's no shame in that **2** *Jur voir* **peine**

infâme [ɛ̃fam] ADJ **1** *(vil ▸ crime)* despicable, loathsome, heinous; *(▸ criminel)* vile, despicable; *(▸ traître)* despicable **2** *(répugnant ▸ odeur, nourriture)* revolting, vile, foul; *(▸ endroit)* disgusting, revolting

infamie [ɛ̃fami] NF **1** *(déshonneur)* infamy, disgrace; **il a couvert sa famille d'i.** he has brought disgrace upon his family
2 *(caractère abject ▸ d'une action, d'une personne)* infamy, vileness
3 *(acte révoltant)* infamy, loathsome deed
4 *(propos)* piece of (vile) slander, smear; **dire des infamies de qn** to vilify *or* to slander sb

infant, -e [ɛ̃fɑ̃, -ɑ̃t] NM,F infante, *f* infanta

infanterie [ɛ̃fɑ̃tri] NF infantry; **soldat d'i.** infantryman, foot soldier; **i. aéroportée/motorisée** airborne/motorized infantry; **i. divisionnaire** tank division; **i. légère** light infantry; **i. de ligne** heavy infantry; **i. de marine** marine corps, marines

infanticide [ɛ̃fɑ̃tisid] ADJ infanticidal
NMF *(personne)* child killer, *Jur & Littéraire* infanticide
NM infanticide

infantile [ɛ̃fɑ̃til] ADJ **1** *Méd & Psy* child *(avant n)*, *Spéc* infantile **2** *Péj (puéril)* infantile, childish; **se comporter de façon i.** to behave childishly

infantiliser [3] [ɛ̃fɑ̃tilize] VT to infantilize; **la télévision infantilise les gens** television reduces people to the level of two-year-olds

infantilisme [ɛ̃fɑ̃tilism] NM **1** *Péj (puérilité)* infantilism, immaturity; **elle a refusé! – c'est de l'i.!** she said no! – how childish! **2** *Méd & Psy* infantilism

infarctus [ɛ̃farktys] NM *Méd* infarct; **avoir un i.** to have a heart attack *or* a coronary

infatigable [ɛ̃fatigabl] ADJ **1** *(toujours dispos)* tireless, untiring, *Sout* indefatigable **2** *(indéfectible ▸ énergie, courage)* inexhaustible, unwavering, unflagging; *(▸ détermination)* dogged, unflagging; *(▸ dévouement)* unstinting, unflagging; **elle a mené une lutte i. contre l'injustice** she fought tirelessly against injustice; *Littéraire* **i. à faire le bien** never wearied in well-doing

infatigablement [ɛ̃fatigabləmɑ̃] ADV tirelessly, untiringly, *Sout* indefatigably

infatuation [ɛ̃fatɥasjɔ̃] NF *Littéraire* conceit, self-importance

infatué, -e [ɛ̃fatɥe] ADJ **1** *Littéraire (vaniteux)* self-satisfied, conceited; **i. de sa personne** self-important, full of oneself **2** *Vieilli (entiché)* **i. de qn/qch** infatuated with sb/sth

infatuer [7] [ɛ̃fatɥe] **s'infatuer** VPR **1** *Littéraire (être content de soi)* to be conceited **2** *Vieilli (s'enticher de)* **s'i. de** to become infatuated with

infécond, -e [ɛ̃fekɔ̃, -ɔ̃d] ADJ *Littéraire* **1** *(sol, femme)* infertile, barren **2** *Fig (pensée)* sterile, barren, unproductive

infécondité [ɛ̃fekɔ̃dite] NF *Littéraire* **1** *(d'un sol, d'une femme)* infertility, infecundity, barrenness **2** *Fig (d'une pensée)* sterility, barrenness, unproductiveness

infect, -e [ɛ̃fekt] ADJ **1** *(répugnant ▸ repas)* rotten, revolting, disgusting; *(▸ odeur)* foul, rank, putrid; *(▸ lieu)* filthy; **il y a une odeur infecte ici** it smells foul in here **2** *Fam (très laid, très désagréable)* foul, appalling, lousy; **c'est un type i.** he's absolutely revolting; **les enfants ont été infects ce matin** the kids were terrible *or* awful this morning; **être i. avec qn** to be rotten to sb

infectant, -e [ɛ̃fektɑ̃, -ɑ̃t] ADJ *Méd* infectious, infective

infecter [4] [ɛ̃fekte] VT **1** *Méd* to infect; **plaie infectée** septic wound
2 *(rendre malsain)* to contaminate, to pollute
3 *Littéraire (empester)* **l'usine infecte toute la région** the factory pollutes the whole area
4 *Ordinat (fichier, disque)* to infect
VPR **s'infecter** *Méd* to become infected, to go septic

infectieux, -euse [ɛ̃feksjø, -øz] ADJ *Méd (maladie)* infectious; **un sujet i.** a carrier

infection [ɛ̃feksjɔ̃] NF **1** *Méd* infection; **i. nosocomiale** nosocomial *or* hospital-acquired infection; **i. nosocomiale à bactéries multi-résistantes** MRSA, *Fam* superbug **2** *(puanteur)* (foul) stench; **c'est une i., ce marché!** this market stinks (to high heaven)! **3** *Ordinat* infection

infectiosité [ɛ̃fektjɔsite] NF *Méd* infectiveness

inféodation [ɛ̃feɔdasjɔ̃] NF **1** *Pol* subservience, subjection (**à** to) **2** *Hist* enfeoffment, infeudation

inféoder [3] [ɛ̃feɔde] VT **1** *(soumettre)* to subjugate; **être inféodé à** to be subservient to **2** *Hist* to enfeoff
VPR **s'inféoder** *Pol* **s'i. à** to become subservient to

inférence [ɛ̃ferɑ̃s] NF inference

inférer [18] [ɛ̃fere] VT *Littéraire* to infer, to gather (**de** from)

inférieur, -e [ɛ̃ferjœr] ADJ **1** *(du bas ▸ étagères, membres)* lower; *(▸ lèvre, mâchoire)* lower, bottom *(avant n)*; **la partie inférieure de la colonne** the bottom *or* lower part of the column
2 *(situé en dessous)* lower down, below; **c'est à l'étage i.** it's on the floor below *or* on the next floor down; **la couche inférieure** the layer below *or* beneath; **être i. à** to be lower than *or* below
3 *(moins bon ▸ niveau)* lower; *(▸ esprit, espèce)* inferior, lesser; *(▸ qualité)* inferior, poorer; **les gens d'un rang i.** people of a lower rank *or* lower in rank; **se sentir i. (par rapport à qn)** to feel inferior (to sb); **i. à** inferior to; **je me sens vraiment inférieure à elle** she makes me feel really inferior; **en physique il est très i. à sa sœur** he's not nearly as good as his sister at physics; **je préfère jouer contre quelqu'un qui ne m'est pas i.** I'd rather play against someone who's at least as good as I am; *Littéraire* **il est i. à sa tâche** he is not equal to the task, he is not up to the job; *Bot & Zool* **animaux/végétaux inférieurs** lower animals/plants
4 *(plus petit ▸ chiffre, salaire)* lower, smaller; *(▸ poids, vitesse)* lower; *(▸ taille)* smaller; **nous (leur) étions inférieurs en nombre** there were fewer of us (than of them); **i. à** *(chiffre)* lower *or* smaller *or* less than; *(rendement)* lower than, inferior to; **A est i. ou égal à 3** A is less than or equal to 3; **des températures inférieures à 10°C** temperatures below 10°C *or* lower than 10°C; **les notes inférieures à douze** marks below twelve
NM,F *(gén)* inferior; *(subalterne)* inferior, subordinate, *Péj* underling; **il les considère comme ses inférieurs** he regards them as his inferiors

inférieurement [ɛ̃ferjœrmɑ̃] ADV *(moins bien)* less well; **i. entretenu/conçu** less well-maintained/-designed

infériorité [ɛ̃ferjɔrite] NF **1** *(inadéquation ▸ en grandeur, en valeur)* inferiority; **i. numérique** *ou* **en nombre** numerical inferiority, inferiority in numbers **2** *(handicap)* weakness, inferiority, deficiency; **être en situation d'i.** to be in a weak position; **je me sens en situation d'i.** I feel that I'm in a weak position

infernal, -e, -aux, -ales [ɛ̃fernal, -o] ADJ **1** *Fam (terrible)* infernal, hellish, diabolical; **cet enfant est i.!** that child's a real terror!; **elle est infernale, à toujours se plaindre** she's really awful, she's always complaining; **il faisait une chaleur infernale** the heat was infernal; **nous dévalions la pente à une vitesse infernale** we hurtled down the slope at breakneck speed; **ils mettent de la musique toute la nuit, c'est i.** they've got music on all night, it's absolute hell **2** *Littéraire (de l'enfer)* infernal; **les puissances infernales** the infernal powers **3** *(diabolique ▸ engrenage, logique)* infernal, devilish, diabolical; **la machination infernale qui devait le conduire à la mort** the diabolical scheme which was to lead him to his death; **cycle i.** vicious circle

infertile [ɛ̃fertil] ADJ *Littéraire* **1** *(terre)* infertile, barren **2** *(imagination, esprit)* infertile, uncreative, sterile

infertilité [ɛ̃fertilite] NF *Littéraire* **1** *(de la terre, de l'imagination)* infertility **2** *(d'une femme)* infertility, barrenness

infestation [ɛ̃festasjɔ̃] NF **1** *Méd (infection)* infection **2** *(de parasites, de moustiques)* infestation

infester [3] [ɛ̃feste] VT **1** *(sujet: rats)* to infest, to overrun; *(sujet: pillards)* to infest; **la région est infestée de sauterelles/moustiques** the area is infested with locusts/mosquitoes; **chien infesté de puces** flea-ridden dog; **rues infestées de marchands de souvenirs** streets swarming with souvenir sellers **2** *Méd* to infest

infeutrable [ɛ̃føtrabl] ADJ *Tex* **ce tissu est i.** this fabric won't mat *or* felt

infibulation [ɛ̃fibylasjɔ̃] NF infibulation

infichu, -e [ɛ̃fiʃy] ADJ *Fam (incapable)* **être i. de faire qch** to be incapable of doing sth ▫

infidèle [ɛ̃fidɛl] ADJ **1** *(gén)* disloyal, unfaithful; *(en amour)* unfaithful, *Littéraire* untrue; *(en amitié)* disloyal; **être i. à sa parole** to go back on one's word **2** *(inexact ▸ témoignage, texte)* inaccurate, unreliable; *(▸ traduction)* unfaithful, inaccurate; *(▸ mémoire)* unreliable **3** *Rel* infidel
NMF *Rel* infidel

infidèlement [ɛ̃fidɛlmɑ̃] ADV *(inexactement)* inaccurately, unfaithfully

infidélité [ɛ̃fidelite] NF **1** *(inconstance)* infidelity, unfaithfulness; *(aventure adultère)* infidelity, affair; **commettre une i.** to be unfaithful; **faire une i. à qn** to be unfaithful to sb; *Hum* **j'ai fait une i. à mon coiffeur** I deserted my usual hairdresser **2** *(déloyauté)* disloyalty, unfaithfulness; **son i. à l'idéal de notre jeunesse** his/her disloyalty to our youthful ideal; **l'i. à la parole donnée** being untrue to *or* breaking one's word **3** *(caractère inexact)* inaccuracy, unreliability; *(erreur)* inaccuracy, error; **le scénario est truffé d'infidélités à Molière** the screenplay is full of departures from Molière's original

infiltration [ɛ̃filtrasjɔ̃] NF **1** *Méd* injection; **se faire faire des infiltrations dans le genou** to have injections in the knee **2** *(gén) & Méd* infiltration; **il y a eu une i. de fluide dans les tissus musculaires** there has been infiltration of fluid into the muscle tissue; **il y a des infiltrations dans le plafond** there are leaks in the ceiling, water is leaking *or* seeping through the ceiling **3** *(d'une idée)* penetration, *Littéraire* percolation; *(d'un agitateur)* infiltration

infiltrer [3] [ɛ̃filtre] VT **1** *Méd* to inject (**dans** into), *Spéc* to infiltrate **2** *(organisation, réseau)* to infiltrate
VPR **s'infiltrer 1** *(air, brouillard, eau)* to seep in; *(lumière)* to filter in; **s'i. dans qch** *(sujet: air, brouillard, eau)* to seep into sth; *(sujet: lumière)* to filter into sth; **quand l'eau s'infiltre dans le sable** when the water seeps (through) into the sand **2** *Fig (pénétrer)* **s'i. dans les lieux** to get into the building; **s'i. dans un réseau d'espions** to infiltrate a spy network; *Littéraire* **un soupçon s'infiltra dans mon esprit** a suspicion crept *or* found its way into my mind

infime [ɛ̃fim] ADJ *(quantité, proportion, différence)* infinitesimal, minute, tiny; *(détail)* minor

infini, -e [ɛ̃fini] ADJ **1** *(étendue)* infinite, vast, boundless; *(ressources)* infinite, unlimited
2 *(extrême ▸ générosité, patience)* infinite, boundless, limitless; *(▸ charme, douceur)* infinite; *(▸ précautions)* infinite, endless; *(▸ bonheur)* infinite, immeasurable; *(▸ difficulté, peine)* immense, extreme; **vous m'avez fait un plaisir i. en venant me voir** you have given me enormous pleasure in coming to see me; **auriez-vous l'infinie bonté de me donner l'heure, monsieur?** would you do me the great kindness of telling me the time, sir?; **mettre un soin i. à faire qch** to take infinite pains to do sth
3 *(interminable)* never-ending, interminable, endless; **j'ai dû attendre un temps i.** I had to wait an interminably long time
4 *Math* infinite
NM **1** *Math, Opt & Phot* infinity; *Phot* **faire la mise au point sur l'i.** to focus to infinity **2** *Phil* **l'i.** the infinite; *Littéraire* **l'i. de cette vaste plaine** the immensity of this endless plain
• **à l'infini** ADV **1** *(discuter, reproduire)* endlessly, ad infinitum; *(varier)* infinitely; *(s'étendre)* endlessly **2** *Math* to *or* towards infinity

infiniment [ɛ̃finimɑ̃] **ADV 1** *(extrêmement ▸ désolé, reconnaissant)* extremely; *(▸ généreux)* immensely, boundlessly; *(▸ agréable, douloureux)* immensely, extremely; *(▸ long, grand)* infinitely, immensely; *(▸ petit)* infinitesimally; **je vous remercie i.** thank you (ever) so much; **je regrette i.** I'm extremely sorry; **c'est i. mieux/pire que la dernière fois** it's infinitely better/worse than last time; **elle est i. plus brillante** she's far *or* infinitely brighter; **avec i. de patience/de précautions** with infinite patience/care **2** *Math* infinitely; **l'i. grand** the infinite, the infinitely great; **l'i. petit** the infinitesimal

infinité [ɛ̃finite] **NF 1** *(très grand nombre)* **une i. de** an infinite number of; **on me posa une i. de questions** I was asked endless *or* a great many questions **2** *Littéraire* **l'i. de l'espace** the infinity of space

infinitésimal, -e, -aux, -ales [ɛ̃finitezimal, -o] **ADJ** infinitesimal

infinitif, -ive [ɛ̃finitif, -iv] **ADJ** *Gram* infinitive
NM infinitive (mood)
• **infinitive NF** infinitive (clause)

infirmation [ɛ̃firmasjɔ̃] **NF** *Jur* invalidation

infirme [ɛ̃firm] **ADJ 1** *(handicapé)* disabled, crippled; **i. du bras gauche** crippled in the left arm; **il est resté i. à la suite de son accident** his accident left him disabled *or* crippled *or* a cripple **2** *Littéraire (faible ▸ esprit, corps, etc)* weak, feeble, frail; **l'esprit est prompt mais la chair est i.** the spirit is willing but the flesh is weak
NMF disabled person; **les infirmes** the disabled; **i. moteur cérébral** person suffering from cerebral palsy, *Vieilli* spastic

infirmer [3] [ɛ̃firme] **VT 1** *(démentir)* to invalidate, to contradict **2** *Jur (arrêt)* to revoke; *(jugement)* to quash

infirmerie [ɛ̃firməri] **NF** *(dans une école, une entreprise)* sick bay *or* room; *(dans une prison, dans une caserne)* infirmary, sick bay; *(sur un navire)* sick bay

infirmier, -ère [ɛ̃firmje, -ɛr] **NM,F** male nurse, *f* nurse; **elle fait un stage d'infirmière** she's doing a nursing course; **i. en chef, infirmière en chef** *Br* charge nurse, *Am* head nurse; **i. militaire** medical orderly; **i. de nuit** night nurse; **infirmière diplômée (d'État)** registered nurse; **infirmière visiteuse** district nurse
ADJ nursing *(avant n)*

infirmité [ɛ̃firmite] **NF 1** *(invalidité)* disability, handicap; **la vieillesse et son cortège d'infirmités** old age and the infirmities that come with it; *Méd* **i. motrice cérébrale** cerebral palsy **2** *Littéraire (faiblesse)* failing, weakness; **i. de l'esprit** weakness of the mind

inflammabilité [ɛ̃flamabilite] **NF** inflammability, flammability

inflammable [ɛ̃flamabl] **ADJ 1** *(combustible)* inflammable, flammable; **gaz i.** flammable gas; **matériaux inflammables** inflammable materials **2** *Littéraire (impétueux)* inflammable; **un tempérament i.** a fiery temperament

inflammation [ɛ̃flamasjɔ̃] **NF** *Méd* inflammation; **j'ai une i. au genou** my knee is inflamed

inflammatoire [ɛ̃flamatwar] **ADJ** *Méd* inflammatory

inflation [ɛ̃flasjɔ̃] **NF 1** *Écon* inflation; **i. par la demande/les coûts** demand-pull/cost-push inflation; **i. fiduciaire** inflation of the currency; **i. galopante** galloping inflation; **i. larvée** creeping inflation; **i. monétaire** monetary inflation; **i. des prix** price inflation; **i. des salaires** wage inflation; **des investissements à l'abri de l'i.** inflation-proof investments **2** *(accroissement ▸ des effectifs)* **l'i. du nombre des bureaucrates** the inflated *or* swelling numbers of bureaucrats

inflationnisme [ɛ̃flasjɔnism] **NM** *Écon* inflationism

inflationniste [ɛ̃flasjɔnist] *Écon* **ADJ** *(tendance)* inflationary; *(politique)* inflationist
NMF inflationist

infléchi, -e [ɛ̃fleʃi] **ADJ 1** *(phonème)* inflected **2** *Archit* **arc i.** inflected arch

infléchir [32] [ɛ̃fleʃir] **VT 1** *(courber)* to bend, to inflect **2** *(influer sur)* to modify, to influence; **i. le cours des événements** to affect *or* to influence the course of events **3** *Bourse (faire diminuer)* to cut, to reduce
VPR s'infléchir 1 *(décrire une courbe ▸ gén)* to bend, to curve (round); *(▸ rayon)* to be inflected *or* bent; *(▸ plancher, poutre)* to sag, to bow; **le chemin s'infléchit à cet endroit** the path curves here **2** *Fig (changer de but)* to shift, to change course; **la politique du gouvernement s'infléchit dans le sens du protectionnisme** government policy is shifting *or* veering towards protectionism **3** *Bourse (diminuer ▸ cours)* to fall

inflexibilité [ɛ̃flɛksibilite] **NF 1** *(d'un matériau)* inflexibility, rigidity **2** *(d'une personne)* inflexibility, firmness, resoluteness

inflexible [ɛ̃flɛksibl] **ADJ 1** *(matériau)* rigid, inflexible **2** *(personne)* inflexible, rigid, unbending; *(volonté)* iron *(avant n)*, unbending; **il est resté i.** he wouldn't change his mind **3** *(loi, morale)* rigid, hard-and-fast; *(règlement, discipline)* strict

inflexiblement [ɛ̃flɛksibləmɑ̃] **ADV** *Littéraire* inflexibly, rigidly

inflexion [ɛ̃flɛksjɔ̃] **NF 1** *(modulation ▸ de la voix)* inflection, modulation
2 *(de courbe, rayon)* inflection
3 *(changement de direction)* shift, change of course; **on constate une i. de la politique vers la détente** there has been a change in policy in favour of détente
4 *Ling* inflection
5 *(inclination)* **avec une gracieuse i. de la tête** with a graceful nod; **une i. du buste** a bow
6 *Bourse (diminution)* reduction, fall

infliger [17] [ɛ̃fliʒe] **VT i. une punition/une défaite/des souffrances/des pertes à qn** to inflict a punishment/a defeat/sufferings/losses on sb; **i. une amende/corvée à qn** to impose a fine/chore on sb; **i. une humiliation à qn** to put sb down, to humiliate sb; **i. sa compagnie** *ou* **présence à qn** to inflict one's company *or* presence on sb

inflight [inflajt] **NM** *Presse* inflight magazine

inflorescence [ɛ̃flɔresɑ̃s] **NF** *Bot* inflorescence

influençable [ɛ̃flyɑ̃sabl] **ADJ** easily influenced *or* swayed

influence [ɛ̃flyɑ̃s] **NF 1** *(marque, effet)* influence; **on voit tout de suite l'i. de Kokoschka dans ses tableaux** it's easy to spot the influence of Kokoschka on *or* in his/her paintings; **cela n'a eu aucune i. sur ma décision** it didn't influence my decision at all, it had no bearing (at all) on my decision **2** *(emprise ▸ d'une personne, d'une drogue, d'un sentiment)* influence; **avoir de l'i. sur qn** to have influence over sb; **avoir une bonne i. sur** to be *or* to have a good influence on; **avoir une grande i. sur** to have a great influence on; **j'ai beaucoup d'i. sur lui** I've got a lot of influence over him; **subir l'i. de qn** to be influenced by sb; **être sous l'i. de la boisson/drogue** to be under the influence of drink/drugs; **être sous l'i. de la jalousie** to be possessed by jealousy; **il a agi sous l'i. de la colère** he acted in the grip of *or* in a fit of anger; **être sous i.** *(drogué)* to be under the influence of drugs **3** *(poids social ou politique)* influence; **avoir de l'i.** to have influence, to be influential

influencer [16] [ɛ̃flyɑ̃se] **VT** to influence; **ne te laisse pas i. par la publicité** don't let advertising influence you, don't let yourself be influenced by advertising; **il se laisse facilement i.** he's easily influenced; **ses arguments m'influençaient toujours au moment du vote** his/her arguments always used to sway me just before a vote; **sa peinture fut très influencée par les fauves** his/her painting was heavily influenced by the Fauvists; **la lune influence les marées** the moon affects the tide

influent, -e [ɛ̃flyɑ̃, -ɑ̃t] **ADJ** influential; **c'est une personne influente** he's/she's a person of influence *or* an influential person; **les gens influents** people in positions of influence, influential people

influer [7] [ɛ̃flye] **influer sur VT IND** to have an influence on, to influence, to affect

influx [ɛ̃fly] **NM** *Physiol* **i. nerveux** nerve impulse

info [ɛ̃fo] *Fam* **NF** info *(UNCOUNT)*; **c'est lui qui m'a donné cette i.** I got the info from him
• **infos NFPL les infos** the news□ *(UNCOUNT)*; **je l'ai entendu aux infos** I heard it on the news

infobulle [ɛ̃fobyl] **NF** *Ordinat* tooltip

infodominance [ɛ̃fodɔminɑ̃s] **NF** *Mil* information dominance

infogérance [ɛ̃foʒerɑ̃s] **NF** facilities management

infographe [ɛ̃fɔgraf] **NMF** graphics artist

Infographie® [ɛ̃fɔgrafi] **NF** computer graphics

infographiste [ɛ̃fɔgrafist] **NMF** graphics artist

in-folio [infɔljo] *Typ* **ADJ INV** folio
NM INV folio

infomercial, -aux [ɛ̃fɔmɛrsjal, -o] **NM** infomercial

infondé, -e [ɛ̃fɔ̃de] **ADJ** unfounded, groundless

informateur, -trice [ɛ̃fɔrmatœr, -tris] **NM,F** *(gén)* informant; *(de police)* informer

informaticien, -enne [ɛ̃fɔrmatisjɛ̃, -ɛn] **ADJ** *voir* **ingénieur**
NM,F *(dans une entreprise)* data processor; *(à l'université)* computer scientist; **son fils est i.** his/her son works in computers

informatif, -ive [ɛ̃fɔrmatif, -iv] **ADJ** informative

information [ɛ̃fɔrmasjɔ̃] **NF 1** *(renseignement)* piece of information; **des informations** (some) information; **on manque d'informations sur les causes de l'accident** we lack information about the cause of the accident; **demander des informations sur** to ask (for information) about, to inquire about; **je vais aux informations** I'll go and find out; **nous vous adressons ce catalogue à titre d'i.** we are sending you this catalogue for your information
2 l'i. *(mise au courant)* information; **réunion d'i.** briefing session; **l'i. circule mal entre les services** there's poor communication between departments; **nous demandons une meilleure i. des consommateurs sur leurs droits** we want consumers to be better informed about their rights; **pour ton i., sache que...** for your (own) information, you should know that…; *Mktg* **i. commerciale** market intelligence; *Mktg* **i. sur le lieu de vente** point-of-sale information; *Mktg* **informations primaires** primary data; *Mktg* **informations secondaires** secondary data
3 *Presse, Rad & TV* news item, piece of news; **voici une i. de dernière minute** here is some last-minute news; **des informations économiques** economic news; **l'i. financière de la journée** the day's financial news; **pour finir, je rappelle l'i. la plus importante de notre journal** finally, here is our main story *or* main news item once again; **l'i.** the news; **la liberté d'i., le droit à l'i.** freedom of information; **qui fait l'i.?** who decides what goes into the news?; **journal d'i.** quality newspaper
4 *Ordinat* **l'i.** data, information; **les sciences de l'i.** information science, informatics *(singulier)*; **protection de l'i.** data protection; **traitement de l'i.** data processing
5 *Aut & Transp* **i. embarquée** on-board information, *(dans une voiture)* in-car information
6 *Jur* **i. (judiciaire)** *(enquête)* inquiry; *(instruction préparatoire)* preliminary investigation; **ouvrir une i.** to set up a preliminary investigation
• **informations NFPL** *Rad & TV (émission)* **les informations** the news (bulletin); **informations régionales** local news; **informations télévisées/radiodiffusées** television/radio news; **c'est passé aux informations** it was on the news; **je l'ai vu/entendu aux informations** I saw/heard it on the news

informatique [ɛ̃fɔrmatik] **ADJ** computer *(avant n)*; **un système i.** a computer system
NF *(science)* computer science, information technology; *(traitement des données)* data processing; **travailler dans l'i.** to work *or* to be in computing; **société/magazine d'i.** computer company/magazine; **cours d'i.** computer course; **i. documentaire** (electronic) information retrieval; **i. d'entreprise** business data processing; **i. familiale** home computing; **i. de gestion** *(dans une administration)* administrative data processing; *(dans une entreprise)* business data processing, business applications; **i. grand public** mass (consumer) computing; **i. individuelle** personal computing

informatiquement [ɛ̃fɔrmatikmɑ̃] **ADV** by *or* on computer; **toutes les données sont traitées i.** all the data is processed by *or* on computer

informatisation [ɛ̃fɔrmatizasjɔ̃] **NF** computerization

informatiser **[3]** [ɛ̃fɔrmatize] **VT** to computerize

VPR s'informatiser to become computerized; **la bibliothèque s'est informatisée** the library catalogue has been computerized; **depuis que je me suis informatisé** since I got a computer

informative [ɛ̃fɔrmativ] *voir* **informatif**

informatrice [ɛ̃fɔrmatris] *voir* **informateur**

informe [ɛ̃fɔrm] **ADJ 1** *(inesthétique ▸ vêtement, sculpture)* shapeless

2 *(qui n'a plus de forme ▸ chaussure)* shapeless, battered

3 *(sans contours nets)* formless, shapeless; *Biol & Chim* amorphous

4 *(ébauché)* rough, unfinished, undeveloped; **ce n'est qu'une esquisse i.** it's only a rough sketch

informé, -e [ɛ̃fɔrme] **ADJ** well-informed, informed; **dans les milieux informés** in informed circles; **les gens bien informés** well-informed people; **de source bien informée** from a well-informed *or* an authoritative source; **c'est son amant – tu m'as l'air bien** *ou* **très i.!** he's her lover – you seem to know a lot!; **nous sommes mal informés** *(peu renseignés)* we don't get enough information, we're not sufficiently informed; *(avec de fausses informations)* we're being misinformed; **se tenir i. de** to keep oneself informed about; **tenir qn i. (de qch)** to keep sb informed (of sth)

NM *Jur* (judicial *or* legal) inquiry; **jusqu'à plus ample i.** pending further information

informel, -elle [ɛ̃fɔrmɛl] **ADJ** *(non officiel, décontracté)* informal

informer **[3]** [ɛ̃fɔrme] **VT 1** *(aviser)* **i. qn de** to inform *or* to tell *or* to advise sb of; **si le notaire téléphone, vous voudrez bien m'en i.** if the solicitor phones, will you please let me know *or* inform me; **elle a démissionné – on vient de m'en i.** she's resigned – I've just been informed of it *or* told about it; **i. qn que** to inform *or* to tell sb that; **l'a-t-on informé qu'il est muté?** has he been informed *or* notified of his transfer?; **nous informons Messieurs les voyageurs que…** passengers are informed that…; **j'ai fait i. son père de votre décision** I've made sure that his/her father has been informed of your decision

2 *(renseigner)* to inform, to give information to; **nous sommes là pour i. le public** our job is to inform the public; **les consommateurs ne sont pas assez informés de** *ou* **sur leurs droits** consumers are not informed enough *or* don't know enough about their rights; **on vous a mal informé, vous avez été mal informé** you've been misinformed *or* wrongly informed

VI *Jur* **i. contre qn** to start investigations concerning sb; **i. sur un crime** to investigate a crime

VPR s'informer 1 *(se renseigner)* to get information, to ask, to inquire; **je me suis informé auprès de mon avocat/de la mairie** I asked my lawyer/at the *Br* town hall *or Am* city hall; **s'i. de** *(droit, horaire, résultats)* to inquire *or* to ask about; **s'i. de la santé de qn** to inquire after sb's health; **s'i. sur** to inform oneself about; **je vais m'i. sur la marche à suivre** I'm going to find out what the procedure is

2 *(se tenir au courant)* to keep oneself informed

informulé, -e [ɛ̃fɔrmyle] **ADJ** unformulated, unspoken

inforoute [ɛ̃fɔrut] **NF** *Can Ordinat* information superhighway, infohighway

infortune [ɛ̃fɔrtyn] **NF** *Littéraire* **1** *(événement)* misfortune; **ce jour-là fut la plus grande i. de ma vie** that day was the greatest misfortune in my life **2** *(malheur)* misfortune; *Euph* **i. conjugale** infidelity

infortuné, -e [ɛ̃fɔrtyne] *Littéraire* **ADJ** *(avant le nom)* unfortunate, luckless

NM,F (unfortunate) wretch

infospectacle [ɛ̃fɔspɛktakl] **NF** infotainment

infosphère [ɛ̃fɔsfɛr] **NF** infosphere

infoutu, -e [ɛ̃futy] **ADJ** *très Fam* **être i. de faire qch** to be downright incapable of doing sth▫

infraction [ɛ̃fraksjɔ̃] **NF 1** *Jur* breach of the law, offence; **i. au code de la route** driving offence; **être en i.** to be in breach of the law; **je n'ai jamais été en i.** I've never committed an *or* any offence; **i. internationale** breach of international law; **i. militaire** military offence; **i. mineure** non-indictable offence; **i. politique** ≃ offence *or* offences against the state **2** *(transgression)* infringement, transgression; **i. à** breach of, transgression against

infranchissable [ɛ̃frɑ̃ʃisabl] **ADJ 1** *(col)* impassable; *(rivière)* which cannot be crossed **2** *(difficulté)* insuperable, insurmountable

infrangible [ɛ̃frɑ̃ʒibl] **ADJ** *Littéraire* infrangible

infrarouge [ɛ̃fraruʒ] **ADJ** infrared

NM infrared (radiation)

infrason [ɛ̃frasɔ̃] **NM** infrasound

infrastructure [ɛ̃frastryktyr] **NF 1** *(ensemble d'équipements)* infrastructure; **i. routière/touristique** road/tourist infrastructure; **l'i. commerciale de la ville** the town's shopping facilities **2** *Constr* substructure

infréquentable [ɛ̃frekɑ̃tabl] **ADJ ils sont infréquentables** they're not the sort of people you'd want to associate with; **tu es i.!** you're a disgrace!

infroissable [ɛ̃frwasabl] **ADJ** crease-resistant

infructueux, -euse [ɛ̃fryktɥø, -øz] **ADJ 1** *(vain)* fruitless, unsuccessful **2** *Vieilli (arbre, terre)* barren

infumable [ɛ̃fymabl] **ADJ** unsmokable

infuse [ɛ̃fyz] *voir* **science**

infuser **[3]** [ɛ̃fyze] **VT 1** *(faire macérer ▸ thé)* to brew, to infuse; *(▸ tisane)* to infuse; **le thé est assez infusé** the tea has brewed *or* infused for long enough **2** *Littéraire (insuffler)* **i. qch à qn** to infuse *or* to inject sb with sth, to infuse *or* to inject sth into sb

VI *(aux être ou avoir) (macérer ▸ thé)* to brew, to infuse; *(▸ tisane)* to infuse; **faire i.** to brew; **laissez i. quelques minutes** leave to infuse for a few minutes

infusible [ɛ̃fyzibl] **ADJ** *Tech* infusible

infusion [ɛ̃fyzjɔ̃] **NF 1** *(boisson)* herbal tea, infusion; **une i. de camomille** some camomile tea, an infusion of camomile **2** *(macération ▸ de thé)* brewing, infusion; *(▸ de tisane)* infusion, infusing; **le thé n'a pas besoin d'être passé après i.** the tea doesn't need straining after brewing

> **SUFFIX**
>
> **-ING**
>
> Although this English suffix has been legitimately integrated into French through the use of whole English words in their original sense (**marketing, shopping, canyoning** etc), it also appears in a lot of "fake" anglicisms which may make an English speaker smile and for which a different word, often not ending in *-ing*, is used, eg:
>
> **un camping** a campsite; **un parking** a car park; **faire le forcing** to put the pressure on; **un pressing** a dry cleaner's; **faire du footing** to go jogging; **un mailing** a mailshot; **le zapping** channel-hopping; **le surbooking** (a hybrid made up of a French prefix and an English word) overbooking, double-booking

ingagnable [ɛ̃gaɲabl] **ADJ** unwinnable, which can't be won; **la partie est i. pour l'Angleterre** England can't win (the game)

ingambe [ɛ̃gɑ̃b] **ADJ** *Littéraire* nimble, spry, sprightly; **il est resté i. jusqu'à la fin** he remained very active to the end

ingénier **[9]** [ɛ̃ʒenje] **s'ingénier VPR s'i. à** to try hard *or* to endeavour *or* to strive to; **s'i. à trouver une solution** to work hard at finding *or* to do all one can to find a solution; **s'i. à plaire** to strive to please; **on dirait qu'il s'ingénie à me nuire** it's as if he's going out of his way to do me down

ingénierie [ɛ̃ʒeniri] **NF** engineering; **i. assistée par ordinateur** computer-assisted engineering; **i. financière** financial engineering; **i. génétique** genetic engineering; **i. informatique** systems engineering; **i. logicielle** software engineering; **i. de systèmes** systems engineering; **i. de systèmes assistée par ordinateur** computer-aided software engineering, CASE

ingénieur [ɛ̃ʒenjœr] **NM** engineer; **i. agronome** agricultural engineer; **i. commercial** sales engineer; **i. électricien** electrical engineer; **i. électronicien** electronics engineer; **i. du génie civil** civil engineer; **i. informaticien** computer scientist; **i. mécanicien** mechanical engineer; **i. de méthodes** methods engineer; **i. des ponts et chaussées** civil engineer; **i. du son** sound engineer; **i. système** systems engineer; **i. des travaux publics** civil engineer

ingénieur-conseil [ɛ̃ʒenjœrkɔ̃sɛj] *(pl* **ingénieurs-conseils)** **NM** engineering consultant, consultant engineer

ingénieuse [ɛ̃ʒenjøz] *voir* **ingénieux**

ingénieusement [ɛ̃ʒenjøzmɑ̃] **ADV** ingeniously

ingénieux, -euse [ɛ̃ʒenjø, -øz] **ADJ** *(personne)* ingenious, clever, inventive; *(plan, appareil, procédé)* ingenious

ingéniosité [ɛ̃ʒenjozite] **NF** ingenuity, inventiveness, cleverness

ingénu, -e [ɛ̃ʒeny] **ADJ** ingenuous, naive

NM,F ingenuous *or* naive person

• **ingénue** **NF** *Théât* ingenue *or* ingénue (role); *Fig* **cesse de jouer les ingénues** stop acting *or* playing the innocent

ingénuité [ɛ̃ʒenɥite] **NF** ingenuousness, naivety

ingénument [ɛ̃ʒenymɑ̃] **ADV** ingenuously, naively

ingérence [ɛ̃ʒerɑ̃s] **NF** interference; *Pol* interference, intervention; *Presse* **i. rédactionnelle** editorial interference

ingérer **[18]** [ɛ̃ʒere] **VT** to absorb, to ingest

VPR s'ingérer s'i. dans to interfere *or* to meddle in; **s'i. dans la vie privée de qn** to meddle in sb's private life; **s'i. dans les affaires intérieures d'un autre pays** to interfere in the domestic affairs of another country

ingestion [ɛ̃ʒɛstjɔ̃] **NF** ingestion

ingouvernable [ɛ̃guvɛrnabl] **ADJ** ungovernable

ingrat, -e [ɛ̃gra, -at] **ADJ 1** *(sans grâce ▸ visage)* unattractive, unpleasant, coarse; **avoir un physique i.** to be unattractive *or* graceless **2** *(tâche, travail, sujet, rôle)* unrewarding; *(terre)* unproductive **3** *(sans reconnaissance ▸ personne)* ungrateful (**avec** *ou* **envers** to, towards)

NM,F ungrateful person

ingratitude [ɛ̃gratityd] **NF 1** *(d'une personne)* ingratitude, ungratefulness; **faire preuve d'i.** to behave with ingratitude **2** *(d'une tâche)* thanklessness

ingrédient [ɛ̃gredjɑ̃] **NM 1** *(dans une recette, un mélange)* ingredient **2** *Fig (élément)* ingredient; **les ingrédients du bonheur** the recipe for happiness

inguérissable [ɛ̃gerisabl] **ADJ** *(malade, maladie)* incurable; *(chagrin)* inconsolable

ingurgitation [ɛgyrʒitasjɔ̃] **NF** swallowing, *Spéc* ingurgitation

ingurgiter **[3]** [ɛ̃gyrʒite] **VT** *Fam* **1** *(avaler ▸ aliments)* to wolf *or* to gulp down; *(▸ boisson)* to gulp down, to knock back **2** *Fig* to take in; **avec tout ce qu'on leur fait i. avant l'examen!** with all the stuff they have to cram (into their heads) before the exam!; **faire i. des faits/dates à qn** to stuff sb's head full of facts/dates

inhabile [inabil] **ADJ 1** *(sans aptitude)* inept, unskilful; **elle n'est pas i. mais elle manque d'expérience** she's not inept but she lacks experience; **i. à** unfit for **2** *(maladroit ▸ mouvement)* clumsy, awkward; *(▸ propos, méthode)* inept, clumsy; **il traça un cercle d'une main i.** he clumsily drew a circle; **une déclaration i.** a bungling statement **3** *Jur* (legally) incapable; **i. à témoigner/à tester** incompetent to stand as a witness/to make a will

inhabileté [inabilte] **NF** *Littéraire* ineptitude, ineptness, clumsiness

inhabilité [inabilite] **NF** *Jur* (legal) incapacity (à to)

inhabitable [inabitabl] **ADJ** *(maison, grenier)* uninhabitable; *(quartier)* unpleasant to live in

> Il faut noter que l'adjectif anglais **inhabitable** est un faux ami. Il signifie **habitable**.

inhabité, -e [inabite] ADJ **1** *(maison, chambre)* uninhabited, unoccupied; *(contrée)* uninhabited; **des villages inhabités** uninhabited villages; **de vastes contrées inhabitées s'étendent vers le nord** vast empty tracts of land lie to the north **2** *Astron (vol)* unmanned

> Il faut noter que l'adjectif anglais **inhabited** est un faux ami. Il signifie **habité**.

inhabituel, -elle [inabitɥɛl] ADJ unusual, odd

inhalateur, -trice [inalatœr, -tris] ADJ inhaling, breathing
NM **1** *(pour inhalations)* inhaler **2** *Aviat* oxygen mask

inhalation [inalasjɔ̃] NF **1** *(respiration)* breathing in, *Spéc* inhalation **2** *(traitement)* (steam) inhalation; **je (me) fais des inhalations avec ce produit** I use this product as an inhalant; **le mieux pour les rhumes, c'est de faire des inhalations** inhaling steam is the best thing for a cold

inhalatrice [inalatris] *voir* **inhalateur**

inhaler [3] [inale] VT to inhale, to breathe in

inharmonieux, -euse [inarmɔnjø, -øz] ADJ *(tons)* inharmonious, jarring; *(musique)* inharmonious, discordant

inhérence [inerɑ̃s] NF inherence

inhérent, -e [inerɑ̃, -ɑ̃t] ADJ inherent; **i. à** inherent in

inhibé, -e [inibe] ADJ inhibited, repressed
NM,F inhibited *or* repressed person

inhiber [3] [inibe] VT to inhibit

inhibiteur, -trice [inibitœr, -tris] ADJ *Physiol & Psy* inhibitive, inhibitory
NM *Pharm & Physiol* inhibitor

inhibition [inibisjɔ̃] NF *Physiol & Psy* inhibition; **le traumatisme a provoqué une i. de la parole chez l'enfant** the child had speech difficulties after the shock

inhibitrice [inibitris] *voir* **inhibiteur**

inhospitalier, -ère [inɔspitalje, -ɛr] ADJ inhospitable

inhumain, -e [inymɛ̃, -ɛn] ADJ inhuman; **un cri i.** an inhuman *or* unearthly cry

inhumainement [inymɛnmɑ̃] ADV inhumanly, inhumanely

inhumanité [inymanite] NF *Littéraire* inhumanity

inhumation [inymasjɔ̃] NF burial, *Sout* interment, inhumation

inhumer [3] [inyme] VT to bury, to inter

inimaginable [inimaʒinabl] ADJ unimaginable; **un paysage d'une beauté i.** an unbelievably beautiful landscape

inimitable [inimitabl] ADJ inimitable

inimité, -e [inimite] ADJ which has still to be imitated, unique

inimitié [inimitje] NF enmity, hostility; **regarder qn avec i.** to look at sb hostilely

ininflammable [inɛ̃flamabl] ADJ *(produit)* nonflammable; *(revêtement)* flame-proof

inintelligemment [inɛ̃teliʒamɑ̃] ADV unintelligently

inintelligence [inɛ̃teliʒɑ̃s] NF **1** *(stupidité)* lack of intelligence; **elle a eu l'i. de photocopier la lettre** rather unintelligently, she photocopied the letter **2** *(incompréhension)* incomprehension, lack of understanding; **une profonde i. des difficultés** a total lack of insight into the problems

inintelligent, -e [inɛ̃teliʒɑ̃, -ɑ̃t] ADJ unintelligent

inintelligibilité [inɛ̃teliʒibilite] NF unintelligibility

inintelligible [inɛ̃teliʒibl] ADJ unintelligible, impossible to understand

inintelligiblement [inɛ̃teliʒibləmɑ̃] ADV unintelligibly

inintéressant, -e [inɛ̃teresɑ̃, -ɑ̃t] ADJ uninteresting

ininterrompu, -e [inɛ̃terɔ̃py] ADJ *(série, flot)* unbroken, uninterrupted; *(bruit, bavardage)* continuous, ceaseless; *(tradition)* continuous, unbroken; *(efforts)* unremitting, steady; **une nuit de sommeil i.** a night of unbroken sleep; **nous diffusons aujourd'hui cinq heures de musique ininterrompue** today we are broadcasting five hours of non-stop *or* uninterrupted music

inique [inik] ADJ *Littéraire* iniquitous, unjust, unfair

iniquement [inikmɑ̃] ADV *Littéraire* iniquitously, unjustly, unfairly

iniquité [inikite] NF *Littéraire* iniquity, injustice; **commettre des iniquités** to commit wrongs

initial, -e, -aux, -ales [inisjal, -o] ADJ initial; **le choc i.** the initial shock
• **initiale** NF *(première lettre)* initial; **il a signé le document de ses initiales** he signed the document with his initials, he initialled the document

initialement [inisjalmɑ̃] ADV initially, at first, originally

initialisation [inisjalizasjɔ̃] NF *Ordinat* initialization

initialiser [3] [inisjalize] VT *Ordinat* to initialize

initiateur, -trice [inisjatœr, -tris] ADJ initiatory
NM,F **1** *(maître)* initiator; **elle a été son initiatrice en amour/musique** it was thanks to her that he/she discovered love/music **2** *(novateur)* pioneer; **les initiateurs de la biologie/du structuralisme** the founders of biology/of structuralism

initiation [inisjasjɔ̃] NF **1** *(approche)* initiation, introduction; **son i. à l'amour eut lieu à l'âge de 20 ans** he/she was initiated into the ways of love when he/she was 20; **i. à la psychologie/au russe** introduction to psychology/to Russian **2** *(en anthropologie)* initiation

initiatique [inisjatik] ADJ *(rite)* initiatory, initiation *(avant n)*

initiative [inisjativ] NF **1** *(esprit de décision)* initiative; **avoir de l'i.** to have initiative *or* drive; **manquer d'i.** to lack initiative; **faire preuve d'i.** to show great initiative; **esprit d'i.** initiative; **plein d'i.** enterprising **2** *(idée)* initiative; **l'i. du concert est venue d'elles** the original idea for the concert came from them; **à** *ou* **sur l'i. de qn** on sb's initiative; **il a été hospitalisé sur mon i.** he was sent to hospital on my initiative; **les négociations ont été organisées à l'i. du Brésil** the negotiations were initiated by Brazil *or* organized on Brazil's initiative; **prendre l'i. de qch** to initiate sth, to take the initiative for sth; **prendre l'i. de faire qch** to take the initiative in doing sth; *Mil* **i. de défense stratégique** strategic defence initiative; **i. gouvernementale** governmental prerogative to propose legislation; **i. parlementaire** parliamentary prerogative to legislate; **i. populaire** democratic right to petition; **i. privée** *Écon* private initiative; *Jur & Pol* initiative **3** *(action spontanée)* initiative; **faire qch de sa propre i.** to do sth on one's own initiative; **prendre une i.** to take an initiative; **prendre des initiatives** to show initiative; **elle nous laisse prendre des initiatives** she allows us freedom of action; **prendre l'i. de faire qch** to take the initiative in doing sth; *Pol* **i. de paix** peace initiative *or* overture

initiatrice [inisjatris] *voir* **initiateur**

initié, -e [inisje] ADJ initiated
NM,F **1** *(connaisseur)* initiated person, initiate; **les initiés** the initiated; **pour les initiés** not for the uninitiated **2** *(en anthropologie)* initiate **3** *Bourse* insider

initier [9] [inisje] VT **1** *(novice)* to initiate; **i. qn à qch** to initiate sb into sth, to introduce sb to sth **2** *(en anthropologie)* to initiate **3** *(faire démarrer)* to initiate, to get going; **i. un processus** to initiate a process
VPR **s'initier s'i. à qch** to learn the basics of sth, to get to know sth; **j'ai besoin de deux semaines pour m'i. au traitement de texte** I need two weeks to teach myself *or* to learn how to use a word processor

injectable [ɛ̃ʒɛktabl] ADJ injectable

injecté, -e [ɛ̃ʒɛkte] ADJ **1** *(rougi)* **yeux injectés de sang** bloodshot eyes **2** *Méd* injected

injecter [4] [ɛ̃ʒɛkte] VT **1** *Méd* to inject (**dans** into); **on cherche des cobayes qui acceptent de se faire i. le virus** we're looking for people who would agree to be injected with the virus **2** *(introduire)* to inject, to infuse, to instil; *Fin (argent, capitaux)* to inject (**dans** into); **il faudrait i. quelques idées nouvelles dans ce projet** we need to inject *or* to infuse a few new ideas into the project; **i. de l'enthousiasme à une équipe** to instil enthusiasm into a team; **i. des millions dans une affaire** to inject *or* to pump millions into a business **3** *Tech* to inject
VPR **s'injecter** *(yeux)* to become bloodshot

injecteur, -trice [ɛ̃ʒɛktœr, -tris] ADJ injection *(avant n)*
NM injector

injection [ɛ̃ʒɛksjɔ̃] NF **1** *Méd* injection **2** *Fin (apport ▸ d'argent)* injection (**dans** into) **3** *Tech* injection; **à i.** (fuel) injection *(avant n)*

injectrice [ɛ̃ʒɛktris] *voir* **injecteur**

injoignable [ɛ̃ʒwaɲabl] ADJ **j'ai essayé de l'appeler toute la matinée mais il était i.** I tried to phone him all morning, but I couldn't get through (to him) *or* get hold of him

injonction [ɛ̃ʒɔ̃ksjɔ̃] NF **1** *(ordre)* order; **sur l'i. de qn** at sb's behest; *Bourse* **i. à la vente** sell order **2** *Jur* injunction, (judicial) order; **i. de faire** mandatory injunction; **i. de payer** order to pay; **i. thérapeutique** drug rehabilitation order, *Br* ≃ Drug Treatment and Testing Order

injouable [ɛ̃ʒwabl] ADJ unplayable; **la sonate est i.** the sonata is impossible to play; **la balle est i.** the ball is unplayable

injure [ɛ̃ʒyr] NF **1** *(insulte)* insult, abuse *(UNCOUNT)*; **un chapelet d'injures** a stream of abuse *or* insults; **il se mit à lâcher des injures** he started hurling abuse; **accabler** *ou* **couvrir qn d'injures** to heap abuse on sb **2** *(affront)* affront, insult; **c'est une i. à la nation** it's an insult to our country; **vous me feriez i. en refusant** you would offend me by refusing; **il m'a fait l'i. de refuser mon invitation** he insulted me by refusing my invitation **3** *Littéraire (dommage)* **l'i. du temps** the ravages of time

> Il faut noter que le nom anglais **injury** est un faux ami. Il signifie le plus souvent **blessure**.

injurier [9] [ɛ̃ʒyrje] VT **1** *(adresser des insultes à)* to insult, to abuse; **il n'arrête pas de l'i.** he's always insulting him/her; **on s'est carrément fait i. par la voisine** we came in for a real stream of abuse from our neighbour **2** *Littéraire (offenser moralement)* to be an insult to; **il injurie la mémoire de son père** he is an insult to his father's memory
VPR **s'injurier** to insult each other; **les chauffeurs de taxi se sont injuriés** the taxi drivers hurled insults at each other *or* swore at one another

> Il faut noter que le verbe anglais **to injure** est un faux ami. Il signifie le plus souvent **blesser**.

injurieux, -euse [ɛ̃ʒyrjø, -øz] ADJ abusive, insulting, offensive; **des propos i.** abusive *or* offensive language; **être i. envers qn** to be abusive *or* insulting to sb; **cela n'a rien d'i.!** no offence meant *or* intended!

injuste [ɛ̃ʒyst] ADJ **1** *(décision)* unjust, unfair; **une sentence i.** an unjust sentence; **ce que vous dites est i.** what you're saying is unfair **2** *(personne)* unfair, unjust; **ne sois pas i.!** be fair!, don't be unfair!; **être i. envers qn** to do sb an injustice

injustement [ɛ̃ʒystəmɑ̃] ADV **1** *(avec iniquité)* unfairly, unjustly; **punir i.** to punish unjustly **2** *(sans raison)* without reason; **se plaindre i.** to complain without just cause *or* for no good reason

injustice [ɛ̃ʒystis] NF **1** *(caractère inique)* injustice, unfairness; **l'i. sociale** social injustice; **c'est l'i. du sort!** that's the luck of the draw! **2** *(acte inique)* injustice, wrong; **commettre une i. envers qn** to do sb wrong *or* an injustice; **c'est une i.!** that's unfair!

injustifiable [ɛ̃ʒystifjabl] ADJ unjustifiable

injustifié, -e [ɛ̃ʒystifje] ADJ *(critique, punition)* unjustified, unwarranted; *(crainte)* unfounded, groundless; *(absence)* unexplained

inlassable [ɛ̃lasabl] ADJ *(infatigable ▸ personne)* indefatigable, tireless, untiring; *(▸ énergie)* tireless; **elle est d'un dévouement i.** her devotion is untiring

inlassablement [ɛ̃lasabləmɑ̃] ADV indefatigably, tirelessly, untiringly; **elle répétait i. le même**

mot she kept repeating the same word over and over again

inné, -e [ine] ADJ 1 *(don)* inborn, innate 2 *Phil* innate

innervant [inɛrvɑ̃] ADJ M **gaz i.** nerve gas

innervation [inɛrvasjɔ̃] NF *Physiol* innervation

innerver [3] [inɛrve] VT *Physiol* to innervate

innocemment [inɔsamɑ̃] ADV innocently; **j'ai posé la question i.** I asked the question in all innocence, I meant no harm by my question

innocence [inɔsɑ̃s] NF 1 *(gén)* innocence; **en toute i.** in all innocence, quite innocently 2 *Jur* innocence; **établir** *ou* **prouver l'i. de qn** to establish *or* to prove sb's innocence

innocent, -e [inɔsɑ̃, -ɑ̃t] ADJ 1 *(non responsable ▸ inculpé, victime)* innocent; *Jur* **déclarer qn i.** to find sb innocent *or* not guilty; **être i. de qch** to be innocent of sth

2 *(plaisanterie, question, plaisirs)* innocent, harmless; *(baiser, jeune fille)* innocent

3 *(candide ▸ enfant, âge)* innocent; **on est encore i. à cet âge** they're still innocent at that age; **i. comme l'agneau** *ou* **l'enfant qui vient de naître** as innocent as a newborn lamb *or* a babe in arms

4 *(niais)* innocent, simple

NM,F 1 *(personne non coupable)* innocent person 2 *(personne candide)* innocent; **faire l'i.** to play *or* to act the innocent; **ne joue pas l'i.** *ou* **les innocents avec moi!** don't act *or Br* come the innocent with me!; **tu as été un bel i. de la croire!** you were pretty naive to believe her!; **aux innocents les mains pleines** the meek shall inherit the earth 3 *(niais)* simpleton; **l'i. du village** the village idiot

innocenter [3] [inɔsɑ̃te] VT 1 *Jur (sujet: jury)* to clear, to find innocent *or* not guilty; *(sujet: témoignage, document)* to prove innocent, to show to be innocent; **il réussit à faire i. son client** he managed to get his client cleared 2 *(excuser)* to excuse; **i. la conduite de qn** to excuse sb's behaviour

innocuité [inɔkɥite] NF harmlessness, inoffensiveness, *Méd & Sout* innocuousness

innombrable [inɔ̃brabl] ADJ innumerable, countless; **une foule i.** a vast *or* huge crowd

innomé, -e [inɔme] ADJ *(sans nom)* unnamed

innommable [inɔmabl] ADJ unspeakable, loathsome, nameless

innovant, -e [inɔvɑ̃, -ɑ̃t] ADJ innovative

innovateur, -trice [inɔvatœr, -tris] ADJ innovative, groundbreaking

NM,F innovator; *Mktg* **i. continu** continuous innovator; *Mktg* **i. tardif** laggard

innovation [inɔvasjɔ̃] NF 1 *(créativité)* innovation 2 *(changement)* innovation; **il y a eu des innovations ici depuis que tu es parti** there have been a few changes around here since you left 3 *Com* innovation; *Mktg* **i. continue** continuous innovation; **i. de produit** product innovation; **i. technologique** technological innovation

innovatrice [inɔvatris] *voir* **innovateur**

innover [3] [inɔve] VI to innovate, to break new ground; **depuis des années, les banques n'ont pas innové** the banks haven't come up with any new ideas *or* haven't innovated for years

inobservable [inɔpsɛrvabl] ADJ 1 *(imperceptible par la vue)* unobservable 2 *(inexécutable)* **des recommandations inobservables** recommendations that cannot be observed *or* carried out

inobservance [inɔpsɛrvɑ̃s] NF *Littéraire* **l'i. des traditions** disregard for tradition; **l'i. du règlement** non-compliance with the regulations

inobservation [inɔpsɛrvasjɔ̃] NF *Littéraire & Jur* **i. d'une loi** non-compliance *or* failure to comply with a law; **i. d'un contrat** breach of contract

inobservé, -e [inɔpsɛrve] ADJ *Littéraire & Jur* unobserved

inoccupé, -e [inɔkype] ADJ 1 *(vide ▸ maison, local)* unoccupied, empty 2 *(vacant ▸ poste)* unoccupied, vacant, available; *(▸ taxi, fauteuil)* empty, free; **choisissez parmi les places/tables inoccupées** take one of the empty seats/tables 3 *(inactif)* inactive, unoccupied, idle; **ne laisse pas les enfants inoccupés** don't leave the children with nothing to do

inoculation [inɔkylasjɔ̃] NF *Méd (vaccination)* inoculation; *(contamination)* infection

inoculer [3] [inɔkyle] VT 1 *Méd* to inoculate; **on inocule le virus à un cobaye** a guinea pig is injected with the virus; **les volontaires se font i. le vaccin** the volunteers are injected with the vaccine 2 *(transmettre ▸ enthousiasme, manie)* to infect, to pass on to; **elle m'a inoculé la passion du jeu** she passed on her love of gambling to me

inodore [inɔdɔr] ADJ 1 *(sans odeur)* odourless 2 *(sans intérêt)* uninteresting, commonplace

inoffensif, -ive [inɔfɑ̃sif, -iv] ADJ *(personne)* harmless, inoffensive; *(animal)* harmless; *(remarque)* innocuous

inondable [inɔ̃dabl] ADJ liable to flooding

inondation [inɔ̃dasjɔ̃] NF 1 *(eau)* flood, flooding, *Sout* inundation; *(action)* flooding, *Sout* inundation 2 *Fig* flood, deluge; *(du marché)* flooding; **on assiste à une i. du marché par les voitures étrangères** foreign cars are flooding *or* inundating the market

inondé, -e [inɔ̃de] ADJ 1 *(champ, maison, cave)* flooded; **populations inondées** flood victims 2 *Fig* **être i. de réclamations/de mauvaises nouvelles** to be inundated with complaints/with bad news; **une pièce inondée de soleil** a room flooded with *or* bathed in sunlight; **être i. de joie** to be overcome *or* overwhelmed by joy; **le visage i. de larmes** with tears streaming down his/her face

NM,F flood victim

inonder [3] [inɔ̃de] VT 1 *(champs, maison, ville)* to flood, *Sout* to inundate; **j'ai été inondé par les gens du dessus** my apartment has been flooded by the people upstairs 2 *(tremper)* to soak; **les larmes inondaient ses joues** his/her cheeks were streaming with *or* bathed in tears; **les yeux inondés de pleurs** his/her eyes full of *or* swimming with tears; **le front inondé de sueur** his/her forehead bathed in sweat 3 *Fig (envahir ▸ marché)* to flood (**de** with); *(▸ sujet: foule)* to flood into, to swarm; *(▸ sujet: lumière)* to flood *or* to pour into, to bathe; *(▸ sujet: bonheur)* to flood; **ses fans l'inondent de lettres** he/she is inundated with fan mail; **le marché des produits de luxe est inondé de contrefaçons** the luxury goods market is flooded with imitation products

VPR **s'inonder s'i. de qch** to flood *or* to douse oneself in *or* with sth; **chaque matin il s'inonde d'eau de Cologne** every morning he douses himself with eau de Cologne

inopérable [inɔperabl] ADJ *Méd* inoperable

inopérant, -e [inɔperɑ̃, -ɑ̃t] ADJ inoperative, ineffective

inopiné, -e [inɔpine] ADJ *(inattendu)* unexpected

inopinément [inɔpinemɑ̃] ADV unexpectedly

inopportun, -e [inɔpɔrtœ̃, -yn] ADJ ill-timed, inopportune, untimely; **sa remarque était plutôt inopportune** he/she timed his/her remark rather badly

inopportunément [inɔpɔrtynemɑ̃] ADV *Littéraire* inopportunely

inopportunité [inɔpɔrtynite] NF *Littéraire* inopportuneness, untimeliness

inorganique [inɔrganik] ADJ inorganic

inorganisé, -e [inɔrganize] ADJ 1 *(désordonné)* disorganized, unorganized 2 *(non syndiqué)* unorganized

NM,F *(travailleur non syndiqué)* non-union member, unorganized worker

inoubliable [inublijabl] ADJ unforgettable, never to be forgotten

inouï, -e [inwi] ADJ 1 *(incroyable)* incredible, amazing, unbelievable; **il a une assurance inouïe** it's incredible *or* extraordinary how confident he is; **c'est i. ce que cet enfant peut faire comme dégâts!** you wouldn't believe how much havoc that child can cause!; **tu es i.!** you're incredible *or* unbelievable! 2 *Littéraire (sans précédent ▸ prouesse, performance)* unheard of, unprecedented

Inox® [inɔks] ADJ INV stainless steel *(avant n)*

NM INV stainless steel; **couverts en I.** stainless steel cutlery

inoxydable [inɔksidabl] ADJ 1 *(qui résiste à l'oxydation)* stainless; **couteau i.** stainless steel knife 2 *Fam (inaltérable)* enduring; **les dessins animés de Tex Avery, c'est i., c'est toujours aussi amusant qu'il y a 50 ans** Tex Avery's cartoons have stood the test of time; they're as funny now as they were 50 years ago

NM stainless steel

INPI [iɛnpei] NM *(abrév* **Institut national de la propriété intellectuelle***)* French National Patent Office

input [input] NM *Écon* input

inqualifiable [ɛ̃kalifjabl] ADJ unspeakable; **un acte i.** an unspeakable act; **ce que tu as fait est i.** there are no words for what you've done

in-quarto [inkwarto] *Typ* ADJ INV quarto

NM INV quarto

inquiet, -ète [ɛ̃kjɛ, -ɛt] ADJ 1 *(personne)* worried, anxious, concerned; *(regard)* worried, uneasy, nervous; *(attente)* anxious; *(sommeil)* uneasy, troubled, broken; **elle est inquiète de ne pas avoir de nouvelles** she's worried *or* anxious at not having any news; **tu es toujours inquiète!** you're always worried!, you're such a worrier!; **être i. de qch** to be worried about sth; **il est i. de la montée du racisme** he's worried about the rise of racism 2 *Littéraire (activité, curiosité)* restless

NM,F worrier

inquiétant, -e [ɛ̃kjetɑ̃, -ɑ̃t] ADJ 1 *(alarmant)* worrying, disquieting, disturbing; **la situation est inquiétante** the situation is worrying *or* gives cause for concern 2 *(qui effraie ▸ air, sourire)* frightening; **la drogue provoquait des fantasmes inquiétants** the drug caused disturbing fantasies

inquiéter [18] [ɛ̃kjete] VT 1 *(troubler ▸ sujet: personne, situation)* to worry, to trouble; **son état de santé m'inquiète** I'm worried about his/her state of health; **son silence m'inquiète beaucoup** his/her silence is worrying me; **qu'est-ce qui t'inquiète?** what are you worried about?, what's worrying you?

2 *(ennuyer, harceler)* to disturb, to bother, to harass; **s'ils viennent t'i. chez toi, préviens-moi** if they come to bother *or* harass you at home, let me know; **ils ont vidé les coffres sans être inquiétés** they were able to empty the safes without being disturbed *or* interrupted; **il n'a jamais inquiété le champion du monde** he's never posed any threat to the world champion; **c'est la première fois que notre gardien de but est sérieusement inquiété** it's the first time that our goalkeeper has been really worried *or* in real trouble

USAGE ABSOLU *(troubler)* **ces nouvelles ont de quoi i.** this news is quite disturbing *or* worrying *or* alarming

VPR **s'inquiéter** 1 *(être soucieux)* to worry, to be worried; **il y a de quoi s'i.** that's something to be worried about, there's real cause for concern; **s'i. au sujet de** *ou* **pour qn** to be worried *or* concerned about sb; **ne t'inquiète pas pour elle!** don't (you) worry about her!; **je m'inquiète beaucoup de le savoir seul** it worries *or* troubles me a lot to know that he's alone

2 **s'i. de** *(tenir compte de)* to bother *or* to worry about; **elle achète sans s'i. du prix** she buys things regardless of the price *or* without worrying about the price

3 **s'i. de** *(s'occuper de)* to see to sth; **et son cadeau? – je m'en inquiéterai plus tard** what about his/her present? – I'll see about that *or* take care of that later; **elle ne s'est jamais inquiétée de savoir si j'avais besoin de quelque chose** she never bothered *or* troubled *or* took the trouble to find out if I needed anything; *Fam* **où tu vas? – t'inquiète!** where are you off to? – mind your own business! *or* what's it to you?

4 **s'i. de** *(se renseigner sur)* to inquire *or* to ask about

inquiétude [ɛ̃kjetyd] NF 1 *(souci)* worry, anxiety, concern; **avec i.** anxiously, fretfully, nervously; **un sujet d'i.** a cause for concern *or* anxiety; **n'ayez aucune i., soyez sans i.** rest easy, have no fear; **avoir des inquiétudes** to be worried *or* concerned 2 *Arch (agitation)* agitation, restlessness

inquisiteur, -trice [ɛ̃kizitœr, -tris] ADJ inquisitive, prying

NM inquisitor

inquisition [ɛ̃kizisjɔ̃] NF 1 *Hist* **la (Sainte) I.** the (Holy) Inquisition 2 *Péj (ingérence)* inquisition

inquisitorial, -e, -aux, -ales [ɛ̃kizitɔrjal, -o] **ADJ 1** *(méthode)* inquisitorial, high-handed **2** *Hist* inquisitorial, Inquisition *(avant n)*

inquisitrice [ɛ̃kizitris] *voir* **inquisiteur**

INRA, Inra [inra] **NM** *(abrév* **Institut national de la recherche agronomique**) = national institute for agronomic research

inracontable [ɛ̃rakɔ̃tabl] **ADJ** *(trop grivois)* unrepeatable; *(trop compliqué)* too complicated for words; **je me suis débattu avec le fisc, c'est i.!** I can't even begin to tell you what a struggle I had with the tax people!

inratable [ɛ̃ratabl] **ADJ** *(spectacle)* unmissable

insaisissable [ɛ̃sezisabl] **ADJ 1** *(imprenable ▸ terroriste, voleur)* elusive

2 *(imperceptible)* imperceptible, intangible; **elle distingue des détails pour moi insaisissables** she picks out details I can't even see

3 *(fuyant)* unfathomable, elusive; **caractère i.** elusiveness; **c'est quelqu'un d'i., tu n'auras pas de réponse nette de sa part** he's/she's very evasive, you won't get a straight answer from him/her

4 *Jur* exempt from seizure

insalissable [ɛ̃salisabl] **ADJ** stain-resistant

insalubre [ɛ̃salybr] **ADJ** *(immeuble)* insalubrious; *(climat)* insalubrious, unhealthy

insalubrité [ɛ̃salybrite] **NF** *(d'un immeuble)* insalubrity; *(du climat)* insalubrity, unhealthiness

insanité [ɛ̃sanite] **NF 1** *(folie)* insanity **2** *(remarque)* insane *or* nonsensical remark; *(acte)* insane act, insane thing to do; **proférer des insanités** to say insane things; **tu n'es pas forcé d'écouter ses insanités** you don't have to listen to his/her ravings

insatiabilité [ɛ̃sasjabilite] **NF** insatiability

insatiable [ɛ̃sasjabl] **ADJ** insatiable; **d'une curiosité i.** insatiably curious

insatiablement [ɛ̃sasjabləmɑ̃] **ADV** insatiably

insatisfaction [ɛ̃satisfaksjɔ̃] **NF** dissatisfaction

insatisfaisant, -e [ɛ̃satisfəzɑ̃, -ɑ̃t] **ADJ** unsatisfactory

insatisfait, -e [ɛ̃satisfe, -et] **ADJ 1** *(inassouvi ▸ curiosité, besoin)* unsatisfied, frustrated **2** *(mécontent ▸ personne)* unsatisfied, dissatisfied, displeased; **être i. de** to be unhappy about

NM,F discontented person; **les insatisfaits** the discontented; **c'est un éternel i.** he's never satisfied *or* happy

inscriptible [ɛ̃skriptibl] **ADJ** inscribable

inscription [ɛ̃skripsjɔ̃] **NF 1** *(ensemble de caractères)* inscription, writing *(UNCOUNT)*; **il y avait une i. sur le mur** there was an inscription *or* something written on the wall; **des tablettes portant des inscriptions** inscribed tablets; **i. comptable** accounting entry

2 *(action d'écrire)* **l'i. d'un slogan sur un mur** daubing *or* writing a slogan on a wall; **l'i. d'une épitaphe sur une tombe** inscribing *or* engraving an epitaph on a tombstone

3 *(action d'inclure ▸ dans un journal, un registre)* entering, recording; **une question dont l'i. à l'ordre du jour s'impose** a question which must go (down) *or* be placed on the agenda; **l'i. des dépenses au budget** the listing of expenses in the budget

4 *(formalité)* **i. à** *(cours, concours)* registration for, enrolment in; *(club, parti)* enrolment in, joining (of); **i. à l'université** university registration *or* enrolment, *Br* university matriculation; **i. sur les listes électorales** *Br* registration on the electoral roll, *Am* voter registration; **au moment de l'i. de votre enfant à l'école** when it's time to enrol *or* to register your child for school; **j'ai demandé mon i. sur une liste d'attente** I've asked for my name to go on *or* to be added to a waiting list; **dernière date pour les inscriptions** *(à l'université)* closing date for enrolment *or* registration; *(dans un club)* closing date for enrolment; *Univ* **dossier d'i.** admission form, *Br* ≃ UCAS form; *Univ* **droits d'i.** registration fees; *Univ* **service des inscriptions** admissions office

5 *(personne inscrite)* **il y a une trentaine d'inscriptions au club/pour le rallye** about 30 people have joined the club/entered the rally

6 *Jur* **i. de faux** challenge *(to the validity of a document)*; **i. hypothécaire** mortgage registration

7 *Fin* scrip; **i. de rente** *ou* **sur le grand-livre** Treasury scrip

8 *Bourse* quotation (privilege); **i. à la cote** quotation on the (official) list

9 *Compta (dans un livre de comptes)* entry; **i. comptable** accounting entry

inscrire [99] [ɛ̃skrir] **VT 1** *(écrire ▸ chiffre, détail)* to write *or* to note (down); *(▸ en gravant)* to engrave, to inscribe; **inscrivez votre adresse ici** write down *or* enter your address here; **quelqu'un avait inscrit une phrase à la peinture sur le mur** somebody had painted some words on the wall; **les données inscrites sur l'écran** the data displayed on (the) screen; **je ferai i. son nom sur la tombe** I'll have his/her name engraved *or* inscribed on the tombstone; *Fig* **son visage reste inscrit dans ma mémoire** his/her face remains etched in my memory

2 *(enregistrer ▸ étudiant)* to register, to enrol; *(▸ électeur, membre)* to register; *Ordinat (▸ logiciel)* to register; **i. un enfant à l'école** to register *or* to enrol a child for school, to put a child's name down for school; **il faut vous (faire) i. à l'université avant le 15 octobre** you must register *or* enrol for university before 15 October; **les étudiants inscrits à l'examen** the students entered for the exam, *Br* the students sitting the exam; **les étudiants inscrits en droit** the students enrolled *Br* on *or Am* in the law course; **se faire i. sur les listes électorales** to register as a voter, to put one's name on the electoral register; **je vais l'i. au cours de danse** I'm putting him/her down for the dance class; **être inscrit à un club** to be a member of a club; **i. qn pour un rendez-vous** to put sb *or* sb's name down for an appointment; **je vous inscris sur la liste d'attente** I'll put your name *or* you (down) on the waiting list; **et la liste des passagers? – il n'y est pas inscrit non plus** what about the passenger list? – he's not listed there *or* his name's not on it either

3 *(inclure)* to list, to include; **i. qch au budget** to include sth in the budget; **ces sommes sont inscrites au budget de la culture** these amounts are listed in the arts budget; **son style l'inscrit dans la tradition italienne** his/her style places *or* situates him/her within the Italian tradition; **i. un prix littéraire/un disque d'or à son palmarès** to add a literary prize/a gold disc to one's list of achievements; **on n'a fait qu'i. dans la législation une coutume solidement établie** all they have done is to write a firmly established custom into the legislation; **i. une question à l'ordre du jour** to put *or* to place a question on the agenda

4 *Sport (but, essai)* to score

5 *Math* to inscribe (**dans** in)

VPR s'inscrire 1 s'i. à *(club, parti)* to join, to enrol as a member of; *(bibliothèque)* to join; *(université)* to register *or* to enrol at; *(concours, rallye)* to enter *or* to put one's name down for; *(cours, atelier)* to put oneself *or* one's name down for, to enrol for; **s'i. au chômage** to register as unemployed; **s'i. sur une liste électorale** to register to vote, to have one's name put on the electoral roll

2 *(apparaître)* to appear, to come up; **le numéro de téléphone va s'i. sur vos écrans** the phone number will come up *or* be displayed *or* appear on your screens; *Fig* **l'âge s'inscrit sur nos visages** age leaves its mark on our faces

3 *Jur* **s'i. en faux contre** to lodge a challenge against; *Fig* **s'i. en faux contre une politique/des allégations** to strongly denounce a policy/deny allegations

4 *Bourse* **s'i. en hausse/baisse** to be (marked) up/down; **les valeurs industrielles s'inscrivent en baisse de 13 points à la clôture** industrial shares closed 13 points down

5 *(appartenir)* **cette mesure s'inscrit dans le cadre de notre campagne** this measure comes *or* lies within the framework of our campaign; **son action s'inscrit tout à fait dans la politique de notre parti** his/her action is totally in keeping *or* in line with our party's policy; **il s'inscrit dans la lignée des grands metteurs en scène réalistes** he is in the tradition of the great realist directors; **son œuvre s'inscrit dans la tradition romantique** his/her work belongs to the Romantic tradition

inscrit, -e [ɛ̃skri, -it] **ADJ 1** *(étudiant, membre d'un club)* enrolled, registered, *Br* matriculated; *(chômeur)* registered; *Pol (candidat, électeur)* registered; *(orateur)* scheduled

2 *Banque & Fin* registered

3 *Math* inscribed

4 *Bourse* **i. à la cote officielle** listed; **non inscrite** unlisted

NM,F *(sur une liste)* registered person; *(à un club, à un parti)* registered member; *(étudiant)* registered student; *(candidat)* registered candidate; *(électeur)* registered elector; **au consulat, nous avons de moins en moins d'inscrits chaque année** fewer and fewer people register with the consulate each year; *Pol* **les inscrits au prochain débat** the scheduled speakers for the next debate; *Naut* **i. maritime** registered seaman

inscrivait *etc voir* **inscrire**

insécable [ɛ̃sekabl] **ADJ** indivisible

insecte [ɛ̃sɛkt] **NM** insect

insecticide [ɛ̃sɛktisid] **ADJ** insecticide *(avant n)*, insecticidal; **poudre i.** insecticide *or* insect powder

NM insecticide

insectifuge [ɛ̃sɛktifyʒ] **NM** insect repellent

insectivore [ɛ̃sɛktivɔr] **ADJ** insectivorous

NM insectivore

insécurité [ɛ̃sekyrite] **NF 1** *(manque de sécurité)* lack of safety; **l'i. qui règne dans les grandes villes** the collapse of law and order in big cities, the climate of fear reigning in big cities; **le gouvernement veut prendre des mesures contre l'i.** the government wants to introduce measures to improve public safety **2** *(précarité ▸ de l'emploi)* insecurity, precariousness; *(▸ de l'avenir)* uncertainty **3** *(angoisse)* insecurity

INSEE, Insee [inse] **NM** *(abrév* **Institut national de la statistique et des études économiques**) = French national institute for statistical and economic studies

inséminateur, -trice [ɛ̃seminatœr, -tris] **ADJ** inseminating

NM,F inseminator

insémination [ɛ̃seminasjɔ̃] **NF** insemination; **i. artificielle** artificial insemination

inséminatrice [ɛ̃seminatris] *voir* **inséminateur**

inséminer [3] [ɛ̃semine] **VT** to inseminate

insensé, -e [ɛ̃sɑ̃se] **ADJ 1** *(déraisonnable ▸ projet, initiative)* foolish, insane; *(▸ espoir)* unrealistic, mad; **ses idées sont littéralement insensées** his/her ideas are literally crazy; **il est complètement i. de penser que...** it is utterly foolish *or* absurd to think that…; **c'est i.!** this is absurd *or* preposterous!; **c'est i. ce qu'il peut boire!** it's crazy the amount he can drink! **2** *(excessif)* enormous, considerable; **une somme insensée** an excessive *or* a ludicrous amount of money; **un travail i.** an enormous *or* unbelievable amount of work

NM,F *Littéraire* madman, *f* madwoman

insensibilisation [ɛ̃sɑ̃sibilizasjɔ̃] **NF** local anaesthesia

insensibiliser [3] [ɛ̃sɑ̃sibilize] **VT 1** *Méd* to anaesthetize; **il m'a insensibilisé la mâchoire** he anaesthetized my jaw **2** *(endurcir)* to harden; **être insensibilisé aux souffrances d'autrui** to be hardened *or* to have become immune to the sufferings of others

insensibilité [ɛ̃sɑ̃sibilite] **NF 1** *(absence de réceptivité)* **i. à** insensitiveness *or* insensitivity to; **i. à la beauté/musique** lack of receptiveness to beauty/music; **i. à la souffrance des autres** insensitivity to the suffering of others **2** *Méd* insensitivity, numbness

insensible [ɛ̃sɑ̃sibl] **ADJ 1** *(privé de sensation, de sentiment)* **i. à** insensitive to; **i. à la douleur** insensitive to pain; **elle est i. au froid** she's insensitive to *or* she doesn't feel the cold; **elle est i. à mes reproches** she's impervious *or* immune to my reproaches; **elle demeura i. à ses prières** she remained indifferent to *or* unmoved by his/her pleas **2** *(imperceptible)* imperceptible

insensiblement [ɛ̃sɑ̃sibləmɑ̃] **ADV** imperceptibly, gradually

inséparable [ɛ̃separabl] **ADJ** inseparable; **ces deux-là, ils sont inséparables** those two are inseparable; **le vice et le crime sont inséparables** vice and crime are inseparable *or* go hand in hand

• **inséparables NMF PL** *(personnes)* **deux insépa-**

rables a pair of inseparable friends **NMPL** *Orn* **un couple d'inséparables** a pair of lovebirds

inséparablement [ɛ̃separabləmɑ̃] **ADV** inseparably

insérable [ɛ̃serabl] **ADJ** insertable

insérer **[18]** [ɛ̃sere] **VT 1** *(ajouter ▸ chapitre, feuille)* to insert (**dans/entre** into/between); *(mettre ▸ publicité, annonce)* to place (**dans** in); **faire i. une clause dans un contrat** to have a clause added to *or* put in *or* inserted into a contract; **i. une annonce dans un journal** to insert *or* to put an advertisement in a paper **2** *(introduire ▸ clé, lame)* to insert; **i. qch dans** to insert sth into **3** *Ordinat* to insert

VPR s'insérer 1 s'i. dans *(socialement)* to become integrated into; **les jeunes ont souvent du mal à s'i. dans le monde du travail** young people often find it difficult to find their place in *or* to fit into a work environment; **être bien/mal inséré dans la société** to be well/poorly integrated into society **2 s'i. dans** *(s'inscrire dans)* to be part of; **ces mesures s'insèrent dans le cadre d'une politique globale** these measures come within *or* are part of an overall policy

INSERM, Inserm [inserm] **NM** *(abrév* **Institut national de la santé et de la recherche médicale**) = national institute for medical research

insert [ɛ̃ser] **NM** *Cin & TV* cut-in, insert

insertion [ɛ̃sersjɔ̃] **NF 1** *(introduction)* insertion, introduction; **i. d'une page dans un livre** inserting a page into a book

2 *(intégration)* integration; **l'i. des jeunes dans le monde du travail** the integration of young people into a work environment; **i. sociale** social integration

3 *Presse & Mktg* advertisement; **i. publicitaire** advertisement; **tarif des insertions** advertising rates; **frais d'i.** advertising charge

4 *Ordinat* insertion; **mode d'i.** insert mode; **i. de caractères** character insert; **i. de ligne** line insert

insidieuse [ɛ̃sidjøz] *voir* **insidieux**

insidieusement [ɛ̃sidjøzmɑ̃] **ADV** insidiously

insidieux, -euse [ɛ̃sidjø, -øz] **ADJ 1** *(perfide ▸ question)* insidious, treacherous; *Littéraire (▸ personne)* insidious; **un raisonnement i.** a specious argument **2** *(sournois ▸ odeur, poison)* insidious **3** *Méd* insidious

insigne [ɛ̃siɲ] **ADJ** *Littéraire (remarquable)* remarkable, noteworthy; **faveur i.** signal favour; **j'ai eu l'i. honneur d'être invité à sa table** I had the great honour of being invited to his/her table; **pour les services insignes rendus à la Couronne** for outstanding services to the Crown; **mensonge/calomnie i.** unparalleled lie/slander

NM *(marque distinctive ▸ d'un groupe)* badge, emblem, symbol; *(▸ d'une dignité)* insignia; **les insignes de la royauté** royal insignia

insignifiance [ɛ̃siɲifjɑ̃s] **NF** insignificance, unimportance

insignifiant, -e [ɛ̃siɲifjɑ̃, -ɑ̃t] **ADJ 1** *(sans intérêt)* insignificant, trivial; **nous parlions de choses insignifiantes** we were engaged in idle chatter; **des gens insignifiants** insignificant *or* unimportant people **2** *(minime ▸ gén)* insignificant, negligible; *(▸ erreur)* unimportant; *(▸ somme)* trifling, petty

insincère [ɛ̃sɛ̃sɛr] **ADJ** *Littéraire* insincere, hypocritical

insinuant, -e [ɛ̃sinɥɑ̃, -ɑ̃t] **ADJ** *(personne, ton)* ingratiating; **il avait un odieux sourire i.** he had a horrible fawning smile

insinuation [ɛ̃sinɥasjɔ̃] **NF** *(allusion)* insinuation, innuendo; **quelles sont ces insinuations?** what are you hinting at *or* insinuating *or* trying to suggest?; **il procède toujours par i.** he always speaks in innuendos

insinuer **[7]** [ɛ̃sinɥe] **VT** to insinuate; **que veut-elle i.?** what's she hinting at *or* trying to insinuate?; **insinuez-vous que je mens?** are you insinuating *or* implying that I'm lying?

VPR s'insinuer elle parvient à s'i. partout she gets everywhere; **s'i. dans** *(sujet: arôme, gaz)* to creep in; *(sujet: eau)* to filter *or* to seep in; *(sujet: personne)* to make one's way in, to infiltrate, to penetrate; **il a réussi à s'i. jusque dans les plus hautes sphères du pouvoir** he managed to worm his way into the higher reaches of power; **s'i. dans les bonnes grâces de qn** to insinuate oneself into sb's favour, to curry favour with sb; **le doute/une idée diabolique s'insinua en lui** doubt/an evil thought crept into his mind

insipide [ɛ̃sipid] **ADJ 1** *(sans goût)* insipid, tasteless; **l'eau est i.** water has no taste *or* doesn't taste of anything **2** *Fig (sans relief ▸ personne)* insipid, bland; *(▸ conversation, livre)* uninteresting, dull

insipidité [ɛ̃sipidite] **NF 1** *(absence de goût)* insipidness, tastelessness **2** *Fig (ennui)* insipidness, tediousness

insistance [ɛ̃sistɑ̃s] **NF** *(obstination)* insistence; **il lui demanda avec i. de chanter** he insisted that he/she should sing; **regarder qn avec i.** to stare at sb insistently; **son i. à refuser** his/her insistence on refusing

insistant, -e [ɛ̃sistɑ̃, -ɑ̃t] **ADJ 1** *(persévérant)* insistent; **elle se faisait de plus en plus insistante** she was growing more and more insistent *or* demanding **2** *(fort ▸ parfum)* pervasive, intrusive

insister **[3]** [ɛ̃siste] **VI 1** *(persévérer)* to insist; **je ne vous dirai rien, inutile d'i.!** I'm not telling you anything, so there's no point pressing me any further!; **ça ne répond pas – insistez!** there's no answer – keep trying *or* try again!; **il a tellement insisté que j'ai fini par accepter** he was so insistent about it that I ended up accepting; **il était en colère, alors je n'ai pas insisté** he was angry, so I didn't push the matter (any further) *or* I didn't insist; **elle a essayé la planche à voile mais elle n'a pas insisté** she tried windsurfing but soon gave (it) up; **insiste, sinon la tache ne partira jamais** keep rubbing or the stain will never come out; **très bien, si vous insistez!** all right, if you insist! **2** *(demander instamment)* to insist; **j'insiste pour que vous m'écoutiez jusqu'au bout** I insist that you hear me out; **elle a insisté pour que nous dormions sur place** she insisted on our staying the night; **vous devez i. auprès du directeur pour qu'on vous accorde un congé** you have to talk to the manager and insist that you get leave

• **insister sur VT IND 1** *(mettre l'accent sur ▸ idée, problème)* to stress, to emphasize, to underline; **on ne saurait trop i. sur cette différence** this difference cannot be overemphasized; **si j'étais toi, je n'insisterais pas trop sur le salaire** if I were you, I wouldn't lay too much emphasis on the salary; **dans notre école, nous insistons beaucoup sur la discipline** in our school, we attach great importance to *or* lay great stress on discipline **2** *(s'attarder sur ▸ anecdote)* to dwell on; *(▸ tache, défaut)* to pay particular attention to; **mes années d'école, sur lesquelles je n'insisterai pas** my school years, which I'd rather not dwell on; **appliquez ce produit sur votre tapis en insistant bien sur les taches** apply the product to your carpet, paying particular attention to stains

in situ [insity] **ADV** in situ

insituable [ɛ̃sitɥabl] **ADJ** unclassifiable, uncategorizable; **c'est un artiste i.** he's an artist who cannot be categorized *or* pigeonholed

insociable [ɛ̃sɔsjabl] **ADJ** *(farouche)* unsociable; *(asocial)* antisocial

insolation [ɛ̃sɔlasjɔ̃] **NF 1** *Méd* sunstroke, *Spéc* insolation; **attraper une i.** to get sunstroke **2** *Météo* sunshine, *Spéc* insolation; **avoir une faible i.** to get very little sunshine **3** *Phot* exposure (to the light)

insolemment [ɛ̃sɔlamɑ̃] **ADV 1** *(avec arrogance)* insolently, arrogantly **2** *(avec effronterie)* unashamedly

insolence [ɛ̃sɔlɑ̃s] **NF 1** *(irrespect)* insolence; **il était d'une telle i. que nous l'avons renvoyé** he was so insolent that we fired him; **avec i.** insolently **2** *(remarque)* insolent remark; *(acte)* insolent act **3** *(orgueil)* arrogance

insolent, -e [ɛ̃sɔlɑ̃, -ɑ̃t] **ADJ 1** *(impoli)* insolent; **d'un ton i.** insolently, impertinently, impudently **2** *(arrogant)* arrogant; **l'insolente arrogance de l'argent** the arrogance that comes with wealth **3** *(extraordinaire ▸ luxe, succès)* outrageous; **vous avez eu une chance insolente** you've been incredibly lucky

NM,F insolent person; **petit i.!/petite insolente!** you impudent *or* impertinent little boy/girl!

insolite [ɛ̃sɔlit] **ADJ** unusual, strange

NM l'i. the unusual, the bizarre

insolubilité [ɛ̃sɔlybilite] **NF** *(d'une substance)* insolubility; *(d'un problème)* insolvability

insoluble [ɛ̃sɔlybl] **ADJ 1** *Chim* insoluble **2** *(problème)* insoluble, insolvable; **le problème est i. si l'on utilise de telles méthodes** the problem can't be solved with such methods; **c'est une situation i.** there's no solution to this situation

insolvabilité [ɛ̃sɔlvabilite] **NF** insolvency

insolvable [ɛ̃sɔlvabl] **ADJ** insolvent

NMF insolvent

insomniaque [ɛ̃sɔmnjak] **ADJ** insomniac

NMF insomniac

insomnie [ɛ̃sɔmni] **NF** insomnia *(UNCOUNT)*; **des nuits d'i.** sleepless nights; **avoir des insomnies** to have insomnia; **souffrir d'insomnies** to suffer from insomnia

insondable [ɛ̃sɔ̃dabl] **ADJ 1** *(impénétrable ▸ desseins, mystère)* unfathomable, impenetrable; *(▸ regard, visage)* inscrutable **2** *(très profond)* unfathomable; **une crevasse i.** a seemingly bottomless crevasse **3** *(infini)* abysmal; **il est d'une bêtise i.** he's abysmally stupid

insonore [ɛ̃sɔnɔr] **ADJ** soundproof, *Spéc* sound-insulated

insonorisation [ɛ̃sɔnɔrizasjɔ̃] **NF** soundproofing, (sound) insulation

insonoriser **[3]** [ɛ̃sɔnɔrize] **VT** to soundproof, to (sound) insulate; **studio d'enregistrement insonorisé** soundproof recording studio; **pièce mal insonorisée** inadequately soundproofed room

insouciance [ɛ̃susjɑ̃s] **NF** lack of concern, carefree attitude; **avec i.** blithely, casually; **vivre dans l'i.** to live a carefree *or* an untroubled existence; **en ce qui concerne l'argent, elle est d'une totale i.** she's got a totally carefree attitude towards money; **son i. à l'égard de ses études** his/her lack of concern for his/her studies; **l'i. de la jeunesse** the frivolity of youth

insouciant, -e [ɛ̃susjɑ̃, -ɑ̃t] **ADJ 1** *(nonchalant)* carefree, unconcerned, casual; **êtes-vous toujours aussi i. lorsqu'il s'agit d'argent?** are you always so casual with money? **2** *(indifférent)* **i. du danger** oblivious of *or* to the danger; **i. de l'avenir** indifferent to *or* unconcerned about the future; **i. de sa santé** unconcerned about one's health

insoucieux, -euse [ɛ̃susjø, -øz] **ADJ** *Littéraire* carefree, unconcerned; **être i. du lendemain** to be heedless of what tomorrow may bring

insoumis, -e [ɛ̃sumi, -iz] **ADJ 1** *(indiscipliné ▸ jeunesse, partisan)* rebellious; *(▸ enfant)* unruly **2** *(révolté ▸ tribu)* rebel, rebellious; *(▸ pays)* unsubdued, undefeated, rebellious **3** *Mil* **soldat i.** *(réfractaire au service militaire)* draft-dodger; *(déserteur)* soldier absent without leave

NM *(réfractaire au service militaire)* draft-dodger; *(déserteur)* soldier absent without leave

insoumission [ɛ̃sumisjɔ̃] **NF 1** *(indiscipline)* rebelliousness, insubordination **2** *(révolte)* rebelliousness, rebellion **3** *Mil (objection)* draft-dodging; *(désertion)* absence without leave

insoupçonnable [ɛ̃supsɔnabl] **ADJ 1** *(personne)* above suspicion; **il est d'une probité i.** his integrity is beyond question **2** *(invisible ▸ retouche, sous-vêtement)* invisible

insoupçonné, -e [ɛ̃supsɔne] **ADJ** *(vérité)* unsuspected; *(richesses)* undreamt-of, unheard-of; **des trésors d'une valeur insoupçonnée** treasure which nobody expected to be so valuable

insoutenable [ɛ̃sutnabl] **ADJ 1** *(insupportable ▸ douleur, scène, température)* unbearable, unendurable; *(▸ lumière)* blinding **2** *(impossible à soutenir ▸ concurrence, lutte)* unsustainable **3** *(indéfendable ▸ opinion, thèse)* unsustainable; *(▸ position)* indefensible

NM l'i. the unbearable; **à la limite de l'i.** verging on the unbearable

inspecter **[4]** [ɛ̃spɛkte] **VT 1** *(contrôler ▸ appartement, bagages, engin, travaux)* to inspect, to examine; *(▸ marchandises)* to examine; *(▸ troupes)* to review, to inspect; *(▸ école, professeur)* to inspect **2** *(scruter)* to inspect, to examine; **i. qn des pieds à la tête** to examine sb from head to foot

inspecteur, -trice [ɛ̃spɛktœr, -tris] **NM,F 1** *(contrôleur)* inspector; **i. des contributions directes** tax inspector; **i. des contributions indirectes** customs and excise official; *Mil* **i. général** inspector general; **i. (général) des Finances** *Br* ≃ general auditor *(of the Treasury, with special responsibilities), Am* ≃ Comptroller General; *Fin* **i. des impôts** tax inspector; **i. des mines** inspector of mines; **i. du travail** factory inspector; *Fig Hum* **c'est un vrai i. des travaux finis!** he always turns up when the work's done!; **i. sanitaire (public)** health inspector; **i. de la TVA** VAT inspector **2** *(policier)* inspector, detective; **excusez-moi i.** excuse me, inspector; **i. de la police judiciaire** = inspector belonging to the criminal investigation department, *Br* ≃ CID inspector; **i. de police** *Br* detective sergeant, *Am* lieutenant; **i. principal** ≃ detective inspector **3** *Scol* **i. d'Académie** *Br* ≃ inspector of schools, *Am* ≃ Accreditation officer; **i. de l'Éducation nationale** = education inspector (mainly for the primary sector); **I. pédagogique régional** = locally-based education inspector

inspection [ɛ̃spɛksjɔ̃] **NF 1** *(vérification)* inspection; *(surveillance)* overseeing, supervising; **faire l'i. de** to inspect; **ils se livrèrent à une i. de la voiture** they inspected the car; **ils se livrèrent à une i. détaillée du véhicule** they searched the vehicle thoroughly; **après i., le dossier se révéla être un faux** on inspection, the file turned out to be a forgery; **passer une i.** *(l'organiser)* to carry out an inspection, to inspect; *(la subir)* to undergo an inspection, to be inspected; **passer l'i.** *(être en règle)* to pass (the test) **2** *Admin* inspectorate; **i. académique** *Br* ≃ Schools Inspectorate, *Am* ≃ Accreditation Agency; **entrer à l'i. académique** to become a school inspector; **i. générale des Finances** = government department responsible for monitoring the financial affairs of state bodies; **I. générale de la police nationale** = police disciplinary body, *Br* ≃ Police Committee; **I. générale des services** = police disciplinary body for Paris, *Br* ≃ Metropolitan Police Commission; **i. des impôts** *Br* ≃ Inland Revenue, *Am* ≃ Internal Revenue Service; **i. du travail** *Br* ≃ Health and Safety Executive, *Am* ≃ Labor Board **3** *(inspectorat)* inspectorship

inspectorat [ɛ̃spɛktɔra] **NM** *(charge)* inspectorate; *(durée)* inspectorship; **pendant son i.** while he/she was an inspector

inspectrice [ɛ̃spɛktris] *voir* **inspecteur**

inspirateur, -trice [ɛ̃spiratœr, -tris] **ADJ 1** *(inspirant)* inspiring **2** *Anat* inspiratory; **muscles inspirateurs** inspiratory muscles

NM,F 1 *(guide)* inspirer; **la religion est la principale inspiratrice de leur mouvement** religion is the main driving force behind their movement **2** *(instigateur)* instigator; **l'i. d'un complot** the instigator of *or* the person behind a plot

• **inspiratrice NF** *(égérie)* muse, inspiration

inspiration [ɛ̃spirasjɔ̃] **NF 1** *(esprit créatif)* inspiration; **tirer son i. de, trouver son i. dans** to draw (one's) inspiration from; **elle a manqué d'i.** she lacked inspiration *or* wasn't much inspired; **je n'ai pas d'i. ce matin** I don't feel inspired *or* I don't have any inspiration this morning; **elle est pour lui une source d'i.** she's his muse; **musique pleine d'i.** inspired music

2 *(idée, envie)* inspiration, (bright) idea; **agir selon l'i. du moment** to act on the spur of the moment; **j'ai eu l'i. de rentrer au bon moment** I had the bright idea of coming home at the right time

3 *(influence)* influence, instigation; **l'architecture d'i. nordique** architecture with a Scandinavian influence, Scandinavian-inspired architecture

4 *Physiol* breathing in, *Spéc* inspiration

inspiratrice [ɛ̃spiratris] *voir* **inspirateur**

inspiré, -e [ɛ̃spire] **ADJ 1** *(artiste, air, livre)* inspired **2** *(avisé)* **j'ai été bien i. de lui résister** I was well-advised to resist him, I did the right thing in resisting him; **tu as été bien i. de venir me voir aujourd'hui** you did well to come and see me today

NM,F 1 *(mystique)* mystic, visionary **2** *Péj (illuminé)* eccentric

inspirer [3] [ɛ̃spire] **VT 1** *(provoquer ▸ décision, sentiment)* to inspire; *(▸ remarque)* to inspire, to give rise to; *(▸ conduite)* to prompt; *(▸ complot)* to instigate; **i. de la haine/du mépris à qn** to inspire sb with hatred/with contempt; **i. de l'admiration à qn** to fill sb with admiration; **i. confiance à qn** to inspire confidence in sb, to inspire sb with confidence; **cette viande ne m'inspire pas confiance!** I don't much like the look of that meat!; **i. le respect** to inspire respect; **son état n'inspire pas d'inquiétude** his/her health gives no cause for concern; **cette réponse lui a été inspirée par la jalousie** his/her answer was inspired *or* prompted by jealousy; **le texte m'inspire plusieurs réflexions** the text leads me to make several remarks; **ma fille m'a inspiré mes plus belles chansons** my daughter inspired me to write my best songs **2** *(influencer ▸ œuvre, personne)* to inspire; **le fait historique qui l'a inspiré pour ce dessin** the historical event which inspired him to do this drawing; **le sujet de dissertation ne m'inspire guère!** the subject of the essay doesn't really inspire me *or* fire my imagination!; **une toile inspirée de Bosch** a painting inspired by Bosch; **l'histoire est largement inspirée de la vie du grand homme** the story is largely drawn from *or* based upon the great man's life **3** *(aspirer ▸ air, gaz)* to breathe in, *Spéc* to inspire

VI to breathe in, *Spéc* to inspire

VPR s'inspirer s'i. de to draw one's inspiration from, to be inspired by

instabilité [ɛ̃stabilite] **NF 1** *(précarité ▸ d'une situation, d'un emploi)* instability, precariousness; *(▸ d'un régime politique, d'un marché, des prix, de la personnalité, d'une population)* instability; *(▸ du temps)* unsettled nature **2** *Chim, Phys & Psy* instability

instable [ɛ̃stabl] **ADJ 1** *(branlant)* unsteady, unstable; *(glissant ▸ terrain)* unstable, shifting; **être en équilibre i.** to be balanced precariously **2** *(précaire ▸ situation, emploi)* unstable, precarious; *(▸ régime politique, marché, prix, personnalité)* unstable; *(▸ population)* shifting, unsettled, unstable; *(▸ temps)* unsettled; **la paix est encore i.** the peace is still fragile *or* uncertain **3** *Chim, Phys & Psy* unstable

NMF unreliable *or* unsteady person; *Psy* unstable person

installateur, -trice [ɛ̃stalatœr, -tris] **NM,F** *(d'appareils sanitaires)* fitter; *Élec, Rad & TV* installer

installation [ɛ̃stalasjɔ̃] **NF 1** *(dispositif, équipement)* installation; *(aménagement)* set-up; **une i. de fortune** a makeshift set-up; **i. électrique** wiring; **i. informatique** computer facility; **i. téléphonique** telephone installation

2 *(d'un dentiste, d'un médecin)* setting up (practice); *(d'un ecclésiastique, d'un magistrat)* installation, induction; *(d'un commerçant)* opening, setting up (shop); *(d'un locataire)* moving in; **je fais une fête pour célébrer mon i.** I'm having a housewarming (party); **comment s'est passée votre i.?** how did the move go?

3 *(mise en service ▸ de l'électricité, du gaz, du chauffage)* installation, installing, putting in; *(▸ d'un appareil ménager)* installation, installing; *(▸ d'une grue)* setting up; *(▸ d'une antenne)* installing; *(▸ d'une cuisine, d'un atelier, d'un laboratoire)* fitting out; **qui a fait l'i. de la prise/du lave-linge?** who wired the socket/plumbed in the washing machine?; **refaire l'i. électrique (d'une maison)** to rewire (a house)

4 *(implantation ▸ d'une usine)* setting up

5 *Ordinat* installation; **programme d'i.** installation program; **i. en réseau** network installation

6 *(œuvre d'art)* installation; **i. vidéo** video installation

• **installations NFPL** *(dans une usine)* machinery and equipment; *(complexe, bâtiment)* installations; **installations portuaires** port installations; **installations sanitaires** sanitary installations *or* fittings

installatrice [ɛ̃stalatris] *voir* **installateur**

installé, -e [ɛ̃stale] **ADJ 1** *(aisé)* well-off, established; **les gens installés** the comfortably well-off **2** *(aménagé)* **un laboratoire bien/mal i.** a well/badly equipped laboratory; **elle est bien installée** she has a really nice house/flat/*etc*; **ils sont mal installés** they have a really uncomfortable house/flat/*etc*

INSTALLER [3] [ɛ̃stale]

VT
- to install **1, 8**
- to put in **1, 2**
- to set up **2, 5, 7**
- to put **3, 6**
- to fit out **4**

VPR
- to sit down **1**
- to be set up **2**
- to set up **2, 3**
- to become established **4**

VT 1 *(mettre en service ▸ chauffage, eau, gaz, électricité, téléphone)* to install, to put in; *(▸ appareil ménager, logiciel)* to install; **nous avons dû faire i. l'eau/le gaz/l'électricité** we had to have the water laid on/the gas put in/the house wired

2 *(mettre en place ▸ meuble)* to put in; *(▸ tente)* to put up, to pitch; *(▸ barrière)* to put up, to erect; *(▸ campement)* to set up; *(▸ troupes)* to position; **j'ai installé deux appliques au-dessus du lit** I've put in *or* fixed *or* installed two wall-lamps above the bed; **où va-t-on i. le buffet?** where are we going to put the sideboard?; **il a installé son ordinateur dans sa chambre à coucher** he set up *or* put his computer in his bedroom

3 *(faire asseoir, allonger)* to put, to place; **n'installez pas les enfants sur la banquette avant** don't put the children in the front; **une fois qu'il est installé devant la télévision, il n'y a plus moyen de lui parler** once he's settled himself down *or* installed (himself) in front of the TV, there's no talking to him

4 *(pièce, logement ▸ aménager)* to fit out; *(▸ disposer)* to lay out; *(usine, atelier ▸ équiper)* to fit up *or* out, to equip; **nous avons installé la salle de jeu au grenier** we've turned the attic into a playroom; **comment le dortoir est-il installé?** how is the dormitory laid out?

5 *(établir ▸ jeune couple)* to set up

6 *(loger)* to put; **je les ai installés dans la chambre bleue** I've put them in the blue room

7 *(implanter ▸ usine)* to set up

8 *Admin* to install; **i. qn dans ses fonctions** to install sb in his/her post

VPR s'installer 1 *(s'asseoir, s'allonger)* **il s'est installé à la terrasse d'un café** he sat down outside a pavement café; **installez-vous comme il faut, je reviens tout de suite** make yourself comfortable *or* at home, I'll be right back; **s'i. dans un canapé/devant la télévision** to settle down on a couch/in front of the television

2 *(s'implanter ▸ cirque, marché)* to (be) set up; *(▸ usine)* to be set up; **s'i. à la campagne** *(emménager)* to set up house *or* to go and live *or* to settle in the country; **s'i. dans une maison** to move into a house; **je m'installai dans un petit hôtel** I put up at a small hotel; **s'i. dans de nouveaux bureaux** *(entreprise)* to move into new offices; *(employés)* to move into one's new offices; **si ça continue, elle va finir par s'i. chez moi!** if this goes on, she'll end up moving in (permanently)!

3 *(pour exercer ▸ médecin, dentiste)* to set up a practice; *(▸ commerçant)* to set up shop; **s'i. à son compte** to set up one's own business *or* on one's own; **quand je me suis installé, la clientèle était rare** when I started, there weren't many customers

4 *(se fixer ▸ statu quo)* to become established; *(▸ maladie)* to take hold; *(▸ doute, peur)* to creep in; *(▸ silence)* to take over; **il s'est installé dans le mensonge** he's become an habitual liar, he's well used to lying; **un climat d'insécurité s'est installé dans le pays** a climate of insecurity has taken hold of the country; **le pays s'installe peu à peu dans la crise** the country is sliding *or* sinking into a recession

instamment [ɛ̃stamɑ̃] **ADV** insistently; **je vous demande i. de revenir sur votre décision** I beg *or* urge you to reconsider your decision

instance [ɛ̃stɑ̃s] **NF 1** *(organisme)* authority; **les instances économiques/communautaires** the economic/EU authorities; **les plus hautes instances du parti** the leading bodies of the party; **le dossier sera traité par une i. supérieure** the file will be dealt with at a higher level *or* by a higher authority **2** *Jur* (legal) proceedings; **introduire une i.** to start *or* to institute proceedings; **en première i.** on first hearing; **en seconde i.** on appeal; **i. d'ap-**

pel appeal proceedings **3** *Littéraire (insistance)* insistence; **avec i.** earnestly, with insistence
• **instances** NFPL entreaties; **sur** *ou* **devant les instances de son père, il finit par accepter** in the face of his father's entreaties *or* pleas, he eventually accepted
• **en dernière instance** ADV in the last analysis
• **en instance** ADJ *(dossier)* pending, waiting to be dealt with; *Jur (affaire)* pending, *Br* sub judice; *(courrier)* ready for posting
• **en instance de** PRÉP **être en i. de divorce** to be waiting for a divorce *or* in the middle of divorce proceedings; **prisonnier en i. de libération** prisoner waiting for *or* pending release

> Il faut noter que le nom anglais **instance** est un faux ami. Il signifie **exemple**.

instant[1] [ɛ̃stɑ̃] NM **1** *(courte durée)* moment, instant; **il a eu un i. d'inattention** he had a momentary lapse of concentration; **nous n'avons pas un i. à perdre** we don't have a moment to lose; **pendant un i., j'ai cru que c'était elle** for a moment *or* an instant, I thought it was her; **il s'arrêta un i.** he stopped for a moment; **j'ai pensé, pendant un i.** *ou* **l'espace d'un i., que...** for half a minute *or* for a split second, I thought that…; **as-tu pensé un i. au danger?** didn't it cross your mind for one moment that it was dangerous?; **il ne s'est pas demandé un i. ce qui pouvait arriver** he never asked himself once what might happen; **je n'en doute pas un seul i.** I don't doubt it at all, I've never doubted it for a minute; **(attendez) un i.!** just a moment!, just a second!; **je reviens dans un i.** I'll be right back, I'll be back in a minute; **c'est l'affaire d'un i.** it won't take a minute; **c'est prêt en un i.** it's ready in an instant *or* in no time at all **2** *(moment précis)* moment
• **à chaque instant** ADV all the time
• **à l'instant (même)** ADV this instant, this minute; **je suis rentré à l'i. (même)** I've just come in this minute *or* second; **je l'apprends à l'i. (même)** I've just this moment heard about it; **nous devons partir à l'i. (même)** we must leave right now *or* this instant *or* this very minute; **à l'i. (même) où je m'apprêtais à partir** just as I was about to leave
• **à tout instant** ADV *(continuellement)* all the time; *(d'une minute à l'autre)* any time (now), any minute
• **dans l'instant** ADV at this moment, instantly
• **de tous les instants** ADJ constant
• **dès l'instant que** CONJ *(si)* if; *(puisque)* since; *(aussitôt que)* as soon as, from the moment
• **d'un instant à l'autre** ADV any moment now
• **par instants** ADV at times, from time to time
• **pour l'instant** ADV for the moment, for the time being

instant[2], **-e** [ɛ̃stɑ̃, -ɑ̃t] ADJ *Littéraire* **1** *(imminent ▸ péril)* pressing **2** *(pressant ▸ prière)* pressing, insistent

instantané, -e [ɛ̃stɑ̃tane] ADJ **1** *(immédiat)* instantaneous; **la mort a été instantanée** death was instantaneous; **sa réponse a été instantanée** his/her answer was immediate **2** *(soluble ▸ café, soupe)* instant **3** *Phot* **cliché i.** snapshot
NM snap, snapshot

instantanément [ɛ̃stɑ̃tanemɑ̃] ADV instantly, instantaneously

instar [ɛ̃star] **à l'instar de** PRÉP following (the example of); **à l'i. de ses parents, il sera enseignant** like his parents, he's going to be a teacher

instaurateur, -trice [ɛ̃stɔratœr, -tris] NM,F *Littéraire* founder, creator

instauration [ɛ̃stɔrasjɔ̃] NF institution, foundation

instauratrice [ɛ̃stɔratris] *voir* **instaurateur**

instaurer [3] [ɛ̃stɔre] VT *(système, régime, contrôle)* to introduce, to set up; *(dialogue)* to initiate, to institute; *(mode)* to introduce, to start; **i. le couvre-feu dans une ville** to impose a curfew in a town; **afin d'i. un climat de confiance** to create an atmosphere of trust
VPR **s'instaurer** to be established

instigateur, -trice [ɛ̃stigatœr, -tris] NM,F instigator; **il nie être l'i. du crime** he denies being behind the crime *or* being the instigator of the crime; **l'association ainsi créée sera l'instigatrice d'une nouvelle politique** the association thus created will initiate new policy decisions

instigation [ɛ̃stigasjɔ̃] NF instigation; **à** *ou* **sur l'i. de qn** at sb's instigation

instigatrice [ɛ̃stigatris] *voir* **instigateur**

instiguer [3] [ɛ̃stige] VT *Belg* to incite

instillation [ɛ̃stilasjɔ̃] NF instillation

instiller [3] [ɛ̃stile] VT **1** *Méd* to instil; **i. un liquide dans l'œil** to drop a liquid into the eye **2** *Littéraire (insuffler)* to instil; **i. le doute dans l'esprit de qn** to instil doubt in sb's mind

instinct [ɛ̃stɛ̃] NM **1** *Psy & Zool* instinct; **i. de conservation** self-preservation instinct; **i. maternel** maternal instinct **2** *(intuition)* instinct; **il eut l'i. de parer le coup** he instinctively fended off the blow; **se fier à son i.** to trust one's instincts *or* intuition **3** *(don)* instinct; **elle a l'i. de la scène** she has a natural talent for the stage
• **d'instinct** ADV instinctively, by instinct
• **par instinct** ADV **1** *Psy & Zool* instinctively, by instinct **2** *(intuitivement)* instinctively

instinctif, -ive [ɛ̃stɛ̃ktif, -iv] ADJ **1** *(inconscient ▸ réaction, antipathie)* instinctive; **si je vois un gâteau, je le mange, c'est i.!** if I see a cake, I eat it, I can't help it! **2** *(impulsif)* instinctive, impulsive; **c'est un être i.** he's/she's a creature of instinct
NM,F instinctive person

instinctivement [ɛ̃stɛ̃ktivmɑ̃] ADV instinctively

instit [ɛ̃stit] NMF *Fam (de maternelle)* (nursery school) teacher▫; *(d'école primaire)* (primary school) teacher▫

instituer [7] [ɛ̃stitɥe] VT **1** *(règlement, système)* to introduce, to establish; *(impôt)* to institute; *(commission d'enquête)* to set up **2** *(désigner ▸ héritier)* to institute, to appoint; *(▸ évêque, cardinal)* to institute
VPR **s'instituer 1** *(se désigner)* to set oneself up; **il s'est institué (comme) arbitre de leur querelle** he set himself up as the arbitrator of their quarrel **2** *(s'établir)* to be *or* to become established; **des relations durables se sont instituées entre les deux pays** a lasting relationship was established between the two countries

institut [ɛ̃stity] NM *(organisme)* institute; **i. de recherches/scientifique** research/scientific institute; **i. de beauté** beauty salon; *Banque* **i. d'émission** central note-issuing authority; **i. monétaire** lender of last resort; **i. de sondage** polling company; **l'I. catholique de Paris** = large private university in Paris; **l'I. d'Études politiques** = "grande école" for political sciences in Paris, commonly known as "Sciences-Po"; **I. européen d'administration** = European business school in Fontainebleau; *Mktg* **I. français d'opinion publique** = French market research institute; **I. français de recherche pour l'exploitation de la mer** = French research establishment for marine resources; **l'I. de France** the Institut de France, *Br* ≃ the Royal Society, *Am* ≃ the National Science Foundation; **I. géographique national** = French national geographical institute, *Br* ≃ Ordnance Survey, *Am* ≃ United States Geological Survey; **l'I. du Monde Arabe** = Arab cultural centre and library in Paris holding regular exhibitions of Arab art; **l'I. monétaire européen** the European Monetary Institute; **I. national d'agronomie** = "grande école" for agricultural studies; **I. national de l'audiovisuel** = national television archive; **I. national de la consommation** = French consumer research organization; **I. national d'études démographiques** = national institute for demographic research; **I. national de la recherche agronomique** = national institute for agronomic research; **I. national de la santé et de la recherche médicale** = national institute for medical research; **I. national de la statistique et des études économiques** = French national institute of statistics and information about the economy; **I. universitaire de formation des maîtres** = teacher-training college; **I. universitaire professionnel** = business school; **I. universitaire de technologie** = vocational higher education college

instituteur, -trice [ɛ̃stitytœr, -tris] NM,F **1** *(de maternelle)* (nursery school) teacher; *(d'école primaire)* (primary school) teacher; **demande à ton institutrice** ask your teacher **2** *Vieilli (précepteur, gouvernante)* tutor, *f* governess

institution [ɛ̃stitysjɔ̃] NF **1** *(établissement)* institution; **i. pour les aveugles** institution *or* school for the blind; **ils ont mis la vieille dame dans une i.** they put the old lady into a home; **i. religieuse** *(catholique)* Catholic school; *(autre)* denominational school, *Br* faith school; **i. financière** financial institution
2 *(coutume)* institution; **l'i. du mariage** the institution of marriage
3 *(mise en place)* institution, establishment; *(d'une loi)* introduction; *(d'une règle)* laying down
4 *(désignation ▸ d'un héritier)* appointment, institution; *(▸ d'un évêque, d'un cardinal)* institution
• **institutions** NFPL institutions; **les institutions politiques** political institutions

institutionnalisation [ɛ̃stitysjɔnalizasjɔ̃] NF institutionalization

institutionnaliser [3] [ɛ̃stitysjɔnalize] VT to institutionalize

institutionnel, -elle [ɛ̃stitysjɔnɛl] ADJ institutional
NMPL institutional investors

institutrice [ɛ̃stitytris] *voir* **instituteur**

instructeur, -trice [ɛ̃stryktœr, -tris] NM,F instructor
ADJ M *Jur* **juge i.** examining magistrate; *Mil* **sergent i.** drill sergeant

instructif, -ive [ɛ̃stryktif, -iv] ADJ informative, instructive; **j'ai trouvé l'émission instructive** I thought the programme was informative *or* instructive; *Hum* **c'est très i. d'écouter aux portes!** you learn a lot listening at keyholes!

instruction [ɛ̃stryksjɔ̃] NF **1** *Vieilli (culture)* (general) education; **il a une solide i.** he has a good general level of education; **elle a beaucoup d'i.** she's well-educated; **manquer d'i.** to be uneducated, to lack education
2 *(formation)* education, teaching; **il se charge de l'i. de ses enfants** he is taking care of his children's education himself; **l'i. que j'ai reçue à l'école** the teaching *or* education I was given at school; **i. civique** civics; *Mil* **i. militaire** military training; **i. primaire** primary education; **i. professionnelle** vocational training; **i. religieuse** religious instruction; **i. secondaire** secondary education
3 *Jur* preliminary investigation *or* inquiry *(of a case by an examining magistrate)*; **qui est chargé de l'i.?** who's setting up the inquiry?
4 *Ordinat* instruction; **jeu d'instructions** instruction set
5 *(ordre)* instruction; **donner/recevoir des instructions** to give/to receive instructions; **sur les instructions de ses supérieurs** following orders from his/her superiors
6 *Admin (circulaire)* directive
• **instructions** NFPL *(d'un fabricant)* instructions, directions; **instructions de montage** instructions *or* directions for assembly; **conformément aux instructions** as directed

instructive [ɛ̃stryktiv] *voir* **instructif**

instructrice [ɛ̃stryktris] *voir* **instructeur**

instruire [98] [ɛ̃strɥir] VT **1** *(enseigner à)* to teach, to instruct; *(former)* to educate; *Mil (recrue)* to train; **une émission destinée à i. en distrayant** a programme designed to be both entertaining and educational; **instruit par l'expérience** taught by experience **2** *(aviser)* **i. qn de qch** to inform sb of sth, to acquaint sb with sth; **il était à peine instruit de la situation** he was barely acquainted with the situation **3** *Jur* **i. une affaire** *ou* **un dossier** to set up a preliminary inquiry
VI *Jur* **i. contre qn** to set up a preliminary inquiry against sb
VPR **s'instruire 1** *(se cultiver)* to educate oneself; **il s'est instruit tout seul** he's self-educated **2** *(apprendre)* to learn; **on s'instruit à tout âge** it's never too late to learn **3 s'i. de qch** to obtain information about sth, to find out about sth; **s'i. de qch auprès de qn** to ask sb about sth, to inquire of sb about sth

instruit, -e [ɛ̃strɥi, -it] **ADJ** well-educated, educated

instrument [ɛ̃strymɑ̃] **NM 1** *(outil, matériel)* instrument; **i. tranchant** edged *or* cutting tool; **naviguer aux instruments** to fly on instruments; **instruments de bord** instruments; **i. de mesure/d'observation** measuring/observation instrument; **un i. de torture** an instrument of torture; **i. de travail** tool; **c'est un de mes instruments de travail** it's a tool of my trade; **i. de vente** sales tool; **c'est un i. d'analyse de l'inflation** it's a tool for analysing inflation
2 *Mus* **i. (de musique)** (musical) instrument; **i. à cordes/à percussion/à vent** string/percussion/wind instrument
3 *Fig (agent)* instrument, tool; **la télévision est-elle un i. de propagande?** is television an instrument of propaganda?; **être l'i. de qn** to be sb's instrument *or* tool; **être l'i. de** to bring about; **il fut l'i. de leur ruine** he brought about their ruin; **il fut l'un des instruments de leur ruine** he was instrumental in their ruin
4 *(document, acte authentique)* instrument; *Jur* (legal) instrument; **i. de commerce** instrument of commerce; **i. de couverture** hedging instrument; **i. de crédit** instrument of credit; **i. dérivé** derivative; **i. financier** financial instrument; **i. financier à terme** financial future; **i. négociable** negotiable instrument; **i. de négociation** trading instrument; **i. de placement** investment instrument

instrumentaire [ɛ̃strymɑ̃tɛr] *voir* **témoin**

instrumental, -e, -aux, -ales [ɛ̃strymɑ̃tal, -o] **ADJ** instrumental
NM *Ling* instrumental (case)

instrumentalisation [ɛ̃strymɑ̃talizasjɔ̃] **NF** instrumentalization

instrumentaliser [3] [ɛ̃strymɑ̃talize] **VT** to use for one's own ends

instrumentation [ɛ̃strymɑ̃tasjɔ̃] **NF 1** *Mus* orchestration, instrumentation **2** *Tech* instrumentation

instrumenter [3] [ɛ̃strymɑ̃te] **VI** *Jur* to draw up an official document; **i. contre qn** to order proceedings to be taken against sb
VT 1 *Mus* to orchestrate, to score (for instruments) **2** *(en travaux publics)* to instrument

instrumentiste [ɛ̃strymɑ̃tist] **NMF** *Mus* instrumentalist

insu [ɛ̃sy] **à l'insu de PRÉP 1** *(sans être vu de)* without the knowledge of, unbeknown *or* unbeknownst to; **sortir à l'i. de ses parents** to go out without one's parents knowing *or* one's parents' knowledge; **à l'i. de tout le monde, il s'était glissé dans la cuisine** he'd slipped unnoticed into the kitchen **2 à mon/son i.** *(sans m'en/s'en apercevoir)* unwittingly, without being aware of it

insubmersible [ɛ̃sybmɛrsibl] **ADJ** *(canot)* insubmersible; *(jouet)* unsinkable

insubordination [ɛ̃sybɔrdinasjɔ̃] **NF** insubordination

insubordonné, -e [ɛ̃sybɔrdɔne] **ADJ** insubordinate

insuccès [ɛ̃syksɛ] **NM** failure; **l'i. de la pièce** the failure of the play; **son i. aux élections l'a découragé** his/her poor performance at the polls has discouraged him/her

insuffisamment [ɛ̃syfizamɑ̃] **ADV** insufficiently, inadequately; **i. nourri** underfed; **la lettre était i. affranchie** the letter had insufficient postage; **des vêtements i. rincés** clothes that haven't been thoroughly rinsed

insuffisance [ɛ̃syfizɑ̃s] **NF 1** *(manque)* insufficiency, deficiency; **i. de ressources** lack of *or* insufficient resources; **l'i. de la production industrielle** the shortfall in industrial production; **i. de capitaux** insufficient capital; **i. d'espèces** cash shortage; **i. de personnel** staff shortage; **i. de provision** insufficient funds *(to meet cheque)* **2** *(point faible)* weakness, deficiency; **ses insuffisances en matière de pathologie** his/her lack of knowledge of pathology **3** *Méd* deficiency; **elle est morte d'une i. cardiaque** she died from heart failure; **i. hormonale** hormone deficiency; **i. rénale** kidney failure *or Spéc* insufficiency; **i. respiratoire** respiratory insufficiency *or* failure

insuffisant, -e [ɛ̃syfizɑ̃, -ɑ̃t] **ADJ 1** *(en quantité)* insufficient; **nous avons des effectifs insuffisants** our numbers are too low, we're understaffed; **c'est i. pour ouvrir un compte** it's not enough to open an account; **nous disposons de médicaments mais en quantité insuffisante** we have drugs at our disposal but not enough of them **2** *(en qualité)* inadequate; **des résultats insuffisants en mathématiques** inadequate results in mathematics **3** *(inapte)* incompetent; **on l'a jugé i. pour ce travail** he's been deemed incompetent *or* unfit for this job; **la plupart de nos élèves sont insuffisants en langues** most of our pupils are poor *or* weak at languages

insufflateur [ɛ̃syflatœr] **NM** *Méd* insufflator

insufflation [ɛ̃syflasjɔ̃] **NF** *Méd* insufflation

insuffler [3] [ɛ̃syfle] **VT 1** *Méd* to insufflate; **i. de l'air dans un corps** to blow *or* to insufflate air into a body **2** *(inspirer)* **i. qch à qn** to instil sth in sb, to infuse sb with sth; **la terreur lui insuffla du courage** terror inspired him/her to be brave; **ce succès a insufflé un nouvel élan à l'entreprise** this success gave the company a new lease of life *or* breathed new life into the company

insulaire [ɛ̃sylɛr] **ADJ** island *(avant n)*, insular; **la population i.** the population of the island, the island population
NMF islander

> Il faut noter que l'adjectif anglais **insular** signifie le plus souvent **borné, étriqué**.

insularité [ɛ̃sylarite] **NF 1** *Géog* insularity; **leur i. en fait des gens à part** the fact that they live on an island sets them apart **2** *Péj (étroitesse d'esprit)* insularity

insuline [ɛ̃sylin] **NF** insulin

insulinodépendant, -e [ɛ̃sylinɔdepɑ̃dɑ̃, -ɑ̃t] **ADJ** insulin-dependent

insulinothérapie [ɛ̃sylinɔterapi] **NF** insulin *or* insulin-based treatment *(for diabetes)*

insultant, -e [ɛ̃syltɑ̃, -ɑ̃t] **ADJ** insulting; **c'est i. pour moi** I'm insulted; **il s'est comporté de façon insultante à mon égard** the way he treated me was an insult

insulte [ɛ̃sylt] **NF 1** *(parole blessante)* insult; **je n'ai pas relevé l'i.** I didn't react; **lancer des insultes à qn** to hurl abuse at sb **2** *Fig (atteinte, outrage)* insult; **c'est une i. à sa mémoire** it's an insult to his/her memory; **une i. au bon sens** an insult to common sense; **il nous a fait l'i. de refuser** he insulted us by refusing

insulté, -e [ɛ̃sylte] **ADJ** insulted; **tu crois qu'elle s'est sentie insultée?** do you think she felt insulted *or* offended?
NM,F l'i. the injured party

insulter [3] [ɛ̃sylte] **VT** to insult; **il m'a insulté** he insulted me; **se faire i.** to be insulted
VPR s'insulter to exchange insults, to insult each other

insupportable [ɛ̃sypɔrtabl] **ADJ 1** *(insoutenable ▸ démangeaison, douleur, vision, bruit)* unbearable; *(▸ lumière)* unbearably bright; *(▸ situation)* intolerable; **il fait une chaleur i.** it's unbearably hot; **sans toi, la vie m'est i.** without you, life is more than I can bear *or* is too hard to bear; **l'idée de tuer un animal lui est i.** he/she can't bear the idea of killing an animal **2** *(turbulent ▸ enfant, élève)* impossible, insufferable, unbearable; **tu es i., si tu continues tu vas au lit!** you're being impossible, if you don't stop you're off to bed!

insupportablement [ɛ̃sypɔrtabləmɑ̃] **ADV** unbearably

insurgé, -e [ɛ̃syrʒe] **ADJ** insurgent *(avant n)*
NM insurgent

insurger [17] [ɛ̃syrʒe] **s'insurger VPR s'i. contre qn** to rise up *or* to rebel against sb; **s'i. contre qch** *(se rebeller)* to rebel against sth; *(critiquer)* to protest strongly against sth; **la nature humaine ne peut que s'i. devant un tel crime** human nature cannot but rise up in protest before such a crime

insurmontable [ɛ̃syrmɔ̃tabl] **ADJ 1** *(infranchissable ▸ obstacle)* insurmountable, insuperable **2** *(invincible ▸ aversion, angoisse)* uncontrollable, unconquerable; **il m'inspire un dégoût i.** I cannot overcome *or* conquer the disgust I feel for him

insurpassable [ɛ̃syrpasabl] **ADJ** unsurpassable

insurrection [ɛ̃syrɛksjɔ̃] **NF 1** *(révolte)* insurrection; **i. armée** armed insurrection **2** *Littéraire (indignation)* revolt

insurrectionnel, -elle [ɛ̃syrɛksjɔnɛl] **ADJ** insurrectionary, insurrectional

intact, -e [ɛ̃takt] **ADJ** *(réputation, économies)* intact; **le paquet est arrivé i.** the parcel arrived in one piece *or* intact; **je veux garder mon capital i.** I want to keep my capital intact, I don't want to touch my capital; **le problème reste i.** the problem remains unsolved

intaille [ɛ̃taj] **NF** intaglio

intangibilité [ɛ̃tɑ̃ʒibilite] **NF** intangibility

intangible [ɛ̃tɑ̃ʒibl] **ADJ 1** *(impalpable)* intangible **2** *(inviolable)* sacred, sacrosanct

intarissable [ɛ̃tarisabl] **ADJ 1** *(inépuisable ▸ source)* inexhaustible, unlimited; *(▸ imagination)* inexhaustible, boundless, limitless; *(▸ bavardage)* endless **2** *(bavard)* unstoppable; **sur le vin, il est i.** if you get him talking on wine, he'll go on for ever

intarissablement [ɛ̃tarisabləmɑ̃] **ADV** inexhaustibly; **il discourait i.** he was going on and on (and on)

intégrable [ɛ̃tegrabl] **ADJ** *Math* integrable

intégral, -e, -aux, -ales [ɛ̃tegral, -o] **ADJ 1** *(complet)* complete; **édition intégrale des poèmes de Donne** collected poems of Donne; **remboursement i. d'une dette** full *or* complete repayment of a debt; **la somme intégrale de vos dépenses s'élève à 480 euros** your expenses amount to 480 euros; **paiement i.** payment in full; **texte i.** unabridged version; **version intégrale** *(film)* uncut version **2** *Hum (en intensif)* utter, complete; **c'est un parasite i.** he's a complete parasite
• **intégrale NF 1** *(œuvre)* complete works; **l'intégrale des œuvres de Shakespeare** the complete works of Shakespeare; **l'intégrale des quatuors à cordes de Chostakovitch** the complete set of Shostakovich string quartets **2** *Math* integral

intégralement [ɛ̃tegralmɑ̃] **ADV** in full, fully, completely; **vous serez i. remboursé** you'll get all your money back, you'll be fully reimbursed; *Fin* **i. libéré** fully paid up

intégralité [ɛ̃tegralite] **NF** whole; **l'i. de la dette** the entire debt, the debt in full; **l'i. de son salaire a été payée aujourd'hui** his/her whole *or* entire salary was paid today; **la presse dans son i. protesta** the press protested as a body *or* en bloc

intégrant, -e [ɛ̃tegrɑ̃, -ɑ̃t] **ADJ partie intégrante de** integral part of; **faire partie intégrante de qch** to be an integral part of sth

intégrateur [ɛ̃tegratœr] **NM** integrator

intégration [ɛ̃tegrasjɔ̃] **NF 1** *(insertion)* integration; **i. raciale** racial integration
2 *(entrée dans une école, une organisation)* entry
3 *Math, Phys & Psy* integration
4 *Écon* integration; **i. en amont** *ou* **ascendante** backward integration; **i. en aval** forward integration; **i. descendante** forward integration; **i. économique** economic integration; **i. européenne** European integration; **i. financière** financial integration; **i. horizontale** horizontal integration; **i. latérale** lateral integration; **i. sociale** social integration; **i. verticale** vertical integration
5 *Ordinat* integration; **i. de bases de données** database integration

intègre [ɛ̃tɛgr] **ADJ 1** *(honnête)* honest **2** *(équitable, impartial)* upright, upstanding

intégré, -e [ɛ̃tegre] **ADJ 1** *(appareil)* built-in **2** *(entreprise)* integrated **3** *Ordinat (fax, modem)* integrated; **traitement i. de l'information** integrated (data) processing

intégrer [8] [ɛ̃tegre] **VT 1** *(inclure)* to integrate (**à** *ou* **dans** in), to incorporate, to include (**à** *ou* **dans** in); **i. un nouveau paragraphe dans un chapitre** to insert a new paragraph into a chapter; **notre société intègre différents secteurs d'activité** our company takes in *or* covers various areas of activity; **des activités destinées à i. les petits à la classe** activities designed to bring *or* to integrate the younger children into the group
2 *(assimiler ▸ enseignement, notion)* to assimilate; **j'ai complètement intégré les préceptes de mes parents** I've totally assimilated the principles my parents taught me

3 *Math* to integrate
4 *(entrer à ▸ école)* to get into, to enter; *(▸ entreprise)* to enter; *(▸ club)* to join; **i. les Mines** to be admitted to the School of Mining Engineers
VI *Fam Arg scol* = to get into a "Grande École"; **i. aux Mines** to get into the School of Mining Engineers
VPR s'intégrer 1 *(élément d'un kit)* to fit; **s'i. à** to fit into; **les pièces s'intègrent les unes aux autres** the pieces fit together **2** *(personne)* to become integrated *or* assimilated; **ils se sont mal intégrés à la vie du village** they never really fitted into village life

intégrisme [ɛ̃tegrism] **NM** *Rel* fundamentalism

intégriste [ɛ̃tegrist] *Rel* **ADJ** fundamentalist
NMF fundamentalist

intégrité [ɛ̃tegrite] **NF 1** *(totalité)* integrity; **dans son i.** as a whole, in its integrity
2 *(état originel)* soundness, integrity; **malgré son âge, elle a conservé l'i. de ses facultés** despite her age, she is still of sound mind
3 *(honnêteté)* integrity, honesty
4 *Ordinat* **i. des données** data integrity

intellect [ɛ̃telɛkt] **NM** intellect, understanding

intellectualiser [3] [ɛ̃telɛktɥalize] **VT** to intellectualize

intellectualisme [ɛ̃telɛktɥalism] **NM** intellectualism

intellectualiste [ɛ̃telɛktɥalist] **ADJ** intellectualistic
NMF intellectualist

intellectualité [ɛ̃telɛktɥalite] **NF** intellectuality

intellectuel, -elle [ɛ̃telɛktɥel] **ADJ 1** *(mental ▸ capacité)* intellectual, mental; **facultés intellectuelles** intellectual faculties; **puissance intellectuelle** brainpower **2** *(cérébral ▸ personne)* intellectual, cerebral; **c'est une approche très intellectuelle de la mise en scène** it's a very intellectual approach to directing **3** *(non manuel ▸ travail)* non-manual
NM,F intellectual

intellectuellement [ɛ̃telɛktɥɛlmɑ̃] **ADV** intellectually

intelligemment [ɛ̃teliʒamɑ̃] **ADV** intelligently, cleverly

intelligence [ɛ̃teliʒɑ̃s] **NF 1** *(intellect, discernement)* intelligence; **il n'est pas d'une grande i.** he's not very intelligent *or* bright *or* clever; **ils ont l'i. vive** they are sharp-witted *or* quick, they have sharp minds; **elle est d'une i. supérieure** she's of above-average intelligence; **avec i.** intelligently; **il a eu l'i. de ne pas recommencer** he was intelligent enough not to try again
2 *(personne)* **c'est une grande i.** he's/she's a great mind *or* intellect
3 *(compréhension)* **pour l'i. de ce qui va suivre** in order to understand *or* to grasp what follows; **elle a l'i. des affaires** she has a good understanding *or* grasp of business; **avoir l'i. du cœur** to be highly intuitive
4 *(relation)* **vivre en bonne/mauvaise i. avec qn** to be on good/bad terms with sb
5 *Ordinat* **i. artificielle** artificial intelligence
6 *Mktg* **i. marketing** marketing intelligence
• **intelligences NFPL** contacts; **elle a des intelligences dans le milieu** she has contacts in the underworld; **entretenir des intelligences avec qn** to have secret dealings *or* contacts with sb
• **d'intelligence ADJ** *(complice)* **regard/sourire d'i.** knowing look/smile; **faire des signes d'i. à qn** to give sb a knowing look **ADV** in collusion; **être d'i. avec qn** to be in collusion *or* in league with sb; **agir d'i. avec qn** to act in (tacit) agreement with sb

intelligent, -e [ɛ̃teliʒɑ̃, -ɑ̃t] **ADJ 1** *(gén)* intelligent, bright, clever; **enfin une analyse intelligente!** an intelligent analysis at last!; *Ironique* **c'est i.!** brilliant!, that was clever! **2** *Ordinat* intelligent; **terminal i.** intelligent terminal **3** *Mil* smart; **armes intelligentes** smart weapons

intelligentsia [ɛ̃teliʒensja, ɛteligensja] **NF l'i.** the intelligentsia

intelligibilité [ɛ̃teliʒibilite] **NF** intelligibility, *Sout* intelligibleness

intelligible [ɛ̃teliʒibl] **ADJ 1** *(compréhensible ▸ explication, raisonnement)* intelligible, comprehensible; **je ne sais pas si mes propos sont intelligibles** I don't know if what I'm saying makes sense to you; **il ne s'exprime pas de façon très i.** he doesn't express himself very clearly **2** *(audible)* intelligible, clear, audible; **parler à haute et i. voix** to speak loudly and clearly

intelligiblement [ɛ̃teliʒibləmɑ̃] **ADV 1** *(de façon compréhensible)* intelligibly **2** *(de façon audible)* intelligibly, clearly, audibly

intello [ɛ̃telo] *Fam Péj* **ADJ** highbrow[□]
NMF intellectual[□], egghead

intempérance [ɛ̃tɑ̃perɑ̃s] **NF 1** *Littéraire (de comportement)* immoderation, intemperance, excess; **ses intempérances de langage** his/her immoderate *or* excessive *or* unrestrained language **2** *(dans la vie sexuelle)* debauchery, intemperance; *(dans le manger, le boire)* lack of moderation, intemperance

intempérant, -e [ɛ̃tɑ̃perɑ̃, -ɑ̃t] **ADJ** excessive, intemperate

intempéries [ɛ̃tɑ̃peri] **NFPL** bad weather; **exposé aux i.** exposed to the elements

intempestif, -ive [ɛ̃tɑ̃pestif, -iv] **ADJ** inopportune, untimely; **sa remarque était intempestive** his/her comment was out of place

intemporalité [ɛ̃tɑ̃pɔralite] **NF 1** *(immuabilité)* timelessness **2** *(immatérialité)* immateriality

intemporel, -elle [ɛ̃tɑ̃pɔrel] **ADJ 1** *(immuable)* timeless **2** *(immatériel)* immaterial

intenable [ɛ̃tənabl] **ADJ 1** *(insupportable)* unbearable, intolerable **2** *(indiscipliné)* uncontrollable, unruly, badly-behaved **3** *(non défendable ▸ thèse)* untenable; *(▸ position)* indefensible

intendance [ɛ̃tɑ̃dɑ̃s] **NF 1** *Mil (pour l'ensemble de l'armée de terre)* Supply Corps; *(dans un régiment)* quartermaster stores **2** *Scol (service, bureau)* (domestic) bursar's office; *(gestion)* school management; **nous avons eu des problèmes d'i.** we had supply problems **3** *(gestion ▸ d'un domaine)* stewardship; *(▸ des finances)* management

intendant, -e [ɛ̃tɑ̃dɑ̃, -ɑ̃t] **NM,F 1** *(administrateur)* steward, bailiff **2** *Univ* bursar
NM *Mil* quartermaster
• **intendante NF** *(d'un couvent)* Mother Superior

intense [ɛ̃tɑ̃s] **ADJ 1** *(extrême ▸ chaleur, froid)* intense, extreme; *(▸ son)* loud, intense; *(▸ lumière)* intense, bright; *(▸ plaisir, désir, passion)* intense; *(▸ douleur)* intense, severe, acute; *(▸ regard)* intent, intense; **vivre de façon i.** to be intense **2** *(très vif ▸ couleur)* intense, bright, strong; **rouge i.** bright red; **des yeux d'un bleu i.** intensely blue eyes, deep blue eyes **3** *(abondant, dense ▸ circulation, bombardement)* heavy

intensément [ɛ̃tɑ̃semɑ̃] **ADV** intensely

intensif, -ive [ɛ̃tɑ̃sif, -iv] **ADJ 1** *(soutenu)* intensive; **cours intensifs** crash *or* intensive course **2** *Agr & Écon* intensive

intensification [ɛ̃tɑ̃sifikasjɔ̃] **NF** *(gén)* intensification; *(d'échanges commerciaux)* strengthening

intensifier [9] [ɛ̃tɑ̃sifje] **VT** *(gén)* to intensify, to step up; *(échanges commerciaux)* to increase, to step up
VPR s'intensifier *(passion, recherche)* to intensify, to become *or* to grow more intense; *(douleur)* to become more intense, to worsen; *(bombardements, circulation)* to become heavier

intensité [ɛ̃tɑ̃site] **NF 1** *(de la chaleur, du froid)* intensity; *(d'un son)* loudness; *(de la lumière)* intensity, brightness; *(d'une douleur)* intensity, acuteness; *(d'une couleur, d'une émotion)* intensity, depth, strength; *(d'un regard)* intentness, intensity; *(des bombardements)* heaviness, severity; **l'i. de la circulation** the heavy traffic; **l'i. de la lumière était telle que…** the light was so intense *or* bright that…; **il y a dans ce spectacle des moments d'une grande i.** there are some very intense moments in the show **2** *Opt & Phys* intensity; **i. d'un champ magnétique** magnetic field strength *or* intensity; *Géol* **i. d'un tremblement de terre** earthquake magnitude *or* intensity; **i. acoustique** intensity level; *Élec* **i. de courant** current; **i. énergétique** radiant intensity; **i. lumineuse/de rayonnement** luminous/radiant intensity; **i. lumineuse d'un télescope/microscope** light-transmitting capacity of a telescope/microscope; *Rad, Tél & TV* **i. du signal** signal strength

intensive [ɛ̃tɑ̃siv] *voir* **intensif**

intensivement [ɛ̃tɑ̃sivmɑ̃] **ADV** intensively

intenter [3] [ɛ̃tɑ̃te] **VT i. une action en justice à** *ou* **contre qn** to bring an action against sb; **i. un procès à** *ou* **contre qn** to institute (legal) proceedings against sb, to take sb to court

intention [ɛ̃tɑ̃sjɔ̃] **NF** intention; **quelles sont vos intentions?** what are your intentions?, what do you intend to do?; **avoir de bonnes/mauvaises intentions** to be well-/ill-intentioned, to have good/bad intentions; **il est plein de bonnes intentions** he's full of good intentions; **elle vous a offert ces fleurs dans la meilleure i.** she gave you these flowers with the best of intentions; **c'est l'i. qui compte** it's the thought that counts; **avoir l'i. de faire qch** to intend to do sth, to have the intention of doing sth; **elle a la ferme i. de rester ici** she's determined to stay here, she's intent on staying here; **il n'a pas l'i. de se laisser faire** he doesn't intend to be cheated; **n'avoir aucune i. de faire qch** to have no intention of doing sth; **il n'est pas** *ou* **il n'entre pas dans mes intentions de l'acheter maintenant** I have no intention of buying it now; **dans l'i. de faire qch** with the intention of *or* with a view to doing sth; **avec i.** on purpose, intentionally; **sans i.** without meaning to, unintentionally; *Jur* **i. délictueuse** criminal intent; *Jur* **sans i. de donner la mort** without intent to kill; *Jur* **sans i. de nuire** with no ill intent; *Mktg* **i. d'achat** intention to buy; **intentions de vote** voting intentions; **ils enregistrent 28 pour cent des intentions de vote** 28 percent of those polled said that they would vote for them
• **à cette intention ADV** for that purpose, with this intention
• **à l'intention de PRÉP** for; **film à l'i. des enfants** film for *or* aimed at children; **collecte à l'i. des aveugles** fund-raising for (the benefit of) *or* in aid of the blind; **messe/prière à l'i. du défunt** mass/prayer for the deceased; **ils ont organisé un banquet à l'i. de leurs invités** they organized a banquet in honour of their guests

intentionné, -e [ɛ̃tɑ̃sjɔne] **ADJ bien/mal i.** well-/ill-intentioned

intentionnel, -elle [ɛ̃tɑ̃sjɔnel] **ADJ** intentional, deliberate

intentionnellement [ɛ̃tɑ̃sjɔnɛlmɑ̃] **ADV** intentionally, deliberately; **c'est i. que je ne l'ai pas invitée** I deliberately didn't invite her, I didn't invite her on purpose

inter [ɛ̃ter] **NM 1** *Vieilli Tél* long-distance call, *Br* trunk call; **j'ai eu du mal à obtenir l'i.** I had trouble getting the long-distance operator *or Br* making a trunk call; **faire l'i.** to make a long-distance call, *Br* to put in a trunk call **2** *Sport* inside-forward; **i. droit/gauche** inside right/left

interactif, -ive [ɛ̃teraktif, -iv] **ADJ 1** *(gén)* interactive **2** *Ordinat* interactive

interaction [ɛ̃teraksjɔ̃] **NF** *(gén)* interaction, interplay

interactive [ɛ̃teraktiv] *voir* **interactif**

interactivité [ɛ̃teraktivite] **NF** interactivity

interafricain, -e [ɛ̃terafrikɛ̃, -ɛn] **ADJ** Pan-African

interallié, -e [ɛ̃teralje] **ADJ** allied

interaméricain, -e [ɛ̃teramerikɛ̃, -ɛn] **ADJ** Pan-American, Inter-American

interarabe [ɛ̃terarab] **ADJ** Pan-Arab

interarmées [ɛ̃terarme] **ADJ INV opération i.** interservice *or* joint service operation; **état-major i.** joint staff

interarmes [ɛ̃terarm] **ADJ INV** *(opération, manœuvre)* combined

interbancaire [ɛ̃terbɑ̃ker] **ADJ** *(relations)* interbank; **le marché i.** the money markets

interblocage [ɛ̃terblɔkaʒ] **NM** *Ordinat* deadlock

intercalaire [ɛ̃terkaler] **ADJ 1** *(feuille)* **feuillet i.** inset, insert; **fiche i.** divider **2** *(date)* **jour/année i.** intercalary day/year
NM 1 *(feuillet)* inset, insert **2** *(fiche)* divider

intercalation [ɛ̃tɛrkalasjɔ̃] NF **1** *(dans le calendrier)* intercalation **2** *(de feuilles)* insertion; *(de termes)* interpolation

intercaler [3] [ɛ̃tɛrkale] VT **1** *Typ* to insert, to inset **2** *(insérer)* to insert, to fit *or* to put in; **des coupures de journaux intercalées dans un dossier** newspaper clippings inserted into a file; **la fédération a intercalé trois jours de repos entre les matches** the league fitted in three rest days between the matches **3** *(dans le calendrier)* to intercalate

VPR **s'intercaler s'i. entre** to come (in) *or* to fit in between; **la voiture s'est intercalée entre deux ambulances** the car came *or* slipped in between two ambulances

intercantonal, -e, -aux, -ales [ɛ̃tɛrkɑ̃tɔnal, -o] ADJ *Suisse (entre cantons)* inter-canton, between cantons; *(qui concerne plusieurs cantons)* cross-canton

intercéder [8] [ɛ̃tɛrsede] VI **i. (auprès de qn) en faveur de qn** to intercede (with sb) for *or* on behalf of sb

intercepter [4] [ɛ̃tɛrsɛpte] VT **1** *(arrêter ▸ véhicule)* to stop; *(▸ lettre, message)* to intercept; *(▸ fugitif)* to stop, to intercept; **le store intercepte la lumière** the blind blocks out the light *or* stops the light coming in **2** *Mil (avion)* to intercept **3** *Sport (ballon)* to intercept

intercepteur [ɛ̃tɛrsɛptœr] NM *Mil* interceptor

interception [ɛ̃tɛrsɛpsjɔ̃] NF interception; **avion d'i.** interceptor (aircraft)

intercesseur [ɛ̃tɛrsesœr] NM *Littéraire* intercessor

intercession [ɛ̃tɛrsesjɔ̃] NF *Littéraire* intercession

> Do not confuse with **intersession**.

interchangeable [ɛ̃tɛrʃɑ̃ʒabl] ADJ interchangeable

interclasse [ɛ̃tɛrklas] NM *Scol Br* break, *Am* recess; **à l'i.** at *or* during *Br* break *or Am* recess

interclassement [ɛ̃tɛrklasmɑ̃] NM *Ordinat* merging

interclasseuse [ɛ̃tɛrklasøz] NF collator

intercom [ɛ̃tɛrkɔm] NM *Can Joual* entryphone

intercommunalité [ɛ̃tɛrkɔmynalite] NF = co-operation between neighbouring communes

intercommunication [ɛ̃tɛrkɔmynikasjɔ̃] NF intercommunication

interconnexion [ɛ̃tɛrkɔnɛksjɔ̃] NF **1** *Élec* interconnection **2** *(de réseaux, systèmes)* interconnectivity

intercontinental, -e, -aux, -ales [ɛ̃tɛrkɔ̃tinɑ̃tal, -o] ADJ intercontinental

intercostal, -e, -aux, -ales [ɛ̃tɛrkɔstal, -o] ADJ *(muscle)* intercostal; **il a des douleurs intercostales** he has a pain in his side

NM intercostal muscle

intercours [ɛ̃tɛrkur] NM *Belg Scol Br* break, *Am* recess; **à l'i.** at *or* during *Br* break *or Am* recess

interculturel, -elle [ɛ̃tɛrkyltyrɛl] ADJ cross-cultural

interdépartemental, -e, -aux, -ales [ɛ̃tɛrdepartəmɑ̃tal, -o] ADJ interdepartmental

interdépendance [ɛ̃tɛrdepɑ̃dɑ̃s] NF interdependence

interdépendant, -e [ɛ̃tɛrdepɑ̃dɑ̃, -ɑ̃t] ADJ *(gén)* interdependent, mutually dependent; *(problèmes)* linked, related

interdiction [ɛ̃tɛrdiksjɔ̃] NF **1** *(prohibition ▸ résultat)* ban; *(▸ action)* banning; **passer outre à/lever une i.** to ignore/to lift a ban; **malgré l'i. des ventes** in spite of the ban on sales *or* of sales being prohibited; **i. d'exportation** export ban; **i. d'importation** import ban; **l'i. du livre en 1953 a assuré son succès** the banning of the book in 1953 guaranteed its success; **obtenir l'i. du site aux touristes** to get an order forbidding tourists access to the site; **et maintenant, i. d'utiliser la voiture!** and now you're banned from driving the car!; **i. m'avait été faite d'en parler** I'd been forbidden to talk about it; **i. est faite aux employés de passer par la grande porte** employees are not allowed through *or* are forbidden to use the main entrance; **i. de faire demi-tour** *(sur panneau)* no U-turn; **i. de marcher sur les pelouses** *(sur panneau)* keep off the grass, do not walk on the grass; **i. de pêcher** *(sur panneau)* fishing prohibited; **i. de stationner** *(sur panneau)* no parking; **i. de déposer des ordures** *(sur panneau)* no dumping; **i. (formelle** *ou* **absolue) de fumer** *(sur panneau)* (strictly) no smoking, smoking (strictly) prohibited; **et i. absolue de toucher à mon ordinateur!** and don't touch my computer!

2 *(suspension ▸ d'un fonctionnaire)* suspension (from duty); *(▸ d'un aviateur)* grounding; *(▸ d'un prêtre)* interdict, interdiction; **frapper un prêtre d'i.** to place a priest under (an) interdict *or* interdiction; **i. bancaire** stopping of payment on all cheques; **vous risquez une i. bancaire** you could have your chequebook taken away; *Ordinat* **i. d'écriture** write lockout; **le document est en i. d'écriture** the document is write-protected; *Jur* **i. légale** (temporary) deprivation of legal rights; **i. de séjour** banning order

interdigital, -e, -aux, -ales [ɛ̃tɛrdiʒital, -o] ADJ interdigital

interdire [103] [ɛ̃tɛrdir] VT **1** *(défendre)* to forbid; **i. l'alcool/le tabac à qn** to forbid sb to drink/to smoke; **i. à qn de faire qch** *(sujet: personne)* to forbid sb to do sth; *(sujet: règlement)* to prohibit sb from doing sth; **le règlement du bureau nous interdit de fumer** office rules prohibit smoking *or* prohibit us from smoking; **ils ont décidé d'i. l'accès du club aux femmes/aux mineurs** they've decided to ban women/minors from the club; **je lui ai interdit ma porte** *ou* **ma maison** I will not allow him/her into my home, I have banned him/her from my home

2 *(tournure impersonnelle)* **il est interdit de...** it's forbidden to...; **il m'est interdit d'en dire plus** I am not allowed *or* at liberty to say any more; **il est interdit de fumer ici** smoking is forbidden *or* isn't allowed here

3 *(prohiber ▸ circulation, stationnement, arme à feu, médicament)* to prohibit, to ban; *(▸ manifestation, revue, parti politique)* to ban; **i. qch d'exportation/d'importation** to impose an export/import ban on sth; **la loi l'interdit, c'est interdit par la loi** it's illegal, *Sout* it's prohibited by law; **le gouvernement a fait i. toute manifestation de rue** the government issued a ban on all street demonstrations

4 *(empêcher)* to prevent, to preclude; **le mauvais temps interdit toute opération de sauvetage** bad weather is preventing any rescue operations; **sa maladie lui interdit tout effort** his/her illness doesn't allow him/her to make any physical effort

5 *(suspendre ▸ magistrat)* to suspend; *(▸ prêtre)* to (lay under an) interdict

VPR **s'interdire s'i. l'alcool/le tabac** to abstain from drinking/smoking; **elle s'interdit tout espoir de la revoir** she denies herself all hope of seeing her again; **il s'interdit d'y penser** he doesn't let himself think about it

interdisciplinaire [ɛ̃tɛrdisiplinɛr] ADJ interdisciplinary

interdisez *etc voir* **interdire**

interdit, -e [ɛ̃tɛrdi, -it] PP *voir* **interdire**

ADJ **1** *(non autorisé)* forbidden; **ne t'assieds pas sur la pelouse, c'est i.** don't sit on the lawn, it's not allowed; **décharge/baignade interdite** *(sur panneau)* no dumping/bathing; **affichage i.** *(sur panneau)* (stick *or* post) no bills; **zone interdite** *(sur panneau)* no-go area; **le pont est i. aux voyageurs** the bridge is closed to passengers; **la zone piétonne est interdite aux véhicules** vehicles are not allowed in the pedestrian area; **i. au public** *(sur panneau)* no admittance; *Cin* **i. aux moins de 18 ans** adults only, *Br* ≃ 18, *Am* ≃ NC-17; *Cin* **i. aux moins de 13 ans** *Br* ≃ PG, *Am* ≃ PG-13

2 *(privé d'un droit) Jur* **i. de séjour en France** banned *or* prohibited from entering France; **être i. bancaire** *ou* **de chéquier** to have one's *Br* chequebook facilities *or Am* checking privileges withdrawn; *Ordinat* **i. d'écriture** *(disquette)* write-protected; **appareil/pilote i. de vol** grounded aircraft/pilot

3 *(frappé d'interdiction ▸ film, revue)* banned

4 *(stupéfait)* dumbfounded, flabbergasted; **laisser qn i.** *(très surpris)* to take sb aback; *(perplexe)* to disconcert sb; **elle le dévisagea, interdite** she stared at him in bewilderment; **ils étaient là, interdits, devant les ruines de leur maison** they stood speechless before the wreckage of their home

NM,F *Jur* **i. de séjour en Suisse** person banned from *or* not allowed to enter Switzerland

NM **1** *(de la société)* (social) constraint; *(tabou)* taboo; **il brave tous les interdits** he defies all social taboos; **lever un i.** to lift a restriction

2 *(condamnation)* **jeter l'i. sur** *ou* **contre qn** to cast sb out, to exclude sb

3 *(en anthropologie)* prohibition

4 *Rel* interdict; **des interdits alimentaires** food forbidden by dietary law

5 *Banque* **i. bancaire** ban on writing cheques; **être frappé d'i. bancaire** to have one's *Br* chequebook facilities *or Am* checking privileges withdrawn

intéressant, -e [ɛ̃teresɑ̃, -ɑ̃t] ADJ **1** *(conversation, œuvre, personne, visage etc)* interesting; **de manière intéressante** interestingly; **elle cherche toujours à se rendre intéressante** she's always trying to attract attention, she's an attention-seeker; **il n'est vraiment pas i.** he's not worth bothering with; *Hum Vieilli* **être dans une situation intéressante** *ou* **dans un état i.** *ou* **dans une position intéressante** to be in the family way **2** *(avantageux)* attractive, favourable; *(lucratif)* profitable, worthwhile; **c'est une affaire très intéressante** it's a very good deal; **cette carte n'est intéressante que si tu voyages beaucoup** this card is only worth having if you travel a lot; **il serait plus i. pour vous de changer de banque** you'd be better off banking with somebody else; **pas i.** *(offre, prix)* not attractive, not worthwhile; *(activité)* not worthwhile, unprofitable

NM,F *Péj* **faire l'i.** *ou* **son i.** to show off

> Il faut noter que l'adjectif anglais **interesting** ne signifie jamais **avantageux**.

intéressé, -e [ɛ̃terese] ADJ **1** *(égoïste ▸ personne)* self-interested, self-seeking, calculating; *(▸ comportement, conseil)* motivated by self-interest; **amour i.** cupboard love; **je ne suis pas du tout i.** I'm not doing it out of self-interest **2** *(concerné)* concerned, involved; **les parties intéressées** *(gén)* the people concerned *or* involved; *Jur* the interested parties **3** *(financièrement)* **être i. dans une affaire** to have a stake *or* a financial interest in a business

NM,F **l'i.** the person concerned; **les premiers/principaux intéressés** the persons most closely concerned *or* most directly affected; **elle est la première** *ou* **principale intéressée** she's the person principally involved *or* concerned; **les intéressés** the persons concerned, the interested parties

intéressement [ɛ̃terɛsmɑ̃] NM **i. (aux résultats)** profit-sharing scheme; **l'i. des salariés aux bénéfices de l'entreprise** profit-sharing

intéresser [4] [ɛ̃terese] VT **1** *(passionner ▸ sujet: activité, œuvre, professeur etc)* to interest; **la politique les intéresse peu** they're not very interested in politics, politics doesn't interest them very much; **notre offre peut peut-être vous i.** our offer might interest you *or* might be of interest to you; **le débat ne m'a pas du tout intéressé** I didn't find the debate at all interesting; **elle sait i. ses élèves** she knows how to gain her pupils' interest *or* how to interest her pupils; **continue, tu m'intéresses!** go on, you're starting to interest me!; **j'ai l'impression que ma sœur l'intéresse beaucoup!** I've got the feeling that he's very interested in my sister!; **ça m'intéresserait de savoir ce qu'il en pense** I'd be interested to know what he thinks; **je revends mon ordinateur, ça t'intéresse?** I'm selling my computer, are you interested?

2 *(concerner ▸ sujet: loi, réforme)* to concern, to affect; **ces mesures intéressent essentiellement les mères célibataires** these measures mainly affect single mothers; **un problème qui intéresse la sécurité du pays** a problem which is relevant to *or* concerns national security

3 *Écon & Fin* **i. qn aux bénéfices** to give sb a share of the profits; **notre personnel est intéressé aux bénéfices** our staff gets a share of our profits, we operate a profit-sharing scheme; **être intéressé dans une entreprise** to have a stake *or* a financial interest in a company

4 *(dans un jeu)* **jouons un euro le point, pour i. la partie** let's play for one euro per point, to make the game more interesting

VPR s'intéresser s'i. à qn/qch to be interested in sb/sth; **elle ne s'intéresse à rien** she is not interested *or* she takes no interest in anything; **à quoi vous intéressez-vous?** what are your interests (in life)?; **je m'intéresse vivement à sa carrière** I take great *or* a keen interest in his/her career; **elle s'intéresse énormément à mon frère** she's very interested in my brother, she shows a great deal of interest in my brother; **un jeune romancier qui mérite qu'on s'intéresse à lui** a young novelist who merits some attention; **personne ne s'intéresse à moi!** nobody cares about me!, nobody's interested in me!; **ce n'est pas facile de les faire s'i. à ce sujet** it's not easy getting them interested in this subject

intérêt [ɛ̃terɛ] **NM 1** *(attention, curiosité)* interest; *(bienveillance)* interest, concern; **avoir** *ou* **éprouver de l'i. pour qch** to be interested *or* to take an interest in sth; **je n'éprouve aucun i. pour le théâtre** I'm not at all interested in the theatre, the theatre doesn't interest me at all; **manifester de l'i. pour qn/qch** to show an interest in sb/sth; **prendre de l'i. à qch** to take an interest in sth; **j'ai pris (un) grand i. à suivre votre émission, j'ai suivi votre émission avec (un) grand i.** I watched your programme with great interest; **elle a perdu tout i. pour son travail** she has lost all interest in her work; **porter de l'i. à qn** to take an interest in sb; **témoigner de l'i. à qn** to show an interest in sb, to show concern for sb

2 *(ce qui éveille l'attention)* interest; **une architecture/ville pleine d'i.** architecture/a town of great interest; **son essai offre peu d'i.** his/her essay is of no great interest

3 *(utilité)* point, idea; **l'i. d'un débat est que tout le monde participe** the point *or* idea of having a debate is that everybody should join in; **je ne vois pas l'i. de continuer cette discussion** I see no point in carrying on this discussion

4 *(importance)* importance, significance; **ses observations sont du plus haut** *ou* **grand i.** his/her comments are of the greatest interest *or* importance

5 *(avantage)* interest; **elle sait où se trouve son i.** she knows what's in her best interests; **agir dans/contre son i.** to act in/against one's own interest; **il n'est pas dans ton i. de vendre maintenant** it's not in your interest to sell now; **dans l'i. général** in the general interest; **dans l'i. de tous** in the interest of everyone; **dans l'i. public** in the public interest; **dans l'i. de mon travail/ma santé** in the interest of my job/my health; **d'i. public** of public interest; **elle a tout i. à se taire** she'd be well-advised to remain silent; **quel i. aurait-elle à te nuire?** why should she want to harm you?; **je n'ai aucun i. à le faire** it's not at all in my interest; **on a i. à réserver si on veut avoir des places** we'd better book if we want seats; *Fam* **tu as i. à te faire tout petit!** you'd be well advised to *or* you'd better keep your head down!; *Fam* **t'as i. à te grouiller!** you *or* you'd better get a move on!; *Fam* **si elle va me rembourser? (il) y a i.!** will she pay me back? you bet (she will)!; **i. du consommateur** consumer welfare

6 *(égoïsme)* self-interest

7 *Écon & Banque* interest; **laisser courir des intérêts** to allow interest to accumulate; **payer des intérêts** to pay interest; **rapporter des intérêts** to yield *or* to bear interest; **placer son argent à 7 pour cent d'i.** to invest one's money at 7 percent interest; **prêt à i.** loan with interest, interest-bearing loan; **prêt sans i.** interest-free loan; **emprunter/prêter à i.** to borrow/to lend at interest; **cela rapporte des intérêts** it yields *or* bears interest; **intérêts arriérés** back interest; **i. bancaire** bank interest; **i. du capital** interest on capital; **intérêts compensatoires** damages; **i. composé** compound interest; **i. conventionnel** contractual interest rate; **intérêts courus** accrued interest; **intérêts débiteurs** debit interest; **intérêts dus** interest due; **intérêts échus** accrued interest; **intérêts exigibles** interest payable; **i. fixe** fixed interest; **i. légal** statutory (rate of) interest; **intérêts moratoires** default interest, penalty interest; **i. négatif** negative interest; *Bourse* **i. de report** contango; **i. de retard** interest on arrears; **i. simple** simple interest; **i. à taux flottant** floating-rate interest; **i. variable** variable-rate interest

• **intérêts NMPL** *(d'une personne, d'un pays)* interests; **nos intérêts économiques/vitaux** our economic/vital interests; **servir les intérêts de qn/d'une société** to serve sb's/a company's interests; *Écon & Fin* **avoir des intérêts dans une société** to have a stake *or* a financial interest in a company

• **sans intérêt ADJ** *(exposition, album)* uninteresting, of no interest, devoid of interest; **que disais-tu? – c'est sans i.** what were you saying? – it's not important *or* it doesn't matter; **c'est sans i. pour la suite de l'enquête** it's of no importance for *or* relevance to the rest of the inquiry **ADV** uninterestedly, without interest; **je fais mon travail sans i.** I take no interest in my work

intereuropéen, -enne [ɛ̃terøropeɛ̃, -ɛn] **ADJ** Pan-European

interfaçage [ɛ̃tɛrfasaʒ] **NM** *Ordinat* interfacing

interface [ɛ̃tɛrfas] **NF 1** *Ordinat* interface; **i. commune de passerelle** common gateway interface, CGI; **i. de communication** communication interface; **i. graphique** graphics interface; **i. d'imprimante** printer interface; **i. numérique** digital interface; **i. parallèle** parallel interface; **i. série** serial interface; **i. utilisateur** user interface; **i. utilisateur graphique** graphical user interface; **i. vidéo numérique** digital video interface; **i. WIMP** WIMP **2** *(intermédiaire)* interface

interfacer **[16]** [ɛ̃tɛrfase] **VT** *Ordinat* to interface

interférence [ɛ̃tɛrferɑ̃s] **NF 1** *Météo, Rad & Phys* interference *(UNCOUNT)*; **il y a des interférences** there is interference **2** *(interaction)* interaction; **il y a i. entre l'évolution climatique et l'équilibre écologique de la région** there's an interaction between climatic changes and the ecological balance of the area

interférent, -e [ɛ̃tɛrferɑ̃, -ɑ̃t] **ADJ** interfering, interference *(avant n)*

interférer **[18]** [ɛ̃tɛrfere] **VI 1** *Phys* to interfere **2** *(se mêler)* to interact, to combine; **le courant A risque d'i. avec le courant B** current A may interact *or* combine with current B; **les deux courants interfèrent** the two currents interact with each other **3** *(intervenir)* **i. dans la vie de qn** to interfere *or* to meddle in sb's life

interféron [ɛ̃tɛrferɔ̃] **NM** interferon

interfolier **[9]** [ɛ̃tɛrfɔlje] **VT** to interleave

intergalactique [ɛ̃tɛrgalaktik] **ADJ** intergalactic

intergénérationnel, -elle [ɛ̃tɛrʒenerasjɔnɛl] **ADJ** intergenerational

intergouvernemental, -e, -aux, -ales [ɛ̃tɛrguvɛrnəmɑ̃tal, -o] **ADJ** intergovernmental

intergroupe [ɛ̃tɛrgrup] **NM** *Pol* joint committee

INTÉRIEUR, -E [ɛ̃terjœr]

ADJ
- inside **1**
- interior **1**
- domestic **3**
- inner **1, 2**
- internal **1, 3, 4**
- inland **5**

NM
- inside **1**
- home **3**
- interior **1–4**

ADJ 1 *(du dedans ▸ escalier)* inside, inner; *(▸ cour)* inner; *(▸ poche)* inside; *(▸ partie)* inside, internal; **la pochette intérieure du disque** the inner sleeve of the record; **l'emballage i.** the inside wrapping; **les peintures intérieures de la maison** the interior decoration of the house

2 *(sentiment, vie)* inner; **un grand calme/bonheur i.** a great (feeling of) inner peace/happiness; **des voix intérieures** inner voices

3 *(national ▸ ligne aérienne, politique)* domestic; *(▸ marché)* domestic, home; *(▸ vol)* domestic, internal; **le gouvernement est aux prises avec des difficultés intérieures** the government is battling against difficulties at home *or* domestic problems; **la dette intérieure** the national debt

4 *(interne)* internal; **les problèmes intérieurs d'un parti** a party's internal problems

5 *Géog (désert, mer)* inland

NM 1 *(d'un bâtiment, d'un véhicule)* inside, interior; *(d'un four, d'un récipient, d'une boîte)* inside; **ne pas utiliser de tampon abrasif pour nettoyer l'i.** do not use abrasive pads to clean the inside; **i. cuir** *(de voiture)* leather trim

2 *(d'un pays, d'une région)* interior; **l'i. (des terres)** the interior; **l'i. de l'île** the interior of the island, the hinterland; **dans l'i. du pays** inland; **les villages de l'i.** inland villages

3 *(foyer, décor)* interior, home; **un i. douillet** a cosy interior *or* home; **son i. est parfaitement bien tenu** his/her housekeeping is perfect; **visiter un i. 1900 reconstitué** to visit a recreated 1900s interior; **femme d'i.** houseproud housewife; **scène d'i.** interior; **veste d'i.** indoor jacket

4 *Cin* interior (shot); **entièrement tourné en i.** shot entirely indoors

5 *Fam* **le Ministère de l'I., l'I.** *Br* ≃ the Home Office, *Am* ≃ the Department of the Interior

6 *Sport* inside-forward; **i. droit/gauche** inside right/left

• **à l'intérieur ADV 1** *(dedans)* inside; **il y a une graine à l'i.** there's a seed inside **2** *(dans la maison)* inside, indoors; **à l'i. il fait plus frais** it's cooler inside *or* indoors

• **à l'intérieur de PRÉP 1** *(lieu)* in, inside; **la pluie pénètre à l'i. du garage** the rain is coming into the garage; **reste à l'i. de la voiture** stay in *or* inside the car; **à l'i. des frontières** within *or* inside the frontiers; **à l'i. des terres** inland **2** *(groupe)* within; **à l'i. d'une famille/d'un petit groupe** within a family/small group

• **de l'intérieur ADV 1** *(d'un lieu)* from (the) inside; **verrouiller la portière de l'i.** to lock the door from (the) inside **2** *(d'un groupe)* from the inside, from within; **il veut transformer le parti de l'i.** he wants to change the party from the inside *or* from within

intérieurement [ɛ̃terjœrmɑ̃] **ADV 1** *(à l'intérieur)* inside, within **2** *(secrètement)* inwardly; **il se félicitait i.** he was congratulating himself inwardly

intérim [ɛ̃terim] **NM 1** *(période)* interim (period); **dans l'i.** meanwhile, in the meantime, *Sout* in the interim **2** *(remplacement)* *Pol* **assurer l'i.** to take over on a caretaker basis; **j'assure l'i. de la secrétaire en chef** I'm deputizing *or* covering for the chief secretary **3** *(emploi)* temporary work, temping; **faire de l'i.** to do temporary work, to temp; **agence d'i.** temping agency

• **par intérim,** *Belg* **ad intérim, ad interim ADJ** *(président, trésorier)* interim *(avant n)*, acting *(avant n)*; *(secrétaire)* acting *(avant n)*; *(gouvernement)* caretaker *(avant n)* **ADV** in a temporary capacity, temporarily; **gouverner par i.** to govern in the interim *or* for an interim period

intérimaire [ɛ̃terimɛr] **ADJ 1** *(assurant l'intérim ▸ directeur, trésorier, ministre)* acting; *(▸ personnel, employé)* temporary; *(▸ gouvernement, cabinet)* caretaker; **secrétaire i.** temporary secretary, temp **2** *(non durable ▸ fonction)* interim *(avant n)*; *(▸ commission)* provisional, temporary

NMF *(cadre)* deputy; *(secrétaire)* temp; **travailler comme i.** to temp, to do temping work; **elle a beaucoup travaillé comme i.** she's done a lot of temping

intériorisation [ɛ̃terjɔrizasjɔ̃] **NF** internalization, interiorization

intérioriser **[3]** [ɛ̃terjɔrize] **VT 1** *Psy* to internalize, to interiorize **2** *(garder pour soi)* to internalize, to keep in; **elle a intériorisé sa colère** she kept her anger in, she bottled up her anger

interjectif, -ive [ɛ̃tɛrʒɛktif, -iv] **ADJ** interjectional

interjection [ɛ̃tɛrʒɛksjɔ̃] **NF 1** *(exclamation)* interjection **2** *Jur* **i. d'appel** lodging of an appeal

interjective [ɛ̃tɛrʒɛktiv] *voir* **interjectif**

interjeter **[27]** [ɛ̃tɛrʒəte] **VT i. appel** to lodge an appeal

interlettrage [ɛ̃tɛrletraʒ] **NM** *Typ* leading

interlettrer **[3]** [ɛ̃tɛrletre] **VT** *Typ* to letterspace

interlignage [ɛ̃tɛrliɲaʒ] **NM** *Typ* leading, line spacing; **i. double** double spacing; **i. simple** single spacing

interligne [ɛ̃tɛrliɲ] **NM 1** *(blanc)* space (between the lines); *Ordinat & Typ* line spacing; **simple/double i.** single/double spacing; **tapé en simple/double i.** typed with single/double spacing, single-/double-spaced; **i. réglable** adjustable line space **2** *(ajout)* interlineation **3** *Mus* space

NF *Typ (lame)* lead

interligner [3] [ɛ̃tɛrliɲe] **VT 1** *(séparer)* to space **2** *(écrire)* to interline, to interlineate, to write between the lines; **i. un mot dans le texte** to interline a word in the text

interlinéaire [ɛ̃tɛrlineɛr] **ADJ** *Typ (texte)* interlinear

interlocuteur, -trice [ɛ̃tɛrlɔkytœr, -tris] **NM,F 1** *(gén)* = person speaking or being spoken to; *Ling* speaker, *Sout* interlocutor; *(dans un débat)* speaker; **mon i. n'avait pas compris** the man I was talking to hadn't understood **2** *(dans une négociation)* negotiating partner; **les États-Unis ont toujours été l'i. privilégié de la Grande-Bretagne** the United States has always had a special relationship with Great Britain; **nous ne considérons plus le ministre comme un i. valable** we no longer consider the minister to be an acceptable negotiating partner; **nous avions un i. de premier plan** we were dealing with a first-rate negotiator

interlocutoire [ɛ̃tɛrlɔkytwar] **ADJ** interlocutory

NM interlocutory judgement

interlocutrice [ɛ̃tɛrlɔkytris] *voir* **interlocuteur**

interlope [ɛ̃tɛrlɔp] **ADJ 1** *(frauduleux)* unlawful, illegal, illicit; **commerce i.** illicit trade **2** *(louche)* shady, dubious; **relations** *ou* **amitiés interlopes** underworld connections

interloquer [3] [ɛ̃tɛrlɔke] **VT** *(décontenancer)* to take aback, to disconcert; *(stupéfier)* to stun; **cette réponse l'a interloqué** the answer stunned *or* nonplussed him; **elle resta interloquée** she was dumbfounded *or* flabbergasted *or* stunned

interlude [ɛ̃tɛrlyd] **NM** interlude

intermède [ɛ̃tɛrmɛd] **NM 1** *Mus* interlude, intermedio, *Spéc* intermezzo; *Théât* interlude, interval piece **2** *Fig* interlude, interval; **notre liaison ne fut qu'un agréable i.** our affair was just a pleasant interlude

intermédiaire [ɛ̃tɛrmedjɛr] **ADJ 1** *(moyen ▸ gén)* intermediate, intermediary; *(▸ pointure)* in between; **couleur i. entre le bleu et le vert** colour halfway between blue and green; **solution i.** compromise (solution) **2** *Scol* intermediate; **niveau i.** intermediate level

NMF 1 *(médiateur)* intermediary, go-between; **servir d'i.** to act as an intermediary *or* as a go-between

2 *Com* intermediary, middleman; **les fournisseurs et les intermédiaires** the suppliers and the middlemen; **i. agréé** authorized dealer; **i. négociateur** trading member

3 *Banque* **i. agréé** authorized intermediary; **i. financier** financial intermediary

4 *Bourse* market maker; **i. remisier (en Bourse)** intermediate broker

• **par l'intermédiaire de PRÉP** *(personne)* through, via; **par votre i.** through you; **il a appris l'anglais par l'i. de la radio** he learnt English from the radio

• **sans intermédiaire ADV** *(directement)* directly; **vendre sans i.** to sell directly to the customer

intermédiation [ɛ̃tɛrmedjasjɔ̃] **NF** intermediary financing

intermezzo [ɛ̃tɛrmedzo] **NM** intermezzo

interminable [ɛ̃tɛrminabl] **ADJ** interminable, neverending, endless; **la route lui paraissait i.** he/she thought the road would never end

interminablement [ɛ̃tɛrminabləmɑ̃] **ADV** interminably, endlessly, without end

interministériel, -elle [ɛ̃tɛrministerjɛl] **ADJ** interdepartmental, *Br* joint ministerial

intermission [ɛ̃tɛrmisjɔ̃] **NF 1** *Méd* (period of) remission, intermission **2** *Can Théât Br* interval, *Am* intermission

intermittence [ɛ̃tɛrmitɑ̃s] **NF 1** *(irrégularité ▸ gén)* intermittence, irregularity; *(▸ de la production)* irregularity **2** *Méd* intermission, remission

• **par intermittence ADV** intermittently; **travailler par i.** to work in fits and starts *or* intermittently

intermittent, -e [ɛ̃tɛrmitɑ̃, -ɑ̃t] **ADJ 1** *(irrégulier ▸ tir)* intermittent, sporadic; *(▸ travail)* casual, occasional; *(▸ pulsation)* irregular, periodic; *(▸ éclairage)* intermittent; *(▸ averses)* occasional **2** *Méd* **pouls i.** irregular pulse

NM les intermittents du spectacle = people working in the performing arts (and thus entitled to social security benefits designed for people without regular employment)

intermoléculaire [ɛ̃tɛrmɔlekylɛr] **ADJ** intermolecular

internalisation [ɛ̃tɛrnalizasjɔ̃] **NF** *Écon* internalization; **i. du recrutement** recruiting in-house, in-house *or* internal recruitment

internaliser [3] [ɛ̃tɛrnalize] **VT** *Écon* to internalize

internat [ɛ̃tɛrna] **NM 1** *Scol (école)* boarding school; *(régime)* boarding school system **2** *Méd (concours)* = competitive examination for *Br* a housemanship *or Am* an internship; *(stage)* hospital training, *Br* time as a houseman, *Am* internship

international, -e, -aux, -ales [ɛ̃tɛrnasjɔnal, -o] **ADJ 1** *(gén)* international **2** *Archit* **style i.** international style

NM,F international (player *or* athlete)

NM *Écon* **l'i.** world markets; **ces entreprises réalisent tout leur chiffre d'affaires à l'i.** these companies make all their profits in international trade *or* on the international market

• **internationaux NMPL** *Sport* internationals; **les internationaux de France de tennis** the French Open

internationalement [ɛ̃tɛrnasjɔnalmɑ̃] **ADJ** internationally

internationalisation [ɛ̃tɛrnasjɔnalizasjɔ̃] **NF** internationalization

internationaliser [3] [ɛ̃tɛrnasjɔnalize] **VT** to internationalize

VPR s'internationaliser to take on an international dimension

internationalisme [ɛ̃tɛrnasjɔnalism] **NM** internationalism

internationaliste [ɛ̃tɛrnasjɔnalist] **ADJ** internationalist

NMF internationalist

internationalité [ɛ̃tɛrnasjɔnalite] **NF** internationality

internaute [ɛ̃tɛrnot] **NMF** Internet user, (Net) surfer; **i. novice** Internet novice, *Fam* newbie

interne [ɛ̃tɛrn] **ADJ 1** *(intérieur ▸ paroi)* internal, inside; *(▸ face, structure, conflit, difficultés)* internal; *(▸ raison, cause, logique)* internal, inner; *(de l'entreprise ▸ personnel)* in-house; **il a fallu radiographier le côté i. de la jambe/du pied** the inner part of the leg/foot had to be X-rayed **2** *Méd (hémorragie, organe)* internal

NMF 1 *Méd* **i. (des hôpitaux)** *Br* houseman, junior hospital doctor, *Am* intern; **i. en pharmacie** student pharmacist *(in a hospital)* **2** *Scol* boarder; **il est i.** he's at boarding school

• **en interne ADV** *(dans l'entreprise)* in-house, on an in-house basis

interné, -e [ɛ̃tɛrne] **ADJ 1** *Méd* committed, *Br Spéc* sectioned **2** *(emprisonné)* interned

NM,F 1 *Méd* committed *or Br Spéc* sectioned patient **2** *(prisonnier)* internee

internégatif [ɛ̃tɛrnegatif] **NM** internegative

internement [ɛ̃tɛrnəmɑ̃] **NM 1** *Méd* commitment, *Br* sectioning **2** *(emprisonnement)* internment; **i. abusif** illegal internment; **i. administratif** internment without trial

interner [3] [ɛ̃tɛrne] **VT 1** *Méd* to commit, *Br* to section **2** *Pol* to intern

Internet [ɛ̃tɛrnɛt] **NM** Internet; **sur (l')I.** on the Internet; **naviguer sur (l')I.** to surf the Internet; **acheter/vendre qch sur (l')I.** to buy/to sell sth on *or* over the Internet

interocéanique [ɛ̃tɛrɔseanik] **ADJ** interoceanic

interopérabilité [ɛ̃tɛrɔperabilite] **NF** interoperability

interparlementaire [ɛ̃tɛrparləmɑ̃tɛr] **ADJ** interparliamentary; **commission i.** joint committee

interpellateur, -trice [ɛ̃tɛrpelatœr, -tris] **NM,F 1** *Pol (questionneur)* questioner, *Spéc* interpellator **2** *(personne qui apostrophe)* = person calling out; **mon i.** the person calling out to me

interpellation [ɛ̃tɛrpelasjɔ̃] **NF 1** *(apostrophe)* call, shout **2** *(par la police)* (arrest for) questioning; **la police a procédé à plusieurs interpellations** several people were detained *or* taken in by police for questioning **3** *Pol* question, *Spéc* interpellation

interpellatrice [ɛ̃tɛrpelatris] *voir* **interpellateur**

interpeller [26] [ɛ̃tɛrpəle] **VT 1** *(appeler)* to call out to, to hail

2 *(sujet: police)* to stop for questioning

3 *(concerner)* to touch; *Hum* **ça m'interpelle quelque part** I can relate to that

4 *Pol* to put a question to

VPR s'interpeller *(s'appeler)* to call out to *or* to hail one another

interpénétration [ɛ̃tɛrpenetrasjɔ̃] **NF** interpenetration

interpénétrer [18] [ɛ̃tɛrpenetre] **s'interpénétrer VPR** to interpenetrate, to penetrate mutually; **des cultures qui s'interpénètrent** intermingling cultures

Interphone® [ɛ̃tɛrfɔn] **NM** *(dans un bureau)* intercom; *(à l'entrée d'un immeuble)* entry *or* security phone

interplanétaire [ɛ̃tɛrplanetɛr] **ADJ** interplanetary; **voyage i.** space flight

interpolation [ɛ̃tɛrpɔlasjɔ̃] **NF** interpolation, insertion

interpoler [3] [ɛ̃tɛrpɔle] **VT 1** *(texte)* to insert, to fit in *or* into, *Spéc* to interpolate; **i. un paragraphe dans un texte** to insert a paragraph into a text **2** *Math* to interpolate

interposer [3] [ɛ̃tɛrpoze] **VT** to place, to insert (**entre** between); **ils ont pu se contacter par personne interposée** they were able to make contact through an intermediary

VPR s'interposer 1 *(faire écran)* **s'i. entre** to stand between; **il s'est interposé entre la lumière et mon appareil** he stood between the light and my camera **2** *(intervenir)* to intervene, to step in, *Sout* to interpose oneself; **il s'est interposé pour l'empêcher de me frapper** he stepped in *or* intervened to stop him/her hitting me

interposition [ɛ̃tɛrpozisjɔ̃] **NF 1** *(d'un objet, de texte)* interposition, interposing **2** *(intervention)* interposition, intervention; *Mil* **forces d'i.** intervention forces

interprétable [ɛ̃tɛrpretabl] **ADJ** interpretable; **c'est i. de deux façons** this may be interpreted *or* taken in two ways

interprétariat [ɛ̃tɛrpretarja] **NM** interpreting; **diplôme d'i.** diploma in interpreting; **faire de l'i.** to work as an interpreter

interprétatif, -ive [ɛ̃tɛrpretatif, -iv] **ADJ 1** *(explicatif)* expository, interpretative, interpretive **2** *Ordinat* interpretive

interprétation [ɛ̃tɛrpretasjɔ̃] **NF 1** *(exécution ▸ d'une œuvre musicale)* interpretation, performance; *(▸ d'un rôle)* interpretation; *(▸ d'un texte)* reading

2 *(analyse)* interpretation, analysis; **c'est une drôle d'i. de la situation** it's a strange way of looking at *or* interpreting the situation; **il a donné une fausse i. de mes déclarations** he gave an incorrect interpretation of *or* he misinterpreted my statements

3 *(interprétariat)* interpreting

4 *Psy* **i. des rêves** interpretation of dreams

5 *Ordinat* interpretation

interprétative [ɛ̃tɛrpretativ] *voir* **interprétatif**

interprète [ɛ̃tɛrprɛt] **NMF 1** *(musicien, acteur)* performer, player; *(chanteur)* singer; *(danseur)* dancer; **l'i. de Giselle** the dancer of the title role in Giselle; **les interprètes** *(d'un film, d'une pièce)* the cast; **il est devenu l'i. par excellence de Beckett** he became the foremost interpreter of Beckett's work; **l'i. de Cyrano n'était pas à la hauteur** the actor playing Cyrano wasn't up to the part; **les interprètes de ce concerto sont...** the concerto will be played by... **2** *(traducteur)* interpreter; **servir d'i. à** to act as interpreter for; **i. de conférence** conference interpreter **3** *(représentant)* spokesperson, spokesman, *f* spokeswoman;

être *ou* **se faire l'i. de qn auprès des autorités** to speak to the authorities on sb's behalf

interpréter **[18]** [ɛ̃tɛrprete] **VT 1** *(exécuter, jouer)* to perform, *Sout* to interpret; **i. un rôle** to play a part; **elle interprète Madame Butterfly** she plays (the part of) Madame Butterfly; **i. une sonate au piano** to play a sonata on the piano; **j'aime la façon dont il interprète Hamlet/la cantate** I like the way he performs Hamlet/the cantata; **i. un air** to perform *or* to sing a tune **2** *(comprendre ▸ texte, paroles, rêve, geste)* to interpret; **mal i. qch** to misinterpret sth; **i. qch en bien/mal** to take sth well/the wrong way **3** *(traduire)* to interpret

VPR s'interpréter *(être compris)* to be interpreted; **son refus peut s'i. de plusieurs façons** his/her refusal can be interpreted in several ways

interpréteur [ɛ̃tɛrpretœr] **NM** *Ordinat* interpreter

interprofessionnel, -elle [ɛ̃tɛrprɔfesjɔnel] **ADJ** interprofessional

interrègne [ɛ̃tɛrrɛɲ] **NM** interregnum

interro [ɛ̃tero] **NF** *Fam Arg scol (abrév* **interrogation)** test

interrogateur, -trice [ɛ̃terɔgatœr, -tris] **ADJ** *(regard)* inquiring, questioning; **d'un air i.** interrogatively, questioningly; **sur un ton i.** questioningly, searchingly

NM,F *Scol* (oral) examiner

interrogatif, -ive [ɛ̃terɔgatif, -iv] **ADJ 1** *(interrogateur)* questioning, inquiring; **d'un ton i.** questioningly **2** *Ling* interrogative

NM interrogative (word); **l'i.** the interrogative

• **interrogative NF** interrogative *or* question clause

interrogation [ɛ̃terɔgasjɔ̃] **NF 1** *(questionnement ▸ gén)* questioning; *(▸ d'un témoin)* questioning, interrogation; **sur son visage se lisait une muette i.** there was a questioning expression on his/her face

2 *Scol* test; **i. écrite/orale** written/oral test

3 *Ling* **i. directe/indirecte** direct/indirect question

4 *Ordinat (d'une base de données)* inquiry, query; *(activité)* interrogation; **i. à distance** remote access

> Do not confuse with **interrogatoire**.

interrogative [ɛ̃terɔgativ] *voir* **interrogatif**

interrogativement [ɛ̃terɔgativmɑ̃] **ADV 1** *Ling* interrogatively **2** *(en demandant)* questioningly, inquiringly

interrogatoire [ɛ̃terɔgatwar] **NM 1** *(par la police ▸ d'un prisonnier, d'un suspect)* interrogation, questioning; **subir un i. en règle** to undergo a thorough questioning *or* interrogation; *Fam* **faire subir à qn un i. serré** to grill sb; *Fam* **faire subir à qn un i. musclé** to work sb over *(to obtain information)* **2** *Jur (dans un procès)* examination, cross-examination; *(par un juge d'instruction)* hearing; *(procès-verbal)* statement

> Do not confuse with the French word **interrogation**.

interrogatrice [ɛ̃terɔgatris] *voir* **interrogateur**

interrogeable [ɛ̃terɔʒabl] **ADJ i. à distance** *(répondeur)* with remote-access facility

interroger **[17]** [ɛ̃terɔʒe] **VT 1** *(questionner ▸ ami)* to ask, to question; *(▸ guichetier)* to ask, to inquire of; *(▸ suspect)* to question, to interrogate, to interview; **i. qn pour savoir si...** to ask sb whether..., *Sout* to inquire of sb whether...; **i. qn sur qch** to ask sb questions about sth; **i. qn du regard** to look questioningly *or* inquiringly at sb; **il y a là un monsieur qui m'a interrogé à votre sujet** there is a gentleman here inquiring about you *or* asking questions about you; **ils l'ont interrogé sans ménagement** they put him through a gruelling interrogation

2 *Fig (sa conscience)* to examine; **i. sa mémoire** to try to remember

3 *Mktg (par un questionnaire)* to interview, to poll, to question; **60% des personnes interrogées ont déclaré n'avoir jamais entendu parler de ce produit** 60% of those questioned said that they had never heard of this product; **personne interrogée** respondent

4 *Scol & Univ (avant l'examen)* to test, to quiz; *(à l'examen)* to examine; **j'ai été interrogé sur la guerre de 14–18** I was asked questions on the 1914–18 war; **être interrogé par écrit/oral** to be given a written/an oral test *or* exam

5 *Ordinat* to interrogate, to query

6 *Jur* to examine, to cross-examine

VPR s'interroger s'i. sur qch to wonder about sth; **je ne sais pas si je vais l'acheter, je m'interroge encore** I don't know whether I'll buy it, I'm still wondering (about it) *or* I haven't made up my mind yet

interrompre **[78]** [ɛ̃terɔ̃pr] **VT 1** *(perturber ▸ personne, conversation, études)* to interrupt; **il fut interrompu par l'arrivée de son père** he was interrupted by the arrival of his father; **je ne voulais pas vous i. dans votre travail** I didn't want to interrupt you while you were working; **n'interrompez pas la conversation** don't interrupt the conversation; **j'en ai assez de me faire i.!** I'm fed up with being interrupted!

2 *(faire une pause dans ▸ débat)* to stop, to suspend; *(▸ session)* to interrupt, to break off; *(▸ voyage)* to break; **l'athlète a interrompu son entraînement pendant deux mois** the athlete stopped training for two months; **i. ses études pendant un an** to take a year off from one's studies

3 *(définitivement)* to stop; **i. sa lecture/son repas** to stop reading/eating; **le match a été interrompu par la pluie** rain stopped play; **i. une grossesse** to terminate a pregnancy

4 *Com (produit)* to discontinue

VPR s'interrompre *(dans une conversation)* to break off, to stop; *(dans une activité)* to break off

interrupteur, -trice [ɛ̃teryptœr, -tris] **NM,F** *Littéraire (personne)* interrupter

NM *(dispositif)* switch; **i. à bascule** toggle switch; *Ordinat* **i. DIP** *ou* **à plusieurs positions** DIP switch; **i. horaire** time switch; **i. principal** master switch

interruption [ɛ̃terypsjɔ̃] **NF 1** *(arrêt définitif ▸ de négociations, de relations diplomatiques)* breaking off; **sans i.** continuously, uninterruptedly, without stopping; **ouvert sans i. de 9 h à 20 h** *(sur la vitrine d'un magasin)* open all day 9 a.m. to 8 p.m.; *Méd* **i. illégale de grossesse** illegal abortion; **i. volontaire de grossesse** termination *(of pregnancy)*

2 *(pause ▸ dans un spectacle)* break; **après une brève i., le spectacle reprit** after a short break, the show started up again

3 *(perturbation)* interruption; **des interruptions continuelles l'empêchaient de travailler** continual interruptions prevented him/her from working; **veuillez nous excuser pour cette i. momentanée de l'image/du son** we apologize for the momentary loss of picture/of sound; *Élec* **i. de courant** power cut

4 *Ordinat* **fonction d'i.** interrupt fonction

interruptrice [ɛ̃teryptris] *voir* **interrupteur**

intersaison [ɛ̃tersezɔ̃] **NF** off season

interscolaire [ɛ̃terskɔlɛr] **ADJ** interschools

intersecté, -e [ɛ̃tersekte] **ADJ** *Archit* intersecting; *Géom* intersected

intersection [ɛ̃terseksjɔ̃] **NF 1** *(de routes)* intersection, junction; **à l'i. des deux routes** where the two roads intersect *or* meet; **à l'i. de plusieurs courants politiques** where several different political tendencies meet *or* come together **2** *Math (de droites, de plans)* intersection; *(d'ensembles)* set

intersession [ɛ̃tersesjɔ̃] **NF** *Pol* recess

> Do not confuse with **intercession**.

intersidéral, -e, -aux, -ales [ɛ̃tersideral, -o] **ADJ** intersideral; **espace i.** deep space

interstellaire [ɛ̃tersteler] **ADJ** interstellar; **espace i.** deep space

interstice [ɛ̃terstis] **NM** crack, chink, *Sout* interstice

interstitiel, -elle [ɛ̃terstisjel] **ADJ** interstitial

NM interstitial

intersyndical, -e, -aux, -ales [ɛ̃tersɛ̃dikal, -o] **ADJ** interunion, joint union

• **intersyndicale NF** interunion committee

intertexte [ɛ̃tertekst] **NM** *Littérature* intertext

intertextualité [ɛ̃tertekstɥalite] **NF** *Littérature* intertextuality

intertitre [ɛ̃tertitr] **NM 1** *Presse* subheading **2** *Cin* insert title

intertropical, -e, -aux, -ales [ɛ̃tertrɔpikal, -o] **ADJ** intertropical

interurbain, -e [ɛ̃teryrbɛ̃, -ɛn] **ADJ** *(gén)* intercity, interurban; *Vieilli Tél* long-distance *(avant n)*, *Br* trunk *(avant n)*

NM *Vieilli* long-distance telephone service, *Br* trunk call service

intervalle [ɛ̃terval] **NM 1** *(durée)* interval; **un i. de trois heures** a three-hour interval *or* gap; **ils se sont retrouvés à trois mois d'i.** they met again after an interval of three months; **à intervalles réguliers** at regular intervals; **par intervalles** intermittently, at intervals, now and again; **dans l'i., je ferai le nécessaire** meanwhile *or* in the meantime I'll do what has to be done; **dans l'i., j'étais revenu** I had come back by then *or* by that time

2 *(distance)* interval, space; **laissez deux mètres d'i. entre chaque piquet** leave a gap of two metres *or* a two-metre gap between each stake; **l'i. entre les deux maisons** the distance between the two houses

3 *(brèche)* gap

4 *Math, Mil & Mus* interval

intervenant, -e [ɛ̃tervənɑ̃, -ɑ̃t] **ADJ** intervening

NM,F 1 *(dans un débat, un congrès)* participant, speaker; **i. principal** keynote speaker **2** *Jur* intervening party **3** *Mktg* **i. sur le marché** market participant

intervenir **[40]** [ɛ̃tervənir] **VI 1** *(agir)* to intervene, to step in; **i. en faveur de qn** to intercede *or* to intervene on sb's behalf; **i. auprès de qn pour** to intercede with sb in order to; **il était temps d'i.** it was time to do something about it *or* to act; **on a dû faire i. la police** the police had to be brought in *or* called in; **l'État a dû i. pour renflouer la société** the state had to intervene to keep the company afloat

2 *Méd* to operate

3 *(prendre la parole)* to speak; **vous ne devez pas i. dans ce débat** you mustn't speak in this debate

4 *(jouer un rôle ▸ circonstance, facteur)* **i. dans** to influence, to affect; **le prix n'intervient pas dans mon choix** the price has no bearing on *or* doesn't affect my choice

5 *(survenir ▸ accord, décision)* to be reached; *(▸ incident, changement)* to take place; **le changement/la mesure intervient au moment où...** the change/measure comes at a time when...

intervention [ɛ̃tervɑ̃sjɔ̃] **NF 1** *(entrée en action)* intervention; **il a fallu l'i. des pompiers** the fire brigade had to be called in *or* brought in; **malgré l'i. rapide des secours** despite swift rescue action; **malgré son i. auprès du ministre** despite his/her having spoken to the minister; **i. en faveur de qn** intervention in sb's favour; **grâce à votre bienveillante i.** thanks to your good offices

2 *Mil* intervention; **l'i. des forces armées** military intervention; **i. aérienne** air strike; **i. armée** armed intervention

3 *(ingérence)* interference; *Pol* intervention; **i. de l'État** state intervention; **i. gouvernementale** government intervention

4 *(discours)* talk, *Univ* paper; **faire une i. dans un colloque** to give a talk *or* paper at a conference; **i. principale** keynote speech; **j'ai fait deux interventions** I spoke twice; **j'ai approuvé son i.** I agreed with his/her contribution *or* what he/she said

5 *Méd* **i. (chirurgicale)** (surgical) operation, surgery *(UNCOUNT)*; **procéder à une i. chirurgicale** to operate

6 *Agr & Écon* **beurre d'i.** subsidized butter; **prix d'i.** intervention price

interventionnisme [ɛ̃tervɑ̃sjɔnism] **NM** interventionism

interventionniste [ɛ̃tervɑ̃sjɔnist] **ADJ** interventionist; **non i.** non-interventionist

NMF interventionist

intervenu, -e [ɛ̃tervəny] **PP** *voir* **intervenir**

interversion [ɛ̃terversjɔ̃] **NF** inversion; **i. des rôles** role reversal

intervertébral, -e, -aux, -ales [ɛ̃tervertebral, -o] **ADJ** intervertebral

intervertir **[32]** [ɛ̃tɛrvɛrtir] **VT** to invert (the order of); **i. les rôles** to reverse roles

intervient *etc voir* **intervenir**

interview [ɛ̃tɛrvju] **NF OU NM** *Presse & TV* interview; **une i. exclusive** an exclusive (interview); **i. radio/télévisée** radio/television interview

interviewé, -e [ɛ̃tɛrvjuve] *Presse & TV* **ADJ** interviewed

NM,F interviewee

interviewer[1] **[3]** [ɛ̃tɛrvjuve] **VT** *Presse & TV* to interview

interviewer[2] [ɛ̃tɛrvjuvœr] **NM** *Presse & TV* interviewer

intervieweur, -euse [ɛ̃tɛrvjuvœr, -øz] **NM,F** *Presse & TV* interviewer

intervint *etc voir* **intervenir**

intervocalique [ɛ̃tɛrvɔkalik] **ADJ** intervocalic

intestat [ɛ̃tɛsta] **ADJ INV** intestate; **mourir i.** to die intestate

NMF intestate

intestin[1] [ɛ̃tɛstɛ̃] **NM** *Anat* intestine, bowel; **les intestins** the intestines, the bowels; **i. grêle** small intestine; **gros i.** large intestine; **cancer de l'i.** bowel cancer

intestin[2]**, -e** [ɛ̃tɛstɛ̃, -in] **ADJ** *(interne)* internal; **luttes intestines** internecine struggles

intestinal, -e, -aux, -ales [ɛ̃tɛstinal, -o] **ADJ** intestinal; **douleurs intestinales** stomach pains

intifada [intifada] **NF** intifada

intimation [ɛ̃timasjɔ̃] **NF 1** *(d'un ordre)* notification **2** *Jur (assignation)* summons *(before a high court)*; **signifier une i.** to issue *or* to serve a summons; **i. d'appel** notice of appeal

intime [ɛ̃tim] **ADJ 1** *(proche)* close; **un ami i.** a close friend, *Sout* an intimate; **ils sont (très) intimes** they are (very) close

2 *(privé ▸ pensée, vie)* intimate; **conversation i.** private conversation; **avoir des relations intimes avec qn** to be intimate with sb, to be on intimate terms with sb; **univers i.** secret world

3 *Euph (génital)* **hygiène i.** personal hygiene; **parties intimes** private parts

4 *(discret)* quiet, intimate; **cérémonie/mariage i.** quiet ceremony/wedding; **soirée i.** *(entre deux personnes)* quiet dinner; *(entre plusieurs)* quiet get-together

5 *(profond)* inner, intimate; **les recoins les plus intimes de l'âme** the innermost *or* deepest recesses of the soul; **le sens i. d'un texte** the underlying *or* deeper meaning of a text; **il a une connaissance i. de la langue** he has a thorough knowledge of the language, he knows the language inside out

6 *(avant le nom)* **j'ai l'i. conviction qu'il ment** I am utterly convinced that he's lying

NMF *(ami)* close friend, *Sout* intimate; **ses intimes** his/her closest friends (and relations); **moi, c'est Madeleine, Mado pour les intimes** I'm Madeleine, Mado to my friends *or* my friends call me Mado

> Il faut noter qu'en anglais **to be intimate with someone** signifie le plus souvent **avoir des rapports sexuels avec quelqu'un.**

intimé, -e [ɛ̃time] **ADJ partie intimée** respondent party

NM,F respondent

intimement [ɛ̃timmɑ̃] **ADV** *(connaître)* intimately; **ces deux faits sont i. liés** these two facts are closely connected; **i. convaincu** *ou* **persuadé** utterly convinced

intimer **[3]** [ɛ̃time] **VT 1** *(signifier)* **i. à qn l'ordre de faire qch** to order sb to do sth **2** *Jur (en appel)* to summon; *(faire savoir)* to notify

intimidable [ɛ̃timidabl] **ADJ** easily intimidated

intimidant, -e [ɛ̃timidɑ̃, -ɑ̃t] **ADJ** intimidating

intimidateur, -trice [ɛ̃timidatœr, -tris] **ADJ** intimidating

intimidation [ɛ̃timidasjɔ̃] **NF** intimidation; **céder à des intimidations** to give in to intimidation

intimidatrice [ɛ̃timidatris] *voir* **intimidateur**

intimider **[3]** [ɛ̃timide] **VT 1** *(faire pression sur)* to intimidate; **vous croyez m'i.?** do you think you can frighten me? **2** *(troubler)* to intimidate, to overawe; **il s'est laissé i. par elle** he allowed her to intimidate him; **elle ne se laisse pas facilement i.** she is not easily intimidated

intimisme [ɛ̃timism] **NM** *Beaux-Arts & Littérature* intimism

intimiste [ɛ̃timist] **ADJ** *Beaux-Arts & Littérature* intimist; **un film i.** a film that explores the world of feelings

intimité [ɛ̃timite] **NF 1** *(vie privée, caractère privé)* privacy; **l'i. du foyer** the privacy of one's own home; **envahir l'i. de qn** to invade sb's privacy; **nous fêterons son succès dans l'i.** we'll celebrate his/her success with just a few close friends; **ils se sont mariés dans la plus stricte i.** they were married in the strictest privacy

2 *(familiarité)* intimacy; **l'i. conjugale** the intimacy of married life; *Euph* **vivre dans l'i. avec qn** to be on intimate terms with sb

3 *(confort)* intimacy, cosiness; **dans l'i. de la cuisine** in the warmth of the kitchen

4 *Littéraire (profondeur)* intimacy; **dans l'i. de la prière** in the privacy *or* intimacy of prayer; **dans l'i. de nos âmes** in the innermost depths of our souls

intitulé [ɛ̃tityle] **NM 1** *(d'un livre)* title; *(d'un chapitre)* heading; *(d'un article)* title **2** *(d'un compte)* name

intituler **[3]** [ɛ̃tityle] **VT** to call; **comment a-t-il intitulé le roman?** what did he call the novel?, what title did he give the novel?; **un film intitulé 'M'** a film called *or* entitled 'M'; **un article intitulé…** an article headed…, an article with the heading…

VPR s'intituler 1 *(personne)* to give oneself the title of, to call oneself **2** *(œuvre)* to be entitled *or* called

intolérable [ɛ̃tɔlerabl] **ADJ 1** *(insupportable)* intolerable, unbearable **2** *(inadmissible)* intolerable, inadmissible, unacceptable; **vos retards sont intolérables** your lateness will not be tolerated; **il est i. que seul l'aîné y ait droit** it's unacceptable that only the older one should be entitled to it

intolérablement [ɛ̃tɔlerabləmɑ̃] **ADV** intolerably

intolérance [ɛ̃tɔlerɑ̃s] **NF 1** *(sectarisme)* intolerance; **i. politique/religieuse** political/religious intolerance **2** *Méd* intolerance; **i. aux analgésiques** intolerance to painkillers; **i. à l'alcool** lack of tolerance to alcohol; **i. alimentaire** food allergy *or* intolerance

intolérant, -e [ɛ̃tɔlerɑ̃, -ɑ̃t] **ADJ** intolerant

NM,F intolerant person, bigot

intonation [ɛ̃tɔnasjɔ̃] **NF** *(inflexion de la voix)* tone, intonation; **une voix aux intonations très douces** a very soft voice

intouchable [ɛ̃tuʃabl] **ADJ** *(qui ne peut être ▸ touché, sanctionné)* untouchable; *(▸ critiqué)* untouchable, beyond criticism

NMF *(paria)* untouchable

intox [ɛ̃tɔks] **NF** *Fam* propaganda▫, brainwashing▫; **tout ça, c'est de l'i.** all that's just propaganda

intoxicant, -e [ɛ̃tɔksikɑ̃, -ɑ̃t] **ADJ** poisonous, toxic

intoxication [ɛ̃tɔksikasjɔ̃] **NF 1** *Méd* poisoning; **i. alimentaire** food poisoning **2** *Fig (propagande)* propaganda, brainwashing

intoxiqué, -e [ɛ̃tɔksike] **ADJ 1** *Méd* poisoned; *(par un aliment)* suffering from food poisoning; **i. par l'alcool** intoxicated, drunk; **il fume beaucoup trop, il est complètement i.!** he smokes far too much, he's totally addicted! **2** *(manipulé)* indoctrinated, brainwashed

NM,F 1 *(drogué)* (drug) addict **2** *(endoctriné)* indoctrinated *or* brainwashed person

> Il faut noter que l'adjectif anglais **intoxicated** signifie le plus souvent **ivre.**

intoxiquer **[3]** [ɛ̃tɔksike] **VT 1** *Méd* to poison **2** *Fig* to brainwash, to indoctrinate; **une propagande qui intoxique les esprits** propaganda which poisons the mind

VPR s'intoxiquer to poison oneself; **s'i. avec de la viande/des crevettes** to get food poisoning from (eating) meat/prawns

intracellulaire [ɛ̃traselylɛr] **ADJ** *Biol* intracellular

intracommunautaire [ɛ̃trakɔmynotɛr] **ADJ** *UE* intra-Community

intradermique [ɛ̃tradɛrmik] **ADJ** *Anat* intradermal, intracutaneous

NF *Méd* intradermal *or* intracutaneous injection

intrados [ɛ̃trado] **NM 1** *Aviat* lower surface *(of a wing)* **2** *Archit* intrados

intraduisible [ɛ̃tradɥizibl] **ADJ 1** *(texte, mot)* untranslatable; **c'est i.** it's impossible to translate, it can't be translated; **le mot est i.** there is no translation for the word **2** *(indicible)* inexpressible, indescribable

intraitable [ɛ̃trɛtabl] **ADJ** uncompromising, inflexible; **il est resté i. sur ce point** he remained adamant on this point; **il est i. sur le chapitre de la propreté** he is a stickler for cleanliness

intrajournalier, -ère [ɛ̃traʒurnalje, -ɛr] **ADJ** *Bourse* intra-day

intra-muros [ɛ̃tramyros] **ADJ INV quartiers i.** districts within the city boundaries; **Vérone i.** the walled city of Verona; **Londres i.** inner London

ADV habiter i. to live in the city itself

intramusculaire [ɛ̃tramyskylɛr] **ADJ** intramuscular

NF intramuscular injection

Intranet [ɛ̃tranɛt] **NM** Intranet

intransférable [ɛ̃trɑ̃sferabl] **ADJ** untransferable, not transferable; *Jur (droit)* unassignable

intransigeance [ɛ̃trɑ̃ziʒɑ̃s] **NF** intransigence; **faire preuve d'i.** to be uncompromising *or Sout* intransigent

intransigeant, -e [ɛ̃trɑ̃ziʒɑ̃, -ɑ̃t] **ADJ** *(personne)* uncompromising, *Sout* intransigent; *(code moral, ligne de conduite)* uncompromising, strict; **se montrer i. envers** *ou* **vis-à-vis de qn** to take a hard line *or* to be uncompromising with sb; **il est i. sur la discipline** he's a stickler for discipline

NM,F hardliner, uncompromising person

intransitif, -ive [ɛ̃trɑ̃zitif, -iv] **ADJ** intransitive

NM intransitive (verb)

intransitivement [ɛ̃trɑ̃zitivmɑ̃] **ADV** intransitively

intransitivité [ɛ̃trɑ̃zitivite] **NF** intransitivity, intransitiveness

intransmissible [ɛ̃trɑ̃smisibl] **ADJ 1** *Biol* intransmissible **2** *Jur* untransferable, nontransferable, unassignable

intransportable [ɛ̃trɑ̃spɔrtabl] **ADJ 1** *(objet)* untransportable; **c'est i.** it can't be moved *or* transported **2** *(blessé)* **il est i.** he shouldn't be moved, he's unfit to travel

intrant [ɛ̃trɑ̃] **NM** *Écon* input

intra-utérin, -e [ɛ̃trayterɛ̃, -in] *(mpl* **intra-utérins**, *fpl* **intra-utérines) ADJ** intrauterine; **la vie intra-utérine** life in the womb, *Soul* life in utero

intraveineux, -euse [ɛ̃travenø, -øz] **ADJ** intravenous

• **intraveineuse NF** intravenous injection

intrépide [ɛ̃trepid] **ADJ 1** *(courageux)* intrepid, bold, fearless **2** *(persévérant)* unashamed, unrepentant; **un buveur i.** a hardened drinker; **un menteur i.** a barefaced liar

NMF intrepid *or* brave person

intrépidement [ɛ̃trepidmɑ̃] **ADV** intrepidly, boldly, fearlessly

intrépidité [ɛ̃trepidite] **NF 1** *(courage)* intrepidness, boldness, *Sout* intrepidity; **il s'était battu avec i.** he had fought fearlessly **2** *(persévérance)* **mentir avec i.** to lie shamelessly

intrigant, -e [ɛ̃trigɑ̃, -ɑ̃t] **ADJ** scheming, conniving

NM,F schemer, plotter

intrigue [ɛ̃trig] **NF 1** *(scénario)* plot; **i. policière** detective story; **i. secondaire** subordinate plot, sub-plot **2** *(complot)* intrigue, plot, scheme; **déjouer une i.** to foil a plot; **nouer une i. contre qn** to hatch a plot against sb; **intrigues politiques** political intrigues **3** *Littéraire (liaison amoureuse)* (secret) love affair

intriguer **[3]** [ɛ̃trige] **VT** to intrigue, to puzzle; **son appel m'a intrigué** his/her call puzzled me

VI to scheme, to plot

intrinsèque [ɛ̃trɛ̃sɛk] **ADJ** intrinsic

intrinsèquement [ɛ̃tʀɛ̃sɛkmɑ̃] **ADV** intrinsically

intro [ɛ̃tʀo] **NF** *Fam (abrév* **introduction**) intro; *(musicale)* theme tune

introducteur, -trice [ɛ̃tʀɔdyktœʀ, -tʀis] **NM,F 1** *(auprès de quelqu'un)* **il fut mon i. auprès de Michel** he was the person who introduced me to Michel **2** *(d'une idée, d'une mode)* initiator; **il fut l'i. du tabac en Europe** he introduced tobacco (in)to Europe

introductif, -ive [ɛ̃tʀɔdyktif, -iv] **ADJ** introductory; **cours i.** foundation course; **discours i.** opening *or* introductory remarks

introduction [ɛ̃tʀɔdyksjɔ̃] **NF 1** *(préambule)* introduction; **une i. à la littérature** an introduction to literature; **quelques mots d'i.** a few introductory remarks; **un cours d'i.** an introductory lecture

2 *(contact)* introduction; **après leur i. auprès de l'attaché** after they were introduced to the attaché

3 *(importation)* importing; *(adoption ▸ d'un mot, d'un règlement)* introduction; **i. en France de techniques nouvelles/de drogues dures** introducing new techniques/smuggling hard drugs into France

4 *(insertion)* insertion (**dans** into)

5 *Bourse (de valeurs)* introduction; **i. en Bourse** flotation, listing on the Stock Market, *Am* initial public offering

6 *Ordinat* **i. de données** data input

7 *(au rugby)* put-in

introductive [ɛ̃tʀɔdyktiv] *voir* **introductif**

introductrice [ɛ̃tʀɔdyktʀis] *voir* **introducteur**

introduire [98] [ɛ̃tʀɔdɥiʀ] **VT 1** *(insérer)* to insert (**dans** into); **i. une clé dans une serrure** to put *or* to insert a key into a lock

2 *(faire adopter ▸ idée, mot)* to introduce, to bring in; *(▸ règlement)* to institute; *(▸ mode, produit)* to introduce, to launch; *(illégalement)* to smuggle in; **i. un sujet dans une conversation** to introduce a topic into a conversation; *Jur* **i. une instance** to institute legal proceedings; **i. des valeurs en Bourse** to list shares on the stock market; **i. clandestinement** *(marchandises)* to smuggle in; **i. des armes dans un pays** to smuggle *or* to bring weapons into a country

3 *(présenter)* to introduce; *(faire entrer ▸ visiteur)* to show in; **i. qn auprès de** to introduce sb to; **il l'a introduit dans un petit cercle d'amis** he introduced him to a small circle of friends; **on introduisit le visiteur dans la pièce** the visitor was let into *or* shown into the room; **veuillez i. cette dame** please show the lady in

4 *Ordinat* **i. des données** to input *or* to enter data

5 *Sport* **i. le ballon** to put the ball in

VPR s'introduire 1 s'i. dans *(pénétrer dans ▸ sujet: clé, piston)* to go *or* to fit into; *(▸ sujet: eau)* to filter *or* to seep into; *(▸ sujet: cambrioleur)* to break into; *Fig (▸ sujet: erreur)* to creep into; **le doute s'est peu à peu introduit dans mon esprit** I began to have doubts; *Ordinat* **s'i. en fraude dans un réseau** to hack into a network **2 s'i. dans** *(être accepté par ▸ sujet: idée)* to penetrate (into), to spread throughout, *Péj* to infiltrate; **l'expression s'est introduite dans la langue** the expression entered the language **3 s'i. dans** *(se faire admettre dans ▸ sujet: postulant)* to gain admittance to; *(▸ sujet: intrigant)* to worm one's way into, to infiltrate

> Il faut noter que le verbe anglais **to introduce oneself** est un faux ami. Il signifie **se présenter**.

intromission [ɛ̃tʀɔmisjɔ̃] **NF** intromission

intronisation [ɛ̃tʀɔnizasjɔ̃] **NF 1** *(d'un roi, d'un évêque)* enthronement **2** *Fig (mise en place ▸ d'un système, d'une politique)* establishment

introniser [3] [ɛ̃tʀɔnize] **VT 1** *(roi, évêque)* to enthrone **2** *Fig (établir)* to establish; **i. une mode** to establish a fashion

introspectif, -ive [ɛ̃tʀɔspɛktif, -iv] **ADJ** introspective

introspection [ɛ̃tʀɔspɛksjɔ̃] **NF** introspection

introspective [ɛ̃tʀɔspɛktiv] *voir* **introspectif**

introuvable [ɛ̃tʀuvabl] **ADJ** *(objet égaré)* nowhere to be found; **elle reste i.** she's still missing, her whereabouts are still unknown; **ces pendules sont introuvables aujourd'hui** you can't get hold of these clocks anywhere these days

introversion [ɛ̃tʀɔvɛʀsjɔ̃] **NF** introversion

introverti, -e [ɛ̃tʀɔvɛʀti] **ADJ** introverted

NM,F introvert

intrus, -e [ɛ̃tʀy, -yz] **ADJ** intrusive

NM,F intruder; **elle considère son gendre comme un i.** she treats her son-in-law like an outsider *or* an unwelcome guest; **cherchez l'i.** *(dans une liste de mots)* find the odd one out

intrusion [ɛ̃tʀyzjɔ̃] **NF 1** *(ingérence)* intrusion; **c'est une i. dans ma vie privée** it's an intrusion into my privacy; **faire i. dans une réunion** to interrupt a meeting; **faire i. dans la vie privée de qn** to intrude upon *or* to invade sb's private life **2** *Géol* intrusion

intubation [ɛ̃tybasjɔ̃] **NF** *Méd* intubation

intuber [3] [ɛ̃tybe] **VT** *Méd* to intubate

intuitif, -ive [ɛ̃tɥitif, -iv] **ADJ** intuitive, instinctive

NM,F intuitive person; **c'est un i.** he's very intuitive

intuition [ɛ̃tɥisjɔ̃] **NF 1** *(faculté)* intuition; **suivre son i.** to follow one's intuition; *Fam* **j'y allais à l'i.** I was acting intuitively; **par i.** intuitively, by intuition; **l'i. féminine** feminine intuition **2** *(pressentiment)* **avoir l'i. d'un drame** to have a premonition of tragedy; **il en a eu l'i.** he knew it intuitively, **j'ai l'i. qu'il est rentré** I have a suspicion *or* an inkling *or* a hunch (that) he's home

intuitive [ɛ̃tɥitiv] *voir* **intuitif**

intuitivement [ɛ̃tɥitivmɑ̃] **ADV** intuitively, instinctively

intuitivité [ɛ̃tɥitivite] **NF** *Ordinat (de logiciel, interface)* intuitiveness

intumescence [ɛ̃tymesɑ̃s] **NF** swelling, *Spéc* intumescence

intumescent, -e [ɛ̃tymesɑ̃, -ɑ̃t] **ADJ** swelling, *Spéc* intumescent

inuit [inɥit] **ADJ INV** Inuit

• **Inuit NMF INV** Inuit; **les I.** the Inuit *or* Inuits

inusable [inyzabl] **ADJ** which will never wear out, hardwearing; **achetez-en une paire, c'est i.!** buy a pair, they'll last (you) forever!

inusité, -e [inyzite] **ADJ 1** *Ling (mot)* uncommon, not in use (any longer); **le terme est i. de nos jours** the word is no longer used **2** *Littéraire (inhabituel)* unusual, uncommon; **un bruit i.** an uncommon *or* a strange noise

in utero [inytero] **ADJ** in utero

ADV in utero

inutile [inytil] **ADJ 1** *(qui ne sert à rien ▸ objet)* useless; *(▸ digression, argument)* pointless; *(▸ effort)* useless, pointless, vain; *(▸ remède)* useless, ineffective; **(il est) i. de m'interroger** there's no point in questioning me; **i. de mentir!** it's no use lying!, lying is useless!; **j'ai écrit, téléphoné, tout s'est révélé i.** I wrote, I phoned, (but) all to no avail **2** *(superflu)* needless, unnecessary; **ces précautions sont inutiles** these precautions serve no purpose; **quelques précisions ne seront pas inutiles** a few explanations will come in useful; **ne me raccompagne pas, c'est i.** you don't have to bring me back, there's no need; **i. de préciser qu'il faut arriver à l'heure** I hardly need to point out that *or* needless to say you have to turn up on time; **i. d'insister, je ne viendrai pas** don't go on about it, I'm not coming

NMF *Péj* useless person; **c'est un i.** he's no use

inutilement [inytilmɑ̃] **ADV** needlessly, unnecessarily

inutilisable [inytilizabl] **ADJ** unusable, useless; **après l'accident, la voiture était i.** the car was *Br* a write-off *or Am* totaled after the accident

inutilisé, -e [inytilize] **ADJ** *(gén)* unused; *(ressources)* untapped, unused

inutilité [inytilite] **NF** *(d'un objet)* uselessness; *(d'une digression, d'un argument)* pointlessness; *(d'un effort)* uselessness, pointlessness; *(d'un remède)* uselessness, ineffectiveness

• **inutilités NFPL** *(futilités)* useless information *(UNCOUNT)*

invaincu, -e [ɛ̃vɛ̃ky] **ADJ** *(équipe)* unbeaten, undefeated; *(armée)* unvanquished, undefeated

invalidant, -e [ɛ̃validɑ̃, -ɑ̃t] **ADJ** incapacitating, disabling

invalidation [ɛ̃validasjɔ̃] **NF** *(d'une élection)* invalidation, quashing; *(d'une décision juridique)* quashing; *(d'un contrat)* nullification; *(d'un élu)* removal from office

invalide [ɛ̃valid] **ADJ 1** *(infirme)* disabled **2** *Jur* invalid, null and void **3** *Ordinat (mot de passe, nom du fichier)* invalid

NMF *(infirme)* disabled person, invalid; **i. du travail** = person disabled in an industrial accident

NM grand i. civil = officially recognized severely disabled person; **(grand) i. de guerre** = officially recognized war invalid

invalider [3] [ɛ̃valide] **VT** *(élection)* to invalidate, to make invalid, to nullify; *(décision juridique)* to quash; *(élu)* to remove from office

invalidité [ɛ̃validite] **NF** disability, disablement

invariabilité [ɛ̃vaʀjabilite] **NF** invariability

invariable [ɛ̃vaʀjabl] **ADJ 1** *(constant)* invariable, unchanging; **d'une i. bonne humeur** invariably good-humoured; **rester i. dans ses opinions** to remain unchanging *or* unswerving in one's opinions **2** *Gram* invariable

invariablement [ɛ̃vaʀjabləmɑ̃] **ADV** invariably

invariance [ɛ̃vaʀjɑ̃s] **NF** invariance, invariancy

invasif, -ive [ɛ̃vazif, -iv] **ADJ** *Méd (traitement)* invasive

invasion [ɛ̃vazjɔ̃] **NF 1** *Mil* invasion; **armée/troupes d'i.** invading army/troops **2** *(arrivée massive)* invasion, influx; **une i. de rats** an invasion of rats; **l'i. de produits étrangers sur le marché** the flooding of the market by foreign products; **une i. de touristes dans les hôtels** an influx of tourists into the hotels

invasive [ɛ̃vaziv] *voir* **invasif**

invective [ɛ̃vɛktiv] **NF** invective *(UNCOUNT)*, insult; **il s'est répandu en invectives contre moi** he started hurling abuse at me

invectiver [3] [ɛ̃vɛktive] **VT** to curse, to insult, to heap insults *or* abuse upon

• **invectiver contre VT IND** to curse

invendable [ɛ̃vɑ̃dabl] **ADJ** unsaleable, unmarketable; **vous m'apportez toujours des marchandises invendables** you always bring me goods that don't sell

invendu, -e [ɛ̃vɑ̃dy] **ADJ** unsold

NM *(gén)* unsold article *or* item; *(journal)* unsold copy

inventaire [ɛ̃vɑ̃tɛʀ] **NM 1** *(liste)* inventory; **faire** *ou* **dresser un i.** to draw up an inventory; **nous avons fait l'i. avec la propriétaire** we went through the inventory with the landlady; **l'i. de ses biens** the inventory *or* a detailed list of his/her possessions; **faire l'i. des ressources d'un pays** to assess a country's resources; *Fig* **si je fais l'i. de mes souvenirs** if I take stock of my memories; **i. supplémentaire des monuments historiques** register of listed buildings

2 *Com (procédure)* stocktaking; *(liste)* stocklist, *Am* inventory; **faire** *ou* **dresser un i.** *Br* to stocktake, *Am* to take the inventory; **faire l'i. de la marchandise** to take stock of the goods; **i. d'entrée/de sortie** incoming/outgoing inventory; **i. extracomptable** stocks, *Br* stock-in-trade, *Am* inventories; **i. intermittent** periodical inventory; **i. périodique** periodic inventory; **i. permanent** perpetual inventory; **i. physique** physical inventory; **i. théorique** theoretical inventory; **livre d'i.** inventory *or* stock book

3 *Compta* **i. (comptable)** book inventory; **i. de fin d'année** accounts for the end of the *Br* financial *or Am* fiscal year

4 *Fin (d'un portefeuille de titres)* valuation

inventer [3] [ɛ̃vɑ̃te] **VT 1** *(créer ▸ machine)* to invent; *(▸ mot)* to coin; **il n'a pas inventé la poudre** *ou* **l'eau chaude** *ou* **l'eau tiède** *ou* **le fil à couper le beurre** he'll never set the world alight **2** *(imaginer ▸ jeu)* to think up, to make up, to invent; *(▸ système)* to think up, to dream up, *Péj* to concoct; **je ne sais plus quoi i. pour les amuser** I've run out of ideas trying to keep them amused; *Fam* **ils ne savent plus quoi i.!** what will they think of next!; **qu'est-ce que tu vas i. là?** whatever gave you that idea?, where on earth did you get that idea from? **3** *(forger)* to think up, to make up, to invent; **invente une excuse!** just make up *or* invent some excuse!; **une histoire inventée de toutes pièces** an entirely made-up story, a complete fabrication

VPR s'inventer 1 ça ne s'invente pas *(ça ne peut qu'être vrai)* you couldn't make it up **2 s'i. un passé/de multiples maîtresses** to invent a past/several mistresses for oneself

inventeur, -trice [ɛ̃vɑ̃tœr, -tris] **NM,F 1** *(d'un appareil, d'un système)* inventor **2** *(de fausses nouvelles)* fabricator

inventif, -ive [ɛ̃vɑ̃tif, -iv] **ADJ** inventive, creative, resourceful; **les enfants sont très inventifs** children have a lot of imagination

invention [ɛ̃vɑ̃sjɔ̃] **NF 1** *Tech & (gén)* invention; **quelle formidable i.!** what a wonderful invention!; **grâce à l'i. du laser** thanks to the invention of lasers

2 *(créativité)* inventiveness, creativeness; **avoir de l'i.** to be inventive *or* creative; **manquer d'i.** to be unimaginative; **de mon/son/***etc* **i.** invented by me/him/her/*etc*; **un modèle de mon i.** a pattern I designed myself, one of my own designs

3 *(idée)* invention; **leur liaison est une i. de l'auteur** their love affair was made up by the author *or* is the author's own invention

4 *(mensonge)* invention, fabrication; **c'est (de la) pure i.** it's all made up *or* sheer invention *or* pure fabrication; **elle n'en est pas à une i. près pour justifier ses retards** she'll make up any excuse to justify being late

inventive [ɛ̃vɑ̃tiv] *voir* **inventif**

inventivité [ɛ̃vɑ̃tivite] **NF** inventiveness

inventorier [9] [ɛ̃vɑ̃tɔrje] **VT 1** *(gén)* to make an inventory of, *Sout* to inventory **2** *Com* to make a stocklist *or* inventory of

inventrice [ɛ̃vɑ̃tris] *voir* **inventeur**

invérifiable [ɛ̃verifjabl] **ADJ** unverifiable, uncheckable

inverse [ɛ̃vɛrs] **ADJ 1** *(opposé)* opposite; **les voitures qui viennent en sens i.** cars coming the other way *or* from the opposite direction; **dans l'ordre i.** in (the) reverse order, the other way round; **dans le sens i. des aiguilles d'une montre** *Br* anticlockwise, *Am* counterclockwise **2** *Math* inverse; **en proportion** *ou* **raison i. de** inversely proportional *or* in inverse proportion to

NM 1 *(contraire)* **l'i.** the opposite, the reverse; **c'est l'i.** it's the other way round; **c'est parce que sa femme l'a quitté qu'il s'est mis à boire et non l'i.** he started drinking because his wife left him and not the other way round *or* and not vice versa; **j'aurais dû faire l'i.** I should have done the opposite (of what I did); **supposons l'i. de cette théorie** let's consider the converse of this theory **2** *Math* inverse; **l'i. d'un nombre** the inverse *or* reciprocal of a number

• **à l'inverse ADV** conversely

• **à l'inverse de PRÉP** contrary to, unlike; **à l'i. de ce que tu crois** contrary to what you think; **à l'i. de mon collègue, je pense que...** unlike my colleague, I think that...

inversé, -e [ɛ̃vɛrse] **ADJ 1** *Phot* reverse, reversed **2** *Aviat & Géog* inverted

inversement [ɛ̃vɛrsəmɑ̃] **ADV 1** *(gén)* conversely; **vous pouvez l'aider, et i. il peut vous renseigner** you can help him, and in return he can give you some information; **i., on pourrait conclure que...** conversely, you could conclude that...; **...ou i.** ...or the other way round, ...or vice versa **2** *Math* inversely; **i. proportionnel à** inversely proportional to

inverser [3] [ɛ̃vɛrse] **VT 1** *(intervertir ▸ ordre, tendance)* to reverse; *(▸ deux mots)* to invert; *(▸ rôles)* to swap; **les rôles ont été totalement inversés** there's been a complete role reversal **2** *Élec & Phot* to reverse

inverseur [ɛ̃vɛrsœr] **NM 1** *Élec* reversing switch; **i. de pôles** pole changing switch **2** *Tech* **i. (de marche)** reversing gear

inversion [ɛ̃vɛrsjɔ̃] **NF 1** *(changement)* reversal, inversion; **i. des rôles** role reversal

2 *Élec* reversal

3 *Ordinat* **i. vidéo** reverse mode; *Phot* **pellicule par i.** reversal film

4 *Psy & Vieilli* inversion, homosexuality

invertébré, -e [ɛ̃vɛrtebre] **ADJ** invertebrate

NM invertebrate

inverti, -e [ɛ̃vɛrti] **ADJ** *Chim* **sucre i.** invert sugar

NM,F *Vieilli (homosexuel)* homosexual, invert

invertir [32] [ɛ̃vɛrtir] **VT 1** *(inverser)* to reverse, to invert **2** *Chim* to invert

investigateur, -trice [ɛ̃vɛstigatœr, -tris] **ADJ 1** *(avide de savoir)* inquiring, inquisitive, probing; **un esprit fin et i.** a sharp, inquisitive mind **2** *(scrutateur ▸ regard)* searching, scrutinizing

NM,F investigator

investigation [ɛ̃vɛstigasjɔ̃] **NF** investigation; **investigations** *(policières)* inquiries, investigation; *(scientifiques)* research, investigations

investigatrice [ɛ̃vɛstigatris] *voir* **investigateur**

investir [32] [ɛ̃vɛstir] **VT 1** *Fin* to invest (**dans** in); **capital investi** invested capital

2 *(engager ▸ ressources, temps, énergie)* to invest; **j'avais beaucoup investi dans notre amitié** I had invested a lot into our friendship

3 *(d'un pouvoir, d'une fonction)* **i. qn d'une dignité** to invest sb with a function; **i. qn de sa confiance** to place one's trust in sb; **par l'autorité dont je suis investi** by the authority vested in *or* conferred upon me; **elle se sentait investie d'une mission** she felt she'd been entrusted with a mission

4 *(encercler ▸ sujet: armée)* to surround, to besiege; *(▸ sujet: police)* to block off, to surround

USAGE ABSOLU *Fin* **i. à court/long terme** to make a short-/long-term investment; **i. dans la pierre** to invest (money) *Br* in bricks and mortar *or Am* in real estate; *Hum* **il est temps que j'investisse dans l'achat d'une nouvelle cravate** it's time I invested in a new tie

VPR s'investir s'i. dans qch to put a lot into sth; **s'i. dans son métier** to be involved *or* absorbed in one's job; **une actrice qui s'investit entièrement dans ses rôles** an actress who throws herself heart and soul into every part she plays; **je me suis énormément investie dans le projet** I really put *or* invested a lot into the project

investissement [ɛ̃vɛstismɑ̃] **NM 1** *Fin (action)* investing, investment; *(somme)* investment; **un gros i. de départ** a big initial investment *or* outlay; *Fig* **ne te plains pas d'avoir appris l'arabe, c'est un i. (pour l'avenir)** don't be sorry that you learnt Arabic, it'll stand you in good stead (in the future); **i. de capitaux** capital investment; **i. à court terme** short-term investment; **i. direct** direct investment; **i. éthique** ethical investment; **i. à l'étranger** outward *or* foreign investment; **i. de l'étranger** inward investment; **i. étranger direct** foreign direct investment; **i. immobilier** investment in real estate, property investment; **i. indirect** indirect investment; **i. institutionnel** institutional investment; **i. locatif** investment in rental property; **i. privé** private investment; **i. de productivité** productivity investment; **i. à revenu fixe** fixed-rate investment; **i. à revenu variable** floating-rate investment; **i. en valeurs de redressement** *ou* **de retournement** failure investment **2** *(effort)* investment, commitment **3** *Mil (encerclement)* surrounding, siege

• **d'investissement ADJ** *Fin (société, banque)* investment *(avant n)*; *(dépenses)* capital *(avant n)*

investisseur, -euse [ɛ̃vɛstisœr, -øz] **ADJ** investing

NM investor; **i. à contre-courant** contrarian investor; **i. institutionnel** institutional investor; **i. minoritaire** minority investor; **i. privé** private investor; **i. providentiel** business angel

investiture [ɛ̃vɛstityr] **NF 1** *Pol (d'un candidat)* nomination, selection; *(d'un gouvernement)* vote of confidence **2** *Hist & Rel* investiture

invétéré, -e [ɛ̃vetere] **ADJ** *(mal, habitude)* ingrained, deep-rooted; *(préjugé)* deeply-held, deep-seated, confirmed; *(buveur)* inveterate, habitual; *(coureur)* inveterate, incorrigible

invincibilité [ɛ̃vɛ̃sibilite] **NF** invincibility, invincibleness

invincible [ɛ̃vɛ̃sibl] **ADJ 1** *(imbattable ▸ héros, nation)* invincible, unconquerable; **avec un courage i.** with invincible *or* indomitable courage **2** *(insurmontable ▸ dégoût)* insuperable, insurmountable; *(▸ passion)* irresistible **3** *(irréfutable ▸ argument)* invincible, unbeatable

invinciblement [ɛ̃vɛ̃sibləmɑ̃] **ADV** invincibly, irresistibly

inviolabilité [ɛ̃vjɔlabilite] **NF 1** *(gén)* inviolability

2 *Pol* immunity; **l'i. parlementaire** *Br* parliamentary privilege, *Am* congressional immunity; **i. diplomatique** diplomatic immunity

3 *Jur* **l'i. du domicile** inviolability of the home

4 *Ordinat (de données)* (data) protection

inviolable [ɛ̃vjɔlabl] **ADJ 1** *(droit, serment)* inviolable **2** *(parlementaire, ministre)* untouchable, immune **3** *(imprenable)* impregnable, *Sout* inviolable

inviolé, -e [ɛ̃vjɔle] **ADJ 1** *(non enfreint ▸ loi)* inviolate, unviolated **2** *(non forcé ▸ lieu)* unforced, inviolate; *(▸ forêt)* virgin; **le sommet i. de la montagne** the unconquered summit of the mountain

invisibilité [ɛ̃vizibilite] **NF** invisibility

invisible [ɛ̃vizibl] **ADJ 1** *(imperceptible)* invisible; **i. à l'œil nu** invisible *or* not visible to the naked eye **2** *(occulte)* hidden, secret; **une menace i.** a hidden threat **3** *(non disponible)* unavailable; **tu es devenu i. dernièrement** you've been rather elusive recently

• **invisibles NMPL** *Écon* **les invisibles** *(échanges)* invisibles, invisible trade; *(exportations)* invisibles, invisible exports; **la balance des invisibles** the balance of invisible trade

invisiblement [ɛ̃vizibləmɑ̃] **ADV** invisibly

invitant, -e [ɛ̃vitɑ̃, -ɑ̃t] **ADJ puissance invitante** host country

invitation [ɛ̃vitasjɔ̃] **NF 1** *(requête)* invitation; **une i. à un cocktail** an invitation to a cocktail party; **à** *ou* **sur l'i. de nos amis** at the invitation of our friends; **venir sans i.** to come uninvited; **répondre à une i.** to reply to an invitation; **sur i.** by invitation only; **carton d'i.** invitation card; **lettre d'i.** letter of *or* written invitation **2** *(incitation)* invitation, provocation; **ton sac grand ouvert est une i. au vol** leaving your bag wide open is an (open) invitation to thieves; **ce film est une i. au voyage** this film makes you want to travel

invite [ɛ̃vit] **NF 1** *(invitation)* invitation, request **2** *Cartes* lead **3** *Ordinat* prompt; **i. du DOS** DOS prompt; **i. du système** system prompt

invité, -e [ɛ̃vite] **NM,F** guest; **i. de marque** distinguished guest; **i. d'honneur** guest of honour

inviter [3] [ɛ̃vite] **VT 1** *(ami, convive)* to invite; **i. qn à déjeuner** to invite *or* to ask sb to lunch; **i. qn chez soi** to invite sb (over) to one's house; **je ne les inviterai plus** I won't invite *or* ask them again; **demain nous sommes invités** we've been invited out tomorrow; **je regrette, je suis déjà invité** I'm sorry, but I have a previous engagement; **puis-je vous i. à danser?** may I have this dance?; **on s'est fait i. à la première par un copain** we were invited to the premiere by a friend; **tu ne peux pas t'arranger pour te faire i.?** can't you swing it so that you get invited? **2** *(inciter)* **i. qn à entrer** to ask sb (to come) in; **d'un signe de la tête, il m'invita à me taire** he nodded to me to keep quiet; **je vous invite à observer une minute de silence** I call upon you to observe a minute's silence; **j'invite tous les locataires mécontents à écrire à l'association** may I suggest that all dissatisfied tenants write to the association; **vous êtes invités à me suivre** would you be so kind as to follow me; **les passagers à destination de Rome sont invités à se présenter à la porte d'embarquement numéro deux** passengers for Rome are requested to proceed to gate number two; **i. à la réflexion** to be thought-provoking; **ce temps invite à la paresse** this weather tends to make you feel lazy

USAGE ABSOLU *Fam (payer)* **allez, c'est moi qui invite!** it's on me!

VI *Cartes* to lead

VPR s'inviter to invite oneself

in vitro [invitro] **ADJ INV** in vitro

ADV in vitro

invivable [ɛ̃vivabl] **ADJ 1** *(personne)* impossible, unbearable, insufferable **2** *(situation)* unbearable, intolerable **3** *(habitation)* **cette maison est devenue i.** this house has become impossible to live in

in vivo [invivo] **ADJ INV** in vivo

ADV in vivo

invocation [ɛ̃vɔkasjɔ̃] **NF** invocation

invocatoire [ɛ̃vɔkatwaʀ] **ADJ** invocatory

involontaire [ɛ̃vɔlɔ̃tɛʀ] **ADJ 1** *(machinal)* involuntary; **j'eus un mouvement de recul i.** I recoiled involuntarily *or* instinctively
2 *(non délibéré)* unintentional; **c'était i.** it was unintentional, I didn't do it on purpose
3 *(non consentant)* unwilling, reluctant; **j'ai été le témoin i. de sa déchéance** I was the reluctant witness of his/her downfall
4 *Anat & Physiol* involuntary
5 *Jur* involuntary

involontairement [ɛ̃vɔlɔ̃tɛʀmɑ̃] **ADV** unintentionally, unwittingly, without meaning to; **être i. mêlé à une affaire de contrebande** to be unwittingly involved in a smuggling operation; **si je vous ai vexé, c'est tout à fait i.** if I've offended you, it really wasn't intentional *or* I really didn't mean to

involution [ɛ̃vɔlysjɔ̃] **NF** involution

invoquer **[3]** [ɛ̃vɔke] **VT 1** *(avoir recours à ▸ argument, prétexte)* to put forward; *(▸ article de loi)* to refer to, to cite; **i. son ignorance** to plead ignorance **2** *(en appeler à ▸ personne)* to invoke, to appeal to; *(▸ dieu, esprit)* to invoke; *(▸ aide)* to call upon

invraisemblable [ɛ̃vʀesɑ̃blabl] **ADJ 1** *(improbable ▸ hypothèse, excuse)* unlikely, improbable, implausible
2 *(incroyable ▸ histoire)* incredible, unbelievable, amazing
3 *(bizarre ▸ tenue, personne)* weird, incredible, extraordinary
4 *(en intensif)* **elle a un toupet i.!** she has an amazing cheek!
NM l'i. the incredible

invraisemblablement [ɛ̃vʀesɑ̃blabləmɑ̃] **ADV** improbably, incredibly, unbelievably

invraisemblance [ɛ̃vʀesɑ̃blɑ̃s] **NF 1** *(caractère improbable)* unlikelihood, unlikeliness, improbability **2** *(fait)* improbability; **le scénario est truffé d'invraisemblances** the script is filled with implausible details

invulnérabilité [ɛ̃vylneʀabilite] **NF** invulnerability

invulnérable [ɛ̃vylneʀabl] **ADJ** invulnerable; **i. aux critiques** immune *or* impervious to criticism; **du fait de ses relations, il est i.** because of his contacts he is unassailable

iode [jɔd] **NM** *Chim* iodine

iodé, -e [jɔde] **ADJ** *Chim* iodized, iodated

ioder **[3]** [jɔde] **VT** *Chim* to iodize, to iodate

iodique [jɔdik] **ADJ M** *Chim* iodic

iodler [jɔdle] = **jodler**

iodoforme [jɔdɔfɔʀm] **NM** *Méd & Pharm* iodoform

iodure [jɔdyʀ] **NM** *Chim* iodide

ion [jɔ̃] **NM** ion

ionien, -enne [jɔnjɛ̃, -ɛn] **ADJ** *(de l'Ionie ▸ gén)* Ionian; *(▸ dialecte)* Ionic
NM *(dialecte)* Ionic
• **Ionien, -enne NM,F** Ionian

ionique [jɔnik] **ADJ 1** *(de l'Ionie)* Ionic
2 *Archit* Ionic
3 *Chim & Phys* ionic
4 *Élec* ionic, ion *(avant n)*

ionisant, -e [jɔnizɑ̃, -ɑ̃t] **ADJ** *Chim & Phys* ionizing

ionisation [jɔnizasjɔ̃] **NF** *Chim & Phys* ionization

ioniser **[3]** [jɔnize] **VT** *Chim & Phys* to ionize

ionosphère [jɔnɔsfɛʀ] **NF** ionosphere

ionotropique [jɔnɔtʀɔpik] **ADJ** *Physiol (récepteur)* ionotropic

iota [jɔta] **NM INV** iota; **ne changez pas votre article d'un i.** *ou* **un i. dans votre article** don't change your article one iota *or* a thing in your article; **il n'a pas bougé d'un i.** *(dans ses convictions)* he didn't shift *or* budge an inch

iourte [juʀt] = **yourte**

IPC [ipese] **NM** *Mktg (abrév* **indice des prix à la consommation***)* CPI

ipéca [ipeka], **ipécacuan(h)a** [ipekakwana] **NM** ipecac, ipecacuanha

iPod® [ipɔd] **NM** iPod®

IPR [ipeɛʀ] **NM** *(abrév* **Inspecteur pédagogique régional***)* = locally-based education inspector

ipso facto [ipsofakto] **ADV** ipso facto, by that very fact

Ipsos [ipsos] **NM** = French market research institute

> **-IQUE** SUFFIX
>
> This suffix containing the idea of RELATING TO, BELONGING TO is a very productive one, especially in the areas of science and technology, where it is used to create words that can sometimes be both adjectives and nouns.
>
> • It can be added to a noun, itself sometimes ending in the suffix **-ie** or **-isme**, and is often, in that case, translated by the English suffix *-ic*, eg:
> **économique** (from *économie*) economical, economic; **bureaucratique** (from *bureaucratie*) bureaucratic; **sadique** (from *sadisme*) sadistic; **alcoolique** (from *alcool*) alcoholic
>
> • It can also be found at the end of a noun to form a feminine noun from the field of science or technology. The English equivalent is often *-ics*, eg:
> **robotique** robotics; **domotique** home automation; **avionique** avionics
>
> • The suffixation can be based directly on a Latin or Greek radical. The English translation often sounds less specialized than the French word, eg:
> **domotique** (from the Latin *domus*, house) home automation; **ludique** (from the Latin *ludus*, game) play *(adj)*; **bionique** (from the Greek *bios*, life) bionics
>
> • The suffix **-ique** is used quite productively in French slang to form derogatory adjectives such as:
> **merdique** rubbish, shitty; **chiatique: t'es vraiment chiatique!** you're a bloody pain!; **bordélique** messy, chaotic

ira *etc voir* **aller**[2]

Irak [iʀak] **NM l'I.** Iraq

irakien, -enne [iʀakjɛ̃, -ɛn] **ADJ** Iraqi
NM *(langue)* Iraqi
• **Irakien, -enne NM,F** Iraqi

Iran [iʀɑ̃] **NM l'I.** Iran

iranien, -enne [iʀanjɛ̃, -ɛn] **ADJ** Iranian
NM *(langue)* Iranian
• **Iranien, -enne NM,F** Iranian

Iraq [iʀak] = **Irak**

iraquien [iʀakjɛ̃] = **irakien**

irascibilité [iʀasibilite] **NF** irritability, testiness, *Sout* irascibility

irascible [iʀasibl] **ADJ** short-tempered, testy, *Sout* irascible

IRC [iɛʀse] **NM** *Ordinat (abrév* **Internet Relay Chat***)* IRC

ire [iʀ] **NF** *Littéraire* ire, wrath

iridescent, -e [iʀidesɑ̃, -ɑ̃t] **ADJ** iridescent

iridié, -e [iʀidje] **ADJ** *Chim* iridic

iridium [iʀidjɔm] **NM** *Chim* iridium

iris [iʀis] **NM 1** *Anat* iris
2 *Bot* iris, flag
3 *Phot* iris (diaphragm)
4 *Littéraire (arc-en-ciel)* iris, rainbow

irisation [iʀizasjɔ̃] **NF** *Opt* iridescence, *Spéc* irisation

irisé, -e [iʀize] **ADJ** iridescent

iriser **[3]** [iʀize] **VT** to make iridescent, *Spéc* to irisate
VPR s'iriser to become iridescent

irlandais, -e [iʀlɑ̃dɛ, -ɛz] **ADJ** Irish
NM *(langue)* Irish
• **Irlandais, -e NM,F** Irishman, *f* Irishwoman; **les I.** the Irish; **un I. du Nord** = a Northern Irish person; **les I. du Nord** the Northern Irish

Irlande [iʀlɑ̃d] **NF l'I.** Ireland; **l'I. du Nord/Sud** Northern/Southern Ireland; **la mer d'I.** the Irish Sea; **la République d'I.** the Irish Republic

IRM [iɛʀɛm] **NF** *Méd (abrév* **imagerie par résonance magnétique***)* MRI

IRMf [iɛʀɛmɛf] **NF** *Méd (abrév* **imagerie par résonance magnétique fonctionnelle***)* fMRI

IRMN [iɛʀɛmɛn] **NF** *Méd (abrév* **imagerie par résonance magnétique nucléaire***)* NMRI

ironie [iʀɔni] **NF** irony; **l'i. du sort a voulu que je le rencontre** as fate would have it, I bumped into him

ironique [iʀɔnik] **ADJ** ironic, ironical; **regarder qn d'un air i.** to look at sb quizzically

ironiquement [iʀɔnikmɑ̃] **ADV** ironically; **répondre i. à une question** to answer a question tongue-in-cheek *or* ironically

ironiser **[3]** [iʀɔnize] **VI** to be sarcastic; **i. sur** to be sarcastic about; **il ne cesse d'i. sur les intentions du parti** he keeps being sarcastic about the party's intentions

ironiste [iʀɔnist] **NMF** ironist

iroquois, -e [iʀɔkwa, -az] **ADJ** Iroquois, Iroquoian
NM *(langue)* Iroquoian
• **Iroquois, -e NM,F** Iroquois
• **iroquoise NF** mohican (hairstyle); **coiffé à l'iroquoise** with a mohican (hairstyle)

irrachetable [iʀaʃtabl] **ADJ** unredeemable, unreturnable

irradiation [iʀadjasjɔ̃] **NF 1** *(rayonnement)* radiation, irradiation
2 *(exposition ▸ d'une personne, d'un tissu)* irradiation, exposure to radiation; **il y a des risques d'i.** there is a risk of irradiation *or* of being exposed to radiation
3 *Méd (traitement)* irradiation
4 *Phot* halation

irradier **[9]** [iʀadje] **VI 1** *Phys* to radiate; **les rayons du foyer lumineux irradient de tous côtés** light waves radiate in all directions **2** *(se propager)* to spread; **la douleur irradiait dans toute la jambe** the pain spread to the whole leg **3** *Littéraire (se diffuser ▸ bonheur)* to radiate; **la joie irradie autour d'elle** she radiates joy
VT 1 *(soumettre à un rayonnement)* to irradiate; **se faire i.** to be exposed to radiation **2** *Littéraire (répandre ▸ bonheur)* to radiate

irraisonné, -e [iʀezɔne] **ADJ** unreasoned, irrational

irrationalisme [iʀasjɔnalism] **NM** irrationalism

irrationalité [iʀasjɔnalite] **NF** irrationality

irrationnel, -elle [iʀasjɔnɛl] **ADJ** *(gén) & Math* irrational; **de façon irrationnelle** irrationally
NM 1 *(gén)* **l'i.** the irrational **2** *Math* irrational (number)

irrattrapable [iʀatʀapabl] **ADJ** *(erreur)* irredeemable, which cannot be rectified; *(retard)* which cannot be made up

irréalisable [iʀealizabl] **ADJ** *(ambition)* unrealizable, unachievable; *(idée, projet)* unworkable, unfeasible, impracticable; *Fin (valeurs)* unrealizable

irréalisé, -e [iʀealize] **ADJ** unrealized, unachieved

irréalisme [iʀealism] **NM** lack of realism

irréaliste [iʀealist] **ADJ** unrealistic
NMF unrealistic person, (pipe) dreamer

irréalité [iʀealite] **NF** unreality

irrecevabilité [iʀəsəvabilite] **NF 1** *(d'un argument)* unacceptability **2** *Jur* inadmissibility

irrecevable [iʀəsəvabl] **ADJ 1** *(inacceptable)* unacceptable **2** *Jur* inadmissible

irréconciliable [iʀekɔ̃siljabl] **ADJ** *(ennemis, adversaires)* irreconcilable, unreconcilable; *(haine)* implacable; **ils sont irréconciliables** nothing can reconcile them

irrécouvrable [iʀekuvʀabl] **ADJ** irrecoverable

irrécupérable [iʀekypeʀabl] **ADJ 1** *(argent)* irrecoverable **2** *(irréparable ▸ objet)* beyond repair **3** *(personne)* irremediable, beyond redemption

irrécusable [iʀekyzabl] **ADJ 1** *(indéniable ▸ signe, vérité)* undeniable; *(▸ preuves)* indisputable **2** *Jur (témoignage, juge)* unimpeachable

irréductibilité [iʀedyktibilite] **NF 1** *(d'un obstacle)* insurmountability, intractability; *(d'un ennemi)* implacability **2** *Chim & Math* irreducibility

irréductible [iʀedyktibl] **ADJ 1** *(insurmontable ▸ conflit, différence)* insurmountable, intractable, insoluble; (▸ *obstacle*) insurmountable **2** *(inflexible)* invincible, implacable, uncompromising; **il s'est fait quelques ennemis irréductibles** he's made himself a few implacable enemies; **derrière cette réussite, il y a la détermination i. d'une femme** this success is based on the invincible *or* indomitable determination of a woman **3** *Math & Chim* irreducible

NMF diehard, hardliner; **les irréductibles de (la) gauche/droite** the left-wing/right-wing diehards

irréel, -elle [ireɛl] **ADJ** unreal

NM 1 *(gén) & Phil* **l'i.** the unreal **2** *Gram* **l'i. du présent/passé** the hypothetical present/past

irréfléchi, -e [irefleʃi] **ADJ** *(acte, parole)* rash, reckless; *(geste, mouvement)* instinctive; *(personne)* unthinking, rash, reckless

irréflexion [irefleksjɔ̃] **NF** rashness, recklessness; **faire preuve d'i.** to be rash *or* reckless

irréformable [irefɔrmabl] **ADJ** *Jur (décision)* final, unchallengeable

irréfragable [irefragabl] **ADJ** indisputable, *Sout* irrefragable

irréfutabilité [irefytabilite] **NF** irrefutability, indisputability

irréfutable [irefytabl] **ADJ** irrefutable, indisputable; **il a prouvé de manière i. que...** he proved irrefutably *or* indisputably that...

irréfutablement [irefytabləmɑ̃] **ADV** indisputably, irrefutably

irréfuté, -e [irefyte] **ADJ** unrefuted

irrégularité [iregylarite] **NF 1** *(de forme, de rythme)* irregularity, unevenness; *(d'un terrain, d'une surface)* unevenness; **une i. du rythme cardiaque** an irregular heartbeat

2 *(en qualité)* unevenness, patchiness; **l'i. de son visage** the irregularity of his/her features; **l'i. de votre travail ne permet pas le passage dans le groupe supérieur** (the quality of) your work is too uneven *or* erratic for you to move up into the next group

3 *(surface irrégulière* ▸ *bosse)* bump; (▸ *creux)* hole; **les irrégularités du sol** the unevenness of the ground; **les irrégularités du relief** the hilliness of the area

4 *(infraction)* irregularity; **il y a des irrégularités dans les comptes** there are a few irregularities *or* discrepancies in the accounts; **i. comptable** accounting irregularity

irrégulier, -ère [iregylje, -ɛr] **ADJ 1** *(dessin, écriture, rythme)* irregular, uneven; *(terrain, surface)* uneven; *(visage, traits)* irregular; *(pouls, respiration)* erratic, irregular; *(expansion)* uneven, erratic; **je m'entraîne de façon irrégulière** I train intermittently *or* sporadically; **nous avons des horaires irréguliers** we don't work regular hours

2 *(qualité, travail)* uneven; **vos prestations sont irrégulières** your work is uneven *or* erratic; **j'étais un étudiant i.** my work was erratic when I was a student

3 *(illégal)* irregular; **ils sont en situation irrégulière dans le pays** their residence papers are not in order; **des retraits de fonds irréguliers** unauthorized withdrawals

4 *Mil* irregular; **les soldats des troupes irrégulières** the irregulars

5 *Gram* irregular

NM *Mil* irregular (soldier)

irrégulièrement [iregyljɛrmɑ̃] **ADV 1** *(de façon non uniforme)* irregularly, unevenly **2** *(de façon illégale)* irregularly, illegally **3** *(de façon inconstante)* irregularly, erratically

irréligieux, -euse [ireliʒjø, -øz] **ADJ** irreligious

irréligion [ireliʒjɔ̃] **NF** irreligion

irremboursable [irɑ̃bursabl] **ADJ** *(obligation)* irredeemable

irrémédiable [iremedjabl] **ADJ** *(rupture)* irreparable, irretrievable; *(dégâts)* irreparable, irreversible; *(maladie)* incurable, fatal; **son mal est i.** his/her illness is incurable *or Sout* irremediable; **les conséquences pour l'environnement sont irrémédiables** the effects on the environment are irreparable *or* irreversible

NM l'i. a été commis irreversible harm has been done

irrémédiablement [iremedjabləmɑ̃] **ADV** irremediably, irretrievably; **tout espoir de le retrouver est i. perdu** we have definitely lost all hope of (ever) finding him

irrémissible [iremisibl] **ADJ** *Littéraire* **1** *(impardonnable)* unpardonable **2** *(inexorable)* implacable, inexorable

irremplaçable [irɑ̃plasabl] **ADJ** irreplaceable

irréparable [ireparabl] **ADJ 1** *(montre, voiture)* unrepairable, beyond repair **2** *(erreur, tort, perte)* irreparable; *(affront)* unpardonable

NM commettre l'i. to go beyond the point of no return

irréparablement [ireparabləmɑ̃] **ADV** *(définitivement)* irreparably; **sa réputation est i. atteinte** his/her reputation has suffered an irreparable blow

irrépréhensible [irepreɑ̃sibl] **ADJ** *Littéraire* irreproachable, irreprehensible

irrépressible [irepresibl] **ADJ** irrepressible

irréprochable [ireprɔʃabl] **ADJ 1** *(personne, conduite)* irreproachable; **personne n'est i.** nobody's beyond *or* above reproach **2** *(tenue)* impeccable; *(travail)* impeccable, faultless; **d'une propreté i.** immaculate

irréprochablement [ireprɔʃabləmɑ̃] **ADV** irreproachably, impeccably, faultlessly

irrésistible [irezistibl] **ADJ 1** *(séduisant)* irresistible **2** *(irrépressible* ▸ *besoin)* compelling, pressing; (▸ *envie)* irresistible, uncontrollable, compelling

irrésistiblement [irezistibləmɑ̃] **ADV** irresistibly

irrésolu, -e [irezɔly] **ADJ 1** *(personne)* indecisive, unresolved, *Sout* irresolute **2** *(problème)* unsolved, unresolved

NM,F irresolute person, *Péj* ditherer

irrésolution [irezɔlysjɔ̃] **NF** irresoluteness, indecisiveness

irrespect [irɛspɛ] **NM** disrespect, lack of respect; **leur i. envers leur mère/l'autorité** their lack of respect for their mother/of authority

irrespectueuse [irɛspɛktɥøz] *voir* **irrespectueux**

irrespectueusement [irɛspɛktɥøzmɑ̃] **ADV** disrespectfully

irrespectueux, -euse [irɛspɛktɥø, -øz] **ADJ** disrespectful, lacking in respect (**envers** towards)

irrespirable [irɛspirabl] **ADJ 1** *(air* ▸ *trop chaud)* stifling, stuffy; (▸ *toxique)* unsafe, not fit to breathe; **aère ta chambre, c'est i. ici!** air your room, it's stifling in here! **2** *(oppressant* ▸ *ambiance)* unbearable, stifling; **j'ai trouvé l'ambiance i. à la maison** I found the atmosphere unbearable at home

irresponsabilité [irɛspɔ̃sabilite] **NF 1** *(légèreté)* irresponsibility; **agir avec une totale i.** to behave totally irresponsibly **2** *(du chef de l'État)* non-accountability; **i. du chef de l'État** = immunity of the Head of State; **i. parlementaire** *Br* parliamentary privilege, *Am* congressional immunity

irresponsable [irɛspɔ̃sabl] **ADJ 1** *(inconséquent)* irresponsible; **de manière i.** irresponsibly **2** *Jur* (legally) incapable

NMF irresponsible person; **espèce d'i.!** you irresponsible idiot!

irrétrécissable [iretresisabl] **ADJ** unshrinkable

irrévérence [ireverɑ̃s] **NF 1** *(irrespect)* irreverence; **avec i.** irreverently **2** *(remarque)* irreverent remark; *(acte)* irreverent act

irrévérencieuse [ireverɑ̃sjøz] *voir* **irrévérencieux**

irrévérencieusement [ireverɑ̃sjøzmɑ̃] **ADV** irreverently

irrévérencieux, -euse [ireverɑ̃sjø, -øz] **ADJ** irreverent

irréversibilité [ireversibilite] **NF** irreversibility

irréversible [ireversibl] **ADJ** *(gén) & Chim & Phys* irreversible; **le processus est i.** the process is irreversible

irréversiblement [ireversibləmɑ̃] **ADV** irreversibly

irrévocabilité [irevɔkabilite] **NF** irrevocability, finality

irrévocable [irevɔkabl] **ADJ** *(gén)* irrevocable; *(verdict)* irrevocable, final

irrévocablement [irevɔkabləmɑ̃] **ADV** irrevocably

irrigable [irigabl] **ADJ** irrigable, suitable for irrigation

irrigateur [irigatœr] **NM** *Agr & Méd* irrigator

irrigation [irigasjɔ̃] **NF 1** *Agr & Méd* irrigation **2** *Physiol* **l'i. des tissus par les vaisseaux sanguins** the supply of blood to the tissues by blood vessels

irriguer [3] [irige] **VT 1** *Agr & Méd* to irrigate **2** *Physiol* **si le cerveau n'est pas irrigué pendant plus de trois minutes** if there is no blood supply to the brain for more than three minutes

irritabilité [iritabilite] **NF 1** *(irascibilité)* irritability, quick temper **2** *Méd* irritability

irritable [iritabl] **ADJ 1** *(colérique)* irritable, easily annoyed **2** *Méd* irritable

irritant, -e [iritɑ̃, -ɑ̃t] **ADJ 1** *(agaçant)* irritating, annoying, aggravating **2** *Méd* irritant

NM *Méd* irritant

irritation [iritasjɔ̃] **NF 1** *(agacement)* irritation, annoyance; **avec i.** irritably, petulantly **2** *Méd* irritation; **i. cutanée** skin irritation

irrité, -e [irite] **ADJ 1** *(exaspéré)* irritated, annoyed (**contre** with); **d'un ton i.** irritably, peevishly **2** *Méd* irritated

irriter [3] [irite] **VT 1** *(agacer)* to irritate, to annoy; **ses petites manies m'irritent** his/her little quirks get on my nerves **2** *Méd* to irritate **3** *Littéraire (exacerber* ▸ *passion, désir)* to inflame, to arouse; (▸ *curiosité)* to excite

VPR s'irriter 1 *(s'énerver)* to get annoyed *or* irritated (**contre qn/de qch** with sb/at sth) **2** *Méd* to become irritated

irruption [irypsjɔ̃] **NF 1** *(entrée)* breaking *or* bursting *or* storming in; **ils n'ont pas pu empêcher l'i. des spectateurs sur le terrain** they were unable to stop spectators from storming *or* invading the *Br* pitch *or Am* field; **l'i. des eaux dans les cultures** the (sudden) flooding of the fields; **faire i. chez qn** to burst in on sb; **faire i. dans** to burst *or* to barge into **2** *(émergence)* upsurge, sudden development

Do not confuse with **éruption**.

IRSM [iɛresem] **NM** *Mktg (abrév* **impact sur la rentabilité de la stratégie marketing)** PIMS

ISA [iesa] **NM** *Mktg (abrév* **imprimé sans adresse)** mailshot

Isaac [izaak] **NPR** *Bible* Isaac

isabelle [izabɛl] **ADJ INV** *(cheval)* Isabella-coloured

NM Isabella-coloured horse

ISAF [izaf] **NF** *(abrév* **International Sailing Federation)** ISAF

Isaïe [izai] **NPR** *Bible* Isaiah

-ISANT, -ISANTE SUFFIX

This suffix is used to form adjectives and – more rarely – nouns with the idea of having a TENDENCY or a LEANING towards, mostly, an ideology. In English, the suffix *-istic* can sometimes be used as an equivalent, eg:

communisant(e) Communistic, with Communist sympathies; **socialisant(e)** left-leaning, with left-wing tendencies; **fascisant(e)** fascistic, pro-fascist

isard [izar] **NM** *Zool* izard, Pyrenean chamois

-ISATION, -ISER SUFFIX

• Like their English equivalents (*-ization, -ize*), these two suffixes are widely used to suggest a TRANSFORMATION, either in noun or verb form. A noun ending in **-isation** often corresponds to a verb ending in **-iser**, which can be transitive or reflexive. The base for derivation is either an adjective or a noun, the idea being that of "becoming...", eg:

se clochardiser (to become destitute/to be made homeless) and **clochardisation** (becoming destitute/making homeless); **diaboliser** (to demonize) and **diabolisation**

(demonization); **(se) marginaliser** (to marginalize/to become marginalized) and **marginalisation** (marginalization); **ringardiser** (to make tacky) and **ringardisation** (making/becoming tacky)

• A particular trend in recent times has been to add **-isation** to a proper noun, often from the political or cultural arena, eg:

l'hollywoodisation du cinéma mondial the Hollywoodization of world cinema; **la disneylandisation d'un lieu** the Disneyfication of a place; **la macdonaldisation de l'alimentation** the McDonaldization of food; **la lepénisation des esprits** the influence of Le Pen (the French far-right politician) on people's ideas

ISBN [isbeen] **NM** *(abrév* **International standard book number) (numéro) I.** ISBN

-iser [ize] *voir* **-isation**

Islam [islam] **NM l'I.** *(civilisation)* Islam

islamique [islamik] **ADJ** Islamic

islamisation [islamizasjɔ̃] **NF** Islamization

islamiser [3] [islamize] **VT** to Islamize

islamisme [islamism] **NM** Islamism

islamiste [islamist] **ADJ** Islamic
NMF Islamic fundamentalist

islamité [islamite] **NF** Islamism

islamophobe [islamɔfɔb] **ADJ** Islamophobic
NMF Islamophobe

islamophobie [islamɔfɔbi] **NF** Islamophobia

islandais, -e [islɑ̃dɛ, -ɛz] **ADJ** Icelandic
NM *(langue)* Icelandic
• **Islandais, -e NM,F** Icelander

Islande [islɑ̃d] **NF l'I.** Iceland

-ISME, -ISTE SUFFIX

• The main use of these suffixes, whose English equivalents are, in many cases, *-ism* and *-ist*, consists in forming nouns and adjectives relating to ATTITUDES, social, political or religious MOVEMENTS or DOCTRINES and to their FOLLOWERS. The base for suffixation can be an adjective, a noun, a proper noun or even a verb, eg:

libéralisme (from *libéral*) liberalism/free-market economics; **racisme/raciste** (from *race*) racism/racist; **catholicisme** (from *catholique*) Catholicism; **narcissisme** (from *Narcisse*) narcissism; **gaullisme** (from *General de Gaulle*) Gaullism; **arrivisme/arriviste** (from *arriver*) pushiness/careerist; **dirigisme/dirigiste** (from *diriger*) state intervention/interventionist

• A recent, humorous and colloquial trend has been to add **-isme** or **-iste** to a whole expression, which is held together with hyphens, eg:

je-m'en-foutisme (from *je m'en fous!* = I don't give a damn!) couldn't-care-less attitude; **il est très je-m'en-foutiste** he's a couldn't-give-a-damn sort of person; **jusqu'au-boutisme** (from *jusqu'au bout* = to the end) hard-line attitude; **les jusqu'au-boutistes** the hard-liners; **à-quoi-bonisme** (from *à quoi bon?* = what's the point?) what's-the-point attitude; **une génération d'à-quoi-bonistes** a generation who don't see the point of anything

• The term **âgisme** (ageism) is a modern coinage due to the influence of the word **racisme**, both in form and meaning. **Jeunisme**, however, although similar in form, has the opposite idea: it refers to the cult of youth rather than discrimination against young people.

ISO [izo] **NF** *Phot (abrév* **International Standards Organization)** ISO

isobare [izɔbar] **ADJ** *Météo & Phys* isobaric
NM *Phys* isobar
NF *Météo* isobar

isocèle [izɔsɛl] **ADJ** isosceles; **triangle i.** isosceles triangle

isochrone [izɔkron] **ADJ** isochronal, isochronous
NF isochron, isochronal line

isoclinal, -e, -aux, -ales [izɔklinal, -o] **ADJ** *Géol* isoclinal

isocline [izɔklin] *Phys* **ADJ** *(ligne)* isoclinal
NF isocline, isoclinal line

isolable [izɔlabl] **ADJ** isolable, isolatable; **un virus difficilement i.** a virus (which is) difficult to isolate

isolant, -e [izɔlɑ̃, -ɑ̃t] **ADJ 1** *(thermique, électrique)* insulating; *(acoustique)* soundproofing; **bouteille isolante** vacuum flask **2** *Ling* isolating
NM *(thermique, électrique)* insulating material; *(acoustique)* soundproofing (material); **i. thermique/électrique** thermal/electrical insulator

isolateur, -trice [izɔlatœr, -tris] **ADJ** insulating
NM *Élec & Phys* insulator

isolation [izɔlasjɔ̃] **NF 1** *Constr* insulation; **i. thermique** heat *or* thermal insulation; **i. phonique** *ou* **acoustique** soundproofing, sound insulation **2** *Élec* insulation **3** *Psy* isolation

Do not confuse with **isolement**.

isolationnisme [izɔlasjɔnism] **NM** isolationism

isolationniste [izɔlasjɔnist] **ADJ** isolationist
NMF isolationist

isolatrice [izɔlatris] *voir* **isolateur**

isolé, -e [izɔle] **ADJ 1** *(unique ▸ cas, exemple)* isolated; **généraliser à partir d'un ou deux cas isolés** to generalize from one or two isolated examples
2 *(coupé du monde ▸ personne)* isolated; *(▸ hameau, maison)* isolated, cut-off, remote; *(▸ forêt)* remote, lonely; **il vit trop i.** he lives too much in isolation, he leads too isolated a life; **quelques arbres isolés visibles à l'horizon** a few lonely trees dotted along the horizon
3 *(seul ▸ activiste)* maverick
4 *Géom & Phys* isolated
NM,F 1 *(personne)* isolated individual **2** *Pol* maverick, isolated activist; **ce sont les revendications de quelques isolés** only a few isolated people are putting forward these demands

isolement [izɔlmɑ̃] **NM 1** *(éloignement ▸ géographique)* isolation, seclusion, remoteness; *(▸ affectif)* isolation, loneliness; *(sanction)* solitary (confinement); *Écon & Pol* isolation; **vivre dans l'i.** to live in isolation
2 *Biol & Méd* isolation; **l'i. du virus** isolating the virus
3 *Élec* insulation
4 *Constr (contre le bruit)* insulation, soundproofing; *(contre le froid, la chaleur)* insulation; **i. thermique** (thermal) insulation

Do not confuse with the French word **isolation**.

isolément [izɔlemɑ̃] **ADV** *(l'un de l'autre)* separately, individually; **le malfaiteur a agi i.** the criminal acted in isolation *or* alone

isoler [3] [izɔle] **VT 1** *(séparer)* to isolate, to separate off *or* out, to keep separate (**de** from); **i. une citation de son contexte** to lift a quotation out of context, to isolate a quotation from its context
2 *(couper du monde ▸ personne, endroit)* to isolate, to cut off; **sa maladie l'isole** his/her illness cuts him/her off from other people; **les inondations ont isolé des dizaines de villages** dozens of villages have been cut off by the flood
3 *(distinguer)* to isolate, to single *or* to pick out; **on n'a pas pu i. la cause de la déflagration** it was not possible to identify the cause of the explosion; **i. un cas parmi d'autres** to pick out an isolated case
4 *Constr (du froid, de la chaleur)* to insulate; *(du bruit)* to insulate (against sound), to soundproof
5 *Élec* to insulate
6 *Méd (malade, virus)* to isolate
7 *Admin (prisonnier)* to put into *or* to place in solitary confinement
VPR s'isoler to isolate oneself, to cut oneself off; **s'i. pour travailler** to find somewhere private to work; **s'i. dans son bureau** to shut oneself (up) in one's office; **le jury s'isola pour délibérer** the jury withdrew to consider its verdict; **pourrions-nous i. un instant?** is there somewhere we could talk privately *or* in private for a moment?

isoloir [izɔlwar] **NM** *Pol* voting booth, polling booth

isomère [izɔmɛr] *Chim & Phys* **ADJ** isomeric
NM isomer

isométrique [izɔmetrik] **ADJ** isometric

isomorphe [izɔmɔrf] **ADJ** *Biol, Chim, Math & Ling* isomorphic, isomorphous
NM *Biol & Chim* isomorph

isomorphisme [izɔmɔrfism] **NM** *Biol, Chim, Math & Ling* isomorphism

Isorel® [izɔrɛl] **NM** hardboard

isotherme [izɔtɛrm] **ADJ** isothermal; **bouteille i.** vacuum flask; **sac i.** cool bag
NF isotherm

isotope [izɔtɔp] *Phys* **ADJ** isotopic
NM isotope

isotrope [izɔtrɔp] **ADJ** *Chim & Phys* isotropic, isotropous

Israël [israɛl] **NM** Israel

israélien, -enne [israeljɛ̃, -ɛn] **ADJ** Israeli
• **Israélien, -enne NM,F** Israeli

israélite [israelit] **ADJ 1** *(juif)* Jewish **2** *Bible* Israelite
• **Israélite NMF 1** *(juif)* Jew, *f* Jewess **2** *Bible* Israelite

-ISSIME SUFFIX

• This very productive suffix is derived from Latin or Italian and acts as a SUPERLATIVE when added to adjectives. Its use always gives a slightly humorous tone to the sentence, especially when the resulting adjective is entirely made up and does not appear in dictionaries. As there is no direct equivalent in English, the translation will have to include a similarly superlative turn of phrase, usually with an adverb, eg:

richissime fantastically wealthy; **rarissime** extremely rare; **nullissime** completely useless; **simplissime** easy as pie; **élégantissime** incredibly elegant; **ringardissime** unbelievably tacky; **glamourissime** amazingly glamorous (It is worth noting that, contrary to the other words listed above, the adjectives *richissime* and *rarissime* have existed for a very long time and have no humorous or colloquial overtones.)

• It is also possible to add **-issime** to a proper noun when describing something or somebody as typical of what the person represents, especially in the field of arts or literature, eg:

un film allenissime (from the American director Woody Allen) a Woody Allen-ish film; **une description proustissime** (from the XIXth century French writer Marcel Proust) a Proustian description

ISSN [iɛsɛsɛn] **NM** *(abrév* **International standard serial number) (numéro) I.** ISSN

issu, -e[1] [isy] **ADJ être i. de** *(résulter de)* to stem *or* to derive *or* to spring from; **la révolution est issue du mécontentement populaire** the revolution stems from popular discontent; **être i. d'une famille pauvre/nombreuse** to be born into a poor/large family; **enfant i. d'un second mariage** child from a second marriage; **cousins issus de germains** second cousins

issue[2] [isy] **NF 1** *(sortie)* exit; *(déversoir)* outlet; **i. de secours** emergency exit **2** *(solution)* solution, way out; **trouver** *ou* **se ménager une i.** to find a way out *or* a loophole; **il n'y a pas d'autre i. que de se rendre** there's no other solution *or* we have no alternative but to surrender **3** *(fin)* outcome; **cet épisode a eu une i. heureuse/tragique** the incident had a happy/tragic ending
• **à l'issue de PRÉP** at the end *or* close of; **à l'i. du cinquième round** at the end of the fifth round
• **sans issue ADJ 1** *(sans sortie)* with no way out; **ruelle sans i.** dead end; **sans i.** *(sur une porte)* no exit **2** *(voué à l'échec)* hopeless, doomed; *(discussions)* deadlocked; **une situation sans i.** a dead end

Il faut noter que le nom anglais **issue** est un faux ami. Il signifie le plus souvent **problème, question**.

IST [ieste] NF *(abrév* **infection sexuellement transmissible)** STI

Istanbul [istɑ̃bul] NF Istanbul

-iste [ist] *voir* **-isme**

isthme [ism] NM *Anat & Géog* isthmus

isthmique [ismik] ADJ isthmian

italianisant, -e [italjanizɑ̃, -ɑ̃t] ADJ *(style)* Italianate

NM,F **1** *Univ* Italianist, Italian scholar **2** *Beaux-Arts* Italianizer

italianiser [3] [italjanize] VT to Italianize

italianisme [italjanism] NM Italianism

Italie [itali] NF **l'I.** Italy

italien, -enne [italjɛ̃, -ɛn] ADJ Italian

NM *(langue)* Italian

• **Italien, -enne** NM,F Italian

• **à l'italienne** ADJ **1** *Culin (sauce)* à l'italienne *(cooked with mushrooms, ham and herbs)*; *(pâtes)* al dente **2** *Typ* landscape; **imprimer qch à l'i.** to print sth in landscape

italique [italik] ADJ **1** *Typ* italic **2** *Hist & Ling* Italic

NM **1** *Typ* italics; **écrire un mot en i.** to write a word in italics, to italicize a word **2** *Hist & Ling* Italic

SUFFIX

-ITE

• The feminine suffix **-ite** originally belongs to the medical world, and means INFLAMMATION of the organ referred to by the noun base. Its equivalent in English is *-itis*, eg:

gastrite gastritis; **appendicite** appendicitis; **pharyngite** pharyngitis

• It has also been given a humorous twist in words like **réunionnite** or **espionnite**, with the implication of some sort of MANIA or obsession, eg:

une réaction contre la réunionnite des années 90 a reaction against the meeting mania of the 90s; **une vague d'espionnite aigüe** a strong wave of spymania

• Note the use of **aigu** in the last example, which emphasizes the fake medical tone of the expression. It can also be found in **flemmingite aigüe**, a colloquial way of describing a bout of laziness, eg:

j'ai fait une pause de plusieurs heures pour cause de flemmingite aigüe I took a few hours' break due to an attack of laziness

SUFFIX

-ITÉ

• When added to adjectives, this suffix is used to create feminine nouns referring to the QUALITY expressed by the root word. In the majority of cases, its English equivalent is *-ity*, but note also the use of *-ness* in some examples below, eg:

féminité femininity; **masculinité** masculinity, manliness; **la laïcité** secularism; **la mixité** coeducational system (in schools); **la parité** parity, equality; **la francité** Frenchness; **la latinité** Latinity/the Latin world

• With the advent of all things electronic, a number of words have been coined or resurrected with a new meaning, often under the influence of English, eg:

jouabilité playability (of a computer game); **connectivité, connectabilité** connectivity, connectability; **fonctionnalités** functions, features (of a piece of software, a website etc)

which refer to national or racial identity, as did **négritude** (negritude, blackness), coined in the 1970s by L.S. Senghor, A. Césaire and other black writers. Those words sometimes have an equivalent in **-ité** with the same meaning, like **francité** (Frenchness). In both cases, the English equivalent is usually **-ness**, eg:

la francitude Frenchness; **l'anglitude** Englishness

item¹ [item] ADV *Com* ditto

item² [item] NM *Ling & Psy* item

itératif, -ive [iteratif, -iv] ADJ **1** *(répété)* repeated, reiterated, *Sout* iterated **2** *Ordinat & Ling* iterative

itération [iterasjɔ̃] NF **1** *(répétition)* iteration, repetition **2** *Typ & Ling* iteration

itérative [iterativ] *voir* **itératif**

Ithaque [itak] NF Ithaca

itinéraire [itinerɛr] NM **1** *(trajet)* itinerary, route; **i. bis** = alternative route recommended when roads are highly congested, especially at peak holiday times; **i. de dégagement** alternative route; **i. touristique** tourist route; **i. vert** nature trail **2** *(cheminement ▸ professionnel)* career, path; **i. politique** political career; **il a eu un i. sentimental mouvementé** his love life has had its ups and downs

itinérance [itinerɑ̃s] NF *Tél* roaming

itinérant, -e [itinerɑ̃, -ɑ̃t] ADJ *(main-d'œuvre)* itinerant, travelling; *(ambassadeur)* roving; *(comédien, exposition)* travelling; **camp i.** = children's holiday camp which moves between various locations

itinérer [18] [itinere] VI **1** *(se déplacer)* to travel from place to place **2** *Tél* to roam

itou [itu] ADV *Fam Vieilli* likewise, ditto; **et moi i.!** me too!

SUFFIX

-ITUDE

• This suffix is similar in meaning to **-ité**, in that it denotes a QUALITY or STATE, mostly based on an adjective but also sometimes on a Latin radical ending in **-i**, eg:

altitude altitude; **aptitude** ability, aptitude; **ingratitude** ingratitude, ungratefulness; **certitude** certainty

• One recent, colloquial word formed on this model is **branchitude**, ie all that is *branché* or trendy, eg:

un haut lieu de la branchitude parisienne one of the hippest hangouts in Paris; **Berlin, capitale de la branchitude** Berlin, capital of cool

• There is also a series of words in **-itude**

IUFM [iyɛfɛm] NM *(abrév* **Institut universitaire de formation des maîtres)** = teacher-training college

IUT [iyte] NM *(abrév* **Institut universitaire de technologie)** = institute of technology offering two-year vocational courses leading to the DUT qualification

IV [ive] ADJ *Méd (abrév* **intra-veineux)** IV

IVG [iveʒe] NF *Méd (abrév* **interruption volontaire de grossesse)** termination *(of pregnancy)*

ivoire [ivwar] NM **1** *(matière)* ivory *(UNCOUNT)*; **statuette d'i.** *ou* **en i.** ivory statuette **2** *(objet)* (piece of) ivory **3** *Bot* **i. végétal** vegetable ivory, ivory nut

• **d'ivoire** ADJ *Littéraire* **1** *(blanc)* ivory *(avant n)*, ivory-coloured **2** *(ayant l'aspect de l'ivoire)* ivory-like

ivoirien, -enne [ivwarjɛ̃, -ɛn] ADJ of/from the Ivory Coast

• **Ivoirien, -enne** NM,F = inhabitant of or person from the Ivory Coast

ivoirier, -ère [ivwarje, -ɛr] NM,F ivory sculptor

ivraie [ivrɛ] NF **1** *Bot* **i. vivace** rye grass **2** *(locution)* **séparer le bon grain de l'i.** to separate the wheat from the chaff

ivre [ivr] ADJ **1** *(saoul)* drunk, intoxicated; **i. mort** blind drunk **2** *Fig* **être i. de joie** to be deliriously happy; **i. de haine** blinded by hatred; **être i. de colère/bonheur** to be beside oneself with anger/happiness; **i. de fatigue** dead tired; **être i. de sang** to be thirsting for blood

ivresse [ivrɛs] NF **1** *(ébriété)* drunkenness, intoxication; **il était en état d'i.** he was drunk *or* intoxicated **2** *(excitation)* ecstasy, euphoria, exhilaration; **la vitesse procure un sentiment d'i.** speed is exhilarating; **emporté par l'i. des mots** *(poésie)* enraptured by these words; *(discours politique)* carried away by this heavy talk *or* rhetoric; **dans l'i. du moment** in the excitement of the moment **3** *Sport* **i. des profondeurs** (diver's) staggers

ivressomètre [ivrɛsɔmɛtr] NM *Can Br* breathalyser, *Am* Breathalyzer®

ivrogne [ivrɔɲ] NMF drunk, drunkard

ivrognerie [ivrɔɲri] NF drunkenness

ixième [iksjɛm] ADJ umpteenth, nth; **pour la i. fois** for the umpteenth time

j

J[1], j [ʒi] **NM INV** *(lettre)* J, j; **J comme Joseph** ≃ J for John

J[2] [ʒi] **NM** *(abrév* **jour***)* day; *Hist & Fig* **le jour J** D-day

J[3] *(abrév écrite* **joule***)* J

j' [ʒ] *voir* **je**

jabot [ʒabo] **NM 1** *Orn* crop **2** *(ornement)* ruffle, frill

jacasse [ʒakas] **NF** *Orn* magpie

jacassement [ʒakasmɑ̃] **NM** *(d'une pie, d'une personne)* chatter *(UNCOUNT)*; **leurs incessants jacassements** their constant chatter

jacasser [3] [ʒakase] **VI** *(pie, personne)* to chatter

jacasserie [ʒakasri] **NF** *Péj* chatter *(UNCOUNT)*; **leurs incessantes jacasseries** their constant chatter *or* prattle

jachère [ʒaʃɛr] **NF** fallow (land); **mettre la terre en j.** to let the land lie fallow; **rester en j.** to lie fallow; **laisser en j.** *(talent)* to leave undeveloped *or* untapped

jacinthe [ʒasɛ̃t] **NF** hyacinth; **j. sauvage** *ou* **des bois** bluebell, wild hyacinth

jack [dʒak] **NM 1** *Tél* jack **2** *Tex* jack (lever)

jackpot [dʒakpɔt] **NM 1** *(combinaison)* jackpot; *aussi Fig* **toucher le j.** to hit the jackpot **2** *(machine)* slot machine

jaco [ʒako] = **jacquot**

Jacob [ʒakɔb] **NPR** *Bible* Jacob

jacobin, -e [ʒakɔbɛ̃, -in] **ADJ 1** *Hist* Jacobin *(avant n)* **2** *Pol* radical, Jacobin *(avant n)* **3** *Rel* Dominican

NM,F Dominican

• **Jacobin NM** *Hist* Jacobin

jacobinisme [ʒakɔbinism] **NM** Jacobinism

jacobite [ʒakɔbit] **ADJ** Jacobite

NMF Jacobite

jacot [ʒako] = **jacquot**

jacquard [ʒakar] **NM 1** *(pull)* Jacquard sweater; *(tissu)* Jacquard weave **2** *Tex (machine)* Jacquard loom

ADJ pull j. Jacquard

jacquerie [ʒakri] **NF** peasants' revolt; *Hist* **la J.** the Jacquerie *(peasant uprising in Picardy against the nobility in May 1358)*

Jacques [ʒak] **NPR** *(roi d'Angleterre)* James; **saint J.** Saint James; **Maître J.** Jack-of-all-trades

NM 1 *Hist (rebelle)* = peasant taking part in "la Jacquerie" **2** *Vieilli (paysan)* peasant

jacquet [ʒake] **NM** *(jeu)* backgammon; *(tablette)* backgammon (board)

jacquot [ʒako] **NM** *Orn* African grey parrot

jactance [ʒaktɑ̃s] **NF 1** *très Fam (baratin)* chattering❑ **2** *Littéraire (infatuation)* conceit *(UNCOUNT)*, self-praise *(UNCOUNT)*, *Arch* vainglory *(UNCOUNT)*

jacter [3] [ʒakte] *très Fam* **VI** *(parler)* to chatter❑, *Br* to witter (on), to natter

Jacuzzi® [ʒakuzi] **NM** Jacuzzi®

jade [ʒad] **NM 1** *(matière)* jade; **bague de j.** jade ring **2** *(objet)* jade (object)

jadis [ʒadis] *Littéraire* **ADV** long ago, in bygone days; **il y avait j. un prince** once upon a time there was a prince; **la ville a conservé sa splendeur de j.** the town has kept its former splendour

ADJ au temps j. in days of old, in bygone days; **contes du temps j.** tales of long ago

jaguar [ʒagwar] **NM** *Zool* jaguar

jaillir [32] [ʒajir] **VI 1** *(personne, animal)* to spring *or* to shoot out; **il jaillit de derrière le mur** he sprang *or* leapt out from behind the wall; **ils jaillissaient de tous les coins de rue** they were pouring out of all the side streets **2** *(liquide, sang, source)* to spurt (out), to gush (forth), to spout; *(flamme)* to leap *or* to shoot up; *(larmes)* to gush, to start flowing; **la lumière d'un projecteur jaillit dans l'obscurité** a spotlight suddenly shone out in the darkness; **des étincelles jaillissaient du moteur** sparks were flying from the engine; *Fig* **les gratte-ciel jaillissent au-dessus de la ville** skyscrapers soar *or* tower above the city **3** *(surgir* ▸ *doute)* to spring up, to arise (suddenly); *(*▸ *rires)* to burst out *or* forth; **une pensée jaillit dans son esprit** a thought suddenly came into his/her mind; **des réponses jaillirent de tous côtés** there was a volley of replies

jaillissant, -e [ʒajisɑ̃, -ɑ̃t] **ADJ** *(liquide)* spurting, gushing; *(étincelles)* flying, shooting

jaillissement [ʒajismɑ̃] **NM** *(jet)* spurting *(UNCOUNT)*, gushing *(UNCOUNT)*; **un j. d'idées** an outpouring of ideas

jaïnisme [ʒainism] **NM** Jainism

jais [ʒɛ] **NM** *Minér* jet; **des perles de j.** jet beads; *Fig* **des yeux de j.** jet-black eyes

Jakarta [dʒakarta] = **Djakarta**

jalon [ʒalɔ̃] **NM 1** *(piquet)* marker **2** *(référence)* milestone, landmark; **cette décision est un j. dans l'histoire des relations est-ouest** this decision is a landmark *or* a watershed in East-West relations; *Fig* **poser les jalons d'un accord** to pave the way for *or* to prepare the ground for an agreement

jalonnement [ʒalɔnmɑ̃] **NM 1** *(de terrain)* marking *or* staking out **2** *Mil* marking

jalonner [3] [ʒalɔne] **VT 1** *(terrain)* to mark out *or* off **2** *(longer)* to line; **de charmants petits villages jalonnent le littoral** the coastline is dotted with lovely little villages; **la route est jalonnée de jolies maisons** the road is lined with pretty houses; **une carrière jalonnée de succès** a career punctuated by a series of successes **3** *Mil* to mark

jalouse [ʒaluz] *voir* **jaloux**

jalousement [ʒaluzmɑ̃] **ADV 1** *(avec jalousie)* jealously; **regarder qn j.** to watch sb jealously **2** *(soigneusement)* jealously; **un secret j. gardé** a closely *or* jealously guarded secret

jalouser [3] [ʒaluze] **VT** to be jealous of

jalousie [ʒaluzi] **NF 1** *(envie)* jealousy, envy; *(possessivité)* jealousy; **éprouver de la j. envers qn** to be *or* to feel jealous of sb **2** *(store)* venetian blind, jalousie

jaloux, -ouse [ʒalu, -uz] **ADJ 1** *(possessif)* jealous; **être j. de qn** to be jealous of sb; **j. comme un tigre** horribly jealous **2** *(envieux)* jealous, envious (**de** of); **elle est jalouse de moi parce que je pars en Italie** she's jealous (of me) because I'm off to Italy

NM,F jealous person; **faire des j.** to make people jealous *or* envious

jamaïcain, -e, jamaïquain, -e [ʒamaikɛ̃, -ɛn] **ADJ** Jamaican

• **Jamaïcain, -e, Jamaïquain, -e NM,F** Jamaican

Jamaïque [ʒamaik] **NF la J.** Jamaica

JAMAIS [ʒame] **ADV 1** *(sens négatif)* never; **il n'est j. trop tard** it's never too late; **il n'a j. su à quoi s'en tenir** he never knew where he stood; **il n'a j. fait aussi froid** it has never been this cold; **je suis heureuse comme j. je ne l'avais été** I'm happier than I have ever been; **il travaille sans j. s'arrêter** he works without ever stopping; *Fam* **j. tu dis bonjour?** don't you ever say hello?❑; **vous ne le verrez plus j.** you'll never (ever) see him again; **comme plus j.** *ou* **j. plus vous n'en reverrez** the like of which you'll never see again; **ah non! plus j. ça!** oh no, never again!; **j. je n'aurais pensé ça de lui** I would never have thought it of him; **j. (une) si grande émotion ne m'avait envahi** never before had I been so overcome with emotion; *Littéraire* **j. homme ne fut plus comblé** there was never a happier man; **n'as-tu j. aimé?** haven't you ever *or* have you never loved?; **la maison est très calme: j. un bruit** the house is very quiet: (there's) never a noise; **presque j.** hardly ever, almost never; **on ne le voit presque j.** we hardly ever see him; **une équipe j. vaincue** an undefeated team; **un rêve j. réalisé** an unfulfilled dream; **c'est du j. vu!** it's never happened before!, it's totally unheard of!; **c'est le moment ou j.!, c'est maintenant ou j.!** it's now or never!; **on ne sait j.!** you never know!, who knows?; **tu lui pardonneras? – j.!** will you forgive him/her? – never!; **vous prenez un petit verre, commissaire? – j. pendant le service!** you'll have a quick one, superintendent? – never while I'm on duty!; **j. deux sans trois** everything comes in threes, if it's happened twice, it'll happen a third time; **j. de la vie!** not on your life!; **j., au grand j.!** never in a month of Sundays!; **j., au grand j., je n'ai fait une telle promesse!** I never ever made such a promise!, I never made such a promise, never on your life!; **il ne faut j. dire j.** never say never

2 *(sens positif)* ever; **a-t-on j. vu pareille splendeur?** have you ever seen such splendour?; **si j'ai j. eu peur, c'est bien cette fois-là** if I was ever frightened, it was that time (then); **c'est à se demander si tu as j. appris à lire** it makes me wonder if you ever learnt to read; **je désespère de j. y arriver** I've lost all hope of ever succeeding; **si j. tu le rencontres, dis-lui de m'appeler** if ever you meet him, tell him to call me; **si j. vous venez** if ever you come, if you ever come; **si j. il revenait** if he ever came back, if ever he came back; **si j. il reste des places, tu en veux?** if by any chance there are tickets left, do you want any?; **si j. je t'y reprends!** if I ever catch you at it again!; **plus/moins/pire que j.** more/less/worse than ever; **on s'amuse plus que j.** we're having more fun than ever, we're enjoying ourselves more than ever; **il est moins que j. décidé à changer d'entreprise** he is less decided than ever about changing firms; **le seul/le plus beau que j'aie j. vu** the only one/the most beautiful I have ever seen

3 *(en corrélation avec "que")* **ce n'est j. qu'à 20 minutes à pied** it's only 20 minutes' walk; **ce n'est j. qu'un film** it's only a film (after all); **ce n'est j. qu'un homme (comme vous et moi)** he's only human (after all); **il n'a j. fait qu'obéir aux ordres** all he did was follow orders, he was only following orders; **elle n'a j. fait que se plaindre toute sa vie** she's done nothing *or* never done anything but complain all her life

• **à jamais** ADV for good, forever; **c'est fini à j.** it's finished for ever *or* for good; **ils se sont dit adieu à j.** they said goodbye forever; **des souvenirs à j. envolés** memories gone forever

• **à tout jamais** ADV forever, *Littéraire* for evermore; **il y a renoncé à tout j.** he has given it up forever *or Littéraire* for evermore; **je renonce à tout j. à connaître le fin mot de l'histoire** I've given up ever trying to get to the bottom of the matter; **nous avons à tout j. perdu l'espoir de le revoir** we have lost all hope of ever seeing him again

• **pour jamais** ADV forever; **il partit pour j.** he left forever *or* never to return

---

jambage [ʒɑ̃baʒ] NM **1** *(de porte, de fenêtre, de cheminée etc)* jamb **2** *(trait d'une lettre ▸ vers le bas)* downstroke; *(▸ vers le haut)* upstroke; *(▸ au-dessous de la ligne)* tail, descender

jambe [ʒɑ̃b] NF **1** *Anat* leg; **avoir de grandes** *ou* **longues jambes** to have long legs; **avoir les jambes nues** to be bare-legged; **elle est tout en jambes** she's all legs; **il a (encore) des jambes de vingt ans** he's still very spry; **j. artificielle/de bois** artificial/wooden leg; *Sport* **il a un bon jeu de jambes** his footwork is good; **je n'ai plus de** *ou* **je ne sens plus mes jambes** I'm totally exhausted, my legs have gone; **avoir dix kilomètres dans les jambes** to have walked ten kilometres; *Fam* **en avoir plein les jambes** to be *Br* knackered *or Am* beat; **il avait les jambes en coton** his legs were like jelly *or* cotton wool; **il est toujours dans mes jambes** *(enfant)* he's always under my feet *or* in my way; **ça me/lui fait une belle j.!** a fat lot of good that does me/him/her!; **la peur lui donnait des jambes** fear drove him/her on; **prendre ses jambes à son cou** to take to one's heels; **détaler** *ou* **s'enfuir à toutes jambes** to make a bolt for it; **se mettre en jambes** to warm up, to do a warm-up; *Fam* **tenir la j. à qn** to drone on (and on) at sb; **tirer dans les jambes à qn** to aim (a shot) at sb's legs; *Fig* to create (all sorts of) problems for sb; **traiter qn par-dessus la j.** to treat sb offhandedly; **un travail fait par-dessus la j.** sloppy *or* slipshod work; *très Fam* **une partie de jambes en l'air** a bit of nooky

2 *(de pantalon)* (trouser) leg

3 *(d'un compas)* leg

4 *Constr* prop; **j. de force** *(d'une poutre)* strut; *(d'un comble)* joist stay

5 *Aut* radius rod

jambier [ʒɑ̃bje] ADJ M leg *(avant n)*

NM **1** *Anat* leg muscle; **j. antérieur/postérieur** anterior/posterior leg muscle **2** *(à l'abattoir)* gambrel

• **jambière** NF *(de joueur)* (shin) pad

• **jambières** NFPL *(grandes chaussettes)* over-the-knee socks; *(sans pied, en laine)* legwarmers

jambon [ʒɑ̃bɔ̃] NM **1** *(viande)* ham; **j. de Bayonne** Bayonne ham; **j. blanc** boiled *or* cooked ham; **j. cru** cured ham; **j. fumé** salted/smoked ham; **j. de Paris** boiled *or* cooked ham; **j. de Parme** Parma ham; **j. de pays** cured ham; **j. salé** salted ham; **j. d'York** boiled ham on the bone; **un j. beurre** a ham sandwich *(in buttered baguette)*; **un j. fromage** a ham and cheese sandwich *(in buttered baguette)* **2** *Fam (cuisse)* thigh▫

jambonneau, -x [ʒɑ̃bɔno] NM *(petit jambon)* knuckle of ham

jamboree [ʒɑ̃bɔri] NM jamboree

janissaire [ʒanisɛr] NM janissary

jansénisme [ʒɑ̃senism] NM Jansenism

janséniste [ʒɑ̃senist] ADJ Jansenist

NMF Jansenist

jante [ʒɑ̃t] NF (wheel) rim; *Aut* **jantes en aluminium** (aluminium) alloy wheels; *Fam Fig* **rouler sur la j.** to be losing one's marbles

janvier [ʒɑ̃vje] NM January; *voir aussi* **mars**

Japon [ʒapɔ̃] NM **le J.** Japan

japonais, -e [ʒapɔnɛ, -ɛz] ADJ Japanese

NM *(langue)* Japanese

• **Japonais, -e** NM,F Japanese (person); **les J.** Japanese people, the Japanese

japonaiserie [ʒapɔnɛzri], **japonerie** [ʒapɔnri] NF Japanese curio *or* artefact

japonisant, -e [ʒapɔnizɑ̃, -ɑ̃t] NM,F specialist in Japanese studies

jappement [ʒapmɑ̃] NM yelp, yap; **des jappements** yelping *(UNCOUNT)*, yapping *(UNCOUNT)*

japper [3] [ʒape] VI *(chien)* to yelp, to yap

jaquette [ʒakɛt] NF **1** *(vêtement ▸ d'homme)* morning coat; *(▸ de femme)* jacket

2 *(de livre)* (dust) cover *or* jacket

3 *(couronne dentaire)* crown

4 *Can (chemise de nuit)* nightdress

5 *Suisse (en tricot)* cardigan

6 *très Fam* = offensive term used to refer to male homosexuals; **la j. (flottante)** *Br* poofs, *Am* fags; **être** *ou* **refiler de la j. (flottante)** to be one of them

jardin [ʒardɛ̃] NM *(terrain clos ▸ gén)* garden; *(▸ d'une maison)* garden, *Am* yard; **il est dans le** *ou* **au j.** he's in the garden; **les jardins du château de Windsor** the grounds of Windsor Castle; **j. d'acclimatation** zoological garden *or* gardens, zoo; **j. à l'anglaise** landscape garden; **j. botanique** botanical garden *or* gardens; **j. à la française** formal garden; **j. fruitier** orchard; **j. d'hiver** winter garden; **j. japonais** miniature (Japanese) garden; **j. maraîcher** market garden; *Bible* **le j. des Oliviers** the Garden of Gethsemane; **j. ouvrier** allotment; **j. paysager** landscaped garden; **j. potager** vegetable *or* kitchen garden; **j. public** park, public garden *or* gardens; **j. de rapport** market garden; **c'est mon j. secret** that's my little secret; **jardins suspendus** hanging gardens; **mobilier de j.** garden furniture; **le J. des Plantes** *(à Paris)* = botanical garden in Paris with a small zoo (la Ménagerie) and Natural History Museum

• **jardin d'enfants** NM kindergarten, playgroup, *Br* pre-school nursery

jardinage [ʒardinaʒ] NM gardening

• **de jardinage** ADJ *(outil, magasin)* gardening *(avant n)*, garden *(avant n)*

jardiner [3] [ʒardine] VI to garden; **j'aime j.** I like gardening; **elle est dehors en train de j.** she's out doing some gardening

jardinerie [ʒardinri] NF garden centre

jardinet [ʒardinɛ] NM small garden

jardinier, -ère [ʒardinje, -ɛr] ADJ *Hort* garden *(avant n)*

NM,F gardener

• **jardinière** NF **1** *(sur un balcon)* window box; *(pour fleurs coupées)* jardinière; *(meuble)* plant holder **2** *Culin* **jardinière (de légumes)** (diced) mixed vegetables, jardinière

• **jardinière d'enfants** NF nursery-school *or* kindergarten teacher

jargon [ʒargɔ̃] NM **1** *(langage incorrect)* jargon; *(langage incompréhensible)* jargon, mumbo jumbo **2** *(langue spécialisée)* jargon; **le j. administratif** officialese, official jargon; **le j. communautaire** Eurospeak; **le j. des journalistes** journalese; **le j. judiciaire** legalese, legal jargon

jargonner [3] [ʒargɔne] VI *(s'exprimer ▸ en jargon)* to talk (in) jargon; *(▸ de façon incompréhensible)* to talk gibberish

jargonneux, -euse [ʒargɔnø, -øz] ADJ *Péj* jargonish, full of jargon

Jarnac [ʒarnak] NPR **coup de J.** stab in the back

jarre [ʒar] NF (earthenware) jar

jarret [ʒarɛ] NM *Anat* back of the knee, ham; *Zool* hock; *Culin* **j. de veau** knuckle of veal, veal shank; **j. de bœuf** shin of beef; *Fam* **avoir des jarrets d'acier** *ou* **du j.** to have a good, sturdy pair of legs

jarretelle [ʒartɛl] NF *Br* suspender, *Am* garter

jarretière [ʒartjɛr] NF garter

jars [ʒar] NM *Zool* gander

jasant, -e [ʒazɑ̃, -ɑ̃t] ADJ *Can Fam (bavard)* chatty; *(cancanier)* gossipy

jase [ʒaz] = **jasette**

jaser [3] [ʒaze] VI **1** *(médire)* to gossip (**sur** about); **ça va faire j. dans le quartier** that'll set the neighbours' tongues wagging **2** *Fam (avouer)* **3** *(gazouiller ▸ pie, geai)* to chatter; *(▸ ruisseau, bébé)* to babble

jasette [ʒazɛt] NF *Can Fam* chat, conversation▫

jaseur, -euse [ʒazœr, -øz] NM,F *(bavard)* chatterbox; *(mauvaise langue)* gossip

ADJ *(personne ▸ qui bavarde)* chattering; *(▸ qui médit)* gossipy

NM *Orn* waxwing

jasmin [ʒasmɛ̃] NM jasmine

jaspe [ʒasp] NM **1** *Minér* jasper; **j. noir** touchstone; **j. sanguin** bloodstone **2** *(objet en jaspe)* jasper object

jasper [3] [ʒaspe] VT to marble, to mottle

jaspiner [3] [ʒaspine] VI *très Fam* to rattle on, to chatter away; **ça a fait j. toute l'école** it had *or* set the whole school talking

jaspure [ʒaspyr] NF marbling *(UNCOUNT)*, mottling *(UNCOUNT)*

jass [jas] NM *Suisse* = popular Swiss card game

JAT [ʒiate] ADJ *(abrév* **juste à temps***)* JIT

jatte [ʒat] NF **1** *(petite)* bowl; *(grande)* basin; **une j. de lait** a bowl of milk **2** *Belg (récipient)* coffee cup; *(contenu)* cup of coffee

jattée [ʒate] NF *(petite)* bowlful; *(grande)* basinful

jauge [ʒoʒ] NF **1** *(pour calibrer)* gauge; **j. d'épaisseur** thickness *or* feeler gauge **2** *(indicateur)* gauge; *Aut* **j. d'essence** *Br* petrol gauge, *Am* gas gauge; *Aut* **j. (de niveau) d'huile** *(sur le tableau de bord)* oil-level indicator; *(manuelle)* dipstick **3** *(contenance ▸ d'un réservoir)* capacity; *(tonnage)* tonnage, burden; **j. brute/nette** gross/net (registered) tonnage

jaugeage [ʒoʒaʒ] NM gauging, measuring; *Naut* measurement (of tonnage)

jauger [17] [ʒoʒe] VT **1** *(mesurer ▸ fil)* to gauge; *(▸ réservoir)* to gauge (the capacity of); *(▸ liquide)* to gauge (the volume of); *(▸ navire)* to measure the tonnage *or* burden of **2** *Littéraire (juger ▸ dégâts)* to assess; *(▸ personne)* to size up; *(▸ situation)* to size up, to weigh up

jaunâtre [ʒonatr] ADJ *(couleur)* yellowish, yellowy; *(teint)* yellowish, sallow

jaune [ʒon] ADJ yellow; **avoir le teint j.** to look yellow *or* sallow; **j. canari** canary yellow; **j. citron** lemon yellow; **j. moutarde** mustard-coloured; **j. d'or** golden yellow; **j. paille** straw-coloured; **j. comme un citron** *ou* **un coing** (as) yellow as a lemon

NMF *(non-gréviste)* strikebreaker

NM **1** *(couleur)* yellow; **elle aime s'habiller en j.** she likes to wear yellow **2** *Culin* **j. (d'œuf)** (egg) yolk **3** *Fam (apéritif anisé)* pastis▫

• **Jaune** NMF *très Fam Vieilli* Oriental, = offensive term used to refer to an Oriental person

jauni, -e [ʒoni] ADJ *(par le temps, le soleil etc)* yellowed

jaunir [32] [ʒonir] VT to turn yellow; **le soleil a jauni les pages** the sun has made the pages go *or* turn yellow

VI **1** *(devenir jaune)* to turn *or* to become yellow, to yellow **2** *(se défraîchir)* to fade

jaunissant, -e [ʒonisɑ̃, -ɑ̃t] ADJ yellowing; **blés jaunissants** ripening corn

jaunisse [ʒonis] NF *Méd* jaundice; **le bébé a la j.** the baby has jaundice; *Fam* **tu ne vas pas en faire une j.!** there's no need to get into a state *or* to get worked up about it!

jaunissement [ʒonismɑ̃] NM yellowing

Java [ʒava] NF Java

java [ʒava] NF **1** *(danse)* = type of popular waltz **2** *Fam (fête)* party▫, shindig, *Br* knees-up; **faire la j.** to party▫

javanais, -e [ʒavanɛ, -ɛz] ADJ Javanese

NM *Ling* **1** *(langue indonésienne)* Javanese **2** *(argot)* = slang using -av- or -ad- as an infix before each vowel sound **3** *Fam (langage incompréhensible)* **c'est du j.** that's gobbledegook

• **Javanais, -e** NM,F Javanese; **les J.** the Javanese

Javel [ʒavɛl] NF **de l'eau de J., de la J.** bleach

javeline [ʒavlin] NF javelin

javelle [ʒavɛl] NF swath

javellisation [ʒavelizasjɔ̃] NF *Chim* chlorination

javelliser [3] [ʒavelize] VT *Chim* to chlorinate

javelot [ʒavlo] NM javelin

jazz [dʒaz] NM jazz; **le j. classique** traditional *or* mainstream jazz

jazzman [dʒazman] (*pl* **jazzmans** *ou* **jazzmen** [dʒazmɛn]) **NM** jazzman, jazz player *or* musician

J.-C. (*abrév écrite* **Jésus-Christ**) J.C.; **en (l'an) 180 avant/après J.** in (the year) 180 BC/AD 180

je [ʒə]

> j' is used before a word beginning with a vowel or h mute.

PRON I; **j'y vais demain** I'm going there tomorrow; **puis-je me joindre à vous?** may I join you?; **que vois-je?** what do I see?; **puissé-je me tromper!** let us hope I am wrong!; *Fam* **et que je me fais un petit café...** (*pour commenter les actions d'autrui*) and there he/she was, chatting away, making coffee...

NM INV le je *Ling* the first person; *Phil* the self

Jean [ʒɑ̃] **NPR** *Bible* John

jean [dʒin] **NM 1** (*tissu*) **(toile de) j.** denim; **un blouson en j.** a denim jacket **2** (*pantalon*) (pair of) jeans

jean-foutre [ʒɑ̃futr] **NM INV** *très Fam* layabout, *Br* waster

Jeanne [ʒan] **NPR J. d'Arc** *ou* **la Pucelle** Joan of Arc; **elle est coiffée à la J. d'Arc** she wears her hair in a pageboy cut

jeannette [ʒanɛt] **NF 1** (*pour repasser*) sleeve-board

2 (*croix*) gold cross (*worn around the neck*); (*chaîne*) gold chain

3 (*scout*) *Br* Brownie, *Am* Girl Scout

4 (*plante*) **j. jaune** daffodil

Jeannot [ʒano] **NM** *Fam* **J. lapin** bunny (rabbit)

jeans [dʒins] = **jean 2**

Jeep® [dʒip] **NF** Jeep®

Jéhovah [ʒeɔva] **NPR** Jehovah; **les témoins de J.** the Jehovah's Witnesses

jéjunostomie [ʒeʒynɔstɔmi] **NF** *Méd* jejunostomy

jéjunum [ʒeʒynɔm] **NM** *Anat* jejunum

je-m'en-fichisme [ʒmɑ̃fiʃism] (*pl* **je-m'en-fichismes**) **NM** *Fam* couldn't-care-less attitude; **faire preuve de j.** to show one couldn't care less

je-m'en-fichiste [ʒmɑ̃fiʃist] (*pl* **je-m'en-fichistes**) *Fam* **ADJ** couldn't-care-less (*avant n*)

NMF couldn't-care-less type

je-m'en-foutisme [ʒmɑ̃futism] (*pl* **je-m'en-foutismes**) **NM** *Fam* couldn't-care-less attitude; **regarde comment il a écrit ça, c'est vraiment du j.!** look how he's written that, he really couldn't give a damn

je-m'en-foutiste [ʒmɑ̃futist] (*pl* **je-m'en-foutistes**) *Fam* **ADJ** couldn't-care-less (*avant n*)

NMF couldn't-care-less type

je-ne-sais-quoi [ʒənsekwa] **NM INV un j.** a certain je ne sais quoi, a certain something; **un j. de qch** a hint of sth

jennérien, -enne [ʒenerjɛ̃, -ɛn] **ADJ** Jennerian

jenny [dʒeni] **NF** *Tex* spinning jenny

jérémiades [ʒeremjad] **NFPL** (*lamentations*) wailing; **assez de j.!** stop moaning *or* complaining!

Jérémie [ʒeremi] **NPR** *Bible* Jeremiah

jerez [gzerɛs] = **xérès**

Jéricho [ʒeriko] **NM** Jericho

jerk [dʒɛrk] **NM** (*danse*) jerk

jéroboam [ʒerɔbɔam] **NM** jeroboam

jerrican(e), jerrycan [ʒerikan] **NM** jerrycan

Jersey [ʒɛrzɛ] **NF** Jersey

jersey [ʒɛrzɛ] **NM** (*tissu*) jersey, jersey knit; **j. de laine** wool jersey

jersiais, -e [ʒɛrzjɛ, -ɛz] **ADJ** of/from Jersey; **vache jersiaise** Jersey (cow)

• **Jersiais, -e NM,F** = inhabitant of or person from Jersey

• **jersiaise NF** Jersey (cow)

Jérusalem [ʒeryzalɛm] **NF** Jerusalem; **la J. céleste** the New Jerusalem

jésuite [ʒezɥit] **ADJ 1** *Rel* Jesuit **2** *Péj* (*hypocrite*) jesuitical

NMF *Péj* (*hypocrite*) Jesuit, casuist; **agir en vrai j.** to be as crafty as a Jesuit

NM *Rel* Jesuit; **les jésuites** the Jesuits

jésuitique [ʒezɥitik] **ADJ 1** *Rel* Jesuit **2** *Péj* (*hypocrite*) jesuitical, casuistic

jésuitisme [ʒezɥitism] **NM 1** (*système moral*) Jesuitism **2** *Péj* (*hypocrisie*) casuistry, jesuitry

Jésus [ʒezy] **NPR** Jesus; **le petit J.** baby Jesus; **(doux) J.!, J. Marie!** sweet Jesus!

jésus [ʒezy] **NM 1** (*représentation*) (figure of the) infant Jesus **2** *Culin* pork liver sausage (*from Franche-Comté and Switzerland*); **j. de Lyon** ≃ pork salami **3** *Typ* **grand j.** ≃ imperial; **petit j.** ≃ super royal

Jésus-Christ [ʒezykri] **NPR** Jesus Christ; **en (l'an) 180 avant/après J.** in (the year) 180 BC/AD 180

jet¹ [dʒɛt] **NM** *Aviat* jet (plane)

jet² [ʒɛ] **NM 1** (*embout*) nozzle; (*lance* ▸ *de pompier*) nozzle, fire (hose); (▸ *de jardinier*) (garden) hose; **laver** *ou* **passer qch au j.** to hose sth down

2 (*jaillissement* ▸ *de flammes, de sang*) spurt, jet; (▸ *d'eau, de vapeur*) jet, gush; (▸ *de gaz*) gush; **un j. de salive** a jet of saliva

3 (*lancer* ▸ *de cailloux, d'une balle etc*) throwing (*UNCOUNT*); **des jets de pierres** stone-throwing; **à un j. de pierre** a stone's throw away

4 *Sport* throw

5 (*ébauche*) **premier j.** (*d'un tableau, d'un dessin*) first *or* rough sketch; (*d'une œuvre littéraire*) first *or* rough draft

6 *Aviat* jet

7 *Métal* (*coulage*) cast, casting

8 *Belg* (*pousse*) **j. de pomme de terre** eye; **j. de soja** (soya) bean sprouts

• **à jet continu ADV** non-stop, without a break

• **d'un (seul) jet ADV** *Métal* in one piece; *Fig* in one go; **elle nous raconta tout d'un seul j.** she told us everything in one go *or* breath

• **jet d'eau NM** (*filet d'eau*) fountain, spray; (*mécanisme*) fountain

jetable [ʒətabl] **ADJ** (*couche, briquet, gobelet etc*) disposable

jeté¹ [ʒəte] **NM 1** (*danse*) jeté

2 *Sport* jerk

3 (*maille*) **j. (simple), 1 j.** make 1

4 (*couverture*) **j. de lit** bedspread; **j. de table** table runner

jeté², **-e**¹ [ʒəte] **ADJ** *Fam* crazy, nuts

jetée² [ʒəte] **NF 1** (*en bord de mer*) pier, jetty **2** (*dans une aérogare*) passageway

JETER [27] [ʒəte]

VT	
• to throw **1, 2, 6**	• to cast **1, 3, 10**
• to throw out **3, 7**	• to give out **3**
• to jot down **5**	• to lay **9**
VPR	
• to throw oneself **2, 4**	• to rush **3**
• to run **5**	

VT 1 (*lancer* ▸ *balle, pierre*) to throw; (▸ *filets, dés*) to cast; **elle m'a jeté la balle** she threw me the ball, she threw the ball to me; **j. qch par terre** to throw sth on the ground; **ne jetez pas de papiers par terre** don't drop litter; **il a jeté le ballon par-dessus le mur** he threw the ball over the wall; **il a jeté son hochet** he threw down his rattle; **elle lui a jeté sa lettre à la figure** she threw the letter in his/her face; *Fig* **j. l'éponge** to throw in the sponge *or* towel; *Fam* **n'en jetez plus (la cour est pleine)!** you're making me blush!, don't overdo it!; *Ironique* give it a rest!

2 (*avec un mouvement du corps*) to throw; **l'enfant jeta ses bras autour de mon cou** the child threw *or* flung his/her arms around my neck; **j. la tête/les épaules en arrière** to throw one's head/one's shoulders back; **j. la jambe en l'air** to kick one's leg up; **j. un (coup d')œil sur** *ou* **à qch** to cast a glance *or* to have a (quick) look at sth; **jette un œil sur les enfants** have a quick look *or* check to see if the children are all right; **j. les yeux** *ou* **un regard sur qn/qch** to glance at sb/sth

3 (*émettre* ▸ *étincelle*) to throw *or* to give out; (▸ *lumière*) to cast, to shed; (▸ *ombre*) to cast; (▸ *son*) to let *or* to give out; **j. un cri** to let out *or* to utter a cry; *Fam* **elle en jette, ta moto!** that's some *or Am* a neat bike you've got there!; *Fam* **elle en jetait dans sa robe de satin noir!** she looked really something in her black satin dress!

4 (*dire brusquement*) **"venez!", me jeta-t-elle de son bureau** "come here!" she called out to me from her office; **elle leur jeta à la figure qu'ils étaient des incapables** she told them straight (to their faces) that they were incompetent; **j. des injures à la tête de qn** to hurl *or* to fling insults at sb; **il nous jeta quelques ordres secs** he barked out a few orders at us

5 (*écrire rapidement*) to jot down, to scribble (down); **elle jeta quelques remarques sur le papier** she scribbled down a few notes

6 (*mettre*) to throw; **j. qn dehors** *ou* **à la porte** to throw sb out; **j. qn à terre** to throw sb down *or* to the ground; **j. qn en prison** to throw sb into jail *or* prison; **j. qn à la rue** to throw sb out into the street; **j. qn à l'eau** (*à la piscine, sur la plage*) to throw sb in *or* into the water; (*d'un bateau*) to throw sb overboard; **il a jeté sa voiture contre un mur** he ran his car into a wall; **j. une lettre à la boîte** to drop *or* to pop a letter into the postbox; **j. un châle sur ses épaules** to throw on a shawl; **j. bas** to throw *or* to cast *or* to hurl down; **la statue du dictateur a été jetée bas** the dictator's statue was hurled to the ground; *Fig* **ils ont jeté bas les idoles** they threw down their idols

7 (*mettre au rebut* ▸ *ordures, vêtements*) to throw away *or* out; **j. qch à la poubelle** to throw sth into the *Br* dustbin *or Am* trashcan; **j. qch au feu** to throw sth into *or* on the fire; **il jeta la boulette de papier dans les flammes** he threw *or* tossed the crumpled piece of paper into the fire; **jette l'eau dans le caniveau** pour the water (out) into the gutter; **il n'y a rien à j. dans ce livre** this book's as good as you'll get; **c'est bon à j.** it's fit for the *Br* dustbin *or Am* trashcan; *Fig* **j. le bébé avec l'eau du bain** to throw the baby out with the bathwater

8 (*plonger*) **j. qn dans l'embarras** to throw *or* to plunge sb into confusion; **j. qn dans le désarroi** to plunge sb into despair; **j. qn dans de terribles fureurs** to drive sb into paroxysms of anger

9 (*établir* ▸ *fondations*) to lay; (▸ *passerelle*) to set up; (▸ *pont*) to throw; **j. les fondements d'une loi/politique** to lay the foundations of a law/policy; **le traité jette les bases de la nouvelle Europe** the treaty lays the foundations for the new Europe

10 (*répandre* ▸ *doute*) to cast; **cela a jeté la consternation dans la famille** it filled the whole family with dismay; **j. le discrédit sur qn/qch** to discredit sb/sth, to bring sb/sth into disrepute; **j. le doute dans les esprits** to sow *or* to cast doubt in people's minds

11 *Fam* (*expulser*) **se faire j.** to get kicked out; **on a essayé d'aller en boîte mais on s'est fait j. par un videur** we tried to get into a nightclub but the bouncer kicked us out; **il s'est fait j. par sa copine** he's been dumped by his girlfriend

VI 1 *Belg* (*graine*) to germinate; (*bulbe, tubercule*) to shoot, to sprout

2 *Fam* **ça jette!** it looks fantastic!

VPR se jeter 1 (*être jetable*) **un rasoir qui se jette** a disposable razor

2 (*sauter*) to throw *or* to hurl oneself, to leap; **se j. à bas de son cheval** to leap from one's horse; **se j. dans le vide** to throw oneself into the void; **se j. par la fenêtre** to throw oneself out of the window; **un homme s'est jeté sous la rame** a man threw himself *or* hurled himself in front of the train; **se j. de côté** to leap aside, to take a sideways leap; **se j. à l'eau** to leap into the water; *Fig* to take the plunge; **jette-toi à l'eau, propose-lui le mariage** go on, take the plunge and ask him/her to marry you

3 (*se précipiter*) to rush (headlong); **se j. aux pieds de qn** to throw oneself at sb's feet; **se j. dans la foule** to plunge into the crowd; **se j. sur qn** to set about *or* to pounce on sb; **les chiens se sont jetés sur la viande** the dogs devoured the meat; **ne vous jetez pas sur les biscuits!** don't eat the biscuits all at once!; **elle se jeta sur son lit** she threw herself on (to) her bed; **le canot s'est jeté dans les rapides** the canoe plunged into the rapids; **elle se jeta dans un taxi** she leapt into a taxi; **elles se jetèrent sous le premier porche venu** they scurried *or* rushed into the nearest doorway; **vous vous êtes tous jetés sur la question B** you all went for question B; **se j. à la tête de qn** to throw oneself at sb

4 (*entreprendre*) **se j. dans qch** to throw *or* to fling oneself into sth; **se j. à corps perdu dans une**

aventure to fling oneself body and soul into an adventure

5 *(cours d'eau)* **se j. dans** to run *or* to flow into

6 *très Fam (locution)* **s'en j. un (derrière la cravate)** to have a quick drink *or* a quick one; **on s'en jette un dernier?** let's have one for the road!

jeteur, -euse [ʒətœr, -øz] **NM,F j. de sort** wizard, *f* witch

jeton [ʒətɔ̃] **NM 1** *(pièce)* token; **j. de téléphone** token for the telephone

2 *(au jeu)* counter; *(à la roulette)* chip, counter

3 *(dans une entreprise)* **j. (de présence)** director's fees; **il n'est là que pour toucher ses jetons** he's just a timeserver, all he does is draw his salary

4 *très Fam (coup de poing)* whack; **(se) prendre un j.** to get a whack in the face

• **jetons NMPL** *très Fam* **avoir les jetons** to be scared stiff; **foutre les jetons à qn** to give sb the willies, *Br* to put the wind up sb

jet-set [dʒɛtsɛt] *(pl* **jet-sets)** **NF OU NM** jet set; **membre de la j.** jet-setter

jet-ski [dʒɛtski] *(pl* **jet-skis)** **NF** jet ski; **faire du j.** to go jet-skiing

jet society [dʒɛtsɔsajti] **NF = jet-set**

jet-stream [dʒɛtstrim] *(pl* **jet-streams)** **NM** *Météo* jet stream

jette *etc voir* **jeter**

JEU, -X [ʒø]

- game **1, 4–6, 8**
- set **3**
- acting **9**
- hand **2**
- play **5, 11, 13**
- gambling **10**

NM 1 *(gén)* game; **le j.** *(activité)* play; **ce n'est qu'un j.!** it's only a game!; **c'est le j.!** it's fair (play)!; **ce n'est pas de** *ou* **du j.!** that's not fair!; **le j. d'échecs** the game of chess; **l'enfant s'exprime par le j.** a child expresses himself/herself through play; **par j.** for fun, in play; **j. d'adresse** game of skill; **j. éducatif** educational game; **j. électronique** computer game; **j. de hasard** game of chance; **j. interactif** interactive game; **j. de l'oie** ≃ snakes and ladders; **j. de plein air** outdoor game; **j. radiophonique** (radio) game show; *(avec questions)* (radio) quiz (show); **j. de rôle** role playing; **jeux de société** *(charades, devinettes)* parlour games; *(petits chevaux, jeu de l'oie)* board games; **j. télévisé** game show; *(avec questions)* (television) quiz (show); **j. vidéo** video game; **c'est un j. d'enfant!** this is child's play!; **se faire un j. de faire qch** to make light *or* easy work of doing sth; **jeux de mains, jeux de vilains** all this fooling around is going to end in tears

2 *(cartes)* hand; **avoir du j.** *ou* **un bon j.** to have a good hand; **ne pas avoir de j., avoir un mauvais j.** to have a bad hand; **il avait tout le j.** he had all the good cards; **elle nous a joué** *ou* **sorti le grand j.** she pulled out all the stops with *or* on us; **avoir beau j. (de faire qch)** to have no trouble (in doing sth), to find it easy (to do sth); **il a eu beau j. de montrer qu'elle avait tort** it was easy for him to prove her wrong; *Fig* **montrer** *ou* **dévoiler son j.** to show one's hand; *Fig* **il a bien caché son j.** he played (his cards) very close to his chest

3 *(ensemble de pièces)* set; **j. de (32/52) cartes** *Br* pack *or Am* deck of (32/52) cards; **un j. de dames/d'échecs** a draughts/chess set; **un j. de clés/tournevis** a set of keys/screwdrivers; *Ordinat* **j. de fiches** card index; *Mus* **j. d'orgue** organ stop

4 *(manigances)* game; **qu'est-ce que c'est que ce petit j.?, à quel j. joues-tu?** *(ton irrité)* what are you playing at?, what's your game?; **entrer dans le j. de qn** to go along with sb; **faire le j. de qn** to play into sb's hands; **se (laisser) prendre au j.** to get caught up *or* involved in what's going on; **voir clair** *ou* **lire dans le j. de qn** to see through sb's little game, to see what sb is up to

5 *(activité sportive, partie)* game; *(action)* play; **les jeux d'équipe** team games; **le j. à XIII** rugby league; **où en est le j.?** what's the score?; **notre équipe a fait tout le j.** our team had the upper hand; **faire j. égal** to be evenly matched; **il a fait j. égal avec le champion** the champion met his match in him

6 *(au tennis)* game; **j., set et match** game, set and match

7 *(terrain)* **la balle est sortie du j.** the ball has gone out (of play); **j. de boules** *(sur gazon)* bowling green; *(de pétanque)* ground *(for playing boules)*; **j. de quilles** skittle alley

8 *(style d'un sportif)* game, way of playing; **elle a un j. de fond de court** she's got a base line game; **il a un bon j. de volée** he's a good volleyer, he volleys well

9 *(interprétation ▸ d'un acteur)* acting; *(▸ d'un musicien)* playing; **la pièce exige un j. tout en nuances** the play requires subtle acting

10 *(activité du parieur)* **le j.** gambling; **elle a tout perdu au j.** she gambled her entire fortune away; **j. de Bourse** gambling on the Stock Exchange, Stock Exchange speculation

11 *(effets)* play; **j. d'eau** fountain; **j. de jambes** *(d'un boxeur, d'un joueur de tennis)* footwork; **jeux de lumière** *(naturels)* play of light; *(artificiels)* lighting effects; **j. de mots** play on words, pun; **j. d'ombres** play of shadows

12 *(espace)* **la vis a** *ou* **prend du j.** the screw is loose; **il y a du j.** there's a bit of play *or* of a gap; **donner du j. à qch** to loosen sth up; *Fig* **donner** *ou* **laisser du j. à qn** to allow sb (some) freedom *or* leeway

13 *(action)* play; **le j. du piston dans le cylindre** the action of the piston inside the cylinder; *Littéraire* **le j. des vagues sur les rochers** the play of waves on the rocks; **c'est un j. de ton imagination/ta mémoire** it's a trick of your imagination/your memory; **laisser faire le j. de la concurrence** to allow the free play of competition; **le marché s'est agrandi grâce au j. de forces économiques nouvelles** the market has expanded because new economic forces have come into play

14 *Compta* **j. d'écritures** paper transaction; **par un j. d'écritures** by some creative accounting

15 *Littérature* = tragedy or comedy in verse, performed during the Middle Ages

• **jeux NMPL 1** *(mise)* **faites vos jeux (, rien ne va plus)** place your bets, faites vos jeux (rien ne va plus); **les jeux sont faits** no more bets, les jeux sont faits; *Fig* the die is cast, there's no going back now **2** *Sport* **les Jeux, les jeux Olympiques** the Olympic Games, the Olympics; **les jeux Olympiques pour handicapés, les jeux Paralympiques** the Paralympics

• **en jeu ADJ** at stake; **l'avenir de l'entreprise n'est pas en j.** the company's future is not at stake *or* at risk; **les forces en j. sur le marché** the competing forces *or* the forces at work on the market; **les intérêts en j.** the interests at stake *or* at issue *or* involved **ADV 1** *Ftbl* **mettre le ballon en j.** to throw in the ball **2** *(en pariant)* **mettre une somme en j.** to place a bet; **mettre qch en j.** *(risquer qch)* to put sth at stake; **mettre son avenir en j.** to put one's future at stake, to stake one's future; **entrer en j.** *(intervenir)* to come into play; **les institutions religieuses sont entrées en j. pour s'opposer à l'avortement** the religious institutions entered the fray to oppose abortion

• **jeu de massacre NM** Aunt Sally; *Fig* **le débat s'est transformé en j. de massacre** the debate turned into a slanging match

jeu-concours [ʒøkɔ̃kur] *(pl* **jeux-concours)** **NM** competition

jeudi [ʒødi] **NM** Thursday; **le J. noir** Black Thursday *(day of the Wall Street Crash, 1929)*; **le J. saint** Holy Thursday, *Br* Maundy Thursday; *Fam* **la semaine des quatre jeudis,** *Can* **dans la semaine des trois jeudis** never in a month of Sundays; *voir aussi* **mardi**

jeun [ʒœ̃] **à jeun ADJ il est à j.** *(il n'a rien mangé)* he hasn't eaten anything; *(il n'a rien bu)* he's sober

ADV on an empty stomach; **venez à j.** don't eat anything before you come; **trois comprimés à j.** three tablets to be taken on an empty stomach

JEUNE [ʒœn]

ADJ
- young **1, 4, 5–7**
- early **4**
- youthful **5**
- younger **2**
- young-looking **5**
- new **6, 7**

NM
- young man

NF
- young girl

ADJ 1 *(peu avancé en âge ▸ personne, génération, population)* young; **mourir j.** to die young; **il n'est plus très j.** he's not that young any more; **j. arbre** sapling, young tree; **un j. homme** a young man, a youth; **eh bien, j. homme, où vous croyez-vous?** I say, young man, where do you think you are?; **une j. femme** a young woman; **un j. garçon** *(enfant)* a boy, a youngster; *(adolescent)* a youth, a teenager; **une j. fille** a girl, a young woman; **j. oiseau** fledgling, young bird; **j. fille au pair** au pair (girl); **j. personne** young lady; **jeunes gens** *(garçons)* young men; *(garçons et filles)* youngsters, young people; **un j. Français/Anglais** a French/an English boy; **une j. Indienne** an Indian girl; **être plus/moins j. que** to be younger/older than; **je suis plus j. que lui de deux mois** I'm two months younger than him; **ils font j.** *ou* **jeunes** they look young; **faire** *ou* **paraître plus j. que son âge** to look younger than one's years *or* one is; *Fam* **c'est j., ça ne sait pas!** he's/she's (still) young *or* wet behind the ears, he'll/she'll learn!

2 *(en comparaison)* younger; **mon j. frère** my younger brother

3 *(débutant)* **être j. dans le métier** to be new to the trade *or* business

4 *(du début de la vie)* young, early; **mes jeunes années** my youth; **étant donné son j. âge** given his/her youth *or* how young he/she is; *Fam* **dans mon j. temps** when I was a youngster[□]

5 *(d'aspect ▸ personne)* young, young-looking, youthful; *(▸ apparence, allure)* youthful; *(▸ couleur, coiffure)* young, youthful; **pour avoir l'air toujours j., pour rester j.** to stay young *or* young-looking; **être j. d'esprit** *ou* **de caractère** to be young at heart; **être j. d'allure** to be youthful-looking

6 *(récent ▸ discipline, entreprise, État)* new, young; **les jeunes États d'Afrique** the new *or* young African States

7 *(vin)* young, new; *(fromage)* young

8 *Fam (juste)* **ça fait** *ou* **c'est un peu j.!** *(somme d'argent)* that's a bit mean!; *(temps)* that's cutting it a bit fine!; *(dimensions)* that's a bit on the small side!; *(poids)* that's a bit on the light side!; **c'est un peu j. comme argument** it's a bit of a flimsy argument

ADV *(comme les jeunes)* **s'habiller j.** to wear young-looking clothes; **se coiffer j.** to wear one's hair in a youthful style

NM *(garçon)* young man, youngster; *Fam* **petit j.** young guy

NF *(fille)* (young) girl; *Fam* **petite j.** young girl[□]

• **jeunes NMPL** *(garçons et filles)* **les jeunes** youngsters, young people, the young; **les jeunes d'aujourd'hui** young people today, the youth of today

jeûne [ʒøn] **NM 1** *(période)* fast; **le j. du ramadan** the fasting at Ramadan **2** *(pratique)* fast, fasting *(UNCOUNT)*; **observer une semaine de j.** to fast for a week

jeûner [3] [ʒøne] **VI 1** *Rel* to fast **2** *(ne rien manger)* to go without food

jeunesse [ʒœnɛs] **NF 1** *(juvénilité ▸ d'une personne)* youth, youthfulness; *(▸ d'une génération, d'une population)* youthfulness, young age; *(▸ d'un arbre, d'un animal)* young age; **elle m'a rendu ma j.** she made me feel young again; **j'apprécie la j. d'esprit** I appreciate a youthful outlook *or* frame of mind; **l'important c'est d'avoir la j. du cœur** what matters is to remain young at heart

2 *(enfance ▸ d'une personne)* youth; *(▸ d'une science)* early period, infancy; **dans ma** *ou* **au temps de ma j.** in my youth, when I was young; **la génétique est encore dans sa j.** genetics is still in its infancy; **il n'est plus de la première j.** *(personne)* he's not as young as he was, he's getting on a bit; *(objet)* it's seen better days; *Prov* **il faut que j. se passe** youth will have its fling

3 *(jeunes gens)* **la j.** young people, the young; **émissions pour la j.** *TV* programmes for young viewers; *Rad* programmes for young listeners; **la j. dorée** bright young things, gilded youth; *Prov* **si j. savait, si vieillesse pouvait** if youth but knew and age but could

4 *Vieilli (jeune fille)* (young) girl; **ce n'est plus une j.** she's no longer young

5 *Can Fam (jeune personne)* young person[□]

6 *(d'un vin)* youthfulness, greenness

7 *(groupe)* **J. agricole chrétienne** = Christian youth organization; **J. communiste révolutionnaire** = Communist youth movement

• **jeunesses** NFPL *(groupe)* youth; **les jeunesses hitlériennes** the Hitler Youth; **les jeunesses communistes/socialistes** Young Communists/Socialists

• **de jeunesse** ADJ **ses amours/œuvres/péchés de j.** the loves/works/sins of his/her youth

jeunet, -ette [ʒœnɛ, -ɛt] ADJ youngish, rather young; **elle est un peu jeunette pour faire ce travail** she's a bit on the young side to do this job

jeûneur, -euse [ʒønœr, -øz] NM,F faster

jeunot, -otte [ʒœno, -ɔt] ADJ youngish, rather young

NM,F youngster; **un petit j.** a young lad

JF, jf 1 *(abrév écrite* **jeune fille***)* girl 2 *(abrév écrite* **jeune femme***)* young woman

JH, jh *(abrév écrite* **jeune homme***)* young man

jihadiste [dʒiadist] NM jihadi

jingle [dʒingœl] NM jingle

jinisme [ʒinizm] = **jaïnisme**

jiu-jitsu [ʒjyʒitsy] NM ju-jitsu, jiu-jitsu

JJ [ʒiʒi] *Bourse (abrév* **au jour le jour***)* overnight

JO [ʒio] NM *Admin (abrév* **Journal Officiel***)* = French government publication giving information to the public about new laws, parliamentary debates, government business and new companies, *Am* ≃ Federal Register; *voir aussi l'encadré sous* **journal**

NMPL *(abrév* **jeux Olympiques***)* Olympic Games

joaillerie [ʒɔajri] NF 1 *(art)* **la j.** jewelling; **la j. du XVème siècle** the art of the jeweller in the 15th century

2 *(commerce)* **la j.** the jewel trade, jewellery

3 *(magasin) Br* jeweller's shop, *Am* jeweler's store

4 *(articles)* **la j.** jewellery

joaillier, -ère [ʒɔaje, -ɛr] ADJ jewel *(avant n)*

NM,F jeweller

Job [ʒɔb] NPR *Bible* Job; **pauvre comme J.** as poor as Job, as poor as a church mouse

job [dʒɔb] NM *Fam (emploi)* job□

NF *Can Joual (travail)* job□; **il a fait une bonne j. sur sa maison** he's done a good job on his house

jobard, -e [ʒɔbar, -ard] *Fam* ADJ *(très naïf)* gullible, naive□

NM,F sucker, *Br* mug

jobarderie [ʒɔbardri], **jobardise** [ʒɔbardiz] NF *Fam (crédulité)* gullibility, naivety□

jobine [jɔbin], **jobinette** [jɔbinet] NF *Can Fam* casual job□; **faire des jobines** to do odd jobs *or* casual work□

jobiste [ʒɔbist] NMF *Belg Fam* student with a casual job□

JOC, Joc [ʒiose] NF *(abrév* **Jeunesse ouvrière chrétienne***)* = Christian youth organization

jockey [ʒɔkɛ] NM jockey

Joconde [ʒɔkɔ̃d] NF **la J.** the Mona Lisa

jodler [3] [jɔdle] VI to yodel

joggeur, -euse [dʒɔgœr, -øz] NM,F jogger

jogging [dʒɔgiŋ] NM 1 *(activité)* jogging; *(course)* run; **faire du j.** to go jogging, to jog; **faire son j. matinal** to go for one's morning jog 2 *(survêtement)* tracksuit

Johannesburg [ʒɔanɛsbur] NM Johannesburg

joice [ʒwas] *très Fam* = **jouasse**

joie [ʒwa] NF 1 *(bonheur)* joy, delight; **être fou de j.** to be wild with joy; **elle ne se sentait plus de j.** she was beside herself with joy; **sauter** *ou* **bondir de j.** to jump *or* to leap for joy; **être au comble de la j.** to be overjoyed; **travailler dans la j. et la bonne humeur** to work cheerfully and good-humouredly; **pour la plus grande j. de ses parents, elle a obtenu la bourse** much to the delight of her parents *or* to her parent's great delight, she won the scholarship; **j. de vivre** joie de vivre, enjoyment of life; *Fam* **c'est pas la j. à la maison** life at home isn't much fun 2 *(plaisir)* pleasure; **avec j.!** with great pleasure!; **nous avons la j. d'avoir M. Dupont parmi nous** we have the pleasure of having Mr Dupont with us; **nous avons la j. de vous annoncer la naissance de Charles** we are delighted to announce the birth of Charles; **quand vais-je avoir la j. de faire sa connaissance?** when will I have the pleasure of making his/her acquaintance?; **je suis tout à la j. de revoir mes amis** I'm overjoyed at the idea of seeing my friends again; **des films qui ont fait la j. de millions d'enfants** films which have given pleasure to *or* delighted millions of children; **la petite Émilie fait la j. de sa mère** little Émilie is the apple of her mother's eye *or* is her mother's pride and joy; **il se faisait une telle j. de venir à ton mariage** he was so delighted at the idea of *or* so looking forward to coming to your wedding; **cette nouvelle l'a mis en j.** he is delighted by the news; **tu m'as fait une fausse j.** you got me all excited for nothing; **ne me fais pas de fausse j.** don't build up my hopes

• **joies** NFPL *(plaisirs)* joys; **les joies de la vie/retraite** the joys of life/retirement

joignable [ʒwaɲabl] ADJ **je suis j. à ce numéro** I can be reached at this number

JOINDRE [82] [ʒwɛ̃dr]

> VT
> • to join **1** • to put together **2**
> • to link **3, 5** • to add **4**
> • to enclose **4** • to attach **4**
> • to combine **5** • to contact **6**
>
> VPR
> • to get through to each other **1** • to make contact **1**
> • to join **3**

VT 1 *(attacher ▸ ficelles, tuyaux)* to join (together); *(▸ câbles)* to join, to connect; *Fig* **j. les deux bouts** to make ends meet

2 *(rapprocher)* to put *or* to bring together; **j. les mains** *(pour prier)* to put one's hands together

3 *(points, lieux)* to link

4 *(ajouter)* to add (**à** to); *(dans une lettre, un colis)* to enclose (**à** with); *Ordinat (à un courrier électronique)* to attach (**à** to); **veuillez j. CV et photo d'identité** please enclose *or* attach a copy of your *Br* CV *or Am* résumé and a photograph; **l'échantillon joint à votre lettre** the sample enclosed with your letter; **je joins à ce pli un chèque de 300 euros** please find enclosed a cheque for 300 euros; **voulez-vous j. une carte aux fleurs?** would you like to send a card with the flowers?; **j. sa voix aux protestations** to add one's voice to *or* to join in the protests

5 *(associer)* to combine, to link; **le bon sens joint à l'intelligence** common sense combined with intelligence

6 *(contacter)* to contact, to get in touch with; **j. qn par téléphone** to get through to sb on the phone, to contact sb by phone; **j. qn par lettre** to contact sb in writing; **où pourrai-je vous j.?** how can I get in touch with you *or* contact you?

VI *(porte, planches, battants)* **des volets qui joignent bien/mal** shutters that close/don't close properly; **des lattes de plancher qui joignent bien** tightly fitting floorboards

VPR **se joindre** 1 *(se contacter ▸ par téléphone)* to get through to each other; *(▸ par lettre)* to make contact

2 *(se nouer)* **leurs mains se sont jointes** their hands came together *or* joined

3 **se j. à** *(s'associer à)* to join; **tu veux te j. à nous?** would you like to join us?; **se j. à une conversation/partie de rami** to join in a conversation/game of rummy; **puis-je me j. à vous pour acheter le cadeau de Pierre?** may I contribute to Pierre's present?; **Lisa se joint à moi pour vous souhaiter la bonne année** Lisa and I wish you *or* Lisa joins me in wishing you a happy New Year

joint, -e [ʒwɛ̃, -ɛ̃t] ADJ 1 *(rapproché)* **agenouillé, les mains jointes** kneeling with his hands (clasped) together 2 *(attaché)* **planches mal/solidement jointes** loose-/tight-fitting boards 3 *(documents, échantillons)* enclosed, attached

NM 1 *Constr & Menuis (garniture d'étanchéité)* joint; *(ligne d'assemblage)* join; **les joints d'un mur** the pointing of a wall; **j. saillant** raised joint

2 *Tech (ligne d'assemblage)* joint; **j. abouté** butt joint; **j. articulé** knuckle (joint); **j. biseauté** scarf joint; **j. à brides** flange joint; **j. brisé** universal *or* cardan joint, coupling; **j. de cardan** universal *or* cardan joint, coupling; *Aut* **j. de culasse** (cylinder) head gasket; **j. à rotule** ball(-and-socket) joint; **j. universel** universal joint

3 *Tech* **j. (d'étanchéité)** seal, gasket; **j. à lèvre** lip seal

4 *Rail* (rail) joint

5 *(de robinet)* washer

6 *Fam (moyen)* **trouver le j.** to come up with a solution□; **il cherche un j. pour payer moins d'impôts** he's trying to find a clever way of paying less tax

7 *(intermédiaire)* **faire le j. (entre deux personnes)** to act as a go-between (between two people)

8 *Fam (drogue)* joint

jointif, -ive [ʒwɛ̃tif, -iv] ADJ *Menuis* butt-jointed

jointure [ʒwɛ̃tyr] NF 1 *Anat* joint; *(chez le cheval)* pastern joint, fetlock; **jointures des doigts** knuckles 2 *(assemblage)* joint; *(point de jonction)* join

joint-venture [dʒɔjntvɛntʃər] *(pl* **joint-ventures***)* NM joint venture

jojo [ʒɔʒo] *Fam* ADJ INV *(beau, correct)* **pas j.** not very nice□; **il est pas j. son petit ami** his/her boyfriend's no oil painting; **c'est pas j. ce qu'il a fait là** what he did there wasn't very nice

NM *(enfant)* **ce gamin est un affreux j.** that child is a little horror

jojoba [ʒɔʒɔba] NM jojoba

joker [ʒɔkɛr] NM 1 *Cartes* joker; *Fig* **sortir son j.** to play one's trump card 2 *Ordinat* wild card

joli, -e [ʒɔli] ADJ 1 *(voix, robe, sourire)* pretty, lovely, nice; *(poème)* pretty, lovely; *(voyage, mariage)* lovely, nice; *(personne)* pretty; **ces deux bleus ensemble, ça n'est pas j.** these two blues don't look nice together; **il est j. garçon** he's good-looking *or* attractive; **le j. mois de mai** the merry month of May; *Fam* **ce n'était pas j. à voir, ce n'était pas j., j.** it wasn't a pretty *or* pleasant sight; **ce n'est pas j. de mentir** it's not nice to tell lies; **être j. comme un cœur** *ou* **j. à croquer** to be (as) pretty as a picture; **faire le j. cœur** to flirt 2 *(considérable)* **une jolie (petite) somme, un j. (petit) pécule** a nice *or* tidy (little) sum of money; **elle s'est taillé un j. succès** she's been most *or* very successful; **de très jolis résultats** very good *or* fine results 3 *(usage ironique)* **elle est jolie, la politique!** what a fine *or* nice thing politics is, isn't it?; *Fam* **tu nous as mis dans un j. pétrin** you got us into a fine mess *or* pickle; **j. monsieur!** what a charming individual!; **tout ça c'est bien j., mais...** that's all very well *or* that's all well and good, but...

NM,F lovely; **viens, ma jolie!** come here, honey *or* darling *or* lovely!

NM *Ironique* 1 *(action blâmable)* **tu l'as cassé? c'est du j.!** you broke it? that's great!; **c'est du j. d'avoir filé!** that's nice, running away! 2 *(locution)* **quand il va voir les dégâts, ça va faire du j.!** when he sees the damage, there'll be all hell to pay!

ADV **faire j.** to look nice *or* pretty

> Il faut noter que l'adjectif anglais **jolly** est un faux ami. Il signifie **joyeux**.

joliesse [ʒɔljɛs] NF *Littéraire* prettiness, charm, grace

joliment [ʒɔlimɑ̃] ADV 1 *(élégamment)* prettily, nicely; **j. dit** nicely *or* neatly put 2 *Fam (en intensif)* pretty, *Br* jolly; **c'est j. compliqué** it's pretty *or* awfully complicated; **elle est j. énervée!** she's really *or Am* darn annoyed!; **elle s'est j. fait enguirlander** she got a real *or Br* right telling-off 3 *Ironique (très mal)* **on s'est fait j. accueillir!** a fine *or* nice welcome we got there!; **te voilà j. arrangé!** you're in a right mess *or* state!

jonc [ʒɔ̃] NM 1 *Bot* rush; **j. à balais** broom; **j. des chaisiers** bulrush 2 *(canne)* (Malacca) cane, rattan 3 **j. d'or** *(bague)* gold ring; *(bracelet)* gold bangle *or* bracelet; *Can Vieilli (alliance)* (gold) wedding ring

joncher [3] [ʒɔ̃ʃe] VT *(couvrir)* to strew; **les corps jonchaient le sol** the bodies lay strewn on the ground; **jonché de détritus** littered with rubbish; **jonché de pétales** strewn with petals

jonchet [ʒɔ̃ʃɛ] NM spillikin; **jouer aux jonchets** to play spillikins

jonction [ʒɔ̃ksjɔ̃] NF 1 *(réunion ▸ action)* joining; *(▸ résultat)* junction; **opérer la j. de deux câbles** to join up two cables; **opérer la j. de deux armées** to combine two armies; **(point de) j.** meeting point *or* junction; **à la j. des deux routes** at the junction (of the two roads) 2 *Jur* **j. d'instance** joinder (of causes of action) **3** *Électron, Ordinat, Rail & Tél* junction

jongler **[3]** [ʒɔ̃gle] **VI 1** *(avec des balles)* to juggle; *Ftbl* **j. avec le ballon** to juggle with the ball **2** *Fig* **j. avec** *(manier avec aisance)* to juggle with; **elle aime j. avec les mots** she likes to juggle *or* to play with words **3** *Can (rêvasser)* to daydream

jonglerie [ʒɔ̃gləri] **NF** juggling

jongleur, -euse [ʒɔ̃glœr, -øz] **ADJ** *Can (rêveur)* dreamy; *(pensif)* pensive, thoughtful

NM,F 1 *(qui fait des tours)* juggler **2** *Can (rêveur)* daydreamer

NM *Hist* (wandering) minstrel, jongleur

jonque [ʒɔ̃k] **NF** junk

jonquille [ʒɔ̃kij] **NF** *Bot* (wild) daffodil, jonquil

ADJ INV bright *or* daffodil yellow

Jordanie [ʒɔrdani] **NF la J.** Jordan

jordanien, -enne [ʒɔrdanjɛ̃, -ɛn] **ADJ** Jordanian

• **Jordanien, -enne NM,F** Jordanian

Josué [ʒɔzɥe] **NPR** *Bible* Joshua

jouabilité [ʒwabilite] **NF** *(d'un jeu vidéo)* playability

jouable [ʒwabl] **ADJ 1** *Mus* playable; *Théât (pièce)* stageable, that can be performed; **sa dernière pièce n'est pas j.** his/her last play can't be staged **2** *Sport (coup)* which can be played, feasible; **le coup n'est pas j.** it's not feasible, it's impossible

joual [ʒwal] **NM** joual, = dialectal form of Canadian French

ADJ *(origines)* working-class

jouasse [ʒwas] **ADJ** *Fam* pleased[□], *Br* chuffed; **qu'est-ce que t'as, t'es pas j.?** got a problem?

joubarbe [ʒubarb] **NF** *Bot* houseleek, sempervivum

joue [ʒu] **NF 1** *Anat* cheek; **j. contre j.** cheek to cheek; **ce bébé a de bonnes joues** this baby's got really chubby cheeks

2 *Culin* **j. de bœuf** ox cheek

3 *Tech (d'une poulie)* cheek; *(d'un rabot)* fence

4 *(d'un fauteuil, d'un canapé)* side

• **joues NFPL** *Naut* bows

• **en joue ADV coucher un fusil en j.** to take aim with *or* to aim a rifle; **coucher** *ou* **mettre qn/qch en j.** to (take) aim at sb/sth; **tenir qn/qch en j.** to hold sb/sth in one's sights; **en j.!** take aim!

JOUER **[6]** [ʒwe]

VI	
• to play **1, 2, 5, 9**	• to gamble **3**
• to act **4**	• to perform **4, 5**
• to be of consequence **6**	• to apply **6**
• to warp **7**	• to work **8**
VT	
• to play **1, 4**	• to bet (on) **2**
• to stake **2, 3**	• to act **4**
• to perform **4**	• to put on **5**
• to fool **6**	
VPR	
• to be on **1**	• to be performed **1**
• to be played **1–3**	
• to play **4**	

VI 1 *(s'amuser)* to play; **j. avec qn** to play with sb; **j. au ballon/au train électrique/à la poupée** to play with a ball/an electric train/a doll; **j. aux petits soldats** to play (at) soldiers; **j. à la marchande/au docteur** to play (at) shops/doctors and nurses; **j. aux charades** to play (at) charades; **on ne joue pas avec un fusil!** a gun isn't a toy!; **elle jouait avec ses cheveux** she was playing *or* fiddling with her hair; *Can Fam* **j. dans les cheveux de qn** to pull a fast one on sb; *Fam* **ne joue pas dans mes plates-bandes** mind your own business; **j. avec les sentiments de qn** to play *or* to trifle with sb's feelings; **tu joues avec ta santé/vie** you're gambling with your health/life; **il a passé sa soirée à faire j. le chien avec la balle** he spent the evening throwing the ball around for the dog; **je ne joue plus** I'm not playing any more; *Fig* I don't want to have any part in this any more; **comme un chat joue avec une souris** as a cat plays with a mouse

2 *Sport & (aux cartes, à un jeu de société)* to play; **j. au golf/football/squash** to play golf/football/squash; **j. aux cartes/au billard** to play cards/billiards; **il joue à l'avant/à l'arrière** he plays up front/in defence; **j. ailier droit** to play on the right wing; **(c'est) à toi de j.** *(aux cartes)* (it's) your turn; *(aux échecs)* (it's) your move; *Fig* it's up to you; **bien/mal j.** to be a good/bad player, to play well/badly; **j. contre qn/une équipe** to play (against) sb/a team; **à quel jeu joues-tu?** what do you think you're playing at?; **j. au plus fin** *ou* **malin avec qn** to try to outsmart sb; **ne joue pas au plus fin avec moi!** don't try to be smart *or* clever with me!; *très Fam* **j. au con** to act like a *Br* prat *or Am* jerk

3 *(parier ▸ au casino)* to gamble; *(▸ aux courses)* to bet; **j'ai joué dans la deuxième course** I had a bet on the second race; **j'ai joué sur le 12** I played (on) number 12; **j. à la roulette** to play roulette; **j. aux courses** to bet on horses; **j. au loto sportif** *Br* ≃ to do the pools, *Am* ≃ to play the pools; **j. à la Bourse** to gamble on *or* to speculate on the Stock Exchange; **j. à la hausse** to gamble on a rise in prices, to bull the market; **j. à la baisse** to gamble on a fall in prices, to bear the market; **je ne joue jamais** *(au casino)* I'm not a gambler, I never gamble; *(aux courses)* I never bet, I'm not a betting man/woman

4 *Cin & Théât (acteur)* to act; *(troupe)* to perform; **elle joue dans une pièce de Brecht** she's got a part in *or* she's in a Brecht play; **bien/mal j.** *(gén)* to be a good/bad actor; *(dans un film, une pièce)* to give a good/bad performance; **elle joue vraiment bien** she's a really good actress

5 *Mus* to play, to perform; **bien/mal j.** *(gén)* to be a good/bad musician; *(dans un concert)* to play well/badly; **j. d'un instrument** to play an instrument; **j. de l'accordéon/du violon** to play the accordeon/the violin

6 *(intervenir ▸ facteur)* to be of consequence *or* of importance; *(▸ clause)* to apply; **l'âge joue peu** age is of little consequence; **les événements récents ont joué dans leur décision** recent events have been a factor in *or* have influenced their decision; **faire j. ses relations** to make use of one's connections; **il a fait j. ses relations pour obtenir le poste** he pulled some strings to get the job; **j. pour** *ou* **en faveur de qn** to work in sb's favour; **j. contre** *ou* **en défaveur de qn** to work against sb; **le temps joue en notre faveur/défaveur** time is on our side/is against us; **ma jeunesse a joué en ma défaveur** the fact that I'm young worked against me *or* put me at a disadvantage

7 *(se déformer ▸ bois)* to warp; *(avoir du jeu)* to work loose; **le bois a joué sous l'effet de l'humidité** the wood has warped with the damp; **les chevilles ont joué** the dowels have worked loose

8 *(fonctionner)* to work; **faire j. une clé (dans une serrure)** *(pour ouvrir la porte)* to turn a key (in a lock); *(pour l'essayer)* to try a key (in a lock); **fais j. le pêne** get the bolt to slide; **faire j. un ressort** to trigger a spring

9 *(faire des effets)* to play; **le soleil jouait sur le lac** the sunlight was playing *or* dancing on the lake

10 *(s'appliquer)* to be operative, to operate; **l'augmentation des salaires joue depuis le 1er janvier** the rise in salaries has been effective since 1 January

11 *Suisse (convenir)* to be all right; **cela ne joue pas** it's not right

VT 1 *Sport (match, carte)* to play; *(pièce d'échecs)* to move, to play; **j. la finale** to play in the final; **j. la revanche/belle** to play the return match/decider; **ils ont joué le ballon à la main** they passed the ball; **j'ai joué cœur** I played hearts; **bien joué!** *Cartes & Sport* well played!; *(à un jeu)* good move!; *Fig* well done!; *Fig* **il joue un drôle de jeu** he's playing a strange *or* funny (little) game; **laisse-la j. son petit jeu, nous ne sommes pas dupes** let her play her little game, she won't fool us; **j. le jeu** to play the game; **rien n'est encore joué** nothing has been decided yet

2 *(au casino ▸ somme)* to stake, to wager; *(▸ numéro)* to bet on; *(au turf ▸ somme)* to bet, to stake; *(▸ cheval)* to bet on, to back; **je ne joue jamais d'argent** I never play for money; **il joue d'énormes sommes** he plays for high stakes *or* big money; **j'ai joué 20 euros sur le 12** I bet *or* put 20 euros on number 12; *aussi Fig* **j. gros jeu** to play for high stakes *or* big money; *Bourse* **j. la livre à la baisse/à la hausse** to speculate on a falling/rising pound

3 *(risquer ▸ avenir, réputation)* to stake; *Fam* **je joue ma peau** I'm risking my neck

4 *(interpréter ▸ personnage)* to play (the part of), to act; *(▸ concerto)* to play, to perform; **l'intrigue est passionnante mais c'est mal joué** the plot is gripping but the acting is poor; **j. Brecht** *(acteur)* to play Brecht, to be in a Brecht play; *(troupe)* to play Brecht, to put on a Brecht play; **j. du Chopin** to play (some) Chopin; **il joue toujours les jeunes premiers** he always plays the lead *or* gets the leading role; *Fig* **j. les martyrs** to play *or* to act the martyr; **ne joue pas les innocents!** don't play the innocent *or* don't act innocent (with me)!; **j. l'étonnement/le remords** to pretend to be surprised/sorry; *Mus* **j. sa partie** to play one's part; *aussi Fig* **j. un rôle** to play a part; **la lecture joue un grand rôle dans l'acquisition de l'orthographe** reading plays a large part in learning to spell

5 *(montrer ▸ film, pièce)* to put on, to show; **qu'est-ce qu'on joue en ce moment?** what's on at the moment?; **on ne joue rien d'intéressant** there's nothing interesting on; **la pièce a toujours été jouée en anglais** the play has always been performed in English; *Fam* **où t'as vu j. ça?** are you mad??

6 *(berner)* to fool, to deceive; **nul n'a jamais pu le j.** no one could ever get the better of him

• **jouer de VT IND 1** *(se servir de)* to make use of, to use; **j. du couteau/marteau** to wield a knife/hammer; **elle joue de son infirmité** she plays on *or* uses the fact that she's disabled; *très Fam* **j. des jambes** *ou* **flûtes** *(s'enfuir)* to take to one's heels, *Br* to scarper, *Am* to hightail (it); *(courir)* to run *Br* like the clappers *or Am* like the dickens; **j. des poings** to use one's fists **2** *(être victime de)* **j. de malchance** *ou* **malheur** to be dogged by misfortune *or* bad luck

• **jouer sur VT IND** *(crédulité, sentiment)* to play on; **ils jouent sur la naïveté des gens** they play on *or* exploit people's gullibility; **j. sur les mots** to play with words

VPR se jouer 1 *(film)* to be on, to be shown; *(pièce)* to be on, to be performed; *(morceau de musique)* to be played *or* performed; **qu'est-ce qui se joue actuellement?** what's on at the moment?

2 *(sport, jeu)* to be played; **le match se jouera la semaine prochaine** the match will be played next week

3 *(être en jeu)* **des sommes considérables se jouent chaque soir** huge amounts of money are played for every night; *Fig* **son sort est en train de se j.** his/her fate is hanging in the balance; **l'avenir du pays se joue dans cette négociation** the fate of the country hinges *or* depends on the outcome of these negotiations

4 *(produire un effet)* to play; **la surface lisse du lac où se joue un rayon de lune** the still surface of the lake on which a moonbeam is dancing *or* playing

5 *Fam* **se la j.** to show off, to pose

6 se j. de *(ignorer)* to ignore; **se j. des lois/du règlement** to pay no heed to the law/rules; **se j. des obstacles** to make light of the difficulties

7 *(locution)* **(comme) en se jouant** with the greatest of ease

jouet [ʒwɛ] **NM 1** *(d'enfant)* toy **2** *(victime)* plaything; **il croyait être le j. des dieux** he felt he was a plaything for the gods; **j'ai été le j. de leur machination** I was a pawn in their game; **tu as été le j. d'une illusion** you've been the victim of an illusion

jouette [ʒwɛt] **ADJ** *Belg* playful, fun-loving

joueur, -euse [ʒwœr, -øz] **ADJ 1** *(chaton, chiot)* playful **2** *(parieur)* **être j.** to be fond of gambling

NM,F 1 *Mus & Sport* player; **j. de basket/flûte** basketball/flute player; **joueurs de cartes/d'échecs** card/chess players; **j. de golf/cricket** golfer/cricketer; **j. de tambour** drummer; **être beau/mauvais j.** to be a good/bad loser *or* sport **2** *(pour de l'argent)* gambler

joufflu, -e [ʒufly] **ADJ** *(bébé)* chubby-cheeked; **un visage j.** a chubby face

NM *Fam (postérieur)* butt, *Br* bum, *Am* fanny

joug [ʒu] **NM 1** *Agr* yoke **2** *Littéraire (assujettissement)* yoke; **être sous le j. d'un tyran** to be under the yoke of a tyrant; **secouer le j.** to throw off the yoke **3** *(d'une balance)* beam

jouir **[32]** [ʒwir] **VI 1** *(sexuellement)* to have an orgasm, *Fam* to come **2** *Fam (prendre du plaisir)* **ça**

me fait j. I get a kick out of it **3** *Fam (souffrir)* to go through hell

• **jouir de** **VT IND 1** *(profiter de ▸ vie, jeunesse)* to enjoy, to get pleasure out of **2** *(se réjouir de ▸ victoire)* to enjoy, to delight in **3** *(avoir ▸ panorama)* to command; *(▸ensoleillement, droit)* to enjoy, to have; *(▸ privilège, réputation)* to enjoy; **j. d'une bonne santé** to enjoy good health; **il ne jouit pas de toutes ses facultés** he isn't in full possession of his faculties

jouissance [ʒwisɑ̃s] **NF 1** *(plaisir)* enjoyment, pleasure; *(orgasme)* climax, orgasm; **les jouissances de la vie** life's pleasures **2** *Jur (usage)* use; **avoir la j. de qch** to have the use of sth; **entrer en j. de qch** to enter *or* to come into possession of sth; **à vendre avec j. immédiate** *(dans une petite annonce)* for sale with immediate possession; **avoir la (pleine) j. de ses droits** to enjoy one's (full) rights; **j. en commun** *(d'un bien)* communal tenure; **j. locative** tenure; **la période de j. est de sept ans** the period of tenure is seven years; *Fin* **j. d'intérêts** entitlement to interest

jouisseur, -euse [ʒwisœr, -øz] **NM,F** pleasure-seeker, sensualist

jouissif, -ive [ʒwisif, -iv] **ADJ** *Fam* fun; *Ironique* **je suis allée chez le dentiste, c'était j.!** I went to the dentist's, what a barrel of laughs!

joujou, -x [ʒuʒu] **NM** *(jouet)* toy, plaything; *Fam* **faire j. avec** to play with; **va faire j.** go and play

joule [ʒul] **NM** joule

JOUR [ʒur]

- day **A1–4**
- light **B2**
- opening **C2, 4**
- daylight **B1**
- gap **C1**

NM A. *DIVISION TEMPORELLE* **1** *(division du calendrier)* day; **les jours de la semaine** the days of the week; **j. de semaine** weekday; **un j. de deuil/joie** a day of mourning/joy; *Admin* **j. chômable, j. chômé** public holiday; **j. de congé** day off; **j. férié** public holiday; *Fin* **jours d'intérêt** interest days; *Com* **j. ouvrable** working day; **j. de paie** pay day; **un j. de repos** a rest day; **un j. de travail** a workday, *Br* a working day; **il me reste des jours à prendre avant la fin de l'année** I still have some (days') leave (to take) before the end of the year; **à dix jours de là** ten days later; **dans deux/quelques jours** in two/a few days' time; **il est resté des jours entiers sans sortir** he didn't go out for days on end; **il y a deux/dix jours** two/ten days ago; **tout le j.** all day long; **tous les jours** every day; **au j. le j.** *(sans s'occuper du lendemain)* from day to day; *(précairement)* from hand to mouth; **de j. en j.** *(grandir)* daily, day by day; *(varier)* from day to day, from one day to the next; **d'un j. à l'autre** *(incessamment)* any day (now); *(de façon imprévisible)* from one day to the next; **j. après j.** *(constamment)* day after day; *(graduellement)* day by day; **j. par j.** day by day; **cela fait deux ans j. pour j.** it's two years to the day

2 *(exprime la durée)* day; **c'est à un j. de marche/voiture** it's one day's walk/drive away; **nous avons eu trois jours de pluie** we had rain for three days *or* three days of rain; **j'en ai pour deux jours de travail** the work's going to take me two days; **il nous reste deux jours de vivres/d'eau/de munitions** we've got two days' (worth of) food/water/ammunition left; **emporte trois jours de ravitaillement** take enough provisions for three days; *Littéraire* **leur beauté n'est que d'un j.** their beauty is ephemeral *or* short-lived

3 *(date précise)* day; **fixer un j. pour qch/pour faire qch** to fix a day *or* date for sth/for doing sth; **quel j. sommes-nous?** what day (of the week) is it (today)?; **depuis ce j.** since that day, from that day on *or* onwards; **l'autre j.** the other day; **le j. où** the day *or* time that; **le j. où on a besoin de lui, il est malade!** the (one) day *or* time you need him, he's ill!; **le j. précédent** *ou* **d'avant** the previous day, the day before; **le j. suivant** *ou* **d'après** the following day, the next day, the day after; **dès le premier j.** from the very first day; **le j. est loin où j'étais heureux** it's a long time since I've been happy; **le j. n'est pas loin où tu pourras y aller tout seul** it won't be long before you can go alone; **le j. viendra où...** the day will come when...; **un j. que...** one day when...; *Scol* **le j. de la rentrée** the first day (back) at school; *Scol* **le j. de la sortie** the last day of school; **le j. de mes 20 ans** my 20th birthday; **le j. de l'an** New Year's Day; **le j. des Cendres** Ash Wednesday; **le j. des élections** election *or* polling day; **le j. du Jugement dernier** doomsday, Judgement Day; **le j. des morts** All Souls' Day; **le j. de Noël** Christmas Day; **le j. de la Pentecôte** Whit Sunday; **le j. des Rameaux** Palm Sunday; **le j. des Rois** Twelfth Night, Epiphany; **le j. du scrutin** election *or* polling day; **le j. du Seigneur** the Lord's Day, the Sabbath; **mon/son (grand) j.** my/his/her (big) day; **le grand j. pour elle/lui** her/his big day; **son manteau des grands jours** the coat he/she wears on important occasions; **de tous les jours** every day *(avant n)*; **mes chaussures de tous les jours** my everyday *or* ordinary shoes, the shoes I wear everyday; **elle attend son j.** she's biding her time *or* marking time; **ce n'est pas mon j.!** it's not my day!; *Ironique* **ce n'est (vraiment) pas le j.!, tu choisis bien ton j.!** you really picked your day!; **il est dans un bon/mauvais j.** he's having one of his good/bad days; **je t'invite, c'est mon j. de bonté** my treat, I'm feeling generous today; *Fam* **il y a les jours avec et les jours sans** there are good days and (there are) bad days, there are days when everything goes right and others when everything goes wrong; **un beau j.** one (fine) day; **un de ces jours, un j. ou l'autre** one of these days; **à un de ces jours!** see you soon!; **à ce j.** to this day, to date; **à ce j. la facture que nous vous avons envoyée reste impayée** to date the invoice we sent you remains unpaid; **intérêts à ce j.** interest to date; *Fam* **au j. d'aujourd'hui** in this day and age; **du j. au lendemain** overnight

4 *Bourse* day; **j. de Bourse** trading day; **j. de grâce** day of grace; **j. de la liquidation** account day, settlement day; **j. de paiement, j. de règlement** payment day, settlement day; **j. du terme** term day; **j. de valeur** value day

B. *CLARTÉ* **1** *(lumière)* daylight; **un faible j. éclairait la cuisine/la scène** the kitchen/the stage was dimly lit; **le j. baisse** it's getting dark; **il fait (encore) j.** it's still light; **l'été, il fait j. à 4h30** in the summer it gets light at 4.30; **il faisait grand j.** it was broad daylight; *Fig* **faire qch au grand j.** to do sth openly; **l'affaire fut étalée au grand j.** the affair was brought out into the open; **le j. se lève** the sun is rising; **avant le j.** before dawn *or* daybreak; **au petit j.** at dawn *or* daybreak; **j. et nuit, nuit et j.** day and night, night and day; **je dors le j.** I sleep during the day *or* in the daytime; **examine-le au** *ou* **en plein j.** look at it in the daylight; **vous me cachez le j.** you're in my light; **mets-toi face au j.** face the light; **j. artificiel** artificial daylight; **elle et son mari, c'est le j. et la nuit** she and her husband are like chalk and cheese

2 *(aspect)* light; **présenter qn/qch sous un j. favorable** to show sb/sth in a favourable light; **le marché apparaît sous un j. défavorable** the market does not look promising; **apparaître sous un meilleur j.** to appear in a better light; **enfin, il s'est montré sous son vrai j.!** he's shown his true colours at last!; **voir qn sous son vrai** *ou* **véritable j.** to see what sb's really like; **voir qch sous son vrai** *ou* **véritable j.** to see sth in its true light; **sous un faux j.** in a false light; **pendant longtemps, nous l'avons vue sous un faux j.** for a long time we didn't see her for what she really was

3 *(locutions)* **donner le j. à** *(enfant)* to give birth to, to bring into the world; *(projet)* to give birth to; *(mode, tendance)* to start; **jeter un j. nouveau sur** to throw *or* to cast new light on; **mettre au j.** to bring to light; **voir le j.** *(bébé)* to be born; *(journal)* to come out; *(théorie, invention)* to appear; *(projet)* to see the light of day

C. *OUVERTURE* **1** *(interstice ▸ entre des planches)* gap, chink; *(▸dans un feuillage)* gap; **il fallut percer un j. dans le mur de devant** an opening had to be made in the front wall

2 *Archit* opening; *Beaux-Arts* light; **balcon à j.** openwork balcony

3 *(fenêtre)* **j. de souffrance** window *(looking on to an adjacent property and subject to legal specifications)*; **faux j.** interior window

4 *Couture* opening *(made by drawing threads)*; **des jours** openwork, drawn work; **à jours** *(passementerie, tricot, chemisier)* openwork

5 *(locution)* **se faire j.** to emerge, to become clear; **pour que la vérité se fasse j.** for the truth to emerge *or* to come out; **l'idée s'est fait j. dans son esprit** the idea dawned on him/her

• **jours** **NMPL 1** *(vie)* days, life; **il a fini ses jours dans l'opulence** he ended his days *or* life a wealthy man; **mettre fin à ses jours** to put an end to one's life; **ses jours sont comptés** his/her days are numbered; **ses jours ne sont plus en danger** we no longer fear for his/her life

2 *(époque)* **de la Rome antique à nos jours** from Ancient Rome to the present day; **passer des jours heureux** to have a good time; **les mauvais jours** *(les moments difficiles)* unhappy days, hard times; *(les jours où rien ne va)* bad days; **il a sa tête des mauvais jours** it looks like he's in a bad mood; **ce manteau a connu des jours meilleurs** this coat has seen better days; **ses vieux jours** his/her old age; **de nos jours** these days, nowadays; **de nos jours on n'en fait plus des comme ça** they don't make them anymore nowadays *or* these days; **les beaux jours** *(printemps)* springtime; *(été)* summertime; **ah, c'étaient les beaux jours!** *(jeunesse)* ah, those were the days!

• **à jour** **ADJ** *(cahier, travail)* kept up to date; *(rapport)* up-to-date, up-to-the-minute; **être à j. de ses cotisations** to have paid one's subscription **ADV** up to date; **tenir/mettre qch à j.** to keep/to bring sth up to date; **mettre son journal intime à j.** to update one's *Br* diary *or Am* journal, to bring one's *Br* diary *or Am* journal up to date; **mettre sa correspondance à j.** to catch up on one's letter writing; **ce qui presse le plus, c'est la mise à j. des registres** updating the ledgers is the most urgent task

• **de jour** **ADJ** *(hôpital, unité)* day, daytime *(avant n)*; *(infirmière)* day *(avant n)*; *Mil (officier)* duty *(avant n)* **ADV** *(travailler)* during the day; *(conduire)* in the daytime, during the day; **être de j.** to be on day duty *or* on days; **de j. comme de nuit** day and night

• **du jour** **ADJ** *(mode, tendance, préoccupation)* current, contemporary; *(homme)* of the moment; **as-tu lu le journal du j.?** have you read today's paper?; **quelles sont les nouvelles du j.?** what's today's news?; **un œuf du j.** a freshly laid egg; **le poisson est-il du j.?** is the fish fresh (today)?

• **d'un jour** **ADJ** short-lived, *Sout* ephemeral, transient

• **par jour** **ADV** a day, per day; **travailler cinq heures par j.** to work five hours a day; **trois fois par j.** three times a day

Jourdain [ʒurdɛ̃] **NM le J.** the (River) Jordan

journal, -aux [ʒurnal, -o] **NM 1** *(publication)* paper, newspaper; *(spécialisé)* journal; **j. du matin/soir** morning/evening paper *or* newspaper; **c'est dans** *ou* **sur le j.** it's in the paper; **j. d'annonces** advertising newspaper; **j. sur CD-ROM** CD-ROM newspaper; *Presse* **j. électronique** electronic newspaper; **j. d'entreprise** staff magazine, company magazine; **j. grand format** broadsheet; **j. gratuit** free paper, freesheet; **j. interne** *(du personnel)* staff magazine *or* newsletter; *(de l'entreprise)* company magazine *or* newsletter; *Can* **j. jaune** scandal sheet; **j. en ligne** electronic newspaper; *Pol* **le J. officiel (de la République Française)** = French government publication giving information to the public about new laws, parliamentary debates, government business and new companies, *Br* ≃ Hansard, *Am* ≃ Federal Register; **j. professionnel** trade journal; **j. à scandale** *ou* **à sensation** scandal sheet

2 *(bureau)* office, paper; *(équipe)* newspaper (staff)

3 *Rad & TV (informations)* **j. parlé/télévisé** radio/television news; **ce j. est présenté par...** the news is presented *or Br* read by...; *Fam* **ils l'ont dit au j.** they said so on the news

4 *(carnet) Br* diary, *Am* journal; *Ordinat* log; **j. (intime)** *Br* diary, *Am* journal; **tenir un j.** to keep a diary; *Naut* **j. de bord** log, logbook; *Belg* **j. de classe** *(d'élève)* homework *Br* diary *or Am* journal; *(de professeur)* (work) record book; **j. de voyage** travel diary

5 *Compta* ledger, account book; **j. des achats** purchase ledger, bought ledger; *Fin* **j. de banque** bank book; **j. des effets à payer** bills payable ledger; **j. des effets à recevoir** bills receivable ledger;

j. de paie wages ledger; **j. de trésorerie** cash book; **j. des ventes** sales ledger

LE JOURNAL OFFICIEL

This bulletin prints information about new laws and summaries of parliamentary debates, and informs the public of any important government business. When new companies are established, they are obliged by law to publish an announcement in the "Journal officiel".

journaleux, -euse [ʒurnalø, -øz] **NM,F** *Fam Péj* hack (journalist)

journalier, -ère [ʒurnalje, -ɛr] **ADJ** daily
NM,F *Agr* day labourer

journaliser [3] [ʒurnalize] **VT** *Compta* to enter, to write up in the books

journalisme [ʒurnalism] **NM** journalism; **faire du j.** to be a journalist; **je fais un peu de j. de temps en temps** I write the odd article; **j. électronique** electronic news gathering; **j. d'investigation, j. d'enquête** investigative journalism; **j. de radio** radio journalism; **j. sportif** sports journalism; **j. de télévision** television journalism

journaliste [ʒurnalist] **NMF** journalist; **elle est j. au Monde** she's a journalist for *or* with Le Monde; **assaillie par les journalistes** mobbed by reporters; **les journalistes de la rédaction** the editorial staff; **j. politique/sportif** political/sports correspondent *or* journalist; **j. embarqué** *ou* **incorporé** *ou* **intégré** embedded journalist; **j. d'investigation** investigative journalist; **j. parlementaire** parliamentary correspondent

journalistique [ʒurnalistik] **ADJ** journalistic

journée [ʒurne] **NF 1** *(durée)* day; **par une belle j. d'été** on a beautiful summer's day; **à quoi occupes-tu tes journées?** how do you spend your days?, what do you do during the day?; **je n'ai rien fait de la j.** I haven't done a thing all day; **dans la j.** in the course of the day, during the day; **en début de j.** early in the morning *or* day; **en fin de j.** at the end of the day, in the early evening; **toute la j.** all day (long), the whole day; **bonne j.!** have a good *or* nice day!; **à une j./deux journées d'ici** one day's/two days' journey away; **j. verte/orange/rouge/noire** = day with little/some/severe/very severe traffic congestion

2 *Écon & Ind* **une j. de travail** a day's work; **la j. de huit heures** the eight-hour day; **faire des journées de 12 heures** to work a 12-hour day *or* 12 hours a day; **faire de longues journées** to work long hours; **embauché/payé à la j.** employed/paid on a daily basis; **j. de travail** working day; **faire des journées (chez)** *(femme de ménage)* to work as *Br* a daily *or Am* a maid (for); **j. d'action** day of (industrial) action; **j. comptable** accounting day; **faire la j. continue** *(entreprise)* to work a continuous shift; *(magasin)* to stay open over the lunch hour; *(personne)* to work through lunch; **journées de travail perdues** lost working days

3 *(salaire)* day's pay *or* wages

4 *(activité organisée)* day; **la j. des enfants/du cinéma** children's/film day; **les journées du cancer** *(séminaire)* the cancer (research) conference; *(campagne)* cancer research (campaign) week; *Pol* **les journées (parlementaires) du parti** *Br* ≃ the (Parliamentary) Party conference, *Am* ≃ the party convention; **j. d'appel de préparation à la défense** = day during which young people are introduced to issues connected with national security; **j. d'études** study day; **j. portes ouvertes** *Br* open day, *Am* open house; **les Journées du Patrimoine** European Heritage Day, *Br* ≃ Doors Open Day

Il faut noter que le nom anglais **journey** est un faux ami. Il signifie **voyage, trajet.**

journellement [ʒurnɛlmɑ̃] **ADV 1** *(chaque jour)* daily, every day **2** *(fréquemment)* every day

joute [ʒut] **NF 1** *Hist* joust, tilt; *Sport* **j. nautique** *ou* **lyonnaise** water jousting **2** *Littéraire (rivalité)* joust; *(dialogue)* sparring match; **j. oratoire** debate; **j. d'esprit** battle of wits

jouter [3] [ʒute] **VI 1** *(combattre)* to joust **2** *Littéraire (rivaliser)* to spar

jouteur, -euse [ʒutœr, -øz] **NM,F 1** *Hist* jouster, tilter; *Sport* water jouster **2** *Fig* adversary, opponent

jouvence [ʒuvɑ̃s] *voir* **bain, eau, fontaine**

jouvenceau, -x [ʒuvɑ̃so] **NM** *Hum* youngster, youth, stripling

jouvencelle [ʒuvɑ̃sɛl] **NF** *Hum* damsel, maiden

jouxter [3] [ʒukste] **VT** to be adjacent to, to adjoin

jovial, -e, -als *ou* **-aux, -ales** [ʒɔvjal, -o] **ADJ** *(visage)* jovial, jolly; *(rire)* jovial, hearty

jovialement [ʒɔvjalmɑ̃] **ADV** jovially

jovialité [ʒɔvjalite] **NF** joviality, cheerfulness; **sa j. le rendait très populaire** his cheerful manner made him very popular

joyau, -x [ʒwajo] **NM 1** *(bijou)* gem, jewel; **les joyaux de la couronne** the crown jewels **2** *Fig (monument)* gem; *(œuvre d'art)* jewel; **le j. de la marine française** the jewel *or* showpiece of the French Navy; **le manoir de Luré, véritable petit j. de la Renaissance** the Manor at Luré, a real little Renaissance gem

joyeuse [ʒwajøz] *voir* **joyeux**

joyeusement [ʒwajøzmɑ̃] **ADV** joyfully, happily; **elle accepta j.** she gladly accepted

joyeux, -euse [ʒwajø, -øz] **ADJ** joyful, joyous, merry; **une joyeuse nouvelle** glad tidings; *Ironique* **et elle vient avec lui? c'est j.!** so she's coming with him? great!; **c'est un j. drille** he's a jolly fellow; **j. anniversaire!** happy birthday!

• **joyeuses NFPL** *Vulg (testicules)* balls, nuts, *Br* bollocks

JT [ʒite] **NM** *(abrév* **journal télévisé***)* TV news

jubé [ʒybe] **NM** jube, rood screen

jubilaire [ʒybilɛr] **ADJ** jubilee *(avant n)*; **année j.** jubilee year

jubilation [ʒybilasjɔ̃] **NF** jubilation, exultation; **avec j.** jubilantly

jubilé [ʒybile] **NM** jubilee

jubiler [3] [ʒybile] **VI** to be jubilant, to rejoice, to exult; *(méchamment)* to gloat; **il jubilait de me voir humilié** he gloated over my humiliation

jucher [3] [ʒyʃe] **VT** to perch; **juchée sur les épaules de son père** perched on her father's shoulders; **une casquette juchée sur le crâne** a cap perched on his/her head
VI *(faisan, poule)* to perch
VPR se jucher se j. sur to perch (up) on

juchoir [ʒyʃwar] **NM** *(endroit)* roost(ing place); *(perche)* perch

judaïcité [ʒydaisite] **NF** Jewishness

judaïque [ʒydaik] **ADJ** Judaic, Jewish

judaïser [3] [ʒydaize] **VT** to Judaize

judaïsme [ʒydaism] **NM** Judaism

judas [ʒyda] **NM 1** *(ouverture)* judas (hole); **j. optique** peephole **2** *(traître)* Judas

Judée [ʒyde] **NF la J.** Judaea, Judea

judéité [ʒydeite] **NF** Jewishness

judéo-chrétien, -enne [ʒydeɔkretjɛ̃, -ɛn] *(mpl* **judéo-chrétiens**, *fpl* **judéo-chrétiennes***)* **ADJ** Judaeo-Christian

• **Judéo-Chrétien, -enne NM,F** Judaeo-Christian

judiciaire [ʒydisjɛr] **ADJ** *(pouvoir, enquête, acte)* judicial; *(aide, autorité, frais)* legal; **vente j.** sale by order of the court

judiciairement [ʒydisjɛrmɑ̃] **ADV** judicially

judiciarisation [ʒydisjarizasjɔ̃] **NF** judicialization; **on assiste à une j. des conflits familiaux** we're seeing more and more family disputes being taken to court

judiciariser [3] [ʒydisjarize] **VT** to judicialize; **j. un conflit** to take a dispute to court; **il faut éviter de j. la relation entre un parent et un enfant** we should avoid turning parent-child relationships into a legal issue

judicieuse [ʒydisjøz] *voir* **judicieux**

judicieusement [ʒydisjøzmɑ̃] **ADV** *(décider)* judiciously, shrewdly; *(agencer, organiser)* cleverly

judicieux, -euse [ʒydisjø, -øz] **ADJ** *(personne, esprit)* judicious, shrewd; *(manœuvre, proposition, décision)* shrewd; *(choix)* judicious; *(plan)* well thought-out; **peu j.** ill-advised; **il serait j. de téléphoner avant d'y aller** it would be sensible *or* wise to phone before going

judo [ʒydo] **NM** judo

judoka [ʒydɔka] **NMF** judoka

juge [ʒyʒ] **NMF 1** *Jur* judge; **Madame/Monsieur le J. X** *Br* ≃ Mrs/Mr Justice X, *Am* ≃ Judge X; **jamais, Monsieur le j.!** never, Your Honour!; **les juges** ≃ the Bench; **être nommé j.** to be appointed judge, *Am* ≃ to be appointed to the Bench; **aller/se retrouver devant le j.** to appear/to end up in court; **j. aux affaires familiales** family court judge; **j. aux affaires matrimoniales** divorce court judge; **j. de l'application des peines** = judge responsible for the terms and conditions of sentences; **j. consulaire** = judge in a commercial court; **j. des enfants** children's judge, *Br* juvenile magistrate; *Vieilli* **j. d'instance** Justice of the Peace; **j. d'instruction** investigating judge, *Br* ≃ examining magistrate *or* justice, *Am* ≃ committing magistrate; **j. des libertés et de la détention** = judge empowered to grant or refuse bail; **j. de la mise en état** pre-trial judge; **j. de paix** stipendiary magistrate; **j. rapporteur** judge rapporteur; **j. des référés** ≃ judge in chambers; **on ne peut être à la fois j. et partie** you can't both judge and be judged

2 *(personne compétente)* **j'en suis seul j.** I am sole judge (of the matter); **je te laisse j. de la situation** I'll let you be the judge of the situation; **être bon/mauvais j. en matière de** to be a good/bad judge of

3 *Sport* judge; **j. de chaise** umpire; **j. de ligne** linesman; **j. de touche** *Ftbl* linesman; *(au rugby)* linesman, touch judge

4 *Bible* **le Livre des Juges, les Juges** the (Book of) Judges

jugé [ʒyʒe] **au jugé ADV** at a guess; **au j., je dirais que…** at a guess, I would say that…; **tirer au j.** to fire blind

jugeable [ʒyʒabl] **ADJ** *Jur* judicable

jugement [ʒyʒmɑ̃] **NM 1** *Jur (procès)* trial; *(verdict)* sentence, ruling, decision; **j. demain** the sentence will be passed tomorrow, a decision is expected tomorrow; **prononcer** *ou* **rendre un j.** to pass sentence, to give a ruling; **faire passer qn en j.** to bring sb to (stand) trial; **passer en j.** to stand trial; **j. avant dire droit** interlocutory judgment; **j. constitutif** = judgment creating or altering status; **j. contentieux** judgment in disputed matter; **j. contradictoire** = judgment rendered in the presence of the parties involved; **j. déclaratif de faillite** adjudication in bankruptcy; **j. déclaratoire** declaratory judgment; **j. par défaut** judgment in absentia *or* default; **j. définitif** final judgment; **j. en dernier ressort** judgment of last resort; **j. exécutoire** enforceable judgment; **j. mis en délibéré** reserved judgment; **j. en premier ressort** trial court judgment; **j. préparatoire** preparatory judgment; **j. provisoire** interlocutory judgment

2 *Rel* **le j. dernier** the Last Judgment, the Day of Judgment, Judgment Day; **le j. de Dieu** the Ordeal

3 *(discernement)* judgment, flair; **erreur de j.** error of judgment; **faire preuve/manquer de j.** to show/lack good judgment; **elle a du/n'a aucun j. (en matière de…)** she's a good/no judge (of…)

4 *(opinion)* judgment; **un j. téméraire** a rash judgment; **formuler un j. sur qn/qch** to express an opinion about sb/sth; **porter un j. sur qn/qch** to pass judgment on sb/sth; **soumettre qch au j. de qn** to submit sth to sb for his/her judgment; **c'est un j. sans appel** it's a harsh verdict; **le j. de l'histoire/la postérité** the verdict of history/posterity; **j. de valeur** value judgment

jugeote [ʒyʒɔt] **NF** *Fam* common sense□

juger [17] [ʒyʒe] **VT 1** *Jur (accusé)* to try; *(affaire)* to judge, to try; **être jugé pour vol** to be tried *or* to stand trial for theft; **elle a été jugée coupable/non coupable** she was found guilty/not guilty; **il s'est fait j. pour atteinte à la vie privée** he had to stand trial for violation of privacy

2 *(trancher)* to judge, to decide; **à toi de j. (si/quand…)** it's up to you to decide *or* to judge (whether/when…); **j. un différend** to arbitrate in a dispute

3 *(se faire une opinion de)* to judge; **vous n'avez pas le droit de me j.!** you have no right to judge me!; **j. qn/qch à sa juste valeur** to form a correct opinion of sb/sth

4 *(considérer)* to consider, to judge; **j. qch utile/nécessaire** to consider *or* to judge sth to be useful/necessary; **son état est jugé très préoccupant** his/her condition is believed to be serious; **jugé bon pour le service** declared fit to join *or* fit for the army; **mesures jugées insuffisantes** measures deemed inadequate; **j. qn bien/mal** to have a good/poor opinion of sb; **vous me jugez mal** *(à tort)* you're misjudging me; **j. bon de faire qch** to think fit to do sth; **agissez comme vous jugerez bon** do as you think fit *or* appropriate; **j. que** to think *or* to consider that, to be of the opinion that

USAGE ABSOLU l'histoire/la postérité jugera history/posterity will judge; **moi, je ne juge pas** I'm not in a position to judge; **j. par soi-même** to judge for oneself; **il ne faut pas j. sur** *ou* **d'après les apparences** don't judge from *or* go by appearances

• **juger de VT IND** to judge; **à en j. par son large sourire** if his/her broad smile is anything to go by; **autant qu'on puisse en j.** as far as one can judge; **si j'en juge par ce que j'ai lu** judging from *or* by what I've read, if what I've read is anything to go by; **jugez-en vous-même** judge *or* see for yourself; **jugez de mon indignation** imagine how indignant I felt

VPR se juger 1 *(se considérer)* **les commerçants se jugent lésés** shopkeepers consider *or* think themselves hard done by **2** *(se mesurer)* to be judged; **le succès d'un livre se juge aux ventes** a book's success is judged by the numbers of copies sold; *Jur* **l'affaire se jugera mardi** the case will be heard on Tuesday

jugulaire [ʒygylɛr] **ADJ** *Anat* jugular

NF 1 *Anat* jugular (vein) **2** *(bride)* chin strap

juguler [3] [ʒygyle] **VT 1** *(arrêter ▸ hémorragie, maladie)* to halt, to check; *(▸ sanglots)* to suppress, to repress; *(▸ chômage, inflation)* to curb, to check **2** *(étouffer ▸ révolte)* to quell

juif, -ive [ʒɥif, -iv] **ADJ** Jewish

NM *Fam* **le petit j.** the funny bone

• **Juif, -ive NM,F** Jew

juillet [ʒɥijɛ] **NM** July; **la monarchie de j.** the July Monarchy; **le quatorze j.** *(fête nationale)* Bastille Day; *voir aussi* **mars**

LA FÊTE DU 14 JUILLET

The celebrations to mark the anniversary of the storming of the Bastille begin on 13 July with outdoor public dances ("les bals du 14 Juillet") and firework displays, and continue on the 14th with a military parade in the morning. Firework displays are also held in the evening of "Bastille Day".

juillettiste [ʒɥijetist] **NMF** = person who goes on holiday in July

juin [ʒɥɛ̃] **NM** June; *voir aussi* **mars**

juive [ʒɥiv] *voir* **juif**

jujube [ʒyʒyb] **NM 1** *(fruit)* jujube (fruit) **2** *Can (friandise)* jujube, gumdrop

jujubier [ʒyʒybje] **NM** jujube (tree)

juke-box [dʒukbɔks] *(pl* **inv** *ou* **juke-boxes)** **NM** jukebox

julep [ʒylɛp] **NM** *Vieilli Pharm* julep

Jules [ʒyl] **NPR** *(pape)* Julius; **J. César** Julius Caesar

jules [ʒyl] **NM** *très Fam* **1** *(amant)* boyfriend[□], man, *Br* bloke; *(mari)* old man **2** *(souteneur)* pimp

julien, -enne[1] [ʒyljɛ̃, -ɛn] **ADJ** *(année, période)* Julian *(avant n)*

julienne[2] [ʒyljɛn] **NF 1** *Culin* **j. (de légumes)** *(garniture)* (vegetable) julienne; *(soupe)* julienne (consommé) **2** *Ich* ling **3** *Bot* dame's violet

jumbo-jet [dʒœmbodʒɛt] *(pl* **jumbo-jets)** **NM** jumbo (jet)

jumeau, -elle, -aux, -elles[1] [ʒymo, -ɛl] **ADJ 1** *Biol* twin *(avant n)*; *(fruits)* double **2** *(symétrique)* twin *(avant n)*, identical; **les flèches jumelles de la cathédrale** the twin spires of the cathedral

NM,F 1 *Biol* twin; **vrais/faux jumeaux** identical/fraternal twins **2** *(sosie)* double

NM 1 *Anat* gemellus muscle **2** *Culin* neck of beef

jumelage [ʒymlaʒ] **NM 1** *(association)* twinning **2** *Rail* paired running

jumelé, -e [ʒymle] **ADJ 1** *(fenêtres)* double; *(colonne)* twin *(avant n)*; **villes jumelées** twin *or* twinned towns/cities, *Am* sister cities **2** *Naut* twin *(avant n)*

jumeler [24] [ʒymle] **VT 1** *(villes)* to twin, *Am* to make sister cities; **être jumelé à** to be twinned with, *Am* to be a sister city with **2** *(moteurs)* to couple; *(poutres)* to join

jumelle [ʒymɛl] **ADJ F** *voir* **jumeau**

NF *(sœur, sosie) voir* **jumeau**

jumellerai *etc voir* **jumeler**

jumelles[2] [ʒymɛl] **ADJ FPL** *voir* **jumeau**

NFPL *Opt* binoculars; **visible aux j.** visible through binoculars; **j. de théâtre** *ou* **spectacle** opera glasses; **j. de campagne** field glasses

jument [ʒymɑ̃] **NF** mare; **j. poulinière** brood mare

jumping [dʒœmpiŋ] **NM** *Équitation* showjumping

jungle [ʒœ̃gl] **NF 1** *Géog* jungle **2** *Fig* jungle; **c'est une vraie j.** *(le monde du travail etc)* it's a jungle out there, it's dog-eat-dog

junior [ʒynjɔr] **ADJ INV 1** *(fils)* junior; **Douglas Fairbanks j.** Douglas Fairbanks Junior **2** *(destiné aux adolescents ▸ mode)* junior; **les nouveaux blousons j.** the new jackets for teenagers **3** *(débutant)* junior

ADJ *Sport* junior; **les équipes juniors** the junior teams

NMF *Sport* junior

junk bond [dʒœ̃kbɔnd] *(pl* **junk bonds)** **NM** *Fin* junk bond

junkie [dʒœnki] **NMF** *très Fam* junkie, junky

Junon [ʒynɔ̃] **NPR** *Myth* Juno

junte [ʒœ̃t] **NF** junta

jupe [ʒyp] **NF 1** *(vêtement)* skirt; **j. droite/plissée/évasée** straight/pleated/flared skirt; **il est toujours dans les** *ou* **accroché aux jupes de sa mère** he's tied to his mother's apron strings **2** *Tech (d'un aéroglisseur)* skirt, apron; *(d'un piston, d'un rouleau)* skirt

jupe-culotte [ʒypkylɔt] *(pl* **jupes-culottes)** **NF** (pair of) culottes

jupette [ʒypɛt] **NF** short skirt; **j. de tennis** tennis skirt

Jupiter [ʒypitɛr] **NF** *Astron* Jupiter

NPR *Myth* Jupiter, Jove

jupon [ʒypɔ̃] **NM** petticoat, slip, underskirt

Jura [ʒyra] **NM le J.** *(chaîne montagneuse)* the Jura (Mountains); *(département)* the Jura

jurassien, -enne [ʒyrasjɛ̃, -ɛn] **ADJ** of/from the Jura

• **Jurassien, -enne NM,F** = inhabitant of or person from the Jura

jurassique [ʒyrasik] **ADJ** Jurassic

NM le j. the Jurassic period

juratoire [ʒyratwar] *voir* **caution**

juré, -e [ʒyre] **ADJ 1** *(assermenté ▸ expert, traducteur)* sworn **2** *(ennemi)* sworn; **je ne recommencerai plus – (c'est) j.?** I won't do it again – do you swear?

NM,F *Jur* member of a jury, juror; **les jurés ont délibéré** the jury has *or* have reached a verdict; **elle a été convoquée comme j.** she's had to report for *Br* jury service *or Am* jury duty

jurer [3] [ʒyre] **VT** *aussi Jur (promettre)* to swear; **je ne l'ai jamais vue, je le jure!** I've never seen her, I swear it!; **j. allégeance/obéissance à qn** to swear *or* to pledge allegiance/obedience to sb; **il a juré ma perte** he has sworn *or* vowed to bring about my downfall; **je te jure que c'est vrai** I swear it's true; **je jurerais que c'est vrai** I'd swear to it; **j'aurais juré que c'était elle** I could have sworn it was her; **j. de faire qch** to swear to do sth; **j'ai juré de garder le secret** I'm sworn to secrecy; **elle m'a fait j. de garder le secret** she swore me to secrecy; **jurez-vous de dire la vérité, toute la vérité, rien que la vérité?** do you swear to tell the truth, the whole truth and nothing but the truth?; **dites je le jure – je le jure** do you so swear? – I swear *or* I do; **j. ses grands dieux que...** to swear to God that...

USAGE ABSOLU j. sur la Bible/devant Dieu to swear on the Bible/to God; **j. sur l'honneur** to swear on one's honour; **je ne l'ai jamais vu, je le jure sur la tête de mon fils** I swear on my mother's grave I've never seen him

VI 1 *(blasphémer)* to swear, to curse; **j. après qn/qch** to curse *or* to swear at sb/sth; **j. comme un charretier** to swear like a trooper **2** *(détonner ▸ couleurs, architecture)* to clash, to jar; **le foulard jure avec la robe** the scarf clashes with the dress **3** *Fig* **j. par** to swear by; **ils ne jurent que par leur nouvel entraîneur** they swear by their new coach

• **jurer de VT IND 1** *(affirmer)* **j. de sa bonne foi** to swear that one is sincere; **il ne faut j. de rien** you never can tell **2** *(au conditionnel)* **j'en jurerais** I'd swear to it; **c'est peut-être mon agresseur, mais je n'en jurerais pas** he might be the man who attacked me but I wouldn't swear to it

VPR se jurer 1 *(l'un l'autre)* **se j. fidélité** to swear *or* to vow to be faithful to each other **2** *(à soi-même)* **se j. de faire** to swear *or* to vow to do; **se j. que** to swear *or* to vow that

juridiction [ʒyridiksjɔ̃] **NF 1** *(pouvoir)* jurisdiction; **exercer sa j.** to exercise one's power; *Jur* **tomber sous la j. de** to come under the jurisdiction of; **j. commerciale** commercial jurisdiction **2** *(tribunal)* court (of law); *(tribunaux)* courts (of law); **j. administrative** administrative court; **j. d'attribution** = administrative court of limited jurisdiction; **j. de droit commun** ordinary courts, courts of general jurisdiction; **j. d'instruction** examining courts; **j. de jugement** penal courts; **j. judiciaire** judicial courts; **j. militaire** ≃ military courts; **j. de la libération conditionnelle** parole jurisdiction; **j. obligatoire** compulsory jurisdiction; **j. de l'ordre judiciaire** ordinary court; **j. de premier degré** court of first instance; **j. de second degré** *Br* ≃ Court of Appeal, *Am* ≃ Appellate Court

juridictionnel, -elle [ʒyridiksjɔnɛl] **ADJ** jurisdictional

juridique [ʒyridik] **ADJ** *(vocabulaire)* legal, juridical; *(conseiller, texte, frais)* legal; *(système, environnement)* legal, judicial; **il a une formation j.** he studied law; **situation j.** legal situation

juridiquement [ʒyridikmɑ̃] **ADV** legally, juridically

jurisconsulte [ʒyriskɔ̃sylt] **NM** jurisconsult

jurisprudence [ʒyrisprydɑ̃s] **NF** *(source de droit)* case law; **faire j.** *(décision, jugement, arrêt)* to set *or* to create a (legal) precedent; **cas/affaire qui fait j.** test case

juriste [ʒyrist] **NMF** *(qui pratique)* lawyer, *Am* jurist; *(auteur)* jurist; **j. d'entreprise** company lawyer

juron [ʒyrɔ̃] **NM** swear word, oath; **proférer des jurons** to swear, to curse

jury [ʒyri] **NM 1** *Jur* jury; **membre du j.** juror, member of the jury; **il fait partie du j.** he sits on the jury

2 *Scol* board of examiners, jury

3 *Beaux-Arts & Sport* panel *or* jury *(of judges)*

4 *Mktg* **j. de consommateurs** focus group

jus [ʒy] **NM 1** *(boisson)* juice; **j. de citron/tomate** lemon/tomato juice; **j. de fruit** *ou* **fruits** fruit juice; **le j. de la treille** wine

2 *Culin (de viande)* juice(s); *(sauce)* gravy; *très Fam* **cuire** *ou* **mijoter dans son j.** to stew in one's (own) juice; *Fam* **c'est du j. de chaussettes, leur café** their coffee tastes like dishwater; *Can Fam* **j. de bras** elbow grease

3 *Fam (café)* coffee[□]; **tu prends un j.?** are you having a cup (of coffee)?

4 *Fam (courant électrique)* juice; **attention, tu vas prendre le j.!** watch out, you'll get a shock!

5 *Fam (eau)* **tout le monde au j.!** everybody in (the water)![□]; **ils ont mis Paul au j.** they've thrown Paul in *or* into the water

6 *Fam (locution)* **être au j.** *(au courant)* to know[□]; **ça vaut le j.** it's really something!

jusant [ʒyzɑ̃] **NM** ebb tide

jusqu'au-boutisme [ʒyskobutism] *(pl* **jusqu'au-boutismes)** **NM** *Fam (d'un individu)* hardline attitude; *Pol* hardline policy

jusqu'au-boutiste [ʒyskobutist] *(pl* **jusqu'au-boutistes)** *Fam* **ADJ** hardline

NMF *Pol* hardliner; **c'est un j.** he's a hardliner

JUSQUE [ʒyskə]

- as far as **1**
- up to **1**
- until **2**
- even **3**

jusqu', or in literary language **jusques**, is used before a word beginning with a vowel or h mute.

PRÉP 1 *(dans l'espace)* **elle m'a suivi j. chez moi** she followed me all the way home; **les nuages s'étendront j. vers la Bourgogne** the clouds will spread as far as Burgundy; **je suis monté jusqu'en haut de la tour** I climbed (right) up to the top of the tower; *Littéraire* **du haut jusques en bas** from top to bottom; **jusqu'où?** how far?; **jusqu'où iront-ils?** (just) how far will they go?; **jusqu'où peut aller la bêtise/cruauté!** (just) how stupid/cruel can people be! **jusques et y compris** up to and including; **jusques et y compris la page 15** up to and including page 15

2 *(dans le temps)* until, till; **j'attendrai j. vers 11 heures** I'll wait till *or* until about 11 o'clock; **jusqu'en avril** until *or* till April; **jusqu'alors** (up) until *or* till then; **j. tard** until *or* till late; **j. tard dans la nuit** until *or* till late at night

3 *(même, y compris)* even; **il y avait du sable j. dans les lits** there was even sand in the beds; **j'ai cherché j. sous les meubles** I even looked underneath the furniture

• **jusqu'à PRÉP 1** *(dans l'espace)* **jusqu'à Marseille** as far as Marseilles; **le train va-t-il jusqu'à Nice?** does the train go all the way to Nice *or* as far as Nice?; **lisez jusqu'à la page 30 incluse** read up to and including page 30; **il a rempli les verres jusqu'au bord** he filled the glasses (right up) to the brim; **jusqu'au bout de la rue** (right) to the end of the street; **le sous-marin peut plonger jusqu'à 3000 m de profondeur** the submarine can dive (down) to 3,000m; **elle avait de l'eau jusqu'aux genoux** she was up to her knees in water, she was knee-deep in water; **il y a 300 m de chez nous jusqu'à la gare** it's 300 m from our house to the station

2 *(dans le temps)* until; **la pièce dure jusqu'à quelle heure?** what time does the play finish?; **jusqu'à 15 ans** up to the age of 15, up to 15 (years old); **jusqu'à quand peut-on s'inscrire?** when's the last (possible) date for registering?; **tu vas attendre jusqu'à quand?** how long are you going to wait?; **il ne veut pas porter de casque, jusqu'au jour où il aura un accident!** he won't wear a helmet, until he has an accident one day!; **jusqu'à nouvel ordre** until further notice; **jusqu'à preuve du contraire** as far as I know; **jusqu'à plus ample informé** pending further information, until further information is available; **de lundi jusqu'à mardi** from Monday to *or* until *or* till Tuesday; **de 15 h jusqu'à 18 h** from 3 p.m. to *or* until *or* till 6 p.m.; **j'ai jusqu'à demain pour finir mon rapport** I've got (up) until *or* till tomorrow to finish my report; **jusqu'à hier** (up) until *or* till yesterday; **jusqu'à maintenant, jusqu'à présent** up to now, until now, till now

3 *(indiquant le degré)* **jusqu'à quel point peut-on lui faire confiance?** to what extent *or* how far can we trust him/her?; **jusqu'à un certain point** up to a certain point, to a certain extent; **jusqu'à 60 pour cent de réduction sur les fourrures!** up to 60 percent discount on furs!; **un amour maternel qui allait jusqu'à l'adoration** motherly love bordering on adoration; **il se montrait sévère jusqu'à la cruauté** he was severe to the point of cruelty; **aller jusqu'à faire qch** to go as far as to do sth; **j'irais jusqu'à dire que c'était délibéré** I would go as far as to say it was done on purpose; **j'irai jusqu'à 30 euros, pas plus** I'll go up to 30 euros, no more; **jusqu'à concurrence de 1000 euros** up to 1,000 euros maximum, up to (a limit of) 1,000 euros; *Fam* **il nous aura embêtés jusqu'à la fin** *ou* **la gauche!** he will have been a nuisance to us (right) to the bitter end!

4 *(même, y compris)* even; **il n'est pas jusqu'aux enfants qui ne se battent** even the children are fighting; **ils ont tout emporté, jusqu'aux meubles** they took everything away, even the furniture *or* furniture and all; **tout en lui, jusqu'à son sourire, a changé** everything about him, right down to *or* even his smile, has changed; **il a mangé tous les bonbons jusqu'au dernier** he's eaten every last *or* single sweet

• **jusqu'à ce que CONJ** until; **je les aiderai jusqu'à ce qu'ils soient tirés d'affaire** I'll help them until they've sorted themselves out; **tout allait bien jusqu'à ce qu'il arrive** everything was going fine until he turned up

• **jusqu'à tant que CONJ** until

• **jusqu'au moment où CONJ** until; **je t'ai attendu jusqu'au moment où j'ai dû partir pour mon rendez-vous** I waited for you until I had to go to my meeting

• **jusque-là ADV 1** *(dans le présent)* up to now, (up) until *or* till now; *(dans le passé)* up to then, (up) until *or* till then; **j.-là, tout va bien** so far so good; **tout s'était bien passé j.-là** everything had gone well up until *or* till *or* to then **2** *(dans l'espace)* **je ne suis pas allé j.-là pour rien** I didn't go all that way for nothing; **ils sont arrivés j.-là et puis ils sont repartis** they got so far and then they went back; **on avait de l'eau j.-là** the water was up to here; **je n'ai pas encore lu j.-là** I haven't got *or* read that far yet; *Fam* **j'en ai j.-là de tes caprices!** I've had it up to here with your whims!, I'm sick and tired of your whims!; *Fam* **s'en mettre j.-là** to stuff one's face *or* oneself

• **jusqu'ici ADV 1** *(dans l'espace)* (up) to here, as far as here; **approchez-vous jusqu'ici** come as far as here; **je ne suis pas venu jusqu'ici pour rien!** I haven't come all this way *or* as far as this for nothing! **2** *(dans le temps)* so far, until now, up to now; **nous n'avons pas eu de nouvelles jusqu'ici** up to now *or* so far we haven't had any news; **jusqu'ici, rien de grave** nothing serious so far

justaucorps [ʒystokɔr] **NM 1** *(de gymnaste, de danseur)* leotard **2** *Hist* jerkin

JUSTE [ʒyst]

ADJ

- fair **1**
- just **2**
- legitimate **2**
- right **3, 4, 7**
- accurate **3**
- tight **5**
- relevant **7**
- good **8**
- in tune **9**

ADV

- correctly **1**
- exactly **2**
- just **2, 3**
- only **3**

NM

- just man

ADJ 1 *(équitable ▸ partage, décision, personne)* fair; **être j. envers** *ou* **avec qn** to be fair to sb; **elle n'a pas eu de chance, soyons justes!** she hasn't had any luck, let's be fair!; **pour être j. envers elle** in fairness to her, to be fair to her; *Fam* **c'est pas j.!** it's not fair *or* right!

2 *(justifié ▸ cause, récompense, punition)* just; *(▸ requête)* legitimate; *(▸ colère)* righteous, legitimate; **il est en colère, et à j. titre!** he's angry, and quite rightly (so) *or* and with good reason!

3 *(exact ▸ calcul, compte, réponse)* right; *(▸ horloge)* accurate, right; *(▸ balance)* accurate, true; **as-tu l'heure j.?** have you got the right *or* exact time?; **à l'heure j.** right on time

4 *(précis ▸ terme, expression)* appropriate, right

5 *(serré ▸ habit)* tight; *(▸ chaussures)* tight, small; **la nappe est un peu j. en longueur/largeur** the tablecloth is a bit on the short/narrow side

6 *(qui suffit à peine)* **trois bouteilles pour sept personnes, c'est un peu j.!** three bottles for seven people, that's not very much!; **une heure pour aller à l'aéroport, c'est trop j.** an hour to get to the airport, that's cutting it a bit fine; **ses notes sont trop justes pour que vous le laissiez passer** his marks are too borderline for you to pass him; **elle a réussi l'examen, mais c'était j.** she passed her exam, but it was a close thing; *Fam* **on est un peu justes en ce moment** *(financièrement)* we're a bit pushed for money *or* strapped for cash at the moment

7 *(sensé, judicieux ▸ raisonnement)* sound; *(▸ objection, observation)* relevant, apt; **ta remarque est tout à fait j.!** your comment is quite right!; **très j.!** quite right!, good point!

8 *(compétent)* good; **avoir l'oreille/le coup d'œil j.** to have a good ear/eye

9 *Mus (voix, instrument)* true, in tune; *(note)* true, right; **le piano n'est pas j.** the piano is out of tune

10 *(approprié)* **apprécier qch à son j. prix** to appreciate the true value *or* worth of sth; **apprécier qn à sa j. valeur** to appreciate the true worth *or* value of sb

ADV 1 *(avec justesse)* **chanter j.** to sing in tune; **deviner j.** to guess correctly *or* right; **tu as vu** *ou* **deviné j.!** you guessed correctly *or* right!; **tomber j.** to guess right, to hit the nail on the head; **sa remarque a touché** *ou* **frappé j.** his/her remark struck home

2 *(exactement)* exactly, just; **il a fait j. ce qu'il fallait** he did just *or* exactly what he had to; **arriver à dix heures j.** to arrive at exactly ten o'clock, to arrive at ten o'clock sharp; **arriver j. à l'heure** to arrive just in time *or* in the nick of time; **le train part à deux h j.** the train leaves at two o'clock exactly; **ça fait j. huit euros, ça fait huit euros tout j.** that comes to exactly eight euros; **la balle est passée j. à côté du poteau** the ball went just past the post; **c'est j. là** it's just there; **j. au milieu** right in the middle; **c'est j. ce qu'il me fallait** it's just what I wanted; **tu arrives j. à temps** you've come just in time; **j. quand** *ou* **comme le téléphone sonnait** just as *or* when the phone was ringing; **il s'est fait renvoyer? – tout j.!** so he was dismissed? – he was indeed!

3 *(à peine, seulement)* just, only; **il vient j. d'arriver** he's just arrived (this minute); **il est j. neuf heures, vous n'allez pas partir déjà** it's only nine o'clock, you're not going to leave already; **je voudrais j. de quoi faire une jupe** I'd like just enough to make a skirt; **j'ai bu j. une gorgée pour goûter** I just *or* only drank a mouthful to get the taste; **c'est j. que je ne voulais pas te déranger** it's only *or* just that I didn't want to disturb you; **j'ai tout j. le temps de prendre un café** I've just about enough *or* I've just got enough time to have a cup of coffee; **j'ai tout j. eu le temps de m'abriter** I only just had (enough) time to run for cover; **ils ont (tout) j. fini de manger** they've only just finished eating; **c'est tout j. s'il ne m'a pas frappé** he very nearly *or* all but hit me; **c'est tout j. s'il sait lire** he can only just *or* he can barely read; **il ne manque jamais son train, mais c'est tout j.** he never misses his train, but he cuts it fine

4 *(en quantité insuffisante)* **un gâteau pour huit, ça fait (un peu) j.** one cake for eight people, that won't go very far; **voir** *ou* **prévoir** *ou* **calculer trop j.** not to allow enough, to allow too little

5 *Com* **j. à temps** *(achat, distribution, production)* just-in-time

NM just man; **les justes** the just

• **au juste ADV** exactly; **combien sont-ils au j.?** how many (of them) are there exactly?

• **au plus juste ADV calculer qch au plus j.** to calculate sth to the nearest penny; **le budget a été calculé au plus j.** the budget was calculated down to the last penny

• **comme de juste ADV** of course, needless to say; **comme de j., elle avait oublié** she'd forgotten, of course

• **juste ciel, juste Dieu EXCLAM** good heavens!, heavens (above)!

justement [ʒystəmɑ̃] **ADV 1** *(à ce moment précis, d'ailleurs)* **voilà j. Paul** talking of Paul, here he is; **j'ai j. besoin d'une secrétaire** actually *or* as it happens, I need a secretary; **j'allais j. te téléphoner** I was just going to phone you

2 *(pour renforcer un énoncé)* quite, just so; **il se met vite en colère – j., ne le provoque pas!** he loses his temper very quickly – quite *or* exactly *or* that's right, so don't provoke him!; **tu ne vas pas partir sans lui dire au revoir? – si, j.!** you're not going without saying goodbye to him/her? – that's precisely *or* exactly what I'm doing *or* indeed I am!

3 *(exactement)* exactly, precisely; **j'ai j. ce qu'il vous faut** I've got exactly *or* just what you need; **c'est j. pour cela que je lui en veux** that's precisely *or* exactly why I'm annoyed with him/her

4 *(pertinemment)* rightly, justly; **comme tu l'as dit si j.** as you (so) rightly said

5 *(avec justice)* rightly, justly; **elle fut j. récompensée/condamnée** she was justly rewarded/condemned

justesse [ʒystɛs] **NF 1** *(d'un raisonnement, d'un jugement)* soundness; *(d'une observation, d'un terme)* appropriateness, aptness; **elle raisonne avec j.** her reasoning is sound **2** *Math & Mus* ac-

curacy; *(d'un mécanisme, d'une horloge, d'une balance)* accuracy, precision
• **de justesse** **ADV** just, barely, narrowly; **j'ai eu mon permis de j.** I only just passed my driving test; **il a gagné de j.** he won by a narrow margin *or* by a hair's breadth; **on a eu le train de j.** we caught the train with only moments to spare, we only just caught the train; **on a évité la collision de j.** we very nearly had a crash

justice [ʒystis] **NF 1** *(équité)* justice, fairness; **avec j.** *(agir)* fairly, justly, with fairness; **en bonne j.** in all fairness; **ce n'est que j.** it's only fair; *Hum* **il n'y a pas de j.!** there's no justice (in the world)!; **j. sociale** social justice **2** *Jur* **la j.** the law; **rendre la j.** to dispense justice; **avoir des démêlés avec la j.** to fall foul of the law; **il a fait des aveux à la j.** he confessed to the law; **j. expéditive** *ou* **sommaire** summary justice; **la j. civile/militaire/administrative** civil/military/administrative law; **j. de paix** Justice of the Peace **3** *(réparation)* justice; **demander j.** to ask for justice to be done; **obtenir j.** to obtain justice; **nous voulons que j. soit faite!** we want justice to be done!; **faire j.** *(venger une faute)* to take the law into one's own hands; **j. est faite** justice is done; **faire j. de qch** *(montrer que c'est nocif)* to prove sth to be bad; *(le réfuter)* to prove sth wrong, to give the lie to sth; **se faire j.** *(se venger)* to take the law into one's own hands; *(se tuer)* to take one's (own) life; **rendre** *ou* **faire j. à qn** to do sb justice; **rendons-lui cette j. qu'elle a fait beaucoup d'efforts** she made a big effort, let's be fair *or* let's grant her that; **j. immanente** poetic justice
• **de justice** **ADJ un homme de j.** a man of the law
• **en justice** **ADV** *Jur* **aller en j.** to go to court; **passer en j.** to stand trial, to appear in court

justiciable [ʒystisjabl] **ADJ 1** *(responsable)* **j. de** answerable for, responsible for; **pour ses électeurs, il est j. de sa politique** he is answerable to the electorate for his policies **2 j. de** *(qui requiert)* requiring; **maladie j. d'hydrothérapie** illness requiring hydrotherapy **3** *Jur* **il est j. des tribunaux pour enfants** he is subject to *or* comes under the jurisdiction of the juvenile courts
NMF person liable *or* subject to trial; **les justiciables** those due to be tried

justicier, -ère [ʒystisje, -ɛr] **ADJ 1** *(qui rend la justice)* justiciary *(avant n)* **2** *(qui fait justice lui-même)* **le jury a condamné le mari j.** the jury found the husband who had taken the law into his own hands guilty
NM,F *(redresseur de torts)* righter of wrongs; **il faut toujours qu'elle s'érige en justicière** she's always setting herself up as a righter of wrongs

justifiable [ʒystifjabl] **ADJ** justifiable; **sa négligence n'est pas j.** his/her negligence is unjustifiable *or* cannot be justified

justificateur, -trice [ʒystifikatœr, -tris] **ADJ** *(témoignage)* justifying, justificatory
NM *Typ & Ordinat* justifier

justificatif, -ive [ʒystifikatif, -iv] **ADJ** *(rapport)* justificatory, supporting; *(facture)* justificatory; **document j. d'identité** (written) proof of one's identity
NM 1 *Admin* written proof *or* evidence; *Compta* receipt; **à adresser à la Comptabilité avec justificatifs** to be sent to the accounts department with all necessary receipts; **j. de domicile** proof of address **2** *Presse* free copy *(of newspaper sent to those who have an advertisement or a review etc in it)*

justification [ʒystifikasjɔ̃] **NF 1** *(motivation ▸ d'une attitude, d'une politique)* justification; **il n'y a pas de j. possible à un acte aussi barbare** there is no possible justification for such a barbaric act
2 *(explication)* justification, reason; **demander/chercher des justifications** to demand/to seek justification; **vos justifications ne m'intéressent pas** I'm not interested in your reasons *or Péj* excuses
3 *Admin* (written) proof *(of expenses incurred)*; **j. d'identité** proof of identity; **j. de paiement** proof of payment
4 *Ordinat & Typ* justification; **j. à droite/gauche** right/left justification; *Typ* **j. de tirage** limitation notice; **j. verticale** vertical justification

justificative [ʒystifikativ] *voir* **justificatif**

justificatrice [ʒystifikatris] *voir* **justificateur**

justifié, -e [ʒystifje] **ADJ** *(conduite, réaction, colère)* justified, justifiable

justifier **[9]** [ʒystifje] **VT 1** *(motiver ▸ conduite, mesure, dépense)* to justify; **rien ne saurait j. de tels propos** there's no possible justification for speaking in such terms
2 *(confirmer ▸ crainte, théorie)* to justify, to confirm
3 *(prouver ▸ affirmation)* to prove, to justify; *(▸ versement)* to give proof *or* evidence of
4 *(innocenter)* to vindicate
5 *Typ & Ordinat* to justify; **le paragraphe est justifié à gauche/droite** the paragraph is left-/right-justified
• **justifier de** **VT IND j. de son identité** to prove one's identity; **pouvez-vous j. de ce diplôme?** can you provide evidence that you are the holder of this qualification?
VPR se justifier to justify oneself; **je n'ai pas à me j. devant toi** I don't have to justify myself to you, I don't owe you any explanations; **se j. d'une accusation** to clear oneself of an accusation, to clear one's name

jute [ʒyt] **NM** jute; **de** *ou* **en j.** jute *(avant n)*

juter **[3]** [ʒyte] **VI** *(fruit)* to be very juicy, to ooze with juice; *(viande)* to drip (with) juice

juteux, -euse [ʒytø, -øz] **ADJ 1** *(fruit, viande)* juicy **2** *Fam (transaction)* lucrative▫; **c'est une affaire bien juteuse!** that business is a real gold mine!
NM *Fam Arg mil Br* warrant officer class II▫, *Am* warrant officer (junior grade)▫

juvénile [ʒyvenil] **ADJ 1** *(jeune ▸ silhouette)* young, youthful; *(▸ ardeur, enthousiasme)* youthful; **il avait toujours gardé une passion j. pour les motos** he'd never lost his youthful passion for motorbikes **2** *Physiol* juvenile

juvénilité [ʒyvenilite] **NF** *Littéraire* youthfulness

juxtalinéaire [ʒykstalineɛr] **ADJ** line-by-line, (placed) parallel

juxtaposer **[3]** [ʒykstapoze] **VT** to juxtapose, to place side by side; **j. un mot à un autre** to juxtapose two words

juxtaposition [ʒykstapozisjɔ̃] **NF** juxtaposition

k

K[1], k[1] [ka] NM INV *(lettre)* K, k; **K comme Kléber** ≃ K for Kevin

K[2] *Ordinat (abrév écrite* **kilo-octet***)* K

k[2] *(abrév écrite* **kilo***)* k

K7 [kasɛt] NF *(abrév* **cassette***)* cassette; **radio-K7** radiocassette

kabbale [kabal] = **cabale 2**

kabbaliste [kabalist] = **cabaliste**

kabbalistique [kabalistik] = **cabalistique**

Kaboul, Kabul [kabul] NF Kabul

kabyle [kabil] ADJ Kabyle
NM *(langue)* Kabyle
• **Kabyle** NMF Kabyle

Kabylie [kabili] NF **la K.** Kabylia; **la Grande K.** Great Kabylia

kafkaïen, -enne [kafkajɛ̃, -ɛn] ADJ Kafkaesque

Kaiser [kajzɛr] NM **le K.** the Kaiser

kakatoès [kakatɔɛs] = **cacatoès**

kaki [kaki] ADJ INV *(couleur)* khaki
NM **1** *(couleur)* khaki **2** *Bot (arbre)* (Japanese) persimmon, kaki; *(fruit)* persimmon, sharon fruit

kakou [kaku] NMF *Fam* **faire le k.** to act smart

kalachnikov [kalaʃnikɔf] NM OU NF kalashnikov

Kalahari [kalaari] NM **le (désert du) K.** the Kalahari Desert

kaléidoscope [kaleidɔskɔp] NM *Opt & Fig* kaleidoscope

kaléidoscopique [kaleidɔskɔpik] ADJ kaleidoscopic

kalmouk, -e [kalmuk] ADJ Kalmuck
NM *(langue)* Kalmuck
• **Kalmouk, -e** NM,F Kalmuck; **les Kalmouks** the Kalmucks *or* Kalmuck

kamikaze [kamikaz] ADJ kamikaze; *Fig* **être k.** to have a death wish
NM kamikaze

Kampuchéa [kɑ̃putʃea] NM **le K.** Kampuchea

kan [kɑ̃] = **khan**

kanak, -e [kanak] = **canaque**

kangourou [kɑ̃guru] NM **1** *Zool* kangaroo **2** *(comme adj)* **(sac) k.** baby carrier; *Rail* **technique k.** railroad transport

kantien, -enne [kɑ̃sjɛ̃, -ɛn] ADJ Kantian

kantisme [kɑ̃tism] NM Kantianism

kaolin [kaɔlɛ̃] NM kaolin

kaolinisation [kaɔlinizasjɔ̃] NF kaolinization

kapok [kapɔk] NM kapok

kapokier [kapɔkje] NM ceiba (tree), kapok tree

Kaposi [kapozi] NPR *Méd* **maladie** *ou* **sarcome de K.** Kaposi's sarcoma

kaput [kaput] ADJ *Fam* kaput; **la téloche est k.; impossible de regarder le match!** the TV's kaput, we can't watch the match!

karakul [karakyl] = **caracul**

karaoké [karaɔke] NM karaoke

karaté [karate] NM karate

karatéka [karateka] NMF karate expert, karateka

karbau, -x [karbo] NM water buffalo

Karcher® [karʃɛr] NM pressure washer

karité [karite] NM *(arbre)* shea (tree); *(substance)* shea; **beurre de k.** shea butter

karma [karma], **karman** [karman] NM karma

karst [karst] NM *Géol* karst

karstique [karstik] ADJ *Géol* karstic

kart [kart] NM kart, go-kart

karting [kartiŋ] NM karting, go-karting; **faire du k.** to go-kart, to go karting

kasba(h) [kazba] NF = **casbah**

kascher [kaʃɛr] ADJ INV *Rel* kosher

Katmandou [katmɑ̃du] NF Katmandu, Kathmandu

kayak [kajak] NM *(embarcation)* kayak; *(sport)* kayaking; **faire du k.** to go kayaking;

kayakiste [kajakist] NMF kayaker

kazakh, -e [kazak] ADJ Kazakh
NM *(langue)* Kazakh
• **Kazakh, -e** NM,F Kazakh

Kazakhstan [kazakstɑ̃] NM **le K.** Kazakhstan

Kb *(abrév écrite* **kilobit***)* Kb

KE [kaə] NM *(abrév* **kiloeuro***)* thousand euros

keffieh [kefje] NM keffiyeh, kaffiyeh

kéfir [kefir] = **képhir**

keiretsu [kejretsu] NM *Écon* keiretsu

kelvin [kɛlvin] NM *Phys* kelvin

kendo [kɛndo] NM kendo

Kenya [kenja] NM **le K.** Kenya

kényan, -e [kenjɑ̃, -an] ADJ Kenyan
• **Kényan, -e** NM,F Kenyan

képhir [kefir] NM kefir, kephir

képi [kepi] NM kepi

kérabau, -x [kerabo] NM *Zool* water buffalo

kératine [keratin] NF *Biol* keratin

kératite [keratit] NF *Méd* keratitis

kératoplastie [keratɔplasti] NF *Méd* keratoplasty

kératose [keratoz] NF *Méd & Physiol* keratosis

Kerguelen [kergelɛn] NFPL **les (îles) K.** the Kerguelen Islands

kermesse [kɛrmɛs] NF **1** *Belg* kermis, kirmess **2** *(de charité)* charity fête, bazaar; **k. de l'école** school fête

kérosène [kerɔzɛn] NM kerosene, kerosine

ket [kɛt] NM *Belg Fam (enfant)* kid[□] *(from Brussels)*

ketch [kɛtʃ] NM ketch

ketchup [kɛtʃœp] NM ketchup

keuf [kœf] NM *très Fam (verlan de* **flic***)* cop; **les keufs** the fuzz, the cops

keum [kœm] NM *Fam (verlan de* **mec***)* guy, *Br* bloke

Kevlar® [kevlar] NM Kevlar®

keynésianisme [kenezjanism] NM *Écon* Keynesianism

keynésien, -enne [kenezjɛ̃, -ɛn] ADJ Keynesian

KF [kaɛf] NM *Anciennement (abrév* **kilofranc***)* thousand francs; **son salaire annuel est de 100 KF** he/she earns 100,000 francs a year

kg *(abrév écrite* **kilogramme***)* kg

KGB [kaʒebe] NM KGB

khâgne [kaɲ] NF *Fam Arg scol* = second year of a two-year preparatory humanities course for entrance to the "École normale supérieure"

khâgneux, -euse [kaɲø, -øz] NM,F *Fam Arg scol* = student in "khâgne"

khalifat [kalifa] = **califat**

khalife [kalif] = **calife**

khamsin [xamsin] NM khamsin

khan [kɑ̃] NM *(titre, abri)* khan

Khartoum [kartum] NF Khartoum

khédive [kediv] NM khedive

khmer, -ère [kmɛr] ADJ Khmer
NM *(langue)* Khmer
• **Khmer, -ère** NM,F Khmer; **les Khmers** the Khmers; **les Khmers rouges** the Khmer Rouge

khôl [kol] NM kohl

kibboutz [kibuts] *(pl inv ou* **kibboutzim** [-tsim]*)* NM kibbutz

kick [kik] NM kick-starter, kick-start; **j'ai démarré au k.** I kick-started the motorbike

kickboxing [kikbɔksiŋ] NM kick boxing

kick-starter [kikstartɛr] NM = **kick**

kidnapper [3] [kidnape] VT *(personne)* to kidnap

kidnappeur, -euse [kidnapœr, -øz] NM,F kidnapper

kidnapping [kidnapiŋ] NM kidnapping

Kiev [kjɛv] NF Kiev

kif [kif] NM *(haschisch)* kif, kef

kiffer [3] [kife] VT *Fam* **1** *(prendre du plaisir à)* to get a kick out of **2** *(aimer)* to be crazy about

kiki [kiki] NM *Fam* **1** *(cou)* neck[□]; *(gorge)* throat[□]; **serrer le k. à qn** to throttle *or* to strangle sb[□] **2** *(en langage enfantin* ▸ *pénis)* willy **3** *(locution)* **c'est parti, mon k.!** here we go!

kil [kil] NM *très Fam* bottle (of wine)[□]; **un k. de rouge** a bottle of cheap red wine *or Br* (red) plonk

Kilimandjaro [kilimɑ̃dʒaro] NM **le (mont) K.** (Mount) Kilimanjaro

kilo [kilo] NM *Fam (abrév* **kilogramme***)* kilo

kilobar [kilɔbar] NM kilobar

kilobaud [kilɔbo] NM *Ordinat* kilobaud

kilobit [kilɔbit] NM *Ordinat* kilobit

kilocalorie [kilɔkalɔri] NF kilocalorie

kilocycle [kilɔsikl] NM *Ordinat* kilocycle

kiloeuro [kilɔøro] NM thousand euros

kilofranc [kilɔfrɑ̃] NM *Anciennement* a thousand francs

kilogramme [kilɔgram] NM kilogramme

kilohertz [kilɔɛrts] NM kilohertz

kilojoule [kilɔʒul] NM kilojoule

kilométrage [kilɔmetraʒ] NM **1** *(d'un véhicule)* ≃ mileage; **k. illimité** ≃ unlimited mileage **2** *(d'une voie)* marking out *(in kilometres)*

kilomètre [kilɔmɛtr] NM **1** *(distance)* kilometre; **100 kilomètres à l'heure, 100 kilomètres-heure** 100 kilometres per *or* an hour; *Fig* **des kilomètres de pellicule** miles of film; **avoir dix kilomètres dans les jambes** to have walked ten kilometres; **k. carré** square kilometre; **kilomètres alimentaires** food miles; *Sport* **k. arrêté** standing-start kilometre **2** *Ordinat* **frappe** *ou* **saisie au k.** straight keying

kilomètre-passager [kilɔmetrpasaʒe] (*pl* **kilomètres-passagers**) **NM** passenger-kilometre

kilométrer [18] [kilɔmetre] **VT** to mark with kilometric reference points

kilomètre-voyageur [kilɔmetrvwajaʒœr] (*pl* **kilomètres-voyageurs**) **NM** passenger-kilometre

kilométrique [kilɔmetrik] **ADJ au point k. 21** at km 21; **distance k.** distance in kilometres

kilo-octet [kilɔɔkte] (*pl* **kilo-octets**) **NM** *Ordinat* kilobyte

kilotonne [kilɔtɔn] **NF** kiloton

kilovolt [kilɔvɔlt] **NM** kilovolt

kilowatt [kilɔwat] **NM** kilowatt

kilowattheure [kilɔwatœr] **NM** kilowatt-hour

kilt [kilt] **NM** *(d'Écossais, de femme)* kilt

kimono [kimɔno] **NM** kimono

ADJ INV manches k. kimono *or* loose sleeves

kinase [kinaz] **NF** *Biol & Chim* kinase

kiné [kine] **NMF** *Fam (abrév* **kinésithérapeute***)* physio

kinésithérapeute [kineziterapøt] **NMF** *Br* physiotherapist, *Am* physical therapist

kinésithérapie [kineziterapi] **NF** *Br* physiotherapy, *Am* physical therapy

kinesthésie [kinestezi] **NF** *Méd* kinaesthesia, kinaesthesis

king-charles [kiŋʃarl] **NM INV** King Charles spaniel

kinkajou [kɛ̃kaʒu] **NM** *Zool* kinkajou

Kinshasa [kinʃasa] **NF** Kinshasa

kiosque [kjɔsk] **NM 1** *(boutique)* **k. à journaux** newspaper stand, newsstand; **k. à fleurs** flower stall

2 *(édifice ▸ dans un jardin)* pavilion; **k. à musique** bandstand

3 *Naut (d'un navire)* wheelhouse; *(d'un sous-marin)* conning tower

4 *Tél* **K.®** *(d'un Minitel®)* ≃ (telephone) viewdata service

5 *Can (stand de foire)* stand *(at an exhibition)*

kip [kip] **NM** *(monnaie)* kip

kippa [kipa] **NF** kippa

kipper [kipœr] **NM** kipper

kir [kir] **NM** kir *(white wine with crème de cassis)*; **k. royal** kir royal *(champagne with crème de cassis)*

kirghiz, -e [kirgiz] **ADJ** Kirghiz, Kirgiz

NM *(langue)* Kirghiz

• **Kirghiz, -e NM,F** Kirghiz, Kirgiz; **les K.** the Kirghiz *or* Kirgiz

Kirghizistan [kirgizistɑ̃] **NM le K.** Kirghizia, Kirgizia

kirsch [kirʃ] **NM** kirsch

kit [kit] **NM** kit; **meubles en k.** flatpack furniture, furniture for self-assembly; **vendu en k.** sold in kit form *or* for self-assembly; **acheter une table en k.** to buy a table in kit form *or* for self-assembly; *Pharm* **k. de dépistage** home testing kit; *Ordinat* **k. d'accès, k. de connexion** connection kit; **k. d'extension** *ou* **d'évolution** upgrade kit; **k. de téléchargeur** download kit

kitch [kitʃ] = **kitsch**

kitchenette [kitʃənɛt] **NF** kitchenette

kitsch [kitʃ] **ADJ INV** kitsch *(avant n)*, kitschy

NM INV kitsch

kiwi [kiwi] **NM 1** *Bot (fruit)* kiwi (fruit); *(arbre)* kiwi tree **2** *Orn* kiwi

Klaxon® [klaksɔn] **NM** horn; **coup de K.** *(fort)* hoot; *(moins fort)* toot, beep; **donner un coup de K.** to sound *or* honk one's horn, *Br* to hoot (one's horn)

klaxonner [3] [klaksɔne] **VI** to sound *or* honk one's horn, *Br* to hoot (one's horn)

VT il m'a klaxonné he honked *or Br* hooted at me

klébard [klebar] **NM** *Fam* mutt

Kleenex® [klineks] **NM** (paper) tissue, Kleenex®

kleptomane [klɛptɔman] **NMF** kleptomaniac

kleptomanie [klɛptɔmani] **NF** kleptomania

klystron [klistrɔ̃] **NM** *Électron* klystron

km *(abrév écrite* **kilomètre***)* km

km/h *(abrév écrite* **kilomètre par heure***)* kmph

knack [knak] **NF** *Culin* Strasburg sausage

knickerbockers [nikœrbɔkœr], **knickers** [nikœr] **NMPL** *Br* knickerbockers, *Am* knickers

knock-out [nɔkawt] **NM INV** knockout; **k. technique** technical knockout

ADJ INV knocked out, out for the count; **mettre qn k.** to knock sb out

knout [knut] **NM** knout

K-O [kao] *(abrév* **knock-out***)* **NM INV** KO; **K. technique** technical knockout

ADJ INV 1 *Sport* KO'd; **mettre qn K.** to knock sb out; **être K.** to be out for the count **2** *Fam (épuisé)* all in, dead beat, *Br* shattered; **mettre qn K.** to exhaust sb[□]

KO [kao] **NM** *Ordinat (abrév* **kilo-octet***)* K, KB; **une disquette de 720 KO** a 720K disquette

koala [kɔala] **NM** *Zool* koala (bear)

kobold [kɔbɔld] **NM** *Myth* kobold

kola [kɔla] **NM** cola, kola

kolatier [kɔlatje] **NM** cola (tree), kola (tree)

kolkhoz(e) [kɔlkoz] **NM** kolkhoz

kolkhozien, -enne [kɔlkozjɛ̃, -ɛn] **ADJ** kolkhoz *(avant n)*

NM,F kolkhoznik

Komintern [kɔmintɛrn] **NM** Comintern

kommandantur [kɔmɑ̃dɑtur] **NF** German military command

komsomol [kɔmsɔmɔl] **NMF** Komsomol member

kopeck [kɔpɛk] **NM** kopeck; *Fam* **ça ne vaut pas un k.** it's not worth *Br* a brass farthing *or Am* a red cent

Koran [kɔrɑ̃] **NM le K.** the Koran

korrigan, -e [kɔrigɑ̃, -an] **NM,F** mischievous dwarf *or* goblin *(in Breton legends)*, ≃ leprechaun

ko/s *Ordinat (abrév écrite* **kilo-octets par seconde***)* kbps

kosovar [kɔsɔvar] **ADJ** Kosovan

• **Kosovar NMF** Kosovan

Kosovo [kɔsɔvo] **NM le K.** Kosovo

kot [kɔt] **NM** *Belg* **1** *(chambre d'étudiant)* bedroom *(for student)* **2** *(abri)* shack, hut

koteur, -euse [kɔtœr, -øz] **NM,F** *Belg Fam* = student in rented accommodation[□]

kouglof [kuglɔf] **NM** *Culin* kugelhopf

kouign-amann [kwigaman] **NM INV** *Culin* = Breton cake rich in butter

koukri [kukri] **NM** kukri, Gurkha knife

koulak [kulak] **NM** kulak

Kouriles [kuril] **NFPL les (îles) K.** the Kuril *or* Kurile Islands

Koursk [kursk] **N** Kursk

Koweït [kɔwɛjt] **NM 1** *(pays)* **le K.** Kuwait, Koweit **2** *(ville)* Kuwait, Kuwait City, Koweit

koweïtien, -enne [kɔwɛjtjɛ̃, -ɛn] **ADJ** Kuwaiti

• **Koweïtien, -enne NM,F** Kuwaiti

kraal [kral] **NM** kraal

krach [krak] **NM** *Fin* crash; **k. (boursier)** (stock market) crash; **le k. de Wall Street** the Wall Street Crash

kraft [kraft] **NM** brown wrapping paper, kraft paper

ADJ INV papier k. brown wrapping paper, kraft paper

kraken [krakɛn] **NM** *Myth* kraken

Kremlin [krɛmlɛ̃] **NM le K.** the Kremlin

kremlinologie [krɛmlinɔlɔʒi] **NF** Kremlinology, Kremlin watching

kremlinologue [krɛmlinɔlɔg] **NMF** Kremlinologist, Kremlin watcher

kriek [krik] **NF** *Belg* kriek, = beer made from cherries

krill [kril] **NM** krill

kriss [kris] **NM** kris

kroumir [krumir] **NM** *(chausson)* pump

krypton [kriptɔ̃] **NM** *Chim* krypton

ksar [ksar] (*pl* **ksour** [ksur]) **NM** = North African fortified village

kugelhof [kuglɔf] = **kouglof**

kumquat [kumkwat] **NM** kumquat

kung-fu [kuŋfu] **NM INV** kung fu

kurde [kyrd] **ADJ** Kurdish

NM *(langue)* Kurdish

• **Kurde NMF** Kurd

Kurdistan [kyrdistɑ̃] **NM le K.** Kurdistan

kvas [kvas] **NM** kvass, kvas

kW *(abrév écrite* **kilowatt***)* kW

kwas [kvas] **NM** kvass, kvas

K-way® [kawe] **NM INV** cagoule; **pantalon de K.-way** waterproof leggings

kWh *(abrév écrite* **kilowattheure***)* kW/hr

kyat [kjat] **NM** kyat

Kyrie [kirije] **NM INV** *Rel* Kyrie (eleison)

kyrielle [kirjɛl] **NF** *Fam* **une k. de bambins** a whole bunch *or* swarm of kids; **une k. d'insultes** a string of insults; **une k. de mensonges** a pack of lies; **elle a toute une k. d'amis** she has masses of friends

kyste [kist] **NM** *Méd* cyst; **k. sébacé** sebaceous cyst, *Spéc* wen

kystique [kistik] **ADJ** *Méd* cystic

L, l[1] [ɛl] **NM INV 1** *(lettre)* L, l; **L comme Louis** ≃ L for Larry **2** *(forme)* L (shape) **3** *Can Univ* **L ès L** *(abrév* **licencié ès lettres***)* *Br* ≃ BA, *Am* ≃ AB
• **en L ADJ** L-shaped

l[2] *(abrév écrite* **litre***)* l

l' [l] *voir* **le**[1, 2]

-là [la] **ADV 1** *(lié à un nom introduit par un adjectif démonstratif) (singulier)* that; *(pluriel)* those; **ce stylo-là** that pen; **cette femme-là** that woman; **dans ces endroits-là** in those places **2** *(lié à un pronom)* **quel livre voulez-vous? – celui-là** which book do you want? – that one

la[1] [la] *voir* **le**[1, 2]

la[2] [la] **NM INV** *Mus* A; *(chanté)* lah; **donner le la** to give the *or* an A; *Fig* to set the tone

LÀ [la] **ADV 1** *(dans l'espace ▸ là-bas)* there; *(▸ ici)* here; **elle habite Paris maintenant, c'est là qu'elle a trouvé du travail** she lives in Paris now, that's where she found work; **il est à la poste? – qu'est-ce qu'il fait là?** he's at the post office? – what's he doing there?; **c'est là, je reconnais la maison** there it is (over there), I recognize the house; **de là au village il y a un kilomètre** it's one kilometre from there to the village; **à quelques kilomètres de là** a few kilometres away; **là où vous êtes** where you are; **là en bas/en haut** down/up there; **déjà là?** (are you) here already?; **je ne peux rien faire, il est toujours là** I can't do anything, he's always around; **viens là!** come here!; **est-ce qu'il est là?** is he in?; **ne t'inquiète pas, je suis là pour t'aider si tu en as besoin** don't worry, I'm here to help you if you need me; **je ne suis là pour personne** if anybody asks I'm not in *or* here; **je suis là pour vous répondre** it's my job to answer your questions; **allez, on n'est pas là pour bavarder** come on now, we're not here to chat

2 *(dans le temps)* **c'est là que j'ai paniqué** that's when I panicked; **attendons demain et là nous déciderons** let's wait until tomorrow and then (we'll) decide; **à partir de là** from then on, from that moment on; **là, je n'ai pas le temps de lui en parler** I don't have time to tell him/her about it right now; **à quelque temps de là** some time after; **à quelques jours/mois de là** a few days/months later; **c'est là où tu m'as le plus étonné** that's where you most surprised me

3 *(dans cette situation)* **là tu exagères** now you're exaggerating; **vous n'avez fait là que ce qui était nécessaire** you only did what you had to, you only did what was necessary; **c'est justement là où je ne vous suis plus** that's just where you've lost me; **nous n'en sommes pas encore là** we haven't reached that stage yet; **pour l'instant nous en sommes là** that's how things stand at the moment; **comment en es-tu arrivé là?** how did you manage to let things go so far?; **je n'ai pas l'intention d'en rester** *ou* **demeurer là** I don't intend leaving it at that

4 *(dans cela)* **il n'y a là rien d'étonnant** there's nothing surprising about that; **je ne vois là aucune raison de s'inquiéter** I don't see that there's anything to worry about; **ne voyez là aucune malice de ma part** please don't take it the wrong way; **c'est bien là le problème** that's the problem; **la santé, tout est là** (good) health is everything

5 *(pour renforcer)* **ce sont là mes amis** those are my friends; **c'est là mon intention** that's my intention *or* what I intend to do; **c'est là la difficulté** that's where the difficulty lies

6 *(emploi expressif)* **oui, j'ai refusé ce travail, là, tu es content?** yes, I turned down the job, now are you satisfied?; **alors là, je ne sais pas!** well that I really don't know!; **alors là, tu exagères!** you've got a nerve!; **c'est une belle grippe que tu as là!** that's a nasty dose of flu you've got there!; *Fam* **que me chantes-tu là?** what are you on about?; **malheureux, qu'as-tu fait là!** what have you gone and done now?; **qu'est-ce que je vois là? mais ce sont mes gants!** if it isn't my gloves!; **là, là, calme-toi!** now, now *or* there, there, calm down!; **hé là!** *ou* **oh là! doucement!** gently does it!
• **de là ADV 1** *(dans l'espace)* from there; **de là jusqu'à la poste il y a 500 m** it's 500 m from there to the post office; *Fig* **de là à dire que c'est un criminel, il y a loin** there's a big difference between that and saying he's a criminal; **mais de là à dire qu'ils sont tous antipathiques!** but I wouldn't go as far as to say they're all unpleasant!; **mais de là à ce qu'il nous donne son accord…** but as to giving us his agreement… **2** *(marquant la conséquence)* **de là son amertume** that's why he's/she's bitter, that explains his/her bitterness, hence his/her bitterness; **on peut déduire de là que…** from that we can deduce that…
• **là contre ADV c'est votre droit, je n'ai rien à dire là contre** it's your right, I have nothing to say in opposition
• **par là ADV 1** *(dans l'espace)* **c'est par là** it's over there; **quelque part par là** somewhere around here/there; **vous devriez passer par là** you should go that way **2** *Fig* **si tu vas par là** if you go along that road; **qu'entendez-vous** *ou* **que voulez-vous dire par là?** what do you mean by that?; **il faut en passer par là!** there's no alternative!, it can't be helped!

là-bas [laba] **ADV 1** *(en bas)* down *or* under there; **l. dans la vallée** down there in the valley **2** *(en un lieu éloigné)* there; **une fois arrivés l., nous nous arrangerons** we'll sort it out when we get there

label [labɛl] **NM 1** *(étiquette)* label; **l. NF** *ou* **norme française** French industry standards label; **l. d'origine** label of origin; **l. de garantie** guarantee label; **l. de qualité/d'exportation** quality/export label **2** *(maison de disques)* label; **l. indépendant** independent *or* indie record label **3** *Ordinat* **l. de volume** volume label

labéliser [3] [labelize] **VT** to label

labeur [labœr] **NM** *Littéraire (travail pénible)* toil, labour; *(effort)* hard work; **une vie de l.** a life of toil

labial, -e, -aux, -ales [labjal, -o] **ADJ 1** *Anat* lip *(avant n)*, labial **2** *Ling* labial
• **labiale NF** labial (consonant)

labialisation [labjalizasjɔ̃] **NF** *(d'une voyelle)* rounding; *(d'une consonne)* labialization

labialiser [3] [labjalize] **VT** *(voyelle)* to round; *(consonne)* to labialize

labié, -e [labje] **ADJ** *Bot* labiate

labiodental, -e, -aux, -ales [labjɔdɑ̃tal, -o] **ADJ** labiodental
• **labiodentale NF** labiodental (consonant)

labo [labo] **NM** *Fam (abrév* **laboratoire***)* lab; **l. de langues** language lab; **l. photo** darkroom

laborantin, -e [labɔrɑ̃tɛ̃, -in] **NM,F** laboratory assistant, *Am* laboratory operator

laboratoire [labɔratwar] **NM 1** *(lieu)* laboratory; *(équipe)* (research) team; **l. d'analyses (médicales)** analytical laboratory; **L. européen pour la physique des particules** European laboratory for particle physics; **l. expérimental** testing laboratory; **l. de recherche** research laboratory; **l. d'idées** think tank

2 *Scol* **l. de langues** language laboratory

3 *Métal* heating chamber

4 *Phot (salle)* processing room; *(usine)* processing works; *Cin & Phot* **l. de film** film laboratory
• **en laboratoire ADV** in the laboratory, under laboratory conditions; **embryon végétal obtenu en l.** plant embryo obtained under laboratory conditions

laborieuse [labɔrjøz] *voir* **laborieux**

laborieusement [labɔrjøzmɑ̃] **ADV** *(péniblement)* laboriously, with great difficulty

laborieux, -euse [labɔrjø, -øz] **ADJ 1** *(long et difficile ▸ procédure, tâche, manœuvre)* laborious **2** *(lourd ▸ style)* heavy, laboured; **trois heures pour faire une lettre, ce fut l.!** three hours to write a letter, that's slow going!; **j'ai réussi à la convaincre, mais ça a été l.!** I managed to convince her but it was hard work *or* but it was heavy going!; **dans un anglais l.** in halting English **3** *(industrieux)* hardworking, industrious; **la classe laborieuse** the working *or* labouring class

labour [labur] **NM 1** *Agr* tilling *(UNCOUNT)*, ploughing *(UNCOUNT)*; **les labours** the ploughed fields; **commencer les labours** to start ploughing **2** *Hort* digging (over)

labourable [laburabl] **ADJ** ploughable; **des terres labourables** arable land

labourage [laburaʒ] **NM 1** *Agr* tilling, ploughing **2** *Hort* digging over

labourer [3] [labure] **VT 1** *Agr* to plough; *Hort* to dig (over) **2** *(entailler)* to dig into, to lacerate, to scratch; **les sangles labouraient les flancs du cheval** the straps were digging into the horse's flanks; **un visage labouré de rides** a face furrowed with wrinkles; **les policiers lui ont labouré les côtes** the cops beat him/her up

laboureur [laburœr] **NM 1** *Littéraire* ploughman **2** *Hist* husbandman, ≃ yeoman

Labrador [labradɔr] **NM le L.** Labrador

labrador [labradɔr] **NM** *Zool* labrador

labyrinthe [labirɛ̃t] **NM 1** *(dédale)* labyrinth; *Fig* maze **2** *Anat* labyrinth

labyrinthique [labirɛ̃tik] **ADJ** labyrinthine

lac [lak] **NM** lake; **l. artificiel** *(pièce d'eau)* artificial lake; *(pour fournir de l'eau)* reservoir; **la région des Lacs** the Lakes, the Lake District; **les lacs d'Écosse** the Scottish lochs; *Fig* **c'est tombé dans le l.** it has fallen through; **le l. de Côme/Garde** Lake Como/Garda; **le l. Érié** Lake Erie; **le l. Léman** Lake Geneva; **le l. de Tibériade** the Sea of Galilee

laçage [lasaʒ] **NM** *(de chaussures, de bottes)* lacing up, tying up; *(de vêtement)* lacing (up)

lacer [16] [lase] **VT** *(vêtement)* to lace (up); *(chaussure)* to lace up, to tie up
VPR se lacer to lace (up); **comment cette botte se lace-t-elle?** how do you lace (up) this boot?

lacération [laserasjɔ̃] **NF 1** *Méd* laceration, gash **2** *(fait de déchirer ▸ gén)* ripping, tearing, slashing; *(▸ de sièges)* slashing

lacérer **[18]** [lasere] **VT 1** *(affiche, rideau, siège)* to slash; **le chat a lacéré le fauteuil avec ses griffes** the cat has clawed the armchair to pieces **2** *(blesser)* to lacerate, to gash; **la douleur lui lacère le dos** he/she has a lacerating pain in his/her back

lacet [lasɛ] **NM 1** *(de chaussure, de corset)* lace
2 *(piège)* snare; **poser** *ou* **tendre des lacets** to set snares
3 *(d'une route)* hairpin bend; **faire des lacets** *(route)* to twist and turn
4 *Aviat* yaw
5 *Couture* tie
• **à lacets** **ADJ** *(chaussure)* with laces, lace-up *(avant n)*
• **en lacets** **ADJ** *(route)* winding, twisting **ADV la route monte en lacets** the road winds *or* twists upwards

lâchage [lɑʃaʒ] **NM 1** *(rupture)* failure; **c'est dû au l. des freins** it's due to brake failure **2** *Fam (abandon)* **c'est un l. en règle de leur part** they've really let us down

lâche [lɑʃ] **ADJ 1** *(poltron)* cowardly, spineless; **se montrer l.** to behave like a coward
2 *(avant le nom) (méprisable)* cowardly; **un l. attentat** a cowardly *or* despicable attack
3 *(non serré ▸ nœud)* loose, slack; *(▸ vêtement)* loose, baggy
4 *(imprécis ▸ dialogue, scénario)* weak; *(▸ raisonnement)* woolly, slipshod
5 *(sans rigueur ▸ règlement, discipline)* lax, overlenient
6 *Tex (étoffe)* loose, loosely woven; *(tricot)* loose-knit
NMF coward

lâchement [lɑʃmɑ̃] **ADV 1** *(sans courage)* in a cowardly manner **2** *(sans tension)* loosely, slackly

lâcher **[3]** [lɑʃe] **VT 1** *(desserrer)* to loosen, to slacken; **il a lâché sa ceinture d'un cran** he let out *or* he loosened his belt a notch; **l. la vapeur** to let off steam; **l. la bride à un cheval** to give a horse its head; *Fig* **l. la bride à qn** to allow sb more freedom of movement
2 *(cesser de tenir)* to let go of; *(laisser tomber)* to drop; **l. la pédale du frein** to take one's foot off the brake (pedal); **elle a lâché la pile d'assiettes** she dropped the pile of plates; **il roule en lâchant le guidon** he rides with no hands; **lâche-moi!** let me go!, let go of me!; **ne lâche pas la rampe, l'escalier est glissant** don't let go of the banister, the stairs are slippery; **elle ne la lâchait pas des yeux** *ou* **du regard** she didn't take her eyes off her for a moment; **l. prise** to let go; **cette idée ne m'a pas lâché** I couldn't get this idea out of my mind; *Fam* **il ne m'a pas lâché d'une semelle** he stuck to me like a leech; *Fam* **lâche-moi les baskets!** leave me alone!, get off my back *or* case!; *Fam* **les l.** *(payer)* to fork out; *Fam* **il les lâche avec un élastique** he's a stingy *or* tight-fisted old so-and-so; **l. la proie pour l'ombre** to chase rainbows; *aussi Fig* **l. pied** to give way
3 *Aviat (bombe)* to drop; *(ballon)* to launch
4 *Ordinat (icône)* to drop
5 *(libérer ▸ oiseau)* to let loose, to release, to let go; *(▸ chien)* to let off, to unleash; *(▸ animal dangereux)* to set loose; *(▸ meute, faucon)* to slip; **l. les chiens sur qn** to set the dogs on sb; *Fam* **le prof nous a lâchés plus tôt** the teacher let us out early
6 *Fam (abandonner ▸ ami)* to drop; *(▸ amant, mari, famille)* to walk out on□; *(▸ emploi)* to chuck in; **l. ses études** to drop out of school; **le moteur nous a lâchés le deuxième jour** the engine died *or* packed in on us on the second day
7 *(émettre ▸ cri, juron)* to let out; *(▸ plaisanterie, sottise)* to come out with; **l. un soupir de soulagement** to let out a sigh of relief; *Fam* **l. un pet** to fart
8 *Sport (distancer ▸ concurrent)* to leave behind, to get a lead on; **l. le peloton** to leave the rest of the field behind, to break from the pack
VI *(se casser ▸ câble)* to snap, to break, to give (way); *(▸ embrayage, frein)* to fail; *Fam (▸ organe)* to give out, to pack in; **les freins ont lâché** the brakes failed; **ses nerfs ont fini par l.** he/she eventually cracked up *or* had a breakdown

NM 1 *(fait de laisser partir)* release; **ils ont fait un l. de ballons/de colombes** they released balloons/a flock of doves **2** *Ordinat* **l. d'icônes** icon drop

lâcheté [lɑʃte] **NF 1** *(manque de courage)* cowardice **2** *(procédé vil)* act of cowardice, cowardly act; **commettre une l.** to do something despicable

lâcheur, -euse [lɑʃœr, -øz] **NM,F** *Fam* **quel l., il n'est pas venu!** what an unreliable so-and-so, he didn't come!

lacis [lasi] **NM 1** *(labyrinthe)* maze, web; **un l. de ruelles** a maze of little streets **2** *(de nerfs, fils etc)* network; **l. veineux** network of veins

laconique [lakɔnik] **ADJ** *(lettre, réponse)* terse, *Sout* laconic; *(personne)* laconic

laconiquement [lakɔnikmɑ̃] **ADV** tersely, *Sout* laconically

laconisme [lakɔnism] **NM** terseness, *Sout* laconism

lacrymal, -e, -aux, -ales [lakrimal, -o] **ADJ** *(conduit)* tear *(avant n)*, *Spéc* lachrymal

lacrymogène [lakrimɔʒɛn] **ADJ** *(gaz)* tear *(avant n)*, *Spéc* lacrymogenic; *(grenade)* tear-gas *(avant n)*

lacs [la] **NM 1** *(piège)* snare **2** *aussi Hér* **l. d'amour** *(motif décoratif)* love knot, true-lover's knot

lactaire [laktɛr] **ADJ** *Physiol* lacteal
NM *Bot* milk cap; **l. délicieux** saffron milk cap

lactation [laktasjɔ̃] **NF** lactation

lacté, -e [lakte] **ADJ 1** *(contenant du lait) (produit, alimentation)* milk *(avant n)*; **farine lactée** milk-enriched cereal; **régime l.** milk diet **2** *Littéraire (pareil au lait)* milky, lacteous

lactescent, -e [laktesɑ̃, -ɑ̃t] **ADJ 1** *(contenant du lait)* lactescent **2** *Littéraire (d'un blanc laiteux)* milky-white, lacteous

lactifère [laktifɛr] **ADJ** lactiferous

lactique [laktik] **ADJ** *Chim* lactic

lactose [laktoz] **NM** lactose

lacunaire [lakynɛr] **ADJ 1** *(incomplet)* incomplete, *Littéraire* lacunary **2** *Anat & Bot (système)* lacunar; *(tissu)* lacunal

lacune [lakyn] **NF 1** *(omission)* gap; **de vieux manuscrits pleins de lacunes** old manuscripts with many parts missing *or* full of gaps; **il y a des lacunes dans cette encyclopédie** there are some omissions in this encyclopedia; **j'ai des lacunes en mathématiques** there are gaps in my knowledge of mathematics; **cette loi n'est pas sans lacunes** there are loopholes in this law **2** *Anat, Biol & Géol* lacuna

lacuneux, -euse [lakynø, -øz] **ADJ 1** *Littéraire (incomplet)* lacunary **2** *Bot* lacunose

lacustre [lakystr] **ADJ 1** *Biol & Bot* lacustrine **2** *Constr & Archit* **cité l.** lakeside pile-dwelling settlement; **habitation l.** lakeside dwelling

lad [lad] **NM** stableboy, *Br* stable lad

là-dedans [laddɑ̃] **ADV** *(ici)* in here; *(là-bas)* in there; **le tiroir est sens dessus dessous, je ne trouve rien l.** the drawer is in a mess, I can't find anything in here; **il y a du vrai l.** there's some truth in it; **ça ne m'étonnerait pas qu'elle soit impliquée l.** it wouldn't surprise me if she was involved (in it); **il n'a rien à voir l.!** he's got nothing to do with it!; **debout l.!** rise and shine!; *Fam Hum* **il y en a, l.!** he's/she's got a lot up top!

là-dessous [ladsu] **ADV 1** *(sous cet objet-ci)* under here; *(sous cet objet-là)* under there **2** *(dans cette affaire)* **il y a quelque chose de bizarre l.** there's something strange *or* odd about all this; **qu'est-ce qui se cache l.?** what's behind all this *or* behind it all?

là-dessus [ladsy] **ADV 1** *(sur cet objet-ci)* on here; *(sur cet objet-là)* on there; **ne t'appuie pas l.!** don't lean on it! **2** *(sur ce sujet)* **je n'en sais pas plus que toi l.** I don't know any more than you about it; **nous reviendrons l.** we'll come back to that; **c'est l. qu'il faut se concentrer** that's what you/we/*etc* have to concentrate on **3** *(sur ce)* **l. je vous dis bonsoir** at this point *or* with that, I'll say goodnight; **l., elle se tut** at which point *or Sout* whereupon, she stopped talking

ladite [ladit] *voir* **ledit**

ladre [ladr] **ADJ 1** *Vét* measly, measled **2** *Littéraire (avare)* miserly **3** *Arch (lépreux)* leprous

NMF 1 *Littéraire (avare)* miser, skinflint **2** *Arch (lépreux)* leper

ladrerie [ladrəri] **NF 1** *Littéraire (avarice)* miserliness **2** *Vét* measles **3** *Arch (lèpre)* leprosy; *(léproserie)* leper hospital *or* house

lagon [lagɔ̃] **NM** (coral reef) lagoon

lagopède [lagɔpɛd] **NM** *Orn* **l. des Alpes** ptarmigan; **l. (rouge) d'Écosse** (red) grouse; **l. d'Écosse femelle** moorhen

lagune [lagyn] **NF** lagoon

là-haut [lao] **ADV 1** *(au-dessus)* up there; *(à l'étage)* upstairs; **leur maison est l. sur la colline** their house is up there on the hill; **tout l.** way up there, all the way up there **2** *(aux cieux)* up there, (up) in Heaven

lai, -e [lɛ] **ADJ** *Rel* **frère l.** lay brother; **sœur laie** lay sister
NM *Littérature* lay

laïc, laïque [laik] **ADJ 1** *(non clérical)* secular, lay; **habit l.** lay dress **2** *(indépendant du clergé)* secular; **l'école laïque** secular education; **un État l.** a secular state; **l'esprit l.** secularism
NM,F layman, *f* laywoman; **les laïcs** the laity
• **laïque** **NF** *Vieilli* state; **la laïque** = the state educational system (in France)

laîche [lɛʃ] **NF** sedge

laïcisation [laisizasjɔ̃] **NF** secularization, laicization

laïciser **[3]** [laisize] **VT** to secularize, to laicize

laïcisme [laisism] **NM** secularism

laïcité [laisite] **NF** secularism; **la défense de la l.** defence of secular education *(in France)*

laid, -e [lɛ, lɛd] **ADJ 1** *(inesthétique ▸ bâtisse)* ugly, unsightly; *(▸ personne, vêtement, tableau)* ugly, unattractive; **il est/c'est très l.** he's/it's hideous; **l. comme un pou** *ou* **un singe, l. à faire peur** *ou* **fuir** (as) ugly as sin **2** *(impoli)* rude, unseemly; **c'est l. de faire des grimaces aux gens** it's rude *or* not nice to pull faces at people
NM *(valeur esthétique)* **le l.** ugliness

laidement [lɛdmɑ̃] **ADV 1** *(de façon laide)* unattractively **2** *(ignoblement)* basely, dishonestly

laideron [lɛdrɔ̃] **NM** ugly girl

laideur [lɛdœr] **NF 1** *(physique ▸ d'une personne, d'une chose)* ugliness **d'une l. repoussante** repulsively ugly **2** *(morale ▸ d'un crime)* heinousness; *(▸ d'une accusation)* meanness, *Littéraire* baseness; **il a dépeint l'hypocrisie dans toute sa l.** he portrayed hypocrisy in all its ugliness

laie [lɛ] **NF 1** *Zool* wild sow **2** *Agr (trouée)* (compartment) line; *(sentier)* forest path

lainage [lɛnaʒ] **NM 1** *Tex (tissu)* woollen fabric *or* material; *(procédé)* napping **2** *(pull)* woollen jumper *or* sweater, *(gilet)* wool cardigan; **mets un l.** put on a jumper *or* sweater; **des lainages** woollens **3** *(toison)* fleece

laine [lɛn] **NF 1** *(poil ▸ du mouton, de l'alpaga etc)* wool; **l. vierge** new wool; **il se laisserait manger** *ou* **tondre la l. sur le dos** he'd let you take the shirt off his back
2 *Tex (tissu)* wool; **l. peignée** worsted;
3 *Fam (vêtement)* **(petite) l.** sweater□, *Br* woolly
4 *(isolant)* **l. de bois** wood wool *or* fibre; **l. de verre** glass wool
• **de laine** **ADJ** wool *(avant n)*, woollen; **bonnet/chaussettes de l.** woollen hat/socks

lainer **[4]** [lɛne] **VT** *Tex (tissu)* to nap

lainerie [lɛnri] **NF 1** *(fabrication)* manufacture of woollens **2** *(usine, atelier)* woollen mill **3** *(magasin de gros)* (wholesale) wool shop

laineur, -euse[1] [lɛnœr, -øz] **NM,F** napper
• **laineuse** **NF** napping machine, raising machine

laineux, -euse[2] [lɛnø, -øz] **ADJ** *(tissu)* woollen; *(mouton, cheveux)* woolly

lainier, -ère [lɛnje, -ɛr] **ADJ** *(production)* wool *(avant n)*; *(usine)* wool-producing
NM,F 1 *(industriel)* wool manufacturer **2** *(ouvrier)* wool worker **3** *(commerçant)* wool stapler

laïque [laik] *voir* **laïc**

lais [lɛ] **NMPL** (exposed) foreshore

laisse [lɛs] **NF 1** *(lien)* leash, lead; **tenir un chien en l.** to keep a dog on the leash *or* lead; *Fig* **mener** *ou* **tenir qn en l.** to keep a tight rein on sb **2** *Géog* *(partie de plage)* foreshore; *(ligne)* tidemark, high-water mark; **l. de basse/haute mer** low/high tidemark

laissé-pour-compte, laissée-pour-compte [lesepurkɔ̃t] *(mpl* **laissés-pour-compte,** *fpl* **laissées-pour-compte)** ADJ *Com (article, marchandise)* rejected, returned

NM,F *(personne)* social reject *or* outcast; **les laissés-pour-compte de l'industrialisation** the casualties *or* victims of industrialization

NM *Com* reject, return

LAISSER [4] [lese]

VT
- to leave **A1–4, 6, 7, B1, 2, 4, 5, C**
- to let **D1, 2**
- to lose **A5**
- to let have **B3**
- to allow **D1, 2**

VPR
- to let oneself

VT **A.** *ABANDONNER* **1** *(ne pas prendre, renoncer à)* to leave; **elle a laissé son dessert** she left her pudding (untouched), she didn't touch her pudding; **laisse quelques fruits pour eux** leave them some fruit, leave some fruit for them; **c'est à prendre ou à l.** (it's) take it or leave it; **il y a à prendre et à l.** *(il y a du bon et du mauvais)* you have to pick and choose; *(il y a du vrai et du faux)* you have to be selective; **laissez toute espérance, vous qui entrez** abandon hope all ye who enter here

2 *(quitter momentanément ▸ personne, chose)* to leave; **j'ai laissé mes enfants chez mon frère** I left my children at my brother's; **n'oubliez pas de l. vos manteaux au vestiaire** don't forget to leave your coats in the cloakroom; **j'ai laissé la voiture à la maison** I left the car at home; **laisse-nous à la gare** drop us off *or* leave us at the station; **laisse-nous, nous avons à parler** leave us (alone), we have things to talk about; **merci, vous pouvez nous l.** thank you, that will be all; **allez, je vous laisse** I'll be off now; **je vous laisse** *(au téléphone)* I must hang up *or* go now; *(dans une lettre)* that's all for now, I'll leave you now; **l. là qn** to leave sb in the lurch

3 *(quitter définitivement)* to leave, to abandon; *(après sa mort ▸ famille)* to leave; **il s'est expatrié, laissant sa famille, ses amis** he emigrated, leaving his family and his friends; **il a laissé femme et enfants** he abandoned his wife and children, he walked out on his wife and children; **il laisse une femme et deux enfants en bas âge** he leaves a wife and two young children

4 *(oublier)* to leave; **j'ai laissé mon sac à la maison** I left my bag at home; **ne laissez rien dans les voitures** don't leave anything in your car; **l. des fautes dans un texte** to leave mistakes in a text

5 *(perdre ▸ membre, personne, bien matériel)* to lose; **il a laissé sa fortune dans cette aventure** he lost all his money in this affair, this affair has lost him all his money; **il y a laissé beaucoup d'argent** he lost a lot of money in it; **y l. la vie** *ou* **sa vie** to lose one's life; **y l. sa santé** to ruin one's health

6 *(derrière soi ▸ trace, marque)* to leave; **la mer a laissé des algues sur la plage** the tide left some seaweed (behind) on the beach; **l. une marque/auréole** to leave a mark/ring; **ce vin laisse un arrière-goût désagréable** this wine has an unpleasant aftertaste; **l. une impression** to leave *or* to make an impression; **il laisse un bon/un mauvais souvenir** we have good/bad memories of him; **elle laisse le souvenir d'une femme énergique** she will be remembered as an energetic woman; **partir sans l. d'adresse** to go away without leaving one's address; **il est mort sans l. de descendance** *ou* **d'héritiers** he died without leaving any heirs; **il laisse beaucoup de dettes** he has left considerable debts (behind him); **elle a laissé une œuvre considérable** she left (behind her) a vast body of work

7 *(négliger)* to leave; **laisse ton livre et viens avec moi** put down *or* leave your book and come with me; **laissez la direction de Paris sur la gauche et tournez à droite** go past the road to Paris on your left and turn right; **laisse tes soucis et viens avec nous** forget your worries and come with us; **laissons les détails et occupons-nous de l'essentiel** let's leave the details aside and concentrate on the essentials

8 *Littéraire* **cette déclaration ne laisse pas d'être inquiétante** one cannot but be worried by this statement; **l'intérêt qu'il me manifeste ne laisse pas de me flatter** the interest he shows in me is nothing if not flattering (to me); **cette réponse ne laisse pas de m'étonner** I can't help but be surprised by this answer

B. *DONNER, CÉDER* **1** *(accorder)* to leave; **l. qch à qn** to leave sth for sb, to leave sb sth; **laisse-moi un peu de gâteau** leave some cake for me; **l. un pourboire au garçon** to leave the waiter a tip; **ils ont laissé les enfants à la grand-mère** they left the children with their grandmother; **le juge lui a laissé les enfants** the judge gave him/her custody of the children; **c'est tout ce que les cambrioleurs m'ont laissé** it's all the burglars left me (with); **après l'insurrection, il dut l. le pouvoir à son fils** after the rebellion, he had to hand over power to his son; **laissez la priorité à droite** give way to the right; **laissez le passage à l'ambulance** let the ambulance through; **l. sa place à qn** *(siège)* to give up one's seat to sb; **laisse-nous un peu de place!** let us have *or* leave us some room!; **laisse-lui le temps de le faire** leave *or* give him/her time to do it; **ils m'ont laissé une semaine pour le finir** they left *or* allowed me a week in which to finish it

2 *(confier)* to leave; **l. des consignes à qn** to leave instructions with sb, to leave sb with instructions; **l. un message à la secrétaire** to leave a message with the secretary; **laissez les clés chez le gardien** drop the keys off at the caretaker's, leave the keys with the caretaker; **il m'a laissé sa voiture pendant son absence** he left me his car while he was away; *Vieilli* **l. sa carte** to leave one's card; **je lui laisse les travaux pénibles** I leave him/her the heavy work, I leave the heavy work to him/her; **tu me laisses tout le travail!** you're leaving me with all the work!; **l. qch à faire à qn** to leave sb to do sth, to leave sth for sb to do; **je vous laisse les lettres à envoyer** I'll leave you to send the letters

3 *(vendre)* to let have; **je vous le laisse pour dix euros** I'll let you have it for ten euros

4 *(léguer)* to leave, *Sout* to bequeath; **il a laissé d'immenses propriétés à sa famille** he left his family vast estates; **elle a laissé tous ses biens à une œuvre de charité** she left *or Sout* bequeathed all her property to charity

5 *(réserver)* to leave; **laissez une marge pour les corrections** leave a margin for corrections; **l. qch pour la fin** to leave sth till last *or* till the end; **l. le meilleur pour la fin** to leave *or* save the best till last

6 **l. à penser que** *(sujet: chose)* to make one think *or* suppose that, to lead one to believe that; **cette note laisse à penser qu'elle est fâchée** this message would lead you to believe *or* from this message you would think she's angry; **ta lettre laisse à penser que tu ne pourras pas venir** your letter implies that you won't be coming; **je vous laisse à imaginer s'ils étaient surpris** I'll leave you to imagine how surprised they were; *aussi Ironique* **je vous laisse à penser comme cela nous a fait plaisir** I hardly need to tell you *or* you can just imagine how pleased we were; **elle n'est pas là, cela laisse à penser** she's not here, it makes you wonder

C. *DANS UN ÉTAT, UNE SITUATION (faire demeurer)* to leave; **elle a laissé son mari planté sur le trottoir** she left her husband standing on the pavement looking like a fool; **laisse la fenêtre fermée/ouverte** leave the window shut/open; **l. un crime impuni** to let a crime go unpunished, to leave a crime unpunished; **ceci me laisse sceptique** I remain sceptical (about it); **cela me laisse froid** *ou* **indifférent** it leaves me cold *or* unmoved; **vous n'allez pas me l. tout seul?** you're not going to leave me (all) on my own?; **l. qn tranquille** *ou* **en paix** to leave sb alone *or* in peace; **l. qch tranquille** to leave sth alone; **je vous laisse libre d'agir** you are free to do as you like; **l. qn dans l'ignorance de qch** to let sb remain ignorant of sth, to leave sb in the dark about sth; **je ne peux pas te l. dans cet état-là!** I can't leave you in this state!; **je ne te laisserai pas dans la misère** I won't let you want for anything; **l. une maison à l'abandon** to let a house go to rack and ruin; **laissez le nom en blanc** leave the name blank, do not write the name in; **l. des terres en friche** to let land lie fallow; **l. qn/qch sans surveillance** to leave sb/sth unattended; **les corps ont été laissés sans sépulture** the bodies remained *or* were left unburied; *aussi Fig* **l. derrière soi** to leave behind; **l. derrière soi tous ses concurrents** to leave all one's competitors behind; **il a laissé le peloton loin derrière** he left the pack well behind him; **elle laisse les autres loin derrière elle** *(elle les surpasse)* she puts all the others to shame, she leaves all the others way behind; **l. la bride sur le cou à un cheval** to give a horse its head; *Fig* **l. la bride sur le cou à qn** to give sb free rein

D. *SUIVI D'UN INFINITIF* **1** *(autoriser)* to let, to allow; **l. qn faire qch** to let sb do sth, to allow sb to do sth; **le gardien les laisse jouer dans la cour** the caretaker lets them play *or* allows them to play in the yard; **ils ne m'ont pas laissé lui parler** they didn't allow me to *or* they didn't let me speak to him/her

2 *(ne pas empêcher de)* to let, to allow; **l. qn faire** to let sb do, to leave sb to do, to allow sb to do; **laisse-le dormir** let him sleep, leave him to sleep; **laissez-moi passer** let me past *or* through; **laissez-le faire!** leave it to him!, let him get on with it!; **laisse-moi le lui dire** let me tell him/her (about it); **je te laisse imaginer la suite** I'll leave the rest to your imagination; **le toit laissait passer la pluie** the roof let the rain in; **l. tomber qch** to drop sth; **l. voir qch à qn** *(lettre, photo)* to let sb have a look at sth, to let sb see sth; **l. voir** *(montrer)* to show, to reveal; **son décolleté laissait voir une peau satinée** her plunging neckline revealed skin like satin; **l. voir son émotion** to show one's emotion; **l. voir ses intentions** to reveal one's intentions; **ils ont laissé le prisonnier s'échapper** they let the prisoner escape; **l. condamner un innocent** to allow an innocent man to be punished; **tu me laisseras aller avec toi, dis?** let me come with you, go on!; **l. échapper un cri de douleur** to let out a cry of pain; **elle laissa échapper un soupir** she gave a sigh; **l. sécher la colle** to leave *or* to allow the glue to dry; **laissez bouillir quelques secondes** let it boil for a few seconds; **elle laisse trop paraître ses sentiments** she doesn't hide her feelings enough; **il ne laisse rien paraître de ses intentions** it's impossible to know what he has in mind; **ne rien l. deviner** to give nothing away; **l. vieillir un vin** to allow a wine to age; **ceci laisse supposer que…** this implies that…, this makes one think that…

3 *(locutions) Fam* **laisse aller, ce n'est pas grave** don't worry, it doesn't matter; *Fam* **laisse courir** leave it, forget it; **laissez dire et faites ce que vous avez à faire** let them talk and do what you have to do; **bien faire et l. dire, c'est ma devise** do what you think best and don't worry about what people say, that's my motto; **on n'y peut rien, il faut l. faire** there's nothing we can do (about it), you just have to let things take their course; **laisse faire, ce n'est pas grave!** don't worry, it doesn't matter!; **tu t'imagines que je vais l. faire ça?** do you think I'm just going to stand by and watch while this happens?; **l. faire le temps** to let time take its course; *Fam* **l. tomber qn** *(ami)* to drop sb; *(petit ami)* to dump sb; *Fam* **tu devrais l. tomber, ça ne marchera jamais** you should give up *or* drop it *or* forget it, it'll never work; *Fam* **je te dois encore cinq euros – laisse tomber** I still owe you five euros – forget it

USAGE ABSOLU *(s'abstenir d'intervenir)* **laisse, je vais le faire** leave it, I'll do it myself; **laisse, ça va aller** I'll be all right; **laissez, je vous en prie** please don't bother (with that); **laisse, c'est moi qui paie** put your money away, I'll pay for this; **laisse, c'est ma tournée** no, it's my round

VPR **se laisser** to let oneself; **elle s'est laissé accuser injustement** she allowed herself to be *or* she let herself be unjustly accused; **il ne s'est pas laissé accuser** he refused to let them pin the blame on him; **se l. décourager** to let oneself be discouraged; **il refuse de se l. photographier** he refuses to be photographed; **il s'est laissé séduire** he let himself be seduced; **il s'est laissé mourir** he just gave up living; **ils se sont laissé surprendre par la nuit** they were caught out by nightfall; **se l. tomber sur une chaise/dans un fauteuil** to collapse onto a chair/into an armchair; **se l. aller** *(se négliger)* to let oneself go; *(se détendre)* to let oneself go, to relax; **depuis la mort de sa femme, il se laisse aller** since his wife's death, he's let himself go; **se l. aller au découragement** to let oneself become discouraged; **se l. aller au pessimisme** to give way to pessimism; **se l. aller à faire qch** to go as *or* so far as to do sth; **il s'est laissé aller à injurier son père** he went so far as to insult his father; **se l. dire que** to have heard (it said) that; **je me suis laissé dire qu'elle avait démissionné** I heard she'd resigned; **on l'accuse injustement et elle se laisse faire** she's unjustly accused, and she just stands by and lets it happen; **ne te laisse pas faire!** stand up for yourself!, don't let yourself be taken advantage of!; **la proposition est tentante, je crois que je vais me l. faire** it's an attractive offer, I think I'll give in to temptation; **laisse-toi faire, ça nous fait plaisir de te l'offrir** do take it *or* come on, we'd love to give it to you; *Fam* **se l. vivre** to take life as it comes; **ça se laisse regarder** *(à la télévision)* it's watchable; **il se laisse boire, ton petit vin** your wine goes down nicely *or* is very drinkable; **ça se laisse manger** it's rather tasty

laisser-aller [lesеale] **NM INV 1** *(désinvolture)* casualness **2** *(relâchement ▸ dans le travail)* carelessness, sloppiness; **il y a du l. dans ce bureau!** things are a bit too easy-going *or* slack in this office!

laisser-faire, laissez-faire [lesefɛr] **NM INV** *Écon* laissez-faire, non-interventionism

laissez-passer [lesepase] **NM INV** *(autorisation)* pass

lait [lɛ] **NM 1** *(des mammifères)* milk; **avec ou sans l.?** with or without milk?, *Br* black or white?; *Belg* **l. battu** buttermilk; **l. caillé** curdled milk; **l. concentré** *ou* **condensé non sucré** evaporated milk; **l. concentré** *ou* **condensé sucré** (sweetened) condensed milk; **l. cru** unpasteurized milk; **l. demi-écrémé** *Br* semi-skimmed milk, *Am* two percent milk; **l. écrémé** *Br* skimmed milk, *Am* skim milk; **l. entier** whole milk, *Br* full-cream milk; **l. longue conservation** long-life milk; **l. maternel** mother's *or* breast milk; **l. maternisé** baby formula (milk); **l. en poudre** dried *or* powdered milk; **l. stérilisé** sterilized milk

2 *(de certains fruits)* milk; **l. de coco** coconut milk

3 *(boisson préparée)* **l. de palme** date palm leaf syrup; **l. de poule** eggnog

4 *(pour la toilette)* milk; **l. démaquillant** *ou* **de toilette** cleansing milk

5 *Constr* **l. de chaux** slaked lime wash

• **au lait ADJ** with milk

• **de lait ADJ 1** *(ayant la même nourrice ▸ frère, sœur)* foster **2** *(qu'on allaite encore ▸ cochon)* suckling **3** *(semblable au lait ▸ teint)* milky, milk-white

laitage [letaʒ] **NM** dairy product

laitance [letɑ̃s] **NF 1** *Ich* milt **2** *Culin* (soft) roe

laité, -e [lete] **ADJ** *(poisson)* soft-roed

laiterie [lɛtri] **NF 1** *(fabrique, ferme, magasin)* dairy **2** *(secteur d'activité)* dairy industry *or* farming

laiteron [lɛtrɔ̃] **NM** *Bot* sow thistle, milkweed

laiteux, -euse [letø, -øz] **ADJ 1** *(semblable au lait)* milky; **un liquide l.** a milky *or* cloudy liquid **2** *(de la couleur du lait ▸ teint)* milk-white, milky

laitier, -ère [letje, -ɛr] **ADJ 1** *(du lait)* dairy *(avant n)*; **des produits laitiers** dairy produce **2** *(bête)* milk *(avant n)*

NM,F 1 *(livreur)* milkman, *f* milkwoman; **l'heure du l.** *(l'aurore)* the crack of dawn **2** *(crémier)* dairyman, *f* dairywoman **3** *(éleveur)* dairy farmer

NM *Métal* slag

• **laitière NF 1** *(ustensile)* milk pail, *Br* milk can, *Am* milk bucket **2** dairy cow; **ces vaches sont de bonnes laitières** these cows are good milkers

laiton [letɔ̃] **NM** brass; **un fil de l.** a piece of brass wire

laitue [lety] **NF** lettuce; **l. pommée** round lettuce

laïus [lajys] **NM** *Fam* long spiel, long-winded speech; **ne me fais pas tout un l.!** give me the short version!

lama [lama] **NM 1** *Rel* lama; **le Grand l.** the Dalai Lama **2** *Zool* llama

lamantin [lamɑ̃tɛ̃] **NM** manatee

lamaserie [lamazri] **NF** lamasery

lambada [lɑ̃bada] **NF** lambada

lambda [lɑ̃bda] **ADJ INV** *Fam* **un individu l.** your average person◻ *or Br* bloke *or Am* Joe; **le contribuable l.** the average *or* ordinary taxpayer◻

NM INV *(lettre)* lambda

lambeau, -x [lɑ̃bo] **NM** *(morceau)* scrap, strip, bit; **des lambeaux de chair** strips of flesh; **des lambeaux de conversation** scraps *or* fragments of conversation

• **en lambeaux ADJ** *(déchiré)* in tatters, in shreds; **le tapis est en lambeaux** the carpet is in tatters *or* in shreds **ADV les affiches partent** *ou* **tombent en lambeaux** the posters are getting really tattered; **mettre qch en lambeaux** to tear sth to shreds *or* to pieces

lambin, -e [lɑ̃bɛ̃, -in] *Fam* **ADJ** dawdling, slow◻; **ce qu'il peut être l.!** he can be such a dawdler *or Br* slowcoach *or Am* slowpoke!

NM,F dawdler, *Br* slowcoach, *Am* slowpoke

lambiner [3] [lɑ̃bine] **VI** *Fam* to dawdle

lambineur, -euse [lɑ̃binœr, -øz], **lambineux, -euse** [lɑ̃binø, -øz] *Can* = **lambin**

lambourde [lɑ̃burd] **NF 1** *Bot* fruit-tree shoot **2** *Constr (pour solives)* wall plate; *(frise)* (joist) backing strip

lambrequin [lɑ̃brəkɛ̃] **NM 1** *(motif décoratif)* lambrequin **2** *Constr* (eaves) cornice **3** *(d'un lit)* valance; *(d'une fenêtre) Br* pelmet, *Am* lambrequin

• **lambrequins NMPL** *Hér* mantle, mantling

lambris [lɑ̃bri] **NM 1** *(en bois)* panelling *(UNCOUNT)*; **l. de chêne** oak panelling; **sous les l. dorés du ministère** in the gilded halls of the ministry **2** *(en marbre, en stuc)* casing *(UNCOUNT)*

lambrissage [lɑ̃brisaʒ] **NM** *(en bois)* panelling, wainscot(t)ing; *(en marbre, en stuc)* casing

lambrisser [3] [lɑ̃brise] **VT** *(en bois)* to panel, to wainscot; *(en marbre, en stuc)* to case; **lambrissé de chêne** oak-panelled

lambswool [lɑ̃bswul] **NM** lambswool

lame [lam] **NF 1** *(de couteau, d'épée)* blade; *(de scie)* web; *(de tournevis)* shaft; **l. de rasoir** razor blade; **il a le visage en l. de couteau** he is hatchet-faced

2 *Littéraire (épée)* sword; **une bonne** *ou* **fine l.** *(personne ▸ homme)* a fine swordsman; *(▸ femme)* a fine swordswoman

3 *Aut (de ressort)* leaf

4 *Constr (de store)* slat; *(en bois)* lath, strip; **l. de parquet** floorboard

5 *Géol* **l. mince** thin plate *or* section

6 *Opt* slide

7 *(de champignon)* lamella, gill

8 *Tex (de lisses)* leaf

9 *(vague)* wave; *aussi Fig* **l. de fond** ground swell; **une l. de fond électorale** a ground swell of electoral support

lamé, -e [lame] **ADJ** lamé

NM lamé; **une robe en l.** a lamé dress; **l. or** gold lamé

lamellaire [lamelɛr] **ADJ** lamellar, lamellate

lamelle [lamɛl] **NF 1** *Bot* lamella, gill

2 *Culin (de viande)* thin strip; *(de fromage, de pomme)* thin slice, sliver; **couper en (fines) lamelles** to cut into (wafer-)thin slices

3 *(de fer, de plastique etc)* thin strip; *(de minéral)* flake, *Spéc* lamella

4 *Opt* coverslip, cover glass

lamellé, -e [lamɛle] **ADJ** lamellated

lamentable [lamɑ̃tabl] **ADJ 1** *(désolant ▸ accident)* deplorable, frightful; *(pitoyable ▸ plainte, vie)* pitiful; *(▸ état)* awful, terrible **2** *(mauvais ▸ performance, résultat)* pathetic, appalling **3** *(triste ▸ voix, ton)* mournful, woeful

lamentablement [lamɑ̃tabləmɑ̃] **ADV** miserably, dismally

lamentation [lamɑ̃tasjɔ̃] **NF 1** *(pleurs)* wailing *(UNCOUNT)*, lamentation **2** *(récrimination)* moaning *(UNCOUNT)*, complaining *(UNCOUNT)*; **cesse tes lamentations** stop your moaning *or* complaining

• **lamentations NFPL** *Rel* **le livre des Lamentations** the Book of Lamentations

lamenter [3] [lamɑ̃te] **se lamenter VPR 1** *(gémir)* to moan, to whine; **se l. sur qch** to moan about sth, *Sout* to bemoan sth; **se l. sur son sort** to bemoan *or* to lament one's fate; **elle se lamentait d'avoir perdu son bracelet** she was moaning about having lost her bracelet, she was bemoaning the loss of her bracelet **2** *(pleurer)* to wail

lamento [lamento] **NM** lament

laminage [laminaʒ] **NM 1** *(du plastique, du métal, du verre)* rolling, laminating; *(du caoutchouc, du papier)* calendering; **l. à chaud/à froid** hot-/cold-rolling **2** *(réduction ▸ des revenus)* erosion; *(▸ des effectifs)* decimation **3** *Fam (anéantissement ▸ d'un parti)* near annihilation◻

laminaire [laminɛr] **NF** *(algue)* oarweed, laminarian

laminer [3] [lamine] **VT 1** *(plastique, métal, verre)* to roll, to laminate; *(caoutchouc, papier)* to calender **2** *(réduire ▸ revenus)* to erode; *(▸ effectifs)* to decimate **3** *Fam (personne ▸ épuiser)* to exhaust; **la gauche a été laminée aux législatives** the left were nearly annihilated in the parliamentary elections◻

lamineur, -euse [laminœr, -øz] **ADJ** laminating; **cylindre l.** roller

NM,F millhand *(in a roller mill)*

• **lamineuse NF** roller *(for glass)*

laminoir [laminwar] **NM 1** *Métal* rolling mill; *Fig* **(faire) passer qn au l.** to put sb through the mill **2** *(à papier)* calender

lampadaire [lɑ̃padɛr] **NM 1** *(dans une maison) Br* standard lamp, *Am* floor lamp **2** *(dans la rue)* streetlamp, streetlight

lampant, -e [lɑ̃pɑ̃, -ɑ̃t] **ADJ** lamp *(avant n)*; **pétrole l.** paraffin (oil), *Am* kerosene

lamparo [lɑ̃paro] **NM 1** *(lampe)* (fishing) lamp; **aller à la pêche au l.** to go fishing by lamplight **2** *(bateau)* lamplight fishing boat

lampe [lɑ̃p] **NF 1** *(luminaire)* lamp, light; **à la lumière de la l.** by lamplight; **l. à acétylène** acetylene lamp *or Am* torch; **l. à arc** arc lamp *or* light; **l. (d')architecte** *ou* **articulée** anglepoise lamp; **l. de bureau** desk lamp; **l. de chevet** bedside lamp; **l. à gaz** gaslight; **l. halogène** halogen lamp; **l. à huile** oil lamp; **l. à incandescence** incandescent lamp; **l. au néon** fluorescent *or* neon light; *Br* **l. à pétrole** paraffin lamp, *Am* kerosene lamp; **l. de poche** *Br* torch, *Am* flashlight; **à la lumière d'une l. de poche** *Br* by torchlight, *Am* by flashlight; **l. témoin** warning light

2 *(appareil)* **l. à alcool** spirit lamp; **l. à bronzer** sunlamp; **l. à souder** *Br* blowlamp, *Am* blowtorch

3 *Mines* **l. de sûreté** safety lamp

4 *Rad* valve (tube)

5 *Fam* **s'en mettre** *ou très Fam* **s'en foutre plein la l.** to stuff oneself *or* one's face

lampée [lɑ̃pe] **NF** *Fam* swig, gulp; **boire qch à grandes lampées** to gulp sth down

lamper [3] [lɑ̃pe] **VT** *Fam* to swig, to gulp down

lampe-tempête [lɑ̃ptɑ̃pɛt] *(pl* **lampes-tempête)** **NF** hurricane lamp, storm lantern

lampion [lɑ̃pjɔ̃] **NM** paper *or* Chinese lantern; **scander des slogans sur l'air des lampions** to chant slogans

lampiste [lɑ̃pist] **NM 1** *Vieilli (d'un théâtre)* light maintenance man; *(des chemins de fer)* lampman **2** *Fam (subalterne)* underling, menial; **ce sont toujours les lampistes qui trinquent** it's always the little people that get the blame

lampisterie [lɑ̃pistəri] **NF** *Vieilli* = place where lamps are stored and repaired in a mine

lamproie [lɑ̃prwa] **NF** *Ich* lamprey; **l. de rivière** lampern, river lamprey

lance [lɑ̃s] **NF 1** *(pique)* spear; **transpercer qn d'un coup de l.** to spear sb, to run sb through with a spear **2** *(tuyau)* **l. d'arrosage** water hose; **l. à eau** hose, pipe; **l. d'incendie** fire hose

lance-bombe, lance-bombes [lɑ̃sbɔ̃b] *(pl* **lance-bombes)** **NM** bomb-dropping gear

lance-flamme, lance-flammes [lɑ̃sflam] *(pl* **lance-flammes)** **NM** flame-thrower

lance-fusée, lance-fusées [lɑ̃sfyze] *(pl* **lance-fusées)** **NM** rocket launcher

lance-grenade, lance-grenades [lɑ̃sgrənad] *(pl* **lance-grenades)** **NM** grenade launcher

lancement [lɑ̃smɑ̃] **NM 1** *Astron & Naut* launch, launching; **rampe de l.** launching ramp

2 *Tech (d'un pont)* throwing

3 *(en publicité ▸ opération)* launching; *(▸ cérémonie, réception)* launch; *(d'un projet, d'une société, d'un produit)* launch; *Mktg* **l. sur le marché** market entry

4 *Bourse (d'une société)* flotation; *(de titres boursiers, d'un emprunt)* issuing, issue; *(d'une souscription)* start

5 *(projection)* throwing

6 *Ordinat (d'impression)* start

lance-missile, lance-missiles [lɑ̃smisil] *(pl* **lance-missiles)** **NM** missile launcher

lancéolé, -e [lɑ̃seɔle] **ADJ 1** *Bot* lanceolate **2** *Archit* **arc l.** lancet arch

lance-pierre, lance-pierres [lɑ̃spjɛr] *(pl* **lance-pierres)** **NM 1** *(fronde)* catapult **2** *Fam (locutions)* **déjeuner/manger au** *ou* **avec un lance-pierres** to gulp one's lunch/meal (down); **être payé au** *ou* **avec un l.** to be paid peanuts *or Am* chump change

lancequiner [3] [lɑ̃skine] **VI** *très Fam* **1** *(pleuvoir)* **il lancequine** it's pissing down **2** *(uriner)* to pee, to piss

LANCER [16] [lɑ̃se]

VT
- to throw **A1, 2, 6**
- to shoot **A2**
- to launch **A2, B2, 4, 7**
- to let out **A3**
- to send out **A4**
- to issue **A4**
- to cast **A7**
- to get going **B3, 5**

NM
- casting **1**
- throw **2**

VPR
- to throw at one another **1**
- to throw oneself **2**
- to take up **6**
- to embark on **5**

VT A. *ENVOYER, ÉMETTRE* **1** *(jeter)* to throw; **elle m'a lancé la balle** she threw me the ball, she threw the ball to me; **lancez les bras en arrière puis en avant** swing *or* throw your arms backwards then forwards; **l. la jambe en l'air** to kick one's leg up; **l. des pierres à qn** to throw stones at sb; **l. le disque/javelot/marteau** to throw the discus/javelin/hammer; **l. le poids** to put the shot; **l. un regard haineux à qn** to shoot sb a look of hatred; **ils nous lançaient des regards curieux** they looked at us curiously; **l. qch à la figure à qn** to throw sth in sb's face; **l. son poing dans la figure à qn** to smash one's fist into sb's face

2 *(flèche)* to shoot; *(fusée, torpille)* to launch; *(bombe)* to drop; *(grenade)* to throw, to launch; **l. des flèches avec un arc** to fire (off) *or* to shoot arrows from a bow; **l. un projectile téléguidé** to fire a remote-controlled missile; **l. des bombes sur un objectif** to drop bombs on a target; **l. un signal de détresse** to fire off *or* to send out a distress signal

3 *(émettre ▸ cri)* to let out; *(▸ remarque)* to make; *(▸ proposition, idée)* to throw out; *(▸ juron)* to let out; *(▸ étincelles, flammes)* to throw out; **l. un cri de terreur** to let out a cry of terror; **les mouettes lançaient leurs appels aigus** the gulls were screeching *or* were crying shrilly; **l. un bon mot** to crack a joke; **l. des injures à qn** to hurl insults at sb; **l. des questions** to fire questions; **les joyaux lançaient mille feux** the jewels were sparkling brightly; **ses yeux lançaient des éclairs** his/her eyes flashed

4 *(diffuser ▸ décret, consigne)* to send out, to put out, to issue; **l. des invitations** *(par courrier)* to send invitations; *(oralement)* to give out invitations; **l. un SOS/un appel à la radio** to send out an SOS/an appeal on the radio; **l. un appel d'offres** to invite tenders; **l. un ultimatum** to issue an ultimatum; **l. un emprunt** to issue a loan

5 *Bourse (société)* to float; *(titres boursiers, emprunt)* to issue; *(souscription)* to start; **l. des titres sur le marché** to issue shares

6 *Constr* to throw; **l. un pont** to throw a bridge

7 *Pêche* to cast; **l. sa ligne** to cast one's line

B. *METTRE EN MARCHE, FAIRE DÉBUTER* **1** *(faire partir brusquement)* **les cavaliers lancèrent leurs chevaux** the riders set off at full speed on their horses; **ils lancèrent les chiens sur les rôdeurs** they set the dogs on the prowlers; **l. des troupes à l'attaque** to send troops into the attack

2 *(mettre en train ▸ campagne)* to launch; *(▸ affaire)* to set up; *(▸ idée)* to float; *(▸ mode)* to start; **l. un mouvement de protestation** to launch a protest campaign, to get a protest campaign going

3 *(faire fonctionner ▸ gén)* to get going *or* started, to start; *Ordinat (programme, impression)* to start, to run; **l. un balancier** to set a pendulum swinging; **l. un moteur** to start an engine; **une fois le moteur lancé** once the engine is running; **le train était lancé à 150 km/h quand…** the train was hurtling along at 150 km/h when…

4 *(faire connaître ▸ projet, société, produit, modèle)* to launch; **l. un nouveau produit sur le marché** to launch a new product on the market; **c'est ce roman/cette émission qui l'a lancé** this novel/programme made him famous; **une fois lancé dans le cyclisme professionnel** once he'd embarked on his career as a professional cyclist; **maintenant qu'il est lancé il pourra demander plus cher** now that he's made a name for himself he can ask for more money

5 *Fam (orienter ▸ discussion)* to get going; **une fois qu'il est lancé sur ce sujet, on ne peut plus l'arrêter** once he gets going on the subject, there's no stopping him; **si on le lance sur la course automobile, il est intarissable** if you start him off on motor racing, there's no stopping him

6 *(engager)* to lead; **vous lancez le pays dans l'aventure** you're leading the country into unknown territory

7 *Mil* to launch; **l. une attaque** to launch an attack

NM 1 *Pêche* casting; **l. léger/lourd** fixed/free reel casting

2 *Sport* throw; *(au base-ball)* pitch; **pratiquer le l. du disque/javelot** to throw the discus/javelin; **pratiquer le l. du poids** to put the shot; **l. franc** *(au basket)* free throw

VPR se lancer 1 *(mutuellement)* to throw at one another; **ils se lançaient des assiettes à la figure** they were throwing plates at each other; **elles se lançaient des injures** they were hurling insults at each other, they were exchanging insults

2 *(se précipiter)* to throw oneself; *(courir)* to rush (headlong), to dash; **se l. à l'attaque** to throw oneself into the attack; **se l. à la poursuite de** to set off in pursuit of; **le malheureux s'est lancé dans le vide** the poor wretch threw himself into the abyss

3 *(se mettre à parler)* **se l. sur un sujet** to get going on a topic

4 *(prendre l'initiative)* **allez, lance-toi et demande une augmentation** go on, take the plunge and ask for a rise; **allez, lance-toi, tu verras ce n'est pas si difficile** go on, off you go, you'll soon see it's not so hard

5 **se l. dans** *(s'aventurer dans ▸ explication, aventure)* to embark on; **ne te lance pas dans de grosses dépenses** don't go spending a lot of money; **se l. dans une entreprise hasardeuse** to embark on a dangerous undertaking; **il s'est lancé dans des digressions interminables** he went off into endless digressions

6 *(débuter)* **se l. dans la politique/la peinture** to take up politics/painting; **puis il a décidé de se l. dans les affaires** then he decided to set up as a businessman

7 *Com & Mktg* **se l. sur le marché** to enter the market

lance-roquette, lance-roquettes [lɑ̃srɔkɛt] *(pl* **lance-roquettes)** **NM** (hand-held) rocket launcher *or* gun

lance-satellites [lɑ̃ssatəlit] **NM INV** satellite launcher

lance-torpille, lance-torpilles [lɑ̃stɔrpij] *(pl* **lance-torpilles)** **NM** torpedo (launching) tube

lancette [lɑ̃sɛt] **NF** *Archit & Méd* lancet, lance

lanceur, -euse [lɑ̃sœr, -øz] **NM,F 1** *Sport (au base-ball)* pitcher; *(au cricket)* bowler; **l. de javelot** javelin thrower; **l. de poids** shot putter **2** *(promoteur)* promoter, originator; **un l. d'affaires** a business promoter

NM *Astron* launch vehicle, launcher

lanceur-d'engins [lɑ̃sœrdɑ̃ʒɛ̃] **NM INV** nuclear warhead submarine, missile launcher

lanceuse [lɑ̃søz] *voir* **lanceur**

lancier [lɑ̃sje] **NM 1** *Mil* lancer **2 les lanciers** *(quadrille)* the lancers

lancinant, -e [lɑ̃sinɑ̃, -ɑ̃t] **ADJ 1** *(douleur)* throbbing **2** *(obsédant ▸ souvenir)* haunting; *(▸ regret)* nagging **3** *(répétitif)* nerve-shattering; **une musique lancinante** pounding music

lanciner [3] [lɑ̃sine] **VT** *(obséder)* to haunt, to plague; *(tourmenter)* to harass

lançon [lɑ̃sɔ̃] **NM** *Ich* launce, sand eel *or* lance

landais, -e [lɑ̃dɛ, -ɛz] **ADJ** of/from the Landes

• **Landais, -e NM,F** = inhabitant of or person from the Landes

landau, -s [lɑ̃do] **NM 1** *(pour bébés) Br* pram, *Am* baby carriage **2** *(attelage)* landau

lande [lɑ̃d] **NF** *(terre)* moor; **la l. bretonne** the moors of Brittany; **les Landes** the Landes (region) *(in south-west France)*

Landernau, Landerneau [lɑ̃dɛrno] **N cela fera du bruit dans L.** it'll be the talk of the town

landier [lɑ̃dje] **NM** firedog, andiron

Land Rover® [landrɔvɛr] **NF** *Aut* Land Rover®

langage [lɑ̃gaʒ] **NM 1** *Ling & Psy* language; **l'acquisition du l.** language acquisition; **le l. enfantin** baby talk; **troubles du l.** speech *or* language disorders

2 *(code)* language; **le l. des abeilles** the language of bees; **le l. du corps** body language; **le l. des fleurs** the language of flowers; **le l. de la peinture** the idiom of painting; **le l. des signes** *ou* **le l. des sourds-muets** sign language

3 *(jargon)* language; **l. administratif/technique** administrative/technical language

4 *(style)* language; **l. familier/populaire** colloquial/popular language; **l. argotique** slang; **l. poétique** poetic language; **il a un l. très grossier** his language is very coarse; **qu'est-ce que c'est que ce l.?** what kind of language is that?; **le beau l.** educated speech

5 *(discours)* language, talk; **tu tiens un drôle de l. depuis quelque temps** you've been coming out with *or* saying some very odd things recently; **tenir un tout autre l.** to change one's tune; **voilà un l. qui me plaît!** that's what I like to hear!; **parler le l. de la franchise/vérité** to speak frankly/truthfully; **c'est le l. de la raison** that's a sensible thing to say

6 *Ordinat & Tél* language; **l. assembleur** *ou* **d'assemblage** assembly language; **l. auteur** authoring language; **l. chiffré** cipher; **l. de commande** command language; **l. évolué** high-level language; **l. d'interrogation** query language; **l. JavaScript®** JavaScript®; **l. machine** internal *or* machine language; **l. naturel** natural language; **l. à objets** object-oriented language; **l. de programmation** programming language; **l. source** source language; **l. utilisateur** user language

Do not confuse with **langue**.

langagier, -ère [lɑ̃gaʒje, -ɛr] **ADJ** linguistic, language *(avant n)*

lange [lɑ̃ʒ] **NM** *(pour bébé)* baby blanket

• **langes NMPL** swaddling clothes

• **dans les langes ADJ** *Fig (à ses débuts)* in its/their infancy; **le cinéma était encore dans les langes** cinema was still in its infancy

langer [17] [lɑ̃ʒe] **VT 1** *(emmailloter)* to swaddle **2** *(changer ▸ bébé)* to change

langoureuse [lɑ̃gurøz] *voir* **langoureux**

langoureusement [lɑ̃gurøzmɑ̃] **ADV** languorously

langoureux, -euse [lɑ̃gurø, -øz] **ADJ** languid, languorous

langouste [lɑ̃gust] **NF** *Zool* (sea) crayfish *or Am* crawfish; *Culin* (spiny) lobster

langoustine [lɑ̃gustin] **NF** langoustine, Dublin bay prawn

langue [lɑ̃g] **NF A.** *ORGANE* **1** *Anat* tongue; **se mordre/se brûler la l.** to bite/to burn one's tongue; **avoir la l. blanche** *ou* **chargée** to have a coated *or* furred tongue; *Fig* **une mauvaise l., une l. de vipère** a malicious gossip; **mauvaise l.!** that's a rather nasty thing to say!; **les langues vont bon train** tongues are wagging; **tirez la l. et dites ah** put *or* stick your tongue out and say aah; **tirer la l. à qn** to stick one's tongue out at sb; *Fam Fig* **tirer la l.** *(avoir soif)* to be gasping (for a drink); *(avoir du mal)* to have a hard *or* rough time; *(être fatigué)* to be worn out; *(être dans le besoin)* to be short of funds *or Br* strapped for cash; **tu as avalé** *ou* **perdu ta l.?** have you lost *or* (has the) cat got your tongue?; *Fam* **avoir la l. bien affilée** *ou* **bien pendue** to have the gift of the gab; *Fig* **avoir la l. trop longue** to have a big mouth; **coup de l.** lick; **donner des coups de l. à qn/qch** to lick sb/sth; *Fig Littéraire* **coups de l.** spiteful gossip; **délier** *ou* **dénouer la l. à qn** to loosen sb's tongue; *Fam* **elle n'a pas la l. dans sa poche** she's never at a loss for something to say *or* for words; **donner sa l. au chat** to give up (guessing); **prendre l. avec qn** to contact sb, to make contact with sb; **il ne sait pas tenir sa l.** he can't keep a secret; *Fam* **tourne sept fois ta l. dans ta bouche avant de parler** think twice before you open your mouth

2 *Culin* tongue; **l. de bœuf** *(chaude)* boiled ox tongue; *(froide)* (cold) tongue

B. *Ling* **1** *(moyen de communication)* language, *Littéraire* tongue; **l. commune** common language; **décrire une l.** to describe a language; **ce métier exige la connaissance des langues** this job requires a knowledge of languages; **un professeur de langues** a (foreign) language teacher; **l'anglais est la l. internationale** English is the international language; **les passagers de l. anglaise** English-speaking passengers; **dans la l. de Molière/Shakespeare** in English/French; **langues anciennes** classical languages; **l. cible** *ou* **d'arrivée** target language; **l. écrite** written language; **langues étrangères** foreign languages; *Univ* **langues étrangères appliquées** = applied modern languages; **l. maternelle** mother tongue; **langues mortes** dead languages; *Hist* **l. d'oc** = medieval French dialect spoken in southern France; *Hist* **l. d'oïl** = medieval French dialect spoken in northern France; **l. officielle** official language; **l. parlée** spoken language; **dans la l. parlée** colloquially; **l. des signes française** = official name of the sign language used in France; **langues sœurs** sister languages; **l. source** *ou* **de départ** source language; **l. de travail** working language; **l. véhiculaire** lingua franca; **la l. vernaculaire** the vernacular; **les langues vivantes** *Scol* modern languages; *(utilisées de nos jours)* living languages

2 *(jargon)* language; **dans la l. du barreau** in the language of the courts, *Sout* in legal parlance; **la l. littéraire** literary language; **la l. populaire** popular language; **l. de bois** hackneyed phrases; **la l. de bois des politiciens** the clichés politicians come out with; *Hist* **l. savante** *(latin)* language of learning; **la l. verte** slang; *Hist* **l. vulgaire** *(langue du peuple)* vernacular

C. *FORME* **1** *(gén)* tongue; **des langues de feu léchaient le mur** tongues of flame were licking the wall

2 *Géog* **une l. de terre** a strip of land, a narrow piece of land; **une l. glaciaire** a spur of ice

> Do not confuse with the French word **langage**.

langue-de-bœuf [lɑ̃gdəbœf] *(pl* **langues-de-bœuf)** **NF** *Bot* beefsteak fungus

langue-de-chat [lɑ̃gdəʃa] *(pl* **langues-de-chat)** **NF** *Culin* langue de chat, thin finger biscuit

languedocien, -enne [lɑ̃gdɔsjɛ̃, -ɛn] **ADJ** of/from the Languedoc (region)

• **Languedocien, -enne NM,F** = inhabitant of or person from the Languedoc (region)

languette [lɑ̃gɛt] **NF 1** *(petite bande)* strip;

2 *(de chaussure)* tab, stem

3 *(d'une canette)* ring-pull, tab

4 *(de balance)* pointer

5 *Tech (tenon)* tongue

6 *Mus (d'orgue)* languet; *(d'instrument à anche)* reed

7 *Ordinat* slider

langueur [lɑ̃gœr] **NF 1** *(apathie)* languidness **2** *(mélancolie douce, rêverie)* languor; **un sourire plein de l.** a languid *or* languorous smile

languide [lɑ̃gid] **ADJ** *Littéraire* languid, languishing

languir **[32]** [lɑ̃gir] **VI 1** *Littéraire (personne, animal)* to languish, to pine; **la petite fille languit loin de sa mère** the little girl is pining for her mother; **l. d'amour** to be lovesick; **l. en prison** to languish in prison

2 *(plante)* to wilt

3 *(conversation, situation)* to flag; **la conversation languissait** the conversation was flagging; **les affaires languissent** business is slack

4 *(attendre)* **faire l. qn** to keep sb waiting; *Littéraire* **je languis d'être avec vous** I am longing *or* pining to be with you

• **languir après VT IND** to languish *or* to pine for

VPR se languir *(personne)* to pine; **il se languit de toi** he's pining for you; **je me languis de la Provence** I'm longing to go back to Provence

languissamment [lɑ̃gisamɑ̃] **ADV** *Littéraire* languidly

languissant, -e [lɑ̃gisɑ̃, -ɑ̃t] **ADJ 1** *Littéraire (qui dépérit)* failing, dwindling; **santé languissante** failing health

2 *Littéraire (amoureux)* lovelorn, lovesick

3 *(sans vigueur)* languid, listless

4 *(morne ▸ conversation)* dull; **le commerce est l.** business is slack

lanière [lanjɛr] **NF 1** *(bande)* strap; **découper qch en lanières** to cut sth into strips **2** *(d'un fouet)* lash

lanifère [lanifɛr], **lanigère** [laniʒɛr] **ADJ** *Zool & Bot* wool-bearing

lanoline [lanɔlin] **NF** lanolin, lanoline

lanterne [lɑ̃tɛrn] **NF 1** *(lampe)* lantern; **l. chinoise** Chinese lantern; **l. sourde/vénitienne** dark/Chinese lantern; **les aristocrates à la l.!** string the aristocrats up!

2 *Cin* projector

3 *Archit* lantern

4 *Phot* **l. magique** magic lantern

• **lanternes NFPL** *Aut Br* sidelights, *Am* parking lights

• **lanterne rouge NF 1** *Rail* rear *or* tail light **2** *(locution)* **être la l. rouge** *(gén)* to bring up the rear; *Sport (dans une course)* to come (in) last; *(équipe)* to get the wooden spoon; *(à l'école)* to be bottom of the class

lanterneau, -x [lɑ̃tɛrno] **NM** skylight, roof light

lanterner **[3]** [lɑ̃tɛrne] **VI** *Fam* **1** *(perdre son temps)* to dawdle, to drag one's feet **2** *(attendre)* **faire l. qn** to keep sb hanging about *or* waiting

Laos [laos] **NM le L.** Laos

laotien, -enne [laɔsjɛ̃, -ɛn] **ADJ** Laotian

NM *(langue)* Lao, Laotian

• **Laotien, -enne NM,F** Laotian

La Palice [lapalis] **NPR une vérité de L.** a truism

lapalissade [lapalisad] **NF** truism; **c'est une l.** that's self-evident, that's stating the obvious

laparoscopie [laparɔskɔpi] **NF** *Méd* laparoscopy

lapement [lapmɑ̃] **NM** lapping *(UNCOUNT)*

laper **[3]** [lape] **VT** to lap (up)

VI to lap

lapereau, -x [lapro] **NM** young rabbit

lapidaire [lapidɛr] **ADJ 1** *(concis)* terse, *Sout* lapidary; **un style l.** a pithy *or* succinct style **2** *Minér* lapidary; **art l.** lapidary art

NM 1 *(artisan)* lapidary **2** *(commerçant)* gem merchant

lapidation [lapidasjɔ̃] **NF** stoning, *Sout* lapidation

lapider **[3]** [lapide] **VT 1** *(jeter des pierres à)* to stone, to throw stones at; *(tuer)* to stone to death, *Sout* to lapidate **2** *Littéraire (critiquer)* to lambast

lapin [lapɛ̃] **NM 1** *Zool* rabbit; **l. mâle** buck (rabbit); **l. de choux** *ou* **de clapier** *ou* **domestique** tame *or* domestic rabbit; **l. de garenne** wild rabbit; *(aux États-Unis)* cottontail (rabbit); *Culin* **civet/pâté de lapin** rabbit stew/paté; *Fam* **poser un l. à qn** to stand sb up; *Can Fam* **en criant l.** in a flash **2** *(fourrure) Br* rabbit(skin), *Am* cony (skin) **3** *Fam (terme d'affection)* pet, *Br* poppet **ça va, mon petit l.?** all right, honey *or Br* poppet?

lapine [lapin] **NF** doe (rabbit); *Fam Fig* **c'est une vraie l.** she breeds like a rabbit

lapiner **[3]** [lapine] **VI** to litter

lapinière [lapinjɛr] **NF** rabbit hutch

lapis-lazuli [lapislazyli], **lapis** [lapis] **NM INV** lapis lazuli

lapon, -e *ou* **-onne** [lapɔ̃, -ɔn] **ADJ** Lapp, Lappish

NM *(langue)* Lappish, Lapp

• **Lapon, -e** *ou* **-onne NM,F** Lapp, Laplander

Laponie [lapɔni] **NF la L.** Lapland

Laponne, laponne [lapɔn] *voir* **lapon**

laps [laps] **NM un l. de temps** a lapse of time, a while

lapsus [lapsys] **NM 1** *(faute)* **l. (linguae)** slip (of the tongue); **l. (calami)** slip of the pen **2** *Psy* Freudian slip; **l. révélateur** Freudian slip

laquage [lakaʒ] **NM 1** *Tech* lacquering **2** *Méd* **l. du sang** haemolysis

laquais [lakɛ] **NM 1** *(valet)* footman **2** *Littéraire Péj (homme servile)* lackey, flunkey

laque [lak] **NF 1** *(vernis)* lacquer; **en l.** lacquered; **l. de Chine** japan

2 *(pour cheveux)* hairspray

3 *(peinture)* gloss (paint)

4 lac

NM *(objet)* piece of lacquerwork; **des laques** lacquerware *(UNCOUNT)*, lacquerwork *(UNCOUNT)*

laqué, -e [lake] **ADJ 1** *Beaux-Arts* lacquered

2 *(peint)* **cuisine laquée (en) rouge** kitchen in red gloss

3 *(cheveux)* lacquered

4 *Culin voir* **canard**

NM *(peinture)* (high) gloss paint; *(enduit) Br* varnish, *Am* enamel

laquelle [lakɛl] *voir* **lequel**

laquer **[3]** [lake] **VT 1** *(objet, meuble)* to lacquer; *(ongles)* to varnish **2** *(cheveux)* to put hairspray on

larbin [larbɛ̃] **NM** *Fam Péj aussi Fig* flunkey

larcin [larsɛ̃] **NM 1** *(petit vol)* petty theft; **commettre de menus larcins** to engage in petty theft **2** *(objet volé)* **le grenier était plein de ses larcins** the attic was filled with his/her spoils *or* booty

lard [lar] **NM 1** *Culin* bacon; **omelette au l.** bacon omelette; **l. fumé** smoked bacon; **l. gras, gros l.** fat bacon; **l. maigre, petit l., l. de poitrine** streaky bacon; **l. salé** salt pork **2** *Fam (locutions)* **faire du l.** to sit around and get fat; **avec eux, on se demande** *ou* **on ne sait pas si c'est du l. ou du cochon** with that lot, you never know where you are; **rentrer dans le l. à qn** to lay into sb; *très Fam* **un gros l.** a fatso, a fat slob

> Il faut noter que le nom anglais **lard** est un faux ami. Il signifie **saindoux**.

larder **[3]** [larde] **VT 1** *Culin* to lard **2** *(poignarder)* **l. qn de coups de couteau** to stab sb repeatedly **3** *(truffer)* **l. une lettre de citations** to pepper a letter with quotations

lardoire [lardwar] **NF 1** *Culin* larding needle *or* pin **2** *Fam (épée)* sword

lardon [lardɔ̃] **NM 1** *Culin* piece of diced bacon, lardon **2** *très Fam (enfant)* kid

lare [lar] **ADJ dieux lares** lares

NM household god; *Littéraire* **transporter ailleurs ses lares et pénates** to move with all one's belongings

largable [largabl] **ADJ** releasable; **réservoir l.** releasable tank

largage [largaʒ] **NM 1** *(par parachute)* dropping; *(de troupes, de matériel)* dispatching, dropping; **opération de l.** drop; **point de l.** drop point **2** *(d'une bombe)* dropping, releasing

large [larʒ] **ADJ 1** *(grand ▸ gén)* broad, wide; *(▸ plaine)* big, wide; *(▸ rue)* broad; *(▸ tache)* large; **l. de 5 cm** 5 cm wide; **un nez l.** a broad nose; **un chapeau à larges bords** a wide-brimmed hat; **l. d'épaules** broad-shouldered; **d'un geste l.** with a sweeping gesture; **peindre à larges traits** to paint with broad brushstrokes; **un l. sourire** a broad smile

2 *(ample ▸ vêtement)* big, baggy; *(▸ chaussures)* wide

3 *(considérable)* large; **elle a une l. part de responsabilité** she must bear a large *or* major share of the blame; **ils font une part très l. à l'esprit d'initiative** they attach a lot of importance to initiative; **jouissant d'une l. autonomie** enjoying a large amount of independence; **jouissant d'une l. diffusion** widely distributed; **avoir un l. vocabulaire** to have a wide *or* wide-ranging vocabulary; **les journaux ont publié de larges extraits de son discours** the papers quoted extensively from his/her speech

4 *(général)* **prendre un mot dans son sens l.** to take a word in its broadest sense

5 *(généreux)* generous; **elle est l. avec le personnel** she's generous with the staff; **de larges gratifications** generous bonuses

6 *(ouvert)* open; **leur père a l'esprit l.** their father is open-minded *or* broadminded

7 *(excessif)* **ton estimation était un peu l.** your estimate was a bit wide of the mark

NM 1 *(dimension)* width; **ici la rivière a** *ou* **fait 2 km de l.** here the river is 2 km wide; **être au l.** to have plenty of room; *(financièrement)* to be well off **2** *Naut* **le l.** the open sea; **respirer l'air du l.** to breathe the sea air; **vent du l.** offshore wind; **au l. de Hong Kong** off Hong Kong; *Fig* **se tenir au l. de qch** to stand clear of sth; **gagner** *ou* **prendre le l.** to head for the open sea; *Fam Fig* **il est temps de prendre le l.** it's time we beat it; *Fam* **du l.!** beat it!, clear off!

ADV calculer *ou* **prévoir l.** to allow a good margin for error; **voir l.** to think big; **cette robe taille l.** this dress is loose-fitting

• **en large ADV** widthways; **mets les tables en l.** turn the tables widthways

> Il faut noter que l'adjectif anglais **large** signifie **grand, important**.

largement [larʒəmɑ̃] **ADV 1** *(amplement)* **gagner l. sa vie** to make a good living; **avoir l. le temps** to have plenty of time; **elle a l. 60 ans** she's well over 60; **il y en a l. assez** there's more than enough; **des pouvoirs l. accrus** considerably increased powers; **une opinion l. répandue** a widely held opinion; **il s'est l. inspiré de Rabelais** he drew a great deal of inspiration from Rabelais; **il vit l. au-dessus de ses moyens** he lives well beyond his means

2 *(généreusement)* generously; **on l'a l. récompensé** he has been amply *or* handsomely rewarded

3 *(de beaucoup)* greatly; **la demande excède l. notre capacité** demand greatly exceeds our capacity

4 *(facilement)* easily; **il vaut l. son frère** he's easily as good as his brother; **je gagne l. le double** I make at least *or* I easily earn twice that

5 *(en grand)* **ouvrir l. une porte** to open a door wide

> Il faut noter que l'adverbe anglais **largely** est un faux ami. Il signifie **en grande partie**.

largesse [larʒɛs] **NF** *(magnanimité)* generosity, *Sout* largesse; **il fait toujours preuve de l.** he's always very generous; **traiter qn avec l.** to be generous to sb

• **largesses NFPL** *(présents)* gifts, *Sout* liberalities; **il ne faisait pas de telles largesses avec tous** he wasn't so generous to everybody

largeur [larʒœr] **NF 1** *(dimension ▸ gén)* width; *(▸ d'une voie ferrée)* gauge; **quelle est la l. de la pièce?** how wide is the room?; **la route a une l. de 5 m** *ou* **a 5 m de l.** the road is 5 metres wide; **une remorque barrait la route dans** *ou* **sur toute sa l.** there was a trailer blocking the entire width of the road; **déchiré dans** *ou* **sur toute la l.** torn all the way across; *Ordinat* **l. de papier** paper width

2 *Fig* broadness, breadth; **l. d'esprit** *ou* **de vues** broadness of mind, broadmindedness

3 *Typ* breadth, set, width; **l. de la colonne** column width

4 *Ordinat* **l. de bande** bandwidth

• **dans les grandes largeurs ADV** *Fam* **dans les grandes largeurs** in a big way, well and truly; **on s'est fait avoir dans les grandes largeurs!** we were well and truly taken for a ride!

• **en largeur ADV** widthways, crosswise; **la table fait 30 cm en l.** the table is 30 cm widthways *or* across

largo [largo] *Mus* **ADV** largo

NM largo

largue [larg] *Naut* **ADJ** *(cordage)* loose, slack; *(vent)* free

NM grand l. quartering wind

largué, -e [large] **ADJ** *Fam* **être l.** *(ne pas comprendre)* to be lost; *(plus à la page)* to be out of touch

larguer [3] [large] **VT 1** *Naut (voile)* to let out, to unfurl; *(amarre)* to slip **2** *Aviat (bombe, charge, parachutiste)* to drop; *(réservoir)* to jettison; *(fusée)* to release **3** *très Fam (abandonner ▸ poste)* to quit□, to walk out on, *Br* to chuck (in); *(▸ vieillerie, projet) Br* to chuck, to bin, *Am* to trash; *(▸ amant)* to dump; *(▸ personne avec qui l'on vit, associé)* to walk out on; **se faire l.** to be dumped

USAGE ABSOLU *Naut* **larguez!** let go!

VI *très Fam (émettre des gaz intestinaux)* to fart, *Br* to let off

larigot [larigo] *voir* **tire-larigot**

larme [larm] **NF 1** *Physiol* tear; **être en larmes** to be in tears; **être au bord des larmes** to be on the verge of tears; **avec des larmes dans la voix** in a tearful voice; **ça vous fait venir les larmes aux yeux** it brings tears to your eyes; **il y a de quoi vous arracher** *ou* **vous tirer des larmes** it's enough to make you burst into tears; **avoir les larmes aux yeux** to have tears in one's eyes; **il a toujours la l. à l'œil, il a la l. facile** he cries easily; **pleurer** *ou* **verser des larmes de joie** to cry for joy, to shed tears of joy; **il y est allé de sa (petite) l.** he shed a tear; **une grosse l.** a big tear; **larmes de crocodile** crocodile tears; *Littéraire* **larmes de sang** tears of blood **2** *(petite quantité)* **une l. (de)** a drop (of); **une l. de cognac** a drop of brandy

larmichette [larmiʃɛt] **NF** *Fam* tiny drop□

larmier [larmje] **NM 1** *Archit* dripstone, larmier **2** *Zool (du cerf)* tear pit; *(du cheval)* temple **3** *Anat* inner corner of the eye, *Spéc* inner canthus

larmoie *etc voir* **larmoyer**

larmoiement [larmwamɑ̃] **NM** *Physiol* watering

• **larmoiements NMPL** *Littéraire (pleurnicheries)* tears, snivelling *(UNCOUNT)*

larmoyant, -e [larmwajɑ̃, -ɑ̃t] **ADJ 1** *Physiol* watery **2** *Péj (éploré)* **le récit l. de ses malheurs** the sorry tale of his/her misfortunes; **d'une voix larmoyante, elle nous annonça...** she told us in a tearful voice... **3** *(sentimental ▸ film, mélo)* mawkish; **comédie larmoyante** sentimental comedy

larmoyer [13] [larmwaje] **VI 1** *Physiol (œil)* to water **2** *Péj (se lamenter)* to snivel

larron [larɔ̃] **NM 1** *Arch (voleur)* robber, thief **2** *Bible* thief; **le bon l. et le mauvais l.** the penitent thief and the impenitent thief

larsen [larsen] **NM effet l.** feedback

larvaire [larvɛr] **ADJ 1** *Zool* larval **2** *Fig* embryonic, rudimentary

larve [larv] **NF 1** *Zool (d'amphibien, de poisson)* larva; *(d'insecte)* grub

2 *Fam (fainéant)* lazybones, slob

3 *Péj* **l. (humaine)** worm

4 *Antiq* spectre

larvé, -e [larve] **ADJ 1** *Méd* latent, *Spéc* larvate **2** *(latent)* latent; **une guerre larvée** a latent war

larver [3] [larve] **VI** *Fam* to veg (out), to slob about *or* around; **j'ai passé la journée à l. devant la télé** I spent the day vegging (out) in front of the TV

laryngé, -e [larɛ̃ʒe] **ADJ** *Anat* laryngal, laryngeal

laryngectomie [larɛ̃ʒɛktɔmi] **NF** *Méd* laryngectomy

laryngien, -enne [larɛ̃ʒjɛ̃, -ɛn] **ADJ** *Anat* laryngal, laryngeal

laryngite [larɛ̃ʒit] **NF** *Méd* laryngitis

laryngologie [larɛ̃gɔlɔʒi] **NF** *Méd* laryngology

laryngologiste [larɛ̃gɔlɔʒist], **laryngologue** [larɛ̃gɔlɔg] **NMF** *Méd* throat specialist, *Spéc* laryngologist

laryngoscope [larɛ̃gɔskɔp] **NM** *Méd* laryngoscope

laryngotomie [larɛ̃gɔtɔmi] **NF** *Méd* laryngotomy

larynx [larɛ̃ks] **NM** *Anat* voice box, *Spéc* larynx

las¹ [lɑs] **EXCLAM** *Littéraire* alas!

las², lasse [lɑ, lɑs] **ADJ** weary; **être l. de qch/de faire qch** to be weary of sth/of doing sth

lasagnes [lazaɲ] **NFPL** lasagne *(UNCOUNT)*

lascar [laskar] **NM** *Fam (individu rusé)* rogue; *(individu quelconque)* fellow, character; **un drôle de l.!** a shady character; **tu vas le regretter, mon l.!** *(homme)* you'll be sorry, pal!; *(enfant)* you'll be sorry, you little rascal! **un grand l.** a big chap

lascif, -ive [lasif, -iv] **ADJ** lascivious

lascivement [lasivmɑ̃] **ADV** lasciviously, lustfully

lascivité [lasivite], **lasciveté** [lasivte] **NF 1** *(sensualité)* wantonness, lasciviousness **2** *(lubricité)* lust, lewdness

laser [lazɛr] **NM** laser; **traitement au l.** laser treatment; **enregistrement l.** *(procédé)* laser recording; *(disque)* laser disc; **faisceau l.** laser beam

lassant, -e [lasɑ̃, -ɑ̃t] **ADJ** tedious; **tu es l. à la fin!** you're beginning to irritate me!

lasse [las] *voir* **las²**

lasser [3] [lase] **VT 1** *(exténuer)* to weary; **lassée par ce long voyage** weary after that long journey **2** *(importuner)* to bore, to tire; **parlons d'autre chose, ne lassons pas nos invités** let's talk about something else, let's not bore our guests **3** *(décourager)* to tax, *Sout* to fatigue; **l. la patience de qn** to try sb's patience

USAGE ABSOLU ses jérémiades finissent par l. his/her moaning gets a bit trying after a while

VPR se lasser to get tired, *Sout* to (grow) weary; **se l. de qn/qch/de faire qch** to get tired of sb/sth/of doing sth; **je ne me lasse pas d'écouter du Mozart** I never get tired of listening to Mozart; **sans se l.** tirelessly

lassitude [lasityd] **NF 1** *(fatigue)* tiredness *(UNCOUNT)*, weariness *(UNCOUNT)*, *Littéraire* lassitude *(UNCOUNT)* **2** *(découragement)* weariness

lasso [laso] **NM** lasso, *Am* lariat; **attraper** *ou* **prendre une bête au l.** to lasso an animal

lasure [lazyr] **NF** varnish, wood sealant

lasurer [3] [lazyre] **VT** to varnish

latence [latɑ̃s] **NF** latency; **période de l.** latency period

latent, -e [latɑ̃, -ɑ̃t] **ADJ** latent; **à l'état l.** in the making

latéral, -e, -aux, -ales [lateral, -o] **ADJ 1** *(sur le côté)* lateral, side *(avant n)*; **porte/rue latérale** side door/street **2** *(annexe)* minor; **canal l.** minor canal **3** *Ling* **consonne latérale** lateral (consonant)

• **latérale NF** *Ling* lateral

latéralement [lateralmɑ̃] **ADV** sideways, laterally; **se déplacer l.** to move sideways *or* crabwise; **la lumière de la bougie l'éclairait l.** the light from the candle fell on him/her from the side

latéralisation [lateralizasjɔ̃] **NF** lateralization; **l. à droite/à gauche** right-/left-handedness

latex [lateks] **NM** latex

latifundium [latifɔ̃djɔm] *(pl* **latifundia** [-dja]) **NM** latifundium

latin, -e [latɛ̃, -in] **ADJ 1** *Antiq* Latin; **le monde l.** the Latin world

2 *Ling (appartenant au latin)* Latin; *(issu du latin)* Romance *(avant n)*; **les langues latines** the Romance *or* Latin languages

3 *(en sociologie)* Latin; **le tempérament l.** the Latin temperament

4 *Rel* Latin; **l'Église latine** the Latin Church

5 *(à Paris)* **le Quartier l.** the Latin Quarter *(area on the Left Bank of the Seine, traditionally associated with students and artists)*

NM *(langue)* Latin; **l. classique** classical Latin; **bas l.** low Latin; **l. de cuisine** dog Latin

• **Latin, -e NM,F** Latin; **les Latins** the Latin people, the Latins

latinisation [latinizasjɔ̃] **NF** Latinization

latiniser [3] [latinize] **VT** to Latinize

latinisme [latinism] **NM 1** *(idiotisme du latin)* Latinism **2** *(emprunt au latin)* Latin phrase

latiniste [latinist] **NMF** *(spécialiste)* Latin scholar, Latinist; *(étudiant)* Latin student, student of Latin

latinité [latinite] **NF 1** *(caractère)* Latinity **2** *(civilisation)* Latin world

latino [latino] *Fam* **ADJ** Latino□

NMF Latino□

latino-américain, -e [latinoamerikɛ̃, -ɛn] *(mpl* **latino-américains**, *fpl* **latino-américaines**) **ADJ** Latin American

• **Latino-Américain, -e NM,F** Latin American

latitude [latityd] **NF 1** *(liberté)* latitude, scope; **j'ai toute l. pour mener mon enquête** I have full scope *or* a free hand to conduct my enquiry;

vous avez toute l. de dire oui ou non you are completely free *or* at liberty to say yes or no **2** *Astron & Géog* latitude; **cette ville est à 70° de l. Nord** this city is situated at latitude 70° North; **par 70° de l. Nord** in latitude 70° North; **basses/hautes latitudes** low/high latitudes **3** *(région, climat)* **sous d'autres latitudes** in other parts of the world

latitudinaire [latitydinɛr] **ADJ** latitudinarian
NMF latitudinarian

lato sensu [latosɛ̃sy] **ADV** loosely *or* broadly speaking

latrines [latrin] **NFPL** latrine

lattage [lataʒ] **NM 1** *(action)* lathing, battening **2** *(lattis)* lathwork *(UNCOUNT)*

latte [lat] **NF 1** *Constr* lath; *(pour chevronnage)* roof batten; **l. de plancher** floorboard
2 *Naut* batten
3 *très Fam (pied)* foot▫; *(chaussure)* shoe▫; **prendre un coup de l.** to get kicked
4 *Belg (règle plate)* ruler
5 *Belg Ftbl (barre)* crossbar; *(passe)* cross

latter [3] [late] **VT 1** *Constr* to lath, to batten **2** *Fam* to kick▫, *Br* to put the boot into

lattis [lati] **NM** *Constr* lathwork *(UNCOUNT)*

laudanum [lodanɔm] **NM** *Pharm* laudanum

laudateur, -trice [lodatœr, -tris] **NM,F** *Littéraire* laudator

laudatif, -ive [lodatif, -iv] **ADJ** *(discours, article)* laudatory; **il a été très l.** he was full of praise

laudatrice [lodatris] *voir* **laudateur**

lauréat, -e [lɔrea, -at] **ADJ** prizewinning
NM,F prizewinner, laureate; **l. du prix Nobel** Nobel prizewinner; **l. du prix Goncourt** winner of the prix Goncourt

lauréole [lɔreɔl] **NF** *Bot* daphne

laurier [lɔrje] **NM 1** *Bot* (bay) laurel, (sweet) bay **2** *Culin* **mettre du l. dans une sauce** to flavour a sauce with bay leaves; **feuille de l.** bay leaf
• **lauriers NMPL** *(gloire)* laurels; **s'endormir** *ou* **se reposer sur ses lauriers** to rest on one's laurels; **il est revenu couvert de lauriers** he came home covered in glory

laurier-rose [lɔrjeroz] *(pl* **lauriers-roses)** **NM** *Bot* rosebay, oleander

laurier-sauce [lɔrjesos] *(pl* **lauriers-sauce)** **NM** *Bot* bay tree

LAV [ɛlave] **NM** *Méd (abrév* **lymphadenopathy associated virus)** LAV

lavable [lavabl] **ADJ** washable; **l. en machine** machine-washable

lavabo [lavabo] **NM 1** *(évier) Br* washbasin, *Am* washbowl **2** *Rel* lavabo
• **lavabos NMPL** *(toilettes)* toilets, *Am* washroom

lavage [lavaʒ] **NM 1** *(nettoyage* ▸ *du linge)* washing *(UNCOUNT)*; *(*▸ *d'une surface)* scrubbing *(UNCOUNT)*; **faites deux lavages séparés pour la laine et le coton** wash wool and cotton separately; **il a fallu trois lavages pour venir à bout des taches** it took three washes to get rid of the stains; **son jean a besoin d'un bon l.** his/her jeans need a good wash; **l. à grande eau** sluicing; **l. en machine** *(sur l'étiquette d'un vêtement)* machine wash; **l. à la main** *(sur l'étiquette d'un vêtement)* hand wash (only) **2** *Méd* lavage; **l. d'estomac** pumping out (of) the stomach, *Spéc* gastric lavage; **faire un l. d'estomac à qn** to pump out sb's stomach; **l. interne** douche **3** *Métal & Tex* washing
• **au lavage ADV** in the wash; **tes chemises sont au l.** your shirts are in the wash; **la tache est partie/n'est pas partie au l.** the stain came out/didn't come out in the wash; **ma chemise a rétréci au l.** my shirt has shrunk in the wash
• **lavage de cerveau NM** brainwashing *(UNCOUNT)*; **faire un l. de cerveau à qn** to brainwash sb

lavallière [lavaljɛr] **NF** = necktie with a large bow

lavande [lavɑ̃d] **NF** *Bot* lavender; **(eau de) l.** lavender water; **l. de mer** sea lavender
ADJ INV lavender blue

lavandière [lavɑ̃djɛr] **NF 1** *Littéraire (blanchisseuse)* washerwoman **2** *Orn* (white) wagtail

lavaret [lavarɛ] **NM** *Ich* powan

lavasse [lavas] *Péj* **ADJ** *(sans éclat)* watery
NF *Fam (café, bière, soupe)* dishwater; **son café, c'est de la l.** his/her coffee tastes like dishwater

lave [lav] **NF** lava
• **de lave ADJ** lava *(avant n)*

lavé, -e [lave] **ADJ 1** *(délayé* ▸ *couleur)* faded, washed-out; **un bleu un peu l.** a slightly washed-out blue **2** *Beaux-Arts* **dessin l.** wash drawing

lave-auto [lavoto] *(pl* **lave-autos)** **NM** *Can* car wash

lave-dos [lavdo] **NM INV** back-scrubber

lave-glace [lavglas] *(pl* **lave-glaces)** **NM** *Br* windscreen washer, *Am* windshield washer

lave-linge [lavlɛ̃ʒ] **NM INV** washing machine

lave-mains [lavmɛ̃] **NM INV** *Br* wash-hand basin, *Am* small washbowl

lavement [lavmɑ̃] **NM 1** *Méd (remède)* enema; **l. baryté** barium enema **2** *Méd (procédé)* lavage

laver [3] [lave] **VT 1** *(vêtement, tissu)* to wash; *(tache)* to wash out *or* off; *(surface)* to wash down; *(avec une brosse)* to scrub; **l. à grande eau** to swill out *or* down; **l. qch à l'éponge** to sponge sth (down); **la voiture a besoin d'être lavée** the car needs washing *or* a wash; **l. la vaisselle** to do the dishes, *Br* to wash up, to do the washing-up; *Fig* **il vaut mieux l. son linge sale en famille** don't wash your dirty linen in public
2 *(faire la toilette de)* to wash; **l. la tête** *ou* **les cheveux à qn** to wash sb's hair; *Fam Fig* **l. la tête à qn** to give sb a good dressing-down
3 *(expier* ▸ *péché)* to wash away; *(dégager)* to clear; **l. sa conscience** to clear one's conscience; **laver qn d'une accusation/de tout soupçon** to clear sb of an accusation/of all suspicion; **l. qn d'une faute** to forgive sb an offence; **l'affront a été lavé dans le sang** the insult was avenged in blood
4 *Beaux-Arts (dessin)* to wash; *(couleur)* to dilute, to wash
5 *Méd (plaie)* to bathe, to cleanse; *(estomac)* to pump out
6 *(minerai)* to wash
USAGE ABSOLU *(nettoyer)* **cette lessive lave très bien** this powder washes very well; **l. en machine** *(sur l'étiquette d'un vêtement)* machine wash; **l. à la main** *(sur l'étiquette d'un vêtement)* hand wash (only)
VPR se laver 1 *(emploi réfléchi)* to (have a) wash; **se l. la figure/les mains** to wash one's face/hands; **se l. les dents** to clean *or* to brush one's teeth; *Fig* **je m'en lave les mains** I wash my hands of the entire matter **2** *(emploi passif)* **ça se lave très bien** it's very easy to wash, it washes very well **3 se l. d'un soupçon** to clear oneself of suspicion; **se l. de ses péchés** to cleanse oneself of one's sins

laverie [lavri] **NF 1** *(blanchisserie)* **l. (automatique)** self-service laundry, *Br* launderette, *Am* Laundromat® **2** *Mines* washing plant

lave-tête [lavtɛt] **NM INV** shampoo basin

lavette [lavɛt] **NF 1** *(chiffon)* dishcloth; *(brosse) Br* washing-up brush, *Am* dish mop **2** *Fam (personne)* drip, wimp **3** *Belg & Suisse (gant de toilette) Br* face flannel, *Am* washcloth

laveur, -euse [lavœr, -øz] **NM,F** *(de vaisselle)* washer, dishwasher; *(de linge)* washerman, *f* washerwoman; *(de voiture)* car washer; **l. de carreaux** *ou* **de vitres** window cleaner
NM *Tech* washer

lave-vaisselle [lavvesel] **NM INV** dishwasher

lave-vitre [lavvitr] *(pl* **lave-vitres)** **NM** *Aut Br* windscreen *or Am* windshield washer

lavis [lavi] **NM 1** *(technique)* washing *(UNCOUNT)* **2** *(dessin)* wash drawing

lavoir [lavwar] **NM 1** *(établissement)* washhouse; *(bassin)* (cement) washtub **2** *Mines (atelier)* washing plant; *(machine)* washer **3** *Belg (blanchisserie)* **l. (automatique)** self-service laundry

lavomatic [lavomatik] **NM** *Br* launderette, *Am* Laundromat®

laxatif, -ive [laksatif, -iv] **ADJ** laxative
NM laxative *(UNCOUNT)*

laxisme [laksism] **NM 1** *(tolérance excessive)* laxity, permissiveness **2** *Rel* laxism

laxiste [laksist] **ADJ 1** *(trop tolérant)* soft, lax **2** *Rel* laxist
NMF 1 *(gén)* overlenient person **2** *Rel* laxist

layette [lɛjɛt] **NF** baby clothes, layette; *Com* babywear; **bleu/rose l.** baby blue/pink

layon [lɛjɔ̃] **NM** *Agr (division)* (compartment) line; *(sentier)* forest path

lazaret [lazarɛ] **NM** *(lieu d'isolement)* lazaretto, lazaret

lazariste [lazarist] **NM** Lazarist (priest)

lazulite [lazylit] **NF** *Minér* lazulite

lazzi [ladzi] *(pl* **inv** *ou* **lazzis)** **NM** jeer, gibe

l/c *Banque (abrév écrite* **lettre de crédit)** L/C

LCD [ɛlsede] **NM** *Électron (abrév* **liquid crystal display)** LCD; **écran LCD** LCD screen

LCR [ɛlseɛr] **NF 1** *Fin (abrév* **lettre de change relevé)** bills of exchange statement **2** *Pol (abrév* **ligue communiste révolutionnaire)** = militant Trotskyist organization

LDL-cholestérol [ɛldeɛlkɔlesterɔl] **NM** *Méd (abrév* **low-density lipoprotein-cholesterol)** LDL-cholesterol

LE[1], LA[1], LES[1] [lə, la, le]

- the **1, 2, 10, 12**
- what a **6**
- a **3–5**
- one's **7**

l' is used instead of **le** or **la** before a word beginning with a vowel or h mute.

ART DÉFINI 1 *(avec un nom commun)* the; **le soleil, la lune et les étoiles** the sun, the moon and the stars; **ouvre la fenêtre** open the window; **le chemin le plus court** the shortest route; **l'arbre qui est derrière la maison** the tree behind the house; **l'été de la sécheresse** the summer there was a drought; **l'idée qu'il allait partir...** the idea that he was going to leave...; **la salade du chef** the chef's salad
2 *(dans le temps)* **le sixième jour** the sixth day; **la troisième fois** the third time; **pendant les vacances** during the holidays; **l'été dernier** last summer; **l'été 1976** the summer of 1976; **le premier juillet** the first of July; **le 15 janvier 1991** 15 January 1991; **il est passé nous voir le 15 août** he came to see us on the 15th of August *or* on August the 15th; *(par écrit)* he came to see us on 15 August
3 *(dans les fractions)* a; **le quart/tiers de** a quarter/third of; **la moitié de** (a) half of
4 *(avec un sens distributif)* **j'y vais le soir** I go there in the evening; **elle vient deux fois la semaine** she comes twice a week; **2 euros le kilo** 2 euro a *or* per kilo; **le docteur reçoit le lundi et le vendredi** *ou* **les lundis et vendredis** the doctor sees patients on Monday and Friday *or* Mondays and Fridays
5 *(avec valeur d'adjectif démonstratif)* **l'affaire est grave** it's a serious matter; **on sait que le problème est difficile** we know that it's a difficult problem
6 *(avec une valeur expressive)* what a; **la belle moto!** what a beautiful bike!; **l'idiot!** what an idiot!, (the) idiot!; **alors, les amis, comment ça va?** well, folks, how are you?; **debout, les enfants!** time to get up, children!
7 *(avec les parties du corps)* **le chapeau sur la tête** his/her/*etc* hat on his/her/*etc* head; **se laver les mains** to wash one's hands; **il est parti le livre sous le bras** he went off with the book under his arm; **elle a les yeux bleus** she has blue eyes; **elle ferma les yeux** she closed her eyes
8 *(avec une valeur généralisante)* **les hommes et les femmes** men and women; **tous les hommes** all men; **la femme est l'égale de l'homme** woman is man's equal; **les jeunes** young people; **le cheval, comme d'autres mammifères...** the horse *or* horses, like other mammals...; **le cauchemar chez l'enfant de six à dix ans** nightmares in children between six and ten years old; **j'apprends le français** I'm learning French; **j'étudie l'économie/la physique** I'm studying economics/physics; **aimer la musique/la littérature/le football** to like music/literature/football; **aller au théâtre/au cinéma** to go to the theatre/the cinema; **la paresse est un des sept péchés capitaux** sloth is one of the seven deadly sins; **les petits et les grands** *(par la taille)* small people and tall people; **ne fais pas l'idiot** don't be an idiot
9 *(marquant l'approximation)* **ça vaut dans les 100 euros** it's worth around 100 euros; **vers les quatre heures** about *or* around four o'clock; **il va sur la quarantaine** he's getting on for forty

10 *(avec un nom propre)* the; **nous sommes invités chez les Durand** we are invited to the Durands' (house); **les Bourbons** the Bourbons; **ce n'est plus la Sophie que nous avons connue** she's no longer the Sophie (that) we used to know; **la Callas** Callas; **le Descartes/Sophocle du XXème siècle** the Descartes/Sophocles of the 20th century; **le Paris de l'après-guerre/que nous aimions** post-war Paris/the Paris we knew and loved; **l'Amérique de Mark Twain n'existe plus** Mark Twain's America no longer exists; **les Raphaël des Offices** the Raphaels in the Uffizi

11 *(avec les jours de fête)* **la Toussaint** All Saints' Day; **quand tombe la Saint-Simon?** what day does Saint Simon's day fall on?; *Fam* **à la Noël** at Christmas

12 *(avec un adjectif)* the; I'll give you the new books and take back the old ones; **tu préfères la rouge ou la jaune?** do you prefer the red (one) or the yellow (one)?

LE², LA², LES² [lə, la, le]

> **l'** is used instead of **le** or **la** before a word beginning with a vowel or h mute.

PRON 1 *(complément d'objet ▸ homme)* him; *(▸ femme, nation, bateau)* her; *(▸ chose, animal)* it; *(▸ nouveau-né, animal domestique mâle)* him, it; *(▸ nouveau-née, animal domestique femelle)* her, it; **l'addition? je l'ai payée** the bill? I've paid it; **ce bordeaux, je l'ai déjà goûté** I've already tasted this *or* that Bordeaux; **Jean est malade, je vais l'appeler** Jean is ill, I'm going to call him; **il l'a probablement oublié, ton livre** he's probably forgotten your book *or* that book of yours; **combien de fois on l'a vu, ce garçon?** how many times have we seen that boy?

2 *(représentant une proposition)* **elle est partie hier soir, du moins je l'ai entendu dire** she left last night, at least that's what I've heard; **il m'a insulté mais, crois-moi, il ne le refera pas** he insulted me but, believe me, he won't do it again; **elle a été récompensée comme elle le mérite** she got her just deserts; **allez, dis-le-lui** go on, tell him (about it); **je le pense aussi** I think so too; **il est plus riche que vous ne le pensez** he's richer than you think (he is); **puisque je te le disais que ce n'était pas possible!** but I TOLD you it was impossible!

3 *(comme attribut)* **son frère est médecin, il voudrait l'être aussi** his brother is a doctor, he would like to be one too; **malheureux, je l'étais certainement** I certainly was unhappy; **pour être timide, ça, il l'est!** boy, is he shy!, talk about shy!

lé [le] **NM 1** *(d'un tissu, d'un papier peint)* width **2** *(d'une jupe)* gore

leader [lidœr] **NM 1** *(chef)* leader; **le l. du parti socialiste** the leader of the socialist party

2 *Com (entreprise, produit)* (market) leader; **le l. mondial de la micro-informatique** the world leader in microcomputing; **l. sur le marché** market leader

3 *Presse* leader, leading article

4 *Sport* **le l. du championnat de France** the team at the top of the French league

leasing [liziŋ] *Banque* **NM** leasing

• en leasing ADV on lease, as part of a leasing contract

léchage [leʃaʒ] **NM 1** *(gén)* licking; *Fam* **l. de bottes** bootlicking **2** *Fam (fignolage)* finishing touches[□]

lèche [lɛʃ] **NF** *très Fam* bootlicking; **faire de la l.** to be a bootlicker; **faire de la l. à qn** to suck up to sb, to lick sb's boots

lèche-bottes [lɛʃbɔt] **NMF INV** *Fam* bootlicker

lèche-cul [lɛʃky] **NMF INV** *Vulg* brown-nose, *Br* arse-licker, *Am* ass-licker

lèchefrite [lɛʃfrit] **NF 1** *(pour recevoir le jus de viande) Br* dripping pan, *Am* broiler pan **2** *Can (moule à gâteau)* cake tin; *(moule à pain)* loaf tin **3** *Can (marmite)* maple syrup boiler

lèchement [lɛʃmɑ̃] = **léchage**

lécher [18] [leʃe] **VT 1** *(passer la langue sur)* to lick; **l. ses plaies** to lick one's wounds; *Fam* **l. les bottes à qn** to lick sb's boots; *Vulg* **l. le cul à qn** to lick sb's *Br* arse *or Am* ass

2 *(confiture, miel)* to lick up; *(lait, crème)* to lap up; **l'enfant lécha la cuillère** the child licked the spoon clean

3 *Fam (perfectionner)* to polish up; **trop léché** overdone, overpolished

4 *(effleurer ▸ sujet: feu)* to lick at; **les flammes léchaient déjà le mur** the flames were already licking at the wall; **les vagues léchaient le sable** the waves were lapping on the sand

VPR se lécher to lick oneself; **le chiot se léchait les pattes** the puppy was licking its paws; **se l. les doigts** to lick one's fingers; **c'est à s'en l. les doigts** *ou* **les babines!** it's scrumptious!, it's really yummy!

lécheur, -euse [leʃœr, -øz] **NM,F** *Fam Péj* bootlicker, groveller[□]

lèche-vitrines [lɛʃvitrin] **NM INV** window-shopping; **faire du l.** to go window-shopping

lécithine [lesitin] **NF** *Chim* lecithin

leçon [ləsɔ̃] **NF 1** *Scol (cours)* lesson; **donner/prendre des leçons de français** to give/to take French lessons; **la couture en 15 leçons** needlework in 15 (easy) lessons; **l. de conduite** driving lesson; **tu ne vas pas me faire une l. de morale?** you're not going to start lecturing me are you?; **leçons particulières** private lessons, private tuition

2 *(devoirs)* homework *(UNCOUNT)*; **apprendre sa l.** *ou* **ses leçons** to do one's homework; *Fig* **ils avaient bien appris leur l.** they had learnt their lines well, they had rehearsed what to say very well

3 *(conseil)* advice; **je n'ai de leçons à recevoir de personne!** I don't need advice from you or anybody else!; **en matière de politesse, il pourrait te donner des leçons** as far as being polite is concerned, he could easily teach you a thing or two; **faire la l. à qn** to tell sb what to do

4 *(avertissement)* lesson; **donner une (bonne) l. à qn** to teach sb a lesson; **ça lui donnera une (bonne) l.!, ça lui servira de l.!** that'll teach him/her!; **que ceci vous serve de l.!** let this *or* that be a lesson to you!; *Fig* **recevoir une (bonne) l.** to learn one's lesson

5 *(de manuscrit)* reading

6 *Rel* lesson

lecteur, -trice [lɛktœr, -tris] **NM,F 1** *(personne qui lit)* reader; **l. de journaux** newspaper reader; **c'est un grand l. de BD** he reads a lot of comics **2** *Scol* foreign language assistant *(at university)* **3** *Typ* proofreader

NM 1 *(de sons, de disques)* player; **l. de cassettes** cassette player; **l. de CD** CD player; **l. de disques compacts** *ou* **laser** CD player; **l. de DVD** DVD player; **l. MP3** MP3 player **2** *Ordinat* reader; *(de disques, de disquettes)* drive; **l. de bandes** tape drive *or* reader; **l. de cartes magnétiques** magnetic card reader; **l. de carte à mémoire** smart card reader, card reader; **l. de carte à puce** smart card reader; **l. de CD-ROM** CD-Rom drive; **l. de code (à) barres** bar code reader; **l. de courrier** mail reader; **l. de disque dur** hard disk drive; **l. de disque optique** CD-ROM drive; **l. de disquettes** disk drive; **l. optique** optical reader *or* scanner; **l. optique de caractères** optical character reader; **l. de pages** page scanner; **l. Zip®** Zip drive

lecteur-encodeur [lɛktœrɑ̃kɔdœr] *(pl* **lecteurs-encodeurs)** **NM** *Ordinat* reader-encoder

lectorat [lɛktɔra] **NM 1** *Presse* readership, readers **2** *Scol* foreign language assistantship

lectrice [lɛktris] *voir* **lecteur**

lecture [lɛktyr] **NF 1** *(déchiffrage ▸ d'un texte, d'une carte)* reading; **j'aime la l.** I like reading; **seule une l. attentive permet de s'en apercevoir** you'll only notice it if you read it carefully; **il est occupé à la l. du scénario** he's busy reading the script; **à la l. de sa lettre, elle a souri** on reading his/her letter, she smiled; **un livre d'une l. agréable** a book that makes pleasant reading; *Typ* **l. des épreuves** proofreading; **l. rapide** speed reading

2 *(capacité)* reading; **l'apprentissage de la l.** learning to read; **leçon de l.** reading lesson

3 *(à voix haute)* reading; **une l. publique de qch** a public reading of sth; **donner l. de qch** to read sth out; **faire la l. à qn** to read (aloud) to sb

4 *(interprétation)* reading, interpretation; **une l. psychanalytique d'un film** a psychoanalytical interpretation *or* reading of a film

5 *(ce qu'on lit)* reading matter, something to read; **un peu de l., monsieur?** would you like something to read, sir?; **à cette époque mes lectures étaient plutôt classiques** at that time I was mostly reading the classics; **il a de mauvaises lectures** he reads things he shouldn't

6 *(de sons, de disques)* reading

7 *Ordinat* reading; **l. optique** optical reading, optical character recognition; **l. au scanner** scan; **en l. seule** in read-only mode

8 *Mus* reading; **l. à vue** sight-reading

9 *Pol* reading; **le texte a été adopté en première l.** the bill was passed on its first reading

10 *Rel* reading; **faire une l.** to do a reading

> Il faut noter que le nom anglais **lecture** est un faux ami. Il signifie **conférence** ou **cours à l'université**.

lecture-écriture [lɛktyrekrityr] **NF** *Ordinat* read-write (mode); **en l.** in read-write mode

lèdge [lɛdʒ] **ADJ** *Fam (excuse)* lame; **deux bouteilles pour quatre, ça va faire un peu l., non?** two bottles for four people, that's going to be cutting it a bit fine, don't you think?

ledit, ladite [lədi, ladit] *(mpl* **lesdits** [ledi], *fpl* **lesdites** [ledit]) **ADJ** *Jur* the aforementioned, the aforesaid

légal, -e, -aux, -ales [legal, -o] **ADJ** *Jur (disposition, procédure)* legal; *(héritier)* lawful; **est-il l. de vendre des biens sans payer d'impôts?** is it legal to sell goods without paying taxes?; **employer des moyens légaux contre qn** to take legal action against sb; **monnaie légale** legal tender

légalement [legalmɑ̃] **ADV** legally, lawfully

légalisation [legalizasjɔ̃] **NF 1** *(action de légaliser)* legalization **2** *(authentification)* certifying, *Sout* ratification

légaliser [3] [legalize] **VT 1** *(rendre légal)* to legalize **2** *(authentifier)* to certify, to authenticate; **une signature légalisée** a certified signature

légalisme [legalism] **NM** legalism

légaliste [legalist] **ADJ** legalistic, legalist

NMF legalist

légalité [legalite] **NF 1** *(caractère légal)* legality; **l. d'un acte/d'une procédure** legality of an act/a procedure **2** *(actes autorisés par la loi)* **la l.** the law; **rester dans/sortir de la l.** to keep within/to break the law

légat [lega] **NM 1** *Antiq* legate **2** *Rel* **l. du Pape** papal legate; **l. a latere** legate a latere

légataire [legatɛr] **NMF** legatee; **l. universel** sole legatee

légation [legasjɔ̃] **NF 1** *(représentation diplomatique)* legation **2** *(résidence)* legation, legate's residence

legato [legato] **ADV** legato

NM legato

légendaire [leʒɑ̃dɛr] **ADJ 1** *(mythique)* legendary; **un héros l.** a legendary hero **2** *(connu de tous)* **elle est d'une discrétion l.** she's well-known for her discretion

légende [leʒɑ̃d] **NF 1** *(récit mythique)* legend, tale; **légendes irlandaises** Irish legends *or* folk tales; **entrer dans la l.** to become a legend **2** *(commentaire ▸ d'un dessin, d'une photo)* caption; *(▸ d'une carte)* legend, key **3** *(d'une médaille, d'une monnaie)* legend, inscription

• de légende ADJ fairytale *(avant n)*; **un mariage de l.** a fairytale wedding

légender [3] [leʒɑ̃de] **VT** *(photo, dessin)* to caption; *(plan, carte)* to provide with a key; **voir photo légendée** see photo with caption

LÉGER, -ÈRE [leʒe, -ɛr]

- light **1–7, 10**
- moderate **5**
- slight **5, 6**
- minor **6**
- irresponsible **8**
- thin **3**
- faint **5**
- mild **6, 7**
- weak **7**

ADJ 1 *(de peu de poids)* light; **construction trop légère** flimsy building; **d'un cœur l.** with a light heart; **l. comme une plume** *ou* **bulle** (as) light as a feather

2 *(gracieux ▸ danseur)* light, nimble; *(▸ démarche)* light, springy

3 *(fin ▸ couche)* thin; *(▸ brouillard)* light; *(▸ robe)* light, flimsy

4 *(mobile ▸ artillerie, industrie, matériel)* light; **escadre légère** flotilla

5 *(modéré ▸ consommation)* moderate; *(▸ bruit, odeur)* faint, slight; *(▸ ondée, brise)* light, slight; *(▸ maquillage)* light, discreet; **une légère tristesse/ironie** a hint of sadness/irony; **le beurre a un l. goût de rance** the butter tastes slightly rancid

6 *(sans gravité ▸ blessure, perte)* minor; *(▸ peine)* light; *(▸ responsabilité)* light, undemanding; *(▸ erreur)* slight, minor; *(▸ douleur, picotement)* slight; *(▸ grippe)* mild; **il n'y a eu que des blessés légers** there were only minor injuries

7 *(peu concentré ▸ café, thé)* weak; *(▸ crème, vin)* light; *(▸ tabac)* mild; **un repas l.** a snack, a light meal

8 *(irresponsable ▸ personne, conduite)* irresponsible, thoughtless; *(insuffisant ▸ excuse, justification, raison)* flimsy; **vous avez été un peu l.** it was a bit thoughtless *or* careless of you; **c'est un peu l. comme résultat** there's not much to show for it

9 *(immoral ▸ femme, mœurs)* loose; *(▸ plaisanterie)* risqué; *(▸ ton)* light-hearted

10 *Mus (opéra, ténor)* light

ADV manger l. to avoid rich food, to eat lightly

• **à la légère ADV agir à la légère** to act thoughtlessly *or* rashly; **prendre qch à la légère** to make light of sth, to treat sth lightly

légèrement [leʒɛrmɑ̃] **ADV 1** *(un peu)* slightly; **l. blessé/teinté** slightly hurt/tinted; **loucher/boiter l.** to have a slight squint/limp; **il est l. paranoïaque** he's a bit paranoid; **un gâteau l. parfumé au citron** a cake with a hint of lemon flavouring

2 *(avec grâce)* nimbly, gracefully

3 *(avec désinvolture)* lightly; **on ne peut pas parler du cancer l.** one cannot talk lightly about cancer; **agir l.** to act thoughtlessly *or* without thinking

4 *(frugalement)* **déjeuner/manger l.** to have a light lunch/meal

5 *(avec des vêtements légers)* **être habillé l.** to be wearing light clothes

légèreté [leʒɛrte] **NF 1** *(poids)* lightness

2 *(grâce)* lightness, nimbleness; **marcher avec l.** to walk lightly

3 *(finesse ▸ de la dentelle, d'une pâtisserie, d'un vin)* lightness; *(▸ d'un parfum)* subtlety

4 *(désinvolture)* casualness; **il a fait preuve d'une certaine l. dans ses propos** what he said was somewhat irresponsible; **avec l.** casually

5 *(faiblesse ▸ d'une blessure)* slightness; *(▸ de la brise)* lightness, gentleness; *(▸ du tabac)* mildness; *(▸ du thé, du café)* weakness; *(▸ d'un son, d'une nuance)* faintness

6 *(clémence ▸ d'une punition)* lightness

leggings [legiŋs] **NFPL** leggings

légiférer [18] [leʒifere] **VI** to legislate

légion [leʒjɔ̃] **NF 1** *Mil* **la L. (étrangère)** the (French) Foreign Legion

2 *(décoration)* **la L. d'honneur** the Légion d'Honneur, the Legion of Honour

3 *Antiq* legion

4 *(grand nombre)* **une l. de cousins** an army of cousins; **ses admirateurs sont l.** his/her admirers are legion

> **LÉGION D'HONNEUR**
>
> This prestigious award was created in 1802 by Napoleon Bonaparte to replace the honorific awards of the **ancien régime** (see box at **ancien**) that had been abolished during the revolution. Intended to reward not only acts of military bravery but also outstanding civilian achievements, the Legion of Honour is the highest distinction that can be conferred by the French state and can be awarded regardless of the nationality of its recipients. It is divided into five ranks ("chevalier","officier","commandeur","grand officier" and "grand-croix"). The order of the Legion of Honour is currently made up of one-third civilians and two-thirds soldiers.

légionnaire [leʒjɔnɛr] **NM 1** *(de la Légion étrangère)* legionnaire **2** *Antiq* legionary

NMF *(membre de la Légion d'honneur)* member of the Légion d'honneur

législateur, -trice [leʒislatœr, -tris] **ADJ** lawmaking

NM,F lawmaker, legislator

NM le l. the legislature

législatif, -ive [leʒislatif, -iv] **ADJ 1** *(qui fait les lois)* legislative; **les instances législatives** legislative bodies **2** *(de l'Assemblée) Br* ≃ parliamentary, *Am* ≃ Congressionary

NM le l. the legislature

• **législatives NFPL** *Br* ≃ general election, *Am* ≃ Congressional election

législation [leʒislasjɔ̃] **NF** legislation; **l. européenne** EU legislation; **l. fiscale** tax laws; **la l. française/anglaise** French/English legislation *or* laws; **l. du travail** labour laws

législative [leʒislativ] *voir* **législatif**

législatives [leʒislativ] *voir* **législatif**

législatrice [leʒislatris] *voir* **législateur**

législature [leʒislatyr] **NF 1** *(durée du mandat)* term (of office); **les crises qui ont agité la précédente l.** the crises in the previous administration **2** *(corps)* legislature, legislative body

légiste [leʒist] **ADJ** *voir* **médecin**

NMF legist

légitimation [leʒitimasjɔ̃] **NF 1** *Jur (d'un enfant)* legitimization **2** *(reconnaissance)* recognition; *(justification)* justification

légitime [leʒitim] **ADJ 1** *(légal ▸ gén)* lawful, legal; *(▸ mariage)* lawful; *(▸ enfant)* legitimate **2** *(justifié ▸ revendication)* legitimate; **son refus l. d'obéir** his/her rightful refusal to obey; **une colère l.** a justifiable *or* justified anger; **il est tout à fait l. de se plaindre** he is/they are/*etc* quite justified in complaining

NF *très Fam (épouse)* missus; **ma l.** the missus, my old lady

• **légitime défense NF** self-defence; **il était en état de l. défense** he was acting in self-defence

légitimement [leʒitimmɑ̃] **ADV 1** *(justement)* legitimately, justifiably; **vous auriez l. pu vous plaindre** you would have been justified in complaining **2** *Jur* legitimately, lawfully

légitimer [3] [leʒitime] **VT 1** *Jur (enfant)* to legitimate; *(accord, union, titre)* to (make) legitimate, to legitimize, to legitimatize **2** *(justifier)* to justify, to legitimate; **n'essaie pas de l. son comportement** don't try to find excuses for *or* to justify his/her behaviour

légitimiste [leʒitimist] **ADJ** legitimist

NMF legitimist

légitimité [leʒitimite] **NF 1** *Jur & Pol* legitimacy **2** *(bien-fondé)* rightfulness; **tu ne peux nier la l. de ses réclamations** you cannot say that his/her complaints aren't justified *or* well-founded

legs [lɛg] **NM 1** *Jur* legacy, bequest; **faire/recevoir un l.** to leave/receive a legacy; **faire un l. à qn** to leave a legacy to sb, to leave sb a legacy; **l. à titre particulier** specific bequest *or* legacy; **l. à titre universel** residuary bequest *or* legacy, residue of one's estate **2** *Fig (héritage)* legacy, heritage

léguer [18] [lege] **VT 1** *Jur* to bequeath, to leave; **l. qch à qn** to bequeath *or* to leave sth to sb; **son père lui a légué une énorme fortune** his/her father bequeathed *or* left him/her a huge fortune **2** *Fig* to hand down, to pass on; **il lui a légué son goût pour la musique** he passed on his love of music to him/her

légume [legym] **NM 1** *Bot & Culin* vegetable; **soupe de légumes** vegetable soup; **légumes secs** dried vegetables; **légumes verts** green vegetables, greens **2** *Fam (personne)* vegetable

NF *Fam* **grosse l.** bigwig, big shot

légumier, -ère [legymje, -ɛr] **ADJ** vegetable *(avant n)*

NM,F 1 vegetable grower **2** *Belg (commerçant)* greengrocer

NM *(plat)* vegetable dish

légumineux, -euse [legyminø, -øz] *Bot* **ADJ** leguminous

• **légumineuse NF** leguminous plant

• **légumineuses NFPL** Leguminosae

lei [lɛ] *voir* **leu**

leitmotiv [lajtmɔtif, lɛjtmɔtiv] *(pl* **leitmotivs** *ou* **leitmotive**) **NM 1** *Littérature & Mus* leitmotiv, leitmotif **2** *Fig* hobbyhorse

lem [lɛm] **NM** *Astron* lunar excursion module, LEM

Léman [lemɑ̃] **NM le lac L.** Lake Geneva

lemme [lɛm] **NM** *Math & Phil* lemma

lemming [lemiŋ] **NM** *Zool* lemming

lémure [lemyr] **NM** *Antiq* lemur

lémurien [lemyrjɛ̃] **NM** *Zool* lemurine

lendemain [lɑ̃dmɛ̃] **NM 1** *(le jour suivant)* **le l.** the next *or* the following day, the day after; **le l. matin** the next *or* the following morning; **le l. de son arrestation** the day after he/she was arrested; *Prov* **il ne faut pas remettre au l. ce qu'on peut faire le jour même** never put off till tomorrow what you can do today **2** *(futur)* **le l.** tomorrow, the future; **il dépense son argent sans penser au l.** he spends his money without thinking of the future

• **lendemains NMPL 1** *(avenir)* future; **son arrivée au pouvoir annonçait de sombres lendemains** his/her coming to power heralded a dark future *or* dark days to come; **délinquant à onze ans, ça nous promet de beaux lendemains!** eleven years old and already a delinquent, he's got a bright future ahead of him!; **des lendemains difficiles** a bleak future; **des lendemains qui chantent** a brighter future **2** *(conséquences)* consequences; **avoir d'heureux lendemains** to have happy consequences

• **au lendemain de PRÉP au l. de la Révolution** immediately *or* just after the Revolution; **au l. de son élection** in the days (immediately) following his/her election

• **sans lendemain ADJ** short-lived

lénifiant, -e [lenifjɑ̃, -ɑ̃t] **ADJ 1** *Méd* calming **2** *Fig (images, paroles)* soothing, lulling

lénifier [9] [lenifje] **VT 1** *Méd* to calm **2** *Fig (calmer)* to soothe, *Sout* to assuage

Lénine [lenin] **NPR** Lenin

léninisme [leninism] **NM** Leninism

léniniste [leninist] **ADJ** Leninist

NMF Leninist

lénitif, -ive [lenitif, -iv] **ADJ 1** *Méd* calming **2** *Fig Littéraire* soothing

lent, -e[1] [lɑ̃, lɑ̃t] **ADJ 1** *(pas rapide ▸ mouvement, film)* slow; *(▸ circulation)* slow, sluggish; *(▸ animal)* slow-moving; **à combustion lente** slow-burning; **avoir l'esprit l.** to be slow-witted; **la justice est tellement lente!** the legal system is so slow!; **il est l. à comprendre** he's slow on the uptake; **la fin est lente à venir** the end is a long time coming; *Can* **l. comme la mort** painfully slow **2** *(progressif ▸ agonie)* lingering; *(▸ effritement, évolution)* slow, gradual; *(▸ poison)* slow-acting

lente[2] [lɑ̃t] **NF** *Entom* nit

lentement [lɑ̃tmɑ̃] **ADV** slowly; **marcher l.** to walk slowly *or* at a slow pace; **il travaille l.** he's a slow worker; **l. mais sûrement** slowly but surely

lenteur [lɑ̃tœr] **NF** slowness; **avec l.** slowly; **d'une l. désespérante** appallingly slow; **l. d'esprit** slow-wittedness; **tu es d'une l.!** you're so slow!; **lenteurs administratives** administrative delays; **les lenteurs de la justice** the slowness of the courts, the slow course of justice

lentigine [lɑ̃tiʒin] **NF** freckle, *Spéc* lentigo

lentigo [lɑ̃tigo] **NM** freckle, *Spéc* lentigo

lentille [lɑ̃tij] **NF 1** *Bot & Culin* lentil; **l. d'eau** duckweed *(UNCOUNT)* **2** *Opt & Phys* lens; **lentilles cornéennes** *ou* **de contact** contact lenses; **lentilles souples** soft (contact) lenses; *Can Phot* **l. télescopique** telescopic lens

lento [lento] *Mus* **ADV** lento

NM lento

léonin, -e [leɔnɛ̃, -in] **ADJ 1** *Jur (commission, partage)* unfair, one-sided; *(contrat)* leonine **2** *(de lion)* leonine **3** *(vers)* Leonine

léopard [leɔpar] **NM 1** *Zool* leopard; **l. de mer** leopard seal; **l. des neiges** snow leopard, ounce **2** *(fourrure)* leopard skin; **veste en l.** leopard-skin jacket **3** *(en apposition)* leopard-skin *(avant n)*; *Mil* **tenue l.** camouflage battle dress

LEP, Lep [lɛp] **NM 1** *Anciennement (abrév* **lycée d'enseignement professionnel**) = former name for a "lycée professionnel" **2** *Banque (abrév* **livret d'épargne populaire**) = special tax-exempt savings account

lepeniste [ləpenist] **NMF** *Pol* = supporter of Jean-Marie Le Pen *(leader of France's extreme right-wing Front national party)*

lépidoptère [lepidɔptɛr] *Entom* **ADJ** lepidopteran, lepidopterous

NM lepidopteran
• **lépidoptères NMPL** the Lepidoptera

lépidoptériste [lepidɔpterist] **NMF** *Entom* lepidopterist

lèpre [lɛpr] **NF 1** *Méd* leprosy **2** *Littéraire (moisissure)* **mur rongé par la l.** wall eaten away by damp **3** *Fig (fléau)* blight, scourge; **la drogue, l. de notre époque** drugs, the scourge of our age

lépreux, -euse [leprø, -øz] **ADJ 1** *Méd* leprous **2** *Littéraire (mur)* flaking, peeling
NM,F *Méd* leper; **traiter qn comme un l.** to ostracize sb, *Br* to send sb to Coventry

léproserie [leprozri] **NF** leper hospital, leprosarium

leptine [lɛptin] **NF** *Biol* leptin

leptotène [lɛptɔtɛn] **NM** *Biol* leptotene

LEQUEL, LAQUELLE [ləkɛl, lakɛl] *(mpl* **lesquels** [lekɛl], *fpl* **lesquelles** [lekɛl])

> **lequel** and **lesquel(le)s** contract with **à** to form **auquel** and **auxquel(le)s**, and with **de** to form **duquel** and **desquel(le)s**.

PRON RELATIF 1 *(sujet ▸ personne)* who; *(▸ chose)* which; **il était avec sa sœur, laquelle m'a reconnu** he was with his sister, who recognized me; **elle habitait une ferme, laquelle n'existe plus** she lived in a farmhouse which is no longer there
2 *(complément ▸ personne)* whom; *(▸ chose)* which; **un ami auprès duquel trouver un réconfort** a friend (who) one can find comfort with, a friend with whom one can find comfort; **un ami avec l. il sort souvent** a friend with whom he often goes out, a friend (who) he often goes out with; **la dame chez laquelle je l'ai rencontré** the lady at whose house I met him; **l'ami sans l. il n'aurait pas réussi** the friend without whom he wouldn't have succeeded; **une réaction à laquelle je ne m'attendais pas** a reaction (which *or* that) I wasn't expecting; **la maison dans laquelle j'ai grandi** the house where *or* in which I grew up, the house (that) I grew up in; **le moyen par l. il compte réussir** the means by which he intends to succeed; **il y avait là beaucoup de jeunes gens parmi lesquels...** there were a lot of young people there, amongst whom...; **c'est une personne dans laquelle je n'ai aucune confiance** he/she is someone (who) I have no confidence in, he/she is someone in whom I have no confidence; **les gens au nom desquels je parle** the people on whose behalf I am speaking; **un dispositif au moyen duquel on peut...** a device whereby *or* by means of which it is possible to...; **l'homme sans l'avis duquel on ne peut rien faire** the man without whose advice one can do nothing; **le livre à la rédaction duquel il se consacre** the book that he is writing
ADJ RELATIF il avait contacté un deuxième avocat, l. avocat avait également refusé de le défendre he contacted another lawyer who also refused to defend him; **auquel cas** in which case; **il se pourrait que j'échoue, auquel cas je repasserai l'examen l'année prochaine** I might possibly fail, in which case I'll resit the exam next year
PRON INTERROGATIF which (one); **l. est-ce?** which (one) is it?; **l. d'entre vous a gagné?** which (one) of you won?; **l. de ces chapeaux préférez-vous?** which (one) of these hats do you prefer?; **laquelle veux-tu?** which (one) would you like?; **laquelle est ta valise?** which is your suitcase?, which suitcase is yours?; **difficile de dire laquelle me plaît le plus** difficult to say which (one) I like best; **j'ai rencontré un de ses collaborateurs, je ne sais plus l.** I met one of his/her colleagues, I can't remember which (one); **de laquelle de ces deux régions êtes-vous originaire?** which (one) of these two regions do you come from?

lerche [lɛrʃ] **ADV** *Fam* **il y en a pas l.** there isn't much/aren't many$^{\square}$

lérot [lero] **NM** *Zool* garden dormouse

les [le] *voir* **le**[1, 2]

lesbianisme [lɛsbjanism] **NM** lesbianism

lesbien, -enne [lɛsbjɛ̃, -ɛn] **ADJ** lesbian
• **lesbienne NF** lesbian

lesdites [ledit], **lesdits** [ledi] *voir* **ledit**

lèse-majesté [lɛzmaʒɛste] **NF INV** lese-majesty, lèse-majesté

léser [18] [leze] **VT 1** *(désavantager ▸ personne)* to wrong; *(▸ intérêts)* to prejudice; **elle s'estime lésée par rapport aux autres** she feels badly done by *or* unfavourably treated compared with the others **2** *Jur* **l. les droits de qn** to encroach *or* to infringe upon sb's rights; **partie lésée** injured party **3** *Méd* to injure

lésine [lezin] **NF** *Littéraire* miserliness, stinginess

lésiner [3] [lezine] **lésiner sur VT IND** to skimp on; **ils lésinent sur tout** they're stingy with everything; **ne pas l. sur** to be generous with, not to skimp on; **tu n'as pas lésiné sur le sel!** you got a bit carried away with *or* you were a bit too generous with the salt!; **il n'a pas lésiné sur les critiques!** he didn't spare his criticism!

lésineur, -euse [lezinœr, -øz] *Vieilli* **ADJ** miserly, niggardly
NM,F miser, niggard

lésion [lezjɔ̃] **NF 1** *Méd* injury, *Spéc* lesion; **à appliquer sur les lésions tous les soirs** *(sur la notice d'une pommade ou d'une lotion)* apply to the affected area every evening; **l. par écrasement/souffle** crush/blast injury **2** *Jur* wrong

lesquels, lesquelles [lekɛl] *voir* **lequel**

lessivable [lesivabl] **ADJ** washable

lessivage [lesivaʒ] **NM 1** *(d'un mur, d'un plancher)* scrubbing, washing; *(du linge)* washing; *Fig* **c'est le grand l. dans la société** a lot of staff in the company are being let go **2** *Géol* leaching

lessive [lesiv] **NF 1** *(poudre)* detergent, washing *or* soap powder; *(liquide)* (liquid) detergent
2 *(linge)* washing *(UNCOUNT)*, laundry *(UNCOUNT)*; *(contenu d'une machine)* (washing-machine) load; **étendre la l.** to hang out the washing; **je t'ai apporté ma l.** I've brought you my washing *or* my laundry
3 *(lavage)* wash; **faire la l.** to do the washing *or* the laundry; **faites deux lessives séparées pour la laine et le coton** wash wool and cotton separately; **j'ai fait trois lessives ce matin** I've done three washes this morning
4 *Fam (épuration)* clean-up (operation)
5 *Chim* lye

lessiver [3] [lesive] **VT 1** *(laver ▸ vêtement, tissu)* to wash; *(▸ mur)* to wash down
2 *Fam (épuiser)* to wear out; **je suis lessivé** I'm washed out *or* all in
3 *Fam (ruiner)* to clean out
4 *très Fam (éliminer)* **se faire l.** to get knocked out
5 *Chim & Géol* to leach (out)

lessiveuse [lesivøz] **NF 1** *Anciennement* boiler *(for clothes)* **2** *Belg (machine à laver)* washing machine

lessiviel, -elle [lesivjɛl] **ADJ** detergent *(avant n)*, *Spéc* detersive

lest [lɛst] **NM** *Aviat & Naut* ballast; **navire sur l.** ship in ballast; **jeter** *ou* **lâcher du l.** to dump ballast; *Fig* **lâcher du l.** to make concessions, to yield some ground

lestage [lestaʒ] **NM** *Aviat & Naut* ballasting

leste [lɛst] **ADJ 1** *(souple et vif ▸ personne)* nimble; *(▸ animal)* agile, nimble; *(▸ mouvement)* brisk, nimble; **il est encore l. malgré son âge** he's still sprightly for his age **2** *(désinvolte ▸ ton)* offhand, disrespectful **3** *(libre ▸ plaisanterie, propos)* risqué, crude

lestement [lestəmɑ̃] **ADV 1** *(avec souplesse)* nimbly **2** *(avec désinvolture)* offhandedly, casually **3** *(hardiment)* **il plaisantait un peu l.** he was making rather risqué jokes

lester [3] [leste] **VT 1** *Aviat & Naut* to ballast **2** *Fam (charger)* **l. qch de** to fill *or* to cram sth with; **les poches lestées de bonbons** pockets filled *or* crammed with sweets
VPR se lester *Fam* **se l. (l'estomac)** to stuff oneself

létal, -e, -aux, -ales [letal, -o] **ADJ** *Méd* lethal

letchi [lɛtʃi] **NM** lychee, litchi

léthargie [letarʒi] **NF 1** *Méd* lethargy; **tomber en l.** to fall into a lethargic state, to become lethargic **2** *Fig (mollesse ▸ physique)* lethargy; **tirer qn de sa l.** to shake sb out of his/her lethargy

léthargique [letarʒik] **ADJ** *Méd & Fig* lethargic

lette [lɛt] **NM** *(langue)* Latvian, Lettish

letton, -e *ou* **-onne** [lɛtɔ̃, -ɔn] **ADJ** Latvian
NM *(langue)* Latvian, Lettish
• **Letton, -e** *ou* **-onne NM,F** Latvian, Lett

Lettonie [lɛtɔni] **NF la L.** Latvia

Lettonne, lettonne [letɔn] *voir* **letton**

lettrage [letraʒ] **NM** *Typ* lettering

lettre [lɛtr] **NF A.** *CARACTÈRE* **1** *(d'un alphabet)* letter; **un mot de neuf lettres** a nine-letter word; **l. majuscule** capital (letter); **l. minuscule** small letter; **écrit en lettres de feu** written in letters of fire; **c'est gravé en lettres d'or** it's forever engraved in my/our/*etc* memory; **cette page d'histoire est imprimée en lettres de sang dans notre mémoire** this page of history has left a bloody impression in our memory
2 *Typ (forme en plomb)* character, letter; **l. ornée** initial
B. *ÉCRIT* **1** *(correspondance)* letter; **suite à votre l. du...** further to your letter of...; **pas de lettres pour moi?** no mail *or* no letters for me?; **mettre une l. à la poste** to post a letter; *Fam* **passer comme une l. à la poste** *(boisson, aliment)* to go down a treat; *(demande, mesure)* to go off without a hitch, to go off smoothly; **la nouvelle est passée comme une l. à la poste** the news was received without any fuss; **l. d'accompagnement** covering letter; *Bourse* **l. d'allocation** letter of allotment; **l. d'amour** love letter; **l. anonyme** anonymous letter; **l. d'avis** advice note, letter of advice; **l. de château** thank-you letter; **l. commerciale** business letter; **l. de démission** resignation letter; **l. d'embauche** written offer of employment; **apportez une l. d'excuse de vos parents** bring a note from your parents; **l. exprès** express letter; **l. d'injures** abusive letter; **l. d'introduction** letter of introduction; **l. de licenciement** letter of dismissal; **l. de menace** threatening letter; *Belg* **l. de mort** announcement of death; **l. de motivation** covering letter *(sent with job application)*; **l. de rappel** reminder; **l. de réclamation** letter of complaint; **l. de recommandation** letter of recommendation, reference; **l. recommandée** *Br* recorded delivery letter, *Am* letter sent by certified mail; *(avec objets de valeur)* registered letter; **l. recommandée avec accusé de réception** = recorded delivery letter with confirmation of receipt; *(avec objets de valeur)* = registered letter with confirmation of receipt; **l. de référence** letter of reference; **l. de relance** follow-up letter; **l. de remerciements** letter of thanks, thank-you letter; **elle m'a écrit une l. de rupture** she wrote to tell me she was leaving me; **l. type** *(pour mailing)* form letter; **l. de vente** sales letter
2 *Banque & Fin* **l. accréditive** letter of credit; **l. de change** bill of exchange; **l. de change à l'extérieur** foreign bill; **l. de change relevé** bills of exchange statement; **l. de créance** letter of credit; **l. de crédit** letter of credit; **l. de crédit documentaire** documentary letter of credit; **l. de gage** debenture bond; *(pour hypothèque)* mortgage bond; **l. de garantie** letter of guarantee; **l. de garantie bancaire** bank guarantee; **l. de garantie d'indemnité** letter of indemnity; **l. de nantissement** letter of hypothecation; **l. de relance des impayés** debt-chasing letter; *Bourse* **l. de souscription** letter of application
3 *Jur* **l. d'intention** letter of intent; **l. de voiture** waybill, consignment note
4 *Hist* **l. de cachet** letter of cachet, = order under the King's private seal; **lettres de noblesse** letters patent (of nobility); *Fig* **conquérir** *ou* **recevoir ses lettres de noblesse** to gain respectability; **lettres patentes** letters patent
5 *Pol* **lettres de créance** credentials
6 *Presse* **l. ouverte (à)** open letter (to)
C. *SENS STRICT* letter; **respecter la l. de la loi** to respect *or* to observe the letter of the law; **rester l. morte** to go unheeded, to be disregarded; **le cessez-le-feu est devenu l. morte** the ceasefire is no longer being observed
• **lettres NFPL 1** *Scol* **les lettres** the arts, the humanities; **étudiant en lettres** arts student; **faculté de lettres** faculty of arts *or* humanities; **lettres classiques** classics, Latin and Greek; **lettres modernes** modern literature; **lettres supérieures** = preparatory class leading to the "École normale supérieure" and lasting two years **2** *Littérature* **les lettres** literature; **le monde des lettres** the literary world; **avoir des lettres** to be well-read; **un homme/une femme de lettres** a man/a woman of letters

• **à la lettre, au pied de la lettre** ADV *(suivre)* to the letter; **suivez l'ordonnance du médecin à la l.** follow the doctor's prescription to the letter; **ne prends pas ce qu'il dit au pied de la l.** don't take what he says at face value

• **avant la lettre** ADV **c'était un surréaliste avant la l.** he was a surrealist before the term was ever invented

• **en toutes lettres** ADV **1** *(entièrement)* in full; **écrire qch en toutes lettres** to write sth (out) in full **2** *(très clairement)* clearly, plainly; **c'est écrit en toutes lettres dans le contrat** it's written in black and white *or* it's spelt out plainly in the contract

lettré, -e [letre] ADJ *(cultivé)* well-read

NM,F **c'est un fin l.** he's extremely well-read *or* scholarly

lettrine [letrin] NF **1** *Ordinat & Typ* drop cap **2** *(d'un dictionnaire)* running initial

leu [lø] *(pl* **lei** [lɛ]) NM *(monnaie)* leu; **15 lei** 15 lei

leucémie [løsemi] NF *Méd* leukaemia; **l. myéloblastique** myeloblastic leukaemia

leucémique [løsemik] *Méd* ADJ leukaemic

NMF leukaemia sufferer

leucoblaste [løkɔblast] NM *Biol* leucoblast

leucocytaire [løkɔsitɛr] ADJ *Biol* leucocytic

leucocyte [løkɔsit] NM *Biol* leucocyte

leucocytose [løkɔsitoz] NF *Méd* leucocytosis

leucome [løkom] NM *Méd* leucoma, albugo

leucorrhée [løkɔre] NF *Méd* leucorrhoea

leucose [løkoz] NF *Méd* leucosis

leur [lœr] PRON to them; **je voudrais l. parler avant qu'ils ne partent** I'd like to speak to them before they leave; **je l. ai donné la lettre** I gave them the letter, I gave the letter to them; **je l. ai serré la main** I shook their hands; **il l. a jeté une pierre** he threw a stone at them; **je la l. ai montrée** I showed it to them, I showed them it; **donnez-le-l.** give it to them, give them it; **ça ne l. rapporte rien** they aren't getting anything out of it; **il l. est difficile de venir** it's difficult for them to come

ADJ POSSESSIF their; **c'est l. tour** it's their turn; **l. oncle et l. tante** their uncle and aunt; **ce sont leurs enfants** these are their children; **une de leurs amies** a friend of theirs, one of their friends; **ils ont eu l. vendredi** they got Friday off; **avec cette aisance qui a toujours été l.** with that characteristic ease of theirs; **ils ont fait l. la langue anglaise** they made the English language their own

• **le leur, la leur, les leurs** PRON theirs; **c'est notre problème, pas le l.** it's our problem, not theirs; **nos enfants et les leurs** our children and theirs; **ils ont pris une valise qui n'était pas la l.** they took a suitcase that wasn't theirs *or* their own; **ils n'en ont pas besoin, ils ont le l.** they don't need it, they've got their own; **les leurs** *(leur famille)* their family; **être (un) des leurs** to belong to their group, to be one of them; **je ne me suis jamais senti l'un des leurs** I never felt that I was one of them; **serez-vous aussi des leurs dimanche?** will you be there on Sunday too?; **ils ont été aidés, mais ils y ont mis beaucoup du l.** they were helped, but they put a lot of effort into it (themselves)

leurre [lœr] NM **1** *(illusion)* delusion, illusion; **ce serait un l. d'espérer qu'il réponde à votre demande** you would be deceiving yourself if you thought that he might comply with your demands

2 *(tromperie)* deception; **son grand projet n'est qu'un l.** his/her great plan is just a trick

3 *Mil* decoy; **l. thermique** heat decoy

4 *Chasse* decoy, lure; *(en fauconnerie)* lure

5 *Pêche* lure; *(vivant)* bait

leurrer [5] [lœre] VT **1** *(tromper)* to deceive, to delude; **ne te laisse pas l. par ses beaux discours** do not be deceived *or* taken in by his/her fine words **2** *(en fauconnerie)* to lure

VPR **se leurrer** *(se laisser abuser)* to delude oneself (**sur** about); **ne te leurre pas, elle ne t'aime plus** don't delude yourself, she doesn't love you any more; **il ne faut pas se l., on va perdre** let's not fool ourselves, we're going to lose

lev [lɛv] *(pl* **leva** [leva]) NM *(monnaie)* lev

levage [ləvaʒ] NM **1** *Tech* lifting; **appareil de l.** lifting tackle *(UNCOUNT) or* appliance **2** *Culin* raising, rising

levain [ləvɛ̃] NM **1** *Culin (substance, pâte)* leaven, leavening; **pain au/sans l.** leavened/unleavened bread **2** *Fig Littéraire* **le l. de la révolte** the seeds of revolt

levant [ləvɑ̃] ADJ *voir* **soleil**

NM **le l.** the east; **baie exposée au l.** east-facing bay; **du l. au couchant** from east to west

levantin, -e [ləvɑ̃tɛ̃, -in] ADJ Levantine

• **Levantin, -e** NM,F Levantine

levé, -e[1] [ləve] ADJ *Belg Fam* **bien/mal l.** in a good/bad mood

NM survey; **faire le l. d'un champ** to survey a field

levée[2] [ləve] NF **1** *(ramassage ▸ du courrier, des impôts)* collection; **il y a deux levées par jour** the *Br* post *or Am* mail is collected twice a day, there are two collections a day

2 *(cessation ▸ de sanctions)* lifting; *(▸ d'une séance)* adjournment; **il a demandé la l. de l'embargo** he asked for the embargo to be lifted; **demander la l. de la séance** to ask for an adjournment; **cela nécessiterait la l. de son immunité parlementaire** this would involve withdrawing his/her *Br* parliamentary *or Am* Congressional immunity

3 *Jur* **l. d'écrou** release (from prison); **l. de jugement** transcript (of the verdict); **l. des scellés** removal of the seals

4 *Cartes* trick; **son roi de pique fait la l.** his/her king of spades takes *or* wins the trick

5 *Géol* levee

6 *Constr* **l. de terre** levee

7 *Mil (de troupes)* levying; *(d'un siège)* raising; **l. en masse** levy en masse; *Fig* **l. de boucliers** outcry, uproar

8 *Fin* **l. d'option/d'actions** taking up of the option/stock; *Banque* **levées de compte** personal withdrawals

9 *(cérémonie)* **la l. du corps** removal of the remains *(for the funeral)*

lève-glace [lɛvglas] *(pl* **lève-glaces**) NM window winder; **l. électrique** electric window

lever[1] [ləve] NM **1** *(apparition)* **le l. du soleil** sunrise; **le l. du jour** daybreak, dawn

2 *(fait de quitter son lit)* **il se met au travail dès son l.** he starts working as soon as he gets up; **le l. du roi** the levee of the king

3 *Théât* **au l. de rideau** when the curtain goes up *or* rises; **un l. de rideau** *(pièce)* a curtain raiser

4 *(d'un plan)* survey

LEVER[2] [19] [ləve]

VT
- to raise **A1, 2, B1, C3**
- to lift **A1, 2, B4**
- to get up **A3**
- to collect **B1**
- to draw (up) **B2**
- to close **B4**
- to remove **B4**
- to pick up **B6, C2**

VI
- to come up **1**
- to rise **2**

VPR
- to go up **1**
- to stand up **2**
- to rise **2–4, 6**
- to get up **3**
- to break **4, 5**

VT **A. 1** *(faire monter)* to raise, to lift; *(soulever)* to lift; **lève la vitre** close the window; **l. une barrière** to raise a barrier; **lève ton verre pour que je puisse te servir** lift your glass so that I can serve you; **levons nos verres à sa réussite** let's raise our glasses to *or* let's drink to his/her success; **je lève mon verre à votre réussite/aux futurs époux** here's to your success/the happy couple; *Théât* **l. le rideau** to raise the curtain; **l. l'ancre** to weigh anchor; *Fig (partir)* to take off, to hit the road, to go; *Fig* **l. l'étendard de la révolte** to rise up in revolt; *Fig* **l. haut son drapeau** *(défendre publiquement ses opinions)* to nail one's colours to the mast

2 *(diriger vers le haut ▸ partie du corps)* to lift, to raise; **l. la tête** to lift *or* to raise one's head; **en entendant la sonnette, elle leva la tête** she looked up *or* she raised her head when she heard the bell; **l. les yeux** *(de son livre)* to look up; **l. les yeux au ciel** to lift up *or* to raise one's eyes to heaven; **lève les pieds quand tu marches** lift *or* don't drag your feet when you walk; **l. le pied** *(automobiliste)* to drive slowly; **l. la main pour prêter serment** to raise one's hand to take an oath; **l. le doigt** *ou* **la main avant de prendre la parole** to put up *or* to raise one's hand before speaking; **l. la main sur qn** to raise *or* to lift one's hand to sb; **l. les bras au ciel** to throw up one's hands; **l. le cœur à qn** to turn sb's stomach; **la puanteur qui s'en échappe vous lève le cœur** the stench coming from it is nauseating; **lève** *Fam* **tes fesses** *ou très Fam* **ton cul de là!** shift (yourself)!

3 *(sortir du lit)* **l. qn** to get sb up, to get sb out of bed; **nous levons les pensionnaires à huit heures** we rouse the boarders at eight o'clock

B. 1 *(ramasser ▸ filets de pêche)* to raise; *(▸ courrier, impôt)* to collect

2 *(dessiner ▸ carte)* to draw (up); **il faudra l. le plan du domaine** a plan of the estate will have to be drawn up

3 *Culin (viande)* to carve; **l. les filets d'un poisson** to fillet a fish

4 *(faire cesser ▸ blocus, interdiction, embargo)* to lift; *(▸ audience, séance)* to close; *(▸ scrupules, ambiguïté)* to remove; *(▸ punition)* to lift; *(▸ obstacle)* to get rid of, to remove; *Mil (▸ siège)* to raise; *Jur* **la séance est levée** the court is adjourned

5 *Bourse* **l. une valeur/une option** to take up a security/an option

6 *Cartes* to pick up; **l. les cartes** to take *or* to pick up a trick

C. 1 *Chasse (gibier, perdreaux)* to flush out

2 *très Fam (séduire)* to pick up, *Br* to pull

3 *Mil (mobiliser)* to raise; **l. des troupes** to raise troops

VI **1** *(pousser ▸ blé, avoine)* to come up

2 *Culin* to rise; **laisser l. la pâte** to let the dough rise

VPR **se lever 1** *(monter)* to go up; **je vois une main qui se lève au fond de la classe** I see a hand going up at the back of the class; **tous les yeux** *ou* **regards se levèrent vers elle** all eyes turned towards her; **le rideau se lève sur un salon bourgeois** the curtain rises on a middle-class drawing room

2 *(se mettre debout)* to stand up, to rise; **le public se leva pour l'applaudir** the public stood up *or* rose to applaud him/her; **se l. de sa chaise** to get up *or* to rise from one's chair; **ne te lève pas de table!** don't leave the table!; *Fig* **se l. contre** to rise up against; **le peuple s'est levé contre l'oppression** the people rose up against oppression

3 *(sortir du lit ▸ dormeur)* to get up, *Littéraire* to rise; *(▸ malade)* to get out of bed; **il est l'heure de se l.!** time to get up!; **il ne s'est levé que la semaine dernière** *(malade)* he only got out of bed last week; **j'ai du mal a le faire se l. aujourd'hui** I'm having trouble getting him out of bed this morning; **se l. avec le soleil** to be up with the lark; *Fig* **pour la prendre en défaut il faut se l. tôt** *ou* **de bonne heure!** you'd have to be on your toes to catch her out!; **pour trouver du bon pain ici, tu peux te l. de bonne heure** you've got your work cut out finding *or* you'll be a long time finding good bread round here

4 *(apparaître ▸ astre)* to rise; *(▸ jour)* to dawn, to break; **le soleil se levait quand nous partîmes** the sun was rising as we left; **au moment où la lune se lève** at the rising of the moon

5 *Météo (vent)* to get up; *(orage)* to break; *(brume)* to lift, to clear; **le temps se lève** the sky's clearing (up); **le vent se lève** the wind's getting up; **la mer se lève** the sea's getting up *or* getting rough

6 *Littéraire (surgir, naître)* to rise (up); **l'espoir commença à se l. dans tous les cœurs** hope welled up in everyone's heart

lève-tard [lɛvtar] NMF INV late riser

lève-tôt [lɛvto] NMF INV early riser, early bird

lève-vitre [lɛvvitr] *(pl* **lève-vitres**) NM window winder; **l. électrique** electric window

levier [ləvje] NM **1** *Tech* lever; **faire l. sur qch** to lever sth up *or* off; **soulever/ouvrir qch avec un l.** to prise *or* to lever sth up/open

2 *(manette)* lever; **l. (de changement) de vitesse** *Br* gear lever, *Am* gearshift; **l. de frein à main** handbrake lever; **l. de commande** control (lever); **être aux leviers de commande** to be at the controls; *Fig* to be in command *or* in the driver's seat

3 *Fig (moyen de pression)* means of pressure, lever; **la grève peut être un puissant l. politique** strike action can be a powerful political lever

4 *Écon* **effet de l.** leverage, gearing

lévitation [levitasjɔ̃] NF levitation; **être en l.** to be levitating

lévite [levit] **NM** *Hist* Levite

levraut [ləvro] **NM** leveret

lèvre [lɛvr] **NF 1** *(de la bouche)* lip; **elle avait le sourire aux lèvres** she had a smile on her lips; **lire sur les lèvres** to lip-read; **l. inférieure/supérieure** lower/upper lip; **être pendu** *ou* **suspendu aux lèvres de qn** to be hanging upon sb's every word; **son nom est sur toutes les lèvres** his/her name is on everybody's lips

2 *(de la vulve)* lip, labium; **les lèvres** the labia; **grandes/petites lèvres** labia majora/minora

3 *Géol* edge, rim

4 *Méd (d'une plaie)* lip

5 *Bot* lip, *Spéc* labium

levrette [ləvrɛt] **NF 1** *(chien)* greyhound bitch; **l. (d'Italie)** Italian greyhound **2** *très Fam (locution)* **en l.** doggy-fashion

lévrier [levrije] **NM** *(chien)* greyhound; **l. afghan** Afghan hound; **l. barzoï** borzoi, Russian wolfhound; **l. d'Irlande** *ou* **irlandais** Irish wolfhound; **l. d'Italie** *ou* **italien** Italian greyhound; **l. russe** borzoi, Russian wolfhound

levure [ləvyr] **NF** yeast; **l. de bière** brewer's yeast, dried yeast; **l. de boulanger** fresh *or* baker's yeast; **l. (chimique)** baking powder

lewisite [lewisit] **NF** *Chim* lewisite

lexème [lɛksɛm] **NM** *Ling* lexeme

lexical, -e, -aux, -ales [lɛksikal, -o] **ADJ** *Ling* lexical

lexicalisation [lɛksikalizasjɔ̃] **NF** *Ling* lexicalization

lexicalisé, -e [lɛksikalize] **ADJ** *Ling* lexicalized

lexicographe [lɛksikɔgraf] **NMF** lexicographer

lexicographie [lɛksikɔgrafi] **NF** lexicography

lexicographique [lɛksikɔgrafik] **ADJ** lexicographical

lexicologie [lɛksikɔlɔʒi] **NF** lexicology

lexicologique [lɛksikɔlɔʒik] **ADJ** lexicological

lexicologue [lɛksikɔlɔg] **NMF** lexicologist

lexie [lɛksi] **NF** *Ling* lexical item *or* unit

lexique [lɛksik] **NM 1** *(ouvrage)* glossary, lexicon **2** *(d'une langue)* lexis, vocabulary; *(d'un auteur)* vocabulary

lézard [lezar] **NM 1** *Zool* lizard; **l. vert/des murailles** green/wall lizard; **faire le l.** to bask in the sun **2** *(peau)* lizardskin; **ceinture en l.** lizardskin belt **3** *Fam (difficulté)* **il y a pas de lézards** no problem, no sweat

lézarde [lezard] **NF** crack, crevice

lézarder [3] [lezarde] **VI** *Fam (au soleil)* to bask in the sun; *(paresser)* to laze about, to lounge (about)

VT *(fissurer)* to crack; **mur lézardé** cracked wall, wall full of cracks

VPR se lézarder to crack

LFAJ [ɛlɛfaʒi] **NF** *(abrév* **Ligue française des auberges de jeunesse)** French youth hostel association

liais [ljɛ] **NM** *Constr* hard limestone

liaison [ljɛzɔ̃] **NF 1** *(contact)* contact; **être en l. avec qn** to be in contact with sb; **assurer la l. entre deux services** to liaise between two departments

2 *Tél* communications link; **la l. téléphonique n'est pas très bonne** the line is not very good; **nous sommes en l. directe avec notre correspondant** we have our correspondent on the line; **l. radio** radio contact; **l. par satellite** satellite link *or* link-up; *TV* **l. video** video link

3 *Transp* link; **un train/car assure la l. entre Édimbourg et Glasgow** there is a train/coach service operating between Edinburgh and Glasgow; **toutes les liaisons Paris–Téhéran sont suspendues** all services between Paris and Tehran have been suspended; **l. aérienne/maritime/ferroviaire** air/sea/rail link

4 *(rapport)* connection, link; **des idées sans l.** unconnected ideas; **son départ est sans l. avec la dispute d'hier** his/her departure is in no way linked to yesterday's argument

5 *Littéraire (relation)* relationship; **ils ont une l. d'affaires** they have a business relationship; **avoir une l. (amoureuse) avec qn** to have an affair with sb

6 *Chim* bond; **l. de covalence** covalent bond; **l. hydrogène** hydrogen bond

7 *Constr* joint

8 *Culin (pour une sauce)* thickening; *(pour farce)* binding

9 *Ordinat* link; **l. par modem** modem link; **l. spécialisée** dedicated line

10 *Ling* liaison; **faire la l.** to make *or* to sound the liaison

11 *Mus (pour tenir une note)* tie; *(pour lier plusieurs notes)* phrase mark, slur

• **en liaison ADV** in touch, in contact; **être/rester en l. (avec qn)** to be/to remain in contact (with sb); **travailler en l. avec qn** to liaise with sb, to work closely with sb

liaisonner [3] [ljɛzɔne] **VT** *Constr* to bond

liane [ljan] **NF** *(vigne, lierre)* creeper; *(en forêt équatoriale)* liana

liant, -e [ljɑ̃, -ɑ̃t] **ADJ** sociable; **il n'est pas très l.** he's not very sociable, he doesn't make friends easily

NM 1 *Littéraire (affabilité)* **avoir du l.** to be sociable **2** *Chim & Constr* binder **3** *(souplesse)* flexibility, pliability

liard [ljar] **NM 1** *Hist* = coin worth three "deniers", *Br* ≃ farthing **2** *Vieilli (très petite quantité)* **il n'a pas un l. de bon sens** he hasn't an ounce *or* a grain of common sense

lias [ljas] **NM** *Géol* Lias

liasse [ljas] **NF** *(de billets)* wad; *(de documents)* bundle

libage [libaʒ] **NM** *Constr* bastard ashlar

Liban [libɑ̃] **NM le L.** (the) Lebanon

libanais, -e [libanɛ, -ɛz] **ADJ** Lebanese

• **Libanais, -e NM,F** Lebanese (person); **les L.** the Lebanese

libanisation [libanizasjɔ̃] **NF** Balkanization

libation [libasjɔ̃] **NF** *Antiq* libation

• **libations NFPL faire de joyeuses libations** to drink copious amounts (of alcohol)

libelle [libɛl] **NM** lampoon; **écrire des libelles contre qn** to lampoon sb

libellé [libele] **NM** *(d'une lettre, d'un acte, d'un contrat)* wording; *Compta (d'une écriture)* particulars; **le l. du chèque est incorrect** the cheque is not made out correctly

libeller [4] [libele] **VT 1** *(lettre, acte, contrat)* to word; *Admin (texte juridique)* to word, to draw up; **libellé comme suit...** worded as follows... **2** *(chèque)* to make out; **libellez votre chèque au nom** *ou* **à l'ordre de...** make your cheque payable to...; **je n'avais pas libellé le chèque** I hadn't put the name of the payee on the cheque; **être libellé au porteur** to be made out to bearer; *Fin* **libellé en dollars** *(chèque)* made out in dollars; *(cours)* quoted *or* given in dollars

libellule [libelyl] **NF** *Entom* dragonfly

libérable [liberabl] **ADJ 1** *Mil (militaire, contingent)* dischargeable; **permission l.** demob leave **2** *Jur (prisonnier)* eligible for release

libéral, -e, -aux, -ales [liberal, -o] **ADJ 1** *(aux idées larges)* liberal, broad-minded

2 *Écon* free-market *(avant n)*, free-enterprise *(avant n)*; **l'économie libérale** the free-market economy

3 *Hist* liberal

4 *Pol (en Grande-Bretagne, au Canada)* Liberal; *(en France)* favouring the free-market economy

NM,F 1 *Pol (en Grande-Bretagne, au Canada)* Liberal; *(en France)* free-marketeer **2** *(personne tolérante)* liberal, broad-minded person

libéralement [liberalmɑ̃] **ADV 1** *(généreusement)* liberally, generously **2** *(avec tolérance)* broad-mindedly, liberally

libéralisation [liberalizasjɔ̃] **NF 1** *Pol* liberalization **2** *Écon* deregulation; **l. du commerce** deregulation of trade, easing of trade restrictions; **la l. complète de l'économie** the application of free-market principles throughout the economy

libéraliser [3] [liberalize] **VT 1** *(mœurs, régime)* to liberalize **2** *Écon (commerce)* to deregulate, to ease restrictions on; **l. l'économie** to reduce state intervention in the economy

VPR se libéraliser *(régime)* to become (more) liberal; *(mœurs)* to become freer

libéralisme [liberalism] **NM 1** *Pol* liberalism **2** *Écon* free-market economics, free enterprise **3** *(tolérance)* broad-mindedness, liberal-mindedness

libéralité [liberalite] **NF 1** *(générosité)* generosity, *Sout* liberality **2** *Jur* gift

• **libéralités NFPL** *(dons)* (cash) donations, liberalities; **je ne tiens pas à vivre de vos libéralités** I do not want to live off your generosity; **faire des libéralités à qn** to give liberally *or* freely to sb

libérateur, -trice [liberatœr, -tris] **ADJ 1** *(rire, geste)* liberating, *Littéraire* cathartic **2** *Pol* liberating; **l'armée libératrice** the liberating army, the army of liberation

NM,F liberator

libération [liberasjɔ̃] **NF 1** *(d'un pays)* liberation; *(d'un prisonnier, d'un otage)* release; *(d'un soldat)* discharge; *Hist* **la L.** the Liberation (of France); **à la L.** when France was liberated

2 *Jur (d'un détenu)* release; **l. anticipée** early release; **l. conditionnelle** (release on) parole

3 *(émancipation)* liberation; *Fig* **éprouver un sentiment de l.** to feel liberated; **la l. de la femme** women's liberation

4 *Écon & Fin (d'une dette)* payment in full, discharge; *(d'une action, du capital)* paying up; *(d'un débiteur)* discharge, release; *(d'un garant)* discharge; **la l. des échanges commerciaux** the deregulation of trade; **la l. des prix** the deregulation of prices, the removal of price controls

5 *Presse* **L.** = French left-of-centre daily newspaper

6 *Chim, Phys, Méd & Physiol* release; **à l. prolongée** slow-release

libératoire [liberatwar] **ADJ paiement l.** payment in full discharge; **avoir force l.** to be legal tender

libératrice [liberatris] *voir* **libérateur**

libéré, -e [libere] **ADJ 1** *(en liberté, émancipé)* liberated **2** *Fin (action)* (fully) paid-up; **un titre de 1000 euros l. de 750 euros** *ou* **l. à 75 pour cent** a 1,000-euro share of which 750 euro are paid up; **l. d'impôt** tax paid

LIBÉRER [18] [libere]

VT
- to free **1–3**
- to relieve **4**
- to vacate **6**
- to discharge **11**
- to release **2, 3, 7, 8**
- to let go **5**
- to lift restrictions on **9**

VPR
- to free oneself **1**
- to become vacant **5**
- to become more liberated **4**

VT 1 *(délivrer ▸ personne)* to free; *(▸ pays, peuple)* to liberate; **quand les Alliés libérèrent Paris** when the Allies liberated Paris; **l. qn de qch** to free sb from sth; **l. qn de ses chaînes** to free sb from his/her chains

2 *(remettre en liberté ▸ prisonnier)* to release, to (set) free

3 *(décharger)* **l. qn d'une promesse** to free *or* to release sb from a promise; **l. qn de la responsabilité légale** to relieve sb of legal liability

4 *(soulager ▸ conscience)* to relieve, to salve; **tu me libères d'un gros souci** *ou* **d'un gros poids** you've taken a load off my mind; **l. son cœur** to unburden one's heart

5 *(laisser partir ▸ élèves, employés)* to let go; **on nous a libérés avant l'heure** we were allowed to leave *or* they let us go early

6 *(rendre disponible ▸ appartement, chambre d'hôtel)* to vacate, to move out of; *(▸ étagère)* to clear; **libérez le passage** clear the way; **je n'arrive même pas à l. une heure pour jouer au tennis** I can't even find a free hour *or* an hour to spare to play tennis; **les postes libérés par les mises à la retraite anticipée** vacancies created by early retirement

7 *(débloquer ▸ mécanisme, émotions)* to release

8 *Chim & Phys (gaz, hormone, énergie, chaleur)* to release

9 *Écon (prix, salaires)* to lift restrictions on, to deregulate

10 *Fin* **l. entièrement une action** to make a share fully paid-up, to pay up a share in full

11 *Mil (conscrit)* to discharge

VPR se libérer 1 *(se délivrer)* to free oneself; **se l. de ses chaînes** to free oneself from one's chains

2 *(se dégager)* **se l. de qch** *(dette)* to redeem sth, to liquidate sth; *(engagement)* to free oneself from sth

3 (dans un emploi du temps) essaie de te l. pour demain try to make some time tomorrow; je ne pourrai pas me l. avant 17 heures I won't be able to get away before 5 o'clock

4 (s'émanciper ▸ femmes) to become more liberated

5 (emploi, appartement) to become vacant or available; il y a une place qui s'est libérée au coin de la rue somebody's just left a parking space at the corner of the street

Liberia [liberja] NM le L. Liberia

libérien, -enne [liberjɛ̃, -ɛn] ADJ Liberian
• **Libérien, -enne** NM,F Liberian

libero, libéro [libero] NM Ftbl sweeper

libertaire [libertɛr] ADJ & NMF libertarian, anarchist

liberté [liberte] NF 1 (gén) & Jur freedom; rendre la l. à un otage to release a hostage; rendre la l. à un oiseau to set a bird free; le pays de la l. the land of the free or of freedom; défenseur de la l. defender of freedom or liberty; l. individuelle personal freedom; l. provisoire ou sous caution release on bail; l. conditionnelle ou sur parole (release on) parole; mettre qn en l. conditionnelle ou sur parole to release sb on parole; l. surveillée probation; mettre qn en l. surveillée to release sb on probation; la statue de la L. the Statue of Liberty

2 (droit) right, freedom; l. d'association/du travail right of association/to work; l. du culte/d'opinion freedom of worship/thought; libertés civiques ou du citoyen civil liberties; l. d'aller et venir right of access; l. d'entreprise free enterprise; libertés individuelles individual freedom; l. de la presse/d'expression freedom of the press/of speech; L., Égalité, Fraternité Liberty, Equality, Fraternity (motto of the French Revolution and, today, of France)

3 (indépendance) freedom; l. de pensée freedom of thought; avoir toute l. d'action to have a free hand or complete freedom of action; on lui laisse trop peu de l. he's/she's given too little freedom; avoir toute l. pour décider to be totally free or to have full freedom to decide; prendre la l. de faire to take the liberty of doing; reprendre sa l. (sentimentalement) to regain one's freedom

4 (temps libre) free time; jour de l. free day, day off; tous mes moments de l. all my free time; je n'ai pas un instant de l. I haven't got a minute to myself

5 (désinvolture, irrévérence) il y a une trop grande l. dans la traduction the translation is not close enough to the original or is too free; l. de langage overfree use of language

6 Écon l. des prix freedom from price controls; instaurer la l. des prix to end or to abolish price controls; l. du commerce freedom of trade; l. d'entreprise (right of) free enterprise; l. syndicale freedom to join a union, union rights
• **libertés** NFPL 1 (droits légaux) liberties, freedom (UNCOUNT); atteinte aux libertés attack on civil liberties; les libertés publiques civil liberties 2 (privautés) prendre ou se permettre des libertés avec qn to take liberties with sb; j'ai pris quelques libertés avec la recette I took a few liberties with or I didn't stick entirely to the recipe
• **en liberté** ADV free; être en l. (personne) to be free or at large; (animal) to be free or in the wild; un parc national où les animaux vivent en l. a national park where animals roam free; Jur (re)mettre qn en l. to release sb, to set sb free
• **en toute liberté** ADV freely; vous pouvez vous exprimer en toute l. you can talk freely; agir en toute l. to act quite freely

libertel [libertɛl] NF Ordinat freenet

libertin, -e [libertɛ̃, -in] ADJ 1 Littéraire (personne) dissolute, debauched; (propos, publication) licentious 2 Hist & Rel libertine, freethinking
NM,F 1 Littéraire (personne dissolue) libertine 2 Hist & Rel libertine, freethinker

libertinage [libertinaʒ] NM 1 Littéraire (comportement) debauchery, Sout libertinism 2 Hist & Rel libertine philosophy, libertinism

Liberty® [liberti] NM INV Liberty® print material; une housse de coussin en L. a Liberty® cushion cover

libidineux, -euse [libidinø, -øz] ADJ (vieillard) lecherous; (regard) lustful, Sout libidinous

libido [libido] NF libido; avoir une forte l. to have a high libido

libraire [librɛr] NMF bookseller

> Il faut noter que le nom anglais **librarian** est un faux ami. Il signifie **bibliothécaire**.

libraire-éditeur [librɛreditœr] (pl libraires-éditeurs) NM publisher and bookseller

librairie [librɛri] NF 1 (boutique) Br bookshop, Am bookstore; paraîtra en l. le 3 juin due out on 3 June, in the bookshops from 3 June; l. d'art/d'occasion art/second-hand bookshop 2 la l. (commerce) bookselling; (profession) the book trade

> Il faut noter que le nom anglais **library** est un faux ami. Il signifie **bibliothèque**.

librairie-papeterie [librɛripapetri] (pl librairies-papeteries) NF stationer's and bookseller's

LIBRE [libr]

• free 1, 2, 4–6, 8–12	• available 2
• vacant 2	• unattached 3
• daring 5	• deregulated 6
• independent 7	• private 7

ADJ 1 (gén) & Pol free; Hist la France l. Free France; si j'ai envie de la voir, je suis bien l.! if I feel like seeing her, it's up to me or that's my affair!; laisser qn l. d'agir to leave sb a free hand, to leave sb free to act; il nous laisse libres de partir he lets us go when we want; être l. de tout souci to be free from care, to be carefree; être l. de ses mouvements to be free to do what one likes; être l. comme l'air to be as free as a bird; l. d'impôt tax-free; l. à toi/à elle de refuser you're/she's free to say no; j'y vais? – alors là, l. à toi! shall I go? – well, that's entirely up to you or you're (entirely) free to do as you wish!

2 (disponible ▸ personne, salle) free, available; (▸ appartement, maison, chambre) available; (▸ place de parking) free, unoccupied; (▸ poste, siège) vacant, free; (▸ table) free; (▸ toilettes) vacant; (▸ passage) clear; la ligne n'est pas l. (au téléphone) the line is Br engaged or Am busy; la voie est l. the way is clear; l. (sur un taxi) for hire; studio à louer, l. de suite (annonce) studio Br flat or Am apartment to rent, available immediately; il faut que j'aie la tête ou l'esprit l. pour prendre une décision I have to have a clear head before I'm able to make a decision; le directeur des ventes n'est pas l. en ce moment the sales manager isn't free or available at the moment; êtes-vous l. à l'heure du déjeuner? are you free for lunch?; j'ai deux après-midi (de) libres par semaine I've got two afternoons off or two free afternoons a week; le lundi est mon jour (de) l. Monday is my day off, I have Mondays free; je n'ai pas eu une minute de l. aujourd'hui I haven't had a spare minute today

3 (sentimentalement) unattached; je ne suis pas l. I'm already seeing somebody; je préfère rester l. I prefer to remain unattached

4 (franc) free, open; je suis très l. avec elle I am quite free (and easy) or open with her

5 (désinvolte, inconvenant ▸ attitude) free, daring; ses remarques un peu libres nous ont choqués his/her somewhat coarse remarks shocked us; il se montre un peu trop l. avec ses secrétaires he is a bit overfamiliar or too free with his secretaries

6 (non réglementé ▸ prix, marché) free, deregulated; leurs honoraires sont libres there are no restrictions on their fees; l. accès open access; en l. accès open-access; bibliothèque en l. accès public library; l'entrée de l'exposition est l. entrance to the exhibition is free; l. circulation free movement; l. concurrence free competition; par le l. jeu de la concurrence through free competition; la l. entreprise free enterprise

7 (privé ▸ radio, télévision) independent; (▸ école, enseignement) private (in France, mostly Catholic)

8 (non imposé ▸ improvisation, style) free; je leur ai donné un sujet l. I left it up to them to choose the subject; escalade l. free climbing; vers l. free verse

9 (non entravé ▸ mouvement, membre) free, unrestrained; le bandage laisse les doigts libres the bandage leaves the fingers free; elle porte les cheveux libres she wears her hair down or loose

10 (non fidèle ▸ adaptation) free; dans une traduction un peu l. de Brecht in a rather free or loose translation of Brecht

11 Chim & Math free

12 Tech (engrenage) free, disengaged

ADV ça sonne l. ou occupé? is it ringing or Br engaged or Am busy?

libre-échange [librəʃɑ̃ʒ] (pl libres-échanges) NM Écon free trade

libre-échangiste [librəʃɑ̃ʒist] (pl libre-échangistes) Écon ADJ (politique, économie) free-trade (avant n); (idée, personne) in favour of free trade
NMF free trader, advocate of free trade

librement [librəmɑ̃] ADV freely

libre-pensée [librəpɑ̃se] (pl libres-pensées) NF freethinking

libre-penseur [librəpɑ̃sœr] (pl libres-penseurs) NM freethinker

libre-service [librəservis] (pl libres-services) NM 1 (principe) self-service 2 (magasin) self-service Br shop or Am store; (cantine) self-service canteen; (restaurant) self-service restaurant; (station-service) self-service Br petrol or Am gas station
• **en libre-service** ADJ self-service

librettiste [librɛtist] NMF librettist

libretto [librɛto] NM libretto

Libreville [librəvil] NF Libreville

Libye [libi] NF la L. Libya; le désert de L. the Libyan Desert

libyen, -enne [libjɛ̃, -ɛn] ADJ Libyan
• **Libyen, -enne** NM,F Libyan

lice [lis] NF 1 Sport (bordure de piste) line; (en hippisme) rail 2 Hist (palissade) lists; (terrain) tilt-yard
• **en lice** ADV aussi Fig entrer en l. to enter the lists; Fig (intervenir dans une discussion) to enter the fray; les deux candidats encore en l. the two candidates still in the running

licence [lisɑ̃s] NF 1 Littéraire (liberté excessive) licence; (débauche) licentiousness; avoir toute ou pleine l. de faire qch to be at liberty or quite free to do sth

2 Littérature l. poétique poetic licence

3 Univ (bachelor's) degree; passer sa l. to sit or to take one's degree exams or one's finals; l. d'économie degree in economics; l. de russe/de droit Russian/law degree; l. ès lettres arts degree, Br ≃ BA, Am ≃ AB; l. ès sciences science degree, Br ≃ BSc, Am ≃ BS

4 Jur (permis) licence; Ordinat (pour l'utilisation d'un logiciel) registration card; accorder une l. à qn to license sb; l. d'importation/d'exportation import/export licence; l. de débit de boissons, Can l. Br licence for the sale of alcohol, Am liquor license; l. exclusive exclusive licence; l. d'exploitation d'un brevet licence to use a patent; l. de fabrication manufacturing licence; Ordinat l. individuelle d'utilisation single user licence; l. de pêche fishing licence; l. de vente selling licence

5 Sport membership card (allowing entry into official competitions)
• **sous licence** ADJ licensed ADV fabriqué sous l. made or manufactured under licence

licencié, -e [lisɑ̃sje] ADJ 1 Univ graduate; il est l. he's a graduate 2 Can Joual (établissement) licensed (to sell alcohol)
NM,F 1 Univ (university) graduate; l. ès lettres/ès sciences arts/science graduate; l. en droit law graduate 2 Sport registered member; seuls les licenciés bénéficient des tarifs réduits (dans le cadre d'un club sportif) discount for club members only 3 (chômeur ▸ pour raisons économiques) laid off or Br redundant employee; (▸ pour faute professionnelle) dismissed employee; il y a eu quatre licenciés four employees were laid-off or Br made redundant

licenciement [lisɑ̃simɑ̃] NM (structurel) layoff, Br redundancy; (pour faute professionnelle) dismissal; depuis mon l. since I was laid off or Br made redundant; avis ou lettre de l. letter of dismissal; l. abusif unfair dismissal; l. collectif mass redundancies; **l. sec** = redundancy without any form of statutory compensation

licencier [9] [lisɑ̃sje] VT *(pour raison économique)* to lay off, *Br* to make redundant; *(pour faute)* to dismiss, to fire, *Br* to sack; **se faire l.** to be made redundant

licencieuse [lisɑ̃sjøz] *voir* **licencieux**

licencieusement [lisɑ̃sjøzmɑ̃] ADV *Litt* licentiously

licencieux, -euse [lisɑ̃sjø, -øz] ADJ licentious, lewd

lichen [likɛn] NM *Bot* lichen

lichette [liʃɛt] NF **1** *Fam (petite quantité)* **une l. de vin/de lait** a (teeny) drop of wine/of milk; **une l. de gâteau** a sliver *or* (tiny) bit of cake **2** *Belg (cordon)* loop, tag

licite [lisit] ADJ licit, lawful

licitement [lisitmɑ̃] ADV licitly, lawfully

licol [likɔl] = **licou**

licorne [likɔrn] NF **1** *Myth* unicorn **2 l. de mer** *(narval)* sea unicorn, narwhal

licou [liku] NM halter; **passer le l. à un cheval** to put the halter on a horse

LICRA [likra] NF *(abrév* **Ligue internationale contre le racisme et l'antisémitisme**) = anti-racist movement

licteur [liktœr] NM *Antiq* lictor

lidar [lidar] NM *Tech (abrév* **light detection and ranging**) lidar

lido [lido] NM sandbar; **le L.** *(à Paris)* = famous cabaret on the Champs-Élysées in Paris

lie [li] NF **1** *(dépôt)* dregs, lees; **l. de vin** wine dregs; **il y a de la l. au fond de la bouteille** there's some sediment at the bottom of the bottle; *Fig* **boire la coupe** *ou* **le calice jusqu'à la l.** to drink one's cup of sorrow to the dregs **2** *(rebut)* dregs, rejects; **la l. de la société** the dregs of society

lié, -e [lje] ADJ **1** *(en relation étroite)* **être (très) l. avec qn** to be (great) friends with sb, to be (very) close to sb; **nous sommes très liés** we are great friends, we are very close **2** *Mus (notes différentes)* slurred; *(note tenue)* tied **3** *Math* bound

lied [lid] *(pl* **lieds** *ou* **lieder** [lidœr]) NM lied; **un récital de lieds** *ou* **de lieder** a lieder recital

liège [ljɛʒ] NM cork; **de** *ou* **en l.** cork; **bouchon de** *ou* **en l.** cork

liégeois, -e [ljeʒwa, -az] ADJ **1** *(personne)* of/from Liège **2** *Culin* **café/chocolat l.** coffee/chocolate sundae *(topped with whipped cream)*

• **Liégeois, -e** NM,F = inhabitant of or person from Liège

lien [ljɛ̃] NM **1** *(entre des choses)* link, connection; **l. de cause à effet** causal relationship, relationship of cause and effect

2 *(entre des gens)* link, connection; **nouer des liens d'amitié** to make friends, to become friends; **les liens conjugaux** *ou* **du mariage** marriage bonds *or* ties; **je vous déclare unis par les liens du mariage** = I now pronounce you man and wife; **l. de parenté** family ties; **ils ont un vague l. de parenté** they're distantly related; **les liens du sang** blood ties; **la crise du l. social** the breakdown of a sense of community in society

3 *(lanière)* tie; **il s'est libéré de ses liens** he freed himself (from his bonds)

4 *Ordinat* link; **l. hypertexte** hypertext link

lier [9] [lje] VT **1** *(attacher ▸ cheveux, paquet, fagot)* to tie up, to bind; **on les lia au poteau** they were tied (up) to the post

2 *Méd* **l. une veine** to ligate a vein

3 *(logiquement)* to link, to connect; **les deux faits ne sont pas liés** the two facts are not connected, there is no connection between the two facts; **tout est lié** everything's interconnected, it all fits together

4 *(enchaîner ▸ gestes)* to link together

5 *(par contrat)* to bind; **votre contrat ne vous lie pas à la société** your contract does not bind you to the company

6 *(associer volontairement)* **l. son sort à qn** to join forces with sb; **l. son sort à qch** to stick with sth for better or worse

7 *(unir par des sentiments)* to bind, to unite; **leur passé commun les lie** they are united by their common past; **l'amitié qui nous lie** the friendship which binds us

8 *(commencer)* **l. amitié** to become friends; **l. connaissance/conversation avec qn** to strike up an acquaintance/a conversation with sb

9 *Constr* to bind

10 *Culin (sauce)* to thicken; *(farce)* to bind

11 *Ling* to link *(with liaisons)*

12 *Mus (notes)* to slur

VPR **se lier se l. (d'amitié)** to become friends; **se l. (d'amitié) avec qn** to strike up a friendship with sb, to become friends with sb; **il se lie facilement** he makes friends easily

lierre [ljɛr] NM *Bot* ivy; **l. terrestre** ground ivy

liesse [ljɛs] NF *Littéraire* jubilation, exhilaration; **en l.** jubilant

lieu[1] [ljø] NM *Ich* hake; **l. jaune** pollack; **l. noir** coalfish

lieu[2], **-x** [ljø] NM **1** *(endroit)* place; **ce n'est pas le l. pour une dispute** this is no place *or* this isn't the place to have an argument; **l. de culte** place of worship; **l. de départ** point of departure; *Fin* **l. d'émission** place of issue; **l. de livraison** place of delivery, point of delivery; **l. de naissance** birthplace, place of birth; **l. de paiement** place of payment; **lieux de passage** *(dans une ville)* thoroughfares; **cette ville n'est qu'un l. de passage** people merely pass through this town; **l. de pèlerinage** place of *or* centre for pilgrimage; **l. de perdition** den of iniquity; **leur l. de promenade habituel** the place where they usually go for a walk; **l. public** public place; **l. de rassemblement** place of assembly, assembly point; **l. de rencontre** meeting place; **l. de rendez-vous** meeting place; **fixons un l. de rendez-vous** let's decide on somewhere to meet *or* on a meeting place; **l. de résidence** (place of) residence; **l. saint** shrine; *Cin* **l. de tournage** location; **sur le l. de travail** in the workplace; **sur votre l. de travail** at your place of work; **l. de vente** point of sale

2 *Gram* **adverbe/complément (circonstanciel) de l.** adverb/complement of place

3 *Géom* **l. géométrique** locus

4 *Ling* **l. commun** commonplace, platitude

5 *(locutions)* **avoir l.** *(entrevue, expérience, spectacle)* to take place; *(accident)* to happen; *(erreur)* to occur; **avoir l. de** *(avoir des raisons de)* to have (good) reasons to; **j'ai tout l. de croire que...** I have good *or* every reason to believe that...; **vous n'aurez pas l. de vous plaindre** you won't find any cause *or* any reason for complaint; **tes craintes n'ont pas l. d'être** your fears are groundless *or* unfounded; **il n'y a pas l. de s'affoler** there's no need to panic; **s'il y a l.** if necessary, should the need arise; **il y a tout l. de croire...** there is every reason to believe...; **donner l. à** *(querelle, problèmes)* to cause, to give rise to; **son retour a donné l. à une réunion de famille** his/her return was the occasion for a family gathering; **tout donne l. de croire que...** everything leads me/us/*etc or* there is every reason to believe that...; **son chien lui tient l. d'enfant** his/her dog is a substitute for a child; **ça tiendra l. de champagne!** that will do instead of champagne!

• **lieux** NMPL **1** *(endroit précis)* scene; **les lieux de l'accident/du crime** the scene of the accident/of the crime; **la police est déjà sur les lieux (du crime)** the police are already at the scene of the crime; **pour être efficace, il faut être sur les lieux 24 heures sur 24** if you want to do things properly, you have to be on the spot 24 hours a day; **rendez-vous immédiatement sur les lieux** go there immediately; **les Lieux saints** the Holy Places **2** *(bâtiments)* premises; **quitter** *ou* **vider les lieux** to vacate the premises; **quand nous serons dans les lieux** when we're in occupation *or* in residence; *Euph* **les lieux d'aisances** *Br* the lavatory, *Am* the bathroom

• **au lieu de** PRÉP instead of; **au l. de faire qch** instead of doing sth

• **au lieu que** CONJ instead of, rather than; **je préfère ranger moi-même mon bureau au l. que tu viennes tout changer de place** I prefer to tidy my desk myself instead of *or* rather than having you changing everything around

• **en dernier lieu** ADV finally, lastly; **n'ajoutez le sucre qu'en tout dernier l.** do not add the sugar until the last moment

• **en haut lieu** ADV in high places; **ça se décidera en haut l.** the decision will be made at a high level

• **en lieu et place de** PRÉP *(de la part de)* on behalf of; *(à la place de)* in lieu of; **le président n'étant pas là, j'ai assisté à l'enterrement en ses l. et place** as the president wasn't available, I attended the funeral on his behalf; **en l. et place d'honoraires/de préavis** in lieu of fees/of notice

• **en lieu sûr** ADV in a safe place

• **en premier lieu** ADV in the first place, firstly, first of all

• **en tous lieux** ADV everywhere; **sa politique est critiquée en tous lieux** his/her policy is under criticism in all quarters *or* everywhere

lieu-dit [ljødi] *(pl* **lieux-dits**) NM *(avec maisons)* hamlet; *(sans maisons)* place; **à La Folie** at the place called La Folie

lieue [ljø] NF **1** *(mesure)* league; **l. marine** league **2** *(locutions)* **nous étions à cent lieues de penser que...** it would never have occurred to us that..., we never dreamt that...; **à cent lieues à la ronde** for miles (and miles) around

lieur, -euse [ljœr, -øz] NM,F *Arch (de gerbes, de bottes)* binder

• **lieuse** NF *(machine)* (sheaf) binder

lieutenant [ljøtnɑ̃] NM **1** *Mil (de l'armée de terre, de la marine)* ≃ lieutenant; *(de l'armée de l'air) Br* ≃ flying officer, *Am* ≃ first lieutenant

2 *(de la marine marchande)* mate; **l. de vaisseau** ≃ lieutenant

3 *Suisse Mil* second lieutenant

4 *(proche collaborateurt)* right-hand man, second in command

lieutenant-colonel [ljøtnɑ̃kɔlɔnɛl] *(pl* **lieutenants-colonels**) NM *(de l'armée de terre)* ≃ lieutenant-colonel; *(de l'armée de l'air) Br* ≃ wing commander, *Am* ≃ lieutenant colonel

lièvre [ljɛvr] NM **1** *Zool* hare; **lever un l.** to start a hare; *Fig* to touch on a sore point; **l. arctique** arctic hare **2** *(fourrure)* hareskin **3** *Sport* pacemaker, pacesetter

lift [lift] NM *Sport* topspin; **faire un l.** to put topspin on the ball

lifter [3] [lifte] VT **1** *Sport* **l. une balle** to give a ball topspin, to put topspin on a ball **2** *(faire un lifting à)* to perform a face lift on; *Fig (rénover)* to give a face lift to

liftier, -ère [liftje, -ɛr] NM,F *Br* lift attendant, *Am* elevator attendant

lifting [liftiŋ] NM **1** *(de la peau)* facelift; **se faire faire un l.** to have a facelift **2** *Fam (rénovation ▸ d'une institution, d'un bâtiment)* facelift

ligament [ligamɑ̃] NM *Anat* ligament

ligature [ligatyr] NF **1** *Méd (opération, fil)* ligature, ligation; **l. des trompes (de Fallope)** tubal ligation **2** *Typ* ligature, tied letter **3** *Hort (processus)* tying up; *(attache)* tie

ligaturer [3] [ligatyre] VT **1** *(attacher)* to tie on **2** *Méd* to ligate, to ligature; **se faire l. les trompes** to have one's (Fallopian) tubes tied **3** *Hort* to tie up

lige [liʒ] ADJ **1** *Hist* liege **2** *Sout* **être l'homme l. de qn** to be totally devoted to sb

ligérien, -enne [liʒerjɛ̃, -ɛn] ADJ of/from the Loire

light [lajt] ADJ *(plat, préparation)* low-fat; *(boisson)* diet *(avant n)*, low-cal

lignage [liɲaʒ] NM **1** *(ascendance)* lineage; **de haut l.** of noble lineage **2** *Typ* linage, lineage

LIGNE [liɲ]

• line **1–3, 5–11, 13, 14, 16**	• outline **4**
• row **5**	• figure **4**
• fishing line **12**	• range **10**

NF **1** *(gén) & Géom* line; **tracer** *ou* **tirer une l.** to draw a line; **les lignes de la main** the lines of the hand; **l. de cœur/de tête/de vie** heart/head/life line; **l. pointillée/brisée** dotted/broken line; **l. droite** straight line; **une l. droite** *(route)* a straight stretch of road; **avancer en l. droite** to advance in a straight line; *Fam* **une l. de coke** a line of coke

2 *(texte)* line; **le prof m'a donné cent lignes** *(punition)* the teacher gave me a hundred lines; **il est payé à la l.** he is paid by the *or* per line; **elle m'a juste envoyé deux lignes** she just dropped me a line; **je vous envoie ces quelques lignes pour vous donner les dernières nouvelles** this is just a note to give you the latest news; **aller à la l.** to begin a new line *or* a new paragraph; **(allez) à la l.!** new

paragraph!; *Presse* **tirer à la l.** to pad (out) an article; *Ordinat* **l. d'impression** print line; *Ordinat & Typ* **l. orpheline** orphan; *Mus* **l. supplémentaire** ledger line; *Ordinat & Typ* **l. veuve** widow
3 *(limite)* line; **tracer les lignes d'un court** to mark out a court; **passer la l. (de l'équateur)** to cross the line; **l. d'arrivée** finishing line; *Sport* **l. de ballon mort** dead-ball line; **l. blanche/jaune** white/yellow line *(on roads)*; *Sport* **l. de but** goal line; *Naut* **l. de charge** load line; **l. continue** continuous line; *Sport* **lignes de côté** *(au tennis)* tramlines; **l. de démarcation** *(gén)* boundary; *Mil* demarcation line; **l. de départ** starting line; **l. discontinue** *(sur la route)* broken line; **l. d'eau** *Natation* (swimming) lane; *Naut* waterline; *Géol* **l. de faille** fault line; **l. de faîte** watershed, crest line; *Sport* **l. de faute** foul line; *Naut* **l. de flottaison** waterline; **l. de flottaison en charge** Plimsoll line; *Sport* **l. de fond** *(au tennis)* baseline; **l. d'horizon** skyline; **l. de mire** line of sight; **l. de partage** dividing line; **l. de partage des eaux** watershed; *Sport* **l. de service** *(au tennis)* service line; **l. de tir** line of fire; **l. de touche** touchline; **l. de visée** line of sight
4 *(silhouette* ▸ *d'un objet)* outline; *(*▸ *d'une personne)* figure; **avoir la l.** to be slim; **je surveille ma l.** I look after *or* watch my figure; **garder la l.** to keep one's figure; **la l. de l'été sera très épurée** this summer's look will be very simple; **la l. élégante d'une voiture** the elegant lines of a car
5 *(rangée)* line, row; **plantés en l.** planted in a line *or* row; **se mettre en l.** to line up, to form a line; *Sport* **la l. d'avants/d'arrières** the forwards/backs; *Mil* **l. d'attaque** line of attack; *Mil* **l. de bataille** line of battle, battle line; **l. de défense** line of defence; **l. de front** front line; **les lignes ennemies** the enemy lines; *Mil & Fig* **être/monter en première l.** to be in/to go to the front line; *Sport* **un première/deuxième/troisième l.** a front-row/second-row/back-row forward
6 *(orientation)* line; *Pol* **l. du parti** party line; **suivre la l., être dans la l.** to follow *or* to toe the party line; **sa décision est dans la droite l. de la politique gouvernementale** his/her decision is completely in line with government policy; **redéfinir sa l. d'action** to adopt a different line *or* course of action; **l. de conduite** line of conduct; **l. directrice** main line; **lignes de force** *(grandes lignes)* dominating *or* guiding principles; *Phys* lines of force; **elle a décrit la situation dans ses grandes lignes** she gave a broad outline of the situation, she outlined the situation
7 *(généalogique)* line; **l. directe/collatérale** direct/collateral line; **descendre en l. directe de** to be directly descended from
8 *Transp* line; **l. aérienne** *(société)* airline (company); *(service)* air service, air link; *(itinéraire)* route; **l. d'autobus** *(service)* bus service; *(itinéraire)* bus route; **lignes de banlieue** suburban lines; **il n'y a que deux lignes de bus qui fonctionnent la nuit** there are only two late-night bus services; **l. de chemin de fer** *Br* railway line, *Am* railroad line; **lignes intérieures** *ou Can* **domestiques** *(aériennes)* domestic flights; **l. maritime** shipping line; **l. de métro** *Br* underground line, *Am* subway line; **l. secondaire** branch line; **les grandes lignes** the main lines; *Rail* **départ grandes lignes** mainline departures
9 *Élec & Tél* line; **la l. est occupée** the line is *Br* engaged *or Am* busy; **la l. est en dérangement** the line is out of order; **la l. a été coupée** I've/we've/*etc* been cut off; **l. directe/intérieure/extérieure** direct/internal/outside line; *Élec* **l. à haute tension** high-voltage line; **l. spécialisée** dedicated line; **l. télégraphique** telegraph line; **l. téléphonique** telephone line
10 *Com* line, range; **l. pour hommes** range for men; **une nouvelle l. de produits** a new line *or* range of products
11 *TV (d'une image)* line
12 *Pêche* fishing line; **l. de fond** ground *or* ledger line; **l. volante** fly line
13 *Banque* **l. de crédit** line of credit, credit line; **l. de cotation** line of quotation; **l. de découvert** line of credit, credit line
14 *Ordinat* line; **hors l.** offline; **l. de commande** command line
15 *Belg (raie des cheveux) Br* parting, *Am* part
16 *Can Vieilli (mesure)* line, = 2.3 mm
17 *(locution)* **entrer en l. de compte** to come *or* to be taken into consideration; **le coût doit entrer en l. de compte** the cost has to be taken into account *or* consideration; **le prix n'a pas à entrer en l. de compte** the cost doesn't come into it
• **en ligne** ADV **1** *(en rang)* **mettez-vous en l.!** line up!, get into line!; **en l. pour le départ!** line up ready for the start!
2 *Ordinat* online
3 *Mil* **monter en l.** *(aller à l'assaut)* to advance (for the attack)
4 *Tél* **restez en l.!** hold the line!; **parlez, vous êtes en l.** go ahead, you're through *or* you're connected; **elle est en l., vous patientez?** her line's engaged, will you hold?
• **hors ligne** ADJ *(hors pair)* unrivalled, matchless
• **sur toute la ligne** ADV **gagner sur toute la l.** to win hands down; **se tromper sur toute la l.** to be completely mistaken

lignée [liɲe] NF **1** *(descendance)* descendants; **avoir une nombreuse l.** to have many descendants; **le premier/dernier d'une longue l.** the first/last of a long line (of descent)
2 *(extraction, lignage)* stock, lineage; **être de noble l.** to be of noble lineage
3 *(tradition)* line, tradition; **elle s'inscrit dans la l. des romancières féministes** she is in the tradition of feminist novelists
4 *Biol* line, stock

ligneux, -euse [liɲø, -øz] ADJ ligneous, woody

lignite [liɲit] NM *Mines* brown coal, lignite

ligoter [3] [ligɔte] VT to bind, to tie up; **ligoté à sa chaise** tied to his chair

ligue [lig] NF **1** *(morale, de défense)* league, pressure group; **l. antialcoolique** temperance league; **la L. nationale contre le cancer** = cancer research charity; **L. pour la protection des oiseaux** = society for the protection of birds, *Br* ≃ RSPB
2 *Hist & Pol* **la (Sainte) L.** the (Holy Catholic) League; **la L. arabe** the Arab League

liguer [3] [lige] VT **être ligué contre** to be united against
VPR **se liguer se l. contre** to join forces against

ligueur, -euse [ligœr, -øz] NM,F **1** *Pol* member *(of a league)* **2** *Hist* member of the (Catholic) League

lilas [lila] NM *(arbre)* lilac (tree); *(fleur)* lilac
ADJ INV lilac *(avant n)*, lilac-coloured

lilliputien, -enne [lilipysjɛ̃, -ɛn] ADJ Lilliputian, tiny
• **Lilliputien, -enne** NM,F Lilliputian

lillois, -e [lilwa, -az] ADJ of/from Lille
• **Lillois, -e** NM,F = inhabitant of or person from Lille

Lima [lima] NF Lima

limace [limas] NF **1** *Zool* slug **2** *Fam Péj (personne) Br* slowcoach, *Am* slowpoke; **le bus se traîne comme une l.** the bus is crawling along **3** *Fam (chemise)* shirt[□]

limaçon [limasɔ̃] NM **1** *Zool* snail **2** *Anat* cochlea

limage [limaʒ] NM *(d'une clé)* filing; *(d'une rugosité)* filing off or away; *(d'une pièce de métal, de bois)* filing down; *(d'un cadenas, d'un barreau)* filing through

limaille [limaj] NF filings; **l. de fer** iron filings

limande [limɑ̃d] NF *Ich* dab; **fausse l.** megrim, scaldfish

limande-sole [limɑ̃dsɔl] *(pl* **limandes-soles)** NF *Ich* lemon sole

limbe [lɛ̃b] NM **1** *(d'un cadran)* limb **2** *Astron* limb **3** *Bot* limb, lamina

limbes [lɛ̃b] NMPL **1** *Rel* limbo; **dans les l.** in limbo **2** *(état vague, incertain)* **être dans les l.** to be in (a state of) limbo

lime [lim] NF **1** *(outil)* file; **l. à ongles** nail file; **l. sourde** dead-smooth file **2** *Bot & Culin* lime **3** *Zool (mollusque)* lima

limer [3] [lime] VT **1** *(clé)* to file; *(rugosité)* to file off *or* away; *(pièce de métal, de bois)* to file down; *(cadenas, barreau)* to file through; **le cadenas a été limé** the padlock has been filed through **2** *Vulg (posséder sexuellement)* to screw
VPR **se limer se l. les ongles** to file one's nails

limier [limje] NM **1** *Zool (chien)* bloodhound, sleuthhound **2** *Fam (policier)* **fin l.** sleuth

liminaire [liminɛr] ADJ *(discours)* introductory, preliminary; **un discours l.** a keynote speech

limitatif, -ive [limitatif, -iv] ADJ *(liste)* restrictive, limitative; *(clause)* restrictive; **une liste non limitative** an open-ended list

limitation [limitasjɔ̃] NF limitation, restriction; **l. des armements** arms control *or* limitation; **l. des naissances** birth control; **l. des prix** price restrictions *or* controls; *Jur* **l. de responsabilité** limitation of responsibility; **l. des salaires** wage restraint; **l. de vitesse** speed limit *or* restrictions; **ce test se fait sans l. de temps** there is no time limit for the test

limitative [limitativ] *voir* **limitatif**

limite [limit] NF **1** *(maximum ou minimum)* limit; **l. de temps** time limit; **fixer** *ou* **mettre une l. à qch** to set a limit to sth, to limit sth; **entrée gratuite dans la l. des places disponibles** *(à l'entrée d'un spectacle)* free admission subject to availability; **dans la l. des stocks disponibles** while stocks last; **dans les limites du possible** as far as is humanly possible; **nos dépenses sont restées dans les limites du raisonnable** our expenses stayed within reasonable bounds; **dans une certaine l.** up to a point, to a certain extent; **c'est dans la l. de mes moyens** it's within my means; **ma patience a des limites!** there's a limit to my patience!; **il y a des limites!** there are limits!; **sa haine ne connaît pas de limites** his/her hatred knows no bounds; **l. d'âge** age limit; **l. de crédit/d'endettement** credit/debt limit
2 *(frontière* ▸ *d'un bois)* border, edge; *(*▸ *d'un pays)* boundary, border; **les limites d'un terrain de football** the boundary (lines) of a football pitch; **essaie de jouer dans les limites du court!** try to keep the ball inside the court!
3 *Math* limit
4 *Boxe* **avant la l.** inside *or* within the distance; **tenir jusqu'à la l.** to go the (full) distance
5 *Bourse* limit; **l. de la baisse/hausse** limit down/up
ADJ **1** *(maximal)* **âge/vitesse l.** maximum age/speed **2** *Fam (juste)* **j'ai réussi l'examen, mais c'était l.** I passed the exam, but only just; **je ne lui ai pas mis une claque, mais c'était l.** I didn't slap him/her but I came very close to it *or* it was touch and go; **je suis un peu l. côté fric** I'm a bit short of funds *or Br* strapped for cash; **question propreté, c'était l.** hygiene-wise, it was a bit iffy *or Br* dodgy **3** *Fam (grivois)* **des plaisanteries un peu l.** jokes bordering on the offensive; **ta remarque était un peu l.** your remark was a bit near the knuckle
• **limites** NFPL *(physiques, intellectuelles)* limitations; **je connais mes limites** I know my limitations
• **à la limite** ADV **à la l., on peut toujours dormir dans la voiture** if the worst comes to the worst we can always sleep in the car; **à la l., je lui prêterais l'argent** if necessary *or* if it came to the crunch, I'd lend him/her the money; **à la l. je préférerais rester ici** I'd almost prefer to stay here
• **à la limite de** PRÉP **c'était à la l. du mauvais goût/de l'insolence** it was verging on bad taste/on impertinence

limité, -e [limite] ADJ **1** *(influence, connaissances)* limited; *(nombre, choix, durée)* limited, restricted; **en temps l.** in a limited amount of time; **d'une importance limitée** of limited *or* minor importance **2** *Fam (personne)* **être l.** to have limited abilities[□], to be of limited ability[□]; **il est assez l. en maths** he's rather weak *or* poor at maths

limiter [3] [limite] VT **1** *(réduire* ▸ *dépenses, nombre)* to limit, to restrict; *(*▸ *temps, influence)* to limit; **la vitesse n'est pas limitée** there is no speed limit; *aussi Fig* **essayez de l. les dégâts** try and limit the damage; **l. qch à** to limit *or* to restrict sth to; **j'ai limité mon budget à 200 euros par semaine** I've limited *or* restricted my weekly budget to 200 euros **2** *(circonscrire)* to mark the limit of, to delimit; **des haies limitent la propriété** hedges mark out the limits of the estate
VPR **se limiter 1** *(emploi réfléchi)* **il ne sait pas se l.** he's incapable of self-restraint; **quand il commence à boire, il est incapable de se l.** once he starts drinking he doesn't know when to stop **2 se l. à** *(se résumer à)* to be restricted to, to be confined to; **l'exposé s'est limité à l'aspect historique** the talk only dealt with *or* was restricted to the

historical aspect; **sa fortune se limite à peu de chose** his/her fortune does not amount to very much **3 se l. à** *(se contenter de)* to limit oneself to; **il se limite à faire ce qu'on lui dit** he only does *or* he limits himself to doing what he's told to do

limiteur [limitœr] NM limiter

limitrophe [limitrɔf] ADJ *(comté)* neighbouring, adjoining; *(pays)* bordering; **les pays limitrophes de la Belgique** the countries bordering on Belgium

limogeage [limɔʒaʒ] NM dismissal

limoger [17] [limɔʒe] VT to dismiss; **il s'est fait l.** he was dismissed

limon [limɔ̃] NM **1** *Géol* silt, alluvium; *Fig Littéraire* **le l. du vice** the slough of vice
2 *Agr* loam
3 *(d'attelage)* shaft
4 *(d'escalier)* stair stringer, stringboard

limonade [limɔnad] NF (fizzy) lemonade

limonadier, -ère [limɔnadje, -ɛr] NM,F **1** *(cafetier)* café owner **2** *(fabricant)* soft drinks manufacturer

limoner [3] [limɔne] VI *Can Fam* **1** *(se plaindre)* to moan, to whinge; *(pleurnicher)* to whinge **2** *(hésiter)* to dither

limoneux, -euse [limɔnø, -øz] ADJ silty, siltladen

limousin, -e[1] [limuzɛ̃, -in] ADJ of/from the Limousin
NM *(dialecte)* Limousin dialect
• **Limousin, -e** NM,F = inhabitant of or person from the Limousin

limousine[2] [limuzin] NF *(automobile)* limousine

limpide [lɛ̃pid] ADJ **1** *(pur ▸ lac, miroir, regard)* limpid, clear; **pierre d'un bleu l.** clear blue stone **2** *(intelligible ▸ discours, style)* clear, lucid; *(▸ affaire)* clear

limpidité [lɛ̃pidite] NF **1** *(d'une eau, d'un regard, d'un diamant)* clearness, *Littéraire* limpidity **2** *(d'un texte)* lucidity; *(d'une affaire)* clarity, clearness

lin [lɛ̃] NM **1** *Bot* flax; **l. des marais** cotton grass **2** *Tex* linen, flax; **en l.** linen *(avant n)*

linceul [lɛ̃sœl] NM shroud

linéaire [linear] ADJ **1** *Électron, Ling & Math* linear **2** *(simple ▸ discours, exposé)* reductionist, one-dimensional; *(▸ récit)* linear
NM *Com* shelf space; *(étalage)* shelf display

linge [lɛ̃ʒ] NM **1** *(pour l'habillement et la maison)* linen *(UNCOUNT)*; *(lavé)* washing *(UNCOUNT)*; **étendre/repasser le l.** to hang out/to iron the washing; **faire sécher le l.** to dry the washing; **pour un l. plus blanc, employez X** for a whiter wash, use X; **le l. blanc** household linen; **l. de corps** underwear *(UNCOUNT)*, underclothes; **l. de maison** household linen; **l. de table** table linen; **linges d'autel** altar cloth; **du petit l.** small items (of laundry); **du gros l.** big items (of laundry); *Fam* **il ne fréquente que du beau l.** he only mixes in high circles *or* with the upper crust **2** *(chiffon)* cloth **3** *Suisse* towel

lingère [lɛ̃ʒɛr] NF *(d'une institution)* laundry supervisor

lingerie [lɛ̃ʒri] NF **1** *(sous-vêtements)* lingerie *(UNCOUNT)*, women's underwear *(UNCOUNT)*; **l. fine** lingerie **2** *(lieu)* linen room

lingette [lɛ̃ʒɛt] NF wipe; *(pour bébés)* babywipe

lingot [lɛ̃go] NM **1** *Fin* ingot; **l. d'or** gold ingot *or* bar; **or en l.** *ou* **en lingots** gold bullion *(UNCOUNT)* **2** *Typ* space

lingual, -e, -aux, -ales [lɛ̃gwal, -o] ADJ lingual

linguiste [lɛ̃gɥist] NMF linguist

linguistique [lɛ̃gɥistik] ADJ linguistic
NF linguistics *(singulier)*; **l. descriptive** descriptive linguistics

linguistiquement [lɛ̃gɥistikmɑ̃] ADV linguistically

liniment [linimɑ̃] NM liniment

lino [lino] NM *Fam (abrév* **linoléum***)* linoleum❑, *Br* lino

linoléum [linɔleɔm] NM linoleum

linon [linɔ̃] NM *Tex* lawn

linotte [linɔt] NF *Orn* linnet

Linotype® [linɔtip] NF *Typ* Linotype®

linotypie [linɔtipi] NF *Typ* Linotype® setting

linotypiste [linɔtipist] NMF *Typ* linotypist

linteau, -x [lɛ̃to] NM lintel

lion [ljɔ̃] NM *(animal) & Fig* lion; **l. de mer** sea lion; **tourner comme un l. en cage** to pace up and down (like a caged lion)

lionceau, -x [ljɔ̃so] NM (lion) cub

lionne [ljɔn] NF lioness

lipase [lipaz] NF *Biol & Chim* lipase

lipide [lipid] NM *Biol & Chim* lipid

lipo [lipo] NF *Fam (abrév* **liposuccion***)* lipo

liposome [lipɔzom] NM *Biol* liposome

liposuccion [lipɔsyksjɔ̃, lipɔsysjɔ̃] NF liposuction

lippe [lip] NF **1** *(lèvre inférieure)* lower lip **2** *Fam (locutions)* **faire la** *ou* **sa l.** *(faire la moue)* to pout; *(bouder)* to sulk

lippu, -e [lipy] ADJ *(personne, bouche)* thick-lipped; *(lèvres)* thick

liquéfaction [likefaksjɔ̃] NF liquefaction

liquéfiable [likefjabl] ADJ liquefiable

liquéfiant, -e [likefjɑ̃, -ɑ̃t] ADJ **1** *Chim & Pétr* liquefying **2** *Fam (épuisant)* exhausting❑, *Br* knackering

liquéfier [9] [likefje] VT **1** *Chim, Métal & Pétr* to liquefy; **plomb liquéfié** liquefied lead **2** *Fam (épuiser ▸ personne)* to exhaust❑, *Br* to knacker; **cette chaleur m'a liquéfié** this heat has knocked me out
VPR **se liquéfier 1** *(plomb, gaz)* to liquefy, to be liquefied **2** *Fam (s'amollir)* to collapse in a heap

liquette [likɛt] NF *Fam (chemise)* shirt❑

liqueur [likœr] NF **1** *(boisson)* liqueur; **l. de fruit** fruit liqueur; **bonbon à la l.** liqueur-filled *Br* sweet *or Am* candy **2** *Pharm* solution; **l. de Fehling** Fehling's solution **3** *Can Joual* **l. (douce)** soft drink; **l. forte** strong drink, hard liquor

> Il faut noter que le terme **liquor**, utilisé en anglais américain, est un faux ami. Il signifie **alcool**.

liquidateur, -trice [likidatœr, -tris] NM liquidator; **l. judiciaire** official liquidator

liquidation [likidasjɔ̃] NF **1** *(règlement)* settling; **la l. de la crise ministérielle** the settling of the ministerial crisis
2 *Fam (assassinat)* liquidation, elimination
3 *Bourse* settlement; *(d'une position)* liquidation; **l. en espèces** cash settlement; **l. de fin de mois** end-of-month settlement
4 *Com (d'un stock)* selling off, clearance; *(d'un commerce)* closing down, *Am* closing out; **l. totale** *(sur panneau)* closing down sale, everything must go
5 *Fin & Jur (d'une société)* liquidation; *(d'un impôt, d'une dette)* settlement, payment; **l. de biens** selling (off) *or* liquidation of assets; **l. (par décision) judiciaire** official receivership; **l. forcée/volontaire** compulsory/voluntary liquidation
• **en liquidation** ADV *Jur* **être en l.** to have gone into liquidation; **entrer en l.** to go into liquidation; **l'entreprise a été mise en l.** the firm was put into liquidation

liquidatrice [likidatris] *voir* **liquidateur**

liquide [likid] ADJ **1** *(qui coule)* liquid; **des aliments liquides** fluids, liquid foods
2 *(trop fluide)* watery, thin; **soupe trop l.** watery soup
3 *Fin (déterminé ▸ créance)* liquid; **dette l.** liquid debt; **peu l.** illiquid
4 *(argent)* **argent l.** cash
5 *Ling* liquid
NM **1** *(substance fluide)* liquid, fluid; **un l. huileux** an oily liquid; **l. correcteur** correction fluid; **l. de freins** brake fluid; **l. de refroidissement** coolant, coolant fluid; **l. vaisselle** washing-up liquid, *Am* dish soap
2 *(aliment)* fluid; **pour le moment, ne lui donnez que des liquides** only give him/her fluids for the moment
3 *Physiol* fluid; **l. amniotique** amniotic fluid; **l. céphalo-rachidien** spinal fluid
4 *(espèces)* cash; **je n'ai pas de l.** I haven't got any cash (on me); **payer en l.** to pay cash
NF *Ling* liquid (consonant)

liquider [3] [likide] VT **1** *Fin & Jur (marchandises, société, biens)* to liquidate; *(succession, compte)* to settle; *(dette)* to settle, to pay off; *Bourse (position)* to liquidate
2 *Com (volontairement ▸ stock)* to sell off, to clear; *(▸ commerce)* to close down, *Am* to close out; **on liquide** *(sur la vitrine d'un magasin)* closing down sale, everything must go
3 *Fam (éliminer ▸ problème)* to get rid of, to scrap
4 *(expédier ▸ travail)* to finish off; *(▸ client)* to deal with (quickly); *(▸ affaire)* to settle
5 *Fam (nourriture)* to scoff, to guzzle; *(boisson)* to sink, to down
6 *Fam (tuer)* to liquidate, to bump off

liquidité [likidite] NF *Chim & Fin* liquidity; **l. du portefeuille** portfolio liquidity
• **liquidités** NFPL *Fin* liquid assets; **liquidités excédentaires** excess liquidities; **liquidités obligatoires** mandatory liquid assets

liquoreux, -euse [likɔrø, -øz] ADJ syrupy

lire[1] [lir] NF *(monnaie)* lira

LIRE[2] **[106]** [lir] VT **1** *(texte, thermomètre, carte)* to read; **avez-vous des choses à l. pour le voyage?** have you got something to read for the journey?; **à l. ce mois-ci** this month's selection; **l. attentivement la notice** *(sur l'emballage d'un médicament)* read instructions carefully; **je l'ai lu dans le magazine** I read (about) it in the magazine; **vous êtes beaucoup lu** many people read your works; **elle a beaucoup lu** she's well read; **en espérant vous l. bientôt** *(dans la correspondance)* hoping to hear from you soon; **lu et approuvé** *(sur un contrat)* read and approved; **allemand lu et parlé** *(dans un curriculum)* fluent German; **il faut l. 50 au lieu de 500** 500 should read 50
2 *(déceler)* to read; **on lisait la déception dans ses yeux** you could read *or* see the disappointment in his/her eyes; **l. les lignes de la main à qn** to read sb's palm; **l. l'avenir dans le marc de café** ≃ to read (the future in the) tea leaves
3 *(interpréter)* to interpret; **on peut l. son rapport de deux façons** his/her report can be interpreted *or* read in two ways
4 *Ordinat (disquette)* to read; *(signes)* to sense; *(images)* to scan
USAGE ABSOLU **apprendre à l.** to learn to read; **elle lit bien maintenant** she can read well now; **l. sur les lèvres** to lip-read; *Fig* **l. entre les lignes** to read between the lines
• **lire dans** VT IND **l. dans les pensées de qn** to read sb's thoughts *or* mind
VPR **se lire 1** *(être déchiffré)* to read; **ça se lit facilement** it's easy to read; **ce roman se lit en une soirée** this novel can be read in an evening; **l'hébreu se lit de droite à gauche** Hebrew reads *or* you read Hebrew from right to left **2** *(apparaître)* to show; **l'inquiétude se lisait sur son visage** anxiety showed on *or* was written all over his/her face

lis [lis] NM **1** *Bot* lily; **l. d'eau** water lily; **l. des vallées** lily of the valley; **un teint de l.** a lily-white complexion **2** *Zool* **l. de mer** sea lily

lisait *etc voir* **lire**[2]

Lisbonne [lisbɔn] NF Lisbon

liseré [lizre], **liséré** [lizere] NM edging

liseron [lizrɔ̃] NM bindweed, *Spéc* convolvulus

liseur, -euse [lizœr, -øz] NM,F reader
• **liseuse** NF **1** *(veste)* bed jacket **2** *(couvre-livre)* dust jacket **3** *(lampe)* reading light

lisibilité [lizibilite] NF *(d'une écriture)* legibility; *(d'un texte, d'un fichier informatique)* readability

lisible [lizibl] ADJ **1** *(écriture, signe)* legible; *Ordinat* **l. par ordinateur** machine-readable **2** *(roman)* readable

lisiblement [liziblәmɑ̃] ADV legibly

lisière [lizjer] NF **1** *(d'une forêt)* edge **2** *Tex* selvage, selvedge

lissage [lisaʒ] NM **1** *Tech (de papier)* glazing; *(d'un cuir)* sleeking; *Tex* smoothing **2** *Écon & Math* smoothing (out) **3** *Ordinat* **l. de courbes/des caractères** curve/character smoothing

lissant, -e [lisɑ̃, -ɑ̃t] ADJ softening, smoothing

lisse [lis] ADJ *(planche, peau, pâte)* smooth; *(che-*

veux, fourrure) sleek; (pneu) bald; rendre qch l. to smooth sth (down)

NF Naut (membrures) ribband; (garde-fou) handrail

lisser [3] [lise] VT (barbe, mèche) to smooth (down); (nappe, feuille) to smooth out; (plumes) to preen; Tech (papier) to glaze; (cuir) to sleek; Tex to smooth; le canard lissait sa queue the duck was preening its tail

VPR se lisser se l. la moustache/les plumes to preen one's moustache/its feathers

lisseur, -euse [lisœr, -øz] NM,F Tex smoother

NM Ordinat l. de fontes font smoother

listage [listaʒ] NM Offic listing

liste [list] NF 1 (énumération ▸ de noms, de chiffres) list; faire ou dresser une l. to make (out) or to draw up a list; tu as la l. des courses (à faire)? have you got the shopping list?; j'ai fait la l. des avantages et des inconvénients I have listed the or made a list of the pros and cons; tu n'es pas sur la l. you're not on the list, your name isn't listed; la l. des invités the guest list; l. d'adresses mailing list, address list; l. d'attente waiting list; l. civile civil list; Com l. de colisage packing list; l. de contrôle checklist; Com l. de diffusion mailing list; Ordinat distribution or discussion or mailing list; l. d'envoi mailing list; Mus l. de lecture playlist; l. de mariage wedding list; l. de naissance = list of presents requested by the parents of a newborn baby; l. noire blacklist; elle est sur la l. noire she has been blacklisted; l. ouverte/close open/closed list; CanJoual l. de paie payroll▫; l. de(s) prix price list; l. de publipostage mailing list; Tél être sur l. rouge Br to be ex-directory, Am to have an unlisted number; Com l. des tarifs price list, tariff

2 Pol l. électorale electoral roll; être inscrit sur les listes électorales to be on the electoral roll; la l. d'opposition the list of opposition candidates; l. commune joint list (of candidates); l. bloquée set list of candidates (which electors cannot modify); l. panachée = ballot paper in which a voter votes for candidates from different lists rather than for a list as a whole

3 Ordinat list; l. de fichiers à imprimer print list, print queue; l. rapide draft; l. de signets bookmark list

4 Aviat l. de vérification checklist

listeau, -x [listo], **listel** [listel] NM 1 Archit listel, fillet 2 (d'une pièce de monnaie) rim

lister [3] [liste] VT 1 (mettre en liste) to list 2 Ordinat to list (out)

listériose [listerjoz] NF Méd listeriosis

listing [listiŋ] NM 1 (gén) list 2 Ordinat printout, listing

lit [li] NM 1 (meuble) bed; Fam un canapé qui fait l. a sofa bed; garder le l., rester au l. to stay or to be in bed; aller au l. to go to bed; envoyer/mettre qn au l. to send/to put sb to bed; se mettre au l. to get into bed; maintenant, au l.! come on now, it's bedtime!; tirer ou sortir qn du l. to drag sb out of bed; je ne te tire ou ne te sors pas du l., au moins? I hope I didn't get you out of bed; faire l. à part to sleep in separate beds; faire le l. de qn to make sb's bed; mourir dans son l. to die in one's bed; l. à baldaquin four-poster (bed); l. bateau = bed with curved sides, higher at the ends; l. de jour ou de repos daybed; l. breton ou clos box bed; l. de camp Br camp bed, Am cot; le l. conjugal the marriage bed; l. d'enfant, petit l. Br cot, Am crib; l. à une place single bed; l. à deux places, grand l. double bed; l. pliant folding bed; l. en portefeuille Br apple-pie bed, Am short-sheeted bed; sur son l. de mort on his/her deathbed; sur son l. de douleur on his/her sickbed; lits gigognes stowaway beds; lits jumeaux twin beds; lits superposés bunk beds, bunks; faire le l. de qch to pave the way for sth; en cédant au chantage, on fait le l. du terrorisme by giving in to blackmail, you play into the hands of terrorists; Prov comme on fait son l. on se couche as you make your bed, so you must lie in it

2 Jur (mariage) enfant d'un premier/deuxième l. child of a first/second marriage

3 (couche) bed, layer; l. de feuilles/mousse bed of leaves/moss; posez la viande sur un l. de légumes verts place the meat on a bed of green vegetables

4 Géog bed; la rivière est sortie de son l. the river has burst or overflowed its banks

5 Naut le l. du courant ou de marée the tideway; le l. du vent the set of the wind, the wind's eye

litanie [litani] NF (longue liste) une l. de plaintes a litany of complaints; (avec lui, c'est) toujours la même l.! he never stops moaning!

• **litanies** NFPL Rel litanies

litchi [litʃi] NM 1 (arbre) lychee, litchi 2 (fruit) lychee, litchi, lichee

liteau, -x [lito] NM 1 (sur linge) coloured stripe 2 (tasseau) bracket 3 (bois débité) batten

litée [lite] NF 1 (groupe d'animaux ▸ lions) pride; (▸ loups) pack 2 (portée d'une laie) wild sow's litter

literie [litri] NF bedding

lithiase [litjaz] NF Méd lithiasis

lithine [litin] NF Chim lithia

lithiné [litine] ADJ eau lithinée lithia water

• **lithinés** NMPL lithium salts

lithium [litjɔm] NM Chim lithium

litho [lito] NF Fam (abrév lithographie) litho

lithographe [litɔgraf] NMF lithographer

lithographie [litɔgrafi] NF 1 (procédé) lithography 2 (estampe) lithograph

lithographier [9] [litɔgrafje] VT to lithograph

lithographique [litɔgrafik] ADJ lithographic

lithosphère [litɔsfɛr] NF lithosphere

lithotomie [litɔtɔmi] NF Méd lithotomy

litière [litjer] NF (pour animaux, palanquin) litter; l. pour chats cat litter

litige [litiʒ] NM 1 (différend) dispute; question en l. contentious or controversial question; objet de l. bone of contention 2 Jur dispute; objet ou point de l. subject of the action; être en l. to be in dispute or involved in litigation; l. commercial commercial dispute

litigieux, -euse [litiʒjø, -øz] ADJ contentious, Sout litigious

litote [litɔt] NF understatement, Spéc litotes (UNCOUNT); quand je dis que ce n'est pas fameux, c'est une l. when I say it's not all that good, that's an understatement

litre [litr] NM 1 (unité) litre 2 (bouteille) litre bottle

litron [litrɔ̃] NM Fam bottle of wine▫

littéraire [literɛr] ADJ (style, œuvre, prix) literary; il fera des études littéraires he's going to study literature

NMF (étudiant) arts student; (professeur) arts teacher; (amateur de lettres) literary person

littérairement [litermɑ̃] ADV in literary terms, literarily

littéral, -e, -aux, -ales [literal, -o] ADJ (transcription, traduction) literal, word-for-word; (sens) literal

littéralement [literalmɑ̃] ADV literally; c'est l. du chantage! that's sheer blackmail!

littéralité [literalite] NF literality

littérateur [literatœr] NM Péj hack (writer)

littérature [literatyr] NF 1 la l. (art, œuvres) literature; (activité) writing; faire carrière dans la l. to make a career in writing; Péj les discours des politiciens, c'est de la l. the politicians' speeches are just (a lot of) fine words 2 (documentation) literature, material; il y a toute une l. là-dessus you'll find a lot of material or literature on the topic

littoral, -e, -aux, -ales [litɔral, -o] ADJ coastal, Spéc littoral

NM coastline, Spéc littoral

Lituanie [litɥani] NF la L. Lithuania

lituanien, -enne [litɥanjɛ̃, -ɛn] ADJ Lithuanian

NM (langue) Lithuanian

• **Lituanien, -enne** NM,F Lithuanian

liturgie [lityrʒi] NF liturgy

liturgique [lityrʒik] ADJ liturgical

livarot [livaro] NM livarot (cheese)

livide [livid] ADJ 1 (pâle ▸ visage, teint) pallid, sallow; (▸ malade, blessé) whey-faced 2 Littéraire (d'une couleur plombée) livid

lividité [lividite] NF lividness

living [liviŋ] (pl livings), **living-room** [liviŋrum] (pl living-rooms) NM living room

livrable [livrabl] ADJ 1 (marchandises) which can be delivered; les marchandises ne sont pas livrables à domicile goods cannot be delivered 2 Bourse deliverable

livraison [livrezɔ̃] NF 1 Com (action, marchandises) delivery; payer à la l. to pay cash on delivery; prendre l. de qch to take delivery of sth; faire ou effectuer une l. to make a delivery; l. à domicile (sur panneau) home delivery, door-to-door delivery; l. franco à domicile free home delivery; l. franco par nos soins carriage paid; l. le jour même same-day delivery; l. contre remboursement Br cash on delivery, Am collect on delivery 2 Typ instalment 3 Bourse delivery; l. à terme future delivery, forward delivery

livre [livr] NM 1 (œuvre, partie d'une œuvre) book; parler comme un l. to talk like a book; l. audio audiobook; l. cartonné ou relié hardback (book); l. électronique e-book; l. d'images/de prières picture/prayer book; l. de classe ou scolaire schoolbook, textbook; c'est mon l. de chevet it's a book I read and re-read; l. de cuisine cookbook, Br cookery book; livres pour enfants children's books; l. d'heures book of hours; l. de messe hymn-book, missal; l. de poche paperback (book); l. spécimen desk copy; il est pour moi comme un l. ouvert I can read him like a book

2 le l. (l'édition) the book trade; l'industrie du l. the book industry; les ouvriers du l. the printworkers

3 (registre) book; Compta l. d'achats purchase ledger; l. d'actionnaires register of shareholders; l. de bord logbook; Compta l. de caisse cash book; Compta l. de commandes order book; Compta l. de comptabilité, l. de comptes (account) book, ledger; Compta l. des créanciers accounts payable ledger; Compta l. des débiteurs accounts receivable ledger; Compta l. de dépenses cash book; Mktg l. d'échantillons sample book; Compta l. d'échéance bill book; Compta l. des effets à payer bills payable ledger; Compta l. des effets à recevoir bills receivable ledger; Compta l. des entrées purchase ledger; Jur l. foncier Land Register; Compta l. des inventaires stock book; Compta l. journal daybook, journal; l. d'or visitors' book; Ordinat guestbook; Compta l. de paie pay ledger; Compta l. de petite caisse petty cash book; Compta l. des réclamations claims book; Compta l. des rendus returns ledger; Compta l. des sorties sales ledger; Compta l. de trésorerie générale general cash book; Compta l. des ventes sales ledger; Compta grand l. ledger

4 Pol l. blanc white paper

NF 1 (unité de poids) half a kilo, ≃ pound; Can pound 2 Fin pound; ça coûte trois livres it costs three pounds; Anciennement l. irlandaise Irish pound, punt; l. sterling pound (sterling) 3 Hist livre

• **à livre ouvert** ADV at sight; elle lit/traduit le grec à l. ouvert she can read/translate Greek at sight

livre-cassette [livrəkaset] (pl livres-cassettes) NM audio book

livrée [livre] NF 1 (de domestique) livery; chauffeur en l. liveried chauffeur 2 Zool (pelage) coat; (plumage) plumage

livre-jeu [livrəʒø] (pl livres-jeux) NM activity book

livre-journal [livrəʒurnal] (pl livres-journaux [-o]) NM day book

LIVRER [3] [livre]

VT
- to hand over 1
- to give away 2
- to deliver 3, 4

VPR
- to give oneself up 1, 4
- to confide 2
- to hold 3
- to conduct 3
- to be engaged in 3
- to abandon oneself to 4

VT 1 (abandonner ▸ personne, pays, ville) to hand over; l. qn à la justice to deliver or to hand over sb to the authorities; vous le livrez à la mort you are sending him to his death; il a livré son complice à la police he handed his accomplice over to the police; le pays est livré à la corruption the country has been given over to or has sunk into corruption; son corps fut livré aux flammes his/

her body was committed to the flames; **bateau livré à la tempête** boat at the mercy of the storm; **être livré à soi-même** to be left to oneself *or* to one's own devices

2 *(révéler)* **l. un secret** to give away *or* to betray a secret; **l'épave du Titanic n'a pas encore livré tous ses secrets** the wreck of the Titanic still hasn't given up *or* yielded all its secrets; **dans ses romans, elle livre peu d'elle-même** she doesn't reveal much about herself in her novels

3 *Com (article, commande)* to deliver; *(client)* to deliver to; **l. qch à domicile** to deliver sth *(to the customer's home)*; **nous livrons à domicile** *(sur panneau)* we deliver to your door; **livré franco domicile** delivered free; **nous vous livrerons** *ou* **vous serez livré demain** you will receive delivery tomorrow

4 *Fin & Bourse* to deliver; **l. à terme fixe** to deliver at a fixed term; **prime pour l.** seller's option; **vente à l.** sale for delivery

5 *(locutions)* **l. bataille** *ou* **combat (à)** to wage *or* to do battle (with); **l. passage à** to make way for

VPR se livrer 1 *(se rendre)* to give oneself up **(à** to); **se l. à la police** to give oneself up to the police

2 *(faire des confidences)* to confide **(à** in); **elle ne se livre jamais** she never confides in anybody, she never opens up

3 se l. à *(faire ▸ enquête)* to hold, to conduct; *(▸ recherches, chantage)* to be engaged in; *(▸ suppositions)* to make; **se l. à l'étude** to devote oneself to one's studies; **elle s'est livrée à des commentaires désobligeants** she made some rather insulting remarks

4 se l. à *(s'abandonner à ▸ débauche)* to abandon oneself to; *(▸ sentiment)* to give oneself up to; **se l. à la violence** to commit acts of violence; **une fois seul, je me livrai à ma peine** as soon as I found myself alone, I gave way to my sorrow

5 *Littéraire* **se l. à** *(amant)* to give *or* to offer oneself to

livresque [livrɛsk] **ADJ** *(connaissances)* acquired from books; *(esprit, exposé)* bookish

livret [livrɛ] **NM 1** *(carnet)* notebook

2 *Banque* **l. (de caisse) d'épargne** savings book, passbook; **l. de compte** bank book; **l. de dépôt** deposit book, passbook; **l. d'épargne logement** *Br* ≃ building society passbook, *Am* ≃ savings and loan association passbook; **compte sur l.** savings account

3 *Jur* **l. de famille** *ou* **de mariage** family record book *(in which dates of births and deaths are registered)*

4 *Scol* **l. scolaire** school report (book)

5 *Mil* **l. militaire** army *or* military record

6 libretto

7 *Suisse* multiplication table

livreur, -euse [livrœr, -øz] **NM,F** deliveryman, *f* deliverywoman

LJM *Com (abrév écrite* **livraison le jour même***)* same-day delivery

LMD [ɛlɛmde] **ADJ** *Univ (abrév* **licence, master, doctorat***)* **système (européen) L.** European Bachelors, Masters, Doctorate system *(aimed at standardizing university qualifications across the EU)*

LOA [ɛlɔa] **NF** *Com (abrév* **location avec option d'achat***)* lease financing

lob [lɔb] **NM** *Sport* lob; **faire un l.** to hit a lob, to lob; **l. lifté** topspin lob

lobby [lɔbi] *(pl* **lobbys** *ou* **lobbies***)* **NM** lobby, pressure group

lobbying [lɔbiiŋ], **lobbyisme** [lɔbiism] **NM** lobbying

lobbyiste, lobbyist [lɔbiist] **NMF** lobbyist

lobe [lɔb] **NM 1** *Anat & Bot* lobe; **l. de l'oreille** earlobe **2** *Archit* foil

lobé, -e [lɔbe] **ADJ 1** *Bot* lobed **2** *Archit* foiled

lobectomie [lɔbɛktɔmi] **NF** *Méd* lobectomy

lobélie [lɔbeli] **NF** *Bot* lobelia

lober [3] [lɔbe] *Sport* **VT** to lob

VI to lob

lobotomie [lɔbɔtɔmi] **NF** lobotomy; **on lui a fait une l.** he's/she's been lobotomized

lobulaire [lɔbylɛr] **ADJ** lobular

lobule [lɔbyl] **NM** lobule

local, -e, -aux, -ales [lɔkal, -o] **ADJ** *(anesthésie, élu, radio)* local; *(averses)* localized

NM 1 *(à usage déterminé)* premises; **l. d'habitation** domestic premises; **l. professionnel** premises used for professional purposes; **locaux commerciaux** *ou* **à usage commercial** business premises **2** *(sans usage déterminé)* place; **je cherche un l. pour faire une fête** I'm looking for a place to hold a party **3** *Can Tél* extension

• **locale NF** *Journ* local news

> Il faut noter que le nom anglais **local** ne désigne jamais une pièce ou un bâtiment.

localement [lɔkalmɑ̃] **ADV 1** *(à un endroit)* locally **2** *(par endroits)* in places; **demain, le ciel sera l. nuageux** tomorrow there will be patchy cloud *or* it will be cloudy in places

localier [lɔkalje] **NM** *Journ* local affairs correspondent

localisable [lɔkalizabl] **ADJ** localizable

localisation [lɔkalizasjɔ̃] **NF 1** *(détection, emplacement)* location; *(d'un appel téléphonique)* tracing

2 *Astron* location, tracking; *(limitation)* localization, confinement

3 *Anat* **l. cérébrale** cerebral localization

4 *Ordinat* **l. de logiciel** software localization

localisé, -e [lɔkalize] **ADJ 1** *(déterminé)* located **2** *(limité)* local, localized; **combats localisés** localized fighting

localiser [3] [lɔkalize] **VT 1** *(situer)* to locate; *(appel téléphonique)* to trace; **il a fallu l. la fuite** we had to locate the leak **2** *(limiter)* to confine, to localize **3** *Ordinat* to localize

localité [lɔkalite] **NF** *(petite)* village; *(moyenne)* small town; **dans toute la l.** throughout the town, all over town

locataire [lɔkatɛr] **NMF** *(d'un appartement, d'une maison)* tenant; *(d'une chambre chez le propriétaire)* lodger; *Jur* **l. (à bail)** lessee

locateur, -euse [lɔkatœr, -øz] **NM,F** *Jur* lessor

locatif, -ive [lɔkatif, -iv] **ADJ 1** *(concernant le locataire, la chose louée)* **le marché l.** the property rental market; **réparations locatives** repairs incumbent upon the tenant; **valeur locative** rental value **2** *Suisse (habitation)* to rent, rental *(avant n)*; **immeuble l.** rented apartment building **3** *Ling* **préposition locative** locative preposition

NM 1 *Ling* locative (case) **2** *Suisse (immeuble)* rented apartment building

location [lɔkasjɔ̃] **NF 1** *(par le propriétaire ▸ d'un logement)* renting (out), *esp Br* letting; *(▸ de matériel, d'appareils)* renting (out), rental, *esp Br* hiring (out); *(▸ de costumes, de skis)* rental, *esp Br* hire; *(▸ d'un navire, d'un avion)* leasing; **l. de voitures** car rental, *Br* car hire

2 *(par le locataire ▸ d'un logement)* renting; *(▸ d'une machine)* renting, *esp Br* hiring; *(▸ d'un navire, d'un avion)* leasing; **l. avec option d'achat** lease financing

3 *(logement)* rented accommodation; **désolé, nous n'avons pas de locations** sorry, we have no accommodation for rent; **l. meublée** furnished accommodation

4 *(réservation)* booking; *Cin* **l. en bloc** block booking

5 *(période)* lease; **(contrat de) l. de deux ans** two-year rental *or* lease *or* tenancy agreement

6 *(prix ▸ d'un logement)* rent; *(▸ d'un appareil)* rental

• **en location ADJ être en l.** *(locataire)* to be renting; *(appartement)* to be available for rent, to be up for rent; **j'ai un appartement, mais il est en l.** *(déjà loué)* I've got a *Br* flat *or Am* apartment but it is rented out **ADV donner** *ou* **mettre une maison en l.** to rent (out) *or* to let a house; **prendre une maison en l.** to rent a house

> Il faut noter que le nom anglais **location** est un faux ami. Il signifie **endroit, emplacement.**

location-gérance [lɔkasjɔ̃ʒerɑ̃s] *(pl* **locations-gérances***)* **NF** *Com* = agreement with a liquidator to manage a company in liquidation

locative [lɔkativ] *voir* **locatif**

loch [lɔk] **NM 1** *Géog* loch **2** *Naut* log

loche [lɔʃ] **NF 1** *Ich (de rivière)* loach; *(de mer)* rockling **2** *(limace)* slug **3** *très Fam (sein)* tit, boob

locked-in syndrome [lɔktinsɛ̃drom] **NM** *Méd* locked-in syndrome

lock-out [lɔkaut] **NM INV** *Ind* lockout

lock-outer [3] [lɔkaute] **VT** *Ind* to lock out

locks [lɔks] **NFPL** *Fam* dreads, dreadlocks▫

lock-up [lɔkœp] **NM INV** *Aut* lock-up

loco [loko] **NF** *Fam (abrév* **locomotive***)* loco

locomoteur, -trice [lɔkɔmɔtœr, -tris] **ADJ 1** *Tech* locomotive *(avant n)* **2** *Anat* locomotive *(avant n)*, locomotor *(avant n)*; **ataxie locomotrice** locomotor ataxia

NM motor unit

• **locomotrice NF** *Rail* electric engine

locomotion [lɔkɔmɔsjɔ̃] **NF** locomotion

locomotive [lɔkɔmɔtiv] **NF 1** *Tech* locomotive, (railway) engine **2** *Fam (d'un parti, d'une économie)* driving force **3** *Sport* pacemaker, pacesetter

locomotrice [lɔkɔmɔtris] *voir* **locomoteur**

locus [lɔkys] **NM INV** *Biol* locus

locuteur, -trice [lɔkytœr, -tris] **NM,F** *Ling* speaker; **l. natif** native speaker

locution [lɔkysjɔ̃] **NF 1** *(expression)* phrase, locution; **une l. figée** *ou* **toute faite** a set phrase, an idiom **2** *Gram* phrase; **l. adverbiale/nominale** adverbial/noun phrase

locutrice [lɔkytris] *voir* **locuteur**

loden [lɔdɛn] **NM 1** *Tex* loden **2** *(manteau)* loden coat

lodge [lɔdʒ] **NF** lodge *(hotel)*

lœss [løs] **NM** loess, löss

lof [lɔf] **NM** *Naut* windward side; **aller au l.** to luff; **virer l. pour l.** to wear

lofer [3] [lɔfe] **VI** *Naut* to luff

loft [lɔft] **NM** loft (conversion)

logarithme [lɔgaritm] **NM** logarithm; **l. népérien** *ou* **naturel** natural logarithm

logarithmique [lɔgaritmik] **ADJ** logarithmic

loge [lɔʒ] **NF 1** *(d'artiste)* dressing room; *(de candidats)* exam room; *Belg* **l. foraine** stall

2 *(de concierge, de gardien)* lodge

3 *(de francs-maçons)* lodge; **la Grande L.** the Grand Lodge

4 *Théât* box; **premières/secondes loges** dress/upper circle boxes; *Fig* **être aux premières loges** to have a ringside *or* front seat

5 *Archit* loggia

6 *Biol & Bot* loculus

logeable [lɔʒabl] **ADJ cet appartement est l., je suppose** I suppose I/we/*etc* could live in this *Br* flat *or Am* apartment; **c'est l. dans le placard** there's room for it in the cupboard

logement [lɔʒmɑ̃] **NM 1** *(habitation)* accommodation *(UNCOUNT)*; **un l. de trois pièces** *(appartement)* a three-room *Br* flat *or Am* apartment; *(maison)* a three-room house; **chercher un l.** to look for accommodation *or* somewhere to live; **ils ont construit des logements pour leurs employés** they have built accommodation for their employees; **l. locatif** rented accommodation; **logements sociaux** *Br* local authority housing, council housing, *Am* housing projects

2 *Mil (chez l'habitant)* billet; *(sur une base)* (married) quarters

3 *(hébergement)* housing *(UNCOUNT)*; **la crise du l.** the housing shortage

4 *Tech* housing, casing

LOGER [17] [lɔʒe]

VT
- to put up **1**
- to accommodate **3**
- to put **3, 4**
- to find accommodation for **2**
- to track down **5**

VI
- to live **1**
- to stay **2**

VPR
- to find somewhere to live **1**
- to lodge itself **3**
- to find somewhere to stay **2**
- to fit **5**

VT 1 *(recevoir ▸ ami, visiteur)* to put up; **nous pouvons vous l. pour une nuit ou deux** we can put you up for a night or two; **je suis bien/mal logé** I'm comfortably/badly housed; **être logé, nourri et blanchi** to get board and lodging with laundry (service) included; *Fig* **on est tous logés à la même enseigne** we're all in the same boat

2 *(trouver un logement pour ▸ gén)* to find accommodation for; *(▸ soldats)* to billet; **on a logé le régiment chez l'habitant** the regiment was billeted with the local population

3 *(contenir ▸ personnes)* to accommodate; *(▸ choses)* to put; **l'école peut l. cinq cents élèves** the school can accommodate five hundred pupils; **où allons-nous l. tout ça?** where are we going to put all that stuff?; **le placard peut l. trois grosses valises** the cupboard can take *or* hold three big suitcases

4 *(mettre)* to put; **j'ai réussi à l. ton sac entre les deux valises** I managed to put *or* fit your bag between the two cases; **l. une balle dans la tête à qn** to put a bullet in sb's head; **l. une idée dans la tête à qn** to put an idea into sb's head

5 *Fam (repérer)* to track down

VI 1 *(habiter)* to live; **où logez-vous?** where do you live?; **elle loge chez sa tante/à l'hôtel/rue de la Paix** she lives with her aunt/in a hotel/on rue de la Paix; **les étudiants logent tous en cité** all the students are accommodated at *or* live in halls of residence

2 *(séjourner)* to stay; **les touristes logeaient chez l'habitant** the tourists were staying in boarding houses *or* in bed-and-breakfasts; **les soldats logeaient chez l'habitant** the soldiers were billeted with the local population

VPR se loger 1 *(à long terme ▸ couple, famille)* to find somewhere to live; **ils se marient dans une semaine et n'ont pas encore trouvé à se l.** they're getting married in a week and they still haven't found anywhere to live

2 *(provisoirement ▸ touriste, étudiant)* to find accommodation *or* somewhere to stay; **nous avons trouvé à nous l.** we've found accommodation, we've found somewhere to stay

3 *(pénétrer)* to lodge itself; **un éclat de verre s'était logé dans son œil droit** a splinter of glass had lodged itself in his/her right eye; **mon ballon est allé se l. entre l'antenne de télé et la cheminée** my ball got stuck *or* lodged itself between the television *Br* aerial *or Am* antenna and the chimney

4 *(se mettre)* **il s'est logé une balle dans la tête** he put a bullet through his head, he shot himself in the head

5 *Tech* to fit, to be housed

logeur, -euse [lɔʒœr, -øz] **NM,F** landlord, *f* landlady *(of furnished apartments)*

loggia [lɔdʒja] **NF** loggia

logiciel, -elle [lɔʒisjɛl] **ADJ** software *(avant n)*

NM software; **ils viennent de sortir un nouveau l.** they've just brought out a new software package; **l. d'application** application *or* software package; **l. auteur** authoring software; **l. de base** systems teaching software; **l. de bureautique** business software; **l. client** client software; **l. de communication** communications package, communications software; **l. de compression de données** data compression software; **l. de comptabilité** accounts software; **l. de conception assistée par ordinateur** computer-aided design package; **l. contributif** shareware; **l. de conversion** conversion software; **l. de courrier électronique** e-mail software; **l. de décompression** decompression software, decompressor; **l. de dessin** art package, drawing program; **l. du domaine public** public domain software; **l. espion** spyware; **l. d'exploitation** operating system software; **l. de filtrage** filtering software; **l. grapheur** graphics software; **l. graphique** illustration software; **l. intégré** integrated software; **l. de jeux** games program; **l. de lecture de nouvelles** news reader; **l. libre** freeware, open source (software); **l. de mise en page** desktop publishing package; **l. multi-utilisateur** multi-user software; **l. de navigation** browser; **l. de PAO** DTP software; **l. de planification** scheduler; **l. de présentation** presentation software; **l. public** public domain software; **l. de reconnaissance de caractères** OCR software, character recognition software; **l. de reconnaissance vocale** voice recognition software; **l. de réseau** network software; **l. de SGBD** DBMS software; **l. système** system software; **l. de système d'exploitation** operating system software; **l. de télémaintenance** remote-access software; **l. de traitement de texte** word-processing software, word-processing software package, WP package; **l. utilisateur** user software; **l. utilitaire** utility program

logicien, -enne [lɔʒisjɛ̃, -ɛn] **NM,F** logician

logique [lɔʒik] **ADJ 1** *Phil* logical

2 *(cohérent, clair)* sensible, logical; **soyons logiques** let's be logical *or* sensible about this; **tu n'es pas l.!** you're being illogical!; **ce n'est pas l.** it doesn't make sense; **sois l. avec toi-même, tu veux qu'elle vienne ou pas?** you can't have it both ways, do you want her to come or not?

3 *(normal, compréhensible)* logical, normal, natural; **c'est dans la suite l. des événements** it's part of the normal course of events; **il est tout à fait l. que tu n'aies pas envie de le revoir** it's quite natural that you don't want to see him again

4 *Ordinat* logic

NF 1 *Phil* logic; **l. déductive** deductive reasoning, deduction; **l. floue** fuzzy logic; **l. formelle** *ou* **pure** formal logic **2** *(cohérence)* logic; **ton raisonnement manque de l.** your argument isn't very logical *or* consistent; **nous sommes entrés dans une l. de guerre** war is inevitable, war is the next logical step; **il n'y a aucune l. là-dedans** none of this makes sense; **c'est dans la l. des choses** it's in the nature of things; **en toute l., voilà ce qui devrait se passer** logically, that's what ought to happen **3** *Ordinat* logic; **l. binaire/câblée** binary/wired logic

logiquement [lɔʒikmɑ̃] **ADV 1** *(avec cohérence)* logically; **procédons l.** let's proceed logically **2** *(normalement)* **l., il devrait déjà être là** he should be here by now

logis [lɔʒi] **NM** *Littéraire* dwelling, abode; **il n'y avait personne au l.** there was nobody (at) home

logistique [lɔʒistik] **ADJ 1** *Mil* logistic, logistical **2** *(organisationnel)* **les élus locaux apportent un important soutien l. au parti** local councillors make an important contribution to the running of the party

NF logistics *(singulier)*; *Mktg* **l. commerciale** marketing mix

logo [logo] **NM** logo

logomachie [lɔgɔmaʃi] **NF 1** *(discussion)* logomachy, semantic argument **2** *(suite de mots creux)* bombast

logopède [lɔgɔpɛd], **logopédiste** [lɔgɔpedist] **NMF** *Belg & Suisse* speech therapist

logorrhée [lɔgɔre] **NF** logorrhoea

logotisé, -e [lɔgɔtize] **ADJ** *Mktg* branded

LOI [lwa] **NF A. 1** *(règles publiques)* law; **les lois de notre pays** the law of the land; **selon la l. en vigueur** according to the law as it stands; **la l. salique** the Salic law

2 *Jur (décret)* act, law; **la l. Dupont a été votée la nuit dernière** the Dupont Act was passed last night; **l. du 28 juillet 1882, défense d'afficher** *(sur un mur)* ≃ billposters will be prosecuted; *Com* **l. antitrust** antitrust *or Br* anti-monopoly law; *Journ & TV* **l. de censure** censorship law; **l. de conservation** conservation law; **l. constitutionnelle** *(loi de révision de la constitution)* constitutional amendment; **la l. constitutionnelle** *(la constitution)* the Constitution; **l. d'exception** emergency legislation; **l. de finances** Finance Act; **l. d'habilitation** enabling Act; **l. Informatique et Libertés** = French law regulating the protection of computer privacy, *Br* ≃ Data Protection Act; **l. martiale** martial law; **l. d'ordre public** public policy; **l. d'orientation** = act laying down the basic principles for government action in a given field; **l. de pleins pouvoirs** enabling act; **l. de police** public order act; **l. référendaire** = laws passed by means of a referendum; **l. répressive** criminal law; **lois scélérates** pernicious legislation; *Hist* **la l. du talion** lex talionis; *Fig* **dans ce cas-là, c'est la l. du talion** in that case, it's an eye for an eye (and a tooth for a tooth)

3 *(légalité)* **la l.** the law; **ça devrait être interdit par la l.!** there ought to be a law against it!; **je suis désolé mais c'est la l.** I'm sorry but that's the law *or* the law's the law; **avoir la l. pour soi** to have the law on one's side; **tomber sous le coup de la l.** to be covered by the law

B. 1 *(devoir)* rule; **les lois de la guerre** the laws of war; **les lois de l'hospitalité/du savoir-vivre** the rules of hospitality/etiquette; **les lois de l'honneur** the code of honour; **se faire une l. de faire qch** to make a point of doing sth

2 *Rel* law; **la l. divine** divine law; **la l. mosaïque** *ou* **de Moïse** the Mosaic Law

C. 1 *(domination)* law, rule; **tenir qn/un pays sous sa l.** to rule sb/a country; **dicter** *ou* **imposer sa l., faire la** *ou* **sa l.** to lay down the law; **c'est elle qui fait la l. ici** she's the one who lays down the law around here; **l'équipe de Bordeaux a dicté** *ou* **imposé sa l. à celle de Marseille** Bordeaux dominated Marseilles

2 *(règles d'un milieu)* **la l. du milieu** the law of the underworld; **c'est la l. de la nature** it's nature's way; **la l. de la jungle** the law of the jungle; **dans la cour de récréation c'est la l. du plus fort** it's the law of the jungle in the *Br* playground *or Am* schoolyard

D. *PRINCIPE* law; **la l. de la gravitation universelle** *ou* **de la pesanteur** *ou* **de la chute des corps** the law of gravity; **les lois de Mendel** Mendel's laws; *Hum* **la l. du moindre effort** the line of least resistance; **la l. de l'offre et de la demande** the law of supply and demand; **les lois de la perspective** the laws of perspective; **l. de probabilité** law of probability; **l. des rendements décroissants** law of diminishing returns

loi-cadre [lwakadr] *(pl* **lois-cadres)** **NF** parent act

LOIN [lwɛ̃] **ADV 1** *(dans l'espace)* far (away); **ils habitent l.** they live a long way away; **c'est l. l'hôtel?** is the hotel far away?, is it far to the hotel?; **en avion ce n'est pas l.** it's not far by plane; **ils se sont garés un peu plus l.** they parked a bit further on; **le prisonnier s'est échappé mais il n'est pas allé bien l.** the prisoner escaped but he didn't get very far; **il n'y a pas l. entre Paris et Versailles** it's not far from Paris to Versailles; **elle est l. derrière nous** she is far *or* way behind us; **aussi l. (que)** as far (as); **aussi l. que l'œil peut porter** as far as the eye can see; **moins l. (que)** not as *or* so far (as); **plus l. (que)** further *or* farther (than); **voir plus l.** *(dans un texte)* see below; **cette arme porte l.** this weapon has a long range

2 *(dans le temps)* far (away), a long way off; **Noël n'est plus très l.** Christmas isn't very far away now; **c'est l. tout ça!** *(dans le passé)* that was a long time ago!, that seems a long way off now!; *(dans le futur)* that's a long way off!

3 *Fig* far; **il y a l. entre ce qu'on dit et ce qu'on fait** there's a big difference between words and deeds; **de là à lui faire confiance, il y a l.** there is a big difference between that and trusting him/her; **d'ici à l'accuser de mensonge, il n'y a pas l.** that comes close to calling him/her a liar; **aller l.** to go far; **il est brillant, il ira l.** he's brilliant, he'll go far; **aller un peu** *ou* **trop l.** to go (a bit) too far; **là, tu vas un peu l.** come on now, you're taking things a bit far *or* you're going a bit too far; **ça va (très) l. ce que vous dites** that's taking things a bit far; **j'irai plus l. et je dirai que...** I'd go even further and say that...; **étouffons l'affaire, il ne faut pas que ça aille plus l.** let's hush up this business, it mustn't go any further; **une analyse qui ne va pas très l.** an analysis lacking in depth; **il ne va pas aller bien l. sans argent** he won't get very far without any money; **avec 20 euros, on ne va pas l.** you can't get very far on 20 euros; **cette affaire risque de vous mener l.** this affair could land you in serious trouble; **ces quelques preuves ne vont pas nous mener très l.** these few scraps of evidence won't get us very far; **ce conflit peut nous entraîner très l.** this dispute could lead to a very serious situation; **la possession de stupéfiants, ça peut mener l.** possession of drugs can lead to serious trouble; **je trouve que vous poussez un peu l.** I think you're going a bit far; **voir l.** to be far-sighted; **elle ne voit pas plus l. que le bout de son nez** she can't see further than the end of her nose; *Prov* **il y a l. de la coupe aux lèvres** there's many a slip 'twixt cup and lip

4 *Suisse (absent)* **il est l.** he's not here

• **au loin ADV** in the distance; **le bateau disparut au l.** the boat disappeared into the distance; **on voyait, au l., une rangée de peupliers** a row of poplars could be seen in the far distance *or* far off in the distance

• **d'aussi loin que** CONJ **il lui fit signe d'aussi l. qu'il la vit** he signalled to her as soon as he saw her in the distance; **d'aussi l. que je me souvienne** as far back as I can remember

• **de loin** ADV **1** *(depuis une grande distance)* from a long way, from a distance; **je vois mal de l.** I can't see very well from a distance; **la tour se voyait de (très) l.** the tower could be seen from a long way off; **avec sa chevelure rousse, on la reconnaît de l.** you can recognize her from a long way off thanks to her red hair; **vue de l., cette histoire n'a pas l'air bien grave** from a distance, this business doesn't seem all that serious; **tu verras mieux d'un peu plus l.** you'll see better from a bit further away; **ils sont venus d'assez l. à pied** they came a fair distance *or* quite a long way on foot; **admirer qn de l.** to admire sb at *or* from a distance *or* from afar; **ils sont parents, mais de l.** they are only distantly related; *Fam* **je l'ai vu venir de l.** I saw him coming a mile off **2** *(assez peu)* **il ne s'intéresse que de l. à la politique** he's only slightly interested in politics; **suivre les événements de l.** to follow events from a distance **3** *(de beaucoup)* far and away, by far; **c'est de l. le meilleur cognac** it's far and away *or* it's by far the best brandy; **je le préfère à ses collègues, et de l.** I much prefer him to his colleagues

• **de loin en loin** ADV **1** *(dans l'espace)* at intervals, here and there **2** *(dans le temps)* from time to time, every now and then

• **du plus loin que** CONJ **il lui fit signe du plus l. qu'il l'aperçut** he signalled to him/her as soon as he saw him/her in the distance; **du plus l. qu'il se souvienne** as far back as he can remember

• **loin de** PRÉP **1** *(dans l'espace)* a long way *or* far (away) from; **quand je suis l. de toi** when I'm far (away) from you; **pas l. d'ici** not far from *or* quite close to here; **l. de là** far from there; **c'est assez l. d'ici** it's quite a long way *or* distance from here; **ils vivent l. de l'agitation des villes** they live far away *or* a long way from the hustle and bustle of towns

2 *Fig* far from; **elle est l. d'être bête** she is far from stupid; **je suis encore l. d'avoir fini** I'm still far from finished; **je ne suis pas l. de leur dire le fond de ma pensée** I have a good mind to tell them what I really think; **je ne suis pas l. de penser que...** I've more or less come to the conclusion that...; **j'étais l. de me douter que...** I never imagined...; **vous êtes l. du sujet** you've gone (way) off the subject; **j'étais l. de la vérité, ça a coûté 300 euros!** I was way out (in my calculations), it cost 300 euros!; **l. de moi l'idée de t'accuser** far be it from me to accuse you; **l. de moi cette idée!** nothing could be further from my mind!; **l. de là** far from it; **je ne veux pas, l. de là** I'm not angry with you, far from it; *Prov* **l. des yeux, l. du cœur** out of sight, out of mind

3 *(dans le temps)* a long way (away) from; **la Première Guerre mondiale est bien l. de nous maintenant** the First World War is a long time ago now *or* is a long way away from us now; **nous ne sommes plus l. de la fin de l'année maintenant** we're not far off the end of the year now

4 *(au lieu de)* **l. de m'aider** far from helping me; **l. de leur en vouloir, il leur en était reconnaissant** far from being angry with them, he was very grateful

• **pas loin de** ADV *(presque)* nearly, almost; **il n'est pas l. de midi** it's getting on for midday, it's nearly midday; **ça ne fait pas l. de quatre ans qu'ils sont mariés** they've been married nearly four years

---

lointain, -e [lwɛ̃tɛ̃, -ɛn] ADJ **1** *(dans l'espace)* distant, far-off; *(île)* remote; **il était une fois, dans un pays l....** once upon a time, in a far-off *or* distant land...; **un l. son de flûte** the distant *or* far-off sound of a flute

2 *(dans le temps ▸ passé)* distant, far-off; *(▸ futur)* distant; **mes souvenirs les plus lointains** my earliest recollections; **aux jours lointains de notre enfance** in the far-off days of our childhood; **dans un l. avenir** in the distant *or* remote future

3 *(indirect ▸ parent, cousin)* remote

4 *(absent ▸ air, sourire)* faraway; **je l'ai trouvée un peu lointaine** *(préoccupée)* she seemed to have something on her mind; *(distraite)* I found her rather vague

5 *(dans la pensée ▸ lien, rapport)* remote, distant; *(▸ ressemblance)* vague; **il n'y a qu'un l. rapport entre...** there's only the remotest connection between...

NM **1** *(fond)* **dans le** *ou* **au l.** *(vers l'horizon)* in the distance **2** *Beaux-Arts* **les lointains** the background

loi-programme [lwaprɔgram] *(pl* **lois-programmes)** NF (framework) legislation, *Br* ≃ Command Paper

loir [lwar] NM *Zool* dormouse

Loire [lwar] NF **1** *(fleuve)* **la L.** the (River) Loire **2** *(région)* **la L.** the Loire (area) *or* valley; **les châteaux de la L.** the châteaux of the Loire **3** *(département)* **la L.** Loire

loisible [lwazibl] ADJ **il est l. de...** it is permissible to...; **il vous est tout à fait l. de partir** you are totally at liberty *or* quite entitled to go

loisir [lwazir] NM **1** *(temps libre)* spare time, free time, leisure time; **comment occupez-vous vos heures de l.?** what do you do in your spare time?; **avoir beaucoup de loisirs** to have a lot of spare time; **il consacre tous ses loisirs à l'écriture** he spends all his spare time writing **2** *(possibilité)* **avoir (tout) le l. de** to have the time *or* the opportunity to; **ils ont eu tout le l. de préparer leur réponse** they've had ample time to prepare their answer; **on ne lui a pas donné** *ou* **laissé le l. de s'expliquer** he/she was not allowed (the opportunity) to explain his/her actions

• **loisirs** NMPL *(activités)* leisure *(UNCOUNT)*, spare-time activities; **nous vivons de plus en plus dans une société de loisirs** we live in a society where leisure is taking on more and more importance

• **(tout) à loisir** ADV at leisure; **faites-le (tout) à l.** do it at (your) leisure

lokoum [lɔkum] = **loukoum**

lolette [lɔlɛt] NF *Suisse Br* dummy, *Am* pacifier

lolo [lolo] NM **1** *Fam (lait)* milk **2** *très Fam (sein)* boob, jug

lombago [lɔ̃bago] = **lumbago**

lombaire [lɔ̃bɛr] *Anat* ADJ lumbar
NF lumbar vertebra

lombalgie [lɔ̃balʒi] NF *Méd* lumbago

lombard, -e [lɔ̃bar, -ard] ADJ Lombardic
NM *(dialecte)* Lombard dialect

• **Lombard, -e** NM,F Lombard

Lombardie [lɔ̃bardi] NF **la L.** Lombardy

lombes [lɔ̃b] NFPL *Anat* lower back, *Spéc* lumbus; **douleur dans les l.** lower back pain

lombric [lɔ̃brik] NM *Zool* earthworm, *Spéc* lumbricus

Lomé [lɔme] NF Lomé

londonien, -enne [lɔ̃dɔnjɛ̃, -ɛn] ADJ of/from London, London *(avant n)*; **les bus londoniens** the London buses

• **Londonien, -enne** NM,F Londoner

Londres [lɔ̃dr] NM London; **le Grand L.** Greater London

londrès [lɔ̃drɛs] NM *Vieilli* Havana cigar

LONG, LONGUE [lɔ̃, lɔ̃g]

ADJ	
• long **A1–3, 5, B1–3, 5**	• thin **A4**
• long-standing **B3**	• long-term **B4**
NM	
• in length **1**	

ADJ **A.** *DANS L'ESPACE* **1** *(grand)* long; **une longue rangée d'arbres** a long row of trees; **un vieillard l. et maigre le regardait fixement** an old man, tall and thin, was staring at him; **chat/chien à poil l.** long-haired cat/dog; **ils se servent de longs bâtons** they use long sticks; **l'âne a de longues oreilles** donkeys have long ears; **une fille aux longues jambes** a long-legged girl, a girl with long legs; **avoir de longs bras** to have long arms; **c'est l. de sept mètres** it's seven metres long

2 *Bot (feuille)* elongated; *(tige)* long

3 *(vêtement)* long; **les jupes seront longues cet hiver** this winter, skirts will be (worn) long; **ton jupon est trop l., il dépasse** your slip's too long, it's showing; **à manches longues** long-sleeved; **porter des pantalons longs** to wear long trousers; **une robe longue** a full-length *or* long dress

4 *Culin* thin; **une sauce longue** a thin sauce

5 *Cartes* long; **couleur longue** long suit

B. *DANS LE TEMPS* **1** *(qui dure longtemps)* long; **c'est un travail l. et difficile** it's a long and difficult job; **un l. soupir** a long-drawn *or* lengthy sigh; **boire à longs traits** to drink in long gulps *or* draughts; **de longues négociations** protracted *or* long negotiations; **une longue bataille** a long *or* long drawn-out battle; **je suis fatigué, la journée a été longue** I'm tired, it's been a long day; **je suis restée de longs mois sans nouvelles de lui** I had no word from him for months and months; **dix jours, c'est l.** ten days is a long time; **obligé d'attendre un l. quart d'heure** kept waiting for a good quarter of an hour; **notre émission de ce soir est plus longue que d'habitude** our programme this evening is longer than usual; **une longue explication** *(détaillée)* a long explanation; *(verbeuse)* a long-winded *or* lengthy explanation; **le film est trop l.** the film is too long *or* is overlong; **vous êtes trop l. dans la dernière partie** you are too long-winded *or* too wordy in the last part; **ne sois pas trop longue ou personne ne t'écoutera jusqu'à la fin** don't take too long *or* don't speak for too long or nobody will listen to you all the way through; **les longues soirées d'hiver** the long winter evenings; **arrivé au terme d'une longue vie** (having arrived) at the end of a long life; **chômage de longue durée** long-term unemployment; **j'ai trouvé le temps l.** the time seemed to go (by) really slowly; **ce voyage/discours est l. comme un jour sans pain** this journey/speech seems to be lasting forever *or* dragging on forever; **une attente longue de trois heures** a three-hour wait; *Can* **à l'année/à la journée longue** all year/day long, throughout the year/day

2 *(qui tarde ▸ personne)* **je ne serai pas l.** I won't be long; **ce ne sera pas l.** it won't take long; **qu'est-ce que tu es l.!** you're so slow!, you're taking forever!; **il s'en sortira, mais ce sera l.** he'll recover but it'll take a long time *or* it will be a slow process; **ne soyez pas trop l. à me répondre** don't take too long answering me; **je n'ai pas été longue à comprendre qu'elle mentait** it didn't take me long to see that she was lying; **l'eau est longue à bouillir** the water is taking a long time to boil; **il est l. à venir, ce café!** that coffee's a long time coming!; **être l. à réagir** to be slow to react

3 *(qui existe depuis longtemps)* long, long-standing; **sa longue expérience de journaliste** his/her many years spent *or* his/her long experience as a journalist; **une longue amitié** a long-standing friendship; **un ami de longue date** an old friend, a friend of long standing

4 *(dans le futur)* **à longue échéance, à l. terme** *(prévision)* long-term; **faire des prévisions à longue échéance** to make long-term forecasts; **ce sera rentable à l. terme** it will be profitable in the long term; **à plus ou moins longue échéance** sooner or later; **emprunt à l. terme** long-term loan; **quels sont tes projets à l. terme?** what are your long-term plans?

5 *Ling & Littérature* long; **une voyelle longue** a long vowel; **"a" l.** long "a"

NM **1** *(longueur)* **le terrain a** *ou* **fait 100 mètres de l.** the plot is 100 metres long *or* in length; **une table de deux mètres de l.** a table two metres long; **faire une mine** *ou* **une tête de dix pieds de l.** *(par déconvenue)* to pull a long face; *(par mauvaise humeur)* to have a long face

2 le l. *(vêtements)* long styles; **la mode est au l.** long styles are in fashion

ADV **1** *(avec des vêtements longs)* **elle s'habille l.** she wears long skirts *or* dresses

2 *(beaucoup)* **geste/regard qui en dit l.** eloquent gesture/look; **une remarque qui en dit l. sur ses intentions** a remark which says a lot about *or* speaks volumes about his/her intentions; **elle pourrait vous en dire l. sur cette affaire** she could tell you a few things about this business; **demande-le-lui, il en sait l.** ask him, he knows all about it; **elle en connaît déjà l. sur la vie** she knows a thing or two about life

• **longue** NF **1** *Cartes* long suit; **longue à pique/trèfle** long suit of spades/clubs **2** *Ling & Littérature* long syllable **3** *Mus* long note

• **à la longue** ADV *(avec le temps)* in the long term *or* run, eventually; **à la longue, tout se sait** everything comes out in the end; **tu oublieras tout ceci à la longue** you'll forget all this eventually

• **au long** ADV in full, fully; **elle a écrit le titre au l.** she wrote the title out in full

• **au long de** PRÉP **1** *(dans l'espace)* along; **des touristes flânaient au l. des rues** tourists were wandering lazily down *or* along the streets **2** *(dans le temps)* during; **il s'est aguerri au l. de ces années difficiles** he's become tougher during *or* over these difficult years

• **de long en large** ADV back and forth, up and down; **j'ai arpenté le hall de la gare de l. en large** I paced back and forth across *or* I paced up and down the main hall of the station

• **de tout son long** ADV **tomber de tout son l.** to fall flat on one's face; **il était étendu de tout son l.** he was stretched out at full length

• **en long** ADV lengthwise, lengthways; **fends-les en l.** split them lengthwise *or* down the middle

• **en long, en large et en travers, en long et en large** ADV **1** *(examiner)* from every (conceivable) angle **2** *(raconter)* in the minutest detail, at some considerable length

• **le long de** PRÉP **1** *(horizontalement)* along; **en marchant le l. de la rivière** walking along the river bank **2** *(verticalement ▸ vers le haut)* up; *(▸ vers le bas)* down; **grimper/descendre le l. de la gouttière** to climb up/down the drainpipe

• **tout au long** ADV *(en détail)* in detail; **il nous a fait tout au l. le récit de son entretien** he gave us a detailed description of his interview

• **tout au long de** PRÉP **1** *(dans l'espace)* all along; **les policiers postés tout au l. du parcours** policemen positioned all along the route **2** *(dans le temps)* throughout, all through; **il est resté calme tout au l. de la discussion** he remained calm throughout *or* all through the discussion; **tout au l. de l'année** all year long, throughout the year

• **tout du long** ADV **1** *(dans l'espace)* **nous avons parcouru la rue tout du l.** we travelled the whole length of the street; **ils ont descendu le fleuve tout du l.** they went all the way down the river **2** *(dans le temps)* all along; **il m'a rabâché la même chose tout du l.** he kept on repeating the same thing all along *or* the whole time

• **tout le long de** PRÉP **1** *(dans l'espace)* all (the way) along; **il y a des arbres tout le l. de la route** there are trees all (the way) along the road; **nous avons chanté tout le l. du chemin** we sang all the way **2** *(dans le temps)* throughout, all through; **tout le l. du jour/de la nuit** all day/night long, throughout *or* all through the day/night

longanimité [lɔ̃ganimite] NF *Littéraire* forbearance

longboard [lɔ̃gbɔrd] NM **1** *(planche)* longboard **2** *(sport)* longboarding

long-courrier [lɔ̃kurje] *(pl* **long-courriers)** ADJ **1** *Aviat (vol)* long-distance, long-haul; *(avion)* long-haul **2** *Naut* ocean-going

NM **1** *Aviat* long-haul aircraft; **compagnie de l.** long-haul operator **2** *Naut (navire ▸ marchand)* ocean-going ship *or* freighter; *(▸ avec passagers)* ocean liner, oceaner; *(matelot)* foreign-going seaman

longe [lɔ̃ʒ] NF **1** *(demi-échine)* loin **2** *(lien ▸ pour attacher)* tether; *(▸ pour mener)* lunge

longer [17] [lɔ̃ʒe] VT **1** *(avancer le long de ▸ gén)* to go along, to follow; *(▸ mur, côte)* to follow, to hug; **ils ont longé la plage à pied/à bicyclette** they walked/cycled along the edge of the beach **2** *(border)* to run along(side), to border; **un bois de hêtres longe la route** a beech wood borders the road

longeron [lɔ̃ʒrɔ̃] NM **1** *(en travaux publics)* (longitudinal) girder

2 *Rail (d'un wagon)* (side) frame (member), bar

3 *Aviat (du fuselage)* longeron, longitudinal; *(d'une aile)* spar

4 *Aut* side member *or* rail

longévité [lɔ̃ʒevite] NF **1** *(longue vie ▸ d'une personne, d'une espèce)* longevity **2** *(durée de vie)* life expectancy **3** *(d'un produit, des capitaux)* life

longiligne [lɔ̃ʒiliɲ] ADJ slender

longitude [lɔ̃ʒityd] NF longitude; **par 30° de l. est/ouest** at longitude 30° east/west; **le bureau des Longitudes** = scientific organization founded in 1795, specializing in astronomy and related fields

longitudinal, -e, -aux, -ales [lɔ̃ʒitydinal, -o] ADJ **1** *(en longueur)* lengthwise, lengthways, *Spéc* longitudinal **2** *Électron* longitudinal; **onde longitudinale** longitudinal wave

longitudinalement [lɔ̃ʒitydinalmɑ̃] ADV lengthwise, lengthways, *Spéc* longitudinally

long-métrage *(pl* **longs-métrages), long métrage** [lɔ̃metraʒ] NM feature *or* full-length film

longrine [lɔ̃grin] NF **1** *Constr* longitudinal beam *or* girder *or* member **2** *Rail* longitudinal sleeper

longskate [lɔ̃gsket] NM **1** *(planche)* longboard **2** *(sport)* longboarding

LONGTEMPS [lɔ̃tɑ̃] ADV **1** *(exprimant une durée)* for a long time; **j'ai attendu l. avant d'entrer** I waited for a long time before going in; **ça fait l. que tu attends?** have you been waiting long?; *Ironique* **tu peux attendre l.** you'll have a long wait; **on a l. pensé que...** it was long thought that..., it was thought for a long time that...; **il faut l. pour...** it takes a long time *or* a while to...; **pas de l.** *ou* **d'ici l.** not for a (long) while *or* long time; **on ne le verra pas d'ici l.** we won't see him for a long time *or* while; **je ne pensais pas le revoir de l.** I didn't expect to see him again for a long time *or* while; **aussi l. que tu veux** as long as you wish; **nous avons attendu assez/très/trop l.** we waited long enough/for ages/too long; **moins l. (que)** for a shorter time (than); **plus l. (que)** longer (than); **mettre** *ou* **prendre l.** to take a while *or* a long time; **elle a mis** *ou* **ça lui a pris l.** she took *or* was a long time (over it); **je n'en ai pas pour l.** I won't be long, it won't take me long; **il n'en a plus pour l.** *(pour finir)* he won't be much longer; *(à vivre)* he won't last much longer, he hasn't got much longer to live; *Fam* **d'ici à ce qu'il pleuve, il n'y en a pas pour l.!** it won't be long till the rain starts!□; **avec moi, il ne va pas y en avoir pour l., tu vas voir!** I'll have this sorted out in no time (at all), just you see!; **ça va durer (encore) l.?** *(ton irrité)* is this going to go on for much longer?, have you quite finished?; **il a été absent pendant l.** he was away for a long time; **avant l.** before long; **je ne reviendrai pas avant l.** I won't be back for a long time; **il restera ici encore l.** he'll be here for a while *or* a long time (yet); **l. avant** long *or* a long time before (that), much earlier; **l. après** much later, long after (that), a long time after (that)

2 *(avec "il y a", "depuis")* **il y a l. (de ça)** ages *or* a long time ago; **il n'y a pas l.** not long ago; **il n'y a pas l. qu'elle est partie** she went not long ago; **il y a l. que** *ou* **cela fait l. que nous sommes amis** we've been friends for a long time (now); **il y a l.** *ou* **cela fait l. que je l'ai lu** it's been a long time since I read it; **il y a l. qu'il est mort** he's long dead, he's been dead for a long time; **il y a l. que j'ai arrêté de fumer** I stopped smoking long *or* ages ago; **il y a** *ou* **cela fait l. que je ne l'ai pas vu** it's a long time *or* ages since I saw him; *Fam* **tiens, il y avait l.!** *(qu'on ne t'avait pas vu)* long time no see!; *(que tu n'avais pas parlé de ça)* here we go again!; **nous ne nous sommes pas vus depuis l.** we haven't seen each other for ages *or* for a long time

longue [lɔ̃g] *voir* **long**

longuement [lɔ̃gmɑ̃] ADV **1** *(longtemps)* for a long time; **les jurés ont l. délibéré** the jurors deliberated for a long time; **il a l. insisté pour que je vienne** he kept on insisting that I should come; **parler l. avec qn** to have a (good) long talk with sb **2** *(en détail ▸ expliquer, commenter)* in detail, in depth; *(▸ scruter)* at length; **il faudrait analyser plus l. les personnages** the characters should be analysed in greater detail

longuet, -ette [lɔ̃gɛ, -ɛt] ADJ *Fam* a bit long, a bit on the long side; **il est l., ce film!** it's dragging on a bit, this film!

NM breadstick

longueur [lɔ̃gœr] NF **1** *(dimension)* length; **mesure de l.** linear measurement; **unité de l.** unit of length; **un ruban de 10 cm de l.** *ou* **d'une l. de 10 cm** a ribbon 10 cm long *or* in length; **le jardin est tout en l.** the garden is long and narrow; **un visage tout en l.** a long thin face; **quelle est la l. de l'Amazone?** how long is the Amazon?; **j'ai traversé l'île dans toute sa l.** *(à pied)* I walked the whole length of the island

2 *(unité de mesure)* length; **une l. de fil** a length of cotton

3 *(dans une course, en natation)* length; **faire des longueurs** to do lengths; **il l'a emporté d'une l.** he won by a length; *Fig* **avoir une l. d'avance (sur)** to be well ahead (of)

4 *Sport* **saut en l.** long jump

5 *Ordinat* length, size; **l. de bloc/de mot** block/word length

6 *Opt* **l. optique** optical path

7 *Rad* **l. d'onde** wavelength; *Fig* **être sur la même l. d'onde** to be on the same wavelength

8 *(dans le temps)* length; **le film était d'une l.!** the film was incredibly long *or* dragged on forever; **d'une l. désespérante** sickeningly long

9 *Typ* **l. de ligne** line width; **l. de page** page length

• **longueurs** NFPL overlong passages; **il y a des longueurs dans le film** the film is a little tedious in parts; **il y avait des longueurs** some passages were a little boring

• **à longueur de** PRÉP **à l. de semaine/d'année** all week/year long; **il se plaint à l. de temps** he's forever complaining, he complains all the time

longue-vue [lɔ̃gvy] *(pl* **longues-vues)** NF telescope, field-glass

look [luk] NM *Fam* **1** *(style)* look, fashion; **le l. des années 30** the 30s look; **t'as le l., coco!** you look great, baby! **2** *(présentation)* image; **le magazine a changé de l.** the magazine has changed its image; **soigner son l.** to cultivate one's image

looké, -e [luke] ADJ *Fam* **être l. punk/grunge** to have a punky/grungy look *or* image

looping [lupiŋ] NM *Aviat* loop; **faire des loopings** to loop the loop

lope [lɔp], **lopette** [lɔpɛt] NF *très Fam Péj* **1** *(homme veule)* wimp **2** *(homosexuel)* fairy, *Br* poof, *Am* fag, = offensive term used to refer to a male homosexual

lopin [lɔpɛ̃] NM **1** *(parcelle)* **l. (de terre)** patch *or* plot (of land) **2** *Métal (cylindre ▸ grand)* bloom; *(▸ petit)* billet

loquace [lɔkas] ADJ talkative, *Sout* loquacious; **tu n'es pas très l. aujourd'hui!** you've not got much to say for yourself today!

loquacité [lɔkasite] NF talkativeness, *Sout* loquacity; **elle a retrouvé sa l. d'autrefois** she's her old talkative self again

loque [lɔk] NF **1** *(haillon)* rag **2** *(personne)* **l. (humaine)** wreck; **n'être qu'une l.** to be a shadow of one's former self **3** *Belg (serpillière)* mop

• **en loques** ADJ tattered, in tatters; **ses vêtements tombaient en loques** his/her clothes were all in rags *or* tatters

loquet [lɔkɛ] NM latch, catch bolt

loqueteau, -x [lɔkto] NM small catch, hasp

loqueteux, -euse [lɔktø, -øz] ADJ **1** *(personne)* dressed in rags, in tatters **2** *(manteau)* ragged, tattered

NM,F ragamuffin

lord [lɔr, lɔrd] NM lord

lord-maire [lɔrdmɛr] *(pl* **lords-maires)** NM Lord Mayor

lordose [lɔrdoz] NF *Méd* lordosis

lorgner [3] [lɔrɲe] VT **1** *(regarder ▸ personne)* to ogle, to eye (up); *(▸ objet)* to eye; **l. qn/qch du coin de l'œil** to cast sidelong glances at sb/sth **2** *(convoiter ▸ héritage, poste)* to have one's (beady) eye on

lorgnette [lɔrɲɛt] NF *(lunette)* spyglass; *(jumelles de théâtre)* opera glasses

lorgnon [lɔrɲɔ̃] NM *(à main)* lorgnette, lorgnon; *(à ressort)* pince-nez

loriot [lɔrjo] NM *Orn* oriole; **l. jaune** golden oriole

lorrain, -e [lɔrɛ̃, -ɛn] ADJ of/from Lorraine

NM *(dialecte)* Lorraine dialect

• **Lorrain, -e** NM,F = inhabitant of or person from Lorraine

lorry [lɔri] *(pl* **lorries** *ou* **lorrys)** NM (platelayer's) trolley, lorry

lors [lɔr] **lors de** PRÉP *(pendant)* during; *(au moment de)* at the time of; **l. de la Première Guerre mondiale** during the First World War; **l. de sa mort** at the time of his/her death

• **lors même que** CONJ *Littéraire* even if, even though; **l. même que nous ferions tous les efforts possibles, nous ne serions pas sûrs d'y parvenir** even if we made every possible effort, we still couldn't be sure of succeeding

lorsque [lɔrsk]

> **lorsqu'** is used before a word beginning with a vowel or h mute.

CONJ when; **nous allions partir lorsqu'on a sonné** we were about to leave when the doorbell rang; **il faut agir lorsqu'il est encore temps** we must act while there is still time

losange [lɔzɑ̃ʒ] **NM** *(forme)* diamond, *Spéc* lozenge; *Géom* rhombus; *Hér* lozenge; **en forme de l.** diamond-shaped, rhomboid

losangé, -e [lɔzɑ̃ʒe] **ADJ** *(frise)* with a diamond pattern

loser [luzœr] **NM** *Fam* loser

lot [lo] **NM 1** *(prix)* prize; **l. de consolation** consolation prize; *aussi Fig* **gagner le gros l.** to win *or* to hit the jackpot

2 *(part ▸ d'objets)* share; *(▸ de terre)* plot, lot; **diviser une propriété en plusieurs lots** to divide an estate into several plots; **à chacun son l. d'infortunes** to each of us his share of misfortunes

3 *Jur* lot; **en lots** lot by lot

4 *(ensemble ▸ de livres)* collection; *(▸ de vaisselle, de linge)* set; *(▸ de savons, d'éponges)* (special offer) pack; *(▸ aux enchères)* lot; *Com (de marchandises)* batch; **vendus par lots** *(torchons, couverts)* sold in sets; **dans le l., il y aura bien un fort en maths** there must be at least one person who's good at maths among them; **à vendre en un seul l.** for sale as a job lot; **se dégager** *ou* **se détacher du l.** to stand out from the rest; **être au-dessus du l.** to be a cut above the rest; **l. dépareillé** odd lot

5 *Ordinat* batch; **traitement par lots** batch processing

6 *Littéraire (destin)* lot, fate; **tel est notre l. commun** such is our common fate

7 *Bourse (d'actions)* parcel

lote [lɔt] = **lotte**

loterie [lɔtri] **NF 1** *(jeu)* lottery, draw; **l. nationale** national lottery **2** *(hasard)* lottery; **c'est une vraie l.!** it's the luck of the draw!

loti, -e [lɔti] **ADJ être bien/mal l.** to be well/badly off; **tu n'es pas mieux l. que moi** you're no better off than I am; *Fam Ironique* **la voilà bien lotie avec ce type-là!** she really hit the jackpot with that guy!

lotion [losjɔ̃] **NF** lotion; **l. après-rasage** after-shave lotion; **l. capillaire** hair lotion; **l. tonique** toning lotion, toner

lotionner [3] [losjɔne] **VT** *(cuir chevelu)* to rub lotion into; *(épiderme)* to apply lotion to

lotir [32] [lɔtir] **VT 1** *(terrain ▸ partager)* to portion off, to divide into plots; *(▸ vendre)* to sell by plots; *(immeubles)* to divide into lots; **à l.** *(sur panneau)* to be divided up for sale **2** *(attribuer à)* **l. qn de qch** *(immeuble, parcelle)* to allot sth to sb

lotissement [lɔtismɑ̃] **NM 1** *(terrain ▸ à construire)* building plot, site *(for a housing development)*; *(▸ construit)* housing development, *Br* (housing) estate **2** *(partage ▸ d'un terrain)* division into lots, parcelling out; *(▸ d'immeubles)* dividing into lots

loto [lɔto] **NM 1** *(jeu)* lotto; *(boîte)* lotto set **2 le L.** ≃ the (French state-run) lottery *(similar to the British National Lottery)*; **le L. sportif** *Br* ≃ the football pools, *Am* ≃ the soccer sweepstakes

> **LE LOTO**
>
> "Loto" is a popular game of chance with large cash prizes. Printed grids ("bulletins") are available at tobacconists or special kiosks. Players mark six numbers on the grid and pay a fee. The twice-weekly prize draw is broadcast on television. "Loto Sportif" is a version of "Loto" in which players bet on the football results.

lotte [lɔt] **NF** *Ich (de rivière)* burbot; **l. (de mer)** monkfish, angler fish

lotus [lɔtys] **NM** lotus

louable [lwabl] **ADJ 1** *(comportement, décision)* praiseworthy, commendable, laudable **2** *(appartement, maison)* rentable, up for rent; **difficilement l.** difficult to rent

louage [lwaʒ] **NM** *(cession)* letting; *(jouissance)* renting; **prendre qch à l.** to rent sth; **l. de services** contract of employment, work contract

louange [lwɑ̃ʒ] **NF** praise; **faire un discours à la l. de qn** to make a speech in praise of sb; *Littéraire* **nous dirons à sa l. que…** to his/her credit, it must be said that…

• **louanges NFPL** praise; **digne de louanges** *(personne)* praiseworthy; *(action)* praiseworthy, commendable; **chanter** *ou* **célébrer les louanges de qn** to sing sb's praises; **couvrir qn de louanges** to heap praise on sb

louanger [17] [lwɑ̃ʒe] **VT** *Littéraire* to praise

louangeur, -euse [lwɑ̃ʒœr, -øz] **ADJ** *Littéraire* laudatory; **paroles louangeuses** words of praise

NM,F *Littéraire* laudator

loubard [lubar] **NM** *Fam Br* yob, *Am* hood

louche[1] [luʃ] **ADJ 1** *(douteux ▸ personne)* shifty, shady, *Br* dodgy; *(▸ attitude, passé)* shady; *(▸ affaire)* shady, sleazy, *Br* dodgy *(▸ endroit)* sleazy; **un individu l.** a shady character; **j'ai repéré son manège l.** I've spotted his/her shady little game; **n'y va pas, c'est l.** don't get involved, there's something fishy about it **2** *(trouble ▸ couleur, lumière)* murky; *(▸ liquide)* cloudy

NM il y a du l. là-dessous! there's something fishy going on!, I smell a rat!

louche[2] [luʃ] **NF 1** *(ustensile)* ladle **2** *très Fam (main)* mitt, paw; **serrer la l. à qn** to shake hands with sb[□]

loucher [3] [luʃe] **VI 1** *Méd* to (have a) squint; **il louche** he has a squint, he's cross-eyed **2** *(volontairement)* to go cross-eyed

• **loucher sur VT IND** *Fam (convoiter ▸ personne)* to ogle, to eye (up); *(▸ biens)* to have an eye on; **ils louchent tous sur les millions de leur oncle** they all have an eye *or* their (beady) eyes on their uncle's millions

loucherie [luʃri] **NF** squinting *(UNCOUNT)*

loucheur, -euse [luʃœr, -øz] **NM,F** cross-eyed person, person with a squint

louer[1] [6] [lwe] **VT** *(glorifier)* to praise; **louons le Seigneur** praise the Lord; **Dieu soit loué** thank God; **loués soient les philanthropes qui…** praise be to the philanthropists who…; **l. qn de** *ou* **pour qch** to praise sb for sth; **on ne peut que vous l. d'avoir agi ainsi** you deserve nothing but praise for having acted in this way

VPR se louer *(se féliciter)* **se l. de qch** to be pleased with sth; **je n'ai qu'à me l. de votre ponctualité/travail** I have nothing but praise for your punctuality/work; **se l. d'avoir fait qch** to congratulate oneself on having done sth; **je peux me l. d'avoir vu juste** I can congratulate myself for having got it right

louer[2] [6] [lwe] **VT 1** *(donner en location ▸ logement)* to rent, *Br* to let (out); *(▸ appareil, véhicule)* to rent (out), *Br* to hire (out); *(▸ usine)* to lease (out); **l. qch à qn** to rent sth to sb, to rent sb sth; **le propriétaire me le loue pour 200 euros** the landlord rents it out to me for 200 euros; **désolé, la maison est déjà louée** sorry, but the house is already let

2 *(prendre en location ▸ logement)* to rent (à from); *(▸ appareil, véhicule)* to rent, *Br* to hire (à from); *(▸ usine)* to lease (à from); **on a loué le hall d'exposition à une grosse société** we've leased the exhibition hall from a big firm

3 *(réserver)* to book; **pour ce spectacle, il est conseillé de l. les places à l'avance** advance booking is advisable for this show

4 *Vieilli (engager ▸ personne)* to engage; **l. du personnel d'entretien** to engage cleaning staff

USAGE ABSOLU elle ne loue pas cher she doesn't ask for very much (by way of) rent; **l'été nous préférons l.** we prefer renting accommodation for our summer holidays; **vous êtes propriétaire? – non, je loue** do you own your house? – no, I rent *or* I'm a tenant

VPR se louer 1 *(travailleur)* to hire oneself out; **il s'est loué à un fermier pour la moisson** he got hired by a farmer for the harvest **2** *(logement)* to be rented *or Br* let; **cette chambre se louerait aisément** you'd have no problem letting this room *or* finding somebody to rent this room; **les locaux situés au centre de la capitale se louent à prix d'or** city centre premises are very expensive to rent **3** *(appareil)* to be rented *or Br* hired

• **à louer ADJ** *Br* to let, *Am* for rent; **chambres à l. à la semaine** *(sur panneau)* rooms *Br* to let *or Am* to rent weekly; **voitures à l.** *(sur panneau) Br* cars for hire, *Am* cars for rent

loueur, -euse [lwœr, -øz] **NM,F** *Jur* lessor; *(entreprise)* rental *or Br* hire company; **l. de bateaux/costumes** person who rents (out) *or Br* hires (out) boats/costumes

louf [luf], **loufedingue** [lufdɛ̃g] **ADJ** *Fam* crazy; **il est complètement l.!** he's completely crazy *or Br* off his rocker!

loufiat [lufja] **NM** *très Fam* waiter[□]

loufoque [lufɔk] **ADJ 1** *(fou)* crazy, nuts; **il est devenu un peu l. après la guerre** he went a bit crazy after the war **2** *(invraisemblable ▸ récit, histoire)* weird, bizarre **3** *(burlesque)* **un film l.** a zany comedy

NMF crank, *Am* screwball

loufoquerie [lufɔkri] **NF** *(caractère, acte)* eccentricity

lougre [lugr] **NM** *Naut* lugger

louis [lwi] **NM** louis d'or

Louisiane [lwizjan] **NF la L.** Louisiana; **en L.** in Louisiana

loukoum [lukum] **NM** piece of Turkish delight; **des loukoums** Turkish delight

loulou[1] [lulu] **NM 1** *(chien)* spitz; **l. de Poméranie** Pomeranian (dog) **2** *Fam (voyou) Br* yob, *Am* hood

loulou[2], **-oute** [lulu, -ut] **NM,F** *Fam* **1** *(en appellatif)* **mon l., ma louloute** (my) darling **2** *(personne)* hoodlum, hooligan

loup [lu] **NM 1** *(mammifère)* wolf; **l. à crinière** maned wolf; **l. doré** Indian jackal; **faire entrer le l. dans la bergerie** to set the fox to mind the geese; *Fig* **avoir vu le l.** to have lost one's virginity; **il est connu comme le l. blanc** everybody knows him; **à pas de l.** stealthily; *Prov* **les loups ne se mangent pas entre eux** there is honour among thieves; **quand on parle du l. on en voit la queue** talk of the devil (and he's sure to appear); **l'homme est un l. pour l'homme** man is capable of great brutality towards his fellow man

2 *(personne)* **jeune l.** *(en politique)* young Turk; *(en affaires)* go-getter; **un vieux l. de mer** an old sea-dog *or* salt

3 *Fam (en appellatif)* **mon (petit** *ou* **gros) l.** my (little) darling *or* love *or* sweetheart

4 *(masque)* (eye) mask

5 *Ich* (European) sea bass

6 *Tech (défaut)* flaw

loup-cervier [luservje] *(pl* **loups-cerviers) NM 1** *Zool* (European) lynx **2** *(fourrure)* lucern

loupe [lup] **NF 1** *Opt* magnifying glass; **observer qch à la l.** to look at sth through a magnifying glass; *Fig* to put sth under a microscope, to scrutinize sth **2** *Méd* wen **3** *Bot* knur; **l. d'érable/de noyer** burr maple/walnut

louper [3] [lupe] *Fam* **VT 1** *(examen)* to fail[□], to flunk; *(dessin, discours, tarte)* to botch, to bungle, to make a mess of; **l. son coup** to bungle it **2** *(laisser échapper ▸ train, personne)* to miss; **je t'ai loupé de cinq minutes** I (just) missed you by five minutes; **l. une occasion** to let an opportunity slip, to pass up an opportunity **3** *(locutions)* **ne pas l. qn** *(le punir)* to sort sb out; **si elle recommence, il ne la loupera pas!** if she does that again he'll sort her out!; **il n'en loupe pas une!** *(il est gaffeur)* he's always putting his foot in it!

VI si tu continues comme ça tu vas tout faire l. if you carry on like that you'll mess everything up *or* make a mess of everything; **ça ne va pas l.** it's bound to happen, it (just) has to happen; **elle lui avait dit que ça ne marcherait pas et ça n'a pas loupé!** she told him/her it wouldn't work and sure enough it didn't!

VPR se louper 1 *(ne pas se rencontrer)* **on s'est loupés de quelques secondes** we missed each other by (just) a few seconds **2** *(manquer son suicide)* **elle s'est loupée pour la troisième fois** that's her third (unsuccessful) suicide attempt; **cette fois, il ne s'est pas loupé** this time he meant business; **tu as vu son maquillage? elle ne s'est pas loupée!** have you seen her make-up? she's put it on with a trowel!; **il s'est coupé les cheveux tout seul et il s'est pas loupé!** he cut his own hair and made some job of it!

loup-garou [lugaru] *(pl* **loups-garous)** **NM 1** *Myth* werewolf **2** *(personnage effrayant)* bogeyman; **si tu n'arrêtes pas, j'appelle le l.** *(à un enfant)* if you don't stop, the bogeyman will come and get you

loupiot, -e[1] [lupjo, -ɔt] **NM,F** *Fam (enfant)* kid, *Br* nipper

loupiote[2] [lupjɔt] **NF** *(lampe)* (small) light

LOURD, -E[1] [lur, lurd]

ADJ	
• heavy **1–5, 7–9, 11**	• deep **1**
• rich **3**	• thick **4, 5**
• sultry **6**	• strong **7**
• clumsy **9**	• high **11**
• serious **11**	
ADV	
• close **1**	

ADJ 1 *(pesant ▸ gén)* heavy; *(▸ sommeil)* heavy, deep; **ma valise est trop lourde** my suitcase is too heavy; **démarche lourde** heavy gait; **d'un pas l.** with a heavy tread *or* step; **le vol l. des corbeaux** the clumsy flight of the crows; **j'ai la tête lourde/les jambes lourdes** my head feels/my legs feel heavy; **les paupières lourdes de sommeil** eyes heavy with sleep; **avoir le sommeil l.** to be a heavy *or* deep sleeper

2 *(complexe ▸ artillerie, chirurgie, industrie)* heavy

3 *(indigeste)* heavy, rich; **des repas trop lourds** excessively rich meals

4 *(compact ▸ sol, terre)* heavy, thick; **terrain l. aujourd'hui à Longchamp** the going is heavy today at Longchamp

5 *(chargé)* heavy, thick; **de lourds nuages** thick *or* dense clouds; **l. de** heavy with; **des branches lourdes de fruits** branches heavy with *or* bowed down with fruit; **un ciel l. de nuages** a heavy sky; **son ton est l. de menace** the tone of his/her voice is ominous *or* menacing; **il régnait dans l'assistance un silence l. d'angoisse** people sat there in anxious silence; **incident l. de conséquences** incident fraught with consequences

6 *(accablant ▸ atmosphère, temps)* sultry, oppressive

7 *(entêtant ▸ odeur)* heavy, strong

8 *(sans grâce ▸ bâtiment, façade)* heavy, heavy-looking; **un visage aux traits lourds** a coarse-featured face

9 *(sans finesse ▸ remarque)* clumsy, heavy-handed; *(▸ mouvement, style)* heavy, ponderous; **des plaisanteries plutôt lourdes** rather unsubtle jokes; **certains passages sont lourds** some passages are a bit laboured *or* tedious; **avoir l'esprit l.** to be slow(-witted) *or* dull-witted

10 *Fam (agaçant)* **sans vouloir être l., je te rappelle que ça doit être fini dans 15 minutes** I don't want to nag but don't forget that you have to finish in 15 minutes; **t'es l. avec tes questions** you're such a pain with all your questions

11 *(important ▸ chiffres)* high; *(▸ horaire, tâche, dépenses)* heavy; *(▸ perte)* heavy, serious, severe; *(▸ dette)* heavy, serious; *(▸ faute)* serious, grave; **notre facture d'électricité a été lourde l'hiver dernier** we had a big electricity bill last winter; **les effectifs des classes sont trop lourds** class sizes are too big; **tu as là une lourde responsabilité** that is a heavy responsibility for you; **l. bilan pour la catastrophe aérienne d'hier** heavy death toll in yesterday's air disaster; **elle a une lourde hérédité** she's got an unfortunate background

ADV 1 *(chaud)* **il fait très l.** it's very close

2 *Fam (beaucoup)* **tu n'en fais pas l.** you don't exactly kill yourself; **ça ne fait pas l.** it's not much to show for it; **je ne gagne pas l.** I don't earn very much; **il n'en sait pas l. sur l'histoire de son pays** he doesn't know much about the history of his country▫

lourdaud, -e [lurdo, -od] **ADJ** oafish, clumsy
NM,F oaf, nitwit

lourde[2] [lurd] **ADJ F** *voir* **lourd**
NF *Fam (porte)* door▫

lourdement [lurdəmɑ̃] **ADV 1** *(très)* heavily; **l. chargé** heavily laden **2** *(sans souplesse)* heavily; **il tomba l. à terre** he fell heavily to the ground; **marcher l.** to tread heavily, to walk with a heavy step **3** *(beaucoup)* greatly; **tu te trompes l.!** you are greatly mistaken!; **cet investissement grève l. le budget** this investment puts a serious strain on the budget; **insister l. sur qch** to be most emphatic about sth

lourder [3] [lurde] **VT** *très Fam* **1** *(congédier)* to kick out, to throw out **2** *(importuner)* to piss off; **tu commences à me l. avec tes histoires** you're starting to piss me off with all your nonsense

lourdeur [lurdœr] **NF 1** *(d'un fardeau, d'une valise)* heaviness; *Fig* **la l. de la tâche m'effraie** the workload frightens me; *Fig* **la l. de l'appareil du parti** the unwieldiness of the party structure

2 *(d'un mouvement)* heaviness, clumsiness; **danser avec l.** to dance heavily *or* clumsily

3 *(douleur)* heavy feeling; **avoir des lourdeurs d'estomac** to feel bloated; **j'ai des lourdeurs dans les jambes** my legs feel heavy

4 *(du temps)* closeness, sultriness

5 *(des formes, des traits)* heaviness; *(d'un bâtiment, d'une architecture)* heaviness, massiveness

6 *(d'un propos, d'un comportement)* bluntness, clumsiness; **l. d'esprit** dull-wittedness; **il est d'une telle l. d'esprit!** he's such an oaf!

7 *(gravité ▸ d'une peine, d'une punition)* severity; *(▸ d'un crime)* gravity; *(▸ d'une responsabilité)* weight

• **lourdeurs NFPL** *(maladresses)* **idées intéressantes mais trop de lourdeurs** interesting ideas, but clumsily expressed

lourdingue [lurdɛ̃g] **ADJ** *très Fam* **1** *(physiquement)* clumsy▫, awkward▫ **2** *(peu subtil ▸ personne)* dim-witted, *Br* thick; *(▸ plaisanterie, réflexion)* pathetic, stupid; *(▸ style)* heavy

loustic [lustik] **NM** *Fam* **1** *(individu louche)* shady character; **drôle de l.** oddball **2** *(farceur)* joker, funny guy; **faire le l.** to play the fool, to fool around

loutre [lutr] **NF 1** *Zool* otter; **l. de mer** sea otter **2** *(fourrure)* otter skin *or* pelt; **manteau de l.** otter-skin coat

louvart [luvar] **NM** *Zool* young wolf

louve [luv] **NF** *Zool* she-wolf, bitch

louvet, -ette [luvɛ, -ɛt] **ADJ** dun

louveteau, -x [luvto] **NM 1** *Zool* (wolf) cub **2** *(scout)* cub, Cub Scout

louvoie *etc voir* **louvoyer**

louvoiement [luvwamɑ̃], **louvoyage** [luvwajaʒ] **NM 1** *Naut* tacking **2** *Fig (manœuvre)* subterfuge

louvoyer [13] [luvwaje] **VI 1** *Naut* to tack (about) **2** *(biaiser)* to hedge, to equivocate

Louvre [luvr] **NM le (palais du) L.** the Louvre

> **LE LOUVRE**
>
> This former royal palace became a museum in 1791–93. It houses one of the richest art collections in the world. The museum was extended in 1989, with the construction of the glass "pyramide du Louvre" in the main courtyard, and again in 1993 when the Richelieu wing, formerly occupied by the ministry of finance, was inaugurated.

lover [3] [ləve] **VT** *Naut* to coil
VPR se lover *(serpent)* to coil up; *(personne)* to curl up

low-cost [lokɔst] **NM OU NF** *(pl* **inv** *ou* **low-costs)** low-cost airline

loxodromique [lɔksɔdrɔmik] **ADJ** *Naut (courbe, navigation)* loxodromic; **navigation l.** plane sailing, loxodromics *(singulier)*

loyal, -e, -aux, -ales [lwajal, -o] **ADJ 1** *(fidèle)* loyal, faithful; **un compagnon l.** a loyal *or* faithful companion; **20 ans de bons et loyaux services** 20 years' unstinting devotion **2** *(honnête ▸ personne)* honest, fair; *(▸ adversaire)* honest; *(▸ combat)* clean; **il a été l. avec moi** he was honest *or* straight with me; **être l. en affaires** to be straightforward *or* honest in one's business dealings; **un procédé l.** honest behaviour, upright conduct; **un jeu l.** a fair game

• **à la loyale ADV se battre à la loyale** to fight fairly

loyalement [lwajalmɑ̃] **ADV 1** *(fidèlement)* loyally, faithfully; **servir qn l.** to serve sb faithfully **2** *(honnêtement ▸ se conduire, agir)* honestly; *(▸ se battre)* cleanly

loyalisme [lwajalism] **NM 1** *(fidélité)* loyalty **2** *Pol* loyalism, Loyalism

loyaliste [lwajalist] **ADJ** *(fidèle)* loyal
NMF loyal supporter

loyauté [lwajote] **NF 1** *(fidélité)* loyalty, faithfulness **2** *(honnêteté)* honesty, fairness

loyer [lwaje] **NM 1** *(d'un logement)* rent; **j'ai trois loyers de retard** I'm three months behind with my rent; **devoir trois mois de l.** to owe three months' rent; **donner à l.** to rent (out), *Br* to let (out); **prendre à l.** to rent; *Can* **être à l.** to be a tenant, to be in rented accommodation **2** *Fin* **le l. de l'argent** the interest rate, the price of money

LP [ɛlpe] **NM 1** *(abrév* **lycée professionnel)** vocational high school **2** *(abrév* **Long Playing)** LP

LSD [ɛlɛsde] **NM** *(abrév* **lysergic acid diethylamide)** LSD

LTA [ɛltea] **NF** *Com (abrév* **lettre de transport aérien)** AWB

lu, -e [ly] **PP** *voir* **lire**[2]

lubie [lybi] **NF** whim; **c'est sa dernière l.** it's his/her latest whim; **encore une de ses lubies!** another one of his/her crazy ideas!

lubricité [lybrisite] **NF** *(d'une personne, d'un regard)* lustfulness, lechery; *(d'un propos, d'une conduite)* lewdness

lubrifiant, -e [lybrifjɑ̃, -ɑ̃t] **ADJ** lubricating
NM lubricant

lubrification [lybrifikasjɔ̃] **NF** lubrication

lubrifier [9] [lybrifje] **VT** to lubricate

lubrique [lybrik] **ADJ** *Littéraire (personne, regard)* lustful, lecherous; *(attitude, propos)* lewd, libidinous

lubriquement [lybrikmɑ̃] **ADV** lecherously, lewdly

Luc [lyk] **NPR** *Bible* Luke

lucane [lykan] **NM** *Entom* stag beetle, *Spéc* lucanid

lucaniste [lykanist], **lucanophile** [lykanɔfil] **NMF** kite-flyer, kite fan

lucarne [lykarn] **NF 1** *(fenêtre)* skylight; **l. faîtière** skylight; **l. pignon** dormer (window) **2** *Ftbl* top corner (of the net)

lucide [lysid] **ADJ 1** *(clairvoyant ▸ personne)* lucid, clear-headed; *(▸ esprit, raisonnement)* lucid, clear; *(▸ critique)* perceptive; **elle ne se fait pas d'illusion sur ce qui l'attend, elle est l.** she has no illusions about what lies in store for her, she sees things clearly **2** *(éveillé)* conscious; *(qui a toute sa tête)* lucid

lucidement [lysidmɑ̃] **ADV** clearly, lucidly

lucidité [lysidite] **NF 1** *(clairvoyance ▸ d'une personne)* lucidity, clear-headedness; *(▸ de l'esprit, d'un raisonnement)* lucidity, clarity; **avec l.** lucidly; **une critique d'une grande l.** a very perceptive criticism **2** *(possession des facultés)* lucidity; **dans ses moments de l.** in his/her lucid moments

Lucifer [lysifɛr] **NPR** Lucifer

luciférien, -enne [lysiferjɛ̃, -ɛn] **ADJ** Luciferian
NM,F *Hist* Satanist

luciole [lysjɔl] **NF** *Zool* firefly, *Am* lightning bug

Lucques [lyk] **NM** *Géog* Lucca

lucratif, -ive [lykratif, -iv] **ADJ** lucrative, profitable

lucrativement [lykrativmɑ̃] **ADV** lucratively

lucre [lykr] **NM** profit, *Sout* lucre; **faire qch par goût du l.** to do sth out of love for money

ludiciel [lydisjɛl] **NM** computer game *(software)*

ludion [lydjɔ̃] **NM** Cartesian diver

ludique [lydik] **ADJ** play *(avant n)*, *Spéc* ludic; **il y a un côté l. dans ses mises en scène** his/her productions have a playful quality to them

ludo-éducatif, -ive [lydɔedykatif, -iv] *(mpl* **ludo-éducatifs,** *fpl* **ludo-éducatives)** **ADJ** edutainment *(avant n)*

ludospace [lydɔspas] **NM** *Aut* people carrier

ludothèque [lydɔtɛk] **NF** toys and games library

luette [lɥɛt] **NF 1** *Anat* uvula **2** *Can Fam* **se mouiller** *ou* **se rincer la l.** *(prendre un verre)* to wet one's whistle, to have a drink; *(se soûler)* to get sloshed *or* drunk

lueur [lɥœr] **NF 1** *(lumière ▸ de l'âtre, du couchant)* glow; *(▸ de la lune, d'une lampe)* light; *(▸ d'une lame)* gleam; **une faible l.** a glimmer; **les lueurs rougeoyantes de l'incendie** the reddish glow of the fire; **l. vacillante** flicker; **à la l. d'une bougie** by candlelight; **aux premières lueurs de l'aube** in the first light of dawn; *Fig* **à la l. des derniers événements** in the light of recent events **2** *Fig (éclat)* glimmer, glint; **une l. d'intelligence/d'espoir** a glimmer of intelligence/of hope

luge [lyʒ] **NF 1** *(gén)* toboggan, *Br* sledge, *Am* sled; **faire de la l.** to toboggan, *Br* to go sledging, *Am* to go sledding **2** *Sport* luge **3** *Suisse* = large sledge used to carry loads

lugeur, -euse [lyʒœr, -øz] **NM,F 1** *(gén)* tobogganer, *Br* sledger, *Am* sledder **2** *Sport* luger

lugubre [lygybr] **ADJ** *(personne, mine, pensées)* gloomy, lugubrious; *(endroit, atmosphère, soirée)* gloomy; *(son, cri)* doleful, mournful

lugubrement [lygybrəmɑ̃] **ADV** lugubriously, gloomily

lui[1] [lɥi] **PP** *voir* **luire**

LUI[2] [lɥi]

- (to) him/her/it **A1**
- it **B1, 3**
- himself **B4**
- he **B1, 2**
- him **B2, 3**

PRON A. *REPRÉSENTANT LE GENRE MASCULIN OU FÉMININ* **1** *(complément ▸ homme)* (to) him; *(▸ femme)* (to) her; *(▸ chose, animal)* (to) it; *(▸ nouveau-né, animal domestique mâle)* (to) him, (to) it; *(▸ nouveau-née, animal domestique femelle)* (to) her, (to) it; **je l. ai parlé** I spoke to him/her; **je l. ai serré la main** I shook his/her hand; **ils l. ont jeté des pierres** they threw stones at him/her; **il a rencontré Hélène et (il) l. a plu** he met Hélène and she liked him; **pensez-vous que cela puisse l. nuire?** do you think that can harm him/her?; **il entend qu'on l. obéisse** he means to be obeyed; **il le l. a présenté** he introduced him to him/her; **qui le l. a dit?** who told him/her?; **je le l. ai reproché** I reproached him/her for it; **donne-le-l.** give it to him/her; **il l. est difficile de venir** it's difficult for him/her to come

2 *(se substituant à l'adjectif possessif)* **il l. a serré la main** he shook his/her hand; **le bruit l. donne mal à la tête** the noise gives him/her a headache

B. *REPRÉSENTANT LE GENRE MASCULIN* **1** *(sujet ▸ personne)* he; *(▸ chose, animal)* it; *(▸ nouveau-né, animal domestique)* he, it; **elle aime le cinéma, l. non** she likes the cinema, he doesn't; **nous travaillons et l., en attendant, il se repose** we're working and meanwhile, HE'S having a rest; **l. ne voulait pas en entendre parler** HE didn't want to hear anything about it; **Paul et l. sont rentrés ensemble** he and Paul went back together; **il sait de quoi je parle, l.** HE knows what I'm talking about; **mon frère, l., n'est pas venu** as for my brother, he didn't come; **si j'étais l.…** if I were him…; **quant à l., il n'était pas là** as for him, he wasn't there; **qui ira avec elle? – l.** who'll go with her? – he will; **l.? il ne ferait jamais ça!** him? he'd never do that!; **l. aussi se pose des questions** he is wondering about it too; **il doit suivre un régime: il est malheureux, l. qui est si gourmand!** he has to go on a diet, and loving his food as he does, he's not happy about it; **l. seul pourrait te le dire** only he could tell you

2 *(avec un présentatif)* **c'est l. qui vous le demande** HE'S asking you; **c'est l. qui nous a présentés** he's the one who introduced us, HE introduced us; **des deux frères, c'est l. que je connais le mieux** of the two brothers I know him *or* it's him I know best; **c'est encore l.?** is it him again?; **c'est tout l.!** that's typical of him!, that's him all over!

3 *(complément ▸ personne)* him; *(▸ chose, animal)* it; *(▸ nouveau-né, animal domestique)* him, it; **elle n'écoute que l.** she will only listen to him; **elle ne veut que l. pour avocat** he's the only lawyer she will accept, she won't have any lawyer but him; **on l'a vu, l.** we saw him; **l., tout le monde le connaît** everybody knows HIM; **elle est plus jeune que l.** she's younger than him, she's younger than he (is); **j'apprécie Marie plus que l.** *(plus qu'il ne l'apprécie)* I like Marie more than he does *or* than him; *(je préfère Marie)* I like Marie more than him; **avez-vous pensé à l.?** have you thought about him?; **elle ne l. a pas plu, à l.** he didn't like her at all; **cette valise n'est pas à l.?** isn't that his suitcase?, doesn't that suitcase belong to him?; **une amie à l.** a friend of his; **il a réussi à le soulever à l. (tout) seul** he managed to lift it on his own *or* without any help; **à l. seul, il possède la moitié de la ville** he owns half of the town himself; **sans l., tout était perdu** without him *or* if it hadn't been for him, all would have been lost; **je vais chez l.** I'm going to his house; **l'enfant n'est pas de l.** the child is not his

4 *(en fonction de pronom réfléchi)* himself; **il est content de l.** he's pleased with himself; **il ne pense qu'à l.** he only thinks of himself

lui-même [lɥimɛm] **PRON** *(une personne)* himself; *(une chose)* itself; **M. Dupont? – l.** Mr Dupont? – at your service; *(au téléphone)* Mr Dupont? – speaking; **il me l'a dit l.** he told me himself; **l. paraissait surpris** he himself seemed surprised; **il se coupe les cheveux l.** he cuts his own hair, he cuts his hair himself; **de l., il a parlé du prix** he mentioned the price without being prompted *or* asked; **il n'a qu'à venir voir par l.** all he has to do is come and see for himself; **il pensait en l. que…** he thought to himself that…

luire [97] [lɥir] **VI 1** *(briller ▸ métal, eau, yeux)* to gleam; *(▸ surface mouillée)* to glisten; *(▸ bougie, lumignon)* to glimmer; *(▸ feu)* to glow; *(▸ soleil, étoile)* to shine; **des larmes luisaient dans leurs yeux** their eyes were glistening with tears, tears were glistening in their eyes **2** *Fig* to shine, to glow; **un faible espoir luit encore** there is still a glimmer of hope

luisant, -e [lɥizɑ̃, -ɑ̃t] **ADJ** *(métal)* gleaming; *(soleil, étoile)* shining; *(flamme)* glowing; *(pavé, pelage)* glistening; **front l. de sueur** forehead glistening with sweat; **les yeux luisants de colère** with eyes ablaze, with eyes blazing with anger; **un manteau l. d'usure** a coat shiny with wear

NM *(d'une étoffe, d'un meuble)* sheen; *(d'une fourrure)* gloss

luisent *etc voir* **luire**

lumbago [lœbago, lɔ̃bago] **NM** *Méd* lumbago

lumen [lymen] **NM** *Phys* lumen

lumière [lymjɛr] **NF 1** *(naturelle ▸ gén)* light; *(▸ du soleil)* sunlight; **la l. du jour** daylight; **la l. des étoiles** starlight; **à la l. de la lune/d'une bougie** by moonlight/candlelight; **l'atelier reçoit la l. du nord** the studio faces north; **sans l.** *(pièce)* dark; **revoir la l.** *(recouvrer la vue)* to be able to see again; *(en sortant d'un lieu sombre)* to see daylight again; *(retrouver la liberté)* to be free again; *Fig* **voir** *ou* **apercevoir la l. au bout du tunnel** to see (the) light at the end of the tunnel

2 *(artificielle)* light; **j'ai vu de la l. et je suis entré** I saw a light (on) so I went in; **allumer la l.** to turn *or* to switch on the light; **éteindre la l.** to turn *or* to switch off the light; **il reste une l. allumée** there's still a light on; **les lumières de la ville** the lights of the city, the city lights

3 *(éclaircissement)* light; **jeter une l. nouvelle sur qch** to throw *or* to shed new light on sth; **toute la l. sera faite** we'll get to the bottom of this

4 *(génie)* genius, luminary; **une des lumières de la littérature contemporaine** one of the leading lights of contemporary literature; **cet enfant n'est pas une l.!** that child is hardly a genius *or* is not very bright!

5 *Astron & Opt* light; **l. blanche** white light; **l. cendrée** earthshine; **l. froide** blue light; **l. noire** *ou* **de Wood** (ultraviolet) black light

6 *Beaux-Arts* light

7 *Rel* **la l. éternelle** *ou* **de Dieu** divine light; **cacher la l. sous le boisseau** to hide one's light under a bushel; **que la l. soit!** let there be light!

8 *Tech (orifice ▸ dans un instrument)* opening; **l. d'admission/d'échappement** inlet/exhaust port

9 *Can (ampoule électrique)* light bulb; *Can Joual (feu de circulation)* traffic light

10 *Cin & TV* **l. de base** key light; **l. diffuse** scattered light; **l. naturelle** available light

• **lumières NFPL 1** *(connaissances)* insight *(UNCOUNT)*, knowledge *(UNCOUNT)*; **elle a des lumières sur le problème** she has (some) insight into the problem; **j'ai besoin de tes lumières** I need the benefit of your wisdom; *Hist* **les Lumières** the Enlightenment **2** *Aut* lights; **les lumières sont restées allumées toute la nuit** the lights stayed on all night

• **à la lumière de PRÉP** *(étant donné)* in (the) light of; **à la l. de ce que tu me dis** in (the) light of what you're telling me

• **en lumière ADV mettre qch en l.** to bring sth out, to shed light on sth

lumignon [lymiɲɔ̃] **NM 1** *(bougie)* candle end **2** *(petite lampe)* small light

luminaire [lyminɛr] **NM 1** *(lampe)* light, lamp; **magasin de luminaires** lighting shop **2** *Astrol* luminary **3** *Rel* lighting *(UNCOUNT)*

luminance [luminɑ̃s] **NF** luminance

luminescence [lyminesɑ̃s] **NF** luminescence

luminescent, -e [lyminesɑ̃, -ɑ̃t] **ADJ** luminescent

lumineuse [lyminøz] *voir* **lumineux**

lumineusement [lyminøzmɑ̃] **ADV** luminously, clearly; **il a très l. exposé les faits** he gave a very lucid presentation of the facts

lumineux, -euse [lyminø, -øz] **ADJ 1** *(qui émet de la lumière)* luminous

2 *(baigné de lumière ▸ journée, appartement)* sunny

3 *(éclatant ▸ couleur)* bright, brilliant

4 *(radieux ▸ teint, sourire, regard)* radiant

5 *(lucide ▸ esprit)* **il a une intelligence lumineuse** he is very insightful

6 *(clair ▸ exposé)* limpid, crystal clear; **son explication était lumineuse** his/her explanation was crystal clear

7 *(de génie ▸ idée)* brilliant

luminosité [lyminozite] **NF 1** *(éclat)* brightness, radiance

2 *(clarté)* luminosity; **la l. est insuffisante pour prendre une photo** there is insufficient light (available) for taking a photo

3 *(d'un écran)* brightness

4 *Astron* luminosity

lump [lœp] **NM** *Ich* lumpfish, lumpsucker

lunaire [lyner] **ADJ 1** *Astron (de lune)* lunar; **paysage l.** lunar landscape; **un visage l.** a moonface **2** *Littéraire (chimérique)* **un projet l.** a fanciful *or* an outlandish plan

NF *Bot* honesty, *Spéc* lunaria

lunaison [lynezɔ̃] **NF** lunar month, *Spéc* synodic month, lunation

lunatique [lynatik] **ADJ** moody, temperamental

NMF temperamental *or* capricious person

Il faut noter que l'adjectif anglais **lunatic** est un faux ami. Il signifie **fou, dément**.

lunch [lœʃ, lœntʃ] *(pl* **lunchs** *ou* **lunches***)* **NM** cold buffet *(served at lunchtime for special occasions)*

lundi [lœdi] **NM** Monday; **le l. de Pâques/Pentecôte** Easter/Whit Monday; *voir aussi* **mardi**

lune [lyn] **NF 1** *Astron* moon; **pleine/nouvelle l.** full/new moon; **nuit sans l.** moonless night; **l. de miel** honeymoon; *Fig* honeymoon (period); **l. rousse** April frost *(at night)*; **être dans la l.** to have one's head in the clouds; **pardon, j'étais dans la l.** sorry, I was miles away *or* my mind was elsewhere; **promettre la l. à qn** to promise sb the moon *or* the earth; **demander** *ou* **vouloir la l.** to ask for the moon; **tomber de la l.** to be flabbergasted; *très Fam* **il est con comme la l.** he's *Br* as thick as two short planks *or Am* dead from the neck up

2 *Fam (fesses)* behind

3 vieilles lunes *(idées dépassées)* old-fashioned *or* outmoded ideas

4 *Arch ou Littéraire (mois)* moon, month

5 *Ich* **l. (de mer)** sunfish, moonfish

6 *(nymphéa)* white water lily

luné, -e [lyne] **ADJ** *Fam* **bien/mal l.** in a good/bad mood

lunetier, -ère [lyntje, -ɛr] **ADJ** spectacle *(avant n)*

NM,F 1 *(fabricant)* *Br* spectacle *or Am* eyeglass manufacturer **2** *(marchand)* optician

lunette [lynɛt] **NF 1** *Opt* telescope; **l. d'approche** refracting telescope, *Arch* spyglass; **l. astronomique** astronomical telescope; **l. de pointage** sighting telescope

2 *(d'une montre)* bezel

3 *(des toilettes ▸ ouverture)* rim; *(▸ siège)* seat
4 *Archit, Beaux-Arts & Constr* lunette
5 *(de guillotine)* lunette
6 *Aut* **l. (arrière)** rear window
• **lunettes** NFPL **1** *(verres correcteurs)* glasses; **une paire de lunettes** a pair of glasses; **porter des lunettes** to wear glasses; **un petit garçon à lunettes** a little boy wearing glasses; **lunettes de vue** *ou* **correctrices** spectacles; **lunettes bifocales** bifocals; **lunettes noires** dark glasses; **lunettes de soleil,** *Belg* **lunettes solaires** sunglasses **2** *(verres protecteurs)* goggles; **lunettes de plongée/ski** swimming/skiing goggles

lunetterie [lynetri] NF **1** *(industrie) Br* spectacle *or Am* eyeglass manufacture **2** *(commerce) Br* spectacle *or Am* eyeglass trade

lunule [lynyl] NF **1** *Anat* half-moon, *Spéc* lunule **2** *Géom* lune

lupanar [lypanar] NM *Littéraire* brothel, house of ill repute

lupin [lypɛ̃] NM *Bot* lupin

lupus [lypys] NM *Méd* lupus; **l. vulgaire** lupus vulgaris

lurette [lyrɛt] NF *Fam* **il y a belle l.** ages ago; **il y a belle l. qu'elle est partie** *(depuis des années)* she left donkey's years ago *or* ages go; *(depuis des heures)* she left hours ago *or* ages ago

luron, -onne [lyrɔ̃, -ɔn] NM,F *Fam* **c'est un gai** *ou* **joyeux l.** he's a bit of a lad; **c'est une gaie luronne** she's quite a girl

lusitanien, -enne [lyzitanjɛ̃, -ɛn] ADJ Lusitanian
• **Lusitanien, -enne** NM,F Lusitanian

lusophone [lyzɔfɔn] ADJ Portuguese-speaking
NMF Portuguese speaker

lustrage [lystraʒ] NM *(d'une poterie, d'un tissu, d'une peau)* lustring; *(d'une peinture)* glazing; *(d'une voiture)* polishing

lustre [lystr] NM **1** *(lampe ▸ de Venise, en cristal)* chandelier; *(▸ simple)* (ceiling) light
2 *(reflet ▸ mat)* glow; *(▸ brillant)* shine, polish
3 *Tech (d'une poterie, d'un tissu, d'une peau)* lustre; *(d'une peinture)* glaze, gloss; *(du papier)* calendering; *(d'un métal)* polish
4 *Littéraire (prestige)* brilliance, glamour; **sans l.** lacklustre; **rendre** *ou* **redonner du l. à qch** to restore sth to its former glory
• **lustres** NMPL **il y a des lustres de ça!** it was ages ago!; **depuis des lustres** for ages

lustré, -e [lystre] ADJ **1** *Tech (tissu, peau)* lustred; *(peinture)* glazed, glossy; *(poterie)* lustred; **poterie lustrée** lustreware **2** *(brillant ▸ pelage)* sleek; *(▸ cheveux)* glossy, shiny **3** *(usé)* shiny (with wear)

lustrer [3] [lystre] VT **1** *Tech (poterie, tissu, peau)* to lustre; *(peinture)* to glaze **2** *(faire briller ▸ voiture)* to polish; **le chat lustre son pelage** the cat is cleaning its coat; **le temps a lustré la pierre** the stone is shiny (and worn) with age

lustrerie [lystrəri] NF *(lampes)* chandeliers; *(commerce, fabrication)* lighting industry

lustrine [lystrin] NF **1** *(soie)* lustring **2** *(percaline)* lustre **3** *(coton)* glazed cotton

lut [lyt] NM *Tech* lute, luting

Lutèce [lytɛs] NF Lutetia

lutéine [lytein] NF *Biol & Chim* lutein

luter [3] [lyte] VT *Tech* to lute

luth [lyt] NM **1** *Mus* lute **2** *Zool* **(tortue) l.** leatherback, leathery turtle

luthéranisme [lyteranism] NM *Rel* Lutheranism

lutherie [lytri] NF **1** *(fabrication)* stringed-instrument manufacture **2** *(commerce)* stringed-instrument trade **3** *(boutique)* stringed-instrument maker's shop *or* workshop

luthérien, -enne [lyterjɛ̃, -ɛn] ADJ Lutheran
• **Luthérien, -enne** NM,F Lutheran

luthier, -ère [lytje, -ɛr] NM,F **1** *(fabricant)* stringed-instrument maker **2** *(marchand)* stringed-instrument dealer

luthiste [lytist] NMF lutenist, lute-player

lutin, -e [lytɛ̃, -in] ADJ *Littéraire* impish, mischievous
NM **1** *(démon ▸ gén)* elf, goblin, imp; *(▸ en Irlande)* leprechaun **2** *Arch (enfant)* (little) imp

lutiner [3] [lytine] VT *Littéraire* to fondle

lutrin [lytrɛ̃] NM *(pupitre)* lectern; *(sur un bureau)* reading *or* book stand; *Mktg (pour un livre)* plinth

lutte [lyt] NF **1** *(affrontement)* struggle, fight, conflict; **la l. est inégale** they are unfairly matched; **se livrer à une l. acharnée** to fight tooth and nail; **une l. d'influence** a fight for domination
2 *Pol* struggle; **luttes politiques/religieuses** political/religious struggles; **l. armée** armed struggle; **la l. des classes** the class struggle *or* war; **L. Ouvrière** = militant Trotskyist organization
3 *(efforts ▸ contre un mal)* fight; **l. contre les incendies** fire-fighting *(UNCOUNT)*; **la l. contre l'alcoolisme/le sida** the fight against alcoholism/AIDS
4 *(résistance)* struggle; **la l. d'un malade contre la mort** a sick person's struggle for life *or* battle against death; **sa vie n'a été qu'une longue l. contre l'adversité** his/her life was just one long struggle against adversity; *Biol* **la l. pour la vie** the struggle for life
5 *(antagonisme)* fight; **la l. entre le bien et le mal** the fight between good and evil
6 *Agr* control *(UNCOUNT)*; **l. biologique** biological (pest) control; **l. génétique** genetic control
7 *Sport* wrestling *(UNCOUNT)*; **faire de la l.** to wrestle; **l. libre/gréco-romaine** all-in/Graeco-Roman wrestling
• **de haute lutte, de vive lutte** ADV after a hard fight
• **en lutte** ADJ **les travailleurs en l. ont défilé hier** the striking workers demonstrated yesterday; **nos camarades en l.** our struggling comrades; **être en l. contre qn** to be at loggerheads with sb

lutter [3] [lyte] VI **1** *(se battre)* **l. contre** to fight (against); **l. contre la bêtise** to fight stupidity; **ils luttent contre le gouvernement** they are struggling against *or* fighting the government; **l. contre la mort** to fight for one's life; **l. contre l'alcoolisme** to fight against *or* to combat alcoholism; **l. contre le sommeil** to fight off sleep; **l. pour** to fight for; **ils luttent pour leurs droits** they are fighting for their rights **2** *(rivaliser)* **ils ont lutté de vitesse** each strove to be faster than the other; **elles luttaient d'adresse** they were trying to outwit each other **3** to wrestle (**contre** with)

lutteur, -euse [lytœr, -øz] NM,F **1** *Sport* wrestler, *f* female wrestler **2** *(battant)* fighter; **c'est une lutteuse, elle s'en remettra** she's a fighter, she'll get over it

lux [lyks] *(pl* **inv** *ou* **luxes)** NM *Phys* lux

luxation [lyksasjɔ̃] NF *Méd* dislocation, *Spéc* luxation

luxe [lyks] NM **1** *(faste)* luxury, wealth; **vivre dans le l.** to live in (the lap of) luxury; **c'est le (grand) l. ici!** it's the height of luxury *or* it's luxurious in here!
2 *(plaisir)* expensive treat, luxury, indulgence; **son seul l. c'est une cigarette après le déjeuner** the only treat he/she allows himself/herself is a cigarette after lunch; **je ne peux pas m'offrir le l. de partir en vacances** I can't afford the luxury of a holiday; *Fig* **elle ne peut pas s'offrir** *ou* **se payer le l. de dire ce qu'elle pense** she can't afford to speak her mind
3 *(chose déraisonnable)* **la viande, c'est devenu un l.** buying meat has become a luxury; *Fam* **ils ont nettoyé la moquette, ce n'était pas du l.!** they cleaned the carpet, (and) it was about time too!
4 **un l. de** *(beaucoup de)* a host *or* a wealth of; **avec un l. de détails** with a wealth of detail
• **de luxe** ADJ **1** *(somptueux)* luxury *(avant n)* **2** *Com (voiture, hôtel)* deluxe, luxury *(avant n)*; *(modèle, édition)* de luxe; *(appartement, boutique)* luxury

Luxembourg [lyksɑ̃bur] NF *(ville)* Luxembourg; **à L.** in (the city of) Luxembourg
NM **1** *(pays)* **le L.** Luxembourg **2** *(à Paris)* **le L., les jardins du L.** the Luxembourg Gardens; **le (palais du) L.** the (French) Senate

luxembourgeois, -e [lyksɑ̃burʒwa, -az] ADJ of/from Luxembourg
• **Luxembourgeois, -e** NM,F = inhabitant of or person from Luxembourg

luxer [3] [lykse] VT *Méd* to dislocate, *Spéc* to luxate
VPR **se luxer se l. le genou/l'épaule** to dislocate one's knee/shoulder

luxueuse [lyksɥøz] *voir* **luxueux**

luxueusement [lyksɥøzmɑ̃] ADV luxuriously

luxueux, -euse [lyksɥø, -øz] ADJ luxurious

luxure [lyksyr] NF *Littéraire* lechery, lust

> Il faut noter que le nom anglais **luxury** est un faux ami. Il signifie **luxe**.

luxuriance [lyksyrjɑ̃s] NF *Littéraire* luxuriance

luxuriant, -e [lyksyrjɑ̃, -ɑ̃t] ADJ *Littéraire* **1** *(végétation)* luxuriant, lush; *(chevelure)* luxuriant **2** *(imagination)* fertile

luxurieux, -euse [lyksyrjø, -øz] ADJ *Littéraire* lascivious, lustful

luzerne [lyzɛrn] NF *Bot Br* lucerne, *Am* alfalfa

lycaon [likaɔ̃] NM *Zool* wild dog; *(en Afrique)* Cape hunting dog

lycée [lise] NM **1** *(gén) Br* ≃ secondary school, *Am* ≃ high school *(providing three years' teaching after the "collège", in preparation for the baccalauréat examination)*; **l. d'enseignement général et technologique, l. polyvalent** *Br* secondary school, *Am* high school *(for both general and technical studies)*; **l. professionnel** vocational high school; *Anciennement* **l. d'enseignement professionnel** = former name for a "lycée professionnel"; **l. hôtelier** catering college **2** *Belg (de filles)* girls' *Br* secondary *or Am* high school

lycéen, -enne [liseɛ̃, -ɛn] NM,F *Br* ≃ secondary school pupil, *Am* ≃ high school student; **un groupe de lycéens** a group of school students; **ce groupe attire surtout les lycéens** this group is mainly a success with teenagers
ADJ school *(avant n)*; **le mouvement l.** the school students' movement

lychee [litʃi] = **litchi**

Lycra® [likra] NM Lycra®

lymphadénectomie [lɛ̃fadenɛktɔmi] NF *Méd* lymphadenectomy

lymphadénite [lɛ̃fadenit] NF *Méd* lymphadenitis

lymphadénopathie [lɛ̃fadenɔpati] NF *Méd* lymphadenopathy

lymphatique [lɛ̃fatik] ADJ **1** *Biol* lymphatic **2** *(apathique)* apathetic, lethargic
NM lymphatic vessel

lymphe [lɛ̃f] NF lymph

lymphocyte [lɛ̃fɔsit] NM *Biol* lymphocyte; **l. T4** T4-lymphocyte

lymphoïde [lɛ̃fɔid] ADJ lymphoid

lymphome [lɛ̃fɔm] NM *Méd* lymphoma; **l. hodgkinien** Hodgkin's lymphoma

lynchage [lɛ̃ʃaʒ] NM lynching

lyncher [3] [lɛ̃ʃe] VT to lynch; **se faire l.** to be *or* to get lynched

lynx [lɛ̃ks] NM **1** *Zool* lynx; *Fig* **avoir des yeux de l.** to have eyes like a hawk **2** *(fourrure)* lynx fur, lucern

Lyon [ljɔ̃] NF Lyon, Lyons

lyonnais, -e [ljɔnɛ, -ɛz] ADJ of/from Lyon
NM *(dialecte)* Lyon dialect
• **Lyonnais, -e** NM,F = inhabitant of or person from Lyon
• **à la lyonnaise** ADJ *Culin* (à la) lyonnaise *(cooked with minced onions stewed in butter)*

lyophilisation [ljɔfilizasjɔ̃] NF freeze-drying, *Spéc* lyophilization

lyophiliser [3] [ljɔfilize] VT to freeze-dry, *Spéc* to lyophilize

lyre [lir] NF *Mus* lyre

lyrique [lirik] ADJ **1** *Littérature (poésie)* lyric; *(inspiration, passion)* lyrical **2** *Mus & Théât (ténor, soprano)* lyric *(avant n)*; **l'art l.** opera; **artiste l.** opera singer
NM lyric poet

lyrisme [lirism] NM lyricism; **avec l.** lyrically; *Fig* **parler de qch avec l.** to wax lyrical about sth

lys [lis] = **lis**

lysergique [lizɛrʒik] ADJ lysergic

Lysol® [lizɔl] NM *Pharm* Lysol®

M

M¹, m¹ [em] **NM INV** *(lettre)* M, m

M² **1** *(abrév écrite* **million***)* M **2** *(abrév écrite* **masculin***)* M **3** *(abrév écrite* **méga***)* M

M. *(abrév écrite* **Monsieur***)* Mr

m² **1** *(abrév écrite* **mètre***)* **60 m** 60 m **2** *(abrév écrite* **milli***)* m

m' [m] **PRON** *voir* **me**

ma [ma] *voir* **mon**

maboul, -e [mabul] *Fam* **ADJ** crazy, bananas
NM,F (raving) loony

mac [mak] **NM** *Fam (abrév* **maquereau***)* pimp, *Am* mack

Macabées [makabe] = **Macchabées**

macabre [makabr] **ADJ** *(découverte)* macabre, gruesome; *(spectacle)* gruesome, macabre, grisly; *(humour)* macabre; **un goût pour ce qui est m.** a taste for the macabre

macache [makaʃ] **ADV** *Fam Vieilli* **m. (bono)!** no way (José)!, *Br* nothing doing!

macadam [makadam] **NM 1** *(matériau, surface)* macadam; **m. goudronné** tarmacadam; **route en m.** tarmac road **2** *(route)* road, roadway, *Spéc* macadam; *Fam* **faire le m.** to walk the streets

macadamiser **[3]** [makadamize] **VT** to macadamize

macaque [makak] **NM** *Zool* macaque; **m. rhésus** rhesus monkey
NMF *Fam (personne laide)* pig; **un vieux m.** an old baboon

macareux [makarø] **NM** *Orn* puffin

macaron [makarɔ̃] **NM 1** *Culin* macaroon
2 *(vignette ▸ officielle)* badge; *(▸ publicitaire)* sticker; *Journ* **m. de presse** press badge
3 *Fam (décoration honorifique)* rosette▫; **il a eu son m.** he got his decoration▫
4 *(de cheveux)* coil; **porter des macarons** to wear (one's hair in) coils
5 *Fam (coup)* blow▫, biff

macaroni [makarɔni] **NM 1** *Culin* piece of macaroni; **des macaronis** macaroni; **gratin de macaronis** *Br* macaroni cheese, *Am* macaroni and cheese **2** *très Fam (Italien)* wop, Eyetie, = offensive term used to refer to an Italian

macchabée [makabe] **NM** *Fam (cadavre)* stiff

Macchabéen, -enne [makabeɛ̃, -ɛn] **ADJ** *Hist* Maccabean

Macchabées [makabe] **NMPL** *Hist* **les M.** the Maccabees

MacDo [makdo] **NM** *Fam* McDonalds▫

macdonaldisation [makdɔnaldizasjɔ̃] **NF** Mcdonaldization

macdonaldiser **[3]** [makdɔnaldize] **VT** to Mcdonaldize

Macédoine [masedwan] **NF** *Géog* **la M.** Macedonia

macédoine [masedwan] **NF** *Culin* **m. de fruits** fruit salad; **m. de légumes** (diced) mixed vegetables

macédonien, -enne [masedɔnjɛ̃, -ɛn] **ADJ** Macedonian
NM *(langue)* Macedonian
• **Macédonien, -enne** **NM,F** Macedonian

macération [maserasjɔ̃] **NF 1** *Culin* maceration, steeping **2** *Pharm* maceration

macérer **[18]** [masere] **VI 1** *Culin* to macerate, to steep; **faire m. le poisson cru dans du jus de citron** macerate *or* steep the raw fish in lemon juice; **les oranges ont macéré 24 heures** the oranges have been macerating for 24 hours; **la viande doit m. plusieurs jours** the meat should be left to steep *or* soak for several days **2** *Pharm* to macerate **3** *Fig Fam* **laisse-le m. dans son jus** let him stew in his (own) juice
VT 1 *Culin* to macerate, to steep **2** *Pharm* to macerate

Mach [mak] **NPR** *Aviat* Mach

mâche [maʃ] **NF** corn salad, lamb's lettuce

mâchefer [maʃfɛr] **NM** *(du charbon)* clinker, slag

mâchement [maʃmɑ̃] **NM** chewing, *Sout* mastication

mâcher **[3]** [maʃe] **VT 1** *(aliment)* to chew; *(sujet: animal)* to champ, to chomp; **mâche-le bien** chew it well; **ne fais pas tant de bruit quand tu mâches** don't munch so loudly; *Fig* **il ne mâche pas ses mots** he doesn't mince his words **2** *Fam (tâche)* **m. le travail** *ou* **la besogne à qn** to spoon-feed sb

machette [maʃɛt] **NF** machete

Machiavel [makjavɛl] **NPR** Machiavelli

machiavélique [makjavelik] **ADJ** Machiavellian

machiavélisme [makjavelism] **NM** Machiavellianism

mâchicoulis [maʃikuli] **NM** machicolation
• **à mâchicoulis** **ADJ** machicolated

machin [maʃɛ̃] **NM** *Fam* **1** *(chose)* thing▫, thingy; **c'est quoi, ce m.?** what's this thing? **2** *(personne ▸ en s'adressant à la personne)* what's-your-name; *(homme ▸ en parlant de lui)* what's-his-name; *(femme ▸ en parlant d'elle)* what's-her-name; **M. Chouette** what's-his-name, *f* what's-her-name; **monsieur M.** Mr What's-his-name, what-d'you-call-him; **madame M.** Mrs What's-her-name, what-d'you-call-her

machinal, -e, -aux, -ales [maʃinal, -o] **ADJ** *(geste)* involuntary, unconscious; *(réaction)* automatic, instinctive; **un travail m.** mechanical work; **faire qch de façon machinale** to do sth automatically

machinalement [maʃinalmɑ̃] **ADV 1** *(involontairement)* automatically, without thinking; **m., il lui rendit son sourire** he smiled back at him/her automatically; **excuse-moi, je l'ai fait m.** sorry, I did it automatically *or* without thinking **2** *(mécaniquement)* mechanically, without thinking; **elle fait son travail m.** she does her work mechanically *or* without thinking

machination [maʃinasjɔ̃] **NF** plot, conspiracy, machination; **des machinations** plotting *(UNCOUNT)*, machinations

machine [maʃin] **NF 1** *(appareil)* machine, piece of machinery; **l'âge des machines** *ou* **de la m.** the machine age, the age of the machine; *Fam* **aller en m.** *(vêtement)* to be machine-washable▫; **m. à calculer** calculator; *(plus grande)* adding machine, calculating machine; **m. à adresser** addressing machine; **m. à affranchir** *Br* franking machine, *Am* postal meter; **m. agrafeuse** stapling machine, stapler; **m. à aléser** boring machine, fine borer; **m. à battre** threshing machine; **m. de bureau** office machine; **m. à café** coffee machine; *Typ* **m. à composer** typesetting machine; **m. comptable** accounting machine; **m. à coudre** sewing machine; **m. à écrire** typewriter; **m. à écrire à mémoire** memory typewriter; **m. à fraiser** milling machine; **m. de guerre** *Hist* engine of war; *Fig* war machine; **m. infernale** explosive device, *Arch* infernal machine; **m. interprète de cartes perforées** punch-card reader; **m. à laver**, *Belg* **m. à lessiver** washing machine; **m. à laver séchante** washer-dryer; **m. à laver la vaisselle** dishwasher; **m. à plier les documents** paper folding machine; **m. poinçonneuse** *(de cartes perforées)* punch; **m. à polycopier** duplicating machine; **m. à rayons X** X-ray machine; *Tech* **m. de rectification** grinding machine; **m. à repasser** steam press; **m. simple/composée** simple/compound machine; **m. à sous** one-armed bandit, *Br* fruit machine; **m. de traitement de l'information** data processor; **m. à** *ou* **de traitement de texte** word processor; **m. à tricoter** knitting machine; **m. trieuse** sorter; **m. à vapeur** steam engine; **m. volante** flying machine
2 *(véhicule)* machine; *Fam (moto)* machine; **machines agricoles** agricultural machinery
3 *(locomotive)* locomotive, engine
4 *Naut (moteur)* engine; **arrêtez** *ou* **stoppez les machines!** stop all engines!; **chambre** *ou* **salle des machines** engine room; **faire m. arrière** to go astern; *Fig* to backtrack
5 *(organisation)* machine, machinery; **les lourdeurs de la m. judiciaire** the cumbersome legal machine; *Pol* **m. du parti** party machine
6 *Théât* machine, piece of theatre machinery; **pièce à machines** play with stage effects
7 *Fig Péj (automate)* machine; **il n'est qu'une m. à faire de l'argent** he's nothing but a money-making machine
8 *Can Joual (voiture)* car▫, wheels, *Br* motor
9 *Fig Hum* **la m. est usée** *(le corps humain)* the old body is tired
10 *Fam (femme ▸ en s'adressant à elle)* what's-your-name; *(▸en parlant d'elle)* what's-her-name
• **à la machine** **ADV** **(fait) à la m.** *(objets)* machine-made; *(opération)* done by machine; **coudre qch à la m.** to sew sth on the machine, to machine *or* to machine-sew sth; **laver qch à la m.** *ou* **en m.** to machine-wash sth, to wash sth in the machine; **taper qch à la m.** to type sth; **tricoter qch à la m.** to machine-knit sth, to make sth on the knitting machine; **travailler le métal à la m.** to machine metal

machine-outil [maʃinuti] *(pl* **machines-outils***)* **NF** machine tool; **l'industrie de la m.** the machine-tool industry **m. à commande numérique** numerically controlled machine tool

machiner **[3]** [maʃine] **VT** *Fam (préparer ▸ complot)* to hatch; *(▸ affaire, histoire)* to plot; **ils ont machiné toute l'histoire afin de l'éliminer** they engineered the whole thing to get rid of him/her

machinerie [maʃinri] **NF 1** *(machines)* machinery, equipment, plant; **c'est la m. qui coûte le plus cher** most of the money goes on equipment **2** *(salle)* machine room; *Naut* engine room **3** *Théât* machinery

machinisme [maʃinism] **NM** mechanization

machiniste [maʃinist] **NMF 1** *Théât* stagehand, scene shifter; **les machinistes** (the) stage staff
2 *Cin & TV* **m. (de plateau)** grip; **m. caméra** dolly

operator; **m. de travelling** tracker
3 *Transp (chauffeur)* driver; **faire signe au m.** *(sur panneau)* ≃ request stop
4 *Belg (conducteur de train)* train driver
5 *Ind* machine tool operator

machisme [matʃism] NM *Péj* male chauvinism

machiste [matʃist] *Péj* ADJ male chauvinist *(avant n)*
NM male chauvinist

machmètre [makmɛtr] NM *Aviat* machmeter

macho [matʃo] *Fam Péj* ADJ male chauvinist□ *(avant n)*
NM male chauvinist□

mâchoire [mɑʃwar] NF **1** *Anat* jaw; **m. inférieure/supérieure** lower/upper jaw; *Fam* **jouer** *ou* **travailler des mâchoires** *(manger avec appétit)* to get stuck in **2** *Zool* jaw; *(d'insectes)* mandible
• **mâchoires** NFPL *(d'un outil)* jaws; *(d'une poulie)* flange; **mâchoires de frein** brake shoes

mâchonnement [mɑʃɔnmɑ̃] NM **1** *(fait de mâcher)* chewing *(UNCOUNT)*; **des mâchonnements bruyants** munching *(UNCOUNT)*, chomping *(UNCOUNT)* **2** *Méd* bruxism

mâchonner [3] [mɑʃɔne] VT **1** *(mâcher ▸ aliment)* to chew; *(▸ brin d'herbe, crayon)* to chew *or* to nibble (at); *(▸ cigare)* to chew (on); *(sujet: âne, cheval)* to munch; **m. son crayon** to chew (the end of) one's pencil; **un âne mâchonnait de la paille** a donkey was munching some straw **2** *Fig (marmonner)* to mumble; **en mâchonnant des injures** mumbling insults

mâchouiller [3] [mɑʃuje] VT *Fam (aliment)* to chew (away) at□; *(brin d'herbe)* to chew *or* to nibble (away) at□; **arrête de m. des bonbons!** stop chewing sweets all the time!

mâchure [mɑʃyr] NF *Tex* flaw

mâchurer[1] [3] [mɑʃyre] VT *Typ* to mackle, to blur

mâchurer[2] [3] [mɑʃyre] VT *(écraser)* to crush, to squash, to mash; *Tech (partie métallique d'un étau)* to dent, to bruise

macis [masi] NM *Culin* mace

Mackenzie [makenzi] NM *Géog* **le M.** *(fleuve)* the Mackenzie

macle [makl] NF *(de cristaux)* macle

mâcon [makɔ̃] NM Mâcon (wine)

maçon, -onne [masɔ̃, -ɔn] ADJ *Zool* mason *(avant n)*; **guêpe maçonne** mason wasp
NM,F *(franc-maçon)* Mason
NM *Constr (entrepreneur)* builder; *(ouvrier) Br* bricklayer, *Am* mason; *(qui travaille la pierre)* (stone)mason

maçonnage [masɔnaʒ] NM **1** *(travail)* building, bricklaying; *(de pierres)* laying of stones **2** *(ouvrage)* masonry

maçonner [3] [masɔne] VT **1** *(construire)* to build
2 *(réparer)* to rebuild, to redo the brickwork of
3 *(revêtir ▸ gén)* to line; *(▸ avec des briques)* to brickline, to line with bricks; *(▸ avec des pierres)* to face with stone
4 *(boucher ▸ gén)* to block up; *(▸ avec des briques)* to brick up *or* over; *(▸ porte, fenêtre)* to wall up; **ça a été bien maçonné** *(gén)* the masonry's good; *(pierres)* the stonework's good; *(briques)* the brickwork's good

maçonnerie [masɔnri] NF **1** *(ouvrage ▸ en pierres, en moellons)* stonework, masonry; *(▸ en briques)* brickwork; **entreprise de m.** building *or* construction firm; **m. sèche** *ou* **en pierres sèches** dry masonry; **2** *(travaux)* **grosse m.** work on the superstructure; **petite m.** interior building work
3 *(franc-maçonnerie)* Freemasonry

maçonnique [masɔnik] ADJ Masonic

macramé [makrame] NM macramé; **en m.** macramé *(avant n)*

macre [makr] NF water chestnut

macreuse[1] [makrøz] NF *Orn* scoter (duck); **m. brune** velvet scoter; **m. noire** common scoter

macreuse[2] [makrøz] NF *Culin* shoulder of beef

macrobiotique [makrɔbjɔtik] ADJ macrobiotic
NF macrobiotics *(singulier)*

macrocéphale [makrɔsefal] ADJ macrocephalic, macrocephalous
NMF person suffering from macrocephaly

macroclimat [makrɔklima] NM macroclimate

macrocommande [makrɔkɔmɑ̃d] NF *Ordinat* macro (command)

macrocosme [makrɔkɔsm] NM macrocosm

macrodéchets [makrodeʃɛ] NMPL = large items of rubbish polluting the sea

macroéconomie [makrɔekɔnɔmi] NF macroeconomics *(singulier)*

macroéconomique [makrɔekɔnɔmik] ADJ macroeconomic

macroenvironnement [makrɔɑ̃virɔnmɑ̃] NM *Mktg* macroenvironment

macrolangage [makrɔlɑ̃gaʒ] NM *Ordinat* macro language

macromarketing [makrɔmarketiŋ] NM macromarketing

macromolécule [makrɔmɔlekyl] NF *Chim* macromolecule

macro-ordinateur [makrɔɔrdinatœr] *(pl* **macro-ordinateurs)** NM mainframe

macrophotographie [makrɔfɔtɔgrafi] NF macrophotography

macropode [makrɔpɔd] NM *Ich* paradise fish

macroscopique [makrɔskɔpik] ADJ macroscopic

macrostructure [makrɔstryktyr] NF macrostructure

macula [makyla] NF *Anat* macula

maculage [makylaʒ] NM **1** *Typ* mackle **2** *Littéraire (fait de salir)* dirtying, soiling; *(salissures)* stains, marks, dirt

maculature [makylatyr] NF *Typ (pour l'emballage)* waste sheet; *(feuille tachée)* smudged *or* mackled sheet; *(feuille intercalaire)* interleaf

macule [makyl] NF **1** *Méd* macula, macule **2** *Typ (pour l'emballage)* waste sheet; *(feuille tachée)* smudged *or* mackled sheet; *(tache)* mackle, smudge; *(feuille intercalaire)* interleaf

maculer [3] [makyle] VT **1** *Littéraire (tacher)* to dirty, to spatter (**de** with); **maculé de sang** bloodstained; **maculé de boue** spattered with mud; **maculé de taches d'encre** smeared with ink stains **2** *Typ* to mackle

Madagascar [madagaskar] NF *Géog* Madagascar; **la République démocratique de M.** the Democratic Republic of Madagascar

Madame [madam] *(pl* **Mesdames** [medam]*)* NF **1** *(au début d'une lettre)* **M.** Dear Madam; **Chère M.** Dear Madam; **M. le Maire** Dear Madam, *Sout* Madam
2 *(sur une enveloppe)* **M. Duval** Mrs Duval; **M. Marie Duval** Mrs Marie Duval; **Mesdames Duval et Lamiel** Mrs Duval and Mrs Lamiel; **M. la Présidente Duval** Mrs Duval
3 *(terme d'adresse)* Madam; **Mesdames** ladies; **bonjour M.** good morning(, Madam); **bonjour M. Duval** good morning, Mrs Duval; **bonjour Mesdames** good morning(, ladies); **merci, M.** thank you; **M. la Présidente, je proteste!** Madam Chairman, I must raise an objection!; **Mesdames, Mesdemoiselles, Messieurs!** Ladies and Gentlemen!; **et voilà, M., une belle laitue fraîche** here you are, Madam, a nice fresh lettuce; *Sout ou Hum* **M. est servie** *(au dîner)* dinner is served(, Madam); *(pour le thé)* tea is served(, Madam); **M. a sonné?** you rang, Madam?; **vous n'y pensez pas, chère M.!** you can't be serious, my dear lady *or* Madam!; **bonjour M., je voudrais la comptabilité s'il vous plaît** *(au téléphone)* hello, I'd like to speak to someone in the accounts department, please
4 *(en se référant à une tierce personne)* **adressez-vous à M. Duval** go and see Mrs Duval; **M. veuve Duval** Mrs Duval, widow of Mr Duval; *Sout* **comment va M. votre mère?** how is your mother?; **Monsieur le docteur Duval et M.** *(pour annoncer)* Doctor (Duval) and Mrs Duval; **M. la Présidente regrette de ne pas pouvoir venir** the chairwoman regrets she is unable to come; **M. est sortie** Madam is not at home; **c'est le chapeau de M.** it's the lady's hat; **M. se plaint que...** *(dit par vendeur)* the lady *or* this lady is complaining that...
5 *Scol* **M., j'ai fini mon addition!** (please) Miss, I've finished my sums!
6 *Fam Ironique* **et en plus, M. exige des excuses!** and so Her Ladyship wants an apology as well, does she?

madame [madam] *(pl* **madames)** NF lady; **jouer à la m.** *(femme)* to put on airs; *(enfant)* to play at being grown up

Madeleine [madlɛn] NPR *Bible* Magdalen(e)

madeleine [madlɛn] NF *Culin* madeleine; **pour moi, ce fut (comme) la m. de Proust** it brought back (a flood of) old memories

Mademoiselle [madmwazɛl] *(pl* **Mesdemoiselles** [medmwazɛl]*)* NF **1** *(dans une lettre)* **M.** Dear Madam; **Chère M.** Dear Madam
2 *(sur une enveloppe)* **M. Duval** Miss Duval; **M. Anne Duval** Miss Anne Duval; **Mesdemoiselles Duval** the Misses Duval; **Mesdemoiselles Duval et Jonville** Miss Duval and Miss Jonville
3 *(terme d'adresse)* Miss, *Sout ou Hum* Miss, Madam; **Mesdemoiselles** ladies; **bonjour M.** good morning(, Miss); **bonjour Mesdemoiselles** good morning(, ladies); **bonjour M. Duval** good morning, Miss Duval; **bonjour Mesdemoiselles Duval** good morning, (young) ladies; **merci m.** thank you, *Sout* thank you, Miss; *(à une femme qui s'appelle Martin)* thank you, Miss Martin; **et voilà, M., une belle laitue pommée!** here you are, Miss, a nice round lettuce!; **M., vous attendrez votre tour comme tout le monde!** you'll have to wait your turn like everybody else, young lady!; **Mesdemoiselles, un peu de silence, s'il vous plaît!** *(à des fillettes)* girls, please be quiet!; *(à des jeunes filles)* ladies, would you please be quiet!; **M. désire-t-elle voir nos derniers modèles?** would Madam like to see our latest designs?; *Sout ou Hum* **M. est servie** *(au dîner)* dinner is served(, Miss); *(pour le thé)* tea is served(, Miss); **M. a sonné?** you rang, Miss?; **le frère de M. attend en bas** *(à une roturière)* your brother is waiting downstairs, Miss *or Sout* Madam; *(à une jeune femme titrée)* Your Ladyship's brother is waiting downstairs; **vous n'y pensez pas, chère M.!** you can't be serious, dear *or* young lady!
4 *(en se référant à une tierce personne)* **c'est M. Duval qui s'en occupe** Miss Duval is dealing with it; **M. votre sœur** your good *or* dear sister; *Vieilli Sout* **comment va M. votre cousine?** how is your cousin?; **Monsieur le docteur Duval et M.** *(pour annoncer)* Doctor (Duval) and Miss Duval; **Mesdemoiselles, Messieurs!** Ladies and Gentlemen!; **c'est le chapeau de M.** it's the young lady's hat; **peux-tu prêter un moment ton stylo à M.?** could you lend the young lady your pen for a minute?
5 *Scol* **M., j'ai fini mon dessin!** Miss, I've finished my drawing!
6 *Fam Ironique* **et en plus, M. se plaint!** so, Her Ladyship is complaining as well, is she?; **alors, M. la spécialiste, qu'en penses-tu?** what does Her Ladyship think, then?

Madère [madɛr] NM Madeira; **à M.** in Madeira

madère [madɛr] NM *(vin)* Madeira (wine)

madone [madɔn] NF **1** *Beaux-Arts* Madonna; **les madones de Raphaël** Raphael's Madonnas; **un visage de m.** a Madonna-like face; **une m. à l'enfant** a Madonna and Child **2** *(statuette)* Madonna, statue of the Virgin Mary **3** *Rel* **la M.** the Madonna, the Virgin Mary

madras [madras] NM **1** *(étoffe)* madras (cotton) **2** *(foulard)* madras scarf

madré, -e [madre] ADJ **1** *(bois)* knotty **2** *Littéraire (rusé)* crafty, cunning
NM,F *Littéraire* crafty person; **c'est une petite madrée!** she's a sly one!; **c'est un vieux m.!** he's a crafty *or* cunning old devil!

madrépore [madrepɔr] NM madrepore

Madrid [madrid] NF Madrid

madrier [madrije] NM (piece of) timber; *(façonné)* thick board *or* plank; *(poutre)* beam

madrigal, -aux [madrigal, -o] NM *Mus & Littérature* madrigal

madrilène [madrilɛn] ADJ of/from Madrid
• **Madrilène** NMF = inhabitant of or person from Madrid

maelström [maelstrɔm] NM **1** *Géog* maelstrom **2** *Fig (agitation)* maelstrom, whirlpool

maestria [maɛstrija] NF (great) skill, mastery, brilliance; **avec m.** masterfully, brilliantly

maestro [maɛstro] **NM** *Mus* maestro; *Fig* maestro, master

maffia [mafja] *voir* **mafia**

maffieux, -euse [mafjø, -øz] *voir* **mafieux**

maffioso [mafjozo] *voir* **mafioso**

mafflu, -e [mafly] **ADJ** *Littéraire (personne)* chubby-cheeked, chubby-faced; *(visage)* chubby

mafia [mafja] **NF 1** *(en Sicile, aux États-Unis)* **la M.** the Mafia **2** *(bande)* gang; **il s'était formé toute une m. de petits commerçants** the shopkeepers had formed themselves into a real little gang **3** *Péj (groupe fermé)* clique; **le milieu du cinéma est une véritable m.** the cinema world is very cliquey

mafieux, -euse [mafjø, -øz] **ADJ le milieu m.** the Mafia; *Fig* **des méthodes mafieuses** Mafia-like methods
NM,F mafioso

mafioso [mafjozo] *(pl* **mafiosi** *ou* **maffiosi** [-zi]) **NM** mafioso

maganer [3] [magane] **VT** *Can Fam* **1** *(user)* to wear out□ **2** *(réprimander)* **m. qn** to lay into sb, to bawl sb out

magasin [magazɛ̃] **NM 1** *(boutique) esp Br* shop, *esp Am* store; **faire** *ou* **courir les magasins** to go round the shops, to go shopping; **elle tient un m. en face de l'église** she has *or* keeps a shop opposite the church; **vous trouverez ça dans n'importe quel m.** you'll find it anywhere; **m. d'ameublement/de jouets** furniture/toy shop; **m. d'alimentation** *Br* food shop, *Am* grocery store; **un petit m. d'alimentation** *Br* a grocer's shop, *Am* a grocery (store); **grand m.** department store; **m. (d'articles) de sport** *Br* sports shop, *Am* sporting goods store; **m. de détail** retail shop *or* outlet; **m. détaxé** duty-free shop; **m. de discount** discount store; *Ordinat* **m. électronique** on-line shop; **m. d'exposition** showroom; **m. franchisé** franchise; **m. sous franchise exclusive** tied outlet; *Can Fam* **m. général** general store□; **m. à grande surface** hypermarket; **m. hors taxe** duty-free shop; **m. d'informatique** computer store; *Mktg* **m. laboratoire** = test-shop used to monitor consumer behaviour; **m. de luxe** luxury goods shop; **m. minimarge** discount store; *Vieilli* **m. de nouveautés** *Br* draper's shop, *Am* dry goods store; **m. de proximité** local shop; *Can Fam* **m. à rayons** department store□; **m. à succursales (multiples)** chain *or* multiple store; **m. de tissus** drapery; **m. d'usine** factory shop, factory outlet; **m. de vente au détail** retail shop; **m. de vêtements** *Br* clothes shop, *Am* clothing store; **m. vidéo** video shop
2 *(entrepôt ▸ industriel)* warehouse, store, storehouse; *(▸ d'une boutique)* storeroom; *(▸ d'une unité militaire)* quartermaster's store, magazine; **avoir qch en m.** to have sth in stock; *Mil* **m. d'armes** armoury; *Mil* **m. d'explosifs** explosives store *or* magazine; **m. à grains** silo; *Douanes* **magasins généraux** bonded warehouse; *Mil* **m. à poudre** (powder) magazine
3 *Théât* **m. des accessoires** prop room; **m. de décors** scene dock
4 *Phot & (d'une arme)* magazine
5 *Ordinat* **m. à papier** *(d'une imprimante)* paper tray

magasinage [magazinaʒ] **NM 1** *Com (mise en magasin)* warehousing, storing; **frais** *ou* **droits de m.** warehouse *or* storage (charges) **2** *Can (courses)* shopping; **faire du m.** to go shopping

magasiner [3] [magazine] *Can* **VI** to shop; **aller m.** to go shopping; **m. en ligne** to shop online
VT to shop around for

magasinier [magazinje] **NM** *(dans une usine)* storekeeper, storeman; *(dans un entrepôt)* warehouseman

magazine [magazin] **NM 1** *(de presse écrite)* magazine; **m. d'actualités** current affairs magazine; **m. de bandes dessinées** comic book; **m. féminin** women's magazine; **m. d'information** news magazine; **m. littéraire** literary magazine *or* review; **le M. littéraire** = French monthly literary magazine; **un m. médical** a medical journal; **m. people** celebrity magazine; **m. à sensation** trashy magazine **2** *Rad & TV* magazine (programme); **m. d'actualités** news programme; *Ordinat* **m. électronique** ezine, e-zine; **m. d'information** current affairs magazine (programme); *TV* **m. télé, m. télévisé** magazine programme

magdalénien, -enne [magdalenjɛ̃, -ɛn] **ADJ** Magdalenian
NM Magdalenian

mage [maʒ] **NM 1** *Antiq & Rel* magus **2** *Fig (voyant)* seer

magenta [maʒɛ̃ta] **ADJ INV** magenta
NM magenta

Maghreb [magrɛb] **NM le M.** the Maghreb

maghrébin, -e [magrebɛ̃, -in] **ADJ** North African
• **Maghrébin, -e NM,F** North African

> **MAGHRÉBIN**
>
> This term usually refers to people from Algeria, Morocco and Tunisia, although it can also refer to Libyans and Mauritanians. It has a particular resonance in contemporary France, where immigrants from these countries constitute the largest ethnic minority in France.

magicien, -enne [maʒisjɛ̃, -ɛn] **NM,F 1** *(illusionniste)* magician **2** *(sorcier)* magician, wizard; **Circé la magicienne** Circé the sorceress **3** *Fig (virtuose)* **un m. de** a master of; **vous êtes un m. du dessin/de la cuisine!** your art work/your cooking is magic!

magie [maʒi] **NF 1** *(sorcellerie)* magic; **m. blanche/noire** white/black magic; **comme par m.** as if by magic; *Ironique* **alors, ce bracelet, il a disparu comme par m.?** so this bracelet just disappeared by magic, did it? **2** *(charme)* magic; **la m. du printemps/du verbe** the magic of spring/language

magique [maʒik] **ADJ 1** *(surnaturel)* magical, magic; *(formule, baguette)* magic **2** *(féerique)* magical, wonderful; **un monde m. les attendait dans la vitrine de Noël** a wonderland was waiting for them in the Christmas window display

magiquement [maʒikmɑ̃] **ADV** magically

magister [maʒistɛr] **NM 1** *Arch (maître d'école)* (village) schoolmaster **2** *Péj (pédant)* pedant

magistère [maʒistɛr] **NM 1** *Univ* post-graduate vocational qualification **2** *(titre)* **le M. de l'Ordre de Malte** the Grand Master of the Order of Malta

magistral, -e, -aux, -ales [maʒistral, -o] **ADJ 1** *(remarquable)* brilliant, masterly; *(réussite)* brilliant, resounding; **une œuvre magistrale** a masterpiece, a masterwork
2 *(docte)* authoritative, masterful, *Sout* magisterial; **il prend toujours un ton m.** he always adopts an authoritative tone
3 *Scol* **cours m.** lecture; **enseignement m.** lecturing
4 *Pharm* specific, *Spéc* magistral; **préparation magistrale** = prescribed medication specially made up by the pharmacist for the particular patient
5 *(en intensif)* huge; *(erreur)* colossal, monumental; **une engueulade magistrale** a huge *or* massive row; **une claque magistrale** a great slap; **elle lui a cloué le bec de façon magistrale** she really shut him/her up in style

magistralement [maʒistralmɑ̃] **ADV** *aussi Hum* brilliantly, magnificently

magistrat [maʒistra] **NM 1** *Jur (qui rend la justice)* judge; *(qui applique la loi) Br* public prosecutor, *Am* prosecuting attorney; **m. inspecteur** visiting magistrate; **m. instructeur** investigating judge; **m. à la cour** *Br* public prosecutor, *Am* prosecuting attorney; **m. du parquet** ≃ member of the State Counsel's Office; **m. du siège** judge
2 *Admin & Pol* = any high-ranking civil servant with judicial authority; **m. municipal** *Br* town councillor, *Am* city councillor; **il est le premier m. de France** he is France's supreme judicial officer
3 *Mil* **m. militaire** judge advocate
4 *Antiq* magistrate

magistrature [maʒistratyr] **NF 1** *(personnes)* **la m.** the judicial authorities; **entrer dans la m.** *(devenir juge)* to be appointed a judge; *(devenir fonctionnaire public)* to be appointed a public prosecutor; *Jur* **la m. assise** the Bench *or* judges; *Jur* **la m. debout** *Br* the (body of) public prosecutors, *Am* the (body of) prosecuting attorneys; **la m. du parquet** ≃ the State Counsel's Office; **la m. du siège** ≃ the Bench, the judges of the ordinary courts; **la m. suprême** the presidency **2** *(fonction)* office; **pendant sa m.** during his/her period in office

magma [magma] **NM 1** *Chim & Géol* magma **2** *Fig Péj (mélange confus)* jumble; **un m. informe de boue et de pierres** a shapeless heap *or* pile of mud and stones

magnanerie [maɲanri] **NF 1** *(activité)* silkworm breeding **2** *(lieu)* silkworm nursery

magnanier, -ère [maɲanje, -ɛr] **NM,F** silkworm breeder

magnanime [maɲanim] **ADJ** magnanimous; **se montrer m.** to show magnanimity, to be magnanimous

magnanimement [maɲanimmɑ̃] **ADV** magnanimously

magnanimité [maɲanimite] **NF** magnanimity; **elle a fait preuve de m. à leur égard** she displayed magnanimity *or* she was magnanimous towards them

magnat [maɲa] **NM 1** *(grand patron)* magnate, tycoon; **m. des médias** media mogul *or* magnate *or* tycoon; **m. de la presse** press baron; **m. du pétrole** oil tycoon **2** *Hist (de Pologne, de Hongrie)* magnate, grandee

magner [3] [maɲe] **se magner VPR** *Fam* **se m. (le train** *ou* **le popotin)** to get a move on, to get one's skates on, *Am* to get it in gear; *très Fam* **se m. le cul** to move *or* to shift one's *Br* arse *or Am* ass

magnésie [maɲezi] **NF** *Chim* magnesia; *(pour l'escalade)* chalk; *Pharm* **sulfate de m.** Epsom salts

magnésite [maɲezit] **NF** *Minér* **1** *(carbonate)* magnesite **2** *(silicate)* meerschaum

magnésium [maɲezjɔm] **NM** *Chim* magnesium; **éclair de m.** magnesium light *or* flash

magnétique [maɲetik] **ADJ 1** *Ordinat & Phys* magnetic **2** *Fig* magnetic; **exercer un pouvoir m. (sur)** to exert a hypnotic *or* magnetic power (on *or* over); **une attraction m. les poussa l'un vers l'autre** they were irresistibly drawn to each other

magnétiquement [maɲetikmɑ̃] **ADV** magnetically

magnétisable [maɲetizabl] **ADJ 1** *Phys* magnetizable **2** *(personne)* hypnotizable

magnétisation [maɲetizasjɔ̃] **NF 1** *Phys* magnetization **2** *(fascination)* fascination, mesmeric effect

magnétiser [3] [maɲetize] **VT 1** *Phys* to magnetize **2** *(fasciner)* to mesmerize, to fascinate, to hypnotize; **il sait m. les foules** he hypnotizes audiences, he has a mesmerizing effect on audiences

magnétiseur, -euse [maɲetizœr, -øz] **NM,F** hypnotist

magnétisme [maɲetism] **NM 1** *Phys* magnetism **2** *(fascination, charisme)* magnetism, charisma; **le m. de son sourire** the magnetism of his/her smile, his/her magnetic smile **3** *(fluide)* **m. animal** animal magnetism

magnétite [maɲetit] **NF** magnetite

magnéto [maɲeto] **NM** *Fam* **1** *(magnétophone)* tape recorder□, cassette player□ **2** *(magnétoscope) Br* video, *Am* VCR
NF *Électron* magneto

magnétocassette [maɲetɔkasɛt] **NM** cassette deck *or* recorder

magnétoencéphalographie [maɲetɔɑ̃sefalɔgrafi] **NF** *Méd* magnetoencephalography

magnétomètre [maɲetɔmɛtr] **NM** magnetometer

magnétophone [maɲetɔfɔn] **NM** tape recorder; **m. à cassette(s)** cassette recorder; **m. à bande(s)** audio tape recorder; **m. à bobines** reel-to-reel tape recorder; **je l'ai enregistré sur** *ou* **au m.** I've taped *or* tape-recorded it

magnétoscope [maɲetɔskɔp] **NM** *Br* video, videorecorder, *Am* VCR; **enregistrer un film au m.** to video a film, to record a film on video; **m. d'enregistrement** recording deck; **m. de lecture** playback deck; **m. à cassette** video cassette recorder,

VCR; **m. à cassette vidéo numérique** digital video recorder

magnétoscoper [3] [maɲetɔskɔpe] **VT** to videotape, to video

magnificat [maɲifikat] **NM INV** Magnificat

magnificence [maɲifisɑ̃s] **NF 1** *(faste)* luxuriousness, magnificence, splendour **2** *Littéraire (prodigalité)* munificence, lavishness

magnifier [9] [maɲifje] **VT 1** *(célébrer)* to glorify, *Sout* to magnify; **m. le Seigneur** to magnify the Lord **2** *(élever)* to exalt, to idealize

magnifique [maɲifik] **ADJ 1** *(très beau ▸ vue, nuit, robe)* magnificent, splendid, superb; **il faisait un temps m.** the weather was gorgeous *or* glorious; **elle était m. dans sa robe de mariée** she looked magnificent *or* wonderful in her wedding dress; **un bébé m.** a beautiful baby

2 *(de grande qualité)* magnificent, excellent, wonderful; **mon boucher a de la viande m.** my butcher has excellent *or* first-rate meat; **elle a une situation m. chez un agent de change** she has a fantastic *or* marvellous job with a stockbroker

3 *(remarquable ▸ découverte, progrès)* remarkable, wonderful

4 *(somptueux ▸ appartement, repas)* splendid, magnificent; **la m. salle du trône** the magnificent *or* grandiose throne room

5 *Vieilli (généreux, prodigue ▸ personne)* liberal, munificent; **Laurent le M.** Lorenzo il Magnifico

magnifiquement [maɲifikmɑ̃] **ADV 1** *(somptueusement)* magnificently, lavishly, gorgeously; **m. illustré** lavishly illustrated; **m. vêtu** beautifully dressed **2** *(bien)* superbly; **il se porte m.** he's in great shape; **la journée avait m. commencé** the day had begun gloriously; **un morceau de musique m. exécuté** a brilliantly performed piece of music

magnitude [maɲityd] **NF 1** *Géol* magnitude; **un séisme de m. 5 sur l'échelle de Richter** an earthquake measuring 5 on the Richter scale **2** *Astron* **m. absolue/apparente/photographique** absolute/apparent/photographic magnitude

magnolia [maɲɔlja] **NM** magnolia (tree)

magnum [magnɔm] **NM** magnum *(bottle)*

magot[1] [mago] **NM 1** *(singe)* Barbary ape, magot **2** *(figurine orientale)* magot; **les Deux Magots** = famous café on the boulevard Saint-Germain in Paris, a meeting-place for Parisian "café society" after the Second World War

magot[2] [mago] **NM** *Fam* **1** *(argent caché)* stash; **où t'as mis le m.?** where've you stashed the loot? **2** *(argent)* loot, pile; **il a dû amasser un joli m.** he must have built up a nice little nest egg *or* a nice little pile; *Hum* **on partage le m.** let's share the loot

magouillage [magujaʒ] **NM** = **magouille**

magouille [maguj] **NF** *Fam* scheme; **magouilles électorales** vote-rigging

magouiller [3] [maguje] *Fam* **VT il magouille quelque chose** he's up to something

VI to scheme, to wheel and deal; **il est toujours en train de m.** he's always wheeling and dealing, he's always scheming; **il l'a eu en magouillant** he wangled it; **elle a dû m. pour avoir ce poste** she had to do some scheming to get the job

magouilleur, -euse [magujœr, -øz] *Fam* **ADJ** scheming

NM,F schemer, wheeler-dealer

magret [magrɛ] **NM m. (de canard)** magret of duck, fillet of duck breast

magyar, -e [magjar] **ADJ** Magyar

• **Magyar, -e NM,F** Magyar

maharadjah, maharaja [maaradʒa] **NM** maharajah, maharaja

maharané [maarane], **maharani** [maarani] **NF** maharani, maharanee

mahatma [maatma] **NM** mahatma

mah-jong [maʒɔ̃g] **NM** mah-jongg, mahjong

Mahomet [maɔmɛ] **NPR** Mahomet, Mohammed

mahométan, -e [maɔmetɑ̃, -an] *Vieilli* **ADJ** Mohammedan

• **Mahométan, -e NM,F** Mohammedan

mahométisme [maɔmetism] **NM** *Vieilli* Mohammedanism

mahous, -ousse [maus] = **maous**

mai [mɛ] **NM 1** *(mois)* May; **le premier m.** *(fête)* May Day; **le huit m.** *(fête)* VE Day; *Prov* **en m., fais ce qu'il te plaît** = in May, you don't need to wear winter clothes any more; **(les événements de) m. 1968** May 1968; *voir aussi* **mars 2** *Hist (arbre)* may *or* maypole tree

> **MAI 68**
>
> The events of May 1968 came about when student protests, coupled with widespread industrial unrest, culminated in a general strike and rioting. De Gaulle's government survived the crisis, but the issues raised made the events a turning point in French social history.

MAIF [maif] **NF** *(abrév* **Mutuelle assurance des instituteurs de France)** = mutual insurance company for primary-school teachers in France

maigre [mɛgr] **ADJ 1** *(très mince)* thin; **des bras/jambes maigres** thin arms/legs; **un visage m.** a thin face; **tu deviens trop m.** you're getting too thin; **un homme grand et m.** a tall, thin man; **m. comme un hareng saur** *ou* **un clou** *ou* **un coucou** as thin as a rake; *Can Fam* **m. comme un chicot** *ou* **un manche à balai** as thin as a rake

2 *Culin* **une soupe m.** a clear soup; **du fromage/yaourt m.** low-fat cheese/yoghurt; **viande/poisson m.** lean meat/fish; **régime m.** low-fat diet

3 *Rel* **jour m.** fast day

4 *Agr (terres, pâturages)* poor; **végétation m.** sparse vegetation

5 *(insuffisant ▸ gên)* thin, poor; *(▸ ration, repas)* small; *(▸ récolte, résultats, revenus)* meagre, poor; *(▸ barbe)* straggly, sparse; **un m. feu** a meagre *or* small fire; **un m. filet d'eau** a thin stream of water; **un m. filet de voix** a thin voice; **les bénéfices sont maigres** the profits are low *or* meagre *or* *Péj* paltry; **de maigres économies** (very) small savings; **de maigres ressources** meagre *or* scant resources; **un m. espoir** a slim *or* slight hope; **quelques maigres idées** a few flimsy ideas

6 *Fam (peu)* **8 euros après deux heures de collecte, c'est m.!** 8 euros after collecting for two hours, that's not much!; **c'est un peu m. comme prétexte!** that's a pretty poor excuse!

7 *Typ* roman, light, light-face(d); **caractères maigres** roman type, light-face(d) type

NMF thin person; **c'est une fausse m.** she isn't as thin as she looks

NM 1 *(d'une viande)* lean part

2 *Rel* **faire m.** to go without meat, to eat no meat; **le vendredi, on faisait m.** we never ate meat on Fridays

3 *Typ* roman *or* light *or* light-face(d) type

4 *Ich* meagre, maigre

• **maigres NMPL** *Géol* shallows

maigréchine [mɛgreʃin] **ADJ** *Can Fam* scrawny, skinny

maigrelet, -ette [mɛgrəlɛ, -ɛt] *Fam* **ADJ** (a bit) thin▫ *or* skinny

NM,F skinny *or* thin▫ person

maigrement [mɛgrəmɑ̃] **ADV** meagrely, poorly; **il est m. payé** he gets meagre wages

maigreur [mɛgrœr] **NF 1** *(minceur excessive)* thinness, leanness; **la m. de son visage** the thinness of his/her face; **le malade était d'une m. effrayante** the sick man was dreadfully thin **2** *(insuffisance)* thinness, meagreness, scantiness; *(de végétation)* sparseness, scantiness

maigrichine [mɛgriʃin] = **maigréchine**

maigrichon, -onne [mɛgriʃɔ̃, -ɔn] *Fam* **ADJ** skinny; **il est tout m.** he's scrawny; **des jambes maigrichonnes** skinny legs

NM,F skinny person

maigrir [32] [mɛgrir] **VI** to get *or* to grow thinner; **tu n'as pas besoin de m.** you don't need to lose (any) weight; **j'ai maigri de dix kilos** I've lost ten kilos; **elle a beaucoup maigri du visage** her face has got a lot thinner; **produits pour m.** diet *or* *Br* slimming aids; **faire m. qn** to make sb lose weight; **ces régimes ne (vous) font pas m.** these diets don't help you lose weight; *Fig* **mes économies maigrissent à vue d'œil** my savings are just vanishing *or* disappearing by the minute

VT 1 m. qn *(maladie)* to make sb thin *or* thinner; *(vêtement)* to make sb look thin *or* thinner; **ce costume le maigrit** this suit makes him look thinner **2** *(pièce de bois)* to thin

mail[1] [maj] **NM 1** *(allée)* mall; **sur le m.** along the mall **2** *Hist (jeu)* mall, pall-mall; *(maillet)* mallet

mail[2] [mɛl] = **e-mail**

mailing [mɛliŋ] **NM 1** *(procédé)* mailing, mail canvassing; **ce sont des clients que nous avons eus par m.** we acquired these customers through a mailshot **2** *(envoi de prospectus)* mailshot; **faire un m.** to do *or* send a mailshot

maillage [majaʒ] **NM 1** *Pêche* meshing **2** *Électron* grid

maillant [majɑ̃] *voir* **filet**

maille [maj] **NF 1** *(d'un filet)* mesh; **filet à mailles fines/larges** close-/wide-mesh(ed) net; *aussi Fig* **passer à travers les mailles du filet** to slip through the net

2 *Couture* stitch; **m. filée** *Br* ladder, *Am* run; **m. à l'endroit/à l'envers** plain/purl stitch; **tricoter une m. à l'endroit, une m. à l'envers** knit one, purl one

3 *(vêtements en maille)* knitwear; **une robe en m. de coton** a knitted cotton dress; **l'industrie de la m.** the knitwear industry

4 *(d'une chaîne)* link

5 *Électron* mesh

6 *Naut* frame space

7 *(sur le plumage)* speckle

8 *Fam (argent)* cash, *Br* dosh, *Am* bucks

9 *(locution)* **avoir m. à partir avec** to be at odds with; **il a eu m. à partir avec la justice** he's been in trouble *or* he's had a brush with the law

maillechort [majʃɔr] **NM** nickel *or* German silver

mailler [3] [maje] **VT 1** *(fil)* to net, to mesh

2 *Naut* to shackle

3 *(organiser en réseau)* to network

4 *Suisse (tordre, fausser)* to warp

VI 1 *Pêche* to be netted **2** *Suisse (s'énerver, se mettre en colère)* to get worked up

VPR se mailler *Suisse (se tordre)* **se m. la cheville/le genou** to twist one's ankle/one's knee; *Fig* **se m. de rire** to kill oneself (laughing), to be in stitches

maillet [majɛ] **NM 1** *(marteau)* mallet, maul **2** *Sport (au croquet)* mallet; *(au polo)* polo stick

mailloche [majɔʃ] **NF 1** *Tech (maillet, outil chauffant)* beetle; *(de mouleur)* rake **2** *Mus* bass drumstick

maillon [majɔ̃] **NM 1** *(chaînon)* link; **m. tournant** swivel; *Fig* **n'être qu'un m. de la chaîne** to be just one link in the chain **2** *Naut* shackle

maillot [majo] **NM 1** *(tee-shirt)* T-shirt, tee shirt; *(pour la danse)* leotard; *(de footballeur, d'équipe)* shirt, jersey; *(de coureur, de rameur)* vest, singlet; **m. (de bain)** *(de femme)* bathing *Br* costume *or Am* suit, *Br* swimming costume; *(d'homme)* (swimming *or* bathing) trunks; **m. une pièce/deux pièces** one-piece/two-piece swimsuit; **m. brassière** tankini; **la nouvelle collection de maillots** the new swimwear collection; **m. de corps** undershirt, *Br* vest, singlet; **le m. jaune** the yellow jersey; *(cycliste)* the leading cyclist in the Tour de France; **être m. jaune** to be the overall leader of the Tour de France; **le m. vert** the green jersey; *(cycliste)* the leading sprinter in the Tour de France **2** *Hist (pour bébé)* swaddling clothes

MAIN [mɛ̃] **NF 1** *(partie du corps)* hand; **avoir/tenir qch dans la m.** to have/hold sth in one's hand; **donner la m. à qn** to hold sb's hand; *Fig (en français régional) (l'aider)* to give sb a hand; **donne-moi la m.** give me your hand, hold my hand; **les enfants, tenez-vous par** *ou* **donnez-vous la m.** hold hands, children; **ils se donnaient la m., ils se tenaient (par) la m.** they were holding hands; *Fig* **ils peuvent se donner la m.!** they're as bad as each other!; **prendre qn par la m.** to take sb's hand, to take sb by the hand; *Fig* **tendre la m.** *(faire l'aumône)* to hold out one's hand, to beg; **tendre la m. (à qn)** to hold out *or* to stretch out one's hand (to sb); *Fig (pour l'aider)* to hold out *or* to stretch out a hand (to sb); *Fig* **tendre la m. à qn** *(lui pardonner)* to hold out one's hand to sb (in forgiveness); *Fig* **tenir la m. de qn** to hold sb's hand; **porter la m. à son chapeau** *(pour saluer)* to touch one's hat, to tip one's hat; *Fig* **mettre la m. à la poche** to put one's hand in one's pocket; *Fig* **on ne le voit pas souvent mettre la m. à son portefeuille** you don't often see him putting his hand in his pocket; **lève la m.** *(à l'école)* put your hand up, raise your hand; *Fig* **lever la m. sur qn** to raise one's hand to sb; **tu veux ma m. sur la figure?** do you want a slap?, you're asking for a slap!; **les mains en l'air!, haut les mains!** hands up!; **les mains derrière le dos/au-dessus de la tête!** hands behind your back/above your head!; **il m'a arraché le sac des mains** he snatched the bag out of my hands *or* from my hands; **la tasse lui a échappé des mains** the cup slipped *or* fell from his/her hands; **d'une m. assurée/tremblante** with a steady/trembling hand; **faire qch d'une m. habile** *ou* **experte** *ou* **exercée** to do sth skilfully; **travailler de ses mains** to work with one's hands; **ne rien savoir faire de ses mains** to be hopeless with one's hands; **écrire une lettre de sa propre m.** to write a letter in one's own hand; **prendre un plateau à deux mains** to take a tray in both hands; **empoigner** *ou* **prendre qch à pleines mains** to grab sth with both hands; **il prenait des bonbons à pleines mains** he was taking handfuls of sweets; *Mus* **à quatre mains** *(morceau)* for four hands; *(jouer)* four-handed; **mettre la m. sur qch** *(trouver ce que l'on cherchait)* to lay *or* to put one's hand(s) on sth; *(trouver par hasard)* to come across sth, to find sth; **je n'arrive pas à mettre la m. dessus** I can't find it, I can't lay my hands on it; *Hum* **je n'ai que deux mains** I only have one pair of hands; **il y a m.!** *(au football)* handball!

2 *(savoir-faire)* **avoir la m.** to have the knack; **il avait gardé la m.** he hadn't lost the knack *or* his touch; **se faire la m.** to practise; **perdre la m.** to lose one's touch; *(sportif, musicien)* to be out of practice

3 *Fig (intervention)* hand; **la m. de Dieu/du diable/du destin** the hand of God/of the Devil/of fate; **certains y voient la m. des services secrets** some people believe that the secret service have a hand in it; **reconnaître la m. de qn** to recognize sb's touch; **on reconnaît la m. du maître** this is obviously the work of a master

4 *Vieilli (permission d'épouser)* **demander/obtenir la m. d'une jeune fille** to ask for/to win a young lady's hand (in marriage); **elle m'a refusé sa m.** she refused my offer of marriage; **m'accorderez-vous votre m.?** will you give me your hand (in marriage)?

5 *Cartes* **m. pleine** full house *(at poker)*; **avoir la m.** *(faire la donne)* to deal; *(jouer le premier)* to lead; **céder** *ou* **passer la m.** to pass the deal; *Fig* to step *or* to stand down; *Fig* **passer la m. à son fils** to hand over the reins to one's son

6 *(gant de cuisine)* (oven) glove

7 *(ornement)* **m. de Fatma** hand of Fatima (pendant); **m. de justice** (hand-shaped) sceptre

8 *Couture* **petite m.** apprentice

9 *Typ (quantité)* ≃ quire *(of 25 sheets)*; **papier qui a de la m.** *(tenue)* paper which has bulk *or* substance

10 *Constr (poignée)* handle; **m. courante** handrail

11 *Compta* **m. courante** daybook; **m. courante de caisse** counter cash book; **m. courante de dépenses** paid cash book; **m. courante de justice** *(de commissariat de police)* incident book; **m. courante de recettes** received cash book

12 *Aut* **m. de ressort** dumb iron

13 *Équitation* **mener un cheval en m.** to lead a horse; **le cheval est dans** *ou* **sur la m.** the horse is well in hand; **mettre un cheval sur la m.** to put a horse on the bit; **rendre la m. à un cheval** to give a horse its head; **en arrière de la m.** behind the bit

14 *Écon* **m. invisible** invisible hand

15 *(locutions) Vieilli* **de longue m.** for a long time (past); **à m. levée** *(voter)* by a show of hands; *(dessiner)* freehand; **à mains nues** barehanded; **combattre à mains nues** to fight barehanded *or* with one's bare hands; **combat à mains nues** bare-fisted *or* bare-knuckle fight; **grand comme la m.** tiny; **un jardin grand comme la m.** a pocket-handkerchief-sized garden; **mener** *ou* **régenter qch d'une m. de fer** to rule sth with an iron hand; **une m. de fer dans un gant de velours** an iron fist in a velvet glove; **la m. sur le cœur** with one's hand on one's heart, in perfect good faith; **chercher une m. secourable** to look for a helping hand *or* for help; **aucune m. secourable ne se présenta** nobody came forward to help; **de m. de maître** masterfully, brilliantly; **un concerto exécuté de m. de maître** a masterfully performed concerto; **la cérémonie a été organisée de m. de maître** the ceremony was a masterpiece of organization; **c'est fait de m. de maître** it's a masterpiece; **passer aux mains de…** to pass *or* fall into the hands of…; **la décision est entre les mains du juge** the decision rests with *or* is in the hands of the judge; **le carnet est entre les mains de la police** the notebook is in the hands of the police; **mon avenir est entre vos mains** my future is in your hands; **la décision est entre vos mains** the decision is in your hands *or* is up to you *or* is yours; **être en bonnes mains, être entre de bonnes mains** to be in good hands; **j'ai laissé l'affaire en de bonnes mains** I left the matter in good hands; *Fig* **avoir/garder les mains libres** to have/to keep a free hand; **un téléphone avec fonction mains libres** a phone with hands-free option; **laisser les mains libres à qn** to give sb carte blanche *or* a free hand; *Fig* **j'ai les mains liées** my hands are tied; **arriver/rentrer les mains vides** to turn up/to go home empty-handed; *Fam Fig* **les mains dans les poches** with not a care in the world, free and easy; **pourquoi s'inquiéter? moi j'y vais les mains dans les poches!** why worry? I'm easy about the whole thing!; **gagner haut la m.** to win hands down; **avoir la haute m. sur** to have total *or* absolute control over; **avoir la m. heureuse** to be lucky; **tu as eu la m. heureuse, j'adore les œillets!** you've struck lucky, I love carnations!; **avoir la m. malheureuse** to be unlucky; **avoir la m. légère** *(être clément)* to be lenient; *(en cuisine)* to underseason; **avoir la m. leste** to be quick with one's hands; **avoir la m. lourde** *(être sévère)* to be harsh *or* heavy-handed; *(en cuisine)* to be heavy-handed (with the seasoning); **avoir la m. verte** to have *Br* green fingers *orAm* a green thumb; *Fam* **avoir qn à sa m.** to have sb under one's thumb; **avoir qch sous la m.** to have sth handy *or* within easy reach *or* close at hand; **garder qch sous la m.** to keep sth at *or* to hand; **j'ai ce qu'il me faut sous la m.** I have what I need at *or* to hand; **en venir aux mains** to come to blows; **faire m. basse sur** *(palais)* to raid, to ransack; *(marchandises, documents)* to get one's hands on; *Hum* **c'est toi qui as fait m. basse sur les chocolats?** are you the one who's been at the chocolates?; **j'en mettrais ma m. au feu** *ou* **à couper** I'd swear to it; **c'est lui, j'en mettrais ma m. au feu** that's him, I'd stake my life on it; **elle n'y est pas allée de m. morte** *(en frappant ou insultant quelqu'un)* she didn't pull her punches; *(exagérer)* she overdid it; **attention, la m. me démange!** watch it or you'll get a slap!; **mettre la m. à l'ouvrage** *ou* **à la pâte** to lend a hand; **mettre** *ou* **prêter la m. à** to have a hand *or* to take part in; **des spécialistes ont prêté la m. à la préparation du documentaire** experts had a hand in *or* participated in the making of the documentary; **mettre la dernière m. à qch** to put the finishing touches to sth; **c'est une photo à ne pas mettre entre toutes les mains** this photo mustn't fall into the wrong hands; **ce sont des documents qu'on ne peut pas mettre entre toutes les mains** these documents are not for general distribution; *Fam* **passer la m. dans le dos à qn** to butter sb up; **prendre qn la m. dans le sac** to catch sb red-handed; *Hum* **ah, ah, je te prends la m. dans le sac!** ha! I've caught you at it!; **tu ne trouveras pas de travail si tu ne te prends pas par la m.** you won't find a job unless you get a grip on yourself *or Br* you pull your socks up; **tomber dans les** *ou* **entre les** *ou* **aux mains de** to fall into the hands *or Péj* clutches of; **tomber aux mains de l'ennemi** to fall into enemy hands; **la première chemise qui me tombe sous la m.** the first shirt that comes to hand

ADV *(fabriqué, imprimé)* by hand; **fait/tricoté/cousu m.** hand-made/-knitted/-sewn; **trié m.** hand-picked

• **à la main** **ADV** **1** *(artisanalement)* **faire qch à la m.** to do sth by hand; *(fabriquer)* to make sth by hand; **fait à la m.** hand-made **2** **écrit à la m.** handwritten; **notes écrites à la m.** handwritten notes **3** *(dans les mains)* **avoir** *ou* **tenir qch à la m.** to hold sth in one's hand; **la fourchette à la m.** with one's fork in one's hand, fork in hand; **mourir les armes à la m.** to die on the battlefield

• **à main** **ADJ** *(levier, outil)* hand *(avant n)*, manual

• **à main droite** **ADV** on the right-hand side; **à m. droite, vous avez le lac** the lake is to *or* on your right

• **à main gauche** **ADV** on the left-hand side; **à m. gauche, vous avez l'église** the church is to *or* on your left

• **de la main** **ADV** with one's hand; **faire qch de la m. droite/gauche** to do sth right-handed/left-handed *or* with one's right/left hand; **saluer qn de la m.** *(pour dire bonjour)* to wave (hello) to sb; *(pour dire au revoir)* to wave (goodbye) to sb, to wave sb goodbye; **dire adieu de la m. à qn** to wave goodbye to sb; **de la m., elle me fit signe d'approcher** she waved me over

• **de la main à la main** **ADV** directly, without any middleman; **j'ai payé le plombier de la m. à la m.** I paid the plumber cash in hand

• **de la main de** **PRÉP** **1** *(fait par)* by; **une toile de la m. de Warhol** a canvas (painted) by Warhol; **la lettre est de la m. même de Proust** the letter is in Proust's own hand; **la lettre est de votre m.** the letter is in your handwriting **2** *(donné par)* from (the hand of); **elle a reçu son prix de la m. du président** she received her award from the President himself

• **de main en main** **ADV** from hand to hand, from one person to the next; **passer de m. en m.** *(objet)* to pass *or* be passed from hand to hand *or* from person to person; *Fig (maison, entreprise)* to go *or* pass through several hands

• **de première main** **ADJ** *(information)* first-hand; *(travail, recherche)* original **ADV** **nous tenons de première m. que…** we have it on reliable authority that…

• **de seconde main** **ADJ** *(information, voiture)* secondhand

• **d'une main** **ADV** *(ouvrir, faire)* with one hand; *(prendre)* with *or* in one hand; **prenant d'une m. la bouteille et de l'autre le tire-bouchon** taking the bottle in one hand and the corkscrew in the other; **donner qch d'une m. et le reprendre de l'autre** to give sth with one hand and take it back with the other

• **en main** **ADJ** **l'affaire est en m.** the matter is in hand *or* is being dealt with; **le livre est actuellement en m.** *(il est consulté)* the book is being consulted at the moment **ADV** **avoir** *ou* **tenir qch en m.** to be holding sth; *Fig* **avoir** *ou* **tenir qch (bien) en m.** to have sth well in hand *or* under control; **quand tu auras la voiture bien en m.** when you've got the feel of the car; *Fig* **prendre qch en m.** to take control of *or* over sth; **prendre une affaire/une situation en m.** to take a matter/a situation in hand; **j'ai la situation en m.** I've got the situation in hand *or* under control; *Fig* **reprendre qch en m.** to regain control of *or* over sth; **la société a été reprise en m.** the company was taken over; *Fig* **prendre qn en m.** to take sb in hand; *Fig* **se prendre en m.** to take oneself in hand

• **en main propre, en mains propres** **ADV** *(directement)* personally; **remettre qch à qn en m. propre** *ou* **en mains propres** to deliver sth to sb in person

• **la main dans la main** **ADV** *(en se tenant par la main)* hand in hand; *Fig* together; *Péj* hand in glove

• **mains libres** **ADJ** *Tél* hands-free

mainate [mɛnat] **NM** *Orn* (hill) mynah bird

main-d'œuvre [mɛ̃dœvr] *(pl* **mains-d'œuvre)** **NF** **1** *(travail)* labour; **le prix de la m.** the cost of labour, labour costs; **une m. bon marché** cheap labour; **industrie de m.** labour-intensive industry **2** *(personnes)* workforce, labour force; **les besoins en m. ont augmenté** manpower requirements have increased; **embaucher de la m.** to take on workers; **réserve** *ou* **réservoir de m.** labour pool *or* reservoir; **m. contractuelle** contract labour; **m. directe** direct labour; **m. étrangère** foreign labour; **m. féminine** female labour; **m. indirecte** indirect labour; **m. occasionnelle** casual labour; **m. peu qualifiée** unskilled labour; **m. productive** productive labour; **m. qualifiée** skilled labour; **m. spécialisée** semi-skilled labour; **m. syndiquée** organized labour

main-forte [mɛ̃fɔrt] **NF** **prêter m. à qn** to give sb a (helping) hand

mainlevée [mɛ̃ləve] **NF** *Jur* withdrawal; *(d'une hypothèque)* discharge, cancellation; **m. de la saisie** replevin, restoration of goods taken in distraint

mainmise [mɛ̃miz] **NF** *(appropriation)* seizure

(**sur** of); *(emprise)* grip, hold (**sur** on); **la m. de Hitler sur les Balkans** Hitler's seizure *or* takeover of the Balkans; *Fig* **la m. du gouvernement sur les médias** the government's hold on the media; **la m. d'une seule société sur le marché du logiciel en inquiète plus d'un** many people are worried about a single company having a stranglehold on the software market

maint, -e [mɛ̃, mɛ̃t] **ADJ** *Littéraire* many a, a great many; **mainte personne** many a person, a great many people; **maints pays** many a country, a great many countries; **maintes et maintes fois, à maintes reprises, en maintes et maintes occasions** time and time again; **je l'ai mis en garde à maintes reprises** I've warned him many a time *or* time and time again

maintenance [mɛ̃tnɑ̃s] **NF 1** *(de matériel, d'un bien)* upkeep; *(d'un appareil, d'un véhicule)* maintenance, servicing; **m. sur site** on-site maintenance **2** *Mil (moyens)* maintenance unit; *(processus)* maintenance

maintenant [mɛ̃tnɑ̃] **ADV 1** *(à présent)* now; **je me sens mieux m.** I feel better now; **m., on peut y aller** we can go now; **à vous m.** now it's your turn; **il y a m. trois ans que cela dure** this has been going on for three years now; **c'est m. que tu arrives?** what time do you call this?; **l'avion a sûrement décollé m.** the plane must have taken off (by) now; **ils sont sûrement arrivés depuis longtemps m.** they must have arrived a long time ago (now); **il est huit heures, ils ne viendront plus m.** it's eight o'clock, they'll never come now; **m. tu sauras à quoi t'en tenir** now *or* from now on you'll know what to expect; **à partir de m.** from now on *or* onwards; **c'est m. ou jamais** it's now or never; **les jeunes de m.** today's youth, young people today **2** *(cela dit)* now; **je l'ai lu dans le journal, m. si c'est vrai ou faux, je n'en sais rien** I read it in the paper, but *or* now whether or not it's true, I don't know; **vous connaissez mon point de vue, m. faites ce que vous voulez** you know what I think, now (you) do what you want; **m. on va voir si les employés voudront reprendre le travail** the question now is whether the employees will be willing to go back to work

• **maintenant que CONJ** now (that); **m. que tu me le dis, je m'en souviens** now (that) you say so *or* tell me, I remember; **m. que Durand est chef du département,...** with Durand now head of department,...

mainteneur [mɛ̃tnœr] **NM** *Bourse* **m. de marché** market maker

MAINTENIR [40] [mɛ̃tnir]

VT	
• to hold firm **1**	• to hold back **2**
• to keep **3, 4**	• to maintain **4, 5**
• to uphold **4**	
VPR	
• to remain	• to hold steady

VT 1 *(tenir)* to hold firm *or* in position; **des rivets maintiennent l'assemblage** the structure is held tight *or* together by rivets; **les colonnes maintiennent la voûte** the columns hold up *or* support the vault; **le pantalon est maintenu par une ceinture** the trousers are held *or* kept up by a belt; **couvrez les pots de morceaux d'étamine maintenus par des élastiques** cover the jars with pieces of muslin held in place by rubber bands; **nous sommes maintenus au sol par la pesanteur** the force of gravity is what keeps us on the ground; **les muscles maintiennent le corps en équilibre** muscles ensure that the body retains its balance; **m. qn assis/debout** to keep sb seated/standing; **une sangle la maintenait sur son lit** a strap held her to her bed, she was strapped to her bed; **il a fallu trois hommes pour le m. allongé** three men were needed to keep him down

2 *(empêcher d'avancer ▸ foule)* to hold back; **m. qn à distance** to keep sb at a distance

3 *(garder)* to keep; **m. l'eau à ébullition** keep the water boiling; **m. la température à 5** keep the temperature at 5; **m. au frais** keep in a cool place; **m. qn en vie** to keep sb alive; **m. les yeux fermés** to keep one's eyes shut; **m. la tête sous l'eau** to keep one's head under water; **m. un membre dans une attelle** to keep a limb strapped up

4 *(conserver ▸ statu quo, tradition)* to maintain, to uphold; *(▸ prix)* to keep in check, to hold steady; *(▸ loi)* to uphold; *(▸ paix, discipline)* to maintain, to keep; *(▸ décision)* to abide by; **m. une entreprise en activité** to keep a company operating; **des traditions qui maintiennent les clivages sociaux** traditions which sustain *or* perpetuate divisions in society; **les ordres sont maintenus** the original orders remain unchanged; **m. l'ordre** to keep order; **punitions maintenues!** punishments upheld!; **m. sa candidature** *(pour un emploi)* to maintain one's application; *Pol* to continue to stand; **m. qn dans ses fonctions** to maintain *or* to keep sb in office; **m. sa position** to maintain one's position; **nos programmes sont maintenus malgré la grève** the normal programmes will be shown despite the strike

5 *(continuer à dire)* to maintain; **il dit que tu as tort et il le maintient** he says you're wrong and he's standing by it; **je maintiens que c'est possible** I maintain that it's possible; **m. une accusation** to stand by *or* to maintain an accusation; **l'accusée a maintenu sa version des faits** the defendant stuck to *or* maintained her story

VPR se maintenir to remain; *(prix, monnaie, taux de change, cours de la Bourse)* to remain steady, to hold up *or* steady; **la monarchie se maintient encore dans quelques pays** monarchy lives on *or* survives in a few countries; **le beau temps se maintiendra** the weather will stay *or* remain fine; **la livre se maintient à 1,50 euros** the pound is remaining steady at 1.50 euros; **la livre se maintient par rapport au dollar** the pound is holding its own against the dollar; *Bourse* **ces actions se maintiennent à 6,55 euros** these shares remain firm at 6.55 euros; **le niveau des commandes se maintient** orders are holding up *or* steady; *Pol* **il se maintient au second tour** he's decided to stand again in the second round; **pourra-t-elle se m. dans les dix premiers?** will she be able to remain in the top ten?; **se m. à flot** *(dans l'eau)* to stay afloat; *(dans son travail)* to keep one's head above water; **se m. en équilibre** to keep one's balance; **se m. en bonne santé** to stay in good health; *Fam* **comment ça va? – on** *ou* **ça se maintient** how's everything going? – so-so *or* not so bad *or* bearing up

maintien [mɛ̃tjɛ̃] **NM 1** *(conservation)* maintenance, upholding; *(de la loi, d'un principe)* upholding; *(de la discipline)* maintenance, keeping; **comment garantir le m. du libre-échange?** how is it possible to uphold *or* to preserve free trade?; **le m. du pouvoir d'achat des salariés doit être une priorité** maintaining wage-earners' purchasing power must be a priority; *Jur* **m. dans les lieux** right of tenancy; **le m. de l'ordre** the maintenance of law and order; **assurer le m. de l'ordre** to maintain law and order; **m. de la paix** peacekeeping; **force de m. de la paix** peacekeeping force; **assurer le m. de la paix** to keep the peace; *Ordinat* **m. majuscule** caps lock **2** *(port)* bearing, deportment; **cours/professeur de m.** lesson in/teacher of deportment **3** *(soutien)* support; **ce soutien-gorge assure un bon m.** this bra gives good support

maintient *etc voir* **maintenir**

maire [mɛr] **NM** *(d'une commune, d'un arrondissement)* ≃ mayor; *(d'une grande ville) Br* ≃ (lord) mayor, *Am* ≃ mayor, *Scot* ≃ provost; **monsieur/madame le m.** the Mayor, His/Her Worship (the Mayor); *(en s'adressant à lui/elle)* Your Worship; *Hum* **passer devant monsieur le m.** to tie the knot, to get hitched; **m. adjoint** deputy mayor

> **MAIRE**
>
> In France, the mayor has obligations not only to the community but also to national government. He or she is responsible for promulgating national law as well as supervising the local police and officiating at civic occasions. Mayors are elected by the "conseil municipal" (and thus indirectly by the town's residents).

mairesse [mɛrɛs] **NF 1** *(femme maire)* (lady) mayor **2** *(épouse du maire)* mayoress

mairie [meri] **NF 1** *(fonction)* office of mayor, *Sout* mayoralty; **il brigue la m. de Paris** he's running for the office of Mayor of Paris; **la m. l'occupe beaucoup** his/her duties as Mayor/Mayoress keep him/her very busy **2** *(administration ▸ gén)* town council; *(▸ d'une grande ville)* city council; **organisé par la m. de Lyon** sponsored by Lyons city council; **la m. a organisé un voyage pour les personnes âgées de la ville** *Br* the council *or Am* city hall has organized a trip for the town's senior citizens; **m. d'arrondissement** *(de Paris, Lyon ou Marseille)* district council **3** *(édifice)* town hall; **demandez une attestation à la m.** you must apply to the town hall for a certificate; **m. de quartier** *(de Paris, Lyon ou Marseille)* local town hall; **m. du village** village *or* town hall

> **MAIRIE**
>
> Also called the "hôtel de ville", this is the centre of municipal government. The "mairie" serves as a vital information source for town residents. People go there to ask about taxes, to get married in a civil ceremony, to enrol in certain community-sponsored classes, etc.

mais [mɛ] **CONJ 1** *(servant à opposer deux termes)* **finalement je n'en veux pas un m. deux** actually, I want two not one; **ce n'est pas bleu, m. vert** it's not blue, it's green; **non, ce n'est pas 123 m. 124** no, it's not 123, it's (actually) 124

2 *(introduisant une objection, une restriction, une précision)* but; **une famille riche m. honnête** a rich but honest family; **m. pourtant vous connaissez le dossier?** but you are familiar with the case, aren't you?; **oui, m....** yes, but...; **m. ce n'est pas du tout ce que j'ai dit!** (but) that's not what I said at all!; **j'aime bien cette jupe m. je la préfère en vert** I like that skirt but I prefer it in green; **ces chaussures sont jolies m. trop chères** these shoes are nice, but they're too expensive; **j'ai trouvé le même, m. moins cher** I found the same thing, only *or* but cheaper

3 *(introduisant une transition)* **m. revenons à notre sujet** but let's get back to the point; **m. tu l'as déjà vu?** what, you've already seen it?; **m. dis-moi, ton frère, il ne pourrait pas m'aider?** I was thinking, couldn't your brother help me?; **m. alors, vous ne partez plus?** so you're not going any more?; **m. qu'avez-vous donc?** whatever's the matter?; **m. j'y pense, je ne l'ai pas encore appelé!** I've just thought, I haven't rung him yet!

4 *(renforçant des adverbes)* **m. oui!** oh yes!, of course!, *Am* sure!; **m. non!** oh no!, not at all!, of course not!; **vous êtes d'accord? – m. oui, tout à fait** do you agree? – yes, absolutely; **tu pleures? – m. non, m. non...** are you crying? – no, no, it's all right...; **tu as peur? – m. non!** are you scared? – of course not!; **tu m'aimes? – m. bien sûr que je t'aime!** do you love me? – of course I love you!; **vous venez aussi? – m. bien sûr!** are you coming as well? – of course (I am/we are)!; **tu m'accompagneras à la gare? – m. certainement** will you come with me to the station? – of course (I will); **nous allons à Venise, m. aussi à Florence et à Sienne** we're going to Venice, and to Florence and Siena too; **nous exportons en Allemagne, m. aussi en Suède et aux Pays-Bas** we export to Germany, but also to Sweden and the Netherlands; **c'est joli, m. encore trop cher** it's nice, but it's still too expensive; **...m. bon, il ne veut rien entendre** ...but he just won't listen; **m. enfin!** well really!; **m. enfin je te l'avais bien dit!** I TOLD you!; **je sais, m. enfin, qu'est-ce qu'on peut dire dans ces cas-là?** I know, but (after all) what can you say in a situation like that?; **elle ne fait rien de la journée, m. vraiment rien** she does nothing all day, absolutely nothing

5 *(employé exclamativement ▸ avec une valeur intensive)* **cet enfant est nerveux, m. nerveux!** that child is highly-strung, and I mean highly-strung!; **j'ai faim, m. faim!** I'm SO hungry!; **il a pleuré, m. pleuré!** he cried, how he cried!; **c'était une fête, m. une fête!** what a party that was!, that was a real party!

6 *(exprimant l'indignation, l'impatience)* **non m. des fois!** (but) really!; **non m. ça ne va pas!** you're/he's/*etc* mad!; **m. vous êtes fou!** you're mad!; **non m. pour qui tu me prends?** who do you take me for anyway?; **m. dis donc, tu n'as pas honte?** well really, aren't you ashamed of yourself?; **m. enfin, en voilà une manière de traiter les**

gens! well *or* I must say, that's a fine way to treat people!; **non m. tu plaisantes?** you can't be serious!, you must be joking!; **m. puisque je te le dis!** it's true I tell you!; **m. écoute-moi un peu!** will you just listen to me a minute!; *Fam* **m. tu vas te taire, bon sang!** for God's sake, will you shut up!; **m. c'est pas un peu fini ce vacarme?** have you quite finished making that racket?; **m. ça suffit maintenant!** that's enough now!

7 *(exprimant la surprise)* **m. tu saignes!** you're bleeding!; **m. c'est Paul!** hey, it's Paul!; **m. dis donc, tu es là, toi?** what (on earth) are you doing here?

NM but; **il n'y a pas de m. (qui tienne), j'ai dit au lit!** no buts about it, I said bed!; **il y a un m.** there's one snag, there's a but; **je vais t'aider, cependant il y a un m.** I'll help you, but on one condition; **je ne veux pas de si ni de m.** I don't want any ifs and buts

maïs [mais] **NM** *Bot Br* maize, *Am* corn; *Culin* sweetcorn; **m. en épi** corn on the cob

MAISON [mɛzɔ̃]

NF
- house **A1, 2, B3, C2, D**
- home **A2**
- family **B1**
- household **B2, 4**
- firm **C1**

ADJ INV
- home-made **1**
- in-house **2**
- first-rate **3**

NF A. 1 *(bâtiment)* house; **maisons (d'habitation)** private dwellings; **m. bourgeoise** substantial house *or Sout* residence; **m. de campagne** *(gén)* house *or* home in the country; *(rustique)* (country) cottage; **m. individuelle** *(non attenante)* detached house; **m. de maître** *(en bien propre)* owner-occupied house; *(cossue)* large house; *(en Belgique)* (fine) town house; **m. de poupée** doll's house; **m. préfabriquée** prefabricated house; *Fam* **gros comme une m.** plain for all to see; *Fam* **un mensonge gros comme une m.** a whopping great lie; *Fam* **il te drague, c'est gros comme une m.** he's flirting with you, it's as plain as the nose on your face

2 *(foyer, intérieur)* home, house; **sa m. est toujours propre** his/her house *or* home is always clean; **je l'ai cherché dans toute la m.** I've looked for it all over the house; **il a quitté la m. à 16 ans** he left home when he was 16; **déménager/changer (toute) la m.** to move/to change everything but the kitchen sink; **tenir une m.** to look after a house, to keep house; **les dépenses de la m.** household expenditure; **à la m.** at home; **cet après-midi, je suis à la m.** I'm (at) home this afternoon; **rentre à la m.!** *(locuteur à l'extérieur)* go home!; *(locuteur à l'intérieur)* come *or* get back in!; **tout pour la m.** *(sur la vitrine d'un magasin)* household goods; **chez eux c'est la m. du bon Dieu** they are very hospitable, their door is always open

B. 1 *(famille, groupe)* family; **quelqu'un de la m.** a member of the family; **visiblement, vous n'êtes pas de la m.** you obviously don't work here; **toute la m. dort** the whole house is asleep

2 *(personnel)* household

3 *(dynastie)* house; **la m. des Tudor** the House of Tudor; **être le descendant d'une grande m.** to be of noble birth

4 *(lieu de travail ▸ d'un domestique)* household *(where a person is employed as a domestic)*; **vous avez combien d'années de m.?** how long have you been in service?

C. 1 *Com (entreprise)* firm, company, business; **la réputation de la m.** the firm's good name; **une m. de renom** a company of high repute; **il a servi la m. pendant 30 ans** he worked with the firm for 30 years; **j'ai 20 ans de m.** I've been with the company for 20 years; **un habitué de la m.** a regular (customer); **la m. ne fait pas crédit** *(sur panneau)* no credit given; **la m. n'accepte pas les chèques** *(sur panneau)* no cheques (accepted); *Banque* **m. d'acceptation** *Br* accepting house, *Am* acceptance house; **m. affiliée** affiliated company, *Am* affiliate; **m. de commerce** (commercial) firm *or* company; **m. de courtage** brokerage house; **m. de couture** fashion house; **m. de détail** retail company; **m. d'édition** publishing house; **m. de gros** wholesale company; **m. d'import-export** import-export firm *or* company *or* business; **m. mère** parent *or Br* mother company; **M. de la presse** newsagent's; **m. de prêt** loan office *or* company; **m. à succursales multiples** chain store; *Bourse* **m. de titres** securities company; **m. de vente par correspondance** mail-order company

2 *Rel* **la m. de Dieu** *ou* **du Seigneur** the house of God, the Lord's house; **m. mère** mother house; **m. religieuse** convent

3 *(lieu spécialisé) Vieilli* **m. close** *ou* **de tolérance** brothel; *Hist* **m. de correction** *ou* **de redressement** reformatory, *Br* remand home, borstal; **la m. du marin/soldat** the Seamen's/Servicemen's hostel; **m. d'arrêt** remand centre; **m. centrale** (long-stay) prison, *Am* State penitentiary; **m. de convalescence** convalescent home; **m. de la culture** ≃ arts *or* cultural centre; **m. d'éducation surveillée** reformatory, *Br* approved school; **m. d'enfants** (residential) holiday centre for children, *Am* camp; **m. familiale** *Br* holiday home, *Am* vacation home *(for low-income families)*; *Péj* **m. de fous** madhouse; **m. de jeu** gambling *or* gaming house; **m. des jeunes et de la culture** ≃ youth and community centre; **m. maternelle** family home; **m. de passe** sleazy hotel *(used by prostitutes)*; **m. du peuple** ≃ trade union and community centre; **la M. de la radio** = Parisian headquarters and studios of French public radio, *Br* ≃ Broadcasting House; **m. de rendez-vous** lovenest; **m. de repos** rest *or* convalescent home; **m. de retraite** old people's home, retirement home; **m. de santé** nursing home

D. *Astrol* house, mansion

ADJ INV 1 *(fabrication)* home-made; **tous nos desserts sont (faits) m.** all our desserts are home-made; **spécialité m.** speciality of the house

2 *(employé)* in-house; **nous avons nos traducteurs m.** we have our own translators in-house; **ingénieur m.** self-taught engineer; **syndicat m.** company union

3 *Fam (en intensif)* first-rate, top-notch; **une engueulade/raclée m.** an almighty ticking-off/thrashing

Maison-Blanche [mɛzɔ̃blɑ̃ʃ] **NF la M.** the White House

maisonnée [mɛzɔne] **NF** household; **son cri réveilla toute la m.** his/her scream woke up the whole household *or* everyone in the house

maisonnette [mɛzɔnɛt] **NF** small house; *(à la campagne)* cottage

maistrance [mɛstrɑ̃s] **NF la m.** the (ship's) petty officers

MAÎTRE, MAÎTRESSE [mɛtr, mɛtrɛs]

ADJ
- main **1, 2**
- master **4**

NM,F
- master, mistress **1**
- teacher **2**

NM
- master **1–5**

NF
- mistress

ADJ 1 *(après le nom) (essentiel)* main, central, major; **l'idée maîtresse du texte** the main theme *or* central idea in the text; **sa qualité maîtresse est le sang-froid** a cool head is his/her outstanding *or* chief quality

2 *(après le nom) (le plus important)* main; **branche maîtresse** largest *or* main branch; *Cartes & Fig* **carte maîtresse** trump card; **cheville maîtresse** kingpin; **poutre maîtresse** *(en bois)* main beam; *(en métal)* main girder

3 *(avant le nom)* **le m. mot** the key word; **maîtresse femme** powerful woman

4 *(dans des noms de métiers)* master; **m. boulanger/forgeron** master baker/blacksmith; **m. charpentier** master carpenter; **m. coq** *ou* **queux** chef; **m. de forges** ironmaster; **m. maçon** master builder *or* mason; **m. sonneur** head *or* chief bell-ringer

NM,F 1 *(personne qui contrôle)* master, *f* mistress; **maîtres et esclaves** masters and slaves; **ce chien n'obéit qu'à sa maîtresse** this dog only obeys his mistress; **être m. chez soi** to be master in one's own house; **ils sont maintenant installés en maîtres chez nous** they now rule the roost in our own house; **agir en m.** to behave as though one were master; **être/rester m. de soi** to be/to remain self-possessed, to be/to remain in control of one's emotions; **il faut rester m. de soi** you must keep your self-control; **il n'était plus m. de lui-même** he lost control (of himself); **rester m. de ses émotions** to keep one's emotions under control; **être m. d'une situation/de son véhicule** to be in control of a situation/of one's vehicle; **le conducteur n'était plus m. de son véhicule** the driver (had) lost control of the car; **les maîtres du monde** the world's rulers; **un dictateur fou qui veut devenir le m. du monde** a mad dictator who wants to take over *or* rule the world; **se rendre m. de** *(d'un pays)* to take *or* seize control of; *(d'une personne)* to make oneself master of; *(d'un incendie)* to get under control; **à la maison, c'est lui le m.** he's (the) boss at home; **être son (propre) m.** to be one's own master *or* boss; **il est son propre m.** he's his own man; **elle est son propre m.** she's her own woman; **être** *ou* **rester m. de faire qch** to be free to do sth; **m. jacques** factotum; **le m. de ces lieux** *ou* **de céans** the master of the house; **m. de maison** host; **pourrais-je parler au m. de maison?** could I speak to the man *or* the master of the house?; **maîtresse de maison** lady of the house, hostess; **pourrais-je parler à la maîtresse de maison?** could I speak to the lady of the house?; *Prov* **les bons maîtres font les bons valets** a good master makes a good servant; *Prov* **tel m. tel valet** like master, like man

2 *(professeur)* **m. (d'école), maîtresse (d'école)** *Br* primary school teacher, *Am* elementary school teacher; **elle fait très maîtresse d'école** she's very schoolmarmish; **Maîtresse, j'ai trouvé!** *Br* Miss *or Am* teacher, I've found the answer!; **m. d'internat** house *Br* master *or Am* director *(responsible for boarders after school)*; **m./maîtresse de ballet** ballet teacher, *Br* ballet master/mistress; **m. de musique** music teacher

NM 1 *(dans des noms de fonctions)* **grand m. (de l'ordre)** grand master; **grand m. de l'Université** *Br* ≃ Secretary of State for Education, *Am* ≃ Secretary of Education; **m. d'armes** fencing master; *Anciennement* **m. auxiliaire** *Br* supply *or Am* substitute teacher; **m. de cérémonie** master of ceremonies; **m. de chapelle** choirmaster; **m. de conférences** *Br* ≃ senior lecturer, *Am* ≃ assistant professor; *Belg* **m. de conférences** *ou* **de conférence** ≃ part-time lecturer; **m. d'équipage** *Hist & Naut* boatswain; **m. de manège** *(directeur)* riding school director; *(moniteur)* riding instructor; **m. d'ouvrage** *(particulier)* client *(of an architect)*; *(organisme public)* contracting authority; **m. de recherches** research director; **m. des requêtes** ≃ government *Br* counsel *or Am* attorney; *Ordinat* **m. de poste** postmaster

2 *(expert)* master; **être passé m. dans l'art de** to be a past master in the art of; **elle est passée m. dans l'art de tromper son monde** she is a past master in the art of misleading people

3 *Beaux-Arts, Littérature & Phil* master; **les grands maîtres de la peinture flamande** the great masters of Flemish painting; **les grands maîtres de la musique** the great composers; **dans le style des maîtres de l'écriture classique** in the classical style; **le m. de Moulins/Madrid** the Master of Moulins/Madrid; *Fig* **trouver son m.** to meet one's master *or* more than one's match; **m. à penser** mentor, guru

4 *Rel* **le m. de l'Univers** *ou* **du monde** the Master of the Universe; *Fig* **se croire le m. du monde** to feel invincible

5 *Cartes* **être m. à carreau** to hold the master *or* best diamond

6 *(titre)* **M. Suzanne Thieu** Mrs/Miss Suzanne Thieu; **M. Dulles, avocat à la cour** ≃ Mr Dulles *Br* QC *or Am* member of the Bar; **cher M., à vous!** *(à un artiste)* Maestro, please!; *Hum* **M. Chat/Renard** Mister Cat/Fox

7 *Naut Br* ≃ chief petty officer, *Am* ≃ petty officer first class; **m. principal** *Br* ≃ fleet chief petty officer, *Am* ≃ master chief petty officer; **premier m.** *Br* ≃ chief petty officer, *Am* ≃ petty officer first class; **second m.** *Br* ≃ petty officer, *Am* ≃ petty officer second class; **être le seul m. à bord** to be sole master on board; *Fig* to be free to choose, to be free to do whatever one wants

8 *Zool* **m. de la brousse** *(serpent)* bushmaster

• **maîtresse NF** *(d'un homme)* mistress; **devenir la maîtresse de qn** to become sb's mistress

• **de maître ADJ 1** *(qui appartient à un riche par-*

ticulier) **chauffeur de m.** (personal) chauffeur; **voiture de m.** expensive car **2** *(exécuté par un grand artiste)* **un tableau** *ou* **une toile de m.** an old master; *Fig* **un coup de m.** a masterstroke; **pour un coup d'essai, c'est un coup de m.** for a first attempt, it was brilliant
• **maître chanteur NM** blackmailer
• **maître couple NM 1** *(de navire)* main frame **2** *Phys* frontal area
• **maître d'hôtel NM** *(dans un restaurant)* maître (d'hôtel), head waiter, *Am* maitre d'; *(chez un particulier)* butler; *Naut* chief steward **ADJ** *Culin* **beurre m. d'hôtel** parsley butter, maître d'hôtel butter
• **maître d'œuvre NM 1** *Constr* main contractor **2** *Fig* **ce volume a eu Diderot lui-même pour m. d'œuvre** Diderot himself took overall responsibility for the compilation of this volume; **le Premier ministre est le m. d'œuvre de l'accord signé hier** the Prime Minister was the architect of the agreement that was signed yesterday

maître-assistant, -e [metrasistɑ̃, -ɑ̃t] *(mpl* **maîtres-assistants,** *fpl* **maîtres-assistantes) NM,F** *Anciennement Br* ≃ (senior) lecturer, *Am* ≃ assistant professor

maître-autel [metrotɛl] *(pl* **maîtres-autels) NM** high altar

maître-nageur [metrənaʒœr] *(pl* **maîtres-nageurs) NM** swimming teacher *or* instructor; **m. sauveteur** lifeguard

maîtresse [metres] *voir* **maître**

maîtrisable [metrizabl] **ADJ 1** *(que l'on peut dominer* ▸ *sentiment, douleur)* controllable **2** *(que l'on peut apprendre)* **ces nouvelles techniques sont facilement maîtrisables** these new techniques are easy to master

maîtrise [metriz] **NF 1** *(contrôle)* mastery, control; **avoir la m. des mers** to have complete mastery of the sea; **sa m. du japonais est étonnante** he/she has an amazing command of Japanese; **avoir la m. d'un art** to have mastered an art; **elle exécuta le morceau avec une grande m.** she performed the piece masterfully *or* with great skill; **m. de la colère** anger management; **m. de soi** self-control, self-possession
2 *(dans une entreprise)* supervisory staff
3 *Univ* ≃ master's degree; **elle a une m. de géographie** she has a master's (degree) *or* an MA in geography, *Am* she mastered in geography
4 *Rel (chœur)* choir; *(école)* choir school

maîtriser [3] [metrize] **VT 1** *(personne)* to overpower; *(adversaire)* to get the better of; *(élèves, animal)* to control; **le chien avait la rage, il n'y avait pas moyen de le m.** the dog had rabies, there was no controlling it; **il a fallu trois hommes pour le m.** three men were needed to bring him under control *or* to overpower him; **c'est un adversaire difficile, mais je le maîtriserai** he's a tough opponent, but I'll get the better of him **2** *(danger, situation)* to bring under control; *(flammes, opposition)* to subdue; *(incendie, épidémie)* to control, to get under control; *(sentiment)* to master, to control; *(passion, impatience)* to control, to curb, to contain; *(peur)* to master, to overcome; **l'incendie a été rapidement maîtrisé** the fire was quickly brought under control; **ils maîtrisent maintenant la situation** they now have the situation (well) in hand *or* under control; **il était trop bouleversé pour m. ses larmes** he was too overcome to hold back his tears; **je réussis à m. ma colère** I managed to contain my anger; **m. ses nerfs** to control *or* to contain one's temper **3** *(technique, savoir)* to master; **m. son sujet** to master one's subject; **il ne maîtrise pas la langue** he hasn't mastered the language; **elle maîtrise bien les déclinaisons latines** she has a good mastery *or* grasp of Latin declensions
VPR se maîtriser to control oneself; **ne pas savoir se m.** to have no self-control; **je sais que tu as du chagrin, mais il faut te m.** I know you're upset, but you must get a grip on yourself; **sous l'influence de l'alcool, on n'arrive plus à se m.** under the influence of alcohol, one loses (all) control

Maïzena® [maizena] **NF** *Br* cornflour, *Am* cornstarch

majesté [maʒeste] **NF 1** *(grandeur)* majesty, grandeur; *(de port)* majesty, dignity, stateliness; **le mont Fuji se dressait devant nous dans toute sa m.** Mount Fuji stood before us in all its majesty; **m. divine/royale** divine/royal majesty **2** *(titre)* **M.** Majesty; **Sa M. (le Roi)** His Majesty (the King); **Sa M. (la Reine)** Her Majesty (the Queen); **Sa Très Gracieuse M., la reine Élisabeth** Her Most Gracious Majesty, Queen Elizabeth; **Leurs Majestés veulent-elles bien me suivre?** will Their Majesties kindly follow me?
• **en majesté ADJ** *Beaux-Arts (Christ, saint, Vierge)* in majesty, enthroned

majestueuse [maʒestɥøz] *voir* **majestueux**

majestueusement [maʒestɥøzmɑ̃] **ADV** majestically

majestueux, -euse [maʒestɥø, -øz] **ADJ** majestic, stately; *(silhouette)* majestic, imposing; **il avait en toute circonstance un port m.** his bearing was at all times majestic *or* noble *or* regal; **le paon est un oiseau m.** peacocks are majestic birds; **un palais m.** a stately palace

majeur, -e [maʒœr] **ADJ 1** *(très important)* major, greatest; **une des réalisations majeures de notre siècle** one of our century's major *or* greatest *or* main achievements; **le bonheur de mon fils est mon souci m.** my son's happiness is my major *or* principal concern; **la raison majeure de qch** the main *or* chief reason for sth; **être absent pour raison majeure** to be unavoidably absent; **y a-t-il un obstacle m. à sa venue?** is there any major reason why he/she shouldn't come? **la majeure partie de son temps/énergie** the major part of his/her time/energy; **la majeure partie des gens** the majority of people, most people
2 *(adulte)* **être m.** to be of age; **tu auras une voiture quand tu seras m.** you'll have a car when you come of age *or Sout* when you reach your majority; *Fig* **il est m., il sait ce qu'il fait** he's old enough *or* grown up, he knows what he's doing; *Fam* **je n'ai pas besoin de tes conseils, je suis m. (et vacciné)** I don't want your advice, I'm old enough to look after myself now
3 *Cartes (couleur)* major; **tierce/quarte majeure** tierce/quart major
4 *Mus* major; **concerto en la m.** concerto in A major; **gamme majeure** major scale; **le mode m.** the major key *or* mode
5 *Rel* **causes majeures** causae majores
NM 1 *(doigt)* middle finger
2 *Ling* major term
3 *Mus* major key *or* mode
4 *Jur* **m. incapable** mentally incompetent person; **m. protégé** protected person of full age
• **majeure NF 1** *Cartes* major suit **2** *Ling* major premise
• **en majeure partie ADV** for the most (part); **son œuvre est en majeure partie hermétique** the major part *or* the bulk of his/her work is abstruse

majolique [maʒɔlik] **NF** majolica

major [maʒɔr] **ADJ** *(supérieur par le rang)* chief *(avant n)*, head *(avant n)*
NM 1 *(dans la marine)* ≃ warrant officer
2 *(dans l'armée de l'air) Br* ≃ warrant officer, *Am* ≃ master sergeant
3 *(dans l'armée de terre) Br* ≃ warrant officer first class, *Am* ≃ chief warrant officer 4–5; **m. du camp** camp commandant; **(médecin) m.** medical officer; **m. général** chief of staff *(of a commander-in-chief in the field)*
4 *Belg, Can & Suisse Mil* ≃ major
5 *Univ* top student *(in the final examination at a "grande école")*; **être m. de promotion** = to be top of one's year; **elle était le m. de la promotion de 58** she came out first in her year in 1958
6 *Suisse* **m. de table** master of ceremonies
NF *(société)* major (company)

majoration [maʒɔrasjɔ̃] **NF 1** *(hausse* ▸ *de prix)* rise, increase (**de** in); *(pour plus de bénéfices)* markup; *(*▸ *d'une facture)* surcharge, additional charge (**de** on); **procéder à une m. des prix** to increase prices; **ils demandent une m. de leurs salaires** they're asking for a wage increase; **m. fiscale, m. d'impôts** surcharge on taxes; **m. pour retard de paiement** additional charge *or* surcharge for late payment **2** *(surestimation)* overestimation

majordome [maʒɔrdɔm] **NM** butler, majordomo

majorer [3] [maʒɔre] **VT 1** *(augmenter* ▸ *prix)* to increase, to raise (**de** by); *(pour faire plus de bénéfices)* to mark up; *(*▸ *facture)* to put a surcharge *or* an additional charge on; **les allocations familiales seront majorées de 15 pour cent** family credit is to be increased by 15 percent; **tous les impôts impayés avant la fin du mois seront majorés de 5 pour cent** there will be a 5 percent surcharge *or* penalty charge on all taxes not paid by the end of the month; **m. une facture de 10 pour cent** to put a surcharge of 10 percent on an invoice, to increase an invoice by 10 percent **2** *Math (suite)* to majorize; *(sous-ensemble)* to contain

majorette [maʒɔrɛt] **NF** (drum) majorette

majoritaire [maʒɔritɛr] **ADJ 1** *(plus nombreux)* majority *(avant n)*; **être m.** to be in the majority; **les femmes sont majoritaires dans l'enseignement** women outnumber men *or* are in the majority in the teaching profession; **vote/parti m.** majority vote/party; **quel est le parti m. au Parlement?** which party has the majority *or* which is the majority party in Parliament?; **coton m.** *(sur l'étiquette d'un vêtement)* cotton-rich **2** *Écon & Bourse (actionnaire, participation)* majority *(avant n)*; **se rendre m.** to acquire a majority interest *or* shareholding
NMF member of a majority group; *Bourse* majority shareholder; **voter avec les majoritaires** to vote with the majority

majorité [maʒɔrite] **NF 1** *(le plus grand nombre)* majority; **la m. de** the majority of, most; **la m. des personnes interrogées...** the majority of (the) people *or* most (of the) people questioned...; **la m. des spectateurs était choqués par la pièce** the majority of *or* most spectators were shocked by the play; **décision prise à la m. (des voix)** decision taken by a majority, majority decision; **dans la m. des cas** in most cases; **nous sommes une m. à vouloir combattre ce fléau** the *or* a majority of us want to fight against this scourge; **la m. silencieuse** the silent majority; *Mktg* **m. conservatrice/innovatrice** late/early majority; *Mktg* **m. précoce/tardive** early/late majority
2 *Pol (à l'issue d'élection)* majority; **avoir la m.** to have the majority; **remporter la m. des suffrages** to win a *or* the majority of the votes, to win a majority; **élu avec dix voix de m.** elected by a majority of ten; **ils ont gagné avec une faible/une écrasante m.** they won by a narrow/an overwhelming margin; **m. absolue/simple** *ou* **relative** absolute/relative majority; **être élu à la m. absolue** to be elected with an absolute majority; **m. qualifiée** qualified majority
3 *Parl (parti)* majority party; **la m.** *(parti)* the majority, the party in power, the governing party; **m. gouvernementale** parliamentary majority; **être dans la m.** to be a member of the majority party
4 *(âge légal)* majority; **atteindre sa m.** to come of age, *Sout* to reach one's majority; **à ta m.** *(dans l'avenir)* when you come of age; *(dans le passé)* when you came of age; **m. civile** (attainment of) voting age; **m. légale** (minimum) voting age; **m. pénale** legal majority
• **en majorité ADJ** in the majority; **nous sommes en m.** we are in the majority **ADV les citoyens pensent en m. que...** the majority of citizens *or* most citizens think that...

Majorque [maʒɔrk] **NF** Majorca

majorquin, -e [maʒɔrkɛ̃, -in] **ADJ** Majorcan
• **Majorquin, -e NM,F** Majorcan

majuscule [maʒyskyl] **ADJ 1** *(gén)* capital; **B m.** capital B **2** *Typ* upper-case; **les lettres majuscules** upper-case letters
NF 1 *(gén)* capital, block letter; **majuscules d'imprimerie** block letters, block capitals; **écrivez votre nom en majuscules** write your name in capitals, print your name (in block letters); **mettez une m. à Rome** write Rome with a capital, *Sout* capitalize Rome **2** *Typ* upper case, upper-case letter

majuscule-clic [maʒyskylklik] *(pl* **majuscules-clics) NM** *Ordinat* shift-click

majuscule-glisser [maʒyskylglise] *(pl* **majuscules-glisser) NM** *Ordinat* shift-drag

making-of [mekiŋɔv] **NM** *Cin* special feature, featurette

MAL[1] [mal] (*pl* **maux** [mo])

- pain **1, 4**
- illness **2**
- sickness **2**
- harm **3**
- ill **5**
- evil **5, 7**
- trouble **6**
- difficulty **6**

NM 1 *(souffrance physique)* pain; **m. de dents** toothache; **m. de dos** backache; **m. de gorge** sore throat; **m. de tête** headache; **maux de tête** headaches; **maux d'estomac** stomach pains; **contre les maux d'estomac** for stomach pain; **avoir des** *ou* **souffrir de maux de tête/ventre** to get *or* to suffer from headaches/stomach aches; **où as-tu m.?** where does it hurt?, where is the pain?; **j'ai m. là** it hurts *or* it's painful here; **j'ai m. aux dents** I've got *Br* toothache *or Am* a toothache; **j'ai m. aux oreilles** I've got *Br* earache *or Am* an earache; **j'ai m. à la tête** I've got a headache; **avoir m. à la cheville/à la gorge/au pied** to have a sore ankle/throat/foot; **avoir m. au dos** to have backache *or* a sore back; **il a m. au ventre** he has a stomach ache; **j'ai m. au bras** I have a sore arm, my arm hurts *or* aches; *Fam* **avoir m. aux cheveux** to have a hangover▫; **faire (du) m. à** to hurt; **sa chaussure lui fait m.** his/her shoe is hurting him/her; **le dentiste ne te fera pas (de) m.** the dentist won't hurt you; **la piqûre ne vous fera pas m.** the injection won't hurt (you); **ça vous fait encore m.?** does it still hurt?, is it still hurting you?; **mon genou me fait m.** my knee hurts; **se faire m.** to hurt oneself; **je me suis fait m. à la main** I've hurt my hand; *Fam* **ça te ferait m. de t'excuser?** it wouldn't hurt you to apologize!; *Fam très Fam* **ça me ferait m. aux seins** it would kill me!; *Fam Fig* **un spectacle qui fait m. (au cœur** *ou* **au ventre)** a painful sight; *Fam* **ça fait m. au ventre de voir des choses pareilles!** it makes you sick *or* it's sickening to see things like that!; *Fam Fig* **ça va faire m.!** we're in for it now!; *Fam* **attention, c'est à moi de jouer, ça va faire m.!** watch out, it's my turn, this is going to be something!; **il n'y a pas de m.!** *(après un heurt)* no broken bones!; *(après une erreur)* no harm done!; **mettre qn à m.** *ou* **à m. qn** to manhandle *or* to maltreat sb

2 *(maladie, malaise)* illness, sickness; *Fam* **tu vas attraper** *ou* **prendre du m.** watch you don't get a cold; *Arch* **le m. français** *ou* **napolitain** syphilis; **m. de l'air** airsickness; **avoir le m. de l'air** to be airsick; **avoir m. au foie** to feel liverish; **m. blanc** whitlow; **m. de mer** seasickness; **avoir le m. de mer** *(en général)* to suffer from seasickness; *(au cours d'un voyage)* to be seasick; **m. des montagnes** altitude sickness; **m. du pays** homesickness; **avoir le m. du pays** to be homesick; **m. de Pott** Pott's disease; **m. des rayons** radiation sickness; **m. de la route** carsickness; **m. des transports** travel sickness

3 *(dommage, tort)* harm; **s'en tirer sans aucun m.** to escape uninjured *or* unhurt *or* unscathed; **le m. est fait** the damage is done (now); **faire du m.** to do harm; **faire du m. à qn** to do sb harm, to harm sb; **bois du lait, ça ne peut pas te faire de m.** drink some milk, it can't do you any harm; *Fam* **allez, un p'tit coup de gnôle, ça n'a jamais fait de m. à personne!** go on, a little tipple never did anyone any harm!; **ne bougez pas et aucun m. ne vous sera fait** don't move and nobody will get hurt; **faire du m. à qch** to do harm to sth, to harm *or* to damage sth; **les insecticides font-ils plus de m. que de bien?** do insecticides do more harm than good?; **vouloir du m. à qn** to wish sb ill *or* harm; **je ne leur veux aucun m.** I don't wish (to cause) them *or* I don't mean them any harm; **il n'y a pas de m. à demander** there's no harm in asking; **il n'y a pas de m. à cela** there's no harm in that; **quel m. y a-t-il à cela?** what harm can that do?, what harm is there in it?; **et si j'en ai envie, où est le m.?** and if that's what I feel like doing, what harm is there in that?; **dire du m. de qn** to gossip about sb, to speak ill of sb; **parler en m. de qn** to speak ill of sb; **penser du m. de qn** to think badly of sb; **m. lui en a pris** he's/she's had cause to regret it; **ne le provoquez pas ouvertement, m. vous en prendrait** don't provoke him or you'll live to regret it; **mettre qch à m.** to damage sth

4 *(douleur morale)* pain; **faire (du) m. à qn** to hurt sb, to make sb suffer; **quand j'y repense, ça me fait du** *ou* **ça fait m.** it hurts to think about it; **n'essaie pas de la revoir, ça te ferait du m.** don't try to see her again, it'll only cause you pain *or* upset you

5 *(affliction, inconvénient)* ill, evil; **c'est un m. nécessaire** it's a necessary evil; **souffrir de trois grands maux** to suffer from three great evils; **les maux dont souffre leur génération** the ills that plague their generation; *Littéraire* **le m. du siècle** world-weariness, Romantic melancholy; **la dépression est le nouveau m. du siècle** depression is the new scourge of the century; **m. de vivre** weariness with life; **avoir le m. de vivre** to be tired of life; *Prov* **entre deux maux, il faut choisir le moindre** always choose the lesser of two evils

6 *(difficulté, tracas)* trouble *(UNCOUNT)*, difficulty *(UNCOUNT)*; **avoir du m. à faire qch** to have difficulty (in) *or* trouble doing sth; **avoir le plus grand m. à faire qch** to have the utmost *or* a great deal of difficulty doing sth; **avoir de plus en plus de m. à faire qch** to find it harder and harder to do sth; **j'ai eu beaucoup de m. à te contacter** I've had a lot of trouble getting in touch with you; **j'ai de plus en plus de m. à me souvenir des noms** I'm finding it harder and harder to remember names; **non sans m.** not without difficulty; **donner du m. à qn** to give sb trouble; **se donner du m. pour faire qch** to go to a lot of trouble to do sth, to take pains to do sth; **je me suis vraiment donné du m. pour que la soirée soit réussie** I really went to a lot of trouble *or* I took great pains to make the party a success; **je me suis donné beaucoup de m. pour faire cette traduction** I worked really hard on this translation; **il a réussi sans se donner de m.** he succeeded without much trouble; *Ironique* **tu ne t'es pas donné trop de m., à ce que je vois!** I see you didn't exactly take a lot of trouble over it!; **ne vous donnez pas tant de m. pour moi** please don't go to all this trouble on my behalf; **ils s'étaient pourtant donné du m. pour dissimuler leurs traces** and yet they had gone to great lengths to cover their tracks; **on n'a rien sans m.** you don't get anything easily

7 *(par opposition au bien)* **le m.** evil; **le bien et le m.** right and wrong, good and evil; **il n'a jamais fait le m.** he has never committed any evil act *or* done any evil; *Rel* **faire le m.** to do evil; **faire le m. pour le m.** to commit evil for evil's sake; **rendre le m. pour le m.** to give as good as one gets, to answer evil by evil; **voir le m. partout** to see the bad side of everything; **il ne pense pas à m.** he doesn't mean any harm, he means well; **il a changé en m.** he has changed for the worse

MAL[2] [mal]

ADV
- wrong **1**
- unwell **2**
- badly **3–6**
- not properly **4**
- uncomfortably **7**

ADJ INV
- wrong **1**
- unwell **2**
- bad **3**

ADV 1 *(désagréablement)* wrong; **tout va m.** everything's going wrong; **ça commence m., c'est m. parti** things are off to a bad start; **il a m. fini** *(délinquant)* he came to a bad end; **ça va finir m.** *ou* **m. finir** *(gén)* it'll end in disaster; *(à des enfants turbulents)* it'll all end in tears; **leur histoire a m. fini** their story had a sad *or* an unhappy ending; **ça tombe m.** *(au mauvais moment)* it comes at a bad time; **il sera là aussi, ça tombe m.** he'll be there too, which is unfortunate; **tu tombes m.** you've come at a bad time

2 *(en mauvaise santé)* **aller m., se porter m.** to be ill *or* unwell, to be in poor health; **il est** *ou* **il va très m.** he's in a very bad way; **comment va-t-elle? – m.** how is she? – not (very) well at all *or* (very) ill

3 *(défavorablement)* badly; **prendre m. qch, m. prendre qch** to take sth badly, to take exception to sth; **elle a très m. pris que je lui donne des conseils** she reacted badly *or* she took exception to my giving her advice; **il prend tout m.** he takes exception to everything; **ne le prends pas m. mais...** I hope you won't be offended but..., don't take it the wrong way but...; *Fam* **être/se mettre m. avec qn** to be/to get on the wrong side of sb

4 *(de façon incompétente ou imparfaite)* badly, not properly; **la porte est m. fermée** the door is not closed properly; **c'est du travail m. fait** it's a shoddy piece of work; **être m. fait (de sa personne)** to be misshapen; **elle n'est pas m. faite** she's got quite a good figure; **vous ne feriez peut-être pas m. de...** it wouldn't be a bad thing (if you were) to..., it might not be a bad idea to...; **cette veste/le vert me va m.** this jacket/green doesn't suit me; **ça lui va m. de donner des conseils** he's/she's hardly in a position to hand out advice; **je le connais m.** I don't know him very well; **s'ils croient que je vais me laisser faire, ils me connaissent m.!** if they think I'm going to take it lying down, they don't know me very well!; **m. comprendre** to misunderstand; **m. interpréter qch** to misinterpret sth, to misconstrue sth; **je dors m.** I have trouble sleeping; **il mange m.** *(salement)* he's a messy eater; *(trop peu)* he doesn't eat enough; *(mal équilibré)* he doesn't eat well; **qu'est-ce qu'on mange m. ici!** the food's really bad here!; **il parle m.** he can't talk properly; **elle parle m. l'allemand** her German isn't very good; **elle chante m.** she's a bad singer; **tu te tiens m.** *(tu es voûté)* you've got poor posture; *(à table)* you don't have any table manners; **elle a m. vécu sa grossesse** she had a bad time with her pregnancy; **cette lampe éclaire m.** this lamp doesn't give much light; *Fig* **on voit m. comment...** it's difficult *or* not easy to see how...; *Fam* **je me vois m. en bermuda/avec un mari comme le sien!** I just can't really see myself in a pair of Bermuda shorts/with a husband like hers!; *Fam* **elle se voyait m. allant lui réclamer l'argent** she couldn't quite imagine going to ask him/her for the money; **s'y prendre m.** to go about it the wrong way; **je m'y prends m.** I'm not going about this the right way; **donne l'aiguille, tu t'y prends horriblement m.** give me the needle, you're getting in a terrible mess; **tu t'y es m. pris pour assembler la bibliothèque** you've gone the wrong way about assembling the bookcase; **s'y prendre m. avec qn** to handle sb the wrong way; **elle s'y prend m. avec les enfants** she's not very good with children; **m. choisir** to make the wrong choice, to choose wrongly; **tu as m. choisi ton jour pour te plaindre** you've chosen the wrong day to complain; **m. dessiné** badly drawn; **il a été m. élevé** he was brought up *or* raised badly; **m. élevé** bad-mannered, impolite; **m. habillé** badly dressed, poorly dressed; **m. vu** *(peu aimé)* poorly thought of

5 *(insuffisamment)* badly, poorly; **m. approvisionné** poorly stocked; **être m. nourri** *(trop peu)* to be underfed *or* undernourished; *(avec de la mauvaise nourriture)* to be badly fed; **m. payé** badly *or* poorly paid

6 *(malhonnêtement ▸ agir)* badly; **vous avez m. agi** you did wrong, you acted badly; **m. tourner** *(situation)* to turn sour; *(dispute)* to turn ugly; *(personne)* to go to the dogs; **à seize ans, il a commencé à m. tourner** when he was sixteen, he started going to the bad

7 *(inconfortablement)* uncomfortably; **être m. assis** to be uncomfortably seated *or* uncomfortable; **on dort m. dans ton canapé-lit** your sofa bed isn't very comfortable

8 *(locutions)* *Fam* **ça la fiche m.** it looks pretty bad; *très Fam* **ça la fout m.** it looks bloody awful; *Fam* **si je n'y vais pas, ça la fiche m.** if I don't go, it looks really bad

ADJ INV 1 *(immoral)* wrong; **c'est m. de tricher** it's wrong to cheat; **c'est très m. de faire ça** *(en parlant à un enfant)* it's very naughty to do that; **je n'ai rien dit/fait de m.** I haven't said/done anything wrong

2 *(malade)* ill, unwell, not well; **il est très m.** he's in a (very) bad way; **se sentir m.** to feel unwell; **se trouver m.** *(s'évanouir)* to faint, to pass out, *Littéraire* to swoon

3 *(peu satisfaisant)* **ça n'était pas si m.** it wasn't that bad; **ce n'était pas m. du tout** it wasn't at all bad; *Fam* **elle n'est pas m.** *(plutôt jolie)* she's quite good-looking; **qu'est-ce que tu penses de ce pull? – pas m.** what do you think of this pullover? – it's not bad *or* it's OK

• **au plus mal** **ADJ 1** *(très malade)* very sick, desperately ill, critical **2** *(fâché)* **être au plus m. avec qn** to be at loggerheads with sb; **ils sont au plus m. (l'un avec l'autre)** they're at loggerheads (with each other)

• **de mal en pis** **ADV** from bad to worse

• **en mal de** **PRÉP** **être en m. de qch** to be yearning *or* desperate for sth, to be badly in need of sth; **être en m. d'affection** to be longing *or* yearning for love; **être en m. d'inspiration** to be short of *or* lacking inspiration; **une femme en m. d'enfants** a woman desperate for children *or* to have children

• **mal à l'aise** ADJ uncomfortable, ill at ease; **m. à l'aise dans ses vêtements usés** feeling uncomfortable in his/her shabby clothes; **je suis m. à l'aise devant elle** I feel ill at ease with her

• **mal à propos** ADV at the wrong time; **ils sont arrivés m. à propos** they timed their arrival badly, they arrived at the wrong moment; **faire une intervention m. à propos** to speak out of turn

• **mal portant, -e** ADJ unwell, in poor health; **elle a toujours été m. portante** she's never been very healthy

mal³, -e [mal] ADJ *Littéraire (locution)* **à la male heure** *(à l'heure de la mort)* upon the hour of death

> **MAL-** PREFIX
>
> **Mal-** is an adverb of Latin origin often used as a prefix, always with a NEGATIVE connotation, but in several different ways.
>
> • This prefix can be added to an adjective (without a hyphen) to form its opposite. The English translation sometimes includes an equivalent prefix such as *un-* or *dis-*, eg:
>
> **malpropre** unclean; **malpoli(e)** rude, impolite; **malhonnête** dishonest; **maladroit(e)** clumsy; **malintentionné(e)** spiteful
>
> • **Mal-** can precede a past participle to create a noun. The hyphen is sometimes optional, eg:
>
> **les mal-logés** the badly housed, the poorly housed
>
> • A number of words prefixed with **mal-** have recently become very popular in the media. Some of them, like **mal-être**, were actually old words which have enjoyed a new lease of life with a different meaning. They are based on nouns, eg:
>
> **le mal-être des adolescents** teenage angst; **le mal-vivre des cités** the poor living conditions on council estates; **le mal-parler** sloppy language
>
> In the same vein, the word **malbouffe** was coined in the 90s and has since been widely used to refer to junk food and poor diet.
>
> • **Mal-** is also a prefix used in the area of social work and disability to refer to certain things in a euphemistic way, eg:
>
> **les malvoyants** the partially sighted; **les malentendants** the hearing-impaired

malabar [malabar] NM *Fam (colosse)* hulk

malachite [malakit] NF malachite

malade [malad] ADJ **1** *(souffrant)* ill, sick, unwell; **une personne m.** a sick person; **un enfant toujours m.** a sickly child; **gravement m.** gravely *or* seriously ill; **m. de la fièvre typhoïde** ill with typhoid; **tomber m.** to fall ill; *Belg* **il fait m.** *(lourd)* the weather is close; **se faire porter m.** to call in *or* to report sick; **être m.** *très Fam* **à crever** *ou Fam* **comme un chien** *ou Fam* **comme une bête** *(souffrir)* to be incredibly ill *or* at death's door; *(vomir)* to be sick as a dog *or* violently ill

2 *(atteint d'une lésion)* bad, diseased; **avoir une dent m.** to have a bad *or* rotten tooth; **avoir une jambe m.** to have a bad *or Br* gammy leg; **avoir le cœur m., être m. du cœur** to have a heart condition, to have heart trouble; **j'ai les intestins malades, je suis m. des intestins** I have trouble with my intestines; **une vigne m.** a diseased vine; **cette année, les pommiers sont malades** the apple trees have got a disease this year

3 *(nauséeux)* sick; **je suis m. en bateau/voiture/avion** I suffer from seasickness/carsickness/airsickness; **rendre qn m.** to make sb sick *or* ill

4 *(dément)* (mentally) ill *or* sick; **avoir l'esprit m.** to be mentally ill

5 *(en mauvais état)* decrepit, dilapidated; *(industrie)* ailing; **nous avons une économie m.** our economy is sick *or* shaky *or* ailing

6 *(affecté moralement)* ill, sick; **m. de jalousie** sick with jealousy, horribly jealous; **m. de peur** sick with fear; **m. d'inquiétude** sick *or* ill with worry; **ça me rend m. de la voir si démunie** it makes me ill to see her so penniless; **et pourtant c'est elle qui a eu le poste – tais-toi, ça me rend** *ou* **j'en suis m.!** all the same, she's the one who got the job – don't, it makes me sick!; **quand j'ai su qu'il n'y avait plus de place, j'en étais m.** when I heard there were no seats left I could have cried

7 *Fam (déraisonnable)* mad[□], crazy; **t'es pas un peu m.?** are you right in the head?, are you off your rocker?; **ne hurle pas comme ça, tu es m. ou quoi?** stop yelling like that, are you off your head?; **du whisky avec de la vodka, il est m., celui-là** whisky mixed with vodka, that guy's sick *or* out of his mind!; **ils veulent en plus qu'on paie la TVA, ils sont malades!** and what's more they want us to pay VAT, they're off their heads *or* they're crazy!

NMF **1** *(patient ▸ gén)* sick person, sick man, *f* woman; *(▸ d'un hôpital, d'un médecin)* patient; *(sujet atteint)* sufferer; **un grand m.** a seriously ill person; **les grands malades** the seriously ill; **les malades en phase terminale** terminal patients; **dans les cas aigus, le m. ressent une vive douleur** in acute cases, the sufferer feels a sharp pain; **faire le m.** to pretend to be ill, to malinger; **c'est un m. imaginaire** he's a hypochondriac

2 *(dément)* **m. (mental)** mentally ill *or* sick person; *(d'un hôpital)* a mental patient; **l'accusé est un m.** the defendant is a sick man *or Péj* has a sick mind *or Jur* is mentally ill

3 *Fam (fou)* maniac, headcase, *Br* nutter, *Am* screwball; **comme un m.** *(travailler, courir, pousser)* like mad *or* crazy; **on a bossé comme des malades pour finir à temps** we worked like mad *or* crazy to finish on time; **il conduit comme un m.** he drives like a maniac; **il a flippé comme un m.** he totally flipped *or* freaked out; **c'est un m., ce mec!** that guy isn't right in the head!

4 *Fam (fanatique)* nut, freak; **un m. de la vitesse** a speed fiend *or* freak; **ce sont des malades du golf** they're golf-crazy

maladie [maladi] NF **1** *(mauvaise santé)* illness, ill health, sickness; **il n'a jamais pu réintégrer son service à cause de la m.** due to ill-health, he never went back to his job

2 *Méd & Vét (mal spécifique)* illness, disease; **attraper une m.** to catch a disease; **une petite m.** an ailment, a minor illness; **une m. bénigne** a minor illness; **une m. grave** a serious illness; **il est mort des suites d'une longue m.** he died after a long illness; **quelle est l'évolution probable de cette m.?** how is this illness likely to develop?; *Fam* **cet hiver, le petit nous a fait toutes les maladies** this winter our boy's had all the diseases under the sun; **la m. peut avoir des suites** there may be complications; **la m. qui l'a emportée** her last *or* fatal illness; **fermé pour cause de m.** *(sur la vitrine d'un magasin)* closed due to illness; *Fam* **être en congé m.** *ou* **en m.** to be on sick leave *or* off sick; *Fam* **je vais me mettre en m.** I'm going to take some sick leave *or* time off sick; **être en longue m.** to be on indefinite sick leave; **la m. d'Alzheimer** Alzheimer's disease; **la m. de Basedow** Graves' *or* Basedow's disease; **la m. bleue** cyanosis, blue disease; **la m. du charbon** anthrax; **la m. de Creutzfeldt-Jakob** Creutzfeldt-Jakob disease; **la m. de Crohn** Crohn's disease; **la m. de Hodgkin** Hodgkin's disease; **la m. du légionnaire** legionnaire's disease; **la m. de Parkinson** Parkinson's disease; **m. chronique** chronic illness *or* condition; **m. de cœur** heart complaint *or* disease; **m. contagieuse** contagious disease; **m. de foie** liver complaint *or* disease; **m. infantile** childhood illness, infantile disorder; **m. infectieuse** infectious disease; **maladies infectieuses émergentes** emerging infectious diseases, EID; **m. héréditaire** hereditary disease; **m. mentale** mental illness *or* disorder; **m. mortelle** fatal disease *or* illness; **m. orpheline** orphan disease *or* illness; **m. de peau** skin disease; **m. professionnelle** occupational *or* industrial disease; **m. sexuellement transmissible** sexually transmitted disease; **m. du sommeil** sleeping sickness; **m. vasculaire** vascular disease; **m. vénérienne** venereal disease, VD

3 *Bot* disease; **les pruniers ont tous eu la m.** all the plum trees got diseased *or* the disease; **m. de l'encre** ink disease

4 *Vét (des chiens)* (canine) distemper; **m. de Carré** (canine) distemper; **m. du dépérissement chronique** chronic wasting disease, CWD; **la m. de la vache folle** mad cow disease

5 *Fig (obsession)* obsession; **la peur du noir peut devenir une m.** fear of the dark can turn into a phobia; *Hum* **elle a encore rangé tous mes journaux, c'est une m. chez elle!** she's tidied up all my papers again, it's an obsession with her!; *Hum* **j'adore le fromage, c'est une véritable m.!** I love cheese, I just can't get enough of it!; *Fam* **en faire une m.** to make a song and dance about it; **il n'y a pas de quoi en faire une m.!** no need to make a song and dance about it *or* to throw a fit!

maladif, -ive [maladif, -iv] ADJ **1** *(personne)* puny, sickly; *(teint)* sickly-looking, unhealthy; *(constitution)* weak; **il a toujours un air m.** he always looks rather unhealthy *or* ill; **elle était d'une pâleur maladive** she was unhealthily pale

2 *(compulsif)* obsessive, pathological; **d'une sensibilité maladive** acutely sensitive; **d'une jalousie maladive** pathologically *or* obsessively jealous; **d'une curiosité maladive** obsessively inquisitive; **elle est d'une inquiétude maladive** she's a pathological *or* an obsessive worrier; **il adore les jeux d'argent, c'est m.** he's a compulsive gambler *or* he can't stop gambling, it's like a disease (with him)

maladivement [maladivmɑ̃] ADV *(à l'excès)* pathologically, morbidly; *(inquiet, ordonné)* obsessively; **être m. timide** to be excessively shy

maladresse [maladrɛs] NF **1** *(manque de dextérité)* clumsiness, awkwardness; **ne le laisse pas porter les verres, il est d'une telle m.!** don't let him carry the glasses, he's so clumsy!

2 *(manque de tact)* clumsiness, tactlessness; **quelle m. de lui avoir dit que tu n'aimais pas sa robe!** how tactless of you to tell her that you didn't like her dress

3 *(remarque, acte)* blunder, gaffe, *Sout* faux pas; **ses maladresses étaient devenues légendaires** *(remarques)* he'd/she'd become famous for his/her tactless remarks *or* for (always) saying the wrong thing; *(actes)* he'd/she'd become famous for his/her blunders; **le but a été marqué sur une m. de la défense** the goal was the result of a blunder *or* slip-up by the defence

4 *Scol* **bon devoir, mais des maladresses** good work, if somewhat awkward in places; **il y a quelques maladresses de style** there are a few awkward *or* clumsy turns of phrase

maladroit, -e [maladrwa, -at] ADJ **1** *(manquant de dextérité)* clumsy, awkward **2** *(manquant de savoir-faire)* clumsy, inept; *(manquant d'assurance)* clumsy, awkward, gauche; *(manquant de tact)* clumsy, tactless, heavy-handed; **une initiative maladroite** a clumsy *or* bungling initiative

NM,F **1** *(de ses mains)* clumsy person; **attention, m., tu as failli lâcher la tasse!** look out, butterfingers, you nearly dropped the cup! **2** *(gaffeur)* blunderer, blundering fool; *(incompétent)* blithering idiot

maladroitement [maladrwatmɑ̃] ADV **1** *(sans adresse)* clumsily, awkwardly; **ils s'y sont pris m.** they set about it the wrong way **2** *(sans tact)* clumsily, tactlessly, heavy-handedly

mal-aimé, -e [maleme] *(mpl* **mal-aimés**, *fpl* **mal-aimées)** NM,F outcast; **c'est le m. de la famille** he's the unpopular one in the family; **il a été le m. de cette génération de réalisateurs** he was the forsaken member of that generation of (film) directors; **les mal-aimés de la société** social outcasts

malais, -e¹ [malɛ, -ez] ADJ Malay, Malayan, Malaysian

NM *(langue)* Malay

• **Malais, -e** NM,F Malay, Malayan, Malaysian

malaise² [malez] NM **1** *(indisposition)* (sudden) weakness, faintness, *Sout* malaise; *(évanouissement)* fainting fit, blackout; *(étourdissement)* dizzy spell; **avoir un m., être pris d'un m.** to feel weak/faint/dizzy

2 *(désarroi, angoisse)* uneasiness (UNCOUNT), anxiety (UNCOUNT), disquiet (UNCOUNT); **ce genre de film provoquait toujours chez elle un m. profond** this sort of film always disturbed her deeply

3 *(mécontentement)* discontent, anger; **il y a un m. croissant chez les viticulteurs** there's mounting tension *or* discontent among wine growers; **m. social** social unrest

4 *(gêne)* unease, awkwardness; **la remarque a créé un m.** the remark caused a moment of unease *or* embarrassment

5 *Fam (problème)* **il y a comme un m.** there's a bit of a snag *or* a hitch

malaisé, -e [maleze] ADJ difficult, hard, arduous; **certains auteurs sont d'une traduction malaisée** certain authors are difficult to translate

malaisément [malezemɑ̃] ADV with difficulty

Malaisie [malezi] NF *Géog* **la M.** Malaya

malandrin [malɑ̃drɛ̃] NM *Littéraire (voleur)* robber, thief; *(bandit de grand chemin)* highwayman; **une bande de malandrins** a band of miscreants

malappris, -e [malapri, -iz] *Vieilli* NM,F boor, lout; **eh bien, jeune m., allez-vous me laisser passer!** well, you ill-bred young lout, are you going to let me past or not?; **cette petite malapprise me tirait la langue!** that rude little minx stuck her tongue out at me!

ADJ boorish, loutish, ill-mannered

malard [malar] NM drake

malaria [malarja] NF *Méd* malaria

malart [malar] = **malard**

malavenant, -e [malavənɑ̃] *Can* ADJ *(désagréable)* unpleasant; *(hargneux)* grumpy; *(peu serviable)* disobliging

NM,F *(personne désagréable)* unpleasant person; *(personne hargneuse)* grump, grumpy person; *(personne peu serviable)* disobliging person

malavisé, -e [malavize] ADJ unwise, ill-advised, misguided; **être m. de faire qch** to be ill-advised *or* unwise to do sth; **tu as été m. de ne pas venir** it was unwise of you *or* you were ill-advised not to come

Malawi [malawi] NM *Géog* **le M.** Malawi

malaxage [malaksaʒ] NM *(d'une pâte)* kneading; *(d'un mélange)* mixing; *(de beurre)* creaming

malaxer **[3]** [malakse] VT *(mélanger)* to mix, to blend; *(pétrir ▸ pâte)* to knead; *(▸ beurre)* to cream; **m. le beurre pour le ramollir** work the butter until soft

malaxeur [malaksœr] NM *(gén)* mixer, mixing machine; *(de béton)* cement mixer; *(de beurre)* butter creamer; *(de sucre)* mixer, agitator

mal-baisée [malbeze] *(pl* **mal-baisées***)* NF *Vulg* **c'est une m.** she needs a good fuck

malbouffe [malbuf] NF *Fam* unhealthy eating

malchance [malʃɑ̃s] NF **1** *(manque de chance)* bad luck, misfortune; **il a eu la m. de...** he was unlucky *or* unfortunate enough to..., he had the misfortune to...; **jouer de m.** to be dogged by ill fortune **2** *(mésaventure)* mishap, misfortune; **une série de malchances** a run of bad luck, a series of mishaps *or* misfortunes

• **par malchance** ADV unfortunately, as ill luck would have it

malchanceux, -euse [malʃɑ̃sø, -øz] ADJ unlucky, luckless; **spéculateurs m.** unlucky *or* luckless *or* hapless speculators; **il a toujours été m.** he's never had any luck; **être m. au jeu/en amour** to be unlucky at gambling/in love

NM,F unlucky person, unlucky man, *f* woman

malcommode [malkɔmɔd] ADJ **1** *(appareil)* impractical; *(fauteuil, position)* uncomfortable; *(horaire, système)* inconvenient, awkward **2** *Can (personne ▸ indiscipliné)* unruly; *(▸ hargneux)* cantankerous

Maldives [maldiv] NFPL *Géog* **les (îles) M.** the Maldive Islands, the Maldives

maldonne [maldɔn] NF **1** *Cartes* misdeal; **tu as fait m.** you misdealt **2** *Fam* **il y a m.** something's gone wrong somewhere

mâle [mal] ADJ **1** *Biol, Zool & Bot* male; **le sexe m.** the male sex; **m. alpha** alpha male

2 *(viril)* virile, masculine, manly; **son beau visage m.** his handsome, manly face; **avec une m. assurance** with robust confidence; **une belle voix m.** a fine manly voice

3 *Tech* male; **vis/connexion m.** male screw/connection; **pièce m.** male component; **prise m.** plug

4 *Zool (avec des noms d'animaux)* male; *(oiseau)* cock; **antilope m.** male antelope; **canard m.** drake; **chat m.** tom, tomcat; **cygne m.** male swan, cob; **éléphant m.** bull elephant; **hamster m.** male hamster; **hérisson m.** male hedgehog; **lapin m.** buck rabbit; **loup m.** male wolf, he-wolf; **ours m.** male bear, he-bear; **pigeon m.** cock pigeon; **renard m.** dog fox

NM male; **le m. de l'espèce** the male of the species; **est-ce un m. ou une femelle?** it is a he or a she?; **le jars est le m. de l'oie** a gander is a male goose; **la tigresse est à la recherche d'un m.** the tigress is looking for a mate; *Fam Hum* **quel m.!** what a man!; **un beau m.** *(animal)* a beautiful male specimen; *Hum (homme)* a real he-man

> Il faut noter qu'en anglais le terme **male** signifie également **masculin**.

malédiction [malediksjɔ̃] NF **1** *(imprécation)* curse, *Sout* malediction; **donner sa m. à qn** to call down a curse upon sb, to curse sb; **que la m. te poursuive!** a curse on you *or* on your head!; **cette m. poursuivra la famille pendant trois générations** this curse will hang over the family for three generations; **une m. pèse sur elle** she is under a curse, a curse is hanging over her **2** *(malheur)* malediction; **encourir la m. divine** to incur the wrath of God; **comme si le sort les poursuivait de sa m.** as if fate had cast her evil eye on them

EXCLAM *Hum* curses!, curse *or* damn it!; **m., le revoilà!** curses, here he comes again!

maléfice [malefis] NM evil spell *or* charm; **jeter un m. sur qn** to cast an evil spell on sb; **écarter un m.** to ward off an evil spell

maléfique [malefik] ADJ *Littéraire (charme, signe, personne)* evil, malevolent; *(émanation, influence)* evil, cursed; *(étoile, planète)* unlucky; **les puissances maléfiques** the forces of evil

malencontreuse [malɑ̃kɔ̃trøz] *voir* **malencontreux**

malencontreusement [malɑ̃kɔ̃trøzmɑ̃] ADV ill-advisedly; **ayant m. gardé ses lettres** having ill-advisedly kept *or* having been ill-advised enough to have kept his/her letters

malencontreux, -euse [malɑ̃kɔ̃trø, -øz] ADJ *(fâcheux ▸ retard, tentative, visite)* ill-timed, inopportune; *(▸ remarque)* unfortunate, untoward; *(mal choisi ▸ parole)* inopportune, ill-advised, unfortunate; **un m. incident diplomatique** an unfortunate diplomatic incident; **par un hasard m.** by a stroke of ill luck

malengueulé, -e [malɑ̃gøle] *Can Fam* ADJ vulgar□, uncouth□

NM,F vulgar *or* uncouth person□

mal en point, mal-en-point [malɑ̃pwɛ̃] ADJ INV in a bad way; **être très/un peu m.** to be in a very bad/a bit of a bad way

malentendant, -e [malɑ̃tɑ̃dɑ̃, -ɑ̃t] ADJ hearing-impaired

NM,F hearing-impaired person; **les malentendants** the hearing-impaired

malentendu [malɑ̃tɑ̃dy] NM misunderstanding; **je répète pour qu'il n'y ait pas de m.** I'll say it again so there's no misunderstanding; **attends, je crois qu'il y a un m. (entre nous)** wait, I think we're at cross purposes

mal-en-train [malɑ̃trɛ̃] ADJ INV *Can* unwell, *Br* poorly; **avoir l'air m.** to look unwell *or Br* poorly

mal-être [malɛtr] NM INV malaise

malfaçon [malfasɔ̃] NF defect

malfaisance [malfəzɑ̃s] NF *Littéraire* maleficence, evil-mindedness

malfaisant, -e [malfəzɑ̃, -ɑ̃t] ADJ **1** *(qui cherche à nuire)* evil, wicked; **un homme m.** an evil man **2** *(néfaste, pernicieux)* evil, pernicious, noxious; *(influence)* evil, harmful; **on dit que cette pierre a un pouvoir m.** this stone is said to have evil powers; **des idées malfaisantes** pernicious ideas

malfaiteur [malfetœr] NM criminal

mal famé, -e *(mpl* **mal famés,** *fpl* **mal famées***)*, **malfamé, -e** [malfame] ADJ disreputable; **des lieux mal famés** places of ill repute

malformation [malfɔrmasjɔ̃] NF *Biol & Méd* malformation, abnormality; **m. (congénitale)** (congenital) malformation

malfrat [malfra] NM *Fam* gangster, crook, hoodlum

malgache [malgaʃ] ADJ Madagascan, Malagasy

NM *(langue)* Madagascan, Malagasy

• **Malgache** NMF Madagascan, Malagasy; **les Malgaches** the Madagascans, the Malagasy *or* Malagasies

malgracieux, -euse [malgrasjø, -øz] ADJ *Littéraire (qui manque d'élégance)* inelegant, ungainly, clumsy

malgré [malgre] PRÉP in spite of, despite; **il est sorti m. la pluie** he went out in spite of *or* despite the rain; **il a pénétré dans l'enceinte m. les ordres** he entered the area against orders; **m. sa fortune, il n'a jamais été heureux** for all his wealth, he's never been happy; **m. soi** *(involontairement)* unwillingly, in spite of oneself; *(à contrecœur)* reluctantly, against one's better judgment; *(forcé)* against one's will; **il a laissé voir m. lui à quel point il était gêné** he revealed in spite of himself *or* he unwillingly revealed how embarrassed he was; **j'ai consenti, bien m. moi** I agreed, very reluctantly *or* much against my better judgment; **on l'a conduit m. lui au poste de police le plus proche** they took him against his will *or* by force to the nearest police station

• **malgré que** CONJ *Fam (bien que)* although□, despite the fact that□; **m. qu'il fasse froid** despite the fact that *or* although it's cold

• **malgré tout** ADV **1** *(en dépit des obstacles)* in spite of *or* despite everything; **je réussirai m. tout** I'll succeed in spite of everything; **m. tout, ils ont réuni la somme nécessaire** despite everything, they raised the required amount **2** *(pourtant)* all the same, even so; **c'était m. tout un grand champion** all the same, he was a great champion; **il faut dire une chose m. tout...** even so, one thing has to be said...; **c'est convaincant mais m. tout je n'y crois pas** it's convincing but all the same *or* nevertheless *or* even so, I don't believe it

malhabile [malabil] ADJ **1** *(maladroit)* clumsy; **elle est m. de ses doigts** she's all fingers and thumbs **2** *Littéraire (inapte)* **il a toujours été m. à marchander** he's always lacked skill *or* been bad at haggling

malhabilement [malabilmɑ̃] ADV clumsily, awkwardly

MALHEUR [malœr]

- misfortune **1, 2**
- accident **1**
- sorrow **3**
- trouble **4**

NM **1** *(incident)* misfortune; *(accident)* accident; **un grand m.** a (great) tragedy *or* catastrophe; **le pays a eu** *ou* **connu beaucoup de malheurs à cette époque** the country experienced great misfortune *or* hardship at that time; **ils ont eu des malheurs** they have been through difficult times; *Ironique* **eh bien, tu en as des malheurs!** oh dear, it's not your day, is it?; **depuis quelques années, il ne m'arrive que des malheurs** for some years now I've had nothing but misfortune; **si jamais il lui arrive (un) m.** if (ever) anything happens to him/her; **en cas de m.** if anything awful should happen; **quel m.!** what a tragedy!; **un petit m.** a (slight) mishap; *Hum* **il n'arrête pas de me raconter ses petits malheurs** he's forever telling me (about) all his petty cares and woes; *Fam* **ne le laissez pas rentrer ou je fais un m.** don't let him in or I won't be responsible for my actions; **elle passait en première partie, et c'est elle qui a fait un m.** she was only the supporting act but she brought the house down; **cette chanson a fait un m. en son temps** that song was a huge success in its day; **son bouquin a fait un m. en librairie** his/her book was a runaway success in the bookshops; **sa nouvelle pièce fait un m.** his/her latest play is a big hit; **les rollers font un m. en France** roller blades are all the rage in France; **je verrouille la grille quand les enfants sont dans le jardin, un m. est si vite arrivé!** I lock the gate when the children are in the garden, you can't be too careful!; **pose cette tasse, un m. est si vite arrivé!** put that cup down before there's an accident!; *Fam* **je crois qu'on va déménager à Londres – parle pas de m.!** I think we're moving to London – God forbid! *or* Lord save us!; **ils veulent tous venir chez toi – parle pas de m.!** they all want to come to your place – oh please no!; *Prov* **un m. ne vient** *ou* **n'arrive jamais seul** it never rains but it pours; **et maintenant, j'apprends qu'il est malade, un m. ne vient jamais seul!** and now I hear he's ill, if it's not one thing (then) it's another!

2 *(malchance)* **le m.** misfortune, bad luck; **le m. a voulu que...** as bad luck would have it...; **le m. c'est que...** the unfortunate thing is that...; **avoir le m. de** to be unfortunate enough to, to have the misfortune to; **j'ai eu le m. de perdre mon père jeune** I had the *or* it was my misfortune to lose my father when I was young; **j'ai eu le m. de lui dire que je n'étais pas d'accord avec lui** I made the mistake of telling him that I didn't agree with him; **une vie marquée par le m.** a life of misfortune *or* sorrow; **être dans le m.** to suffer misfortunes *or* hard times; **il est resté très digne dans le m.** he remained very dignified in (his) adversity; **montrer du courage dans le m.** to show courage in the face of adversity *or* hardship; **faire l'expérience du m.** to taste misfortune; **porter m. à qn** to bring sb bad luck; **arrête, ça porte m.!** stop, it brings bad luck!; **je l'ai bien connu, pour mon m.** I knew him well, more's the pity; **pour son m., il était l'aîné de six enfants** unfortunately for him, he was the oldest of six; *Prov* **c'est dans le m. qu'on connaît ses vrais amis** a friend in need is a friend indeed

3 *(désespoir)* **faire le m. de qn** to cause sb unhappiness, to bring sorrow to sb; **elle avait rencontré l'homme qui allait faire son m.** she'd met the man who was to be the curse *or* bane of her life; *Prov* **le m. des uns fait le bonheur des autres** one man's joy is another man's sorrow

4 *(inconvénient)* trouble, problem; **le m., c'est que j'ai perdu l'adresse** unfortunately *or* the trouble is I've lost the address; **son mari ne l'a jamais crue, c'est là le m.!** her husband never believed her, there's the tragedy (of it)!; **sans permis de travail, pas de possibilité d'emploi, c'est ça le m.** without a work permit you can't get a job, that's the snag *or* the problem; **quel m. que je ne l'aie pas su!** what a pity *or* shame I didn't know (about it)

EXCLAM damn!; **m., mon lait qui se sauve!** oh, damn, the milk's boiling over!; **m. à eux!** woe betide them!; **m. à toi et à toute ta descendance!** a curse on you and all your family!; *Bible* **m. à l'homme par qui le scandale arrive** woe to that man by whom the offence cometh; **m. aux vaincus!** vae victis!, woe to the vanquished!

• **de malheur** ADJ *Fam Hum* accursed, wretched; **je ne remonterai plus sur ce vélo de m.** I'll never ride that wretched *or* accursed bike again

• **par malheur** ADV unfortunately; **par m., j'ai laissé la porte ouverte** unfortunately, I left the door open; **par m., son fils est né avec la même maladie** sadly, his/her son was born with the same disease

malheureuse [malœrøz] *voir* **malheureux**

malheureusement [malœrøzmɑ̃] ADV unfortunately; **je ne retrouve m. pas mon agenda** unfortunately *or* I'm afraid I can't lay my hands on my diary; **m. pour toi, il ne reste plus de petites tailles** you're out of luck, there are no small sizes left

malheureux, -euse [malœrø, -øz] ADJ **1** *(peiné)* unhappy, miserable, wretched; *(expression, air, regard)* unhappy, sad, miserable; **il est m. s'il ne peut pas sortir** he's miserable *or* unhappy when he can't go out; **je suis m. de ne pouvoir l'aider** I feel sad *or* wretched at not being able to help him/her; **leur air m. en disait long** their unhappy *or* miserable faces spoke volumes; **rendre qn m.** to make sb miserable *or* unhappy; **il l'a rendue malheureuse toute sa vie** he made her life a misery, he caused her lifelong unhappiness; **n'y pense plus, tu ne fais que te rendre m.** don't think about it any more, you're only making yourself miserable; **m. en ménage** unhappily married; **être m. comme une pierre** *ou* **les pierres** to be dreadfully unhappy

2 *(tragique ▸ enfance)* unhappy; *(▸ destin)* cruel; **sans le savoir, nous entrions dans une époque malheureuse** without knowing it, we were entering an unhappy period

3 *(malchanceux)* unfortunate, unlucky; **les candidats m. recevront une montre digitale** the unlucky contestants will receive a digital watch; **le candidat m. verra ses frais de déplacement remboursés** the unsuccessful candidate will have his travel expenses paid; **il est m. au jeu/en amour** he has no luck with gambling/women; **avoir la main malheureuse** to be unlucky; **des amours malheureuses** unhappy love affairs; **les m. réfugiés/sinistrés** the unfortunate *or* hapless refugees/victims; **la malheureuse femme ne savait rien de la catastrophe** nobody had told the poor *or* unfortunate *or* wretched woman about the catastrophe

4 *(infructueux ▸ initiative, effort)* thwarted; *(▸ amour)* unrequited; *(malencontreux ▸ tentative)* unfortunate, ill-fated; *(▸ conséquences)* unfortunate, unhappy; *(▸ incident)* unfortunate; **son intervention a eu des suites malheureuses** his/her action had some unfortunate *or* unhappy consequences; **oublions tout de ce m. incident** *ou* **de cet incident m.** let's forget this unfortunate incident; **par un m. hasard** by an unfortunate coincidence, as bad luck would have it

5 *(regrettable ▸ geste, mot)* unfortunate

6 *(avant le nom) (insignifiant)* **pleurer ainsi pour un m. parapluie perdu/une malheureuse piqûre!** all these tears for a stupid lost umbrella/a tiny little injection!; **ne nous battons pas pour quelques m. cents** let's not fight over a few measly cents; **sur le plat, il n'y avait qu'un m. poulet et deux poireaux** on the dish there was just a pathetic-looking chicken and a couple of leeks

7 *(dans des tournures impersonnelles)* **il est m. que vous ne l'ayez pas rencontré** it's unfortunate *or* a pity *or* a shame you didn't meet him; **il est m. que le gouvernement n'ait pas compris cet appel** it is to be regretted that the Government didn't hear that plea; **ce serait m. de ne pas en profiter** it would be a pity *or* shame not to take advantage of it; **c'est m. à dire, mais c'est la vérité** it's an awful thing to say, but it's the truth; **c'est m. à dire, mais je m'ennuie** I hate to say so but I'm bored; *Fam* **si c'est pas m. (de voir/d'entendre ça)!** it's a (crying) shame (to see/to hear that)!; *Fam* **ce n'est pas m.!** about time too!, not a moment too soon!

NM,F **1** *(indigent)* poor *or* needy man, *f* woman; **secourir les m.** to help the poor *or* the needy *or* those in need **2** *(personne pitoyable)* unfortunate *or* wretched man, *f* woman; **il est bien seul maintenant, le m.** he's very much on his own now, the poor devil; **le m. ne comprenait rien à ce qui se passait** the poor wretch *or* soul didn't understand anything that was going on; **faire un m.** *(attrister quelqu'un)* to make someone unhappy; **elle a fait plus d'un m. quand elle s'est mariée** she made more than one man unhappy *or* broke quite a few hearts when she got married; **attention, petit m.!** careful, you wretched boy *or* little wretch!; **qu'as-tu dit là, m.!** honestly, what a thing to say!; **m.! qu'avez-vous fait?** you wretch! what have you done?

malhonnête [malɔnɛt] ADJ **1** *(sans scrupules)* dishonest, crooked; **des procédés malhonnêtes** underhand *or* dishonest methods; **c'est m. de sa part** it's dishonest of him/her **2** *Suisse ou Vieilli (impoli)* rude, impolite **3** *Vieilli (indécent ▸ geste)* indecent; *(▸ suggestion)* improper

NMF **1** *(personne sans scrupules)* cheat, crook **2** *Suisse (personne impolie)* rude person

malhonnêtement [malɔnɛtmɑ̃] ADV *(sans probité)* dishonestly

malhonnêteté [malɔnɛtte] NF *(manque de probité)* dishonesty, crookedness; **la m. de ses procédés** the underhandedness *or* the dishonesty of his/her methods; **m. intellectuelle** intellectual dishonesty

Mali [mali] NM *Géog* **le M.** Mali

malice [malis] NF **1** *(espièglerie)* mischievousness, impishness, prankishness; **un regard plein** *ou* **pétillant de m.** an impish *or* a mischievous look **2** *Vieilli (méchanceté)* malice, spitefulness; **ne pas entendre m. à qch** *(ne voir rien de mal à quelque chose)* to see no harm in sth; *(ne pas avoir l'intention de faire du mal)* to mean no harm by sth; **je suis sûre qu'elle n'y entendait pas m.** I'm sure she didn't mean any harm (by it); **il n'y a vu aucune m. de leur part** he didn't think they meant anything by it

• **à malices** ADJ **sac/boîte à malices** bag/box of tricks

• **sans malice** ADJ guileless, innocent ADV **je me suis moqué de lui, mais c'était sans m.** I made fun of him but it wasn't serious

> Il faut noter que le terme anglais **malice** est un faux ami. Il signifie **méchanceté** ou **préméditation**, selon le contexte.

malicieuse [malisjøz] *voir* **malicieux**

malicieusement [malisjøzmɑ̃] ADV mischievously, impishly

malicieux, -euse [malisjø, -øz] ADJ **1** *(espiègle ▸ personne, sourire, remarque)* mischievous, impish; *(▸ solution)* clever, smart **2** *Vieilli (méchant)* malicious

> Il faut noter que l'adjectif anglais **malicious** est un faux ami. Il signifie **méchant**.

malien, -enne [maljɛ̃, -ɛn] ADJ Malian
• **Malien, -enne** NM,F Malian

maligne [maliɲ] *voir* **malin**

malignement [maliɲmɑ̃] ADV *(avec méchanceté)* spitefully; *(par méchanceté)* out of spite

malignité [maliɲite] NF **1** *(d'une action, d'une personne)* malice, spitefulness, spite; *(du sort)* cruelty **2** *Méd* malignancy

malin, -igne *ou Fam* **-ine** [malɛ̃, -iɲ, -in] ADJ **1** *(rusé)* cunning, crafty, shrewd; **elle avait un petit air m.** she had a wily *or* cunning look about her; **être m. comme un singe** to be as cunning as a fox; **jouer au plus m. avec qn** to try and outsmart *or* outwit sb

2 *(intelligent)* bright, clever, *esp Am* smart; **il est plus m. que ça** he knows better; *Fam* **elle n'est pas bien maligne** *ou* **maline** she's not very clever *or* not all that bright; **tu te crois m.?** do you think you're clever?; **tu te crois m. d'avoir copié sur les autres?** so you think cribbing from the others was a clever thing to do?; *Ironique* **c'est m.!** very clever!; **ce n'était pas très m. (de ta part)** that wasn't very bright, was it?; **c'est pas bien m.!** that's dead easy!, that's simple!; **alors, 224 multiplié par 2, ce n'est pourtant pas bien m.!** so, 224 times 2, that's not so hard *or* that's not taxing your brain too much, is it?; **bien m. qui comprendra** it'll take a genius to understand that

3 *Méd (tumeur)* malignant

4 *(malveillant ▸ plaisir)* malicious; *Arch (▸ influence)* malignant, evil; **elle mettait une joie maligne à me poser les questions les plus difficiles** she would take a perverse pleasure in asking me the most difficult questions; **éprouver un m. plaisir à faire qch** to experience (a) malicious pleasure in doing sth

5 *Can (méchant, irascible)* irritable, bad-tempered; **un chien m.** a vicious dog

NM,F clever person; **c'est un m., il trouvera bien une solution** he's a bright spark, he'll find a way; *Fam Ironique* **gros m., va!** very clever!; *Fam Ironique* **alors, gros m., montre-nous ce que tu sais faire** OK, wise guy, show us what you can do; **un petit m.** a smart aleck, *Br* a clever dick; ; *Fam* **c'est une petite maligne** *ou* **maline** she's a sly one, she's a little imp; *Ironique* **les petits malins qui doublent sur une ligne blanche** the smart alecks *or Br* clever dicks who overtake on a solid white line; **la petite maligne avait tout prévu** the crafty little so-and-so had thought of everything; **faire le m.** to show off, to try to be smart; **arrêtez de faire les malins!** stop messing about!; **fais pas le m. avec moi** don't (you) get smart with me; *Prov* **à m., m. et demi** = there's always somebody cleverer than you somewhere

• **Malin** NM **le M.** the Devil, the Evil One

malingre [malɛ̃gr] ADJ puny, sickly, frail

malintentionné, -e [malɛ̃tɑ̃sjɔne] ADJ nasty, spiteful; **des propos malintentionnés** malicious *or* spiteful remarks; **être m. à l'égard de** *ou* **envers qn** to be ill-disposed towards sb

mal-jugé [malʒyʒe] *(pl* **mal-jugés***)* NM *Jur* miscarriage of justice

malle [mal] NF **1** *(valise)* trunk; **faire sa m.** *ou* **ses malles** to pack one's bags; *Fam* **se faire la m.** *(partir)* to beat it, *Br* to clear off, *Am* to book it; *Fam* **allez, on se fait la m.!** come on, let's get out of here!

2 *Vieilli Aut Br* boot, *Am* trunk; **m. arrière** luggage compartment, load area

3 *Hist (voiture de la poste)* mail coach; **la M. des Indes** the Indian Mail; *Can Fam* **mettre une lettre à la m.** to mail a letter❑, *Br* to post a letter❑

4 *Belg Transp* **la M. d'Anvers** the Antwerp ferry

malléabilité [maleabilite] **NF 1** *(souplesse)* flexibility, malleability, pliability **2** *Métal* malleability

malléable [maleabl] **ADJ 1** *(cire)* soft; *(caractère, personnalité)* easily influenced *or* swayed; **elle n'est pas très m.** she's rather rigid *or* inflexible **2** *Métal* malleable

malle-poste [malpɔst] *(pl* **malles-poste)** **NF** *Hist* mailcoach

mallette [malɛt] **NF 1** *(valise)* suitcase; *(porte-documents)* attaché case, briefcase **2** *Belg (musette d'ouvrier)* (canvas) haversack; *(sacoche)* bag; *(cartable d'écolier)* satchel

mal-logé, -e [malloʒe] *(mpl* **mal-logés**, *fpl* **mal-logées)** **NM,F** person living in bad housing; **les mal-logés** the badly housed, the poorly housed

mal-logement [malloʒmɑ̃] **NM** poor housing (conditions), substandard accommodation

malmener **[19]** [malməne] **VT 1** *(brutaliser)* to manhandle, to treat roughly; **arrête de m. cet enfant** stop being so rough with that child

2 *(objet)* to handle *or* to treat roughly; *(matériel, véhicule)* to mistreat; **m. la grammaire** to misuse grammar, to make grammatical mistakes

3 *Fig (traiter sévèrement)* to bully, to push around; **un metteur en scène réputé pour m. ses acteurs** a director renowned for giving actors a rough *or* hard time; **malmené par la critique** panned by the critics

4 *Sport* **m. un adversaire** to give an opponent a hard time, to maul an opponent

malnutrition [malnytrisjɔ̃] **NF** malnutrition

malodorant, -e [malɔdɔrɑ̃, -ɑ̃t] **ADJ** foul-smelling, smelly, *Sout* malodorous

malotru, -e [malɔtry] **NM,F** boor, lout, oaf

malouin, -e [malwɛ̃, -in] **ADJ** of/from Saint-Malo

• **Malouin, -e NM,F** = inhabitant of or person from Saint-Malo

Malouines [malwin] **NFPL les (îles) M.** the Falkland Islands, the Falklands, the Malvinas; **un habitant des M.** a Falkland Islander

mal-pensant [malpɑ̃sɑ̃] *(pl* **mal-pensants)** **NM** dissenter

malpoli, -e [malpɔli] *Fam* **ADJ** rude□, impolite□, bad-mannered□; **c'est m.!** that's rude!

NM,F lout, boor; **petit m.!** you rude (little) boy!; **petite malpolie!** you rude (little) girl!

malpropre [malprɔpr] **ADJ 1** *(crasseux)* dirty, filthy, unclean; *(apparence)* slovenly, untidy; **des mains malpropres** dirty *or* grubby hands

2 *(mal fait ▸ ouvrage)* shoddy, sloppily done; **cette serrure, c'est du travail m.** that lock is a shoddy piece of work

3 *(inconvenant, impudique)* dirty, filthy, smutty

4 *(malhonnête)* obnoxious, dishonest, unsavoury

NMF filthy swine; **se faire traiter comme un m.** to be treated like dirt; **se faire chasser** *ou* **renvoyer comme un m.** to be sent packing

malproprement [malprɔprəmɑ̃] **ADV** *(manger)* messily; *(travailler)* shoddily, sloppily; *(agir)* vilely, sordidly

malpropreté [malprɔprəte] **NF 1** *(aspect sale)* dirtiness, filthiness, uncleanliness **2** *Fig (acte malhonnête)* low *or* dirty *or* filthy trick **3** *Fig (propos indécent)* dirty *or* smutty remark; **dire des malpropretés** to talk smut; **où as-tu appris ces malpropretés?** where did you learn such filthy *or* disgusting language?

malsain, -e [malsɛ̃, -ɛn] **ADJ 1** *(nuisible à la santé)* unhealthy; **climat m.** unhealthy climate; **nourriture malsaine** unhealthy *or* unwholesome food

2 *Fig (qui va mal ▸ industrie)* ailing

3 *Fig (pervers ▸ personne)* unwholesome; *(▸ ambiance, curiosité, esprit)* unhealthy; *(▸ littérature)* unwholesome; **ils ont des rapports malsains** they have an unhealthy relationship

4 *Fam (dangereux)* **c'est plutôt m. par ici** it's a bit dodgy around here; **je sentais que ça allait devenir m.** I could sense things would soon turn nasty

malséant, -e [malseɑ̃, -ɑ̃t] **ADJ** *Littéraire (contraire aux conventions)* unseemly, improper, indecorous; *(contraire à la décence)* indecent, improper; **il serait m. que tu m'accompagnes** it would be quite unseemly *or* unbecoming for you to accompany me

malsonnant, -e [malsɔnɑ̃, -ɑ̃t] **ADJ** *Littéraire (inconvenant)* offensive; *Hum* **après un échange de propos malsonnants** after exchanging a few uncomplimentary remarks

malt [malt] **NM** malt

maltage [maltaʒ] **NM** malting

maltais, -e [maltɛ, -ɛz] **ADJ** Maltese

NM 1 *(langue)* Maltese **2** *(chien)* Maltese (dog)

• **Maltais, -e NM,F** Maltese; **les M.** the Maltese

• **maltaise NF** Maltese (blood orange)

Malte [malt] **NF** *Géog* **(l'île de) M.** Malta

malter **[3]** [malte] **VT** to malt

malterie [maltəri] **NF** *(usine)* maltings

malthusianisme [maltyzjanism] **NM** Malthusianism

malthusien, -enne [maltyzjɛ̃, -ɛn] **ADJ** Malthusian

NM,F Malthusian

maltose [maltoz] **NM** *Chim* maltose

maltraitance [maltretɑ̃s] **NF** (physical) abuse

maltraitant, -e [maltretɑ̃, -ɑ̃t] **ADJ** abusive; **des parents maltraitants** abusive parents

maltraiter **[4]** [maltrete] **VT 1** *(brutaliser)* to ill-treat, to mistreat, to maltreat; *(verbalement)* to attack; **les otages n'ont pas été maltraités par leurs ravisseurs** the hostages were not mistreated by their kidnappers; **m. sa femme/ses enfants** to batter one's wife/one's children **2** *Fig (malmener)* to misuse; **les accords internationaux sont bien maltraités** international agreements are being ignored *or* trampled on; **la pièce a été maltraitée par la critique** the play was mauled by the critics

malus [malys] **NM** *Assur* surcharge, extra premium

malveillance [malvejɑ̃s] **NF 1** *(méchanceté)* malevolence, spite, malice; **avec m.** malevolently, spitefully, maliciously; **par pure m.** out of sheer spite *or* malice; **ne voyez là aucune m. de ma part** please do not think there is any ill will on my part; **c'était sans m. de sa part** he/she meant no ill **2** *(intention criminelle)* criminal intent; **un incident dû à la m.** a malicious incident

malveillant, -e [malvɛjɑ̃, -ɑ̃t] **ADJ** *(personne, propos)* malicious, spiteful; *(sourire)* malevolent, malicious

NM,F malicious *or* malevolent person

malvenu, -e [malvəny] **ADJ 1** *(inopportun)* untimely, inopportune; **votre remarque était malvenue** your remark was untimely **2** *Littéraire* **être m. à** *ou* **de faire qch** to be in no position to do sth; **il serait m. à** *ou* **de se plaindre** he's hardly in a position to complain; **il serait tout à fait m. de le critiquer** it would be quite inappropriate to criticize him **3** *(mal formé ▸ arbre)* underdeveloped, malformed

malversation [malversasjɔ̃] **NF** embezzlement (UNCOUNT); **il est coupable de malversations** he is guilty of embezzlement *or* misappropriation of funds

malvoisie [malvwazi] **NM 1** *(vin)* malmsey **2** *(cépage)* malvasia, malmsey grape

maman [mamɑ̃] **NF 1** *(terme d'appellation) Br* mum, mummy, *Am* mom **2** *(mère)* mother, *Br* mum, *Am* mom; **toutes les mamans sont invitées** all mothers *or Br* mums *or Am* moms are invited; **la plus belle récompense d'une m.** the finest reward a mother could ask for

mambo [mɑ̃mbo] **NM** mambo

mamelle [mamɛl] **NF 1** *Vieilli (sein)* breast; *Littéraire* **un enfant à la m.** a suckling (child) **2** *(de vache)* udder; *(de chienne, de truie)* teat, dug

mamelon [mamlɔ̃] **NM 1** *Anat & Zool (d'une femme)* nipple **2** *(colline)* hillock, hummock

mamelonné, -e [mamlɔne] **ADJ 1** *Anat, Zool & Méd Br* mamillated, *Am* mammillated **2** *Géog* hummocky

mamelouk, mameluk [mamluk] **NM** *Hist* Mameluke

m'amie, mamie[1] [mami] **NF** *Arch (mon amie)* my beloved

mamie[2] [mami] **NF** *Fam* **1** *(grand-mère)* granny, grannie **2** *(vieille dame)* old lady□

mamillaire [mamilɛr] **ADJ** mamillary

NF *Bot* nipple cactus

mammaire [mamɛr] **ADJ** mammary

mammalogie [mamalɔʒi] **NF** mammalogy

mammectomie [mamɛktɔmi] **NF** *Méd* mastectomy

mammifère [mamifɛr] **NM** mammal; **les grands mammifères** the higher mammals

mammographie [mamɔgrafi] **NF** *Méd* **1** *(cliché)* mammogram, mammograph **2** *(technique)* mammography

mammouth [mamut] **NM** mammoth

mammy [mami] = **mamie**[2]

mamours [mamur] **NMPL** *Fam* cuddle; **faire des m. à qn** to cuddle sb; **se faire des m.** to cuddle

mam'selle [mamzɛl] **NF** *Fam* Miss; **alors, ma petite m., ça va?** and how's my little Miss?

mamy [mami] = **mamie**[2]

mam'zelle [mamzɛl] = **mam'selle**

MAN [emaen] **NMF** *Can Pol (abrév* **Membre de l'Assemblée Nationale)** MNA

Man [man] *voir* **île**

manade [manad] **NF** = herd of horses or bulls in the Camargue

management [manadʒmɛnt] **NM** *Com & Sport* management

manager[1] **[17]** [manadʒe] **VT** *Com & Sport* to manage

manager[2] [manadʒœr] **NM** *Com & Sport* manager

managérial, -e, -aux, -ales [manadʒerjal, -o] **ADJ** managerial

manant [manɑ̃] **NM 1** *Hist (villageois)* villager; *(paysan)* peasant, villein **2** *Littéraire (mufle)* churl, boor

manceau, -elle [mɑ̃so, -ɛl] **ADJ** of/from Le Mans

• **Manceau, -elle NM,F** = inhabitant of or person from Le Mans

Manche [mɑ̃ʃ] **NF la M.** the (English) Channel; *(en Espagne)* La Mancha

manche[1] [mɑ̃ʃ] **NM 1** *(d'outil)* handle; *(de poignard)* handle, haft; *(de club de golf)* shaft; *(de fouet)* stock; **à m. court** short-handled; **à m. long** long-handled; **couteau à m. d'ivoire** ivory-handled knife, knife with an ivory handle; **m. de pioche** pickaxe handle *or* shaft; **m. de** *ou* **à balai** broomstick; *Fam* **être** *ou* **se mettre du côté du m.** to side with the winner; *Prov* **il ne faut jamais jeter le m. après la cognée** never say die

2 *Fam (personne maladroite)* clumsy oaf, *Br* cack-handed idiot, *Am* klutz; *(personne incapable)* useless idiot, *Br* pillock, *Am* lame; **s'y prendre comme un m.** to make a right mess of things; **tu t'y prends comme un m.** you're making a right mess of it; **pour l'organisation du dîner, vous vous êtes débrouillés** *ou* **vous vous y êtes pris comme des manches** you made a right mess of organizing the dinner; **avec les femmes, il s'y prend comme un m.** he's absolutely useless with women; **il conduit/danse comme un m.** he's a lousy *or* hopeless driver/dancer

3 *très Fam (obstacle)* **tomber sur un m.** to hit a snag

4 *Fam Aviat & Ordinat* **m. à balai** joystick

5 *Culin (de côtelette, de gigot)* bone; **m. à gigot** leg of mutton holder

6 *Mus (de violon, de guitare)* neck

manche[2] [mɑ̃ʃ] **NF 1** *(de vêtement)* sleeve; **sans manches** sleeveless; **à manches courtes/longues** short-/long-sleeved; **être en manches de chemise** to be in one's shirt-sleeves; **relever** *ou* **retrousser ses manches** to roll up one's sleeves; *Fig* to roll up one's sleeves, to get down to work; *Fam Fig* **avoir qn dans sa m.** to have sb in one's pocket; **il a le conseil municipal dans sa m.** he's well in with the local council; **m. bouffante/trois-quarts** puff/three-quarter sleeve; **m. gigot/raglan** leg-of-mutton/raglan sleeve; **m. ballon** puff sleeve; **m. chauve-souris** batwing sleeve; **manches kimono** kimono sleeves

2 *(conduit ▸ de ballon)* neck; **m. à air** *Aviat* windsock; *Naut* windsail; **m. à vent** wind sock

3 *(dans un jeu)* round; *(au bridge)* game; *Sport (gén)* leg; *(au tennis)* set; *Fig* **gagner la première m.** to win the first round

4 *Fam (locution)* **faire la m.** *(mendiant)* to beg□; *(musicien, mime)* to perform in the streets□, *Br* to busk

manchego [mɑ̃tʃego] NM *(fromage)* manchego

manchette [mɑ̃ʃɛt] NF **1** *(rabat de manche ▸ décoratif)* cuff; *(▸ de protection)* oversleeve

2 *Presse* (front-page) headline; **la nouvelle a fait la m. de tous les journaux** the news made the headlines *or* the story was headline news in all the papers

3 *Typ (note)* side note

4 *Sport* forearm smash; *Escrime* slash on the sword wrist; *(au volley-ball)* dig

manchon [mɑ̃ʃɔ̃] NM **1** *(fourreau pour les mains)* muff; *(guêtre)* gaiter **2** *Tech (de protection)* sleeve, casing; *(pour axe, arbre)* sleeve; *(de palier)* bush (ing); *(pour pivot)* socket; **m. d'accouplement** coupling sleeve; *Aut & Tech* **m. d'embrayage** clutch; **m. à gaz** *ou* **à incandescence** incandescent mantle **3** *Culin* **manchons de canard** duck drumsticks

manchot, -e [mɑ̃ʃo, -ɔt] ADJ *(d'un bras)* one-armed; *(d'une main)* one-handed; *(des deux bras)* armless, with no arms; *(des deux mains)* with no hands; *Fam* **il n'est pas m.** *(il est habile de ses mains)* he's clever with his hands; *(il est efficace)* he knows how to go about things; *(il peut le faire lui-même)* he's got hands, hasn't he?

NM,F *(d'un bras)* one-armed person; *(d'une main)* one-handed person; *(des deux bras)* armless person, person with no arms; *(des deux mains)* person with no hands

NM *Orn* penguin; **m. empereur** emperor penguin

manchou, -e [mɑ̃dʃu] = **mandchou**

mandala [mɑ̃dala] NM mandala

mandale [mɑ̃dal] NF *Fam* clout, slap□; **filer une m. à qn** to clout *or* slap sb; **tu veux une m.?** do you want a clip round the ear?

mandant, -e [mɑ̃dɑ̃, -ɑ̃t] NM,F **1** *Jur* principal **2** *Pol (gén)* voter; *(d'un député)* constituent

mandarin [mɑ̃darɛ̃] NM **1** *Hist* mandarin

2 *Fig Péj (personnage influent)* mandarin

3 *(langue)* Mandarin Chinese

4 *Orn* mandarin duck

mandarinal, -e, -aux, -ales [mɑ̃darinal, -o] ADJ mandarin *(avant n)*, mandarinic

mandarinat [mɑ̃darina] NM **1** *Hist* mandarinate **2** *Fig Péj (élite)* **le m. littéraire/politique** the literary/political establishment

mandarine [mɑ̃darin] NF **1** *(fruit)* mandarin (orange) **2** *TV & Cin (éclairage)* redhead

mandarinier [mɑ̃darinje] NM mandarin tree

mandat [mɑ̃da] NM **1** *Jur (procuration)* power of attorney, proxy; *(ordre)* warrant; **donner m. à qn (pour faire qch)** to give sb power of attorney (to do sth); **choisissez une personne à qui donner votre m.** choose a proxy; **m. d'action** receiving order (in bankruptcy); **m. d'amener** = warrant for a suspect or witness; **m. d'arrêt** (arrest) warrant; **un m. d'arrêt à l'encontre de...** a warrant for the arrest of...; **m. de comparution** summons *(singulier)*; **m. de contrôle** watching brief; **m. de dépôt** committal (order); **placer qn sous m. de dépôt** to commit sb; **m. d'expulsion** eviction order; **m. de justice** (police) warrant; **m. de perquisition** search warrant

2 *Pol (fonction)* mandate; *(durée)* term of office; **m. de député** member's (electoral) mandate; **m. politique** political mandate; **m. présidentiel** president's *or* presidential term of office; **ces prérogatives n'entrent pas dans son m.** he/she does not have a mandate to exercise these prerogatives; **solliciter le renouvellement de son m.** to seek re-election; **elle a rempli son m.** *(gén)* she's done what she was asked to do; *Pol* she's fulfilled her mandate

3 *Fin* **m. (de paiement)** order to pay; **m. international** international money order; **m. postal** *Br* postal order, *Am* money order; **m. télégraphique** telegraphic money order; **m. du Trésor** Treasury warrant; **m. de virement** transfer order

4 *(autorité)* mandate; **m. international** international mandate; **les pays sous m. (international)** mandated countries, mandates

mandataire [mɑ̃datɛr] NMF **1** *Jur* attorney, proxy; **constituer un m.** to appoint a proxy **2** *Pol* representative **3** *Com* authorized agent

NM *Ordinat* proxy

mandatement [mɑ̃datmɑ̃] NM **1** *Jur* appointment, commissioning; **m. d'office** establishment of a commission **2** *Fin* order to pay

mandater [3] [mɑ̃date] VT **1** *(députer)* to appoint, to commission **2** *Pol* **m. qn** to elect sb, to give sb a mandate; **m. des délégués pour un congrès** to mandate delegates to a conference **3** *Fin* to pay by *Br* postal order *or Am* money order

mandchou, -e [mɑ̃dʃu] ADJ Manchu, Manchurian

NM *(langue)* Manchu

• **Mandchou, -e** NM,F Manchu; **les Mandchous** the Manchus *or* Manchu

Mandchourie [mɑ̃dʃuri] NF **la M.** Manchuria

mandement [mɑ̃dmɑ̃] NM **1** *Hist* command, mandate, order **2** *Rel* pastoral (letter)

mander [3] [mɑ̃de] VT *Vieilli & Littéraire* **1** *(faire venir)* to send for **2** *(ordonner)* **m. à qn de faire qch** to instruct sb to do sth **3** *(informer)* **m. une nouvelle à qn** to convey news to sb

mandibule [mɑ̃dibyl] NF *Anat & Zool* mandible

• **mandibules** NFPL *Fam* **jouer des mandibules** to munch away

mandoline [mɑ̃dɔlin] NF **1** *Mus* mandolin, mandoline **2** *(hachoir)* (vegetable) slicer, mandolin, mandoline

mandragore [mɑ̃dragɔr] NF mandrake, mandragora

mandrill [mɑ̃dril] NM *Zool* mandrill (ape)

mandrin [mɑ̃drɛ̃] NM **1** *(pour soutenir ▸ sur un tour)* mandril, mandrel; *(▸ sur une machine-outil)* chuck **2** *(pour percer)* punch; *(pour agrandir des trous)* drift

manécanterie [manekɑ̃tri] NF *Vieilli* parish choir school

manège [manɛʒ] NM **1** *Équitation (salle)* manege; *(école)* riding school, manege; *(exercices)* riding exercises, manege work; **faire du m.** to do riding exercises *or* manege work; **heures de m.** = hours spent riding in a manege

2 *(attraction)* **m. (de chevaux de bois)** merry-go-round, roundabout

3 *Fig (manigances)* (little) game; **j'observai quelques instants ce m.** I watched these goings-on for a few minutes; **je ne comprenais rien à leur m.** I couldn't figure out what they were up to

4 *(en danse)* manège

5 *(piste de cirque)* ring

mânes [man] NMPL **1** *Antiq* manes **2** *Littéraire* spirits

maneton [mantɔ̃] NM crankpin

manette [manɛt] NF (hand) lever, (operating) handle; *Aviat* **m. des gaz** throttle (control *or* lever); **m. de jeux** joystick; *Fam* **à fond les manettes** at full speed□, *Br* like the clappers, *Am* like sixty

manga [mɑ̃ga] NM manga

manganate [mɑ̃ganat] NM *Chim* manganate

manganèse [mɑ̃ganɛz] NM *Chim* manganese

manganite [mɑ̃ganit] *Chim* NM manganite (salt)

NF manganite (hydroxide)

mangeable [mɑ̃ʒabl] ADJ **1** *(comestible)* edible **2** *(médiocre)* (just about) edible *or* eatable; **c'est bon? – c'est m.** is it good? – it's edible

mangeaille [mɑ̃ʒaj] NF **1** *Vieilli (pâtée d'animaux ▸ gén)* feed; *(▸ pour cochons)* (pig) swill **2** *Fam Péj (nourriture)* grub, *Br* nosh

mange-disque [mɑ̃ʒdisk] *(pl* **mange-disques***)* NM slotfeed record player

mangeoire [mɑ̃ʒwar] NF *(pour le bétail)* trough, manger; *(pour les animaux de basse-cour)* trough; *(pour des oiseaux en cage)* feeding dish

manger¹ [mɑ̃ʒe] NM food, meal; **je ne pourrai pas rentrer avant m.** I won't be able to get back before lunch/dinner/*etc*; **à prendre après m.** *(sur étiquette)* to be taken after meals; **je suis en train de lui faire son m.** I'm getting his/her food ready (for him/her); **on peut apporter son m.** customers *or* patrons are allowed to consume their own food on the premises

manger² [17] [mɑ̃ʒe] VT **1** *(pour s'alimenter)* to eat; **m. un sandwich** to eat a sandwich; *(au lieu d'un repas)* to have a sandwich; **m. un morceau** to have a bite to eat; **m. du poisson** to eat fish; **je ne mange pas de poisson** I don't eat fish; **elle mange de tout** she'll eat anything, she's not a fussy eater; **elle a tout mangé** she's eaten it all up; **mange ta soupe** eat (up) *or* drink (up) your soup; **qu'est-ce qu'on mange?** what are we having to eat?, what's for lunch/dinner/*etc*?; **qu'est-ce que vous avez mangé aujourd'hui à la cantine, les enfants?** what did you have (to eat) for dinner at school today, children?; **faire m. qch à qn** to give sb sth to eat; *Fam Fig* **on s'est fait m. par les moustiques** we were bitten to death *or* eaten alive by mosquitoes; *Fam* **m. de la vache enragée** to have a hard time of it; *Fam* **il a mangé du lion aujourd'hui** he's full of beans today; *Can Fam* **m. des bêtises** *(se faire insulter)* to take abuse□; *(se faire réprimander)* to get told off; *Can Fam* **m. de la misère** *(vivre misérablement)* to lead a hand-to-mouth existence□, to live in dire poverty□; *(avoir une vie difficile)* to have a hard time of it; **il ne mange pas de ce pain-là** he doesn't go in for that sort of thing, that's not his cup of tea; *Fam* **il peut me m. la soupe sur la tête** *(il est beaucoup plus grand)* he's a head taller than me□; *(il est bien meilleur)* he's miles better than me; *Fam* **m. la laine sur le dos à qn** to sponge shamelessly off sb; *Fam* **m. les pissenlits par la racine** to be pushing up (the) daisies; **m. son pain blanc le premier** to have it easy for a while; **m. son pain noir le premier** to get the worst part over with first; *Fam* **m. du curé** to be violently anticlerical□; **dis-moi ce que tu manges, je te dirai qui tu es** tell me what you eat and I'll tell you who you are, you are what you eat

2 *Fig* to eat; **elle le mangeait des yeux** *(personne)* she (just) couldn't take her eyes off him; *(objet)* she gazed longingly at it; **m. qn de baisers** to smother sb with kisses; *Hum* **elle ne va pas te m.!** she's not going to eat *or* to bite you!

3 *(ronger)* **des couvertures mangées aux mites** *ou* **par les mites** moth-eaten blankets; **une statue mangée par l'air marin** a statue eaten away by the sea air; **la rouille mange l'acier** rust eats into steel

4 *(prendre toute la place dans)* **tes cheveux te mangent la figure** your hair is hiding your face; **elle avait de grands yeux qui lui mangeaient le visage** her eyes seemed to take up her whole face

5 *(négliger)* **m. ses mots** *ou* **la moitié des mots** to swallow one's words, to mumble, to mutter; *Belg* **m. sa parole** to break one's promise, to fail to keep one's word

6 *(dépenser)* to get through; **m. son capital** to eat up one's capital; **la chaudière mange un stère de bois tous les cinq jours** the boiler gets through *or* eats up *or* consumes a cubic metre of wood every five days; **l'imprimante mange du papier** the printer is heavy on paper; **m. son blé en herbe** to spend one's money even before one gets it; *Fam* **ça ne mange pas de pain** it doesn't cost anything; **on peut toujours essayer, ça ne mange pas de pain** we can always have a go, it won't cost us anything

VI **1** *(s'alimenter)* to eat; **m. dans une assiette** to eat off a plate; **il ne sait pas m. avec une fourchette/des baguettes** he doesn't know how to eat with a fork/with chopsticks; **apprends-lui à m. correctement à table** teach him/her some (proper) table manners; **il a bien mangé** *(en quantité ou en qualité)* he's eaten well; **nous avons bien mangé** we had a very good meal; **j'ai mal mangé** *(insuffisamment)* I didn't eat enough, I didn't have enough to eat; *(de la mauvaise qualité)* I didn't have a very good meal; **il faut m. léger** you should eat light meals; **m. à sa faim** to eat one's fill; **nous ne mangions pas tous les jours à notre faim** we didn't always have enough food *or* enough to eat; **le bébé/chat mange toutes les trois heures** the baby/cat has to be fed once every three hours; **faire m. qn** to feed sb; *Fam* **m. comme un cochon** to eat like a pig; *Fam* **m. comme quatre** *ou* **comme un ogre** *ou* **comme un chancre** to eat like a horse; **m. comme un moineau** *ou* **comme un oiseau** to eat like a sparrow; **m. du bout des dents** to pick at one's food; *Fig* **il lui mange dans (le creux de) la main** he eats out of his/her hand; **m. sur le pouce** to have a snack, to grab a bite to eat; *Péj* **il mange à tous les râteliers** he's got a finger in every pie; **ce journaliste politique mange à tous les râteliers** this political journalist jumps on every passing bandwagon; *Hum* **c'est tellement propre chez elle qu'on mangerait par terre** her house is so clean you could eat off the floor; **il faut m. pour vivre et non pas vivre pour m.** one must eat to live and not live to eat

2 *(participer à un repas)* to eat; **venez m.!** *(à table!)* come and get it!; **venez m. demain soir** come to dinner tomorrow evening; **vous mangerez bien avec nous?** won't you (have something to) eat with us?; **ils m'ont demandé de rester m.** they asked me to stay for a meal; **j'ai mangé avec eux** I had a meal *or* I ate with them; **inviter qn à m.** *(chez soi)* to ask sb round for a meal; *(au restaurant)* to ask sb out for a meal; *Fam* **on a eu les Michaud à m.** we had the Michauds round for a meal; **m. à la carte** to eat à la carte *or* from the à la carte menu; **m. dehors** *(en plein air)* to eat outside; *(ailleurs que chez soi)* to eat out, to go out for a meal; **m. au restaurant** to eat out; **m. chez soi** to eat in *or* at home; **c'est un restaurant simple mais on y mange bien** it's an unpretentious restaurant, but the food is good

3 *(comme locution nominale)* **je veux à m.** I want something to eat; **as-tu eu assez à m.?** have you had enough to eat?; **les pays qui n'ont pas assez à m.** the countries where people don't have enough food *or* enough to eat; **donner à m. à qn** to feed sb, to give sb something to eat; **donner à m. à un animal/bébé** to feed an animal/a baby; **faire à m. à qn** to make something to eat for sb; **que veux-tu que je fasse à m. ce soir?** what would you like me to make for dinner (tonight)?

VPR **se manger 1** *(emploi passif)* to be eaten; **ça se mange avec de la mayonnaise** you eat it *or* it is served with mayonnaise; **les huîtres se mangent crues** oysters are eaten raw; **cette partie ne se mange pas** you don't eat that part, that part shouldn't be eaten *or* isn't edible **2** *Fam (se disputer)* to have a set-to; to quarrel; **se m. le nez** to quarrel; **toujours à se m. le nez, ces deux-là!** these two are always at each other's throats! **3** *Fam* **se m. qch** *(percuter)* to go head-first into sth

mange-tout [mɑ̃ʒtu] NM INV *Bot (haricot) Br* runner bean, *Am* string bean; *(petit pois)* mange-tout, sugar pea

mangeur, -euse [mɑ̃ʒœr, -øz] NM,F eater; **c'est un gros m.** he's a big eater, he eats a lot; **les Asiatiques sont de gros mangeurs de riz** people from Asia eat a lot of rice *or* are big rice-eaters; **mangeurs d'hommes** cannibals, man-eating savages; **tigre/requin m. d'hommes** man-eating tiger/shark; *Fam* **mangeuse d'hommes** man-eater; **attention, c'est une mangeuse d'hommes** watch out, she's a man-eater *or* she eats men for breakfast; *Can Fam* **m. de curés** *ou* **de soutanes** = violently anti-clerical person; *Can Fam Péj* **m./mangeuse de balustrades** Holy Joe, *f* Mary

manglier [mɑ̃glije] NM mangrove (tree)

mangoustan [mɑ̃gustɑ̃] NM mangosteen (fruit)

mangouste [mɑ̃gust] NF **1** *Zool* mongoose **2** *(fruit)* mangosteen

mangue [mɑ̃g] NF *Bot* mango

manguier [mɑ̃gje] NM mango (tree)

maniabilité [manjabilite] NF **1** *(d'un outil)* manageability, practicability; *(d'une voiture)* handling ability, manoeuvrability; *(d'un avion)* manoeuvrability; *(d'un logiciel)* user-friendliness; **une caméra d'une grande m.** a camera which is very easy to handle; **critiqué par les consommateurs pour son manque de m.** criticized by consumers for its unwieldiness **2** *(plasticité ▸ de l'argile)* plasticity; *(▸ du béton)* workability

maniable [manjabl] ADJ **1** *(facile à utiliser ▸ outil)* handy, easy to use *or* to handle; *(facile à travailler ▸ cuir)* easy to work **2** *(manœuvrable ▸ voiture)* easy to drive; *(▸ avion)* easy to control, easy to manoeuvre; *(▸ tondeuse)* easy to handle, easy to manoeuvre **3** *Naut* **temps m.** fine weather; **vent m.** moderate wind

maniaco-dépressif, -ive [manjakɔdepresif, -iv] *(mpl* **maniaco-dépressifs**, *fpl* **maniaco-dépressives)** ADJ manic-depressive; **psychose maniaco-dépressive** manic depression

NM,F manic-depressive

maniaque [manjak] ADJ **1** *(obsessionnel)* fussy, fastidious; **il range ses livres avec un soin m.** he's obsessively *or* fanatically tidy about his books **2** *(exigeant)* fussy; **elle est si m. pour les chaussures qu'elle les fait faire sur mesure** she's so particular *or* fussy when it comes to shoes that she has them made to measure **3** *Psy* manic; **état m.** mania

NMF **1** *(personne ▸ trop difficile)* fussy person; *(▸ qui a une idée fixe)* fanatic; **c'est un m. de l'hygiène/de l'ordre** he's fanatical about *or* obsessed with hygiene/tidiness; **mon médecin est un m. des antibiotiques** my doctor prescribes antibiotics for everything; **enfin, un logiciel pour les maniaques de l'orthographe/des mots croisés!** at last, a software package for spelling/crossword buffs! **2** *(dément)* maniac; **m. sexuel** sexual pervert, sex maniac

> Il faut noter que le terme anglais **maniac** ne signifie jamais **pointilleux**.

maniaquerie [manjakri] NF fussiness; **son exactitude frôle la m.** there's something almost obsessive about his/her punctuality

manichéen, -enne [manikeɛ̃, -ɛn] ADJ **1** *Rel* Manichean **2** *Fig* **il est très m.** he sees everything in very black-and-white terms

NM,F Manichean

manichéisme [manikeism] NM **1** *Rel* Manicheism **2** *Fig* rigid *or* uncompromising approach to things; **faire du m.** to see things in black and white

manicle [manikl] NF *(pour la cuisine)* oven glove; *Tech* protective glove

manie [mani] NF **1** *(habitude)* odd habit; *(idée fixe)* obsession, quirk; **avoir la m. de la propreté** to be obsessively clean *or* a stickler for cleanliness; **il a la m. de fermer toutes les portes** he has a habit of always closing doors; **chacun a ses petites manies** everyone has their own peculiar ways *or* little quirks; **c'est une m. chez elle de dire du mal des autres** it's become a habit with her to run other people down; **c'est une m., chez toi!** it's an obsession with you!; **c'est ta nouvelle m., de fumer la pipe?** is that your latest fad *or* craze, smoking a pipe?; **ça tourne à la m.** it's getting to be a fixation *or* an obsession **2** *Psy* mania

maniement [manimɑ̃] NM *(manipulation)* handling, operating; **nous cherchons à simplifier le m. de nos appareils** we're trying to make our equipment easier to handle *or* to operate; **montre-lui le m. de la télécommande** show him/her how to use *or* to work the remote control; *Fig* **le m. de la langue lui a toujours paru facile** he's/she's always found it easy to speak the language *or* had an easy command of the language; *Fig* **rompu au m. des affaires/des foules** used to handling business/manipulating crowds; **à l'armée ils sont initiés au m. des armes** in the army they learn how to use a gun; *Mil* **m. d'armes** (arms) drill

manier [9] [manje] VT **1** *(manipuler ▸ objet, somme)* to handle; **vers dix mois, il commencera à vouloir m. les objets** at ten months, he'll want to start handling *or* manipulating objects; **facile/difficile à m.** easy/difficult to handle; **m. qch avec délicatesse** to handle sth gently; **m. de grosses sommes** to handle large sums (of money)

2 *(diriger, contrôler ▸ hommes, cheval)* to handle, to manage; *(▸ avion)* to control, to manoeuvre; **m. les avirons** to ply *or* pull the oars

3 *(utiliser)* to use, to operate; **avez-vous déjà manié un télescope/micro?** have you ever used a telescope/microphone?; **une imprimante portative très facile à m.** an easy-to-use portable printer; **elle sait m. la caméra** she's good with a cine camera; **il savait m. la plume** he was a fine writer; **il sait m. l'ironie** he knows how *or* when to use irony

4 *(modeler ▸ pâte)* to knead; *(▸ argile)* to handle, to fashion

VPR **se manier** *Fam* to get a move on, to get one's skates on

MANIÈRE [manjɛr] NF **1** *(façon, méthode)* way, manner; **d'une m. ridicule** in a ridiculous manner, ridiculously; **d'une m. bizarre** in a strange manner, strangely; **d'une m. assez particulière** in a rather unusual way *or* manner; **de m. habile** skilfully; **il y a différentes manières d'accommoder le riz** there are many ways of preparing rice; **quelle est la meilleure m. d'aborder le sujet?** what's the best way of approaching the subject?; **nous ne faisons pas les choses de la même m.** we don't do things (in) the same way; **la m. qu'elle a de regarder les gens par en dessous** the furtive way she has of looking at people; **de quelque m. qu'on s'y prenne, on obtient toujours le même résultat** however you go about it you always get the same result; **user de** *ou* **employer la m. forte** to use strong-arm tactics; **m. de voir** *ou* **de penser** way of looking at things; **c'est une m. de parler** it's just a manner of speaking; **il fallait bien que je lui dise la vérité – oui mais il y a m. et m.** I had to tell him/her the truth – yes, but there are ways and ways (of doing it)

2 *Gram* manner; **adjectif/adverbe de m.** adjective/adverb of manner

3 *(savoir-faire)* **je comprends qu'il t'ait critiqué, mais il y a la m.** I can understand him criticizing you, but there are ways of doing these things; **il faut avoir la m.** you've got to have the knack; **refusez, mais mettez-y la m.** say no, but do it with tact; *Fam* **avec les gosses, il a la m.** he's got a way *or* he's good with kids

4 *(style)* way, style; **elle ne se plaindra pas, ce n'est pas dans sa m.** she won't complain, it's not her way *or* style; **c'est ma m. d'être** that's the way I am; **sa m. de marcher/s'habiller** his/her way of walking/dressing, the way he/she walks/dresses; **il a une drôle de m. de recevoir les gens** he has a funny way of welcoming people

5 *Beaux-Arts & Cin* manner, style; **un tableau dans la m. de Watteau** a painting in the manner *or* style of Watteau; **un Truffaut première/dernière m.** an early/late Truffaut

6 une m. de *(une sorte de)* a *or* some sort of, a *or* some kind of; **c'est une m. de poème épique** it's a sort of (an) epic *or* an epic of sorts; **le silence est parfois une m. de mensonge** silence is sometimes a way of lying

• **manières** NFPL *(façons de se comporter)* manners; **belles manières** social graces; **bonnes manières** (good) manners; **je vais t'apprendre les bonnes manières, moi!** I'll teach you to be polite *or* to behave yourself!; **mauvaises manières** bad manners; *Péj* **qu'est-ce que c'est que ces** *ou* **en voilà des manières!** what a way to behave!; **faire des manières** *(être poseur)* to put on airs and graces; *(se faire prier)* to stand on ceremony, to make a fuss; *Péj* **cesse de faire des manières et prends un chocolat** stop pussyfooting around and have a chocolate; **sans manières** without (a) fuss; **elle a pris l'argent sans (faire de) manières** she took the money without any fuss, she made no bones about taking the money; **venez dîner ce soir, mais vous savez, ce sera sans manières** come and have dinner tonight, but you know, it'll only be a simple meal

• **à la manière** ADV **à la m. paysanne** in the peasant way *or* manner

• **à la manière de** PRÉP **1** *(dans le style de)* in the manner *or* style of; **un tableau à la m. de Degas** a painting after (the manner of) Degas; **une chanson à la m. de Cole Porter** a song à la Cole Porter; **sauce tomate à la m. de tante Flo** tomato sauce like Auntie Flo used to make it **2** *(comme nom) Beaux-Arts & Littérature* **un à la m. de** a pastiche

• **à ma/sa/***etc* **manière** ADV in my/his/her/*etc* (own) way; **elle dit qu'elle l'aime à sa m.** she says she loves him in her own way; **laissez-moi faire à ma m.** let me do it my (own) way

• **de cette manière** ADV (in) this *or* that way; **je conserve tous les reçus, de cette m. je sais combien j'ai dépensé** I keep all the receipts, that way I know how much I've spent

• **de la belle manière, de la bonne manière** ADV *Ironique* properly, well and truly; **il s'est fait expulser de la bonne m.!** he was thrown out good and proper!

• **de la manière que** CONJ as; **tout s'est passé de la m. que l'on avait prévu** everything turned out as planned

• **de la même manière** ADV in the same way

• **de manière à** CONJ so as to, so that, in order to; **j'ai écrit aux parents de m. à les rassurer** I wrote to father and mother in order to reassure them

• **de manière (à ce) que** CONJ *(pour que)* so

(that); **laisse la porte ouverte, de m. que les gens puissent entrer** leave the door open so people can come in

• **de manière que** CONJ *(ce qui fait que)* in such a way that; **tu dis cela de m. que tu déplais à tout le monde** the way you say that upsets everybody

• **de telle manière que** CONJ in such a way that; **rabattez le pan A de telle m. qu'il se pose sur la figure B** fold over flap A so that it rests on figure B

• **de toute manière, de toutes les manières** ADV anyway, in any case *or* event, at any rate; **de toute m., tu as tort** in any case, you're wrong; **de toutes les manières, la promenade lui aura fait du bien** at any rate *or* anyway, the walk will have done him/her good

• **d'une certaine manière** ADV in a way; **j'étais d'une certaine m. prisonnière** I was what you might call a prisoner; **d'une certaine m., je suis content que ce soit fini** in a way, I'm glad it's over

• **de manière générale, d'une manière générale** ADV **1** *(globalement)* on the whole; **d'une m. générale, il réussit plutôt bien** he does quite well on the whole **2** *(le plus souvent)* generally, as a general rule; **d'une m. générale, je ne bois pas de vin** as a general rule, I don't drink wine

• **d'une manière ou d'une autre** ADV somehow (or other), one way or another; **d'une m. ou d'une autre il devra accepter** he's going to have to agree one way or another; **avertie ou pas, d'une m. ou d'une autre elle va s'inquiéter** whether she's told about it or not she's going to worry

• **en aucune manière** ADV in no way, on no account, under no circumstances; **est-ce de sa faute? – en aucune m.** is it his/her fault? – no, not in the slightest *or* least; **avez-vous eu connaissance des documents? – en aucune m.** did you get to see the documents? – no, not at all *or* no, I didn't at all

• **en manière de** PRÉP by way of; **elle n'était pas mon genre, se dit-il en m. de consolation** she wasn't my type, he told himself by way of consolation; **une boîte en carton en m. d'abri** a cardboard box by way of a shelter

• **en quelque manière** ADV in a way, as it were; **elle était en quelque m. ma fille** she was like a daughter to me

• **par manière de** = **en manière de**

---

maniéré, -e [manjere] ADJ **1** *(personne)* affected; **elle est tellement maniérée dans sa façon de parler!** she has such an affected way of speaking! **2** *Beaux-Arts & Littérature (style)* mannered

maniérisme [manjerism] NM **1** *(comportement)* affectation, *Sout* mannerism **2** *Beaux-Arts & Littérature* mannerism, Mannerism

manieur, -euse [manjœr, -øz] NM,F **m. d'argent** businessman; **manieuse d'argent** businesswoman; **c'est un m. d'hommes** he's a leader of men *or* a born leader

manif [manif] NF *Fam (abrév* **manifestation***)* demo

manifestant, -e [manifestɑ̃, -ɑ̃t] NM,F demonstrator

manifestation [manifestasjɔ̃] NF **1** *Pol* demonstration; **une m. contre le nucléaire** an anti-nuclear demonstration; **participer** *ou* **prendre part à une m.** to take part in a demonstration

2 *(marque)* expression; **des manifestations de joie** expressions of joy; **il n'y a eu aucune m. de mécontentement** nobody expressed any dissatisfaction; **sa pièce est la m. d'un grand trouble intérieur** his/her play is the expression of *or* expresses a deep-seated malaise

3 *(événement)* event; **m. artistique/culturelle/sportive** artistic/cultural/sporting event

4 *Méd* sign, symptom; **les manifestations précoces de la maladie** early symptoms of the disease

5 *Rel* revelation

manifeste[1] [manifest] ADJ *(évident)* obvious, evident, *Sout* manifest; **n'est-ce pas une preuve m. de son innocence?** isn't it clear proof of his/her innocence?; **il est m. que ses études ne l'intéressent pas** it's obvious that he/she isn't interested in his/her studies; **il est d'une incompétence m.** he is obviously *or* manifestly incompetent; **une erreur m.** an obvious error

manifeste[2] [manifest] NM **1** *Littérature & Pol* manifesto **2** *Aviat* manifest; *Naut* (ship's) manifest; **m. de douane** customs manifest; **m. d'entrée** inward manifest; **m. de sortie** outward manifest

manifestement [manifɛstəmɑ̃] ADV evidently, obviously, plainly; **il n'a m. pas envie de venir avec nous** he clearly *or* plainly doesn't feel like coming with us; **m., elle nous a menti** she has plainly been lying to us

manifester [3] [manifeste] VT **1** *(exprimer)* to express, to show; **m. son étonnement** to express one's surprise; **m. son mécontentement à qn** to indicate *or* to express one's dissatisfaction to sb; **je lui manifeste mon amour tous les jours** I show my love for him/her every day; **m. sa volonté** to make one's wishes clear; **m. son soutien à qn** to assure sb of one's support; **a-t-elle manifesté le désir d'être enterrée près de son mari?** was it her wish that she should be buried near her husband? **2** *(révéler)* to show, to demonstrate; **rien ne manifestait son désespoir intérieur** nothing indicated his/her inner despair; **sans m. la moindre irritation/admiration** without the slightest show of anger/admiration

VI to demonstrate; **m. contre qch** to demonstrate against sth

VPR **se manifester 1** *(personne)* to come forward; *Rel* to become manifest; **aucun témoin ne s'est manifesté** no witnesses came forward; **que le gagnant se manifeste, s'il vous plaît!** would the (lucky) winner step forward *or* come forward please!; **bon élève, mais devrait se m. plus/moins souvent en classe** good student, but should contribute more/be quieter in class; **ça fait très longtemps qu'il ne s'est pas manifesté** he hasn't been in touch for ages, I/we/*etc* haven't heard from him for ages; **je n'ai pas osé me m.** I didn't dare (to) show myself **2** *(sentiment)* to show (**par** in); *(phénomène)* to appear (**par** in); **sa joie de vivre se manifeste dans toutes ses toiles** his/her joie de vivre is expressed *or* expresses itself in every one of his/her paintings; **de petites plaques rouges se manifestent vers le troisième jour** small red spots come up *or* appear around the third day

manigance [manigɑ̃s] NF *(souvent au pl)* scheme, trick; **manigances** scheming *(UNCOUNT)*, schemes; **victime de toutes sortes de manigances** victim of all kinds of scheming

manigancer [16] [manigɑ̃se] VT to scheme, to plot; **m. une évasion** to plot *or* to engineer an escape; **l'affaire a été manigancée pour déshonorer le ministre** the whole affair was set up to discredit the minister; **qu'est-ce qu'ils manigancent?** what's their (little) game?, what are they up to?; **je me demande ce que les enfants sont en train de m.** I wonder what the children are up to; **toujours en train de m. quelque chose** always up to some little game; **je ne sais pas ce que je vais pouvoir m. pour ne pas le rencontrer** I don't know what I'll be able to come up with to avoid meeting him

Manille [manij] NF Manila

manille[1] [manij] NM *(cigare)* Manila (cigar)

manille[2] [manij] NF *Tech* shackle, clevis; *Naut* shackle; **m. lyre** harp shackle

manille[3] [manij] NF *(jeu)* manille *(French card game)*; *(carte)* ten

manillon [manijɔ̃] NM *Cartes* ace

manioc [manjɔk] NM manioc, cassava; **farine de m.** cassava

manip, manipe [manip] NF *Fam* **1** *(coup monté)* frame-up **2** *Scol* practical[□], experiment[□] **3** *(manipulation)* manipulation[□]

manipulateur, -trice [manipylatœr, -tris] NM,F **1** *(opérateur)* technician; *(de machine)* operator; *(d'argent, de biens)* handler; **m. de laboratoire** laboratory technician; **m. radio(graphe)** X-ray technician *or* assistant **2** *Péj* manipulator; **le comité est la proie de manipulateurs** the committee has fallen prey to a group of manipulators **3** *(prestidigitateur)* conjurer, conjuror

NM **1** *Tech* **m. à distance** remote-control manipulator **2** *Tél* sending *or* signalling key; **m. automatique** automatic key

manipulation [manipylasjɔ̃] NF **1** *(maniement)* handling; *Fig* **s'exercer à la m. des concepts mathématiques** to learn to handle *or* to manipulate mathematical concepts

2 *Scol & (en sciences)* experiment, piece of practical work; **m. génétique, manipulations génétiques** genetic engineering *(UNCOUNT)*

3 *Méd* manipulation; **m. vertébrale** (vertebral) manipulation; **un ostéopathe m'a fait des manipulations** an osteopath manipulated my spine

4 *(en prestidigitation)* conjuring trick

5 *Péj (intervention)* interference, manipulation; **manipulations électorales** *(coup monté)* vote rigging; **le nouvel organisme risque d'être victime des pires manipulations** the new organization risks falling victim to the worst kinds of manipulation; **nous craignons la m. des statistiques de l'emploi** we are afraid the employment figures might be interfered with *or* massaged; **à travers son journal, il orchestre la m. de l'opinion publique** he manipulates public opinion through his newspaper

6 *Ordinat* manipulation; **m. de colonnes** column handling; **m. de documents** document handling; **m. de données** data manipulation

7 *Fin* **m. monétaire** currency manipulation

manipulatrice [manipylatris] *voir* **manipulateur**

manipuler [3] [manipyle] VT **1** *(manier ▸ objet, somme)* to handle; *(▸ outil compliqué)* to manipulate; **m. de grosses sommes** to handle large sums of money **2** *Péj (influencer ▸ personne, électeurs)* to manipulate; *(▸ scrutin)* to rig; *(▸ statistiques)* to massage; *(▸ comptes)* to fiddle; **l'opinion publique est plus difficile à m. qu'ils ne le croient** public opinion is not as easily swayed *or* manipulated as they think; **il a prétendu que la police l'avait manipulé** he claimed that the police had manipulated him; **elle s'est fait complètement m. par ce type** she allowed the guy to twist her around his little finger **3** *Ordinat* to manipulate

manique [manik] NF *(pour la cuisine)* oven glove; *Tech* protective glove

manitou [manitu] NM **1** *(chez les Algonquins)* manitu, manitou **2** *Fam Fig* **(grand) m.** big shot *or* chief; **les grands manitous du pétrole** oil magnates[□] *or* tycoons[□]; **c'est un grand m. de la finance** he's a big shot in finance

manivelle [manivɛl] NF **1** *Tech* crank; *(pour un moteur)* crank (handle); *Aut* starting handle; *(de lève-glace)* window winder; **j'ai dû donner plusieurs tours de m.** I had to turn the handle a few times; **démarrer à la m.** to crank (up) the engine; **m. de mise en marche** starting handle **2** *(de pédalier)* pedal crank **3** *Cin (sur les anciennes caméras)* winding handle

manne[1] [man] NF **1** *Bible* manna **2** *Fig (aubaine)* godsend, manna **3** *Can Entom* mayfly, dayfly

manne[2] [man] NF *(panier)* (large) wicker basket

mannequin[1] [mankɛ̃] NM **1** *(personne)* model; **m. de charme** glamour model; **m. homme** male model; **elle est m. chez Zoot** she works as a model for Zoot **2** *(de vitrine)* dummy, mannequin; *(de couture)* dummy **3** *Beaux-Arts* lay figure

mannequin[2] [mankɛ̃] NM *(panier)* small (two-handled) basket

mannequinat [mankina] NM modelling

manœuvrabilité [manœvrabilite] NF manoeuvrability

manœuvrable [manœvrabl] ADJ *(maniable)* easy to handle, manoeuvrable; **cette voiture est peu m.** the car is not at all easy to manoeuvre *or* handle

manœuvre[1] [manœvr] NF **1** *(maniement)* operation, handling; **du sol, elle surveillait la m. de la grue** from the ground, she was checking the handling of the crane *or* how the crane was being operated; **apprendre la m. d'un fusil/d'un télescope** to learn how to handle a rifle/to operate a telescope

2 *(en voiture)* manoeuvre; **m. de stationnement** parking manoeuvre; **faire une m.** to (do a) manoeuvre; **faire une fausse m.** to manoeuvre badly; **j'ai manqué ma m. en essayant de me garer** I messed up my manoeuvre when I was parking

3 *aussi Fig (opération)* **fausse m.** wrong move; *Fig* **faire une fausse m.** to get it wrong; **une fausse m. au clavier et tu risques d'effacer ton document** one simple keying error is enough to erase your document

4 *Mil (instruction)* drill; *(simulation)* exercise; *(mouvement)* movement; *Vieilli* **les manœuvres, les grandes manœuvres** (army) manoeuvres; **être en manœuvres** *(à petite échelle)* to be on exercise; *(à grande échelle)* to be on manoeuvres; **m. d'encerclement** encircling movement; **m. de repli** (movement of) withdrawal
5 *Naut (action)* manoeuvre; **le bateau a commencé sa m. d'accostage** the ship has started docking
6 *Naut (cordage)* rope; **manœuvres dormantes** standing rigging; **manœuvres courantes** running rigging; **fausses manœuvres** preventer rigging *or* stays
7 *Fig* **laisser à qn une grande liberté de m.** to give sb freedom of action; **vous avez toute liberté de m.** you have a completely free hand, you have complete freedom of action
8 *Fig Péj (machination)* manoeuvre; **manœuvres** scheming *(UNCOUNT)*, manoeuvring *(UNCOUNT)*; *Bourse* **manœuvres boursières** stock market manipulation; **manœuvres électorales** electioneering; *Jur* **manœuvres frauduleuses** embezzling
9 *Méd* manipulation; **une m. obstétricale a été réalisée** the baby had to be turned
10 *Rail Br* shunting, *Am* switching; **voie de m.** *Br* shunting *or Am* switching track

manœuvre[2] [manœvr] **NM** *(ouvrier)* unskilled worker; *Constr & (en travaux publics)* labourer; **m. agricole** farm labourer *or* hand; **m. qualifié** skilled worker; **m. saisonnier** seasonal worker; **m. spécialisé** skilled worker; **travail de m.** unskilled work

manœuvrer **[5]** [manœvre] **VT1** *(faire fonctionner)* to work, to operate; **le monte-charge est manœuvré à la main** the hoist is hand-operated **2** *(faire avancer et reculer ▸ véhicule)* to manoeuvre; *Rail (▸ wagons à plate-forme)* to shunt, to marshal **3** *(influencer)* to manipulate
USAGE ABSOLU **une manœuvrez jamais sur une route à grande circulation** don't manoeuvre *or* do any manoeuvring on a busy road; **il se laisse m. par sa femme** he lets himself be manipulated *or* manoeuvred by his wife
VI1 *(agir)* to manoeuvre; *Fig* to manoeuvre, to scheme; *Péj* **ils manœuvrent tous pour devenir chef du parti** they're all jockeying for the position of party leader; **bien manœuvré!** clever *or* good move!; **m. dans l'ombre** to work behind the scenes **2** *Mil (s'exercer)* to drill; *(simuler)* to be on manoeuvres; **faites-les m. dans la cour** drill them in the yard; **ils sont partis m. sur la lande** they're off to the moors on manoeuvres

manœuvrier [manœvrije] **NM** *Naut* able *or* expert seaman

manoir [manwar] **NM** manor (house), (country) mansion

manomètre [manɔmɛtr] **NM** pressure gauge; *(en forme de U)* manometer; *Aut* **m. de compression** cylinder compression gauge; *Aut* **m. de pression d'huile** oil pressure gauge

manométrique [manɔmetrik] **ADJ** manometric, manometrical

manouche [manuʃ] **ADJ** gypsy *(avant n)*, gipsy *(avant n)*
NMF gypsy, gipsy

manquant, -e [mɑ̃kɑ̃, -ɑ̃t] **ADJ** missing; **la pièce manquante** the missing part; **les deux pages manquantes** the two missing pages; **les soldats manquants à l'appel** the soldiers missing at roll-call
NM,F missing one; **les manquants** *(élèves)* the absent pupils; **nous avons trouvé toutes les factures, les manquantes étaient dans le tiroir** we've found all the invoices, the missing ones were in the drawer
NM *Com* shortfall; **éviter des manquants dans la marchandise** to prevent short delivery; **m. en caisse** cash shortage; **m. en stock** stock shortage

manque[1] [mɑ̃k] **NM1** *(insuffisance)* **m. de** *(imagination, place, sommeil)* lack of; *(appartements, denrées)* shortage of, scarcity of; *(personnel)* lack of, shortage of; **ce serait un m. de respect** it would be lacking in respect, it would show lack of respect; **par m. de** *(originalité, audace)* for lack of, for want of; *(main-d'œuvre)* through lack *or* shortage of; **être en m. d'affection** to be starved of affection; **souffrir d'un m. affectif** to suffer from a lack of affection; **m. de chance** *ou Fam* **de bol** *ou Fam* **de pot** hard *or* tough luck; *Fam* **m. de bol, j'ai du travail** it's just (my) tough *or* rotten luck that I've got work to do
2 *(absence ▸ d'une personne)* gap; **quand il sera parti, il y aura un m.** his departure will leave a gap
3 *(de drogue)* **être en (état de) m.** to have *or* to feel withdrawal symptoms
4 *Écon & Jur* **m. à gagner** loss of (expected) income *or* earnings; **il y aura un m. à gagner de 200 euros** there will be a shortfall of 200 euros; *Compta* **m. de caisse** cash unders
5 *(à la roulette)* manque
• **manques NMPL** *(insuffisances)* failings, shortcomings; *(lacunes)* gaps; **avoir conscience de ses manques** to be aware of one's shortcomings *or* failings; **il y a beaucoup de manques dans ce rapport** there's a lot missing from this report

> Do not confuse with **manquement**.

manque[2] [mɑ̃k] **à la manque ADJ** *Fam* useless, pathetic; **qu'est-ce que c'est que cette histoire à la m.?** what kind of a pathetic story is that?

manqué, -e [mɑ̃ke] **ADJ1** *(non réussi ▸ attentat)* failed; *(▸ vie)* wasted; *(▸ occasion)* missed, lost; *(▸ rendez-vous)* missed; *(▸ tentative)* failed, abortive, unsuccessful; *(▸ photo, sauce)* spoilt; **je vais essayer de toucher la pomme – m.!** I'll try and hit the apple – missed! **2** *(personne)* **c'est un cuisinier/un médecin m.** he should've been a cook/a doctor
NM *Culin* = almond-flavoured cake

manquement [mɑ̃kmɑ̃] **NM** breach (à of); **m. à la discipline** breach of *or* lapse in discipline; **m. à un devoir** dereliction of duty; **m. aux bonnes manières** breach of etiquette; **m. à une règle** breach *or* violation of a rule

> Do not confuse with **manque**.

MANQUER **[3]** [mɑ̃ke]

> **VT**
> • to miss **1, 2, 4** • to fail **3**
> • to spoil **3**
> **VI**
> • to be missing **1** • to be away **1**
> • to be lacking **3** • to want **5**
> • to fail **6**

VT1 *(laisser échapper ▸ balle)* to miss, to fail to catch; *(▸ marche, autobus)* to miss; **j'ai manqué le train de trois minutes** I missed the train by three minutes; **l'église est à droite, vous ne pouvez pas la m.** the church is on the right, you can't miss it; *Sport* **m. le but** to miss the goal; *Fig* **m. son but** to fail to reach one's goal; **m. la cible** *Mil* to miss the target; *Fig* to miss one's target, to fail to hit one's target, to shoot wide; **il l'a manquée de peu** *(la cible)* he just missed it; **m. son coup** to miss; *Fig* to miss one's chance; *Fig* **elle s'est moquée de moi mais je ne la manquerai pas!** she made a fool of me but I'll get even with her!; **je n'ai pas vu cet opéra – tu n'as rien manqué/tu as manqué quelque chose!** I didn't see that opera – you didn't miss anything/you really missed something there!; **c'est une émission à ne pas m.** this programme shouldn't be missed *or* is a must; **il ne faut surtout pas m. ça** you really mustn't miss it; **m. une occasion** to miss (out on) an opportunity; *Hum* **tu as manqué une bonne occasion de te taire** why couldn't you have just kept your mouth shut for once?; *Fam* **il n'en manque jamais une!** *(il remarque tout)* he never misses a trick!; *(il est gaffeur)* (you can always) trust him to put his foot in it!
2 *(ne pas rencontrer)* to miss; **vous l'avez manquée de peu** you've just missed her
3 *(ne pas réussir ▸ concours)* to fail; *(▸ photo, sauce)* to spoil, to make a mess of; *aussi Hum* **tu as manqué ta vocation** you've missed your vocation; **moi qui croyais lui faire plaisir, j'ai vraiment manqué mon coup!** and here's me thinking I would make him/her happy, (just) how wrong can you get!
4 *(ne pas aller à)* to miss; **m. un cours** *(volontairement)* to miss *or* to skip *or* to jump a class; *(involontairement)* to miss a class; **j'ai bien envie de m. la gym** I feel like skipping gym; **il a manqué la messe, dimanche?** did he miss Mass on Sunday?

VI1 *(être absent ▸ fugueur, bouton, argenterie)* to be missing; *(▸ employé, élève)* to be away *or* off *or* absent; **le bouton qui manque à ma veste** the button that's missing from my jacket, the missing button on my jacket; **une pièce manque au puzzle** there's a piece missing from the jigsaw puzzle, a piece of the jigsaw puzzle is missing; **j'ai suivi tous les cours et je n'ai pas manqué une seule fois** I attended all the classes and never missed one *or* and I was never absent once; **elle a beaucoup manqué le mois dernier** she was off (school) a lot *or* missed a lot of classes last month; **m. à l'appel** *Mil* to be absent (at roll call); *Fig Hum* to be missing
2 *Ironique (tournure impersonnelle)* **il ne manquait plus qu'elle!** she's all we/I/*etc* need *ou* needed!; **il ne manquait plus que ça!** that's all we/I/*etc* need!; **il ne manquerait plus qu'elle tombe enceinte!** it would be the last straw if she got pregnant!
3 *(être insuffisant)* to be lacking, to be in short supply; **commencer à m.** to begin to run short *or* run out; **quand le pain vint à m., ils descendirent dans la rue** when they ran short of *or* ran out of bread, they took to the streets; **les occasions de te rendre utile ne manqueront pas** there will be no shortage of opportunities to make yourself useful; **la pluie/le travail, ce n'est pas ce qui manque!** there's no shortage of rain/work!; *Fam* **il n'y a pas d'eau chaude et ça manque!** there's no hot water and don't we know it!; **le pied m'a manqué** I lost my footing; **le temps m'a manqué** I didn't have enough time, I was short of time; **la place me manque** I don't have enough room; **l'argent leur a toujours manqué** they've always been short of money *or* lacked money; **la force/le courage lui manqua** (his/her) strength/courage failed him/her; *Littéraire* **le cœur lui manqua** his/her heart failed him/her; **les mots me manquent** words fail me, I'm at a loss for words; **la voix me manqua** words failed me; **ce n'est pas l'envie qui m'en manque, mais...** not that I don't want to *or* I'd love to, but...; **les occasions ne manquent pas, ce ne sont pas les occasions qui manquent** there's no lack of opportunity
4 *(tournure impersonnelle)* **il manque une bouteille/un bouton** there's a bottle/a button missing; **il nous manque trois joueurs** *(ils sont absents)* we have three players missing; *(pour jouer)* we're three players short; **il me manque trois euros** I'm three euros short, I need another three euros; **il lui manque un bras** he/she has only one arm, he/she has lost an arm; **il ne manquait plus rien à son bonheur** his/her happiness was complete; **il ne manque pas de gens pour dire que...** there is no lack *or* shortage of people who say that...; **il ne lui manque que la parole** *(animal)* the only thing it can't do is speak; *(machine)* it does everything but talk; *Fam* **il lui manque une case** he's/she's got a screw loose
5 *(être pauvre)* to want; **elle a toujours peur de m.** she's always afraid of having to go without
6 *(échouer)* to fail; **ça ne manquera pas** it's sure *or* bound to happen; **j'ai dit qu'elle reviendrait et ça n'a pas manqué!** I said she'd come back and sure enough(, she did)!; **je serai là sans m.** I'll be there without fail
• **manquer à VT IND1** *(faillir à)* **m. à son devoir/son honneur** to fail in one's duty/one's honour; **m. à ses devoirs** to neglect one's duties; *Hum* **je manque à tous mes devoirs!** I'm neglecting my duties!; **m. à sa parole/promesse** to fail to keep one's word/promise, to break one's word/promise; **m. à la consigne** to disregard orders; **m. au règlement** to break the rules; **m. aux usages** to defy *or* to flout convention; **m. à ses engagements financiers** to fail to meet one's financial liabilities
2 *(être regretté par)* **elle manque à ses enfants** her children miss her; **il me manque** I miss him; **ma famille me manque** I miss my family
• **manquer de VT IND1** *(ne pas avoir assez de)* to lack, to be short of; **m. de temps** to be short of time; **m. de courage** to lack courage; **m. de métier/d'expérience** to lack experience; **m. de personnel** to be short-staffed, to be short of staff; **je manque de sommeil** I'm not getting enough sleep; **nous manquons de l'essentiel** we lack *or* we're short of the basics; **ils manquent de tout** they're short of *or* they lack everything; **nous**

n'avons jamais manqué de rien we never went short of anything; **ta soupe manque de sel** your soup needs salt; **la chambre manque de lumière** the room doesn't get enough light, the room is lacking in *or* lacks light; **on commence à m. d'eau** we're beginning to run out of water; **ils ont fini par m. d'air et mourir** they finally ran out of air and died; **tu ne manques pas d'audace** *ou* **d'air** *ou Fam* **de culot!** you've (certainly) got some nerve!; *Fam* **ça manque de pain!** we're a bit short of bread!; *Fam* **ça manque de musique!** we could do with some music!

2 *(oublier de)* **vous viendrez? – je n'y manquerai pas** will you come? – definitely *or* without fail; **ne manquez pas de me le faire savoir** be sure to let me know, do let me know; **ne manquez pas de nous écrire** be sure to write to us, mind you write to us; **il n'a pas manqué de faire remarquer mon retard** he didn't fail to point out that I was late; **elle ne manquera pas de t'en faire la remarque** she'll be quite sure *or* she's bound to point it out to you

3 *(s'empêcher de)* **on ne peut m. de constater/penser...** one can't help but notice/think...; **personne ne peut m. d'observer...** no one can fail to notice...; **vous ne manquerez pas d'être frappé par cette coïncidence** you're bound to be struck by this coincidence; **tu ne manqueras pas d'être surpris** you're sure *or* bound to be surprised; **il n'a pas manqué d'être étonné** he couldn't help but be surprised

4 *(faillir)* **elle a manqué (de) se noyer** she nearly *or* almost drowned (herself)

VPR se manquer 1 *(emploi réciproque)* **nous nous sommes manqués à l'aéroport** we missed each other at the airport **2** *(emploi réfléchi)* to fail (in one's suicide attempt); **il s'est manqué pour la troisième fois** that's his third (unsuccessful) suicide attempt; **la deuxième fois, elle ne s'est pas manquée** her second suicide attempt was successful **3** *(tournure impersonnelle)* **il s'en manque de beaucoup** far from it

mansarde [mɑ̃sard] **NF 1** *(chambre)* garret, attic (room) **2** *Archit* **comble en m.** mansard roof

mansardé, -e [mɑ̃sarde] **ADJ** *(chambre, étage)* attic *(avant n)*; *(toit)* mansard *(avant n)*; **une pièce mansardée** an attic room, a room with a sloping ceiling

mansuétude [mɑ̃sɥetyd] **NF** *Littéraire* indulgence, goodwill, mansuetude

mante [mɑ̃t] **NF 1** *Entom* **m. (religieuse)** (praying) mantis **2** *Fig Hum* **m. religieuse** man-eater

manteau, -x [mɑ̃to] **NM 1** *(vêtement de ville)* coat; *(capote)* greatcoat; **m. de fourrure** fur coat; **m. de pluie** raincoat

2 *Zool (dos)* back; *(membrane ▸ d'un mollusque)* mantle

3 *Archit* **m. de cheminée** mantelpiece, mantel

4 *Théât* **m. d'Arlequin** proscenium arch

5 *Géol* mantle; **m. neigeux** snow mantle

6 *(locutions)* **sous le m.** unofficially, on the sly; **faire qch sous le m.** to do sth secretly *or Sout* clandestinely; **sous le m. de la nuit** under (the) cover of darkness

mantelé, -e [mɑ̃tle] **ADJ** *Zool (corbeau)* hooded

mantelet [mɑ̃tlɛ] **NM** *(cape ▸ de femme)* mantelet; *(▸ de prélat)* mantelletta

mantille [mɑ̃tij] **NF** mantilla *(scarf)*

manucure [manykyr] **NMF** manicurist

NF manicure; **se faire faire une m.** to have a manicure

manucuré, -e [manykyre] **ADJ** manicured

manuel, -elle [manɥɛl] **ADJ 1** *(métier, travailleur)* manual; *(outil)* hand-held; **je ne suis pas m. pour deux sous** I'm no good at all with my hands; **corrections manuelles** corrections by hand, manual corrections **2** *(non automatique)* manual; **commande manuelle** hand *or* manual control; **à commande manuelle** manually controlled; *Aviat* **passer en m.** to switch (over) to manual

NM,F 1 *(personne habile de ses mains)* practical person; **c'est une manuelle** she's good with her hands **2** *(travailleur)* manual worker

NM *(mode d'emploi, explications)* manual, handbook; **m. d'histoire/de géographie** history/geography book *or* textbook; **m. scolaire** (school) textbook; **m. d'entretien** service manual, maintenance manual, workshop manual; **m. d'installation** installation manual; **m. de style** *(dans l'édition)* style book; **m. d'utilisation, m. de l'utilisateur** instruction book *or* manual; *Aviat* **m. de vol** flight manual

manuellement [manɥelmɑ̃] **ADV** manually, by hand; **un dispositif qui fonctionne m.** a manually operated device

manufacture [manyfaktyr] **NF 1** *(atelier)* factory; *Hist* manufactory; **m. de soie/pipes** silk/pipe factory; **la m. des Gobelins** the Gobelins tapestry workshop; **la M. de porcelaine de Sèvres** the Sèvres porcelain factory **2** *(fabrication)* manufacture, manufacturing

manufacturer [3] [manyfaktyre] **VT** to manufacture

manufacturier, -ère [manyfaktyrje, -ɛr] **ADJ** manufacturing

NM,F *Arch* industrialist, factory owner

manu militari [manymilitari] **ADV 1** *(par la violence)* by force; **être expulsé m.** to be forcibly expelled **2** *Jur (par les forces de l'ordre)* by the forces of law and order

manuscrit, -e [manyskri, -it] **ADJ** *(lettre)* handwritten; *(page, texte)* manuscript *(avant n)*

NM 1 *(texte écrit à la main)* handwritten text **2** *(texte à publier)* manuscript; **m. dactylographié** manuscript, typescript; **sous forme de m.** in manuscript (form) **3** *(texte ancien)* **m. (ancien)** ancient manuscript; *(sous forme de rouleau)* scroll; **un m. du XIIIe siècle** a 13th-century manuscript; **les manuscrits de la mer Morte** the Dead Sea Scrolls

manutention [manytɑ̃sjɔ̃] **NF 1** *(manipulation)* handling **2** *(entrepôt)* warehouse, store house

manutentionnaire [manytɑ̃sjɔnɛr] **NMF** *(homme)* warehouseman, warehouse worker; *(femme)* warehouse worker; **il est m. dans une fabrique de meubles** he's a packer in a furniture factory

manutentionner [3] [manytɑ̃sjɔne] **VT** *(déplacer)* to handle; *(emballer)* to pack

maoïsme [maɔism] **NM** Maoism

maoïste [maɔist] **ADJ** Maoist

NMF Maoist

maori, -e [maɔri] **ADJ** Maori

NM *(langue)* Maori

• **Maori, -e NM,F** Maori; **les Maoris** the Maoris *or* Maori

maous, -ousse [maus] **ADJ** *Fam* ginormous, humongous

mappemonde [mapmɔ̃d] **NF** *(globe)* globe; *(carte)* map of the world *(showing both hemispheres)*; **m. céleste** planisphere

maquer [3] [make] **VT 1** *Belg (frapper)* to beat up; *Fig (abasourdir)* to stun, to astound **2** *Fam* **je pense pas qu'elle soit maquée** I don't think she's got a man; **elle est maquée avec lui** she's shacked up with him; **on a réussi à les m. ensemble** we managed to fix them up with each other

VPR se maquer *Fam (se marier)* to get hitched *or* spliced, to tie the knot; *(s'établir en couple)* to shack up together; **se m. avec qn** *(se marier)* to get hitched to sb; *(s'établir en couple)* to shack up with sb

maquereau, -x [makro] **NM 1** *Ich* mackerel **2** *Fam (souteneur)* pimp, *Am* mack

maquerelle [makrɛl] **NF** *Fam* **(mère) m.** madam *(in brothel)*

maquette [makɛt] **NF 1** *(modèle réduit)* (scale) model; **m. d'avion/de village** model aircraft/village; **faire des maquettes** to make models

2 *Beaux-Arts (d'une sculpture)* model, maquette; *(d'un dessin)* sketch

3 *Théât (de mise en scène)* model

4 *Typ (de pages)* paste-up, layout; *(de livre)* dummy

5 *Ind* mock-up, (full-scale) model

maquettiste [makɛtist] **NMF 1** *(modéliste)* model maker **2** *Typ* layout artist

maquignon [makiɲɔ̃] **NM 1** *(marchand ▸ de chevaux)* horse trader; *(▸ de bestiaux)* cattle trader **2** *Péj (entremetteur)* trickster

maquignonnage [makiɲɔnaʒ] **NM 1** *(vente ▸ de chevaux)* horse trading; *(▸ de bétail)* cattle trading **2** *Péj (manœuvre douteuse)* shady dealing, wheeling and dealing

maquignonner [3] [makiɲɔne] **VT 1** *(bétail, cheval)* to deal *or* to trade *or* to traffic in **2** *Péj (manœuvrer)* **ils ont maquignonné cette affaire entre eux** they've cooked this business up between them

maquillage [makijaʒ] **NM 1** *(cosmétiques)* make-up; *(application)* making up, putting on make-up; **elle met beaucoup de soin dans son m.** she takes a lot of care with her make-up **2** *(falsification ▸ d'un passeport, d'un texte)* falsifying, faking; *(▸ de photos)* faking; *(▸ de preuves, de comptes)* falsifying; *(▸ d'un véhicule)* respraying

maquiller [3] [makije] **VT 1** *(visage)* to make up; **être bien/mal maquillé** to be nicely/badly made up; **être trop maquillé** to be wearing too much make-up; **qui vous a maquillé?** who did your make-up?; **elle est allée se faire m. dans un institut de beauté** she went to a beauty parlour to get her make-up done **2** *(falsifier ▸ passeport, texte)* to falsify, to fake; *(▸ photos)* to fake; *(▸ preuves, comptes)* to falsify; *(▸ véhicule)* to respray; **m. un crime en suicide** to make a murder look like a suicide

VPR se maquiller se m. (le visage) to make up (one's face), to put on one's make-up; **se m. les yeux** to put one's eye make-up on; **elle se maquille trop** she uses too much make-up, she puts too much make-up on

maquilleur, -euse [makijœr, -øz] **NM,F** make-up artist, make-up man, *f* girl; *TV* **passer chez le m.** to have one's make-up put on; *Cin, TV* **elle est maquilleuse de studio** she works at a studio as a make-up artist

maquis [maki] **NM 1** *Géog* scrub, scrubland, maquis **2** *Hist* **le M.** the Maquis *(French Resistance movement in WWII)*; **prendre le m.** *Hist* to take to the maquis; *Fig* to go underground; **les m. d'Afghanistan** the Afghan freedom fighters **3** *Fig (labyrinthe)* **dans le m. des lois/de la finance internationale** in the jungle of law/of international finance

maquisard [makizar] **NM 1** *Hist* maquis, French Resistance fighter *(in WWII)* **2** *(guérillero)* guerrilla fighter

marabout [marabu] **ADJ INV** *Can* bad-tempered, grumpy

NM 1 *(oiseau, plume)* marabou, marabout

2 *(ermite, tombeau)* marabout

3 *(sorcier)* witchdoctor

4 *Can (personne acariâtre)* bad-tempered person

marabouter [3] [marabute] **VT** *(en Afrique francophone)* to put the evil eye on

maraca [maraka] **NF** maraca

maracuja [marakuʒa, -kyʒa], **maracudja** [marakudʒa] **NM 1** *(fruit)* passion fruit, maracuja **2** *(cocktail)* batida de maracuja *(Brazilian passion fruit cocktail)*

maraîchage [marɛʃaʒ] **NM** *Br* market gardening *(UNCOUNT)*, *Am* truck farming *or* gardening *(UNCOUNT)*

maraîcher, -ère [marɛʃe, -ɛr] **NM,F** *Br* market gardener, *Am* truck farmer

ADJ vegetable *(avant n)*; **produits maraîchers** *Br* market garden produce, *Am* truck

marais [marɛ] **NM 1** *(terrain recouvert d'eau)* marsh, swamp; **m. maritime** tidal marsh; **m. salant** salt marsh, salina **2** *(région)* marsh, marshland, bog **3** *(terrain consacré à la culture maraîchère) Br* market garden, *Am* truck farm

marasme [marasm] **NM 1** *Écon* slump, stagnation; **l'économie des pays d'Asie traverse actuellement une période de m.** Asian economies are currently going through a period of stagnation; **dans le m. économique actuel** in the present economic slump; **nous sommes en plein m.** we're going through a slump, our economy's in the doldrums **2** *Méd* marasmus, cachexia

marasque [marask] **NF** marasca cherry

marasquin [maraskɛ̃] **NM** maraschino; **cerises au m.** maraschino cherries

marathon [maratɔ̃] **NM 1** *Sport* marathon; **courir un m.** to run a marathon; **m. de danse** dance marathon **2** *Fig* **m. diplomatique/électoral** diplomatic/electoral marathon **3** *(comme adj inv; avec ou sans trait d'union)* marathon *(avant n)*; **discussion/séance m.** marathon discussion/session

marathonien, -enne [maratɔnjɛ̃, -ɛn] **NM,F** marathon runner

marâtre [marɑtr] **NF 1** *(méchante mère)* unnatural *or* wicked mother **2** *(belle-mère)* stepmother

maraud, -e [maro, -od] **NM,F** *Vieilli* rascal, rapscallion

maraudage [marodaʒ] **NM** pilfering *(of food)*

maraude [marod] **ADJ F** *voir* **maraud**

NF *(vol)* pilfering *(of food)*

• **en maraude ADJ un taxi en m.** a cruising taxi

marauder [3] [marode] **VI 1** *(personne)* to filch *or* to pilfer (food); *(soldat)* to maraud **2** *(taxi)* to cruise

maraudeur, -euse [marodœr, -øz] **NM,F** *(gén)* pilferer; *(soldat)* marauder

ADJ *(renard)* on the prowl; *(oiseau)* thieving

marbre [marbr] **NM 1** *Minér* marble; **un escalier/une statue en m.** a marble staircase/statue; **un mur en faux m.** a marbleized wall; *Fig* **ce n'est pas écrit dans le m.** it's not set in stone, it's not written in (tablets of) stone;

2 *(plateau ▸ de cheminée, meuble)* marble top

3 *Beaux-Arts (statue)* marble (statue); *(plaque)* marble plate

4 *Typ* (forme) bed; *Journ* reserve feature; **mettre sur le m.** *(journal)* to put to bed; *(livre)* to put on the press; *Fam* **avoir du m.** to have copy over; **rester sur le m.** to be excess copy

5 *Tech* surface plate

6 *Can Joual (bille)* marble▫

• **de marbre ADJ 1** *(insensible)* insensitive; **avoir un cœur de m.** to have a heart of stone; **il resta de m.** he remained impassive; **la mort de sa mère l'a laissé de m.** his mother's death left him cold *or* unmoved **2** *(impassible)* impassive; **un visage de m.** a poker face; **il est resté de m. pendant qu'on lui arrachait ses galons** he remained impassive while they tore off his stripes

marbré, -e [marbre] **ADJ** *(tacheté)* marbled, mottled; *(veiné)* veined; **peau marbrée** blotchy skin; **il avait la peau toute marbrée de coups** his skin was all marked with bruises

marbrer [3] [marbre] **VT 1** *(papier, tranche de livre)* to marble **2** *(peau)* to mottle, to blotch; **jambes/joues marbrées par le froid** legs/cheeks mottled with the cold

marbrerie [marbrəri] **NF 1** *(industrie)* marble industry **2** *(atelier)* marble (mason's) yard **3** *(métier, art)* marble work; **m. funéraire** monumental (marble) masonry

marbrier, -ère [marbrije, -ɛr] **ADJ** marble *(avant n)*

NM marbler; **m. (funéraire)** monumental mason

• **marbrière NF** marble quarry

marbrure [marbryr] **NF 1** *(aspect marbré)* marbling; *(imitation)* marbleizing, marbling **2** *(de peau)* mottling

• **marbrures NFPL** blotches, streaks, veins

marc[1] [mar] **NM 1** *(résidu de fruit)* marc **2** *(eau-de-vie)* marc (brandy) **3 m. (de café)** coffee grounds *or* dregs; **lire l'avenir dans le m. de café** ≃ to read the future in tea leaves

marc[2] [mar] **NM 1** *(monnaie, poids)* mark; **un m. d'or/d'argent** *(monnaie)* a gold/silver mark; *(poids)* a mark of gold/silver **2** *Jur* **au m. le franc** pro rata, proportionally

marcassin [markasɛ̃] **NM** young wild boar, squeaker

marcassite [markasit] **NF** *Minér* marcasite

marcel [marsɛl] **NM** singlet, *Br* vest

marchand, -e [marʃɑ̃, -ɑ̃d] **NM,F** *(négociant) Br* shopkeeper, *Am* storekeeper; *(▸ en vin)* merchant; *(▸ de meubles, de chevaux)* dealer; *(▸ sur un marché)* stallholder; **m. ambulant** (street) pedlar; *Péj* **m. de canons** arms dealer; **m. de charbon** coal merchant; **m. de chaussures** *Br* shoe-shop owner, *Am* shoe-store owner; **m. de couleurs** hardware store owner, *Br* ironmonger; **m. au détail** retailer; **m. d'esclaves** slave trader; **m. de fleurs** florist; **m. de fromage** cheese merchant; **m. de fruits** fruiterer; **m. en gros** wholesaler, wholesale dealer; *Péj* **m. d'illusions** dealer in false promises; **m. de journaux** *(en boutique)* newsagent; *(en kiosque)* newsstand man, newsvendor; **m. de légumes** *Br* greengrocer, *Am* vegetable seller; **m. de poisson** fishmonger; **m. des quatre-saisons** *Br* costermonger, *Am* fruit and vegetable seller; *Péj* **m. de sommeil** rack-renter, slumlord; **m. de tabac** tobacconist; **m. de tableaux** art dealer; **m. de tapis** carpet dealer; *Fig Péj* haggler; *Fig Péj* **des discussions de marchands de tapis** haggling; **m. de vin** wine merchant, vintner; **le m. de sable est passé** the sandman's coming

ADJ 1 *(valeur, prix)* market *(avant n)*; *(denrée)* marketable; *(qualité)* standard; **un tableau sans aucune valeur marchande** a painting of no saleable *or* marketable value **2** *(rue)* shopping *(avant n)*; *(quartier, ville)* commercial **3** *(marine, navire)* merchant *(avant n)*

marchandage [marʃɑ̃daʒ] **NM 1** *(discussion d'un prix)* haggling, bargaining; **faire du m.** to haggle **2** *Péj (tractation)* wheeler-dealing **3** *Jur* subcontracting

marchander [3] [marʃɑ̃de] **VT 1** *(discuter le prix de)* to bargain *or* to haggle over; **m. qch avec qn** to haggle *or* bargain with sb over sth **2** *(au négatif) (lésiner sur)* to spare; **ils n'ont pas marchandé leur effort** they spared no effort; **la presse n'a pas marchandé ses éloges pour sa dernière pièce** the press wasn't sparing of its praise for his/her last play **3** *Jur* to subcontract

VI to haggle, to bargain

marchandeur, -euse [marʃɑ̃dœr, -øz] **NM,F** haggler

NM *Jur* subcontractor

marchandisage [marʃɑ̃dizaʒ] **NM** merchandizing

marchandisation [marʃɑ̃dizasjɔ̃] **NF** merchandization

marchandise [marʃɑ̃diz] **NF 1** *(produit)* commodity; **marchandises** goods, merchandise *(UNCOUNT)*; **marchandises au détail** retail goods; **marchandises en entrepôt** warehoused goods, goods in storage; *Douanes* bonded goods, goods in bond; **marchandises en gros** wholesale goods; **marchandises en magasin** stock in hand; **marchandises périssables** perishable goods, perishables; **marchandises en souffrance** unclaimed goods; **marchandises en vrac** bulk goods

2 *(fret, stock)* **la m.** the goods, the merchandise; **la m. sera livrée à Londres** the merchandise will be delivered in London; **on lui a volé toute sa m.** all his/her goods were stolen; **notre boucher a de la bonne m.** our butcher sells good-quality meat

3 *Fam aussi Fig* **tromper** *ou* **voler qn sur la m.** to swindle sb; *Fig* **vanter** *ou* **étaler** *ou* **faire valoir sa m.** to make the most of oneself

4 *Fam Hum (organes sexuels masculins)* family jewels, *Br* tackle

marchandiser [3] [marʃɑ̃dize] **VT** to merchandize

marchandiseur [marʃɑ̃dizœr] **NM** merchandizer

MARCHE [marʃ]

• walking **1**	• walk **2**
• march **3–5**	• pace **6**
• step **6, 11**	• running **7–9**
• working **8, 9**	

NF 1 *(activité, sport)* walking; **la m. (à pied)** walking; **la m. en montagne** hill walking; **m. nordique** Nordic walking; **j'en ai fait de la m. aujourd'hui!** I've done quite a bit of walking today!; **elle fait de la m.** *(comme sport)* she goes walking; **aimer la m.** to be fond of walking; **poursuivre sa m.** to keep (on) *or* to carry on walking, to walk on; **la frontière n'est qu'à une heure de m.** the border is only an hour's walk away

2 *(promenade)* walk; **nous avons fait une m. de huit kilomètres** we did an eight kilometre walk; *Can* **prendre une m.** to go for a walk

3 *(défilé)* march; **m. silencieuse/de protestation** silent/protest march; **m. pour la paix** peace march; **ouvrir la m.** to lead the way; **fermer la m.** to bring up the rear

4 *Mus* march; **m. nuptiale/funèbre/militaire** wedding/funeral/military march

5 *Mil* march; **colonne en m.** column on the march; **ordre(s) de m.** marching orders; **en avant, m.!** forward, march!; **faire m. sur une citadelle** to march on *or* upon a citadel; **m. forcée** forced march; *Hist* **la Longue M.** the Long March; *Hist* **la M. sur Rome** the March on Rome

6 *(allure)* pace, step; **ralentir sa m.** to slow (down) one's pace; **accélérer sa m.** to increase *or* to step up one's pace

7 *(déplacement ▸ d'un train, d'une voiture)* running; *(▸ de bateaux)* sailing, running; *(▸ d'une étoile)* course; **dans le sens de la m.** *(dans un train)* facing the engine; *(dans un bus)* facing forward; **dans le sens contraire de la m.** *(dans un train)* (with one's) back to the engine; *(dans un bus)* facing backwards; *Aut* **m. avant/arrière** forward/reverse gear; **entrer/sortir en m. arrière** to reverse in/out, to back in/out; **faire m. arrière** *(conducteur)* to reverse, to back up; *Fig* to backpedal, to backtrack; **en voyant le prix, j'ai fait m. arrière** when I saw the price I backed out of buying it; *Cin & TV* **m. arrière** reverse motion

8 *(fonctionnement ▸ d'une machine)* running, working; **m., arrêt** on, off; **en (bon) état de m.** in (good) working order; **être en m.** *(machine)* to be running; *(fourneau)* to be in blast

9 *(d'une entreprise, d'un service)* running, working, functioning; **pour assurer la bonne m. de notre coopérative** to ensure the smooth running of our co-op; **la privatisation est-elle un obstacle à la bonne m. de l'entreprise?** is privatization an obstacle to the proper working *or* functioning of the company?

10 *(progression)* **la m. du temps** the passing *or Sout* march of time; **la m. de l'histoire** the course of history; **la m. des événements** the course *or Sout* march of events; **la révolution est en m.** revolution is on the march *or* move

11 *(degré ▸ d'un escalier)* step, stair; *(▸ d'un marchepied)* step; *(▸ d'un métier à tisser)* treadle; *(▸ d'un orgue)* pedal; **la première/dernière m.** *(en montant)* the bottom/top step; *(en descendant)* the top/bottom step; **descendre/monter les marches** to go down/up the stairs; **attention à la m.** *(sur panneau)* mind the step

12 m. à suivre *(instructions)* directions (for use); *(pour des formalités)* procedure, form

13 *Bourse* **m. aléatoire** random walk

• **en marche ADV monter/descendre d'un train en m.** to get on/off a moving train; **je suis descendue du bus en m.** I got off the bus while it was still moving; **mettre en m.** *(moteur, véhicule)* to start (up); *(appareil)* to switch *or* to turn on; **se mettre en m.** *(machine)* to start; **le four se mettra automatiquement en m. dans une heure** the oven will turn *or* switch itself on automatically in an hour **ADJ** moving, in motion; **navire en m.** ship under way

marché[1] [marʃe] **NM 1** *(lieu de vente)* market; **aller au m.** to go to the market; **je l'ai acheté au m.** I bought it at the market; **faire son m.** to go (grocery) shopping; **faire les marchés** *(commerçant)* to go round *or* to do the markets; **jour de m.** market day; **m. aux fleurs/à la volaille** flower/poultry market; **m. aux poissons/bestiaux** fish/cattle market; **m. aux puces** flea market; **m. couvert** covered market; **m. en plein air** open-air market; **m. d'intérêt national** wholesale market for agricultural produce

2 *Com & Écon* market; **m. des matières premières/du sucre/du café** raw materials/sugar/coffee market; **m. du travail** labour market; **mettre** *ou* **lancer un nouveau produit sur le m.** to put *or* to launch a new product on the market; **retirer qch du m.** to take sth off the market; **conquérir un m.** to break into a market; **arriver sur le m.** to come onto the market; **le vaccin n'est pas encore sur le m.** the vaccine is not yet (available) on the market; **il n'y a pas de m. pour ce type d'habitation** there is no market for this type of housing; **ils ont ouvert leur m. aux produits japonais** they've opened their markets to Japanese products; **le M. unique (européen)** Single (European) Market; **étude/économie de m.** market research/economy; **m. d'acheteurs** buyers' market; **m. à la baisse** buyers' market; **m. captif** captive market; **m. cible** target market; **le M. commun** the Common Market; **m. des consommateurs** *ou* **de la consommation** consumer market; **m. effectif** available market; **m. d'équipement** capital goods market; **m. à l'export** *ou* **à l'exportation** export market; **m.**

extérieur foreign *or* overseas market; **m. générique** generic market; **m. global** global market; **m. grand public** consumer market, mass market; **m. gris** grey market; **m. industriel** industrial market; **m. intérieur** home *or* domestic market; **m. libre** free market; **m. monopolistique** monopoly market; **m. national** national market, home market; **m. noir** black market; **faire du m. noir** to buy and sell on the black market; **m. officiel** official market; **m. parallèle** parallel market, black market; **m. principal** core market; **m. de référence** core market; *Mktg* **m. témoin** control market, test market; *Mktg* **m. test** test market; **le M. unique (européen)** the Single (European) Market; *Mktg* **m. utile** addressable market; **m. vendeur** sellers' market; **m. visé** target market

3 *Bourse & Fin* market; **m. des actions** stock market; **m. de l'argent** money market; **m. boursier** stock market; **m. cambiste** foreign exchange market; **m. des capitaux** capital market; **m. des changes** foreign exchange; **m. au comptant** spot market; **m. de cotation** securities market; **m. en coulisse** outside market; **m. des devises (étrangères)** foreign exchange market; **m. du disponible** spot market; **m. électronique privé** ECN, electronic communications network; **m. de l'eurodevise** *ou* **des eurodevises** euromarket; **m. financier** capital *or* financial market; **m. de gré à gré entre banques** interbank wholesale market; **m. à la hausse, m. haussier** sellers' market; **m. hors cote** unlisted securities market, *Am* over-the-counter market; **m. hypothécaire** mortgage market; **m. interbancaire** interbank market; **m. monétaire** money market; **m. du neuf** primary market; **m. obligataire** bond market; **m. à** *ou* **des options** options market; **m. secondaire** off-exchange market, OFEX; **m. à terme** futures market; **m. des titres** stock market; **m. des valeurs mobilières** share market

4 *(accord)* deal, bargain; *(plus officiel)* contract; **faire** *ou* **passer un m. (avec qn)** to strike a deal *or* bargain (with sb), to clinch a deal (with sb); **conclure un m. (avec qn)** to make a deal (with sb); **m. conclu!** it's a deal!, that's settled!; **c'est un m. de dupes** it's a con; **mettre le m. en main à qn** to force sb to take it or leave it

5 *Fam (locution)* **par-dessus le m.** into the bargain, what's more; **il est jeune, intelligent et beau par-dessus le m.** he's young, intelligent and handsome into the bargain; **et il se plaint, par-dessus le m.!** and what's more he's complaining!

• **à bon marché** ADV cheaply; **fabriqué à bon m.** cheaply made; **je l'ai eu à bon m.** I got it cheap

• **bon marché** ADJ cheap, inexpensive ADV **faire bon m. de qch** to treat sth lightly; **il a fait bon m. de mes conseils** he took no notice of my advice

• **meilleur marché** ADJ INV cheaper; **je l'ai eu meilleur m. à Paris** I got it cheaper in Paris

marché[2] [marʃe] NM *(au basket-ball)* travelling

marchéage [marʃeaʒ] NM *Mktg* marketing mix *or* spectrum; **m. de distribution** retailing mix

marchéisation [marʃeizasjɔ̃] NF marketization

marchepied [marʃəpje] NM **1** *(d'un train)* step, steps; *(d'un camion)* footboard; *(d'une voiture)* running board **2** *Fig (tremplin)* stepping stone; **ce petit rôle lui a servi de m. pour devenir célèbre** this small role put him/her on the road to fame **3** *(estrade)* dais; *(banc)* footstool; *(escabeau)* pair of steps

MARCHER [3] [marʃe]

- to walk **1**
- to step **3**
- to run **4**
- to go along with things **7**
- to march **2**
- to work **4, 5**
- to be working out **5**
- to fall for it **8**

VI **1** *(se déplacer à pied)* to walk; **m. tranquillement** to amble along; **descendre une avenue en marchant lentement/rapidement** to stroll/to hurry down an avenue; **m. à grands pas** *ou* **à grandes enjambées** to stride (along); **m. à petits pas** to take small steps; **m. à quatre pattes** to walk on all fours; **m. à reculons** to walk backwards; **m. de long en large (dans une salle)** to walk up and down (a room); **m. sur la pointe des pieds** to walk on tiptoe; **m. sur les mains** to walk on one's hands; **boiter en marchant** to walk with a limp; **il a une drôle de façon de m.** he has a funny walk; **m. sur les traces de qn** to follow in sb's footsteps; *Fig* **m. vers le succès** to be on the road to success; *Fig* **un peuple qui marche vers la liberté** a people marching *or* on the march towards liberty *or* freedom; *Fig* **l'État marche à la ruine** the State is heading for ruin; **m. droit** to walk straight *or* in a straight line; *Fig* to toe the line; **m. sur des œufs** *(marcher avec précaution)* to walk gingerly; *(devoir être prudent)* to tread carefully; *Fam* **c'est marche ou crève!** it's do or die!, it's sink or swim!

2 *Mil* to march; **m. au pas** to march in step; **m. sur une ville/sur l'ennemi** to march on a city/against the enemy

3 *(poser le pied)* **m. sur** to step *or* to tread on; **m. dans** *(flaque, saleté)* to step *or* to tread in; **ne marche pas sur les fleurs!** keep off the flowers!, don't walk on the flowers!; **tu marches sur tes lacets** you're treading on your laces; **m. sur les pieds à qn** to tread *or* to stand *or* to step on sb's feet; **il ne faut pas se laisser m. sur les pieds** you shouldn't let people walk all over you

4 *(fonctionner ▸ machine)* to work, to function; *(▸ moteur)* to run; **m. au gaz** to work on gas; **m. à l'électricité** to work *or* to run on electricity; **le jouet marche à piles** the toy is battery-operated; **comment ça marche?** how does it work?; **ma montre ne marche plus** my watch isn't working *or* going; *Fam* **les trains ne marchent pas aujourd'hui** the trains aren't running today[□]; **faire m.** *(machine)* to work

5 *(donner de bons résultats ▸ manœuvre, ruse)* to come off, to work; *(▸ projet, essai)* to be working (out), to work; *(▸ activité, travail)* to be going well; **ses études marchent bien/mal** he's/she's doing well/not doing very well at college; *Fam* **elle marche bien en chimie/au tennis** she's doing well in chemistry/at tennis; *Fam* **un jeune athlète qui marche très fort** an up-and-coming young athlete; **la répétition a bien/mal marché** the rehearsal went well/badly; **les affaires marchent mal/très bien** business is slack/is going well; **ça fait m. les affaires** *ou* **le commerce** it's good for business *or* for trade; **tout a très bien marché jusqu'ici** everything's gone very well until now; **et le travail, ça marche?** how's work (going)?; **ça marche comme ça?** *(arrangement, rendez-vous)* is that OK with you?; **ça marche pour ce soir? – ça marche!** is it OK for this evening *or* are we on for this evening? – definitely *or* sure!; **on partage les bénéfices 50/50, ça marche?** we'll share the profits 50/50, (is that) agreed *or* OK?; **si ça marche, je monterai une exposition** if it works out, I'll organize an exhibition; **leur couple/commerce n'a pas marché** their relationship/business didn't work out; **ça a l'air de bien m. entre eux** they seem to be getting on fine together, things seem to be going well between them

6 *(au restaurant)* **ça marche!** coming up!

7 *Fam (s'engager, accepter)* to go along with things; **OK, je marche!** OK, count me in!; **je ne marche pas!** nothing doing!, count me out!; **elle ne marchera jamais** she'll never agree

8 *Fam (croire naïvement)* to fall for it, to swallow it; *Hum* **je lui ai dit que ma tante était malade et il n'a pas marché, il a couru** I told him that my aunt was ill and he bought the whole story *or* and he swallowed it hook, line and sinker; **faire m. qn** *(le taquiner)* to pull sb's leg, *Br* to wind sb up; *(le berner)* to take sb for a ride, to lead sb up the garden path; **ce n'est pas vrai, tu me fais m.?** are you pulling my leg?, *Br* are you having me on?

9 *(au basket-ball)* to travel

marchette [marʃɛt] NF *Can (chariot d'enfant)* baby-walker; *(support de marche)* walking frame, Zimmer® frame

marcheur, -euse [marʃœr, -øz] ADJ **1** *Orn* **oiseaux marcheurs** flightless birds **2 navire bon m.** fast ship

NM,F *(gén) & Sport* walker

marcottage [markɔtaʒ] NM layering

marcotte [markɔt] NF layer

marcotter [3] [markɔte] VT to layer

mardi [mardi] NM Tuesday; **Nice, le m. 10 août** Nice, Tuesday 10 August; **je suis né un m. 18 avril** I was born on Tuesday 18 April; **nous sommes m. aujourd'hui** today's Tuesday; **je reviendrai m.** I'll be back on Tuesday; **je suis revenu m.** I came back on Tuesday; **m. dernier/prochain** last/next Tuesday; **ce m., m. qui vient** this (coming) Tuesday, Tuesday next, next Tuesday; **m. en huit** a week on Tuesday, Tuesday week; **m. en quinze** *Br* a fortnight on Tuesday, *Am* two weeks from Tuesday; **il y aura huit jours m.** a week on Tuesday; **tous les mardis** every Tuesday, on Tuesdays; **l'autre m.** *(dans le passé)* (the) Tuesday before last; *(dans l'avenir)* Tuesday after this; **le premier/dernier m. du mois** the first/last Tuesday of the month; **tous les deuxièmes mardis du mois** every second Tuesday in the month; **un m. sur deux** every other *or* every second Tuesday; **m. matin/après-midi** Tuesday morning/afternoon; **m. midi** Tuesday lunchtime, Tuesday (at) noon; **m. soir** Tuesday evening *or* night; **m. dans la nuit** Tuesday (during the) night; **dans la nuit de m. à mercredi** Tuesday night; **la séance/le marché du m.** the Tuesday session/market; **M. gras** *Rel* Shrove Tuesday; *(carnaval)* Mardi Gras; *Fam* **ce n'est pas M. gras, aujourd'hui!** what do you think this is, a carnival or something?

MARDI GRAS

This is a very popular festival, falling on the eve of Ash Wednesday, at the end of the carnival. On this day, crêpes are prepared and eaten, and children dress up at school.

mare [mar] NF **1** *(pièce d'eau)* pond; **m. aux canards** duck pond **2** *(de sang, d'essence)* pool

marécage [marekaʒ] NM *Géog* marsh, bog; *(dans un pays chaud)* swamp; *(terres marécageuses)* marshland

marécageux, -euse [marekaʒø, -øz] ADJ **1** *(région)* marshy, boggy; *(dans un pays chaud)* swampy **2** *(plante)* marsh *(avant n)*

maréchal, -aux [mareʃal, -o] NM **1** *Mil (en France)* marshal; *(en Grande-Bretagne)* field marshal; *(aux États-Unis)* five star general, general of the army; **M. de France** Marshal of France; **m. des logis** sergeant; **m. des logis-chef** *Br* ≃ staff sergeant, *Am* ≃ top sergeant **2** *Hist & Mil* marshal *(in a royal household)*

maréchalat [mareʃala] NM marshalcy, marshalship

maréchale [mareʃal] NF *Mil (en France)* marshal's wife; *(en Grande-Bretagne)* field marshal's wife; *(aux États-Unis)* general's wife

maréchalerie [mareʃalri] NF **1** *(métier)* blacksmith's trade, smithery, *Br Spéc* farriery **2** *(atelier)* blacksmith's (shop), smithy, *Br Spéc* farriery

maréchal-ferrant [mareʃalferɑ̃] *(pl* **maréchaux-ferrants)** NM blacksmith, *Br Spéc* farrier

maréchaussée [mareʃose] NF **1** *Hist* mounted police *or Br* constabulary **2** *Fam Hum* **la m.** the police[□], *Br* the boys in blue

marée [mare] NF **1** *Géog* tide; **(à) m. haute/basse** (at) high/low tide; **changement de m.** turn *or* turning of the tide; **horaire des marées** tide tables; **grande/faible m.** spring/neap tide; **m. montante** flowing *or* flood tide; **m. descendante** ebb tide; **lorsque la m. monte/descend** when the tide is rising/ebbing, when the tide comes in/goes out; *Écol* **m. noire** oil slick; *Fig* **une m. humaine** a flood of people; *Can Fig* **manquer la m.** to be left on the shelf, to stay unmarried **2** *(poissons, crustacés etc)* (fresh) seafood; **arriver comme m. en carême** to come as surely as night follows day

marelle [marɛl] NF *(jeu)* hopscotch; *(figure)* (set of) hopscotch squares; **jouer à la m.** to play hopscotch

marémoteur, -trice [maremɔtœr, -tris] ADJ tidal; **usine marémotrice** tidal power station

marengo [marɛ̃go] ADJ INV *Culin voir* **veau**

NM *Tex* = black cloth flecked with white

marennes [marɛn] NF (Marennes) oyster

mareyage [marɛjaʒ] NM fish trade

mareyeur, -euse [marɛjœr, -øz] NM,F fish and seafood wholesaler

margaille [margaj] NF *Belg Fam* **1** *(rixe)* fight[□], *Br* ruck **2** *(tapage)* row

margarine [margarin] NF margarine

marge [marʒ] NF **1** *(espace blanc)* margin; **laisser une grande/petite m.** to leave a wide/narrow margin; **laissez une m. de trois centimètres** leave a margin of three centimetres; **écrire qch dans la m.** to write sth in the margin; **m. de droite/gauche** right-/left-hand margin, right/left margin; *Typ* **m. extérieure** outside margin; **m. du haut** *ou* **supérieure** top margin; **m. inférieure** *ou* **du bas** bottom margin; **m. intérieure** back *or* inside *or* inner margin; **m. de pied** tail; **m. de reliure** inside margin; **m. de tête** head *or* top margin

2 *Fig (liberté d'action)* leeway; **avoir de la m.** to have some leeway; *(temps)* to have time to spare; **je vous donne deux mètres de tissu/deux mois, comme ça, vous avez de la m.** I'll give you two metres of cloth/two months, that'll be more than enough; **laisser à qn une m. de liberté** to give sb some latitude *or* leeway; **prévoir une m. d'erreur de 40 centimètres/de dix euros** to allow for a margin of error of 40 centimetres/of ten euros; **m. de manœuvre** room for manoeuvre; **m. de sécurité** safety margin; **m. de tolérance** (range of) tolerance

3 *Com* margin; **avoir une faible/forte m.** to have a low/high (profit) margin; **nous faisons 30 pour cent de m. sur ce produit** we make a 30 percent margin on this product; **m. avant impôt** pre-tax margin; **m. bénéficiaire** profit margin; **m. brute** gross margin; **m. brute d'autofinancement** gross cashflow; **m. commerciale brute/nette** gross/net profit margin; *Compta* **m. sur coûts variables** contribution; **m. de crédit** credit margin; **m. du détaillant** retailer margin; **m. du distributeur** distributor's margin; **m. du grossiste** wholesaler margin; **m. de l'importateur** importer's margin; **m. avant impôt** pre-tax margin; **m. initiale** initial margin; **m. nette** net margin; **m. nette d'exploitation** operating margin; **m. de profit** profit margin; **m. sectorielle** segment margin; **m. supplémentaire** additional margin

4 *Bourse* **appel de m.** margin call

• **en marge** ADJ *(original)* fringe *(avant n)*; **un artiste en m.** an unconventional *or* a fringe artist

ADV **1** *(d'une feuille de papier)* in the margin; **faites vos annotations en m.** write your notes in the margin **2** *(à l'écart)* **vivre en m.** to live on the fringe *or* fringes (of society); **il est toujours resté en m.** he's always been a loner; **elle a fait une carrière en m.** she made an unconventional career for herself

• **en marge de** PRÉP **vivre en m. de la société** to live on the fringe *or* margin *or* edge of society; **les événements en m. de l'histoire** footnotes to history, marginal events in history; **il y a une grande exposition de photos en m. du festival** there's a big exhibition of photographs as a fringe event

margelle [marʒɛl] NF *(d'un puits, d'une fontaine)* edge, *Br* kerb, *Am* curb

marger [17] [marʒe] VT **1** *Typ* to feed in, to lay on **2** *Ordinat* **m. une page** to set the page margins

VI to set the margin/margins; **m. à droite/à gauche** to set the right/left margin

margeur, -euse [marʒœr, -øz] NM **1** *Typ* (paper) feed **2** *(sur une machine à écrire)* margin setter

marginal, -e, -aux, -ales [marʒinal, -o] ADJ **1** *(secondaire ▸ problème, rôle)* marginal, minor, peripheral; **ce problème n'a qu'une importance marginale** this problem is of only marginal importance

2 *(à part ▸ personne, mode de vie)* on the fringes of society; **groupe m.** *Pol* fringe group; *(en sociologie)* marginal group

3 *Écon* marginal

4 *(annotation)* marginal

5 *Géog (récif)* fringing

NM,F dropout; **les marginaux** the fringe elements of society; **ça a toujours été un m.** he's always been a bit of a dropout

marginalisation [marʒinalizasjɔ̃] NF marginalization

marginaliser [3] [marʒinalize] VT to marginalize

VPR **se marginaliser** to become marginalized; *(rôle, fonction)* to become marginalized *or* irrelevant

marginalité [marʒinalite] NF **1** *(d'un problème, d'un rôle)* minor importance, insignificance, marginality **2** *(d'une personne)* nonconformism; **vivre** *ou* **être dans la m.** to live on the fringe *or* fringes of society; **ils ont préféré vivre dans la m.** they preferred to opt out

marginer [3] [marʒine] VT to write notes in the margin of

margoulette [margulet] NF **1** *Fam* **se casser la m.** to fall flat on one's face **2** *Can (pomme d'Adam)* Adam's apple

margoulin [margulɛ̃] NM *Fam Péj* **1** *(escroc)* crook, swindler **2** *(incompétent)* prat, *Br* pillock, *Am* lame

marguerite [margərit] NF **1** *Bot* daisy; **grande m.** oxeye daisy, marguerite **2** *Typ* daisy wheel

marguillier [margije] NM *Hist* churchwarden

mari [mari] NM husband; *Fam* **son petit m.** her hubby

mariable [marjabl] ADJ marriageable

mariage [marjaʒ] NM **1** *(union)* marriage; *(état)* marriage, matrimony; **proposer le m. à qn** to propose (marriage) to sb; **il m'avait promis le m.** he had promised to marry me; **donner sa fille en m.** to give one's daughter in marriage; **je ne pense pas encore au m.** I'm not thinking about getting married yet; **elle a fait un mauvais m.** she made a bad marriage; **faire un m. d'amour** to marry for love, to make a love match; **faire un m. d'argent** *ou* **d'intérêt** to marry for money; **m. arrangé** arranged marriage; **m. blanc** unconsummated marriage, marriage in name only; **faire un m. blanc** to enter into a marriage of convenience *(primarily in order to acquire nationality)*; **m. de convenance** *ou* **de raison** marriage of convenience; **m. homosexuel** gay marriage; **m. mixte** mixed marriage; **enfants (nés) d'un premier m.** children from a first marriage; **enfants nés hors du m.** children born out of wedlock

2 *(vie commune)* married life, *Sout* matrimony; **leur première année de m.** their first year of married life *or* marriage

3 *(cérémonie)* wedding; *(cortège)* wedding procession; **m. en blanc** white wedding; **m. civil** civil wedding; *Can* **m. forcé, m. obligé** shotgun wedding; **m. religieux** church wedding; **de m.** wedding *(avant n)*; **anniversaire de m.** wedding anniversary; **ils ont fêté leurs 25 ans de m.** they celebrated their 25th wedding anniversary *or* their silver wedding

4 *Fig (d'arômes, de saveurs)* blend, mixture; *(de couleurs)* combination; *(d'associations, d'organisations)* merging; **cette fille, c'est le m. de l'intelligence et de la beauté** this girl is a combination of *or* combines intelligence and beauty; *Fam* **c'est le m. de la carpe et du lapin** they make strange bedfellows

5 *Cartes* king and queen *(of a suit)*; *(au bésigue)* marriage

> Attention: ne pas confondre **marriage** et **wedding** lorsque l'on traduit **mariage**. **Wedding** se rapporte uniquement à la cérémonie, alors que **marriage** se rapporte à l'institution.

> **MARIAGE**
>
> In France, a civil ceremony (which takes place at the "mairie") is required of all couples wishing to marry, though some choose to have a church wedding as well. The traditional wedding involves a long and sumptuous meal at which the wedding cake, a "pièce montée", is served.

Marianne [marjan] NF *(figure)* Marianne *(personification of the French Republic)*

Marie [mari] NPR **1** *Rel* Mary; **la Vierge M.** the Virgin Mary **2** *Hist* **M. Stuart** Mary Queen of Scots, Mary Stuart; **M. de Médicis** Maria de Medici

marié, -e [marje] ADJ married; **non m.** unmarried, single; **il est m. avec Maud** he's married to Maud; **je suis m. depuis trois ans** I've been married for three years

NM **le (jeune) m.** the groom, the bridegroom; **le futur m.** the bridegroom-to-be

• **mariée** NF **la (jeune) mariée** the bride; **la future mariée** the bride-to-be; **une robe de mariée** a wedding dress; *Fig* **tu te plains que la mariée est trop belle!** you don't know how lucky you are!

• **mariés** NMPL **les mariés** *(le jour de la cérémonie)* the bride and groom *or* bridegroom; **les futurs mariés** the bride and groom-to-be; **les jeunes mariés** the newly-weds; **féliciter les mariés** to congratulate the bride and groom *or* the married couple

Marie-Chantal [mariʃɑ̃tal] NF INV *Fam Br* ≃ Sloane (Ranger), *Am* ≃ preppy

Marie-couche-toi-là [marikuʃtwala] NF INV *Fam* slut, *Br* tart

marie-jeanne [mariʒan] NF INV *Fam Arg drogue (cannabis)* Mary Jane, pot

marier [9] [marje] VT **1** *(unir)* to marry, *Littéraire* to wed; **le maire/le prêtre les a mariés hier** the mayor/the priest married them yesterday

2 *(donner en mariage)* to marry; **ils marièrent leur fille à un médecin** they married their daughter to a doctor; **elle a encore un fils/une fille à m.** she still has a son/a daughter to marry off; **elle est bonne à m.** she's of marriageable age

3 *(parfums, couleurs)* to blend, to combine, *Sout* to marry; *(styles, sons)* to harmonize, to combine, *Sout* to marry; *(vêtements, styles de meubles)* to harmonize; **il marie l'égoïsme à la plus parfaite indifférence** he is a combination of selfishness and total indifference

4 *Belg (épouser)* to marry

VPR **se marier 1** *(personnes)* to get married, to marry, *Littéraire* to wed; **se m. à** *ou* **avec qn** to marry sb, to get married to sb; **il veut se m. à l'église** he wants to have a church wedding *or* to get married in church **2** *(couleurs, arômes, styles)* to go together; **ça se marie bien avec le vert** it goes nicely with the green

marie-salope [marisalɔp] *(pl* **maries-salopes***)* NF **1** *(péniche)* hopper (barge); *(drague)* dredger **2** *très Fam (souillon)* slut

marieur, -euse [marjœr, -øz] NM,F *Fam* matchmaker

marigot [marigo] NM **1** *(bras de fleuve)* side channel, backwater, marigot **2** *(région inondable)* flood lands

marihuana [marirwana], **marijuana** [mariʒɥana] NF marijuana

marin, -e[1] [marɛ̃, -in] ADJ *(air, courant, sel)* sea *(avant n)*; *(animal, carte)* marine, sea *(avant n)*; *(plante, vie)* marine; **paysage m.** seascape; **navire m.** seaworthy ship; **monstres marins** sea monsters

NM **1** *(gén)* seaman, seafarer; **un peuple de marins** a seafaring nation **2** *Mil & Naut* seaman, sailor; **costume/béret de m.** sailor suit/hat; **simple m.** able *or* able-bodied seaman; **marins marchands** *ou* **du commerce** merchant seamen; **m. pêcheur** (deep-sea) fisherman; *Hum* **m. d'eau douce** Sunday sailor

marina [marina] NF marina

marinade [marinad] NF **1** *(saumure)* pickle; *(mélange aromatique)* marinade; **viande en m.** marinated *or* marinaded meat **2** *Can* **marinades** pickles

marine[2] [marin] ADJ F *voir* **marin**

ADJ INV *(bleu marine)* navy (blue)

NF **1** *Naut* navy; **la M. nationale** the (French) Navy; **m. marchande** merchant navy *or* marine

2 *Mil* **m. (de guerre)** navy; **le musée de la M.** = the Paris Naval Museum, in the Palais de Chaillot

3 *(navigation)* seamanship; **terme de m.** nautical term

4 *Beaux-Arts* seascape

NM **1** *(fusilier marin ▸ britannique)* Royal Marine; *(▸ des États-Unis)* (US) Marine; **les Marines** *Br* the Royal Marines, *Am* the US Marine Corps, the Marines **2** *(couleur)* navy (blue)

mariner [3] [marine] VT *(pour assaisonner)* to marinate, to marinade; *(dans une saumure)* to pickle, to souse; **des harengs marinés** pickled herrings

VI **1** *Culin* to marinate; **laissez la viande m.** *ou* **faites m. la viande pendant plusieurs heures** allow the meat to marinate for several hours **2** *Fam (personne)* to wait⁼, to hang around *or Br* about; **il marine en prison** he's rotting in prison; **laisse-la m.!** let her stew for a while!; **ne nous fais pas m.!** don't keep us hanging around!; **il m'a fait m. pendant deux heures** he kept me hanging around for two hours

maringouin [marɛ̃gwɛ̃] NM *Can* mosquito; **m. domestique** northern house mosquito

marinier [marinje] NM *Br* bargee, *Am* bargeman

marinière [marinjɛr] **NF 1** *(blouse)* sailor blouse; *(maillot rayé)* (white and navy blue) striped jersey **2** *Culin* **(à la) m.** in a white wine sauce

mariole, mariolle [marjɔl] *Fam* **ADJ** *(astucieux)* smart, clever

NM smart aleck, *Br* clever dick, *Am* wise guy; **faire le m.** to act smart

marionnette [marjɔnɛt] **NF 1** *(poupée)* **m. (à fils)** puppet, marionette; **m. (à gaine)** (hand *or* glove) puppet; **spectacle/théâtre de marionnettes** puppet show/theatre; **on va aux marionnettes** we're going to the puppet show; *Fam* **faire les marionnettes** = to move one's hands and sing in order to amuse a young child **2** *Péj (personne)* puppet

marionnettiste [marjɔnɛtist] **NMF** puppeteer

marital, -e, -aux, -ales [marital, -o] **ADJ** *Jur* **1** *(relatif au mari)* marital; **l'autorisation maritale** the husband's authorization; **les biens maritaux** the husband's possessions **2** *(relatif à l'union libre)* **au cours de leur vie maritale** while they lived together (as man and wife)

maritalement [maritalmɑ̃] **ADV vivre m.** to live as husband and wife; **vivre m. avec qn** to cohabit with sb

maritime [maritim] **ADJ 1** *(du bord de mer* ▸ *village)* coastal, seaside *(avant n)*, *Am* seaboard *(avant n)*; **province m.** maritime *or* coastal province; *Admin* **région m.** coastal area; **ville m.** seaside town **2** *(naval* ▸ *hôpital, entrepôt)* naval; *(*▸ *commerce)* seaborne, maritime; **puissance m.** maritime *or* sea power **3** *Jur (législation, droit)* maritime, shipping *(avant n)*; *(agent)* shipping *(avant n)*; *(assurance)* marine

maritorne [maritɔrn] **NF** *Littéraire* sloven, slattern

marivaudage [marivodaʒ] **NM** *Littéraire* light-hearted banter

marivauder [3] [marivode] **VI** *Littéraire* to banter, to exchange gallantries

marjolaine [marʒɔlɛn] **NF** *Bot* marjoram

mark [mark] **NM** *Anciennement Fin* mark

marketing [marketiŋ] **NM** marketing; **faire du m.** *(étudier)* to do marketing; *(avoir pour profession)* to be in marketing; **m. "à la carte"** customized *or* tailored marketing; **m. ciblé** niche marketing, target marketing; **m. électronique** on-line marketing, e-marketing; **m. global** global marketing; **m. international** global marketing; **m. de masse** mass marketing; **m. mix** marketing mix; **m. relationnel** relationship marketing; **m. de réseau** multi-level marketing; **m. stratégique** strategic marketing; **m. téléphonique** telemarketing; **m. terrain** grass roots marketing; **m. de la valeur** value marketing; **m. vert** green marketing; **m. viral** viral marketing

marlot [marlo] **NM** *Can Fam* good-for-nothing

marlou [marlu] **NM** *Fam* **1** *(voyou)* hoodlum **2** *(souteneur)* pimp, *Am* mack

marmaille [marmaj] **NF** *Fam Péj* brood, kids; **elle est venue avec toute sa m.** she came with her whole brood

marmelade [marmәlad] **NF** *Culin* compote; **m. de fraises** strawberry compote; **m. de pommes** stewed apple *or* apples, apple compote; *(pour viande)* apple sauce; **m. d'oranges** (orange) marmalade

• **en marmelade ADJ 1** *Culin* stewed; *(trop cuit, écrasé)* mushy **2** *Fam (en piteux état)* **j'ai les pieds en m.** my feet are absolutely killing me; **elle avait le visage en m.** her face was all smashed up

marmite [marmit] **NF 1** *Culin (contenant)* pot, cooking pot; *(contenu)* pot, potful; **m. norvégienne** haybox **2** *Géol* **m. torrentielle** *ou* **de géants** pothole

marmiton [marmitɔ̃] **NM** young kitchen hand

marmonnement [marmɔnmɑ̃] **NM** mumbling, muttering

marmonner [3] [marmɔne] **VI** to mumble, to mutter; **la vieille femme marmonnait dans son coin** the old woman was muttering (away) to herself

VT to mumble, to mutter; **qu'est-ce que tu marmonnes encore?** what's that you're muttering *or* mumbling (now)?

marmoréen, -enne [marmɔreɛ̃, -ɛn] **ADJ** *Littéraire* marmoreal, marble *(avant n)*

marmot [marmo] **NM** *Fam* (little) kid, *Br* nipper

marmotte [marmɔt] **NF 1** *Zool* marmot; **m. d'Amérique** *ou* **du Canada, m. commune** woodchuck; *Fig* **tu es une vraie m.!** you're a *Br* real *or Am* regular dormouse! **2** *(fourrure)* marmot; **de** *ou* **en m.** marmot *(avant n)*

marmottement [marmɔtmɑ̃] **NM** mumbling, muttering

marmotter [3] [marmɔte] **VI** to mutter, to mumble

VT to mutter, to mumble

marnage[1] [marnaʒ] **NM** *Agr* marling

marnage[2] [marnaʒ] **NM** *(d'un plan d'eau)* tidal range

marne [marn] **NF** marl

marner [3] [marne] **VT** *Agr* to marl

VI *Fam (personne)* to slog, to sweat blood

Maroc [marɔk] **NM** *Géog* **le M.** Morocco

marocain, -e [marɔkɛ̃, -ɛn] **ADJ** Moroccan

NM *(langue)* Moroccan (Arabic)

• **Marocain, -e NM,F** Moroccan

maronite [marɔnit] **NMF** Maronite

ADJ Maronite

maronner [3] [marɔne] **VI** *Fam* **1** *(maugréer)* to grumble, to grouch; *(être en colère)* to be fuming; **ne la fais pas m.** don't get her back up **2** *(attendre)* to hang about *or* around; **il nous fait toujours m.** he always has us hanging about *or* around waiting

maroquin [marɔkɛ̃] **NM 1** *(peau)* morocco **2** *Fam (ministère)* minister's portfolio

maroquinerie [marɔkinri] **NF 1** *(commerce)* leather trade; *(industrie)* leather craft; *(magasin)* leather (goods) *Br* shop *or Am* store **2** *(articles)* (small) leather goods **3** *(atelier)* tannery; *(tannage)* tanning

maroquinier, -ère [marɔkinje, -ɛr] **ADJ ouvrier m.** leather worker; **marchand m.** leather merchant

NM,F *(ouvrier)* tanner; *(artisan)* leather craftsman; **je l'ai acheté chez un m.** I bought it from a leather (goods) *Br* shop *or Am* store

marotte [marɔt] **NF 1** *Fam (passe-temps)* pet hobby; *(manie)* fad, craze; **c'est sa m.** it's his/her pet hobby *or* thing; **il a la m. des mots croisés** crosswords are his pet hobby **2** *(sceptre)* fool's bauble **3** *(de coiffeur, de modiste)* dummy head

marouflage [maruflaʒ] **NM** *Beaux-Arts* backing

maroufler [3] [marufle] **VT** *Beaux-Arts* to back

marquage [markaʒ] **NM 1** *Sport* marking **2** *(de linge)* marking; *(d'animaux)* marking, branding; *Com* branding, labelling; **m. de marchandises** marking of goods; *Aut* **m. au sol** road markings; **m. en zig-zag** zig-zag marking **3** *Phys* **m. radioactif** radioactive labelling *or* tracing

marquant, -e [markɑ̃, -ɑ̃t] **ADJ 1** *(personne)* prominent, outstanding; **les personnalités marquantes de ce siècle** this century's most influential figures **2** *(détail, trait)* striking; *(fait, épisode)* significant; **un événement particulièrement m.** an event of particular *or* outstanding importance; *Littérature* **passages marquants** highlights, purple passages

MARQUE [mark]

- mark **1–3, 5**
- make **4**
- hallmark **5**
- marker **2, 9, 12**
- brand **4**
- score **6, 7**

NF 1 *(trace)* mark; *(cicatrice)* mark, scar; **marques de coups** marks of blows; **on voit encore la m. du coup qu'elle a reçu** you can still see where she was hit; **marques de doigts** *(sales)* fingermarks; *(empreintes)* fingerprints; **les marques de la vieillesse** marks *or* traces of old age; **les brûlures n'ont laissé aucune m. sur son bras** the burns left no marks *or* scars on his/her arm; **faire une m. au couteau sur qch** to make a mark with a knife *or* a knife mark on sth, to mark sth with a knife; **le cintre a fait une m. sur ce vêtement** the coat-hanger has left a mark on this garment

2 *(signet)* marker, book mark; *(trait)* mark; **m. au crayon/à la craie** pencil/chalk mark; *Com* **marques d'expédition** shipping marks

3 *Fig (preuve)* mark; **comme m. d'amitié/d'estime/de confiance** as a token of friendship/esteem/trust; **c'est là la m. d'une grande générosité** that's the sign *or* mark of real generosity

4 *Com (de produits manufacturés)* make, brand; *(de produits alimentaires et chimiques)* brand; *(de voitures)* make, marque; *(sur l'article)* trademark; *(nom du fabricant)* logo; **voiture de m. française** French-made *or* French-built car; **j'ai eu des voitures de trois marques différentes** I've had three different makes of car; **grande m.** famous make, well-known brand; *(dans la mode)* designer label; **les grandes marques d'électroménager** the main brands of electrical appliance(s); **c'est une grande m. de cigarettes/de voitures** *(célèbre)* it's a well-known brand of cigarette/make of car; *(de luxe)* it's a brand of luxury cigarette/a make of luxury car; **produits de grande m.** top brand *or* name products; **m. commerciale, m. de commerce** trademark, brand (name); **m. déposée** registered trademark; **m. de détaillant** retailer brand; **m. de distributeur** distributor's brand name, own brand; **m. économique** economy brand; **m. d'enseigne** retailer brand, shop's own brand; **m. de fabricant** manufacturer's brand (name); **m. de fabrique** trademark, brand (name); **m. générique** generic brand; **m. globale** global brand; **m. grand public** consumer brand; **m. de magasin** store brand; **m. multiple** multi-brand; **m. ombrelle** umbrella brand; **m. d'origine** origin of goods label; **m. de tête** brand leader

5 *(identification* ▸ *sur bijoux)* hallmark; *(*▸ *sur meubles)* stamp, mark; *(*▸ *sur animaux)* brand; *Vét* **m. de l'inspection vétérinaire** Health Officer's inspection stamp; **un produit qui porte la m. de la douane** goods that have been stamped at customs; *Fig* **il a dessiné ces jardins, il est facile de reconnaître sa m.** he designed these gardens, it's easy to recognize his style; *Fig* **porter la m. du génie** to bear the stamp *or* the hallmark of genius; *Fig* **on reconnaît la m. du génie** that's the hallmark *or* stamp of genius

6 *(dans un jeu* ▸ *jeton)* chip; *(*▸ *décompte)* score; **tenir la m.** to keep (the) score

7 *Sport (score)* score; **mener à la m.** to be ahead, to be in the lead

8 *Sport (au rugby)* **m.!** mark!

9 *Ling* marker; **en français, le e est souvent la m. du féminin** in French the letter e often indicates that the word is in the feminine form; **porter la m. du féminin/pluriel** to be in the feminine/plural form

10 *Typ* **m. d'imprimeur** printer's colophon

11 *Naut* **la m. de l'amiral** the admiral's flag

12 *Ordinat* marker, flag, tag; **m. d'insertion** insertion marker; **m. de paragraphe** paragraph mark

• **marques NFPL** *Sport* **prendre ses marques** *(coureur)* to take one's marks; *(sauteur)* to pace out one's run up; *Fig* **chercher ses marques** to try to find one's bearings; **à vos marques! prêts! partez!** on your marks! get set! go!, ready! steady! go!

• **de marque ADJ** *(produit)* branded; *(hôte)* distinguished; **articles de m.** branded goods; **produits de m. courante** well-known branded goods; **personnage de m.** VIP

marqué, -e [marke] **ADJ 1** *(visible* ▸ *différence)* marked, distinct; *(*▸ *préférence)* marked, obvious; *(*▸ *accent)* marked, broad, strong; *(*▸ *traits)* pronounced; **il a le visage très m.** *(par des blessures)* his face is covered with scars; *(par la maladie)* illness has left its mark on his face; **visage m. par la petite vérole** pockmarked face; **visage m. par l'âge** face lined with age; **robe à la taille marquée** dress fitted at the waist

2 *Fig (impressionné)* **j'ai été très m. par ce film** the film made a strong impression on me; **il est m. à vie par cette expérience** he has been marked for life by the experience

3 *Fig (engagé)* **il est très m. politiquement** politically he is very committed

4 *(écrit)* **il n'y a rien (de) m. dessus** there's nothing marked *or* written on it; **il est m. qu'il faut une pièce d'identité** it says that some form of identification is required; **qu'est-ce qui est m.** *ou* **qu'est-ce qu'il y a de m. sur l'enveloppe?** what does it say on the envelope?, what's written on the envelope?

marque-page [markpaʒ] **NM INV** bookmark

marquer [3] [marke] **VT 1** *(montrer)* to mark; **m. la**

limite de qch to mark sth (off), to mark the limit of sth; **les lignes bleues marquent les frontières** the blue lines show *or* indicate where the border is; **l'horloge marque trois heures** the clock shows *or* says three o'clock; **la balance marque 3 kg** the scales register *or* read 3 kg; **le thermomètre marque 40°C** the thermometer shows *or* registers 40°C

2 *(signaler ▸ passage d'un texte)* to mark; *(▸ bétail)* to brand, to mark; *(▸ arbre)* to blaze; *(▸ linge)* to label, to tag; **marque-le à ton nom** mark it with your name; **marquez-le d'un tiret/d'une flèche/d'une croix** mark it with a dash/an arrow/a cross; **m. au fer rouge** to brand; *Fig* **cet événement a marqué la fin de son adolescence** this event marked the end of his/her adolescence; *Fig* **ce jour est à m. d'une pierre blanche** this will go down as a red-letter day

3 *(témoigner de)* to mark, to show; **pour m. sa confiance** as a token *or* mark of his/her trust

4 *(événement, date)* to mark; **de nombreuses manifestations ont marqué le bicentenaire** a number of events marked *or* commemorated the bicentenary; *Fam* **m. le coup** *(fêter quelque chose)* to mark the occasion□; *(réagir)* to react□

5 *(prendre en note)* to write *or* to take *or* to note (down); *(tracer)* to mark, to write; **marquez votre nom en haut à gauche** write your name in the top left-hand corner; **tu l'as marqué?** have you made a note of it?; **marqué à l'encre/à la craie/au crayon sur le mur** marked in ink/chalk/pencil on the wall, inked/chalked/pencilled on the wall; **m. les prix** to mark prices

6 *(sujet: difficulté, épreuve)* to mark; **le chagrin a marqué son visage** his/her face is lined *or* furrowed with sorrow; **la guerre l'a beaucoup marqué** the war certainly left its mark on him *or* left a deep impression on him; **ces années de pauvreté l'ont marquée (à jamais)** those years of poverty have left their (indelible) mark on her; **cette expérience l'a marqué à vie** he was scarred for life by this experience; **le choc a marqué la carrosserie** the bodywork was marked *or* damaged in the collision

7 *(impressionner)* to mark, to affect, to make an impression on; **ça m'a beaucoup marqué** it made a big *or* lasting impression on me; **il a profondément marqué les musiciens de son époque** he made a deep impression on the musicians of the period; **c'est un film qui ne m'a pas marqué** I wasn't very struck by the film

8 *Sport & (dans un jeu)* **m. un point/but** to score a point/goal; **m. 30 points** to score 30 (points); **ne m. aucun point** to fail to score (a single point); **m. les points** to note *or* to keep the score; *Fig* **l'argument est judicieux, vous marquez un point** the argument is valid, that's one to you *or* you've scored a point; **m. un joueur** to mark a player

9 *(rythmer)* **il marquait la cadence du pied** he beat time with his foot; *Mus* **m. la mesure** to keep the beat; **m. un temps d'arrêt** to pause *(for a moment)*; **m. le pas** to mark time

10 *Couture* **manteau qui marque bien la taille** coat that shows off the waist

11 *Can Fam* **m. un achat** to charge a purchase (to one's account)□, to have a purchase put on one's tab; **elle fait m. et paie pour tout à la fin du mois** she charges everything to her account and pays for it all at the end of the month

12 *Ordinat* to mark, to flag, to tag

VI 1 *(événement)* to stand out; *(personne)* to make one's mark; **les grands hommes qui ont marqué dans l'histoire** the great men who have left their mark on history; **sa mort a marqué dans ma vie** his/her death had a great effect *or* impact on my life **2** *(crayon, objet)* **ce feutre ne marque plus** this felt-tip pen doesn't write any more; **attention, ça marque!** careful, it'll leave a mark!; **le verre a marqué sur la table** the glass left a mark on the table, the glass marked the table **3** *Sport* to score

marqueté, -e [markəte] **ADJ** *(meuble)* inlaid

marqueterie [marketri] **NF 1** *(décoration)* marquetry, inlay; **un panneau en m.** a marquetry panel; **un guéridon en m.** an inlaid pedestal table; **bois de m.** marquetry wood **2** *(métier)* marquetry

marqueteur, -euse [markətœr, -øz] **NM,F** inlayer

marqueur, -euse [markœr, -øz] **NM,F 1** *(de documents)* stamper; *(de bétail)* brander **2** *(qui compte les points)* scorekeeper, scorer; *(qui gagne les points)* scorer; **m. automatique** *(au bridge)* scoreboard

NM 1 *(gros feutre)* marker (pen); *(surligneur)* highlighter; **la phrase indiquée au m.** the highlighted sentence

2 *Biol, Ling & Méd* marker

3 *Nucl* tracer

4 *Ordinat* marker, flag; **m. de fin de texte** end of text marker

• **marqueuse NF** *Com* marking *or* stamping machine

marquis [marki] **NM** marquess, marquis; **merci, Monsieur le M.** thank you, your Lordship

marquisat [markiza] **NM** *(rang, fief)* marquessate, marquisate

marquise [markiz] **NF 1** *(titre ▸ gén)* marchioness, *(▸ en France)* marquise; **merci, Madame la M.** thank you, your Ladyship; **elle est maintenant m.** she's now a marchioness

2 *(abri de toile)* awning; *(auvent vitré)* (glass) canopy; *(de gare)* glass roof

3 *(bijou)* marquise ring

4 *Culin* **m. glacée** iced marquise

Marquises [markiz] **NFPL les (îles) M.** the Marquesas Islands; **aux (îles) M.** in the Marquesas Islands

marraine [marɛn] **NF 1** *Rel* godmother **2** *(d'un bateau)* christener, namer; **elle fut choisie comme m. du bateau** she was chosen to launch *or* to name the ship **3** *(d'un nouveau membre)* sponsor; **m. de guerre** soldier's wartime penfriend *or* penpal

Marrakech [marakɛʃ] **NF** Marrakech, Marrakesh

marrant, -e [marɑ̃, -ɑ̃t] *Fam* **ADJ 1** *(drôle)* funny□; **il est (trop) m.!** he's a hoot *or* scream!; **elle n'est pas marrante, sa femme** his wife is no fun!; **je ne veux pas y aller – t'es pas m.!** I don't want to go – you're no fun!; **vous êtes marrants, je n'ai pas que ça à faire!** come on, I've got other things to do, you know! **2** *(bizarre)* funny□, odd□, strange□; **c'est m. qu'elle ne soit pas encore là** funny (that) she hasn't arrived yet

NM,F joker, funny guy, *f* girl; **être un m.** to be fun, to be a laugh *or* a riot; **son père, c'est pas un m.** his dad's not much fun *or* not much of a laugh; **le nouveau directeur, c'est vraiment pas un m.** the new manager doesn't fool around; **c'est un petit m. qui se croit tout permis** he's a little joker who thinks he can do as he likes

marre [mar] **ADV** *Fam* **en avoir m. (de)** to be fed up (with) *or* hacked off (with); **en avoir m. de faire qch** to be fed up *or* sick and tired of doing sth; **il en a m. de ses études** he's fed up with *or* sick and tired of studying; **je commence à en avoir plus que m. de tes mensonges** I've just about had enough of your lies, I'm sick and tired of your lies; **j'en ai m. que ce soit toujours moi qui fasse les courses** I'm fed up with always having to do the shopping; **j'en ai m.!** I've had enough!; **il y en a m. (de)** that's enough (of); **il y en a m. de te voir ne rien faire** I'm sick (and tired) of seeing you lie around doing nothing

marrer [3] [mare] *Fam* **VI faire m. qn** to make sb laugh□; *aussi Ironique* **me fais pas m.** don't make me laugh

VPR se marrer to have a (good) laugh; **on s'est drôlement marrés hier soir** we really had a good laugh *or* a great time last night; **elle ne doit pas se m. tous les jours avec ce type-là** she can't have much fun with that guy; *Ironique* **alors là, je me marre!** that's a laugh!, don't make me laugh!; *Ironique* **qu'est-ce qu'on se marre!** this is great fun, not! *or* I don't think!

marri, -e [mari] **ADJ** *Arch (contrarié, fâché)* **être (fort) m.** to be (most) aggrieved

marron¹ [marɔ̃] **NM 1** *Bot* chestnut; **m. d'Inde** horse chestnut, *Fam* conker; **marrons chauds** roast *or* roasted chestnuts; **marrons glacés** marrons glacés, crystallized *or* candied chestnuts; **crème de m.** chestnut purée; *Fig* **tirer les marrons du feu** to do all the dirty work **2** *(couleur)* brown; **j'aime le m.** I like brown **3** *Fam (coup)* belt, wallop; **flanquer** *ou* **coller un m. à qn** to belt *or* wallop sb one; **il s'est pris de ces marrons!** he got a real thumping *or* walloping!

ADJ INV *(brun)* brown; **m. clair** light brown

ADJ *Fam (dupé)* **être m.** *(avoir été dupé)* to have been taken in *or* for a ride, *Am* to have been rooked; **faire qn m.** to take sb in *or* for a ride, *Am* to rook sb; **zut, voilà le contrôleur, on est marrons!** *(on est coincés)* oh, no, we've had it now, here comes the ticket collector!

> Il faut noter que le mot anglais **maroon** est un faux ami. Lorsqu'il désigne une couleur, il signifie **bordeaux**.

marron², -onne [marɔ̃, -ɔn] **ADJ** *(malhonnête)* crooked; **amateurisme m.** shamateurism; **avocat m.** crooked lawyer; **esclave m.** escaped slave; **médecin m.** quack

marronnier [marɔnje] **NM** chestnut tree; **m. d'Inde** horse chestnut (tree)

Mars [mars] **NF** *Astron* Mars

NPR *Myth* Mars

mars [mars] **NM** *(mois)* March; **en m.** in March; **au mois de m.** in (the month of) March; **nous y allons tous les ans en m.** *ou* **au mois de m.** we go there every (year in) March; **au début du mois de m., début m.** at the beginning of March, in early March; **au milieu du mois de m., à la mi-m.** in the middle of March, in mid-March; **à la fin du mois de m., (à la) fin m.** at the end of March, in late March; **en m. dernier/prochain** last/next March; **Nice, le 5 m. 2006** Nice, 5 March 2006; **la commande vous a été livrée le 31 m.** your order was delivered on 31 March; **j'attendrai jusqu'au (lundi) 4 m.** I'll wait until (Monday) 4 March; *Fig* **arriver comme m. en carême** to come as surely as night follows day

marseillais, -e [marsejɛ, -ɛz] **ADJ** of/from Marseilles

• **Marseillais, -e NM,F** = inhabitant of or person from Marseilles

• **Marseillaise NF** *Mus* **la Marseillaise** the Marseillaise *(the French national anthem)*

Marseille [marsej] **NF** Marseilles, Marseille

marsouin [marswɛ̃] **NM 1** *Zool* porpoise **2** *Fam Arg mil* Marine□ **3** *Can Fam (malin)* rascal□

marsupial, -e, -aux, -ales [marsypjal, -o] **ADJ** marsupial

NM marsupial

marte [mart] = **martre**

marteau, -x [marto] **NM 1** *(maillet)* hammer; **coup de m.** blow with a hammer; **enfoncer un clou à coups de m.** to hammer a nail home *or* in; **travailler le fer au m.** to work iron with a hammer; *Fig* **être entre le m. et l'enclume** to be stuck in the middle; **le m. du commissaire-priseur** the auctioneer's hammer *or* gavel; **m. à panne fendue** claw hammer; **m. piqueur** *ou* **pneumatique** pneumatic drill; **m. perforateur** hammer drill

2 *(pièce ▸ d'une horloge)* striker, hammer; *(▸ d'une porte)* knocker, hammer; *(▸ dans un piano)* hammer

3 *Anat* hammer, *Spéc* malleus

4 *Sport* hammer

5 *(poisson)* hammerhead shark

6 *Métal* **m. à emboutir** embossing hammer

7 *Suisse & (en français régional) (molaire)* molar

ADJ *Fam (fou)* nuts, crazy; **être m.** to be not all there, to have a screw *or Br* a slate loose

martel [martɛl] **NM se mettre m. en tête** to be worried sick; **ne te mets pas m. en tête pour si peu** don't get worked up about such a small thing

martelage [martəlaʒ] **NM** *Métal* hammering

martelé, -e [martəle] **ADJ 1** *Métal (travaillé au marteau)* hammered; **argent m.** beaten silver **2** **paroles martelées** hammered-out words

martèlement [martɛlmɑ̃] **NM** *(bruit ▸ d'un marteau)* hammering; *(▸ de pas, de bottes)* pounding; **j'entends le m. de la pluie sur le toit de zinc** I can hear the rain beating on the zinc roof

marteler [25] [martəle] **VT 1** *Métal* to hammer; **m. à froid** to cold-hammer **2** *Fig (frapper)* to hammer (at), to pound (at); **il martelait la table de ses poings** he was hammering with *or* banging his fists on the table; **la douleur lui martelait la tête** his/her head was throbbing with pain **3** *Fig (scander)* to hammer out; **m. ses mots** to hammer out one's words

martial, -e, -aux, -ales [marsjal, -o] ADJ **1** *Littéraire (guerrier)* martial, warlike; **un discours m.** a warlike speech

2 *Sport* **arts martiaux** martial arts

3 *(résolu, décidé)* resolute, determined; **une démarche/voix martiale** a firm tread/voice

4 *Jur* **cour martiale** court martial; **passer devant la cour martiale pour haute trahison** to be court-martialled for high treason; **loi martiale** martial law; **code m.** articles of war

martialement [marsjalmɑ̃] ADV martially

martien, -enne [marsjɛ̃, -ɛn] ADJ Martian

• **Martien, -enne** NM,F Martian

martinet¹ [martinɛ] NM **1** *(fouet)* strap, cat-o'-nine-tails; **tu vas avoir six coups de m.** you'll get six of the strap *or* of the best **2** *Métal* (small) drop hammer

martinet² [martinɛ] NM *Orn* swift

martingale [martɛ̃gal] NF **1** *(ceinture)* half belt **2** *Équitation (sangle)* martingale **3** *(au jeu ▸ façon de jouer)* doubling-up, ≃ martingale; *(▸ combinaison)* winning formula

martiniquais, -e [martinikɛ, -ɛz] ADJ Martinican

• **Martiniquais, -e** NM,F Martinican

Martinique [martinik] NF *Géog* **la M.** Martinique

martin-pêcheur [martɛ̃pɛʃœr] *(pl* **martins-pêcheurs)** NM *Orn* kingfisher

martre [martr] NF **1** *Zool* marten; **m. d'Amérique** American marten; **m. du Canada** mink **2** *(fourrure)* sable

martyr, -e [martir] ADJ martyred; **un peuple m.** a martyred people; **les enfants martyrs** battered children

NM,F **1** *(personne qui se sacrifie)* martyr; **les martyrs chrétiens** the Christian martyrs; **les martyrs de la Résistance** the martyrs of the Resistance **2** *Hum* martyr; **arrête de jouer les martyrs** *ou* **de prendre des airs de m.** stop being a *or* playing the martyr!

NM **1** *(supplice)* martyrdom; **le martyre des premiers chrétiens** the martyrdom of the early Christians; *Fig* **mettre qn au martyre** to torture sb **2** *Fig (épreuve)* torture, martyrdom; *(douleur)* agony; **souffrir le martyre** to be in agony; **cette visite a été un véritable martyre!** that visit was sheer torture!

martyriser [3] [martirize] VT **1** *(supplicier ▸ gén)* to martyrize; *Rel* to martyr **2** *Fig (maltraiter ▸ animal)* to ill-treat, to torture; *(▸ enfant)* to beat, to batter; *(▸ collègue, élève)* to bully; **on n'imagine pas le nombre d'enfants qui se font m. à l'école** you'd be amazed how many children are bullied at school

marxisme [marksism] NM Marxism

marxisme-léninisme [marksismleninism] NM Marxism-Leninism

marxiste [marksist] ADJ Marxist

NMF Marxist

marxiste-léniniste [marksistleninist] *(pl* **marxistes-léninistes)** ADJ Marxist-Leninist

NMF Marxist-Leninist

MAS [mas] NF *(abrév* **Maison d'accueil spécialisée)** = nursing home for severely disabled people

mas [ma(s)] NM = traditional country house or farm in Provence

mascara [maskara] NM mascara; **(se) mettre du m.** to put mascara on

mascarade [maskarad] NF **1** *(bal)* masked ball, masquerade **2** *Péj (accoutrement)* **qu'est-ce que c'est que cette m.?** what on earth is that outfit you're wearing? **3** *Fig (simulacre)* farce, mockery; **le candidat ayant déjà été choisi, l'entrevue ne fut qu'une m.** the candidate had already been selected so the interview was a complete farce *or* charade

mascaret [maskarɛ] NM **1** *(vague)* (tidal) bore, mascaret **2** *(raz de marée)* tidal wave

mascaron [maskarɔ̃] NM *Beaux-Arts* grotesque mask, *Spéc* mascaron

Mascate [maskat] N *Géog* Muscat

mascotte [maskɔt] NF mascot

masculin, -e [maskylɛ̃, -in] ADJ **1** *(propre à l'homme)* male; *(qui a les caractères de l'homme ▸ trait, orgueil)* masculine; *(▸ femme)* masculine, mannish; **le sexe m.** the male sex; **la mode masculine** men's fashion; **un métier m.** a male profession; **une voix masculine** *(d'homme)* a male *or* man's voice; *(de femme)* a masculine voice; **c'est bien un préjugé m.!** that's a typical male prejudice! **2** *(composé d'hommes)* **une équipe masculine** a men's team; **main-d'œuvre masculine** male workers **3** *Ling* masculine; **nom m.** masculine noun

NM *Ling* masculine; **au m.** in the masculine

masculinisation [maskylinizasjɔ̃] NF **1** *Méd* masculinization **2 la m. d'une profession** the increase in the number of men in a profession

masculiniser [3] [maskylinize] VT **1 m. qn** *(vêtement, coupe)* to make sb look masculine; **m. une profession** to increase the number of men in a profession, to attract more and more men to a profession **2** *Biol* to produce male characteristics in, to masculinize

VPR **se masculiniser** *(profession)* to attract more and more men; *(population)* to become predominantly male

masculinité [maskylinite] NF *(comportement)* masculinity, virility, manliness

maskinongé [maskinɔ̃ʒe] NM *Ich* muskellunge

maso [mazo] *Fam (abrév* **masochiste)** ADJ masochistic; **t'es complètement m. d'avoir accepté!** you must be a masochist *or* a glutton for punishment if you agreed!

NMF masochist; **c'est un m.** he's a glutton for punishment *or* a masochist

masochisme [mazɔʃism] NM masochism

masochiste [mazɔʃist] ADJ masochist, masochistic

NMF masochist

masquage [maskaʒ] NM *(gén) & Ordinat & Phot* masking

masque [mask] NM **1** *(déguisement, protection)* mask; **l'homme au m. de fer** the man in the iron mask; **m. de carnaval** *ou* **de Mardi gras** (carnival) mask; **m. funéraire** *ou* **mortuaire** death mask; **m. d'escrime/de plongée/de ski** fencing/diving/ski mask; **m. d'anesthésie/à oxygène/stérile** anaesthetic/oxygen/sterile mask; **m. de chirurgien** operating *or* surgeon's mask; **m. de soudeur** welding mask; **m. à gaz** gas mask

2 *(pour la peau)* **m. (de beauté)** face pack *or* mask; **m. à l'argile** mudpack

3 *Méd* **m. de grossesse** (pregnancy) chloasma

4 *Fig (apparence)* mask, front; **sous ce m. jovial, elle cache son amertume** under that jovial facade *or* appearance, she conceals her bitterness; **sous le m. de la vertu** under the mask of *or* in the guise of virtue; **sa bonté n'est qu'un m.** his/her kindness is just a front *or* is only skin-deep; **lever** *ou* **tomber le m., jeter (bas) son m.** to unmask oneself, to show one's true colours, to take off one's mask

5 *Mus & Théât* mask, masque

6 *(en acoustique)* **effet de m.** (audio) masking

7 *Électron, Typ & Phot* mask

8 *Ordinat* mask; **m. d'écran** screen mask; **m. d'entrée, m. de saisie** input mask

masqué, -e [maske] ADJ **1** *(voleur)* masked, wearing a mask; *(acteur)* wearing a mask, in a mask **2** *Mil* **tir m.** hidden *or* concealed fire

masquer [3] [maske] VT **1** *(dissimuler ▸ obstacle, ouverture)* to mask, to conceal; *(▸ lumière)* to shade, to screen (off), to obscure; *(▸ difficulté, intentions, sentiments)* to hide, to conceal, to disguise; *(▸ saveur, goût)* to mask, to disguise, to hide; *Naut (navire)* to darken; **le mur masque la vue** the wall blocks out *or* masks the view; **la colline masquait les chars ennemis** the enemy tanks were hidden *or* concealed by the hill; **son arrogance lui servait à m. sa lâcheté** he/she hid *or* concealed his/her cowardice under a mask of arrogance; *Mil* **m. une batterie** to conceal *or* to hide a battery; *Naut* **naviguer à feux masqués** to sail without lights **2** *(déguiser ▸ personne)* to put a mask on

VI *Naut* to back the sails

VPR **se masquer** *(se déguiser)* to put a mask on, to put on a mask

massacrante [masakrɑ̃t] ADJ F *Fam* **être d'une humeur m.** to be in a foul *or* vile mood

massacre [masakr] NM **1** *(tuerie)* massacre, slaughter; **envoyer des troupes au m.** to send troops to the slaughter; *Bible* **le m. des Innocents** the Massacre of the Innocents

2 *Fam (d'un adversaire)* massacre, slaughter; **5 à 0, c'est un m.!** 5 nil, it's a massacre!; **il a fait un m. dans le tournoi** he massacred *or* slaughtered *or* made mincemeat of all his opponents in the tournament

3 *Fam (travail mal fait)* **c'est du** *ou* **un m.** *(gâchis)* it's a mess; *(bâclage)* it's a botch-up *or Am* botch; **quel m., son 'Phèdre'!** she's managed to murder 'Phèdre'; **regarde comment il m'a coupé les cheveux, c'est un vrai m.!** look at the mess he's made of my hair!; **attention en découpant le gâteau, quel m.!** watch how you cut the cake, you're making a pig's ear *or* a real mess of it!

4 *Fam (succès)* **faire un m.** to be a runaway success, to be a smash (hit); **elle fait actuellement un m. sur la scène de la Lanterne** she's currently bringing the house down at the Lanterne theatre; **une chanson qui a fait un m. à sa sortie** a song which was a smash (hit) when it first came out

5 *Chasse (trophée)* stag's antlers *or* attire

massacrer [3] [masakre] VT **1** *(tuer ▸ animal, personne)* to slaughter, to massacre, to butcher; **ils vont se faire m. s'ils restent là!** they're going to be slaughtered if they stay there!

2 *Fam (vaincre facilement ▸ adversaire)* to make mincemeat of, to massacre, to slaughter; **notre équipe s'est fait m.** our team was massacred; **jouer aux échecs avec lui? tu vas te faire m.!** you're going to play chess with him? he'll wipe the floor with you!

3 *Fam (critiquer)* to pan, *Br* to slate; **la pièce s'est fait m.** the play got torn to pieces *or Br* slated; **ils l'ont massacré dans les journaux** they made mincemeat out of him *or* tore him to pieces in the papers; **lors du débat, il s'est vraiment fait m. par son interlocuteur** he was really savaged by his opponent in the debate

4 *Fam (gâcher ▸ concerto, pièce de théâtre)* to murder, to make a mess of; *(▸ langue)* to murder; *(▸ vêtements)* to ruin; **écoute-le m. la langue française** listen to him massacring *or* murdering the French language

5 *Fam (bâcler ▸ travail)* to make a mess *or* hash of, to botch (up), to make a pig's ear (out) of

massacreur, -euse [masakrœr, -øz] NM,F **1** *(tueur)* slaughterer, butcher **2** *Fam (mauvais exécutant ▸ d'un concerto, d'une pièce)* murderer; *(bâcleur)* botcher, bungler

massage [masaʒ] NM massage; **faire un m. à qn** to massage sb, to give sb a massage; **se faire faire un m.** to have a massage *Méd* **m. cardiaque** cardiac *or* heart massage; **m. thaïlandais** Thai massage

masse¹ [mas] NF **1** *(bloc informe)* mass; **m. de cheveux/terre** mass of hair/earth; **m. de nuages** bank of clouds; **m. d'eau** body of water; *(en mouvement)* mass of water; *Météo* **m. d'air** mass of air; **il vit une m. sombre sur le sol** he saw a dark mass *or* a great dark shape on the ground; **sculpté** *ou* **taillé dans la m.** carved from the block; *Fam* **un grand type taillé dans la m.** a big, heavily-built sort of chap; **s'abattre** *ou* **s'écrouler** *ou* **s'affaisser comme une m.** to collapse *or* to slump heavily

2 *Fam (grande quantité)* **une m. de** *(objets)* heaps *or* masses of; *(gens)* crowds *or* masses of; **il y avait des masses de livres** there were masses (and masses) of books; **il (n')y en a pas des masses** *(se rapportant à un indénombrable)* there aren't masses of them; *(se rapportant à un dénombrable)* there isn't masses (of it); **pas des masses** *(se rapportant à un indénombrable)* not that much; *(se rapportant à un dénombrable)* not that many; **des amis, il n'en a pas des masses** he hasn't got that many friends; **vous vous êtes bien amusés? – pas des masses!** did you have fun? – not that much!

3 *(groupe social)* **la m.** the masses; **communication/culture de m.** mass communication/culture; **les masses (populaires)** the mass (of ordinary people); **les masses laborieuses** the toiling masses

4 *(ensemble)* body, bulk; *(majorité)* majority; *Ordinat (d'informations)* bulk; **la grande m. des étudiants ne se sent pas concernée** the great majority of the students don't feel concerned; la m. des connaissances the total sum of knowledge **5** *Écon & Fin* fund, stock; la m. des créanciers/obligataires the body of creditors/bondholders; m. active assets; m. monétaire money supply; m. passive liabilities; m. salariale wage bill; il faut établir la m. d'équipement dans le budget de cette année we have to establish the total amount of (money allowed for) capital goods in this year's budget

6 *Électron Br* earth, *Am* ground; mettre à la m. *Br* to earth, *Am* to ground; mise à la m. *Br* earthing, *Am* grounding

7 *Chim & Phys* mass; le kilogramme est l'unité de m. the kilogram is the unit of mass; m. atomique/moléculaire atomic/molecular mass; m. critique critical mass; m. volumique relative density

• **à la masse** ADJ *Fam* être à la m. to be rather slow on the uptake

• **en masse** ADJ *(licenciements, production)* mass *(avant n)* ADV **1** *(en grande quantité)* produire *ou* fabriquer en m. to mass-produce; la population a approuvé en m. le projet de réforme the reform bill gained massive support; arriver en m. *(lettres, personnes)* to pour in; se déplacer en m. to go in a body *or* en masse; arrivée en m. des estivants sur les plages *(titre dans un journal)* holidaymakers invade the beaches *or* take to the beaches in droves; les villageois se préparent à une arrivée en m. des touristes villagers are bracing themselves for a tourist invasion; *Fam* avoir des bijoux en m. to have stacks *or* masses *or* loads of jewellery **2** *Com (en bloc)* in bulk

masse² [mas] NF **1** *(outil)* sledgehammer, beetle; m. en bois beetle

2 *(d'huissier)* (ceremonial) mace; *Mil* m. d'armes mace

3 *(de queue de billard)* butt

4 *Fam Fig* coup de m. (very) nasty shock; ça a été le coup de m. it came as a (very) nasty shock

masselotte [maslɔt] NF **1** *(sur pièce de fonderie)* sprue **2** *(dans un mécanisme)* bob weight

massepain [maspɛ̃] NM marzipan

masser¹ [3] [mase] VT **1** *(réunir ▸ enfants)* to gather *or* to bring together; *(▸ soldats)* to mass; *(▸ livres, pièces)* to put together **2** *Beaux-Arts* to group, to arrange into groups **3** *(au billard)* m. une bille to play a massé shot

VPR se masser to gather, to assemble, to mass; les enfants se massèrent dans la cour de l'école the children assembled *or* gathered in the *Br* school playground *or Am* schoolyard; les manifestants se massèrent devant l'hôtel de ville the demonstrators massed *or* gathered in front of the town hall

masser² [3] [mase] VT *(membre, muscle)* to massage; m. qn to massage sb, to give sb a massage; se faire m. to be massaged, to have a massage; masse-moi le bras rub *or* massage my arm

VPR se masser se m. le genou/le bras to massage one's knee/one's arm; elle se masse les tempes quand elle a mal à la tête she rubs her temples when she has a headache

massette [masɛt] NF **1** *(outil)* two-handed hammer **2** *Bot* bulrush, reed mace

masseur, -euse [masœr, -øz] NM,F masseur, *f* masseuse

NM *(appareil)* (vibro)massager

masseur-kinésithérapeute, masseuse-kinésithérapeute [masœrkineziterapøt, masøzkineziterapøt] *(mpl* masseurs-kinésithérapeutes, *fpl* masseuses-kinésithérapeutes) NM,F *Br* physiotherapist, *Am* physical therapist

massicot¹ [masiko] NM *(d'imprimeur)* guillotine; *(pour papier peint)* trimmer

massicot² [masiko] NM *Chim* massicot

massicoter [3] [masikɔte] VT *(papier)* to guillotine; *(papier peint)* to trim

massif, -ive [masif, -iv] ADJ **1** *Menuis & (en joaillerie)* solid; argent/or m. solid silver/gold; armoire en acajou m. solid mahogany wardrobe **2** *(épais)* massive, heavy-looking, bulky; une bâtisse au fronton m. a building with a massive pediment; sa silhouette massive his/her huge frame **3** *Fig (en grand nombre)* mass *(avant n)*, massive; *(en grande quantité)* massive, huge; des migrations massives vers le Nouveau Monde mass migrations to the New World; un apport m. d'argent liquide a massive cash injection; une réponse massive de nos lecteurs an overwhelming response from our readers

NM **1** *Géog & Géol* m. (montagneux) mountainous mass, massif; m. ancien primary *or* Caledonian massif; le M. central the Massif Central; le M. éthiopien the Ethiopian Hills; le m. du Hoggar the Hoggar Mountains **2** *Hort* m. (de fleurs) flowerbed; un m. de roses a rosebed, a bed of roses; m. d'arbustes clump of bushes; les rhododendrons font de jolis massifs rhododendrons look nice planted together in groups

massique [masik] ADJ **1** *Phys* mass *(avant n)* **2** *Tech* puissance m. power-to-weight ratio, power-weight ratio

massive [masiv] *voir* massif

massivement [masivmɑ̃] ADV *(en grand nombre)* massively, en masse; ils ont voté m. pour le nouveau candidat they voted overwhelmingly for the new candidate; les Français ont voté m. the French turned out in large numbers to vote

mass media, mass-média(s) [masmedja] NMPL mass media

massue [masy] NF **1** *(gourdin)* club; *(à pointes)* mace; un coup de m. a blow with a club; *Fig (événement imprévu)* staggering blow, bolt from the blue; *(prix excessif)* rip-off **2** *(comme adj)* un argument m. a sledgehammer argument

mastaire [mastɛr] NM *Univ* = postgraduate qualification

mastard [mastar] NM *Fam* hulk

mastectomie [mastɛktɔmi] NF *Méd* mastectomy

master [mastɛr] NM *Univ* ≃ masters (degree), two-year postgraduate qualification

master class [mastɛrklas] NF masterclass

mastère [mastɛr] NM *Univ (d'ingénieur)* DEng; *(de commerce)* MBA

mastic [mastik] ADJ INV putty-coloured

NM **1** *Constr* mastic; *(pour vitrier)* putty; *(pour menuisier)* filler; m. de colmatage filler paste **2** *Typ* transposition; faire un m. to (accidentally) transpose characters **3** *Bot* mastic

masticage [mastikaʒ] NM *Constr (d'une vitre)* puttying; *(d'une lézarde, d'une cavité)* filling

masticateur, -trice [mastikatœr, -tris] ADJ masticatory

mastication [mastikasjɔ̃] NF *(d'aliments)* chewing, *Spéc* mastication

masticatoire [mastikatwar] *Méd* ADJ masticatory

NM masticatory

masticatrice [mastikatris] *voir* masticateur

mastiquer¹ [3] [mastike] VT *(pain, viande)* to chew, *Spéc* to masticate

mastiquer² [3] [mastike] VT *(joindre ▸ lézarde, cavité)* to fill (in); *(▸ vitre)* to putty; couteau à m. putty knife

mastite [mastit] NF *Méd* mastitis

mastoc [mastɔk] ADJ INV *Fam* **1** *(lourd ▸ personne)* hefty; *(▸ objet)* bulky; *(▸ construction)* cumbersome **2** *Belg (fou ▸ personne)* crazy, nuts

mastodonte [mastɔdɔ̃t] NM **1** *Zool* mastodon **2** *Fam (personne)* colossus, enormous man, *f* woman; c'est un m. he's/she's built like the side of a house **3** *Fam (objet)* hulking great thing; *(camion) Br* juggernaut, *Am* tractor-trailer

mastoïde [mastɔid] ADJ *Anat* mastoid

mastoïdien, -enne [mastɔidjɛ̃, -ɛn] ADJ *Anat* mastoid

mastose [mastoz] NF *Méd* mastosis

mastroquet [mastrɔkɛ] NM *Fam Vieilli* **1** *(cafetier)* bar owner, *Br* publican **2** *(bistro)* bar, *Br* pub

masturbation [mastyrbasjɔ̃] NF masturbation; c'est de la m. intellectuelle it's intellectual self-indulgence *or* masturbation

masturbatoire [mastyrbatwar] ADJ masturbatory

masturber [3] [mastyrbe] VT to masturbate

VPR se masturber **1** *(emploi réfléchi)* to masturbate **2** *(emploi réciproque)* to masturbate each other

m'as-tu-vu [matyvy] ADJ INV showy, flashy; leur maison est très m. their house is very showy; qu'est-ce qu'elle est m.! what a show-off she is!; ce genre de voiture, ça fait très m. it's a really flashy type of car

NMF INV show-off; faire le *ou* son m. to show off

masure [mazyr] NF shack, hovel

mat¹ [mat] NM *Fam* morning; deux/trois heures du m. two/three a.m. *or* in the morning

mat, -e [mat] ADJ **1** *(couleur)* dull, matt; *(surface)* unpolished; *(peinture)* matt; *Phot* matt **2** *(teint)* olive **3** *(son)* un son m. a thud, a dull sound

NM **1** *Échecs* checkmate, mate; être sous le m. to be under the threat of checkmate *or* mate **2** *Tex* mat

ADJ INV *Échecs* checkmated, mated; le roi est m. the king is checkmated *or* in checkmate; tu es m. (you're) checkmate; faire m. en trois coups to mate *or* checkmate in three; il m'a fait m. en trois coups he mated *or* checkmated me in three moves

mât [mɑ] NM **1** *(poteau)* pole, post; *(en camping)* pole; m. de cocagne greasy pole

2 *(hampe)* flagpole

3 *Tech* m. de charge cargo beam, derrick; m. de levage lift mast

4 *Naut* mast; m. d'artimon mizzen, mizzenmast; m. de beaupré bowsprit; m. de charge cargo boom, derrick; m. de hune topmast; m. de misaine foremast; grand m. main mast; navire à trois mâts three-masted ship, three-master

5 *Rail* m. (de signal) signal post

matador [matadɔr] NM matador

mataf [mataf] NM *Fam (matelot)* tar, sailor

matamore [matamɔr] NM braggart; faire le m. to boast, to brag

match [matʃ] *(pl* matchs *ou* matches) NM match, *Am* game; disputer un m. to play a match; on fait un m.? shall we have *or* play a match?; m. de boxe boxing match; m. de tennis tennis match, game of tennis; m. aller/retour first/second leg (match); m. amical friendly (match); m. de barrage play-off, decider; m. de championnat league match; m. d'improvisation = live improvisation contest between two teams, the winning team being decided by the audience; m. nul draw; faire m. nul to draw, *Am* to tie; ils ont fait m. nul they drew *or Am* tied, the match ended in a draw *or Am* tie; m. de sélection trial

maté [mate] NM **1** *Bot* maté (tree) **2** *(boisson)* maté

matelas [matla] NM **1** *(d'un lit)* mattress; m. à ressorts/de laine spring/wool mattress; m. de mousse foam-rubber mattress; m. pneumatique air mattress **2** *(couche ▸ de feuilles mortes, de neige)* layer, carpet; *Fam* un m. de billets de banque *(liasse)* a wad *or* roll of *Br* banknotes *or Am* bills; *(fortune)* a pile (of money)

matelassé, -e [matlase] ADJ **1** *(fauteuil)* padded; enveloppe matelassée padded envelope, Jiffy bag® **2** *Couture (doublé)* lined; *(rembourré)* quilted, padded **3** *Tex (avec du matelassé)* covered with quilted material

NM quilted material; du m. de soie quilted silk

matelasser [3] [matlase] VT **1** *(fauteuil)* to pad **2** *Couture (doubler)* to line; *(rembourrer)* to quilt; matelassé de soie silk-lined **3** *(recouvrir de matelassé)* to cover with quilted material

matelassure [matlasyr] NF padding, mattress filling

matelot [matlo] NM **1** *(de la marine ▸ marchande)* sailor, seaman; *(▸ militaire)* sailor; servir comme simple m. to sail before the mast; m. de (breveté) première/deuxième/troisième classe leading/able/ordinary seaman; m. breveté *Br* able rating, *Am* seaman apprentice **2** *(bâtiment)* ship, vessel; m. d'avant/d'arrière ship ahead/astern

matelotage [matlɔtaʒ] NM **1** *(solde)* sailor's pay **2** *(travaux, connaissances)* seamanship

matelote [matlɔt] NF *Culin* matelote, fish stew *(with wine, onion and mushroom sauce)*; m. d'anguilles stewed eels *(in red wine sauce)*; sauce m. red wine and onion sauce

mater¹ [3] [mate] VT **1** *Échecs* to mate, to checkmate **2** *Fig (dompter ▸ personne, peuple)* to bring to heel; *(▸ révolte)* to quell, to curb, to put down; m. l'orgueil de qn to humble sb, to crush sb's pride; *Fam* **petit morveux, je vais te m., moi!** you little swine, I'll show you who's boss!

USAGE ABSOLU *Échecs* to mate, to checkmate; **m. en six coups** to mate *or* checkmate in six moves

mater[2] **[3]** [mate] **VT 1** *(dépolir)* to matt **2** *Métal* to caulk

mater[3] **[3]** [mate] *Fam* **VT 1** *(vérifier)* to check out; **mate un peu si le prof arrive** keep your eyes peeled, see if the teacher's coming **2** *(regarder avec convoitise)* to ogle, to eye up; **mate un peu la gonzesse!** just take a look at *or* get an eyeful of that chick!; **mate-moi ça!** check it out!, *Br* get a load of that!; **t'as fini de le m.?** have you quite finished (checking him out)?; **qu'est-ce qu'on s'est fait m. à la plage!** we got eyed up so much at the beach!

VI to eye up *or* ogle (the) women/men; **qu'est-ce que ça mate, ici!** all these men/women eyeing us up!

mâter [3] [mate] **VT 1** *Naut (pourvoir de mâts)* to mast **2** *Can (dresser)* to set upright

VPR se mâter *Can (animal)* to rear up (on its hind legs); *Fig Vieilli (personne)* to lose one's temper, to get one's dander up

matérialisation [materjalizasjɔ̃] **NF** *(réalisation)* materialization; **c'est la m. de tous mes rêves** it's a dream come true for me

matérialisé, -e [materjalize] **ADJ** *Admin* **voie matérialisée** = section of road delimited by a white line; **voie non matérialisée pendant 1 km** *(sur panneau)* no markings *or* roadmarkings for 1 km

matérialiser [3] [materjalize] **VT 1** *(concrétiser)* to materialize; **m. un projet** to carry out *or* to execute a plan **2** *(indiquer)* to mark out, to indicate **3** *(symboliser)* to symbolize, to embody

VPR se matérialiser to materialize

matérialisme [materjalism] **NM** materialism; **m. dialectique/historique** dialectical/historical materialism

matérialiste [materjalist] **ADJ 1** *Phil* materialist **2** *(personne, esprit, civilisation)* materialistic

NMF materialist

matérialité [materjalite] **NF 1** *(caractère de ce qui est réel, matériel)* materiality **2** *(matérialisme)* materialism

matériau, -x [materjo] **NM** *(substance)* material; **m. composite** composite

• **matériaux NMPL 1** *Constr* material, materials; **matériaux de construction** building *or* construction material(s) **2** *Fig (éléments)* components, elements; **rassembler des matériaux pour une enquête** to assemble (some) material for a survey

Do not confuse with **matériel**.

matériel, -elle [materjel] **ADJ 1** *(réel ▸ preuve)* material; **c'est une impossibilité matérielle** it's a physical impossibility; **je n'ai pas le temps m. de faire l'aller et retour** I simply don't have the time to go there and back; **il n'a pas le pouvoir m. de le faire** he doesn't have the means to do it

2 *(pécuniaire, pratique ▸ difficulté, aide)* material; **nos besoins matériels** our material needs; **sur le plan m., il n'a pas à se plaindre** from a material point of view, he has no grounds for complaint; **l'organisation matérielle de la fête a posé de gros problèmes** the practical organization of the party posed great problems

3 *(physique)* material; **être dans l'impossibilité matérielle de bouger** to find it physically impossible to move; **pour mon confort m.** for my material well-being; **les plaisirs matériels** material pleasures

4 *(matérialiste ▸ esprit, civilisation)* material

5 *Phil (être, univers)* physical, material

6 *Math & Tech (point)* material, physical

NM 1 *(équipement, machines)* equipment; **m. agricole** agricultural equipment; **m. de bureau** office equipment; **m. de camping** camping equipment *or* gear; **m. d'exploitation** working plant; **m. ferroviaire** *Br* railway *or Am* railroad equipment; **m. hi-fi** hi-fi equipment; **m. industriel** industrial equipment; **m. lourd** heavy equipment; **m. de pêche** fishing tackle *or* gear; **m. de peinture** painting equipment *or* gear; *Rail* **m. roulant** rolling stock

2 *(documentation)* material; **m. pédagogique** teaching materials; *Mktg* **m. de PLV** point-of-sale material; *Mktg* **m. de présentation** display material; **m. de promotion** promotional material; **m. publicitaire** advertising material; **m. scolaire** school materials

3 *Mil* **m. de guerre** weaponry, matériel; **arme** *ou* **service du m.** Ordnance Corps

4 *Écon* **le m. humain** the workforce, human material

5 *Biol & Psy* material

6 *Ordinat* hardware; **m. informatique** computer hardware

7 *Can Joual (tissu)* material, cloth

Do not confuse with **matériau**.

matériellement [materjelmɑ̃] **ADV 1** *(concrètement)* materially; **il m'est m. impossible de le faire** it's physically impossible for me to do it; **je n'ai m. pas le temps de venir te voir** I simply don't have time to come and see you; **une tâche m. impossible à effectuer** a physically impossible task **2** *(financièrement)* materially, financially

maternage [materna3] **NM** mothering

maternel, -elle [maternel] **ADJ 1** *(propre à la mère ▸ autorité, instinct)* maternal, motherly; *(▸ soins, gestes)* motherly; **il craignait la colère maternelle** he feared his mother's anger; **elle est très maternelle avec ses collègues** she acts in a very maternal *or* motherly way towards her colleagues **2** *(qui vient de la mère)* maternal; **grand-mère maternelle** maternal grandmother; **du côté m.** on the mother's *or* maternal side; **il y a de l'asthme dans ma famille du côté m.** there is asthma on my mother's side of the family

• **maternelle NF** *(école)* nursery school, kindergarten, *Br* infant school

> **MATERNELLE**
>
> Nursery education for children from two to six years old is provided by the state and is available to all families in France. Although it is not compulsory, the vast majority of children attend and are thus well-prepared for entry into primary school.

maternellement [maternelmɑ̃] **ADV** maternally; **elle s'occupait de lui m.** she cared for him like a mother *or* in a motherly fashion

materner [3] [materne] **VT** to mother; **tu ne vas pas m. ton fils jusqu'à 30 ans, non?** you're not going to mollycoddle *or* baby your son until he's 30, are you?; **il aime se faire m.** he likes to be mothered *or* mollycoddled

materné [materne] **ADJ M** *voir* **lait**

maternité [maternite] **NF 1** *(clinique)* maternity hospital *or* home; *(service)* maternity ward

2 *(fait d'être mère)* motherhood; **ça te va bien, la m.!** being a mother suits you!

3 *(grossesse)* pregnancy; **un corps déformé par des maternités successives** a body misshapen by successive pregnancies

4 *Jur* maternity; **action en recherche de m. naturelle** maternity suit

5 *Beaux-Arts* mother and child

mateur, -euse [matœr, -øz] **NM,F** *Fam* ogler; **c'est un sacré m.** he's always eyeing up women

math [mat] **NFPL = maths**

mathématicien, -enne [matematisjɛ̃, -ɛn] **NM,F** mathematician

mathématique [matematik] **ADJ 1** *Math* mathematical **2** *Fig (précis, exact)* mathematical; *(esprit)* logical **3** *Fig (inévitable)* inevitable; **elle était sûre de perdre, c'était m.** she was sure to lose, it was *Br* a dead cert *or Am* a surefire thing

• **mathématiques NFPL** mathematics *(singulier)*

mathématiquement [matematikmɑ̃] **ADV 1** *Math* mathematically **2** *Fig (objectivement)* mathematically, absolutely; **c'est m. impossible** it's mathematically *or* utterly impossible **3** *Fig (inévitablement)* inevitably; **m., il devait perdre** he was bound to lose

matheux, -euse [matø, -øz] **NM,F** *Fam* **1** *(gén)* **c'est un m.** he's a wizard at *Br* maths *or Am* math; **demandez à Jeanne, c'est elle, la matheuse** ask Jeanne, she's the *Br* maths *or Am* math brain **2** *(étudiant)* *Br* maths *or Am* math student

maths [mat] **NFPL** *Fam Br* maths, *Am* math; **m. sup/spé** = first/second year of a two-year science course preparing for entrance to the "Grandes Écoles"

Mathusalem [matyzalem] **NPR** *Bible* Methuselah; *Fam* **ça date de M.** it's out of the ark, it's as old as the hills; *Fam* **vieux comme M.** as old as Methuselah

MATIÈRE [matjɛr]

> • matter **1, 2, 4, 5** • material **1, 3** • subject **3, 5**

NF 1 *(substance)* matter, material; *Typ* matter; **c'est en quelle m.?** what's it made of?; *Nucl* **m. fissile/nucléaire** fissile/nuclear material; **m. plastique, matières plastiques** plastic, plastics; **m. première, matières premières** raw material *or* materials; **m. synthétique** synthetic material

2 *Biol, Chim, Phil & Phys* **la m.** matter; **m. organique/inorganique** organic/inorganic matter; **m. inanimée/vivante** inanimate/living matter; **matières (fécales)** faeces; **m. grasse, matières grasses** fat; **60 pour cent de matières grasses** 60 percent fat content; **sans matières grasses** fat-free, non-fat; *Fam* **m. grise** grey matter; **fais travailler ta m. grise!** use your brains *or* head!

3 *Fig (contenu ▸ d'un discours, d'un ouvrage)* material, subject matter; *(▸ de conversation)* subject, topic, theme; **je n'avais pas assez de m. pour en faire un livre** I didn't have enough material to write a book; **entrer en m.** to tackle a subject; **une entrée en m.** an introduction, a lead-in

4 *Fig (motif, prétexte)* matter; **donner m. à qch** to give cause for sth; **il n'y a pas là m. à rire** *ou* **plaisanter** this is no laughing matter; **il y a m. à discussion** there are a lot of things to be said about that; **cela donne m. à réfléchir** *ou* **à réflexion** this is a matter for serious thought, this matter requires some serious thinking; **y a-t-il là m. à dispute/procès?** is this business worth fighting over/going to court for?

5 *Fig (domaine)* matter, subject; *Scol* subject; **je suis incompétent en la m.** I'm ignorant on the subject; **il est mauvais/bon juge en la m.** he's a bad/good judge of this subject; **en m. philosophique/historique** in the matter of philosophy/history, as regards philosophy/history; **le latin est ma m. préférée** Latin is my favourite subject; **les matières à l'écrit/à l'oral** the subjects for the written/oral examination

6 *Fin* **m. imposable** taxable income

• **en matière de PRÉP** as regards; **en m. de cuisine** as far as cooking is concerned, as regards cooking

MATIF, Matif [matif] **NM 1** *Bourse (abrév* **Marché à terme international de France**) = body regulating activities on the French stock exchange, *Br* ≃ LIFFE, *Am* ≃ CBOE **2** *Fin (abrév* **Marché à terme des instruments financiers**) financial futures market

matifier [9] [matifje] **VT** to mattify

Matignon [matiɲɔ̃] **NM** **(l'hôtel) M.** = building in Paris which houses the offices of the Prime Minister; **les accords (de) M.** the Matignon Agreements; *Hum* **le locataire de M.** the (French) Prime Minister; **M. a décidé que...** the Prime Minister's office has decided that...

> **MATIGNON**
>
> The name of the Prime Minister's offices is often used to refer to the Prime Minister and his or her administrative staff, for example "L'Élysée et Matignon ont fini par se mettre d'accord".

matin [matɛ̃] **NM 1** *(lever du jour)* morning; **de bon** *ou* **grand m., le m. de bonne heure** in the early morning, early in the morning; **partir au petit m.** to leave early in the morning; **rentrer au petit m.** to come home in the early *or* small hours; **du m. au soir** all day long, from morning till night; **l'étoile/la rosée du m.** the morning star/dew **2** *(matinée)* morning; **ce m.,** *Can* **à m.** this morning; **par un m. d'été/de juillet** one summer/July morning; *Fam* **un beau m., un de ces (quatre) matins** one fine day, one of these (fine) days; **le m. du 8, le 8 au m.** on the morning of the 8th; **il est trois heures du m.** it's three a.m. *or* 3 (o'clock) in the morning;

je suis du m. *(actif le matin)* I'm an early riser; *(de service le matin)* I'm on *or* I do the morning shift, I'm on mornings; **il travaille le m.** he works mornings *or* in the morning; **le docteur visite le m.** the doctor does his house-calls in the morning; **à prendre m., midi et soir** to be taken three times a day **3** *Littéraire* **au m. de sa vie** in the morning of his/her life

ADV **1** *Littéraire (de bonne heure)* early in the morning, in the early hours (of the morning); **se lever très m.** to get up very early **2** *(durant la matinée)* **demain/hier m.** tomorrow/yesterday morning; **tous les dimanches m.** every Sunday morning

ADJ *Can* = **matinal 1**

mâtin, -e [matɛ̃, -in] NM,F *Fam Vieilli* imp, monkey; **le m., il a filé!** the little devil *or* rascal has taken off!; **ah, la mâtine!** oh, the cheeky little hussy!

NM *(chien)* mastiff, guard dog

EXCLAM *Fam Vieilli* by Jove!, great Scott!

matinal, -e, -aux, -ales [matinal, -o] ADJ **1** *(du matin)* morning *(avant n)*; **promenade/brise matinale** morning walk/breeze **2** *(du petit matin)* **heure matinale** early hour **3** *(personne)* **être m.** to be an early riser; **je suis assez m.** I'm quite an early riser; **vous êtes bien m. aujourd'hui** you're up early today

mâtiné, -e [matine] ADJ crossbred; *Fig* **m. de qch** mixed with sth; **c'est un berger allemand m. de lévrier** it's an Alsatian crossed with a greyhound, it's a cross between an Alsatian and a greyhound; *Fig* **un français m. d'italien** French peppered with Italian words; *Fig* **il parle un français m. d'anglais** his French is full of anglicisms; *Fig* **un humour m. d'une touche de mépris** humour tinged with scorn

matinée [matine] NF **1** *(matin)* morning; **je vous verrai demain dans la m.** I'll see you sometime tomorrow morning; **en début/fin de m.** at the beginning/end of the morning; **j'ai travaillé toute la m.** I've worked all morning; **j'ai passé toute ma m. à l'attendre/au lit** I spent the whole morning waiting for him/in bed; **je ne l'ai pas vu de toute la m.** I haven't seen him all morning; **une m. de lecture** a morning (spent) reading; **par une belle m. de printemps/de juillet** on a fine spring/July morning **2** *Théât & Cin* matinee; **y a-t-il une séance en m.?** is there an afternoon *or* matinee performance?; **on joue ce film en m.** the film is showing as a matinée

matines [matin] NFPL matins, mattins

matir [32] [matir] VT to matt, to dull

matité [matite] NF **1** *(aspect mat ▸ gén)* matt look; (▸ *d'une peinture)* matt finish **2** *(d'un son)* dullness

matois, -e [matwa, -az] *Littéraire* ADJ sly, cunning, wily

NM,F cunning person; **c'est un fin m.** he's a cunning old fox

maton[1] [matɔ̃] NM *Belg (lait caillé)* curdled milk

maton[2], -onne [matɔ̃, -ɔn] NM,F *Fam Arg crime (gardien de prison)* screw, *Am* hack, bull

matos [matos] NM *Fam* gear, stuff; **ils ont un sacré m.** they've got amazing gear

matou [matu] NM *Fam* tom, tomcat; *Can Fig (individu lubrique)* sex fiend *or* maniac

matraquage [matrakaʒ] NM **1** *(dans une bagarre)* bludgeoning, clubbing; *(dans une manifestation) Br* truncheoning, *Am* clubbing **2** *Fam (propagande)* **m. publicitaire** hype; **le m. d'un disque** the plugging of a record; **tu as vu le m. qu'ils font pour le bouquin/le concert?** have you seen all the hype about the book/the concert?

matraque [matrak] NF **1** *(de police) Br* truncheon, *Am* billy club, night stick; **il a reçu un coup de m.** he was hit with a *Br* truncheon *or Am* billy club; *Fam Fig* **100 euros, c'est le coup de m.!** 100 euros, that's a bit steep! **2** *(de voyou)* club, *Br* cosh; **tué à coups de m.** bludgeoned *or* clubbed to death

matraquer [3] [matrake] VT **1** *(frapper ▸ sujet: malfaiteur)* to bludgeon, to club; (▸ *sujet: agent de police) Br* to truncheon, *Am* to club; **les manifestants se sont fait m. par la police** the demonstrators were beaten by the police **2** *Fam Fig (auditeur, consommateur)* to bombard; *(disque, chanson)* to plug, to hype **3** *Fam Fig* **on se fait m. dans ce restaurant!** they really rip you off *or Am* soak you in this restaurant!

matriarcal, -e, -aux, -ales [matrijarkal, -o] ADJ matriarchal

matriarcat [matrijarka] NM matriarchy

matricaire [matrikɛr] NF *Bot* feverfew

matrice [matris] NF **1** *(moule ▸ gén)* mould, die, *Spéc* matrix; (▸ *d'un caractère d'imprimerie)* mat, matrix; **m. d'un disque/d'une bande** matrix record/tape; **coulé en m.** die-cast

2 *Math* matrix; **m. carrée** square matrix

3 *Ordinat* matrix; *(de données)* array; **m. active/passive** active/passive matrix; **m. d'aiguilles** dot matrix; **m. de vérité** truth table

4 *Admin* **m. du rôle des contributions** original list of taxpayers

5 *Vieilli (utérus)* womb

matricide [matrisid] NMF *(personne)* matricide

NM *Littéraire (crime)* matricide

matriciel, -elle [matrisjel] ADJ **1** *Admin* tax-assessment *(avant n)* **2** *Math* **calcul m.** matrix calculation **3** *Ordinat (écran)* dot matrix *(avant n)*

• **matricielle** NF *Ordinat* dot matrix

matricule [matrikyl] ADJ reference *(avant n)*; **numéro m.** reference number

NM **1** *Admin* reference number **2** *Mil* roll number

NF **1** *Admin* register; *(de prison, d'hôpital)* roll, register, list; *Mil* (regimental) roll; *(immatriculation)* registration **2** *(extrait)* registration certificate

matrimonial, -e, -aux, -ales [matrimɔnjal, -o] ADJ matrimonial

matrone [matrɔn] NF **1** *(femme ▸ respectable)* staid *or* upright woman, matron; (▸ *corpulente)* stout *or* portly woman **2** *Antiq* matron **3** *Can (gardienne de prison) Br* prison officer, *Am* prison guard

maturation [matyrasjɔ̃] NF **1** *Bot* maturation; *Fig* **son talent est arrivé à m.** his/her talent has reached its peak

2 *Méd* maturation; **m. sexuelle** sexual maturation

3 *(du fromage)* ripening, maturing

4 *Agr* maturation, ripening

mature [matyr] ADJ **1** *Ich* ripe **2** *(développé)* mature

mâture [mɑtyr] NF *Naut (mâts)* masts; **dans la m.** aloft

maturité [matyrite] NF **1** *(d'un fruit)* ripeness; *Fig (de personne, d'animal, de pensée, du marché)* maturity; **venir** *ou* **parvenir à m.** to become ripe, to ripen; *Fig* to become mature, to reach maturity; **manquer de m.** to be immature; **cette jeune femme ne manque pas de m.** that young woman is very mature; **attendons qu'elle ait une plus grande m. d'esprit** *ou* **de jugement** let's wait until she's more intellectually mature **2** *(âge)* prime (of life); **l'artiste fut frappée en pleine m.** the artist was struck down at the height of her powers *or* of her creative genius **3** *Suisse (baccalauréat)* school-leaving diploma *(from a "gymnase", granting admission to university)*

matutinal, -e, -aux, -ales [matytinal, -o] ADJ *Littéraire* morning *(avant n)*

maudire [104] [modir] VT **1** *Rel* to damn **2** *(vouer à la calamité)* to curse; **m. le destin** to curse fate; **je maudis le jour où je l'ai rencontré** I curse the day (when) I met him

maudit, -e [modi, -it] ADJ **1** *(damné)* cursed; **sois m.!** curse you! *Littéraire* **m./maudite soit...** a curse *or* plague on...; *Littéraire* **m. sois-tu!** a curse on you!

2 *(mal considéré)* accursed; **c'est un livre m.** the book has been censured; **peintre m.** accursed painter; **poète m.** damned *or* cursed poet

3 *(avant le nom) Fam (dans des exclamations)* cursed, blasted, damned; **encore ce m. temps!** this damn weather again!; **maudite bagnole!** blasted *or Am* goddamn car!

4 *Can très Fam (très)* **c'est une maudite belle fille!** she's a damn good-looking girl!, she's one hell of a good-looking girl!

NM *Rel* **le M.** Satan, the Fallen One; **les maudits** the Damned

EXCLAM *Can très Fam* shit!, *Br* bloody hell!

• **en maudit** ADV *Can* **1** *très Fam (en colère)* in a foul temper **2** *(en intensif)* **c'est un beau film en m.** it's a damn *or Br* bloody good film; **il court vite en m.** he's a damn *or Br* bloody fast runner

maugréer [15] [mogree] VI to grumble; **m. contre qch** to grumble about sth

maure [mɔr] ADJ Moorish

• **Maure** NM Moor; **les Maures** the Moors

mauresque [mɔresk] ADJ Moorish

NF **1** *(motif)* moresque, Moresque **2** *(boisson)* = pastis with barley water and water

• **Mauresque** NF Moorish woman

Maurice [moris] NF *Géog* **l'île M.** Mauritius

mauricien, -enne [morisjɛ̃, -ɛn] ADJ Mauritian

• **Mauricien, -enne** NM,F Mauritian

Mauritanie [moritani] NF *Géog* **la M.** Mauritania

mauritanien, -enne [moritanjɛ̃, -ɛn] ADJ Mauritanian

• **Mauritanien, -enne** NM,F Mauritanian

mausolée [mozɔle] NM mausoleum

maussade [mosad] ADJ **1** *(de mauvaise humeur)* glum, sullen; **elle l'accueillit d'un air m.** she greeted him/her sullenly **2** *(triste ▸ temps)* gloomy, dismal

maussaderie [mosadri] NF *Littéraire* moroseness, glumness

MAUVAIS, -E [movɛ, -ɛz]

ADJ
- bad **A1–3, B1–3, C2, D1, 3, 4**
- unpleasant **B1, D2**
- inconvenient **C2**
- poor **A1, 3**
- wrong **A2, C1, 2**
- nasty **B1, D1, 2**

NM,F
- bad person

NM
- bad

ADV
bad

ADJ **A.** *EN QUALITÉ* **1** *(médiocre)* bad, poor; **son deuxième roman est plus/moins m. que le premier** his/her second novel is worse than his/her first/ is not as bad as his/her first; **en m. état** in bad *or* poor condition; **un produit de mauvaise qualité** a poor quality product; **du m. travail** bad *or* poor *or* shoddy work; **la récolte a été mauvaise cette année** it was a bad *or* poor harvest this year; **la route est mauvaise** the road is bad *or* in a bad state; **j'ai une mauvaise vue** *ou* **de m. yeux** I've got bad eyesight; **il s'exprimait dans un m. français** he spoke in bad French; **de m. résultats** *(dans une entreprise)* poor results; *(à un examen)* bad *or* poor *or* low grades; **ce n'est pas un m. conseil qu'il t'a donné là** that's not a bad piece of advice he's just given you; **m. goût** *(d'une image, d'une personne, d'une idée)* bad taste; **c'est de m. goût** it's in bad taste; **il porte toujours des cravates de m. goût** he always wears such tasteless ties; **elle a très m. goût** she has very bad *or* poor taste

2 *(défectueux)* bad, wrong, faulty; **la ligne est mauvaise** *(téléphone)* the line is bad; *Sport* **la balle est mauvaise** the ball is out; *Sport* **le service est m.** it's a bad *or* faulty serve

3 *(incompétent)* bad, poor; **un m. mari** a bad husband; **il a été m. à la télévision hier** he was bad on TV yesterday; **je suis mauvaise en économie** I'm bad *or* poor at economics

B. *DÉSAGRÉABLE* **1** *(odeur, goût)* bad, unpleasant, nasty; **prends ton sirop – c'est m.!** take your cough mixture – it's nasty!; **je n'irai plus dans ce restaurant, c'était trop m.** I won't go to that restaurant again, it was too awful; **il n'est pas si m. que ça, ton café** your coffee isn't that bad; **le poisson a une mauvaise odeur** the fish smells bad; **les mauvaises odeurs** bad *or* unpleasant smells; **elle a mauvaise haleine** she has bad breath; **m. goût** *(de la nourriture, d'un médicament)* bad *or* nasty *or* unpleasant taste; **jette ça, c'est m.** *(pourri)* throw that away, it's gone bad; **enlève ce qui est m.** *(dans un fruit)* take off the bad bits

2 *(éprouvant)* bad; **passer un m. hiver** to have a bad winter; **j'ai eu une mauvaise expérience du ski** I had a bad experience skiing; **le m. temps** bad weather; *Fam* **la trouver** *ou* **l'avoir mauvaise** to be hacked off *or* bummed; **tirer qn d'un m. pas** to get sb out of a fix

3 *(défavorable)* bad; **je vous apporte de mauvaises nouvelles** I've got some bad news for you;

mauvaise nouvelle, elle ne vient plus bad news, she's not coming any more; **tu as fait une mauvaise affaire** you've got a bad deal (there); **faire de mauvaises affaires** to get some bad deals

C. *NON CONFORME* **1** *(erroné, inapproprié)* wrong; **tu vas dans la mauvaise direction** you're going the wrong way; **prendre qch dans le m. sens** to take sth the wrong way; *Fig* **faire un m. calcul** to miscalculate

2 *(inopportun)* bad, inconvenient, wrong; **j'ai téléphoné à un m. moment** I called at a bad *or* an inconvenient time; **tu as choisi le m. jour pour me parler d'argent** you've picked the wrong day to talk to me about money; **il ne serait pas m. de la prévenir** it wouldn't be a bad idea to warn her

D. *NÉFASTE* **1** *(dangereux)* bad, nasty; **une mauvaise égratignure** a nasty scratch; **un m. rhume** a bad *or* nasty cold; **elle est retombée dans une mauvaise position et s'est tordu la cheville** she landed badly and sprained her ankle; **c'est m. pour les poumons/plantes** it's bad for your lungs/for the plants; **ne bois pas l'eau, elle est mauvaise** don't drink the water, it's unsafe *or* not safe; **je trouve m. que les enfants regardent trop la télévision** I think it's bad *or* harmful for children to watch too much television

2 *(malveillant)* nasty, unpleasant; **un rire/sourire m.** a nasty laugh/smile; **m. coup** *(de poing)* nasty blow *or* punch; *(de pied)* nasty kick; **faire un m. coup** to get up to no good; **faire un m. coup à qn** to play a dirty trick on sb; **avoir l'air m.** to look nasty; **si on la contrarie, elle devient mauvaise** when people annoy her, she gets vicious *or* turns nasty; **en fait, ce n'est pas un m. homme/une mauvaise femme** he/she means no harm(, really)

3 *(immoral)* bad; **de mauvaises influences** bad influences

4 *(funeste)* bad; **c'est (un) m. signe** it's a bad sign; **m. présage** bad *or* ill omen

NM,F *(personne méchante)* bad person; **oh, le m./la mauvaise!** *(à un enfant)* you naughty boy/girl!

NM *(ce qui est critiquable)* **il n'y a pas que du m. dans ce qu'il a fait** what he did wasn't all bad; **il y a du bon et du m. dans leur proposition** there are some good points and some bad points in their proposal

ADV *Météo* **il fait m.** the weather's bad *or* nasty

mauve [mov] **ADJ** mauve

NM mauve

NF *Bot* mallow

mauviette [movjet] **NF 1** *Fam (gringalet)* weakling; *(lâche)* sissy, wimp **2** *Orn* lark

maux [mo] *voir* **mal**[1]

MAV [emave] **NM** *Mktg (abrév* **marketing après-vente***)* after-sales marketing

max [maks] **NM** *Fam (abrév* **maximum***)* **1** *(peine)* maximum sentence❑; **il a écopé du m.** he got the maximum sentence *or Am* rap, *Br* he copped the full whack **2** *(locution)* **un m.** loads, lots; **ça va te coûter un m.** it's going to cost you a packet *or Br* a bomb; **il en a rajouté un m.** he went completely overboard; **assurer un m.** to do brilliantly; **sur scène ils assurent un m.** they really rock on stage; **un m. de fric** loads of money; **un m. de monde/de voitures** stacks *or* a ton of people/cars

maxi [maksi] **ADJ INV 1** *(long)* maxi; **un m. 45 tours** a twelve-inch single **2** *Fam (maximum)* **vitesse m.** top *or* full speed❑

ADV *Fam (au maximum)* max, tops; **on sera 20 m.** there'll be 20 of us max *or* tops; **ça prendra deux heures m.** it'll take two hours max *or* tops

> **MAXI-** PREFIX
>
> • This prefix conveys the idea of LARGENESS. It is used before a noun, mostly in the language of fashion and advertising where it often contrasts with **mini-**. As far as spelling is concerned, there seems to be some hesitation as to the use of the hyphen, eg:
>
> **une maxi(-)jupe** a maxi skirt; **un maxi tee-shirt** a baggy *or* an oversized T-shirt; **un maxi(-)écran** a giant screen
>
> • **Maxi-** can also refer to something large in terms of volume or importance, and is even used, in colloquial French, as an INTENSIFIER in the same vein as **super-** or **méga-** (see entries), eg:
>
> **une maxi dose de café** a mega dose of coffee; **maxi promo sur toute la gamme!** prices slashed across the whole range!

maxidiscompte [maksidiskɔ̃t] **NM** *Com* hard discount

maxillaire [maksilɛr] *Anat* **ADJ** maxillary; **os m.** jawbone, *Spéc* maxilla

NM jaw, jawbone, *Spéc* maxilla; **les maxillaires** the maxillae; **m. supérieur/inférieur** upper/lower jaw

maxillofacial, -e, -aux, -ales [maksilɔfasjal, -o] **ADJ** *Méd* maxillofacial

maxima [maksima] *voir* **maximum**

maximal, -e, -aux, -ales [maksimal, -o] **ADJ** *(le plus grand)* maximal, maximum *(avant n)*; **pour un confort m.** for maximum comfort; **à la vitesse maximale** at top speed; **vitesse maximale autorisée: 60 km/h** speed limit: 60 km/h; **température maximale** highest *or* maximum temperature

maxime [maksim] **NF** maxim

maximum [maksimɔm] *(pl* **maximums** *ou* **maxima** [-ma]*)* **ADJ** maximum; **pressions maxima** maximum pressures; **vitesse m.** maximum *or* top speed; **des rendements maximums** maximum *or* top production figures

NM 1 *(le plus haut degré)* maximum; **le m. saisonnier** the maximum temperature for the season; **en rentrant, on a mis le chauffage au m.** when we got home, we turned the heating on full; **le thermostat est réglé sur le m.** the thermostat is on the highest setting; **la crue était à son m.** the river had risen to its highest level *or* was in full spate; **nous ferons le m. le premier jour** we'll do as much as we can on the first day; **je ferai le m. pour finir dans les temps** I'll do my utmost *or* I'll do all I can to finish on time **2** *Fam (en intensif)* **un m.** *(beaucoup)* loads; **un m. de** an enormous amount of; **un m. de gens** *(le plus possible)* as many people as possible❑; *(énormément)* loads of people; **on a eu un m. d'ennuis** everything went wrong; **il y a eu un m. de visiteurs le premier jour** we/they/*etc* had an enormous number of visitors the first day; **pour ça, il faut un m. d'organisation** that sort of thing needs a huge amount of *or* needs loads of organization; **je voudrais un m. de silence pendant le film** I want total silence during the film; **ça rendra un m. sur papier brillant** it will come up great on gloss paper **3** *(peine)* **le m.** the maximum sentence; **il a eu le m.** he got the maximum sentence

ADV at the most *or* maximum; **il fait 3°C m.** the temperature is 3°C at the most *or* at the maximum

• **au maximum ADV 1** *(au plus)* at the most *or* maximum; **deux jours au m.** two days at the most; **au grand m.** at the very most **2** *(le plus possible)* **un espace utilisé au m.** an area used to full advantage; **porter la production au m.** to increase production to a maximum, to maximize production

maya[1] [maja] **ADJ** Maya, Mayan

NM *(langue)* Maya, Mayan

• **Maya NMF** Maya, Mayan; **les Mayas** the Maya *or* Mayas, the Mayans

maya[2] [maja] **NF** *Rel* maya

Mayence [majɑ̃s] **NF** Mainz

mayonnaise [majɔnɛz] **NF** *Culin* mayonnaise; **crabe à la m.** crab in mayonnaise; **œufs m.** egg mayonnaise; **la m. ne prend pas** the mayonnaise won't set; *Fam Fig* **la m. n'a pas pris** it didn't work❑; **la m. a pris** it worked❑; *Fam* **la m. ne prend pas entre eux** they don't see eye to eye; *Fam Fig* **faire monter la m.** to stir things up

mazagran [mazagrɑ̃] **NM** = glazed earthenware cup for drinking coffee

mazette [mazɛt] **EXCLAM** *Vieilli Hum* my (word)!

mazout [mazut] **NM** (fuel) oil; **chauffage central au m.** oil-fired central heating

mazouté, -e [mazute] **ADJ** *(plage)* oil-polluted, polluted with oil; *(oiseau)* oil-covered, covered in oil, oiled

mazurka [mazyrka] **NF** mazurka

Mb *Ordinat (abrév écrite* **mégabit***)* Mb

MBA[1] [ɛmbea] **NF** *Compta (abrév* **marge brute d'autofinancement***)* cashflow, funds generated by operations

MBA[2] [ɛmbie] **NM** *(abrév* **Master of Business Administration***)* MBA

Mbps *Ordinat (abrév écrite* **mégabits par seconde***)* mbps

MDD [ɛmdede] **NF** *Com (abrév* **marque de distributeur***)* distributor's brand name, own brand

MDR *Ordinat & Tél (abrév écrite* **mort de rire***)* LOL

M^{e} *(abrév écrite* **Maître***)* = title for lawyers

me [mə]

> m' is used before a word beginning with a vowel or h mute.

PRON 1 *(avec un verbe pronominal)* myself; **je me suis fait mal** I've hurt myself; **je me suis évanoui** I fainted; **je ne m'en souviens plus** I don't remember any more; **je me disais que...** I thought to myself...

2 *(objet direct)* me; **il me connaît** he knows me; **il est venu me chercher** he came to fetch me; **ça me regarde** that's my business; **me voici** here I am

3 *(objet indirect)* (to) me; **il m'a écrit** he wrote to me; **il me l'a donné** he gave it (to) me, he gave me it; **donnez-m'en** give me some; **ton idée me plaît** I like your idea; **ton amitié m'est précieuse** your friendship is precious *or* means a lot to me; **ça me soulève le cœur** it makes me sick; **il m'a fait lire ce livre** he made me read this book; *Fam* **il me court après depuis un certain temps** he's been chasing me for some time

4 *Fam (emploi expressif)* **tu veux bien m'éteindre la lumière?** would you switch off the light (for me)?; **va me fermer cette porte** shut that door, will you?; **va me faire tes devoirs** go and get that homework done; **qu'est-ce qu'ils m'ont encore fait comme bêtises?** what kind of stupid tricks have they got up to now?; **où est-ce que tu m'as mis le sucre?** now where have you hidden the sugar?

> **MÉ-** PREFIX
>
> When added to verbs, nouns or adjectives, the prefix **mé-** has a generally NEGATIVE connotation – it expresses the opposite of what the verb, noun or adjective represents. It is often translated by an equivalent prefix, either *mis-* or *dis-*, eg:
>
> **méconnaître** to misjudge, to misunderstand; **mécontent(e)** displeased; **médire de quelqu'un** to speak ill of somebody; **se méfier de quelqu'un** to distrust somebody; **par mégarde** inadvertently; **se méprendre** to be mistaken; **mépriser** to despise; **une mésaventure** a misadventure, a misfortune

mea culpa [meakylpa] **NM INV 1** *Rel* mea culpa; **faire** *ou* **dire son m.** to say one's mea culpa **2** *Fig* **ils ont fait leur m.** they acknowledged responsibility, they admitted it was their fault; **le journal a publié hier un m. en première page** yesterday the paper published a front page apology

EXCLAM *Hum* it's my fault!, mea culpa!

méandre [meɑ̃dr] **NM** *Archit & Géog* meander; *(de route)* bend; **le fleuve fait des méandres** the river meanders *or* twists and turns; *Fig* **les méandres de sa pensée** the twists and turns of his/her thoughts; **se perdre dans les méandres d'un raisonnement** to get lost in the intricacies of an argument

mec [mɛk] **NM** *Fam* **1** *(homme)* guy, *Br* bloke; **un beau m.** a good-looking guy; **c'est un drôle de m.** he's a strange guy; **pauvre m., va!** you creep!; **écoute, petit m.!** look, (you little) punk!; *Hum* **ça, c'est un vrai m.!** there's a real man for you!; **salut les mecs!** hi, guys! **2** *(petit ami)* boyfriend❑, man; **elle est venue sans son m.** she came without her man

mécanicien, -enne [mekanisjɛ̃, -ɛn] **NM,F 1** *(monteur, réparateur)* mechanic; *Naut* engineer; *Aviat* **m. (de bord)** *ou* **navigant** (flight) engineer; **ouvrier m.** mechanic **2** *(physicien)* mechanical engineer **3** *Rail Br* engine driver, *Am* engineer

• **mécanicienne NF** *Couture* machinist

mécanicien-dentiste [mekanisjɛ̃dɑ̃tist] *(pl* **mécaniciens-dentistes***)* **NM** *Vieilli* dental technician

mécanique [mekanik] **ADJ 1** *(de la mécanique)* mechanical

2 *(non manuel ▸ tapis, tissage)* machine-made; *(▸ abattage, remblayage)* mechanical, machine *(avant n)*
3 *(non électrique, non électronique ▸ commande)* mechanical; *(▸ jouet)* clockwork; *(▸ montre)* wind-up
4 *(non chimique)* **moyens mécaniques de contraception** barrier methods of contraception
5 *(du moteur)* engine *(avant n)*; **nous avons eu un incident m.** *ou* **des ennuis mécaniques** we had engine trouble
6 *(machinal)* mechanical; **je n'aime pas faire mon travail de façon m.** I don't like working like a robot *or* machine; **c'est un travail très m.** it's very mechanical work; **gestes mécaniques** mechanical gestures
NF 1 *(science)* mechanics *(singulier)*; *Ind & Tech* mechanical engineering; **m. quantique/relativiste** quantum/relativistic mechanics; **m. des fluides** fluid mechanics; **m. ondulatoire** wave mechanics **2** *Aut* car mechanics *(singulier)*; **il aurait voulu faire de la m.** he'd have liked to have been a (car) mechanic **3** *(machine)* piece of machinery; *(dispositif)* mechanism; *(d'une imprimante laser)* engine; **marcher** *ou* **tourner comme une m. bien huilée** to work like a well-oiled machine; **une belle m.** *(moto, voiture)* a fine piece of engineering

> Il faut noter que le nom anglais **mechanic** est un faux ami. Il signifie **mécanicien**.

mécaniquement [mekanikmɑ̃] **ADV** mechanically

mécanisation [mekanizasjɔ̃] **NF** mechanization; **l'ère de la m.** the machine age

mécaniser **[3]** [mekanize] **VT** to mechanize

mécanisme [mekanism] **NM 1** *(processus)* mechanism; *(dispositif)* mechanism, device; **le m. de la violence** the mechanism of violence; **le m. du corps humain** the human mechanism; **elle étudie le m.** *ou* **les mécanismes de la finance** she's studying the workings of finance; **m. administratif** administrative machinery; **grâce à des mécanismes bancaires spécifiques** thanks to specific banking mechanisms; **m. budgétaire** budgetary mechanism; *UE* **m. de change** Exchange Rate Mechanism; *UE* **m. de change européen** European Exchange Rate Mechanism; *Psy* **mécanismes de défense** defence mechanisms; **mecanismes économiques** economic machinery; **m. de l'offre et de la demande** supply and demand mechanism; **m. des prix** price mechanism; *UE* **m. des taux de change** Exchange Rate Mechanism **2** *Tech (d'une serrure, d'une horloge)* mechanism; *(d'un fusil)* mechanism, workings; *Aut* **m. d'avance automatique** automatic advance mechanism; *Aut* **m. d'avance centrifuge** centrifugal advance mechanism; *Aut* **m. de basculement** tipping gear; *Aut* **m. de direction** steering gear **3** *Phil* mechanism; *(de la pensée, de la parole)* mechanics

mécano [mekano] **NM** *Fam* **1** *Aut* mechanic◻ **2** *Rail Br* engine driver◻, *Am* engineer◻

mécanographe [mekanɔgraf] **NMF** punch card (machine) operator

mécanographie [mekanɔgrafi] **NF 1** *(procédé)* data processing *(with punch card machines)* **2** *(service)* data processing department

mécanographique [mekanɔgrafik] **ADJ** **service m.** (mechanical) data processing department, punch card department; **fiche m.** punch *or* punched card

mécatronique [mekatrɔnik] *Ind* **ADJ** mechatronic
NF mechatronics *(singulier)*

Meccano® [mekano] **NM** Meccano® (set)

mécénat [mesena] **NM** *(par une personne)* patronage, sponsorship; *(par une société)* sponsorship; **le m. d'entreprise** corporate sponsorship

mécène [mesen] **NM** *(personne)* patron, sponsor; *(société)* sponsor

méchamment [meʃamɑ̃] **ADV 1** *(avec cruauté)* nastily, spitefully, wickedly; **il ne l'a pas fait m.** he didn't do it nastily **2** *Fam (très, beaucoup)* really◻, *Br* dead, *Am* real; **être m. déçu/embêté** to be *Br* dead *or Am* real disappointed/annoyed; **il est rentré m. bronzé** he came back with a fantastic tan; **ça a m. cartonné hier au bar** there was one hell of a punch-up in the bar yesterday

méchanceté [meʃɑ̃ste] **NF 1** *(volonté de nuire)* spite, malice, nastiness; **par pure m.** out of sheer spite; **soit dit sans m., elle n'est pas futée** without wishing to be unkind, she is not very bright **2** *(caractère méchant)* maliciousness, nastiness, spitefulness; **la m. se lit dans son regard** you can see the malice in his/her eyes **3** *(acte, propos)* spiteful *or* nasty action/remark; **dire des méchancetés à qn** to say nasty *or* horrible things to sb; **faire des méchancetés à qn** to be nasty *or* horrible to sb; **c'était la pire m. qu'il pouvait faire** it was the nastiest *or* meanest thing he could have done

méchant, -e [meʃɑ̃, -ɑ̃t] **ADJ 1** *(cruel ▸ animal)* nasty, vicious; *(▸ personne)* wicked; *(haineux)* nasty, spiteful, wicked; *(remarque)* spiteful, nasty, malicious; **un regard m.** a nasty *or* wicked look; **il n'est pas m.** *(pas malveillant)* there's no harm in him, he's harmless; *(pas dangereux)* he won't do you any harm; **en fait, ce n'est pas une méchante femme** she means no harm *or* she's not that bad, really; **je ne voudrais pas être m., mais vous avez une sale tête aujourd'hui!** I don't want to be nasty, but you look dreadful today!
2 *(très désagréable)* horrible, horrid, nasty; **ne sois pas si m. avec moi** don't be so nasty *or* horrible to me; **de fort méchante humeur** in a (really) foul mood; **il s'est mis sur le dos une méchante affaire** *ou* **querelle** he's got himself into some nasty business
3 *(enfant)* naughty, bad; **la dame me dira si vous avez été méchants** the lady will tell me if you've been naughty
4 *(grave)* nasty, very bad; **il a attrapé une méchante grippe** he caught a nasty dose of flu; *Fam* **ça n'était pas bien m., finalement, cette piqûre/ce permis?** the injection/driving test wasn't that bad after all, was it?
5 *(avant le nom) Fam (formidable)* amazing, terrific, great; **j'avais une méchante envie de dormir/lui casser la figure** I had an incredible urge to sleep/to smash his face in
6 *(avant le nom) (pitoyable)* pathetic, wretched, miserable; **elle essayait de vendre deux ou trois méchantes salades** she was trying to sell a couple of pathetic-looking lettuces
7 *Can Fam (mauvais)* foul, awful; **la soupe n'est pas méchante** the soup isn't bad at all◻, *Br* the soup isn't half bad; **il fait m.** the weather's lousy
8 *Can Fam (incorrect)* wrong◻; **le m. numéro** the wrong number
NM,F 1 *(en langage enfantin)* naughty child; **la poupée, c'est une méchante!** naughty dolly!; **faire le m.** to turn nasty **2** *(dans un film, dans un livre)* baddy, bad guy **3** *Can Fam* **faire sortir le m.** *(se défouler)* to let it all out

mèche [mɛʃ] **NF 1** *(de cheveux)* lock; **se faire (faire) des mèches** to have highlights *or* streaks put in; **mèches folles** wispy curls; **une m. rebelle** a wayward strand of hair; **une m. dans les yeux** (a strand of) hair in his/her eyes
2 *(pour lampe, bougie, explosifs, feu d'artifice)* wick; *(pour canon)* match; *(de mine)* fuse; *Fam* **découvrir** *ou* **éventer la m.** to uncover the plot◻
3 *Tech (de perceuse)* bit
4 *(de câble etc)* core, heart; *(de fouet)* lash; *Élec* **charbon à m.** cored carbon
5 *Menuis* auger, gimlet; **m. anglaise** *ou* **à trois pointes** centre bit; **m. hélicoïdale** twist bit, twist drill
6 *Méd (pour coaguler)* pack; *(pour drainer)* (gauze) wick
7 *Fam (locutions)* **être de m. avec qn** to be in league *or* in cahoots with sb; **ils sont de m. avec les dignitaires du coin** they're hand in glove with the local dignitaries; **ils étaient de m.** they were in it together; **il n'y a pas m.** no way, no chance; *Can* **il y a une m.** ages ago, a long time ago◻; *Can* **à une m. de** far away from◻, quite a distance from◻

méchoui [meʃwi] **NM** *(repas)* barbecue *(of a whole sheep roasted on a spit)*; *(fête)* barbecue (party)

mécompte [mekɔ̃t] **NM 1** *Littéraire (désillusion)* disappointment, disillusionment **2** *Vieilli (erreur)* miscalculation, error

méconium [mekɔnjɔm] **NM** *Méd* meconium

méconnais *etc voir* **méconnaître**

méconnaissable [mekɔnɛsabl] **ADJ** *(à peine reconnaissable)* hardly recognizable; *(non reconnaissable)* unrecognizable; **sans sa barbe il est m.** you wouldn't recognize him without his beard; **dix ans après, elle était m.** ten years later she had changed beyond recognition

méconnaissait *etc voir* **méconnaître**

méconnaissance [mekɔnɛsɑ̃s] **NF 1** *(ignorance)* ignorance, lack of knowledge; **il a fait preuve d'une totale m. du sujet** he displayed a complete lack of knowledge of the subject; **par m. des faits** through ignorance of the facts, through not being acquainted with the facts; **la m. du règlement vous exposerait à des poursuites** ignorance of the regulations may render you liable to prosecution **2** *(incompréhension)* lack of comprehension *or* understanding **3** *(refus de reconnaître comme valable ▸ d'un droit, d'une loi)* disregard

méconnaître **[91]** [mekɔnɛtr] **VT** *Littéraire* **1** *(ignorer)* to be unaware of
2 *(ne pas reconnaître)* to fail to recognize; **sans vouloir m. ce qu'ils ont fait pour nous** while not wishing to minimize *or* to underestimate what they have done for us; **il était méconnu de ses contemporains** he went unrecognized by his contemporaries
3 *(mal comprendre)* to fail to understand; *(personne)* to misunderstand, to misjudge; **c'est m. le milieu universitaire!** you're/he's/*etc* misjudging the academic world!; **c'est le m. que de le croire chauvin** if you think he's chauvinistic, you don't really know him
4 *(négliger ▸ devoir)* to disregard

méconnu, -e [mekɔny] **ADJ** *(incompris)* unappreciated, unrecognized; *(peu connu)* obscure; **un coin m. mais très joli de la Bretagne** a little-known but very pretty part of Brittany; **rester m.** *(non apprécié)* to go unrecognized, to remain unappreciated; *(sans gloire)* to remain unknown; **malgré son grand talent, il est mort pauvre et m.** in spite of his great talent he died penniless and in obscurity; **mes mérites sont méconnus** my merits have never been acknowledged

méconnut *etc voir* **méconnaître**

mécontent, -e [mekɔ̃tɑ̃, -ɑ̃t] **ADJ 1** *(insatisfait)* displeased (**de** with); **elle est très mécontente du travail du plombier** she is very dissatisfied with the plumber's work; **je ne suis pas mécontente de mes résultats** I am not altogether dissatisfied *or* unhappy with my results; **nous ne sommes pas mécontents que tout soit terminé** we are not sorry that it's all over **2** *(fâché)* annoyed; **il s'est montré très m. de ma décision** he was very annoyed at my decision
NM,F 1 *(gén)* complainer, grumbler, moaner **2** *Pol* **les mécontents** the discontented, the disgruntled; **cette politique va faire des mécontents** this measure is going to displease quite a few people

mécontentement [mekɔ̃tɑ̃tmɑ̃] **NM 1** *(agitation sociale)* discontent, unrest; **il y a un m. croissant chez les étudiants** there is growing discontent *or* unrest amongst students; **cela risque de provoquer le m. des agriculteurs** that might anger the farmers; **c'est un sujet de m.** it's a source of discontent *or* dissatisfaction; **m. populaire** popular unrest **2** *(agacement)* annoyance; **marquer** *ou* **exprimer son m.** to show *or* express one's annoyance *or* displeasure

mécontenter **[3]** [mekɔ̃tɑ̃te] **VT** *(déplaire à)* to fail to please, to displease; *(irriter)* to annoy, to irritate; **la réforme risque de m. les milieux d'affaires** the reform might anger business circles

Mecque [mɛk] **NF 1** *Géog* **La M.** Mecca **2** *Fig* **la M. des surfeurs** a mecca for surfers

mécréant, -e [mekreɑ̃, -ɑ̃t] *Littéraire* **ADJ** infidel, unbelieving
NM,F infidel, miscreant

> Il faut noter que le nom anglais **miscreant** est un faux ami. Il signifie **scélérat**.

mecton [mɛktɔ̃] **NM** *Fam* guy, *Br* bloke

MÉDAF [medaf] **NM** *Fin (abrév* **modèle d'évaluation des actifs***)* CAPM

médaille [medaj] **NF 1** *(pour célébrer, récompenser)* medal; **m. d'or/d'argent/de bronze** gold/silver/bronze medal; **être m. d'or** *(sportif)* to be a gold medallist, to be a gold medal winner; **détenir la m. du 60 mètres** to hold the medal for the 60 metres; **m. d'honneur** = medal for honourable service in a profession; **m. du travail** medal for long service; *Prov* **toute m. a son revers** every rose has its thorn **2** *(pour identifier)* (official) badge; *(de chat, de chien)* (identity) disc *or* tag **3** *(bijou)* pendant; **une m. de la Vierge** a medal of the Virgin Mary; **m. pieuse** holy medal

médaillé, -e [medaje] **ADJ** *(soldat)* decorated; *Sport* medal-holding *(avant n)*

NM,F 1 *Admin & Mil* medal-holder; **les médaillés du travail** holders of long-service medals **2** *Sport* medallist; **les médaillés olympiques** the Olympic medallists

médaillier [medaje] **NM 1** *(collection)* medal collection **2** *(meuble)* medal cabinet

médaillon [medajɔ̃] **NM 1** *(bijou)* locket
2 *Culin* medallion
3 *(élément décoratif)* medallion
4 *TV, Cin & Journ* inset

médecin [medsɛ̃] **NM 1** *(docteur)* doctor, physician; **aller chez le m.** to go to the doctor('s); **une femme m.** a woman doctor; **m. agréé** = doctor whose fees are partially reimbursed by the social security system; **m. des armées** army medical officer; **m. de bord** ship's doctor; **m. de campagne** country doctor; **m. consultant** consultant; **m. conventionné** = doctor who meets the French social security criteria, *Br* ≃ NHS doctor; **m. de famille** family doctor; **m. généraliste** *Br* general practitioner, GP, *Am* family doctor *or* physician; **m. des hôpitaux** hospital doctor; **m. légiste** forensic expert *or* scientist, *Am* medical examiner; **m. de quartier** local doctor; **m. spécialiste** specialist (physician); **m. traitant** attending physician; **qui est votre m. (traitant)?** who is your (regular) doctor?; **m. du travail** *(dans le privé)* company doctor; *(dans le secteur public)* health *or Br* medical officer; **Médecins du monde, Médecins sans frontières** = organizations providing medical aid to victims of war and disasters, especially in the Third World **2** *Fig Littéraire* **m. de l'âme** *ou* **des âmes** *(confesseur)* confessor

médecine [medsin] **NF 1** *(gén)* medicine; **exercer la m.** to practise medicine; **docteur en m.** doctor of medicine, MD; **médecines alternatives, médecines douces** alternative medicine; **m. générale** general practice; **m. par les herbes** herbalism; **m. homéopathique** homeopathic medicine, homeopathy; **m. interne** internal medicine; **m. légale** forensic medicine; **m. opératoire** surgery; **médecines parallèles** alternative medicine; **m. préventive** preventive *or* preventative medicine; **m. sportive** sports medicine; **m. traditionnelle** traditional medicine; **m. du travail** industrial *or* occupational medicine **2** *Univ* medicine, medical studies; **étudiant en m.** medical student; **il fait (sa) m., il est en m.** he's studying medicine, he's a medical student; **elle est en troisième année de m.** she's in her third year at medical school, she's a third-year medical student **3** *Arch (remède)* medicine, remedy

> Il faut noter que le nom anglais **medicine** signifie également **médicament, remède**.

Medef [medɛf] **NM** *(abrév* **Mouvement des Entreprises de France)** French employers' association, *Br* ≃ CBI

média [medja] **NM** medium; **les médias** the media; **faire campagne dans tous les médias** to carry out a media-wide advertising campaign; **médias électroniques** electronic media; **m. de masse** mass media; **médias numériques** digital media; **médias numériques interactifs** interactive digital media; **m. publicitaire** advertising media; **médias de télécommunication** telecommunications media; **les nouveaux médias** new media

médial, -ale, -aux, -ales [medjal, -o] **ADJ** *Ling (lettre)* medial
• **médiale NF** *(en statistique)* median

médian, -e [medjɑ̃, -an] **ADJ 1** *Géom* median **2** *Ling* medial
• **médiane NF 1** *(en statistique)* median **2** *Ling* mid vowel

médiateur, -trice [medjatœr, -tris] **ADJ** mediating, mediatory

NM,F intermediary, go-between, mediator; **servir de m.** to act as a go-between; **le président sert de m. entre les deux factions** the president is mediating *or* arbitrating between the two factions

NM 1 *Ind* arbitrator, mediator **2** *Admin & Pol* mediator, ombudsman; **le M. européen** the European Ombudsman; **le M. (de la République)** *Br* ≃ the Parliamentary Commissioner, ≃ the Ombudsman
• **médiatrice NF** *Géom* midperpendicular

médiathèque [medjatɛk] **NF** media library

médiation [medjasjɔ̃] **NF** *(entremise) & Pol* mediation; *Ind* arbitration; **il a fallu la m. de l'évêque** the bishop had to mediate

médiatique [medjatik] **ADJ** media *(avant n)*; **un événement m.** a media *or Péj* a media-staged event; **il est très m.** *(il passe bien à la télévision)* he comes over well on television; *(il exploite les médias)* he uses the media very successfully

médiatisation [medjatizasjɔ̃] **NF** *(popularisation)* media coverage; **la m. d'un événement** the media coverage *or* attention given to an event; **on assiste à une m. croissante de la production littéraire** literary works are getting more and more media exposure; **nous déplorons la m. de la politique** it's a shame to see politics being turned into a media event

médiatiser [3] [medjatize] **VT** *(populariser)* to popularize through the (mass) media; *(événement)* to give media coverage to; **m. les élections/la guerre** to turn elections/the war into a media event

médiator [medjatɔr] **NM** *Mus* plectrum

médiatrice [medjatris] *voir* **médiateur**

médical, -e, -aux, -ales [medikal, -o] **ADJ** medical

médicalement [medikalmɑ̃] **ADV** medically

médicalisation [medikalizasjɔ̃] **NF 1** *(d'une région)* **la m. des pays pauvres** the provision of health care to poor countries **2** *(d'un état, d'une pathologie)* medicalization; **la m. croissante de la grossesse** the increasing reliance on medical intervention during pregnancy

médicalisé, -e [medikalize] **ADJ** medicalized; **accouchement m.** medicalized childbirth; **maison de retraite médicalisée** nursing home *(providing medical care)*

médicaliser [3] [medikalize] **VT 1** *(région, pays)* to provide with health care **2** *(maternité, vieillesse)* to medicalize, to increase medical intervention in

médicament [medikamɑ̃] **NM** medicine, drug; **prends tes médicaments** take your medicine; **est-ce que vous prenez des médicaments?** are you on any kind of medication?; **m. de confort** = pharmaceutical product not considered to be essential and not fully reimbursed by the French social security system; **m. délivré sans ordonnance, m. en vente libre** medicine issued without a prescription, over-the-counter drug; **m. délivré** *ou* **en vente sur ordonnance** drug available on prescription, prescription drug; **m. homéopathique** homeopathic drug; **m. préventif** *ou* **prophylactique** preventive

médicamenteux, -euse [medikamɑ̃tø, -øz] **ADJ** medicinal

médication [medikasjɔ̃] **NF** medication, (medicinal) treatment

médicinal, -e, -aux, -ales [medisinal, -o] **ADJ** medicinal

medicine-ball [medisinbol] *(pl* **medicine-balls)** **NM** medicine ball

médico-éducatif, -ive [medikoedykatif, -iv] *(mpl* **médico-éducatifs**, *fpl* **médico-éducatives)** **ADJ** **institut m.** special needs school

médico-légal, -e [medikɔlegal] *(mpl* **médico-légaux** [-o], *fpl* **médico-légales)** **ADJ** forensic, medico-legal; **institut m.** institute of forensic medicine

médico-pédagogique [medikɔpedagɔʒik] *(pl* **médico-pédagogiques)** **ADJ** **institut m.** special school *(for children with special needs or learning disabilities)*

médico-social, -e [medikɔsɔsjal] *(mpl* **médico-sociaux** [-o], *fpl* **médico-sociales)** **ADJ** medico-social; **centre m.** health centre; **équipe médico-sociale** health and social services team; **services médico-sociaux** health and social services network

médiéval, -e, -aux, -ales [medjeval, -o] **ADJ** medieval; **l'époque médiévale** the medieval period, the Middle Ages

médiéviste [medjevist] **NMF** medievalist

médina [medina] **NF** medina

médiocre [medjɔkr] **ADJ 1** *(rendement, efficacité, qualité etc)* mediocre, poor; **cette année les rendements en blé ont été médiocres** wheat production has been mediocre *or* poor this year; **elle est m. en mathématiques** she's pretty mediocre at mathematics; **temps m. sur toute la France** poor weather throughout France **2** *(quelconque)* second-rate, mediocre; **il a fait une carrière m.** his career has been unsuccessful **3** *(avant le nom) (piètre)* poor; **un livre de m. intérêt** a book of little interest

NMF *(personne)* nonentity; **dans cette classe, il n'y a que des médiocres** there are only mediocrities in this class

NM *(médiocrité)* mediocrity; **se complaire dans le m.** to revel in mediocrity

médiocrement [medjɔkrəmɑ̃] **ADV** indifferently, poorly; **un enfant m. doué pour les langues** a child with no great gift for languages; **m. satisfait, il décida de recommencer** not very satisfied, he decided to start again; **j'ai répondu assez m. à l'examen oral** my answers in the oral exam were rather poor; **elle chante très m.** she's a very mediocre singer; **la station n'est que m. équipée** the resort's facilities are below average

médiocrité [medjɔkrite] **NF 1** *(chose)* mediocrity, poor quality **2** *(personne)* nonentity

médire [103] [medir] **médire de VT IND** *(critiquer)* to speak ill of, to run down; *(calomnier)* to spread scandal about, to malign

USAGE ABSOLU **arrête de m.!** stop criticizing!

médisance [medizɑ̃s] **NF 1** *(dénigrement)* gossip, scandalmongering; **c'est de la m.!** that's slander!; **victime de la m.** victim of (malicious) gossip; **les gens qui se livrent à la m.** scandalmongers **2** *(propos)* gossip; **les médisances de ses collègues lui ont fait du tort** his/her colleagues' (malicious) gossip has damaged his/her good name

médisant, -e [medizɑ̃, -ɑ̃t] **ADJ** slanderous; *(personne)* scandalmongering; **qu'est-ce que tu peux être m.!** what a scandalmonger you are!; **sans vouloir être m., je dois dire que je le trouve un peu naïf** no malice intended, but I have to say that I find him a bit naïve

NM,F *(auteur de ragots)* gossip, gossipmonger, scandalmonger; *(auteur de diffamation)* slanderer

médisez *etc voir* **médire**

médit [medi] **PP** *voir* **médire**

méditatif, -ive [meditatif, -iv] **ADJ** meditative, contemplative, thoughtful

NM,F thinker

méditation [meditasjɔ̃] **NF 1** *Psy & Rel* meditation; **faire de la m.** to meditate; **m. transcendantale** transcendental meditation **2** *(réflexion)* meditation, thought; **plongé dans la m.** lost in thought; **le fruit de mes méditations** the fruit of my meditation *or* meditations

méditative [meditativ] *voir* **méditatif**

méditer [3] [medite] **VT 1** *(réfléchir à)* to reflect on *or* upon, to ponder (upon); **elle veut encore m. sa décision** she wants to think some more about her decision; **m. une vengeance** to contemplate vengeance **2** *(projeter)* to plan; **qu'est-ce qu'ils méditent encore?** what are they planning now?; **m. de faire qch** to be contemplating doing sth

VI to meditate; **m. sur** to meditate on, to think about

Méditerranée [mediterane] **NF la (mer) M.** the Mediterranean (Sea); **en M.** in the Mediterranean; **une croisière sur la M.** a Mediterranean cruise

méditerranéen, -enne [mediteraneɛ̃, -ɛn] **ADJ** Mediterranean

• **Méditerranéen, -enne** **NM,F** **1** *(de la Méditerranée)* Mediterranean, Southern European *(from the Mediterranean area)* **2** *(en France)* Southerner

médium [medjɔm] **NMF** *(spirite)* medium
NM **1** *Mus* middle register **2** *(support)* medium **3** *(liant)* medium, vehicle

médius [medjys] **NM** middle finger

médoc[1] [medɔk] **NM** Médoc (wine)

médoc[2] [medɔk] **NM** *Fam* medicine[□], meds

médullaire [medyler] **ADJ** *Anat* medullary

méduse [medyz] **NF** jellyfish, *Spéc* medusa

méduser **[3]** [medyze] **VT** to astound, to stun, to stupefy; **sa réponse m'a médusé** his/her reply stunned me

meeting [mitiŋ] **NM** (public) meeting; **m. aérien** air show; **m. d'athlétisme** athletics *Br* meeting *or Am* meet

méfait [mefɛ] **NM** *(mauvaise action)* misdeed, wrong, wrongdoing; *(délit)* offence; *Jur* misdemeanour
• **méfaits** **NMPL** *(ravages)* **les méfaits du temps/de la guerre** the ravages of time/war; **les méfaits du laxisme parental** the damaging effects of a lack of parental discipline; **les méfaits de l'alcoolisme** the ill effects of *or* the damage done by alcoholism; **les méfaits de la télévision** the harm caused by television

méfiance [mefjɑ̃s] **NF** *(manque de confiance)* distrust; *(suspicion)* mistrust, suspicion; **avoir de la m. envers qn** to distrust sb; *(avoir de la suspicion)* to mistrust sb, to be suspicious of sb; **avoir de la m. envers tout ce qui est nouveau** to be distrustful of *or* to be wary of *or* to distrust anything new; **sa m. envers les étrangers** his/her distrust of foreigners; **éveiller la m. de qn** to make sb suspicious; **il renifla le paquet avec m.** he warily sniffed the parcel; **elle est sans m.** she has a trusting nature; **m.!** be careful!, be on your guard!; *Prov* **m. est mère de sûreté** better safe than sorry

méfiant, -e [mefjɑ̃, -ɑ̃t] **ADJ** *(n'ayant pas confiance)* distrustful; *(suspicieux)* mistrustful, suspicious; **m. de nature** naturally distrustful; **il n'est pas assez m.** he is too unsuspecting *or* trusting; **être m. envers qch** to be sceptical of sth; **on n'est jamais assez m.** you can never be too careful
NM,F doubter, suspicious *or* doubting person

méfier **[9]** [mefje] **se méfier** **VPR** **1** *(faire attention)* to be careful *or* wary; **on ne se méfie jamais assez** you can't be too careful; **méfie-toi!** be careful!, watch out!, be on your guard! **2** **se m. de qn** to distrust sb; *(avoir de la suspicion)* to mistrust sb, to be suspicious of sb; **se m. de qch** to be wary of sth, to be on one's guard against sth; **il se méfie même de ses proches** he is even suspicious of *or* he even mistrusts his own family; **méfie-toi de lui/de son air doux** don't trust him/his mild manners; **méfiez-vous des pickpockets** beware of pickpockets; **il faut se m. des apparences** you shouldn't trust appearances; *Fam* **méfiez-vous qu'ils ne se sauvent pas** watch out *or* mind they don't run away

méforme [mefɔrm] **NF** unfitness, lack of fitness; **après quelques jours de m.** after a few days off form

MEG [emɔʒe] **NM** *Méd (abrév* **magnétoencéphalographie)** MEG

méga [mega] **NM** *Fam Ordinat* megabyte[□], meg

> **MÉGA-** PREFIX
>
> • This prefix of scientific origin has come to prominence with the advent of mass computing and its *megabytes* (**mégaoctets**) and *megaflops* (**mégaflops**). It has since passed into colloquial language as an INTENSIFIER:
> **méga-promo sur toute la gamme!** prices slashed across the whole range!; **on a fait une méga-teuf** we had a massive party; **ce film, c'est le méga délire!** this film is absolutely brilliant!; **c'est méga cool!** wicked!
>
> As far as spelling is concerned, there seems to be some hesitation as to the use of the hyphen.
>
> • It is worth noting that, in colloquial computing speak, **mégaoctet** or **mégabit** are often abbreviated to just **méga** *(meg* in English), eg:
> **100 mégas d'espace Web perso** 100 megs of personal Web space; **accès ADSL jusqu'à 8 mégas** broadband access up to 8 megs

mégabit [megabit] **NM** *Ordinat* megabit; **mégabits par seconde** megabits per second

mégacycle [megasikl] **NM** megacycle

mégaflop [megaflɔp] **NM** *Ordinat* megaflop

mégahertz [megaerts] **NM** megahertz

mégajoule [megaʒul] **NM** megajoule

mégalithe [megalit] **NM** megalith

mégalithique [megalitik] **ADJ** megalithic

mégalomane [megalɔman] **ADJ** megalomaniac
NMF megalomaniac

mégalomanie [megalɔmani] **NF** megalomania

mégalopole [megalɔpɔl], **mégalopolis** [megalɔpɔlis] **NF** megalopolis

méga-octet [megaɔktɛ] *(pl* **méga-octets)** **NM** *Ordinat* megabyte

mégaphone [megafɔn] **NM** megaphone, *Br* loud-hailer, *Am* bullhorn

mégapixel [megapiksel] **NM** *Ordinat* megapixel

mégarde [megard] **par mégarde** **ADV** *(par inattention)* inadvertently, by accident, accidentally; *(par erreur)* by mistake, inadvertently; *(sans le vouloir)* unintentionally, inadvertently, accidentally

mégastore [megastɔr] **NF** megastore

mégatonne [megatɔn] **NF** megaton

mégawatt [megawat] **NM** megawatt

mégère [meʒɛr] **NF** shrew, harridan

mégot [mego] **NM** *(de cigarette)* cigarette butt *or* end; *(de cigare)* cigar butt

mégotage [megɔtaʒ] **NM** *Fam* skimping, scrimping (and saving); **avec lui, c'était des mégotages sur tout** he was always scrimping and saving *or* always pinching and scraping

mégoter **[3]** [megɔte] **VI** *Fam* to skimp, to scrimp; **on ne va pas m. pour quelques euros** let's not quibble about a few euros; **arrête de m., achète du vrai Champagne!** don't be stingy, buy real champagne!; **m. sur qch** to skimp *or* to scrimp on sth; **il a pas mégoté sur le piment** he didn't skimp on the chilli

méhari [meari] *(pl* **méharis** *ou* **méhara** [-ra]) **NM** racing camel *or* dromedary, mehari

méhariste [mearist] **NMF** dromedary rider
NM = mounted soldier of the French Camel Corps in North Africa

meilleur, -e [mejœr] **ADJ** **1** *(comparatif)* better; **elle est meilleure que lui** she is better than him *or* than he is; **il est m. en anglais qu'en allemand** he is better at English than German; **il est m. père que mari** he is a better father than he is a husband; **il est m. danseur que coureur** he is a better dancer than he is a runner, he is better at dancing than running; **je ne connais rien de m.** I don't know anything better; **il n'y a rien de m., il n'y a pas m.** there's nothing to beat it, there's nothing better; **c'est m. avec de la crème** it's better *or* it tastes better with cream; **c'est m. marché** it's cheaper; *Suisse* **avoir m. temps de faire qch** to be better off doing sth; **t'as m. temps de te taire** you'd be better off keeping quiet **2** *(superlatif)* **le m. élève** *(de tous)* the best pupil; *(de deux)* the better pupil; **son m. ami** his/her best friend; **c'est le m. des maris** he's the best husband in the world; **nous sommes les meilleurs amis du monde** we're the best of friends; **avec la meilleure volonté** with the best will in the world; **dans le m. des mondes** in the best of all possible worlds; **meilleurs vœux** best wishes; **meilleurs vœux de prompt rétablissement** get well soon; **m. souvenir de Cannes** *(sur une carte postale)* greetings from Cannes; *(en fin de lettre)* best wishes from Cannes; **information prise aux meilleures sources** information from the most reliable sources; **il appartient au m. monde** he moves in the best circles
NM,F **le m.** *(de tous)* the best; *(des deux)* the better; **seuls les meilleurs participeront à la compétition** only the best (players) will take part in the competition; **que le m. gagne!** may the best man win!
NM **le m.** *(de tous)* the best; *(des deux)* the better; **garder le m. pour la fin** to save the best till last; **mange-le, c'est le m.** eat it, it's the best part; **il a donné** *ou* **il y a mis le m. de lui-même** he gave his all, he gave of his best; **et le m. de l'histoire, c'est que c'est lui qui m'avait invité** and the best part of it is that he's the one who'd invited me; **pour le m. et pour le pire** for better or for worse; *Sport* **prendre le m. sur son adversaire** to get the better of one's opponent
ADV **il fait m. aujourd'hui** the weather's *or* it's better today; **il fait m. dans la chambre** *(plus chaud)* it's warmer in the bedroom; *(plus frais)* it's cooler in the bedroom
• **meilleure** **NF** *Fam* **tu ne connais pas la meilleure** *(fin de l'histoire)* you haven't heard the best bit yet; *(histoire)* wait until I tell you this one; **ça alors, c'est la meilleure (de l'année)!** that's the best (one) I've heard in a long time!; **ça c'est la meilleure!** that just tops it all!; **j'en passe, et des meilleures** and I could go on

méiose [mejoz] **NF** *Biol* meiosis

méiotique [mejɔtik] **ADJ** *Biol* meiotic

méjuger **[17]** [meʒyʒe] *Littéraire* **VT** to misjudge
• **méjuger de** **VT IND** to underestimate, to underrate
VPR **se méjuger** to underestimate oneself

mél [mel], **mel** [mel] **NM** *(adresse électronique)* e-mail address; *(courrier électronique)* e-mail

melæna [melena] **NM** *Méd* melaena

mélamine [melamin] **NF** melamine

mélaminé, -e [melamine] **ADJ** melamine
NM melamine

mélancolie [melɑ̃kɔli] **NF** **1** *(tristesse)* melancholy; **j'y pense avec m.** I feel melancholy when I think about it; **avoir un accès de m.** to be feeling a bit melancholy **2** *Psy & Arch* melancholia

mélancolique [melɑ̃kɔlik] **ADJ** **1** *(triste, désenchanté)* melancholy **2** *Psy* melancholic
NMF melancholic

Mélanésie [melanezi] **NF** **la M.** Melanesia

mélanésien, -enne [melanezjɛ̃, -ɛn] **ADJ** Melanesian
NM *(langue)* Melanesian
• **Mélanésien, -enne** **NM,F** Melanesian

mélange [melɑ̃ʒ] **NM** **1** *(processus)* mixing; *(de thés, de parfums, de tabacs)* blending
2 *(résultat)* mixture; *(de thés, de parfums, de tabacs)* blend; **c'est un m. de plusieurs thés/parfums** it's a blend of several teas/perfumes; **ma famille et mes collègues, ça donne un curieux m.!** my family and my colleagues, that makes for a strange mixture!; **un m. de fermeté et de gentillesse** a mixture of strictness and kindness; **pas de whisky après le vin, je ne fais pas de mélanges** no whisky after my wine, I don't mix my drinks
3 *Aut* mixture; **m. détonant/pauvre/riche** explosive/poor/rich mixture; **m. air/carburant** air/fuel mixture; **m. carburé** explosive mixture; **m. gazeux** gas mixture
4 *(en acoustique)* mixing
5 *Chim* **m. racémique** racemate
• **sans mélange** **ADJ** *(joie)* unalloyed; *(admiration)* unmitigated

mélangé, -e [melɑ̃ʒe] **ADJ** mixed; **c'est un coton m.** it's a cotton mixture

mélanger **[17]** [melɑ̃ʒe] **VT** **1** *(remuer ▸ cartes)* to shuffle; *(▸ salade)* to toss; **ajoutez le lait et mélangez** add the milk and mix (well); **m. le citron à la crème** to mix the lemon (in) with the cream **2** *(mettre ensemble)* to mix; *(thés, vins, tabacs)* to blend; *(idées, documents)* to mix up; **m. des couleurs** to blend colours; **ils ne veulent pas m. les filles et les garçons** they want to keep boys and girls separate; **mélangez les œillets rouges avec les blancs** mix the red carnations with the white ones **3** *(confondre)* to mix up; **ne mélange pas tout** don't get everything (all) mixed *or* jumbled *or* muddled up; **on a un peu trop mélangé les genres** it's a mixture of too many different styles; *Fig Hum* **il ne faut pas m. les torchons et les serviettes** (don't get them mixed up,) they're in a different class
VPR **se mélanger** **1** *(se fondre)* **se m. avec** to mix

with; **l'eau et l'huile ne se mélangent pas bien** water and oil don't mix well; **les nouveaux venus ne se mélangent pas avec les habitués du club** the newcomers don't mix *or* socialize with the regular club members **2** *(devenir indistinct)* to get mixed up; **tout se mélange dans ma tête** I'm getting all mixed up *or* muddled up **3** *Fam* **se m. les pédales** *ou* **les pinceaux (dans qch)** to get (oneself) into a muddle (with sth), to get (sth) muddled up

mélangeur [melɑ̃ʒœr] **NM 1** *(robinet) Br* mixer tap, *Am* mixing faucet **2** *(de son)* mixer **3** *TV & Cin* **m. (de production)** production mixer *or* switcher; **m. numérique** digital mixer; **m. de son** dubbing *or* sound mixer; **m. vidéo** vision mixer

mélanine [melanin] **NF** *Physiol* melanin

mélanome [melanom] **NM** *Méd* melanoma

mêlant, -e [melɑ̃, -ɑ̃t] **ADJ** *Can* **c'est pas m.** there's no doubt about it

mélasse [melas] **NF 1** *(sirop)* molasses *(singulier)*, *Br* (black) treacle **2** *Fam (brouillard)* peasouper; *Fig* **être dans la m.** *(avoir des ennuis)* to be in a jam *or* a fix *or* a pickle; *(être sans argent)* to be hard up

Melba [melba] **ADJ INV pêche/poire M.** peach/pear Melba

mêlé, -e [mele] **ADJ 1** *(mélangée)* mixed (**de** with); **du vin m. d'eau** wine mixed with water; **une société mêlée** a mixed society; **des sentiments (très) mêlés** (very) mixed feelings; **un chagrin m. de pitié** sorrow mixed *or* mingled with pity **2** *(emmêlé)* **dans cette histoire, la politique et le crime sont très mêlés** politics and crime are closely linked in this business; **tout est m. dans son suicide: la drogue, sa célébrité déclinante...** everything played a part in his/her suicide: drugs, his/her declining fame... **3** *Can (désorienté)* disoriented; *(embrouillé)* mixed-up; **être m. dans ses papiers** to be confused *or* mixed-up

• **mêlée NF 1** *(combat)* fray, melee; *Fig* **être au-dessus de la mêlée** to be above the fray; *Fig* **rester au-dessus de la mêlée** to stay above the fray, to remain aloof; *Fig* **entrer dans la mêlée** to join *or* enter the fray; **elle reste à l'écart de la mêlée politique** she keeps out of the hurly-burly of politics **2** *(bousculade)* scuffle, free-for-all; *(désordre)* commotion, confusion; **j'ai perdu mon parapluie dans la mêlée** I lost my umbrella in the general confusion; **il y a eu une mêlée générale** there was a general free-for-all **3** *(au rugby)* scrum, scrummage; **effondrer/tourner la mêlée** to collapse/to wheel the scrum; **mêlée ouverte** *(gén)* loose scrum; *(balle par terre)* ruck; *(balle en main)* maul

méléna [melena] = **melæna**

mêler [4] [mele] **VT 1** *(mélanger)* to mix (**à** *or* **avec** with); **m. deux races de chien** to cross two breeds of dog; **je n'aime pas m. les styles de mobilier** I don't like mixing different styles of furniture

2 *(allier* ▸ *sujet: personne)* to combine; *(*▸ *sujet: chose)* to be a mixture *or* combination of; **elle mêle la rigueur à la fantaisie** she combines *or* mixes seriousness with light-heartedness; **son sourire mêlait la fausseté et la veulerie** his/her smile was a mixture of falseness and cowardly indecision

3 *(embrouiller* ▸ *documents, papiers)* to mix *or* to muddle *or* to jumble up; *(*▸ *cartes, dominos)* to shuffle; **j'ai mêlé tous les dossiers** I've got all the files mixed up

4 *(impliquer)* **m. qn à** to involve sb in, to get sb involved in; **m. qn à la conversation** to bring sb into the conversation; **être mêlé à un scandale** to be involved in *or* linked with a scandal

VPR se mêler 1 *(se mélanger)* to mix, to mingle; *(sons, parfums)* to blend; **les styles se mêlent harmonieusement** the styles blend well together

2 se m. à *ou* **avec** *(s'unir)* to mix *or* to mingle with; **ses cris se mêlèrent au bruit de la foule** his/her shouts mingled with the noise of the crowd; **se m. à la foule** to mingle with *or* blend into the crowd

3 se m. à *(participer à)* to take part in, to join in; **se m. à la conversation** to take part *or* to join in the conversation; **se m. à un cortège/une manifestation** to take part in a procession/a demonstration

4 se m. de *(de manière inopportune)* to interfere *or* to meddle in, to get mixed up in; **se m. des affaires d'autrui** to meddle *or* to interfere in other people's business; **elle se mêle de ce qui ne la regarde pas** she is interfering in things that are no concern of hers; **mêlez-vous de ce qui vous regarde** mind your own business; **de quoi se mêle-t-il?** what business is it of his?; *Fam* **de quoi je me mêle?** mind your own business!; **si le mauvais temps s'en mêle, la récolte est perdue** if the weather decides to turn nasty, the crop will be ruined; **il se mêle de tout** he is very nosy; *Péj* **il se mêle de poésie maintenant!** so he's started dabbling in poetry now, has he?

mélèze [melez] **NM** *Bot* larch

méli-mélo [melimelo] *(pl* **mélis-mélos)NM** *(d'objets)* mess, jumble; *(d'idées, de dates)* mishmash, *Br* hotchpotch, *Am* hodgepodge; **quel m.!** what a mess!

mélioratif, -ive [meljɔratif, -iv] **ADJ** meliorative

NM meliorative

mélisse [melis] **NF** *Bot* (lemon) balm

mélo [melo] *Fam* **ADJ** *(qui tient du mélodrame)* melodramatic[□], over-the-top, *Br* OTT; *(qui donne dans la sensiblerie)* sentimental[□], mushy, *Am* schmaltzy

NM melodrama[□]; **nous sommes en plein m.!** this is melodramatic *or* blood-and-thunder stuff!

mélodie [melɔdi] **NF 1** *(air de musique)* melody, tune; *(en composition)* melody, song **2** *Fig (d'une langue)* melodiousness; **la m. des vers de Lamartine** the melodic quality of Lamartine's verse

mélodieuse [melɔdjøz] *voir* **mélodieux**

mélodieusement [melɔdjøzmɑ̃] **ADV** melodiously, tunefully

mélodieux, -euse [melɔdjø, -øz] **ADJ** *(son)* melodious; *(air)* tuneful; *(voix)* melodious, musical; **de sa voix mélodieuse** in his/her melodious *or* musical voice

mélodique [melɔdik] **ADJ** melodic

mélodiste [melɔdist] **NMF** melodist

mélodramatique [melɔdramatik] **ADJ** melodramatic

mélodrame [melɔdram] **NM** melodrama; **nous sommes en plein m.!** this is like (something out of) a melodrama!

mélomane [melɔman] **ADJ** music-loving; **êtes-vous m.?** do you like music?, are you musical?

NMF music lover

melon [məlɔ̃] **NM 1** *Bot* melon; **m. d'eau** watermelon; **m. d'Espagne** honeydew melon **2** *(chapeau) Br* bowler (hat), *Am* derby **3** *Fam (Maghrébin)* = offensive term used to refer to a North African Arab

melonnière [məlɔnjer] **NF** *Hort* melon bed *or* patch

mélopée [melɔpe] **NF 1** *(mélodie)* lament, threnody **2** *Antiq* melopoeia

MEM [mɛm] **NF** *Ordinat (abrév* **mémoire morte)** ROM

membrane [mɑ̃bran] **NF 1** *Biol* membrane **2** *Mus* membrane, skin **3** *Tél* diaphragm

membraneux, -euse [mɑ̃branø, -øz] **ADJ** membranous

membre [mɑ̃br] **NM 1** *Anat* limb; **m. inférieur/supérieur** lower/upper limb; **m. (viril)** (male) member; *Méd* **m. fantôme** phantom limb

2 *Zool* limb; **m. antérieur** foreleg, fore limb; **m. postérieur** back leg, rear limb

3 *(adhérent)* member; **m. d'un comité** committee member; **m. du conseil d'administration** member of the board, board member; **être m. d'un syndicat** to belong to *or* to be a member of a union; **devenir m. d'une association** to join an association; **envoyer une lettre à tous les membres** to send a letter to (all) the members *or* to the entire membership; **elle a été élue m. de l'Académie** she was elected to the Academy; **ils le considèrent comme un m. de la famille** they treat him as one of the family; **tous les membres de la famille** the whole family; *Can* **M. de l'Assemblée Nationale** Member of the National Assembly; **les États membres** the member states; **les pays membres** the member countries; **m. bienfaiteur** supporter; **m. fondateur** founder, founding member; **m. honoraire** honorary member; **m. du Parlement** member of Parliament; **m. du Parlement européen** Member of the European Parliament, MEP, Euro-MP; **m. du parti** party member; **m. permanent** permanent member; **m. suppléant** deputy member

4 *Math* member; **premier/second m. d'une équation** left-hand/right-hand member of an equation

5 *Gram* **m. de phrase** member *or* clause of a sentence

6 *Archit & Géol* member

7 *Naut* timber, rib

membré, -e [mɑ̃bre] **ADJ** *Littéraire* **bien m.** strong-limbed; **mal m.** weak-limbed

membrure [mɑ̃bryr] **NF 1** *(d'un corps humain)* limbs; **homme à forte m.** strong-limbed *or* powerfully built man **2** *Constr* member; *Menuis* frame **3** *Naut (en bois)* rib; *(en métal)* frame

MÊME [mɛm]

ADJ
• same **1, 2**
• myself/yourself/*etc* **4**
• very **3**

PRON INDÉFINI
• same

ADV
• even

ADJ INDÉFINI 1 *(avant le nom) (identique, semblable)* same; **elles sont nées le m. jour** they were born on the same day; **mettre deux choses sur le m. plan** to put two things on the same level; **en m. temps** at the same time

2 *(en corrélation avec "que")* **il a le m. âge que moi** he's the same age as me; **j'utilise le m. parfum que toi** I use the same perfume as you (do); **j'ai la m. voiture qu'elle** I have the same car as her *or* as she does

3 *(après le nom) (servant à souligner)* **elle est la bonté m.** she is kindness itself; **ce sont ses paroles mêmes** those are his/her very words; **ils sont repartis le soir m.** they left that very evening; **je l'ai fait le jour m.** I did it that (very) same day; **aujourd'hui m.** this very day; **il habite ici m.** he lives in this very place/house; **la dernière version, celle-là m. qui est arrivée hier** the latest version, the one which arrived yesterday; **c'est le titre m. que vous avez à traduire** it's the title itself *or* the actual title that you have to translate; **c'est cela m. que je cherchais** it's the very thing I was looking for; **c'est cela m.** *(c'est exact)* that's it exactly

4 moi-m. myself; **toi-m.** yourself; **lui-m.** himself/itself; **elle-m.** herself/itself; **soi-m.** oneself; **nous-mêmes** ourselves; **vous-mêmes** yourselves; **eux-/elles-mêmes** themselves; **moi-m., quand j'y pense, j'en ai des frissons** I get shivers myself when I think about it; **par toi-m.** by yourself; **j'ai dû y aller car elle-m. ne peut plus se déplacer** I had to go because she can't get about herself any more; **il l'a fait lui-m.** he did it himself; **faire qch de soi-m.** to do sth of one's own accord; **c'est lui-m. qui me l'a dit, il me l'a dit lui-m.** he told me himself; **je l'ai trouvée pareille à elle-m.** I found she hadn't changed, I found her the same as ever; **rester/être égal à soi-m.** to remain/to be true to form; **égale à elle-m., elle est restée très calme** typically *or* true to form, she remained calm; **la chose n'est pas mauvaise en elle-m.** the thing is not bad in itself *or* per se; **je pensais en moi-m. que...** I was thinking to myself that...; **menteur! – toi-m.!** liar! – liar yourself!

PRON INDÉFINI le m. the same; **elle est toujours la m.** she's still the same; **ce sont toujours les mêmes qui gagnent** it's always the same ones who win; **depuis quelque temps, leurs rapports ne sont plus les mêmes** for some time their relationship has not been the same; **cela** *ou* **ça revient (strictement) au m.** it comes to *or* amounts to (exactly) the same thing

ADV even; **m. les savants** *ou* **les savants m. peuvent se tromper** even scientists can make mistakes; **m. Paul est d'accord** even Paul agrees; **j'ai écrit, j'ai téléphoné, et j'ai m. envoyé un télégramme** I wrote, I phoned and I even sent a telegram; **je le pense et m. j'en suis sûr** I think so, in fact I'm sure of it; **elle ne va m. plus au cinéma** she doesn't even go to the cinema any more; **je ne sais m. pas l'heure qu'il est** I don't even know what time it is; **t'a-t-elle remercié? – m. pas!** did she thank you? – not even (that)!; **il y va m. quand il pleut** he goes (there) even when it rains; **il a toujours rêvé de faire ce métier, m. lorsqu'il était enfant** he always dreamed of doing this job, even when he was a child

• **à même** PRÉP **dormir à m. le sol** to sleep on the floor; **boire à m. la bouteille** to drink straight from the bottle; **je ne supporte pas la laine à m. la peau** I can't stand wool next to my skin; **des marches taillées à m. le roc** steps hewn out of the rock

• **à même de** PRÉP able to, in a position to; **être à m. de faire qch** to be able *or* in a position to do sth; **elle est à m. de vous aider** she can help you; **il n'est pas à m. de faire le voyage** he's not up to making the journey; **je serai bientôt à m. de vous en dire plus** I shall soon be able to tell you more

• **de même** ADV1 *(pareillement)* **faire de m.** to do likewise *or* the same, to follow suit; **il est parti avant la fin, moi de m.** he left before the end, and so did I; **je vous souhaite le bonsoir – moi de m.** I wish you goodnight – likewise; **Joyeux Noël – vous de m.** Merry Christmas – same to you; **il en est de m. des autres** it's the same for the others, the same is true *or* holds good for the others; **il en va de m. pour vous** the same is true for you **2** *Can (comme cela)* like this, (in) this way; **place tes mains de m. et pousse** place your hands like this and push; **quel dommage, cet accident, une belle fille de m.!** what a tragic accident, a lovely girl like that!; **qui croirait une histoire de m.?** who could believe such a story *or* a story like that?

• **de même que** CONJ just as; **de m. que qn** just like sb; **de m. que qch** just like sth; *(aussi bien que)* as well as sth; **il a refusé de travailler pour eux, de m. qu'il avait refusé de le faire pour moi** he refused to work for them, just as *or* just like he had refused to for me; **je déteste la Bretagne de m. que la Normandie** I hate Brittany just as much as Normandy

• **même que** CONJ *Fam* so much so that□; **elle roulait très vite, m. que la voiture a failli déraper** she was driving so fast that the car nearly skidded; **il va venir, m. qu'il me l'a promis!** he'll come, what's more he promised me he would!

• **même si** CONJ even if; **m. s'il me le demandait, je n'accepterais pas** even if he asked me, I wouldn't accept; **m. s'il pleut** even if it rains

mémé [meme] *Fam* NF1 *(en appellatif) (grand-mère)* grandma, granny, *Br* gran **2** *(vieille dame)* old dear; **une petite m.** an old dear **3** *Péj* old woman□

ADJ INV *Péj* dowdy, frumpy, grannyish; **elle fait très m. avec cette coiffure** that hairstyle makes her look so dowdy; **elle fait m., ta robe!** that dress makes you look like an old granny!, you look like an old frump in that dress!

mémento [memẽto] NM1 *(agenda)* diary **2** *Scol* revision notes; **m. d'histoire** history revision notes **3** *Rel* memento

mémèrage [memɛraʒ] NM *Can Fam* gossip□

mémère [memɛr] *Fam* NF1 *(en appellatif) (grand-mère)* grandma, granny, *Br* gran **2** *Péj (femme d'un certain âge)* old biddy, *Br* old dear; **une grosse m.** a fat old bag; *Hum* **le petit chien-chien à sa m.** mummy's little doggie-woggie

ADJ *Péj (style, vêtements)* dowdy, frumpy, grannyish; **faire m.** *(style, femme, vêtements)* to look dowdy *or* frumpy; **ça fait m. chez elle** her place is like an old granny's house; **tu fais m. avec cette robe!** that dress makes you look dowdy *or* frumpy! **il fait m., ton chemisier** that blouse makes you look dowdy *or* frumpy

mémérer [18] [memere] VI *Can Fam* to gossip□

mémo [memo] NM1 *(carnet)* memo pad, note book, notepad **2** *(note de service)* memo

mémoire[1] [memwar] NF1 *(faculté)* memory; **avoir (une) mauvaise m.** to have a poor *or* bad memory; **avoir (une) bonne m.** to have a good memory; **si j'ai bonne m.** if I remember correctly; **si ma m. ne me trompe pas** if my memory serves me right, if I remember correctly; **avoir la m. des noms/dates** to have a good memory for names/dates; *Fam* **avoir une m. d'éléphant** to have a memory like an elephant; **perdre la m.** to lose one's memory; **il n'a plus de m.** he's lost his memory; **il n'a pas de m.** he's got a bad memory; **je n'ai aucune m.!** I can never remember anything!; **tu as la m. courte!** you've got a short memory!; **fais un effort de m.** try hard to remember, search (your memory) hard; **rappeler qch à la m. de qn, remettre qch en m. à qn** to remind sb of sth; **se remettre qch en m.** to recall sth; **je n'ai plus son nom en m.** his/her name has slipped my memory, his/her name escapes me; **une vieille expression me revint** *ou* **remonta à la m.** an old saying came (back) to me; **son nom est resté dans toutes les mémoires** his/her name is remembered by everyone; **ce détail est resté à jamais** *ou* **s'est gravé dans ma m.** this detail has stayed with me ever since *or* has forever remained engraved in my memory; **réciter qch de m.** to recite sth from memory; **la m. collective** collective memory

2 *(souvenir)* memory; **honorer la m. de qn** to honour the memory of sb; **faire un travail de m.** = to come to terms with atrocities committed by one's country in the past and accept one's share of collective responsibility; **en ces temps de triste m.** in those days of bitter memory; **de sinistre m.** *(personne, événement, lieu)* notorious, infamous; *(date, jour)* dark, tragic

3 *Ordinat* memory, storage; **m. de 40 méga-octets** 40 megabyte memory; **m. centrale** *ou* **principale** main memory *or* storage; **mettre un dossier en m.** to write a file to memory; **m. cache** cache memory; **mettre en m. cache** to cache; **m. disponible** available memory; **m. à disque** disk memory, RAM disk; **m. écran** screen memory; **m. étendue** extended memory; **m. expansée** expanded memory; **m. externe** external memory; **m. haute** high memory; **m. d'images** picture memory; **m. intermédiaire** buffer memory; **m. morte** read-only memory; **m. non effaçable** non-erasable memory; **m. paginée** expanded memory; **m. RAM dynamique** dynamic RAM; **m. de stockage** mass memory; **m. tampon** buffer (storage); **m. tampon de données** data buffer; **m. tampon d'imprimante** *ou* **pour imprimante** printer buffer; **m. vidéo** video memory; **m. virtuelle** virtual memory; **m. vive** random access memory; **m. vive dynamique** DRAM, dynamic random access memory; **m. vive statique** SRAM, static RAM, static random access memory; **m. volatile** volatile memory

• **à la mémoire de** PRÉP in memory of, to the memory of; **faire qch à la m. de qn** to do sth in memory of sb

• **de mémoire** ADV from memory

• **de mémoire de** PRÉP **de m. de sportif** in all my/his/*etc* years as a sportsman; **de m. d'homme** in living memory

• **en mémoire de** = **à la mémoire de**

• **pour mémoire** ADV *Com & Fig* for the record; **je signale, pour m., que…** I might mention, for the record, that…; **je vous signale pour m. que…** I would remind you that…

mémoire[2] [memwar] NM1 *(rapport)* report, paper

2 *Univ* thesis, dissertation; **m. de maîtrise** ≃ MA thesis *or* dissertation

3 *Jur* statement of case

4 *Com & Fin* bill, statement (of account)

• **Mémoires** NMPL memoirs; **écrire ses Mémoires** to write one's memoirs

mémorable [memɔrabl] ADJ memorable

mémorandum [memɔrɑ̃dɔm] NM **1** *(note)* memorandum; *Naut* **m. de combat** battle orders **2** *(carnet)* notebook

mémorial, -aux [memɔrjal, -o] NM **1** *(texte)* memoir; *Pol* memorial **2** *(monument)* memorial

• **Mémorial** NM *(Mémoires)* memoirs

mémorisation [memɔrizasjɔ̃] NF1 *(processus)* memorization; *Mktg* recall **2** *Ordinat* storage, writing to memory

mémoriser [3] [memɔrize] VT1 *(apprendre par cœur)* to memorize; **il a mémorisé les conjugaisons** he has learnt the verb tables by heart **2** *Ordinat* to store, to write to memory

menaçant, -e [mənasɑ̃, -ɑ̃t] ADJ1 *(comminatoire* ▸ *personne, geste, ton)* menacing, threatening; **de façon menaçante** threateningly; **d'un ton m.** menacingly **2** *(inquiétant* ▸ *signe, silence, nuage)* menacing, threatening, ominous; *(*▸ *ciel)* threatening; **le temps est m.** the weather's looking ominous

menace [mənas] NF1 *(source de danger)* threat; **une m. pour l'ordre public** a danger *or* threat to law and order; **m. de tempête/d'épidémie** threat of a storm/an epidemic **2** *(acte, parole)* threat; *Jur* **menaces** intimidation; **comment, des menaces maintenant!** so it's threats now, is it?; **des menaces en l'air** idle threats; **mettre ses menaces à exécution** to carry out one's threats; **des menaces de mort** death threats; **la victime avait reçu des menaces de mort** the victim had been threatened with death *or* had received death threats; **ils ont même essayé la m.** they even tried threats; **sous la m.** under duress; **sous la m. de** under (the) threat of; **sous la m. de la torture** under (the) threat of torture; **sous la m. d'une arme** at gunpoint; **sous la m. de sanctions** under threat of sanctions; **un geste de m.** a threatening *or* menacing gesture; **ton lourd** *ou* **plein de m.** tone heavy *or* fraught with menace

menacé, -e [mənase] ADJ threatened, under threat, endangered; **le groupe le plus m.** the group under the heaviest threat; **ses jours sont menacés** his/her life is in danger; **espèce menacée** endangered species

menacer [16] [mənase] VT1 *(mettre en danger)* to threaten, to menace; **un danger mortel le menace** he's in mortal danger; **rien ne la menace** she's in no danger; **l'apoplexie le menace** he's in danger of having a stroke; **une nouvelle crise nous menace** a new crisis is threatening us *or* looming; **les fluctuations du dollar menacent notre système monétaire** fluctuations in the dollar are a threat to our monetary system; **se faire m.** to be threatened **2** *(pour impressionner, contraindre)* to threaten (**de** with); **m. qn du doigt/poing** to shake one's finger/fist at sb; **m. qn d'un procès** to threaten sb with legal proceedings; **m. qn de mort** to threaten to kill sb; **il est menacé de mort** he's being threatened with death

VI *(crise)* to threaten; *(tempête, orage, révolution)* to be brewing; **l'orage menace** there's a storm brewing; **la pluie menace** it's threatening to rain, it looks like rain

• **menacer de** VT IND **m. de faire qch** to threaten to do sth; **elle menace d'annuler le concert si ses exigences ne sont pas satisfaites** she's threatening to cancel the concert if her demands aren't met; **le procès menace d'être long** the trial threatens to be lengthy; **le conflit menace de s'étendre** there is a (real) danger of the conflict spreading; **le mur menace de s'écrouler** the wall is in danger of collapsing; **cette étagère menace de tomber** that shelf looks like it will fall

ménage [menaʒ] NM1 *(couple)* couple; *(en sociologie)* household; **être heureux en m.** to be happily married; **leur m. marche mal** their marriage isn't going very well; **faire bon/mauvais m. avec qn** to get on well/badly with sb; **ils se sont mis en m.** they've moved in together; **ils sont en m.** they live together; **monter son m.** to set up house; **un m. sans enfants** a childless couple; **m. à trois** ménage à trois

2 *(économie domestique)* housekeeping

3 *(nettoyage)* housework, cleaning; **faire le m.** to do the housework, *Am* to clean house; **faire le m. en grand** *ou* **à fond** to clean the house from top to bottom; **faire le m. dans une armoire** to clean out a wardrobe; **faire le m. dans un bureau** to tidy an office; **demain, je fais du/mon m.** tomorrow I'm going to do some/my housework; *Fig* **le directeur a fait le (grand) m. dans son service** the manager has shaken up *or* spring-cleaned his department; **faire des ménages** to clean for people, to go out cleaning

4 *(meubles) Vieilli* **m. de poupée** set of doll's furniture; *Can* **avoir du beau m.** to have nice furniture

• **de ménage** ADJ *Vieilli* **1** *(fabriqué à la maison)* homemade **2** *(pour l'entretien)* household *(avant n)*, cleaning *(avant n)*

ménagement [menaʒmɑ̃] NM care, caution, circumspection; *(tact)* thoughtfulness, consideration, *Sout* solicitude

• **avec ménagement** ADV carefully, cautiously; *(avec tact)* tactfully, gently; **traite ma voiture avec m.** treat my car with care, take (good) care of my car; **traiter qn avec le plus grand m.** to treat sb with great consideration

• **sans ménagement** ADV *(annoncer)* bluntly; *(éconduire, traiter)* unceremoniously

ménager[1] [17] [menaʒe] VT1 *(économiser)* to be sparing with; **sans m. ses efforts** *ou* **sa peine** tirelessly; **elle ne ménage pas ses efforts** *ou* **sa peine** she spares no effort; **m. ses forces** to conserve one's strength; **sans m. ses paroles** without mincing one's words

2 *(traiter avec soin)* to treat *or* to handle carefully; *(personne)* to treat tactfully *or* with consideration; **m. sa santé** to take care of one's health; **je prends l'ascenseur pour m. mes vieilles jambes** I take the *Br* lift *or Am* elevator to spare my old legs; **ménage ton foie, ne bois pas d'alcool** take care of *or* look after your liver, don't drink alcohol; **ménagez-le, il a le cœur malade** treat him gently, he has a weak heart; **m. son cheval** not to tire one's horse

3 *(respecter)* to spare; **ménage sa susceptibilité** humour him/her; **ménage sa fierté** spare his/her pride; *Fig* **m. la chèvre et le chou** to sit on the fence, to run with the hare and hunt with the hounds

4 *(arranger ▸ passage, escalier)* to put in; *(▸ entretien, rencontre)* to organize, to arrange; **m. une sortie** to provide an exit; **j'ai ménagé un espace pour planter des légumes** I've left some space for growing vegetables; **nous avons ménagé une ouverture pour accéder directement au garage** we knocked a door through to the garage; **m. une surprise à qn** to prepare a surprise for sb

VPR se ménager 1 *(prendre soin de soi)* to save oneself; **elle ne se ménage pas assez** she drives herself too hard; **ménage-toi** take it easy, don't overdo it; **elle se ménage pour le troisième set** she's saving herself *or* conserving her energy for the third set **2 se m. qch** *(se réserver qch)* to set sth aside for oneself; **se m. une sortie** to provide oneself with a way out; **se m. des temps de repos dans la journée** to set aside rest periods for oneself during the day

ménager², -ère [menaʒe, -ɛr] **ADJ 1** *(de la maison)* domestic *(avant n)*, household *(avant n)*; **équipement m.** domestic *or* household appliances **2** *Can (économe)* thrifty, careful (with money)

NM *Com* **le gros/petit m.** major/small household appliances

• **ménagère NF 1** *(femme)* housewife; **elle est bonne ménagère** she's a good housekeeper **2** *(couverts)* canteen (of cutlery); **une ménagère en argent** a canteen of silver cutlery

ménagerie [menaʒri] **NF** menagerie; *Fig* **c'est une vraie m. ici!** it's like a zoo in here!

ménarche [menarʃ] **NM** *Physiol* menarche

mendélien, -enne [mɛ̃deljɛ̃, -ɛn] **ADJ** Mendelian

mendélisme [mɛ̃delism] **NM** Mendelianism, Mendelism

mendiant, -e [mɑ̃djɑ̃, -ɑ̃t] **NM,F** *(clochard)* beggar

NM *Culin* = almond, fig, hazelnut and raisin biscuit

ADJ M *Rel* mendicant

mendicité [mɑ̃disite] **NF 1** *(action)* begging; **vivre de m.** to beg for a living **2** *(état)* beggary, *Sout* mendicity, mendicancy; **être réduit à la m.** to be reduced to begging

mendier [9] [mɑ̃dje] **VI** to beg

VT *(argent, sourire)* to beg for; **m. des votes** to canvass for votes

mendigot, -e [mɑ̃digo, -ɔt] **NM,F** *très Fam Vieilli* beggar[□], *Am* panhandler

meneau, -x [məno] **NM** *(horizontal)* transom; *(vertical)* mullion

menées [məne] **NFPL** *(intrigues)* intrigues, machinations; **des m. subversives** subversive activities; **les m. de l'opposition** the opposition's intrigues *or* scheming; **déjouer les m. de qn** to thwart *or* outwit sb

MENER [19] [məne]

VT	
• to take **1, 2**	• to lead **1–6**
• to run **4**	• to conduct **4**
VI	
• to be in the lead	

VT 1 *(conduire ▸ personne)* to take, to lead (à to); **m. qn à sa chambre** to take *or* to show sb to his/her room; **comment mènes-tu tes enfants à l'école?** how do you take your children to school?; *Fig* **elle mènera son club à la victoire** she'll lead her club to victory; **son inconscience le mène au désastre** his thoughtlessness is leading him to disaster; **cette petite somme ne te mènera pas bien loin** that won't get you very far

2 *(sujet: escalier, passage, route)* to take, to lead; **le bus te mènera jusqu'à l'hôtel** the bus will take you (right) to the hotel

3 *(être à la tête de ▸ cortège, course)* to lead; **le champion mène le peloton** the champion is leading the pack

4 *(diriger ▸ groupe, équipe)* to lead; *(▸ combat, négociation)* to carry on; *(▸ affaire, projet)* to run, to manage; *(▸ enquête)* to conduct, to lead; *(▸ campagne)* to conduct; *(▸ débat)* to lead, to chair; **m. la danse** *ou* **le bal** to lead the dance; *Fig* to call the tune; **m. le jeu** *Sport* to be in the lead; *Fig* to have the upper hand, to call the tune; **m. qch à bien** *ou* **à terme** *ou* **à bonne fin** *(finir)* to see sth through successfully; **je mènerai les fouilles à terme** *ou* **à bonne fin** I'll see the dig through to the end; **sauras-tu m. à bien cette entrevue?** will you be able to get through this interview?; **m. de front plusieurs projets** to run *or* manage several projects at once

5 *(vie)* to lead; **m. la vie dure à qn** to give sb a hard time; **laissez-la m. sa vie** let her live her life

6 *(contrôler)* **il se laisse trop facilement m.** he's too easily led; *Fig* **m. qn par le bout du nez** to lead sb by the nose; **se laisser m. par le bout du nez** to let oneself be led

7 *(locution)* **il n'en menait pas large avant la publication des résultats** his heart was in his boots before the results were released

USAGE ABSOLU *(conduire)* **le chemin qui mène à la ville** the road that leads to the town; **la ligne nº 1 mène à Neuilly** line No. 1 takes you *or* goes to Neuilly; **la deuxième année mène au dessin industriel** after the second year, you go on to technical drawing; *Fig* **cela ne mène à rien** this is getting us nowhere

VI to (be in the) lead; **l'équipe locale mène par 3 buts à 0** the local team is leading by 3 goals to 0; **le skieur italien mène avec 15 secondes d'avance sur le Suisse** the Italian skier has a 15-second lead *or* advantage over the Swiss; **de combien on mène?** what's our lead?

ménestrel [menɛstrɛl] **NM** minstrel

ménétrier [menetrije] **NM 1** *Arch (violoneux)* fiddler **2** *Hist* musician

meneur, -euse [mənœr, -øz] **NM,F 1** *(dirigeant)* leader; **c'est un m. d'hommes** he's a born leader (of men); **m. de jeu** *Sport* play maker; *TV & Rad* quiz master, question-master; **meneuse de revue** chorus-line leader; *Can Sport* **meneuse de claque** cheerleader **2** *Péj (agitateur)* ringleader, leader, agitator

menhir [menir] **NM** menhir

méninge [menɛ̃ʒ] **NF** *Anat* meninx; **méninges** meninges

• **méninges NFPL** *Fam* brains; **il ne se fatigue pas** *ou* **ne se creuse pas les méninges!** he's in no danger of wearing his brain out!; **se remuer les méninges** to rack *or Am* cudgel one's brains; **fais travailler tes méninges** use your brains

méningé, -e [menɛ̃ʒe] **ADJ** meningeal

méningite [menɛ̃ʒit] **NF** *Méd* meningitis

ménisque [menisk] **NM** *Anat, Opt & Phys* meniscus

ménopause [menɔpoz] **NF** menopause; *Fam* **faire sa m.** to go through the menopause[□]

ménopausée [menɔpoze] **ADJ F une femme m.** a post-menopausal woman

ménorragie [menɔraʒi] **NF** *Méd* menorrhagia

menotte [mənɔt] **NF** *(main)* tiny (little) hand

• **menottes NFPL** handcuffs; **passer les menottes à qn** to handcuff sb; **menottes aux poignets** handcuffed, in handcuffs

mens *etc voir* **mentir**

mensonge [mɑ̃sɔ̃ʒ] **NM 1** *(action)* **le m.** lying, untruthfulness; **détester le m.** to hate lying *or* lies; **vivre dans le m.** to live a lie **2** *(propos)* lie; **faire** *ou* **dire un m.** to tell a lie; **dire des mensonges** to tell lies; **un m. par omission** a lie of omission; **elle n'a raconté que des mensonges** she just told a pack of lies; *Fam* **c'est vrai, ce m.?** are you having me on?; **petit m., pieux m.** white lie; **gros m.** downright lie

mensonger, -ère [mɑ̃sɔ̃ʒe, -ɛr] **ADJ** untruthful, *Sout* mendacious; *(promesse)* false, empty; *(publicité)* misleading; **des déclarations mensongères** untruthful statements

menstruation [mɑ̃stryasjɔ̃] *Physiol* **NF** menstruation, menstruating

menstruel, -elle [mɑ̃stryɛl] **ADJ** menstrual

menstrues [mɑ̃stry] **NFPL** *Vieilli* menses

mensualisation [mɑ̃sɥalizasjɔ̃] **NF** *(des salaires, des impôts, du personnel)* monthly payment; **pour vos règlements, pensez à la m.** don't forget that you can pay in monthly instalments

mensualiser [3] [mɑ̃sɥalize] **VT** to pay on a monthly basis; **être mensualisé** *(pour les impôts)* = to pay one's income tax in advance monthly instalments, the amount paid being an estimation based on previous years; *(pour un salaire)* to be paid monthly

mensualité [mɑ̃sɥalite] **NF 1** *(somme perçue)* monthly payment; *(somme versée)* monthly instalment; **m. de remboursement** monthly repayment **2** *(salaire)* monthly salary

• **par mensualités ADV** monthly, on a monthly basis; **payer par mensualités** to pay by monthly instalments

mensuel, -elle [mɑ̃sɥɛl] **ADJ** monthly

NM,F worker paid by the month

NM *Journ* monthly (magazine)

mensuellement [mɑ̃sɥɛlmɑ̃] **ADV** monthly, every month

mensuration [mɑ̃syrasjɔ̃] **NF** measurement, mensuration

• **mensurations NFPL** measurements; **prendre les mensurations de qn** to take sb's measurements; **elle a des mensurations à faire rêver** her vital statistics are out of this world; *Jur* **mensurations judiciaires** height and weight (as shown on one's criminal record)

> **-MENT** SUFFIX
>
> This suffix appears in many adverbs formed from an adjective. Whatever its connotations, *-ly* is usually the corresponding suffix in English.
>
> • In most cases, they are adverbs of manner, equivalent in meaning to IN A ... MANNER where "..." is the adjective on which the adverb is based, eg:
> **simplement** simply; **gentiment** kindly; **rapidement** quickly, rapidly; **bêtement** foolishly, stupidly; **il mange salement** he's a messy eater
>
> • Some adverbs ending in **-ment** are adverbs of INTENSITY, some of which can be colloquial, eg:
> **énormément** enormously, a great deal; **extrêmement** extremely; **légèrement** slightly; **totalement** totally; **drôlement** awfully; **vachement** really; **sacrément** damn, bloody
>
> • A number of adverbs ending in **-ment** are equivalent to FROM A ... POINT OF VIEW, where "..." is the adjective used as a basis, eg:
> **économiquement** economically; **politiquement** politically; **moralement** morally

mental, -e, -aux, -ales [mɑ̃tal, -o] **ADJ** mental

NM le m. the mind, the mental state; **un m. d'acier** a positive mental attitude

mentalement [mɑ̃talmɑ̃] **ADV** mentally; **j'ai préparé m. ce que j'allais lui répondre** I prepared in my head the answer I was going to give him/her

mentalité [mɑ̃talite] **NF** mentality; **avoir une m. de petit bourgeois** to have a lower middle-class mentality; **avoir une sale m.** to have a nasty mind; **faire changer les mentalités** to change people's mentality *or* the way people think; **les mentalités ont évolué** (people's) attitudes have changed; **quelle (sale) m. dans ce bureau!** what an atmosphere *or* a nasty atmosphere there is in this office!; *Ironique* **belle** *ou* **jolie m.!** that's a nice attitude!; **l'histoire des mentalités** the history of mentalities

menteur, -euse [mɑ̃tœr, -øz] **ADJ** *(personne)*

untruthful, lying; *(discours, compliments)* deceitful; **enfant, il était très m.** he used to tell lies all the time when he was a child

NM,F liar; *Fam* **sale m.!** you fibber!

NM *(jeu)* **jouer au m.** to play cheat

menthe [mɑ̃t] NF **1** *Bot* mint; **m. poivrée** peppermint; **m. verte** spearmint

2 *(tisane)* mint tea; **je prendrai une verveine m.** I'll have verbena and mint tea

3 *(sirop)* **m. à l'eau** peppermint cordial; **boire** *ou* **prendre une m. à l'eau** to drink a glass of peppermint cordial

4 *(essence)* peppermint; **parfumé à la m.** mint-flavoured; **bonbons à la m.** mints, peppermints; **pastilles de m.** mints, peppermints

menthol [mɑ̃tɔl] NM menthol; **bonbons/cigarettes au m.** menthol(ated) sweets/cigarettes

mentholé, -e [mɑ̃tɔle] ADJ mentholated, menthol *(avant n)*

mention [mɑ̃sjɔ̃] NF **1** *(référence)* mention; **faire m. de qch** to refer to *or* to mention sth

2 *(texte)* note, comment; **apposez votre signature précédée de la m. manuscrite "lu et approuvé"** append your signature after adding in handwriting "read and approved"; **l'enveloppe portait la m. "urgent"** the word "urgent" appeared *or* was written on the envelope; **mentions obligatoires** *(sur formulaire)* essential information

3 *Scol & Univ* distinction; **être reçu avec m.** to pass with distinction; **être reçu sans m.** to get an ordinary pass; **décrocher une m.** to pass with distinction; **m. très bien** *Br* ≃ first class honours, *Am* ≃ grade A; **m. bien** *Br* ≃ upper second class honours, *Am* ≃ grade B; **m. assez bien** *Br* ≃ lower second-class honours, *Am* ≃ grade C; **m. passable** = minimum pass grade; **m. honorable** = first level of distinction for a PhD; **m. très honorable** = second level of distinction for a PhD; **m. très honorable avec les félicitations du jury** = highest level of distinction for a PhD

4 *Cin* **m. spéciale** special mention

mentionner **[3]** [mɑ̃sjɔne] VT to mention; **le nom du traducteur n'est pas mentionné** the translator's name does not appear; **le service mentionné ci-dessus** the above-mentioned department, the department mentioned above; *TV & Cin* **m. au générique** to acknowledge *or* feature in the credits

mentir **[37]** [mɑ̃tir] VI *(gén)* to lie; *(une fois)* to tell a lie; *(plusieurs fois)* to tell lies; **m. à qn** to lie to sb, to tell sb a lie/lies; **elle ment à son mari** she is deceiving her husband; **tu mens (effrontément)!** you're lying (shamelessly)!, you're a (barefaced) liar!; **et je ne mens pas!** and that's the truth!; **sans m.!** honestly!; **sans m., elle me l'a dit quinze fois** without a word of a lie, she told me fifteen times; **m. par omission** to lie by omission; *Fam* **elle ment comme elle respire** *ou* **comme un arracheur de dents** she lies through her teeth; **si je mens je vais en enfer** cross my heart and hope to die

• **mentir à** VT IND *Littéraire (manquer à)* to belie; **m. à sa réputation** not to live up to one's reputation

VPR **se mentir 1** *(emploi réfléchi)* **se m. à soi-même** to fool oneself **2** *(emploi réciproque)* to lie to each other, to tell each other lies

menton [mɑ̃tɔ̃] NM chin; **m. en galoche/pointu/rond** protruding/pointed/round chin; **avoir un m. volontaire** to have a firm *or* determined chin

mentonnier, -ère[1] [mɑ̃tɔnje, -ɛr] ADJ of the chin

mentonnière[2] [mɑ̃tɔnjɛr] NF **1** *(d'un chapeau)* chin strap; *(d'un casque)* chin piece **2** *Méd* chin bandage **3** *Mus* chin rest

mentor [mɛ̃tɔr] NM **1** *Littéraire* mentor **2** *Can (guide)* mentor

menu[1] [məny] NM **1** *(repas)* menu; **composer son m.** to plan one's meal; **qu'y a-t-il au m. aujourd'hui?** what's on the menu today?; *Fig* what's on the agenda for today? **2** *(au restaurant)* set meal; **deux menus à 20 euros** two 20-euro menus *or* set meals; **m. enfant** children's menu; **m. à prix fixe** set menu, fixed-price menu **3** *Ordinat* menu; **contrôlé par m.** *ou* **menus** menu-driven; **m. d'aide** help menu; **m. de césure** hyphenation menu; **m. déroulant** pull-down menu; **m. fichier** file menu; **m. flottant** tear-off menu; **m. hiérarchique** hierarchical menu; **m. d'impression** print menu; **m. local** pop-up menu, pop-up; **m. pomme** Apple menu; **menus en cascade** pull-down menus, cascading menus

menu[2]**, -e** [məny] ADJ **1** *(attaches, silhouette)* slim, slender; *(voix)* small, thin; *(écriture)* small, tiny; *(enfant)* tiny; *(femme)* petite; **à pas menus** with minute *or* tiny steps **2** *(avant le nom) (petit)* small, tiny; **couper qch en menus morceaux** to cut sth into small pieces **3** *(avant le nom) (négligeable)* small; **il fait les menus travaux** he does odd jobs; **menues dépenses** out-of-pocket expenses; **menus frais** minor expenses; **de la menue monnaie** small change; **m. fretin** *Ich* fry; *Fig* small fry; **les menus plaisirs** life's little pleasures; **voici un peu d'argent pour tes menus plaisirs** here's a little pin money

ADV *(couper, hacher)* thoroughly, finely; **écrire m.** to write small

• **par le menu** ADV *(raconter)* in (great) detail; *(vérifier)* thoroughly

menuet [mənɥɛ] NM *Mus* minuet

menuiserie [mənɥizri] NF **1** *(activité)* joinery **2** *(atelier)* (joiner's) workshop **3** *(boiseries)* woodwork

menuisier, -ère [mənɥizje, -ɛr] NM,F joiner

méphistophélique [mefistɔfelik] ADJ Mephistophelian, Mephistophelean

méphitique [mefitik] ADJ noxious, mephitic, mephitical

méplat [mepla] NM *(pièce méplate)* flat surface; *(de rocher)* ledge

méprendre **[79]** [meprɑ̃dr] **se méprendre** VPR to make a mistake, to be mistaken (**sur** *ou* **quant à** about); **je me suis mépris sur ses intentions réelles** I was mistaken about *or* I misunderstood his/her real intentions; **se m. sur qn** to misjudge sb; **on dirait de la soie, c'est à s'y m.** it feels just like silk; **on dirait ta sœur, c'est à s'y m.** she looks just like your sister

mépris [mepri] NM contempt, disdain, scorn; **avoir** *ou* **éprouver du m. pour** to be filled with contempt for, to despise; **paroles/regard de m.** contemptuous words/look; **avec m.** scornfully, contemptuously; **avoir** *ou* **tenir qn en m.** to hold sb in contempt; **le m. de** *(convenances, tradition)* contempt for, lack of regard for; **avoir le m. de l'argent/des conventions** to scorn *or* to despise money/convention

• **au mépris de** PRÉP with no regard for, regardless of; **au m. du danger/du règlement** regardless of the danger/the rules; **au m. des convenances** spurning convention

méprisable [meprizabl] ADJ contemptible, despicable

méprisant, -e [meprizɑ̃, -ɑ̃t] ADJ contemptuous, disdainful, scornful

méprise [mepriz] NF mistake, error; **victime d'une m.** victim of a misunderstanding; **il y a m. sur le destinataire** it has been delivered to the wrong person

• **par méprise** ADV by mistake

mépriser **[3]** [meprize] VT **1** *(dédaigner)* to look down on, to despise, to scorn; **je le méprise d'être si lâche** I despise him for being such a coward; **elle méprise l'argent** she thinks nothing of *or* scorns money **2** *(braver ▸ conventions, règlement)* to disregard, to defy; *(▸ mort, danger)* to defy; *(▸ conseil, offre)* to disregard

mer [mɛr] NF **1** *Géog* sea; **mettre un canot à la m.** *(d'un navire)* to lower *or* to launch a boat; *(de la terre)* to get out a boat; **jeter qch à la m.** *(d'un navire)* to throw sth overboard; *(de la terre)* to throw sth into the sea; **un homme à la m.!** man overboard!; **ils sont partis en m.** they've gone out to sea; **perdus en m.** lost at sea; **en haute** *ou* **pleine m.** (out) at sea; **sous/sur la m.** under/on the sea; **vers la m.** seawards, towards the sea; **voyager par m.** to travel by sea; **prendre la m.** to put out to sea; **ce capitaine/navire n'a pas pris la m. depuis 20 ans** this captain/boat hasn't been to sea for 20 years; **état de la m.** sea conditions; **m. calme/belle/peu agitée** calm/smooth/moderate sea; **m. très grosse, grosse m.** very heavy *or* stormy sea; **par grosse m.** when the sea is heavy; **m. agitée devenant forte** sea moderate becoming heavy; **la m. est mauvaise** the sea is rough; **m. d'huile** sea as calm as a millpond; **m. intérieure** inland sea; **m. territoriale** territorial waters; **droit de la m.** maritime law; **coup de m.** heavy swell; **essuyer un coup de m.** to be struck by a heavy sea; *Fam* **ce n'est pas la m. à boire** it's not that hard, it's no big deal; **la m. Adriatique** the Adriatic Sea; **la m. des Antilles** the Caribbean Sea; **la m. d'Aral** the Aral Sea; **la m. d'Azov** the Sea of Azov; **la m. Baltique** the Baltic Sea; **la m. de Barents** the Barents Sea; **la m. de Beaufort** the Beaufort Sea; **la m. de Béring** the Bering Sea; **la m. Blanche** the White Sea; **la m. Caraïbe** *or* **des Caraïbes** the Caribbean Sea; **la m. Caspienne** the Caspian Sea; **la m. de Chine** the China Sea; **la m. de Corail** the Coral Sea; **la m. Égée** the Aegean Sea; **la m. du Groenland** the Greenland Sea; **la m. Intérieure** the Inland Sea; **la m. Ionienne** the Ionian Sea; **la m. d'Irlande** the Irish Sea; **la m. Jaune** the Yellow Sea; **la m. de Marmara** the Sea of Marmora; **la m. Méditerranée** the Mediterranean Sea; **la m. Morte** the Dead Sea; **la m. Noire** the Black Sea; **la m. du Nord** the North Sea; **la m. d'Oman** the Arabian Sea; **la m. Rouge** the Red Sea; **la m. Tyrrhénienne** the Tyrrhenian Sea

2 *(marée)* tide; **à quelle heure la m. sera-t-elle haute/basse?** what time is high/low tide?

3 *(région côtière)* seaside; **à la m.** at *or* by the seaside; **aller à la m.** to go to the seaside; **au bord de la m.** at *or* by the seaside, by the sea

4 *Fig (grande étendue)* **m. de glace** glacier; **m. de sable** ocean of sand, sand sea

5 *Astron* mare

mer-air [mɛrɛr] ADJ INV *Mil* **missile m.** sea-to-air missile

mercanti [mɛrkɑ̃ti] NM *Péj* shark, profiteer

mercantile [mɛrkɑ̃til] ADJ **1** *Péj (intéressé)* mercenary, self-seeking, venal **2** *(commercial)* mercantile

mercantilisme [mɛrkɑ̃tilism] NM **1** *Littéraire (attitude)* mercenary *or* self-seeking attitude **2** *Écon (théorie)* mercantilism; *(système)* mercantile system

mercaphonie [mɛrkafɔni] NF *Mktg* telemarketing, telephone marketing

mercaticien, -enne [mɛrkatisjɛ̃, -ɛn] NM,F marketing expert

mercatique [mɛrkatik] NF marketing

mercenaire [mɛrsənɛr] ADJ *Littéraire (troupe)* mercenary; *(travail)* paid

NM mercenary

mercerie [mɛrsəri] NF **1** *(magasin)* *Br* haberdasher's shop, *Am* notions store **2** *(industrie, articles)* *Br* haberdashery, *Am* notions; **des articles de m.** sewing materials

merceriser **[3]** [mɛrsərize] VT to mercerize; **coton mercerisé** mercerized cotton

merchandisage [mɛrʃɑ̃dizaʒ], **merchandising** [mɛrʃɑ̃dajziŋ] NM merchandizing

merci [mɛrsi] NM thank you; **dites-lui un grand m. pour son aide** give him/her a big thank you *or* all our thanks for his/her help

EXCLAM thank you, thanks; **m. de votre cadeau/amabilité** thank you *or* thanks for your present/kindness; **m. de** *ou* **pour votre offre** thank you for your offer; **m. d'avoir répondu aussi vite** thank you for replying so promptly; **dire m.** to say thank you *or* thanks; **as-tu dit m. à la dame?** did you thank the lady *or* say thank you to the lady?; **m. bien, m. beaucoup** thank you very much, thanks a lot; *Ironique* **m'excuser? m. bien, après ce qu'il m'a fait!** apologize? no way *or* no thanks, not after what he did to me!; **m. mille fois** thank you so much *or* very much; **mille mercis pour votre invitation** thank you so much *or* many thanks for your invitation; **voulez-vous du fromage? – (non) m., je n'ai pas faim** would you like some cheese? – no thank you *or* thanks, I'm not hungry; **un café? – m., volontiers** would you like a coffee? – (yes,) thanks, I'd love one; *Fam* **m., très peu pour moi!** thanks but no thanks!; *Ironique* **m. du compliment!** thanks for the compliment!; *Fam* **m. qui? m. mon chien!** don't bother to say thank you!

NF *Littéraire* mercy; **demander m.** to ask for

mercy

• **à la merci de** PRÉP at the mercy of; **tenir qn à sa m.** to have sb at one's mercy *or* in one's power

• **sans merci** ADJ merciless, pitiless, ruthless; **une lutte sans m.** a merciless struggle ADV mercilessly, pitilessly, ruthlessly

mercier, -ère [mɛrsje, -ɛr] NM,F *Br* haberdasher, *Am* notions dealer

Mercosur [mɛrkosyr] NM *Écon (abrév* **Marché commun du cône sud**) Mercosur

mercredi [mɛrkrədi] NM Wednesday; **le m. des Cendres** Ash Wednesday; *voir aussi* **mardi**

EXCLAM *Euph* sugar!

mercure [mɛrkyr] NM *Chim* mercury

mercuriale¹ [mɛrkyrjal] NF *Littéraire (accusation)* remonstrance, admonition

mercuriale² [mɛrkyrjal] NF *Bourse* market price list, commodity price list

mercuriale³ [mɛrkyrjal] NF *Bot* mercury

mercuriel, -elle [mɛrkyrjɛl] ADJ *Chim* mercurial

merde [mɛrd] *très Fam* NF **1** *(excrément)* shit, crap; **une m. de chien** a dog turd; **tu as de la m. sous tes pompes** you've got shit on your shoes; *Fig* **traîner qn dans la m.** to drag sb's name through the mud; *Fig* **il a de la m. dans les yeux** he never sees a thing, he can't see what's going on right in front of him; **il ne se prend pas pour une** *ou* **pour de la m.** *Br* he thinks the sun shines out of his arse, *Am* he thinks he's God's gift to the world

2 *(chose de mauvaise qualité)* shit, crap; **une m. à 10 euros** some cheap rubbish costing 10 euros; **ce film/bouquin est une vraie m.** this film/book is a load of crap; **de la m.** (a load of) shit; **c'est de la m., ce rasoir!** this razor's (a load of) shit!; **de m.** shitty; **ce temps de m.** this shitty weather; **un boulot/un quartier de m.** a shit *or* shitty job/area; **tu vas éteindre ta radio de m., oui?** will you turn that *Br* bloody *or Am* goddamn radio off!

3 *(désordre) Br* bloody *or Am* godawful mess; **foutre** *ou* **semer la m.** to create havoc; **chaque fois que ce gosse est dans ma classe, il fout la** *ou* **sa m.** whenever that kid is in my classroom, it's total chaos; **c'est la m. dans le pays en ce moment** the country's a *Br* bloody *or Am* goddamn mess *or* shambles at the moment

4 *(ennuis)* **c'est la m.!** it's hell!; **être dans la m. (jusqu'au cou)** to be (right) in the shit, to be up shit creek (without a paddle); **mettre** *ou* **foutre qn dans la m.** to drop sb in the shit

5 *(mésaventure)* shitty mess; **il m'arrive encore une m.** I've got another *Br* bloody *or Am* goddamn problem; **et si il nous arrivait une m.?** what if we ended up in the shit?

EXCLAM shit!; **m. alors!** oh shit!; **et m., j'en ai marre!** to hell with it *or Br* sod it, I've had enough!; *Fig* **dire m. à qn** to tell sb to piss off *or Br* bugger off; **(je te dis) m.!** *(ton agressif)* to hell with you!; *(pour souhaiter bonne chance)* break a leg!; **alors, tu viens, oui ou m.?** are you coming or not, for Christ's sake?; **avoir un œil qui dit m. à l'autre** to have a squint□

merder [3] [mɛrde] *très Fam* VI to screw up, *Br* to cock up; **mon imprimante merde depuis trois jours** my printer's been on the blink for the last three days; **j'ai complètement merdé en littérature anglaise** I completely screwed up the English Lit paper; **j'ai envie de partir en vacances, mais j'ai l'impression que ça va m.** I want to go on holiday, but I've a feeling it won't work out; **ça merde entre eux** things between them are really screwed up

VT *(rater)* to screw up, *Br* to cock up; **il a merdé son examen** he made a complete *Br* balls-up *or Am* ball-up of his exam

merdeux, -euse [mɛrdø, -øz] *très Fam* ADJ *(coupable)* shitty, crappy; **se sentir m.** to feel shit *or* shitty

NM,F **1** *(personne méprisable)* shit **2** *(enfant)* little shit; **un m. de 14 ans** a 14-year old brat

merdier [mɛrdje] NM *très Fam* **1** *(désordre)* pigsty; **range un peu tes affaires, c'est le m. ici** it's like a pigsty in here, tidy up your things **2** *(situation confuse)* **je suis dans un sacré m.** I'm really in the shit; **on s'est retrouvé dans un beau m. après son départ** we were in one hell of a mess after he/she left

merdique [mɛrdik] ADJ *très Fam* shit, shitty, crappy; **leur voiture est complètement m.** their car's complete rubbish

merdouiller [3] [mɛrduje], **merdoyer** [13] [mɛrdwaje] VI *très Fam* to screw up, *Br* to cock up; **j'ai complètement merdouillé à l'oral** I made *Br* a right cock-up *or Am* a real screw-up of the oral

mère [mɛr] NF **1** *(génitrice)* mother; **elle est m. de cinq enfants** she is a mother of five; **c'est une m. pour lui** she's like a mother to him; **frères/sœurs par la m.** half-brothers/half-sisters on the mother's side; **il l'a rendue m. au bout de dix ans de mariage** he gave her a child after ten years of marriage; **veau élevé sous la m.** calf nourished on its mother's milk; **m. adoptive** adoptive mother; **m. biologique** biological mother; **m. célibataire** unmarried mother; **m. de famille** mother; **elle est m. de famille** she is a wife and mother; **m. nourricière** foster mother; **m. porteuse** *ou* **de substitution** surrogate mother; *aussi Fig* **m. poule** mother hen

2 *Fam (madame)* **la m. Vorel** old mother Vorel; **alors la petite m., on a calé?** stalled, have you, *Br* missus *or Am* ma'am?

3 *très Fam (insulte)* **ta m.!** fuck off!, *Br* piss off!; *Vulg* **enculé de ta m.!** you fucking prick!; *Vulg* **niquer sa m. à qn** to kick sb's fucking head in, *Am* to punch sb out

4 *Rel* Mother; **m. Élisabeth** Mother Elizabeth; **oui, ma m.** yes, Mother; **la m. supérieure** the Mother Superior

5 *Littéraire (origine)* mother; **m. patrie** mother country; **la Grèce, m. de la démocratie** Greece, mother of democracy

6 *Tech* mould

7 *(comme adj) Ordinat* **carte m.** motherboard; *Biol* **cellule m.** mother cell; *Com* **maison m.** headquarters, head office; *Com* **société m.** parent company

mérengué [merenge] NM *(danse, musique)* merengue

merguez [mɛrgɛz] NF merguez *(spicy North African sausage)*

méridien, -enne [meridjɛ̃, -ɛn] ADJ **1** *Littéraire (de midi)* meridian; **l'heure méridienne** noon, midday; **chaleur méridienne** midday heat; **ombre méridienne** shadow at noon **2** *Astron* meridian

NM *Astron & Météo* meridian; **m. international** *ou* **origine** prime *or* Greenwich meridian

• **méridienne** NF **1** *Math* meridian (section); *Géog* meridian line; *Géol* triangulation line **2** *Littéraire (sieste)* siesta **3** *(lit)* chaise longue

méridional, -e, -aux, -ales [meridjɔnal, -o] ADJ **1** *(du Sud)* southern, *Sout* meridional **2** *(du sud de la France)* of/from the South of France

NM,F **1** *(du Sud)* Southerner **2** *(du sud de la France)* = inhabitant of or person from the South of France; **les méridionaux** Southern French people

meringue [mərɛ̃g] NF meringue

meringuer [3] [mərɛ̃ge] VT to cover with meringue; **tarte au citron meringuée** lemon meringue pie

mérinos [merinos] NM **1** *Zool* merino **2** *Tex* **(laine) m.** merino wool **3** *Fam Hum* **laisser pisser le m.** to let things take their course□

merise [məriz] NF wild cherry, merise

merisier [mərizje] NM **1** *(arbre)* wild cherry (tree) **2** *(bois)* cherry (wood)

méritant, -e [meritɑ̃, -ɑ̃t] ADJ worthy, deserving; **peu m.** undeserving; **les élèves les plus méritants ont été récompensés** the most deserving pupils were given a reward

mérite [merit] NM **1** *(vertu)* merit, worth; **gens de m.** people of merit; **avoir du m.** to be deserving of *or* to deserve praise; **il a bien du m.!** you have to take your hat off to him!; **tu as du m. de t'occuper d'eux** it is greatly to your credit that you take such care of them; **je n'ai aucun m.** I deserve no credit, I can't take any credit (for it) **2** *(gloire)* credit; **s'attribuer le m. de qch** to take the credit for sth; **tout le m. de l'affaire vous revient** all the credit for the deal is yours, you deserve all the credit for the deal; **tu n'as même pas le m. de l'avoir fait tout seul** you can't even take credit for doing it yourself **3** *(qualité)* merit; **sa déclaration a au moins le m. d'être brève** his/her statement at least has the merit of being brief; **selon ses mérites** according to his/her merits; **par ordre de m.** in order of merit; **au seul m.** on merit alone

mériter [3] [merite] VT **1** *(sujet: personne)* to deserve, *Sout* to merit; **tu mérites une fessée** you deserve to be spanked; **tu mérites qu'on te fasse la même chose** you deserve to have the same thing happen to you; **tu l'as bien mérité!** it serves you right!, you got what you deserve!; **il n'a que ce qu'il mérite!** he's got what he deserves, it serves him right; **ils ne méritent pas qu'on s'intéresse à eux** they are not worth bothering with; **tu mériterais que je te laisse là tout seul** it would serve you right if I left you there on your own; **un repos bien mérité** a well-deserved rest; **son renvoi, il l'a bien mérité** he fully deserved to be fired **2** *(sujet: objet, idée)* to be worth, to deserve, *Sout* to merit; **une exposition qui mérite d'être vue** an exhibition worth seeing *or* which deserves to be seen; **la proposition mérite réflexion** the proposal is worth thinking about **3** *(valoir)* **voilà ce qui lui a mérité cette renommée** this is what earned him/her this fame

• **mériter de** VT IND **avoir bien mérité de la patrie** to have served one's country well

VPR **se mériter 1** *(ne pas être donné)* **un cadeau pareil, ça se mérite** you have to do something special to get a present like that **2** *Can (recevoir)* **se m. un prix/une récompense** to be awarded *or* to receive a prize/a reward

méritocratie [meritɔkrasi] NF meritocracy

méritoire [meritwar] ADJ commendable, praiseworthy, *Sout* meritorious

merlan [mɛrlɑ̃] NM **1** *Ich* whiting; *Fam* **faire des yeux de m. frit à qn, regarder qn avec des yeux de m. frit** *(sans comprendre)* to gaze blankly at sb□, to gape at sb□; *(amoureusement)* to make sheep's eyes at sb **2** *Culin Br* topside, *Am* top round

merle [mɛrl] NM **1** *Orn* **m. (noir)** blackbird **2** *(individu désagréable)* **un vilain m., ton propriétaire!** what a nasty piece of work that landlord of yours is!

• **merle blanc** NM **1** *Orn* white crow **2** *(personne)* rare bird, exceptional person; **chercher le m. blanc** to ask for the moon **3** *(objet)* rarity

merlin [mɛrlɛ̃] NM *Naut* marline

merlu [mɛrly] NM hake

merluche [mɛrlyʃ] NF **1** *Ich* hake **2** *Com & Culin* dried (unsalted) cod, stockfish

mer-mer [mɛrmɛr] ADJ INV *Mil* **missile m.** sea-to-sea missile

mérou [meru] NM *Ich* grouper

mérovingien, -enne [merɔvɛ̃ʒjɛ̃, -ɛn] ADJ Merovingian *(dynasty of Frankish kings, 481–751)*

• **Mérovingien, -enne** NM,F Merovingian

mer-sol [mɛrsɔl] ADJ INV *Mil* **missile m.** sea-to-ground missile

merveille [mɛrvɛj] NF **1** *(chose remarquable)* marvel, wonder, treasure; **cette liqueur est une m.** this liqueur is amazing; **ce bracelet est une m.** this bracelet is marvellous; **ma couturière est une m.** my seamstress is a treasure; **une m. d'ingéniosité** a marvel of ingenuity; **les merveilles de la technologie** the marvels *or* wonders of technology; **sa fille est une m. de patience** his/her daughter has the patience of a saint; **faire des merveilles, faire m.** to work wonders **2** *Culin* ≃ type of sweet fritter

• **à merveille** ADV wonderfully, marvellously; **ils s'entendent à m.** they get on marvellously (well) *or* like a house on fire; **se porter à m.** to be in perfect health; **ce travail lui convient à m.** this job suits him/her down to the ground; **ce chèque tombe à m.** this cheque couldn't have come at a better time; **elle s'y est adaptée à m.** she took to it like a duck to water

merveilleuse [mɛrvejøz] *voir* **merveilleux**

merveilleusement [mɛrvɛjøzmɑ̃] ADV wonderfully, marvellously; **il fait m. beau** it's marvellous *or* wonderful weather, the weather's marvellous *or* wonderful; **aller m. bien** to be wonderfully well, to be in excellent health; **elle a m. réussi son examen** she passed her exam with excellent results

merveilleux, -euse [mɛrvejø, -øz] ADJ **1** *(formidable)* wonderful, marvellous, amazing **2** *(après le nom) (fantastique)* magic; **une histoire merveilleuse** a wondrous tale; **la lampe merveilleuse** the magic lamp

NM **1** *(surnaturel)* **le m.** the supernatural *or* marvellous; *Cin & Littérature* **l'emploi du m.** the use of the fantastic element **2** *(caractère extraordinaire)* **le m. de l'histoire, c'est qu'il est vivant** the amazing thing about the whole story is that he's still alive **3** *Belg Culin* = meringue coated with chocolate and cream

• **merveilleuse** NF *Hist* merveilleuse, fine lady

mes [me] *voir* **mon**

mésadapté, -e [mezadapte] *Can* ADJ *(enfant)* with special needs, maladjusted

NM,F *(adulte)* person with social difficulties; *(enfant)* child with special needs, maladjusted child

mésalliance [mezaljɑ̃s] NF misalliance, mismatch; **faire une m.** to marry beneath oneself *or* one's station

mésallier [9] [mezalje] **se mésallier** VPR to marry beneath oneself *or* one's station

mésange [mezɑ̃ʒ] NF tit, titmouse; **m. bleue** blue tit; **m. charbonnière** great tit; **m. noire** coal tit

mésaventure [mezavɑ̃tyr] NF misadventure, misfortune, mishap

mescal [mɛskal] NM mescal

mescaline [mɛskalin] NF mescalin, mescaline

Mesdames [medam] *voir* **Madame**

Mesdemoiselles [medmwazɛl] *voir* **Mademoiselle**

mésentente [mezɑ̃tɑ̃t] NF disagreement, difference of opinion; **oublions notre m. passée** let's forget our past disagreements

mésestimation [mezɛstimasjɔ̃] NF *Littéraire (mépris)* lack of respect, low esteem *or* regard; *(fait de sous-estimer)* underestimation, underrating

mésestime [mezɛstim] NF *Littéraire* lack of respect, low esteem *or* regard; **tenir qn en m.** to hold sb in low esteem, to have little regard for sb

mésestimer [3] [mezɛstime] VT *Littéraire (mépriser)* to have a low opinion of; *(sous-estimer)* to underestimate, to underrate

mésintelligence [mezɛ̃teliʒɑ̃s] NF *Littéraire* disagreement, lack of (mutual) understanding, discord

mesmérisme [mɛsmerism] NM mesmerism

Mésopotamie [mezɔpɔtami] NF **la M.** Mesopotamia

mésopotamien, -enne [mezɔpɔtamjɛ̃, -ɛn] ADJ Mesopotamian

• **Mésopotamien, -enne** NM,F Mesopotamian

mésothérapie [mezɔterapi] NF mesotherapy, = treatment of cellulite, circulation problems, rheumatism etc involving the use of tiny needles

mésozoïque [mezɔzɔik] *Géol* ADJ Mesozoic

NM Mesozoic

mesquin, -e [mɛskɛ̃, -in] ADJ **1** *(médiocre)* mean, petty; **des préoccupations mesquines** petty concerns; **laissons cela aux esprits mesquins** let's not waste our time on such petty concerns **2** *(parcimonieux)* mean, stingy, niggardly; **une portion mesquine** a stingy portion

mesquinement [mɛskinmɑ̃] ADV **1** *(selon des vues étroites)* pettily, small-mindedly **2** *(avec parcimonie)* meanly, stingily

mesquinerie [mɛskinri] NF **1** *(étroitesse d'esprit)* meanness, petty-mindedness, pettiness **2** *(parcimonie)* meanness, stinginess; **connu pour sa m.** renowned for his stinginess

mess [mɛs] NM mess; **le m. des officiers** the officers' mess

message [mesaʒ] NM **1** *(information)* message; **prendre un m.** to take a message; **faire parvenir un m. à qn** to send a message to sb; **veuillez laisser un m. après le signal sonore** *(sur répondeur)* please leave a message after the tone; **m. codé** coded message; **m. de détresse** distress message; **m. enregistré** recorded message; *Ordinat* **m. instantané** instant message; *Mktg* **m. principal** core message; **m. publicitaire** advertisement; *Tél* **m. téléphoné** *Br* ≃ Telemessage®, *Am* ≃ telegram *(delivered on the telephone)*; **m. téléphonique** telephone message; **m. télex** telex (message); *Tél* **m. texte** text message; **envoyer un m. texte à qn** to text sb, to text-message sb

2 *(déclaration)* speech; **un m. de bienvenue** a message of welcome

3 *(pensée)* message; **le m. de l'Évangile** the message of the Gospel

4 *Biol* **m. génétique** genetic information *or* code; **m. nerveux** nerve impulse *or* message

5 *Ordinat* **m. d'accueil** welcome message; **m. d'aide** help message; **m. d'alerte** warning message, alert box; **m. d'attente (du système)** (system) prompt; **m. électronique** e-mail; **envoyer un m. électronique à qn** to e-mail sb; **m. d'erreur** error message; **m. d'invite** *(du système)* prompt

• **à message** ADJ with a message; **un livre/une chanson à m.** a book/a song with a message

messager, -ère [mesaʒe, -ɛr] NM,F **1** *(personne qui transmet)* messenger; **m. de malheur** bearer of bad news; **je me ferai votre m. auprès de lui** I'll speak to him on your behalf **2** *Littéraire (annonciateur)* **m. de bonheur** harbinger of happiness

NM **1** *Hist* messenger; *Myth* **Mercure, le m. des dieux** Mercury, the messenger of the gods **2** *Orn* carrier pigeon **3** *(de colis, de cargaison)* courier

messagerie [mesaʒri] NF *Ordinat & Tél* **m. de dialogue en direct** chat; **m. électronique** e-mail; **m. instantanée** instant messaging, IM; **m. vocale** voice mail; **les messageries télématiques videotex** messaging services; **les messageries roses** = interactive Minitel® services enabling individuals seeking companionship to make contact

• **messageries** NFPL parcels service; **messageries aériennes** air freight company; **messageries de presse** newspaper distributing service; **messageries maritimes** shipping line; **bureau de(s) messageries** *Naut* shipping office; *Rail* parcel(s) office; *Hist* stagecoach office

messe [mɛs] NF **1** *Rel* Mass; **aller à la m.** to go to Mass; **célébrer** *ou* **dire la m.** to celebrate *or* to say Mass; **faire dire une m. pour qn** to have a Mass said for sb; **des messes ont été dites pour la paix dans le monde** Masses were held for world peace; *Fig* **la m. est dite** the die is cast; **m. basse** Low Mass; *Fig* **faire** *ou* **dire des messes basses** to whisper; *Fig* **pas de messes basses, s'il vous plaît!** no whispering, please!; **m. de minuit** midnight Mass; **m. des morts** *ou* **de requiem** Mass for the dead, Requiem; **m. noire** black mass; *Can* **il y a du monde à la m.!** the place is jam-packed! **2** *Mus* mass

Messeigneurs [mesɛɲœr] *voir* **Monseigneur**

messeoir [67] [meswar] **messeoir à** VT IND *Littéraire* **1** to be unbecoming to, to ill befit; **cela messied à votre âge** that doesn't become you at your age **2** *(tournure impersonnelle)* **il ne messied pas parfois d'avoir un esprit critique** there are times when it behoves one to have a critical mind

messianique [mesjanik] ADJ messianic

messianisme [mesjanism] NM messianism

messidor [mesidɔr] NM = 10th month of the French Revolutionary calendar, from 19 or 20 June to 18 or 19 July

messie [mesi] NM messiah; **le M.** the Messiah; *Fig* **attendre qn comme le M.** to wait eagerly for sb; *Can* **attendre le M.** *(attendre un enfant)* to be expecting a child; *(attendre l'impossible)* to expect the impossible

messied *etc voir* **messeoir**

Messieurs [mesjø] *voir* **Monsieur**

messieurs [mesjø] *voir* **monsieur**

messin, -e [mesɛ̃, -in] ADJ of/from Metz

• **Messin, -e** NM,F = inhabitant of or person from Metz

messire [mesir] NM *Hist* my lord; **m. Thomas** my lord Thomas

mestrance [mɛstrɑ̃s] = **maistrance**

mesurable [məzyrabl] ADJ measurable

mesurage [məzyraʒ] NM measurement, measuring

MESURE [məzyr]

- measurement **1, 2, 4**
- moderation **5**
- step **7**
- time **9**
- metre **10**
- measure **2, 3, 6, 7, 11**
- extent **8**
- bar **9**

NF **1** *(évaluation d'une dimension)* measuring *(UNCOUNT)*, measurement; *(résultat)* measurement; **prendre les mesures de qch** to take the measurements of sth

2 *(valeur)* measure, measurement; **unité de m.** unit of measurement; **m. de surface/longueur** measure of surface area/of length; **m. de volume** cubic measure; *Fig* **sans commune m.** unrivalled; *Fig* **il n'y a pas commune m. entre ces deux vins** there is no comparison between the two wines

3 *(récipient)* measure; **verser une m. de vin à qn** to pour sb out a measure of wine; **de vieilles mesures en étain** old pewter measures; **m. de capacité** *(pour liquides)* (liquid) measure; *(pour le grain, les haricots)* (dry) measure; *Com* **faire bonne m.** to give good measure; **il m'a donné deux pommes pour faire bonne m.** he gave me two apples for good measure; *Hum* **et pour faire bonne m., j'ai perdu ma clef** and to cap it all, I've lost my key

4 *Couture* measurement; **prendre les mesures d'un client** to take a customer's measurements

5 *(retenue)* moderation; **manquer de m.** to be excessive, to lack moderation; **garder une juste m.** to keep a sense of moderation; **rester dans la juste m.** to keep within bounds; **avoir le sens de la m.** to have a sense of moderation; **tu passes** *ou* **dépasses la m.** you're going too far; **leur cynisme passe la m.** they're excessively cynical; **oublier toute m.** to fling aside all restraint, to lose all sense of moderation *or* proportion; **dépenser avec/sans m.** to spend with/without moderation; **ambition sans m.** unbounded *or* limitless ambition; **un homme plein de m.** a man with a sense of moderation

6 *(qualité)* measure; *Fig* **donner toute sa m.** to show what one is capable of; **il ne donne (toute) sa m. que dans la dernière scène** he only displays the full measure of his talent *or* only shows what he's capable of in the last scene; **prendre la m. d'un adversaire** to size up an opponent

7 *Admin, Jur & Pol* measure, step; **prendre des mesures** to take measures *or* steps *or* action; **prendre des mesures contre qch** to take action against sth; **prendre des mesures pour faire qch/pour que…** to take measures *or* steps to do sth/so that…; **m. conservatoire** protective measure; **mesures déflationnistes** deflationary measures; **m. économique** economic measure; **m. incitative** initiative; *Jur* **m. d'instruction** investigative measure; **m. préventive** preventative measure *or* step; **m. de rétorsion** retaliatory measure, reprisal; **m. de sécurité** safety measure; **m. de sûreté** security measure, preventive measure; **m. d'urgence** emergency measure; **par m. d'hygiène** in the interest of hygiene; **par m. de salubrité** as a health mesure; **par m. de sécurité** as a safety precaution; **par m. d'économie** as a cost-saving measure, for reasons of economy

8 *(degré)* extent; **son attitude donne la m. de son cynisme** his/her behaviour shows just how cynical he/she really is; **prendre la (juste) m. de qch** to understand the full extent of sth; **être en m. de** to be able *or* in a position to; **elle n'est pas en m. de te payer** she's not in a position to *or* she can't pay you; **dans la m. de mes possibilités** insofar as I am able; **dans la m. du possible** as far as possible; **je vous aiderai dans la m. de mes forces** *ou* **du possible** I'll help you to the best of my ability *or* as much as I can *or* as best I can; **ces dépenses ne sont pas dans la m. de mes moyens** this expenditure is beyond my means; **dans la m. où cela peut lui être agréable** insofar as *or* inasmuch as he/she might enjoy it; **dans une certaine m.** to some *or* a certain extent; **dans quelle m.?** to what extent *or* degree?

9 *Mus (rythme)* time, tempo; *(division)* bar; **battre la m.** to beat time; **être en m.** to be in time; **en m., s'il vous plaît!** (keep in) time, please!; **m. composée/simple** compound/simple time; **m. à qua-**

tre temps four-four time *or* measure, common time *or* measure

10 *Littérature* metre

11 *Escrime* measure, reach

• **à la mesure de** PRÉP worthy of; **être à la m. de qn/qch** to measure up to sb/sth; **des aspirations qui ne sont pas à la m. de l'homme** aspirations which are beyond the scope of human achievement; *Sport & Fig* **trouver un adversaire à sa m.** to meet one's match; **elle a un adversaire à sa m.** she's got an opponent worthy of her *or* who is a match for her

• **à mesure** ADV as one goes along

• **à mesure que** CONJ as; **à m. que le temps passe** as time goes by

• **dans une large mesure** ADV to a great *or* large extent

• **sur mesure** ADJ **1** *Couture* made-to-measure; **fabriquer des vêtements sur m.** to make clothes to measure; **fait sur m.** custom-made; **costume (fait) sur m.** made-to-measure suit; **j'ai trouvé un travail sur m.** I've found the ideal job (for me); **le producteur lui a trouvé un rôle sur m.** the producer found him/her a role that was tailor-made for him/her **2** *(comme nom)* **c'est du sur m.** *Couture* it's made to measure; *Fig* it fits the bill

---

mesuré, -e [məzyre] ADJ **1** *(lent)* measured; **à pas mesurés** at a measured pace **2** *(modéré)* steady, moderate; *(langage, personne)* moderate, restrained; **il emploie toujours un ton m.** he never raises his voice

mesurément [məzyremɑ̃] ADV in moderation

mesurer [3] [məzyre] VT **1** *(déterminer la dimension ou le volume de)* to measure; *(tissu)* to measure off *or* out; **m. qch en hauteur/largeur** to measure the height/width of sth; **m. qn** to take sb's measurements, to measure sb (up); **je vais te m. pour voir si tu as grandi** I'm going to measure you to see if you've grown

2 *(difficulté, qualité)* to assess; **il ne mesure pas sa force** *ou* **ses forces** he doesn't know his own strength; **m. ses paroles** to be careful what one says; **mesure-t-elle la portée de ses paroles?** is she aware of the consequences of what she's saying?; **il n'a pas entièrement mesuré les risques** he didn't fully consider *or* assess the risks; **on mesure le travail au résultat** the work is measured by results

3 *(limiter)* to limit; **m. la nourriture à qn** to ration sb's food; **m. l'argent à qn** to ration out money to sb; **on nous mesure les crédits** our funds are limited; **il ne mesure pas sa peine** he doesn't spare his efforts; **et pourtant, je mesure mes mots** and I'm choosing my words carefully; **le temps vous sera mesuré pour cette épreuve** you will have a limited amount of time for this test

4 *(adapter)* **m. qch à** to adapt sth to; **m. le châtiment à l'offense** to make the punishment fit the crime

VI to measure; **combien mesures-tu?** how tall are you?; **il mesure presque deux mètres** he's almost two metres tall; **le sapin ne mesure que deux mètres** the fir tree is only two metres high; **la cuisine mesure deux mètres sur trois** the kitchen is *or* measures two metres by three

VPR **se mesurer 1** *(emploi réciproque)* **se m. des yeux** *ou* **du regard** to size each other up, to look each other up and down **2 se m. à** *(lutter avec)* to have a confrontation with, to pit oneself against; **je n'ai pas envie de me m. à lui** I don't feel like tackling him

mesurette [məzyrɛt] NF **1** *(cuillère)* measuring spoon **2** *Fam Péj (petite réforme)* petty reform[□]

mesureur [məzyrœr] NM **1** *(agent)* measurer **2** *(instrument)* gauge, measure

ADJ M **verre m.** measuring cup *or* jug

mésuser [3] [mezyze] **mésuser de** VT IND *Littéraire* to misuse; **m. de son talent** to misuse one's talent; **m. de son pouvoir** to abuse one's power

met *etc voir* **mettre**

métabolique [metabɔlik] ADJ *Physiol (du métabolisme)* metabolic

métabolisme [metabɔlism] NM *Physiol* metabolism

métacarpe [metakarp] NM *Anat* metacarpus

métacarpien, -enne [metakarpjɛ̃, -ɛn] *Anat* ADJ metacarpal

NM metacarpal

métairie [meteri] NF sharecropping farm, metairie

métal, -aux [metal, -o] NM metal; **m. en barres/lingots** metal in bars/ingots; **m. blanc** white metal; **m. déployé/en feuilles** expanded/sheet metal; **m. précieux** precious *or* noble metal; **le m. jaune** gold; **métaux lourds** heavy metals; **métaux vils** base metals

métalangage [metalɑ̃gaʒ] NM metalanguage

métalangue [metalɑ̃g] NF metalanguage

métallifère [metalifɛr] ADJ metal-bearing, metalliferous

métallique [metalik] ADJ **1** *(en métal)* metal *(avant n)*; **câble m.** wire rope **2** *(semblable au métal)* metallic, steel *(avant n)*, steely; **un bruit/une voix m.** a metallic noise/voice; **rendre un son m.** to clang, to clank; **bleu m.** steel *or* steely blue **3** *Fin* **réserve m.** bullion reserve

métallisation [metalizasjɔ̃] NF plating, metal-plating, metallization

métallisé, -e [metalize] ADJ *(couleur, finition)* metallic; *(papier)* metallized; **voiture bleu m.** metallic blue car

métalliser [3] [metalize] VT to metallize

métallo [metalo] NM *Fam (ouvrier)* metalworker[□]; *(dans une aciérie)* steelworker[□]

métallurgie [metalyrʒi] NF metallurgy

métallurgique [metalyrʒik] ADJ *(procédé)* metallurgical; *(atelier ▸ gén)* metalworking *(avant n)*; *(▸ dans une aciérie)* steelworking *(avant n)*

métallurgiste [metalyrʒist] NM **1** *(ouvrier)* metalworker; *(dans une aciérie)* steelworker **2** *(industriel, expert)* metallurgist

métamorphique [metamɔrfik] ADJ metamorphic, metamorphous

métamorphiser [3] [metamɔrfize] VT to metamorphose

métamorphisme [metamɔrfism] NM metamorphism

métamorphose [metamɔrfoz] NF **1** *Biol & Myth* metamorphosis **2** *Fig (transformation)* metamorphosis, transformation

métamorphoser [3] [metamɔrfoze] VT **1** *Myth* **m. qn en** to change *or* to turn sb into **2** *Fig (transformer)* to transform, to change; **ses vacances l'ont métamorphosé** his holiday has really changed him

VPR **se métamorphoser 1** *Myth* **se m. en** to turn into, to be metamorphosed into **2** *Fig (se transformer)* to change, to transform; **en 20 ans, la télévision s'est métamorphosée** television has undergone a transformation over the last 20 years

métamoteur [metamɔtœr] NM *Ordinat* **m. (de recherche)** metasearch engine

métaphore [metafɔr] NF metaphor; **parler par métaphores** to speak in metaphors; **m. filée** extended metaphor

métaphorique [metafɔrik] ADJ metaphoric, metaphorical, figurative

métaphoriquement [metafɔrikmɑ̃] ADV metaphorically, figuratively

métaphysicien, -enne [metafizisjɛ̃, -ɛn] NM,F metaphysician, metaphysicist

métaphysique [metafizik] ADJ **1** *Phil* metaphysical **2** *(spéculatif)* metaphysical, abstruse, abstract

NF **1** *Phil* metaphysics *(singulier)*; *(système de pensée)* metaphysic **2** *(spéculations)* abstractness, abstruseness; *Fam* **il ne s'embarrasse pas de m.** he doesn't let anything get in his way

métaphysiquement [metafizikmɑ̃] ADV metaphysically

métapsychique [metapsiʃik] *Vieilli* ADJ psychic

NF parapsychology

métastase [metastaz] NF *Méd* metastasis; **former des métastases** to metastasize

métatarse [metatars] NM *Anat* metatarsus

métatarsien, -enne [metatarsjɛ̃, -ɛn] *Anat* ADJ metatarsal

NM metatarsal

métathèse [metatez] NF metathesis

métayage [metɛjaʒ] NM sharecropping

métayer, -ère [meteje, -ɛr] NM,F sharecropper, sharecropping tenant

métazoaire [metazɔɛr] *Zool* NM metazoan

• **métazoaires** NMPL Metazoa

métempsycose [metɑ̃psikoz] NF metempsychosis

météo [meteo] ADJ INV weather *(avant n)*, meteorological; **bulletin m.** weather report; **prévisions m.** (weather) forecast; **station m.** meteorological *or* weather station

NF *(service) Br* Met Office, *Am* Weather Bureau; *(temps prévu)* weather forecast; **la m. a dit que...** the weather forecast said...; **Monsieur M.** the weatherman

météore [meteɔr] NM **1** *Astron* meteor **2** *Fig* nine days' wonder

météorique [meteɔrik] ADJ **1** *Astron* meteoric **2** *(éphémère)* meteoric, short-lived, fleeting

météorite [meteɔrit] NF **1** *(météoroïde)* meteoroid **2** *(aérolithe)* meteorite

météorologie [meteɔrɔlɔʒi] NF **1** *(science)* meteorology **2** *(organisme) Br* Met Office, *Am* Weather Bureau

météorologique [meteɔrɔlɔʒik] ADJ meteorological, weather *(avant n)*

météorologiste [meteɔrɔlɔʒist], **météorologue** [meteɔrɔlɔg] NMF meteorologist

métèque [metɛk] NM *Hist* metic

NMF *Fam* = offensive term used to refer to any dark-skinned foreigner living in France, especially one from the Mediterranean

méthadone [metadɔn] NF *Pharm* methadone

méthamphétamine [metɑ̃fetamin] NF *Pharm* methamphetamine

méthane [metan] NM *Chim* methane (gas)

méthanier [metanje] NM methane tanker *or* carrier

méthanol [metanɔl] NM *Chim* methanol

méthode [metɔd] NF **1** *(façon de procéder)* method; *Tech* method, technique; **c'est une bonne m. pour apprendre l'anglais** it's a good way of learning English; **j'ai ma m. pour le convaincre** I have my own way of convincing him; **c'est quoi ta m. pour rester aussi mince?** how do you manage to stay so slim?; **je vais changer de m.** I'm going to change my methods; **leur m. de vinification** their wine-making techniques; *Compta* **m. des coûts variables** direct costing; **m. de financement** funding method; **m. de gestion** management technique; *Scol* **m. globale** = method of teaching children literacy that emphasizes word recognition and reading for meaning, ≃ whole language approach; *Scol* **m. mixte** = method of teaching children literacy that combines phonics and meaning-based techniques; *Mktg* **m. des quotas** quota sampling method; *Scol* **m. semi-globale** = method of teaching children literacy that combines phonics and meaning-based techniques; *Scol* **m. syllabique** phonics method; **m. de travail** method, modus operandi; *Mktg* **m. de vente** sales *or* selling technique

2 *(organisation)* method; **vous manquez de m.** you lack method, you aren't methodical enough; **avec m.** methodically; **sans m.** unmethodically

3 *Fam (astuce)* **faut avoir la m.** you've got to have the knack; **tu as vraiment la m. avec les enfants!** you really have a way with *or* know how to handle children!; **lui, il a trouvé la m.!** he's got the hang of it!

4 *(manuel)* **m. d'anglais** English course book; **m. d'apprentissage** course book; **m. de lecture** primer; **m. de solfège** music handbook *or* manual; **m. de piano** piano tutor; **m. de relaxation** (book of) relaxation techniques

méthodique [metɔdik] ADJ methodical; **de façon m.** methodically

méthodiquement [metɔdikmɑ̃] ADV methodically

méthodisme [metɔdism] NM Methodism

méthodiste [metɔdist] ADJ Methodist

NMF Methodist

méthodologie [metɔdɔlɔʒi] NF methodology

méthodologique [metɔdɔlɔʒik] ADJ methodological

méthyle [metil] NM *Chim* methyl

méthylène [metilɛn] NM *Chim* methylene; *Com* methyl alcohol

méthylique [metilik] ADJ *Chim* methyl *(avant n)*

méticuleuse [metikyløz] *voir* **méticuleux**

méticuleusement [metikyløzmɑ̃] ADV meticulously

méticuleux, -euse [metikylø, -øz] ADJ **1** *(minutieux ▸ personne)* meticulous; *(▸ enquête)* probing, searching **2** *(scrupuleux)* meticulous, scrupulous; **d'une propreté méticuleuse** spotlessly *or* scrupulously clean

méticulosité [metikylozite] NF *Littéraire* meticulousness

métier [metje] NM **1** *(profession)* trade; **mon m.** my job *or* occupation *or* trade; **le m. de banquier** the banking profession, banking; **les métiers manuels** the manual trades; **les métiers d'art** (arts and) crafts; **quel est votre m.?** what do you do (for a living)?, what's your job?; **faire** *ou* **exercer le m. de chimiste** to work as a chemist; **j'ai fait tous les métiers** I've done every sort of job there is; **qu'est-ce que tu feras comme m. plus tard?** what do you want to be when you grow up?; **j'exerce le m. de journaliste** I'm a journalist (by profession); **changer de m.** to change career; **elle a un bon m.** she has a good job; **études qui ne mènent à aucun m.** course with no job prospects; **la soudure ne tiendra pas, et je connais mon m.!** the welding won't hold, and I know what I'm talking about; **apprendre son m. à qn** to teach sb one's trade; **ce n'est pas toi qui vas m'apprendre mon m.!** don't teach me my business!, I know what I'm doing!; **le m. de mère** a mother's job; **le m. de roi est chose difficile** being a king is not easy *or* no easy job; **quel m. de fou!** you don't have to be crazy to do this job but it helps!; *Euph* **le plus vieux m. du monde** the oldest profession in the world; *Littéraire* **il n'y a pas de sot m.(, il n'y a que de sottes gens)** there's no such thing as a worthless trade; **chacun son m. (et les vaches seront bien gardées)** you do your job and I'll do mine

2 *(expérience)* skill, experience; **avoir du m.** to have job experience; **elle manque encore un peu de m.** she still lacks experience; **c'est le m. qui rentre** it shows you're learning

3 *(machine)* **m. à filer/tricoter** spinning/knitting machine; **m. à broder** embroidery frame, tambour frame; **m. à tisser** loom; **m. à tisser mécanique** power loom; **m. à tapisserie** tapestry frame *or* loom; *Fig* **avoir qch sur le m.** to have sth lined up

• **de métier** ADJ *(homme, femme, armée)* professional; *(argot)* technical; *(technique)* of the trade ADV **avoir 15 ans de m.** to have been in the job *or* business for 15 years

• **de son métier** ADV by trade; **être boulanger de son m.** to be a baker by trade; **être journaliste de son m.** to be a journalist by profession

• **du métier** ADJ of the trade; **les gens du m.** people of the trade *or* in the business; **quand on est du m.** *(membre de la profession)* when you're in the business; *(expert)* when you're an expert at the job; **demande à quelqu'un du m.** ask a professional *or* an expert

métis, -isse [metis] ADJ **1** *(personne)* of mixed race; **un enfant m.** a mixed-race child **2** *Zool* crossbred, hybrid, cross; *(chien)* crossbred **3** *Bot* hybrid

NM,F **1** *(personne)* person of mixed race; **les M.** = aboriginal ethnic group in Canada **2** *Zool* crossbreed, hybrid, cross; *(chien)* crossbreed **3** *Bot* hybrid

NM *Tex* (heavy) linen-cotton mixture

métissage [metisaʒ] NM **1** *Biol (de personnes)* interbreeding; *(d'animaux)* crossbreeding, hybridization; *(de plantes)* hybridization **2** *(en sociologie)* intermarrying; *Fig* **le m. culturel** multiculturalism; **le m. de la salsa et du rock** the fusion of salsa and rock music

métisser [3] [metise] VT *Zool* to cross, to crossbreed; *Bot* to hybridize; **une population très métissée** a highly intermixed population; **musique métissée** crossover *or* fusion music

métonymie [metɔnimi] NF *Ling* metonymy

métrage [metraʒ] NM **1** *(prise de mesures)* measurement; *Constr* quantity surveying **2** *(longueur)* length; *Couture* length, yardage; **grand/petit m.** *(tissu)* cut lengthways/crossways; **vous le voulez en quel m.?** what width would you like?; **quel m. faut-il pour un manteau?** how many yards are needed to make an overcoat? **3** *Cin* footage, length; **long m.** feature(-length) film; **moyen m.** medium-length film; **court m.** short (film)

mètre[1] [mɛtr] NM **1** *(unité)* metre; **m. carré/cube** square/cubic metre; **m. par seconde** metre per second **2** *Sport* **le 400 mètres** the 400 metres, the 400-metre race; **il court le 100 mètres en dix secondes** he runs the 100 metres in ten seconds **3** *(instrument)* (metre) rule; **m. pliant** folding rule; **m. à ruban** tape measure, measuring tape

mètre[2] [mɛtr] NM *Littérature* metre

métré [metre] NM **1** *(mesure)* measurement **2** *Constr (devis)* bill *or* schedule of quantities

métrer [8] [metre] VT **1** *(mesurer)* to measure *(in metres)* **2** *Constr* to survey, to do a quantity survey of

métreur [metrœr] NM **m. (vérificateur)** quantity surveyor

métrique[1] [metrik] *Math* ADJ metric; **adopter le système m.** to adopt the metric system

métrique[2] [metrik] *Littérature* ADJ metrical

NF prosody, metrics *(singulier)*

métro [metro] NM *Br* underground, *Am* subway; **le m. parisien/de Montréal** the Paris/Montreal metro; **le m. londonien** *ou* **de Londres** the London underground (system), *Fam* the tube; **le premier m.** the first *or* milk train; **le dernier m.** the last train; **m. aérien** elevated *or* overhead railway; **au m. Charonne** at Charonne metro (station); **prendre le m.** to take the *Br* underground *or Am* subway; **je préfère y aller en m.** I'd rather go by *Br* underground *or Am* subway; *Fam Fig* **elle a toujours un m. de retard** she's always the last one to know what's going on; *Fam* **m., boulot, dodo** the daily grind, the nine-to-five routine; **depuis que j'habite à Paris, ma vie c'est vraiment m., boulot, dodo** life has become very humdrum *or* routine since I moved to Paris

métrologie [metrɔlɔʒi] NF metrology

métrologique [metrɔlɔʒik] ADJ metrological

métrologiste [metrɔlɔʒist] NMF metrologist

métronome [metrɔnɔm] NM metronome; **avec la régularité d'un m.** like clockwork, (as) regular as clockwork

métropole [metrɔpɔl] NF **1** *(ville)* metropolis **2** *Admin* mother country; **les Français de la m.** the metropolitan French **3** *Rel* metropolis

métropolitain, -e [metrɔpɔlitɛ̃, -ɛn] ADJ *Admin & Rel* metropolitan; *(église)* archiepiscopal; **troupes métropolitaines** home troops

NM **1** *Vieilli (métro) Br* underground (railway), *Am* subway **2** *Rel* metropolitan (primate)

métrosexuel, -elle [metrɔsɛksɥɛl] ADJ metrosexual

NM metrosexual

mets [mɛ] NM *(aliment)* dish; **des m. de grande qualité** gourmet fare

mettable [metabl] ADJ *(vêtement)* wearable; **la veste est encore m.** the jacket's still wearable; **je n'ai plus rien de m.** I don't have anything decent left to wear

metteur [metœr] NM *Cin & Théât* **m. en scène** director; *Tech* **m. au point** adjuster, setter; *Typ* **m. en pages** layout artist

METTRE [84] [metr]

VT	
• to put **1, 2, 6, 11**	• to lay **2**
• to set **4**	• to put on **7**
• to wear **7**	• to turn on **8**
• to put in **9**	• to take **10**
• to give **13**	
VPR	
• to go **1–3**	• to get **3, 4**
• to put on **5, 10**	• to wear **5, 10**
• to start **12**	

VT **1** *(placer)* to put; **m. des verres dans un placard** to put glasses (away) in a cupboard; **m. la main sur le bras de qn** to lay *or* to put one's hand on sb's arm; **m. l'amour avant l'argent** to put *or* to place love before money; **m. qn parmi les grands** to rate *or* to rank sb among the greats; **m. sa confiance/tout son espoir en** to put one's trust/all one's hopes in; **m. la confusion dans un service** to throw a department into confusion; **j'avais mis beaucoup de moi-même dans le projet** I'd put *or* invested a lot into the project; **elle a mis son talent au service des défavorisés** she used her talent to help the underprivileged; **ne mets pas les coudes sur la table!** don't put your elbows on the table!; **m. une pièce à l'affiche** to bill a play; **m. une lettre à la poste** to post a letter; **m. un enfant au lit** to put a child to bed; **on l'a mise à un poste clé** she was put in *or* appointed to a key position; **on m'a mis au standard** they put me on the switchboard; **je n'ai pas pu la m. à l'école du quartier** I couldn't get her into the local school; **m. qn dans l'avion/le train** to put sb on the plane/the train; **m. ses enfants dans le privé** to send one's children to a private school; **m. un enfant en pension** to put a child in a *or* to send a child to boarding school; **m. qn en prison** to put sb in prison; **m. 20 euros sur un cheval** to put *or* to lay 20 euros on a horse; **m. de l'argent sur son compte** to put *or* to pay some money into one's account; *Fam* **m. qn en boîte** to pull sb's leg

2 *(poser horizontalement)* to lay, to put; **mets les cartes face dessous** lay *or* put *or* place the cards face down; **il mit le tapis par terre** he laid *or* put the carpet down on the floor; **m. qch à plat** to lay sth down flat; **il mit le dossier devant moi** he set *or* laid the file down in front of me

3 *(disposer)* **m. le loquet** to put the latch down; *Fam* **mets le store** *(tire-le)* pull the blind (down)

4 *(ajuster)* to set; **m. qch droit** to set sth straight; **m. une pendule à l'heure** to set a clock to the right time; **mets le magnétoscope sur la deuxième chaîne** set the *Br* video *or Am* VCR on channel two; **mets la sonnerie à 20 h** set the alarm for 8 p.m.

5 *(établir ▸ dans un état, une situation)* **m. un étang à sec** to drain a pond; **m. le nom au pluriel** to put the noun into the plural; **m. qn au régime** to put sb on a diet; **m. qn au travail** to set sb to work, to get sb working; **m. qn dans la confidence** to let sb in on *or* into the secret; **m. qn dans l'embarras** *(perplexité)* to put sb in a predicament; *(pauvreté)* to put sb in financial difficulty; **m. qn dans l'obligation de faire qch** to oblige sb to do sth; **m. qn dans une situation délicate** to put sb in an awkward position; **m. une maison en vente** to put a house up for sale; **m. du vin en bouteilles** to put wine into bottles, to bottle wine; **mis en bouteille au château** *(sur une bouteille de vin)* chateau-bottled; **m. des fruits en bocaux** to put fruit into jars, to bottle fruit; *Jur* **m. qn en examen** to indict sb; **m. qch en œuvre** to implement sth; **m. une plante en pot** to pot a plant; **m. une plante en terre** to put a plant into the soil; **m. qch en miettes** to smash sth to bits; **m. un poème en musique** to set a poem to music; *Typ* **m. qch en page** to make sth up; **m. qch en vigueur** to bring sth into force *or* operation; **m. qch à cuire** to put sth on to cook; **m. qch à réchauffer** to heat sth up (again); **m. de l'eau à chauffer** to put some water on to heat (up); **m. du linge à sécher** *(dans la maison)* to put *or* to hang clothes up to dry; *(à l'extérieur)* to put *or* to hang clothes out *or* up to dry; **m. des fleurs à sécher** to leave flowers to dry, to dry flowers; **m. qch à tremper** to put sth to soak, to soak sth; **m. qn sous tranquillisants** to put sb on tranquillizers

6 *(fixer, ajouter)* to put; **m. une pièce à un pantalon** to put a patch on *or* to patch a pair of trousers; **m. un bouton à sa veste** to sew a button on one's jacket; **il faut lui m. des piles** you have to put batteries in it; **j'ai fait m. de nouveaux verres à mes lunettes** I had new lenses put in my glasses

7 *(se vêtir, se coiffer, se chausser de)* to put on; *(porter régulièrement)* to wear; **m. son manteau/une robe** to put on one's coat/a dress; **m. du fond de teint/du parfum** to put on some foundation/some perfume; **j'ai du mal à m. mes souliers** I find it difficult to get my shoes on; **mets tes skis/ta casquette** put your skis/your cap on; **mets une barrette** put a (hair) slide in; **tu devrais m. une ceinture avec cette robe** you should wear a belt with that dress; **je n'ai plus rien à m.** I've nothing to wear; **je lui ai mis son manteau/ses gants** I put his/her coat/his/her gloves on (for him/her)

8 *(faire fonctionner ▸ appareil)* to turn *or* to put *or* to switch on; **m. le chauffage** to put *or* to switch *or* to turn the heating on; **m. un disque** to put a record on; **mets de la musique** put some music on, play some music; **m. la radio plus fort** to turn up the radio; *Fam* **mets les sports/la première chaîne** put on the sports channel/channel one

9 *(installer)* to put in, to install; **faire m. l'électricité** to have electricity put in; **faire m. le chauffage central** to have central heating put in *or* installed; **faire m. l'eau et le gaz** to have water and gas put in; **m. la table** *ou* **le couvert** to lay *or* set the table; **m. des rideaux aux fenêtres** to put curtains at the windows, to put up curtains; **m. des étagères** to put up shelves; **m. du papier peint/de la moquette dans une pièce** to wallpaper/to carpet a room; **nous avons mis du gazon dans le jardin** we turfed the garden; **ça mettra de la couleur dans la pièce** it will give the room a bit of colour

10 *(consacrer ▸ temps)* to take; **m. du temps à faire qch** to take time to do sth; **il a mis trois heures à faire ses devoirs** he took three hours to do *or* he spent three hours over his homework; **elle a mis trois mois à me répondre** she took three months *or* it took her three months to answer me; **combien de temps met-on pour y aller?** how long does it take to get there?; **nous y mettrons le temps/le prix qu'il faudra** we'll spend as much time/money as we have to; **tu en a mis du temps pour te décider!** you took some time to make up your mind!; **m. de l'argent dans une voiture** to put money in *or* into a car; **m. de l'argent sur un cheval** to put money on a horse, to back a horse; **m. 500 euros dans qch** to spend 500 euros on sth; **m. 10 000 euros dans une affaire** to sink 10,000 euros into a business venture; **je serais prêt à m. tout ce que j'ai dans cette entreprise** I'd be willing to put everything I have into this venture; **m. toute son énergie/tout son enthousiasme à faire qch** to put all one's energy/enthusiasm into doing sth; **j'y mettrai tous mes soins** I'll give it my full attention

11 *(écrire)* to put; **que faut-il m. dans les cases de droite?** what do you have to put *or* write in the right-hand boxes?; **on met un accent sur le "e"** "e" takes an accent; **on met deux m à "pomme"** "pomme" has two m's; *Fam* **mets qu'il a refusé de signer** write *or* put down that he refused to sign; **tu veux lui m. un petit mot?** *(sur la carte, lettre)* do you want to write him/her a little note?; **je ne sais pas quoi m. sur la carte de vœux** I don't know what to put *or* to write on the (greetings) card; **tu n'as qu'à m. que je le remercie** *(dans une lettre)* tell him thanks, give him my thanks; **je t'ai mis sur la liste des invités** I've put you on the guest list

12 *(supposer)* **mettons** (let's) say; **et mettons que tu gagnes?** suppose *or* let's say you win?; **il faut, mettons, deux mètres de tissu** we need, (let's) say *or* shall we say, two metres of material; **mettons que ça fasse 50 euros** (let's) call it *or* say 50 euros; **mettons que j'ai mal compris!** *(acceptation)* let's just say I got it wrong!; **mettez que je n'ai rien dit** pretend I didn't say anything

13 *(donner)* to give; **vous me mettrez trois douzaines d'huîtres** give me *or* let me have three dozen oysters; **je vous mets un peu plus de la livre** I've put in a bit more than a pound; **le prof m'a mis 18** ≃ the teacher gave me an A

14 *Fam (infliger)* **qu'est-ce qu'il m'a mis au ping-pong!** he really hammered me at table tennis!; **on leur a mis cinq buts en première mi-temps** we hammered in five goals against them in the first half; **m. son poing dans la figure de qn** to punch sb in the face; **je lui ai mis une bonne claque** I gave *or* landed him/her a good slap; **qu'est-ce que son père va lui m.!** his/her father is really going to give it to him/her!

15 *Vulg (posséder sexuellement)* to fuck, to screw, *Br* to shag; **se faire m.** to get fucked *or* laid; **va te faire m.!** up yours!, fuck off!

16 *Naut* **m. une voile au vent** to hoist *or* to set a sail

17 *(locutions)* **m. les bouts** *ou* **les voiles** to make tracks, to hit the road

VI *Naut* **m. à la voile** to set sail

VPR se mettre 1 *(dans une position, un endroit ▸ chose)* to go; **où se mettent les tasses?** where do the cups go?; **les pieds, ça ne se met pas sur la table!** tables aren't made to put your feet on!

2 *(aller ▸ vêtement)* to go; **le noir se met avec tout** black goes with everything

3 *(s'installer, s'établir ▸ dans une position)* **se m. derrière un arbre** to go *or* get behind a tree; **se m. contre un mur** to stand *or* lean against a wall; **se m. devant qn** *(debout)* to stand in front of sb; *(assis)* to sit in front of sb; **se m. au lit** to get into bed; **se m. à table** to sit down at the table; **se m. au soleil/à l'ombre** to sit in the sunshine/shade; **se m. debout** to stand up; **se m. sur le dos/ventre** to lie (down) on one's back/stomach; **mets-toi sur cette chaise** sit on that chair; **mets-toi près de la fenêtre** *(debout)* stand near the window; *(assis)* sit near the window; **mettez-vous près du feu** sit (down) by the fire; **mettez-vous en cercle** arrange yourselves into *or* form a circle; **mettez-vous autour de grand-mère pour la photo** gather round grandma for the photo; **mets-toi là et ne bouge plus** stand/sit there and don't move; **je me mets dehors pour travailler** I go outside to work; **mettez-vous dans la position du lotus** get into the lotus position; *Belg* **mettez-vous!** take a seat!, sit down!; *Fig* **je ne savais plus où me m.** I didn't know where to put myself; **se m. entre les mains d'un spécialiste** to place oneself in the hands of a specialist

4 *(entrer ▸ dans un état, une situation)* **ne te mets pas dans un tel état!** don't get (yourself) into such a state!; **il s'est mis dans une position difficile** he's got *or* put himself in a difficult situation

5 *(s'habiller)* **se m. en** to put on; **se m. en pantalon** to put on a pair of trousers; **se m. en civil** to dress in civilian clothes; **se m. en uniforme** to put on one's uniform; **elle se met toujours en jupe** she always wears a skirt; **elle ne se met jamais en pantalon/en rouge** she never wears trousers/red

6 *(s'unir)* **se m. avec qn** *(pour un jeu)* to team up with sb; *(dans une discussion)* to side with sb; *Fam (pour vivre)* to move in with sb; **se m. avec qn pour faire qch** to join forces with sb to do sth; **on a dû se m.** *ou* **s'y m. à trois pour bouger l'armoire** it took three of us to move the wardrobe; **on s'est tous mis ensemble pour acheter le cadeau** we all clubbed together to buy the present; **on s'est mis par équipes de six** we split up into *or* we formed teams of six (people)

7 *Vulg* **son contrat, il peut se le m. quelque part!** he can shove his contract up his *Br* arse *or Am* ass!

8 *Fam (nourriture)* **s'en m. jusque-là** to stuff oneself *or* one's face; **qu'est-ce qu'on s'est mis!** we really stuffed ourselves *or* our faces!

9 *Fam* **qu'est-ce qu'ils se sont mis!** *(dans une bagarre)* they really laid into each other!, they were going at it hammer and tongs!

10 se m. qch to put sth on; **se m. une belle robe/du parfum** to put on a nice dress/some perfume; **se m. un nœud dans les cheveux** to put a bow in one's hair; **se m. du vernis à ongles** to put on nail varnish, to paint *or* varnish one's nails; **je n'ai rien à me m.!** I haven't got anything to wear *or* to put on!; **se m. de la crème sur les mains** to put some cream on one's hands; **je me suis mis de la peinture dans les cheveux/de la confiture sur les doigts** I've got paint in my hair/jam on my fingers; **se m. nu** to undress, to strip off

11 *(pour indiquer une évolution)* **quand le feu se met au rouge** when the lights turn *or* go red; **le temps se met au beau** it's getting sunny; **le temps se met au froid/à la pluie** it's getting *or* turning cold/starting to rain

12 se m. à faire qch *(commencer)* to start doing sth; **se m. à rire/chanter/pleurer** to begin *or* start to laugh/sing/cry, to start laughing/singing/crying; **il s'est mis à boire après le dessert** he started drinking after dessert; **c'est quand sa femme est morte qu'il s'est mis à boire** he started drinking *or* took to drink after his wife died; **se m. au régime** to put oneself on a diet, to go on a diet; **se m. au judo** to take up judo; **se m. à l'allemand** to start (learning) German; **se m. à l'ouvrage** *ou* **au travail** to set to work, to get down to work; **voilà qu'il se met à pleuvoir!** now it's started to rain *or* raining!; **s'y m.** *(au travail)* to get down to it; *(à une activité nouvelle)* to have a try; **si tu veux avoir l'examen, il faut que tu t'y mettes sérieusement!** if you want to pass the exam, you've really got to get down to some work!; **je n'ai jamais fait de piano, mais j'ai bien envie de m'y m.** I've never played the piano, but I'd quite like to have a try; *Fam* **elle est insupportable quand elle s'y met** she's unbearable once she gets started *or* going; *Fam* **si le (mauvais) temps s'y met, il faut annuler la kermesse** if the weather decides to turn bad, we'd better cancel the fête

meublant, -e [mœblɑ̃, -ɑ̃t] *voir* **meuble NM 2**

meuble [mœbl] **ADJ 1** *Agr & Hort* loose, light **2** *Géol* crumbly, friable; **formation m.** crumb **3** *Jur* **biens meubles** movables, movable assets, personal estate

NM 1 *(élément du mobilier)* **un m.** a piece of furniture; **des meubles** furniture; **les meubles du salon** the furniture in the living room; **être dans ses meubles** to have a place of one's own; **quelques pauvres meubles** a few sticks of furniture; **m. de rangement** cupboard; **je manque de meubles de rangement** I don't have much storage space; **m. d'angle** corner unit; **meubles de bureau** office furniture; **des meubles de salon** living room furniture; **des meubles de style** period furniture; *Fam* **faire partie des meubles** to be part of the furniture

2 *Jur* movable; **meubles corporels** tangible assets *or* movables; **meubles à demeure** fixtures; **meubles incorporels** intangible assets *or* movables; **les meubles meublants** (household) furniture, movables

> Do not confuse with **mobilier**.

meublé, -e [mœble] **ADJ** furnished; **une maison meublée/non meublée** a furnished/an unfurnished house

NM *(une pièce)* furnished room; *(plusieurs pièces)* furnished *Br* flat *or Am* apartment; **habiter** *ou* **vivre en m.** to live in furnished accommodation

meubler [5] [mœble] **VT 1** *(garnir de meubles)* to furnish; **ils ont meublé leur maison en Louis XIII** they furnished their home in the Louis XIII style; **ils sont entièrement meublés en chêne** all their furniture is oak; **comment vas-tu m. la cuisine?** what sort of furniture are you going to put in the kitchen?; **une cellule meublée d'un lit et d'une table** a cell furnished with a bed and a table **2** *(remplir)* to fill; **m. le silence/sa solitude** to fill the silence/one's solitude; **pour m. la conversation** to stop the conversation from flagging, for the sake of conversation; **m. ses soirées en lisant** to spend one's evenings reading

VPR se meubler to buy (some) furniture; **meublez-vous chez Caudin** buy your furniture at Caudin's

meuf [mœf] **NF** *Fam (verlan de* **femme***)* **1** *(fille)* chick, *Br* bird **2** *(compagne)* girlfriend ᵒ, woman, *Br* bird

meuglement [møgləmɑ̃] **NM un m.** a moo; **le m. des vaches** the mooing of the cows; **des meuglements** mooing

meugler [5] [møgle] **VI** to moo

meuh [mø] **NM** moo; **faire m.** to moo

meulage [mølaʒ] **NM** grinding

meule [møl] **NF 1** *Agr* stack, rick; **mettre en meules** to stack, to rick; **m. de foin** hayrick, haystack; **m. de paille** stack of straw

2 *Tech* (grinding) wheel; **m. à aiguiser** *ou* **affûter** grindstone; **m. à polir/à rectifier** polishing/trueing wheel

3 *Culin* **une m. de fromage** a (whole) cheese

4 *(d'un moulin)* millstone

5 *Suisse Fam (chose, personne fastidieuse)* bore, drag; **faire la m.** *ou* **des meules à qn** to hassle sb

6 *Fam (mobylette®)* moped

• **meules NFPL** *Fam (postérieur)* butt, *Br* bum, *Am* fanny

meuler [5] [møle] **VT** *(pour aiguiser)* to grind; *(pour éliminer)* to grind down; **machine/roue à m.** grinding machine/wheel

meulette [mølɛt] **NF** *Agr (de foin, de paille)* small stack *or* rick; *(de maïs)* stook, shock

meulière [møljɛr] **ADJ F pierre m.** millstone (grit)

NF 1 *(carrière)* millstone quarry **2** *(pierre)* millstone grit

meunerie [mønri] **NF 1** *(activité)* (flour) milling **2** *(commerce)* flour *or* milling trade **3** *(usine)* flour works *(singulier)*

meunier, -ère [mønje, -ɛr] **ADJ** flour-milling *(avant n)*, milling *(avant n)*

NM 1 *(artisan)* miller; **échelle** *ou* **escalier de m.**

narrow flight of steps **2** *Ich* miller's thumb, bullhead **3** *Orn (martin-pêcheur)* kingfisher
• **meunière** NF **1** *(épouse du meunier)* miller's wife **2** *Culin* **sole (à la) meunière** sole meunière *(coated with flour and fried in butter)*
meuron [mœrɔ̃] NM *Suisse Bot* mulberry
meurt *etc voir* **mourir**
meurtre [mœrtr] NM murder; **crier au m.** to scream blue murder; **m. avec préméditation** premeditated murder, *Am* ≃ first-degree murder; **m. sans préméditation** murder, *Am* ≃ second-degree murder
meurtri, -e [mœrtri] ADJ *(bras, fruit)* bruised; **visage m.** bruised *or* battered face; *(par la fatigue)* ravaged face; **être tout m.** to be black and blue all over; **il avait les mains meurtries par le froid** his hands were blue with cold; *Fig* **m. par l'indifférence de son fils** wounded by his son's indifference; *Fig* **elle est sortie très meurtrie de cette expérience** she was bruised by the experience, it was a very bruising experience for her
meurtrier, -ère [mœrtrije, -ɛr] ADJ **1** *(qui tue ▸ engin, lame)* deadly, lethal, murderous; *(▸ guerre, attentat)* murderous; *(▸ avalanche)* deadly, fatal; *(▸ route)* lethal, murderous; *(▸ folie, passion)* murderous; *(▸ épidémie)* deadly; **humour m.** lethal *or* devastating humour; **le lundi de Pâques est souvent m.** there are often a lot of deaths on the road on Easter Monday **2** *Arch (personne)* murderous, guilty of murder
NM,F murderer, *f* murderess
• **meurtrière** NF *Archit* (arrow) loophole
meurtrir [32] [mœrtrir] VT **1** *(contusionner)* to bruise **2** *Fig Littéraire* to hurt, to wound **3** *(poire, fleur)* to bruise
meurtrissure [mœrtrisyr] NF **1** *(contusion)* bruise **2** *Fig Littéraire* scar, wound; **les meurtrissures du cœur** sorrows of the heart **3** *(tache)* bruise; **des poires pleines de meurtrissures** pears covered in bruises
Meuse [møz] NF **la M.** the Meuse
meut *etc voir* **mouvoir**
meute [møt] NF *(de chiens)* pack; *Fig (de gens)* mob, crowd; **lancer la m.** to loose the pack *or* hounds; **une m. de paparazzi** a crowd *or* mob of paparazzi
meuvent *etc voir* **mouvoir**
MEV [mev] NF *Ordinat (abrév* **mémoire vive**) RAM
mévente [mevɑ̃t] NF **1** *(baisse des ventes)* slump (in sales), slack period **2** *Vieilli (vente à perte)* selling at a loss
mexicain, -e [mɛksikɛ̃, -ɛn] ADJ Mexican
• **Mexicain, -e** NM,F Mexican
Mexico [mɛksiko] NM Mexico City
Mexique [mɛksik] NM **le M.** Mexico; **le golfe du M.** the Gulf of Mexico
mézigue [mezig] PRON *Fam* yours truly, *Br* muggins (here); **et qui est-ce qui va casquer? c'est m.!** and who's going to pay? yours truly *or Br* muggins here!
mezzanine [mɛdzanin] NF **1** *Archit (entresol)* mezzanine; *(fenêtre)* mezzanine window **2** *Théât (corbeille)* dress circle
mezze [medze] NMPL *Culin* meze
mezzo-soprano [mɛdzosɔprano] *(pl* **mezzo-sopranos**) NM *(voix)* mezzo-soprano
NF *(cantatrice)* mezzo-soprano
MF[1] [ɛmɛf] NF *Rad (abrév* **modulation de fréquence**) FM
MF[2] *Anciennement (abrév écrite* **million de francs**) a million francs, one million francs; **3 MF** 3 million francs
mg *(abrév écrite* **milligramme**) mg
Mgr. *Rel (abrév écrite* **Monseigneur**) Mgr
mi [mi] NM INV **1** *(note)* E; *(chanté)* mi, me **2** *(d'un violon)* first string, E string

> PREFIX
> **MI-**
> This particle suggesting an INTERMEDIARY STATE is a very productive one, with several grammatical functions.
> • It can be combined with adjectives to form a new adjectival expression, eg:
> **des cheveux mi-longs** shoulder-length hair; **les yeux mi-clos** with eyes half-closed
> The adjective in **mi-** is often part of a succession of two such words, ie **mi-..., mi-...**, in combination with adjectives or nouns. The English equivalent can be *half-..., half-...*, but sometimes it is necessary to use a different turn of phrase, eg:
> **il la regardait, mi-amusé, mi-intrigué** he was looking at her half-amused, half-puzzled; **une créature mi-homme, mi-bête** a creature that is half-man, half-beast; **un sourire mi-figue, mi-raisin** a quizzical smile
> • **Mi-** can be attached to a noun and preceded with **à** or **jusqu'à**, thus forming an adverbial expression, usually relating to DISTANCE or LEVEL. The translation often includes the word *halfway*, eg:
> **à mi-chemin** halfway; **à mi-course** halfway through the race; **à mi-pente** halfway up/down the hill; **à mi-parcours** halfway along (the route); **elle avait de l'eau jusqu'à mi-jambe** the water came halfway up her legs
> • When joined to a noun, **mi-** can be used to form feminine nouns relating to TIME, eg:
> **la première mi-temps** the first half (of the game); **à la mi-juillet** mid-July

miam [mjam], **miam-miam** [mjamjam] EXCLAM *Fam* yum(-yum)!; **m., ça a l'air bon** that looks yummy
miaou [mjau] NM miaow; **faire m.** to miaow
miasmatique [mjasmatik] ADJ *Littéraire* miasmatic
miasme [mjasm] NM *Littéraire* miasma; **des miasmes** miasmas, miasmata
miaulement [mjolmɑ̃] NM miaowing, mewing
miauler [3] [mjole] VI to miaow, to mew
miauleur, -euse [mjolœr, -øz] ADJ miaowing, mewing
mi-bas [miba] NM INV *(en laine)* knee-high *or* knee-length sock; *(en voile)* popsock
mica [mika] NM *(roche)* mica
mi-carême [mikarɛm] *(pl* **mi-carêmes**) NF **à la m.** on the third Thursday of Lent
micaschiste [mikaʃist] NM mica schist
miche [miʃ] NF **1** *(pain)* round loaf **2** *Belg & Suisse (petit pain)* (bread) roll
• **miches** NFPL *Fam (fesses)* butt, *Br* bum, *Am* fanny; *(seins)* knockers, boobs; **vire tes miches** move yourself, move your backside; **gare à tes miches** mind yourself
Michel-Ange [mikɛlɑ̃ʒ] NPR Michelangelo
micheline [miʃlin] NF railcar
mi-chemin [miʃmɛ̃] **à mi-chemin** ADV halfway, midway; **s'arrêter à m.** to stop halfway; **nous sommes à m.** we're halfway there
• **à mi-chemin de** PRÉP halfway to; **à m. de Lyon** halfway to Lyons; **à m. de l'église et de l'école** halfway *or* midway between the church and the school
micheton [miʃtɔ̃] NM *Fam Arg crime esp Br* punter, *Am* john; **elle s'est fait cinq michetons dans la soirée** she turned five tricks that evening
michetonner [3] [miʃtɔne] VI *Fam Arg crime* to turn the occasional trick
Michigan [miʃigɑ̃] NM *Géog* **le M.** Michigan; **au M.** in Michigan; **le lac M.** Lake Michigan
mi-clos, -e [miklo, -kloz] ADJ half-closed
micmac [mikmak] NM *Fam* **1** *(affaire suspecte)* funny *or* fishy business, strange carry-on; **des micmacs financiers** financial wheeler-dealing **2** *(complications)* muddle, shambles; **ça a été tout un m. pour pouvoir entrer** trying to get in was a real performance **3** *Can Fam (désordre)* mess; **as-tu nettoyé le m. dans ta chambre?** have you cleaned up the mess in your room?
mi-corps [mikɔr] **à mi-corps** ADV *(à partir du bas)* up to the waist; *(à partir du haut)* down to the waist; **l'eau nous arrivait à m.** the water came up to our waists
mi-côte [mikot] **à mi-côte** ADV *(en partant du bas)* halfway up the hill; *(en partant du haut)* halfway down the hill
mi-course [mikurs] **à mi-course** ADV halfway through the race, at the halfway mark
micro [mikro] NM **1** *(microphone)* mike; *(tenu à la main)* baton *or* stick mike; **parler dans le m.** to speak into the mike; **m. caché** concealed mike; **m. canon** rifle *or* gun mike; **m. directionnel** directional mike; **m. sur perche** boom mike; **m. sur pied** stand mike; **m. portatif** hand mike; **m. à ruban** ribbon mike; **m. sans fil** radio mike; **m. suspendu** hung *or* hanging *or* slung mike; **m. de table** desk mike **2** *Fam (micro-ordinateur)* PC
NF *Fam* microcomputing
microampère [mikroɑ̃pɛr] NM microampere
microanalyse [mikroanaliz] NF microanalysis
microbalance [mikrɔbalɑ̃s] NF microbalance
microbe [mikrɔb] NM **1** *Biol* germ, *Spéc* microbe; **attraper un m.** to catch a bug **2** *Fam (personne)* shrimp, (little) runt *or* pipsqueak
microbicide [mikrɔbisid] *Vieilli* ADJ bactericidal, germ-killing
NM bactericide, germ-killer
microbien, -enne [mikrɔbjɛ̃, -ɛn] ADJ *Biol (relatif aux microbes)* microbial, microbic; *(causé par les microbes)* bacterial
microbiologie [mikrɔbjɔlɔʒi] NF microbiology
microbiologique [mikrɔbjɔlɔʒik] ADJ microbiological
microbiologiste [mikrɔbjɔlɔʒist] NMF microbiologist
microbrasserie [mikrɔbrasri] NF *Can (brasserie artisanale)* microbrewery; *(établissement où l'on consomme de la bière)* = pub attached to a microbrewery
microcéphale [mikrosefal] ADJ microcephalic
NMF microcephalic
microchirurgie [mikrɔʃiryrʒi] NF microsurgery
microcircuit [mikrɔsirkɥi] NM *Ordinat* microcircuit; **microcircuits** microcircuitry
microclimat [mikrɔklima] NM microclimate
microcosme [mikrɔkɔsm] NM microcosm
microcosmique [mikrɔkɔsmik] ADJ microcosmic
microcoupure [mikrokupyr] NF *Électron* power blip
microcrédit [mikrokredi] NM *Fin* microcredit
microcyte [mikrɔsit] NF *Physiol* microcyte
microdermabrasion [mikrodɛrmabrazjɔ̃] NF microdermabrasion
microdisquette [mikrodiskɛt] NF *Ordinat* microfloppy
microéconomie [mikrɔekɔnɔmi] NF microeconomics *(singulier)*
microéconomique [mikrɔekɔnɔmik] ADJ microeconomic
microédition [mikrɔedisjɔ̃] NF desktop publishing
microélectronique [mikrɔelɛktrɔnik] ADJ microelectronic
NF microelectronics *(singulier)*
microentreprise [mikroɑ̃trəpriz] NF microenterprise, microbusiness
microenvironnement [mikrɔɑ̃virɔnmɑ̃] NM micro-environment
microfiche [mikrɔfiʃ] NF microfiche
microfilament [mikrɔfilamɑ̃] NM *Biol* microfilament
microfilm [mikrɔfilm] NM microfilm
microfilmer [3] [mikrɔfilme] VT to microfilm
microfinance [mikrɔfinɑ̃s] NF microfinance
micrographie [mikrɔgrafi] NF **1** *(science)* micrography **2** *(photographie)* micrograph **3** *Métal* microstructural microscopy
micrographique [mikrɔgrafik] ADJ micrographic
micro-informatique [mikrɔɛ̃fɔrmatik] *(pl* **micro-informatiques**) NF microcomputing
micromarketing [mikromarketiŋ] NM micromarketing
micromètre [mikrɔmɛtr] NM **1** *(instrument)* micrometer **2** *(unité)* micrometre
micrométrique [mikrɔmetrik] ADJ micrometric, micrometrical
micron [mikrɔ̃] NM micron

Micronésie [mikrɔnezi] **NF** *Géog* **la M.** Micronesia

micronisation [mikrɔnizasjɔ̃] **NF 1** *Ordinat* downsizing **2** *Phys* micronization

microniser [3] [mikrɔnize] **VT 1** *Ordinat* to downsize **2** *Phys* to micronize

micro-onde [mikrɔɔ̃d] (*pl* **micro-ondes**) **NF** microwave

• **micro-ondes NM INV** microwave (oven); **faites dégeler au micro-ondes** defrost in the microwave; **faire cuire qch au micro-ondes** to cook sth in the microwave, to microwave sth

micro-ordinateur [mikrɔɔrdinatœr] (*pl* **micro-ordinateurs**) **NM** microcomputer; **m. de bureau** desktop computer; **m. portable** laptop (computer)

micro-organisme [mikrɔɔrganism] (*pl* **micro-organismes**) **NM** *Biol* microorganism

micro-paiement [mikrɔpemɑ̃] (*pl* **micro-paiements**) **NM** *Ordinat* micropayment

microphone [mikrɔfɔn] **NM** microphone; **m. à condensateur** condenser microphone; **m. sur pied** stand microphone

microphotographie [mikrɔfɔtɔgrafi] **NF 1** (*technique*) microphotography **2** (*image*) microphotograph

microphotographique [mikrɔfɔtɔgrafik] **ADJ** microphotographic, photomicrographic

microphysique [mikrɔfizik] **NF** microphysics (*singulier*)

micropilule [mikrɔpilyl] **NF** minipill

microplaquette [mikrɔplakɛt] **NF** *Électron* chip

microprocesseur [mikrɔprɔsesœr] **NM** *Ordinat* microprocessor; **m. en tranches** bit slice microprocessor

microprogramme [mikrɔprɔgram] **NM** *Ordinat* microprogram, firmware

microscope [mikrɔskɔp] **NM** microscope; **visible au m.** visible under the microscope; **étudier qch au m.** to examine sth under *or* through a microscope; *Fig* to put sth under the microscope; **m. électronique** electron microscope; **m. électronique à balayage** scanning electron microscope; **m. optique** optical *or* light microscope

microscopie [mikrɔskɔpi] **NF** microscopy

microscopique [mikrɔskɔpik] **ADJ** microscopic; *Fig* (*petit*) microscopic, tiny, minute

microseconde [mikrɔsəgɔ̃d] **NF** microsecond

microserveur [mikrɔsɛrvœr] **NM** *Ordinat* microserver

microsillon [mikrɔsijɔ̃] **NM** (*sillon*) microgroove; (*disque*) **m. record**

microsociologie [mikrɔsɔsjɔlɔʒi] **NF** microsociology

microsome [mikrɔsɔm] **NF** *Biol* microsome

microtome [mikrɔtɔm] **NM** *Biol* microtome

micro-trottoir [mikrɔtrɔtwar] (*pl* **micros-trottoirs**) **NM** street interview, *Br Fam* vox pop

miction [miksjɔ̃] **NF** urination, *Spéc* micturition

mi-cuit, -e [mikɥi, -kɥit] (*mpl* **mi-cuits**, *fpl* **mi-cuites**) *Culin* **ADJ** half-cooked, partially-cooked

NM m. au chocolat melting chocolate pudding

MidCAC [midkak] **NM** *Bourse* **le M., l'indice M.** = Paris stock exchange index comprising 100 medium-range shares, ≃ MidCap

midi[1] [midi] **NM 1** (*milieu du jour*) midday, lunchtime, noon; **en plein m.** at the height of noon; **qu'est-ce que tu fais, ce m.?** what are you doing at lunchtime *or* for lunch?; **je m'arrête à m.** I stop at lunchtime; (*pour déjeuner*) I stop for lunch; **je joue au squash à m.** (*pendant la pause*) I play squash during *or* at lunchtime; **tous les midis** every day at lunchtime, every lunchtime; **il mange des pâtes tous les midis** he has pasta for lunch every day **2** (*heure*) midday, twelve (o'clock), (twelve) noon; **il est m.** it's midday, it's twelve (noon); **il est m. passé** it's after twelve, it's past midday; **m. et demi** half-past twelve; **m. et quart** a quarter past twelve; **m. moins vingt** twenty to twelve; **entre m. et deux (heures)** between twelve and two, during lunch *or* lunchtime; **fermé de m. à 14 h** closed from 12 to 2 p.m.; **vers m.** round (about) twelve *or* midday; **sur le coup de m.** on the stroke of twelve **3** (*sud*) south; **exposé au m.** south-facing, facing south

• **Midi NM** (*région du sud*) South; **le M. (de la France)** the South of France; **du M.** Southern, southern; **le climat du M.** the Southern climate; **l'accent du M.** southern (French) accent

• **de midi ADJ** (*repas, informations*) midday (*avant n*); **la pause de m.** the lunch break

midi[2] [midi] **ADJ INV** (*de taille moyenne*) **chaîne m.** midi system

midinette [midinɛt] **NF 1** *Fam Vieilli* (*cousette*) dressmaker's apprentice, seamstress **2** *Péj* (*jeune fille*) starry-eyed girl; **des amours de m.** the loves of some starry-eyed young girl; **des lectures de m.** slushy novels

mi-distance [midistɑ̃s] **à mi-distance ADV** halfway, midway

• **à mi-distance de PRÉP** halfway *or* midway between; **nous sommes à m. de notre but** we are halfway to our goal

midship [midʃip] **NM** *Fam Naut* middy

mie[1] [mi] **NF** (*de pain*) white *or* soft *or* doughy part; **mettez de la m. de pain à tremper** soak some bread, having removed the crusts

mie[2] [mi] **NF** *Arch & Littéraire* (*femme*) truelove, ladylove; **ma m.** my beloved; **venez, ma m.** come, fair damsel

miel [mjɛl] **NM 1** (*d'abeilles*) honey; **m. liquide/solide** clear/set honey; **m. d'acacia** acacia honey **2** (*locutions*) **faire son m. de qch** to make capital out of sth; **il est (tout sucre) tout m.** he's a sweet talker

• **au miel ADJ** honey (*avant n*), honey-flavoured

miellé, -e [mjele] **ADJ** *Littéraire* (*parfum*) honeyed; (*boisson*) tasting of honey; **du thé m.** honey-sweetened tea

mielleuse [mjɛløz] *voir* **mielleux**

mielleusement [mjɛløzmɑ̃] **ADV** smarmily; **sourire m.** to give a sweet, sugary smile; **il s'exprime m.** he's a sweet talker

mielleux, -euse [mjɛlø, -øz] **ADJ 1** *Péj* (*doucereux*) sickly sweet; (*personne*) sugary; **un sourire m.** a saccharine smile; **d'un ton m.** in a syrupy voice; **un discours m.** a speech oozing with insincerity **2** (*relatif au miel*) honey (*avant n*), honeylike

mien [mjɛ̃], (*f* **mienne** [mjɛn], *mpl* **miens** [mjɛ̃], *fpl* **miennes** [mjɛn]) **ADJ** *Littéraire* **c'est un principe que j'ai fait m. depuis longtemps** it has long been a principle of mine; **j'ai fait m. ce mot d'ordre** I've adopted this slogan as my own; **je fais miennes les félicitations qu'il vous adresse** I join (with) him in congratulating you; **une mienne cousine** a cousin of mine

• **le mien** (*f* **la mienne**, *mpl* **les miens**, *fpl* **les miennes**) **PRON** mine; **je te prête le m.** you can borrow mine; **puis-je prendre ta voiture? la mienne est au garage** may I take your car? mine is at the garage; **je suis parti avec une valise qui n'était pas la mienne** I left with a suitcase that wasn't mine *or* that didn't belong to me; **il ressemble au m.** it looks like mine; **je veux bien te donner du m.** please have some of mine; **tes enfants sont plus âgés que les miens** your children are older than mine (are); **vos préoccupations sont aussi les miennes** I share your anxieties; **ton jour/ton prix sera le m.** name the day/your price; **les deux miens** my two, both of mine; (*en insistant*) my own two; **je lui ai laissé deux des miens** I gave him/her two of mine; *très Fam* **le m. de bébé est plus intelligent** my baby is more intelligent□; *Fam* **à la mienne!** (*en buvant*) here's to me! **NM j'y mets du m.** (*en faisant des efforts*) I'm making an effort; (*en étant compréhensif*) I'm trying to be understanding; *Fam* **j'ai encore fait des miennes!** I've (gone and) done it again!

• **les miens NMPL** (*ma famille*) my family, *Am* my folks; (*mes partisans*) my followers; (*mes coéquipiers*) my team-mates

miette [mjɛt] **NF 1** (*d'aliment*) crumb; **une m. de pain** a crumb of bread; **des miettes de pain** breadcrumbs; **des miettes de crabe/de thon** crab/tuna flakes **2** (*petite quantité*) **pas une m. de** not a shred of; **tu n'en auras pas une m.!** you're not getting any of it!; **ils n'en ont pas laissé une m.** they didn't leave a crumb, they ate the lot; **elle n'a pas perdu une m. de la conversation** not one scrap of the conversation escaped her *or* passed her by; **une m. de** a little bit of **3** *Belg* (*locution*) **une m.** a bit, a little

• **miettes NFPL 1** (*restes*) leftovers, crumbs, scraps; **après le partage, ma cousine n'a eu que des miettes** my cousin had to make do with what little was left over after the inheritance was shared out **2** (*morceaux*) piece, fragment, bit; **mettre** *ou* **réduire qch en miettes** (*objet*) to smash sth to pieces *or* bits *or* smithereens; **sa voiture est en miettes** his/her car's a wreck; **son rêve est en miettes** his/her dream is in shreds *or* tatters

MIEUX [mjø]

ADV
• better **A1, 2, B, C** • best **B**
ADJ
• better **1–3**
NM
• improvement **1** • best **2**

ADV A. *COMPARATIF DE "BIEN"* **1** (*d'une manière plus satisfaisante*) better; **tout va m.** things are better (now); **elle va m.** she's better; **il travaille m. depuis quelque temps** he's been working better for some time *or* a while now; **cette jupe te va m.** (*d'aspect*) that skirt suits you better; (*de taille*) that skirt fits you better; **le vert me va m.** green suits me better; **qui dit m.?** (*aux enchères*) any advance (on that)?, any more bids?; *Fig* who can top that?; **repassez demain, je ne peux pas vous dire m.** come again tomorrow, that's the best *or* all I can tell you; **je m'y prends m. depuis** I'm handling it better now, I've got better at it since; **il s'y prend m. avec lui maintenant** he deals with *or* handles him better now; **cette fois-ci, elle a m. pris la plaisanterie** this time she took the joke better; **m. payé** better paid; **m. assis** (*plus confortablement*) sitting more comfortably; (*au spectacle*) in a better seat; **un peu m.** a little *or* a bit better; **beaucoup** *ou* **bien m.** a lot *or* much better; **vraiment m.** much better; **se sentir m.** to feel better; **moins je le vois, m. je me porte!** the less I see of him, the better I feel!; **plus je le lis, m. je le comprends** the more I read it, the better I understand it; **il parle italien m. que je ne pensais** he speaks Italian better than I thought; **il ne lit pas m. qu'il ne parle** he doesn't read any better than he speaks

2 (*conformément à la raison, à la morale*) better; **pas m.** no better; **son frère ne fait que des bêtises, et elle ce n'est pas m.** her brother is always misbehaving and she's no better; **il ferait m. de travailler/de se taire** he'd do better to work/to keep quiet; **il pourrait m. faire** he could do better; **on ne peut pas m. dire** you can't say better *or* fairer than that

B. *SUPERLATIF DE "BIEN"* **le m.** (*de deux*) the better; (*de plusieurs*) the best; **c'est le mannequin le m. payé** (*des deux*) she's the better-paid model; (*de plusieurs*) she's the best-paid model; **voilà ce qui me convient le m.** this is what suits me best; **des deux, qui est la m.?** who's the better of the two?; **la m. de toutes** the best of them all; **le m. qu'il peut** the best he can; **le m. possible** as well as possible; **j'ai classé les dossiers le m. possible** I filed everything as best I could; **le m. du monde** beautifully; **s'entendre le m. du monde avec qn** to be on the best of terms with sb

C. *EMPLOI NOMINAL* better; **c'est pas mal, mais il y a m.** it's not bad, but there's better; **en attendant/espérant m.** while waiting/hoping for better (things); **il s'attendait à m., il attendait m.** he was expecting (something) better; **faute de m., je m'en contenterai** since there's nothing better, I'll make do with it; **c'est sa mère en m.** she's like her mother, only better-looking; **changer en m.** to take a turn for *or* to change for the better

ADJ 1 (*plus satisfaisant*) better; **voilà, c'est déjà beaucoup m.!** there, it's already much *or* a lot better!; **on ne se voit plus, c'est m. ainsi** we don't see each other any more, it's better that way; **c'était m. que jamais** it was better than ever; **c'est m. que rien** it's better than nothing; **le dernier modèle est m. que le précédent** the latest model is better than *or* is an improvement on the previous one

2 (*du point de vue de la santé, du bien-être*) better; **il est m.** he's better; **on sent qu'il est m. dans sa peau** you can tell he's feeling better about himself; **tu seras m. en pantalon** you'd be better in trousers; **on est m. dans ce fauteuil** this armchair is more comfortable

3 *(plus beau)* better; **elle est m. avec les cheveux courts** she looks better with short hair; **prends cette robe, elle est m. que l'autre** take this dress, it's better than the other (one); **elle est m. que sa sœur** she's better-looking than her sister

NM **1** *(amélioration)* improvement; **il y a du m.** things have got better, there's some improvement; **il y a un m.** there is an improvement; **la situation connaît un léger m.** the situation has improved slightly, there's been a slight improvement in the situation

2 *(ce qui est préférable)* **le m. est de ne pas y aller** it's best not to go; **le m., c'est de partir un peu plus tôt** it's best to leave a bit earlier; **faire de son m.** to do one's (level) best; **il a fait de son m.** he did his best; *Prov* **le m. est l'ennemi du bien** the best is the enemy of the good

• **à qui mieux mieux** ADV **les enfants répondaient à qui m. m.** the children were trying to outdo each other in answering

• **au mieux** ADV **faire au m.** to do whatever's best, to act for the best; **ils sont au m. (l'un avec l'autre)** they're on very good terms; **vous l'aurez lundi, en mettant les choses au m.** you'll get it on Monday at the very earliest; **au m. de sa forme** on top form, in prime condition; **j'ai agi au m. de vos intérêts** I acted in your best interest

• **de mieux** ADJ *(de plus satisfaisant)* **c'est ce que nous avons de m.** it's the best we have; **si tu n'as rien de m. à faire, viens avec moi** if you've got nothing better to do, come with me

• **de mieux en mieux** ADV better and better; **elle joue de m. en m.** she plays better and better; *Ironique* **de m. en m.!** it gets better!

• **des mieux** ADV **j'ai un ami qui est des m. placé** *ou* **placés au ministère** I have a friend who's high up in the Ministry

• **on ne peut mieux** ADV extremely well; **il s'exprime on ne peut m.** he expresses himself extremely well; **le stage va on ne peut m.** the course couldn't be going better

• **pour le mieux** ADV for the best; **tout va pour le m.** everything is for the best; **faire pour le m.** to act for the best

• **qui mieux est** ADV even better, better still

---

mieux-disant [mjødizɑ̃] *(pl* **mieux-disants)** NM elite

mieux-être [mjøzɛtr] NM INV better quality of life

mieux-vivre [mjøvivr] NM INV better *or* higher standard of living; **la lutte pour le m.** the struggle for a better *or* higher standard of living

mièvre [mjɛvr] ADJ *Péj* **1** *(fade)* insipid, vapid, bland; *(sentimental)* mawkish, syrupy; **un roman m.** a mawkish novel **2** *(maniéré)* mawkish, precious; **avec une grâce un peu m.** demurely; **sa façon un peu m. de dire bonjour** his/her slightly simpering *or Br* twee way of saying hello **3** *(joli sans vrai talent* ▸ *dessin)* pretty-pretty, flowery

mièvrerie [mjɛvrəri] NF *Péj* **1** *(fadeur)* insipidness; *(sentimentalité)* mawkishness; *(caractère maniéré)* sickly affectation; *(joliesse)* floweriness, insipid prettiness **2** *(acte)* mawkish behaviour *(UNCOUNT)*; *(propos)* mawkish *or Br* twee remark; **ces mièvreries qu'on nous sert à la télé** these stupid programmes *or* the pap they show on TV

mi-fin, -e [mifɛ̃, -fin] *(mpl* **mi-fins,** *fpl* **mi-fines)** ADJ *Com* medium

mignard, -e [miɲar, -ard] ADJ *Littéraire (gracieux)* dainty; *Péj (affecté)* affected

mignardise [miɲardiz] NF **1** *Littéraire (grâce)* daintiness; *Péj (affectation)* affectedness **2** *Bot* **(œillet) m.** garden pink

mignon, -onne [miɲɔ̃, -ɔn] ADJ **1** *(joli* ▸ *enfant, chiot)* sweet, cute; *(*▸ *femme)* pretty; **elle est plus mignonne avec les cheveux courts** she's prettier with short hair; **il est m., ton appartement** you've got a lovely little *Br* flat *or Am* apartment; **c'est m. comme tout chez eux** they have a delightful *or* charming home; *Fam* **c'est m. tout plein à cet âge-là** children are as cute as anything at that age; *Fam* **un mec super m.** a great-looking guy **2** *Fam (gentil)* sweet, nice, lovely; **il m'a apporté des fleurs, c'était m. comme tout** he brought me flowers, it was so sweet of him; **allez, sois mignonne, va te coucher** come on, be a darling *or* sweetie and go to bed

NM,F *Fam (terme d'affection)* darling, sweetie; **ma mignonne** darling, sweetie

NM *Hist* minion, favourite

mignonnet, -ette [miɲɔnɛ, -ɛt] ADJ pretty-pretty

• **mignonnette** NF **1** *Bot (réséda)* mignonette; *(saxifrage)* London pride; *(œillet mignardise)* garden pink; *(chicorée sauvage)* wild chicory **2** *(poivre)* coarse-ground pepper **3** *(gravillon)* small gravel **4** *(bouteille miniature)* miniature (bottle) **5** *Tex* mignonette lace

migraine [migrɛn] NF *(mal de tête)* bad headache; *Méd* migraine; **avoir la m.** to have a bad headache; **avoir des migraines** to get bad headaches/migraines; **m. ophtalmique** headache caused by eyestrain

migraineux, -euse [migrenø, -øz] *Méd* ADJ migrainous

NM,F migraine sufferer

migrant, -e [migrɑ̃, -ɑ̃t] ADJ migrant *(avant n)*

NM,F migrant

migrateur, -trice [migratœr, -tris] ADJ *Biol & Zool* migratory

NM *(oiseau)* migrator, migrant

migration [migrasjɔ̃] NF **1** *(des oiseaux, des travailleurs)* migration; *Fig* **les grandes migrations estivales vont commencer** the mass summer migrations are about to begin **2** *Chim & Géol* migration

migratoire [migratwar] ADJ migratory

migratrice [migratris] *voir* **migrateur**

migrer [3] [migre] VI to migrate (**vers** to); *Ordinat* **faire m.** to transmit

mi-jambe [miʒɑ̃b] **à mi-jambe** ADV *(à partir du bas)* up to the knees; *(à partir du haut)* down to the knees; **on était dans la neige à m.** we were knee-deep in snow

mijaurée [miʒɔre] NF *(pimbêche)* (stuck-up) little madam; **ne fais pas la** *ou* **ta m.!** don't give yourself such airs!

mijoter [3] [miʒɔte] VT **1** *Culin (faire cuire)* to simmer; *(préparer avec soin)* to cook up; **m. des petits plats** to spend time preparing delicious meals **2** *Fam (coup, plan)* to plot, to cook up; **qu'est-ce que tu mijotes?** what are you up to?; **elle mijote quelque chose** she's got something up her sleeve; **ils ont mijoté ça entre eux** they cooked it up between them

VI **1** *Culin* to simmer, to stew gently; **continuez à faire** *ou* **laissez m. jusqu'à ce que la viande soit cuite** (allow to) simmer until the meat is cooked **2** *Fam Fig* **laisse-la m. dans son coin** *ou* **jus** leave her a while to stew in her own juice

VPR **se mijoter** *Fam (coup, plan)* to be cooking *or* brewing, to be afoot

mikado [mikado] NM **1** *(titre)* mikado **2** *(jeu)* mikado, spillikins *(singulier)*

mil[1] [mil] ADJ INV *(mille)* thousand *(used only in writing out AD dates)*; **l'an m. neuf cent quatre-vingt-dix** (the year) nineteen hundred and ninety

mil[2] [mil] NM *(céréale)* millet

milady [miledi] *(pl* **miladys)** NF *(titre)* my Lady; *(noble)* titled (English) lady

milan [milɑ̃] NM *Orn* kite; **m. royal** red kite

milanais, -e [milanɛ, -ɛz] ADJ Milanese

• **Milanais, -e** NM,F Milanese; **les M.** the Milanese

mildiou [mildju] NM *(gén)* mildew; *(de la pomme de terre)* potato blight; *(de la vigne)* brown rot

mildiousé, -e [mildjuze] ADJ mildewy, mildewed

mile [majl] NM (statute) mile

miliaire [miljer] *Méd* ADJ miliary

NF prickly heat, *Spéc* miliaria

milice [milis] NF **1** *Hist* militia **2** *(organisation paramilitaire)* militia; **m. privée** private militia **3** *Belg (service militaire)* military service; **la m.** *(armée)* the army

milicien, -enne [milisjɛ̃, -ɛn] NM,F militiaman, *f* militia woman

NM *Belg Br* conscript, *Am* draftee

milieu, -x [miljø] NM **1** *(dans l'espace)* middle, centre; **une nappe déchirée/décorée en son m.** a tablecloth torn/decorated in the middle; **sciez-la par le** *ou* **en son m.** saw it through *or* down the middle; **la table du m.** the middle table; **celui du m.** the one in the middle, the middle one

2 *(dans le temps)* middle; **l'incendie s'est déclaré vers le m. de la nuit** the fire broke out in the middle of the night; **en m. de trimestre** in mid-term; **il est entré en plein m. d'une discussion** he came in right in the middle of a discussion

3 *(moyen terme)* middle way *or* course; **le juste m.** the happy medium; **il faut trouver un juste m.** we have to find a happy medium; **tenir le m. entre... et...** to steer a middle course between... and...

4 *(entourage)* environment, milieu; **l'influence du m. familial** *ou* **d'origine sur la réussite scolaire** the influence of the home background *or* environment on achievement at school; **m. socioculturel** (social) background; **des gens de tous les milieux** people from all walks of life *or* backgrounds; **c'est un m. très snob** it's a very snobbish environment; **les milieux scientifiques** scientific circles; **les milieux bien informés** well-informed circles; **dans les milieux financiers** in financial circles; **se sentir/ne pas se sentir dans son m.** to feel at home/out of place; **je n'appartiens pas à leur m., je ne suis pas de leur m.** I don't belong to *or* I'm not part of their set *or* circle, I don't move in their circles; **en m. ouvert** *(éducation, réhabilitation)* in the community

5 *Biol (environnement)* environment, habitat; **dans un m. acide** in an acid medium; **m. de culture** culture medium; **m. naturel** natural habitat; **en m. stérile** in a sterile environment

6 *Phys* medium

7 *Ind & (en sciences)* **en m. réel** in the field

8 *(pègre)* **le m.** the underworld

9 *Math* midpoint, midrange

• **au beau milieu de** PRÉP right in the middle of

• **au (beau) milieu** ADV (right) in the middle, (right) in the centre; **et là, au m., il y avait un puits** and there, right in the middle, was a well

• **au milieu de** PRÉP **1** *(dans l'espace)* in the middle of, in the centre of; **au m. de la pièce** in the middle *or* centre of the room **2** *(dans le temps)* in the middle of; **au m. de la journée/nuit** in the middle of the day/night; **au m. du mois** in the middle of the month; **au m. de l'hiver/l'été** in midwinter/midsummer; **au m. du mois de mars** in mid-March; **au m. du trimestre** in mid-term; **vers le m. du mois** about the middle of the month; **elle est partie au m. de mon cours** she left in the middle of *or* halfway through my lesson **3** *(parmi)* amongst, in the midst of, surrounded by; **mourir au m. des siens** to die amongst *or* surrounded by one's loved ones; **au m. de la foule** in the middle *or* in the midst of the crowd; **il quitta la scène au m. des huées** he was booed off the stage

• **milieu de terrain** NM *Sport (zone)* midfield (area); *(joueur)* midfield player

militaire [militer] ADJ *(gén)* military; *(de l'armée de terre)* army *(avant n)*, service *(avant n)*; *(de l'armée de l'air, de la marine)* service *(avant n)*; **tous les personnels militaires** all service personnel

NM *(soldat* ▸ *gén)* soldier; *(*▸ *de l'armée de terre)* soldier, serviceman; *(*▸ *de l'armée de l'air, de la marine)* serviceman; **c'est un ancien m.** he's an ex-serviceman; **m. du contingent** national serviceman; **m. de carrière** professional soldier; **les militaires** the military, the armed forces, the services

militairement [militɛrmɑ̃] ADV **saluer m.** to salute in military fashion; **les bases ennemies sont occupées m.** the enemy bases are occupied by the military; **il nous faut intervenir m.** we have to resort to military intervention

militance [militɑ̃s] NF militancy

militant, -e [militɑ̃, -ɑ̃t] ADJ militant

NM,F militant, activist; **les militants de base sont d'accord** the grassroots militants agree; **m. syndical** trade union militant *or* activist

militantisme [militɑ̃tism] NM militancy, militantism

militarisation [militarizasjɔ̃] NF militarization

militariser [3] [militarize] VT to militarize

militarisme [militarism] NM militarism

militariste [militarist] ADJ militaristic
NMF militarist

militer [3] [milite] VI 1 *(agir en militant)* to be a militant *or* an activist; **m. au** *ou* **dans le parti socialiste** to be a socialist party activist; **m. pour/contre qch** to fight for/against sth 2 *Fig (plaider)* to militate; **ces témoignages ne militent pas en votre faveur** this evidence goes *or* militates against you; **les derniers bilans militent en faveur d'une refonte de la société** the latest balance sheets are a good argument *or* make a good case for restructuring the company

milk-shake [milkʃɛk] *(pl* **milk-shakes)** NM milkshake; **m. à la fraise** strawberry milkshake

millage [milaʒ] NM *Can* mileage

mille[1] [mil] ADJ INV 1 *(dix fois cent)* a *or* one thousand; **m. hommes** a thousand men, one thousand men; **m. un** a thousand and one, one thousand and one; **dix/cent m.** ten/a hundred thousand; **m. fois trois égale trois m.** one thousand times three is three thousand; **en l'an m. cinquante** in the year one thousand and fifty; **l'an m. neuf cent avant J.-C.** (the year) nineteen hundred BC; **c'est à m. kilomètres d'ici** it's a thousand kilometres from here 2 *(beaucoup de* ▸ *exemples, raisons)* countless, numerous, many; **je vous l'ai dit m. fois** I've told you a thousand times, I've told you time and time again; **vous avez m. fois raison** you are so right; **c'est m. fois trop grand** it's miles too big; **ton énigme est m. fois trop compliquée pour moi** your riddle is far too difficult for me; **m. baisers** lots *or* tons of kisses; **m. mercis, merci m. fois** many thanks; **m. excuses** *ou* **pardons si je t'ai blessé** I'm dreadfully sorry if I've hurt you; **voilà un exemple entre m.** here's just one of the countless examples I could choose, here's an example taken at random; **en m. morceaux** in pieces; **il y a m. et une manières de réussir sa vie** there are thousands of ways *or* a thousand and one ways of being successful in life; **endurer** *ou* **souffrir m. morts** to go through agonies; **(m. milliards de) m. sabords!** ≃ shiver me timbers!
NM INV 1 *(nombre)* a *or* one thousand; **ils sont morts par centaines de m.** they died in (their) hundreds of thousands; **il y a une chance sur m. que ça marche** there's a one-in-a-thousand chance that it'll work; **les chances de guérison sont de dix pour m.** there's a one in a hundred chance of a cure; **un taux de natalité de 5 pour m.** a birthrate of 0.5 percent; **par m. de briques vendu(es)** per thousand bricks sold, for every thousand bricks sold; *Fam* **des m. et des cents** loads of money; **il ne gagne pas des m. et des cents** he doesn't exactly earn a fortune 2 *(centre d'une cible)* bull's eye; *Fam* **mettre** *ou* **taper (en plein) dans le m.** to hit the bull's-eye◻; *Fig* to score a bull's-eye, to be bang on target

mille[2] [mil] NM 1 *Naut* **m. (marin** *ou* **nautique)** nautical mile 2 *Can Anciennement* **m. (anglais)** (statute) mile

mille-feuille [milfœj] *(pl* **mille-feuilles)** NF *Bot* yarrow, milfoil
NM *Culin* millefeuille, *Am* napoleon

millénaire [milener] ADJ thousand-year-old; **un arbre m.** a thousand-year-old tree; **des traditions (plusieurs fois) millénaires** age-old *or* time-honoured traditions; **cette superstition est plusieurs fois m.** the superstition has existed for several thousands of years
NM 1 *(période)* millennium; **au cours du troisième m. avant Jésus-Christ** in the third millennium BC; **dater du premier m. av. J.-C.** to date from the first millennium BC; **cette tradition est vieille d'au moins un m.** the tradition has existed for at least a thousand years 2 *(anniversaire)* millennium, thousandth anniversary; **l'année du m. capétien** the millennium of the foundation of the Capetian dynasty

millénarisme [milenarism] NM millenarianism

millénariste [milenarist] ADJ millenarian
NMF millenarian

millenium [milenjɔm] NM *Rel* millennium

mille-pattes [milpat] NM INV *Entom* millipede, centipede

millepertuis [milpɛrtɥi] NM *Bot* St John's wort

milleraies [milrɛ] NM INV needlecord
ADJ INV **velours m.** needlecord

millésime [milezim] NM 1 *(date)* date, year 2 *(en œnologie* ▸ *date de récolte)* year, vintage; **le m. 1976 est l'un des meilleurs** the 1976 vintage is among the best; **il ne boit que de grands millésimes** he only drinks vintage wine

millésimé, -e [milezime] ADJ 1 *(vin)* vintage *(avant n)*; **un bourgogne m. 1970** a 1970 (vintage) Burgundy; **une bouteille millésimée 1880** a bottle dated 1880 2 *(pièce)* dated

millet [mijɛ] NM millet; **(grains de) m.** birdseed, canary seed

milliampère [miliɑ̃pɛr] NM milliamp, milliampere

milliard [miljar] NM billion, *Br Vieilli* thousand million; **cela a coûté deux milliards (d'euros)** it cost two billion (euros); **des milliards de globules rouges** billions of red corpuscles

milliardaire [miljardɛr] ADJ **sa famille est plusieurs fois m.** his/her family is worth billions
NMF billionaire

milliardième [miljardjɛm] ADJ billionth, *Br Vieilli* thousand millionth
NMF 1 *(personne)* billionth, *Br Vieilli* thousand millionth 2 *(objet)* billionth (one), *Br Vieilli* thousand millionth (one)
NM *(partie)* billionth, *Br Vieilli* thousand millionth

millibar [milibar] NM *Météo* millibar

millième [miljɛm] ADJ thousandth
NMF 1 *(personne)* thousandth 2 *(objet)* thousandth (one)
NM *(partie)* thousandth; **elle ne connaît pas le m. de mes sentiments** she can't begin to have an idea of my feelings; **il ne fournit pas le m. du travail nécessaire** he isn't doing a fraction of the work that has to be done; *voir aussi* **cinquième**

millier [milje] NM thousand; **un m. de livres ont été vendus** a thousand books have been sold; **des milliers de** thousands of
• **par milliers** ADV *(arriver)* in their thousands; *(envoyer, commander)* by the thousand; **des ballons ont été lâchés par milliers** thousands (upon thousands) of balloons have been released

milligramme [miligram] NM milligram, milligramme

millilitre [mililitr] NM millilitre

millimètre [milimɛtr] NM millimetre

millimétré, -e [milimetre], **millimétrique** [milimetrik] ADJ millimetric; **échelle millimétrée** millimetre scale

million [miljɔ̃] NM 1 *(quantité)* million; **un m. de personnes** a *or* one million people; **quatre millions d'hommes** four million men; **des millions de** millions of; *Fig* **il n'y en a pas des millions à s'appeler comme ça** there can't be too many people with a name like that 2 *(somme)* **dix millions d'euros** ten million euros; *Anciennement Fam* **la maison vaut 35 millions** *(de centimes de franc)* the house is worth 350,000 francs; *Anciennement Fam* **un m. cinq** *(de centimes de franc)* 15,000 francs; *(de francs)* 1.5 million francs

millionième [miljɔnjɛm] ADJ millionth
NMF 1 *(personne)* millionth 2 *(objet)* millionth (one)
NM *(partie)* millionth

millionnaire [miljɔnɛr] ADJ millionaire, millionnaire; **être/devenir m.** to be/to become a millionaire; **elle est plusieurs fois m. (en dollars)** she's a (dollar) millionaire *or* millionairess several times over
NMF millionaire, *f* millionairess

milliseconde [milisəgɔ̃d] NF millisecond

millivolt [milivɔlt] NM millivolt

milliwatt [miliwat] NM milliwatt

milord [milɔr] NM 1 *(en appellation)* lord; **après vous, m.** after you, my lord 2 *Fam Vieilli (homme riche)* toff 3 *(véhicule)* victoria

mi-lourd [milur] *(pl* **mi-lourds)** *Boxe* ADJ M light heavyweight *(avant n)*
NM light heavyweight

mime [mim] NMF 1 *(artiste)* mime (artist) 2 *(imitateur)* mimic
NM 1 *(art)* mime; **faire du m.** to be a mime (artist); **un spectacle de m.** a mime show 2 *(action de mimer)* miming *(UNCOUNT)*

mimer [3] [mime] VT 1 *Théât* to mime 2 *(imiter)* to mimic

mimétique [mimetik] ADJ *Biol, Beaux-Arts & Littérature* mimetic

mimétisme [mimetism] NM 1 *Biol* mimetism, mimesis 2 *(imitation)* mimicry, mimicking; **ils le font tous par m.** they can't help copying each other, they can't help mimicking each other

mimi [mimi] ADJ INV *Fam (mignon)* lovely◻, sweet◻, cute
NM 1 *(en langage enfantin* ▸ *chat)* pussy (cat) 2 *Fam (bisou)* kiss◻; *(caresse)* cuddle◻, hug◻; **fais m. à ta sœur** give your sister a kiss; **faire un gros m. à qn** to give sb a big kiss; **elle adore faire des mimis à son petit frère** she loves cuddling her little brother 3 *Fam (terme d'affection)* darling, sweetie, honey; **qu'est-ce qui ne va pas, mon m.?** what's wrong, sweetie-pie?

mimique [mimik] ADJ **langage m.** sign language
NF 1 *(gestuelle)* gesture; **il fit une m. de désespoir** he made a despairing gesture 2 *(grimace)* facial expression; **il a fait une curieuse m.** he made a strange face

mimodrame [mimɔdram] NM dumb show

mimolette [mimɔlɛt] NF Mimolette (cheese)

mimosa [mimɔza] NM 1 *Bot* mimosa 2 *Culin* **œuf m.** egg mayonnaise *(topped with crumbled yolk)*

mi-moyen [mimwajɛ̃] *(pl* **mi-moyens)** *Boxe* ADJ M welterweight *(avant n)*
NM welterweight

min *(abrév écrite* **minute)** min

minable [minabl] *Fam* ADJ 1 *(pauvre* ▸ *logement)* shabby, grotty
2 *(mesquin)* **une petite vengeance m.** petty revenge; **c'est m., ce que tu lui as fait** that was a rotten trick you played on him/her
3 *(insuffisant* ▸ *salaire, repas)* pathetic, lousy
4 *(sans envergure)* small-time, third-rate; **un escroc m.** a small-time crook
NMF loser, no-hoper, dead loss; **tu n'es qu'un m.!** you're so pathetic!; **pauvre m., va!** you pathetic loser!; **quelle bande de minables!** what a pathetic *or* useless bunch!

minaret [minarɛ] NM minaret

minauder [3] [minode] VI to mince, to simper; **elle répondait aux questions en minaudant** she answered the questions with a simper; **arrête de m.!** don't be such a poser!

minauderie [minodri] NF 1 *(préciosité)* (show of) affectation 2 *(acte, propos)* affectation; **minauderies** simpering

minaudier, -ère [minodje, -ɛr] ADJ affected, simpering, mincing

mince [mɛ̃s] ADJ 1 *(sans épaisseur)* thin; **une m. couche de vernis** a thin layer of varnish; **une m. tranche de bacon** a sliver *or* a thin slice of bacon; **des lèvres minces** thin lips; **un m. filet d'eau** a thin trickle of water; **m. comme une feuille de papier à cigarette** paper-thin, wafer-thin 2 *(personne* ▸ *svelte)* slim, slender; **être m.** to be slim *or* slender; **m. comme un fil** as thin as a rake 3 *Fig (négligeable)* slim, slender; **de minces bénéfices** slender profits; **les preuves sont bien minces** the evidence is rather slim; **mes connaissances dans ce domaine sont trop minces** I know too little about this field, my knowledge in this field is too scanty; **ce n'est pas une m. affaire** this is no small affair; **ce n'est pas une m. responsabilité** it's no small responsibility; **un demi-chapitre sur la Révolution, c'est un peu m.** half a chapter on the French Revolution is a bit feeble; **c'est un peu m. comme excuse!** it's a bit of a poor excuse!
ADV thinly
EXCLAM *Fam (pour exprimer l'exaspération) Br* blast!, *Am* darn!; *(pour exprimer la surprise)* wow!, *Br* blimey!, *Am* gee (whiz)!; **m. alors, qui l'aurait cru!** wow *or Br* blimey *or Am* gee (whiz), who'd have thought it!

minceur [mɛ̃sœr] NF 1 *(finesse)* slimness, thinness 2 *(sveltesse)* slimness, slenderness 3 *Fig (insuffisance)* weakness, feebleness; **étant donné la m. de mes revenus** since my income is so small

mincir [32] [mɛ̃sir] VI *(personne)* to get slimmer *or* thinner; **elle essaie de m.** she's trying to lose weight

VT *(sujet: vêtement, couleur)* **cette robe te mincit** that dress makes you look slimmer

mine[1] [min] NF **1** *(apparence)* appearance, exterior; **sous sa m. respectable** under his/her respectable exterior; **elle fit m. de raccrocher, puis se ravisa** she made as if to hang up, then changed her mind; **ne fais pas m. de ne pas comprendre** don't act as if *or* pretend you don't understand; *Fam* **m. de rien, ça finit par coûter cher** it may not seem much but in the end it all adds up; **m. de rien, elle était furieuse** although *or* though she didn't show it, she was furious; **il est 4 heures du matin, m. de rien** it's hard to believe *or* you wouldn't think it, but it's four in the morning; **m. de rien, l'affaire progresse** the work is progressing, though you wouldn't think so to look at it; **m. de rien, essaie de vérifier** try to check on it without letting on (what you're up to) **2** *(teint)* **avoir bonne m.** to look well; **il a mauvaise m.** he doesn't look very well; *Fig Ironique* **nous avons bonne m. maintenant!** we look really good now, don't we!; **avoir une m. superbe** *ou* **resplendissante** to be the (very) picture of health; *Fam* **avoir une sale m.** to look dreadful *or* awful; *Fam* **avoir une petite m.** to look out of sorts *or* off-colour; *Fam* **avoir une m. de papier mâché** *ou* **de déterré** to look like death warmed up; **je lui trouve meilleure m.** I think he/she looks better *or* in better health **3** *(visage, contenance)* look, countenance; **m. boudeuse** sulky expression; **il ne faut pas vous fier à sa m. de petite fille sage** don't trust that butter-wouldn't-melt-in-my-mouth expression of hers; **avoir une m. réjouie** to beam, to be beaming; **prendre une m. contrite** to look offended; **faire grise** *ou* **triste** *ou* **piètre m.** to make *or Br* to pull a long face

• **mines** NFPL *(manières ▸ de bébé)* gestures, expressions; **faire des mines** to simper; **il m'énerve à toujours faire des mines** he irritates me, always simpering around

mine[2] [min] NF **1** *Géol* deposit; *(installations ▸ de surface)* pithead; *(▸ en sous-sol)* pit; *(gisement)* mine; **travailler à la m.** to work in the mine, to be a miner; **mon fils n'ira pas à la m.** my son isn't going down the mine *or* pit; **m. de charbon** *ou* **de houille** coal mine; **m. à ciel ouvert** opencast mine; *aussi Fig* **une m. d'or** a gold mine

2 *Fig (source importante)* **une m. de** a mine *or* source of; **une m. de renseignements** a mine of information

3 *(d'un crayon)* lead; **crayon à m. grasse/dure** soft/hard pencil; **m. de plomb** graphite *or* black lead

4 *Mil (galerie)* mine, gallery, sap; *(explosif)* mine; **poser** *ou* **mouiller une m.** to lay a mine; **faire jouer une m.** to fire a blast *or* a mine; **m. aérienne/sous-marine/terrestre** aerial/submarine/land mine

5 *(explosif)* **coup de m.** blast; **attention, coups de m.!** *(sur panneau)* danger, blasting

• **mines** NFPL **1** *Géog* mining area, mines; *Écon* mining industry **2** *Admin* **les Mines** = government department responsible for supervising all construction projects involving tunnelling; **École des Mines, les Mines** = "grande école" of engineering studies; **service des Mines** = government department which verifies the roadworthiness of cars

miner [3] [mine] VT **1** *(terrain)* to mine; **danger! zone minée** *(sur panneau)* beware of mines **2** *(ronger)* to undermine, to erode, to eat away (at) *or* into; **l'humidité a miné les fondations** the damp has eaten into the foundations **3** *Fig (affaiblir)* to undermine, to sap; **l'opposition cherche à m. les efforts du gouvernement** the opposition is trying to undermine the government's work; **ces ennuis la minent** these problems are wearing her down; **m. les forces/la santé de qn** to sap sb's strength/health; **la froideur de son accueil m'a miné le moral** the cold reception he/she gave me sapped my spirits; **miné par le chagrin** consumed with *or* worn down by grief

minerai [minrɛ] NM ore; **m. de fer/d'uranium** iron/uranium ore; **m. riche/pauvre** high-grade/low-grade ore; **m. brut** crude ore

minéral, -e, -aux, -ales [mineral, -o] ADJ mineral *(avant n)*

NM mineral

minéralier [mineralje] NM ore carrier

minéralisation [mineralizasjɔ̃] NF mineralization

minéraliser [3] [mineralize] VT *(métal, eau)* to mineralize

minéralogie [mineralɔʒi] NF mineralogy

minéralogique [mineralɔʒik] ADJ **1** *Géol* mineralogical **2** *Aut* **numéro m.** *Br* registration *or Am* license number

minéralogiste [mineralɔʒist] NMF mineralogist

Minerve [minɛrv] NPR *Myth* Minerva

minerve [minɛrv] NF *Méd* neck brace, (surgical) collar

minestrone [minɛstrɔn] NM minestrone

minet, -ette [mine, -ɛt] NM,F *Fam* **1** *(jeune garçon)* trendy young guy, pretty boy; *(jeune femme)* babe, trendy young chick **2** *(chat)* puss, pussy (cat) **3** *(terme d'affection)* sweetie, honey; **mon m., ma minette** sweetie, honey

• **minette** NF *très Fam (sexe de la femme)* pussy, snatch

mineur, -e [minœr] ADJ **1** *(secondaire)* minor; **d'un intérêt m.** of minor interest **2** *Jur* below the age of criminal responsibility; **enfants mineurs** under age children, minors; **être m.** to be under age *or* a minor **3** *Mus* minor; **concerto en sol m.** concerto in G minor; **accord parfait m.** minor chord

NM,F *Jur* minor; **interdit aux mineurs** *(film)* adults only; **cet établissement est interdit aux mineurs** these premises are banned to persons under 18; **délinquant m.** juvenile offender; **détournement** *ou* **enlèvement de m.** abduction

NM **1** *(ouvrier)* miner, mineworker; **famille de mineurs** mining family; **grève/maladie des mineurs** miners' strike/disease; **m. de fond** underground worker; **m. de houille** coalminer, *Br* collier **2** *Mil* sapper, miner **3** *Mus* **en m.** in the minor mode *or* key

• **mineure** NF *Ling* minor premise

mini [mini] ADJ INV **la mode m.** the mini-length *or* thigh-length fashion; **la mode m. est de retour** the mini is back (in fashion)

ADV **s'habiller m.** to wear miniskirts

NM *(mode courte)* mini; **le m. est de retour** minis *or* miniskirts are back

miniature [minjatyr] ADJ miniature; **un train m.** a model *or* miniature train

NF **1** *(modèle réduit)* small-scale replica *or* model **2** *Beaux-Arts* miniature; **peintre de miniatures** miniature painter, miniaturist

• **en miniature** ADJ miniature *(avant n)*; **c'est un jardin en m.** it's a model *or* miniature garden

miniaturisation [minjatyrizasjɔ̃] NF miniaturization

miniaturiser [3] [minjatyrize] VT to miniaturize

VPR **se miniaturiser** to become miniaturized; **la hi-fi se miniaturise** sound systems are getting much smaller

miniaturiste [minjatyrist] ADJ **un peintre m.** a miniaturist

NMF miniaturist

minibar [minibar] NM **1** *(dans le train)* trolley; **un service de m. est assuré dans ce train** there is a trolley service on the train **2** *(à l'hôtel)* minibar

minibus [minibys], **minicar** [minikar] NM minibus

minicassette [minikasɛt] NF (small) cassette

NM (small) cassette recorder

minichaîne [miniʃɛn] NF mini (stereo) system

MiniDisc® [minidisk] NM MiniDisc®

mini-disquette [minidiskɛt] *(pl* **mini-disquettes)** NF minidisk, mini-floppy

minidose [minidoz] NF individual sachet; *(de café)* capsule; *(de détergent lave-linge)* doser

mini-écouteur [miniekutœr] *(pl* **mini-écouteurs)** NM earbud, in-ear headphone

minier, -ère [minje, -ɛr] ADJ mining *(avant n)*

minigolf [minigɔlf] NM crazy golf, miniature golf

minijupe [miniʒyp] NF miniskirt

minima [minima] *voir* **minimum**

minimal, -e, -aux, -ales [minimal, -o] ADJ **1** *(seuil, peine)* minimum *(avant n)*; *(art)* minimal; **température minimale** minimal *or* minimum temperature **2** *Math* minimal

minimalisme [minimalism] NM minimalism

minimaliste [minimalist] ADJ minimalist

NM minimalist

minime [minim] ADJ *(faible)* minimal, minor; *(rôle)* minor; *(perte)* trivial; *(valeur)* trifling; **l'intrigue n'a qu'une importance m.** the plot is of only minor importance; **la différence est m.** the difference is negligible

NMF *Sport* (school) Junior

NM *Rel* Minim

minimessage [minimesaʒ] NM *Tél* text message; **envoyer un m. à qn** to text sb, to send sb a text message

minimisation [minimizasjɔ̃] NF minimization, minimizing; **m. des pertes** mitigation of damages

minimiser [3] [minimize] VT *(rôle)* to minimize, to play down; *(risque)* to minimize, to cut down; **sans vouloir m. sa contribution** without wishing to minimize *or* play down his/her contribution

minimum [minimɔm] *(pl* **minimums** *ou* **minima** [-ma]) ADJ minimum; **poids/service m.** minimum weight/service; *Électron* **charge m.** base *or* minimum load; **prix m.** minimum *or* bottom price; *(aux enchères)* reserve price

NM **1** *(le plus bas degré)* minimum; **températures proches du m. saisonnier** temperatures approaching the minimum *or* the lowest recorded for the season; **dépenser le m.** to spend as little as possible; **réduire les frais au m.** to reduce expenses to a minimum; **mets le chauffage au m.** turn the heating down as low as it will go; **j'ai réduit les matières grasses au m.** I've cut down on fat as much as possible, I've cut fat down to a minimum; **la rivière était à son m.** the river was at its lowest level; **ils n'ont même pas le m. vital** they don't even have the bare minimum, they're living below the breadline

2 *Jur (peine la plus faible)* **le m.** the minimum sentence

3 *(petite quantité)* **un m. (de)** a minimum (of); **un m. de temps** a minimum amount of time; **en un m. de temps** in as short a time as possible; *Fam* **je n'y resterai que le m. de temps** I'll make it as brief as I can; **avec un m. d'efforts** with a minimum of effort; **s'il avait un m. de bon sens/d'honnêteté** if he had an ounce of common sense/of decency; **nous exigeons un m. de garanties** we demand the minimum guarantees; **tu as vraiment fait un m.!** you really have done just the bare minimum!; **c'est vraiment le m. que tu puisses faire pour elle** it's the least you can do for her; **trois mois, c'est un m. pour s'habituer au climat** three months is the minimum it takes *or* it takes at least three months to get used to the climate

4 *Fin & Admin* **m. imposable** tax threshold; **m. vieillesse** basic state pension; **les minima sociaux** = basic income support

ADV minimum; **il fait 3°C m.** the minimum temperature is 3°C

• **au minimum** ADV *(au moins)* at the least; **deux jours au m.** at least two days, a minimum of two days; **au m. cinq ans d'expérience** at least five years' experience, a minimum of five years' experience

mini-ordinateur [miniɔrdinatœr] *(pl* **mini-ordinateurs)** NM minicomputer

minipilule [minipilyl] NF minipill

mini-séjour [miniseʒur] *(pl* **mini-séjours)** NM mini-break, short break

mini-série [miniseri] *(pl* **mini-séries)** NF *TV* mini-series

mini-slip [minislip] *(pl* **mini-slips)** NM tanga

ministère [ministɛr] NM **1** *Pol (charge) Br* ministry, *Am* administration; **elle a refusé le m. qu'on lui proposait** she turned down the government position she was offered; **sous le m. de M. Thiers** when M. Thiers was (the) minister, under M. Thiers' *Br* ministry *or Am* secretaryship

2 *(cabinet)* government, ministry; **former un m.** to form a government; **entrer au m.** to take over as a minister, *Am* to take a position in the ad-

ministration
3 *(bâtiment) Br* ministry, *Am* department (offices); *(département) Br* ministry, *Am* department; **m. des Affaires étrangères** *ou* **des Relations extérieures** Ministry of Foreign Affairs, *Br* ≃ Foreign Office, *Am* ≃ State Department; **m. de l'Agriculture** Ministry *or* Department of Agriculture; **m. du Commerce** Ministry of Trade, *Br* ≃ Department of Trade and Industry, *Am* ≃ Department of Commerce; **m. de la Culture** Ministry of Culture, Ministry for the Arts; **m. de la Défense** *Br* ≃ Ministry of Defence, *Am* ≃ Department of Defense; **m. de l'Économie et des Finances** Ministry of Finance, *Br* ≃ Treasury, *Am* ≃ Treasury Department; **m. de l'Éducation nationale** ≃ Department of Education; **m. de l'Environnement** Ministry of the Environment, *Br* ≃ Department of the Environment, Transport and the Regions, *Am* ≃ Department of the Environment; **m. de l'Intérieur** Ministry of the Interior, *Br* ≃ Home Office, *Am* ≃ Department of the Interior; **m. de la Justice** Department of Justice; **m. de la Santé et de la Sécurité Sociale** *Br* ≃ Department of Social Security, *Am* ≃ Department of Health and Human Services; **m. du Travail** Ministry for Employment, *Br* ≃ Department of Education and Employment, *Am* ≃ Department of Labor
4 *Jur* **m. public** public prosecutor's department, *Br* ≃ Crown Prosecution Service, *Am* ≃ District Attorney's office
5 *Rel* ministry; **exercer un m.** to serve as minister, to perform one's ministry

ministériel, -elle [ministerjel] **ADJ 1** *(émanant d'un ministre) Br* ministerial, *Am* departmental **2** *(concernant le gouvernement)* cabinet *(avant n)*, *Br* ministerial

ministrable [ministrabl] **ADJ** in line for a government *or Br* ministerial position; **elle est m.** she's a likely candidate for *Br* a ministerial post *or Am* a post in the administration
NMF potential secretary of state, *Br* ministerial hopeful

ministre [ministr] **NM 1** *Pol Br* minister, *Am* secretary; **m. d'État** secretary of state, *Br* minister; **m. sans portefeuille** minister without portfolio; **m. des Affaires étrangères** *ou* **des Relations extérieures** Minister of Foreign Affairs, *Br* ≃ Foreign Secretary, *Am* ≃ Secretary of State; **m. de l'Agriculture** Agriculture Minister, Minister for Agriculture; **m. du Commerce** *Br* ≃ Secretary of State for Trade and Industry, *Am* ≃ Secretary of Commerce; **m. de la Culture** Minister for the Arts; **m. de la Culture et de la Communication** Minister of Culture and Communication; **m. de la Défense (nationale)** ≃ Secretary of State for Defence, Minister of Defence; **m. de l'Économie et des Finances** Finance Minister, *Br* ≃ Chancellor of the Exchequer, *Am* ≃ Secretary of the Treasury; **m. de l'Éducation nationale** ≃ Secretary of State for Education; **m. de l'Environnement** *Br* ≃ Secretary of State for the Environment, *Am* ≃ Secretary of the Environment; **m. de l'Intérieur** Minister of the Interior, *Br* ≃ Home Secretary, *Am* ≃ Secretary of the Interior; **m. de la Justice** Minister of Justice, *Br* ≃ Lord (High) Chancellor, *Am* ≃ Attorney General; **m. de la Santé et de la Sécurité Sociale** *Br* ≃ Secretary of State for Social Security, *Am* ≃ Secretary for Health and Human Services; **m. des Transports** *Br* ≃ Secretary of State for the Environment, Transport and the Regions, *Am* ≃ Transportation Secretary; **m. du Travail** *Br* ≃ Secretary of State for Education and Employment, *Am* ≃ Labor Secretary
2 *(ambassadeur)* **m. plénipotentiaire (auprès de)** minister plenipotentiary (to)
3 *Rel (pasteur)* **m. du culte** minister
4 *Arch ou Littéraire (de Dieu, d'un prince)* servant, agent

Minitel® [minitel] **NM** viewdata service, *Br* ≃ Prestel®, *Am* ≃ Minitel®; **sur M.** on viewdata, *Br* ≃ on Prestel®, *Am* ≃ on Minitel®; **M. rose** erotic viewdata service

> **MINITEL®**
>
> The domestic viewdata service run by France Télécom was launched in the early 1980s and was for many years a familiar part of French life. The basic monitor and keyboard were given free of charge and the subscriber charged for the services used on his or her phone bill. A precursor to the Internet, some Minitel® services were purely informative (such as a full telephone directory, news, information on the weather, road conditions, stock prices and so on) while others were more interactive, enabling users to carry out bank transactions, make purchases, book travel tickets and even chat to each other. Although the service has largely been discontinued in favour of the Internet, the service is still available in some post offices.

minitéliste [minitelist] **NMF** Minitel® user

mini-tour [minitur] *(pl* **mini-tours***)* **NF** *Ordinat* mini tower

minium [minjɔm] **NM 1** *Chim* red lead, minium **2** *(peinture)* red lead paint

minivague [minivag] **NF** light perm

minois [minwa] **NM** pretty little face

minoration [minɔrasjɔ̃] **NF 1** *(baisse)* reduction, cut; **une m. de cinq pour cent du tarif de base** a five percent cut in the basic rate; **procéder à une m. des loyers** to reduce *or* to lower rents **2** *(minimisation)* minimizing

minorer [3] [minɔre] **VT 1** *(baisser)* to reduce, to cut, to mark down; **m. les prix de 2 pour cent** to cut prices by 2 percent **2** *(minimiser)* to minimize, to downplay the importance of

minoritaire [minɔriter] **ADJ 1** *(moins nombreux)* minority *(avant n)*; **parti m.** minority party; **ils sont minoritaires à l'Assemblée** they are in the minority in the Assembly; **les femmes sont minoritaires dans cette profession** women are a minority in this profession; **très minoritaires** very much in the minority **2** *(non reconnu)* minority *(avant n)*; **opinion m.** minority opinion
NMF member of a minority (group); *Bourse* minority shareholder; **les minoritaires** the minority

minorité [minɔrite] **NF 1** *(le plus petit nombre)* minority; **une m. de** a minority of
2 *(groupe)* minority (group); **m. ethnique** ethnic minority; **m. nationale** national minority; **m. agissante** active minority
3 *(âge légal)* minority; *Jur* nonage; **pendant sa m.** before he/she came of age, while he/she was under age; **m. pénale** nonage
4 *Écon* **m. de blocage** blocking minority
• **en minorité ADJ** in a *or* the minority; **nous sommes en m.** we're in a minority **ADV mettre le gouvernement en m.** to defeat the government; **la gauche a été mise en m. lors des dernières élections** the left became the minority party at the last elections

Minorque [minɔrk] **NF** Minorca

minorquin, -e [minɔrkɛ̃, -in] **ADJ** Minorcan
• **Minorquin, -e NM,F** Minorcan

minoterie [minɔtri] **NF 1** *(lieu)* flourmill **2** *(activité)* flour-milling

minotier [minɔtje] **NM** miller, (flour) millowner

minou [minu] **NM 1** *Fam (chat)* pussy, pussy cat; **m.! m.! m.!** puss! puss!, kitty! kitty!
2 *Fam (chéri)* darling, sweetie, honey
3 *très Fam (sexe de la femme)* pussy
4 *Can (bourgeon de saule)* pussy willow
5 *Can (boule de poussière)* piece of fluff, *Am* dustball, dust kitten

minuit [minɥi] **NM 1** *(milieu de la nuit)* midnight **2** *(heure)* midnight, twelve midnight, twelve o'clock (at night); **il est m.** it's twelve (midnight), it's midnight; **il est m. passé** it's after *or* past midnight; **m. et demi** half-past twelve at night; **m. et quart** a quarter *Br* past twelve *or Am* after midnight; **m. moins vingt** twenty to twelve *or* to midnight; **à m.** at midnight, at twelve o'clock (at night); **vers m., vers les m.** about twelve *or* midnight; **sur le coup de m.** on the stroke of twelve *or* of midnight; *Hum* **m., l'heure du crime!** midnight, the witching hour!
• **de minuit ADJ** midnight *(avant n)*

minus [minys] **NMF** *Fam* **1** *(nabot)* midget, shortie, runt **2** *(incapable)* loser

minuscule [minyskyl] **ADJ 1** *(très petit)* minute, minuscule, tiny **2** *Typ* **un b m.** a small *or Typ* lower-case b; **lettre** *ou* **caractère m.** small *or Typ* lower-case letter
NF small letter; *Typ* lower-case letter; **écrire en minuscules** to write in small *or Typ* lower-case letters

minutage [minytaʒ] **NM** timing

minute [minyt] **NF 1** *(mesure du temps)* minute; **une m. de silence** a minute's silence, a minute of silence; **chaque m. compte** every minute counts; **il n'y a pas une m. à perdre** there's not a minute to lose; **à la m. près** on the dot, right on time; *Fam* **on n'est pas à la m. près** *ou* **à la m.!** there's no hurry!; **à deux minutes (de voiture/de marche) de chez moi** two minutes('drive/walk) from my house
2 *(moment)* minute, moment; **revenez dans une petite m.** come back in a minute *or* moment (or two); **il y a une m.** *ou* **il n'y a pas même une m., tu disais tout le contraire** just a minute *or* moment ago, you were saying the very opposite; **il est parti il y a deux minutes** he left a couple of minutes ago; **de m. en m.** by the minute; **ne pas avoir une m. de répit** not to have a moment's *or* minute's rest; **ne pas avoir une m. à soi** not to have a minute *or* a moment to oneself; **as-tu une m.? j'ai à te parler** do you have a minute? I have to talk to you; **la m. de vérité** the moment of truth
3 *(comme adj inv) (instantané)* **nettoyage m.** same-day cleaning; **talon m.** on-the-spot shoe repair, *Br* heel bar; **clés m.** key bar; **steak m.** minute steak; **repas m.** convenience meal
4 *Jur (d'un document)* original; *(de contrat)* minute, draft; *(d'acte, de jugement)* record; **les minutes** *(d'une réunion)* minutes
EXCLAM *Fam* wait a minute *or* moment!; **m., papillon!** hold your horses!, not so fast!
• **à la minute ADV 1** *(il y a un instant)* a moment ago; **elle est sortie à la m.** she's just this minute gone out **2** *(sans attendre)* this minute *or* instant; **faire qch à la m.** to do sth at a minute's *or* a moment's notice; **je veux que ce soit fait à la m.** I want it done this instant **3** *(toutes les 60 secondes)* per minute; **45 tours à la m.** 45 revolutions a *or* per minute
• **d'une minute à l'autre ADV** any time; **il sera là d'une m. à l'autre** he'll be here any minute (now), he won't be a minute; **les choses peuvent changer d'une m. à l'autre** things may change at any moment

minuter [3] [minyte] **VT 1** *(spectacle, cuisson)* to time; **sa journée de travail est soigneusement minutée** he/she works to a very tight *or* strict schedule **2** *(accord)* to draw up, to draft; *(acte, jugement)* to record, to enter

minuterie [minytri] **NF 1** *Élec* time switch, timer; **il y a une m. dans l'escalier** the stair light is on a time switch **2** *(d'une horloge)* motion work; *(d'un compteur)* counter mechanism; **as-tu mis en route la m. du four?** did you set the oven timer?

minuteur [minytœr] **NM** timer

minutie [minysi] **NF 1** *(application)* meticulousness, thoroughness; **avec m.** *(travailler)* meticulously, carefully; *(examiner)* in minute detail, thoroughly **2** *Vieilli (détail)* minute detail; **minuties** trifles, petty details, *Sout* minutiae

minutieuse [minysjøz] *voir* **minutieux**

minutieusement [minysjøzmɑ̃] **ADV 1** *(avec précision)* meticulously, carefully **2** *(en détail)* in minute detail

minutieux, -euse [minysjø, -øz] **ADJ 1** *(personne)* meticulous, thorough **2** *(travail)* meticulous, detailed, thorough; *(dessin, sculpture)* detailed; **enquête/recherche minutieuse** thorough investigation/research; **la broderie est un travail très m.** embroidery demands close work *or* attention to detail

miocène [mjɔsɛn] **ADJ** Miocene
NM le m. the Miocene (period)

mioche [mjɔʃ] **NMF** *Fam* kid, *Br* nipper

mi-pente [mipɑ̃t] **à mi-pente ADV** halfway up/down the hill

MIPS [mips] **NM** *Ordinat (abrév* **million d'instructions par seconde***)* MIPS

mirabelle [mirabɛl] **NF** *(fruit)* mirabelle (plum); *(liqueur)* mirabelle *(plum brandy)*

mirabellier [mirabelje] **NM** mirabelle plum tree

miracle [mirakl] **NM 1** *(intervention divine)* miracle; **sa guérison tient du m.** his/her recovery is (nothing short of) a miracle
2 *(surprise)* miracle, marvel; **et le m. se produisit, l'enfant parla enfin** and the miracle happened, the child at last spoke; **c'est (un) m. que…** + *subjonctif* it's a miracle *or* a wonder that…; **faire des miracles** to work miracles *or* wonders; **le m. de l'amour** the miracle *or* wonder of love; **les miracles de la science** the wonders *or* marvels of science; **m. économique** economic miracle; **un m. d'architecture** a marvel *or* miracle of architecture
3 *Théât* miracle play
4 *(comme adj; avec ou sans trait d'union)* miracle *(avant n)*, wonder *(avant n)*; **médicament m.** miracle *or* wonder drug; **une crème m. contre la cellulite** a cream that works miracles *or* wonders on cellulite; **la solution-m. à vos problèmes de rangement** the miracle solution to your storage problems; **je ne crois pas aux solutions-m.** I don't believe in miracle cures
• **par miracle ADV** by a *or* some miracle, miraculously; **échapper à qch par m.** to have a miraculous escape from sth; **comme par m.** as if by a *or* some miracle; **mais par m., j'avais pensé à fermer le gaz** but, miraculously *or* amazingly enough, I'd remembered to turn off the gas

miraculé, -e [mirakyle] **ADJ** *(d'une maladie)* miraculously cured; *(d'un accident)* miraculously saved
NM,F 1 *Rel* **c'est un m. de Lourdes** he was miraculously cured at Lourdes **2** *(survivant)* miraculous survivor; **une des rares miraculées du tremblement de terre** one of the few (people) who miraculously survived the earthquake; **c'est un m.** he's lucky to be alive

miraculeuse [mirakyløz] *voir* **miraculeux**

miraculeusement [mirakyløzmɑ̃] **ADV** miraculously, (as if) by a *or* some miracle

miraculeux, -euse [mirakylø, -øz] **ADJ 1** *(qui tient du miracle)* miraculous, miracle *(avant n)*; **cela n'a rien de m.!** there's nothing miraculous *or* special about it! **2** *(prodigieux)* miraculous, miracle *(avant n)*; **produit/sauvetage m.** miracle product/rescue

mirador [miradɔr] **NM 1** *Archit* mirador **2** *Mil* watchtower, mirador

mirage [miraʒ] **NM 1** *(illusion optique)* mirage **2** *(chimère)* mirage, delusion; **je m'étais laissé prendre au m. de l'amour** I had fallen for the illusion of perfect love **3** *(d'un œuf)* candling

miraud [miro] = **miro**

mire [mir] **NF 1** *(de fusil)* **point de m.** aim, target; *Fig* **pendant les Jeux, la ville sera le point de m. du monde entier** the eyes of the world will be on the city during the Games **2** *(d'un téléviseur)* **m. (de réglage)** test card, *Spéc* test pattern **3** *Tech (pour niveler)* levelling rod *or* staff; *(piquet)* (surveyor's) ranging pole

mirer **[3]** [mire] **VT 1** *(œuf)* to candle **2** *Littéraire (voir se refléter)* **le saule mire ses branches dans la rivière** the willow branches are reflected *or* mirrored in the river **3** *Arch (regarder)* to watch; *(viser)* to aim at, to take aim at
VPR se mirer *Littéraire* **1** *(se regarder)* to gaze at oneself **2** *(se refléter)* to be mirrored *or* reflected; **les saules se miraient dans le lac** the willows were mirrored *or* reflected in the lake

mirettes [mirɛt] **NFPL** *Fam* eyes⌑, peepers, *Am* baby blues; **on s'en est pris plein les m.** we feasted our eyes on it

mirifique [mirifik] **ADJ** *Hum* fabulous, amazing, staggering

mirliflor, mirliflore [mirliflɔr] **NM** *Hum Vieilli* dandy, fop

mirliton [mirlitɔ̃] **NM** *Mus* kazoo, mirliton; **une musique de m.** second-rate music; **des vers de m.** doggerel, bad verse

mirmidon [mirmidɔ̃] **NM** *Vieilli* whippersnapper, pipsqueak, little runt

miro [miro] **ADJ** *Fam (myope)* short-sighted⌑; **sans mes lunettes, je suis complètement m.** I'm as blind as a bat without my glasses

mirobolant, -e [mirɔbɔlɑ̃, -ɑ̃t] **ADJ** *Fam (mirifique)* fabulous, stupendous, amazing; **il touche un salaire m.** he earns an absolute fortune; **des promesses mirobolantes** extraordinary *or* grandiose promises

miroir [mirwar] **NM 1** *(verre réflecteur)* mirror; **m. déformant/grossissant** distorting/magnifying mirror; **m. à main/à barbe** hand/shaving mirror; **m. (pliant) à trois faces** triple mirror; **m. aux alouettes** *Chasse* decoy; *Fig* trap for the unwary; *Aut* **m. de courtoisie** vanity mirror **2** *Littéraire (image, reflet)* mirror, reflection; **les yeux sont le m. de l'âme** the eyes are the windows of the soul

miroitant, -e [mirwatɑ̃, -ɑ̃t] **ADJ 1** *(luisant)* glistening, gleaming **2** *(chatoyant)* shimmering

miroité, -e [mirwate] **ADJ** *(cheval, robe)* dappled

miroitement [mirwatmɑ̃] **NM 1** *(lueurs)* glistening, gleaming **2** *(chatoiement)* shimmering

miroiter **[3]** [mirwate] **VI 1** *(luire)* to glisten, to gleam; *(chatoyer)* to shimmer **2** *Fig* **faire m. qch à qn** to (try and) lure sb with the prospect of sth; **on lui a fait m. une augmentation** they dangled the prospect of a rise before him/her

miroton [mirɔtɔ̃], **mironton** [mirɔ̃tɔ̃] **NM (bœuf) m.** = sliced beef and onions stewed in white wine

Mis *(abrév écrite* **Marquis**) Marquis, Marquess

mis, -e¹ [mi, miz] **PP** *voir* **mettre**
ADJ *(vêtu)* **bien m.** well dressed, nicely turned out

misaine [mizɛn] **NF (voile de) m.** foresail

misanthrope [mizɑ̃trɔp] **ADJ** misanthropic
NMF misanthrope, misanthropist

misanthropie [mizɑ̃trɔpi] **NF** misanthropy

misanthropique [mizɑ̃trɔpik] **ADJ** *Littéraire* misanthropic

miscible [misibl] **ADJ** miscible

M^ise^ *(abrév écrite* **Marquise**) Marchioness

mise² [miz] **ADJ F** *voir* **mis**
NF 1 *Cartes & (au jeu)* stake; *(à une vente aux enchères)* bid; **augmenter la m.** to up the stakes; **doubler sa m.** to double one's stake
2 *(tenue)* attire, dress; **soigner sa m.** to take care over one's appearance; **on voit à sa m. qu'elle n'est pas très riche** you can see from the way she dresses *or* the clothes she wears that she's not very rich
3 *Suisse (vente)* auction (sale)
4 *(dans des expressions) Fig* **m. à l'abri** putting in a safe place; **m. à l'affiche** *(d'un film)* screening; *(d'un concert, d'une pièce)* putting on, billing; *Naut* **m. à l'eau** launch; **m. à exécution** carrying out, implementation; **m. à feu** *(de fusée etc)* firing; **m. à l'heure** setting (to the right time); **m. à jour** *(réactualisation)* updating, update, bringing up to date; *(résultat)* update, updated version; *Ordinat* upgrading; **m. à mort** *(gén)* putting to death; *(en tauromachie)* execution; *Chasse* kill, *Spéc* mort; *Chasse* **au moment de la m. à mort** at the kill; **m. à neuf** renovation; *Ordinat* **m. à niveau** upgrade; *Scol* **faire une m. à niveau en maths** = to catch up in maths *(after switching to another specialization)*; **m. à pied** *(disciplinaire)* suspension; *(économique)* laying off; **donner trois jours de m. à pied à qn** to give sb three days' suspension, to suspend sb for three days; **m. à la retraite** pensioning off; **m. à la retraite anticipée** early retirement; **m. à sac** *(d'une ville)* sacking; *(d'un appartement)* ransacking; **se livrer à une m. à sac** *(voyous)* to go on a looting spree; **m. au courant** informing; **m. au monde** birth; **m. au pas** *Équitation* reining in (to a walk); *(d'une personne, de l'économie)* bringing into line; **m. au propre** making a fair copy, tidying up *(of a document)*; **m. au tombeau** entombment; **m. en accusation** indictment; **m. en application** implementation; **m. en attente** postponing, shelving; *Ordinat & Tél* hold; *Tél* **m. en attente d'appels** call holding; *Ordinat* **m. en attente des fichiers à imprimer** printer spooling; **m. en bière** placing in the coffin; **assister à la m. en bière** to be present when the body is placed in the coffin; *Cin & Rad* **m. en boîte** editing; **m. en bouteilles** bottling; **m. en branle** starting up, getting going; **m. en cause** *(d'une personne)* implication; *(d'une idée)* calling into question; *Fin* **m. en circulation** issue; **m. en condition** *(du corps)* getting fit; *(de l'esprit)* conditioning; **m. en conserve** canning; *Jur* **m. en délibéré** = adjourning for further consultation of judges; **m. en demeure** injunction, formal notification; *(de paiement)* formal demand; *Com* **m. en dépôt** warehousing; *Jur* **m. en détention provisoire** detention pending trial; **m. en disponibilité** leave of absence; **demander sa** *ou* **une m. en disponibilité** to ask for leave of absence; **m. en doute** putting into doubt, questioning; **m. en état** *Jur* preparation for hearing; *(d'un engin)* getting into working order; *(d'un local)* renovation; *Jur* **m. en examen** indictment; **m. en exploitation** *(d'une machine)* commissioning; **m. en forme** *(d'un chapeau)* shaping; *Ordinat* formatting; *Typ* imposition; *Sport* fitness training; **m. en garde** warning; **m. en jeu** *(au début) Sport* kick-off; *(au hockey)* bully-off; *(à la touche) Ftbl* throw-in; *(au rugby)* line-out; *Fig* bringing into play; *Jur* **m. en liberté** release; *Jur* **m. en liberté conditionnelle** conditional discharge; *Jur* **m. en liberté provisoire** release on bail; *Ordinat* **m. en ligne** putting on-line; **m. en marche** starting up; *Ordinat* **m. en mémoire** storing *or* saving (in the memory); **m. en mouvement** setting in motion; **m. en musique d'un poème** setting a poem to music; **m. en œuvre** implementation; **m. en orbite** putting into orbit; **depuis sa m. en orbite** since it was put into orbit; **m. en ordre** *(d'un local)* tidying up; *Ordinat (d'un fichier)* sequencing; *(d'un programme)* housekeeping; *Math* ordering; *Fin* **m. en paiement** *(d'un dividende)* payment; **m. en place** setting up, organization; **la m. en place du nouveau réseau demandera plusieurs mois** it will take several months to set up the new system *or* to get the new system up and running; **m. en pratique** carrying out, putting into practice; **m. en question** questioning, challenging; *Ordinat* **m. en relation** *(avec un service)* log-on; *Ordinat* **m. en relief** highlighting; *Ordinat* **m. en réseau** networking; **m. en retraite** pensioning (off), retirement on a pension; **m. en route** starting up; **m. en service** putting into service; **sa m. en service ne se fera qu'en septembre** it won't come into service until September; *Fin* **m. en terre** burial; **m. en train** *(d'un projet)* starting up; *Sport* warming up; *(d'une soirée)* breaking the ice; **m. en valeur** *(d'un sol, d'une région)* development; *(de biens)* improvement; *(d'un investissement)* turning to account; *(de qualités)* setting off, enhancement; **m. en vente** (putting up for) sale; *(d'un produit)* bringing onto the market, launching; **m. en vigueur** bringing into force, implementation; **m. hors circuit** *Électron* disconnection; *Tech* disabling; *Fam Fig* **la m. hors circuit du champion** knocking the champion out of the race; *Jur* **m. sous séquestre** sequestration; *Jur* **m. sous scellés** affixing the official seals; **m. sous surveillance** putting under surveillance; **m. sous tension** supplying with electricity; *(d'un ordinateur, d'une turbine)* power-up; **m. sur écoutes** (phone) tapping; **m. sur pied** setting up
• **de mise ADJ** appropriate; **si tu y vas, sache que la cravate est de m.** if you go, you'll have to wear a tie, mind; **le tutoiement n'est pas de m.** it's not the done thing to say "tu"
• **mise à feu NF** *Mil* firing; *Astron* blast-off, launch; *Mines & Tech* firing, ignition
• **mise à prix NF** *Br* reserve *or Am* upset price
• **mise au point NF 1** *Opt & Phot* focusing, focussing
2 *Tech* tuning, adjustment; *(d'un moteur)* tuning
3 *Ordinat* trouble-shooting, debugging
4 *Fig* clarification, correction; *(d'un document, d'un rapport)* finalization, finalizing; *(d'un produit)* development; **après cette petite m. au point** now that the record has been set straight; **je voudrais faire une m. au point** I'd like to clarify something
• **mise de fonds NF** capital investment; **m. de fonds initiale** *(pour un achat)* initial outlay; *(pour monter une affaire)* initial investment, seed money
• **mise en page, mise en pages NF 1** *Typ (maquette)* page design *or* layout; *(composition)* make-up, making up **2** *Ordinat* editing; **je n'aime pas la m. en page de la revue** I don't like the layout of the magazine
• **mise en plis NF** set; **faire une m. en plis à qn** to set sb's hair, to give sb a set
• **mise en scène NF** *Cin & Théât* direction; **c'est elle qui a signé la m. en scène** she was responsible for staging the play; *Fig* **toute cette histoire**

n'était en fait qu'une vaste m. en scène the entire story was just one big set-up

miser [3] [mize] VT **1** *(parier)* to stake, to bet (**sur** on); **j'ai misé cinq euros sur le numéro 29** I've staked five euros on number 29 **2** *Suisse (acheter)* to buy *(at an auction)*; *(vendre)* to put up for auction

• **miser sur** VT IND **1** *(cheval)* to bet on, to back; *(numéro)* to bet on; *Fig* **m. sur les deux tableaux** to back both horses, to hedge one's bets; *Bourse* **m. sur une hausse/une baisse** to speculate on a rising/falling market **2** *(compter sur ▸ quelque chose)* to bank *or* to count on; *(▸ quelqu'un)* to count on

misérabilisme [mizerabilism] NM *Cin & Littérature* miserabilism

misérabiliste [mizerabilist] *Cin & Littérature* ADJ miserabilist

NMF miserabilist

misérable [mizerabl] ADJ **1** *(après le nom) (sans ressources)* impoverished, poverty-stricken, poor; **quartier m.** poor *or* poverty-stricken district; **tout le pays est m.** the whole country is wretchedly *or* miserably poor

2 *(pitoyable)* pitiful, miserable, wretched; **une cabane m.** a wretched little shack; **elle me fit le récit de sa m. existence** she told me the tale of her wretched life

3 *(insignifiant)* miserable, paltry; **elles se disputent pour un m. vase** they're arguing over a stupid vase; **travailler pour un salaire m.** to work for a pittance; **pour la m. somme de dix euros** for a paltry ten euros

4 *Littéraire (méprisable)* despicable, mean

NMF **1** *Sout ou Hum (malheureux)* **m., qu'as-tu fait là!** what have you done, you wretch! **2** *Littéraire (miséreux)* pauper, wretch **3** *Littéraire (canaille) (vile)* rascal *or* scoundrel

> Il faut noter que l'adjectif anglais **miserable** est un faux ami. Il signifie le plus souvent **malheureux, triste**.

misérablement [mizerabləmɑ̃] ADV **1** *(pauvrement)* in poverty, wretchedly **2** *(lamentablement)* pitifully, miserably, wretchedly

misère [mizer] NF **1** *(indigence)* poverty, *Sout* destitution; **être dans la m.** to be destitute *or* poverty-stricken; **ils sont dans une m. noire** they have nothing, they are quite destitute; **vivre dans la m.** to live in poverty; **tomber dans la m.** to become destitute; **réduire qn à la m.** to reduce sb to poverty; *Can Fam* **avoir de la m. à faire qch** to have trouble doing sth▫; *Can Fam* **faire de la m. à qn** to give sb a hard time, to make sb's life a misery▫

2 *Fig* poverty; **il y avait une grande m. culturelle pendant la dictature** there was great cultural poverty under the dictatorship; **m. sexuelle** sexual deprivation *or* misery

3 *(malheur)* **c'est une m. de les voir se séparer** it's pitiful *or* it's a shame to see them break up

4 *(somme dérisoire)* pittance; **gagner une m.** to earn a pittance; **je l'ai eu pour une m.** I got *or* bought it for next to nothing; **10 euros? une m.!** 10 euros? a mere nothing!

5 *Cartes* misère

6 *Bot* tradescantia

7 *Belg (locution)* **chercher m. à qn** to try to pick a quarrel with sb

EXCLAM oh Lord!; *Hum* **m. de moi!** woe is me!

• **misères** NFPL *Fam* **des misères** *(broutilles)* trifles, minor irritations▫; *(ennuis de santé)* aches and pains; **les petites misères de la vie conjugale** *(ennuis)* the little upsets of married life; **faire des misères à qn** to torment sb▫; **raconte-moi tes misères** tell me all your woes; **il te fait des misères?** has he been horrible to you?

• **de misère** ADJ **un salaire de m.** a starvation wage, a pittance

> Il faut noter que le nom anglais **misery** est un faux ami. Il signifie **malheur** ou **tristesse**.

miserere [mizerere] NM INV miserere

miséréré [mizerere] NM = **miserere**

miséreux, -euse [mizerø, -øz] ADJ *Vieilli (pauvre)* poverty-stricken, destitute

NM,F poor person, pauper; **aider** *ou* **secourir les m.** to help the poor

miséricorde [mizerikɔrd] NF *Littéraire (pitié)* mercy, forgiveness; **implorer m.** to beg *or* to cry for mercy; **m. divine** divine mercy; *Vieilli ou Hum* **m.!** heaven help us!, mercy on us!

miséricordieux, -euse [mizerikɔrdjø, -øz] ADJ *Littéraire* merciful, forgiving; **être m. envers qn** to show mercy towards sb; **soyez m.** have mercy

misogyne [mizɔʒin] ADJ misogynous, misogynistic

NMF misogynist, woman-hater

misogynie [mizɔʒini] NF misogyny

miss [mis] *(pl* **inv** *ou* **misses** [mis]*)* NF **1** *Vieilli (gouvernante)* governess **2** *Fam Hum* **ça va, la m.?** how's things, babe?; **et comment va m. Martin?** and how is Miss Martin?; *(en s'adressant directement à la personne)* and how are we today, Miss Martin?

• **Miss** NF INV *(reine de beauté)* beauty queen; **M. Japon/Monde** Miss Japan/World

missel [misɛl] NM missal

missile [misil] NM missile; **m. air-air** air-to-air missile; **m. antiaérien** antiaircraft missile; **m. antichar** antitank missile; **m. antimissile** antimissile missile; **m. de croisière** cruise missile; **m. sol-sol** ground-to-ground missile; **m. stratégique** strategic missile; **m. à tête chercheuse à infrarouge** heat-seeking missile

mission [misjɔ̃] NF **1** *(charge)* mission, assignment; *(dans le cadre d'une entreprise)* assignment; *(dossier)* brief; **envoyer qn en m. aux États-Unis** to send sb to the United States; **recevoir pour m. de faire qch** to be commissioned to do sth; **j'ai pour m. de...** my job *or* task is to...; **être en m.** to be on an assignment; **ministre en m. spéciale à Paris** minister on a special mission to Paris; **m. vous avait été confiée de faire...** you were given the job of doing..., *Sout* you were assigned the task of doing...; *Mil* **m. de reconnaissance** reconnaissance mission; **être en m. de reconnaissance** to be on reconnaissance duty; **m. accomplie** mission accomplished

2 *(devoir)* mission, task; **la m. de notre organisation est de défendre les droits de l'homme** our organization's mission is to defend human rights; **la m. du journaliste est d'informer** a journalist's task is to inform; **il s'était donné pour m. de sauver les enfants** he had taken it upon himself to save the children

3 *(groupe)* mission; **m. commerciale** business assignment; *(gouvernementale)* trade mission; **m. diplomatique** diplomatic mission; **m. scientifique** scientific mission; **partir en m. au pôle Nord** to go on an expedition to the North Pole

4 *Rel (organisation)* mission; **missions étrangères** foreign missions; *(lieu)* mission (station); **la M. de France** = Catholic evangelical organization

missionnaire [misjɔnɛr] ADJ missionary *(avant n)*; **la vocation m.** the vocation of a missionary

NMF missionary

Mississippi [misisipi] NM *Géog* **1** *(fleuve)* **le M.** the Mississippi (River) **2** *(État)* **le M.** Mississippi; **au M.** in Mississippi

missive [misiv] ADJ F missive *(avant n)*

NF *Littéraire* missive

mistigri [mistigri] NM *Fam (chat)* puss

mistoufle [mistufl] NF *très Fam Vieilli* **1** *(misère)* **être dans la m.** to be down at heel **2** *(méchanceté)* **faire des mistoufles à qn** to play dirty tricks on sb

mistral, -als [mistral] NM mistral

mit *etc voir* **mettre**

mitaine [mitɛn] NF fingerless glove; *Can & Suisse (moufle)* mitten

mitan [mitɑ̃] NM *Vieilli* **1** *(centre)* middle, centre **2** *Fam Arg crime* **le m.** the underworld, gangland

mitard [mitar] NM *Fam Arg crime (cachot)* disciplinary cell▫, cooler; **être au m.** to be in solitary *or* in the cooler; **se retrouver au m.** to end up in solitary *or* in the cooler

mite [mit] NF **1** *(papillon)* (clothes) moth; **rongé par les** *ou* **aux mites** moth-eaten **2** *(ciron)* **m. du fromage** cheese-mite

mité, -e [mite] ADJ moth-eaten

mi-temps [mitɑ̃] NF INV *Sport* **1** *(moitié)* half; **la première/seconde m.** the first/second half; *Hum* **la troisième m.** the post-match celebrations **2** *(pause)* half-time; **le score est de zéro à zéro à la m.** the half-time score is nil-nil; **siffler la m.** to blow the whistle for half-time

NM INV part-time job; **chercher un m.** to look for a part-time job; **faire un m.** to work part-time; *Scol* **m. pédagogique** part-time teaching position

• **à mi-temps** ADJ part-time; **travailleur à m.** part-timer, part-time worker ADV **travailler** *ou* **être à m.** to work part-time; **elle travaille à m. comme serveuse** she's a part-time waitress

miter [3] [mite] **se miter** VPR to become moth-eaten

miteux, -euse [mitø, -øz] *Fam* ADJ **1** *(costume, chambre, hôtel)* shabby, grotty; *(personne)* seedy-looking, shabby, down-at-heel **2** *(situation, salaire)* pathetic; *(escroc)* small-time

NM,F *(incapable)* nonentity, loser, *Br* no-hoper; *(indigent)* bum, *Br* dosser

Mithridate [mitridat] NPR Mithridates

mithridatiser [3] [mitridatize] VT *Littéraire* to mithridatize

mitigation [mitigasjɔ̃] NF mitigation; **la m. d'une peine** the mitigation of a sentence

mitigé, -e [mitiʒe] ADJ *(modéré)* mixed; **des critiques mitigées** mixed reviews; **manifester un enthousiasme m.** to be reserved in one's enthusiasm; **j'avais des sentiments mitigés à son égard** I had mixed feelings about him; **le public était assez m.** the public was quite mixed in its reaction

mitiger [17] [mitiʒe] VT *Vieilli* to mitigate; *(peine)* to reduce, to mitigate; *(règlement, loi)* to relax; **m. qch de** to mix *or* to temper sth with

mitigeur [mitiʒœr] NM *Br* mixer tap, *Am* mixing faucet; **m. de douche** shower mixer

mitochondrie [mitɔkɔ̃dri] NF *Biol* mitochondrion

mitonner [3] [mitɔne] VT **1** *Culin* to simmer, to slow-cook; **je vous ai mitonné une petite recette à moi** I've cooked you one of my tasty little recipes **2** *Fig (coup, plan)* to plot, to cook up; **j'ai bien mitonné ma vengeance** I carefully plotted my revenge

VI *Culin* to simmer, to stew gently; **laissez m. la viande** leave the meat to simmer

mitose [mitoz] NF *Biol* mitosis

mitoyen, -enne [mitwajɛ̃, -ɛn] ADJ **1** *(commun)* common, shared; **puits m. entre les deux maisons** well shared by *or* common to the two houses; **cloison mitoyenne** dividing wall *(between two rooms)* **2** *(jouxtant)* bordering, neighbouring; **les champs sont mitoyens** the fields are adjacent to each other; **le jardin m. du nôtre** the garden (immediately) next to ours, the neighbouring garden (to ours); **deux maisons mitoyennes** semi-detached houses **3** *(en copropriété)* commonly owned, jointly owned; **mur m.** party wall

mitoyenneté [mitwajɛnte] NF **1** *(copropriété)* common *or* joint ownership **2** *(contiguïté)* adjacency

mitraillade [mitrajad] NF volley of shots

mitraillage [mitrajaʒ] NM machinegunning

mitraille [mitraj] NF **1** *Mil* grapeshot; *(décharge)* volley of shots **2** *Fam (petite monnaie)* small *or* loose change▫, *Br* coppers

mitrailler [3] [mitraje] VT **1** *Mil* to machinegun **2** *Fam (photographier)* to snap (away) at; **se faire m. par les photographes** to be besieged by photographers **3** *Fig (assaillir)* **m. qn de questions** to fire questions at sb, to bombard sb with questions

mitraillette [mitrajɛt] NF submachine-gun, machine pistol

mitrailleur [mitrajœr] NM machine-gunner

mitrailleuse [mitrajøz] NF machine gun

mitral, -e, -aux, -ales [mitral, -o] ADJ mitral

mitre [mitr] NF **1** *Rel* mitre; **recevoir la m.** to be mitred **2** *Constr* (chimney) cowl

mitré, -e [mitre] ADJ mitred

mitron [mitrɔ̃] NM **1** *(garçon pâtissier)* pastry cook's apprentice *or* boy; *(garçon boulanger)* baker's apprentice *or* boy **2** *Constr* chimney cowl seating *or* head

mi-voix [mivwa] **à mi-voix** ADV in a low *or* hushed voice, in hushed tones; **chanter à m.** to sing softly; **parler à m.** to speak quietly *or* in a low voice

mix [miks] **NM** *Mktg (marchéage)* mix; **m. média** media mix; **m. de produits** product mix

mixage [miksaʒ] **NM** *Rad, TV & Mus* mixing; **m. final** master soundtrack

mixer¹ [3] [mikse] **VT1** *Culin* to blend, to liquidize **2** *Mus* to mix

mixer², mixeur [miksœr] **NM** blender, liquidizer

mixité [miksite] **NF1** *(gén)* mixed nature **2** *Scol* coeducation, coeducational system

mixte [mikst] **ADJ1** *(des deux sexes)* mixed; *Scol* **classe m.** mixed class; *Sport* **double m.** mixed doubles; **école m.** mixed *or* coeducational school; **équipe m.** mixed team **2** *(de nature double)* mixed; **billet m.** combined rail and road ticket; **commission m.** joint commission; **train m.** composite train *(goods and passengers)* **3** *(à double usage)* **cuisinière m.** combined gas and electric *Br* cooker *or Am* stove

NM *Sport* mixed doubles match

mixtion [mikstjɔ̃] **NF** *Pharm (action)* blending, compounding; *(médicament)* mixture

mixture [mikstyr] **NF1** *Chim & Pharm* mixture **2** *(boisson, nourriture)* mixture, concoction; **on nous a servi une m. infâme** they served us a vile concoction

mizuna [mizuna] **NM** *Bot & Culin* mizuna

MJC [ɛmʒise] **NF** *(abrév* **maison des jeunes et de la culture**) community centre

ml *(abrév écrite* **millilitre**) ml

MLF [ɛmɛlɛf] **NM** *(abrév* **Mouvement de libération de la femme**) = women's movement, *Am* ≃ NOW

Mlle *(abrév écrite* **Mademoiselle**) Miss

Mlles *(abrév écrite* **Mesdemoiselles**) Misses

MM. *(abrév écrite* **Messieurs**) Messrs

mm *(abrév écrite* **millimètre(s)**) mm

Mme *(abrév écrite* **Madame**) *(femme mariée)* Mrs; *(femme mariée ou célibataire)* Ms

Mmes *(abrév écrite* **Mesdames**) Ladies

MMS [ɛmɛmɛs] **NM** *Tél (abrév* **multimedia message service**) MMS

mnémonique [mnemɔnik] **ADJ** mnemonic; **procédé** *ou* **moyen m.** mnemonic

mnémotechnie [mnemɔtɛkni] **NF** mnemonics *(singulier)*

mnémotechnique [mnemɔteknik] **ADJ** mnemonic; **formule m.** mnemonic

NF mnemonics *(singulier)*

M° *(abrév écrite* **métro**) metro

Mo [ɛmo] **NM** *Ordinat (abrév* **mégaoctet**) MB

mob¹ [mɔb] **NF** *Fam (Mobylette®)* moped

mob² [mɔb] **NF** *Suisse Hist* = mobilization of the Swiss reserve army during the First and Second World Wars

mobile [mɔbil] **ADJ1** *(qui se déplace ▸ pont, cible)* moving; *(▸ main-d'œuvre, population, personne âgée)* mobile; *(▸ organe, cartilage)* mobile, having freedom of movement; *(▸ panneau)* sliding; *(amovible)* movable, removable; *(feuillets)* loose; **trois étagères mobiles et deux fixes** three movable *or* removable shelves and two fixed ones; **carnet à feuilles mobiles** loose-leaf notepad; **le boxeur est très m.** the boxer is very nimble *or* quick on his feet; *Tech* **organes mobiles** sliding *or* working *or* moving parts

2 *Mil (unité)* mobile

3 *Vieilli (humeur)* changeable

4 *Typ (à valeur non fixe)* **caractère m.** movable character

NM1 *(de sculpteur, pour enfant) & Beaux-Arts* mobile; *Mktg* **m. publicitaire** advertising mobile

2 *Phys* moving object

3 *(motif)* motive; **le m. d'un crime** the motive for a crime; **quel m. l'a poussé à agir ainsi?** what motivated *or* prompted him to act this way?

4 *(téléphone portable) Br* mobile (phone), *Am* cellphone

mobile home [mɔbilom] *(pl* **mobile homes**) **NM** mobile home

mobilier, -ère [mɔbilje, -ɛr] **ADJ** *Jur (propriété)* personal, movable; *(titre)* transferable; **biens mobiliers** personal property *(UNCOUNT)*; **effets mobiliers** chattels

NM1 *(d'une habitation)* furniture, furnishings; **du m. Louis XIII/Renaissance** Louis XIII/Renaissance (style) furniture; **le m. de la salle à manger** the dining room furniture; **M. national** = state-owned furniture (in France)

2 *(pour un usage particulier)* **m. de bureau/jardin** office/garden furniture; **m. scolaire** school furniture *or* furnishings; **m. de présentation** display stands

3 *Jur* movable property, movables

4 **m. urbain** street fittings, street furniture

> Do not confuse with **meuble**.

mobilisable [mɔbilizabl] **ADJ1** *Mil* liable to be called up, mobilizable; **les jeunes de moins de 18 ans ne sont pas mobilisables** young people under 18 are not eligible for call-up **2** *(disponible)* available **3** *Fin (capital)* realizable; *(actif, biens immobiliers)* mobilizable

mobilisateur, -trice [mɔbilizatœr, -tris] **ADJ** mobilizing; **un slogan m.** a rallying cry; **c'est un thème très m. en ce moment** it's an issue which is stirring a lot of people into action at the moment

mobilisation [mɔbilizasjɔ̃] **NF1** *Mil (action)* mobilization, mobilizing, calling up; *(état)* mobilization; **m. générale/partielle** general/partial mobilization; **ordre de m. générale** general mobilization order

2 *(d'une force politique)* mobilization; *(d'énergie, de volonté)* mobilization, summoning up; **il appelle à la m. de tous les syndicats** he is calling on all the unions to mobilize; **les syndicats comptent beaucoup sur la m. des enseignants contre ce projet de réforme** the unions are relying heavily on the teachers to rally against this proposed reform

3 *Fin (de capital)* realization; *(d'actif, de biens immobiliers)* mobilization; *(de fonds)* raising

4 *Méd & Physiol* mobilization

mobilisatrice [mɔbilizatris] *voir* **mobilisateur**

mobilisé, -e [mɔbilize] **ADJ** *(troupes)* mobilized; *(réservistes)* called up

NM,F serviceman, *f* servicewoman; **un m. de la guerre de 14** a soldier in the First World War

mobiliser [3] [mɔbilize] **VT1** *Mil (population)* to call up, to mobilize; *(armée)* to mobilize; *(réservistes)* to call up; *Fig Hum* **nous avons tous été mobilisés pour l'aider à déménager** we were all marshalled *or* mobilized into helping him/her move; *Fig* **toute la famille a été mobilisée pour préparer la fête** the whole family was put to work to organize the party

2 *(syndicalistes, consommateurs, moyens techniques)* to mobilize; *(volontés)* to mobilize, to summon up; **m. toute son énergie** to summon up all one's energy; **m. qn pour faire qch** to mobilize sb into doing sth; **m. l'opinion en faveur des réfugiés politiques** to rally public opinion for the cause of the political refugees; **m. les forces vives d'une nation** to call upon the full resources of a nation

3 *Fin (capital)* to realize; *(actif, biens immobiliers)* to mobilize; *(fonds)* to raise

4 *Méd & Physiol (membre, articulation)* to mobilize

VPR se mobiliser to mobilize (**contre/en faveur de** against/in support of); **tout le village s'est mobilisé contre le projet** the whole village rose up in arms against the plan *or* mobilized to fight the plan

mobilité [mɔbilite] **NF1** *(dans l'espace ▸ d'une personne, d'une population)* mobility; *(dans le travail)* willingness to move *or* relocate; *(des organes)* freedom of movement **2** *(expression ▸ d'un regard)* expressiveness; *Fig (de caractère, d'humeur)* changeability **3** *(dans une hiérarchie)* mobility; **m. professionnelle** professional mobility; **m. sociale** social mobility

mobinaute [mɔbinot] **NMF** mobile Internet user

Mobylette® [mɔbilɛt] **NF** Mobylette®, moped; **faire de la M.** to ride a moped; **elle y va en** *ou* **à M.** she goes there on her moped

mocassin [mɔkasɛ̃] **NM1** *(chaussure)* moccasin **2** *(serpent)* (water) moccasin

moche [mɔʃ] **ADJ** *Fam* **1** *(laid ▸ personne)* ugly◻; *(▸ objet, vêtement)* ugly◻, awful, horrible; **t'as vu ses chaussures? ce qu'elles sont moches!** have you seen her shoes? they're hideous *or* awful!

2 *(moralement répréhensible)* lousy, rotten; **c'est m., ce qu'elle lui a fait** it was rotten, what she did to him/her

3 *(regrettable)* rotten; **c'est m., ce qui lui est arrivé** it was rotten *or* terrible what happened to him/her; **c'est trop m. de mourir à 20 ans** it's terrible to die at 20

4 *(pénible)* **tu ne peux pas prendre de congé? c'est m., dis donc!** can't you take any time off? that's terrible!

mocheté [mɔʃte] **NF** *Fam* **1** *(laideur)* ugliness◻; **c'est d'une m.!** what an eyesore!, it's absolutely hideous!; **la mode de cet été est d'une m.!** this summer's fashions are hideous! **2** *(homme laid)* horror; *(femme laide)* dog, hag, horror; *(objet)* eyesore; **c'est une vraie m.!** she's as ugly as sin!; **quelle m., cette lampe!** what an eyesore that lamp is!, that lamp's absolutely hideous!

mod [mɔd] **NM** *Ordinat* mod

modal, -e, -aux, -ales [mɔdal, -o] **ADJ** *Ling & Mus* modal

NM *Ling* modal (auxiliary)

modalité [mɔdalite] **NF1** *(façon)* mode, method; *(d'application d'une loi)* mode; *Jur* **modalités** (restrictive) clauses; *Scol* **modalités de contrôle** methods of assessment; **modalités de financement** financing terms *or* conditions; **modalités de paiement** *(conditions)* conditions *or* terms of payment; *(liquide, chèque etc)* methods of payment; **modalités de remboursement** terms of repayment **2** *(circonstances)* **les modalités de l'accord** the terms of the agreement; *Jur* **modalités d'application d'un décret** modes of enforcement of a ruling; *Écon* **modalités d'une émission** terms and conditions of an issue **3** *Ling, Mus & Phil* modality; **adverbe de m.** modal adverb

mode¹ [mɔd] **NF1** *(vêtements)* **la m.** fashion; **la m. (de) printemps/(d')hiver** the spring/winter fashion; **la m. est aux couleurs pastel** pastels are in (fashion); **la m. des pantalons pattes d'éléphant est revenue** flares are back (in fashion); **c'est la m. des bas résille** fishnet stockings are in fashion *or* in vogue; **c'est la dernière** *ou* **c'est la grande m.** it's the latest fashion; **passer de m.** to go out of fashion; **c'est passé de m.** it's out of fashion, it's no longer fashionable; **ceux qui font la m.** trendsetters, fashionsetters; **lancer une m.** to set a fashion *or* a trend; **il a lancé la m. de la fausse fourrure** he launched the fashion for imitation fur; **suivre la m.** to follow fashion

2 *(activité)* **la m.** *(gén)* the fashion industry *or* business; *(stylisme)* fashion designing; **un professionnel de la m.** a fashion professional; **journal de m.** fashion magazine

3 *(goût du jour)* fashion; **c'était la m. de faire du jogging** jogging was all the rage then; **ce n'est plus la m. de se marier** marriage is outdated *or* has gone out of fashion; **la m. des années quatre-vingt-dix** the style of the nineties

4 *Vieilli (coutume)* custom, fashion; **c'était l'ancienne m.!** those were the days!

5 *Arch* **modes** *(vêtements)* fashions; **gravures de modes** fashion plates; **magasin de modes** milliner's shop

ADJ INV *(coloris, coupe)* fashion *(avant n)*, fashionable; **c'est très m.** it's very fashionable, it's very much in fashion; **il ne porte que des choses très m.** he only wears things that are the height of fashion

• **à la mode ADJ** *(vêtement)* fashionable, in fashion; *(personne, sport)* fashionable; *(chanson)* (currently) popular; **être à la m.** *(vêtement, objet)* to be in fashion *or* in vogue; **ce n'est plus à la m.** it's out of fashion; **dans un café à la m.** in a fashionable café; **ce sont des gens à la m.** they're very fashionable **ADV se mettre à la m.** to follow the latest fashion; **revenir à la m.** to come back into fashion

• **à la mode de PRÉP1** *(suivant l'usage de)* in the fashion of; **je les fais toujours à la m. de chez nous** I always do them like we do at home **2** *(locutions)* **cousin à la m. de Bretagne** distant cousin, first cousin once removed; **neveu/oncle à la m. de Bretagne** nephew/uncle six times removed

mode² [mɔd] **NM1** *(méthode)* **m. de** *(méthode)* mode *or* method of; *(manière personnelle)* way of; **m. d'action** form *or* mode of action; **m. de classement** filing system; **m. de codification** coding method; **m. de cuisson** cooking instructions; **m. d'emploi** directions *or* instructions for use; **m. d'existence** way of living; **m. d'expédition** method of delivery; **m. d'expression** means of expression; **m. de fonctionnement** method of operation; **m. de gestion** management method *or* style; **m. de paiement** mode *or* method of payment; **m. de pensée** way of thinking; **m. de production** mode of production; **m. de règlement** mode *or* method of payment; **m. de scrutin** voting system; **m. de transport** method of transport; **m. de vie** *(gén)* lifestyle, way of life; *(en sociologie)* pattern of living

2 *Ling* mood, mode

3 *Ordinat* mode; **m. d'accès** access mode; **m. ajout** append mode; **m. autonome** off-line mode; **m. brouillon** draft mode; **m. connecté** on-line mode; **m. continu** continuous mode; **m. différé** delayed mode, non real-time mode; **m. édition** edit mode; **m. en ligne** on-line mode; **m. graphique** graphics mode; **m. hors ligne** off-line mode; **m. d'impression rapide** draft mode; **m. d'insertion** insert mode; **m. lecture seule** read-only mode; **m. local** off-line mode; **m. maître** master mode; **m. multitâche** multitasking mode; **m. paysage** landscape mode; **en m. point** *(image)* bitmapped, bitmap; **m. portrait** portrait mode; **m. rapide** draft mode; **m. texte** text mode; **m. de transmission** data communication mode; **m. utilisateur** user mode

4 *Math, Mus & Phil* mode

5 *Typ* **m. à la française** portrait mode; **m. à l'italienne** landscape mode

6 *Aut* **m. de conduite hiver** winter driving mode; **m. de sélecteur de vitesses** gear selector; **m. dégradé** limp-home mode

modelage [mɔdəlaʒ] **NM 1** *(action)* modelling **2** *(objet)* sculpture

modèle [mɔdɛl] **NM 1** *(référence à reproduire ▸ gén)* model; *(▸ de tricot, de couture)* pattern; **prendre m. sur qch** to use sth as a model; **construire qch sur le m. de** to build sth on the model of; *Beaux-Arts* **dessiner d'après un m.** to draw from life; **j'ai pris ton pull comme m.** I used your sweater as a pattern; **m. de lettre** standard letter; **m. de signature** specimen signature

2 *Scol (corrigé)* model answer; **résumez le texte en vous aidant du m.** summarize this text along the same lines

3 *(bon exemple)* model, example; **elle est un m. pour moi** she's my role model; **prendre qn pour m.** to model oneself on sb; **servir de m. à qn** to serve as a model for sb, to be a model to sb; **c'est le m. du parfait employé** he's a model employee; *Fam* **ta sœur, c'est pas un m.!** your sister is no example to follow!; **c'est un m. de discrétion** he's/she's a model of discretion; **c'est un m. du genre** it's a perfect example of its type; **un m. de vertu** a paragon of virtue; **le m. américain/japonais** the American/Japanese model

4 *Com (prototype, version ▸ gén)* model; *(▸ vêtement)* model, style, design; **grand/petit m.** large-scale/small-scale model; *Aut* **m. sport/deux portes** sports/two-door model; **une voiture dernier m.** a car of the latest design; **c'est un ancien m.** it's an old model; **vous avez ce m. en 38?** do you have this one in a 38?; **m. de démonstration** demonstration model; **m. déposé** registered design; *Tech* **m. de fabrique** factory prototype; **m. familial** family model

5 *(maquette)* model; **m. réduit** scale model; **m. réduit d'avion** model aeroplane; **un m. au 1/10** a 1 to 10 (scale) model

6 *Beaux-Arts (personne qui pose)* model; **servir de m. à un artiste** to sit *or* to model for an artist

7 *Ordinat* model; **m. client-serveur** client-server model

8 *Ling* pattern

9 *Com & Math (représentation schématique)* model; **m. économique** economic model; **m. d'entreprise** corporate model

ADJ 1 *(parfait)* model *(avant n)*; **il a eu un comportement m.** he was a model of good behaviour **2** *(qui sert de référence)* **ferme/prison m.** model farm/prison

modelé [mɔdəle] **NM 1** *(sur tableau)* relief; *(d'une sculpture, d'un buste)* contours, curves **2** *Géog* (surface) relief

modeler [25] [mɔdle] **VT 1** *(argile)* to model, to shape, to mould; *(figurine)* to model, to mould, to fashion; **m. des animaux en terre** to mould *or* to model animals in clay; **l'eau/l'érosion a modelé le relief de la côte** water/erosion has shaped the coastline; **les glaciers ont modelé le paysage** the glaciers moulded the landscape **2** *Fig (idées, caractère, opinion publique)* to shape, to mould; **m. sa conduite sur qn** *ou* **celle de qn** to model one's behaviour on sb *or* sb's

VPR se modeler se m. sur to model oneself on

modeleur, -euse [mɔdlœr, -øz] **NM,F 1** *Beaux-Arts* modeller **2** *Métal* pattern-maker

modélisation [mɔdelizasjɔ̃] **NF** modelling

modélisme [mɔdelism] **NM** scale model making

modéliste [mɔdelist] **NMF 1** *(de maquettes)* model maker **2** *Couture* (dress) designer

modem [mɔdɛm] **NM** modem; **envoyer qch à qn par m.** to modem sth to sb, to send sth to sb by modem; **m. externe** external modem; **m. fax** fax modem; **m. interne** internal modem; **m. nul** null modem; **m. Numéris** ISDN modem; **m. RNIS** ISDN modem

modem-câble [mɔdɛmkɑbl] *(pl* **modems-câbles)** **NM** *Ordinat* cable modem

modérateur, -trice [mɔderatœr, -tris] **ADJ** *(élément, présence)* moderating, restraining

NM,F mediator, moderator; **jouer un rôle de m.** to have a moderating influence

NM 1 *Tech* regulator, moderator **2** *Nucl & Rel* moderator **3** *(dans un forum Internet)* regulator

modération [mɔderasjɔ̃] **NF 1** *(mesure)* moderation, restraint; **avec m.** *(boire, manger, utiliser)* in moderation; *(agir)* moderately, with moderation; **une réponse pleine de m.** a very restrained answer **2** *(réduction ▸ de dépenses)* reduction, reducing; *(atténuation ▸ d'un sentiment)* restraint, restraining

modératrice [mɔderatris] *voir* **modérateur**

modéré, -e [mɔdere] **ADJ 1** *(prix)* moderate, reasonable; *(vent, température)* moderate; *(enthousiasme, intérêt, succès)* moderate, reasonable; *Météo* **mer modérée à belle** sea moderate to good **2** *(mesuré, raisonnable)* moderate; *(plein de retenue)* moderate, restrained; **être m. dans ses propos** to be moderate in what one says **3** *Pol* moderate

NM,F *Pol* moderate; **les modérés** the moderates

modérément [mɔderemɑ̃] **ADV 1** *(sans excès)* in moderation **2** *(relativement)* moderately, relatively; **je ne suis que m. surpris** I'm only moderately surprised, I'm not really all that surprised; *Ironique* **j'ai m. apprécié sa remarque** I didn't much appreciate his/her remark; *Ironique* **j'apprécie m. qu'on mette le nez dans mes affaires** I'm not very keen on people sticking their noses into my business

modérer [18] [mɔdere] **VT** *(ardeur, enthousiasme, impatience, dépenses)* to moderate, to restrain, to curb; *(vitesse)* to reduce; *(exigences)* to moderate, to restrain; **elle voulait un gros salaire mais elle a dû m. ses prétentions** she wanted a high salary but she had to set her sights a bit lower; **modérez vos propos!** please tone down *or* moderate your language!; *Hum* **modère tes ardeurs!** control yourself!

VPR se modérer 1 *(se contenir)* to restrain oneself **2** *(se calmer)* to calm down

moderne [mɔdɛrn] **ADJ 1** *(actuel, récent ▸ mobilier, bâtiment, technique, théorie)* modern; **les temps modernes, l'époque m.** modern times; **le mode de vie m.** modern living, today's way of life

2 *(progressiste ▸ artiste, opinions, théoricien)* modern, progressive; **la femme m. travaille** the modern woman goes out to work; **c'est une grand-mère très m.** she's a very modern *or* up-to-date grandmother

3 *Beaux-Arts* modern, contemporary

4 *Scol (maths)* modern, new; *(études, histoire)* modern, contemporary

5 *Ling (langue, sens)* modern; **grec m.** Modern Greek

NM 1 *Beaux-Arts* modern artist; *Littérature* modern writer **2 le m.** *(genre)* modern style; *(mobilier)* modern furniture; **mélanger le m. et l'ancien** to mix old and new

modernisation [mɔdɛrnizasjɔ̃] **NF** modernization, modernizing, updating; **un effort de m. de l'enseignement** an attempt to modernize education

moderniser [3] [mɔdɛrnize] **VT** to modernize, to bring up to date

VPR se moderniser to modernize

modernisme [mɔdɛrnism] **NM** modernism

moderniste [mɔdɛrnist] **ADJ** modernist

NMF modernist

modernité [mɔdɛrnite] **NF** modernity

modern style [mɔdɛrnstil] **ADJ INV** modern style *(avant n)*, art nouveau *(avant n)*; **une glace m.** an art nouveau mirror

NM INV modern style, art nouveau

modeste [mɔdɛst] **ADJ 1** *(logement)* modest; *(revenu)* modest, small; *(goût, train de vie)* modest, unpretentious; *(tenue)* modest, simple; **une pièce aux dimensions modestes** a small room, a room of modest dimensions

2 *(milieu)* modest, humble; **être d'origine très m.** to come from a very modest *or* humble background

3 *(avant le nom) (modique)* modest, humble, small; **ce n'est qu'un m. présent** it's only a very modest *or* small gift, it's just a little something; **je ne suis qu'un m. commerçant** I'm only a shopkeeper

4 *(sans vanité)* modest

5 *Vieilli (pudique ▸ air, jeune fille)* modest

NMF faire le/la m. to put on a show of modesty; **allons, ne fais pas la** *ou* **ta m.!** come on, don't be (so) modest!; **elle joue les modestes** she's acting modest

modestement [mɔdɛstəmɑ̃] **ADV 1** *(simplement)* modestly, simply; **ils vivent très m.** they live very modestly, they lead a very simple life **2** *(sans vanité)* modestly **3** *Vieilli (avec réserve)* modestly, unassumingly; *(avec pudeur)* modestly

modestie [mɔdɛsti] **NF 1** *(humilité)* modesty; **faire preuve de m.** to be modest; **ce n'est pas la m. qui l'étouffe!** you can't say he's/she's overmodest!; **en toute m.** in all modesty; **fausse m.** false modesty; *Ironique* **allons, pas de fausse m.!** come on, don't be so modest! **2** *Vieilli (réserve)* modesty, self-effacement; *(pudeur)* modesty **3** *(d'exigences, d'ambitions, de revenus)* modesty

modeux, -euse [mɔdø, -øz] **NM,F** *Fam* fashionista

modicité [mɔdisite] **NF** *(de prix, de rémunération)* smallness; **malgré la m. du loyer** despite the low rent; **la m. de leur salaire ne leur permet pas de partir en vacances** they can't go on holiday because they earn so little

modifiable [mɔdifjabl] **ADJ** modifiable; **après cela, le texte ne sera plus m.** after that, the text cannot be amended

modificateur, -trice [mɔdifikatœr, -tris] **ADJ** modifying, modificatory

NM *Biol, Gram & Ordinat* modifier

modificatif, -ive [mɔdifikatif, -iv] **ADJ** modifying

modification [mɔdifikasjɔ̃] **NF 1** *(processus)* modification, modifying, changing; *(altération)* modification, alteration, change; *(à une loi, un contrat)* amendment; **apporter** *ou* **faire une m. à qch** to make an alteration to sth, to modify sth; **apporter une m. à la loi** to change the law **2** *Ordinat* alteration, modification; **m. d'adresse** address modification

modificative [mɔdifikativ] *voir* **modificatif**

modificatrice [mɔdifikatris] *voir* **modificateur**

modifier [9] [mɔdifje] **VT 1** *(transformer ▸ politique, texte)* to modify, to change, to alter; *(▸ loi)* to amend, to change; **j'ai modifié la disposition des meubles** I've moved *or* changed the furniture around; *Naut* **m. la route** to alter course **2** *Gram* to modify **3** *Ordinat* to alter, to modify; **m. la configuration de qch** to reconfigure sth

VPR se modifier to change, to alter, to be modified

modique [mɔdik] **ADJ** *(peu élevé ▸ prix, rémunération)* modest, small; **et pour la m. somme de 20 euros, mesdames, je vous donne deux couvertures!** and for the modest sum of 20 euros, ladies, I'll give you two blankets!; *Ironique* **sa voiture a**

coûté la m. somme de 20 000 euros his/her car cost a cool 20,000 euros

modiquement [mɔdikmɑ̃] **ADV** *(rétribuer)* poorly, modestly, meagrely

modiste [mɔdist] **NMF 1** *(fabricant ou vendeur de chapeaux)* milliner **2** *Can Vieilli (couturière)* seamstress, dressmaker

modulable [mɔdylabl] **ADJ** *(équipement, installation)* modular, flexible; *(horaires, tarif)* flexible; *(chauffage, éclairage)* adjustable; **bibliothèque composée d'éléments modulables** bookshelves made of versatile *or* modular units

modulaire [mɔdylɛr] **ADJ** modular

modulateur, -trice [mɔdylatœr, -tris] **ADJ** modulating *(avant n)*

NM *Ordinat & Tél* modulator; **m. de fréquence** converter

modulation [mɔdylasjɔ̃] **NF 1** *(tonalité ▸ de la voix)* modulation; *Mus & (en acoustique)* modulation

2 *Électron, Ordinat, Rad & Tél* modulation; **m. d'amplitude/de fréquence** amplitude/frequency modulation

3 *Fig (nuance)* modulation, variation

4 *Fig (ajustement)* adjustment

modulatrice [mɔdylatris] *voir* **modulateur**

module [mɔdyl] **NM 1** *(élément ▸ gén)* module, unit; *Archit & Constr* module; **m. (d'enseignement)** module; *Astron* **m. de commande** command module **2** *Math & Phys* modulus **3** *Ordinat* module; **m. d'extension** plug-in

moduler [3] [mɔdyle] **VT 1** *Tech* to modulate **2** *(adapter)* to adjust (**en fonction de** in relation to) **3** *(nuancer)* to vary; *(voix)* to inflect, to modulate

VI *Mus* to modulate

modus vivendi [mɔdysvivɛ̃di] **NM INV** modus vivendi; **trouver un m. avec** to come to a working arrangement with

moé [mwe] **PRON** *Can Fam* me□

moelle [mwal] **NF 1** *Anat* marrow, *Spéc* medulla; **m. épinière** spinal cord; **m. osseuse/jaune/rouge** bone/yellow/red marrow; *Fig* **jusqu'à la m.** to the core; **être gelé** *ou* **transi jusqu'à la m. des os** to be frozen to the marrow *or* to the bone **2** *Culin* (bone) marrow **3** *Bot* pith

moelleuse [mwaløz] *voir* **moelleux**

moelleusement [mwaløzmɑ̃] **ADV** *(s'installer)* comfortably, snugly, luxuriously; **s'enfoncer m. dans un coussin de plumes** to snuggle down into a feather cushion; **être m. installé dans un fauteuil/sous une couette** to be snuggled up in an armchair/under an eiderdown

moelleux, -euse [mwalø, -øz] **ADJ 1** *(au toucher)* soft; **des coussins m.** soft *or* comfortable cushions

2 *(à la vue, à l'ouïe)* mellow, warm; **une voix moelleuse** a mellow voice

3 *(au palais ▸ vin)* mellow, well-rounded; *(▸ viande)* tender; *(▸ gâteau)* moist; *(▸ fromage)* smooth

4 *Littéraire (gracieux)* soft; **une courbe moelleuse** a soft *or* gentle *or* graceful curve

NM softness, mellowness; *(d'un vin)* mellowness; **un vin qui a du m.** a mellow *or* smooth wine

moellon [mwalɔ̃] **NM** *Constr* rubble, rubblestone, moellon; **construction en moellons** rubble work; **m. d'appareil** ashlar; **m. brut** quarry stone

mœurs [mœr, mœrs] **NFPL 1** *(comportement social)* customs, habits, *Sout* mores; *(d'animaux)* habits; **les m. politiques** political practice; **c'est entré dans les m.** it's become part of everyday life; **les m. de notre temps** the social mores of our time; **autres temps, autres m.** times have changed

2 *(comportement personnel)* manners, ways; **elle a des m. vraiment bizarres** she behaves in a really odd way; **quelles drôles de m.!** what a strange way to behave!

3 *(style de vie)* lifestyle; **avoir des m. simples** to have a simple lifestyle *or* way of life, to lead a simple life

4 *(principes moraux)* morals, moral standards; **avoir des m. très strictes** to have very strict moral standards *or* morals; **avoir des m. dissolues** to lead a dissolute life, to have loose morals; *Euph* **des m. particulières** particular tastes; **une femme de m. légères** a woman of easy virtue; **les bonnes m.** morality; **c'est contraire aux bonnes m.** it goes against accepted standards of behaviour; *Fam* **la police/brigade des m., les M.** ≃ the vice squad

5 *Zool* habits

• **de mœurs ADJ 1** *(sexuel)* **affaire de m.** sex case **2** *Littérature* **comédie/roman de m.** comedy/novel of manners

mofette[1] [mɔfɛt] **NF** *Géol* mofette

mofette[2] [mɔfɛt] **NF** *Zool* skunk

mogette [mɔʒɛt] **NF** = type of bean from the Vendée area

mohair [mɔɛr] **NM** mohair; **un pull en m.** a mohair sweater

Mohican [mɔikɑ̃] **NM** Mohican; **les Mohicans** the Mohicans, the Mohican

moi [mwa] **PRON 1** *(sujet)* **qui est là? – m.** who's there? – me; **je l'ai vue hier – m. aussi** I saw her yesterday – so did I *or* me too; **elle est invitée, et m. aussi** she's invited, and so am I; **je n'en sais rien – m. non plus** I have no idea – neither do I *or* me neither; **m.? je n'ai rien dit!** me? I didn't say a word!; **m., je n'y comprends rien!** I don't understand a thing (about it)!; **m. m'sieur, m. m'sieur, je connais la réponse!** me sir, me sir, I know the answer!; **m. qui vous parle, je l'ai vu de mes propres yeux** I'm telling you, I saw him with my very own eyes; **et vous voulez que m., j'y aille?** you want ME to go?; **et m. qui te faisais confiance!** and to think (that) I trusted you!; **il faisait nuit, et m. qui ne savais pas où aller!** it was dark, and there was me, not knowing where to go!; **les enfants et m., nous rentrons** the children and I are going back; **m. seul possède la clef** I'm the only one with the key; *Fam* **m., les femmes, c'est fini!** I've had my fill of women!, I'm finished with women!

2 *(avec un présentatif)* **c'est m. qui lui ai dit de venir** I was the one who *or* it was me who told him/her to come; **salut, c'est m.!** hi, it's me!; **c'est m. qui te le dis!** I'm telling you!; **je vous remercie – non, c'est m.** thank you – thank YOU

3 *(complément)* **dites-m.** tell me; **donne-le-m.** give it to me; **attendez-m.!** wait (for me)!; **et m.? vous m'oubliez?** what about me? have you forgotten me?; **vous me soupçonnez, m.?** you suspect ME?; **il nous a invités, ma femme et m.** he invited both my wife and me

4 *(avec une préposition)* **avec/pour/sans m.** with/for/without me; **ce livre est à m.** this book is mine *or* belongs to me; **c'est à m. qu'il a confié cette tâche** he gave ME this task, it was me he gave this task to; **c'est à m. qu'il l'a donné** he gave it to ME; **c'est à m. qu'il a fait cette confidence** he confided this to ME; **qu'est-ce que ça peut me faire, à m.?** what difference does that make to ME?; **il me l'a dit, à m.** he told ME; **une chambre à m. tout seul** a room of my own; *Fam* **un ami à m.** a friend of mine□; **à m.!** *(au secours)* help!; *(de jouer)* it's my turn!; *(d'essayer)* let me have a go!; **parlez-lui de m.** mention my name to him/her; **ça ne vient pas de m.** it isn't from me; **ces vers ne sont pas de m.** these verses are not mine; **c'est de m., cette lettre?** is this letter from me?, is this letter one of mine?, is this one of my letters?; **c'est en m.** it's in me; **c'est pour m.** it's for me; *(je vais payer l'addition)* I'll get this, it's on me; **comptez sur m.** you can count on me

5 *(dans les comparaisons)* **il est plus âgé que m.** he is older than me *or* than I am; **tu as d'aussi bonnes raisons que m.** you have just as good reasons as me *or* as I have

6 *(en fonction de pronom réfléchi)* myself; **je suis contente de m.** I'm pleased with myself; **je devrais penser un peu plus à m.** I ought to think of myself a bit more

7 *(emploi expressif)* **regardez-m. ça!** just look at that!; **rangez-m. ça tout de suite!** put that away right now!; **sors-m. ce chien de là!** get that dog out of here!

NM *Phil* **le m.** the self; *Psy* the ego; **la psychanalyse nous aide à découvrir notre vrai m.** psychoanalysis helps us discover our true selves; *Psy* **le m. idéal** the ego ideal

moignon [mwaɲɔ̃] **NM** stump *(of a limb)*

moi-même [mwamɛm] **PRON** myself; **j'ai m. vérifié** I checked it myself; **mon épouse et m.** my wife and I; **je préfère vérifier par m.** I prefer to check for myself; **j'y suis allé de m.** I went there on my own initiative; **c'est m.** *(au téléphone) Br* speaking, *Am* this is he/she

moindre [mwɛ̃dr] **ADJ 1** *(comparatif) (perte)* lesser, smaller; *(qualité)* lower, poorer; *(quantité)* smaller; *(prix)* lower; **de m. gravité** less serious; **de m. importance** less important, of lesser importance; **son talent est bien m.** he's/she's far less gifted; **c'est un m. mal** it's the lesser evil; **c'est couvert par l'assurance, ce qui est un m. mal** it's covered by the insurance, so things aren't as bad as they might have been; **de deux maux, il faut choisir le m.** you have to choose the lesser of two evils

2 *(superlatif)* **le/la m.** *(de deux)* the lesser; *(de trois ou plus)* the least, the slightest; **le m. mouvement/danger** the slightest movement/danger; **pas la m. chance** not the slightest *or* remotest chance; **il n'y a pas le m. espoir de les retrouver vivants** there isn't the slightest hope of finding them alive; **je ne lui ai pas fait le m. reproche** I didn't reproach him/her in the slightest *or* in the least; **il n'a pas fait la m. remarque** he didn't say a single word; **je n'en ai pas la m. idée** I haven't got the slightest *or* faintest *or* remotest idea; **jusqu'au m. détail** down to the last *or* smallest detail; **c'est la m. des choses** it's the least I/we/*etc* can do; **ce serait la m. des politesses** it would be only common courtesy; **un expert, et non des moindres** no mean expert; **c'est une pianiste, et non des moindres!** she's a pianist, and a good one at that!; **c'est là son m. défaut** that's the least of his/her faults; **au m. reproche, il se met à pleurer** he bursts into tears at the slightest reproach

3 *Suisse Fam (malade)* ill□; **se sentir m.** to feel ill

4 *Suisse Fam* **la m.** a bit□, a little□; **parlons la m. de vous** let's talk a bit about you

moindrement [mwɛ̃drəmɑ̃] **ADV** *Littéraire ou Can* **il n'était pas le m. gêné** he wasn't embarrassed in the least *or* in the slightest; **sans être le m. intéressé** without being in the least bit interested

moine [mwan] **NM 1** *Rel* monk, friar

2 *Zool* Mediterranean (monk) seal

3 *Orn (macareux)* puffin

4 *Arch (bassinoire)* bed warmer

5 *Can (toupie)* (spinning) top

6 *Can Vulg (pénis)* prick, dick

moineau, -x [mwano] **NM 1** *Orn* sparrow; *Fam* **avoir une cervelle** *ou* **tête de m.** to be bird-brained *or* scatterbrained **2** *Fam (individu)* bird, customer, fellow; **c'est un drôle de m.!** he's an odd *Br* fish *or Am* bird!

moinillon [mwanijɔ̃] **NM** *(jeune moine)* young monk

MOINS [mwɛ̃]

ADV
• less **A1–2** • least **B1–2**
PRÉP
• less **1** • minus **1, 3**
• to **2**
NM
• minus sign

ADV A. COMPARATIF D'INFÉRIORITÉ 1 *(avec un adjectif, un adverbe)* less; **cinq fois m. cher** five times less expensive; **deux fois m. cher** half as expensive, twice as cheap; **les fraises sont m. sucrées** the strawberries are less sweet *or* aren't as sweet; **elle voit m. bien depuis l'opération** her sight hasn't been as good since the operation; **c'est Venise en m. ensoleillé** it's like Venice minus *or* without the sunshine; **c'est m. bien que l'an dernier** it's not as good as last year; **c'est le même appartement, en m. bien/grand** it's the same flat, only not as nice/big; **il est bien m. beau maintenant** he's much less *or* not as handsome now; **beaucoup/un peu m.** a lot/a little less; **il est m. riche qu'eux** he is not as rich as they are; **je suis m. enthousiaste que toi** I'm less enthusiastic than you, I'm not as enthusiastic as you; **c'est elle la m. intelligente des deux** she's the less intelligent of the two; **un peu m. beau que...** a bit less handsome than..., not quite as handsome as...; **il est m. timide que réservé** he's not so much shy as reserved; **il n'en est pas m. vrai que...** it is nonetheless true that...; **non m. charmante que...** just as charming as..., no less charming than...

2 *(avec un verbe)* less, not... so *or* as much; **je souffre m.** I'm not in so much *or* I'm in less pain; **parle m.!** don't speak so much!; **tu devrais demander m.** you shouldn't ask for so much; **m. tu parles, mieux ça vaut** the less you speak, the better; **j'y pense m. que tu ne le crois** I think about it less than you think; **il travaille m. que sa sœur** he works less than his sister

B. *SUPERLATIF D'INFÉRIORITÉ* **1** *(avec un adjectif, un adverbe)* **c'est lui le m. riche des trois** he's the least wealthy of the three; **c'est le sommet le m. élevé** it's the lowest peak; **c'est le modèle le m. cher qu'on puisse trouver** it's the least expensive (that) you can find; **le m. possible** as little as possible; **il travaille le m. possible** he works as little as possible; **tremper le tissu le m. souvent possible** soak the material as little as possible; **c'est lui qui habite le m. loin** he lives the least far away *or* the nearest; **je ne suis pas le m. du monde surpris** I'm not at all *or* not in the least bit surprised; **je vous dérange? – mais non, pas le m. du monde** am I disturbing you? – of course not *or* not in the slightest

2 *(avec un verbe)* **le m.** (the) least; **c'est le dernier-né qui crie le m.** the youngest is the one who cries (the) least; **c'est ce qui coûte/rapporte le m.** this is the least expensive/makes the least profit; **le m. qu'on puisse faire, c'est de les inviter** the least we could do is invite them; **le m. que l'on puisse dire, c'est qu'il manque de talent** the least one can say is that he lacks talent; **c'est le m. qu'on puisse dire!** that's the least you can say!

PRÉP 1 *(en soustrayant)* minus, less; **dix m. huit font deux** ten minus *or* less eight makes two; **on est seize: m. les enfants, ça fait douze** there are sixteen of us, twelve not counting the children

2 *(indiquant l'heure)* to; **il est m. vingt** it's twenty to; **il est trois heures m. le quart** it's quarter *or* a quarter to three; *Fam* **il était m. une** *ou* **cinq** that was a close call *or* shave

3 *(introduisant un nombre négatif)* minus; **m. 50 plus m. 6 égalent m. 56** minus 50 plus minus 6 is *or* makes minus 56; **il fait m. 25** it's 25 below *or* minus 25; **plonger à m. 300 m** to dive to a depth of 300 m

NM minus, minus sign; **mets un m. avant le chiffre 4** put a minus sign in front of the figure 4

• **à moins ADV j'étais terrifié – on le serait à m.!** I was terrified – and lesser things have frightened me!

• **à moins de PRÉP 1** *(excepté)* **à m. d'un miracle** short of *or* barring a miracle; **nous n'arriverons pas à temps, à m. de partir demain** we won't get there on time unless we leave tomorrow **2** *(pour moins de)* for less than; **vous n'en trouverez pas à m. de 30 euros** you won't find any for under *or* for less than 30 euros **3** *(dans le temps, l'espace)* **il habite à m. de dix minutes/500 m d'ici** he lives less than ten minutes/500 m from here

• **à moins que CONJ** unless; **j'irai au tribunal à m. qu'il ne me rembourse** I'll go to court unless he pays me back; **à m. que vous ne vouliez le faire vous-même** unless you wanted to do it yourself

• **au moins ADV 1** *(en tout cas)* at least; **dis-moi ce qui t'est arrivé, au m.!** at least tell me what happened to you!; **embrasse au m. ta mère** at least kiss your mother; **il va partir, (tout) au m. c'est ce qu'il dit** he's leaving, at least that's what he says **2** *(au minimum)* at least; **il y a au m. vingt personnes qui attendent** there are at least twenty people waiting; **ça fait au m. un mois qu'on ne l'a pas vu** we haven't seen him for at least a month

• **de moins ADV il y a dix euros de m. dans le tiroir** there are ten euros missing from the drawer; **je me sens dix ans de m.** I feel ten years younger; **j'ai un an de m. qu'elle** I'm a year younger than her; **j'ai une tête de m. qu'elle** I'm shorter than her by a head

• **de moins en moins ADV** less and less; **nous nous voyons de m. en m.** we see less and less of each other *or* each other less and less; **de m. en m. souvent** less and less often

• **de moins en moins de DÉT** *(suivi d'un nom comptable)* fewer and fewer; *(suivi d'un nom non comptable)* less and less; **de m. en m. de gens** fewer and fewer people; **il y a de m. en m. de demande pour ce produit** there is less and less demand for this product; **elle a de m. en m. de fièvre** her temperature is falling

• **des moins ADV un accueil des m. chaleureux** a less than warm welcome; **vos amis sont des m. discrets** your friends aren't the most discreet of people

• **du moins ADV** at least; **il lui devait de l'argent, du m. c'est ce que je croyais** he owed him/her money, at least that's what I thought; **ils devaient venir samedi, c'est du m. ce qu'ils nous avaient dit** they were supposed to come on Saturday, at least that's what they told us

• **en moins ADV il y a une chaise en m.** there's one chair missing, we're one chair short

• **en moins de PRÉP** in less than; **en m. d'une heure** in less than an hour, in under an hour; **en m. de temps qu'il n'en faut pour le dire** before you can say Jack Robinson; **en m. de rien** in no time at all; *Fam* **en m. de deux** in a jiffy, in two ticks

• **moins de DÉT 1** *(comparatif) (avec un nom comptable)* fewer; *(avec un nom non comptable)* less; **ils étaient m. de cent** there were fewer than a hundred of them; **m. de beurre** less butter; **m. de bouteilles** fewer *or* not so many bottles; **je l'ai payé un peu m. de 20 euros** I paid just under *or* a little less than 20 euros for it; **il a m. de dix-huit ans** he's under eighteen; **les m. de dix-huit ans** the under-eighteens; **il ne me faudra pas m. de trois heures pour tout faire** I'll need at the very least three hours to do everything; **il y avait m. d'enfants que d'habitude** there were fewer children than usual; **il a m. de patience que son frère** he's less patient than his brother **2** *(superlatif)* **le m. de** *(avec un nom comptable)* the fewest; *(avec un nom non comptable)* the least; **c'est lui qui fait le m. de bruit** he makes the least noise; **c'est ce qui consomme le m. d'énergie** it uses the least amount of energy; **c'est à la montagne qu'il y a le m. de monde** it's in the mountains where you find the least number of people; **c'est avec cette voiture que j'ai eu le m. de pannes** this is the car I've had the fewest breakdowns in

• **moins... moins ADV** the less... the less; **m. il travaillera, m. il aura de chances de réussir à son examen** the less he works, the less chance he'll have of passing his exam; **m. on mange, m. on grossit** the less you eat, the less weight you put on

• **moins... plus ADV** the less... the more; **m. tu dors, plus tu seras énervé** the less you sleep, the more on edge you'll be

• **moins que rien ADV** next to nothing; **il m'a fait payer 15 euros, c'est m. que rien** he charged me 15 euros, which is next to nothing **NMF INV** nobody; **c'est un/une m. que rien** he's/she's a nobody; **des m. que rien** a useless bunch (of individuals)

• **on ne peut moins ADV elle est on ne peut m. honnête** she's as honest as they come; **c'est on ne peut m. loin!** it couldn't be nearer!; **c'est on ne peut m. compliqué!** it couldn't be less complicated!

• **pour le moins ADV** at the very least, to say the least; **il y a pour le m. une heure d'attente** there's an hour's wait at the very least; **c'est pour le m. étonnant** it's surprising, to say the least

> Attention: ne pas confondre **fewer** et **less** lorsque l'on traduit **moins. Fewer** s'utilise uniquement avec des termes dénombrables; **less** s'utilise avec des termes indénombrables ou dénombrables (bien que ce dernier emploi soit contesté).

moins-disant [mwɛ̃dizɑ̃] *(pl* **moins-disants)** **NM** lowest bidder

moins-perçu [mwɛ̃pɛrsy] *(pl* **moins-perçus)** **NM** amount due

moins-value [mwɛ̃valy] *(pl* **moins-values)** **NF 1** *(dépréciation)* depreciation, capital loss **2** *(déficit du fisc)* (tax) deficit, shortfall

moirage [mwaraʒ] **NM 1** *(effet)* watered effect *or* finish

2 *(technique)* watering

3 *(sur une image)* cross-hatching

4 *(sur un disque)* moiré (effect)

moire [mwar] **NF 1** *(tissu)* moire, watered fabric; **m. de soie** watered *or* shot silk **2** *Littéraire (irisation)* iridescence, irisation

moiré, -e [mware] **ADJ 1** *Tex* moiré, watered **2** *(irisé)* iridescent, irisated, moiré

NM 1 *Tex* moiré, watered effect *or* finish **2** *Métal* **m. métallique** etching

moirer [3] [mware] **VT 1** *(tissu)* to moiré, to water **2** *(métal, papier)* to moiré **3** *Littéraire (iriser)* to make iridescent, to irisate

moirure [mwaryr] **NF** *Littéraire (irisation)* iridescence, irisation

• **moirures NFPL** *Tex* moiré (effect), watered effect *or* finish; *Métal* moiré (effect)

mois [mwa] **NM 1** *(division du calendrier)* month; **le m. de mai/décembre** the month of May/December; **au m. de mars** in (the month of) March; **au début/à la fin du m. d'avril** in early/late April; **au milieu du m. d'août** in mid-August *or* the middle of August; **les m. en r** months with an r in them; *Com* **le 15 de ce** *ou* **du m.** the 15th of this month, *Br* the 15th inst *or* instant; **m. commercial** thirty days (month); *Bourse* **m. d'échéance** trading month; *Jur* **m. légal** thirty days (month) **2** *(durée)* month; **tous les m.** every *or* each month, monthly; **le comité se réunit tous les m.** the committee meets on a monthly basis; **dans un m.** in a month, in a month's time; **pendant mes m. de grossesse/d'apprentissage** during the months when I was pregnant/serving my apprenticeship; **un m. de préavis** a month's notice; **un m. de vacances/salaire** a month's holiday/wages **3** *(salaire)* monthly wage *or* salary *or* pay; *(versement)* monthly instalment; **je vous dois trois m.** *(de salaire)* I owe you three months' wages; *(de loyer)* I owe you three months' rent; **toucher son m.** to receive one's (monthly) salary; **m. double, treizième m.** = extra month's salary paid as an annual bonus

• **au mois ADV** by the month, monthly, on a monthly basis; **les intérêts sont calculés au m.** interest is worked out on a monthly basis; **louer qch au m.** to hire sth by the month

• **du mois ADJ avez-vous le numéro du m.?** do you have this month's issue?

Moïse [mɔiz] **NPR** *Bible* Moses

moïse [mɔiz] **NM** Moses basket

moisi, -e [mwazi] **ADJ** *(papier, tissu)* mildewy, mouldy; *(fruit, pain)* mouldy; *(logement)* mildewy, fusty

NM *(moisissure)* mildew, mould; **odeur de m.** musty *or* fusty smell; **avoir un goût de m.** to taste mouldy *or* musty; **ça sent le m.** it smells musty; *Fam Fig* I can smell trouble

moisir [32] [mwazir] **VT** to make (go) mouldy

VI 1 *(pourrir)* to go mouldy; *(mur, livre)* to go mildewed; **le pain a moisi** the bread's gone mouldy **2** *Fam (s'éterniser)* to rot; **je ne vais pas m. ici jusqu'à la fin de mes jours!** I'm not going to stay and rot here forever!

moisissure [mwazisyr] **NF** *(champignon)* mould, mildew; *(tache)* patch of mould; **moisissures** mouldy bits, mould *(UNCOUNT)*; **une forte odeur de m.** a strong musty smell

moisson [mwasɔ̃] **NF 1** *Agr (récolte, époque)* harvest; **faire la m.** *ou* **les moissons** to harvest (the crops); **engranger** *ou* **rentrer la m.** to bring in the harvest **2** *(grande quantité)* **une m. de** an abundance *or* a wealth of

moissonnage [mwasɔnaʒ] **NM** harvesting

moissonner [3] [mwasɔne] **VT 1** *Agr* to harvest, to reap; *(champ)* to reap; *(récoltes)* to harvest, to gather (in); **m. les blés** to harvest the corn

2 *Fig (recueillir ▸ informations, documents)* to amass; **m. des renseignements** to collect *or* to gather information

3 *Fig (remporter ▸ récompense)* to carry off

4 *Littéraire (décimer)* to decimate; **la guerre a moissonné toute leur génération** the war decimated their entire generation

moissonneur, -euse [mwasɔnœr, -øz] **NM,F** harvester, reaper

• **moissonneuse NF** *(machine)* harvester

moissonneuse-batteuse [mwasɔnøzbatøz] *(pl* **moissonneuses-batteuses)** **NF** combine (harvester)

moissonneuse-lieuse [mwasɔnøzljøz] *(pl* **moissonneuses-lieuses)** **NF** reaper, reaper-binder, self-binder

moite [mwat] **ADJ** *(air)* muggy, clammy; *(chaleur)* moist; *(mains)* sticky, sweaty; *(front)* damp, sweaty; **une journée m. et oppressante** a muggy, stifling day

moiteur [mwatœr] NF *(sueur)* stickiness, sweatiness; *(humidité)* dampness, moistness; *(de l'air)* mugginess

moitié [mwatje] NF **1** *(part)* half; **une m. de** *ou* **la m. d'un poulet** half a chicken; **la m. des élèves** half (of) the pupils; **la m. de ses revenus est consacrée** *ou* **sont consacrés à sa maison** half (of) his/her income is spent on his/her house; **quelle est la m. de douze?** what's half of twelve?; **arrivé à la m. du livre** halfway through the book; **nous ferons la m. du trajet** *ou* **chemin ensemble** we'll do half the journey together; **partager qch en deux moitiés** to divide sth in half *or* into (two) halves, to halve sth **2** *(comme modificateur)* half; **m. riant, m. pleurant** half laughing, half crying; **je suis m. français, m. canadien** I'm half French, half Canadian; **m. déçu, m. soulagé** half disappointed, half relieved; **il mange m. moins que moi** he eats half as much as me; **m. moins gros/cher** 50 percent smaller/cheaper; **m. moins de monde** 50 percent fewer people; **c'est m. moins gros que l'autre** it's half the size of the other one; **ça m'a coûté m. moins cher** it cost me half the price; **il n'est pas m. aussi méchant qu'on le dit** he's not half as nasty as people say **3** *Fam Hum (épouse)* **sa/ma (tendre) m.** his/my better half

• **à moitié** ADV half; **à m. mort/cuit/nu/endormi** half-dead/-cooked/-naked/-asleep; **il l'a à m. assommé** he half *or* almost knocked him out; **la bouteille était à m. pleine/vide** the bottle was half full/empty; **je ne suis qu'à m. surpris** I'm not completely surprised; **faire les choses à m.** to do things by halves; **le travail n'est fait qu'à m.** only half the work's been done, the work's only half done; **vendre à m. prix** to sell (at) half-price

• **de moitié** ADV by half; **réduire qch de m.** to reduce sth by half, to halve sth; **l'inflation a diminué de m.** inflation has been halved *or* cut by half

• **par la moitié** ADV through *or* down the middle

• **par moitié** ADV in two, in half

• **pour moitié** ADV partly; **il est pour m. responsable** he is equally *or* just as much to blame, half the responsibility is his; **tu es pour m. dans son échec** you're half *or* partly responsible for his failure

moitié-moitié [mwatjemwatje] ADV **1** *(à parts égales)* half-and-half; **faire m.** *(dans une affaire)* to go halves *or* fifty-fifty; *(au restaurant)* to go halves, to split the bill **2** *Fam (ni bien ni mal)* so-so; **elle est contente? – m.** is she pleased? – so-so

moitir [32] [mwatir] VT *Vieilli* to dampen, to moisten

mojette [mɔʒɛt] = **mogette**

mojito [mɔito] NM *(cocktail)* mojito

moka [mɔka] NM **1** *(gâteau)* mocha cake, coffee cream cake **2** *(café)* mocha (coffee)

mol [mɔl] *voir* **mou**

molaire[1] [mɔlɛr] NF *(dent)* molar

molaire[2] [mɔlɛr] ADJ *Chim* molar

molasse [mɔlas] NF molasse

moldave [mɔldav] ADJ Moldavian

• **Moldave** NMF Moldavian

Moldavie [mɔldavi] NF **la M.** Moldavia

Moldova [mɔldɔva] NF **la M.** Moldova

mole [mɔl] NF *Chim* mole

môle [mol] NM *(jetée)* mole, (stone) jetty *or* breakwater

NF **1** *Ich* sunfish **2** *Méd* mole

moléculaire [mɔlekylɛr] ADJ molecular

molécule [mɔlekyl] NF molecule

molécule-gramme [mɔlekylgram] *(pl* **molécules-grammes***)* NF gram-molecule

molène [mɔlɛn] NF *Bot* mullein

moleskine [mɔlɛskin] NF **1** *Tex* moleskin **2** *(imitation cuir)* imitation leather

molester [3] [mɔlɛste] VT to maul, to manhandle, to molest; **la police a molesté les manifestants** the demonstrators were manhandled by the police; **plusieurs journalistes se sont fait m. par les forces de l'ordre** several journalists were manhandled by the police

> Il faut noter que le verbe anglais **to molest** est un faux ami. Il signifie le plus souvent **faire subir des sévices sexuels.**

moletage [mɔltaʒ] NM milling, knurling

moleter [27] [mɔlte] VT to mill, to knurl

molette [mɔlɛt] NF **1** *(pièce cylindrée)* toothed wheel; **m. de réglage** control knob

2 *(dans un briquet)* wheel

3 *(de verrier)* cutting wheel

4 *Menuis (roulette)* beading roller; *(fraise)* (beading) reamer

5 *(d'un éperon)* rowel

6 *(de jumelles)* focus wheel

Molière [mɔljɛr] NPR Molière; **les Molières** = French theatre awards

moliéresque [mɔljerɛsk] ADJ Molieresque; **une satire sociale toute m.** a social satire worthy of *or* in the style of Molière

mollachu, -e [mɔlaʃy] *Suisse* ADJ slow▫, sluggish▫

NMF lazy so-and-so

mollah [mɔla] NM mullah, mollah

mollard [mɔlar] NM *très Fam* gob, *Br* gob of spit

mollarder [3] [mɔlarde] VI *très Fam* to spit▫, *Br* to gob

mollasse [mɔlas] ADJ **1** *Fam (apathique)* drippy, wimpish, *Br* wet; *(moralement)* spineless; **qu'il est m.!** he's such a drip! **2** *(flasque)* flabby, flaccid, limp; **une poignée de main m.** a limp handshake

NMF *Fam* wimp, drip

mollasson, -onne [mɔlasɔ̃, -ɔn] *Fam* ADJ slow▫, sluggish▫

NM,F lazy so-and-so

molle [mɔl] *voir* **mou**

mollement [mɔlmɑ̃] ADV **1** *(sans énergie)* listlessly, limply; **il m'a serré m. la main** he gave me a limp handshake; **m. allongé sur un divan** lying languidly *or* limply on a sofa **2** *(sans conviction)* feebly, weakly; **elle protesta m.** she protested feebly, she made a feeble protest

mollesse [mɔlɛs] NF **1** *(d'une substance, d'un objet)* softness; *(des chairs)* flabbiness; *(d'une poignée de main)* limpness **2** *(d'un relief)* soft shape; *Péj* **la m. d'un dessin** the lifelessness of a drawing **3** *(apathie)* feebleness, weakness; **c'est la m. de l'opposition qui est en cause** the opposition's spinelessness is to blame; **devant la m. de ces protestations** faced with such feeble protests

mollet[1] [mɔlɛ] NM *Anat* calf; *Fam* **avoir des mollets de coq** to have legs like matchsticks, to have spindly legs

mollet[2], **-ette** [mɔlɛ, -ɛt] ADJ *Littéraire (moelleux)* soft; *(œuf)* soft-boiled; **pain m.** (soft) bread roll

molletière [mɔltjɛr] ADJ F *voir* **bande**

NF puttee

molleton [mɔltɔ̃] NM **1** *(tissu ► en coton)* flannelette; *(► en laine)* flannel **2** *(sous-nappe)* table-felt

molletonné, -e [mɔltɔne] ADJ *(garni)* covered with fleece; *(doublé)* fleece-lined

molletonner [3] [mɔltɔne] VT *(garnir)* to cover with fleece; *(doubler)* to line with fleece

mollette [mɔlɛt] *voir* **mollet**[2]

mollir [32] [mɔlir] VI **1** *(chanceler)* **j'ai senti mes jambes m.** I felt my legs give way (under me); **le sol mollissait sous mes pieds** the ground was giving way beneath my feet **2** *(vent)* to drop, *Sout* to abate **3** *(courage, volonté)* to flag; *(forces)* to diminish

VT *Naut (cordage)* to slacken; *(barre)* to ease

mollo [mɔlo] ADV *Fam* easy; **y aller m.** to take it easy; **vas-y m. sur cette route!** take it easy on that road!; **m. avec le chocolat!** go easy on the chocolate!

mollusque [mɔlysk] NM **1** *Zool* mollusc **2** *Fam (personne)* drip, wimp

molosse [mɔlɔs] NM *(chien)* watchdog

molybdène [mɔlibdɛn] NM *Chim* molybdenum

Mombasa [mɔ̃basa] NM Mombasa

môme [mom] *Fam* NMF *(enfant)* kid; **sale m.!** you little brat!

NF *Vieilli (fille)* chick, *Br* bird; *(compagne)* girlfriend▫, *Br* bird

ADJ **quand j'étais (tout) m.** when I was (just) a kid

moment [mɔmɑ̃] NM **1** *(laps de temps)* moment, while; **restez avec moi un m.** stay with me a moment *or* a while; **laisse-moi un m. pour réfléchir** give me a moment *or* minute to think it over; **il y a un (bon) m. que j'attends** I've been waiting for (quite) a while; **pendant un bon m.** for quite some time; **j'en ai pour un (petit) m.** I'll be a (little) while

2 *(instant)* moment, minute; **c'est l'affaire d'un m.** it'll only take a minute *or* moment; **attends-moi, je n'en ai que pour un m.** wait for me, I'll be finished in a minute *or* moment; **je n'ai pas un m. à moi** I don't have a minute *or* moment to myself; **dans un m. de colère** in a moment of anger; **il eut un m. d'hésitation** he hesitated for a moment; **(attends) un m.!** just (wait) a moment!

3 *(période)* moment, time; **attendre le dernier m.** to wait till the last minute; **nous avons passé** *ou* **eu de bons moments** we had some good times; **elle a ses bons et ses mauvais moments** she has her off days; **c'est un mauvais m. à passer** it's just a difficult spell *or Br* a bad patch; **les grands moments de l'histoire** the great moments of history; **les derniers moments de sa vie** the last moments of his/her life; **il l'a assistée jusqu'aux derniers moments** he was by her side until the end; **à mes moments perdus** in my spare time; **à quel m. de l'année?** at what time of the year?; **à quel m. de l'histoire/sa vie?** at what stage of *or* point in the story/his/her life?; **dans ces moments-là, on ne réfléchit pas** at times like that you don't think

4 *(occasion)* moment, opportunity; **à quel m.?** when?; **choisis un autre m. pour lui parler** choose another time to speak to him/her; **c'est le m. d'intervenir** now's the time to speak up; *Ironique* **c'est bien le m.!** what a time to pick!; **c'est le m. ou jamais** it's now or never; **c'est le m. ou jamais de lui demander** ask him/her, it's now or never; **c'est le m. ou jamais de lui dire ce que tu penses** now's the time (if ever there was one) to tell him/her what you think; **à quel m. voulez-vous venir?** (at) what time would you like to come?; **le m. venu** when the time comes; **le m. venu, il ne sut plus quoi dire** when the time came, he was at a loss for words; **arriver au bon m.** to come at the right time; *Ironique* **il arrive toujours au bon m., celui-là!** he really picks his moments!; **au mauvais m.** at the wrong time; **le m. crucial du film/match** the crucial point in the film/match

5 *Phys* momentum; **m. cinétique** kinetic moment; **m. magnétique** magnetic moment

• **à aucun moment** ADV at no time; **à aucun m. il ne s'est plaint** at no time *or* point did he complain

• **à ce moment-là** ADV **1** *(dans le temps)* at that time, then **2** *Fig (dans ce cas)* in that case, if that's so; **à ce m.-là, tu aurais dû me le dire!** in that case *or* if that was the case, you should have told me!

• **à tout moment** ADV **1** *(n'importe quand)* (at) any time *or* moment; **il peut téléphoner à tout m.** I/we/*etc* can expect a call from him any time now **2** *(sans cesse)* constantly, all the time; **elle s'interrompait à tout m.** she was constantly stopping, she kept stopping

• **au moment de** PRÉP **au m. de son départ** when he/she was leaving; **au m. de partir** just as I/he/*etc* was leaving *or* was about to leave; **au m. de mon divorce** when I was getting divorced, at the time of my divorce; **au m. de sa naissance/de l'accident** at the time of his/her birth/of the accident; **il me l'a dit au m. de mourir** he told me as he died

• **au moment où** CONJ as, when; **au m. où il allait démissionner** as he was about to resign; **juste au m. où le téléphone a sonné** just when *or* as the phone rang

• **à un moment donné** ADV at a certain point; **à un m. donné, il a refusé** at one point he refused

• **dès le moment où** CONJ **1** *(dans le temps)* from the time *or* moment that, as soon as **2** *(dans un raisonnement)* as soon as, once; **dès le m. où on accepte l'idée d'immortalité** once you accept the idea of immortality

• **du moment** ADJ **l'homme du m.** the man of the moment; **le succès/l'idole du m.** the current hit/idol; **un des sujets du m.** one of the issues of the day

• **du moment que** CONJ *(puisque)* since; **du m.**

qu'il a signé, tu es garanti seeing that *or* since he's signed, you're safe; *Fam* du m. que je te le dis! you can take my word for it!

• **d'un moment à l'autre** ADV *(très prochainement)* any moment *or* minute *or* time now; **il peut téléphoner d'un m. à l'autre** he may phone any minute now

• **en ce moment** ADV at the moment, just now

• **en un moment** ADV in a moment

• **par moments** ADV at times, every now and then, every so often

• **pour le moment** ADV for the moment, for the time being

• **sur le moment** ADV at the time; **sur le m., ça n'a pas fait mal** it didn't hurt at the time

momentané, -e [mɔmɑ̃tane] ADJ momentary, brief; **il y aura des pannes d'électricité momentanées** there will be temporary *or* brief power cuts; **sa passion n'a été que momentanée** his/her passion was only short-lived

momentanément [mɔmɑ̃tanemɑ̃] ADV **1** *(en ce moment)* for the time being, for the moment; **il est m. absent** he's temporarily absent, he's absent for the moment **2** *(provisoirement)* momentarily, for a short while; **les émissions sont m. interrompues** we will be temporarily off the air

momerie [mɔmri] NF *Littéraire & Vieilli* mummery; *(pratique insincère)* insincerity

mômerie [momri] NF *(gén pl) Fam* childishness[❑], childish behaviour[❑]

momie [mɔmi] NF mummy

momification [mɔmifikasjɔ̃] NF mummification

momifier [9] [mɔmifje] VT to mummify

VPR **se momifier** *(personne)* to become mummified; *Fig (esprit)* to become fossilized

mon, ma, mes [mɔ̃, ma, me]

> **ma** becomes **mon** before a word beginning with a vowel or h mute.

ADJ POSSESSIF **1** *(indiquant la possession)* my; **m. ami/amie** my friend; **m. meilleur ami/ma meilleure amie** my best friend; **mes frères et sœurs** my brothers and sisters; **un de mes amis** a friend of mine, one of my friends; **un professeur de mes amis** a teacher friend of mine; **j'ai mis m. chapeau et mes gants** I put on my hat and (my) gloves; *Fam* **j'aurai ma chambre à moi** I'll have my own room[❑]

2 *(dans des appellatifs)* **m. cher Pierre** my dear Pierre; **m. Père** Father; **m. capitaine** Captain; **(oh) m. Dieu!** (oh) my God!; **viens, m. enfant** come here, child; *Fam* **alors là, ma grande, c'est ton problème!** well that, my dear, is your problem!; *Fam* **mais m. pauvre vieux, vous n'y arriverez jamais!** you'll never manage it, old chap!

3 *(emploi expressif)* **j'ai m. vendredi** I've got Friday off; *Fam* **je gagne mes 1000 euros par mois** I earn 1,000 euros a month[❑]; *Fam* **m. imbécile de frère** my idiot of a brother; *Fam* **m. artiste de mari** my husband, the artist[❑]; *Fam* **alors, tu veux le rencontrer, m. artiste?** do you want to meet this artist of mine, then?; *Fam* **mais ma Jacqueline, elle n'était pas du tout d'accord!** but our Jacqueline wasn't going along with that!; *Fam* **et voilà m. Simon qui se met à rouspéter** then old Simon starts grumbling; **m. bonhomme n'était pas du tout content!** I don't mind telling you (that) the fellow wasn't at all pleased!; *très Fam* **ah ben, m. salaud** *ou* **cochon!** lucky bastard!

monacal, -e, -aux, -ales [mɔnakal, -o] ADJ monastic, *Sout* monachal

monachisme [mɔnaʃism] NM monasticism, *Sout* monachism

Monaco [mɔnako] NM *Géog* **(la principauté de) M.** (the principality of) Monaco

monade [mɔnad] NF monad

monarchie [mɔnarʃi] NF monarchy; **la m. absolue/constitutionnelle/parlementaire** absolute/constitutional/parliamentary monarchy; **la m. de droit divin** monarchy by divine right; **la m. de Juillet** the July Monarchy

monarchique [mɔnarʃik] ADJ monarchic, monarchical, monarchial

monarchisme [mɔnarʃism] NM monarchism

monarchiste [mɔnarʃist] ADJ monarchist, monarchistic

NMF monarchist

monarque [mɔnark] NM monarch

monastère [mɔnastɛr] NM *(de moines)* monastery; *(de religieuses)* convent

monastique [mɔnastik] ADJ monastic

monaural, -e, -aux, -ales [mɔnɔral, -o] ADJ monaural

monceau, -x [mɔ̃so] NM *(amas)* heap, pile

mondain, -e [mɔ̃dɛ̃, -ɛn] ADJ **1** *(de la haute société)* society *(avant n)*; **il mène une vie très mondaine** he moves in society circles; **carnet m., rubrique mondaine** society *or* gossip column; **soirée mondaine** society *or* high-society evening

2 *(qui aime les mondanités)* **elle est très mondaine** she likes moving in fashionable circles *or* society, she's a great socialite

3 *Rel* worldly; *Phil* mundane

4 la brigade mondaine ≃ the vice squad

NM,F socialite, society person

• **la Mondaine** NF *Fam* ≃ the vice squad[❑]

> Il faut noter que l'adjectif anglais **mundane** est un faux ami. Il signifie **terre-à-terre.**

mondanité [mɔ̃danite] NF **1** *(style)* society life **2** *Rel* worldliness

• **mondanités** NFPL **1** *(réunions)* fashionable gatherings; *(politesses)* social chitchat *(UNCOUNT)*, polite conversation *(UNCOUNT)*; **il aime les mondanités** he likes society life **2** *Presse* society news *(UNCOUNT)*, gossip column

monde [mɔ̃d] NM **1** *(univers)* world; **parcourir** *ou* **courir le m. (à la recherche de)** to travel the world (in search of); **le m. entier** the whole world; **dans le m. entier** all over the world; **il est connu dans le m. entier** he's known worldwide *or* the world over; **venir au m.** to come into the world; **mettre un enfant au m.** to bring a child into the world; **elle n'était pas de ce m.** she was not of this world; **il n'est plus de ce m.** he's no longer with us, he's gone to the next world; **en ce bas m.** here on earth, here below; **l'autre m.** the next world; **elle est dans son m.** she's in her own little world; **elle s'est créé un petit m. à elle** she's created her own little world for herself; **le m. est petit!** it's a small world!; **depuis que le m. est m.** since the beginning of time, since time began; **c'est le m. renversé** *ou* **à l'envers!** what's the world coming to?

2 *(humanité)* world; **le m. entier attend cet événement** the whole world is awaiting this event; **il faut de tout pour faire un m.** it takes all sorts (to make a world); **ainsi va le m.** it's the way of the world; **refaire le m.** to put the world to rights

3 *(pour intensifier)* **il y a un m. entre l'agneau importé et l'agneau de notre région** there's a world of difference between imported lamb and our local lamb; **le plus célèbre au** *ou* **du m.** the most famous in the world; **les meilleurs amis du m.** the best friends in the world; **c'est la femme la plus charmante du m.** she's the most charming woman you could wish to meet; **le plus simplement/gentiment du m.** in the simplest/kindest possible way; **c'est ce que j'aime/je veux le plus au m.** it's what I love/want most in the world; **je vous dérange? – pas le moins du m.!** am I interrupting? – not in the least!; **je ne m'ennuie pas le moins du m.** I'm not in the least bit bored; **ils s'entendent le mieux du m.** they get on famously; **tout s'est déroulé le mieux du m.** everything went off very smoothly; **rien au m. ne pourrait me faire partir** nothing in the world would make me leave; **pour rien au m.** not for anything, not for the world; **nul** *ou* **personne au m.** nobody in the world; **on m'a dit tout le bien du m. de ce nouveau shampooing** I've been told the most wonderful things about this new shampoo

4 *(communauté)* world; **le m. des affaires** the business world; **le m. de la finance** the world of finance, the financial world; **le m. du spectacle** (the world of) show business; **le m. chrétien/musulman** the Christian/Muslim world; **le m. libre** the Free World; **le m. animal/végétal** the animal/plant world

5 *(gens)* people; **il y a un m. fou, c'est noir de m.** the place is swarming *or* alive with people; **il y a trop de m.** it's too crowded, there are too many people; *Fam* **il y a plein de m. à la foire** there are loads of people at the fair; **il n'y avait pas grand m. au spectacle** there weren't many people at the show; **je viens de m'installer, je ne connais pas encore beaucoup de m.** I've just settled in, I don't know (very) many people yet; **tu attends du m.?** are you expecting people *or* company?; **il ne voit plus beaucoup de m.** he doesn't socialize very much any more; *Fam* **j'ai du m. à dîner** I've got people coming for dinner; **ne t'en fais pas, je connais mon m.!** don't worry, I know who I'm dealing with!; **grand-mère aime bien avoir tout son petit m. autour d'elle** grandmother likes to have all her family *or Hum* brood around her; *Can* **le grand m.** the grown-ups, the adults; *Fam Hum* **il y a du m. au balcon!** she's well-endowed!; *Fam* **tu te moques** *ou* **te fiches du m.!** you've got a nerve *or* a cheek!; *Fam* **ils se fichent vraiment du m.!** they really must think we're stupid![❑]

6 *(société)* world; *(groupe social)* circle, set; **se retirer du m.** to withdraw from society; **les plaisirs du m.** worldly pleasures; *Rel* **le m.** the world; **elle n'appartient pas à notre m.** she's not one of us, she doesn't belong to our circle; **ils ne sont pas du même m.** they don't move in the same circles; **le m., le beau m., le grand m.** *(classes élevées)* high society; **aller dans le m.** to mix in society; **ses premiers pas dans le m.** his/her introduction to (high) society; **fréquenter le beau** *ou* **le grand m.** to mix with high society *or* in society; **femme du m.** socialite; **homme du m.** man-about-town; **gens du m.** socialites, society people; *Ironique* **embarquez-moi tout ce joli m. dans le panier à salade** throw this bunch *or* crew into the back of the van

7 *(domaine)* world, realm; **le m. de l'imaginaire** the realm of imagination; **le m. du rêve** the world *or* realm of dreams; *Littéraire* **le m. du silence** the silent world (under the sea)

8 *Arch (domestiques)* servants, men, hands

9 *Presse* **Le M.** = French daily broadsheet newspaper, whose political leanings are left-of-centre

10 *Fam (locutions)* **pourquoi ne ranges-tu jamais tes affaires, c'est un m. tout de même!** why in the world *or* why oh why don't you ever put your things away?; **se faire (tout) un m. de qch** to get worked up about sth; **il se fait tout un m. de rencontrer son beau père** he's making a big thing about meeting his father-in-law; **ne te fais pas un m. d'un rien** don't make a mountain out of a molehill

• **tout le monde** PRON everybody, everyone; **tout le m. est là?** is everybody here?; **tout le m. n'est pas arrivé** not everybody's here (yet)

mondial, -e, -aux, -ales [mɔ̃djal, -o] ADJ worldwide, global, world *(avant n)*; **production mondiale de blé** world wheat production; **une crise à l'échelle mondiale** a worldwide crisis, a crisis on a world scale; **une vedette de renommée mondiale** a world-famous star

NM *Ftbl* **le M.** the World Cup

mondialement [mɔ̃djalmɑ̃] ADV throughout *or* all over the world; **m. renommé** famous all over the world, world-famous

mondialisation [mɔ̃djalizasjɔ̃] NF globalization; **la m. libérale** liberal globalization

mondialiser [3] [mɔ̃djalize] VT to globalize

VPR **se mondialiser** to become globalized; **la crise s'est rapidement mondialisée** the crisis has rapidly taken on an international dimension

mondovision [mɔ̃dɔvizjɔ̃] NF worldwide satellite broadcasting; **en m.** broadcast all over the world by satellite

monégasque [mɔnegask] ADJ Monegasque, Monacan

• **Monégasque** NMF Monegasque, Monacan

monème [mɔnɛm] NM *Ling* moneme

MONEP [mɔnɛp] NM *Bourse (abrév* **marché des options négociables à Paris**) MONEP *(Paris traded options exchange), Br* ≃ LIFFE, *Am* ≃ CBOE

monétaire [mɔnetɛr] ADJ monetary; **marché/masse m.** money market/supply; **politique/système/unité m.** monetary policy/system/unit

monétarisme [mɔnetarism] NM monetarism

monétariste [mɔnetarist] ADJ monetarist

NMF monetarist

Monétique® [mɔnetik] NF electronic banking, e-banking

monétisation [mɔnetizasjɔ̃] NF monetization

monétiser [3] [mɔnetize] VT to monetize

mongol, -e [mɔ̃gɔl] ADJ **1** *(de Mongolie)* Mongol, Mongolian **2** *très Fam Péj* moronic
NM *(langue)* Mongolian
• **Mongol, -e** NM,F **1** *(de Mongolie)* Mongol, Mongolian **2** *très Fam Péj* moron

Mongolie [mɔ̃gɔli] NF **la M.** Mongolia; *Anciennement* **la M.-Extérieure** Outer Mongolia; **la M.-Intérieure** Inner Mongolia

mongolien, -enne [mɔ̃gɔljɛ̃, -ɛn] *Méd* ADJ **être m.** to have Down's syndrome
NM,F = person with Down's syndrome

mongolique [mɔ̃gɔlik] ADJ Mongolic, Mongolian

mongolisme [mɔ̃gɔlism] NM Down's syndrome

mongoloïde [mɔ̃gɔlɔid] ADJ **1** *(de type mongol)* Mongoloid **2** *Méd (individu)* affected by Down's syndrome; **être m.** to have Down's syndrome

moniteur, -trice [mɔnitœr, -tris] NM,F *Sport* instructor, *f* instructress; *(de colonie de vacances)* (group) supervisor *or* leader, *Am* (camp) counselor; **m. d'auto-école** driving instructor; **m. de ski** ski instructor
NM **1** *Ordinat (écran)* display unit; *(dispositif matériel ou logiciel)* monitor; **m. couleur** RGB *or* colour monitor; **m. à cristaux liquides** liquid crystal monitor; **m. à écran plat** flat screen monitor; **m. SVGA** SVGA monitor; **m. vidéo** video monitor **2** *Méd* monitor **3** *Belg* **M. (belge)** = Belgian government publication, *Br* ≃ Hansard, *Am* ≃ Federal Register

monitorage [mɔnitɔraʒ] = **monitoring**

monitorat [mɔnitɔra] NM *(enseignement)* instruction; *(de colonie de vacances)* group leading, *Am* camp counseling; *(fonction)* instructorship; *(période de formation)* training to be an instructor

monitoring [mɔnitɔriŋ] NM monitoring; **elle est sous m.** she's been placed on a monitor

monitrice [mɔnitris] *voir* **moniteur**

monnaie [mɔnɛ] *voir* **monnayer**
NF **1** *Écon & Fin (d'un pays)* currency; **frapper la m., battre m.** to coin *or* mint money; **les monnaies étrangères** foreign currencies; **le yen est la m. du Japon** the yen is Japan's (unit of) currency *or* monetary unit; *UE* **m. commune** common currency; **m. de compte** account *or* near money; **m. de compte (convertible)** (convertible) money of account; **m. courante** legal currency; *Fig* **c'est m. courante** it's common practice, it's a common *or* an everyday occurrence; *Fig* **m. d'échange** bargaining counter; **m. électronique** electronic money, e-money, e-cash; **m. étrangère** foreign currency; **m. faible** soft currency; **m. fiduciaire** fiduciary money *or* issue, paper money, *Am* fiat money; **m. flottante** floating currency; **m. forte** hard currency; **m. légale** legal tender; **m. métallique** metal money; **m. non convertible** blocked currency; **m. de papier** paper money; **m. de réserve** reserve currency; **m. scripturale** bank money; *Fam* **m. de singe** Monopoly money; *Fam* **payer qn en m. de singe** to fob sb off; **m. unique** single currency; **m. verte** green currency; **fausse m.** counterfeit *or* false money **2** *(appoint)* change; **faire de la m.** to get (some) change; **faire de la m. à qn** to give sb some change; **faire la m. de 50 euros** to get change for 50 euros, to change a 50-euro note; **je vais te faire** *ou* **te donner la m. de 20 euros** I'll change 20 euros for you, I'll give you change for 20 euros; **vous auriez de la m. pour le parcmètre?** do you have some change for the parking meter?; **vous auriez la m. de 20 euros?** could you give me change for a 20-euro note?, could you change a 20-euro note for me?; **rendre la m. à qn** to give sb change; **il m'a rendu la m. sur 10 euros** he gave me the change out of *or* from 10 euros; **m. d'appoint** (correct) change; **menue/petite m.** small/loose change; *Fig* **je lui rendrai la m. de sa pièce!** I'll give him/her a taste of his/her own medicine! **3** *(argent)* cash, *Br* dosh, *Am* bucks

> Il faut noter que le nom anglais **money** est un faux ami. Il signifie **argent**.

monnaie-du-pape [mɔnedypap] *(pl* **monnaies-du-pape)** NF *Bot* honesty

monnayable [mɔnɛjabl] ADJ convertible into money; **ton expérience est m.** you could make money out of your experience

monnayage [mɔnɛjaʒ] NM minting, coining

monnayer [11] [mɔneje] VT **1** *(convertir en monnaie)* to mint **2** *(vendre)* to sell, to make money out of; **m. son expérience/savoir-faire** to cash in on one's experience/know-how; **il refusa de m. son silence** he refused to sell his silence **3** *(échanger)* to exchange; **il a monnayé ses services contre une lettre d'introduction** he asked for a letter of introduction in exchange for his services
VPR **se monnayer tu devrais savoir que le talent se monnaie** you ought to know there's money to be made out of talent; **ici tout se monnaie** money can buy (you) anything here, everything here has its price

monnayeur [mɔnɛjœr] NM **1** *(pour faire la monnaie)* change machine; *(pour payer)* coin box **2** *(ouvrier)* coiner, minter

mono [mɔno] *Fam* ADJ INV *(disque)* mono
NF INV mono; **en m.** in mono
NMF **1** *Sport* instructor[□], *f* instructress[□] **2** *(de colonie de vacances)* (group) supervisor[□] *or* leader[□], *Am* (camp) counselor[□]
NM monoski[□]

monoacide [mɔnɔasid] NM *Chim* monoacid

monobloc [mɔnɔblɔk] ADJ *(fusil)* cast en bloc, solid; *(cylindre, moteur, roue)* monobloc

monocaméral, -e, -aux, -ales [mɔnɔkameral, -o] ADJ *Pol* unicameral

monochrome [mɔnɔkrom] ADJ monochrome

monochromie [mɔnɔkrɔmi] NF monochromaticity

monocle [mɔnɔkl] NM (single) eyeglass, monocle

monocoque [mɔnɔkɔk] ADJ *Aviat, Naut & Aut* monocoque; **avion m.** monocoque; **bateau m.** monohull
NM *Naut* monohull

monocorde [mɔnɔkɔrd] ADJ **1** *Mus (instrument)* single-stringed **2** *(son, ton, voix)* monotonous, droning; **parler d'un ton m.** to speak in a monotone
NM monochord

monocorps [mɔnɔkɔr] *Aut* ADJ monobox
NM monobox

monocotylédone [mɔnɔkɔtiledɔn] *Bot* NF monocotyledon
ADJ monocotyledonous
• **monocotylédones** NFPL Monocotyledoneae

monoculaire [mɔnɔkylɛr] ADJ monocular; **cécité m.** blindness in one eye

monoculture [mɔnɔkyltyr] NF monoculture

monocycle [mɔnosikl] NM unicycle

monocylindre [mɔnosilɛ̃dr] ADJ single-cylinder *(avant n)*
NM single-cylinder engine

monocylindrique [mɔnɔsilɛ̃drik] ADJ single-cylinder *(avant n)*

monoéthylèneglycol [mɔnoetilɛnglikɔl] NM *Chim* monoethylene glycol

monogame [mɔnɔgam] ADJ monogamous
NMF monogamist

monogamie [mɔnɔgami] NF monogamy

monogamique [mɔnɔgamik] ADJ monogamous

monogramme [mɔnɔgram] NM monogram; **marquer qch d'un m.** to monogram sth

monographie [mɔnɔgrafi] NF monograph

monohydrate [mɔnɔidrat] NM *Chim* monohydrate

monoï [mɔnɔj] NM INV Monoi, = scented coconut oil

mono-insaturé, -e [mɔnoɛ̃satyre] *(mpl* **mono-insaturés,** *fpl* **mono-insaturées)** ADJ *(lipide)* monounsaturated

monokini [mɔnɔkini] NM monokini, topless swimsuit; **faire du m.** to go topless; **m. interdit** *(sur panneau)* no topless bathing

monolingue [mɔnɔlɛ̃g] ADJ monolingual
NMF monoglot

monolinguisme [mɔnɔlɛ̃gɥism] NM monolingualism

monolithe [mɔnɔlit] ADJ *Géol* monolithic
NM *Géol & Fig* monolith

monolithique [mɔnɔlitik] ADJ *Géol & Fig* monolithic

monologue [mɔnɔlɔg] NM **1** *(discours)* monologue; *Théât* monologue, soliloquy **2** *Littérature* **m. intérieur** stream of consciousness, interior monologue

monologuer [3] [mɔnɔlɔge] VI *(monopoliser la parole)* to carry on a monologue; *Théât* to soliloquize; **il monologue des heures durant** *(en public)* he can go on (talking) for hours; *(tout seul)* he talks to himself for hours

monomaniaque [mɔnɔmanjak] *Psy* ADJ monomaniac *(avant n)*
NMF monomaniac

monomanie [mɔnɔmani] NF *Psy* monomania

monôme [mɔnom] NM *Math* monomial

monométallisme [mɔnɔmetalism] NM *Fin* monometallism

monomoteur [mɔnɔmɔtœr] ADJ M single-engine *(avant n)*, single-engined
NM single-engine *or* single-engined aircraft

mononucléose [mɔnɔnykleoz] NF *Méd* mononucleosis; **m. infectieuse** *Br* glandular fever, *Spéc* mononucleosis, *Am* mononucleosis

monoparental, -e, -aux, -ales [mɔnɔparɑ̃tal, -o] ADJ single-parent *(avant n)*

monoparentalité [mɔnoparɑ̃talite] NF single parenthood

monophasé, -e [mɔnɔfaze] ADJ single-phase, monophase
NM single-phase (current)

monophonique [mɔnɔfɔnik] ADJ *Mus* monophonic; *(système électroacoustique)* monophonic, monaural

monoplace [mɔnɔplas] ADJ one-seater *(avant n)*, single-seater *(avant n)*
NM one-seater *or* single-seater (vehicle)
NF single-seater racing car

monoplan [mɔnɔplɑ̃] NM monoplane

monopole [mɔnɔpɔl] NM **1** *Écon* monopoly; **avoir le m. de qch** to have a monopoly on sth; **exercer un m. sur un secteur** to monopolize a sector; **m. d'achat** buyer's monopoly; **m. de droit** legal monopoly; **m. d'embauche** closed shop; **m. d'émission** issuing monopoly; **m. d'État** state monopoly; **m. d'exploitation** operating monopoly; **m. de fabrication** manufacturing monopoly; **m. de fait** monopoly; **m. des prix** price monopoly; **m. de vente** sales monopoly **2** *Fig* monopoly; **vous pensez avoir le m. de la vérité?** do you think you have a monopoly on the truth?

monopoleur, -euse [mɔnɔpɔlœr, -øz] ADJ monopolist
NM,F monopolist

monopolisateur, -trice [mɔnɔpɔlizatœr, -tris] NM,F monopolizer

monopolisation [mɔnɔpɔlizasjɔ̃] NF monopolization

monopolisatrice [mɔnɔpɔlizatris] *voir* **monopolisateur**

monopoliser [3] [mɔnɔpɔlize] VT *Écon* to monopolize, to have a monopoly on; *Fig* to monopolize; **m. l'antenne** *(sujet: parti politique, groupe de pression etc)* to rule *or* to monopolize the airwaves; **il a monopolisé l'antenne pendant la majeure partie du débat** he dominated the discussion for most of the programme; **m. la parole** not to let anyone else speak, to monopolize the conversation; **m. le téléphone/la salle de bains** to hog the phone/the bathroom; **ne monopolisez pas notre jeune amie** don't keep our young friend to yourself

monoposte [mɔnopɔst] NM *Ordinat* standalone

monorail [mɔnoraj] ADJ monorail *(avant n)*
NM monorail

monoski [mɔnɔski] NM *(planche)* monoski; *(activité)* monoskiing; **faire du m.** to monoski; **m. nautique** *(planche)* wakeboard; *(activité)* wakeboarding

monospace [mɔnɔspas] NM people carrier, people mover

monosyllabe [mɔnɔsilab] *Ling* ADJ monosyllabic

NM monosyllable

monosyllabique [mɔnɔsilabik] ADJ *Ling* monosyllabic

mono-tâche [mɔnɔtaʃ] ADJ INV *Ordinat* single-tasking *(avant n)*

monothéisme [mɔnɔteism] NM monotheism

monothéiste [mɔnɔteist] ADJ monotheistic, monotheist *(avant n)*

NMF monotheist

monotone [mɔnɔtɔn] ADJ **1** *(voix, bruit)* monotonous **2** *(discours, style)* monotonous, dull **3** *(vie)* monotonous, dreary, humdrum; *(paysage)* monotonous, dreary

monotonie [mɔnɔtɔni] NF monotony, dullness, dreariness; **rompre la m.** to break the monotony

Monotype® [mɔnɔtip] NF *Typ* Monotype®

monovalent, -e [mɔnɔvalɑ̃, -ɑ̃t] ADJ *Chim* monovalent

monoxyde [mɔnɔksid] NM *Chim* monoxide; **m. de carbone** carbon monoxide

Monseigneur [mɔ̃sɛɲœr] *(pl* **Messeigneurs** [mesɛɲœr]) NM **1** *(terme d'adresse ▸ archevêque, duc)* Your Grace; *(▸ évêque)* My Lord (Bishop); *(▸ cardinal)* Your Eminence; *(▸ prince)* Your Royal Highness **2** *(titre ▸ archevêque, duc)* His Grace; *(▸ évêque)* His Lordship; *(▸ cardinal)* His Eminence (Cardinal); *(▸ prince)* His Royal Highness; **M. l'évêque de...** the Lord Bishop of...

Monsieur [məsjø] *(pl* **Messieurs** [mesjø]) NM **1** *(dans une lettre)* **M.** Dear Sir, *Sout* Sir; **Cher M. Duval** Dear Mr Duval; **M. et cher Confrère, M. et cher Collègue** *(qui s'appelle Martin)* Dear Mr Martin; **Messieurs** Dear Sirs; **M. le Maire** Dear Sir; **M. le Vicomte** My Lord

2 *(sur une enveloppe)* **M. Duval** Mr Duval; **M. Robert Marceau** Mr Robert Marceau, *Sout* R. Marceau Esq; **Messieurs Thon et Lamiel** Messrs Thon and Lamiel; **Messieurs Marceau et Cie** Messrs Marceau and Co

3 *(terme d'adresse)* **bonjour M.!** good morning!; **bonjour M. Leroy!** good morning, Mr Leroy!; **bonjour M. le Ministre!** good morning, Sir!; **bonjour M. le Consul!** good morning, Sir *or* Your Excellency!; **bonjour M. le Marquis!** good morning, Your Lordship!; **bonjour M. le Duc!** good morning, Your Grace!; **bonjour Messieurs** good morning(, gentlemen); **bonjour Messieurs Duval!** good morning, gentlemen!; *Fam* **(bonjour) Messieurs Dames!** morning, all *or* everybody!; *Vieilli ou Hum* **M. Robert** *(à un petit garçon)* Master Robert; **M. le Président, et l'inflation?** *(au chef de l'État)* Sir *or Am* Mr President, what about inflation?; *(au directeur)* Sir *or* Mr Chairman, what about inflation?; *Br* **Messieurs les députés, vous êtes priés de vous asseoir!** will the Honourable Members please be seated!; **Mesdames, Mesdemoiselles, Messieurs!** Ladies and Gentlemen!; **Messieurs, un peu de silence, s'il vous plaît!** *(à des garçonnets)* boys, please be quiet!; *(à des jeunes gens)* gentlemen, would you please be quiet!; **et voilà, M., une laitue bien fraîche!** here you are, Sir, a nice fresh lettuce!; **M. désirerait voir les pantalons?** would you like to see the trousers, Sir?; *Sout ou Hum* **M. est servi** *(au dîner)* dinner is served(, Sir); *(pour le thé)* tea is served(, Sir); **M. a sonné?** you rang, Sir?; **le frère de M. attend en bas** *(à un roturier)* your brother is waiting downstairs, Sir; *(à un homme titré)* Your Lordship's brother is waiting downstairs; **que prendront ces messieurs?** what will you have, gentlemen?; **vous n'y pensez pas, cher** *ou* **mon bon** *ou* **mon pauvre M.!** my dear Sir, you can't be serious!; **peux-tu prêter un instant ton stylo à M.?** could you lend the gentleman your pen for a minute?; **bonjour M., je voudrais parler à quelqu'un de la comptabilité, s'il vous plaît** *(au téléphone)* hello, I'd like to speak to somebody in the accounts department, please

4 *(en se référant à une tierce personne)* **adressez-vous à M. Duval** apply to Mr Duval; **M. votre père** your father; **le docteur Duval et M.** *(pour annoncer)* Doctor Duval and Mr Duval; **M. le Président regrette de ne pas pouvoir venir** *(chef de l'État)* the President regrets he is unable to come; *(directeur)* the Chairman *or* Mr X regrets he is unable to come; **je voudrais parler à m. le Directeur** *(d'un magasin, d'un service)* I would like to speak to the manager; *(d'une école)* I would like to speak to the *Br* headmaster *or Am* principal; **M. le Marquis est arrivé** His Lordship has arrived; **M. le Duc est arrivé** His Grace has arrived; **M. se plaint que...** *(dit par vendeur)* the gentleman *or* this gentleman is complaining that...; **c'est le chapeau de M.** it's the gentleman's hat; **M. est sorti** His Lordship is not at home

5 *Scol* **M., j'ai fini mon addition!** (please) Sir, I've finished my sum!

6 *Fam (en appellatif)* **alors, M. le frimeur, tu es satisfait?** so, are you pleased with yourself, Mr Big Shot?; **et en plus, M. exige des excuses!** His Lordship wants an apology as well, does he?

7 *Hist* Monsieur *(title given to the King of France's younger brother)*

8 *(locutions)* **il a été nommé M. sécurité routière** he was made road safety czar; **M. Tout-le-Monde** the man in the street, *Hum Br* Joe Public, *Am* Joe Blow; **m. je-sais-tout** Mr Know-all, Mr Know-it-all; **il va encore nous jouer son m. je-sais-tout** here he goes again, the know-all *or* know-it-all

monsieur [məsjø] *(pl* **messieurs** [mesjø]) NM man, gentleman; **un m. vous a demandé** a man *or* a gentleman's been asking for you; **le jeune m. prendra-t-il une orangeade?** will the young gentleman have an orange juice?; *Péj* **il se prend pour un m.** he thinks he's a gentleman; **c'est un vilain m.** he's a wicked man

monstre [mɔ̃str] NM **1** *Biol, Myth & Zool* monster; **le m. du Loch Ness** the Loch Ness Monster; **les monstres marins** the monsters of the deep; *Fig* **m. sacré** superstar; **James Dean était un m. sacré du cinéma hollywoodien** James Dean was a Hollywood screen idol

2 *(chose énorme)* monster

3 *(personne laide)* monster, monstrously ugly *or* hideous person; *(brute)* monster, brute; **un m. d'ingratitude/d'égoïsme** an ungrateful/a selfish brute

4 *Fam (enfant insupportable)* monster, little terror, *Br* perisher; **sortez d'ici, petits monstres!** out of here, you little monsters!

ADJ *Fam (erreur, difficulté, déficit)* monstrous, enormous, colossal; *(rassemblement)* monstrous, mammoth; *(répercussions, succès, effet)* tremendous, enormous; *(soldes)* gigantic, huge, colossal; **il y a une queue m. chez le boucher** there's a huge *or* massive queue at the butcher's; **j'ai un boulot m.!** I've got loads *or* tons *or* piles of work to do!; **il a un culot m.!** he's got a damned nerve *or Br* a bloody cheek!

monstrueuse [mɔ̃stryøz] *voir* **monstrueux**

monstrueusement [mɔ̃stryøzmɑ̃] ADV *(laid)* monstrously, hideously; *(intelligent)* prodigiously, stupendously

monstrueux, -euse [mɔ̃stryø, -øz] ADJ **1** *(difforme)* monstrous, deformed; **un être m., une créature monstrueuse** a freak

2 *(laid)* monstrous, hideous, ghastly

3 *(abject, cruel)* monstrous, wicked, vile; **elle est d'un égoïsme m.** she is a selfish monster; **un crime m.** a heinous *or* monstrous crime

4 *Fam (très grave)* monstrous, dreadful, ghastly

monstruosité [mɔ̃stryozite] NF **1** *(difformité)* deformity **2** *(acte, crime)* monstrosity; **commettre/dire des monstruosités** to do/to say the most terrible things

mont [mɔ̃] NM **1** *Géog* mountain; *Littéraire* mount; **m. sous-marin** seamount; **aller par monts et par vaux** to wander up hill and down dale; *Fig* **il est toujours par monts et par vaux** he's always on the move; *Fig* **promettre monts et merveilles à qn** to promise sb the earth *or* the moon; **les monts Appalaches** the Appalachian Mountains; **le m. Ararat** Mount Ararat; **le m. Aventin** the Aventine Hill; **le m. Blanc** Mont Blanc; **les monts Cantabriques** the Cantabrian Mountains; **le m. Capitolin** the Capitoline Hill; **le m. Carmel** Mount Carmel; **le m. Cassin** Monte Cassino; **le m. Everest** Mount Everest; **le m. Fuji-Yama** Mount Fuji; **le m. des Oliviers** the Mount of Olives; **le m. Olympe** Mount Olympus; **le m. Palatin** the Palatine Hill; **le m. Parnasse** Mount Parnassus; **le m. Sinaï** Mount Sinai **2** *Anat* **le m. de Vénus** mons veneris

montage [mɔ̃taʒ] NM **1** *(assemblage ▸ d'un meuble, d'un kit)* assembly, assemblage; *(▸ d'une tente)* pitching, putting up; *(▸ de porte)* hanging; *(▸ d'un vêtement)* assembling, sewing together; *(▸ d'un col)* setting in; *(▸ de bijou)* setting, mounting; *Typ* (page) make-up, pasting up

2 *(installation ▸ d'un appareil)* installing, fixing; *(▸ d'une pierre précieuse)* mounting, setting; *(▸ de pneus)* fitting

3 *Fin* **m. de crédit** credit *or* loan arrangement; **m. financier** financial arrangement; **le m. financier a été difficile** it wasn't easy getting the money together; **le m. financier du projet sera le suivant** money for the project will be provided as follows

4 *Cin & (dans l'audiovisuel ▸ processus)* editing; *(▸ avec effets spéciaux)* montage; *(▸ résultat)* montage; **m. réalisé par X** *(d'un film)* film editing by X; *(du son)* sound editing by X; **couper qch au m.** to edit sth out; **premier m.** rough cut; **m. alterné** *(processus)* cross-cutting; *(résultat)* cross-cut; **m. audiovisuel** sound slide show; **m. définitif** final cut; **m. original** edited master; *Cin, Rad & TV* **m. sonore** sound editing; *(avec truquage)* sound montage; **m. vidéo** video(tape) editing, tape editing; *Cin* **salle de m.** cutting room

5 *Phot* mounting; *(image truquée)* montage; **m. de photos** photomontage

6 *Élec & Électron* wiring, connecting, connection; **m. en parallèle/série** connection in parallel/in series

7 *(de matériaux de construction)* taking up, carrying up

montagnard, -e [mɔ̃taɲar, -ard] ADJ mountain *(avant n)*, highland *(avant n)*

NM,F mountain dweller; **les montagnards** mountain people

• **Montagnard** NM *Hist* **les Montagnards** the Montagnards, the members of the Mountain

montagne [mɔ̃taɲ] NF **1** *(mont)* mountain; **les montagnes Rocheuses** the Rocky Mountains, the Rockies; *Fig* **déplacer** *ou* **soulever des montagnes** to move heaven and earth; **(se) faire une m. de qch** to make a great song and dance about sth; **(se) faire une m. de rien** *ou* **d'un rien** to make a mountain out of a molehill; **c'est la m. qui accouche d'une souris!** what a lot of fuss about nothing!; *Prov* **il n'y a que les montagnes qui ne se rencontrent pas** there are none so distant that fate cannot bring together; *Prov* **si la m. ne va pas à Mahomet, Mahomet ira à la m.** if the mountain will not come to Mohammed, Mohammed must go to the mountain

2 *(région)* **la m.** the mountains; *(en Écosse)* the highlands; **à la m.** *ou* **en m.** in the mountains; **de m.** mountain *(avant n)*; **faire de la m.** to go mountaineering; **la basse/haute/moyenne m.** the low mountains/high mountains/uplands; **de basse m.** low-mountain *(avant n)*; **de haute m.** high-mountain *(avant n)*; **de moyenne m.** upland *(avant n)*; **en basse m.** in the foothills; **en haute m.** high in the mountains; **en moyenne m.** in the uplands; **ce n'est que de la m. à vaches** it's only hills

3 *(grosse quantité)* **une m. de** lots *or* mountains *or* a mountain of; **une m. de détritus/spaghettis** a mountain of refuse/spaghetti; **une m. de repassage** a huge pile of ironing; **m. de blé** wheat mountain

4 montagnes russes *(attraction foraine)* roller-coaster, *Br* big dipper

5 *Hist* **la M.** the Mountain

montagneux, -euse [mɔ̃taɲø, -øz] ADJ mountainous

montant, -e [mɔ̃tɑ̃, -ɑ̃t] ADJ **1** *(qui grimpe ▸ sentier)* rising, uphill; **la génération montante** the rising generation

2 *Naut* upstream *(avant n)*; *Transp* up *(avant n)*

3 *(col)* high; *(corsage)* high-necked, high-neckline *(avant n)*; **chaussures montantes** ankle boots

4 *Mil voir* **garde**

NM **1** *(d'une échelle, d'un châssis)* upright; *(d'une tente)* pole; *(d'une porte, d'une fenêtre)* jamb; *(d'un portail, d'un lit)* post; *Sport* **m. (de but)** (goal)post

2 *Fin* amount, sum, total; **écrivez le m. en toutes lettres** write out the sum in full; **le m. du découvert** the amount of the overdraft, the total overdraft; **quel est le m. du chèque/de la facture?** how much is the cheque/invoice for?; **chèque/facture d'un m. de 500 euros** cheque/invoice for 500 euros; **un cadeau d'un m. total de 150 euros** a present worth 150 euros; **cinq versements d'un m. de 100 euros** five payments of 100 euros (each); **le m. total des réparations s'élève à..., les réparations s'élèvent à un m. total de...** the total cost of the repairs adds up to...; **m. brut** gross amount; *UE* **montants compensatoires (monétaires)** (compensatory) subsidies, (monetary) compensatory amounts; **m. forfaitaire** lump sum; **m. net** net total; **m. à régler** *(sur une facture)* amount due; *Compta* **m. à reporter** amount brought forward; **m. du retour net** net return; **m. total** total (amount)

3 *Culin* spiciness, tang

4 *(en œnologie)* **vin qui a du m.** wine with a strong bouquet

mont-blanc [mɔ̃blɑ̃] *(pl* **monts-blancs)** **NM** = chestnut cream dessert

mont-de-piété [mɔ̃dpjete] *(pl* **monts-de-piété)** **NM** (state-owned) pawnshop; **mettre qch au m.** to pawn sth

monte [mɔ̃t] **NF 1** *Équitation (technique)* horsemanship **2** *(participation à une course)* mounting; **j'ai eu trois montes dans la journée** I had three mounts today; **partants et montes probables** probable runners and riders **3** *Vét (accouplement)* covering; *(époque de l'accouplement)* breeding *or* mating season; **mener une jument à la m.** to take a mare to be covered

monté, -e [mɔ̃te] **ADJ 1** *(pourvu)* provided, equipped; *Fam Ironique* **tu es bien montée avec un pareil mari!** you've married a good *or Br* a right one there!

2 *(à cheval ▸ police, troupes)* mounted

3 *(bijou)* set, mounted; **m. sur or** gold-mounted; **médaille montée en pendentif** medal mounted as a pendant; **photographies non montées** unmounted photographs

4 *Fam (irrité)* **être m. contre qn** to be angry with sb[□]; **les ouvriers sont très montés** the workers are up in arms; **elle est très montée, ne lui en parle pas aujourd'hui** she's pretty wound up, don't talk to her about it today

5 *Couture* made-up; **manche montée** made-up *or* fitted sleeve

6 *(plante)* seeded, gone to seed, bolted

7 *Culin* **œufs montés en neige** beaten egg whites

8 *Fam* **être bien m.** to be well hung; *très Fam* **être m. comme un âne** *ou* **un bourricot** *ou* **un taureau** to be hung like a horse *or* a donkey

• **montée NF 1** *(pente)* climb, uphill *or* upward slope; **en haut de la montée** at the top of the hill; **méfiez-vous, la montée est raide!** watch out, it's quite a steep climb!

2 *(ascension)* climb; *(d'un avion)* ascent; **la montée jusqu'au chalet** the climb up *or Sout* the ascent to the chalet; **la montée des escaliers lui fut très pénible** he/she climbed *or* struggled up the stairs with great difficulty; **pendant la montée du col** as he was/we were/*etc* going uphill; *Aut & Aviat* **essai de montée** climbing test; *Aviat* **vitesse en montée** climbing speed; *Aut & Rail* speed on a gradient

3 *(élévation ▸ d'une fusée, d'un dirigeable)* ascent; *(▸ de la sève)* rise; **la montée des eaux** the rise in the water level

4 *(augmentation ▸ de violence)* rise; *(▸ de mécontentement, du nationalisme)* rise, increase, growth; **la montée des prix/températures** the rise in prices/temperatures; **face à la montée en flèche des prix du pétrole** faced with rocketing *or* soaring oil prices; **devant la montée de la violence/du racisme** faced with the rising tide of violence/racism

5 *(accession)* rise, *Sout* ascension; **sa montée au pouvoir** his/her rise to power

6 *Archit* height

7 *Physiol* **montée de lait** onset of lactation

monte-charge [mɔ̃tʃarʒ] *(pl inv ou* **monte-charges)** **NM** hoist, *Br* goods lift, *Am* freight elevator

montée [mɔ̃te] *voir* **monté**

monte-en-l'air [mɔ̃tɑ̃lɛr] **NM INV** *Fam Vieilli* cat burglar

Monténégro [mɔtenegro] **NM le M.** Montenegro

monte-plat, monte-plats [mɔ̃tpla] *(pl* **monte-plats)** **NM** dumb waiter, *Br* service lift

MONTER **[3]** [mɔ̃te]

VI

- to go up **1, 4, 6, 9**
- to rise **1, 4, 6, 8**
- to board **2, 7**
- to climb **1**
- to get on **2**
- to increase **4**

VT

- to go up **1**
- to put up **3, 4, 6**
- to assemble **6**
- to mount **7, 8, 12**
- to organize **9**
- to take up **2**
- to turn up **4**
- to set up **6, 9, 10**
- to fit **7, 13**

VPR

- to be ridden **2**
- to wind oneself up **3**

VI *(aux être)* **1** *(personne, animal ▸ vu d'en bas)* to go up; *(▸ vu d'en haut)* to come up; *(avion)* to climb; *(soleil)* to rise; *(oiseau)* to soar, to fly up; *(drapeau)* to go up; *(rideau de théâtre, air, fumée)* to go up, to rise; *(chemin)* to go up, to rise, to climb; **m. en courant/en rampant** to run/crawl up; **m. se coucher** to go (up) to bed; **m. au grenier** to go up to *or* into the attic; **m. à** *ou* **sur un arbre/une échelle** to climb (up) (into) a tree/(on to) a ladder; **m. sur une chaise** to stand *or* to get on a chair; **m. dans sa chambre** to go up to one's room; **m. chez qn** to go up to sb's place; **monte par l'ascenseur** go up in *or* use the lift; **Anna est arrivée? faites-la m.** Anna's here? tell her to come up; **le cortège est monté jusqu'en haut de la colline** the procession went *or* climbed to the top of the hill; **le premier de cordée continuait à m.** the leader continued to climb *or* continued the ascent; **es-tu déjà montée au dernier étage de la tour Eiffel?** have you ever been up to the top of the Eiffel Tower?; **m. en pente douce** to climb gently (upwards); **m. en pente raide** to climb steeply *or* sharply; **ça monte trop, passe en première** it's too steep, change down into first; *Naut* **faire m. tous les hommes** to order all hands on deck; **m. de** *(sujet: odeur, bruit)* to rise (up) from, to come from; **des clameurs montèrent de la place** a clamour rose up from the square

2 *(dans un moyen de transport)* **m. dans** *(avion, train)* to get on *or* on to, to board; *(bus)* to get on, to board; *(voiture)* to get into; **tous les jours quand je monte dans le train** every day as I get on *or* as I board the train; **où êtes-vous monté?** where did you get on?; **m. en voiture** to get into a car; **tu montes (avec moi)?** *(dans ma voiture)* are you coming with me (in my car)?; **m. sur un** *ou* **à bord d'un bateau** to board a ship; **est-ce que tout le monde est monté à bord?** is everybody aboard *or* on board?; **m. sur un cheval** to get on *or* to mount a horse; **m. sur une bicyclette** to get on a bicycle; **ça fait longtemps que je ne suis pas monté sur une bicyclette** it's a long time since I've been on a bicycle; **m. à cheval** to ride, to go riding; *Équitation* to ride; **elle monte régulièrement à Vincennes** she rides regularly in Vincennes; **m. à bicyclette** to ride a bicycle

3 *(apparaître après une émotion)* **les larmes lui sont montées aux yeux** tears welled up in his/her eyes, his/her eyes filled with tears; **ça m'a fait m. les larmes aux yeux** it brought tears to my eyes; **le rouge lui est monté aux joues** the colour rose to his/her cheeks; **le sang lui monta au visage** the blood rushed to his/her face

4 *(s'élever ▸ température)* to rise, to go up; *(▸ soleil, ballon, fièvre)* to rise; *(▸ prix, taux)* to rise, to go up, to increase; *(▸ action, rivière)* to rise; *(▸ mer, marée)* to come in; *(▸ anxiété, mécontentement)* to grow, to increase; **dès dix heures du matin, la chaleur commence à m.** it starts getting hot around ten in the morning; **faire m.** *(tension, peur)* to increase; **faire m. les prix** *(surenchère)* to send *or* to put prices up; *(marchand)* to put up *or* to increase prices; **empêcher les prix de m.** to keep prices down; **les loyers ont monté de 25 pour cent** rents have gone up *or* increased by 25 percent; *Fam* **le thermomètre monte** it's *or* the weather's getting warmer[□]; **le lait monte** *(chez une femme qui allaite)* lactation has started; **attendez que l'écume monte à la surface de la confiture** wait for the scum to come *or* to rise (up) to the top of the jam; *Culin* **faire m. des blancs en neige** to whisk up egg whites; **le soufflé a bien monté/n'a pas monté** the soufflé rose beautifully/didn't rise; **le ton montait** *(de colère)* voices were being raised, the discussion was becoming heated; *(d'animation)* the noise level was rising

5 *(atteindre un certain niveau)* **la cloison ne monte pas assez haut** the partition isn't high enough; **m. à** *ou* **jusqu'à** *(sujet: eau, vêtement, chaussures)* to come up to; **son plâtre monte jusqu'au genou** his leg is in a plaster cast up to the knee; **les pistes de ski montent jusqu'à 3000 m** the ski runs go up to *or* as high as 3,000 m; **la rue va en montant** the street climbs; **la fièvre est montée à 40°C** his/her temperature has gone up to *or* reached 40°C; *Fam* **je peux m. jusqu'à 200 km/h** I can do up to 200 km/h; **le pain est monté à trois euros** bread has gone up to three euros; **l'hectare de vigne peut m. jusqu'à 5000 euros** one hectare of vineyard can cost up to *or* fetch as much as 5,000 euros

6 *Mus (voix)* to go up, to rise; **il peut m. jusqu'au si** he can go *or* sing up to B

7 *(pour attaquer) Naut* **m. à l'abordage** to board; *Mil* **m. à l'attaque** *ou* **à l'assaut** to go into the attack; **m. à l'assaut de** to launch an attack on; **m. au front** *ou* **en ligne** to go into action, to go up to the front (line); **m. au filet** *(au tennis, au volley-ball)* to go up to the net

8 *(dans une hiérarchie)* to rise; **m. en grade** to be promoted; **un chanteur qui monte** an up-and-coming singer; **la génération qui monte** *(dans le temps)* the rising *or* new generation

9 *(aller vers le nord)* **je monte à Paris demain** I'm going (up) to Paris tomorrow; **quand vous monterez à Paris, venez coucher à la maison** when you come (up) to Paris, come and stay with us; **prendre le train qui monte à Bordeaux** to take the train (up) to Bordeaux; **il a dû m. à Lyon pour trouver du travail** he had to move (up) to Lyons in order to find work

10 *(pousser)* to go to seed, to bolt; **les salades sont montées** the lettuces have gone to seed *or* have bolted

11 *Cartes* **m. sur le valet de trèfle** to play a club higher than the jack

VT *(aux avoir)* **1** *(gravir)* to go up; *(colline, escalier)* to go/come up, to climb (up); **m. l'escalier** to go *or* to climb up the stairs, to go upstairs; **m. une marche** to go up a *or* one step; **m. les marches** to go up *or* to climb the steps; **m. la rue en courant** to run up the street; **la voiture a du mal à m. la côte** the car has difficulty getting up the hill; *Mus* **m. la gamme** to go up *or* to climb the scale

2 *(porter en haut ▸ bagages, colis)* to take *or* to carry up; **m. du vin de la cave** to fetch *or* to bring wine up from the cellar; **monte-moi mes lunettes** bring my glasses up for me; **je lui ai monté son journal** I took the newspaper up to him/her; **peut-on se faire m. le repas dans les chambres?** is it possible to have meals brought up to the room?

3 *(mettre plus haut)* **monte l'étagère d'un cran** put the shelf up a notch; **monte un peu le tableau** put the picture up a bit; **monte la vitre, j'ai froid** wind up the (car) window, I'm cold

4 *(augmenter ▸ son)* to turn up; *(▸ prix)* to put up; *Fam* **monte la télé** turn the TV up; **l'hôtel a monté ses prix** the hotel has put up its prices; *Beaux-Arts* **m. une couleur** to heighten a colour

5 *(mettre en colère)* **m. (la tête à) qn contre qn** to set sb against sb; **ils ont monté les ouvriers contre la direction** they've turned the workers against the management

6 *(assembler ▸ kit)* to assemble, to put together; *(▸ tente)* to pitch, to put up; *(▸ abri)* to rig up; *(▸ appareil, machine)* to set up, to erect; *(▸ porte)* to hang; *Élec* to connect up, to wire (up); **les voitures sont montées à l'usine de Flins** the cars are assembled at the Flins plant; *Typ* **m. une page** to make up *or* to paste up *or* to lay out a page; *Élec* **m. en parallèle/série** to connect in parallel/series

7 *(fixer ▸ radiateur)* to fit, to mount; *(▸ pneu)* to fit (on); *(▸ store)* to put up, to mount; *(▸ photo)* to mount; **il a monté un moteur plus puissant sur sa voiture** he has put a more powerful engine into his car

8 *(bijou)* to mount, to set; **rubis monté sur or** ruby set *or* mounted in gold

9 *(organiser ▸ gén)* to organize; *(▸ pièce, spectacle)* to put on, to stage, to produce; *(▸ canular)* to think up; *(▸ machination)* to set up; **m. une entreprise** to set up a business; **m. un magasin** to set up *or* to open a shop; **l'institut monte une expédition océanographique** the institute is organizing an ocean-survey expedition; **m. un atelier de poterie** to set up a pottery workshop; **il avait monté tout un scénario dans sa tête** he'd thought up some weird and wonderful scheme; **m. un complot** to hatch a plot; **m. un coup** to plan a job; *Fam* **m. le coup à qn** to take sb in, to take sb for a ride

10 *(pourvoir ▸ bibliothèque, collection, cave)* to set up; **m. son ménage** *ou* **sa maison** to set up house

11 *Équitation* **m. un cheval** to ride a horse

12 *Cin (bobine)* to mount; *(film)* to edit

13 *Couture* to fit (on); **m. une manche** to sew on *or* to attach a sleeve; **le pantalon est prêt à être monté** the trousers are ready to assemble *or* to be made up; **le devant est monté n'importe comment** the front's been sewn together any old how

14 *Tricot* **m. les mailles** to cast on (the stitches)

15 *Culin* **m. des blancs en neige** to beat egg whites; **m. une mayonnaise** to make some mayonnaise

16 *Vét & Zool* to cover, to serve

VPR se monter 1 *(s'assembler)* **cette bibliothèque se monte facilement** these bookshelves are easy to assemble

2 *(d'un cheval)* to be ridden; **Flicka se monte facilement** Flicka is easy to ride

3 *Fam (s'énerver)* to wind oneself up (to a pitch)

4 se m. à *(coût, dépenses)* to come *or* to amount *or* to add up to; **à combien se monte tout cela?** how much does all this come to *or* add up to *or* amount to?

5 se m. en to equip *or* to provide oneself with; **se m. en linge/vaisselle** to build up one's supplies of linen/crockery; **se m. en vins** to stock (up) one's cellar

monteur, -euse [mɔ̃tœr, -øz] **NM,F 1** *Ind & Tech* fitter **2** *Cin* editor; **m. son** sound editor **3** *(de bijoux)* setter

Montevideo [mɔ̃tevideo] **NM** Montevideo

montgolfière [mɔ̃gɔlfjɛr] **NF** hot-air balloon, montgolfier (balloon)

monticule [mɔ̃tikyl] **NM 1** *(colline)* hillock, mound, *Sout* monticule **2** *(tas)* heap, mound; **un m. de pierres** a heap *or* pile of stones **3** *Sport (au base-ball)* pitcher's mound

montoir [mɔ̃twar] **NM** *Équitation (de cheval)* mounting block; **(côté du) m.** near side *(of a horse)*; **côté hors (du) m.** off side

montrable [mɔ̃trabl] **ADJ** *(objet)* exhibitable; *(spectacle)* fit to be seen

montre [mɔ̃tr] **NF 1** *(instrument)* watch; **il est onze heures à ma m.** it's eleven o'clock by my watch; **il a mis une heure m. en main** it took him *or* he took exactly one hour (by the clock); **jouer la m.** to play for time; **m. étanche** waterproof watch; **m. de plongée** diver's watch; **m. de précision** precision watch; **m. à quartz** quartz watch **2** *(preuve)* **faire m. de prudence** to show caution, to behave cautiously; **faire m. d'audace** to show *or* to display one's boldness; *Littéraire* **faire qch pour la m.** to do sth merely for show **3** *(vitrine)* shop window, display window; *(dans un meuble)* showcase; **mettre qch en m.** to put sth in the window *or* on show *or* on display

Montréal [mɔ̃real] **NF** Montreal, Montréal

montréalais, -e [mɔ̃realɛ, -ɛz] **ADJ** of/from Montreal

• **Montréalais, -e NM,F** Montrealer

montre-bracelet [mɔ̃trəbraslɛ] *(pl* **montres-bracelets) NF** wristwatch

montrer [3] [mɔ̃tre] **VT 1** *(gén)* to show; *(passeport, ticket)* to show, to produce; *(document secret)* to show, to disclose; *(spectacle, œuvre)* to show, to exhibit; **m. qch à qn** to show sth to sb, to show sb sth; **m. la ville à qn** to show sb round the town; **il m'a montré son usine** he showed me (round) his factory; **montrez-moi votre bras** let me see *or* show me your arm; **il faudrait que tu montres ta fille/cette vilaine blessure à un médecin** you should let a doctor have a look at *or* see your daughter/that nasty wound; **peux-tu me m. comment ça marche?** can you show me how it works?; **les toiles ne sont pas encore prêtes à être montrées** the paintings aren't ready to go on show yet; **m. le poing à qn** to shake one's fist at sb; *Fig* **m. patte blanche** to produce one's credentials; *aussi Fig* **m. ses cartes** to show one's hand

2 *(exhiber ▸ partie du corps)* to show; *(▸ bijou, richesse, talent)* to show off, to parade, to flaunt; **une robe décolletée qui montre les épaules** a low-cut dress which leaves the shoulders bare *or* which exposes the shoulders; **tu n'as pas besoin de m. ta science!** no need to show off your knowledge!; **elle a montré ce qu'elle savait faire** she showed what she was capable of

3 *(faire preuve de ▸ courage, impatience, détermination)* to show, to display; *(laisser apparaître ▸ émotion)* to show; **pour m. sa bonne volonté** to show one's goodwill; **j'essayais de ne pas trop m. ma déception/surprise** I tried not to show my disappointment/surprise too much; **il a montré un grand courage** he showed *or* displayed great courage

4 *(signaler)* to point out, to show; **m. la sortie** *(de la tête)* to nod towards the exit; *(du doigt)* to point to the exit; *(de la main)* to gesture towards the exit; **montre-moi de qui tu parles** show me who you mean; **m. la porte à qn** to show sb the door; *aussi Fig* **m. le chemin à qn** to show sb the way; **m. la voie** *ou* **le chemin** to lead *or* to show the way; **m. l'exemple** to set an example, to give the lead; **m. qn du doigt** to point at sb; *Fig* to point the finger of shame at sb; **m. qch du doigt** to point sth out, to point to *or* at sth; *Fig* to point the finger at sth; **il s'est fait m. du doigt dans le village** everyone in the village is pointing at him

5 *(marquer ▸ sujet: aiguille, curseur, cadran)* to show, to point to; *(▸ sujet: écran)* to show, to display; **l'astérisque montre la somme restant à payer** the asterisk shows *or* indicates the sum outstanding

6 *(prouver)* to show, to prove; **comme le montrent ces statistiques** as these statistics show; **ce qui montre bien qu'il était coupable** which goes to show *or* which shows *or* which proves that he was guilty; *Fam* **ça montre bien que...** it (just) goes to show that...; **cela te montre qu'il faut être prudent** that (just) shows that you have to be careful

7 *(évoquer)* to show, to depict; **la vie des galériens, si bien montrée dans son roman** the lives of the galley slaves, so clearly depicted in his/her novel

8 *(enseigner ▸ technique, procédé)* to show, to demonstrate; *(▸ recette, jeu)* to demonstrate; **m. comment faire qch** to show how to do sth; **la brochure montre comment s'en servir** the booklet explains *or* shows how to use it; **il m'a montré une nouvelle danse** he showed me a new dance, he demonstrated a new dance step for me

VPR se montrer 1 *(se présenter)* to show oneself, to appear (in public); **je ne peux pas me m. dans cet état!** I can't let people see me like this!; **il n'ose plus se m.** he doesn't dare show himself *or* his face; **le voilà, ne te montre pas!** here he is, stay out of sight!; **elle ne s'est même pas montrée au mariage de sa fille** she never even showed up *or* showed her face *or* turned up at her daughter's wedding; **se m. à son avantage** to show oneself in a good light *or* to advantage

2 *(s'afficher)* to appear *or* to be seen (in public); **elle se montrait beaucoup dans les milieux politiques** she was often seen in political circles; **il se montre partout à son bras** he parades everywhere with him/her on his arm

3 *(se révéler)* **se m. d'un grand égoïsme** to display great selfishness; **ce soir-là, il s'est montré odieux/charmant** he was obnoxious/charming that evening; **elle s'est montrée très gentille/courageuse** she was very kind/courageous, she showed great kindness/courage; **finalement, elle s'est montrée digne/indigne de ma confiance** she eventually proved (to be) worthy/unworthy of my trust; **il s'est montré incapable de faire face à la situation** he proved (to be) *or* he was incapable of facing up to the situation

montreur, -euse [mɔ̃trœr, -øz] **NM,F m. de marionnettes** puppeteer; **m. d'ours** bearkeeper

montueux, -euse [mɔ̃tɥø, -øz] **ADJ** *Littéraire* hilly

monture [mɔ̃tyr] **NF 1** *(d'une pierre précieuse)* setting; *(de lunettes)* frame; **des lunettes à m. d'écaille/de plastique** horn-/plastic-rimmed glasses; **des lunettes sans m.** rimless glasses

2 *(d'un vase, d'un miroir)* mounting

3 *Équitation* mount; *Prov* **qui veut voyager loin ménage sa m.** slow and steady wins the race

4 *Mil (d'un fusil)* stock; *(d'une épée)* guard

monument [mɔnymɑ̃] **NM 1** *(stèle, statue)* monument; **élever un m. à la mémoire de qn** to erect a monument in memory of *or* to the memory of sb; **m. funéraire** (funerary) monument; **m. aux morts** war memorial

2 *(édifice)* monument, building; **m. historique** historic monument *or* building; **être classé m. historique** to be a listed building; **m. public** civic building

3 *Littéraire (travail admirable)* monument, masterpiece; **elle a écrit un m.** she's written a monumental work

4 *Fam Fig* **ce type est un m. de naïveté/lâcheté** that guy is the ultimate dupe/coward

monumental, -e, -aux, -ales [mɔnymɑ̃tal, -o] **ADJ 1 plan m. de la ville** *(plan touristique)* city map showing buildings of interest

2 *(grandiose)* monumental, incredible; **une œuvre monumentale** a monumental piece of work

3 *Fam (canular, erreur)* monumental, phenomenal, mammoth *(avant n)*; **d'une stupidité monumentale** monumentally *or* astoundingly stupid

4 *Archit* monumental

mooniste [munist] **NMF** *(membre de la secte Moon)* Moonie

mop [mɔp] **NF** *Belg & Can Joual* mop; *Fig (personne molle)* wimp, pushover

moppe [mɔp] *Can Joual* = **mop**

mopper [3] [mɔpe] **VT** *Belg & Can Joual* to mop

moque [mɔk] **NF 1** *Naut* cringle **2** *Suisse Fam (morve)* snot

moquer [3] [mɔke] **VT** *Littéraire* to mock (at)

VPR se moquer 1 *Littéraire* to jest; **vous vous moquez!** you jest!

2 se m. de *(railler)* to laugh at, to mock (at), to make fun of; **les gens vont se m. d'elle** people will laugh (at her)

3 se m. de *(ignorer ▸ danger, conseil)* to disregard, to ignore

4 se m. de *(être indifférent à)* not to care about; **je me/il se moque de tout ça** I/he couldn't care less about all that; **je me moque de ce que les gens pensent** I couldn't care less what people think; **je me moque que tu sois mécontent** I don't care if you're not pleased; **elle s'en moque pas mal** she couldn't care less; *Fam* **il se moque du tiers comme du quart** he doesn't care *or* give a damn about anybody or anything; *Fam* **je m'en moque comme de l'an quarante** *ou* **comme de ma première chemise** I don't give a damn, I don't care two hoots *or* a tinker's cuss

5 se m. de *(duper)* to dupe, to deceive, to trick; **il s'est moqué de toi** he's pulled a fast one on you; **on s'est moqué de toi** you've been taken for a ride; *Fam* **elle ne s'est pas moquée de toi!** *(repas, réception)* she did you proud (there)!; *(cadeau)* she didn't skimp on your present!; *Fam* **ce type se moque du monde!** that guy's got a real nerve!; **vous vous moquez** *ou* **c'est se m. du monde!** you've got a nerve!

moquerie [mɔkri] **NF** mockery *(UNCOUNT)*, jeering *(UNCOUNT)*; **leurs moqueries continuelles** their constant mockery *or* jeering *or* ridicule; **il était en butte à des moqueries continuelles** he was always being mocked *or* made fun of

moquette [mɔkɛt] **NF** (wall-to-wall) carpet, *Br* fitted carpet; *Tex* moquette; **faire poser de la** *ou* **une m.** to have a (wall-to-wall) carpet laid

moquetter [4] [mɔkete] **VT** to carpet, *Br* to lay a (fitted) carpet in

moqueur, -euse [mɔkœr, -øz] **ADJ 1** *(remarque, rires)* mocking; **d'un ton m.** mockingly, derisively; **d'un air m.** mockingly **2** *(personne)* given to mockery; **elle est très moqueuse** she likes to make fun of people

NM,F mocker; **les moqueurs** mocking *or* jeering people

NM *Orn* mockingbird

moraillon [mɔrajɔ̃] NM hasp

moraine [mɔrɛn] NF *Géog* moraine

moral, -e, -aux, -ales [mɔral, -o] ADJ **1** *(éthique ▸ conscience, jugement)* moral; **il n'a aucun sens m.** he has no moral sense *or* no sense of morality; **je me sens dans l'obligation morale de l'aider** I feel morally obliged to *or* I feel I have a moral obligation to help him/her; **prendre l'engagement m. de faire qch** to be morally committed to do sth **2** *(édifiant ▸ auteur, conte, réflexion)* moral; **la fin de la pièce n'est pas très morale!** the end of the play is rather immoral! **3** *(spirituel ▸ douleur)* mental; *(▸ soutien, victoire, résistance)* moral; **elle a une grande force morale** she has great moral strength *or* fibre

NM morale, spirits; **toutes ces épreuves n'ont pas affecté son m.** all these ordeals failed to shake her morale; **comment va le m.?** are you in good spirits?; **son m. est bas** his/her spirits are low, he's/she's in low spirits; **avoir le m., avoir bon m.** to be in good *or* high spirits; **il n'a pas le m. en ce moment** he's a bit depressed *or* he's in the doldrums at the moment; **allez, il faut garder le m.!** come on, keep your chin *or* spirits up!; **remonter le m. à qn** *(consoler)* to raise sb's spirits, to give sb's morale a boost; *(égayer)* to cheer sb up; **retrouver le m.** to perk up; **avoir un m. d'acier** to be a tower of strength; **avoir le m. au beau fixe** to be in fine spirits; *Fam* **avoir le m. à zéro** to feel down in the dumps; **au physique comme au m., elle nous bat tous!** physically as well as mentally, she's in better shape than all of us!; **c'est bon pour le m.** it's good for morale

• **morale** NF **1** *(règles ▸ de la société)* moral code *or* standards, morality; *(▸ d'une religion)* moral code, ethic; *(▸ personnelles)* morals, ethics; **contraire/conforme à la morale** immoral/moral; **faire la morale à qn, faire une leçon de morale à qn** to lecture sb, to preach at sb **2** *Phil* moral philosophy, ethics *(singulier)* **3** *(d'une fable, d'une histoire)* moral

moralement [mɔralmɑ̃] ADV **1** *(du point de vue de la morale)* morally; **je me sens m. obligé de...** I feel duty-bound *or* morally bound to...; **être m. responsable de...** to be morally responsible for... **2** *(sur le plan psychique)* **m., elle va mieux** she's in better spirits

moralisant, -e [mɔralizɑ̃, -ɑ̃t] ADJ moralizing, moralistic

moralisateur, -trice [mɔralizatœr, -tris] ADJ **1** *(personne, propos)* moralizing, moralistic; **parler à qn sur un ton m.** to speak to sb sanctimoniously **2** *(histoire, principes)* edifying

NM,F moralizer

moralisation [mɔralizasjɔ̃] NF moralization

moralisatrice [mɔralizatris] *voir* **moralisateur**

moraliser [3] [mɔralize] VT **1** *(rendre conforme à la morale)* to moralize **2** *(réprimander)* to lecture

VI *(prêcher)* to moralize, to preach

moraliste [mɔralist] ADJ moralistic

NMF moralist

moralité [mɔralite] NF **1** *(éthique)* morality, ethics *(singulier)*; **d'une m. douteuse** of questionable morals; **être d'une m. irréprochable** to have impeccable moral standards; **quelqu'un d'une m. au-dessus de tout soupçon** someone with high/impeccable moral standards

2 *(comportement)* morals, moral standing *or* standards; **certificat de m.** character reference

3 *(conclusion)* **m., il faut toujours...** and the moral (of the story) is, you must always...; *Fam* **m., on ne l'a plus revu** and the result was, we never saw him again

4 *Hist & Théât* morality play

morasse [mɔras] NF *Presse* final proof

moratoire [mɔratwar] ADJ moratory; *(paiement)* delayed by agreement; **intérêts moratoires** interest on overdue payments, moratorial interest

NM moratorium

moratorium [mɔratɔrjɔm] NM *Jur* moratorium

morbide [mɔrbid] ADJ **1** *(malsain)* morbid, unhealthy **2** *Méd* morbid

morbidité [mɔrbidite] NF **1** *Littéraire (d'une obsession)* morbidity, morbidness, unhealthiness **2** *Méd & (en sociologie)* morbidity rate

morbier [mɔrbje] NM **1** *(fromage)* Morbier (cheese) **2** *Suisse (horloge)* grandfather clock

morbleu [mɔrblø] EXCLAM *Arch* zounds!, ye gods!

morce [mɔrs] NF *Suisse* mouthful; **manger une m.** to have a bite to eat

morceau, -x [mɔrso] NM **1** *(de nourriture)* piece, bit; *(de viande)* cut, piece; **m. de sucre** lump of sugar, sugar lump; **sucre en morceaux** lump sugar; **m. de choix** choice morsel, *Br* titbit, *Am* tidbit; **bas morceaux** *(de viande)* cheap(er) cuts; **aimer les bons morceaux** to like good things (to eat); **je vous le donne dans quel m.?** which cut would you like?; *Can* **m. des dames** *Br* parson's nose, *Am* pope's nose; *Fam Fig* **c'est le gros m.** *(examen, matière)* this is the big one; **tu reprendras bien un petit m.!** come on, have another bit *or* piece!; *Fam* **si on allait manger un m.?** how about going for a bite to eat?; *Fam Fig* **cracher** *ou* **lâcher** *ou* **casser** *ou* **manger le m.** to spill the beans; *Fam Fig* **emporter** *ou* **enlever le m.** to get one's own way[□]

2 *(de bois, de métal ▸ petit)* piece, bit; *(▸ gros)* lump, chunk; *(de papier, de verre)* piece; *(d'étoffe, de câble ▸ gén)* piece; *(▸ mesuré)* length; **il y a des petits morceaux de bouchon dans mon verre** I've got little bits *or* pieces of cork in my glass; **assembler les morceaux de qch** to piece sth together; **en morceaux** in bits *or* pieces; **mettre en morceaux** *(papier, étoffe)* to tear up; *(jouet)* to pull to pieces *or* bits; **tomber en morceaux** to fall apart, to fall to pieces

3 *(extrait)* passage, extract, excerpt; **m. d'anthologie** anthology piece; **cette scène est un véritable m. d'anthologie** it's a truly memorable scene; **m. de bravoure** purple passage; **(recueil de) morceaux choisis** (collection of) selected passages *or* extracts

4 *Mus (fragment)* passage; *(œuvre)* piece; **jouemoi un m. de piano** play something on the piano for me; **m. pour trombone** piece for trombone

5 *Fam (personne)* **un beau m.** a babe, a knockout

morceler [24] [mɔrsəle] VT **1** *(partager)* to parcel out; *(démembrer)* to divide (up), to break up **2** *Mil* to split up

morcellement [mɔrsɛlmɑ̃] NM **1** *(d'un terrain)* dividing (up); *(d'un héritage)* parcelling (out) **2** *Mil* splitting (up)

morcellera *etc voir* **morceler**

mordacité [mɔrdasite] NF *Littéraire* mordancy

mordant, -e [mɔrdɑ̃, -ɑ̃t] ADJ **1** *(caustique)* biting, caustic, scathing **2** *(froid)* biting, bitter

NM **1** *(dynamisme ▸ d'une personne)* drive, spirit, punch; *(▸ d'un style, d'une publicité)* punch, bite; *(▸ de troupes, d'équipe)* keenness; **une campagne qui a du m.** a campaign which really packs a punch; **l'équipe a perdu de son m.** the team has lost its punch **2** *(d'une lame, d'une lime)* bite **3** *(en gravure, teinture, dorure)* mordant

mordée [mɔrde] NF *Can* bite; **prendre une m. dans qch** to take a bite out of sth, to bite sth

mordicus [mɔrdikys] ADV *Fam* stubbornly, doggedly; **il soutient m. que c'est vrai** he absolutely insists that it's true

mordieu [mɔrdjø] EXCLAM *Arch* death!, zounds!

mordillage [mɔrdijaʒ], **mordillement** [mɔrdijmɑ̃] NM nibbling

mordiller [3] [mɔrdije] VT to nibble *or* to chew (at)

mordoré, -e [mɔrdɔre] ADJ golden brown, bronze

mordorer [3] [mɔrdɔre] VT *Littéraire* to bronze

mordorure [mɔrdɔryr] NF *Littéraire* golden brown, bronze

mordre [76] [mɔrdr] VT **1** *(sujet: animal, personne)* to bite; **m. un fruit** to bite into a piece of fruit; **m. qn au bras** to bite sb's arm, to bite sb on the arm; **m. qn jusqu'au sang** to bite sb and draw blood; **se faire m.** to get bitten; **il s'est fait m. à la main** he was bitten on the hand; *Hum* **prends la serpillière, elle ne mord pas** *ou* **elle ne te mordra pas!** take the mop, it won't bite (you)!; *Fig* **m. la poussière** to bite the dust; *Fig* **faire m. la poussière à qn** to make sb bite the dust

2 *(sujet: scie, vis)* to bite into; *(sujet: acide)* to eat into; *(sujet: pneus cloutés)* to grip; *(sujet: ancre)* to grip, to bite; *(sujet: froid)* to bite; **le froid lui mordait les doigts** the cold was nipping *or* biting his/her fingers

3 *(empiéter sur)* **m. la ligne** *(au saut en longueur)* to cross the (take-off) board; *(sur la route)* to cross the white line

4 *Beaux-Arts* **m. une planche** to etch a plate

USAGE ABSOLU **il ne va pas m., ton chien?** your dog won't bite, will he?

VI **1** *Pêche* to bite; **ça mord?** are the fish biting?; *aussi Fig* **m. (à l'appât** *ou* **à l'hameçon)** to rise (to the bait), to bite; *Fam Fig* **il** *ou* **ça n'a pas mordu** he wasn't taken in, he didn't fall for it

2 *Tech* to mesh

3 *(gravure)* to bite; *(teinture)* to take

4 *(accrocher)* to bite; **lime/vis qui mord** file/screw that bites *or* has a good bite; **l'ancre ne mord pas** the anchor won't hold *or* grip

• **mordre à** VT IND *Fam* **1** *(prendre goût à)* to take to, to fall for, to be hooked by **2** *(être trompé par)* to be taken in by, to fall for

• **mordre dans** VT IND to bite into

• **mordre sur** VT IND *(ligne, marge)* to go *or* to cross over; *(économies)* to make a dent in, to eat into; *(période)* to overlap; *Sport* **m. sur la ligne** *(au tennis)* to have one's foot (just) over the line

VPR **se mordre** to bite oneself; *aussi Fig* **se m. la langue** to bite one's tongue; **se m. les lèvres pour ne pas rire/pour ne pas hurler** to bite one's lip so as not to laugh/scream; *Fig* **je m'en suis mordu les doigts** I could have kicked myself; *Fig* **il va s'en m. les doigts** he'll be sorry he did it, he'll live to regret it; **se m. la queue** to chase one's tail; *Fig* to go round in circles

mordu, -e [mɔrdy] ADJ **1** *Fam (passionné)* **il est m. de jazz** he's mad *or* crazy about jazz **2** *Fam (amoureux)* madly in love, completely smitten

NM,F *Fam (passionné)* fan, addict; **un m. de cinéma/d'opéra** a film/an opera buff; **un m. de football** a football fan; **les mordus de la télé** TV addicts

more [mɔr] = **maure**

morelle [mɔrɛl] NF *Bot* nightshade

moresque [mɔrɛsk] = **mauresque** ADJ

morfal, -e, -als, -ales [mɔrfal] NM,F *Fam Br* pig, gannet, *Am* hog

morfler [3] [mɔrfle] *Fam* VT **1** *(recevoir)* to get[□] **2** *(se voir infliger une peine de)* to get[□], to cop

VI **1** *(être abîmé)* to get smashed up; *(être blessé)* to get injured[□] **2** *(être puni, pâtir)* to catch it, *Br* to cop it

morfondre [75] [mɔrfɔ̃dr] **se morfondre** VPR **1** *(languir)* to mope; **il se morfondait en attendant les résultats du test** he waited anxiously *or* fretfully for the results of the test **2** *Can (s'épuiser)* to wear oneself out

morfondu, -e [mɔrfɔ̃dy] ADJ *Littéraire* gloomy, dejected

morganatique [mɔrganatik] ADJ morganatic

morgue[1] [mɔrg] NF *(établissement)* morgue; *(dans un hôpital) Br* mortuary, *Am* morgue

morgue[2] [mɔrg] NF *(arrogance)* arrogance, haughtiness, disdainfulness

moribond, -e [mɔribɔ̃, -ɔ̃d] ADJ dying, *Sout* moribund

NM,F dying person; **les moribonds** the dying

moricaud, -e [mɔriko, -od] *Fam Péj* ADJ darkskinned[□], swarthy[□]

NM,F **1** *(personne de race noire)* darkie, nigger, *Br* wog, = racist term used to refer to a black person **2** *(personne à la peau foncée)* dark-skinned *or* swarthy person[□]

morigéner [18] [mɔriʒene] VT to chide, to rebuke, to upbraid

morille [mɔrij] NF morel

morillon [mɔrijɔ̃] NM **1** *(raisin)* small black grape **2** *Orn* tufted duck **3** *(émeraude)* small rough emerald

mormon, -e [mɔrmɔ̃, -ɔn] ADJ Mormon

• **Mormon, -e** NM,F Mormon

mormonisme [mɔrmɔnism] NM Mormonism

morne [mɔrn] ADJ **1** *(triste ▸ personne, regard)* glum, gloomy; *(▸ silence)* gloomy

2 *(monotone ▸ discussion)* dull; *(▸ paysage)* bleak, drab, dreary; **d'un ton m.** in a dreary voice

3 *(maussade ▸ climat)* dull, dreary, dismal; **une journée m.** a dreary day

4 *(terne ▸ couleur, style)* dull

NM *(aux Antilles)* mound, hill

mornifle [mɔrnifl] NF *Fam Vieilli (gifle)* slap, cuff

morose [mɔroz] ADJ **1** *(individu, air, humeur, vie)* glum, morose; *(temps, année)* miserable **2** *(économie)* sluggish, slack

morosité [mɔrozite] NF **1** *(d'une personne)* glumness, sullenness, moroseness; *(d'un climat)* miserableness; *(d'un paysage)* gloominess; **la m. de son humeur** his/her glumness *or* sullenness *or* moroseness **2** *(d'un marché)* slackness, sluggishness

Morphée [mɔrfe] NPR *Myth* Morpheus; *Fig* **dans les bras de M.** in the arms of Morpheus

morphème [mɔrfɛm] NM *Ling* morpheme

morphine [mɔrfin] NF *Pharm* morphine, morphia

morphing [mɔrfiŋ] NM *Cin* morphing

morphinisme [mɔrfinism] NM *Méd* morphinism

morphinomane [mɔrfinɔman] *Méd* ADJ addicted to morphine

NMF morphine addict, *Spéc* morphinomaniac

morphinomanie [mɔrfinɔmani] NF *Méd* morphine addiction, *Spéc* morphinism

morphogénétique [mɔrfɔʒenetik] ADJ *Biol* morphogenetic, morphogenic

morphologie [mɔrfɔlɔʒi] NF *Biol* morphology

morphologique [mɔrfɔlɔʒik] ADJ *Biol* morphological

morphologiquement [mɔrfɔlɔʒikmɑ̃] ADV *Biol* morphologically

morphologue [mɔrfɔlɔg] NMF *Biol* morphologist

morphopsychologie [mɔrfɔpsikɔlɔʒi] NF *Psy* morphopsychology

morphose [mɔrfoz] NF *Biol* morphosis

morpion [mɔrpjɔ̃] NM **1** *Fam Péj (enfant)* brat **2** *Fam (pou du pubis)* crab **3** *(jeu) Br* ≃ noughts and crosses, *Am* ≃ tic-tac-toe

mors [mɔr] NM **1** *(d'un cheval)* bit; **prendre le m. aux dents** *(sujet: cheval)* to take the bit in its teeth; *Fig* to take the bit in between one's teeth, to swing into action **2** *(d'un étau)* jaw, chop; *(d'une pince)* jaw, pincer **3** *(d'un livre)* joint, groove

morse[1] [mɔrs] NM *Zool* walrus

morse[2] [mɔrs] NM *(code)* Morse (code); **en m.** in Morse (code)

morsure [mɔrsyr] NF **1** *(d'un animal)* bite; **une m. de chien** a dog bite; **une m. de serpent** a snakebite **2** *Beaux-Arts (de l'acide)* biting **3** *Fig (de la jalousie, du remords)* pang; **les morsures du froid** the biting cold

mort, -e [mɔr, mɔrt] PP *voir* **mourir**

ADJ **1** *(décédé ▸ personne)* dead; **il est m.** he's dead; **il est m. hier** he died yesterday; **elle est morte depuis longtemps** she died a long time ago, she's been dead (for) a long time; **il est m. dans un accident de voiture** he died *or* was killed in a car crash; **elle était comme morte** she looked as if she were dead; **si tu fais un geste, tu es un homme m.** one move and you're a dead man; **laisser qn pour m.** to leave sb for dead; *aussi Fig* **m. et enterré, m. et bien m.** dead and buried, dead and gone, long dead; **m. sur le champ de bataille** *ou* **au champ d'honneur** killed in action; **m. pour la France** killed in action *(annotation on a French death certificate, giving certain entitlements to the relatives of the dead person)*; **m. ou vif** dead or alive; **être plus m. que vif** *(à demi mort)* to be more dead than alive; *(très effrayé)* to be half-dead with fright; *Prov* **morte la bête, m. le venin** = a dead enemy is no longer a threat

2 *(arbre, cellule, dent)* dead; **des branches mortes** dead branches

3 *(en intensif)* **m. de peur/d'inquiétude/de froid** frightened/worried/freezing to death; **il était m. de fatigue** he was dead tired; **être m. de rire** to be killing oneself (laughing)

4 *(passé ▸ amour, désir)* dead; *(▸ espoir)* dead, buried, long gone

5 *(inerte ▸ regard)* lifeless, dull; *(▸ quartier, bistrot)* dead; *(▸ eau)* stagnant; *Fam* **c'est m. par ici le dimanche** it's dead around here on Sundays

6 *Fam (hors d'usage ▸ appareil, voiture)* dead, finished; **mon sac est m.** my bag's had it

7 *Fam (épuisé)* **je suis m.!** I'm dead!

NM,F **1** *(personne)* dead person; **les morts** the dead; **le nombre des morts sur la route** the number of deaths on the roads; **l'épidémie n'a pas fait de morts** no one died in the epidemic; **les émeutes ont fait trois cents morts** three hundred people died *or* were killed in the rioting; **l'accident a fait trois morts** the accident claimed three lives, three people died *or* were killed in the accident; **c'est un m. vivant** *(mourant)* he's at death's door; **les morts vivants** the living dead; **jour** *ou* **fête des morts** All Souls' Day; **messe/prière des morts** mass/prayer for the dead; **faire le m.** to pretend to be dead, to play dead; *Fam Fig* **je lui ai écrit il y a trois semaines, mais depuis, il fait le m.** I wrote to him three weeks ago, but since then he's been as silent as the grave *or* I haven't heard a thing **2** *(dans un jeu)* dummy; **faire le m.** to be dummy; **je suis le m.** I'm dummy

• **mort** NF **1** *(décès)* death; **la m.** death; **à la m. de son père** on his/her father's death; **envoyer qn à la m.** to send sb to his/her death; **frôler la m.** to have a brush with death; **il a vu la m. de près** he saw death staring him in the face; **se donner la m.** to commit suicide, to take one's own life; **trouver la m.** to meet one's death, to die; **trouver la m. dans un accident** to die in an accident; **les émeutes ont entraîné la m. de trente personnes** the riots led to the death *or* deaths of thirty people; **il n'y a pas eu m. d'homme** nobody was killed, there was no loss of life; **(mourir d'une) m. subite/lente** (to die a) sudden/slow death; **périr de m. violente** to die a violent death; **il a eu une m. douce** he died painlessly; **m. cérébrale** *ou* **clinique** brain death; **m. accidentelle** *(gén)* accidental death; **m. naturelle** natural death; *Jur* death from natural causes; **il est m. de m. naturelle** he died from natural causes; **m. subite du nourrisson** cot death, *Spéc* sudden infant death syndrome, SIDS; *Sport* **m. subite** *(au football)* sudden death; *Littéraire* **la petite m.** (the moment of) climax; **avoir la m. dans l'âme** to have a heavy heart; **je partis la m. dans l'âme** I left with a heavy heart; **souffrir m. et passion** to suffer agonies; *Fam* **vous allez attraper la m.!** you'll catch your death (of cold)!; *Fam* **c'est pas la m. (du petit cheval)!** it's not the end of the world!; **la foule scandait "à m., à m.!"** the crowd was chanting "kill, kill!" *or* "kill him, kill him!"; **m. aux traîtres!, à m. les traîtres!** death to the traitors!; *Fam* **m. aux vaches!** down with the cops!

2 *(économique)* end, death; **c'est la m. des cinémas de quartier** it's the end of local cinemas; **le monopole est la m. de l'industrie** monopoly means the end *or* is the ruin of industry

3 *Bot* **m. aux loups** wolfsbane; **m. aux poules** henbane

• **à mort** ADJ *(lutte, combat)* to the death ADV **1** *Fam (en intensif)* **haïr qn à m.** to hate sb's guts, to loathe and detest sb; **en vouloir à m. à qn** to have a huge grudge against sb; **je lui en veux à m.** I hate his/her guts; **je lui en veux à m. d'avoir dit ça** I'll never forgive him/her for saying that; **j'ai freiné à m.** I braked like hell, I slammed on the brakes; **ils sont brouillés** *ou* **fâchés à m.** they're enemies for life; *très Fam* **déconner à m.** to talk complete crap *or Br* bollocks **2** *(mortellement)* **blesser qn à m.** to mortally wound sb; **frapper qn à m.** to strike sb dead; **mettre qn à m.** to put sb to death; **mettre un animal à m.** to kill an animal

• **de mort** ADJ *(silence, pâleur)* deathly, deathlike; **être en danger** *ou* **péril de m.** to be in mortal danger; **menace/pulsion de m.** death threat/wish

• **jusqu'à ce que mort s'ensuive** ADV *Vieilli Jur* until he/she be dead; *Hum* to the bitter end

• **jusqu'à la mort** ADV to the death; *Fig* to the bitter end; **je m'en souviendrai jusqu'à la m.** I'll remember it until my dying day

mortadelle [mɔrtadɛl] NF mortadella

mortaise [mɔrtɛz] NF **1** *Menuis* mortise, mortice **2** *(de clavette)* keyway; *(de serrure)* mortise

mortaiser [4] [mɔrteze] VT **1** *Menuis* to mortise, to mortice **2** *Tech* to slot

mortalité [mɔrtalite] NF **1** *(gén)* mortality; *(dans des statistiques)* death rate, mortality (rate); **m. infantile** child *or* infant mortality **2** *Arch (condition mortelle)* mortal nature

mort-aux-rats [mɔrora] NF INV rat poison

mort-bois [mɔrbwa] *(pl* **morts-bois)** NM underwood, brushwood

morte-eau [mɔrto] *(pl* **mortes-eaux** [mɔrtəzo]) NF neap tide, neap

mortel, -elle [mɔrtɛl] ADJ **1** *(qui tue ▸ accident, maladie)* fatal; *(▸ dose, poison)* deadly, lethal; *(▸ coup, blessure)* fatal, lethal, *Sout* mortal; *(▸ champignon)* poisonous, deadly; *(péché)* deadly; **il a fait une chute mortelle** he had a fatal fall; *Fig* **c'est un coup m. porté à notre petite communauté** this is a death-blow for our small community; *Fam Fig* **son revers est m.!** his/her backhand is lethal!; *Fam Fig* **tu as raté l'examen, mais ça n'est pas m.!** you've failed the exam, but it's not the end of the world!

2 *(acharné ▸ ennemi)* mortal, deadly; *(▸ haine)* deadly

3 *(qui rappelle la mort ▸ pâleur, silence)* deathly

4 *(qui n'est pas éternel)* mortal

5 *Fam (ennuyeux)* deadly dull, deadly boring; **d'un ennui m.** deadly dull, dead boring

6 *Fam (excellent)* cool, *Br* wicked, *Am* awesome

7 *Fam (très mauvais)* hellish, *Am* gnarly

NM,F *(être humain)* mortal

ADV *Fam* **on s'est éclatés m.!** we had a wicked time!; *très Fam* **on s'est fait chier m.** we were bored shitless

EXCLAM cool!, *Br* wicked!, *Am* awesome!

mortellement [mɔrtɛlmɑ̃] ADV **1** *(à mort)* **m. pâle** deathly pale; **être m. blessé** to be fatally *or Sout* mortally wounded **2** *(en intensif)* **s'ennuyer m.** to be bored to death, to be bored rigid; **le film est m. ennuyeux** the film is deadly boring; **tu l'as m. offensé** you've mortally offended him

morte-saison [mɔrtsɛzɔ̃] *(pl* **mortes-saisons)** NF slack *or* off season; **à la m.** in the off season

mortier [mɔrtje] NM **1** *(récipient)* mortar

2 *Mil* mortar; **tirs de m.** mortar fire; **attaque au m.** mortar attack

3 *Constr* mortar; **planche à m.** mortarboard

4 *(bonnet)* judge's cap *(worn by certain judges in France)*

mortifiant, -e [mɔrtifjɑ̃, -ɑ̃t] ADJ mortifying, humiliating

mortification [mɔrtifikasjɔ̃] NF **1** *Rel* mortification **2** *(humiliation)* mortification, humiliation **3** *Culin (faisandage)* hanging *(of game meat)*

mortifié, -e [mɔrtifje] ADJ mortified

mortifier [9] [mɔrtifje] VT **1** *Rel* to mortify **2** *(humilier)* to mortify, to humiliate; **elle en a été mortifiée** she was mortified **3** *Culin (faisander)* to (leave to) hang

VPR **se mortifier** to mortify oneself

mortinatalité [mɔrtinatalite] NF stillbirth rate

mort-né, -e [mɔrne] *(mpl* **mort-nés,** *fpl* **mort-nées)** ADJ *aussi Fig* stillborn

NM,F stillborn baby

mortuaire [mɔrtɥɛr] ADJ **1** *(rituel)* mortuary *(avant n)*, funeral *(avant n)*; *(cérémonie, couronne)* funeral *(avant n)*; **chambre m.** death chamber; **drap m.** pall **2** *Admin* **acte m.** death certificate; **registre m.** register of deaths

NF *Belg (maison)* house of the deceased; *(chambre mortuaire)* death chamber

mort-vivant, morte-vivante [mɔrvivɑ̃, -ɑ̃t] *(mpl* **morts-vivants,** *fpl* **mortes-vivantes)** NM,F member of the living *or* walking dead; **les morts-vivants** the living *or* walking dead

morue [mɔry] NF **1** *Culin & Ich* cod **2** *très Fam (prostituée)* whore, hooker **3** *très Fam (femme)* tart, *Br* slapper

morutier, -ère [mɔrytje, -ɛr] ADJ cod-fishing *(avant n)*

NM **1** *(navire)* cod-fishing boat **2** *(marin)* cod-fisherman

morve [mɔrv] NF **1** *(mucus)* nasal mucus **2** *Vét* glanders *(singulier)*

morveux, -euse [mɔrvø, -øz] ADJ **1** *(sale)* snotty-nosed; *(nez)* runny; *Prov* **qui se sent m., qu'il se mouche** if the cap fits, wear it **2** *Vét* glandered

NM,F *Fam* **1** *(enfant)* (snotty-nosed) little kid **2** *(jeune prétentieux)* snotty *or* snotty-nosed little upstart

MOS [ɛmoɛs] NM *(abrév* **métal oxyde semiconducteur)** MOS

mosaïque[1] [mɔzaik] NF **1** *Beaux-Arts* mosaic; **sol en m.** mosaic floor **2** *Fig (mélange ▸ de cou-*

leurs) patchwork, mosaic; *(▸ de cultures)* mixture, mosaic; *(▸ de populations)* medley; *Ordinat* **afficher en m.** *(fenêtres)* to tile **3** *Bot* mosaic (disease)

mosaïque[2] [mɔzaik] **ADJ** *Rel* Mosaic

mosaïste [mɔzaist] **NMF** mosaicist

Moscou [mɔsku] **NF** Moscow

moscovite [mɔskɔvit] **ADJ** Muscovite
• **Moscovite NMF** Muscovite

mosquée [mɔske] **NF** mosque

mot [mo] **NM 1** *Ling* word; **un m. à la mode** a buzzword; **"orgueilleux", c'est bien le m.** "arrogant" is the (right) word; **"riche" n'est pas vraiment le m.** "rich" isn't exactly the word I would use; *Euph* **le m. de Cambronne** *ou* **de cinq lettres** = the word "merde"; **m. clé** key word; **m. composé** compound (word); **m. d'emprunt** loanword; **le m. juste** the right *or* appropriate word; **m. de passe** password; **m. vedette** headword; **gros m.** swearword; **ne dis pas de gros mots!** don't swear!; *Belg Péj* **m. à soixante-quinze** *ou* **septante-cinq centimes, m. à un franc soixante-cinq** *ou* **septante-cinq centimes, m. à deux/trois/***etc* **francs soixante-cinq** *ou* **septante-cinq centimes** interminably long word
2 *Ordinat* **m. binaire** binary word; **m. d'état** status word; **m. machine** computer word; **m. mémoire** storage *or* memory word
3 *(parole)* word; **il n'a pas dit un m. de toute la soirée** he didn't say a (single) word the entire evening; **dire un m. à qn** to have a word with sb; **pourriez-vous nous dire un m. sur ce problème?** could you say a word (or two) *or* a few words about this problem for us?; **il n'a pas dit un seul m. en ta faveur** he didn't put in a single good word for you; **qui ne dit m. consent** silence is tantamount to consent; **dire deux mots à qn** to have a word with sb; **dire un m. de travers** to say something wrong, to put a foot wrong; **il n'a jamais un m. plus haut que l'autre** he never raises his voice; **je vais lui en toucher** *ou* **je lui en toucherai un m.** I'll have a word with him/her about it; **pas un m.!** don't say a word!; **pas un m. à qui que ce soit!** not a word to anybody!; **les mots manquent** words are not enough; **les mots manquent pour décrire la beauté de ce matin-là** there are no words to describe *or* words cannot describe the beauty of that particular morning; **les mots me manquent** words fail me; **les mots me manquent pour vous remercier** I'm at a loss for words to express my gratitude; **je ne trouve pas les mots (pour le dire)** I cannot find the words (to say it); **chercher ses mots** to try to find *or* to search for the right words; **manger** *ou* **avaler ses mots** to mumble; **je ne pouvais pas placer un m.** I couldn't get a word in edgeways; **ce ne sont que des mots!** words, words, words!, all that's just talk!; **à ces mots** at these words; **sur ces mots** with these words; **sur ces mots, il nous quitta** with these words *or* so saying, he left us; **m. d'ordre** slogan; *Mil* watchword; **m. d'ordre de grève** call for strike action; **c'est mon dernier m.** it's my last *or* final offer; **avoir le dernier m.** to have the last word; **"voleur", c'est un bien grand m.** "thief", that would be putting it a bit too strongly *or* going a bit too far; **"l'amour", le grand m. est lancé** "love", that's the word we've been waiting for; **avec toi, c'est tout de suite** *ou* **toujours les grands mots** you're always exaggerating; **mots doux** words of love, sweet nothings; **avoir des mots (avec qn)** to have words (with sb); **on a eu des mots** we had words *or* a row; **avoir son m. à dire** to have a *or* one's say; **moi aussi, j'ai mon m. à dire là-dessus** I've got a say in the matter as well; **il faut toujours qu'elle ait son m. à dire** she always has to have her say (in the matter); **tu n'as qu'un m. à dire** just say the word, you just have to say the word; **avoir toujours le m. pour rire** to be a (great) laugh *or* joker; **pas le premier** *ou* **un traître m. de** not a single word of; **je ne sais pas un (traître) m. de russe** I don't know a word of Russian; **prendre qn au m.** to take sb at his/her word; **se donner** *ou* **se passer le m.** to pass the word around; **tout le monde s'était donné le m.** word had been passed around
4 *(parole mémorable)* saying; **m. d'esprit, bon m.** witticism, witty remark; **m. d'auteur** (author's) witty remark; **m. d'enfant** child's remark; **m. de la fin** concluding message, closing words; **mots célèbres** famous sayings *or* quotes
5 *(message écrit)* note, word; **il m'a laissé un m. sur mon bureau** he left a note on my desk; **ce petit m. pour vous dire que je suis bien arrivé** just a note to say that I've arrived safely; **écrire un m. à qn** to write sb a note, to drop sb a line; **m. d'absence** note *(explaining absence)*; **m. d'excuse** word of apology; **m. de remerciements** thank-you note
• **à mots couverts ADV** in veiled terms; **dire qch à mots couverts** to hint at sth, to say sth in a roundabout manner; **faire comprendre qch à qn à mots couverts** to give sb to understand sth in a roundabout manner
• **au bas mot ADV** at least, at the very least
• **en d'autres mots ADV** in other words
• **en un mot ADV** in a word; **en un m. comme en cent** *ou* **mille** *(en bref)* in a nutshell, to cut a long story short; *(sans détour)* without beating about the bush
• **mot à mot ADV** *(littéralement)* word for word; *(comme nom)* **faire du m. à m., traduire m. à m.** to translate word for word
• **mot pour mot ADV** word for word; **répéter qch m. pour m.** to repeat sth word for word *or* verbatim; **c'est ce qu'elle a dit, m. pour m.** those were her very words, that's what she said, word for word
• **sans mot dire ADV** without (uttering) a word

motard, -e [mɔtar, -ard] **NM,F** *Fam* motorcyclist□, biker
NM *(policier)* motorcycle policeman; **voiture escortée de motards** car with a motorcycle escort

motel [mɔtɛl] **NM** motel

motet [mɔtɛ] **NM** *Mus* motet

moteur, -trice [mɔtœr, -tris] **ADJ 1** *Tech (force)* driving; **voiture à quatre roues motrices** four-wheel-drive car; **roue motrice** driving wheel; **temps m.** power stroke; **unité motrice** power pack *or* unit **2** *Anat (nerf, neurone, muscle)* motor *(avant n)*
NM 1 *Tech* motor, engine; **m. ACT** ohc engine; **m. à allumage par bougie** spark-ignition engine; **m. à allumage par compression** compression-ignition engine; **m. d'avion** aero-engine; **m. à combustion** combustion engine; **m. à deux temps** two-stroke engine; **m. Diesel** diesel engine; **m. électrique** electric motor; **m. à essence** petrol engine; **m. à explosion** internal combustion engine; **m. à gaz** gas engine; **m. hydrogène** hydrogen engine; **m. à injection** fuel injection engine; **m. en ligne** in-line engine; **m. pas à pas** stepper motor; **m. à pistons** piston engine; **m. à quatre temps** four-stroke engine; **m. à réaction** jet engine; **m. à refroidissement par air** air-cooled engine; **m. seize soupapes** sixteen-valve engine; **m. thermique** heat engine; **m. turbo-diesel** turbo-diesel engine; **m. en V** vee engine; **m. V6** V6 (engine); **m. à vapeur** steam engine
2 *Fig (cause)* mainspring, driving force; **être le m. de qch** to be the driving force behind sth
3 *Cin* **m.!** camera!
4 *Ordinat* **m. d'impression** *(d'une imprimante laser)* printer engine; **m. de recherche** search engine
• **motrice NF** motor unit
• **à moteur ADJ** power-driven, motor *(avant n)*; **bateau à m.** motorboat; **à moteurs multiples, à plusieurs moteurs** *(avion)* multi-engine *(avant n)*, multi-engined

motif [mɔtif] **NM 1** *(raison)* reason; **venons-en au m. de votre visite** let's turn to the reason for your visit; **quel m. avez-vous de vous plaindre?** what cause *or* grounds have you for complaint?; **le crime avait-il un m.?** did the crime have a motive?, was there a motive to the crime?; **le m. de mon absence** the reason for my absence; **m. de licenciement** grounds for dismissal; **m. de mécontentement** cause *or* grounds for discontent; **m. de réclamation** reason for claim; **il a agi sans m.** he did it for no reason; **peur/soupçons sans motifs** groundless fear/suspicions
2 *Jur (jugement)* grounds
3 *(intention)* motive; **les motifs qui l'animent** his/her motivation *or* motives
4 *(dessin)* pattern, design; **un m. à petites fleurs** a small flower pattern *or* design; **robe à motifs/à grands motifs** patterned/large-pattern dress; **une veste avec des motifs noirs et blancs** a jacket with a black and white design
5 *Beaux-Arts (élément)* motif; *(sujet)* subject
6 *Mus* motif

motion [mosjɔ̃] **NF** motion; **voter une m.** to pass a motion; **la m. a été adoptée** the motion was carried; **m. de censure** vote of no confidence

motivant, -e [mɔtivɑ̃, -ɑ̃t] **ADJ** *(travail, résultat)* motivating; *(salaire, rémunération)* attractive

motivation [mɔtivasjɔ̃] **NF 1** *(justification)* motivation, justification, explanation; *(raison)* motivation, motive, reason; **quelles sont vos motivations?** what motivates you?; **joindre une lettre de m. à votre CV** send a *Br* covering letter *or Am* cover letter with your *Br* CV *or Am* résumé
2 *Ling* = relationship between the signifier and the signified
3 *Com & Mktg* motivation, incentive; **étude de m.** motivation *or* motivational research; **m. d'achat** buying *or* purchasing motive
4 *Psy* motivation

motivé, -e [mɔtive] **ADJ 1** *(personne)* motivated; **élève très m.** very keen *or* motivated pupil; **le personnel n'est plus m.** the staff isn't motivated any longer **2** *(justifié)* well-founded, justified; **un refus m.** a justifiable refusal; **non m.** unjustified, unwarranted; **sa peur n'est pas motivée** his/her fears are groundless; *Jur* **sentence arbitrale motivée** = award stating the reasons on which it is based; *Jur* **avis m.** counsel's opinion

motiver [3] [mɔtive] **VT 1** *(inciter à agir)* to spur on, to motivate; **motivé par l'appât du gain** spurred on by greed; **des crimes motivés par l'argent** crimes motivated by money *or* with money as the motive; **l'ambition les motive** they are motivated by ambition **2** *(causer)* to be the reason for; **qu'est-ce qui a motivé votre retard?** what's the reason for your being late? **3** *(justifier)* to justify, to explain; **m. un refus** to give grounds for a refusal

moto [mɔto] **NF** motorbike, bike; **faire de la m.** to ride a motorbike; **aller au travail à** *ou* **en m.** to go to work on a motorbike, to ride a motorbike to work; **m. tout terrain** *ou* **verte** trail bike

motocross [mɔtɔkrɔs] **NM** motocross, *Br* (motorcycle) scramble

motocrotte [mɔtɔkrɔt] **NF** *Fam* = motorized scooter with an attachment for cleaning up dog dirt in the street

motoculteur [mɔtɔkyltœr] **NM** *Agr* (motor) cultivator

motoculture [mɔtɔkyltyr] **NF** motorized *or* mechanized agriculture

motocycle [mɔtɔsikl] **NM** motorbicycle

motocyclette [mɔtɔsiklet] **NF** *Vieilli* motorcycle

motocycliste [mɔtɔsiklist] **NMF** motorcyclist

motomarine [mɔtɔmarin] **NF** *Can* jet ski; **faire de la m.** to go jet skiing

motonautique [mɔtɔnotik] **ADJ réunion/sport m.** speedboat event/racing

motonautisme [mɔtɔnotism] **NM** speedboat *or* motorboat racing

motoneige [mɔtɔnɛʒ] **NF** *Can* snowmobile, skidoo

motopompe [mɔtɔpɔ̃p] **NF** motor pump

motorisation [mɔtɔrizasjɔ̃] **NF** motorization

motorisé, -e [mɔtɔrize] **ADJ 1** *(agriculture)* motorized; *(troupes)* motorized, mechanized **2** *Fam (personne)* **être m.** to have *Br* transport *or Am* transportation; **tu es m.?** have you got a car?

motoriser [3] [mɔtɔrize] **VT 1** *(mécaniser)* to motorize, to mechanize; **m. l'agriculture** to mechanize agriculture **2** *(doter d'automobiles)* to motorize; **m. un régiment** to motorize a regiment

motoriste [mɔtɔrist] **NMF** *(industriel)* engine manufacturer; *(technicien)* engine technician

mot-outil [mouti] *(pl* **mots-outils)** **NM** *Ling* form word, link word

motrice [mɔtris] *voir* **moteur**

motricité [mɔtrisite] **NF** *Physiol* motor functions

motte [mɔt] **NF 1** *Agr* **m. (de terre)** clod *or* clump (of earth); **m. de tourbe** (turf of) peat; **m. de gazon** sod **2** *Hort* ball; **plantation en m.** ball planting **3** *Culin* **m. de beurre** slab of butter; **beurre à la m.** butter in blocks

motteux [mɔtø] **NM** wheat ear

motus [mɔtys] **EXCLAM** *Fam* **m. (et bouche cousue)!** not a word (to anybody)!, mum's the word!

mou, molle [mu, mɔl]

> **mol** is used before masculine singular nouns beginning with a vowel or h mute.

ADJ **1** *(souple ▸ pâte, cire, terre, fruit)* soft; *(▸ fauteuil, matelas)* soft; **les biscuits sont tout mous** the biscuits have gone all soft; **devenir m.** to soften, to go soft; **être m. au toucher** to be soft to the touch
2 *(sans tenue ▸ étoffe, vêtement)* limp; *(▸ joues, chair)* flabby; *(▸ corde)* slack
3 *(sans vigueur physique ▸ mouvement)* limp, lifeless, feeble; *(▸ poignée de main)* limp; *(▸ geste)* lifeless, limp; **mon revers est trop m.** my backhand is too weak *or* lacks power; *Fam* **j'ai les jambes toutes molles** my legs feel all weak *or* feel like jelly; *Fam* **je me sens tout m.** I feel washed out; **ce qu'il peut être m.!** God, he's feeble *or* useless!; *Fam* **allez, rame plus vite, c'est m. tout ça!** come on, pull on those oars, let's see some effort!
4 *(estompé ▸ contour)* soft; **des collines au relief m.** rolling hills
5 *(sans conviction ▸ protestation, excuse, tentative)* feeble, weak; *(▸ doigté, style)* lifeless, dull; *(▸ élève)* apathetic, lethargic
6 *(sans force de caractère)* spineless; *Fam* **être m. comme une chiffe** *ou* **une chique** to be a real wimp
7 *(trop tolérant ▸ parents, gouvernement)* lax, soft
8 *Ling* soft
9 *Anat* **parties molles** soft tissue *(UNCOUNT)*
10 *Phys* **rayonnements mous** soft radiation *(UNCOUNT)*
NM,F *Fam* **1** *(moralement)* wimp **2** *(physiquement)* weak *or* feeble individual❑
ADV **1 elle joue trop m.** she doesn't put enough verve into her playing **2** *Fam Vieilli (doucement)* **y aller m.** to go easy, to take it easy; **vas-y m. avec le piment** go easy on *or* take it easy with the chilli
NM **1** *(jeu)* slack, give, play; **avoir du m.** *(sujet: cordage)* to be slack; *(sujet: vis, charnière)* to be loose, to have a bit of play; **donner du m. à un câble** to give a cable some slack; **donner du m. à un cordage** to slacken a rope; **prendre du m.** *(sujet: corde)* to slacken **2** *(abats)* lights, lungs **3** *Fam (locutions)* **bourrer le m. à qn** to pull the wool over sb's eyes; **rentrer dans le m. à qn** *(agresser)* to go for sb, to lay into sb

mouais [mwɛ] EXCLAM *Fam* well, yeah!; **alors, t'as aimé le film? – m., j'ai vu pire** did you like the movie, then? – well, yeah, I've seen worse; **m., ce n'est pas mal** it's all right, I suppose

mouchage [muʃaʒ] NM **1** *(de nez)* blowing **2** *(de chandelles)* snuffing (out)

mouchard, -e [muʃar, -ard] NM,F *Fam Péj* **1** *(à l'école)* snitch, *Br* sneak, tell-tale **2** *(indic)* informer❑, *Br* grass, *Am* fink
NM **1** *(enregistreur ▸ d'un avion)* black box, flight recorder; *(▸ d'un camion)* tachograph; *(contrôleur)* watchman's clock
2 *Aviat & Mil* spy plane
3 *Ordinat* **m. électronique** cookie
4 *Fam (sur une porte)* Judas(-hole)❑, spyhole

moucharder [3] [muʃarde] *Fam Péj* VT **1** *(sujet: enfant)* to snitch on, *Br* to sneak on, to tell tales on **2** *(sujet: indic)* to squeal on, *Br* to grass on, *Am* to fink on
VI **1** *(enfant)* to snitch, *Br* to sneak, to tell tales **2** *(indic)* to squeal, *Br* to grass, *Am* to rat

mouche [muʃ] NF **1** *Entom* fly; **m. bleue** bluebottle; **m. domestique** housefly; *Can* **m. à feu** firefly; **m. à merde** *très Fam* dung fly; *Can Fig Vulg (personne ennuyeuse)* pain in the *Br* arse *or Am* ass; **m. à miel** honey bee; *Can* **m. noire** black fly; **m. tsé-tsé** tsetse fly; **m. du vinaigre** fruit fly; **il ne ferait pas de mal à une m.** he wouldn't hurt a fly; *Fam* **quelle m. te pique?** what's up *or* wrong with you (all of a sudden)?; *Fam* **tomber comme des mouches** to drop like flies; *Fam* **prendre** *ou* **Suisse piquer la m.** to hit the *Br* roof *or Am* ceiling; **elle prend facilement la m.** she's very touchy; **on aurait entendu une m. voler** you could have heard a pin drop; *Belg Prov* **on ne prend** *ou* **n'attrape pas les mouches avec du vinaigre** you don't get anywhere by being unpleasant
2 *Pêche* **m. (artificielle)** (artificial) fly; **m. mouillée** wet fly; **m. à saumon** salmon fly; **pêche à la m.** fly-fishing; **pêche à la m. sèche** dry-fly fishing
3 *(sur la peau)* beauty spot, patch; *(poils)* tuft of hair *(under the lower lip)*, soul patch
4 *(de cible)* bull's-eye; *Escrime* button; **faire m.** to hit the bull's-eye, to score a bull's-eye; *Fig* to hit the nail on the head
5 *Méd* **mouches (volantes)** floaters, *Spéc* muscae volitantes
6 *Arch (tache)* spot, speck; *(sur vêtement)* stain

moucher [3] [muʃe] VT **1** *(nettoyer)* **m. son nez** to blow one's nose; **m. qn** to blow sb's nose; **je mouche du sang** there's blood on my handkerchief when I blow my nose **2** *Fam (rabrouer)* **m. qn** to put sb in his/her place, to teach sb a lesson; **se faire m.** to be put in one's place **3** *(chandelle)* to snuff (out)
VPR **se moucher** to blow one's nose; *Fam* **elle ne se mouche pas du pied** *ou* **du coude** she thinks she's the cat's whiskers *or* the bee's knees

moucheron [muʃrɔ̃] NM *Entom* midge

moucheronner [3] [muʃrɔne] VI *(poisson)* to jump *or* to rise (for flies)

moucheté, -e [muʃte] ADJ **1** *(œuf, fourrure, laine)* mottled, flecked; *(tissu)* speckled; *(cheval)* dappled; **rouge m. de blanc** red flecked with white; **nez m. de taches de rousseur** freckled nose
2 *Escrime* buttoned

moucheter [27] [muʃte] VT **1** *(couvrir de taches)* to speckle; *(parsemer de taches)* to fleck **2** *Escrime* to button

mouchette [muʃɛt] NF **1** *Archit (de fenêtre)* outer fillet, mouchette; *(de larmier)* lip **2** *Menuis (rabot)* beading plane; *(moulure)* beading
• **mouchettes** NFPL *(ciseaux)* (pair of) candle snuffers

moucheture [muʃtyr] NF *(d'un pelage, d'un plumage)* speckling; *(d'un tissu)* flecks, flecking; **une écharpe blanche avec des mouchetures noires** a white scarf with black flecks, a white scarf specked *or* flecked with black

mouchoir [muʃwar] NM handkerchief; **m. en papier** (paper) tissue, kleenex; **m. en tissu** handkerchief; **leur jardin est grand comme un m. de poche** their garden is the size of a pocket handkerchief

mouchure [muʃyr] NF (nasal) mucus

moudjahidin, moudjahidine [mudʒaidin] NMPL mujahedin

moudre [85] [mudr] VT *(café, poivre)* to grind; *(blé)* to mill, to grind

moue [mu] NF pout; **m. boudeuse** sulk; **faire une m. de dégoût** to screw one's face up in disgust; **faire une m. de dépit** to pull a face; **faire la m.** to pout

mouette [mwɛt] NF *Orn* gull, seagull; **m. rieuse** black-headed gull

moufeter [3] [mufte] = **moufter**

moufette, mouffette [mufɛt] NF *Zool* skunk

moufle [mufl] NF **1** *(gant)* mitt, mitten **2** *(poulie)* pulley block
NM *Tech (four, récipient)* muffle

mouflet, -ette [muflɛ, -ɛt] NM,F *Fam* kid, *Br* sprog

mouflon [muflɔ̃] NM mouflon, moufflon; **m. d'Amérique** *ou* **du Canada** bighorn (sheep); **m. à manchettes** Barbary sheep

moufter [3] [mufte] VI *(à l'infinitif et au participe passé seulement) Fam* **ne pas m.** to keep one's mouth shut, *Br* to keep shtum; **sans m.** without a peep

mouillage [mujaʒ] NM **1** *(du linge)* dampening
2 *Naut (emplacement)* anchorage, moorings, moorage; *(manœuvre)* anchoring, mooring; *(de bouée)* putting down; **être au m.** to be riding at anchor; **prendre son m.** to anchor
3 *(du vin, du lait)* watering down
4 *Mil* **m. de mines** mine laying

mouillé, -e [muje] ADJ **1** *(surface, vêtement, cheveux)* wet, damp; **je suis tout m.** I'm all wet **2** *(voix)* tearful; *(regard)* tearful, watery; **elle le regarda, les yeux mouillés de larmes** she looked at him with tears in her eyes **3** *Ling* palatalized
NM **ça sent le m.** it smells of damp

mouillement [mujmɑ̃] NM *Ling* palatalization

mouiller [3] [muje] VT **1** *(accidentellement ▸ vêtement, personne)* to wet; **ne mouille pas tes chaussons!** don't get your slippers wet!; *Euph* **il mouille encore son lit** he still wets his *or* the bed; **se faire m.** *(par la pluie)* to get wet; *Fam* **m. sa chemise** *ou* **son maillot** to slog away
2 *(humecter ▸ doigt, lèvres)* to moisten; *(▸ linge)* to dampen
3 *Fam (compromettre)* to drag in; **il a cherché à nous m. dans cette affaire** he tried to drag us into this affair
4 *Can Fam (fêter)* **il va falloir m. ça!** we'll have to have a drink to celebrate!❑, this calls for a celebration!❑
5 *Naut (ancre)* to cast, to drop; *(bouée)* to put down; *Mil (mine)* to lay; *Pêche (ligne)* to cast
6 *Ling* to palatalize
7 *(vin, boisson alcoolisée, lait)* to dilute, to water down
USAGE ABSOLU *Culin* **mouillez avec du vin/du bouillon** moisten with wine/stock
VI **1** *Naut (jeter l'ancre)* to cast *or* to drop anchor; *(stationner)* to ride *or* to lie *or* to be at anchor; **mouillez!** let go (the anchor)!
2 *très Fam (avoir peur)* to wet oneself
3 *Can & (régional en France) Fam (pleuvoir)* to rain❑; *Can* **m. à siau** *ou* **à verse** *ou* **à boire debout** to rain buckets
4 *Vulg (être excitée sexuellement)* to be wet
VPR **se mouiller 1** *(volontairement)* **se m. les cheveux** to wet one's hair
2 *(accidentellement)* to get wet; **se m. les pieds** to get one's feet wet
3 *(yeux)* to fill with tears
4 *Fam (prendre un risque)* to stick one's neck out
5 *Can Fam* **se m. la dalle** *ou* **le gargoton** *ou* **le canayen** to get pissed *or Br* legless
• **en mouiller** V IMPERSONNEL *Can* **des imbéciles comme lui, il en mouille** there's no shortage of idiots like him around, there are loads of idiots like him around

mouillette [mujɛt] NF *(de pain)* finger of bread *(for dunking)*, *Br* soldier

mouilleur [mujœr] NM **1** *(de timbres)* (stamp) sponge damper **2** *Naut* anchor stopper **3** *Mil* **m. de mines** mine-layer

mouillure [mujyr] NF **1** *(marque)* wet mark *or* patch **2** *Ling* palatalization

mouise [mwiz] NF *Fam (misère)* poverty❑; *(ennuis)* grief, hassle, *Br* aggro; **être dans la m.** *(être dans la misère)* to be hard up *or* broke *or Br* skint; *(avoir des ennuis)* to be in a hole, *Am* to be behind the eightball; **tirer** *ou* **sortir qn de la m.** to get sb out of a hole

moujik [muʒik] NM muzhik, mujik, moujik

moujingue [muʒɛ̃g] NMF *très Fam* kid

moukère [mukɛr] NF *très Fam (femme maghrébine)* Maghrebi woman❑; *(femme)* female

moulage¹ [mulaʒ] NM **1** *Beaux-Arts (processus)* casting
2 *(reproduction)* cast; **un m. en plâtre/bronze de Beethoven** a plaster/bronze cast of Beethoven
3 *Métal* casting, moulding
4 *(d'un fromage)* moulding

moulage² [mulaʒ] NM *(du grain)* grinding, milling

moulait *etc voir* **moudre**

moulant, -e [mulɑ̃, -ɑ̃t] ADJ tight-fitting, clingy

moule¹ [mul] NM **1** *(récipient, matrice)* mould; **m. à gâteau** *Br* cake *or* baking tin, *Am* cake *or* baking pan; **m. à gaufre** *ou* **gaufres** waffle iron; **m. à manqué** *Br* sandwich tin, *Am* deep cake pan; **m. à tarte** *Br* flan case, *Am* pie pan; *Fam* **être coulé dans le même m.** to be cast in the same mould; *Fam* **on n'en fait plus des comme lui, on a cassé le m.** they broke the mould when they made him
2 *Fig (modèle imposé)* mould; **refuser d'entrer dans le m.** to refuse to conform; **être coulé dans le même m.** to be cast in the same mould; **être fait au m.** to be very shapely *or* perfectly shaped

moule² [mul] NF **1** *(mollusque)* mussel; **moules frites** mussels and *Br* chips *or Am* French fries *(speciality of Belgium and the north of France)*; **moules marinières** moules marinières, mussels in white wine; *Belg* **moules parquées** = mussels served raw **2** *Fam (personne)* drip **3** *Vulg (sexe de la femme)* pussy, snatch

moulé, -e [mule] ADJ **1** *(pain)* baked in a *Br* tin *or Am* pan
2 *(écriture)* neat, well-shaped; *(lettre)* printed, copperplate

3 *(statue)* cast, moulded; **statue de plâtre m.** plaster cast

4 *Méd (matières fécales)* well-shaped, consistent

mouler [3] [mule] VT **1** *(former ► buste, statue)* to cast; *(► brique, lingot, fromage)* to mould

2 *(prendre copie de ► visage, empreinte)* to take *or* to make a cast of; **m. qch en plâtre/cire** to take a plaster/wax cast of sth

3 *Fig (adapter)* **m. ses pensées/son mode de vie sur** to mould *or* to model one's thoughts/lifestyle on

4 *Fig (serrer ► hanches, jambes)* to hug, to fit closely (round); **cette jupe te moule trop** this skirt is too tight *or* tight-fitting for you; **un pantalon qui moule** close-fitting *or* tight-fitting *or* skin-tight trousers; **ses hanches moulées dans une jupe en cuir** her hips moulded in a leather skirt

moules-frites [mulfrit] NM INV *Belg* **1** *Culin* mussels and *Br* chips *or Am* French fries *(speciality of Belgium and the north of France)* **2** *(restaurant)* = restaurant specializing in mussels and *Br* chips *or Am* French fries

mouleur, -euse [mulœr, -øz] NM,F caster, moulder

moulière [muljɛr] NF mussel bed

moulin [mulɛ̃] NM **1** *(machine, bâtiment)* mill; **m. à eau** water mill; **m. à vent** windmill; *Fig* **se battre contre des moulins à vent** to tilt at windmills; *Fig* **on y entre comme dans un m.** anyone can just walk in; **ce n'est pas un m. ici!** you can't just walk in *or* breeze in as if you owned the place!; *Fam* **m. à paroles** windbag, chatterbox; **le M. Rouge** = famous cabaret in Paris **2** *(instrument)* **m. à café** coffee grinder; **m. à légumes** vegetable mill; **m. à poivre** peppermill; *Rel* **m. à prières** prayer wheel; *Can* **m. à viande** mincer **3** *Fam (moteur)* engine▫

mouliner [3] [muline] VT **1** *(aliment)* to mill **2** *Pêche* to reel in

VI *Fam (pédaler)* to pedal▫

moulinet [mulinɛ] NM **1** *Pêche* reel

2 *Tech* winch

3 *(mouvement)* **faire des moulinets avec un bâton** to twirl *or* to whirl a stick around; **il faisait des moulinets avec ses bras** he was whirling *or* waving his arms around

4 *(tourniquet)* turnstile

Moulinette® [mulinɛt] NF **1** *Culin* (hand-held) vegetable mill, Moulinette®; **passer de la viande à la M.** to put some meat through a/the food mill **2** *Fam Fig* **passer qch à la M.** to make mincemeat of sth

moult [mult] ADV *Hum ou Vieilli* **avec m. détails** with a profusion of details; **avec m. remerciements** with many thanks

moulu, -e [muly] PP *voir* **moudre**

ADJ **1** *(en poudre)* ground; **café fraîchement m.** freshly ground coffee **2** *Fam (épuisé)* **m. (de fatigue)** dead beat, all in

moulure [mulyr] NF moulding

moulurer [3] [mulyre] VT to mould; **profils moulurés** mouldings

moulut *etc voir* **moudre**

moumoute [mumut] NF *Fam* **1** *(perruque)* wig▫, rug **2** *(veste)* sheepskin jacket▫ *or* coat▫

mouquère [mukɛr] = **moukère**

mourant, -e [murɑ̃, -ɑ̃t] ADJ **1** *(personne, animal, plante)* dying **2** *(lumière, son)* dying, fading; *(voix)* faint

NM,F dying man, *f* woman; **les mourants** the dying

mourir [42] [murir] VI **1** *(personne, animal, plante)* to die; **il est mort hier** he died yesterday; **il est mort assassiné** he was murdered; **il est mort de vieillesse** he died of old age; **m. empoisonné** to die of poisoning *or* from poison; **m. d'une crise cardiaque/d'un cancer** to die of a heart attack/of cancer; **m. de chagrin** to die of grief; **m. de mort naturelle** *ou* **de sa belle mort** to die a natural death; **m. de faim** to die of starvation, to starve to death; **m. de soif/chaleur** to die of thirst/heat; **m. de froid** to freeze to death; **il mourut de ses blessures** he died from his wounds; **m. sous les coups** to be beaten to death; **m. sur le coup** to die instantly; **m. à la tâche** to die in harness; **m. en héros** to die a hero's death *or* like a hero; **m. avant l'âge** to die before one's time; **je l'aime à en m.** I'm desperately in love with him/her; **faire m. qn** to kill sb; *Fig* **faire m. qn à petit feu** to kill sb slowly; **au moment de m.** in the hour of death; **au moment de m., il a fait venir toute sa famille** just before he died, he sent for his entire family; *Fam* **tu n'en mourras pas!** it won't kill you!; *Fam* **plus débile/macho, tu meurs!** they don't come any more stupid/macho than that!

2 *(disparaître ► culture)* to die out; *(► flamme, bougie)* to die out *or* down; *(► bruit)* to die away *or* down; **les vagues qui viennent m. sur la plage** the waves which break and spend themselves on the beach

3 *Fig (pour intensifier)* **m. de faim** to be starving *or* famished; **m. de soif** to be dying of thirst, to be parched; **m. de chaleur** to be boiling hot; **m. de froid** to be freezing cold; **m. de peur** to be scared to death; **m. d'ennui, s'ennuyer à m.** to be bored to death *or* to tears; **m. d'envie de faire qch** to be dying to do sth; **je meurs d'envie de boire un thé** I'm dying for a cup of tea; **vous me faites m. d'impatience** the suspense is killing me; **j'ai cru m. de rire** I thought I would die laughing, I nearly died laughing; **être à m. de rire** *(sujet: film, roman, personne)* to be hilarious; **la pièce est à m. de rire** the play's hilarious *or* a scream; **elle me fait m. de rire!** she really cracks me up!

V IMPERSONNEL **il meurt des milliers d'enfants chaque jour** thousands of children die every day

VPR **se mourir** *Littéraire* **1** *(personne)* to be dying; *Fig* **se m. d'amour pour qn** to pine for sb **2** *(civilisation, coutume)* to die out; *(d'un feu)* to die down; **une tradition qui se meurt** a dying tradition

mouroir [murwar] NM *Péj* (old people's) home; **certains foyers pour personnes âgées ne sont que des mouroirs** some homes are just places where old people are left to die

mouron [murɔ̃] NM *Fam (locution)* **se faire du m.** to worry oneself sick; **te fais pas de m. pour lui!** don't (you) worry about him!

mourra *etc voir* **mourir**

mousquet [muskɛ] NM musket

mousquetaire [muskətɛr] NM musketeer; **gants (à la) m.** gauntlets

mousqueterie [muskɛtri] NF *Vieilli* musketry

mousqueton [muskətɔ̃] NM **1** *(anneau)* snap hook *or* clasp; *(en alpinisme)* karabiner **2** *Mil* carbine

moussage [musaʒ] NM *Chim* foaming

moussaillon [musajɔ̃] NM *Fam* (young) cabin boy

moussaka [musaka] NF moussaka

moussant, -e [musɑ̃, -ɑ̃t] ADJ *(crème à raser)* lathering; *(shampooing, gel)* foaming

mousse [mus] ADJ **1** *Tex* **collant m.** stretch tights **2** *Chim* **caoutchouc m.** foam rubber

NM **1** *(apprenti marin)* cabin boy, ship's boy **2** *Can Fam (en appellatif)* darling, sweetheart

NF **1** *(bulles ► de shampooing, de crème à raser)* lather, foam; *(► d'un bain)* bubbles, foam; *(► de savon)* suds, lather; *(► de champagne, de cidre)* bubbles; *(► de bière)* froth; **m. à raser** shaving foam; **faire de la m.** *(savon, crème à raser)* to lather; *Fam* **se faire de la m.** to worry oneself sick

2 *Culin* mousse; **m. au chocolat** chocolate mousse; **m. de saumon** salmon mousse

3 *Fam (bière)* (glass of) beer▫; **on se boit une m.?** fancy a *Br* pint *or Am* brew?

4 *(dans les matériaux synthétiques)* foam; **m. de Nylon®** stretch nylon; **balle en m.** rubber ball

5 *Bot* moss; **couvert de m.** mossy

mousseline [muslin] NF *(de coton)* muslin; *(de soie, de Nylon®, de laine)* chiffon, mousseline; **m. de soie** chiffon; **foulard en m.** muslin *or* chiffon scarf

ADJ INV **pommes m.** puréed potatoes; **sauce m.** mousseline sauce

mousser [3] [muse] VI **1** *(champagne, cidre)* to bubble, to sparkle; *(bière)* to froth; *(savon, crème à raser)* to lather; *(détergent, shampooing)* to foam, to lather; **ce savon ne mousse pas beaucoup** this soap doesn't lather very well *or* doesn't give much of a lather; **ce champagne mousse beaucoup** there are a lot of bubbles in this champagne, this champagne is very fizzy; **j'ai une méthode infaillible pour faire m. le chocolat chaud** I have an infallible method for making hot chocolate frothy **2** *Fam Fig* **faire m. qn** *(le mettre en colère)* to wind sb up, to rile sb; *(le mettre en valeur)* to sing sb's praises; **faire m. qch** to sing the praises of sth; **se faire m.** to blow one's own trumpet

mousseron [musrɔ̃] NM St George's mushroom

mousseux, -euse [musø, -øz] ADJ **1** *(vin, cidre)* sparkling; *(bière, lait)* frothy; *(eau)* foamy; *(sauce, jaune d'œuf)* (light and) frothy; **un chocolat m.** a cup of frothy hot chocolate **2** *Bot* mossy

NM sparkling wine

moussoir [muswar] NM whisk

mousson [musɔ̃] NF monsoon

moussu, -e [musy] ADJ mossy

moustache [mustaʃ] NF **1** *(d'un homme)* moustache; **porter la m.** *ou* **des moustaches** to have a moustache; **elle a de la m.** she's got a bit of a moustache; **m. en brosse** toothbrush moustache; **m. (à la) gauloise** walrus moustache **2** *Zool* whiskers

moustachu, -e [mustaʃy] ADJ **un homme m.** a man with a moustache; **il est m.** he's got a moustache

NM man with a moustache

moustiquaire [mustikɛr] NF *ou Belg* NM *(d'un lit)* mosquito net; *(d'une ouverture)* mosquito screen; *(de fenêtre)* screen

moustique [mustik] NM **1** *Entom* mosquito **2** *Fam (gamin)* kid, mite; *(petite personne)* (little) squirt

moût [mu] NM *(de raisin)* must; *(de bière)* wort

moutard [mutar] NM *Fam* kid

moutarde [mutard] NF **1** *Bot* mustard; **graines de m.** mustard seeds **2** *Culin* mustard; **m. à l'ancienne** grain mustard; **m. de Dijon** Dijon mustard; **m. forte** Dijon mustard **3** *Fam (locutions)* **la m. lui est montée au nez** he/she lost his/her temper, he/she saw red; **je sens que la m. me monte au nez** I can feel my temper starting to rise

ADJ INV **1** *(jaune)* mustard *(avant n)*, mustard-coloured **2** *Mil* **gaz m.** mustard gas

moutardier [mutardje] NM **1** *(récipient)* mustard pot **2** *(fabricant)* mustard maker *or* manufacturer **3** *(marchand)* mustard seller

moutier [mutje] NM *Vieilli* monastery

mouton, -onne [mutɔ̃, -ɔn] NM **1** *(animal)* sheep; *Fig* **m. à cinq pattes** rare bird; **chercher le m. à cinq pattes** to seek the impossible; *Fig* **le m. noir de la famille** the black sheep of the family; *Fig* **compter les moutons** to count sheep; **ils ont tous suivi comme des moutons** they all followed like sheep; *Fig* **revenons** *ou* **retournons à nos moutons** let's get back to the point

2 *(fourrure, cuir)* sheepskin; **veste en (peau de) m.** sheepskin jacket

3 *Culin* mutton; **côte de m.** mutton chop; **ragoût de m.** mutton stew

4 *Fam (individu)* sheep; **c'est un vrai m. de Panurge** he's easily led, he follows the herd

5 *Métal* drop hammer

6 *(en travaux publics)* pile driver

7 *Fam Arg crime (espion) Br* grass, *Am* fink

8 *Can* **m. noir** *(nuage)* rain cloud

ADJ *Fig* sheep-like

• **moutons** NMPL *(poussière)* bits of fluff, fluff *(UNCOUNT)*; *(nuages)* fleecy *or* fluffy clouds; *(écume sur la mer)* white horses

moutonné, -e [mutɔne] ADJ **1** *(ciel)* flecked *or* dotted with fleecy clouds **2** **tête moutonnée** curly head of hair

moutonnement [mutɔnmɑ̃] NM *(de la mer)* frothing

moutonner [3] [mutɔne] VI *(mer)* to froth, to break into white horses; *(ciel)* to become covered with small fleecy clouds

moutonneux, -euse [mutɔnø, -øz] ADJ *(mer)* flecked with white horses; *(ciel)* spotted *or* dotted with fleecy clouds

moutonnier, -ère [mutɔnje, -ɛr] ADJ **1** *Agr* ovine, sheep *(avant n)* **2** *Fig (trop docile)* sheep-like, easily led

mouture [mutyr] NF **1** *(version)* version; **ma première m. était meilleure** my first draft was better

2 *Péj (copie, reprise)* rehash

3 *Agr & Culin (des céréales)* milling, grinding; *(du café)* grinding

4 *Fig Vieilli* **tirer deux moutures d'un sac** to profit twice over from sth

mouv' [muv] **NM** *Fam (abrév* **mouvement)** **c'est dans le m.** it's dead hip, it's totally cool

mouvance [muvɑ̃s] **NF** *(domaine d'influence)* circle of influence; **dans la m. surréaliste** in surrealist circles; **ils se situent dans la m. socialiste** they belong to the socialist camp

mouvant, -e [muvɑ̃, -ɑ̃t] **ADJ 1** *(en mouvement ▸ foule)* moving, surging; *(▸ cible)* moving **2** *(instable ▸ surface)* unsteady, moving; *(▸ terrain)* unstable **3** *(changeant ▸ situation)* unstable, unsettled

mouvement [muvmɑ̃] **NM 1** *(geste)* movement; **faire un m.** to move; **un m. de tête** *(affirmatif)* a nod; *(négatif)* a shake of the head; **répondre d'un m. de tête** *(pour dire non)* to answer with a shake of the head, to shake one's head; *(pour dire oui)* to answer with a nod, to nod; **elle me fit signe d'entrer d'un m. de tête** she signalled to me to come/go in; **un léger m. de surprise** a start *or* a movement of surprise; **m. vers l'arrière** backward movement *or* motion; **avoir un m. de recul** to start (back); **avoir un m. de dégoût** to recoil in disgust; **des mouvements pour soulager son mal de dos** exercises to relieve backache; **il y eut un m. de foule** a ripple ran through the crowd; **faire un faux m.** to pull something

2 *(impulsion)* **mon premier m. fut de...** my first impulse was to...; **m. de colère** fit *or* burst of anger; **m. d'humeur** outburst (of temper); **avoir un bon m.** to make a nice gesture; **allez! un bon m.!** go on, be generous!

3 *(déplacement ▸ d'un astre, d'un pendule)* movement; *(▸ de personnes)* movement; *Phys* motion; **surveiller les mouvements de qn** to monitor sb's movements; **m. perpétuel** perpetual motion; *Banque* **mouvements de compte** account transactions; *Admin* **m. de personnel** staff transfer *or* changes; **m. de repli** withdrawal; **amorcer un m. de repli** to start falling back; **m. de retraite** retreat; **mouvements de marchandises** movement of goods; **mouvements de troupes** troop movements; *Aut* **m. de caisse** body roll

4 *(évolution ▸ des prix, des taux)* trend, movement; *(▸ du marché, des devises)* fluctuation; *Écon* **m. ascensionnel** upward trend; **m. en baisse/en hausse** downward/upward trend; **m. boursier** stock market movement; *Compta* **m. de caisse** cash transaction; *Écon* **m. des capitaux** movement *or* flow of capital; *Bourse* **m. des cours** price fluctuation; *Fin* **m. des devises** currency fluctuation; **m. de la population** demographic changes; *Bourse* **m. des valeurs** share movements; *Fam* **être dans le m.** to be with it, to be up to date

5 *Pol (action collective)* movement; **m. de grève** strike (movement); **reconduire un m. de grève** to extend a strike; **lancer un m. de grève/révolte** to instigate a strike/revolt; **m. indépendantiste** independence *or* separatist movement; **M. de libération de la femme** Women's Liberation Movement; **M. National Républicain** = right-wing French political party; **le m. ouvrier** the labour movement; **m. pacifiste** peace movement; **m. de protestation** protest rally; **m. séparatiste** separatist *or* independence movement; **m. social** industrial action; **le m. syndical** the *Br* trade-union *or Am* labor-union movement;

6 *(animation ▸ d'un quartier)* bustle, liveliness; *(▸ dans un aéroport, un port)* activity, traffic; **eh bien, il y a du m. chez vous!** it's all go at your place!; **il aime le m.** he likes change, he likes to move around, he can't stay in one place

7 *Géog* **m. de terrain** undulation

8 *(impression de vie ▸ d'une peinture, d'une sculpture)* movement; *(▸ d'un vers)* flow, movement; *(▸ d'une robe)* drape; *(▸ de draperies, d'un cou, de reins)* line, lines; *(▸ d'un paysage)* undulations

9 *Mus (rythme)* tempo; *(section d'un morceau)* movement; **m. perpétuel** moto perpetuo, perpetuum mobile; **presser/ralentir le m.** to quicken/to slow the tempo

10 *(mécanisme)* movement

• **en mouvement** **ADJ** *(athlète)* moving, in motion; *(population, troupes)* on the move; **cet enfant est toujours en m.!** that child never stops *or* is always on the go!; **c'est une ville toujours en m.** it's a bustling *or* very lively city; **pièces en m.** *(de machine)* moving parts **ADV** **mettre un mécanisme en m.** to set a mechanism going *or* in motion; **le balancier se mit en m.** the pendulum started moving; **le cortège se mit en m.** the procession started *or* set off

• **sans mouvement** **ADJ** *(personne)* inert

mouvementé, -e [muvmɑ̃te] **ADJ 1** *(débat)* (very) lively, heated, stormy; *(voyage, vie, journée)* eventful; *(match)* (very) lively, eventful **2** *(paysage)* rolling, undulating

mouvoir [54] [muvwar] **VT** *Littéraire* **1** *(bouger ▸ membre, objet)* to move; **mécanisme mû par un ressort** spring-operated mechanism **2** *(activer ▸ machine)* to drive, to power; **mû par l'électricité** electrically driven, electrically powered; **mû par la vapeur** steam-driven **3** *Fig (pousser)* to move, to prompt; **mû par l'intérêt/le désir/la jalousie** prompted by self-interest/desire/jealousy; **mû par la sympathie** moved by sympathy

VPR se mouvoir *(se déplacer)* to move

MOYEN[1] [mwajɛ̃] **NM 1** *(méthode)* way, means; **il n'y a qu'un (seul) m. de s'échapper** there is only one way to escape; **il n'y a pas d'autre m.** there's no other way *or* solution; **il y a toujours un m. de se faire de l'argent** there are always ways of getting money; **par quel m. peut-on le contacter?** how can he be contacted?; **il y a m. de la contacter par l'intermédiaire de ses parents** she can be contacted through her parents; **j'emploierai tous les moyens** I'll use whatever means *or* do whatever I have to; **nous avons les moyens de vous faire parler!** we have ways of making you talk!; **je l'aurais empêché, si j'en avais eu les moyens** I would have stopped him, if I'd been able to; **trouver un m. de faire qch** to find a way *or* a means of doing sth; **trouver le m. de faire qch** to discover *or* to find out how to do sth; **il a encore trouvé le m. de se faire dispenser** he's managed to get out of it again; *Ironique* **elle a trouvé le m. de se mettre mal avec tous ses collègues** she's managed to get *or* she's succeeded in getting on bad terms with all her colleagues; **et en plus, tu trouves le m. d'être en retard!** not only that, but you've managed to be late as well!; **trouver m. de faire qch** to manage to do sth; **le chien a encore trouvé m. de s'échapper** the dog's managed to escape again; **m. de défense/d'existence** means of defence/existence; **m. de locomotion** *ou* **de transport** means of *Br* transport *or Am* transportation; **m. d'action** means of action; **m. d'expression** means of expression; **m. de production** means of production; **m. de subsistance** means of subsistence; **employer** *ou* **utiliser les grands moyens** to take drastic steps; **tous les moyens lui sont bons** he'll/she'll stop at nothing

2 *(pour intensifier)* **il n'y a pas m.** it can't be done, it's impossible; **il n'y a pas m. d'ouvrir la porte!** there's no way of opening the door!, the door won't open!; *Fam* **pas m. de dormir ici!** it's impossible to get any sleep around here!; **il n'y a pas m. de le faire obéir!** he just won't do what *or* as he's told!; **j'ai tout fait pour le convaincre, mais il n'y a pas eu m.** I did everything I could to convince him, but it was impossible *or* but I couldn't budge him; *Fam* **je voulais me reposer, mais non, pas m.!** I wanted to get some rest, but no such luck!; **est-ce qu'il y a m. d'avoir le silence?** can we please have some silence around here?; **y a-t-il m. d'éviter le centre-ville?** is there any way of avoiding the centre of town?; **y aurait-il m. d'avoir un vol moins cher/d'avoir un peu de pain avec mon fromage?** is there any chance of a cheaper flight/a bit of bread with my cheese?

3 *Gram* **adverbe de m.** adverb of means

4 *Can* **avoir le m., être en m.** to be very well-off

• **moyens** **NMPL 1** *(financiers)* means; **je n'ai pas les moyens de m'acheter un ordinateur** I haven't got the means to *or* I can't afford to buy a computer; **je n'en ai pas les moyens** I can't afford it; **ils ont les moyens** they're well-off, they can afford it; **c'est facile d'être généreux quand on a les moyens!** it's easy to be generous when you're well-off *or* when you can afford to be!; **j'ai de tout petits moyens** I have a very small income; **avoir de gros moyens** to be very well-off; **je peux te payer une bière, c'est encore dans mes moyens** I can buy you a beer, I can just about manage that; **c'est au-dessus de mes moyens** it's beyond my means, I can't afford it; **vivre au-dessus de ses moyens** to live beyond one's means; **dans la mesure de mes moyens** to the best *or* to the utmost of my ability, as best I can; **moyens de paiement** means of payment

2 *(intellectuels, physiques)* **perdre (tous) ses moyens** to go to pieces; **une fois sur scène, j'ai perdu tous mes moyens** once on the stage, I just went blank *or* to pieces; **faire perdre tous ses moyens à qn** to make sb lose his/her head; **faire qch par ses propres moyens** to do sth on one's own *or* unaided; **je suis venu par mes propres moyens** I made my own way here

3 *(pratiques)* **moyens de production** means of production; **moyens de communication** means of communication; **avec les moyens du bord** with the means at one's disposal; **nous avons fait avec les moyens du bord** we made do with what we had; **il faudra faire avec les moyens du bord** we'll have to manage with what we've got; **si tu veux réussir, il faut t'en donner les moyens** if you want to succeed, you have to equip yourself to do so

• **au moyen de** **PRÉP** by means of, with; **il a calé la table au m. d'un ticket de métro** he wedged the table with a metro ticket

• **par tous les moyens** **ADV** by all possible means; *(même immoraux)* by fair means or foul; **j'ai essayé par tous les moyens** I've tried everything

moyen[2], -enne[1] [mwajɛ̃, -ɛn] **ADJ 1** *(assez grand, intermédiaire)* medium; **de dimensions moyennes** medium-sized; **être de taille moyenne** *(chose)* to be medium-sized; *(personne)* to be of average height; **les tailles/pointures moyennes** the medium (clothes) sizes/shoe sizes; **cadres moyens** middle-ranking executives; **classes moyennes** middle classes; **m. terme** *Phil* middle term; *(solution)* compromise, middle course; **trouver un m. terme** to find a happy medium; **moyenne saison** *(en tourisme)* shoulder period; **à moyenne échéance** in the medium term

2 *(résultant d'un calcul ▸ prix, consommation, distance)* average; *(▸ température)* average, mean

3 *(médiocre ▸ aptitudes, niveau, service)* average; *(▸ qualité)* average, medium; **ses notes sont trop moyennes** his/her marks are too poor; **il est m. en maths** he's average at maths; **la nourriture était moyenne** the food was average; *Péj* **vin d'une qualité très moyenne** very average wine, wine of a very indifferent quality

4 *(ordinaire)* **le spectateur/lecteur m.** the average spectator/reader; **le Français m.** the average Frenchman

5 *Mus* **voix moyenne** middle voice

6 *Géog* **le cours m. du Rhône** the middle course of the Rhône

Moyen Âge [mwajɛnɑʒ] **NM** **le M.** the Middle Ages

moyenâgeux, -euse [mwajɛnɑʒø, -øz] **ADJ** medieval; *Hum* **ils utilisent des techniques moyenâgeuses** they use methods out of the Dark Ages

moyen-courrier [mwajɛ̃kurje] *(pl* **moyen-courriers)** **NM** medium-haul aeroplane

moyen-métrage *(pl* **moyens-métrages)**, **moyen métrage** [mwajɛ̃metraʒ] **NM** medium-length movie *or Br* film

moyennant [mwajɛnɑ̃] **PRÉP** (in return) for; **elle garde ma fille m. 20 euros** she looks after my daughter for 20 euros; **m. finance** for a fee *or* a consideration; **faire qch m. finance** to do sth in return for payment *or* for a consideration; **m. paiement** in exchange for payment, subject to payment; **m. quoi** in return for which; **je l'ai aidé à faire son devoir d'anglais, m. quoi il...** I helped him with his English homework, and in return he...

moyenne[2] [mwajɛn] **ADJ F** *voir* **moyen[2]**

NF 1 *(gén)* average; **la m. des précipitations/températures** the average rainfall/temperature; **la m. d'âge des candidats est de 21 ans** the average age of the applicants is 21; **calculer** *ou* **faire la m. de** to work out the average of; **supérieure/inférieure à la m.** above/below average, higher/lower than average; *Compta* **m. mobile** moving average; *Compta* **m. pondérée** weighted average

2 *Math* mean, average

3 *(vitesse moyenne)* **m. (horaire)** (hourly) average; *Aut* average (speed); **faire une m. de 90 km/h** to average 90 km/h

4 *Scol (absolue)* *Br* pass mark, *Am* passing grade *(of 50 percent)*; *(relative)* average (*Br* mark *or* *Am* grade); **notes au-dessus/au-dessous de la m.** *Br* marks *or* *Am* grades above/under half; **j'ai eu tout juste la m.** *(à un examen)* I just got a pass; **la m. de la classe est (de) 8 sur 20** the average *Br* mark *or* *Am* grade for the class is 8 out of 20; **j'ai 8/20 de m. en mathématiques** ≃ I averaged 40 percent in maths; **j'ai 13 de m. générale** my average (mark) is 13 out of 20

5 *(ensemble)* **la m. des gens** most people, the vast majority of people; **d'une intelligence au-dessus de la m.** of above-average intelligence

• **en moyenne** ADV on average; **je m'entraîne en m. quatre heures par jour** I train for an average of four hours a day; **c'est ce que la voiture consomme en m.** that's what the car consumes on average, that's what the car's average consumption is

moyennement [mwajɛnmɑ̃] ADV moderately, fairly; *Ironique* **c'est m. drôle** it's not that funny; *Ironique* **il a m. apprécié** he didn't find it very funny; *Ironique* **j'ai m. aimé ce qu'elle a dit** I didn't think much of what she said

Moyen-Orient [mwajɛnɔrjɑ̃] NM **le M.** the Middle East; **au M.** in the Middle East

moyen-oriental, -e [mwajɛnɔrjɑ̃tal] (*mpl* **moyen-orientaux** [-o], *fpl* **moyen-orientales**) ADJ Middle Eastern

moyette [mwajɛt] NF *Agr* shock

moyeu, -x [mwajø] NM **1** *(d'une roue ▸ de voiture)* (wheel) hub; *(▸ de charrue)* nave **2** *(d'une hélice)* boss, hub

mozambicain, -e [mɔzɑ̃bikɛ̃, -ɛn] ADJ Mozambican

• **Mozambicain, -e** NM,F Mozambican

Mozambique [mɔzɑ̃bik] NM *Géog* **le M.** Mozambique

mozzarella [mɔdzarela], **mozzarelle** [mɔdzarɛl] NF mozzarella

MRAM [ɛmram] NF *Ordinat* (*abrév* **magnetic random access memory**) MRAM

MRAP [mrap] NM (*abrév* **Mouvement contre le racisme, l'antisémitisme et pour la paix**) = pacifist anti-racist organization

MS-DOS [ɛmɛsdɔs] NM *Ordinat* (*abrév* **Microsoft Disk Operating System**) MS-DOS

MST[1] [ɛmɛste] NF (*abrév* **maladie sexuellement transmissible**) STD

MST[2] [ɛmɛste] NF *Univ* (*abrév* **maîtrise de sciences et techniques**) = master's degree in science and technology; **M. hôtellerie-restauration** = higher vocational qualification in hotel management and catering

mû, -ue[1] [my] PP *voir* **mouvoir**

muance [mɥɑ̃s] NF *Vieilli (à la puberté)* breaking of the voice

mucilage [mysilaʒ] NM mucilage

mucilagineux, -euse [mysilaʒinø, -øz] ADJ mucilaginous

mucoïde [mykɔid] NM *Chim* mucoid

mucosité [mykozite] NF mucus

mucoviscidose [mykovisidoz] NF *Méd* cystic fibrosis

mucus [mykys] NM mucus

mue[2] [my] PP *voir* **mouvoir**

NF **1** *Zool (transformation ▸ d'un reptile)* sloughing; *(▸ d'un volatile, d'un crustacé)* moulting; *(▸ d'un mammifère à poils)* shedding hair, moulting; *(▸ d'un mammifère sans poils)* shedding *or* casting (of skin); *(▸ d'un cerf)* shedding (of antlers)

2 *Physiol (de la voix)* breaking, changing

3 *(dépouille ▸ d'un reptile)* slough; *(▸ d'un volatile)* moulted feathers; *(▸ d'un crustacé)* discarded shell; *(▸ d'un mammifère à poils)* shed hair; *(▸ d'un mammifère sans poils)* shed skin; *(▸ d'un cerf)* shed antlers

4 *(époque)* moulting season

5 *Fig (métamorphose)* change, transformation

6 *(cage ▸ pour volaille)* (hen) coop; *(pour faucons)* mew

muer [7] [mɥe] VI **1** *Zool (reptile)* to slough, to moult; *(volatile, crustacé)* to moult; *(mammifère à poils)* to shed hair, to moult; *(mammifère sans poils)* to shed skin, to moult; *(cerf)* to shed (its antlers) **2** *Physiol (voix)* to break, to change; **il mue** his voice is breaking

VPR **se muer** *Littéraire* **se m. en** to change *or* to turn into

muesli [mɥesli] NM muesli

muet, -ette [mɥe, -ɛt] ADJ **1** *(qui ne parle pas)* dumb; **m. de naissance** dumb from birth

2 *Fig (silencieux)* silent, mute, dumb; **le ministre préfère rester m. à ce sujet** the Minister prefers to remain silent on this matter; **m. d'admiration** in mute admiration; **m. de stupeur** dumbfounded; **j'écoutais, m. d'étonnement** I listened, speechless with astonishment, I listened in mute astonishment; **m. de colère** speechless with anger; **elle est restée muette comme une carpe toute la soirée** she never opened her mouth all evening; **je serai m. comme une tombe** my lips are sealed, I won't breathe a word

3 *(non exprimé ▸ douleur, reproche)* unspoken, mute, silent; **les grandes douleurs sont muettes** great sorrow is often silent

4 *Cin (film, cinéma)* silent; *(rôle, acteur)* nonspeaking, walk-on

5 *Ling* mute, silent

6 *(sans indication ▸ touche, carte)* blank; **piano m.** dumb piano, dummy keyboard

NM,F *(personne)* mute, dumb person

NM *Cin* **le m.** the silent *Br* cinema *or* *Am* movies

muezzin [mɥedzin] NM *Rel* muezzin

mufle [myfl] NM **1** *Zool (d'un ruminant)* muffle; *(d'un félin)* muzzle **2** *Fam Péj (malotru)* boor, lout

muflée [myfle] NF *Fam* **prendre une m.** to get wasted *or* *Br* legless; **il tenait une sacrée m.** he was totally wasted *or* *Br* legless

muflerie [myflәri] NF *Fam* **1** *(caractère)* boorishness, loutishness, churlishness **2** *(action)* boorish behaviour; **lassée de ses mufleries** tired of his boorish behaviour *or* boorishness **3** *(parole)* boorish remark

muflier [myflije] NM *Bot* snapdragon, antirrhinum

mufti [myfti] NM mufti

mug [mœg] NF *(grande tasse)* mug

muge [myʒ] NM *Ich* grey mullet

mugir [32] [myʒir] VI **1** *(vache)* to moo, to low; *(taureau)* to bellow **2** *Littéraire (vent)* to howl, to roar; *(océan)* to roar, to thunder; *(torrent)* to roar; *(sirène)* to wail

mugissement [myʒismɑ̃] NM **1** *(d'une vache)* mooing, lowing; *(d'un taureau)* bellowing **2** *Littéraire (du vent)* howling, roaring; *(des flots)* roar, thundering; *(d'un torrent)* roaring; *(d'une sirène)* wailing

muguet [myge] NM **1** *Bot* lily of the valley **2** *Méd* thrush, *Spéc* candidiasis

> **MUGUET**
>
> On May Day in France, bunches of lily of the valley are sold in the streets and given as presents. The flowers are supposed to bring good luck.

mulâtre, -esse [mylɑtr, mylɑtrɛs] NM,F mulatto

• **mulâtre** ADJ INV mulatto

mule[1] [myl] NF **1** *Zool* mule *(female)* **2** *Fam (personne entêtée)* mule **3** *Fam Arg drogue (passeur de drogue)* mule

mule[2] [myl] NF *(chausson)* mule; **la m. du pape** the Pope's slipper; **baiser la m. du pape** to kiss the Pope's toe

mulet[1] [mylɛ] NM **1** *Zool* mule *(male)* **2** *Fam (voiture)* back-up car[□]

mulet[2] [mylɛ] NM *Ich* mullet

muletier, -ère [myltje, -ɛr] ADJ **chemin** *ou* **sentier m.** (mule) track

NM,F muleteer, mule driver

mulot [mylo] NM field mouse

multiangle [myltiɑ̃gl] ADJ *Cin (plan, scène)* multiangle

multicantonal, -e, -aux, -ales [myltikɑ̃tɔnal, -o] ADJ *Suisse* involving many cantons

multicarte [myltikart] ADJ *(voyageur de commerce)* = representing several companies

multicellulaire [myltiselylɛr] ADJ multicellular

multicéréale [myltisereal] ADJ multigrain

multicolore [myltikɔlɔr] ADJ multicoloured, many-coloured

multicoque [myltikɔk] ADJ **bateau m.** multihull *or* multihulled boat

NM multihull

multicritère [myltikritɛr] ADJ *Ordinat* **recherche m.** multisearch

multiculturalisme [myltikyltyralism] NM multiculturalism

multiculturel, -elle [myltikyltyrɛl] ADJ multicultural

multidevise [myltidәviz] ADJ *Fin* multicurrency

multidimensionnel, -elle [myltidimɑ̃sjɔnɛl] ADJ multidimensional; *Fig (expérience, compétence)* multifaceted

multidisciplinaire [myltidisiplinɛr] ADJ multidisciplinary

multi-écran [myltiekrɑ̃] (*pl* **multi-écrans**) NM *TV* multiscreen, split screen

multiemploi [myltiɑ̃plwa] NM = holding several jobs at the same time

multiflore [myltiflɔr] ADJ *Bot* multiflora

multifonction, multifonctions [myltifɔ̃ksjɔ̃] ADJ multifunction *(avant n)*, multifunctional

multiforme [myltifɔrm] ADJ *(aspect, créature)* multiform; *Fig (question, personnalité)* many-sided, multifaceted

multigrade [myltigrad] ADJ multigrade *(avant n)*

multijoueur [myltiʒwœr] ADJ multiplayer

multilatéral, -e, -aux, -ales [myltilateral, -o] ADJ multilateral

multilatéralisme [myltilateralism] NM multilateralism

multimarque [myltimark] NF multibrand

multimédia [myltimedja] ADJ multimedia *(avant n)*

NM **le m.** multimedia

multimilliardaire [myltimiljardɛr] ADJ multimillionaire *(avant n)*

NMF multimillionaire

multinational, -e, -aux, -ales [myltinasjɔnal, -o] ADJ multinational

• **multinationale** NF multinational, multinational company

multinorme [myltinɔrm] ADJ multistandard, multisystem

multipare [myltipar] ADJ multiparous

NF multipara

multipartisme [myltipartism] NM multiparty system

multipartite [myltipartit] ADJ multiparty *(avant n)*, multipartite

multiplateforme [myltiplatfɔrm] ADJ *Ordinat* cross-platform *(avant n)*

multiple [myltipl] ADJ **1** *(nombreux ▸ exemples, incidents, qualités)* many, numerous; *(▸ fractures)* multiple; **à usages multiples** multipurpose; **à de multiples reprises** repeatedly, time and (time) again; *Ordinat* **à accès m.** multi-access

2 *(divers ▸ raisons, intérêts)* many, multiple, *Sout* manifold; **personnalité aux multiples facettes** many-sided *or* multifaceted personality; **femme aux talents multiples** multitalented woman; **les causes sont multiples** the reasons are many *or* *Sout* manifold

3 *(complexe ▸ problème, difficulté)* many-sided, multifaceted, complex

4 *Math* **9 est m. de 3** 9 is a multiple of 3

NM *Math* multiple; **prenez un m. de 3** choose any multiple of 3; **le plus petit commun m.** the lowest common multiple

multiplex [myltiplɛks] *Rad, Tél & TV* ADJ multiplex *(avant n)*

NM multiplex; **une émission en m.** a multiplex programme

multiplexage [myltiplɛksaʒ] NM *Rad, Tél & TV* multiplexing

multiplexe [myltiplɛks] NM multiplex (cinema)

multiplexer [3] [myltiplɛkse] VT to multiplex

multiplexeur [myltiplɛksœr] NM multiplexer

multipliable [myltiplijabl] ADJ multipliable, multiplicable

multiplicande [myltiplikɑ̃d] NM multiplicand

multiplicateur, -trice [myltiplikatœr, -tris] ADJ multiplying *(avant n)*

NM *Math* multiplier

multiplicatif, -ive [myltiplikatif, -iv] ADJ multiplicative

multiplication [myltiplikasjɔ̃] NF 1 *Biol, Math & Nucl* multiplication; **m. asexuée** monogenesis; *Fig* **la m. des accidents** the increase in the number of accidents 2 *Rel* **la m. des pains** the miracle of the loaves and fishes 3 *Tech* gear ratio; **grande/petite m.** high/low gear; **m. du levier** leverage

multiplicative [myltiplikativ] *voir* **multiplicatif**

multiplicatrice [myltiplikatris] *voir* **multiplicateur**

multiplicité [myltiplisite] NF multiplicity; **la m. des choix qui nous sont offerts** the (very) many choices open to us

multiplier [10] [myltiplije] VT 1 *(contrôles, expériences, efforts)* to multiply, to increase; **m. les erreurs** to make mistake after mistake; **nous avons multiplié les avertissements** we have issued repeated warnings; **le chef de l'État a multiplié les appels au calme** the Head of State has called repeatedly for calm 2 *Math* to multiply (**par** by); **2 multiplié par 3** 2 multiplied by 3; *Fig* **la production a été multipliée par trois** output has tripled 3 *Tech* **m. la vitesse de révolution** to gear up

VPR **se multiplier** 1 *(attentats, menaces)* to multiply, to increase; **les crimes se multiplient** crime is on the increase 2 *Biol (se reproduire)* to multiply 3 *Fig* to be everywhere (at once); **je ne peux pas me m.** I can't be everywhere at once

multipolaire [myltipɔlɛr] ADJ multipolar

multipostage [myltipɔstaʒ] NM volume mailing

multiposte [myltipɔst] ADJ multiple-station *(avant n)*

NM multiple-station computer

multiprocesseur [myltiprɔsesœr] ADJ M multiprocessing *(avant n)*

NM multiprocessor, multiprocessor system

multiprogrammation [myltiprɔgramasjɔ̃] NF *Ordinat* multiprogramming, multiple programming

multipropriété [myltiprɔprijete] NF timeshare, time-sharing; **investir dans la m.** to invest in a time-share; **acheter une maison en m.** to buy a time-share (house)

multiracial, -e, -aux, -ales [myltirasjal, -o] ADJ multiracial

multirécidiviste [myltiresidivist] *Jur* ADJ reoffending

NMF persistent *or* habitual offender

multirisque [myltirisk] ADJ *Assur* multiple risk *(avant n)*; **assurance m.** comprehensive insurance

multisalle, multisalles [myltisal] ADJ INV **complexe m.** *Br* multiplex (cinema), *Am* movie theater complex

NM INV *Br* multiplex (cinema), *Am* movie theater complex

multisoupapes [myltisupap] ADJ multivalve

multistandard [myltistɑ̃dar] ADJ multistandard, multisystem

multitâche [myltitɑʃ] ADJ *Ordinat* multitasking, multitask *(avant n)*

multithérapie [myltiterapi] NF *Méd* combination therapy, multitherapy

multitraitement [myltitrɛtmɑ̃] NM *Ordinat* multiprocessing

multitude [myltityd] NF 1 *(grande quantité)* **une m. de** a multitude of, a vast number of; **une m. de gens** hosts *or* crowds *or* swarms of people; **il y avait sur la cheminée une m. de bibelots** the mantelpiece was crowded with ornaments 2 *Littéraire (foule)* **la m.** the multitude, the masses

multiutilisateurs [myltiytilizatœr] ADJ INV *Ordinat* multiuser *(avant n)*

Mumbai [mumbai] NM *Géog* Mumbai, *Anciennement* Bombay

munichois, -e [mynikwa, -az] ADJ of/from Munich

• **Munichois, -e** NM,F 1 *(personne)* = inhabitant of or person from Munich 2 *Hist* **les M.** the men of Munich

municipal, -e, -aux, -ales [mynisipal, -o] ADJ *(élection, conseil)* local, municipal; *(bibliothèque, parc, théâtre)* public, municipal

• **municipales** NFPL *Pol* local *or Br* council elections

> **MUNICIPALES**
>
> These are the elections where residents choose the town councils. Electors vote for a list of council members whose leader or "**tête de liste**" will become the mayor, a ceremonial and political post.

municipalisation [mynisipalizasjɔ̃] NF municipalization

municipaliser [3] [mynisipalize] VT to municipalize

municipalité [mynisipalite] NF 1 *(communauté)* town, municipality 2 *(représentants)* ≃ (town) council

munificence [mynifisɑ̃s] NF *Littéraire* munificence

munificent, -e [mynifisɑ̃, -ɑ̃t] ADJ *Littéraire* munificent

munir [32] [mynir] VT **m. qn de** to provide *or* to supply sb with; **les visiteurs furent munis de casques** the visitors were provided with *or* given helmets; **munissez les enfants de vêtements de pluie** kit out the children in rainproof clothing; **munie d'un plan de la ville, elle se mit en route** equipped *or* armed with a map of the town, she set off; **muni de ces quelques conseils** armed with this advice; **muni des sacrements de l'Église** fortified with the rites of the Church; **m. qch de** to equip *or* to fit sth with; **la voiture est munie de phares réglementaires** the car is equipped *or* fitted with regulation headlights

VPR **se munir se m. de qch** to take sth; **se m. de vêtements chauds/d'un parapluie** to equip oneself with warm clothes/with an umbrella; **munissez-vous de votre passeport** carry your passport *or* take your passport with you

munitions [mynisjɔ̃] NFPL ammunition *(UNCOUNT)*, munitions

munster [mœ̃stɛr] NM Munster (cheese)

muon [myɔ̃] NM *Phys* muon

muphti [myfti] = **mufti**

muqueux, -euse [mykø, -øz] ADJ mucous

• **muqueuse** NF mucous membrane

mur [myr] NM 1 *(construction)* wall; **il a passé la journée entière entre quatre murs** he spent the whole day shut up inside; **j'en ai marre de rester entre quatre murs toute la journée** I'm tired of being cooped up all day; **les cambrioleurs n'ont laissé que les (quatre) murs** the burglars took everything but the kitchen sink, the burglars stripped the place bare; **je serai dans mes murs la semaine prochaine** I'll have moved in by next week; **c'est comme si tu parlais à un m.** it's (just) like talking to a brick wall; **se heurter à un m.** to come up against a brick wall; *Fam* **faire le m.** *(soldat, interne)* to go *or* to jump over the wall; **les murs ont des oreilles** walls have ears; **gros murs** main walls; **m. d'appui** parapet; **m. aveugle** blank *or* windowless wall; **le m. de Berlin** the Berlin Wall; **m. de clôture** enclosing wall; *Ordinat* **m. coupe-feu** firewall; **m. d'enceinte** outer *or* surrounding wall; **le m. des Fédérés** = wall in the Père-Lachaise cemetery in front of which the last remaining defendants of the Paris Commune were executed in 1871; **le m. des Lamentations** the Wailing Wall; **m. mitoyen** party wall; **m. portant** *ou* **porteur** load-bearing wall; **m. de séparation** dividing wall; **m. de soutènement** retaining *or* breast wall

2 *(escarpement)* steep slope; **m. artificiel** rock-climbing *or* artificial wall; **m. d'escalade** climbing wall

3 *Fig (de flammes, de brouillard, de pluie)* wall, sheet; *(de silence)* wall; *(de haine, d'incompréhension)* wall, barrier

4 *Aviat* **m. sonique** *ou* **du son** sound barrier; **passer** *ou* **franchir le m. du son** to break the sound barrier

5 *Ftbl* wall

• **murs** NMPL 1 *(remparts)* (city) walls; **l'ennemi est dans nos murs** the enemy is within the gates 2 **les murs** *(d'un commerce)* the building; **il est à présent dans nos murs** *(en visite ▸ dans notre ville)* he is in town at the moment; (▸ *dans nos locaux)* he is on the premises at the moment

• **mur à mur** ADJ *Can Joual* **tapis m. à m.** wall-to-wall carpeting[◻], *Br* (fitted) carpet[◻]; *Can Fam* **la salle était pleine m. à m.** the room was jam-packed; *Can Fam* **il est fédéraliste m. à m.** he's an out-and-out federalist *or* a federalist through and through

mûr, -e[1] [myr] ADJ 1 *(fruit, graine, abcès)* ripe; **trop m.** overripe, too ripe; **pas m.** unripe, not ripe 2 *(personne)* mature; **elle est très mûre pour son âge** she is very mature for her age; **pas m.** immature

3 *(prêt ▸ révolte, plan)* ripe, ready; **après mûre réflexion** after careful thought *or* consideration

4 *très Fam (saoul)* smashed

murage [myraʒ] NM *(de porte, fenêtre)* walling up, blocking up

muraille [myrɑj] NF 1 *(d'une ville, d'un château, de rocs)* wall; **la Grande M. (de Chine)** the Great Wall of China 2 *Naut (de la coque)* side, dead work

mural, -e, -aux, -ales [myral, -o] ADJ wall *(avant n)*; **carte/pendule murale** wall map/clock; *Archit* **console murale** wall bracket; **peinture murale** mural

• **mural, -als** NM *(peinture)* mural

• **mural, -aux** NM *Com* wall (display) unit

mûre[2] [myr] ADJ F *voir* **mûr**

NF *(fruit)* mulberry; **m. sauvage** blackberry, bramble

mûrement [myrmɑ̃] ADV **un projet m. réfléchi** a carefully thought-out plan; **après avoir m. réfléchi** after careful thought *or* consideration

murène [myrɛn] NF *Ich* moray (eel)

murer [3] [myre] VT 1 *(entourer de murs)* to wall in 2 *(boucher ▸ porte, fenêtre)* to wall up, to block up; **m. une fenêtre avec des briques** to brick up a window 3 *(enfermer ▸ personne, chat)* to wall in *or* up

VPR **se murer** to shut oneself away; *Fig* **se m. dans le silence** to retreat *or* to withdraw into silence, to build a wall of silence around oneself

muret[1] [myrɛ] NM low (dry-stone) wall

muret[2] [myrɛ] NM *Belg Bot* wallflower, gillyflower

murge [myrʒ] NF *Fam* **prendre une m.** to get wasted *or Br* legless; **il tenait une sacrée m.** he was totally wasted *or Br* legless

murger [17] [myrʒe] **se murger** VPR *Fam (s'enivrer)* to get wasted *or Br* legless

mûrier [myrje] NM mulberry tree *or* bush; **m. blanc** white mulberry; **m. sauvage** bramble (bush), blackberry bush

mûrir [32] [myrir] VI 1 *Bot* to ripen; **faire m.** to ripen

2 *(en œnologie)* to mature, to mellow

3 *(abcès)* to come to a head

4 *Fig (évoluer ▸ pensée, projet)* to mature, to ripen, to develop; (▸ *personne)* to mature; **elle a beaucoup mûri** she has greatly matured, she has become much more mature

VT 1 *(fruit)* to ripen 2 *Fig (pensée, projet, sentiment)* to nurture, to nurse; **une année à l'étranger l'a mûri** a year abroad has made him more mature; **laisser m. une idée** to give an idea time to gestate

mûrissant, -e [myrisɑ̃, -ɑ̃t] ADJ 1 *Bot* ripening 2 *(personne)* of mature years

mûrissement [myrismɑ̃] NM 1 *Bot* ripening 2 *Fig (d'une pensée, d'un plan)* maturing, development

murmure [myrmyr] NM 1 *(d'une personne)* murmur; *Littéraire (d'une source, de la brise)* murmur, murmuring; *(d'un ruisseau)* babbling 2 *(commentaire)* **un m. de protestation/d'admiration** a murmur of protest/of admiration

• **murmures** NMPL *(plaintes)* murmurs, murmurings

murmurer [3] [myrmyre] VI 1 *(parler à voix basse)* to murmur 2 *Littéraire (source, brise)* to murmur; *(ruisseau)* to babble 3 *(se plaindre)* **m. entre ses dents** to mutter

VT *(dire à voix basse)* to murmur; **m. des mots tendres à l'oreille de qn** to whisper sweet nothings in sb's ear; **on murmure qu'il va démissionner** rumour has it *or* there are rumours that he's going to resign

mûron [myrɔ̃] NM *Bot* wild raspberry

mus *voir* **mouvoir**

musaraigne [myzarɛɲ] NF *Zool* shrew

musard, -e [myzar, -ard] *Vieilli* ADJ dawdling

NM,F dawdler

musarder [3] [myzarde] VI *(flâner)* to wander around; *(ne rien faire)* to lounge around

musc [mysk] NM musk

muscade [myskad] NF **1** *Bot & Culin* nutmeg; **fleur de m.** mace **2** *(d'escamoteur)* vanishing ball **3** *(locution)* **passez m.!** hey presto!

muscadier [myskadje] NM nutmeg tree

muscadin [myskadɛ̃] NM *Hist* muscadin; *Arch (dandy)* dandy, fop

muscardin [myskardɛ̃] NM dormouse

muscat [myska] ADJ muscat *(avant n)*; **raisin m.** muscat grape, muscatel grape; **vin m.** muscatel (wine)

NM *(fruit)* muscat grape; *(vin)* muscat, muscatel (wine)

muscle [myskl] NM muscle; *Fam* **avoir des muscles** *ou* **du m.** to be muscular; **prendre du m.** to develop one's muscles; *Fam* **être tout en m.** to be all muscle; **m. cardiaque** cardiac *or* heart muscle

musclé, -e [myskle] ADJ **1** *(corps, personne)* muscular **2** *Fam (énergique)* powerful□, forceful□; **une campagne électorale musclée** a punchy electoral campaign; **mener une politique musclée contre qch** to take a hard line *or* a tough stance on sth; **l'intervention musclée de la police** the strong-arm tactics of the police **3** *(vif ▸ style)* robust, vigorous, powerful; *(▸ discours)* forceful, powerful

muscler [3] [myskle] VT **1** *Sport* **m. ses jambes/épaules** to develop one's leg/shoulder muscles **2** *Fig (renforcer)* to strengthen

VI *Fam* **le sport, ça muscle** sport builds up your muscles□

VPR **se muscler** to develop (one's) muscles; **se m. les bras** to develop one's arm muscles

muscu [mysky] NF *Fam (abrév* **musculation***)* body-building (exercises)□

musculaire [myskylɛr] ADJ muscular, muscle *(avant n)*; **fibre m.** muscle fibre

musculation [myskylasjɔ̃] NF body-building (exercises); **faire de la m.** to do body-building

musculature [myskylatyr] NF musculature, muscles

musculeux, -euse [myskylø, -øz] ADJ *(athlète)* muscular, brawny; *(bras)* muscular

muse [myz] NF *(inspiratrice)* muse; **invoquer sa m.** to invoke *or* to call on one's muse

• **Muse** NF **1** *Myth* Muse; **les (neuf) Muses** the (nine) Muses **2** *Fig Littéraire* **la M., les Muses** the Muse, the Muses; **taquiner la M.** to dabble in poetry, to court the Muse

museau, -x [myzo] NM **1** *Zool (d'un chien, d'un ours)* muzzle; *(d'un porc)* snout; *(d'une souris)* nose **2** *Fam (figure)* face□, mug; **vilain m.** ugly mug **3** *Culin* **m. (de porc)** *Br* brawn, *Am* headcheese; **m. vinaigrette** = brawn in vinaigrette

musée [myze] NM **1** *(d'œuvres d'art) Br* art gallery, *Am* museum; *(des sciences, des techniques)* museum; **le m. de l'homme** the Museum of Mankind; *Hum* **c'est le m. des horreurs!** it's a dump! **2** *(comme adj; avec ou sans trait d'union)* **une ville m.** a historical town

muséifier [9] [myzeifje] VT *Péj (quartier, ville)* to museumify

museler [24] [myzle] VT **1** *(chien)* to muzzle **2** *(presse, opposition)* to muzzle, to gag, to silence

muselière [myzəljɛr] NF muzzle; **mettre une m. à un chien** to muzzle a dog

muselle *etc voir* **museler**

musellement [myzɛlmɑ̃] NM **1** *(d'un chien)* muzzling **2** *(de contestataires, de la presse)* muzzling, gagging, silencing

muséographie [myzeɔgrafi] NF museography

muser [3] [myze] VI **1** *Littéraire (se promener)* to dawdle, to saunter; *(ne rien faire)* to dilly-dally **2** *Belg (fredonner)* to hum

muserolle [myzrɔl] NF *Équitation* noseband

musette [myzɛt] ADJ INV **bal m.** dance (with accordion music); **orchestre m.** band (with accordions); **valse m.** waltz (played on the accordion)

NM (popular) accordion music

NF **1** *Mus (hautbois, gavotte)* musette **2** *(d'un cheval)* nosebag **3** *(d'un enfant)* satchel; *(d'un soldat)* haversack; *(d'un ouvrier)* (canvas) haversack; *(d'un chasseur)* game bag

muséum [myzeɔm] NM **m. (d'histoire naturelle)** natural history museum; **le M. national d'histoire naturelle** = the Paris Natural History Museum, in the Jardin des Plantes

musical, -e, -aux, -ales [myzikal, -o] ADJ *(voix, événement)* musical; **critique m.** music critic

musicalement [myzikalmɑ̃] ADV musically

musicalité [myzikalite] NF musicality

music-hall [myzikol] *(pl* **music-halls***)* NM *(local)* music hall; **le m.** *(activité)* variety, music hall; **numéro de m.** variety act; **faire du m.** to do variety *or Br* music hall *or Am* vaudeville

musicien, -enne [myzisjɛ̃, -ɛn] ADJ musical

NM,F musician

musicographe [myzikɔgraf] NMF musicographer

musicologie [myzikɔlɔʒi] NF musicology

musicologue [myzikɔlɔg] NMF musicologist

musicos [myzikos] NM *Fam* muso

musicothérapie [myzikɔterapi] NF musicotherapy

musique [myzik] NF **1** *(gén)* music; **m. de X** music by X; **je mets de la m.?** shall I put some music on?; **ils dansaient sur une** *ou* **de la m. rock** they were dancing to (the sound of) rock music; **mettre des paroles en m.** to set words to music; **texte mis en m.** text set *or* put to music; **faire de la m.** *(personne)* to play (an instrument); *(objet)* to play a tune; **lire la m.** to read music; **étudier/dîner en m.** to study/to have dinner with music playing; *Can* **faire face à la m.** to face the music; **la grande m.** classical music; **m. d'ambiance** background music; *TV & Cin* **m. d'archives** stock music; **m. de chambre** chamber music; **m. classique** classical music; **m. contemporaine** contemporary music; **une m. de film** a movie *or Br* film theme; **il a composé beaucoup de musiques de film** he has composed a lot of movie *or Br* film scores; **il veut acheter la m. du film** he wants to buy the soundtrack of the movie *or Br* film; *TV & Cin* **m. de fin** playout music; **m. folk** folk music; **m. folklorique** folk music; **m. de fond** background music; *TV & Cin* **m. de générique** title music, theme tune; *TV & Cin* **m. de générique de fin** playout music; **m. légère** light music; **m. militaire** military music; **m. religieuse** church music; **m. sacrée** sacred music; *Fam* **ça va, je connais la m.** I've heard it all before; *Fam* **c'est toujours la même m. avec lui!** it's always the same old story with him!; *Fam* **en avant la m.!** let's get started!; **la m. adoucit les mœurs** music has charms to soothe a savage breast **2** *(musiciens)* band; **ils entrent dans le village, m. en tête** they come into the village, led by the band **3** *Belg, Suisse & Can* **m. à bouche** harmonica, mouth organ

musiquette [myzikɛt] NF **on entendait une m.** we heard a simple little tune

musli [mysli] = **muesli**

musoir [myzwar] NM pier-head, jetty head

musqué, -e [myske] ADJ **1** *(parfum, saveur)* musky **2** *Zool* **bœuf m.** musk ox; **canard m.** Muscovy duck, musk duck; **rat m.** muskrat

must [mœst] NM *Fam* must; **c'est un m.** it's a must; **ce film est un m.** this film is compulsory viewing□ *or* a must

mustang [mystɑ̃g] NM mustang

musulman, -e [myzylmɑ̃, -an] ADJ Muslim

NM,F Muslim

mutabilité [mytabilite] NF mutability

mutable [mytabl] ADJ mutable

mutant, -e [mytɑ̃, -ɑ̃t] ADJ mutant

NM,F mutant

mutation [mytasjɔ̃] NF **1** *(d'une entreprise, d'un marché)* change, transformation; **industrie en pleine m.** industry undergoing major change *or* a radical transformation; **le secteur sidérurgique a subi de profondes mutations** the steel industry has undergone extensive change *or* changes **2** *Admin* transfer; **il a demandé/obtenu sa m. pour raison de santé** he asked for/obtained a transfer for health reasons **3** *Biol* mutation

muter [3] [myte] VT *Admin* to transfer, to move; **il s'est fait m. en province** he's been transferred to the provinces

VI *Biol* to mutate

mutilateur, -trice [mytilatœr, -tris] ADJ mutilative, mutilatory; *Fig (expérience)* crippling

NM,F *Littéraire* mutilator

mutilation [mytilasjɔ̃] NF **1** *(du corps)* mutilation **2** *(d'une œuvre)* mutilation

mutilatrice [mytilatris] *voir* **mutilateur**

mutilé, -e [mytile] NM,F disabled person; **mutilés de guerre** disabled ex-servicemen; **m. du travail** industrially disabled person

mutiler [3] [mytile] VT **1** *(personne, animal)* to mutilate, to maim; **il a eu la main mutilée dans un accident du travail** his hand was badly injured in an industrial accident **2** *(film, poème)* to mutilate; *(statue, bâtiment)* to mutilate, to deface; *(paysage)* to disfigure

VPR **se mutiler** to mutilate oneself

mutin, -e [mytɛ̃, -in] ADJ *Littéraire* **1** *(espiègle ▸ enfant)* impish, mischievous, cheeky; *(▸ air)* mischievous **2** *Arch (désobéissant)* disobedient, unruly, unbiddable

NM rebel, mutineer; *Hist* **les mutins de 1917** = the French soldiers who refused to keep on fighting during World War I, following the disastrous offensive of the "Chemin des Dames", some of whom were executed

mutiné, -e [mytine] ADJ mutinous, rebellious

NM,F mutineer, rebel

mutiner [3] [mytine] **se mutiner** VPR *(marin, soldat)* to mutiny, to rebel, to revolt (**contre** against); *(employés, élèves, prisonniers)* to rebel, to revolt (**contre** against)

mutinerie [mytinri] NF *(de marins, de soldats)* mutiny, revolt, rebellion; *(d'employés, de prisonniers)* rebellion, revolt

mutique [mytik] ADJ mute

mutisme [mytism] NM **1** *(silence)* silence; **s'enfermer dans un m. complet** to retreat into absolute silence **2** *Méd* muteness, dumbness; *Psy* mutism

mutité [mytite] NF *Méd & Psy* mutism

mutualisme [mytɥalism] NM **1** *Zool* mutualism, symbiosis **2** *Écon* mutualism

mutualiste [mytɥalist] ADJ **1** *Biol* symbiotic, mutualistic **2** *Écon* mutualistic; **société** *ou* **groupement m.** mutual benefit insurance company, *Br* ≃ friendly society, *Am* ≃ benefit society; **pharmacie m.** = chemist associated with private insurance company, which may offer reduced rates on certain items to members of the company

NMF mutualist, member of a mutual benefit (insurance) company

mutualité [mytɥalite] NF *(système)* mutual (benefit) insurance company; **la m. française** *(ensemble des sociétés mutualistes)* the French mutual (benefit) insurance system

mutuel, -elle [mytɥɛl] ADJ **1** *(partagé, réciproque)* mutual **2** *(sans but lucratif)* mutual

• **mutuelle** NF mutual (benefit) insurance company, *Br* ≃ friendly society, *Am* ≃ benefit society; **prendre une mutuelle** to take out private insurance

> **MUTUELLE**
>
> A "mutuelle" is a non-profit-making health insurance company which provides insurance complementary to that of the "**Sécurité sociale**". Often these companies are set up for a particular profession: there is a "mutuelle" for students, one for teachers etc.

mutuellement [mytɥɛlmɑ̃] ADV one another, each other

Myanmar [mjanmar] NM *Géog* **le M.** Myanmar

Mycènes [misɛn] NF Mycenae

mycénien, -enne [misenjɛ̃, -ɛn] ADJ Mycenaean, Mycenian

NM *(langue)* Mycenaean, Mycenian

• **Mycénien, -enne** NM,F *Hist* Mycenaean, Mycenian

mycologie [mikɔlɔʒi] NF mycology

mycose [mikoz] NF *(gén)* fungal infection, thrush *(UNCOUNT)*, *Spéc* mycosis *(UNCOUNT)*; *(aux orteils)* athlete's foot

myéline [mjelin] NF *Physiol* myelin

myélite [mjelit] NF *Méd* myelitis

myélome [mjelɔm] NM *Méd* myeloma

mygale [migal] NF *Entom* tarantula, *Spéc* mygale

myocarde [mjɔkard] NM *Anat* myocardium

myocardite [mjɔkardit] NF *Méd* myocarditis

myologie [mjɔlɔʒi] NF *Méd* myology

myome [mjom] NM *Méd* myoma

myopathe [mjɔpat] *Méd* ADJ myopathic
NMF = person with muscular dystrophy

myopathie [mjɔpati] NF *Méd* myopathy; *(dystrophie musculaire)* muscular dystrophy

myope [mjɔp] ADJ *Br* short-sighted, *Am* nearsighted, *Spéc* myopic; *Fam* **m. comme une taupe** (as) blind as a bat
NMF *Br* short-sighted *or Am* nearsighted person, *Spéc* myope

myopie [mjɔpi] NF *Br* short-sightedness, *Am* nearsightedness, *Spéc* myopia

myosotis [mjɔzɔtis] NM *Bot* forget-me-not, *Spéc* myosotis

myriade [mirjad] NF myriad

myrmidon [mirmidɔ̃] NM *Littéraire* pipsqueak

myrrhe [mir] NF myrrh

myrte [mirt] NM *Bot* myrtle

myrtille [mirtij] NF blueberry, *Br* bilberry

mystère [mister] NM **1** *(atmosphère)* mystery; **entouré de m.** shrouded *or* cloaked in mystery; *Fam* **où est-elle? – m. et boule de gomme!** where is she? – I haven't (got) a clue!
2 *(secret)* mystery; **cet homme est un m.** that man's a mystery; **ne fais pas tant de mystères** don't be so mysterious; **si tu avais travaillé, tu aurais réussi l'examen, il n'y a pas de m.!** if you'd worked, you'd have passed your exam, it's as simple as that!; **ça reste un m.** that remains a mystery; **ce n'est un m. pour personne** it's no secret, it's an open secret; **faire un m. de qch** to make a mystery out of sth; **je n'en fais pas (un) m.** I make no mystery *or* secret of it
3 *Rel* mystery
4 *Hist & Théât* mystery (play); **m. de la Passion** Passion play
5 *Culin* **M.** = ice cream filled with meringue and coated with crushed almonds

mystérieuse [misterjøz] *voir* **mystérieux**

mystérieusement [misterjøzmɑ̃] ADV mysteriously

mystérieux, -euse [misterjø, -øz] ADJ **1** *(inexplicable)* mysterious, strange; **un crime m.** a mysterious crime
2 *(surnaturel)* mysterious
3 *(confidentiel)* secret; **ils se sont rencontrés dans un endroit resté m.** they met in a place which has been kept secret
4 *(énigmatique)* mysterious
NM **le m.** the mysterious

mysticisme [mistisism] NM mysticism

mystifiable [mistifjabl] ADJ gullible

mystifiant, -e [mistifjɑ̃, -ɑ̃t] ADJ mystifying, deceiving

mystificateur, -trice [mistifikatœr, -tris] ADJ **une lettre mystificatrice** a hoax letter; **avoir un côté m.** to have a mischievous streak
NM,F hoaxer

mystification [mistifikasjɔ̃] NF **1** *(canular)* hoax, practical joke **2** *(tromperie)* mystification, deception; **m. collective** mass deception **3** *(imposture)* myth

mystificatrice [mistifikatris] *voir* **mystificateur**

mystifier [9] [mistifje] VT **1** *(duper, se jouer de)* to fool, to take in **2** *(leurrer)* to fool, to deceive

> Il faut noter que le verbe anglais **to mystify** est un faux ami. Il signifie **déconcerter, laisser perplexe.**

mystique [mistik] ADJ mystic, mystical
NMF mystic
NF *Rel* **la m.** mysticism; *Fig* **la m. de la démocratie/paix** the mystique of democracy/peace

mystiquement [mistikmɑ̃] ADV mystically

mythe [mit] NM myth; **elle fut un m. vivant** she was a legend in her own lifetime, she was a living legend

mythique [mitik] ADJ mythic, mythical

mytho [mito] *Fam* ADJ **il est complètement m.** you can't believe anything *or* a word he says
NMF compulsive liar

mythologie [mitɔlɔʒi] NF mythology

mythologique [mitɔlɔʒik] ADJ mythological

mythologue [mitɔlɔg] NMF mythologist

mythomane [mitɔman] ADJ mythomaniac; **il est un peu m.** he has a tendency to make things up
NMF compulsive liar; *Psy* mythomaniac

mythomanie [mitɔmani] NF compulsive lying; *Psy* mythomania

mytiliculteur, -trice [mitilikyltœr, -tris] NM,F mussel farmer

mytiliculture [mitilikyltyr] NF mussel farming

myxœdème [miksedem] NM *Méd* myxoedema

myxomatose [miksɔmatoz] NF *Vét* myxomatosis

N¹, n [ɛn] NM INV **1** *(lettre)* N, n **2** *Math* n

N² **1** *(abrév écrite* **newton***)* N **2** *(abrév écrite* **nord***)* N

n' [n] *voir* **ne**

na [na] EXCLAM *Fam* **(et) na!** so there!, and that's that!

naan [nan] NM *Culin* naan (bread)

nabab [nabab] NM **1** *Fam (homme riche)* nabob **2** *Hist* nabob

nabot, -e [nabo, -ɔt] NM,F *Péj* dwarf, midget

Nabuchodonosor [nabykɔdɔnɔzɔr] NPR Nebuchadnezzar

nacelle [nasɛl] NF **1** *(d'un aérostat)* basket, gondola; *(d'un avion)* pod; *(d'un landau ▸ détachable)* carrycot; *(▸ fixe)* carriage; *(pour un ouvrier)* basket **2** *Littéraire (bateau)* (rowing) wherry

nacre [nakr] NF **la n.** mother-of-pearl, *Spéc* nacre; **un collier de** *ou* **en n.** a mother-of-pearl necklace

nacré, -e [nakre] ADJ pearly, *Spéc* nacreous

nacrer [3] [nakre] VT **1** *(bijou)* to give a pearly gloss to **2** *Littéraire* to cast a pearly shimmer over

nadir [nadir] NM nadir

nævus [nevys] *(pl* **nævi** [-vi]*)* NM *Méd* naevus

nage [naʒ] NF **1** *Sport (activité)* swimming; *(style)* stroke; **n. indienne** sidestroke; **n. libre** freestyle; **faire la n. du petit chien** to doggy-paddle; **le 100 mètres quatre nages** the 4 x 100 metres relay **2** *Naut* rowing stroke; **n. à couple** sculling; **banc de n.** thwart

• **à la nage** ADV **s'éloigner à la n.** to swim off *or* away; **traverser un lac à la n.** to swim across a lake

ADJ *Culin* à la nage *(cooked in a court-bouillon)*

• **en nage** ADJ **être en n.** to be dripping with sweat

nageoire [naʒwar] NF **1** *Zool (de poisson)* fin; *(d'otarie, de phoque, de dauphin)* flipper; **n. anale** anal fin; **n. caudale** tail *or* caudal fin; **n. dorsale** dorsal fin; **n. pectorale** pectoral fin; **n. pelvienne** pelvic fin **2** *Aviat (flotteur)* fin

nager [17] [naʒe] VI **1** *Sport* to swim; **n. vers la côte** to swim for the shore; **tu viens n.?** are you coming for a swim?; **il ne sait pas/sait n.** he can't/can swim; **elle nage très bien** she's a very good swimmer; **n. comme un fer à repasser** to swim like a brick; **n. comme un poisson** to swim like a fish; *Fig* **savoir n.** to know one's way around, to know how to take care of oneself

2 *(flotter ▸ objet)* to float

3 *Fig* **la viande nageait dans la sauce** the meat was swimming in gravy; **il nageait dans son sang** he was bathed in (his own) blood; **n. dans l'opulence** to be rolling in money; **n. dans le bonheur** to be blissfully *or* deliriously happy; **on nageait dans le mystère** we were totally bewildered; *Fam* **tu nages dans ce pantalon!** those trousers are miles too big for you!

4 *Fig Littéraire (vapeurs, nuages, effluves)* to drift

5 *Fam (ne rien comprendre)* to be completely lost, not to have a clue; **il nage complètement en physique** he doesn't have a clue in physics

6 *Naut* to row; **n. à couple** to row double-banked; **n. en arrière** *ou* **à culer** to back water; **n. en pointe** to row single-banked; **n. plat** to feather; **nagez partout!** pull away!

VT **n. le crawl** to swim *or* to do the crawl; **n. la brasse** to swim *or* to do (the) breast-stroke; **n. le 200 mètres** to swim (in) the 200 metres

nageur, -euse [naʒœr, -øz] NM,F **1** *(personne)* swimmer; **être bon/mauvais n.** to be a good/bad swimmer, to swim well/badly; **n. de combat** naval frogman **2** *Naut* rower; **n. de l'avant** bowman; **n. de l'arrière** stroke

ADJ *(animal)* swimming *(avant n)*

naguère [nager] ADV *Littéraire (autrefois)* long ago, formerly; *(il y a peu de temps)* not long ago

naïade [najad] NF *Myth* naiad; *Littéraire* nymph

naïf, -ïve [naif, -iv] ADJ **1** *(candide ▸ enfant, remarque)* innocent, naive, ingenuous **2** *(trop crédule)* naive, gullible; **ne sois pas si n., il ne te rendra pas l'argent** don't be so naive, he won't give you your money back **3** *Beaux-Arts* naive, primitive

NM,F gullible *or* naive fool; **vous me prenez pour un n.!** what sort of a fool do you take me for?; **jouer les naïfs/les naïves** to act *or* to play the innocent

NM naive *or* primitive painter

nain, -e [nɛ̃, nɛn] ADJ dwarf *(avant n)*; **caniche n.** toy poodle; **poule naine** bantam

NM,F dwarf

NM **1** *(jeu)* **n. jaune** Pope Joan *(card game)* **2** **n. de jardin** garden gnome

• **naine** NF *Astron* dwarf; **naine blanche/rouge** white/red dwarf

Nairobi [nɛrɔbi] NM Nairobi

nais *etc voir* **naître**

naissain [nesɛ̃] NM *Zool* spat

naissait *etc voir* **naître**

naissance [nesɑ̃s] NF **1** *(d'une personne, d'un animal)* birth; **à ta n.** at your birth, when you were born; **donner n. à** to give birth to; **n. multiple** multiple birth; **contrôle** *ou* **limitation** *ou* **régulation des naissances** birth control **2** *(début ▸ d'un sentiment, d'une idée)* birth; *(▸ d'un mouvement, d'une démocratie, d'une ère)* birth, dawn; **à la n. du jour** at daybreak; **donner n. à qch** to give birth *or* rise to sth; **prendre n.** *(mouvement)* to arise, to originate; *(idée)* to originate, to be born; *(sentiment)* to arise, to be born; *Littéraire* **la n. du printemps** the birth of spring; *Littéraire* **la n. du jour** dawn, daybreak, the break of day **3** *(endroit ▸ de langue, d'ongle)* root; *Archit (de pilier, d'arche)* spring; **la n. d'un fleuve** the source of a river; **la n. du cou** the base of the neck; **à la n. des seins** at the top of one's cleavage; **cicatrice à la n. des cheveux** scar just where the hair begins *or* at the hairline

• **à la naissance** ADV at birth

• **de naissance** ADV **1** *(congénitalement)* congenitally, from birth; **elle est aveugle de n.** she was born blind, she's been blind from birth; *Fam* **il est bête, c'est de n.!** he was born stupid!; **qu'est-ce que tu es paresseuse! – oui, je sais, chez moi, c'est de n.** you're so lazy! – I know, I was born that way *or* I've been like that since the day I was born **2** *(d'extraction)* **italien de n.** Italian by birth; **être de bonne** *ou* **haute n.** to be of noble birth; **d'obscure n.** of humble birth

naissant, -e [nesɑ̃, -ɑ̃t] ADJ **1** *(révolte)* incipient; *(sentiment)* growing, budding; *(beauté)* budding, nascent; *(jour)* dawning; **à l'aube naissante** at break of day; **une barbe naissante** the beginnings of a beard; **ses seins naissants** her budding breasts **2** *Chim* **(à l'état) n.** nascent

naître [92] [nɛtr] VI *(aux être)* **1** *(personne, animal)* to be born; **il naquit/est né en 1880** he was born in 1880; **quand tu es né** when you were born; **je l'ai vu n.** I have known him from birth *or* since he was a baby; **enfant à n.** unborn child; **mon bébé devrait n. en mars** my baby is due in March; **le bébé qui vient de n.** the newborn baby; **une fille lui/leur est née** a girl was born to her/them; **il est né de parents inconnus** he is of unknown parentage; **il est né de** *ou* **d'une mère hongroise** he was born of a Hungarian mother; **né de parents anglais** born of English parents, of English parentage; **enfant né d'un premier mariage** child born of a first marriage; **elle est née musicienne** she's a born musician, she was born a musician; **je ne suis pas né d'hier** *ou* **de la dernière couvée** *ou* **de la dernière pluie** I wasn't born yesterday; **il est né coiffé** *ou* **sous une bonne étoile** he was born under a lucky star; *Hum* **il n'est pas encore né, celui qui me fera manger des escargots!** the man who can make me eat snails hasn't been born yet!

2 **être né pour** *(être destiné à)* to be born *or* destined *or* meant to; **il était né pour aimer/souffrir** he was born to love/to suffer; *Fam* **elle est née pour emmerder le monde** it seems to be her mission in life to get up people's noses

3 *Littéraire* **n. à** *(s'ouvrir à)* to awaken to

4 *(apparaître ▸ sentiment, doute, espoir)* to arise, *Sout* to be born; *(▸ peur)* to rise, to arise; *(▸ problème)* to crop *or* to come up; *(▸ projet, idée)* to originate (**de** in), to arise (**de** out of); *(▸ communauté, entreprise)* to spring up; *(▸ mouvement)* to spring up, to arise; **la légende/l'idée était née** the legend/the idea was born; **une idée naquit dans son esprit** an idea dawned on him/her; **faire n. qch** *(soupçons, sympathie)* to arouse sth; *(doute, espoir)* to give rise to sth; *(sourire)* to raise sth; **n. de** *(provenir de)* to arise *or* to spring from; **cette peur du noir est née du fait qu'enfant il avait été laissé seul** his fear of the dark originates *or* arises from his being left alone as a child; **de là sont nées toutes nos difficultés** that's the cause of all our difficulties; **l'espoir de paix est né de la rencontre des deux présidents** the meeting between the two presidents has given rise to hopes of peace

5 *Littéraire (fleur)* to spring *or* to come up; *(jour)* to break, to dawn

6 *(tournure impersonnelle)* **il naît un enfant toutes les secondes** a child is born every second

naïve [naiv] *voir* **naïf**

naïvement [naivmɑ̃] ADV **1** *(innocemment)* innocently, naively, ingenuously **2** *(avec crédulité)* naively, gullibly

naïveté [naivte] NF **1** *(innocence)* innocence, naivety **2** *(crédulité)* naivety, gullibility; **j'ai eu la n. de lui faire confiance** I was naive enough to trust him/her **3** *(remarque)* naive remark

Namibie [namibi] NF *Géog* **la N.** Namibia

namibien, -enne [namibjɛ̃, -ɛn] ADJ Namibian

• **Namibien, -enne** NM,F Namibian

nana [nana] NF *Fam (femme)* chick, *Br* bird; *(petite amie)* girlfriend ᵅ, *Br* bird

nanar [nanar] NM *Fam* **1** *(film)* lousy film, *Am* turkey **2** *(marchandise sans valeur)* junk, *Am* garbage

nandou [nɑ̃du] NM *Orn* nandu, rhea

nanisme [nanism] NM *(d'une personne)* dwarfism

Nanjing [nɑ̃ʒiŋ], **Nankin** [nɑ̃kɛ̃] NF Nanking, Nanjing

nankin [nɑ̃kɛ̃] NM nankeen

nanoélectronique [nanoelektrik] NF *Électron* nanoelectronics *(singulier)*

nanomètre [nanomɛtr] NM nanometer

nanorobot [nanorɔbo] NM nanobot

nanoseconde [nanosəgɔ̃d] NF nanosecond

nansouk [nɑ̃suk] NM nainsook

nanti, -e [nɑ̃ti] ADJ *(riche)* affluent, well-to-do, well-off

NM,F affluent person; **les nantis** the well-to-do

nantir [32] [nɑ̃tir] VT **1** *(doter)* **n. qn de** to provide sb with; **être bien nanti** to be well off *or* well provided for **2** *Fin & Jur (prêt)* to secure; *(créancier)* to give security to; **n. des valeurs** to deposit shares as security; **entièrement/partiellement nanti** *(créancier)* fully/partly secured

VPR **se nantir se n. de** to equip oneself with

nantissement [nɑ̃tismɑ̃] NM **1** *(objet)* security, pledge **2** *(contrat)* security; **emprunter sur n.** to borrow on security; **déposer des titres en n.** to lodge stock as security; *Bourse* **n. d'actions** lien on shares; *Banque* **n. flottant** *ou* **général** floating charge

napalm [napalm] NM napalm; **bombe au n.** napalm bomb

naphtaline [naftalin] NF *Chim* **(boules de) n.** mothballs; **ça sent la n.** it smells of mothballs; *Fig* it's a bit antiquated; *Can Fig* **sortir qch de la n.** to take sth out of mothballs

naphte [naft] NM *Chim* naphtha, mineral oil; **n. de goudron** coal-tar naphtha

Napoléon [napoleɔ̃] NPR Napoleon; **N. Bonaparte** Napoleon Bonaparte

napoléonien, -enne [napoleonjɛ̃, -ɛn] ADJ Napoleonic

napolitain, -e [napolitɛ̃, -ɛn] ADJ Neapolitan

NM *(dialecte)* Neapolitan

• **Napolitain, -e** NM,F Neapolitan

nappage [napaʒ] NM topping

nappe [nap] NF **1** *(linge)* tablecloth; **mettre/ôter la n.** to lay/to remove the cloth; **n. d'autel** altar-cloth

2 *(couche)* **n. de brouillard** blanket of fog; **n. d'eau** *(en surface)* stretch *or* expanse *or* sheet of water; *(souterraine)* ground water; **n. de feu** sheet of flames; **n. de gaz** layer of gas; **n. de pétrole** *(souterraine)* layer of oil; *(de marée noire)* oil slick

3 *Géol* **n. éruptive** lava flow; **n. phréatique** ground water (table), phreatic layer

4 *Tech* **n. d'armature** belt, bracing ply; **n. carcasse** casing ply

napper [3] [nape] VT **1** *Culin* **n. qch de** to coat sth with; **glace à la vanille nappée de chocolat** vanilla ice cream topped with chocolate *or* with chocolate topping **2** *(recouvrir ▸ table)* to cover with a cloth

napperon [naprɔ̃] NM mat; **n. individuel** place mat

naquit *etc voir* **naître**

Narcisse [narsis] NPR *Myth* Narcissus

narcisse [narsis] NM **1** *Bot* narcissus; **n. des poètes** poet's narcissus; **n. sauvage** *ou* **des prés** daffodil **2** *Littéraire* narcissistic person, narcissist

narcissique [narsisik] ADJ narcissistic

narcissisme [narsisism] NM narcissism

narcodollars [narkodɔlar] NMPL narcodollars, drug money

narcolepsie [narkɔlɛpsi] NF *Méd* narcolepsy

narcoleptique [narkɔlɛptik] ADJ *Méd* narcoleptic

narcose [narkoz] NF *Méd* narcosis

narcotique [narkɔtik] *Pharm* ADJ narcotic

NM narcotic

narcotrafic [narkotrafik] NM drug trafficking

narcotrafiquant, -e [narkotrafikɑ̃, -ɑ̃t] NM,F drug trafficker

nard [nar] NM *Bot & Pharm* nard, spikenard

narguer [3] [narge] VT **1** *(se moquer de, provoquer)* to taunt, to mock **2** *(braver, mépriser)* to scorn, to spurn, to deride

narine [narin] NF nostril

narquois, -e [narkwa, -az] ADJ taunting, mocking

narquoisement [narkwazmɑ̃] ADV tauntingly, mockingly

narrateur, -trice [naratœr, -tris] NM,F narrator

narratif, -ive [naratif, -iv] ADJ narrative

narration [narasjɔ̃] NF **1** *(exposé)* narrative, narration **2** *(partie du discours)* narration

narrative [narativ] *voir* **narratif**

narratrice [naratris] *voir* **narrateur**

narrer [3] [nare] VT *Littéraire (conte)* to narrate, to tell; *(événements)* to narrate, to relate

narval, -als [narval] NM *Zool* narwhal, narwal

nasal, -e, -aux, -ales [nazal, -o] ADJ nasal

• **nasale** NF *Ling* nasal

nasaliser [3] [nazalize] VT *Ling* to nasalize

Nasdaq® [nasdak] NM *Fin (abrév* **National Association of Securities Dealers Automated Quotation**) Nasdaq®

nase [nɑz] *Fam* ADJ **1** *(épuisé) Br* knackered, *Am* beat

2 *(hors d'usage)* kaput, bust, *Br* clapped-out

3 *(stupide)* dense, *Am* dumb

4 *(de mauvaise qualité)* crap, lousy

NMF *(personne stupide)* idiot, *Am* jerk; **c'est un n., ce mec** this guy's hopeless, *Br* this guy's bloody useless

naseau, -x [nazo] NM *Zool* nostril; *Fam* **naseaux** *(nez)* hooter

nasillard, -e [nazijar, -ard] ADJ *(ton)* nasal; *(radio, haut-parleur)* tinny; **parler d'une voix nasillarde** to talk through one's nose *or* with a (nasal) twang

nasillement [nazijmɑ̃] NM **1** *(d'une voix)* (nasal) twang; *(d'un haut-parleur)* tinny sound **2** *(d'un canard)* quacking

nasiller [3] [nazije] VI **1** *(personne)* to speak with a (nasal) twang; *(radio)* to have a tinny sound **2** *(canard)* to quack

nasique [nazik] NM *Zool* proboscis monkey

nasse [nas] NF **1** *Pêche* (conical) lobster pot **2** *(pour oiseaux)* hoop net **3** *Fig* **tomber dans la n.** to fall into the trap

natal, -e, -als, -ales [natal] ADJ *(pays, ville)* native; **sa maison natale** the house where he/she was born

> Do not confuse with **natif**.

nataliste [natalist] ADJ **politique n.** policy to increase the birth rate

natalité [natalite] NF birth rate, *Am* natality; **forte/faible n.** high birth rate; **courbe de n.** birth-rate curve

natation [natasjɔ̃] NF swimming; **club de n.** swimming club; **faire de la n.** to swim; **n. synchronisée** *ou* **artistique** synchronized swimming

natatoire [natatwar] ADJ swimming *(avant n)*, *Spéc* natatory

Natel® [natel] NM INV *Suisse (abrév* **national Telefon**) *Br* mobile (phone), *Am* cellphone

natif, -ive [natif, -iv] ADJ **1** *(originaire)* native; **je suis n. de Paris/Pologne** I was born in Paris/Poland **2** *Littéraire (inné)* native **3** *Métal* native

NM,F native

> Do not confuse with **natal**.

nation [nasjɔ̃] NF nation; **n. commerçante** mercantile nation; **n. la plus favorisée** most favoured nation; **les Nations unies** the United Nations; **n. en voie de développement** developing nation

national, -e, -aux, -ales [nasjɔnal, -o] ADJ **1** *(de la nation)* national; **funérailles** *ou* **obsèques nationales** state funeral; **la presse nationale en a parlé** the national newspapers *or* the nationals carried stories about it **2** *(nationaliste ▸ parti, politique)* nationalist

• **nationale** NF *Br* ≃ A road, *Am* ≃ interstate highway

• **nationaux** NMPL nationals

nationalisation [nasjɔnalizasjɔ̃] NF nationalization

nationalisé, -e [nasjɔnalize] ADJ nationalized

nationaliser [3] [nasjɔnalize] VT to nationalize

nationalisme [nasjɔnalism] NM nationalism

nationaliste [nasjɔnalist] ADJ nationalist, nationalistic

NMF nationalist

nationalité [nasjɔnalite] NF nationality; **être de n. française/nigériane** to be French/Nigerian; **quelle est sa n., de quelle n. est-il?** what nationality is he?; **les personnes de n. française** people of French nationality, French nationals

national-populisme [nasjɔnalpɔpylism] NM national populism

national-socialisme [nasjɔnalsɔsjalism] NM National Socialism

national-socialiste [nasjɔnalsɔsjalist] *(pl* **nationaux-socialistes** [nasjonɔsɔsjalist]) ADJ National Socialist

NMF National Socialist

native [nativ] *voir* **natif**

nativité [nativite] NF **1** *Rel* **la N.** the Nativity **2** *Beaux-Arts* Nativity scene

natron [natrɔ̃], **natrum** [natrɔm] NM *Chim* natron

natte [nat] NF **1** *(tapis de paille)* (straw *or* rush) mat **2** *(de cheveux) Br* plait, *Am* braid; **porter des nattes** to wear one's hair in *Br* plaits *or Am* braids; **porter** *ou* **avoir une n.** to have a *Br* plait *or Am* braid

natter [3] [nate] VT **1** *(cheveux)* to braid, to plait **2** *(fils, osier)* to plait, to weave **3** *(mur)* to cover with mats

naturalisation [natyralizasjɔ̃] NF **1** *Admin, Bot & Ling* naturalization **2** *(empaillage)* stuffing

naturalisé, -e [natyralize] ADJ naturalized

NM,F naturalized person

naturaliser [3] [natyralize] VT **1** *Admin* to naturalize; **il s'est fait n. français** he was granted French citizenship **2** *Bot & Ling* to naturalize **3** *(empailler)* to stuff

naturalisme [natyralism] NM naturalism

naturaliste [natyralist] ADJ naturalistic

NMF **1** *Bot & Zool* naturalist **2** *(empailleur)* taxidermist

NATURE [natyr]

NF	
• nature **1–3, 5**	• country(side) **2**
• type **4, 5**	• life **6**
ADJ INV	
• plain **1**	• natural **2**

NF **1** *(univers naturel)* **la n.** nature; **les lois de la n.** the laws of nature; **à l'état de n.** in the natural state; **la n. fait bien les choses** nature works wonders; **laisser faire** *ou* **agir la n.** to let nature take its course; **des formes qui n'existent pas dans la n.** shapes which do not occur in nature; **la n. a horreur du vide** nature abhors a vacuum

2 *(campagne)* **la n.** nature, the country, the countryside; **une n. luxuriante s'offrit à nos yeux** a luxuriant landscape opened up before us; **elle vit quelque part en pleine n.** she lives somewhere right out in the countryside; **tomber en panne en pleine n.** to break down in the middle of nowhere; **une maison perdue dans la n.** a house out in the wilds; **se promener dans la n.** to go for a walk in the country; *Fig* **disparaître** *ou* **s'évanouir dans la n.** to vanish into thin air; **il n'a pourtant pas disparu dans la n., ce piano!** that piano can't just have walked off *or* vanished!; *Fam* **partir dans la n.** to run into a ditch/a field[❑]; *Fig* **la voiture a fait une embardée et ils se sont retrouvés dans la n.** the car swerved and they ended up in a ditch

3 *(caractère)* nature; **la n. du sol** the nature of the soil; **être d'une n. douce** to have a gentle nature; **ce n'est pas dans sa n.** it's not like him/her, it's not in his/her nature; **ce** *ou* **il n'est pas dans sa n. d'être aussi agressive** it's not like her *or* it's not in her nature to be so aggressive; **c'est dans la n. des choses** it's in the nature of things, that's the way the world is; **la n. humaine** human nature

4 *(type de personne)* type, sort; **une bonne n.** a

good sort; **une heureuse n.** a happy person; **c'est une n. violente** he's/she's a violent sort; **c'est une petite n.** he's/she's a bit feeble

5 *(sorte)* nature, type, sort; **un programme de cette n.** a programme of this kind *or* nature; **les raisonnements de cette n.** this kind of argument, arguments of this kind

6 *(réalité)* **plus grand que n.** larger than life; *Beaux-Arts* **d'après n.** from life; *Beaux-Arts* **n. morte** still life

ADJ INV 1 *(bœuf, choucroute)* plain, with no trimmings; *(salade, avocat)* plain, with no dressing; **riz n.** (plain) boiled rice

2 *Fam (simple)* natural, unaffected

• **contre nature ADJ** against nature, unnatural; **des sentiments/penchants contre n.** unnatural feelings/leanings; **c'est contre n.** it's not natural, it goes against nature

• **de nature ADV** by nature; **il est généreux de n.** he's generous by nature, it's (in) his nature to be generous; **elle est anxieuse de n.** she's the worrying kind *or* anxious type

• **de nature à CONJ** likely *or* liable to; **une découverte de n. à révolutionner la science** a discovery likely to revolutionize science; **ce genre de détail n'est pas de n. à les inquiéter** that kind of detail is unlikely to bother them

• **de toute nature ADJ** of all kinds *or* types; **il y avait des arbustes de toute n.** there were all sorts of shrubs

• **en nature ADV** in kind; *aussi Fig* **payer en n.** to pay in kind

• **par nature ADV je suis conservateur par n.** I'm naturally conservative, I'm conservative by nature

naturel, -elle [natyrɛl] **ADJ 1** *(du monde physique ▸ phénomène, ressource, frontière)* natural

2 *(physiologique ▸ fonction, processus)* natural, bodily; **les défenses naturelles de l'organisme** the body's natural defences

3 *(inné ▸ disposition, talent)* natural, inborn; *(▸ boucles, blondeur)* natural; **il a une grâce naturelle** he is naturally graceful

4 *(sans affectation)* natural; **tu n'as pas l'air n. sur cette photo** you don't look natural in this photo

5 *(normal)* natural; **son inquiétude est tout à fait naturelle** it's only natural that he/she should be worried; **je vous remercie – je vous en prie, c'est tout n.!** thank you – please don't mention it, it's the least I could do!; **trouver n. de faire qch** to think nothing of doing sth

6 *(pur ▸ fibre)* pure; *(▸ nourriture)* natural; *Com* natural, organic; **soie naturelle** *(sur l'étiquette d'un vêtement)* pure *or* 100% silk

7 *Ling, Mus, Phil & Rel* natural

8 *(illégitime)* natural; **il était le fils n. du roi** he was the natural son of the king

NM 1 *(tempérament)* nature; **elle est d'un n. généreux/peureux/jaloux** she has a generous/timid/jealous nature, she is generous/timid/jealous by nature; **être d'un bon n.** to be good-natured **2** *(authenticité)* naturalness; **manque de n.** affectation, artificiality; **ce que j'aime chez elle, c'est son n.** what I like about her is she's so natural; **avec n.** naturally; **elle est mieux au n. qu'à la télévision** she's better in real life than on TV

• **au naturel ADJ 1** *Culin* plain; **poires au n.** pears in natural fruit juice **2** *Beaux-Arts* **peindre qch au n.** to paint sth from life

naturellement [natyrelmɑ̃] **ADV 1** *(de façon innée)* naturally; **n. timide** naturally shy, shy by nature; **ça lui vient n.** it comes naturally to him/her **2** *(simplement)* naturally, unaffectedly; **c'est le plus n. du monde qu'on nous a reçus** they welcomed us as if it were the most natural thing in the world **3** *(bien sûr)* naturally, of course; **vous viendrez? – n.!** will you be coming? – naturally *or* of course I will!

naturisme [natyrism] **NM 1** *(nudisme)* naturism; **adepte du n.** naturist, nudist **2** *Méd* naturopathy

naturiste [natyrist] **ADJ** *(nudiste)* naturist; **centre n.** nudist colony *or* camp

NMF *(nudiste)* naturist, nudist

naufrage [nofraʒ] **NM 1** *(d'un navire)* wreck, shipwreck; **faire n.** *(personne)* to be shipwrecked; *(navire)* to be wrecked; **périr dans un n.** to be lost at sea; **lors du n. du Titanic** when the Titanic sank **2** *Fig (ruine)* ruin, wreckage; *(d'entreprise)* failure; **faire n.** *(entreprise, mariage)* to fail, to collapse

naufragé, -e [nofraʒe] **ADJ** *(personne ▸ gén)* shipwrecked; *(▸ sur une île)* castaway *(avant n)*; *(navire)* wrecked

NM,F *(gén)* shipwreck victim; *(sur une île)* castaway

naufrageur, -euse [nofraʒœr, -øz] **NM,F** *aussi Fig* wrecker; **bateau n.** wrecker

naupathie [nopati] **NF** *Méd* seasickness

nauséabond, -e [nozeabɔ̃, -ɔ̃d] **ADJ 1** *(qui sent mauvais)* putrid, foul, foul-smelling; *(personne, pièce)* foul-smelling **2** *Fig (répugnant)* nauseating, sickening, repulsive

nausée [noze] **NF 1** *(envie de vomir)* nausea; **avoir la n.** to feel sick; **avoir des nausées** *(gén)* to have bouts of sickness; *(femme enceinte)* to have morning sickness; **donner la n. (à)** to nauseate; **à vous donner la n.** *(odeurs, images)* nauseating **2** *Fig (dégoût)* **une telle hypocrisie me donne la n.** such hypocrisy makes me sick

nauséeux, -euse [nozeø, -øz] **ADJ 1** *(odeur)* nauseating; *(état)* nauseous; **se sentir n.** to feel sick *or* nauseous **2** *Fig Littéraire (révoltant)* nauseating, sickening

nautile [notil] **NM** *Zool* nautilus

nautique [notik] **ADJ** nautical; **carte n.** nautical chart; **le salon n.** ≃ the Boat Show

nautisme [notism] **NM** water sports, aquatics *(singulier)*

naval, -e, -als, -ales [naval] **ADJ** naval; **architecture navale** naval architecture; **construction navale** shipbuilding (industry)

• **Navale NF** *Fam* **faire Navale** ≃ to attend naval college

navarin [navarɛ̃] **NM** navarin *(mutton and vegetable stew)*

navel [navɛl] **NF** navel orange

navet [navɛ] **NM 1** *Bot* turnip **2** *Fam (œuvre)* **c'est un n.** it's (a load of) nonsense *or Br* rubbish; *(film)* it's a lousy movie *or Br* film, *Am* it's a turkey

navette[1] [navɛt] **NF 1** *Aviat & Transp* shuttle; **faire la n. (entre)** to shuttle back and forth *or* to and fro (between); **un bus fait la n. entre la gare et l'aéroport** there is a shuttle bus (service) between the station and the airport; **il fait la n. entre Paris et Marseille** he shuttles back and forth between Paris and Marseilles; **n. de transfert** transfer bus; **n. gratuite** courtesy bus; **la n. parlementaire** = successive readings of bills by the "Assemblée nationale" and the "Sénat"

2 *(fusée)* **n. (spatiale)** (space) shuttle

3 *Rel* incense holder

4 *Tex* shuttle

navette[2] [navɛt] **NF** *Bot* rape

navetteur, -euse [navɛtœr, -øz] **NM,F** *Belg* commuter

navigabilité [navigabilite] **NF 1** *(d'un cours d'eau)* navigability, navigableness **2 (état de) n.** *Naut* seaworthiness; *Aviat* airworthiness; **en état de n.** *Naut* seaworthy; *Aviat* airworthy

navigable [navigabl] **ADJ** *(cours d'eau)* navigable

navigant, -e [navigɑ̃, -ɑ̃t] **ADJ** *Naut* seafaring; *Aviat* **personnel n.** flight personnel, aircrew, crew

NM,F les navigants *Naut* the crew; *Aviat* the aircrew, the crew

navigateur, -trice [navigatœr, -tris] **NM,F 1** *Naut (voyageur)* sailor, seafarer; *(membre de l'équipage)* navigator; **n. solitaire** single-handed yachtsman, *f* yachtswoman **2** *Aviat* navigator, copilot *(in charge of navigation)* **3** *Aut* navigator

NM 1 *(appareil)* navigator **2** *Ordinat* browser

ADJ M seafaring, seagoing

navigation [navigasjɔ̃] **NF 1** *Naut* navigation, sailing; **la n. est dangereuse ici** sailing is dangerous *or* it's dangerous to sail around here; **après un mois de n.** after a month at sea; **n. côtière** coastal navigation; **n. à l'estime** navigation by dead reckoning; **n. extérieure** high seas navigation; **n. fluviale** inland navigation; **n. intérieure** inland navigation; **n. au long cours** deep-sea *or* ocean navigation; **n. maritime** high seas navigation; **n. de plaisance** yachting, pleasure sailing; **n. à voile** sailing **2** *Aviat* navigation, flying; **n. aérienne** aerial navigation; **n. spatiale** space flight *or* travel; **n. à vue** contact flying **3** *Ordinat* **n. sur (l')Internet** browsing the Internet, Internet surfing; **n. rapide/sécurisée** rapid/secure browsing

• **de navigation ADJ** *(registre)* navigational; *(terme, école)* nautical; *(instrument)* navigation *(avant n)*; **compagnie de n.** *Naut* shipping company; *Aviat* airline company; **permis de n.** ship's passport, sea letter

navigatrice [navigatris] *voir* **navigateur**

naviguer [3] [navige] **VI 1** *Naut* to sail (**vers** to); **n. au compas/à l'estime** to navigate by compass/by dead reckoning

2 *Aviat* to fly; **n. à vue** to use contact flight rules, to fly visually

3 *Ordinat* **n. sur (l')Internet** to surf the Net, to browse the Web

4 *Fig (se déplacer)* to get about; **le dossier a navigué entre les différents responsables du projet** the file moved around *or* was passed from project manager to project manager; **savoir n.** to know one's way around

navire [navir] **NM** ship, vessel; **n. de charge** freighter, cargo ship; **n. de commerce** merchant ship; **n. de forage** drilling ship; **n. frigorifique** refrigerated vessel; **n. de guerre** warship; **n. de haute mer** ocean-going ship; **n. au long cours** ocean-going ship; **n. marchand** merchant ship; **n. mixte** mixed passenger and cargo ship; **n. de passagers** passenger ship; **n. porte-conteneurs** container ship; **n. à voiles** sailing ship

navire-citerne [navirsitɛrn] *(pl* **navires-citernes)** **NM** (oil) tanker

navire-école [navirekɔl] *(pl* **navires-écoles)** **NM** training ship

navire-hôpital [navirɔpital] *(pl* **navires-hôpitaux** [navirɔpito]) **NM** hospital ship

navire-jumeau [navirʒymo] *(pl* **navires-jumeaux)** **NM** sister ship

navire-usine [naviryzin] *(pl* **navires-usines)** **NM** factory ship

navrant, -e [navrɑ̃, -ɑ̃t] **ADJ 1** *(attristant ▸ spectacle)* distressing, upsetting; **tu es n.!** you're pathetic *or* hopeless!; **sa bêtise est navrante** he's/she's hopelessly stupid; **un film n. de bêtise** a hopelessly stupid movie *or Br* film **2** *(regrettable)* **c'est n., mais il n'y a rien à faire** it's a terrible shame, but there's nothing we can do

navré, -e [navre] **ADJ** *(personne, expression, ton)* distressed; **être n. de qch** to be very *or* terribly sorry about sth; **je suis n. (de l'apprendre)** I'm terribly *or* very sorry (to hear that); **n. de vous avoir fait attendre** sorry to have kept you waiting

navrer [3] [navre] **VT** to upset, to distress

nazaréen, -enne [nazareɛ̃, -ɛn] **ADJ** *Géog* Nazarene

• **Nazaréen, -enne NM,F** *Géog* Nazarene; *Rel* **le N.** *(Jésus)* the Nazarene

naze [naz] = **nase**

nazi, -e [nazi] **ADJ** Nazi

NM,F Nazi

nazillon, -onne [nazijɔ̃, -ɔn] **NM,F** *Fam* little Nazi

nazisme [nazism] **NM** Nazism

NB *(abrév écrite* **nota bene)** NB

NbP *Typ (abrév* **note de bas de page)** footnote

NCM [ɛnseem] **NFPL** *(abrév* **négociations commerciales multilatérales)** multilateral trade negotiations

NDLR *(abrév écrite* **note de la rédaction)** Ed.

NdT NF *(abrév* **note du traducteur)** translator's note

NE [nə] **ADV A.** *EN CORRÉLATION AVEC UN MOT NÉGATIF* **aucun d'eux ne peut venir** none of them can come; **je ne l'ai dit à personne** I haven't told anyone; **je n'ai vu personne** I saw nobody, I didn't see anybody; **je n'ai rien vu** I saw nothing, I didn't see anything; **nul n'est parfait** nobody's perfect; **ce n'est ni bleu ni vert** it's neither blue nor green; **je n'en parlerai ni à l'un ni à l'autre** I won't speak about it to either of them; **je ne vois guère comment t'aider** I don't really see how I can help you; **le temps n'est guère prometteur** the weather is not very promising; **il ne répond jamais au téléphone** he never answers the phone; **le téléphone**

ne marche plus the telephone doesn't work any more; **ne le dérange pas!** don't disturb him!; **parlez tout bas pour ne pas réveiller le bébé** speak softly so as not to wake the baby; **il ne la voit pas plus dans ce rôle-là que dans l'autre** he can't see *or* imagine her in that role any more than in the other

B. *EN CORRÉLATION AVEC "QUE"* **ils ne font que répéter ce qu'on leur a dit** all they (ever) do is repeat what they've been told; **je ne fais que d'arriver** I've only just arrived; **il n'a pas que des amis** not everybody likes him; **je n'ai pas que cette idée-là** that's not the only idea I have; **il n'y a pas que toi sur terre!** you're not the only person in the world(, you know)!; **tu ne sais dire que des mensonges** all you ever do is tell lies; **vous n'avez qu'à lui en parler** all you have to do is speak to him/her (about it); **je n'ai pas d'autre solution que celle-là** I have no other solution but that

C. *EMPLOYÉ SEUL* **1** *(avec une valeur négative)* **je ne puis** I cannot; **il n'ose** he dare not; **il ne cesse de m'appeler** he won't stop calling me; **il n'ose le lui dire** he doesn't dare tell him/her; **je ne sais quoi faire** I don't know what to do; **qui n'agirait ainsi dans de telles circonstances?** who wouldn't do the same in such circumstances?; **quel père n'aiderait son fils?** what father would refuse to help his son?; **beaucoup de choses ont changé depuis que je ne t'ai vu** many *or* a lot of things have changed since I last saw you; **voilà trois jours que je ne l'ai vue** I haven't seen her for three days; **il y a six jours qu'il n'est venu** he hasn't been for six days; **il n'y a rien qu'il ne fasse pour vous** there's nothing he wouldn't do for you; **je n'avais rien qui ne lui appartînt aussi** I had nothing that didn't also belong to him/her; **prenez garde qu'on ne vous voie** be careful (that) nobody sees you; **que ne le disais-tu plus tôt?** why didn't you say so earlier?, if only you had said so earlier!; **que ne dit-elle ce qu'elle en pense?** why doesn't she say what she thinks (about it)?; **que ne ferais-je pour vous?** what wouldn't I do for you?; **n'ayez crainte, je le préviendrai** don't worry, I'll tell him

2 *(avec une valeur explétive)* **je crains qu'elle n'en parle** I'm frightened she'll talk (about it); **je crains qu'il n'accepte** I'm afraid he might say yes; **sa seule crainte, c'était qu'on ne le renvoyât** all he was afraid of *or* his only fear was of being dismissed; **je tremble qu'il ne soit trop tard** I'm afraid it might be too late; **on redoute que l'épidémie ne s'étende** there are fears that the epidemic might spread; **de peur qu'elle ne le voie** for fear she might see him; **évite qu'il ne te rencontre** try to avoid meeting him; **je ne doute pas qu'il ne soit sympathique** I don't doubt (that) he's nice; **peu s'en faut qu'il n'ait réussi** he very nearly succeeded; **à moins qu'il ne vous le dise** unless he tells you; **avant que je ne parte** before I go; **sans que je ne le dise** without me *or* my saying it; **il se porte mieux que je ne croyais** he's better than I'd imagined; **c'est moins efficace que je ne l'espérais** it's not as effective as I'd hoped

---

né, -e [ne] **PP** *voir* **naître**

ADJ born; **né d'une famille bourgeoise** born into a middle-class family; **enfant né d'un premier mariage** child from a first marriage; *Fig* **un film né de la rencontre d'un réalisateur et d'une actrice** a film born of *or* that grew out of a meeting between a director and an actress; **Clara Brown, née Moore** Clara Brown, née Moore; **c'est une musicienne née** she's a born musician, she was born (to be) a musician; **être bien né** to be well born *or* of noble birth

Néandertal [neɑ̃dɛrtal] *voir* **homme**

néanmoins [neɑ̃mwɛ̃] **ADV** nevertheless, nonetheless; **ce travail est bon, n. vous pouvez mieux faire** this work is good, nevertheless *or* yet you can do better; **il est brillant et n. très modeste** he is brilliant but nonetheless *or* nevertheless very modest

néant [neɑ̃] **NM 1** *(non-être)* nothingness; **une voix sortie du n.** a voice that seemed to come from nowhere **2** *(superficialité)* vacuousness; **dans tous leurs discours, je ne trouve que le n.** I find all their speeches totally vacuous **3** *Admin* **enfants: n.** children: none

nébuleux, -euse [nebylø, -øz] **ADJ 1** *(nuageux)* cloudy, clouded **2** *Fig (obscur)* obscure, nebulous

• **nébuleuse NF 1** *Astron* nebula **2** *Fig (amas confus)* **leur projet était encore à l'état de nébuleuse** their plan was still pretty vague, they still had only the bare outlines of a plan **3** *(conglomérat)* business conglomerate

nébuliseur [nebylizœr] **NM** nebulizer

nébulosité [nebylozite] **NF 1** *(nuage)* haze, nebulosity **2** *Météo* cloud cover; **forte n.** heavy cloud cover **3** *Fig Littéraire (imprécision)* haziness, nebulousness

nécessaire [nesesɛr] **ADJ 1** *(indispensable)* necessary; **un mal n.** a necessary evil; **cela ne sera pas n.** that won't be necessary; **si (c'est) n.** if necessary, if need be; **je viendrai si c'est vraiment n.** I'll come if it's really necessary; **est-il n. de la mettre** *ou* **qu'elle soit au courant?** does she have *or* need to know?; **il n'est pas n. d'être impoli** there is no need to be rude; **il n'est pas n. de passer par le standard** there is no need *or* it is not necessary to go through the switchboard; **il est n. que vous y alliez en personne** you need to *or* you must go there in person; **ils n'ont pas jugé n. de venir s'excuser** they didn't think *or* consider it necessary to come and apologize; **n. à** *ou* **pour qn/qch** necessary *or* required for sb/sth; **l'eau est n. aux plantes** plants need water; **cette introduction est n. à la compréhension du texte** you have to read this introduction to understand the text **2** *(requis ▸ aptitude)* necessary, requisite; **toutes les qualités nécessaires** all the necessary qualities **3** *(logique, inévitable)* necessary, unavoidable, inevitable

NM 1 *(choses indispensables)* bare necessities; **n'emportez que le strict n.** just take the basic essentials *or* what's absolutely necessary; **il ne fait que le strict n.** he does no more than which is strictly necessary; **manquer du n.** to lack the necessities *or* basics of life

2 *(démarche requise)* **je vais faire le n.** I'll see to it; **je ferai le n. pour vos réservations** I'll see to your reservations; **merci de faire le n. pour qu'on vienne le chercher à l'aéroport** thank you for arranging for him to be met at the airport

3 *(trousse, étui)* **n. à chaussures** shoe-cleaning kit; **n. à couture** sewing kit; **n. à ongles** manicure set; **n. à ouvrage** workbox; **n. de toilette** toilet bag; **n. de voyage** travel *or Br* overnight bag

4 *Littéraire (serviteur)* servant, domestic, indispensable person

nécessairement [nesesɛrmɑ̃] **ADV 1** *(inévitablement)* necessarily, unavoidably, inevitably; **n., il devait y avoir collision** the crash was unavoidable **2** *(obligatoirement)* necessarily, *Sout* of necessity; **pas n.** not necessarily; **ce n'est pas n. vrai** it's not necessarily true

nécessité [nesesite] **NF 1** *(caractère nécessaire)* necessity, need; **être dans la n. de faire qch** to find it necessary to do sth, to have no choice but to do sth; **la n. de dormir** the need to sleep; **la crise nous a mis dans la n. de renvoyer la moitié du personnel** the crisis made it necessary for us *or* gave us no choice but to lay off half the staff; **quelle n. y avait-il de le faire?** what need was there to do it? **2** *(chose indispensable)* necessity; **c'est une n.** it's essential; **faire de n. vertu** to make a virtue out of necessity; *Prov* **n. fait loi** needs must (where the devil drives) **3** *Vieilli (indigence)* destitution, poverty; **être dans la n.** to be in need

• **nécessités NFPL les nécessités de la vie** the necessities of life; **les nécessités du service** the operational requirements; **nécessités militaires** military requirements

• **de première nécessité ADJ** *(dépenses, fournitures)* basic; *(objets, denrées)* essential; **ne prenez que des objets de première n.** take only what's absolutely necessary

• **de toute nécessité ADV vous devez de toute n. réparer le toit** it's absolutely imperative *or* essential that you repair the roof

• **par nécessité ADV** of necessity, necessarily, unavoidably

nécessiter [3] [nesesite] **VT** to require, to demand; **cela nécessite que vous veniez** that means you have to come; **ce travail nécessite beaucoup de patience** this job requires a lot of patience

nécessiteux, -euse [nesesitø, -øz] **ADJ** needy, in need

NM,F needy person; **les n.** the needy

nec plus ultra [nɛkplyzyltra] **NM INV** last word, ultimate; **le n. du confort** the last word in comfort

nécrologe [nekrɔlɔʒ] **NM** necrology, death roll

nécrologie [nekrɔlɔʒi] **NF 1** *(liste)* necrology **2** *(notice biographique)* obituary **3** *(rubrique)* obituary column

nécrologique [nekrɔlɔʒik] **ADJ** obituary *(avant n)*

nécromancie [nekrɔmɑ̃si] **NF** necromancy

nécromancien, -enne [nekrɔmɑ̃sjɛ̃, -ɛn] **NM,F** necromancer

nécrophage [nekrɔfaʒ] **ADJ** necrophagous

nécrophile [nekrɔfil] **ADJ** necrophiliac *(avant n)*, necrophile *(avant n)*

NMF necrophiliac, necrophile

nécrophilie [nekrɔfili] **NF** necrophilia, necrophilism

nécrophore [nekrɔfɔr] **NM** *Entom* burying beetle

nécropole [nekrɔpɔl] **NF** necropolis

nécrose [nekroz] **NF** *Méd* necrosis

nécroser [3] [nekroze] *Méd* **VT** to necrose

VPR se nécroser to necrose

nectaire [nɛktɛr] **NM** *Bot* nectary

nectar [nɛktar] **NM** *(gén)* nectar; **n. de poire/d'abricot** pear/apricot nectar

nectarine [nɛktarin] **NF** nectarine

née [ne] *voir* **né**

néerlandais, -e [neɛrlɑ̃dɛ, -ɛz] **ADJ** Dutch

NM *(langue)* Dutch

• **Néerlandais, -e NM,F** Dutchman, *f* Dutchwoman; **les N.** the Dutch

nef [nɛf] **NF 1** *Archit* nave; **n. centrale** nave; **n. latérale** (side) aisle **2** *Arch ou Littéraire (vaisseau)* vessel, craft

néfaste [nefast] **ADJ 1** *(nuisible)* harmful; **une influence n.** a bad influence **2** *Littéraire (tragique)* ill-fated

nèfle [nɛfl] **NF 1** *Bot* medlar; **n. du Japon** loquat **2** *Fam (locution)* **des nèfles!** no way!, no chance!

néflier [neflije] **NM** *Bot* medlar (tree); **n. du Japon** loquat (tree)

négateur, -trice [negatœr, -tris] *Littéraire* **ADJ** negative

NM,F decrier, detractor

négatif, -ive [negatif, -iv] **ADJ 1** *(réponse, attitude)* negative **2** *Élec, Ling & Méd* negative **3** *Math* **un nombre n.** a negative *or* minus number

EXCLAM *Fam* nope!

NM *Phot* negative

• **négative NF dans la négative** if not; **répondre par la négative** to give a negative answer, to answer in the negative

négation [negasjɔ̃] **NF 1** *(gén) & Phil* negation **2** *Gram* negative (form)

négationnisme [negasjɔnism] **NM** revisionism *(denying that the Holocaust ever happened)*

négationniste [negasjɔnist] **ADJ** revisionist *(denying that the Holocaust ever happened)*

NMF revisionist *(who denies that the Holocaust ever happened)*

négative [negativ] *voir* **négatif**

négativement [negativmɑ̃] **ADV** *(réagir)* negatively; *(répondre)* in the negative

négativisme [negativism] **NM** negativism

négatrice [negatris] *voir* **négateur**

négligé, -e [negliʒe] **ADJ 1** *(peu soigné ▸ tenue, personne)* sloppy, scruffy, slovenly; *(▸ coiffure)* unkempt, untidy; *(▸ travail, devoir, style)* slovenly, careless **2** *(délaissé)* neglected

NM 1 *(débraillé, laisser-aller)* scruffiness, slovenly *or* untidy appearance **2** *(robe d'intérieur)* negligee, negligée

négligeable [negliʒabl] **ADJ** *(différence, quantité, risque)* negligible, insignificant; *(détail)* unimportant; **un avantage non n.** a not inconsiderable advantage; **une quantité non n. de** a significant quantity of

négligemment [negliʒamɑ̃] **ADV 1** *(sans soin)* negligently, carelessly **2** *(avec nonchalance)* negligently, casually; **un foulard n. noué autour du cou** a scarf casually tied around his/her neck

négligence [negliʒɑ̃s] **NF 1** *(manque de soin)*

negligence, carelessness; (d'un devoir) neglect; habillé avec n. sloppily or carelessly dressed; n. de style stylistic error, error of style
2 (manque d'attention) negligence, neglect; (oubli) oversight; la n. du conducteur the driver's negligence; l'accident est dû à une n. the accident was due to carelessness; par (pure) n. through (sheer) carelessness or negligence
3 (nonchalance) negligence, casualness, nonchalance; il me répondit avec n. qu'il viendrait peut-être he casually or nonchalantly replied that he would perhaps come
4 Jur n. coupable ou criminelle criminal negligence; n. professionnelle professional negligence, malpractice

négligent, -e [negliʒɑ̃, -ɑ̃t] ADJ 1 (peu consciencieux) negligent, careless, neglectful 2 (nonchalant) negligent, casual, nonchalant; d'un geste n., il ramassa le livre he casually picked up the book

négliger [17] [negliʒe] VT 1 (se désintéresser de ▸ études, santé, personne) to neglect; si tu négliges ce rhume, il ne fera qu'empirer if you don't take care of that cold, it'll only get worse; il néglige sa tenue ces derniers temps he hasn't been taking care of his appearance lately 2 (dédaigner) to disregard; (élément, détail) to overlook, to disregard; il ne faut rien n. you mustn't leave anything to chance; il ne faut pas n. son offre don't disregard his/her offer 3 (omettre) to neglect; n. de faire qch to neglect or to fail to do sth
VPR se négliger 1 (être mal habillé) to neglect one's appearance, to let oneself go 2 (se désintéresser de sa santé) to be neglectful of or to neglect one's health

négoce [negɔs] NM 1 (activité) business, trade, trading; faire du n. to be in trade; le n. international international trade or trading; le n. du vin the wine trade; Bourse n. de titres share-dealing 2 (entreprise) business; un petit n. a small business

négociabilité [negɔsjabilite] NF negotiability

négociable [negɔsjabl] ADJ negotiable; Fin (bon, traite) negotiable, transferable, tradeable; non n. non-negotiable; n. en banque bankable; n. en Bourse negotiable on the Stock Exchange

négociant, -e [negɔsjɑ̃, -ɑ̃t] NM,F 1 (commerçant) merchant, trader; n. exportateur export merchant; n. en gros wholesaler; n. en vins wine merchant 2 (grossiste) wholesaler 3 Bourse trader

négociateur, -trice [negɔsjatœr, -tris] NM,F Com & Pol negotiator

négociation [negɔsjasjɔ̃] NF 1 (discussions) negotiation; entamer des négociations (sur qch) to enter into negotiations (on sth); les deux pays ont engagé des négociations the two countries have begun negotiations; être en n. (sujet: conditions, contrat, salaire) to be under negotiation; être en n. avec qn to be in negotiation with sb; UE négociations d'adhésion accession negotiations; négociations collectives joint negotiations; (au sein d'une entreprise) collective bargaining (UNCOUNT); négociations commerciales trade negotiations; négociations pour la paix peace negotiations; négociations salariales wage bargaining (UNCOUNT) 2 Fin & Bourse negotiation, transaction; négociations de Bourse Stock Exchange transactions; négociations de change exchange transactions; négociations au comptant spot trading (UNCOUNT); n. à la criée open-outcry trading; négociations à prime options trading (UNCOUNT); négociations à terme futures trading (UNCOUNT)

négociatrice [negɔsjatris] voir négociateur

négocier [9] [negɔsje] VT 1 Com, Fin & Pol to negotiate (avec with); Bourse to trade; prix à n. price negotiable 2 Aut n. un virage to negotiate a bend
VI 1 (discuter) to negotiate (avec with) 2 Arch (faire du commerce) to trade
VPR se négocier les actions se négocient ce matin à 7,75 euros shares are trading at 7.75 euros this morning

nègre, négresse [negr, negres] NM,F Negro, f Negress; (avec une connotation raciste) nigger, = racist term used to refer to a black person; Fam travailler comme un n. to work like a slave; n. blanc (à peau claire) White Negro
NM 1 Fam (écrivain) ghost (writer); être le n. de qn to ghost for sb 2 Culin n. en chemise = chocolate dessert coated with whipped cream
ADJ 1 Beaux-Arts & Mus Negro 2 (personne) Negro; (avec une connotation raciste) nigger, = offensive term used to refer to a black person
• nègre blanc ADJ INV propos n. blanc double-talk

négrier, -ère [negrije, -ɛr] ADJ slave (avant n); navire n. slave ship, slaver
NM 1 (marchand d'esclaves) slave trader, slaver 2 (bateau) slave ship, slaver 3 Péj (employeur) slave-driver

négrillon, -onne [negrijɔ̃, -ɔn] NM,F piccaninny, = racist term referring to a black child

négritude [negrityd] NF negritude

négro [negro] NM Negro, nigger, = offensive term used to refer to a black person

négroïde [negrɔid] ADJ Negroid
NMF Negroid

neige [nɛʒ] NF 1 Météo snow; n. artificielle artificial snow; les neiges éternelles permanent snow; n. fondue (pluie) sleet; (boue) slush; n. poudreuse powdery snow; Ski n. pourrie hazardous or crumbly snow; n. tôlée crusted snow; chute ou giboulée de n. snowfall; Can banc de n. snow bank, snowdrift
2 Chim n. carbonique dry ice
3 Fam Arg drogue (cocaïne) snow
4 Culin battez les blancs en n. whisk the whites until they form peaks; œufs (battus) en n. stiffly beaten egg whites
• à la neige ADV aller à la n. to go on a skiing Br holiday or Am vacation

neiger [23] [neʒe] V IMPERSONNEL il neige it's snowing

neigeux, -euse [nɛʒø, -øz] ADJ 1 (cime) snow-capped, snow-clad; (toit, pente) snow-covered 2 (hiver, temps) snowy 3 Fig (barbe, chevelure) snow-white, snowy

nem [nɛm] NM = type of Vietnamese spring roll

nématode [nematɔd] NM Zool roundworm, threadworm, Spéc nematode

néné [nene] NM Fam (sein) boob, tit

nénette [nenɛt] NF Fam 1 (femme, fille) chick, Br bird 2 (petite amie) girlfriend□, Br bird 3 (tête) se casser la n. (à faire qch) to go to a lot of bother (to do sth)□; tu ne t'es pas trop cassé la n. pour faire ta rédaction you didn't exactly strain yourself or exert yourself over your essay; te casse pas la n. don't worry about it□, don't let it bother you□

nénuphar [nenyfar] NM Bot waterlily, pond lily; n. jaune ou des étangs yellow waterlily or pond lily

néo- [neo] PRÉF neo-

néo-calédonien, -enne [neɔkaledɔnjɛ̃, -ɛn] (mpl néo-calédoniens, fpl néo-calédoniennes) ADJ New Caledonian
• Néo-Calédonien, -enne NM,F New Caledonian

néocapitalisme [neɔkapitalism] NM neocapitalism

néocapitaliste [neɔkapitalist] ADJ neo-capitalist
NMF neo-capitalist

néoclassicisme [neɔklasisism] NM neoclassicism

néoclassique [neɔklasik] ADJ neoclassic, neoclassical

néocolonial, -e, -aux, -ales [neɔkɔlɔnjal, -o] ADJ neocolonial

néocolonialisme [neɔkɔlɔnjalism] NM neocolonialism

néoconservateur, -trice [neɔkɔ̃sɛrvatœr, -tris] ADJ neoconservative
NM,F neoconservative

néofascisme [neofaʃism] NM Neofascism

néofasciste [neofaʃist] ADJ Neofascist
NMF Neofascist

néogothique [neɔgɔtik] ADJ Neo-Gothic
NM Neo-Gothic (style)

néo-hébridais, -e [neɔebride, -ɛz] (mpl inv, fpl néo-hébridaises) Anciennement ADJ from the New Hebrides, Vanuatuan
• Néo-Hébridais, -e NM,F Vanuatuan

néo-impressionnisme [neoɛ̃presjɔnism] NM Neo-Impressionism

néolibéral, -e, -aux, -ales [neɔliberal, -o] Pol ADJ neoliberal
NM,F neoliberal

néolibéralisme [neɔliberalism] NM neoliberalism

néolithique [neɔlitik] ADJ Neolithic
NM Neolithic (period)

néologisme [neɔlɔʒism] NM Ling & Psy neologism

néon [neɔ̃] NM 1 (gaz) neon 2 (éclairage) neon (lighting); (lampe) neon (lamp); (tube) neon tube; (enseigne) neon sign

néonatal, -e, -als, -ales [neɔnatal] ADJ neonatal

néonazi, -e [neonazi] ADJ neo-Nazi
NM,F neo-Nazi

néonazisme [neonazism] NM neo-Nazism, neo-Naziism

néophyte [neɔfit] NMF 1 (nouvel adepte) novice 2 Rel neophyte, novice

Néoprène® [neɔprɛn] NM neoprene

néoréalisme [neɔrealism] NM Cin neorealism

néoréaliste [neɔrealist] Cin ADJ neorealist
NMF neorealist

néorural, -e, -aux, -ales [neɔryral, -o] ADJ neo-rural
NM,F = former city-dweller who has relocated to the countryside

néo-zélandais, -e [neɔzelɑ̃dɛ, -ɛz] (mpl inv, fpl néo-zélandaises) ADJ of/from New Zealand; agneau n. New Zealand lamb
• Néo-Zélandais, -e NM,F New Zealander

Népal [nepal] NM Géog le N. Nepal

népalais, -e [nepalɛ, -ɛz] ADJ Nepalese, Nepali
NM (langue) Nepali
• Népalais, -e NM,F Nepalese (person), Nepali; les N. the Nepalese, the Nepalis or Nepali

népérien, -enne [neperjɛ̃, -ɛn] ADJ (logarithme) natural, Napierian

néphrétique [nefretik] ADJ Anat nephritic

néphrite [nefrit] NF 1 Méd nephritis; n. chronique Bright's disease, chronic nephritis 2 Minér nephrite

néphrologie [nefrɔlɔʒi] NF Méd nephrology

néphron [nefrɔ̃] NM Anat nephron

néphrosclérose [nefrɔskleroz] NF Méd nephrosclerosis

népotisme [nepɔtism] NM nepotism

Neptune [nɛptyn] NPR Myth Neptune

néréide [nereid] NF Zool nereis

nerf [nɛr] NM 1 Anat nerve; n. moteur/sensitif/mixte motor/sensor/mixed nerve; n. gustatif gustatory nerve
2 (toujours singulier) (énergie) elle manque de n. pour diriger l'entreprise she hasn't got what it takes to run the company; son style manque de n. his/her style is a bit weak; ça, c'est une voiture qui a du n.! now that's what I call a responsive car!; allez, un peu de n. ou du n.! come on, put some effort into it!; l'argent est le n. de la guerre money is the sinews of war
3 (tendon) piece of gristle; une viande pleine de nerfs a gristly or stringy piece of meat
4 Vieilli un grand athlète tout en n. a tall, sinewy athlete
5 (de reliure) rib
• nerfs NMPL (système nerveux) nerves; Vieilli être malade des nerfs, avoir les nerfs malades to suffer from nerves, to have bad nerves; ses nerfs ont fini par lâcher she eventually cracked; Fam avoir les nerfs à cran ou en boule ou en pelote to be wound up, to be on edge; avoir les nerfs à fleur de peau ou à vif to be a bundle of nerves; avoir les nerfs solides ou des nerfs d'acier to have nerves of steel; Fam avoir les nerfs to be hacked off; il a ses nerfs en ce moment he's a bag of nerves or rather on edge at the moment; être sur les nerfs to be worked up; on est tous sur les nerfs depuis ce matin we've all been on edge since this morning; il est toujours ou il vit sur les nerfs he's highly-strung, he lives on his nerves; Fam c'est un paquet ou une boule de nerfs he's/she's a bundle or a bag of nerves; Fam ne passe pas tes nerfs sur

moi don't take it out on me; *Fam* **porter** *ou* **taper sur les nerfs à qn** to get on sb's nerves; **tu commences à me taper sur les nerfs!** you're starting to get on my nerves *or Br* wick!; *Fam* **foutre les nerfs à qn** to hack sb off, to get sb's back up
• **nerf de bœuf** NM bludgeon

nerprun [nɛrprœ̃] NM *Bot* buckthorn

nervation [nɛrvasjɔ̃] NF venation, nervation, nervature

nerveuse [nɛrvøz] *voir* **nerveux**

nerveusement [nɛrvøzmɑ̃] ADV **1** *Méd* nervously; **elle est fatiguée n.** she's suffering from nervous exhaustion **2** *(de façon agitée)* nervously, restlessly

nerveux, -euse [nɛrvø, -øz] ADJ **1** *Anat & Méd (système, maladie)* nervous; *(centre, influx)* nerve *(avant n)*
2 *(énervé ▸ de nature)* nervous, highly-strung; *(▸ passagèrement)* nervous, on edge; **le café me rend n.** coffee makes me hyper
3 *(toux, rire)* nervous
4 *(mains, corps)* sinewy
5 *(énergique ▸ personne)* dynamic, energetic; *(▸ cheval)* spirited, vigorous; *(▸ style)* energetic, forceful, vigorous; *(▸ voiture)* responsive; *(▸ conduite)* dynamic; **une conduite nerveuse** a jerky way of driving
6 *(dur ▸ viande)* gristly, stringy
NM,F nervous *or* highly-strung person

nervi [nɛrvi] NM *(tueur)* hired killer, hitman; *(homme de main)* henchman, thug

nervosité [nɛrvozite] NF **1** *Méd* nervosity
2 *(excitation)* nervousness; **donner des signes de n.** to show signs of agitation; *Fig* **la n. des marchés financiers** the nervousness *or* jitteriness of the financial markets
3 *(irritabilité)* irritability, touchiness
4 *(vigueur)* responsiveness; **un moteur d'une grande n.** a highly responsive engine

nervure [nɛrvyr] NF **1** *Bot* vein, nervure
2 *Entom* vein
3 *Aviat & Métal* rib
4 *(de reliure)* rib
5 *Tech* flange; *(de radiateur)* gill
6 *Couture* piping; **nervures** pin tucks
7 *Archit & Constr* rib

nervuré, -e [nɛrvyre] ADJ *(feuille, aile)* veined; *(vêtement)* ribbed

n'est-ce pas [nɛspɑ] ADV **1** *(sollicitant l'acquiescement)* **vous viendrez, n.?** you'll come, won't you?; **elle a téléphoné, n.?** she did phone, didn't she?; **nous pouvons compter sur vous, n.?** we can count on you, can't we?; **n. qu'ils sont mignons?** aren't they cute *or* sweet? **2** *(emploi expressif)* **la question, n., reste ouverte** the question, of course, remains unanswered; **le problème, n., c'est qu'il est déjà tard** the problem is, you see, that it's already late

Net [nɛt] NM **le N.** the Net, the Internet

NET, NETTE [nɛt]

ADJ	
• clean **1, 2**	• neat **1, 2**
• clear **1, 3, 4**	• sharp **4, 6**
• distinct **5**	• net **7**
ADV	
• frankly **2**	• net **3**

ADJ **1** *(propre)* clean, neat; *Fig* **j'ai la conscience nette** I have a clear conscience, my conscience is clear
2 *(ordonné)* (clean and) tidy, neat (and tidy)
3 *(pur ▸ peau, vin)* clear; *Littéraire* **n. de** free from; **être n. de tout soupçon** to be above suspicion; **être n. de tout blâme** to be blameless
4 *(bien défini ▸ gén)* clear; *(▸ contour)* sharp; *(▸ réponse)* plain, straight; **une écriture nette** neat handwriting; **la cassure est nette** the break is clean; **elle a une diction nette** she speaks *or* articulates clearly; **une réponse nette** a straight answer; **sa position est nette** his/her position is clear-cut; **un refus n.** a flat refusal; **j'ai la nette impression que...** I have the distinct *or* clear impression that...; **elle a gardé des souvenirs très nets de sa petite enfance** she remembers her childhood quite clearly *or* vividly
5 *(évident)* distinct, definite; **il a fait de nets progrès** he's made distinct *or* definite progress; **il y a une nette amélioration** there's a marked improvement; **il fait plus froid ici, c'est très n.** it's noticeably *or* definitely colder here
6 *Phot* sharp; **l'image n'est pas nette** the picture isn't very clear
7 *Com & Fin* net; **n. d'impôt** tax-free; **n. de tout droit** exempt *or* free from duty; **le montant n.** the net amount
8 *Fam (locution)* **pas n.** *(louche)* shady, *Br* dodgy; *(ivre, drogué)* wasted, wrecked; *(pas complètement sain d'esprit)* not all there
ADJ INV *Sport* **la balle est n.** (it's a) let
ADV **1** *(brutalement)* **s'arrêter n.** to stop dead; **se casser n.** to break clean through; **être tué n.** to be killed outright; *Fam* **couper** *ou* **casser n. avec qn** to break with sb completely
2 *(sans mentir)* frankly, plainly; *(sans tergiverser)* frankly, bluntly; **refuser (tout) n.** to refuse point-blank *or* flatly; **je vous le dis tout n.** I'm telling you straight
3 *Com & Fin* net; **je gagne 1000 euros n. par semaine** *ou* **1000 euros par semaine n.** I take home *or* my take-home pay is 1,000 euros a week
NM *Compta* **n. commercial** net profit; **n. financier** *(revenu)* net interest income; *(à payer)* net interest charges; **n. à payer** net payable
• **au net** ADV **mettre qch au n.** to make a fair copy of sth

netcam [nɛtkam] NF *Ordinat* netcam, webcam

netéconomie [nɛtekɔnɔmi] NF *Écon & Ordinat* Internet economy

netiquette [nɛtikɛt] NF *Ordinat (sur l'Internet)* netiquette

netsurfer [nɛtsœrfœr] NM *Ordinat* net surfer

nette [nɛt] *voir* **net**

nettement [nɛtmɑ̃] ADV **1** *(distinctement)* clearly, distinctly; **on voit n. la forme du bec** you can clearly see the shape of the beak; **il apparaît n. qu'il est en tort** it's clear that he's in the wrong
2 *(avec franchise)* clearly, frankly, bluntly
3 *(incontestablement)* definitely, markedly; **je travaille n. mieux à la maison qu'ici** I work much better at home than here
4 *(beaucoup)* much, distinctly; **ça va n. mieux comme ça** it's a lot *or* much better like this; **il est n. plus fort que Paul** he's much stronger than Paul

netteté [nɛtte] NF **1** *(propreté)* cleanness, cleanliness **2** *(clarté)* clearness, clarity; **n. des idées** clear thinking **3** *(précision ▸ de l'écriture)* neatness, clearness; *(▸ d'une image, d'un contour)* sharpness, clearness; *(▸ de souvenir)* clearness, clarity; *(▸ de rupture)* cleanness; **offensé par la n. de son refus** offended by the flatness of his/her refusal

nettoie *etc voir* **nettoyer**

nettoiement [nɛtwamɑ̃] NM **1** *(des rues)* cleaning; **service du n.** refuse collection service **2** *Agr* clearing

nettoyage [nɛtwajaʒ] NM **1** *(d'une maison, d'un vêtement)* cleaning; *Fam* **porter sa robe au n.** to take one's dress to the cleaner's; **n. à sec** dry cleaning; *(sur une étiquette)* dry clean only; **entreprise de n.** cleaning firm; **produits de n.** cleaning products; **(grand) n. de printemps** spring-cleaning; **faire le n. par le vide** to make a clean sweep; **avant de déménager, j'ai fait un n. par le vide** before moving, I had a big clean-out **2** *Fam Fig (d'un quartier, d'une ville)* clean-up; *(par la police)* cleaning *or* clearing out; **les policiers ont opéré un véritable n. du quartier** the police officers really cleaned out *or* cleared out the district; *Mil* **opérations de n.** mopping-up operations; *Pol* **n. ethnique** ethnic cleansing

nettoyant, -e [nɛtwajɑ̃, -ɑ̃t] ADJ cleaning *(avant n)*
NM *(gén)* cleaning product; *(détachant)* stain remover

nettoyer [13] [nɛtwaje] VT **1** *(rendre propre ▸ gén)* to clean; *(▸ plaie)* to clean, to cleanse; *Naut (pont)* to swab; **n. une maison à fond** to spring-clean a house; **donner un vêtement à n.** to have a garment cleaned, to take a garment to the cleaner's; **n. à sec** to dry-clean
2 *(enlever ▸ tache)* to remove
3 *Fam (vider)* to clean out; **les cambrioleurs ont tout nettoyé** the burglars cleaned the place out; **je me suis fait n. au poker** I got cleaned out at poker; *Mil* **n. les poches de résistance** to mop up
4 *Fam (quartier)* to clean up *or* out
5 *Fam (épuiser)* to wear out; **ça suffit pour aujourd'hui, les magasins, je suis nettoyé!** enough shopping for today, I'm worn out!
6 *Fam Arg crime (tuer)* to bump off
VPR **se nettoyer 1 se n. les mains/ongles** to clean one's hands/nails **2** *(emploi passif)* **ça se nettoie facilement** it's easy to clean **3 le four se nettoie automatiquement** the oven cleans itself automatically *or* is self-cleaning

nettoyeur, -euse [nɛtwajœr, -øz] ADJ *(d'entretien)* cleaning *(avant n)*
NM,F *(employé)* cleaner

neuf[1] [nœf] ADJ INV **1** *(gén)* nine **2** *(dans des séries)* ninth; **page/numéro n.** page/number nine
PRON nine
NM INV **1** *(gén)* nine
2 *(numéro d'ordre)* number nine
3 *(chiffre écrit)* nine
4 *Cartes* nine; *voir aussi* **cinq**

neuf[2], **neuve** [nœf, nœv] ADJ **1** *(n'ayant jamais servi)* new; **flambant** *ou* **tout n.** brand-new; **à l'état n.** as new; *(timbre postal, livre)* in mint condition, unused; **état n.** *(dans une annonce)* as new; **comme n.** as good as new **2** *(récemment créé ▸ pays)* new, young; **notre démocratie est encore neuve** democracy is still in its infancy in our country; **une ville neuve** a new town **3** *(original ▸ point de vue, idée)* new, fresh, original; **porter un regard n. sur qn/qch** to take a fresh look at sb/sth; **il est encore (un peu) n. en matière de...** he's still (relatively) new *or* a (relative) newcomer to...
NM **1** *(objets nouveaux)* **faire le n. et l'occasion** to sell new and second-hand goods; **acheter du n.** *(dans l'immobilier)* to buy new; **meublé de** *ou* **en n.** newly furnished; **vêtu de n.** (dressed) in new clothes **2** *(informations nouvelles)* **tu as du n. pour ton visa?** any news about your visa?, have you heard anything about your visa?; **qu'est-ce qu'il y a de** *ou* **quoi de n.?** what's new?; **rien de n. depuis la dernière fois** nothing new since last time
• **à neuf** ADV **remettre qch à n.** to make sth as good as new; *(machine)* to recondition sth, to renovate sth; **j'ai remis** *ou* **refait la maison à n.** I did up the house like new
• **coup de neuf** NM **donner un coup de n. à qch** to spruce sth up

neurasthénie [nørasteni] NF *Méd & Psy* neurasthenia; *Fam* **faire de la n.** *(de la dépression)* to be depressed

neurasthénique [nørastenik] ADJ *Méd & Psy* neurasthenic; *Vieilli (dépressif)* depressed
NMF *Méd & Psy* neurasthenic; *Vieilli (dépressif)* depressed person

neurobiologie [nørobjɔlɔʒi] NF neurobiology

neuroblaste [nøroblast] NM neuroblast

neurochirurgie [nøroʃiryrʒi] NF neurosurgery

neurochirurgien, -enne [nøroʃiryrʒjɛ̃, -ɛn] NM,F neurosurgeon

neurodégénératif, -ive [nørodeʒeneratif, -iv] ADJ *Méd* neurodegenerative

neuroleptique [nørɔlɛptik] ADJ neuroleptic
NM neuroleptic; **être sous neuroleptiques** to be on tranquillizers

neurologie [nørɔlɔʒi] NF neurology

neurologiste [nørɔlɔʒist], **neurologue** [nørɔlɔg] NMF neurologist

neuromusculaire [nøromyskylɛr] ADJ neuromuscular

neuronal, -e, -aux, -ales [nørɔnal, -o] ADJ neuronal; **réseau n.** neural net

neurone [nørɔn] NM neuron, neurone

neuronique [nørɔnik] ADJ neuronic

neuropathologie [nøropatɔlɔʒi] NF neuropathology

neuropsychiatrie [nøropsikjatri] NF neuropsychiatry

neuropsychologie [nøropsikɔlɔʒi] NF neuropsychology

neurovégétatif, -ive [nøroveʒetatif, -iv] ADJ *Anat* **système nerveux n.** autonomic nervous system

neutralisation [nøtralizasjɔ̃] **NF** neutralization; *Mil* **tir de n.** neutralizing fire

neutraliser [3] [nøtralize] **VT 1** *(atténuer)* to tone down
2 *(annuler)* to neutralize, to cancel out
3 *(maîtriser)* to overpower, to bring under control
4 *(contrecarrer)* to neutralize, to thwart
5 *(bloquer)* to close; **la voie rapide est neutralisée dans le sens Paris-province** the fast lane is closed to traffic leaving Paris
VPR se neutraliser to neutralize; **les deux forces se neutralisent** the two forces cancel each other out

neutralisme [nøtralism] **NM** neutralism

neutraliste [nøtralist] **ADJ** neutralist, neutralistic
NMF neutralist

neutralité [nøtralite] **NF 1** *(d'une attitude)* neutrality; **observer la n.** to remain neutral; **sortir de sa n.** to take sides; *Pol* to abandon one's neutrality *or* one's neutral position; **violer la n. d'un État** to violate a state's neutrality **2** *Chim & Phys* neutrality

neutre [nøtr] **ADJ 1** *(couleur, décor, attitude, pays)* neutral; **d'une voix n.** in a neutral *or* an expressionless voice; **je veux rester n.** I don't want to take sides; *Mil* **la zone n.** no-man's-land **2** *Chim, Élec & Phys* neutral **3** *Ling & Entom* neuter
NMF *Pol* **les neutres** the neutral countries
NM 1 *Ling* neuter; **au n.** in the neuter **2** *Élec* neutral (wire) **3** *Can Aut* neutral; **se mettre sur le n.** to go into neutral

neutrino [nøtrino] **NM** *Phys* neutrino

neutron [nøtrɔ̃] **NM** neutron

neuvaine [nœvɛn] **NF** *Rel* novena

neuve [nœv] *voir* **neuf**[2]

neuvième [nœvjɛm] **ADJ** ninth; **le n. art** cartoons
NMF 1 *(personne)* ninth **2** *(objet)* ninth (one)
NM 1 *(partie)* ninth **2** *(étage) Br* ninth floor, *Am* tenth floor **3** *(arrondissement de Paris)* ninth (arrondissement)
NF 1 *Anciennement Scol Br* = third year of primary school, *Am* ≃ third grade **2** *Mus* ninth; *voir aussi* **cinquième**

neuvièmement [nœvjɛmmɑ̃] **ADV** ninthly, in ninth place

névé [neve] **NM 1** *(dans un glacier)* névé **2** *(plaque)* bank of snow

neveu, -x [nəvø] **NM** nephew; *Fam* **un peu, mon n.!** you bet (your sweet life)!

névralgie [nevralʒi] **NF** neuralgia; **avoir une n.** *(un mal de tête)* to have a headache; **avoir des névralgies** to suffer from neuralgia

névralgique [nevralʒik] **ADJ 1** *Méd* neuralgic **2** *Fig voir* **point**[2]

névrite [nevrit] **NF** *Méd* neuritis

névritique [nevritik] **ADJ** *Méd* neuritic

névropathe [nevrɔpat] **NMF** *Méd* neuropath

névrose [nevroz] **NF** *Psy* neurosis; **n. obsessionnelle** obsessive compulsive disorder, OCD; **n. post-traumatique** post-traumatic stress disorder

névrosé, -e [nevroze] **ADJ** neurotic
NM,F neurotic

névrotique [nevrɔtik] **ADJ** neurotic

new-look [njuluk] **NM INV** New Look
ADJ INV New Look *(avant n)*

newsgroup [njuzgrup] **NM** *Ordinat* newsgroup

new-yorkais, -e [nujɔrkɛ, -ɛz] *(mpl* **inv,** *fpl* **new-yorkaises)** **ADJ** of/from New York; **les musées n.** the museums in New York
• **New-Yorkais, -e NM,F** New Yorker

nez [ne] **NM 1** *(partie du corps)* nose; **avoir le n. bouché** to have a stuffed-up *or* blocked nose; **avoir le n. qui coule** to have a runny nose; **avoir le n. qui saigne, saigner du n.** to have a nosebleed; **avoir le n. fin** *(avoir un bon odorat)* to have a good nose *or* a keen sense of smell; **se faire refaire le n.** to have a nose job; **n. camus** pug nose; **n. en trompette** turned-up nose; **avoir un n. grec** to have a Grecian nose; **avoir un n. en pied de marmite** to have a turned-up nose; **respirer du n.** to breathe through one's nose; **parler du n.** to talk *or* to speak through one's nose
2 *Fig (jugement)* flair, good judgement *(UNCOUNT)*, intuition *(UNCOUNT)*; **avoir du n.** to have good judgement; **elle a du n. pour la qualité des tissus** she's a good judge of fabric, she knows good fabric when she sees it; **il a du n. pour acheter des antiquités** he's got a flair for buying antiques; **avoir le n. fin** *ou* **creux** to be shrewd; **j'ai eu du n.** *ou* **le n. fin** *ou* **le n. creux** my intuition was good; **tu vois, j'ai eu le n. fin de partir avant minuit** you see, I was right to trust my instinct and leave before midnight
3 *(odorat* ▸ *d'une personne)* sense of smell; *(*▸ *d'un chien)* scent; **avoir du n.** to have a good nose
4 *(en parfumerie* ▸ *personne)* nose
5 *Aviat* nose; **sur le n.** tilting down
6 *Constr* (tile) nib; **n. de marche** nosing *(of a stair)*
7 *Géog* edge, overhang
8 *Naut* nose, bow; **sur le n.** down by the bows, on the bows
9 *(d'un vin)* nose; **un vin qui a du n.** a wine with a good nose
10 *Tech* shank; *(de moteur)* nosepiece; **n. de broche** spindle shank
11 *Com* **n. de caisse** checkout display
12 *(locutions)* **le n. en l'air** looking upwards; *Fig (sans souci)* without a care in the world; *(en rêvant)* with one's head in the clouds; **partir/se promener le n. au vent** to stroll *or* to dawdle off/along; **il a toujours le n. dans une BD** he's always got his nose buried in a comic; **sans lever le n. de son travail** without looking up from his/her work; **travailler sans lever le n.** to work without a break, to keep one's head down; **montrer (le bout de) son n.** to show one's face, to put in an appearance; **le voisin/soleil n'a pas montré son n. de la semaine** the man next door/sun hasn't come out all week; **fermer/claquer la porte au n. à qn** to shut/to slam the door in sb's face; **raccrocher au n. à qn** to hang up on sb, to put the phone down on sb; **au** *ou* **sous le n. de qn, au n. et à la barbe de qn** under sb's nose; **dérober qch au n. et à la barbe de qn** to steal sth from right under sb's nose; **tu as le n. dessus!, il est sous ton n.!** it's right under your nose!; **le dernier billet m'est passé sous le n.** I just missed the last ticket; **ça m'est passé sous le n.** it slipped through my fingers; **regarder qn sous le n.** to stare at sb; **se trouver n. à n. avec qn** to find oneself face to face with sb; **l'ayant critiquée dans sa rubrique, il eut le désagrément de se trouver n. à n. avec elle** after criticizing her in his column, he had the unpleasant experience of meeting her face to face; *Fam* **ce type, je l'ai dans le n.** I can't stand *or* stomach that guy, *Br* that guy gets right up my nose; **ton n. remue** *ou* **s'allonge!** *(tu mens)* you're lying!, your nose is growing (longer)!; **tu aurais vu le n. qu'il a fait!** you should have seen his face!; **ça se voit comme le n. au milieu de la figure** it's as plain as the nose on your face; **elle est jalouse, ça se voit comme le n. au milieu de la figure** she's jealous, it's written all over her face; **cela te pend au n.** you've got it coming (to you); *Belg* **faire de son n.** to make a fuss; *Fam* **se manger** *ou* **se bouffer le n.** to be at each other's throats; **avoir un verre** *ou* **un coup dans le n.** to be a bit merry *or* tipsy; **elle ne met jamais le n. ici** she never shows her face in here; **je n'ai pas mis le n. dehors de la journée** I didn't set foot outside the door all day; *Fam* **mettre** *ou* **fourrer son n. dans les affaires de qn** to poke *or* to stick one's nose in sb's business; **mettre à qn le n.** *Fam* **dans son caca** *ou très Fam* **dans sa merde** to call sb to order, to pull sb up
• **à plein nez ADV ça sent le fromage à plein n.** there's a strong smell of cheese; *Fig* **ça sent l'entourloupe à plein n.** there's some dirty business going on

NF [ɛnɛf] **NF** *(abrév* **Norme française)** = label indicating compliance with official French standards, *Br* ≃ BS, *Am* ≃ US standard

NfD NF *Typ (abrév* **note de fin de document)** endnote

ni [ni] **CONJ** nor; **je ne peux ni ne veux venir** I can't come and I don't want to either, I can't come, nor do I want to; **elle ne me parle plus, ni même ne me regarde** she doesn't talk to me any more, nor even look at me; **sans argent ni bagages** without money or luggage, with neither money nor luggage; **il est sorti sans pull ni écharpe** he went out without either his jumper or his scarf; **il ne mange ni ne boit** he neither eats nor drinks; **je n'ai jamais rien mangé ni bu d'aussi bon** I have never eaten or drunk anything so good; **ni moi** *(moi non plus)* nor me (either), *Sout* nor I
• **ni... ni CONJ** neither... nor; **ni Pierre ni Henri ne sont venus** neither Pierre nor Henri came; **je n'ai ni femme ni enfant ni amis** I have neither wife nor child nor friends; **ni lui ni elle ne sont prêts à céder** neither of them is willing to give way; **je ne veux voir ni lui ni elle** I don't want to see either of them; **ni toi ni moi ne pouvons l'aider** neither you nor I can help him, neither of us can help him; **ni l'un ni l'autre** neither of them *or* neither one nor the other; **ni l'un ni l'autre n'est tout à fait innocent** neither (one) of them is completely innocent; **ni ici ni ailleurs** neither here nor elsewhere; **il n'a répondu ni oui ni non** he didn't say yes and he didn't say no; **c'était comment? – ni bien ni mal** how was it? – OK; **ni fleurs ni couronnes** *(dans faire-part de décès)* no flowers, by request; **ni vu ni connu** without anybody noticing; **et ni vu ni connu, il a empoché les pièces** quick as a flash, he pocketed the coins and nobody was any the wiser; **ni plus ni moins** neither more nor less

niacoué, -e [njakwe] **NM,F** *très Fam Br* slant-eye, *Am* gook, = offensive term used to refer to an oriental person

niais, -e [njɛ, njɛz] **ADJ** *(sot)* simple, inane; *(sourire)* inane, silly
NM,F simpleton, fool; **espèce de grand n.!** you silly fool!

niaisage [njɛzaʒ] **NM** *Can* idleness

niaisement [njɛzmɑ̃] **ADV** inanely, stupidly; **rire n.** to give a silly laugh, to laugh inanely

niaiser [3] [njeze] *Can Fam* **VT n. qn** *(faire tourner en bourrique)* to drive sb crazy; *(se moquer de) Br* to wind sb up, *Am* to razz sb; *(raconter des histoires à)* to pull sb's leg, *Br* to wind sb up
VI *(hésiter)* to dither; *(ne rien faire)* to loaf about

niaiserie [njɛzri] **NF 1** *(caractère)* simpleness, inanity, foolishness **2** *(parole)* stupid *or* inane remark; **dire des niaiseries** to talk nonsense

niaiseux, -euse [njezø, -øz] *Can Fam* **ADJ** silly□
NM,F moron, jerk

niaque [njak] **NF** *Fam* fighting spirit□, drive□; **avoir la n., être plein de n.** to have plenty of drive

nibard [nibar] **NM** *très Fam (sein)* tit, boob

Nicaragua [nikaragwa] **NM** *Géog* **le N.** Nicaragua

nicaraguayen, -enne [nikaragwajɛ̃, -ɛn] **ADJ** Nicaraguan
• **Nicaraguayen, -enne NM,F** Nicaraguan

Nicée [nise] **NF** *Antiq* Nicaea; **le symbole de N.** the Nicene Creed

niche[1] [niʃ] **NF 1** *(renfoncement)* niche, (small) alcove
2 *Mktg* (market) niche
3 *Géog* niche, recess
4 *(pour chien) Br* kennel, *Am* doghouse; **à la n.!** into your kennel!

niche[2] [niʃ] **NF** *Fam (espièglerie)* trick□; **faire des niches à qn** to play pranks on sb

nichée [niʃe] **NF 1** *(d'oiseaux)* nest, brood **2** *(de chiots, de chatons)* litter **3** *Fam (enfants)* **il est arrivé avec toute sa n.** he turned up with all his brood

nicher [3] [niʃe] **VI 1** *(faire son nid)* to nest (**dans** in) **2** *Fam (habiter)* to crash, *Br* to doss; **elle niche chez moi pour l'instant** she's crashing at my place just now **3** *(couver)* to brood
VT to nestle; **n. sa tête au creux de l'épaule de qn** to nestle one's head on *or* against sb's shoulder
VPR se nicher 1 *(faire son nid)* to nest **2** *(se blottir)* to nestle; **niché dans un fauteuil** curled up in an armchair; **je rêve d'un petit chalet niché dans la montagne** I dream of a little chalet nestling among the mountains **3** *Fam (se cacher)* **où est-elle allée se n.?** where's she hiding herself?; **où ce chat a-t-il bien pu se n.?** where's the cat got to?

nichet [niʃɛ] **NM** nest egg

nichoir [niʃwar] **NM** nest-box

nichon [niʃɔ̃] **NM** *très Fam* boob, tit

nickel [nikel] **NM** nickel
ADJ INV *Fam* **1** *(très propre)* spotless□, gleaming; **2** *(parfait)* perfect□, just the thing, *Br* spot-on; **c'est n., comme appareil, pour se mettre à la photo** it's the perfect camera for someone just taking up photography

ADV *Fam (très bien)* **faire qch n. (chrome)** to do sth really well□

nickelage [nikla3] NM nickel-plating, nickelling

nickelé, -e [nikle] ADJ nickel-plated, nickelled; *Fam Vieilli* **avoir les pieds nickelés** *(être trop paresseux pour marcher)* to be too lazy to walk anywhere□; *(avoir de la chance)* to be lucky□ *or Br* jammy

nickeler [24] [nikle] VT to plate with nickel, to nickel

niçois, -e [niswa, -az] ADJ of/from Nice
NM *Ling* Nice dialect
• **Niçois, -e** NM,F = inhabitant of or person from Nice

nicotine [nikɔtin] NF nicotine

nicotinisme [nikɔtinism] NM *Méd* nicotinism

nictation [niktasjɔ̃] NF nictation, nictitation

nictitant, -e [niktitɑ̃, -ɑ̃t] ADJ *Zool* nictitating

nid [ni] NM **1** *(d'oiseau, de guêpes)* nest; **n. d'aigle** eyrie, eagle's nest; *Fig* eyrie **2** *Fig (habitation)* (little) nest; **n. d'amour** love nest; **un (petit) n. douillet** a cosy little nest **3** *(concentration)* nest; **n. de brigands/d'espions** den of thieves/spies; **n. à poussière** dust trap; **n. à rats** slum, hovel; **n. de résistance** pocket of resistance; **un n. de vipères** a vipers' nest
• **nid d'ange** *Br* baby's sleeping bag, *Am* bunting bag

nid-d'abeilles [nidabɛj] *(pl* **nids-d'abeilles***)* NM **1** *(tissu)* waffle; *(point de broderie)* smocking; **une robe à n.** a smocked dress **2** *Aut* **radiateur à n.** honeycomb (radiator) **3** *Tech (matériau)* honeycomb

nid-de-pie [nidpi] *(pl* **nids-de-pie***)* NM **1** *Mil* lodgement **2** *Naut* crow's nest

nid-de-poule [nidpul] *(pl* **nids-de-poule***)* NM pothole

nièce [njɛs] NF niece

nielle[1] [njɛl] NF **1** *(plante)* corncockle **2** *(maladie)* **n. des blés** blight, smut

nielle[2] [njɛl] NM *(incrustation)* niello

nieller[1] **[4]** [njele] VT *Agr* to blight, to smut

nieller[2] **[4]** [njele] VT *(incruster)* to niello

niellure[1] [njelyr] NF *Agr* blight, smut

niellure[2] [njelyr] NF *Beaux-Arts* niello work

nier [9] [nje] VT *(démentir)* to deny; **je nie l'avoir vue** I deny having seen her; **elle nie être coupable** she denies that she's guilty; **cela, on ne peut le n.** that cannot be denied; **je ne nie pas que j'ai parfois tort** I don't deny that I'm sometimes wrong; **on ne peut pas n. que...** there's no denying *or* one can't deny *or* it's undeniable that...
VI **il continue de n.** he continues to deny it; **l'accusé nie** the accused denies the charge

niet [njɛt] EXCLAM no way!, not a chance!

nigaud, -e [nigo, -od] ADJ simple, stupid
NM,F idiot, halfwit; **gros n.!** you great *or* big idiot!

nigelle [niʒɛl] NF *Bot* nigella, love-in-a-mist

Niger [niʒɛr] NM *Géog* **1** *(fleuve)* **le N.** the River Niger **2** *(État)* **le N.** Niger

Nigeria [niʒerja] NM *Géog* **le N.** Nigeria

nigérian, -e [niʒerjɑ̃, -an] ADJ Nigerian
• **Nigérian, -e** NM,F Nigerian

nigérien, -enne [niʒerjɛ̃, -ɛn] ADJ Nigerien
• **Nigérien, -enne** NM,F Nigerien

nihilisme [niilism] NM nihilism

nihiliste [niilist] ADJ nihilist, nihilistic
NMF nihilist

Nil [nil] NM **le N.** the Nile

nilgaut [nilgo] NM *Zool* nilgai

nilotique [nilɔtik] ADJ *Ling* of the Nile, Nilotic

nimbe [nɛ̃b] NM **1** *Beaux-Arts & Rel* nimbus, aureole *(round the head)* **2** *Littéraire* halo, nimbus

nimbé, -e [nɛ̃be] ADJ haloed

nimbus [nɛ̃bys] NM INV *Météo* nimbus

n'importe [nɛ̃pɔrt] ADV **1** *(indique l'indétermination)* **quel pull mets-tu? – n.** which jumper are you going to wear? – any of them **2** *(introduit une opposition)* **son roman est très discuté, n., il a du succès** him/her novel is highly controversial, but it's successful all the same
• **n'importe comment** ADV **1** *(sans soin)* any old how; **il m'a coupé les cheveux n. comment** he cut my hair anyhow *or* any old how **2** *(de toute façon)* anyhow, anyway; **n. comment, il est trop tard pour l'appeler** anyhow *or* anyway, it's too late to call him
• **n'importe lequel, n'importe laquelle** PRON INDÉFINI any; **n. lequel d'entre eux** any (one) of them; **tu veux le rouge ou le vert? – n. lequel** do you want the red one or the green one? – either *or* I don't mind
• **n'importe où** ADV anywhere; **ne laisse pas traîner tes affaires n. où** don't just leave your things anywhere
• **n'importe quand** ADV whenever you/we/*etc* like
• **n'importe quel, n'importe quelle** ADJ INDÉFINI any; **n. quel débutant sait ça** any beginner knows that
• **n'importe qui** PRON INDÉFINI anybody, anyone; *Fam* **ce n'est pas n. qui!** he/she is not just anybody!; **demande à n. qui dans la rue** ask the first person you meet in the street
• **n'importe quoi** PRON INDÉFINI anything; **il ferait n. quoi pour obtenir le rôle** he'd do anything *or* he would go to any lengths to get the part; **tu dis vraiment n. quoi!** you're talking absolute nonsense!; *Fam* **c'est un bon investissement – n. quoi!** that's a good investment – don't talk nonsense *or esp Br* rubbish!; **une table Louis XIII d'époque, ce n'est pas n. quoi** a genuine Louis XIII table is no ordinary table

ninas [ninas] NM INV (French) cigar

nipper [3] [nipe] *Fam* VT to rig out, to dress up□; **elle est drôlement bien nippée ce soir!** she's dressed up to the nines tonight!
VPR **se nipper** to get dressed□; **il sait pas se n.** he's got no dress sense□

nippes [nip] NFPL *Fam (vêtements)* gear, togs

nippon, -e *ou* **-onne** [nipɔ̃, ɔn] ADJ Japanese
• **Nippon, -e** *ou* **-onne** NM,F Japanese

nique [nik] NF **faire la n. à qn** *(faire un geste de bravade, de mépris à)* to thumb one's nose at sb; *(se moquer de)* to poke fun at sb

niquer [3] [nike] VT **1** *Vulg (posséder sexuellement)* to fuck, to screw; **va te faire n.!, nique ta mère!** fuck off!, go fuck yourself!
2 *très Fam (duper)* to shaft, to screw; **se faire n.** to get shafted; **c'est un faux, tu t'es fait n.!** it's a fake, you've been shafted *or* screwed!
3 *très Fam (attraper)* to nab, to collar; **il s'est fait n. par les contrôleurs** he got nabbed *or* collared by the ticket collectors
4 *très Fam (endommager)* to bust, *Br* to knacker, to bugger; **je vais lui n. sa gueule!** I'm going to waste his/her fucking face!
VI *Vulg* to fuck, to screw

niquet [nikɛ] NM *Belg Fam* snooze, nap□

nirvana [nirvana] NM nirvana

nissart [nisar] NM = dialect of langue d'oc spoken in the area around Nice

nitrate [nitrat] NM nitrate; **n. de potassium** nitre

nitre [nitr] NM *Vieilli Chim* nitre, saltpetre

nitré, -e [nitre] ADJ nitrated; **composé n.** nitro compound

nitrer [3] [nitre] VT to nitrate

nitreux, -euse [nitrø, -øz] ADJ nitrous

nitrifier [9] [nitrifje] VT to nitrify
VPR **se nitrifier** to nitrify

nitrique [nitrik] ADJ nitric

nitrobenzène [nitrobɛ̃zɛn] NM nitrobenzene

nitroglycérine [nitrogliserin] NF nitroglycerin, nitroglycerine

nitrure [nitryr] NM nitride; **n. de fer** iron nitride

nitrurer [3] [nitryre] VT *Métal* to nitride

niveau, -x [nivo] NM **1** *(hauteur)* level; **n. d'eau/d'huile** water/oil level; **n. des basses/hautes eaux** low-water/high-water mark; **la Saône n'avait jamais atteint un n. aussi haut** the Saône had never reached such a high level *or* had never been so high; **les deux cadres ne sont pas au même n.** the two frames are not level (with each other); **fixer les étagères au même n. que la cheminée** put up the shelves level with *or* on the same level as the mantelpiece
2 *(étage)* level, storey; **un parking à trois niveaux** a *Br* car park *or Am* parking lot on three levels; **un immeuble à dix niveaux** a ten-storey building; **le supermarché se trouve au troisième n.** the supermarket is on the third level; **n. arrivée/départ** *(d'un aéroport)* arrivals/departures level
3 *(degré)* level; **maintenir les prix à un n. élevé** to maintain prices at a high level; **la production atteint son plus haut n.** production is reaching its peak; **la production n'avait jamais atteint un n. aussi haut** production had never reached such a high level *or* had never been so high; **la natalité n'est jamais tombée à un n. aussi bas** the birth-rate is at an all-time low *or* at its lowest level ever; **la décision a été prise au plus haut n.** the decision was made at the highest level; **au plus haut n. de la hiérarchie** at the highest level of the hierarchy, at the very top; *Fig* **au plus bas n. de l'échelle** at the very bottom of the ladder; **les salaires augmentent régulièrement à tous les niveaux** there are regular salary increases for all grades *or* at all levels; **n. social** social level; **ils sont d'un n. social différent** they are from different social backgrounds; **n. des besoins** need level; **n. d'entrée** *(à un poste)* entry level; *Ling* **n. de langue** register; **n. d'occupation** *(d'un hôtel)* occupancy level; **n. de prix** price level; **n. des stocks** inventory *or* stock level
4 *(étape)* level, stage; **méthode d'apprentissage à plusieurs niveaux** learning method in several stages *or* steps
5 *(qualité)* level, standard; **n. scolaire** academic standard; **son n. scolaire est-il bon?** is he/she doing well at school?; **quel est son n. en anglais?** what is his/her standard in English?; **j'ai un bon n./un n. moyen en russe** I'm good/average at Russian; **les élèves sont tous du même n.** the pupils are all at the same level; **avoir le n. (requis)** to be up to standard; **je ne peux pas nager avec toi, je suis loin d'avoir ton n.** I can't swim with you, I'm not up to your standard; **évaluer le n. des candidats** to evaluate the candidates' level of ability; **nous recherchons un candidat n. baccalauréat/maîtrise** we are looking for a candidate of baccalauréat/master's degree standard; **n. de vie** standard of living
6 *(instrument)* level (tube); **n. d'eau** water level; **n. à bulle (d'air)** spirit level; **n. de maçon** plumb level; **n. à plomb** vertical *or* plumb level
7 *Ordinat* **n. d'accès** *(dans un réseau)* access level; **n. de gris** grey scale; **n. de sécurité** security level
8 *Bourse* **n. de cours des actions** stock price level; **n. de dépôt requis** margin requirement
• **au niveau** ADJ up to standard, of the required level; **dans deux mois, vous serez au n.** in two months' time, you'll have caught up ADV **1 se mettre au n.** to catch up **2 au n. régional/local** at regional/local level; *Fam* **au n. matériel** on the financial front, where finance is concerned
• **au niveau de** PRÉP **1** *(dans l'espace)* **au n. de la mer** at sea level; **l'eau lui arrivait au n. du genou** the water came up to his/her knees; **au n. du carrefour, vous tournez à droite** when you come to the crossroads, turn right; **j'habite à peu près au n. de l'église** I live by the church **2** *(dans une hiérarchie)* on a par with, at the level of; **cet élève n'est pas au n. de sa classe** this pupil is not on a par with the rest of his class; **ce problème sera traité au n. du syndicat** this problem will be dealt with at union level **3** *aussi Fig* **se mettre au n. de qn** to come down to sb's level
• **de niveau** ADJ level; **un sol de n.** a level floor; **mettre qch de n.** to make sth level; **les deux terrains ne sont pas de n.** the two plots of land are not level (with each other)

nivelage [nivla3] NM equalizing, levelling (out)

niveler [24] [nivle] VT **1** *(aplanir)* to level (off); **nivelé par l'érosion** worn (away) by erosion **2** *Fig (égaliser)* to level (off), to even out; **leur but est de n. les revenus des Français** their aim is to reduce salary differentials in France; **n. par le bas** *ou* **au plus bas** to level down; **n. par le haut** *ou* **au plus haut** to level up **3** *Tech* to (measure with a spirit) level

niveleur, -euse [nivlœr, -øz] NM,F leveller
NM *Hist* Leveller
• **niveleuse** NF *Constr* grader, motor grader

nivelle *etc voir* **niveler**

nivellement [nivɛlmɑ̃] NM **1** *(aplanissement)* evening out, levelling (out) *or* off **2** *Géog* (erosion) denudation 3 *Fig (égalisation)* equalizing, levelling; **le n. des revenus** income redistribution; **n. par le bas/haut** levelling down/up

nivéole [niveɔl] NF *Bot* snowflake

nivôse [nivoz] NM = 4th month of the French Revolutionary calendar (from 21 December to 20 January)

NNTP [enentepe] NM *Ordinat (abrév* **Network News Transfer Protocol**) NNTP

nobélisable [nɔbelizabl] ADJ *(chercheur, écrivain)* potential Nobel prize-winning

NMF potential Nobel prize-winner

nobéliser [3] [nɔbelize] VT *(décerner un prix Nobel à)* to award the Nobel prize to

nobiliaire [nɔbiljɛr] ADJ nobiliary; **particule n.** nobiliary particle; **titre n.** title

NM peerage list

noble [nɔbl] ADJ 1 *(de haute naissance)* noble 2 *Fig* noble; **un geste n.** a noble deed; **le n. art** the noble art 3 *(en œnologie)* noble, of noble vintage

NMF noble, nobleman, *f* noblewoman; **les nobles** the nobility

noblement [nɔbləmɑ̃] ADV nobly

noblesse [nɔblɛs] NF 1 *(condition sociale)* nobleness, nobility; **famille de n. récente** recently ennobled family; *Hist* **n. de robe** *ou* **d'office** = nobility acquired after having fulfilled specific judicatory duties; **n. d'épée** old nobility; **n. héréditaire** hereditary peerage; **n. terrienne** landed gentry; **la haute n.** the nobility; **la petite n.** the gentry; **n. oblige** (it's a case of) noblesse oblige 2 *(générosité)* nobleness, nobility; **par n. de cœur/d'esprit** through the nobleness of his/her heart/spirit

nobliau, -x [nɔblijo] NM *Péj* petty nobleman

noce [nɔs] NF 1 *(cérémonie)* wedding; *(fête)* wedding festivities; **être de la n., être invité à la n.** to be invited to the wedding; *Fam* **être à la n.** to have the time of one's life, to have a whale of a time; *Fam* **elle n'avait jamais été à pareille n.** she had the time of her life; *Fam* **on n'était pas à la n.** it was no picnic; *Fam* **faire la n.** to live it up 2 *(ensemble des invités)* wedding party

• **noces** NFPL wedding; **le jour des noces** the wedding day; **le jour de ses noces** his/her wedding day; **elle l'a épousé en troisièmes noces** he was her third husband; **noces d'argent/d'or/de diamant** silver/golden/diamond wedding (anniversary)

• **de noces** ADJ wedding *(avant n)*; **nuit de noces** wedding night; **repas de noces** wedding breakfast

noceur, -euse [nɔsœr, -øz] *Fam* ADJ **ils sont très noceurs** they like to party, they like to live it up

NM,F reveller, *Am* partyer

nocif, -ive [nɔsif, -iv] ADJ noxious, harmful

nocivité [nɔsivite] NF noxiousness, harmfulness

noctambule [nɔktɑ̃byl] NMF night owl

noctuelle [nɔktɥɛl] NF *Entom* owlet moth, *Spéc* noctuid, noctua

nocturne [nɔktyrn] ADJ 1 *(gén)* nocturnal, night *(avant n)*; *(attaque, visite)* night *(avant n)*; **évasion n.** escape by night; **vision n.** night vision 2 *Bot & Zool* nocturnal

NM 1 *Mus* nocturne 2 *Rel* nocturn 3 *Orn (rapace)* nocturnal bird (of prey)

NF 1 *Sport* evening *Br* fixture *or Am* meet 2 *Com* late-night opening; **le magasin fait n.** *ou* **ouvre en n. le jeudi** the shop stays open late on Thursdays

nodal, -e, -aux, -ales [nɔdal, -o] ADJ *(point, ligne)* nodal

NM *TV* master control room

nodosité [nɔdozite] NF *Bot & Méd (nodule)* node, nodule; *(état)* nodosity

nodule [nɔdyl] NM 1 *Méd* nodule, node 2 *Géol* nodule

Noé [nɔe] NPR Noah

Noël [nɔɛl] NM 1 *(fête)* Christmas; **à N.** at Christmas (time); **la nuit** *ou* **la veille de N.** Christmas Eve; **le jour de N.** Christmas Day; **joyeux N.!** Merry Christmas! 2 *(période)* Christmas time; **passer N. en famille** to spend Christmas with the family

NF **la N.** *(fête)* Christmas; *(période)* Christmas time

nœud [nø] NM 1 *(lien)* knot; **faire un n.** to tie *or* to make a knot; **faire un n. à ses lacets** to do up *or* to tie (up) one's shoelaces; **faire un n. de cravate** to knot *or* to tie a tie; **tu as des nœuds dans les cheveux** your hair is (all) tangled, you've got lots of knots *or* tangles in your hair; **n. coulant** *(pour serrer)* slipknot, running knot; *(pour étrangler)* noose; *Tech* **n. de grappin** fisherman's bend; **n. en huit** figure of eight; **n. plat** reef knot; **couper** *ou* **trancher le n. gordien** to cut the Gordian knot; *Fig* **avoir un n. dans l'estomac** to have a knot in one's stomach; *Fig* **avoir un n. dans la gorge** to have a lump in one's throat

2 *(étoffe nouée)* bow; **porter un n. noir dans les cheveux** to wear a black bow *or* ribbon in one's hair; **n. papillon,** *Fam* **n. pap** bow tie

3 *(ornement)* bow; **n. de diamants/d'émeraudes** diamond/emerald bow

4 *Naut (vitesse)* knot

5 *Fig (point crucial)* crux; **le n. du problème** the crux *or* heart of the problem; *Théât* **le n. d'une pièce** the crux *or* knot of a play

6 *Anat* node; **n. lymphatique** lymph node; **n. vital** vital centre

7 *Bot (bifurcation)* node; *(dans le bois)* knot

8 *(de serpent)* coil; *aussi Fig* **n. de vipères** nest of vipers

9 *Astron* **n. ascendant/descendant** ascending/descending node

10 *Ordinat, Ling, Math & Phys* node

11 *(en travaux publics)* **n. ferroviaire** rail junction; **n. routier** interchange

12 *Vulg (pénis)* cock, dick; **à la mords-moi le n.** lousy, crappy

noie *etc voir* **noyer**[2]

noir, -e [nwar] ADJ 1 *(gén)* black; **n. comme de l'ébène** jet-black, ebony; **n. comme un corbeau** *ou* **du charbon** (as) black as soot, pitch-black; **n. de jais** jet-black; **n. de suie** black with soot; *Fig* **n. de monde** teeming with people

2 *(très sombre ▸ gén)* black, dark; *(▸ cheveux, yeux, lunettes)* dark; **un ciel n.** a dark *or* leaden sky; **dans les rues noires** in the pitch-black *or* pitch-dark streets; *Fam* **elle est revenue noire d'Italie** *(bronzée)* she was black when she came back from Italy

3 *(plongé dans l'obscurité ▸ nuit, cellule)* dark

4 *(sale)* black, dirty, grimy; **avoir les ongles noirs** to have dirty fingernails; **être n. comme du charbon** to be as black as soot; **être n. de crasse** to be black with grime

5 *Fig (maléfique)* black; *Littéraire (crime)* heinous, foul; **lancer un regard n. à qn** to shoot sb a black look; **il m'a regardé d'un œil n.** he gave me a black look; **de noirs desseins** dark intentions

6 *(pessimiste)* black, gloomy, sombre; **faire** *ou* **peindre un tableau très n. de la situation** to paint a very black *or* gloomy picture of the situation; **le lundi/jeudi n.** Black Monday/Thursday; **rien n'est jamais tout blanc ou tout n.** nothing is completely black and white

7 *(extrême)* **saisi d'une colère noire** livid with rage; **être d'une humeur noire** to be in a black *or* foul mood; **être dans une misère noire** to live in abject poverty

8 *(en anthropologie)* black; **le problème n. aux États-Unis** the race problem in the United States

9 *(illégal)* **travail n.** moonlighting

10 *Fam (ivre)* plastered, wasted

11 *Géog* **la mer Noire** the Black Sea

NM 1 *(couleur)* black; **n. de carbone** carbon black; **n. de Chine** Indian ink, *Am* India ink; **n. de fumée** carbon black; **d'un n. d'ébène** jet-black, ebony-black; **être vêtu de n., être en n.** to be dressed (all) in black; **se mettre du n. aux yeux** to put on eyeliner; **le n. et blanc** *Cin & Phot* black and white photography; *TV* black and white transmissions; *Fig* **c'était écrit n. sur blanc** it was there in black and white

2 *(saleté)* dirt, grime; **nettoie le n. sous tes ongles** clean the dirt from under your fingernails; **tu as du n. sur la joue** you've got a dirty mark on your cheek

3 *(obscurité)* darkness; **dans le n.** in the dark, in darkness; **avoir peur du n.** *ou* **dans le n.** to be afraid *or* scared of the dark; *Fig* **être dans le n. le plus complet** to be totally in the dark

4 *(dans un jeu)* black; **le n. est sorti** black came up; **les noirs jouent et font mat en trois coups** black to play and mate in three

5 *(technique)* **n. au blanc** *Typ* reverse printing; *Ordinat* reverse video; *Typ* **n. au gris** black-on-tone, BOT

6 *Fam (café)* (black) coffee; **un petit n., s'il vous plaît** a cup of black coffee, please

7 *Mil (d'une cible)* bull's-eye

ADV dark; **il fait n. de bonne heure** it's getting dark early; **il fait n. comme dans un four** *ou* **tunnel ici** it's pitch-dark *or* pitch-black in here

• **Noir, -e** NM,F Black, black man, *f* woman; **les Noirs** (the) Blacks; **N. américain** African American

• **noire** NF *Mus Br* crotchet, *Am* quarter note

• **au noir** ADJ **travail au n.** moonlighting ADV *(illégalement)* **je l'ai eu au n.** I got it on the black market; **travailler au n.** to moonlight; **acheter/vendre au n.** to buy/sell on the black market

• **en noir** ADJ *Belg* **travail en n.** moonlighting ADV 1 *(colorié, teint)* black; **habillé en n.** dressed in black, wearing black 2 *Fig* **voir tout en n.** to look on the dark side of things 3 *Belg* **travailler en n.** to moonlight; **acheter/vendre en n.** to buy/sell on the black market

noirâtre [nwarɑtr] ADJ blackish

noiraud, -e [nwaro, -od] ADJ dark, dark-skinned, swarthy

NM,F dark *or* swarthy person

noirceur [nwarsœr] NF 1 *(couleur noire)* blackness, darkness 2 *Littéraire (d'un acte, d'un dessein)* blackness, wickedness; *(d'un crime)* heinousness, foulness 3 *Can (obscurité)* dark, darkness; **dans la n.** in the dark *or* darkness; **avoir peur dans la n.** to be afraid of the dark

noircir [32] [nwarsir] VT 1 *(rendre noir)* to blacken; **noirci par le charbon** blackened with coal; **les parois noircies par la crasse** walls black with dirt *or* grime; *Fam* **n. du papier** to write pages and pages *or* page after page; **tout ce qu'il est capable de faire, c'est n. du papier** the only thing he's good at is putting ink on paper 2 *Fig (dramatiser)* **n. la situation** *ou* **le tableau** to make the situation out to be darker *or* blacker than it is 3 *Fig (dénigrer)* **n. la réputation de qn, n. qn** to blacken sb's reputation

VI to go black, to darken; *(légumes, fruits)* to go black; **le ciel noircit à l'horizon** the sky is darkening on the horizon

VPR **se noircir** 1 *(se grimer)* **se n. le visage** to blacken one's face; *Théât* to black up 2 *(s'assombrir)* to darken; **notre avenir se noircit** our future is looking blacker 3 *Fam (s'enivrer)* to get blind drunk

noircissement [nwarsismɑ̃] NM 1 *(gén)* blackening, darkening 2 *Métal* facing, blacking

noircissure [nwarsisyr] NF black stain

noise [nwaz] NF *Littéraire* **chercher n.** *ou* **des noises à qn** to try to pick a quarrel with sb

noisetier [nwaztje] NM *(plante)* hazel, hazelnut tree; *(bois)* hazel (wood)

noisette [nwazɛt] NF 1 *Bot* hazelnut

2 *(petite portion)* **une n. de beurre** a knob of butter; **une n. de pommade** a small dab of ointment; **une n. de gel** a small amount of gel

3 *Culin* **n. d'agneau** noisette of lamb; **beurre à la n.** brown butter

4 *(café)* = small coffee with a drop of milk

ADJ INV hazel; *Culin* **beurre n.** brown butter

noix [nwa] NF 1 *Bot* walnut; **n. du Brésil** Brazil nut; **n. de cajou** cashew (nut); **n. de coco** coconut; **n. de kola** cola nut; **n. de macadamia** macadamia nut; **n. (de) muscade** nutmeg; **n. de pécan** pecan (nut); *Fam* **des n.!** tripe!, hogwash!

2 *Culin* **n. de bœuf, n. de côtelette, n. de gigot** pope's eye; **n. de veau** cushion of veal

3 *(petite quantité)* **une n. de beurre** a knob of butter

4 *Fam (imbécile)* nut; **quelle n., ce type!** he's such a fool!

5 *Fam (camarade)* **salut, vieille n.!** hi, buddy *or Br* old chap!

• **à la noix, à la noix de coco** ADJ *Fam* lousy, crummy; **des excuses à la n.** *ou* **à la n. de coco** lousy excuses

nolisation [nɔlizasjɔ̃] NF chartering

nolisement [nɔlizmɑ̃] NM chartering

noliser [3] [nɔlize] VT to charter

nom [nɔ̃] **NM 1** *(patronyme)* name; *(prénom)* first name; **un homme du n. de Pierre** a man by the name of Pierre; **n.... prénom...** *(sur formulaire)* surname... first name...; **n. et prénoms** full name; **vos n., prénoms et adresse** your full name and address; **elle porte le n. de sa mère** *(prénom)* she was named after her mother; *(patronyme)* she has *or* uses her mother's surname; **tu porteras le n. de ton mari?** will you take your husband's name?; **Bosch, c'est un n. que tout le monde connaît** Bosch is a household name; **quelqu'un du n. de** *ou* **qui a pour n. Kregg vous demande** someone called Kregg *or* someone by the name of Kregg is asking for you; **je n'arrive pas à mettre un n. sur son visage** I can't put a name to his/her (face); **je la connais de n.** I (only) know her by name; **je ne te dirai pas son n.** I won't tell you who he/she is, I won't tell you his/her name; **quelqu'un dont je tairai le n.** someone who shall remain nameless; **j'écris sous le n. de Kim Lewis** I write under the name of Kim Lewis; **on le connaissait sous le n. de Leduc** he went by *or* was known by the name of Leduc; **sous un faux n.** under a false *or* an assumed name; **il veut laisser un n. dans l'histoire** he wants his name to go down in history; **un grand n. de la musique** one of the great names of music; **Louis, onzième du n.** Louis, the eleventh of that name; **en mon/ton n.** in my/your name, on my/your behalf; **parler en son n.** to speak for oneself; **parle-lui en mon n.** speak to him/her on my behalf *or* for me; **n. à particule** *ou Fam* **à rallonges** *ou* **à tiroirs** *ou* **à courants d'air** aristocratic surname, ≃ double-barrelled name; **un n. à coucher dehors** a mouthful; **il a un n. à coucher dehors** his name's a real mouthful; **n. de baptême,** *Fam* **petit n.** first name, *Am* given name; **n. de code** code name; **n. d'emprunt** assumed name; *Bourse* nominee name; **n. de famille** surname; **n. de guerre** nom de guerre, alias; **n. de jeune fille** maiden name; **traiter** *ou* **appeler qn de tous les noms** to call sb all the names under the sun; **je lui ai donné tous les noms d'oiseaux** I called him/her every name under the sun; **n. patronymique** patronymic (name); **n. de plume** nom de plume, pen name; **n. de scène** *ou* **de théâtre** stage name; **faire un n. à qn** to help make a name for sb; **se faire un n.** to make a name for oneself; *Bible* **que ton n. soit sanctifié** hallowed be thy name

2 *(appellation ▸ d'une rue, d'un animal, d'un objet, d'une fonction)* name; **comme son n. l'indique** as its name indicates; **cet arbre porte le n. de peuplier** this tree is called a poplar; **il n'est roi que de n.** he is king in name only; **d'empereur, il ne lui manquait que le n.** he was emperor in all but name; **cruauté/douleur sans n.** unspeakable cruelty/pain; **une censure qui ne dit pas son n.** hidden *or* disguised censorship; **c'est du racisme qui n'ose pas dire son n.** it's racism by any other name; **appeler** *ou* **nommer les choses par leur n.** to call a spade a spade; **n. scientifique/vulgaire** *(d'une plante)* scientific/common name; *Ordinat* **n. de champ** field name; **n. commercial** trade name; *Com* **n. déposé** registered trademark; *Ordinat* **n. de domaine** domain name; *Mktg* **n. de famille global** blanket family name; *Ordinat* **n. de fichier** file name; *Mktg* **n. générique** generic name; **n. de lieu** place name; **n. de marque** brand name; *Ordinat* **n. de l'utilisateur** user name

3 *Gram & Ling* noun; **n. de chose** concrete noun; **n. commun** common noun; **n. composé** compound (noun); **n. comptable** countable noun; **n. numéral** *ou* **de nombre** numeral; **n. propre** proper noun *or* name

EXCLAM *Fam* **n. de n.!, n. d'un petit bonhomme!, n. d'une pipe!** for goodness' sake!, *Br* blimey!, *Am* gee (whiz)!; **n. d'un chien!** hell!; **n. de Dieu!** for Christ's sake!, Christ (Almighty)!; **je t'avais pourtant dit de ne pas y toucher, n. de Dieu!** for Christ's sake, I did tell you not to touch it!

• **au nom de PRÉP** in the name of; **faire une proposition au n. de qn** to make a proposal for sb *or* on behalf of sb; **faire qch au n. de l'amitié/la justice** to do sth in the name of friendship/justice; **au n. de la loi, je vous arrête** I arrest you in the name of the law; **au n. de toute l'équipe** on behalf of the whole team; **au n. du ciel!** in heaven's name!; **au n. du Père, du Fils et du Saint-Esprit** in the name of the Father, the Son and the Holy Ghost

nomade [nɔmad] **ADJ 1** *(peuple)* nomad *(avant n)*, nomadic **2** *Zool* migratory

NMF nomad; *Jur (gitan)* traveller; *Comput & Tél* road warrior

NF *Entom* Nomada

nomadisme [nɔmadism] **NM** nomadism

nombre [nɔ̃br] **NM 1** *Math (gén)* number; *(de 0 à 9)* number, figure; **un n. de trois chiffres** a three-digit *or* three-figure number; **n. complexe** complex number; **n. décimal** decimal (number); **n. entier** whole number, integer; **n. naturel** natural number; **n. parfait** perfect number; **n. premier** prime (number); **n. rationnel** rational number; **n. réel** real number; **grands nombres** large numbers

2 *(quantité)* number; **inférieur/supérieur en n.** inferior/superior in number *or* numbers; **nous sommes en n. suffisant** there are enough of us; *(dans une réunion)* we have a quorum; **les exemplaires sont en n. limité** there's a limited number of copies; **les voitures/manifestants convergeaient en très grand n. vers le centre de la ville** the cars/demonstrators were converging in huge numbers on the town centre; *Littéraire* **en n. écrasant** by an overwhelming majority; **un n. de** a number of; **un bon n. de** a good many; **je te l'ai déjà dit (un) bon n. de fois** I've already told you several times; **un grand n. de** a lot of, a great number of, a great many; **elle avait un grand n. d'invités** she had a great number of guests; **un grand/petit n. d'entre nous** many/a few of us; **le plus grand n. d'entre eux a accepté** the majority of them accepted; **un certain n. de** a (certain) number of; **il y a eu un certain n. de gens** there was a (fair) number of people; *Typ* **n. de caractères** character count; *Presse* **n. de lecteurs** readership; **n. de mots** word count, number of words; *Typ* **n. de pages** extent

3 *(masse)* numbers; **vaincre par le n.** to win by sheer weight *or* force of numbers; **venir en n.** to come in large *or* great numbers; **dans le n., il y en aura bien un pour te raccompagner** there's bound to be one of them who will take you home; **sur le n.** among *or* out of (all) those; **ils finirent par succomber sous le n. des assaillants** they were finally overcome by the sheer number of their attackers; **tu subiras la loi du n.** you'll be overwhelmed by sheer weight of numbers; **tous ceux-là n'ont été invités que pour faire n.** those people over there have just been invited to make up the numbers

4 *Astron, Biol & Phys* number; **n. atomique** atomic number; **n. d'Avogadro** Avogadro's number; **n. chromosomique** chromosome number; **n. d'or** golden section *or* mean

5 *Gram* number

• **Nombres NMPL** *Bible* **le livre des Nombres** (the Book of) Numbers

• **au nombre de PRÉP les invités sont au n. de cent** there are a hundred guests; **ils sont au n. de huit** there are eight of them; **être au n. des élus** to be one of *or* among the elect; *Sout* **mettre** *ou* **compter qn au n. de ses intimes** to number sb among one's friends

• **du nombre de PRÉP** amongst; **étiez-vous du n. des invités?** were you amongst *or* one of those invited?

• **sans nombre ADJ** countless, innumerable; *(foule)* huge, vast

nombreux, -euse [nɔ̃brø, -øz] **ADJ 1** *(comportant beaucoup d'éléments ▸ famille, armée, groupe)* large; **une foule nombreuse** a large *or* huge crowd **2** *(en grand nombre)* many, numerous; **avoir de n. clients** to have a great number of *or* many *or* numerous customers; **ils sont trop n.** there are too many of them; **ils étaient peu n.** there weren't many of them; **les étudiants sont plus n. qu'avant** there are more students than before; **les fumeurs sont de moins en moins n.** there are fewer and fewer smokers, the number of smokers is decreasing; **vous avez été n. à nous écrire** many of you have written to us; **venir (très) n.** to come in (very) large numbers; **venez n.!** all (are) welcome!, everyone (is) welcome!

nombril [nɔ̃bril] **NM 1** *Anat* navel; **une chemise ouverte jusqu'au n.** a shirt open to the waist **2** *Bot* hilum **3** *Fam (locutions)* **il se prend pour le n. du monde** he thinks he's the centre of the universe; **il aime bien se contempler** *ou* **se regarder le n.** he's very self-obsessed▫, he spends a lot of time navel-gazing; *Can* **ne pas avoir le n. sec** to be (still) wet behind the ears

nombrilisme [nɔ̃brilism] **NM** navel-gazing, self-obsession; **faire du n.** to contemplate one's navel

nomenclature [nɔmɑ̃klatyr] **NF 1** *(ensemble de termes techniques)* nomenclature **2** *(liste ▸ gén)* list; *(▸ d'un dictionnaire)* word list; *(▸ d'une voiture etc)* parts list; **n. douanière** *ou* **générale des produits** customs nomenclature

nominal, -e, -aux, -ales [nɔminal, -o] **ADJ 1** *(sans vrai pouvoir)* nominal; **il n'est que le chef n.** he's just the nominal leader, he's the leader in name only

2 *(par le nom)* of names, *Sout* nominal; **appel n.** roll call; **contrôle n.** name check; **liste nominale** list of names, name list

3 *Gram* nominal

4 *Bourse, Écon & Fin* **salaire n.** nominal wage *or* salary; **valeur nominale** *(d'une obligation)* par value; *(d'une action)* face *or* nominal value

5 *Ind* rated; **vitesse nominale** rated speed

NM *(d'une action)* nominal value; *(d'une obligation)* par value

nominalement [nɔminalmɑ̃] **ADV 1** *(sans vrai pouvoir)* nominally, formally; **il dirige n. l'entreprise** he's the nominal head of the business, he's the head of the business in name only **2** *(par le nom)* by name; **être désigné n.** to be mentioned by name **3** *Gram (comme un nom)* nominally, as a noun

nominalisme [nɔminalism] **NM** nominalism

nominatif, -ive [nɔminatif, -iv] **ADJ 1** *(contenant les noms)* **liste nominative** list of names **2** *Bourse (liste)* nominal; *(titres, actions)* registered **3** *(ticket, carte)* non-transferable; **votre carte bancaire est nominative** *(inscription sur carte)* this banker's card may be used only by the authorized signatory *or* by the person whose name it bears; **les places de concert ne sont pas nominatives** the seats for the concert are transferable

NM *Gram* nominative (case); **au n.** in the nominative (case)

nomination [nɔminasjɔ̃] **NF 1** *(à un poste)* appointment, nomination (**à** to); **attendre sa n.** to expect to be appointed; **elle a obtenu** *ou* **reçu sa n. au poste de directrice** she was appointed (to the post of) manager **2** *(pour un prix, une récompense)* nomination (**à** for); **ce film a trois nominations aux Césars** this film has received three César nominations **3** *Ling & Phil* naming

nominative [nɔminativ] *voir* **nominatif**

nominativement [nɔminativmɑ̃] **ADV** by name

nominer [3] [nɔmine] **VT** to nominate

nommage [nɔmaʒ] **NM** *Ordinat (de site Internet)* designation

nommé, -e [nɔme] **ADJ** *(appelé)* named; **deux enfants, nommés Victor et Marie** two children, named *or* called Victor and Marie

NM,F le n. Antoine the man named *or* called Antoine; **la nommée Chantal** the woman named *or* called Chantal; **elle fréquente un n. Paul** she's going out with someone *or* a man called Paul

nommément [nɔmemɑ̃] **ADV 1** *(par le nom ▸ citer, féliciter, accuser)* by name; **il est n. mis en cause** he, in particular, is implicated; **ces deux éléments, n. le cuivre et le zinc** these two elements, namely copper and zinc **2** *(spécialement)* especially, in particular

nommer [3] [nɔme] **VT 1** *(citer)* to name, to list; **ils refusent de n. leurs complices** they refuse to name their accomplices; **un homme que je ne nommerai pas** a man who shall remain nameless *or* whom I won't (mention by) name; *Ironique* **c'est la faute de Nina, pour ne pas la n.** without mentioning any names *or* naming no names, it's Nina's fault

2 *(prénommer)* to name, to call; **ils la nommèrent Aurore** they named her Aurore

3 *(dénommer)* to name, to call, to term; **on nomme aumôniers les prêtres attachés à un régiment** priests attached to a regiment are called chaplains

4 *(désigner à une fonction)* to appoint (**à** to); *Mil (officier)* to commission; **n. des experts** to appoint experts; **n. qn directeur** to appoint sb manager; **n. qn son héritier** to appoint sb as one's heir; **être nommé à Paris** to be appointed to a post in Paris; **être nommé au grade supérieur** to be promoted

VPR se nommer 1 *(s'identifier)* to give one's name; *(se présenter)* to introduce oneself; **elle ne s'est même pas nommée** she didn't even introduce herself *or* say who she was **2** *(s'appeler)* to be called *or* named; **comment se nomme-t-il?** what's his name?, what's he called?

non [nɔ̃] **ADV 1** *(en réponse négative)* no; **veux-tu venir? – n.** do you want to come? – no; **n. merci!** no, thank you!; **mais n.!** no!, absolutely not!; **mais n., voyons!** no, of course not!; **mais bien sûr que n.!** of course not!; **certes n.!** most definitely not!; **ma foi n.!** my goodness me, no!; **tu es content? – ma foi n.!** are you happy? – certainly not *or* far from it!; **ah ça n.!** definitely not!; **ah n. alors!** oh no!; **oh que n.!** definitely not!, certainly not!; *Vieilli Hum* **dame n.!, mon Dieu n.!, que n.!** certainly not!, definitely not!; **n., n. et n.!** no, no and no again!; **alors, ton augmentation? – c'est n.** what about your pay rise? – I didn't get it

2 *(pour annoncer ou renforcer la négation)* no; **n., je ne veux pas y aller** no, I don't want to go there; **n., il n'en est pas question** no, it's out of the question

3 *(dans un tour elliptique)* **il part demain, moi n.** he's leaving tomorrow, I'm not; **je me demande si je dois recommencer ou n.** I wonder whether I should start again or not; **que tu le veuilles ou n.** whether you like it or not; **venez-vous ou n.?** are you coming or not?

4 *(comme complément du verbe)* **il me semble que n.** I think not, I don't think so; **je pense que n.** I don't think so, I think not; **je dis que n.** I say no; **il a fait signe que n.** *(de la main)* he made a gesture of refusal; *(de la tête)* he shook his head; **il voulait traverser la rue, mais sa mère lui fit signe que n.** he was about to cross the road, but his mother signalled to him not to; **il paraît que n.** it would seem not, apparently not; **il a répondu n.** he answered no; **faire n. de la tête** to shake one's head

5 *(en corrélation avec "pas")* **n. pas** not; **il l'a fait par gentillesse et n. (pas) par intérêt** he did it out of kindness and not out of self-interest; **elle a été élevée n. (pas) par ses parents mais par ses grands-parents** she was brought up by her grandparents, not by her parents; **n. (pas) pour moi, mais pour lui** not for me, but for him; *Littéraire* **n. pas!** not so!, not at all!

6 *(en corrélation avec "plus")* **je m'adresse à vous n. plus en tant que ministre mais en tant que citoyen** I'm speaking to you not as a Minister but as a fellow citizen; **le problème est cette fois n. plus d'ordre économique mais social** the problem is now not economic but social; **je n'irai pas – moi n. plus** I'm not going – neither *or* nor am I

7 *(n'est-ce pas)* **il devait prendre une semaine de vacances, n.?** he was supposed to take a week's holiday, wasn't he?; **il n'est plus tout jeune, n.?** he's not that young any more, is he?

8 *(emploi expressif)* **n.!** never!, no!; **n.! pas possible!** no *or* never! I don't believe it!; **il est parti – n.!** he has left – really?; **n. mais (des fois)!** honestly!, I ask you!; **n. mais celui-là, pour qui il se prend?** who on earth does he think he is?; *Belg* **n. peut-être!** you bet!

9 *(devant un nom, un adjectif, un participe, un adverbe)* **la n.-observation du règlement** failure to comply with the regulations; **n. coupable** not guilty; **un débiteur n. solvable** an insolvent debtor; **un bagage n. réclamé** an unclaimed piece of luggage; **il a bénéficié d'une aide n. négligeable** he received not insubstantial help; **n. content de conduire sans permis, l'individu était ivre** not content with driving without a licence, the man was also drunk; **n. loin de la ville** not far from the town; **n. sans raison** not without reason

NM INV 1 *(réponse)* no; **elle m'a opposé un n. catégorique** she flatly refused; **les n. de la majorité** the noes of the majority **2** *Ordinat & Math* not

• **non que, non pas que CONJ** not that; **n. que je ne vous plaigne** not that I don't pity you

> **NON-** PREFIX
>
> **Non-** is a very productive prefix in French. It conveys an idea of OPPOSITION, and can be added to adjectives or nouns.
>
> • In the first case, the general rule is not to use a hyphen, although some adjectives starting with **non-** have become so lexicalized that they appear in dictionaries in hyphenated form. Nouns starting with **non-** normally carry a hyphen.
>
> • Besides well-established nouns occurring in dictionaries, recent usage has also created countless words with **non-**, mostly belonging to the field of philosophy or social affairs and carrying a distinctly euphemistic tone.
>
> • In many instances, the same prefix can be used in English, but sometimes the translator will need to paraphrase slightly, eg:
>
> **il a été déclaré non coupable** he was found not guilty; **une boisson non(-)alcoolisée** a non-alcoholic drink; **les pays non-alignés** nonaligned countries; **un pacte de non-agression** a non-aggression pact; **les non-fumeurs** non-smokers; **un état de non-droit** a situation in which law and order have broken down; **le non-respect de la loi** failure to observe the law; **le non-bonheur** unhappiness; **la non-liberté d'expression** lack of freedom of speech

non-acceptation [nɔnakseptasjɔ̃] **NF** *Banque (d'une lettre de change)* non-acceptance

non-accomplissement [nɔnakɔ̃plismɑ̃] **NM** *(d'un contrat)* non-fulfilment

non-activité [nɔnaktivite] **NF** *Mil* inactivity; **être en n.** to be temporarily off duty; *Admin* **mettre en n.** *(employé)* to suspend; *Mil (officier)* to put on half-pay; **mise en n.** *(d'un employé)* suspension; *Mil (d'un officier)* putting on half-pay

nonagénaire [nɔnaʒenɛr] **ADJ** nonagenarian; **être n.** to be in one's nineties

NMF person in his/her nineties

non-agression [nɔnagresjɔ̃] **NF** non-aggression

non-alcoolisé, -e [nɔnalkɔlize] *(mpl* **non-alcoolisés,** *fpl* **non-alcoolisées)** **ADJ** non-alcoholic

non-aligné, -e [nɔnaliɲe] *(mpl* **non-alignés,** *fpl* **non-alignées)** **ADJ** non-aligned

NM,F non-aligned country

non-alignement [nɔnaliɲmɑ̃] **NM** non-alignment

nonantaine [nɔnɑ̃tɛn] **NF** *Belg & Suisse* **1** *(quantité)* **une n.** around *or* about ninety, ninety or so; **une n. de voitures** around *or* about ninety cars; **elle a une n. d'années** she's around *or* about ninety (years old) **2** *(âge)* **avoir la n.** to be around *or* about ninety; **quand on arrive à** *ou* **atteint la n.** when you hit ninety

nonante [nɔnɑ̃t] *Belg & Suisse* **ADJ 1** *(gén)* ninety **2** *(dans des séries)* ninetieth; **page/numéro n.** page/number ninety

PRON ninety

NM INV 1 *(gén)* ninety **2** *(numéro d'ordre)* number ninety **3** *(chiffre écrit)* ninety; *voir aussi* **cinquante**

nonantième [nɔnɑ̃tjɛm] *Belg & Suisse* **ADJ** ninetieth

NMF 1 *(personne)* ninetieth **2** *(objet)* ninetieth (one)

NM 1 *(partie)* ninetieth **2** *(étage) Br* ninetieth floor, *Am* ninety-first floor; *voir aussi* **cinquième**

non-assistance [nɔnasistɑ̃s] **NF** *Jur* **n. à personne en danger** failure to assist a person in danger

non-autorisé, -e [nɔnɔtɔrize, nɔ̃ɔtɔrize] *(mpl* **non-autorisés,** *fpl* **non-autorisées)** **ADJ** *Ordinat (nom de fichier etc)* illegal

non-belligérance [nɔ̃beliʒerɑ̃s] **NF** non-belligerence

non-belligérant, -e [nɔ̃beliʒerɑ̃, -ɑ̃t] *(mpl* **non-belligérants,** *fpl* **non-belligérantes)** **ADJ** non-belligerent

NM,F non-belligerent

nonce [nɔ̃s] **NM** nuncio; **n. apostolique** papal nuncio

non-cessible [nɔ̃sesibl] *(pl* **non-cessibles)** **ADJ** *(billet)* not transferable

nonchalamment [nɔ̃ʃalamɑ̃] **ADV** *(avec insouciance)* nonchalantly; *(lentement)* listlessly

nonchalance [nɔ̃ʃalɑ̃s] **NF** *(insouciance)* nonchalance; *(lenteur)* listlessness; **avec n.** nonchalantly

nonchalant, -e [nɔ̃ʃalɑ̃, -ɑ̃t] **ADJ** *(insouciant)* nonchalant; *(lent)* listless

nonciature [nɔ̃sjatyr] **NF 1** *(charge d'un nonce)* nunciature **2** *(résidence)* nuncio's residence

non-combattant, -e [nɔ̃kɔ̃batɑ̃, -ɑ̃t] *(mpl* **non-combattants,** *fpl* **non-combattantes)** **ADJ** non-combatant

NM,F non-combatant

non-comparution [nɔ̃kɔ̃parysjɔ̃] **NF** non-appearance *or* defaulting *(in court)*

non-conciliation [nɔ̃kɔ̃siljasjɔ̃] **NF** *Jur* irretrievable breakdown

non-conformisme [nɔ̃kɔ̃fɔrmism] **NM 1** *(originalité)* nonconformism **2** *Rel* Nonconformism

non-conformiste [nɔ̃kɔ̃fɔrmist] *(pl* **non-conformistes)** **ADJ 1** *(original)* nonconformist **2** *Rel* Nonconformist

NMF 1 *(original)* nonconformist **2** *Rel* Nonconformist

non-conformité [nɔ̃kɔ̃fɔrmite] **NF** nonconformity

non-connecté, -e [nɔ̃kɔnekte] *(mpl* **non-connectés,** *fpl* **non-connectées)** **ADJ** *Ordinat* off-line

non-consigné, -e [nɔ̃kɔ̃siɲe] *(mpl* **non-consignés,** *fpl* **non-consignées)** **ADJ** non-returnable

non-coté, -e [nɔ̃kɔte] *(mpl* **non-cotés,** *fpl* **non-cotées)** **ADJ** *Bourse* unquoted

non-cumul [nɔ̃kymyl] **NM** *Jur* **n. des peines** concurrence of sentences; *Pol* **il faut renforcer les règles de n. des mandats** the laws prohibiting politicians from holding more than one post at a time need to be reinforced

non-dit [nɔ̃di] *(pl* **non-dits)** **NM le n.** the unsaid; **il y avait trop de n. dans notre famille** too much was left unsaid in our family; **un film riche en non-dits** a film full of meaningful silences

non-droit [nɔ̃drwa] **NM zone de n.** area in which law and order have broken down; **état de n.** situation in which law and order have broken down

none [nɔn] **NF 1** *Antiq (heure)* ninth hour **2** *Rel (office de 15 heures)* nones

• **nones NFPL** *Antiq (jour)* Nones

non-encaissé, -e [nɔnɑ̃kese] *(mpl* **non-encaissés,** *fpl* **non-encaissées)** **ADJ** *(chèque)* uncashed

non-engagé, -e [nɔnɑ̃gaʒe] *(mpl* **non-engagés,** *fpl* **non-engagées)** **ADJ** *(personne)* neutral; *(nation)* non-aligned

NM,F *(personne)* neutral person; *(nation)* non-aligned country

non-engagement [nɔnɑ̃gaʒmɑ̃] **NM** *(d'une personne)* neutrality, non-commitment; *(d'une nation)* non-alignment

non-être [nɔnɛtr] **NM INV** nonbeing

non-événement, non-évènement [nɔnevɛnmɑ̃] *(pl* **non-événements** *ou* **non-évènements)** **NM** non-event

non-exécution [nɔnegzekysjɔ̃] **NF** *(d'un contrat)* non-fulfilment

non-existence [nɔnegzistɑ̃s] **NF** non-existence

non-ferreux [nɔ̃ferø] **NM INV** *Métal & Minér* non-ferrous metal

non-figuratif, -ive [nɔ̃figyratif, -iv] *(mpl* **non-figuratifs,** *fpl* **non-figuratives)** *Beaux-Arts* **ADJ** non-figurative

NM,F nonfigurative artist, abstractionist

non-formaté, -e [nɔ̃fɔrmate] *(mpl* **non-formatés,** *fpl* **non-formatées)** **ADJ** *Ordinat* unformatted

non-fumeur, -euse [nɔ̃fymœr, -øz] *(mpl* **non-fumeurs,** *fpl* **non-fumeuses)** **ADJ** non-smoking

NM,F non-smoker; **compartiment non-fumeurs** non-smoking *or* no-smoking compartment

non-gage [nɔ̃gaʒ] **NM** *Aut* **certificat de n.** certificate of ownership

non-ingérence [nɔnɛ̃ʒerɑ̃s] **NF** *(par une personne)* non-interference; *(par une nation)* non-interference, non-intervention

non-initialisé, -e [nɔninisjalize, nɔ̃inisjalize]

(*mpl* **non-initialisés,** *fpl* **non-initialisées**) **ADJ** *Ordinat* uninitialized

non-initié, -e [noninisje] (*mpl* **non-initiés,** *fpl* **non-initiées**) **ADJ** uninitiated
NM,F uninitiated person

non-inscrit, -e [nonɛ̃skri, -it] (*mpl* **non-inscrits,** *fpl* **non-inscrites**) **ADJ** independent, non-party
NM,F independent member of parliament

non-intervention [nonɛ̃tɛrvɑ̃sjɔ̃] **NF** non-intervention

non-interventionniste [nonɛ̃tɛrvɑ̃sjɔnist] (*pl* **non-interventionnistes**) **ADJ** non-interventionist
NMF non-interventionist

non-jouissance [nɔ̃ʒwisɑ̃s] **NF** non-enjoyment

non-justifié, -e [nɔ̃ʒystifje] (*mpl* **non-justifiés,** *fpl* **non-justifiées**) **ADJ** *Typ* unjustified, non-justified; **n. à droite** ragged right; **n. à gauche** ragged left

non-lieu [nɔ̃ljø] (*pl* **non-lieux**) **NM** *Jur* **(ordonnance** *ou* **arrêt de) n.** no grounds for prosecution; **bénéficier d'un n.** to be discharged through lack of evidence

non-livraison [nɔ̃livrɛzɔ̃] **NF** *Com* non-delivery

non-modifiable [nɔ̃mɔdifjabl] (*pl* **non-modifiables**) **ADJ** (*billet*) not alterable

nonne [nɔn] **NF** *Vieilli* nun

non-négociable [nɔ̃negɔsjabl] (*pl* **non-négociables**) **ADJ** non-negotiable

nonnette [nɔnɛt] **NF 1** *Vieilli & Rel* young nun **2** *Orn* **n. (cendrée)** marsh tit **3** *Culin* iced gingerbread (*biscuit*)

non-nuisible [nɔ̃nɥizibl] **ADJ n. à l'environnement** environmentally friendly, environment-friendly

nono, -ote [nono, -ɔt] **NM,F** *Can Fam* (*idiot*) jerk

nonobstant [nɔnɔpstɑ̃] **PRÉP** *Jur ou Hum* notwithstanding, despite; **ce n.** this notwithstanding

nonote [nɔnɔt] *voir* **nono**

non-paiement [nɔ̃pemɑ̃] **NM** *Jur* non-payment, failure to pay

nonpareil, -eille [nɔ̃parɛj] **ADJ** *Vieilli* peerless

non-partant [nɔ̃partɑ̃] (*pl* **non-partants**) **NM** (*cheval*) non-starter

non-polluant, -e [nɔ̃pɔlɥɑ̃, -ɑ̃t] (*mpl* **non-polluants,** *fpl* **non-polluantes**) **ADJ** non-polluting

non-prolifération [nɔ̃prɔliferasjɔ̃] **NF** non-proliferation

non-recevoir [nɔ̃rəsəvwar] *voir* **fin**

non-récupérable [nɔ̃rekyperabl] (*pl* **non-récupérables**) **ADJ** *Ordinat* non-recoverable

non-remboursable [nɔ̃rɑ̃bursabl] (*pl* **non-remboursables**) **ADJ** non-refundable

non-représentation [nɔ̃rəprezɑ̃tasjɔ̃] **NF** *Jur* **n. d'enfant** non-restitution of a child (to its custodian), non-compliance with a custodianship order

non-résident [nɔ̃rezidɑ̃] (*pl* **non-résidents**) **NM** foreign national, non-resident

non-respect [nɔ̃rɛspɛ] **NM** failure to respect; (*d'une loi*) failure to observe

non-retour [nɔ̃rətur] **NM point de n.** point of no return

non-salarié, -e [nɔ̃salarje] (*mpl* **non-salariés,** *fpl* **non-salariées**) **ADJ** unsalaried
NM,F self-employed person; **les non-salariés** the self-employed

non-sens [nɔ̃sɑ̃s] **NM INV 1** (*absurdité*) nonsense; **cette situation est un n.** this situation is nonsensical *or* a nonsense **2** *Ling* meaningless word/phrase (*in a translation*)

non-spécialiste [nɔ̃spesjalist] (*pl* **non-spécialistes**) **ADJ** non-specialized
NMF non-specialist

non-stop [nɔnstɔp] **ADJ INV** non-stop
ADV non-stop

non-suspendu [nɔ̃syspɑ̃dy] (*pl* **non-suspendus**) **ADJ M** *Aut* (*freins*) outboard

non-syndiqué, -e [nɔ̃sɛ̃dike] (*mpl* **non-syndiqués,** *fpl* **non-syndiquées**) **ADJ** non-union, non-unionized
NM,F non-union *or* non-unionized worker

non-taxable [nɔ̃taksabl] **ADJ** non-dutiable

non-tissé [nɔ̃tise] (*pl* **non-tissés**) **NM** non-woven fabric

non-usage [nɔnyzaʒ] **NM 1** (*gén*) non-use **2** *Jur* non-usage

non-valeur [nɔ̃valœr] (*pl* **non-valeurs**) **NF 1** *Péj* (*chose*) valueless thing; (*personne*) nonentity **2** *Jur* (*état*) unproductiveness; (*bien*) unproductive asset; **terres en n.** unproductive land (*UNCOUNT*) **3** *Fin* (*créance*) bad debt; *Bourse* worthless security

non-vérifié, -e [nɔ̃verifje] (*mpl* **non-vérifiés,** *fpl* **non-vérifiées**) **ADJ** *Compta* unaudited

non-viable [nɔ̃vjabl] (*pl* **non-viables**) **ADJ 1** *Méd* nonviable **2** *Fig* unfeasible

non-violence [nɔ̃vjɔlɑ̃s] **NF** non-violence

non-violent, -e [nɔ̃vjɔlɑ̃, -ɑ̃t] (*mpl* **non-violents,** *fpl* **non-violentes**) **ADJ** non-violent
NM,F non-violent protester

non-voyant, -e [nɔ̃vwajɑ̃, -ɑ̃t] (*mpl* **non-voyants,** *fpl* **non-voyantes**) **NM,F** unsighted person, visually impaired person; **les non-voyants** the unsighted, the visually impaired

nopal, -als [nɔpal] **NM** *Bot* nopal, prickly pear

noquette [nɔkɛt] **NF** *Belg* **une n. de beurre** a knob of butter

noradrénaline [nɔradrenalin] **NF** *Biol & Chim* noradrenalin, noradrenaline

nord [nɔr] **NM INV 1** (*point cardinal*) north; **au n.** in the north; **où est le n.?** which way is north?; **la partie la plus au n. de l'île** the northernmost part of the island; **le vent vient du n.** it's a north *or* northerly wind, the wind is coming from the north; **un vent du n.** a northerly wind; **le vent du n.** the north wind; **aller au** *ou* **vers le n.** to go north *or* northwards; **les trains qui vont vers le n.** trains going north, northbound trains; **rouler vers le n.** to drive north *or* northwards; **aller droit vers le n.** to head due north; **la cuisine est plein n.** *ou* **exposée au n.** the kitchen faces due north; **n. géographique** true *or* geographic north; **n. magnétique** magnetic north; *Fam* **perdre le n.** to go crazy, to lose it **2** (*partie d'un pays, d'un continent*) north, northern area *or* regions; (*partie d'une ville*) north; **le n. de l'Italie** northern Italy, the north of Italy; **elle habite dans le n.** she lives in the north; **il habite dans le n. de Paris** he lives in the north of Paris; **elle est du n.** she's from the north
ADJ INV north (*avant n*), northern; (▸ *côte, face*) north (*avant n*); (▸ *banlieue, partie, région*) northern; **la façade n. d'un immeuble** the north-facing wall of a building; **la chambre est côté n.** the bedroom faces north; **dans la partie n. de la France** in the north of France, in northern France; **suivre la direction n.** to head *or* to go northwards

• **Nord ADJ INV** North **NM 1** *Géog* **le N.** the North; **le grand N.** the Far North; **la mer du N.** the North Sea **2** (*département*) **le N.** Nord

• **au nord de PRÉP** (to the) north of; **il habite au n. de Paris** he lives to the north of Paris

nord-africain, -e [nɔrafrikɛ̃, -ɛn] (*mpl* **nord-africains,** *fpl* **nord-africaines**) **ADJ** North African
• **Nord-Africain, -e NM,F** North African

nord-américain, -e [nɔramerikɛ̃, -ɛn] (*mpl* **nord-américains,** *fpl* **nord-américaines**) **ADJ** North American
• **Nord-Américain, -e NM,F** North American

nord-coréen, -enne [nɔrkɔreɛ̃, -ɛn] (*mpl* **nord-coréens,** *fpl* **nord-coréennes**) **ADJ** North Korean
• **Nord-Coréen, -enne NM,F** North Korean

nord-est [nɔrɛst] **NM INV** north-east
ADJ INV north-east (*avant n*)

nordicité [nɔrdisite] **NF** *Can* northerliness, nordicity

nordique [nɔrdik] **ADJ** (*pays, peuple*) Nordic; (*langue*) Nordic, Scandinavian
NM (*langue*) Norse
• **Nordique NMF** Nordic

nordir [32] [nɔrdir] **VI** *Naut* to veer north *or* northward

nordiste [nɔrdist] **ADJ 1** (*du Nord des États-Unis*) Northern, Yankee (*avant n*) **2** *Am Hist* (*pendant la guerre de Sécession*) Northern, Yankee
• **Nordiste NMF 1** (*du Nord des États-Unis*) Northerner, Yankee **2** *Am Hist* (*pendant la guerre de Sécession*) Northerner, Yankee

nord-nord-est [nɔrnɔrɛst] **NM INV** north-north-east
ADJ INV north-north-east (*avant n*)

nord-nord-ouest [nɔrnɔrwɛst] **NM INV** north-north-west
ADJ INV north-north-west (*avant n*)

nord-ouest [nɔrwɛst] **NM INV** north-west
ADJ INV north-west (*avant n*)

nord-vietnamien, -enne [nɔrvjetnamjɛ̃, -ɛn] (*mpl* **nord-vietnamiens,** *fpl* **nord-vietnamiennes**) **ADJ** North Vietnamese
• **Nord-Vietnamien, -enne NM,F** North Vietnamese

NOREX [nɔrɛks] **NM** *Com* = source of information on standards and rules governing goods for export

noria [nɔrja] **NF 1** (*machine hydraulique*) bucket elevator, noria **2** *Fig* (*série de véhicules*) endless stream

normal, -e, -aux, -ales [nɔrmal, -o] **ADJ 1** (*ordinaire* ▸ *vie, personne*) normal; (▸ *taille, poids*) normal, standard; (▸ *accouchement, procédure*) normal, straightforward; **la situation est redevenue normale** the situation is back to normal; **tu trouves ça n., toi?** do you think that's all right *or* OK?; **la lampe ne s'allume pas, ce n'est pas n.** the light isn't coming on, there's something wrong; **vitesse normale** normal *or Spéc* rated speed
2 (*habituel*) normal, usual; **elle n'était pas dans son état n.** she wasn't her normal self; **c'est le prix n.** that's the usual *or* standard price; **en temps n.** in normal circumstances, normally
3 (*compréhensible*) normal, natural; **c'est tout à fait n. que la jeunesse se rebelle** it's only normal *or* natural for young people to rebel; **mais c'est bien n., voyons** it's only natural, don't worry about it; *Fam* **c'est pas n.!** it's not on!
4 *Fam* (*mentalement*) normal; **elle n'est pas très normale, celle-là!** she's not quite normal!
5 *Chim* normal; **solution** *ou* **liqueur normale** normal solution
6 *Typ* roman
• **normale NF 1** (*situation*) normal (situation); **un retour à la normale** a return to normal
2 *Météo* normal; **température au-dessous de la normale (saisonnière)** temperature below the (seasonal) average
3 (*moyenne*) average; **intelligence supérieure à la normale** above average intelligence
4 *Scol* **Normale (Sup)** = "grande école" for teacher-training

normalement [nɔrmalmɑ̃] **ADV 1** (*de façon ordinaire*) normally **2** (*sauf changement*) if all goes well; **n., nous partirons en juin** if all goes well, we'll be leaving in June; **n., elle devrait être arrivée** she should be here by now **3** (*habituellement*) normally, usually, generally; **n., elle rentre à trois heures** she normally *or* generally comes home at three (o'clock)

> Il faut noter que l'adverbe anglais **normally** ne s'emploie jamais dans le sens de "si tout va bien".

normalien, -enne [nɔrmaljɛ̃, -ɛn] **NM,F 1** (*de l'École normale*) student at an "École normale"; (*ancien de l'École normale*) graduate of an "École normale" **2** (*de l'École normale supérieure*) student at the "École normale supérieure"; (*ancien de l'École normale supérieure*) graduate of the "École normale supérieure"

normalisation [nɔrmalizasjɔ̃] **NF 1** (*d'un produit*) standardization **2** (*d'une situation*) normalization; **jusqu'à la n. de la situation** until the situation becomes normal

normalisé, -e [nɔrmalize] **ADJ** standardized

normaliser [3] [nɔrmalize] **VT 1** (*produit*) to standardize **2** (*rapport, situation*) to normalize
VPR se normaliser to return to normal

normalité [nɔrmalite] **NF** normality, *Am* normalcy

normand, -e [nɔrmɑ̃, -ɑ̃d] **ADJ 1** (*de Normandie*) Normandy (*avant n*); **je suis n.** I'm from Normandy **2** *Hist* Norman
NM (*langue*) Norman French
• **Normand, -e NM,F** (*en France*) Norman; **les Normans** the Normans

Normandie [nɔrmɑ̃di] **NF la N.** Normandy

norme [nɔrm] NF **1** *Ind* norm, standard; **n. de production** production norm; **n. de productivité** productivity norm; **produit conforme aux normes de fabrication/sécurité** product conforming to manufacturing/safety standards; **n. française (homologuée)** French standard (of manufacturing), *Br* ≃ British Standard, *Am* ≃ US Standard; **normes européennes** European standards; **normes d'application obligatoires/volontaires** compulsory/voluntary standards; **normes publicitaires** advertising standards; **n. technique** technical standard; **n. de travail** work standard **2** *(règle)* **la n.** the norm, the rule; **échapper à la n.** to be an exception **3** *Math* norm

normographe [nɔrmɔgraf] NM stencil

norois[1] [nɔrwa] NM *(vent)* northwester

norois[2], **-e** [nɔrwa, -az] *Ling* ADJ Norse
NM Norse

noroît [nɔrwa] = **norois**[1]

norrois, -e [nɔrwa, -az] = **norois**[2]

Norvège [nɔrvɛʒ] NF *Géog* **la N.** Norway

norvégien, -enne [nɔrveʒjɛ̃, -ɛn] ADJ Norwegian
NM *(langue)* Norwegian
• **Norvégien, -enne** NM,F Norwegian
• **norvégienne** NF Norway yawl

nos [no] *voir* **notre**

nosocomial, -e, -aux, -ales [nozokɔmjal, -o] ADJ *Méd (maladie, infection)* nosocomial

nostalgie [nɔstalʒi] NF **1** *(regret)* nostalgia; **penser à qch avec n.** to think of sth nostalgically *or* with nostalgia; **avoir la n. de** to feel nostalgic about; **j'ai la n. de ces temps-là** I look back on that time with nostalgia, I feel nostalgia for that time **2** *(mal du pays)* homesickness; **avoir la n. du pays** to be homesick

nostalgique [nɔstalʒik] ADJ nostalgic
NMF nostalgic person; **les nostalgiques des années 60** people who pine for the 60s, people who are nostalgic for the 60s

nota bene [nɔtabene], **nota** [nɔta] NM INV nota bene

notabilité [nɔtabilite] NF notable, worthy

notable [nɔtabl] ADJ *(fait)* notable; *(différence)* appreciable, noticeable
NM notable, worthy; **tous les notables de la ville** all the town notables *or* worthies

notablement [nɔtabləmɑ̃] ADV notably, considerably

notaire [nɔtɛr] NM *(qui reçoit actes et contrats)* notary (public), lawyer; *(qui surveille les transactions immobilières)* lawyer, *Br* solicitor

notamment [nɔtamɑ̃] ADV especially, in particular, notably

notarié, -e [nɔtarje] ADJ legally drawn up, authentic; **acte n.** notarized deed

notation [nɔtasjɔ̃] NF **1** *(remarque)* note
2 *Chim, Ling, Math & Mus* notation; **la n. phonétique** phonetic symbols
3 *Scol (d'un travail, d'un élève) Br* marking, *Am* grading
4 *Ordinat* **n. hexadécimale** hex *or* hexadecimal code
5 *(gén) & Fin & Bourse* rating; *Bourse* **n. AA** double-A rating; *Bourse* **n. AAA** triple-A rating

note [nɔt] NF **1** *Mus (son)* note; *(touche)* key; **sais-tu lire les notes?** can you read music?; **dans la n.** in tune *or* key; *aussi Fig* **être dans la n.** to hit just the right note; **donner la n.** *Mus* to give the keynote; *Fig* to give the lead; **fausse n.** *Mus* wrong note; *Fig* false note; *Mus* **faire une fausse n.** *(pianiste)* to hit a wrong note *or* key; *(violoniste)* to play a wrong note; *(chanteur)* to sing a wrong note; **la n. juste** the right note
2 *(annotation)* note; **prendre des notes** to take notes; **voilà les notes rapides que j'ai prises** here are the notes I jotted down; **prendre qch en n., prendre n. de qch** to make a note of sth, to note sth down; **prendre bonne n. de qch** to take due *or* good note of sth; **n. de l'auteur** author's note; **n. explicative** explanatory note; **n. de** *ou* **en bas de page** footnote; **n. de l'éditeur** editor's note; *Ordinat* **n. de fin de document** endnote; **n. marginale** marginal note; **n. de la rédaction** editor's note; **n. de renvoi** cross-reference; **n. du traducteur** translator's note
3 *(communication)* **n. diplomatique/officielle** diplomatic/official note; **n. d'information** *ou* **de service** memo, memorandum; *Douanes* **n. de détail** details, description *(of parcel)*
4 *Scol & Univ Br* mark, *Am* grade; **notes trimestrielles** (end-of-term) report; **avoir la meilleure n.** to get the best *or* highest *or* top *Br* mark *or Am* grade; **carnet** *ou* **relevé de notes** *Br* school report, *Am* report card
5 *(nuance)* note, touch, hint; **une n. d'originalité** a touch *or* note of originality; **apporter une n. personnelle à qch** to give sth a personal touch; **mettre une n. de gaieté dans une pièce** to lend a cheerful note to a room; **finir sur une n. positive** to end on a positive note
6 *(facture)* bill, *Am* check; **n. de téléphone** phone bill; **n. de restaurant** restaurant bill; **mettez-le sur ma n.** charge it to my account, put it on my bill; **régler la n.** to pay the bill; *Com* **n. d'avis** advice note; **n. d'avoir** credit note; **n. de commission** commission note, fee note; **n. de crédit** credit note; **n. de débit** debit note; **n. de frais** expense account; *(présentée après coup)* expenses claim form; **présenter sa n. de frais** to claim for expenses; **mettre qch sur sa n. de frais** to put sth on one's expense account; *Com* **n. de fret** freight note; **n. d'honoraires** invoice *(for work done by self-employed person)*; **n. de rappel** reminder
7 *(d'un parfum)* note
• **notes** NFPL *(précis)* study notes *(for works of literature)*

noté, -e [nɔte] ADJ **1 être bien/mal n.** *(élève, employé)* to have a good/bad record; *(devoir)* to have received a good/poor *Br* mark *or Am* grade **2** *Bourse* **n. AA/AAA** double-A/triple-A rated

notebook [nɔtbuk] NM *Ordinat* notebook

noter [3] [nɔte] VT **1** *(prendre en note)* to note *or* to write (down); **je note votre nom** I'll make a note of *or* I'll write down your name; **veuillez n. notre nouvelle adresse** please note *or* make a note of our new address; **notez que chaque enfant doit apporter un vêtement chaud** please note that every child must bring something warm to wear; **n. une commande** to log *or* to note an order
2 *(faire ressortir ► gén)* to mark; *(► en cochant)* to tick; *(► en surlignant)* to highlight; **n. qch d'une croix** to put a cross next to sth
3 *(remarquer)* to note, to notice; **j'ai noté une erreur dans votre article** I noticed a mistake in your article; **notez que je ne dis rien** please note that I'm making no comment; **il est à n. que...** it should be noted *or* borne in mind that...; **à n.: les bus ne circulent pas le dimanche** note: there are no buses on Sundays; **très bien, chef, c'est noté** OK, boss, I've got it; *Fam* **je ne veux pas que tu recommences, c'est noté?** I don't want you to do it again, do you understand *or* have you got that *or* is that clear?; **notez bien cela** take good note of this, note this well; **notez bien, il a fait des progrès** mind you, he's improved
4 *Scol & Univ (travail, examen) Br* to mark, *Am* to grade; *(élève) Br* to give a mark to, *Am* to grade
USAGE ABSOLU **1** *(prendre en note) Fam* **très bien, chef, je note** OK, boss, I've got it **2** *Scol (évaluer)* **elle note généreusement/sévèrement** she gives high/low *Br* marks *or Am* grades

notice [nɔtis] NF **1** *(résumé)* note; **n. bibliographique** bibliographical details; **n. biographique** biographical note; **n. nécrologique** obituary (notice); **n. publicitaire** *(brochure)* advertising brochure; *(annonce)* advertisement **2** *(instructions)* instruction book *or* booklet, handbook, manual; **n. du constructeur** manufacturer's instructions; **n. explicative** *ou* **d'emploi** directions for use **3** *(préface de livre)* note

> Il faut noter que le nom anglais **notice** est un faux ami. Il signifie le plus souvent **avertissement**, **écriteau** ou **attention**, selon le contexte.

notification [nɔtifikasjɔ̃] NF *(avis)* notification; **donner à qn n. de qch** to give sb notification of sth, to notify sb of sth; **recevoir n. de qch** to receive notification *or* to be notified of sth

notifier [9] [nɔtifje] VT *(apprendre)* **n. qch à qn** to notify sb of sth; **on vient de lui n. son renvoi** he's/she's just received notice of his/her dismissal, he's/she's just been notified of his/her dismissal; *Jur* **n. son consentement à qn** to signify one's consent to sb; **on lui notifia qu'il aurait à déménager dans les vingt-quatre heures** he received notice to quit within twenty-four hours
USAGE ABSOLU **veuillez n. par courrier** please inform us in writing

notion [nosjɔ̃] NF *(idée)* notion; **perdre la n. du temps** to lose all sense of time, to lose track of time; **perdre la n. de la réalité** to lose all sense of reality
• **notions** NFPL *(rudiments)* **notions de base** fundamentals, basic knowledge; **il a quelques notions de physique** he has some knowledge of physics; **anglais: notions** *(sur un CV)* basic knowledge of English

notoire [nɔtwar] ADJ recognized; *Péj* notorious; *(fait)* well-known; **son sens politique est n.** his/her political acumen is acknowledged by all, he's/she's famous for his/her political acumen; **être d'une avarice n.** to be notoriously miserly

> Il faut noter que l'adjectif anglais **notorious** signifie "tristement célèbre".

notoirement [nɔtwarmɑ̃] ADV manifestly, *Péj* notoriously; **fait n. faux** manifestly false fact; **un malfrat n. connu** a notorious gangster

notoriété [nɔtɔrjete] NF **1** *(renommée)* fame, renown; **cela lui a valu une certaine n.** that brought *or* earned him/her a certain reputation; **il est de n. publique que...** it's public *or* common knowledge that... **2** *Mktg* awareness; **n. assistée** aided recall; **n. de la marque** brand awareness; **n. du produit** product awareness; **n. publicitaire** advertising awareness; **n. spontanée** spontaneous recall **3** *Jur* **acte de n.** sworn affidavit

> Il faut noter que le nom anglais **notoriety** signifie uniquement "mauvaise réputation".

notre [nɔtr] *(pl* **nos** [no]) ADJ POSSESSIF **1** *(indiquant la possession)* our; **n. ami/amie** our friend; **nos enfants** our children; **n. père et n. mère,** *Littéraire* **nos père et mère** our father and mother; **ils ont mis nos chapeaux et nos gants** they put on our hats and (our) gloves; **nous avons pris n. sac** *(il n'y a qu'un sac)* we took our bag; *(chacun a son sac)* we took our bags; **un de nos amis** a friend of ours, one of our friends; **n. société** our society; *Fam* **nous aurons n. chambre à nous** *(il y a une chambre)* we will have our own room[☐]; *Fam* **nous avons n. vendredi** we've got Friday off[☐]
2 *Rel* **N. Père** Our Father; **le N. Père** the Lord's Prayer
3 *(se rapportant au "nous" de majesté ou de modestie)* **car tel est n. bon plaisir** for such is our pleasure
4 *(emploi expressif)* our; **comment se porte n. petit malade?** how's our little invalid, then?; *Fam* **n. imbécile de frère** our idiot of a brother; *Fam* **nos artistes de maris** our artist husbands; **nous retrouvons n. héros dix ans plus tard...** we meet our hero again ten years later...

nôtre [notr] ADJ *Littéraire* ours; **un n. cousin** a cousin of ours; **ces espoirs qui furent nôtres** these hopes which were ours; **nous ferons nôtres ses principes** we shall adopt these principles of his/hers; **nous faisons nôtres les félicitations qu'ils vous adressent** we join them in congratulating you
PRON POSSESSIF **le n./la n./les nôtres** ours; **cette valise n'est pas la n.** this isn't our case, this case isn't ours; **un sort tel que le n.** a fate such as ours; **il ressemble au n.** it looks like ours; **nous voulons bien te donner du n.** you can have some of ours; **amenez vos enfants, les nôtres ont le même âge** bring your children, ours are the same age; **cette histoire qui est la n.** this story which is ours; **les deux nôtres** our two, the two of ours, both of ours; *(en insistant)* our own two
NM **les nôtres** *(notre famille)* our family, *Am* our folks; *(nos partisans)* our followers; *(nos coéquipiers)* our team-mates; **c'est un des nôtres** he's one of us; **serez-vous des nôtres demain soir?** will you be joining us tomorrow evening?; **vous n'étiez pas des nôtres pour le réveillon de Noël?** weren't you at our Christmas Eve party?; **il faut y mettre du n.** we must do our bit, we should make an effort; **à la (bonne) n.!** cheers!

Notre-Dame [nɔtrədam] NF *Rel (titre)* Our Lady;

(église) **N. de Paris** *(cathédrale)* Notre Dame; **la fête de N.** the feast of the Assumption

nouba [nuba] **NF 1** *Fam (fête)* **faire la n.** to party, to have a wild time **2** *(musique)* (Algerian) military band

noue¹ [nu] **NF** *(terre grasse)* marshy meadow, water meadow

noue² [nu] **NF** *Constr (arête)* valley *(of roof)*; *(bande de plomb ou zinc)* flashing; **pièce de n.** valley tile

nouer [6] [nwe] **VT 1** *(attacher ensemble ▸ lacets, cordes)* to tie *or* to knot (together); **elle noua ses bras autour de mon cou** she wrapped her arms round my neck **2** *(faire un nœud à)* to tie (up), to knot; **n. qch serré** to knot sth tightly, to make a tight knot in sth; **n. sa cravate** to knot one's tie; **n. son tablier** to tie one's apron; **il a noué le foulard autour de sa taille** he tied the scarf around his waist; **n. ses cheveux** to tie up one's hair; *Fig* **la peur lui nouait la gorge/les entrailles** his/her throat/stomach tightened with fear **3** *(établir)* **n. des relations avec qn** to enter into a relationship with sb; **n. conversation avec qn** to enter into conversation with sb; **n. une intrigue** to hatch a plot

VI *Bot* to set

VPR se nouer 1 *(emploi réfléchi)* **se n. les cheveux** to tie up one's hair

2 *(emploi passif) (ceinture)* to fasten, to do up; **les cheveux se nouent d'abord sur la nuque** first tie your hair back at the neck

3 *(s'entrelacer)* to intertwine; **nos doigts se nouèrent** our fingers intertwined

4 *(s'instaurer)* to develop, to build up; **c'est à cet âge que beaucoup d'amitiés se nouent** it's at that age that a lot of friendships are made

5 *(prendre forme ▸ intrigue)* to take shape; **l'action ne se noue que dans le dernier chapitre** only in the last chapter does the plot come to a head *or* climax

noueux, -euse [nwø, -øz] **ADJ 1** *(tronc, bois)* knotty, gnarled **2** *(doigt, mains, tronc d'arbre)* gnarled; **un vieux paysan n.** a wizened old farmer

nougat [nuga] **NM 1** *Culin* nougat **2** *Fam (locutions)* **c'est du n.!** it's a cinch!, it's as easy as pie!; **c'est pas du n.!** it's not as easy as it looks!

• **nougats NMPL** *Fam (pieds)* feet▫, *Br* plates, *Am* dogs

nougatine [nugatin] **NF** nougatine

nouille [nuj] **ADJ INV 1** *Fam (niais)* dumb, silly

NF 1 *Culin* noodle **2** *Fam (nigaud)* dimwit, dumbo; *(mollasson)* drip, wimp

• **nouilles NFPL** noodles; *Fam (pâtes en général)* pasta▫ *(UNCOUNT)*

noumène [numen] **NM** noumenon

nounou [nunu] **NF** *Fam* nanny

nounours [nunurs] **NM** *Fam* teddy (bear)▫

nourri, -e [nuri] **PP** *voir* **nourrir**

ADJ 1 *(dense ▸ fusillade)* sustained, heavy **2** *(ininterrompu ▸ applaudissements)* prolonged, sustained **3** *(riche ▸ style)* rich, full; *(ligne en dessin)* broad, firm; **discussion nourrie** heated debate, lively discussion

nourrice [nuris] **NF 1** *(qui allaite)* wet nurse **2** *(qui garde) Br* childminder, *Am* nurse, nursemaid; **mettre un enfant en n.** to leave a child with a childminder; **n. agréée** registered childminder **3** *Aut (bidon)* spare can; *(réservoir)* service tank

nourricier, -ère [nurisje, -ɛr] **ADJ 1** *Littéraire (qui nourrit)* **notre terre nourricière** mother Earth **2** *Anat* nutrient *(avant n)* **3** *Bot* nutritive

nourrir [32] [nurir] **VT 1** *(alimenter)* to feed, *Sout* to nourish; **n. sa famille** to provide for *or* to feed one's family; **n. qn (de** *ou* **avec qch)** to feed sb (on sth); **n. un bébé au sein/au biberon** to breastfeed/to bottle-feed a baby; **poulet nourri au grain** corn-fed chicken; **être bien nourri** to be well-fed; **être mal nourri** *(sous-alimenté)* to be undernourished

2 *(sujet: crème, lotion ▸ peau, visage, cuir)* to nourish; *(feu)* to feed

3 *(faire subsister)* to feed; **j'ai trois enfants à n.** I've got three mouths to feed; **la Brie nourrit la capitale** the Brie area provides the capital with food; **la chanson/sculpture ne nourrit pas son homme** you can't live off singing/sculpture alone; **le métier est dangereux, mais il nourrit son homme** it's a dangerous job, but it brings in the money *or* it pays well

4 *Fig* **l'art contemporain ne me nourrit pas** I don't get anything out of modern art; **un roman nourri des souffrances de l'auteur** a novel inspired by the author's own suffering; *Mus* **n. le son** to give fullness *or* body to the tone

5 *Littéraire (pensée)* to entertain; *(illusion, rancœur, haine)* to harbour, to nurse, *Sout* to nourish; *(espoir)* to entertain, to cherish; *(projet)* to nurse; **il nourrit une vive rancœur contre elle** he harbours a feeling of great resentment towards her; **je nourris l'espoir de le revoir** I cherish the hope of seeing him again

USAGE ABSOLU le lait nourrit (bien) milk is nourishing

VPR se nourrir 1 *(s'alimenter)* to feed (oneself); *(manger)* to eat; **il est trop petit pour se n. tout seul** he's too young to feed himself; **il se nourrit mal** he doesn't eat properly; **il refuse de se n.** he won't eat; **se n. de lait/fruits** to live on milk/fruit; **il gagne juste de quoi se n.** he earns just enough to live on; **chasser pour se n.** to hunt for one's food **2** *Fig* **se n. d'illusions** to revel in illusions

nourrissant, -e [nurisɑ̃, -ɑ̃t] **ADJ** nourishing, nutritious; **crème nourrissante** nourishing cream

nourrisseur [nurisœr] **NM 1** *(éleveur ▸ de bétail)* stock breeder; *(▸ de vaches)* dairyman **2** *(appareil)* feeder

nourrisson [nurisɔ̃] **NM** *(bébé)* baby, infant; **consultation de nourrissons** baby clinic

nourriture [nurityr] **NF 1** *(alimentation)* food; **donner à qn une n. saine** to provide sb with a healthy diet; **le maïs sert à la n. du bétail** maize is used as a foodstuff for cattle *or* used as cattle-feed

2 la n. *(aliments)* food; **il refuse toute n. depuis trois jours** he has been refusing food *or* refusing to eat for three days; **priver qn de n.** to starve sb, to deprive sb of food

3 *(aliment)* food; **le lait est une n. riche en calcium** milk is a food rich in calcium

4 *Littéraire (de l'esprit, du cœur)* nourishment; **c'est bon pour leur n. intellectuelle** it will stimulate their minds

nous [nu] **PRON 1** *(sujet ou attribut d'un verbe)* we; **elle et moi, n. partons** she and I are leaving; **c'est n. qui déciderons** we are the ones who'll decide; **n., n. restons** *ou* *Fam* **on reste là** we are staying here; *Fam* **n. sommes allés au restaurant avec mon mari** *(lui et moi)* me and my husband went to the restaurant; **partons, rien que n. trois** let's leave, just us three *or* the three of us; **coucou, c'est n.!** hello, it's us!; **n. autres médecins pensons que…** we doctors think that…

2 *(complément d'un verbe ou d'une préposition)* us; **il ne n. connaît pas** he doesn't know us; **il n. a serré la main** he shook our hands; **les enfants n. ont jeté des pierres** the children threw stones at us; **elle n. en a parlé** she spoke to us about it; **lisez-le-n.** read it to us; **et n., tu n. oublies?** and what about us, have you forgotten us?; **elle n'aime que n. deux** she only loves us two *or* the two of us; **c'est à n. deux qu'il l'a demandé** he asked the two of us *or* (the) both of us; **à n. six, on a fini la paella** between the six of us, we finished the paella; **à n. deux!** *(sur un ton menaçant)* I want a word with you!; **c'est de la part de n. tous** it's from us all; **un ami à n.** a friend of ours; **notre voilier à n.** our (own) yacht; **ces anoraks ne sont pas à n.** these anoraks aren't ours *or* don't belong to us; **chez n.** *(dans notre foyer)* at home, in our house; *(dans notre pays)* at *or* back home; **il était avec n.** he was with us; **entre n.** between us; **entre n. (soit dit), elle ment** between us *or* between you and me, she's lying

3 *(sujet ou complément, représentant un seul locuteur)* we; **dans notre thèse, n. traitons le problème sous deux aspects** in our thesis, we deal with the problem in two ways; **alors, comment allons-n. ce matin?** *(à un malade, un enfant)* and how are we this morning?

PRON 1 *(emploi réfléchi)* **n. n. réchauffons** we are warming ourselves; **n. n. sommes versé du vin** we poured ourselves some wine; **n. n. amusons beaucoup** we're having a great time, we're really enjoying ourselves **2** *(emploi réciproque)* each other; **n. n. aimons** we love each other; **n. n. battions avec l'ennemi** we were fighting the enemy

NM le n. de majesté the royal we

nous-même [numɛm] **PRON** *(après "nous" de majesté, de modestie)* ourself

nous-mêmes [numɛm] **PRON** ourselves; **nous l'avons fait n.** we did it ourselves

NOUVEAU, -ELLE, -AUX, -ELLES [nuvo, -ɛl]

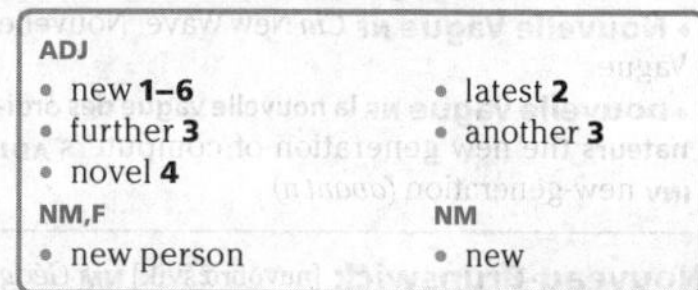

ADJ	
• new **1–6**	• latest **2**
• further **3**	• another **3**
• novel **4**	
NM,F	**NM**
• new person	• new

nouvel is used before masculine singular nouns beginning with a vowel or h mute.

ADJ 1 *(récent ▸ appareil, modèle)* new; *(▸ pays)* new, young; **il est n., ce manteau?** is this coat new?; **notre démocratie est encore nouvelle** democracy is still in its infancy in our country; **je suis n. dans le métier** I'm new to this business; **c'est tout n., ça vient de sortir** *(livre)* it's hot off the press; *(appareil)* it's brand-new, it's just come out; *Fig* **c'est n., ça vient de sortir** that's a new one on me; **la nouvelle génération** the new *or* rising generation; **les nouveaux arrivants** the newcomers; **nouvelle économie** new economy; **les nouveaux mariés** the newlyweds, the newly married couple; **les nouveaux pauvres** the new poor; **les nouveaux pères** modern fathers; **mots nouveaux** new words; *Pol* **nouvel État indépendant** newly independent state; **n. pays industrialisé** newly industrialized country; **n. riche** nouveau riche; *Mktg* **nouvel utilisateur** first-time user; *Méd* **n. variant de la maladie de Creutzfeldt-Jakob** new variant CJD; **n. venu/nouvelle venue** newcomer; *Cin* **nouvelle version** remake; *Fin* **nouvelle émission** *(d'actions)* new issue; *Fin* **nouveaux emprunts** new borrowings

2 *(dernier en date)* new, latest; **la nouvelle mode** the latest fashion; **ce nouvel attentat a fait 52 morts** this latest bomb attack leaves 52 dead; **elle se prend pour la nouvelle Marilyn Monroe** she thinks she's another *or* the new Marilyn Monroe; **nouvelle technologie** new technology; **techniques nouvelles** new *or* up-to-date techniques; **nouveaux élus** *(députés)* new *or* newly elected deputies; **herbe nouvelle** young grass; **carottes nouvelles** spring carrots; **pommes de terre nouvelles** new potatoes; **le beaujolais n.** the new Beaujolais *or* Beaujolais nouveau; **nouvel an, nouvelle année** New Year; **la nouvelle Europe** New Europe; **le N. Monde** the New World; **le N. Testament** the New Testament

3 *(autre)* further, new; **une nouvelle raison/hausse des prix** a further *or* an additional *or* another reason/price rise; **se faire de nouveaux amis** to make new friends; **faire de nouveaux efforts** to make fresh efforts; **faire à qn un n. procès** to retry sb; **écrire un n. chapitre** to write another chapter; **de nouvelles négociations sont prévues** further negotiations are scheduled to take place; **une nouvelle fois, je tiens à vous remercier** let me thank you once more *or* again

4 *(original ▸ découverte, idée)* new, novel, original; **un esprit/un son n. est né** a new spirit/sound is born; **une conception nouvelle** a novel *or* fresh approach; **porter un regard n. sur qn/qch** to take a fresh look at sb/sth; **elle est mécontente – ce n'est pas n.!** she's not happy – nothing new about that!

5 *(inhabituel)* new; **ce dossier est n. pour moi** this case is new to me, I'm new to this case

6 *(novateur)* **nouvelle critique** new criticism; **nouvelle cuisine** nouvelle cuisine; **n. roman** nouveau roman, new novel

NM,F *(adulte)* new person, new man, *f* new woman; *(élève)* new boy, *f* new girl

NM qu'est-ce qu'il y a de n.? what's new?; **rien de n. depuis la dernière fois** nothing new *or* special since last time; **il n'y a rien de n. sous le soleil** there's nothing new under the sun; **il y a quelqu'un de n. au bureau** there's someone new in the office; **j'ai du n. au sujet de…** I've got news about…

• **à nouveau ADV 1** *(de façon différente)* anew, afresh; **faites le plan à n.** redraft the plan, draft the plan again; **recommence à n.** start anew *or* afresh **2** *(encore)* (once) again, once more; **on**

entendit à n. le même bruit we heard the same noise (once) again **3** *Banque* **porter à n.** to carry forward

• **de nouveau** ADV again, once again, once more; **tu as fait de n. la même bêtise** you've made the same mistake again;

• **Nouvelle Vague** NF *Cin* New Wave, Nouvelle Vague

• **nouvelle vague** NF **la nouvelle vague des ordinateurs** the new generation of computers ADJ INV new-generation *(avant n)*

Nouveau-Brunswick [nuvobrœsvik] NM *Géog* **le N.** New Brunswick

Nouveau-Mexique [nuvomɛksik] NM *Géog* **le N.** New Mexico

nouveau-né, -e [nuvone] *(mpl* **nouveau-nés,** *fpl* **nouveau-nées)** ADJ newborn; **une fille nouveau-née** a newborn baby girl

NM,F **1** *(bébé)* newborn baby **2** *(appareil, technique)* new arrival; **un n. dans la gamme des ordinateurs portables** a new addition to the family of portable computers

nouveauté [nuvote] NF **1** *(chose nouvelle)* novelty, new thing; *(produit)* new product, innovation; *(livre)* new publication; *(invention)* new invention; **les nouveautés discographiques/littéraires** new releases/books; **tu fais de la musculation, c'est une n.!** you've taken up body-building, that's new!; **le racisme a toujours existé, ce n'est pas une n.** racism has always existed, there's nothing new *or* recent about it **2** *(originalité)* novelty, newness; **recherche constante de la n.** constant search for something new *or* for novelty **3** *Couture* fashion; **le commerce/l'industrie de la n.** the fashion trade/industry; **nouveautés de printemps** new spring fashions; *Vieilli* **magasin de nouveautés** draper's shop, *Am* dry goods store

nouvel [nuvɛl] *voir* **nouveau**

nouvelle [nuvɛl] ADJ F *voir* **nouveau**

NF **1** *(information)* news *(UNCOUNT)*, piece of news; **c'est une n. intéressante** that's an interesting piece of news, that's interesting news; **j'ai une bonne/mauvaise n. pour toi** I have (some) good/bad news for you; **voici une excellente n.!** this is good news!; **une n. plutôt décevante** a rather disappointing piece of news; **tu ne connais pas la n.? elle est renvoyée** haven't you heard (the news)? she's been fired; **la n. de sa mort** the news of his/her death; **fausse n.** false report; **répandre des fausses nouvelles** to spread false rumours; **première n.!** that's news to me! **2** *Littérature* short story, novella

• **nouvelles** NFPL **1** *(renseignements)* news *(UNCOUNT)*; **je n'ai pas eu de ses nouvelles depuis** I haven't had any news from him/her *or* heard from him/her since; **donne vite de tes nouvelles** write soon; **Paul m'a demandé de tes nouvelles** Paul was asking after you; **prendre des nouvelles de qn** to ask after sb; **j'ai eu des nouvelles de Pierre** *(par lui-même)* I've had news from *or* I've heard from Pierre; *(par quelqu'un d'autre)* I've had news about *or* of Pierre; **j'ai eu de tes nouvelles par ta sœur** your sister told me how you were getting on; **on n'eut plus jamais de leurs nouvelles** they were never heard of again; **je suis sans nouvelles de lui** *(directement)* I've had no news from him, I've not heard from him; *(indirectement)* I've had no news of *or* about him; **on est sans nouvelles des trois alpinistes** there's been no news of the three climbers; **aller aux nouvelles** to go and find out what's (been) happening; **je venais aux nouvelles** I just wanted to find out what's been happening; **les nouvelles vont vite** news travels fast; **aux dernières nouvelles, il était à Lima** he was last heard of in Lima; *Fam* **goûte-moi cette mousse, tu m'en diras des nouvelles** have a taste of this mousse, I think you'll like it; *Prov* **pas de nouvelles, bonnes nouvelles** no news is good news **2** *Rad & TV* news *(UNCOUNT)*; **les dernières nouvelles** the latest news; **à quelle heure sont les nouvelles?** when's the news on?

> Il faut noter que le nom anglais **novel** est un faux ami. Il signifie **roman**.

Nouvelle-Angleterre [nuvɛlɑ̃glətɛr] NF *Géog* **la N.** New England

Nouvelle-Calédonie [nuvɛlkaledɔni] NF *Géog* **la N.** New Caledonia

Nouvelle-Écosse [nuvɛlekɔs] NF *Géog* **la N.** Nova Scotia

Nouvelle-Galles du Sud [nuvɛlgaldysyd] NF *Géog* **la N.** New South Wales

Nouvelle-Guinée [nuvɛlgine] NF *Géog* **la N.** New Guinea

nouvellement [nuvɛlmɑ̃] ADV newly, recently, freshly; **n. élu/nommé** newly elected/appointed

Nouvelle-Orléans [nuvɛlɔrleɑ̃] NF *Géog* **La N.** New Orleans

Nouvelles-Hébrides [nuvɛlzebrid] NFPL *Anciennement* **les N.** the New Hebrides

Nouvelle-Zélande [nuvɛlzelɑ̃d] NF *Géog* **la N.** New Zealand

nouvelliste [nuvelist] NMF short story writer

nova [nɔva] NF nova

novateur, -trice [nɔvatœr, -tris] ADJ innovative

NM,F innovator

novélisation [nɔvelizasjɔ̃] NF novelization

novembre [nɔvɑ̃br] NM November; **le premier n.** (on) the first of November, (on) November the first; **le onze n.** *(fête) Br* Armistice Day, *Am* Veterans Day; *voir aussi* **mars**

novice [nɔvis] ADJ inexperienced, green; **être n. dans** *ou* **en qch** to be inexperienced in *or* a novice at sth

NMF **1** *(débutant)* novice, beginner **2** *Rel* novice

noviciat [nɔvisja] NM *Rel (période, lieu)* noviciate

Novocaïne® [nɔvɔkain] NF *Pharm* Novocaine®

noyade [nwajad] NF **1** *(fait de se noyer)* drowning *(UNCOUNT)*; **sauver qn de la n.** to save sb from drowning **2** *(accident)* drowning; **être témoin d'une n.** to witness a drowning **3** *Hist* execution by drowning

noyau, -x [nwajo] NM **1** *(de fruit)* stone, *Am* pit; **n. de cerise/pêche** cherry/peach stone; **enlever le n. d'un fruit** to pit a fruit, to remove the stone from a fruit

2 *(centre)* nucleus; **n. familial** family nucleus

3 *(petit groupe)* small group; **un n. d'opposants/d'irréductibles** a small group of opponents/hardliners; **le n. dur** *(d'un parti, de l'actionnariat)* the hard core; **n. de résistance** pocket *or* centre of resistance

4 *Anat, Astron, Biol & Phys* nucleus

5 *Élec, Géol & Nucl* core; *Géol* **n. volcanique** volcanic bomb

6 *Métal* (mould) core

7 *Chim* nucleus, ring

8 *Ordinat* node

noyautage [nwajotaʒ] NM *Pol* infiltration

noyauter [3] [nwajote] VT *Pol* to infiltrate

noyé, -e [nwaje] PP *voir* **noyer**[2]

ADJ **1** *(personne)* drowned; **mourir n.** to drown **2** *(moteur)* flooded **3** *Fig* **les yeux noyés** *ou* **le regard n. de larmes** his/her eyes swimming with *or* full of tears; **être n. dans la brume** to be shrouded in mist; **être n. dans la foule** to be lost in the crowd; **après l'invasion, le pays fut n. dans le sang** after the invasion, the country was awash with blood; **la maisonnette est noyée dans la verdure** the cottage is lost in the greenery; **l'essentiel est n. dans les détails** the essentials have been buried *or* lost in a mass of detail; *Fam* **être n.** *(ne rien comprendre)* to be out of one's depth

NM,F drowned person; **les noyés** the drowned; **on a repêché un n. dans la rivière** a drowned man was fished out of the river

noyer[1] [nwaje] NM **1** *(arbre)* walnut (tree); **n. (blanc) d'Amérique** hickory **2** *(bois)* walnut

noyer[2] [13] [nwaje] VT **1** *(personne, animal)* to drown; *(terre, champs)* to swamp; *(moteur, soute, vallée)* to flood; **les polders ont été noyés sous des mètres cubes d'eau** the polders were submerged under several cubic metres of water; **n. son chagrin (dans l'alcool)** to drown one's sorrows (in drink); *Pêche* **n. le poisson** to play the fish; *Fam Fig* **ne cherche pas à n. le poisson** don't try to confuse the issue; *Prov* **qui veut n. son chien l'accuse de la rage** give a dog a bad name (and hang him)

2 *(mouiller abondamment)* **les larmes noyaient son visage** his/her face was drenched with tears; **les larmes noyaient ses joues** tears poured down his/her cheeks

3 *(faire disparaître)* **une épaisse brume noie la vallée** the valley is shrouded in fog; **le piano est noyé par les violons** the violins are drowning out the piano

4 *Culin (sauce)* to water down, to thin (out) too much; *(vin)* to water down

5 *Menuis* to sink in cement; *(vis)* to countersink; **n. un clou** to drive a nail right in

VPR **se noyer 1** *(se suicider)* to drown oneself; **elle a essayé de se n.** she tried to drown herself

2 *(accidentellement)* to drown

3 *Fig* **se n. dans** *(se plonger dans)* to bury *or* to absorb oneself in; **quand j'ai des ennuis, je me noie dans le travail** when I have problems, I throw myself into my work *or* bury myself in work

4 *Fig* **se n. dans** *(s'empêtrer dans)* to get tangled up *or* bogged down *or* trapped in; **tu te noies dans tes mensonges** you're getting tangled up in your (own) lies; *Hum* **se n. dans un verre d'eau** to make a mountain out of a molehill

NPI [ɛnpei] NM *(abrév* **nouveau pays industrialisé)** NIC

NMPL *(abrév* **nouveaux pays industrialisés)** NICs

NTI [ɛntei] NFPL *(abrév* **nouvelles technologies de l'information)** NIT

nu, -e[1] [ny] ADJ **1** *(sans habits ▸ personne)* naked, nude; **une femme nue** a naked *or* nude woman; **être nu** to be naked *or* in the nude; **il était nu jusqu'à la ceinture** he was stripped to the waist; **être tout nu** to be stark naked; **se baigner tout nu** to bathe in the nude; **une plage où l'on peut se baigner (tout) nu** a beach where nude bathing is allowed; **se mettre (tout) nu** to take off all one's clothes, to strip naked; **être à demi nu** *ou* **à moitié nu** to be half-naked; **revue nue** nude show; **être nu comme un ver** *ou* **la main** to be stark naked

2 *(découvert ▸ partie du corps)* bare; **avoir les bras nus/fesses nues** to be bare-armed/bare-bottomed; **avoir le crâne nu** to be bald-headed; **se promener les jambes nues** to walk about bare-legged *or* with bare legs; **être pieds nus** to be barefoot *or* barefooted; **n'y va pas pieds nus** don't go there with bare feet; **avoir les seins nus** to be topless, to have bare breasts; **se baigner seins nus** to sunbathe topless; **la tête nue** bareheaded, without a hat on; **il travaillait torse nu** he was working without a shirt on; **mettez-vous torse nu** strip to the waist; **visible à l'œil nu** visible to the naked eye

3 *Fig (dégarni ▸ sabre)* naked; *(▸ paysage, mur, pièce, arbre)* bare; *(▸ style)* plain, unadorned; **la vérité (toute) nue** the plain *or* naked truth; *Élec* **fil nu** bare wire

NM **1** *Beaux-Arts (personne, œuvre)* nude; **le nu** *(genre)* the nude; **une photo de nu** a nude photo **2** *Constr* **nu de mur** plain of a wall

• **à nu** ADJ bare; **le fil est à nu** *(accidentellement)* the wire is bare; *(exprès)* the wire has been stripped; **mon âme était à nu** my soul had been laid bare ADV **mettre à nu** to expose; **mettre un fil électrique à nu** to strip a wire; **mettre son cœur à nu** to bare one's soul; *Vieilli Équitation* **monter un cheval à nu** to ride (a horse) bareback

nuage [nɥaʒ] NM **1** *Météo* cloud; **ciel chargé de nuages** cloudy *or* overcast sky; **n. de fumée/poussière** cloud of smoke/dust; **n. radioactif** radioactive cloud; **n. de sauterelles** cloud of locusts; **n. toxique** toxic cloud; **n. de chaleur** heat haze; **n. d'orage** storm cloud

2 *Fig (menace, inquiétude)* cloud; **un n. passa dans ses yeux/sur son visage** his/her eyes/face clouded over; **un n. de tristesse assombrissait son front** his/her face was clouded with sadness

3 *Fig (rêverie)* **être dans les nuages** to have one's head in the clouds, to be daydreaming; **être sur un** *ou* **son petit n.** to be on cloud nine

4 *Fig (masse légère)* **un n. de tulle** a mass *or* swathe of tulle

5 *Fig (petite quantité)* **un n. de lait** a drop of milk

6 *(en joaillerie)* cloud

7 *Phys* **n. (électronique)** electron cloud

• **sans nuages** ADJ **1** *Météo* cloudless; **sous un ciel sans nuages** under cloudless blue skies **2** *Fig (amitié)* untroubled, perfect; *(bonheur)* unclouded, perfect

nuageux, -euse [nɥaʒø, -øz] ADJ **1** *Météo*

(temps) cloudy; **ciel n.** cloudy *or* overcast sky; **masse nuageuse** cloudbank; **système n.** cloud system; **zone nuageuse** area of cloud **2** *Fig (confus ▸ esprit, idée)* hazy, nebulous, obscure

nuance [nɥɑ̃s] **NF 1** *(différence ▸ de couleur)* shade, hue; *(▸ de son)* nuance; **des nuances de bleu** shades of blue; **n. de sens** shade of meaning, nuance; **je ne saisis pas la n.** I don't quite see the difference; **j'ai dit "peut-être", pas "oui", n.!** I said "perhaps", not "yes", there's a slight difference! **2** *(subtilité)* nuance, subtlety; **toutes les nuances de sa pensée** the many subtleties *or* all the finer aspects of his/her thinking; **il joue du piano sans nuances/avec n.** his piano-playing lacks subtlety/displays a good sense of musical shading **3** *(trace légère)* touch, tinge; **une n. de regret/mépris** a touch of regret/contempt; **il y avait une n. d'amertume dans sa voix** there was a touch *or* hint of bitterness in his/her voice

nuancé, -e [nɥɑ̃se] **ADJ** *(couleur, ton)* subtle; *Fig (discours, propos, attitude)* full of nuances; **ses réponses sont toujours très nuancées** he always qualifies his answers a lot

nuancer **[16]** [nɥɑ̃se] **VT 1** *(couleur)* to shade; *(mélanger)* to blend (**de** with); *(musique)* to nuance; *Mus* **n. son jeu** to introduce light and shade into one's playing **2** *(critique, jugement)* to nuance, to qualify **3** *Tex* to grade, to tone

nuancier [nɥɑ̃sje] **NM** colour chart; *Com* sample card *or* chart

nubile [nybil] **ADJ** nubile; **l'âge n.** ≃ the age of consent

nubilité [nybilite] **NF** nubility

nucléaire [nykleɛr] **ADJ** *Biol, Mil & Phys* nuclear; **particule n.** elementary particle

NM le n. *(énergie)* nuclear power *or* energy; *(industrie)* the nuclear industry

nucléarisation [nyklearizasjɔ̃] **NF** *Ind* = introduction of nuclear power to replace conventional energy sources; *Mil* nuclearization

nucléariser **[3]** [nyklearize] **VT** *Ind* to supply with nuclear power; *Mil* to supply with nuclear weapons, to nuclearize

VPR se nucléariser to go nuclear

nucléé, -e [nyklee] **ADJ** *Biol* nucleate, nucleated

nucléique [nykleik] **ADJ acide n.** nucleic acid

nucléole [nykleɔl] **NM** *Biol* nucleolus

nucléon [nykleɔ̃] **NM** nucleon

nucléonique [nykleɔnik] **ADJ** nucleonic

NF nucleonics *(singulier)*

nucléus, nucleus [nykleys] **NM** nucleus

nude [njud] **ADJ** *(maquillage)* nude, natural

nudisme [nydism] **NM** nudism, naturism; **pratiquer le n., faire du n.** to practise nudism

nudiste [nydist] **ADJ** nudist *(avant n)*

NMF nudist; **camp de nudistes** nudist camp

nudité [nydite] **NF 1** *(d'une personne)* nakedness, nudity; *Fig* **l'horreur étalée dans toute sa n.** the horror displayed in all its starkness; *Fig* **ses crimes furent étalés dans toute leur n.** his/her crimes were exposed for all to see **2** *(d'un lieu)* bareness; **la n. des murs rend la pièce glaciale** the bare walls make the room feel very cold **3** *Beaux-Arts* nude

nue[2] [ny] **ADJ F** *voir* **nu**

NF *Arch & Littéraire* high cloud(s); **les nues** the skies; **l'oiseau fendait les nues** the bird was cleaving its way through the skies; *Fig* **porter qn/qch aux nues** to laud *or* to praise sb/sth to the skies; *Littéraire* **se perdre dans les nues** to have one's head (completely) in the clouds, to be lost in the clouds *or* in daydreams; *Fig* **tomber des nues** to be flabbergasted, to be thunderstruck

nuée [nɥe] **NF 1** *Littéraire* thick cloud; **n. d'orage** storm cloud, thundercloud **2** *Géol* **n. ardente** nuée ardente **3** *(multitude)* horde, host; **une n. de paparazzi/d'admirateurs** a horde of paparazzi/admirers; **n. d'insectes** horde *or* swarm of insects

nue-propriétaire [nyprɔprijetɛr] *voir* **nu-propriétaire**

nue-propriété [nyprɔprijete] *(pl* **nues-propriétés)** **NF** bare ownership

nuire **[97]** [nɥir] **nuire à VT IND** *(être néfaste pour)* **n. à qn** to harm *or* to injure sb; **n. à qch** to be harmful to *or* to damage *or* to harm sth; **n. aux intérêts de qn** to prejudice *or* to harm *or* to damage sb's interests; **le tabac nuit à la santé** smoking damages your health; **ne fais rien qui puisse n. à ta carrière** don't do anything that might damage *or* harm your career; **les grèves nuisent à la reprise économique** strikes are a threat to economic recovery; **mettre qn hors d'état de n.** *(en lieu sûr)* to put sb out of harm's way

VPR se nuire to do oneself harm

nuisance [nɥizɑ̃s] **NF** (environmental) nuisance; **n. acoustique** noise pollution; **n. chimique** chemical pollution

nuisette [nɥizɛt] **NF** short *or* baby-doll nightie

nuisibilité [nɥizibilite] **NF** harmfulness

nuisible [nɥizibl] **ADJ** harmful (**à** to); **gaz/fumées nuisibles** noxious gases/fumes; **des individus nuisibles à la société** individuals harmful to society; **animaux nuisibles** pests; **plantes nuisibles** noxious plants

• **nuisibles NMPL** *Zool* vermin, pests

nuisons *etc voir* **nuire**

nuit [nɥi] **NF 1** *(obscurité)* night *(UNCOUNT)*, dark, darkness; **il fait n.** it's dark; **il fait n. noire** it's pitch-dark *or* pitch-black; **il commence à faire n.** it's getting dark; **la n. tombe** it's getting dark, night is falling; **l'hiver, la n. tombe plus tôt** it gets dark earlier in winter; **rentrer avant la n.** to get back before nightfall *or* dark; **à la n. tombante, à la tombée de la n.** at nightfall, at dusk; **une fois la n. tombée, à n. tombée, à la n. tombée** after dark; **remonter à la n. des temps** to go back to the dawn of time; **se perdre dans la n. des temps** to be lost in the mists of time; *Littéraire* **la n. de l'ignorance** the darkness of ignorance; *Littéraire* **entrer dans la n. éternelle** *ou* **la n. du tombeau** to descend into the darkness of the grave; *Littéraire* **l'homme ne sait rien, il est dans la n.** man knows nothing, he struggles in the dark; **c'est le jour et la n.!** it's like night and day!

2 *(intervalle entre le coucher et le lever du soleil)* night, night-time; **une n. étoilée** a starry night; **je dors la n.** I sleep at *or* during the night; **son état a empiré pendant la n.** his/her condition worsened during the night; **faire sa n.** to sleep through the night; **le bébé fait ses nuits** the baby sleeps through the night; **bonne n.!** goodnight!; **passer une bonne n.** *(sujet: malade)* to have a comfortable night; **as-tu passé une bonne n.?** did you have a good night?; **passer la n. à l'hôtel** to spend *or* stay the night at a hotel; **il ne passera pas la n.** he won't last the night; **une n. de marche/repos/travail** a night's walk/rest/work; **une n. d'insomnie** a sleepless night; **une n. de sommeil ininterrompu** a night of unbroken sleep; *Prov* **la n. porte conseil** = it would be best to sleep on it

3 *(dans des expressions de temps)* **la n. dernière** last night; **cette n.** *(d'aujourd'hui)* tonight; *(passée)* last night; **que s'est-il passé cette n.?** what happened last night?; **nous partons cette n.** we're leaving tonight; **des nuits entières** nights on end; **en pleine n.** in the middle of the night; **en une n.** *(pendant la nuit)* in one night; *(vite)* overnight; **il y a deux nuits** the night before last; **il y a trois nuits** three nights ago; **ne sors pas seul la n.** don't go out alone at night; **la n. de mardi/vendredi** Tuesday/Friday night; **dans la n. de mardi à mercredi** during Tuesday night, during the night of Tuesday to Wednesday; **la n. où ils ont disparu** the night (that) they disappeared; **la n. précédente** *ou* **d'avant** the previous night, the night before; **la n. suivante** *ou* **d'après** the next night, the night after; **l'autre n.** the other night; **n. et jour, de n. comme de jour** night and day; **stationnement interdit n. et jour** *(sur panneau)* no parking day or night; **toute la n.** all night (long), through the night; **toutes les nuits** nightly, every night; *Prov* **la n., tous les chats sont gris** all cats are grey in the dark

4 *(dans des noms de dates)* **la n. de cristal** kristallnacht; **la n. des longs couteaux** the Night of the Long Knives; **la n. de Noël** Christmas night; **la n. de la Saint-Jean** Midsummer Night; **la n. de la Saint-Sylvestre** New Year's Eve (night)

5 *(nuitée)* **n. d'hôtel** *(dans l'hôtellerie)* bed-night; **payer une n. d'hôtel** to pay for a night at a hotel; **payer sa n.** to pay for the night; **c'est combien la n.?** how much is it for one night?; **c'est 300 euros la n.** it's 300 euros a night

• **de nuit ADJ 1** *Zool* **animaux/oiseaux de n.** nocturnal animals/birds **2** *(pharmacie)* night *(avant n)*, all-night *(avant n)*, twenty-four hour *(avant n)* **3** *(qui a lieu ou qui sert la nuit)* night *(avant n)*; **garde/vol de n.** night watch/flight; **train/bateau/voyage de n.** night train/boat *or* ferry/journey; **conduite de n.** night-driving, driving at night; **être de n.** to work night shifts, to be on nights; **aujourd'hui, je suis de n. à l'hôpital** I'm on night-duty at the hospital tonight; **vêtements de n.** nightwear **ADV travailler de n.** to work nights *or* the night shift *or* at night; **conduire de n.** to drive at *or* by night; **voyager de n.** to travel by night *or* at night; **nous arriverons plus vite en faisant la route de n.** we'll arrive earlier if we drive at night

• **nuit américaine NF** *Cin* day for night; **tourné en n. américaine** shot in day for night

• **nuit blanche NF** sleepless night; **passer une n. blanche** *(par insomnie)* to spend a sleepless night; *(volontairement)* to stay up all night

• **nuit bleue NF** night of bomb attacks

nuitamment [nɥitamɑ̃] **ADV** *Littéraire ou Hum* at *or* by night

nuitée [nɥite] **NF** overnight stay; **le gérant de l'hôtel nous a facturé deux nuitées** the hotel manager charged us for two nights

nul[1], **nulle**[1] [nyl] **ADJ 1** *(inexistant)* nil, non-existent; **les bénéfices sont presque nuls** the profits are almost non-existent *or* nil *or* zero; **le solde est n.** the balance is nil

2 *Fam (très mauvais ▸ gén)* crap, garbage, *Br* rubbish; *(▸ personne)* useless, hopeless, clueless; **leur dernière chanson est nulle** their latest song is crap; **être n. en maths** to be hopeless *or* useless at maths; **t'es n.!** *(mauvais)* you're useless!; *(méchant)* you're pathetic!; *Vulg* **c'est n. à chier!** it's fucking awful!

3 *Math* null

4 *Jur* null; **n. et non avenu** invalid, null and void; **rendre n.** to nullify, to annul; **bulletin n.** *(d'élection)* spoilt (ballot) paper

5 *Sport* nil; **le score est n.** *(en fin de match)* the game is drawn, the result is a draw; *(à la mi-temps)* neither team has scored yet, the game so far is drawn; **score n., zéro (à) zéro** *(en fin de match)* match drawn nil-nil; *(à la mi-temps)* score nil-nil

NM,F *Fam* useless idiot, *Br* prat

nul[2], **nulle**[2] [nyl] **ADJ INDÉFINI** *(avant le nom)* no, not any; **n. autre que lui n'aurait pu y parvenir** nobody (else) but he could have done it; **à n. autre pareil, à nulle autre pareille** peerless, unrivalled; **elle n'a nulle envie de me voir** she has no desire (whatsoever) to see me; **sans n. doute** undoubtedly, without any doubt; **n. doute qu'il tiendra sa promesse** there is no doubt that he will keep his promise

PRON INDÉFINI no one, nobody; **n. mieux que lui n'aurait su analyser la situation** no one could have analysed the situation better than him; **n. n'est venu** no one *or* nobody came; **n. n'est parfait** nobody's perfect; **n. n'est censé ignorer la loi** ignorance of the law is no defence; *Prov* **n. n'est prophète en son pays** no man is a prophet in his own country

• **nulle part ADV** nowhere; **on ne l'a trouvé nulle part** he was nowhere to be found; **je ne les vois nulle part** I can't see them anywhere; **il n'a nulle part où aller** he has nowhere to go; **nulle part ailleurs** nowhere else

nullard, -e [nylar, -ard] *Fam* **ADJ** thick, *Am* dumb

NM,F useless idiot, *Br* prat

nulle [nyl] *voir* **nul**[1, 2]

nullement [nylmɑ̃] **ADV** *Littéraire* not at all, not in the least; **elle n'avait n. honte de ce qu'elle avait fait** she wasn't in the least ashamed of what she'd done; **je n'ai n. l'intention d'y aller** I haven't the slightest *or* least intention of going; **ça vous gêne que je fume? – n.** do you mind my smoking? – not at all *or* not in the least

nullissime [nylisim] **ADJ** *Fam* totally useless, pathetic

nullité [nylite] **NF 1** *(manque de valeur)* incompetence, uselessness; *(de remarque, plaisanterie)* crassness; **cette fille est d'une n. totale** this girl's totally useless *or* incompetent **2** *(personne)* useless idiot, *Br* prat; **c'est une n.** he's/she's completely useless **3** *Jur* nullity; **action en n.** action for (a) voidance of contract; **frapper une clause de n.** to render a clause void; **s'agissant du mariage, la bigamie est cause de n.** bigamy is grounds for the annulment of a marriage

nûment [nymɑ̃] **ADV** *Littéraire* frankly, without embellishment

numéraire [nymerer] **ADJ espèces numéraires** legal tender *(UNCOUNT)*, legal currency *(UNCOUNT)*; **valeur n.** face value
NM specie, cash; **payer en n.** to pay in specie, to pay cash; **n. fictif** paper money

numéral, -e, -aux, -ales [nymeral, -o] **ADJ** numeral
NM numeral

numérateur [nymeratœr] **NM** numerator

numération [nymerasjɔ̃] **NF 1** *(dénombrement)* numeration, numbering *(UNCOUNT)*; *(signes)* notation; **n. décimale/binaire** decimal/binary notation **2** *Méd* **n. globulaire** blood count; **n. et formule sanguine** full blood count

numérique [nymerik] **ADJ 1** *(gén)* numerical; **dans l'ordre n.** in numerical order **2** *Math* numerical **3** *Ordinat (ordinateur, donnée)* digital; **balance à affichage n.** digital scales; **enregistrement/disque n.** digital recording/record
NM *Ordinat* **le n.** digital technology; *TV* **n. hertzien** *ou* **n. terrestre** digital terrestrial (broadcasting)

numériquement [nymerikmɑ̃] **ADV 1** *(en nombre)* numerically **2** *Ordinat* digitally

numérisation [nymerizasjɔ̃] **NF** digitization

numériser [3] [nymerize] **VT** to digitize

numériseur [nymerizœr] **NM** digitizer; **n. d'image** image digitizer

numéro [nymero] **NM 1** *(nombre)* number; *Naut* **n. d'appel, n. d'attente** *(dans une file d'attente)* number; **prenez un n. d'appel** *ou* **d'attente** please take a ticket and wait for your number to be called; **n. de chambre** room number; *Banque* **n. de chèque** cheque number; *Com* **n. de commande** order number; *Banque* **n. de compte** account number; **n. d'enregistrement** booking number; **n. de fabrication** serial number; *Can* **n. d'identification personnel** PIN (number), personal identification number; *Banque* **n. d'identité bancaire** bank sort code; *Aut* **n. d'immatriculation** *Br* registration number, *Am* license number; *Ordinat* **n. Internet** Internet number; *Ordinat* **n. IP** IP number; *Ordinat* **n. de licence** registration number; **n. matricule** number; **n. d'ordre** *(dans une file d'attente)* number; **n. de page** page number; *Typ* folio; *Suisse* **n. postal** *Br* postcode, *Am* zip code; **n. de référence** reference number; **n. de sécurité sociale** social security number; **n. de série** serial number; **n. de sociétaire** *(d'une assurance)* insurance *or* policy number; **n. de vol** flight number
2 *Tél* **n. (de téléphone** *ou* **d'appel)** (telephone) number; **n. d'appel gratuit** *Br* ≃ 0800 number, Freefone® number, *Am* ≃ toll-free number, 800 number; **n. azur** = telephone number for a call charged at the local rate irrespective of the actual distance covered; **n. de fax** fax number; **n. de poste** extension number; **n. d'urgence** emergency number; *Br* **n. vert** ≃ 0800 number, Freefone® number, *Am* ≃ toll-free number, 800 number; **donne-moi ton n.** give me your number; **refais le n.** dial (the number) again; **j'ai changé de n.** my number has changed; **faire un faux n.** to dial a wrong number; **il n'y a pas d'abonné au n. que vous avez demandé** ≃ the number you have dialled has not been recognized
3 *(habitation, place)* number; **j'habite au n. 10** I live at number 10
4 *(exemplaire)* issue, number (**sur** on *or* about); *(d'une émission)* edition; **n. du jour/de la semaine/du mois, dernier n.** current issue *or* number; **ancien n., n. déjà paru** back issue *or* number; **n. spécial** special issue; **deux numéros en un** double issue; **acheter un magazine au n.** to buy a magazine as it appears; **il faudra chercher dans de vieux numéros** we'll have to look through some back issues
5 *Mus* number; *(dans un spectacle)* act, turn; **n. de cirque** circus act; **il fait le n. le plus important du spectacle** he's top of the bill; **elle a fait son n. habituel** she went into her usual routine; *Fam* **il aime faire son petit n.** he likes doing his little act; *Fam* **il lui a fait un n. de charme terrible** he really turned on the charm with him/her
6 *(dans un jeu ▸ nombre)* number; **un n. gagnant** a winning number; **n. complémentaire** = extra number in Loto, used as a joker; **tirer le bon/mauvais n.** to draw a lucky/an unlucky number; *Fig* **lui, il a tiré le bon n.!** he's really struck it lucky!
7 *(personne)* **n'être qu'un n.** to be just a number; **le n. un/deux russe** the Russian number one/two; *Fam* **quel n.!** *(hurluberlu)* what a character!; *Fam* **c'est un drôle de n.!** he's/she's a strange character!
8 *(comme adj; après le nom)* **le lot n. 12** lot 12; **la chambre n. 20** room (number) 20

numérologie [nymerɔlɔʒi] **NF** numerology

numérotage [nymerɔtaʒ] **NM** *(attribution d'un numéro)* numbering; *Typ* **n. de pages** page numbering, pagination

numérotation [nymerɔtasjɔ̃] **NF 1** *(attribution d'un numéro)* numbering; **la n. des pages** pagination, page numbering **2** *Tél* dialling; **n. abrégée** speed dial

numéroter [3] [nymerɔte] **VT** to number; **n. les pages d'un livre** to paginate a book, to number the pages of a book; **les places ne sont pas numérotées** the seats aren't numbered; *Mil* **numérotez-vous (à partir de la droite)!** (from the right) number!
VI *Tél* to dial

numéroteur [nymerɔtœr] **NM** numbering device

numismate [nymismat] **NMF** numismatist, numismatologist

numismatique [nymismatik] **NF** numismatics *(singulier)*, numismatology
ADJ numismatic

nummulaire [nymyler] **NF** *Bot* moneywort, creeping Jenny

nunuche [nynyʃ] *Fam* **ADJ** *Br* daft, *Am* dumb
NF dope, halfwit

nu-pieds [nypje] **ADV** barefoot
NMPL sandals

nu-propriétaire, nue-propriétaire [nyprɔprijeter] *(mpl* **nus-propriétaires,** *fpl* **nues-propriétaires) NM,F** bare owner

nuptial, -e, -aux, -ales [nypsjal, -o] **ADJ** *(de mariage)* wedding *(avant n)*; *(chambre, cortège)* bridal *(avant n)*; **robe nuptiale** wedding dress, bridal gown

nuptialité [nypsjalite] **NF** marriage rate, nuptiality

nuque [nyk] **NF** nape (of the neck); **une coiffure qui dégage la n.** a hairstyle that is short at the back; **saisir qn par la n.** to grab sb by the scruff of the neck

nurse [nœrs] **NF** *Vieilli* nanny, governess

nursery [nœrsəri] *(pl* **nurserys** *ou* **nurseries) NF** nursery

nutation [nytasjɔ̃] **NF** nutation

nu-tête [nytet] **ADV** bareheaded

nutritif, -ive [nytritif, -iv] **ADJ 1** *(nourrissant ▸ aliment)* nourishing, nutritious; **substance nutritive** nutrient **2** *(relatif à la nutrition)* nutritive, nutritional; **valeur nutritive** nutritional value

nutrition [nytrisjɔ̃] **NF** nutrition, feeding; **une mauvaise n.** a bad *or* an unbalanced diet

nutritionniste [nytrisjɔnist] **NMF** nutritionist, dietary expert

nutritive [nytritiv] *voir* **nutritif**

nyctalope [niktalɔp] **ADJ 1** *Zool* **la chouette est un oiseau n.** the owl has good nocturnal vision **2** *(personne)* having good night vision

Nylon® [nilɔ̃] **NM** nylon; **en** *ou* **de N.** nylon; **des bas N.** nylon stockings, nylons

nymphe [nɛ̃f] **NF 1** *Myth* nymph **2** *Entom* nymph

nymphéa [nɛ̃fea] **NM** *Bot* white water lily

nymphette [nɛ̃fɛt] **NF** nymphet

nympho [nɛ̃fo] **ADJ** *Fam* nympho

nymphomane [nɛ̃fɔman] **ADJ F** nymphomaniac *(avant n)*
NF nymphomaniac

nymphomanie [nɛ̃fɔmani] **NF** nymphomania

O[1], **o** [o] **NM INV** *(lettre)* O, o

O[2] [o] *(abrév écrite* **Ouest**) W

ô [o] **EXCLAM** *Littéraire* oh!, O!

-o — SUFFIX

The suffix **-o** is widely used in French slang as a way to ABBREVIATE words.

• It is not to be confused with the final **-o** of a truncated word which already contains an o (**biologique ▸ bio**; **écologique ▸ écolo**; **catholique ▸ catho**; **information ▸ info**; **interrogation ▸ interro**; **personnel ▸ perso**; **homosexuel ▸ homo**), although in both cases the register is colloquial, eg:

alcoolo (from *alcoolique*) alkie; **apéro** (from *apéritif*) aperitif, drink; **facho** (from *fasciste*) fascist; **gaucho** (from *gauchiste*) lefty; **intello** (from *intellectuel*) intellectual, egghead; **proprio** (from *propriétaire*) landlord, landlady; **romano** (from *romanichel*) gippo

• Even first names can be abbreviated in this way, eg:

Frédéric ▸ Frédo; **Madeleine ▸ Mado**

• Note that the radical is sometimes altered when the truncation occurs, eg:

clochard ▸ clodo; **directeur ▸ dirlo**; **travesti ▸ travelo**; **hôpital ▸ hosto**

OAA [ɔaa] **NF** *(abrév* **Organisation des Nations unies pour l'alimentation et l'agriculture**) FAO

OACI [ɔasei] **NF** *(abrév* **Organisation de l'aviation civile internationale**) ICAO

OAS [ɔaɛs] **NF** *Hist (abrév* **Organisation armée secrète**) OAS *(French terrorist organization which opposed Algerian independence in the 1960s)*

oasien, -enne [ɔazjɛ̃, -ɛn] **ADJ** oasis *(avant n)*

NM,F oasis dweller

oasis [ɔazis] **NF** oasis; *Fig* haven, oasis

OAT [ɔate] **NF** *Fin (abrév* **obligation assimilable du Trésor**) = French government bond

obédience [ɔbedjɑ̃s] **NF 1** *(adhésion)* allegiance; **pays d'o. socialiste** socialist *or* socialist-run countries; **des communistes d'o. trotskiste** Communists of the Trotskyist tendency **2** *Rel* obedience; **musulman de stricte o.** devout Muslim; **o. religieuse** religious persuasion

Il faut noter que le nom anglais **obedience** signifie le plus souvent **obéissance**.

obéir [32] [ɔbeir] **USAGE ABSOLU 1** *(se soumettre)* **refuser d'o.** to refuse to obey; **vas-tu o.?** will you do as you're told! **2** *(répondre)* **le moteur obéit bien** the engine responds well; **soudain, les freins ont cessé d'o.** all of a sudden, the brakes stopped responding

• **obéir à VT IND 1** *(se soumettre à)* **o. à qn/qch** to obey sb/sth; **o. à qn au doigt et à l'œil** to be at sb's beck and call; **savoir se faire o. de qn** to command *or* to compel obedience from sb; **il a fini par se faire o.** he was finally obeyed; **c'était un professeur très obéi de ses élèves** as a teacher, he commanded (great) obedience from his pupils; **o. à un ordre** to comply with *or* to obey an order; **o. à un règlement/une loi** to obey a rule/a law, to abide by a rule/a law **2** *(être régi par)* **o. à qch** to submit to *or* to obey sth; **o. à la force/une contrainte** to yield to force/a constraint; **o. à une théorie/un principe** to obey *or* to follow a theory/a principle; **le marché obéit à la loi de l'offre et de la demande** the market is governed by *or* follows the law of supply and demand; **o. à une impulsion** to follow an impulse; **obéissant à une soif de vengeance** moved *or* prompted by a thirst for revenge; **o. à sa conscience** to follow the dictates of *or* to obey one's conscience **3** *(réagir à ▸ sujet: mécanisme)* **o. à qch** to respond to sth; *Naut* **o. à la barre** to answer the helm; *Aviat* **o. aux commandes** to respond to the controls

obéissance [ɔbeisɑ̃s] **NF 1** *(action d'obéir)* obedience, submission (à to); **jurer o. au roi** to swear allegiance to the king; **devoir o. à qn** to owe sb obedience *or* allegiance; **on exige d'eux une o. aveugle** they are expected to be blindly obedient; **o. à une règle** adherence to a rule **2** *(discipline)* obedience; **les professeurs se plaignent du manque d'o. des élèves** the teachers complain of the pupils' disobedience; **refus d'o.** insubordination **3** *Rel* obedience

obéissant, -e [ɔbeisɑ̃, -ɑ̃t] **ADJ** obedient; **être** *ou* **se montrer o. envers qn** to be obedient to *or* towards sb

obélisque [ɔbelisk] **NM** obelisk

obérer [18] [ɔbere] **VT 1** *(accabler financièrement)* to be a burden on, to weigh down; **la facture pétrolière obère le budget de l'État** the oil bill is a burden on the country's budget; **très** *ou* **fort obéré** heavily burdened with debt, deeply in debt, debt-ridden **2** *(compromettre)* to compromise; **cette décision obère l'avenir** this decision compromises the future

obèse [ɔbɛz] **ADJ** obese

NMF obese person

obésité [ɔbezite] **NF** obesity; **o. morbide** morbid obesity

obier [ɔbje] **NM** *Bot* guelder rose

objecter [4] [ɔbʒɛkte] **VT 1** *(opposer ▸ un argument)* **o. qch à qn** to put sth forward as an argument against sb; **o. des arguments à une théorie** to put forward arguments against a theory; **n'avoir rien à o. à qch** to have no objection to sth; **il n'a rien eu à o. à ce que j'ai dit** he raised no objections to what I said; **que peut-on lui o.?** what arguments can we put forward against him/her?; **on nous objectera le coût trop élevé de l'opération** they will object to the high cost of the operation; **o. que…** to object that…; **on vous objectera que…** they will object that… **2** *(prétexter)* **on lui objecta sa jeunesse** they took exception to his/her youth, his/her youth counted *or* was held against him/her; **il objecta son incompétence pour se débarrasser de la corvée** he pleaded incompetence to get out of doing the chore; **ils peuvent m'o. que je suis trop jeune** they may object that I am too young

objecteur [ɔbʒɛktœr] **NM o. de conscience** conscientious objector

objectif, -ive [ɔbʒɛktif, -iv] **ADJ 1** *(impartial)* objective, unbiased; **témoin o.** unbiased witness **2** *(concret, observable)* objective; **la fièvre est un signe o. de maladie** fever is an objective symptom of disease **3** *Gram & Phil* objective

NM 1 *(but à atteindre)* objective, goal, aim; *Com (de croissance, de production)* target; **se fixer/atteindre un o.** to set oneself/to reach an objective; **o. de chiffre d'affaires** sales target; **o. marketing** marketing goal; **o. de production** production target; **o. de profit** profit target; **o. publicitaire** advertising goal; **o. de vente** sales target; **o. lointain/à terme** long-term/short-term objective **2** *Mil (cible)* target, objective **3** *Opt & Phot* lens, objective; *(de microscope)* object glass, objective; **braquer son o. sur qch** to train one's camera on sth; **fixer l'o.** to look into the camera; *Phot* **régler l'o.** to adjust the focus; **elle est très naturelle devant l'o.** she's very natural in front of a camera; *TV & Cin* **o. à courte focale** short-focus lens; *TV & Cin* **o. à distance focale variable** zoom lens; *Phot* **o. fish-eye** fish-eye lens; *TV & Cin* **o. à focale fixe** prime lens; *Phot* **o. grand angle** wide-angle lens; *Phot* **o. normal** normal angle lens; *Phot* **o. ultra grand angle** fish-eye lens; *Phot* **o. zoom** zoom lens

objection [ɔbʒɛksjɔ̃] **NF 1** *(gén)* objection; **faire** *ou* **soulever** *ou* **formuler une o. (à qch)** to make *or* to raise an objection (to sth); **tu as** *ou* **tu y vois une o.?** do you have any objection?; **je ne vois pas d'o. à continuer le débat/à ce que vous partiez** I have no objection to our continuing the debate/to your leaving; **on me fit l'o. que…** they objected *or* argued that…; **o. de conscience** conscientious objection **2** *Jur* **o.!** objection!; **o. accordée/refusée** objection sustained/overruled

objective [ɔbʒɛktiv] *voir* **objectif**

objectivement [ɔbʒɛktivmɑ̃] **ADV** objectively; **vous n'avez pas rendu compte des faits o.** you didn't report the facts objectively, you didn't give an objective account of the facts

objectiver [3] [ɔbʒɛktive] **VT 1** *Psy* to objectify, to objectivize **2** *(sentiment, idée)* to verbalize

objectivisme [ɔbʒɛktivism] **NM** objectivism

objectivité [ɔbʒɛktivite] **NF** objectivity; **l'o. d'un rapport/journaliste** the objectivity of a report/journalist, a report's/journalist's objectivity; **manque d'o.** lack of objectivity; **en toute o.** (quite) objectively

objet [ɔbʒɛ] **NM 1** *(chose)* object, item; **traiter qn comme un o.** to treat sb like an object *or* a thing; **je ne suis pas un o. dont on dispose** I refuse to be treated like an object; **o. d'art** objet d'art, art object; **o. de luxe** luxury item; **objets personnels** personal belongings *or* effects; **o. sexuel** sex object; **objets de toilette** toiletries; **objets trouvés** lost property *(UNCOUNT)*; **o. volant non identifié** unidentified flying object; **c'est un homme-o.** he's a sex object

2 *(thème)* subject; **l'o. de leurs discussions était toujours la politique** politics was always the subject of their discussions; **ceci sera l'o. d'une conférence** there will be a conference on this subject; **quel est l'o. de la thermodynamique?** what does thermodynamics cover?; **o. (construit)** construct; **o. mathématique** mathematical construct; *Com* **o.: confirmation de demande** *(dans une lettre)* re: confirmation of order

3 *(personne)* object; *(raison)* cause; **o. de pitié/haine** object of pity/hatred; **l'o. de sa haine/curiosité** the object of his/her hatred/curiosity; **l'o. de toute cette agitation** the object *or* cause of all this excitement; **l'o. de mes pensées entra soudain** the object of my thoughts suddenly came in

4 *(but)* object, purpose, aim; **mon o. est de** *ou* **j'ai pour o. de vous convaincre** my purpose *or* goal is to convince you; **l'o. de l'émission est de divertir** the purpose *or* aim *or* object of the programme is to entertain; **exposer l'o. de sa visite** to explain the purpose of *or* reason for one's visit; **ma visite a pour o. de...** the object of my visit is to...; **le congrès a rempli son o., qui était d'informer** the congress has achieved its aim *or* purpose, which was to inform; **cet appareil/cette nouvelle mesure remplit tout à fait son o.** the device/the new measure does exactly what it's supposed to; **faire** *ou* **être l'o. de soins particuliers** to receive *or* to be given special care; **les enfants sont l'o. de nombreux soins** children receive a lot of care; **faire l'o. d'une fouille corporelle** to be subjected to a body search; **faire l'o. d'attaques répétées** to be the victim of repeated attacks; **faire l'o. de controverses** to be a controversial subject; **faire l'o. de vives critiques** to be the object *or* target of sharp criticism; **votre requête fera l'o. de toute notre attention** your request will receive our full attention; **l'ancien ministre fait actuellement l'o. d'une enquête** the former minister is currently being investigated; **cela fera l'o. d'une recherche approfondie** this will be the subject of a thorough investigation

5 *Gram* object; **o. direct/indirect** direct/indirect object

6 *Phil* object

7 *Jur* matter; **l'o. du litige** the matter at issue; **l'o. de la plainte** the matter of the complaint; **l'o. d'un contrat** the subject matter of a contract; **l'o. désigné dans le contrat** the object of the contract

8 *Ordinat* object

• **sans objet** ADJ **1** *(sans but)* aimless, pointless; **des rêveries sans o.** aimless daydreaming **2** *(non justifié)* unjustified, groundless, unfounded; **votre démarche est désormais sans o.** you are no longer justified in taking this step; **ces arguments sont maintenant sans o.** these arguments no longer apply *or* are no longer applicable

objurgations [ɔbʒyrgasjɔ̃] NFPL *Littéraire* **1** *(reproches)* objurgations, castigations **2** *(prières)* entreaties, pleas

oblat, -e [ɔbla, -at] NM,F *Rel* oblate

oblation [ɔblasjɔ̃] NF *Rel* oblation, offering

obligataire [ɔbligatɛr] ADJ bonded, debenture *(avant n)*; **dette o.** bonded *or* debenture debt; **emprunt/créancier o.** bonded loan/creditor

NMF debenture holder, bondholder

NM debenture bond

obligation [ɔbligasjɔ̃] NF **1** *(contrainte)* obligation; **la vie communautaire crée certaines obligations** communal life creates certain obligations; **vous pouvez contribuer, mais il n'y a pas d'o.** *ou* **ce n'est pas une o.** you can give money if you wish, but you don't have to *or* there's no obligation; **je suis** *ou* **je me vois dans l'o. de vous expulser** I'm obliged *or* forced to evict you; **je me sens dans l'o. de vous avertir** I feel obliged to warn you; **avoir l'o. de faire qch** to be under an obligation to do sth, to be obliged to do sth; **faire o. à qn de** to oblige *or* to require sb to; **la loi vous fait o. de vous présenter en personne** the law requires you to appear in person; **sans o. de votre part** without any obligation (on your part); **sans o. d'achat** *(dans un jeu ou un concours)* no purchase necessary; **o. de réserve** duty of confidentiality

2 *(devoir)* obligation, duty, commitment; **mes obligations de président de la société** my duties as the chairman of the company; **remplir ses obligations** to meet one's obligations; **tu manques à toutes tes obligations** you're not facing up to any of your responsibilities; **avoir/se sentir des obligations envers qn** to be/to feel under an obligation to sb; **obligations familiales** family obligations *or* commitments; **obligations militaires** military obligations *or* duties; **être dégagé des obligations militaires** to have done one's military service; **l'o. scolaire** compulsory education

3 *Jur* obligation; **o. alimentaire** alimony, *Br* maintenance (order); **contracter une o. irrévocable** to enter into a binding agreement; **contracter une o. envers qn** to enter into an agreement with sb; **faire honneur à ses obligations** to fulfil one's obligations, to carry out one's duties

4 *Bourse & Fin* bond, debenture; **obligations** bonds, loan stock *or* notes; **o. portant un intérêt de 6 pour cent** bond bearing interest at 6 per cent; **o. amortissable** redeemable bond; **o. assimilable du Trésor** = French government bond; **o. cautionnée** guaranteed bond; **o. convertible** convertible bond; **o. échangeable** convertible bond; **o. échue** matured bond; **o. d'entreprise** bond, *Br* debenture (stock); **o. d'État** (government) bond; **o. garantie** guaranteed bond; **o. hypothécaire** mortgage bond; **o. indexée** indexed *or* index-linked bond; **o. à intérêt variable** floating-rate bond; **o. à lots** prize bond, lottery bond; **o. multimarchés** global bond; **o. négociable** marketable bond; **o. nominative** registered bond; **o. non amortissable** irredeemable bond; **o. non garantie** unsecured bond; **o. or** gold bond; **o. au porteur** bearer bond; **o. de premier ordre, o. à prime** prime bond; **o. privilégiée** preference *or* preferment bond; **o. remboursable** redeemable bond; **o. à revenu fixe** fixed-rate bond; **o. à revenu variable** floating-rate bond; **o. de société** corporate bond; **o. à taux progressif** step-up bond; **o. à taux variable** variable-income bond, floating-rate bond; **o. transférable, o. transmissible** transferable bond

5 *Littéraire (gratitude)* obligation

obligatoire [ɔbligatwar] ADJ **1** *(exigé, imposé)* compulsory, obligatory; **lectures/exercices obligatoires** compulsory texts/exercises; **(le port de) la ceinture de sécurité est o.** the wearing of seat belts is compulsory; **le vaccin est o. pour entrer à la maternelle** children must be vaccinated before being admitted to *Br* infant school *or Am* kindergarten; **l'école est gratuite et o.** education is free and compulsory; **tenue de soirée o.** *(sur un carton d'invitation)* formal dress required **2** *Fam (inéluctable)* **un jour ou l'autre ils en viendront aux mains, c'est o.** one of these days, they're bound to come to blows

obligatoirement [ɔbligatwarmɑ̃] ADV **1** *(par nécessité)* **vous devez o. montrer votre passeport** you are required to show your passport; **il doit o. avoir la licence pour s'inscrire** he must have a degree to enrol; **nous devons o. fermer les portes à huit heures** we're obliged *or* required to close the doors at eight o'clock; **est-ce qu'il faut porter une robe habillée? – pas o.** do you have to wear an evening dress? – not necessarily **2** *Fam (immanquablement)* inevitably[□]; **il va o. tout aller lui répéter** he's bound to go and tell him/her everything[□]; **alors, o., il a pensé qu'on lui cachait des choses** so he inevitably thought we were hiding things from him[□]

obligé, -e [ɔbliʒe] ADJ **1** *(contraint)* obliged, compelled (**de faire qch** to do sth); **tu y es allé? – (bien) o.!** did you go? – I had to! *or* I didn't have a choice!

2 *(nécessaire ▸ conséquence)* necessary; **c'est un passage o.** it's something that has to be done

3 *Fam (inévitable)* **c'était o.!** it was bound to happen![□]; **c'est o. qu'il rate son examen** he's bound to fail his exam

4 *Sout (reconnaissant)* obliged, grateful (**de** for); **je vous serais o. de...** I would be much obliged if you would...

5 *Jur* **être o. envers un créancier** to be under an obligation to a creditor

6 *Mus* obbligato, obligato

NM,F *Jur* obligee; **je suis votre o. en cette affaire** I'm obliged to you in this matter

obligeamment [ɔbliʒamɑ̃] ADV obligingly; **elle distribuait les bonnes notes un peu trop o.** she was a little too free with high *Br* marks *or Am* grades

obligeance [ɔbliʒɑ̃s] NF **veuillez avoir l'o. de me répondre rapidement** please be so kind as to *or* be kind enough to reply as quickly as possible; **un jeune homme d'une extrême o.** an extremely obliging young man

obligeant, -e [ɔbliʒɑ̃, -ɑ̃t] ADJ obliging, kind; **des remarques peu obligeantes** rather unkind remarks

obliger [17] [ɔbliʒe] VT **1** *(mettre dans la nécessité de)* to oblige, to force; **o. qn à faire qch** to force sb to do sth; **ne m'oblige pas à te punir** don't force me to *or* don't make me punish you; **ce travail m'oblige à me lever à cinq heures tous les matins** this job means I have to get up at five o'clock every morning; **une force intérieure l'obligeait à tuer** an inner force compelled him to kill; **son état de santé l'oblige à de longs moments de repos** the state of his/her health means he/she has to rest for long periods; **le devoir/l'honneur m'oblige à révéler mes sources** I'm duty-bound/honour-bound to reveal my sources; **rien ne t'y oblige** you don't have to, nobody's forcing you; **on ne t'y oblige pas** nobody's forcing you; **personne ne t'oblige à aller travailler à l'étranger** nobody's forcing you to go and work abroad; **être obligé de faire qch** to be forced to do sth, to have to do sth; **je suis bien obligé de suivre** I have no option *or* choice but to follow; **ne te sens pas obligé de le faire** don't feel obliged *or* compelled to do it, don't feel you have to do it; **se croire obligé de faire qch** to feel obliged to do sth; *Ironique* **ne te crois pas obligé de tout boire!** don't feel obliged to drink it all!

2 *(contraindre moralement ou juridiquement)* **la loi oblige les candidats à se soumettre à un test** applicants are legally required to take a test; **la loi m'y oblige** I'm required to by law, the law requires me to; **votre signature vous oblige** your signature is legally binding

3 *Sout (faire plaisir à)* to oblige; **vous m'obligeriez en venant** *ou* **si vous veniez** I would be obliged if you came; **nous vous sommes très obligés de votre soutien** we are very grateful to you for your support; **je vous serais obligé de bien vouloir m'expédier les articles avant le 31 mai** I would be (greatly) obliged if you would kindly send the items before 31 May

USAGE ABSOLU **j'ai mis une cravate, réunion oblige** I had to wear a tie, what with the meeting and all

VPR **s'obliger 1 s'o. à** *(se forcer à)* to force oneself to; **elle s'oblige à marcher un peu** *ou* **à un peu de marche chaque jour** she forces herself to *or* she makes herself walk a little every day

2 s'o. à *(s'engager à)* to commit oneself to; **par ce contrat, je m'oblige à évacuer les lieux avant le 21** in this contract, I commit myself to leaving *or* I undertake to leave the premises by the 21st

oblique [ɔblik] ADJ **1** *(ligne)* oblique; *(pluie, rayon)* slanting; *(regard)* sidelong; *Fig* **manœuvre o.** *(malhonnête)* underhand move **2** *Ling* oblique; **cas o.** oblique case **3** *Anat* **muscle o.** oblique muscle

NM *Anat* oblique (muscle)

NF *Géom* oblique (line)

• **en oblique** ADV diagonally

obliquement [ɔblikmɑ̃] ADV **1** *(de biais)* obliquely, diagonally, at an angle; **regarder qn o.** to look sideways *or* sidelong at sb **2** *Fig (hypocritement)* obliquely, indirectly; **il agit toujours o.** he never acts openly

obliquer [3] [ɔblike] VI to turn *or* to veer off; **la voiture obliqua dans une ruelle étroite** the car swerved (off) into a narrow alley; **la route oblique à gauche** the road veers left; **obliquez à gauche/à droite!** bear left/right!

obliquité [ɔblikɥite] NF obliquity, obliqueness

oblitérateur, -trice [ɔbliteratœr, -tris] ADJ cancelling *(avant n)*

NM cancelling machine; *(pour timbres)* franker

oblitération [ɔbliterasjɔ̃] NF **1** *(apposition d'une marque)* cancellation; *(marque ▸ sur un timbre)* postmark; *(▸ sur un ticket)* stamp; **o. premier jour** first-day cover; **cachet d'o.** postmark **2** *Littéraire (altération)* fading **3** *Méd* obturation

oblitératrice [ɔbliteratris] *voir* **oblitérateur**

oblitérer [18] [ɔblitere] VT **1** *(timbre)* to postmark, to cancel; **la lettre n'a pas été oblitérée** the letter hasn't been postmarked; **timbre oblitéré** used stamp **2** *Littéraire (effacer)* to obliterate, to erase, to efface **3** *Méd* to obturate

VPR **s'oblitérer** *Littéraire* **peu à peu, le passé s'oblitérait dans sa mémoire** little by little, every trace of the past disappeared from his/her memory

oblong, -ongue [ɔblɔ̃, -ɔ̃g] ADJ **1** *Géom* oblong; *Typ* **format o.** oblong format **2** *(visage, pelouse)* oblong, oval; **un coquillage de forme oblongue** an oblong shell

obnubiler [3] [ɔbnybile] VT **1** *(obséder)* to obsess; **être obnubilé par une idée** to be obsessed by an idea; **ça l'obnubile** he's/she's obsessed by it **2** *Fig (obscurcir)* to cloud, to obnubilate

obole [ɔbɔl] NF **1** *(somme d'argent)* (small) contribution *or* donation; *(dans la Bible)* widow's mite; **chacun apporte** *ou* **verse son o.** each person is making a contribution; *Littéraire* **il ne m'a pas fait l'o. d'un sourire** he didn't deign to smile at me **2** *Hist (monnaie ▸ grecque)* obol; *(▸ française)* obole

obscène [ɔpsɛn] ADJ *(licencieux)* obscene, lewd; *(livre, langage)* obscene

obscénité [ɔpsenite] NF **1** *(caractère licencieux)* obscenity, lewdness; *(d'un livre, du langage)* obscenity **2** *(parole, geste)* obscenity; **raconter** *ou* **dire des obscénités** to utter obscenities, to make obscene remarks

obscur, -e [ɔpskyr] ADJ **1** *(sombre)* dark; **une nuit obscure** a pitch-black night; *Fig* **des forces obscures dominaient leur planète** obscure forces *or* forces of darkness ruled their planet

2 *(incompréhensible)* obscure, abstruse; **pour quelque raison obscure** for some obscure reason

3 *(indéfini)* obscure, vague, indefinite; *(impression, sentiment)* vague; **un o. pressentiment** a vague premonition

4 *(peu connu)* obscure; **références à d'obscurs auteurs** *ou* **des auteurs obscurs du XIXème siècle** references to obscure nineteenth-century writers

5 *(humble ▸ naissance)* lowly, humble; **une vie obscure** a modest existence

obscurantisme [ɔpskyrɑ̃tism] NM obscurantism

obscurantiste [ɔpskyrɑ̃tist] ADJ obscurantist
NMF obscurantist

obscurcir [32] [ɔpskyrsir] VT **1** *(priver de lumière)* to darken, to make dark; **yeux obscurcis par les larmes** eyes misty *or* dim with tears; **une grande tenture obscurcissait la pièce** a large hanging made the room dark *or* darkened the room; **de gros nuages vinrent o. le ciel** large clouds darkened the sky **2** *(rendre confus ▸ discours, raisonnement)* to make obscure; **le jugement obscurci par l'alcool** his/her judgement clouded *or* obscured *or* confused by drink

VPR **s'obscurcir 1** *(ciel)* to darken; *(pièce, paysage)* to darken, to grow dark; *(vue)* to grow dim; **soudain, tout s'obscurcit et je m'évanouis** suddenly everything went dark *or* black and I fainted; *Fig* **son esprit s'obscurcit avec la maladie** the illness is dulling his/her mind; **son visage s'obscurcit à ces mots** at these words, his/her face clouded (over) *or* darkened; **son regard s'obscurcit** his/her face clouded over *or* darkened **2** *(se compliquer)* to become (more) obscure; **le mystère s'obscurcit** the plot thickens; **dans le dernier chapitre, son message s'obscurcit** in the last chapter, his/her meaning becomes obscure

obscurcissement [ɔpskyrsismɑ̃] NM **1** *(d'un lieu)* darkening **2** *(de l'esprit)* obscuring, clouding over; *(de la vue)* dimming; **l'o. progressif de ses facultés** the gradual weakening *or* loss of his/her faculties

obscurément [ɔpskyremɑ̃] ADV **1** *(vaguement)* obscurely, vaguely, dimly; **je me souviens o. d'une scène** I vaguely remember a scene; **nous sentions o. que...** we had a vague *or* an obscure feeling that... **2** *(de façon inconnue)* **mourir o.** to die in obscurity

obscurité [ɔpskyrite] NF **1** *(manque d'éclairage)* dark, darkness; **avoir peur de l'o.** to be afraid of the dark; **dans l'o.** in darkness, in the dark; **être plongé dans l'o.** to be plunged into darkness; **dans l'o., on voyait luire les yeux du chat** you could see the cat's eyes glowing in the dark; **faire l'o. dans une salle** to make a room dark, to darken a room; **soudain, l'o. se fit dans la chambre** it suddenly became *or* went dark in the room

2 *(caractère complexe)* obscurity, *Sout* abstruseness

3 *(remarque, expression)* obscure *or* abstruse remark, obscurity; **langage/projet de loi plein d'obscurités** language/bill full of obscurities

4 *Littéraire (anonymat)* **vivre/tomber dans l'o.** to live in/to fall into obscurity; **sortir de l'o.** to emerge from obscurity

obsédant, -e [ɔpsedɑ̃, -ɑ̃t] ADJ *(souvenir, musique)* haunting, obsessive; *(besoin, pensée)* obsessive

obsédé, -e [ɔpsede] ADJ *(gén)* obsessed; *(sexuel)* (sexually) obsessed; **être o. par qch** to be obsessed by *or* with sth; **o. par la pensée de la mort** obsessed *or* gripped with the idea of death

NM,F **1** *(victime d'obsessions)* obsessive; **o. sexuel** sex maniac **2** *Fam (fanatique)* fanatic; **c'est un o. de la moto** he's a motorbike fanatic; **les obsédés de la vitesse/de l'hygiène** speed/hygiene freaks

obséder [18] [ɔpsede] VT **1** *(sujet: image, peur)* to haunt, to obsess; **son souvenir m'obsède** I'm obsessed by the memory of him/her; **le cauchemar de l'autre nuit ne cesse de m'o.** I can't stop thinking about the nightmare I had the other night; **c'est un problème, mais ne te laisse pas o.** it's a problem, but don't become obsessed by it *or* don't let it become an obsession **2** *Littéraire (sujet: personne)* to importune, to bother

obsèques [ɔpsɛk] NFPL funeral; **faire à qn des o. nationales** to hold a state funeral for sb

obséquieuse [ɔpsekjøz] *voir* **obséquieux**

obséquieusement [ɔpsekjøzmɑ̃] ADV obsequiously

obséquieux, -euse [ɔpsekjø, -øz] ADJ obsequious

obséquiosité [ɔpsekjozite] NF obsequiousness

observable [ɔpsɛrvabl] ADJ observable; **le phénomène est o. à l'œil nu** the phenomenon can be observed with the naked eye

observance [ɔpsɛrvɑ̃s] NF *(d'un rite, d'une loi)* observance; **bénédictin d'ancienne o.** Benedictine of the old school; **communiste de stricte o.** hardline communist

observateur, -trice [ɔpsɛrvatœr, -tris] ADJ *(perspicace)* observant; **avoir un esprit très o.** to be very observant *or* perceptive; **rien n'échappe à l'œil o. du peintre** nothing can escape the painter's perceptive eye

NM,F **1** *(témoin)* observer; **tous les observateurs s'accordent à trouver le président fatigué** (all) observers agree that the president looks tired **2** *Pol* observer; **un o. de l'ONU** a UN observer **3** *Mil* spotter

observation [ɔpsɛrvasjɔ̃] NF **1** *(remarque)* observation, remark, comment; **faire des observations** to make observations *or* remarks *or* comments; **avez-vous des observations à faire sur ce premier cours?** do you have any comments to make about this first class?; **si je puis me permettre une o.** if I may make an observation *or* say something; **la réponse du ministre appelle plusieurs observations** the minister's answer calls for some comment *or* several observations

2 *(critique)* (piece of) criticism, critical remark; **je te prie de garder tes observations pour toi** please keep your remarks to yourself; **ma secrétaire est toujours en retard et je lui en ai fait l'o.** my secretary's always late and I've had a word with her about it; **faire des observations** to make *or* to pass remarks; **il faisait toujours des observations à ses élèves** he was always finding fault with his pupils; **j'ai horreur qu'on me fasse des observations** I hate people criticizing me *or* making remarks to me; **à la moindre o. de ma part, elle se met en colère** the slightest remark from me and she gets angry, she gets angry if I make the slightest remark; **à la première o., vous sortez!** *(à un élève)* if I have to say one (more) word to you, you're out!

3 *(investigation, exposé ▸ scientifique)* observation; **observations météorologiques/par satellite** meteorological/satellite observations

4 *(compte-rendu)* observation; **j'ai lu vos observations sur la danse des abeilles** I read your account of *or* observations on the dance of the bees

5 *(méthode d'étude)* observation, observing; **l'o. de la nature/d'une réaction chimique** observing nature/a chemical reaction; **avoir l'esprit d'o.** to be observant; *Mktg* **o. en situation** personal observation

6 *Mil* observation; **o. aérienne/terrestre** aerial/ground observation; **o. sous-marine** underwater observation

7 *(observance)* observance, observing, keeping

8 *Méd (description)* notes; *(surveillance)* observation; **mettre un malade en o.** to put a patient under observation; **être/rester en o.** to be/to remain under observation

• **d'observation** ADJ **1** *Aviat, Astron & Mil* observation *(avant n)*; **avion d'o.** spotter plane **2** *(scientifique)* **techniques/erreur d'o.** observation techniques/error

observatoire [ɔpsɛrvatwar] NM **1** *Astron & Météo* observatory **2** *Mil & Fig* observation *or* lookout post **3** *Écon* **O. français des conjonctures économiques** = economic research institute; **o. des prix** price-monitoring watchdog

observatrice [ɔpsɛrvatris] *voir* **observateur**

observer [3] [ɔpsɛrve] VT **1** *(examiner ▸ gén)* to observe, to examine; *(▸ scientifiquement)* to observe; **o. qch à la loupe** to examine sth under a magnifying glass; **elle adore o. les gens dans le métro** she loves watching people *or* she loves to people-watch in the metro; **il passait des heures à o. les oiseaux** he spent hours bird-watching

2 *(surveiller)* to watch, to keep a watch *or* an eye on; **attention, on nous observe** careful, we're being watched; **se sentir observé** to feel one is being watched; **o. qn avec attention/du coin de l'œil** to watch sb attentively/out of the corner of one's eye; **il était chargé d'o. le prisonnier** his job was to watch over the prisoner

3 *(respecter ▸ accord)* to observe, to respect, to abide by; *(▸ règlement)* to observe, to keep (to), to comply with; **o. une minute de silence** to observe a minute's silence; **o. le sabbat** to observe *or* to keep the Sabbath; **o. le code de la route** to observe *or* to follow the Highway Code; **faire o. la loi** to enforce (obedience to) the law

4 *(conserver)* **o. une attitude digne** to maintain *or* to keep a dignified attitude; **o. la plus stricte neutralité** to observe *or* to maintain the strictest neutrality

5 *(constater)* to observe, to notice, to note; **nous observons un retour à...** we are seeing *or* witnessing a return to...; **on observe un changement d'attitude chez les jeunes** there is a noticeable change in attitude amongst young people; **on observe une tache noire dans le poumon droit** a dark patch can be seen in the right lung; **faire o. qch à qn** to draw sb's attention to sth, to point sth out to sb; **je te ferai o. que tu t'es trompé** let me point out that you were wrong; **j'observe que cela n'a pas encore été fait** I see that this has not yet been done

6 *(dire)* to observe, to remark; **"tu ne portes plus d'alliance", observa-t-il** "you're not wearing a wedding ring any more," he observed *or* remarked

USAGE ABSOLU **c'est comme ça qu'il apprend, en observant** that's how he learns, by watching; **je ne critique pas, je ne fais qu'o.** this isn't a criticism, just an observation

VPR **s'observer 1** *(emploi réfléchi)* to keep a check on oneself **2** *(emploi réciproque)* to observe *or* to watch each other; **elles s'observèrent pendant longtemps** they observed *or* examined each other for some time **3** *(emploi passif)* to be seen *or* observed; **ce phénomène s'observe surtout par temps sec** this phenomenon is mainly seen *or* encountered in dry weather

obsession [ɔpsesjɔ̃] NF **1** *(hantise)* obsession; **beaucoup de femmes ont l'o. de grossir** many women are obsessed with the idea of putting on weight; **il croit qu'on veut le tuer, c'est devenu une o.** he believes people want to kill him, it's become a real obsession (with him) **2** *(idée fixe)* obsession; **il ne faut pas en faire une o.** it shouldn't become an obsession; **ça tourne à l'o.** it's becoming an obsession; **c'est une o. chez lui!** it's a real obsession with him!; **mais c'est une o.** *ou* **de l'o.!** you're/he's/she's/*etc* obsessed (with the idea)!

obsessionnel, -elle [ɔpsesjɔnɛl] ADJ **1** *(répétitif)* obsessive, obsessional **2** *Psy (comportement)* obsessive; *(névrose)* obsessional; **de manière obsessionnelle** obsessively

NM,F obsessive

obsidienne [ɔpsidjɛn] NF obsidian

obsolescence [ɔpsɔlesɑ̃s] NF obsolescence; **le taux d'o. des ordinateurs est très élevé** the obsolescence rate of computers is very high, computers very quickly become obsolete; **o. calculée** *ou* **planifiée** *ou* **prévue** built-in *or* planned obsolescence

obsolescent, -e [ɔpsɔlesɑ̃, -ɑ̃t] ADJ obsolescent

obsolète [ɔpsɔlɛt] ADJ obsolete

obstacle [ɔpstakl] NM **1** *(objet bloquant le pas-*

sage) obstacle; **des troncs ont fait o. à l'écoulement normal du ruisseau** tree trunks have blocked *or* obstructed the normal flow of the stream; **l'immeuble d'en face fait o. au soleil** the building opposite blocks (out) *or* obstructs the sun **2** *Sport* hurdle; *Équitation* fence; **tourner l'o.** *(sujet: cheval)* to run out (at the fence); *Fig* to get round the problem **3** *Fig (difficulté)* obstacle, difficulty, problem; **il y a un gros o.** there's a big problem; **le plus gros o. a été le directeur régional** the main obstacle was the area manager; **buter sur** *ou* **se heurter à un o.** to come up against an obstacle; **être un** *ou* **faire o. à** to be an obstacle to, to hinder, to impede; **la cécité n'est pas un o. à une carrière dans l'enseignement** being blind is no obstacle *or* impediment to a teaching career; **plus rien ne fait o. à notre amour** nothing stands in the way of our love any longer; **plus rien ne fait o. à ce que vous l'épousiez** there's no longer any reason why you shouldn't marry her; **je n'y vois pas d'o.** I don't see any difficulty *or* problem (about it); **mettre un o. aux ambitions de qn** to put an obstacle in the way of sb's ambitions

obstétrical, -e, -aux, -ales [ɔpstetrikal, -o] **ADJ** obstetric, obstetrical

obstétricien, -enne [ɔpstetrisjɛ̃, -ɛn] **NM,F** obstetrician

obstétrique [ɔpstetrik] **NF** obstetrics *(singulier)*

obstination [ɔpstinasjɔ̃] **NF 1** *(persévérance)* persistence, perseverance **2** *(entêtement)* obstinacy, obstinateness, stubbornness

obstiné, -e [ɔpstine] **ADJ 1** *(entêté)* obstinate, stubborn; *(persévérant)* persevering, determined **2** *(incessant)* persistent, relentless **3** *(assidu)* obstinate; *(résistance, efforts)* stubborn, dogged; *(refus, silence)* stubborn

NM,F c'est un o. *(qui persévère)* he's very determined; *(qui s'entête)* he's very stubborn *or* obstinate

obstinément [ɔpstinemɑ̃] **ADV 1** *(avec entêtement)* obstinately, stubbornly; *(refuser, répondre)* stubbornly; **l'enfant tenait o. à rester avec sa mère** the child was stubbornly determined to stay with his/her mother **2** *(avec persévérance)* perseveringly, persistently; *(travailler, avancer)* determinedly, doggedly

obstiner [3] [ɔpstine] **s'obstiner VPR** to persist, to insist; **ne t'obstine pas, abandonne le projet** don't be so stubborn, give the project up; **on ne cesse de te dire d'arrêter, mais toi, tu t'obstines** we keep telling you to stop, but you won't listen; **s'o. à faire qch** *(continuer)* to persist in doing sth; *(vouloir)* to be set *or Sout* bent on doing sth; **elle s'obstine à vouloir partir** she persists in wanting to leave *or* insists on leaving; **il s'obstinait à ne rien dire** he obstinately *or* stubbornly refused to talk; **s'o. dans son silence** to remain stubbornly *or* obstinately silent; **s'o. dans ses idées/convictions** to cling stubbornly *or* doggedly to one's ideas/convictions; **la vague de froid semble s'o. sur toute l'Europe** the cold spell seems to have set in all over Europe

obstruction [ɔpstryksjɔ̃] **NF 1** *(obstacle)* obstruction, blockage; *(blocage)* obstruction, obstructing, blocking; **faire o. à** to block, to obstruct **2** *(action délibérée)* **faire de l'o.** *(gén)* to be obstructive; *Pol* to obstruct (legislation); *Ftbl* to obstruct **3** *Méd* obstruction

obstructionnisme [ɔpstryksjɔnism] **NM** obstructionism

obstructionniste [ɔpstryksjɔnist] **ADJ** obstructionist

NMF obstructionist

obstruer [7] [ɔpstrye] **VT 1** *(passage)* to obstruct, to block; *(tuyau)* to block; **le corridor était obstrué par des piles de livres** the corridor was blocked *or* obstructed by piles of books; **une tour obstrue maintenant la vue** now a tower blocks (out) the view **2** *Méd* to obstruct; **il a des artères obstruées** he has blocked arteries

VPR s'obstruer to become blocked *or* obstructed

obtempérer [18] [ɔptɑ̃pere] **USAGE ABSOLU le soldat s'empressa d'o.** the soldier hurriedly obeyed; *Jur* **refus d'o.** obstruction

• **obtempérer à VT IND 1** *(se soumettre à)* to comply with; **le ministre a obtempéré à l'avis du président** the minister complied with the president's opinion; **o. à un ordre** to obey an order **2** *Jur* to obey; **o. à une sommation** to obey a summons

obtenir [40] [ɔptənir] **VT 1** *(acquérir ▸ baccalauréat, licence, note, point)* to obtain, to get; *(▸ prix, nomination)* to receive, to win, to get; *(▸ consentement)* to get, to win; *(▸ prêt, promesse)* to secure, to obtain, to get; *(▸ accord)* to reach, to obtain, to get; **essayer d'o. une amélioration** to try to bring about an improvement; **o. la garde d'un enfant** to get *or* to win custody of a child; **o. le droit de vote** to win the right to vote, to get the vote; **le numéro de trapèze obtient toujours un grand succès** the trapeze act is always a big success; **o. qch de qn** to obtain *or* to get sth from sb; **o. de qn une permission** to obtain *or* to get permission from sb; **n'espère plus rien o. de moi** don't expect (to get) anything else from me; **j'ai obtenu d'elle qu'elle vérifie tout** I got her to agree to check everything

2 *(procurer)* **o. qch à qn** to obtain *or* to get sth for sb; **elle lui a obtenu une augmentation** she got him/her a raise; **c'est lui qui m'a fait o. ces renseignements** he's the one who got (hold of) *or* obtained the information for me

3 *(arriver à ▸ résultat)* to obtain, to get, to achieve; *(▸ effet, succès)* to achieve; **les résultats obtenus par l'équipe nationale** the national team's results; **si on mélange ces deux substances, qu'obtient-on?** what do you get if you mix these two substances?; **fouettez jusqu'à o. une crème onctueuse** whip into a smooth cream; **ils ont fini par o. la libération des otages** they finally secured the release of the hostages; **j'ai travaillé sur ce dossier pendant trois mois et qu'ai-je obtenu? – rien!** I've worked on this case for three months and what have I got to show for it *or* what have I achieved? – nothing!; **en divisant par deux, on obtient 24** if you divide by two, you get 24; **cette technique lui permet d'o. un son très pur** this technique allows him/her to achieve great purity of sound; **j'ai obtenu qu'elle revienne** I arranged for her to come back; **j'ai enfin obtenu qu'elle mette ses gants pour sortir** I eventually got her to wear her gloves to go out

• **obtenir de VT IND il a obtenu de repousser le rendez-vous** he managed to get the meeting postponed; **j'ai obtenu de le voir** I obtained *or* got permission to see him

VPR s'obtenir le résultat demandé s'obtient en multipliant 3 par 5 to arrive at *or* to reach the required result, multiply 3 by 5

obtention [ɔptɑ̃sjɔ̃] **NF 1** *(acquisition)* obtaining, getting; **depuis l'o. de son diplôme** since obtaining his/her diploma, since he/she got his/her diploma; **pour l'o. de qch** (in order) to obtain sth **2** *(production)* creation, production; **l'o. d'une nouvelle variété de poire** the creation of a new variety of pear; **ajoutez du blanc jusqu'à o. de la couleur désirée** add white until the desired colour is obtained

obtenu, -e [ɔptəny] **PP** *voir* **obtenir**

obtient *etc voir* **obtenir**

obturateur, -trice [ɔptyratœr, -tris] **ADJ 1** *Tech* obturating *(avant n)*, shutting *(avant n)* **2** *Anat* obturator *(avant n)*; **artère obturatrice** obturator artery; **muscle o.** obturator muscle

NM 1 *Phot* shutter; **armer/déclencher l'o.** to set/to release the shutter; **o. focal** focal plane shutter; **o. d'objectif/à rideau** between-lens/roller-blind shutter; **o. de plaque** focal-plane shutter; **o. au diaphragme** diaphragm shutter

2 *Tech* shut-off

3 *Anat & Méd (d'une ouverture)* obturator

4 *Aut* throttle

obturation [ɔptyrasjɔ̃] **NF 1** *Tech* sealing, stopping up **2** *Méd* **l'o. d'une dent** the filling of a tooth

obturatrice [ɔptyratris] *voir* **obturateur**

obturer [3] [ɔptyre] **VT 1** *Tech (boucher)* to seal, to stop up **2** *Méd* to fill

obtus, -e [ɔpty, -yz] **ADJ 1** *Math* obtuse **2** *Fig (borné)* obtuse, dull, slow-witted

obus [ɔby] **NM 1** *Mil* shell; **o. à mitraille** *ou* **à balles** shrapnel (shell); **o. à mortier/à gaz/fumigène** mortar/gas/smoke shell; **o. traçant** tracer shell **2** *(comme adj)* **homme o./femme o.** human cannonball

obusier [ɔbyzje] **NM** howitzer

obvier [19] [ɔbvje] **obvier à VT IND** *Littéraire (parer à)* to obviate, to ward off; **o. à un danger/un accident** to forestall a danger/an accident

OC *Rad (abrév écrite* **ondes courtes***)* SW

oc [ɔk] *voir* **langue**

ocarina [ɔkarina] **NM** *Mus* ocarina

occase [ɔkaz] *Fam* **NF 1** *(circonstance favorable)* opportunity◻, chance◻

2 *(affaire)* steal, *Br* snip; **profites-en, c'est une o.!** make the most of it, it's a real steal!

3 *(article de seconde main)* second-hand item◻; **elle est neuve, ta voiture? – non, c'est une o.** is your car new? – no, it's second-hand

4 *(moment)* moment◻; **à la première o.** asap, as soon as possible◻; **j'attends la bonne o.** I'm waiting for the right moment

• **d'occase ADV** *Fam* second-hand◻; **je l'ai acheté d'o.** I bought it second-hand

occasion [ɔkazjɔ̃] **NF 1** *(circonstance favorable)* opportunity, chance; **si l'o. se présente** if the opportunity arises, *Sout* should the opportunity arise; **l'o. ne se représentera pas** there won't be another chance like that; **laisser passer l'o.** to let the opportunity slip (by); **saisir l'o. (au vol), sauter sur l'o.** to seize the opportunity, to jump at the chance; **profiter de l'o. pour faire qch** to take the opportunity to do sth; **à la première o.** at the first *or* earliest opportunity; **je le lui dirai à la première o.** I'll tell him/her as soon as I get a chance; **ça te donnera l'o. de la rencontrer** it'll give you the opportunity *or* the chance to meet her; **avoir l'o. de faire qch** to have the opportunity *or* chance of doing *or* to do sth; **je n'ai jamais eu l'o. de me plaindre de lui** I've never had cause to complain about him; **ne manque pas l'o. de le lui dire** don't miss your chance of telling him/her; **il ne perd jamais une o. de se faire remarquer** he never misses an opportunity to get himself noticed; *Fam* **il a manqué** *ou* **perdu** *ou* **raté une belle o. de se taire** he could have kept his mouth shut; *Fam* **c'est l'o. ou jamais de le faire** now's the time to do it◻; *Fam* **c'était l'o. ou jamais de changer de boulot!** if ever there was a time to change jobs, it was then!; *Prov* **l'o. fait le larron** opportunity makes a thief; *Mktg* **o. d'entendre** opportunity to hear; *Mktg* **o. de voir** opportunity to see; *Fin* **o. de profit** profit opportunity

2 *(moment)* occasion; **à deux occasions** twice; **à trois/quatre occasions** three/four times; **en toute o.** on every occasion; **en plusieurs/maintes occasions** several/many times, on several/many occasions; **à cette o.** at that point, on that occasion; **en pareille o.** in circumstances like these, in similar circumstances; **dans les grandes occasions** on big *or* important *or* special occasions; **pour les grandes occasions** for special occasions; **être l'o. de qch** to be the occasion of sth; **sa mort a été l'o. de changements importants** significant changes took place after his/her death; **ces retrouvailles furent l'o. de grandes réjouissances** there were great festivities to celebrate this reunion; **ce sera l'o. de faire la fête** that will be a good excuse for a party

3 *(article de seconde main)* second-hand *or* used article; **acheter qch d'o.** to buy sth second-hand; **elle est neuve, ta voiture? – non, c'est une o.** is your car new? – no, it's second-hand; **l'o.** the second-hand trade; **l'o. se vend bien** there's a brisk trade in second-hand goods; **le marché de l'o.** the second-hand market

4 *(bonne affaire)* bargain; **à** *ou* **pour ce prix-là, c'est une o.!** it's a (real) bargain at that price!

• **à l'occasion ADV 1** *(un de ces jours)* one of these days **2** *(éventuellement)* should the opportunity arise; **à l'o., passez nous voir** drop by some time *or* if you get the chance **3** *(de temps en temps)* on occasion; **elle peut être très virulente à l'o.** she can be very harsh on occasion

• **à l'occasion de PRÉP** on the occasion of, upon; **à l'o. de sa venue** upon his/her arrival; **à l'o. de votre départ à la retraite** on the occasion of your retirement; **je l'ai rencontré à l'o. d'un concert** I met him at a concert; **je m'en suis rendu compte à l'o. d'une visite de routine** I realized it during a routine visit

• **d'occasion ADJ 1** *(non neuf)* second-hand; **voiture d'o.** second-hand *or* used car **2** *(improvisé)*

des amours d'o. chance *or* casual (love) affairs ADV *(acheter, vendre)* second-hand; **j'ai fini par le trouver d'o.** in the end, I found a second-hand one

• **pour l'occasion** ADV for the occasion

occasionnel, -elle [ɔkazjɔnɛl] ADJ **1** *(irrégulier)* casual, occasional; *(aide)* casual; **je vais parfois au restaurant, mais cela reste très o.** I sometimes eat out, but only very occasionally; *Fam* **je ne trouve que des (petits) boulots occasionnels** I can only get casual work **2** *(fortuit)* chance *(avant n)*; **rencontre occasionnelle** chance meeting

occasionnellement [ɔkazjɔnɛlmɑ̃] ADV occasionally, from time to time

occasionner [3] [ɔkazjɔne] VT *(causer)* to cause, to bring about, *Sout* to occasion; **le verglas sur les routes a occasionné bon nombre d'accidents** icy roads have caused numerous accidents; **un déménagement occasionne de nombreux frais** moving house is a costly business; **o. des ennuis à qn** to cause trouble for sb, to get sb into trouble

occident [ɔksidɑ̃] NM **1** *Géog* west **2** *Pol* **l'O.** the West, *Sout* the Occident

occidental, -e, -aux, -ales [ɔksidɑ̃tal, -o] ADJ **1** *Géog* west *(avant n)*, western; **côte occidentale** west coast; **l'Europe occidentale** Western Europe **2** *Pol* Western, *Sout* Occidental; **les pays occidentaux, le monde o.** Western countries, the West

• **Occidental, -e** NM,F *Pol* Westerner, *Sout* Occidental

• **à l'occidentale** ADV **vivre à l'occidentale** to live like a Westerner; **s'habiller à l'occidentale** to wear Western-style clothes

occidentalisation [ɔksidɑ̃talizasjɔ̃] NF westernization, *Sout* occidentalization

occidentaliser [3] [ɔksidɑ̃talize] VT to westernize, *Sout* to occidentalize

VPR **s'occidentaliser** to become westernized *or* *Sout* occidentalized

occipital, -e, -aux, -ales [ɔksipital, -o] *Anat* ADJ occipital

NM occipital (bone)

occiput [ɔksipyt] NM *Anat* occiput

occire [ɔksir] VT *Arch (à l'infinitif et au participe passé seulement)* to slay

occitan, -e [ɔksitɑ̃, -an] ADJ *(de la région)* of/from Occitanie; *(langue, littérature)* of/from the langue d'oc

NM *(langue)* langue d'oc *(language spoken in parts of southern France)*

• **Occitan, -e** NM,F = inhabitant of or person from Occitanie

occlusif, -ive [ɔklyzif, -iv] ADJ occlusive

• **occlusive** NF *Ling* occlusive (consonant)

occlusion [ɔklyzjɔ̃] NF *Chim, Ling & Méd* occlusion; **o. intestinale** bowel obstruction, *Spéc* ileus

occlusive [ɔklyziv] *voir* **occlusif**

occultation [ɔkyltasjɔ̃] NF **1** *Astron* occultation **2** *Rail* occulting *(UNCOUNT)*; **feu à occultations** intermittent *or* occulting light **3** *Littéraire (obscurcissement)* obscuring, concealment, hiding

occulte [ɔkylt] ADJ **1** *(surnaturel)* occult **2** *(secret)* occult, secret; *(cause)* hidden; *(rôle)* clandestine, covert; **financements occultes** secret *or* mystery funding *(UNCOUNT)*; **fonds** *ou* **réserves occultes** slush funds

occulter [3] [ɔkylte] VT **1** *Astron & Rail* to occult; *(signal lumineux)* to block out, *Spéc* to occult **2** *(ville, région)* to black out, to black out TV programmes in **3** *Fig (réalité, problème)* to cover up, to hush up, to gloss over; *(sentiment, émotion)* to deny; **votre récit occulte un détail essentiel** your story glosses over *or* overlooks an essential detail

occultisme [ɔkyltism] NM occultism

occupant, -e [ɔkypɑ̃, -ɑ̃t] ADJ occupying *(avant n)*; **la puissance occupante** the occupying power

NM,F **1** *(d'un véhicule)* occupant; *(d'un lieu, d'une maison)* occupant, occupier; *(d'un poste)* occupant **2** *Mil* occupier, occupying force; **collaborer avec l'o.** to collaborate with the occupying forces **3** *Jur* **premier o.** first occupant

occupation [ɔkypasjɔ̃] NF **1** *(professionnelle)* occupation, job; *(de loisirs)* occupation; **avoir de l'o.** to be busy, to have things to do; **la pêche à la ligne, voilà mon o. favorite** angling is my favourite occupation; **je n'aime pas qu'il soit** *ou* **reste sans occupations** I don't like seeing him with nothing to do; *Admin* **o. principale** main occupation

2 *(d'un endroit)* occupancy, occupation; *(d'une maison)* possession; **l'o. de l'université par les étudiants** the student sit-in at the university; **o. des lieux** occupancy; **grève avec o. des lieux** sit-down strike, sit-in

3 *(dans un hôtel)* **o. des chambres/des lits** room/bed occupancy; **o. double** double occupancy; **o. maximale** capacity occupancy

4 *Mil* occupation; **les troupes d'o.** the occupying troops

5 *Hist* **l'O.** the (German) Occupation (of France); **la vie sous l'O.** life in occupied France

occupé, -e [ɔkype] ADJ **1** *(non disponible ▸ ligne de téléphone) Br* engaged, *Am* busy; *(▸ toilettes) Br* engaged, *Am* occupied; *Fam* **ça sonne o.** *Br* I'm getting the engaged tone, *Am* the line is busy; **ces places sont occupées** these seats are taken **2** *Mil & Pol* occupied **3** *(personne)* busy; **une femme très occupée** a very busy woman; **o. aux préparatifs du départ** busy with the preparations for departure, busy getting ready to leave; **j'ai des journées très occupées** my days are full

occuper [3] [ɔkype] VT **1** *(donner une activité à)* **o. qn** to keep sb busy *or* occupied; **cela l'occupe beaucoup** it takes up a lot of his/her time; **les enfants m'occupent toute la journée** the children keep me busy all day; **on pourrait o. les petits à des jeux de sable** we could keep the little ones busy playing in the sand; **fais un peu de ménage, ça t'occupera!** do a bit of housework, that'll pass *or* fill the time!; **le textile occupait toute la région** the textile industry used to provide work for *or* to employ people throughout the region; **la question qui nous occupe** the matter in hand; **la lecture de ce livre m'a occupé toute la soirée** reading this book took up my entire evening *or* kept me busy all evening; **ces problèmes m'ont occupé pendant un certain temps** these problems have kept me busy *or* kept me occupied *or* given me something to think about for some time; **être occupé à faire qch** to be busy doing sth

2 *(envahir)* to occupy, to take over; **les rebelles occupent tout le Nord** the rebels have occupied the entire northern area; **o. le terrain** *Mil & Fig* to have the field; *Com* to make one's presence felt in the market

3 *(remplir ▸ espace)* to take up, to occupy; **le bar occupe le fond de la pièce/trop de place** the bar stands at the back of the room/takes up too much space; **les livres d'art occupent trois étagères de la bibliothèque** the art books take up *or* occupy *or* fill three shelves of the bookcase; **les grévistes occupent les bureaux** the strikers have occupied the offices; **o. le devant de la scène** to be in the foreground

4 *(remplir ▸ temps)* to fill, to occupy; **faire qch pour o. le temps** to do sth to fill *or* occupy the time; **les enfants occupent la majeure partie de mon temps** the children take up the greater part of my time

5 *(consacrer)* to spend; **o. sa journée à faire qch** to spend one's day doing sth; **j'occupe mes loisirs à lire** I spend my free time reading; **à quoi peut-on o. ses dimanches?** what is there to do on Sundays?

6 *(habiter)* to occupy, to live in; **qui occupe la maison d'en face?** who lives in *or* occupies the house opposite?

7 *(détenir ▸ poste, place)* to hold, to occupy; **il occupe un poste important** he holds an important position; **Liverpool occupe la seconde place du championnat** Liverpool are (lying) second in the league table

USAGE ABSOLU **ça occupe!** it keeps me/him/her/*etc* busy; *Fam* **la télé, ça occupe** watching TV helps to pass the time

VPR **s'occuper 1** *(passer le temps)* to keep oneself busy *or* occupied, to occupy oneself; **s'o. en lisant** to spend one's time reading; **je m'occupe en faisant du crochet** I keep myself busy by crocheting; **s'o. à faire qch** to be busy doing sth, to be occupied in doing sth; **à quoi s'occupent les citadins au mois d'août?** how do city dwellers spend their time in August?; **il va falloir qu'elle s'occupe** she'll have to find something to keep her occupied; **tu n'as donc pas de quoi t'o.?** haven't you got something to be getting on with?; **on trouve toujours à s'o.** there's always something to do; **je trouverai bien de quoi m'o. en attendant** I'll find something to keep me busy while I'm waiting; *Fam* **c'est juste histoire de m'o.** it's just for something to do

2 s'o. de *(avoir pour responsabilité ou tâche)* to deal with, to be in charge of, to take care of; **je m'occupe de jeunes délinquants** I'm in charge of young offenders; **qui s'occupe de votre dossier?** who's dealing with *or* handling your file?; **nous allons maintenant nous o. du bilan** we will now turn (our attention) to the balance sheet; **je m'en occupe** I'll see to it, I'll take care of it; **je m'en occuperai plus tard** I'll see to it later; **je m'en occuperai dès demain matin** I'll attend to *or* take care of that first thing in the morning; **t'es-tu occupé des réservations?** did you see about the reservations?; **je m'occupe de te faire parvenir ton courrier** I'll see about having your mail sent on to you; **cette maison s'occupe surtout d'argenterie** this firm specializes in silverware; *Fam* **occupe-toi de tes affaires** *ou* **oignons** *ou* **de ce qui te regarde** mind your own business; *Fam* **t'occupe!** mind your own business!, keep your nose out!, butt out!

3 s'o. de *(entourer de soins)* to look after, to care for; **s'o. d'un malade** to care for a patient; **s'o. d'un bébé** to look after a baby; **peux-tu t'o. des invités pendant que je me prépare?** would you look after *or* see to the guests while I get ready?; **on s'occupe de vous, Madame?** are you being attended to *or* served, Madam?; **il ne s'occupe pas assez d'elle** he doesn't pay her enough attention

occurrence [ɔkyrɑ̃s] NF **1** *(cas)* case; **en pareille o., il faut appeler la police** in such a case *or* in such circumstances, the police must be called **2** *Ling* token, occurrence **3** *Ordinat (lors d'une recherche sur l'Internet)* hit

• **en l'occurrence** ADV as it happens; **il voulait s'en prendre à quelqu'un, en l'o. ce fut moi** he wanted to take it out on somebody, and it happened to be me *or* and as it happened, it was me; **mais, en l'o., tu as tort** but in this case *or* but this time *or* but as it happens, you're wrong

OCDE [ɔsedeə] NF *(abrév* **Organisation de coopération et de développement économiques**) OECD

océan [ɔseɑ̃] NM **1** *Géog* ocean; **l'o. Atlantique/Antarctique/Indien/Pacifique** the Atlantic/Antarctic/Indian/Pacific Ocean; **l'o. (Glacial) Arctique** the Arctic Ocean **2** *Fig* **un o. de larmes** floods of tears; **un o. de couleurs** a sea of colour

océane [ɔsean] ADJ F **1** *Culin (salade, sauce)* seafood *(avant n)* **2** *Littéraire (de l'Océan)* **une brise o.** a sea breeze; *Arch* **la mer o.** the ocean sea, the Atlantic

• **Océane** NF **l'O.** *(autoroute)* = the Paris–Nantes motorway

Océanie [ɔseani] NF **l'O.** Oceania, the (central and) South Pacific

océanien, -enne [ɔseanjɛ̃, -ɛn] ADJ Oceanian, Oceanic

• **Océanien, -enne** NM,F Oceanian, South Sea Islander

océanique [ɔseanik] ADJ oceanic

océanographe [ɔseanɔgraf] NMF oceanographer

océanographie [ɔseanɔgrafi] NF oceanography

océanographique [ɔseanɔgrafik] ADJ oceanographic

océanologie [ɔseanɔlɔʒi] NF oceanology

ocelle [ɔsɛl] NM *Zool* **1** *(œil)* ocellus **2** *(tache)* ocellus, eyespot

ocelot [ɔslo] NM **1** *(animal)* ocelot **2** *(fourrure)* ocelot (fur)

SUFFIX

-OCHE

This slang suffix lends a PEJORATIVE or simply HUMOROUS tone to the new word created from an adjective, noun or verb radical. There is not always a slang equivalent for these words in English, eg:

cantoche (from *cantine*) canteen; **cinoche** (from *cinéma*) cinema, movies; **fastoche** (from *facile*) dead easy; **pelloche** (from *pel-*

licule) film, flick; **avoir la pétoche** (from *péter*) to be scared stiff; **pistoche** (from *piscine*) (swimming) pool; **téloche** (from *télévision*) TV, telly; **valoche** (from *valise*) suitcase/bag under the eyes

OCR [oseɛr] NF *(abrév* **optical character recognition)** OCR

ocre [ɔkr] NF ochre; **o. jaune** yellow ochre; **o. rouge** ruddle
ADJ INV ochre
NM ochre

ocré, -e [ɔkre] ADJ ochry

ocreux, -euse [ɔkrø, -øz] ADJ ochreous

octaèdre [ɔktaɛdr] ADJ octahedral
NM octahedron

octaédrique [ɔktaedrik] ADJ octahedral

octal, -e, -aux, -ales [ɔktal, -o] ADJ octal

octane [ɔktan] NM octane

octave [ɔktav] NF *Mus* octave; **à l'o. inférieure/supérieure** one octave lower/higher; **jouer à l'o.** *(plus haut)* to play an octave higher; *(plus bas)* to play an octave lower

octet [ɔktɛ] NM *Ordinat* octet, (eight-bit) byte; **milliard d'octets** gigabyte; **o. de contrôle** check byte

octobre [ɔktɔbr] NM October; *voir aussi* **mars**

octogénaire [ɔktɔʒenɛr] ADJ octogenarian; **être o.** to be in one's eighties
NMF person in his/her eighties

octogonal, -e, -aux, -ales [ɔktɔgɔnal, -o] ADJ octagonal

octogone [ɔktɔgɔn] ADJ octagonal
NM octagon

octopode [ɔktɔpɔd] ADJ octopod
NM octopod

octosyllabe [ɔktɔsilab] ADJ octosyllabic
NM octosyllable

octosyllabique [ɔktɔsilabik] ADJ octosyllabic

octroi [ɔktrwa] NM **1** *(don)* granting, bestowing; *Com* **o. de licence** licensing **2** *Hist (taxe, administration)* octroi

octroyer [13] [ɔktrwaje] VT *(accorder)* to grant; **o. qch à qn** *(faveur, permission, congé)* to grant sb sth; **o. sa grâce à un condamné a mort** to reprieve a condemned man; **le ministère a fait o. une prime aux soldats du contingent** the ministry gave instructions for a bonus to be paid to the conscripts
VPR **s'octroyer s'o. un congé** to take a day off *(without permission)*; **il s'est octroyé un jour de vacances supplémentaire** he gave himself *or* awarded himself an extra day's holiday; **s'o. le droit de faire qch** to assume the right to do sth

octuor [ɔktɥɔr] NM octet

octuple [ɔktypl] ADJ octuple; *(montant)* eightfold
NM octuple

oculaire [ɔkylɛr] ADJ ocular; **hygiène o.** eye care, care of the eyes
NM *Opt* ocular, eyepiece; **o. de visée** *(d'une caméra)* eyepiece

oculiste [ɔkylist] NMF oculist

odalisque [ɔdalisk] NF **1** *Hist* odalisque **2** *Littéraire (courtisane)* courtesan, odalisque

ode [ɔd] NF ode

odeur [ɔdœr] NF **1** *(de nourriture)* smell, odour; *(de fleur, de parfum)* smell, fragrance, scent; **bonne o.** lovely *or* pleasant smell; **mauvaise o.** bad *or* unpleasant smell; **une forte o. de brûlé/chocolat venait de la cuisine** a strong smell of burning/chocolate was coming from the kitchen; **il a une drôle d'o., ce poisson** this fish has a funny smell *or* smells funny; **ce médicament a une mauvaise o.** this medicine smells bad *or* has a bad smell; **chasser les mauvaises odeurs** to get rid of (nasty *or* unpleasant) smells; **sans o.** odourless; **ça n'a pas d'o.** it has no smell, it doesn't smell; **o. corporelle** body odour **2** *Rel* **mourir en o. de sainteté** to die in the odour of sanctity; *Fig* **être en o. de sainteté auprès de qn** to be in sb's good books; *Fig* **ne pas être en o. de sainteté** to be in sb's bad books, to be out of favour; **il n'est pas en o. de sainteté dans le parti** he is out of favour in the party

odieuse [ɔdjøz] *voir* **odieux**

odieusement [ɔdjøzmɑ̃] ADV odiously, hatefully, obnoxiously

odieux, -euse [ɔdjø, -øz] ADJ **1** *(atroce ▸ comportement)* odious; *(▸ crime)* heinous; **je me dois de répondre à ces odieuses accusations** it's my duty to answer these monstrous charges **2** *(désagréable ▸ personne)* hateful, obnoxious; **l'examinateur a été o. avec moi** the examiner was obnoxious *or* vile to me; **elle a deux enfants o.** she has two unbearable *or* obnoxious children; **cela m'est o.** I absolutely loathe it

odomètre [ɔdɔmɛtr] NM *(pour véhicule)* odometer; *(pour piéton)* pedometer

odontologie [ɔdɔ̃tɔlɔʒi] NF odontology

odorant, -e [ɔdɔrɑ̃, -ɑ̃t] ADJ **1** *(qui a une odeur)* odorous **2** *(parfumé)* fragrant, sweet-smelling; **leur jardin était lumineux et o.** their garden was bright and fragrant

odorat [ɔdɔra] NM (sense of) smell; **avoir l'o. développé** to have a keen sense of smell; **manquer d'o.** to have no sense of smell

odoriférant, -e [ɔdɔriferɑ̃, -ɑ̃t] ADJ *Littéraire (parfumé)* sweet-smelling, fragrant, odoriferous

odyssée [ɔdise] NF odyssey; **nous attendions avec impatience le récit de son o.** we were looking forward to hearing the story of his epic journey

OEA [ɔəɑ] NF *(abrév* **Organisation des États américains)** OAS

OEB [ɔəbe] NM *(abrév* **Office européen des brevets)** EPO

œcuménique [ekymenik] ADJ ecumenical

œcuménisme [ekymenism] NM ecumenicalism, ecumenicism

œcuméniste [ekymenist] ADJ ecumenic, ecumenical
NMF ecumenist

œdème [edem] NM *Méd* oedema; **o. aigu du poumon** acute pulmonary oedema; **avoir un o. aux poumons** to have pulmonary oedema

Œdipe [edip] NPR *Myth* Oedipus

œil [œj] *(pl sens* **1–7**, **9 yeux** [jø], *pl sens* **8 œils)** NM **1** *Anat* eye; **j'ai le soleil dans les yeux** the sun's in *or* I've got the sun in my eyes; **fermer/ouvrir les yeux** to close/to open one's eyes; *Fig* **fermer les yeux à qn** to be present at sb's death; **j'ai les yeux qui se ferment (tout seuls)** I can't keep my eyes open; **les yeux fermés** with one's eyes closed; **ouvrir un o.** to half-open one's eyes; **ouvrir de grands yeux** to look surprised; **faire** *ou* **ouvrir des yeux ronds** to stare wide-eyed; **baisser les yeux** to lower one's eyes *or* gaze, to look down; **avoir de grands yeux** to have large eyes; **avoir de gros yeux** to have bulbous eyes; **avoir de petits yeux** to have small eyes; *Fig* to look (all) puffy-eyed *or* puffy round the eyes; **avoir les yeux verts/marron** to have green/brown eyes; **avoir l'o. humide** to have tearful eyes *or* a tearful gaze; **aux yeux de biche** doe-eyed; **elle a des yeux de biche** she's got doe-eyes; **avoir les yeux battus** to have (dark) rings *or* bags under one's eyes; **il n'a qu'un o.** he's one-eyed, he's only got one eye; **je vois mal d'un o.** one of my eyes is weak; **il ne voit plus que d'un o.** he can only see with one eye now; **je l'ai de mes yeux vu, je l'ai vu de mes propres yeux** I saw it with my own eyes; **o. artificiel/de verre** artificial/glass eye; *Biol* **o. composé** *ou* **à facettes** compound eye; *Littéraire* **l'o. intérieur** the inner eye; **le mauvais o.** the evil eye; **jeter le mauvais o. à qn** to give sb the evil eye; *Fam* **mon o.!** my eye!, my foot!; **généreux, mon o.!** generous, my foot!; *Fam* **attention les yeux!** get an eyeful of that!; **il a une petite amie/une bagnole, attention les yeux!** you should see his girlfriend/car!; *Fam* **avoir un o. poché** *ou* **au beurre noir** to have a black eye *or Br* a shiner; **elle avait les yeux qui lui sortaient de la tête** her eyes were popping out of her head; *Fam* **il/ça me sort par les yeux de la tête** I can't stand him/it; **il faudrait avoir des yeux derrière la tête!** you'd need (to have) eyes in the back of your head!; *Hum* **avoir un o. qui dit** *Fam* **zut** *ou très Fam* **merde à l'autre,** *Fam* **avoir les yeux qui se croisent les bras, avoir un o. qui joue au billard et l'autre qui compte les points, avoir un o. à Paris et l'autre à Pontoise** to have a squint[□], to be cross-eyed[□], *Br* to be boss-eyed; *Fam* **coûter les yeux de la tête** to cost a fortune[□] *or* an arm and a leg; *Fam* **viens me lire ça, petit, j'ai besoin d'yeux** come and read this for me, son, I need (somebody with) a good pair of eyes; **faire les gros yeux à un enfant** to look sternly *or* reprovingly at a child; **maman va te faire les gros yeux!** Mummy's going to tell you off!; **faire qch pour les beaux yeux de qn** to do sth for the love of sb; **je ne travaille pas pour les beaux yeux de mon patron!** I don't do this job for the love of it!; *Fam* **entre quat'z yeux** in private[□]; *Fam* **il n'a pas froid aux yeux** he's got plenty of nerve, he's not backward in coming forward; *Fam* **tu as les yeux plus grands que le ventre** *(tu es trop gourmand)* your eyes are bigger than your belly *or* your stomach; *(tu as été trop ambitieux)* you've bitten off more than you can chew; *Bible* **o. pour o.(, dent pour dent)** an eye for an eye (and a tooth for a tooth)
2 *(vision)* sight, eyesight; **avoir de bons yeux** to have good eyesight; **avoir de mauvais yeux** to have bad *or* poor eyesight; **avoir des yeux de lynx** to be eagle-eyed; **il la suivait de son o. d'aigle** he was watching her every move like a hawk; **il a des yeux de chat** he can see like a cat in the dark; **je n'ai plus mes yeux de vingt ans** I can't see as well as I used to; **s'user** *ou* **s'abîmer les yeux** to ruin one's eyes *or* eyesight; **fatiguer les yeux** to strain one's eyes; **cette lumière me fatigue les yeux** I'm straining my eyes in this light
3 *(regard)* **ne me fais pas ces yeux-là!** don't look *or* stare at me like that!; **les yeux dans les yeux** *(tendrement)* looking into each other's eyes; *(avec franchise)* looking each other straight in the eye; **regarder qn dans les yeux** to look sb in the eye; **regarder qn avec les yeux de l'amour** to look at sb through the eyes of love; **chercher qn des yeux** to look around for sb; **suivre qn des yeux** to follow sb with one's eyes; **jeter les yeux sur qch** to cast a glance at sth; **dès que j'eus jeté les yeux sur lui** as soon as I had set eyes on him; **jeter un o. à** to have a quick look at; **veux-tu y jeter un o. en vitesse?** do you want to have a quick look at it?; **lever les yeux sur qn/qch** to look up at sb/sth; **sans lever les yeux de son livre** without looking up *or* raising his/her eyes from his/her book; **lever les yeux au ciel** *(pour regarder)* to look up at the sky; *(par exaspération)* to raise one's eyes heavenwards; **poser un o. sur** to have a look at; **elle posait sur tout un o. curieux** she was curious about everything; **n'ayant jamais posé les yeux sur de telles splendeurs** never having laid *or* set eyes on such fabulous sights; **devant les yeux de** before (the eyes of); **les clefs sont devant tes yeux** the keys are right in front of you; *Littéraire* **sous les yeux de, sous l'o. de** under the eye *or* gaze of; **sous l'o. amusé/jaloux de son frère** under the amused/jealous gaze of her brother; **sous mes yeux** *(devant moi)* right in front of me; *(effrontément)* before my very eyes; **il l'a volé sous nos yeux** he stole it from under our very eyes; **elle dépérissait sous mes yeux** I could see her wasting away before my very eyes; **j'ai votre dossier sous les yeux** I've got your file right here in front of me *or* before me; **à l'abri des yeux indiscrets** away from prying eyes; **n'avoir d'yeux que pour** to only have eyes for; **il n'avait d'yeux que pour elle** he only had eyes for her
4 *(expression, air)* look; **son o. malicieux/interrogateur** her mischievous/inquiring look; **elle est arrivée, l'o. méchant** *ou* **mauvais** she arrived with a nasty look on her face *or* looking like trouble; **il m'a regardé d'un o. noir/furieux** he gave me a black/furious look; **elle se taisait, mais ses yeux parlaient pour elle** she said nothing, but her eyes did the talking; *Fam* **faire de l'o. à qn** *(pour aguicher)* to give sb the eye, to make eyes at sb; *(en signe de connivence)* to wink knowingly at sb; **arrête de faire de l'o. à tous les garçons!** stop giving all the boys the eye!; **faire les yeux doux** *ou* **des yeux de velours à qn** to make sheep's eyes at sb
5 *(vigilance)* **rien n'échappait à l'o. du professeur** nothing escaped the teacher's notice; **avoir l'o.** to be vigilant *or* watchful; **aie l'o.!** be on the lookout!; **elle a l'o. à tout** she keeps an eye on everything; **il faut avoir l'o. à tout avec les enfants** you've got to keep an eye on everything when children are around; **il a l'o. du maître** *(rien ne lui échappe)* he doesn't miss a thing; **avoir l'o. sur qn** to keep an eye *or* a close watch on sb; **être tout**

yeux to be all eyes; **ils étaient tout yeux et tout oreilles** they were all eyes and ears; **ouvrir les yeux à qn sur qch** to open sb's eyes to sth; *Fam* **ouvrir l'o. (et le bon)** to keep one's eyes open *or* peeled *or* skinned; **sauter aux yeux,** *Fam* **crever les yeux** to be blindingly *or* glaringly obvious; *Fam* **il n'a pas les yeux en face des trous** *(il est mal réveillé)* he hasn't come to yet, his brain isn't in gear yet; *(il n'est pas observateur)* he's as blind as a bat, he never sees what's going on right in front of him; *Fam* **elle n'a pas les yeux dans sa poche** she keeps her eyes open, she's very observant□

6 *(état d'esprit, avis)* **voir qch d'un bon/mauvais o.** to look favourably/unfavourably upon sth; **considérer** *ou* **voir qch d'un o. critique** to look critically at sth; **considérer** *ou* **voir qch d'un o. neuf** to look at sth with a fresh eye; **voir les choses du même o. que qn** to see eye to eye with sb; **nous voyons ça du même o.** we see eye to eye (with each other) about it; **nous ne voyons pas du tout les choses de cet o.-là** we don't see things in that light at all; **il voit tout par les yeux de sa femme** he sees everything through his wife's eyes; **il voit avec les yeux de la foi/de l'amour** he sees things through the eyes of a believer/of love; **aux yeux de** in the eyes of; **aux yeux de tous, il passait pour fou** he was regarded by everyone as a madman; **à mes yeux** in my eyes, in my opinion; **ça n'a aucun intérêt à mes yeux** it's of no interest to me; **aux yeux de la loi** in the eyes of the law

7 *(trou* ▸ *dans une porte)* spyhole, Judas(-hole), spyhole; *(*▸ *au théâtre)* peep hole; *(*▸ *d'une aiguille)* eye; *(d'une charnière)* (screw-)hole; *Météo (d'un cyclone)* eye, centre

8 *Typ* face; **o. du caractère** typeface

9 *Tech* **o. magique** magic eye

• **yeux** NMPL **1** *Fam Hum (lunettes)* glasses□, *Br* specs; **j'ai oublié mes yeux** I've forgotten my specs **2** *Culin (du pain, du gruyère)* hole; **les yeux du bouillon** the fat *(floating on the surface of the stock)*

• **à l'œil** ADV *Fam* **1** *(gratis)* (for) free□, for nothing□; **j'ai voyagé à l'o.** I travelled for free; **ce soir-là, j'ai chanté à l'o.** that night, I sang for free; **j'ai eu deux tickets à l'o.** I got two tickets gratis *or* (for) free *or* on the house **2** *(locution)* **avoir** *ou* **tenir qn à l'o.** to have one's eye on sb, to keep an eye on sb; **toi, je t'ai à l'o.!** I've got my eye on you!

• **coup d'œil** NM **1** *(regard)* look, glance; **elle s'en rendit compte au premier coup d'o.** she noticed straight away *or* immediately *or* at a glance; **donner** *ou* **jeter un (petit) coup d'o. à** to have a quick look *or* glance at; **d'un coup d'o., il embrassa le tableau** he took in the situation at a glance; **avoir le coup d'o.** *(savoir regarder)* to have a good eye; **pour les coquilles, elle a le coup d'o.** she has a good *or* keen eye for misprints; **valoir le coup d'o.** to be (well) worth seeing **2** *(panorama)* view; **de là-haut, le coup d'o. est unique** the view up there is unique

œil-de-bœuf [œjdəbœf] *(pl* **œils-de-bœuf***)* *Archit* NM *(oculus)* oculus; *(lucarne)* bull's-eye

œil-de-chat [œjdəʃa] *(pl* **œils-de-chat***)* NM *Minér* cat's-eye

œil-de-perdrix [œjdəperdri] *(pl* **œils-de-perdrix***)* NM **1** *Anat* (soft) corn **2** *(du bois)* small knot **3** *(vin)* oeil-de-perdrix, = Swiss rosé wine made from Pinot Noir grapes

œillade [œjad] NF wink; **jeter** *ou* **lancer des œillades à qn** to give sb the (glad) eye; *Hum* **une o. assassine** a provocative wink

œillère [œjɛr] NF **1** *(de cheval) Br* blinker, *Am* blinder; *Fig* **avoir des œillères** to be blinkered, to have a blinkered attitude; *(être borné)* to be narrow-minded **2** *(coupelle)* eyebath

œillet [œjɛ] NM **1** *Bot (plante)* carnation, pink; *(fleur)* carnation; **o. des fleuristes** carnation; **o. de poète** sweet william **2** *(perforation)* eyelet hole **3** *(anneau* ▸ *de papier gommé)* reinforcement ring; *(*▸ *de métal)* eyelet, grommet

œilleton [œjtɔ̃] NM **1** *Bot* eye **2** *Opt* eyepiece shade **3** *(d'une porte)* Judas(-hole), spyhole

œillette [œjɛt] NF oil poppy, opium poppy; **huile d'o.** poppy seed oil

œnologie [enɔlɔʒi] NF oenology; **un stage d'o.** a wine-tasting course

œnologique [enɔlɔʒik] ADJ oenological

œnologue [enɔlɔg] NMF oenologist, wine specialist

œsophage [ezɔfaʒ] NM *Anat* oesophagus

œstre [ɛstr] NM *Entom* gadfly, warble fly

œstrogène [ɛstrɔʒɛn] NM *Biol & Chim* oestrogen

œstrus [ɛstrys] NM *Biol* oestrus

œuf [œf] *(pl* **œufs** [ø]*)* NM **1** *Culin* egg; **œufs brouillés** scrambled eggs; **o. en chocolat** chocolate egg; **o. (en) cocotte** coddled egg; **o. (à la) coque** boiled egg; *Belg* **o. cuit dur** hard-boiled egg; **o. dur** hard-boiled egg; **o. du jour** new-laid egg; **œufs au lait** ≃ egg custard; **o. mayonnaise** egg mayonnaise; **o. (au) miroir** fried egg; **o. mollet** soft-boiled egg; **œufs à la neige** floating islands; **œufs en neige** beaten egg whites; **o. de Pâques** Easter egg; **o. sur le plat** *ou* **au plat** fried egg; *Fam* **œufs sur le plat** *(seins)* fried eggs; **elle n'a que des œufs sur le plat** she's as flat as a pancake; **o. poché** poached egg; *Fig* **sortir de l'o.** to be still wet behind the ears; *Fig* **écraser** *ou* **étouffer** *ou* **tuer qch dans l'o.** to nip sth in the bud; **c'est comme l'histoire de l'o. et de la poule** it's a chicken and egg situation; **c'est comme l'o. de Christophe Colomb, il fallait y penser** it's easy when you know how; *Prov* **il ne faut pas mettre tous ses œufs dans le même panier** never put all your eggs in one basket

2 *Fam (imbécile)* oaf, blockhead; **tête d'o.!** you nincompoop!

3 *Biol* (egg) cell, egg; *Zool (d'insecte, de poisson)* egg; *(de homard)* berry; *Ich* **œufs de poisson** spawn; *Culin* fish roe

4 *Couture* **o. à repriser** darning egg

5 *(télécabine)* cable car

6 *Ordinat* **o. de Pâques** Easter egg

œufrier [œfrije] NM egg holder *(for boiling eggs)*

œuvre[1] [œvr] NM **1** *Archit & Constr* **une construction dans o./hors (d')o.** a construction within/without the perimeter; **mesure dans/hors o.** inside/outside measurement; **gros o.** carcass, fabric; **le gros o. est enfin terminé** the main building work is finished at last; **second o.** finishing (jobs) **2** *Beaux-Arts* works; **son o. gravé et son o. peint** his paintings and his etchings **3** *(en alchimie)* **le Grand o.** the Great Work, the Magnum Opus

œuvre[2] [œvr] NF **1** *(travail)* work; **o. de longue haleine** long-term undertaking; **ce tabouret est l'o. d'un artisan** this stool is the work of a craftsman; *Ftbl* **le troisième but a été l'o. de Bergova** the third goal was the work of Bergova; **cette rencontre était son o.** *(grâce à lui)* it was thanks to him that they met; *(à cause de lui)* it was because of him that they met; **elle a fait o. durable/utile** she's done a lasting/useful piece of work; **la vieillesse a fait son o.** old age has done its work; **quand le médecin arriva, la mort avait déjà fait son o.** by the time the doctor arrived, the patient had already died; **mettre qch en o.** to bring sth into play; **mettre tout en o. pour que** to do all in one's power to ensure that; **nous avons mis tous les moyens** *ou* **tout en o. pour juguler l'incendie** we did everything we could to bring the fire under control; **elle a mis tout en o. pour être sélectionnée** she pulled out all the stops in order to get selected; **o. maîtresse** magnum opus; **mise en o.** *(en joaillerie)* mounting; **faire o. de rénovateur** to act as a renovator

2 *Beaux-Arts, Littérature & Mus* work; **toute son o.** the whole of her works; **couronné pour l'ensemble de son o.** rewarded for his overall achievement; **o. d'art** work of art; **œuvres choisies/complètes de Molière** selected/complete works of Molière; **o. de jeunesse** early work

3 *(charité)* **o. (de bienfaisance)** charitable organization; **je fais la collecte pour une o.** I'm collecting for charity; **(bonnes) œuvres** charity *(UNCOUNT)*

• **œuvres** NFPL **1** *Admin* **œuvres sociales** community service *(UNCOUNT)* **2** *Naut* **œuvres mortes** dead work *(UNCOUNT)*, topsides; *Naut* **œuvres vives** quickwork *(UNCOUNT)*; *Fig* **la France, blessée dans ses œuvres vives** France, cut to the quick

• **à l'œuvre** ADV at work; **être à l'o.** to be at work; **se mettre à l'o.** to get down to *or* to start work; **voir qn à l'o.** to see sb at work

œuvrer [5] [œvre] VI to work, to strive; **nous voulons la paix, et nous allons o. pour cela** we want peace, and we will do our utmost to achieve it

off [ɔf] ADJ INV **1** *Cin* offscreen; **voix o.** voice off **2** *(festival)* fringe *(avant n)*

NM **le o.** the Fringe festival; **dans le o.** on the Fringe (festival); **au programme du o.** on the Fringe (festival programme)

offensant, -e [ɔfɑ̃sɑ̃, -ɑ̃t] ADJ offensive

offense [ɔfɑ̃s] NF **1** *(affront)* insult; **faire o. à** to offend, to give offence to; **soit dit sans o., tu n'es plus tout jeune non plus** no offence intended *or* meant, but you're not that young either; **c'est une o. au bon goût** it's an offence *or* a crime against good taste; *Fam* **il n'y a pas d'o.** no offence taken **2** *Rel* trespass, transgression **3** *Jur* **o. à la cour** contempt of court

offensé, -e [ɔfɑ̃se] ADJ offended, insulted; **air o.** offended *or* outraged look

NM,F offended *or* injured party

offenser [3] [ɔfɑ̃se] VT **1** *(blesser)* to offend, to give offence to; **je l'ai offensé sans le vouloir** I offended him unintentionally; **tu l'offenserais en ne l'invitant pas** you'd offend him if you didn't invite him; **sans vouloir t'o., Jean-Pierre, j'ai bien l'impression que...** no offence (intended), Jean-Pierre, *or* I don't wish to offend, Jean-Pierre, but I get the feeling that…; **o. la mémoire de qn** to offend sb's memory **2** *(enfreindre)* to violate; **o. un principe** to fly in the face of a principle; *Rel* **o. Dieu** to offend God, to trespass against God **3** *Littéraire (bon goût, délicatesse)* to offend against; **o. les regards** to be an eyesore, to offend the eye

VPR **s'offenser** *(se vexer)* to take offence; **s'o. de la moindre critique** to take exception to the slightest criticism; **elle s'est offensée qu'il ait oublié son anniversaire** she was offended because he forgot her birthday

offenseur [ɔfɑ̃sœr] NM offender

offensif, -ive [ɔfɑ̃sif, -iv] ADJ offensive; **l'équipe a adopté un jeu très o.** the team has opted to play an attacking game; **arme/guerre offensive** offensive weapon/war

• **offensive** NF *Mil & Fig* offensive; **passer à/prendre l'offensive** to go on/to take the offensive; **mener une offensive** to carry out *or* to conduct an offensive; **le club lillois revient à l'offensive contre Bordeaux** the Lille team is back on the offensive *or* is making a fresh attack against Bordeaux; *Fig* **offensive de charme** charm offensive; *Fig* **offensive du froid** sudden cold spell, cold snap; *Pol* **offensive de paix** peace offensive

offert, -e [ɔfɛr, -ɛrt] PP *voir* **offrir**

offertoire [ɔfɛrtwar] NM offertory

office [ɔfis] NM **1** *(gén) & Hist* office; **dans son o. de gouvernante** in her position as governess; **le secrétaire n'a pas rempli son o.** the secretary didn't carry out his duties; **le signal d'alarme n'a pas rempli son o.** the alarm didn't (fulfil its) function; **la pénicilline a rempli son o.** the penicillin did its job; **faire o. de président** to act as chairman; **qu'est-ce qui peut faire o. de pièce d'identité?** what could serve as proof of identity?; **pendant le voyage, j'ai dû faire o. de cuisinier** I had to act as cook during the trip; **o. ministériel** ministerial office

2 *Rel* service; **aller à/manquer l'o.** to go to/to miss the church service; **l'o. des morts** funeral service; **o. du soir** evening service

3 *(agence)* agency, bureau; **o. de publicité** advertising agency; **o. du tourisme espagnol** Spanish tourist office *or* bureau; **O. européen des brevets** European Patent Office; **O. du commerce extérieur** foreign trade office; *Suisse* **o. de poste** post office

4 les Offices *(à Florence)* the Uffizi

5 *Com (dans l'édition)* **exemplaire d'o.** copy sent on sale or return

NM OU *Vieilli* NF *(d'une cuisine)* pantry; *(d'un hôtel, d'une grande maison)* kitchen, kitchens; **tous les verres sont rangés dans l'o.** all the glasses are stored in the pantry; **enfant, je dînais à l'o.** as a child, I used to eat with the servants

• **offices** NMPL **accepter les bons offices de qn** to accept sb's good offices; **proposer ses bons offices** to offer to act as mediator; **grâce aux bons offices de M. Prat/du gouvernement allemand** thanks to Mr Prat's good offices/to the good offices of the German government; *Fam* **monsieur bons offices** mediator□

• **d'office** ADV automatically; il a été promu d'o. au rang de général he was automatically promoted to (the rank of) general; je vous mets d'o. parmi les altos I'll put you in straight away with the altos; avocat commis d'o. (officially) appointed lawyer

officialisation [ɔfisjalizasjɔ̃] NF officialization

officialiser [3] [ɔfisjalize] VT to make official, to officialize

officiant [ɔfisjɑ̃] ADJ M officiating *(avant n)*
NM officiant

officiel, -elle [ɔfisjɛl] ADJ 1 *(public)* official; communiqué o. official communiqué; la version officielle est le suicide the official version is suicide; rien de ce que je vous dis là n'est o. everything I'm telling you is unofficial *or* off the record; il a rendu officielle sa décision de démissionner he made public *or* he officially announced his decision to resign; congé o. official holiday; milieux officiels official circles; langage *ou* jargon o. officialese 2 *(réglementaire)* formal; tenue officielle formal attire; notre rencontre n'avait aucun caractère o. our meeting took place on an informal *or* unofficial basis
NM *(représentant)* official; les officiels du Parti the Party officials

officiellement [ɔfisjɛlmɑ̃] ADV officially; je dépose plainte o. I'm making an official complaint; o., il a donné sa démission, mais... officially, he resigned, but...; il a donné sa démission o. he formally resigned

officier[1] **[9]** [ɔfisje] VI 1 *Rel* to officiate 2 *Fig Hum* to preside; qui officie aux fourneaux ce soir? who's in charge *or* presiding in the kitchen tonight?

officier[2] [ɔfisje] NM 1 *Mil* officer; o. d'active regular officer; o. de l'armée de terre army officer; o. général *Mil* general officer; *Naut* flag officer; o. de liaison liaison officer; o. de marine naval officer; o. d'ordonnance orderly; o. de paix senior police officer; o. de permanence duty officer, officer of the day, *Br* orderly officer; *Naut* o. de pont deck officer; o. de port harbour master; o. de réserve reserve officer; o. en second second-in-command; o. de service duty officer; o. subalterne *Br* junior *or Am* company officer; o. supérieur field officer 2 *(titulaire ▸ d'une fonction, d'une distinction)* o. de l'état civil ≃ registrar; o. de la Légion d'honneur Officer of the Legion of Honour; o. ministériel = member of the legal or allied professions; *(notaire)* notary (public); *(huissier)* officer of the court; o. de police judiciaire = police officer in the French Criminal Investigation Department; o. de renseignements intelligence officer

officieuse [ɔfisjøz] *voir* officieux

officieusement [ɔfisjøzmɑ̃] ADV unofficially, informally

officieux, -euse [ɔfisjø, -øz] ADJ unofficial, informal; à titre o. unofficially

officinal, -e, -aux, -ales [ɔfisinal, -o] ADJ *(plante)* medicinal; *(remède)* officinal; préparation officinale patent medicine

officine [ɔfisin] NF 1 *Pharm* dispensary, pharmacy 2 *Fig Péj* o. d'espionnage den of spies

off-line [ɔflajn] ADJ INV *Ordinat* off-line

offrande [ɔfrɑ̃d] NF 1 *Rel (don)* offering; *(cérémonie)* offertory; o. votive votive offering 2 *(contribution)* offering; apporter son *ou* une o. (à) to make a donation (to); verser une o. à une œuvre to give to a charity

offrant [ɔfrɑ̃] NM bidder; vendre qch au plus o. to sell sth to the highest bidder; on me propose deux emplois et j'ai décidé de dire oui au plus o. I've got two job offers and I've decided to accept the one offering the most money

offre [ɔfr] NF 1 *(proposition)* offer; *(dans un appel d'offres)* tender, bid; *(dans une vente aux enchères)* bid; *(action)* offering; recevoir/accepter une o. to receive/to accept an offer; ils lui ont fait une o. avantageuse they made him/her a worthwhile offer; faire une o. à 1000 euros to make an offer of 1,000 euros; *(aux enchères)* to bid 1,000 euros; cette o. est valable jusqu'au 31 mai this offer is valid until 31 May; o. de base basic offer; o. de bon de réduction coupon offer; o. d'emploi job offer, offer of employment; offres d'emploi *(dans le journal)* situations vacant; il y a très peu d'offres d'emploi there are very few job offers *or* openings; o. d'essai trial offer; o. export export bid; o. globale package deal; o. de lancement introductory offer; o. à prix réduit reduced-price offer; o. promotionnelle promotional offer; o. de remboursement money-back offer; offres de service offer to help; faire des offres de service à qn to offer to help sb; *Com* to solicit orders from sb; o. spéciale special offer, *Am* special 2 *Écon* supply; o. excédentaire excess supply; o. de monnaie/devises money/currency supply; l'o. et la demande supply and demand; lorsque l'o. excède la demande, les prix ont tendance à baisser when supply exceeds demand, prices have a tendency to fall 3 *Fin* o. de concours competitive (state) tender; o. publique d'achat takeover bid; faire *ou* lancer une o. publique d'achat (sur) to make a takeover bid (for); o. publique d'échange exchange offer, takeover bid for shares; o. publique de retrait public buy-out offer; o. publique de vente public offering, public share offer

offreur, -euse [ɔfrœr, -øz] NM,F *Écon* seller

OFFRIR [34] [ɔfrir]

VT
- to give 1, 2
- to offer 2–4
- to present 1, 4

VPR
- to offer oneself 1
- to offer one's services 2
- to give each other 3
- to treat oneself to 5

VT 1 *(faire cadeau de)* to give; o. qch en cadeau à qn to give sb sth as a present; on lui offrit une médaille they presented him/her *or* he/she was presented with a medal; je vous offre un café/un verre? can I buy you coffee/a drink?; ils (nous) ont offert le champagne they treated us to champagne; pour finir ce journal, nous vous offrons quelques images de la première neige dans Paris and now to end the news, we bring you some shots of the first snow of the year in Paris; elle s'est fait o. une voiture pour ses 25 ans she was given a car for her 25th birthday; il s'est fait o. un repas au restaurant he managed to get himself taken out for a meal

2 *(donner ▸ choix, explication, hospitalité)* to give, to offer; o. une récompense to offer a reward; je vous offre une nouvelle chance I'm giving you a second chance; o. son assistance *ou* son aide à qn to offer to help sb; o. à qn la possibilité de faire qch to offer *or* to give sb the chance of doing sth

3 *(proposer)* to offer; o. son bras à qn to offer *or* to lend sb one's arm; je lui ai montré mon autoradio, il m'en offre 100 euros I showed him my car radio and he's offering me 100 euros for it; on lui a offert une place de mécanicien he was offered a job as a mechanic; o. de faire qch to offer to do sth

4 *(présenter ▸ spectacle, vue)* to offer, to present; la conversation n'offrait qu'un intérêt limité the conversation was of only limited interest; cette solution offre l'avantage d'être équitable this solution has *or* presents the advantage of being fair; le sommet offre un panorama de toute beauté the summit offers *or* affords the most stupendous views; le vieil homme/le jardin dévasté offrait un piteux spectacle the old man/the ruined garden was a pathetic sight; l'histoire en offre plusieurs exemples history gives *or Sout* affords several examples of it; o. une résistance acharnée to put up stiff *or* fierce resistance

USAGE ABSOLU pourriez-vous me faire un paquet-cadeau, c'est pour o. could you gift-wrap it for me, please, it's a present; c'est pour o.? shall I gift-wrap it for you?; c'est moi qui offre it's on me, I'll pay; o. à déjeuner à qn to offer sb lunch

VPR **s'offrir** 1 *(sexuellement)* to offer *or* to give oneself; s'o. aux regards *(personne)* to expose oneself to the public gaze

2 *(proposer ses services)* to offer one's services; s'o. comme guide to offer to act as a guide, to offer oneself *or* one's services as a guide; il s'est offert pour un emploi de manutentionnaire he applied for a job as a packer; s'o. à payer les dégâts to offer to pay for the damage; l'article s'offre à orienter le lecteur dans le marché de la hi-fi the article aims to help the reader find his way in the world of hi-fi

3 *(emploi réciproque)* to give *or* to buy each other; à Noël, on s'offre des cadeaux at Christmas, people give each other presents

4 *(se présenter ▸ occasion)* un seul moyen s'offrait à moi there was only one course of action open to me; plein d'enthousiasme pour la journée qui s'offrait à lui full of enthusiasm for the day that lay ahead of him; un panorama exceptionnel s'offre au regard an amazing view meets your eyes

5 *(se faire cadeau de)* to treat oneself to; s'o. le luxe de manger du caviar to indulge in the luxury of eating caviar; et si on s'offrait à boire? shall we have a drink?; tu ne peux vraiment pas t'o. une soirée au cinéma? can you really not afford a night out at the cinema?; je ne peux pas m'o. une secrétaire I can't afford (the luxury of) a secretary

offset [ɔfsɛt] *Typ* ADJ INV offset
NM INV offset (process)
NF INV offset (printing) machine

off-shore, offshore [ɔfʃɔr] ADJ INV *Banque, Pétr & Sport* offshore; bateau o. speedboat, powerboat; course o. speedboat *or* powerboat race; plate-forme o. offshore oil rig
NM INV 1 *Pétr* offshore technology 2 *Sport (activité)* powerboat racing; *(bateau)* powerboat; faire du o. to go powerboat racing

offusquer [3] [ɔfyske] VT to offend, to upset, to hurt
VPR **s'offusquer** s'o. de to take offence at, to take umbrage at; s'o. d'un rien to be easily offended, to be quick to take offence

ogival, -e, -aux, -ales [ɔʒival, -o] ADJ *(structure)* ogive *(avant n)*, ogival; *(art, style)* gothic

ogive [ɔʒiv] NF 1 *Archit* ogive, diagonal rib 2 *Mil & Nucl* warhead; *(d'une roquette)* nose cone; o. nucléaire nuclear warhead 3 *Géom* ogive

OGM [ɔʒeɛm] NM *(abrév* organisme génétiquement modifié*)* GMO

ogre, -esse [ɔgr, ɔgrɛs] NM,F *(dans les contes) & Fam Fig* ogre, *f* ogress

oh [o] EXCLAM 1 *(pour indiquer ▸ la surprise, l'admiration, l'indignation)* oh!; oh là là! my goodness!; oh là là, qu'est-ce qu'il fait chaud! my goodness, it's hot!; oh là là, qu'est-ce qu'on va faire? oh dear, what are we going to do?; oh, quelle horreur! oh, how awful!; oh oh, est-ce que j'aurais deviné juste? oho, could I be right? 2 *(pour interpeller)* hey!; oh là, qu'est-ce que tu fais? hey, what are you doing?
NM INV ooh!, oh!; pousser des oh et des ah devant qch to ooh and aah at sth

ohé [ɔe] EXCLAM hey!; o.! vous, là-bas hey, you over there!

ohm [om] NM *Élec* ohm

ohmique [omik] ADJ *Élec* ohmic

ohmmètre [ommɛtr] NM *Élec* ohmmeter

oie [wa] NF 1 *Orn* goose
2 *(jeu)* jeu de l'o. ≃ snakes and ladders
3 *Mil* pas de l'o. goosestep; défiler *ou* marcher au pas de l'o. to goosestep
4 *Péj (personne)* silly goose; c'est une o. blanche she's (wide-eyed and) innocent

oignon [ɔɲɔ̃] NM 1 *Culin* onion; soupe à l'o. onion soup; o. blanc spring onion; petits oignons baby onions; *Fam* un week-end aux petits oignons a great *or* first-rate weekend; *Fam* soigner qn aux petits oignons to look after sb really well□; *Fam* être soigné aux petits oignons to get the VIP treatment; *Fam* c'est pas tes oignons! it's none of your business!; *Fam* mêle-toi *ou* occupe-toi de tes oignons mind your own business
2 *Hort (bulbe)* bulb; oignons à fleurs flowering bulbs
3 *Méd* bunion
4 *(montre)* fob watch, turnip watch
5 *Vulg (anus) Br* arsehole, *Am* asshole; l'avoir dans l'o. to have been shafted *or* screwed

oïl [ɔjl] *voir* langue

oilpé [walpe] **à oilpé** ADV *Fam (verlan de* à poil*)* stark naked, in the buff, *Br* starkers

oindre [82] [wɛ̃dr] VT 1 *(enduire)* to rub with oil 2 *Rel* to anoint

oint, -e [wɛ̃, wɛ̃t] ADJ anointed
NM l'o. du Seigneur the Lord's anointed

oiseau, -x [wazo] NM **1** *Orn* bird; **o. marin** *ou* **de mer** seabird; **o. migrateur** migratory bird; **o. nocturne** *ou* **de nuit** night bird; **o. de paradis** bird of paradise; **o. de proie** bird of prey; **o. de volière** aviary bird, cage bird; **o. des îles** tropical bird; *Fig* exotic creature; *Fig* **o. de mauvais augure** *ou* **de malheur** bird of ill omen; **o. de passage** bird of passage; *Fig* **ce n'était qu'un o. de passage** he was just a ship that passed in the night; *Fig* **il est parfait pour cet emploi, tu as vraiment déniché l'o. rare** he's perfect for this job, you've found a rare bird there; **elle cherche l'o. rare** *(comme époux)* she's looking for the ideal man; *(comme employé)* she's looking for the ideal employee; **être comme l'o. sur la branche** to be in a very precarious situation; **le petit o. va sortir!** *(photo)* watch the birdie!; *Prov* **petit à petit, l'o. fait son nid** slow and steady wins the race **2** *Fam (individu douteux)* customer; **c'est un drôle d'o.** *ou* **un vilain o.** he's an odd character, he's a funny old bird; **quand la police arriva, l'o. s'était envolé** by the time the police arrived the bird had flown

oiseau-lyre [wazolir] *(pl* **oiseaux-lyres)** NM *Orn* lyrebird

oiseau-mouche [wazomuʃ] *(pl* **oiseaux-mouches)** NM *Orn* hummingbird

oiseleur [wazlœr] NM bird catcher

oiselier, -ère [wazəlje, -ɛr] NM,F bird seller

oiselle [wazel] NF *Littéraire (oiseau femelle)* hen bird; *Fam Fig* naive young girl

oisellerie [wazelri] NF **1** *(boutique)* bird shop **2** *(commerce)* bird selling

oiseux, -euse [wazø, -øz] ADJ **1** *(futile)* futile; **des occupations oiseuses** futile occupations; **des rêveries oiseuses** daydreaming *(UNCOUNT)* **2** *(qui ne mène à rien)* irrelevant, pointless; *(conversation)* idle; *(explication)* unsatisfactory

oisif, -ive [wazif, -iv] ADJ *(personne, vie)* idle
NM,F man of leisure, *f* woman of leisure; **les oisifs** the idle rich

oisillon [wazijɔ̃] NM fledgling

oisive [waziv] *voir* **oisif**

oisivement [wazivmɑ̃] ADV idly; **vivre o.** to live in idleness

oisiveté [wazivte] NF idleness; **vivre dans l'o.** to live in idleness; *Prov* **l'o. est la mère de tous les vices** the devil finds work for idle hands

oison [wazɔ̃] NM **1** *Orn* gosling **2** *Vieilli (personne)* gullible *or* credulous person

OIT [oite] NF *(abrév* **Organisation internationale du travail)** ILO

OK [ɔke] EXCLAM *Fam* OK, okay; **OK! pour moi c'est bon!** OK, that's fine by me!

okapi [ɔkapi] NM *Zool* okapi

olé [ɔle] EXCLAM olé!

oléagineux, -euse [ɔleaʒinø, -øz] ADJ oil-producing, *Spéc* oleaginous; **graines oléagineuses** oilseeds
NM oil-producing *or Spéc* oleaginous plant

oléiculteur, -trice [ɔleikyltœr, -tris] NM,F **1** *(cultivateur)* olive grower **2** *(fabricant d'huile* ► *d'olive)* olive oil manufacturer; *(*► *d'autres oléagineux)* vegetable oil manufacturer

oléiculture [ɔleikyltyr] NF *(culture* ► *des olives)* olive growing; *(*► *des oléagineux)* oil-crop growing

oléifère [ɔleifɛr] ADJ oil-producing, *Spéc* oleiferous

oléine [ɔlein] NF *Chim* olein

oléique [ɔleik] ADJ *Chim* oleic

oléoduc [ɔleɔdyk] NM (oil) pipeline

olé olé [ɔleɔle] ADJ INV *Fam* **être un peu o.** *(de mœurs légères)* to be a bit loose; *(peu respectueux)* to be a bit too laid back; **elle est très o. depuis qu'elle a divorcé** she's been leading a pretty wild life since her divorce; **il y a quelques scènes o.** some of the scenes are a bit close to the bone *or* risqué *or Br* near the knuckle

oléopneumatique [ɔleopnømatik] ADJ air/hydraulic

olfactif, -ive [ɔlfaktif, -iv] ADJ *Physiol* olfactory

olibrius [ɔlibrijys] NM *Fam Péj* oddball

olifant [ɔlifɑ̃] NM *Hist* oliphant

oligarchie [ɔligarʃi] NF oligarchy

oligarchique [ɔligarʃik] ADJ oligarchic, oligarchical

oligarque [ɔligark] NM oligarch

oligoélément [ɔligɔelemɑ̃] NM trace element

oligopole [ɔligɔpɔl] NM *Écon* oligopoly

oligopolistique [ɔligɔpɔlistik] ADJ *Écon* oligopolistic

oligopsone [ɔligɔpsɔn] NM *Écon* oligopsony

oliphant [ɔlifɑ̃] NM *Hist* oliphant

olivaie [ɔlivɛ] NF olive grove

olivâtre [ɔlivatr] ADJ olive-greenish; *(teint)* sallow

olive [ɔliv] NF **1** *Bot* olive; **o. noire/verte** black/green olive **2** *Élec* switch
ADJ INV *(couleur)* **(vert) o.** olive, olive-green

oliveraie [ɔlivrɛ] NF olive grove

olivette [ɔlivɛt] NF **1** *(tomate)* plum tomato **2** *(raisin)* (olive-shaped) grape **3** *(olivaie)* olive plantation *or* grove

olivier [ɔlivje] NM **1** *Bot* olive tree **2** *(bois)* olive (wood)

olographe [ɔlɔgraf] ADJ *Jur* holograph

OLP [oelpe] NF *(abrév* **Organisation de libération de la Palestine)** PLO

Olympe [ɔlɛ̃p] NM *Géog & Myth* **l'O.** Olympus; **les dieux de l'O.** the Olympic deities, the Olympians; **le mont O.** Mount Olympus

olympiade [ɔlɛ̃pjad] NF **1** *(événement)* Olympic Games; **à la dernière o.** during the last Olympics **2** *(quatre ans)* olympiad
• **olympiades** NFPL **les olympiades** the Olympic Games

olympien, -enne [ɔlɛ̃pjɛ̃, -ɛn] ADJ *Myth & Hum* Olympian; *Fig* **un calme o.** an Olympian calm

olympique [ɔlɛ̃pik] ADJ Olympic; **stade/piscine o.** Olympic stadium/pool; **les jeux Olympiques** the Olympic Games, the Olympics

Oman [ɔman] NM *Géog* Oman; **le golfe d'O.** the Gulf of Oman

ombelle [ɔ̃bɛl] NF *Bot* umbel; **en o.** umbellate

ombellifère [ɔ̃belifɛr] *Bot* ADJ umbelliferous
NF umbellifer, member of the Umbelliferae

ombilic [ɔ̃bilik] NM **1** *Anat* navel, *Spéc* umbilicus **2** *Bot (renflement)* hilum; *(plante)* navelwort

ombilical, -e, -aux, -ales [ɔ̃bilikal, -o] ADJ **1** *Anat* umbilical **2** *Astron* **mât o.** umbilical cord

omble [ɔ̃bl] NM *Ich* **o. (chevalier)** char

ombrage [ɔ̃braʒ] NM **1** *(ombre)* shade; **ces arbres donnent** *ou* **font un o. agréable à la terrasse** these trees pleasantly shade the terrace
2 *(feuillage)* canopy, foliage
3 *Littéraire* **prendre o. de qch** to take offence *or* umbrage at sth; **porter** *ou* **faire o. à qn** to cause offence to sb, to offend sb
4 *Ordinat* shading

ombragé, -e [ɔ̃braʒe] ADJ shady

ombrager [17] [ɔ̃braʒe] VT **1** to shade **2** *Fig Littéraire* to overshadow

ombrageux, -euse [ɔ̃braʒø, -øz] ADJ **1** *(susceptible)* touchy, easily offended **2** *(cheval)* skittish, nervous, jumpy

ombre¹ [ɔ̃br] NM *Ich* grayling

ombre² [ɔ̃br] NF **1** *(pénombre)* shade; **projeter une o.** to cast a shadow; **dans l'o. des sous-bois** in the shadowy undergrowth; **le gratte-ciel fait de l'o. à tout le quartier** the skyscraper casts a shadow over the whole area *or* leaves the whole area in shadow; **faire de l'o. à qn** to be in sb's light; *Fig* to be in sb's way; **sortir de l'o.** to emerge from the dark *or* darkness *or* shadows; *Fig (artiste)* to emerge from obscurity, to come into the public eye; *Fig* **jeter une o. sur la fête** to cast a shadow *or* a gloom over the festivities; *Fig* **une zone d'o.** a grey area
2 *(forme* ► *d'une personne, d'un arbre, d'un mur)* shadow; **j'aperçois une o. dans le jardin** I can see a (vague) shadow *or* shadowy shape in the garden; *Hum* **avoir peur de son o.** to be afraid of one's own shadow; **il n'est plus que l'o. de lui-même** he's a shadow of his former self; **avec l'adolescence, une o. est apparue sur sa lèvre supérieure** in adolescence, a thin shadow appeared on his upper lip; **o. propre** shade
3 *(trace* ► *de jalousie, de surprise)* hint; *(*► *d'un sourire)* hint, shadow; **pas l'o. d'un remords/d'une preuve** not a trace of remorse/shred of evidence; **pas l'o. d'un reproche** not the slightest hint of blame; **sans l'o. d'un doute** without a shadow of a doubt; **cela ne fait pas** *ou* **il n'y a pas l'o. d'un doute** there's not a shadow of a doubt; **elle n'a pas l'o. d'un scrupule!** she's totally unscrupulous!
4 *Beaux-Arts* shade, shadow; *Fig* **il y a une o. au tableau** there's a fly in the ointment
5 *(obscurité)* darkness; *Fig (anonymat)* obscurity; **ils disparurent dans l'o. de la nuit** they were swallowed up by the darkness; **leurs agissements délictueux se faisaient dans l'o. de la nuit** their criminal schemes were carried out under cover of darkness
6 *Astron* umbra
• **ombres** NFPL **1** *Théât* **ombres chinoises** shadow play; **théâtre d'ombres** shadow theatre; **leurs profils se projetaient sur le mur en ombres chinoises** their profiles were silhouetted on the wall **2** *Antiq* shadows, departed souls; **le royaume des ombres** the netherworld
• **à l'ombre** ADV **1** *(à l'abri du soleil)* in the shade; **il fait 30°C à l'o.** it's 30°C in the shade; *Fam* **marche à l'o.!** *(conseil)* keep a low profile!; *(menace)* stay out of my sight! **2** *Fam (en prison)* inside; **mettre qn/être à l'o.** to put sb/to be behind bars *or* inside
• **à l'ombre de** PRÉP in the shade of; *Fig Littéraire* under the protection of; **à l'o. des lois** protected by the law; *Fig* **elle a grandi à l'o. de la Tour Eiffel** she grew up in the shadow of *or* within a stone's throw of the Eiffel Tower
• **dans l'ombre** ADV **1** *(dans la pénombre)* in the shade; **le jardin/balcon est dans l'o.** the garden/balcony is in the shade **2** *Fig (dans le secret)* **elle a préféré vivre dans l'o.** she chose a life of obscurity; **rester dans l'o.** *(raison)* to remain obscure *or* unclear; *(personne)* to remain unknown; **laisser qch dans l'o.** to keep sth dark; **l'enquête n'a rien laissé dans l'o.** the enquiry left no stone unturned; **travailler dans l'o.** to work behind the scenes; **ceux qui œuvrent dans l'o. pour la paix** those who work behind the scenes to bring about peace; **vivre dans l'o. de qn** to live in sb's shadow
• **ombre à paupières** NF eyeshadow

> Attention: ne pas confondre **shadow** et **shade** lorsque l'on traduit **ombre**. **Shadow** décrit une forme projetée par un objet se trouvant dans une source de lumière, alors que **shade** s'applique simplement à un lieu se trouvant à l'abri du soleil.

ombre³ [ɔ̃br] NF **terre d'o.** umber

ombré [ɔ̃bre] NM *Ordinat* shading

ombrelle [ɔ̃brɛl] NF **1** *(parasol)* parasol **2** *(d'une méduse)* umbrella

> Il faut noter que le nom anglais **umbrella** est un faux ami. Il signifie **parapluie**.

ombrer [3] [ɔ̃bre] VT **1** *Beaux-Arts* to shade; **o. un sujet pour le faire ressortir/pour l'intégrer dans l'arrière-plan** to shade out/in a subject **2** *Littéraire (faire de l'ombre à* ► *sujet: arbre, store)* to shade; **un grand chapeau ombrait son visage** a large hat shaded his/her face **3** *(assombrir* ► *sujet: couleur)* to darken, to shade; **un maquillage violet ombrait ses paupières** he/she was wearing purple eyeshadow

ombreux, -euse [ɔ̃brø, -øz] ADJ *Littéraire* shady

Ombrie [ɔ̃bri] NF **l'O.** Umbria

ombudsman [ɔmbydsman] NM ombudsman

OMC [oemse] NF *(abrév* **Organisation mondiale du commerce)** WTO

oméga [ɔmega] NM INV omega

omelette [ɔmlɛt] NF omelette; **o. aux champignons/au fromage/au jambon** mushroom/cheese/ham omelette; **o. aux fines herbes** omelette with herbs, omelette (aux) fines herbes; **une o. baveuse** a runny omelette; **o. norvégienne** *ou* **surprise** baked Alaska; **o. soufflée** soufflé omelette; *Prov* **on ne fait pas d'o. sans casser des œufs** you can't make an omelette without breaking eggs

omettre [84] [ɔmɛtr] VT to omit, to leave out;

sans o. un seul détail without leaving out a single detail; **n'omets personne sur ta liste** don't miss anyone off your list; **o. de faire qch** to fail *or* to neglect *or* to omit to do sth; **ils ont omis de nous informer** they failed *or* neglected to inform us

OMI [ɔemi] **NF** *(abrév* **Organisation maritime internationale)** IMO

omis, -e [ɔmi, -iz] **PP** *voir* **omettre**

omission [ɔmisjɔ̃] **NF** *(oubli)* omission; *(oubli)* oversight; **l'o. d'un mot** leaving out *or* omitting a word; **j'ai relevé plusieurs omissions dans la liste** I noticed that several things are missing *or* have been omitted from the list; **péché/mensonge par o.** sin/lie of omission; **pécher/mentir par o.** to sin/lie by omission

omnibus [ɔmnibys] **NM 1** *Rail Br* slow *or* stopping train, *Am* local (train) **2** *Arch (bus)* omnibus

ADJ INV le train est o. entre Melun et Sens the train calls at all stations between Melun and Sens

omnidirectionnel, -elle [ɔmnidirɛksjɔnɛl] **ADJ** omnidirectional

omnipotence [ɔmnipɔtɑ̃s] **NF** omnipotence; **l'o. de l'État** the omnipotence of the state

omnipotent, -e [ɔmnipɔtɑ̃, -ɑ̃t] **ADJ** omnipotent

omnipraticien, -enne [ɔmnipratisjɛ̃, -ɛn] **ADJ médecin o.** general practitioner

NM,F general practitioner

omniprésence [ɔmniprezɑ̃s] **NF** omnipresence

omniprésent, -e [ɔmniprezɑ̃, -ɑ̃t] **ADJ** *(souci, souvenir)* omnipresent; *(publicité, pollution)* ubiquitous; **il est o. dans l'usine** he's everywhere (at once) in the factory

omniscience [ɔmnisjɑ̃s] **NF** omniscience

omniscient, -e [ɔmnisjɑ̃, -ɑ̃t] **ADJ** omniscient

omnisports [ɔmnispɔr] **ADJ INV rencontre o.** allround sports event; **salle o.** sports centre; **terrain o.** sports field

omnium [ɔmnjɔm] **NM** *Vieilli* **1** *Écon* combine; *Bourse* **o. de valeurs** = investment trust **2** *Sport* open; *Courses de chevaux* open handicap

omnivore [ɔmnivɔr] **ADJ** omnivorous

NM omnivore

omoplate [ɔmɔplat] **NF** *Anat* shoulder blade, *Spéc* scapula; **il lui avait pointé un fusil entre les omoplates** he'd shoved a gun in his/her back

OMS [oɛmɛs] **NF** *(abrév* **Organisation mondiale de la santé)** WHO

on [ɔ̃]

> **on** may be preceded by the article **l'** in formal contexts.

PRON INDÉFINI 1 *(indéterminé)* you, people, *Sout* one; **on lui a retiré son passeport** they took his/her passport away (from him/her), his/her passport was confiscated; **on construit une nouvelle école** a new school is being built; **il y a dix ans, on ne connaissait pas cette maladie** this illness was unknown ten years ago; **on vit de plus en plus vieux en Europe** people in Europe are living longer and longer; **partout où l'on trouve de ces fossiles** wherever these fossils are found

2 *(avec une valeur généralisante)* you, *Sout* one; **souvent, on n'a pas le choix** often you don't have any choice, often there's no choice; **on n'a pas le droit de fumer ici** you can't smoke in here; **on n'arrive pas à dormir avec cette chaleur** it's impossible to sleep in this heat; **on ne sait jamais (ce qui peut arriver)** you never know *or Sout* one never knows (what could happen); **on n'en sait rien** nobody knows anything about it; **on dirait qu'il va pleuvoir** it looks like rain; **on ne croirait pas qu'il est malade** you wouldn't think he was ill; **on parlait très peu au déjeuner** we didn't talk much over lunch; **on était le sept mars** it was the seventh of March

3 *(les gens)* people, they; **on jasait** people were talking, there was a lot of talk; **on s'était rué sur les derniers billets** there'd been a rush for the last tickets; **on dit que la vie là-bas n'est pas chère** they say that the cost of living over there is cheap; **on dit qu'elle est folle** it's said *or* they say *or* people say that she's mad, she's said to be mad; **on rapporte que...** it is said that...

4 *(désignant un nombre indéterminé de personnes)* they; **en Espagne, on dîne plus tard** in Spain they eat later; **dans ce bureau, on se moque de vos problèmes** they don't care about your problems in this department; **on m'a dit que vous partiez bientôt** I've been told you're leaving soon; **qu'est-ce qu'on en dit chez toi?** what do your folks have to say about it?, what do they have to say about it at your place?

5 *(quelqu'un)* **on frappe à la porte** someone's *or* somebody's (knocking) at the door, there's a knock at the door; **on sonne** there's the (door) bell, there's someone *or* somebody at the door; **on vous a appelé ce matin** somebody called you *or* there was a (phone) call for you this morning; **on m'a volé mon sac** my bag has been stolen, someone's stolen my bag; **est-ce qu'on t'a vu?** did anyone see you?; **est-ce qu'on vous sert, Monsieur?** are you being served, sir?; **est-ce qu'on pourrait me servir, s'il vous plaît?** could somebody serve me, please?

6 *Fam (nous)* we; **on n'a pas grand-chose à se dire** we don't have much to say to one another; **nous, on en a marre, on s'en va** we've had enough of this, we're off; **allez viens, on va bien s'amuser** go on, come with us, it'll be great fun; **on était très déçus** we were very disappointed; **on est dix en tout** there are ten of us in all; **on est allés au cinéma avec les parents** we went to the *Br* cinema *or Am* movies with our parents

7 *(se substituant à d'autres pronoms personnels)* **dans ce premier chapitre, on a voulu montrer...** in this first chapter, the aim has been to show...; *Fam* **ça va, on a compris!** all right, I've got the message!; *Fam* **il faut qu'on vous le répète?** do I have to repeat myself?; *Fam* **on est bien habillé, aujourd'hui!** we are dressed up today, aren't we?; *Fam* **alors, on ne répond pas au téléphone?** aren't you going to answer the phone?; *Fam* **alors les gars, on cherche la bagarre?** are you guys looking for a fight?; **alors, on s'en va comme ça?** are you really leaving just like that?; *Fam* **on a tout ce qu'il faut et on passe son temps à se plaindre!** he/she has got everything and he/she still complains all the time!

8 *(dans des annonces)* **on cherche un vendeur** salesman wanted *or* required; **ici on parle allemand** *(à l'entrée d'un magasin, d'un restaurant, d'un hôtel)* German spoken (here); **on est prié de laisser sa clé à la réception** keys must be left at reception

onagre¹ [ɔnagr] **NF** *Bot* evening primrose, oenothera

onagre² [ɔnagr] **NM** *Mil & Zool* onager

onanisme [ɔnanism] **NM** onanism

once¹ [ɔ̃s] **NF** *(mesure)* ounce; **il n'a pas une o. de bon sens** he doesn't have an ounce of common sense

once² [ɔ̃s] **NF** *Zool* ounce, snow leopard

oncle [ɔ̃kl] **NM** uncle; **o. d'Amérique** rich uncle; **l'O. Sam** Uncle Sam

oncogène [ɔ̃kɔʒɛn] **ADJ** *Méd* oncogenic

onction [ɔ̃ksjɔ̃] **NF 1** *Méd & Rel* unction **2** *Littéraire (douceur* ▸ *attendrissante)* sweetness, gentleness; *Péj* (▸ *hypocrite)* unctuousness, unctuosity

onctueuse [ɔ̃ktɥøz] *voir* **onctueux**

onctueusement [ɔ̃ktɥøzmɑ̃] **ADV** smoothly, *Sout* unctuously

onctueux, -euse [ɔ̃ktɥø, -øz] **ADJ 1** *(huileux)* smooth, *Sout* unctuous **2** *Culin* creamy; **un fromage o.** a creamy cheese **3** *Littéraire (personne)* smooth, unctuous

onctuosité [ɔ̃ktɥozite] **NF** *(d'un dessert)* creaminess; *(d'une crème)* smoothness

onde [ɔ̃d] **NF 1** *Phys* wave; **o. cérébrale** brainwave; **o. de choc** shock wave; **ondes courtes** short wave; **sur ondes courtes** on short wave; **ondes entretenues** continuous waves; **ondes hertziennes** Hertzian waves; **ondes longues, grandes ondes** long wave; **sur grandes ondes** on long wave; **o. lumineuse** light wave; **ondes moyennes** medium wave; **sur ondes moyennes** on medium wave; **o. porteuse** carrier wave; **o. radio(électrique)** radio wave; **ondes très courtes** very high frequency; **ondes ultra-courtes** ultra-high frequency; *Fam Fig* **nous ne sommes pas sur la même longueur d'o.** we're not on the same wavelength

2 *Fig (vague)* wave; **une o. de bonheur l'envahit** a wave of happiness washed over him/her

3 *Littéraire* **l'o.** *(l'eau)* the waters, the deep; **l'o. limpide du ruisseau** the clear waters of the stream

4 *Métal* corrugation

• **ondes NFPL** *Rad* **mettre en ondes** to produce; **sur les ondes** on the air; **passer sur les ondes** *(sujet: émission)* to be broadcast; *(sujet: personne)* to be on air *or* radio

ondé, -e¹ [ɔ̃de] **ADJ** *Littéraire (cheveux)* wavy; *(soie)* watered

ondée² [ɔ̃de] **NF** shower *(of rain)*; **temps à ondées** showery weather; *Littéraire* **une brusque o. de tristesse** a sudden pang of sadness

ondemètre [ɔ̃dmɛtr] **NM** wavemeter

ondin, -e [ɔ̃dɛ̃, -in] **NM,F** *Myth* water sprite, undine

on-dit [ɔ̃di] **NM INV je ne me soucie guère des o.** I don't care about what people say; **ce ne sont que des o.** it's only hearsay

ondoie *etc voir* **ondoyer**

ondoiement [ɔ̃dwamɑ̃] **NM 1** *Littéraire (du blé, des cheveux)* undulation, swaying motion; *(d'un ruisseau)* undulation **2** *Rel* summary baptism

ondoyant, -e [ɔ̃dwajɑ̃, -ɑ̃t] **ADJ** *Littéraire* **1** *(blé)* undulating, rippling; *(flamme)* dancing, wavering; *(lumière, ruisseau)* rippling; *(cheveux)* wavy; *(foule, mouvement)* swaying **2** *(personne)* changeable

ondoyer [13] [ɔ̃dwaje] **VI** *(champ de blé)* to undulate, to ripple; *(flamme)* to dance, to waver; *(lumière, ruisseau)* to ripple; *(surface de l'eau)* to undulate; *(drapeau)* to wave

VT *Rel* to baptize summarily

ondulant, -e [ɔ̃dylɑ̃, -ɑ̃t] **ADJ 1** *(terrain)* undulating; *(route, rivière)* twisting (and turning), winding; *(chevelure)* flowing; *(façon de marcher)* swaying; **avoir une démarche ondulante** to swing one's hips **2** *Méd (pouls)* irregular

ondulation [ɔ̃dylasjɔ̃] **NF 1** *(de l'eau, du terrain)* undulation; **les ondulations de la plaine** the rolling *or* undulating plain

2 *(du corps)* undulation, swaying *(UNCOUNT)*; **les ondulations de la danseuse** the undulations *or* the swaying of the dancer

3 *(des cheveux)* wave; **les ondulations de sa chevelure** his/her wavy hair

4 *Littéraire (d'une ligne, d'une mélodie)* undulation

5 *TV* **o. de l'image** picture weave

ondulatoire [ɔ̃dylatwar] **ADJ 1** *(forme)* undulatory **2** *Phys (mouvement)* undulatory, wave *(avant n)*

ondulé, -e [ɔ̃dyle] **ADJ** *(sol)* undulating; *(cheveux)* wavy; *(tôle, carton)* corrugated; **route ondulée** switchback road; **trait o.** wavy line

onduler [3] [ɔ̃dyle] **VI 1** *(eau, vagues, champs)* to ripple, to undulate **2** *(cheveux)* to be wavy **3** *(personne)* to sway; **la danseuse ondulait des hanches** the dancer swayed her hips

VT *(friser)* **se faire o. les cheveux** to have one's hair waved *or* permed

onduleur [ɔ̃dylœr] **NM** *Élec* inverter; *Ordinat* uninterruptible power supply, UPS

onduleux, -euse [ɔ̃dylø, -øz] **ADJ** *Littéraire* **1** *(houleux* ▸ *flots)* swelling **2** *(souple)* undulating; **elle avait une démarche onduleuse** her body swayed as she walked **3** *(paysage)* undulating, rolling; *(sentier, rivière)* twisting, winding

onéreux, -euse [ɔnerø, -øz] **ADJ** costly, expensive; **à titre o.** subject to payment

> Il faut noter que l'adjectif anglais **onerous** est un faux ami. Il signifie **lourd, pénible**.

ONF [oɛnɛf] **NM** *(abrév* **Office national des forêts)** the French Forestry commission, *Br* ≃ the Forestry Commission, *Am* ≃ the Forestry Service

ONG [oɛnʒe] **NF** *(abrév* **organisation non gouvernementale)** NGO

ongle [ɔ̃gl] **NM 1** *Anat (des doigts de la main)* nail, fingernail; *(des orteils)* toenail; **se faire les ongles** *(les couper)* to cut one's nails; *(les vernir)* to do *or* to paint one's nails; *Fig* **connaître** *ou* **savoir qch sur le bout des ongles** to know sth perfectly; **il est français jusqu'au bout des ongles** he's French to his fingertips, he's every inch a Frenchman; *Fig*

avoir les ongles crochus to be mean; *Fam* **avoir les ongles en deuil** to have dirty nails **2** *Zool* claw; *(de rapace)* talon

• **à ongles** ADJ *(ciseaux, lime, vernis)* nail *(avant n)*

onglée [ɔ̃gle] NF **j'avais l'o.** the tips of my fingers were numb with cold

onglet [ɔ̃glɛ] NM **1** *(entaille)* thumb index; *(d'un canif)* thumbnail groove; **o. à fenêtre** *(d'une fiche)* window tab

2 *Constr* mitred angle; **tailler à** *ou* **en o.** to mitre

3 *Typ (béquet)* tab; *(d'un livre)* guard, stub; **dictionnaire à onglets** thumb-indexed dictionary

4 *Culin* flank; **o. à l'échalote** = long, narrow steak served fried with chopped shallots

onglier [ɔ̃glije] NM **1** *(nécessaire)* manicure set **2** *(ciseaux)* (nail) scissors

onguent [ɔ̃gɑ̃] NM ointment, salve

ongulé, -e [ɔ̃gyle] *Zool* ADJ hoofed, *Spéc* ungulate

NM ungulate

onirique [ɔnirik] ADJ **1** *Psy* oneiric **2** *Fig* **une vision o.** a dreamlike vision

onirisme [ɔnirism] NM **1** *Psy* hallucinations **2** *Fig* **des dessins à l'o. troublant** drawings with a disturbing dreamlike quality

onirologie [ɔnirɔlɔʒi] NF interpretation of dreams

ONN [oenen] NM *(abrév* **Office national de la navigation)** French national shipping and inland waterways office

onomasiologie [ɔnɔmazjɔlɔʒi] NF *Ling* onomasiology

onomastique [ɔnɔmastik] *Ling* ADJ onomastic

NF onomastics *(singulier)*

onomatopée [ɔnɔmatɔpe] NF onomatopoeia

onomatopéique [ɔnɔmatɔpeik] ADJ onomatopoeic

on-shore, onshore [ɔnʃɔr] ADJ *Fin (fonds, investissements, société)* onshore

ont [ɔ̃] *voir* **avoir**[2]

Ontario [ɔ̃tarjo] NM **l'O.** Ontario; **le lac O.** Lake Ontario

ontogenèse [ɔ̃tɔʒənɛz] NF *Biol* ontogenesis, ontogeny

ontogénétique [ɔ̃tɔʒenetik] ADJ *Biol* ontogenetic, ontogenic

ontogénie [ɔ̃tɔʒeni] NF *Biol* ontogenesis, ontogeny

ontologie [ɔ̃tɔlɔʒi] NF *Phil* ontology

ontologique [ɔ̃tɔlɔʒik] ADJ *Phil* ontological

ONU, O.N.U. [ony, oenuy] NF *(abrév* **Organisation des Nations unies)** UN, UNO

ONUDI, Onudi [onydi] NF *(abrév* **Organisation des Nations unies pour le développement industriel)** UNIDO

onusien, -enne [onyzjɛ̃, -ɛn] ADJ **projet/expert o.** UN project/expert

onyx [ɔniks] NM onyx

onze [ɔ̃z] ADJ **1** *(gén)* eleven **2** *(dans des séries)* eleventh; **page/numéro o.** page/number eleven

PRON eleven

NM INV **1** *(gén)* eleven

2 *(numéro d'ordre)* number eleven

3 *(chiffre écrit)* eleven

4 *Ftbl* **le o. tricolore** the French eleven *or* team; *voir aussi* **cinq**

onzième [ɔ̃zjɛm] ADJ eleventh; **les ouvriers de la o. heure** last-minute helpers

NMF **1** *(personne)* eleventh **2** *(objet)* eleventh (one)

NM **1** *(partie)* eleventh **2** *(étage)* *Br* eleventh floor, *Am* twelfth floor **3** *(arrondissement de Paris)* eleventh (arrondissement)

NF *Mus* eleventh; *voir aussi* **cinquième**

onzièmement [ɔ̃zjɛmmɑ̃] ADV in eleventh place

oolite, oolithe [ɔɔlit] NM *Géol* oolite

oolithique [ɔɔlitik] ADJ *Géol* oolitic

OPA [opea] NF *Fin (abrév* **offre publique d'achat)** takeover bid; **lancer une O. (sur)** to make a takeover bid (for); **être l'objet d'une O.** to be the subject of a takeover bid; **O. amicale** friendly takeover bid; **O. hostile** *ou* **inamicale** *ou* **sauvage** hostile takeover bid

opacification [ɔpasifikasjɔ̃] NF opacifying

opacifier [9] [ɔpasifje] VT to opacify, to make opaque

VPR **s'opacifier** to opacify

opacité [ɔpasite] NF **1** *Littéraire (ombre)* shadow, darkness; *(d'une forêt)* darkness, denseness

2 *Littéraire (inintelligibilité)* opaqueness, opacity

3 *Phys (d'un corps)* opacity, opaqueness; *(d'un liquide)* cloudiness

4 *Méd* **o. radiologique** X-ray shadow

opale [ɔpal] NF opal

ADJ **verre o.** opal glass; *Élec* **ampoule o.** pearl bulb

opalescence [ɔpalesɑ̃s] NF *Littéraire* opalescence

opalescent, -e [ɔpalesɑ̃, -ɑ̃t] ADJ *Littéraire* opalescent

opalin, -e [ɔpalɛ̃, -in] ADJ opaline

• **opaline** NF opaline

opaque [ɔpak] ADJ **1** *Phys* opaque; **collant o.** opaque *Br* tights *or Am* pantihose; **o. aux rayons X** impervious to X-rays **2** *(sombre)* dark, impenetrable; *(forêt)* dark, dense; **dans la nuit o.** in the pitch-dark *or* jet-black night **3** *Fig (incompréhensible)* opaque, impenetrable

op art [ɔpart] NM op art

OPCVM [opeseveem] NM *Bourse (abrév* **organisme de placement collectif en valeurs mobilières)** collective investment fund, *Br* ≃ unit trust, *Am* ≃ mutual fund; **O. actions** ≃ equity-based *Br* unit trust *or Am* mutual fund

OPE [opeə] NF *Fin (abrév* **offre publique d'échange)** exchange offer, takeover bid for shares

opéable [opeabl] ADJ likely to be the target of a takeover bid, vulnerable to takeover bids

open [ɔpɛn] ADJ INV *(billet, tournoi)* open

NM *Sport* open; **o. de tennis** open tennis championship *or* tournament

OPEP, Opep [ɔpɛp] NF *(abrév* **Organisation des pays exportateurs de pétrole)** OPEC

opéra [ɔpera] NM **1** *Mus (œuvre)* opera; *(genre)* opera; **aller à l'o.** to go to the opera; **écouter de l'o.** to listen to opera; **o. bouffe** comic opera, opera buffa; **o. rock** rock opera **2** *(bâtiment)* opera (house); **l'O. (de Paris)** the Paris Opera House

opérable [ɔperabl] ADJ operable; **la malade n'est plus o.** the patient is no longer operable *or* is beyond surgery

opéra-comique [ɔperakɔmik] *(pl* **opéras-comiques)** NM light opera, opéra comique

opérande [ɔperɑ̃d] NM *Math & Ordinat* operand

opérant, -e [ɔperɑ̃, -ɑ̃t] ADJ **1** *(effectif)* effective; **notre action a été opérante** our action proved to be effective

opérateur, -trice [ɔperatœr, -tris] NM,F **1** *Cin & TV* **o. banc-titre** rostrum cameraman; **o. magnétoscope** videotape operator; **o. de mixage** vision mixer; **o. de prises de vues** cameraman; **o. du son** sound technician; **o. steadicam** steadicam operator; **o. vidéo** video operator; **o. de la vision** video control operator

2 *Tél (employé)* (telephone) operator; *(exploitant)* telephone company; **pour l'étranger, il faut passer par l'o.** to phone abroad, you have to go through the operator; *Tél* **o. historique** ILEC, incumbent local exchange carrier; **o. radio** radio operator

3 *Typ* operative, operator; **o. de PAO** DTP operator

4 *Tech* **o. (sur machine)** (machine) operator; *Com* **o. de transport multimodal** multi-modal operator

5 *Ordinat* operator; **o. de saisie** keyboarder; **o. de comparaison** comparator; **o. booléen** Boolean operator; **o. logique** logical operator; **o. relationnel** relational operator; **o. système** systems operator, SYSOP

6 *Bourse* operator, dealer; **o. à la baisse** operator for a fall, bear; **o. boursier** stock-exchange dealer; **o. en couverture** hedger; **o. sur écran** screen trader; **o. à la hausse** operator for a rise, bull; **o. d'un jour** day trader

NM *Ling & Math* operator

opération [ɔperasjɔ̃] NF **1** *Méd* operation; **pratiquer une o.** to carry out surgery *or* an operation; **subir une grave/petite o.** to undergo major/minor surgery, to have a major/minor operation; **une o. (chirurgicale)** surgery, a surgical operation; **o. à chaud/froid** emergency/interval surgery; **o. à cœur ouvert** open-heart surgery

2 *Math* operation; **poser une o.** to do a calculation; *Scol* **connais-tu les quatre opérations?** do you know how to add, subtract, multiply and divide?

3 *Banque & Bourse* operation, transaction; **en la vendant à moitié prix, j'ai encore fait une belle o.!** even selling it at half price, I still got a really good deal!; **en acceptant de la recevoir pour trois semaines, tu n'as pas fait une bonne o.!** it wasn't very smart of you to agree to put her up for three weeks!; **o. à la baisse/hausse** bull/bear transaction; **o. bancaire** *ou* **de banque** bank transaction; **o. blanche** break-even transaction; **o. boursière** *ou* **de Bourse** stock exchange transaction *or* dealing; *Banque* **opérations de caisse** counter transactions; *Compta* **o. en capital** capital transaction; **o. de change** exchange transaction *or* deal; **o. de clearing** clearing transaction; **opérations de clôture** late trading, trading at the finish; **o. commerciale** business operation; **o. comptable** accounting operation; **o. au comptant** *(gén)* cash transaction; *Bourse* spot *or* cash deal; *Compta* **opérations courantes** normal business transactions; *Bourse* **opérations de couverture** hedging; *Bourse* **o. à découvert** short position; *Bourse* **opérations sur écran** screen trading; **o. d'escompte** discount operation; **o. de face à face** back-to-back loan; **o. financière** financial transaction; **opérations fermes** firm transactions; **opérations internationales** international operations; *Bourse* **o. de journée** day trade; *Bourse* **o. jumbo** jumbo trade; *Bourse* **opérations à option** option dealing *or* trading; *Banque* **o. de prêt** loan transaction; *Bourse* **o. à prime** option deal; *Bourse* **opérations à terme** futures trading

4 *(manœuvre)* operation; **nous faisons appel à lui pour des opérations ponctuelles** we call upon his services when we need a specific job carried out; **o. prix cassés** *(sur la vitrine d'un magasin)* prices slashed; **o. de commando/de sauvetage** commando/rescue operation; *Com* **o. en commun** joint venture; **la police a effectué une o. coup de poing dans le quartier** the police swooped on the area; **o. coup de poing sur les chaînes hi-fi** *(sur la vitrine d'un magasin)* hi-fi prices slashed; **une o. escargot a perturbé la circulation hier** a *Br* go-slow *or Am* slowdown by drivers disrupted traffic yesterday; **o. de police** police operation; **o. portes ouvertes à l'Université** *Br* open day *or Am* open house at the University

5 *(campagne)* operation, campaign; **o. marketing** marketing campaign; **o. publicitaire** advertising campaign

6 *(démarche)* process; **les opérations de l'esprit** mental processes, the workings of the mind

7 par l'o. du Saint-Esprit *Rel* through the workings of the Holy Spirit; *Fig Hum* by magic; *Hum* **crois-tu que tu y arriveras par l'o. du Saint-Esprit?** do you think you'll succeed just waiting for things to happen?

8 *(ensemble de travaux)* process, operation; **les opérations de fabrication de l'acier** steel making processes; **la machine exécute 18 opérations différentes** the machine performs 18 different operations

9 *Ordinat* operation; **o. "si-alors"** if-then operation

opérationnel, -elle [ɔperasjɔnɛl] ADJ **1** *(en activité)* operational; **les nouveaux ateliers ne seront opérationnels que l'année prochaine** the new workshops won't be operational until next year **2** *(fournissant le résultat optimal)* efficient, operative

opératoire [ɔperatwar] ADJ **1** *Math* operative **2** *Méd (chirurgical)* operating *(avant n)*, surgical; *(postopératoire)* post-operative; **médecine o.** surgery

opératrice [ɔperatris] *voir* **opérateur**

opercule [ɔpɛrkyl] NM **1** *Bot & Zool* operculum **2** *(dans un emballage)* lid **3** *Naut* **o. de hublot** deadlight

operculé, -e [ɔpɛrkyle] ADJ **1** *Bot & Zool* operculated **2** *(emballage, pot)* with a lid

opéré, -e [ɔpere] NM,F patient (who has undergone surgery); **le chirurgien est passé voir son dernier o.** the surgeon came round to see the last person he operated on; **les grands opérés** (post-operative) intensive care patients; **c'est un grand o.** he's had major surgery

opérer **[18]** [ɔpere] **VT 1** *Méd (blessé, malade)* to operate on; **o. qn des amygdales** to take sb's tonsils out; **elle a été opérée de l'appendicite** she was operated on for appendicitis, she had her appendix removed; **il vient juste d'être opéré** he's just had an operation; **se faire o.** to undergo *or* to have surgery; **se faire o. des amygdales** to have one's tonsils taken out; **se faire o. d'une tumeur** to have an operation to remove a tumour

2 *(procéder à ▸ modification, réforme, restructuration)* to carry out; *(▸ miracle, retour en arrière)* to bring about; *(▸ paiement, virement, distinction)* to make; *Chim (▸ synthèse)* to perform; **tu dois o. un choix** you have to choose *or* to make a choice; **le pays tente d'o. un redressement économique** the country is attempting to bring about an economic recovery

USAGE ABSOLU *Méd* **le chirurgien a opéré toute la matinée** the surgeon was in the operating theatre all morning

VI 1 *(faire effet)* to work; **le médicament a opéré** the medicine worked; **son charisme n'a pas opéré sur moi** his/her charisma had no effect *or* didn't work on me

2 *(intervenir)* to act, to operate; **la police opère souvent la nuit** the police often operate at night; **la façon dont les cambrioleurs ont opéré** the way the burglars went to work; **je ne sais pas comment il opère en de telles circonstances** I don't know how he proceeds in such circumstances

3 *Bourse* **o. à découvert** to take a short position, to go short

VPR s'opérer 1 *(emploi passif)* **ce genre de lésion ne s'opère pas** this type of lesion can't be operated on

2 *(avoir lieu)* to take place; **un grand changement s'est opéré depuis ton départ** a major change has taken place since you left; **une transformation s'opéra en elle** she underwent a transformation

opérette [ɔperɛt] **NF** operetta; **chanteuse d'o.** operetta singer

• **d'opérette ADJ le colonel n'est qu'un soldat d'o.** the colonel is just a tin soldier; **une armée d'o.** a caricature of an army

ophidien [ɔfidjɛ̃] **NM** *Zool* ophidian

ophite [ɔfit] **NM** ophite, serpentine

ophrys [ɔfris] **NM** *Bot* ophrys; **o. abeille/mouche** bee/fly orchid

ophtalmie [ɔftalmi] **NF** ophthalmia; **o. des neiges** snow blindness

ophtalmique [ɔftalmik] **ADJ** ophthalmic

ophtalmo [ɔftalmo] **NMF** *Fam (abrév* **ophtalmologiste**) eye specialist[□]

ophtalmologie [ɔftalmɔlɔʒi] **NF** ophthalmology

ophtalmologiste [ɔftalmɔlɔʒist], **ophtalmologue** [ɔftalmɔlɔg] **NMF** ophthalmologist, eye specialist

ophtalmoscope [ɔftalmɔskɔp] **NM** ophthalmoscope

opiacé, -e [ɔpjase] **ADJ 1** *(qui contient de l'opium)* opiate, opiated **2** *(qui sert d'opium)* opiate, opium-scented

NM opiate

opiner **[3]** [ɔpine] **VI** *Littéraire* **o. sur qch** to express an opinion about sth; **o. pour/contre qch** to come down in favour of/against sth

VT *Littéraire* **o. que...** to be of the opinion that...

• **opiner à VT IND** *Littéraire* to consent to; **elle opina à ce mariage** she gave her assent *or* consent to this marriage

• **opiner de VT IND o. de la tête** *ou* **du bonnet** *ou* **du chef** to nod one's assent *or* agreement, to nod in agreement

opiniâtre [ɔpinjatr] **ADJ 1** *(personne)* stubborn, obstinate **2** *(haine, opposition, lutte)* relentless, obstinate; *(résistance)* stubborn, dogged; *(détermination)* dogged **3** *(toux)* persistent

opiniâtrement [ɔpinjatrəmɑ̃] **ADV 1** *(avec entêtement)* stubbornly, obstinately **2** *(avec ténacité)* relentlessly, persistently, doggedly

opiniâtreté [ɔpinjatrəte] **NF** *Littéraire* **1** *(entêtement)* stubbornness, obstinacy **2** *(ténacité)* relentlessness, doggedness

opinion [ɔpinjɔ̃] **NF 1** *(point de vue)* opinion (**de** of; **sur** about, on); **j'ai mon o. sur lui** I have my own opinion about him; **se faire soi-même une o.** to make up one's own mind; **se faire une o. sur qch** to make up one's mind about sth, to form an opinion about sth; **mon o. est faite** I've made up my mind; **je ne partage pas votre o.** I don't agree with you, I don't share your views; **partager les opinions de qn** to share sb's opinions *or* views, to think the same way as sb; **au dernier moment, elle changea brusquement d'o.** she suddenly changed her mind at the last minute; **je vais vous donner mon o.** let me tell you what I think; **c'est une affaire d'o.** it's a matter of opinion; **journal d'o.** = political weekly/monthly (with a particular stance); *Journ* **libre o.** editorial; **opinions politiques/subversives** political/subversive views; **l'o. (publique)** public opinion; **informer l'o.** to inform the public; **sans o.** *(dans un sondage)* don't know; **les sans o.** *(sondés)* the don't knows **2** *(jugement)* opinion; **avoir une bonne/mauvaise/haute o. de qn** to have a good/bad/high opinion of sb; **je me moque de l'o. d'autrui** I don't care what others may think

opiomane [ɔpjɔman] **NMF** opium addict

opium [ɔpjɔm] **NM** opium; *Fig* **la religion est l'o. du peuple** religion is the opium of the people

opossum [ɔpɔsɔm] **NM** *Zool* opossum

opportun, -e [ɔpɔrtœ̃, -yn] **ADJ** opportune, timely; *(moment, jour)* right; **ton arrivée était plus qu'opportune** you came at just the right time; **je vous donnerai ma réponse en temps o.** I'll give you my answer in due course; **il serait o. de prendre une décision** it's time to make a decision; **il lui est apparu o. de partir avant elle** he/she found it appropriate *or* advisable to leave before her

opportunément [ɔpɔrtynemɑ̃] **ADV** opportunely; **la police est arrivée o.** the police arrived at just the right moment

opportunisme [ɔpɔrtynism] **NM** opportunism

opportuniste [ɔpɔrtynist] **ADJ** opportunist; *(maladie)* opportunistic

NMF opportunist

opportunité [ɔpɔrtynite] **NF 1** *(à-propos)* appropriateness; *(d'une arrivée)* timeliness, *Sout* opportuneness; *(d'un projet, d'une décision)* advisability **2** *(occasion)* opportunity; **o. commerciale** market opportunity; **o. marketing** marketing opportunity

opposable [ɔpozabl] **ADJ** opposable (**à** to); **rien n'est o. à ses arguments** there is no answer to his/her arguments, nothing can be said against his/her arguments

opposant, -e [ɔpozɑ̃, -ɑ̃t] **ADJ 1** *(adverse)* opposing **2** *Jur* opposing **3** *Anat* **muscles opposants** opponens

NM,F *(adversaire)* opponent (**à** of); *Pol* member of the Opposition; **les opposants au régime** the opponents of the regime; **les opposants à la politique actuelle** those who oppose current policy

NM *Anat* **les opposants** the opponens

opposé, -e [ɔpoze] **ADJ 1** *(en vis-à-vis)* opposite; **il est arrivé du côté o.** he came from the other *or* opposite side; **sur le mur o.** on the opposite wall; *(par rapport au locuteur)* on the wall facing us

2 *(contraire ▸ sens, direction)* opposite, other; *(▸ mouvement, équipe)* opposing; *(▸ goût, caractère)* different; *(▸ avis)* opposite; *(▸ intérêt)* conflicting; **je suis d'une opinion opposée (à la vôtre)** I am of a different opinion

3 *(contrastant ▸ couleur, ton)* contrasting

4 *Géom & Math (côté, angle)* opposite

5 *(contre)* **être o. à une mesure** to oppose *or* to be opposed to *or* to be against a measure; **je suis o. à ce qu'une centrale soit construite dans cette région** I'm opposed to *or* I'm against a power station being built in this area

NM 1 *(direction)* opposite; **quel est l'o. du sud?** what's the opposite of south? **2** *(contraire)* opposite, reverse; **chaque fois que je te dis quelque chose, tu soutiens l'o.!** whenever I say anything, you say the opposite *or* you contradict it!; **il est tout l'o. de sa sœur** he's the exact opposite of his sister **3** *Math (nombre)* opposite number

• **à l'opposé ADV 1** *(dans l'espace)* opposite, on the other side; *Fig* on the other hand; **la gare est à l'o.** the station is in the opposite direction **2** *(en désaccord)* **il est de droite et je suis tout à l'o.** his views are right-wing but mine are completely the opposite

• **à l'opposé de PRÉP 1** *(dans l'espace)* opposite; **à l'o. de la gare** opposite the station **2** *(en contradiction avec)* unlike, contrary to; **à l'o. de sa mère, elle n'aimait pas la peinture** unlike her mother, she didn't like painting; **mon avis est à l'o. du sien** my opinion is the opposite of his/hers; **à l'o. de ce que nous attendions** contrary to expectation *or* to what we expected; **cela va à l'o. de ce que l'on m'avait promis/de notre politique** that goes against what I was promised/our policy

opposer **[3]** [ɔpoze] **VT 1** *(objecter ▸ argument)* **je n'ai rien à o. à cette objection** I've nothing to say against that objection; **que peut-il t'o.?** what objection can he have to that?, what can he say against that?; **o. des arguments valables à une théorie** to put forward valid arguments against a theory; **il a opposé à ma théorie des raisons intéressantes** he put forward some interesting objections to my theory; **elle m'a opposé qu'elle n'avait pas le temps de s'en occuper** she objected that she didn't have time to take care of it

2 *(mettre en confrontation ▸ adversaires, armées, pays)* to bring into conflict (with each other); **deux guerres ont opposé nos pays** two wars have brought our countries into conflict; **qui peut-on o. au président sortant?** who can we put up against the outgoing president?; **cette course oppose les meilleurs athlètes d'Europe** this race will see Europe's finest athletes competing against each other; **la finale opposera le joueur français au joueur américain** the final will pit the French player against the American; **la finale opposera la France à l'Italie** France will meet Italy *or* come up against Italy in the final; **à l'idéalisme de son père, Renaud opposa une approche plus pragmatique** Renaud countered his father's idealism with a more pragmatic approach; **nous opposerons nos méthodes** we'll test our methods against each other; **o. Mozart à Debussy** to contrast Mozart with Debussy

3 *Phys* **o. une pression de sens contraire** to apply pressure from the opposite direction; **o. une résistance** to resist, to be resistant; *Fig* to put up a resistance; *Fig* **o. une résistance vigoureuse** to put up *or* to offer vigorous resistance

4 *(disposer vis-à-vis)* to set *or* to place opposite each other

VPR s'opposer 1 s'o. à *(être contre)* to object to, to oppose; **quelqu'un s'oppose-t-il à cette nomination?** are there any objections to this appointment?; **nous nous opposons à ce que la centrale soit construite** we oppose the building of the power station, we are opposed to *or* are against the power station being built; **le règlement/ma religion s'y oppose** it goes against the rules/my religion; **les conditions météo s'opposent à toute navigation aérienne aujourd'hui** weather conditions are making flying inadvisable today; **nous nous opposons à ce qu'il arrête ses études** we are against *or* we are opposed to the idea of him giving up his studies; **rien ne s'oppose à votre projet** nothing stands in the way of your plan; **rien ne s'oppose à ce que vous fassiez ce que vous souhaitez** there's nothing to stop you doing what you want to

2 s'o. à *(être en désaccord avec)* to oppose; **je m'oppose à lui sur la politique étrangère** I'm against him *or* I oppose him on foreign policy

3 s'o. à *(affronter)* to oppose, to be against; **il s'opposera ce soir au président dans un débat télévisé** he'll face the president tonight in a televised debate; **les meilleurs joueurs d'échecs s'opposent dans ce tournoi** this tournament pits the best chess players against one another, the best chess players come up against each other in this tournament

4 s'o. à *(contraster avec ▸ couleur, notion, mot)* to be the opposite of; **le noir s'oppose au blanc** black is the opposite of white

opposite [ɔpozit] **NM** *Arch ou Littéraire* opposite, contrary; **il est tout l'o. de son frère** he is the exact opposite of his brother; **il pense tout l'o. de ce qu'il dit** he thinks quite the reverse of what he says

• **à l'opposite** ADV **leurs maisons sont à l'o.** their houses are opposite (each other)

• **à l'opposite de** PRÉP **à l'o. de l'église, vous trouverez le monument** you'll see the monument opposite the church

opposition [ɔpozisjɔ̃] NF **1** *(désaccord)* opposition; *(contraste)* contrast, difference; **o. de** *ou* **entre deux styles** clash of *or* between two styles; **couleurs en o.** contrasting colours

2 *(résistance)* opposition; **le ministre a fait** *ou* **mis o. au projet** the minister opposed the plan; **l'o. de la plupart des citoyens à la guerre n'est pas prouvée** it has not been proved that most citizens are opposed to *or* against the war; **nous avons rencontré une forte o.** we encountered strong opposition; **la loi est passée sans o.** the bill went through unopposed; **il fait de l'o. systématique à tout ce qu'on lui propose** he's automatically against everything you suggest

3 *Pol* **l'o.** the Opposition; **les dirigeants/les partis de l'o.** the leaders/the parties of the Opposition

4 *Jur* caveat; **o. sur titre** attachment against securities; **jugement susceptible d'o.** judgment liable to stay of execution; **faire o. à une décision** to appeal against a ruling; **faire o. à un chèque** to stop a cheque; **faire o. à un mariage** to raise an objection to *or* to enter a caveat to a marriage

5 *Astrol & Astron* opposition; **planète en o.** *Astrol* planet in opposition; *Astron* planet at opposition

• **en opposition avec** PRÉP against, contrary to, in opposition to; **agir en o. avec ses principes** to act against one's principles; **c'est en o. totale avec les principes qu'il expose dans ses livres** it is in complete contrast to *or* is totally at odds with *or* totally contradicts the principles that he puts forward in his books; **tout cela est en o. totale avec ce que je pense** all that is the complete opposite of what I think; **je me suis trouvée en o. avec elle sur plusieurs points** I found myself at odds *or* at variance with her on several points

• **par opposition à** PRÉP as opposed to, in contrast with

oppositionnel, -elle [ɔpozisjɔnɛl] ADJ *Pol* oppositional, opposition *(avant n)*

NM,F oppositionist

oppressant, -e [ɔpresɑ̃, -ɑ̃t] ADJ oppressive

oppresser [4] [ɔprese] VT **1** *(situation, atmosphère)* to oppress; **l'obscurité/la chaleur m'oppresse** I find the darkness/the heat oppressive; **elle était oppressée par l'angoisse** she was gripped *or* choked with anxiety; **ils sont oppressés par le remords** they are weighed down with remorse **2** *Littéraire (peuple, nation)* to oppress

> Do not confuse with **opprimer**.

oppresseur [ɔpresœr] NM oppressor

ADJ M *(régime)* oppressive

oppressif, -ive [ɔpresif, -iv] ADJ oppressive

oppression [ɔpresjɔ̃] NF **1** *(domination)* oppression **2** *(suffocation)* suffocation, oppression; **o. de la poitrine** tightness of the chest, difficulty in breathing

oppressive [ɔpresiv] *voir* **oppressif**

opprimé, -e [ɔprime] ADJ oppressed

NM,F oppressed person; **elle prend toujours le parti des opprimés** she always sides with the underdog

opprimer [3] [ɔprime] VT **1** *(asservir)* to oppress **2** *(censurer)* to suppress, to stifle; **o. la presse** to gag the press

> Do not confuse with **oppresser**.

opprobre [ɔprɔbr] NM *Littéraire* **1** *(honte)* shame, opprobrium; **jeter l'o. sur qn, accabler** *ou* **couvrir qn d'o.** to heap shame *or* opprobrium on sb; **il est l'o. de sa famille** he's a disgrace to his family **2** *(avilissement)* shame, infamy; **vivre dans l'o.** to live in infamy

optatif, -ive [ɔptatif, -iv] ADJ optative

NM optative (mode)

opter [3] [ɔpte] VI **o. entre deux choses** to choose between two things

• **opter pour** VT IND to opt for; **vous devez o. pour une de ces deux possibilités** you'll have to choose between these two possibilities; **j'ai opté pour les cheveux courts** I opted for a short haircut

opticien, -enne [ɔptisjɛ̃, -ɛn] NM,F optician

optimal, -e, -aux, -ales [ɔptimal, -o] ADJ optimal, optimum *(avant n)*; **pour un rendement o.** for optimal results

optimalisation [ɔptimalizasjɔ̃] NF optimization; *Fin* **o. du profit** *ou* **des profits** profit optimization

optimisation [ɔptimizasjɔ̃] NF optimization; *Fin* **o. du profit** *ou* **des profits** profit optimization

optimiser [3] [ɔptimize] VT to optimize; *Ordinat (matériel, système)* to upgrade

optimiseur [ɔptimizœr] NM *Ordinat* optimizer

optimisme [ɔptimism] NM optimism; **avec o.** optimistically

optimiste [ɔptimist] ADJ optimistic; **nous ne sommes pas très optimistes quant à la guérison de ce malade** we're not very optimistic about the patient's chances of recovery *or* that the patient will recover

NMF optimist; **c'est un éternel o.** he's an eternal optimist

optimum [ɔptimɔm] *(pl* **optimums** *ou* **optima** [-a]) ADJ optimum *(avant n)*, optimal; **la température o. ne dépasse pas 5 degrés** the optimum temperature does not exceed 5 degrees

NM optimum; **o. écologique** optimum ecological conditions; **o. de peuplement** optimum population

option [ɔpsjɔ̃] NF **1** *(choix)* option, choice; **je n'ai pas d'autre o.** I have no other alternative *or* choice

2 *Scol* **(matière à) o.** optional subject; **il avait le latin en o. au baccalauréat** he took Latin as an option *or* an optional subject *or* an elective subject for the baccalauréat

3 *Fin & Bourse* **o. d'achat** call option; **o. d'achat d'actions** stock option; **o. sur actions** option on shares; **o. américaine** American-style option; **o. à l'argent** at-the-money option; **o. de change** foreign currency option; **o. sur contrats à terme** futures option; **o. cotée** traded option; **o. au cours** at-the-money option; **o. du double** call of more; **o. d'échange** swap option; **o. européenne** European-style option; **o. sur indice** index option; **o. à la monnaie** at-the-money option; **o. négociable** traded option; **o. sur titre** stock option; **o. de vente** put option

4 *Com & Jur* option; **prendre une o. sur qch** to take (out) an option on sth; **o. d'achat/de vente** option to buy/to sell

5 *(accessoire facultatif)* optional extra; **en o.** as an (optional) extra; **le flash est en o.** the flash is optional *or* is an optional extra

6 *Ordinat* **o. d'impression** print option; **o. de menu** menu option; **o. de sauvegarde** save option

7 *Pol* **o. zéro** zero option

optionnel, -elle [ɔpsjɔnɛl] ADJ optional

optique [ɔptik] ADJ **1** *Anat* optic; **nerf o.** optic nerve

2 *Opt* optical

3 *Phys* optic; **angle o.** optic angle

4 *Ordinat* optical

NF **1** *(science)* optics *(singulier)*; **o. électronique** electron optics; **transmettre par o.** to communicate by visual signals **2** *Tech* (set of) lenses; *(d'un projecteur)* optical system **3** *(point de vue)* perspective; **mon o. est différente** I see it from a different angle *or* point of view; **dans cette o.** from this perspective *or* viewpoint; **nous ne travaillons pas dans la même o.** we're working towards different aims; *Mktg* **o. marketing** marketing orientation; *Mktg* **o. produit** product orientation; **o. publicitaire** advertising approach; *Mktg* **o. vente** sales orientation

• **d'optique** ADJ optical

optométrie [ɔptɔmetri] NF optometry

optométriste [ɔptɔmetrist] NMF optometrist

opulence [ɔpylɑ̃s] NF **1** *(richesse)* opulence, affluence; **vivre dans l'o.** to live an opulent life *or* a life of plenty **2** *Littéraire (ampleur)* fullness, ampleness; **l'o. de ses formes** the fullness of her figure

opulent, -e [ɔpylɑ̃, -ɑ̃t] ADJ **1** *(riche)* affluent, wealthy, opulent; *(moisson, pâturage)* abundant **2** *(physiquement ▸ personne)* corpulent; *(▸ forme)* generous, full; **une poitrine opulente** an ample *or* full bosom; **son opulente chevelure** his/her luxuriant hair

opus [ɔpys] NM opus

opuscule [ɔpyskyl] NM *(petit ouvrage)* opuscule; *(brochure)* brochure

OPV [opeve] NF *Fin (abrév* **offre publique de vente)** public offering, public share offer

or[1] [ɔr] CONJ *(pour introduire une précision)* now; *(pour introduire une opposition)* well; **il faut tenir les délais; or, ce n'est pas toujours possible** deadlines must be met; now this is not always possible; **avant de le lire, je pensais que le livre était bon, or, il ne l'était pas** before reading it, I thought the book was good, well, it wasn't; **je devais y aller, or au dernier moment, j'ai eu un empêchement** I was supposed to go, but then at the last moment something came up; **il n'achète jamais de chocolats, or…** he never buys chocolates, but…; **or…, donc…** now…, therefore…

or[2] [ɔr] NM **1** *(métal)* gold; **le cours de l'or** the price of gold; **or monnayé/au titre/sans titre** coined/essayed/unessayed gold; **or en barre** gold bullion; *Fam* **ces actions, c'est de l'or en barre** these shares are a rock-solid investment; **or blanc** white gold; **l'or blanc** *(les sports d'hiver)* the winter sports bonanza; **or bleu** blue gold, water; **or brut** gold nuggets; **or jaune** yellow gold; **or rouge** red gold; **l'or noir** black gold; **l'or vert** "green gold", forest resources; **or massif** solid gold; **la montre est en or massif** the watch is solid gold; **or pur/fin** pure/fine gold; **la valeur or** value in gold, gold exchange value; *Fig* **pour tout l'or du monde** for all the money in the world, for all the tea in China; **il/ça vaut son pesant d'or** he's worth his/it's worth its weight in gold; **parler d'or** to speak with the voice of wisdom **2** *(couleur)* gold, golden colour **3** *Jur* **clause or** gold clause

ADJ INV gold *(avant n)*, gold-coloured

• **d'or** ADJ **1** *Minér & (en joaillerie)* gold *(avant n)* **2** *(doré ▸ cheveux)* golden, gold *(avant n)*; *(▸ cadre)* gold *(avant n)* **3** *(locutions)* **un cœur d'or** a heart of gold; *Littéraire* **le siècle d'or** the golden age

• **en or** ADJ **1** *(fait d'or ▸ bijou)* gold *(avant n)*; **une bague en or** a gold ring **2** *(excellent)* **une mère en or** a wonderful mother; **une affaire en or** *(occasion)* a real bargain; *(entreprise)* a goldmine; **c'est une occasion en or** it's a golden opportunity

oracle [ɔrakl] NM *Antiq & Fig* oracle; **rendre un o.** to pronounce an oracle; **parler d'un ton d'o.** to speak with assurance

orage [ɔraʒ] NM **1** *Météo* storm, thunderstorm; **un temps d'o.** stormy *or* thundery weather; **par temps d'o.** in stormy weather; **le temps est à l'o.** there's thunder in the air; **il va y avoir un o.** there's a storm brewing, there's going to be a storm; **o. magnétique/de chaleur** magnetic/heat storm; **pluie d'o.** rainstorm **2** *Fig (dispute)* row, argument; **depuis des semaines, je sentais venir l'o.** I'd known for weeks that trouble was brewing; **il y a de l'o. dans l'air** there's trouble brewing; **laisser passer l'o.** to let the storm blow over **3** *Littéraire (déchirement, tourmente)* upheaval, tumult; **les orages de l'amour** the turmoil of love

orageuse [ɔraʒøz] *voir* **orageux**

orageusement [ɔraʒøzmɑ̃] ADV stormily, tempestuously

orageux, -euse [ɔraʒø, -øz] ADJ **1** *Météo (ciel)* stormy, thundery; *(chaleur, averse)* thundery; **le temps est o.** it's thundery *or* stormy, the weather's thundery *or* stormy **2** *Fig (tumultueux ▸ jeunesse, séance)* stormy, turbulent; *(▸ discussion)* stormy, heated

oraison [ɔrɛzɔ̃] NF **1** *Rel (prière)* prayer; **l'o. dominicale** the Lord's Prayer **2** *Littérature* **o. funèbre** funeral oration

oral, -e, -aux, -ales [ɔral, -o] ADJ **1** *(confession, déposition)* verbal, oral; *(message, tradition)* oral; *Scol (épreuve)* oral **2** *Anat & Ling* oral

NM **1** *(examen ▸ gén)* oral (examination); *(▸ à l'université)* oral (examination), *Br* viva (voce); **notes d'o.** oral *Br* marks *or Am* grades; **j'ai raté l'o. de physique** I failed the physics oral **2** *Scol & Univ* **l'o.** *(l'expression orale)* **il n'est pas très bon à l'o.** his oral work isn't very good

oralement [ɔralmɑ̃] ADV orally, verbally

orange [ɔrɑ̃ʒ] NF orange; **o. amère/douce** bitter/ sweet orange; **o. sanguine** blood orange; **une o. pressée** a glass of freshly squeezed orange juice

NM *(couleur)* orange; *Aut* **passer à l'o.** to go through the lights on amber; **le feu était à l'o.** the lights were at amber

ADJ INV *(coloré)* orange, orange-coloured

orangé, -e [ɔrɑ̃ʒe] ADJ orangey, orange-coloured

NM orangey colour

orangeade [ɔrɑ̃ʒad] NF orange drink

oranger [ɔrɑ̃ʒe] NM orange tree

orangeraie [ɔrɑ̃ʒrɛ] NF orange grove

orangerie [ɔrɑ̃ʒri] NF **1** *(serre)* orangery **2** *(plantation)* orange grove

orangisme [ɔrɑ̃ʒism] NM *Pol* Orangism

orangiste [ɔrɑ̃ʒist] NMF **1** *(en Irlande du Nord)* Orangeman, *f* Orangewoman **2** *Hist* Orangist

ADJ Orange *(avant n)*

orang-outan, orang-outang [ɔrɑ̃utɑ̃] *(pl* **orangs-outans** *ou* **orangs-outangs)** NM *Zool* orang-outang, orang-utan

orateur, -trice [ɔratœr, -tris] NM,F **1** *(rhétoricien)* orator **2** *(gén)* speaker; **c'est un excellent o.** he is an excellent speaker

oratoire[1] [ɔratwar] ADJ *(style, talent)* oratorical; **passage o.** oration; **prendre des précautions oratoires** to choose one's words carefully; **l'art o.** (the art of) oratory, public speaking

oratoire[2] [ɔratwar] NM **1** *(chapelle)* oratory **2** *Rel* **l'O. de France** the French Oratory

oratorio [ɔratɔrjo] NM oratorio

oratrice [ɔratris] voir **orateur**

orbe[1] [ɔrb] ADJ *Archit* **mur o.** blind wall

orbe[2] [ɔrb] NM **1** *Astron* orbit **2** *Littéraire (globe)* orb, globe, sphere; *(cercle)* circle, coil, ring; **l'o. rouge du soleil** the red orb of the sun

orbitaire [ɔrbitɛr] ADJ orbital

orbital, -e, -aux, -ales [ɔrbital, -o] ADJ *Astron* orbital

• **orbitale** NF *Phys* **orbitale atomique** atomic orbital; **orbitale moléculaire** molecular orbital

orbite [ɔrbit] NF **1** *Anat* (eye) socket, *Spéc* orbit; *Fig* **il était tellement en colère que les yeux lui sortaient des orbites** he was so angry that his eyes were popping out (of their sockets)

2 *(d'un vaisseau spatial, d'un électron) & Astron* orbit; **o. géostationnaire** geostationary orbit; **être sur** *ou* **en o.** to be in orbit; **être en o. autour de qch** *(sujet: astre, engin)* to be in orbit round sth, to orbit sth; **satellite en o. autour de la Terre** Earth-orbiting satellite; **le satellite est en o. basse** the satellite is on a low orbit; **mettre en** *ou* **placer sur o.** to put into orbit

3 *Phys* orbital

4 *Fig (d'une personne, d'un pays)* sphere of influence, orbit

orbiter [3] [ɔrbite] VI to orbit; **o. autour de** to orbit (round)

Orcades [ɔrkad] NFPL **les O.** the Orkney Islands, the Orkneys

orchestral, -e, -aux, -ales [ɔrkɛstral, -o] ADJ orchestral, orchestra *(avant n)*; **la partition orchestrale** the orchestral *or* orchestra score

orchestration [ɔrkɛstrasjɔ̃] NF **1** *Mus* orchestration; **faire une nouvelle o. d'un morceau** to reorchestrate a piece **2** *Fig (organisation)* orchestration, organization

orchestre [ɔrkɛstr] NM **1** *Mus (classique)* orchestra; *(de jazz)* band, orchestra; **grand o.** full orchestra; **o. symphonique/de chambre** symphony/chamber orchestra; **o. de cuivres** brass band; **o. philharmonique** philharmonic (orchestra) **2** *Cin & Théât Br* stalls, *Am* orchestra; **nous sommes à l'o.** we have seats in the stalls

orchestrer [3] [ɔrkɛstre] VT **1** *Mus (composer)* to orchestrate; *(adapter)* to orchestrate, to score **2** *Fig (préparer)* to orchestrate, to organize

orchidée [ɔrkide] NF orchid

ordalie [ɔrdali] NF *Hist* ordeal; **o. par l'eau/le feu** ordeal by water/fire

ordi [ɔrdi] NM *Fam* computer[□], puter

ordinaire [ɔrdinɛr] ADJ **1** *(habituel ▸ journée)* ordinary, normal; *(▸ procédure)* usual, standard, normal; *(▸ comportement)* ordinary, usual, customary; *Jur & Pol (▸ session)* ordinary; **elle parlait avec son arrogance o.** she was talking with her usual *or* customary arrogance; **en temps o.** usually, normally; **peu** *ou* **pas o.** *(attitude, méthode, journée)* unusual; *(volonté)* unusual, extraordinary; **nous nous sommes couchés à 22 heures, rien que de très o.** we went to bed at 10, nothing unusual about that; **il n'a même pas téléphoné – voilà qui n'est pas o.!** he didn't even phone – that's odd *or* that's not like him!

2 *(de tous les jours ▸ habits, vaisselle)* ordinary, everyday *(avant n)*

3 *Com (qualité, modèle)* standard; *(produit)* ordinary

4 *(banal ▸ cuisine, goûts)* ordinary, plain; *(▸ gens)* ordinary, common; *(▸ spectacle)* ordinary, run-of-the-mill; *(▸ conversation)* run-of-the-mill, commonplace; **c'est quelqu'un de très o.** he's/ she's a very ordinary person; **elle mène une existence très o.** she leads a very humdrum existence; **voilà une chose qui n'est pas o.!** that's not something you see every day!

NM **1** *(norme)* **l'o.** the ordinary; **voilà ce qui fait l'o. de son existence** that's how he/she generally spends his/her time; **sortir de l'o.** to be out of the ordinary, to be unusual; **son mari sort vraiment de l'o.!** her husband is one of a kind!

2 *(repas habituel)* everyday *or* ordinary fare; **pour améliorer l'o. des soldats** in order to improve the soldiers' ordinary fare; **auberge où l'o. est excellent** inn where the food is excellent; *Hum* **voulez-vous partager notre o.?** will you share our humble repast?

3 *(essence) Br* ≃ two-star petrol, *Am* ≃ regular

4 *Mil* (company) mess

• **à l'ordinaire** ADV **plus intéressant qu'à l'o.** more interesting than usual; **comme à l'o., il arriva en retard** as usual, he turned up late

• **d'ordinaire** ADV usually, ordinarily, normally; **plus tôt que d'o.** earlier than usual; **une attitude plus franche que d'o.** an unusually honest attitude

ordinairement [ɔrdinɛrmɑ̃] ADV usually, ordinarily, normally

ordinal, -e, -aux, -ales [ɔrdinal, -o] ADJ *(adjectif, nombre)* ordinal

NM **1** *(nombre)* ordinal (number) **2** *(adjectif)* ordinal (adjective)

ordinateur [ɔrdinatœr] NM **1** *(machine)* computer; **mettre qch sur o.** to computerize sth, to put sth on computer; **o. analogique** analog computer; **o. autonome** stand-alone (computer); **o. bloc-notes** notebook (computer); **o. de bord** *Aut* trip computer; *Naut* shipboard computer; **o. de bureau** desktop computer; **o. central** mainframe (computer); **o. domestique** home computer; **o. dorsal** back-end computer; **o. à écran tactile** touch-screen computer; **o. embarqué** onboard computer; **o. familial** family computer; **o. frontal** front-end computer; **o. de gestion** business computer; **o. hôte** host computer; **o. individuel** home *or* personal computer, PC; **o. multimédia** multimedia computer; **o. numérique** digital computer; **o. personnel** home *or* personal computer, PC; **o. de poche** palmtop (computer); **o. portable** portable computer; **o. portatif** laptop computer; **o. de réseau** network computer; **o. sans clavier** keyboardless computer; **o. serveur** host computer, server; **o. de table** desktop (PC); **o. vectoriel** vector processor **2** *Rel* ordainer, ordinant

ordination [ɔrdinasjɔ̃] NF **1** *Rel (d'un prêtre)* ordination; *(consécration)* consecration **2** *Math* ordering

ordinogramme [ɔrdinɔgram] NM (process) flow chart *or* flow diagram

ordonnance [ɔrdɔnɑ̃s] NF **1** *(disposition)* organization, order, arrangement; **l'o. des mots dans une phrase** the arrangement *or* order of words in a sentence; **je ne veux pas déranger l'o. de vos papiers** I don't want to disturb your papers

2 *Archit* layout, disposition

3 *Méd* prescription; **un médicament vendu sans o.** a drug that can be bought over the counter; **délivré seulement sur o.** available on prescription only

4 *Jur (loi)* ordinance, statutory instrument; *(jugement)* order, ruling; *(de police)* (police) regulation *or* order; **o. d'amnistie** amnesty order; **o. d'interdiction temporaire** restraining order; **o. de mise en détention** detention order; **o. de non-lieu** non-suit; **rendre une o. de non-lieu** to dismiss a case for lack of evidence; **o. de renvoi** committal for trial; **o. de saisie** writ of execution

5 *Hist* ordinance (law), decree

6 *Fin* **o. de paiement** order to pay, authorization of payment

7 *Mil* orderly; **revolver d'o.** service pistol; **bottes d'o.** standard issue boots; **officier d'o.** aide-de-camp; *Naut* flag lieutenant

ordonnancement [ɔrdɔnɑ̃smɑ̃] NM **1** *Ind (organisation des phases)* sequencing; *(prévision des délais)* timing, scheduling **2** *Fin* order to pay **3** *Ordinat* scheduling

ordonnancer [16] [ɔrdɔnɑ̃se] VT **1** *(agencer)* to arrange, to organize **2** *Fin (déclarer bon à payer)* to authorize **3** *Ordinat* to schedule

ordonnancier [ɔrdɔnɑ̃sje] NM *(de pharmacien)* prescription book *or* register; *(de médecin)* prescription pad

ordonnateur, -trice [ɔrdɔnatœr, -tris] NM,F **1** *(organisateur)* organizer; **le comité sera l'o. de la cérémonie** the committee will be in charge of *or* will organize the ceremony; **o. des pompes funèbres** funeral director **2** *Fin* = official in charge of overseeing public expenditure

ordonné, -e[1] [ɔrdɔne] ADJ **1** *(méthodique ▸ personne)* tidy, neat; *(▸ esprit)* methodical, systematic

2 *(rangé ▸ chambre)* tidy, neat, orderly

3 *(régulier ▸ existence, mode de vie)* orderly, well-ordered

4 *Math* ordered

ordonnée[2] [ɔrdɔne] NF *Math* ordinate

ordonner [3] [ɔrdɔne] VT **1** *(commander ▸ silence, attaque, enquête)* to order; *Méd (▸ traitement, repos)* to prescribe; **ils ont ordonné le secret sur l'affaire** they've ordered that the matter (should) be kept secret; **o. à qn de faire qch** to order *or* to command sb to do sth; **o. à qn de se taire** to tell sb to be quiet; **o. à qn d'entrer/de sortir** to order sb in/out; **qui a ordonné qu'on les fusille?** who gave orders for them to be shot? **2** *(agencer ▸ documents)* to (put in) order; *(▸ arguments, idées)* to (put into) order, to arrange; *(▸ chambre)* to tidy (up); *Math (▸ nombres, suite)* to (arrange in) order; **o. des nombres du plus petit au plus grand/du plus grand au plus petit** to list numbers in ascending/descending order; **il faut davantage o. votre argumentation** you need to organize your arguments a bit more, you need to get more order into your arguments **3** *Rel* to ordain; **o. qn prêtre** to ordain sb

VPR **s'ordonner** *(faits)* to fall into order *or* place; **les indices s'ordonnaient dans mon esprit** the clues began to fall into place in my mind

ORDRE [ɔrdr]

- order **A1, 2, B1, 3–4, C1, 3–5**
- tidiness **B2**
- command **A1**
- sequence **B1**
- nature **C4**

NM **A. INSTRUCTION 1** *(directive, injonction)* order; *Mil* order, command; **c'est un o.!** (and) that's an order!; **donner un o.** *(parent)* to give an order; *(officiel, policier, officier)* to issue *or* to give an order; **donner (l')o. de** to give the order to; **donner à qn l'o. de faire qch** to order sb to do sth, to give sb the order to do sth; **qui a donné l'o. d'attaquer?** who gave the order to attack?, who ordered the attack?; **donner des ordres à qn** to give sb orders; *Fig* to order sb around; **je n'aime pas qu'on me donne des ordres** I don't like being ordered about; **il aime bien donner des ordres** he likes giving orders; **recevoir des ordres** to receive *or* to take orders; **je n'aime pas recevoir d'ordres!** I don't like to be ordered about!; **recevoir l'o. de faire qch** to be ordered *or* to receive the order to do sth; **j'ai reçu l'o. formel de ne pas le déranger** I've been formally instructed not to disturb him; **par** *ou* **sur o. de** by order of, on the orders of; **être sous les ordres de qn** to be under sb's command; **être aux ordres de qn** to take orders from sb; **je ne suis pas à tes ordres!** I'm not at your beck and call!; *Mil* **o. d'appel** *Br* call-up papers, *Am* draft notice;

o. d'exécution death warrant; **o. de grève** strike call; **o. d'incorporation** draft card; *Mil* **o. de mission** orders (for a mission); *Mil* **o. de route** marching orders; *Mil ou Hum* **à vos ordres!** yes, sir!

2 *Banque & Bourse* **à l'o. de** payable to, to the order of; **chèque à mon o.** cheque made out *or* payable to me; **c'est à quel o.?** who shall I make it payable to?; **o. d'achat** *(gén)* purchase order; *Bourse* buy order; **o. de Bourse** stock exchange order; **o. au comptant** cash order; *Bourse* **o. conditionnel** contingent order; *Bourse* **o. environ** discretionary order; *Bourse* **o. lié** straddle; *Bourse* **o. de négociation** trading order; *Banque* **o. de paiement** payment order; *Banque* **o. permanent** standing order; *Banque* **o. de prélèvement (permanent)** direct debit; *Bourse* **o. à révocation** good-till-cancelled order; *Bourse* **o. stop** stop order, stop loss order; *Bourse* **o. à terme** futures order; *Bourse* **o. tout ou rien** all-or-none order; *Banque* **o. de transfert permanent** banker's order, *Br* standing order; *Bourse* **o. de vente** selling order, order to sell; *Banque* **o. de virement** transfer order; *Banque* **o. de virement automatique, o. de virement bancaire** banker's order, *Br* standing order

3 *Jur* **o. d'exécution** death warrant

B. *HIÉRARCHIE, AGENCEMENT* **1** *(succession)* order, sequence; **l'o. des mots dans la phrase** the word order in the sentence; **par o. de grandeur/d'importance** in order of size/importance; **par o. alphabétique/chronologique/croissant/décroissant** in alphabetical/chronological/ascending/descending order; *Mil* **en o. de bataille/de marche** in battle/marching order; *Mil* **en o. dispersé/serré** in extended/close order; *Aut* **o. d'allumage** firing sequence; **par o. d'apparition à l'écran** in order of appearance; **par o. d'entrée en scène** in order of appearance; *TV* **o. de passage** running order; **par o. de préséance** in order of precedence; **o. utile** ranking (of creditor); *Jur* **o. de succession** intestate succession

2 *(rangement)* tidiness, neatness; **j'aimerais qu'il y ait un peu plus d'o. dans ta chambre** I'd like to see your room a little tidier; **attends, j'essaie de mettre de l'o. dans mes cartes** wait a minute, I'm trying to tidy up *or* to order my cards; **sans o.** *(maison, personne)* untidy; **la pièce était en o.** the room was tidy; **mettre qch en o.** to put sth in order; **mets tes vêtements en o.** sort out your clothes; **remettre qch en o.** to tidy sth up; **tenir une maison en o.** to keep a house tidy; **avoir de l'o.** *(sens du rangement)* to be tidy; **manquer** *ou* **ne pas avoir d'o.** to be untidy; **manque d'o.** untidiness

3 *(organisation méthodique ▸ de documents)* order; **mettre qch en o., mettre de l'o. dans qch** *(documents, comptabilité)* to set sth in order, to tidy sth up; **mettre de l'o. dans ses idées** to order one's ideas; **mettre ses affaires en o.** *(avant de mourir)* to settle one's affairs, to put one's affairs in order; **il a laissé ses papiers/ses comptes en o. avant de partir** he left his papers/accounts in order before leaving; **remettre de l'o. dans sa vie** to sort out one's life; **mettre bon o. à qch** to sort sth out; **il abuse de vous, vous devez y mettre bon o.** he's taking advantage of you, you must sort that out

4 *(discipline sociale)* **l'o.** order; **faire régner l'o.** to keep *or* to maintain order; **rappeler qn à l'o.** to call sb to order; **se faire rappeler à l'o.** *(dans une assemblée)* to be called to order; *(dans une classe)* to get told off; **la police est chargée du maintien de l'o.** it's the police's job to keep law and order; **l'o. établi** the established order; **l'o. public** public order, law and order; **puis tout est rentré dans l'o.** then order was restored, then everything went back to normal

C. *CLASSIFICATION, DOMAINE* **1** *Rel* order; **l'o. des dominicains/des capucins** the order of Dominicans/Capuchins; **les ordres monastiques** the monastic orders; **les saints ordres** the holy orders; **entrer dans les ordres** to take (holy) orders

2 *(confrérie)* **l'o. administratif** the administrative court system; **l'o. des avocats** *Br* ≃ the Bar, *Am* ≃ the Bar Association; **l'o. judiciaire** the ordinary court system, the non-administrative court system; **l'o. juridique** the legal system; **l'o. des médecins** *Br* ≃ the British Medical Association, *Am* ≃ the American Medical Association; **o. professionnel** professional body; *Hist* **les trois ordres** the three orders

3 *(association honorifique)* **l'O. de la Jarretière** the Order of the Garter; **l'O. national du Mérite** = the French Order of Merit

4 *(nature, sorte)* nature, order; **des problèmes d'o. professionnel** problems of a professional nature; **mes raisons sont d'o. différent** my reasons are of a different order; **dans le même o. d'idées** similarly; **dans un autre o. d'idées** in another connection; **du même o.** *(proposition, responsabilités)* similar, of the same nature; **pour un salaire du même o.** for a similar salary; **de l'o. de** in the region *or* order of; **une augmentation de 5 pour cent? – oui, de cet o.** a 5 percent rise? – yes, roughly *or* in that region; **donner un o. de grandeur** to give a rough estimate; **des sommes du même o. de grandeur** sums of the same order, similar sums of money; **c'est dans l'o. des choses** it's in the order *or* nature of things

5 *Archit & Biol* order

• **de dernier ordre** ADJ third-rate

• **de premier ordre** ADJ first-rate

• **de second ordre** ADJ *(question)* of secondary importance; *(artiste, personnalité)* second-rate

• **ordre du jour** NM **1** *(d'un comité)* agenda; *Parl* order of the day; **être à l'o. du jour** to be on the agenda; *Fig* to be in the news; **mettre qch à l'o. du jour** to put *or* to place sth on the agenda **2** *Mil* general orders, order of the day; **cité à l'o. du jour** mentioned in dispatches

ordré, -e [ɔrdre] ADJ *Suisse (ordonné)* tidy, orderly, neat

ordure [ɔrdyr] NF **1** *très Fam (individu méprisable)* scumbag, *Br* rotter, *Am* stinker **2** *Littéraire (fange)* **l'o.** filth, mire; **se vautrer dans l'o.** to wallow in filth

• **ordures** NFPL **1** *(déchets)* refuse *(UNCOUNT)*, *Br* rubbish *(UNCOUNT)*, *Am* garbage *(UNCOUNT)*, trash *(UNCOUNT)*; **ramasser les ordures** to collect the *Br* rubbish *or Am* garbage *or* trash; **vider les ordures** to empty (out) the *Br* rubbish *or Am* garbage *or* trash; **jeter** *ou* **mettre qch aux ordures** to throw sth into the *Br* rubbish bin *or Am* garbage can *or* trash can; **c'est bon à mettre aux ordures!** it's fit for *Br* the dustbin *or Am* the trash!; **mets-le aux ordures** throw it away; **ordures ménagères** household refuse **2** *(excréments)* dirt *(UNCOUNT)*, filth *(UNCOUNT)*; **faire ses ordures sur le trottoir** *(chien)* to make a mess on the pavement **3** *Fam (obscénités)* obscenities[□], filth *(UNCOUNT)*; **elle ne dit que des ordures** she always uses filthy language; **dire/écrire des ordures sur qn** to talk/to write filth about sb

ordurier, -ère [ɔrdyrje, -ɛr] ADJ foul, filthy, obscene

orée [ɔre] NF *Littéraire* edge; **à l'o. du bois** on the edge of the wood

oreillard, -e [ɔrɛjar, -ard] ADJ long-eared

NM **1** *(chauve-souris)* long-eared bat **2** *(lièvre, âne)* long-eared animal **3** *(d'un fauteuil)* wing

oreille [ɔrɛj] NF **1** *(partie du corps)* ear; **j'ai mal aux oreilles** I've got earache, my ears are hurting; **avoir les oreilles décollées** to have protruding *or* sticking-out ears; **avoir les oreilles en feuille de chou** to have cauliflower ears; **avoir les oreilles qui bourdonnent** *ou* **des bourdonnements d'o.** to have a buzzing in one's ears; **chien aux oreilles courtes/longues** short-eared/long-eared dog; **coucher les oreilles** *(d'un cheval)* to set *or* to lay its ears back; **elle n'entend pas de l'o. gauche** she's deaf in the left ear; *Fig* **il ne l'entend pas de cette o.** he won't hear of it; **mettre** *ou* **porter son chapeau sur l'o.** to wear one's hat over one ear; **o. interne/moyenne** inner/middle ear; **o. externe** outer *or* external ear; *Fig Hum* **les oreilles ont dû lui siffler** his/her ears must have been burning; **elle est repartie l'o. basse** she left with her tail between her legs; *Fig* **frotter les oreilles à qn** to box sb's ears; *Fig* **montrer le bout de l'o.** to show (oneself in) one's true colours; **tirer les oreilles à qn** to pull sb's ears; *Fig (réprimander)* to tell sb off; *Fig* **tu vas te faire tirer les oreilles** you'll get told off, you'll get a telling-off; *Fig* **se faire tirer l'o.** to need a lot of persuading; **il ne s'est pas fait tirer l'o. pour accepter** he didn't have to be asked twice *or* to have his arm twisted before saying yes; *Fam* **chauffer** *ou* **échauffer les oreilles à qn** to get on sb's nerves, to annoy sb

2 *(ouïe)* (sense of) hearing; **avoir l'o. fine** to have an acute sense of hearing; **avoir de l'o.** *ou* **l'o. musicale** to have a good ear for music; **avoir l'o. absolue** to have perfect pitch

3 *(pour écouter)* ear; **dresser** *ou* **tendre l'o.** to prick up one's ears; **écouter une conversation d'une o. distraite** to listen to a conversation with only half an ear; **écouter de toutes ses oreilles, être tout oreilles** to be all ears; **ouvrir ses oreilles toutes grandes** to listen very carefully; **ouvrez bien vos oreilles!** listen very carefully!; **venir** *ou* **parvenir aux oreilles de qn** to come to *or* to reach sb's ears; **l'histoire étant parvenue à mes oreilles, je lui téléphonai** when I got wind of the story, I called him/her; **dire** *ou* **souffler qch à l'o. de qn** *ou* **dans le creux de l'o. de qn** to whisper sth in sb's ear; **je n'en crois pas mes oreilles** I can't believe my ears *or* what I'm hearing; *Fam* **ça rentre par une o. et ça sort par l'autre** it goes in one ear and out the other; *Fam* **ce n'est pas tombé dans l'o. d'un sourd!** it hasn't fallen on deaf ears!

4 *(d'une cocotte)* handle; *(d'un écrou)* wing; *(d'une casquette)* earflap; **fauteuil à oreilles** wing chair

5 *Journ* position to right/left of headline

oreiller [ɔreje] NM pillow; **sur l'o.** in bed; **confidences sur l'o.** pillow talk

oreillette [ɔrɛjɛt] NF **1** *Anat* auricle **2** *(d'une casquette)* earflap; **fauteuil à oreillettes** wing chair **3** *(d'un baladeur)* earphone

oreillette-micro [ɔrɛjɛtmikro] *(pl* **oreillettes-micros)** NF wireless headset

oreillon [ɔrɛjɔ̃] NM **1** *Archéol* ear-piece, cheek-piece **2** *Anat & Zool* tragus

• **oreillons** NMPL *Méd* mumps; **avoir les oreillons** to have (the) mumps

Orénoque [ɔrenɔk] NM **l'O.** the Orinoco

ores [ɔr] **d'ores et déjà** ADV already

orfèvre [ɔrfɛvr] NM **1** *(artisan qui travaille ▸ l'or)* goldsmith; *(▸ l'argent)* silversmith **2** *(locution)* **être o. en la matière** to be an expert in the matter

orfèvrerie [ɔrfɛvrəri] NF **1** *(métier ▸ de l'or)* goldsmithing, gold work; *(▸ de l'argent)* silversmithing, silver work; **l'o.** *(produits ▸ en or)* gold plate; *(▸ en argent)* silver plate **2** *(boutique ▸ d'objets d'or)* goldsmith's *Br* shop *or Am* store; *(▸ d'objets d'argent)* silversmith's *Br* shop *or Am* store

orfraie [ɔrfrɛ] NF white-tailed eagle

organdi [ɔrgɑ̃di] NM organdie; **d'o., en o.** organdie

organe [ɔrgan] NM **1** *Anat* organ; **organes génitaux** *ou* **sexuels** genitals, genitalia; **organes vocaux** *ou* **de la parole** speech *or* vocal organs; *Méd* **o. cible** receptor; **organes des sens** sense organs

2 *(voix)* voice; **avoir un bel o.** to have a fine voice

3 *Tech* part, component; **organes de commande** controls; **organes de transmission** transmission system; *Ordinat* **o. d'entrée** input unit; *Ordinat* **o. périphérique** peripheral device

4 *(institution)* organ; **les organes de l'État** the apparatus of the state; **o. de presse** newspaper, publication; **les organes de presse** the press

5 *(porte-parole, publication)* mouthpiece, organ; **l'o. officiel du parti** the official organ *or* mouthpiece of the party

6 *(instrument)* medium, vehicle; **o. de publicité** advertising medium

organigramme [ɔrganigram] NM **1** *(structure)* organization *or* organizational chart, organigram **2** *Ordinat (de programmation)* flow chart *or* diagram; **o. de production** production flow chart

organique [ɔrganik] ADJ organic

organiquement [ɔrganikmɑ̃] ADV organically

organisateur, -trice [ɔrganizatœr, -tris] ADJ *Biol* organizing *(avant n)*

NM,F organizer; *(d'une rencontre sportive)* promoter, organizer; **o. de conférences/de congrès** conference organizer; **o. d'événements** event co-ordinator *or* organizer; **o. de mariages** wedding planner; **o. de voyages** tour operator

organisation [ɔrganizasjɔ̃] NF **1** *(organisme)* organization; **O. de l'alimentation et l'agriculture** Food and Agriculture Organization; *Hist* **O. de l'armée secrète** Secret Army Organization *(right-wing group opposed to Algerian independence)*; **O. de l'aviation civile internationale** International Civil Aviation Authority; **O. de coopération et de développement économique** Organization for Economic Cooperation and Development; **O.**

européenne de coopération économique Organization for European Economic Cooperation; **o. gouvernementale** governmental organization; **o. humanitaire** aid agency; **o. internationale** international organization *or* agency; **O. internationale de normalisation** International Standards Organization; **O. internationale du travail** International Labour Organization; **O. de libération de la Palestine** Palestine Liberation Organization; **O. maritime internationale** International Maritime Organization; **O. mondiale du commerce** World Trade Organization; **O. mondiale de la santé** World Health Organization; **O. des Nations unies** United Nations Organization; **O. des Nations unies pour le développement industriel** United Nations Industrial Development Organization; **O. des Nations unies pour l'éducation, la science et la culture** United Nations Educational, Scientific and Cultural Organization; **O. de la navigation maritime consultative et intergouvernementale** Intergovernmental Maritime Consultative Organization; **o. non gouvernementale** non-governmental organization; **o. patronale** employers' organization *or* association; **O. des pays exportateurs de pétrole** Organization of Petroleum Exporting Countries; **o. de solidarité** aid organization; **o. de solidarité internationale** international aid organization; **o. syndicale** trade union; **O. du traité de l'Atlantique Nord** North Atlantic Treaty Organization; **o. de travailleurs** workers' organization; **O. de l'unité africaine** Organization of African Unity

2 *(mise sur pied ▸ d'une fête, d'une réunion, d'un service, d'une manifestation)* organization; *(▸ d'un attentat)* organization, planning; **l'o. du temps de travail** the organization of working hours; **o. d'événements** event management

3 *(structure ▸ d'un discours, d'une association, d'un système)* organization, structure; *(▸ du travail)* organization; *Ordinat* **o. des données** data organization; *Com* **o. scientifique du travail** organization and methods, time and motion studies

4 *(méthode)* organization; **avoir de l'o.** to be organized; **ne pas avoir d'o.** to be disorganized

5 *Biol (du corps humain)* structure

organisationnel, -elle [ɔrganizasjɔnel] **ADJ** organizational

organisatrice [ɔrganizatris] *voir* **organisateur**

organisé, -e [ɔrganize] **ADJ 1** *(regroupé ▸ consommateurs, groupe)* organized

2 *(aménagé)* **bien/mal o.** well-/badly-organized

3 *(méthodique ▸ personne)* organized, well-organized, methodical

4 *Biol* **êtres organisés** organisms

organiser [3] [ɔrganize] **VT 1** *(mettre sur pied ▸ gén)* to organize; *Mil (attaque)* to plan **2** *(agencer ▸ association, journée, tâche)* to organize; *(▸ temps, emploi du temps)* to organize, to plan; **le service est organisé en plusieurs sections** the department is organized into several divisions; **j'ai organisé mon emploi du temps de façon à pouvoir partir plus tôt** I've organized *or* planned my schedule so that I can leave earlier

VPR s'organiser 1 *(se préparer)* to be planned; **un voyage, ça s'organise longtemps à l'avance** trips have to be organized *or* planned well in advance **2** *(personne)* to get (oneself) organized, to organize oneself; **il suffit de s'o.** all you need is some organization; **la société s'est vite organisée en classes sociales** society rapidly became organized into social classes

organiseur [ɔrganizœr] **NM** *(agenda, logiciel)* organizer; **o. électronique** electronic organizer

organisme [ɔrganism] **NM 1** *Biol (animal, végétal)* organism; *(humain)* body, organism; **les réactions de l'o.** bodily reactions; **c'est mauvais pour l'o.** it's bad for your health *or* for you; **o. génétiquement modifié** genetically modified organism

2 *(organisation)* organization, body; **o. d'aide** aid organization; **o. de charité** charity (organization); **o. de contrôle** *ou* **de surveillance** watchdog; **o. de crédit** credit organization *or* institution; **o. de défense des consommateurs** consumer organization; **o. de gestion** management body; **o. international** international organization; **o. de normalisation** standards committee; *Fin* **o. de placement collectif** collective investment scheme; *Fin* **o. de placement collectif en valeurs mobilières** *Br* ≃ unit trust, *Am* ≃ mutual fund; **o. professionnel** professional body

organiste [ɔrganist] **NMF** organist

organoleptique [ɔrganɔleptik] **ADJ** organoleptic

orgasme [ɔrgasm] **NM** orgasm

orge [ɔrʒ] **NF** barley

NM barley; **o. mondé/perlé** hulled/pearl barley

orgeat [ɔrʒa] **NM** orgeat

orgelet [ɔrʒəle] **NM** sty, stye

orgiaque [ɔrʒjak] **ADJ** orgiastic

orgie [ɔrʒi] **NF 1** *(débauche)* orgy; **faire une o.** to have an orgy; *Fig* **j'ai fait une o. de foie gras** I gorged myself on foie gras **2** *(abondance)* riot, profusion; **une o. de roses** a profusion of roses; **une o. de bleus et de rouges** a riot of blues and reds

orgue [ɔrg] **NM 1** *Mus* organ; **jouer de l'o.** to play the organ; **o. électrique/électronique/de chœur** electric/electronic/choir organ; **o. de Barbarie** barrel organ; **o. à plein jeu** full organ; **buffet d'o.** organ case; **grand o.** great organ; **point d'o.** pause

• **orgues NFPL 1** *Mus* organ; **les grandes orgues de la cathédrale** the great organ of the cathedral; *Fig* **faire donner les grandes orgues** to be pompous **2** *Géol* columnar structure *or* structures; **orgues de basalte** basalt columns

orgueil [ɔrgœj] **NM 1** *(fierté)* pride **2** *(amour-propre)* pride; **il a trop d'o. pour faire des excuses** he's too proud *or* he has too much pride to apologize; **c'est de l'o. mal placé** it's just misplaced pride; **gonflé** *ou* **bouffi d'o.** puffed up *or* bursting with pride **3** *(sujet de fierté)* pride; **j'étais l'o. de ma mère** I was my mother's pride and joy; **le "Nautilus", o. de la flotte** the "Nautilus", the pride of the fleet

orgueilleuse [ɔrgœjøz] *voir* **orgueilleux**

orgueilleusement [ɔrgœjøzmɑ̃] **ADV 1** *(avec arrogance)* proudly, arrogantly **2** *(avec fierté)* proudly

orgueilleux, -euse [ɔrgœjø, -øz] **ADJ 1** *(arrogant)* conceited, arrogant **2** *(fier ▸ personne)* proud **3** *Littéraire (majestueux ▸ démarche, navire)* proud

NM,F 1 *(prétentieux)* arrogant *or* conceited person **2** *(fier)* proud person

oriel [ɔrjel] **NM** oriel (window), bay window

orient [ɔrjɑ̃] **NM 1** *(est)* east, orient; **parfum/tapis d'o.** oriental scent/carpet; *Littéraire* **génie à son o.** rising *or* budding genius

2 *Géog* **l'O.** the East *or* Orient; **en O.** in the East

3 *(d'une perle)* orient

4 le Grand O. *(maçonnique)* the Grand Orient

orientable [ɔrjɑ̃tabl] **ADJ 1** *(antenne, rétroviseur)* adjustable **2** *(lampe)* rotating, swivel *(avant n)*

oriental, -e, -aux, -ales [ɔrjɑ̃tal, -o] **ADJ 1** *Géog* eastern, east *(avant n)*; **la plaine orientale** the eastern plain **2** *(de l'Orient ▸ art, cuisine, civilisation)* oriental, eastern; *(langue)* oriental

NM,F Oriental, Easterner

• **à l'orientale ADV** in the oriental style

orientalisme [ɔrjɑ̃talism] **NM** orientalism

orientaliste [ɔrjɑ̃talist] **ADJ** orientalist

NMF orientalist

orientateur, -trice [ɔrjɑ̃tatœr, -tris] *voir* **orienteur, -euse NM,F 1**

orientation [ɔrjɑ̃tasjɔ̃] **NF 1** *(direction ▸ d'une enquête, de recherches)* direction, orientation; *(▸ d'un mouvement)* orientation; *(▸ d'une politique)* thrust; **l'o. de notre entreprise doit changer** our firm must adopt a new outlook; **o. stratégique d'une société** corporate strategic orientation; **o. politique** *(d'un journal, d'une personne)* political leanings *or* tendencies; *(d'un parti)* political direction

2 *Scol (conseil ▸ pour des études)* academic counselling; *(▸ vers un métier)* careers guidance; *(direction ▸ des études)* course; *(▸ du métier)* career; **choisir une o.** to choose a course of study; **o. en fin de cinquième** = determination of future course of studies at the end of one's second year; **o. professionnelle** careers advice *or* guidance

3 *(position ▸ d'un édifice)* direction; **l'o. plein sud de l'appartement est un de ses principaux atouts** one of the *Br* flat's *or Am* apartment's main assets is that it faces due south

4 *(positionnement ▸ d'un faisceau, d'une lampe)* directing; *(▸ d'un rétroviseur)* adjustment; *(▸ d'une grue, d'une antenne)* positioning; **o. d'un canon** training of a gun; **à o. libre** free-moving, adjustable; *Aut* **o. de la roue** wheel alignment, tracking

5 *(aptitude)* **avoir le sens de l'o.** to have a good sense of direction; **course** *ou* **parcours d'o.** orienteering course

6 *Biol & Math* orientation

7 *(tendance)* **o. de la Bourse** stock market trend; *Mktg* **o. clientèle** customer orientation; **o. économique** economic direction; *Mktg* **o. marché** market orientation *or* trend; **o. du marché à la baisse/hausse** downward/upward market trend

orienté, -e [ɔrjɑ̃te] **ADJ 1** *(positionné)* **o. à l'ouest** *(édifice)* facing west, with a western aspect; *(radar)* directed towards the west; **local bien/mal o.** well-/badly-positioned premises

2 *(idéologiquement ▸ discours, journal)* biased, slanted; **analyse orientée à droite** analysis with a right-wing bias

3 *Scol* **élève bien/mal o.** pupil who has taken the right/wrong academic advice

4 *Math* **surface orientée** oriented surface

5 *Géog (carte)* orientated

6 *Bourse* **o. à la baisse** *(marché)* bearish, falling; **o. à la hausse** *(marché)* bullish, rising

7 *Ordinat* **o. bloc** block-orientated; **o. ligne** line-orientated; **o. objet** object-orientated; **o. problème** problem-orientated; **o. procédure** procedure-orientated

orienter [3] [ɔrjɑ̃te] **VT 1** *(antenne, haut-parleur, spot, téléscope)* to direct, to turn, to point; *(rétroviseur)* to adjust, to position; *(plante)* to position; *(canon, fusil)* to train (**vers** on); **orientez votre tente à l'est** pitch your tent so that it faces east; **o. un faisceau vers qch** to direct a beam towards sth; **oriente ton flash vers le plafond** point *or* turn your flashlight towards the ceiling; **la chambre est orientée plein nord** the bedroom faces due north

2 *(mettre sur une voie)* **o. vers** *(enquête, recherches)* to direct *or* to orientate towards; *(discussion)* to turn round to; *(passant)* to direct to; **il m'a demandé où était la gare mais je l'ai mal orienté** he asked where the station was, but I misdirected him; **on l'a orienté vers un spécialiste** he was referred to a specialist; **j'ai essayé d'o. la conversation sur toi** I tried to bring *or* to steer the conversation round to you; **o. ses études vers qch** to direct one's studies towards sth; **elle a été orientée vers une école technique** she was advised to go to a technical school; *Scol* **on l'a mal/bien orienté** he was given the wrong/right academic advice

3 *(rendre partial ▸ discours)* to give a bias *or* a slant to; **ses cours sont politiquement orientés** his/her lectures are coloured by his/her political convictions

4 *(carte, plan, bâtiment)* to orientate

5 *Math* to orient; **o. une droite** to indicate the direction of a straight line

VPR s'orienter 1 *(se repérer)* to take one's bearings; **j'ai toujours du mal à m'o.** I've got no sense of direction; **s'o. sur l'étoile polaire** to take one's bearings from the polar star **2 s'o. vers** *(sujet: enquête, recherches)* to be directed towards; *(sujet: discussion)* to turn round to; *(sujet: parti, entreprise)* to move towards; *(sujet: étudiant)* to turn to; **il s'oriente vers une carrière commerciale** he's got his sights set on a career in sales; **s'o. vers la vente de produits écologiques** to specialize in the sale of environmentally-friendly products

orienteur, -euse [ɔrjɑ̃tœr, -øz] **NM,F 1** *Scol* academic counsellor **2** *(conseiller professionnel)* careers adviser, careers guidance officer

ADJ M officier o. interviewing officer

NM *(instrument)* orientator

orifice [ɔrifis] **NM 1** *(ouverture)* hole, opening; *(d'un puits, d'une galerie)* mouth; *Tech* port **2** *Anat* orifice **3** *Aut* **o. d'admission** intake port, inlet port; **o. de remplissage** filling hole; **o. d'air** air port; **o. d'alimentation** feed hole; **o. d'arrivée d'essence** petrol port; **o. d'écoulement d'huile** oil drain hole; **o. de sortie** outlet port

oriflamme [ɔriflam] NF **1** *(bannière d'apparat)* banner, standard **2** *Hist* oriflamme

origami [ɔrigami] NM origami

origan [ɔrigɑ̃] NM *Bot & Culin* oregano

originaire [ɔriʒinɛr] ADJ **1** *(natif)* **être o. de** *(personne)* to be a native of; *(coutume, plat)* to originate from; **ma mère est o. de Paris** my mother was born in *or* comes from Paris; **animal/plante o. des pays tropicaux** animal/plant native to tropical countries **2** *(originel)* innate, inherent; *(membre)* original, founding

originairement [ɔriʒinɛrmɑ̃] ADV originally, at first

original, -e, -aux, -ales [ɔriʒinal, -o] ADJ **1** *(nouveau ▸ architecture, idée, système)* original, novel; *(▸ cadeau, film, style, personne)* original; **il n'y a rien d'o. dans son dernier roman** there's nothing original in his/her latest novel **2** *(excentrique ▸ personne)* odd, eccentric **3** *(d'origine ▸ document, manuscrit)* original

NM,F *(excentrique)* eccentric, character

NM **1** *(d'une œuvre)* original; *(d'un document, d'une disquette)* original *or* master (copy); *(d'un texte)* top copy, original; *(d'un objet, d'un personnage)* original; **copier qch d'après l'o.** to copy sth from the original; **il ne possède que des originaux** he owns only original works of art **2** *(texte à traduire)* original; **je préfère presque la traduction à l'o.** I like the translation almost more than the original

> Do not confuse with **originel**.

originalité [ɔriʒinalite] NF **1** *(caractère)* originality, novelty; **cet artiste manque d'o.** there is nothing new *or* original in this artist's work **2** *(extravagance)* eccentricity; **ses originalités la mettaient au ban de notre petite société** her strange *or* odd ways excluded her from our little group **3** *(nouveauté)* original feature; **cette robe est une des originalités de notre collection** this dress is one of the outstanding features of our collection

origine [ɔriʒin] NF **1** *(cause première ▸ d'un feu, d'une maladie, d'une querelle)* origin; **si nous remontons à l'o. du scandale** if we go back to the origin of the scandal; **avoir son o. dans, tirer son o. de** to have one's origins in, to originate in; **avoir qch pour o.** to be caused by sth; **la guerre a-t-elle eu pour o. l'assassinat de l'archiduc?** was the archduke's assassination the cause of the war?; **être à l'o. d'un projet de loi** *(personne)* to be behind a bill; **ces erreurs judiciaires ont été à l'o. du projet de loi** these miscarriages of justice were the impetus for the bill; **être à l'o. d'une querelle** *(personne)* to be behind *or* to be the cause of an argument; *(malentendu)* to be at the origin *or* at the root of an argument; **symptômes d'o. cardiaque** symptoms due to heart problems

2 *(début)* origin, beginning; **les origines de la civilisation** the origins of civilization; **les vêtements, des origines à nos jours** *(dans un livre, dans un musée)* clothes, from their origins to the present day; **dès l'o.** from the (very) beginning, from the outset; **dès l'o., il y eut un malentendu** there was a misunderstanding right from the very start; **le travail du bronze, dès l'o., fut ornemental** bronze-working had a decorative function from its inception

3 *(source ▸ d'un terme)* origin, root; *(▸ d'une tradition)* origin; *(▸ d'un produit manufacturé)* origin; **tirer son o. de qch** to originate from sth, to have its origins in sth; **le mot tire son o. du latin** the word originates *or* derives from the Latin; **l'o. de cette coutume est...** the custom has its origins in...; **la police connaît l'o. des appels** the police know who made the calls; **quelle est l'o. de ces pêches?** where are these peaches from?

4 *(d'une personne)* origin; **il ne sait rien de ses origines** he doesn't know anything about his origins *or* where he comes from; **elle fait remonter ses origines à Louis-Philippe** she traces her origins back to Louis-Philippe; **d'o. modeste** of humble origin *or* birth; **d'o. espagnole** of Spanish origin; **il a des origines anglaises** he is of English extraction *or* has English origins; **la colonie devait son o. aux baleiniers** the colony was founded by *or* owed its origins to whalers

5 *Géom* origin; *Math* **(point) o.** zero point

• **à l'origine** ADV originally, initially, at the beginning; **à l'o., je voulais écrire une chanson** I started off intending to *or* originally I wanted to write a song

• **d'origine** ADJ *(pays)* of origin; *(couleur, emballage, nom, monnaie)* original; **ma voiture a encore son moteur d'o.** my car has still got its original engine; **vins d'o.** vintage wines

originel, -elle [ɔriʒinɛl] ADJ **1** *(primitif ▸ innocence)* original **2** *(premier)* original; *(cause)* original, primary; **sens o. d'un mot** original *or* primary meaning of a word

> Do not confuse with the French adjective **original**.

originellement [ɔriʒinɛlmɑ̃] ADV *(dès l'origine)* from the (very) start *or* beginning, from the outset; *(au début)* originally, at first

orignal, -aux [ɔriɲal, -o] NM *Zool* moose

oripeaux [ɔripo] NMPL *Littéraire (vêtements)* tawdry rags

ORL [oɛrɛl] *Méd* NMF *(abrév* **oto-rhino-laryngologiste)** ENT specialist

NF *(abrév* **oto-rhino-laryngologie)** ENT

orléaniste [ɔrleanist] *Hist* ADJ Orleanist

NMF Orleanist

Orlon® [ɔrlɔ̃] NM Orlon®

ormaie [ɔrmɛ] NF elm grove

orme [ɔrm] NM **1** *(arbre)* elm (tree); **o. blanc, o. de (s) montagne(s)** wych-elm; **o. champêtre** *ou* **à petites feuilles** common elm, English elm; **maladie des ormes** Dutch elm disease **2** *(bois)* elm (wood)

ormeau[1]**, -x** [ɔrmo] NM *Bot* young elm (tree)

ormeau[2]**, -x** [ɔrmo] NM *Zool (mollusque)* earshell, ormer, abalone

orné, -e [ɔrne] ADJ *(style)* ornate, florid; **lettre ornée** illuminated letter

ornement [ɔrnəmɑ̃] NM **1** *(objet)* ornament

2 *Beaux-Arts* embellishment, adornment; **sans o.** plain, unadorned; **architecture surchargée d'ornements** ornate architecture; **plafonds riches en ornements** ceilings rich in ornament *or* ornamentation

3 *Mus* ornament

4 *Rel* **ornements sacerdotaux** vestments

• **d'ornement** ADJ *(plantes, poupée)* ornamental; *Mus* **notes d'o.** grace notes, ornaments

ornemental, -e, -aux, -ales [ɔrnəmɑ̃tal, -o] ADJ *(motif)* ornamental, decorative; *(plante)* ornamental

ornementation [ɔrnəmɑ̃tasjɔ̃] NF ornamentation

ornementer **[3]** [ɔrnəmɑ̃te] VT to ornament; **o. qch de qch** *ou* **avec qch** to ornament *or* to decorate sth with sth

orner **[3]** [ɔrne] VT **1** *(décorer ▸ sujet: personne)* to decorate; *(▸ sujet: dessin, plante, ruban)* to adorn, to decorate, to embellish; **des bouquets ornaient la table** the table was decorated with bunches of flowers; **o. avec qch** *ou* **de qch** to decorate with sth; **sa chambre était ornée de trophées de guerre** his/her room was adorned *or* decorated with war trophies; **o. une robe de dentelle** to trim a dress with lace; **sabre orné de joyaux** sword set with jewels **2** *(enjoliver ▸ texte)* to embellish; *(▸ vérité)* to adorn, to embellish; *Littéraire* **o. son esprit** to enrich one's mind

ornière [ɔrnjɛr] NF **1** *(trou)* rut **2** *Fig (routine)* **suivre l'o.** to get into a rut; **sortir de l'o.** to get out of a rut **3** *Fig (impasse)* **tirer qn de l'o.** to help sb out of a difficulty; **sortir de l'o.** to get oneself out of trouble

ornithologie [ɔrnitɔlɔʒi] NF ornithology

ornithologique [ɔrnitɔlɔʒik] ADJ ornithological

ornithologiste [ɔrnitɔlɔʒist], **ornithologue** [ɔrnitɔlɔg] NMF ornithologist

ornithorynque [ɔrnitɔrɛ̃k] NM *Zool* (duck-billed) platypus, *Spéc* ornithorynchus

orogène [ɔrɔʒɛn] NM *Géol* orogeny

orogenèse [ɔrɔʒənɛz], **orogénie** [ɔrɔʒeni] NF *Géol* orogenesis, orogeny

orogénique [ɔrɔʒenik] ADJ *Géol* orogenic, orogenetic

orographie [ɔrɔgrafi] NF *Géol* orography

oronge [ɔrɔ̃ʒ] NF *Bot* Caesar's mushroom; **fausse o.** fly agaric

orpaillage [ɔrpajaʒ] NM gold washing *or* panning

Orphée [ɔrfe] NPR *Myth* Orpheus

orphelin, -e [ɔrfəlɛ̃, -in] ADJ **1** *(enfant)* orphan *(avant n)*, orphaned; **être o. de père/de mère** to be fatherless/motherless, to have lost one's father/mother; **être o. de père et de mère** to have lost both one's parents, to be an orphan **2** *Typ* **ligne orpheline** orphan

NM,F orphan

• **orpheline** NF *Typ* orphan

• **orphelines** NFPL *très Fam (testicules)* balls, nuts, *Br* bollocks

orphelinat [ɔrfəlina] NM *(bâtiment)* orphanage; *(personnes)* orphans

orphéon [ɔrfeɔ̃] NM **1** *(fanfare)* band **2** *(chœur ▸ d'hommes)* male choir; *(▸ d'enfants)* (mixed) children's choir

orphéoniste [ɔrfeɔnist] NMF **1** *(d'une fanfare)* band member **2** *(chanteur ▸ adulte)* male singer *or* chorister; *(▸ enfant)* (little) chorister

orphie [ɔrfi] NF *Ich* garfish, needlefish

orphisme [ɔrfism] NM *Antiq & Beaux-Arts* Orphism

orpiment [ɔrpimɑ̃] NM *Minér* orpiment

orque [ɔrk] NF *Zool* killer whale

Orsay [ɔrsɛ] NM **le musée d'O.** = museum of 19th-century and early 20th-century art in Paris

ORSEC, Orsec [ɔrsɛk] ADJ *(abrév* **Organisation des secours) plan O.** = disaster contingency plan; **plan O.-Rad** = disaster contingency plan in case of nuclear accident

> **LE PLAN ORSEC**
>
> This scheme is set in motion whenever there is a major disaster in France, such as flooding or forest fires. Under the provisions of the scheme, the "préfet", or chief of police, is empowered to mobilize both public and private resources to deal with a civil emergency.

orteil [ɔrtɛj] NM toe; **gros o.** big toe; **petit o.** little toe

ORTF [oɛrteɛf] NM *Anciennement (abrév* **Office de radiodiffusion télévision française)** = former French broadcasting corporation

orthochromatique [ɔrtɔkrɔmatik] ADJ orthochromatic

orthodontie [ɔrtɔdɔ̃si] NF orthodontics *(singulier)*, dental orthopaedics *(singulier)*

orthodontique [ɔrtɔdɔ̃tik] ADJ orthodontic

orthodontiste [ɔrtɔdɔ̃tist] NMF orthodontist

orthodoxe [ɔrtɔdɔks] ADJ **1** *Rel* Orthodox **2** *Fig (méthode, pratique)* orthodox; **pas très** *ou* **peu o.** rather unorthodox

NMF **1** *Rel* person of orthodox beliefs; *(de l'Église orthodoxe)* member of the Orthodox church; **les orthodoxes** the Orthodox **2** *(disciple)* **les orthodoxes de...** the orthodox followers of...

orthodoxie [ɔrtɔdɔksi] NF orthodoxy

orthogénie [ɔrtɔʒeni] NF *Méd* birth control

orthogonal, -e, -aux, -ales [ɔrtɔgɔnal, -o] ADJ orthogonal

orthogonalement [ɔrtɔgɔnalmɑ̃] ADV orthogonally, at right angles

orthographe [ɔrtɔgraf] NF *(graphie)* spelling; *(règles)* spelling system, *Spéc* orthography; *(matière)* spelling, *Spéc* orthography; **il y a deux orthographes possibles** there are two ways of spelling it *or* two possible spellings; **je ne connais pas l'o. de ce mot** I don't know how to spell this word *or* how this word is spelt; **avoir une bonne/mauvaise o.** to be good/bad at spelling

orthographier **[9]** [ɔrtɔgrafje] VT to spell; **mal/bien orthographié** wrongly/correctly spelt; **savoir o.** to be good at spelling

VPR **s'orthographier comment s'orthographie votre nom?** how do you spell your name?; **son nom s'orthographie avec deux L** his/her name is spelt with two L's

orthographique [ɔrtɔgrafik] ADJ spelling *(avant n)*, orthographic

orthopédie [ɔrtɔpedi] NF orthopaedics *(singulier)*

orthopédique [ɔrtɔpedik] ADJ orthopaedic; **chaussures/semelles orthopédiques** orthopaedic shoes/built-up soles

orthopédiste [ɔrtɔpedist] NMF *(médecin)* orthopaedist; *(fabricant)* maker of orthopaedic apparatus

ADJ **chirurgien o.** orthopaedic surgeon

orthophonie [ɔrtɔfɔni] NF speech therapy

orthophoniste [ɔrtɔfɔnist] NMF speech therapist

orthoptie [ɔrtɔpsi] NF orthoptics *(singulier)*

orthoptiste [ɔrtɔptist] NMF orthoptist

ortie [ɔrti] NF *Bot* (stinging) nettle; **o. brûlante** stinging nettle

ortolan [ɔrtɔlɑ̃] NM *Orn* ortolan

orvet [ɔrvɛ] NM *Zool* slowworm, blindworm

oryx [ɔriks] NM *Zool* oryx

OS [oɛs] NM *(abrév* **ouvrier spécialisé***)* skilled worker

os [ɔs, *pl* o] NM **1** *Anat & Zool* bone; **j'ai de gros/petits os** I'm big-boned/small-boned; **il s'est coupé jusqu'à l'os** he cut himself (through) to the bone; **os de seiche** cuttlebone; **cuiller en os** bone spoon; *Fam* **jusqu'à l'os** totally[a], completely[a]; *Fig* **être gelé/trempé jusqu'aux os** to be frozen to the marrow/soaked to the skin; *Fig* **être pourri jusqu'à l'os** to be thoroughly corrupt; **il ne fera pas de vieux os!** he's not long for this world!; **elle est tellement maigre qu'on lui voit les os** she's a bag of bones; **c'est un sac** *ou* **paquet** *ou* **tas d'os** he's/she's a bag of bones, he's/she's just skin and bones; *très Fam* **il l'a eu dans l'os!** *(il n'a pas réussi)* he got egg on his face!; *(il s'est fait escroquer)* he's been had! **2** *Culin* bone; **viande avec os** meat on the bone; **viande sans os** meat off the bone, boned meat; **poulet sans os** boneless chicken, boned chicken; **os à moelle** marrowbone; **acheter du jambon à l'os** to buy ham off the bone; **donner un os à ronger à qn** to give sb sth to keep him/her quiet **3** *Fam (problème)* snag, hitch; **il y a un os** there's a snag *or* a hitch; **elle est tombée sur** *ou* **elle a trouvé un os** she hit a snag

> **-OS** SUFFIX
>
> The suffix **-os** has proved rather productive in French slang, especially in recent decades. It is used mostly to create adjectives and, more rarely, adverbs or nouns, by replacing the last letters of the word, eg:
>
> **rapidos** (from *rapidement*) quickly; **craignos** (from *craindre*) dodgy, hideous, crap; **nullos** useless idiot (from *nul*); **calmos!** (from *calme*) chill out!, take it easy!; **matos** (from *matériel*) gear, stuff

oscar [ɔskar] NM **1** *Cin* Oscar; **elle a reçu l'o. du meilleur second rôle** she won the Oscar for the best supporting role **2** *(récompense)* **l'o. de la meilleure publicité** the award for the best commercial

oscarisé, -e [ɔskarize] ADJ *Cin* Oscar-winning; **l'acteur o. pour 'Gladiator'** the actor who won an Oscar for 'Gladiator'

oscariser [3] [ɔskarize] VT *Cin* to award an Oscar to

OSCE [oɛssəe] NF *(abrév* **Organisation pour la sécurité et la coopération en Europe***)* OSCE

oscillant, -e [ɔsilɑ̃, -ɑ̃t] ADJ **1** *(qui balance)* oscillating

2 *(incertain)* oscillating, fluctuating

3 *Méd (fièvre)* irregular

4 *Élec (décharge)* oscillating

5 *Phys* **circuit o.** oscillating circuit

oscillateur [ɔsilatœr] NM oscillator

oscillation [ɔsilasjɔ̃] NF **1** *(balancement)* swaying, rocking; **les oscillations du téléphérique** the swaying *or* swinging of the cable car

2 *Fig (variation)* fluctuation, variation; **oscillations des prix** price variations; **oscillations saisonnières** seasonal fluctuations

3 *Élec & Phys* oscillation; **oscillations amorties/entretenues** damped/sustained oscillations

4 *Tech* vibration

oscillatoire [ɔsilatwar] ADJ oscillatory

osciller [3] [ɔsile] VI **1** *(bouger* ▸ *pendule, objet suspendu)* to oscillate, to swing, to sway; *(*▸ *branche, corde)* to sway, to swing; *(*▸ *arbre, statue)* to sway; *(*▸ *aiguille aimantée)* to flicker; *(*▸ *personne, tête, bateau)* to rock; **la brise faisait o. les roseaux** the reeds were swaying in the breeze; **le choc a fait o. les immeubles pendant de longues secondes** the buildings shook for several seconds under the impact of the blast; **le courant d'air fit o. la flamme** the flame was flickering in the draught **2** *(varier)* **o. entre** to vary *or* to fluctuate between; **o. entre deux options** to waver *or* to hesitate between two options **3** *Fin (marché)* to fluctuate

oscillogramme [ɔsilɔgram] NM oscillogram

oscillographe [ɔsilɔgraf] NM oscillograph; **o. cathodique** cathode ray tube

oscilloscope [ɔsilɔskɔp] NM oscilloscope

osé, -e [oze] ADJ **1** *(audacieux* ▸ *tentative)* bold, daring **2** *(choquant* ▸ *histoire)* risqué, racy **3** *(téméraire* ▸ *personne)* bold, intrepid

oseille [ozɛj] NF **1** *Bot & Culin* sorrel **2** *Fam (argent)* dough, *Br* dosh, *Am* bucks; **avoir de l'o.** to have bags *or* pots of money, to be loaded

oser [3] [oze] VT **1** *(avoir l'audace de)* **o. faire qch** to dare (to) do sth; **elle n'ose pas parler** she doesn't dare (to) speak, she daren't speak; **je voudrais qu'il vienne mais je n'ose l'espérer** I'd like him to come but I daren't hope *or* I don't dare hope that he will; **comment oses-tu répondre à ton père!** how dare you answer your father back!; **quand quelqu'un osait l'interrompre** if anybody dared to *or* was bold enough to interrupt him/her; *Littéraire* **o. qch** to dare sth

2 *(suggestion, réponse)* to risk; **ils furent trois à o. l'ascension** three of them risked the climb *or* were bold enough to climb

3 *(dans les tournures de politesse)* **j'ose croire/espérer que...** I trust/hope that...; **si j'ose dire** if I may say so; **si j'ose m'exprimer ainsi** if I may say so, if I may put it that way

4 *Suisse (avoir la permission de)* **est-ce que j'ose entrer?** may I come in?

USAGE ABSOLU **comment oses-tu!** how dare you!; **vous n'oseriez pas!** you wouldn't dare!; **il faut o. dans la vie!** one has to take risks in life!; **si j'osais, je l'inviterais chez moi** if I dared *or* if I were bold enough, I'd invite him/her over to my place; **il veut me parler? qu'il ose un peu!** he wants to talk to me? just let him dare!; **approchez si vous osez!** come over here if you dare!

oseraie [ozrɛ] NF osier bed, osiery

OSI [oɛsi] NF *(abrév* **organisation de solidarité internationale***)* international aid organization

osier [ozje] NM **1** *Bot* willow, osier; **brin d'o.** withy **2** *(matériau)* wicker, wickerwork; **chaise en o.** wicker *or* wickerwork *or* basketwork chair

Oslo [ɔslo] NM Oslo

osmonde [ɔsmɔ̃d] NF *Bot* osmund, osmunda; **o. royale** royal fern

osmose [ɔsmoz] NF **1** *Biol & Chim* osmosis **2** *Fig* osmosis; **une o. s'est produite entre les deux civilisations** the two civilizations have merged into one another

ossature [ɔsatyr] NF **1** *Anat (d'une personne)* frame, skeleton; *(du visage)* bone structure; **d'une o. puissante** powerfully built, of powerful build **2** *Constr (d'un avion, d'un immeuble)* frame, framework, skeleton; *(d'un pont)* main girders; **pont à o. métallique** bridge with a metal frame *or* framework **3** *(d'un discours)* framework, structure

osselet [ɔslɛ] NM **1** *Anat* ossicle; *Zool* knucklebone **2** *(jeu)* jack, knucklebone; **jouer aux osselets** to play jacks

ossements [ɔsmɑ̃] NMPL remains, bones

osseux, -euse [ɔsø, -øz] ADJ **1** *Anat* bone *(avant n)*, *Spéc* osseous

2 *Méd* **greffe osseuse** bone graft; **maladie osseuse** bone disease

3 *(aux os apparents)* bony

4 *Ich* **poissons o.** bony fish

ossification [ɔsifikasjɔ̃] NF ossification

ossifier [9] [ɔsifje] VT **1** *(transformer en os)* to ossify **2** *Fig Littéraire (rendre insensible)* to harden

VPR **s'ossifier 1** *Anat* to ossify **2** *Littéraire (sensibilité)* to harden

ossu, -e [ɔsy] ADJ *Littéraire* big-boned

ossuaire [ɔsɥɛr] NM ossuary

OST [oɛste] NF *Com (abrév* **organisation scientifique du travail***)* organization and methods, time and motion studies

ostensible [ɔstɑ̃sibl] ADJ conspicuous, open, clear; **avec un mépris o. pour les conventions** with open contempt for convention

> Il faut noter que le terme anglais **ostensible** est un faux ami. Il signifie **prétendu, apparent**.

ostensiblement [ɔstɑ̃sibləmɑ̃] ADV conspicuously, openly, clearly; **il manifesta o. son ennui** he made it quite clear that he was bored

> Il faut noter que le terme anglais **ostensibly** est un faux ami. Il signifie **prétendument, en apparence**.

ostensoir [ɔstɑ̃swar] NM monstrance, ostensory

ostentation [ɔstɑ̃tasjɔ̃] NF *(affectation, vanité)* ostentation; **avec o.** with ostentation, ostentatiously; **sans o.** without ostentation, unostentatiously; *Littéraire* **faire o. de qch** to parade sth

ostentatoire [ɔstɑ̃tatwar] ADJ ostentatious

ostéoarthrite [ɔsteɔartrit] NF *Méd* osteoarthritis

ostéoarthrose [ɔsteɔartroz] NF *Méd* osteoarthrosis

ostéoarticulaire [ɔsteɔartikylɛr] ADJ *Méd* joint *(avant n)*, *Spéc* osteoarticular; **douleurs ostéoarticulaires** joint pain

ostéologie [ɔsteɔlɔʒi] NF *Anat* osteology

ostéomyélite [ɔsteɔmjelit] NF *Méd* osteomyelitis

ostéopathe [ɔsteɔpat] NMF *Méd* osteopath

ostéoporose [ɔsteɔpɔroz] NF *Méd* osteoporosis

ostracisme [ɔstrasism] NM **1** *Antiq* ostracism **2** *(exclusion)* ostracism; **être victime d'o.** to be ostracized; **frapper qn d'o.** to ostracize sb

ostréicole [ɔstreikɔl] ADJ *(région)* oyster farming; *(industrie)* oyster *(avant n)*; **parc o.** oyster bed; **la région est l'un des plus grands parcs ostréicoles de la France** it is one of the largest oyster-producing regions in France

ostréiculteur, -trice [ɔstreikyltœr, -tris] NM,F oyster farmer, oysterman, *f* oysterwoman

ostréiculture [ɔstreikyltyr] NF oyster farming

ostrogot, -e, ostrogoth, -e [ɔstrogo, -ɔt] ADJ Ostrogothic

NM *Fam (homme malappris)* boor; **un drôle d'o.** a funny *or* a strange customer

• **Ostrogot, -e** NM,F Ostrogoth

> **-OT, -OTTE** SUFFIX
>
> When added to adjectives, this suffix has a DIMINUTIVE function, sometimes with an affectionate overtone, eg:
>
> **pâlot(te)** peaky, pale; **jeunot(te)** youngish, rather young; **fiérot(te)** proud; **vieillot(te)** old-fashioned

otage [ɔtaʒ] NM hostage; **prendre qn en o.** to take sb hostage

otalgie [ɔtalʒi] NF *Méd* otalgia

OTAN, Otan [ɔtɑ̃] NF *(abrév* **Organisation du traité de l'Atlantique Nord***)* NATO

otarie [ɔtari] NF *Zool* sea lion; **o. à fourrure** fur seal

OTASE [ɔtaz] NF *(abrév* **Organisation du traité de l'Asie du Sud-Est***)* SEATO

ôter [3] [ote] VT **1** *(retirer)* to take off, to remove (from); *(vêtement)* to take off; *(tache)* to remove, to get out; *(assiettes)* to clear away; **ôtez votre veste** take your jacket off; **ô. des épingles d'un chignon** to take hairpins out of *or* to remove hairpins from a bun; **ôte tes pieds du fauteuil** take *or* get your feet off the armchair; **ô. son masque** to take off *or* to remove one's mask; *Fig* to unmask oneself; **ôte-moi d'un doute, tu ne vas pas accep-**

ter! wait a minute, you're not actually going to say yes!; **cela n'ôte rien à sa valeur/à notre amitié** that in no way detracts from its value/from our friendship

2 *(mettre hors de portée)* to take away; **ô. qch à qn** to take sth away from sb; **personne n'a pensé à lui ô. son arme** nobody thought to take his/her weapon (away) from him/her; **ô. un enfant à ses parents** to take a child away from its parents; *Fig* **ô. le pain de la bouche à qn** to take the bread out of sb's mouth

3 *(supprimer)* to remove (from); **un nouveau produit chimique a ôté à l'eau son mauvais goût** a new chemical removed the bad taste from the water; **ô. à qn l'envie de faire qch** to deprive sb of all desire of doing sth; **ô. la vie à qn** to take sb's life; *Fig* **cela m'ôte un poids** that's a weight off my mind; **son attitude m'a ôté mes dernières illusions** his/her attitude rid me of my last illusions; **on ne m'ôtera pas de l'idée que...** I can't help thinking that...; **cela lui a ôté l'appétit** it has taken away his/her appetite; **cela lui a ôté toute sa force** it has drained him/her of all his/her strength

4 *Math* to take away; **20 ôté de 100 égale 80** 20 (taken away) from 100 leaves 80

VPR s'ôter 1 *(s'enlever)* to come off, to be removed; **ces bottes s'ôtent facilement** these boots are easy to take off **2 elle ne peut pas s'ô. de l'idée que...** she can't get it out of her head that...; **ôte-toi cette idée de la tête** get that idea out of your head **3 ôte-toi de là (que je m'y mette)** budge up (for me); **ôtez-vous de là, vous gênez le passage** move, you're in the way; *Fig* **ôte-toi de mon soleil** get out of my way

otique [ɔtik] **ADJ** *Anat* otic

otite [ɔtit] **NF** *Méd* earache, *Spéc* otitis

OTM [oteɛm] **NM** *Com (abrév* **opérateur de transport multimodal***)* multi-modal operator

otologie [ɔtɔlɔʒi] **NF** *Méd* otology

otoplastie [ɔtɔplasti] **NF** *Méd* otoplasty

oto-rhino [ɔtɔrino] *(pl* **oto-rhinos***)* **NMF** *Fam* ear, nose and throat specialist

oto-rhino-laryngologie [ɔtɔrinɔlarɛ̃gɔlɔʒi] **NF** otorhinolaryngology

oto-rhino-laryngologiste [ɔtɔrinɔlarɛ̃gɔlɔʒist] *(pl* **oto-rhino-laryngologistes***)* **NMF** ear, nose and throat specialist, *Spéc* otorhinolaryngologist

otoscope [ɔtɔskɔp] **NM** otoscope, auriscope

OTSI *(abrév écrite* **Office du tourisme-syndicat d'initiative***)* tourist office

Ottawa [ɔtawa] **NM** Ottawa

-otte [-ɔt] *voir* **-ot**

ottoman, -e [ɔtɔmɑ̃, -an] **ADJ** Ottoman

NM *Tex* ottoman *(rib)*

• **Ottoman, -e NM,F** Ottoman

• **ottomane NF** *(siège)* ottoman *(seat)*

ou [u] **CONJ 1** *(indiquant une alternative ou une équivalence)* or; **le rouge ou le bleu, peu importe** red or blue, it doesn't matter which; **tu viens ou quoi?** are you coming or not?; **tu peux venir aujourd'hui ou demain** you can come (either) today or tomorrow; **que tu le veuilles ou non** whether you like it or not; **c'est l'un ou l'autre** it's one or the other; **le patronyme ou nom de famille** the patronymic or surname **2** *(indiquant une approximation)* or; **ils étaient cinq ou six** there were five or six of them **3** *(indiquant la conséquence)* or (else); **rends-le moi, ou ça ira très mal** give it back, or (else) there'll be trouble

• **ou (bien)... ou (bien) CONJ** either... or; **ou c'est lui ou c'est moi!** it's either him or me!; **ou bien tu viens et tu es aimable, ou bien tu restes chez toi!** either you come along and be nice, or you stay at home!

où [u] **PRON RELATIF 1** *(dans l'espace)* where; **la maison où j'habite** the house I live in *or* where I live; **le pays où je suis né** the country where I was born; **nous cherchons un village où passer nos vacances** we're looking for a village where we can spend our holidays; **pose-le là où tu l'as trouvé** put it back where you found it; **j'irai où vous voudrez** I'll go where(ever) you wish; **partout où vous irez** everywhere you go; **d'où j'étais, je voyais la cathédrale** from where I was, I could see the cathedral; **le pays d'où je viens** the country which *or* where I come from; **les villes par où nous passerons** the towns which we will go through

2 *(dans le temps)* **le jour où je suis venu** the day (that) I came; **à la seconde où elle est entrée** the second (that) she came in; **à l'époque où...** in the days when...

3 *Fig* **là où je ne vous suis plus, c'est lorsque vous dites...** the bit where I lose track is when you say...; **c'est une spécialité où il excelle** it's a field in which he excels; **dans l'état où elle est** in her state, in the state she is; **au prix où elle est payée, elle refuse de travailler le soir** she refuses to work nights for the money she gets; **au prix où c'est** at that price; **à l'allure où tu vas** (at) the speed you're going; **au point où nous en sommes** (at) the point we've reached

ADV RELATIF 1 *(dans l'espace)* where; **je vais où je veux** I go where *or* wherever I please; **où que vous alliez** wherever you go; **où que vous soyez** wherever you are; **d'où que tu viennes** wherever you come from; **par où que tu passes** whichever route you take, whichever way you go

2 *Fig* **où je ne le comprends pas, c'est lorsque...** where I don't understand him is when...

ADV INTERROGATIF where; **où habite-t-il?** where does he live?; **où vas-tu?** where are you going?; **d'où viens-tu?** where have you come from?; **d'où viens-tu en Angleterre?** whereabouts are you from in England?; **par où voulez-vous passer?** which way do you want to go?, which route do you want to take?; **par où commencer?** where to begin?, where should I begin?; **par où est-il passé?** which way did he go?; **jusqu'où les a-t-il suivis?** how far did he follow them?; **où en êtes-vous?** how far have you got (with it)?; **où voulez-vous en venir?** what are you trying to say?; **dites-moi vers où il est allé** tell me which direction he went in; **je me demande où je l'ai mis** I wonder where I put it

• **d'où CONJ d'où on conclut que...** which leads us *or* one to the conclusion that...; **d'où il suit que...** from which it follows that...; **je ne savais pas qu'il était déjà arrivé, d'où ma surprise** I didn't know that he'd already arrived, which is why I was so surprised; **d'où sa tristesse** hence his/her sadness

OUA [oya] **NF** *(abrév* **Organisation de l'unité africaine***)* OAU

ouache [waʃ] **NF** *Can* bear's den

ouah [wa] **ONOMAT o.! o.!** *(chien)* woof! woof!

ouailles [waj] **NFPL** *Littéraire ou Hum* flock

ouais [wɛ] **EXCLAM** *Fam* yeah!; *(sceptique)* oh yeah?

ouananiche [wananiʃ] **NF** *Can Zool* Atlantic salmon

ouaouaron [wawarɔ̃] **NM** *Can Zool* bullfrog

ouate [wat] **NF 1** *(coton)* cotton wool **2** *Tex* wadding, padding; **un manteau doublé d'o.** a quilted coat **3** *Fig* **l'o.** *ou* **la o. des nuages** fleecy clouds; **avoir été élevé dans la o.** to have been brought up in cotton wool

ouaté, -e [wate] **ADJ 1** *(doublé)* quilted **2** *(assourdi)* muffled **3** *(douillet)* cocooned

ouater **[3]** [wate] **VT 1** *(vêtement)* to quilt; *(couverture)* to wad, to pad **2** *Littéraire (estomper)* to muffle

ouatine [watin] **NF** quilting (material)

ouatiné, -e [watine] **ADJ** *(tissu)* quilted

ouatiner **[3]** [watine] **VT** to quilt

oubli [ubli] **NM 1** *(fait de ne pas se rappeler)* forgetting, neglecting; **l'o. d'un nom sur une liste peut avoir de graves conséquences** leaving a name off a list can have serious consequences; **l'o. d'un accent sur un mot coûte un point** forgetting *or* neglecting to put an accent on a word will lose you one point

2 *(lacune)* omission; **page 45, il y a un o.** there's an omission on page 45; **il y a beaucoup d'oublis dans sa liste** he/she left a lot of items off his/her list, there are a lot of gaps in his/her list; **réparer un o.** to rectify an omission

3 *(trou de mémoire)* oversight, lapse of memory; **ce n'est qu'un o.** it's just an oversight

4 *(isolement)* **l'o.** oblivion; **arracher qch à** *ou* **tirer qch de l'o.** to snatch *or* to rescue sth from oblivion; **tomber dans l'o.** to sink into oblivion

5 *(consolation)* **l'o. viendra avec le temps** time is a great healer

6 *Littéraire (indifférence)* **l'o. de soi** selflessness, self-denial; **pratiquer l'o. des injures** to forgive and forget

oublier **[10]** [ublije] **VT 1** *(ne pas se remémorer* ▸ *nom, rue, date)* to forget; **j'ai oublié son nom** I've forgotten his/her name, his/her name has slipped my mind; **n'oublie pas le rendez-vous** don't forget (that) you have an appointment; **mon Dieu, le dentiste, je l'ai oublié!** God, the dentist, I'd forgotten all about him!; **o. son texte** to forget one's lines; **n'oublie pas que c'est son anniversaire** remember *or* don't forget that it's his/her birthday; **o. où/quand/qui...** to forget where/when/who...; **o. de faire qch** to forget to do sth; *Hum* **il a oublié d'être bête** he's not lacking in brains, he's as clever as they come

2 *(ne pas reconnaître* ▸ *mélodie)* to forget; **j'ai oublié son visage** I've forgotten what he/she looks like; **un visage que je n'oublierai jamais** a face I will never forget

3 *(ne plus penser à* ▸ *héros, injure, souci)* to forget (about); **les preneurs de son sont souvent oubliés par les jurys de prix** sound technicians are often ignored by award juries; **j'ai oublié l'heure** I forgot the time; **n'oubliez pas le guide!** don't forget the guide!; **oublions ce malentendu** let's forget (all) about this misunderstanding; **o. le passé** to forget the past; **oublions le passé** let's let bygones be bygones; **n'oublie pas à qui tu parles!** don't (you) forget who you're talking to!; *Fam* **oublie-moi un peu, veux-tu?** get off my back *or* case, will you?; **sortir me fait o. mes soucis** going out helps me to forget my troubles; **se faire o.** to keep a low profile, to stay out of the limelight

4 *(omettre)* to leave out; **je ferai en sorte de l'o. dans mon testament/sur le registre** I'll make sure she's left out of my will/left off the register

5 *(négliger)* to forget (about); **n'oubliez pas les consignes de sûreté préconisées par la gendarmerie** don't forget the safety precautions recommended by the police; **depuis son mariage, il nous oublie** he's been neglecting us *or* he's forgotten (about) us since he got married

6 *(ne pas prendre)* to forget, to leave (behind); **j'ai oublié mes lunettes chez toi** I've left my glasses (behind) at your place; **j'ai oublié la lettre à la maison** I left the letter at home

7 *(ne pas mettre)* to forget; **tu as oublié le citron dans la sauce** you forgot to put lemon in the sauce

USAGE ABSOLU to forget; **qu'a-t-elle dit? j'ai oublié** what did she say? I've forgotten; **il boit pour o.** he drinks to forget

VPR s'oublier 1 *(emploi passif)* **les langues étrangères s'oublient facilement quand on ne les pratique pas** foreign languages are easily forgotten when you don't use them; **des choses pareilles ne doivent jamais s'o.** things like that must never be forgotten; **c'est comme le vélo, ça ne s'oublie pas!** it's like riding a bike, once you learn you never forget; **la politesse s'oublie à présent** politeness is becoming a thing of the past

2 *(s'exclure)* to forget oneself; *Hum* **tu ne t'es pas oublié, à ce que je vois!** I see you've not forgotten yourself!; *Fam* **il ne s'oublie pas** he always looks after himself, he always takes care of number one

3 *(se relâcher)* to forget oneself; **vous vous oubliez, retirez ce que vous venez de dire** you're forgetting yourself, take back what you've just said

4 *Euph (animal, enfant)* to have an accident

oubliette [ublijet] **NF** *(fosse)* oubliette

• **oubliettes NFPL** *(cachot)* dungeon, black hole; *Fig* **le projet est tombé dans les** *ou* **aux oubliettes** the project has been shelved

oublieux, -euse [ublijø, -øz] **ADJ** *Littéraire* forgetful; **o. de ses devoirs** forgetful of one's duty

OUC [oyse] **NF** *Rad (abrév* **ondes ultra-courtes***)* USW

ouèbe [wɛb] **NM** *Ordinat* **l'o.** the Web

oued [wɛd] **NM** wadi

Ouessant [wɛsɑ̃] **NF** Ushant

ouest [wɛst] **NM INV 1** *(point cardinal)* west; **à l'o.** in the west; **où est l'o.?** which way is west?; **la partie la plus à l'o. de l'île** the westernmost part of the island; **le vent vient de l'o.** it's a west *or* westerly wind, the wind is coming from the west; **un vent d'o.** a westerly wind; **le vent d'o.** the west wind; **aller au** *ou* **vers l'o.** to go west *or* westwards; **les trains qui vont vers l'o.** trains going west, westbound trains; **rouler vers l'o.** to drive west *or* westwards; **aller droit vers l'o.** to head due west; **la cuisine est plein o.** *ou* **exposée à l'o.** the kitchen faces due west; **le soleil se couche à l'o.** the sun sets in the west **2** *(partie d'un pays, d'un continent)* west, western area *or* regions; *(partie d'une ville)* west; **l'o. de l'Italie** western Italy, the west of Italy; **elle habite dans l'o.** she lives in the west; **il habite dans l'o. de Paris** he lives in the west of Paris; **elle est de l'o.** she's from the west; **les gens de l'o.** people who live in the west **3** *Fig* **être à l'o.** to be lost, to be all at sea; **je ne sais pas me servir d'un ordinateur alors je suis carrément à l'o. dans mon nouveau boulot** I don't know how to use a computer, so I'm all at sea *or* totally lost in my new job; **ça fait plusieurs nuits que je ne dors pas alors je suis un peu à l'o.** I haven't slept for several nights so I hardly know if I'm coming or going

ADJ INV *(gén)* west *(avant n)*, western; *(côte, face)* west; *(banlieue, partie, région)* western; **la façade o. d'un immeuble** the west-facing wall of a building; **la chambre est côté o.** the bedroom faces west; **dans la partie o. de la France** in the West of France, in western France; **suivre la direction o.** to head *or* to go westwards

• **Ouest ADJ INV** West **NM** *Géog* **l'O.** the West

• **à l'ouest de PRÉP** (to the) west of; **il habite à l'o. de Paris** he lives to the west of Paris

ouest-allemand, -e [westalmɑ̃, -ɑ̃d] *(mpl* **ouest-allemands,** *fpl* **ouest-allemandes)** *Anciennement* **ADJ** West German

• **Ouest-Allemand, -e NM,F** West German

ouf [uf] **EXCLAM** phew!; **je n'ai pas eu le temps de dire o.** I didn't even have time to catch my breath

NM pousser un o. de soulagement to heave a sigh of relief

Ouganda [ugɑ̃da] **NM l'O.** Uganda

ougandais, -e [ugɑ̃dɛ, -ɛz] **ADJ** Ugandan

• **Ougandais, -e NM,F** Ugandan

ougrien, -enne [ugrijɛ̃, -ɛn] *Ling* **ADJ** Ugric

• **Ougrien, -enne NM,F** Ugric

oui [wi] **ADV 1** *(en réponse affirmative)* yes; **viendra-t-il? – o.** will he come? – yes; **tu en veux? – o., s'il te plaît** do you want some? – (yes) please; **voulez-vous prendre X pour époux? – o.** do you take X to be your lawful wedded husband? – I do; **Michel! – o., o., voilà, j'arrive!** Michel! – yes *or* all right, I'm coming!; **tu comprends? – o. et non** do you understand? – yes and no *or* I do and I don't; **alors c'est o. ou c'est non?** so is it yes or no?; **mais o.** yes, of course; **o., bien sûr** yes, of course; **il est audacieux – certes o.** he's rather daring – he certainly is; **o. assurément** yes indeed; **c'est vraiment injuste! – ah ça o.!** that's really unfair! – you said it *or* that's for sure!; *Fam* **tu vas déposer une plainte? – ah ça o.!** are you going to lodge a complaint? – you bet I am!; *Fam* **tu vas la laisser faire? – oh que o.!** are you going to let her go ahead? – you bet!; *Mil* **o., mon capitaine!** (yes,) sir!; *Naut* **o., mon commandant!** aye aye Captain!

2 *(en remplacement d'une proposition)* **il semblerait que o.** it would seem so; **tu vas voter? – je crois que o.** are you going to vote? – (yes) I think so *or* I think I will; **bien sûr que o.** (yes,) of course; **elle n'a dit ni o. ni non** she didn't say either yes or no, she was very noncommittal; **faire o. de la tête** to nod; **faire signe que o., faire o. de la tête** to nod (one's head); **tu les connais? – lui non, mais elle o., très bien** do you know them? – him no, but her yes, very well; **elle vient aussi? si o., je reste** will she be there too? if so *or* if she is I'll stay

3 *(emploi expressif)* **o., je veux bien y aller** yes, I'd really like to go; **o., j'ai entendu!** yes, I heard!; **eh o., c'est bien moi!** yes, it's me alright!; **o., évidemment, elle a un peu raison** of course, she's right in a way; **eh bien o., c'est moi qui le lui ai dit!** yes, I was the one who told her!; **je suis déçu, o., vraiment déçu!** I'm disappointed, really disappointed!; **le nucléaire o., mais pas à n'importe quel prix!** yes to nuclear energy, but not at any cost!; **tu viens, o.?** are you coming then?; **tu me le donnes, o. ou non?** are you going to give it to me or not *or* aren't you?; **tu viens, o. ou non?** are you coming or not?; *très Fam* **tu viens, o. ou merde?** are you coming or not, for Christ's sake?; **tu me réponds, o.?** answer me will you?, will you answer me?; **elle va se dépêcher, o.?** is she going to hurry up or isn't she?

NM INV je voudrais un o. définitif I'd like a definitive yes; **un o. franc et massif** a solid yes vote; **les o. et les non** the yesses *or* ayes and the noes; **il y a eu 5 o.** *(dans un vote)* there were 5 votes for *or* 5 ayes; **le o. de la mariée s'entendit à peine** the bride could barely be heard when she said "I do"; **répondre par o. ou non** to answer yes or no; **pleurer pour un o., pour un non** to cry at the least (little) thing; **il change d'avis pour un o. pour un non** he changes his mind at the drop of a hat

ouï-dire [widir] **NM INV** hearsay; **cette histoire n'est fondée que sur des o.** this story is just based on hearsay

• **par ouï-dire ADV** by hearsay, through the grapevine

ouïe[1] [wi] **NF 1** *Anat* (sense of) hearing; **avoir l'o. fine** to have a keen ear; *Hum* **continue, je suis tout o.** go on, I'm all ears

2 *Ich* gill

3 *Mus* sound hole

4 *Tech (d'un ventilateur)* ear; *Aut* louvre

ouie[2], **ouille** [uj] **EXCLAM** ouch!

> SUFFIX
>
> **-OUILLE/-OUILLER**
>
> Although **-ouille** is used to form nouns and **-ouiller** is used to form verbs, they both have the same PEJORATIVE or DIMINUTIVE function. Words featuring these two suffixes are often colloquial in register, eg:
>
> **merdouille** mess/load of shit; **glandouille** loafing about; **glandouiller** to loaf about; **grattouiller** to itch; **mâchouiller** to chew at; **merdouiller** to screw up, to cock up

ouïr [51] [wir] **VT 1** *Littéraire ou Hum* to hear (tell); **j'ai ouï dire que tu avais déménagé** I heard tell that you had moved; **j'ai souvent ouï dire que...** I have often heard it said that...; *Arch ou Hum* **oyez, oyez braves gens** hear ye, good people **2** *Jur* **o. des témoins** to hear witnesses

ouistiti [wistiti] **NM 1** *Zool* marmoset **2** *Fam (personne)* **drôle de o., celui-là!** he's a bit of a weirdo, that one!

oukase [ukaz] = **ukase**

ouragan [uragɑ̃] **NM 1** *Météo* hurricane; **il est entré comme un o. et s'est mis à hurler** he burst in like a whirlwind and started yelling **2** *Fig (tumulte)* storm, uproar; **son discours provoqua un o. de protestations** his/her speech caused a storm of protest *or* an uproar

Oural [ural] **NM 1** *(fleuve)* **l'O.** the Ural **2** *(montagnes)* **l'O.** the Urals, the Ural mountains

ourdir [32] [urdir] **VT 1** *Littéraire (complot)* to hatch, to weave; *(intrigue)* to weave **2** *Tech (tissage)* to warp; *(vannerie)* to weave

ourdissage [urdisaʒ] **NM** *Tex* warping

ourdou [urdu] = **urdu**

ourlé, -e [urle] **ADJ** *Couture* hemmed; **des oreilles délicatement ourlées** delicately shaped ears; **elle a des lèvres bien ourlées** her lips are well-defined

ourler [3] [urle] **VT 1** *Couture* to hem; **o. à jour** to hemstitch **2** *Littéraire (border)* to fringe; **des paupières ourlées de longs cils** eyelids fringed with long eyelashes

ourlet [urlɛ] **NM 1** *Couture* hem; **faire un o. à une jupe** to hem a skirt; **faux o.** false hem; **point d'o.** hemstitch **2** *(repli, rebord ▸ d'un cratère)* edge; *(▸ de l'oreille)* rim, *Spéc* helix **3** *Métal (de feuilles de métal)* lap joint, hem

ours [urs] **NM 1** *Zool* bear; **o. blanc** polar bear; **o. brun** brown bear; **o. des cavernes** cave bear; **o. gris d'Amérique** grizzly bear; **o. kodiak** Kodiak bear, Alaskan brown bear; **o. à lunettes** spectacled bear; **o. marin** sea bear, fur seal; **o. noir** black bear; **o. polaire** polar bear; **arrête de tourner en rond comme un o. en cage!** stop pacing up and down like a caged animal!

2 *Fam (personne)* **il est un peu o.** he's a bit grumpy *or* gruff; **quel o. mal léché!** grumpy old thing!

3 *(jouet)* **o. (en peluche)** teddy bear

4 *Journ* masthead

5 *Typ* credits page *(where contributors to a book are acknowledged)*

6 *Fam* **avoir ses o.** *(d'une femme)* to have the curse, to have one's period[□]

oursin [ursɛ̃] **NM** *Zool* sea urchin

ourson [ursɔ̃] **NM** (bear) cub

> SUFFIX
>
> **-OUSE, -OUZE**
>
> This is a suffix used in French SLANG to form feminine nouns. It can either be added to a noun or replace its ending. Note the two spelling options in some cases, eg:
>
> **bagouse** (from *bague*) ring; **partouze, partouse** (from *partie*) orgy; **perlouse, perlouze** (from *perle*) pearl; **piquouse** (from *piqûre*) shot, jab; **tantouze, tantouse** (from *tante*) fairy (male homosexual)

Oussama Ben Laden [usamabenladen] **NPR** Osama Bin Laden

oust, ouste [ust] **EXCLAM** *Fam* out!, scram!; **allez, o., tout le monde dehors!** come on, get a move on, everybody out!

out [awt] **ADV 1** *Sport (au tennis, au badminton etc)* out; **la balle est o.** the ball is out **2** *Boxe* out, knocked out

ADJ INV out

outarde [utard] **NF** *Orn* **1** bustard **2** *(bernache du Canada)* Canada goose

outer [3] [awte] **VT** *(révéler l'homosexualité de)* to out

outil [uti] **NM 1** *(pour travailler)* tool; **cabane/boîte à outils** tool shed/box; **outils de jardinage** garden implements *or* tools; **o. coupant** *ou* **de coupe** *ou* **tranchant** cutting tool; *(pour bords ou bordures)* edging tool **2** *(moyen, aide)* tool; **o. d'aide à la décision** decision-making tool; *Ordinat* **o. auteur** authoring tool; *Ordinat* **o. de création de pages Web** web authoring tool; **o. de gestion** management tool; *Fig* **savoir utiliser l'o. informatique** to know how to use computers; **o. de marketing** marketing tool; *Fig* **les outils mathématiques** mathematical tools; *Ordinat* **o. de navigation sur le Web** web browser; **outils pédagogiques** teaching aids; **o. de production** production tool; **o. de recherche** research tool; **o. de travail** tool, work instrument; *Bourse* **o. de spéculation** trading instrument **3** *Fam Hum (pénis)* tool

outillage [utijaʒ] **NM 1** *(ensemble d'outils)* (set of) tools; *(pour un jardinier)* (set of) tools *or* implements **2** *(industrie)* toolmaking *(UNCOUNT)* **3** *(dans une usine)* (machine) tool workshop

outiller [3] [utije] **VT** *(ouvrier)* to supply with tools; *(atelier, usine)* to equip, to fit with tools

VPR s'outiller *(usine)* to equip itself; *(bricoleur)* to equip oneself with tools; **vous auriez dû mieux vous o.** you should have made sure you were better equipped

outing [awtiŋ] **NM** *(d'un homosexuel)* outing

outrage [utraʒ] **NM 1** *(offense)* insult (**à** to); **subir les outrages de qn** to be insulted by sb; **faire o. à l'honneur de qn** to insult sb's honour; *Euph* **faire subir les derniers outrages à une femme** to violate a woman; **les outrages du temps** *ou* **des ans** the ravages of time **2** *Jur* **o. à agent** insulting behaviour; **o. aux bonnes mœurs** affront to public decency; **o. à magistrat** (criminal) contempt of court; **o. (public) à la pudeur** indecent exposure

outrageant, -e [utraʒɑ̃, -ɑ̃t] **ADJ** *(proposition, refus)* insulting; *(plaisanterie, propos)* offensive; *(accusation)* outrageous

outrager [17] [utraʒe] **VT 1** *(offenser)* to offend, to insult, to abuse; **o. une femme dans son honneur** to insult a woman's honour **2** *Littéraire (porter atteinte à ▸ la vérité)* to violate; *(▸ la raison, le bon goût)* to offend against; *Fig* **o. le bon sens** to be an insult to *or* to offend common sense

VPR s'outrager parle franchement, personne ne s'outragera de tes propos speak freely, your remarks will shock *or* outrage no one

outrageuse [utraʒøz] *voir* **outrageux**

outrageusement [utraʒøzmɑ̃] **ADV** excessively, extravagantly, outrageously

outrageux, -euse [utraʒø, -øz] **ADJ** *Littéraire* insulting, offensive, outrageous

outrance [utrɑ̃s] **NF 1** *(exagération)* excessiveness, extravagance, outrageousness; **l'o. de sa remarque lui ôte toute crédibilité** his/her remark is so outrageous that it loses all credibility **2** *(acte)* extravagance; *(parole)* extravagant *or* immoderate language

• **à outrance** ADJ **combat à o.** all-out fight; **industrialisation à o.** all-out industrialization ADV excessively, extravagantly, outrageously

outrancier, -ère [utrɑ̃sje, -ɛr] ADJ excessive, extravagant, extreme

outre[1] [utr] NF **1** *(pour transporter des liquides)* wine skin; *(en peau de chèvre)* goatskin bottle **2** *Zool* **o. de mer** sea squirt

outre[2] [utr] PRÉP *(en plus de)* besides, as well as; **o. le fait que...** besides the fact that...; **o. cette somme** besides *or* in addition to that sum; **o. leur cousin, ils hébergent une amie en ce moment** as well as *or* besides their cousin they have a friend staying at the moment

ADV **passer o. à qch** to disregard sth; **passer o. à une interdiction/une objection** to disregard a ban/an objection; **elle a passé o. malgré l'interdiction** she carried on regardless of *or* she disregarded the ban

• **en outre** ADV besides, furthermore, moreover; **j'ai en o. plusieurs remarques à vous faire** I have moreover several things to say to you

• **outre mesure** ADV excessively; **je n'ai pas l'intention d'insister o. mesure** I'm not going to push the matter; **il ne s'est pas inquiété o. mesure** he didn't worry unduly; **je n'y crois pas o. mesure** I don't set much store by it; **ils ne s'aiment pas o. mesure** they're not overly *or* excessively keen on each other

• **outre que** CONJ apart from; **o. (le fait) qu'il est riche** apart from the fact that he's rich, apart from *or* besides *or* in addition to being rich; **o. qu'il est très serviable, il est aussi très efficace** apart from being obliging he's also very efficient, not only is he obliging but he's also very efficient

outré, -e [utre] ADJ **1** *Littéraire (exagéré)* excessive, exaggerated, overdone; **des compliments outrés** excessive *or* exaggerated compliments; **comédien dont le jeu est o.** actor who overacts **2** *(choqué)* indignant, shocked, outraged

outre-Atlantique [utratlɑ̃tik] ADV across the Atlantic

outrecuidance [utrəkɥidɑ̃s] NF *Littéraire* **1** *(fatuité)* overconfidence, self-importance **2** *(impertinence)* impudence, impertinence

outrecuidant, -e [utrəkɥidɑ̃, -ɑ̃t] ADJ *Littéraire* **1** *(fat, prétentieux)* overconfident, self-important **2** *(impertinent)* arrogant, impudent, impertinent

outre-Manche [utrəmɑ̃ʃ] ADV across the Channel

outre-mer [utrəmɛr] ADV overseas; **la France d'o.** France's overseas territories and departments; *Admin* **territoires d'o.** overseas territories

outremer [utrəmɛr] ADJ INV ultramarine

NM *Minér* lapis lazuli; *(teinte)* ultramarine

outrepasser [3] [utrəpase] VT *(droit)* to go beyond; *(ordre)* to exceed; *(pouvoirs)* to abuse

outrer [3] [utre] VT **1** *Littéraire (exagérer)* to exaggerate, to magnify **2** *(révolter)* to outrage

outre-Rhin [utrərɛ̃] ADV across the Rhine

outre-Sarine [utrəsarin] ADV *Suisse* in German-speaking Switzerland

outre-tombe [utrətɔ̃b] **d'outre-tombe** ADJ INV **une voix d'o.** a voice from beyond the grave

outsider [awtsajdœr] NM outsider

ouvert, -e [uvɛr, -ɛrt] PP *voir* **ouvrir**

ADJ **1** *(porte, tiroir)* open; **entre, la porte est ouverte** *ou* **c'est o.** come in, the door's open; **grand o., grande ouverte** wide open; **je vis une porte grande ouverte** I saw a door that was wide open; **un robinet o. peut causer une inondation** a *Br* tap *or Am* faucet that's been left on can cause flooding; **il avait la chemise ouverte** his shirt was open (to the waist) *or* undone; **n'achetez pas de tulipes ouvertes** don't buy tulips that are already open; **elle s'avança la main ouverte** she moved forward with her hand open

2 *(bouche, yeux)* open; **dormir la bouche ouverte** to sleep with one's mouth open; **ne reste pas là la bouche ouverte!** don't just stand there gawping!; **il était dans son lit, les yeux ouverts** he was lying in bed with his eyes open; **garder les yeux (grands) ouverts** to keep one's eyes (wide) open; *Fig* to keep one's eyes peeled, to be on the lookout

3 *(coupé)* cut, open; **elle a eu la lèvre ouverte** her lip was cut; **il gisait là, le ventre o./la gorge ouverte** he lay there with his stomach slashed open/his throat cut; **plaie ouverte** open *or* gaping wound; **il a le crâne/le genou o.** he has a gaping wound in his skull/knee, his skull/knee has been split open

4 *(magasin, bureau, restaurant, maison)* open; **en ville, je n'ai rien trouvé d'o.** in town none of the shops were open; **vous restez o.?** will you stay open?; **o. de 10 heures à 5 heures** open (from) 10 to 5; *Fam* **l'épicier du coin reste o. jusqu'à minuit** the grocer on the corner stays open till midnight; **les jardins sont ouverts au public** the gardens are open to the public; **ils laissent toujours (tout) o.** *(ne ferment pas à clé)* they never lock the house; *(ne ferment pas les fenêtres)* they always leave the windows open; **une voiture ouverte est une tentation pour les voleurs** a car left unlocked *or* open is an invitation to burglars

5 *(qui a commencé)* **la séance est ouverte** I declare the meeting open; **la chasse/la campagne électorale est ouverte depuis ce matin** the hunting season/the election campaign began *or* started this morning; **les paris sont ouverts** *Courses de chevaux* bets are being taken; *Fig* it's anyone's guess

6 *(réceptif)* open; **un visage o.** an open face; **o. (d'esprit)** open-minded; **avoir l'esprit o.** to be open-minded, to have an open mind; **être o. à** to be open to; **nous sommes ouverts aux idées nouvelles** we are open to new ideas

7 *(non caché)* open; **être en guerre ouverte avec qn** to be openly at war with sb; **c'est la guerre ouverte contre les fumeurs** it's open war on smokers; **en conflit o. avec ses parents** in open conflict with his/her parents

8 *Ordinat* open; *(système)* open-ended

9 *Math* open; *Géom* wide

10 *Sport (imprévisible)* **un match très o.** a (wide) open game; **un jeu o.** an open game; *Ski* **porte ouverte** open flags; *Golf* **tournoi o.** open tournament, golf open

11 *Élec (circuit)* open; *(machine)* uninsulated

12 *Fin* **à capital o.** with an open *or* a fluctuating authorized capital

ouvertement [uvɛrtəmɑ̃] ADV openly

ouverture [uvɛrtyr] NF **1** *(trou)* opening; **une o. dans le mur** an opening *or* a hole in the wall; *Fig* **l'événement représente une véritable o. pour ces pays** this development will open up real opportunities for these countries; *Fig* **avoir une o. avec qn** to have a chance with sb

2 *(action d'ouvrir)* **l'o. des grilles a lieu à midi** the gates are opened *or* unlocked at noon; **pour ne pas faire la queue, j'étais là avant même l'o.** to avoid queuing I was there even before it *or* the doors opened; **o. des portes à 20 heures** doors open at 8; *Com* **les plus belles affaires se font à l'o.** the best bargains are to be had when the shop opens; **o. en nocturne le jeudi** late closing *or* open late on Thursdays; **heures/jours d'o.** opening hours/days; **nous attendons avec impatience l'o. du tunnel** we can hardly wait for the tunnel to open; **l'o. du coffre se fera devant témoins** the safe will be opened *or* unlocked in front of witnesses

3 *(mise à disposition)* **pour faciliter l'o. d'un compte courant** to make it easier to open a current account; **l'o. de vos droits ne date que de février dernier** you were not entitled to claim benefit before last February; **o. de crédit** (bank) credit arrangement

4 *(d'une session, d'un festival)* opening; **je tiens le rayon parfumerie depuis le jour de l'o.** I've been in charge of the perfume department since the day we opened; **discours d'o.** opening speech; *Bourse* **à l'o.** at start of trading; *Bourse* **depuis l'o.** since trading began *or* opened (this morning); *Bourse* **cours d'o.** opening price; **heures d'o.** opening hours; *Jur* **o. des débats** opening of proceedings; *Ordinat* **o. de session** log-on

5 *Chasse & Pêche* opening; **demain, on fait l'o. ensemble** tomorrow we're going out together on the first (official) day of the open season

6 *(écartement ▸ d'une voûte)* width, span; *(des branches d'un compas)* spread

7 *Fig Pol* **l'o. vers la gauche/la droite** broadening the base of government to the left/right; **la politique d'o.** consensus politics; **o. d'esprit** open-mindedness

8 *Sport* opening up; *Boxe* opening

9 *Cartes & (dans un jeu)* opening; **avoir l'o.** to have the opening move; **avoir l'o. à trèfle** to lead clubs

10 *Mus* overture

11 *Phot* aperture; **o. du diaphragme** f-stop

12 *Aut (des roues)* toe-out; **o. sans clé** keyless entry

13 *Élec* opening, breaking

14 *Presse* front-page article

15 *Mktg* opening, window of opportunity; **l'o. de nouveaux débouchés** the opening up of new markets

• **ouvertures** NFPL overtures; **faire des ouvertures de paix** to make peace overtures

ouvrable [uvrabl] ADJ **heures ouvrables** business hours, shop hours; **pendant les heures ouvrables** *Com* during opening hours; *Admin* during office hours; **jour o.** workday, *Br* working day

ouvrage [uvraʒ] NM **1** *(travail)* work; **se mettre à l'o.** to get down to work, to start work

2 *(œuvre)* (piece of) work; **le gros de l'o. a été exécuté par un jeune artiste** the bulk of the work was done by a young artist; *Archit & Constr* **o. d'art** construction works; **ouvrages de maçonnerie** masonry; **menus ouvrages** finishing (jobs); *Fig* **une rencontre qui est l'o. du hasard** a meeting which is due to chance, a chance meeting; *Fig* **l'o. du temps** the work of time

3 *(tricot, broderie)* work; *Vieilli* **o. de dames** needlework

4 *(livre)* book; **un o. de philosophie** a work of philosophy, a philosophy book; **l'o. se compose de trois volumes** the book is in three volumes; **o. de référence** reference work *or* book, work of reference

NF *Hum* **c'est de la belle o.!** that's a nice piece of work!

ouvragé, -e [uvraʒe] ADJ *(nappe)* finely embroidered; *(bijou)* finely worked; *(construction)* elaborate, ornate

ouvrager [17] [uvraʒe] VT *(nappe)* to embroider finely; *(métal, bijou)* to work finely

ouvrant, -e [uvrɑ̃, -ɑ̃t] ADJ opening, moving

NM *Beaux-Arts (d'un triptyque)* panel

ouvré, -e [uvre] ADJ **1** *(bois, fer)* ornate, elaborate, elaborately decorated; *(nappe)* (finely *or* elaborately) embroidered, finely worked **2** *Tech (fer)* wrought; **produits ouvrés et semi-ouvrés** finished and semi-finished products **3** *Admin & Com* **jour o.** workday, *Br* working day

ouvre-boîte, ouvre-boîtes [uvrəbwat] *(pl* **ouvre-boîtes)** NM can opener, *Br* tin opener

ouvre-bouteille, ouvre-bouteilles [uvrəbutɛj] *(pl* **ouvre-bouteilles)** NM bottle opener

ouvre-huître, ouvre-huîtres [uvrɥitr] *(pl* **ouvre-huîtres)** NM oyster knife

ouvrer [3] [uvre] VT *(bois)* to decorate (elaborately); *(linge)* to embroider, to work (finely)

ouvreur, -euse [uvrœr, -øz] NM,F **1** *Cartes & (dans un jeu)* opener **2** *Cin & Théât* usher, *f* usherette **3** *Sport* forerunner

• **ouvreuse** NF *Tex* opening machine

ouvrez-moi [uvremwa] NM INV *Ordinat* read-me document

ouvrier, -ère [uvrije, -ɛr] ADJ **1** *(quartier, condition)* working-class; **solidarité ouvrière** working-class solidarity; **agitation ouvrière** industrial unrest; **la classe ouvrière** the working class **2** *Entom* **abeille ouvrière** worker bee; **fourmi ouvrière** worker ant

NM,F (manual) worker; **les ouvriers sur le chantier** the workmen on the site; **une famille d'ouvriers** a working-class family; *Fig Littéraire* **il est l'o. de sa fortune** he is a self-made man; *Littéraire* **le grand o., l'éternel o.** God, the great Architect of the universe; **o. agricole** agricultural worker, farm labourer; **o. du bâtiment** builder; **o. à domicile** home worker; **o. à façon** outworker; **o. hautement qualifié** highly-skilled worker; **o. à la journée** day labourer; **o. mécanicien** garage mechanic; **o. non qualifié** unqualified worker *or* labourer; **o. professionnel** skilled worker; **o. qualifié** skilled worker; **o. spécialisé** semi-skilled worker; **o. du textile** mill worker *or* hand; **o. en bois/sur métaux** woodworker/metalworker

• **ouvrière** **NF** *(abeille)* worker (bee); *(fourmi)* worker (ant)

ouvriérisme [uvrijerism] **NM** *Pol (autogestion)* worker control; *(syndicalisme)* trade unionism

OUVRIR **[34]** [uvrir]

VT	
• to open **1–8, 10–14**	• to open up **2, 3, 6, 10**
• to unlock **1**	• to begin **5**
• to undo **4**	• to turn on **8**
• to clear **6**	• to cut open **10**
• to lead **9**	
USAGE ABSOLU	
• to answer the door **1**	• to open **2, 3**
VI	
• to be open **1**	• to open **1, 2**

VT 1 *(portail, tiroir, capot de voiture, fenêtre)* to open; *(porte fermée à clé)* to unlock, to open; *(porte verrouillée)* to unbolt, to open; *(loquet)* to unfasten; *(avec une clef)* to unlock; **o. une fenêtre tout grand** to open a window wide; **il ouvrit la porte d'un coup d'épaule** he shouldered the door open, he forced the door (open) with his shoulder; **il ouvrit la porte d'un coup de pied** he kicked the door open; **o. une porte par effraction** to force a door; **o. sa porte à qn** to throw open one's house to sb; *Fig* **o. la porte à qch** to open the door to sth

2 *(bouteille, pot, porte-monnaie)* to open; *(coquillage)* to open (up); *(paquet)* to open, to unwrap; *(enveloppe)* to open, to unseal; **allez, on ouvre une bouteille de champagne!** come on, let's open *or* crack open a bottle of champagne!; **ils ont ouvert le coffre-fort au chalumeau** they used a blowtorch to break open *or* into the safe; **o. un pot de peinture avec un levier** to prise the lid off a pot of paint

3 *(déplier ▸ éventail)* to open; *(▸ carte routière)* to open (up), to unfold; *(▸ livre)* to open (up); **ouvrez votre manuel page 15** open your book *Br* on *or Am* to page 15; **les fleurs ouvrent leurs corolles au soleil du matin** the flowers open their petals in the morning sun

4 *(desserrer, écarter ▸ compas, paupières)* to open; *(▸ rideau)* to open, to draw back; *(▸ aile, bras)* to open (out), to spread (out); *(▸ mains)* to open (out); *(déboutonner ▸ veste)* to undo, to unfasten; **o. les bras** *(en signe d'affection)* to open one's arms; **o. les yeux** to open one's eyes; **le matin, j'ai du mal à o. les yeux** *(à me réveiller)* I find it difficult to wake up in the morning; **o. l'œil** to open one's eye; *Fig* to keep one's eyes open; **cette rencontre avec lui m'a ouvert les yeux** meeting him was a real eye-opener for me; **o. de grands yeux** *(être surpris)* to be wide-eyed; **ouvrez grands vos yeux** *(soyez attentifs)* keep your eyes peeled; **o. l'esprit à qn** to broaden sb's outlook; *Fam* **l'o.**, *très Fam* **o. sa gueule** *(parler)* to open one's big mouth; *Fam* **il n'a pas ouvert la bouche, il ne l'a pas ouverte** he didn't open his mouth; **tu ferais mieux de ne pas l'o.!** you'd better keep your mouth *or* trap shut!

5 *(commencer ▸ hostilités)* to open, to begin; *(▸ campagne, récit, enquête)* to open, to start; *(▸ bal, festival, conférence, saison de chasse)* to open; **la scène qui ouvre la pièce** the opening scene of the play; **l'indice qui a ouvert la séance à la Bourse** the opening share prices on the Stock Exchange today; **voici le candidat qui ouvre notre grand concours** here's the first contestant to enter our competition; *Ordinat* **o. une session** to log in, to log on

6 *(rendre accessible ▸ chemin, voie)* to open (up), to clear; *(▸ frontière, filière)* to open; **il ouvrait un sentier au coupe-coupe** he cleared a path with a machete; *Can* **o. un chemin** *(dégager la neige)* to clear snow from a road; *(en coupant des arbres)* to cut down trees to make way for a new road; **des policiers lui ont ouvert un passage parmi ses fans** policemen cleared a way for him/her through the crowd of fans; **o. son pays** *ou* **ses frontières aux réfugiés politiques** to open up one's country *or* to open one's borders to political refugees; **ils refusent d'o. leur marché aux produits européens** they refuse to open up their market to European products; **il faut o. l'université à tous** universities must be open to all; **ce sont des professions que nous voulons o. aux femmes** they are professions that we want to open up to women; **pourquoi ne pas o. cette formation à de jeunes chômeurs?** why not make this form of training available to young unemployed people?; **le diplôme vous ouvre de nombreuses possibilités** the diploma opens up a whole range of possibilities for you

7 *(créer ▸ boutique, cinéma, infrastructure)* to open; *(▸ entreprise)* to open, to set up

8 *(faire fonctionner ▸ radiateur, robinet)* to turn on; *(▸ circuit électrique)* to open; *Fam* **ouvre la télé** turn *or* switch the TV on; *Fam* **o. l'eau/l'électricité/le gaz** to turn on the water/the electricity/the gas

9 *(être en tête de ▸ défilé, procession)* to lead; **o. la marche** to lead the march, to walk in front; **c'est son nom qui ouvre la liste** his/her name is (the) first on the list

10 *(inciser ▸ corps)* to open (up), to cut open; *(▸ panaris)* to lance, to cut open; *Fam* **ils l'ont ouvert de la cheville au genou** they opened up *or* cut open his leg from the ankle to the knee

11 *Sport* **o. le jeu** to open play; **essayez d'o. un peu plus la partie** try to play a more open game; **o. la marque** *ou* **le score** *(gén)* to open the scoring; *Ftbl* to score the first goal; **il vient d'o. la marque pour son équipe** he's just put his team on the board

12 *Banque (compte bancaire, portefeuille d'actions)* to open; *(emprunt)* to issue, to float; **o. un crédit à qn** to give sb credit facilities; **o. un droit à qn** *(dans les assurances)* to entitle sb to a claim

13 *Cartes & (dans un jeu)* to open

14 *Élec* to break, to open

USAGE ABSOLU 1 je suis allé o. chez les Loriot avant qu'ils rentrent de voyage I went and opened up the Loriots' house before they came back from their trip; **va o.** go and answer the door; **on a sonné, je vais o.** there's someone at the door, I'll go; **c'est moi, ouvre** it's me, open the door *or* let me in; **o. à qn** to open the door to sb, to let sb in; **va leur o.** go and let them in

2 *(commencer)* to open; **la scène ouvre par un chœur** the scene opens with a chorus; *TV & Cin* **o. en fondu** to fade in; *TV & Cin* **o. par un volet** to wipe on

3 *Cartes* **o. à cœur** to open (the bidding) in hearts; *(commencer le jeu)* to open *or* to lead with a heart

VI 1 *(boutique, restaurant, spectacle)* to (be) open; *Bourse* to open; **le supermarché ouvre de 9 heures à 22 heures** the supermarket is open *or* opens from 9 a.m. to 10 p.m.; **les magasins n'ouvrent pas les jours de fête** the shops don't open *or* aren't open on public holidays; **le musée ouvrira bientôt au public** the museum will soon be open to the public; **la chasse au faisan/la conférence ouvrira en septembre** the pheasant season/the conference will open in September; *Bourse* **o. en baisse/en hausse** to open down/up; *Bourse* **les valeurs pétrolières ont ouvert ferme** oils opened firm

2 *(couvercle, fenêtre, porte)* to open; **le portail ouvre mal** the gate is difficult to open *or* doesn't open properly; **la porte n'ouvre que de l'intérieur** the door can only be opened from the inside, the door only opens from the inside

• **ouvrir sur** **VT IND 1** *(déboucher sur)* to open onto; **nos fenêtres ouvrent sur la piazza** our windows open out onto *or* have a view of the piazza **2** *(commencer par)* to open with; **le colloque ouvrira sur sa communication** his/her paper will open the conference, the conference will open with his/her paper **3** *Sport* **o. sur qn** to pass (the ball) to sb; **o. sur l'aile gauche** to release the ball to the left wing

VPR s'ouvrir 1 *(boîte, valise)* to open; *(chemisier, fermeture)* to come undone; **le toit s'ouvre en coulissant** the roof slides open; **la tente s'ouvre des deux côtés avec une fermeture à glissière** the tent can be unzipped on both sides; **la fenêtre de ma chambre s'ouvre mal** the window in my room is difficult to open *or* doesn't open properly

2 *(être inauguré)* to open; **la nouvelle ligne Paris–Bordeaux s'ouvrira en décembre** the new Paris to Bordeaux line will open *or* be opened in December

3 *(se couper ▸ personne)* **je me suis ouvert le pied sur un bout de verre** I've cut my foot (open) on a piece of glass; **s'o. les veines** to slash *or* to cut one's wrists

4 *(se ménager)* **s'o. un chemin à travers la foule** to push one's way through the crowd

5 *(se desserrer, se déplier ▸ bras, fleur, huître, main)* to open; *(▸ aile)* to open (out), to spread, to unfold; *(▸ bouche, œil, paupière, livre, rideau)* to open

6 *(se fendre ▸ foule, flots)* to part; *(▸ sol)* to open up; *(▸ melon)* to open, to split (open); **la cicatrice s'est ouverte** the scar has opened up; **les flots s'ouvrirent** the sea parted; **un gouffre s'ouvrait sous mes pieds** a chasm opened up *or* yawned under my feet

7 *(boîte, valise ▸ accidentellement)* to (come) open

8 *(fenêtre, portail)* to open; **la fenêtre s'ouvrit brusquement** the window flew *or* was flung *or* was thrown open; **la porte s'ouvrit en coup de vent** the door flew open; **la porte s'ouvre sur la pièce/dans le couloir** the door opens into the room/out into the corridor

9 *(s'épancher)* to open up; **sans s'o. entièrement, elle m'a confié que...** without opening up completely to me, she confided that...; **il éprouvait le besoin de s'o.** he felt the need to talk to somebody; **s'o. à qn** to unburden oneself to sb, to confide in sb; **s'o. à qn de qch** to open one's heart to sb about sth, to confide in sb about sth; **elle ne s'en est jamais ouverte à moi** she's never confided in me *or* she's never opened her heart to me about it; **s'o. de qch** to open up about sth; **il finit par s'o. de ses problèmes** he eventually talked openly *or* opened up about his problems

10 *(débuter ▸ bal, conférence)* **s'o. par** to open *or* to start with

11 *(se présenter ▸ carrière)* to open up; **un avenir radieux s'ouvrait devant nous** a bright future opened up before us

12 s'o. à *(des idées, des influences)* to open up to; **s'o. à des cultures nouvelles** to become aware of new cultures; **leur pays s'ouvre peu à peu au commerce extérieur** their country is gradually opening up to foreign trade; **carrières qui s'ouvrent de plus en plus aux femmes** careers that are opening up more and more to women; **s'o. à de nouvelles technologies** to open (up) one's mind to new technologies

ouvroir [uvrwar] **NM** *(dans un couvent)* workroom; *(dans une paroisse)* sewing room

ouzbek [uzbɛk] **ADJ** Uzbek

NM *(langue)* Uzbek

• **Ouzbek** **NMF** Uzbek; **les Ouzbeks** the Uzbeks *or* Uzbek

Ouzbékistan [uzbekistɑ̃] **NM l'O.** Uzbekistan

-ouze [uz] *voir* **-ouse**

ovaire [ɔvɛr] **NM** *Anat* ovary; *Méd* **cancer de l'o.** ovarian cancer; *Méd* **kyste de l'o.** ovarian cyst

ovale [ɔval] **ADJ** *(en surface)* oval; *(en volume)* egg-shaped, ovoid

NM *(forme)* oval; **son visage était d'un o. parfait** his/her face was a perfect oval; **en o.** oval

ovalien, -enne [ɔvaljɛ̃, -ɛn] **ADJ** rugby *(avant n)*; **le monde o.** the world of rugby

ovalisation [ɔvalizasjɔ̃] **NF** *Tech* ovalization

ovaliser **[3]** [ɔvalize] **VT** to make oval, to turn into an oval; *Tech* **l'usure ovalise les cylindres** cylinders become ovalized through wear

ovariectomie [ɔvarjɛktɔmi] **NF** *Méd* ovariectomy, oophorectomy

ovarien, -enne [ɔvarjɛ̃, -ɛn] **ADJ** *Anat* ovarian

ovation [ɔvasjɔ̃] **NF** ovation; **ils se sont tous levés pour lui faire une o.** he/she got a standing ovation

ovationner **[3]** [ɔvasjɔne] **VT o. qn** to give sb an ovation; **le groupe s'est fait o. pendant dix minutes** the group were given a ten-minute standing ovation

ové, -e [ɔve] **ADJ** egg-shaped, ovate

overbooké, -e [ɔvœrbuke] **ADJ** *Fam (personne)* booked-up, busy[□]; **je peux pas te voir cette semaine, je suis complètement o.** I can't see you this week, I've got a really hectic schedule

overdose [ɔvœrdoz] **NF 1** *(surdose)* overdose; **mourir d'une o.** to die of *or* from an overdose **2** *Fam Fig* overdose, OD; **j'ai eu une o. de chocolat à Noël** I overdosed on chocolate at Christmas

overdrive [ɔvœrdrajv] **NM** *Aut* overdrive

ovidés [ɔvide] **NMPL** *Zool & Agr* Ovidae

oviducte [ɔvidykt] **NM** oviduct

ovin, -e [ɔvɛ̃, -in] **ADJ** ovine
NM ovine, sheep

ovipare [ɔvipar] **ADJ** egg-laying, *Spéc* oviparous
NMF egg-laying *or Spéc* oviparous animal

OVNI, Ovni [ɔvni] **NM** *(abrév* **objet volant non identifié***)* UFO

ovocyte [ɔvɔsit] **NM** *Biol* oocyte

ovoïde [ɔvɔid], **ovoïdal, -e, -aux, -ales** [ɔvɔidal, -o] **ADJ** egg-shaped, *Spéc* ovoid; *Élec* **maillon o.** egg insulator

ovovivipare [ɔvɔvivipar] **ADJ** ovoviviparous
NMF ovoviviparous animal

ovulaire [ɔvylɛr] **ADJ** ovular

ovulation [ɔvylasjɔ̃] **NF** ovulation

ovule [ɔvyl] **NM 1** *Physiol* ovum **2** *Bot & Zool* ovule **3** *Pharm* pessary

ovuler [3] [ɔvyle] **VI** to ovulate

oxalate [ɔksalat] **NM** *Chim* oxalate; **o. de fer** oxalate of iron, ferrous oxalate

oxalide [ɔksalid] **NF** *Bot* oxalis, wood sorrel

oxalique [ɔksalik] **ADJ acide o.** oxalic acid

oxford [ɔksfɔrd] **NM** Oxford (cloth); **une chemise en o.** an Oxford shirt
ADJ flanelle o. Oxford

oxhydrique [ɔksidrik] **ADJ** *Chim* oxyhydrogen *(avant n)*

oxyacétylénique [ɔksiasetilenik] **ADJ** oxyacetylene

oxycoupage [ɔksikupaʒ] **NM** *Métal* oxygen cutting

oxydable [ɔksidabl] **ADJ** liable to rust, oxidizable; **facilement o.** which rusts easily

oxydant, -e [ɔksidɑ̃, -ɑ̃t] *Chim* **ADJ** oxidizing
NM oxidant, oxidizer, oxidizing agent

oxydation [ɔksidasjɔ̃] **NF** *Chim* oxidation, oxidization

oxyde [ɔksid] **NM** *Chim* oxide; **o. d'azote** nitrogen oxide; **o. de carbone** carbon monoxide; **o. métallique** metallic oxide; **o. nitrique** nitric oxide

oxyder [3] [ɔkside] *Chim* **VT** to oxidize
VPR s'oxyder to become oxidized

oxygénation [ɔksiʒenasjɔ̃] **NF** *Chim* oxygenation

oxygène [ɔksiʒɛn] **NM 1** *Chim* oxygen **2** *Fig* **j'ai besoin d'o.** I need some fresh air

oxygéné, -e [ɔksiʒene] **ADJ** *Chim* oxygenated; **cheveux oxygénés** peroxide blonde hair, bleached hair

oxygéner [18] [ɔksiʒene] **VT 1** *Chim & Physiol* to oxygenate, to oxygenize **2** *(cheveux)* to bleach, to peroxide
VPR s'oxygéner *Fam* to get some fresh air

oxymore [ɔksimɔr], **oxymoron** [ɔksimɔrɔ̃] **NM** oxymoron

oxyton [ɔksitɔ̃] **NM** *Ling* oxytone

oxyure [ɔksjyr] **NM** pinworm, *Spéc* oxyuris

oyat [ɔja] **NM** lyme grass

Ozalid® [ɔzalid] **NM** *Typ Br* Ozalid®, *Am* blues

ozone [ozɔn] **NM** ozone; **couche d'o.** ozone layer; **diminution de l'o.** ozone depletion

ozonisation [ozɔnizasjɔ̃] **NF** *Chim* ozonization

ozoniser [3] [ozɔnize] **VT** *Chim* to ozonize

P, p [pe] **NM INV** *(lettre)* P, p; **P comme Pierre** ≃ P for Peter; *Mktg* **les quatre P** *(le marketing mix)* the four Ps

PAC, Pac [pak] **NF** *UE (abrév* **politique agricole commune***)* CAP

PACA, Paca [paka] **NF** *(abrév* **Provence-Alpes-Côte d'Azur***)* = region of south-eastern France

pacage [pakaʒ] **NM 1** *(lieu)* pasture, grazing-land; **p. d'été** summer pasture **2** *(action)* grazing; *Jur* **droit de p.** grazing rights

pacager [17] [pakaʒe] **VI** to graze
VT to (put out to) graze

pacane [pakan] **NF** *Bot* pecan (nut)

pacemaker [pesmekœr] **NM** (cardiac) pacemaker

pacha [paʃa] **NM 1** *Hist* pasha **2** *Fam Fig* **mener une vie de p.** to live like a lord ◻, to live a life of ease ◻; **tu ne vas pas faire le p. tout le week-end!** don't expect to be waited on hand and foot all weekend!

pachyderme [paʃidɛrm] **NM 1** *Zool* pachyderm; **de p.** *(allure, démarche)* elephantine, lumbering; *(grâce)* elephantine **2** *(personne)* (great) elephant

pacificateur, -trice [pasifikatœr, -tris] **ADJ** *(réconciliateur)* pacifying; *Pol* peacemaking
NM,F pacifier, peacemaker; *Pol* peacemaker

pacification [pasifikɑsjɔ̃] **NF** *(gén) & Pol* pacification

pacificatrice [pasifikatris] *voir* **pacificateur**

pacifier [9] [pasifje] **VT** to pacify

pacifique [pasifik] **ADJ 1** *Pol (pays, gouvernement)* peace-loving **2** *(non militaire)* peaceful, non-military **3** *(fait dans le calme)* peaceful; **mener une existence p.** to lead a quiet *or* peaceful life
NMF peace-loving person
• **Pacifique NM le P.** the Pacific (Ocean)

pacifiquement [pasifikmɑ̃] **ADV** peacefully; **le changement de régime s'est fait p.** the change of regime was achieved by peaceful means

pacifisme [pasifism] **NM** pacifism

pacifiste [pasifist] **ADJ** pacifist
NMF pacifist

pack [pak] **NM 1** *Sport* pack **2** *Géog* pack ice **3** *Com* pack; **acheter des yaourts en p.** to buy a pack of yoghurts; **acheter de la bière en p. de six** to buy a six-pack (of beer)

package [pakɛdʒ] **NM** *(gén) & Ordinat* package

packaging [pakadʒiŋ] **NM** packaging

pacotille [pakɔtij] **NF** *(camelote)* cheap junk
• **de pacotille ADJ** cheap; **des bijoux de p.** baubles, trinkets; *Fig* **un exotisme de p.** bogus exoticism

Pacs [paks] **NM** *(abrév* **Pacte civil de solidarité***)* civil solidarity pact *(law introduced in France in 1999 extending the legal rights of married couples to unmarried heterosexual couples and to homosexual couples, particularly with regard to inheritance and taxation)*; **faire** *ou* **conclure un P.** to enter into a Pacs agreement

pacser [3] [pakse] *Fam* **VI** = to sign a "Pacs" contract, to enter into a civil solidarity pact
VPR se pacser = to sign a "Pacs" contract, to enter into a civil solidarity pact

pacson [paksɔ̃] **NM** *Fam* **1** *(colis)* parcel ◻, package ◻ **2** *(somme d'argent)* **toucher le p.** *(dans une affaire)* to make a bundle *or Br* a packet; *(au jeu)* to win a bundle *or Br* a packet

pacte [pakt] **NM 1** *(gén)* agreement; **conclure** *ou* **faire** *ou* **sceller un p. (avec qn)** to make an agreement (with sb); **signer un p. avec le diable** to sign a pact with the Devil **2** *Pol* pact, treaty, agreement; **p. de non-agression** non-aggression pact; *UE* **P. de stabilité et de croissance** Stability and Growth Pact; *Hist* **le P. de Varsovie** the Warsaw Pact **3** *Jur* **P. civil de solidarité** civil solidarity pact *(law introduced in France in 1999 extending the legal rights of married couples to unmarried heterosexual couples and to homosexual couples, particularly with regard to inheritance and taxation)*

pactiser [3] [paktize] **pactiser avec VT IND 1** *(conclure un accord avec)* to make a deal *or* pact with; **p. avec le diable** to make a pact with the devil **2** *(transiger avec)* to collude with, to connive at; **p. avec le crime** to condone crime

pactole [paktɔl] **NM 1** *Fig (source de profit)* gold mine; **ce travail est un vrai p.** this type of work is a real gold mine **2** *(somme)* **elle a touché un joli p. quand son grand-père est mort** she came into a nice *or* tidy little sum when her grandfather died; **on peut se faire un joli p. dans le pétrole** there are rich pickings to be had in the oil business **3** *(gros lot)* jackpot

paddle [padœl] **NM** *Sport* paddle tennis

paddock [padɔk] **NM 1** *(enclos)* paddock **2** *Fam (lit)* bed ◻, *Br* pit; **se mettre** *ou* **aller au p.** to hit the sack *or* hay

paddy [padi] **NM** paddy (rice)

Padoue [padu] **NM** Padua

paella [paela] **NF** paella

PAF [paf] **NF** *(abrév* **police de l'air et des frontières***)* airport and border police
NM *Rad & TV (abrév* **paysage audiovisuel français***)* French broadcasting

paf[1] [paf] **ADJ INV** *Fam (ivre)* wasted, plastered
NM *très Fam (pénis)* dick, *Br* knob

paf[2] [paf] **ONOMAT** bam, wham

PAG [peaʒe] **NF** *Com (abrév* **procédure accélérée générale de dédouanement***)* accelerated customs clearance procedure

pagaie [pagɛ] *voir* **pagayer**
NF *(rame)* paddle

pagaille, pagaïe [pagaj] *Fam* **NF 1** *(désordre)* mess, shambles; **il y a une drôle de p., dans ce bureau** this office looks as if a bomb has hit it *or* is a real pigsty; **pour mettre la p., t'es champion** when it comes to making a mess, you're unbeatable; **arrête de mettre la p. dans mes affaires** stop messing up my things **2** *(confusion)* chaos; **c'est la p. dans les rues de Paris** the streets of Paris are absolute chaos; **semer la p. dans/parmi...** to cause havoc in/among...
• **en pagaille ADJ** *(maison, chambre)* in a mess; *(affaires, papiers)* all jumbled up, in a mess **ADV 1** *(en désordre)* **mettre qch en p.** to mess sth up **2** *(en quantité)* **ils ont de l'argent en p.** they've got loads *or* bags of money, they're rolling in money

paganisme [paganism] **NM** paganism

pagaye [pagaj] = **pagaille**

pagayer [11] [pageje] **VI** to paddle

pagayeur, -euse [pagejœr, -øz] **NM,F** paddler

page[1] [paʒ] **NM** *Hist* page (boy); **il avait les cheveux coupés à la p.** he had a page-boy haircut

page[2] [paʒ] = **pageot**

page[3] [paʒ] **NF 1** *(rectangle de papier)* page; **p. blanche** blank page; **arracher les pages d'un livre** to tear pages *or* leaves out of a book; **ouvrez vos livres à la p. 10** open your books at page 10, open your books and turn to page 10; **en première p. des journaux** on the front page of the newspapers; **faire la première p. des journaux** to hit the headlines; **suite de l'article en p. 5** (article) continued on page 5; **c'est en bas de p.** it's at the bottom of the page; **une lettre de huit pages** an eight-page letter; *Typ* **mettre en pages** to design, to lay out; **p. centrale** centre page; *Typ* **p. de copyright** copyright page; **pages financières** financial *or Br* City pages; **p. de garde** flyleaf; *(d'un fax)* cover sheet *or* page; *Tél* **les Pages Jaunes®** the Yellow Pages®; *Typ* **p. de titre** title page; **tourner une p.** to turn (over) a page; *Fig* to turn over a new leaf; **une p. politique vient d'être tournée avec la mort du sénateur** the death of the senator marks the end of a political era; *Fig* **tourner la p.** to make a fresh start
2 *(extrait)* passage, excerpt; **des pages inoubliables** unforgettable passages; **quelques très belles pages de Proust** some very beautiful passages *or* excerpts from Proust; *Rad* **et maintenant, une p. musicale** and now for some music; *Rad & TV* **une p. de publicité** a commercial break; **pages choisies** selected (prose) passages
3 *(épisode)* page, chapter; **quelques pages de notre histoire** some pages *or* chapters in our history
4 *Ordinat* page; **p. d'accueil** home page; **p. perso, p. personnelle** personal home page; **p. précédente** page up; **p. de résultats** results page; **p. suivante** page down; **p. web** Web page
• **à la page ADJ** *Fam (fashion, people)* with-it; **être à la p.** to be with it; **tu n'es plus à la p. du tout!** you're completely out of touch *or* out of it!; **il faut te mettre à la p.** you're going to have to get with it
ADV *(être payé)* by the page

page-écran [paʒekrɑ̃] *(pl* **pages-écrans***)* **NF** *Ordinat* screen page

pageot [paʒo] **NM** *Fam* bed ◻, *Br* pit; **se mettre** *ou* **aller au p.** to hit the sack *or* hay

pagination [paʒinɑsjɔ̃] **NF 1** *Typ* pagination, page numbering; **il y a une erreur de p.** the pages have been numbered wrongly **2** *Ordinat* page numbering, paging

paginer [3] [paʒine] **VT** to paginate, to number the pages of

pagne [paɲ] **NM** *(en tissu)* loincloth, pagne; *(en rafia)* grass skirt

pagnoter [3] [paɲɔte] **se pagnoter VPR** *Fam Vieilli (se coucher)* to hit the sack *or* hay

pagode [pagɔd] **NF 1** *Archit* pagoda; **toit en p.** pagoda roof **2** *Couture* **(manche) p.** pagoda sleeve **3** *(figurine à tête mobile)* mandarin

Pagsi [paksi] **NM** *(abrév* **Programme d'action gouvernemental pour la société de l'information***)* = government scheme to promote the use of the Internet in education and in public services

paie [pɛ] *voir* **payer**

NF **1** *(salaire)* pay, wages; **toucher sa p.** to be paid; **c'est le jour de p.** it's payday **2** *Fam (locution)* **ça fait une p. que je ne l'ai pas vu** I haven't seen him for ages□; **quand vous êtes-vous rencontrés? – ça fait une p.!** when did you meet? – donkey's years ago!

paiement [pɛmɑ̃] NM payment; *(d'un compte)* payment, settlement; **faire** *ou* **effectuer un p.** to make a payment; **contre p. de 100 euros** on payment of 100 euros; *aussi Fig* **c'est tout ce qu'il a reçu en p. de son travail** that's all he got (as payment) for his work; **p. par anticipation** payment in advance; **p. arriéré** payment in arrears; **p. d'avance** payment in advance, advance payment; **p. par carte** card payment, payment by card; **p. par chèque** payment by cheque; **p. à la commande** cash with order; **p. (au) comptant** cash payment, payment in cash; **p. contre documents** payment against documents; **p. différé** deferred payment; **à p. différé** deferred; **p. échelonné** staggered payment; **p. électronique** electronic payment, payment by electronic transfer; **p. en espèces** payment in cash, cash payment; **p. exceptionnel** windfall payment; **p. de l'indu** payment made in error; **p. intégral** payment in full; **p. par intervention** payment on behalf of a third party; **p. libératoire** payment in full discharge from debt; **p. en liquide** payment in cash, cash payment; **p. à la livraison** *Br* cash on delivery, *Am* collect on delivery; **p. mensuel** monthly payment; **p. en nature** payment in kind; **p. partiel** part payment; **paiements périodiques** periodic payments; **p. préalable** prepayment; **p. progressif** graduated *or* increasing payments; **p. au prorata** payment pro rata; *Ordinat* **p. sécurisé** secure (electronic) transaction; **p. en souffrance** overdue *or* outstanding payment; **p. à tempérament** payment by *or* in instalments; **p. à terme** payment by *or* in instalments

païen, -enne [pajɛ̃, -ɛn] ADJ pagan, heathen

NM,F pagan, heathen; **jurer comme un p.** to swear like a trooper

paierie [pɛri] NF local treasury office

paillage [pajaʒ] NM *Hort* (straw) mulching

paillard, -e [pajar, -ard] ADJ *(personne)* bawdy, coarse; *(chanson, histoire)* dirty

NM,F libertine

paillardise [pajardiz] NF **1** *(caractère)* bawdiness, coarseness **2** *(histoire)* dirty story

paillasse[1] [pajas] NF **1** *(matelas grossier)* straw *or* straw-filled mattress **2** *(d'un évier)* drainer, draining board; *(de laboratoire)* (laboratory) bench **3** *Fam (ventre)* stomach□, belly, guts; **trouer la p. à qn** to knife sb in the guts

paillasse[2] [pajas] NM clown

paillasson [pajasɔ̃] NM **1** *(d'une entrée)* doormat **2** *Fam Fig (personne)* doormat; **elle le traite comme un p.** she treats him like a doormat **3** *Hort* (straw) mulch

paille [paj] NF **1** *(chaume)* straw; **p. de blé** wheat straw; **p. de riz** rice straw; *Hum* **sur la p. humide des cachots** behind bars; *Fam* **être/finir sur la p.** to be/end up completely broke *or Br* on one's uppers *or Am* without a dime; *Fam* **mettre qn sur la p.** to ruin sb□; *Fam* **une p.!** *(peu de chose)* chickenfeed!, peanuts!

2 *(tige)* piece of straw, straw; *Bible* **voir la p. dans l'œil du prochain et ne pas voir la poutre dans le sien** to see the mote in one's brother's eye but not the beam in one's own; **tirer à la courte p.** to draw lots

3 *(pour boire)* (drinking) straw; **boire avec une p.** to drink through a straw

4 *Tech (défaut)* flaw

5 p. de fer steel wool

ADJ INV straw-coloured

paillé, -e [paje] ADJ **1** *(siège)* straw-bottomed **2** *(métal, pierre précieuse)* flawed **3** *(couleur)* straw-coloured

NM stable litter

pailler[1] [paje] NM *(grenier)* straw loft; *(cour)* straw yard; *(meule)* straw stack

pailler[2] [3] [paje] VT **1** *(siège)* to straw-bottom **2** *Hort* to (straw) mulch

paillet [pajɛ] NM *Naut* mat, fender; **p. d'abordage** *ou* **makarov** collision mat

pailleté, -e [pajte] ADJ *(robe)* sequined; *(maquillage)* glittery, sparkly

pailleter [27] [pajte] VT *(vêtement)* to spangle; *(maquillage, coiffure)* to put glitter on

paillette [pajɛt] NF **1** *Couture* sequin, spangle; **une robe à paillettes** a sequined dress **2** *(parcelle ▸ d'or)* speck; *(▸ de quartz, de mica)* flake; *(▸ de savon)* flake **3** *(d'une pierre précieuse)* flaw

• **paillettes** NFPL *(de maquillage)* glitter

pailleux, -euse [pajø, -øz] ADJ **1** *(fumier)* strawy **2** *Métal* flawed

paillis [paji] NM *Agr* mulch

paillote [pajɔt] NF straw hut

pain [pɛ̃] NM **1** *(substance)* bread; **un peu de p.** a bit *or* piece of bread; **gagner son p.** to earn one's *or* make a living; **mettre qn au p. sec et à l'eau** to put sb on dry bread and water; **p. azyme** unleavened bread; **p. bénit** consecrated bread; *Fig* **c'est p. bénit** that's a godsend; **p. blanc** white bread; *Fig* **manger son p. blanc le premier** to have it easy for a while; **p. brioché** brioche-like bread; **p. complet** *Br* wholemeal *or Am* wholewheat bread; **p. doré** French toast; **p. d'épice** ≃ gingerbread; **p. grillé** toast; *Can* **p. d'habitant** *ou* **de famille** *ou* **du pays** homemade bread; **p. de mie** sandwich bread; **p. noir** black bread; **p. perdu** French toast; **p. de seigle** rye bread; **p. de son** *Br* wholemeal *or Am* wholewheat bread; **gros p.** farmhouse bread *(sold by weight)*; **notre p. quotidien** our daily bread; **la maladie, les soucis d'argent, c'était son p. quotidien** illness and money worries were his/her daily lot; **être bon comme du bon p.** to be the salt of the earth; **long comme un jour sans p.** interminable, endless; **avoir du p. sur la planche** to have one's work cut out; **enlever** *ou* **retirer** *ou* **ôter le p. de la bouche à qn** to take the bread out of sb's mouth; *Fam* **ça mange pas de p.** it doesn't cost anything; **du p. et des jeux** bread and circuses

2 *(individuel ▸ gén)* loaf; *(▸ pain long)* baguette, *Br* French stick; *(▸ boule)* round loaf (of bread), cob; *Belg* **p. baguette** baguette, *Br* French stick; **p. bis,** *Can* **p. de blé entier, p. brun** brown loaf, *Br* wholemeal *or Am* wholewheat loaf; **p. au chocolat** pain au chocolat *(chocolate-filled pastry)*; **p. de campagne** farmhouse loaf; **p. complet** *Br* wholemeal *or Am* wholewheat loaf; *Can* **p. français** baguette, *Br* French stick; **p. de Gênes** ≃ Genoa cake; *Belg* **p. intégral** *Br* wholemeal *or Am* wholewheat loaf; **p. au lait** finger roll *(made with milk)*; **p. au levain** sourdough loaf; **p. de ménage** homemade loaf; **p. moulé** large tin loaf; **p. parisien** thick French loaf; **p. platine, p. à** *ou* **sur platine** large tin loaf; **p. aux raisins** = circular pastry made from sweetened dough and raisins; **p. de seigle** rye loaf; **p. de son** *Br* wholemeal *or Am* wholewheat loaf; **p. viennois** Vienna loaf; **petit p.** (bread) roll

3 *(préparation)* loaf; **p. de poisson** fish loaf; **p. de courgettes** courgette loaf

4 *(bloc)* **p. savon** bar of soap; **p. de glace** block of ice; *Culin* **p. de sucre** sugarloaf; *Géog* **le P. de Sucre** Sugarloaf Mountain

5 *Fam (coup)* smack; **je lui ai filé un de ces pains!** I socked him/her one!

• **pain brûlé** ADJ INV *(tissu, peinture)* dark brown; *(peau)* brown as a berry

pair[1] [pɛr] NM **1** *(noble)* peer

2 *(égal)* peer; **être jugé par ses pairs** to be judged by one's peers; *Littéraire* **traiter qn de p. à compagnon** to treat sb as an equal

3 *Bourse* par (value); *Fin* par (rate of exchange); **emprunt émis au-dessus du p.** loan issued above par

4 *(au jeu)* even numbers; **jouer p.** to bet on the even numbers

• **au pair** ADJ **jeune fille au p.** au pair (girl) ADV **1** *(en échange du logement)* **travailler** *ou* **être au p.** to work as *or* to be an au pair **2** *Fin* at par

• **de pair** ADV **aller de p.** to go together, to go hand in hand; **la méchanceté va souvent de p. avec la bêtise** nastiness often goes together *or* hand in hand with stupidity

• **hors pair, hors de pair** ADJ unequalled, outstanding; **c'est un traducteur hors p.** as a translator he's second to none *or* in a class of his own

pair[2]**, -e**[1] [pɛr] ADJ **1** *(nombre, jour)* even; **jouer un chiffre p.** to bet on an even number; **habiter du côté p.** to live on the even-numbered side of the street; **stationnement les jours pairs seulement** parking on even-numbered dates only **2** *Anat (organes)* paired

paire[2] [pɛr] NF **1** *(de ciseaux, de chaussures, de chaussettes)* pair; *(de draps)* set; *(de faisan, de pistolets)* brace; **si tu continues, tu vas recevoir une p. de gifles** if you go on like that, you'll get your face slapped; *Fam* **une belle p. de seins** a great pair; *Fam* **une belle p. de fesses** a nice butt *or Br* bum; **vous êtes une belle p. d'hypocrites!** you're a right pair of hypocrites!; *Fam* **c'est une autre p. de manches** that's a different kettle of fish; *Fam* **se faire la p.** *(s'enfuir)* to take off, to make oneself scarce, *Br* to scarper; *(s'évader)* to break out; *(faire une fugue)* to run away□, *Br* to do a bunk **2** *Ling* **p. minimale** minimal pair

pairesse [pɛrɛs] NF **1** *(en Grande-Bretagne)* peeress **2** *(épouse d'un pair)* wife of a peer

pairie [pɛri] NF peerage; **p. à vie** life peerage

paisible [pezibl] ADJ **1** *(doux)* peaceful, quiet

2 *(serein)* quiet, calm, peaceful; **le bébé dort d'un sommeil p.** the baby is sleeping peacefully

3 *(silencieux)* calm, quiet; **nous habitons un quartier très p.** we live in a very quiet part of town

4 *Jur* **p. possesseur d'un bien** uncontested owner of a piece of property

paisiblement [pezibləmɑ̃] ADV **1** *(dormir)* peacefully, quietly **2** *(parler, discuter)* calmly

paissait *etc voir* **paître**

paître [91] [pɛtr] VI *(animaux)* to graze; **faire p. le bétail** to graze the cattle, to put the cattle out to graze; **envoyer qn p.** to tell sb where to go, *Br* to send sb packing

VT **1** *(sujet: animal)* to feed on, to graze (on) **2** *Arch ou Littéraire (bétail)* to feed, to graze

paix [pɛ] NF **1** *Mil & Pol* peace; **demander la p.** to sue for peace; **pourparlers/offres de p.** peace talks/proposals; **négocier la p.** to negotiate peace; **en temps de p.** in peacetime; **faire la p.** to make peace; **signer/ratifier un traité de p.** to sign/to ratify a peace treaty; **p. armée** armed peace; **p. séparée** separate peace; **la p. des braves** an honourable peace; *Prov* **si tu veux la p., prépare la guerre** if you wish for peace, prepare for war

2 *(ordre)* peace; **troubler la p. publique** to disturb public order *or* the peace; **favoriser la p. sociale** to promote social peace

3 *(entente)* peace; **vivre en p. (avec qn)** to live in peace (with sb), to be at peace (with sb); **être en p. avec sa conscience** to have a clear conscience, to be at peace with one's conscience; **faire la p. avec qn** to make one's peace with sb, to make up with sb; **on fait la p.?** let's make up, let's be friends again

4 *(repos)* peace, quiet; **avoir besoin de p. pour se concentrer** to need peace and quiet to concentrate; **j'ai enfin la p. depuis qu'il est parti** I've at last got some peace and quiet now that he's left; **il ne me laissera pas en p. tant que je ne lui aurai pas tout avoué** he won't give me any peace until I tell him everything; **laisse-moi en p.!** leave me alone!; *Fam* **fiche-moi la p.!** get lost!; *Fam* **je veux qu'on me fiche la p.** I want to be left alone□; *très Fam* **fous-moi la p.!** get the hell out of here!, *Br* sod off!; *Fam* **la p.!** quiet!, shut up!

5 *(sérénité)* peace; **trouver la p. de l'âme** to find inner peace; **la p. du tombeau** the quiet of the grave; **avoir la conscience en p.** to have a clear conscience; **p. à ses cendres** God rest his soul; **qu'il repose en p., p. à son âme** may he *or* his soul rest in peace; **allez en p.** go in peace

6 *(harmonie)* peace, peacefulness; **la p. du soir à la campagne** peaceful evenings in the countryside

pajot [paʒo] = **pageot**

Pakistan [pakistɑ̃] NM **le P.** Pakistan

pakistanais, -e [pakistanɛ, -ɛz] ADJ Pakistani

• **Pakistanais, -e** NM,F Pakistani

PAL, Pal [pal] ADJ *TV (abrév* **Phase Alternation Line)** PAL

pal, -als [pal] NM **1** *(pieu)* stake, pale; **le supplice du p.** torture by impalement **2** *(plantoir)* planter, dibber

palabre [palabr] NF OU NM *Hist* palaver

• **palabres** NMPL OU NFPL *Péj (discussion oiseuse)* endless discussion; **après de longues palabres** after a lengthy discussion

palabrer [3] [palabre] **VI** *Péj* to talk endlessly; **vous ne faites que p.** all you ever do is talk

palace [palas] **NM** luxury hotel; **tu verrais sa maison, c'est un vrai p.** you should see his/her house, it's palatial *or* luxurious

> Il faut noter que le terme anglais **palace** est un faux ami. Il signifie **palais**.
>
> Do not confuse with **palais**.

paladin [paladɛ̃] **NM 1** *Hist* paladin **2** *Littéraire (redresseur de torts)* knight in shining armour, righter of wrongs

palais [palɛ] **NM 1** *(bâtiment)* palace; **p. des congrès** convention centre; **p. des expositions** exhibition hall; **p. des sports** sports stadium
2 *(monument)* **le P. Brongniart** = the Paris Stock Exchange; **le p. Garnier** = the (old) Paris opera house; **le p. des Papes** = the Papal Palace in Avignon *(the most prestigious venue of the Avignon Festival)*; **le Grand P., le Petit P.** = galleries built for the Exposition universelle in 1900, now used for art exhibitions
3 *Jur* **le P. de justice, le P.** the law courts; **le P. du Luxembourg** = the seat of the French Senate
4 *Anat* palate; **p. dur** hard palate; **p. fendu** cleft palate; **p. mou** soft palate
5 *(organe du goût)* palate; **elle a le p. fin** she has a refined palate; **un goût qui flatte le p.** a flavour that delights the taste buds *or* palate

> Do not confuse with the French word **palace**.

Palais-Bourbon [palɛburbɔ̃] **NM le P.** the French National Assembly

palan [palɑ̃] **NM** *Tech* hoist; **p. manuel** block and tackle

palanche [palɑ̃ʃ] **NF** *Tech* yoke

palanque [palɑ̃k] **NF** (timber) stockade

palanquée [palɑ̃ke] **NF 1** *Naut* load **2** *Fig (multitude)* **une p. de…** a raft of…

palanquer [3] [palɑ̃ke] **VT 1** *(lever avec un palan)* to hoist **2** *(munir de palanques)* to stockade

palanquin [palɑ̃kɛ̃] **NM** *(chaise)* palanquin

palatal, -e, -aux, -ales [palatal, -o] **ADJ 1** *Ling (voyelle)* front; *(consonne)* palatal **2** *Anat* palatal
• **palatale NF** *Ling (consonne)* palatal consonant; *(voyelle)* front vowel

palatalisation [palatalizasjɔ̃] **NF** *Ling* palatalization

palataliser [3] [palatalize] *Ling* **VT** to palatalize
VPR se palataliser to be palatalized

palatin, -e [palatɛ̃, -in] **ADJ 1** *(du palais)* palace *(avant n)* **2** *(du Palatinat)* Palatine *(avant n)* **3** *Anat* palatine, palatal
NM *Hist* Palatine

Palatinat [palatina] **NM** *Hist* **le P.** the Palatinate

pale [pal] **NF 1** *(d'une hélice, d'une rame)* blade; *(d'un bateau à aube)* paddle **2** *(vanne)* paddle, sluice(-gate)

pâle [pɑl] **ADJ 1** *(clair)* pale; *(exsangue)* pale, pallid; **elle est toute p.** she's very pale; **p. de colère** livid with rage; **être p. comme la mort** to be deathly pale; **être p. comme un linge** to be as white as a sheet; *Fam Arg mil* **se faire porter p.** to go *or* to report sick□ **2** *(couleur, lumière)* pale; **la p. lueur de l'aube** the pale light of dawn **3** *(insipide)* pale, weak; *(style)* colourless; **elle nous a fait un p. sourire** she smiled weakly *or* faintly at us; **son spectacle n'est qu'une p. imitation du livre** his/her show is nothing but a pale *or* poor imitation of the book; **mes aventures semblent bien pâles auprès des vôtres** my adventures pale in comparison with yours

palefrenier, -ère [palfrənje, -ɛr] **NM,F** groom; *Arch (d'auberge)* ostler

palefroi [palfrwa] **NM** *Arch* palfrey

paléoanthropologie [paleoɑ̃trɔpɔlɔʒi] **NF** paleoanthropology

paléoanthropologue [paleoɑ̃trɔpɔlɔg] **NMF** paleoanthropologist

paléographe [paleɔgraf] **ADJ** paleographic
NMF paleographer

paléographie [paleɔgrafi] **NF** paleography

paléographique [paleɔgrafik] **ADJ** paleographic

paléolithique [paleɔlitik] **ADJ** Paleolithic
NM le p. the Paleolithic

paléontologie [paleɔ̃tɔlɔʒi] **NF** paleontology

paléontologique [paleɔ̃tɔlɔʒik] **ADJ** paleontological

paléontologiste [paleɔ̃tɔlɔʒist], **paléontologue** [paleɔ̃tɔlɔg] **NMF** paleontologist

paléozoïque [paleɔzɔik] **ADJ** Paleozoic
NM le p. the Paleozoic (era)

Palerme [palɛrm] **NM** Palermo

paleron [palrɔ̃] **NM** chuck steak

Palestine [palɛstin] **NF la P.** Palestine

palestinien, -enne [palɛstinjɛ̃, -ɛn] **ADJ** Palestinian
• **Palestinien, -enne NM,F** Palestinian

palet [palɛ] **NM 1** *Sport (pour hockey sur glace)* puck; *(pour curling)* stone **2** *(à la marelle)* quoit

paletot [palto] **NM 1** *(pardessus)* (short) jacket **2** *Fam* **tomber sur le p. à qn** *(attaquer)* to jump on sb, to go for sb; *(pour lui parler)* to buttonhole sb

palette [palɛt] **NF 1** *Beaux-Arts* palette; *Fig (choix)* choice, range; *Fig* **la p. de Cézanne** Cézanne's palette *or* range of colours; **proposer toute une p. d'articles** to offer a wide choice *or* range of articles; *Ordinat* **p. graphique** graphics palette; *Ordinat* **p. d'outils** tool palette
2 *Culin* shoulder
3 *(d'une roue à aubes)* paddle
4 *Tech (pour la manutention)* pallet
5 *(pour battre le linge)* (washerwoman's) beetle

palettisation [paletizasjɔ̃] **NF** *Tech* palletization

palettiser [3] [paletize] **VT** *Tech* to palletize

palettiseur [paletizœr] **NM** *Tech* palletizing machine

palétuvier [paletyvje] **NM** *Bot* mangrove

pâleur [pɑlœr] **NF 1** *(d'une couleur, de la lumière)* paleness; *(du teint)* pallor **2** *Fig (du style)* colourlessness

pâlichon, -onne [pɑliʃɔ̃, -ɔn] **ADJ** *Fam* a bit pale□, on the pale side□

palier [palje] **NM 1** *(plate-forme)* landing; **p. de repos** half-landing
2 *(niveau)* stage, level; *(d'un graphique)* plateau; **atteindre un p.** to reach a plateau, to level off; **à partir d'un certain p., le taux change** the rate changes at a certain point
3 *Constr* level, flat
4 *Aviat* **voler en p.** to fly level
5 *Tech* bearing; **p. lisse/à roulement** plain/rolling bearing
• **par paliers ADV** in stages, step by step; **la tension monte par paliers** tension is gradually mounting

palière [paljɛr] **ADJ F porte p.** landing door, door opening onto the landing; **marche p.** top step

palimpseste [palɛ̃psɛst] **NM** palimpsest

palindrome [palɛ̃drom] **NM** palindrome

palinodie [palinɔdi] **NF 1** *Littérature* palinode **2** *Littéraire (revirement)* volte-face

pâlir [32] [pɑlir] **VI 1** *(personne)* to (turn *or* go) pale; **p. de froid/peur** to turn pale with cold/fear; **p. de rage/de colère** to become livid with rage/anger; **p. de jalousie/d'envie** to go green with jealousy/envy; **elle a une voiture/un salaire à faire p.** her car/salary is enough to make anyone green with envy **2** *(couleur, lumière, étoile)* to grow dim *or* pale, to fade; **le soleil a fait p. le tissu du canapé** the sun has faded the couch material **3** *(gloire)* to fade (away), to grow faint *or* fainter, to dim
VT *Littéraire* to make pale

palis [pali] **NM** *(alignement)* fence, paling; *(pieu)* stake, pale; *(enclos)* enclosure

palissade [palisad] **NF 1** *(clôture ► de pieux)* fence, paling, palisade; *(► de planches)* hoarding; *(► d'arbres)* hedgerow **2** *Mil* palisade

palissader [3] [palisade] **VT 1** *(clôturer)* to fence in, to put a fence round **2** *Mil* to palisade

palissandre [palisɑ̃dr] **NM** rosewood, palissander

pâlissant, -e [pɑlisɑ̃, -ɑ̃t] **ADJ** *(lumière)* fading, growing *or* becoming dim

palladium [paladjɔm] **NM** *Chim & Myth* palladium

palliatif, -ive [paljatif, -iv] **ADJ** palliative
NM 1 *Méd* palliative **2** *(expédient)* stopgap measure, palliative

pallier [9] [palje] **VT 1** *(manque, erreur, inconvénient)* to make up for **2** *(difficultés)* to overcome; *(crise)* to resolve **3** *Méd (douleur)* to palliate
• **pallier à VT IND** to make up for

palmarès [palmarɛs] **NM 1** *(liste ► de lauréats)* prize list, list of prizewinners; *(► de sportifs)* winners' list, list of winners; *(► de chansons)* charts; **être** *ou* **figurer au p.** to be among the prizewinners; *(de la chanson)* to be in the charts; **être premier au p.** to be number one, to top the charts **2** *(succès)* **avoir de nombreuses victoires à son p.** to have numerous victories to one's credit; **avoir un beau p.** to have an excellent track record

palme [palm] **NF 1** *Bot (feuille)* palm leaf; *(palmier)* palm tree; **huile/vin de p.** palm oil/wine **2** *(distinction)* palm; **la p. du martyre** the crown of martyrdom; **la P. d'Or** = trophy awarded for best film at the Cannes film festival; **remporter la p.** *(être le meilleur)* to win; *Ironique* to win hands down **3** *Sport* flipper
• **palmes NFPL palmes (académiques)** = decoration for services to education, the arts or science

palmé, -e [palme] **ADJ 1** *Bot* palmate; *Zool* webbed, *Spéc* palmate **2** *Fam Hum (locution)* **les avoir palmées** to be bone idle *or* a complete layabout

palmer [palmɛr] **NM** *(instrument)* micrometer

palmeraie [palmərɛ] **NF** palm grove

palmier [palmje] **NM 1** *Bot* palm (tree); **p. dattier** date palm **2** *(pâtisserie)* palmier *(heart-shaped biscuit made of flaky pastry)*

palmipède [palmipɛd] **ADJ** palmiped
NM palmiped

palmiste [palmist] **NM** *Bot* cabbage palm

Palm Pilot® [palmpajlɔt] **NM** *Ordinat* Palm Pilot®

palombe [palɔ̃b] **NF** *Orn* ringdove, wood pigeon

palonnier [palɔnje] **NM 1** *Aviat* rudder (bar) **2** *(d'un véhicule)* rocking lever; *Aut* **p. de freinage** compensator

palot [palo] **NM** *(outil)* = narrow spade used for digging worms, shells etc out of the sand

pâlot, -otte [pɑlo, -ɔt] **ADJ** *Fam* peaky, pale□, on the pale side□

palourde [palurd] **NF** *Zool* clam

palpable [palpabl] **ADJ 1** *(évident)* palpable; **des preuves palpables** palpable proof *or* evidence **2** *(que l'on peut toucher)* palpable, tangible

palpation [palpɑsjɔ̃] **NF** *Méd* palpation

palper [3] [palpe] **VT 1** *Méd* to palpate **2** *(tâter)* to feel **3** *Fam (recevoir)* **elle a palpé une belle somme** she came into a tidy sum
USAGE ABSOLU *Fam* to get one's money□, to collect; **qu'est-ce qu'il a dû p.!** he must have made a mint!

palpeur [palpœr] **NM** sensor

palpitant, -e [palpitɑ̃, -ɑ̃t] **ADJ 1** *(passionnant)* thrilling, exciting **2** *(qui palpite ► cœur, pouls)* palpitating, fluttering; *Fig* **p. d'émotion/d'angoisse** quivering *or* trembling with emotion/anxiety
NM *Fam (cœur)* ticker

palpitation [palpitɑsjɔ̃] **NF** *(du cœur)* pounding; *(des artères)* throbbing; *(des flancs)* heaving; *(des paupières)* fluttering
• **palpitations NFPL** palpitations; **avoir des palpitations** *(une fois)* to have palpitations; *(souvent)* to suffer from palpitations

palpiter [3] [palpite] **VI** *(artère)* to throb; *(paupière)* to flutter; *(flancs)* to quiver, to heave; **son cœur palpitait violemment** his/her heart was beating fast *or* pounding; **sa poitrine palpitait** her bosom was heaving

paltoquet [paltɔkɛ] **NM** *Fam* **1** *Vieilli (rustre)* boor, peasant **2** *(personne insignifiante)* pipsqueak

paluche [palyʃ] **NF** *Fam* hand□, paw, mitt

paludéen, -enne [palydeɛ̃, -ɛn] **ADJ 1** *Méd* malarial, paludal **2** *(des marais)* marsh *(avant n)*, paludal

paludisme [palydism] NM *Méd* malaria, paludism

palustre [palystr] ADJ **1** *Méd* malarial **2** *(des marais)* marsh *(avant n)*, paludal

PAM [pam] NM *(abrév* **programme alimentaire mondial**) WFP

pâmer [3] [pame] **se pâmer** VPR *Littéraire ou Hum* to swoon; **se p. d'aise** to be as pleased as Punch, to be tickled pink; **se p. de rire** to be convulsed with laughter; **se p. d'admiration devant** to be in raptures over, to be overcome with admiration for; **se p. devant qn** to swoon over sb

pâmoison [pɑmwazɔ̃] NF *Littéraire ou Hum* swoon, fainting fit; **tomber en p. (devant)** to swoon (over)

pampa [pɑ̃pa] NF pampas

pamphlet [pɑ̃flɛ] NM *(écrit satirique)* lampoon, pamphlet

> Il faut noter que le terme anglais **pamphlet** est un faux ami. Il désigne le plus souvent une brochure.

pamphlétaire [pɑ̃fletɛr] ADJ *(ton, esprit)* pamphleteering

NMF lampoonist, pamphleteer

pamplemousse [pɑ̃pləmus] NM grapefruit, *Am* pomelo

pampre [pɑ̃pr] NM *Bot* vine branch

Pan [pɑ̃] NPR *Myth* Pan

pan[1] [pɑ̃] EXCLAM *(gifle)* wham!, whack!; *(coup de feu)* bang!; **et p., le voilà qui entre!** and then, would you believe it, in he comes!; **je vais te faire p. p. (cucul)!** *(langage enfantin)* I'll smack your bottom!

pan[2] [pɑ̃] NM **1** *(d'un vêtement)* tail; *(d'une nappe)* fold; **se promener en p. de chemise** to wander about in one's shirt-tails

2 *Constr* **p. de bois/fer** wood/metal framing; *Archit* **à pans coupés** canted, with a cut-off corner; **p. de mur** (section of) wall

3 *(morceau)* section, piece; **un p. de ciel bleu** a patch of blue sky

4 *Tech* side, face

panacée [panase] NF panacea

panachage [panaʃaʒ] NM **1** *(mélange)* blend, blending, mixing **2** *Pol* = voting for candidates from different lists rather than for a list as a whole

panache [panaʃ] NM **1** *(plume)* plume, panache; *Fig* **p. de fumée** plume of smoke **2** *(brio)* panache, style, verve; **avec p.** with great panache; **avoir du p.** to have panache, to show great verve

panaché, -e [panaʃe] ADJ **1** *(mélangé* ▸ *sélection, salade)* mixed; *(*▸ *fleurs)* variegated; **un demi p.** a (lager) shandy; **glace panachée** assorted ice-cream **2** *Pol* **liste panachée** = ballot paper in which a voter votes for candidates from different lists rather than for a list as a whole

NM (lager) shandy

panacher [3] [panaʃe] VT **1** *(mélanger)* to blend, to mix **2** *Pol* **p. une liste électorale** = to vote for candidates from different lists rather than for a list as a whole

panade [panad] NF **1** *Culin* bread soup **2** *Fam (locution)* **être dans la p.** to be penniless❑ *or Br* on one's uppers

panafricain, -e [panafrikɛ̃, -ɛn] ADJ Pan-African

panafricanisme [panafrikanism] NM Pan-Africanism

panais [pane] NM parsnip

Panama [panama] NM **1** *(pays)* **le P.** Panama; **le canal de P.** the Panama Canal; **l'isthme de P.** the Isthmus of Panama **2** *(ville)* Panama City; **à P.** in Panama City

Paname [panam] NM *Fam* = nickname given to Paris

panaméen, -enne [panameɛ̃, -ɛn] ADJ Panamanian

• **Panaméen, -enne** NM,F Panamanian

panaméricain, -e [panamerikɛ̃, -ɛn] ADJ Pan-American

panaméricanisme [panamerikanism] NM Pan-Americanism

panamien, -enne [panamjɛ̃, -ɛn] = **panaméen**

panarabe [panarab] ADJ Pan-Arab

panarabisme [panarabism] NM Pan-Arabism

panard, -e [panar, -ard] ADJ cow-hocked

NM *Fam* **1** *(pied)* foot❑ **2** *(plaisir intense)* **quel p.!** great!, terrific!, fantastic!; **ce n'est pas le p.** it's not exactly a load of laughs *or* a barrel of fun

panaris [panari] NM felon, whitlow

panavision [panavizjɔ̃] NF panavision

pan-bagnat [pɑ̃baɲa] *(pl* **pans-bagnats**) NM filled roll *(containing tomatoes, onions, green peppers, olives, tuna and anchovies and seasoned with olive oil)*

pancake [pankɛk] NM *Eng* Scotch pancake, *Am & Scot* pancake

pancarte [pɑ̃kart] NF *(gén)* sign, notice; *(dans une manifestation)* placard;

pancréas [pɑ̃kreas] NM *Anat* pancreas

pancréatique [pɑ̃kreatik] ADJ *Anat* pancreatic

panda [pɑ̃da] NM *Zool* panda; **grand p., p. géant** giant panda

pandémie [pɑ̃demi] NF *Méd* pandemic

pandémique [pɑ̃demik] ADJ *Méd* pandemic

pandémonium [pɑ̃demɔnjɔm] NM *Littéraire* pandemonium

pandit [pɑ̃dit] NM pandit

Pandore [pɑ̃dɔr] NPR *Myth* Pandora; **la boîte de P.** Pandora's box

pané, -e [pane] ADJ breaded

panégyrique [paneʒirik] NM panegyric, eulogy; **faire le p. de qn** to extol sb's virtues, to eulogize sb

ADJ panegyrical

panégyriste [paneʒirist] NMF panegyrist

panel [panɛl] NM **1** *(de spécialistes)* panel **2** *Mktg (échantillon)* panel, sample group; **p. ad hoc** ad hoc panel; **p. de consommateurs** consumer panel, shopping panel; **p. de détaillants** retail panel

panéliste [panelist] NMF panel member

paner [3] [pane] VT to coat with breadcrumbs

panetière [pantjɛr] NF bread box

paneuropéanisme [panøropeanism] NM pan-Europeanism

paneuropéen, -enne [panøropeɛ̃, -ɛn] ADJ pan-European

pangermanisme [pɑ̃ʒɛrmanism] NM pan-Germanism

pangermaniste [pɑ̃ʒɛrmanist] ADJ pan-Germanist

NMF pan-Germanist

panier [panje] NM **1** *(corbeille)* basket; **p. à bouteilles** bottle case *or* carrier; **p. à couverts** cutlery basket; **p. à diapositives** slide tray; **p. à frites** *Br* chip basket, *Am* French fry basket; **p. à linge** linen basket; **p. à ouvrage** workbasket; **p. à pain** bread basket; **p. à pique-nique** picnic basket; **p. à provisions** shopping basket; **p. à salade** salad shaker; *Fam (fourgon cellulaire) Br* police van❑, Black Maria, *Am* police wagon❑, paddy wagon; **mettre** *ou* **jeter qch au p.** to throw sth out; **bon à mettre** *ou* **jeter au p.** fit for the *Br* bin *or Am* trash can; **il ne faut pas tous les mettre dans le même p.** you can't lump them all together, they're not all tarred with the same brush; **être un (véritable) p. percé** *(être dépensier)* to be a (real) spendthrift; *Can Fam (être indiscret)* to be a blabbermouth; *Fam* **mettre la main au p. à qn** to goose sb

2 *(quantité)* **un (plein) p. de** a basketful of

3 *Sport* basket; **réussir** *ou* **marquer un p.** to score a basket

4 *Écon* basket; **p. de la ménagère** shopping basket; **la hausse du beurre se répercute sur le p. de la ménagère** the increase in the price of butter makes a difference to the housekeeping bill; *Bourse* **p. d'actions** basket of shares; **p. de monnaies** *ou* **de devises** basket of currencies

5 *Mktg (présentoir)* dump bin; **p. de présentation en vrac, p. présentoir** dump bin; **p. à la sortie** check-out display; **p. vrac** dump bin

6 *(nasse)* lobster pot; **c'est un (véritable) p. de crabes** they're always at each other's throats

7 *(de crinoline)* hoop

panier-repas [panjerəpa] *(pl* **paniers-repas**) NM *Br* packed lunch, *Am* brown bag lunch

panifiable [panifjabl] ADJ *(céréale)* suitable for making bread; **farine p.** bread flour

panifier [9] [panifje] VT to make bread from

panique [panik] NF *(terreur)* panic; **ne pas céder à la p.** not to panic, not to give way to panic; **il s'est enfui, pris de p.** he fled in panic; **les passagers étaient pris de p.** the passengers were panic-stricken; **il y a eu un mouvement de p.** there was a wave of panic; *Fam* **c'était la p.!** it was panic stations!; **pas de p.!** don't panic!, there's no need to panic!

ADJ **peur p.** panic

paniquer [3] [panike] *Fam* VT *(angoisser)* to panic❑, to throw into a panic❑; **elle était complètement paniquée** she was completely panic-stricken, she was in a complete panic

VI to panic❑; **la nouvelle les a fait p.** the news panicked them

VPR **se paniquer** to panic❑

panislamique [panislamik] ADJ pan-islamic

panislamisme [panislamism] NM pan-islamism

panne [pan] NF **1** *(de voiture)* breakdown; **vous êtes à l'étranger et soudain c'est la p., que faites-vous?** suppose you're abroad and you suddenly break down, what do you do?; **trouver la p.** to find the problem, to find the cause of the problem; **p. d'électricité** *ou* **de courant** power cut *or* failure; **avoir une p. d'essence** to run out of *Br* petrol *or Am* gas; **p. de moteur** engine failure; *Fam Hum* **j'ai eu une p. d'oreiller** I overslept❑; **p. de secteur** local mains failure; *Fam* **il a essayé de me faire le coup de la p.** he tried to pull the old running-out-of-petrol trick on me

2 *Ordinat* failure, crash; **p. logicielle** software crash; **p. matérielle** hardware crash; **p. du système** system crash

3 *Tex* panne

4 *(d'un cochon)* pig's fat *or* lard

5 *(d'un marteau)* peen

6 *(d'un bâtiment)* purlin, purline

• **en panne** ADJ **des automobilistes en p.** drivers whose cars have broken down; **en p.** out of order; **la machine/voiture est en p.** the machine/car has broken down; **je suis en p.** *(automobiliste)* I've broken down; *Fam Fig* **je suis en p. de poivre/d'idées** I've run out of *or* I'm out of pepper/ideas

ADV **mettre un voilier en p.** to heave a sailing ship to; **tomber en p.** *(voiture, machine)* to break down; *(automobiliste)* to break down, to have a breakdown; *(ordinateur)* to crash

panneau, -x [pano] NM **1** *(pancarte)* sign; *(pour afficher)* board; **p. d'affichage** notice board; *Ordinat* bulletin board; *Ordinat* **p. de configuration** control panel; **p. indicateur** signpost; **p. publicitaire** billboard, *Br* hoarding; **p. de signalisation** roadsign

2 *(plaque)* panel; **p. de particules** chipboard, particleboard; **p. solaire** solar panel

3 *Couture* panel; **une jupe à trois panneaux** a three-panelled skirt

4 *Chasse* (game) net; **tomber** *ou* **donner dans le p.** to fall into the trap

panneton [pantɔ̃] NM bit, web *(of a key)*

pano [pano] NM *Fam Cin & TV* pan❑

panonceau, -x [panɔ̃so] NM **1** *(plaque)* plaque, sign; *(écriteau)* sign; **p. publicitaire** advertisement, *Br* advert **2** *Hist* escutcheon

panoplie [panɔpli] NF **1** *(ensemble d'instruments)* (complete) set; **la p. du bricoleur** do-it-yourself equipment *or* kit

2 *(déguisement)* outfit; **une p. de Zorro/d'infirmière** a Zorro/nurse's outfit

3 *Fig (d'arguments)* battery; **toute une p. de mesures contre les chauffards** a full array of measures against dangerous drivers

4 *Hist (armure complète)* panoply

panorama [panɔrama] NM **1** *(vue)* panorama, view **2** *Fig (vue d'ensemble)* survey, overview; **pour terminer ce p. de l'actualité musicale** to end this round-up of current musical events **3** *Beaux-Arts* panorama

panoramique [panɔramik] ADJ *(écran, vue)* panoramic; *(restaurant)* with panoramic views; *Rail* **wagon** *ou* **car p.** observation car

NM *Cin & TV* pan (shot); **faire un p.** to pan; **faire un p. horizontal/vertical** to pan/tilt

panoramiquer [panɔramike] VI *Cin & TV* to pan; **p. vers le bas/le haut** to pan down/up

panosse [panɔs] **NF** *Suisse* mop

panosser [3] [panɔse] **VT** *Suisse* to mop

panouille [panuj] **NF** *Fam* **1** *(personne stupide)* idiot, fool **2** *(petit rôle)* bit-part

pansage [pɑ̃saʒ] **NM** grooming

panse [pɑ̃s] **NF 1** *Zool* paunch, rumen **2** *Fam (d'une personne)* paunch, belly; **s'en mettre plein la p., se remplir la p.** to make a pig of oneself, to stuff one's face **3** *(d'un vase)* belly

pansement [pɑ̃smɑ̃] **NM** *(action)* dressing; *(objet)* dressing, bandage; **il lui a fait un p. à la jambe** he put a dressing on his/her leg; **elle lui a refait son p.** she changed his/her dressing; **il est couvert de pansements** he's all bandaged up; **p. (adhésif)** *Br* (sticking) plaster, Elastoplast®, *Am* Band Aid®; **p. gastrique** *(liquide)* = milk of magnesia; *(poudre)* stomach powder

panser [3] [pɑ̃se] **VT 1** *Méd (personne blessée)* to dress the wounds of; *(blessure)* to dress, to put a dressing on; *(membre)* to put a dressing on, to bandage; *Fig* **le temps panse tous les maux** time is a great healer; *Fig* **p. ses blessures** to lick one's wounds **2** *(toiletter ▸ animal)* to groom

panslavisme [pɑ̃slavism] **NM** Pan-Slavism

pansu, -e [pɑ̃sy] **ADJ 1** *Fam (ventripotent)* paunchy, potbellied **2** *(renflé ▸ cruche, bouteille)* potbellied

pantacourt [pɑ̃takur] **NM** cropped trousers, three-quarter (length) trousers

pantagruélique [pɑ̃tagryelik] **ADJ** *(appétit)* enormous; *(repas)* gargantuan, pantagruelian

pantalon [pɑ̃talɔ̃] **NM** (pair of) *Br* trousers *or Am* pants; **mon p.** my *Br* trousers *or Am* pants; **deux pantalons** two pairs of *Br* trousers *or Am* pants; **p. bouffant** baggy *Br* trousers *or Am* pants; **p. cargo** cargo *Br* trousers *or Am* pants; **p. cigarette** *Br* drainpipe trousers, *Am* straight-leg pants; **p. de golf** plus fours; **p. jazz** jazz pants; **p. multi-poches** combat trousers, combats; **p. de pyjama** pyjama *Br* trousers *or* bottoms *or Am* pants; **p. de ski** ski pants

pantalon-jupe [pɑ̃talɔ̃ʒyp] *(pl* **pantalons-jupes***)* **NM** culottes

pantalonnade [pɑ̃talɔnad] **NF 1** *(hypocrisie)* hypocrisy *(UNCOUNT)*, pretence *(UNCOUNT)* **2** *Théât* (second-rate) farce, slapstick comedy

pantelant, -e [pɑ̃tlɑ̃, -ɑ̃t] **ADJ 1** *(haletant)* panting, gasping for breath; *Fig* **être p. de terreur** to be panting *or* gasping with terror **2** *(palpitant)* **chair pantelante** twitching flesh

panteler [24] [pɑ̃tle] **VI** *Littéraire* **1** *Vieilli (haleter)* to pant **2** *(palpiter)* to twitch

panthéisme [pɑ̃teism] **NM** pantheism

panthéiste [pɑ̃teist] **ADJ** pantheistic
NMF pantheist

panthéon [pɑ̃teɔ̃] **NM 1** *Antiq & Rel* pantheon; **le P.** the Pantheon **2** *Fig* pantheon, hall of fame; **je le place au p. des accordéonistes** I consider him to be one of the greatest accordion players of all time; **son nom est resté au p. de l'histoire** his/her name went down in history

panthère [pɑ̃tɛr] **NF 1** *Zool* leopard; **p. des neiges** snow leopard; **p. noire** panther **2** *(fourrure)* leopard; **un manteau en (peau de) p.** a leopard-skin coat **3** *Pol* **les Panthères noires** the Black Panthers

pantin [pɑ̃tɛ̃] **NM 1** *(jouet)* jumping jack **2** *Fig* puppet; **n'être qu'un p. entre les mains de qn** to be sb's puppet

pantographe [pɑ̃tɔgraf] **NM** *Tech* pantograph

pantois, -e [pɑ̃twa, -az] **ADJ** speechless, dumbstruck; **elle en est restée pantoise** it left her speechless, she was dumbstruck *or* speechless

pantomime [pɑ̃tɔmim] **NF 1** *(jeu de mime)* mime; *Théât (pièce)* mime show **2** *Péj (comédie)* scene, fuss

> Il faut noter que le terme anglais **pantomime** est un faux ami. Il désigne un spectacle de Noël inspiré d'un conte de fées.

pantouflard, -e [pɑ̃tuflar, -ard] *Fam* **ADJ ils sont très pantouflards** they're real homebodies, they never go out□
NM,F homebody, stay-at-home

pantoufle [pɑ̃tufl] **NF** slipper; **p. de vair** *(dans Cendrillon)* glass slipper; **être en pantoufles** to be in one's slippers

pantoufler [3] [pɑ̃tufle] **VI** *Fam* = to leave a civil service post and work for the private sector

pantoute [pɑ̃tut] **ADV** *Can Fam (pas du tout)* absolutely not□, no way; *(jamais de la vie)* never in a million years

panure [panyr] **NF** breadcrumbs *(for coating)*

Panurge [panyrʒ] **NPR** *Littérature* = the faithful companion of Pantagruel, best known for the incident where he throws a sheep into the sea, causing the rest of the flock to follow; *voir* **mouton**

panurgisme [panyrʒism] **NM** *Péj* herd mentality

PAO [peao] **NF** *(abrév* **publication assistée par ordinateur***)* *Ordinat* DTP

paon [pɑ̃] **NM 1** *Orn* peafowl; **p. (bleu)** peacock; **fier** *ou* **orgueilleux** *ou* **vaniteux comme un p.** (as) proud as a peacock; **faire le p.** to strut about (like a peacock) **2** *Entom* **p. de jour** peacock; **p. de nuit** emperor moth

paonne [pan] **NF** *Orn* peahen

paonneau, -x [pano] **NM** peachick

PAP [pap] **NM** *(abrév* **prêt d'accession à la propriété***)* = loan for first-time homebuyers

papa [papa] **NM 1** *(père ▸ gén)* dad; *(▸ en langage enfantin)* daddy; **jouer au p. et à la maman** to play mummies and daddies **2** *Fam (homme d'un certain âge)* **alors, p., tu traverses?** come on, granddad, get across!

• **à la papa** **ADV** *Fam (tranquillement)* leisurely□; **on va faire ça à la p.** we'll take it easy, we'll do it at our own pace

• **à papa** **ADJ** *Fam* **c'est un fils/une fille à p.** he's/she's got a rich daddy

• **de papa** **ADJ** *Fam* old-fashioned□

papal, -e, -aux, -ales [papal, -o] **ADJ** papal

paparazzi [paparadzi] **NMPL** paparazzi

paparazzo [paparadzo] **NM** paparazzo

papauté [papote] **NF** papacy

papaye [papaj] **NF** papaya, pawpaw

papayer [papaje] **NM** papaya (tree), pawpaw (tree)

pape [pap] **NM 1** *Rel* pope; **le p. Benoît XVI** Pope Benedict XVI **2** *Fig (chef de file)* high priest, guru

papelard¹ [paplar] **NM** *Fam* **1** *(bout de papier)* paper□ **2** *Journ* article□, piece **3 papelards** *(papiers d'identité)* ID

papelard², -e [paplar, -ard] **ADJ** *Littéraire (personne)* unctuous; **..., dit-il d'un air p.** ..., he said smoothly

paperasse [papras] **NF** *Péj* papers, *Br* bumf; **je n'ai pas le temps de remplir toute cette p.** I don't have the time to fill in all these forms; **je passe mon temps à m'occuper de la p.** I spend all my time doing paperwork

paperasserie [paprasri] **NF** *Péj* **1** *(formulaires ▸ gén)* paperwork; *(▸ administratifs)* red tape; **toute cette p. va sûrement retarder le projet** all this red tape is bound to delay the project **2** *(amoncellement)* papers

paperassier, -ère [paprasje, -ɛr] *Péj* **ADJ** *(personne)* who loves filling in forms, who loves paperwork
NM,F *Br* penpusher, *Am* pencilpusher

papet [papɛ] **NM** *Suisse* = Swiss dish made with potatoes, leeks and sausages

papeterie [papɛtri] **NF 1** *(boutique)* stationer's (*Br* shop *or Am* store)
2 *(matériel)* stationery
3 *(usine)* paper mill
4 *(fabrication)* paper manufacturing; *(secteur)* paper industry

papetier, -ère [paptje, -ɛr] **ADJ** paper *(avant n)*, stationery *(avant n)*
NM,F 1 *Com* stationer **2** *Ind* paper-maker

papetier-libraire [paptjelibrɛr] *(pl* **papetiers-libraires***)* **NM** *Com* bookseller and stationer

papi [papi] **NM** *Fam (grand-père)* granddad

papier [papje] **NM 1** *(matière)* paper; *Fig* **barbouiller** *ou* **noircir du p.** to fill page after page; **toujours à gratter** *ou* **noircir du p.** always scribbling something or other; **sur le p.** on paper; **sur le p., le projet paraît réalisable** on paper, the project seems feasible; **jeter qch sur le p.** to jot sth down; **p. d'aluminium,** *Fam* **p. alu** *Br* aluminium *or Am* aluminum foil; **p. d'argent** silver foil *or* paper; **p. avion** airmail paper; *Ordinat* **p. à bandes perforées** perforated paper; **p. bible** bible paper; **p. brouillon** rough paper; **p. buvard** blotting paper; **p. cadeau** wrapping paper; **p. carbone** carbon (paper); **p. à cartouche** cartridge paper; **p. à cigarette** cigarette paper; **fin comme du p. à cigarette** *(usé)* like tissue paper; **p. collant** *(adhésif)* adhesive tape; *(gommé)* gummed paper *or* strip; **p. contact** contact paper; *Ordinat* **p. (en) continu** continuous paper *or* stationery, listing paper; **p. couché** *Ordinat* coated paper; *Beaux-Arts* art paper; **p. crépon** crêpe paper; *très Fam* **p. cul, p. Q** *Br* bog roll, *Am* TP; **p. à dessin** drawing paper; **p. d'emballage** (brown) wrapping paper; **p. à en-tête** headed paper *or* notepaper; **p. d'étain** tinfoil; **p. glacé** glazed paper; **sur p. glacé** *(magazine)* glossy; **p. huilé** oil-paper; **p. hygiénique** toilet paper; *Ordinat* **p. d'impression** printer paper; **p. journal** newspaper, newsprint; **p. kraft** brown paper; **p. à lettres** writing paper; **le contrat a été rédigé sur p. libre** the contract was drawn up on a sheet of plain paper; **envoyer une lettre sur p. libre** to apply in writing; *Ordinat* **p. listing** listing paper; **p. mâché** papier-mâché; **p. machine** typing paper; **p. millimétré** graph paper; **p. ministre** official paper; *Ordinat* **p. multiple** multi-part stationery; **p. à musique** music paper; **p. paraffiné** wax paper; **p. peint** wallpaper; **p. pelure** onion skin (paper); **p. photographique** photographic paper; **p. quadrillé** squared paper; **p. de riz** rice paper; **p. en rouleau** web *or* reel paper; *Can* **p. sablé** sandpaper; **p. sans bois** woodfree paper; **p. de soie** tissue paper; **p. sulfurisé** *Br* greaseproof *or Spéc* sulphurized paper, *Am* sulphurized paper; *Ordinat* **p. thermique** *ou* **thermosensible** thermal paper; **p. timbré** stamped paper *(for official use)*; **p. toilette,** *Can* **p. de toilette** toilet paper; **p. torchon** torchon paper; **p. de verre** sandpaper; **p. vélin** vellum *or Br* wove paper
2 *(morceau)* piece of paper; *(page)* sheet of paper, piece of paper; **as-tu un p. et un crayon?** do you have a piece of paper and a pencil?; **p. de bonbon** *Br* sweet *or Am* candy wrapper; **être dans les petits papiers de qn** to be in sb's good books
3 *Journ* article, piece; **faire un p. sur** to do a piece *or* an article on
4 *Admin* **papiers** papers; **les papiers du véhicule, s'il vous plaît** may I see your (vehicle) registration papers *or Br* logbook, please?; **les papiers de la vente** the sale documents; **papiers (d'identité)** (identity) papers; **mes papiers sont en règle** my papers are in order; **vos papiers, s'il vous plaît!** can I see your identity papers, please?; **faux papiers** false *or* forged papers
5 *Fin* **p. bancable** bankable paper; **p. de commerce** commercial paper; **p. sur l'étranger** foreign bill; **p. financier** *ou* **de crédit** bank credit note; **p. négociable** negotiable paper; **p. à ordre** instrument to order; **p. au porteur** bearer paper; **papiers valeurs** paper securities; **p. à vue** sight paper

• **de papier, en papier** **ADJ** paper *(avant n)*; **lanterne en p.** paper lantern

• **papiers gras** **NMPL** litter

> **PAPIERS**
>
> All French citizens are required by law to carry a "carte d'identité" (featuring a photograph, address and details of one's physical appearance) at all times. In order to guarantee a cheque, French people are also often required to present some form of identity (whether an identity card, a passport, a residence permit or a driving licence). When voting in elections, French voters must be in possession of a "carte d'électeur" issued by the town hall or "mairie". In the "livret de famille" which is presented to newly married couples at their civil wedding ceremony and is often needed for administrative procedures, details of marriages, divorces and births are recorded. The red tape associated with French bureaucracy is, however, gradually being simplified.

papier-calque [papjekalk] (*pl* **papiers-calque**) **NM** tracing paper

papier-émeri [papjeemri] (*pl* **papiers-émeri**) **NM** emery paper

papier-filtre [papjefiltr] (*pl* **papiers-filtres**) **NM** filter paper

papier-monnaie [papjemɔnɛ] (*pl* **papiers-monnaies**) **NM** paper money

papillaire [papilɛr] **ADJ** *Anat* papillary, papillate

papille [papij] **NF** *Anat* papilla; **papilles gustatives** taste buds

papillon [papijɔ̃] **NM 1** *Entom* butterfly; **p. de nuit** moth
2 *Fam (contravention)* (parking) ticket[□]
3 *(dans un livre)* inset; *(publicité)* leaflet
4 *Fig (esprit volage)* **c'est un (vrai) p.** he's flighty
5 *Tech (écrou)* butterfly *or* wing nut; *(obturateur, clapet)* butterfly valve; *Aut* **p. des gaz** throttle
6 *Natation* **(brasse) p.** butterfly (stroke); **nager le p.** to do the butterfly

papillonnage [papijɔnaʒ] = **papillonnement**

papillonnant, -e [papijɔnɑ̃, -ɑ̃t] **ADJ 1** *(versatile, instable ▸ esprit)* flight, **2** *(insecte)* fluttering

papillonnement [papijɔnmɑ̃] **NM 1** *(versatilité, inconstance)* flightiness **2** *(volettement)* fluttering

papillonner [3] [papijɔne] **VI 1** *(voltiger)* to flit *or* to flutter about; *Fig (d'un lieu à un autre, d'une personne à une autre)* to flit about **2** *(être volage)* to be flighty

papillotage [papijɔtaʒ] **NM** *(des yeux)* blinking; *(d'une lumière, d'un reflet)* flickering, dancing; *(des paupières)* fluttering

papillote [papijɔt] **NF 1** *(bigoudi)* curlpaper; *Fig* **ta dissertation, tu peux en faire des papillotes** your essay isn't worth the paper it's written on **2** *Culin (pour gigot)* frill; **en papillotes** en papillote *(cooked in foil or paper parcels)* **3** *(papier de bonbon) Br* sweet *or Am* candy wrapper

papillotement [papijɔtmɑ̃] **NM 1** *(clignement ▸ des yeux)* blinking; *(▸ des paupières)* fluttering **2** *(scintillement ▸ d'une lumière, d'un reflet)* flickering, flashing, dancing **3** *Cin & TV* flicker

papilloter [3] [papijɔte] **VI 1** *(œil)* to blink; *(paupière)* to flicker, to flutter **2** *(lumière, reflet)* to flicker, to flash, to dance
VT *Culin (dans du papier)* to wrap in buttered paper; *(dans de l'aluminium)* to wrap in foil

papisme [papism] **NM** papism, popery

papiste [papist] **ADJ** papist
NMF papist

papoter [3] [papɔte] **VI** *Fam* to chat, *Br* to natter; **nous avons passé la journée à p.** we spent the day chatting *or Am* shooting the breeze

papou, -e [papu] **ADJ** Papuan
• **Papou, -e NM,F** Papuan

Papouasie-Nouvelle-Guinée [papwazinuvelgine] **NF la P.** Papua New Guinea

papouilles [papuj] **NFPL** *Fam* **faire des p. à un bébé** to give a baby a little tickle; **faire des p. à qn** to pet sb; **se faire des p.** to pet (each other)

paprika [paprika] **NM** paprika

papule [papyl] **NF** papule

papy [papi] **NM** *Fam (grand-père)* grandad

papy-boom [papibum] **NM** *Hum* grandpa boom, elderly boom

papyrus [papirys] **NM** papyrus

paqson [paksɔ̃] = **pacson**

pâque [pɑk] **NF** *(agneau pascal)* paschal lamb

paquebot [pakbo] **NM** liner

pâquerette [pɑkrɛt] **NF** daisy; *Fam* **voler au ras des pâquerettes** *(conversation, plaisanterie)* to be a bit lowbrow

Pâques [pɑk] **NM** Easter; **à P. ou à la Trinité** never in a month of Sundays; **l'île de P.** Easter Island
• **pâques NFPL joyeuses p.** Happy Easter; **faire ses p.** to take communion (at Easter); **p. fleuries** Palm Sunday

> **PÂQUES**
>
> In France, Easter is traditionally symbolized not only by eggs but also by bells; according to legend, church bells fly to Rome at Easter. At this time of the year, people offer each other chocolate eggs, bells, fish or hens.

paquet [pakɛ] **NM 1** *(colis)* parcel, package; *(ballot, liasse)* bundle; **faire un p.** to make up a parcel
2 *Com (marchandise emballée ▸ gén)* packet, pack; *(▸ de sucre, de farine)* bag, packet; *(▸ de café, de pâtes, de lessive)* packet; *(▸ de cigarettes) Br* packet, *Am* pack; **du riz/du café en p.** prepacked *or* packaged rice/coffee; **p. échantillon** sample pack; **p. économique** economy pack; **p. familial** family-size pack; **p. géant** giant-sized pack; **p. de présentation** presentation pack
3 *(valise)* bag; **mets tes paquets là** put your bags down here; **faire ses paquets** to pack one's bags
4 *Fam (quantité importante)* **tout un p. de** a pile *ou* stack of; **il y a un p. d'erreurs dans ce texte** there are a ton of mistakes in this text; *Fig* **mettre le p.** to pull out all the stops, to go all out; **lâcher le p.** to get things off one's chest, to unburden oneself; **toucher le p.** to make a packet *or* mint *or* pile
5 *(masse)* **les manifestants arrivent par petits paquets** the demonstrators are arriving in clusters *or* in small groups; **j'ai reçu un p. de neige sur la tête** a lump of snow fell on my head; **il tombait des paquets d'eau** the rain was coming down in sheets; *Naut* **un p. de mer** a big wave; *Fam* **sa mère est un p. de nerfs** his/her mother's a bundle *or* bag of nerves
6 *Sport* **p. (d'avants)** pack
7 *Ordinat* packet
8 *Bourse (d'actions, de valeurs)* parcel, block
9 *Écon & Fin* **p. fiscal** tax package

paquetage [paktaʒ] **NM** *Mil* kit, pack; **faire son p.** to get one's kit ready

paquet-cadeau [pakɛkado] (*pl* **paquets-cadeaux**) **NM** gift-wrapped purchase; **je vous fais un p.?** shall I gift-wrap it for you?

paqueté, -e [pakte] **ADJ** *Can Fam (ivre) Br* pissed, *Am* bombed

paquet-poste [pakɛpɔst] (*pl* **paquets-poste**) **NM** mail parcel

par¹ [par] **NM** *Golf* par

PAR² [par]

• by **1, 4, 6**	• through **1**
• on **2**	• out of **5**
• per **7**	• with **8, 9**

PRÉP 1 *(indiquant la direction, le parcours)* by; *(en traversant un lieu)* through; **il est entré p. la porte de derrière** he came in by the back door; **il est arrivé p. la route** he came by road; **sors p. la fenêtre** go out by *or* through the window; **il est arrivé p. la gauche/p. la droite/p. le nord** he arrived from the left/the right/the north; **faut-il passer p. Paris?** do we have to go through *or* via Paris?; **il est passé p. la maison avant de ressortir** he dropped in before going off again; **il allait p. les rues** he was walking through the streets; **la nouvelle s'est répandue p. la ville** the news spread throughout the town
2 *(indiquant la position)* **elle est assise p. terre** she's sitting on the ground; **la neige avait fondu p. endroits** the snow had melted in places; *Naut* **p. 45 de latitude nord** lying at a latitude of 45 north; *Naut* **p. 10 brasses d'eau** in 10 fathoms of water; *Naut* **p. bâbord avant/arrière** on the port bow/stern
3 *(pendant)* **p. un beau jour d'été** on a fine summer's day; **p. une belle matinée de septembre** on a fine morning in September; **p. grand froid/grosse chaleur** in extreme cold/intense heat; **p. le passé** in the past; **p. moments** at times, from time to time; **p. les temps qui courent** these days; **p. deux fois** twice; **p. trois fois** three times, *Littéraire* thrice
4 *(indiquant le moyen, la manière)* by; **prends le couteau p. le manche** take the knife by the handle; **tenir qn p. la taille** to hold sb by the waist; **attraper qn p. les cheveux** to grab sb by the hair; **envoyer qch p. avion** to send sth by airmail; **p. air/terre/mer** by air/land/sea; **voyager p. bateau/le train** to travel by boat/train; **voyager p. avion** to travel by plane, to fly; **je l'ai appris p. la radio** I heard it on the radio; **répondre p. oui ou p. non/p. la négative** to answer yes or no/in the negative; **obtenir qch p. la force/la douceur** to obtain sth by force/through kindness; **je suis avec toi p. la pensée** I'm thinking of you, my thoughts are with you
5 *(indiquant la cause, l'origine)* **faire qch p. habitude/caprice/plaisir/paresse** to do sth out of habit/on a whim/for the pleasure of it/out of laziness; **il n'a pas répondu p. négligence/manque de temps** he didn't answer out of carelessness/because he didn't have the time; **différer p. ses habitudes** to differ in one's habits; **je l'ai rencontré p. hasard** I met him by chance; **je le sais p. expérience** I know it from experience; **fidèle p. devoir** faithful out of duty; **nous sommes cousins p. ma mère** we're cousins on my mother's side (of the family); **une tante p. alliance** an aunt by marriage
6 *(introduisant le complément d'agent)* by; **les récoltes ont été dévastées p. la grêle** the crops were ruined by the hail; **le logiciel est protégé p. un code** the software is protected by *or* with a code; **faire faire qch p. qn** to have sth done by sb; **je l'ai découvert p. son intermédiaire** I discovered it through him/her; **je l'ai appris p. elle** I heard it from her, I learned of it through her; **ils veulent le faire p. eux-mêmes** they want to do it by *or* for themselves; **elles se sont rencontrées p. son intermédiaire** they met through him/her; **les deux appareils sont reliés p. un fil** the two devices are connected by a wire; **le 'Discours de la méthode', p. Descartes** the 'Discourse on Method' by Descartes
7 *(emploi distributif)* **une heure p. jour** one hour a *or* per day; **100 euros p. personne** 100 euros per person; **une fois p. an** once a year; **un p. un** one by one; **heure p. heure** hour by hour; **mettez-vous deux p. deux** line up in twos; **ils arrivaient p. petits groupes/centaines** they arrived in small groups/in their hundreds
8 *(avec les verbes "commencer" et "finir")* **ça finira p. arriver/p. ressembler à quelque chose** it will end up happening/looking like something; **commence p. travailler** start (off) by working; **il a fini p. avouer** he eventually owned up; **le concert débuta p. une sonate de Mozart** the concert opened with a sonata by Mozart; **notre programme se terminera p. les informations à 23 heures 40** our programmes for the evening will end with the news at 11.40
9 *(suivi d'un verbe)* **il se fatigue p. trop écrire** he tires himself with writing too much
• **de par PRÉP 1** *(par l'ordre de)* **de p. la loi** according to the law; **de p. le roi** in the name of the king **2** *Littéraire (dans l'espace)* throughout; **de p. le monde** all over *or* throughout the world **3** *(du fait de)* by virtue of; **de p. son éducation, il est tout à fait à l'aise dans ce milieu** by virtue of his upbringing, he is perfectly at ease in this environment
• **par-ci par-là ADV 1** *(dans l'espace)* here and there; **des livres traînaient p.-ci p.-là** books were lying around here and there **2** *(dans le temps)* now and then, from time to time, every now and then *or* again **3** *(marquant la répétition)* **avec lui, c'est mon yacht p.-ci, mon avion personnel p.-là** it's my yacht this, my plane that, all the time with him

para [para] **NM** *Fam (gén)* parachutist[□]; *Mil* para

paraben [parabɛn] **NM** *Chim* paraben

parabole [parabɔl] **NF 1** *Littérature & Rel* parable **2** *Math* parabola **3** *Tél (antenne)* satellite dish, parabolic dish, *Am* dish antenna

parabolique [parabɔlik] **ADJ 1** *Littérature & Rel* parabolic, parabolical **2** *Math* parabolic **3** *(miroir)* parabolic; **radiateur p.** electric fire *(with parabolic reflector)*

paracétamol [parasetamɔl] **NM** paracetamol; **deux cachets de p.** two paracetamol

parachèvement [paraʃɛvmɑ̃] **NM** *(action)* completion; *(résultat)* crowning

parachever [19] [paraʃve] **VT** to complete; **p. un travail** to complete a piece of work; **p. un tableau** to put the finishing touches to a painting

parachutage [paraʃytaʒ] **NM 1** *(de soldats)* parachuting, parachute drop; *(de vivres, matériel)* parachute drop **2** *Fam (d'un candidat)* = bringing in a candidate from outside the constituency **3** *Fam (dans une entreprise)* parachuting in, = bringing an outsider into a firm

parachute [paraʃyt] **NM** parachute; **faire du p.** to go parachuting; **p. ascensionnel** *(tracté par véhicule)* parascending; *(tracté par bateau)* parasailing; **p. dorsal** back-pack parachute; **p. ventral** lap-pack *or* chest-pack parachute

parachuter [3] [paraʃyte] **VT 1** *Mil & Sport* to parachute **2** *Fam (candidat)* to parachute in **3** *Fam (dans une entreprise)* **il a été parachuté directeur dans une succursale** he was pitchforked *or* parachuted into the job of branch manager

parachutisme [paraʃytism] **NM** parachuting; **faire du p.** to go parachuting; **p. ascensionnel** parascending; **p. en chute libre** skydiving

parachutiste [paraʃytist] **NMF 1** *Sport* parachutist **2** *Mil* paratrooper; **parachutistes** *(corps d'armée)* paratroops, paratroopers

ADJ troupes parachutistes paratroops, paratroopers

parade [parad] **NF 1** *(défilé)* parade; **faire p. de** *(connaissances, richesse)* to show off, to parade, to display

2 *Zool* **p. nuptiale** courtship display

3 *Boxe* parry; *Escrime* parade, parry; *Équitation* pulling up; *Ftbl* save

4 *(riposte)* retort, reply, riposte; **nous devons trouver la p.** we must find a way of counterattacking

• **de parade ADJ 1** *(ornemental)* ceremonial **2** *(feint)* **une amabilité de p.** an outward show of friendliness

parader [3] [parade] **VI 1** *(troupes)* to parade **2** *Équitation* to execute a dressage **3** *(personne)* to show off, to pose, to strut about

paradigmatique [paradigmatik] **ADJ** paradigmatic

NF *Ling* paradigmatics *(singulier)*

paradigme [paradigm] **NM** paradigm

paradis [paradi] **NM 1** *Rel* paradise, heaven; **ce petit village est un véritable p.** this little village is heaven on earth *or* paradise; **aller au p.** to go to heaven; **p. fiscal** tax haven; **le P. terrestre** the Garden of Eden *or* Earthly Paradise; *Fig* heaven on earth **2** *Théât* **le p.** the (top) gallery, *Br* the gods

paradisiaque [paradizjak] **ADJ** heavenly, *Sout* paradisiacal; **une île p.** a paradise island

paradisier [paradizje] **NM** bird of paradise

paradoxal, -e, -aux, -ales [paradɔksal, -o] **ADJ 1** *(contradictoire)* paradoxical; **il a l'esprit p.** he's got a perverse way of looking at things **2** *(déconcertant)* unexpected, paradoxical; **sa présence parmi eux était paradoxale** it was surprising to find him/her among them

paradoxalement [paradɔksalmɑ̃] **ADV** paradoxically

paradoxe [paradɔks] **NM** paradox

parafe [paraf] = **paraphe**

parafer [parafe] = **parapher**

parafeur [parafœr] = **parapheur**

paraffinage [parafinaʒ] **NM** paraffining

paraffine [parafin] **NF** *Chim* paraffin (wax)

paraffiner [3] [parafine] **VT** to paraffin

parafiscal, -e, -aux, -ales [parafiskal, -o] **ADJ** *(taxe)* exceptional, special

parafiscalité [parafiskalite] **NF** indirect taxation, special taxation

parage [paraʒ] **NM** *Vieilli (extraction)* **de haut p.** of high lineage, high-born

parages [paraʒ] **NMPL 1** *(environs)* area, surroundings; **il habite (quelque part) dans les p.** he lives around here somewhere; **est-ce qu'il est dans les p.?** is he around?; **il est dans les p.** he's around somewhere; **dans les p. de...** in the vicinity of..., near... **2** *Naut* waters; **les p. du cap Horn** the waters off Cape Horn

paragraphe [paragraf] **NM 1** *(passage)* paragraph **2** *(signe typographique)* paragraph (sign), par

Paraguay [paragwɛ] **NM le P.** Paraguay

paraguayen, -enne [paragwejɛ̃, -ɛn] **ADJ** Paraguayan

• **Paraguayen, -enne NM,F** Paraguayan

para-hôtellerie NF serviced accommodation industry

parais *etc voir* **paraître**[2]

paraître[1] [parɛtr] **NM le p.** appearance, appearances; **l'être et le p.** appearance and reality

paraître[2] **[91]** [parɛtr] **VI 1** *(se montrer ▸ soleil)* to appear, to come out; *(▸ émotion)* to show; *(▸ personne attendue)* to appear, to turn up; *(▸ dignitaire, prince)* to appear, to make a public appearance; *(▸ acteur)* to appear; **il n'a pas paru au bureau depuis huit jours** he hasn't turned up *or* appeared at the office for a week now; **laisser p. son émotion** to let one's emotion show

2 *(figurer)* to appear; **l'usine nous appartient, mais notre logo n'y paraît pas** the factory belongs to us, but our logo isn't (displayed) on it

3 *(être publié ▸ livre)* to be published, to come out, to appear; **faire p. une petite annonce dans un journal** to put an advertisement in a paper; **à p.** *(livre)* forthcoming; **vient de p.** just published

4 *(sembler)* to appear, to seem, to look; **il ne paraît pas très à l'aise dans son costume** he doesn't seem (to be) very comfortable in his suit; **p. plus jeune que l'on n'est** to seem *or* to look *or* to appear younger than one is; **il paraît moins fatigué qu'hier** he looks less tired than he did yesterday; **il parut céder** he looked as though he was giving in; **paraît-il** apparently; **tu as retrouvé du travail, paraît-il** I hear you've got a new job

5 *(se donner en spectacle)* to show off; **il cherche toujours à p.** he's always showing off

VT 75 ans? vous ne les paraissez pas 75 years old? you don't look it

V IMPERSONNEL ça ne paraît pas (mais...) *(ça ne se voit pas)* it doesn't look like it (but...); **elle a 50 ans, ça ne paraît pas** she doesn't look 50, does she?; **il n'y paraît pas** it doesn't show; **il n'y paraît pas, mais le plancher est mouillé** it doesn't look like it, but the floor is wet; **je tâche de l'aider sans qu'il y paraisse** I try to help him without letting it show; **il me paraît préférable de se décider maintenant** I think it's better *or* it seems better to make up our minds now; **vous êtes renvoyé? – il paraît** have you been fired? – it looks like it *or* so it seems; **il paraît que...** I've heard (that)..., it would seem (that)...; *Fam* **paraît que tu vas te marier!** I hear you're getting married!; **à ce qu'il paraît** apparently

paralangage [paralɑ̃gaʒ] **NM** paralanguage

paralinguistique [paralɛ̃gɥistik] **ADJ** paralinguistic

NF paralinguistics *(singulier)*

paralittéraire [paraliterɛr] **ADJ les productions paralittéraires** minor literary works

paralittérature [paraliteratyr] **NF** literature with a small "l", minor literary works

parallaxe [paralaks] **NF** *Astron, Géom & Phot* parallax; **erreur de p.** parallax error

parallèle [paralɛl] **ADJ 1** *Géom, Sport & Ordinat* parallel (**à** to); **la droite AB est p. à la droite CD** line AB is parallel to line CD

2 *(comparable ▸ données, résultats)* parallel, comparable, similar; **nous avons eu des carrières parallèles** we had similar careers

3 *(non officiel ▸ festival)* unofficial, fringe *(avant n)*; *(▸ marché, transaction)* unofficial; *(▸ police)* unofficial, secret; **mener une vie p.** to live a double life

4 *Ordinat (port, imprimante, interface)* parallel

NM 1 *Astron & Géog* parallel; **p. de latitude** parallel of latitude **2** *(comparaison)* parallel; **établir un p. entre deux phénomènes** to draw a parallel between two phenomena **3** *Sport* parallel turning *or* skiing

NF *Géom* parallel (line)

• **en parallèle ADV 1** *(en balance)* **mettre deux faits en p.** to draw a parallel between *or* to compare two facts; **mettre qch en p. avec qch** to compare sth with sth **2** *Ordinat* (in) parallel

parallèlement [paralɛlmɑ̃] **ADV 1** *Géom* **p. à** in a parallel to **2** *(simultanément)* at the same time; **p. à** at the same time as

parallélépipède [paralelepipɛd] **NM** *Géom* parallelepiped

parallélisme [paralelism] **NM 1** *Géom* parallelism **2** *Aut* wheel alignment; **il y a un défaut de p.** there's something wrong with the alignment, the wheels aren't properly aligned **3** *(concordance)* parallel, concordance; **établir un p. entre deux faits** to draw a parallel between two facts

parallélogramme [paralelɔgram] **NM** *Géom* parallelogram

paralympique [paralɛ̃pik] **ADJ** Paralympic

paralysant, -e [paralizɑ̃, -ɑ̃t] **ADJ** *Méd & Fig* paralysing

paralysé, -e [paralize] **ADJ** paralysed; **elle a le bras droit p.** her right arm is paralysed; **être p. de peur** to be petrified, to be paralysed with fear; **nous sommes paralysés par l'insuffisance des fonds** we are hamstrung by a lack of funds

NM,F *Méd* paralytic

paralyser [3] [paralize] **VT 1** *Méd* to paralyse **2** *(figer, inhiber ▸ gén)* to paralyse; *(▸ économie, pays)* to cripple; *(▸ circulation)* to bring to a standstill; **la ville est paralysée par la grève** the town is paralysed by the strike; **ce genre de situation me paralyse** I'm petrified in that kind of situation; **paralysé par le froid** paralysed *or* numb with cold; **paralysé par la peur** petrified, paralysed with fear; **paralysé par le brouillard/la neige** fog-/snow-bound

paralysie [paralizi] **NF 1** *Méd* paralysis; **p. de Bell** Bell's palsy; **p. cérébrale** cerebral palsy; **p. faciale** facial palsy; **p. générale (progressive)** creeping paralysis **2** *(arrêt)* paralysis, paralysation

paralytique [paralitik] *Méd* **ADJ** paralytic

NMF paralytic

paramédical, -e, -aux, -ales [paramedikal, -o] **ADJ** paramedical; **personnel p.** paramedics

paramétrable [parametrabl] **ADJ** *Ordinat* configurable; **p. par l'utilisateur** user-definable

paramétrage [parametraʒ] **NM** *Ordinat* configuration

paramètre [paramɛtr] **NM 1** *Math* parameter **2** *(élément variable)* parameter, factor **3** *Ordinat* parameter, setting; *(du DOS)* switch

paramétrer [18] [parametre] **VT** *Ordinat* to configure

paramilitaire [paramiliter] **ADJ** paramilitary

NMF paramilitary

parangon [parɑ̃gɔ̃] **NM** *Littéraire* paragon; **p. de vertu** paragon of virtue

parano [parano] *Fam* **ADJ** *(abrév* **paranoïaque)** paranoid[□]

NMF *(abrév* **paranoïaque)** *(personne)* paranoid person[□]; **c'est un/une p.** he's/she's paranoid[□]

NF *(abrév* **paranoïa)** *(maladie)* paranoia[□]; **tu es en pleine p.!** you're being completely paranoid![□]; **arrête ta p.!** stop being paranoid![□]

paranoïa [paranɔja] **NF** paranoia; **tu es en pleine p.!** you're being completely paranoid![□]

paranoïaque [paranɔjak] **ADJ** paranoiac, paranoid

NMF paranoiac

paranoïde [paranɔid] **ADJ** paranoid

paranormal, -e, -aux, -ales [paranɔrmal, -o] **ADJ** paranormal

NM le p. the paranormal

parapente [parapɑ̃t] **NM** *(activité)* paragliding; *(parachute)* paraglider; **faire du p.** to go paragliding

parapet [parapɛ] **NM** *Constr* parapet

parapharmaceutique [parafarmasøtik] **ADJ produits parapharmaceutiques** toiletries and cosmetics

parapharmacie [parafarmasi] **NF 1** *(produits)* (non-pharmaceutical) *Br* chemist's *or Am* druggist's merchandise **2** *(magasin)* = chemist selling personal hygiene products, ≃ *Am* drugstore

paraphe [paraf] **NM 1** *(pour authentifier)* initials; *(pour décorer)* flourish, paraph **2** *Jur ou Sout (signature)* signature

parapher [3] [parafe] **VT 1** *(pour authentifier) Br* to initial, *Am* to initialize **2** *Jur ou Sout (signer)* to sign

parapheur [parafœr] **NM** *(classeur)* signature book

paraphrase [parafraz] **NF** paraphrase; **faire de la p.** to paraphrase

paraphraser [3] [parafraze] **VT** to paraphrase

paraplégie [parapleʒi] **NF** *Méd* paraplegia

paraplégique [parapleʒik] *Méd* **ADJ** paraplegic

NMF paraplegic

parapluie [paraplɥi] **NM 1** *(accessoire)* umbrella; **p. de golf** golf umbrella **2** *Pol* **p. nucléaire** *ou* **atomique** nuclear umbrella

parapsychologie [parapsikɔlɔʒi] **NF** parapsychology

parapublic, -ique [parapyblik] ADJ *(entreprise)* part government-owned

parasciences [parasjɑ̃s] NFPL sciences of the paranormal

parascolaire [paraskɔlɛr] ADJ *(activité)* extra-curricular; *(édition, ouvrage)* self-study

parasitaire [paraziter] ADJ *Biol & Fig* parasitic

parasite [parazit] ADJ **1** *Biol* parasitic, parasitical **2** *Élec* **bruit p.** interference **3** *Fig (superflu)* unnecessary, superfluous

NM **1** *Biol* parasite **2** *(personne)* parasite, scrounger

• **parasites** NMPL *Rad, TV & Tél* interference *(UNCOUNT)*, *Br* atmospherics; *Tél* noise, static; **il y a des parasites sur la ligne** the line's bad, there's static on the line

parasiter [3] [parazite] VT **1** *Biol* to live as a parasite on, to be parasitic on, to parasitize; *Fig* **p. la société** to be a parasite on society **2** *Rad, TV & Tél* to interfere with, to cause interference on

parasitique [parazitik] ADJ parasitic(al)

parasitisme [parazitism] NM **1** *Biol* parasitism **2** *Fig* parasitical behaviour, parasitism

parasitologie [parazitɔlɔʒi] NF *Biol* parasitology

parasitologique [parazitɔlɔʒik] ADJ *Méd* parasitological

parasitose [parazitoz] NF *Méd* parasitosis

parasol [parasɔl] NM *(en ville, dans un jardin)* parasol, sunshade; *(pour la plage)* beach umbrella, parasol

parasympathique [parasɛ̃patik] *Méd* ADJ parasympathetic

NM parasympathetic nervous system

parataxe [parataks] NF *Gram* parataxis

paratonnerre [paratɔnɛr] NM lightning conductor

paratyphoïde [paratifɔid] *Méd* ADJ paratyphoid

NF paratyphoid (fever)

paravalanche [paravalɑ̃ʃ] NM avalanche barrier

paravent [paravɑ̃] NM **1** *(écran)* (folding) screen *or* partition **2** *Fig* (smoke) screen, cover; **cette société leur sert de p. pour d'autres activités** the company is a screen *or* front for their other activities

parbleu [parblø] EXCLAM *Vieilli* by Jove!

parc [park] NM **1** *(enclos ▸ à bétail)* pen, enclosure; *(▸ à moutons)* fold; *(▸ pour bébé)* pen, playpen; **p. à bestiaux** cattle pen; **p. de stationnement** *Br* car park, *Am* parking lot

2 *Pêche* bed; **p. à huîtres** oyster bed

3 *(jardin public)* park; *(domaine privé)* park, grounds; **p. animalier** safari park; **p. aquatique** water park; **p. d'attractions** amusement park; **p. de loisirs** leisure park; **p. national** national park; **p. naturel** nature reserve; **le p. des Princes** = large sports stadium in Paris, formerly used for international football and rugby matches; **p. régional** regional park; **p. à thème** theme park; **p. zoologique** zoo, zoological gardens

4 *Com* **p. des expositions** exhibition centre; **p. d'activités** *(zone)* business park

5 *(unités d'équipement)* **p. automobile** *(dans une entreprise)* fleet of cars; **le p. automobile français** the total number of cars in France; **p. immobilier** housing stock; **p. informatique** computer park; **p. d'ordinateurs** computer population, total number of computers in service; **p. technologique** technology park

6 *Ind (entrepôt)* depot; *Can* **p. industriel** industrial *Br* estate *or Am* park

7 p. éolien, p. d'éoliennes wind farm

parcage [parkaʒ] NM **1** *(enfermement ▸ d'animaux)* penning in *or* up; *(▸ de prisonniers)* confining **2** *Ordinat (de disque dur)* parking; **effectuer le p. d'un disque** to park a disk

parcellaire [parselɛr] ADJ **1** *Admin & Jur* **cadastre** *ou* **plan p.** cadastral survey **2** *(fractionné ▸ connaissances, tâche)* fragmented; *Ind* **travail p.** division of labour

parcellarisation [parselarizasjɔ̃] = **parcellisation**

parcellariser [parselarize] = **parcelliser**

parcelle [parsɛl] NF **1** *Admin* parcel, plot; *(lopin)* plot (of land) **2** *(morceau ▸ d'or)* particle **3** *Fig (petite partie)* **une p. de liberté** a (tiny) bit of freedom; **pas une p. de vérité** not a grain *or* shred of truth; **pas la moindre p. d'intelligence/de vérité** not an ounce of intelligence/truth

parcellisation [parselizasjɔ̃] NF **1** *(gén)* fragmentation, division **2** *Ind* **p. des tâches** division of labour

parcelliser [3] [parselize] VT *(gén)* to fragment, to divide; *(travail)* to break down into individual operations

parce que [parskə] CONJ because; **elle n'est pas venue parce qu'elle se sentait fatiguée** she didn't come because she was feeling tired; **ce n'est pas parce qu'on a eu une dispute que je ne vais plus te parler** just because we've had an argument doesn't mean I'm never going to speak to you again; **il ne répondit rien p. très gêné** he didn't reply because he was so embarrassed; *Fam* **pourquoi pleures-tu? – p.!** why are you crying? – because!; **d'accord, mais c'est bien p. c'est vous!** OK, but only because it's you!

parchemin [parʃəmɛ̃] NM **1** *(peau, document)* parchment **2** *Fam Vieilli (diplôme)* diploma, degree **3** *(titre de noblesse)* title of nobility

parcheminé, -e [parʃəmine] ADJ **1** *(papier)* with a parchment finish **2** *(peau)* wrinkled; *(visage)* wizened

parcheminer [3] [parʃəmine] VT *(papier)* to give a parchment finish to

VPR **se parcheminer** *(peau)* to shrivel up, to become shrivelled

par-ci, par-là [parsiparla] ADV *voir* **par**[2]

parcimonie [parsimɔni] NF parsimony, parsimoniousness

• **avec parcimonie** ADV parsimoniously, sparingly; **il distribue les compliments avec p.** he's sparing with his praise

parcimonieuse [parsimɔnjøz] *voir* **parcimonieux**

parcimonieusement [parsimɔnjøzmɑ̃] ADV parsimoniously, sparingly; **distribuer les compliments p.** to be sparing with one's compliments

parcimonieux, -euse [parsimɔnjø, -øz] ADJ parsimonious, sparing

parcmètre [parkmɛtr] NM (parking) meter

parcourir [45] [parkurir] VT **1** *(distance ▸ gén)* to cover; *(▸ en courant)* to run; *(▸ en marchant)* to walk; *(▸ à cheval, à vélo)* to ride; **la distance à p. par les chevaux** the distance to be run *or* covered by the horses; **il reste deux kilomètres/un long chemin à p.** there are two kilometres/there is a long way to go; **chemin parcouru** distance covered

2 *(pour visiter)* to travel through; *(dans une quête)* to scour, to search (all over); **ils ont parcouru toute l'Amérique** they've travelled the length and breadth of America; **p. les mers** *(marin, bateau)* to sail the seas; **je parcourais la ville à la recherche d'un emploi** I was searching all over town for a job

3 *(traverser ▸ sujet: douleur, frisson)* to run through; **un murmure de protestation parcourut la salle** a murmur of protest ran through the room; **le pays est parcouru de canaux** the country has a network of canals

4 *(jeter un coup d'œil à ▸ journal, roman, notes de cours)* to skim *or* to leaf through; *(▸ lettre)* to glance at; *(▸ document informatique)* to scroll through; **elle parcourut la liste des reçus** she scanned the list of successful students

5 *Ordinat (document)* to scroll through

parcours [parkur] NM **1** *(trajet ▸ d'une personne)* way, journey; *(▸ d'un fleuve)* course; *Transp* route; **elle m'a questionné pendant tout le p.** she asked me questions all the way; **il a effectué le p. en deux heures** he did the trip *or* journey in two hours; **le car fait le p. entre la ville et la côte** the bus runs between the town and the coast; **je fais le p. à pied dans les deux sens** I walk both ways **2** *Fig (évolution personnelle)* career, record, path; **son p. scolaire a été irréprochable** he/she had a faultless school record; **après le service militaire, nos p. ont été très différents** after we'd done our national service, we took very different paths **3** *Sport (de golf, de course à pied)* course; *(de course automobile)* circuit; **les chevaux font un p. de 20 kilomètres** the horses run over a distance of 20 kilometres; **p. du combattant** *Mil* assault course; *Fig* obstacle course

parcouru, -e [parkury] PP *voir* **parcourir**

par-delà [pardəla] PRÉP beyond

par-derrière [parderjer] PRÉP behind, round the back of; **passe p. la maison** go round the back of the house

ADV **1** *(par l'arrière)* from behind, at the rear; **on entre dans la cuisine p.** you get into the kitchen from behind *or* round the back; **ça se boutonne p.** it buttons at the back **2** *Fig (sournoisement)* **il me critique p.** he criticizes me behind my back; **il fait ses coups p.** he operates behind people's backs

par-dessous [pardəsu] PRÉP under, underneath

ADV underneath; **je suis passé p.** I crept underneath; **prendre qch p.** to get hold of sth underneath

par-dessus [pardəsy] PRÉP **1** *(en franchissant)* over, above; **passe p. la grille** go over the railings **2** *(sur)* **porter un manteau p. sa veste** to wear an overcoat on top of one's jacket **3** *Fig* over; **elle est passée p. le directeur des ventes** she went over the head of the sales manager

ADV *(dans l'espace)* over; **j'ai mis un tee-shirt avec une chemise p.** I wore a T-shirt with a shirt on top *or* with a shirt over it

• **par-dessus tout** ADV most of all, above all

pardessus [pardəsy] NM overcoat

par-devant [pardəvɑ̃] PRÉP *Admin & Jur* **tout a été fait p. notaire** everything was done in the proper legal way

ADV *(passer)* round the front

par-devers [pardəver] PRÉP **1** *Jur (en présence de)* before, in the presence of **2** *(en la possession de)* **garder qch p. soi** to keep sth in one's possession *or* to oneself

pardi [pardi] EXCLAM of course!

pardieu [pardjø] EXCLAM *Vieilli* by Jove!

pardon [pardɔ̃] NM **1** *(rémission)* forgiveness, *Sout* pardon; **demander p. à qn** to apologize to sb, to ask for sb's forgiveness; **je lui accordai mon p.** I forgave him/her; **demander le p. de ses fautes** to beg mercy for one's sins; **demande p. à la dame** say sorry to *or* apologize to the lady; **p.?** *(pour faire répéter)* sorry?, (I beg your) pardon?; **p., auriez-vous un crayon?** excuse me, do you have a pencil?; **oh, p.!** *(pour s'excuser)* sorry!, excuse me!; *Ironique* (so) sorry!; **ah p., ce n'est pas ce que j'ai dit!** excuse me *or* pardon me, but that's NOT what I said; *Fam* **la mère est déjà désagréable, mais alors la fille, p.!** the mother's bad enough, but the daughter!; *Fam* **qu'est-ce qu'on a bien mangé, alors là, p.!** you should have seen how well we ate, it was something else!; **elle a de ces jambes, p.!** you should see the legs on her! **2** *(en Bretagne)* religious festival **3** *Rel* **le Grand P., le jour du P.** Yom Kippur, the Day of Atonement

pardonnable [pardɔnabl] ADJ excusable, forgivable, pardonable; **à son âge, on est p.!** it's excusable at that age!; **tu es p. d'avoir oublié** you can be forgiven for forgetting; **je ne suis pas p.!** I have no excuse!

pardonner [3] [pardɔne] VT **1** *(oublier ▸ offense)* to forgive, to excuse; *(▸ péché)* to forgive, to pardon; **p. qch à qn** to forgive sb for sth; **allez, je te pardonne tout** all right, you're forgiven; **p. ses péchés à qn** to forgive sb (for) his sins; **il ne me pardonne pas d'avoir eu raison** he won't forgive me for having been right; **est-ce que tu me pardonnes?** do you forgive me?, am I forgiven?; **se faire p.** to be forgiven, to win forgiveness; **pour me/te/etc faire p.** to make it up; **pour se faire p. son retard** as a way of saying sorry for being late; *Rel* **pardonne-nous nos offenses** forgive us our trespasses **2** *(dans des formules de politesse)* to forgive, to excuse; **pardonnez-moi d'insister** excuse me for being so insistent; **pardonnez-moi, mais vous oubliez un détail d'importance** excuse me, but you've forgotten an important point

USAGE ABSOLU to forgive; **apprendre à p.** to learn forgiveness *or* to forgive; **une distraction au volant, ça ne pardonne pas!** one slip in concentration at the wheel is fatal!

VPR **se pardonner 1** *(emploi réfléchi)* **je ne me le**

pardonnerai jamais I'll never forgive myself; **je ne me pardonnerai jamais de lui avoir menti** I'll never forgive myself for lying to him/her **2** *(emploi passif)* to be excused *or* forgiven; **une traîtrise ne se pardonne pas** treachery cannot be forgiven **3** *(emploi réciproque)* to forgive one another; **ils se sont pardonné leurs mensonges** they forgave each other's lies

pare-avalanches [paravalɑ̃ʃ] **NM INV** avalanche barrier *or* wall

pare-balles [parbal] **ADJ INV** bulletproof
NM INV bullet-shield

pare-boue [parbu] **NM INV** mudflap

pare-brise [parbriz] **NM INV** *Br* windscreen, *Am* windshield; **p. feuilleté** laminated *Br* windscreen *or Am* windshield

pare-buffle [parbyfl] **NM INV** *Aut* bull bars

pare-chocs [parʃɔk] **NM INV** *Aut* bumper; **nous étions** *ou* **roulions p. contre p.** we were bumper to bumper
NMPL *Fam Hum (seins)* knockers, *Am* hooters

pare-éclats [parekla] **NM INV** *Mil* shellproof screen

pare-étincelles [paretɛ̃sɛl] **NM INV** *(écran)* sparkguard, fireguard

pare-feu [parfø] **ADJ INV porte p.** fire door
NM INV 1 *(en forêt)* firebreak **2** *(d'une cheminée)* fireguard **3** *Ordinat* firewall

pare-fumée [parfyme] **ADJ INV** *voir* **écran**
NM INV smoke extractor

parégorique [paregɔrik] **ADJ** paregoric

pareil, -eille [parej] **ADJ 1** *(identique)* the same; **leurs bagues sont presque pareilles** their rings are almost identical *or* the same; **il n'y en a pas deux (de) pareils** no two are alike; **vous êtes (bien) tous pareils!** you're all alike *or* the same!; **et lui, qu'est-ce qu'on lui donne? – p., une orange** and what will we give him? – the same (thing), an orange; **comment vas-tu? – toujours p.!** how are you? – same as ever!; **c'est toujours p., personne n'ose se plaindre!** it's always the same, nobody ever dares complain!; **l'an dernier à pareille époque** this time last year; *Fam* **si ça ne te plaît pas, c'est p.** too bad if you don't like it
2 *(similaire)* the same; **tu as vu ses chaussures? – oui, j'en ai de pareilles** have you seen her shoes? – yes, I have a pair just like them; **p. à** the same as, just like; **toujours p. à lui-même** the same as always; *Fam* **p. que** (the) same as□; **ta jupe est pareille que la mienne** your skirt's the same as mine
3 *(de cette nature)* such (a); **un talent p.** *ou* **un p. talent est très rare** such talent is very rare; **comment peux-tu lire un journal p.?** how can you read such a paper?; **mais je n'ai jamais dit une chose pareille!** but I never said any such thing!; **je n'ai jamais rien vu de p.** I've never seen anything like it; **tu ne vas pas croire une chose pareille!** you're not going to believe something like that!; **on n'avait jamais vu (un) p. scandale!** there'd never been such a scandal!; **qui peut bien téléphoner à une heure pareille?** who could be phoning at this hour *or* time?; **en p. cas** in such a case; **en pareilles circonstances** in such circumstances; **dans de pareils moments, dans des moments pareils** at times like these
NM,F ne pas avoir son p. to be second to none; **elle n'a pas sa pareille pour arriver au mauvais moment!** there's nobody quite like her for turning up at the wrong moment!; *Vieilli* **son p./sa pareille** *(personne semblable)* another one like him/her; *(chose semblable)* another one like it; *Vieilli* **impossible de trouver le p.** it's impossible to find another one like it
NM *Fam* **c'est du p. au même** it's six of one and half a dozen of the other, same difference
ADV *Fam* **1** *(pareillement)* the same□; **on a tous fait p.** we all did the same (thing); **je grossis, pourtant je mange p.** I'm putting on weight, but I'm not eating any differently; **on n'a pas dû comprendre p.** we can't have understood the same thing; **ils sont habillés p.** they're dressed the same **2** *Can (quand même)* all the same, nevertheless **3** *Can (exactement)* **p. comme** just like, just the same as; **c'est p. comme si j'étais au ciel!** it's just like being in heaven!
• **pareille NF rendre la pareille à qn** *(se venger)* to get one's own back on sb, to pay sb back; *(faire preuve de reconnaissance)* to repay sb, to pay sb back; **si on me frappe, je rends la pareille** if anyone hits me I hit them back; *Belg* **(en) dire/faire une pareille** *ou* **de pareilles** to say/do such an outlandish thing
• **pareils NMPL nos pareils** *(semblables)* our fellow men; *(égaux)* our equals *or* peers; **vous et vos pareils!** you and your kind!
• **sans pareil, sans pareille ADJ** *(éclat, beauté, courage, talent)* unrivalled, unequalled; *(artiste, cuisinière)* unequalled, *Sout* peerless

pareillement [parɛjmɑ̃] **ADV 1** *(de la même manière)* in the same way; **ils s'habillent p.** they dress the same *or* in the same way **2** *(aussi)* equally, likewise; **j'ai été p. surprise** I was equally surprised, I was surprised too; **bonne soirée! – et à vous p.!** have a nice evening! – you too!

parement [parmɑ̃] **NM 1** *Couture* facing; *(de manche)* cuff **2** *Constr (surface)* facing, face; *(revêtement)* facing, dressing **3** *Rel* **p. (d'autel)** (altar) frontal

parent, -e [parɑ̃, -ɑ̃t] **ADJ 1** *(de la même famille)* related; **je suis parente avec eux, nous sommes parents** I'm related to them **2** *(analogue)* similar; **ces deux interprétations sont parentes** the two interpretations are similar
NM,F *(personne de la même famille)* relative, relation; **un proche p., un p. proche** a close relative *or* relation; **un lointain p., un p. éloigné** a distant relative *or* relation; **un p. du côté paternel/maternel** a relation on the father's/mother's side; **ce sont des parents en ligne directe/par alliance** they're blood relations/related by marriage; **p. pauvre** poor relation; **c'est le p. pauvre de l'opéra** it's opera's poor relation
NM *(père ou mère)* parent
• **parents NMPL 1** *(père et mère)* parents, father and mother; **la relation parents-enfant** the parent-child relationship; **parents adoptifs** adoptive parents; **parents biologiques** biological parents; **parents d'élèves** (pupils') parents; **association de parents d'élèves** parent-teacher association **2** *Littéraire (aïeux)* **nos parents** our forebears *or* ancestors

parental, -e, -aux, -ales [parɑ̃tal, -o] **ADJ** parental; **les responsabilités parentales** parental duties

parenté [parɑ̃te] **NF 1** *(lien familial)* relationship, kinship; **il n'y a aucune p. entre eux** they're not related in any way; **p. par alliance** relationship by marriage; **p. directe** blood relationship **2** *(ressemblance)* relationship, connection; **il y avait une p. de caractère entre les deux amis** the two friends had similar temperaments **3** *(famille)* family; **soyez maudits, toi et toute ta p.!** a curse upon you and all your kin!

parenthèse [parɑ̃tɛz] **NF 1** *(signe)* parenthesis, *Br* bracket; **ouvrir/fermer la p.** to open/to close the parentheses *or Br* brackets; *Typ* **p. ouvrante** opening parenthesis *or Br* bracket; **p. fermante** closing parenthesis *or Br* bracket **2** *Fig (digression)* digression, parenthesis; **mais c'est une p.** but that's a digression *or* an aside; *Fig* **je voudrais ouvrir une p.** *(pour aborder cette question)* I would like to digress for a moment; **je voudrais vous dire, dans une p.** *ou* **par p., que ...** I would like to say by way of digression *or* parenthetically that ...; **fermons la p.** anyway, enough of that; **cette époque n'a été qu'une p. dans sa vie** that period was only an interlude in his life **3** *Gram* parenthesis, parenthetical clause
• **entre parenthèses ADJ** *(mot, phrase)* in parentheses, in *or* between brackets **ADV 1** *(mot, phrase)* **mettre qch entre parenthèses** to put sth in parentheses, to put sth in *or* between brackets; *Fig* **il a dû mettre sa vie privée entre parenthèses** he had to put his private life on hold **2** *Fig (à propos)* incidentally, by the way;
• **par parenthèse ADV** *Fig* incidentally, by the way

paréo [pareo] **NM** *(tahitien)* pareo; *(pour la plage)* sarong

parer[1] **[3]** [pare] **VT 1** *Littéraire (embellir ▸ pièce)* to decorate, to deck out, to adorn; *(▸ personne)* to deck out, to adorn; *(vêtir)* to dress; **l'autel paré de lys** the altar bedecked with lilies; **elle arriva enfin, parée de fourrures/bijoux** she finally arrived, attired in furs/bedecked in jewels; **elle ne sort que parée de ses plus beaux atours** she only goes out attired in her best finery
2 *(attribuer à)* **p. qn de toutes les vertus** to attribute every virtue to sb, to endow sb with every virtue
3 *Naut (préparer ▸ ancre)* to clear
4 *Culin (poisson, volaille)* to dress; *(rôti)* to trim
VPR se parer 1 *(s'habiller avec élégance)* to put one's finery on; **se p. de** *(bijoux, fourrures)* to adorn oneself with; *(titres, honneurs)* to assume **2** *Can (se préparer)* to get ready

parer[2] **[3]** [pare] **VT 1** *(éviter ▸ coup, danger)* to ward *or* to fend *or* to stave off; *(▸ attaque)* to stave off, to parry; *Naut (cap)* to round; *Boxe & Escrime* to parry **2** *(protéger)* **p. qn contre qch** to shield *or* to protect sb against sth; **je suis paré contre le froid/l'hiver** I'm prepared for the cold/the winter
• **parer à VT IND 1** *(faire face à)* to cope *or* to deal with, to handle; *(prévenir)* to guard against; **pour p. à toute difficulté/à tout retard** in order to guard against any difficulties/delay; **p. à toute éventualité** to prepare for *or* to guard against any contingency; **p. au plus pressé** *(en voyageant, en emménageant)* to deal with basic necessities (first); **je n'ai pu que p. au plus pressé** *(après un incident)* I could only employ stopgap measures **2** *(se défendre contre ▸ tir, attaque)* to ward off
VPR se parer se p. contre to protect oneself against; **je me suis paré contre les rigueurs de l'hiver** I prepared for the rigours of winter

pare-soleil [parsɔlɛj] **NM INV 1** *(de voiture)* sun visor **2** *Phot* lens hood

paresse [parɛs] **NF 1** *(fainéantise)* laziness, idleness; **avoir la p. de faire qch** to be too lazy *or* idle to do sth; **elle est d'une p. incroyable** she's incredibly lazy; **p. intellectuelle** intellectual laziness **2** *(apathie)* indolence, laziness **3** *Méd* **p. intestinale** sluggishness of the digestive system

paresser [4] [parese] **VI** to laze (about *or* around)

paresseuse [parɛsøz] *voir* **paresseux**

paresseusement [parɛsøzmɑ̃] **ADV 1** *(avec paresse)* lazily, idly; **elle s'étira p.** she stretched lazily **2** *(avec lenteur)* lazily, idly, sluggishly

paresseux, -euse [parɛsø, -øz] **ADJ 1** *(sans ardeur)* lazy, idle; **c'est un élève très p.** he's a very lazy pupil; **c'est un esprit p.** he's/she's got a lazy mind; **être p. comme un loir** *ou* **une couleuvre** to be *Br* bone-idle *or Am* a goldbricker **2** *(lent)* lazy, slow, indolent; **le cours p. de la rivière** the river's sluggish waters **3** *Méd (digestion)* sluggish
NM,F lazy person
NM *Zool* sloth

parfaire [109] [parfɛr] **VT 1** *(peaufiner)* to perfect; **p. une œuvre** to add the finishing touches to a work **2** *(compléter ▸ opération)* to round off; *(▸ somme)* to make up

parfait, -e [parfɛ, -ɛt] **ADJ 1** *(sans défaut ▸ beauté, crime, harmonie, conditions)* perfect; *(▸ argumentation, diamant, maquillage)* perfect, flawless; *(▸ scolarité, savoir-vivre, personne)* perfect, faultless; **son russe est p.** his/her Russian is perfect *or* flawless, he/she speaks perfect Russian; **personne n'est p.** nobody's perfect
2 *Biol* mature; *Bot* perfect; *Math (cercle)* perfect
3 *(en intensif)* perfect, utter; **c'est le p. homme du monde** he's a perfect gentleman; **c'est un p. goujat/idiot** he's an utter boor/fool
4 *(complet, total ▸ bonheur, calme, entente)* perfect, complete, total; *(▸ ressemblance)* perfect, exact; **elle s'est montrée d'une parfaite délicatesse** she showed exquisite *or* perfect tact; **dans la plus parfaite indifférence** in utter *or* complete *or* total indifference; **nous sommes en p. accord** we're in full *or* perfect agreement
5 *(excellent)* perfect, excellent; **en p. état/parfaite santé** in perfect condition/health; **il a été p.** he was perfect *or* marvellous; **le rôle est p. pour lui** the part is ideal *or* made for him; **10 heures, ça vous va? – c'est p.!** would 10 o'clock suit you? – that's perfect *or* (just) fine!; **p., maintenant passons à autre chose** fine *or* good, now let's go on to something else
NM 1 *(crème glacée)* parfait; **p. au café** coffee parfait **2** *Gram* **le p.** the perfect (tense); **au p.** in the perfect (tense)

parfaitement [parfɛtmɑ̃] **ADV 1** *(très bien)* perfectly, impeccably, faultlessly; **elle parle p. (l')anglais** she speaks English perfectly, she speaks perfect English; **cela m'ira p.** that will suit me perfectly *or* just fine; **ce vin accompagne p. le poisson** this wine is the perfect accompaniment for fish; **j'avais p. entendu!** I heard all right! **2** *(absolument)* perfectly, absolutely, thoroughly; **c'est p. inadmissible/ridicule!** it's quite unacceptable/ridiculous!; **tu as p. le droit de refuser** you are perfectly entitled to refuse; **je comprends p.** I quite understand; **cela lui est p. indifférent** it's a matter of complete indifference to him/her; **il est p. idiot** he's a perfect *or* complete idiot **3** *(oui)* (most) certainly, definitely; **c'est vrai? – p.!** is that true? – it (most) certainly *or* definitely is!; **oui, p., j'y étais** yes indeed, I was there

parfois [parfwa] **ADV 1** *(quelquefois)* sometimes; **il venait p. nous voir** he sometimes came to see us **2** *(dans certains cas)* sometimes, at times, occasionally; **il était là tous les jours, p. seul, p. accompagné** he was there every day, sometimes alone, sometimes *or* other times not

parfum [parfœ̃] **NM 1** *(odeur ▸ d'une lotion, d'une fleur)* perfume, scent, fragrance; *(▸ d'un mets)* smell, aroma; *(▸ d'un vin)* bouquet, aroma; *(▸ d'un fruit)* smell

2 *Fig* **p. de scandale/d'hérésie** whiff of scandal/heresy

3 *(cosmétique)* perfume, scent

4 *(goût)* flavour; **tu veux une glace à quel p.?** what flavour ice-cream do you want?; **yaourts sans p. artificiel** yoghurts with no artificial flavouring

• **au parfum ADV** *Fam* **être au p.** to be in the know; **mettre qn au p.** to put sb in the picture

parfumé, -e [parfyme] **ADJ 1** *(fleur)* fragrant, sweet-smelling; *(fruit)* sweet-smelling; *(vin, air)* fragrant **2** *(artificiellement ▸ savon, mouchoir)* perfumed, scented; **elle est trop parfumée** *(femme)* she's wearing too much perfume; **glace parfumée au café** coffee-flavoured ice-cream

parfumer [3] [parfyme] **VT 1** *(embaumer)* to perfume; **le gâteau parfume la cuisine** the kitchen smells of cake; **un soupçon de patchouli parfumait son oreiller** her pillow had a faint smell of patchouli **2** *(mettre du parfum sur)* to put *or* to dab perfume on; **être parfumé** *(personne)* to have perfume on, to be wearing perfume; **se faire p.** *(dans un grand magasin)* to try on perfume **3** *Culin* to flavour (**à** with); **un peu de safran pour p. la sauce** a pinch of saffron to flavour the sauce

VPR se parfumer *(une fois)* to put on perfume; *(habituellement)* to wear perfume

parfumerie [parfymri] **NF 1** *(magasin)* perfumery, perfume *Br* shop *or Am* store

2 *(usine)* perfume factory, perfumery

3 *(profession)* perfumery, perfume trade *or* industry

4 *(articles)* perfumes (and cosmetics), perfumery

parfumeur, -euse [parfymœr, -øz] **NM,F** perfumer

pari [pari] **NM 1** *(défi, enjeu)* bet, wager; **faire un p.** to lay a bet, to (have a) bet; **faire un p. avec qn** to make a bet with sb; **je suis prêt à faire le p. que...** I'm willing to bet that...; *aussi Fig* **je tiens le p.!** I'll take you up on it!; **perdre un p.** to lose a bet **2** *(mise)* bet, stake; **il a gagné son p.** he won his bet; *Fig* **les paris sont ouverts** it's anyone's guess; **p. mutuel (urbain)** = French betting authority, *Br* ≃ tote, *Am* ≃ pari-mutuel

paria [parja] **NM 1** *(d'un groupe)* outcast, pariah **2** *(en Inde)* pariah, untouchable

parier [9] [parje] **VT 1** *(somme)* to bet, to lay, to stake; *(repas, bouteille)* to bet **2** *(exprimant la certitude)* to bet; **tu crois qu'il a terminé? – je parie que non** do you think he's finished? – I bet he hasn't; **je te parie qu'il ment** I bet you he's lying; **qu'est-ce que tu paries qu'il va refuser?** how much do you bet he'll say no?; **je te parie tout ce que tu veux que...** I bet you anything (you like)...; **elle a refusé, je parie?** I bet she said no; **il y a fort** *ou* **gros à p. que...** the odds are *or* it's odds on that...; **je l'aurais parié!** I knew it!

VI 1 *(faire un pari)* to (lay a) bet; **p. sur un cheval** to bet on *or* to back a horse; *Fam* **tu paries?, on parie?** want to bet? **2** *(être parieur)* to bet; **p. aux courses** *(de chevaux)* to bet on the horses

pariétal, -e, -aux, -ales [parjetal, -o] **ADJ 1** *Anat* parietal **2** *Beaux-Arts* **art p.** *(sur parois rocheuses)* rock painting; *(dans grottes)* cave painting

NM parietal bone

parieur, -euse [parjœr, -øz] **NM,F 1** *(qui fait un pari)* better **2** *(qui aime parier)* betting man, *f* woman

parigot, -e [parigo, -ɔt] *Fam* **ADJ** Parisian ▫

NM,F Parisian ▫

Paris [pari] **NM** Paris; **la banlieue de P.** the Paris suburbs; *Prov* **P. ne s'est pas fait en un jour** Rome wasn't built in a day

parisianisme [parizjanism] **NM 1** *(attitude)* Paris-centredness; **le p. des médias** the capital-city mentality of the Paris media **2** *(expression)* Parisian (turn of) phrase **3** *(habitude)* Parisian habit *or* quirk

parisien, -enne [parizjɛ̃, -ɛn] **ADJ 1** *(relatif à Paris, sa région)* Paris *(avant n)*; *(natif de Paris, habitant à Paris)* Parisian; **la vie parisienne** life in Paris, Parisian life; **les immeubles parisiens** buildings in Paris **2** *(typique de Paris)* Parisian; **un événement bien p.** a very Parisian occasion

• **Parisien, -enne NM,F** Parisian

paritaire [paritɛr] **ADJ** *(commission)* joint *(avant n)*; **représentation p.** parity of representation, equal representation

parité [parite] **NF 1** *(concordance ▸ entre des rémunérations)* parity, equality; *(▸ entre des monnaies, des prix)* parity; *(▸ entre des concepts)* comparability; **à p.** at parity, at the money; **p. du change** exchange rate parity; **p. euro-dollar** euro-dollar parity; **p. fixe** fixed parity; **p. hommes-femmes** sexual equality; **p. des monnaies** monetary parity; *Bourse* **p. du pouvoir d'achat** purchasing power parity; **p. rampante** crawling peg; **la p. des salaires** equal pay **2** *Math* parity **3** *Ordinat* parity check

parjure [parʒyr] **ADJ** disloyal, treacherous

NMF *(personne)* disloyal person, traitor, betrayer

NM *(acte)* disloyalty, treachery, betrayal; **commettre un p.** to forswear

parjurer [3] [parʒyre] **se parjurer VPR** *(manquer à son serment)* to break one's word *or* promise

parka [parka] **NM OU NF** parka

parking [parkiŋ] **NM 1** *(parc de stationnement) Br* car park, *Am* parking lot; **une place de p.** a parking space; **p. couvert** underground *Br* car park *or Am* parking lot **2** *(action de se garer)* **le p. est interdit** parking is prohibited here; **p. payant** *(sur panneau)* pay and display

Parkinson [parkinsɔn] **NPR** *voir* **maladie**

parkinsonien, -enne [parkinsɔnjɛ̃, -ɛn] *Méd* **ADJ** Parkinson's *(avant n)*, parkinsonian

NM,F person with Parkinson's (disease), Parkinson's sufferer

parkinsonisme [parkinsɔnism] **NM** *Méd* parkinsonism

parkour [parkur] **NM** parkour, free running

parlant, -e [parlɑ̃, -ɑ̃t] **ADJ 1** *(film)* talking *(avant n)*

2 *Fam (bavard)* **il n'est pas très p.** he hasn't got very much to say (for himself)

3 *(significatif ▸ chiffre, exemple, schéma)* which speaks for itself; **leurs statistiques sont parlantes** their figures speak volumes

4 *(expressif ▸ portrait)* lifelike; *(▸ description)* vivid, graphic; *(▸ geste, regard)* eloquent, meaningful

parlé, -e [parle] **ADJ** *(langue, français, anglais, etc ▸ oral)* spoken; *(▸ familier)* colloquial; **ça se dit dans la langue parlée** it's a colloquial term, it's used colloquially

NM *(à l'opéra)* spoken part, dialogue

parlement [parləmɑ̃] **NM 1** *Pol* **le P.** *(en France)* (the French) Parliament; *(en Grande-Bretagne)* (the Houses of) Parliament; **au p.** in Parliament; **P. bicaméral** bicameral *or* two-chamber parliament; **membre du P.** member of Parliament; **le P. européen** the European Parliament; **membre du P. européen** member of the European Parliament, MEP, Euro-MP **2** *Hist (en France)* parliament, parlement *(under the Ancien Régime)*

parlementaire [parləmɑ̃tɛr] **ADJ 1** *(débat, habitude, régime)* parliamentary; **procédure p.** parliamentary procedure **2** *Hist (en Grande-Bretagne)* Parliamentary

NMF 1 *(député)* member of Parliament; *(aux États-Unis)* Congressman, *f* Congresswoman; **p. européen** member of the European Parliament, Euro-MP, MEP **2** *(négociateur)* mediator, negotiator

parlementarisme [parləmɑ̃tarism] **NM** parliamentarianism, parliamentary government

parlementer [3] [parləmɑ̃te] **VI** to negotiate; *Pol* **p. avec** to parley with; **il a dû p. avec l'agent pour qu'il le laisse passer** he had to talk the policeman into letting him through

parler[1] [parle] **NM 1** *(vocabulaire)* speech, way of speaking; **dans le p. de tous les jours** in common parlance **2** *(langue d'une région)* dialect, variety

PARLER[2] **[3]** [parle] **VI A.** *FAIRE UN ÉNONCÉ* **1** *(articuler des paroles)* to talk, to speak; **p. du nez** to talk through one's nose; **p. bas** *ou* **à voix basse** to speak softly *or* in a low voice; **p. haut** *ou* **à voix haute** to speak loudly *or* in a loud voice; *Fig* **les syndicats commencent à p. haut** the unions are beginning to make a lot of noise; **elle parle avec un accent** she talks *or* speaks with an accent; **parle plus fort** speak louder *or* up; **parlez moins fort** keep your voice down, don't speak so loud; **elle a une poupée qui parle** she's got a talking doll; **dans ses fables, il fait p. les animaux** in his fables, he makes the animals talk; **p. par gestes** *ou* **signes** to use sign language; **p. avec les mains** to talk with one's hands

2 *(s'exprimer)* to talk, to speak; **vous pouvez p. librement** you can speak *or* talk freely; **parle donc!** speak up!; **ça m'a fait du bien de p.** it's done me good to talk (things over); **je n'ai pas l'habitude de p. en public** I'm not used to speaking in public *or* to public speaking; **le conseiller a parlé le dernier** the councillor spoke last; **il parle mal** *(improprement)* he doesn't talk correctly; **comme tu parles mal!** *(grossièrement)* (mind your) language!; *Ironique* that's a fine way to talk!; **tu n'as qu'à p. pour être servi** just say the word and you'll be served; **mon père parlait peu** my father was a man of few words; **tu parles en euros?** are you talking in *or* do you mean euros?; **il a parlé à la radio** he spoke *or* talked on the radio; **il a fait p. l'adolescent** he drew the adolescent out of himself, he got the adolescent to talk; **les armes ont parlé** weapons were used; **ne laissons pas p. notre haine** let us not yield to hatred; **laisse p. ton cœur** listen to your heart; **p. pour** *ou* **à la place de qn** to speak for sb *or* on sb's behalf; **ne parle pas tout le temps pour moi!** stop answering for me!; *Fig* **sa franchise parle pour lui** his straightforwardness is a point in his favour; *Fam* **parle pour toi!** speak for yourself!; **p. contre/pour** to speak against/for; **il va p. pour la suppression de la peine de mort** he will be speaking against capital punishment; **politiquement/artistiquement parlant** politically/artistically speaking; **p. à qn** *(lui manifester ses sentiments)* to talk to *or* to speak to *or* to have a word with sb; *Fam* **je vais lui p., moi, à ton copain!** I'm going to have a word with that pal of yours!; **parle-moi!** talk *or* speak to me!; **p. à qn** *(s'adresser à)* to talk *or* to speak to sb; **ne parle pas aux gens que tu ne connais pas** don't talk to strangers; **je ne lui ai parlé que brièvement** I only talked to *or* with him/her for a brief moment; **ne me parle pas sur ce ton!** don't talk to me like that!; **c'est à toi que je parle!** it's you I'm talking to!; **je ne leur parle plus** I'm not on speaking terms with them any more, I don't speak to them any more; **le secrétaire général parlera aux travailleurs demain** the general secretary will talk to *or* address the workers tomorrow; **puis-je p. à Virginie?** *(au téléphone)* could *or* may I speak to Virginie?; **vous pouvez p.!** *(message de l'opératrice)* go ahead, caller!; **p. à qn** *(l'émouvoir, le toucher)* to speak *or* to appeal to sb; **sa musique me parle** his/her music speaks to me; **ses tableaux ne me parlent pas** his/her paintings don't appeal to me *or* don't do anything for me; *Fam* **voilà ce qui s'appelle p.!, ça, c'est p.!** well said!; **il sait ce que p. veut dire** he's not stupid; **parlons peu mais parlons bien** let's be brief but to the point

3 *(discuter)* to talk; **les longues soirées d'hiver où l'on parlait autour du feu** the long winter evenings spent talking *or* chatting around the fire; **ne parle pas sans savoir** don't talk about things you don't know about; **p. pour ne rien dire** to talk for the sake of talking; **assez parlé, allons-y!** that's enough chat, let's go!; **p. de qn/qch** to talk *or* to speak about sb/sth; **je sais de quoi je parle** I know what I'm talking about; **je ne sais pas de quoi tu veux p.** I don't know what you mean; **p. de choses et d'autres** to talk about this and that; **tiens, en parlant de vacances, Luc a une villa à louer** hey, talking of holidays, Luc has a villa to let; **je ne veux pas qu'on parle de ça à table!** I won't have that kind of talk at the table!; **ce professeur va venir p. de Proust** this professor will give a talk on Proust; **qui parle d'Europe parle d'axe franco-allemand** you can't talk about Europe without talking about *or* mentioning the special relationship between France and Germany; **il en sera beaucoup parlé dans les jours qui viennent** everybody's going to be talking about it in the next few days

4 *(jaser)* to talk; **les gens commencent à p.!** people are starting to talk!; **tout le monde en parle** everybody's talking about it; **on ne parle que de cela au village** it's the talk of the village; **faire p. de soi** to get oneself talked about; *(dans la presse)* to get one's name in the papers

5 *(avouer)* to talk; **ses complices ont parlé** his/her accomplices talked; **faire p. qn** to make sb talk, to get sb to talk

6 *(être éloquent)* to speak volumes; **les chiffres/faits parlent d'eux-mêmes** the figures/facts speak for themselves

7 *(dans des jeux)* **à qui de p.?** whose bid is it?; **c'est à toi de p.** it's your bid

B. *LOCUTIONS Fam* **tu parles!** *(absolument)* you're telling me!, absolutely!, *Br* too right!; *(absolument pas)* you must be joking!, are you kidding!; **tu parles comme je peux oublier ça!** as if I could ever forget it!; **tu parles si je sais de quoi elle est capable!** you bet I know what she's capable of!; **ça t'a plu? – tu parles!** *(bien sûr)* did you like it? – you bet!; *(pas du tout)* did you like it? – you must be joking!; **ça t'irait, 200 euros? – tu parles (si ça m'irait)!** would 200 euros be OK? – you bet (it would)!; **tu parles que je vais lui rendre!** *(je vais lui rendre)* you bet I'll give it back to him/her!; *(je ne vais pas lui rendre)* there's no way I'm giving it back to him/her!; *Ironique* **tu parles si c'est agréable/intelligent!** that's really nice/clever!; **tu parles si je m'en fiche!** a fat lot I care!; **tu parles si ça m'aide!** much good that is to me!; **la truite pesait au moins 10 kilos! – tu parles!** the trout was at least 10 kilos! – you must be joking *or Br* pull the other one!; **tu parles d'une veine!** what a stroke of luck!; **tu parles d'une cuisinière! elle est pas fichue de faire cuire un œuf** some cook she is, she can't even boil an egg!; **c'est difficile – ne m'en parle pas!** it's difficult – don't tell me *or* you're telling me!; **quel temps! – ne m'en parlez pas!** what filthy weather! – oh, don't *or* don't even talk about it!; **sa timidité? parlons-en!** his/her shyness? that's a good one *or* you must be joking!; **la chambre du haut, n'en parlons pas** let's *or* we can forget the upstairs bedroom; **n'en parlons plus** let's not mention it again, let's say no more about it

VT 1 *(langue)* to speak; **il parle plusieurs langues** he speaks *or* he can speak several languages; **elle parle chinois couramment** she's fluent in Chinese, she speaks Chinese fluently; **il parle bien (le) russe** he speaks good Russian; **vous connaissez l'allemand? – je le parle un peu** do you know any German? – I can speak (it) a little; **il ne parle pas un mot de polonais** he doesn't *or* can't speak a word of Polish; **elle parle le langage des sourds-muets** she knows sign language; *Fig* **et pourtant je parle français, non?** ≃ don't you understand plain English?; *Fig* **nous ne parlons pas la même langue** *ou* **le même langage** we don't speak the same language; **p. le langage de la raison** to talk sense; **p. affaires/politique** to talk business/politics

2 *(dire d'une façon naturelle)* to speak, to read out; **parle ton texte, ne le déclame pas** just read out your text, don't recite it

• **parler de VT IND 1** *(mentionner)* **vous ne parlez même pas de Dali dans votre thèse** you don't even mention Dali in your thesis; **le livre parle de la guerre** the book is about *or* deals with the war; **tous les journaux en parlent ce matin** it's (mentioned) in all the newspapers this morning; **ils en ont parlé aux informations** they talked about it on the news; **si elle en parle devant toi, fais comme si tu ne savais rien** if she mentions it in front of you, pretend you don't know anything (about it); **p. (de) religion/(de) littérature** to talk religion/literature; **tu ne vas pas déjà p. de départ!** you're not talking about leaving already, are you?; **je ne l'aime pas, alors ne parlons pas de mariage!** I don't like him, so let there be no talk of marriage!; **p. de faire qch** to talk about *or* of doing sth; **elle parle de déménager** she's talking of moving house; **ils parlent de réduire les impôts** they're talking about *or* there's talk of cutting taxes; **qui parle de laisser tomber?** who said anything about giving up?; **on parle d'elle comme d'une candidate possible** she's being talked about *or* billed as a possible candidate; **tu en parles comme d'une catastrophe** you make it sound like a catastrophe; **n'en parle à personne!** don't mention it to anybody!; **après ça, qu'on ne vienne plus me p. de solidarité** after that, I don't want to hear any more about solidarity; **elle nous a parlé de ses projets** she talked to us about her plans; **parlez-moi un peu de vous/de ce que vous avez ressenti** tell me something about yourself/what you felt; **on m'a beaucoup parlé de vous** I've heard a lot about you; **je cherche un travail, alors, si vous pouviez lui p. de moi** I'm looking for a job, so if you could put in a good word for me **2** *Littéraire (rappeler)* to remind of; **tout ici me parle de toi** everything here reminds me of you

VPR se parler 1 *(emploi réciproque)* to talk to one another *or* each other; **il faudrait qu'on se parle tous les deux** I think we two should have a talk **2** *(emploi réfléchi)* to talk to oneself **3** *(emploi passif)* to be spoken; **le français se parle dans plusieurs pays d'Afrique** French is spoken in several African countries

• **sans parler de PRÉP** to say nothing of, not to mention, let alone; **sans p. du fait que...** to say nothing of..., without mentioning the fact that...

---

parler-vrai [parlevʀɛ] *(pl* **parlers-vrai)** **NM** *(gén) & Pol* straight talking *(UNCOUNT)*

parleur, -euse [parlœr, -øz] **NM,F** talker; **c'est un beau p.** he's a smooth talker

parloir [parlwar] **NM 1** *(d'une prison)* visitors' room; *(d'un monastère)* parlour **2** *Belg (salon)* parlour

parlote, parlotte [parlɔt] **NF** *Fam* chitchat, *Br* natter; **faire la p. (avec qn)** to chat (with sb), to have a chat (with sb)

Parme [parm] **NM** Parma

parmentier [parmɑ̃tje] **NM** *Culin (au bœuf)* ≃ cottage pie; *(avec de la viande blanche)* = dish similar to cottage pie, made with white meat; *(au mouton)* ≃ shepherd's pie

parmesan, -e [parməzɑ̃, -an] **ADJ** Parmesan

NM *(fromage)* Parmesan (cheese)

• **Parmesan, -e NM,F** Parmesan

parmi [parmi] **PRÉP** among; **p. eux se trouvait un grand homme maigre** there was a tall, thin man among them; **elle erra p. la foule** she wandered in *or* among the crowd; **il figure p. les meilleurs** he's one of the best, he's among the best; **nous souhaitons vous avoir bientôt p. nous** we hope that you'll soon be with us; **p. tout ce vacarme** in the midst of all this noise; **c'est une solution p. (tant) d'autres** that's one solution

Parnasse [parnas] **NM 1** *Géog* **le P.** (Mount) Parnassus **2** *Littérature & Myth* Parnassus

parnassien, -enne [parnasjɛ̃, -ɛn] **ADJ** Parnassian

• **Parnassien, -enne NM,F** Parnassian *(member of the Parnassian school of French poets)*

parodie [parɔdi] **NF 1** *Littérature* parody **2** *(imitation grossière)* mockery; **une p. de procès** a mockery of a trial

parodier [9] [parɔdje] **VT 1** *Beaux-Arts* to parody **2** *(singer)* to mimic, to parody; **je le parodie un peu, mais c'est ce qu'il a dit** I'm parodying him a little, but that's what he said

parodique [parɔdik] **ADJ** parodic

parodiste [parɔdist] **NMF** parodist

paroi [parwa] **NF 1** *(entre des pièces)* partition (wall); *(d'une pièce, d'un ascenseur)* wall; *(d'une citerne, d'un vase)* inside *or* inner surface **2** *Anat, Biol & Bot* wall; **p. des artères** artery wall; **p. cellulaire** cell wall **3** *Géol & (en alpinisme)* face, wall

paroisse [parwas] **NF** parish

paroissial, -e, -aux, -ales [parwasjal, -o] **ADJ** *(fête, église)* parish *(avant n)*; *(décision, don)* parish *(avant n)*, parochial

paroissien, -enne [parwasjɛ̃, -ɛn] **NM,F 1** *Rel* parishioner **2** *Fam (type)* **c'est un drôle de p.** he's a weird one

NM *(livre* ▸ *gén)* prayer book; *(*▸ *catholique)* missal

parole [parɔl] **NF 1** *(faculté de s'exprimer)* **la p.** speech; **être doué de p.** to be endowed with speech; **perdre/retrouver l'usage de la p.** to lose/to recover the power of speech; **avoir la p. facile** to be a fine talker, to have a way with words; *Prov* **la p. est d'argent, le silence est d'or** speech is silver, silence is golden

2 *(fait de parler)* **demander la p.** to ask for the right to speak; *Jur* to request leave to speak; **les délégués demandent la p.** the delegates want to speak; **prendre la p.** *(gén)* to speak; *(au parlement, au tribunal)* to take the floor; **vous avez la p.** *(à un avocat, un député)* you have the floor; *(dans un débat)* (it's) your turn to speak *or* over to you; **la p. est à la défense** the defence may now speak; **adresser la p. à qn** to talk *or* to speak to sb; **nous ne nous adressons plus la p.** we're not on speaking terms *or* we don't talk to each other any more; **couper la p. à qn** to interrupt sb; **passer la p. à qn** to hand over to sb; **je laisse maintenant la p. à mon collègue** I now hand over to my colleague; **droit de p.** right to speak; **temps de p.** speaking time; **votre temps de p. est révolu** your time is up

3 *Ling* speech, parole; **acte de p.** speech act

4 *(souvent pl) (propos)* word, remark; **des paroles blessantes** hurtful words *or* remarks; **jamais une p. gentille!** never a kind word!; **voilà une bonne p.!** well said!; **prononcer des paroles historiques** to utter historic words; **ce sont ses propres paroles** those are his/her very own words; **elle n'a jamais une p. plus haute que l'autre** she never raises her voice; **ce ne sont que des paroles en l'air** all that's just idle talk; **il s'y connaît en belles paroles** he's full of fine words; **en paroles, ça a l'air simple, mais...** it's easy enough to say it, but...; **en paroles et en actes** in word and deed; **répandre** *ou* **porter la bonne p.** to spread *or* to carry the good word; **la p. de Dieu** the Word of God; **c'est p. d'Évangile** it's the gospel truth

5 *(engagement)* word; **ma p. vaut bien la sienne** my word is as good as his/hers; **c'est votre p. contre la sienne** it's your word against his/hers; **il n'a qu'une p., il est de p.** his word is his bond, he's a man of his word; **tu n'as aucune p.** you never keep your word; **donner sa p. (d'honneur) à qn** to give sb one's word (of honour); **tenir p.** to keep one's word; **reprendre** *ou* **retirer sa p.** to go back on one's word; **c'est un homme de p.** he's a man of his word; **p. d'honneur!** I give you my word (of honour)!; **ma p.!** my word!; **p.!** cross my heart!, I swear to God!

6 *Cartes* **avoir la p.** to be the first to bid; **passer p.** to pass; **p.!** *(je passe)* pass!, your bid!

• **paroles NFPL 1** *(d'une chanson)* words, lyrics **2** *(d'une illustration)* words; **histoire sans paroles** wordless cartoon

• **sur parole ADV** *(prisonnier)* on parole

parolier, -ère [parɔlje, -ɛr] **NM,F** *(d'une chanson)* lyric writer, lyricist; *(d'un opéra)* librettist

paronyme [parɔnim] **ADJ** paronymous

NM paronym

paronymie [parɔnimi] **NF** paronymy

paroxysme [parɔksism] **NM 1** *(d'un état affectif)* paroxysm, height; **le mécontentement a atteint son p.** discontent is at its height; **au p. de la douleur** in paroxysms of pain; **être au p. de la joie** to be ecstatically happy; **les fans étaient au p. du délire** the fans' enthusiasm had reached fever pitch **2** *(d'un phénomène)* height; **l'incendie était à son p.** the fire was at its height **3** *Méd* paroxysm, crisis

parpaing [parpɛ̃] **NM 1** *(pierre de taille)* perpend **2** *(aggloméré) Br* breezeblock, *Am* cinderblock

Parque [park] NF *Myth* **la P.** Fate; **les Parques** the Parcae, the Fates

parquer [3] [parke] VT **1** *(mettre dans un parc ▸ bétail)* to pen in *or* up; *(▸ moutons)* to pen in *or* up, to fold

2 *(enfermer ▸ prisonniers)* to shut in *or* up, to confine; *(▸ foule, multitude)* to pack *or* to cram in; **on parquait les réfugiés dans les camps** the refugees were herded into the camps

3 *(voiture)* to park

4 *Ordinat* to park

parquet [parke] NM **1** *(revêtement de bois)* (wooden) floor *or* flooring; *(à chevrons)* parquet; **refaire le p.** to re-lay *or* to replace the floorboards; **p. à l'anglaise** strip flooring **2** *Jur* public prosecutor's department, *Br* ≃ Crown Prosecution Service, *Am* ≃ District Attorney's office; **déposer une plainte auprès du p.** to lodge a complaint with the public prosecutor **3** *Bourse* **le p.** *(lieu)* the (trading) floor; *(personnes)* the Stock Exchange

parquetage [parkətaʒ] NM *Constr (installation)* laying of parquet flooring; *(sol)* (parquet) flooring

parqueter [27] [parkəte] VT to lay a parquet floor in, to put a parquet floor down in

parqueterie [parketri, -kətri] NF *(installation)* laying of parquet floors; *(fabrication)* manufacture of parquet floors

parqueteur [parkətœr] NM *(fabricant)* parquet maker; *(poseur)* parquet layer

parrain [parɛ̃] NM **1** *Rel* godfather

2 *Com* sponsor

3 *(d'un projet)* promoter; *(d'un enfant du tiers-monde)* sponsor; *(d'une œuvre charitable)* patron; *Pol* proposer, *Am* sponsor

4 *(d'un navire)* namer, christener

5 *(de la mafia)* godfather

parrainage [parenaʒ] NM **1** *Rel* (act of) being a godparent

2 *Com* sponsorship, sponsoring; **p. d'entreprises** corporate sponsorship; **p. télévision** television sponsoring

3 *(d'un projet)* proposing, promoting; *(d'un enfant du tiers-monde)* sponsorship, sponsoring; *(d'une œuvre charitable)* patronage; *Pol* proposing, *Am* sponsoring

4 *(d'un navire)* naming, christening

parrainer [4] [parene] VT **1** *(candidat, postulant)* to propose, *Am* to sponsor; *(projet)* to propose, to support; *(enfant du tiers-monde)* to sponsor; *(œuvre charitable)* to patronize **2** *Com* to sponsor; **se faire p.** to be sponsored **3** *(navire)* to name, to christen

parraineur [parenœr] NM sponsor

parricide [parisid] ADJ parricidal

NMF *(assassin)* parricide

NM *(crime)* parricide

pars *etc voir* **partir**

parsemer [19] [parsəme] VT **1** *(semer, saupoudrer)* **p. qch de qch** to scatter sth with sth **2** *(sujet: fleurs, étoiles)* **le ciel était parsemé d'étoiles** the sky was studded *or* scattered with stars; **un champ parsemé de pâquerettes** a field dotted with daisies; *Littéraire* **des feuilles parsemaient le chemin** the path was scattered *or* strewn with leaves; *Fig* **un texte parsemé de coquilles** a text littered with misprints; **un visage parsemé de taches de rousseur** a freckled face

parsi, -e [parsi] ADJ Parsi, Parsee

NM *(langue)* Parsee

• **Parsi, -e** NM,F Parsi, Parsee

PART [par] NF **1** *(dans un partage ▸ de nourriture)* piece, portion; *(▸ d'un butin, de profits, de travail etc)* share; **une p. de gâteau** a slice of cake; **donnez-moi deux parts de choucroute** I'd like two portions *or* servings *or* helpings of sauerkraut; **à chacun sa p.** share and share alike; **couper qch en parts égales** to cut sth into equal parts *or* portions; **elle a eu sa p. de soucis** she's had her share of worries; **repose-toi, tu as fait ta p.** have a rest, you've done your bit; **avoir p. à** to have a share in, to share (in); **avoir p. aux bénéfices** to share in the profits; **avoir la p. belle** to get a good deal; **faire la p. belle à qn** to give sb a good deal; *Fam aussi Fig* **vouloir sa p. de** *ou* **du gâteau** to want one's share of the cake; **se réserver** *ou* **se tailler la p. du lion** to keep *or* to take the lion's share; *Fam* **p. à deux!** let's go halves!

2 *Jur (pour les impôts)* = basic unit used for calculating personal income tax; **un couple avec un enfant a deux parts et demie** a couple with a child *Br* has a tax allowance worth two and a half *or Am* has two and a half tax exemptions; **p. virile** *(dans un héritage)* lawful share

3 *Écon & Fin* share; **p. de fondateur** founder's share; **p. d'intérêts** partner's share; **p. de marché** market share; **p. patronale** employer's contribution; **p. salariale** employee's contribution; **p. sociale** unquoted share

4 *(fraction)* part, portion; **ce n'est qu'une petite p. de la vérité** it's only a fraction *or* small part of the truth; **en grande p.** for the most part, largely, to a large extent; **les sociétés, pour la plus grande p., sont privatisées** firms, for the most part, are privatized; **elle ne participe que pour une petite p. aux frais d'exploitation** she only pays a fraction *or* small part of the running costs; **il y a toujours une p. d'affabulation dans ce qu'il dit** there's always a touch of fantasy in what he says; **il y a une grande p. de peur dans son échec** his/her failure is due largely to fear; *Rad & TV* **p. d'audience** audience share

5 *(participation)* **prendre p. à** *(discussion, compétition, manifestation)* to take part in; *(cérémonie, projet)* to join in, to play a part in; *(attentat)* to take part in, to play a part in; **prendre p. à la joie/peine de qn** to share (in) sb's joy/sorrow; **un acte où la volonté n'a eu aucune p.** an act in which willpower had no share *or* part; **la chance n'a aucune p. dans sa réussite** luck has nothing to do with his/her success; **il faut faire la p. du hasard/de la malchance** you have to recognize the part played by chance/ill-luck, you have to make allowances for chance/ill-luck; **faire la p. des choses** to take things into consideration; **faire la p. du feu** to cut one's losses

6 *Théât (aparté)* (artist's) cut

7 *(locutions)* **je viens de la p. de Paula** Paula sent me; **donne-le lui de ma p.** give it to him/her from me; **dis-lui au revoir/merci de ma p.** say goodbye/thank you for me; **je vous appelle de la p. de Jacques** I'm calling on behalf of Jacques; **de ta p., cela me surprend beaucoup** I'm surprised at you; **je ne m'attendais pas à une telle audace/mesquinerie de leur p.** I didn't expect such boldness/meanness from them; **c'est très généreux de ta p.** that's very generous of you; **cela demande un certain effort de votre p.** it requires a certain amount of effort on your part; **c'est de la p. de qui?** *(au téléphone, à un visiteur)* who (shall I say) is calling?; **pour ma/sa p.** (as) for me/him/her; **pour ma p., je n'ai rien contre** as for me *or Sout* for my part, I have nothing against it; **d'une p...., d'autre p.** on the one hand..., on the other hand; **nous avons entamé des négociations avec les Américains d'une p. et les Japonais d'autre p.** we have started talks with the Americans and with the Japanese; **faire p. de qch à qn** to announce sth to sb, to inform sb of sth; **prendre qch en bonne p.** to take sth in good part; **prendre qch en mauvaise p.** to take offence at sth, to take sth amiss; **ne le prenez pas en mauvaise p., mais...** don't be offended, but...

• **à part** ADJ **1** *(séparé ▸ comptes, logement)* separate **2** *(original, marginal)* odd; **ce sont des gens à p.** these people are rather special

ADV **1** *(à l'écart)* **elle est restée à p. toute la soirée** she kept herself to herself all evening; **les stagiaires ont l'impression qu'on les met à p.** the trainees feel they're being left on the sidelines; **mets les dossiers bleus à p.** put the blue files to one side; **mis à p. deux ou trois détails, tout est prêt** except for *or* apart from two or three details, everything is ready **2** *(en aparté)* **prendre qn à p.** to take sb aside *or* to one side **3** *(séparément)* separately; **faites cuire la viande à p.** cook the meat separately *or* on its own

PRÉP **1** *(excepté)* except for, apart *or* aside from; **à p. toi, personne ne le sait** nobody knows apart from you; **à p. cela** apart from that, that aside **2 à p. soi** to oneself; **elle se disait à p. soi que...** she said to herself that...

• **à part entière** ADJ **un membre à p. entière de** a full *or* fully paid-up member of; **elle est devenue une actrice à p. entière** she's now a proper *or* a fully-fledged actress

• **à part que** CONJ *Fam* except that[□], if it weren't *or* except for the fact that[□]; **c'est une jolie maison, à p. qu'elle est un peu humide** it's a nice house, except that it's a bit damp

• **de part en part** ADV from end to end, throughout, right through; **la poutre est fendue de p. en p.** the beam is split from end to end

• **de part et d'autre** ADV **1** *(des deux côtés)* on both sides, on either side **2** *(partout)* on all sides; **on entendait dire, de p. et d'autre, que...** people on all sides were saying that...

• **de part et d'autre de** PRÉP on both sides of

• **de toute part, de toutes parts** ADV (from) everywhere, from all sides *or* quarters; **ils accouraient de toutes parts vers le village** they were rushing towards the village from all directions; **l'eau fuyait de toutes parts** water was leaking out everywhere

• **pour une large part** ADV to a great extent

---

partage [partaʒ] NM **1** *(division ▸ d'un domaine)* division, dividing *or* splitting up; *(▸ d'un pays)* partition; *(▸ d'un rôti)* carving; *(▸ d'un gâteau)* slicing, cutting (up); **faire le p. de qch** to divide sth up

2 *(répartition ▸ d'une fortune, des devoirs, des tâches)* sharing out; *(▸ des torts, des fautes)* sharing, apportioning; **p. des bénéfices** profit-sharing; *Aviat* **p. de code** code-sharing; **p. du pouvoir** power sharing; **p. du travail** jobsharing

3 *Littéraire (lot)* lot; **la souffrance est le p. du genre humain** suffering is the lot of mankind

4 *Jur (acte juridique)* partition

5 *Ordinat* **p. des données** data sharing; **p. de fichiers** file sharing; **p. d'imprimantes** printer sharing; **p. de temps** time-sharing

• **en partage** ADV **donner qch en p. à qn** to leave sb sth (in one's will); **il donna en p. à ses fils dix hectares de terre** he left ten hectares of land to be shared out between his sons; *Fig Littéraire* **ce que la nature lui a donné en p.** the gifts bestowed upon him/her by nature

• **sans partage** ADJ *(joie)* unmitigated; *(affection)* undivided; *(engagement, enthousiasme)* thoroughgoing

partagé, -e [partaʒe] ADJ **1** *(opposé)* split, divided; **les avis sont partagés** opinions are divided; **j'ai lu des critiques partagées** I've read mixed reviews

2 *(indécis)* torn; **je suis très p. sur ce point** I have very mixed feelings on the subject; **il était p. entre la joie et la crainte** he was torn between joy and fear

3 *(mutuel ▸ haine)* mutual, reciprocal; *(▸ amour)* mutual

4 *(commun ▸ sentiments, douleur)* shared

5 *Ordinat* **en temps p.** on a time-sharing basis

partageable [partaʒabl] ADJ **1** *(bien, propriété)* which can be shared out *or* divided; *(nombre)* divisible **2** *(point de vue)* that can be shared

partager [17] [partaʒe] VT **1** *(diviser ▸ propriété)* to divide up, to share out; **p. qch en deux/par moitié** to divide sth in two/into two halves; **p. son temps entre deux occupations** to divide *or* split one's time between two occupations

2 *(moralement ▸ pays, société)* to divide; **la question du désarmement partage le pays** the country is divided *or* split over the question of disarmament; **je suis partagée entre l'envie de finir mes études et celle de travailler** I'm torn between finishing my studies and getting a job

3 *(répartir ▸ bénéfices, provisions)* to share out; **ils ont partagé la nourriture entre les deux/trois familles** they shared out the food between both/all three families; **je lui ai proposé de p. mon croissant** I offered him/her a share of my croissant

4 *(avoir en commun)* to share; **p. un lit/une chambre (avec qn)** to share a bed/room (with sb); **p. la joie/peine de qn** to share (in) sb's joy/sorrow/; **je ne partage vraiment rien avec ces gens-là** I really have nothing in common with those people; **le pouvoir est partagé entre les deux assemblées** power is shared *or* split between the two Houses; **p. l'avis de qn** to share sb's opinion; **voici une opinion partagée par beaucoup de gens** this is an opinion shared *or* held by many (people)

5 *Fin* **p. proportionnellement** to divide pro rata

USAGE ABSOLU elle n'aime pas p. she doesn't like to share

VPR se partager 1 *(biens, travail, vivres, butin)* to share (out); *Sport* **Lyon et Marseille se partagent la première place** Lyons and Marseilles share first place *or Br* are equal first

2 *(diviser son temps)* **elles se partagent entre leur carrière et leurs enfants** their time is divided between their professional lives and their families

3 *(se diviser)* to fork, to divide; **se p. en** to be split *or* divided into; **l'association se partage en deux tendances** the association is split into two groups

4 *(être communiqué)* **ces expériences ne se partagent pas facilement** it's not very easy to share such experiences

partageur, -euse [partaʒœr, -øz] **ADJ** willing to share; **cet enfant n'est pas très p.** this child is not good at sharing

partagiciel [partaʒisjɛl] **NM** *Offic Ordinat* shareware

partance [partɑ̃s] **en partance ADJ** *(train, voyageur)* due to leave; *(avion)* about to take off; *(navire)* about to sail; **le dernier train en p.** the last train; **en p. pour** bound for

partant¹ [partɑ̃] **CONJ** *Littéraire* therefore, consequently, thus

partant², -e [partɑ̃, -ɑ̃t] **ADJ être p. pour faire qch** to be willing *or* ready to do sth; **êtes-vous toujours p.?** are you still game?, can I/we/*etc* still count you in?

NM,F *Sport (cheval)* runner; *(cycliste, coureur)* starter

partenaire [partənɛr] **NMF 1** *(gén)* partner; **je suis son p. au tennis** I partner him/her at tennis, I'm his/her tennis partner **2** *Écon* (business) partner; **partenaires commerciaux** trading partners; **les partenaires sociaux** unions and management **3** *Cin & Théât* co-star; **il était mon p. dans la pièce** I acted opposite him in the play

partenariat [partənarja] **NM** partnership; *Mktg* **p. télévision** television tie-in; **p. public-privé** Public-Private Partnership, private finance initiative

parterre [partɛr] **NM 1** *Hort (en bordure)* border; *(plus large)* bed, flowerbed; **un p. de fleurs** a flowerbed **2** *Fam (sol)* floor **3** *Théât (emplacement) Br* stalls, *Am* orchestra; *(spectateurs)* (audience in the) *Br* stalls *or Am* orchestra

parthe [part] **ADJ** Parthian

NM *(langue)* Parthian

• **Parthe NMF** Parthian

parthénogenèse [partenoʒənɛz] **NF** *Biol* parthenogenesis

parthénogénétique [partenoʒenetik] **ADJ** *Biol* parthenogenic, parthenogenetic, parthenogenous

Parthénon [partenɔ̃] **NM le P.** the Parthenon

parti¹ [parti] **NM 1** *Pol* **p. (politique)** (political) party; **le p. (communiste)** the (Communist) Party; **le p. conservateur/démocrate/républicain/socialiste** the Conservative/Democratic/Republican/Socialist Party; **les partis de droite/gauche** the parties of the right/left, the right-wing/left-wing parties; **le système du p. unique** the one-party system

2 *(choix, décision)* decision, course of action; **hésiter entre deux partis** to wonder which course of action to take; **prendre le p. de la modération** to opt for moderation; **prendre le p. de faire qch** to make up one's mind to do sth, to decide to do sth; **j'ai fini par prendre le p. de vendre** I eventually decided to sell; **prendre p.** *(prendre position)* to take sides *or* a stand; **prendre p. pour/contre qch** to come out for/against sth; **prendre p. pour qn** to side *or* to take sides with sb; **prendre p. contre qn** to take sides against sb; **son p. est pris** his/her mind is made up, he's/she's made up his/her mind; **elle ne sera jamais musicienne, il faut que j'en prenne mon/qu'elle en prenne son p.** she'll never be a musician, I'll/she'll just have to accept it

3 *(avantage)* **tirer p. de** *(situation)* to take advantage of; *(équipement)* to put to good use; **tirer p. du matériel** to put the equipment to good use; **elle ne sait pas tirer p. de ses qualifications** she doesn't know how to get the most out of her qualifications; **elle tire p. de tout** she can turn anything to her advantage; **il tire le meilleur p. possible de ses relations** he uses his connections to the best possible advantage

4 *Vieilli ou Hum (personne à marier)* **c'est un beau** *ou* **bon p.** he's/she's a good catch

5 *(locution)* **faire un mauvais p. à qn** to ill-treat sb

• **parti pris NM 1** *(prise de position)* commitment; **avoir un p. pris de modernisme/clarté** to be committed to modernism/clear-thinking **2** *(préjugé)* bias; **je n'ai aucun p. pris contre le tennis professionnel, mais...** I'm not biased against professional tennis, but...; **être de p. pris** to be biased; **faire qch de p. pris** to do sth deliberately *or* on purpose; **être sans p. pris** to be unbiased *or* objective; **je dirais, sans p. pris, qu'elle est la meilleure** without any bias on my part, I'd say that she's the best

parti², -e¹ [parti] **ADJ** *Fam (ivre)* wasted, plastered; **tu étais bien p. hier soir!** you were far gone *or Br* well away last night!

partial, -e, -aux, -ales [parsjal, -o] **ADJ** biased, partial

> Do not confuse with **partiel**.

partialement [parsjalmɑ̃] **ADV** in a biased *or* partial way

partialité [parsjalite] **NF** *(favorable)* partiality; *(défavorable)* bias; **p. en faveur de qn** partiality for sb, bias in favour of sb; **p. contre qn** bias against sb

participant, -e [partisipɑ̃, -ɑ̃t] **ADJ** participant, participating; **les personnes participantes** the participants, the people taking part

NM,F *(gén)* participant; *Sport* competitor; **les participants au congrès** the participants in *or* those taking part in the congress

participation [partisipasjɔ̃] **NF 1** *(engagement, contribution ▸ gén)* participation, involvement (à in); *(▸ en classe)* level of participation; **il nie sa p. à** *ou* **dans l'enlèvement du prince** he denies having participated *or* been involved in the prince's kidnapping; **sa p. aux jeux Olympiques semble compromise** there's a serious question mark hanging over his/her participation in the Olympic Games; **apporter sa p. à qch** to contribute to sth; **cela s'est fait avec leur p.** they were involved in it; **la décision a été prise sans sa p.** the decision was made without him/her being involved *or* having any part in it

2 *(dans un spectacle)* appearance; **avec la p. des frères Jarry** featuring the Jarry Brothers; **avec la p. spéciale de Robert Vann** guest appearance by Robert Vann

3 *(contribution financière)* contribution (to costs); **il y a 20 euros de p. aux frais** you have to pay 20 euros towards costs

4 *Pol* **p. (électorale)** (voter) turnout; **un faible taux de** *ou* **une faible p. aux élections** a poor *or* low turnout at the polls

5 *Écon & Pol (détention de capital)* interest, share; **avoir une p. majoritaire dans une société** to have a majority holding *or* interest in a company; **il détient une p. de 6 pour cent dans l'entreprise** he holds a 6 percent share in the company; **p. aux frais** cost sharing; **prendre des participations dans une entreprise** to buy into a company; **p. aux bénéfices** profit-sharing; **p. croisée** cross-holding; **p. ouvrière** worker participation; **p. des salariés aux bénéfices** profit-sharing scheme

• **en participation ADJ** profit-sharing *(avant n)*

participe [partisip] **NM** *Gram* participle (form); **p. passé/présent** past/present participle

participer [3] [partisipe] **USAGE ABSOLU** *(dans un jeu)* to take part, to join in; *(à l'école)* to contribute (during class); **tu ne participes pas assez (en classe)** you don't contribute enough in class

• **participer à VT IND 1** *(prendre part à ▸ concours, négociation, cérémonie)* to take part in; *(▸ discussion)* to contribute to; *(▸ projet)* to be involved in; *(▸ aventure)* to be involved in, to be part of; *(▸ épreuve sportive)* to take part *or* to be in; *(▸ attentat, vol)* to be involved in, to take part in; *(▸ jeu)* to join in; *(▸ émission)* to take part in; **tous ceux qui ont participé au jeu** all contestants *or* competitors; **c'est le premier rallye/marathon auquel je participe** it's the first rally/marathon I've been in; **elle nie avoir participé au complot** she denies having been involved in the plot

2 *(partager)* to share (in); **p. à la douleur/joie de qn** to share in sb's pain/joy

3 *(financièrement ▸ achat, dépenses)* to share in, to contribute to

4 *Écon & Fin (profits, pertes)* to share (in); **p. aux bénéfices** to share in the profits

• **participer de VT IND** to pertain to; **tout ce qui participe de la philosophie** everything pertaining *or* relating to philosophy

participial, -e, -aux, -ales [partisipjal, -o] *Gram* **ADJ** participial

• **participiale NF** participial clause

particularisation [partikylarizasjɔ̃] **NF** particularization

particulariser [3] [partikylarize] **VT 1** *(restreindre à un cas particulier)* to particularize **2** *(distinguer, singulariser)* to distinguish, to characterize

VPR se particulariser se p. par to be distinguished *or* characterized by

particularisme [partikylarism] **NM** particularism

particularité [partikylarite] **NF 1** *(trait distinctif ▸ d'une personne, d'une culture, d'une langue etc)* particularity, (specific) feature *or* characteristic *or* trait; *(▸ d'une région)* distinctive feature; *(▸ d'une machine)* special feature; **la p. de cet aspirateur, c'est que...** what distinguishes this vacuum cleaner (from all the rest) *or* what is special about this vacuum cleaner is... **2** *(élément)* detail, particular

particule [partikyl] **NF 1** *Géol, Gram & Phys* particle; **p. alpha/bêta** alpha/beta particle; **p. élémentaire** elementary *or* fundamental particle **2** *(dans un nom)* particule *(the preposition "de" in a surname, indicating aristocratic origin)*

particulier, -ère [partikylje, -ɛr] **ADJ 1** *(précis ▸ circonstance, exemple, point)* particular, specific; **j'ai traité un aspect p. de son œuvre** I've dealt with a particular *or* specific aspect of his/her work

2 *(caractéristique ▸ odeur, humour, parler, style)* distinctive, characteristic; **p. à** peculiar to, characteristic of; **il a un humour qui lui est p.** he has his own special brand of humour; **un trait bien p.** a highly distinctive feature; *Littéraire* **une façon de marcher à lui particulière** his own particular way of walking

3 *(exceptionnel)* particular, special, unusual; **porter une attention toute particulière à qch** to pay particular *or* special attention to sth; **elle avait pour cette amie une tendresse toute particulière** she was particularly fond of that friend; **leurs photos n'offrent pas d'intérêt p.** their photographs are of *or* hold no particular interest; **il ne s'est rien passé de p.** nothing special *or* particular happened

4 *(bizarre ▸ comportement, goûts, mœurs)* peculiar, odd; **elle a toujours été un peu particulière** she's always been a bit unusual; **ses tableaux sont très particuliers** his/her pictures are very peculiar

5 *(privé ▸ avion, intérêts)* private; **j'ai une voiture particulière** I've got my own car *or* a car of my own; **cours p., leçon particulière** private lesson; **je donne des cours particuliers de latin** I give private lessons *or Br* tuition in Latin

6 *Can (minutieux)* meticulous, particular

NM 1 *(personne privée)* private individual; **simple p.** ordinary person, private citizen; **vente de p. à p.** private sale **2** *Fam Péj (individu)* character; **un drôle de p.** an odd character **3** *(élément individuel)* **le p.** the particular; **passer du p. au général** to go from the particular to the general

• **en particulier ADV 1** *(essentiellement)* in particular, particularly, especially; **vous avez été très désagréables, toi en p., Jacques** you've been most unpleasant, especially you *or* you in particular, Jacques **2** *(seul à seul)* in private; **puis-je vous parler en p.?** may I have a private word with you?; **recevoir qn en p.** to see sb privately *or* in private

> Attention: ne pas confondre **particular** et **peculiar** lorsque l'on traduit **particulier. Particular** signifie **spécifique**, alors que **peculiar** signifie **bizarre**.

particulièrement [partikyljɛrmɑ̃] **ADV 1** *(sur-*

tout) particularly, specifically, in particular; **j'avais tout p. envie de cette robe-là** I particularly wanted that dress; **leurs enfants sont très beaux, p. leur fille** their children are very good-looking, especially their daughter **2** *(spécialement)* particularly, specially, especially; **il n'est pas p. laid/doué** he's not particularly ugly/gifted; **je n'aime pas p. cela** I'm not particularly keen on it; **je ne la connais pas p.** I don't know her very *or* particularly well; **tu aimes le whisky? – pas p.** do you like whisky? – not particularly

PARTIE[2] [parti]

- part **1, 2, 6, 8, 10**
- game **3**
- field **5**
- party **7**

ADJ F *voir* **parti[2]**

NF 1 *(élément, composant)* part; **les parties du corps** the parts of the body; **les parties constituantes** the component parts; **faire p. de** *(comité)* to be a member of, to be on, to sit on; *(club, communauté)* to be a member of, to belong to; *(équipe)* to belong to, to be one of, to be in; *(licenciés)* to be among, to be one of; *(métier, inconvénients, risques)* to be part of; **tous ceux qui font p. de notre association** all the members of our association; **il ne fait plus p. de notre personnel** he's no longer on our staff, he's not a member of our staff any more; **il fait presque p. de la famille** he's almost one of the family; **faire p. intégrante de** to be an integral part of; **cela fait p. intégrante de la vie quotidienne** it's part and parcel of everyday life; **parties communes/privatives** communal/private areas *(in a building or an estate)*; **parties génitales** *ou* **sexuelles** genitals, private parts; **parties viriles** male (sexual) organs; *Fam* **ses parties** his privates

2 *(fraction, morceau)* part; **couper qch en deux parties** to cut sth into two (parts); **coupez le melon en trois parties** cut the melon into three parts; **la p. visible de la Lune** the visible side of the Moon; **la p. boisée de la colline** the wooded part *or* side of the hill; *Hum* **dans la p. charnue de mon anatomie** in the fleshy part of my anatomy; **ce n'est qu'une p. de la vérité** it's only part of the truth; **une p. de l'héritage** (a) part of the inheritance; **une grande/petite p. de l'électorat** a large/small part of the electorate, a large/small section of the electorate; **il est absent une grande** *ou* **la plus grande p. du temps** he's away much of *or* most of the time; **pendant la plus grande p. du chemin** (for) most of the way; **la plus grande p. de ses concerts** most of his/her concerts; **j'ai lu une p. de ses livres** I've read some of his/her books

3 *Sport & (jeu)* game; **faire une p. de cartes** to have a game of cards; **on fait une p.?** shall we play *or* have a game?; *aussi Fig* **la p. n'est pas égale** it's an uneven match, it's not a fair match; *Fig* **la p. sera difficile à jouer** it's not going to be easy, we've got a tough time ahead of us; **p. d'échecs/de billard/de tennis/de cartes** game of chess/billiards/tennis/cards; **p. de golf** round of golf; *Fig* **abandonner** *ou* **quitter la p.** to give up the fight, to throw in the towel; *Fig* **avoir la p. belle** to be in a favourable position, to be well placed; *Fig* **avoir p. gagnée** to be bound to succeed; *Fig* **la p. est jouée/n'est pas jouée** the outcome is a foregone conclusion/is still wide open

4 *(divertissement à plusieurs)* **p. de chasse/pêche** shooting/fishing party; **p. de campagne** day *or* outing in the country; *Fam* **p. carrée** foursome; *Fam* **p. fine** orgy□; *Fam* **une p. de jambes en l'air** a bit of nooky; **p. de plaisir** pleasure trip; *Fam* **cette course était une véritable p. de plaisir** that race was a piece of cake; *Fam* **ça n'est pas une p. de plaisir!** it's no picnic *or* fun!; **on va lui faire une farce, qui veut être de la p.?** we're going to play a trick on him/her, who wants to join in?; **s'il se met aussi de la p., nous aurons les capitaux nécessaires** if he comes in on it too, we shall have the necessary capital; **ce n'est que p. remise, je me vengerai!** I'll get even some day!

5 *(domaine, spécialité)* field, line; **ce n'est pas ma p.** it's not my field *or* line; **elle est de la p.** it's her line

6 *Mus* part; **la p. de la clarinette/du soprano** the clarinet/soprano part

7 *(participant ▸ gén) & Jur* party; **être p. dans** to be a party to *or* in; **les parties en présence** the parties; **p. adverse/intervenante** opposing/intervening party; **p. appelante** appellant; **parties belligérantes** belligerent *or* warring parties; **p. civile** private party *(acting jointly with the public prosecutor in criminal cases)*, plaintiff *(for damages)*; **se constituer** *ou* **se porter p. civile** to act jointly with the public prosecutor; **p. comparante** appearer; **parties contractantes/intéressées** contracting/interested parties; **p. défaillante** party failing to appear (in court), defaulting party; **p. lésée** aggrieved party; **les parties plaidantes** the litigants; **p. prenante** payee, receiver; *Fig* **être p. prenante dans qch** to be directly involved *or* concerned in sth; **la p. publique** *ou* **poursuivante** the public prosecutor, *Br* ≃ the Crown, *Am* ≃ the District Attorney; **les parties signataires** signatories

8 *Gram* **p. du discours** part of speech

9 *Math* **p. d'un ensemble** subset

10 *Chim* **p. par million** part per million

11 *(locution)* **avoir p. liée avec qn** to be hand in glove with sb; **ils avaient p. liée depuis le début** they were working hand in glove together from the start

12 *Compta* **en p. double** double-entry; **en p. simple** single-entry

13 parties annexes *(d'un ouvrage)* end matter

• **à partie ADV prendre qn à p.** *(s'attaquer à lui)* to set on sb; *(l'interpeller)* to take sb to task

• **en partie ADV** in part, partly, partially; **en p. dû au mauvais temps** partly due to the bad weather; **je ne l'ai cru qu'en p.** I only half believed him; **c'est en p. vrai** it's partly true; **c'est en p. de la fiction et en p. de la réalité** it's part fiction and part truth; **c'est en p. de l'or et en p. de l'argent** it's partly gold and partly silver; **en grande** *ou* **majeure p.** for the most part, largely, mainly; **c'est en grande p. à cause de lui** it's largely because of him

• **pour partie ADV** partly, in part

partiel, -elle [parsjɛl] **ADJ** partial; **contrôle** *ou* **examen p.** mid-term exam; **(emploi à) temps p.** part-time job; **elle ne le fait qu'à temps p.** she only does it part-time

NM 1 *Univ* mid-term exam **2** *Phys* partial

• **partielle NF** *Pol* by-election

Do not confuse with the French word **partial**.

partiellement [parsjɛlmɑ̃] **ADV** partially, partly

PARTIR **[43]** [partir]

- to go **1–4, 9, 10**
- to pass away **1**
- to set out **2**
- to go off **6**
- to come out **9**
- to leave **1, 3, 6**
- to set off **2**
- to start off **2, 7**
- to disappear **9**
- to come off **10**

VI 1 *(s'en aller)* to go, to leave; *Euph (mourir)* to pass on *or* away; **pars, tu vas rater ton train** (off you) go, or you'll miss your train; **il faut que je parte** I must be off, I must go *or* leave; **je peux p. maintenant?** can I go *or* leave now?; **empêche-la de p.** stop her (going), don't let her go; **je ne vous fais pas p., j'espère** I hope I'm not chasing you away; **p. en courant/boitant** to run/to limp off; **p. discrètement** to leave discreetly, to slip off; **laisser p.** *(prisonnier, otage)* to set free, to let go, to release; *(écolier)* to let out; *(employé)* to let go; **laisse-moi p.** let me go; **sa femme est partie pour toujours/avec son meilleur ami** his wife has gone for good/gone off with his best friend; **il est parti avec la caisse** he ran away *or* off with the till; **faites-les p.** ask them to leave; **le climat les a fait p.** the climate drove them away; **tout son argent part en livres** all his/her money goes on books; **p. de** to leave; **je ne peux pas p. du bureau avant 17h30** I can't leave the office before 5.30; **je suis parti de chez moi à 10 heures** I left home at 10; **p. du gouvernement** to leave office *or* the government

2 *(se mettre en route)* to set off *or* out, to start off; **il faut p. de bonne heure pour éviter les bouchons** we must set off early *or* make an early start if we want to beat the traffic jams; **pars devant, je te rattrape** go ahead, I'll catch up with you; *Fam* **regarde cette circulation, on n'est pas encore partis!** by the look of that traffic, we're not off yet!; **le courrier n'est pas encore parti** the post hasn't gone yet; **p. en avion** *(personne)* to fly (off); *(courrier)* to go air mail *or* by air; **p. en bateau** to go (off) by boat, to sail; **p. à bicyclette** to go (off) by bike, to cycle off; **p. en voiture** to go (off) by car, to drive off

3 *(se rendre)* to go, to leave; **je pars à** *ou* **pour Toulon demain** I'm leaving for *or* I'm off to Toulon tomorrow; **dans quelle direction est-elle partie?** which way did she go?; **p. à la campagne/montagne/mer** to go (off) to the countryside/mountains/seaside; **p. vers le sud** to go south

4 *(aller ▸ pour se livrer à une activité)* to go; **elle est partie au tennis/à la danse** she's gone to play tennis/to her dance class; **p. à la chasse/pêche** to go shooting/fishing; **p. à la recherche de** to set off in search of, to go looking for; **p. à la guerre** to go (off) to war; **p. en week-end** to go off *or* away for the weekend; **tu ne pars pas (en vacances) cet été?** aren't you going on *Br* holiday *or Am* vacation this summer?; **p. en congé maternité** to go on maternity leave; **p. skier/se promener** to go skiing/for a walk; **sa tête est partie heurter le buffet** his/her head struck against the sideboard

5 *(s'engager)* **p. dans un discours** to launch into a speech; **p. dans une explication** to embark on an explanation; **p. sur un sujet** to start off on a topic; *Fam* **quand elles sont parties sur leur boulot, c'est difficile de les arrêter** once they start on about their job, there's no stopping them; *Fam* **les voilà partis à refaire toute la maison** there they go doing up the entire house

6 *(démarrer ▸ machine, moteur, voiture)* to start (up); *(▸ avion)* to take off, to leave; *(▸ train)* to leave, to depart; *(▸ fusée)* to go up; *(▸ pétard)* to go off; *(▸ plante)* to take; **ton avion n'est pas encore parti** your plane hasn't left yet; **le coup (de feu) est parti tout seul** the gun went off on its own; **il m'a insulté et la gifle est partie** he insulted me and I just slapped him; **excuse-moi, le mot est parti (tout seul)** I'm sorry, the word just slipped out; **faire p.** *(moteur)* to start (up); *(pétard)* to set *or* to let off; *(fusil)* to let off; *(plante)* to get started

7 *(se mettre en mouvement, débuter ▸ coureur, match, concert)* to start (off); *Sport* **il est parti trop vite** he set *or* went off too fast; **on est partis pour avoir des ennuis!** we're headed for trouble!; **elle est partie pour nous faire la tête toute la soirée** she's all set to sulk the whole evening; **le match est bien/mal parti pour notre équipe** the match has started well/badly for our team; **le projet est bien parti** the project is off to a good start; **elle a l'air bien partie pour remporter l'élection** she seems well set to win the election

8 *(se vendre)* to sell; **le nouveau modèle part bien** the new model is selling well

9 *(disparaître, s'effacer ▸ inscription)* to disappear, to be rubbed off *or* out, to be worn off; *(▸ tache)* to disappear, to go, to come out; *(▸ douleur)* to go, to disappear; *(▸ bouton)* to come off; *(▸ pellicules, odeur)* to go; **ça partira au lavage** it'll wash off, it'll come out in the wash; **faire p.** *(salissure)* to get rid of, to remove; *(odeur)* to get rid of, to clear; *(douleur)* to ease; **ça ne fera pas p. ton mal de gorge** it won't get rid of your sore throat

10 *(se défaire, se détacher ▸ attache, bouton)* to come off, to go; *(▸ maille)* to run; *(▸ étiquette)* to come off

• **partir de VT IND 1** *(dans l'espace)* **pour teindre le cheveu, on part de la racine** to dye hair, you start with the roots; **de petites pousses partent du pied** little sprouts are shooting up from the root; **le ferry/marathon part de Brest** the ferry sails from/the marathon starts in Brest; **la rue part de la mairie** the street starts at the town hall; **c'est le quatrième en partant de la droite/du haut** it's the fourth (one) from the right/top

2 *(dans le temps)* **nous allons faire p. le contrat du 15 janvier** we'll make the contract effective (as) from 15 January; **votre congé part de la fin mai** your holidays begin at the end of May

3 *(dans un raisonnement)* **p. du principe que...** to start from the principle that..., to start by assuming that...; **tu ne devrais pas p. du présupposé que...** you shouldn't start (off) by presupposing that *or* start from the presupposition that...

4 *(provenir de)* **tous les problèmes sont partis de là** all the problems stemmed from that; **ça partait d'un bon sentiment** his/her intentions were good

• **à partir de PRÉP 1** *(dans le temps)* (as) from; **à p. de mardi/d'aujourd'hui** from Tuesday/today onwards, (as) from Tuesday/today; **à p. de 5 heures** from 5 o'clock on *or* onwards; **à p. de (ce moment-)là, il ne m'a plus adressé la parole** from that moment on *or* from then on, he never spoke to me again

2 *(dans l'espace)* (starting) from; **le deuxième à p. de la droite** the second (one) from the right; **comptez cinq espaces à p. de la marge** count five spaces in from the margin; **à p. du carrefour, c'est tout droit** after the crossroads, it's straight on *or* ahead

3 *(numériquement)* **imposé à p. de 2000 euros** taxable from 2,000 euros upwards; **compte à p. de dix** count from ten

4 *(avec, à base de)* from; **c'est fait à p. d'huiles végétales** it's made from *or* with vegetable oils; **j'ai fait un résumé à p. de ses notes** I've made a summary based on his/her notes

partisan, -e [partizɑ̃, -an] **ADJ** *(querelles, esprit)* partisan; *(choix)* biased; **être p. de qch/de faire qch** to be in favour of sth/doing sth; **elle n'est pas partisane de cette thèse** she doesn't favour this theory

NM 1 *(adepte, défenseur)* supporter; **c'est un p. de la censure** he's for *or* in favour of censorship **2** *(dans une guerre)* partisan; **guerre de partisans** guerilla *or* guerrilla warfare

partitif, -ive [partitif, -iv] *Gram* **ADJ** partitive

NM partitive (form)

partition [partisjɔ̃] **NF 1** *Mus (symboles)* score; *(livret)* score, music; **p. d'orchestre** full score **2** *Hist & Pol* partition, partitioning

> Il faut noter que le terme anglais **partition** signifie également **cloison**.

partitionner [partisjɔne] **VT** *Ordinat (disque dur)* to partition

partitive [partitiv] *voir* **partitif**

partouse [partuz] **NF** *Fam* orgy

partouser [3] [partuze] **VI** *Fam* = to take part in an orgy

partout [partu] **ADV 1** *(dans l'espace)* everywhere; **chercher qch p.** to look everywhere for sth; **je ne peux pas être p. à la fois!** I can't be everywhere *or* in two places at the same time!; **il laisse toujours traîner ses affaires p.** he always leaves his things all over the place; **il a voyagé un peu p.** he's been all over the place; **ils ont habité un peu p. en Italie** they've lived all over Italy; **j'ai mal p.** I ache all over; **p. où** everywhere (that), wherever **2** *Sport* **3 buts p.** 3 (goals) all; **15 p.** *(au tennis)* 15 all; **40 p.** *(au tennis)* deuce

partouze [partuz] = **partouse**

partouzer [3] [partuze] = **partouser**

parturiente [partyrjɑ̃t] **NF** parturient

parturition [partyrisjɔ̃] **NF** parturition

paru, -e [pary] **PP** *voir* **paraître²**

parure [paryr] **NF 1** *(ensemble)* set; **p. de berceau** *Br* cot *or Am* crib set; **p. de lit** set of bed linen **2** *(bijoux)* parure, set of jewels; *(colifichets)* matching set of costume jewellery **3** *Littéraire (ornements)* finery; **dans sa plus belle p.** in all her (best) finery

parut *etc voir* **paraître²**

parution [parysjɔ̃] **NF** *(gén)* publication; *(d'une revue)* issue; **juste avant/après la p. du livre** just before/after the book came out; **date de p.** *(d'un livre, article)* date of publication, publication date; *(d'une revue)* date of issue

parvenir [40] [parvənir] **USAGE ABSOLU** *Vieilli (s'élever socialement)* to succeed *or* get on (in life)

• **parvenir à VT IND** *(aux être)* **1** *(atteindre ▸ sujet: voyageur, véhicule, lettre, son)* **p. à** *ou* **jusqu'à** to get to, to reach; **l'ambulance ne put p. jusqu'à lui** the ambulance couldn't get (through) to him; **faire p. un colis à qn** to send sb a parcel; **si cette carte vous parvient** if you get *or* receive this card; **votre demande doit nous p. avant le 4** your application must be in *or* reach us by the 4th

2 *(obtenir ▸ célébrité, réussite)* to achieve; **étant parvenu au faîte de la gloire** having reached *or* achieved the pinnacle of fame

3 *(en venir à)* to reach; **elle était parvenue à un âge avancé** she had reached an advanced age

4 *(réussir à)* **p. à faire qch** to succeed in doing *or* to manage to do sth; **il ne parviendra jamais à la convaincre** he'll never succeed in convincing *or* manage to convince her

parvenu, -e [parvəny] *Péj* **ADJ** parvenu, upstart, nouveau riche

NM,F parvenu, upstart, nouveau riche

parvient, parvint *etc voir* **parvenir**

parvis [parvi] **NM** parvis, square *(in front of church or public building)*

pas¹ [pɑ] **NM 1** *(déplacement)* step; **mes p. me conduisirent à une clairière** my steps took me to a clearing; **je vais faire quelques p. dans le parc** I'm going for a short *or* little walk in the park; **revenir** *ou* **retourner sur ses p.** to retrace one's steps *or* path, to turn back; **arriver sur les p. de qn** to follow close on sb's heels, to arrive just after sb; **avancer à** *ou* **faire de petits p.** to take short steps; **marcher à grands p.** to stride along; **faire un p. sur le côté** to take a step to the *or* to one side; **faire un p. en avant** to step forward, to take a step *or* pace forward; **faire un p. en arrière** to step back; **faire ses premiers p.** to learn to walk; *Fig* **il a fait ses premiers p. de comédien dans un film de Hitchcock** he made his debut as an actor in a Hitchcock film; **marcher à p. de velours** to pad around; *Fig* **marcher sur les p. de qn** to follow in sb's footsteps

2 *Fig (progrès)* **avancer à petits p.** to make slow progress; **avancer à grands p.** *(enquête)* to make great progress; *(technique, science)* to take big steps forward; *(échéance, événement)* to be looming; **avancer à p. comptés** *ou* **mesurés** *(lentement)* to make slow progress; *(prudemment)* to tread carefully; *Fig* to proceed slowly but surely; **faire un p. en avant** *(discussion, négociateur)* to take a step forward; **faire un grand p. en avant** to take a great step *or* leap forward; **faire un p. en arrière** to take a step back *or* backwards; **faire un p. en avant et deux (p.) en arrière** to take one step forward and two steps back *or* backwards; **faire le premier p.** to make the first move; **il n'y a que le premier p. qui coûte** the first step is the hardest; **c'est au moins un p. sur la bonne voie** at least it's a step in the right direction

3 *Fig (étape)* step; **c'est un p. difficile pour lui que de te parler directement** talking to you directly is a difficult step for him to take; **c'est un grand p. à faire** *ou* **franchir** it's a big step to take; **franchir** *ou* **sauter le p.** to take the plunge

4 *(empreinte)* footprint; **des p. sur le sable** footprints in the sand

5 *(allure)* pace; **allonger** *ou* **doubler le p.** to quicken one's step *or* pace; **hâter** *ou* **presser le p.** to hurry on; **ralentir le p.** to slow one's pace, to slow down; **aller du** *ou* **marcher au même p.** to walk at the same pace; **aller** *ou* **marcher d'un bon p.** to walk at a good *or* brisk pace; **avancer** *ou* **marcher d'un p. lent** to walk slowly; **changer de p.** to change pace

6 *(démarche)* gait, tread; **marcher d'un p. alerte/léger/élastique** to walk with a sprightly/light/bouncy tread; **avancer d'un p. lourd** *ou* **pesant** to tread heavily, to walk with a heavy tread

7 *Mil* step; **p. accéléré** = marching step between quick march and double-quick; **p. cadencé** quick march; *Mil* **au p. de charge** at the charge; *Fig* charging along; **au p. redoublé** on the double, at double-quick march; **p. de route** march at ease

8 *(danse)* pas, step; **apprendre le p. du tango** to learn the tango *or* how to (dance the) tango; **esquisser un p.** to dance a few steps, to do a little dance; **p. battu/tombé** pas battu/tombé; **p. de deux/trois** pas de deux/trois

9 *Sport* **au p. de course** at a run; *Fig* at a run, on the double; **au p. de gymnastique** at a jog trot

10 *(mesure)* pace; *(espace approximatif)* pace, step; **comptez trente p.** count thirty steps *or* paces; **à quelques p. de là** a few steps *or* paces away; **le restaurant n'est qu'à deux p. (de la gare)** the restaurant is (only) just round the corner (from the station); **il se tenait à quelques p. de moi** he was standing just a few yards from me; **ne pas quitter qn d'un p.** to follow sb's every footstep

11 *(marche d'escalier)* step; **attention au p. en descendant dans la cuisine** watch the step on the way (down) to the kitchen; **p. de porte** doorstep; **sur tous les p. de porte** on every doorstep; **ne reste pas sur le p. de la porte** don't stand at the door *or* on the doorstep *or* in the doorway

12 *Géog (en montagne)* pass; *(en mer)* strait; **le p. de Calais** the Strait of Dover

13 *Tech (d'une vis)* thread; *(d'une denture, d'un engrenage)* pitch; **p. à droite/gauche** right-hand/left-hand thread

14 *Aviat* pitch

15 *Mil* **p. de tir** *(pour missile)* launching site

16 *(locutions)* **prendre le p. sur qn/qch** to take precedence over sb/sth; **céder le p.** to give way; **se tirer d'un mauvais p.** to get oneself out of a fix

• **à chaque pas ADV 1** *(partout)* everywhere, at every step; **je la rencontre à chaque p.** I meet her everywhere (I go) **2** *(constamment)* at every turn *or* step; **à chaque p. je dois corriger les mêmes erreurs** I keep having to correct the same mistakes

• **au pas ADV 1** *(en marchant)* at a walking pace; **ne courez pas, allez au p.** don't run, walk **2** *Aut* **aller** *ou* **rouler au p.** *(dans un embouteillage)* to crawl along; *(consigne de sécurité)* to go slow, *Br* to go dead slow **3** *Équitation* walking, at a walk; **mettre son cheval au p.** to walk one's horse; **mettre qn/qch au p.** to bring sb/sth to heel

• **de ce pas ADV** straightaway, at once

• **pas à pas ADV 1** *(de très près)* step by step; **il la suivait p. à p.** he followed her step by step **2** *(prudemment)* step by step, one step at a time

pas² [pɑ] **ADV 1** *(avec "ne", pour exprimer la négation)* **elle ne viendra p.** she won't come; **je n'aime p. les légumes** I don't like vegetables; **ils n'ont p. de problèmes/d'avenir** they have no problems/no future, they haven't got any problems/a future; **il a décidé de ne p. accepter** he decided not to accept; **ce n'est p. que je ne veuille p., mais...** it's not that I don't want to, but...

2 *Fam (avec omission du "ne")* **elle sait p.** she doesn't know; **t'en fais p.!** don't (you) worry!; **c'est p. sûr** it's not sure *or* definite

3 *(avec "non", pour renforcer la négation)* **non p.** not; **il était non p. sévère mais ferme** he wasn't strict, (he was) just firm; **elle est non p. belle mais jolie** she's not so much beautiful as pretty

4 *(employé seul)* **sincère ou p.** sincere or not; **les garçons voulaient danser, les filles p.** the boys wanted to dance, the girls didn't; **tu comprends ou p.?** do you understand or not *or* or don't you?; **pourquoi p.?** why not?; *Fam* **p. la peine** (it's) not worth it; **j'ai insisté, mais p. assez** I insisted but not enough

5 *(dans des réponses négatives)* **p. de dessert pour moi, merci** no dessert for me, thank you; **qui l'a pris? – p. moi, en tout cas!** who took it? – not me, that's for sure!; **p. du tout** not at all; **c'est toi qui as fini les chocolats? – p. du tout!** was it you who finished the chocolates? – certainly not!; **je n'en suis p. du tout sûr** I'm not at all sure (about it); **p. le moins du monde** not in the least *or* slightest, not at all; **absolument p.** not at all

6 *Fam (n'est-ce pas)* **on a fait ce qu'on a pu, p.?** we did what we could, didn't we *or* right?

• **pas mal** *Fam* **ADJ INV** not bad; **l'album n'est p. mal** the album isn't bad; **c'est p. mal comme idée** that's not a bad idea **ADV 1** *(bien)* **je ne m'en suis p. mal tiré** I handled it quite well; **on ferait p. mal de recommencer** we'd be better off starting again **2** *(très)* **il est p. mal soûl** he's pretty drunk; **la voiture est p. mal amochée** the car's pretty battered

• **pas mal de ADV** *Fam (suivi d'un nom dénombrable)* quite a few, quite a lot of; *(suivi d'un nom indénombrable)* quite a lot of; **p. mal de mensonges/journalistes** quite a few lies/journalists; **p. mal d'argent** quite a lot of money; **quand? – il y a p. mal de temps** when? – quite a while ago

• **pas plus mal ADV il a maigri – c'est p. plus mal** he's lost weight – good thing too *or* that's not such a bad thing *or* just as well

• **pas un, pas une ADJ** not a (single), not one; **p. une maison n'est restée debout** not a single *or* not one house was left standing; **p. un mot!** not a word! **PRON** not (a single) one; **p. une n'est arrivée à l'heure** not one *or* not a single one (of them) got there on time; **il n'y en a p. un d'acceptable** none of them are acceptable; **il sait faire les crêpes comme p. un** he makes pancakes like nobody else (on earth)

pas-à-pas [pɑzapɑ] **ADJ INV** *Ordinat* step-by-step, single-step

NM INV 1 *Tech* step by step (mechanism) 2 *Ordinat* single-step operation

pascal¹, -e, -als *ou* **-aux, -ales** [paskal, -o] ADJ *Rel (de la fête chrétienne)* Easter *(avant n)*, *Spéc* paschal; *(de la fête juive ▸ gén)* paschal, Passover *(avant n)*; *(▸agneau)* paschal

pascal², -als [paskal] NM 1 *Phys* pascal 2 *Anciennement Fam (billet)* **un p.** a 500-franc note

pascalien, -enne [paskaljɛ̃, -ɛn] ADJ Pascalian, Pascal's; **le pari p.** Pascal's wager

Pas-de-Calais [pɑdəkalɛ] NM **le P.** Pas-de-Calais

pas-de-porte [pɑdpɔrt] NM INV 1 *Com* ≃ commercial lease 2 *Jur* key money

pashmina [paʃmina] NM *(laine, châle)* pashmina

pasionaria [pasjɔnarja] NF militant

paso doble [pasodɔbl] NM INV paso doble

passable [pɑsabl] ADJ 1 *(acceptable)* passable, tolerable; **il écrit des vers passables** he writes quite good poetry 2 *Scol (tout juste moyen)* average

passablement [pɑsabləmɑ̃] ADV 1 *(de façon satisfaisante)* passably well, tolerably (well); **je chante p.** my voice isn't bad 2 *(notablement)* fairly, rather, somewhat; **ils avaient p. bu** they had drunk quite a lot

passade [pɑsad] NF 1 *(amourette)* fling, *Sout* amourette; **entre eux, ce ne fut qu'une p.** they just had a (little) fling 2 *(caprice)* passing fancy, fad

passage [pɑsaʒ] NM A. *MOUVEMENT* 1 *(allées et venues)* **chaque p. du train faisait trembler les vitres** the windows shook every time a train went past; **laisser le p. à qn/une ambulance** to let sb/an ambulance through, to make way for sb/an ambulance; **ils attendaient le p. des coureurs** they were waiting for the runners to go by; **p. de troupeaux** *(panneau sur la route)* cattle crossing

2 *(circulation)* traffic; **il y a peu/beaucoup de p. dans notre ville/rue** there's not much/a lot of traffic in our town/street

3 *(arrivée, venue)* **elle attend le p. de l'autobus** she's waiting for the bus; **guette le p. du facteur** watch out for the *Br* postman *or Am* mailman

4 *(visite)* call, visit; **c'est le seul souvenir qui me reste de mon p. chez eux** that's the only thing I remember of my visit to them; **lors de mon prochain p. à Paris** next time I'm in Paris

5 *(franchissement ▸ d'une frontière, d'un fleuve)* crossing; *(▸d'un col)* passing; *(▸de la douane)* passing (through); **p. interdit** *(sur panneau)* no entry; *Mil* **p. à l'ennemi** going over to the enemy; *Naut* **le p. de la ligne** the crossing of the line

6 *(changement, transition)* change, transition; **le p. de l'hiver au printemps** the change *or* passage from winter to spring

7 *(dans une hiérarchie)* move; **p. d'un employé à l'échelon supérieur** promotion of an employee to a higher grade; *Scol* **le p. dans la classe supérieure** going *or* moving up to the next *Br* class *or Am* grade

8 *(voyage sur mer, traversée)* crossing; **ils travaillaient durement pour payer leur p.** they worked hard to pay for their passage *or* crossing; **pour limiter le nombre des passages clandestins vers les États-Unis** to reduce the number of illegal border crossings into the United States

9 *Astron* transit

10 *Ordinat* **p. machine** run; **p. automatique à la ligne (suivante)** autoflow, wordwrap

11 *Psy* **p. à l'acte** acting out

12 *Rad, Théât & TV* **lors de son dernier p. à la télévision** *(personne)* last time he/she was on TV; *(film)* last time it was shown on TV

13 *Sport* **temps de p.** split time; **p. du témoin** *(au relais)* (baton) changeover

B. *VOIE* 1 *(chemin)* passage, way; **enlève ton sac du p.** move your bag out of the way; **tu es dans le p.!** you're in the way!; **donner** *ou* **livrer p. à qn/qch** to let sb/sth in; **boucher** *ou* **obstruer le p. à qn** to block the way for sb; **le p. du nord-ouest** the Northwest Passage; **p. secret** secret passage

2 *(ruelle)* alley, passage; *(galerie commerçante)* arcade; **p. couvert** passageway

3 *(tapis de couloir)* runner

4 *Aut* **p. de roue** wheel housing

5 *Rail* **p. à niveau** *Br* level crossing, *Am* grade crossing

6 *(voie)* **p. clouté** *ou* **(pour) piétons** *Br* pedestrian *or* zebra crossing, *Am* crosswalk; **p. protégé** priority over secondary roads; **p. souterrain** underpass, *Br* (pedestrian) subway

C. *D'UN FILM, D'UN ROMAN* passage, section; **elle m'a lu quelques passages de la lettre de Paul** she read me a few passages from Paul's letter

• **au passage** ADV 1 *(sur un trajet)* on one's way; **les enfants doivent attraper la cocarde au p.** the children have to catch the ribbon as they go past; **nous visiterons les caves de Reims au p.** we'll visit the cellars at Rheims on our way 2 *(dans le cours de l'action)* in passing 3 *(à propos)* incidentally, by the way; **tiens, au p., je te signale trois fautes page 32** by the way, there are three mistakes on page 32

• **au passage de** PRÉP **au p. du carrosse, la foule applaudissait** when the carriage went past *or* through, the crowd clapped

• **de passage** ADJ *(client)* casual; **être de p.** *(voyageur)* to be passing through; **je suis de p. à Paris** I'm in Paris for a few days

• **sur le passage de** PRÉP **la foule s'est massée sur le p. du marathon** the crowd gathered on the marathon route

• **passage à tabac** NM beating up

• **passage à vide** NM **avoir un p. à vide** *(moralement)* to feel a bit low *or* down; *(intellectuellement)* to have a lapse in concentration

passager, -ère [pasaʒe, -ɛr] ADJ 1 *(momentané ▸ bonheur)* fleeting, short-lived; *(▸ mauvaise humeur, crise)* passing, short-lived; *(▸engouement)* passing; **état p.** passing phase; **ne vous inquiétez pas, ces douleurs seront passagères** don't worry, the pain won't last; **ils ont eu une petite brouille passagère** they fell out momentarily 2 *(très fréquenté)* busy; **des rues très passagères** very busy roads, roads with very heavy traffic

NM,F passenger; **ce sont les passagers à destination d'Athènes qui ont le plus attendu** the people going to Athens waited the longest; **p. clandestin** stowaway; **p. en transit** transit passenger

passagèrement [pasaʒɛrmɑ̃] ADV for a short while, temporarily, momentarily

passant¹, -e [pasɑ̃, -ɑ̃t] ADJ *(voie, route)* busy

NM,F passer-by

passant² [pasɑ̃] NM (belt) loop

passation [pasasjɔ̃] NF 1 *Jur (d'un acte, d'un contrat)* drawing up (and signing) 2 *Pol* **p. des pouvoirs** transfer of power 3 *Compta (d'une écriture)* entering; *(d'un dividende)* payment; **p. d'écriture** journal entry; **p. par pertes et profits** write-off

passavant [pasavɑ̃] NM 1 *Jur* transire 2 *Naut* (fore-and-aft) catwalk, flying bridge

passe [pɑs] NM 1 *(passe-partout)* master *or* pass key 2 *(laissez-passer)* pass

NF 1 *Sport (aux jeux de ballon)* pass; **faire une p.** to pass (the ball), to make a pass; *Ftbl* **p. en avant/en retrait** forward/back pass; *Escrime* **p. d'armes** sparring

2 *Fam (d'une prostituée)* trick; **faire une p.** to turn a trick

3 *(situation)* **être dans une bonne p.** *(commerce)* to be thriving; *(mentalement)* to be going through a good period *or* patch; **leur couple traverse une mauvaise p.** their relationship is going through a rough *or* bad patch

4 *Géog (col)* pass; *(chenal)* pass, channel; **la p. de Khaybar** the Khyber Pass

5 *Tech (sur un tour)* cut

6 *Typ* overs, overplus; **exemplaires de p.** surplus copies, over copies

7 *Fin* **p. de caisse** allowance for cashier's errors

8 *(mise)* stake; *(à la roulette)* passe; **p. anglaise** craps

9 *(sur un cours d'eau)* passage

• **en passe de** PRÉP about to, on the point of; **ils sont en p. de prendre le contrôle des médias** they're poised *or* set to gain control of the media

passé¹ [pase] PRÉP after; **p. minuit** after midnight; **p. le pont, c'est à droite** it's on the right after the bridge; **p. la première impression** once *or* after the first impression has worn off

passé², -e [pase] ADJ 1 *(précédent ▸ année, mois)* last, past; **au cours des mois passés** over the past *or* last few months

2 *(révolu)* **il est 3 heures passées** it's past *or Br* gone 3 o'clock; **elle a 30 ans passés** she's over 30; **à 15 ans passés, il ne savait toujours pas lire** he was over 15 and he still couldn't read

3 *(qui n'est plus)* past, former; **elle songeait au temps p.** she was thinking of times *or* days gone by

4 *(teinte, fleur)* faded

NM 1 *(temps révolu)* **le p.** the past; **oublions le p.** let bygones be bygones, let's forget the past; **dans le p.** in the past; **c'est du p., tout ça** it's all in the past *or* it's all behind us now 2 *(d'une personne, d'une ville)* past; **un pays au p. glorieux/sanglant** a country with a glorious/bloody past; **avoir honte/être fier de son p.** to be ashamed/proud of one's past; **il a un lourd p.** he's a man with a past 3 *Gram* past tense; **au p.** in the past tense; **les temps du p.** past tenses; **p. antérieur** past anterior; **p. composé** (present) perfect; **p. simple** *ou* **historique** simple past, past historic

• **par le passé** ADV in the past; **il est beaucoup plus indulgent que par le p.** he's much more indulgent than before *or* than he used to be

passe-crassane [pɑskrasan] NF INV passe-crassane *(variety of winter pear)*

passe-droit [pɑsdrwa] *(pl* **passe-droits***)* NM privilege, special favour

passéisme [paseism] NM *Péj* attachment to the past, backward-looking attitude

passéiste [paseist] *Péj* ADJ backward-looking

NMF backward-looking person

passe-lacet [pɑslasɛ] *(pl* **passe-lacets***)* NM bodkin; *Fam* **raide comme un p.** completely broke *or Br* skint

passement [pɑsmɑ̃] NM (piece of) braid *or* braiding *or* cord *(used as trimming)*

passementer [3] [pɑsmɑ̃te] VT to braid

passementerie [pɑsmɑ̃tri] NF *(articles)* trimmings, soft furnishings; *(commerce)* soft furnishing trade

passementier, -ère [pɑsmɑ̃tje, -ɛr] ADJ *(commerce, industrie)* soft furnishing *(avant n)*

NM,F soft furnishing manufacturer

passe-montagne [pɑsmɔ̃taɲ] *(pl* **passe-montagnes***)* NM balaclava

passe-partout [pɑspartu] ADJ INV *(robe, instrument)* versatile, all-purpose *(avant n)*; **un discours p.** a speech for all occasions; **une réponse p.** a stock *or* all-purpose reply

NM INV 1 *(clé)* master *or* skeleton key 2 *Beaux-Arts & Typ* passe-partout 3 *(scie)* two-handed saw

passe-passe [pɑspɑs] NM INV **tour de p.** *(tour de magie)* (magic) trick; *(tromperie)* trick

passe-plat [pɑspla] *(pl* **passe-plats***)* NM serving hatch

passepoil [pɑspwal] NM piping *(UNCOUNT)*

passepoiler [3] [pɑspwale] VT *(vêtement)* to trim with piping, to pipe; **poche passepoilée** welted pocket

passeport [pɑspɔr] NM 1 *Admin* passport; **p. biométrique** biometric passport 2 *Fig* passport; **ce diplôme est un p. pour la vie professionnelle** this diploma is a passport to a job

PASSER [3] [pɑse]

VI	
• to pass **A1, 6, 10, 12, B2, 4, 6, 9, D1, 2**	• to pass by **A1**
• to flow **A3**	• to go past **A1, 7, 12**
• to call **A7, 8**	• to go **A5, 11, B3, 5**
• to get through **A9**	• to run **A3, 5**
• to be on **B7**	• to be elected **B6**
• to go by **D1**	• to become **C2**
• to fade **D2**	• to disappear **D2**
• to die down **D2**	• to wear off **D2**
	• to go bad **D3**
VT	
• to cross **A1, 2**	• to pass **A3, 9, B6**
• to go past **A3**	• to take across **A4**
• to put **A6**	• to run **A7**
• to clear **A8**	• to take **B1**
• to have **B1**	• to get through **B2**
• to leave out **B3**	• to give **B6**

- to put through **B6**
- to lend **B8**
- to apply **B9**
- to put on **B9, 11, 13**
- to show **B13**
- to reach **B14**
- to agree on **B14**
- to draw up **B16**
- to spend **C1**
- to get through **C2**

USAGE ABSOLU

- to pass

VI *(aux être)* **A.** *EXPRIME UN DÉPLACEMENT* **1** *(se déplacer ▸ personne, véhicule)* to pass (by), to go *or* to come past; **regarder p. les coureurs** to watch the runners go past; **p. à droite/gauche** to go right/left; **l'avion est passé au-dessus de la maison** the plane flew over the house; **un avion passait dans le ciel** a plane was flying in the sky; **p. devant qch** to go past sth; **puisque tu passes devant la boulangerie, rapporte du pain** seeing as you're going past the baker's, pick up some bread; **passe devant si tu ne vois pas** *(devant moi)* go in front of me if you can't see; *(devant tout le monde)* go to the front if you can't see; **p. sous une échelle** to go under a ladder; **p. sous une voiture** *(se faire écraser)* to get run over (by a car); **p. sur un pont** to go over *or* to cross a bridge

2 *(fugitivement)* **j'ai vu un éclair de rage p. dans son regard** I saw a flash of anger in his/her eyes; **un sourire passa sur ses lèvres** a smile played about his/her lips; **elle dit tout ce qui lui passe par la tête** she says the first thing that comes into her head; **qu'est-ce qui a bien pu lui p. par la tête?** whatever was he/she thinking of?; **le pouvoir n'a fait que p. entre leurs mains** they knew power only briefly; *Fam Hum* **il y a que le train qui lui soit pas passé dessus** she's the town bike

3 *(s'écouler ▸ fluide)* to flow, to run; **il y a de l'air qui passe sous la porte** there's a permanent draught coming under the door

4 *(emprunter un certain itinéraire)* **si vous passez à Paris, venez me voir** come and see me if you're in Paris; **le voleur est passé par la fenêtre** the burglar got in through the window; **passe par l'escalier de service** use the service stairs

5 *(fleuve, route)* to go, to run; **la nouvelle route ne passera pas dans le village** the new road won't go *or* run through the village; **le Rhône passe à Lyon** the Rhone goes *or* flows through Lyons; **le tunnel passera sous la montagne** the tunnel will go under the mountain; **le pont passe au-dessus de l'avenue** the bridge crosses the avenue

6 *Math* to pass; **soit une droite passant par deux points A et B** given a straight line between two points A and B

7 *(sur un parcours régulier ▸ démarcheur, représentant)* to call; *(▸ bateau, bus, train)* to come *or* to go past; **p. chez un client** to call on a client; **le facteur n'est pas encore passé** the *Br* postman *or Am* mailman hasn't been yet; **le bus passe toutes les sept minutes** there's a bus every seven minutes; **le bateau/train est déjà passé** the boat/train has already gone *or* left

8 *(faire une visite)* to call; **p. chez qn** to call at sb's place; **j'ai demandé au médecin de p.** I asked the doctor to call (in) *or* to come *or* to visit; **veuillez p. au commissariat demain** please report to the police station tomorrow; **je ne fais que p.** I'm not stopping; **p. voir qn** to call on sb; **je passerai te chercher** I'll come and fetch you

9 *(franchir une limite)* to get through; **tu ne passeras pas, il y a trop de monde** you won't get through, there are too many people; **ne laissez p. personne** don't let anybody through; **il est passé au rouge** he went through a red light; **ça passe ou ça casse** it's make or break

10 *(s'infiltrer)* to pass; **p. dans le sang** to pass into *or* to enter the bloodstream; **la lumière passe à travers les rideaux** the light shines through the curtains; **le vent et la neige passaient entre les planches disjointes** the wind and snow got in through the gaps in the floorboards

11 *(aller, se rendre)* to go; **où est-il passé?** where's he gone (to)?; **où sont passées mes lunettes?** where have my glasses disappeared to?; **passons à table** let's eat; **passons dans mon bureau** let's go into my office; **p. de Suisse en France** to cross over *or* to go from Switzerland to France; **p. à l'ennemi** to go over to the enemy; **elle est passée à l'opposition** she's gone over to *or* she's joined the opposition; **il est passé du côté du vainqueur** he's switched to the winning side

12 *Chasse* to pass, to go *or* to come past; **ici, les bécasses passent en septembre** woodcock fly over here in September; **là où le gibier passe** where game animals pass

13 *Naut* **p. au vent** to sail to windward; **p. sur l'avant** to cut across the bow

14 *Théât* to cross the stage

B. *EXPRIME UNE ACTION* **1 p. à** *(se soumettre à)* to go for; **p. au scanner** to go for a scan; **p. à la visite médicale** to go for a medical examination; **ce matin, je suis passé au tableau** I was asked to explain something at the blackboard this morning; *Fam* **je ne veux pas me faire opérer – il faudra bien que tu y passes, pourtant!** I don't want to have an operation – you're going to have to!; *Fam* **avec lui, toutes les femmes du service y sont passées** he's had all the women in his department; *Fam* **y p.** *(mourir)* to croak, *Br* to snuff it; **tout le monde a cru que tu allais y p.** everybody thought you were a goner

2 *(être accepté)* to pass; **elle est passée à l'écrit mais pas à l'oral** she got through *or* she passed the written exam but not the oral; **j'ai un bout de pomme qui est passé de travers** a bit of my apple has gone down the wrong way; **sa dernière remarque n'est pas passée** his/her last remark stuck in my throat; **ce genre d'explication ne passera pas avec lui** he won't swallow an explanation like that; **ton petit discours est bien passé** your little speech went down well *or* was well received; **la deuxième scène ne passe pas du tout** the second scene doesn't work at all; **le fascisme ne passera pas!** no to fascism!; **l'injurier, passe encore, mais le frapper!** it's one thing to insult him, but quite another to hit him!

3 *(être transmis)* to go; **la ferme est passée de père en fils depuis cinq générations** the farm has been handed down from father to son for five generations; **la carafe passa de main en main** the jug was passed around; **la locution est passée du latin à l'anglais** the phrase came *or* passed into English from Latin; **le pouvoir est passé de la gauche à la droite** the right has taken over from the left

4 *(entrer)* to pass; **c'est passé dans le langage courant** it's passed into *or* it's now part of everyday speech; **c'est passé dans les mœurs** it's become standard *or* normal practice

5 *(être utilisé, absorbé)* to go; **tout son salaire passe dans la maison** all his/her salary goes on the house; **400 à 500 euros passent chaque mois dans la nourriture** food accounts for 400 to 500 euros a month; **tout le fromage y est passé** every last bit of cheese went (in the end); **les deux bouteilles y sont passées** both bottles were drunk; **toutes ses économies y passent** all his/her savings go towards *or* into it

6 *Pol (être adopté ▸ projet de loi, amendement)* to pass, to be passed; *(être élu ▸ député)* to be elected, to get in; **la loi est passée** the law was passed; **si les socialistes passent** if the socialists get in *or* are elected

7 *Cin & Théât* to be on, to be showing; **son documentaire n'est jamais passé** his/her documentary was never shown; *Rad & TV* **les informations passent à 20 heures** the news is on at 8 pm; **p. à la radio** *(émission, personne)* to be on the radio *or* the air; **p. à la télévision** *(personne)* to be *or* to appear on television; *(film)* to be on television

8 *Jur (comparaître)* **p. devant le tribunal** to come up *or* to go before the court; **p. en correctionnelle** ≃ to go before the magistrate's court; **l'affaire passera en justice le mois prochain** the case will be heard next month

9 *(dans un jeu)* to pass; **je passe** pass

C. *EXPRIME UN CHANGEMENT D'ÉTAT* **1** *(accéder ▸ à un niveau)* **p. dans la classe supérieure** to move up to the next *Br* form *or Am* grade; *Scol* **p. en seconde** ≃ to move up *Br* to the fifth form *or Am* to tenth grade; **p. à** to move to; **il est passé au grade supérieur** he's been promoted to the next highest rank

2 *(devenir)* to become; **p. entraîneur** to become a coach; **il est passé ailier** he plays on the wing now; **p. professionnel** to turn professional

3 *Aut* **p. en troisième** to change into third (gear)

4 *(dans des locutions verbales)* **passons à l'ordre du jour** let us turn to the business on the agenda; **traduisons le texte, puis nous passerons au commentaire** let's translate the text first, then we'll analyse it; **p. à l'action** to take action; **p. de l'état liquide à l'état gazeux** to pass *or* to change from the liquid to the gaseous state; **la lumière passait du rose au mauve** the light changed from pink to mauve; **quand on passe de l'adolescence à l'âge adulte** when you pass from adolescence to adulthood; **la production est passée de 20 à 30/de 30 à 20 tonnes** output has gone (up) from 20 to 30/(down) from 30 to 20 tonnes; **p. du français au russe** to switch from French to Russian; **comment êtes-vous passé du cinéma au théâtre?** how did you move *or* make the transition from the cinema to the stage?; **il passe d'une idée à l'autre** he jumps *or* flits from one idea to another

D. *EXPRIME UNE ÉVOLUTION DANS LE TEMPS* **1** *(s'écouler ▸ temps)* to pass, to go by; **la journée est passée agréablement** the day went off *or* passed pleasantly; **une heure est vite passée** an hour passes quickly; **à mesure que les jours passaient** as the days went by; **comme le temps passe!** how time flies!

2 *(s'estomper ▸ douleur, enthousiasme)* to fade (away), to wear off; *(▸ malaise)* to disappear; *(▸ mode, engouement)* to die out; *(▸ beauté)* to fade, to wane; *(▸ chance, jeunesse)* to pass; *(▸ mauvaise humeur)* to pass, to vanish; *(▸ rage, tempête, averse)* to die down; **mon envie est passée** I don't feel like it any more; **j'aimais regarder la télévision mais cela m'a passé** I used to like watching television but not any more; **ce médicament fait p. la douleur très rapidement** this medicine relieves pain very quickly

3 *(s'altérer ▸ fruit, denrées)* to spoil, to go bad, *Br* to go off; *(se faner ▸ fleur)* to wilt; **le vin est ouvert depuis trop longtemps, il a passé** the wine's been open too long, it's gone off; **les roses sont passées** the roses have wilted

4 *(pâlir ▸ teinte)* **le papier peint a passé au soleil** the sun has faded the wallpaper

5 *(aux avoir) Vieilli Euph (mourir)* **il a passé cette nuit** he passed on *or* away last night

VT *(aux avoir)* **A.** *EXPRIME UN DÉPLACEMENT* **1** *(traverser ▸ pont, col de montagne)* to go over, to cross; *(▸ écluse)* to go through, to cross; **p. une rivière à la nage** to swim across a river; **p. un ruisseau à gué** to ford a stream

2 *(franchir ▸ frontière, ligne d'arrivée)* to cross, to go through; **si je passe cette porte, je ne reviendrai plus jamais** if I go through that door I'll never come back; **nous passerons la frontière à Vintimille** we'll cross the border at Ventimiglia

3 *(dépasser ▸ point de repère)* to pass, to go past; **vous passez l'escalier et c'est à droite** go past the stairs and it's on your right, it's on your right after you pass the stairs; **p. l'arrêt de l'autobus** *(le manquer)* to miss one's bus stop; **quand on passe les 1000 mètres d'altitude** when you go over 1,000 metres high; **l'or a passé les 400 dollars l'once** gold has broken through the $400 an ounce mark

4 *(transporter)* to ferry *or* to take across

5 *(introduire)* **p. de la drogue/des cigarettes en fraude** to smuggle drugs/cigarettes

6 *(engager ▸ partie du corps)* to put; **p. son bras autour de la taille de qn** to put *or* to slip one's arm round sb's waist; **il passa son doigt à travers le grillage** he put *or* he stuck a finger through the wire netting; **je n'arrive pas à p. ma tête dans l'encolure de cette robe** my head won't go through the neck of the dress

7 *(faire aller ▸ instrument)* to run; **p. un peigne dans ses cheveux** to run a comb through one's hair; **p. une éponge sur la table** to wipe the table; **p. un chiffon sur les meubles** to dust the furniture; **p. l'aspirateur** to vacuum, *Br* to hoover; **p. le balai** to sweep up; **passe le balai dans l'escalier** give the stairs a sweep, sweep the stairs

8 *Équitation (haie)* to jump, to clear; **le cheval a passé le fossé** the horse cleared the ditch

9 *Sport (franchir ▸ obstacle, haie)* to jump (over); *(transmettre ▸ ballon)* to pass; *(dépasser ▸ coureurs)* to overtake, to pass; **p. la barre à deux mètres** to clear the bar at two metres; **p. les autres concurrents** to overtake the other competitors; *Fig* **p. tous les obstacles** to overcome *or* to surmount all the obstacles

B. *EXPRIME UNE ACTION* **1** *(se soumettre à ▸ permis de conduire)* to take; *(▸ examen)* to take, *Br* to sit; *(▸ scanner, visite médicale)* to have, to go for; **il passe sa thèse demain** he has his oral *or Br* viva for his thesis tomorrow; **la voiture doit p. un contrôle** the car must go (in) for a test *or* must be tested

2 *Vieilli (réussir ▸ examen)* to pass; *(▸ épreuve éliminatoire)* to get through; **elle a passé sa ceinture noire de karaté** she's got her black belt in karate now; **il a passé l'écrit, mais attendons l'oral** he's passed the written exam, but let's see what happens in the oral

3 *(omettre)* to miss *or* to leave out, to omit; **je passe toutes les descriptions dans ses romans** I miss out *or* I skip all the descriptions in his/her novels

4 *(tolérer)* **elle lui passe tout** she lets him/her get away with anything; **elle est gentille, alors on lui passe le reste** she's so nice that people make allowances (for the rest); **passez-moi l'expression/le mot** if you'll pardon the expression/excuse the term

5 *(soumettre à l'action de)* **p. une plaie à l'alcool** to put alcohol on a cut; **p. les parquets à l'encaustique** to polish the floors; **p. des légumes au mixeur** to put vegetables through the blender, to blend vegetables; **p. qch sous l'eau** to rinse sth *or* to give sth a rinse under the tap; **p. qch au four** to put sth in the oven; *Fam* **p. quelque chose** *Br* to tick sb off, *Am* to chew sb out; *Fam* **se faire p. quelque chose** *Br* to get a good ticking off, *Am* to get a good chewing-out

6 *(donner, transmettre ▸ gén)* to pass, to hand, to give; *(▸ rhume)* to pass on, to give; *(▸ au téléphone)* to put through; **passe-moi le sel** pass me the salt; **fais p. à ton voisin** pass it to your neighbour; **p. la consigne à qn** to pass on orders to sb; **p. ses pouvoirs à son successeur** to hand over one's powers to one's successor; **il a passé sa grippe à tout le bureau** he gave his flu to everybody in the office; **je te passe Fred** here's Fred, I'll hand you over to Fred; **passe-moi Annie** let me talk to Annie, put Annie on

7 *(rendre public ▸ annonce)* **faire p. une petite annonce** to place a small ad

8 *Fam (prêter)* to lend ☐; **peux-tu me p. 50 euros jusqu'à demain?** could you lend me 50 euros till tomorrow?; **je lui passe ma chambre et je dors au salon** he/she can have my room and I'll sleep in the living room

9 *(appliquer ▸ substance)* to apply, to put on; **p. une couche de peinture sur un mur** to apply a coat of paint to a wall; **il faudra p. une deuxième couche** it needs a second coat; **je vais te p. de la crème dans le dos** I'm going to put *or* to rub some cream on your back

10 *(filtrer, tamiser ▸ thé, potage)* to strain; *(▸ farine)* to sieve

11 *(enfiler ▸ vêtement)* to slip *or* to put on; **je passe une robe moins chaude et j'arrive** I'll put on a cooler dress and I'll be with you; **elle passa l'anneau à son doigt** she slipped the ring on her finger

12 *Aut* **p. une vitesse** to put the car in gear; **p. la marche arrière** to go into reverse; **p. la troisième** to change *or* to shift into third gear

13 *Cin & TV (film)* to show, to screen; *(diapositive)* to show; *Rad (émission)* to broadcast; *(cassette, disque)* to play, to put on; **on passe un western au Rex** there's a western on at the Rex

14 *Com (conclure ▸ entente)* to conclude, to come to, to reach; *(▸ marché)* to agree on, to strike, to reach; *(▸ commande)* to place (**de qch** for sth; **à qn** with sb); **passez commande avant le 12** order before the 12th

15 *Compta* to enter, to post; **p. un article en compte** to enter a sale into a ledger; **p. écriture d'un article** to post an entry; **p. une somme au débit/au crédit** to debit/credit an account with a sum; **p. une somme en perte** to charge an amount to an account; **p. une somme en profit** to credit an amount to an account; **p. par pertes et profits** to transfer to profit and loss, to write off

16 *Jur (faire établir ▸ acte juridique)* to draw up; **nous passons le contrat demain** we're drawing up the contract tomorrow; **un acte passé par-devant notaire** a deed drawn up in the presence of a lawyer

C. *EXPRIME UNE NOTION TEMPORELLE* **1** *(employer ▸ durée)* to spend; **j'ai passé un an en Angleterre** I spent a year in England; **passez un bon week-end/une bonne soirée!** have a nice weekend/evening!; **j'ai passé deux heures sur la traduction** I spent two hours on the translation, it took me two hours to do the translation; **p. ses vacances à lire** to spend one's *Br* holidays *or Am* vacation reading; **as-tu passé une bonne nuit?** did you sleep well last night?, did you have a good night?; **pour p. le temps** to pass the time

2 *(aller au-delà de ▸ durée)* to get through, to survive; **s'il arrive à p. la première semaine, il sera tiré d'affaire** if he gets through *or* survives the first week, he'll be out of danger; **elle ne passera pas la nuit** she won't see the night out, she won't last the night

3 *(assouvir ▸ envie)* to satisfy; **p. sa colère sur qn** to work off *or* to vent one's anger on sb; **je passais ma colère en jouant de la batterie** I let off steam by playing the drums; **ne passe pas ta fureur sur moi!** don't take it out on me!

USAGE ABSOLU *(transmettre ▸ ballon)* to pass; **il a passé à l'avant-centre** he passed to the centre forward

• **passer après** VT IND **le directeur commercial passe après lui** the sales manager comes after him; **il faut le faire libérer, le reste passe après** we must get him released, everything else is secondary

• **passer avant** VT IND to go *or* to come before; **ses intérêts passent avant tout** his/her own interests come before anything else; **le travail passe avant le plaisir** work (comes) before pleasure

• **passer par** VT IND **1** *(dans une formation)* to go through; **il est passé par une grande école** he studied at a "grande école"; **elle est passée par tous les échelons** she rose through all the grades **2** *(dans une évolution)* to go through, to undergo; **le pays est passé par toutes les formes de gouvernement** the country has experienced every form of government; **la maladie passe par différentes phases** the illness goes through different stages; **elle est passée par des moments difficiles** she's been through some difficult times **3** *(recourir à)* to go through; **je passe par une agence pour avoir des billets** I get tickets through an agency; **p. par l'opératrice** to go through the operator; **il va falloir en p. par ses exigences** we'll just have to do what he/she says; **je suis passé par là** it's happened to me too, I've been through that too

• **passer pour** VT IND **1** *(avec nom)* to be thought of as; **je vais p. pour un idiot** I'll be taken for *or* people will take me for an idiot; **en te maquillant, tu pourrais facilement p. pour elle** with some make-up on, you could easily pass for her *or* you could easily be taken for her; **se faire p. pour qn** to pass oneself off as sb; **il se fait p. pour un professionnel** he claims to be a professional **2** *(avec adj)* **son livre passe pour sérieux** his/her book is considered to be serious; **il s'est fait p. pour fou** he pretended to be mad **3** *(avec verbe)* **elle passe pour descendre d'une famille noble** she is said to be descended from an aristocratic family

• **passer sur** VT IND *(ne pas mentionner)* to pass over, to skip; *(excuser)* to overlook; **passons sur les détails** let's pass over *or* skip the less important facts; **je passerai sur votre attitude pour cette fois** I'll overlook your attitude this once; **passons!** let's say no more about it!, let's drop it!; **tu me l'avais promis, mais passons!** you promised me, but never mind!

VPR se passer 1 *(s'écouler ▸ heures, semaines)* to go by, to pass; **la soirée s'est passée tranquillement** the evening went by *or* passed quietly; **la journée s'est passée dans l'angoisse pour les parents** it was a day of anguish for the parents; **si la journée de demain se passe sans incident** if everything goes off smoothly tomorrow

2 *(survenir ▸ événement)* to take place, to happen; **l'histoire se passe en Corse/en 1789** the story takes place in Corsica/in 1789; **qu'est-ce qui se passe?** what's happening?, what's going on?; **que s'est-il passé?** what happened?; **qu'est-ce qui va se p. maintenant?** what's going to happen now?; **il se passe que ton frère vient d'être arrêté(, voilà ce qui se passe)!** your brother's just been arrested(, that's what's the matter)!; **il ne se passe rien d'intéressant** nothing interesting's happening; **il ne se passe pas une semaine sans qu'il perde de l'argent aux courses** not a week goes by without him losing money on the horses

3 *(se dérouler ▸ dans certaines conditions)* to go (off); **comment s'est passée ton audition?** how did your audition go?; **l'opération s'est bien/mal passée** the operation went (off) smoothly/badly; **si tout se passe bien, nous y serons demain** if all goes well, we'll be there tomorrow; **tout se passe très bien entre les membres de l'équipe** the team (members) get along very well together; **tout se passe comme prévu** everything's going according to plan *or* going as planned

4 *(s'achever ▸ douleur)* to go, to subside; *(▸ malaise)* to vanish; **bois de l'eau, ton hoquet se passera** drink some water, it'll get rid of your hiccups *or* and your hiccups'll stop

5 *(s'appliquer, se mettre ▸ produit)* to apply, to put on; **se p. de la crème sur les mains** to put some cream on one's hands; **il se passa un peigne/la main dans les cheveux** he ran a comb/his fingers through his hair

6 se p. de *(vivre sans)* to do *or* to go without; **il faudra te p. de jardinier/secrétaire** you'll have to do *or* to go *or* to manage without a gardener/secretary; **il ne peut pas se p. de télévision** he can't live without TV; **les plantes ne peuvent se p. d'eau** plants can't survive without water; **il ne peut se p. de boire** he can't do without drink

7 se p. de *(s'abstenir)* to do without; **je me serais bien passée de garder ses enfants** I could have done without having to look after his/her children; **sa déclaration se passe de tout commentaire** his/her statement needs no comment

• **en passant** ADV **1** *(dans la conversation)* in passing; **faire une remarque en passant** to make a casual remark; **soit dit en passant** it must be said **2** *(sur son chemin)* **il s'arrête de temps à autre en passant** he calls on his way by *or* past from time to time

• **en passant par** PRÉP **1** *(dans l'espace)* via; **l'avion va à Athènes en passant par Londres** the plane goes to Athens via London *or* stops in London on its way to Athens **2** *(dans une énumération)* (and) including; **toutes les romancières de Sand à Sarraute en passant par Colette** every woman novelist from Sand to Sarraute, including Colette

> Il faut noter que l'expression **passer un examen** se traduit par **to sit an exam** ou **to take an exam. To pass an exam** signifie **réussir un examen.**

passereau, -x [pasro] **NM 1** *(oiseau)* passerine **2** *Vieilli (moineau)* sparrow

passerelle [pasrɛl] **NF 1** *(pour piétons)* footbridge; **p. panoramique** skywalk

2 *Naut (plan incliné)* gangway, gangplank; *(escalier)* boarding steps; **la p. de commandement** the bridge; **p. de navigation** navigation bridge

3 *Aviat (amovible)* steps; *(fixe)* passenger bridge

4 *Théât* catwalk

5 *Univ (entre deux cycles)* link; **établir une p. entre deux cursus** to link two courses

6 *Ordinat* gateway

passe-temps [pastɑ̃] **NM INV** pastime, hobby

passe-thé [paste] **NM INV** tea strainer

passeur, -euse [pasœr, -øz] **NM,F 1** *(sur un bac, un bateau etc)* ferryman, *f* ferrywoman **2** *(de contrebande, de gens)* smuggler; **il trouva un p. qui l'aida à gagner les États-Unis** he found someone to get him over the border into the United States

passe-vite [pasvit] **NM INV** *Belg & Suisse* vegetable mill

passible [pasibl] **ADJ p. de** liable to; **p. d'une contravention** liable to be fined; **p. de poursuites** actionable; **p. des tribunaux** liable to prosecution

passif¹ [pasif] **NM** *(dettes)* liabilities; **p. exigible** *ou* **circulant** current liabilities; **l'actif et le p.** assets and liabilities; **p. reporté** deferred liabilities

passif², -ive [pasif, -iv] **ADJ** *(gén) & Chim & Gram* passive

NM *Gram* passive (voice); **au p.** in the passive (voice)

passif-agressif, passive-agressive [pasifagresif, pasifagresiv] *(mpl* **passifs-agressifs,** *fpl* **passives-agressives) ADJ** *Psy* passive-aggressive; **comportement p.** passive aggression, passive aggressivity

passiflore [pasiflɔr] **NF** *Bot* passionflower, *Spéc* passiflora

passing-shot [pasiŋʃɔt] *(pl* **passing-shots)** **NM** passing shot; **faire un p.** to play a passing shot

passion [pasjɔ̃] **NF 1** *(amour fou)* passion, love; **ils ont vécu une grande p.** they had a passionate love affair, they were passionately in love; **aimer qn à la** *ou* **avec p.** to love sb passionately

2 *(du jeu, des voyages etc)* passion; **avoir la p. de qch, avoir une p. pour qch** to have a passion for sth, to be passionately interested in sth; **sa p. pour la musique** his/her passion for music

3 *(exaltation)* passion, feeling; **débattre de qch avec p.** to argue passionately about sth; **sans p.** dispassionately

4 *Rel* **la P. (du Christ)** the Passion; **la semaine de la P.** Passion Week; *Rel* **la P. selon saint Jean** the Passion according to Saint John; *Mus* the (Saint) John Passion

• **passions NFPL** *(sentiments)* passions, emotions, feelings; **savoir dominer ses passions** to be able to control one's emotions

passionnant, -e [pasjɔnɑ̃, -ɑ̃t] **ADJ** *(voyage, débat)* fascinating, exciting; *(personne)* fascinating; *(récit)* fascinating, enthralling, gripping; **ce boulot n'est pas très p.** this job's not very exciting

passionné, -e [pasjɔne] **ADJ 1** *(aimant ▸ amant, lettre)* passionate **2** *(très vif ▸ caractère, tempérament)* passionate, emotional; *(▸ discours)* passionate, impassioned; *(▸ débat)* heated, impassioned; *(▸ intérêt, sentiment)* passionate, keen **3** *(intéressé ▸ lecteur, joueur d'échecs etc)* avid, keen; **être p. de qch** to be mad about sth

NM,F 1 *(en amour)* passionate person **2** *(fervent)* enthusiast, devotee; **c'est une passionnée de moto** she's mad about motorbikes, she's a motorbike fanatic; **pour les passionnés de flamenco** for flamenco lovers

passionnel, -elle [pasjɔnɛl] **ADJ** passionate

passionnément [pasjɔnemɑ̃] **ADV 1** *(avec passion)* passionately, with passion **2** *(en intensif)* keenly, fervently, ardently; **je désire p. que tu réussisses** I very much hope that you will succeed

passionner [3] [pasjɔne] **VT 1** *(intéresser ▸ sujet: récit)* to fascinate, to enthral, to grip; *(▸ sujet: discussion, idée)* to fascinate, to grip; **la politique la passionne** politics is her passion, she has a passion for politics **2** *(animer ▸ débat)* **elle ne sait pas parler politique sans p. le débat** every time she talks about politics it becomes very heated

VPR se passionner se p. pour qch *(idée)* to feel passionately about sth; *(activité)* to have a passion for sth

passive [pasiv] *voir* **passif**[2]

passivement [pasivmɑ̃] **ADV** passively

passivité [pasivite] **NF** *(attitude)* passivity, passiveness

passoire [pɑswar] **NF 1** *(à petits trous)* sieve; *(à gros trous)* colander; **p. à thé** tea strainer; *Fam* **avoir la tête** *ou* **la mémoire comme une p.** to have a memory like a sieve; *Fam* **transformer qn en p.** to pump sb full of lead, to riddle sb with bullets **2** *Fam (personne, institution négligente)* **cette frontière est une vraie p.** this border doesn't keep anyone in or out

pastel [pastɛl] **NM 1** *(crayon)* pastel; *(dessin)* pastel (drawing); **dessiner au p.** to draw in pastels **2** *(teinte douce)* pastel (shade) **3** *Bot* pastel woad

ADJ INV pastel; **tons p.** pastel shades

pastelliste [pastelist] **NMF** pastellist

pastèque [pastɛk] **NF** watermelon

pasteur [pastœr] **NM 1** *Rel (protestant)* minister, pastor; *Vieilli (prêtre)* pastor; **le Bon P.** the Good Shepherd **2** *Littéraire (berger)* shepherd

pasteurisation [pastœrizasjɔ̃] **NF** pasteurization, pasteurizing

pasteuriser [3] [pastœrize] **VT** to pasteurize

pastiche [pastiʃ] **NM** pastiche

pasticher [3] [pastiʃe] **VT** to do a pastiche of

pasticheur, -euse [pastiʃœr, -øz] **NM,F** *(auteur de pastiches)* writer of pastiches

pastille [pastij] **NF 1** *Pharm* pastille, lozenge; **p. pour la gorge** throat lozenge; **p. contre la toux** cough drop *or Br* sweet

2 *Culin* **p. de chocolat** chocolate drop; **p. de menthe** mint

3 *(pois)* polka dot; **un chemisier rouge à pastilles blanches** a red blouse with white polka dots

4 *(disque de papier, de tissu)* disc; **p. verte** = green label on a low-emission vehicle indicating that it may be driven on days when restrictions are placed on traffic due to high levels of atmospheric pollution

pastis [pastis] **NM 1** *(boisson)* pastis **2** *Fam (situation embrouillée)* muddle, mess, fix

pastoral, -e, -aux, -ales [pastɔral, -o] **ADJ** *Littérature, Mus & Rel* pastoral

• **pastorale NF 1** *Littérature* pastoral; *Mus* pastorale **2** *Rel* pastoral

pastorat [pastɔra] **NM** pastorate

pastoureau, -elle, -aux, -elles [pasturo, -ɛl] **NM,F** *Littéraire* shepherd boy, *f* girl

• **pastourelle NF 1** *Littérature* pastourelle **2** *(danse)* fourth figure of the quadrille

pat [pat] *Échecs* **ADJ INV le roi est p.** it's a stalemate

NM stalemate; **éviter le p.** to avoid stalemate

patachon [pataʃɔ̃] **NM** *Fam* **mener une vie de p.** to lead a riotous existence

Patagonie [patagɔni] **NF la P.** Patagonia

patapouf [patapuf] *Fam* **NM** fatty, podge; **un gros p.** a fatso, a fatty

EXCLAM crash!

pataquès [patakɛs] **NM 1** *(faute de liaison)* bad *or* incorrect liaison **2** *(faute de langage)* serious mistake *(in pronunciation etc)* **3** *Fam (situation confuse)* mess, shambles *(singulier)*

patata [patata] *voir* **patati**

patate [patat] **NF 1** *Bot & Culin* **p. (douce)** sweet potato

2 *Fam (pomme de terre)* spud; *Can* **patates frites** *Br* chips, *Am* (French) fries

3 *Fam (coup)* thump, clout

4 *Fam (personne stupide)* dork, *Br* divvy, *Am* putz

5 *Anciennement Fam (dix mille francs)* ten thousand francs☐

6 *Math* = set diagram

7 *Can Fam (cœur)* heart☐, *Br* ticker; **monter les escaliers, c'est dur pour la p.** going up the stairs is hard on the old heart *or Br* ticker

8 *Fam (locutions)* **avoir la p.** to be on top form, to be full of beans; **en avoir gros sur la p.** to be down in the mouth

patati [patati] **et patati, et patata ADV** *Fam* blah blah blah, and so on and so forth

patatras [patatra] **EXCLAM** crash!

pataud, -e [pato, -od] **ADJ** *(maladroit)* clumsy; *(sans finesse)* gauche

NM,F 1 *(chiot)* (big-pawed) puppy **2** *Vieilli (personne ▸ maladroite)* clumsy oaf; *(▸ à l'esprit lent)* oaf

Pataugas® [patogas] **NMPL** = thick-soled hiking boots with canvas uppers

pataugeoire [patoʒwar] **NF** paddling pool

patauger [17] [patoʒe] **VI 1** *(dans l'eau)* to paddle about; *(dans la boue)* to squelch about **2** *(s'empêtrer)* to flounder; **il patauge dans ses réponses** he's getting more and more bogged down trying to answer; *Fam* **p. (dans la semoule)** to be totally lost☐ **3** *(ne pas progresser ▸ enquête)* to get bogged down

patch [patʃ] **NM** *Méd* patch

patchouli [patʃuli] **NM** patchouli; **huile de p.** patchouli oil

patchwork [patʃwœrk] **NM** *Couture (technique)* patchwork; *(ouvrage)* (piece of) patchwork; *Fig* **le pays est un p. de nationalités** the country is a patchwork of different nationalities

• **en patchwork ADJ** patchwork *(avant n)*

pâte [pɑt] **NF 1** *(à base de farine ▸ à pain)* dough; *(▸ à tarte) Br* pastry, *Am* dough; *(▸ à gâteau) Br* mixture, *Am* batter; *(▸ à frire)* batter; **p. à beignets** batter; **p. brisée** *Br* short *or* shortcrust pastry, *Am* pie dough; **p. à crêpes** pancake batter; **p. à choux** choux pastry; **p. feuilletée** flaky pastry, *Br* puff pastry; **p. à foncer** pastry (dough); **p. à frire** batter; **p. sablée** *Br* rich shortcrust pastry, *Am* sweet *or* sugar dough

2 *(pour fourrer, tartiner)* paste; **p. d'amandes** marzipan, almond paste; **p. d'anchois** anchovy paste *or* spread; **p. de coing** quince jelly; **p. de fruits** fruit jelly *(made from thick fruit pulp)*

3 *(en fromagerie)* **(fromage à) p. cuite** cheese made from scalded curds; **(fromage à) p. fermentée/molle** fermented/soft cheese

4 *(tempérament)* **il est d'une p. à vivre cent ans** he's the sort who'll live to be a hundred; **c'est une bonne p., il est bonne p.** he's a good sort; **une p. molle** *(personne sans caractère)* a wimp; *Can (personne paresseuse)* a shirker

5 *Beaux-Arts* paint, colours

6 *(en cosmétologie)* paste; **p. dentifrice,** *Can* **p. à dents** toothpaste

7 *Tech* **p. à bois** wood pulp; **p. à papier** paper pulp

8 p. à modeler Plasticine®, modelling clay

• **pâtes NFPL 1** *Culin* **pâtes (alimentaires)** pasta *(UNCOUNT)*; **pâtes fraîches** fresh pasta **2** *Pharm* **pâtes pectorales** cough lozenges *or* pastilles

pâté [pɑte] **NM 1** *Culin* pâté; **p. de campagne** pâté de campagne *(coarse pâté made with pork)*; **p. en croûte** pâté en croûte, *Br* raised (crust) pie; **p. de foie** liver pâté; **p. impérial** spring roll; **p. à la viande** meat pie

2 *Belg (gâteau)* cake

3 *Fam (tache d'encre)* (ink) blot; **faire des pâtés** *(stylo)* to smudge; *(élève)* to make inkblots

4 *(tas)* **p. de sable** sand pie

• **pâté de maisons NM** block

pâtée [pɑte] **NF 1** *(pour animaux)* food, feed; **p. pour chat/chien** cat/dog food **2** *(nourriture grossière)* pap **3** *Fam* thrashing, hammering; **foutre la p. à qn** *(correction, défaite écrasante)* to give sb a thrashing *ou* a hammering

patelin[1] [patlɛ̃] **NM** *Fam (village)* village☐; *(petite ville)* small town☐

patelin[2]**, -e** [patlɛ̃, -in] **ADJ** *Littéraire* fawning, unctuous

patelle [patɛl] **NF 1** *Zool (mollusque)* limpet **2** *Archéol* patella

patène [patɛn] **NF** paten

patenôtre [patnotr] **NF** *Vieilli ou Littéraire* **1** *(prière)* prayer **2** *(paroles incompréhensibles)* gibberish

patent, -e[1] [patɑ̃, -ɑ̃t] **ADJ 1** *(flagrant, incontestable)* obvious, patent; **il est p. que...** it is patently obvious that... **2** *Hist* patent

patentable [patɑ̃tabl] **ADJ** *Admin* subject to a licence, requiring a licence

patente[2] [patɑ̃t] **NF 1** *Anciennement (taxe)* trading tax; **payer p.** to be duly licensed **2** *Naut* **p. de santé** bill of health

patenté, -e [patɑ̃te] **ADJ 1** *Fam (attesté)* established☐; **un raciste p.** an out-and-out racist **2** *(qui paie patente)* trading under licence, licensed

patenter [3] [patɑ̃te] **VT** to license

pater [pater] **NM 1** *Fam (père)* old man, *Br* pater **2** *Rel* paternoster (bead)

patère [pater] **NF 1** *(à vêtements)* coat peg **2** *(à rideaux)* curtain hook

paternalisme [paternalism] **NM** paternalism

paternaliste [paternalist] **ADJ** paternalist, paternalistic

paterne [patɛrn] **ADJ** *Littéraire* benevolent

paternel, -elle [paternɛl] **ADJ 1** *(du père)* paternal; **cousins du côté p.** cousins on the father's *or* paternal side; **ma grand-mère paternelle** my grandmother on my father's side **2** *(indulgent)* fatherly

NM *Fam Hum (père)* old man, *Br* pater

paternellement [paternɛlmɑ̃] **ADV** paternally, in a fatherly way

paternité [paternite] **NF 1** *(d'un enfant)* fatherhood, *Sout* paternity; **il vit mal sa p.** he's finding fatherhood difficult, he's finding it difficult being a father; *Jur* **p. légitime/naturelle** legitimate/natural paternity **2** *(d'une œuvre)* authorship, *Sout* paternity; *(d'une théorie)* paternity; **revendiquer/désavouer la p. d'un livre** to claim/to repudiate authorship of a book

pâteux, -euse [pɑtø, -øz] **ADJ 1** *(gâteau)* doughy; **avoir la bouche** *ou* **langue pâteuse** to have a furred tongue **2** *(style)* heavy, clumsy, lumbering

pathétique [patetik] **ADJ 1** *(émouvant)* pathetic, moving, poignant; **des descriptions pathétiques** descriptions full of pathos **2** *Anat* **nerf p.** pathetic nerve

NM 1 *(émotion)* pathos 2 *Anat* pathetic nerve

Il faut noter que l'adjectif anglais **pathetic** est un faux ami. Il signifie souvent **lamentable**.

pathétiquement [patetikmɑ̃] ADV pathetically, movingly, poignantly

pathétisme [patetism] NM *Littéraire* pathos

pathogène [patɔʒɛn] *Méd* ADJ pathogenic, pathogenetic
NM pathogen

pathologie [patɔlɔʒi] NF pathology

pathologique [patɔlɔʒik] ADJ 1 *Méd* pathologic, pathological 2 *Fam (excessif, anormal)* pathological

pathologiquement [patɔlɔʒikmɑ̃] ADV pathologically

pathologiste [patɔlɔʒist] ADJ pathologistic
NMF pathologist

pathos [patos] NM pathos

patibulaire [patibylɛr] ADJ sinister; **il avait une mine p.** he looked sinister

patiemment [pasjamɑ̃] ADV patiently

patience [pasjɑ̃s] NF 1 *(calme)* patience, *Sout* forbearance; **avec p.** patiently; **je n'ai aucune p. avec les enfants** I've no patience with children; **aie un peu de p.** be patient for a minute; **prends p.** be patient; **ma p. a des limites** there are limits to my patience; **prendre son mal en p.** to put up with it; **elle a une p. d'ange** she has the patience of a saint *or* of Job
2 *(persévérance)* patience, painstaking care; **sa p. a été récompensée** his/her patience was rewarded
3 *Cartes Br* patience, *Am* solitaire; **faire des patiences** to play *Br* patience *or Am* solitaire; **jeu de p.** puzzle; *Fig (travail minitieux)* test of patience
4 *Bot* dock
EXCLAM hold on!; **p., j'ai presque fini!** hold on *or* just a minute, I've almost finished!

patient, -e [pasjɑ̃, -ɑ̃t] ADJ patient
NM,F *(malade)* patient
NM *Gram (par opposition à agent)* patient

patienter [3] [pasjɑ̃te] VI *(attendre)* to wait; **faites-la p. un instant** ask her to wait for a minute; **p. en lisant le journal** to read the newspaper to while away *or* pass the time; *Tél* **c'est occupé, vous voulez p.?** it's *Br* engaged *or Am* busy, will you hold?

patin [patɛ̃] NM 1 *Sport* skate; *(de luge, de traîneau)* runner; **patins à glace/roulettes** ice/roller skates; **faire du p. à glace/roulettes** to go ice-skating/roller-skating; **sais-tu faire du p. à glace/à roulettes?** can you ice-skate/rollerskate?; *Can Fam* **être vite sur ses patins** to be quick on one's feet[□]; *Can Fam* **accrocher ses patins** *(gén)* to hang up one's hat, to retire[□]; *(sportif)* to hang up one's boots, to retire[□]
2 *(pour marcher sur un parquet)* felt pad *(used to move around on a polished floor)*
3 *très Fam (baiser)* French kiss, *Br* to snog; **rouler un p. à qn** to French kiss *or Br* to snog sb
4 *Aut* **p. de frein** brake shoe; *Fam* **donner** *ou* **filer un coup de p.** *(un coup de frein)* to slam on the brakes
5 *Constr (d'échafaudage)* sole plate *or* piece
6 *Tech* shoe, pad

patinage [patinaʒ] NM 1 *Sport* skating, ice-skating; **p. artistique** figure skating; **p. à roulettes** roller-skating; **p. de vitesse** speed skating 2 *(d'une roue)* spinning; *(de l'embrayage)* slipping 3 *(patine artificielle)* patination

patine [patin] NF sheen, patina; **la p. du temps** the patina of age *or* time

patiner [3] [patine] VI 1 *Sport* to skate 2 *Aut (roue)* to spin; *(embrayage)* to slip; **ça patine!** it's very slippery!, it's like an ice rink *or* a skating rink! 3 *Fig (stagner)* to get nowhere
VT *(un meuble)* to patine, to patinize
VPR **se patiner** to patinate, to become patinated

patinette [patinɛt] NF (child's) scooter

patineur, -euse [patinœr, -øz] NM,F *(sur glace)* skater, ice-skater; *(à roulettes)* roller-skater; *(en rollers)* rollerblader
NM *Can Entom (araignée)* water spider

patinoire [patinwar] NF 1 *Sport* ice *or* skating rink 2 *(surface trop glissante)* **ce trottoir est une véritable p.** this pavement is like an ice rink *or* a skating rink

patio [patjo, pasjo] NM patio

pâtir [32] [pɑtir] **pâtir de** VT IND to suffer from, to suffer as a result of

pâtis [pɑti] NM grazing (ground), pasture

pâtisserie [pɑtisri] NF 1 *(gâteau)* cake, pastry 2 *(activité)* cake-making, pastry-making; **faire de la p.** to make *or* to bake cakes; **elle fait de la bonne p.** she makes good cakes 3 *(boutique)* pâtisserie, cake *Br* shop *or Am* store; **p.-confiserie** confectioner's

pâtissier, -ère [pɑtisje, -ɛr] NM,F pastry cook, confectioner; **son mari est très bon p.** her husband makes very good cakes

patois [patwa] NM patois, dialect; **il parle encore le p.** he still speaks patois *or* the dialect

patoisant, -e [patwazɑ̃, -ɑ̃t] ADJ patois-speaking, dialect-speaking
NM,F patois *or* dialect speaker

patouiller [3] [patuje] *Fam* VI *(patauger)* to slosh *or* to wallow about
VT *(tripoter)* to paw, to mess about with

patraque [patrak] ADJ *Fam (souffrant)* out of sorts, under the weather

pâtre [pɑtr] NM *Littéraire* shepherd

patriarcal, -e, -aux, -ales [patrijarkal, -o] ADJ patriarchal

patriarcat [patrijarka] NM 1 *Rel (dignité, territoire)* patriarchate 2 *(en anthropologie)* patriarchy

patriarche [patrijarʃ] NM *(gén) & Rel* patriarch

patricien, -enne [patrisjɛ̃, -ɛn] ADJ patrician

patrie [patri] NF 1 *(pays natal)* homeland, native country; *(région natale)* native region; *(ville natale)* home town; **morts pour la p.** *(sur monument aux morts)* they gave their lives for their country 2 *(communauté)* home; **trouver une nouvelle p.** to find a new home 3 *Fig* **la p. de** the home *or* birthplace of

patrimoine [patrimwan] NM 1 *(possessions héritées)* inheritance, *Sout* patrimony
2 *Fin (d'un individu)* property, wealth, personal assets; *(actif net)* net assets; **p. immobilier** *Br* property assets, *Am* real-estate assets; **p. social** social assets
3 *(artistique, culturel)* heritage
4 *Biol* **p. génétique** gene pool; **p. héréditaire** genotype

patrimonial, -e, -aux, -ales [patrimɔnjal, -o] ADJ patrimonial

patriotard, -e [patrijɔtar, -ard] *Péj* ADJ jingoistic
NM,F jingoist, chauvinist

patriote [patrijɔt] ADJ patriotic
NMF patriot

patriotique [patrijɔtik] ADJ patriotic

patriotisme [patrijɔtism] NM patriotism

patron[1] [patrɔ̃] NM 1 *Couture* pattern; **p. de jupe** skirt pattern; **(taille) p.** medium size; **demi-p.** small size; **grand p.** large size 2 *Beaux-Arts* template 3 *Typ (plaque)* stencil (plate); **coloriage au p.** stencil-painting

patron[2]**, -onne** [patrɔ̃, -ɔn] NM,F 1 *(d'une entreprise ▸ propriétaire)* owner; *(▸ gérant)* manager; *(▸ directeur)* employer; *(▸ de café, d'auberge)* owner, landlord, *f* landlady; **eh, la patronne, une bière!** a beer please, landlady!; **p. de presse** newspaper proprietor
2 *(maître de maison)* master, *f* mistress
3 *Univ* **p. de thèse** (doctoral) supervisor
4 *(d'un service hospitalier)* senior consultant
5 *Fam (conjoint)* old man; *(conjointe)* old lady
6 *Rel* patron saint; **la patronne des musiciens** the patron saint of musicians
NM *(d'une entreprise ▸ chef)* boss; **être son propre p.** to be one's own boss; *Fam* **c'est moi le p.!** I'm the boss!, I'm in charge!

Il faut noter que le terme anglais **patron** est un faux ami. Il signifie le plus souvent **client**.

patronage [patrɔnaʒ] NM 1 *(soutien officiel)* patronage; **sous le haut p. de...** under the patronage of... 2 *(soutien financier)* sponsorship, sponsoring; **sous le p. de...** sponsored by... 3 *(pour les jeunes)* youth club
• **de patronage** ADJ moralistic; **une mentalité de p.** a Sunday school mentality

patronal, -e, -aux, -ales [patrɔnal, -o] ADJ 1 *Com & Ind* employer's, employers' 2 *Rel* patronal

patronat [patrɔna] NM **le p.** the employers; **le p. français** French employers

patronne [patrɔn] *voir* **patron**[2]

patronner [3] [patrɔne] VT *(parrainer ▸ gén)* to support; *(▸ financièrement)* to sponsor; **p. une entreprise auprès des banques** to secure a company with the banks

patronnesse [patrɔnɛs] ADJ F *voir* **dame**

patronyme [patrɔnim] NM patronymic

patronymique [patrɔnimik] ADJ patronymic

patrouille [patruj] NF patrol; *Aviat* **p. de chasse** fighter patrol; *Naut* **p. maritime** navy patrol; **faire une/être en p.** to go/to be on patrol

patrouiller [3] [patruje] VI to patrol

patrouilleur [patrujœr] NM 1 *Mil* man on patrol; **les patrouilleurs** the patrol 2 *Aviat (de chasse)* (patrolling) fighter; *(de détection)* spotter plane 3 *Naut* patrol ship

patte [pat] NF 1 *(jambe)* leg; *(pied ▸ d'un félin, d'un chien)* paw; *(▸ d'un oiseau)* foot; **donne la p., Rex!** Rex, give a paw!; **être bas** *ou* **court sur pattes** *(animal, personne)* to be short-legged; **être haut sur pattes** to be long-legged; **pattes de devant** *(membres)* forelegs; *(pieds)* forepaws, forefeet; **pattes de derrière** *(membres)* hind legs; *(pieds)* hind paws *or* feet; **p. de lapin** rabbit foot; *(favori)* sideburn, sidewhisker; **pattes de mouche** (spidery) scrawl; *Fam* **pantalon (à) pattes d'éléphant** *ou* **d'éph** bell-bottoms, *Br* flares; **bas les pattes!** *(à un chien)* down!; **faire p. de velours** *(chat)* to sheathe *or* to draw in its claws; *(personne)* to use the velvet glove (approach)
2 *Fam (jambe)* leg[□], *Br* pin, *Am* gam; **se casser une p.** to break one's leg; **il a une p. folle** he's got a *Br* gammy leg *or Am* gimpy leg; **retomber sur ses pattes** to land on one's feet; **tirer dans les pattes à qn** to cause trouble for sb; **ils n'arrêtent pas de se tirer dans les pattes** they're always giving each other a hard time; **se faire faire aux pattes** to get collared
3 *Fam (main)* hand[□], paw; **avoir les pattes sales** to have grubby paws; **un coup de p.** a swipe, a cutting remark; **eh, toi, bas les pattes!** *(à une personne)* hey, you, paws off!, keep your paws to yourself!; **tomber dans** *ou* **entre les pattes de qn** to fall into sb's clutches; **graisser la p. à qn** to grease sb's palm
4 *(savoir-faire ▸ d'un peintre)* (fine) touch; *(▸ d'un écrivain)* talent; **avoir de la p., avoir le coup de p.** *(d'un peintre)* to have a fine touch
5 *Constr (pour fixer)* (metal) tie, (heavy) fastener
6 *(d'un portefeuille, d'une chaussure)* tongue; *(sur l'épaule)* strap; **p. de boutonnage** fly (front)
7 *Naut (d'une ancre)* fluke, palm
8 *Tech (d'un grappin)* claw; **p. d'attache** gusset plate
9 *Suisse & (dans l'est de la France) (torchon)* cloth
• **pattes** NFPL *(favoris)* sideburns, sidewhiskers
• **à pattes** ADV *Fam* **allez, on y va à pattes!** come on, let's hoof it!

patte-d'oie [patdwa] *(pl* **pattes-d'oie**) NF 1 *(ride)* crow's-foot 2 *(carrefour)* crossroads, junction 3 *Bot (Potentilla anserina)* silverweed; *(famille des Chénopodiacées)* goosefoot

pattemouille [patmuj] NF damp cloth *(used when ironing)*

pâturage [pɑtyraʒ] NM 1 *(prairie)* pasture, pastureland 2 *(activité)* grazing

pâture [pɑtyr] NF 1 *(nourriture)* food, feed; **jeter** *ou* **donner qn en p. à qn** to serve sb up to sb 2 *(lieu)* pasture 3 *(pour l'esprit)* food, diet; **la poésie est sa p. favorite** poetry is his/her favourite reading matter

pâturer [3] [pɑtyre] VT to graze
VI to graze

paturon [patyrɔ̃] NM 1 *(du cheval)* pastern 2 *Fam* foot[□], *Br* plate, *Am* dog

paume [pom] NF 1 *Anat* palm 2 *Menuis* halving (lap joint) 3 *Sport* real tennis; **jeu de p.** *(terrain)* real-tennis court

paumé, -e [pome] *Fam* ADJ 1 *(désemparé, indé-*

cis) confused□, mixed-up; *(marginal)* out of it **2** *(isolé)* remote, godforsaken; **un patelin complètement p.** a village in the middle of nowhere *or* in the back of beyond **3** *(perdu)* lost□

NM,F *(marginal)* dropout

paumelle [pomɛl] **NF 1** *Constr (gond)* (lift-off) hinge; *(partie du gond)* (hinge) plate **2** *(gant)* sailmaker's palm

paumer [3] [pome] *Fam* **VT 1** *(égarer)* to lose□ **2** *(recevoir)* to get□, to cop; **il a paumé un gnon dans la figure** he got himself a whack in the face **3** *(attraper ▸ délinquant, fautif)* **se faire p.** to get busted *or Br* nicked

VI *(perdre)* to lose□

VPR se paumer *Fam* to get lost□

paupérisation [poperizasjɔ̃] **NF** pauperization

paupériser [3] [poperize] **VT** to pauperize

VPR se paupériser to become pauperized

paupérisme [poperism] **NM** pauperism

paupière [popjɛr] **NF** eyelid

paupiette [popjɛt] **NF p. (de veau)** paupiette of veal, veal olive

pause [poz] **NF 1** *(moment de repos)* break; **faire une p.** to have *or* to take a break; **la p. de midi** the lunch break; **p.-cigarette** cigarette break; **p.-repas** meal break

2 *(temps d'arrêt ▸ dans une conversation)* pause; **marquer une p.** to pause

3 *(arrêt ▸ d'un processus)* halt; **il a annoncé une p. dans les réformes** he declared a temporary halt to the reforms

4 *(de lecteur de DVD, de CD etc)* pause; **mettre sur pause** to pause

5 *Mus* rest

pause-café [pozkafe] *(pl* **pauses-café)** **NF** coffee break

pause-carrière [pozkarjɛr] *(pl* **pauses-carrière)** **NF** *Belg* career break *(on reduced pay)*

pauvre [povr] **ADJ 1** *(sans richesse ▸ personne, pays, quartier)* poor **2** *(avant le nom) (pitoyable ▸ demeure, décor)* humble, wretched; *(▸ sourire)* weak, thin; *(▸ personne)* poor; *Fam* **ce n'est qu'un p. gosse** he's only a poor kid; **p. femme/homme!** poor woman/man!; *Fam* **c'est la vie, mon p. vieux!** that's life, my friend!; *Fam* **p. crétin!** you idiot!; *Fam* **c'est un p. type** he's a sad case; **p. de moi!** woe is me! **3** *(insuffisant ▸ gén)* poor; *(▸ robe, meubles etc)* shabby; *(▸ excuse, argument)* poor, lame; *(▸ sourire)* weak, thin; *(▸ orateur)* poor, bad; **une végétation p.** sparse vegetation; **souffrir d'une alimentation p.** to suffer from a poor diet; **être p. en qch** to lack sth, to be lacking in sth; **régime p. en calories** low-calorie diet

NMF 1 *(par compassion)* poor thing; **mon p.!** you poor thing! **2** *(en appellatif)* **mais mon p./ma p., il ne m'obéit jamais!** *(pour susciter la pitié)* but my dear fellow/my dear, he never does as I say!

NM poor man, *Littéraire* pauper; **les pauvres** the poor; **c'est le champagne du p.** it's poor man's champagne

pauvrement [povrəmɑ̃] **ADV 1** *(misérablement ▸ décoré, habillé)* poorly, shabbily; **vivre p.** to live in poverty **2** *(médiocrement)* poorly; **il traduit p.** he's a poor translator

pauvresse [povrɛs] **NF** *Vieilli* poor woman, pauperess; **une p. en haillons** a poor ragged woman

pauvret, -ette [povrɛ, ɛt] **ADJ** poor, poor-looking

NM,F le p., la pauvrette the poor (little) dear, the poor (little) thing

pauvreté [povrəte] **NF 1** *(manque d'argent)* poverty; **il a fini ses jours dans la p.** he ended his days in poverty **2** *(médiocrité)* poverty; **son article montre la p. de ses idées** his/her article demonstrates the poverty of his/her ideas **3** *(déficience)* poverty; **la p. du sol ne permet qu'un faible rendement** the poorness of the soil means that the yield is very low

pauvrette [povrɛt] *voir* **pauvret**

pavage [pavaʒ] **NM 1** *(action ▸ gén)* paving; *(▸ aux pavés ronds)* cobbling **2** *(surface ▸ dallée)* paving; *(▸ empierrée)* cobbles, cobblestones

pavane [pavan] **NF** pavane

pavaner [3] [pavane] **se pavaner VPR** to strut about

pavé [pave] **NM 1** *(surface ▸ dallée)* pavement, paving; *(▸ empierrée)* cobbles, cobblestones; **tenir le haut du p.** to be on top; **être sur le p.** *(sans domicile)* to be on the street; *(au chômage)* to be jobless; **jeter** *ou* **mettre qn sur le p.** *(l'expulser de son domicile)* to throw sb out on the streets; *(le licencier)* to throw sb out of his/her job

2 *(pierre ▸ gén)* paving stone; *(▸ ronde)* cobblestone; *Fig* **avoir un p. sur l'estomac** to have a weight on one's stomach; **un** *ou* **le p. dans la mare** a bombshell; **jeter un p. dans la mare** to drop a bombshell, to set the cat among the pigeons

3 *Culin* **p. (de romsteck)** thick rump steak; **un p. au chocolat** a (thick) chocolate cake

4 *Presse & Typ (encart)* block (of text); *(publicité)* (large) display advertisement

5 *Ordinat* pad, keypad; **p. numérique** numeric keypad

6 *Fam (livre)* massive tome, doorstop; *(article)* huge article; *(dissertation)* huge essay

7 *Fam (dent)* tooth□

pavement [pavmɑ̃] **NM** *Constr* flooring *or* paving *(made of flags, tiles or mosaic)*

paver [3] [pave] **VT** *(avec des dalles)* to pave; *(avec des pavés ronds)* to cobble; **cour pavée** *(dallée)* paved (court)yard; *(aux pavés ronds)* cobbled (court)yard; *Can Fig* **être pavé de monde** to be full of *or* packed with people

paveur [pavœr] **NM** *Constr* paver

pavillon [pavijɔ̃] **NM 1** *(maison particulière)* detached house

2 *(belvédère, gloriette)* lodge; **le p. du gardien** the keeper's lodge; **p. de chasse** hunting lodge; **p. de jardin** summerhouse, pavilion

3 *(dans un hôpital)* wing, wards; *(dans une cité universitaire)* house; *(dans une exposition)* pavilion; **il travaille au p. de pédiatrie** he works on the pediatric ward *or* in the pediatric wing

4 *Aut* roof

5 *Anat (des trompes utérines)* pavilion; **p. (auriculaire)** auricle, pinna

6 *Mus (d'un instrument)* bell; *(d'un phonographe, d'un haut-parleur, d'une sirène)* horn

7 *Naut* flag; **p. de complaisance** flag of convenience; **p. de détresse** flag of distress; **p. national** ensign; **p. de quarantaine** quarantine flag, yellow jack; **pavillons de signaux** *ou* **de signalisation** signal flags; **baisser p.** to lower *or* to strike one's flag; *Fig* to back down; **il a baissé p. devant elle!** he let her ride roughshod over him!

pavillonnaire [pavijɔnɛr] **ADJ un quartier p.** an area of low-rise housing; **un hôpital p.** a hospital (constructed) in wings, a multiwing hospital

pavois [pavwa] **NM 1** *Hist* shield; **élever** *ou* **hisser** *ou* **porter qn sur le p.** to raise *or* to carry sb on high **2** *Naut (partie de la coque)* bulwark; *(pavillons)* flags and bunting; **hisser le grand p.** to dress ship *or* full; **hisser le petit p.** to dress (the ship) with masthead flags

pavoiser [3] [pavwaze] **VT 1** *(édifice, rue)* to deck with flags *or* bunting **2** *Naut* to dress (with flags)

VI 1 *(déployer des drapeaux)* to put out flags **2** *Naut* to dress ship **3** *Fam (faire le fier)* **il n'y a pas de quoi p.** that's nothing to crow about

pavot [pavo] **NM** *Bot* poppy; **graines de p.** poppy seeds; **p. somnifère** opium poppy

payable [pɛjabl] **ADJ** payable; **p. à l'ordre de** payable to; **p. le 5 du mois** payable *or* due on the 5th of the month; **p. à l'arrivée** payable on arrival; **p. à la banque** payable at the bank; **p. à la commande** cash with order, payable with order; **p. comptant** payable in cash; **p. sur demande** payable on demand; **p. à l'échéance** payable at maturity; **p. à la livraison** payable on delivery; **p. au porteur** payable to bearer; **p. à vue** payable on sight

payant, -e [pɛjɑ̃, -ɑ̃t] **ADJ 1** *(non gratuit)* **les consommations sont payantes** you have to pay for your drinks; **l'entrée est payante** there is an admission charge *or* a charge for admission; *Can* **téléphone p.** payphone **2** *(qui paie)* paying **3** *Fam (qui produit ▸ de l'argent)* profitable□; *(▸ un résultat)* efficient□; **une spéculation payante** a profitable speculation; *Fig* **ça s'est avéré p.** it turned out to be worth it

paye [pɛj] = **paie**

payement [pɛmɑ̃] = **paiement**

payer [11] [peje] **VT 1** *(solder, régler)* to pay; **j'ai une amende à p.** I've got a fine to pay; **p. sa dette à la société** to pay one's debt to society; **c'est le prix à p. si tu veux réussir** that's the price you have to pay for success; *Hum* **p. son tribut à la nature** to go to meet one's maker

2 *(rémunérer)* to pay; **combien paies-tu ta femme de ménage?** how much do you pay your cleaning lady?; **j'espère que tu t'es fait p. pour ces informations** I hope they paid you *or* you were paid for what you told them; **être payé pour savoir qch** to have learnt sth the hard way

3 *(acheter)* **p. qch à qn** to buy sth for sb; **p. à boire à qn** to buy sb a drink; **je lui ai payé un diamant** I bought him/her a diamond; **j'ai payé ma voiture 10 000 euros** I paid 10,000 euros for my car; **je te paie le théâtre** I'll take you out to the theatre; **combien il t'a fait p.?** how much did he charge?; **il me l'a fait p. trop cher** he overcharged me; **c'est payé?** is it paid for?

4 *Fig (obtenir au prix d'un sacrifice)* **p. qch de** to pay for sth with; **p. sa réussite de sa santé** to succeed at the expense *or* the cost of one's health; **elle me le paiera!** she'll pay for this!; **p. cher qch** to pay a high price for sth; **c'est p. cher la réussite** that's too high a price to pay for success

5 *(subir les conséquences de)* to pay for; **il paie maintenant son laisser-aller** now he's paying for his easy-going attitude; *Fig* **p. les pots cassés** to foot the bill; *Vieilli* **p. les violons** to be out of pocket for nothing

6 *(dédommager)* to compensate, to repay; **p. qn de belles paroles** to fob sb off with smooth talk; **p. qn d'ingratitude** to repay sb with ingratitude; **p. qn de retour** to repay sb in kind

7 *(acheter ▸ criminel)* to hire; *(▸ témoin)* to buy (off); **p. un tueur** to hire a hitman

8 *(compenser)* to pay; **son loyer ne paie même pas mes impôts locaux** his/her rent doesn't even pay *or* cover my local taxes

9 *(être soumis à ▸ taxe)* **certaines marchandises paient un droit de douane** you have to pay duty on some goods, some goods are liable to duty

USAGE ABSOLU p. comptant *ou* **en liquide** *ou* **en espèces** to pay (in) cash; **p. à crédit** to pay by credit; **p. par chèque/carte de crédit** to pay by cheque/credit card; **p. d'avance** to pay in advance; **p. intégralement, p. en totalité** to pay in full; **p. à la livraison** to pay on delivery; **p. à l'ordre de...** *(sur chèque)* pay to the order of...; **payez au porteur** pay to bearer; **p. à présentation** to pay on presentation; **p. à vue** to pay at sight; **les chômeurs ne paient pas** the unemployed don't have to pay; **c'est moi qui paie** *(l'addition)* I'll pay, it's my treat; **p. de ses deniers** *ou* **de sa poche** to pay out of one's own pocket; **p. rubis sur l'ongle** to pay (cash) on the nail; **leur patron paie bien** their boss pays well; *Fig* **vous êtes coupable, vous devez p.** you're guilty, you're going to pay; **p. pour les autres** to be punished for others

VI 1 *(être profitable)* to pay; **c'est un travail qui paie mal** it's badly paid work, it's work that doesn't pay well; **l'honnêteté ne paie plus** it doesn't pay to be honest any more

2 *Fam (prêter à rire)* to be *or* to look a sight; **tu payes avec ces lunettes!** you're an amazing sight with those glasses on!

3 *(locutions) Littéraire* **p. d'audace** to risk one's all; *Fam* **la maison ne paie pas de mine, mais elle est confortable** the house isn't much to look at but it's very comfortable

VPR se payer 1 *(emploi réfléchi)* to compensate oneself; **tenez, payez-vous** here, take what I owe you; **se p. de mots** to talk a lot of fine words

2 *(emploi passif)* to have to be paid for; **la qualité se paie** you have to pay for quality; **tout se paie** everything has its price

3 *Fam (s'offrir)* to treat oneself to; **j'ai envie de me p. une robe** I feel like treating myself to a dress; **se p. la tête** *ou très Fam* **la tronche de qn** *(se moquer de)* to make a fool of sb, *Br* to take the mick *or* the mickey out of sb; *(duper)* to take sb for a ride; **se p. du bon temps,** *très Fam* **s'en p. (une tranche)** to have a fantastic time

4 *Fam (être chargé de)* to be landed *or* saddled with; **je me paie tout le boulot** I end up doing all the work□

5 *Fam (recevoir)* to get□, *Br* to land; **je me suis payé un 2 à l'oral** I got a 2 in the oral

6 *Fam (supporter)* to put up with□; **on s'est payé leurs gosses pendant tout le week-end** we had to put up with their kids for the whole weekend; **il s'est payé une crève carabinée** he came down with a stinking cold

7 *Fam (percuter)* to run *or* to bump into□; **il a brûlé un feu rouge et s'est payé un piéton** he went through a red light and hit a pedestrian□

8 *Fam (agresser)* to go for; **s'il continue à m'énerver, celui-là, je vais me le p.!** if he carries on annoying me, I'm going to swing for him *or* thump him one!

payeur, -euse [pɛjœr, -øz] **ADJ** *(agent, fonctionnaire)* payments *(avant n)*

NM,F payer

NM 1 *Admin (distribuant ▸ les salaires)* wages clerk; *(▸ les remboursements de frais)* firm's accountant **2** *Mil* paymaster **3** *(débiteur)* **mauvais p.** bad debtor, defaulter

pays¹ [pei] **NM 1** *(nation)* country; **les nouveaux p. industrialisés** the newly industrialized countries; **le p. d'accueil** the host country; **p. étranger** foreign country; **p. exportateur** exporting country; **p. d'origine** *ou* **de provenance** country of origin; **les p. les moins avancés** the least developed countries; **les p. riches** affluent countries; **p. en (voie de) développement** developing country; **p. du tiers-monde** Third World country; *Can* **les vieux p.** *(pays d'Europe)* the old countries, the Old World; **ils se conduisent comme en p. conquis** they're acting *or* behaving as if they own the place; **voir du p.** to travel a lot; *Fam* **faire voir du p. à qn** to give sb a hard time

2 *(zone, contrée)* region, area; **p. chaud/sec** hot/dry region; **p. de montagnes/lacs** mountain/lake country; **le P. de la Loire** the Loire (region); **en p. de Loire** in the Loire area *or* valley; **au p. des rêves** *ou* **des songes** in the land of dreams; **être en p. de connaissance** *(avec des gens connus)* to be among familiar faces; *(sur un sujet)* to be on familiar *or* home ground

3 *(agglomération)* village, small town; **un petit p. de 2000 âmes** a small town of 2,000 souls; **ça s'est vite su dans tout le p.** the whole village *or* every man, woman and child in the village soon knew about it

4 *(peuple)* people, country; **s'adresser au p.** to talk to the nation

5 *(région d'origine)* **le p.** *(nation)* one's country; *(région)* one's home (region); *(ville)* one's home (town); **les jeunes quittent le p.** there's an exodus of young people from the region; **on voit bien que tu n'es pas du p.!** it's obvious you're not from around here!; **le mal du p.** homesickness; **avoir le mal du p.** to be homesick

6 *Admin* = group of neighbouring "communes" which have joined together to promote distinctive aspects of the locality

7 *Fig (berceau, foyer)* **le p. des tulipes** the country of the tulip; **l'Espagne, p. de la corrida** Spain, land of the bullfight

• **de** *ou* **du pays ADJ** *(produits)* local; **ils vendent des produits du p.** they sell local produce; **saucisson de p.** traditional *or* country-style sausage

pays², -e [pei, -iz] **NM,F** *Fam Vieilli* **il a rencontré un p. au régiment** he met somebody from back home in the army□

paysage [peizaʒ] **NM 1** *(étendue géographique)* landscape; **p. montagneux/vallonné** hilly/rolling landscape

2 *(panorama)* view, scenery, landscape; **du sommet, le p. est magnifique** the view from the top is beautiful; **cette région offre de merveilleux paysages** this area has marvellous scenery; *Fam Fig* **faire bien dans le p.** to look good

3 *(aspect d'ensemble)* landscape, scene; **p. politique/social** political/social landscape *or* scene; **le p. audiovisuel français** French broadcasting; **p. urbain** townscape, urban landscape

4 *Beaux-Arts* landscape (painting)

5 *Ordinat* **(mode** *ou* **format) p.** landscape (mode); **imprimer qch en p.** to print sth in landscape

paysager, -ère [peizaʒe, -ɛr] **ADJ** landscape *(avant n)*; **parc p.** landscaped gardens

paysagiste [peizaʒist] **ADJ** landscape *(avant n)*

NMF 1 *Beaux-Arts* landscape painter, landscapist **2** *Hort* landscape gardener

paysan, -anne [peizɑ̃, -an] **ADJ 1** *(population)* rural; *Hist & Péj* peasant *(avant n)*; **le monde p.** the farming world **2** *(rustique ▸ décor)* rustic; *(▸ style, vêtements)* rustic, country *(avant n)*; *Péj* peasant

NM,F 1 *(cultivateur)* (small) farmer; *Hist & Péj* peasant; **les paysans veulent des réformes** the farming community wants *or* the farmers want reforms **2** *Péj (rustre)* peasant; **des manières de p.** rough manners

paysannerie [peizanri] **NF** farming community, farmers; *Hist* peasantry

Pays-Bas [peiba] **NMPL les P.** the Netherlands

PC [pese] **NM 1** *(abrév* **parti communiste)** CP, Communist Party **2** *(abrév* **personal computer)** PC **3** *Mil (abrév* **poste de commandement)** HQ

NF *Fin (abrév* **pièce de caisse)** cash voucher

pcc *(abrév écrite* **pour copie conforme)** certified accurate

PCF [peseɛf] **NM** *(abrév* **Parti communiste français)** French Communist Party

PCG [peseʒe] **NM** *Compta (abrév* **plan comptable général)** chart of accounts

PCP [pesepe] **NF** *Chim (abrév* **phencyclidine)** PCP

PCS [peseɛs] **NFPL** *(abrév* **professions et catégories sociales)** socio-economic categories

PCV [peseve] **NM** *Tél (abrév* **à percevoir)** *Br* reverse-charge call, *Am* collect call; **je les ai appelés en P.** *Br* I reversed the charges when I called them, *Am* I called them collect

PDF [pedeɛf] **NM** *Ordinat (abrév* **portable document format)** PDF

P-DG [pedeʒe] **NMF INV** *(abrév* **président-directeur général)** *Br* ≃ MD, *Am* ≃ CEO

PDM [pedeɛm] **NF** *Mktg (abrév* **part de marché)** market share

PDV [pedeve] **NM** *Com (abrév* **point de vente)** POS

PEA [peəa] **NM** *Fin (abrév* **plan d'épargne en actions)** ≃ investment trust, *Br* ≃ ISA

péage [peaʒ] **NM 1** *(taxe)* toll **2** *(lieu ▸ d'autoroute, de pont)* toll (gate); *Hist* tollhouse; **p. à 5 kilomètres** *(panneau sur la route)* toll 5 kilometres **3** *TV* **chaîne à p.** pay channel

péagiste [peaʒist] **NMF** toll collector

peau, -x [po] **NF 1** *Anat* skin; *(autour des ongles)* hangnail; **elle a la p. douce** she has soft skin; **avoir une p. de pêche** to have (soft and) velvety skin; **avoir la p. sèche/grasse** to have dry/greasy skin; **p. mixte** combination skin; **peaux mortes** dead skin; **n'avoir que la p. et les os, n'avoir que la p. sur les os** to be all skin and bone; **prendre qn par la p. du cou** *ou* **du dos** *ou Fam* **des fesses** *ou très Fam* **du cul** to grab sb by the scruff of the neck; **être** *ou* **se sentir bien dans sa p.** to feel good about oneself; **être mal dans sa p.** to be ill at ease with oneself, to feel bad about oneself; **entrer** *ou* **se mettre dans la p. de qn** to put oneself in sb's shoes *or* place; **entrer dans la p. du personnage** to get right into the part; *Fam* **avoir qn dans la p.** to be crazy about sb□, to have sb under one's skin; *Fam* **avoir qch dans la p.** to have sth in one's blood; *Fam* **il sait pas quoi faire de sa p.** he doesn't know what to do with himself; **changer de p.** to change one's look; *Fig* **faire p. neuve** to get a facelift; **l'université fait p. neuve** the university system is being completely overhauled; **c'est dur de faire p. neuve à 50 ans** it's hard to start a new life at 50; **avoir la p. dure** to be thick-skinned; *Fam* **si tu tiens à ta p.** if you value your life *or* hide; *Fam* **y laisser sa p.** to pay with one's life□, to be killed□; *Fam* **un jour, j'aurai ta p.!** I'll get you one of these days!; *Fam* **faire** *ou* **crever la p. à qn** to do sb in, to bump sb off; *Fam* **trouer la p. à qn** to fill *or* to pump sb full of lead; **coûter la p.** *Fam* **des fesses** *ou très Fam* **du cul** to cost an arm and a leg

2 *Zool (gén)* skin; *(fourrure)* pelt; *(cuir ▸ non tanné)* hide; *(▸ tanné)* leather, (tanned) hide; **une valise en p.** a leather suitcase; **le commerce des peaux** the fur and leather trade; **p. d'ours** bearskin; **sac en p. de serpent** snakeskin bag; **cuir pleine p.** full leather; *Fam* **une p. d'âne** *(diplôme)* a diploma□; **p. de chamois** *(chiffon)* chamois leather; *Fam Péj* **vieille p.** old bag; *Fam Péj* **des révolutionnaires en p. de lapin** Mickey Mouse *or* tinpot revolutionaries

3 *(d'un fruit, d'un légume, du lait bouilli, d'un saucisson)* skin; **enlever la p. d'un fruit** to peel a fruit; *aussi Fig* **p. de banane** banana skin

4 *Élec* **effet de p.** skin effect

5 *(locutions) Fam* **p. de balle (et balai de crin),** *Vulg* **p. de zébi** *(refus, mépris)* no way, no chance; **en fin de compte, tout ce qu'on a obtenu c'est p. de balle** in the end we got *Br* sod all *or Am* zilch

• **peau d'orange NF** orange peel; *Méd* orange-peel skin *(caused by cellulite)*

• **peau de vache NF** *Fam (femme)* bitch, *Br* cow; *(homme) Br* swine, *Am* stinker

peaucier [posje] **ADJ M** dermal

NM p. (du cou) platysma

peaufiner [3] [pofine] **VT 1** *(à la peau de chamois)* to shammy-leather **2** *Fig* to put the finishing touches to

peau-rouge [poruʒ] *(pl* **peaux-rouges) ADJ** Red Indian *(avant n)*, redskin *(avant n)*

• **Peau-Rouge NMF** Red Indian, Redskin

peausserie [posri] **NF 1** *(peaux)* leatherwear **2** *(industrie)* leather *or* skin trade

peaussier [posje] **NM 1** *(personne qui prépare les peaux)* skinner **2** *(commerçant)* leather dealer

pébroc, pébroque [pebrɔk] **NM** *Fam* umbrella□, *Br* brolly

pécari [pekari] **NM** peccary

peccadille [pekadij] **NF** peccadillo

pechblende [pɛʃblɛ̃d] **NF** *Minér* pitchblende

pêche¹ [pɛʃ] **NF 1** *(fruit)* peach; **p. abricot** *ou* **jaune/blanche** yellow/white peach; **elle a un teint de p.** she has a peaches and cream complexion; **p. Melba** peach Melba **2** *Fam (énergie)* get-up-and-go; **avoir la p.** to be on (top) form, to be full of beans; **ça va te donner la p.** it'll make you feel on top of the world **3** *Fam (coup)* thump, wallop; **prendre une p.** to get thumped *ou* walloped

ADJ INV peach *(avant n)*, peach-coloured

pêche² [pɛʃ] **NF 1** *(activité)* fishing; **aller à la p.** to go fishing; **p. à la baleine** whaling, whale-hunting; *Can* **p. blanche** ice fishing; **p. au gros** deep-sea fishing; **p. à la ligne** angling; **p. maritime** sea fishing; **p. à la mouche** fly fishing; **p. sous la glace** ice fishing; **aller à la p. aux informations** to go in search of information **2** *(produit de la pêche)* catch; **la p. a été bonne** there was a good catch; *Bible* **p. miraculeuse** miraculous draught of fishes **3** *(lieu)* fishery, fishing ground; **pêches maritimes** sea fisheries; **p. côtière** coastal fishery; **p. gardée** restricted fishing area

péché [peʃe] **NM 1** *(faute)* sin; **p. de (la) chair** sin of the flesh; **p. mortel/véniel** mortal/venial sin; **le p. originel** original sin; **p. de jeunesse** youthful indiscretion; **p. mignon** weakness; **mon p. mignon, c'est le chocolat** I just can't resist chocolate, chocolate is my little weakness; **le p. d'orgueil** the sin of pride; **les sept péchés capitaux** the seven deadly sins; *Prov* **à tout p. miséricorde** = every sin can be forgiven **2** *(état)* sin; **vivre dans le p.** *(gén)* to lead a life of sin *or* a sinful life; *(sans mariage religieux)* to live in sin

pécher [18] [peʃe] **VI 1** *Rel* to sin; **p. par omission** to sin by omission; **p. par orgueil** to commit the sin of pride **2** *(commettre une erreur)* **cette enquête pèche sur un point** the inquiry falls down on one point; **p. par excès de minutie** to be overmeticulous; **elle a péché par imprudence** she was too careless, she was overcareless; **p. contre le bon goût** to go against the rules of good taste

pêcher¹ [peʃe] **NM 1** *(arbre)* peach tree **2** *(bois)* peach wood

pêcher² [4] [peʃe] **VT 1** *Pêche (essayer de prendre)* to fish for; *(prendre)* to catch; **j'ai pêché trois truites** I caught *or* landed three trout; **p. la baleine** to hunt whales, to go whaling; **p. le corail/des perles** to dive for coral/pearls **2** *(tirer de l'eau)* to fish out; **p. une chaussure** to fish out a shoe **3** *Fam (dénicher)* to hunt *or* to track down, to unearth; **où a-t-il été p. que j'avais démissionné?** where did he get the idea that I'd resigned?□

VI *(aller à la pêche)* to fish; **il pêche tous les dimanches** he goes fishing every Sunday; **p. à la ligne** to angle; **p. en mer** to go sea fishing; *Fig* **p. en eau trouble** to fish in troubled waters

pechère [pəʃɛr] = **peuchère**

pécheresse [peʃrɛs] *voir* **pécheur**

pêcherie [pɛʃri] **NF** fishery

pécheur, -eresse [peʃœr, peʃrɛs] **NM,F** sinner

pêcheur, -euse [pɛʃœr, -øz] **NM,F** fisherman, *f*

fisherwoman; **p. de baleines** whaler; **p. à la ligne** angler; *Fig* abstentionist; **p. au chalut** trawlerman; **p. de perles** pearl diver

pêchu, -e [peʃy] **ADJ** *Fam* on (top) form, full of beans

pécloter [3] [peklɔte] **VI** *Suisse Fam* **1** *(être en mauvaise santé) & Fig* to be in a bad way **2** *(mal fonctionner)* to play up

pecnot [pɛkno] = **péquenaud**

PECO [peko] **NM** *(abrév* **pays d'Europe centrale et orientale***)* CEEC

pécore [pekɔr] *Fam Péj* **NMF** *(paysan)* yokel, peasant, *Am* hick

NF quelle p., celle-là! she's so stuck-up!

pectine [pɛktin] **NF** pectin

pectique [pɛktik] **ADJ** pectic

pectoral, -e, -aux, -ales [pɛktɔral, -o] **ADJ 1** *Anat* pectoral **2** *Pharm (pâtes)* cough *(avant n)*; **sirop p.** expectorant

NM *Anat* pectoral muscle; **travailler ses pectoraux** to work on one's pecs

pécule [pekyl] **NM 1** *(petit capital)* savings, nest egg; **se constituer un (petit) p.** to put some money aside **2** *Mil* (service) gratuity **3** *Jur* **p. de libération** prison earnings *(paid on discharge)*

pécuniaire [pekynjɛr] **ADJ** financial, *Sout* pecuniary; **des difficultés pécuniaires** financial *or* money problems

pécuniairement [pekynjɛrmɑ̃] **ADV** financially, *Sout* pecuniarily

PED [peəde] **NM** *(abrév* **pays en développement***)* developing country

pédagogie [pedagɔʒi] **NF 1** *(méthodologie)* educational methods **2** *(pratique)* teaching skills

pédagogique [pedagɔʒik] **ADJ** *(science, manière)* educational, teaching *(avant n)*, *Sout* pedagogical; *(voyage, sortie)* educational; **elle n'a aucune formation p.** she's not been trained to teach *or* as a teacher

pédagogiquement [pedagɔʒikmɑ̃] **ADV** from an educational *or* a pedagogical point of view

pédagogue [pedagɔg] **ADJ il n'est pas très p.** he's not very good at teaching; **elle est très p.** she's a very good teacher

NMF 1 *(enseignant)* teacher **2** *(éducateur)* educationalist

pédale [pedal] **NF 1** *(d'un vélo, d'un pédalo)* pedal; **appuyer sur les pédales** to pedal hard

2 *(d'une poubelle)* pedal; *(d'une machine à coudre, d'un tour)* treadle

3 *Aut* pedal; **p. d'accélérateur** accelerator pedal; **p. d'embrayage** clutch; **appuyer sur la p. du frein** to step on *or* to use the brake pedal

4 *Mus* pedal; **p. douce** soft pedal; **p. forte** loud *or* sustaining pedal; *aussi Fig* **mettre la p. douce** to soft-pedal

5 *Fam (homosexuel)* queer, *Am* fag, = offensive term used to refer to a male homosexual; **il est de la p.** he's a queer *or Am* fag

6 *Fam* **perdre les pédales** to lose one's marbles, *Br* to lose the plot; **s'emmêler les pédales** to get all mixed up, to get hopelessly lost

• à pédales ADJ pedal *(avant n)*; **auto à pédales** *(jouet)* pedal car

pédaler [3] [pedale] **VI 1** *(sur un vélo)* to pedal **2** *Fam (locutions)* **p. dans la choucroute** *ou* **la semoule** *ou* **le yaourt** to get nowhere

pédaleur, -euse [pedalœr, -øz] **NM,F** *Fam* cyclist^◻^

pédalier [pedalje] **NM 1** *(d'une bicyclette)* drive (mechanism) **2** *Mus (d'un orgue)* pedals, pedal board

Pédalo® [pedalo] **NM** pedalo, pedal-boat

pédant, -e [pedɑ̃, -ɑ̃t] **ADJ** *(exposé, ton)* pedantic

NM,F pedant

pédanterie [pedɑ̃tri] **NF** pedantry

pédantesque [pedɑ̃tɛsk] **ADJ** *Littéraire* pedantic

pédantisme [pedɑ̃tism] **NM** = **pédanterie**

pédé [pede] *très Fam* **ADJ** queer, *Br* bent, = offensive term used to refer to a male homosexual; **p. comme un phoque** *Br* as bent as a nine-bob note *or* as a three-pound note, *Am* as queer as a three-dollar bill

NM queer, *Am* fag, = offensive term used to refer to a male homosexual

pédégé [pedeʒe] **NM** *Fam Hum Br* MD^◻^, *Am* CEO^◻^

pédéraste [pederast] **NM 1** *(avec des jeunes garçons)* pederast **2** *(entre hommes)* homosexual

pédérastie [pederasti] **NF 1** *(avec des jeunes garçons)* pederasty **2** *(entre hommes)* homosexuality

pédestre [pedɛstr] **ADJ 1** *voir* **randonnée 2** *voir* **statue**

pédiatre [pedjatr] **NMF** paediatrician

pédiatrie [pedjatri] **NF** paediatrics *(singulier)*

pedibus [pedibys] **ADV** *Fam Hum* **p. (cum jambis)** on foot^◻^, on Shanks's *Br* pony *or Am* mare

pédicelle [pedisɛl] **NM** pedicel

pédicule [pedikyl] **NM 1** *Anat* peduncle **2** *Bot (pédicelle)* pedicle; *(pédoncule)* peduncle

pédicure [pedikyr] **NMF** chiropodist

pédieux, -euse [pedjø, -øz] **ADJ** *Anat* pedal

pedigree [pedigre] **NM** pedigree; **un chien avec p.** a pedigree dog

pédomètre [pedɔmɛtr] **NM** pedometer

pédoncule [pedɔ̃kyl] **NM** *Anat & Bot* peduncle

pédophile [pedɔfil] **ADJ** paedophiliac

NMF paedophile

pédophilie [pedɔfili] **NF** paedophilia

pedzouille [pɛdzuj] **NM** *Fam Péj* yokel, peasant, *Am* hick

PEE [peəə] **NM** *(abrév* **plan d'épargne d'entreprise***)* company savings scheme

peeling [piliŋ] **NM** *(soin de beauté)* exfoliation (treatment); *Méd* dermabrasion; **se faire faire un p.** to have exfoliation treatment; *Méd* to have dermabrasion; **se faire un p.** to exfoliate; **p. chimique** chemical peel

peer-to-peer [pirtupir] **ADJ** *Ordinat* peer-to-peer

pègre [pɛgr] **NF** (criminal) underworld

peignage [pɛɲaʒ] **NM** *Tex (du lin, de la laine)* combing; *(du chanvre)* hackling

peignait *etc* **1** *voir* **peindre 2** *voir* **peigner**

peigne [pɛɲ] **NM 1** *(pour les cheveux)* comb; **se donner un coup de p.** to run a comb through one's hair, to give one's hair a comb; **p. fin** fine-tooth comb; *Fig* **passer une région/un document au p. fin** to go over an area/a document with a fine-tooth comb **2** *Tex (de filage à la main ▸ pour lin, laine)* comb; *(▸ pour chanvre)* hackle; *(d'un métier à tisser)* reed **3** *Zool (mollusque)* scallop, pecten; *(chez l'oiseau)* pecten; *(chez les scorpions)* comb

ADJ *Can Fam Péj (avare)* stingy

peigné, -e[1] [pɛɲe] **ADJ** *(fil)* combed

NM *(tissu)* combed yarn

peigne-cul [pɛɲky] *(pl* **inv** *ou* **peigne-culs***)* **NM** *très Fam Péj (individu méprisable)* jerk, *Br* tosser; *(individu grossier)* pig, boor

peignée[2] [pɛɲe] **NF 1** *Fam (volée de coups)* thrashing, hiding, hammering; **flanquer une p. à qn** to give sb a thrashing *or* hiding *or* hammering; **recevoir une p.** to get a thrashing *or* hiding *or* hammering **2** *Tex* cardful

peigner [4] [pɛɲe] **VT 1** *(cheveux)* to comb; **viens ici que je te peigne** come here so that I can comb your hair; **je suis vraiment mal peignée aujourd'hui** my hair is all over the place today; *Fam* **faire ça ou p. la girafe** we're completely wasting our time **2** *Tex (lin, laine)* to comb; *(chanvre)* to hackle

VPR se peigner *(se coiffer)* to comb one's hair

peignoir [pɛɲwar] **NM 1** *(sortie de bain)* **p. (de bain)** bathrobe **2** *(robe de chambre)* dressing gown, *Am* bathrobe **3** *(chez le coiffeur) Br* cape, *Am* robe

Pei-king [pejkiŋ] = **Pékin**

peinard, -e [penar, -ard] *Fam* **ADJ** *(vie, boulot)* cushy; **rester** *ou* **se tenir p.** to keep one's nose clean; **là-bas, on sera peinards** we'll have it easy there; **il sont peinards dans leur nouvelle baraque** they're nice and comfortable in their new place; **il a trouvé un coin p. pour pioncer** he found a quiet corner to crash out

ADV *(tranquillement)* in peace^◻^, peacefully^◻^

peindre [81] [pɛ̃dr] **VT 1** *(mur, tableau)* to paint; **j'ai peint la porte en bleu** I painted the door blue; **p. à la bombe/au pistolet** to spray-paint; **p. au pinceau/rouleau** to paint with a brush/roller; **p. à l'huile/à l'eau** to paint in oils/in watercolours; *Suisse Fig* **p. le diable sur la muraille** to be pessimistic **2** *(décrire)* to portray, to depict

VI to paint, to be a painter *or* an artist

VPR se peindre 1 *(emploi passif)* to be painted on **2** *(se représenter ▸ en peinture)* to paint one's (own) portrait; *(▸ dans un écrit)* to portray oneself

3 *(se grimer)* **se p. le visage** to paint one's face

4 to show; **la stupéfaction se peignit sur son visage** amazement was written all over his/her face

PEINE [pɛn]

- sentence **A1**
- trouble **B1, C1, 2**
- effort **C1**
- difficulty **C2**
- suffering **A2**
- sadness **B2**
- worth **C1**

NF A. 1 *(châtiment)* sentence; **infliger une lourde p. à qn** to pass a harsh sentence on sb; **la p. capitale** capital punishment, the death penalty; **p. contractuelle** penalty for non-performance (of contract); **p. correctionnelle** = imprisonment for between two months and five years, or a fine; **p. criminelle** = imprisonment for more than five years; **p. de durée indéterminée** indeterminate sentence; **p. d'emprisonnement** prison sentence; **p. incompressible** sentence without remission; **p. infamante** = penalty involving loss of civil rights; **la p. de mort** capital punishment, the death penalty; **p. obligatoire** mandatory sentence; **p. patrimoniale** property penalty, penalty affecting property *(fine and confiscation)*; **p. de police** penalty for minor offences; **p. de prison** prison sentence; **p. de prison avec sursis** suspended (prison) sentence; **p. requise** recommended sentence; **p. de substitution** non-custodial sentence; *Littéraire* **porter la p. de la célébrité** to pay the price of fame

2 *Rel (damnation)* damnation, suffering; **les peines éternelles** eternal damnation *or* suffering, the fires of hell

B. 1 *(tourment, inquiétude)* trouble; **mes amis viennent souvent me raconter leurs peines** my friends often come to tell me their troubles; **faire p. à voir** to be a sorry sight; **se mettre en p. pour qn** to be extremely worried about sb

2 *(tristesse)* sadness, sorrow, grief; **il partageait sa p.** he shared his/her grief; **avoir de la p.** to be sad *or* upset; **faire de la p. à qn** to upset sb; **il me fait vraiment de la p.** I feel really sorry for him

C. 1 *(effort)* effort, trouble; **ce n'est pas la p.** it's not worth it, it's pointless; **ce n'est pas la p. de tout récrire/que tu y ailles** there's no point writing it all out again/your going; **se donner de la p.** to go to a lot of trouble; **il s'est donné beaucoup de p. pour réussir** he went to a lot of trouble to succeed; **prendre** *ou* **se donner la p. de...** to go to *or* to take the trouble to...; **donnez-vous la p. d'entrer** please do come in, *Sout* (please) be so kind as to come in; **si vous voulez bien vous donner la p. d'attendre un instant** if you wouldn't mind waiting a moment; **il ne s'est même pas donné la p. de répondre** he didn't even bother replying; **ne vous donnez pas la p. de me reconduire, je connais le chemin** don't bother to show me out, I know the way; **s'il veut s'en donner la p., il peut très bien réussir** if he can be bothered to make the effort, he's perfectly capable of succeeding; **tu aurais pu prendre la p. de téléphoner** you could at least have phoned; **valoir la p.** to be worth it; **l'exposition vaut la p. d'être vue** the exhibition is worth seeing; **en être pour sa p.** to have nothing to show for one's trouble; **ne pas épargner** *ou* **ménager sa p.** to spare no effort; **n'essaie pas de le convaincre, c'est p. perdue** don't try to persuade him, it's a waste of time *or* you'd be wasting your breath

2 *(difficulté)* **avoir de la p. à marcher** to have trouble *or* difficulty walking; **elle a eu toutes les peines du monde à venir à la réunion** she had a terrible time *or* the devil's own job getting to the meeting; **je serais bien en p. de vous l'expliquer** I'd have a hard job explaining it to you, I wouldn't really know how to explain it to you; **je ne suis pas en p. pour y aller** it's no trouble for me to get there, I'll have no problem getting there

• **à peine** ADV **1** *(presque pas)* hardly, barely, scarcely; **j'arrive à p. à soulever mon sac** I can hardly *or* barely lift my bag; **j'y vois à p.** *(ma vue est mauvaise)* I've very poor sight, I can hardly see; *(il fait sombre)* I can hardly see anything; **c'est à p. si je l'ai entrevu** I only just caught a glimpse of him; *Fam Hum* **je t'assure, je n'ai pas touché au gâteau – à p.!** I swear I didn't touch the cake – a likely story!

2 *(tout au plus)* barely; **il était à p. dix heures** it was only just ten o'clock; **il y a à p. une semaine/deux heures** barely a week/two hours ago

3 *(à l'instant)* just; **je termine à p.** I've only just finished

4 *(aussitôt)* **à p. guérie, elle a repris le travail** no sooner had she recovered than she went back to work

• **avec peine** ADV **1** *(difficilement)* with difficulty; **je l'ai fait avec p.** I had trouble *or* a struggle doing it **2** *Sout (à regret)* **je vous quitte avec p.** it is with deep regret that I leave you

• **sans peine** ADV **1** *(aisément)* without difficulty, easily; **l'italien sans p.** Italian the easy way **2** *(sans regret)* with no regrets, with a light heart

• **sous peine de** PRÉP **défense de fumer sous p. d'amende** *(écriteau dans un lieu public)* smokers will be prosecuted; **sous p. de mort** on pain of death

peiner [4] [pene] VT *(attrister)* to upset, to distress; **sa mort m'a profondément peiné** his/her death greatly grieved *or* distressed me; **je suis peiné par ton attitude** I'm unhappy with your attitude; **d'un ton peiné** in a sad tone

VI **1** *(personne)* to have trouble *or* difficulty; **j'ai peiné pour terminer dans les délais** I had to struggle to finish *or* I had a lot of trouble finishing on time; **il peinait sur son travail** he was toiling at *or* over his work; **p. à marcher** to have trouble *or* difficulty walking; **je peine à comprendre son point de vue** I find it hard to understand his point of view **2** *(machine)* to strain, to labour; **on entendait un moteur p. dans la montée** you could hear a car engine toiling up the hill

peint, -e [pɛ̃, pɛ̃t] PP *voir* **peindre**

peintre [pɛ̃tr] NM **1** *(artiste)* painter **2** *(artisan, ouvrier)* painter; **p. en bâtiment** house painter; **p. en lettres** signwriter **3** *Fig (écrivain)* portrayer; **c'est un excellent p. de la vie à la campagne** his depictions of country life are superb

peinture [pɛ̃tyr] NF **1** *(substance)* paint; **p. laquée/satinée/mate** gloss/satin-finish/matt paint; *Constr* **p. à l'eau** water *or* water-based paint; *Beaux-Arts* **p. à l'huile** oil paint

2 *(action)* painting; **faire de la p.** to paint; **p. en bâtiment** (house) painting

3 *(couche de matière colorante)* paintwork; **donner un petit coup de p. à qch** to freshen sth up; **la porte a besoin d'un petit coup de p.** the door could do with a lick of paint; **p. fraîche** *(sur un écriteau)* wet paint; **refaire la p. d'une porte** to repaint a door; **il faudra refaire les peintures** the paintwork will have to be done; **p. de guerre** warpaint

4 *Beaux-Arts (art, technique)* painting; **faire de la p.** to paint; **p. au doigt** finger-painting

5 *(œuvre)* painting, picture, canvas; **une p. murale** a mural; **peintures rupestres** cave paintings; *Fam* **je ne peux pas la voir en p.** I can't stand *or Br* stick the sight of her

6 *(ensemble d'œuvres peintes)* painting; **la p. figurative** figurative painting; **la p. de Picasso** Picasso's paintings

7 *(description)* portrayal, picture; **une p. de la société médiévale** a picture of medieval society

peinturer [3] [pɛ̃tyre] VT **1** *(barbouiller)* to daub with paint **2** *Can* to paint

peinturlurer [3] [pɛ̃tyrlyre] *Fam* VT to daub with paint

VPR **se peinturlurer elle s'était peinturluré le visage** she'd plastered make-up on her face

péjoratif, -ive [peʒɔratif, -iv] ADJ pejorative, derogatory

NM pejorative (term)

péjoration [peʒɔrasjɔ̃] NF pejoration

péjorative [peʒɔrativ] *voir* **péjoratif**

péjorativement [peʒɔrativmɑ̃] ADV pejoratively, derogatorily

Pékin [pekɛ̃] NM Peking

pékin [pekɛ̃] NM **1** *Tex* Pekin (fabric) **2** *Fam Mil (civil)* civilian□ **3** *Fam (individu)* guy, *Br* bloke

pékinois, -e [pekinwa, -az] ADJ Pekinese, Pekingese

NM **1** *(langue)* Pekinese, Mandarin (Chinese) **2** *(chien)* Pekinese, Pekingese

• **Pékinois, -e** NM,F Pekinese, Pekingese (person)

PEL [peœl] NM *Banque (abrév* **plan (d')épargne logement)** *Br* ≃ building society account, *Am* ≃ savings and loan association account

pelade [pəlad] NF *Méd* alopecia areata, pelada

pelage [pəlaʒ] NM coat, fur

pélagique [pelaʒik] ADJ *Biol* pelagic

pelant, -e [pəlɑ̃, -ɑ̃t] ADJ *Belg Fam (agaçant)* annoying□; *(assommant)* boring□, deadly dull; **c'est p.!** *(agaçant)* it's a real pain in the neck!; *(assommant)* it's a real drag!

pélargonium [pelargɔnjɔm] NM *Bot* pelargonium

pelé, -e [pəle] ADJ **1** *(chat, renard, fourrure)* mangy; *(vêtement)* threadbare **2** *(sans végétation)* bare, treeless

NM *Fam* **1** *(chauve)* bald *or* bald-headed man□, *Br* slaphead **2** *(locution)* **il y avait trois pelés et un tondu** there was hardly a soul there

pêle-mêle [pɛlmɛl] ADV in a jumble; **les draps et les couvertures étaient p. sur le lit** sheets and covers were all jumbled up *or* in a heap on the bed; **les spectateurs se sont engouffrés p. dans la salle** the spectators piled pell-mell into the room

NM INV *(cadre pour photos)* multiple (photo) frame

peler [25] [pəle] VT **1** *(fruit, légume)* to peel **2** *très Fam (locution)* **p. le jonc à qn** to get on sb's nerves *or Br* wick

VI **1** *(peau)* to peel; **j'ai le dos qui pèle** my back's peeling **2** *Fam (locution)* to be freezing (cold)□; **ça pèle** it's freezing (cold) *or Br* brass monkeys

VPR **se peler qu'est-ce qu'on** *Fam* **se pèle** *ou très Fam* **se les pèle ici!** it's freezing in here!□

pèlerin [pɛlrɛ̃] NM **1** *Rel* pilgrim

2 *Ich (requin)* basking shark

3 *Orn* peregrine (falcon)

4 *Fam (individu)* guy, *Br* bloke

pèlerinage [pɛlrinaʒ] NM **1** *(voyage)* pilgrimage; **faire un** *ou* **aller en p. à Lourdes** to go on a pilgrimage to Lourdes **2** *(endroit)* place of pilgrimage

pèlerine [pɛlrin] NF cape

pélican [pelikɑ̃] NM *Orn* pelican

pelisse [pəlis] NF pelisse

pellagre [pelagr] NF *Méd* pellagra

pelle [pɛl] NF **1** *(pour ramasser)* shovel; *(pour creuser)* spade; **p. à charbon** coal shovel; **p. à ordures** dustpan

2 *Culin* **p. à poisson/tarte** fish/cake slice

3 *Constr* **p. mécanique** *(sur roues)* mechanical shovel; *(sur chenilles)* excavator

4 *(extrémité d'un aviron)* (oar) blade

5 *très Fam (baiser)* French kiss, *Br* snog; **rouler une p. à qn** to French kiss sb, *Br* to snog sb

6 *Fam (locutions)* **(se) prendre** *ou* **(se) ramasser une p.** *(tomber, échouer) Br* to come a cropper, *Am* to take a spill

• **à la pelle** ADV **1** *(avec une pelle)* **ramasser la neige à la p.** to shovel up the snow **2** *Fam (en grande quantité)* in spades, by the bucketful; **gagner** *ou* **ramasser de l'argent à la p.** to be raking it in□; **il y en a à la p.** there's masses *or* loads (of it/them)

pelle-pioche [pɛlpjɔʃ] *(pl* **pelles-pioches)** NF = combined pick and hoe

pelletée [pɛlte] NF **1** *(de terre ▸ ramassée)* shovelful; *(▸ creusée)* spadeful **2** *Fam (grande quantité)* heap, pile; **une p. d'injures** a stream of insults

pelleter [27] [pɛlte] VT to shovel (up); *Can* **p. des nuages** to dream up idle schemes

pelleterie [pɛltri] NF **1** *(art)* fur dressing **2** *(peaux)* peltry, pelts **3** *(commerce)* fur trade

pelleteur, -euse [pɛltœr, -øz] NM,F *(personne)* shoveller

• **pelleteuse** NF mechanical shovel *or* digger; **pelleteuse chargeuse** loading shovel, wheel loader

pelletier, -ère [pɛltje, -ɛr] NM,F furrier

pellicule [pelikyl] NF **1** *(peau ▸ gén)* skin, film; *(▸ du raisin)* skin; **une p. s'était formée sur le lait** a skin had formed on the milk **2** *(mince croûte)* film, thin layer; **une p. de glace sur la mare** a thin layer of ice over the pond **3** *Phot* film; **une p.** *(bobine)* a reel (of film); *(chargeur)* a (roll of) film; **p. en bobine** roll film; **p. (en) couleur** colour film; **p. rapide** fast film; **p. vierge** film stock

• **pellicules** NFPL *(dans les cheveux)* dandruff *(UNCOUNT)*; **avoir des pellicules** to have dandruff; **shampooing contre les pellicules** anti-dandruff shampoo

pelloche [pelɔʃ] NF *Fam* film□ *(for camera)*

pélo [pelo] NM *Fam (individu)* guy, *Br* bloke

Péloponnèse [pelɔpɔnɛz] NM **le P.** the Peloponnese

pelotage [pəlɔtaʒ] NM *Fam* (heavy) petting, necking

pelotari [pəlɔtari] NM pelota player, pelotari

pelote [pəlɔt] NF **1** *(de ficelle, de coton)* ball; **une p. de laine** a ball of wool; *Fam* **faire sa p.** to make one's nest egg *or* one's pile; **p. à épingles** pincushion

2 *Can (boule)* **p. de neige** snowball

3 *Couture (coussinet)* pincushion

4 *Sport* pelota; **jouer à la p. (basque)** to play pelota

peloter [3] [plɔte] *Fam* VT to grope, to feel up; **elle s'est fait p. dans le métro** somebody groped her in the metro

VPR **se peloter** to grope each other

peloteur, -euse [plɔtœr, -øz] *Fam* ADJ **il est du genre p.** he can't keep his hands to himself, he's got wandering hands

NM,F **quel p.!** he can't keep his hands to himself!

peloton [plɔtɔ̃] NM **1** *Mil (division)* platoon; *(unité)* squad; **p. de discipline** *ou* **de punition** punishment squad; **p. d'exécution** firing squad; **suivre** *ou* **faire le p. (d'instruction)** to attend the training unit

2 *Sport* pack; **être dans le p. de tête** to be up with the leaders; *Fig* to be among the front runners

3 *(de coton, de laine)* small ball

4 *(d'abeilles, de chenilles)* cluster

pelotonner [3] [pəlɔtɔne] VT *(laine)* to wind up into a ball

VPR **se pelotonner** to curl up; *(pour avoir chaud)* to snuggle up

pelouse [pəluz] NF **1** *(terrain)* lawn; *(herbe)* grass; **arroser/tondre la p.** to water/to mow the lawn; **p. interdite** *(sur panneau)* keep off the grass **2** *Sport* field, *Br* pitch; *(d'un champ de courses)* paddock

peluche [pəlyʃ] NF **1** *(jouet)* cuddly toy **2** *Tex* plush **3** *(poussière)* (piece of) fluff *(UNCOUNT)*

• **en peluche** ADJ **chien/canard en p.** (cuddly) toy dog/duck

peluché, -e [pəlyʃe] ADJ **1** *(à poils longs)* fluffy **2** *(tissu)* pilled

pelucher [3] [pəlyʃe] VI to pill

pelucheux, -euse [pəlyʃø, -øz] ADJ **1** *(tissu)* fluffy **2** *(fruit)* downy

pelure [pəlyr] NF **1** *(peau)* peel *(UNCOUNT)*; **p. d'oignon** onion skin; *(vin)* pale rosé wine **2** *Fam (vêtement)* coat□

pelvien, -enne [pɛlvjɛ̃, -ɛn] ADJ *Anat (cavité, organe)* pelvic

pelvis [pɛlvis] NM *Anat* pelvis

pénal, -e, -aux, -ales [penal, -o] ADJ *(droit)* criminal; *(code, réforme)* penal

pénalement [penalmɑ̃] ADV penally; **être p. responsable** to be liable in criminal law

pénalisation [penalizasjɔ̃] NF **1** *Sport* penalty (for infringement); *Équitation* **points de p.** faults, penalty points **2** *(désavantage)* penalization

pénaliser [3] [penalize] VT **1** *Sport* to penalize **2** *(désavantager)* to penalize, to put *or* to place at a disadvantage; **ces enfants sont pénalisés dès leur**

entrée à l'école these children are disadvantaged from the moment they start school

pénalité [penalite] NF **1** *Fin* penalty; **p. libératoire** full and final penalty payment; **p. de retard** penalty for late *or* overdue payment; *(pour livraison tardive)* late delivery penalty **2** *Sport* penalty; **coup de pied de p.** penalty kick; **jouer les pénalités** to go into injury time

penalty [penalti] *(pl* **penaltys** *ou* **penalties)** NM penalty (kick); **siffler/tirer un p.** to award/to take a penalty

pénard [penar] = **peinard**

pénates [penat] NMPL **1** *Myth* Penates **2** *Fam* **regagner ses p.** to go home□

penaud, -e [pəno, -od] ADJ sheepish, contrite; **prendre un air p.** to look sheepish

penchant [pɑ̃ʃɑ̃] NM **1** *(goût* ▸ *pour quelque chose)* liking, penchant (**pour** for); (▸ *pour quelqu'un)* fondness, liking (**pour** for); **un petit p. pour le chocolat** a weakness for chocolate; **éprouver un p. pour qn** to be fond of sb **2** *(tendance)* tendency, inclination; **de mauvais penchants** evil tendencies **3** *Vieilli ou Littéraire (pente)* slope

penché, -e [pɑ̃ʃe] ADJ **1** *(tableau)* crooked; *(mur, écriture)* sloping, slanting; *(objet)* tilting **2** *(personne)* leaning; **il était p. en avant** he was leaning forward; **il est toujours p. sur ses livres** he's always got his head in a book

pencher [3] [pɑ̃ʃe] VI **1** *(aux être) (être déséquilibré* ▸ *pile)* to lean (over), to tilt; (▸ *bateau)* to list; **la tour/le mur penche vers la droite** the tower/the wall leans to the right; **le miroir penche encore un peu, redresse-le** the mirror is still crooked, straighten it; **ne faites pas p. le bateau** don't rock the boat; *Fig* **faire p. la balance en faveur de/contre qn** to tip the scales in favour of/against sb **2** *(aux être) (être en pente)* to slope (away); **le sol penche** the floor slopes *or* is on an incline **3** *(aux avoir)* **p. pour** *(préférer)* to be inclined to, to favour; **je penche pour cette solution** I favour this solution

VT to tilt, to tip up; **il pencha la tête en arrière pour l'embrasser** he leaned backwards to kiss him/her; **elle pencha la tête au-dessus du parapet** she leaned over the parapet

VPR **se pencher 1** *(s'incliner)* to lean, to bend; **se p. en avant/en arrière** to lean *or* bend forward/backwards; **se p. à** *ou* **par la fenêtre** to lean out (of) the window; **il se pencha sous la table pour ramasser son crayon** he reached under the table to pick up his pencil **2 se p. sur un problème/un dossier** to look into a problem/a file

pendable [pɑ̃dabl] ADJ **1** *Vieilli (passible de la pendaison)* **ce n'est pas un cas p.** it's not a hanging matter **2 jouer un tour p. à qn** to play a rotten trick on sb

pendaison [pɑ̃dɛzɔ̃] NF hanging; **mort par p.** death by hanging

• **pendaison de crémaillère** NF housewarming (party)

pendant¹ [pɑ̃dɑ̃] PRÉP *(au cours de)* during; *(insistant sur la durée)* for; **il est arrivé p. la cérémonie** he came in during the ceremony; **p. l'hiver** during the winter; **quelqu'un a appelé p. l'heure du déjeuner** somebody called while you were at lunch *or* during your lunch break; **il te l'a dit après la réunion? – non, p.** did he tell you after the meeting? – no, during it; **p. ce temps(-là)** in the meantime, meanwhile; **je suis là p. tout l'été** I'm here during the *or* for the whole (of the) summer; **p. une heure** for an hour; **je m'absenterai p. un mois** I'll be away for a month; **je ne l'ai pas vu p. plusieurs années** I didn't see him for several years; **j'y ai habité p. un an** I lived there for a year; **nous avons roulé p. 20 kilomètres** we drove for 20 kilometres

• **pendant que** CONJ **1** *(tandis que)* while; **surveille les valises p. que je vais chercher les billets** look after the suitcases while I go and get the tickets **2** *(tant que)* while; **partons p. qu'il est encore temps** let's go while it's still possible; **p. que tu y es, pourras-tu passer à la banque?** while you're there *or* at it, could you stop off at the bank?; **p. que j'y pense, voici l'argent que je te dois** while I think of it, here's the money I owe you **3** *(puisque)* since, while; **allons-y p. que nous y sommes** let's go, since we're here

pendant², -e [pɑ̃dɑ̃, -ɑ̃t] ADJ **1** *(tombant* ▸ *jambes)* dangling; (▸ *seins, joues)* sagging; **il restait là, les bras pendants** he stood there with his arms hanging at his sides; **la langue pendante** *(de fatigue, de convoitise)* with one's tongue hanging out; **un chien aux oreilles pendantes** a dog with floppy ears **2** *Jur (en cours)* pending

NM **1** *(bijou)* pendant; **p. (d'oreilles)** (pendant) earring **2** *(symétrique* ▸ *d'une chose)* matching piece (**de** to); **faire p. à qch** to match sth; **se faire p.** to match, to be a matching pair

pendard, -e [pɑ̃dar, -ard] NM,F *Fam Vieilli* rogue, rapscallion

pendeloque [pɑ̃dlɔk] NF **1** *(de boucle d'oreille)* pendant, eardrop **2** *(d'un lustre)* pendant, drop

pendentif [pɑ̃dɑ̃tif] NM **1** *(bijou)* pendant **2** *Archit* pendentive

penderie [pɑ̃dri] NF *(meuble)* wardrobe; *(pièce)* walk-in wardrobe *or* closet

pendiller [3] [pɑ̃dije] VI to hang (down), to dangle

pendoir [pɑ̃dwar] NM butcher's *or* meat hook

Pendolino® [pɑ̃dɔlino] NM Pendolino®

pendouiller [3] [pɑ̃duje] VI *Fam* to hang down□, to dangle□

pendre [73] [pɑ̃dr] VT **1** *(accrocher)* to hang (up); **p. un tableau à un clou** to hang a picture from a nail; **p. son linge sur un fil** to hang up one's washing on a line; **p. la crémaillère** to have a housewarming (party) **2** *(exécuter)* to hang; **condamné à être pendu** sentenced to be hanged; **il sera pendu à l'aube** he'll hang *or* be hanged at dawn; **p. qn haut et court** to hang sb (by the neck); **se faire p.** to be hanged; *Fam* **qu'il aille se faire p. ailleurs** he can go to blazes *or* go hang; **je veux bien être pendu si...** I'll be hanged if... **3** *Fig* **être pendu au cou de qn** to cling to sb; **être (toujours) pendu après qn** *ou* **aux basques de qn** to dog sb's every footstep, to hang around sb; *Fam* **être pendu au téléphone** to be never off the phone, to spend one's life on the phone

VI **1** *(être accroché)* to hang; **du linge pendait aux fenêtres** washing was hanging out of the windows; *Fam* **ça te pend au nez** you've got it coming to you **2** *(retomber)* to hang; *(bras, jambes)* to dangle; *(langue d'un animal)* to hang out; **ta jupe pend par derrière** your skirt's hanging down *or* dipping at the back; **avoir les joues/seins qui pendent** to have sagging cheeks/breasts; **des rideaux qui pendent jusqu'à terre** full-length curtains

VPR **se pendre 1** *(se suicider)* to hang oneself **2** *(s'accrocher)* to hang (**à** from); **se p. au cou de qn** to fling one's arms around sb's neck

pendu, -e [pɑ̃dy] NM,F hanged man, *f* woman; **le (jeu du) p.** hangman *(game)*

pendulaire [pɑ̃dylɛr] ADJ oscillating, pendulous; **train p.** tilting train

NMF *Suisse* commuter

pendule [pɑ̃dyl] NM *(instrument, balancier)* pendulum

NF *(horloge)* clock; *Fig* **remettre les pendules à l'heure** to set the record straight; *Fam* **en faire une p.**, *Vulg* **en chier une p.** to make a big fuss

pendulette [pɑ̃dylɛt] NF small clock; **p. de voyage** travel (alarm) clock

pêne [pɛn] NM bolt

pénéplaine [peneplɛn] NF peneplain, peneplane

pénétrabilité [penetrabilite] NF penetrability

pénétrable [penetrabl] ADJ **1** *(où l'on peut entrer)* **une jungle difficilement p.** an impenetrable jungle **2** *Fig (compréhensible)* fathomable; **des poèmes/musiques peu pénétrables** rather abstruse poems/music

pénétrant, -e [penetrɑ̃, -ɑ̃t] ADJ **1** *(humidité)* pervasive; *(pluie)* drenching; *(odeur)* penetrating, pervasive; **le froid était p.** it was bitterly cold **2** *(clairvoyant* ▸ *esprit)* penetrating, sharp; (▸ *regard)* piercing, penetrating; **lancer à qn un regard p.** to give sb a piercing look

• **pénétrante** NF = road leading into the city

pénétration [penetrasjɔ̃] NF **1** *(par un solide)* penetration; *(par un liquide)* seepage, seeping; *(par un corps gras)* absorption **masser doucement jusqu'à p. totale de la crème** gently massage *or* rub in the cream until it has been completely absorbed into the skin

2 *(acte sexuel)* penetration

3 *(invasion)* penetration, invasion; **une tentative de p.** an attempted raid

4 *Fig (perspicacité)* perception

5 *Com (d'un produit)* (market) penetration; *(d'un marché)* penetration

pénétré, -e [penetre] ADJ **1** *(rempli)* **être p. de joie/honte** to be filled with joy/shame; **il se sentit p. de la vérité de ces paroles** he felt convinced of the truth of these words; **un orateur p. de son sujet** a speaker who is completely immersed in his subject; *Péj* **p. de sa propre importance** full of one's own importance **2** *(convaincu)* earnest, serious; **d'un air p.** with an earnest air, earnestly

pénétrer [18] [penetre] VI **1** *(entrer)* to go, to enter; **p. dans les bois** to go into the woods; **ils ont réussi à p. en Suisse** they managed to cross into *or* to enter Switzerland; **l'armée a pénétré en territoire ennemi** the army penetrated enemy territory; **p. dans la maison de qn** *(avec sa permission)* to enter sb's house; *(par effraction)* to break into sb's house; **p. sur un marché** to break into a market **2** *(passer* ▸ *balle)* to penetrate; *(s'infiltrer* ▸ *liquide)* to seep, to penetrate; **la balle a pénétré dans le poumon** the bullet entered *or* penetrated the lung; **l'eau a très vite pénétré dans la cale** water quickly flooded into the hold; **le vent pénètre par la cheminée** the wind comes in by the chimney; **la poussière pénètre partout** dust gets in everywhere **3 p. dans** *(approfondir)* to go (deeper) into; **p. dans les détails d'une théorie** to go into the details of a theory

VT **1** *(traverser)* to penetrate, to go in *or* into, to get in *or* into; **la balle a pénétré l'os** the bullet penetrated *or* pierced the bone; **la pluie m'a pénétré jusqu'aux os** I got soaked to the skin (in the rain); **un froid glacial me pénétra** I was chilled to the bone *or* to the marrow

2 *(imprégner)* to spread into *or* through; **ces idées ont pénétré toutes les couches de la société** these ideas have spread through all levels of society

3 *Com (un marché)* to penetrate, to enter

4 *(sexuellement)* to penetrate

5 *(deviner)* to penetrate, to perceive; **p. un mystère** to get to the heart of a mystery; **p. les intentions de qn** to guess *or* fathom sb's intentions

VPR **se pénétrer 1** *(emploi réciproque)* **les croyances hindoue et bouddhiste se sont mutuellement pénétrées** the Hindu and Buddhist faiths became intertwined **2** *(emploi réfléchi)* **se p. d'une vérité** to become convinced of a truth; **se p. de l'importance de qch** to be fully aware of the importance of sth

pénible [penibl] ADJ **1** *(épuisant* ▸ *voyage, ascension)* hard, tough; (▸ *travail, tâche)* laborious, hard; (▸ *vie)* hard, difficult; (▸ *respiration)* laboured, heavy; **elle trouve de plus en plus p. de monter les escaliers** she finds it more and more difficult *or* harder and harder to climb the stairs **2** *(attristant)* distressing, painful; **il m'est p. de devoir vous annoncer que...** it is my painful duty to inform you that...; **en parler m'est très p.** I find it difficult to talk about (it); **ma présence lui est p.** my being here bothers him **3** *(difficile à supporter)* tiresome; **je trouve ça vraiment p.** I find it a real pain; **tu es p., tu sais!** you're a real pain!

péniblement [penibləmɑ̃] ADV **1** *(avec difficulté)* laboriously, with difficulty; **avancer p. dans la neige** to struggle through the snow; **il respire de plus en plus p.** he's finding it more and more difficult to breathe **2** *(tout juste)* just about; **j'arrive p. à boucler les fins de mois** I barely manage to make ends meet at the end of the month; **il atteint p. la moyenne en allemand** he just about scrapes through in German

péniche [peniʃ] NF *(large)* barge; *(étroite)* narrow boat; *Mil* **p. de débarquement** landing craft

• **péniches** NFPL *Fam (grandes chaussures)* clodhoppers

pénicilline [penisilin] NF *Biol & Pharm* penicillin

péninsulaire [penɛ̃sylɛr] ADJ peninsular

NMF inhabitant of a peninsula

péninsule [penɛ̃syl] NF peninsula; **la p. Ibérique** the Iberian Peninsula

pénis [penis] NM penis

pénitence [penitɑ̃s] NF **1** *Rel (repentir)* penitence; *(punition)* penance; *(sacrement)* penance, sacrament of reconciliation; **faire p.** to repent **2** *(punition)* punishment; **mettre qn en p.** to punish sb; **pour votre p.** as a punishment **3** *(dans un jeu)* forfeit

pénitencier [penitɑ̃sje] NM **1** *(prison)* prison, *Am* penitentiary **2** *Rel* penitentiary; **grand p.** grand penitentiary

pénitent, -e [penitɑ̃, -ɑ̃t] ADJ penitent

NM,F penitent

pénitentiaire [penitɑ̃sjɛr] ADJ prison *(avant n)*

pénitentiel, -elle [penitɑ̃sjɛl] ADJ penitential, penitence *(avant n)*

NM penitential (book)

penne[1] [pɛn] NF **1** *Orn* quill, *Spéc* penna **2** *(d'une flèche)* flight, feather **3** *(d'une antenne)* tip

penne[2] [pene] NMPL *(pâtes)* penne

Pennsylvanie [pɛnsilvani] NF **la P.** Pennsylvania

péno [peno] NM *Fam (abrév* **penalty***)* penalty□, *Br* pen *(in football)*

pénombre [penɔ̃br] NF **1** *(obscurité)* half-light, dim light; **la p. nous empêchait de distinguer les visages** the light was too faint *or* dim to see any faces; **dans la p.** in the half-light; *Fig* in the background, out of the limelight **2** *Astron* penumbra

pensable [pɑ̃sabl] ADJ **à cette époque-là, de telles vitesses n'étaient pas pensables** in those days, such speeds were unthinkable; **cette histoire n'est pas p.!** this story is incredible!

pensant, -e [pɑ̃sɑ̃, -ɑ̃t] ADJ *(être)* thinking; **mal p.** unorthodox

pense-bête [pɑ̃sbɛt] *(pl* **pense-bêtes***)* NM reminder

pensée [pɑ̃se] NF **1** *(idée)* thought, idea; **la seule p. d'une seringue me donne des sueurs froides** the very thought of a needle brings me out in a cold sweat; **la p. que tu seras là me donne du courage** the thought that you'll be there gives me courage; **cette p. me hante** I'm haunted by that thought; **tout à la p. de son rendez-vous, il n'a pas vu arriver la voiture** deeply absorbed in *or* by the thought of his meeting, he didn't see the car (coming); **être tout à** *ou* **perdu dans ses pensées** to be lost in thought; **avoir une p. pour qn** to think of sb; **avoir de mauvaises pensées** *(méchantes)* to have evil thoughts; *(sexuelles)* to have immoral *or* bad thoughts; **avoir de sombres pensées** to have gloomy thoughts

2 *(façon de raisonner)* thought; **avoir une p. claire** to be clear-thinking

3 *(opinion)* thought, (way of) thinking; **j'avais deviné ta p.** I'd guessed what you were thinking; **veux-tu connaître ma p. sur ce livre?** do you want to know what I think of *or* about this book?; **dire sa p.** to speak one's mind, to say what one thinks; **dire le fond de sa p.** to say what one really thinks; **il partage ma p.** he shares my opinion, he thinks the same way I do

4 *(esprit)* mind; **nous sommes avec vous par la** *ou* **en p.** our thoughts are with you; **je les vois en p.** I can see them in my mind *or* in my mind's eye

5 *Phil* thought

6 *(idéologie)* thinking, thought; **la p. marxiste** Marxist thinking, Marxist thought

7 *(dans les formules)* **je vous envoie une tendre p. (à vous et à votre famille)** I send my love (to you and your family); **avec nos affectueuses** *ou* **meilleures pensées** with (all) our love *or* fondest regards

8 *Bot* pansy; **p. sauvage** wild pansy

• **pensées** NFPL *Littérature & Phil* thoughts

PENSER [3] [pɑ̃se]

VT
- to think **1–6**
- to realize **4**
- to think out **7**
- to assume **1**
- to remember **5**

VI
- to think **1**

VT **1** *(croire)* to think, to assume; **qu'en penses-tu?** what do you think of it?; **je ne sais qu'en p.** I don't know what to think *or* I can't make up my mind about it; **je pense que oui** (yes,) I think so; **je pense que non** (no,) I don't think so *or* I think not; **je pense que tu devrais lui dire** I think you should tell him/her; **pas aussi beau qu'on le penserait** not as beautiful as you might think; **on pensait du mal de lui dans le village** in the village, they thought ill of him *or* they had a low opinion of him; **je pense qu'elle viendra demain** I think that she'll come tomorrow; **qu'est-ce qui te fait p. qu'il ment?** what makes you think he's lying?; **j'ai pensé qu'un rôti, ce ne serait pas suffisant** it occurred to me *or* I thought that one joint wouldn't be enough; **quoi qu'on pense** whatever people (may) think; **quoi que tu puisses p.** whatever you (may) think; **je le pensais diplomate** I thought him tactful, I thought he was tactful; **je pensais la chose faisable, mais on me dit que non** I thought it was possible (to do), but I'm told it's not

2 *(escompter)* **je pense partir demain** I'm thinking of *or* planning on *or* reckoning on leaving tomorrow; **je pense avoir réussi** *(examen)* I think I passed

3 *(avoir à l'esprit)* to think; **je ne sais jamais ce que tu penses** I can never tell what you're thinking *or* what's on your mind; **au volant, pensez sécurité** when you're at the wheel, think safety (first); **dire tout haut ce que certains** *ou* **d'autres pensent tout bas** to say out loud what others are thinking in private; *Fam Euph* **ce que je pense** you-know-what; **il a marché dans ce que je pense** he trod in some you-know-what; *Fam Euph* **(là) où je pense** in the *Br* backside *or Am* butt; *Fam* **il peut se le mettre où je pense** he knows where he can stick it; *Fam* **elle lui a fichu un coup de pied où je pense** she gave him/her a kick up the you-know-where

4 *(comprendre)* to think, to realize; **pense qu'elle a près de cent ans** you must realize that she's nearly a hundred

5 *(se rappeler)* to remember, to think; **je n'ai plus pensé que c'était lundi** I forgot *or* I never thought it was Monday

6 *(pour exprimer la surprise, l'approbation, l'ironie)* **je n'aurais/on n'aurait jamais pensé que...** I'd never/nobody'd ever have thought that...; **qui aurait pu p. que...** who'd have thought *or* guessed that...; **quand je pense que j'aurais pu être sa femme!** to think that I could've been his wife!; **quand on pense qu'il n'y avait pas le téléphone à l'époque!** when you think that there was no such thing as the phone in those days!; *Fam* **tu penses!** you bet!; *Ironique* you must be joking!; *Fam* **lui, me dire merci? tu penses** *ou* **penses-tu** *ou* **pense donc!** him? thank me? I should be so lucky *or* you must be joking!; *Fam* **tu penses bien que je lui ai tout raconté!** I told him/her everything, as you can well imagine!; *Fam* **il est content? – je pense** *ou* **tu penses bien!** is he pleased? – you bet!; **tu penses bien que le voleur ne t'a pas attendu!** you can bet your life the thief didn't leave his name and address!

7 *(concevoir)* to think out *or* through; **le projet n'a pas été pensé dans toutes ses implications** the implications of the project weren't thought through (properly); **une architecture bien pensée** a well-planned *or* well-thought out architectural design

8 *Littéraire (être sur le point de)* **je pensai m'évanouir** I all but fainted; **elle pensa devenir folle** she was very nearly driven to distraction

VI **1** *(réfléchir)* to think; **p. tout haut** to think aloud *or* out loud; **donner** *ou* **laisser à p.** to make one think, to start one thinking; **voilà des statistiques qui donnent à p.!** these figures provide food for thought!; *Péj* **p. bien** to have conventional beliefs; **une ville dont les habitants pensent bien** a conservative town

2 *(avoir une opinion)* **je n'ai jamais pensé comme toi** I never did agree with you *or* share your views; **je ne dis rien mais je n'en pense pas moins** I say nothing but that doesn't stop me thinking

• **penser à** VT IND **1** *(envisager)* to think about *or* of; **p. à l'avenir** to think about *or* to ponder the future; **pense un peu à ce que tu dis!** just think for a moment (about) what you're saying!; **oui, c'est faisable, j'y penserai** yes, it can be done, I'll think about *or* I'll consider it; **vous éviteriez des ennuis, pensez-y** you'd save yourself a lot of trouble, think it over!; **c'est simple mais il fallait y p.** it's a simple enough idea but somebody had to think of it (in the first place); **sans y p.** *(par automatisme)* without thinking; **quand tu sauras conduire, tu changeras de vitesse sans y p.** when you know how to drive, you'll change gear without (even) thinking; **sans p. à mal** without *or* not meaning any harm (by it); **tu n'y penses pas** you can't be serious; **me rétracter, tu n'y penses pas!** me, go back on what I said, come off it *or* never!

2 *(rêver à)* to think about *or* of; **à quoi penses-tu?** what are you thinking about?; **je pense à toi** *(dans une lettre)* I'm thinking of you

3 *(se préoccuper de)* to think of, to care about; **elle ne pense qu'à elle** she only cares about herself; **essaye de p. un peu aux autres** try to think of others; *Fam Euph* **il ne pense qu'à ça!** he's got a one-track mind

4 *(se remémorer)* to think *or* to remember to; **as-tu pensé au** *ou* **à apporter le tire-bouchon?** did you think *or* remember to bring the corkscrew?; **et mon livre? – j'y pense, je te le rapporte demain** what about my book? – I haven't forgotten (it), I'll bring it back tomorrow; **tu ne penses à rien!** you've a memory *or* head like a sieve!; **n'y pense plus!** forget (about) it!; **cela me fait p. à mon frère** it reminds me of my brother; **fais-moi p. à l'appeler** remind me to call him/her

---

penseur, -euse [pɑ̃sœr, -øz] NM,F thinker

pensif, -ive [pɑ̃sif, -iv] ADJ thoughtful, pensive; **d'un air p.** thoughtfully

pension [pɑ̃sjɔ̃] NF **1** *(somme allouée)* pension; **toucher une p.** to draw a pension; **p. alimentaire** *Br* maintenance, *Am* alimony; **p. de guerre** war pension; **p. d'invalidité** disability pension; **p. de retraite** (retirement *or* old-age) pension; **p. de réversion** survivor's pension; **p. de veuve** widow's pension; **p. viagère** life annuity

2 *(logement et nourriture)* board and lodging; **la p. est de 100 euros par jour** it's 100 euros a day for room and board *or* board and lodging; **prendre p. chez qn** *(client)* to take board and lodgings with sb; *(ami)* to be staying with sb; **être en p. chez qn** to lodge with sb; **prendre qn en p.** to take sb in as a lodger; **être en p. complète** to be on full board

3 *(hôtel)* **p. (de famille)** ≃ boarding house, guesthouse

4 *(pensionnat)* boarding school; *(élèves)* boarders; **être en p.** to be a boarder *or* at boarding school; **envoyer qn en p.** to send sb to boarding school

5 *Belg (cessation d'activité)* retirement; **l'âge de la p.** retirement age; **prendre sa p.** to retire

pensionnaire [pɑ̃sjɔnɛr] NMF **1** *(d'un hôtel)* guest, resident; *(d'un particulier)* (paying) guest, lodger; *(d'une maison de retraites)* resident; *Fam (d'une prison)* inmate□ **2** *Scol* boarder **3** *(à la Comédie-Française)* = actor or actress on a fixed salary with no share in the profits (as opposed to a "sociétaire")

> Il faut noter que le nom anglais **pensioner** est un faux ami. Il signifie le plus souvent **retraité**.

pensionnat [pɑ̃sjɔna] NM **1** *(école)* boarding school **2** *(pensionnaires)* boarders

pensionné, -e [pɑ̃sjɔne] ADJ **1** *(qui perçoit une pension)* **elle est pensionnée à 75 pour cent** her pension represents 75 percent of her income **2** *Belg (qui est à la retraite* ▸ *gén)* retired; *(*▸ *officier)* on the retired list

NM,F **1** *(personne qui perçoit une pension)* pensioner **2** *Belg (personne ne travaillant plus)* retired person

pensionner [3] [pɑ̃sjɔne] VT **p. qn** to (grant sb a) pension

VI *Can (être en pension)* to be a boarder

pensive [pɑ̃siv] *voir* **pensif**

pensivement [pɑ̃sivmɑ̃] ADV pensively, thoughtfully

pensum [pɛ̃sɔm] NM **1** *Vieilli Scol* imposition, punishment; *(lignes)* lines **2** *(corvée)* chore

pentagonal, -e, -aux, -ales [pɛ̃tagɔnal, -o] ADJ *Géom* pentagonal

pentagone [pɛ̃tagɔn] NM *Géom* pentagon

pentamètre [pɛ̃tamɛtr] NM *Littérature* pentameter

Pentateuque [pɛ̃tatøk] NM le P. the Pentateuch

pentathlon [pɛ̃tatlɔ̃] NM pentathlon

pentatonique [pɛ̃tatɔnik] ADJ *Mus* pentatonic

pente [pɑ̃t] NF 1 *(inclinaison)* slope, incline; **une forte p.** a steep incline *or* slope
2 *(descente, montée)* slope; **gravir une p.** to climb a slope
3 *Constr* slope; *(d'un toit)* pitch; **une p. de 10 pour cent** a 1 in 10 gradient
4 *Math (d'une courbe)* slope
5 *Littéraire (penchant)* inclination, leaning
6 *(locutions)* **être sur une mauvaise p.** to be heading for trouble; **il a bien remonté la p.** *(en meilleure santé)* he's back on his feet again; *(financièrement)* he's solvent again; **être sur une p. glissante** *ou* **savonneuse** to be on a slippery slope
• **en pente** ADJ *(route)* sloping; *(plage, côte)* shelving; **la route est en p.** the road is on a slope *or* an incline; **en p. douce** sloping gently; **en p. raide** on a steep incline ADV **descendre/monter en p. douce** to slope gently down/up; **descendre/monter en p. raide** to slope sharply down/up

Pentecôte [pɑ̃tkot] NF 1 *(fête chrétienne)* Whitsun, Pentecost; **la semaine de la P.** Whit Week, Whitsuntide; **dimanche de P.** Whit Sunday; **lundi de P.** Whit Monday 2 *(fête juive)* Shabuoth

pentoxyde [pɛ̃tɔksid] NM *Chim* pentoxide

pentu, -e [pɑ̃ty] ADJ *(chemin)* steep, sloping; *(toit)* sloping, slanting, pointed; *(comble)* sloping

penture [pɑ̃tyr] NF *Tech (de porte, de volet)* strap hinge; **p. et gond** hook and hinge; *Naut* **pentures du gouvernail** rudder braces

pénultième [penyltjɛm] ADJ penultimate
NF penultimate (syllable)

pénurie [penyri] NF 1 *(pauvreté)* destitution, penury; **vivre dans la p.** to live in poverty 2 *(manque)* **p. de** lack *or* shortage of; **p. d'argent** shortage of money; *Écon* **p. de main-d'œuvre** labour shortage

people [pipœl] *Fam* ADJ INV **la presse p.** the celebrity press□
NM INV *(magazine)* celebrity magazine□
NMF INV celebrity□, celeb; **c'est très à la mode chez les p.** all the celebs are into it

PEP [pɛp] NM *Banque (abrév* **plan d'épargne populaire**) = personal pension plan

pep [pɛp] NM *Fam* pep; **avoir du p.** to be full of pep

pépé [pepe] NM *Fam* 1 *(grand-père)* grandpa, *Br* granddad, *Am* gramps 2 *Péj (vieillard) Br* old codger *or* boy, *Am* old-timer

pépée [pepe] NF *Fam Vieilli* chick

pépère [pepɛr] *Fam* ADJ *(facile ▸ travail)* cushy; *(tranquille ▸ endroit)* quiet□; **un petit boulot p.** a cushy little number *or* job; **une petite vie p.** a cosy little life
ADV leisurely□; **on a fait ça p.** we took it easy, we did it at our own pace□; **rouler p.** to potter along
NM 1 *(grand-père)* grandpa, *Br* granddad, *Am* gramps 2 *Péj (vieillard) Br* old boy *or* codger, *Am* old-timer 3 *Fam (locution)* **gros p.** *(avec affection)* tubby; *(avec mépris)* fat slob

pépette, pépète [pepet] *Fam* NF *Belg* fear□; **avoir la p.** to be scared stiff *or* witless
• **pépettes, pépètes** NFPL 1 *Vieilli (argent)* cash, dough; **t'as des pépettes?** have you got any cash? 2 *Belg (peur)* fear□; **avoir les pépettes** to be scared stiff *or* witless

pépie [pepi] NF 1 *Orn* pip 2 *Fam (soif)* **avoir la p.** to be parched

pépiement [pepimɑ̃] NM chirping, tweeting, twittering

pépier [9] [pepje] VI to chirp, to tweet, to twitter

pépin [pepɛ̃] NM 1 *(de fruit)* pip; **des mandarines sans pépins** seedless tangerines 2 *Fam (problème)* hitch, snag; **il y a un petit p.** there's a slight hitch; **avoir un p.** to have a problem□; **il m'arrive un gros p.** I'm in big trouble 3 *Fam (parapluie)* umbrella□, *Br* brolly

pépinière [pepinjɛr] NF 1 *Bot* (tree) nursery; *Fig* **une p. de futurs prix Nobel** a breeding-ground for future Nobel prizewinners 2 **p. d'entreprise** business incubator

pépiniériste [pepinjerist] ADJ nursery *(avant n)*
NMF nurseryman, *f* nurserywoman

pépite [pepit] NF nugget; **p. d'or** gold nugget; **pépites de chocolat** chocolate chips

péplum [peplɔm] NM 1 *Antiq (vêtement de femme)* peplum 2 *(film)* (historical) epic

PEPS [peɔpeɛs] NM *Com & Compta (abrév* **premier entré, premier sorti**) FIFO

peps [pɛps] NM *Fam* energy□, get-up-and-go; **avoir du p.** to have plenty of get-up-and-go, to be full of life

pepsine [pɛpsin] NF *Biol & Chim* pepsin

peptide [pɛptid] NM *Biol & Chim* peptide

peptique [pɛptik] ADJ *Biol & Chim* peptic

peptone [pɛptɔn] NF *Biol & Chim* peptone

péquenaud, -e [pekno, -od], **péquenot, -otte** [pekno, -ɔt] NM,F *Fam Péj (rustre)* yokel, peasant, *Am* hick

péquin [pekɛ̃] = **pékin 2, 3**

péquiste [pekist] *Can* ADJ = of the Parti québécois
NMF *(membre)* member of the Parti québécois; *(partisan)* supporter of the Parti québécois

PER [peɔɛr] NM 1 *Banque (abrév* **plan d'épargne retraite**) retirement savings plan *or* scheme 2 *(abrév* **price/earnings ratio**) p/e ratio

perborate [pɛrbɔrat] NM *Chim* perborate

perçage [pɛrsaʒ] NM 1 *(d'un trou)* drilling, boring 2 *Tex* punching

percale [pɛrkal] NF percale

percaline [pɛrkalin] NF percaline

perçant, -e [pɛrsɑ̃, -ɑ̃t] ADJ 1 *(voix, cri)* piercing, shrill; *(regard)* piercing, sharp; **avoir une vue perçante** to have a sharp eye; **elle a des yeux perçants** she has a piercing gaze 2 *(froid)* **le froid était p.** it was bitterly cold

perce [pɛrs] NF 1 *(outil)* punch, drill, bore 2 *Mus* bore
• **en perce** ADV **mettre un tonneau en p.** to broach a barrel

percée [pɛrse] NF 1 *(ouverture ▸ gén)* opening; *(▸ dans un mur)* gap, breach; **ouvrir une p. dans un bois** to clear a path through a wood 2 *Sport* break; *Mil* breakthrough; **une p. à travers les lignes ennemies** a breakthrough into enemy lines; **faire une p.** to make a breakthrough, to break through 3 *Écon & Tech* breakthrough; **faire une p. dans un marché** to break into a market; *Mktg* **p. commerciale** market thrust; **p. technologique** technological breakthrough

percement [pɛrsəmɑ̃] NM *(d'une route)* building, opening; *(d'un tunnel)* driving; *(d'un canal)* cutting; *(d'une porte, d'une fenêtre)* opening

perce-muraille [pɛrsmyraj] *(pl* **perce-murailles**) NF *Bot* pellitory-of-the-wall

perce-neige [pɛrsənɛʒ] NF INV OU NM INV *Bot* snowdrop

perce-oreille [pɛrsɔrɛj] *(pl* **perce-oreilles**) NM *Entom* earwig

perce-pierre [pɛrsəpjɛr] *(pl* **perce-pierres**) NF *Bot (saxifrage)* saxifrage; *(criste-marine)* (rock) samphire

percepteur, -trice [pɛrsɛptœr, -tris] NM, F 1 *(receveur des impôts)* tax inspector, taxman 2 *Belg (receveur des postes)* postmaster, *f* postmistress

perceptibilité [pɛrsɛptibilite] NF perceptibility

perceptible [pɛrsɛptibl] ADJ 1 *(sensible)* perceptible; **p. à l'oreille** audible 2 *Jur & Fin* liable for collection *or* to be levied

perceptiblement [pɛrsɛptibləmɑ̃] ADV perceptibly

perceptif, -ive [pɛrsɛptif, -iv] ADJ perceptive

perception [pɛrsɛpsjɔ̃] NF 1 *(par les sens)* perception; *Mktg* **p. de marque** brand perception 2 *(notion)* perception, notion; **avoir une p. claire des problèmes** to be clearly aware of the problems 3 *Fin & Jur (encaissement ▸ gén)* collection, levying; *(▸ d'un impôt)* collection; *(lieu) Br* tax office, *Am* internal revenue office; **p. de dividende** receipt of a dividend; **p. douanière** collection of customs duties; **p. à la source** tax deduction at source

perceptive [pɛrsɛptiv] *voir* **perceptif**

perceptrice [pɛrsɛptris] *voir* **percepteur**

percer [16] [pɛrse] VT 1 *(trouer ▸ gén)* to pierce (through); *(▸ planche)* to drill (a hole) through; *(▸ mur)* to make a hole in; **la pointe a percé le ballon** the nail burst *or* pierced the balloon; **la malle était percée au fond** there was a hole in the bottom of the trunk; **mes chaussures sont percées** I've got holes in my shoes; **se faire p. les oreilles** to have one's ears pierced; **un bruit à vous p. les oreilles** *ou* **tympans** an ear-splitting noise; **p. le cœur/bras à qn d'un coup de couteau** to stab sb through the heart/in the arm
2 *(pratiquer ▸ trou)* to drill; *Constr (route)* to open, to build (**dans** through); *(tunnel)* to drive (**dans** through); *(canal)* to cut (**dans** through); **p. une porte dans un mur** to put a door in *or* into a wall
3 *(pénétrer avec difficulté)* to push through; **le soleil perça enfin le brouillard** at last the sun pierced through the fog; **ses yeux avaient du mal à p. l'obscurité** he/she had trouble making things out in the dark; **p. un mystère** to solve a mystery
4 *(déchirer)* to pierce, to tear, *Littéraire* to rend; **un cri perça le silence/la nuit** a scream rent the silence/night; **p. qn/qch à jour** to see right through sb/sth
5 *(sujet: bébé)* **p. ses dents** to be teething; **p. une dent** to cut a tooth *or* to have a tooth coming through
VI 1 *(poindre)* to come through; **des crocus percent sous la neige** crocuses are coming *or* pushing up through the snow; **le soleil perce enfin** the sun's finally broken through; **ses dents ont commencé à p.** his/her teeth have begun to come through
2 *(abcès)* to burst
3 *(filtrer)* to filter through, to emerge; **rien n'a percé de leur entrevue** nothing came out *or* emerged from their meeting; **il laissa p. son impatience/sa jalousie** he let his impatience/jealousy show
4 *(réussir)* to become famous; **commencer à p.** to be on the way up; **un jeune chanteur en train de p.** an up-and-coming young singer

perceur, -euse [pɛrsœr, -øz] NM,F *(personne)* driller; **p. de coffre-fort** safebreaker, safecracker
• **perceuse** NF *(machine-outil)* drill; **perceuse électrique (portative)** power *or* electric drill; **perceuse radiale/à percussion** radial/hammer drill

percevable [pɛrsəvabl] ADJ *Fin & Jur* liable to be levied *or* for collection

percevoir [52] [pɛrsəvwar] VT 1 *(vibration, sensation, chaleur)* to feel; **j'ai cru p. une nuance de mépris dans sa voix** I thought I detected a note of contempt in his/her voice; **je ne perçois pas la différence** I can't see the difference; **je commençais à p. la vérité** the truth was beginning to dawn on me; **être bien/mal perçu** *(personne)* to be well/badly thought of; *(produit)* to be well/badly perceived 2 *Fin (rente, intérêt)* to receive, to be paid; *(allocation, commission)* to receive; *(impôt)* to collect; **cotisations à p.** contributions still due

perchaude [pɛrʃod] NF *Can Ich* (yellow) perch

perche [pɛrʃ] NF 1 *(pièce de bois)* pole; *(tuteur)* stake; *Rail* coupling pole; *Sport* pole; *(de téléski)* T-bar; **p. à houblon** hop pole; *Fig* **jeter** *ou* **tendre la p. à qn** to throw sb a line, to give sb a helping hand; *Fig* **prendre** *ou* **saisir la p.** to take *or* to rise to the bait
2 *Cin & TV* boom
3 *Fam (personne)* **grande p.** beanpole
4 *Ich* perch

percher [3] [pɛrʃe] VI 1 *(oiseau)* to perch; *(poule)* to roost 2 *Fam (habiter)* to live□
VT *(placer)* to put; **pourquoi as-tu perché le bol sur l'étagère du haut?** why did you put the bowl on the top shelf?; *Fig* **une petite église perchée en haut de la colline** a little church perched on top of the hill
VPR **se percher** 1 *(oiseau)* to perch; *(poule)* to roost 2 *(monter)* to perch; **ils se sont perchés sur le balcon pour mieux voir** they perched on the balcony to get a better view

percheron [pɛrʃərɔ̃] NM *Zool* percheron

percheur, -euse [pɛrʃœr, -øz] ADJ *(oiseau)* perching

perchiste [pɛrʃist] NMF 1 *Sport* pole-vaulter 2 *Cin & TV* boom (operator), boom man

perchlorate [pɛrklɔrat] NM *Chim* perchlorate

perchlorique [pɛrklɔrik] ADJ *Chim* perchloric

perchman [pɛrʃman] NM boom (operator), boom man

perchoir [pɛrʃwar] NM **1** *(pour les oiseaux)* perch; *(pour la volaille)* roost **2** *Pol* = raised platform for the seat of the President of the French National Assembly; **obtenir le p.** to become President of the (French) National Assembly

perclus, -e [pɛrkly, -yz] ADJ crippled, paralysed; **être p. de rhumatismes** to be crippled with rheumatism; **être p. de douleur/terreur/timidité** to be paralysed with pain/fear/shyness

perçoir [pɛrswar] NM *(perceuse)* drill, borer; *(alêne)* awl; *(vrille)* gimlet; *(poinçon)* punch, punching machine

perçoit, perçoivent *etc voir* **percevoir**

percolateur [pɛrkɔlatœr] NM coffee (percolating) machine

perçu, -e [pɛrsy] PP *voir* **percevoir**

percussion [pɛrkysjɔ̃] NF *Méd, Mus & Tech* percussion; **fusil à p.** percussion gun

• **percussions** NFPL percussion ensemble; **aux percussions, Jack** on percussion, Jack

percussionniste [pɛrkysjɔnist] NMF percussionist

perçut *etc voir* **percevoir**

percutané, -e [pɛrkytane] ADJ *Méd* percutaneous

percutant, -e [pɛrkytɑ̃, -ɑ̃t] ADJ **1** *(gén)* percussion *(avant n)*; *Tech* percussive **2** *(argument, formule)* powerful, striking; *(style)* incisive; *(titre de journal)* hard-hitting

percuter [3] [pɛrkyte] VT **1** *(heurter)* to crash *or* to run into; **la moto a percuté le mur** the motorbike crashed into the wall **2** *Mil & Tech* to strike **3** *Méd* to percuss

VI **1** *Mil* to explode **2** *Fam (comprendre)* to catch on

• **percuter contre** VT IND **aller/venir p. contre** to crash into

percuteur [pɛrkytœr] NM **1** *Mil* firing pin, hammer **2** *Archéol* percussion tool

perdant, -e [pɛrdɑ̃, -ɑ̃t] ADJ losing; **être p.** *(gén)* to lose out; *(perdre de l'argent)* to be out of pocket; **partir p.** to start out with low expectations

NM,F loser; **être bon/mauvais p.** to be a good/bad loser

perdition [pɛrdisjɔ̃] NF *Rel* perdition

• **en perdition** ADJ **1** *Naut* in distress **2** *(en danger)* in trouble; **une entreprise en p.** a company in difficulties *or* in trouble

PERDRE [77] [pɛrdr]

VT	
• to lose **1–8**	• to waste **9**
• to ruin **10**	
VI	
• to lose **1, 2**	
VPR	
• to get lost **2, 3**	• to disappear **2, 4**
• to die out **5**	• to go to waste **6**

VT **1** *(égarer ▸ clefs, lunettes)* to lose, to mislay

2 *(laisser tomber)* **p. de l'eau/de l'huile** to leak water/oil; **des sacs de sable qui perdaient leur contenu** sandbags spilling their contents; **la brosse perd ses poils** the brush is losing *or* shedding its bristles; **il perd son pantalon** his trousers are coming down; **tu perds un gant!** you've dropped a glove!

3 *(laisser échapper)* to lose; **p. sa page** to lose one's page *or* place; *aussi Fig* **p. la trace de qn** to lose track of sb; *aussi Fig* **p. qn/qch de vue** to lose sight of sb/sth, to lose track of sb/sth; **je n'ai pas perdu un mot/une miette de leur entretien** I didn't miss a (single) word/scrap of their conversation; **ça ne sera pas perdu pour tout le monde, va!** somebody somewhere will be happy (about it)!; *Fam* **p. les pédales** *(ne plus comprendre)* to be completely lost◻; *(céder à la panique)* to lose one's head; *aussi Fig* **p. pied** to get out of one's depth

4 *(être privé de ▸ bien, faculté)* to lose; **p. sa place** *(dans une réunion)* to lose one's seat; **p. sa fortune au jeu** to lose one's fortune gambling, to gamble one's fortune away; **p. son emploi** *ou* **sa situation** *ou* **sa place** to lose one's job; **n'avoir rien à p.** to have nothing to lose; **p. la mémoire/l'appétit** to lose one's memory/appetite; **p. la parole** *(la voix)* to lose one's voice; *(dans une réunion)* to lose the floor; **p. un œil/ses dents** to lose an eye/one's teeth; **p. du sang/poids** to lose blood/weight; *Méd* **elle a perdu les eaux** her waters broke; **p. le contrôle de** to lose control of; **p. connaissance** to pass out, to faint; **p. le goût/sens de** to lose one's taste for/sense of; **p. espoir** to lose hope; **p. l'habitude de (faire)** to get out of the habit of (doing); **p. patience** to run out of *or* to lose patience; **p. (tous) ses moyens** to panic; **p. la raison** *ou* **la tête** to go mad; *Fam* **p. le nord** *ou* **la boule** to crack up, to go round the bend, *Br* to lose the plot; *Fam* **celui-là, il perd pas le nord!** he's certainly got his head screwed on!; **il en a perdu le boire et le manger** it worried him so much he lost his appetite; **j'y perds mon latin** I'm totally confused *or* baffled

5 *(avoir moins)* to lose; **les actions ont perdu de leur valeur** the shares have partially depreciated; **elle a beaucoup perdu de son anglais** she's forgotten a lot of her English

6 *(être délaissé par)* to lose; **tu vas p. tous tes amis si tu ne changes pas d'attitude** you'll lose all your friends if you don't change your attitude; *Fam* **un de perdu, dix de retrouvés** there's plenty more fish in the sea

7 *(par décès)* to lose; **il a perdu ses parents dans un accident** he lost his parents in an accident

8 *(contre quelqu'un)* to lose; *Sport (set)* to drop, to lose; **p. l'avantage** to lose the *or* one's advantage; **il a perdu la partie** *(dans un jeu)* he lost the game; **p. du terrain** to lose ground

9 *(gâcher ▸ temps, argent)* to waste; **j'ai perdu ma journée** I've wasted the day; **comme ça je n'aurai pas perdu ma journée!** that way my day won't have been wasted after all!

10 *(causer la ruine de)* to ruin (the reputation of); **c'est le jeu qui le perdra** gambling will be the ruin of him *or* his downfall; *Hum* **toi, c'est la curiosité qui te perdra!** you're far too inquisitive for your own good!

11 *(locution)* **tu ne perds rien pour attendre!** just (you) wait and see!

VI **1** *(dans un jeu, une compétition, une lutte etc)* to lose; **c'est le 35 qui est sorti, tu as perdu!** number 35 came up, you've lost!; **p. à la loterie/aux élections** to lose at the lottery/polls; **je vous le vends 100 euros mais j'y perds** I'm selling it to you for 100 euros but I'm losing (money) on it; **p. au change** to lose out (on a deal); *Fig* to lose out; *aussi Fig* **je n'ai pas perdu au change** I've come out of it quite well

2 *(en qualité, psychologiquement)* to lose (out); **ces vins blancs perdent à être conservés trop longtemps** these white wines don't improve with age; **on perd toujours à agir sans réfléchir** you're bound to be worse off if you act without thinking

VPR **se perdre 1** *(emploi réciproque)* **se p. de vue** to lose sight of each other

2 *(emploi passif) (crayon, foulard, clef)* to get lost, to disappear; **si on ne les range pas, ces lunettes vont se p.!** these glasses will get lost if they're not put away!; *Fam* **il y a des paires de claques qui se perdent** somebody needs a good slap

3 *(s'égarer ▸ personne)* to get lost, to lose one's way; *(▸ avion, bateau)* to get lost; **je me suis perdu** I got lost *or* couldn't find my way; **son regard se perdait dans le lointain** he/she had a faraway look in his/her eyes; **se p. dans les détails** to get bogged down in too much detail; **se p. dans ses calculs** to get one's calculations muddled up; **se p. en conjectures** to be lost in conjecture

4 *(disparaître)* to disappear, to become lost, to fade; **les sommets se perdaient dans la brume** the mountain tops were lost *or* shrouded in the mist; **se p. dans la nuit des temps** to be lost in the mists of time

5 *(devenir désuet)* to become lost, to die out; **ce sont des métiers qui se perdent** these trades are dying out

6 *(nourriture, récolte ▸ par pourrissement)* to rot; *(▸ par surabondance)* to go to waste

---

perdreau, -x [pɛrdro] NM **1** *Orn* young partridge **2** *Fam Arg crime (policier)* cop

perdrix [pɛrdri] NF *Orn* partridge; **p. des neiges** ptarmigan

perdu, -e [pɛrdy] PP *voir* **perdre**

ADJ **1** *(balle, coup)* stray; *(heure, moment)* spare; **à temps p.** in a spare moment

2 *(inutilisable ▸ emballage)* disposable; *(▸ verre)* non-returnable

3 *(condamné)* lost; **sans votre intervention, j'étais un homme p.** if you hadn't intervened, I'd have been finished *or* lost

4 *Littéraire (ruiné)* **c'est un homme p. de dettes** he's heavily in debt

5 *(désespéré)* lost; **il est complètement p. depuis la mort de sa mère** he's been completely lost since his mother died

6 *(gâché ▸ vêtement, chapeau)* ruined, spoiled; *(▸ nourriture)* spoiled

7 *(de mauvaise vie)* **femme perdue** loose woman

8 *(isolé ▸ coin, village)* lost, remote, godforsaken

NM,F *Fam* **comme un p.** *(courir)* hell for leather; *(crier)* like a mad thing

perdurer [3] [pɛrdyre] VI to continue (on), to endure, to last

père [pɛr] NM **1** *(géniteur)* father; **tu es un p. pour moi** you're like a father to me; **p. inconnu** *(sur fiche d'état civil)* father unknown; **John Smith p.** John Smith senior; **maintenant que je suis p. de famille** now that I've got a family; **être bon p. de famille** to be a (good) father *or* family man; **en bon p. de famille** carefully; **c'est un investissement de p. de famille** it's a rock-solid *or* copper-bottomed investment; **p. naturel** natural father; *Théât* **jouer les pères nobles** to play elderly noblemen; **p. nourricier** foster father; *Prov* **tel p., tel fils** like father, like son

2 *(innovateur)* father; **le p. de la psychanalyse** the father of psychoanalysis; **p. fondateur** founding father

3 *(homme, enfant) Fam* **tu as vu ce gros p., il peut à peine se remuer** look at that tub of lard *or* fat lump, he can barely move; *Fam* **mon petit p.** (my) little one *or* fellow; *Fam* **il pleure, pauvre petit p.!** he's crying, poor little thing!; **c'est un p. tranquille** he's a quiet sort; *Fam* **moi, je conduis en p. peinard** I like to drive nice and slowly; **le p. Fouettard** the Bogeyman; **le p. Durand** old Durand; **le p. Noël** Santa Claus, Father Christmas

4 *Rel* father; **le p. Lamotte** Father Lamotte; **merci, mon p.** thank you, Father; **il a fait ses études chez les pères** he was educated at a religious institution; **les Pères Blancs** the White Friars, the Carmelites; **le P. éternel** the Heavenly Father; **le P., le Fils et le Saint-Esprit** the Father, the Son and the Holy Ghost *or* Spirit; **notre P. qui êtes aux cieux** our Father who art in Heaven

5 *Zool* sire

• **pères** NMPL *Littéraire (aïeux)* forefathers, fathers

• **de père en fils** ADV **cette tradition s'est transmise de p. en fils** this tradition has been handed down from father to son

pérégrination [peregrinasjɔ̃] NF peregrination

péremption [perɑ̃psjɔ̃] NF *Jur* lapsing; **au bout de trois ans il y a p. et vous ne pouvez plus réclamer la dette** there is a strict time limit of three years on claims after which payment may not be demanded

péremptoire [perɑ̃ptwar] ADJ **1** *(impérieux ▸ ton)* peremptory **2** *(tranchant ▸ argument)* unanswerable

péremptoirement [perɑ̃ptwarmɑ̃] ADV peremptorily

pérenniser [3] [perenize] VT to perpetuate

pérennité [perenite] NF perenniality, lasting quality

péréquation [perekwasjɔ̃] NF *Admin, Écon (d'impôts, de salaires)* equalization; *Rail (de tarifs)* standardizing; *Can Admin* **fonds de p.** equalization fund

perestroïka [perestrɔika] NF perestroika

perfectibilité [pɛrfɛktibilite] NF *Littéraire* perfectibility

perfectible [pɛrfɛktibl] ADJ perfectible

perfectif, -ive [pɛrfɛktif, -iv] *Gram* ADJ perfective

NM perfective aspect

perfection [pɛrfɛksjɔ̃] NF 1 *(qualité)* perfection; **atteindre la p.** to achieve perfection 2 *(trésor)* gem, treasure
• **à la perfection** ADV to perfection, perfectly; **tout marche à la p.** things couldn't be better, everything's perfect

perfectionné, -e [pɛrfɛksjɔne] ADJ sophisticated

perfectionnement [pɛrfɛksjɔnmɑ̃] NM 1 *(d'un art, d'une technique)* perfecting; **notre but est le p. de nos techniques** our aim is to perfect our techniques 2 *(d'un objet matériel)* improvement 3 *(formation)* **stage/cours de p.** advanced course/classes

perfectionner [3] [pɛrfɛksjɔne] VT 1 *(amener au plus haut niveau)* to (make) perfect; **des techniques très perfectionnées** very sophisticated techniques 2 *(améliorer)* to improve (upon)
VPR **se perfectionner** to improve oneself; **il s'est beaucoup perfectionné en français** his French has improved considerably

perfectionnisme [pɛrfɛksjɔnism] NM perfectionism

perfectionniste [pɛrfɛksjɔnist] ADJ **être p.** to be a perfectionist
NMF perfectionist

perfective [pɛrfɛktiv] *voir* **perfectif**

Perfecto® [pɛrfɛkto] NM biker's jacket

perfide [pɛrfid] *Littéraire* ADJ *(personne, conseil)* perfidious, treacherous, faithless; **la p. Albion** perfidious Albion
NMF traitor

perfidement [pɛrfidmɑ̃] ADV *Littéraire* perfidiously, treacherously

perfidie [pɛrfidi] NF *Littéraire* 1 *(caractère)* perfidy, treacherousness 2 *(acte)* piece of treachery, perfidy; *(parole)* perfidious *or* treacherous remark

perforage [pɛrfɔraʒ] NM 1 *Métal* piercing
2 *(du cuir)* punching
3 *Ordinat* punching
4 *Méd* perforating
5 *Mines* drilling

perforant, -e [pɛrfɔrɑ̃, -ɑ̃t] ADJ 1 *(pointe, dispositif)* perforating 2 *(balle, obus)* armour-piercing 3 *Anat (artère)* perforating; *(nerf)* perforans

perforateur, -trice [pɛrfɔratœr, -tris] ADJ perforating
NM,F *Ordinat* punch-card operator
NM 1 *Méd* perforator 2 *(pour documents)* (hole) punch
• **perforatrice** NF 1 *Mines* rock drill 2 *Ordinat* card punch

perforation [pɛrfɔrasjɔ̃] NF 1 *(action)* piercing, perforating; *Ordinat* punching 2 *(trou ► dans du papier, du cuir)* perforation; *(► dans une pellicule)* sprocket hole; *Ordinat* punch (hole) 3 *Méd* perforation; **p. intestinale** perforation of the intestine

perforatrice [pɛrfɔratris] *voir* **perforateur**

perforer [3] [pɛrfɔre] VT 1 *(percer)* to perforate 2 *(titre de transport) & Ordinat* to punch 3 *Méd* to perforate

perforeuse [pɛrfɔrøz] NF *Ordinat* card punch, (key) punch

performance [pɛrfɔrmɑ̃s] NF 1 *(résultat)* result, performance; **moteur haute p.** high-performance engine; **il faut améliorer les performances de notre entreprise** we must improve our company's performance; **les performances de l'année dernière sur le marché japonais** last year's results on the Japanese market 2 *(réussite)* achievement; **elle donne une p. éblouissante dans le rôle d'Antigone** she gives a dazzling performance in the role of Antigone
• **performances** NFPL *(d'ordinateur, de voiture etc)* (overall) performance

performant, -e [pɛrfɔrmɑ̃, -ɑ̃t] ADJ *(machine, système)* high-performance; *(produit, entreprise)* competitive; *(résultats)* outstanding, impressive; *(investissement)* profitable, high-yield; **une voiture très performante** a high-performance car

perfuser [3] [pɛrfyze] VT *Méd* to put on a drip *or Am* an IV

perfusion [pɛrfyzjɔ̃] NF *Méd* drip, *Am* IV, *Spéc* perfusion; **être sous p.** to be on a drip *or Am* an IV; **p. saline** saline drip *or Am* IV

pergola [pɛrgɔla] NF pergola

péricarde [perikard] NM *Anat* pericardium

péricardite [perikardit] NF *Méd* pericarditis

péricliter [3] [periklite] VI to be on a downward slope, to be going downhill; **ses affaires périclitent dangereusement** his business is going downhill fast

péridot [perido] NM *Minér* peridot, chrysolite

péridural, -e, -aux, -ales [peridyral, -o] *Méd* ADJ epidural
• **péridurale** NF epidural; **accoucher sous péridurale** to give birth under an epidural

périf [perif] = **périph**

périgée [periʒe] NM perigee

périglaciaire [periglasjɛr] ADJ periglacial

périhélie [perieli] NM perihelion

péri-informatique [periɛ̃fɔrmatik] *(pl* **péri-informatiques)** ADJ **matériel p.** computer equipment
NF computer environment

péril [peril] NM 1 *(danger)* danger; **au p. de ma/leur/*etc* vie** at great risk to my/their/*etc* (own) life; *Littéraire* **se jeter dans le p.** to rush into peril; *Fig* **il n'y a pas p. en la demeure** it's not a matter of life and death 2 *(menace)* peril; *Péj* **le p. jaune** the yellow peril 3 *Naut* **les périls de la mer** the perils of the sea
• **en péril** ADJ *(monuments, animaux)* endangered; **être en p.** to be in danger *or* at risk ADV **mettre en p.** to endanger, to put at risk

périlleuse [perijøz] *voir* **périlleux**

périlleusement [perijøzmɑ̃] ADV perilously, dangerously

périlleux, -euse [perijø, -øz] ADJ perilous, hazardous, dangerous

périmé, -e [perime] ADJ 1 *(expiré)* out-of-date; **mon passeport est p.** my passport is no longer valid *or* has expired 2 *(aliment)* past its sell-by date 3 *(démodé)* outdated, outmoded; **vous défendez des principes périmés** you're defending outdated principles

périmer [3] [perime] **se périmer** VPR 1 *(expirer)* to expire; **laisser (se) p. un billet** to let a ticket go out of date; **laisser p. de la nourriture** to let food go off *or* bad 2 *Jur* to lapse 3 *(se démoder)* to become outdated *or* outmoded

périmètre [perimɛtr] NM 1 *(contour) & Géom* perimeter; *(surface)* area; **dans un vaste p.** over a vast area; **dans un p. de 50 kilomètres** within a 50-kilometre radius; **p. de sécurité** safety zone 2 *Jur* **p. sensible** ≃ green belt

périnatal, -e, -als *ou* **-aux, -ales** [perinatal, -o] ADJ *Méd* perinatal

périnatalogie [perinatalɔʒi] NF *Méd* perinatal paediatrics

périnée [perine] NM *Anat* perineum

période [perjɔd] NF 1 *(époque)* period, time; **traverser une p. difficile** to go through a difficult period *or* time; **la p. bleue de Picasso** Picasso's blue period; **c'était ma p. opéra** it was the time when I was keen on opera; **elle a eu sa p. jazz** she went through a jazz phase *or* period; **nous avons eu une longue p. de froid** we had a long spell of cold weather; **pendant la p. électorale** during election time; **pendant la p. des fêtes** at Christmas time; *Fin* **p. d'amortissement** depreciation period; *Fin* **p. comptable** financial period, accounting period, *Am* fiscal period; *UE* **p. de double circulation** *(de la monnaie nationale et de l'euro)* double circulation period; **p. d'essai (gratuit)** (free) trial period; **p. d'essor** boom; **p. de grâce** tax holiday; **p. de réflexion** cooling-off period; *Jur* **p. de sûreté** tariff (of imprisonment)
2 *Mil* **p. (d'exercice)** training
3 *Phys, Chim & Mus* period; *Math (d'une fonction)* period; *(d'une fraction)* repetend; **p. (radioactive)** half-life
4 *Transp* **p. bleue/blanche/rouge** = period during which tickets are cheapest/medium-priced/most expensive
5 *Gram* period, complete sentence
NM *Littéraire* **le plus haut p. (de la gloire/de l'éloquence)** the height *or* acme (of glory/of eloquence)
• **périodes** NFPL *Vieilli (règles)* period(s); **avoir ses périodes** to be having one's period
• **par périodes** ADV from time to time, every now and then, every so often

périodicité [perjɔdisite] NF frequency

périodique [perjɔdik] ADJ 1 *Chim, Phys, Psy & Mus* periodic; *Math (fonction)* periodic; *(fraction)* recurring 2 *(publication)* periodical 3 *Méd* recurring
NM periodical

périodiquement [perjɔdikmɑ̃] ADV 1 *Chim, Math & Phys* periodically 2 *(régulièrement)* periodically, every so often

périoste [perjɔst] NM *Anat* periosteum

péripatéticien, -enne [peripatetisjɛ̃, -ɛn] ADJ *Antiq* Peripatetic
NM,F *Antiq* Peripatetic, member of the Peripatetic school
• **péripatéticienne** NF *Littéraire ou Hum* streetwalker

péripétie [peripesi] NF 1 *(événement)* event, episode; *(aventure)* adventure; **une vie pleine de péripéties** an eventful life, a life rich in incident 2 *Littérature* peripeteia

périph [perif] NM *Fam (abrév* **boulevard périphérique)** **le p.** the Paris *Br* ring road *or Am* beltway

périphérie [periferi] NF 1 *(bord)* periphery; **sur la p. de la plaie** on the edges of the wound 2 *(faubourg)* outskirts; **à la p. des grandes villes** on the outskirts of cities

périphérique [periferik] ADJ 1 *(quartier)* outlying 2 *Physiol & Ordinat* peripheral
NM 1 *(boulevard) Br* ring road, *Am* beltway; **le p.** *(à Paris)* the Paris *Br* ring road *or Am* beltway 2 *Ordinat* peripheral; **p. d'entrée/de sortie** input/output device; **p. externe** external device

périphrase [perifraz] NF circumlocution, *Spéc* periphrasis

périphrastique [perifrastik] ADJ circumlocutory, *Spéc* periphrastic

périple [peripl] NM 1 *(voyage d'exploration)* voyage, expedition 2 *(voyage touristique)* tour, trip

périr [32] [perir] VI *Littéraire* 1 *(personne)* to perish; **péri en mer** lost at sea; **p. noyé** to drown, to be drowned; *Fig* **p. d'ennui** to die of boredom; **s'ennuyer à p.** to be bored to death 2 *(souvenir)* to perish; *(idéal, gloire, liberté)* to be destroyed, to perish; **son nom ne périra pas** his/her name will live (on)

périscolaire [periskɔlɛr] ADJ extracurricular

périscope [periskɔp] NM periscope

périscopique [periskɔpik] ADJ periscopic

périssabilité [perisabilite] NF perishability

périssable [perisabl] ADJ perishable

périssoire [periswar] NF canoe

péristaltique [peristaltik] ADJ *Physiol* peristaltic

péristaltisme [peristaltism] NM *Physiol* peristalsis

péristyle [peristil] NM peristyle

Péritel® [peritɛl] ADJ INV **prise P.** scart plug; *(qui reçoit)* scart socket

péritéléphonie [peritelefɔni] NF *Tech* peripheral telephone equipment

péritoine [peritwan] NM *Anat* peritoneum

péritonite [peritɔnit] NF *Méd* peritonitis

périurbain, -e [periyrbɛ̃, -ɛn] ADJ out-of-town

perle [pɛrl] NF 1 *(bijou)* pearl; **p. fine/de culture** natural/cultured pearl; **p. noire** black pearl; **c'est la p. de ma collection** it's the prize piece of my collection; *Fig* **jeter des perles aux pourceaux** to cast pearls before swine
2 *(bille)* bead; **perles de verre** glass beads
3 *(goutte)* drop; **des perles de sueur** beads of sweat; **des perles de rosée** dewdrops; **une p. de sang** a drop of blood
4 *(personne)* gem, treasure; **sa femme est une p.!** his wife is a real gem!; **c'est la p. des maris!** he's the perfect husband!
5 *Fam (bêtise)* howler
6 *très Fam (pet)* fart; **lâcher une p.** to fart
ADJ INV pearl, pearl-grey

perlé, -e [pɛrle] ADJ 1 *(nacré)* pearly, pearl *(avant n)*; **des dents perlées** pearly teeth

2 *(orné de perles)* beaded; **coton p.** *(mercerisé)* pearl *or* perlé cotton
3 *(orge)* pearl *(avant n)*; *(riz)* polished
4 *(rire, son)* rippling

perler **[3]** [pɛrle] VI to bead; **la sueur perlait sur son visage** beads of sweat stood out on his face
VT *Vieilli (travail)* to execute perfectly

perlier, -ère [pɛrlje, -ɛr] ADJ *(barque)* pearling; *(industrie)* pearl *(avant n)*

perlimpinpin [pɛrlɛ̃pɛ̃pɛ̃] NM *voir* **poudre**

perlingual, -e, -aux, -ales [pɛrlɛ̃gwal, -o] ADJ perlingual; **à prendre par voie perlinguale** *(dans mode d'emploi)* to be dissolved under the tongue

perlouse, perlouze [pɛrluz] NF **1** *Fam (perle)* pearl❑ **2** *Vulg (pet)* fart; **lâcher une p.** to fart, *Br* to let off, *Am* to lay one

perm [pɛrm] NF *Fam* **1** *Mil (abrév* **permission**) leave❑; **être en p.** to be on leave **2** *Scol (abrév* **permanence**) *(tranche horaire)* study period❑; *(salle)* study *Br* room *or Am* hall❑; **aller en p.** to go to the study *Br* room *or Am* hall

permanence [pɛrmanɑ̃s] NF **1** *(persistance ▸ gén)* permanence, lasting quality; *(▸ d'une tradition)* continuity
2 *(service de garde)* duty (period); **être de p.** to be on duty *or* call; **une p. est assurée à la mairie le mardi matin** council offices are open on Tuesday mornings; **p. téléphonique** answering service
3 *(local, bureau)* office
4 *Scol* study *Br* room *or Am* hall; **aller en p.** to go to the study *Br* room *or Am* hall; **avoir deux heures de p.** to have a two-hour study period
• **en permanence** ADV permanently

permanent, -e [pɛrmanɑ̃, -ɑ̃t] ADJ **1** *(constant)* permanent; **avec elle, ce sont des reproches permanents** she's forever nagging
2 *(fixe)* permanent; **avoir un emploi p.** to have a permanent job; **armée permanente** standing army
3 *Cin* continuous, non-stop; **cinéma p.** continuous showing
4 *Ordinat* permanent
NM,F *(d'un parti)* official; *(d'une entreprise)* salaried worker, worker on the payroll
• **permanente** NF perm; **se faire faire une permanente** to have a perm, to have one's hair permed

permanenter **[3]** [pɛrmanɑ̃te] VT to perm; **se faire p.** to have a perm, to have one's hair permed

permanganate [pɛrmɑ̃ganat] NM *Chim* permanganate

perméabilité [pɛrmeabilite] NF **1** *Géol & Phys* permeability **2** *(d'une personne)* susceptibility (**à** to)

perméable [pɛrmeabl] ADJ **1** *Géol & Phys* permeable (**à** to) **2** *(personne)* susceptible (**à** to)

PERMETTRE **[84]** [pɛrmɛtr] VT **1** *(sujet: personne)* to allow; *(sujet: chose)* to allow, to permit, to enable; **je ne permettrai aucun écart de conduite** I won't stand for *or* allow any misconduct; **p. à qn de faire qch, p. que qn fasse qch** to allow sb to do sth, to let sb do sth; **je ne vous permets pas de me parler sur ce ton** I won't have you speak to me in that tone of voice; **je ne te permets plus ce genre de commentaire** I won't take that sort of remark from you again; **il ne permettra pas qu'on insulte son frère** he won't allow his brother to be insulted; **le règlement permet de sortir à 5 heures** the regulations allow you to leave at 5; **le train à grande vitesse permettra d'y aller en moins de deux heures** the high-speed train will make it possible to get there in under two hours; **sa lettre permet toutes les craintes** his/her letter gives cause for concern; **votre mission ne permet pas d'erreur** your mission leaves no room for error; **si le temps/sa santé le permet** weather/(his/her) health permitting
2 *(tournure impersonnelle)* **c'est permis?** is it allowed *or* permitted?; **il n'est pas/il est permis de boire de l'alcool** drinking is not/is allowed *or* permitted; **autant qu'il est permis d'en juger** as far as it is possible to judge; **est-il permis d'être aussi mal élevé?** how can anyone be so rude?; *Fam* **elle est belle/insolente comme c'est pas permis** she's outrageously beautiful/cheeky
3 *(dans des formules de politesse)* **il reste un sandwich, vous permettez?** may I have the last sandwich?; **si vous me permettez l'expression** if I may be allowed to say so, if you don't mind my saying; **permettez-moi de ne pas partager votre avis** I beg to differ; **tu n'es pas sincère non plus, permets-moi de te le dire** and you're not being honest either, let me tell you; *Fam* **non, mais tu permets que j'en place une?** I'd like to get a word in, if you don't mind; *Littéraire* **permettez-moi de vous présenter mon frère** let me introduce *or* allow me to introduce my brother
VPR **se permettre 1** *(s'accorder)* to allow *or* to permit oneself; **je me suis permis un petit verre de vin** I allowed myself a small glass of wine
2 *(oser)* to dare; **elle se permettait n'importe quoi** she thought she could get away with anything; **si je peux me p., je ne pense pas que ce soit une bonne idée** if you don't mind my saying so, I don't think it's a very good idea
3 *(pouvoir payer)* to (be able to) afford; **pouvez-vous vous p. 1000 euros de plus?** can you afford 1,000 euros more?
4 **se p. de faire qch** to take the liberty of doing sth; **je me suis permis de vous apporter des fleurs** I took the liberty of bringing you some flowers; **je me permets de vous écrire au sujet de mon fils** I'm writing to you about my son

permis¹ [pɛrmi] NM permit, licence; **p. (de conduire)** *Br* driving licence, *Am* driver's license; **rater/réussir le p. (de conduire)** to fail/to pass one's (driving) test; **p. de conduire international** international driving licence; **p. de construire** building permit *or* licence, *Br* planning permission; **p. de chasse** *(à courre)* hunting permit; *(au fusil)* shooting licence; **p. de débarquement** landing permit; **p. de douane** customs permit; **p. d'embarquement** shipping note; **p. d'exportation** export permit *or* licence; **p. d'inhumer** burial certificate; **p. de port d'armes** firearms licence; **p. de séjour/travail** residence/work permit

permis², -e [pɛrmi, -iz] PP *voir* **permettre**

permissif, -ive [pɛrmisif, -iv] ADJ permissive

permission [pɛrmisjɔ̃] NF **1** *(autorisation)* permission, leave; **demander/accorder la p. de faire qch** to ask/to grant permission to do sth; **si tu veux inviter tes amis, tu as ma p.** you have my permission to invite your friends; **les enfants n'ont la p. de sortir qu'accompagnés** the children don't have permission *or* aren't allowed to go out unaccompanied; **avec votre p., je vais aller me coucher** if you don't mind, I'll go to bed **2** *Mil (congé)* leave, furlough; *(certificat)* pass; **être en p.** to be on leave *or* furlough; **avoir une p. de six jours** to have six days' leave

permissionnaire [pɛrmisjɔnɛr] NM man on leave

permissive [pɛrmisiv] *voir* **permissif**

permissivité [pɛrmisivite] NF permissiveness

permit *etc voir* **permettre**

permutabilité [pɛrmytabilite] NF permutability, interchangeability

permutable [pɛrmytabl] ADJ **1** *(interchangeable)* interchangeable **2** *Math* permutable

permutation [pɛrmytasjɔ̃] NF **1** *(transposition ▸ gén)* permutation; *(▸ de postes)* exchange of posts **2** *Math* permutation

permuter **[3]** [pɛrmyte] VT **1** *(intervertir ▸ gén)* to switch round, to permutate; *(▸ lettres, chiffres)* to switch round **2** *Math* to permute
VI *(changer de place, de poste)* **les deux équipes permutent** the two teams swap shifts; **p. avec** to swap with

pernicieuse [pɛrnisjøz] *voir* **pernicieux**

pernicieusement [pɛrnisjøzmɑ̃] ADV perniciously

pernicieux, -euse [pɛrnisjø, -øz] ADJ **1** *(néfaste)* noxious, injurious, *Sout* pernicious; **des insinuations pernicieuses** insidious suggestions **2** *Méd* pernicious

péroné [perɔne] NM fibula

péronnelle [perɔnɛl] NF scatterbrain

péroraison [perɔrɛzɔ̃] NF *(conclusion)* peroration

pérorer **[3]** [perɔre] VI *Péj (discourir)* to hold forth

Pérou [peru] NM **le P.** Peru; *Fam* **c'est pas le P.** it won't break the bank

peroxyde [pɛrɔksid] NM *Chim* peroxide

peroxydé [pɛrɔkside] ADJ peroxide; **une blonde peroxydée** a peroxide blonde

perpendiculaire [pɛrpɑ̃dikylɛr] ADJ **1** *(gén) & Math* perpendicular (**à** to) **2** *Archit* perpendicular
NF perpendicular; **tirer une p.** to drop *or* draw a perpendicular

perpendiculairement [pɛrpɑ̃dikylɛrmɑ̃] ADV perpendicularly; **p. à la rue** at right angles *or* perpendicular to the street

perpète [pɛrpɛt] NF *Fam Arg crime* **il a pris p.** he got life
• **à perpète** ADV *Fam* **1** *(loin ▸ habiter)* miles away, in the back of beyond; **il m'a envoyée à p.** he sent me miles away **2** *(très longtemps)* **jusqu'à p.** till Doomsday, forever **3** *(à vie)* **être condamné à p.** to get life

perpétration [pɛrpetrasjɔ̃] NF perpetration

perpétrer **[18]** [pɛrpetre] VT to commit, *Sout* to perpetrate

perpette [pɛrpɛt] = **perpète**

perpétuation [pɛrpetɥasjɔ̃] NF perpetuation

perpétuel, -elle [pɛrpetɥɛl] ADJ **1** *(éternel)* perpetual, everlasting; **être condamné à la prison perpétuelle** to be sentenced to life imprisonment; **un monde en p. devenir** a perpetually *or* an ever-changing world **2** *(constant)* perpetual, constant; **de perpétuels reproches** perpetual *or* constant reproaches **3** *(à vie ▸ secrétaire, membre)* permanent

perpétuellement [pɛrpetɥɛlmɑ̃] ADV forever, constantly, perpetually

perpétuer **[7]** [pɛrpetɥe] VT **1** *(tradition, préjugé)* to carry on **2** *(souvenir)* to perpetuate, to pass on
VPR **se perpétuer 1** *(personne)* to perpetuate one's name; **se p. dans sa musique** to live on through *or* in one's music **2** *(tradition)* to live on

perpétuité [pɛrpetɥite] NF *Littéraire* perpetuity; **la p. de l'espèce** the continuation of the species
• **à perpétuité** ADJ **1** *(condamnation)* life *(avant n)* **2** *(concession)* in perpetuity ADV **être condamné à p.** to be sentenced to life imprisonment

perplexe [pɛrplɛks] ADJ perplexed, puzzled; **laisser p.** to perplex, to puzzle; **sa remarque m'a laissé p.** his/her remark perplexed *or* puzzled me

perplexité [pɛrplɛksite] NF confusion, perplexity, puzzlement; **la p. se lisait sur son visage** you could see that he/she was confused; **être dans une profonde p.** to be in a state of great confusion; **être plongé dans la p.** to be perplexed *or* puzzled

perquisition [pɛrkizisjɔ̃] NF search; **procéder à** *ou* **faire une p. chez qn** to carry out *or* to make a search of sb's home; **p. domiciliaire** house search

perquisitionner **[3]** [pɛrkizisjɔne] VI *Jur* to carry out a search, to conduct a search; **p. chez** *ou* **au domicile de qn** to search sb's home, to carry out *or* to conduct a search of sb's home
VT *Jur* to search

perré [pere] NM *Constr (d'une route, d'une digue)* stone pitching *or* facing

perron [perɔ̃] NM steps *(outside a building)*

perroquet [perɔkɛ] NM **1** *Orn* parrot; **apprendre/répéter qch comme un p.** to learn/to repeat sth parrot-fashion; *Ich* **p. de mer** parrot fish **2** *Naut* topgallant (sail) **3** *(boisson)* pastis and mint cocktail

perruche [peryʃ] NF **1** *Orn* parakeet; **p. (ondulée)** budgerigar **2** *Fam (personne)* chatterbox **3** *Naut* mizzen topgallant sail

perruque [peryk] NF **1** *(postiche)* wig; *Hist* periwig, peruke **2** *Pêche* tangled line **3** *Fam (travail clandestin)* **faire de la p.** to work on the side❑ *(during office hours)*

perruquier [perykje] NM wigmaker

pers, -e¹ [pɛr, pɛrs] ADJ *Littéraire* seagreen, perse

persan, -e [pɛrsɑ̃, -an] ADJ Persian
NM **1** *(langue)* Persian **2** *Zool* Persian cat
• **Persan, -e** NM,F Persian

perse[2] [pers] ADJ Persian; **l'Empire p.** the Persian Empire
NM *(langue)* Persian; **moyen/vieux p.** Middle/Old Persian
NF *(tissu)* chintz
• **Perse** NMF Persian

persécuté, -e [persekyte] ADJ persecuted
NM,F **1** *(opprimé)* persecuted person **2** *Psy* persecution maniac

persécuter [3] [persekyte] VT **1** *(opprimer)* to persecute **2** *(harceler)* to torment; **se sentir persécuté** to feel persecuted

persécuteur, -trice [persekytœr, -tris] ADJ tormenting, *Sout* persecutory
NM,F persecutor

persécution [persekysjɔ̃] NF **1** *(oppression)* persecution; **être victime d'une p. religieuse** to suffer religious persecution **2** *(harcèlement)* harassment, harassing, tormenting **3** *Psy* **délire de p.** persecution complex; **manie de p.** persecution mania

persécutrice [persekytris] *voir* **persécuteur**

persévérance [perseverɑ̃s] NF perseverance, persistence

persévérant, -e [perseverɑ̃, -ɑ̃t] ADJ persevering, persistent, tenacious; **être p. (dans qch)** to be persevering *or* to persevere (in sth)

persévérer [18] [persevere] VI to persevere, to persist; **p. dans qch** to continue *or* to carry on doing sth; **si vous persévérez dans cette attitude de refus** if you continue with *or* keep up this negative attitude; *Littéraire* **p. à faire qch** to persevere in doing sth

persicaire [persiker] NF *Bot* persicaria, lady's thumb

persienne [persjen] NF shutter, Persian blind

persiflage [persiflaʒ] NM **1** *(attitude)* scoffing, jeering, mocking **2** *(propos)* taunts, scoffs, jeers

persifler [3] [persifle] VT *Littéraire* to scoff at, to jeer at, to deride

persifleur, -euse [persiflœr, -øz] ADJ *(moqueur)* scoffing, jeering, mocking
NM,F scoffer, mocker

persil [persi] NM parsley; **faux p.** fool's parsley

persillade [persijad] NF = sauce made from chopped parsley and garlic; **p. de bœuf** cold beef sautéd with "persillade"

persillé, -e [persije] ADJ **1** *(plat)* sprinkled with parsley **2** *(viande)* marbled **3 fromage p., fromage à pâte persillée** blue-veined cheese

persique [persik] ADJ *(de l'ancienne Perse)* (Ancient) Persian

persistance [persistɑ̃s] NF **1** *(d'un phénomène)* persistence; **p. rétinienne** persistence of vision **2** *(de quelqu'un ▸ dans le travail)* persistence, perseverance, tenacity; *(▸ dans le refus)* obstinacy, stubbornness, *Sout* obdurateness; **sa p. dans le mensonge** his/her persistent lying
• **avec persistance** ADV *(courageusement)* persistently; *(obstinément)* obstinately, stubbornly

persistant, -e [persistɑ̃, -ɑ̃t] ADJ **1** *(tenace)* persistent, lasting, enduring; **une odeur persistante** a persistent *or* lingering smell **2** *Bot* evergreen; **arbre à feuilles persistantes** evergreen (tree)

persister [3] [persiste] VI **1** *(durer)* to continue, to persist; **la chaleur persistera demain** the hot weather will continue for another day; **il persiste un doute/une interrogation** there remains a doubt/question **2** *(s'obstiner)* to persist; **il faut p.** you must persevere, you must keep at it; **p. à faire qch** to persist in doing sth; **je persiste à croire que tu avais tort** I still think you were wrong; **p. dans sa décision/son choix** to stick to one's decision/choice **3** *Jur* **persiste et signe** I certify the truth of the above; *Hum* **je persiste et signe!** I'm sticking to my guns!

perso [perso] *Fam* ADJ *(abrév* **personnel***)* personal□, private□
ADV *(abrév* **personnellement***)* **il joue trop p.** he hogs the ball too much

persona grata [personagrata] ADJ INV persona grata; **je ne suis plus p.** I'm now persona non grata

personnage [personaʒ] NM **1** *(de fiction)* character; *(dans un tableau)* figure; **un p. de roman/de théâtre** a character in a novel/in a play; **un p. de bande dessinée** a cartoon character; **jouer un p.** *Cin & Théât* to play *or* to act a part; *Fig* to act a part, to put on an act; **p. principal** main *or* leading character
2 *(individu)* character, individual; **sinistre p.** evil character; **grossier p.!** swine!
3 *(personnalité importante)* person of note, important figure, big name; **p. connu** *ou* **célèbre** celebrity; **grands personnages de l'État** state dignitaries; **les grands personnages de l'histoire** the great names of history
4 *(personne remarquable)* character; **ce Frédéric, c'est un p.!** that Frédéric's quite a character!
5 *(image publique)* (public) image, persona; **il s'est construit un p.** he's created an image for himself

personnalisation [personalizasjɔ̃] NF personalization; **la p. d'une tenue** giving an outfit a personal touch

personnaliser [3] [personalize] VT *(papier à lettres)* to personalize; *(voiture, crédit)* to customize; **nous devons p. l'accueil** we must welcome our guests/clients/*etc* in a more personal manner; **comment p. votre cuisine** how to give your kitchen a personal touch

personnalité [personalite] NF **1** *(caractère ▸ d'une personne)* personality, character; *(▸ d'une maison, d'une pièce etc)* character; **un homme sans aucune p.** a man with no personality (whatsoever); **c'est une forte p.** he/she has a strong personality **2** *(personne importante)* personality; **les personnalités du monde du spectacle** personalities *or* celebrities in the entertainment business; **les personnalités politiques** the key political figures **3** *Jur* **p. civile** *ou* **juridique** *ou* **morale** legal personality

personne[1] [pɛrsɔn] NF **1** *(individu)* person; **plusieurs personnes** several people *or Admin* persons; **toute p. intéressée peut** *ou* **les personnes intéressées peuvent me contacter** all those interested *or* all interested parties should contact me; **une p. de ta/sa connaissance** somebody you know/he/she knows; **20 euros par p.** 20 euros each *or* per person *or* a head; **une p. âgée** an elderly person; **les personnes âgées** the elderly; **grande p.** grown-up; **les grandes personnes** grown-ups
2 *(être humain)* **ce qui compte, c'est l'œuvre/le rang et non la p.** it's the work/the rank that matters and not the individual; **la p. humaine** the individual
3 *(femme)* lady; **une jeune p.** a young lady; **une petite p.** a little woman
4 *(corps)* **ma p.** myself; **ta p.** yourself; **sa p.** himself/herself; *Fam* **il s'occupe un peu trop de sa petite p.** he's a little too fond of number one; **ils s'en sont pris à la p. (même) du diplomate** they physically attacked the diplomat; **un attentat sur la p. du Président** an attempt on the President's life; **il trouva en la p. d'Élise une épouse et une inspiratrice** in Élise, he found both a wife and a muse; **en p.** in person; **venir en p.** to come in person; **j'y veillerai en p.** I'll see to it personally; **c'était lui? – en p.!** was it him? – none other!; **c'est la vindicte en p.** he's/she's vindictiveness itself *or* personified; **être bien (fait) de sa p.** to have a good figure
5 *Gram* person; **première/deuxième/troisième p.** first/second/third person; **à la première p. du singulier** in the first person singular
6 *Jur* **p. à charge** dependent; **p. juridique** juristic person; **p. morale** legal entity; **p. physique** natural person; **p. à charge** dependant
• **par personne interposée** ADV through *or* via a third party; **dis-le-lui par p. interposée** have a go-between tell him/her

personne[2] [pɛrsɔn] PRON INDÉFINI **1** *(avec un sens négatif)* no one, nobody; **qui me demande? – p.** who wants to see me? – nobody *or* no one; **p. n'a compris** nobody *or* no one understood; **p. ne peut rien y faire** nobody *or* no one can do anything about it; **p. ne vient jamais me voir** nobody *or* no one ever comes to see me; **que p. ne sorte!** nobody *or* no one leave (the room)!; **p. d'autre que toi** nobody *or* no one (else) but you; *Fam* **p. le sait** nobody knows□; *Fam* **p. en veut** nobody wants any□ **2** *(en fonction de complément)* anyone, anybody; **il n'y a p.** there's no one *or* nobody there, there isn't anyone *or* anybody there; **je ne vois p. que je connaisse** I can't see anyone *or* anybody I know; **je ne connais p. d'aussi gentil qu'elle** I don't know anyone *or* anybody as nice as her; **elle ne parle à p. d'autre** she doesn't speak to anyone *or* anybody else; **je n'y suis** *ou* **je ne suis là pour p.** if anyone *or* anybody calls, I'm not in; *Fam* **quand il s'agit de faire la vaisselle/de payer, il n'y a plus p.** when it's time to do the dishes/to pay, you can't see anyone *or* anybody for dust **3** *(avec un sens positif)* anyone, anybody; **je me demande si p. arrivera un jour à le convaincre** I wonder if anyone *or* anybody will ever manage to convince him; **je doute que p. s'en soit aperçu** I doubt whether anyone *or* anybody noticed; **si tu le montres jamais à p....** if you never show it to anyone *or* anybody...; **sortez avant que p. vous voie** leave before anyone *or* anybody sees you; **il est meilleur conseiller que p.** he's better at giving advice than anyone *or* anybody (else); **y a-t-il p. de plus rassurant que lui?** is there anyone *or* anybody more reassuring than him?; **c'est trop difficile pour laisser p. d'autre que lui s'en charger** it is too difficult to let anyone *or* anybody but him do it; **p. de blessé?** nobody *or* anybody injured?; **tu le sais mieux que p.** you know it better than anyone *or* anybody (else)

personnel[1] [pɛrsɔnɛl] NM *(d'une entreprise)* staff, workforce; *(d'un service)* staff, personnel; *Mil* personnel; **le p. est en grève** the staff is *or* are on strike; **faire partie du p.** to be on the staff; **un membre du p.** a member of staff; **avoir trop/manquer de p.** to be overstaffed/understaffed *or* short-staffed; **p. (de maison)** servants, (domestic) staff; **p. administratif** administrative staff; **p. de bureau** office staff, clerical staff; **p. de cabine** *(d'un avion)* flight personnel, cabin crew *or* staff; **p. dirigeant** managerial staff; **p. d'encadrement** supervisory personnel, management; **p. d'entretien** maintenance staff; **p. intérimaire** temporary staff; **p. navigant** flight personnel *or* staff *or* crew; **p. réduit** reduced *or* skeleton staff; **p. saisonnier** seasonal staff; **p. au sol** ground personnel *or* staff *or* crew; *Mktg* **p. de soutien commercial** sales support staff; **p. à temps partiel** part-time staff; **p. de vente** sales personnel; **p. volant** flight staff

personnel[2], **-elle** [pɛrsɔnɛl] ADJ **1** *(privé ▸ gén)* personal, individual; *(▸ titre de transport, laissez-passer)* non-transferable; **c'est un appel p.** *(n'intéressant pas le travail)* it's a personal call; *(confidentiel)* it's a rather private call; **avoir son hélicoptère p.** to have one's own *or* a private helicopter; **il mène une campagne personnelle contre la pollution** he's conducting a one-man campaign against pollution; *Pol* **le pouvoir p.** (absolute) personal power
2 *(original)* **très p.** highly personal *or Sout* idiosyncratic
3 *(joueur)* selfish
4 *Gram (pronom)* personal

personnellement [pɛrsɔnɛlmɑ̃] ADV personally; **je ne le connais pas p.** I don't know him personally; **p., je suis contre la peine de mort** I'm against the death penalty personally *or* myself

personnification [pɛrsɔnifikasjɔ̃] NF personification, embodiment; **ma mère est la p. de la patience** my mother is patience itself *or* is patience personified

personnifier [9] [pɛrsɔnifje] VT to personify, to be the embodiment of; **l'Oncle Sam personnifie les États-Unis** Uncle Sam personifies the United States; **il personnifie la prudence paysanne** he typifies the cautious nature of the peasant

perspectif, -ive[1] [pɛrspɛktif, -iv] ADJ *(plan, vue)* perspective

perspective[2] [pɛrspɛktiv] NF **1** *Beaux-Arts* perspective; **p. aérienne** aerial perspective; **manquer de p.** to be out of perspective
2 *(point de vue)* angle, viewpoint, standpoint; **dans une p. sociologique** from a sociological standpoint; **analysons maintenant ce texte sous une p. différente** let us now analyse this text from a different viewpoint
3 *(éventualité)* prospect, thought; **elle était très excitée à la p. de faire ce voyage** she was very excited at the prospect of going on the journey; **p. d'avenir** outlook, prospects

4 *(avenir)* (future) prospect, outlook; **perspectives commerciales** market prospects; **perspectives de croissance** prospects for growth; **ouvrir de nouvelles** *ou* **des perspectives (pour)** to open up new horizons (for)

5 *(vue)* view

• **en perspective** ADV **1** *Beaux-Arts* in perspective; **en p. accélérée** in trompe-l'œil perspective **2** *(en vue)* on the horizon, in sight; **pas de reprise du travail en p.** no return to work in sight

perspicace [pεrspikas] ADJ perceptive, *Sout* perspicacious

perspicacité [pεrspikasite] NF insight, perceptiveness, perspicacity; **d'une grande p.** of acute perspicacity

persuader [3] [pεrsɥade] VT **1** *(convaincre)* to persuade, to convince; **il ne se laissera pas p.** he won't be persuaded; **p. qn de qch** to persuade *or* convince sb of sth; **p. qn de faire qch** to persuade sb to do sth; **être persuadé** *(être convaincu)* to be convinced; **les jurés sont persuadés de sa sincérité** the jurors are convinced of his/her sincerity; **j'en suis persuadé** I'm convinced *or* sure of it; **je n'en suis pas persuadé** I'm not convinced (of it) **2** *Vieilli ou Littéraire (faire admettre)* **p. qch à qn** to persuade sb of sth, to make sb believe sth

VPR **se persuader se p. de** to convince oneself of, to become convinced of; **elle s'est persuadée qu'elle est trop grosse** she's convinced herself that she's too fat

persuasif, -ive [pεrsɥazif, -iv] ADJ persuasive

persuasion [pεrsɥazjɔ̃] NF persuasion; **avoir un grand pouvoir de p.** to have great powers of persuasion; **agir par la p.** to use persuasion

persuasive [pεrsɥaziv] *voir* **persuasif**

perte [pεrt] NF **1** *(décès)* loss

2 *(privation ▸ d'une faculté)* **p. de connaissance** fainting, blackout; **p. d'appétit** loss of appetite; **p. de mémoire** (memory) blank; **p. de la vue** loss of eyesight

3 *(disparition, destruction)* loss; **déclarer une p.** to report something lost; **ce n'est pas une grande** *ou* **grosse p.** it's no great loss; **avec pertes et fracas** unceremoniously

4 *(gaspillage)* waste; **quelle p. de temps!** what a waste of time!

5 *(réduction)* loss; **p. de chaleur** heat loss; **p. de charge** *(dans un tuyau)* pressure loss; **p. de poids** weight loss; **p. de compression/de vitesse** loss of compression/of engine speed; **en p. de vitesse** *(avion)* losing speed; *Fig* losing momentum; *Élec* **p. à la terre** earth *or Am* ground leakage

6 *Littéraire (ruine)* ruin, ruination; **courir** *ou* **aller (droit) à sa p.** to be on the road to ruin; **jurer la p. de qn** to vow to ruin sb

7 *Fin* loss, deficit; **travailler** *ou* **fonctionner à p.** to operate at a loss; **vendre qch à p.** to sell sth at a loss; **passer une p. par profits et pertes** to write off a loss; **subir de lourdes pertes** to suffer heavy losses; **l'entreprise a enregistré une p. de 2 millions** the company has chalked up losses of 2 million; **p. de bénéfice** loss of profit; **p. brute** gross loss; **p. en capitaux** capital loss; **p. de change** (foreign) exchange loss; **p. d'intérêts** loss of interest; **p. latente** unrealized loss; **p. nette** net loss; *Compta* **pertes et profits exceptionnels** extraordinary items; **p. sèche** dead loss; *Compta* **p. supportée** loss attributable; **p. totale** total loss; *Compta* **p. transférée** loss transferred

8 *(défaite)* loss; **très affecté par la p. de son procès** very upset at having lost his case; **la p. d'un set** *(au tennis)* the dropping of a set

• **pertes** NFPL **1** *Fin* losses, loss; **pertes et profits** profit and loss; **compte des pertes et profits** profit and loss account; *aussi Fig* **passer qch aux** *ou* **par pertes et profits** to write sth off (as a total loss); **pertes d'exploitation** operating loss **2** *Mil* losses; **les pertes ont été énormes** there were heavy losses, there was a heavy loss of life **3** *Méd* **pertes (blanches)** whites, (vaginal) discharge; **pertes de sang** metrorrhagia

• **à perte** ADV at a loss; **vendre qch à p.** to sell sth at a loss

• **à perte de vue** ADV **1** *(loin)* as far as the eye can see **2** *(longtemps)* endlessly, interminably, on and on

• **en pure perte** ADV for nothing, to no avail; **il a couru en pure p., il a quand même manqué son train** it was a waste of time *or* absolutely no use running, he missed the train all the same

pertinemment [pεrtinamɑ̃] ADV **1** *(à propos)* appropriately, pertinently, fittingly; **elle ajouta p. que...** she added, rather pertinently, that... **2** *(parfaitement)* **je sais p. que ce n'est pas vrai** I know perfectly well *or* for a fact that it's not true

pertinence [pεrtinɑ̃s] NF *(bien-fondé)* pertinence, relevance

pertinent, -e [pεrtinɑ̃, -ɑ̃t] ADJ *(propos)* pertinent, relevant

pertuis [pεrtɥi] NM **1** *Géog (détroit)* straits, channel; *(d'un fleuve)* narrows **2** *Naut* sluice

perturbant, -e [pεrtyrbɑ̃, -ɑ̃t] ADJ disturbing

perturbateur, -trice [pεrtyrbatœr, -tris] ADJ *(élève)* disruptive; *(agent, militant)* subversive

NM,F *(en classe)* troublemaker, rowdy element; *(agitateur)* troublemaker, subversive element

perturbation [pεrtyrbasjɔ̃] NF **1** *(désordre)* disturbance, disruption; **jeter** *ou* **semer la p. dans qch** to disrupt sth

2 *Astron* perturbation

3 *Météo* disturbance; **p. atmosphérique** (atmospheric) disturbance

4 *Tél & Rad* interference

perturber [3] [pεrtyrbe] VT **1** *(interrompre)* to disrupt; **p. le déroulement d'un match** to disrupt a match **2** *(déconcerter)* to disconcert **3** *(affecter)* to upset, to perturb; **la mort de son frère l'a profondément perturbé** he was deeply upset by his brother's death

péruvien, -enne [peryvjε̃, -εn] ADJ Peruvian

• **Péruvien, -enne** NM,F Peruvian

pervenche [pεrvɑ̃ʃ] NF **1** *Bot* periwinkle **2** *Fam (contractuelle)* *Br* (female) traffic warden□, *Am* meter maid□

ADJ INV **(bleu) p.** periwinkle blue

pervers, -e [pεrvεr, -εrs] ADJ **1** *(dépravé)* perverted; **avoir l'esprit p., être p.** to have a perverted *or* twisted mind **2** *Littéraire (malfaisant)* wicked **3** *(effet)* perverse

NM,F pervert; **p. (sexuel)** (sexual) pervert

> Il faut noter que l'adjectif anglais **perverse** signifie également **contrariant**.

perversion [pεrvεrsjɔ̃] NF **1** *Littéraire (corruption)* perversion, corruption **2** *Psy* perversion; **p. sexuelle** sexual perversion

perversité [pεrvεrsite] NF **1** *(caractère)* perversity **2** *(acte)* perverse act

perverti, -e [pεrvεrti] ADJ *(personne)* perverted

NM,F pervert

pervertir [32] [pεrvεrtir] VT **1** *(corrompre ▸ personne)* to pervert, to corrupt **2** *(déformer)* to pervert, to impair, to distort

VPR **se pervertir** to become perverted

pesage [pəzaʒ] NM **1** *(action de peser)* weighing **2** *Sport (vérification)* weigh-in; *(lieu ▸ pour les concurrents)* weighing room; *(▸ pour les spectateurs)* enclosure *(inside race courses)*

pesamment [pəzamɑ̃] ADV heavily; **marcher p.** to walk with a heavy step, to tread heavily; **descendre p. l'escalier** to thump down the stairs; **il s'éloigna p.** he lumbered off

pesant, -e [pəzɑ̃, -ɑ̃t] ADJ **1** *(lourd ▸ gén)* heavy; **marcher à pas pesants** *ou* **d'une démarche pesante** to tread heavily; **il descendit la colline d'un pas p.** he lumbered down the hill; **je me sens les jambes pesantes** my legs feel heavy

2 *(astreignant)* hard, heavy, demanding; **dix heures par jour, c'est trop p. pour elle** ten hours a day is too heavy *or* too much for her

3 *(grave)* heavy, weighty, *Littéraire* burdensome

4 *(trop orné ▸ architecture)* heavy, cumbersome

5 *(peu vivace ▸ esprit)* slow, sluggish

6 *(insupportable)* heavy; **l'ambiance chez eux est toujours pesante** it always feels very oppressive in their house

NM **valoir son p. d'or** to be worth one's weight in gold; *Fam Hum* **son histoire valait son p. de nougat!** that was some story he/she told!

pesanteur [pəzɑ̃tœr] NF **1** *Phys* gravity **2** *(lourdeur ▸ d'un objet)* heaviness, weightiness; *(▸ d'une démarche)* heaviness; *(▸ d'un style)* ponderousness; *(▸ de l'esprit)* slowness, sluggishness; **j'ai une p. d'estomac** there's something lying heavy on my stomach; **les pesanteurs administratives** cumbersome administrative procedures

PESC [peəεse] NF *UE (abrév* **politique étrangère et de sécurité commune***)* CFSP

pèse-alcool [pεzalkɔl] NM INV alcoholometer

pèse-bébé [pεzbebe] *(pl* **inv** *ou* **pèse-bébés)** NM (set of) baby scales

pesée [pəze] NF **1** *(avec une balance)* weighing; **faire la p. d'un paquet** to weigh a parcel

2 *(pression)* **exercer une p. sur qch** to push one's whole weight on sth

3 *Méd* weighing

4 *Sport* weigh-in; **passer à la p.** to (go to the) weigh-in

pèse-lait [pεzlε] NM INV galactometer, lactometer

pèse-lettre [pεzlεtr] *(pl* **inv** *ou* **pèse-lettres)** NM (set of) letter scales

pèse-personne [pεzpεrsɔn] *(pl* **inv** *ou* **pèse-personnes)** NM (set of) bathroom scales

peser [19] [pəze] VT **1** *(avec une balance)* to weigh; **p. qch dans sa main** to feel the weight of sth; **p. une livre de sucre par kilo de fruits** weigh out one pound of sugar per kilo of fruit

2 *Fam (valoir)* **un mec qui pèse 10 millions de dollars** a guy worth 10 million bucks

3 *(évaluer, choisir)* to weigh; **p. ses mots** to weigh *or* to choose one's words; **et je pèse mes mots!** and I'm not saying this lightly!; **p. le pour et le contre** to weigh (up) the pros and cons; **p. les risques** to weigh up the risk, to evaluate the risks; **tout bien pesé** all things considered, all in all

4 *Fig (entreprise)* to be worth; **cette entreprise pèse 20 millions de dollars** this company is worth 20 million dollars

VI **1** *(corps, objet ▸ avoir comme poids)* to weigh; *(▸ être lourd)* to be heavy; **combien pèses-tu/pèse le paquet?** how much do you/does the parcel weigh?; **la valise pesait 30 kilos** the suitcase weighed 30 kilos; *Fam* **ce truc-là pèse une tonne!** that thing weighs a ton!; *Sport* **il pèse 75 kilos** he weighs in at 165 pounds

2 *Fig (personne, opinion)* to weigh; **p. lourd** to weigh a lot; **il ne pèse pas lourd face à lui** he's no match for him; **mon avis ne pèse pas lourd** my opinion doesn't carry much weight *or* count for much; **la question d'argent a pesé très lourd dans mon choix** the question of money was a determining *or* major factor in my choice; **mes raisons ne pèsent pas lourd dans la balance** my arguments don't carry much weight *or* don't matter very much

3 p. sur *(faire pression sur ▸ sujet: masse, poids)* to press (heavily) on; **p. sur un levier** to lean on a lever; *Can Joual* **p. sur les gaz** to step on it, *Am* to hit the gas

4 p. sur *(accabler)* to weigh down, to be a strain on; **les responsabilités qui pèsent sur moi** the responsibilities I have to bear; **un lourd silence pesait sur l'assemblée** a heavy silence hung over the meeting; **une menace qui pèse sur nous** a threat that is hanging over us; **des présomptions pèsent sur elle** she's under suspicion; **ça me pèse sur l'estomac/la conscience** it's lying on my stomach/weighing on my conscience

5 p. sur *(influer sur)* to influence, to affect; **ces actes peuvent p. sur la décision du jury** these acts may influence the jury's decision

6 *Suisse* **p. sur** *(appuyer)* to press

7 p. à *(être pénible pour)* to weigh down *or* heavy on; **ton absence me pèse** I find your absence difficult to bear; **cette ambiance me pèse un peu** I'm finding this atmosphere a bit oppressive; **la solitude ne me pèse pas** being alone doesn't bother me

VPR **se peser 1** *(emploi réfléchi)* to weigh oneself **2** *(emploi passif)* to be weighed; **les mangues ne se pèsent pas** *(au magasin)* mangoes are not sold by weight

peseta [pezeta, peseta] NF *Anciennement* peseta

pèse-vin [pεzvε̃] NM INV oenometer

peso [pezo, peso] NM peso

peson [pəzɔ̃] NM balance

pessaire [pesεr] NM *Méd* pessary

pesse [pεs] NF *Bot* horsetail, *Spéc* equisetum; **p. d'eau** mare's-tail

pessimisme [pesimism] NM pessimism

pessimiste [pesimist] ADJ pessimistic
NMF pessimist

peste [pɛst] NF **1** *Méd* plague; **avoir la p., être atteint de la p.** to have the plague, to be stricken with the plague; **p. bubonique** bubonic plague; *Hist* **la Grande P., la P. noire** the Black Death; *Vét* **p. bovine** rinderpest, cattle plague; *Vét* **p. porcine** swine fever; **fuir qn comme la p.** to avoid sb like the plague; **je me méfie de lui comme de la p.** I don't trust him one little bit, I wouldn't trust him as far as I could throw him **2** *Fam (personne)* pest, pain; **petite p.** little devil, little pest **3** *Vieilli ou Littéraire* **(la) p. soit de toi!, (que) la p. t'étouffe!** a plague on you!
EXCLAM *Vieilli* good gracious!, heavens!

Il faut noter que le terme anglais **pest** est un faux ami. Il ne désigne jamais une maladie.

pester [3] [pɛste] VI **p. contre qn/qch** to complain *or* to moan about sb/sth; **je l'entends qui peste dans sa barbe** I can hear him cursing under his breath

pesticide [pɛstisid] ADJ pesticidal
NM pesticide

pestiféré, -e [pɛstifere] ADJ plague-stricken, plague-ridden
NM,F plague victim; *Fig* **traiter qn comme un p.** to treat sb like a pariah *or* a leper

pestilence [pɛstilɑ̃s] NF stench, foul smell

pestilentiel, -elle [pɛstilɑ̃sjɛl] ADJ foul, stinking, *Sout* pestilential

pet[1] [pɛ] NM *Fam* **1** *(vent)* fart; **lâcher un p.** to fart, to break wind; **ça ne vaut pas un p. de lapin** it's not worth a monkey's fart; **elle a toujours un p. de travers** there's always something wrong with her□; **il n'a pas un p. d'amour-propre** he doesn't have an ounce of self-respect **2** *(bagarre)* **il va y avoir du p.** there's going to be hell to pay **3 faire le p.** *(faire le guet)* to keep watch *or* a lookout□

pet[2] [pɛt] NM *Fam (coup brutal)* wallop, thump; *(trace de choc)* dent; **ma voiture a pris un p. sur le pare-chocs** my car took a thump on the bumper

pétage [petaʒ] NM *très Fam* **le patron nous a fait un p. de plombs quand il l'a su** the boss went totally ballistic *or* totally hit the *Br* roof *or Am* ceiling when he found out; **être au bord du p. de plombs** to be on the verge of cracking up

pétainiste [petenist] ADJ Pétainist; **ils étaient pétainistes** they were Pétain supporters
NMF Pétain supporter, Pétainist

pétale [petal] NM petal; **pétales de maïs** cornflakes

pétanque [petɑ̃k] NF (game of) pétanque

PÉTANQUE

Originally invented in the south of France, where it has become a local institution, this bowling game is equally popular with tourists. The game, which requires two teams and is played up to a score of thirteen points, is played outdoors on a flat sandy or earth surface. Each team consists of two to three players, each of whom has three steel "boules". Each player tosses or rolls their "boule" so that it ends up as near as possible to the "cochonnet" (a small wooden ball thrown from a distance of 6 to 10 metres), at the same time trying to hit the other team's "boules" so as to scatter them. Players take turns, and whoever ends up closest to the "cochonnet" when all balls are played, wins.

pétant, -e [petɑ̃, -ɑ̃t] ADJ *Fam* **à 3 heures pétantes** at 3 (o'clock) sharp *or* on the dot

Pétaouchnock [petauʃnɔk] NF *Fam* = imaginary distant place; **ils l'ont envoyé à P.** they sent him to some place in the back of beyond *or* to Timbuktu

pétaradant, -e [petaradɑ̃, -ɑ̃t] ADJ *Fam* putputting

pétarade [petarad] NF **1** *(d'un cheval)* (succession of) farts **2** *(d'un moteur)* backfiring, putputting; *(d'un feu d'artifice)* crackle, banging

pétarader [3] [petarade] VI **1** *(cheval)* to let off a succession of farts **2** *(feu d'artifice)* to crackle, bang; *(moteur)* to backfire, to put-put

pétard [petar] NM **1** *(explosif ▸ dans les fêtes)* firecracker, *Br* banger; **lancer** *ou* **tirer des pétards** to let off firecrackers; *Fig* **p. mouillé** damp squib
2 *Fam* **faire du p.** *(bruit)* to make a racket *or* a din; *(scandale)* to kick up a fuss, to cause a stink
3 *Fam (pistolet)* shooter, *Am* piece
4 *Fam (cigarette de cannabis)* joint
5 *Fam (postérieur)* butt, *Br* bum, *Am* fanny
• **en pétard** ADJ *Fam* **être en p.** *(en colère)* to be fuming *or* livid; **se mettre en p.** to go ballistic, to hit the *Br* roof *or Am* ceiling

pétasse [petas] NF *très Fam* **1** *(femme vulgaire)* slut, *Br* slapper, scrubber **2** *(prostituée)* whore, hooker **3** *(peur)* **avoir la p.** to be scared stiff

pétaudière [petodjɛr] NF *Fam (lieu)* shambles *(singulier)*; *Fig* disaster area; *(groupe)* motley crew

pet-de-nonne [pɛdnɔn] *(pl* **pets-de-nonne**), *Can* **pet-de-sœur** [pɛdsœr] *(pl* **pets-de-sœur**) NM doughnut

pété, -e [pete] ADJ *très Fam* **1** *(ivre)* shit-faced, wasted; *(drogué)* stoned, high **2** *(cassé)* broken□, bust

péter [18] [pete] *Fam* VI **1** *(faire un pet)* to fart; *très Fam* **il pète plus haut que son cul** *ou Can* **le trou** he thinks he's the bee's knees, he thinks he's all that; *très Fam* **p. dans la soie** to live in the lap of luxury; *très Fam* **envoyer qn p.** to tell sb where to go *or* where to get off
2 *(exploser)* to blow up; **la grenade lui a pété en pleine figure** the grenade blew up right in his/her face; **faire p. qch** *(bâtiment, voiture)* to blow sth up; *(pétards)* to set *or* let off sth; **si ça continue comme ça entre eux, ça va finir par p.** if things carry on the way they are between them, all hell will break loose; **il faut que ça pète (ou que ça dise pourquoi)** let's have it all out in the open
3 *(faire du bruit ▸ bois qui brûle)* to crack, to crackle; *(▸ bouchon)* to pop
4 *(casser ▸ corde, élastique)* to snap; **ma braguette a pété** my zip's bust; *Fig* **p. dans les mains de qn** *(projet, affaire)* to fall through
5 *très Fam* **tu vas la fermer? j'en ai rien à p. de tes histoires!** will you shut up? I don't give a *Br* monkey's *or Am* rat's ass about your nonsense
VT **1** *(casser)* to break□, to bust; **je crois que j'ai pété le magnétoscope** I think I've bust the *Br* video *or Am* VCR; *très Fam* **p. la gueule à qn** to smash sb's face in; **p. les plombs** *(se mettre en colère)* to go ballistic, to hit the *Br* roof *or Am* ceiling; *(craquer)* to crack up; **p. un câble** to crack up; *Can* **p. la cerise** to pop one's cherry
2 *(être plein de)* **p. la santé** to be bursting with health; **p. le feu** *ou* **des flammes** to be bursting with energy, to be full of beans; *Can très Fam* **p. de la broue** to show off□
3 la p. *(avoir très faim)* to be starving *or* ravenous
4 *Belg (recaler ▸ candidat)* to fail□, *Am* to flunk; **il a été pété** he failed *or Am* flunked his exam
VPR **se péter 1 attention, ça va se p.!** watch out, it's going to break!□ **2** *(se casser)* to break; **se p. le poignet/la cheville** to break one's wrist/ankle□ **3** *(locutions)* **se p. la gueule** *très Fam (tomber)* to fall flat on one's face; *(en voiture)* to get smashed up; *Vulg (s'enivrer)* to get shit-faced *or* pissed; *Can* **se p. les bretelles** to brag□, to be full of oneself□; **se la p.** to show off□

pète-sec [pɛtsɛk] *Fam* ADJ INV curt□, snippy
NMF INV curt□ *or* snippy person

péteux, -euse [petø, -øz] *Fam* ADJ **1** *(lâche)* chicken, yellow-bellied **2** *(prétentieux)* stuck-up, snooty
NM,F **1** *(lâche)* chicken; **tu n'es qu'un petit p.!** you're just chicken! **2** *(prétentieux)* upstart; **quel petit p.!** he's so full of himself!

pétillant, -e [petijɑ̃, -ɑ̃t] ADJ **1** *(effervescent ▸ eau, vin)* sparkling, fizzy **2** *(brillant)* **avoir le regard p.** to have a twinkle in one's eye
NM sparkling wine

pétillement [petijmɑ̃] NM **1** *(crépitement)* crackling, crackle **2** *(effervescence)* bubbling, sparkling **3** *(vivacité)* sparkle; **le p. de son regard** the sparkle in his/her eyes

pétiller [3] [petije] VI **1** *(crépiter)* to crackle **2** *(faire des bulles)* to bubble, to fizz **3** *(briller)* to sparkle; **p. d'esprit** to sparkle with wit; **un regard qui pétille de joie/d'intelligence** a look that sparkles with joy/with intelligence

pétiole [pesjɔl] NM *Bot* leafstalk, *Spéc* petiole

petiot, -e [pətjo, -ɔt] *Fam* ADJ tiny, teenyweeny
NM,F (little) kiddy, tiny tot; **ma petiote** my little girl

PETIT, -E [p(ə)ti, -it]

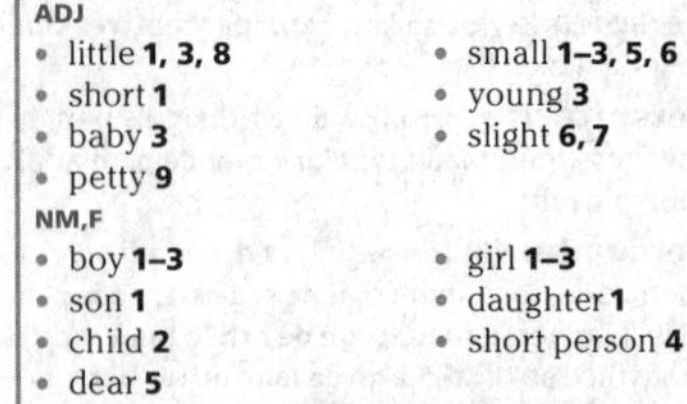

ADJ
• little **1, 3, 8** • small **1–3, 5, 6**
• short **1** • young **3**
• baby **3** • slight **6, 7**
• petty **9**
NM,F
• boy **1–3** • girl **1–3**
• son **1** • daughter **1**
• child **2** • short person **4**
• dear **5**

ADJ **1** *(en hauteur, en largeur)* small, little; *(en longueur)* little, small, short; **une personne de petite taille** a small *or* short person; **un p. gros** a tubby little man; **une petite femme sèche** a skinny little woman; **un homme p. et malingre** a short puny man; **il y a un p. mur entre les deux jardins** there's a low *or* small wall between the two gardens; *Fam* **une toute petite bonne femme** *(femme)* a tiny little woman; *(fillette)* a tiny little girl; **de petites jambes grassouillettes** *(de bébé)* little fat legs; *(d'adulte)* short fat legs; **petite distance** short distance; **à petite distance on voyait une chaumière** a cottage could be seen a short way *or* distance away; **la corde est un peu trop petite** the rope is a bit too short; **elle a de petits pieds** she's got small *or* little feet; **un p. "a"** a small "a"; **je voudrais ce tissu en petite largeur** I'd like that material in a narrow width; **un p. nuage** a small *or* little cloud; **un p. bout de papier** a scrap of paper; **une petite ossature** a small *or* frail bone structure; **une chambre assez petite** a smallish room; **une toute petite maison** a tiny little house; **acheter une petite tour Eiffel** to buy a miniature *or* model Eiffel Tower; **se faire tout p.** *(passer inaperçu)* to make oneself inconspicuous, to keep a low profile; **se faire tout p. devant qn** *(par respect ou timidité)* to humble oneself before sb; *(par poltronnerie)* to cower *or* to shrink before sb; **ça vaut un p. 12 sur 20** it's only worth 12 out of 20; **on y sera dans une petite heure** we'll be there in a bit less than *or* in just under an hour; **dans une petite huitaine** in a little less than a week; **je voudrais un p. kilo de rôti de bœuf** ≃ I'd like just under two pounds of beef for roasting; **il y a un p. kilomètre d'ici à la ferme** ≃ it's no more than *or* just under three quarters of a mile from here to the farm; *Can* **p. suisse** chipmunk
2 *(faible)* small; **petite averse** small *or* light shower; **expédition/émission à p. budget** low-budget expedition/programme; **p. loyer** low *or* moderate rent; **petite retraite/rente** small pension/annuity; **avec un p. effectif** with small numbers (of people)
3 *(jeune ▸ personne)* small, little; *(▸ plante)* young, baby *(avant n)*; *(plus jeune)* little, younger; **quand j'étais p.** when I was little; **je ne suis plus une petite fille!** I'm not a little girl any more!; **les petits Français** French children; **une petite Chinoise** a young *or* little Chinese girl; **il est encore trop p.** he's still too small *or* young; **un p. chien** a puppy; **un p. chat** a kitten; **un p. lion/léopard** a lion/leopard cub; **un p. mouton** a lamb; **un p. éléphant** a baby elephant, an elephant calf
4 *(bref, court)* short, brief; **p. entracte** short *or* brief interval; **petite phrase** *(énoncé)* soundbite; **un p. séjour** a short *or* brief stay; **si on lui faisait une petite visite?** shall we pop in to see him/her?; **elle est partie faire un p. tour en ville** she's gone off for a little walk round the town; **donnez-moi un p. délai** give me a little more time; **un p. répit** a short breathing space
5 *(dans une hiérarchie)* **petite entreprise** small company; **les petites et moyennes entreprises** small and medium-sized businesses; **les petites et moyennes entreprises industrielles** small industrial firms, SMIs; **petite association** small association; **p. commerçant** small trader, shopkeeper; **les petits commerçants** (owners of) small businesses; **le p. commerce** the small retail trade; **la**

petite délinquance petty crime; **la petite industrie** small industry; **les petits agriculteurs/propriétaires** small farmers/landowners; **p. fonctionnaire** minor *or Péj* petty official; **p. peintre/poète** minor painter/poet; **les petits salaires** *(sommes)* low salaries, small wages; *(employés)* low-paid workers; *Com* **p. porteur** small investor *or* shareholder; **il s'est trouvé un p. emploi au service exportation** he found a minor post in the export department

6 *(minime)* small, slight, minor; *(insignifiant)* small, slight; **p. changement** small *or* slight *or* minor change; **une petite touche de peinture** a slight touch of paint; **ce n'est qu'un p. détail** it's just a minor detail; **dans les plus petits détails** down to the last detail; **il y a de petits avantages** there are a few small advantages; **une petite intervention chirurgicale** minor surgery, a small *or* minor operation; **il a fallu lui faire de petites réparations** it had to undergo minor repairs; **un p. malentendu** a small *or* slight misunderstanding; **il y a un p. défaut** there's a slight *or* small *or* minor defect; **j'ai un p. ennui** I've got a bit of a problem; **j'ai eu un p. rhume** I had a bit of a cold *or* a slight cold; **de petites erreurs** small *or* slight mistakes; **j'ai eu une petite peur** I was somewhat frightened, I had a bit of a fright

7 *(léger)* slight; **un p. sourire** a hint of a smile; **un p. soupir** a little sigh; **elle a un p. accent** she's got a slight accent; **... dit-elle d'une petite voix** ... she said in a faint voice; **petite montée** gentle slope; **petite brise** gentle breeze; **ça a un p. goût** it tastes a bit strange; **ça a un p. goût d'orange** it tastes slightly of orange

8 *(avec une valeur affective)* little; **mon p. mignon** (my) little darling; *Fam* **alors, la petite mère, ça va?** all right, *Br* missus *or Am* little lady?; **elle a ses petits préférés** she's got her little favourites; **j'ai trouvé une petite couturière** I've found a very good little seamstress; **il ne faut pas changer ses petites habitudes!** you shouldn't try to change his/her little ways!; **je me suis octroyé un p. congé** I allowed myself a little bit of time off; **fais-moi une petite place** make a little space for me, give me a (little) *or* tiny bit of room; **il aimait faire son p. poker le soir** he was fond of a game of poker in the evening; **elle portait toujours sa petite robe noire en scène** she always wore her little black dress on stage; **tu mets ton p. ensemble?** will you be wearing that nice little suit?; **un p. roman distrayant** an entertaining little novel; **un p. vin sans prétention** an unpretentious little wine; **il y a un p. vent frais pas désagréable** there's a nice little breeze; **ma petite maman** *Br* Mummy, *Am* Mommy, my *Br* Mum *or Am* Mom; **alors, mon p. Paul, comment ça va?** *(dit par une femme)* how's life, Paul, dear?; *(dit par un homme plus âgé)* how's life, young Paul?; **tu mangeras bien une petite glace!** come on, have an ice cream!; **un p. pourboire aiderait à le convaincre** a small tip might persuade him; **je n'ai pas le temps de faire un match – juste un p.!** I've no time to play a match – come on, just a quick one!; **p. débrouillard!** you're smart!, you don't miss a thing!; *Euph* **c'est une petite surprise** it's quite a surprise; **c'est tout de même une petite victoire** still, it's quite a victory; **c'est un p. événement** it's quite an event; **c'est un p. exploit!** it's quite an achievement!; **p. imbécile!** you idiot!; *très Fam* **p. con!** you *Br* arsehole *or Am* asshole!; **mon p. monsieur, je vous prie de changer de ton** look here, my (good) man, I'll thank you not to use that tone with me; **j'en ai assez de ses petits mystères/petites manigances!** I'm fed up with his/her little mysteries/intrigues!

9 *Littéraire (mesquin)* mean, mean-spirited, petty; **il est p.** he's small-minded *or* petty; **il est avare, c'est le côté p. du personnage** he's a skinflint, that's the petty side of his personality; **comme c'est p., ce que vous avez fait là!** that was really mean!

10 *Bot* **petite bardane** lesser burdock; **petite camomille** wild camomile

NM,F 1 *(fils)* little son *or* boy; *(fille)* little daughter *or* girl; **c'est le p. de Monique** it's Monique's son; *Fam* **c'est la petite d'en face** it's the girl from across the street, it's the daughter of the people across the street; **elle va à la même école que le p. (des) Verneuil** she goes to the same school as the Verneuil boy

2 *(enfant)* little *or* small child, little *or* small boy, *f* girl; **quant aux petits, nous les emmènerons au zoo** as for the younger children, we'll take them to the zoo; **la cour des petits** *(garçons ou filles)* the younger children's *or Br* junior playground; **la cour des petites** the younger girls' *or Br* junior playground; **c'est un livre qui fera les délices des petits comme des grands** this book will delight young and old (alike); **tu veux de la pâte à modeler? – c'est pour les petits!** do you want some Plasticine? – that's for children!

3 *Fam (adolescent)* (young) boy, *f* girl; **le p./la petite de la boulangerie** *(employé)* the boy/the girl who works at the baker's

4 *(adulte de petite taille)* short person; *Fam Hum* **alors, le p., tu viens?** coming, shorty?

5 *(avec une valeur affective ▸ à un jeune)* dear; *(▸ à un bébé)* little one; **attention petite, ça brûle!** careful, dear *or* darling, it's boiling hot!; **mon p.** darling; **mon p., je suis fier de toi** *(à un garçon)* young man, I'm proud of you; *(à une fille)* young lady, I'm proud of you; **viens, mon tout p.** come here (my) little one; **ça, ma petite, vous ne l'emporterez pas au paradis!** you'll never get away with it, my dear!; **pauvre p., il a perdu sa mère** the poor little thing's lost his mother; **la pauvre petite, comment va-t-elle faire?** poor thing, however will she manage?

NM 1 *(animal)* baby; **ses petits** *(gén)* her young; *(chatte)* her kittens; *(chienne)* her puppies; *(tigresse, louve)* her cubs; **l'éléphante protège son p.** the elephant cow protects her calf *or* baby; **quand les petits sortent de l'œuf** when the fledglings *or* baby birds hatch out; **faire des petits** *(chienne)* to have pups; *(chatte)* to have kittens; *Fam* **mes économies ont fait des petits** my savings have grown; *Can Fam Fig* **faire ses petits** to pack (up)▫

2 *(dans une hiérarchie)* **c'est toujours les petits qui doivent payer** it's always the little man who's got to pay; **dans la course aux marchés, les petits sont piétinés** in the race to gain markets, small firms *or* businesses get trampled underfoot

3 *(carte au tarot)* lowest trump card

ADV 1 *Com* **c'est un 38 mais ce modèle chausse/taille p.** it says 38 but this style *Br* is a small fitting *or Am* runs small

2 *(juste)* **voir/prévoir p.** to see/to plan things on a small scale; **un seul gâteau, tu as vu p.!** only one cake, you're cutting it fine *or* that's stretching it a bit!

• **en petit ADV** *(en petits caractères)* in small characters *or* letters; *(en miniature)* in miniature; **un univers en tout p.** a miniature universe; **je voudrais cette jupe (mais) en plus p.** I'd like this skirt (but) in a smaller size

• **en petite ADV** *Can Aut* in low gear

• **petit à petit ADV** little by little, gradually

petit-beurre [p(ə)tibœr] (*pl* **petits-beurre**) **NM** petit beurre, butter *Br* biscuit *or Am* cookie, *Br* ≃ rich tea biscuit

petit-bourgeois, petite-bourgeoise [p(ə)tiburʒwa, p(ə)titburʒwaz] (*mpl* **petits-bourgeois**, *fpl* **petites-bourgeoises**) **ADJ** lower-middle class, petit bourgeois

NM,F member of the lower-middle class; **les petits-bourgeois** the lower-middle class, the petty bourgeoisie

petit-déj' [p(ə)tideʒ] (*pl* **petits-déj'**) **NM** *Fam* breakfast▫, *Br* brekkie

petit déjeuner [p(ə)tideʒœne] (*pl* **petits déjeuners**) **NM** breakfast

petit-déjeuner [5] [p(ə)tideʒœne] **VI** *Fam* to have breakfast▫

petite-fille [p(ə)titfij] (*pl* **petites-filles**) **NF** granddaughter

petitement [pətitmɑ̃] **ADV 1** *(modestement)* humbly; **être p. logé** to live in cramped accommodation **2** *(mesquinement)* pettily, meanly; **agir p.** to behave pettily

petite-nièce [p(ə)titnjɛs] (*pl* **petites-nièces**) **NF** great-niece

petitesse [pətitɛs] **NF 1** *(taille ▸ d'un objet)* smallness, small size; *(▸ d'une somme, d'un revenu)* paltriness **2** *(caractère mesquin)* pettiness, meanness; **p. d'esprit** narrow-mindedness **3** *(acte mesquin)* petty act, mean-spirited action

petit-fils [p(ə)tifis] (*pl* **petits-fils**) **NM** grandson

petit-gris [p(ə)tigri] (*pl* **petits-gris**) **NM 1** *(escargot)* garden snail; *Culin* petit-gris **2** *(écureuil)* Siberian grey squirrel; *(fourrure)* squirrel fur

pétition [petisjɔ̃] **NF 1** *(texte)* petition; **adresser une p. à qn** to petition sb; **faire une p.** to organize a petition **2** *Phil* **p. de principe** petitio principii; **vous partez d'une p. de principe** you're assuming that what we're trying to prove is true, you're begging the question

pétitionnaire [petisjɔnɛr] **NMF** petitioner

pétitionner [3] [petisjɔne] **VI** to petition

petit-lait [p(ə)tilɛ] (*pl* **petits-laits**) **NM** whey; **ça se boit comme du p.** it goes down like water; *Fig* **boire du p.** to be lapping it up

petit-maître, petite-maîtresse [p(ə)timɛtr, p(ə)titmɛtrɛs] (*mpl* **petits-maîtres**, *fpl* **petites-maîtresses**) **NM,F** *Vieilli* dandy, fop, *f* young woman of fashion

petit-nègre [p(ə)tinɛgr] **NM** pidgin; *Péj* **ce n'est pas du français, c'est du p.** that isn't French, it's gibberish

petit-neveu [p(ə)tinəvø] (*pl* **petits-neveux**) **NM** great-nephew

petits-enfants [pətizɑ̃fɑ̃] **NMPL** grandchildren

petit-suisse [p(ə)tisɥis] (*pl* **petits-suisses**) **NM** petit suisse, = thick fromage frais sold in small individual portions

pétochard, -e [petɔʃar, -ard] *Fam* **ADJ** *(peureux)* chicken

NM,F *(personne peureuse)* chicken

pétoche [petɔʃ] **NF** *Fam* fear▫; **avoir la p.** to be scared stiff *or* witless; **filer** *ou* **flanquer la p. à qn** to scare the living daylights out of sb

pétocher [3] [petɔʃe] **VI** *Fam* to be scared stiff *or* witless

pétoire [petwar] **NF 1** *(sarbacane)* peashooter **2** *Fam Hum (arme à feu)* old rifle▫

pétole [petɔl] **NF** *Suisse (crotte)* goat shit

peton [pətɔ̃] **NM** *Fam* foot▫, *Br* plate, *Am* dog

pétoncle [petɔ̃kl] **NM** (pilgrim) scallop

pétouiller [3] [petuje] **VI** *Suisse* to loaf about

Pétrarque [petrark] **NPR** Petrarch

pétrel [petrɛl] **NM** *Orn* petrel

pétrifiant, -e [petrifjɑ̃, -ɑ̃t] **ADJ 1** *Littéraire (ahurissant)* stunning, stupefying **2** *Géol* petrifactive

pétrification [petrifikasjɔ̃] **NF** petrification, petrifaction; *Fig (du cœur)* hardening; *(de l'esprit)* sclerosis

pétrifier [9] [petrifje] **VT 1** *(abasourdir)* to petrify, to transfix; **être pétrifié de terreur** to be petrified **2** *Géol* to petrify **3** *(couvrir de calcaire)* to encrust with lime

VPR se pétrifier 1 *(se figer)* **son visage se pétrifia** his/her face froze **2** *Géol* to petrify, to become petrified **3** *Fig* **son esprit se pétrifiait** he/she was developing sclerosis of the mind

pétrin [petrɛ̃] **NM 1** *(à pain)* kneading trough; **p. mécanique** dough mixer, kneading machine **2** *Fam (embarras)* jam, fix; **être dans le p.** to be in a fix *or* a mess; **se fourrer dans un beau** *ou* **sacré p.** to get into a real mess; **on s'est fourrés dans un beau p.!** we're right up the creek (without a paddle)!; **mettre qn dans un beau** *ou* **sacré p.** *Br* to land sb (right) in it, *Am* to land sb in a tough spot

pétrir [32] [petrir] **VT 1** *(malaxer)* to knead; **il lui pétrissait le bras** he was kneading his/her arm **2** *(façonner ▸ esprit, personne)* to mould, to shape **3** *(emplir)* **être pétri d'orgueil** to be filled with pride; **être pétri de préjugés** to be steeped in prejudice; **être pétri de contradictions** to be riddled with contradictions

pétrissage [petrisaʒ] **NM** kneading

pétrisseur, -euse [petrisœr, -øz] **NM,F** *(ouvrier)* **p.** dough mixer

• **pétrisseuse NF** *(machine)* kneading machine

pétrochimie [petrɔʃimi] **NF** petrochemistry

pétrochimique [petrɔʃimik] **ADJ** petrochemical

pétrochimiste [petrɔʃimist] **NMF** petrochemist

pétrodollar [petrɔdɔlar] **NM** petrodollar

pétrographie [petrɔgrafi] **NF** petrography

pétrole [petrɔl] **NM** oil, petroleum; **p. brut** crude (oil); **p. lampant** *Br* paraffin oil, *Am* kerosene; **p. vert** food (processing) industry

ADJ INV *(couleur)* **bleu p.** petrol blue

• **à pétrole** **ADJ** *(lampe, réchaud) Br* oil *(avant n)*, *Am* kerosene *(avant n)*

> Il faut noter que le terme anglais britannique **petrol** est un faux ami. Il signifie **essence**.

pétrolette [petrɔlet] **NF** *Fam Hum (cyclomoteur)* moped□

pétroleuse [petrɔløz] **NF 1** *Hist* female arsonist *(active during the Paris Commune)* **2** *Fam (militante)* militant female political activist□

pétrolier, -ère [petrɔlje, -ɛr] **ADJ** *(industrie, compagnie, choc)* oil *(avant n)*; *(pays)* oil-producing

NM 1 *(navire)* (oil) tanker **2** *(industriel)* oil tycoon **3** *(technicien)* petroleum *or* oil engineer

> Do not confuse with **pétrolifère**.

pétrolifère [petrɔlifɛr] **ADJ** oil-bearing

> Do not confuse with **pétrolier**.

pétromonarchie [petrɔmɔnarʃi] **NF** oil kingdom

pétulance [petylɑ̃s] **NF** exuberance, ebullience

pétulant, -e [petylɑ̃, -ɑ̃t] **ADJ** exuberant, ebullient

> Il faut noter que l'adjectif anglais **petulant** est un faux ami. Il signifie **irascible**.

pétunia [petynja] **NM** petunia

PEU [pø]

- little **A1, B1**
- not very **A2**
- few **B3**
- not much **A1**
- not long **B2**
- a bit, a little **C**

ADV A. *EMPLOYÉ SEUL* **1** *(modifiant un verbe)* little, not much; **il mange/parle p.** he doesn't eat/talk much; **je le connais p.** I don't know him well; **c'est p. le connaître** it just shows how little you know him; **il vient très p.** he comes very rarely, he very seldom comes; **on s'est très p. vus** we saw very little of each other; **j'ai trop p. confiance en elle** I don't trust her enough

2 *(modifiant un adjectif, un adverbe etc)* not very; **un livre p. intéressant** a rather dull book; **une avenue p. fréquentée** a quiet street; **l'affaire est p. rentable** the business isn't very profitable; **il vient p. souvent** he doesn't come very often; **l'alibi est fort p. crédible** the alibi is highly implausible; **p. avant** shortly *or* not long before; **p. après** soon after, shortly *or* not long after; **pas p.** not a little, more than a little; **je ne suis pas p. fier du résultat** I'm more than a little proud of the result

B. *EMPLOI NOMINAL* **1** *(indiquant la faible quantité)* **le p. que tu manges** the little you eat; **il vit de p.** he lives off very little; **il est mon aîné de p.** he's only slightly older than me; *Fam* **il a raté son examen de p.** he just failed his exam□, he failed his exam by a hair's breadth; **c'est p.** it's not much; *Littéraire* **hommes/gens de p.** worthless men/people; **c'est p. (que) de le dire, encore faut-il le faire!** that's easier said than done!; **c'est p. dire** that's an understatement, that's putting it mildly; **ce n'est pas p. dire!** and that's saying something!; *Fam* **très p. pour moi!** not on your life!

2 *(dans le temps)* **ils sont partis il y a p.** they left a short while ago, they haven't long left; **d'ici p.** very soon, before long; **vous aurez de mes nouvelles avant p.** you'll hear from me before long; **je travaille ici depuis p.** I've only been working here for a while, I haven't been working here long

3 *(quelques personnes)* a few (people); **tout le monde en parle, p. le connaissent** everybody's talking about him but few know him; **p. avaient compris** few (people) had understood; **nous étions p. à le croire** only a few of us believed it

C. *PRÉCÉDÉ DE "UN"* **1** *(modifiant un verbe)* **un p.** a little, a bit; **je le connais un p.** I know him a little *or* a bit; **reste un p. avec moi** stay with me for a while; **il ressemble un p. à David Beckham** he looks a bit *or* a little like David Beckham; **veux-tu manger un p.?** do you want something to eat?; **pousse-toi un (tout) petit p.** move up a (little) bit; **viens un p. par là** come here a minute; **pose-lui un p. la question, et tu verras!** just ask him/her and you'll see!; **fais voir un p....** let me have a look...; *Fam* **tu l'as vu? – un p.!** did you see it? – you bet I did *or* and how!; *Fam* **un p. que je vais lui dire ce que je pense!** I'll give him/her a piece of my mind, don't you worry (about that)!

2 *(modifiant un adjectif, un adverbe etc)* **un p.** a little, a bit; **il est un p. fatigué** he is a little *or* a bit tired; **je suis un p. pressée** I'm in a bit of a hurry; **votre devoir était un p. confus** your work was a little *or* a bit confused; **il est un p. poète** he's a bit of a poet; **un p. partout** just about *or* pretty much everywhere; **un p. plus de** *(suivi d'un nom comptable)* a few more; *(suivi d'un nom non comptable)* a little (bit) more; **un p. moins** a little *or* bit less; **un p. moins de** *(suivi d'un nom comptable)* slightly fewer, not so many; *(suivi d'un nom non comptable)* a little (bit) less; **un p. trop** a little *or* bit too (much); **il en fait vraiment un p. trop!** he's really making too much of it!; *Fam* **il est un p. bête, ce mec – un p. beaucoup!** the guy's a bit stupid – more than a bit!; *Fam* **tu as bu un p. beaucoup hier soir** you certainly had a few last night; *Fam* **un p.(, mon neveu)!** you bet!, sure thing!, *Br* too right!; *Fam* **elle est jolie – un p., oui!** she's pretty – just a bit!; *Fam* **il te reproche de lui avoir menti, c'est un (petit) p. ça, non?** he's blaming you for lying to him, isn't that it?□; *Fam* **un p. plus et l'évier débordait!** another minute and the sink would have overflowed!□; *Fam* **un p. plus et je me faisais écraser!** I was within an inch of being run over!; *Fam* **pas qu'un p.** more than a little

• **peu à peu** **ADV** little by little, bit by bit, gradually; **on s'habitue, p. à p.** you gradually get used to things

• **peu de** **DÉT 1** *(suivi d'un nom non comptable)* not much, little; *(suivi d'un nom comptable)* not many, few; **il a p. de travail** he doesn't have much work; **cela a p. d'importance** that is of little importance, that doesn't matter much; **je ne reste que p. de temps** I'm only staying for a short while, I'm not staying long; **p. de temps avant/après** not long before/after; **il y avait p. de neige** there wasn't much snow; **il reste p. de jours** there are only a few days left; **en p. de mots** in a few words; **p. d'écrivains ont abordé cette question** few writers have dealt with this question; **on est p. de chose** what an insignificant thing man is; **ne me remerciez pas, c'est vraiment p. de chose** don't thank me, it's really nothing

2 *(avec un déterminant)* **le p. de** *(suivi d'un nom comptable)* the *or* what few; *(suivi d'un nom non comptable)* the *or* what little; **le p. de connaissances que j'ai** the *or* what few acquaintances I have; **le p. de fois où je l'ai vu** on the few *or* rare occasions when I've seen him; **le p. d'expérience que j'avais** what little experience I had; **son p. d'enthousiasme** his/her lack of enthusiasm; **avec mon p. de moyens** with my limited means

• **peu ou prou** **ADV** *Littéraire* more or less

• **pour peu que** **CONJ** **pour p. qu'il le veuille, il réussira** if he wants to, he'll succeed; **pour p. qu'elle ait compris...** if she's got the message...

• **pour un peu** **ADV** **pour un p. il m'accuserait!** he's all but accusing me!; **pour un p., j'oubliais mes clés** I nearly forgot my keys

• **quelque peu** **ADV 1** *(modifiant un verbe)* just a little; **vous ne trouvez pas que vous exagérez quelque p.?** don't you think you're exaggerating just a little? **2** *(modifiant un adjectif)* somewhat, rather; **il était quelque p. éméché** he was somewhat *or* rather tipsy

• **quelque peu de** **DÉT** not a little; **le chantier a été achevé avec quelque p. de hâte** the site was completed in not a little haste

• **si peu que** **CONJ** **si p. que j'y aille, j'apprécie toujours beaucoup l'opéra** although I don't go very often, I always enjoy the opera very much

• **si peu... que** **CONJ** **si p. informé qu'il soit** however badly informed he may be

• **sous peu** **ADV** before long, in a short while; **vous recevrez sous p. les résultats de vos analyses** you will receive the results of your tests in a short while

• **un peu de** **DÉT** a little (bit) of; **prends un p. de gâteau** have a little *or* some cake; **un p. de tout** a bit of everything; **avec un p. de chance...** with a little luck...; **tu l'as quitté par dépit? – il y a un petit p. de ça** so you left him in a fit of pique? – that was partly it *or* that was part of the reason

peuchère [pøʃɛr] **EXCLAM** *(dans le Midi)* heck!, *Br* strewth!

peuh [pø] **EXCLAM 1** *(avec indifférence)* bah! **2** *(avec dédain)* humph!

peuplade [pœplad] **NF** (small) tribe, people

peuple [pœpl] **NM 1** *(communauté)* people; **un roi aimé de son p.** a king loved by his people *or* subjects; **les peuples d'Asie** the peoples of Asia; *Rel* **le p. élu** the chosen people *or* ones

2 le p. *(prolétariat)* the people; **le pouvoir revient au p.** power belongs to the people; **parti du p.** people's party; **homme du p.** ordinary man; *Vieilli* **le bas** *ou* **petit p.** the lower classes *or Br* orders

3 *Fam (foule)* crowd; **il va y avoir du p.** there's going to be tons of people there

4 *(locutions) Fam* **il se fiche** *ou* **se moque du p.** he's got some nerve; **que demande le p.?** what more could you ask for?

ADJ INV working-class; **se donner un genre p.** to try to look working-class; *Péj* **une expression qui fait p.** a vulgar *or* common turn of phrase

peuplé, -e [pœple] **ADJ** populated; **région peu/très peuplée** sparsely/densely populated region

peuplement [pœpləmɑ̃] **NM 1** *(humain ▸ action)* populating; *(▸ état)* population; **des régions à faible p.** sparsely populated areas **2** *École (d'une forêt)* planting (with trees); *(d'une rivière)* stocking (with fish); *(ensemble ▸ des végétaux)* plant population, *Spéc* stand; *(▸ des arbres)* tree population

peupler [5] [pœple] **VT 1** *(région, ville)* to populate, to people; *(forêt)* to plant (with trees); *(rivière)* to stock (with fish) **2** *(vivre dans)* to live in, to inhabit; **les Indiens qui peuplent ces régions** the Indians who live in these areas; **peuplé de** inhabited by **3** *Fig Littéraire* to fill; **un lieu peuplé de souvenirs** a place full of memories

VPR se peupler *(région, ville)* to become populated, to acquire a population; **la ville nouvelle se peuple petit à petit** people are gradually moving into the new town

peupleraie [pøplərɛ] **NF** poplar grove

peuplier [pøplije] **NM** poplar (tree); **p. tremble** aspen

peur [pœr] **NF 1** *(sentiment)* fear, apprehension, alarm; **la p. lui donnait des ailes** fear gave him/her wings; **avoir p.** to be afraid *or* frightened *or* scared; **on a eu très p.** we were badly frightened; **je n'ai qu'une p., c'est de les décevoir** my one fear is that I might disappoint them; *Fam* **on a sonné tard, j'ai eu une de ces peurs!** someone rang the doorbell late at night and it gave me a terrible fright!; **avoir p. pour qn** to fear for sb; **avoir p. d'un rien** to scare easily, to be easily frightened; **avoir horriblement p. de qch** to have a dread of sth; **avoir grand-p.** to be very frightened *or* scared; **n'aie pas p.** *(ne t'effraie pas)* don't be afraid; *(ne t'inquiète pas)* don't worry; **ça va, tu n'as pas besoin d'avoir p.!** don't you worry about that!, there's nothing to be afraid of!; **j'ai bien p. qu'elle ne vienne pas** I'm really worried (that) she won't come; **j'en ai (bien) p.** I'm (very much) afraid so; **il ne s'en remettra pas – j'en ai bien p.** he won't pull through – I'm very much afraid you might be right; **faire p. à qn** to frighten *or* to scare sb; **le travail ne lui fait pas p.** he's/she's not workshy *or* afraid of hard work; **j'adore les films qui font p.** I love scary movies *or Br* films; **à faire p.** frightening; **une tête à faire p.** a frightening face; **boiter/loucher à faire p.** to have a dreadful limp/squint; **prendre p.** to get frightened, to take fright; **être pris de p.** to be gripped by fear, to be overcome with fear, to take fright; **avoir une p. bleue de** to be scared stiff of; **faire une p. bleue à qn** to give sb a terrible fright; **la p. du gendarme** the fear of authority; **avec eux, il n'y a que la p. du gendarme qui marche** they only understand the language of repression; **avoir la p. au ventre** to be gripped by fear; **être mort** *ou* **vert de p.** to be frightened out of one's wits; **elle était morte de p. à cette idée** that idea scared her out of her wits; **on a eu plus de p. que de mal** we weren't hurt, just scared; **il y a eu plus de p. que de mal** nobody was hurt, but it was frightening; *Fam Ironique* **tu as l'air content, ça fait p.!** you don't exactly look beside yourself with joy! **2** *(phobie)* fear; **avoir p. de l'eau/du noir** to be afraid of water/of the dark; **il a p. en avion** he's afraid of flying

• **dans la peur de** PRÉP **vivre dans la p. de qch** to live in fear *or* in dread of sth

• **de peur de** PRÉP **de p. de faire** for fear of doing; **je ne disais rien de p. de lui faire du mal** I said nothing for fear that I might *or* in case I hurt him/her

• **de peur que** CONJ for fear that; **je préfère éteindre de p. qu'on nous voie** I'd rather switch the light off in case someone sees us; **il partit de p. qu'on ne l'accusât d'ingérence** he left for fear of being *or Sout* lest he should be accused of interfering

• **par peur de** PRÉP out of fear of; **il cèdera au chantage par p. du scandale** the fear of a scandal will make him give in to blackmail

• **sans peur** ADV fearlessly, undaunted; **affronter l'avenir sans p.** to face up to the future bravely

peureuse [pœrøz] *voir* **peureux**

peureusement [pœrøzmɑ̃] ADV fearfully, timorously, apprehensively

peureux, -euse [pœrø, -øz] ADJ *(craintif)* timorous, fearful; **un enfant p.** a fearful child

NM,F *(poltron)* fearful person; **quel p.!** what a coward!

peut-être [pøtetr] ADV maybe, perhaps; **ils sont p. sortis, p. sont-ils sortis** maybe they've gone out, they may *or* might have gone out; **elle est p. efficace, mais guère rapide** she might be efficient, but she is not very quick; **je n'ai p. pas d'expérience, mais j'ai de l'ambition** I may lack experience *or* maybe I lack experience, but I'm ambitious; **tu viendras? – p.** will you come? – maybe *or* perhaps; **p. pas** maybe *or* perhaps not; **il est p. bien déjà parti** he may well have already left; **p. bien, mais...** perhaps *or* maybe so but...; **j'y suis pour quelque chose, p.?** so you think it's my fault, do you!; **je suis ta bonne, p.?** what do you take me for? a maid?

• **peut-être que** CONJ perhaps, maybe; **p. qu'il est malade** perhaps *or* maybe he is ill; **p. (bien) qu'il viendra** he may well come; **tu viendras? – p. bien que oui, p. bien que non** will you come? – perhaps I will, perhaps I won't *or* maybe I will, maybe I won't

p. ex. *(abrév* **par exemple)** eg

pèze [pez] NM *Fam* cash, dough

pff [pf], **pfft** [pft], **pfut** [pfyt] EXCLAM pooh!

pH [peaʃ] NM *Chim (abrév* **potentiel hydrogène)** pH; **savon/shampooing/*etc* (à) p. neutre** pH balanced soap/shampoo/*etc*

phacochère [fakɔʃɛr] NM *Zool* warthog

phaéton [faetɔ̃] NM *(véhicule)* phaeton

phagocyte [fagɔsit] NM *Biol* phagocyte

phagocyter [3] [fagɔsite] VT **1** *Biol* to phagocytose **2** *Fig (absorber)* to engulf, to absorb; **après avoir phagocyté tous ses concurrents** after having swallowed up all its competitors

phagocytose [fagɔsitoz] NF *Biol* phagocytosis

phalange [falɑ̃ʒ] NF **1** *Anat* phalanx

2 *(groupe)* **la P. (espagnole)** the Falange; **les Phalanges libanaises** the (Lebanese) Phalangist Party

3 *Antiq (corps d'armée)* phalanx

4 *Littéraire (armée)* host, army

phalangette [falɑ̃ʒɛt] NF *Anat* top joint *(of finger or toe)*, *Spéc* distal phalanx

phalangien, -enne [falɑ̃ʒjɛ̃, -ɛn] ADJ *Anat* phalangeal

phalangiste [falɑ̃ʒist] ADJ *(en Espagne)* Falangist; *(au Liban)* Phalangist

NMF *(en Espagne)* Falangist; *(au Liban)* Phalangist

phalanstère [falɑ̃stɛr] NM **1** *(de Fourier)* phalanstery **2** *Littéraire (communauté)* community, group

phalène [falɛn] NF *Entom* geometer moth

phallique [falik] ADJ phallic

phallocrate [falɔkrat] ADJ male-chauvinist

NM male chauvinist

phallocratie [falɔkrasi] NF male chauvinism

phalloïde [falɔid] ADJ phalloid

phallus [falys] NM *Anat* phallus

phantasme [fɑ̃tasm] = **fantasme**

pharamineux, -euse [faraminø, -øz] = **faramineux**

pharaon [faraɔ̃] NM **1** *Hist* pharaoh **2** *Cartes* faro

pharaonien, -ienne [faraɔnjɛ̃, -jɛn], **pharaonique** [faraɔnik] ADJ **1** *Hist* Pharaonic **2** *Fig (gigantesque)* huge, enormous

phare [far] NM **1** *Naut* lighthouse; **p. à éclipses** *ou* **occultations** occulting light; **p. à feu fixe/tournant** fixed/revolving light; **p. flottant** lightship

2 *Aut* headlight, *Br* headlamp; **allumer** *ou* **mettre ses phares** to switch one's headlights on; **mettre les phares en code** *Br* to dip *or Am* to dim one's headlights; **p. antibrouillard** fog *Br* lamp *or Am* light; **p. de recul** *Br* reversing *or Am* back-up light

3 *Aviat* light, beacon; **phares d'atterrissage** landing lights

4 *Littéraire (guide)* beacon, leading light

5 *(comme adj; avec ou sans trait d'union) (exemplaire)* flagship *(avant n)*; **industrie p.** flagship *or* pioneering industry; **film-p.** seminal movie *or Br* film; **produit-p.** flagship (product)

pharisaïque [farizaik] ADJ **1** *Hist & Rel* Pharisaic, Pharisaical **2** *Littéraire (hypocrite)* pharisaical

pharisien, -enne [farizjɛ̃, -ɛn] ADJ **1** *Hist & Rel* Pharisaic, Pharisaical **2** *(moralisateur)* self-righteous

NM,F **1** *Hist & Rel* Pharisee **2** *(moralisateur)* self-righteous person **3** *Littéraire* pharisee

pharmaceutique [farmasøtik] ADJ pharmaceutic, pharmaceutical

pharmacie [farmasi] NF **1** *(magasin) Br* chemist's (shop), *Am* pharmacy, drugstore; *(dans un hôpital)* dispensary, pharmacy; **p. de garde** duty *Br* chemist *or Am* pharmacy *or* drugstore; **quelle est la p. de garde ce soir?** which *Br* chemist *or Am* pharmacy *or* drugstore is open all night tonight? **2** *(meuble)* medicine chest *or* cabinet *or Br* cupboard; *(boîte)* first-aid box; **p. de voyage** travelling first-aid kit **3** *Univ* pharmacy, pharmaceutics *(singulier)*

pharmacien, -enne [farmasjɛ̃, -ɛn] NM,F **1** *(diplômé)* pharmacist, *Br* chemist **2** *(vendeur) Br* (dispensing) chemist, *Am* druggist

pharmacodépendance [farmakɔdepɑ̃dɑ̃s] NF (pharmaceutical) drug dependency

pharmacologie [farmakɔlɔʒi] NF pharmacology

pharmacologique [farmakɔlɔʒik] ADJ pharmacological

pharmacopée [farmakɔpe] NF pharmacopeia, pharmacopoeia

pharmacorésistance [farmakorezistɑ̃s] NF resistance to drugs

pharmacovigilance [farmakɔviʒilɑ̃s] NF (pharmaceutical) drug testing and control, pharmaceutical monitoring

pharyngé, -e [farɛ̃ʒe], **pharyngien, -enne** [farɛ̃ʒjɛ̃, -ɛn] ADJ *Méd* pharyngal, pharyngeal

pharyngite [farɛ̃ʒit] NF *Méd* pharyngitis

pharynx [farɛ̃ks] NM *Anat* pharynx

phase [faz] NF **1** *(moment)* phase, stage; **être en p. de croissance/déclin** to be going through a period of growth/decline; **p. critique** critical stage; *Méd* critical phase; **p. de développement** development stage; **p. terminale** terminal phase; **cancer en p. terminale** terminal cancer; **le projet en arrive à sa p. d'exploitation** the project has moved into its first production run; **p. de fabrication** manufacturing stage; *Mktg* **p. de faisabilité** feasibility stage; *Mktg* **p. d'introduction** introduction stage

2 *Élec, Phys & Chim* phase; **différence de p.** difference in phase; **diagramme des phases** phase *or* constitution diagram; **règle des phases** phase rule

3 *Astron* phase; **phases de la Lune** phases of the Moon, lunar phases

4 *Aviat* phase; **p. d'approche** approach phase; **p. d'atterrissage** landing phase; **p. de décollage** take-off phase

• **en phase** ADJ *Élec & Phys* in phase; **les mouvements ne sont plus en p.** the movements are now out of phase; *Fig* **être en p.** to see eye to eye

Phébus [febys] NPR *Myth* Phoebus

Phèdre [fɛdr] NPR *Myth* Phaedra

Phénicie [fenisi] NF **la P.** Phoenicia

phénicien, -enne [fenisjɛ̃, -ɛn] ADJ Phoenician

NM *(langue)* Phoenician

• **Phénicien, -enne** NM,F Phoenician

phénix [feniks] NM **1** *Myth* phoenix **2** *Littéraire (prodige)* paragon **3** *Bot* palm tree

phénol [fenɔl] NM *Chim* phenol, carbolic acid

phénoménal, -e, -aux, -ales [fenɔmenal, -o] ADJ **1** *(prodigieux)* phenomenal, amazing; **son sens des affaires est p.** he/she has phenomenal *or* amazing business acumen; **il a un toupet p.** he's got an outrageous nerve, *Br* he's outrageously cheeky **2** *Phil* phenomenal

phénoménalement [fenɔmenalmɑ̃] ADV phenomenally

phénomène [fenɔmɛn] NM **1** phenomenon; **la grêle et autres phénomènes naturels** hail and other natural phenomena

2 *(manifestation)* phenomenon; **la communication de masse est un p. du XXème siècle** mass communication is a 20th-century phenomenon

3 *(prodige)* prodigy, wonder; **une truite de 10 kilos est un p.** a 10-kilo trout is a rare phenomenon

4 *Fam (excentrique)* character; **un drôle de p.** an odd customer; **cette gamine, quel p.!** that kid is a real character!

5 *(monstre)* **p. (de foire)** freak

phénoménologie [fenɔmenɔlɔʒi] NF phenomenology

Philadelphie [filadɛlfi] NM Philadelphia

philanthrope [filɑ̃trɔp] ADJ philanthropic

NMF philanthropist, philanthrope

philanthropie [filɑ̃trɔpi] NF philanthropy

philanthropique [filɑ̃trɔpik] ADJ philanthropic

philatélie [filateli] NF stamp-collecting, *Spéc* philately

philatélique [filatelik] ADJ philatelic

philatéliste [filatelist] NMF stamp-collector, *Spéc* philatelist

philharmonie [filarmɔni] NF philharmonic *or* musical society

philharmonique [filarmɔnik] ADJ philharmonic

NM **le p. de Boston/Berlin** the Boston/Berlin Philharmonic (Orchestra)

philippin, -e [filipɛ̃, -in] ADJ Filipino

• **Philippin, -e** NM,F Filipino

Philippines [filipin] NFPL **les P.** the Philippines, the Philippine Islands

philistin, -e [filistɛ̃, -in] *Littéraire* ADJ philistine, uncultured

NM,F philistine

philo [filo] NF *Fam (abrév* **philosophie)** philosophy[□]

philodendron [filɔdɛ̃drɔ̃] NM philodendron

philologie [filɔlɔʒi] NF philology

philologique [filɔlɔʒik] ADJ philological

philologue [filɔlɔg] NMF philologist

philosophale [filɔzɔfal] ADJ F *voir* **pierre**

philosophe [filɔzɔf] ADJ philosophical

NMF **1** *(penseur)* philosopher **2** *(sage)* **il a pris la chose en p.** he took it philosophically *or* calmly

philosopher [3] [filɔzɔfe] VI to philosophize (**sur** about)

philosophie [filɔzɔfi] NF **1** *(étude)* philosophy; **faire des études de p.** to study *or Br* to read philosophy; **la p. de l'histoire/des sciences** the philosophy of history/science **2** *(conception, doctrine)* philosophy; **p. de la vie** philosophy of life **3** *(sagesse)* **il est plein de p.** he is very wise

• **avec philosophie** ADV philosophically

philosophique [filɔzɔfik] ADJ philosophical

philosophiquement [filɔzɔfikmɑ̃] ADV philosophically

philtre [filtr] NM **p. (d'amour)** love-potion, philtre

phishing [fiʃiŋ] NM *Ordinat* phishing

phlébite [flebit] NF *Méd* phlebitis

phlébologie [flebɔlɔʒi] NF *Méd* phlebology

phlébologue [flebɔlɔg] NMF *Méd* vein specialist, *Spéc* phlebologist

phlébotomie [flebɔtɔmi] NF *Méd* phlebotomy

phlegmon [flɛgmɔ̃] NM *Méd* phlegmon

phlox [flɔks] NM *Bot* phlox

pH-mètre [peaʃmɛtr] (*pl* **pH-mètres**) NM pH meter

phobie [fɔbi] NF phobia; **avoir la p. de qch** to have a phobia about sth

phobique [fɔbik] ADJ phobic

phocéen, -enne [fɔseɛ̃, -ɛn] ADJ **1** *Antiq* Phocaean **2** *(de Marseille)* of/from Marseilles; **la cité phocéenne** = the city of Marseilles

phœnix [feniks] = **phénix 3**

phonation [fɔnɑsjɔ̃] NF phonation

phonatoire [fɔnatwar] ADJ phonatory

phone [fɔn] NM phon

> **-PHONE** SUFFIX
>
> The most interesting use of this suffix from a translation point of view is the creation, based on a root ending in **-o**, of adjectives and nouns referring to SPEAKERS of a particular language.
>
> Although the equivalent form ending in *-phone* also exists in English in some cases, it is of a more formal register than the French, eg:
>
> **francophone** French-speaking, Francophone; **un francophone** a French speaker, a Francophone; **anglophone** English-speaking, Anglophone; **un anglophone** an English speaker, an Anglophone; **germanophone** German-speaking; **un germanophone** a German speaker; **hispanophone** Spanish-speaking; **un hispanophone** a Spanish speaker

phonématique [fɔnematik] ADJ phonemic, phonematic
NF phonemics *(singulier)*

phonème [fɔnɛm] NM phoneme

phonémique [fɔnemik] ADJ phonemic
NF phonemics *(singulier)*

phonéticien, -enne [fɔnetisjɛ̃, -ɛn] NM,F phonetician

phonétique [fɔnetik] ADJ phonetic
NF phonetics *(singulier)*

phonétiquement [fɔnetikmɑ̃] ADV phonetically

phoniatre [fɔnjatr] NMF speech therapist

phoniatrie [fɔnjatri] NF speech therapy

phonie [fɔni] NF *Tél* **1** *(abrév* **radiotéléphonie***)* radiotelephony **2** *(abrév* **téléphonie***)* telephony

phoning [fɔniŋ] NM *Mktg* telesales

phonique [fɔnik] ADJ **1** *Ling* phonic **2** *(relatif aux sons)* sound *(avant n)*

phono [fɔno] NM *Fam Vieilli (abrév* **phonographe***)* phonograph❑, gramophone❑

phonographe [fɔnɔgraf] NM phonograph, gramophone

phonographique [fɔnɔgrafik] ADJ phonographic

phonologie [fɔnɔlɔʒi] NF *Ling* phonology

phonologique [fɔnɔlɔʒik] ADJ *Ling* phonological

phonologue [fɔnɔlɔg] NMF *Ling* phonologist

phonothèque [fɔnɔtɛk] NF sound archives

phoque [fɔk] NM **1** *Zool* seal; **p. gris** grey seal; **p. moine** monk seal; **p. veau-marin** common *or* harbour seal **2** *(fourrure)* sealskin

phosgène [fɔsʒɛn] NM *Chim* phosgene

phosphatage [fɔsfataʒ] NM *Chim* phosphatization

phosphate [fɔsfat] NM *Chim* phosphate

phosphaté, -e [fɔsfate] ADJ *Chim* phosphated; **des engrais phosphatés** phosphate-enriched fertilizers

phosphater [3] [fɔsfate] VT **1** *Agr* to phosphatize, to treat with phosphates **2** *Métal* to phosphate, to phosphatize

phosphène [fɔsfɛn] NM *Chim* phosphene

phosphore [fɔsfɔr] NM *Chim* phosphorus

phosphoré, -e [fɔsfɔre] ADJ *Chim* phosphorated

phosphorer [3] [fɔsfɔre] VI *Fam (réfléchir)* to think hard❑, *Hum* to cogitate; **qu'est-ce que ça phosphore ici!** I can see those brains are working overtime here!

phosphorescence [fɔsfɔresɑ̃s] NF *Phys* phosphorescence

phosphorescent, -e [fɔsfɔresɑ̃, -ɑ̃t] ADJ **1** *Phys* phosphorescent **2** *(luisant)* luminous, glowing

phosphoreux, -euse [fɔsfɔrø, -øz] ADJ *Chim* phosphorous

phosphorique [fɔsfɔrik] ADJ *Chim* phosphoric

phosphure [fɔsfyr] NM *Chim* phosphide

phot [fɔt] NM *Phys* phot

photo [fɔto] NF **1** *(cliché)* photo, shot; **avez-vous fait des photos?** did you take any photos *or* pictures?; **sur la p.** in the photo; **p. de famille** family portrait; *Fig* **poser pour la traditionnelle p. de famille** *(politiciens, sportifs)* to have the traditional group photograph taken; **p. d'identité** passport photo; **p. souvenir** souvenir photo; *Fam* **tu veux ma p.?** what are you staring at?; *Fam Fig* **y'a pas p.** there's no contest **2** *(activité)* photography; **faire de la p. en amateur/professionnel** to be an amateur/professional photographer; **p. de mode** fashion photography

• **en photo** ADJ on a photograph; **des fleurs en p.** a photo of some flowers ADV **prendre qn en p.** to take sb's photo *or* picture; **prendre qch en p.** to take a photo *or* picture of sth; **il est bien en p.** he photographs well

photobiologie [fɔtobjɔlɔʒi] NF *Biol* photobiology

photochimie [fɔtɔʃimi] NF *Chim* photochemistry

photochimique [fɔtɔʃimik] ADJ *Chim* photochemical

photocomposer [3] [fɔtɔkɔ̃poze] VT *Typ* to photoset, to photocompose, *Br* to filmset

photocomposeuse [fɔtɔkɔ̃pozøz] NF *Typ* photocompositor, *Br* filmsetter

photocompositeur [fɔtɔkɔ̃pozitœr] NM *Typ* photocomposer, phototypesetter, *Br* filmsetter

photocomposition [fɔtɔkɔ̃pozisjɔ̃] NF *Typ* photocomposition, photosetting, *Br* filmsetting

photoconducteur, -trice [fɔtɔkɔ̃dyktœr, -tris] *Électron* ADJ photoconductive
NM photoconductor

photoconduction [fɔtɔkɔ̃dyksjɔ̃] NF *Électron* photoconductivity

photoconductrice [fɔtɔkɔ̃dyktris] *voir* **photoconducteur**

photocopie [fɔtɔkɔpi] NF photocopy; *(action)* photocopying

photocopier [9] [fɔtɔkɔpje] VT to photocopy; **photocopiez-moi ce document en trois exemplaires, s'il vous plaît** please make three photocopies *or* copies of this document for me

photocopieur [fɔtɔkɔpjœr] NM photocopier

photocopillage [fɔtɔkɔpijaʒ] NM = infringement of copyright through excessive use of photocopiers

photodiode [fɔtɔdjɔd] NF *Électron* photodiode

photoélectricité [fɔtɔelɛktrisite] NF *Phys* photoelectricity

photoélectrique [fɔtɔelɛktrik] ADJ *Phys* photoelectric

photo-finish [fɔtɔfiniʃ] (*pl* **photos-finish**) NF *(photographie)* photo finish; *(appareil)* photo-finish camera; **l'arrivée a dû être vérifiée à la p.** it was a photo finish

photogénique [fɔtɔʒenik] ADJ photogenic

photogramme [fɔtɔgram] NM photogram

photogrammétrie [fɔtɔgrametri] NF photogrammetry

photographe [fɔtɔgraf] NMF **1** *(artiste)* photographer; **ils ont posé sur le perron pour les photographes** they had a photo call on the steps; **p. de mode** fashion photographer; *Cin* **p. de plateau** unit photographer; **p. de presse** press photographer **2** *(commerçant)* dealer in photographic equipment; **je vais apporter cette pellicule chez le p.** I'm taking this film to the developer's *or* photo shop

> Il faut noter que le terme anglais **photograph** est un faux ami. Il signifie **photographie**, **cliché**.

photographie [fɔtɔgrafi] NF **1** *(activité)* photography; **faire de la p.** *(professionnel)* to be a photographer; *(amateur)* to be an amateur photographer; **p. aérienne/en couleurs** aerial/colour photography; **p. au flash** flash photography; **p. de mode** fashion photography **2** *(cliché)* photograph, picture; **prendre une p. de qn** to take a photograph *or* a picture of sb; **nos photographies de Grèce** our photographs from Greece; **toutes les photographies du mariage** all the wedding pictures *or* photographs; **p. d'identité** passport photograph; **p. de plateau** still; **p. publicitaire** publicity still; **p. satellite** satellite photograph; **p. de tournage** still **3** *(reproduction)* **ce sondage est une p. de l'opinion** this survey is an accurate reflection *or* snapshot of public opinion

photographier [9] [fɔtɔgrafje] VT **1** *(prendre une photographie de)* to photograph, to take photographs *or* pictures of; **se faire p.** to have one's photograph *or* picture taken **2** *Fig (mémoriser)* to memorize (photographically)

photographique [fɔtɔgrafik] ADJ **1** *Phot* photographic **2** *Fig (fidèle à la réalité)* **il nous a fait une description presque p. des lieux** he described the place in the minutest detail

photographiquement [fɔtɔgrafikmɑ̃] ADV photographically

photograveur [fɔtɔgravœr] NM photoengraver

photogravure [fɔtɔgravyr] NF photoengraving

photo-interprétation [fɔtɔɛ̃tɛrpretasjɔ̃] (*pl* **photos-interprétations**) NF photo-interpretation

photojournalisme [fɔtɔʒurnalism] NM photojournalism

photojournaliste [fɔtɔʒurnalist] NMF photojournalist

photolithographie [fɔtɔlitɔgrafi] NF **1** *(technique)* photolithography **2** *(image)* photolithograph

photolyse [fɔtɔliz] NF *Chim* photolysis

Photomaton® [fɔtɔmatɔ̃] NM photobooth

photomécanique [fɔtɔmekanik] ADJ *Typ* photomechanical

photomètre [fɔtɔmɛtr] NM photometer

photométrie [fɔtɔmetri] NF photometry

photométrique [fɔtɔmetrik] ADJ photometric

photomontage [fɔtɔmɔ̃taʒ] NM photomontage

photon [fɔtɔ̃] NM *Phys* photon

photopériode [fɔtɔperjɔd] NF *Biol* photoperiod

photopériodique [fɔtɔperjɔdik] ADJ *Biol* photoperiodic

photopériodisme [fɔtɔperjɔdism] NM *Biol* photoperiodism

photophobie [fɔtɔfɔbi] NF *Méd* photophobia

photophore [fɔtɔfɔr] NM **1** *(lampe)* reflective lamp *(used by miner)* **2** *(pour bougie)* candle holder with glass shade

photopile [fɔtɔpil] NF photovoltaic cell

photoreportage [fɔtɔrəpɔrtaʒ] NM **1** *(discipline)* photojournalism **2** *(article)* report *(consisting mainly of photographs)*

photo-robot [fɔtɔrɔbo] (*pl* **photos-robots**) NF Photofit® *or* Identikit® (picture)

photosensible [fɔtɔsɑ̃sibl] ADJ photosensitive; **rendre qch p.** to photosensitize sth

Photoshop® [fotoʃɔp] NM Photoshop®

photosphère [fɔtɔsfɛr] NF *Astron* photosphere

photostat [fɔtɔsta] NM *Tech* photostat

photostoppeur, -euse [fɔtɔstɔpœr, -øz] NM,F street photographer

photostyle [fɔtɔstil] NM *Ordinat* light pen

photosynthèse [fɔtɔsɛ̃tɛz] NF *Biol & Bot* photosynthesis; **fabriquer qch par la p.** to photosynthetize sth

photothèque [fɔtɔtɛk] **NF** picture *or* photographic library

photothérapie [fɔtɔterapi] **NF** *Méd* phototherapy

phototransistor [fɔtɔtrɑ̃zistɔr] **NM** phototransistor

phototypie [fɔtɔtipi] **NF** *Typ* phototype (process)

photovoltaïque [fɔtɔvɔltaik] **ADJ** photovoltaic

phragmite [fragmit] **NM 1** *Bot* reed **2** *Orn* **p. aquatique** aquatic warbler; **p. des joncs** sedge warbler

phrase [fraz] **NF 1** *Ling* sentence; *(en grammaire transformationnelle)* phrase **2** *(énoncé)* **sa dernière p.** the last thing he/she said; **laisse-moi finir ma p.** let me finish (what I have to say); **p. célèbre** famous saying *or* remark; **p. toute faite** set phrase; *Pol* **petite p.** soundbite; **faire de grandes phrases** *ou* **des phrases** to talk in flowery language **3** *Mus* phrase
• **sans phrases ADV** straightforwardly

> Il faut noter que le nom anglais **phrase** est un faux ami. Il signifie **expression**.

phrasé [fraze] **NM** *Mus* phrasing

phraséologie [frazeɔlɔʒi] **NF 1** *(style)* phraseology **2** *Littéraire (verbiage)* flowery *or* high-flown language

phraser [3] [fraze] **VT** *Mus* to phrase

phraseur, -euse [frazœr, -øz] **NM,F** *Péj* speechifier, person of fine words

phrastique [frastik] **ADJ** *Ling* sentence *(avant nom)*

phréatique [freatik] **ADJ** phreatic

phrénologie [frenɔlɔʒi] **NF** phrenology

Phrygie [friʒi] **NF la P.** Phrygia

phrygien, -enne [friʒjɛ̃, -ɛn] **ADJ 1** *Antiq* Phrygian **2 bonnet p.** cap of liberty, Phrygian cap
• **Phrygien, -enne NM,F** Phrygian

phtisie [ftizi] **NF** *Vieilli Méd* consumption, *Spéc* phthisis

phylactère [filaktɛr] **NM 1** *Rel* phylactery, tefillah **2** *Beaux-Arts* phylactery, scroll **3** *(dans une bande dessinée)* bubble, balloon

phylloxéra, phylloxera [filɔksera] **NM** *Entom & Bot* phylloxera

phylogenèse [filɔʒenɛz] **NF** *Biol* phylogenesis, phylogeny

physalis [fizalis] **NM** *Bot* winter *or* ground cherry, cape gooseberry, physalis

physicien, -enne [fizisjɛ̃, -ɛn] **NM,F** physicist; **p. nucléaire** nuclear physicist

> Il faut noter que le terme anglais **physician** est un faux ami. Il signifie **médecin**.

physico-chimie [fizikoʃimi] **NF** physical chemistry, physicochemistry

physico-chimique [fizikoʃimik] *(pl* **physico-chimiques)** **ADJ** physicochemical

physico-mathématique [fizikɔmatematik] *(pl* **physico-mathématiques)** **ADJ** physicomathematical

physiocrate [fizjɔkrat] *Hist* **ADJ** physiocratic
NMF physiocrat

physiocratie [fizjɔkrasi] **NF** *Hist* physiocracy

physiologie [fizjɔlɔʒi] **NF** physiology

physiologique [fizjɔlɔʒik] **ADJ** physiological

physiologiquement [fizjɔlɔʒikmɑ̃] **ADV** physiologically

physiologiste [fizjɔlɔʒist] **NMF** physiologist

physionomie [fizjɔnɔmi] **NF 1** *(visage)* features, facial appearance, *Spéc* physiognomy; **il ne faut pas juger les gens sur leur p.** you shouldn't judge by appearances **2** *(aspect ▸ d'une chose)* face, appearance; **la p. des choses** the face of things; **la p. du quartier a changé en dix ans** the appearance of the district has changed in ten years

physionomiste [fizjɔnɔmist] **ADJ** good at remembering faces, observant (of people's faces)
NMF *Vieilli* physiognomist

physiopathologie [fizjɔpatɔlɔʒi] **NF** physiopathology

physiothérapeute [fizjɔterapøt] **NMF** *Can & Suisse Méd* physiotherapist

physiothérapie [fizjɔterapi] **NF** natural medicine

physique[1] [fizik] **NF** physics *(singulier)*; **p. expérimentale** experimental physics; **p. nucléaire** nuclear physics; **p. des particules** particle physics; **p. du sol** soil mechanics

physique[2] [fizik] **ADJ 1** *Phys & Chim (propriété)* physical
2 *(naturel ▸ monde, univers)* physical, natural
3 *(corporel ▸ exercice, force, effort, souffrance)* physical, bodily; *(▸ symptôme)* physical; *Fam* **je ne le supporte pas, c'est p.** I can't stand him, it's a gut feeling
4 *(sexuel ▸ plaisir, jouissance)* physical, carnal
NM 1 *(apparence)* **soigner son p.** to take care of *or* to look after oneself; **avoir un p. ingrat** to be physically unattractive; **avoir un p. avantageux** to have a fine physique; *Théât & Fig* **avoir le p. de l'emploi** to look the part **2** *(constitution)* physical condition; **au p. comme au moral** physically as well as morally speaking

physiquement [fizikmɑ̃] **ADV** physically; **il n'est pas mal p.** he's quite good-looking

phytobiologie [fitɔbjɔlɔʒi] **NF** phytobiology

phytogéographie [fitɔʒeɔgrafi] **NF** phytogeography

phytoplancton [fitɔplɑ̃ktɔ̃] **NM** phytoplankton

phytosanitaire [fitɔsanitɛr] **ADJ** plant-care *(avant n)*, *Spéc* phytosanitary; **produit p.** *(engrais)* plant-care product; *(pesticide)* pesticide

phytothérapie [fitɔterapi] **NF** herbal medicine

pi [pi] **NM INV** *(lettre) & Math* pi

piaf [pjaf] **NM** *Fam (oiseau)* bird▫; *(moineau)* sparrow▫; *Fig* **cervelle** *ou* **crâne** *ou* **tête de p.!** birdbrain!

piaffement [pjafmɑ̃] **NM** pawing (the ground)

piaffer [3] [pjafe] **VI 1** *(cheval)* to paw the ground **2** *(personne)* to stamp one's feet; **p. d'impatience** to be champing at the bit, to be seething with impatience

piaillard, -e [pjajar, -ard] = **piailleur**

piaillement [pjajmɑ̃] **NM 1** *(d'oiseaux)* **un p.** a chirp, a cheep; **le p. des moineaux** the chirping *or* cheeping of the sparrows; **des piaillements** chirping, cheeping **2** *Fam (d'enfants)* squealing▫ *(UNCOUNT)*

piailler [3] [pjaje] **VI 1** *(oiseau)* to chirp, to cheep **2** *Fam (enfant)* to squeal▫

piailleur, -euse [pjajœr, -øz] *Fam* **ADJ** *(enfant)* squealing▫
NM,F *(enfant)* squealer▫

piane-piane [pjanpjan] **ADV** *Fam* slowly▫; **vas-y p.!** take your time!, easy does it!

pianiste [pjanist] **NMF** pianist, piano player; **p. de jazz** jazz pianist

piano [pjano] **NM** *(instrument)* piano; **jouer** *ou* **faire du p.** to play the piano; **se mettre au p.** *(s'asseoir)* to sit at the piano; *(jouer)* to go to the piano (and start playing); *(apprendre)* to take up the piano; **au p., Clara Bell** *(classique)* the pianist is Clara Bell; *(jazz)* on piano, Clara Bell; **p. droit/à queue** upright/grand piano; *Fam* **p. à bretelles** *ou* **du pauvre** squeezebox; **p. de concert** concert grand; **p. crapaud** boudoir grand; **p. demi-queue** baby grand; **p. mécanique** Pianola®, player piano; **p. préparé** prepared piano; **p. quart de queue** miniature grand
ADV 1 *Mus* piano **2** *Fam (doucement)* slowly▫; **vas-y p.(-p.)!** take your time!, there's no rush!

piano-bar [pjanobar] *(pl* **pianos-bars)** **NM** piano bar

pianoforte [pjanofɔrte] **NM** forte-piano

pianotage [pjanɔtaʒ] **NM 1** *(sur un piano)* tinkling (on a piano) **2** *(sur une table)* drumming **3** *Fam (sur un clavier)* tapping away (at a keyboard)

pianoter [3] [pjanɔte] **VI 1** *(jouer du piano)* to tinkle away on the piano **2** *(tambouriner)* to drum one's fingers **3** *Fam (taper sur un clavier)* to tap away; **p. sur un ordinateur** to tap away at a computer
VT *(sur un piano)* to tinkle out on the piano

piastre [pjastr] **NF 1** *(au Proche-Orient)* piastre **2** *Can Fam (dollar)* dollar▫, buck; *(argent)* money▫, cash, *Br* dosh **3** *Hist* piastre, piece of eight

piaule [pjol] **NF** *Fam* **1** *(chambre)* room▫ **2** *(logement)* place

piaulement [pjolmɑ̃] **NM 1** *(d'un oiseau)* cheep; **les piaulements de l'oiseau** the cheeping of the bird **2** *Fam (d'un enfant)* whimpering▫ *(UNCOUNT)*

piauler [3] [pjole] **VI 1** *(oiseau)* to cheep **2** *Fam (enfant)* to whimper▫

PIB [peibe] **NM** *(abrév* **produit intérieur brut)** GDP

pic [pik] **NM 1** *(montagne)* peak
2 *(outil)* pick, pickaxe; **p. à glace** ice-pick
3 *Orn* woodpecker
4 *(d'une courbe)* peak
• **à pic ADJ** *(paroi, falaise)* sheer **ADV 1** *(verticalement)* straight down; **les rochers tombent à p. dans la mer** the sheer rocks go straight down to the sea **2** *Fam (au bon moment)* just at the right time▫, *Br* spot on; **tu tombes** *ou* **tu arrives à p., j'allais t'appeler** you've come just at the right time *or* right on cue, I was about to call you

pica [pika] **NM** *Méd* pica

picador [pikadɔr] **NM** picador

picaillons [pikajɔ̃] **NMPL** *Fam (argent)* dough, bread; **avoir des p.** to be loaded

picard, -e [pikar, -ard] **ADJ** of/from Picardy
NM *(dialecte)* Picard *or* Picardy dialect
• **Picard, -e NM,F** = inhabitant of or person from Picardy

Picardie [pikardi] **NF la P.** Picardy

picaresque [pikarɛsk] **ADJ** picaresque

piccolo [pikɔlo] **NM** piccolo

pichenette [piʃnɛt] **NF** flick; **d'une p., elle envoya la miette par terre** she flicked the crumb onto the ground

pichet [piʃɛ] **NM** jug, pitcher

pickles [pikœlz] **NMPL** pickles

pickpocket [pikpɔkɛt] **NM** pickpocket

pick-up [pikœp] **NM INV 1** *(lecteur)* pick-up (arm); *Vieilli (tourne-disque)* record player **2** *(camion)* pick-up (truck)

picoler [3] [pikɔle] **VI** *Fam (boire)* to booze, to knock it back; **qu'est-ce qu'on a picolé ce soir-là!** we really knocked it back that night!; **il picole pas mal** he's a real boozer

picoleur, -euse [pikɔlœr, -øz] **NM,F** *Fam (buveur)* boozer, alky

picorer [3] [pikɔre] **VT 1** *(oiseau)* to peck (at) **2** *(personne)* to nibble (away) at, to pick at
USAGE ABSOLU *(oiseau)* to pick *or* scratch about; **cette enfant ne fait que p.** that child only picks at his/her food

picoseconde [pikɔsəgɔ̃] **NF** picosecond

picot [piko] **NM 1** *Tech* barb, point **2** *(au crochet, en dentelle)* picot **3** *(sur du bois)* splinter

picotement [pikɔtmɑ̃] **NM** *(dans les yeux)* smarting *or* stinging (sensation); *(dans la gorge, le nez)* tickle; *(sur la peau)* tingle, prickle; **j'ai des picotements dans les doigts** my fingers are tingling; **j'ai des picotements dans les yeux** my eyes are smarting; **ça me donne des picotements partout** it makes my flesh crawl *or* creep

picoter [3] [pikɔte] **VT 1** *(piquer ▸ yeux)* to sting, to smart; *(▸ gorge)* to irritate, to tickle; *(▸ peau, doigt)* to sting; **la fumée lui picotait les yeux** the smoke was stinging his/her eyes; **j'ai les orteils qui me picotent** my toes are tingling **2** *(sujet: oiseau)* to peck at **3** *(faire de petits trous dans)* to prick tiny holes in, to perforate

picotin [pikɔtɛ̃] **NM 1** *(mesure)* peck **2** *(ration)* **p. (d'avoine)** ration of oats

picrate [pikrat] **NM 1** *Chim* picrate **2** *Fam Péj (vin)* wine▫, vino, *Br* plonk

picte [pikt] **ADJ** Pictish
• **Picte NMF** Pict

pictogramme [piktɔgram] **NM** pictogram, pictograph

pictographie [piktɔgrafi] **NF** pictography

pictographique [piktɔgrafik] **ADJ** pictographic

pictural, -e, -aux, -ales [piktyral, -o] **ADJ** pictorial

pic-vert [pivεr] *(pl* **pics-verts***)* = **pivert**

Pie [pi] **NPR** *(pape)* Pius

pie [pi] **ADJ INV** *(couleur)* pied; **cheval p.** piebald (horse); **vache p. noire** black and white cow; **voiture p.** patrol car, *Br* panda car

ADJ F *Littéraire (pieux)* **œuvre p.** pious work

NF 1 *Orn* magpie; **trouver la p. au nid** to make a lucky find **2** *Fam (bavard)* chatterbox

PIÈCE [pjεs]

NF
- piece **1, 2, 6**
- part **2**
- room **4**
- play **6**
- gun **10**
- bit **1**
- patch **3**
- paper, document **5**
- coin **7**

ADV
- each

NF 1 *(morceau)* piece, bit; **une p. de viande** *(flanc)* a side of meat; *(morceau découpé)* a piece *or* cut of meat; **une p. de tissu** *(coupée)* a piece *or* length of cloth; *(sur rouleau)* a roll of cloth; *Fam* **une belle p.** *(femme)* a babe, *Br* a nice bit of stuff, a bit of all right; **mettre qch en pièces** *(briser)* to smash sth to pieces; *(déchirer)* to tear *or* to pull sth to pieces; *(critiquer)* to tear sth to pieces; **p. à p.** piecemeal, gradually; **le domaine constitué p. à p. par mon père** the estate gradually built up by my father; **d'une seule p., tout d'une p.** all of a piece; *Fig* **il est tout d'une p.** he's very blunt *or* straightforward; **il n'a jamais travaillé pour nous, il a monté cela de toutes pièces** he never worked for us, he made up *or* invented the whole thing; **c'est un mensonge monté de toutes pièces** it's an out-and-out lie *or* a lie from start to finish; **fait de pièces et de morceaux** made up of bits and pieces, *Péj* cobbled together

2 *(d'une collection)* piece, item; *(d'un mécanisme)* part, component; *(d'un jeu)* piece; **ménagère de 36 pièces** 36-piece cutlery set; **p. détachée** (spare) part; **en pièces détachées** in separate pieces *or* parts; **le bureau est livré en pièces détachées** the desk comes in kit form; **pièces et main-d'œuvre** parts and labour; **p. maîtresse** centrepiece; **la p. maîtresse d'une argumentation** the main part *or* the linchpin of an argument; *aussi Fig* **p. de musée** museum piece; **p. de rechange** spare *or* replacement part; *aussi Fig* **les pièces d'un puzzle** the pieces of a puzzle

3 *Couture* patch; **je vais y mettre une p.** I'll patch it *or* put a patch on it; **p. rapportée** patch; *Fig (personne)* odd person out

4 *(salle)* room; **un deux-pièces** a one-bedroom *Br* flat *or Am* apartment; **un trois-pièces cuisine** a two-bedroom *Br* flat *or Am* apartment

5 *(document)* paper, document; **p. annexe** attachment; **p. à l'appui** supporting document; *Compta* **p. de caisse** cash voucher; **p. comptable** (accounting) voucher; *Jur* **p. à conviction** exhibit; **p. d'identité** proof of identity, ID; **avez-vous une p. d'identité?** do you have any proof of identity *or* any ID?; **pièces jointes** enclosures; **pièces justificatives** supporting documents; **je vous le démontrerai pièces à l'appui** I'll show you (actual) proof of it

6 *Littérature & Mus* piece; **p. (de théâtre)** play; **petite p.** playlet; **p. écrite pour la télévision** *Br* television play, *Am* play written for TV; **monter une p.** to put on *or* to stage a play

7 *(argent)* **p. (de monnaie)** coin; **une p. de 2 euros** a 2-euro coin *or* piece; **je n'ai que quelques pièces dans ma poche** I've only got some loose change in my pocket

8 *(champ)* **une p. d'avoine** a field sown in oats; **mettre une p. en betteraves** to grow beetroot on a piece of land

9 *Culin* **p. montée** *(gâteau)* ≃ tiered cake; *(pyramide)* = pyramid of caramel-covered profiteroles often served at weddings and other special occasions; **p. de résistance** main dish; *Fig* pièce de résistance

10 *Mil* **p. (d'artillerie)** gun

11 *(locutions)* **faire p. à qn** to set up in opposition to sb; *Belg* **avoir toujours une p. pour mettre sur le trou** *(tout savoir)* to have an answer for everything; *(avoir de la repartie)* to be always ready with an answer; *Belg* **ne plus tenir p. ensemble** to be falling to pieces

ADV *(chacun)* each, apiece; **les roses sont à 3 euros p.** the roses are 3 euros each *or* apiece

• **à la pièce ADV** *(à l'unité)* singly, separately; **vendus à la p.** sold separately *or* individually

• **à la pièce, aux pièces ADV travailler à la p.** to be on *or* to do piecework; **être payé à la p.** to be paid a *or* on piece rate; *Fam* **on n'est pas aux pièces!** we're not on piecework!, there's no great hurry!

• **sur pièces ADV** on evidence; **juger sur pièces** to judge for oneself

• **pièce d'eau NF 1** *(lac)* (ornamental) lake **2** *(bassin)* (ornamental) pond

PIÈCE

Flats in France are referred to in terms of the total number of rooms they have (excluding the kitchen and bathroom). "Un deux-pièces" is a flat with a living room and one bedroom; "un cinq-pièces" is a flat with five rooms.

piécette [pjesεt] **NF** *(monnaie)* small coin

PIED [pje] **NM 1** *(d'une personne, d'un animal)* foot; **pieds nus** barefoot; **marcher/être pieds nus** to walk/to be barefoot; **avoir** *ou* **marcher les pieds en dedans** to be pigeon-toed, to walk with one's feet turned in; **avoir** *ou* **marcher les pieds en dehors** to walk with one's feet turned out, to be splay-footed *or Am* duck-toed; **sauter à pieds joints** to make a standing jump; **le p. m'a manqué** my foot slipped, I lost my footing; **mettre le p. (en plein) dans qch** to step right in sth; *Euph* **je vais lui mettre mon p. quelque part** I'll give him a kick up the backside; **mettre p. à terre** *(à cheval, à moto)* to dismount; **lorsqu'ils mirent le p. sur le sol de France** when they set foot on French soil; *Fam* **je n'ai pas mis les pieds dehors/à l'église depuis longtemps** I haven't set foot outside/in church for a long time▫; **je ne mettrai** *ou* **remettrai plus jamais les pieds là-bas** I'll never set foot there again; *Méd* **avoir les pieds plats** to have flat feet, to be flat-footed; *Fam* **il ne remuait** *ou* **bougeait ni p. ni patte** he stood stock-still *or* didn't move a muscle; **aller** *ou* **avancer** *ou* **marcher d'un bon p.** to go apace; **aller** *ou* **marcher d'un p. léger** to have a spring in one's step; **avoir bon p. bon œil** to be fit as a fiddle; **partir du bon/mauvais p.** to start off (in) the right/wrong way; **l'opération est partie du bon p.** the operation got off to a good start; **leur couple part du mauvais p.** their relationship is off to a bad start *or* off on the wrong foot; **avoir le p. marin** to be a good sailor; **je n'ai pas le p. marin** I'm prone to seasickness; **faire un p. de nez à qn** to thumb one's nose at sb; *Fam* **cette pièce est un p. de nez aux intellos** this play is a real slap in the face for intellectual types; **avoir les (deux) pieds sur terre** to have one's feet (firmly) on the ground *or* one's head screwed on (the right way); **avoir p.** to touch bottom; **au secours, je n'ai plus p.!** help, I'm out of my depth *or* I've lost my footing!; **j'ai déjà un p. dans la place/l'entreprise** I've got a foot in the door/a foothold in the company already; **avoir un p. dans la tombe** to have one foot in the grave; **avoir les deux pieds dans le même sabot** to be lacking in initiative *or* resourcefulness; **elle n'a pas les deux pieds dans le même sabot** there are no flies on her; *Fam* **bien fait pour tes/leurs/***etc* **pieds!, ça te/leur/***etc* **fera les pieds!** serves you/them/*etc* right!; **être pieds et poings liés** to have no room to manoeuvre; **je suis pieds et poings liés** my hands are tied; **faire des pieds et des mains pour** to bend over backwards *or* to pull out all the stops in order to; **faire du p. à qn** *(flirter)* to play footsie with sb; *(avertir)* to kick sb (under the table); **faire le p. de grue** to cool *or Br* to kick one's heels; **les pieds devant** feet first, in one's coffin; **elle en est partie les pieds devant** she left there feet first *or* in a box; *Fam* **avoir le p. au plancher** *(accélérer)* to have one's foot down; *Fam* **lever le p.** *(ralentir)* to ease off (on the accelerator), to slow down▫; *(partir subrepticement)* to slip off; **il n'a pas levé le p. de tout le trajet** he never took his foot off the accelerator once during the whole trip; *Belg Fam* **jouer avec les pieds de qn** *(se moquer de)* to make fun of sb▫, *Br* to take the mick *or* the mickey out of sb; *(duper)* to take sb for a ride; *Can Fam* **mettre qn à p.** *(employé)* to give sb the push; **mettre le p. à l'étrier** to get into the saddle; *Fig* **il a fallu lui mettre le p. à l'étrier** he/she had to be given a leg up; *Fam* **mettre les pieds dans le plat** *(intervenir sans ménagements)* to steam in; *(commettre une maladresse) Br* to put one's foot in it, *Am* to put one's foot in one's mouth; **mettre qch sur p.** to set sth up; **il ne peut plus mettre un p. devant l'autre** *(ivre)* he can't walk in a straight line any more; *(fatigué)* his legs won't carry him any further; **reprendre p.** to get *or* to find one's footing again; *aussi Fig* **retomber sur ses pieds** to fall *or* to land on one's feet; **ne pas savoir sur quel p. danser** to be at a loss to know what to do; **se jeter** *ou* **se traîner aux pieds de qn** to throw oneself at sb's feet, to get down on one's knees to sb; **se lever du p. gauche** to get out of bed on the wrong side; **elle s'est levée du p. gauche aujourd'hui** she got out of bed on the wrong side today; *Fam* **je cuisine comme un p.** *(très mal)* I'm a terrible cook; **il a fait ça comme un p.** he made a pig's ear of it; **il chante/conduit comme un p.** he can't sing/drive to save his life; **on s'est débrouillés comme des pieds** we went about it the wrong way *or Br* in a cack-handed way; *Fam* **prendre son p.** *(s'amuser)* to get one's kicks; *(sexuellement)* to come; **il prend son p. en faisant du jazz!** he gets a real kick out of playing jazz!; *Fam* **c'est le p.** it's great *or* fantastic *or Br* fab *or Am* awesome; *Fam* **on a passé dix jours à Hawaï, quel p.!** we spent ten days in Hawaii, what a blast!; *Fam* **les cours d'anglais, ce n'est pas le p.!** the English class isn't exactly a barrel of laughs!; *Fam* **être bête comme ses pieds** *Br* to be thick (as two short planks), *Am* to have rocks in one's head

2 *(d'un mur, d'un lit)* foot; *(d'une table, d'une chaise)* leg; *(d'une lampe, d'une colonne)* base; *(d'un verre)* stem; *(d'un micro, d'un appareil photo)* stand, tripod

3 *Typ (d'une lettre)* bottom, foot; *Typ* **p. de page** footer

4 *Bot* plant; *(de champignon)* foot; **p. de laitue** head of lettuce

5 *(mesure)* foot; **le mur fait 6 pieds de haut** the wall is 6 feet high; **un mur de 6 pieds de haut** a 6-foot high wall

6 *Tech Aut* **p. à coulisse** calliper rule; **p. milieu** centre pillar

7 *Littérature* foot; **vers de 12 pieds** 12-foot verse *or* line

8 *Culin* **p. de cochon** pig's *Br* trotter *or Am* foot; **p. de mouton/de veau** sheep's/calf's foot

9 *(d'un bas, d'une chaussette)* foot

10 *Cin & TV* **p. de sol** high-hat

• **à pied ADV 1** *(en marchant)* on foot; **on ira au stade à p.** we'll walk to the stadium **2** *(au chômage)* **mettre qn à p.** *(mesure disciplinaire)* to suspend sb; *(mesure économique)* to lay sb off, *Br* to make sb redundant

• **à pied d'œuvre ADJ être à p. d'œuvre** to be ready to get down to the job

• **à pied sec ADV** without getting one's feet wet; **on peut traverser la rivière à p. sec** the river can be forded

• **au petit pied ADJ** *Vieilli* small-time

• **au pied de PRÉP** at the foot *or* bottom of; **au p. de la tour Eiffel** at *or* by the foot of the Eiffel Tower; **au p. des Alpes** in the foothills of the Alps; **être au p. du mur** to be faced with no alternative; **mettre qn au p. du mur** to get sb with his/her back to the wall, to leave sb with no alternative

• **au pied de la lettre ADV** literally; **prendre qch au p. de la lettre** to take *or* to interpret sth literally; **suivre des instructions au p. de la lettre** to follow instructions to the letter

• **au pied levé ADV** at a moment's notice; **il faut que tu sois prêt à le faire au p. levé** you must be ready to drop everything and do it

• **de pied en cap ADV en vert de p. en cap** dressed in green from top to toe *or* head to foot

• **de pied ferme ADV** resolutely; **je t'attends de p. ferme** I'll definitely be waiting for you; **les cambrioleurs, je les attends de p. ferme!** I've got a nasty surprise in store for potential burglars!

• **des pieds à la tête ADV** from top to toe *or* head to foot

• **en pied ADJ** *(photo, portrait)* full-length; *(statue)* full-size standing

• **pied à pied** ADV inch by inch; **lutter** *ou* **se battre p. à p.** to fight every inch of the way
• **sur le pied de guerre** ADV *Mil* on a war footing; *Hum* ready (for action); **dans la cuisine, tout le monde était sur le p. de guerre** it was action stations in the kitchen
• **sur pied** ADJ *(récolte)* uncut, standing; *(bétail)* on the hoof ADV **être sur p.** *(en bonne santé)* to be up and about; **mettre qn sur p.** to set sb on his/her feet; **remettre qn sur p.** to put sb on his/her feet again, to make sb better
• **sur un pied d'égalité** ADV on an equal footing; **être sur un p. d'égalité avec** to stand on equal terms with

pied-à-terre [pjetatɛr] NM INV pied-à-terre

pied-bot [pjebo] *(pl* **pieds-bots)** NMF club-footed person

pied-d'alouette [pjedalwɛt] *(pl* **pieds-d'alouette)** NM *Bot* larkspur

pied-de-biche [pjedbiʃ] *(pl* **pieds-de-biche)** NM **1** *(pince)* nail puller *or* extractor **2** *(levier)* crowbar **3** *(d'une machine à coudre)* foot

pied-de-coq [pjedkɔk] *(pl* **pieds-de-coq)** NM hound's-tooth (check), dogtooth (check)
ADJ INV **un tailleur p.** a hound's-tooth suit

pied-de-poule [pjedpul] *(pl* **pieds-de-poule)** NM hound's-tooth (check), dogtooth (check)
ADJ INV **un tailleur p.** a hound's-tooth suit

pied-de-roi [pjedərwa] *(pl* **pieds-de-roi)** NM *Can* folding rule

pied-droit [pjedrwa] *(pl* **pieds-droits)** NM = **piédroit**

piédestal, -aux [pjedestal, -o] NM pedestal; **mettre qn sur un p.** to put *or* to set *or* to place sb on a pedestal

pied-noir [pjenwar] *(pl* **pieds-noirs)** ADJ pied-noir
NMF pied-noir *(French settler in North Africa, especially Algeria)*

> PIED-NOIR
>
> This is the name given to the French settlers who settled in North Africa (most notably in Algeria) during the period of French colonial expansion. Most of them resettled in France (mainly on the south coast) after the colonies regained their independence. The largest wave of these settlers to arrive in France was in 1962, following the Algerian war.

piédouche [pjeduʃ] NM small pedestal

piédroit [pjedrwa] NM *Archit (d'une voûte)* pier; *(d'une fenêtre)* jamb; *(jambage)* piedroit

piège [pjɛʒ] NM **1** *(dispositif)* trap, snare; **prendre un animal au p.** to trap an animal; **poser** *ou* **tendre un p.** to set a trap; **tendre un p. à qn** to set a trap for sb; **attirer qn dans un p.** to lure sb into a trap; **être pris à son propre p.** to fall into one's own trap, *Sout* to be hoist by one's own petard; **se laisser prendre au p. de l'amour** to be taken in by love; **donner dans le p.** to fall into the trap; *Fam* **p. à cons** con, scam; *Fam* **élections, p. à cons!** election, deception!; **p. à mâchoires** jaw trap; **p. à souris** mousetrap **2** *(difficulté)* trap, snare; **les pièges des contrats d'assurance** the traps hidden in the small print of insurance contracts

piégeage [pjeʒaʒ] NM *Chasse* trapping

piéger [22] [pjeʒe] VT **1** *(animal)* to trap, to ensnare; **la police les a piégés** the police trapped them; **se laisser p.** to fall into a trap, to get trapped; *Fig* **je me suis fait p. comme un débutant** I was taken in *or* caught out like a complete beginner **2** *(voiture, paquet)* to booby-trap

piégeur, -euse [pjeʒœr, -øz] NM,F trapper

pie-grièche [pigrijɛʃ] *(pl* **pies-grièches)** NF *Orn* shrike

pie-mère [pimɛr] *(pl* **pies-mères)** NF *Anat* pia mater

Piémont [pjemɔ̃] NM **le P.** Piedmont

piémontais, -e [pjemɔ̃tɛ, -ɛz] ADJ Piedmontese
NM *(dialecte)* Piedmontese dialect
• **Piémontais, -e** NM,F Piedmontese; **les P.** the Piedmontese

piercé, -e [pirse] ADJ *Fam* pierced□ *(part of body)*

piercing [pirsiŋ] NM **1** *(pratique)* (body) piercing **2** *(bijou)* piercing

piéride [pjerid] NF *Entom* pierid; **p. du chou** cabbage white (butterfly)

pierrade® [pjɛrad] NF *Culin* **1** *(appareil, méthode)* hot stone grill **2** *(mets)* = meal consisting of pieces of meat or fish cooked at the table on a hot stone grill

pierraille [pjɛraj] NF loose stones, scree *(UNCOUNT)*

Pierre [pjɛr] NPR Peter; **P. le Grand** Peter the Great

pierre [pjɛr] NF **1** *(matière)* stone; *(caillou)* stone, *Am* rock; *(rocher)* rock, boulder; **d'un coup** *ou* **jet de p.** by throwing *or* hurling a stone; **tuer qn à coups de pierres** to stone sb to death; *Beaux-Arts* **la p.** stone; **sculpter la p.** to carve in stone; **la p.** *(immobilier)* the property *or Am* real estate business; **investir dans la p.** to invest in property *or* in bricks and mortar; **les vieilles pierres** old buildings; **p. d'achoppement** stumbling block; **p. levée** standing stone; **faire d'une p. deux coups** to kill two birds (with one stone); **jeter une p. à qn** to throw a stone at sb; **jeter la p. à qn** to cast a stone at sb; **qui va (lui) jeter la première p.?** who will cast the first stone?; **c'est une p. dans ton jardin** that remark was (meant) for you; **se mettre une p. autour du cou** to make things difficult for oneself; **la date est à marquer d'une p. blanche** it's a red-letter day; *Prov* **p. qui roule n'amasse pas mousse** a rolling stone gathers no moss
2 *Constr* stone; *aussi Fig* **p. angulaire** keystone, cornerstone; **p. à bâtir** building stone; **mur de** *ou* **en p.** stone wall; **mur de** *ou* **en pierres sèches** drystone wall; **poser la première p. (de)** to lay down the first stone (of); *Fig* to lay the foundations (of)
3 *Minér & (en joaillerie)* stone; **p. brute** rough *or* uncut stone; **p. taillée** cut stone; **p. fine** *ou* **semi-précieuse** semi-precious stone; **p. de lune** moonstone; **p. précieuse** gem, precious stone; *aussi Fig* **p. de touche** touchstone
4 *Géol* **p. calcaire** *ou* **à chaux** limestone; **p. ponce** pumice stone
5 *(instrument)* **p. à affûter** *ou* **aiguiser** whetstone; **p. à briquet** (lighter) flint; **p. à feu** *ou* **fusil** gun flint; **p. à griller** hot stone grill
6 *(stèle)* **p. funéraire** *ou* **tombale** tombstone, gravestone
7 *Hist & Fig* **p. philosophale** philosopher's stone; *Fig* **chercher la p. philosophale** to search for the impossible
• **de pierre** ADJ stony, of stone; **être/rester de p.** to be/to remain icy-cool; **son cœur/visage restait de p.** he/she remained stony-hearted/stony-faced
• **pierre à pierre, pierre par pierre** ADV stone by stone; *Fig* painstakingly; **il a construit sa fortune p. par p.** he built up his fortune from nothing
• **pierre sur pierre** ADV *Littéraire* **après le tremblement de terre, il ne restait pas p. sur p.** not a stone was left standing after the earthquake; **ils n'ont pas laissé p. sur p. de la théorie d'origine** they shot the original theory to pieces

pierreries [pjɛrri] NFPL precious stones, gems

pierreux, -euse [pjɛrø, -øz] ADJ **1** *(terrain)* stony, rocky; *(chemin)* stony; *(lit de rivière)* gravelly **2** *(fruit)* gritty

pierrot [pjero] NM **1** *Théât* Pierrot; *(clown)* pierrot, clown **2** *Fam (moineau)* sparrow□

pietà [pjeta] NF pietà

piétaille [pjetaj] NF **1** *Hum (fantassins)* rank and file **2** *Péj (subalternes)* rank and file; **la direction nous considère comme de la p.** the management just thinks of us as *Br* skivvies *or Am* flunkies **3** *Hum (piétons)* pedestrians

piété [pjete] NF **1** *Rel* piety; **articles de p.** devotional objects **2** *(amour)* devotion, reverence

piétinement [pjetinmɑ̃] NM **1** *(marche sur place)* shuffling about **2** *(bruit)* **le p. des chevaux** the sound of the horses' hooves; **le p. de la foule** the sound of the crowd shuffling about **3** *Fig (stagnation)* **le p. de l'affaire arrange certaines personnes** the lack of progress in the case suits certain people

piétiner [3] [pjetine] VI **1** *(marcher sur place)* to shuffle about; *(avancer péniblement)* to shuffle along **2** *(trépigner)* **p. d'impatience** to stamp one's feet impatiently; *Fig* to be champing at the bit **3** *Fig (stagner)* to fail to make (any) progress *or* headway; **l'enquête piétine** the enquiry is getting nowhere *or* is making no headway; **on piétine, il faut se décider!** we're not getting anywhere *or* we're just marking time, let's make up our minds!
VT **1** *(écraser)* to trample *or* to tread on; **ils sont morts piétinés par la foule** they were trampled to death by the crowd **2** *Fig (libertés, traditions)* to trample underfoot, to ride roughshod over

piétisme [pjetism] NM pietism

piétiste [pjetist] ADJ pietistic, pietistical
NMF pietist

piéton, -onne [pjetɔ̃, -ɔn] ADJ **rue piétonne** pedestrianized street; **zone piétonne** pedestrian precinct
NM,F pedestrian

piétonnier, -ère [pjetɔnje, -ɛr] ADJ pedestrian *(avant n)*; **rue piétonnière** pedestrianized street; **zone piétonnière** pedestrian precinct

piètre [pjɛtr] ADJ *(avant n) (gén)* very poor, mediocre; *(excuse)* lame, paltry; **faire p. figure** to be a sorry sight; **c'est une p. consolation** that's small *or* not much comfort

piètrement [pjɛtrəmɑ̃] ADV very mediocrely; **je suis bien p. récompensée** this is (a) meagre recompense indeed for my effort

pieu, -x[1] [pjø] NM **1** *(poteau ▸ pour délimiter)* post; *(▸ pour attacher)* stake **2** *Fam (lit)* bed□, pit; **aller** *ou* **se mettre au p.** to hit the *Br* sack *or Am* hay **3** *Constr* pile; **p. de fondation** foundation pile

pieuse [pjøz] *voir* **pieux**[2]

pieusement [pjøzmɑ̃] ADV **1** *(dévotement)* piously, devoutly **2** *Littéraire (scrupuleusement)* religiously, scrupulously

pieuter [3] [pjøte] *Fam* VI **1** *(passer la nuit)* to crash (out) **2** **p. avec qn** to bunk down with sb
VPR **se pieuter** to hit the *Br* sack *or Am* hay

pieuvre [pjœvr] NF **1** *Zool* octopus **2** *Fig (personne)* leech

pieux[2]**, -euse** [pjø, -øz] ADJ **1** *(dévot)* pious, devout **2** *(charitable)* **p. mensonge** white lie **3** *(respectueux ▸ silence)* reverent

pif [pif] ONOMAT bang, smack; **p., paf!** bang! bang!
NM *Fam (nez) Br* conk, hooter, *Am* shnozzle; **je l'ai dans le p.** I can't stand the sight of him/her, *Br* he/she gets right up my nose
• **au pif** ADV *Fam* **faire qch au p.** to do sth by guesswork□; **au p., je dirais trois** I'd say three, at a rough guess, off the top of my head I'd say three; **j'ai répondu au p.** I just guessed□; **j'y suis allé au p. et il restait des places** I just went on the off-chance and there were still some seats left; **j'ai pris celui-là au p.** I just took the first one that came to hand

pifer, piffer [3] [pife] VT *Fam (supporter)* **je ne peux pas le p.!** I can't stomach him!, I just can't stand him!□

pifomètre [pifɔmɛtr] **au pifomètre** ADV *Fam* **j'ai dit ça au p.** I was just guessing□; **faire qch au p.** to do sth by guesswork□

pige [piʒ] NF **1** *(tige graduée)* measuring stick
2 *Tech* gauge rod
3 *Fam Journ* **travailler à la p., faire des piges** to work freelance□; **être payé à la p.** to be paid piece rate□ *or* by the line□
4 *(d'un typographe)* take *(amount of copy to be set up in a given time)*
5 *Fam (an)* year□; **elle a déjà 70 piges** she's 70 already□; **pour 40 piges, il est bien conservé** he still looks pretty good for a 40-year-old
6 *Fam (locution)* **faire la p. à qn** to go one better than sb

pigeon [piʒɔ̃] NM **1** *Orn* pigeon; **p. voyageur** carrier *or* homing pigeon
2 *(jeu)* **p. vole** = children's game consisting of a yes or no answer to the question: does X fly?
3 *Constr (plâtre)* handful of plaster; *(chaux)* lump (in lime)

4 *Sport* **p. d'argile** clay pigeon

5 *Fam (dupe) Br* mug, *Am* sucker; **et c'est encore moi le p.!** and yours truly *or Br* muggins here ends up holding the baby as usual!

pigeonnant, -e [piʒɔnɑ̃, -ɑ̃t] **ADJ soutien-gorge p.** uplift bra; **poitrine pigeonnante** full bosom

pigeonne [piʒɔn] **NF** hen pigeon

pigeonneau, -x [piʒɔno] **NM** *Orn* young pigeon, *Spéc* squab

pigeonner [3] [piʒɔne] **VT 1** *Constr* to plaster **2** *Fam (duper)* **p. qn** to take sb in *or* for a ride, to hoodwink sb; **se faire p.** *(tromper)* to be led up the garden path, to be taken for a ride; *(pour de l'argent)* to get ripped off

pigeonnier [piʒɔnje] **NM 1** *(pour pigeons)* dovecote **2** *Fam (mansarde)* garret, attic

piger [17] [piʒe] **VT 1** *Fam (comprendre)* to get it, to catch on, *Br* to twig; **j'ai mis une heure avant de p. ce qu'il disait** it took me an hour to catch on to what he was saying; **pigé?** got it?, got the picture?; **elle pige rien** *ou* **que dalle à l'art** she hasn't got a clue about art; **impossible de lui faire p. quoi que ce soit!** you just can't get through to him/her at all! **2** *(mesurer)* to rule (out)

USAGE ABSOLU to get it; **tu piges?** get it?; **il a fini par p.** he finally got it *or* got the picture, *Br* the penny finally dropped

VI *Fam (travailler à la pige)* to work freelance□

pigiste [piʒist] **NMF 1** *Typ* piece-rate typographer **2** *Journ* freelance journalist, freelancer

pigment [pigmɑ̃] **NM** pigment

pigmentaire [pigmɑ̃tɛr] **ADJ** pigmentary

pigmentation [pigmɑ̃tasjɔ̃] **NF** pigmentation

pigmenter [3] [pigmɑ̃te] **VT** to pigment

pigne [piɲ] **NF 1** *(cône)* pine cone **2** *(graine)* pine kernel

pignon [piɲɔ̃] **NM 1** *Archit (de mur)* gable; *(de bâtiments)* side wall; **avoir p. sur rue** *(personne)* to be well-off (and respectable); *(entreprise)* to be well established **2** *Tech (roue dentée)* cogwheel, gear wheel; *(petite roue)* pinion; *(d'une bicyclette)* rearwheel, sprocket **3** *Bot* pine kernel *or* nut

pignoratif, -ive [piɡnɔratif, -iv] **ADJ** *Jur* with a repurchase option

pignouf [piɲuf] **NM** *Fam (rustre)* slob, boor

pilaf [pilaf] **NM** pilaf, pilau

pilage [pilaʒ] **NM** pounding, grinding

pilaire [pilɛr] **ADJ** pilar, pilary

pilastre [pilastr] **NM** *Archit* pilaster; *(d'escalier)* newel (post); *(d'un balcon)* pillar

Pilate [pilat] **NPR Ponce P.** Pontius Pilate

Pilates [pilat] **NM (la méthode) P.** Pilates; **pratiquer la méthode P.** to do Pilates

pilaw [pilav] = **pilaf**

pilchard [pilʃar] **NM** pilchard

pile [pil] **NF 1** *(tas ▸ désordonné)* pile, heap; *(▸ ordonné)* pile, stack; **mettre en p.** to stack (up), to pile (up)

2 *Ordinat* stack

3 *Constr (appui)* pier; *(pieu)* pile

4 *Élec* battery; **une radio à piles** a radio run on batteries, a battery radio; **marcher avec des** *ou* **sur piles** to work on *or* off batteries; **p. atomique** pile reactor; **p. bouton** button battery; **p. à combustible** fuel cell; **p. sèche** dry battery; **p. solaire** solar cell

5 *(côté d'une pièce)* **le côté p.** the reverse side; **p. ou face?** heads or tails?; **p., je gagne** tails, I win; **jouer** *ou* **tirer à p. ou face** to toss a coin; **tirons à p. ou face** let's toss for it

6 *Fam (coups)* belting, thrashing; **flanquer la p. à qn** to give sb a good thrashing

7 *Fam (défaite)* beating; **recevoir** *ou* **prendre une (bonne) p.** to get a beating *or Br* hammering *or Am* shellacking; **flanquer une p. à une équipe** to hammer *or* to thrash a team

ADV *Fam* **1** *(net)* dead; **s'arrêter p.** to stop dead **2** *(juste)* right; **p. au milieu** right in the middle; **ça commence à 8 heures p.** it begins at 8 o'clock sharp *or* on the dot; **nous étions p. à l'heure** we were (there) right on time *or* on the dot; **il y en a p. 250** there are 250 exactly; **tu es tombé p. sur le bon chapitre** you just hit (on) the right chapter; **vous tombez p., j'allais vous appeler** you're right on cue, I was about to call you

pile-poil [pilpwal] **ADV** *Fam* **ça rentre p.** it fits exactly□; **c'est tombé p.** *(au bon moment)* it came just at the right time□; **je suis arrivée p. à l'heure** I got there on the dot *or* bang on time

piler [3] [pile] **VT 1** *(broyer ▸ gén)* to crush, to grind; *(▸ noix, amandes)* to grind **2** *Fam (vaincre)* to make mincemeat of, to wipe the floor with; **il a pilé ses adversaires** he thrashed his opponents; **on s'est fait p. en beauté au foot!** they wiped the floor with us at football!

VI *Fam (freiner)* to slam on the brakes

pilet [pilɛ] **NM** *Orn* pintail

pileux, -euse [pilø, -øz] **ADJ** *(bulbe, follicule)* hair *(avant n)*

pilier [pilje] **NM 1** *Anat & Constr* pillar **2** *Fig (défenseur)* pillar; *(bastion)* bastion, bulwark; **c'était un p. du socialisme** she was a pillar of socialism; **la constitution, p. de la démocratie** the constitution, one of the pillars of democracy; *Fam Péj* **c'est un p. de bar** *ou* **bistrot** *(habitué) Br* he can always be found propping up the bar, *Am* he's a regular barfly **3** *(au rugby)* prop (forward)

pili-pili [pilipili] **NM INV** bird pepper

pillage [pijaʒ] **NM 1** *(vol)* pillage, looting, plundering; **le p. de la ville par les soldats** the pillaging of the town by the soldiers; **mettre au p.** to pillage **2** *(plagiat)* plagiarism, pirating

pillard, -e [pijar, -ard] **ADJ** pillaging, looting, plundering

NM,F *(d'une ville, d'un village)* pillager, looter, plunderer; *(lors d'une émeute)* looter

piller [3] [pije] **VT 1** *(dépouiller ▸ village, ville)* to pillage, to loot, to plunder; *(▸ magasin)* to loot **2** *(détourner)* to siphon off, *Br* to cream off; **p. les caisses de l'État** to siphon off *or Br* to cream off taxpayers' money **3** *(plagier)* to plagiarize

pilleur, -euse [pijœr, -øz] **NM,F** *(d'une ville, d'un village)* pillager, looter, plunderer; *(lors d'une émeute)* looter

pilon [pilɔ̃] **NM 1** *(de mortier)* pestle; *Tech* pounder

2 *Typ* **mettre un livre au p.** to pulp a book; **on a eu plus de 2000 pilons** we had to pulp more than 2,000 copies

3 *(jambe de bois)* (straight) wooden leg

4 *(de volaille)* drumstick

pilonnage [pilɔnaʒ] **NM 1** *(broyage)* pounding **2** *Typ* pulping **3** *(bombardement)* (heavy) bombardment, shelling; *Fig* **p. publicitaire** barrage of publicity

pilonner [3] [pilɔne] **VT 1** *(broyer)* to pound **2** *Typ* to pulp **3** *(bombarder)* to bombard, to shell

pilori [pilɔri] **NM 1** *Hist* pillory **2** *Fig* **clouer** *ou* **mettre qn au p.** to pillory sb

pilo-sébacé, -e [pilɔsebase] *(mpl* **pilo-sébacés,** *fpl* **pilo-sébacées) ADJ** pilosebaceous

pilosité [pilozite] **NF** pilosity; **p. excessive/normale** excessive/normal hair growth; **p. faciale** facial hair

pilot [pilo] **NM** *Constr* pile; **p. de pont** bridge pile

pilotable [pilɔtabl] **ADJ** *(avion)* flyable; *(bateau)* sailable; *(voiture)* driveable; *(moto)* rideable

pilotage [pilɔtaʒ] **NM 1** *Naut* piloting; **droits de p.** pilotage dues

2 *Aviat* pilotage, piloting; **école de p.** flying school; **p. automatique** automatic piloting; **sur p. automatique** on automatic pilot *or* autopilot; **p. sans visibilité** blind flying

3 *(d'une voiture)* driving; *(d'une moto)* riding

4 *Fig (direction)* **le p. d'une entreprise** running a business

pilote [pilɔt] **NM 1** *Aviat & Naut* pilot; **p. de chasse** fighter pilot; **p. d'essai** test pilot; **p. de ligne** airline pilot

2 *(guide)* guide; **je vais lui servir de p.** I'll show him/her round, I'll act as his/her guide

3 *(de voiture de course)* driver; *(de moto de course)* rider; **p. automobile** *ou* **de course** racing driver

4 *Tech* **p. automatique** autopilot, automatic pilot; *Fig* **je ne me rappelle de rien, j'ai dû rentrer chez moi en** *ou* **sur p. automatique** I don't remember anything, I must have got home on autopilot

5 *Élec* pilot

6 *Ordinat (d'affichage, d'imprimante)* driver; **p. de mise en file d'attente** spooler

7 *Rail* pilot, pilotman

8 *TV* pilot

ADJ 1 *(expérimental)* experimental; *(promotionnel)* promotional; **école p.** experimental school; **usine/installation p.** pilot factory/plant; **produit p.** promotional item, special offer **2** *Mktg (échantillon, étude, prix)* pilot

piloter [3] [pilɔte] **VT 1** *(conduire ▸ avion)* to pilot, to fly; *(▸ bateau)* to pilot; *(▸ voiture)* to drive; *(▸ moto)* to ride

2 *(guider ▸ personne)* to guide, to show around; *(▸ outil)* to guide

3 *Ordinat* to drive; **piloté par ordinateur** computer-driven; **piloté par menu** menu-driven

4 *(étude, campagne)* to pilot

pilotis [pilɔti] **NM** piling; **maison sur p.** house built on piles *or* stilts

pilou [pilu] **NM** flannelette

pilpil® [pilpil] **NM** *Culin* bulgur (wheat)

pils [pils] **NF** *Belg* lager

pilulaire [pilylɛr] **ADJ** pilular

pilule [pilyl] **NF 1** *(médicament)* pill; *Fam* **dorer la p. à qn** to *Br* sugar *or Am* sweeten the pill for sb; *Fam* **se dorer la p.** to catch some rays; *Fam Fig* **faire passer la p.** to get sb to swallow the pill *or* to take their medicine; **il a dit ça pour faire passer la p.** he said it to *Br* sugar *or Am* sweeten the pill; *Fam Fig* **trouver la p. amère** to find it a bitter pill to swallow; *Fin* **p. empoisonnée** *(contre-OPA)* poison pill **2** *(contraceptif)* **p. contraceptive** *ou* **anticonceptionnelle** contraceptive pill; **la p.** the pill; **prendre la p.** to be on the pill; **p. abortive** abortion pill; **p. du lendemain** morning-after pill

pimbêche [pɛ̃bɛʃ] **ADJ** stuck-up; **ce qu'elle peut être p.!** she thinks she's the queen bee *or Br* Lady Muck!

NF c'est une p. she's really stuck-up

piment [pimɑ̃] **NM 1** *Bot & Culin* chili, chilli; **p. doux** (sweet) pepper; **p. rouge** red chili; **p. fort** hot pepper, pimento **2** *(saveur, charme)* **ça met un peu de p. dans la vie!** it adds some spice to life!; **une histoire/vie qui ne manque pas de p.** a story/life that is anything but dull; **cette fille a du p.** she's certainly got character

pimenté, -e [pimɑ̃te] **ADJ** *(sauce)* hot, spicy

pimenter [3] [pimɑ̃te] **VT 1** *Culin* to season with chili, to spice up **2** *(corser)* **p. une histoire** to spice up a story; **p. la vie** to add spice to life

pimpant, -e [pɛ̃pɑ̃, -ɑ̃t] **ADJ** *(net)* spruce, neat, smart; *(frais)* fresh, bright

pimprenelle [pɛ̃prənɛl] **NF** *Bot* salad burnet

PIN [peiɛn] **NM** *Écon (abrév* **produit intérieur net)** NDP

pin [pɛ̃] **NM 1** *(arbre)* pine, pine tree **2** *(bois)* pine, pinewood

pinacle [pinakl] **NM 1** *Archit* pinnacle **2** *Fig* zenith, acme; **être au p.** to be at the top; **mettre** *ou* **porter qn au p.** to praise sb to the skies, to put sb on a pedestal

pinacothèque [pinakɔtɛk] **NF** art gallery

pinaillage [pinɑjaʒ] **NM** *Fam* nitpicking, hairsplitting

pinailler [3] [pinɑje] **VI** *Fam* to split hairs, to nitpick; **p. sur qch** to quibble over sth

pinailleur, -euse [pinɑjœr, -øz] *Fam* **ADJ** nitpicking, quibbling

NM,F nitpicker

pinard [pinar] **NM** *Fam* wine□, vino, *Br* plonk

pinasse [pinas] **NF** (flat-bottomed) pinnace

pinçage [pɛ̃saʒ] **NM** nipping off, pinching out

pince [pɛ̃s] **NF 1** *(outil)* (pair of) pliers *or* pincers; *(pour l'âtre, de forgeron)* tongs; *(pour tenir en place)* clip; **p. à cheveux** hair clip; **p. coupante** wire cutters; **p. crocodile** crocodile clip; **p. à dénuder** wire-strippers; **p. à dessin** bulldog clip; **p. à épiler** (pair of) tweezers; **p. à glaçons** ice tongs; **p. à linge** clothes peg *or Am* pin; **p. multiprise** multiple pliers; **p. à ongles** (nail) clippers; **p. à sucre** sugar tongs; **p. universelle** universal *or* all-purpose pliers; **p. à vélo** bicycle clip

2 *Biol & Méd* **p. (à disséquer)** (dissecting) forceps; **pinces hémostatiques** artery clip, *Spéc* haemostat

3 *Zool (d'un crabe, d'un homard)* claw, pincer; *(d'un sabot de cheval)* toe; *(incisive)* incisor

4 *Couture* dart, tuck; **p. de poitrine** dart
5 *Cin & TV* **p. pour projecteur** gaffer grip
6 *Fam (main)* paw, mitt; **serrer la p. à qn** to shake hands with sb□
• **à pinces** ADJ *Couture* pleated ADV *Fam (à pied)* on foot□, on shanks's *Br* pony *or Am* mare; **j'irai à pinces** I'll hoof it

pincé, -e[1] [pɛ̃se] ADJ **1** *(dédaigneux ▸ sourire)* tight-lipped; **..., répondit-elle d'un ton p.** ..., she answered stiffly **2** *(serré)* tight; **aux lèvres pincées** tight-lipped

pinceau, -x [pɛ̃so] NM **1** *(brosse ▸ de peintre)* paintbrush, brush; *(▸ de maquillage)* brush; **coup de p.** brush stroke; **il a un bon coup de p.** he paints well **2** *(style)* brushwork **3** *(de lumière)* beam, pencil; *Opt* **p. lumineux** light pencil
• **pinceaux** NMPL *Fam (jambes)* legs□, *Br* pins, *Am* gams; *(pieds)* feet□; **s'emmêler les pinceaux** *(trébucher)* to trip up□, to stumble□; *(s'embrouiller)* to tie oneself in knots

pincée[2] [pɛ̃se] ADJ F *voir* **pincé**
NF *(de sel, de tabac à priser etc)* pinch

pincement [pɛ̃smɑ̃] NM **1** *(émotion)* twinge, pang; **j'ai eu un p. au cœur** it tugged at my heartstrings
2 *(fait de serrer)* pinching, nipping
3 *Mus* plucking
4 *Hort* nipping off, *Br* deadheading

pince-monseigneur [pɛ̃smɔ̃seɲœr] *(pl* **pinces-monseigneur)** NF jemmy

pince-nez [pɛ̃sne] NM INV pince-nez

pincer [16] [pɛ̃se] VT **1** *(serrer)* to pinch, to nip; **son grand-père lui pinça la joue** his/her grandfather pinched his/her cheek; **pince-moi, je rêve!** pinch me, I must be dreaming!; **se faire p. les fesses** to have one's bottom pinched; **p. les lèvres** to go tight-lipped; **une veste/robe qui pince la taille** a fitted jacket/dress
2 *(sujet: vent, froid)* to nip at; **le vent pinçait mes joues** the wind nipped at my cheeks
3 *Mus* to pluck
4 *Hort* to nip off, *Br* to deadhead
5 *Fam (arrêter)* to collar, to nab; **un jour, tu vas te faire p. par les flics** one day, you'll get nabbed *or Am* collared
6 *Fam (locution)* **en p. pour qn** to have the hots for sb, *Br* to fancy the pants off sb
USAGE ABSOLU *Fam (faire froid)* **ça pince** it's nippy, there's a nip in the air; **ça pince (dur) aujourd'hui!** it's bitterly *or* freezing cold today!□
VPR **se pincer 1** *(soi-même)* to pinch oneself; **se p. le nez** to hold *or* to pinch one's nose **2** *(par accident ▸ doigt)* to catch; **je me suis pincé le doigt dans le tiroir** I caught my finger in the drawer, my finger got caught in the drawer

pince-sans-rire [pɛ̃ssɑ̃rir] ADJ INV **être p.** to have a dry sense of humour; **répondre d'un air p.** to answer drily *or* deadpan
NMF INV person with a deadpan *or* dry sense of humour

pincette [pɛ̃sɛt] NF **1** *(d'horloger)* (pair of) tweezers **2** *Suisse (pince à linge)* clothes *Br* peg *or Am* pin
• **pincettes** NFPL *(pour attiser)* (fireplace) tongs; *Fam* **il n'est pas à prendre avec des pincettes** *(très énervé)* he's like a bear with a sore head

pinçon [pɛ̃sɔ̃] NM pinch mark

pindarique [pɛ̃darik] ADJ Pindaric

pine [pin] NF *Vulg (pénis)* dick, prick, cock

pinéal, -e, -aux, -ales [pineal, -o] ADJ pineal

Pineau [pino] NM **1** *(vin)* **P. (des Charentes)** Pineau (des Charentes) *(aperitif made from unfermented grape juice and brandy)* **2** *(cépage)* Pineau grape

pinède [pinɛd] NF pinewood, pine grove

pinglot [pɛ̃glo] NM *Fam (pied)* foot□, *Br* plate, *Am* dog

pingouin [pɛ̃gwɛ̃] NM *(alcidé)* auk; *(manchot)* penguin

ping-pong [piŋpɔ̃g] NM *(pl* **ping-pongs)** table tennis, ping-pong

pingre [pɛ̃gr] ADJ *(avare)* stingy, mean, tight-fisted
NMF skinflint, penny-pincher

pingrerie [pɛ̃grəri] NF *(avarice)* stinginess, meanness

pinot [pino] NM pinot

pin's [pins] NM INV *Br* badge, *Am* button

pinson [pɛ̃sɔ̃] NM *Orn* chaffinch

pintade [pɛ̃tad] NF *Orn* guinea fowl

pintadeau, -x [pɛ̃tado] NM *Orn* young guinea fowl

pinte [pɛ̃t] NF **1** *(mesure ▸ française)* ≃ quart *(0.93 litre)*; *(▸ anglo-saxonne)* pint; *(▸ canadienne)* quart
2 *(verre)* pint; **une p. de bière** a pint of beer
3 *Suisse* café-bar
4 *Fam (locutions)* **s'offrir** *ou* **se faire** *ou* **se payer une p. de bon sang** to have a good laugh; *Can* **se faire une p. de mauvais sang** to worry oneself sick

pinter [3] [pɛ̃te] *Fam* VI *(se saouler)* to booze
VT *(boire)* to swill, to knock back
VPR **se pinter** *très Fam* **se p. (la gueule)** to get wasted *or* trashed

pinteur, -euse [pɛ̃tœr, -øz] NM,F *Belg & Suisse Fam* boozer, alky

pin-up [pinœp] NF INV *(photo)* pin-up; *(jolie fille)* sexy-looking girl

pinyin [pinjin] NM *Ling* Pinyin

pioche [pjɔʃ] NF **1** *(outil)* pick, pickaxe, mattock; **ils ont démoli le mur à coups de p.** they demolished the wall with a pick **2** *(aux dominos)* stock; *(aux cartes)* talon, stock

piocher [3] [pjɔʃe] VT **1** *(creuser)* to dig (up) **2** *(tirer)* to draw; **p. une carte/un domino** to draw a card/a domino (from the stock); **p. des prunes dans un compotier** to dig into a bowl for plums **3** *Fam (étudier)* to cram, *Br* to swot at, *Am* to grind away at
VI **1** *(puiser)* to dig (**dans** into); **les cerises sont délicieuses, vas-y, pioche (dans le tas)** the cherries are delicious, go ahead, dig in **2** *(aux dominos, aux cartes)* to draw from the stock; **pioche!** *(aux cartes)* take a card!

piocheur, -euse [pjɔʃœr, -øz] ADJ *Fam* hard-working□
NM,F **1** *(ouvrier)* digger **2** *Fam (étudiant)* *Br* swot, *Am* grind

piolet [pjɔlɛ] NM ice-axe

pion[1] [pjɔ̃] NM **1** *(de jeux de société)* piece; *(de dames)* draughtsman, *Am* checker; *(d'échecs)* pawn **2** *Fig (personne)* **n'être qu'un p. sur l'échiquier** to be just a cog in the machine *or* a pawn in the game

pion[2], **pionne** [pjɔ̃, pjɔn] NM,F *Fam Arg scol (surveillant)* supervisor□

> PION
>
> In French lycées, the "pions" (officially called "surveillants") are responsible for supervising pupils outside class hours; they are often university students who do the job to make a little extra money.

pioncer [16] [pjɔ̃se] VI *Fam* to sleep□, *Br* to kip

pionicat, pionnicat [pjɔnika] NM *Fam Arg scol (activité du surveillant)* = working as a "pion"

pionnier, -ère [pjɔnje, -ɛr] ADJ pioneering; **une entreprise pionnière dans le domaine du multimédia** a pioneering company in the multimedia world
NM,F **1** *(inventeur)* pioneer **2** *(colon)* pioneer; **les pionniers de l'Ouest américain** the pioneers of the Wild West
NM *(société, produit)* pioneer; **entrer en p. sur le marché** to be the first on the market

pipe [pip] NF **1** *(à fumer ▸ contenant)* pipe; *(▸ contenu)* pipe, pipeful; **une p. en bruyère/terre** a briar/clay pipe
2 *Tech* pipe
3 *Vulg (fellation)* blow-job; **faire** *ou* **tailler une p. à qn** to give sb a blow-job
4 *Fam (cigarette)* *Br* fag, *Am* smoke
5 *(futaille)* (large) cask, barrel
6 *(tuyau)* pipe(line) *(for liquid, gas)*
7 *Fam* **casser sa p.** *(mourir)* to croak, to kick the bucket

pipeau, -x [pipo] NM *Mus* (reed) pipe; *Fam Fig* **c'est du p.** it's a load of garbage *or Br* rubbish
• **pipeaux** NMPL *(pour les oiseaux)* birdlimed *or* limed twigs

pipée [pipe] NF bird snaring, bird catching *(with bird calls and limed twigs)*

pipelet, -ette [piplɛ, ɛt] NM,F *Fam* **1** *Vieilli (concierge)* concierge□, *Am* doorman□ **2** *(bavard)* chatterbox, gasbag

pipe-line, pipeline [pajplajn, piplin] *(pl* **pipelines)** NM pipeline

piper [3] [pipe] VT **1** *(truquer ▸ dés)* to load; *(▸ cartes)* to mark; *aussi Fig* **les dés sont pipés** the dice are loaded **2** *(locution)* **ne pas p. (mot)** to keep mum

piperade [piperad] NF piperade *(rich stew of tomatoes and sweet peppers, mixed with beaten eggs and slightly scrambled)*

pipette [pipɛt] NF pipette; *Suisse* **ça ne vaut pas p.** it's not worth a bean *or Am* a red cent

pipeule [pipœl] = **pipole**

pipeulisation [pipœlizasjɔ̃] = **pipolisation**

pipi [pipi] NM *Fam (urine)* pee; **faire p.** to have a pee, to pee; **le chien a fait p. sur le tapis** the dog's made a puddle *or* peed on the carpet; **aller faire p.** to go for a pee, to go to the *Br* loo *or Am* john; **faire p. au lit** to wet the bed; **c'est du p. de chat** *(sans goût)* it's like gnat's pee, it's like dishwater; *(sans intérêt)* it's a load of bilge *or Br* tripe

pipi-room [pipirum] *(pl* **pipi-rooms)** NM *Fam Br* loo, *Am* john

pipistrelle [pipistrɛl] NF *Zool* pipistrelle

pipole [pipɔl] *Fam* ADJ **la presse p.** the celebrity press□
NM *(magazine)* celebrity magazine□
NMF celebrity□, celeb; **c'est très à la mode chez les pipoles** all the celebs are into it

pipolisation [pipɔlizasjɔ̃] NF *Fam* influence of celebrity culture□; **la p. de la vie politique française est un phénomène récent** French politics has become increasingly celebrity-focused recently□

pipoliser [pipɔlize] **se pipoliser** VPR *Fam* **la politique se pipolise** politics is becoming more about celebrity□ *or* increasingly celebrity-focused□

piquage [pikaʒ] NM **1** *Couture* stitching **2** *Tex* punching

piquant, -e [pikɑ̃, -ɑ̃t] ADJ **1** *(plante)* thorny; *(ortie)* stinging; *(barbe)* prickly
2 *(vif ▸ air, vent)* biting
3 *Culin (moutarde, radis)* hot; *(plat, sauce)* hot, spicy
4 *(caustique ▸ remarque, ton)* cutting, biting
5 *(excitant ▸ récit, détail)* spicy, juicy; *(charmant ▸ beauté, brunette)* striking
6 *Fam (eau)* fizzy
NM **1** *(de plante)* thorn, prickle; *(d'oursin, de hérisson)* spine; *(de barbelé)* barb, spike; **couvert de piquants** prickly **2** *(intérêt)* **le p. de l'histoire, c'est qu'elle n'est même pas venue!** the best part of it is that *or* to crown it all she didn't even show up!; **des détails qui ne manquent pas de p.** juicy details; **le changement donne du p. à la vie** variety is the spice of life; **cette fille a du p.** that girl is rather striking *or* is strikingly attractive

pique [pik] NF **1** *(arme)* pike; *(de picador)* pic, lance **2** *(propos)* barb, cutting remark; **envoyer** *ou* **lancer des piques à qn** to make cutting remarks to sb
NM *Cartes* **du p.** spades; **le roi de p.** the king of spades; **jouer à** *ou* **du p.** to play spades

piqué, -e [pike] ADJ **1** *(abîmé ▸ vin)* sour; *(▸ miroir)* mildewed; *(▸ bois)* wormeaten; *(▸ papier)* foxed
2 *Fam (fou)* crazy□, loopy
3 *Mus* staccato; **note piquée** dotted note
4 *(dessus de lit, vêtement)* quilted
5 *(locutions) Fam* **une histoire pas piquée des hannetons** *ou* **des vers** a heck of a good story; **il est pas p. des hannetons** *ou* **des vers, ton frangin!** your brother is really something else!
NM **1** *Tex* piqué **2** *Aviat* nosedive; **attaquer en p.** to dive-bomb; **descendre en p.** to (go into a) nosedive

pique-assiette [pikasjɛt] *(pl* **inv** *ou* **pique-assiettes)** NMF *Fam* sponger, scrounger, freeloader; **jouer les p.** to gatecrash

pique-bœuf [pikbœf] *(pl* **inv** *ou* **pique-bœufs** [pikbø]) NM *Orn* oxpecker

pique-feu [pikfø] *(pl* **inv** *ou* **pique-feux)** NM poker

pique-fleur, pique-fleurs [pikflœr] *(pl* **pique-fleurs)** NM flower holder

pique-nique [piknik] (*pl* **pique-niques**) NM picnic; **faire un p.** to go on *or* for a picnic

pique-niquer [3] [piknike] VI to picnic, to go on *or* for a picnic

pique-niqueur, -euse [piknikœr, -øz] (*mpl* **pique-niqueurs**, *fpl* **pique-niqueuses**) NM,F picnicker

pique-note, pique-notes [piknɔt] (*pl* **pique-notes**) NM spike file, bill file

piquer [3] [pike] VT **1** *Méd (avec une seringue)* **p. qn** to give sb an injection

2 *Vét (tuer)* **p. un animal** to put an animal down, to put an animal to sleep; **faire p. un chien** to have a dog put down

3 *(avec une pointe)* to prick; **p. un morceau de viande avec une fourchette** to stick a fork into a piece of meat; **p. un bœuf avec un aiguillon** to goad an ox

4 *(sujet: animal, plante)* to sting, to bite; **être piqué** *ou* **se faire p. par une abeille** to get stung by a bee; **se faire p. par un moustique** to get bitten by a mosquito; **être piqué par des orties/méduses** to get stung by nettles/jellyfish

5 *(enfoncer)* to stick; **p. une aiguille dans une pelote** to stick a needle into a ball; **p. une photo sur le mur** to pin a picture on *or* onto the wall; **p. une broche sur un chemisier** to pin a brooch on *or* onto a blouse

6 *(brûler)* to tickle, to tingle, to prickle; **ça pique la gorge** it gives you a tickle in your *or* the throat; **le poivre pique la langue** pepper burns the tongue; **la fumée me pique les yeux** the smoke is making my eyes sting; **le vent me pique les joues** the wind is biting *or* stinging my cheeks

7 *(stimuler ▸ curiosité, jalousie)* to arouse, to awaken; *(▸ amour-propre)* to pique; *(▸ intérêt)* to stir (up)

8 *Fam (faire de manière soudaine)* **p. un cent mètres** *ou* **un sprint** to sprint off; *Fig* to take off in a flash; **p. une colère** to go ballistic, to hit the roof; **p. une crise (de nerfs)** to get hysterical; **p. un somme** *ou* **un roupillon** to take a nap, to grab some shut-eye; **p. un fard** to turn red *or* crimson; **p. une tête** *(plonger)* to dive in; *(se baigner)* to have a dip

9 *Fam (dérober)* to pinch, *Br* to nick; **p. une voiture** to pinch *or Br* to nick a car; **p. un porte-monnaie** to snatch a wallet; **il a piqué la femme de son copain** he ran off with his friend's wife; **p. une phrase dans un livre/à un auteur** to lift a sentence from a book/an author; **je me suis fait p. ma voiture ce matin** my car got pinched *or Br* nicked this morning

10 *Fam (arrêter)* to nab, to collar, *Br* to nick; **la police l'a piqué la main dans le sac** he was caught red-handed; **se faire p.** *(arrêter)* to get nabbed *or Am* nailed; *(surprendre)* to get caught

11 *Mus* **p. une note** to dot a note, to play a note staccato

12 *Couture* to sew; *(cuir)* to stitch

13 *Culin* **p. un rôti d'ail** to stick pieces of garlic into a roast; **p. une viande de lardons** to lard a piece of meat

VI **1** *(brûler ▸ barbe)* to prickle; *(▸ désinfectant, alcool)* to sting; *(▸ yeux)* to burn, to smart; **aïe! ça pique!** ouch! that stings!; **tu piques!** *(tu es mal rasé)* you're all prickly!; **radis/moutarde qui pique** hot radish/mustard; *Fam* **eau qui pique** fizzy water[□]; **vin qui pique** sour wine; **odeur qui pique** pungent smell; **gorge qui pique** sore throat **2** *(descendre ▸ avion)* to (go into a) dive; *(▸ oiseau)* to swoop down; *(▸ personne)* to head straight towards; **p. (droit) vers** to head (straight) for **3** *(locutions)* **p. du nez** *(avion)* to (go into a) nosedive; *(bateau)* to tilt forward; *(fleur)* to droop; *(personne)* to (begin to) drop *or* nod off; *Équitation* **p. des deux** to spur; *Fig* to run away full tilt

VPR **se piquer 1** *(avec une seringue ▸ malade)* to inject oneself; *(▸ drogué)* to shoot up; **il se pique à l'héroïne** he shoots *or* does heroin

2 *(par accident)* to prick oneself

3 *(s'abîmer ▸ papier, linge)* to go mouldy; *(▸ métal)* to pit, to get pitted; *(▸ vin)* to turn sour

4 *Fam* **se p. le nez** *ou* **la ruche** to get plastered

5 *Littéraire* **se p. de** to pride oneself on; **il se pique de connaissances médicales** he prides himself on his knowledge of medicine

6 *(locution)* **elle s'est piquée au jeu** it grew on her

piquet [pikɛ] NM **1** *(pieu)* post, stake, picket; *(plus petit)* peg; **planter un p. dans le sol** to drive a stake into the ground; **p. de tente** tent peg; **être planté comme un p.** to stand there like a lemon *or* dummy

2 *(groupe ▸ de soldats, de grévistes)* picket; **p. d'incendie** fire fighting squad; **p. de grève** picket

3 *(coin)* **mettre un enfant au p.** to send a child to stand in the corner; *aussi Hum* **au p.!** go to the back of the class!

4 *(jeu)* piquet; **faire une partie de p.** to play a hand of piquet

piquetage [piktaʒ] NM *(d'une route, d'un chemin)* staking (out), pegging (out)

piqueter [27] [pikte] VT **1** *(route, chemin)* to stake *or* to peg (out) **2** *Littéraire (parsemer)* to stud, to dot; **un ciel piqueté d'étoiles** a sky studded with stars, a star-studded sky

piquette [pikɛt] NF *Fam* **1** *(vin)* cheap wine[□], *Br* plonk **2** *(défaite)* thrashing, pasting; **foutre la p. à qn** to thrash *or* to paste sb **3** *(locution)* **c'est de la p.** it's a mere trifle

piqueur, -euse [pikœr, -øz] ADJ *Entom* stinging *(avant n)*

NM,F **1** *Couture* stitcher; *(dans l'industrie de la chaussure)* upper stitcher **2** *Fam (voleur)* thief[□]; **un p. d'idées** a stealer of ideas[□] **3** *(surveillant d'écurie)* groom

NM *Constr* overseer

piquouse [pikuz] NF *Fam* shot, *Br* jab; **se faire une p.** to have a jab

piqûre [pikyr] NF **1** *(d'aiguille)* prick; **p. d'épingle** pinprick

2 *(de guêpe, d'abeille)* sting; *(de moustique, de puce)* bite; *(de plante)* sting

3 *Méd* injection, shot; **faire une p. à qn** to give sb an injection; **p. de rappel** booster (injection *or* shot)

4 *Couture (point)* stitch; *(rangs, couture)* stitching *(UNCOUNT)*

5 *(altération ▸ du bois)* wormhole; *(▸ du métal)* pit; **piqûres** *(sur une page)* foxing

6 *(tache ▸ de rouille, de moisi)* spot, speck

piranha [piraɲa] NM *Ich* piranha

piratage [prataʒ] NM pirating *(UNCOUNT)*, piracy; **p. informatique** (computer) hacking; **p. de logiciels** software piracy; **p. musical** music piracy; **p. téléphonique** phreaking

pirate [pirat] NM **1** *(sur les mers)* pirate; **p. de l'air** hijacker

2 *(escroc)* swindler, thief

3 *(de logiciels, de cassettes)* pirate; **p. informatique** cracker, hacker; **p. du téléphone** phreaker

4 *(comme adj; avec ou sans trait d'union)* pirate *(avant n)*; **enregistrement p.** pirate *or* bootleg recording

pirater [3] [pirate] VT **1** *Fam (voler)* to rip off, to rob; **p. des idées** to pinch ideas **2** *(copier illégalement)* to pirate; *Ordinat* to hack; **p. un film/une cassette** to make a pirate copy of a movie *or Br* film/a cassette

VI to pirate

piraterie [piratri] NF **1** *(sur les mers ▸ activité)* piracy; *(▸ acte)* act of piracy; **p. aérienne** air piracy, hijacking **2** *(escroquerie)* swindle **3** *(plagiat)* piracy, pirating; **p. audiovisuelle** unauthorized copying *or* reproduction; **p. commerciale** industrial piracy; **p. informatique** hacking

piraya [piraja] = **piranha**

pire [pir] ADJ **1** *(comparatif)* worse; **si je dors, c'est p. encore** if I sleep, it's even worse; **les conditions sont pires que jamais** the conditions are worse than ever; **ça ne pourrait pas être p.** it couldn't be worse; **c'est de p. en p.** it's getting worse and worse; *Prov* **il n'est p. eau que l'eau qui dort** still waters run deep **2** *(superlatif)* worst; **mon p. ennemi** my worst enemy; **la p. chose qui pouvait arriver** the worst thing that could happen

NM **il y a p.** you could find worse, there is *or* are worse; **le p.** the worst; **s'attendre au p.** to expect the worst; **craindre le p.** to fear the worst; **le p. est qu'elle en aime un autre** the worst (part) of it is that she's in love with someone else; **dans le p. des cas, (en mettant les choses) au p.** at worst

piriforme [pirifɔrm] ADJ pear-shaped, *Spéc* pyriform

pirogue [pirɔg] NF pirogue, dugout

piroguier [pirɔgje] NM pirogue boatman

pirouette [pirwɛt] NF **1** *(tour sur soi-même)* pirouette, body spin; **faire une p.** to pirouette, to spin (on one's heels)

2 *Équitation & (en danse)* pirouette

3 *(changement d'opinion)* about-face, about-turn

4 *(dérobade)* **répondre** *ou* **s'en tirer par une p.** to answer flippantly

pirouetter [4] [pirwete] VI **1** *(pivoter)* to pivot; **p. sur ses talons** to turn on one's heels **2** *(faire une pirouette ▸ danseur)* to pirouette

pis[1] [pi] NM *(de vache)* udder

pis[2] [pi] *Littéraire* ADJ worse; **c'est p. que jamais** it's worse than ever

NM **le p.** *(le pire)* the worst; **il y a p.** you could find worse, there is *or* are worse; **dire p. que pendre de qn** to vilify sb; **on m'a dit p. que pendre de cet homme-là** I've been told the most dreadful things about that man; **le nouveau musée? on en dit p. que pendre** the new museum? nobody has a good word to say about it

ADV worse; **il a fait p. encore** he's done worse things still

• **au pis** ADV if the worst comes to the worst

• **au pis aller** ADV at the very worst

• **qui pis est** ADV what's *or* what is worse

pis-aller [pizale] NM INV *(expédient)* last resort; **on va l'engager mais c'est un p.** we'll take him/her on but it's far from ideal, we'll take him/her on, it's the best we can do under the circumstances

piscicole [pisikɔl] ADJ fish-farming *(avant n)*, *Spéc* piscicultural

pisciculteur, -trice [pisikyltœr, -tris] NM,F fish-farmer, *Spéc* pisciculturist

pisciculture [pisikyltyr] NF fish-farming, *Spéc* pisciculture

pisciforme [pisifɔrm] ADJ fish-shaped, *Spéc* piscine

piscine [pisin] NF **1** *(de natation)* (swimming) pool; **p. couverte/découverte** *ou* **en plein air** indoor/outdoor (swimming) pool; **p. à débordement** infinity pool; **p. d'eau de mer** sea-water pool; **p. municipale** public (swimming) pool; **p. olympique** Olympic-size(d) (swimming) pool; **p. à vagues** wave pool **2** *Fam Arg crime* **la p.** = the French secret service

piscivore [pisivɔr] ADJ fish-eating, *Spéc* piscivorous

NMF fish-eating *or Spéc* piscivorous animal

Pise [piz] NM Pisa; **la tour de P.** the Leaning Tower of Pisa

pissaladière [pisaladjɛr] NF = onion, olive and anchovy tart *(from Nice)*

pisse [pis] NF *très Fam* piss; **c'est de la p. d'âne, ta bière!** your beer's like (gnat's) piss!

pisse-copie [piskɔpi] NMF INV *Fam* hack

pisse-froid [pisfrwa] NM INV *Fam* cold fish

pissenlit [pisɑ̃li] NM **1** *Bot* dandelion; *Fam* **manger les pissenlits par la racine** *(être mort)* to be pushing up the daisies **2** *Can Fam (enfant)* bed-wetter[□]

pisser [3] [pise] *très Fam* VI **1** *(uriner)* to piss, to (have a) pee; **je dois aller p.** I've got to have a piss *or* a leak; **le chien a pissé sur le tapis** the dog peed on the carpet; **il a pissé dans sa culotte** he's pissed in *or* peed in *or* wet his pants; **p. au lit** to wet the bed; *Vulg Fig* **je lui pisse dessus** screw him/her; *Vulg* **je te pisse à la raie!** up yours!; **c'est comme si on pissait dans un violon** it's like pissing into the wind, *Br* it's a bloody waste of time; **laisse p. (le mérinos)** bugger it, forget it; **ça ne pisse pas** *ou* **ne va pas p. loin** it's no big deal *or* great shakes; **envoyer p. qn** to tell sb to piss off; **ne plus se sentir p.** to think one's shit doesn't stink; **c'était à p. de rire** it was an absolute scream; **ils en pissaient dans leur culotte** *ou* **froc** they were pissing themselves (laughing); **ça lui a pris comme une envie de p.** the urge just came over him/her **2** *(fuir)* to leak[□]

VT **1** *(uriner)* to piss; **p. du sang** to piss blood; **p. des lames de rasoir** *(souffrir au cour de la miction)* to piss razor blades **2** *(laisser s'écouler)* **ça pissait le sang** there was blood gushing *or* spurting everywhere; **mon nez pissait le sang** I had blood pouring from my nose; **le moteur commençait à p.**

de l'huile oil started to gush from the engine 3 (locution) p. de la copie to churn it out, to write reams

pissette [pisɛt] NF 1 Chim wash(ing) bottle 2 Can Vulg (pênis) dick, prick

pisseur, -euse [1] [pisœr, -øz] très Fam NM,F (gén) person with a weak bladder□; (enfant qui fait au lit) bedwetter□; p. de copie hack (who writes a lot)
• **pisseuse** NF little madam, little brat

pisseux, -euse [2] [pisø, øz] ADJ Fam 1 (imprégné d'urine) urine-soaked□; des draps p. sheets soaked with pee; les couloirs sont p. (sentent mauvais) the corridors reek of pee 2 (délavé) washed-out□; les papiers peints ont fini par devenir p. the wallpaper has faded over the years□; un vert p. a washed-out shade of green□ 3 (jauni) yellowing□

pisse-vinaigre [pisvinɛgr] NM INV Fam 1 (avare) skinflint, miser 2 (rabat-joie) wet blanket

pissoir [piswar] NM Fam public urinal□

pissou, -x [pisu] NM Can Fam chicken, coward□

pistache [pistaʃ] NF pistachio (nut); glace à la p. pistachio ice-cream
ADJ INV (vert) p. pistachio (green)

pistachier [pistaʃje] NM pistachio (tree)

pistage [pistaʒ] NM (de personne) tailing; (d'animal) tracking, trailing

pistard [pistar] NM track cyclist

piste [pist] NF 1 (trace) track, trail; être sur la p. de qn to be on sb's trail; les policiers sont sur sa p. the police are on his/her trail; ils sont sur la bonne/une fausse p. they're on the right/wrong track; jeu de p. treasure hunt
2 (indice) lead; la police cherche une p. the police are looking for leads
3 Sport (de course à pied) running track; (pour les courses de chevaux) (race)course, (race)track; (de patinage) rink; (de course cycliste) cycling track; (de course automobile) racing track; (d'athlétisme) lane; (d'escrime) piste; p. cendrée cinder track; p. de cirque circus ring; p. de danse dance floor; p. de patinage skating rink; p. de ski skirun, run, piste; p. de ski artificielle dry ski slope
4 (chemin, sentier) trail, track; p. cavalière bridle path; p. cyclable (sur la route) cycle lane; (à côté) cycle track
5 Aviat runway; en bout de p. at the end of the runway; p. d'envol/d'atterrissage take-off/landing runway
6 Cin & Ordinat track; magnéto 4 pistes 4-track tape recorder; p. magnétique (sur carte) magnetic strip; p. sonore soundtrack; p. de travail working track
7 Ordinat p. d'amorçage boot track
• **en piste** EXCLAM off you go! ADV entrer en p. to come into play, to join in

pister [3] [piste] VT (suivre ▸ personne) to tail; (▸ animal) to track, to trail

pisteur [pistœr] NM Ski (pour entretien) ski slope maintenance man; (pour surveillance) ski patrolman

pistil [pistil] NM pistil

pistoche [pistɔʃ] NF Fam (swimming) pool□

pistole [pistɔl] NF Hist pistole

pistolet [pistɔlɛ] NM 1 (arme à feu) pistol, gun; p. à air comprimé air pistol; p. automatique pistol; Sport p. de starter starting pistol
2 (instrument) p. agrafeur staple gun; p. à peinture spray gun; Can Fam être en p. to be hopping mad or fuming
3 (de dessinateur) French curve
4 (jouet) p. à bouchon popgun; p. à eau water pistol
5 Fam (urinal) bottle□
6 Fam (type bizarre) un drôle de p. a shady or Br dodgy character
7 Belg (petit pain) bread roll

pistolet-mitrailleur [pistɔlemitrajœr] (pl pistolets-mitrailleurs) NM submachine-gun

pistoleur [pistɔlœr] NM spray gun painter

piston [pistɔ̃] NM 1 Tech piston; p. de frein brake piston; p. plongeur ram, plunger piston 2 Mus (d'un instrument à vent) valve, piston; (cornet) cornet 3 Fam (recommandation, protection) string-pulling; il est rentré par p. he got in by knowing the right people; elle a du p. she has friends in the right places; elle a fait marcher le p. pour se faire embaucher she got somebody to pull a few strings for her to get the job

pistonné, -e [pistɔne] NM,F Fam c'est un p. he got where he is thanks to a bit of string-pulling

pistonner [3] [pistɔne] VT Fam to pull strings for; elle s'est fait p. pour entrer au ministère she used her connections to get into the Ministry□

pistou [pistu] NM (sauce) pesto; (soupe) = vegetable soup with pesto

pita [pita] NF pitta bread

pitahaya [pitaaja] NF Bot dragon fruit, pitahaya

pitance [pitɑ̃s] NF Littéraire sustenance, daily bread; une maigre p. scanty or meagre fare; gagner sa p. to earn a living

> Il faut noter que le terme anglais **pittance** est un faux ami. Il désigne une somme dérisoire.

pitaya [pitaja] NF = pitahaya

pitbull [pitbul] NM pitbull (terrier)

pitcher [3] [pitʃe] VT Cin to pitch

pitchoun, -e [pitʃun], **pitchounet, -ette** [pitʃunɛ, -ɛt] NM,F (dans le Midi) little one; où il est, le p.? where's the little one?

pitchpin [pitʃpɛ̃] NM pitch pine

piteuse [pitøz] voir piteux

piteusement [pitøzmɑ̃] ADV miserably, pathetically

piteux, -euse [pitø, -øz] ADJ 1 (pitoyable) pitiful, piteous; être en p. état to be in a pitiful condition; un manteau en p. état a shabby coat
2 (mauvais, médiocre) poor, mediocre
3 (triste) faire piteuse mine to look crestfallen
4 (honteux) sheepish; elle s'est excusée de façon piteuse she apologized shamefacedly

pithécanthrope [pitekɑ̃trɔp] NM pithecanthropus

pithiviers [pitivje] NM puff-pastry cake (filled with almond cream)

pitié [pitje] NF 1 (compassion) pity; elle l'a fait par p. pour lui she did it out of pity for him; avoir p. de qn (s'apitoyer) to feel pity for or to pity sb; elle me fait p. I feel sorry for her; vous me faites p.! you look awful!; (avec mépris) you're pitiful!; cela faisait p. à voir it was pitiful to see; la pièce? c'était à faire p. the play? it was wretched or pitiful; prendre qn en p. to take pity on sb 2 (désolation) pity; quelle p.!, c'est une p.! what a pity! 3 (clémence) mercy, pity; il a eu p. de ses ennemis he had mercy on or took pity on his enemies; elle avait l'air si fatiguée que j'ai eu p. d'elle et j'ai fait la vaisselle à sa place she looked so tired that I took pity on her and did the dishes for her
EXCLAM (par) p.! (have) mercy!; (avec agacement) for pity's sake!; par p., taisez-vous! for pity's sake, be quiet!
• **sans pitié** ADJ ruthless, merciless; ils ont été sans p. (jurés) they showed no mercy; (terroristes) they were ruthless

piton [pitɔ̃] NM 1 (clou ▸ gén) eye or eye-headed nail; (▸ d'alpiniste) piton 2 Géog p. rocheux rocky outcrop 3 Can Fam (d'une sonnette) button□; (d'un clavier) key□

pitoune [pitun] NF Can 1 (bille de bois) pulpwood bolt
2 Fam (femme bien en chair) plump woman□; grosse p. fat lump (of a woman)
3 Fam Péj (femme de mœurs légères) tramp, tart
4 Fam (terme d'affection) darling, sweetheart

pitoyable [pitwajabl] ADJ 1 (triste ▸ destin) pitiful; c'est p. à voir it's a pitiful or pathetic sight 2 (mauvais ▸ effort, résultat, excuse) pitiful, pathetic

pitoyablement [pitwajabləmɑ̃] ADV 1 (tristement) pitifully 2 (médiocrement) pitifully, deplorably; échouer p. to fail miserably

pitre [pitr] NM 1 (plaisantin) clown; faire le p. to clown or to fool around 2 (bouffon) clown

pitrerie [pitrəri] NF tomfoolery (UNCOUNT); faire des pitreries to clown or to fool around

pittoresque [pitɔrɛsk] ADJ picturesque, colourful
NM picturesqueness

pituitaire [pitɥitɛr] ADJ Anat pituitary

pituite [pitɥit] NF Méd gastrorrhoea

pive [piv] NF Suisse pine cone

pivelé, -e [pivle] ADJ Can (moucheté ▸ gén) spotted; (▸ de taches de rousseur) freckled

pivert [pivɛr] NM Orn (green) woodpecker

pivoine [pivwan] NF Bot peony

pivot [pivo] NM 1 (axe ▸ gén) pivot; (▸ de levier) fulcrum; (▸ de compas, de boussole) centre pin; à p., monté sur p. pivoted, swivelling; Aut p. de fusée kingpin, kingbolt
2 (centre) pivot, hub; le p. de toute son argumentation the crux of his/her argument
3 Sport centre
4 (en dentisterie) post

pivotant, -e [pivɔtɑ̃, -ɑ̃t] ADJ (qui tourne) revolving, swivelling; fauteuil p. swivel chair

pivoter [3] [pivɔte] VI 1 (autour d'un axe ▸ porte) to revolve (sur/autour de on/around); (▸ fauteuil) to swivel; (▸ aiguille) to swivel around, to pivot; faire p. qch to swing sth (round) 2 (personne) to turn; p. sur ses talons to spin round, to pivot on one's heels 3 Mil to wheel round

pixel [piksɛl] NM pixel

pixélisé, -e [pikselise] ADJ Ordinat pixellated (avant n)

pixillation [piksilasjɔ̃] NF Cin & TV pixillation

pizza [pidza] NF pizza

pizzeria [pidzerja] NF pizzeria

pizzicato [pidzikato] (pl pizzicati [-ti]) NM Mus pizzicato

PJ [1] [peʒi] NF Fam (abrév police judiciaire) Br ≃ CID, Am ≃ FBI

PJ [2] (abrév écrite pièces jointes) encl.

placage [plakaʒ] NM 1 (revêtement ▸ de bois) veneering; (▸ de pierre, de marbre) facing, cladding; (▸ de métal) plating; bois de p. veneer 2 Sport tackle 3 Littérature & Mus Fam patchwork (composition)

placard [plakar] NM 1 (armoire) cupboard, Am closet; p. à balais broom cupboard; p. de cuisine kitchen cupboard; p. mural wall cupboard; p. à provisions store cupboard; p. de salle de bains bathroom cabinet; p. à vêtements Br wardrobe, Am closet; avoir un cadavre dans le p. to have a skeleton in the Br cupboard or Am closet; Fam mettre qn au p. (l'écarter) to sideline sb□; Fam mettre qch au p. (le retirer de la circulation) to put sth in cold storage or in mothballs; Fam mettre qn dans un p. doré to kick sb upstairs
2 (affiche) poster; p. publicitaire display advertisement; (grand) large display advertisement; (de pleine page) full-page advertisement
3 Typ galley (proof)
4 Naut patch
5 Fam (prison) slammer, clink; faire 20 ans de p. to do 20 years inside or in the clink; mettre qn au p. to put sb behind bars or inside or away

> Il faut noter que le terme anglais **placard** est un faux ami. Il signifie **pancarte**.

placarder [3] [plakarde] VT 1 (afficher ▸ photo, affiche) to stick up, to put up; j'ai placardé des photos sur les murs I plastered the walls with photos 2 (couvrir ▸ mur) p. qch de qch to cover sth with sth 3 Typ p. un ouvrage to set a book in galleys

placardisation [plakardizasjɔ̃] NF Fam sidelining□

placardiser [3] [plakardize] VT Fam to sideline□

PLACE [plas]

• space 1, 4	• room 1
• place 2, 7	• seat 3
• ticket 3	• square 5
• job, position 6	• rank 7

NF 1 (espace disponible) space (UNCOUNT), room (UNCOUNT); je n'ai pas la p. pour un piano I haven't got enough room or space for a piano; faire de la p. to make room or space; fais une p. sur le bureau pour l'ordinateur make some room or clear a space on the desk for the computer; faites-lui une petite p. give him/her a bit of room; il reste de la p. pour quatre personnes there's enough space or room left for four people; prendre de la p. to take up a lot of space or room; ne prends pas toute la p. (à table, au lit) don't take up so much room; *(sur la page)* don't use up all the space; **laisser la** *ou* **faire p. à** to make room *or* way for; **la machine à écrire a fait p. au traitement de texte** word processors have taken over from *or* superseded typewriters; **ce travail ne laisse aucune p. à la créativité** there's no place *or* room for creativity in this kind of work; **p. aux jeunes!** make room for the younger generation!; **et maintenant, p. aux artistes** and now, on with the show; **la musique tient une grande p. dans ma vie** music is a very important part of my life; **sa famille ne tient qu'une petite p. dans son emploi du temps** he/she devotes very little time to his/her family; **p. au sol** *(d'un ordinateur, d'une voiture)* footprint; **faire p. nette** to tidy up; *Fig* to clear up, to make a clean sweep; **j'ai fait p. nette dans la cuisine** I cleared up the kitchen

2 *(endroit précis)* place, spot; **changer les meubles de p.** to move the furniture around; **mets/remets les clefs à leur p.** put the keys/put the keys back where they belong; **la statue est toujours à la même p.** the statue is still in the same place *or* spot; **ce plateau n'est pas à sa p.** this tray isn't in its proper place *or* doesn't belong here; **est-ce que tout est à sa p.?** is everything in order *or* in its proper place?; **savoir rester à sa p.** to know one's place; **je ne me sens pas à ma p. parmi eux** I feel out of place among them; **ta p. n'est pas ici** you're out of place here; **trouver sa p. dans l'existence** to find one's niche in life; **il a rapidement trouvé sa p. dans notre équipe** he quickly fitted into our team; *Fig* **avoir une** *ou* **sa p. quelque part** to have one's place somewhere; **tu auras toujours une p. dans mon cœur** there'll always be a place in my heart for you; **reprendre sa p.** *(sa position)* to go back to one's place; *(son rôle)* to go back to where one belongs; **notre collègue ne pourra pas reprendre sa p. parmi nous** our colleague is unable to resume his/her post with us; **pour rien au monde je ne donnerais ma p.** I wouldn't swop places for anything in the world; **remettre qn à sa p.** to put sb in his/her place; **se faire une p. au soleil** to make a success of things, to find one's place in the sun; **une p. pour chaque chose et chaque chose à sa p.** a place for everything and everything in its place

3 *(siège)* seat; *(fauteuil au spectacle)* seat; *(billet)* ticket; **retourne à ta p.** go back to your seat; **céder** *ou* **laisser sa p. à qn** to give up *or* to offer one's seat to sb; **avoir la p. d'honneur** *(sur l'estrade)* to sit at the centre of the stage; *(à table)* to sit at the top *or* head of the table; **à la p. du conducteur** in the driver's seat; **à la p. du mort** in the (front) passenger seat; **une voiture à deux places** a two-seater car; **une salle de 500 places** a room that can seat 500 people; **un autobus de 46 places** a 46-seater bus; **réserver une p. d'avion/de train** to make a plane/train reservation; **payer p. entière** to pay full price; **il a pris le train sans payer sa p.** he got on the train without buying a ticket; **j'ai trois places de concert** I have three tickets for the concert; **ça vous ennuierait de changer de p.?** would you mind swopping places?; **est-ce que cette p. est prise?** is anybody sitting here?; **prendre p.** *(s'asseoir)* to sit down; **p. assise** seat; **25 places debout** *(sign)* 25 standing; **il ne reste plus que des places debout** it's now standing room only; **dans le monde du spectacle, les places sont chères** it's difficult to gain a foothold in show business; *aussi Fig* **la p. est toute chaude** the seat's still warm

4 *(dans un parking)* (parking) space; *Suisse* **p. de parc** *(individuel)* parking space; *(collectif)* *Br* car park, *Am* parking lot

5 *(espace urbain)* square; **la p. du marché** the market place, the market square; **la p. du village** the village square; **médecin connu sur la p. de Paris** doctor well-known in Paris; **sur la p. publique** in public; **porter le débat sur la p. publique** to make the debate public; *Suisse* **p. de jeu(x)** playground; *Suisse* **p. de sport** sportsground; **la p. de la Concorde** = one of the biggest and busiest squares in Paris, laid out in the reign of Louis XV; **la p. Rouge** Red Square; **la p. Tian'anmen** Tiananmen Square

6 *(poste, emploi)* position, post; **quitter/perdre sa p.** to leave/to lose one's job; **une bonne p.** a good job; **il y a peu de places libres** there are few situations vacant; **je cherche une p. de secrétaire** I'm looking for a job as a secretary

7 *(rang ▸ dans une compétition)* place, rank; **avoir la première p.** to come first *or* top; **avoir la dernière p.** to come last *or* *Br* bottom; **elle est en bonne p. au dernier tour** she's well placed on the last lap; **être** *ou* **partir en bonne p. pour gagner** to be (all) set to win

8 *Bourse* **p. boursière** stock market; **p. financière** financial centre; **p. financière internationale** money market; **le dollar est à la hausse sur la p. financière de New York** the dollar has risen on the New York exchange

9 *Mil* **p. d'armes** parade ground, *Am* parade; **p. (forte)** fortress, stronghold; **nous voici dans la p.** *(ville assiégée)* here we are, inside the walls (of the city); *(endroit quelconque)* here we are; *Fig* we've now gained a foothold

10 *Belg (pièce d'habitation)* room

• **à la place** ADV instead; **on ira en Espagne à la p.** we'll go to Spain instead; **j'ai rapporté la jupe et j'ai pris un pantalon à la p.** I returned the skirt and exchanged it for a pair of trousers

• **à la place de** PRÉP **1** *(au lieu de)* instead of; **à la p. du documentaire, on a eu un vieux feuilleton** instead of the documentary, we were shown an old series; **j'irai à sa p.** I'll go instead of him/her **2** *(dans la situation de)* **à ma/sa p.** in my/his/her situation; **à ta p., j'irais** if I were you I'd go; **mettez-vous à ma p.** put yourself in my place *or* shoes; **je ne voudrais pas être à sa p.** rather him/her than me

• **de place en place** ADV here and there

• **en place** ADJ *(important)* established; **un homme politique en p.** a well-established politician; **les gens en p. disent que...** the powers that be say that... ADV **1** *(là)* in position; **les forces de police sont déjà en p.** the police have already taken up their position; **est-ce que tout est en p.?** is everything in order *or* in its proper place? **2** *(locutions)* **mettre en p.** *(équipement)* to set up; *(plan)* to set up, to put into action; *(réseau)* to set up; **la méthode sera mise en p. progressivement** the method will be phased in (gradually); **ça va lui mettre/remettre les idées en p.** it'll give him a more realistic view of things/set him thinking straight again; **il ne tient pas en p.** *(il est turbulent)* he can't keep still; *(il est anxieux)* he's nervous; *(il voyage beaucoup)* he's always on the move

• **par places** ADV here and there

• **sur place** ADV there, on the spot; **je serai déjà sur p.** I'll already be there; **tué sur p.** killed on the spot; **s'approvisionner sur p.** to use local suppliers

placé, -e [plase] ADJ **1** *(aux courses)* **cheval p.** placed horse; **arriver p.** to be placed **2** *(situé)* **bien p.** *(magasin, appartement)* well-situated; *(bouton, couture)* well-positioned; **mal p.** *(magasin, appartement)* badly-located; *(bouton, couture)* poorly-positioned; *(coup)* below the belt; *(orgueil)* misplaced; **on était très bien/mal placés** *(au spectacle)* we had really good/bad seats; *Fig* **être bien/mal p. pour faire qch** to be in a good position/no position to do sth; **il est mal p. pour en parler** he's in no position to talk (about it) **3** *(socialement)* **haut p.** well up *or* high up in the hierarchy; **des gens haut placés** people in high places

placebo [plasebo] NM placebo

placement [plasmɑ̃] NM **1** *(investissement)* investment; **faire un p.** to make an investment, to invest; **nous avons acheté la maison pour faire un p.** we bought the house as an investment; **un p. de père de famille** a gilt-edged investment, a blue chip; **p. en actions** equity investment; **p. à court terme/à long terme** short-term/long-term investment; **p. éthique** ethical investment; **p. financier** Stock Market investment; **p. obligataire** bond investment; **p. à revenus fixes** fixed-income *or* fixed-yield investment; **p. à revenus variables** variable-income *or* variable-yield investment

2 *(de chômeurs)* placing

3 *Jur (d'un mineur dans une famille d'accueil ou dans un organisme)* placement; **je m'occupe du p. des jeunes dans les familles** my job is finding homes for young people

4 *(attribution d'un siège)* seating

5 *(internement)* **p. d'office** hospitalization order; **p. volontaire** ≃ voluntary admission *(including detention for observation)*

6 *Mktg* placement; *Cin & TV* **p. de produit** product placement

placenta [plasɛ̃ta] NM placenta

placentaire [plasɛ̃tɛr] *Zool* ADJ placental
NM placental mammal

PLACER [16] [plase]

VT	
• to place **1, 3–5**	• to seat **2**
• to put **3, 5, 8**	• to set **6**
• to locate **7**	• to sell **10**
• to invest **11**	• to find a job for **12**
VPR	
• to stand, to sit **1**	• to consider **3**
• to finish **4**	• to find a job **5**
• to sell **7**	

VT **1** *(mettre dans une position précise)* to place; **p. ses doigts sur le clavier** to place one's fingers on the keyboard; *Sport* **p. la balle** to place the ball

2 *(faire asseoir)* to seat; **l'ouvreuse va vous p.** the usherette will show you to your seats; **p. des convives à table** to seat guests around a table; **pourvu qu'ils ne me placent pas à côté d'Anne!** I hope they don't put me next to Anne!

3 *(établir ▸ dans une position, un état)* to put, to place; **p. qn devant ses responsabilités** to force sb to face up to his/her responsibilities

4 *(établir ▸ dans une institution)* to place; **p. un enfant à l'Assistance publique** to place *or* to put a child in care; **p. qn à l'hospice** to put sb in an old people's home

5 *(classer)* to put, to place; **moi, je le placerais parmi les grands écrivains** I would rate *or* rank him among the great writers

6 *(situer dans le temps)* **il a placé l'action du film en l'an 2000** he set the film in the year 2000

7 *(situer dans l'espace)* to locate; **je n'arrive pas à p. Nice sur la carte** I can't tell you where Nice is on the map

8 *(mettre)* to put; **p. sa confiance en qn** to put one's trust in sb; **elle a placé tous ses espoirs dans ce projet** she's pinned all her hopes on this project

9 *(dans la conversation)* **il essaie toujours de p. quelques boutades** he always tries to slip in a few jokes; **je n'ai pas pu p. un mot** I couldn't get a word in edgeways; *Fam* **je peux en p. une?** can I get a word in?

10 *(vendre)* to sell; **les enfants sont chargés de p. les billets de loterie** the children are to sell the lottery tickets; *Hum* **j'essaie désespérément de p. mon vieux canapé!** I'm desperately trying to find a home for my old sofa!

11 *Fin* to invest; **le banquier s'est chargé de p. mon argent** the banker helped me invest my money; **p. de l'argent sur un compte** to put *or* deposit money in an account

12 *(procurer un emploi à)* to find a job for; **p. les jeunes chômeurs** to find jobs for unemployed young people; **p. qn comme apprenti chez qn** to apprentice sb to sb; **elle a été placée à la direction commerciale** she was appointed head of the sales department

VPR **se placer 1** *(dans l'espace)* **place-toi près de la fenêtre** *(debout)* stand near the window; *(assis)* sit near the window; **placez-vous en cercle** get into a circle; **plaçons-nous plus près de l'écran** let's move closer to the screen

2 *(dans le temps)* **plaçons-nous un instant au début du siècle** let's go back for a moment to the turn of the century

3 *(dans un jugement, une analyse)* to look at *or* to consider things; **si l'on se place de son point de vue** if you look at things from his/her point of view

4 *(occuper un rang)* to rank, to finish; **se p. premier/troisième** to finish first/third

5 *(trouver un emploi)* **elle s'est placée comme infirmière** she found *or* got a job as a nurse

6 *Fam (se présenter avantageusement)* **se p. auprès du patron** to butter up *or* to sweet-talk the boss

7 *(se vendre)* to sell; **ces marchandises se placent facilement** these goods sell easily

placet [plasɛ] NM **1** *Arch (demande écrite)* petition, address **2** *Jur (réquisition d'audience)* (plaintiff's) claim

placette [plasɛt] NF (small) square

placeur, -euse [plasœr, -øz] **NM,F 1** *(dans une salle de spectacle)* usher, *f* usherette **2** *(dans une agence pour l'emploi)* employment agent

placide [plasid] **ADJ** placid, calm

placidement [plasidmɑ̃] **ADV** placidly, calmly

placidité [plasidite] **NF** placidness, calmness

placier [plasje] **NM 1** *(forain)* market superintendent, market pitch agent **2** *(représentant de commerce)* sales representative; *(qui fait du porte-à-porte)* door-to-door salesman, *f* saleswoman

Placoplâtre® [plakoplɑtr] **NM** plasterboard

placoter [3] [plakɔte] **VI** *Can Fam* to gossip

plafond [plafɔ̃] **NM 1** *(d'un bâtiment)* ceiling; *(d'une voiture, d'une galerie)* roof; **faux p.** false ceiling; **p. à caissons** coffered ceiling; **p. flottant** *ou* **suspendu** drop *or* suspended ceiling; **la pièce est basse de p.** the room has got a low ceiling; *Fig* **il est un peu bas de p.** he's a bit slow on the uptake

2 *Aviat* ceiling

3 *Météo* **p. (nuageux)** (cloud) ceiling

4 *(limite supérieure)* ceiling; **le p. des salaires** the wage ceiling, the ceiling on wages; **fixer un p. à un budget** to put a ceiling on a budget, to cap a budget; **p. des charges budgétaires** spending limit, budgetary limit; **p. de crédit** credit ceiling *or* limit; *Banque* **p. de découvert** overdraft limit; **p. de l'impôt** tax ceiling; *Banque* **p. d'autorisation de retrait, p. de retrait** withdrawal limit

5 *(comme adj: avec ou sans trait d'union)* ceiling *(avant n)*; **vitesse p.** maximum speed; **des prix plafonds** ceiling *or* top prices

plafonnage [plafɔnaʒ] **NM** *(d'une pièce)* ceiling installation

plafonnement [plafɔnmɑ̃] **NM p. des salaires/cotisations** *(fait de limiter)* setting a ceiling on wages/contributions; *(fait d'atteindre un plafond)* levelling off of wages/contributions

plafonner [3] [plafɔne] **VT 1** *(pièce, maison)* to put a ceiling in *or* into **2** *(impôts, salaires etc)* to set a ceiling on; **les cotisations sont plafonnées à 12 pour cent** contributions have a ceiling *or* upper limit of 12 percent

VI 1 *(avion)* to fly at the ceiling; *(voiture)* to go at maximum *or* top speed **2** *(ventes, salaires)* to level off; *(taux d'intérêt, prix)* to peak; **la production plafonne** output has reached its ceiling; **je plafonne à 1500 euros depuis un an** my monthly income hasn't exceeded 1,500 euros for over a year

plafonneur [plafɔnœr] **NM** *(plâtrier)* ceiling plasterer

plafonnier [plafɔnje] **NM** *(d'appartement)* ceiling light; *(de véhicule)* (overhead) courtesy *or* guide light

plage [plaʒ] **NF 1** *(grève)* beach; **p. de galets/de sable** pebble/sandy beach; **aller en vacances à la p.** to go on holiday to the seaside

2 *(espace de temps)* **p. horaire** (allotted) slot; **p. publicitaire** commercial break

3 *(écart)* range; **p. de prix** price range; **p. de taux** rate band

4 *Littéraire (surface)* zone, area; **une p. d'ombre** an area of shadow; **une p. de lumière** a sunny area; *Opt* **p. lumineuse** light area, highlight

5 *Naut (d'un cuirassé)* freeboard deck; **p. avant** foredeck; **p. arrière** quarterdeck, afterdeck

6 *Aut* **p. arrière** parcel shelf, back shelf

7 *(d'un disque)* track

• **de plage ADJ** beach *(avant n)*; **serviette de p.** beach towel; **vêtements de p.** beachwear

plagiaire [plaʒjɛr] **NMF** plagiarizer, plagiarist

plagiat [plaʒja] **NM** plagiary, plagiarism

plagier [9] [plaʒje] **VT** *(œuvre, auteur)* to plagiarize

plagiste [plaʒist] **NMF** beach attendant

plaid [plɛd] **NM** *(pièce de tissu)* plaid; *(couverture)* car rug

plaidable [plɛdabl] **ADJ** pleadable

plaidant, -e [plɛdɑ̃, -ɑ̃t] **ADJ** *voir* **avocat**[2], **parti**[1]

plaider [4] [plede] **VI 1** *Jur* to plead; **p. pour qn** to defend sb, to plead for *or* on behalf of sb; **p. contre qn** to plead (the case) against sb **2** *(présenter des arguments) aussi Fig* **p. en faveur de qn/qch** to speak in sb's/sth's favour; *aussi Fig* **p. contre qn/qch** to speak against sb/sth; **ton attitude ne plaide guère en ta faveur** your attitude hardly speaks for you *or* is hardly a strong point in your favour; **nous plaidons ici pour le respect des droits de l'homme** we are here to defend human rights

VT to plead; *Jur* **p. une cause** to plead a case; **l'affaire sera plaidée en juin** the case will be heard in June; **p. coupable/non coupable** to plead guilty/not guilty, to make a plea of guilty/not guilty; **plaidez-vous coupable ou non coupable?** how do you plead(, guilty or not guilty)?; **p. la légitime défense** to plead self-defence; *Fig* **p. la cause de qn** to speak in favour of *or* to defend sb, to plead sb's cause; **p. sa propre cause** to speak in one's own defence

VPR se plaider la cause s'est plaidée hier the case was heard yesterday

plaider coupable, plaider-coupable [plɛdekupabl] **NM** *Jur* plea-bargaining

plaideur, -euse [plɛdœr, -øz] **NM,F** litigant

plaidoirie [plɛdwari] **NF 1** *(exposé) Jur* speech for the defence; *Fig* defence **2** *(action de plaider)* pleading

plaidoyer [plɛdwaje] **NM 1** *Jur* speech for the defence **2** *(supplication)* plea

plaie [plɛ] **NF 1** *(blessure)* wound; **p. profonde/superficielle** deep/surface wound; **une p. vive** an open wound; **le départ de sa femme est resté pour lui une p. vive** his wife's departure scarred him for life

2 *Littéraire (tourment)* wound; *Prov* **p. d'argent n'est pas mortelle** = money isn't everything

3 *Bible* **les dix plaies d'Égypte** the ten plagues of Egypt

4 *Fam (personne ennuyeuse)* pest, pain, nuisance; *(chose ennuyeuse)* pain, nuisance

plaignait *etc voir* **plaindre**

plaignant, -e [plɛɲɑ̃, -ɑ̃t] *Jur* **ADJ la partie plaignante** the plaintiff

NM,F plaintiff

plain [plɛ̃] **ADJ** *Fam Vieilli (terrain, surface)* flat, level, even

NM le p. high tide

plain-chant [plɛ̃ʃɑ̃] *(pl* **plains-chants)** **NM** plainsong, plainchant

plaindre [80] [plɛ̃dr] **VT 1** *(avoir pitié de)* to feel sorry for, to pity; **je plains celle qui l'épousera!** I feel sorry for *or* I pity whoever's going to marry him!; **comme je vous plains** I do feel sorry for you; **il adore se faire p.** he's always looking for sympathy; **il est plus à p. qu'à blâmer** he is more to be pitied than blamed; **avec tout l'argent qu'ils gagnent, ils ne sont vraiment pas à p.** with all the money they're making, they've got nothing to worry about **2** *Vieilli (donner parcimonieusement)* to give grudgingly, to spare; **ne pas p. sa peine** to be unstinting in one's efforts; **je n'ai jamais plaint mon temps passé auprès des enfants** I never begrudged the time I spent with the children

VPR se plaindre 1 *(protester)* to complain; **arrête de te p. tout le temps** stop complaining all the time; *Ironique* **plains-toi (donc)!** my heart bleeds for you!; **se p. de** *(symptôme)* to complain of; *(personne, situation)* to complain about; **le patient se plaint de manquer** *ou* **de son manque d'appétit** the patient is complaining of loss of appetite; **il est venu se p. à moi de sa femme** he came and complained to me about his wife; **elle se plaint de ce qu'on la traite comme une servante** she complains that they treat her like a servant; **ce n'est pas moi qui m'en plaindrai!** I'm not complaining! **2** *(geindre)* to moan, to groan

plaine [plɛn] **NF 1** *(étendue plate)* plain **2** *Belg* **p. de jeux** playground; **p. de(s) sports** sports field *or* ground

plain-pied [plɛ̃pje] **de plain-pied ADV 1** *(au même niveau)* on the same level (**avec** as), on a level (**avec** with); **la chambre et le salon sont de p.** the bedroom and the living room are on the same level *or* on a level; **une maison construite de p.** *(avec le sol extérieur) Br* a bungalow, *Am* a ranch house **2** *(d'emblée)* **entrons de p. dans le sujet** let's get straight to the point **3** *(sur un pied d'égalité)* **être de p. avec qn** to be on an equal footing with sb

plaint, -e [plɛ̃, -ɛ̃t] **PP** *voir* **plaindre**

• **plainte NF 1** *(gémissement ▸ d'un malade)* moan, groan; *Littéraire* **les plaintes du vent** the howling of the wind **2** *(protestation)* complaining *(UNCOUNT)*, moaning *(UNCOUNT)*; **c'est un sujet de plainte assez répandu** it's a common complaint; **je n'ai aucun sujet de plainte** I have no complaints, I have nothing to complain about **3** *Jur* complaint; **déposer une plainte** to lodge *or* to file a complaint; **porter plainte contre qn** to bring an action against sb; **plainte en diffamation** action for libel; **plainte contre X** action against person or persons unknown

plaintif, -ive [plɛ̃tif, -iv] **ADJ** plaintive, mournful; **d'un ton p.** plaintively

plaintivement [plɛ̃tivmɑ̃] **ADV** plaintively, mournfully

plaire [110] [plɛr] **plaire à VT IND 1** *(être apprécié par)* **cela me plaît** I like it; **l'album m'a plu** I liked the album; **le potage ne vous a pas plu?** didn't you like the soup?; **ça vous plaît, le commerce?** how do you like business life?; **le nouveau professeur ne me plaît pas du tout** I really don't like *or* care for the new teacher; **rien ne lui plaît** there's no pleasing him/her; **cette idée ne me plaît pas du tout** I'm not at all keen on this idea; *Fam* **il commence à me p., celui-là!** he's starting to bug me *or Br* get on my wick!; **offre du parfum, ça plaît toujours** give perfume, it's always appreciated

2 *(convenir à)* **si ça me plaît** if I feel like it; **quand ça me plaît** whenever I feel like it; **elle ne lit que ce qui lui plaît** she only reads what she feels like (reading)

3 *(séduire)* to be appealing *or* attractive to; **il cherche à p. aux femmes** he tries hard to make himself attractive to women; **c'est le genre de fille qui plaît aux hommes** she's the kind of girl that men find attractive

USAGE ABSOLU il a vraiment tout pour p.! he's got everything going for him!; *Ironique* he's so marvellous!; **aimer p.** to take pleasure in being attractive; **une robe doit p. avant tout** a dress must above all be appealing

V IMPERSONNEL 1 *(convenir)* **il lui plaît de croire que...** he/she likes to think that...; **te plairait-il de nous accompagner?** would you like to come with us?; **comme** *ou* **tant qu'il te plaira** *(exprime l'indifférence)* see if I care; **tu le prends sur ce ton? comme il te plaira** if you choose to take it like that, see if I care; **plaise à Dieu** *ou* **au ciel que...** *(souhait)* please God that...; **plût à Dieu** *ou* **au ciel que...** *(regret)* if only...

2 *(locutions)* **s'il te plaît, s'il vous plaît** please; **s'il vous plaît!** *(dit par un client)* excuse me!; *Belg (dit par un serveur)* there you go!; **prête-moi un stylo, s'il te plaît** lend me a pen, please; *Fam* **du caviar, s'il vous plaît, on ne se refuse rien!** caviar! my, my, we're splashing out a bit, aren't we?; *Vieilli ou Hum* **plaît-il?** I beg your pardon?

VPR se plaire 1 *(emploi réciproque)* **ces deux jeunes gens se plaisent, c'est évident** it's obvious that those two like each other

2 *(dans un endroit)* **je me plais (bien) dans ma nouvelle maison** I enjoy living in my new house, I like it in my new house; **alors, vous vous plaisez à Paris?** so, how do you like living in *or* like it in Paris?

3 se p. à to enjoy, to delight *or* take pleasure in; **il se plaît à la contredire** he loves *or* enjoys contradicting her; *Ironique* **je me plais à penser que tu as fait tes devoirs avant de sortir** I suppose you've done your homework before going out

plaisamment [plɛzamɑ̃] **ADV 1** *(agréablement)* pleasantly, agreeably **2** *(de façon amusante)* amusingly **3** *(risiblement)* ridiculously, laughably

plaisance [plɛzɑ̃s] **NF** (pleasure) boating

• **de plaisance ADJ** *(navigation, bateau)* pleasure *(avant n)*

plaisancier, -ère [plɛzɑ̃sje, -ɛr] **NM,F** amateur yachtsman, *f* yachtswoman

plaisant, -e [plɛzɑ̃, -ɑ̃t] **ADJ 1** *(agréable)* pleasant, nice; **p. à l'œil** pleasing to the eye, nice to look at **2** *(drôle)* funny, amusing **3** *(ridicule)* ridiculous, laughable

NM 1 *(aspect)* **le p. de l'histoire** the funny part of it; **le p. de cette aventure** the funny thing about this adventure **2** *Vieilli (farceur)* wag, joker **3** **mauvais p.** joker; **un mauvais p. avait débranché la télé** some joker had unplugged the TV

plaisanter [3] [plezɑ̃te] VI 1 *(faire de l'esprit)* to joke; *(faire une plaisanterie)* to (crack a) joke; elle aime bien p. she enjoys a joke; elle n'était pas d'humeur à p. she wasn't in a joking mood; il faut bien p., n'est-ce pas? we all have to have a laugh from time to time, don't we?; p. sur to make fun of; p. sur le nom de qn to make fun of sb's name; en plaisantant jokingly; je l'ai dit pour p. I meant it as a joke 2 *(parler à la légère)* to joke; c'est vrai, je ne plaisante pas it's true, I'm not joking; tu plaisantes! you can't be serious!, you've got to be joking! 3 *(prendre à la légère)* on ne plaisante pas avec ces choses-là you mustn't joke about such things; le patron ne plaisante pas avec la discipline the boss takes discipline very seriously *or* is a stickler for discipline; on ne plaisante pas avec la santé you shouldn't take any chances with your health

VT to make fun of, to tease; ils n'arrêtent pas de le p. sur son accent they're always teasing him about his accent

plaisanterie [plezɑ̃tri] NF 1 *(parole amusante)* joke; faire des plaisanteries to tell *or* crack jokes; lancer une p. to make a joke; c'est une p., j'espère? I trust *or* hope you're joking; c'est une p.! *(ça ne peut être sérieux)* it must be a joke!; la p. a assez duré this has gone far enough; une p. de mauvais goût a joke in bad *or* poor taste; les plaisanteries les plus courtes sont les meilleures brevity is the soul of wit

2 *(humour)* joking; comprendre *ou* entendre la p. to be able to take a joke; elle ne comprend *ou* n'entend pas la p. she can't take a joke; je l'ai dit par p. I meant it as a joke; pousser trop loin la p. to take the joke too far, to go too far; p. à part joking apart; tourner qch en p. to make a joke of sth

3 *(raillerie)* joke, jibe; faire des plaisanteries sur le nom de qn to make fun of sb's name; elle est en butte aux plaisanteries de ses collègues she's the laughing stock of her colleagues; mauvaise p. cruel joke

4 *(chose facile)* child's play *(UNCOUNT)*; c'est une p., cet exercice! this exercise is child's play!

plaisantin [plezɑ̃tɛ̃] NM 1 *(farceur)* joker, clown; quel est le petit p. qui m'a donné un faux numéro? which joker gave me a wrong number? 2 *(fumiste)* ce n'est qu'un p. he's nothing but a fly-by-night

plaisir [plezir] NM 1 *(joie)* pleasure; j'éprouve du p. à écouter du jazz I get pleasure out of listening to jazz; avoir (du) p. *ou* prendre (du) p. à faire qch to take pleasure in doing sth; j'ai eu grand p. à voyager avec vous it was a real pleasure travelling with you; faire p. à qn to please sb; ça va lui faire p. he'll/she'll be pleased *or* delighted (with this); on prend son p. où on le trouve! you only live once!; le bon p. de qn sb's wish *or* desire; on ne déciderait jamais rien s'il fallait attendre son bon p.! we'd never make any decisions if we always had to wait until he/she felt like it!

2 *(dans des formules de politesse)* vous me feriez p. en restant dîner I'd be delighted if you would stay for dinner; cela fait p. de vous voir en bonne santé it's a pleasure to see you in good health; faites-moi le p. d'accepter won't you grant me the pleasure of accepting?; tu me feras le p. de ne plus revoir ce garçon I don't want you to see that boy again; fais-moi le p. d'éteindre cette télévision do me a favour, will you, and turn off the television; elle se fera un p. de vous raccompagner she'll be (only too) glad to take you home; cette chipie se fera un p. de répandre la nouvelle that little minx will take great pleasure in spreading the news; aurai-je le p. de vous avoir parmi nous? will I have the pleasure of your company?; j'ai le p. de vous informer que... I am pleased to inform you that...; tout le p. est pour moi the pleasure is all mine, (it's) my pleasure; au p. (de vous revoir) see you again *or* soon

3 *(agrément)* pleasure; les plaisirs de la vie life's pleasures; elle aime les plaisirs de la table she loves good food

4 *(sexualité)* pleasures; les plaisirs de la chair pleasures of the flesh; les plaisirs défendus forbidden pleasures; *Euph* p. solitaire self-abuse

• **à plaisir** ADV 1 *(sans motif sérieux)* il se tourmente à p. he's a born worrier 2 *(sans retenue)* unrestrainedly; elle ment à p. she lies through her teeth

• **avec plaisir** ADV with pleasure; pourrez-vous m'aider? – avec p.! will you be able to help me? – I'd be delighted (to) *or* with pleasure!

• **par plaisir, pour le plaisir** ADV for its own sake, just for the fun of it

plaisons *etc voir* plaire

PLAN[1] [plɑ̃]

- plan **B, C**
- map **C1**
- plane **A1, 3, 5**
- shot **A4**
- project **B1, 3, 5**
- blueprint **C2, 3**
- surface **A2**

NM **A.** 1 *(surface plane)* plane

2 *Constr (surface)* surface; p. de cuisson hob; p. snack fold-down table; p. de travail *(d'une cuisine)* worktop, working surface

3 *Beaux-Arts & Phot* plane

4 *Cin & TV* shot; gros p., p. serré close-up; très gros p. extreme close-up, detail shot; p. américain American shot, two-shot; p. de détail detail shot; p. éloigné long shot; p. d'ensemble wide shot; p. d'extérieur exterior (shot); p. général long shot; p. de mise en place establishing shot; p. moyen medium shot; p. en plongée high-angle shot, overhead shot, bird's-eye shot; p. rapproché close shot; p. de secours *ou* p. de sécurité cover shot; p. serré close-up, tight shot; p. de situation establishing shot; p. travelling travelling shot; p. de visage face shot

5 *Géom* plane; p. horizontal/incliné/médian/tangent level/inclined/median/tangent plane

6 *Aviat* p. de sustentation aerofoil

B. 1 *(projet)* plan, project; *Fam* ne vous inquiétez pas, j'ai un p. don't worry, I've got a plan□; *Fam* j'ai un bon p. pour les vacances I've got a great idea for the holidays; *Fam* on se fait un p. ciné/resto? shall we go to the *Br* cinema *or Am* movies/go out for a meal?□; p. d'action plan of action; p. de bataille battle plan

2 *(structure)* plan, framework, outline

3 *Admin* plan, project; p. d'aménagement rural rural development plan *or* scheme; p. de modernisation modernization project *or* scheme; p. d'occupation des sols = document laying out local land development plans; p. de santé health scheme; p. de sauvegarde zoning plan; p. d'urbanisme town planning scheme

4 *Écon* plan; *Compta* p. d'amortissement depreciation schedule; *Écon* p. d'austérité austerity programme; *Pol* p. de campagne campaign plan; *Compta* p. comptable ≃ Statement of Standard Accounting Practices; *Compta* p. comptable général, p. de comptes chart of accounts; p. d'échantillonnage *(en statistique)* sample survey; p. d'échéances instalment plan; p. économique economic plan; *Banque* p. d'épargne savings scheme *or* plan; *Banque* p. d'épargne en actions investment trust, *Br* ≃ ISA; p. d'épargne entreprise employee *Br* share *or Am* stock ownership plan; *Banque* p. d'épargne logement *ou* p. épargne-logement *Br* ≃ building society account, *Am* ≃ savings and loan association account; *Banque* p. d'épargne populaire special savings account; *Banque* p. d'épargne retraite = retirement savings plan *or* scheme; *Compta* p. de financement funding *or* financial plan; p. financier financial plan; p. d'investissement investment plan; p. de licenciement planned redundancy scheme; *Bourse* p. d'options sur titres stock option plan; p. quinquennal five-year plan; p. de redressement recovery plan; p. de restructuration restructuring plan; p. de retraite pension plan *or* scheme; p. social *(du gouvernement)* = corporate restructuring plan, usually involving job losses; p. stratégique d'entreprise strategic business plan

5 *Mktg (projet)* plan, project; p. de campagne campaign plan; p. de développement des produits product planning; p. marketing marketing plan; p. média media plan; p. prix price plan

6 *Cin & TV* p. de production production schedule; p. de tournage shooting schedule; p. de travail production schedule

7 *Typ (en publication assistée par ordinateur)* p. de maquette layout card; p. de mise en page(s) page plan

C. 1 *(carte)* map, plan; un p. de Paris a map *or* plan of Paris; p. de métro *Br* underground *or Am* subway map; p. de vol flight plan

2 *Archit (dessin)* plan, *Am* blueprint; acheter un appartement sur plans to buy *Br* a flat from the plans *or Am* an apartment as shown on the blueprint; lever un p. to make a survey; *Fig* tirer des plans sur la comète to build castles in the air

3 *Tech* plan, blueprint

• **de second plan** ADJ *(question)* of secondary importance; *(artiste, personnalité)* second-rate

• **en plan** ADV *Fam* in the lurch; laisser qn en p. to leave sb in the lurch; laisser qch en p. to drop sth; j'ai tout laissé en p. et j'ai filé à l'hôpital I dropped everything and rushed to the hospital; il m'a laissée en p. he left me in the lurch; je suis resté en p. *(seul)* I was left stranded *or* high and dry; tous mes projets sont restés en p. none of my plans came to anything□

• **sur le plan de** PRÉP as regards, as far as... is concerned; sur le p. du salaire, ça me convient as far as the salary is concerned, it suits me fine; sur le p. intellectuel intellectually speaking; sur le p. personnel on a personal level; c'est le meilleur sur tous les plans he's the best whichever way you look at it

• **plan d'eau** NM *(naturel)* stretch of water; *(artificiel)* reservoir; *(ornemental)* (ornamental) lake

• **premier plan** NM 1 *Cin* foreground; au premier p. in the foreground 2 *Fig* au premier p. de l'actualité in the forefront of today's news; de (tout) premier p. *(personnage)* leading, prominent; jouer un rôle de tout premier p. dans qch to play a leading *or* major part in sth

plan[2], **-e** [plɑ̃, plan] ADJ 1 *(miroir)* plane; *(terrain, surface)* flat 2 *Math* plane, planar; surface plane plane

planage [planaʒ] NM *(d'une surface)* planing; *(d'un métal)* planishing; *(pour rendre la forme)* straightening, flattening (out)

planant, -e [planɑ̃, -ɑ̃t] ADJ *Fam (drogue)* relaxing□; *(musique)* mellow

planche [plɑ̃ʃ] NF 1 *(de bois)* plank, board; p. à billets printing press *(for printing banknotes)*; *Fam* recourir à *ou* faire marcher la p. à billets to pump (more) money into the economy□; p. à découper chopping board; p. à dessin drawing board; p. à laver washboard; p. à pain breadboard; *Fam* c'est une p. à pain she's (as) flat as a board *or* a pancake; *Fam* avoir du pain sur la p. to have a lot on one's plate; p. à pâtisserie pastry board; p. à repasser ironing board; p. de salut last hope; *Fam* c'est une p. pourrie he/she can't be relied on□; *Can Fam* conduire à la p. to drive at top speed□ *or* like a maniac; *Can Fam* ça marche à la p. everything's going like clockwork

2 *Naut* gangplank

3 *Fam (ski)* ski□

4 *Typ* plate; planches en couleurs colour plates

5 *Hort (de légumes)* patch; *(de plantes, de fleurs)* bed

6 *Aviat* p. de bord instrument panel

7 *Sport* faire la p. to float on one's back; p. d'appel take-off board; p. à neige snowboard; p. de surf surfboard

• **planches** NFPL 1 *Théât* les planches the boards, the stage; son amour des planches his/her love of the stage; monter sur les planches to tread the boards 2 *(chemin) Br* promenade, *Am* boardwalk

• **planche à roulettes** NF skateboard; faire de la p. à roulettes to go skateboarding, to skateboard

• **planche à voile** NF sailboard, windsurfer; faire de la p. à voile to go windsurfing, to windsurf

planchéiage [plɑ̃ʃejaʒ] NM 1 *(parquetage)* flooring 2 *(lambrissage)* planking, boarding

planchéier [4] [plɑ̃ʃeje] VT 1 *(parqueter)* to floor 2 *(lambrisser)* to board

plancher[1] [plɑ̃ʃe] NM 1 *Archit & Constr* floor; refaire le p. d'une pièce to refloor a room *(with floorboards)*; p. creux/plein hollow/solid floor; *Fam* le p. des vaches dry land□, terra firma□; *Fam* débarrasse-moi le p.! clear off!, get lost!; *Fam* avoir un feu de p. = to be wearing trousers that are too short

2 *Aut* floor

3 *Anat* floor; p. pelvien pelvic floor

4 *(limite inférieure)* floor; une augmentation de 3 pour cent avec un p. de 100 euros a 3 percent rise

with a lower limit *or* a floor of 100 euros; **p. des salaires** wage floor

5 *(comme adj; avec ou sans trait d'union)* minimum; **prix p.** minimum *or* bottom price

plancher² **[3]** [plɑ̃ʃe] **VI** *Fam Arg scol* to have a test□; **demain on planche en maths** we've got a *Br* maths *or Am* math test tomorrow

• **plancher sur** **VT IND** *Fam (travailler sur)* to work on□

planchette [plɑ̃ʃɛt] **NF 1** *(petite planche)* small board; *(étagère)* (small) shelf **2** *(topographique)* plane-table

planchiste [plɑ̃ʃist] **NMF** windsurfer

plançon [plɑ̃sɔ̃] **NM** *(jeune arbre)* sapling; *(plante)* set, slip

plan-concave [plɑ̃kɔ̃kav] *(pl* **plan-concaves)** **ADJ** plano-concave

plan-convexe [plɑ̃kɔ̃vɛks] *(pl* **plan-convexes)** **ADJ** plano-convex

plancton [plɑ̃ktɔ̃] **NM** plankton

plané, -e [plane] **ADJ** *Aviat* **vol p.** gliding; **descendre en vol p.** to glide down; *Fam* **faire un vol p.** *(tomber)* to go flying

planéité [planeite] **NF** planeness, flatness, evenness

planer **[3]** [plane] **VI 1** *(oiseau)* to soar; *(avion)* to glide; *(fumée, ballon)* to float; **laisser son regard** *ou* **ses regards p. sur** to gaze out over

2 *(danger, doute, mystère)* to hover; **p. sur** to hover over, to hang over; **le danger planait sur l'Europe** danger hung *or* hovered over Europe; **le doute plane encore sur cette affaire** this affair is still shrouded in mystery

3 *(être en dehors des réalités)* to be (way) above things; **il plane au-dessus de ces petits détails** he's way above such insignificant details

4 *Fam (être sous l'influence d'une drogue)* to be high, to be spaced out; *(ne pas avoir le sens des réalités)* to have one's head in the clouds; *(penser à autre chose)* to be miles away; **ça plane pour moi!** everything's hunky-dory!

VT *(surface)* to make smooth; *(bois)* to plane; *(métal)* to planish

planétaire [planetɛr] **ADJ 1** *Astron* planetary **2** *(mondial)* worldwide, global; **à l'échelle p.** on a global scale **3** *Phys (électrons)* orbital, orbiting

planétairement [planetɛrmɑ̃] **ADV** worldwide

planétarisation [planetarizasjɔ̃] **NF** globalization; **la p. économique** the growth of a world economy

planétarium [planetarjɔm] **NM** planetarium

planète [planɛt] **NF** planet; **sur la p. tout entière** *(la Terre)* all over the Earth *or* world; **p. naine** dwarf planet

planétoïde [planetɔid] **NM** planetoid

planétologie [planetɔlɔʒi] **NF** planetology

planeur, -euse [planœr, -øz] **NM,F** *(de métal)* planisher

NM *Aviat* glider; **faire du p.** to go gliding

• **planeuse** **NF** *(machine ▸ pour bois)* planing machine; *(▸ pour métal)* planishing machine

planifiable [planifjabl] **ADJ** which can be planned

planificateur, -trice [planifikatœr, -tris] **ADJ** planning *(avant n)*, relating to (economic) planning

NM,F planner

planification [planifikasjɔ̃] **NF** planning; **p. budgétaire** budget planning; **p. à court terme** short-term planning; **p. économique** economic planning; **p. de l'entreprise** company *or* corporate planning; **p. à long terme** long-term planning; **p. des naissances** population control; **p. des opérations** operational planning; *Mktg* **p. du produit** product planning; *Mktg* **p. stratégique** strategic planning; *Ordinat* **p. des systèmes** systems engineering; **p. des ventes** sales planning

planificatrice [planifikatris] *voir* **planificateur**

planifier **[9]** [planifje] **VT** *(gén) & Écon* to plan

planigramme [planigram] **NM** flow chart

planisme [planism] **NM** support for *or Péj* over-reliance on economic planning

planisphère [planisfɛr] **NM** planisphere

planning [planiŋ] **NM** *(programme)* plan, schedule; **le p. de la semaine** the week's schedule; **faire un p.** to work out a schedule; **un p. chargé** a busy schedule; *Compta* **p. des charges** expenditure planning

• **planning familial** **NM** *(méthode)* family planning; *(organisme)* family planning clinic

plan-plan [plɑ̃plɑ̃] **ADJ INV** *Fam* routine□, humdrum

planque [plɑ̃k] **NF** *Fam* **1** *(cachette ▸ d'une personne)* hideout□, hideaway□; *(▸ d'une chose)* hiding place□ **2** *(travail ▸ gén)* cushy job **3** *(guet)* stakeout; **faire une p.** to stake a place out; **la police est en p. devant la maison** the police are staking out the house

planqué, -e [plɑ̃ke] *Fam* **NM,F** = person with a cushy job; **quelle planquée!** what a cushy job she's got!

NM *Mil* draft dodger

planquer **[3]** [plɑ̃ke] *Fam* **VT** *(cacher)* to hide□, to stash

VI *(surveiller)* to keep watch□

VPR se planquer *(se cacher)* to hide□; *(se mettre à l'abri)* to take cover□

plant [plɑ̃] **NM 1** *(jeune plante ▸ gén)* young plant; *(▸ issue d'une graine)* seedling; *(jeune arbre)* sapling **2** *(ensemble ▸ de légumes)* patch; *(▸ de plantes, de fleurs)* bed; *(▸ d'arbres, d'arbustes)* (nursery) plantation

plantage [plɑ̃taʒ] **NM 1** *Fam (erreur)* mistake□, *Br* boob, *Am* goof **2** *Fam (échec)* flop **3** *Fam Ordinat (d'un réseau, d'un logiciel)* crash

plantain [plɑ̃tɛ̃] **NM** *(herbe, bananier)* plantain

plantaire [plɑ̃tɛr] **ADJ** *Anat* plantar

plantard [plɑ̃tar] = **plançon**

plantation [plɑ̃tasjɔ̃] **NF 1** *(opération)* planting **2** *(culture)* plant, crop; **p. d'oranges** orange grove **3** *(exploitation agricole)* plantation

plante¹ [plɑ̃t] **NF** *Bot* plant; **p. verte/à fleurs** green/flowering plant; **p. d'appartement** house *or* pot plant; **p. grasse** succulent plant; **p. grimpante** creeper, climbing plant; **p. d'intérieur** pot plant, indoor plant; **p. médicinale** medicinal herb; **p. potagère** vegetable; **p. de serre** hothouse plant; *Fig (personne)* delicate flower, fragile person; **p. vivace** perennial plant; **médecine par les plantes** herbal medicine, herbalism; **se soigner par les plantes** to use herbal remedies; *Fam* **c'est une belle p.** she's a fine figure of a woman

plante² [plɑ̃t] **NF** *Anat* **la p. du pied** the sole of the foot; **la p. des pieds** the soles of the feet

planté, -e [plɑ̃te] **ADJ 1 bien p.** *(enfant)* lusty, robust; *(dent)* well-positioned, well-placed; **avoir les dents mal plantées** to have crooked *or* uneven teeth; **avoir les cheveux plantés bas/haut** to have a low/receding hairline **2** *Fam Ordinat* **être p.** *(réseau, ordinateur)* to be down

planter **[3]** [plɑ̃te] **VT 1** *Agr & Hort* to plant; **p. des choux** to plant cabbages; *Fam Fig* **aller p. ses choux** to go and live in the country□; **une colline plantée d'arbres** a hill planted with trees

2 *(enfoncer)* to stick *or* to drive in; *(avec un marteau)* to hammer in; **p. un pieu dans le sol** to drive a stake into the ground; **il ne sait même pas p. un clou** he can't even hammer a nail in properly; **p. un couteau dans le dos de qn** to stab sb in the back, to stick a knife in sb's back; **le lion lui a planté ses griffes dans la cuisse** the lion dug its claws into his/her thigh

3 *(tente)* to pitch, to put up; *Fig* **il a fini par p. sa tente en Provence** he finally settled in Provence

4 *(poser résolument)* **p. un baiser sur les lèvres de qn** to kiss sb full on the lips; **il planta ses yeux dans les miens** he stared into my eyes

5 *(dépeindre ▸ personnage)* to sketch (in); **les personnages sont plantés dès la page 20** the characters have all been sketched in by page 20

6 *Fam (abandonner ▸ personne, voiture)* to dump, to ditch; *(▸ travail, projet)* to pack in, to drop; **je l'ai planté là** I just dumped him there; **ne la laissez pas plantée là** don't leave her standing there□; **je crois que je vais tout p. là** I think I'll pack it all in *or* ditch the whole thing

7 *Fam (tuer à l'arme blanche)* to knife to death□; *(blesser à l'arme blanche)* to knife□

VI *Fam Ordinat (réseau, logiciel)* to go down, to crash

VPR se planter 1 *(s'enfoncer)* to become stuck *or* embedded, to embed itself

2 *Fam (se tenir immobile)* to stand□; **j'irai me p. sous leur nez** I'll go and stand right in front of them; **ne reste pas planté là comme une souche** don't just stand there like a fool *or Br* a lemon

3 *Fam (se tromper)* to get it wrong□

4 *Fam (dans un accident)* to have a crash□; **se p. contre un arbre** to smash into a tree□

5 *Fam (échouer)* to fail□; **il s'est planté à son examen** he failed□ *or Am* flunked his exam

6 *Fam (ordinateur)* to go down, to crash

planteur, -euse [plɑ̃tœr, -øz] **NM,F** *Agr* planter

NM 1 *(dans les pays tropicaux)* planter **2** *(cocktail)* **(punch) p.** planter's punch

• **planteuse** **NF** *(machine)* planter, planting machine

plantigrade [plɑ̃tigrad] **ADJ** plantigrade

NM plantigrade

plantoir [plɑ̃twar] **NM** dibble

planton [plɑ̃tɔ̃] **NM** *Mil* orderly; **être de p.** to be on orderly duty; *Fam* **faire le p.** to stand about *or* around (waiting)□

plantureuse [plɑ̃tyrøz] *voir* **plantureux**

plantureusement [plɑ̃tyrøzmɑ̃] **ADV** *Littéraire* copiously, lavishly

plantureux, -euse [plɑ̃tyrø, -øz] **ADJ 1** *(aux formes pleines ▸ femme, beauté)* buxom; *(▸ poitrine)* full, generous **2** *(copieux ▸ repas)* copious, lavish **3** *Littéraire (fertile)* fertile; **la plantureuse province** the lush province

plaquage [plakaʒ] **NM 1** *(revêtement)* cladding, coating **2** *Sport* tackling *(UNCOUNT)*, tackle **3** *Fam (abandon ▸ d'une personne)* ditching, dumping; *(▸ d'une activité)* dropping

plaque [plak] **NF 1** *(surface ▸ de métal)* plate; *(▸ de marbre)* slab; *(▸ de verre)* plate, pane; *(▸ de chocolat)* bar; *(▸ de beurre)* pack; *(revêtement)* plate; *(pour commémorer)* plaque; **p. de blindage** armour plate; **p. de cheminée** fire back; **p. d'égout** manhole cover; **p. minéralogique** *ou* **d'immatriculation** *Br* number plate, *Am* license plate; **p. de plâtre** plasterboard; **p. de propreté** fingerplate; **p. de rue** street name plate, street sign; **p. de verglas** icy patch; *Fam* **être à côté de la p.** to be wide of the mark, to be barking up the wrong tree

2 *(inscription professionnelle)* nameplate, plaque; *(insigne)* badge

3 *(au casino)* chip

4 *Élec* plate; *Électron* plate, anode; **p. d'accumulateur** accumulator plate; **p. de déviation** deflector plate

5 *Phot* plate

6 *Culin (de four)* baking tray; **p. (de cuisson** *ou* **chauffante)** hot plate

7 *Anat & Méd (sur la peau)* patch; **des plaques rouges dues au froid** red blotches due to the cold; **p. dentaire** (dental) plaque; **p. muqueuse** mucous plaque; **plaques d'eczéma** eczema patches

8 *Géol* **p. (lithosphérique)** plate

9 *Typ* **p. gravée** gravure; **p. offset** offset plate

• **en plaques, par plaques** **ADV** **sa peau part en** *ou* **par plaques** his/her skin is flaking

• **plaque tournante** **NF 1** *Rail* turntable **2** *Fig* nerve centre; **la p. tournante du trafic de drogue** the nerve centre of the drug-running industry; **cette ville deviendra la p. tournante de l'Europe** this city will become the hub of Europe

plaqué, -e [plake] **ADJ** plated; **p. d'or** *ou* **or** gold-plated; **p. d'argent** *ou* **argent** silver-plated

NM 1 *(en joaillerie)* **montre en p. or** gold-plated watch; **c'est du p.** *(or)* it's gold-plated; *(argent)* it's silver-plated **2** *Menuis* veneer

plaquemine [plakmin] **NF** (Japanese) persimmon, kaki

plaqueminier [plakminje] **NM** (Japanese) persimmon (tree)

plaquer **[3]** [plake] **VT 1** *Menuis* to veneer

2 *(en joaillerie)* to plate

3 *Métal* to clad

4 *(mettre à plat)* to lay flat; **le vent plaquait ses cheveux sur sa figure** the wind blew his/her hair flat against his/her face; **la sueur plaquait sa chemise contre son corps** his/her shirt was stuck to his/her chest with sweat; **les cheveux plaqués sur le front** hair plastered down on the forehead; **je l'ai plaqué contre le mur/au sol** I pinned him to the wall/ground; **le dos plaqué contre la porte** standing flat against the door; **p. sa cavalière**

contre soi to clasp one's partner to one; **p. un baiser sur la joue de qn** to give sb a smacking kiss on the cheek; **p. sa main sur la bouche de qn** to put one's hand over sb's mouth

5 *(ajouter)* **la conclusion semble plaquée** the conclusion feels as though it's just been tacked on

6 *Fam (abandonner ▸ personne, travail, situation)* to dump, to ditch; *(▸ famille)* to walk out on; **j'ai envie de tout p.** I feel like *Br* packing *or* chucking it all in *or Am* chucking everything; **il s'est fait p. par sa femme** his wife walked out on him

7 *Sport* to tackle; *Fig (personne en fuite)* to rugby-tackle

8 *Mus (accord)* to strike, to play

9 *Belg (coller)* to stick

VPR se plaquer se p. au sol to throw oneself flat on the ground; **se p. contre un mur** to flatten oneself against a wall

plaquette [plakɛt] **NF 1** *(livre)* booklet; **p. publicitaire** (advertising) brochure

2 *Physiol* (blood) platelet, thrombocyte

3 *(petite plaque)* (small) plate; **p. commémorative** commemorative plaque

4 *Com (de beurre)* pack; *(de chocolat)* bar; *(de pilules)* blister-pack

5 *Aut* **p. de frein** brake pad

6 *Ordinat* circuit board

plaqueur [plakœr] **NM 1** *Menuis* veneerer **2** *Métal* plater

plasma [plasma] **NM 1** *Biol* plasma; **p. sanguin** blood plasma **2** *Phys* plasma; **jet de p.** plasma jet

plastic [plastik] **NM** plastic explosive

plasticage [plastikaʒ] = **plastiquage**

plasticien, -enne [plastisjɛ̃, -ɛn] **NM,F 1** *Beaux-Arts* (plastic) artist **2** *Méd* plastic surgeon **3** *Tech* plastics technician

plasticité [plastisite] **NF 1** *(d'un matériau)* plasticity **2** *(du caractère)* pliability, malleability **3** *Beaux-Arts* plastic quality, plasticity

plastie [plasti] **NF** plastic surgery

plastifiant [plastifjɑ̃] **NM** *Chim & Constr* plasticizer

plastifier **[9]** [plastifje] **VT 1** *(recouvrir de plastique)* to cover in *or* with plastic; **une couverture plastifiée** a plastic-coated cover **2** *(ajouter un plastifiant à)* to plasticize **3** *(document)* to laminate

plastination [plastinasjɔ̃] **NF** plastination

plastiner **[3]** [plastine] **VT** to plastinate

plastiquage [plastikaʒ] **NM** bombing, bomb attack *(with plastic explosives)*; **après le p. de l'ambassade** after the embassy was blown up, after the bombing of *or* bomb attack on the embassy

plastique [plastik] **ADJ 1** *(malléable)* plastic **2** *Beaux-Arts* plastic

NM 1 *(matière)* plastic **2** *(explosif)* plastic explosive

NF 1 *Beaux-Arts* (art of) modelling *or* moulding; **la p. grecque** Greek sculpture **2** *(forme du corps)* figure

• **en plastique ADJ** plastic

plastiquement [plastikmɑ̃] **ADV** plastically, in plastic terms

plastiquer **[3]** [plastike] **VT** to blow up, to bomb *(with plastic explosives)*

plastiqueur, -euse [plastikœr, -øz] **NM,F** bomber *(using plastic explosives)*

plastoc, plastoque [plastɔk] **NM** *Fam* plastic□

plastron [plastrɔ̃] **NM 1** *(de chemise ▸ non amovible)* shirtfront; *(▸ amovible)* dickey; **chemise à p.** dinner shirt **2** *(de cuirasse)* plastron, breastplate

plastronner **[3]** [plastrɔne] **VI 1** *(se rengorger)* to throw out one's chest **2** *(parader)* to swagger *or* to strut around

plat[1] [pla] **NM 1** *(contenant)* dish; **p. à gratin** baking dish; **p. de service** serving dish; **p. à tarte** flan dish; **p. à barbe** shaving dish

2 *(préparation culinaire)* dish; **un p. froid/chaud** a cold/hot dish; **p. cuisiné** precooked *or* ready-cooked dish; **p. garni** main dish served with vegetables; **un p. en sauce** a dish cooked *or* made with a sauce; **un petit p.** a delicacy; **elle aime les bons petits plats** she enjoys good food; **je t'ai préparé un bon petit p.** I've cooked something special for you; *Fig* **vendre qch contre un p. de lentilles** to sell something for peanuts; *Fam* **quel p. de nouilles!** what a *Br* berk *or Am* meathead!

3 *(partie du menu)* course; **le p. du jour** today's special, the dish of the day; **le p. principal** *ou* **de résistance** the main course *or* dish

4 *(locutions)* **mettre les petits plats dans les grands** to put on a big spread; *Fam* **faire (tout) un p. de qch** to make a big song and dance *or* a big fuss about sth; **il n'y a pas de quoi en faire tout un p.** it's not worth getting all worked up about; **il en fait un p.** *(il fait très chaud)* it's a scorcher, *Br* it's roasting; *Fam* **faire du p. à qn** *(à une femme)* *Br* to chat sb up, *Am* to give sb a line; *(à son patron)* to sweet-talk sb, *Br* to butter sb up

plat[2], **-e** [pla, plat] **ADJ 1** *(plan, horizontal ▸ terrain)* flat, level; *(▸ mer)* still; **un p. pays** *(plaine)* a plain

2 *(non profond)* flat, shallow; **bateau p.** shallow *or* shallow-bottomed boat

3 *(non saillant)* flat; **avoir un ventre p.** to have a flat stomach; **avoir la poitrine plate** to be flat-chested; *Fam* **elle est plate comme une planche à pain** *ou* **comme une limande** she's (as) flat as a board *or* pancake

4 *(non épais ▸ montre, calculatrice)* slimline; *(▸ écran)* flat

5 *(sans hauteur ▸ casquette)* flat; **ma coiffure est trop plate** my hair lacks body; **chaussures plates** *ou* **à talons plats** flat shoes

6 *(médiocre ▸ style)* flat, dull, unexciting; *(sans saveur ▸ vin)* insipid; **une plate imitation** a pale imitation; **sa vie a été bien plate** he/she led rather a dull existence

7 *(obséquieux)* cringing, fawning; **être p. devant ses supérieurs** to cringe before *or* to kow-tow to one's superiors; **je vous fais mes plus plates excuses** please accept my most humble apologies; **p. comme une punaise** spineless

8 *(non gazeux)* still, non-sparkling

9 *Littérature voir* **rime**

NM 1 *(partie plate ▸ gén)* flat (part); *(▸ d'un aviron)* blade; **le p. de la main/d'une épée** the flat of the hand/a sword

2 *(lieu plan)* **sur le p.** on the flat *or* level

3 *(en sport)* **le p.** the flat; **spécialiste du p.** flat-racing specialist; *Équitation* **(course de) p.** flat race

4 *Fam (plongeon)* belly-flop

5 *Typ* **p. couverture** case cover; **plats** boards

• **à plat ADJ 1** *Fam (fatigué)* (all) washed out; **je suis complètement à p.** I've had it, I feel totally washed out **2** *Fam (déprimé)* down; **il est très à p.** he's feeling very low *or* down **3** *(pneu, batterie, pile)* flat **ADV 1** *(horizontalement)* flat; **couché à p.** lying flat on his back; **dormir à p.** to sleep without a pillow; **les mains à p. sur la table** hands flat on the table; **mettre à p.** *(robe)* to unpick (and lay out the pieces); *(projet, problème)* to examine from all angles; **tomber à p.** *(plaisanterie)* to fall flat **2** *(rouler)* with a flat (tyre)

• **à plat ventre ADV** face down *or* downwards; **couché à p. ventre** lying face downwards; **se mettre à p. ventre** *(après avoir été allongé)* to flop over onto one's stomach; *(après avoir été debout)* to lie face downwards; **tomber à p. ventre** to fall flat on one's face; *Fig* **ils sont tous à p. ventre devant elle** they all bow down to her

platane [platan] **NM** plane tree; *Fam* **rentrer dans un p.** to crash into a tree□

plat-bord [plabɔr] *(pl* **plats-bords)** **NM** *Naut* gunwale, gunnel

plateau, -x [plato] **NM 1** *(présentoir)* tray; **p. de viandes froides** selection of *Br* cold meats *or Am* cold cuts; **p. à fromages** cheeseboard; **p. de fruits de mer** seafood platter; **p. d'argent** silver salver; *Fig* **il attend que tout lui soit apporté sur un p. (d'argent)** he expects everything to be handed to him on a (silver) platter

2 *Théât* stage; *Cin* set; *TV* panel; **sur le p.** *Théât* on stage; *Cin* on set; *TV* **nous avons un beau p. ce soir** we have a wonderful line-up for you in the studio tonight; *Cin* **p. fermé** closed set; *Cin* **p. de tournage** film set

3 *Tech (d'un électrophone, d'un micro-ondes)* turntable; *(d'une balance)* plate, pan; *(d'un véhicule)* platform; **p. de chargement** platform trolley; **p. d'embrayage** pressure plate; **p. de frein** brake backing plate; **p. de pédalier** front chain wheel; *Fig* **mettre qch sur les plateaux de la balance** to weigh sth up

4 *(d'une courbe)* plateau; **faire un** *ou* **atteindre son p.** to reach a plateau, to level off

5 *Géog* plateau, tableland; **hauts plateaux** high plateau; **p. continental** continental shelf

6 *(d'une table)* top

7 *Sport* clay pigeon

8 **p. technique** *(d'un hôpital)* technical equipment

plateau-repas [platorəpa] *(pl* **plateaux-repas)** **NM** *(à la maison)* dinner; *(dans un avion)* in-flight meal

plate-bande [platbɑ̃d] *(pl* **plates-bandes)** **NF 1** *Hort (pour fleurs)* flowerbed, bed; *(pour arbustes, herbes)* bed **2** *Fam (locutions)* **marcher sur** *ou* **piétiner les plates-bandes de qn** to tread on sb's toes; **ne marche pas sur mes plates-bandes** keep off my patch

plate-forme [platfɔrm] *(pl* **plates-formes)** **NF 1** *Transp (d'un train, d'un bus)* platform

2 *Géog* shelf; **p. continentale** *ou* **insulaire** continental shelf; **p. de glace** ice shelf

3 *Pétr* rig; **p. de forage** drilling rig; **p. de forage en mer** offshore oil rig; **p. off-shore** offshore platform; **p. pétrolière** oil rig

4 *Pol* platform; **p. électorale** election platform

5 *(pour armement)* (gun) platform

6 *Constr* **toit en p.** flat roof

7 *Ordinat & TV* platform; **p. numérique** digital platform; **p. satellite** satellite platform

platement [platmɑ̃] **ADV 1** *(banalement)* dully, flatly **2** *(servilement)* cringingly, fawningly; **s'excuser p.** to give a cringing apology

platinage [platinaʒ] **NM** platinization

platine [platin] **ADJ INV** *voir* **blond**

NM *(métal)* platinum

NF 1 *Tech (d'une serrure, d'une horloge)* plate; *(d'un microscope)* stage **2** *Mus* **platines** *(de DJ)* decks; **p. cassette** cassette deck; **p. CD** CD player; **p. disque** *ou* **tourne-disque** record deck; **p. double cassette** twin cassette deck; **p. laser** CD player; **p. de magnétophone** tape deck **3** *Typ* platen

platiné, -e [platine] **ADJ** *(blond ▸ cheveux)* platinum blond; **une blonde platinée** a platinum blonde

platiner **[3]** [platine] **VT** *(recouvrir de platine)* to platinize

platiniste [platinist] **NMF** *Fam* DJ□

platitude [platityd] **NF 1** *(absence d'originalité)* dullness, flatness, triteness; **ce film est d'une p.!** this movie *or Br* film is so dull! **2** *(lieu commun)* platitude, commonplace, trite remark; **débiter des platitudes** to talk in platitudes **3** *Littéraire (obséquiosité)* obsequiousness, grovelling; **elle ne reculera devant aucune p. pour avoir ce poste** she'll stoop to anything to get the job

Platon [platɔ̃] **NPR** Plato

platonicien, -enne [platɔnisjɛ̃, -ɛn] **ADJ** Platonic

NM,F Platonist

platonique [platɔnik] **ADJ 1** *Phil* Platonic **2** *(amour)* platonic **3** *Littéraire (de pure forme)* token; **la France a formulé une protestation p.** France has made a token protest

platoniquement [platɔnikmɑ̃] **ADV 1** *(aimer, admirer)* platonically **2** *Littéraire (sans produire d'effet)* futilely, to no effect

platonisme [platɔnism] **NM** Platonism

plâtrage [plɑtraʒ] **NM** *Constr (action)* plastering; *(ouvrage)* plasterwork

plâtras [plɑtra] **NM** *(débris)* (plaster) rubble *(UNCOUNT)*

plâtre [plɑtr] **NM 1** *Constr* plaster; **plafond en p.** plastered ceiling; *Fam* **ton camembert, c'est du vrai p.** your camembert tastes like chalk (it's so unripe)□ **2** *Méd (matériau)* plaster; *(appareil)* plaster cast; **ils lui ont mis un bras dans le p.** they put his arm in plaster; **être dans le p.** to be in plaster; **il devra garder son p.** he'll have to keep his cast on; **p. de marche** walking cast **3** *Beaux-Arts (matériau)* plaster; *(objet)* plaster cast *or* model; **p. de Paris** *ou* **à modeler** plaster of Paris; **p. à mouler** moulding plaster

• **plâtres NMPL les plâtres** *(revêtements)* the plasterwork

plâtrée [plɑtre] **NF** *Fam* huge helping; **une p. de nouilles** a huge helping of noodles

plâtrer [3] [plɑtre] **VT 1** *Méd (accidenté)* to plaster (up); *(membre)* to put in a cast *or* in plaster; **aura-t-il besoin d'être plâtré?** will he have to have a cast?; **je suis allé à l'hôpital pour me faire p. le bras** I went to hospital to have my arm put in plaster **2** *Constr (couvrir)* to plaster (over); *(colmater)* to plaster over *or* up

plâtrerie [plɑtrəri] **NF 1** *(usine)* plasterworks **2** *(travaux)* plasterwork, plastering

plâtreux, -euse [plɑtrø, -øz] **ADJ 1** *(fromage)* chalky **2** *(mur)* plastered, covered with plaster **3** *(couleur, teint)* pasty

plâtrier [plɑtrije] **NM 1** *(maçon)* plasterer **2** *(industriel)* plaster manufacturer

plâtrière [plɑtrijɛr] **NF 1** *(carrière)* gypsum *or* lime quarry **2** *(usine)* plasterworks **3** *(four)* plaster kiln, gypsum kiln

plausibilité [plozibilite] **NF** plausibility

plausible [plozibl] **ADJ** plausible, credible, believable; **peu p.** implausible

Plaute [plot] **NPR** Plautus

play-back [plɛbak] **NM INV** miming; **il chante en p.** he's miming (to a tape); **c'est du p.** he's/she's/*etc* miming

play-boy [plɛbɔj] *(pl* **play-boys)** **NM** playboy

playlist [plɛlist] **NF** *Mus* playlist

plèbe [plɛb] **NF** *Littéraire Péj* **la p.** the hoi polloi, the plebs

plébéien, -enne [plebejɛ̃, -ɛn] *Antiq & Littéraire Péj* **ADJ** plebeian

NM,F plebeian

plébiscite [plebisit] **NM** plebiscite

plébisciter [3] [plebisite] **VT 1** *(élire* ▸ *par plébiscite)* to elect by (a) plebiscite; *(*▸ *à une large majorité)* to elect by a large majority **2** *(approuver)* to approve (by a large majority); **les spectateurs plébiscitent notre émission** viewers overwhelmingly support our programme

plectre [plɛktr] **NM** plectrum

pléiade [plejad] **NF 1** *Littéraire (grand nombre de)* group, pleiad; **une p. de vedettes** a glittering array of stars **2** *Littérature* **la P.** *(poètes)* = group of seven French poets in the 16th century, including du Bellay and Ronsard; *(édition)* = prestigious edition of literary classics

Pléiades [plejad] **NFPL** *Astron & Myth* Pleiades

PLEIN, -E [plɛ̃, plɛn]

ADJ	
• full **1, 3–5, 7, 9, 10**	• solid **2**
• busy **4**	
NM	**PRÉP**
• full tank **1**	• all over

ADJ 1 *(rempli)* full; **avoir l'estomac** *ou* **le ventre p.** to have a full stomach; **avoir les mains pleines** to have one's hands full; **avoir le nez p.** to have a blocked nose; **verre à demi p.** half full glass; **p. à ras bord** full to the brim; **p. à ras bord de** brimming with; **p. de** full of; **la casserole est pleine d'eau** the pan is full of water; **un roman p. d'intérêt** a very interesting novel; **être p. d'enthousiasme** to show great enthusiasm; *Fam* **p. aux as** loaded, stinking rich; **p. à craquer** *(valise)* bulging, bursting, crammed full; *(salle)* packed; *Fam* **un gros p. de soupe** a tub of lard, a fat slob; *Fam* **être p. comme un œuf** *(valise, salle)* to be chock-a-block; *(personne repue)* to be stuffed; *Fam* **être p. (comme) une barrique** *ou* **une outre** to be plastered, to have had a skinful

2 *(massif)* solid; **une porte pleine** a solid door; **en bois p.** solid-wood; **mur p.** blind wall

3 *(complet)* full; **année/mois pleine** full (calendar) year/month; **p. temps, temps p.** full-time; **être** *ou* **travailler à temps p.** to work full-time; **pleine page** *(gén)* full page; *(en publicité, sur une page)* full-page ad; *(en publicité, sur deux pages)* spread; **pleins pouvoirs** (full) power of attorney; **avoir les pleins pouvoirs** to have full powers

4 *(chargé)* busy, full; **j'ai eu une journée pleine** I've had a busy day; **ma vie a été pleine** I've led a full life; **la pleine saison** the height of the season, the high season

5 *(en intensif)* **une pleine carafe de** a jugful of; **une pleine valise de** a suitcase full of; **de son p. gré** of his/her own volition *or* free will; **obtenir un p. succès** to achieve complete success; **une industrie en p. essor** a booming *or* fast-growing industry; **j'ai pleine conscience de ce qui m'attend** I know exactly what to expect; **être en pleine forme** to be on top form; **couler à pleins bords** to be overflowing; **embrasser qn à pleine bouche** to kiss sb full on the mouth; **manger des mûres à pleine bouche** to eat mouthfuls of blackberries; **ramasser qch à pleins bras** to pick up armfuls of sth; **rire à pleine gorge** to laugh one's head off; **chanter/crier à p. gosier** to sing/to shout at the top of one's voice; **ramasser qch à pleines mains** to pick up handfuls of sth; **sentir qch à p. nez** to reek of sth; **respirer à pleins poumons** to take deep breaths; *Fam* **mettre la radio à p. tube** *ou* **pleins tubes** to put the radio on full blast; *Fam* **foncer/rouler à p. tube** to go/to drive flat out; *très Fam* **déconner à p. tube** *ou* **pleins tubes** to talk a load of crap *or Br* bollocks; **pleine charge moteur** full throttle; **pleins feux sur** spotlight on; **pleins gaz,** *Fam* **pleins pots** full throttle; **allez, vas-y pleins gaz!** go on, put your foot down *or* step on it!; **pleins phares** *Br* full beam, *Am* high beams; **rouler (en) pleins phares** to drive on full headlights *or Br* on full beam *or Am* on high beams

6 *(milieu, cœur)* **en p. air** *(concert, marché)* open-air, outdoor; **des activités de p. air** outdoor activities; **en pleine campagne** right out in the country, in the middle of the countryside; **en p. cœur de la ville** right in the heart of the city; *Fam* **en pleine figure** *ou* **poire** right in the face□; **en p. jour** in broad daylight; **en pleine mer** (out) in the open sea; **en p. midi** at twelve (noon) on the dot; **en pleine nuit** in the middle of the night; **en pleine rue** (right) in the middle of the street; **en p. soleil** in full sunlight; **en pleine terre** in the open ground; **en p. vent** in the wind; **en p. vol** in mid-flight

7 *(arrondi)* full; **avoir des formes pleines** to have a well-rounded *or* full figure; **avoir des joues pleines** to be chubby-cheeked; **avoir le visage p.** to be moon-faced

8 *Zool (vache)* in calf; *(jument)* in foal; *(truie)* in pig; *(brebis)* in lamb; *(chatte)* pregnant

9 *Littéraire (préoccupé)* **ses lettres sont pleines de vous** she talks about nothing but you in her letters; **être p. de soi-même/son sujet** to be full of oneself/one's subject

10 *Astron & Météo* full; **la lune est pleine** the moon is full; **la pleine mer** high tide

NM 1 *(de carburant)* full tank; **on fait le p. une fois par mois au supermarché** *(de courses)* we stock up once a month at the supermarket; **avec un p., tu iras jusqu'à Versailles** you'll get as far as Versailles on a full tank; **faire le p.** to fill up; **le p., s'il vous plaît** fill her *or* it up, please; *Fig* **faire le p. de vitamines/soleil** to stock up on vitamins/sunshine; **il a fait le p. de ses voix** he got as many votes as he's ever likely to get

2 *(maximum)* **donner son p.** *(personne)* to give one's best, to give one's all; **le p. de la lune** the moon at its full; **le p. de la mer** the tide at its highest

3 *(en calligraphie)* downstroke

4 *Constr* solid *or* massive parts

ADV 1 *Fam* **tout p.** *(très)* really□; **il est mignon tout p., ce bébé** this baby's as cute as a button

2 *(non creux)* **sonner p.** to sound solid

PRÉP *(partout dans)* all over; **j'ai des plantes p. ma maison** my house is full of plants, I have plants all over the house; **il a de la boue p. son pantalon** his trousers are covered in mud, he's got mud all over his trousers; *Fig* **avoir de l'argent p. les poches** to have loads of money; *Fam* **il en a p. la bouche, de sa nouvelle voiture** he keeps on about his new car; *Fam* **en avoir p. les bottes de qch** to be fed up with sth; *Fam* **j'en ai p. les bottes** *ou* **pattes** my feet are killing me; **j'en ai p. le** *Fam* **dos** *ou Vulg* **cul** I've had it up to here; *Fam* **s'en mettre p. la lampe** to stuff one's face; *Fam* **en mettre p. la vue à qn** to put on a show for sb; **en prendre p.** *Fam* **les dents** *ou* **les gencives** *ou très Fam* **la gueule** *(se faire reprendre)* to get bawled out, *Br* to get a right rollocking; *(être éperdu d'admiration)* to be bowled over

• **à plein ADV les moteurs/usines tournent à p.** the engines/factories are working to full capacity; **utiliser des ressources à p.** to make full use of resources

• **de plein droit ADV exiger** *ou* **réclamer qch de p. droit** to demand sth as of right *or* as one's right

• **de plein fouet ADJ** head-on **ADV** head-on, full on

• **en plein ADV 1** *(en entier)* in full, entirely; **le soleil éclaire la pièce en p.** the sun lights up the entire room **2** *(complètement, exactement)* **en p. dans/sur** right in the middle of/on top of; **j'ai mis le pied en p. dans une flaque** I stepped right in the middle of a puddle; **donner en p. dans un piège** to fall right into a trap

• **plein de DÉT** *Fam* lots of□; **il y avait p. de gens dans la rue** there were crowds *or* masses of people in the street; **tu veux des bonbons? j'en ai p.** do you want some sweets? I've got lots; **j'ai (p., p.) p. d'argent** I've got lots (and lots) *or* loads (and loads) of money

plein(-)emploi [plɛnɑ̃plwa] **NM** *Écon* full employment

pleinement [plɛnmɑ̃] **ADV** wholly, fully, entirely; **vivre p. sa passion** to live one's passion to the full; **je suis p. convaincu** I'm fully convinced; **profiter p. de qch** to make the most of sth

plein-temps [plɛ̃tɑ̃] *(pl* **pleins-temps)** **ADJ INV** full-time

NM full-time job; **faire un p.** to work full-time, to have a full-time job

• **à plein-temps ADV travailler à p.** to work full-time

pléistocène [pleistɔsɛn] **NM** *Géol* Pleistocene (period)

plénier, -ère [plenje, -ɛr] **ADJ** plenary

plénipotentiaire [plenipɔtɑ̃sjɛr] **ADJ** plenipotentiary

NMF plenipotentiary

plénitude [plenityd] **NF 1** *Littéraire (des formes, d'un son)* fullness; **être dans la p. de son talent** to be at the peak of one's talent **2** *(satisfaction totale)* fulfilment

plénum [plenɔm] **NM** *Pol* plenum

pléonasme [pleɔnasm] **NM** pleonasm

pléonastique [pleɔnastik] **ADJ** pleonastic

plésiosaure [plezjɔzɔr] **NM** plesiosaur

pléthore [pletɔr] **NF** *(excès)* excess, plethora; **p. de** an excess of, a plethora of; **il y a p. de candidats à ce poste** far too many candidates have applied for the post

pléthorique [pletɔrik] **ADJ** *(excessif)* excessive, overabundant

pleur [plœr] **NM** *Vieilli ou Littéraire* tear; **répandre** *ou* **verser des pleurs (sur)** to shed tears (for), to weep (for); **en pleurs** in tears; **il y aura des pleurs et des grincements de dents** there will be a great wailing and gnashing of teeth; *Ironique* **verser un p. pour** to shed a tear for, to weep for

pleurage [plœraʒ] **NM 1** *(basse fréquence)* wow; *(haute fréquence)* flutter **2** *Can (pleurnicherie)* whining *(UNCOUNT)*, *Br* whingeing *(UNCOUNT)*

pleural, -e, -aux, -ales [plœral, -o] **ADJ** *Anat* pleural

pleurant [plœrɑ̃] **NM** *Beaux-Arts* weeping figure, weeper

pleurard, -e [plœrar, -ard] **ADJ 1** *Fam (sanglotant)* whimpering **2** *(plaintif)* whining, *Br* whingeing

NM,F 1 *Fam (qui sanglote)* whimperer **2** *(qui se plaint)* whiner, *Br* whinger

pleurer [5] [plœre] **VI 1** *(verser des larmes)* to cry; **le bébé pleure** the baby's crying; **s'endormir en pleurant** to cry oneself to sleep; **p. de joie/rage** to weep for joy/with rage; **j'en pleurais de rire!** I laughed so much that I cried!; **j'en aurais pleuré** I could have wept *or* cried; **à p.** enough to make you weep *or* cry; **l'histoire est bête/triste à p.** the story is so stupid/sad you could weep; **faire p. qn** to make sb cry; *Ironique* **arrête, tu vas me faire p.!** my heart bleeds for you!; **p. à chaudes larmes** to cry one's eyes out; *Fam* **p. comme une Madeleine** *ou* **comme un veau** *ou* **comme une fontaine** to bawl one's eyes out; **ne laisser à qn que les yeux pour p.** to leave sb nothing but the clothes they stand up in; **il ne lui reste** *ou* **il n'a plus que les yeux pour p.** he has nothing left to his name; *Fam* **aller p.**

dans le gilet de qn to go crying to sb□; **elle pleurait d'un œil et riait de l'autre** she didn't know whether to laugh or cry; **elle n'avait pas assez de ses yeux pour p.** she was grief-stricken

2 *Physiol* to cry; **avoir un œil qui pleure** to have a weepy *or* watery eye

3 *Fam (réclamer)* to beg□; **il est allé p. auprès du directeur pour avoir une promotion** he went cap in hand to the boss *or* went and begged the boss for a promotion; **p. après** to beg for; **p. après des subventions** to go begging for subsidies

4 *(se lamenter)* **p. sur** to lament, to bemoan, to bewail; **p. sur soi-même** *ou* **son sort** to bemoan one's fate

5 *Littéraire (vent)* to wail, to howl; *(animal)* to wail

VT 1 *(répandre)* to cry, to shed, to weep; **p. des larmes de joie** to cry *or* to shed tears of joy; **p. toutes les larmes de son corps** to cry one's eyes out

2 *(être en deuil de)* to mourn; **nous pleurons notre cher père** we're mourning (for) our dear father; **p. la mort de qn** to mourn sb's death

3 *(regretter)* to lament, to bemoan; **p. une occasion perdue** to lament a lost opportunity

4 *Fam (donner à regret)* to begrudge□; **il ne pleure pas sa peine** he doesn't mind putting himself out; **tu ne vas pas p. les quelques euros que tu lui donnes par mois?** surely you don't begrudge him/her the few euros you give her a month?

5 *(se plaindre)* **elle est allée p. qu'on l'avait trompée** she went complaining that she'd been deceived

6 *(locution)* **p. misère** to cry over *or* to bemoan one's lot; **il est allé p. misère chez ses parents** he went to his parents asking for money

pleurésie [plœrezi] **NF** *Méd* pleurisy

pleurétique [plœretik] *Méd* **ADJ** pleuritic

NMF pleurisy sufferer, pleuritic

pleureur, -euse [plœrœr, -øz] **ADJ 1** *(personne)* who cries a lot; **c'est un enfant très p.** he cries a lot **2** *(arbre)* weeping *(avant n)*

NM,F c'est un p. he cries a lot

• **pleureuse NF** *(aux enterrements)* (professional) mourner

pleurite [plœrit] **NF** *Méd* dry pleurisy

pleurnichard, -e [plœrniʃar, -ard] = **pleurnicheur**

pleurnichement [plœrniʃmɑ̃] **NM** = **pleurnicherie**

pleurnicher **[3]** [plœrniʃe] **VI** *(sangloter)* to whimper; *(se plaindre)* to whine, *Br* to whinge; **et après, ne viens pas p.!** and don't come crying to me!; **p. auprès de qn** to go crying to sb

pleurnicherie [plœrniʃri] **NF** whining *(UNCOUNT)*, *Br* whingeing *(UNCOUNT)*

pleurnicheur, -euse [plœrniʃœr, -øz] **ADJ** *(sanglotant)* whimpering; *(plaintif)* whining, *Br* whingeing

NM,F *(qui sanglote)* whimperer; *(qui se plaint)* whiner, *Br* whinger

pleurote [plœrɔt] **NM** oyster mushroom

pleut *voir* **pleuvoir**

pleutre [pløtr] *Littéraire* **ADJ** cowardly, faint-hearted, lily-livered

NM coward

pleuvasser **[3]** [pløvase] **V IMPERSONNEL** *Fam* to drizzle□

pleuvoir **[68]** [pløvwar] **V IMPERSONNEL** to rain; **il pleut** it's raining; **il a plu toute la journée** it's been raining all day; **il pleut à grosses gouttes** it's raining heavily; **il pleut quelques gouttes** there's a spatter of rain; **on dirait qu'il va p.** it looks like rain; *Fam* **il pleut à seaux** *ou* **à verse** *ou Fam* **des cordes** *ou Fam* **des hallebardes** it's raining cats and dogs, *Br* it's bucketing down; *Fam* **il pleut comme vache qui pisse** it's pouring (down); **qu'il pleuve ou qu'il vente** come rain come shine; **des récompenses comme s'il en pleuvait** rewards galore; **elle dépense de l'argent comme s'il en pleuvait** she's spending money like there was no tomorrow; **il pleut, il mouille (c'est la fête à la grenouille)** ≃ it's raining, it's pouring (the old man is snoring)

VI *(coups)* to rain down, to fall like rain; *(insultes)* to shower down; **les coups pleuvaient sur sa tête** blows were raining down upon *or* on his/her head; **faire p. des coups sur qn** to rain blows (down) on sb, to shower sb with blows; **faire p. les malédictions sur qn** to rain curses upon *or* on sb's head

pleuvoter **[3]** [pløvɔte] **V IMPERSONNEL** *Fam* to drizzle□

plèvre [plɛvr] **NF** *Anat* pleura

Plexiglas® [plɛksiglas] **NM** *Br* Perspex®, *Am* Plexiglas®

plexus [plɛksys] **NM** *Anat* plexus; **p. solaire** solar plexus

pli [pli] **NM 1** *(repli ▸ d'un éventail, d'un rideau, du papier)* fold; *(▸ d'un pantalon)* crease; **le drap fait des plis** the sheet is creased *or* rumpled; **un tissu qui ne fait pas de plis** a material that doesn't crease; **faux p.** crease; *Fam* **ça ne fait pas un p.** there's no doubt about it□; **je me doutais qu'il se blesserait, et ça n'a pas fait un p.** I was just waiting for him to hurt himself, and sure enough he did

2 *Couture* pleat; **p. couché** knife pleat; **p. creux** box pleat; **p. plat** flat pleat

3 *(habitude)* habit; **c'est un p. à prendre** you've (just) got to get into the habit; **il a pris le p. de marcher tous les jours** he got into the habit of going for a walk every day; **le p. était pris** I/he/she/*etc* had got used to it

4 *(ride)* wrinkle, line, crease; *(bourrelet)* fold; **des petits plis apparaissent autour de ses yeux** little lines are showing around his/her eyes; **les plis de son ventre** *(petits)* the creases in his/her belly; *(gros)* the rolls of fat on his/her belly; **p. du bras** bend of the arm

5 *(enveloppe)* envelope; *(lettre)* letter; **veuillez trouver sous ce p. le document demandé** please find enclosed the required document; **sous p. cacheté** in a sealed envelope; **la copie vous sera envoyée sous p. séparé** the copy will be sent to you under separate cover; **sous p. recommandé** by registered letter

6 *Cartes* trick; **faire un p.** to win *or* to take a trick

7 *Menuis* ply

• **à plis ADJ** pleated

pliable [plijabl] **ADJ** foldable; **difficilement p.** hard to fold

pliage [plijaʒ] **NM** *(action)* folding; *(objet)* folded-paper model

pliant, -e [plijɑ̃, -ɑ̃t] **ADJ** folding, collapsible

NM folding stool

plie [pli] **NF** *Ich* plaice

plié [plije] **NM** *(en danse)* plié

plier **[10]** [plije] **VT 1** *(journal, carte, drap, vêtement)* to fold; **p. bagage** to pack up and go

2 *(tordre ▸ fil de fer, doigt, genou)* to bend; **p. les jambes/bras** to bend one's legs/arms; **la douleur le plia en deux** he was doubled up in pain; *Fam* **plié en deux** *ou* **en quatre (de rire)** doubled up (with laughter)□

3 *(rabattre ▸ parapluie, chaise)* to fold up *or* away

4 *(soumettre)* **je n'ai jamais pu la p. à mes désirs/pu p. sa volonté** I never managed to get her to submit to my desires/to bend her will; **p. qn à une habitude** to get sb into a habit

5 *Fam (détruire)* to smash up□, to wreck□

6 *Fam* **c'est plié** *(c'est fait)* it's done and dusted; *(les dés sont jetés)* the die is cast

VI 1 *(se courber)* to bend (over), to bow; **les branches pliaient sous le poids des fruits** the branches were weighed down with fruit; **p. sous le poids des responsabilités** to be weighed down by responsibility **2** *(se soumettre)* to yield, to give in, to give way; **tu plieras!** you'll just have to knuckle under!; **p. devant qn** to submit *or* to yield to sb; **faire p. qn** to subdue sb, to make sb give in; **tu ne me feras pas p.** I won't give in (to you)

VPR se plier 1 *(chaise, parapluie)* to fold up *or* away; *(personne, corps)* to bend, to stoop; **se p. en deux** to bend double **2 se p. à** *(se soumettre à)* to submit to; *(s'adapter à)* to adapt to; **il faut se p. aux usages locaux** you have to respect local customs; **se p. à des méthodes nouvelles** to adapt to *or* to accept new methods; **se p. aux caprices/volontés de qn** to give in to sb's whims/wishes

plieur, -euse [plijœr, -øz] **NM,F** *(de papier)* folder

• **plieuse NF** *Typ (machine)* folder, folding machine *or* unit

Pline [plin] **NPR P. l'Ancien/le Jeune** Pliny the Elder/Younger

plinthe [plɛ̃t] **NF 1** *Constr Br* skirting (board), *Am* baseboard **2** *Archit* plinth

pliocène [plijɔsɛn] *Géol* **ADJ** Pliocene *(avant n)*

NM Pliocene (period)

plioir [plijwar] **NM** *(coupe-papier)* paper knife

plissage [plisaʒ] **NM** pleating

plissé, -e [plise] **ADJ 1** *(jupe)* pleated **2** *(ridé ▸ front, visage)* wrinkled, creased

NM *(plis)* pleats

plissement [plismɑ̃] **NM** *(du front, du visage)* wrinkling *(UNCOUNT)*; *(des yeux)* screwing up

plisser **[3]** [plise] **VT 1** *(faire des plis à ▸ volontairement)* to fold; *(▸ involontairement)* to crease **2** *(froncer ▸ yeux)* to screw up; *(▸ nez, front)* to wrinkle; **la contrariété plissait son front** his/her brow was furrowed with worry; **p. la bouche** *ou* **les lèvres** to pucker one's lips **3** *Couture* to pleat

VI *(se froisser ▸ pantalon, robe, nappe)* to crease, to become creased; *(▸ collant)* to wrinkle

VPR se plisser 1 *(se froisser)* to crease **2** *(se rider)* to crease, to wrinkle; **son front se plissa** he/she frowned; **ses yeux se plissent quand elle sourit** her eyes go all crinkly when she smiles

plisseur, -euse [plisœr, -øz] *Tex* **NM,F** *(personne)* pleater

• **plisseuse NF** *(machine)* pleating machine

pliure [plijyr] **NF 1** *(marque)* fold **2** *(pliage)* folding **3** *(du genou, du bras)* bend

ploc [plɔk] **ONOMAT** plop; **on entendait le p. des gouttes d'eau dans l'évier** we could hear the sound of water dripping into the sink

ploie *etc voir* **ployer**

ploiement [plwamɑ̃] **NM** *Littéraire* bending

plomb [plɔ̃] **NM 1** *Métal* lead; **j'ai du p. dans l'estomac** I feel as though I have a lead weight in my stomach; *Fam* **il n'a pas de p. dans la tête** *ou* **cervelle** he's featherbrained, he's got nothing between the ears; **ça te mettra un peu de p. dans la tête** *ou* **cervelle** that'll knock some sense into you

2 *(d'arme à feu)* leadshot, shot; **un p.** a piece of shot; **du gros p.** buckshot; **du petit p.** small shot; **avoir du p. dans l'aile** *(entreprise)* to be in a sorry state *or* bad way; *(personne)* to be in bad shape *or* on one's last legs

3 *Élec* fuse; **un p. a sauté** a fuse has blown; **faire sauter les plombs** to blow the fuses; *Fam* **péter les plombs** *(se mettre en colère)* to go ballistic, to hit the *Br* roof *or Am* ceiling; *(craquer)* to crack up

4 *Pêche* sinker

5 *(de vitrail)* lead, came

6 *(sceau)* lead seal

7 *Typ* type

8 *Naut* **p. (de sonde)** lead

• **à plomb ADJ le mur n'est pas/est à p.** the wall is off plumb/is plumb **ADV mettre qch à p.** to plumb sth

• **de plomb ADJ** *(gouttière, tuyau etc)* lead *(avant n)*; **un ciel de p.** a leaden sky

plombage [plɔ̃baʒ] **NM 1** *(d'une dent)* filling; **faire un p. à qn** to fill sb's tooth; **se faire faire un p.** to have a tooth filled *or* a filling (put in) **2** *(d'un colis)* sealing (with lead) **3** *(de la céramique)* lead glazing

plombagine [plɔ̃baʒin] **NF** graphite, plumbago

plombe [plɔ̃b] **NF** *Fam* hour□; **ça fait des plombes que je t'attends** I've been waiting for you for ages□; **elle met toujours trois plombes à se préparer** she always takes ages to get ready□

plombé, -e [plɔ̃be] **ADJ 1** *(teint)* leaden, pallid; *(ciel)* leaden, heavy

2 *(scellé ▸ colis, wagon)* sealed (with lead)

3 *(dent)* filled

4 *très Fam (atteint par une MST)* **être p.** to have a dose

plomber **[3]** [plɔ̃be] **VT 1** *(dent)* to fill, to put a filling in

2 *(colis)* to seal with lead

3 *Pêche* to weight (with lead), to lead

4 *(mur)* to plumb

5 *(céramique)* to glaze

6 *Littéraire (rendre gris ▸ teint, ciel)* **p. qch** to turn sth the colour of lead

7 *Fam (tuer à l'aide d'une arme à feu)* **p. qn** to fill sb with lead, to pump sb full of lead

8 *très Fam (transmettre une MST à)* **p. qn** to give sb a dose

9 *Fig (handicaper, compromettre)* to jeopardize, to undermine; **un parti plombé par les scandales** a party plagued by scandal

VPR **se plomber** *(ciel)* to turn leaden *or* the colour of lead

plomberie [plɔ̃bri] NF 1 *(installation)* plumbing 2 *(profession)* plumbing 3 *(atelier)* plumber's shop

plombier [plɔ̃bje] NM 1 *(artisan)* plumber 2 *Fam (espion)* spy□ *(who plants bugs)*

plombières [plɔ̃bjɛr] NF tutti-frutti (ice cream)

plonge [plɔ̃ʒ] NF *Fam* washing-up□, washing the dishes□; **faire la p.** to wash dishes□ *(in a restaurant)*

plongeant, -e [plɔ̃ʒɑ̃, -ɑ̃t] ADJ plunging; **il y a une vue plongeante jusqu'à la mer** the view plunges down to the sea

plongée [plɔ̃ʒe] NF 1 *Sport* (underwater) diving; **faire de la p.** to go diving; **il fait de la p. depuis deux ans** he has been diving for two years; **p. en cage** cage diving; **p. sous-marine** skin *or* scuba diving

2 *(de sous-marin)* dive, diving *(UNCOUNT)*, submersion *(UNCOUNT)*; **effectuer sa p.** to dive, to submerge; **être en p.** to be submerged

3 *Cin* high-angle shot

4 *(descente rapide)* swoop, plunge, dive

plongeoir [plɔ̃ʒwar] NM diving board

plongeon [plɔ̃ʒɔ̃] NM 1 *(dans l'eau)* dive; **faire un p.** to dive; **p. de haut vol** high dive; *Fam aussi Fig* **faire le p.** to take a tumble, *Br* to come a cropper; **son entrepôt a brûlé, il a fait le grand p.** his warehouse burned down and he lost everything□ 2 *Ftbl* dive; **faire un p.** to dive 3 *Orn Br* diver, *Am* loon

plonger [17] [plɔ̃ʒe] VI 1 *(dans l'eau)* to dive; *(en profondeur)* to dive, to go skin *or* scuba diving; **il plongea du haut du rocher** he dived off the rock

2 *Ftbl* to dive

3 *(descendre ► avion)* to dive; *(► sous-marin)* to dive; *(► oiseau)* to dive, to swoop; *(► racine)* to go down; *Fig* **le roman plonge dans le suspense dès la première page** the novel plunges (the reader) into suspense from the very first page; **depuis le balcon, la vue plonge dans le jardin des voisins** there's a bird's-eye view of next door's garden from the balcony

4 **p. dans** *(s'absorber dans)* to plunge into, to absorb oneself in; **elle plongea dans la dépression** she plunged into depression

5 **p. dans** *(avoir ses sources dans)* to go back to; **cette tradition plonge dans la nuit des temps** this tradition goes back to the dawn of time

6 *Fam (échouer)* to decline□, to fall off□; *(faire faillite)* to go bankrupt□, to fold; **beaucoup d'élèves plongent au deuxième trimestre** a lot of pupils' work deteriorates in the second term; **de nombreux petits commerçants ont plongé** a lot of small businesses folded; **c'est ce qui l'a fait p.** that's what caused his demise

7 *Fam Arg crime (être envoyé en prison)* to be put inside *or* away, *Br* to be sent down

8 *Fam (prendre une décision importante)* to take the plunge, to go for it

VT 1 *(enfoncer)* to plunge, to thrust; **p. la main dans l'eau** to plunge one's hand into the water; **il plongea la main dans sa poche** he thrust his hand deep into his pocket; **elle lui plongea un couteau entre les épaules** she thrust a knife between his/her shoulder blades; **plongez les crustacés dans l'eau bouillante** plunge the shellfish into a pan of boiling water

2 *(mettre)* to plunge; **la panne a plongé la pièce dans l'obscurité** the power failure plunged the room into darkness; **p. son regard** *ou* **ses regards dans** to look deep *or* deeply into; **p. qn dans l'embarras** to put sb in a difficult spot; **la remarque nous plongea tous dans la consternation** the remark appalled us all; **être plongé dans** to be deep in; **j'étais plongé dans mes pensées/comptes** I was deep in thought/in my accounts; **être plongé dans le désespoir** to be deep in despair; **je suis plongé dans Proust pour l'instant** at the moment I'm completely immersed *or* engrossed in Proust; **plongé dans un sommeil profond, il ne nous a pas entendus** as he was sound asleep, he didn't hear us

VPR **se plonger se p. dans** *(bain)* to sink into; *(études, travail)* to throw oneself into; *(livre)* to bury oneself in

plongeur, -euse [plɔ̃ʒœr, -øz] NM,F 1 *Sport* diver; **p. sous-marin** skin *or* scuba diver 2 *(dans un café) Br* washer-up, *Am* dishwasher

NM *(oiseau) Br* diver, *Am* loon

plot [plo] NM 1 *Élec* contact; *(dans un commutateur)* contact block 2 *(bille de bois)* block; *Suisse* **p. de boucherie** butcher's block 3 *Sport* block

plouc [pluk] NM 1 *Fam Péj* yokel, peasant, *Am* hick; **qu'est-ce qu'il fait p.!** he's so uncouth!□ 2 *Fam Arg mil Br* squaddie, *Am* grunt

plouf [pluf] ONOMAT splash!; **elle a fait p. dans l'eau** she went splash into the water

ploutocrate [plutɔkrat] NMF plutocrat

ploutocratie [plutɔkrasi] NF plutocracy

ploutocratique [plutɔkratik] ADJ plutocratic

ployable [plwajabl] ADJ *Littéraire* pliable, flexible

ployer [13] [plwaje] VT 1 *Littéraire (courber)* to bend, to bow; **le vent ploie la cime des arbres** the wind bends the tops of the trees 2 *(fléchir)* to bend, to flex; **p. les genoux** to bend one's knees; *Fig* to toe the line, to submit

VI *Littéraire* 1 *(arbre)* to bend; *(étagère, poutre)* to sag; **les étagères ploient sous le poids des livres** the shelves are sagging under the weight of the books; **ses jambes ployèrent sous lui** his legs gave way beneath him 2 *Fig* **p. sous le poids des ans** to be weighed down by age; **p. sous le joug** to bend beneath the yoke

plu [ply] PP 1 *voir* **plaire** 2 *voir* **pleuvoir**

pluché, -e [plyʃe] = **peluché**

plucher [3] [plyʃe] = **pelucher**

pluches [plyʃ] NFPL *Fam* 1 *(épluchage)* peeling□; **faire les p.** to peel the veggies *or Br* veg **je suis de p.** *(gén)* I'm peeling the veggies *or Br* veg; *(soldat)* I'm on spud-bashing (duty) 2 *(épluchures)* (vegetable) peelings□

plucheux, -euse [plyʃø, -øz] = **pelucheux**

plug-and-play [plœgɛ̃dple] *Ordinat* ADJ INV plug-and-play

NM plug-and-play

pluie [plɥi] NF 1 *Météo* rain; **le temps est à la p.** it looks like rain; **sous la p.** in the rain; **sous une p. diluvienne** in the pouring rain; **p. battante** driving rain; **p. torrentielle** torrential rain; **(petite) p. fine** drizzle; *Écol* **pluies acides** acid rain; **ennuyeux comme la p.** deadly boring; **triste comme la p.** terribly sad; *Fig* **faire la p. et le beau temps** to rule the roost; **parler de la p. et du beau temps** to talk about this and that; *Prov* **après la p., le beau temps** every cloud has a silver lining 2 *(retombée)* shower; **une p. de cendres s'échappa du volcan** the volcano sent out a shower of ashes; **une p. d'étoiles filantes** a meteor-shower 3 *(série ► de coups, de balles, de pierres)* hail, shower; *(► d'injures, de compliments)* stream

• **en pluie** ADV **les cendres tombaient en p. sur la ville** ashes rained *or* showered down on the town; **verser la farine en p. dans le lait** sprinkle the flour into the milk

plumage [plymaʒ] NM plumage, feathers

plumard [plymar] NM *Fam* bed□, sack; **aller au p.** to hit the *Br* sack *or Am* hay

plume[1] [plym] NF 1 *(d'oiseau)* feather; **un édredon de p.** *ou* **plumes** a feather quilt; **une couette en p.** *ou* **plumes d'oie** a goose-feather quilt *or Br* duvet; *Fam* **j'y ai laissé des plumes** I didn't come out of it unscathed; *Fig Hum* **perdre ses plumes** to go thin on top, to go bald; *Fam* **voler dans les plumes à qn** to go for sb, to let fly at sb

2 *(pour écrire)* quill; *(de stylo)* nib; **dessiner à la p.** to draw in pen and ink; **je prends la p. pour te dire que...** I take up my pen to tell you that...; **je passe la p. à ton frère pour qu'il te donne tous les détails** I'll hand over to your brother who'll give you all the details; *Ironique* **j'ai pris ma plus belle p. pour écrire à la Direction du personnel** I wrote the personnel department a very nice letter; **c'est un critique à la p. acérée** he's a scathing critic; **les idées se pressent sous sa p.** he/she can't write his/her ideas down quickly enough, his/her ideas are coming thick and fast; **p. d'oie** goose quill; **laisser aller** *ou* **courir sa p.** to write as the ideas come; **avoir la p. facile** to have a gift for writing; **vivre de sa p.** to make one's living by writing, to live by one's pen

3 *(écrivain)* pen

4 *Méd* **p. à vaccin** vaccine point

• **à plumes** ADJ 1 *Orn* feathered 2 *(vêtement)* (decorated) with feathers

• **en plumes** ADJ feather *(avant n)*, feathered

plume[2] [plym] NM = **plumard**

plumeau, -x [plymo] NM feather duster

plumer [3] [plyme] VT 1 *(oiseau)* to pluck 2 *Fam (escroquer)* to fleece

plumet [plymɛ] NM plume

plumetis [plymti] NM 1 *(broderie)* **(broderie au) p.** raised satin stitch 2 *Tex* Swiss muslin

plumeux, -euse [plymø, -øz] ADJ *Littéraire* feathery

plumier [plymje] NM pencil box *or* case

plumitif [plymitif] NM 1 *Péj (employé)* pen pusher 2 *Péj (journaliste)* hack; *(écrivain)* bad writer□

plum-pudding [plumpudiŋ] *(pl* **plum-puddings**) NM Christmas pudding, plum pudding

plupart [plypar] **la plupart** NF most; **quelques-uns sont partis mais la p. ont attendu** some left but most (of them) waited

• **la plupart de** PRÉP most (of); **la p. des enfants** *(du monde)* the majority of *or* most children; *(d'un groupe)* the majority *or* most of the children; **la p. des chanteurs étaient anglais** most of the singers were English, the singers were mostly English; **la p. d'entre eux** most of them, the majority of them; **la p. du temps** *(d'habitude)* most of the time; *(en général)* in most cases; **dans la p. des cas** in the majority of *or* in most cases

• **pour la plupart** ADV mostly, for the most part; **les clients sont pour la p. satisfaits** the customers are mostly *or* for the most part satisfied

plural, -e, -aux, -ales [plyral, -o] ADJ plural; **vote p.** plural voting

pluralisme [plyralism] NM pluralism

pluraliste [plyralist] ADJ pluralist, pluralistic

NMF pluralist

pluralité [plyralite] NF plurality

pluriannuel, -elle [plyrianɥɛl] ADJ 1 *Jur* running over several years 2 *Bot (plante)* perennial

pluridisciplinaire [plyridisiplinɛr] ADJ multidisciplinary, joint *(avant n)*; **cursus p.** joint *or* interdisciplinary course

pluridisciplinarité [plyridisiplinarite] NF **la p. de notre formation** the interdisciplinary nature of our training programme; **nous encourageons la p. dans les études universitaires** we encourage students to take up a range of subjects

pluriel, -elle [plyrjɛl] ADJ 1 *Gram* plural 2 *(diversifié)* diverse, multifarious; **une société plurielle** a pluralist society

NM plural; **la troisième personne du p.** the third person plural; **au p.** in the plural; **mettre au p.** to put in *or* into the plural

pluriethnique [plyriɛtnik] ADJ multiethnic

plurihebdomadaire [plyriɛbdɔmadɛr] ADJ published several times weekly

NM = publication appearing several times weekly

plurilingue [plyrilɛ̃g] ADJ multilingual, polyglot

plurilinguisme [plyrilɛ̃gɥism] NM multilingualism

plurinational, -ale, -aux, -ales [plyrinasjɔnal, -o] ADJ multinational

plurinominal, -e, -aux, -ales [plyrinɔminal, -o] *voir* **scrutin**

pluripartisme [plyripartism] NM *Pol* pluralist (party) *or* multiparty system

pluripartite [plyripartit] ADJ *Pol* pluralist, multiparty

PLUS

ADV
- more **A**
- most **B**
- not any more **C1**
- no more **C2**

CONJ
- plus

NM
- plus sign **1**
- plus **2**

ADV [ply] **A.** *COMPARATIF DE SUPÉRIORITÉ* **1** *(suivi d'un adverbe, d'un adjectif)* more; **viens p. souvent** (do) come more often; **p. tôt** earlier; **p. tard** later; **c'est p. loin** it's further *or* farther; **maniez-le p. doucement** handle it more gently *or* with more care; **c'est p. court/petit** it's shorter/smaller; **elle est p. intéressante/sophistiquée** she's more interesting/sophisticated; **tu es p. patient que moi** you're more patient than I am *or* than me; **c'est p. fatigant qu'on ne le croit** it's more tiring than it seems; **c'est p. rouge qu'orange** it's red rather than *or* it's more red than orange; **c'est p. que gênant** it's embarrassing, to say the least; **on a obtenu des résultats p. qu'encourageants** our results were more than encouraging; **elle a eu le prix mais elle n'en est pas p. fière pour ça** she got the award, but it didn't make her any prouder for all that; **je veux la même, en p. large** I want the same, only bigger; **bien p. beau** much more handsome; **bien p. gros** much fatter; **encore p. beau** more handsome still, even more handsome; **ça ira infiniment p. vite** it'll be infinitely faster; **il est autrement p. calme que son père** he's certainly much calmer than his father; **cinq fois p. cher** five times dearer *or* as dear *or* more expensive; **deux fois p. cher** twice as expensive; **il l'a fait deux fois p. vite (qu'elle)** he did it twice as quickly (as she did)

2 *(avec un verbe)* more; **j'apprécie p. son frère** I like his/her brother more *or* better; **je m'intéresse à la question p. que tu ne penses** I'm more interested in the question than you think; **je ne peux vous en dire p.** I can't tell you any more; **la verte coûtait p.** the green one was more expensive

3 *(avec un nom)* **c'est p. qu'un problème, c'est une catastrophe!** it's more than just a problem, it's a disaster!

B. *SUPERLATIF DE SUPÉRIORITÉ* **1** *(suivi d'un adverbe, d'un adjectif)* most; **le p. loin** the furthest *or* farthest; **la montagne la p. haute** the highest mountain; **l'homme le p. riche du monde** the richest man in the world, the world's richest man; **j'ai répondu le p. gentiment que j'ai pu** I answered as kindly as I could; **j'y vais le p. rarement possible** I go there as seldom as possible; **le p. souvent** most of the time; **le p. rouge/laid** the reddest/ugliest; **la p. amusante** the most amusing one; **tu es le p. gentil de tous** you're the kindest of all; **le festival le p. populaire de France** the most popular festival in France; **un de ses tableaux les p. connus** one of his/her best-known paintings; **le p. gros des deux** the bigger of the two; **le p. gros des trois** the biggest of the three; **c'est ce qu'il y a de p. original dans sa collection d'été** it's the most original feature of his/her summer collection; **c'est en hiver que les fleurs sont le p. chères** in winter, flowers are at their dearest *or* most expensive; **choisis les fruits les p. mûrs possible** select the ripest possible fruit; **faites au p. vite** do it the quickest possible way *or* as quickly as possible; **aller au p. pressé** *ou* **urgent** to deal with the most urgent priority first

2 *(précédé d'un verbe)* most; **c'est moi qui travaille le p.** I'm the one who works most *or* the hardest; **ce qui me tourmente le p.** what worries me (the) most; **faites-en le p. possible** do as much as you can

C. *ADVERBE DE NÉGATION* **1** *(avec "ne")* **je n'y retournerai p.** I won't go back there any more; **je ne m'en souviens p.** I don't remember (any more); **je ne les vois p.** I don't see them any more, *Sout* I no longer see them

2 *(tour elliptique)* **p. de** no more; **p. de glace pour moi, merci** no more ice cream for me, thanks; **p. un mot!** not another word!

ADJ [plys] *Scol* **B p.** B plus

CONJ [plys] **1** *Math* plus; **3 p. 3 égale 6** 3 plus 3 is *or* makes 6; **il fait p. 5°** it's 5° above freezing, it's plus 5°

2 *(en sus de)* plus; **le transport, p. le logement, p. la nourriture, ça revient cher** travel, plus *or* and accommodation, plus *or* then food, (all) work out quite expensive; **ça fait 1000 euros, p. la TVA** it's 1,000 euros plus VAT; **p. le fait que...** plus *or* together with the fact that...

NM [plys] **1** *Math* plus (sign); **mets un p. avant le chiffre 4** put a plus sign in front of the figure 4

2 *(avantage, atout)* plus, bonus, asset; **la connaissance de l'anglais est toujours un p.** knowledge of English is always a plus; **la proximité de la gare est un p.** the closeness of the station is an advantage *or* a plus

• **au plus ADV** *(au maximum)* at the most *or* outside; **il a au p. 20 ans** he's 20 at the most, he can't be more than 20; **ça coûtera au p. 50 euros** it'll cost a maximum of 50 euros *or* 50 euros at most; **il y a 15 km au p.** it's 15 km at the outside

• **de plus ADV 1** *(en supplément)* extra, another, more; **mets deux couverts de p.** lay two extra *or* more places; **raison de p. pour y aller** all the more reason for going; **je ne veux rien de p.** I don't want anything more; **il est content, que te faut-il de p.?** he's happy, what more do you want?; **un mot de p. et je m'en allais** another word and I would have left; **10 euros de p. ou de moins, quelle différence?** 10 euros either way, what difference does it make?

2 *(en trop)* too many; **en recomptant, je trouve 30 points de p.** when I add it up again, I get 30 points too many

3 *(en outre)* furthermore, what's more, moreover; **elle fait mal son travail et de p. elle prend trop cher** she doesn't do her work properly, and what's more her fees are too high

• **de plus en plus ADV 1** *(suivi d'un adjectif)* more and more, increasingly; *(suivi d'un adverbe)* more and more; **de p. en p. souvent** more and more often; **de p. en p. dangereux** more and more *or* increasingly dangerous; **ça devient de p. en p. facile/compliqué** it's getting easier and easier/more and more complicated

2 *(précédé d'un verbe)* **les prix augmentent de p. en p.** prices are increasing all the time

• **de plus en plus de DÉT** *(suivi d'un nom dénombrable)* more and more, a growing number of; *(suivi d'un nom non dénombrable)* more and more; **de p. en p. de gens** more and more people, an increasing number of people; **il y a de p. en p. de demande pour ce produit** demand for this product is increasing, there is more and more demand for this product; **elle a de p. en p. de fièvre** her temperature is rising

• **des plus ADV** most; **son attitude est des p. compréhensibles** his/her attitude is most *or* quite understandable

• **en plus ADV 1** *(en supplément)* extra *(avant n)*; **c'est le même appartement avec un balcon en p.** it's the same *Br* flat *or Am* apartment with a balcony as well; **les boissons sont en p.** drinks are extra, you pay extra for the drinks; **ça fait 45 minutes de transport en p.** it adds 45 minutes to the journey; **10 euros en p. ou en moins, quelle différence?** 10 euros either way, what difference does it make?

2 *(en trop)* spare; **tu n'as pas des tickets en p.?** do you have any spare tickets?; **j'ai une carte en p.** *(à la fin du jeu)* I've got one card left over; *(en distribuant)* I've got one card too many

3 *(en cadeau)* as well, on top of that; **et vous emportez une bouteille de champagne en p.!** and you get a bottle of champagne as well *or* on top of that *or* into the bargain!

4 *(en outre)* further, furthermore, what's more; **elle a une excellente technique et en p., elle a de la force** her technique's first-class and she's got strength; *Fam* **mais c'est qu'elle est méchante en p.!** and she's nasty to cap it all *or* to boot!; **et elle m'avait menti, en p.!** not only that but she'd lied to me (as well)!; **c'est lui qui s'est trompé, et en p., il se plaint!** he makes the mistake and, to crown it all, complains about it!

5 *(d'ailleurs)* besides, what's more, moreover; **je ne tiens pas à le faire et, en p., je n'ai pas le temps** I'm not too keen on doing it, and besides *or* what's more, I've no time

• **en plus de PRÉP** *(en supplément de)* besides, on top of, in addition to; **en p. du squash, elle fait du tennis** besides (playing) squash, she plays tennis

• **et plus ADV** over; **deux ans et p.** over two years; **45 kilos et p.** over 45 kilos, 45 odd kilos; **les gens de 30 ans et p.** people aged 30 and over; **des chemisiers à 35 euros et p.** blouses at 35 euros and over *or* more

• **ni plus ni moins ADV** no more no less, that's all; **je te donne une livre, ni p. ni moins** I'll give you one pound, no more no less; **tu t'es trompé, ni p. ni moins** you were mistaken, that's all

• **non plus ADV moi non p. je n'irai pas** I won't go either; **je ne sais pas – moi non p.!** I don't know – neither do I *or* nor do I *or* me neither!

• **on ne peut plus ADV je suis on ne peut p. désolé de vous voir partir** I'm ever so sorry you're leaving; **c'est on ne peut p. compliqué** it couldn't be more complicated; **des gens on ne peut p. charmants** the most charming people you could ever wish to meet

• **plus de DÉT 1** *(comparatif, suivi d'un nom)* more; **nous voulons p. d'autonomie!** we want more autonomy!; **tu as fait p. de fautes que moi** you made more mistakes than I did *or* than me; **je n'ai pas p. de courage qu'elle** I'm no braver than she is *or* her; **c'est p. de l'insouciance que de l'incompétence** it's more (a matter of) carelessness than incompetence

2 *(comparatif, suivi d'un nombre)* more than, over; **il y a p. de 15 ans de cela** it's more than 15 years ago now; **elle a bien p. de 40 ans** she's well over 40; **elle roulait à p. de 150 km/h** she was driving at more than 150 km/h *or* doing over 150 km/h; *Fam* **vous avez un peu p. du kilo** you've got *or* that's a bit over one kilo; **il y en a p. d'un qui s'est plaint** more than one person complained; **il est p. de 5 heures** it's past 5 o'clock *or* after 5

3 *(superlatif, suivi d'un nom)* **le p. de** (the) most; **c'est ce qui m'a fait le p. de peine** that's what hurt me (the) most; **c'est notre équipe qui a le p. de points** our team has (the) most points; **celui qui a le p. de chances de réussir** the one (who's the) most likely to succeed; **le p. possible de cerises** as many cherries as possible; **le p. d'argent possible** as much money as possible; **les p. de 20 ans** people over 20, the over-20s

• **plus... moins** the more... the less; **p. il vieillit, moins il a envie de sortir** the older he gets, the less he feels like going out; **p. ça va, moins je la comprends** I understand her less and less (as time goes on)

• **plus... plus** the more... the more; **p. je réfléchis, p. je me dis que...** the more I think (about it), the more I'm convinced that...; **p. j'attendais, p. j'étais en colère** the longer I waited, the angrier I got; **p. j'avançais, p. la forêt s'épaississait** the further *or* the deeper I went into the forest, the thicker it got; **p. ça va, p. il est agressif** he's getting more and more aggressive (all the time); **p. ça va, p. je me demande si...** the longer it goes on, the more I wonder if...

• **plus ou moins ADV** more or less; **c'est p. ou moins cher, selon les endroits** prices vary according to where you are; **j'ai p. ou moins compris ce qu'elle disait** I understood more or less what she was talking about; **je ne l'ai que p. ou moins cru** I only half believed him; **tous ces partis, c'est p. ou moins la même chose** all these parties amount to more or less the same thing

• **qui plus est ADV** what's *or* what is more

• **sans plus ADV** nothing more; **c'était bien, sans p.** it was nice, but nothing more

• **tout au plus ADV** at the most; **c'est une mauvaise grippe, tout au p.** it's a bad case of flu, at the most

---

plusieurs [plyzjœr] **ADJ INDÉFINI** several; **il y a eu p. témoins** there were several witnesses; **p. fois, à p. reprises** several times

PRON INDÉFINI 1 *(désignant des personnes)* several people; **se mettre à p. pour faire qch** to do sth as a group; **ils s'y sont mis à p.** several people got together; **vous venez à p.?** will there be several of you coming?; **nous serons p. à la réunion** there will be several of us at the meeting; **p. (d'entre eux) ont refusé** several of them refused; **p. parmi les enfants avaient envie de rentrer** several of the children wanted to go back **2** *(reprenant le substantif)* several; **il n'y a pas une seule solution mais p.** there is no single solution, but several; **il ne sera pas le seul intervenant, il y en aura p.** he won't be the only contributor, there will be several of them

plus-que-parfait [plyskəparfɛ] *(pl* **plus-que-parfaits) NM** pluperfect, past perfect

plus-value [plyvaly] *(pl* **plus-values) NF 1** *(augmentation de la valeur)* increase (in value), appreciation

2 *(excédent d'impôts)* (tax) budget surplus

3 *(surcoût)* surplus value

4 *(somme ajoutée au salaire)* bonus

5 *(bénéfice)* capital gain, profit; **réaliser une p.**

sur la vente d'un produit to make a profit on the sale of a product; **p. sur titres** paper profit

plut *etc* **1** *voir* **plaire 2** *voir* **pleuvoir**

Pluton [plytɔ̃] NPR *Myth* Pluto
NF *Astron* Pluto

plutonium [plytɔnjɔm] NM *Chim* plutonium

plutôt [plyto] ADV **1** *(de préférence)* rather; *(à la place)* instead; **p. mourir!** I'd rather die!; **mets p. mon manteau, tu auras plus chaud** put my coat on instead, you'll be warmer; **demande p. à un spécialiste** you'd better ask a specialist; **ne te plains pas, travaille p.!** don't complain, just work!; **p. que** rather than, instead of; **p. que de travailler, je vais aller faire des courses** I'm going to do some shopping instead of working; **p. que de faire les choses en cachette** rather than do things in secret; **p. la mort que l'esclavage!** death before slavery!, rather *or* sooner death than slavery!
2 *(plus précisément)* rather; **la situation n'est pas désespérée, disons p. qu'elle est délicate** the situation is not hopeless, let's say rather that it is delicate; **ce n'était pas une maison de campagne, mais p. un manoir** it wasn't a country house, it was more of a country manor; **elle n'est pas bête, p. étourdie** she's not so much stupid as absent-minded, she's not stupid, just absent-minded; **elle a l'air sévère ou p. austère** she looks severe, or rather austere; **elle le méprise p. qu'elle ne le hait** she doesn't so much hate as despise him
3 *(assez, passablement)* rather, quite; **elle est p. jolie** she's rather pretty; **comment va-t-il? – p. bien** how is he? – quite well; **c'est p. mieux que la dernière fois** it's rather better than last time; **c'est p. une bonne idée, tu ne trouves pas?** it's rather a good idea, isn't it?
4 *(en intensif) Fam* **il est p. collant, ce type!** that guy's a bit of a leech!; **il est idiot, ce film! – p., oui!** it's stupid, this film! – you can say that again!, you're telling me!

pluvial, -e, -aux, -ales [plyvjal, -o] ADJ pluvial; **eau pluviale** rainwater

pluvier [plyvje] NM *Orn* plover

pluvieux, -euse [plyvjø, -øz] ADJ *(temps, journée)* rainy, wet; *(climat)* wet, damp

pluviner [3] [plyvine] V IMPERSONNEL = **pleuvasser**

pluviomètre [plyvjɔmɛtr] NM rain gauge, *Spéc* pluviometer

pluviôse [plyvjoz] NM = 5th month of the French Revolutionary calendar (from 20/21/22 January to 18/19/20 February)

pluviosité [plyvjozite] NF (average) rainfall

PLV [peɛlve] NF *Mktg* (*abrév* **publicité sur le lieu de vente**) point-of-sale promotion

PMA [peɛma] NF (*abrév* **procréation médicalement assistée**) assisted conception
NMPL (*abrév* **pays les moins avancés**) LDCs

PME [peɛmə] NF INV (*abrév* **petite et moyenne entreprise**) small business; **les P.** small and medium-sized enterprises
NM (*abrév* **porte-monnaie électronique**) electronic wallet, electronic purse

PMI [peɛmi] NF INV (*abrév* **petite et moyenne industrie**) small industry; **les P.** small and medium-sized industries

PMU [peɛmy] NM (*abrév* **Pari mutuel urbain**) = French betting authority, *Br* $\simeq$ tote, *Am* $\simeq$ pari-mutuel

PN (*abrév écrite* **Parc National**) National Park

PNB [peɛnbe] NM (*abrév* **produit national brut**) GNP

pneu [pnø] NM **1** *Aut* tyre; **avoir un p. à plat/crevé** to have a flat (tyre)/a puncture; **p. à carcasse biaise** *ou* **croisée** crossply tyre; **p. à carcasse radiale, p. radial** radial (ply) tyre; **p. à chambre à air** tube tyre; **p. sans chambre à air** tubeless *or* solid tyre; **p. clouté** spiked tyre; *Can* **p. d'hiver** winter tyre; **p. neige** snow tyre; **p. pluie** wet-weather tyre; *Can* **p. quatre-saisons** all-season *or* all-weather tyre; **p. taille basse** low-profile tyre; **p. tout-temps** all-weather tyre; **p. tout-terrain** all-terrain tyre **2** *Fam (lettre)* message□ *(sent through a compressed air tube system)*, pneumatic (dispatch)□

pneumatique [pnømatik] ADJ **1** *(gonflable)* inflatable, blow-up *(avant n)* **2** *Phys* pneumatic
NM **1** *Aut* tyre **2** *(lettre)* message *(sent through a compressed air tube system)*, pneumatic (dispatch)

pneumocoque [pnømɔkɔk] NM *Biol & Med* pneumococcus

pneumologie [pnømɔlɔʒi] NF *Méd* pneumology

pneumologue [pnømɔlɔg] NMF *Méd* lung specialist

pneumonie [pnømɔni] NF *Méd* pneumonia; **p. atypique** atypical pneumonia

pneumothorax [pnømɔtɔraks] NM *Méd* pneumothorax

PNN [peɛnɛn] NM *Écon* (*abrév* **produit national net**) NNP

PNUD, Pnud [pnyd] NM (*abrév* **Programme des Nations unies pour le développement**) UNDP

PO 1 *Rad* (*abrév écrite* **petites ondes**) MW **2** *Com* (*abrév* **par ordre**) by order

pochade [pɔʃad] NF **1** *(peinture)* (quick) sketch, thumbnail sketch **2** *(écrit)* sketch

pochard, -e [pɔʃar, -ard] NM,F *Fam* alky, boozer

poche [pɔʃ] NF **1** *(d'un vêtement)* pocket; *(d'un sac)* pocket, pouch; **je n'ai même pas cinq euros en p.** I don't even have five euros on me; **p. intérieure** inside (breast) pocket; **p. plaquée** patch pocket; **p. (de) poitrine** breast pocket; **p. à rabat** flapped pocket; **p. revolver** hip pocket; **avoir les poches percées** to be a spendthrift; **j'ai les poches percées** money just burns a hole in my pocket; *Fam* **se remplir les poches, s'en mettre plein les poches,** *très Fam* **s'en foutre plein les poches** to rake it in; *Fam* **faire les poches à qn** to go through *or* to rifle (through) sb's pockets; *Fam* **j'en ai été de ma p.** I was out of pocket; *Fam* **c'est dans la p.!** it's in the bag!; *Fam* **il a mis tout le monde dans sa p.** he twisted everyone round his little finger, he took everyone in; *Fam* **mets ça dans ta p. (et ton mouchoir par-dessus)!** put that in your pipe and smoke it!; *Fam* **ne pas avoir les yeux dans sa p.** to have eyes in the back of one's head
2 *(boursouflure)* bag; **avoir des poches sous les yeux** to have bags under one's eyes; **faire des poches aux genoux/coudes** to go baggy at the knees/elbows
3 *(amas)* pocket; **p. d'air** air pocket; **p. d'eau/de gaz** pocket of water/gas
4 *Méd* sac; **p. des eaux** (sac of) waters, amniotic sac; **la p. des eaux s'est rompue** her waters broke
5 *Zool (d'un kangourou)* pouch; *(d'un poulpe)* sac; *(d'un oiseau)* crop
6 *(contenant)* **p. plastique** plastic bag; *Culin* **p. à douille** piping bag
7 *(secteur)* pocket; **p. de résistance/pauvreté** pocket of resistance/deprivation
NM *(livre)* paperback (book)
• **de poche** ADJ *(collection, édition)* pocket *(avant n)*; *(cuirassé, théâtre)* pocket *(avant n)*, miniature *(avant n)*
• **en poche** ADV **1** *(avec soi ▸ argent)* on me/you/*etc*; *(▸ diplôme)* under one's belt; **elle est repartie, contrat en p.** she left with the contract signed and sealed **2** *(livre)* in paperback; **il est sorti en p.** it's come out in paperback

poché, -e [pɔʃe] ADJ **1** *(œuf)* poached **2** *(meurtri)* **avoir un œil p.** to have a black eye

pocher [3] [pɔʃe] VT **1** *Culin (œuf, poisson)* to poach **2** *(meurtrir)* **p. un œil à qn** to give sb a black eye **3** *Beaux-Arts (peinture)* to dash off
VI *(vêtement)* to go baggy

pochetron [pɔʃtrɔ̃] NM *Fam* alky, boozer

pochette [pɔʃɛt] NF **1** *(d'un vêtement)* (breast) pocket handkerchief
2 *(sac ▸ de femme)* clutch bag, (small) handbag; *(▸ d'homme)* clutch bag
3 *(sachet ▸ pour documents)* (plastic) wallet, (plastic) document holder; *(▸ d'allumettes)* book
4 *(d'un disque)* sleeve, cover

pochette-surprise [pɔʃɛtsyrpriz] *(pl* **pochettes-surprises)** NF *Br* lucky bag, *Am* surprise pack; *Fam Hum* **tu l'as trouvé dans une p., ton permis de conduire?, tu l'as eu dans une p., ton permis?** did you get your *Br* driving licence *or Am* driver's license in a cornflakes packet *or* in a Christmas cracker?

pochoir [pɔʃwar] NM *(plaque évidée)* stencil; **décor au p.** stencils, stencilled motifs *or* patterns; **faire une frise au p.** to make a wall frieze with stencils, to stencil a wall frieze

pochon [pɔʃɔ̃] NM **1** *(poche)* belt pouch; *(sachet)* (small) bag **2** *(dans l'est de la France et le canton de Genève) (louche)* ladle

pochothèque [pɔʃɔtɛk] NF *(librairie)* paperback *Br* shop *or Am* bookstore; *(rayon)* paperback section

podagre [pɔdagr] *Arch Méd* ADJ gouty
NMF gout sufferer
NF *(goutte)* gout

podcast [pɔdkast] NM *Ordinat* podcast

podcaster [3] [pɔdkaste] VT *Ordinat* to podcast

podcasting [pɔdkastiŋ] NM podcasting

podiatre [pɔdjatr] NMF *Can Br* chiropodist, *esp Am* podiatrist

podium [pɔdjɔm] NM podium; *Sport* **monter sur le p.** to mount the podium; *(à la télévision, dans un jeu)* to step onto the platform

podologie [pɔdɔlɔʒi] NF *Br* chiropody, *esp Am* podiatry

podologue [pɔdɔlɔg] NMF *Br* chiropodist, *esp Am* podiatrist

podomètre [pɔdɔmɛtr] NM pedometer

poêle [pwal] NM **1** *(chauffage)* stove; *(en céramique)* furnace; **p. à accumulation** storage heater; **p. à bois** wood *or* wood-burning stove; **p. à mazout** oil *or* oil-fired stove; **2** *(drap)* pall; **tenir les cordons du p.** to be a pallbearer
NF *(ustensile)* **p. (à frire)** *Br* frying pan *or Am* fry pan; **passer qch à la p.** to fry sth

poêlée [pwale] NF **1** *(contenu d'une poêle)* **une p. de pommes de terre** a *Br* frying pan *or Am* fry pan full of potatoes **2** *Culin* **p. de champignons** pan-fried mushrooms

poêler [3] [pwale] VT **1** *(frire)* to fry **2** *(braiser)* to braise *(in a shallow pan)*

poêlon [pwalɔ̃] NM casserole

poème [pɔɛm] NM **1** *Littérature* poem; **un p. en prose** a prose poem; **un p. en vers** a poem **2** *Mus* **p. symphonique** symphonic *or* tone poem **3** *Fam (locutions)* **ç'a été (tout) un p., pour venir de l'aéroport jusqu'ici!** what a to-do *or* business getting here from the airport!; **ta fille, c'est (tout) un p.!** your daughter's really something else!

poésie [pɔezi] NF **1** *(genre)* poetry; **écrire de la p.** to write poems *or* poetry
2 *(poème)* poem; **des poésies pour enfants** poems *or* verse for children
3 *Littéraire (charme)* poetry; **la p. du vieux Montmartre** the poetic charm of old Montmartre
4 *(sensibilité)* **tu manques de p.** you don't have any soul

poète [pɔɛt] NM *(auteur)* poet; **il est p. à ses heures** he writes the occasional poem
ADJ *(allure, air)* poetic, of a poet

poétesse [pɔetɛs] NF poetess

poétique [pɔetik] ADJ poetic
NF poetics *(singulier)*

poétiquement [pɔetikmɑ̃] ADV poetically

poétiser [3] [pɔetize] VT *Littéraire* to poetize, to poeticize

pogne [pɔɲ] NF *Fam* hand□, mitt

pognon [pɔɲɔ̃] NM *Fam* cash, *Br* dosh, *Am* bucks; **ils ont plein de p.** they're rolling *Br* in it *or Am* in dough

pogrom, pogrome [pɔgrɔm] NM pogrom

poids [pwa] NM **1** *(gén) & Phys* weight; **son p. est de 52 kilos** he/she weighs 52 kilos; **faire attention à** *ou* **surveiller son p.** to watch one's weight; **prendre/perdre du p.** to gain/to lose weight; **reprendre du p.** to put weight back on *or* on again; **je suis tombé de tout mon p. sur le bras** I fell on my arm with all my weight; **p. brut/net** gross/net weight; **p. atomique** atomic weight; **p. en charge** (fully) loaded weight; **p. mort** dead weight; **p. net à l'emballage** net weight when packed; **p. net embarqué** loaded net weight; *Com* **p. rendu** delivered weight; **p. spécifique** unit weight; *Com* **p. de taxation** chargeable weight; **p. utile** *Aviat* useful load; *Astron* payload; **p. à vide** unladen weight, tare; *Com* **faire bon p.** to give good weight; **il y a un kilo de cerises bon p.** there's a little more than or just over a kilo of cherries; faire le p. *Com* to make up the weight; *Fig* to hold one's own; il ne fait pas le p. face aux spécialistes he's no match for *or* not in the same league as the experts; j'ai peur de ne pas faire le p. I'm afraid of being out of my depth

2 *(objet ▸ gén, d'une horloge)* weight; avoir un p. sur l'estomac to feel bloated; *Fam* les p. et mesures weights and measures

3 *(charge pénible)* burden; le p. des impôts the burden of taxation; ça m'a enlevé un p. it's taken a weight off my mind

4 *Sport (lancer)* shotputting, shot; *(instrument)* shot; *(aux courses)* weight; p. et haltères weightlifting; *Boxe* p. coq bantamweight; *Boxe* p. léger lightweight; *Boxe* p. lourd heavyweight; *Fig* un p. lourd de la politique a political heavyweight; *Boxe* p. mi-lourd light heavyweight; *Boxe* p. mi-moyen light middleweight; *Boxe* p. mouche flyweight; *Boxe* p. moyen middleweight; *Boxe* p. plume featherweight; *Fig* c'est un p. plume, cette petite! that little one weighs next to nothing!

5 *(importance)* influence, weight; son avis a du p. auprès du reste du groupe his/her opinion carries weight with the rest of the group; donner du p. à un argument to lend weight to an argument

• **au poids** ADV *(vendre)* by weight

• **au poids de** PRÉP by the weight of

• **de poids** ADJ *(alibi, argument)* weighty; un homme de p. an influential man

• **sous le poids de** PRÉP 1 *(sous la masse de)* under the weight of; courbé sous le p. d'un gros sac bowed down by *or* bent under the weight of a heavy bag 2 *Fig* under the burden of; écrasé sous le p. des responsabilités weighed down by responsibilities

• **poids lourd** NM 1 *Transp* heavy (goods) vehicle *or Br* lorry *or Am* truck 2 *voir* poids *nm* 4

• **poids mort** NM *Tech & Fig* dead weight; *Mktg (produit)* dog, dodo

poignait *voir* poindre

poignant, -e [pwaɲɑ̃, -ɑ̃t] ADJ heartrending, poignant; de façon poignante poignantly

poignard [pwaɲar] NM dagger; coup de p. stab; donner un coup de p. à qn to stab sb; recevoir un coup de p. to get stabbed; *Fig* un coup de p. dans le dos a stab in the back

poignarder [3] [pwaɲarde] VT to stab, to knife; *aussi Fig* p. qn dans le dos to stab sb in the back; se faire p. to be knifed *or* stabbed; c'est comme si on me poignardait *(douleur, angoisse)* it feels as if I were being stabbed

poigne [pwaɲ] NF grip; avoir de la p. to have a strong grip; *Fig* to rule with a firm hand

• **à poigne** ADJ firm, authoritarian, iron-handed

poignée [pwaɲe] NF 1 *(contenu ▸ gén)* handful; *(▸ de billets de banque)* fistful; une p. de riz a handful of rice 2 *(petit nombre)* handful; une p. de manifestants a handful of demonstrators 3 *(pour saisir ▸ gén)* handle; *(▸ d'un sabre, d'une épée)* hilt; *(▸ d'un pistolet)* grip; la p. d'un tiroir/d'une valise a drawer/suitcase handle; p. de porte door handle

• **à poignées** ADV 1 *(en quantité)* prendre des bonbons à poignées to take handfuls of sweets 2 *(avec prodigalité)* hand over fist; dépenser l'argent à poignées to spend money hand over fist

• **par poignées** ADV in handfuls; je perds mes cheveux par poignées my hair's coming out in handfuls

• **poignée de main** NF handshake; distribuer des poignées de main à la foule to shake hands with people in the crowd; donner une p. de main à qn to shake hands with sb, to shake sb's hand

• **poignées d'amour** NFPL *Fam* love handles

poignet [pwaɲɛ] NM 1 *Anat* wrist 2 *(extrémité d'une manche)* cuff; *(bande de tissu)* wristband

poil [pwal] NM 1 *(d'une personne, d'un animal)* hair; le lavabo était plein de poils the washbasin was full of hairs; avoir le p. dur *ou* dru *(barbe)* to have a rough beard; *Fam* je n'ai plus un p. de sec *(mouillé)* I'm soaked through; *(en sueur)* I'm sweating like a pig; *(mort de peur)* I'm in a cold sweat; *Fam* il n'a plus un p. sur le caillou he's bald as an egg *or Br* a coot; p. pubien pubic hair; *Fam* avoir un p. dans la main to be bone-idle; *Fig* avoir du p. au menton to have grown up; même pas encore de p. au menton et monsieur se permet d'avoir un avis! hardly a hair on his lip and he thinks he can have an opinion!; *Fam* avoir du p. aux pattes to have hairy legs; *Fam* être de bon/mauvais p. to be in a good/bad mood▫; *Fam* reprendre du p. de la bête *(guérir)* to perk up again; *(reprendre des forces)* to regain some strength for a fresh onslaught▫; *Fam* tomber sur le p. à qn to jump on sb, to go for sb; d'un seul coup, elle m'est tombée sur le p. she came down on me like a ton of bricks; p. follet down

2 *Fam (infime quantité)* pas un p. de not an ounce of; il n'a pas un p. d'intégrité he doesn't have one ounce *or* a shred of integrity; à un p. près, il était tué he missed being killed by a hair's breadth, he came within an inch of his life; à un p. près il ratait son examen he very nearly failed his exam▫; nous avons payé la même chose à un p. près we paid more or less the same▫; *Fam* un p. plus haut/moins vite a fraction *or* a touch higher/slower

3 *(pelage ▸ long)* hair, coat; *(▸ court)* coat; il a le p. luisant his coat is shiny; chien à p. ras/long smooth-haired/long-haired dog; manteau en p. de chameau camel-hair coat; en poils de sanglier made of bristle

4 *(d'une brosse)* bristle; *(d'un pinceau)* hair, bristle; *(d'un tapis)* pile

5 *Bot* hair; poils absorbants root hairs; p. à gratter itching powder

6 *Fam* torse p. *(homme)* barechested▫; *(femme)* topless▫

• **à poil** *Fam* ADJ stark naked, *Br* starkers ADV stark naked, *Br* starkers; se mettre à p. to strip (off); aller se baigner à p. to go skinny-dipping

• **au poil** *Fam* ADJ terrific, great; être au (petit) p. to be just the ticket; il est au p., ton copain! your friend's terrific! ADV terrifically; ils avaient tout préparé au p. they'd done everything to a T; tu peux venir samedi, au p.! you can come on Saturday, great!; tomber au p. to arrive just at the right moment▫

• **au petit poil, au quart de poil** ADV *Fam* terrifically; ça a marché au petit p. it's all gone exactly according to plan; démarrer au quart de p. to start right away or first time▫

• **de tout poil, de tous poils** ADJ *Fam Hum* of all kinds▫; voleurs et escrocs de tout p. all manner of thieves and crooks

poilant, -e [pwalɑ̃, -ɑ̃t] ADJ *Fam* hysterical, side-splitting

poiler [3] [pwale] se poiler VPR *Fam (rire)* to kill oneself (laughing); *(s'amuser)* to have a ball

poilu, -e [pwaly] ADJ hairy

NM *Hist* les poilus de 14 *ou* de 1914 (French) soldiers in the 1914–18 war

poinçon [pwɛ̃sɔ̃] NM 1 *(marque)* hallmark; marquer une bague au p. to hallmark a ring

2 *(de brodeuse, de couturière)* bodkin; *(de cordonnier)* awl, bradawl; *(de graveur)* stylus; *(de sculpteur)* chisel

3 *Typ* (matrice) punch

4 *Métal* die, stamp

poinçonnage [pwɛ̃sɔnaʒ], **poinçonnement** [pwɛ̃sɔnmɑ̃] NM 1 *(d'un ticket)* punching 2 *(en joaillerie)* hallmarking 3 *Métal* stamping, die-stamping

poinçonner [3] [pwɛ̃sɔne] VT 1 *(ticket)* to punch 2 *(en joaillerie)* to hallmark 3 *Métal* to stamp

poinçonneur, -euse [pwɛ̃sɔnœr, -øz] NM,F 1 *(employé)* ticket puncher 2 *Métal* punching machine operator

• **poinçonneuse** NF *(machine)* punching machine

poindre [82] [pwɛ̃dr] *Littéraire* VI 1 *(lumière, jour)* to break; *(plante)* to appear, to come out; dès que le jour poindra as soon as dawn breaks, at daybreak 2 *(mouvement, idée)* je vis p. un sourire sur son visage I saw the beginnings of a smile on his/her face; une idée commençait à p. dans son esprit an idea was growing in his/her mind

VT 1 *(tourmenter)* to stab; ce souvenir le poignait parfois the memory would stab him painfully from time to time 2 *(stimuler)* to prick, to spur on; le désir de justice ne cessait de la p. she was forever spurred on by the desire for justice

poing [pwɛ̃] NM fist; lever le p. to raise one's fist; montrer le p. à qn to shake one's fist at sb; les poings sur les hanches with arms akimbo; se battre à poings nus to fight with one's bare fists; donner *ou* taper du p. sur la table to bang one's fist on *or* to thump the table; *Fam* mettre son p. dans la figure à qn to punch▫ *or* to smack sb in the face; *très Fam* tu veux (prendre) mon p. dans la gueule? fancy a knuckle sandwich *or Br* a bunch of fives, do you?; ils sont entrés, revolvers/armes au p. they came in, guns/arms at the ready

point[1] [pwɛ̃] *voir* poindre

POINT[2] [pwɛ̃]

- point 1, 3, 6, 7, 9–12
- blob 2
- position 4
- twinge 8
- dot 1, 3, 16
- spot 1, 2, 7
- full stop, period 3
- place 7
- stitch 8, 14, 15

NM 1 *(marque)* point, dot, spot; *(sur un dé, un domino)* pip, spot; un corsage à petits points bleus a blouse with blue polka dots; elle a des petits points blancs dans la gorge she's got small white spots in her throat; je t'ai fait un p. sur la carte pour indiquer où c'est I put a dot on the map to show you where it is; la voiture n'était plus qu'un p. à l'horizon the car was now no more than a speck on the horizon; p. lumineux spot *or* point of light

2 *(petite quantité)* spot, dab, blob; mets-y un p. de colle put a dab of glue on it; p. de rouille speck *or* spot of rust

3 *(symbole graphique ▸ en fin de phrase) Br* full stop, *Am* period; *(▸ sur un i ou un j)* dot; *(▸ en morse, en musique)* dot; *Math* point; *(dans une adresse électronique)* dot; deux points, trois traits two dots, three dashes; a p. b a point b; *Fam Fig* p. barre end of story; tu rentres à minuit ou bien tu n'y vas pas, p. barre you'll be home by midnight or you're not going at all and that's it, end of story; p. d'exclamation *Br* exclamation mark, *Am* exclamation point; p. d'insertion insertion point; *aussi Fig* p. d'interrogation *Br* question mark, *Am* query mark; p. typographique point; points de conduite (dot) leaders; points de suspension ellipsis, suspension points; p. final full stop, *Am* period *(at the end of a piece of text)*; *Fig* j'ai dit non, p. final *ou* un p. c'est tout! I said no and that's that *or* that's final *or* there's an end to it!; mettre un p. final à une discussion to terminate a discussion, to bring a discussion to an end; p., à la ligne! new paragraph!; *Fig* il a fait une bêtise, p. à la ligne! he did something stupid, let's leave it at that!; *Ordinat* gdupont arrobas transex, p., co, p., uk gdupont at transex, dot, co, dot, uk

4 *Aviat & Naut (position)* position; porter le p. sur la carte to mark one's position on the map; p. estimé/observé estimated/observed position; p. fixe run-up; *Naut* faire le p. to take a bearing, to plot one's position

5 *(bilan)* faire le p. to take stock (of the situation); à 40 ans, on s'arrête et on fait le p. when you reach 40, you stand back and take stock of your life; on fera le p. vendredi we'll get together on Friday and see how things are progressing; et maintenant, le p. sur la circulation and now, the latest traffic news; nous ferons le p. sur les matches à Wimbledon we'll bring you a round-up of play at Wimbledon

6 *Géom* point; le p. B point B; par deux points distincts ne passe qu'une seule droite only one line passes through two distinct points; p. d'intersection/de tangence intersection/tangential point

7 *(endroit)* point, spot, place; en plusieurs points de la planète in different places *or* spots on the planet; *Com* p. d'achat point of purchase; *Anat* p. aveugle blind spot; p. de contrôle checkpoint; p. de convergence focus point; quel est le p. culminant des Alpes? what is the highest point of the Alps?; *Com* p. de distribution distribution outlet; p. névralgique *Méd* nerve centre; *Fig* sensitive spot; p. de rencontre meeting point; *Banque* p. retrait *Br* cashpoint, *Am* ATM; *Com* p. de vente point of sale; *Com* p. de vente au détail retail outlet; *Com* p. de vente électronique electronic point of sale; disponible dans votre p. de vente habituel available at your local stockist

8 *(douleur)* twinge, sharp pain; *Méd* pressure point; j'ai un p. au poumon I can feel a twinge (of pain) in my chest; p. de côté stitch

9 *(moment, stade)* point, stage; **à ce p. de la discussion** at this point in the discussion; **à ce p. de nos recherches** at this point *or* stage in our research; **nous nous retrouvons au même p. qu'avant** we're back to where we started; **p. de bascule** tipping point; *Fin* **p. critique** break-even point; *Mktg* **p. mort** break-even point; *Mktg* **p. prix** price point
10 *(degré)* point; **porter qch à son plus haut p.** to carry sth to extremes; **si tu savais à quel p. je te méprise!** if you only knew how much I despise you!; *Fam* **il est radin, mais à un p.!** you wouldn't believe how tightfisted he is!; *Chim* **p. d'éclair** flashpoint; *Chim* **p. de fusion/liquéfaction** melting/liquefaction point; *aussi Fig* **p. de saturation** saturation point
11 *(élément ▸ d'un texte, d'une théorie)* point; *(▸ d'un raisonnement)* point, item; *(▸ d'une description)* feature, trait; **il reste quelques points obscurs dans votre thèse** a few points in your thesis still need clarifying; **le second p. à l'ordre du jour** the second item on the agenda; **un programme social en trois points** a three-point social programme; **voici un p. d'histoire que je souhaiterais éclaircir** I'd like to make clear what happened at that particular point in history; **c'est au moins un p. d'acquis** we all agree on at least one point; **p. d'entente/de désaccord** point of agreement/of disagreement; **p. commun** common feature; **nous n'avons aucun p. commun** we have nothing in common; *Jur* **un p. de droit** a point of law
12 *(unité de valeur ▸ dans un sondage, à la Bourse)* point; *(▸ du salaire de base)* (grading) point; *(▸ sur une carte de fidélité)* point; *Scol* point, *Br* mark; *Sport & (dans un jeu)* point; **sa cote de popularité a gagné/perdu trois points** his/her popularity rating has gone up/down by three points; **il me manquait 12 points pour avoir l'examen** I was 12 marks short of passing the exam; **une faute d'orthographe, c'est quatre points de moins** four marks are taken off for each spelling mistake; **avoir plus de points que qn** to outpoint sb, to have more points than sb; *Boxe* **battu aux points** beaten on points; **elle est à deux points du set** she's two points from winning the set; **faire le p.** *(le gagner)* to win the point; *Scol* **bon p.** *(image)* = card or cardboard picture given to schoolchildren as a reward, ≃ gold star; *(appréciation)* mark *(for good behaviour)*; *Fig Hum* **un bon p. pour toi!** you get a brownie point!, good for *or Br* on you!; *Scol* **mauvais p.** black mark *(against someone's name)*; *Fig Hum* **un mauvais p. pour toi!** go to the back of the class!; **points d'annonce** points in hand; **points cadeau** points *(on a loyalty card)*; *aussi Fig* **marquer un p.** to score a point; **rendre des points à qn** to be way above sb
13 *Astron* **p. gamma** *ou* **vernal** First Point of Aries, vernal equinox
14 *Couture* stitch; **faire un p. à** to put a stitch *or* a few stitches in; **bâtir à grands points** to tack; **coudre à grands points** to sew using a long stitch; **p. de couture/crochet/tricot** sewing/crochet/knitting stitch; **p. arrière** backstitch; **p. de devant** front stitch; **p. de jersey** stocking stitch; **p. mousse** moss stitch; **p. de riz** moss stitch; **tapisserie au petit p.** petit point tapestry; *Fig* **c'est un travail au petit p.** it's a highly demanding piece of work
15 *Méd* **p. de suture** stitch; **il a fallu lui faire dix points de suture au visage** he/she had to have ten stitches in his/her face
16 *Ordinat (unité graphique)* dot; *(emplacement)* **p. d'accès/de retour** entry/reentry point; **p. d'accès Wi-Fi** hot spot; **p. de branchement** branchpoint; **p. de sonde** probing-point
• **à ce point, à un tel point** ADV *(tellement)* so, that; **ton travail est dur à ce p.?** is your job so (very) *or* that hard?; **comment peux-tu être maladroit/paresseux à un tel p.?** how can you be so clumsy/lazy?; **j'en ai tellement assez que je vais démissionner – à ce p.?** I'm so fed up that I'm going to resign – that bad, is it?
• **à ce point que, à (un) tel point que** CONJ so much so that, to such a point that; **il faisait très chaud, à tel p. que plusieurs personnes se sont évanouies** it was very hot, so much so that several people fainted; **les choses en étaient arrivées à un tel p. que...** things had reached such a pitch that...; **elle est déprimée, à ce p. qu'elle ne veut plus voir personne** she's so depressed that she won't see anyone any more
• **à point** ADJ *(steak)* medium; *(rôti)* done to a turn; *(fromage)* ripe, just right; *(poire)* just *or* nicely ripe; *Fam Fig* **ton bonhomme est à p., tu n'as plus qu'à enregistrer ses aveux** your man's nice and ready now, all you've got to do is get the confession down on tape ADV **1** *Culin* **le gâteau est cuit à p.** the cake is just cooked through **2** *(au bon moment)* **tomber à p.** *(personne)* to come (just) at the right time; *(arrivée, décision)* to be very timely
• **à point nommé** ADV **faire qch à p. nommé** to do sth (just) at the right time *or* on time; **arriver à p. nommé** to arrive (just) at the right moment *or* when needed, to arrive in the nick of time
• **au plus haut point** ADV *(énervé, généreux, irrespectueux)* extremely, most; *(méfiant)* highly, extremely; **je le respecte/déteste au plus haut p.** I couldn't respect/hate him more; **elle m'inquiète au plus haut p.** I'm really worried about her
• **au point** ADJ *Phot* in focus; *(moteur)* tuned; *(machine)* in perfect running order; *(technique)* perfected; *(discours, plaidoyer)* finalized; *(spectacle, artiste)* ready; **ton revers n'est pas encore au p.** your backhand isn't good enough *or* up to scratch yet; **le son/l'image n'est pas au p.** the sound/the image isn't right; **quand ma technique sera au p.** when my technique has been refined *or* polished; **mes élèves sont maintenant au p. pour l'examen** my students are now ready for the exam ADV **mettre au p.** *(texte à imprimer)* to edit; *(discours, projet, rapport)* to finalize, to put the finishing touches to; *(spectacle)* to perfect; *(moteur)* to tune; *(appareil photo)* to (bring into) focus; *(affaire)* to settle, to finalize; **mettre les choses au p.** to put the record straight; **mettons les choses au p.: je refuse de travailler le dimanche** let's get things straight: I refuse to work Sundays; **après cette discussion, j'ai tenu à mettre les choses au p.** following that discussion, I insisted on putting the record straight; **tu devrais mettre les choses au p. avec lui** you should sort things out between you
• **au point de** PRÉP **méticuleux au p. d'en être agaçant** meticulous to the point of being exasperating; **il n'est pas stupide au p. de le leur répéter** he's not so stupid as to tell them
• **au point du jour** ADV *Littéraire* at dawn *or* daybreak
• **au point où** CONJ **nous sommes arrivés au p. où...** we've reached the point *or* stage where...; **au p. où j'en suis, autant que je continue** having got this far, I might as well carry on; **au p. où en sont les choses** as things stand, the way things are now
• **au point que** CONJ so much that, so... that; **il était très effrayé, au p. qu'il a essayé de se sauver** he was so frightened that he tried to run away; **ils maltraitaient leur enfant, au p. qu'on a dû le leur retirer** they mistreated their child so much that he had to be taken away from them
• **de point en point** ADV point by point, punctiliously, to the letter
• **point par point** ADV point by point
• **sur le point de** PRÉP **être sur le p. de faire qch** to be about to do *or* on the point of doing *or* on the verge of doing sth; **j'étais sur le p. de partir** I was about to *or* going to leave; **sur le p. de pleurer** on the verge of tears *or* of crying
• **point d'ancrage** NM **1** *Aut* seat-belt anchorage **2** *Fig* cornerstone
• **point d'appui** NM **1** *(d'un levier)* fulcrum **2** *Mil* strongpoint **3** *Fig (soutien)* support
• **point chaud** NM **1** *Géog aussi Fig* hot spot **2** *Ordinat* hotspot
• **point de chute** NM **1** *(d'un objet)* point of impact **2** *Fig* **j'ai un p. de chute à Milan** I have somewhere to stay in Milan
• **point culminant** NM *Astron* zenith; *Géog* peak, summit, highest point; *Fig* acme, apex; **les investissements sont à leur p. culminant** investment has reached a peak
• **point de départ** NM starting point; *aussi Fig* **nous voilà revenus au p. de départ** now we're back where we started
• **point faible** NM weak spot
• **point fort** NM *(d'une personne, d'une entreprise)* strong point; *(d'un joueur de tennis)* best shot; **les maths n'ont jamais été mon p. fort** I was never any good at maths, maths was never my strong point
• **point mort** NM *Aut* neutral; **au p. mort** *Aut* in neutral; *Fig* at a standstill
• **point noir** NM **1** *Méd* blackhead **2** *(difficulté)* difficulty, headache; **un p. noir de la circulation** *(encombré)* a heavily congested area; *(dangereux)* an accident blackspot
• **point sensible** NM **1** *(endroit douloureux)* tender *or* sore spot **2** *Mil* key *or* strategic target **3** *Fig* **toucher un p. sensible** *(chez quelqu'un)* to touch a sore point *or* on a sore spot; *(dans un problème)* to touch on a sensitive area

point[3] [pwɛ̃] ADV *Arch ou Littéraire* **1** *(en corrélation avec "ne")* **je ne l'ai p. encore vu** I haven't seen him yet; **p. n'est besoin de** there's no need to; **p. n'était besoin de partir de si bonne heure** there was no need *or* it was unnecessary to leave so early **2** *(employé seul)* **du vin il y en avait, mais de champagne p.** there was wine, but no champagne *or* not a drop of champagne; **p. de démocratie sans liberté de critiquer** (there can be) no democracy without the freedom to criticize **3** *(en réponse négative)* **p. du tout!** not at all!, not in the least!

pointage [pwɛ̃taʒ] NM **1** *(d'une liste)* ticking off *(UNCOUNT)*, checking (off) *(UNCOUNT)*; *(de votes)* counting **2** *(d'un fusil)* aiming; *(d'un télescope)* pointing, training **3** *(des ouvriers ▸ système)* timekeeping; *(▸ à l'arrivée)* clocking in *or* on; *(▸ à la sortie)* clocking out *or* off

pointe [pwɛ̃t] NF **1** *(extrémité ▸ gén)* point, pointed end, tip; *(▸ d'un cheveu)* tip; *(▸ d'une flèche)* tip, head; *(▸ d'une chaussure)* toe; **la p. du sein** the nipple; **à la p. de l'épée** at the point of a sword; **mets-toi sur la p. des pieds** stand on tiptoe *or* on the tips of your toes; **elle traversa la pièce/monta l'escalier sur la p. des pieds** she tiptoed across the room/up the stairs; **allons jusqu'à la p. de l'île** let's go to the farthest point of the island; **p. d'asperge** asparagus tip; **p. feutre** fibre tip
2 *Géog* **p. (de terre)** headland, foreland
3 *Sport* spike
4 *(foulard)* headscarf *(folded so as to form a triangle)*; *(lange) Br* nappy, *Am* diaper
5 *Mil (avancée)* advanced party; *Fig* **faire** *ou* **pousser une p. jusqu'au village suivant** to push *or* to press on as far as the next village
6 *(accès)* peak, burst; **p. (de vitesse)** burst of speed; **faire une p. à plus de 200 km/h** to put on a burst of speed of over 200 km/h; **avec des pointes à 160 km/h** with a top speed of 160 km/h
7 *(moquerie)* barb, taunt; *(mot d'esprit)* witticism; **lancer des pointes à qn** to taunt sb
8 *(petite quantité ▸ d'ail)* hint; *(▸ d'ironie, de jalousie)* trace, hint, note; **il a une p. d'accent** he's got a slight accent; **il n'a pas une p. d'accent** he hasn't got the slightest trace of an accent
9 p. de lecture *(d'un tourne-disque)* stylus
10 *Beaux-Arts* **p. sèche** *(outil)* dry point; *(procédé)* dry-point (engraving)
11 *(outil de maçon)* point
12 *Élec* surge; **pouvoir des pointes** point effect
13 *(clou)* nail, sprig, brad
14 *Méd* **pointes de feu** ignipuncture
• **pointes** NFPL *(en danse)* points; **faire des pointes** to dance on points
• **à la pointe de** PRÉP to the forefront of; *aussi Fig* **à la p. du combat** in the front line of battle; **à la p. de l'actualité** right up to date; **à la p. du progrès** in the vanguard (of progress)
• **à la pointe du jour** ADV *Littéraire* at daybreak *or* dawn, at the break of day
• **de pointe** ADJ **1** *(puissance, période)* peak *(avant n)*; **heure de p.** rush hour; **vitesse de p.** maximum *or* top speed **2** *(secteur, industrie)* high-tech; *(technologie)* cutting-edge
• **en pointe** ADJ *(menton)* pointed; *(décolleté)* plunging ADV **1** *(en forme de pointe)* to a point; **s'avancer en p.** to taper (to a point); **tailler en p.** *(barbe)* to shape to a point; *(diamant)* to cut to a point **2** *(à grande vitesse)* at top speed; *Fam* **je fais plus de 200 en p.** I can do over 200, *Br* I can do 200 plus top whack

pointeau, -x [pwɛ̃to] NM **1** *Tech* centre punch; *(d'un carburateur)* needle

2 *(pour trouer)* punch
3 *(pour régler une ouverture)* nozzle valve
4 *(surveillant)* timekeeper

pointer[1] [pwɛ̃tœr] **NM** *(chien)* pointer

pointer[2] **[3]** [pwɛ̃te] **VT 1** *(dresser)* **l'animal pointa les oreilles** the animal pricked up its ears; *Fig* **p. son nez** *ou* **sa tête quelque part** to show one's face somewhere
2 *(diriger ▸ arme)* to aim (**sur** *ou* **vers** at); *(▸ télescope)* to point (**sur** *ou* **vers** at), to train (**sur** *ou* **vers** on); *(▸ spot, projecteur)* to train (**sur** *ou* **vers** on); *(▸ doigt)* to point (**vers** at); *Ordinat (▸ curseur)* to position (**sur** on); **p. un mot** to point to a word; **le mot pointé** the word where the cursor is
3 *(marquer ▸ liste)* to check (off), to tick off; *(votes)* to count; **p. la liste des participants** to check *or* to tick off the list of participants
4 *(contrôler ▸ à l'arrivée)* to check in; *(▸ à la sortie)* to check out
VI 1 *(monter en pointe ▸ jeune pousse)* to come up *or* through; **p. vers le ciel** *(arbre, oiseau)* to rise (up) towards the sky
2 *(faire saillie)* to stick *or* to jut out, to protrude; **ses seins pointaient sous son corsage** her nipples showed beneath her blouse
3 *(apparaître ▸ aube, jour)* to be dawning; *(▸ jalousie, remords)* to be breaking *or* seeping through; **j'ai vu une lueur d'effroi p. dans son regard** I saw fear flashing in his/her eyes
4 *(à la pétanque)* to draw (the jack)
5 *(ouvrier ▸ en arrivant)* to clock in *or* on; *(▸ en sortant)* to clock out *or* off; **p. à l'ANPE** *ou* **au chômage** to register unemployed, to *Br* sign on
6 *Ordinat* **p. et cliquer** to point-and-click (**sur** on)
VPR se pointer *Fam* to show (up), to turn up; **il s'est pas pointé** he never showed; **alors, tu te pointes?** are you coming or aren't you?▫

pointeur, -euse [pwɛ̃tœr, -øz] **NM,F 1** *(surveillant)* timekeeper **2** *Sport* scorer, marker
NM *Ordinat & Mil* pointer; **p. laser** laser pointer
• **pointeuse NF** *(horloge)* time clock

pointillage [pwɛ̃tijaʒ] **NM 1** *(d'une surface)* stippling **2** *(d'une ligne)* marking out with dots, dotting

pointillé [pwɛ̃tije] **NM 1** *(trait)* dotted line **2** *(technique de dessin)* stippling; **dessin au p.** stippled design
• **en pointillé ADJ les frontières sont en p. sur la carte** the frontiers are drawn as dotted lines on the map **ADV** *Fig* **une solution lui apparaissait en p.** he/she was beginning to see the outline of a solution; **on pouvait lire en p. des allusions à son passé glorieux** reading between the lines we saw certain allusions to his/her glorious past

pointiller [3] [pwɛ̃tije] **VT 1** *(surface)* to stipple **2** *(ligne)* to dot, to mark with dots
VI to draw in stipple

pointilleux, -euse [pwɛ̃tijø, -øz] **ADJ** *(personne)* fussy, fastidious; *(commentaire)* nitpicking; **il est très p. sur l'horaire** he's very particular about *or* he's a stickler for time-keeping

pointillisme [pwɛ̃tijism] **NM** *Beaux-Arts* pointillism

pointilliste [pwɛ̃tijist] *Beaux-Arts* **ADJ** pointillist
NMF pointillist

pointu, -e [pwɛ̃ty] **ADJ 1** *(effilé)* sharp, pointed
2 *(perspicace ▸ esprit)* sharp, astute; *(▸ étude)* in-depth, astute; **une lecture pointue de l'œuvre** an astute *or* perceptive interpretation of the work; **elle avait un esprit très p.** her mind was razor-sharp
3 *(revêche ▸ air, caractère)* querulous, petulant; **prendre un air p.** to bridle
4 *(aigu ▸ voix, ton)* shrill, sharp; **un accent p.** *(parisien)* a clipped Parisian accent
5 *(spécialisé ▸ formation, marché)* (very) narrowly specialized, narrowly targeted
6 *(aux courses)* **arrivée pointue** bunched finish
ADV parler p. *(en France)* = to talk in a clipped (Parisian) way; *(au Canada)* = to talk in a posh pseudo-French way

pointure [pwɛ̃tyr] **NF 1** *(de chaussures)* size; **quelle est ta p.?** what size do you take? **2** *Fam Fig (personne remarquable en son genre)* **une (grosse) p.** a big name; **une (grosse) p. de la boxe** a big name in boxing

point-virgule [pwɛ̃virgyl] *(pl* **points-virgules***)* **NM** semicolon

poire [pwar] **NF 1** *(fruit)* pear; **nous en avons parlé entre la p. et le fromage** we talked idly about it at the end of the meal; **en forme de p.** pear-shaped; **p. conférence** conference pear; **p. Williams** Williams pear
2 *(alcool)* pear brandy
3 *(objet en forme de poire)* **p. en caoutchouc** rubber syringe; **p. électrique** (pear-shaped) switch; **p. à injections** douche; **p. à lavement** enema
4 *Fam (visage)* face▫, mug; **prendre qch en pleine p.** to get smacked in the face with sth; **il s'est pris le ballon en pleine p.** the ball hit him right in the face▫ *or* between the eyes; **il s'est pris la remarque en pleine p.** the remark hit him where it hurt
5 *Fam (imbécile)* sucker, *Br* mug; **une bonne p.** a real sucker *or Br* mug; **et moi, bonne p., j'ai accepté** and sucker *or Br* mug that I am, I accepted
ADJ *Fam* **ce que tu peux être p.!** you're such a sucker *or Br* mug!
• **en poire ADJ** *(sein, perle)* pear-shaped

poiré [pware] **NM** perry

poireau, -x [pwaro] **NM 1** *(légume)* leek; *Fam* **faire le p.** to hang about *or* around **2** *Vulg (pénis)* dick, cock

poireauter [3] [pwarote] **VI** *Fam* to hang about *or* around; **faire p. qn** to keep sb hanging about *or* around

poirée [pware] **NF** *Bot* white beet

poirier [pwarje] **NM 1** *(arbre)* pear tree **2** *(bois)* pear, pearwood **3** *Sport* **faire le p.** to do a headstand

pois [pwa] **NM 1** *Bot & Culin* pea; **petits p.** (green) peas, garden peas; *(extrafins)* petit pois; **p. cassé** split pea; **p. chiche** chickpea; **p. de senteur** sweet pea **2** *(motif)* (polka) dot, spot; **un corsage à p. blancs** a blouse with white polka dots *or* white spots

poiscaille [pwaskaj] **NF** *Fam* fish▫

poison [pwazɔ̃] **NM 1** *(substance)* poison; **ils avaient mis du p. dans son café** they had poisoned his/her coffee **2** *Fam (corvée)* drag, hassle **3** *Littéraire (vice)* poison; **le p. de l'oisiveté** the poison of idleness
NMF *(enfant, personne insupportable)* pest

poissard, -e [pwasar, -ard] *Vieilli Péj* **ADJ** *(faubourien)* coarse, common, vulgar
• **poissarde NF** fishwife

poisse [pwas] **NF** *Fam* bad *or* rotten luck▫; **quelle p.!** what rotten luck!; **avoir la p.** to be unlucky▫; **porter la p. (à qn)** to bring (sb) bad luck

poisser [3] [pwase] **VT 1** *(rendre poisseux)* **p. qch** to make sth sticky **2** *Fam (attraper)* to nail, to nab; **se faire p.** to get nabbed **3** *(enduire de poix)* to (cover with) pitch

poisseux, -euse [pwasø, -øz] **ADJ** sticky

poisson [pwasɔ̃] **NM 1** *(animal)* fish; **attraper du p.** to catch fish; **p. d'eau douce/de mer** freshwater/saltwater fish; **poissons osseux** bony fish; **les poissons plats** flatfish; **p. rouge** goldfish; **p. volant** flying fish; **être comme un p. dans l'eau** to be in one's element; **être heureux comme un p. dans l'eau** to be as happy as a lark *or Br* as a sandboy *or Am* as a clam; *Fam* **engueuler qn comme du p. pourri** to call sb every name under the sun; *Prov* **petit p. deviendra grand** tall oaks from little acorns grow **2** *Culin* fish; **je n'aime pas le p.** I don't like fish **3** *Entom* **p. d'argent** silverfish
• **poisson d'avril NM 1** *(farce)* April fool; **p. d'avril!** April fool! **2** *(papier découpé)* = cut-out paper fish placed on someone's back as a prank on 1 April
• **Poissons NMPL** *Astron & Astrol* Pisces **être Poissons** to be Pisces *or* a Piscean

POISSON D'AVRIL

In France and other French-speaking countries, on the first of April, children cut fish shapes out of paper and stick them on their unsuspecting classmates' backs, and people play practical jokes on one another before crying out "Poisson d'avril!" ("April fool!"). This custom is referred to in Quebec as "courir le poisson d'avril".

poisson-chat [pwasɔ̃ʃa] *(pl* **poissons-chats***)* **NM** *Ich* catfish

poisson-lune [pwasɔ̃lyn] *(pl* **poissons-lunes***)* **NM** *Ich* sunfish

poissonnerie [pwasɔnri] **NF 1** *(magasin)* fish shop, *Br* fishmonger's; *(au marché)* fish stall; *(marché)* fish market **2** *(industrie)* fish industry

poissonneux, -euse [pwasɔnø, -øz] **ADJ** *(eaux)* full of fish

poissonnier, -ère [pwasɔnje, -ɛr] **NM,F** *(personne) Br* fishmonger, *Am* fish merchant
• **poissonnière NF** *(ustensile)* fish-kettle

poisson-pilote [pwasɔ̃pilɔt] *(pl* **poissons-pilotes***)* **NM** *Ich* pilot fish

poitevin, -e [pwatvɛ̃, -in] **ADJ 1** *(du Poitou)* of/from Poitou **2** *(de Poitiers)* of/from Poitiers
NM *(dialecte du Poitou)* Poitou dialect
• **Poitevin, -e NM,F 1** *(du Poitou)* = inhabitant of or person from Poitou **2** *(de Poitiers)* = inhabitant of or person from Poitiers

poitrail [pwatraj] **NM 1** *Zool* breast **2** *(partie de harnais)* breastplate **3** *Hum (poitrine)* chest

poitrinaire [pwatrinɛr] *Vieilli Méd*
ADJ consumptive
NMF consumptive

poitrine [pwatrin] **NF 1** *(thorax)* chest; *(seins)* bust, chest; **serrer qn contre** *ou* **sur sa p.** to hold *or* press *or* clasp sb to one's breast; **elle a une p. opulente** she's got a big bust *or* bosom; **elle a commencé à avoir de la p. vers 12 ans** she started developing breasts at about 12 years old; **elle n'a pas encore de p.** she's still flat-chested, she hasn't got any bust yet; **elle n'a pas beaucoup de p.** she's quite flat-chested **2** *(poumons)* chest, lungs; **être fragile de la p.** to have weak lungs *or* a weak chest; *Arch* **s'en aller de la p.** to be dying of consumption **3** *Culin* **p. de bœuf** beef brisket, brisket of beef; **p. fumée** ≃ smoked bacon; **p. de porc** belly pork; **p. salée** *Br* ≃ salt belly pork, *Am* ≃ salt pork; **p. de veau** breast of veal

poivrade [pwavrad] **NF** *(sauce)* pepper sauce
• **à la poivrade ADJ** *Culin* with a pepper sauce

poivre [pwavr] **NM** pepper; **p. blanc** white pepper; **p. de Cayenne** Cayenne (pepper); **p. noir** *ou* **gris** (black) pepper; **p. vert** green pepper; **p. en grains** peppercorns, whole pepper; **p. moulu** ground pepper
• **poivre et sel ADJ INV** *(cheveux, barbe)* pepper-and-salt

poivré, -e [pwavre] **ADJ 1** *Culin* peppery
2 *(parfum)* peppery, spicy
3 *(chanson, histoire)* spicy, racy
4 *Fam (ivre)* smashed, wasted

poivrer [3] [pwavre] **VT** *Culin* to pepper; **tu devrais p. un peu plus ta sauce** you should put a little more pepper in your sauce
VPR se poivrer *Fam* to get wasted *or Br* sloshed

poivrier [pwavrije] **NM 1** *Bot* pepper plant **2** *(contenant)* pepper pot; *(moulin)* pepper mill

poivrière [pwavrijɛr] **NF 1** *Archit* pepper box (fortification) **2** *(ustensile)* pepper pot **3** *(plantation)* pepper plantation

poivron [pwavrɔ̃] **NM** (sweet) pepper, capsicum; **p. vert/jaune/rouge** green/yellow/red pepper

poivrot, -e [pwavro, -ɔt] **NM,F** *Fam* alky, boozer

poix [pwa] **NF** pitch

poker [pɔkɛr] **NM** *Cartes* poker; **jouer au p.** to play poker; **faire un p.** *ou* **une partie de p.** to have a game of poker; **p. d'as** *(dés)* poker dice; *(cartes)* four aces; **p. menteur** liar poker

Polac, Polack [pɔlak] **NMF** *Fam* Polack, = offensive term used to refer to a Polish person

polaire [pɔlɛr] **ADJ 1** *Math, Phys & Tech* polar **2** *Tex* **laine p.** fleece, fleecy material; **fourrure p.** fleecy jacket
NF 1 *Phys* polar curve **2** *Math* polar axis

polar [pɔlar] **NM** *Fam (livre, film)* thriller▫, whodunnit

polard, -e [pɔlar, -ard] *Fam* **ADJ être complètement p.** to be a total *Br* swot *or Am* grind
NM,F *Br* swot, *Am* grind

polarimètre [pɔlarimɛtr] **NM** *Opt* polarimeter

polarisable [pɔlarizabl] **ADJ** *Phys* polarizable

polarisant, -e [pɔlarizɑ̃, -ɑ̃t] ADJ *Phys* polarizing

polarisation [pɔlarizasjɔ̃] NF 1 *Phys* polarization 2 *(de l'intérêt, des activités)* focusing, concentrating

polariscope [pɔlariskɔp] NM *Opt* polariscope

polariser [3] [pɔlarize] VT 1 *Phys* to polarize 2 *(concentrer ▸ son attention, son énergie, ses ressources)* to focus; **il a polarisé l'attention de l'auditoire** he made the audience sit up and listen 3 *(faire se concentrer)* **p. qn sur qch** to make sb concentrate (exclusively) on sth; **le programme polarise trop les élèves sur les mathématiques** the syllabus forces the students to concentrate too much on mathematics

VPR **se polariser 1** *Phys* to polarize **2 se p. sur qch** *(se concentrer ▸ personne, attention)* to focus on sth; **il s'est trop polarisé sur sa carrière** he was too wrapped up in his career; **être polarisé sur ses ennuis personnels/ses études** to be obsessed by one's personal problems/one's studies; **être polarisé sur un seul aspect de qch** to focus on a single aspect of sth

polariseur [pɔlarizœr] NM *Opt* polarizer

polarité [pɔlarite] NF polarity

Polaroid® [pɔlarɔid] NM 1 *(appareil)* Polaroid® (camera) 2 *(photo)* Polaroid® (picture)

polatouche [pɔlatuʃ] NM *Zool* flying squirrel

polder [pɔldɛr] NM *Géog* polder

pôle [pol] NM 1 *Phys, Géog & Math* pole; **le p. Nord/Sud** the North/South Pole; **pôles magnétiques** magnetic poles

2 *(extrême)* pole; **le gouvernement a réussi à concilier les deux pôles de l'opinion sur cette question** the government managed to reconcile the two poles of opinion on this subject

3 *Écon* **p. de conversion** special economic zone; **pôles de croissance** main centres of economic growth; **p. économique** economic hub; **Toulouse est devenue le p. (d'attraction) économique de la région** Toulouse has become the focus *or* hub of economic development in the region; **p. de reconversion** development *or* reconversion zone

4 *Élec* pole

polémique [pɔlemik] ADJ 1 *(article)* polemic, polemical, provocative; *(attitude)* polemic, polemical, embattled 2 *(journaliste, écrivain)* provocative

NF controversy; **une vive p. s'ensuivit** a heated argument ensued

polémiquer [3] [pɔlemike] VI to be polemical; **sans vouloir p., je pense que...** I don't want to be controversial, but I think that...

polémiste [pɔlemist] NMF polemist, polemicist

polémologie [pɔlemɔlɔʒi] NF war studies, *Spéc* polemology

polenta [pɔlɛnta] NF polenta

pole position [pɔlpozisjɔ̃] *(pl* **pole positions)** NF pole position; **être en p.** to be in pole position

poli, -e [pɔli] ADJ 1 *(bien élevé)* polite, courteous; **être très p. avec qn** to be very polite *or* very courteous to sb; **ce n'est pas p. de répondre!** it's rude to answer back!; **il est trop p. pour être honnête** he's too sweet to be wholesome 2 *(pierre)* smooth; *(métal)* polished; *(marbre)* glassed

NM *(éclat)* shine, sheen; **la table a un beau p.** the table has a nice shiny finish *or* a high polish *or* a rich sheen

police [pɔlis] NF 1 *(institution)* police; **la p. est alertée** *ou* **prévenue** the police have been called; **entrer dans la p.** to join the police, to go into the police force; **toutes les polices de France sont à ses trousses** the entire French police force are chasing him/her, police throughout France are chasing him/her; *Fam* **je vais à la p.** I'm going to the police❑; *Fig Hum* **tu es de la p. ou quoi?** what is this, the Spanish Inquisition?, what is this, Twenty Questions?; **p.! les mains en l'air!** police! hands up!; **p. administrative** law enforcement; **p. de l'air et des frontières** airport and border police; **p. judiciaire** *Br* ≃ Criminal Investigation Department, *Am* ≃ Federal Bureau of Investigation; **p. militaire** military police; **p. mondaine** *ou* **des mœurs** vice squad; **p. montée** mounted police; **p. municipale** ≃ local police; **la P. nationale** the police force *(excluding "gendarmes")*; **p. parallèle** paramilitary police; **p. du roulage** *Br* traffic police, *Am* state highway patrol; **p. secours** (police) emergency services; **p. secrète** secret police; **la guerre des polices** = rivalry between different police departments; *Fam* **la p. des polices** ≃ the police complaints committee

2 *(maintien de l'ordre)* (enforcement of) law and order; *(par les policiers)* policing; **faire la p. dans les centres commerciaux** to maintain security in shopping *Br* centres *or Am* malls; **il n'a jamais voulu faire la p. chez lui** he never tried to keep his family in order

3 *Typ & Ordinat* **p. (de caractères)** font; **p. bâton** sans serif font; **p. bitmap** *ou* **pixélisée** bitmap font; **p. par défaut** default font

4 *Assur* **p. d'assurance** insurance policy; **p. d'assurance (sur la) vie** life (insurance) policy; **prendre** *ou* **contracter une p. d'assurance** to take out a policy; **p. conjointe** joint policy; **p. individuelle crédit acheteur** individual buyer credit policy; **p. individuelle crédit fournisseur** individual supplier credit policy; **p. ouverte** open policy; **p. tous risques** fully comprehensive policy; **p. universelle** worldwide policy

• **de police** ADJ police *(avant n)*

> POLICE NATIONALE
>
> The "Police nationale" operates under the authority of the Ministry of the Interior, unlike the "Gendarmerie", which is an army corps.

policé, -e [pɔlise] ADJ *Littéraire* highly civilized, urbane

policeman [pɔlisman] *(pl* **policeman** *ou* **policemen** [-mɛn]) NM (British) policeman

policer [16] [pɔlise] VT *Littéraire* to civilize

polichinelle [pɔliʃinɛl] NM 1 *(pantin)* (Punch) puppet; *Fam* **avoir un p. dans le tiroir** to have a bun in the oven 2 *Fam Péj (personne)* clown, buffoon; **arrête de faire le p.** stop clowning around

policier, -ère [pɔlisje, -ɛr] ADJ 1 *(de la police)* police *(avant n)* 2 *(roman, film)* detective *(avant n)*

NM 1 *(agent)* policeman, police officer; **une femme p.** a policewoman, a woman *or* female police officer; **p. en civil** detective; **une femme p. en civil** a woman detective; **plusieurs policiers sont entrés dans l'immeuble** several police officers went into the building 2 *(livre)* detective novel; *(film)* detective film

policlinique [pɔliklinik] NF outpatient clinic

poliment [pɔlimɑ̃] ADV politely

polio [pɔljo] *Méd* NMF polio victim

NF polio

poliomyélite [pɔljɔmjelit] NF *Méd* poliomyelitis

poliomyélitique [pɔljɔmjelitik] ADJ *(gén)* polio *(avant n)*; *(personne)* suffering from polio; **il est p.** he has polio

NMF polio victim

polir [32] [pɔlir] VT 1 *(métal)* to polish (up), to burnish; *(pierre, meuble)* to polish; *(chaussures)* to polish, to clean, to shine; *(ongles)* to buff; **poli par l'érosion/le temps** made smooth by erosion/the passage of time 2 *(parfaire)* to polish, to refine; **p. ses phrases** to polish one's sentences

VPR **se polir se p. les ongles** to polish *or* to buff one's nails

polissage [pɔlisaʒ] NM 1 *(d'un meuble)* polishing; *(des ongles)* buffing 2 *Métal* polishing, burnishing

polisseur, -euse [pɔlisœr, -øz] NM,F *(personne)* polisher

• **polisseuse** NF 1 *(machine ▸ pour la pierre)* glassing *or* polishing machine 2 *Métal* polishing head *or* stick

polissoir [pɔliswar] NM *(machine)* polishing machine; *(outil)* polishing head *or* lathe, polisher; **p. à ongles** (nail) buffer

polisson, -onne [pɔlisɔ̃, -ɔn] ADJ 1 *(taquin)* mischievous, cheeky 2 *(égrillard)* saucy, naughty

NM,F *(espiègle)* little devil *or* rogue *or* scamp

polissonner [3] [pɔlisɔne] VI *Vieilli* 1 *(badiner)* to fool around 2 *(faire des sottises)* to get up to mischief

polissonnerie [pɔlisɔnri] NF 1 *(facétie)* piece of mischief 2 *(parole grivoise)* risqué *or* saucy remark 3 *(acte grivois)* **des polissonneries** naughty goings-on

politesse [pɔlitɛs] NF 1 *(bonne éducation)* politeness, courteousness; **il est toujours d'une grande p.** he is always very polite *or* courteous; **faire/dire qch par p.** to do/to say sth out of politeness; **brûler la p. à qn** to leave sb abruptly 2 *(propos)* polite remark; **échanger des politesses** to exchange polite small-talk; *Ironique* to trade insults 3 *(acte)* polite gesture; **rendre la p. à qn** to pay sb back for a favour; *Ironique* to give sb a taste of his/her own medicine

• **de politesse** ADJ *(lettre, visite)* courtesy *(avant n)*

politicaillerie [pɔlitikajri] NF *Fam Péj* backroom politics❑

politicard, -e [pɔlitikar, -ard] *Fam Péj* ADJ careerist❑

NM,F careerist politician❑

politicien, -enne [pɔlitisjɛ̃, -ɛn] ADJ 1 *(d'habile politique)* political 2 *Péj* scheming

NM,F politician

politico-économique [pɔlitikoekɔnɔmik] *(pl* **politico-économiques)** ADJ politico-economic

politicologie [pɔlitikɔlɔʒi] = **politologie**

politicologue [pɔlitikɔlɔg] = **politologue**

politique [pɔlitik] ADJ 1 *(du pouvoir de l'État ▸ institution, carte)* political

2 *(de la vie publique)* political; **quelles sont ses opinions politiques?** what are his/her politics?; **une carrière p.** a career in politics; **dans les milieux politiques** in political circles; **homme p., femme p.** politician; **les partis politiques** the political parties

3 *Littéraire (diplomate)* diplomatic, politic; **ce n'était pas très p. de le licencier** it wasn't a very wise move to fire him

NF 1 *(activité)* politics; **faire de la p.** to be involved in politics; **je ne fais pas de p.!** *(je refuse de prendre parti)* I don't want to bring politics into this!, no politics please!; **elle se destine à la p.** she wants to go into politics; **parler p.** to talk politics; **p. de juste milieu** middle-of-the-road politics; **p. locale** local politics; **p. minoritaire** minority politics; **p. de parti** party politics; **p. partisane** partisan politics; *Péj* **la p. politicienne** party politics

2 *(stratégie)* policy; **suivre** *ou* **adopter une nouvelle p.** to follow *or* adopt a new policy; **une p. de gauche** a left-wing policy; **c'est de bonne p.** *Pol* it's good political practice; *Fig* it's good practice; *UE* **la p. agricole commune** the Common Agricultural Policy; **p. antiprotectionniste** free-trade policy; **p. d'apaisement** policy of appeasement; **p. d'austérité** austerity policy; **p. budgétaire** budgetary *or* fiscal policy; **p. commerciale** trade policy; **p. de commercialisation** marketing policy; *UE* **p. communautaire** EU policy; **p. commune de la pêche** Common Fisheries Policy; *Mktg* **p. de communication** promotional policy; **p. conjoncturelle** economic policy *(responding to changes in the business cycle)*; **la p. consensuelle** consensus politics; **p. conventionnelle** = policy relating to union-management agreements; **p. à court terme** short-termism; **p. de crédit** credit policy; **p. déflationniste** *ou* **p. de déflation** deflationary policy; **p. de distribution** distribution policy; *Pol* **p. économique** economic policy; **p. d'élargissement européenne** policy of enlarging the European Union; **p. électoraliste** vote-catching policies; **p. étrangère** foreign policy; *UE* **p. étrangère et de sécurité commune** Common Foreign and Security Policy; **p. extérieure** foreign policy; **p. fiscale** fiscal policy; **p. de gestion** business policy; **p. industrielle** industrial policy; **p. inflationniste** inflationary policy; **p. intérieure** domestic policy; **p. d'investissement** investment policy; **p. du laissez-faire** laissez-faire policy; **p. de libre-échange** free-trade policy; **p. à long terme** long-term policy; *Mktg* **p. de marque** brand policy; *Com* **p. en matière de change** exchange policy; **p. monétaire** monetary policy; **p. d'open-market** open-market policy; **p. d'ouverture** consensus politics; **p. de la porte ouverte** open-door policy; **p. des prix** pricing *or* prices policy; *Mktg* **p. de produit** product policy; *Mktg* **p. de promo-**

tion promotional policy; **p. de rigueur** policy of austerity; **p. des salaires** wages policy; **p. sécuritaire** repressive law-and-order policy; **p. de stabilité** stabilizing policy; **p. de la terre brûlée** scorched-earth policy; *Mktg* **p. de vente** sales policy; **pratiquer la p. de l'autruche** to bury one's head in the sand; **pratiquer la p. de la chaise vide** to make a political point by not attending meetings; **pratiquer la p. de la main tendue** to make friendly overtures, to be conciliatory; **la p. du pire** = deliberately worsening the situation to further one's ends

NMF 1 *(politicien)* politician **2** *(prisonnier)* political prisoner

NM politics

> Attention: ne pas confondre **politics** et **policy** lorsque l'on traduit **politique**. **Politics** est un terme indénombrable qui désigne la politique en tant que discipline, alors que le terme **policy** est un terme dénombrable qui désigne un ensemble de mesures.

politique-fiction [pɔlitikfiksjɔ̃] **NF** futuristic political fiction; **un roman de p.** a futuristic political novel

politiquement [pɔlitikmɑ̃] **ADV 1** *Pol* politically; **p. correct** politically correct **2** *Littéraire (adroitement)* diplomatically

politisation [pɔlitizasjɔ̃] **NF** politicization; **la p. du sport** the politicization of sport, bringing politics into sport

politiser [3] [pɔlitize] **VT** to politicize, to bring politics into; **ils sont moins/plus politisés** they are less/more interested in politics; **p. une grève** to give a political dimension to a strike

VPR se politiser to become political

politologie [pɔlitɔlɔʒi] **NF** political science

politologue [pɔlitɔlɔg] **NMF** political scientist

polka [pɔlka] **NF** polka

pollen [pɔlɛn] **NM** pollen

pollinisation [pɔlinizasjɔ̃] **NF** pollination

polliniser [3] [pɔlinize] **VT** to pollinate

polluant, -e [pɔlɥɑ̃, -ɑ̃t] **ADJ** polluting; **un produit p.** a pollutant

NM polluting agent, pollutant

pollué, -e [pɔlɥe] **ADJ** polluted; **région fortement polluée** highly polluted region, region with a high level of pollution

polluer [7] [pɔlɥe] **VT 1** *Écol* to pollute **2** *Fig (souiller)* to pollute, to sully; **la presse à scandale pollue toute la profession** the gutter press is a disgrace to the whole profession

pollueur, -euse [pɔlɥœr, -øz] **ADJ** *(industrie)* polluting

NM,F polluter

pollution [pɔlysjɔ̃] **NF 1** *Écol* pollution; **p. atmosphérique** atmospheric *or* air pollution **2** *Fig* pollution

• **pollutions NFPL** *Méd* **pollutions nocturnes** wet dreams, *Spéc* nocturnal emissions

polo [pɔlo] **NM 1** *Sport* polo **2** *(chemise)* polo shirt

polochon [pɔlɔʃɔ̃] **NM** *Fam* bolster[❑]

Pologne [pɔlɔɲ] **NF la P.** Poland

polonais, -e [pɔlɔnɛ, -ɛz] **ADJ** Polish

NM *(langue)* Polish

• **Polonais, -e NM,F** Pole

• **polonaise NF** *Mus (danse)* polonaise

• **à la polonaise ADJ** *Culin* à la polonaise, = covered with chopped hard-boiled egg yolk, herbs and fried breadcrumbs

polonium [pɔlɔnjɔm] **NM** *Chim* polonium

poltron, -onne [pɔltrɔ̃, -ɔn] **ADJ** cowardly, faint-hearted, lily-livered

NM,F coward, *Littéraire* poltroon

poltronnerie [pɔltrɔnri] **NF** cowardice, faint-heartedness

polyacide [pɔliasid] **NM** *Chim* polyacid

polyamide [pɔliamid] **NM** *Chim* polyamide

polyamour [pɔliamur] **NM** polyamory

polyandre [pɔljɑ̃dr] **ADJ** polyandrous

polyandrie [pɔliɑ̃dri] **NF** polyandry

polyarthrite [pɔliartrit] **NF** *Méd* polyarthritis; **p. rhumatoïde** rheumatoid arthritis

polycentrisme [pɔlisɑ̃trism] **NM** *Pol* polycentrism

polycentriste [pɔlisɑ̃trist] **ADJ** *Pol* polycentrist

polychrome [pɔlikrom] **ADJ** polychromatic, polychrome

polychromie [pɔlikrɔmi] **NF** polychromy

polyclinique [pɔliklinik] **NF** polyclinic

polycopie [pɔlikɔpi] **NF 1** *(procédé)* duplication; **envoyer un texte à la p.** to send a text to be duplicated **2** *(document)* duplicate

polycopié [pɔlikɔpje] **NM** *(gén)* (duplicated) notes; *Univ* handout

polycopier [9] [pɔlikɔpje] **VT** to duplicate

polyculture [pɔlikyltyr] **NF** polyculture, mixed farming

polydactyle [pɔlidaktil] **ADJ** polydactyl, polydactylous

NMF polydactyl

polyèdre [pɔliɛdr] *Géom* **ADJ** polyhedral

NM polyhedron

polyédrique [pɔliedrik] **ADJ** *Géom* polyhedral

polyester [pɔliɛstɛr] **NM** *Chim* polyester

polyéthylène [pɔlietilɛn] **NM** *Chim* polythene, *esp Am* polyethylene

polygame [pɔligam] **ADJ** polygamous

NM polygamist

polygamie [pɔligami] **NF** polygamy

polyglotte [pɔliglɔt] **ADJ** polyglot

NMF polyglot

polygonal, -e, -aux, -ales [pɔlygɔnal, -o] **ADJ** *Géom* polygonal

polygone [pɔligɔn] **NM 1** *Géom* polygon **2** *Mil* **p. de tir** shooting range **3** *(dans des statistiques)* **p. des fréquences** frequency polygon

polygraphe [pɔligraf] **NM** *(écrivain)* versatile writer; *Péj* = writer who writes on too many subjects

polyhandicapé, -e [pɔliɑ̃dikape] *Méd* **ADJ** multiply disabled

NM,F person with multiple disabilities

polyinsaturé, -e [pɔliɛ̃satyre] **ADJ** polyunsaturated

polymère [pɔlimɛr] *Chim* **ADJ** polymeric

NM polymer

polymérisation [pɔlimerizasjɔ̃] **NF** *Chim* polymerization

polymorphe [pɔlimɔrf] **ADJ 1** *(gén) & Biol* polymorphous, polymorphic; **espèce p.** polymorph **2** *Chim* polymorphic

polymorphie [pɔlimɔrfi] **NF** *Chim* polymorphism

Polynésie [pɔlinezi] **NF la P.** Polynesia; **la P. française** French Polynesia

polynésien, -enne [pɔlinezjɛ̃, -ɛn] **ADJ** Polynesian

NM *(langue)* Polynesian

• **Polynésien, -enne NM,F** Polynesian

polynôme [pɔlinom] **NM** *Math* polynomial

polynucléaire [pɔlinykleɛr] *Biol* **ADJ** polynuclear, polynucleate

NM polymorphonuclear leucocyte

polype [pɔlip] **NM 1** *Méd* polyp, polypus **2** *Zool* polyp

polypeux, -euse [pɔlipø, -øz] **ADJ** *Méd & Zool* polypous

polyphasé, -e [pɔlifaze] **ADJ** *Élec* polyphase *(avant n)*

polyphénol [pɔlifenɔl] **NM** *Chim* polyphenol

polyphonie [pɔlifɔni] **NF** *Mus* polyphony

polypropène [pɔliprɔpɛn], **polypropylène** [pɔliprɔpilɛn] **NM** polypropylene

polysémie [pɔlisemi] **NF** *Ling* polysemy

polysémique [pɔlisemik] **ADJ** *Ling* polysemous

polystyrène [pɔlistirɛn] **NM** polystyrene

polysyllabe [pɔlisilab], **polysyllabique** [pɔlisilabik] **ADJ** polysyllabic

NM polysyllable

polytechnicien, -enne [pɔlitɛknisjɛ̃, -ɛn] **NM,F** *(étudiant)* student at the "École Polytechnique"; *(diplômé)* graduate of the "École Polytechnique"

polytechnique [pɔlitɛknik] **ADJ 1** *(polyvalent)* polytechnic **2** *Univ* polytechnic; **(l'École) P.** = "grande école" for engineers

> Il faut noter que le nom anglais **polytechnic** est un faux ami. Jusqu'en 1992 il désignait un établissement d'enseignement supérieur comparable à un IUT en Grande-Bretagne.

> **ÉCOLE POLYTECHNIQUE**
>
> Founded in 1794, this prestigious engineering college has close connections with the Ministry of Defence. Formerly situated in the heart of Paris's 5th arrondissement, the college moved to Palaiseau, near Paris, in the 1970s. It is popularly known as "l'X". Students are effectively enlisted in the army and must repay their education through government service.

polythéisme [pɔliteism] **NM** polytheism

polythéiste [pɔliteist] **ADJ** polytheistic

NMF polytheist

Polythène® [pɔlitɛn] **NM** *Chim* polythene

polytransfusé, -e [pɔlitrɑ̃sfyze] **ADJ** = who has received multiple blood transfusions

NM,F = person who has received multiple blood transfusions

polytraumatisé, -e [pɔlitromatize] *Méd* **ADJ** suffering from multiple trauma

NM,F multiple trauma sufferer

polyuréthane, polyuréthanne [pɔliyretan] **NM** *Chim* polyurethan, polyurethane

polyvalence [pɔlivalɑ̃s] **NF** *(gén)* versatility, adaptability; *Chim* polyvalence, polyvalency

polyvalent, -e [pɔlivalɑ̃, -ɑ̃t] **ADJ** *(gén)* versatile, adaptable; *(salle)* multi-purpose; *Chim* polyvalent

NM,F 1 *Fin & Jur* tax inspector **2** *(dans les services sociaux)* social worker

• **polyvalente NF** *Can (école)* = secondary school offering both general and vocational courses

polyvinyle [pɔlivinil] **NM** polyvinyl

polyvinylique [pɔlivinilik] **ADJ** polyvinyl *(avant n)*

pomelo, pomélo [pɔmelo] **NM** pomelo

Poméranie [pɔmerani] **NF la P.** Pomerania

pommade [pɔmad] **NF 1** *Méd (pour brûlures)* ointment; *(pour foulures)* liniment; **p. pour les lèvres** lip salve *or* balm; *Fam* **passer de la p. à qn** to butter sb up **2** *Culin* cream, paste *(made from pounding various ingredients together)*

pommader [3] [pɔmade] **VT** *(cheveux)* to put cream on, to pomade

pomme [pɔm] **NF 1** *(fruit)* apple; **p. d'api** = variety of small, sweet apple; **p. (de) cajou** cashew apple *or* pear; **p. cannelle** custard apple; **p. à cidre** cider apple; **p. à couteau** dessert *or* eating apple; **p. à cuire** cooking apple, *Br* cooker; **p. de reinette** pippin; *Fig* **la p. de discorde** the bone of contention; *Fam Fig* **tomber dans les pommes** to pass out[❑], to keel over

2 *(légume)* potato; **pommes allumettes** (very thin) fries; **pommes chips** (potato) crisps *or Am* chips; **pommes dauphine/duchesse** dauphine/duchesse potatoes; **pommes frites** *Br* chips, *Am* (French) fries; **pommes noisettes** pommes noisettes, = deep-fried potato balls; **pommes vapeur** steamed potatoes

3 *(cœur ▸ du chou, de la salade)* heart

4 *(objet rond ▸ d'une canne)* knob; **p. d'arrosoir** rose *(of a watering can)*; **p. de douche** shower head

5 *Fam (figure)* face[❑], mug; **t'en fais une drôle de p.!** you're looking funny *or* weird!

6 p. (à l'eau *ou* **à l'huile)** *(naïf)* sucker, *Br* mug; **être bonne p.** to be a sucker *or Br* a mug; **t'es trop bonne p.!** you're such a soft touch *or* a pushover!

7 *Fam (locutions)* **ma p.** *(moi)* yours truly; **ta/sa p.** *(toi/lui/elle)* you[❑]/him[❑]/her[❑]; **et l'addition, c'est encore pour ma p.!** and yours truly *or Br* muggins has to fork out again!; **et les papiers à remplir, ce sera pour sa p.!** and he/she can damn well cope with the paperwork himself/herself!

• **aux pommes ADJ 1** *Culin* apple *(avant n)* **2** *Fam (extraordinaire)* terrific, great

• **pomme d'Adam NF** Adam's apple

• **pomme d'amour NF 1** *(tomate)* tomato **2**

(friandise) toffee apple
• **pomme de pin** NF pine *or* fir cone
• **pomme de terre** NF potato; **pommes de terre à l'eau** boiled potatoes; **pommes de terre frites** *Br* chips, *Am* (French) fries; **p. de terre en robe de chambre** *ou* **en robe des champs** baked potato, jacket potato

pommé, -e [pɔme] ADJ **1** *(salade, chou)* hearty, firm **2** *Fam Vieilli (idiot, gaffe)* complete□, downright□

pommeau, -x [pɔmo] NM *(d'une canne)* knob, pommel; *(d'une selle, d'une épée)* pommel; *(d'un fût de pistolet)* pommel, cascabel; **p. de douche** shower head

pommelé, -e [pɔmle] ADJ **1** *(cheval)* dappled; **gris p.** dapple-grey **2** *(ciel)* mackerel *(avant n)*, dappled

pommeler [24] [pɔmle] **se pommeler** VPR **le ciel se pommelait** the sky was becoming dappled with clouds

pommelle [pɔmɛl] NF drain grating *or* cover

pommer [3] [pɔme] VI *(chou, laitue)* to heart

pommeraie [pɔmrɛ] NF apple orchard

pommette [pɔmɛt] NF *(de la joue)* cheekbone

pommier [pɔmje] NM **1** *(arbre)* apple tree **2** *(bois)* apple wood

pompage [pɔ̃paʒ] NM pumping

pompe [pɔ̃p] NF **1** *(machine)* pump; **prendre de l'eau à la p.** to get some water from the pump; **p. à air/chaleur** air/heat pump; **p. à vide/d'injection** vacuum/injection pump; **p. aspirante** suction pump; **p. à bicyclette** *ou* **à vélo** bicycle pump; **p. à essence** *(distributeur) Br* petrol *or Am* gas pump; *(station) Br* petrol *or Am* gas station; **s'arrêter à une p. (à essence)** to stop at a *Br* petrol *or Am* gas station; **les prix à la p.** pump prices; **p. foulante** force pump; *Aut* **p. à huile** oil pump; **p. à incendie** water pump *(on a fire engine)*; *Fam* **avoir un coup de p.** to suddenly feel *Br* knackered *or Am* bushed

2 *Fam (chaussure)* shoe□; **un coup de p.** a kick□; **être** *ou* **marcher à côté de ses pompes** to be screwed up; **il est à côté de ses pompes aujourd'hui** he's not quite with it today

3 *(apparat)* pomp; **la p. des mariages princiers** the pomp (and circumstance) of royal weddings; **en grande p.** with great pomp and ceremony

4 *Fam Arg mil* **(soldat de) deuxième p.** *Br* squaddie, *Am* grunt

5 *Fam (aide-mémoire) Br* crib, *Am* trot

6 *Fam Arg drogue (seringue)* hype, hypo
• **pompes** NFPL *Sport Br* press-ups, *Am* push-ups
• **à toute(s) pompe(s)** ADV *Fam* like lightning; **il est parti à toutes pompes** he was off like a shot
• **pompes funèbres** NFPL **(entreprise de) pompes funèbres** funeral parlour; **les pompes funèbres sont venues à 9 heures** the undertakers came at 9 o'clock

pompé, -e [pɔ̃pe] ADJ *Fam (épuisé) Br* knackered, *Am* bushed

Pompée [pɔ̃pe] NPR Pompey

Pompéi [pɔ̃pei] NM Pompeii

pompéien, -enne [pɔ̃pejɛ̃, -ɛn] ADJ Pompeiian, Pompeian
• **Pompéien, -enne** NM,F Pompeiian, Pompeian

pomper [3] [pɔ̃pe] VT **1** *(aspirer ▸ pour évacuer)* to pump (out); *(▸ pour faire monter)* to pump up; *(▸ pour boire)* to suck up; **il va falloir p. l'eau du bateau** we'll have to pump the water out of the boat; **p. de l'eau du puits** to pump (up) water from the well; **des parasites qui pompent le sang** parasites that suck blood; *Fam* **p. qn, p. l'air à qn** *(l'importuner)* to get on sb's nerves, to bug sb

2 *(absorber ▸ sujet: éponge)* to soak up; *(▸ sujet: sol)* to soak *or* to drink up

3 *Fam Fig (utiliser ▸ économies, réserves)* to take up□, to eat up; **notre voyage aux Seychelles a pompé toutes nos économies** our trip to the Seychelles just ate up all our savings; **il se fait p. tout son argent par son ex-femme** his ex-wife is bleeding him dry

4 *Fam (fatiguer)* to wear out, to do in; **ce déménagement m'a pompé** that move's done me in

5 *très Fam (boire)* to knock back

6 *Fam Arg scol (copier)* to crib (**sur** from)

VI **1** *(faire marcher une pompe, appuyer)* to pump; **p. sur la pédale du frein** to pump the brake pedal **2** *Fam Arg scol (copier)* to crib (**sur** from)

pompette [pɔ̃pɛt] ADJ *Fam* tipsy, merry

pompeuse [pɔ̃pøz] *voir* **pompeux**

pompeusement [pɔ̃pøzmɑ̃] ADV pompously, bombastically

pompeux, -euse [pɔ̃pø, -øz] ADJ pompous, bombastic

pompidolien, -enne [pɔ̃pidɔljɛ̃, -ɛn] ADJ = relating to the Pompidou era *(1969–74, when Georges Pompidou was French President)*; **l'ère pompidolienne** the Pompidou era; **la France pompidolienne** France under Georges Pompidou

pompier, -ère [pɔ̃pje, -ɛr] ADJ *Beaux-Arts* pompier; *Péj (style, décor)* pretentious, pompous

NM **1** *(sapeur)* fireman; **les pompiers** the fire *Br* brigade *or Am* department **2** *Beaux-Arts (style)* pompier (style); *(artiste)* pompier **3** *Vulg* **faire un p. à qn** to give sb a blow-job, to suck sb off

pompiste [pɔ̃pist] NMF *Br* petrol *or* pump attendant, *Am* gas station attendant

pom-pom girl [pɔmpɔmgœrl] NF cheerleader

pompon [pɔ̃pɔ̃] NM **1** *Tex* pompom; **bonnet à p.** bobble hat **2** *Fam (locutions)* **dans le genre désagréable, il tient le p.!** when it comes to unpleasantness, he certainly takes the *Br* biscuit *or Am* cake!; **ça, c'est le p.!** that's the limit!

pomponner [3] [pɔ̃pɔne] VT **p. qn** to do sb up, to doll sb up; **se faire p.** to get dolled up

VPR **se pomponner** to do oneself up, to doll oneself up

ponçage [pɔ̃saʒ] NM *(au papier de verre ▸ d'un mur)* sanding (down), sandpapering; *(▸ de peinture)* rubbing down; *(avec une ponceuse)* sanding; *(à la pierre ponce)* pumicing

ponce [pɔ̃s] ADJ **pierre p.** pumice (stone)

Ponce Pilate [pɔ̃spilat] *voir* **Pilate**

poncer [16] [pɔ̃se] VT *(polir au papier de verre ▸ mur)* to sandpaper, to sand (down); *(▸ peinture)* to rub down; *(polir avec une ponceuse)* to sand (down); *(polir à la pierre ponce)* to pumice (off)

ponceur, -euse [pɔ̃sœr, -øz] NM,F sander
• **ponceuse** NF *(machine)* sander, sanding machine

poncho [pɔ̃tʃo] NM *(cape)* poncho

poncif [pɔ̃sif] NM *Péj (cliché)* cliché, commonplace

ponction [pɔ̃ksjɔ̃] NF **1** *Méd* puncture; *(de poumon)* tapping; **p. lombaire/du ventricule** lumbar/ventricular puncture **2** *(retrait)* withdrawal; **faire une grosse p. sur un compte** to withdraw a large sum from an account; **c'est une p. importante sur mes revenus** it makes quite a big hole *or* dent in my income; *Admin* **p. fiscale** taxation; **p. sociale** = contributions to the social security scheme, *Br* ≃ National Insurance contributions

ponctionner [3] [pɔ̃ksjɔne] VT **1** *Méd (poumon)* to tap; *(région lombaire)* to puncture **2** *(compte en banque)* to withdraw money from; *(économies)* to make a hole *or* dent in; **on nous ponctionne un tiers de notre salaire en impôts** a third of our salary goes in tax

ponctualité [pɔ̃ktɥalite] NF *(exactitude)* punctuality, promptness; **avec p.** promptly, on time

ponctuation [pɔ̃ktɥasjɔ̃] NF punctuation

ponctuel, -elle [pɔ̃ktɥɛl] ADJ **1** *(exact)* punctual; **être p.** to be on time **2** *(action) Br* one-off, *Am* one-shot; *(problèmes, difficultés)* occasional; *(expérience)* isolated; **ses interventions ponctuelles étaient vitales pour le projet** the contributions he/she made at various stages of the project were invaluable; **l'État accorde une aide ponctuelle aux entreprises en difficulté** the state gives backing to companies to see them through periods of financial difficulty; **les terroristes ne se livraient qu'à des actions ponctuelles** the terrorists made only sporadic attacks **3** *Ling & Math* punctual; *Phys* **source ponctuelle de chaleur** pinpoint flame; **source lumineuse ponctuelle** point source

ponctuellement [pɔ̃ktɥɛlmɑ̃] ADV **1** *(avec exactitude)* punctually **2** *(de façon limitée)* on an ad hoc basis, as the need arises

ponctuer [7] [pɔ̃ktɥe] VT **1** *Gram* to punctuate **2** *Fig* to punctuate; **ses conférences étaient toujours ponctuées de plaisanteries** his/her lectures were always punctuated *or* peppered with jokes; **elle ponctuait les mots importants d'un hochement de tête** she emphasized *or* stressed the important words with a nod **3** *Mus* to phrase

USAGE ABSOLU *Gram* **savoir p.** to know how to use punctuation

pondaison [pɔ̃dɛzɔ̃] NF laying season

pondérable [pɔ̃derabl] ADJ weighable, ponderable

pondéral, -e, -aux, -ales [pɔ̃deral, -o] ADJ weight *(avant n)*

pondérateur, -trice [pɔ̃deratœr, -tris] ADJ stabilizing

pondération [pɔ̃derasjɔ̃] NF **1** *(sang-froid)* level-headedness; **agir/parler avec p.** to act/to speak level-headedly **2** *Bourse & Écon* weighting **3** *Pol (de pouvoirs)* balance, equilibrium

pondératrice [pɔ̃deratris] *voir* **pondérateur**

pondéré, -e [pɔ̃dere] ADJ **1** *(personne)* level-headed, steady; *(esprit)* well balanced **2** *Bourse & Écon* weighted

pondérer [18] [pɔ̃dere] VT **1** *(pouvoirs)* to balance (out), to counterbalance **2** *Bourse & Écon* to weight

pondéreux, -euse [pɔ̃derø, -øz] *Ind* ADJ heavy

NM heavy material; **les p.** heavy goods

pondeur, -euse [pɔ̃dœr, -øz] ADJ *(poule)* laying
• **pondeuse** NF **1** *(poule)* laying hen, layer; **c'est une bonne pondeuse** she's a good layer **2** *Fam Péj ou Hum (femme)* **c'est une vraie pondeuse** she breeds like a rabbit

pondoir [pɔ̃dwar] NM laying place

pondre [75] [pɔ̃dr] VT **1** *(sujet: oiseau)* to lay; **un œuf frais pondu** a new(ly)-laid egg, a freshly-laid egg **2** *Fam Péj (sujet: femme ▸ enfant)* to produce□, to drop **3** *Fam (créer ▸ gén)* to come up with; *(▸ en série)* to churn out; **il pond un article tous les jours** he churns out an article every day; **je n'ai pondu que trois pages sur le sujet** I could only produce *or* come up with three pages on the subject

VI *(poule)* to lay (an egg/eggs); *(moustique, saumon etc)* to lay its eggs

poney [pɔnɛ] NM pony

pongiste [pɔ̃ʒist] NMF table tennis player

pont [pɔ̃] NM **1** *Constr* bridge; **dormir** *ou* **vivre sous les ponts** to be homeless, *Br* to sleep under the arches; **p. autoroutier** *Br* motorway *or Am* freeway flyover; **p. à bascule** *ou* **basculant** bascule *or* balance bridge; **p. ferroviaire** railway bridge; **p. à haubans** cable-stayed bridge; **p. levant** lift bridge; **p. mobile** movable bridge; **p. à péage** toll-bridge; **p. routier** road bridge; **p. suspendu** suspension bridge; **p. tournant** *(routier)* swing bridge; *(ferroviaire)* turntable; **faire/promettre un p. d'or à qn** to offer/to promise sb a golden hello; *Fig* **jeter un p.** to build bridges; **se porter** *ou* **être solide comme le P.-Neuf** to be as fit as a fiddle; **les Ponts** = nickname of the "École des Ponts et Chaussées"

2 *Naut* deck; **bateau à deux/trois ponts** two-/three-decker; **p. arrière** aft *or* after deck; **p. avant** foredeck; **p. d'envol** flight deck; **p. inférieur/principal** lower/main deck; **p. supérieur** upper *or* top deck; **tout le monde sur le p.!** all hands on deck!

3 *(week-end)* long weekend; *(jour)* = day off between a national holiday and a weekend; **faire le p.** *(employé)* = to take the intervening working day or days off; **le 14 juillet tombe un jeudi, je vais faire le p.** the 14th of July falls on a Thursday, I'll take Friday off (and have a long weekend)

4 *(structure de manutention)* **p. de chargement** loading platform; **p. élévateur** *ou* **de graissage** garage ramp, car lift, elevator platform; **p. roulant** gantry *or* travelling crane

5 *Aut* axle; **p. arrière** rear axle (and drive)

6 *Aviat* **p. aérien** airlift

7 p. aux ânes *Géom* pons asinorum; *Fig* old chestnut

8 *Mus* bridge; *Cin & TV* **p. sonore** bridge

9 *Sport* bridge; **faire le p.** to do the crab
• **Ponts et Chaussées** NMPL **les Ponts et Chaus-**

sées *Admin* Department of Civil Engineering; *Univ* College of Civil Engineering

pontage [pɔ̃taʒ] **NM 1** *Méd* bypass (operation); **p. coronarien** heart bypass (operation); **on lui a fait un p.** he's/she's had a bypass, he's/she's had bypass surgery **2** *Constr* (gantry) bridging **3** *Naut* decking

pont-bascule [pɔ̃baskyl] (*pl* **ponts-bascules**) **NM** weighbridge

ponte[1] [pɔ̃t] **NM 1** *Fam (autorité)* **un (grand) p.** a big shot, a bigwig; **ce sont tous de grands pontes de l'université/de la médecine** they're all top-flight academics/high up in the medical profession **2** *(dans les jeux de hasard)* punter

ponte[2] [pɔ̃t] **NF 1** *Zool (action)* laying (of eggs); *(œufs ▸ d'un oiseau)* clutch, eggs; *(▸ d'un insecte, d'un poisson)* eggs **2** *Physiol* **p. ovulaire** ovulation

ponté, -e [pɔ̃te] *Naut* **ADJ** *(à un pont)* single-deck *(avant n)*; *(à plusieurs ponts)* multi-deck *(avant n)*
• **pontée NF** deck load

ponter [3] [pɔ̃te] **VI** *(aux jeux de hasard)* to punt
VT 1 *(miser)* to bet **2** *Naut* to deck

pontier [pɔ̃tje] **NM 1** *(qui manœuvre un pont mobile)* swing-bridge keeper **2** *(qui conduit un pont roulant)* travelling-crane operator

pontife [pɔ̃tif] **NM 1** *Fam (autorité)* pundit, bigwig, big shot **2** *Rel* pontiff

pontifiant, -e [pɔ̃tifjɑ̃, -ɑ̃t] **ADJ** pontificating

pontifical, -e, -aux, -ales [pɔ̃tifikal, -o] *Rel* **ADJ** *(insignes, cérémonie)* pontifical; *(État, trône)* papal
NM pontifical

pontificat [pɔ̃tifika] **NM** pontificate; **sous le p. de Jean-Paul II** during the pontificate of John-Paul II

pontifier [9] [pɔ̃tifje] **VI** to pontificate

pont-l'évêque [pɔ̃levɛk] **NM INV** Pont l'Évêque (cheese)

pont-levis [pɔ̃ləvi] (*pl* **ponts-levis**) **NM** drawbridge

ponton [pɔ̃tɔ̃] **NM 1** *(d'un port de commerce)* pontoon, floating dock; *(d'un port de plaisance)* landing stage, jetty; *(pour nageurs)* (floating) platform **2** *(chaland)* hulk, lighter; *(vieux vaisseau)* hulk

pontonnier [pɔ̃tɔnje] **NM** *Mil* pontonier

pont-promenade [pɔ̃prɔmnad] (*pl* **ponts-promenade** *ou* **ponts-promenades**) **NM** promenade deck

pool [pul] **NM 1** *Écon* pool; **p. d'assurances** insurance pool; **p. bancaire** banking pool; **p. de l'or** gold pool **2** *(équipe)* pool; **p. de dactylos** typing pool; **p. de secrétaires** secretarial pool

pop [pɔp] **ADJ INV** *(art, chanteur, mouvement)* pop; **musique p.** pop (music); **p. électronique** electro-pop
NM OU NF pop (music)

pop art [pɔpart] (*pl* **pop arts**) **NM** pop art

pop-corn [pɔpkɔrn] **NM INV** popcorn

pope [pɔp] **NM** (Eastern Orthodox Church) priest

popeline [pɔplin] **NF** *Tex* poplin

popote [pɔpɔt] *Fam* **NF 1** *(cuisine)* cooking[□]; **faire la p.** to do the cooking **2** *(matériel)* mess kit[□] **3** *Mil (mess)* officers' mess[□]
ADJ INV overly houseproud[□]; **elle est très p.** she's very much the stay-at-home type

popotin [pɔpɔtɛ̃] **NM** *Fam* butt, *Br* bum, *Am* fanny

populace [pɔpylas] **NF** *Fam Péj* rabble, hoi polloi, plebs

populacier, -ère [pɔpylasje, -ɛr] **ADJ** vulgar, common

populage [pɔpylaʒ] **NM** *Bot* marsh marigold

populaire [pɔpylɛr] **ADJ 1** *(ouvrier)* working-class; **les quartiers populaires** the working-class areas; **les classes populaires** the working classes
2 *(tradition, croyance)* popular; **bon sens p.** popular wisdom
3 *Pol (gouvernement)* popular; *(démocratie, tribunal)* people's *(avant n)*; *(soulèvement)* mass *(avant n)*; **la volonté p.** the will of the people
4 *(destiné au peuple)* popular; **art p.** popular art; **romans populaires** popular fiction
5 *(qui a du succès ▸ chanteur, mesures)* popular; **elle s'est rendue très p. auprès des étudiants** she made herself very popular with the students; **la voile devient très p.** sailing is growing in popularity *or* becoming more and more popular
6 *Ling (étymologie)* popular; *(niveau de langue)* colloquial

populairement [pɔpylɛrmɑ̃] **ADV** *Ling* colloquially; **comme on dit p.** as the popular phrase goes

populariser [3] [pɔpylarize] **VT** to popularize

popularité [pɔpylarite] **NF** popularity; **elle jouit d'une grande p. parmi les étudiants** she's very popular with the students; **le président a perdu de sa p.** there's been a decline in the president's popularity

population [pɔpylasjɔ̃] **NF 1** *(nombre d'individus)* population; **p. active/civile** working/civilian population; **p. canine** dog *or* canine population; **p. excédentaire** surplus population; **p. inactive** non-working population; **p. mondiale** world population **2** *(peuple)* people; **la p. locale** the local people, the locals **3** *Mktg* **p. cible** target population; **p. mère** basic population; **p. prévue** projected population

populationnisme [pɔpylasjɔnism] **NM** = policy of population growth

populationniste [pɔpylasjɔnist] **ADJ** encouraging population growth; **politique p.** policy of population growth; **gouvernement p.** government in favour of population growth
NMF = supporter of measures encouraging population growth

populeux, -euse [pɔpylø, -øz] **ADJ** *(quartier)* heavily *or* densely populated, populous; *(place, rue)* crowded, very busy

populisme [pɔpylism] **NM** *Littérature* populism *(literary movement in the 1920s and 1930s that set out to describe the lives of working-class people)*

populiste [pɔpylist] *Littérature* **ADJ** populist
NMF populist (writer) *(member of the literary movement in the 1920s and 1930s that set out to describe the lives of working-class people)*

populo [pɔpylo] **NM** *Fam* **1** *(foule)* crowd[□]; **il y avait un de ces populos en ville** the town was jam-packed *or Br* chock-a-block *or* heaving **2** *(peuple)* **le p.** the plebs, the riff-raff, the rabble

pop-up [pɔpœp] (*pl* **pop-ups**) **NM OU NF** pop-up; *(publicité)* pop-up ad

poquet [pɔkɛ] **NM** *Agr* seed hole

porc [pɔr] **NM 1** *Zool Br* pig, *Am* hog; **manger comme un p.** to eat like a pig; **p. sauvage** wild boar
2 *Culin* pork
3 *(peau)* pigskin
4 *Fam (personne)* pig, swine
• **de porc ADJ 1** *Culin* pork *(avant n)* **2** *(en peau)* pigskin *(avant n)*

porcelaine [pɔrsəlɛn] **NF 1** *(produit)* china, porcelain; **p. phosphatique** *ou* **tendre naturelle** bone china
2 *(pièce)* piece of china *or* porcelain
3 *(ensemble)* **la p.** china, chinaware, porcelain; **p. de Chine** china; **p. de Saxe** Dresden china
4 *Zool (mollusque)* cowrie
• **de porcelaine ADJ 1** *(tasse, objet)* china *(avant n)*, porcelain *(avant n)* **2** *(teint)* porcelain *(avant n)*, peaches-and-cream *(avant n)*

porcelainier, -ère [pɔrsəlenje, -ɛr] **ADJ** china *(avant n)*, porcelain *(avant n)*
NM,F porcelain *or* china manufacturer

porcelet [pɔrsəlɛ] **NM** piglet

porc-épic [pɔrkepik] (*pl* **porcs-épics**) **NM 1** *Zool* porcupine **2** *(personne revêche)* prickly person **3** *Fam (homme mal rasé)* **c'est un vrai p.** he's really bristly

porche [pɔrʃ] **NM** porch

porcher, -ère [pɔrʃe, -ɛr] **NM,F** swineherd

porcherie [pɔrʃəri] **NF** *aussi Fig* pigsty, *Am* pigpen

porcin, -e [pɔrsɛ̃, -in] **ADJ 1** *(industrie, production)* pig *(avant n)* **2** *(yeux, figure)* pig-like, piggy
NM pig; **les porcins** the pig family

pore [pɔr] **NM** pore; **avoir les pores dilatés** to have open pores; *Fig* **elle sue la suffisance par tous les pores** she exudes *or* oozes self-importance

poreux, -euse [pɔrø, -øz] **ADJ** porous

porno [pɔrno] *Fam* **ADJ** *(abrév* **pornographique**) *(film, magazine, scène)* porn *(avant n)*, porno *(avant n)*; **des photos pornos** dirty pictures
NM *(abrév* **pornographie**) **1 le p.** *(genre)* porn; *(industrie)* the porn industry **2** *(film) Br* blue movie, *Br* porn film

pornographe [pɔrnɔgraf] **NMF** pornographer

pornographie [pɔrnɔgrafi] **NF** pornography

pornographique [pɔrnɔgrafik] **ADJ** pornographic

porosité [pɔrozite] **NF** porosity

porphyre [pɔrfir] **NM** *Minér* porphyry

porreau, -x [pɔro] **NM** *Suisse* leek

porridge [pɔridʒ] **NM** porridge

port[1] [pɔr] **NM 1** *(pour bateaux)* harbour; *(plus important, ville)* port; **dans le p. de Dunkerque** in Dunkirk harbour; **sur le p.** on the quayside; **entrer au p.** to come into port *or* harbour; **quitter le p.** to leave port *or* harbour; **p. artificiel** artificial port; **p. d'attache** port of registry, home port; *Fig* home base; **p. de commerce** commercial port; **p. d'embarquement** *(de marchandises)* port of shipment; *(de personnes)* port of embarkation; **p. d'entrée** port of entry; **p. d'escale** port of call; **p. fluvial** river port; **p. franc** free port; **p. de guerre** *ou* **militaire** naval base; **p. maritime** *ou* **de mer** sea port; **p. naturel** natural harbour; **p. de pêche** fishing port; **p. de plaisance** marina; **p. de relâche** port of call; **p. de transit** port of transit; *Fig* **nous touchons** *ou* **arrivons au p.** we're on the home straight; **faire naufrage (en arrivant) au p., échouer en vue du p.** to fall at the last fence **2** *Littéraire (havre, refuge)* haven **3** *Ordinat* port; *(pour Internet)* socket; **p. de communication** comms port, communications port; **p. d'imprimante** printer port; **p. modem** modem port; **p. parallèle** parallel port; **p. série** serial port; **p. série universel** USB, universal serial bus; **p. souris** mouse port
• **à bon port ADV** safely, safe and sound; **nous sommes arrivés à bon p.** we got there safe and sound; **les verres sont arrivés à bon p.** the glasses got there in one piece *or* without mishap

port[2] [pɔr] **NM 1** *(d'une lettre, d'un colis)* postage; **frais de p.** (cost of) postage; **(en) p. dû/payé** postage due/paid; **p. et emballage** postage and packing; **p. franc, p. payé** postage paid; **p. compris** postage included
2 *Transp (de marchandises)* carriage; **p. franc, franco de p.** carriage paid *or* included; **p. avancé** carriage forward, freight collect; **p. dû** carriage forward; **p. payé** carriage paid; **p. payé, assurance comprise** carriage insurance paid
3 *(possession ▸ d'une arme)* carrying; *(▸ d'un uniforme, d'un casque)* wearing; **p. d'armes prohibé** illegal carrying of weapons; *Mil* **se mettre au p. d'armes** to shoulder arms; **le p. du casque est obligatoire** *(sur panneau)* safety helmets must be worn
4 *(maintien)* bearing, deportment; **elle a un p. de tête très gracieux** she holds her head very gracefully; **avoir un p. de reine** to have a regal *or* queenly bearing
5 *Naut* **p. en lourd** dead weight

port[3] [pɔr] **NM** *(mot occitan) (col)* pass *(in the Pyrenees)*

portabilité [pɔrtabilite] **NF** *Ordinat* portability; *Tél* **p. du numéro** number portability

portable [pɔrtabl] **ADJ 1** *(téléviseur, ordinateur)* portable; *(téléphone) Br* mobile *(avant n)*, *Am* cellular **2** *(vêtement)* wearable **3** *Fin* to be paid in person
NM *(ordinateur)* laptop; *(téléphone) Br* mobile, mobile phone, *Am* cell, cellphone

portage [pɔrtaʒ] **NM 1** *(d'équipement)* porterage
2 *Naut* portage
3 *Banque & Écon* piggybacking
4 *(distribution d'un journal à domicile)* home delivery

portail [pɔrtaj] **NM 1** *(d'une église)* portal; *(d'un jardin, d'une école)* gate **2** *Ordinat* portal

portance [pɔrtɑ̃s] **NF 1** *Aviat* lift **2** *(d'un terrain)* bearing capacity

portant, -e [pɔrtɑ̃, -ɑ̃t] **ADJ 1** *Naut* **vent p.** fair wind **2** *(mur)* load-bearing **3** *(locution)* **bien/mal p.** in good/poor health; **il est bien p.** he's very well

NM **1** *Théât* upright, support *(for flats)* **2** *(pour vêtements)* rail, rack **3** *(poignée)* handle

portatif, -ive [pɔrtatif, -iv] ADJ *(gén)* portable; *(ordinateur)* laptop
NM *(ordinateur)* laptop

Port-au-Prince [pɔroprɛ̃s] NM Port-au-Prince

porte [pɔrt] NF **1** *(d'une maison, d'un véhicule, d'un meuble)* door; **on vient de sonner, tu vas ouvrir la p.?** someone's just rung the bell, could you answer *or* open the door?; **le piano est resté coincé dans la p.** the piano got stuck in the door *or* doorway; **fermer** *ou* **interdire** *ou* **refuser sa p. à qn** to bar sb from one's house; **fermer ses portes** *(magasin)* to close down; **ouvrir sa p. à qn** to welcome sb; **ouvrir la p. toute grande à qn** to welcome sb with open arms; **ouvrir ses portes** *(magasin, musée)* to open; **un père ministre, ça ouvre pas mal de portes** a father who happens to be a minister can open quite a few doors; *Aut* **p. arrière** rear passenger door; *Aut* **p. avant** *(côté conducteur)* driver door; *(côté passager)* front passenger door; **p. coupe-feu** firedoor; **p. dérobée** hidden door; **p. de derrière/devant** back/front door; **p. d'entrée** front door; *Belg* **p. de rue** front door; **p. de secours** emergency exit; **p. de service** tradesmen's entrance; **p. de sortie** way out, exit; *Fig* way out, let-out; **trouver une p. de sortie** to find a way out; **ménager à qn une p. de sortie** to leave sb a way out; *aussi Fig* **à ma/sa p.** at my/his/her door, on my/his/her doorstep; **il n'habite pas la p. à côté** he doesn't exactly live round the corner; **elle est entrée dans l'entreprise par la grande p.** she went straight in at the top of the company; **entrer dans une profession par la petite p.** to get into a profession by the back door; **l'équipe quitte le tournoi par la grande p.** the team is leaving the tournament in style; **après le scandale, il est sorti par la petite p.** after the scandal, he made a discreet exit; *Fig* **ouvrir la p. à qch** to pave the way for sth; **ouvrir la p. à l'espoir** to allow a measure of hope; **cette décision ouvre toute grande la p. à l'injustice** this decision throws the door wide open to injustice; **prendre la p.** to leave; **il lui a dit de prendre la p.** he showed him/her the door; **j'y suis allé mais j'ai trouvé p. close** I went round but nobody was in *or* at home; **il a essayé tous les éditeurs, mais partout il a trouvé p. close** he tried all the publishers, but without success; **c'est la p. ouverte à tous les abus** it leaves the door wide open for all kinds of abuses; *Prov* **il faut qu'une p. soit ouverte ou fermée** = it has to be either one way or the other
2 *(passage dans une enceinte)* gate; **les portes de Paris** = the old city gates around Paris; **p. d'écluse** lock gate; **p. d'embarquement** (departure) gate; **les portes de l'enfer** the gates of hell; **les portes du paradis** heaven's gates, the pearly gates
3 *(panneau)* door (panel); **p. basculante/battante** up-and-over/swing door; **p. coulissante** *ou* **roulante** sliding door; **p. à deux battants** double door; **p. coupée** half-door, stable door; **p. escamotable** folding door; **p. palière** landing door; **p. tournante** revolving door; **p. vitrée** glass door
4 *Sport* gate
5 *Ordinat* gate
• **à la porte** ADV **à la p.!** out of here!; **ne reste pas à la p.** don't stay on the doorstep; **je suis à la p. de chez moi** *(sans clefs)* I'm locked out; *(chassé)* I've been thrown out (of my home); **mettre qn à la p.** *(importun)* to throw sb out; *(élève)* to expel sb; *(employé)* to fire *or* to dismiss sb
• **de porte à porte, porte à porte** ADV (from) door to door
• **de porte en porte** ADV from door to door

porté [pɔrte] NM *(en danse)* porté

porte-à-faux [pɔrtafo] NM INV overhang; *Constr* cantilever
• **en porte-à-faux** ADV **être en p.** *(mur)* to be out of plumb, to be out of true; *(roche)* to be in a precarious position; *Fig* to be in an awkward position; **mettre qn en p.** to put sb in an awkward position; **il est en p. par rapport à la politique officielle du parti** he's at odds with the official party line

porte-affiches [pɔrtafiʃ] NM INV noticeboard

porte-aiguille [pɔrteguij] *(pl inv ou* **porte-aiguilles**) NM **1** *Méd* needle holder **2** *Couture (d'une machine)* needle holder; *(étui)* needle case

porte-amarre [pɔrtamar] NM INV line-throwing machine

porte-à-porte [pɔrtapɔrt] NM INV *(pour vendre)* door-to-door selling; *(démarchage électoral)* door-to-door canvassing, doorstepping; **faire du p.** *(pour vendre)* to sell from door to door, to be a door-to-door salesman, *f* saleswoman; *(pour un candidat, un parti)* to go canvassing from door-to-door, to go doorstepping

porte-avions [pɔrtavjɔ̃] NM INV aircraft carrier

porte-bagages [pɔrtbagaʒ] NM INV *(d'un vélo)* rack; *(d'un train)* (luggage) rack; *(d'une voiture)* roof rack

porte-balai [pɔrtbalɛ] *(pl inv ou* **porte-balais**) NM *Élec* brush holder

porte-bébé [pɔrtbebe] *(pl inv ou* **porte-bébés**) NM **1** *(nacelle)* carry-cot **2** *(harnais)* baby sling

porte-billet, porte-billets [pɔrtbijɛ] *(pl* **porte-billets**) NM *Br* wallet, *Am* billfold

porte-bombes [pɔrtbɔ̃b] NM INV *Mil & Aviat* bomb rack

porte-bonheur [pɔrtbɔnœr] NM INV lucky charm; **une patte de lapin p.** a lucky rabbit's foot

porte-bouteille, porte-bouteilles [pɔrtbutɛj] *(pl* **porte-bouteilles**) NM **1** *(châssis)* wine rack **2** *(panier)* bottle-carrier **3** *(d'un réfrigérateur)* bottle rack

porte-carte, porte-cartes [pɔrtəkart] *(pl* **porte-cartes**) NM **1** *(portefeuille)* card-holder, *Br* wallet, *Am* billfold *(with spaces for cards, photos etc)* **2** *(de cartes géographiques)* map holder

porte-chapeaux [pɔrtʃapo] NM INV hat stand

porte-chars [pɔrtəʃar] NM INV *Mil* tank transporter

porte-chéquier [pɔrtəʃekje] *(pl* **porte-chéquiers**) NM cheque *or Am* check book holder

porte-cigare, porte-cigares [pɔrtsigar] *(pl* **porte-cigares**) NM cigar case

porte-cigarette, porte-cigarettes [pɔrtsigarɛt] *(pl* **porte-cigarettes**) NM cigarette case

porte-clefs, porte-clés [pɔrtəkle] NM INV **1** *(anneau)* key ring **2** *(étui)* key case

porte-conteneurs [pɔrtkɔ̃tnœr] NM INV container ship

porte-copie [pɔrtkɔpi] *(pl inv ou* **porte-copies**) NM *Typ* copy holder

porte-couteau [pɔrtkuto] *(pl inv ou* **porte-couteaux**) NM knife rest

porte-croix [pɔrtəkrwa] NM INV cross bearer

porte-document, porte-documents [pɔrtdɔkymɑ̃] *(pl* **porte-documents**) NM briefcase, document case

porte-drapeau [pɔrtdrapo] *(pl inv ou* **porte-drapeaux**) NM *aussi Fig* standard bearer

portée [pɔrte] NF **1** *Mil & Opt* range; *(de la voix)* range, compass; **(à) courte p.** short-range; **(à) grande p.** long-range; **(à) longue p.** long-range; **(à) moyenne p.** medium-range
2 *(champ d'action* ▸ *d'une mesure, d'une loi)* scope; *(impact* ▸ *d'une décision)* impact, significance; *(*▸ *d'un événement)* consequences, repercussions; *(*▸ *d'une déclaration, des mots)* (full) significance *or* import; *(*▸ *d'une publicité, d'une campagne)* reach; **l'incident a eu une p. considérable** the incident had far-reaching consequences; **ces idées furent sans grande p. jusqu'en 1940** these ideas had very little impact until 1940
3 *Zool (gén)* litter; *(d'une truie)* farrow
4 *Mus* staff, stave
5 *Constr (dimension)* span; *(charge)* load
6 *Tech* area of bearing
7 *(d'un navire)* burden, tonnage; **p. en lourd** deadweight (capacity); **p. utile** load-carrying capacity
• **à la portée de** PRÉP **1** *(près de)* close *or* near to; **ne pas laisser à la p. des enfants** *(sur emballage)* keep out of the reach of children **2** *(pouvant être compris par)* **son livre est à la p. de tous** his/her book is easily accessible to the ordinary reader; **l'article n'est pas à ma p.** the article is beyond me; **un jeu à la p. des 10–12 ans** a game suitable for 10–12 year olds **3** *(locution)* **à la p. de toutes les bourses** easily affordable, to suit all pockets; **ce n'est pas à la p. de toutes les bourses** not everyone can afford it
• **à portée de** PRÉP within reach of; **à p. de fusil** within (firing) range, within gunshot; **à p. de canon** within gun range; **à p. de (la) main** within (easy) reach; **avoir** *ou* **garder qch à p. de (la) main** to keep sth handy *or* close at hand *or* within (easy) reach; **gardez la trousse de secours à p. de la main** keep the first-aid kit in a handy place; **à p. de voix** within earshot

porte-étendard [pɔrtetɑ̃dar] *(pl inv ou* **porte-étendards**) NM *(officier)* standard bearer

portefaix [pɔrtəfɛ] NM INV *(porteur)* porter

porte-fenêtre [pɔrtfənɛtr] *(pl* **portes-fenêtres**) NF *Br* French window, *Am* French door

portefeuille [pɔrtəfœj] NM **1** *(étui) Br* wallet, *Am* billfold; *Fam* **avoir le p. rembourré** *ou* **bien garni** to be comfortably off **2** *Fin (ensemble)* portfolio; **p. d'actions** share portfolio; **p. d'activités** business portfolio, portfolio mix; **p. d'assurances** insurance portfolio; *Com* **p. effets** bills in hand, holdings; **p. indexé** indexed portfolio; **p. d'investissements** investment portfolio; **p. avec mandat** discretionary portfolio; *Mktg* **p. de marques** brand portfolio; *Mktg* **p. de produits** product portfolio; **p. de titres** portfolio of securities **3** *Pol* portfolio; **on lui a confié le p. des Affaires étrangères** he/she has been given *or* he/she holds the foreign affairs portfolio

porte-greffe [pɔrtəgrɛf] *(pl inv ou* **porte-greffes**) NM *Hort* stock

porte-hélicoptères [pɔrtelikɔptɛr] NM INV helicopter carrier *or* ship

porte-jarretelles [pɔrtʒartɛl] NM INV *Br* suspender belt, *Am* garter belt

porte-journaux [pɔrtʒurno] NM INV newspaper rack

porte-malheur [pɔrtmalœr] NM INV jinx; **les plumes de paon sont considérées comme un p.** peacock feathers are thought to bring bad luck

portemanteau, -x [pɔrtmɑ̃to] NM **1** *(sur pied)* coat stand, hat stand; *(mural)* coat rack **2** *(cintre)* coathanger **3** *Arch (malle)* portmanteau

portement [pɔrtəmɑ̃] NM **p. de croix** (Christ's) bearing of the Cross

porte-menu [pɔrtməny] *(pl inv ou* **porte-menus**) NM menu holder

portemine [pɔrtəmin] NM propelling pencil

porte-monnaie [pɔrtmɔnɛ] NM INV *Br* purse, *Am* change purse; **p. électronique** electronic purse *or* wallet; *Fam* **avoir le p. rembourré** *ou* **bien garni** to be comfortably off

porte-musique [pɔrtmyzik] NM INV music case

porte-objet [pɔrtɔbʒɛ] *(pl inv ou* **porte-objets**) NM **1** *(de microscope)* slide **2** *(platine)* stage

porte-outil [pɔrtuti] *(pl inv ou* **porte-outils**) NM *(gén)* tool holder; *(d'une perceuse)* chuck; *(d'une raboteuse)* stock; *(d'un tour)* slide rest

porte-papier [pɔrtpapje] NM INV toilet paper holder; *(pour rouleau)* toilet roll holder

porte-parapluie [pɔrtparaplɥi] *(pl inv ou* **porte-parapluies**) NM umbrella stand

porte-parole [pɔrtparɔl] NM INV **1** *(personne)* spokesperson, spokesman, *f* spokeswoman; **se faire le p. de qn** to speak on sb's behalf **2** *(périodique)* mouthpiece, organ

porte-pipes [pɔrtəpip] NM INV pipe rack

porte-plume [pɔrtəplym] *(pl inv ou* **porte-plumes**) NM pen holder

porter[1] [pɔrte] = **porté**

porter[2] [pɔrter] NM *(bière)* porter

PORTER[3] **[3]** [pɔrte]

VT	
• to carry **A1, C1, 4–6**	• to bear **A1, C1, 2, 4, 7**
• to give strength to **A2**	• to bring **B1, 4**
• to take **B1**	• to direct **B4**
• to write down **B3**	• to wear **C1**
• to feel **B6**	• to have **C1, 3**
• to show **C2**	
VI	
• to carry **1**	• to hit home **3**

VT **A.** *TENIR, SUPPORTER* **1** *(soutenir* ▸ *colis, fardeau, meuble)* to carry; *(*▸ *bannière, pancarte, cercueil)* to carry, to bear; **aide-moi à p. le sac jusqu'à la cuisine** help me to carry the bag to the kitchen;

j'ai porté sa malle jusqu'au grenier I carried his/her trunk up to the attic; **tu peux p. combien?** how much can you carry?; **deux piliers portent le toit** two pillars take the weight of *or* support the roof; *Sport* **celui qui porte le ballon** the player with *or* in possession of the ball; *Mil* **portez armes!** shoulder arms!; **p. qn sur son dos/dans ses bras** to carry sb on one's back/in one's arms; **ses jambes ne la portaient plus** her legs couldn't carry her any more; **se laisser p. par le courant** to let oneself be carried (away) by the current; *Fig* **elle porte bien son âge** she looks young for her age; **p. la responsabilité de qch** to bear (the) responsibility for sth; **il a trouvé cette responsabilité bien lourde à p.** this responsibility weighed heavily upon him

2 *(soutenir moralement ▸ sujet: foi, religion)* to give strength to, to support; **c'est l'espoir de le retrouver qui la porte** the hope of finding him again keeps her going

B. *METTRE, AMENER* **1** *(amener)* to take; **p. qch à qn** to take sth to sb; **p. un message à qn** to take *or* to convey a message to sb; **porte-lui ce colis** take him/her this parcel, deliver this parcel to him/her; **p. des fleurs sur la tombe de qn** to take flowers to sb's grave; **portez-le sur le canapé** take *or* carry him to the settee; **se faire p. un repas** to have a meal brought (to one); **p. une œuvre à l'écran/à la scène** to adapt a work for the screen/the stage; **p. le débat sur la place publique** to make the debate public; **p. une affaire devant les tribunaux** to take *or* to bring a matter before the courts; **p. qn au pouvoir** to bring sb to power; **p. une émotion/crise à son paroxysme** to bring an emotion to a peak/a crisis to a head; **p. son art à la perfection** to perfect one's art; **cela porte le total à 210 euros** that brings the total (up) to 210 euros; **les frais d'inscription ont été portés à 35 euros** the registration fees have been increased *or* raised to 35 euros; *Culin* **p. qch à ébullition** to bring sth to the boil

2 *(diriger)* **p. sa** *ou* **la main à sa tête** to raise one's hand to one's head; **il porta la main à sa poche** he put his hand to his pocket; **il porta la main à son revolver** he reached for his gun; **p. une tasse à ses lèvres** to lift *or* to raise a cup to one's lips; **p. le buste en avant** to lean forward; **p. son regard vers** *ou* **sur** to look towards *or* in the direction of; **p. ses pas vers** to make one's way towards, to head for; *Mil* **p. des troupes en avant** to move troops forward

3 *(enregistrer ▸ donnée)* to write down, to put down; **p. sa signature sur un registre** to sign a register; **porte ce point sur le graphique** plot that point onto the graph; **p. qn absent** to report sb absent; **se faire p. absent/malade** to go absent/sick; **p. qn disparu** to report sb missing; **p. qn déserteur** to report *or* to declare sb a deserter; **portez le vin à mon compte** put the wine on my account; *Compta* **p. un achat sur un compte** to enter a purchase on an account; *Fin* **p. une somme au compte clients** to post a sum to accounts receivable; **p. 200 euros au crédit de qn** to credit sb's account with 200 euros, to credit 200 euros to sb's account; **p. 200 euros au débit de qn** to debit 200 euros from sb's account

4 *(appliquer ▸ effort, énergie)* to direct, to bring, to bear; **p. son attention sur** to focus one's attention on, to turn one's attention to; **p. son choix sur** to choose; **p. une accusation contre qn** to bring a charge against sb; **il a fait p. tout son effort** *ou* **ses efforts sur la réussite du projet** he did his utmost to make the project successful; **p. une attaque contre qn** to direct an attack at *or* to attack sb; **p. ses vues sur qn** *(pour accomplir une tâche)* to have sb in mind *(for a job)*; *(pour l'épouser)* to have one's eye on sb

5 *(inciter)* **mon intervention l'a portée à plus de clémence** my intervention prompted her to be more lenient; **le paysage portait à la mélancolie** the scenery elicited feelings of melancholy; **l'alcool peut p. les gens à des excès/à la violence** alcohol can drive people to excesses/induce people to be violent; **qu'est-ce qui vous a porté à faire du théâtre?** what made you take up acting?; **tout porte à croire que...** everything leads one to believe that...; **tous les indices portent à penser que c'est lui le coupable** all the evidence suggests he is the guilty one; **être porté à faire** to be inclined to do; *Fam* **il est porté sur la boisson** *ou* **bouteille** he's fond of the bottle; *Fam Euph* **être porté sur la chose** to have a one-track mind

6 *(éprouver)* **p. de l'intérêt à qn/qch** to be interested in sb/sth; **p. de l'admiration à qn** to admire sb; **je lui porte beaucoup d'amitié** I hold him/her very dear; **l'amour qu'il lui portait** the love he felt for him/her; **la haine qu'il lui portait** the hatred he felt towards him/her *or* bore him/her

C. *AVOIR SUR SOI, EN SOI* **1** *(bijou, chaussures, lunettes, vêtement)* to wear, to have on; *(badge, décoration)* to wear; *(barbe, couettes, moustache, perruque)* to have; *(cicatrice)* to bear, to have, to carry; *(pistolet, stylo)* to carry; **je porte toujours sur moi de quoi écrire** I always carry something to write with; **il porte le dossard numéro 12** he's wearing number 12; **son cheval porte le numéro 5** his/her horse is number 5; **elle porte toujours du noir** she always dresses in *or* wears black; **p. les cheveux longs/courts/relevés** to wear one's hair long/short/up; **je porte bien/mal les pantalons** trousers look good/don't look good on me

2 *(laisser voir ▸ trace)* to show, to bear; *(▸ date, inscription)* to bear; **l'étui portait ses initiales gravées** the case was engraved with his/her initials; **la lettre porte la date du 13 mars** the letter is dated 13 March *or Sout* bears the date 13 March; **le couteau ne porte aucune empreinte** there are no fingerprints on the knife; **la signature que porte le tableau** the signature (which appears *or* is) on the painting; **le rapport portait le nom de plusieurs hauts fonctionnaires** the report bore *or* carried the names of several senior officials; **elle portait la résignation sur son visage** resignation was written on *or* all over her face; *Ling* **la syllabe portant l'accent tonique** the stressed syllable

3 *(nom, prénom, patronyme)* to have; **nous portons le même nom** we have *or* bear the same name; **il porte le nom de Legrand** he's called Legrand; **elle porte le nom de son mari** she has taken her husband's name; **c'est un nom difficile à p.** it's not an easy name to be called by; **le roman et la pièce portent le même titre** the novel and the play have the same title

4 *(en soi)* to carry, to bear; **p. qch en soi** to carry *or* to bear sth within oneself; **l'espoir/la rancune que je portais en moi** the hope/resentment I bore within me

5 *Méd (virus)* to carry; **ceux qui portent le virus** carriers of the virus

6 *(sujet: femme, femelle ▸ enfant, petit, portée)* to carry

7 *Agr & Hort (fruits)* to bear; **la tige porte trois feuilles** there are three leaves on the stem; **lorsque l'arbre porte ses fleurs** when the tree's in bloom; *Fig* **p. ses fruits** to bear fruit

USAGE ABSOLU *(soutenir)* **l'eau de mer porte plus que l'eau douce** sea water is more buoyant than fresh water

VI 1 *(son, voix)* to carry; **sa voix ne porte pas assez** his/her voice doesn't carry well; **aussi loin que porte la vue** as far as the eye can see

2 *(canon, fusil)* **p. à** to have a range of; **le coup de feu a porté à plus de 2 km** the shot carried more than 2 km

3 *(faire mouche ▸ critique, mot, plaisanterie)* to hit *or* to strike home; *(▸ observation)* to be heard *or* heeded; *(▸ coup)* to hit home

4 *(cogner)* **c'est le crâne qui a porté** the skull took the impact *or* the full force; **p. sur** *ou* **contre** to hit; **sa tête a porté sur** *ou* **contre le pilier** his/her head hit the pillar

5 *Naut* **laisser p.** to bear away, to let (her) go; **p. au vent** to stand to windward

• **porter sur VT IND 1** *(concerner ▸ sujet: discussion, discours, chapitre, recherches)* to be about, to be concerned with; *(▸ sujet: critiques)* to be aimed at; *(▸ sujet: loi, mesures)* to concern; *(▸ sujet: dossier, reportage)* to be about *or* on; **le détournement porte sur plusieurs millions d'euros** the embezzlement concerns several million euros **2** *(reposer sur ▸ sujet: charpente)* to rest on; *Ling* **l'accent porte sur la deuxième syllabe** the accent falls on the second syllable, the second syllable is stressed

VPR se porter 1 *(bijou, chaussures, vêtement)* to be worn; **je veux une veste qui se porte avec tout** I want a jacket which can be worn *or* which goes with anything; **les manteaux se porteront longs cet hiver** coats will be (worn) long this winter

2 *(personne)* **comment vous portez-vous?** how do you feel?, how are you (feeling)?; **il se porte très bien maintenant** he's (feeling) fine now; **à bientôt, portez-vous bien!** see you soon, look after yourself!; **il va bientôt s'en aller, je ne m'en porterai que mieux** he's going to leave soon and I'll feel all the better for it; **nos parents ne prenaient pas de congés et ne s'en portaient pas plus mal** our parents never took time off and they were none the worse for it

3 *(se proposer comme)* **se p. candidat** *Br* to stand *or Am* to run as a candidate; **se p. caution** to stand security; **se p. volontaire pour faire** to volunteer to do; **se p. fort pour qn** to act as a guarantor for sb; **se p. fort de qch** to guarantee sth, to vouch for sth

4 *(aller)* to go; **se p. au-devant de qn** to go to meet sb; **se p. en tête d'une procession/course** to take the lead in a procession/race; *Mil* **se p. en avant** to move forward, to advance; **il s'est porté à l'avant du peloton** he went to the head of the pack; **tout son sang s'est porté à sa tête** the blood rushed to his/her head

5 se p. à *(se livrer à)* to give oneself over to, to indulge in; **se p. à des actes de violence** to indulge in violent acts; **comment a-t-il pu se p. à de telles extrémités?** how could he go to such extremes?

6 se p. sur *(sujet: choix, soupçon)* to fall on; *(sujet: conversation)* to turn to; **tous les regards se portèrent sur elle** all eyes turned towards her

porte-revues [pɔrtrəvy] **NM INV** magazine rack

porterie [pɔrtəri] **NF** gatehouse

porte-savon [pɔrtsavɔ̃] *(pl* **inv** *ou* **porte-savons)** **NM** soap dish

porte-serviette[1]**, porte-serviettes** [pɔrtsɛrvjɛt] *(pl* **porte-serviettes)** **NM** *(support)* towel rail

porte-serviette[2] [pɔrtsɛrvjɛt] **NM INV** *(pochette)* napkin holder

porte-skis [pɔrtski] **NM INV** *Aut* ski carrier, ski rack

porte-toasts [pɔrtətost] **NM INV** toast rack

porteur, -euse [pɔrtœr, -øz] **ADJ 1** *(plein d'avenir)* flourishing; **un marché p.** a buoyant market; **un secteur p.** a flourishing *or* booming industry; **une idée porteuse** an idea with great potential

2 *(chargé)* **un vaccin p. d'espoir** a vaccine which brings new hope; **un livre p. de doutes** a book expressing doubt

3 *Tech (essieu)* load-bearing; *(roue)* carrying

4 *Phys* **onde/fréquence porteuse** carrier wave/frequency

5 *Astron (fusée)* booster *(avant n)*

6 *Constr (mur)* load-bearing

7 *Méd* **les individus porteurs du virus** individuals who carry the virus, (individuals who are) carriers of the virus

NM,F 1 *Méd* carrier; **p. sain** (unaffected) carrier

2 *(de bagages)* porter; *(d'un cercueil, d'un brancard, d'un étendard)* bearer; *(d'eau)* carrier; *(de nouvelles, d'une lettre)* bearer; **p. d'eau** water-carrier; **le p. du message attend votre réponse** the messenger *or Sout* the bearer of the message is waiting for your answer; **j'arrivais, p. d'heureuses nouvelles** I arrived bringing *or* bearing good news; **il était p. de faux papiers** he was carrying false papers; **par p.** by messenger

3 *Sport* **le p. du ballon** the player in possession of *or* with the ball

NM *Banque & Bourse* bearer; *(actionnaire)* shareholder, *Am* stockholder; **chèque/obligations au p.** bearer cheque/bonds; **les petits/gros porteurs** small/big investors; **p. d'actions** shareholder, *Am* stockholder; **p. d'actions nominatives** registered shareholder *or Am* stockholder; **p. d'obligations** debenture holder, bondholder; **p. de parts** shareholder, *Am* stockholder; **p. de titres** holder of stock, stockholder; **payable au p.** payable to bearer

• **porteuse NF 1** *Tél* carrier **2** *Can (marraine)* godmother

> Do not confuse with **portier**, which means **doorman**.

porte-vélos [pɔrtəvelo] **NM INV** bicycle rack

porte-vent [pɔrtəvɑ̃] *(pl* **inv** *ou* **porte-vents)** **NM** air duct

porte-voix [pɔrtəvwa] **NM INV** *(simple)* megaphone; *(électrique) Br* loudhailer, *Am* bullhorn; **parler dans un p.** *(simple)* to talk through a megaphone; *(électrique)* to talk through a *Br* loudhailer *or Am* bullhorn; **mettre ses mains en p.** to cup one's hands round one's mouth

portfolio [pɔrtfoljo] **NM** portfolio

portier, -ère [pɔrtje, -ɛr] **ADJ** *Rel* **frère p.** porter; **sœur portière** portress

NM,F 1 *(gardien ▸ d'un établissement public)* doorman, *f* doorwoman; *(▸ d'un hôtel)* commissionaire; **p. de nuit** night porter; **p. électronique** electronic door-entry system **2** *Littéraire (d'un domaine, d'un monastère)* gatekeeper

NM *Rel* porter

• **portière NF 1** *(d'un véhicule)* door **2** *(tenture)* portière, door curtain

Do not confuse with **porteur**.

portillon [pɔrtijɔ̃] **NM** *(d'une porte cochère)* wicket; *(d'un passage à niveaux)* side gate; *(d'une gare)* gate, barrier; **p. automatique** *(dans le métro)* ticket barrier; *Fam* **ça se bouscule au p.** *(il y a affluence)* there's a huge crowd trying to get in; *(il/elle/etc bafouille)* he/she/*etc* can't get his/her/*etc* words out; *Fam Hum* **ça ne se bouscule pas au p.** people are staying away in droves

portion [pɔrsjɔ̃] **NF 1** *(part ▸ de gâteau, de quiche)* portion; *(▸ de viande, de légumes etc)* portion, helping; *(▸ d'argent)* share, cut; **p. congrue** (income providing a) meagre living; **être réduit à la p. congrue** to have just enough to live on, to make a meagre living **2** *(d'un groupe, d'une population)* portion, section **3** *(segment ▸ de ligne, d'autoroute)* stretch

• **en portions ADJ** in individual helpings

portique [pɔrtik] **NM 1** *Archit* portico

2 *Sport* crossbeam

3 *(dispositif de sécurité)* security gate

4 *Rail* **p. à signaux** signal gantry

portland [pɔrtlɑ̃d] **NM (ciment) p.** Portland cement

Porto [pɔrto] **NM** Oporto

porto [pɔrto] **NM** port (wine)

portoricain, -e [pɔrtɔrikɛ̃, -ɛn] **ADJ** Puerto Rican

• **Portoricain, -e NM,F** Puerto Rican

Porto Rico [pɔrtoriko] **NM** Puerto Rico; **à P.** in Puerto Rico

portos [pɔrtos] **NMF INV** *Fam* dago *(from Portugal)*, = offensive term used to refer to a Portuguese

portrait [pɔrtrɛ] **NM 1** *(dessin, peinture, photo)* portrait; **le p. n'est pas très ressemblant** it is not a very good likeness; **faire le p. de qn** *(dessinateur)* to draw sb's portrait; *(peintre)* to paint sb's portrait; *Fam* **se faire tirer le p.** to have one's photo taken□; **p. de famille** family portrait; **être tout le p.** *ou* **le p. vivant de qn** to be the spitting image of sb

2 *Beaux-Arts* **l'art du p., le p.** portraiture

3 *Fam (figure)* **abîmer** *ou* **arranger le p. à qn** to waste sb's face, to rearrange sb's features; **elle s'est fait arranger le p.** she got her face rearranged

4 *(description)* portrayal, description, portrait; **faire** *ou* **tracer le p. de qn** to portray sb

5 *Ordinat* **(mode** *ou* **format) p.** portrait (mode); **imprimer qch en p.** to print sth in portrait

portraitiste [pɔrtretist] **NMF** portraitist

portrait-robot [pɔrtrɛrɔbo] *(pl* **portraits-robots)** **NM 1** *(d'un criminel)* Photofit® *or* Identikit® picture **2** *(caractéristiques)* typical profile

portraiturer [3] [pɔrtretyre] **VT** *Littéraire* to portray, to depict

portuaire [pɔrtɥɛr] **ADJ** port *(avant n)*, harbour *(avant n)*

portugais, -e [pɔrtygɛ, -ɛz] **ADJ** Portuguese

NM *(langue)* Portuguese

• **Portugais, -e NM,F** Portuguese; **les P.** the Portuguese

• **portugaise NF** *(huître)* Portuguese oyster

• **portugaises NFPL** *Fam* ears□, *Br* lugholes; **avoir les portugaises ensablées** to be as deaf as a post

Portugal [pɔrtygal] **NM le P.** Portugal

pose [poz] **NF 1** *(mise en place ▸ d'appareils)* putting in, installing; *(▸ de rideaux)* putting up, hanging; *(▸ de carrelage, de câbles)* laying; *(▸ de moquette)* fitting, laying; *(▸ d'une bombe)* planting; **la p. de la fenêtre vous coûtera 300 euros** it will cost you 300 euros to have the window put in; **la p. de la moquette a pris une demi-journée** it took half a day to fit *or* lay the carpet(s)

2 *(attitude)* position, posture; *(pour un artiste)* pose; **dans une p. peu élégante** in a rather inelegant position *or* posture; **prendre une p. avantageuse** to strike a flattering pose; **prendre la p.** to start posing, to take up a pose; **garder** *ou* **tenir la p.** to hold the pose

3 *Phot (cliché, durée)* exposure; **une pellicule de 24/36 poses** a 24-/36-exposure film

4 *(affectation)* affectation

5 *Typ* **p. de marges** margin setting; **p. de tabulations** tabbing, setting of tabs

posé, -e [poze] **ADJ 1** *(mesuré ▸ personne)* self-possessed, collected, composed; *(▸ manières, ton)* calm, cool, tranquil **2** *Mus* **voix bien/mal posée** steady/unsteady voice

posément [pozemɑ̃] **ADV** calmly, coolly

posemètre [pozmɛtr] **NM** *Phot* exposure meter

poser[1] [poze] **NM** *Mil* landing *(of a helicopter)*

POSER[2] [3] [poze]

VT	
• to put **1**	• to lay **1, 3**
• to place **1, 9**	• to put away **2**
• to put up **3**	• to put in **3**
• to install **3**	• to ask **4**
• to state **5**	• to land **10**
VI	
• to pose **1, 2**	• to put on airs **2, 3**
VPR	
• to land **3**	• to arise **5**

VT 1 *(mettre)* to put, to lay, to place; **p. ses coudes sur la table** to rest *or* to put one's elbows on the table; **je ne sais plus où j'ai posé la clef** I can't remember where I've put *or* left the key; **p. un sac par terre** to put a bag (down) on the floor; **elle avait posé sa bicyclette contre la palissade** she'd leant *or* put her bike against the fence; **elle a posé le pied sur la première marche** she placed *or* put her foot on *or* onto the first step; **j'ai tellement mal que je ne peux plus p. le pied par terre** my foot hurts so much, I can't put my weight on it any longer; **dès que je pose la tête sur l'oreiller, je m'endors** I fall asleep as soon as my head touches the pillow; **il posa un baiser sur ses paupières** he kissed her on the eyelids; *Fam Hum* **je ne sais pas où p. mes fesses** I don't know where to park my *Br* bum *or Am* butt

2 *(cesser d'utiliser)* to put away *or* down; **pose ton ballon et viens dîner** put away your ball and come and have dinner; **posez vos stylos et écoutez-moi** put your pens down and listen to me

3 *(installer ▸ papier peint, cadre, tentures, affiche)* to put up; *(▸ antenne)* to put up, to install; *(▸ radiateur, alarme)* to put in, to install; *(▸ verrou)* to fit; *(▸ cadenas)* to put on; *(▸ moquette)* to fit, to lay; *(▸ carrelage, câble, tuyau)* to lay; *(▸ vitre)* to put in; *(▸ placard)* to put in, to install; *(▸ prothèse)* to fit, to put in; *(▸ bombe)* to plant; **faire p. un double vitrage** to have double-glazing put in *or* fitted; **se faire p. une couronne** to have a crown fitted

4 *(énoncer ▸ question)* to ask; *(▸ devinette)* to ask, to set; **p. une question à qn** to ask sb a question, to put a question to sb; **je peux p. la question autrement** I can put *or* ask the question another way; **p. un problème** *(causer des difficultés)* to raise *or* to pose a problem; *(l'énoncer)* to set a problem; **de la façon dont il m'avait posé le problème...** the way he'd put *or* outlined the problem to me...; **elle me pose de gros problèmes** she's a great problem *or* source of anxiety to me; **si ça ne pose pas de problème, je viendrai avec mon chien** if it's not a problem (for you) I'll bring my dog

5 *(établir ▸ condition)* to state, to lay down; *(▸ principe, règle)* to lay *or* to set down, to state; **une fois posées les bases du projet** once the foundations of the project have been laid down; **p. qch comme condition/principe** to lay sth down as a condition/principle; **si l'on pose que...** if we assume *or* suppose that...; **si l'on pose comme hypothèse que...** if we take as a hypothesis that...; **cela posé, nous pouvons dire que...** taking this as read, we can say that...; **posons cela comme acquis** let's take that as read

6 *Fam (mettre en valeur)* to establish the reputation of□, to give standing to□; **il n'y a rien qui pose un chercheur comme le Nobel** there's nothing quite like the Nobel prize to get a scientist noticed□ *or* to boost a scientist's reputation□; **une voiture comme ça, ça vous pose** that kind of car gives you a certain status□

7 *Math* to put down; **je pose 2 et je retiens 1** put down 2, carry 1; **p. une opération** to set out a sum

8 *Mus* **p. sa voix** to pitch one's voice

9 *Sport* to place; **il a bien posé sa volée** he placed his volley perfectly

10 *Aviat (avion, hélicoptère)* to land, to set down

11 *Can (photographier)* to photograph, to take a photograph *or* picture of

USAGE ABSOLU à toi de p.! *(aux dominos)* your turn!

VI 1 *(pour un peintre, un photographe)* to pose, to sit; **j'ai souvent posé pour elle** I used to pose *or* to sit for her regularly; **p. pour une photo/un magazine** to pose for a photo/magazine; *Fam* **faire p. qn** *(le faire attendre)* to keep sb hanging around

2 *(fanfaronner)* to put on airs, to show off, to pose; **regardez-le p. devant ces dames!** just look at him showing off in front of those ladies!

3 *(faire semblant)* to put on airs, to strike a pose *or* an attitude; **elle n'est pas vraiment malheureuse, elle pose** she's not really unhappy, it's just a façade *or* it's all show; *Fam* **p. au justicier** *(se faire passer pour)* to act the avenger

VPR se poser 1 *(emploi passif)* **se p. facilement** *(chaudière)* to be easy to install; *(moquette)* to be easy to lay

2 *(faire surgir)* **se p. la question** *ou* **le problème de savoir si...** to ask oneself *or* to wonder whether...; **il va finir par se p. des questions** he's going to start having doubts

3 *(descendre ▸ avion, hélicoptère)* to land, to touch down; *(▸ papillon, oiseau)* to land; **se p. en catastrophe** to make an emergency landing; **se p. en douceur** to make a smooth landing; **les hirondelles se posent sur les fils électriques** the swallows land *or* perch on the electric wires; **une plume est venue se p. sur sa tête** a feather floated down onto his/her head; **tous les regards se posèrent sur elle** all eyes turned to her; **il sentit leurs yeux se p. sur lui** he could feel their eyes on him; **sa main se posa sur la mienne** he/she put his/her hand on mine

4 *Fam (s'asseoir)* **pose-toi là** sit yourself down here

5 *(surgir ▸ question, problème)* to arise, to come up; **la question s'est déjà posée plusieurs fois** the question has come up several times already; **la question ne se pose plus maintenant** the question is irrelevant now; **la question qui se pose maintenant est la suivante** the question which must now be asked is the following; **le problème qui se pose à moi** the problem I've got to face *or* to solve; **le problème se pose de savoir si l'on doit négocier** there's the problem of whether or not we should negotiate; **le problème ne se pose pas exactement en ces termes** that's not exactly where the problem lies

6 se p. en *ou* **comme** *(se faire passer pour)* to pass oneself off as; **il veut se p. comme arbitre du goût** he wants to pass himself off as *or* to pose as an arbiter of taste; **je ne me suis jamais posé en expert** I never set myself up to be *or* I never pretended I was an expert

7 *Fam (locutions)* **pour l'intelligence, son frère se pose là!** *(il est brillant)* his/her brother's got quite a brain!; **elle se pose là, leur bagnole!** *(avec admiration)* their car's an impressive bit of machinery!; **comme plombier, tu te poses là!** call yourself a plumber, do you?; **comme enquiquineuse, elle se pose un peu là!** she's such a pain in the neck!; **comme gaffe, ça se pose là!** that's what you might call a blunder!

poseur, -euse [pozœr, -øz] **ADJ** *(prétentieux)* affected, pretentious, mannered

NM,F 1 *(m'as-tu-vu)* show-off, *Br* poseur **2** *(installateur)* **p. de parquet/carrelage/câbles** floor/tile/cable layer; **p. d'affiches** billsticker, billposter;

p. de mines mine layer; **p. de rails** tracklayer, platelayer; **les poseurs de bombes se sont enfuis** those responsible for planting the bombs *or* the bombers ran away

posidonie [pɔzidɔni] **NF** *Bot* neptune-grass

positif, -ive [pozitif, -iv] **ADJ 1** *(constructif ▸ mesures, suggestion, attitude)* positive, constructive; *(▸ réaction, échos, critique)* favourable
2 *(réaliste)* pragmatic, practical-minded
3 *(affirmatif ▸ réponse)* positive; **si sa réponse est positive** if he/she says yes
4 *(certain ▸ fait)* positive, actual
5 *Math, Méd, Phot & Phys* positive
NM 1 *(quelque chose de constructif)* **il nous faut du p.** we need something positive **2** *Ling, Math & Phot* positive; *Typ* **p. en couleur** colour positive

POSITION [pozisjɔ̃] **NF 1** *Mil (lieu d'où l'on mène une action)* position; **une p. dominante** a commanding position; **p. avancée/défensive** advanced/defensive position; **p. clef** key position; **être en p. de combat** to be ready to attack; **des positions fortifiées** a fortified position; *aussi Fig* **p. de repli** fall-back position; **p. retranchée** entrenched *or* dug-in position
2 *(lieu où l'on se trouve)* position; **donnez-nous votre p.** what is your position?; **déterminer sa p.** to find one's bearings; **déterminer la p. de qch** to locate sth
3 *(dans un sondage, une course)* position, place; **nous sommes en dernière/première p. dans le championnat** we're bottom of the league/in the lead in the championship; **arriver en première/dernière p.** *(coureur)* to come first/last; *(candidat)* to come top/be last; **elle est en sixième p.** she's in sixth position *or* place, she's lying sixth; **ils ont rétrogradé en quatrième p. au hit-parade** they went down to number four in the charts
4 *(d'une entreprise, d'un produit)* position; **p. clé** key position; **p. concurrentielle** competitive position; **p. stratégique** strategic position
5 *(posture)* posture, position; **changer de p.** to change (one's) position, to shift; **tu as une mauvaise p.** you've got bad posture; **la p. debout est inconfortable** standing up is uncomfortable; **dans la** *ou* **en p. verticale** when standing up; **dans la** *ou* **en p. allongée** when lying down; **dans la** *ou* **en p. assise** when sitting, in a sitting position; **la p. du missionnaire** the missionary position; **p. de sécurité** brace position
6 *(angle, orientation)* position, setting; **quelle est la p. de l'aiguille?** where is the needle pointing?, what's the position of the needle?; **mettez le siège en p. inclinée** tilt the seat back; **éclairage à plusieurs positions** lamp with several settings
7 *(opinion)* position, stance, standpoint; **prendre p. (sur qch)** to take a stand *or* to take up a position (on sth); **prendre p. pour** *ou* **en faveur de qch** to come down in favour of sth; **prendre p. contre qch** to come out against sth; **rester sur ses positions** to stand one's ground, to stick to one's guns; **quelle est la p. de la France dans ce conflit?** what's France's position on this conflict?; *Pol* **p. commune** common stance; **p. de principe** policy position
8 *(situation)* position, situation; **vous me mettez dans une p. délicate** you're putting me in a difficult situation *or* position; **en p. de force** in a strong position *or* a position of strength; **p. sociale** social standing; *Belg* **être en p., être dans une p. intéressante** to be expecting; **être en p. de faire qch** to be in a position to do sth
9 *(dans une entreprise)* position, post
10 *Banque* balance (of account); *Bourse* position; *Banque* **feuille de p.** interim statement; *Bourse* **liquider une p.** to close (out) a position; *Bourse* **prendre une p. inverse sur le marché** to offset; *Bourse* **p. acheteur** long position, bull position; *Banque* **p. de compte** balance; *Banque* **p. créditrice** credit balance; *Banque* **p. débitrice** debit balance; *Bourse* **p. de place** market position; *Banque* **p. de trésorerie** cash(flow) situation; *Bourse* **p. vendeur** short position, bear position
11 *(en danse)* position

positionnement [pozisjɔnmɑ̃] **NM 1** *Com & Mktg* positioning; **p. concurrentiel** competitive positioning; **p. de la marque** brand positioning; **p. de prix** price positioning; **p. du produit** product positioning; **p. par la qualité** quality positioning; **p. stratégique** strategic positioning **2** *Tech* positioning **3** *Fin (d'un compte)* calculation of the balance

positionner [3] [pozisjɔne] **VT 1** *Com & Mktg (produit)* to position
2 *Tech* to position
3 *(localiser)* to locate, to determine the position of
4 *Fin (compte)* to calculate the balance of
VPR se positionner to position oneself, to get into position; **se p. par rapport à la concurrence** to position oneself in relation to the competition; **se p. à la hausse sur le marché** to move upmarket

positive [pozitiv] *voir* **positif**

positivement [pozitivmɑ̃] **ADV 1** *Élec* positively; **chargé p.** positively charged
2 *(réagir)* positively
3 *(tout à fait)* absolutely, positively; **c'est p. honteux** it's absolutely shameful; **il est p. idiot** he's an absolute *or* perfect idiot
4 *(avec certitude)* **je ne le sais pas p.** I don't know it for certain, I can't be positive about it

positiver [3] [pozitive] **VI** to think positively

positivisme [pozitivism] **NM** *Phil* positivism

positiviste [pozitivist] *Phil* **ADJ** positivist
NMF positivist

positivité [pozitivite] **NF** positivity

positon [pozitɔ̃] **NM** *Phys* positron

posologie [pozɔlɔʒi] **NF** *Méd* **1** *(instructions)* dosage; **respectez la p.** use as directed **2** *(science)* posology

possédant, -e [pɔsedɑ̃, -ɑ̃t] **ADJ** propertied, property-owning
• **possédants NMPL** property owners

possédé, -e [pɔsede] **ADJ** *(par le démon)* possessed
NM,F person possessed; **comme un p.** like a man possessed

posséder [18] [pɔsede] **VT 1** *(détenir ▸ demeure, collection, fortune, terres)* to own, to possess, to have; *(▸ colonies)* to have; *(▸ preuve, document, titre, ticket)* to hold, to have; *(▸ arme, armée)* to possess; **les gens qui ne possèdent rien** those who have nothing; **tu ne possèdes pas la vérité, tu sais** you don't know everything, you know
2 *(être doté de ▸ talent, mémoire)* to possess, to have; **cette région possède de grandes réserves d'eau** this region has large water reserves
3 *Littéraire (maîtriser ▸ art, langue)* to have mastered; **(bien) p. son sujet** to be master of *or* on top of one's subject; **un conférencier qui possède parfaitement son sujet** a lecturer who knows exactly what he's talking about
4 *(habiter ▸ sujet: démon)* to possess; **la jalousie le possède** he's consumed with *or* eaten up with jealousy; **il était possédé par la haine** he was consumed with *or* full of hatred; **être possédé du diable** *ou* **du démon** to be possessed by the devil
5 *Fam (tromper ▸ sujet: escroc)* to con, to have; **je me suis fait p.** I've been conned *or* had
6 *Littéraire (sexuellement)* to possess, to have carnal knowledge of
VPR se posséder *(se dominer)* **je ne me possédais plus** I was not myself any more, I was no longer master of myself; **elle ne se possédait plus de joie/rage** she was beside herself with joy/rage

possesseur [pɔsesœr] **NM 1** *(propriétaire ▸ d'une maison, d'une collection, d'une fortune)* owner, possessor; *(▸ d'un hôtel, d'une ferme)* owner, proprietor; *(▸ d'une charge, d'un ticket, de valeurs, de documents)* holder; *(▸ d'un titre)* incumbent, holder; **être le p. d'une propriété** to own *or* to possess a property **2** *(détenteur ▸ d'une preuve)* possessor

possessif, -ive [pɔsesif, -iv] **ADJ** *Gram & Psy* possessive
NM *Gram* possessive (form)

possession [pɔsesjɔ̃] **NF 1** *(détention ▸ d'une maison, d'un hôtel, d'une collection, d'une fortune)* ownership, possession; *(▸ d'informations)* possession; *(▸ d'actions, d'un diplôme)* holding; *(▸ d'une charge, d'un titre)* possession, holding; *(▸ d'un poste)* tenure; **avoir qch en sa p.** to have sth in one's possession; **être en p. de qch** to be in possession of sth; **prendre p. de** *(maison)* to take possession of; *(fonctions)* to take up; **entrer en p. de** to come into possession of, to come by; **comment êtes-vous entré en p. de ces documents?** how did you come to have *or* come by these documents?; **tomber en la p. de qn** to come into sb's possession
2 *Jur* possession
3 *Fin (d'une société)* assets
4 *(territoire)* possession, dominion
5 *(contrôle)* control; **une force étrange a pris p. de lui** a strange force has gained possession of him; **reprendre p. de soi-même** to regain *or* recover one's self-control *or* composure; **être en p. de toutes ses facultés** to be in (full) possession of one's faculties; **être en pleine p. de ses moyens** to be at the peak of one's powers *or* abilities
6 *Psy & Rel* possession

possessive [pɔsesiv] *voir* **possessif**

possessivité [pɔsesivite] **NF** possessiveness

possessoire [pɔseswar] *Jur* **ADJ** possessory
NM 1 *(droit)* (right of) possession **2** *(action)* possessory action

possibilité [pɔsibilite] **NF 1** *(chose envisageable ou faisable)* possibility; **p. (de) cuisine séparée** *(dans une petite annonce)* separate kitchen possible
2 *(moyen)* possibility; *(occasion)* opportunity; **il n'a pas vraiment la p. de refuser** he can't really refuse; **mon travail me donne la p. de voyager** my job gives me the opportunity of travelling; **on ne m'en a jamais donné la p.** I was never given the opportunity *or* chance
3 *(éventualité)* possibility; **c'est une p. que je n'avais pas envisagée** it's a possibility that I hadn't envisaged; **le syndicat n'a pas nié la p. d'une reprise des négociations** the *Br* trade union *or Am* labor union has not ruled out the possible reopening of negotiations
• **possibilités NFPL 1** *(financières)* means; **50 euros, c'est dans mes possibilités** 50 euros, that's within my means; **chacun doit payer selon ses possibilités** from each according to his means; **la maison était au-dessus de nos possibilités** we couldn't afford the house
2 *(intellectuelles, physiques)* possibilities, potential; **c'est un pianiste qui a de grandes possibilités** this pianist has got great possibilities *or* potential; **écrire une thèse serait au-dessus de mes possibilités** I couldn't cope with writing a thesis; **connaître ses possibilités** to be aware of one's (own) capabilities
3 *(techniques)* facilities; **machine qui offre de multiples possibilités d'utilisation** machine with many features; *Ordinat* **possibilités d'extension** upgradeability

possible [pɔsibl] **ADJ 1** *(réalisable ▸ gén)* possible; *(▸ construction)* feasible; **est-il p. de vivre sur Mars?** is life possible on Mars?; **rendre qch p.** to make sth possible; **il est p. de dire/de faire** it is possible to say/to do; **il est toujours p. d'annuler la réunion** the meeting can always be cancelled; **il ne m'est financièrement pas p. de partir pour l'étranger** I can't afford to go abroad; **j'ai fait tout ce qu'il m'était techniquement p. de faire** I did everything that was technically possible; **ce n'est pas p. d'être aussi maladroit!** how can anyone be so clumsy!; **il faut qu'on divorce, ce n'est pas p. autrement** we've got to get a divorce, it's the only solution; **on a dû le pousser, ce n'est pas p. autrement!** somebody MUST have pushed him!; *Fam* **il est pas p., ce mec!** this guy's just too much!
2 *(probable)* possible; **il est p. que je vous rejoigne plus tard** I may *or* might join you later; **serait-il p. qu'il m'ait menti?** could he (possibly) have lied to me?; **il t'aime – c'est bien p., mais moi pas!** he loves you – quite possibly *or* that's as may be, but I don't love him!; **tu devrais lui écrire – c'est p., mais je n'en ai pas envie** you should write to him/her – maybe (I should), but I don't feel like it
3 *(pour exprimer l'étonnement) Fam* **elle est morte hier – c'est pas p.!** she died yesterday – I can't believe it!; *Fam* **pas p.! c'est ta fille?** is this your daughter? impossible *or* surely not!; *Ironique* **Noël c'est le 25 – pas p.!** Christmas is on the 25th – never *or* you don't say!
4 *(envisageable ▸ interprétation, explication, option)* possible; **le 24 février serait une date p.** 24 February would be a possible date *or* a possibility; **voici la sélection p. pour le match de demain**

here is the possible selection for tomorrow's match

5 *(potentiel)* possible; **je l'ai cherché dans tous les endroits possibles** I looked for it everywhere imaginable *or* in every possible place; **as-tu considéré tous les cas possibles?** have you considered every possible *or* conceivable explanation?; **il a eu tous les problèmes possibles et imaginables pour récupérer son argent** he had all kinds of problems getting his money back; **bougez le moins p.** move as little as possible; **roulez le plus lentement p.** drive as slowly as possible; **je veux un rapport aussi détaillé que p.** I want as detailed a report as possible; **j'ai acheté les moins chers p.** I bought the cheapest I could find; **il mange le plus/le moins de gâteaux p.** *ou* **possibles** he eats as many/as few cakes as possible

NM le p. the possible; **c'est dans le domaine du p.** it's within the bounds of possibility, it's quite possible; **faire (tout) son p.** to do one's best *or* all one (possibly) can *or* one's utmost

• **au possible ADV** in the extreme; **ennuyeux au p.** extremely boring; **elle a été désagréable/serviable au p.** she couldn't have been more unpleasant/helpful

post-achat [pɔstaʃa] (*pl* **post-achats**) **ADJ** post-purchase

post-acheminement [pɔstaʃminmɑ̃] (*pl* **post-acheminements**) **NM** transfer from main airport

postal, -e, -aux, -ales [pɔstal, -o] **ADJ** *(colis)* (sent) by mail *or Br* post; *(frais, service, tarif)* postal; *(train, camion, wagon)* mail *(avant n)*

postcombustion [pɔstkɔ̃bystjɔ̃] **NF 1** *(combustion)* reheat, after-burning **2** *(dispositif)* after-burner

postcommunion [pɔstkɔmynjɔ̃] **NF** *Rel* post-communion

postcommunisme [pɔstkɔmynism] **NM** post-communism

postcure [pɔstkyr] **NF** *Méd* rehabilitation, after-care; **foyer de p.** rehabilitation centre; **elle est en p.** she's in aftercare

postdater [3] [pɔstdate] **VT** to postdate

post-doctoral, -e, -aux, -ales [pɔstdɔktɔral, -o] **ADJ** *Univ* post-doctoral, post-doctorate

post-doctorat [pɔstdɔktɔra] (*pl* **post-doctorats**) **NM** *Univ* post-doctorate

poste[1] [pɔst] **NM 1** *Rad & TV* **p. (de) radio/télévision** radio/television set; *Fam* **ouvrir/fermer le p.** to switch the radio/television on/off□; **p. émetteur/récepteur** transmitting/receiving set; **p. émetteur pirate** pirate station; **p. d'émission** transmitter

2 *Tél (appareil)* telephone; *(d'un standard)* extension; **passez-moi le p. 1421** give me extension 1421; **je vous passe le p.** I'm putting you through; **p. cellulaire** cellphone

3 *(métier)* post, job, position; **un p. à pourvoir** a post to be filled, a (job) vacancy; **présenter sa candidature à un p. de technicien** to apply for a job as a technician; **elle a un p. très élevé au ministère** she has a very senior position *or* post in the ministry; **il a obtenu le p. de directeur financier** he was given the post of *or* he was appointed financial director; **p. d'encadrement** managerial position; **p. évolutif** job with prospects (for promotion)

4 *(local, installation)* **p. d'aiguillage** signal box; **p. de douane** customs post; **p. d'équipage** crew's quarters; **p. d'essence** *Br* petrol *or Am* gas station; **p. d'incendie** fire point; **p. de pilotage** *Aviat* flight deck; *Naut* cockpit; **p. de police** police station; **passer la nuit au p.** to spend the night at the station; **p. de ravitaillement** service station; **p. de secours** first-aid post

5 *Mil* post; *aussi Fig* **être/rester à son p.** to be/to stay at one's post; **à vos postes!** to your posts!, stand by!; **p. avancé** advanced *or* outlying post; **p. de combat** action *or* battle station; **p. de commandement** command post; **p. de contrôle** checkpoint; **p. de garde** guardroom; *aussi Fig* **p. d'observation/d'écoute/de surveillance** observation/listening/look-out post

6 *Fin (d'un compte)* item, entry; *(d'un budget)* item; **p. de bilan** balance sheet item; **p. créditeur/débiteur** credit/debit item; **p. extraordinaire** extraordinary item

7 *Ind (division du temps)* shift; **p. de 10 heures** 10-hour shift; **p. de nuit** nightshift; **p. de travail** *(emplacement)* workplace

8 *Ordinat* **p. autonome** stand-alone; **p. terminal** terminal; **p. de travail** workstation

poste[2] [pɔst] **NF 1** *(établissement)* post office; **p. restante** poste restante **2** *(moyen d'acheminement)* mail, *Br* post; **envoyer qch par la p.** to mail sth, to send sth by mail or *Br* post; **mettre une lettre à la p.** to mail *or Br* to post a letter; **je venais de la mettre à la p. quand je m'aperçus que j'avais oublié le timbre** I'd just dropped it in the mail *or Br* letter box when I realized I hadn't put a stamp on it; **p. aérienne** airmail **3** *Admin* **la p.** ≃ the Post Office; **travailler à la p.** ≃ to work for the Post Office; **les Postes et Télécommunications** = the French postal and telecommunications service; **grève des postes** postal *or* mail strike

posté, -e [pɔste] **ADJ travail p.** shift work; **ouvrier p.** shift worker

poste-à-poste ADJ INV *Ordinat* point-to-point

poste-frontière [pɔstəfrɔ̃tjɛr] (*pl* **postes-frontières**) **NM** customs post

poster[1] [pɔstɛr] **NM** poster

poster[2] [3] [pɔste] **VT 1** *(envoyer* ▸ *colis, courrier)* to mail, *Br* to post; **la lettre a été postée le 2 mai** the letter was sent *or* was mailed *or Br* was posted on 2 May **2** *(placer* ▸ *garde, complice, troupes)* to post, to station; **l'inspecteur fit p. un homme à chaque issue** the inspector gave orders for a man to be stationed at each exit

VPR se poster *(sentinelle)* to station *or* to post *or* to position oneself; **se p. sur le parcours d'une course/d'un cortège** to go and stand on the route of a race/procession

postérieur, -e [pɔsterjœr] **ADJ 1** *(ultérieur* ▸ *date, époque)* later; *(*▸ *fait, invention)* subsequent, later; **le tableau est p. à 1930** the picture was painted after 1930; **la rechute est très postérieure à son opération** the relapse came a long time after his/her operation **2** *(de derrière* ▸ *pattes)* hind, rear, back; *(*▸ *partie)* back, *Sout* posterior

NM *Fam Hum* behind, posterior

postérieurement [pɔsterjœrmɑ̃] **ADV** later, subsequently, at a later date; **p. à** later than, after

postériorité [pɔsterjɔrite] **NF** posteriority

postérité [pɔsterite] **NF 1** *Littéraire (lignée)* posterity, descendants; **mourir sans p.** to die without issue; *Fig* **la p. du nouveau roman** the legacy of the nouveau roman **2** *(générations futures)* posterity; **nous travaillons pour la p.** we are working for posterity; **passer à la p.** *(artiste)* to become famous, to go down in history; *(mot, œuvre)* to be handed down to posterity *or* to future generations

postface [pɔstfas] **NF** postscript, afterword

postglaciaire [pɔstglasjɛr] **ADJ** *Géol* postglacial

posthume [pɔstym] **ADJ** *(enfant, ouvrage)* posthumous; **médaille décernée à titre p.** posthumously awarded medal

postiche [pɔstiʃ] **ADJ 1** *(cheveux, barbe, chignon)* false **2** *(fictif)* sham, spurious

NM hairpiece

postier, -ère [pɔstje, -ɛr] **NM,F** postal worker

postillon [pɔstijɔ̃] **NM 1** *(de salive)* **postillons** spluttering; **envoyer des postillons** to splutter **2** *(cocher)* postilion

postillonner [3] [pɔstijɔne] **VI** to splutter; **"jamais!", dit-il en postillonnant** "never!" he spluttered; **il nous postillonnait dessus** he spluttered all over us

postindustriel, -elle [pɔstɛ̃dystrijɛl] **ADJ** post-industrial

postmoderne [pɔstmɔdɛrn] **ADJ** postmodern

postmodernisme [pɔstmɔdɛrnism] **NM** post-modernism

post mortem [pɔstmɔrtɛm] **ADJ** post-mortem

ADV post mortem

postnatal, -e, -als *ou* **-aux, -ales** [pɔstnatal, -o] **ADJ** postnatal

postopératoire [pɔstɔperatwar] **ADJ** post-operative

post-partum [pɔstpartɔm] **NM INV** postpartum period

postposer [3] [pɔstpoze] **VT 1** *Gram* to place after; **un adjectif postposé** a postpositive adjective, an adjective that comes after the noun **2** *Belg (remettre à plus tard)* to postpone

postposition [pɔstpozisjɔ̃] **NF** *Gram* **1** *(particule)* postposition **2** *(fait de postposer)* **la p. de l'adjectif** placing the adjective after the noun

postproduction [pɔstprɔdyksjɔ̃] **NF** *Cin & TV* postproduction

postscolaire [pɔstskɔlɛr] **ADJ** further education *(avant n)*; **enseignement p.** further education

post-scriptum [pɔstskriptɔm] **NM INV** post-script

postsonorisation [pɔstsɔnɔrizasjɔ̃] **NF** *Cin* post-synchronization, dubbing

postsonoriser [3] [pɔstsɔnɔrize] **VT** *Cin* to post-synchronize, to dub

post-synchro [pɔstsɛ̃kro] **NF** *Cin* post-synching

postsynchronisation [pɔstsɛ̃krɔnizasjɔ̃] **NF** postsynchronization

postsynchroniser [3] [pɔstsɛ̃krɔnize] **VT** to postsynchronize

postulant, -e [pɔstylɑ̃, -ɑ̃t] **NM,F 1** *(à un emploi)* applicant, candidate **2** *Rel* postulant

postulat [pɔstyla] **NM 1** *Math* postulate; **nous partons du p. que...** we take it as axiomatic that... **2** *Rel* postulancy

postuler [3] [pɔstyle] **VT 1** *(poste)* to apply for **2** *Math* to postulate, to assume

VI *Jur* **p. pour un client** to act on behalf of *or* to represent a client

• **postuler à VT IND** *(emploi)* to apply for

posture [pɔstyr] **NF 1** *(position du corps)* posture, position; **prendre une p. comique** to strike a comic pose **2** *(situation)* position; **être en bonne/en mauvaise** *ou* **fâcheuse p.** to be in a good/in an awkward position; **être en p. de faire qch** to be in a position to do sth

pot [po] **NM 1** *(contenant)* pot; **mettre en p.** *(plantes)* to pot; *(fruits, confitures)* to put into jars; **p. à eau/lait** water/milk jug; **p. à** *ou* **de yaourt** yoghurt pot; **p. de chambre** (chamber) pot; **p. à confiture** *ou* **à confitures** jam jar; **p. de fleurs** *(vide)* flower-pot, plant pot; *(planté)* flowers in a pot, potted flowers; **p. à moutarde** mustard pot; **p. à tabac** to-bacco jar; *Fig* tubby little person; **tourner autour du p.** to beat about the bush; *Fam* **être sourd comme un p.** to be as deaf as a post

2 *(contenu)* pot, potful; **p. de confiture/miel** jar of jam/honey; *Ordinat* **p. de miel** *(pour piéger les pirates informatiques)* honeypot; **p. de peinture** pot *or* can of paint; *Péj* **être un vrai p. de peinture** *(très maquillée)* to put one's make-up on with a trowel; **petit p. (pour bébé)** (jar of) baby food

3 *(pour enfant)* pot, potty; **aller sur le p.** to use the potty

4 *Vieilli (marmite)* (cooking) pot

5 *Fam (boisson)* drink□, *Br* jar, *Am* snort; **prendre un p.** to have a drink; **viens, je t'offre un p.** come on, I'll buy you a drink; **ils font un p. pour son départ à la retraite** they're having a little get-together for his retirement; **je suis invité à un p. ce soir** I've been invited out for drinks tonight

6 *Fam (chance)* luck□; **avoir du p.** *(souvent)* to be lucky□; *(à un certain moment)* to be in luck; **il n'a pas de p.** *(jamais)* he's unlucky□; *(en ce moment)* he's out of luck; **pas de p.!** hard *or* tough luck!; **manque de p., la banque était fermée** as (bad) luck would have it, the bank was closed; **coup de p.** stroke of luck

7 *Fam (derrière)* butt, *Br* bum, *Am* fanny

8 *Cartes (talon)* stock; *(enjeux)* pot

9 *Aut* **p. d'échappement** *(silencieux)* silencer, *Am* muffler; *(tuyau) Br* exhaust (pipe), *Am* tail pipe; **p. catalytique** catalytic converter

10 *Fam* **plein p.** *(à toute vitesse) Br* like the clappers, *Am* like sixty

11 *Naut* **p. au noir** doldrums

• **en pot ADJ** *(plante)* pot *(avant n)*, potted; *(confiture, miel)* in a jar

• **pot de colle NM** *Fam Fig* nuisance□; **quel p. de colle!** he/she sticks to you like glue!, you can't shake him/her off *or* get rid of him/her!

potable [pɔtabl] **ADJ 1** *(buvable)* **eau p.** drinking water; **eau non p.** water unsuitable for drinking **2** *Fam (acceptable* ▸ *travail)* reasonable□, just about OK; *(*▸ *vêtement)* wearable

potache [pɔtaʃ] NM *Fam* schoolkid; **blague de p.** schoolboy joke

potage [pɔtaʒ] NM **1** *Culin* soup; **p. aux légumes** vegetable soup; *Fam* **être dans le p.** *(être évanoui)* to be out cold; *(être dans une situation pénible)* to be in the soup **2** *Vieilli ou Littéraire* **n'ayant pour tout p. que son diplôme de masseur** with only his masseur's diploma to his name

potager, -ère [pɔtaʒe, -ɛr] ADJ *(culture)* vegetable *(avant n)*; *(plante)* grown for food, food *(avant n)*; **jardin p.** kitchen garden, vegetable plot

NM *(jardin)* kitchen garden, vegetable plot

potasse [pɔtas] NF *Chim* **1** *(hydroxyde)* potassium hydroxide, (caustic) potash **2** *(carbonate)* (impure) potassium carbonate, potash

potasser [3] [pɔtase] *Fam* VT *(discipline, leçon) Br* to swot up on, *Am* to bone up on; *(examen)* to cram for

VI *Br* to swot, *Am* to bone up

potassique [pɔtasik] ADJ *Chim (gén)* potassium *(avant n)*; *(sel)* potassic

potassium [pɔtasjɔm] NM *Chim* potassium

pot-au-feu [pɔtofø] NM INV *Culin* pot-au-feu, boiled beef with vegetables

ADJ INV *Fam (pantouflard)* **être p.** to be a homebody

pot-de-vin [podvɛ̃] *(pl* **pots-de-vin***)* NM bribe; **verser des pots-de-vin à qn** to grease sb's palm, to bribe sb

pote [pɔt] *Fam* ADJ **être p. avec qn** to be pally with sb; **ils sont très potes** they're very pally

NM pal, *Br* mate, *Am* buddy; **salut mon p.!** hi pal *or Br* mate *or Am* buddy!

poteau, -x [pɔto] NM **1** *(mât)* post, pole; *Belg* **p. d'éclairage** street lamp, streetlight; **p. électrique** electricity pylon; **p. indicateur** signpost; **p. télégraphique** telegraph pole *or* post; **p. (d'exécution)** (execution) stake; **envoyer qn au p.** to sentence sb to execution by firing squad; *Fam* **le proviseur, au p.!** down with the *Br* headmaster *or Am* principal!; *Fam* **avoir des jambes comme des poteaux** to have legs like tree-trunks; **elle a de ces poteaux!** her legs are like tree-trunks!

2 *(support de but)* post, goalpost; **le premier/second p.** the near/back post

3 *(dans une course)* **p. d'arrivée** winning post; **p. de départ** starting post; **rester au p.** *(cheval)* to be left at the starting post; **se faire coiffer au** *ou* **battre sur le p. (d'arrivée)** to be beaten at the (finishing) post; *Fig Br* to be pipped at the post, *Am* to be beaten by a nose

4 *Fam Vieilli (ami) Br* mate, *Am* buddy

potée [pɔte] NF *Culin* pork hotpot *(with cabbage and root vegetables)*

potelé, -e [pɔtle] ADJ plump, chubby

potence [pɔtɑ̃s] NF **1** *(supplice, instrument)* gallows

2 *Constr (d'une charpente)* post and braces; *(d'une lanterne, d'une enseigne)* support; *(d'une perfusion)* stand; **en p.** bracket-shaped, L-shaped

3 *(d'une grue)* crane jib

4 *(pour panneaux de signalisation)* overhead signpost

potentat [pɔtɑ̃ta] NM **1** *(monarque)* potentate **2** *(despote)* despot; **il se comporte en vrai p. avec ses employés** he's a real despot as far as his employees are concerned

potentialisation [pɔtɑ̃sjalizasjɔ̃] NF *Physiol* potentiation

potentialiser [3] [pɔtɑ̃sjalize] VT *Physiol* to potentiate

potentialité [pɔtɑ̃sjalite] NF **1** *Gram* potentiality **2** *(possibilité)* **ce projet offre de multiples potentialités de développement** this project has a lot of potential for development

potentiel, -elle [pɔtɑ̃sjɛl] ADJ potential; **un client p.** a prospective client

NM **1** *Élec, Math, Phys & Physiol* potential; **p. de repos** resting potential **2** *(possibilités)* potential, potentiality; **avoir un certain p.** *(personne)* to have potential; **p. de croissance** growth potential; *Pol* **p. électoral** chances of electoral success; **p. du marché** market potential *(of market)*; **p. sur le marché** market potential *(of product)*; **p. militaire** military potential; **p. de production** production potential *or* capacity; **p. publicitaire** advertising potential; **p. de vente** sales potential **3** *Ling* potential (mood)

potentiellement [pɔtɑ̃sjɛlmɑ̃] ADV potentially

potentille [pɔtɑ̃tij] NF *Bot* potentilla

potentiomètre [pɔtɑ̃sjɔmɛtr] NM potentiometer; **p. général** group fader

poterie [pɔtri] NF **1** *(art)* pottery; **faire de la p.** to do *or* to make pottery

2 *(article)* piece of pottery; **des poteries grecques** Greek pottery

3 *(atelier)* potter's workshop *or* studio; *(usine)* pottery (works)

4 *Métal* **p. d'étain/de cuivre** pewter(ware)/copper(ware)

poterne [pɔtɛrn] NF *(porte)* postern

potiche [pɔtiʃ] NF **1** *(vase)* rounded vase **2** *Fam (personne sans pouvoir)* figurehead▫; **jouer les potiches** *(femme)* to look decorative

potier, -ère [pɔtje, -ɛr] NM,F potter

potin [pɔtɛ̃] NM *Fam (bruit)* racket, din; **faire du p.** *(machine, personne)* to make a racket; *(scandale, affaire)* to cause a furore

• **potins** NMPL *Fam (commérages)* gossip, idle rumours▫; **(rubrique des) potins mondains** society gossip (column)

potiner [3] [pɔtine] VI *Fam* to gossip, to spread rumours▫

potion [posjɔ̃] NF potion, draught; **p. magique** magic potion

potiron [pɔtirɔ̃] NM pumpkin

pot-pourri [popuri] *(pl* **pots-pourris***)* NM **1** *Mus* potpourri, medley **2** *(fleurs)* potpourri

potron-jaquet [pɔtrɔ̃ʒakɛ], **potron-minet** [pɔtrɔ̃minɛ] NM INV *Vieilli ou Hum* **dès p.** at the crack of dawn

pou, -x [pu] NM **1** *(parasite de l'homme)* louse; **des poux** lice; **p. de tête/du corps** head/body louse; **poux du pubis** crab *or* pubic lice, crabs; *Fam Fig* **chercher des poux dans la tête à qn** to pick a quarrel with sb **2** *(locutions) Fam* **être laid** *ou* **moche comme un p.** to be as ugly as sin; **être fier** *ou* **orgueilleux comme un p.** to be as proud as a peacock

pouah [pwa] EXCLAM ugh!, yuck!

poubelle [pubɛl] NF **1** *(récipient à déchets) Br* dustbin, *Am* trash *or* garbage can; **mettre** *ou* **jeter qch à la p.** to put *or* to throw sth in the *Br* dustbin *or Am* trash can; **je vais mettre ces vieilles chaussures à la p.** I'm going to throw these old shoes out; **descendre la p.** to put the *Br* rubbish *or Am* garbage out; **bon pour la p.** fit for the *Br* bin *or Am* trash can; **faire les poubelles** to go scavenging (from the *Br* dustbins *or Am* trash cans); *Fig* **les poubelles de l'histoire** the scrap-heap of history; **p. à pédale** pedal bin

2 *(dépotoir)* dumping-ground, *Br* rubbish *or Am* garbage dump; **ne prenez pas la mer pour une p.** don't use the sea as a dumping-ground

3 *Fam (voiture)* heap, banger, rustbucket

4 *(utilisé en apposition)* **pétrolier p.** = old, poorly-maintained oil tanker which poses a threat to the environment; **usines poubelles** dirty factories, factories which damage the environment; **la télé p.** trash TV

5 *Ordinat* wastebasket, *Am* trash

pouce [pus] NM **1** *Anat (doigt)* thumb; *(orteil)* big toe; *Fam* **se tourner les pouces** to twiddle one's thumbs; *Suisse* **tenir les pouces à qn** to keep one's fingers crossed for sb; *Belg* **sucer de son p.** to guess; *Fam* **et le p.!** and a bit more besides! **2** *(mesure)* inch; *Fig* **on n'avançait pas d'un p. sur la route** the traffic was solid; *Fig* **je ne changerai pas d'un p. les dispositions de mon testament** I won't change one jot *or* iota of my will; *Fig* **ne pas céder un p. de terrain** not to yield *or* budge an inch **3** *Can Fam (locutions)* **avoir les mains pleines de pouces** to be all thumbs; **donner un p.** to give a lift to a hitchhiker▫; **faire du p., voyager sur le p.** to thumb a *Br* lift *or Am* ride

EXCLAM *(dans un jeu) Br* pax!, *Am* time out!

poucer [3] [puse] VI *Can Fam (faire de l'auto-stop)* to thumb a *Br* lift *or Am* ride

Poucet [pusɛ] NPR **le Petit P.** Tom Thumb

poucettes [pusɛt] NFPL = metal rings formerly attached to the thumbs of prisoners

poucier [pusje] NM *(doigtier)* thumbstall

pouding [pudiŋ], **poudingue** [pudɛ̃g] = **pudding**

poudrage [pudraʒ] NM **1** *(gén)* (light) powdering *or* sprinkling **2** *Tech* powdering **3** *Agr* dusting, crop-dusting

poudre [pudr] NF **1** *(aliment, médicament)* powder; *(de craie, d'os, de diamant, d'or)* dust, powder; **mettre** *ou* **réduire qch en p.** to reduce sth to powder, to pulverize *or* to powder sth; **p. à éternuer** sneezing powder; **p. à laver,** *Belg* **p. à lessiver** soap *or Br* washing powder; *Suisse* **p. à lever** baking powder; **p. à récurer** scouring powder

2 *Mil* powder, gunpowder; **p. à canon** gunpowder; **faire parler la p.** to settle the argument with guns; **ça sent la p.** there's talk of war

3 *(cosmétique ▸ pour le visage)* (face) powder; *(▸ pour une perruque)* powder; **p. de riz** face powder; **p. compacte/libre** pressed/loose powder; **se mettre de la p.** to powder one's face *or* nose

4 *Fam Arg drogue (héroïne)* smack, skag; *(cocaïne)* coke, charlie, *Am* nose candy

5 *Vieilli (poussière)* dust

6 *(locutions)* **prendre la p. d'escampette** to decamp; **jeter de la p. aux yeux à qn** to try to dazzle *or* to impress sb; **tout ça c'est de la p. aux yeux** all that's just for show; **p. de perlimpinpin** *(faux remède)* quack remedy; **leur politique, c'est de la p. de perlimpinpin** their policy is just a magic cure-all

• **en poudre** ADJ *(amandes, lait)* powdered; **chocolat en p.** drinking chocolate

poudrer [3] [pudre] VT **1** *(maquiller)* to powder; **une femme poudrée** a woman with a powdered face **2** *Littéraire (saupoudrer)* **la neige poudrait les arbres** the trees had a light powdering *or* sprinkling of snow

VPR **se poudrer** to powder one's nose *or* face

poudrerie [pudrəri] NF **1** *(fabrique)* gun-powder factory **2** *Can (neige)* flurry of snow

poudreux, -euse [pudrø, -øz] ADJ **1** *(terre)* dusty; *(substance, neige)* powdery **2** *Vieilli (couvert de poussière)* dusty

• **poudreuse** NF *(neige)* powdery snow, powder

poudrier [pudrije] NM (powder) compact

poudrière [pudrijɛr] NF **1** *Mil* (gun)powder store; **la maison était une vraie p.** the house was packed with explosives **2** *Fig (région)* powder keg

poudrin [pudrɛ̃] NM spindrift

poudroiement [pudrwamɑ̃] NM *Littéraire (de la neige)* sparkle; *(de la poussière)* fine cloud

poudroyer [13] [pudrwaje] VI *Littéraire (sable, neige)* to rise in clouds; *(soleil, lumière)* to shine hazily; **au loin, la route poudroyait** in the distance, fine clouds of dust could be seen rising up from the road

pouf[1] [puf] NM *(siège)* pouf, pouffe

• **à pouf** ADV *Belg* **1** *(à crédit)* on tick **2 taper à p.** *(au hasard)* to make a wild guess

pouf[2] [puf] ONOMAT *(dans une chute)* thump, bump; **faire p.** to go thump; **et p., par terre!** whoops-a-daisy!

pouffer [3] [pufe] VI **p. (de rire)** to titter

pouffiasse, poufiasse [pufjas] NF *très Fam Péj* **1** *(prostituée)* whore, hooker **2** *(femme aux mœurs légères)* slut, tart **3** *(femme désagréable)* bitch, *Br* cow

pouillerie [pujri] NF *Vieilli* **1** *(pauvreté sordide)* squalor **2** *(lieu)* filthy place, hole

pouilleux, -euse [pujø, -øz] ADJ **1** *(couvert de poux)* covered in lice, lousy, verminous **2** *(pauvre et sale ▸ individu)* grubby, filthy; *(▸ restaurant, quartier)* shabby, seedy **3** *Géog (stérile)* **la Champagne pouilleuse** = the barren part of the Champagne region

NM,F *Péj* grubby person, scruffy wretch

pouillot [pujo] NM *Orn* warbler

poujadisme [puʒadism] NM *Pol & Fig Péj* Poujadism

LE POUJADISME

This short-lived right-wing political movement, drawing support from craftsmen, small shopkeepers and small farmers, was led by Pierre Poujade. Over fifty deputies were elected in 1956. The term typifies a still prevalent attitude of resistance to change amongst traditionalist groups threatened by economic developments.

poujadiste [puʒadist] **NMF** *Pol & Fig Péj* Poujadist

poulaille [pulɑj] **NF** *Fam* **la p.** the cops, *Br* the pigs, the fuzz

poulailler [pulɑje] **NM 1** *(hangar)* hen house; *(cour)* hen run **2** *Fam Théât* **le p.** *Br* the gods, *Am* the peanut gallery; **nous avons des places au p.** we've got seats up in *Br* the gods *or Am* the peanut gallery

poulain [pulɛ̃] **NM 1** *Zool* colt; *(très jeune)* foal **2** *(protégé)* (young) protégé **3** *Tech* **p. (de chargement)** skid

poulaine [pulɛn] **NF 1** *(chaussure)* **(soulier à la) p.** poulaine **2** *Naut* head

poulamon [pulamɔ̃] **NM** *Can* (Atlantic) tomcod

poularde [pulard] **NF** fattened hen, poulard, poularde

poulbot [pulbo] **NM** (Montmartre) urchin

poule [pul] **NF 1** *Orn* hen; **p. d'eau** moorhen; **p. faisane** hen pheasant; **p. pondeuse** laying hen; **la p. aux œufs d'or** the goose that laid the golden eggs; **se coucher avec les poules** to go to bed very early; **p. mouillée** drip; **ton argent, tu le reverras quand les poules auront des dents** you can kiss your money goodbye; **tu crois qu'on va avoir une augmentation? – c'est ça, quand les poules auront des dents!** do you think we're going to have a pay rise? – and pigs might fly!; **une p. n'y retrouverait pas ses poussins** it's an awful mess; **être comme une p. qui a trouvé un couteau** to be all flustered

2 *Culin* (boiling) fowl; **p. au riz** boiled chicken with rice; **p. au pot** = casseroled chicken with vegetables

3 *Fam (maîtresse)* mistress❑; *Vieilli (prostituée)* whore; **p. de luxe** *(prostituée)* high-class whore *or* prostitute

4 *Fam (terme d'affection)* **ma p.** sweetheart, honey

5 *(comme adj)* **c'est une mère p.** she's a real mother hen; **c'est un papa p.** he's a real mother hen

6 *Sport* group, pool; **en p. A, Metz bat Béziers** in group *or* pool A, Metz beat Béziers; *Équitation* **p. d'essai** 1,600 m maiden race

7 *(cagnotte)* pool, kitty

Do not confuse with **poulet**.

poulet [pulɛ] **NM 1** *Culin & Orn* chicken; **p. fermier** free-range chicken; **p. de grain** corn-fed chicken

2 *Fam (policier)* cop, *Br* pig

3 *Fam (terme d'affection)* **mon p.** my pet, (my) love

4 *Fam Vieilli (lettre galante)* love letter❑

Do not confuse with **poule**.

poulette [pulɛt] **NF 1** *Orn* pullet

2 *Fam (terme d'affection)* **ma p.** sweetheart, honey

3 *Fam (femme) Br* bird, *Am* chick

4 *Culin* **sauce (à la) p.** = sauce made from butter, egg yolks and vinegar

pouliche [puliʃ] **NF** filly

poulie [puli] **NF** *(roue)* pulley; *(avec enveloppe)* block

pouliner [3] [puline] **VI** to foal

poulinière [pulinjɛr] **NF** brood mare
ADJ F *voir* **jument**

pouliot [puljo] **NM** *Bot* pennyroyal

poulot, -otte [pulo, -ɔt] **NM,F** *Vieilli* **mon p.** (my) pet, (my) darling

poulpe [pulp] **NM** octopus

pouls [pu] **NM** *Méd* pulse; **prendre le p. à qn** to take sb's pulse; **tâter le p. à qn** to feel sb's pulse; **prendre** *ou* **tâter le p. de** *(électorat)* to feel the pulse of, to sound out; *(entreprise, secteur)* to feel the pulse of

poumon [pumɔ̃] **NM 1** *Anat* lung; **p. artificiel** *ou* **d'acier** artificial *or* iron lung; *Méd* **cancer du p.** lung cancer; **avoir de bons poumons** *ou* **des poumons** *(chanteur)* to have a powerful voice; *(bébé)* to have a good pair of lungs; *Fig* **Central Park, le p. vert de New York** Central Park, New York's green lung *or* main green park **2** *Fam Hum* **poumons** *(seins)* knockers, jugs, *Am* hooters

poupard [pupar] **NM** *Vieilli (bébé)* chubby-cheeked baby

poupe [pup] **NF** *Naut* stern

poupée [pupe] **NF 1** *(figurine)* doll; **jouer à la p.** to play with dolls; **p. de chiffon/porcelaine** rag/china doll; **p. qui parle/marche** talking/walking doll; **p. Barbie®** *ou* **mannequin** Barbie® doll; **p. de son** stuffed doll; **p. gonflable** inflatable *or* blow-up doll; **des poupées gigognes** *ou* **russes** a set of Russian dolls **2** *Fam (fille, femme)* babe, doll **3** *Fam (bandage)* (large) finger bandage❑; **faire une p. à qn** to bandage sb's finger

• **de poupée ADJ une chambre de p.** a doll's bedroom; **un visage de p.** a doll-like face

poupin, -e [pupɛ̃, -in] **ADJ** *(visage, personne)* chubby

poupon [pupɔ̃] **NM 1** *(bébé)* little baby **2** *(jouet)* baby doll

pouponner [3] [pupɔne] **VI** *Fam* to play the doting mother/father

pouponnière [pupɔnjɛr] **NF** nursery *(for babies and toddlers who can neither stay with their parents nor be fostered)*

poupoune [pupun] **NF** *Can Fam* sweetie, honey

POUR [pur]

- for **1–4, 7, 10–12, 14, 16**
- on behalf of **12**
- in favour of **16**
- to **5**
- per **9**
- in order to **15**

PRÉP 1 *(indiquant le lieu où l'on va)* for; **partir p. l'Italie** to leave for Italy; **un billet p. Paris** a ticket for *or* to Paris; **p. Granville, prendre à gauche** turn left for Granville; **le train p. Séville** the train for Seville, the Seville train; **je m'envole p. Rome** I'm flying to Rome; **partir p. la campagne** to go to the country

2 *(dans le temps ▸ indiquant le moment)* for; **pourriez-vous avoir fini p. lundi/demain?** could you have it finished for Monday/tomorrow?; **p. dans une semaine** for a week's time; **p. le 10 mai** for 10 May; **vous partez en Italie p. Pâques?** are you going to Italy for Easter?; **p. la première fois** for the first time; **p. le moment** for the moment; **tu organises quelque chose p. ton anniversaire?** are you doing anything for your birthday?; **j'ai repeint la chambre p. quand tu viendras** I've redecorated the room for when you visit

3 *(dans le temps ▸ indiquant la durée)* for; **partir p. 10 jours** to go away for 10 days; **il n'en a plus p. longtemps** he won't be long now; *(à vivre)* he hasn't got long to live; **j'en ai bien p. cinq heures** it'll take me at least five hours

4 *(exprimant la cause)* for; **je l'ai remercié p. son amabilité** I thanked him for his kindness; **il a été grassement récompensé p. son aide** he was handsomely rewarded for his help; **fermé p. travaux** *(sur vitrine d'un magasin)* closed for repairs; **un restaurant apprécié p. ses fruits de mer** a restaurant famous for its seafood; **ils se querellent p. des broutilles** they quarrel over the slightest thing; **désolé p. dimanche** sorry about Sunday; **il est tombé malade p. avoir mangé trop d'huîtres** he fell ill after eating *or* because he ate too many oysters; **condamné p. vol** found guilty of theft; **elle a obtenu un prix p. son premier film** she won an award for her first movie *or Br* film; **sa bonne constitution y est p. quelque chose** his/her strong constitution had something to do with *or* played a part in it; **elle est p. beaucoup dans le succès de la pièce** the success of the play is to a large extent due to her, she has had a great deal to do with the success of the play; **ne me remerciez pas, je n'y suis p. rien** don't thank me, I didn't have anything to do with it

5 *(exprimant la conséquence)* to; **p. son malheur** to his/her misfortune; **p. la plus grande joie des enfants** to the children's great delight; **il a erré trois heures en forêt p. se retrouver à son point de départ** he wandered for three hours in the forest, only to find he was back where he'd started from; **ses paroles n'étaient pas p. me rassurer** his/her words were far from reassuring to me; **ce n'est pas p. me déplaire** I can't say I'm displeased with it

6 *(capable de)* **je me suis trompé et il ne s'est trouvé personne p. me le dire** I made a mistake and nobody was capable of telling me; **il y a toujours des gens p. rire du malheur des autres** there will always be people who'll laugh at other people's misfortune

7 *(par rapport à)* for; **il est en avance p. son âge** he's advanced for his age; **pas mal p. un début** not bad for a start; **il fait froid p. un mois de mai** it's cold for May; **c'est cher p. ce que c'est** it's expensive for what it is

8 *(avec une valeur emphatique)* **mot p. mot** word for word; **p. un champion, c'est un champion!** that's what I call a (real) champion!; **p. une surprise, c'est une surprise!** well, talk about (a) surprise!; **perdre p. perdre, autant que ce soit en beauté** if we are going to lose, we might as well do it in style; **p. être en colère, je l'étais!** I was SO angry!

9 *(indiquant une proportion, un pourcentage)* per; **cinq p. cent** five percent; **p. mille** per thousand; **il faut 200 g de farine p. une demi-livre de beurre** take 200 grams of flour to or for half a pound of butter

10 *(moyennant)* for; **p. 50 euros** for 50 euros; **p. la somme de** for the sum of; **p. rien** for nothing; **il y en a bien p. 300 euros de réparation** the repairs will cost at least 300 euros

11 *(à la place de)* for; **prendre un mot p. un autre** to mistake a word for another; **on l'a prise p. sa fille** they mistook her for her daughter

12 *(au nom de)* for, on behalf of; **parler p. qn** to speak on sb's behalf *or* for sb; **remercie-le p. moi** thank him from me *or* for me *or* on my behalf; **son tuteur prend toutes les décisions p. lui** his guardian makes all the decisions for him *or* on his behalf; **p. le directeur** *(dans la correspondance)* pp Director

13 *(en guise de, en qualité de)* **prendre qn p. époux/épouse** to take sb to be one's husband/wife; **avoir qn p. ami/professeur** to have sb as a friend/teacher; **j'ai son fils p. élève** his/her son is one of my pupils; **p. tout remerciement voilà ce que j'ai eu** that's all the thanks I got; **avoir p. conséquence** to have as a consequence; **j'ai p. principe que...** I believe on principle that...; **il se fait passer p. un antiquaire** he claims to be an antique dealer; **le livre a p. titre...** the book's title is..., the book is entitled...

14 *(indiquant l'attribution, la destination, le but)* for; **acheter un cadeau p. qn** to buy a present for sb; **il y a quelqu'un p. vous au téléphone** there's someone on the phone for you; **j'ai beaucoup d'admiration p. lui** I've got a lot of admiration for him; **son amour p. moi** his/her love for me; **mes sentiments p. elle** my feelings towards *or* for her; **tant pis p. lui!** that's too bad (for him)!; **c'est p. quoi faire, ce truc?** what's that thing for?; **sirop p. la toux** cough mixture; **un journal p. enfants** a newspaper for children; **des vêtements chauds p. l'hiver** warm clothes for winter; **tout est bon p. son ambition** everything feeds his/her ambition; **il est mort p. la patrie** he died for his country; **voyager p. son plaisir** to travel for pleasure; **l'art p. l'art** art for art's sake; **la discipline p. la discipline c'est idiot** discipline (just) for the sake of discipline is stupid; **p. quatre personnes** *(recette)* serves four; *(couchage)* sleeps four; **c'est fait p.** that's what it's (there) for

15 *(suivi de l'infinitif) (afin de)* (in order) to; **je suis venu p. vous voir** I'm here *or* I've come to see you; **nous sommes là p. vous informer** we're here to inform you; **p. mieux comprendre** in order to understand more clearly; **si tu veux réussir, il faut tout faire p.** if you want to succeed you have to do everything possible

16 *(en faveur de)* for, in favour of; **voter p. qn** to vote for *or* in favour of sb; **manifester p. les droits de l'homme** to demonstrate for *or* in favour of human rights; **il a p. lui de nombreuses qualités** he has a number of qualities in his favour; **être p.** to be in favour; **qui est p.?** who's in favour?; **on est p. ou contre** you're either for or against (it); **ceux qui sont p. cette solution** the supporters of this solution, those who are in favour of this solution; **je suis p. qu'on s'y mette tout de suite** I'm in favour of gettingdown to it immediately

17 *(du point de vue de)* **ça compte peu p. toi, mais**

p. moi c'est tellement important it matters little to you but to *or* for me it's so important; **p. moi, il a dû se réconcilier avec elle** if you ask me, he must have made it up with her; **p. moi, c'est comme s'il était toujours là** to *or* for me, it's as though he's still here *or* around

18 *(en ce qui concerne)* **et p. le salaire?** and what about the salary?; **ne t'en fais pas p. moi** don't worry about me; **p. certains de nos collègues, la situation est inchangée** as far as some of our colleagues are concerned, the situation has not changed; **p. ce qui est de l'avancement, voyez avec le responsable du personnel** as far as promotion is concerned, see the personnel officer

19 *(exprimant la concession)* **p. être gentil il n'en est pas moins bête** he may be kind but he's still stupid, for all his kindness he's no less stupid; **p. être jeune, elle n'en est pas moins compétente** young though she is she's very competent; **p. patient qu'il soit, il ne supportera pas cette situation** for all his patience, he won't put up with this situation

20 *Littéraire (sur le point de)* about to, on the point of; **il était p. partir** he was about to leave *or* on the point of leaving

NM INV il y a du p. et du contre there are things to be said on both sides (of the argument); **peser le p. et le contre** to weigh up the pros and cons; **les p. l'emportent** the argument in favour is overwhelming; *Pol ou Hum* the ayes have it

• **pour que CONJ 1** *(exprimant le but)* so that, *Sout* in order that; **j'ai pris des places non-fumeurs p. que vous ne soyez pas incommodés par la fumée** I've got non-smoking seats so that you won't be bothered by the smoke **2** *(exprimant la conséquence)* **il est assez malin p. qu'on ne l'arrête pas** he is cunning enough to avoid being caught; **mon appartement est trop petit p. qu'on puisse tous y dormir** my *Br* flat *or Am* apartment is too small for us all to be able to sleep there

pourboire [purbwar] **NM** tip; **donner un p. à qn** to give a tip to sb, to tip sb; **j'ai laissé deux euros de p.** I left a two-euro tip; **être payé au p.** to depend on tips for one's pay

pourceau, -x [purso] **NM** *Littéraire* **1** *(porc)* pig, *Am* hog **2** *(homme ▸ sale)* pig; *(▸ vicieux)* animal

pourcentage [pursɑ̃taʒ] **NM 1** *Fin & Math* percentage; **ça fait combien, en p.?** what's the percentage figure? **2** *Com* percentage, commission; **travailler au p.** to work on a commission *or* percentage basis; **être payé au p.** to be paid on commission *or* on a commission basis

pourchasser [3] [purʃase] **VT 1** *(criminel)* to chase, to pursue; **pourchassé par ses créanciers** pursued *or* hounded by his creditors **2** *(erreur, abus)* to track down; **nous pourchasserons les injustices** we'll root out injustice wherever we find it

> Il faut noter que le verbe anglais **to purchase** est un faux ami. Il signifie **acheter**.

pourfendeur, -euse [purfɑ̃dœr, -øz] **NM,F** *Littéraire* **p. d'idées reçues/de l'hypocrisie** declared *or* sworn enemy of received ideas/of hypocrisy

pourfendre [73] [purfɑ̃dr] **VT** *Littéraire* **1** *(avec une épée ▸ ennemi)* to kill (by the sword) **2** *(hypocrisie, préjugés)* to combat

pourlécher [18] [purleʃe] **se pourlécher VPR** to lick one's lips; **se p. les babines** to lick one's lips; *Hum* **je m'en pourlèche les babines à l'avance** my mouth is watering already

pourliche [purliʃ] **NM** *Fam* tip☐ *(in bar, restaurant)*

pourparlers [purparle] **NMPL** negotiations, talks; **être/entrer en p. avec qn** to have/to enter into talks *or* negotiations with sb; **les p. vont reprendre** negotiations will be resumed; *UE* **p. d'adhésion** entry talks; **p. bilatéraux** bilateral talks; **p. de paix** peace talks

pourpier [purpje] **NM** *Bot* purslane

pourpoint [purpwɛ̃] **NM** doublet, pourpoint

pourpre [purpr] **ADJ** crimson; **son visage devint p.** he/she went *or* turned crimson

NM 1 *(couleur)* crimson; **le p. de la honte lui monta au visage** he/she turned crimson with shame **2** *(mollusque)* murex, purple fish **3** *Biol* **p. rétinien** visual purple

NF 1 *(teinte)* purple (dye) **2** *Rel* **la p.** *(robe)* the purple; **né dans la p.** born in *or* to the purple

pourpré, -e [purpre] **ADJ** *Littéraire* crimson

pourquoi [purkwa] **ADV** why; **p. pars-tu?, p. est-ce que tu pars?** why are you going?; **p. m'avoir menti?** why did you lie to me?; **p. cet air triste?** why are you looking so sad?; **p. chercher des difficultés?** why make things more complicated?; **p. lutter?** what's the use of fighting?; **p. tant d'efforts?** why so much effort?; **p. tant de simagrées?** what's the point of all this play-acting?; **mais p.?** but why?; **p. pas?** why not?; **elle a bien réussi l'examen, p. pas moi?** she passed the exam, why shouldn't I?; **p. ça?** why?; **et p. donc?** but why?; **et p., s'il vous plaît?** and why, may I ask?; **je ne sais pas p. tu dis ça** I don't know why you're saying that; **voilà p. je démissionne** that's (the reason) why I am resigning, that's the reason for my resignation; **c'est p. je n'y suis pas allée** that's why I didn't go; **personne ne m'a dit p.** nobody has told me why; **il boude, va savoir** *ou* **comprendre p.!** he's sulking, don't ask me why!; **je l'ai fait sans savoir p.** I did it without knowing why; **c'est une opération délicate, et voici p....** it is a tricky operation and this is why…

NM INV nous ne saurons jamais le p. de cette affaire we'll never get to the bottom of this affair; **il s'interroge toujours sur le p. et le comment des choses** he's always bothered about the whys and wherefores of everything; **dans sa lettre, il explique le p. de son suicide** in his letter, he explains the reason *or* reasons for his suicide

pourri, -e [puri] **ADJ 1** *(nourriture)* rotten, bad; *(planche, arbre, plante)* rotten; *(dent)* rotten, decayed; *(chairs)* decomposed, putrefied; **complètement p.** rotten to the core

2 *Fam (mauvais ▸ climat, saison)* rotten

3 *(en mauvais état)* falling apart, *Br* knackered; **elle est complètement pourrie ta voiture!** your car is a heap of junk *or* a wreck!

4 *(de mauvaise qualité)* crappy, lousy, *Br* rubbish

5 *Fam (corrompu ▸ individu, système, société)* rotten to the core

6 *(trop gâté ▸ enfant)* spoilt

7 *Fam (plein)* **il est p. de fric** he's stinking rich, he's loaded; **il est p. de talent** he's amazingly talented; **il est p. de vices** he's rotten to the core; **être p. d'orgueil/d'ambition** to be eaten up with pride/ambition

NM,F *Fam* **1** *(homme méprisable)* scumbag, *Br* swine, *Am* stinker; *(femme méprisable)* bitch, *Br* cow; **tas de pourris!** you rotten swines! **2** *Belg (paresseux)* lazy so-and-so

NM *(partie pourrie)* rotten *or* bad part; **enlève le p.** cut off the bad bit/bits; **sentir le p.** to stink

pourriel [purjel] **NM** *Ordinat* spam e-mail; **pourriels** spam

pourrir [32] [purir] **VI 1** *(nourriture)* to go rotten, to go bad *or Br* off; *(planche, arbre)* to rot; *(végétation, dent)* to decay, to rot; *(chairs)* to decay, to putrefy; **p. sur pied** to rot on the stalk; **la pluie a fait p. toute la récolte** the rain rotted the entire harvest; *Fig* **laisser p. la situation** to let the situation deteriorate **2** *Fam (croupir ▸ personne)* to rot; **p. en prison** to rot in prison

VT 1 *(nourriture)* to rot, to putrefy; *(végétation, dent)* to decay

2 *(gâter ▸ enfant)* to spoil

3 *(pervertir ▸ individu, société)* to corrupt

4 *(gâcher)* **elle me pourrit l'existence** she's ruining my life

5 *Fam (dire du mal de)* to badmouth, *Br* to slag off

pourrissement [purismɑ̃] **NM 1** *(de fruits, du bois, de la viande)* rotting; *(de chairs)* putrefaction; *(d'une dent, de la végétation)* decay, rotting, decaying **2** *(d'une situation)* deterioration

pourriture [purityr] **NF 1** *(partie pourrie)* rotten part *or* bit

2 *(processus)* rotting, rot, decay; *(état)* rottenness

3 *(corruption)* rottenness, corruption

4 *Fam (personne)* rotten swine

pour-soi [purswa] **NM INV** *Phil* pour-soi

poursuite [pursɥit] **NF 1** *(pour rattraper un animal, un fugitif)* chase; **p. en voiture** car chase; **les voilà partis dans une p. effrénée** off they go in hot pursuit; **ils sont à la p. des voleurs** *(ils courent)* they're chasing the thieves; *(ils enquêtent)* they're on the trail of the thieves; **se mettre** *ou* **se lancer à la p. de qn** to set off in pursuit of sb, to give chase to sb

2 *(prolongation ▸ de pourparlers, d'études, de recherches)* continuation; **la panne d'électricité a empêché la p. de l'opération** the power cut prevented the operation from going on *or* being carried out; **ils ont décidé la p. de la grève** they've decided to carry on *or* to continue with the strike

3 *(recherche ▸ du bonheur, d'un rêve)* pursuit

4 *Sport* pursuit

5 *Théât (projecteur)* follow spot

6 *Jur* **p. disciplinaire** disciplinary action

• **poursuites NFPL** *Jur* **poursuites (judiciaires)** *(en droit civil)* (legal) proceedings; *(en droit pénal)* prosecution; **entamer** *ou* **engager des poursuites contre qn** *(en droit civil)* to institute (legal) proceedings *or* to take legal action against sb; *(en droit pénal)* to prosecute sb; **vous pouvez faire l'objet de poursuites** you're liable to prosecution

poursuiteur, -euse [pursɥitœr, -øz] **NM,F** *Sport* pursuit rider

poursuivant, -e [pursɥivɑ̃, -ɑ̃t] **ADJ** *Jur* **la partie poursuivante** the plaintiff

NM,F 1 *(dans une course)* pursuer **2** *Jur* plaintiff

poursuivre [89] [pursɥivr] **VT 1** *(courir après ▸ animal, voleur, voiture)* to chase (after), *Sout* to pursue; **je me suis fait p. par une bande de voyous/une voiture de police** I was chased by a gang of thugs/a police car; **il sentait leurs regards qui le poursuivaient** he could feel their eyes pursuing *or* following him

2 *(s'acharner contre ▸ sujet: créancier, rival)* to hound, to harry, to pursue; *(▸ sujet: image, passé, remords)* to haunt, to hound, to pursue; **p. qn de ses assiduités** to pester sb with one's attentions; **p. qn de sa haine** to hound sb through hatred; **il est poursuivi par la malchance** he is dogged *or* pursued by misfortune

3 *(continuer ▸ interrogatoire, récit, recherche, voyage)* to go *or* to carry on with, to continue; *(▸ lutte)* to continue, to pursue; **p. son chemin** to press on; **elle poursuivit sa lecture** she carried on reading, she read on; **ils poursuivirent la discussion jusqu'à une heure tardive** they went on talking till late at night; **poursuivez votre travail** get on with your work; **"quelques années plus tard", poursuivit-il** "a few years later," he went on

4 *(aspirer à ▸ objectif)* to pursue, to strive towards; *(▸ rêve)* to pursue; *(▸ plaisirs)* to pursue, to seek

5 *Jur* **p. qn (en justice)** *(en droit civil)* to institute (legal) proceedings against *or* to sue sb; *(en droit pénal)* to prosecute sb; **être poursuivi pour détournement de fonds** to be prosecuted for embezzlement; **être poursuivi en diffamation** to be sued for libel

USAGE ABSOLU *(continuer)* **veuillez p., Monsieur** please proceed, sir; **bien, poursuivons** right, let's go on *or* continue

VPR se poursuivre 1 *(se courir après)* to chase one another *or* each other **2** *(se prolonger ▸ pourparlers, recherches)* to go on, to continue; *(▸ opération)* to go on

pourtant [purtɑ̃] **ADV 1** *(malgré tout)* yet, even so, all the same; **elle est p. bien gentille** and yet she's very nice; **il faut p. bien que quelqu'un le fasse** somebody has to do it all the same; **et p.** and yet; **c'est une avenue résidentielle, et p. bruyante** it's a residential street and yet it's still noisy; **et p., toutes les conditions étaient réunies!** and yet, all the conditions were right! **2** *(emploi expressif)* **c'est p. simple!** but it's quite simple!; **ce n'est p. pas compliqué!** it's not exactly complicated!; **il n'est pas bête, p.!** he's not exactly stupid!; **je t'avais p. prévenu!** I did warn you!; **les instructions étaient p. claires** the instructions were quite clear; **ma montre ne s'est p. pas envolée!** my watch didn't just vanish into thin air!; **c'est p. vrai qu'il est déjà midi!** 12 o'clock already!

pourtour [purtur] **NM 1** *(délimitation ▸ d'un terrain)* perimeter; *(▸ d'un globe)* circumference; **les pays du p. méditerranéen** the countries around the Mediterranean **2** *(bordure ▸ d'un plat)* edge, rim; *(▸ d'une baignoire)* surround

pourvoi [purvwa] **NM** *Jur* appeal; **p. en cassation**

appeal to the final court of appeal; **il a présenté un p. en cassation** he has taken his case to the final court of appeal; **p. en grâce** appeal for clemency; **p. en révision** review

pourvoir [64] [purvwar] **VT 1** *(équiper)* **p. qn de** *ou* **en** *(outils)* to equip *or* to provide sb with; *(vivres, documents)* to provide sb with; **p. qch de** to equip *or* to fit sth with; **p. une maison du chauffage central** to fit out *or* to equip a house with central heating; **la salle est pourvue d'un excellent système acoustique** the auditorium has been fitted with an excellent sound system **2** *(doter)* **p. de** to endow with; **la nature l'a pourvue d'une remarquable intelligence** nature has endowed *or* graced her with extraordinary intelligence; **ses parents l'ont pourvu d'une solide éducation** his parents provided him with a sound education; **la cigogne est pourvue d'un long bec** storks have *or* possess long beaks **3** *(remplir ▸ emploi)* to fill; **le poste est toujours à p.** the post is still vacant *or* is still to be filled

• **pourvoir à VT IND** *(besoin)* to provide *or* to cater for; *(dépense)* to pay for; **nous pourvoirons au transport des médicaments** we will provide for *or* deal with the transport of medicine

VPR se pourvoir 1 *Jur* to appeal; **se p. en cassation** to take one's case to the final court of appeal **2 se p. de** *(outils)* to equip oneself with; *(vivres)* to provide oneself with

pourvoyeur, -euse [purvwajœr, -øz] **NM,F 1** *(d'armes, de marchandises)* supplier; *(de drogue)* dealer **2** *Littéraire* **p. de fausses nouvelles** rumour monger

pourvu que [purvykə] **CONJ 1** *(exprimant un souhait)* **pourvu qu'il vienne!** I hope *or* let's hope he's coming!; **p. ça dure!** let's hope it lasts! **2** *(exprimant une condition)* provided (that), so *or* as long as; **tout ira bien p. vous soyez à l'heure** everything will be fine so long as you're on time

poussage [pusaʒ] **NM** pushing

poussah [pusa] **NM 1** *(figurine)* tumbler (toy) **2** *(homme)* portly (little) man

pousse [pus] **NF 1** *Anat* growth

2 *Bot (bourgeon)* (young) shoot, sprout; *(début de croissance)* sprouting; *(développement)* growth; **une plante à p. lente/rapide** a slow-growing/fast-growing plant; **ma plante fait des pousses** my plant is sprouting new leaves; **pousses de bambou** bamboo shoots; **pousses de soja** beansprouts

3 *Com & Ordinat* **jeune p. (d'entreprise)** start-up

4 *(de la pâte à pain)* proving

poussé, -e[1] [puse] **ADJ 1** *(fouillé ▸ interrogatoire)* thorough, probing, searching; *(▸ recherche, technique)* advanced; *(▸ connaissances)* extensive; *(▸ description)* thorough, extensive, exhaustive; **d'une efficacité très poussée** highly efficient; **elle fera des études poussées** she'll go on to advanced studies; **je n'ai pas fait d'études poussées** I didn't stay in education very long **2** *(exagéré)* excessive; **60 euros pour une coupe, c'est un peu p.!** 60 euros for a haircut is a bit steep!; **la plaisanterie est un peu poussée** that's taking the joke too far **3** *Aut (moteur)* customized

pousse-au-crime [pusokrim] *Fam* **ADJ INV** that encourages crime◻

NM INV 1 *(eau-de-vie)* firewater, rotgut **2 c'est du p.** it encourages crime◻

pousse-café [puskafe] **NM INV** *Fam* liqueur◻, pousse-café◻; **voulez-vous un p.?** would you like a liqueur with your coffee?

poussée[2] [puse] **NF 1** *Constr, Géol, Phys & Aviat* thrust; **centre de p.** *Phys* aerodynamic centre, centre of pressure; *(de liquide)* centre of buoyancy

2 *(pression)* push, shove, thrust; **la barrière a cédé sous la p. des manifestants** the barrier gave way under the pressure of the demonstrators; **écarter qch d'une p.** to push *or* shove sth aside

3 *Méd* eruption, outbreak; **le bébé fait une petite p. de boutons rouges** the baby has a rash; **faire une p. de fièvre** to have a sudden rise in temperature; **une p. d'adrénaline** a surge of adrenalin; **faire une p. de croissance** to shoot up

4 *Bot* **p. radiculaire** root pressure

5 *(progression)* upsurge, rise; **une p. de racisme** an upsurge of racism; **une p. de l'inflation** *ou* **une p. inflationniste** a rise in inflation

6 *(attaque)* thrust; **la p. des troupes hitlériennes contre la Pologne** the thrust *or* offensive of Hitler's troops against Poland

pousse-pousse [puspus] **NM INV 1** *(en Extrême-Orient)* rickshaw **2** *Suisse (poussette) Br* pushchair, *Am* stroller

POUSSER [3] [puse]

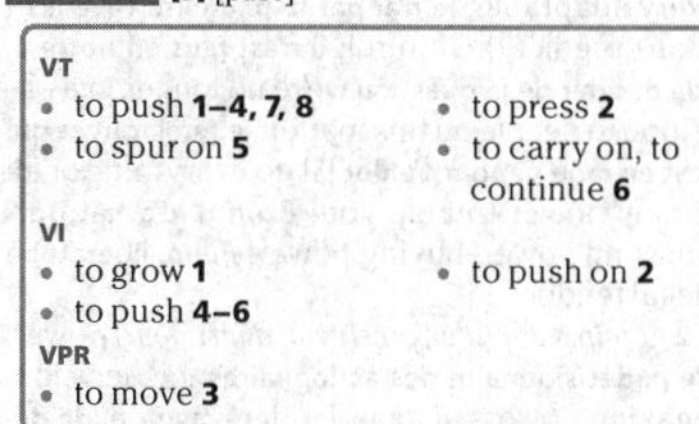
VT
• to push **1–4, 7, 8** • to press **2**
• to spur on **5** • to carry on, to continue **6**
VI
• to grow **1** • to push on **2**
• to push **4–6**
VPR
• to move **3**

VT 1 *(faire avancer ▸ caddie, fauteuil roulant, landau)* to push, to wheel (along); *(▸ moto en panne)* to push, to walk; *(▸ caisse)* to push (along), to push forward; *(▸ pion)* to move forward; **on va p. la voiture** *(sur une distance)* we'll push the car (along); *(pour la faire démarrer)* we'll push-start the car, we'll give the car a push (to start it); **il poussait son troupeau devant lui** he was driving his flock before him; **ils essayaient de p. les manifestants vers la place** they were trying to drive *or* to push the demonstrators towards the square; **le vent pousse le radeau loin de la côte** the wind is pushing the raft away from the coast; **des rafales de vent poussaient les nuages** gusts of wind sent the clouds scudding across the sky; **je me sentais irrésistiblement poussé vers elle** I was irresistibly attracted to her; *Fam* **faut pas p. (mémé** *ou* **mémère dans les orties)** that's pushing it a bit

2 *(enclencher, appuyer sur ▸ bouton, interrupteur)* to push (in), to press; **p. un levier vers le haut/bas** to push a lever up/down; **p. un verrou** *(pour ouvrir)* to slide a bolt out; *(pour fermer)* to slide a bolt in *or* home; **pousse le volet** *(pour l'ouvrir)* push the shutter open *or* out; *(pour le fermer)* push the shutter to; **p. une porte** *(doucement, pour l'ouvrir)* to push a door open; *(doucement, pour la fermer)* to push a door to *or* shut; **la porte à peine poussée, il me racontait ce qu'il avait fait dans la journée** no sooner was he inside the door, than he began telling me all about his day

3 *(bousculer)* to push, to shove; **p. qn du coude** *(pour l'alerter, accidentellement)* to nudge sb with one's elbow; **j'ai été obligé de p. plusieurs personnes pour pouvoir sortir** I had to push past several people to get out; **elle l'a poussé par-dessus bord** she pushed him overboard

4 *(enlever)* to push (away), to push *or* to shove aside; **pousse le vase/ton pied, je ne vois pas la télévision** move the vase/your foot out of the way, I can't see the television; *Fam* **pousse ton derrière de là!** shove over!, *Br* budge up!

5 *(inciter, entraîner ▸ personne)* to spur on, to drive; **c'est l'orgueil qui le pousse** he is spurred on *or* driven by pride; **on n'a pas eu à le p. beaucoup pour qu'il accepte** he didn't need much pressing *or* persuasion to accept; **p. qn à la dépense** to encourage sb to spend more; **p. qn au désespoir/suicide** to drive sb to despair/suicide; **ici, tout pousse à la paresse** this place encourages idleness; **sa curiosité l'a poussé à l'indiscrétion** his curiosity made him indiscreet; **p. qn à faire qch** *(sujet: curiosité, jalousie)* to drive sb to do sth; *(sujet: pitié soudaine)* to prompt sb to do sth; *(sujet: personne)* to incite sb to do *or* to push sb into doing *or* to prompt sb to do sth; **p. qn à se droguer** to push sb into taking drugs; **p. qn à boire** to drive sb to drink; **sa tyrannie les avait poussés à se révolter** his/her tyranny had driven them to revolt; **un désir inexplicable me poussa à y retourner** I was mysteriously compelled to go back there; **mes parents ne m'ont jamais poussé à faire des études** my parents never encouraged me to study; **elle le pousse à divorcer** *(elle l'en persuade)* she's talking him into getting a divorce; **mais qu'est-ce qui a bien pu te p. à lui dire la vérité?** what on earth possessed you to tell him/her the truth?

6 *(poursuivre ▸ recherches)* to press on *or* to carry on with; *(▸ discussion, études, analyse)* to continue, to carry on (with); *(▸ argumentation)* to carry on (with), to push further; *(▸ comparaison, interrogatoire)* to take further; *(▸ avantage)* to press home; **en poussant plus loin l'examen de leur comptabilité** by probing deeper into their accounts; **vous auriez dû p. un peu plus votre réflexion sur ce point** you should have developed that point further; **p. la plaisanterie un peu loin** to take *or* to carry the joke a bit too far; **tu pousses un peu loin le cynisme** you're being a bit too cynical; **p. la promenade jusqu'à** to push on to, to walk as far as; **p. la sévérité jusqu'à la cruauté** to carry severity to the point of cruelty; **elle a poussé l'audace jusqu'à...** she was bold enough to...; **il a poussé le vice jusqu'à ne pas la saluer** his spite was such that he refused even to greet her

7 *(forcer ▸ moteur)* to push; *(▸ voiture)* to drive hard *or* fast; *(▸ chauffage, son)* to turn up; *(exiger un effort de ▸ étudiant, employé)* to push; *(▸ cheval)* to urge *or* to spur on; **je suis à 130, je préfère ne pas p. le moteur** I'm doing 130, I'd rather not push the engine any further; *Fam* **p. la sono à fond** to turn the sound up full (blast); **on ne m'a pas assez poussé quand j'étais à l'école** I wasn't pushed hard enough when I was at school

8 *(encourager ▸ candidat, jeune artiste)* to push; **elle a poussé son fils pour qu'il entre dans l'enseignement** she pushed her son towards a teaching career; **si tu la pousses un peu sur le sujet, tu verras qu'elle ne sait pas grand-chose** if you push her a bit on the subject, you'll see that she doesn't know much about it

9 *(émettre)* **p. un cri** *(personne)* to cry, to utter *or* to let out a cry; *(oiseau)* to call; **p. une exclamation** to cry out; **p. un gémissement** to groan; **p. une plainte** to moan; **p. un soupir** to sigh, to heave a sigh; **p. des cris/hurlements de douleur** to scream/to yell with pain; *Fam* **p. la chansonnette, en p. une** to sing a song◻; **allez, grand-père, tu nous en pousses une?** come on, grandpa, give us a song!

10 *Agr & Bot (plante, animal)* to force

11 *Mil (troupes)* to push forward, to drive on; **p. une charge** to charge; **p. une reconnaissance** to go on a (wide-ranging) reconnaissance; *aussi Fig* **p. une attaque** to drive an attack home

12 *Écon* **p. à la hausse/la baisse** to have an inflationary/a deflationary effect; **poussé par les profits** profit-driven; **p. la vente de qch** to push the sale of sth; **p. qch aux enchères** to up the bidding for sth

VI 1 *(grandir ▸ arbre, poil, ongle)* to grow; *(▸ dent)* to come through; **le banian ne pousse qu'en Inde** banyans only grow *or* are only found in India; **pour empêcher les mauvaises herbes de p.** to stop weeds from growing; **des mauvaises herbes poussées entre les pierres** weeds which have sprung up between the stones; **les plants de tomates poussent bien** the tomato plants are doing well; **ses dents commencent à p.** he's/she's cutting his/her teeth, he's/she's teething; *Fig* **il a poussé trop vite** he's grown too fast; *Fam* **et les enfants, ça pousse?** how're the kids (then), growing *or* shooting up?; **des tours poussent partout dans mon quartier** there are high-rise blocks springing up all over my neighbourhood; **faire p.** *(légumes, plantes)* to grow; **faire p. du blé** to grow *or* to cultivate wheat; **on fait p. de la vigne dans la région** they grow grapes in this region; **mets de l'engrais, ça fera p. tes laitues plus vite** use fertilizer, it'll make your lettuces grow faster; **laisser p.** to grow; **et si tu laissais p. ta barbe?** what about growing *or* why don't you grow a beard?; **elle a laissé p. ses cheveux** she's let her hair grow

2 *(avancer)* to push on; **ils ont poussé jusqu'au manoir** they went on *or* pushed on *or* carried on as far as the manor house

3 *Fam (exagérer)* **deux heures de retard, tu pousses!** you're two hours late, that's a bit much!; **60 euros par personne, ils poussent un peu!** 60 euros per person, that's a bit much *or* steep!; **faut pas p.!** enough's enough!

4 *(bousculer)* to push, to shove; **ne poussez pas, il y en aura pour tout le monde!** stop shoving *or* pushing, there's plenty for everyone!; *Fam* **ça poussait dans la file d'attente** there was a lot of shoving *or* jostling in the queue

5 *(appuyer)* to push; **on a tous poussé en même temps pour désembourber la voiture** we all pushed together to get the car out of the mud; **p. sur un bouton** to push a button; **p. sur ses pieds/jambes** to push with one's feet/legs; **poussez sur vos bâtons dans la descente** use your poles as you go downhill; **p. dans le sens de qn** to push sb's cause

6 *Physiol (à la selle)* to strain; *(dans l'enfantement)* to push; **poussez!** *(femme enceinte)* push!

VPR se pousser 1 *(emploi passif)* to be pushed; **la manette se pousse d'un seul doigt** the lever can be pushed with a single finger

2 *(emploi réciproque)* **les gens se poussaient pour voir arriver le Président** people were pushing and shoving to get a look at the President

3 *(se déplacer)* to move; **tu peux te p. un peu?** *(dans une rangée de chaises)* could you move along a bit *or* a few places?; *(sur un canapé, dans un lit)* could you move over slightly?; **la foule s'est poussée pour laisser passer l'ambulance** the crowd moved out of the way of the ambulance; *Fam* **pousse-toi de là, tu vois bien que tu gênes!** move over *or* shove over, can't you see you're in the way?; *Fam* **pousse-toi de devant la télé!** stop blocking the TV!

4 *Fam (hiérarchiquement)* **se p. dans une entreprise** to make one's way up (the ladder) in a firm ❑; **il faut une fortune pour se p. dans la finance** you need a private fortune to get ahead in the world of finance ❑

5 *Can Fam (s'enfuir)* to run away ❑, *Br* to scarper

poussette [pusɛt] **NF 1** *(pour enfant) Br* pushchair, *Am* stroller; *Suisse (landau) Br* pram, *Am* baby carriage **2** *(à provisions)* shopping *Br* trolley *or Am* cart **3** *Fam* **faire la p. à un coureur cycliste** to give a rider a little push *or* shove

pousseur [pusœr] **NM 1** *Naut* push tug **2** *Astron* booster **3** *Littéraire (de soupirs)* heaver; *(de belles phrases)* utterer

poussier [pusje] **NM** coal dust

poussière [pusjɛr] **NF 1** *(terre sèche, salissures)* dust *(UNCOUNT)*; *(grain)* speck of dust; **la voiture souleva un nuage de p.** the car raised a cloud of dust; **tu en fais de la p. en balayant!** you're making *or* raising a lot of dust with your broom!; **prendre la p.** *ou Belg* **les poussières** to collect dust; **les tapisseries prennent facilement la p.** the wall-hangings are dust traps; **recouvert de p.** dusty, covered with dust; **faire la p.** *ou Belg* **les poussières** to dust, to do the dusting; **essuie la p. sur les meubles/dans ta chambre** dust the furniture/your room; **mettre** *ou* **réduire qch en p.** to smash sth to smithereens; **tomber en p.** to crumble into dust; **les parchemins/os tombent en p.** the pieces of parchment/the bones are crumbling into dust **2** *(dans l'œil)* piece of grit **3** *(particules ▸ de roche, de charbon, d'or)* dust *(UNCOUNT)*; **p. cosmique/interstellaire** cosmic/interstellar dust; **poussières industrielles** industrial dust; **p. lunaire** lunar *or* moon dust; **p. radioactive** radioactive particles *or* dust

• poussières NFPL *Fam* **dix euros et des poussières** just over ten euros ❑; **ça fait trois kilos et des poussières** it's a little over three kilos ❑

poussiéreux, -euse [pusjerø, -øz] **ADJ 1** *(couvert de poussière)* dusty, dust-covered **2** *(dépassé ▸ législation, théorie)* outmoded, outdated

poussif, -ive [pusif, -iv] **ADJ 1** *(essoufflé ▸ cheval)* broken-winded; *(▸ vieillard)* short-winded, wheezy; *(▸ locomotive)* puffing, wheezing **2** *(laborieux ▸ prose)* dull, flat, laboured; *(▸ campagne électorale, émission)* sluggish, dull

poussin [pusɛ̃] **NM 1** *Orn* chick; *Culin* spring chicken, *Br* poussin **2** *Fam (terme d'affection)* **mon p.** my pet *or* darling; **pauvre petit p.!** poor little thing! **3** *Sport* junior *(9 years old)*

poussive [pusiv] *voir* **poussif**

poussivement [pusivmɑ̃] **ADV monter p.** to puff *or* to wheeze (one's way) up; **le train avançait p.** the train was wheezing *or* puffing along

poussoir [puswar] **NM 1** *(d'une montre)* button; *(d'une sonnerie électrique)* (push) button **2** *Tech* tappet

poutou [putu] **NM** *Fam (bise)* kiss ❑

poutrage [putraʒ] **NM** *Constr (de bois)* (framework of) beams; *(de fer, d'acier)* (framework of) girders

poutre [putr] **NF 1** *Constr (en bois)* beam; *(en fer)* girder; **p. armée/en treillis** lattice/trussed girder; **p. apparente** exposed beam; **p. de faîte** ridge beam **2** *Sport* beam

poutrelle [putrɛl] **NF** *Constr (en bois)* small beam; *(en acier)* girder

poutser [3] [putse] **VT** *Suisse Fam* to clean ❑

pouvoir¹ [puvwar] **NM 1** *(aptitude, possibilité)* power; **avoir un grand p. de concentration/de persuasion** to have great powers of concentration/persuasion; **avoir un grand p. d'adaptation** to be very adaptable; **je n'ai pas le p. de lire l'avenir!** I can't predict the future!; **il n'est plus en notre p. de décider de la question** we're no longer in a position to decide on this matter; **je ferai tout ce qui est en mon p. pour t'aider** I'll do everything *or* all in my power to help you; *Écon* **p. d'achat** purchasing power, buying power; *Fin* **p. libératoire** legal tender

2 *Admin & Jur (d'un président, d'un tuteur)* power; **le p. décisionnaire des actionnaires** the decision-making powers of shareholders; **avoir p. de décision** to have the authority to decide; **je n'ai pas p. de vous libérer** I have no authority *or* it is not in my power to release you; **je lui ai donné p. de décider à ma place par-devant notaire** I gave him/her power of attorney; **p. absolu** absolute power; **p. disciplinaire** disciplinary powers

3 *Pol* **le p.** *(exercice)* power; *(gouvernants)* government; **elle est trop proche du p. pour comprendre** she's too close to those in power to understand; **arriver au p.** to come to power; **être au p.** *(parti élu)* to be in power *or* office; *(junte)* to be in power; **les gens au p. ne connaissent pas nos problèmes** those in power *or* the powers that be don't understand our difficulties; **prendre le p.** *(élus)* to take office; *(dictateur)* to seize power; **exercer le p.** to exercise power, to govern, to rule; **le p. central** central government; **p. constituant** constituent power; **le p. exécutif** executive power, the executive; **le p. judiciaire** judicial power, the judiciary; **le p. législatif** legislative power, the legislature; **le p. local** local government, the local authorities

4 *(influence)* power, influence; **avoir du p. sur qn** to have power *or* influence over sb; **il a beaucoup de p. au sein du comité** he's very influential *or* he has a lot of influence within the committee; **avoir qn en son p.** to have sb in one's power; **la ville est tombée en leur p.** the town has fallen into their hands; **le p. de la télévision/des sens** the power of television/the senses

5 *Phys & Tech* power, quality; **p. absorbant** absorbency; **p. calorifique (inférieur/supérieur)** (net/gross) calorific value; **p. isolant** insulating capacity

• pouvoirs NMPL 1 *(fonctions)* powers, authority; **outrepasser ses pouvoirs** to overstep *or* to exceed one's authority; **avoir tous pouvoirs pour faire qch** *(administrateur)* to have full powers to do sth; *(architecte, animateur)* to have carte blanche to do sth; *Pol* **pouvoirs exceptionnels** special powers *(available to the President of the French Republic in an emergency)*; **pouvoirs partagés** shared powers **2** *(gouvernants)* **les pouvoirs constitués** the legally constituted government; **les pouvoirs publics** the authorities **3** *(surnaturels)* powers

POUVOIR² [58] [puvwar] **V AUX 1** *(avoir la possibilité, la capacité de)* **je peux revenir en France** I'm able to *or* I can return to France; **comme vous pouvez le voir sur ces images** as you can see in these pictures; **je peux vous aider?** *(gén, dans un magasin)* can I help you?; **on peut toujours s'arranger** some sort of an arrangement can always be worked out; **si seulement je pouvais me souvenir de son nom** if only I could remember his/her name; **pourriez-vous m'indiquer la gare?** could you tell me the way to the station?; **comment as-tu pu lui mentir!** how could you lie to him/her!; **je te l'apporte dès que je peux** I'll bring it to you as soon as I can *or* as soon as possible; **quand il pourra de nouveau marcher** when he's able to walk again; **c'est plus que je ne peux payer** it's more than I can afford (to pay); **je ne peux (pas) m'empêcher de penser que...** I can't help thinking that...; **ce modèle peut se ranger dans une valise** this model packs *or* can be packed into a suitcase; **je ne peux pas dormir** I'm unable to *or* I can't sleep; **tout le monde ne peut pas le faire!** not everybody can do it!; **le projet ne pourra pas se faire sans sa collaboration** the project can't be carried out without his/her collaboration; **il ne peut pas suivre d'études universitaires** *(il n'est pas assez brillant)* he's not up to going to university; **fais ce que tu veux, je ne peux pas mieux te dire!** do as you please, that's all I can say!; **tu ne peux pas ne pas l'aider** you MUST help him/her, you can't refuse to help him/her; *Fam* **il ne peut pas la voir (en peinture)** he can't stand (the sight of) her

2 *(parvenir à)* to manage *or* to be able to; **avez-vous pu entrer en contact avec lui?** did you manage to contact him?; **c'est construit de telle manière que l'on ne puisse pas s'échapper** it's built in such a way that it's impossible to escape *or* as to make escape impossible

3 *(avoir la permission de)* **vous pouvez disposer** you may *or* can go now; **si je peux** *ou* **si je puis m'exprimer ainsi** if I may use the phrase; **si on ne peut plus plaisanter, maintenant!** it's a pretty sad day if you can't have a laugh any more!

4 *(avoir des raisons de)* **on ne peut que s'en féliciter** one can't but feel happy about it; *Fam* **je suis désolé – ça, tu peux (l'être)!** I'm so sorry – so you should be *or* and with good reason *or* and I should think so too!

5 *(exprime une éventualité, un doute, un risque)* **la maladie peut revenir** the disease can *or* may recur; **attention, tu pourrais glisser** careful, you might *or* could slip; **ça peut exploser à tout moment** it could *or* may *or* might explode at any time; **il a pu les oublier dans le bus** he could *or* may have left them on the bus; **ce ne peut être déjà les invités!** (surely) it can't be the guests already!; **j'aurais pu l'attendre longtemps, elle n'arrive que demain!** I could have waited a long time, she's not coming until tomorrow!; **la gauche pourrait bien ne pas être élue** the left could well not get *or* be elected; **après tout, il pourrait bien ne pas avoir menti** he may well have been telling the truth after all; **d'aucuns pourront mettre sa sincérité en doute** some people might question his/her sincerity; **c'est plus facile qu'on ne pourrait le croire** it's easier than you might think; **elle a très bien pu arriver entre-temps** she may well have arrived in the meantime; **je peux toujours m'être trompé** it's possible I might have got it wrong; **ça aurait pu être pire** it could have been worse; **on a pu dire de lui qu'il était le précurseur du romantisme** some consider him to be the precursor of the Romantic movement; **il pourrait** *(tournure impersonnelle)* it could *or* may (possibly); **il pourrait s'agir d'un suicide** it could *or* may *or* might be suicide; **il peut arriver que...** it may (so) *or* can happen that...; **il ne peut pas y avoir d'erreur** there can't (possibly) be a mistake

6 *(exprime une approximation)* **elle pouvait avoir entre 50 et 60 ans** she could have been between 50 and 60 (years of age); **il pouvait être deux heures quand nous sommes sortis** it could *or* might have been two o'clock when we came out

7 *(exprime une suggestion, une hypothèse)* **tu peux toujours essayer de lui téléphoner** you could always try phoning him/her; **tu pourrais te lever pour donner ta place à la dame, quand même!** you might get up and let the lady have your seat!; **il aurait pu me prévenir!** he could've *or* might've warned me!; **on peut s'attendre à tout avec elle** anything's possible with her

8 *(en intensif)* **où ai-je bien pu laisser mes lunettes?** what on earth can I have done with my glasses?; **qu'a-t-elle (bien) pu leur dire pour les mettre dans cet état?** what can she possibly have said for them to be in such a state!

9 *Littéraire (exprime le souhait)* **puisse-t-il vous entendre!** let us hope he can hear you!; **puissé-je ne jamais revivre des moments pareils!** may I never have to live through that again!

VT *(être capable de faire)* **qu'y puis-je?** what can I do about it?; **tu y peux quelque chose, toi?** can YOU do anything about it?; **on n'y peut rien,** *Belg* **on n'en peux rien** it can't be helped, nothing can be done about it; **que puis-je pour vous?** what can I do for you?; **elle peut beaucoup pour notre cause** she can do a lot for our cause; **j'ai fait tout ce que j'ai pu** I did my all I could; *Fam Hum* **je fais ce que je peux et je peux peu** I do what I can, which isn't very much; **je n'en peux plus** *(physiquement)* I'm exhausted; *(moralement)* I can't take any more *or* stand it any longer; *(je suis rassasié)* I'm full (up); *Fam* **ma voiture n'en peut plus** my car's had it; **je n'en peux plus de l'entendre se plaindre sans**

cesse I just can't take his/her continual moaning any more; *Fam* **regarde-le danser avec elle, il n'en peut plus!** just look at him dancing with her, he's in seventh heaven!

V IMPERSONNEL se pouvoir ça se peut it may *or* could be; **ça se peut, mais...** that's as may be, but...; **il va pleuvoir – ça se pourrait bien!** it's going to rain – that's quite possible!; **est-ce qu'ils vont se marier? – cela se pourrait** are they going to get married? – they might *or* it's possible; **sois calme, et s'il se peut, diplomate** keep calm and, if (at all) possible, be tactful; **il** *ou* **ça se peut qu'il soit malade** he might be ill, maybe he's ill; **il se peut que je vienne** I might come, maybe I'll come; **il se pourrait bien qu'il n'y ait plus de places** it might *or* could well be fully booked

---

pp 1 *(abrév écrite* **pages)** pp **2** *(abrév écrite* **par procuration)** pp

PPCM [pepeseem] **NM** *Math (abrév* **plus petit commun multiple)** LCM

ppm [pepeem] **NFPL 1** *Chim (abrév* **parties par million)** ppm **2** *Ordinat (abrév écrite* **pages per minute)** ppm

PPP [pepepe] **NM** *(abrév* **partenariat public-privé)** PPP

ppp *(abrév écrite* **points par pouce)** dpi

PQ[1] [peky] **NM** *très Fam (abrév* **papier-cul)** *Br* bog roll, *Am* TP

PQ[2] *(abrév écrite* **province de Québec)** PQ

PR[1] [peɛr] **NM** *(abrév* **parti républicain)** = right-wing French political party

PR[2] *(abrév écrite* **poste restante)** PR

pragmatique [pragmatik] **ADJ** *(politique)* pragmatic; *(personne, attitude)* pragmatic, practical

NF pragmatics *(singulier)*

pragmatisme [pragmatism] **NM** pragmatism

pragmatiste [pragmatist] **ADJ** pragmatist

NMF pragmatist

pragois, -e [pragwa, -az] = **praguois**

Prague [prag] **NM** Prague

praguois, -e [pragwa, -az] **ADJ** of/from Prague

• **Praguois, -e NM,F** = inhabitant of or person from Prague

praire [prɛr] **NF** clam

prairial, -als [prɛrjal] **NM** *Hist* = 9th month of the French Republican Calendar (from 20 May to 18 June)

prairie [prɛri] **NF 1** *(terrain)* meadow **2** *(formation végétale)* grassland; **p. artificielle** cultivated grassland **3 la P.** *(aux États-Unis)* the Prairie; **les Prairies** *(au Canada)* the Prairies

pralin [pralɛ̃] **NM** *Culin* praline *(toasted nuts in caramelized sugar)*

praline [pralin] **NF 1** *Culin (amande)* praline; *Belg (chocolat)* (filled) chocolate **2** *Fam (balle d'arme à feu)* slug **3** *Fam (coup)* belt, wallop

praliné, -e [praline] **ADJ** *(glace, entremets)* praline-flavoured; *(amande)* browned in sugar; *(chocolat)* with a praline centre

NM chocolate with a praline centre

praticable [pratikabl] **ADJ 1** *(sentier)* passable, practicable **2** *(réalisable* ▸ *suggestion, solution)* practicable, feasible **3** *(porte, fenêtre)* practicable

NM 1 *Cin & TV* dolly **2** *Théât* platform **3** *Sport* (floor) mat

praticien, -enne [pratisjɛ̃, -ɛn] **NM,F 1** *(médecin, dentiste etc)* practitioner **2** *(technicien)* practitioner **3** *Beaux-Arts* sculptor's assistant

praticité [pratisite] **NF** *(commodité)* convenience; *(utilité)* usefulness

pratiquant, -e [pratikɑ̃, -ɑ̃t] **ADJ** practising; **catholique p.** practising Catholic; **je ne suis pas p.** *(gén)* I'm not religious *or* a believer, I don't practise (my religion); *(chrétien)* I don't attend church regularly, I'm not a (regular) churchgoer; **non p.** nonpractising

NM,F 1 *Rel (catholique)* practising Catholic; *(protestant)* practising Protestant; *(juif)* practising Jew; *(musulman)* practising Muslim **2** *(adepte)* adherent

pratique[1] [pratik] **ADJ 1** *(utile* ▸ *gadget, outil, voiture, dictionnaire)* practical, handy; *(*▸ *vêtement)* practical; **peu p.** not very practical; **quand on a des invités, c'est bien p. un lave-vaisselle!** when you've got guests, a dishwasher comes in handy!; **c'est très p. d'avoir l'école si près de la maison** it's very practical *or* handy to have the school so close to the house

2 *(facile* ▸ *horaires)* convenient; **il faut changer de bus trois fois, ce n'est pas p.!** you have to change buses three times, it's very inconvenient!; **cette crème n'est pas p. à appliquer** this cream isn't easy to apply

3 *(concret* ▸ *application, connaissance, conseil, formation, détail)* practical

4 *(pragmatique)* practical; **avoir le sens** *ou* **l'esprit p.** to have a practical turn of mind, to be practical

pratique[2] [pratik] **NF 1** *(application* ▸ *d'une philosophie, d'une politique)* practice; *(*▸ *de l'autocritique, d'une vertu)* exercise; *(*▸ *d'une technique, de la censure)* application; **mettre en p.** *(conseils, préceptes)* to put into practice; *(vertu)* to exercise; **en** *ou* **dans la p.** in (actual) practice

2 *(d'une activité)* practice; **la p. régulière du tennis/vélo** playing tennis/cycling on a regular basis; **la p. d'un sport est encouragée** sporting activity *or* practising a sport is encouraged; **p. illégale de la médecine** illegal practice of medicine; **la p. religieuse** religious observance

3 *Can (entraînement)* training session; **une p. de hockey** a hockey training session

4 *(expérience)* practical experience; **on voit que tu as de la p.** you've obviously done this before; **j'ai plusieurs années de p.** I have several years' practical experience

5 *(usage)* practice; **des pratiques religieuses** religious practices; **pratiques déloyales** unfair (business) dealings; **pratiques restrictives** restrictive practices; **une p. courante** common practice; **le marchandage est une p. courante là-bas** over there, it's common practice to barter

6 *Jur* **terme de p.** legal term

7 *Naut* **avoir libre p.** to be out of quarantine

pratiquement [pratikmɑ̃] **ADV 1** *(presque)* practically, virtually; **il n'y avait p. personne** there was hardly anybody *or* practically nobody **2** *(concrètement)* in practice; *(en fait)* in practice *or* (actual) fact

pratiquer [3] [pratike] **VT 1** *(faire* ▸ *entaille, incision, ouverture)* to make; *(*▸ *passage)* to open up; *(*▸ *intervention chirurgicale, tests)* to carry out, to perform; **des marches avaient été pratiquées dans la roche** steps had been carved out in the rock; **p. un trou** *(à la vrille)* to bore *or* to drill a hole; *(aux ciseaux)* to cut (out) a hole

2 *(appliquer* ▸ *préceptes, politique)* to practise; *(*▸ *autocritique, vertu)* to practise, to exercise; *(*▸ *technique)* to use, to apply; *(*▸ *censure)* to apply; *(*▸ *sélection)* to make; **je ne pratiquerai jamais ce genre de chantage** I will never resort to *or* use this kind of blackmail; **la vivisection est encore pratiquée dans certains laboratoires** vivisection is still carried out *or* practised in some laboratories

3 *(s'adonner à* ▸ *jeu de ballon)* to play; *(*▸ *art martial, athlétisme)* to do; *(*▸ *art, médecine, religion, charité)* to practise; *(*▸ *langue)* to speak; *(*▸ *humour, ironie)* to use; **p. un sport** to take part in a sporting activity; **est-ce que vous pratiquez un sport?** do you do anything in the way of sport?; **p. la natation** to swim; **p. la boxe** to box

4 *(fréquenter)* **p. un auteur** to read an author's works regularly; *Hum* **ça fait des années que je pratique l'animal** I've known this guy for years

5 *Com (rabais)* to make, to give; **ce sont les prix pratiqués dans tous nos supermarchés** these are the current prices in all our supermarkets

USAGE ABSOLU il a appris le piano mais ne pratique plus beaucoup he learnt the piano but doesn't play it much any more

VI 1 *Rel* to practise (one's religion); **il est catholique, mais il ne pratique pas** he is not a practising Catholic **2** *(travailler* ▸ *médecin, avocat)* to practise

VPR se pratiquer cette coutume se pratique encore dans certains pays this custom still exists in certain countries; **le commerce de l'ivoire se pratique encore** ivory trading still goes on *or* is still practised; **les prix qui se pratiquent à Paris** current Paris prices; **cela se pratique couramment dans leur pays** it is common practice in their country

praxis [praksis] **NF** *Phil* praxis

pré [pre] **NM 1** *Agr* meadow **2** *(locution) Littéraire* **aller sur le p.** to fight a duel

pré-acheminement [preaʃminmɑ̃] *(pl* **pré-acheminements)** **NM** transfer to main airport

préadhésion [preadezjɔ̃] **NF** *UE* pre-accession

préadolescence [preadɔlesɑ̃s] **NF** preteen years

préadolescent, -e [preadɔlesɑ̃, -ɑ̃t] **NM,F** preteen

préalable [prealabl] **ADJ** *(discussion, entrevue, sélection)* preliminary (**à** to); *(travail, formation)* preparatory (**à** to); *(accord, avertissement)* prior (**à** to); **faites un essai p. sur un bout de tissu** test first *or* beforehand on a piece of cloth; **...mais il y a quelques formalités préalables** ...but there are a few formalities to be gone through first; **sans avertissement p.** without prior notice

NM prerequisite, precondition

• **au préalable ADV** first, beforehand

préalablement [prealabləmɑ̃] **ADV** first, beforehand; **appliquer sur la plaie p. nettoyée** apply after cleansing the wound

• **préalablement à PRÉP** prior to, before

préallumage [prealymaʒ] **NM** *Aut* pre-ignition

Préalpes [prealp] **NFPL les P.** the Pre-Alps, the Lower Alps

préalpin, -e [prealpɛ̃, -in] **ADJ** of the Pre-Alps

préambule [preɑ̃byl] **NM 1** *(d'une constitution, d'une conférence)* preamble; **épargnez-nous les préambules!** spare us the preliminaries!, get to the point! **2** *(prémices)* prelude (**de** to); **cet incident a été le p. d'une crise grave** this incident was the prelude to a serious crisis

• **sans préambule ADV** without preliminaries, straight off

préamplificateur [preɑ̃plifikatœr] **NM** preamplifier

PréAO [preao] **NF** *Ordinat (abrév* **présentation assistée par ordinateur)** computer-assisted presentation

préapprentissage [preaprɑ̃tisaʒ] **NM** pre-apprenticeship training

préau, -x [preo] **NM** *(d'une école)* covered part of the playground; *(d'un pénitencier)* yard; *(d'un cloître)* inner courtyard

préavis [preavi] **NM** (advance) notice; **mon propriétaire m'a donné un mois de p.** my landlord gave me a month's notice (to move out); **p. de grève** strike notice, notice of strike action; **déposer un p. de grève** to give notice of strike action; **p. (de licenciement)** notice (of dismissal); *Banque* **dépôt à sept jours de p.** deposit at seven days' notice

• **sans préavis ADV** *Admin* without prior notice *or* notification

prébende [prebɑ̃d] **NF 1** *Rel* prebend **2** *Littéraire (emploi)* sinecure; *(argent)* handsome payment

prébendé [prebɑ̃de] *Rel* **ADJ M** prebendal

NM prebendary, prebend

prébendier [prebɑ̃dje] **NM** *Rel* prebendary, prebend

précaire [prekɛr] **ADJ** *(équilibre)* fragile, precarious; *(vie, situation)* precarious; *(santé)* delicate, frail; *(abri)* precarious, rickety; **il a un emploi p.** he's got no job security

• **précaires NMPL les précaires** people living on the poverty line

précairement [prekɛrmɑ̃] **ADV** precariously

précambrien, -enne [prekɑ̃brijɛ̃, -ɛn] *Géol*

ADJ Precambrian

NM Precambrian (era)

précarisation [prekarizasjɔ̃] **NF on assiste à une p. croissante de l'emploi** we are seeing job security increasingly threatened

précariser [3] [prekarize] **VT p. l'emploi** to threaten job security; **la crise a précarisé leur situation** the recession has made them more vulnerable

précarité [prekarite] **NF** precariousness; **la p. de l'emploi** the lack of job security

précaution [prekosjɔ̃] **NF 1** *(disposition préventive)* precaution; **prendre la p. de faire qch** to take the precaution of doing *or* to be especially careful to do sth; *aussi Euph* **prendre des** *ou* **ses précautions** to take precautions; **prenez des**

précautions avant de vous engager dans cette affaire take all necessary precautions before getting involved; **avec beaucoup de précautions oratoires** in carefully chosen phrases; **précautions d'emploi** caution (before use) **2** *(prudence)* caution, care

• **avec précaution** ADV cautiously, warily

• **par (mesure de) précaution** ADV as a precaution *or* precautionary measure

• **pour plus de précaution** ADV to be on the safe side, to make absolutely certain

• **sans précaution** ADV carelessly, rashly; **elle manipule les produits toxiques sans la moindre p.** she handles toxic substances without taking the slightest precaution

précautionner [3] [prekosjɔne] **se précautionner** VPR *Littéraire* **se p. contre qch** to guard against sth

précautionneuse [prekosjɔnøz] *voir* **précautionneux**

précautionneusement [prekosjɔnøzmɑ̃] ADV **1** *(avec circonspection)* cautiously, warily **2** *(avec soin)* carefully, with care

précautionneux, -euse [prekosjɔnø, -øz] ADJ **1** *(circonspect)* cautious, wary **2** *(soigneux)* careful

précédemment [presedamɑ̃] ADV before (that), previously; **comme je l'ai dit p.** as I have said *or* mentioned before

précédent, -e [presedɑ̃, -ɑ̃t] ADJ previous; **la semaine précédente** the week before, the previous week

NM precedent; **créer un p.** to create *or* set a precedent

• **sans précédent** ADJ without precedent, unprecedented

précéder [18] [presede] VT **1** *(être devant)* to precede; **je vais vous p. dans le tunnel** I'll go into the tunnel first; **le groupe, précédé par le guide** the group, led *or* preceded by the guide; **l'antichambre qui précède le salon** the antechamber leading to the drawing room

2 *(être placé avant)* to precede, to be in front of; **l'adresse doit p. le numéro de téléphone** the address should come before the telephone number; **faire p. son nom de ses initiales** to write one's initials in front of one's name

3 *(avoir lieu avant)* to precede; **le film sera précédé par un** *ou* **d'un documentaire** the film will be preceded by *or* will follow a documentary; **le jour qui précéda son arrestation** the day before *or* prior to his/her arrest; **celui qui vous a précédé à ce poste** the person who held the post before you, your predecessor

4 *(arriver en avance sur)* to precede, to arrive ahead of *or* before; **elle m'a précédé sur le court de quelques minutes** she got to the court a few minutes before me; **il précède le favori de trois secondes** he has a three-second lead over the favourite; **il avait été précédé de sa mauvaise réputation** his bad reputation had preceded him

VI to precede; **as-tu lu ce qui précède?** have you read what comes before?; **les semaines qui précédèrent** the preceding weeks; **faites p. votre signature de la mention "lu et approuvé"** before your signature add the words "lu et approuvé"

précepte [presɛpt] NM precept

précepteur [presɛptœr] NM private *or* home tutor

préceptorat [presɛptɔra] NM private *or* home tutorship

précession [presesjɔ̃] NF precession

préchambre [preʃɑ̃br] NF precombustion chamber

précharge [preʃarʒ] NF *Aut* pre-load

préchargé, -e [preʃarʒe] ADJ *(logiciel)* preloaded

préchauffage [preʃofaʒ] NM *(d'un four)* preheating; *(d'un moteur)* warm-up

préchauffer [3] [preʃofe] VT *(four)* to preheat; *(moteur)* to warm up

prêche [prɛʃ] NM sermon

prêcher [4] [preʃe] VT **1** *Rel (Évangile, religion)* to preach; *(carême, retraite)* to preach for; *(personne)* to preach to; **vous prêchez un converti** you're preaching to the *Br* converted *or Am* choir; *Hum* **p. la bonne parole** to spread the good word **2** *(recommander ▸ doctrine, bonté, vengeance)* to preach; **p. le faux pour savoir le vrai** to make false statements in order to discover the truth

VI *(prêtre, moralisateur)* to preach; **p. d'exemple** *ou* **par l'exemple** to practise what one preaches; **p. dans le désert** to preach in the wilderness; **p. pour son saint** *ou* **son clocher** *ou* **sa paroisse** to look after one's own interests

prêcheur, -euse [prɛʃœr, -øz] ADJ **1** *Fam Péj (sermonneur)* moralizing[□], preachy **2** *Rel* **frères prêcheurs** preaching friars

NM,F **1** *Fam Péj (sermonneur)* moralizer[□] **2** *Rel* preacher

prêchi-prêcha [preʃipreʃa] NM INV *Fam Péj* sermonizing[□], lecturing[□]

précieuse [presjøz] *voir* **précieux**

précieusement [presjøzmɑ̃] ADV **1** *(soigneusement)* preciously; **conserver qch p.** to look after sth very carefully, to take great care of sth **2** *(avec affectation)* **c'est écrit un peu p.** the style is a little bit precious

précieux, -euse [presjø, -øz] ADJ **1** *(de valeur ▸ temps, santé)* precious; *(▸ pierre, métal)* precious; *(▸ ami, amitié)* precious, valued; *(▸ objet, trésor, bijou)* precious, priceless **2** *(très utile)* invaluable; **c'était un p. conseiller** he was an invaluable *or* irreplaceable adviser; **elle m'a été d'un p. secours** her help was invaluable to me **3** *(maniéré)* mannered, affected, precious

• **précieuse** NF *Hist* précieuse *(member of an aristocratic movement of ladies in 17th-century France who espoused refinement in language and social behaviour and held literary salons)*

• **précieuses** NFPL *très Fam Hum (testicules)* balls, nuts

préciosité [presjozite] NF *(maniérisme)* affectedness, mannered style

précipice [presipis] NM **1** *(gouffre)* precipice **2** *(catastrophe)* **être au bord du p.** to be on the brink of disaster

précipitamment [presipitamɑ̃] ADV *(annuler, changer)* hastily, hurriedly; **monter/traverser p.** to dash up/across; **agir trop p.** to be too hasty *or* overhasty, to act too hastily

précipitation [presipitasjɔ̃] NF **1** *(hâte)* haste; **les ouvriers ont quitté l'usine avec p.** the workers rushed *or* hurried out of the factory; **dans ma p., j'ai oublié l'adresse** in the rush, I forgot the address **2** *(irréflexion)* rashness; **agir avec p.** to act rashly **3** *Chim* precipitation

• **précipitations** NFPL *Météo* precipitation; **fortes précipitations sur l'ouest du pays demain** tomorrow, it will rain heavily in the west

précipité, -e [presipite] ADJ **1** *(pressé ▸ pas)* hurried; *(▸ fuite)* headlong **2** *(rapide ▸ respiration)* rapid; **tout cela a été si p.** it all happened so fast **3** *(hâtif ▸ retour)* hurried, hasty; *(▸ décision)* hasty, rash

NM *Chim* precipitate

précipiter [3] [presipite] VT **1** *(faire tomber)* to throw *or* to hurl (down); **ils ont précipité leur voiture dans la mer** they pushed their car into the sea; **le choc précipita les passagers vers l'avant** the shock sent the passengers flying *or* hurtling to the front

2 *Fig (plonger)* to plunge; **p. qn dans le désespoir/le malheur** to plunge sb into despair/misfortune; **p. un pays dans la guerre/crise** to plunge a country into war/a crisis

3 *(faire à la hâte)* **il ne faut rien p.** we mustn't rush (into) things *or* be hasty; **nous avons dû p. notre départ/mariage** we had to leave/get married sooner than planned

4 *(accélérer ▸ pas, cadence)* to quicken, to speed up; *(▸ mouvement, mort)* to hasten

5 *Chim* to precipitate (out)

VI *Chim* to precipitate (out)

VPR **se précipiter 1** *(d'en haut)* to hurl oneself; **il s'est précipité du septième étage** he threw *or* hurled himself from the seventh floor

2 *(se ruer)* to rush (**sur** at); **on s'est tous précipités dehors** we all rushed out; **il s'est précipité dans l'ascenseur** he rushed into the *Br* lift *or Am* elevator; **se p. vers** *ou* **au-devant de qn** to rush to meet sb; **dès qu'il rentre à la maison, il se précipite devant la télévision** as soon as he gets home he throws himself down in front of the television

3 *(s'accélérer ▸ pouls, cadence)* to speed up, to quicken; **depuis peu, les événements se précipitent** things have been moving really fast recently

4 *(se dépêcher)* to rush, to hurry; **on a tout notre temps, pourquoi se p.?** we've got plenty of time, what's the rush?; **ne te précipite pas pour répondre** take your time before answering

précis, -e [presi, -iz] ADJ **1** *(exact ▸ horloge, tir, instrument)* precise, exact; *(▸ description)* precise, accurate; **les dimensions précises de la maison** the exact measurements of the house; **pour être plus p.** to be more precise; **à 20 heures précises** at precisely 8 p.m., at 8 p.m. sharp; **à cet instant p.** at that precise *or* very moment; **il arriva à l'instant p. où je partais** he arrived just as I was leaving **2** *(clair, net)* precise, specific; **instructions précises** precise orders; **je voudrais une réponse précise** I'd like a clear answer; **je n'ai aucun souvenir p. de cette année-là** I don't remember that year clearly at all; **il est très p. dans son travail** he's very meticulous *or* precise *or* exact in his work **3** *(particulier)* particular, specific; **sans raison précise** for no particular reason; **sans but p.** with no specific aim in mind; **rien de p.** nothing in particular; **tu penses à quelqu'un de p.?** do you have a specific person in mind?

NM **1** *(manuel)* handbook; **un p. d'histoire de France** a short history of France **2** *(résumé)* précis, summary

précisément [presizemɑ̃] ADV **1** *(exactement)* precisely; **il nous reste très p. 4,55 euros** we've got precisely *or* exactly 4.55 euros left; **ce n'est pas p. ce à quoi je pensais** that's not exactly what I had in mind; *Euph* **pas p.** not exactly; **ce n'est pas p. une réussite** it's not exactly a success, it's not (exactly) what you'd call a success; **ou plus p....** or more precisely..., or to be more precise... **2** *(justement, par coïncidence)* precisely, exactly; **c'est p. le problème** that's exactly *or* precisely what the problem is; **M. Lebrun? c'est p. de lui que nous parlions** Mr Lebrun? that's precisely who we were talking about **3** *(oui)* that's right

préciser [3] [presize] VT **1** *(clarifier ▸ intentions, pensée)* to make clear; **cette fois-ci, je me suis bien fait p. les conditions d'admission** this time I made sure they explained the conditions of entry clearly to me **2** *(spécifier)* **l'invitation ne précise pas si l'on peut venir accompagné** the invitation doesn't specify *or* say whether you can bring somebody with you; **p. qch à qn** to make sth clear to sb; **j'ai oublié de leur p. le lieu du rendez-vous** I forgot to tell them where the meeting is taking place; **la Maison-Blanche précise que la rencontre n'est pas officielle** the White House has made it clear that this is not an official meeting; **"cela s'est fait sans mon accord", précisa-t-il** "this was done without my agreement," he pointed out

USAGE ABSOLU **vous dites avoir vu quelqu'un, pourriez-vous p.?** you said you saw somebody, could you be more specific?

VPR **se préciser** *(idée, projet)* to take shape; *(situation, menace)* to become clearer; **les vacances se précisent** the holiday plans are taking shape

précision [presizjɔ̃] NF **1** *(exactitude ▸ d'une information, d'une description)* accuracy; *(▸ de mouvements)* preciseness, precision; **avec p.** accurately, precisely **2** *(netteté)* precision, distinctness **3** *(explication)* **apporter une p. à qch** to clarify sth; **demander des précisions sur qch** to ask for more *or* further information *or* details about sth; **je vous remercie de vos précisions** thank you for your informative comments; **raconter qch avec maintes précisions** to recount sth in great detail

• **de précision** ADJ precision *(avant n)*; **instrument de p.** precision instrument

précité, -e [presite] ADJ *(oralement)* aforesaid, aforementioned; *(par écrit)* above-mentioned, aforesaid; **les auteurs précités** the authors quoted above

préclassique [preklasik] ADJ preclassical

précoce [prekɔs] ADJ **1** *(prématuré ▸ surdité, mariage)* premature **2** *(en avance ▸ intellectuellement)* precocious, mature (beyond one's years); *(▸ sexuellement)* precocious; **j'étais un**

garçon p. pour mon âge I was advanced for a boy of my age **3** *Bot & Météo* early; **les gelées précoces** early frost; **poire p.** early *or* early-fruiting pear

précocement [prekɔsmɑ̃] **ADV** prematurely, precociously

précocité [prekɔsite] **NF 1** *(d'un enfant)* precociousness, precocity; *(d'une faculté, d'un talent)* early manifestation, precociousness; **p. sexuelle** sexual precociousness **2** *Bot & Météo* early arrival, earliness

précolombien, -enne [prekɔlɔ̃bjɛ̃, -ɛn] **ADJ** pre-Columbian

précombustion [prekɔ̃bystjɔ̃] **NF** precombustion

pré-commercialisation [prekɔmɛrsjalizasjɔ̃] **NF** *Mktg* pre-marketing

précompte [prekɔ̃t] **NM 1** *(retenue) Br* tax deduction (from one's salary), *Am* withholding tax **2** *(estimation)* (deduction) schedule

précompter [3] [prekɔ̃te] **VT 1** *(déduire)* to deduct; *(cotisations, impôts)* to deduct at source; **vos cotisations sont précomptées sur votre salaire** your contribution is deducted automatically from your salary **2** *(estimer)* to schedule, to estimate

préconception [prekɔ̃sepsjɔ̃] **NF** preconception, prejudice

préconçu, -e [prekɔ̃sy] **ADJ** set, preconceived; **idée préconçue** preconceived idea

préconditionné, -e [prekɔ̃disjɔne] **ADJ** prepacked, pre-packaged

préconditionner [3] [prekɔ̃disjɔne] **VT** to prepack, to pre-package

préconfiguré, -e [prekɔ̃figyre] **ADJ** *Ordinat* preconfigured

préconisation [prekɔnizasjɔ̃] **NF** *(d'un remède)* recommendation; *(d'une solution, d'une méthode)* advocacy

préconiser [3] [prekɔnize] **VT** *(recommander ▸ remède)* to recommend; *(▸ solution, méthode)* to advocate

précontraint, -e [prekɔ̃trɛ̃, -ɛ̃t] *Tech* **ADJ** prestressed

NM prestressed concrete

précuit, -e [prekɥi, -it] **ADJ** precooked, ready-cooked

précurseur [prekyrsœr] **ADJ M** warning *(avant n)*; **signe p.** forewarning, portent

NM forerunner, precursor; **faire figure** *ou* **œuvre de p.** to break new ground

prédateur, -trice [predatœr, -tris] *Bot & Zool* **ADJ** predatory

NM predator

prédécesseur [predesesœr] **NM** predecessor

• **prédécesseurs NMPL** *(ancêtres)* forebears

prédécoupé, -e [predekupe] **ADJ** precut, ready-cut

pré-définition [predefinisjɔ̃] **NF** *Ordinat* **p. des secteurs** hard sectoring

prédélinquant, -e [predelɛ̃kɑ̃, -ɑ̃t] **NM,F** predelinquent

prédestination [predɛstinasjɔ̃] **NF** predestination

prédestiné, -e [predɛstine] **ADJ** *(voué à tel sort)* predestined, fated; **être p. à faire qch** to be predestined *or* fated to do sth; **un nom p.** an appropriate name

NM,F *Rel* chosen *or* predestined one

prédestiner [3] [predɛstine] **VT** *(vouer)* to prepare, to predestine; **rien ne me prédestinait à devenir acteur** nothing marked me out to become an actor *or* for an acting career

prédétermination [predetɛrminasjɔ̃] **NF** predetermination

prédéterminer [3] [predetɛrmine] **VT** to predetermine

prédicant [predikɑ̃] **NM** *Rel* preacher

prédicat [predika] **NM** *Ling (verbe)* predicator; *(adjectif)* predicate

prédicateur, -trice [predikatœr, -tris] **NM,F** preacher

prédicatif, -ive [predikatif, -iv] **ADJ 1** *Ling & (en logique)* predicative **2** *Rel* predicatory, predicant

prédication [predikasjɔ̃] **NF 1** *Ling & (en logique)* predication **2** *Rel* **la p.** *(action)* preaching; *(prêche)* sermon

prédicative [predikativ] *voir* **prédicatif**

prédicatrice [predikatris] *voir* **prédicateur**

prédictif, -ive [prediktif, -iv] **ADJ** predictive; *Tél* **écriture prédictive** predictive texting, predictive text input

prédiction [prediksjɔ̃] **NF** *(prophétie)* prediction

prédictive [prediktiv] *voir* **prédictif**

prédigéré, -e [prediʒere] **ADJ** predigested

prédilection [predilɛksjɔ̃] **NF** predilection, partiality; **avoir une p. pour qch** to be partial to sth, to have a predilection for sth

• **de prédilection ADJ** favourite

prédire [103] [predir] **VT** to predict, to foretell; **ils avaient prédit la guerre** they'd predicted the war *or* that there would be a war; **p. l'avenir** *(par hasard ou estimation)* to predict the future; *(voyant)* to tell fortunes; **elle m'a prédit un grand avenir/ que je voyagerais** she predicted a great future ahead of me/that I would travel; **je lui prédis des jours difficiles** I can see difficult times ahead for him/her

prédisposer [3] [predispoze] **VT 1** *(préparer)* to predispose; **sa taille la prédisposait à devenir mannequin** her height made modelling an obvious choice for her **2** *(incliner)* **être prédisposé en faveur de qn** to be favourably disposed to sb

USAGE ABSOLU cette époque-là ne prédisposait pas à la frivolité that period was not conducive to frivolity

prédisposition [predispozisjɔ̃] **NF 1** *(tendance)* predisposition (**à** to) **2** *(talent)* gift, talent

prédit, -e [predi, -it] **PP** *voir* **prédire**

prédominance [predɔminɑ̃s] **NF** predominance

prédominant, -e [predɔminɑ̃, -ɑ̃t] **ADJ** *(principal ▸ couleur, trait)* predominant, main; *(▸ opinion, tendance)* prevailing; *(▸ souci)* chief, major

prédominer [3] [predɔmine] **VI** *(couleur, trait)* to predominate; *(sentiment, tendance)* to prevail; **le soleil va p. sur presque tout le pays** the weather will be sunny in most parts of the country; **c'est ce qui prédomine dans tous ses romans** that's the predominant feature of all his/her novels

prééclampsie [preeklɑ̃psi] **NF** *Méd* preeclampsia

préélectoral, -e, -aux, -ales [preelɛktɔral, -o] **ADJ** pre-electoral

préemballé, -e [preɑ̃bale] **ADJ** pre-packed, pre-packaged

préemballer [3] [preɑ̃bale] **VT** to pre-pack, to pre-package

pré-embarquement [preɑ̃barkəmɑ̃] **NM** *(à un aéroport)* pre-boarding

pré-embarquer [3] [preɑ̃barke] **VI** *(à un aéroport)* to pre-board

préembryon [preɑ̃brijɔ̃] **NM** *Biol & Méd* preembryo

prééminence [preeminɑ̃s] **NF** pre-eminence, dominance; **donner la p. à qch** to put sth first

prééminent, -e [preeminɑ̃, -ɑ̃t] **ADJ** preeminent; **occuper un rang p.** to hold a prominent position

préempter [3] [preɑ̃pte] **VT** *Jur* to pre-empt

préemption [preɑ̃psjɔ̃] **NF** *Jur* pre-emption

préencollé, -e [preɑ̃kɔle] **ADJ** prepasted

préenregistré, -e [preɑ̃rəʒistre] **ADJ** prerecorded

préenregistrement [preɑ̃rəʒistrəmɑ̃] **NM** prerecording

préétablir [32] [preetablir] **VT** to pre-establish, to establish in advance

préexistant, -e [preɛgzistɑ̃, -ɑ̃t] **ADJ** existing

préexistence [preɛgzistɑ̃s] **NF** preexistence

préexister [3] [preɛgziste] **préexister à VT IND** *(gén)* to exist before; *(loi)* to predate

préfabrication [prefabrikasjɔ̃] **NF** prefabrication

préfabriqué, -e [prefabrike] **ADJ** prefabricated; *Fig* **un sourire p.** an artificial smile

NM 1 *(construction)* prefab **2** *(matériau)* prefabricated material; **en p.** prefabricated

préface [prefas] **NF** preface (**de** to)

préfacer [16] [prefase] **VT** to write a preface to, to preface

préfacier [prefasje] **NM** prefacer, preface writer

préfacturation [prefaktyrasjɔ̃] **NF** *Compta* prebilling

préfectoral, -e, -aux, -ales [prefɛktɔral, -o] **ADJ** *(du préfet)* prefectorial, prefectural; **par arrêté p., par mesure préfectorale** by order

préfecture [prefɛktyr] **NF** *Admin (chef-lieu)* prefecture; *(édifice)* prefecture building; *(services)* prefectural office; *(emploi)* post of prefect; **p. maritime** port prefecture; **p. de police** (Paris) police headquarters

> **PRÉFECTURE**
>
> This refers to the main administrative office of each "département". The word has also come to refer to the town where the office is located. One goes to the "préfecture" to obtain a driving licence or a "carte de séjour", for example.

préférable [preferabl] **ADJ** preferable; **cette solution est nettement p.** that solution is preferable *or* to be preferred; **ne va pas trop loin, c'est p.** it'd be better if you didn't go too far away; **il serait p. de le revoir** *ou* **qu'on le revoie** it would be preferable *or* better to see him again; **p. à** preferable to, better than; **tout est p. à cette vie de reclus** anything is better than this hermit's life

préférablement [preferabləmɑ̃] **ADV** *Littéraire* **p. à** *(de préférence à)* in preference to

préféré, -e [prefere] **ADJ** favourite

NM,F favourite

préférence [preferɑ̃s] **NF 1** *(prédilection)* preference; **par ordre de p.** in order of preference; **donner** *ou* **accorder la p. à** to give preference to; **avoir une p. pour** to have a preference for; **ma p. va aux tissus unis** I prefer *or* have a preference for plain fabrics; **ça m'est égal, je n'ai pas de p.** it doesn't matter to me *or* I don't mind, I've no particular preference; **avoir la p. sur qn** to have preference over sb; **sur 200 candidates, c'est elle qui a eu la p.** she was chosen out of 200 candidates; *Mktg* **p. du consommateur** consumer preference **2** *Jur* **droit de p.** right to preferential treatment **3** *Pol* **la p. nationale** = policy of discrimination in favour of a country's own nationals as opposed to immigrants

• **de préférence ADV** preferably; **donne-moi un verre de vin, et du bon de p.** give me a glass of wine, preferably a good one; **à consommer de p. avant fin 2008** *(sur emballage)* best before end 2008

• **de préférence à PRÉP** in preference to, rather than

préférentiel, -elle [preferɑ̃sjel] **ADJ** *(traitement, tarif, vote)* preferential

préférer [18] [prefere] **VT** to prefer; **ils préfèrent les échecs aux cartes** they prefer chess to playing cards; **je préférerais du thé** I'd prefer tea, I'd rather have tea; **je me préfère avec un chignon** I think I look better with my hair up; **il préférait mourir plutôt que (de) partir** he would rather die than leave; **il y a des moments où l'on préfère rester seul** there are times when one would rather be alone; **je préfère que tu n'en dises rien à personne** I'd prefer it if *or* I'd rather you didn't tell anybody

USAGE ABSOLU si tu préfères, nous allons rentrer if you'd prefer, we'll go home

préfet [prefe] **NM 1** *Admin* prefect; **le p. de Paris** the prefect of Paris; **p. de police** *(en France)* prefect *or* chief of police; *(en Grande-Bretagne)* ≃ chief constable, ≃ head of the constabulary; **p. de région** regional prefect **2** *Naut* **p. maritime** = port admiral overseeing the defence of certain maritime departments **3** *Belg Scol Br* head teacher, *Am* principal *(of a secondary school)*

> **PRÉFET**
>
> In France a "préfet" is a high-ranking official, one of a body of civil servants created by Napoleon in 1800. The "préfet" is the general administrator of the "département", the chief executive officer and the executive chief of police.

préfète [prefɛt] **NF 1** *(épouse)* prefect's wife **2** *(titulaire)* (woman) prefect **3** *Belg Scol Br* headmistress, *Am* principal *(of a secondary school)*

préfiguration [prefigyrasjɔ̃] **NF** prefiguration, foreshadowing

préfigurer [3] [prefigyre] **VT** *(annoncer)* to prefigure

préfinancement [prefinɑ̃smɑ̃] **NM** advance funding, prefinancing

préfixal, -e, -aux, -ales [prefiksal, -o] **ADJ** prefixal, prefix *(avant n)*

préfixation [prefiksasjɔ̃] **NF** prefixing, prefixation; **la p. d'un morphème** the use of a morpheme as a prefix

préfixe [prefiks] **NM** prefix

préfixer [3] [prefikse] **VT** to prefix

préformaté, -e [prefɔrmate] **ADJ** *Ordinat* preformatted

préformater [3] [prefɔrmate] **VT** *Ordinat* to preformat

pré-gardiennat, prégardiennat [pregardjena] *(pl* **pré-gardiennats** *ou* **prégardiennats)** **NM** *Belg (jardin d'enfants) Br* nursery school, *Am* kindergarten

préglaciaire [preglasjɛr] **ADJ** *Géol* preglacial

préhellénique [preelenik] **ADJ** pre-Hellenic

préhenseur [preɑ̃sœr] **ADJ M** prehensile

préhensile [preɑ̃sil] **ADJ** prehensile

préhension [preɑ̃sjɔ̃] **NF** prehension; **doué de p.** able to grip

préhistoire [preistwar] **NF** prehistory

préhistorique [preistɔrik] **ADJ 1** *(ère, temps)* prehistoric, prehistorical **2** *Fam (dépassé)* ancient, prehistoric; **elle est p., sa bagnole!** his/her car's virtually an antique!

pré-impression [preɛ̃presjɔ̃] **NF** *Typ* pre-press

pré-imprimé [preɛ̃prime] *(pl* **pré-imprimés)** **NM** preprinted form

pré-imprimée NF = **pré-imprimé**

préindustriel, -elle [preɛ̃dystrijel] **ADJ** preindustrial

préinscription [preɛ̃skripsjɔ̃] **NF** preregistration

préinstallé, -e [preɛ̃stale] **ADJ** *Ordinat* preinstalled

préinstaller [3] [preɛ̃stale] **VT** *Ordinat* to preinstall

préjudice [preʒydis] **NM** harm *(UNCOUNT)*, wrong *(UNCOUNT)*; **causer un** *ou* **porter p. à qn** to harm sb, to do sb harm; **les magnétoscopes ont-ils porté p. au cinéma?** have *Br* video recorders *or Am* VCRs been detrimental to the cinema?; **p. corporel** bodily harm; *Jur* **p. écologique** environmental damage; **p. financier** financial loss; **p. matériel** material injury; **subir un p. matériel/financier** to sustain damage/financial loss; **p. moral** non-pecuniary damages; **subir un p. moral** to suffer mental distress; **p. personnel** personal injury; **p. psychologique** mental injury

• **au préjudice de PRÉP** *(chose)* to the detriment *or* at the expense of; *(personne)* to the detriment *or Sout* prejudice of

• **sans préjudice de PRÉP** without prejudice to

> Il faut noter que le terme anglais **prejudice** est un faux ami. Il signifie le plus souvent **préjugé**.

préjudiciable [preʒydisjabl] **ADJ** prejudicial, detrimental (**à** to); **de telles déclarations seraient préjudiciables à votre candidature** such statements would be harmful *or* injurious to your candidature

préjudiciel, -elle [preʒydisjel] **ADJ** *(question)* interlocutory; *(action)* prejudicial

préjugé [preʒyʒe] **NM** prejudice; **préjugés raciaux** racial prejudice; **avoir un p. contre qn** to be prejudiced against sb; **avoir un p. favorable pour** *ou* **à l'égard de qn** to be prejudiced in sb's favour, to be biased towards sb; **n'avoir aucun p.** to be totally unprejudiced *or* unbiased

préjuger [17] [preʒyʒe] *Littéraire* **VT** to prejudge; **autant qu'on puisse le p.** as far as one can judge beforehand

• **préjuger de VT IND p. de qch** to judge sth in advance, to prejudge sth; **autant qu'on puisse en p.** as far as one can judge beforehand; **son attitude ne laisse rien p. de sa décision** his/her attitude gives us no indication of what he/she is going to decide; **on ne peut p. de l'avenir** you can't tell what the future has in store; **je crains d'avoir préjugé de mes forces** I'm afraid I've overestimated my strength

prélart [prelar] **NM** *(bâche)* tarpaulin

prélasser [3] [prelase] **se prélasser VPR** to be stretched out, to lounge *or* to laze around; **se p. au soleil** to laze *or* to bask in the sun

prélat [prela] **NM** prelate

prélature [prelatyr] **NF** prelacy

prélavage [prelavaʒ] **NM** prewash

prélèvement [prelɛvmɑ̃] **NM 1** *Méd & Ind (action)* sampling; *(échantillon ▸ gén)* sample; *(▸ sur les tissus)* swab; **il faut faire un p. dans la partie infectée** we have to take a swab of the infected area; **faire des prélèvements à qn** to do tests on sb **2** *Banque (retrait)* withdrawal; **p. automatique** *ou* **bancaire** direct debit; **p. en espèces** cash withdrawal; **faire un p. sur un compte** to debit an account **3** *Fin (retenue ▸ sur le salaire)* deduction; *(▸ sur les biens)* levy; **p. sur le capital** capital levy; **les cotisations sont payées par p. à la source** contributions are deducted at source; **p. à l'exportation** export levy; **prélèvements fiscaux** taxes; **p. à l'importation** import levy; **p. de l'impôt à la source** taxation at source; **prélèvements obligatoires** tax and social security contributions; **p. salarial** deduction from wages; **prélèvements sociaux** social security contributions

prélever [19] [prelǝve] **VT 1** *Méd & Ind (échantillon)* to take; *(organe)* to remove; *(en prévision de transplantations futures)* to harvest; **p. du sang** to take a blood sample **2** *Banque (somme ▸ en espèces)* to withdraw; **la somme sera prélevée sur votre compte tous les mois** the sum will be deducted *or* debited from your account every month **3** *Fin (sur un salaire)* to deduct, to withdraw; **p. qch à la source** to deduct sth at source; **p. une commission de 2 pour cent sur une opération** to charge a 2 percent commission on a transaction

préliminaire [preliminɛr] **ADJ** preliminary

• **préliminaires NMPL** *(préparatifs)* preliminaries; *(discussions)* preliminary talks

prélude [prelyd] **NM 1** *Mus* prelude **2** *(préliminaire)* prelude (**de** *ou* **à** to); **cette première rencontre fut le p. de bien d'autres** this was the first of many meetings

préluder [3] [prelyde] **VI** *Mus* to warm up, to prelude; **p. par des vocalises** to warm up by doing vocal exercises

• **préluder à VT IND** to be a prelude to

prémaquette [premakɛt] **NF** rough layout

prématuré, -e [prematyre] **ADJ 1** *(naissance, bébé)* premature; **être p. de six semaines** to be six weeks premature **2** *(décision)* premature; *(décès)* untimely; **il est p. de dresser un bilan de la situation** it is too early to assess the situation
NM,F premature baby *or* infant

prématurément [prematyremɑ̃] **ADV** prematurely; **il nous a quittés p.** his was an untimely death

prématurité [prematyrite] **NF** prematurity

prémédication [premedikasjɔ̃] **NF** *Méd* premedication

prémédiquer [3] [premedike] **VT** *Méd* to premedicate

préméditation [premeditasjɔ̃] **NF** premeditation; **avec p.** with malice aforethought; **meurtre avec p.** premeditated murder; **meurtre sans p.** unpremeditated murder, murder without premeditation

préméditer [3] [premedite] **VT** *(crime, vol)* to premeditate; **p. de faire qch** to plan to do sth; **ils avaient bien prémédité leur coup** they'd thought the whole thing out really well

prémenstruel, -elle [premɑ̃stryel] **ADJ** premenstrual

prémices [premis] **NFPL 1** *Littéraire (début)* beginnings; **les p. de l'été** the first *or* early signs of summer **2** *Antiq (récolte)* premices, primices, first fruits; *(animaux)* premices, primices

> Il faut noter que le nom anglais **premises** est un faux ami. Il signifie **locaux**.
>
> Do not confuse with **prémisse**.

PREMIER, -ÈRE [prǝmje, -ɛr] **ADJ 1** *(souvent avant le nom) (initial)* early; **les premiers hommes** early man; **ses premières œuvres** his/her early works; **les premiers temps** at the beginning, early on; **il n'est plus de la première jeunesse** he's not as young as he used to be; **un Matisse de la première période** an early Matisse

2 *(proche)* nearest; **je réussis à attraper les premières branches** I managed to grasp the nearest branches; **au p. rang** *Cin & Théât* in the first *or* front row; *Scol* in the first row

3 *(à venir)* next, first; **le p. venu** the first person who comes along; **ce n'est pas le p. venu** he's not just anybody; **le p. imbécile venu pourrait le faire** any idiot could do it; **on s'est arrêtés dans le p. hôtel venu** we stopped at the first hotel we came to *or* happened to come to

4 *(dans une série)* first; **chapitre p.** Chapter One; **à la première heure** first thing, at first light; **à première vue** at first (sight); **au p. abord** at first; **dans un p. temps** (at) first, to start with, to begin with; **de la première à la dernière ligne** from beginning to end; **de la première à la dernière page** from cover to cover; **le p. nom d'une liste** the top name on a list; *Can* **p. nom** first *or* Christian name, *Am* given name; *Fam* **du p. coup** first off, at the first attempt; **faire ses premières armes** to make one's debut; **il a fait ses premières armes à la 'Gazette du Nord'** he cut his teeth at the 'Gazette du Nord'; **j'ai fait mes premières armes dans le métier comme apprenti cuisinier** I started in the trade as a cook's apprentice; **p. amour** first love; **le p. arrivé** the first person to arrive; **p. jet** (first) *or* rough *or* initial draft; *Cin* **première prise** first take *or* shot; **premiers secours** *(personnes et matériel)* emergency services; *(soins)* first aid; **c'est la première fois que...** it's the first time that...; **il y a toujours une première fois** there's always a first time; *Journ* **première page** front page; **faire la première page des journaux** to be headline news; **première partie** *(gén)* first part; *(au spectacle)* opening act; **qui va (lui) jeter** *ou* **lancer la première pierre?** who will cast the first stone?

5 *(principal)* main; **de (toute) première nécessité/urgence** (absolutely) essential/urgent; **c'est vous le p. intéressé** you're the main person concerned *or* the one who's got most at stake; **le p. pays producteur de vin au monde** the world's leading wine-producing country; **la première collection de fossiles au monde** the world's greatest *or* foremost collection of fossils

6 *(haut placé ▸ clerc, commis)* chief; *(▸ danseur)* leading; **le p. personnage de l'État** the country's Head of State; **P. Ministre** Prime Minister

7 *(après le nom) (originel)* first, original, initial; **l'idée première était de...** the original idea was to...

8 *(spontané)* first; **quelles sont vos premières réactions?** what are your first *or* initial reactions?

9 *(après le nom) (fondamental)* first; *Math (nombre)* prime; **principe p.** first *or* basic principle

10 *(moindre)* **et ta récitation, tu n'en connais pas le p. mot!** you haven't a clue about your recitation, have you?; **la robe coûte 300 euros et je n'en ai pas le p. sou** the dress costs 300 euros and I haven't a *Br* penny *or Am* cent to my name

11 *Gram* **première personne (du) singulier/pluriel** first person singular/plural

12 *Culin* **côte/côtelette première** prime rib/cutlet
NM,F 1 *(personne)* **le p.** the first; **entre la première** go in first; **elle a fini dans les cinq premières** she finished amongst the top five; **elle est la première de sa classe/au hit-parade** she's top of her class/the charts; **si c'est moi qui pars le p.** if I go first; *Fam* **mon p. m'a fait une rougeole** my eldest has had measles[□]; *Pol* **le P. (britannique)** the (British) Prime Minister *or* Premier

2 *(chose)* **le p.** the first (one); **de toutes les maisons où j'ai vécu, c'est la première que je regrette le plus** of all the houses in which I have lived, I miss the first (one) most of all

3 le p. *(celui-là)* the former; **plantez des roses ou des tulipes, mais les premières durent plus longtemps** plant roses or tulips, but the former last longer

NM 1 *(dans une charade)* **mon p. sent mauvais** my first has a nasty smell
2 *(étage) Br* first floor, *Am* second floor; **la dame du p.** the lady on the *Br* first floor *or Am* second floor
3 *(dans des dates)* **le p. du mois** the first of the month; **tous les premiers du mois** every first (day) of the month; **Aix, le p. juin** Aix, *Br* 1 June *or Am* June 1; **le P. Mai** May Day; **le p. janvier** *ou* **de l'an** New Year's Day
• **première NF 1** *Cin & Théât* first night, opening night
2 *(exploit)* **c'est une (grande) première chirurgicale** it's a first for surgery; **la première des Grandes Jorasses** the first ascent of the Grandes Jorasses
3 *Scol Br* lower sixth (form), *Am* eleventh grade
4 *Aut* first (gear); **être/passer en première** to be in/to go into first
5 *Transp* first class; **voyager en première** to travel first class; **billet/wagon de première** first-class ticket/carriage
6 *(en danse)* first (position)
7 *Typ (épreuve)* first proof; *(édition ▸ d'un livre)* first edition; *(▸ d'un journal)* early edition
• **de première ADJ** *Fam* first-rate; **un imbécile de première** a prize idiot
• **en premier ADV** first, in the first place, first of all; **je dois m'occuper en p. de mon visa** the first thing I must do is to see about my visa
• **premier degré NM 1** *Scol Br* primary *or Am* elementary education **2** *(phase initiale)* first step; **brûlure au p. degré** first-degree burn **3** *Fig* **des gags à ne pas prendre au p. degré** jokes which mustn't be taken at face value
• **premier prix NM 1** *Com* lowest *or* cheapest price; **dans les premiers prix** at the cheaper *or* lower end of the scale **2** *(récompense)* first prize; **elle a eu le p. prix d'interprétation** she's won the award for best actress

premièrement [prəmjɛrmɑ̃] **ADV 1** *(dans une énumération)* in the first place, first; **p. il faut de l'argent, deuxièmement il faut du temps** first you need the money, then you need the time **2** *(pour objecter)* firstly, in the first place, to start with; **p., ça ne te regarde pas!** to begin *or* to start with, it's none of your business!

premier-ministrable [prəmjeministrabl] *(pl* **premier-ministrables)** **ADJ** *(politicien)* suitable for Prime Minister
NMF potential Prime Minister

premier-né, première-née [prəmjene, prəmjɛrne] *(mpl* **premiers-nés**, *fpl* **premières-nées)**
ADJ first-born
NM,F first-born

prémilitaire [premilitɛr] **ADJ** premilitary

prémisse [premis] **NF** premise

> Do not confuse with **prémices**.

prémix [premiks] **NM** *(boisson)* ready-mixed alcoholic drink

prémolaire [premɔlɛr] **NF** premolar

prémonition [premɔnisjɔ̃] **NF** premonition

prémonitoire [premɔnitwar] **ADJ** premonitory; **j'ai fait un rêve p.** I had a premonition in my dream

prems [prəms] = **preums**

prémunir [32] [premynir] **VT p. qn contre qch** *(protéger)* to protect sb against sth; *(mettre en garde)* to put sb on his/her guard against sth
VPR se prémunir se p. contre qch to protect oneself *or* to guard against sth

prenable [prənabl] **ADJ** pregnable

prenait *etc voir* **prendre**

prenant, -e [prənɑ̃, -ɑ̃t] **ADJ 1** *(captivant)* engrossing, gripping **2** *(qui prend du temps)* time-consuming **3** *(préhensile)* prehensile

prénatal, -e, -als *ou* **-aux, -ales** [prenatal, -o] **ADJ** *Br* antenatal, *Am* prenatal

PRENDRE [79] [prɑ̃dr]

- to take **A1–4, B2–5, 7, 8, C1–3, 6, D2, 3, 5, E1–3, F1, G1–4**
- to pick up **A1**
- to buy **A7**
- to hold **A2**
- to borrow **B2**
- to get **A5-7, D6**
- to drink **B3**
- to use **B1**
- to eat **B3**
- to travel by **B5**
- to catch **B6, C5**
- to capture **C1**
- to take up **C3**
- to come over **C4**
- to consider **E3**
- to write down **F1**
- to have **G1, 3**
- to assume **G5**

VI

- to take **1**
- to catch on **1**
- to set **2**
- to thicken **2**
- to start **4**

VT A. *SAISIR, ACQUÉRIR* **1** *(ramasser)* to pick up; **la chatte prend ses chatons par la peau du cou** the cat picks up her kittens by the scruff of the neck; **elle prit sa guitare sur le sol** she picked her guitar up off the floor; **prends la casserole par le manche** pick the pan up by the handle; **il prit son manteau à la patère** he took his coat off the hook; **p. qch des mains de qn** to take sth off sb; **va p. du persil/des fleurs dans le jardin** go and pick some parsley/flowers in the garden; **p. un peigne dans sa poche/dans un tiroir** to take a comb out of one's pocket/a drawer; **prends le bébé** pick the baby up
2 *(saisir et garder)* to take (hold of), to hold; **tu peux p. mon sac un instant?** could you hold on to *or* take my bag for a minute?; **p. sa tête entre ses mains** to hold one's head in one's hands; **il m'a pris par les épaules et m'a secoué** he took (hold of) me by the shoulders and shook me; **prenez cette médaille qui vous est offerte par tous vos collègues** accept this medal as a gift from all your colleagues; **p. un siège** to take a seat, to sit down
3 *(emporter ▸ lunettes, document, en-cas)* to take; **tu as pris tes papiers (avec toi)?** have you got your papers (with you)?; **p. des vivres pour un mois** to take one month's supply of food; **quand prendrez-vous le colis?** when will you collect the parcel?
4 *(emmener)* to take (along); **l'inspecteur prit trois hommes avec lui** the inspector took three men with him; **je suis passé la p. chez elle à midi** I picked her up at *or* collected her from her home at 12 noon; **p. qn en voiture** to give sb a lift; **p. un auto-stoppeur** to pick up a hitchhiker
5 *(trouver)* to get; **où as-tu pris ce couteau?** where did you get that knife (from)?; **où as-tu pris cette idée?** where did you get that idea?; **où as-tu pris qu'on est plus heureux à la campagne?** where did you get the idea that people are happier in the country?
6 *(se procurer)* **p. des renseignements** to get some information
7 *(acheter ▸ nourriture, billet de loterie)* to get, to buy; *(▸ abonnement, assurance)* to take out; *(réserver ▸ chambre d'hôtel, place de spectacle)* to book; **j'ai pris des artichauts pour ce soir** I've got *or* bought some artichokes for tonight; **je vais vous p. un petit poulet aujourd'hui** I'll have *or* take a small chicken today
8 *(demander ▸ argent)* to charge; **je prends une commission de 3 pour cent** I take a 3 percent commission; *Fam* **mon coiffeur ne prend pas cher** my hairdresser isn't too expensive *or* doesn't charge too much; **je prends 20 euros de l'heure** I charge 20 euros per hour; **elle l'a réparé sans rien nous p.** she fixed it free of charge *or* without charging us (anything) for it
9 *(retirer)* **les impôts sont pris à la source** tax is deducted at source; **p. de l'argent sur son compte** to withdraw money from one's account
B. *AVOIR RECOURS À, SE SERVIR DE* **1** *(utiliser ▸ outil)* to use; **prends un marteau, ce sera plus facile** use a hammer, you'll find it's easier
2 *(emprunter)* to take, to borrow; **je peux p. ta voiture?** can I take *or* borrow your car?
3 *(consommer ▸ nourriture)* to eat, to have; *(▸ boisson)* to drink, to have; *(▸ médicament)* to take; *(▸ sucre)* to take; **je ne prends jamais de somnifères** I never take sleeping pills; **nous en discuterons en prenant le café** we'll discuss it over a cup of coffee; **tu prends du lait?** do you take milk?; **qu'est-ce que tu prends?** what would you like to drink?, what will it be?; **je prendrais bien une bière** I could do with a beer; **si on allait p. un verre?** how about (going for) a drink?; **elle prend de la cocaïne** she takes cocaine; **à p. matin, midi et soir** to be taken three times a day; **elle n'a rien pris depuis trois jours** she hasn't eaten anything for three days; **tu leur as fait p. leurs médicaments?** did you make sure they took their medicine?
4 *(comme ingrédient)* to take; **p. 50 g de beurre et 200 g de farine** take 50 g of butter and 200 g of flour
5 *(se déplacer en)* to take, to go *or* to travel by; **p. l'avion** to take the plane, to fly; **p. le bateau** to take the boat, to sail; **p. le bus/le train** to take the bus/train, to go by bus/train; **p. un taxi** to take *or* to use a taxi; **je ne prends jamais la voiture** I never use the car; **elle prend sa bicyclette pour aller au travail** she goes to work by bike, she cycles to work
6 *(monter dans ▸ bus, train)* to catch, to get on; **elle a pris le vol suivant/le mauvais avion** she caught the next plane/got on the wrong plane
7 *(louer)* to take; **on a pris une chambre dans un petit hôtel** we took a room in a small hotel; **j'ai pris un petit studio** I rented a little studio *Br* flat *or Am* apartment
8 *(suivre ▸ voie)* to take; **prends la première à droite** take the first (on the) right; **prenez la direction de Lille** follow the signs for Lille; **j'ai pris un sens interdit** I drove down a one-way street
C. *PRENDRE POSSESSION DE, CONTRÔLER* **1** *(retenir par la force ▸ fugitif)* to capture; *(▸ prisonnier)* to take; *(▸ animal)* to capture, to catch; *Mil (ville, position)* to take; **p. qn en otage** to take sb hostage
2 *(voler)* to take; **il a tout pris dans la maison** he took everything in the house; **p. une citation dans un livre** *(sans permission)* to lift *or* to poach a quotation from a book; **combien vous a-t-on pris?** how much was taken *or* stolen from you?; **elle m'a pris mon idée/petit ami** she stole my idea/boyfriend; *Littéraire* **la mort lui a pris son fils** death has robbed him/her *or* deprived him/her of his/her son
3 *(occuper ▸ temps)* to take (up), *Sout* to require; *(▸ place)* to take (up); **il prenait le banc à lui tout seul** he was taking up all the space on the bench; **ça prend combien de temps pour y aller?** how long does it take to get there?; **ça (m')a pris deux heures** it took (me) two hours; **chercher un appartement prend du temps** *Br* flat-hunting *or Am* apartment-hunting is time-consuming
4 *(envahir ▸ sujet: malaise, rage)* to come over; *(▸ sujet: peur, doute)* to seize, to take hold of; **quand ses quintes de toux le prennent** when he has a bout of coughing; **la fièvre du jeu la prit** she was gripped by gambling fever; **une douleur le prit dans le dos** he suddenly felt a twinge of pain in his back; **l'envie le** *ou* **lui prit d'aller nager** he felt like going for a swim; **je me suis laissé p. par le charme du lieu** I fell under the spell of the place; **qu'est-ce qui te prend?** what's wrong with *or* what's the matter with *or* what's come over you?; **qu'est-ce qui le** *ou* **lui prend de ne pas répondre?** why on earth isn't he answering?; *Fam* **ça te prend souvent?** do you make a habit of this?; *Fam* **quand ça le** *ou* **lui prend, il casse tout** when he gets into this state, he just smashes everything in sight; **il me prend parfois le désir de tout abandonner** I sometimes feel like giving it all up; **il est rentré chez lui et bien/mal lui en a pris** he went home and it was just as well he did/but he'd have done better to stay where he was; *très Fam* **ça me prend la tête** it's a real pain; **il me prend la tête** he's really getting on my nerves
5 *(surprendre ▸ voleur, tricheur)* to catch; **si tu veux le voir, il faut le p. au saut du lit** if you want to see him, you must catch him as he gets up; **l'orage/la pluie nous a pris en rase campagne** the storm/rain crept up on us *or* caught us unawares in the open countryside; **ils se sont fait p. à la frontière** they were caught at the border; **p. qn à faire qch** to catch sb doing sth; **que je ne te prenne plus à écouter aux portes!** don't let me catch you listening at keyholes again!; **on ne me prendra plus à l'aider!** you'll never catch me helping him/her again!; **je t'y prends, petit galopin!** caught *or* got you, you little rascal!
6 *(pion, dame)* to take; **le roi prend la dame** the King is higher than *or* takes the Queen
7 *Sport* **p. le service de qn** to break sb's service; **il est venu p. la deuxième place** *(pendant la course)* he moved into second place; *(à l'arrivée)* he came in second
8 *Fam (affronter ▸ adversaire)* to take on
D. *ADMETTRE, RECEVOIR* **1** *(recevoir)* **le docteur ne pourra pas vous p. avant demain** the doctor won't be able to see you before tomorrow; **après**

22 heures, nous ne prenons plus de clients after 10 p.m., we don't let any more customers in

2 *(cours)* to take

3 *(accueillir* ▸ *pensionnaire, locataire)* to take in; *(*▸ *passager)* to take; *(admettre par règlement)* to take, to allow; *(engager* ▸ *employé, candidat)* to take on; **le lycée prend des pensionnaires** the school takes boarders; **nous ne prenons pas les cartes de crédit/les bagages en cabine** we don't take credit cards/cabin baggage; **après son opération, je le prendrai dans mon service** after his operation, I'll have him transferred to my department; **p. un comptable** to take on *or* to hire an accountant; **ils ne prennent que des gens qui ont de l'expérience** they only take *or* employ *or* use experienced people; **p. qn à titre d'essai** *ou* **à l'essai** to take sb (on) *or* to employ sb on a trial basis; **p. qn comme stagiaire** to take sb on as a trainee; **on l'a prise comme assistante de direction** she's been taken on as (an) executive assistant

4 *(acquérir, gagner)* **p. de l'avance/du retard** to be earlier/later than scheduled; **j'ai pris trois centimètres de tour de taille** I've put on three centimetres round the waist; **quand le gâteau commence à p. une jolie couleur dorée** when the cake starts to take on a nice golden colour; **le projet commence à p. forme** *ou* **tournure** the project's starting to take shape

5 *(terminaison)* to take; **"gaz" ne prend pas d's au pluriel** "gaz" doesn't take an s in the plural; **le a prend un accent circonflexe** there's a circumflex on the a

6 *(subir)* to get; **p. un coup de soleil** to get sunburnt; *Vieilli* **p. froid** *ou* **du mal** to catch *or* to get a cold; *Fam* **tu vas p. une fessée/claque!** you'll get a smack/a clout!; **p. des coups de pied** to get kicked; *Sport & Fig* **il prend bien les coups** he can take a lot of punishment; **j'ai pris la tuile en plein sur la tête** the tile hit me right on the head; *Fam* **c'est elle qui a tout pris** *(coups, reproches)* she got the worst *or* took the brunt of it; *(éclaboussures)* she got most *or* the worst of it; *Fam* **qu'est-ce qu'on a pris!, on a pris quelque chose!** *(averse)* we got soaked *or* drenched!; *(réprimande)* we got a real dressing down!; *(critique)* we got panned!; *(défaite)* we got thrashed!; *Fam* **qu'est-ce que le gouvernement a pris dans les journaux du matin!** the government got a roasting in the morning papers!; *Fam* **il en a pris pour 15 ans** he got 15 years, he got put away for 15 years

E. *CONSIDÉRER DE TELLE MANIÈRE* **1** *(accepter)* to take; **il faut p. les choses comme elles viennent/sont** you've got to take things as they come/are; **il a essayé de le p. avec le sourire** *ou* **en souriant** he tried to pass it off with a smile; **elle a pris sa défaite avec le sourire** she accepted her defeat with a smile; **bien/mal p. qch** to take sth well/badly; **elle prend très mal la critique** she doesn't take kindly to being criticized

2 *(interpréter)* to take; **ne prends pas ça pour toi** *(ne te sens pas visé)* don't take it personally; **p. qch en bien/en mal** to take sth as a compliment/badly; **elle a pris mon silence pour de la désapprobation** she took my silence as a criticism

3 *(considérer)* to take, to consider; **prenons un exemple** let's take *or* consider an example; **prends Pierre, il n'est pas brillant, et pourtant il a réussi** take Pierre, he's not very bright but he's got on in life; **p. qn en amitié** to grow fond of sb; **p. qn en pitié** to take pity on sb; **j'ai pris cette maison en horreur** I grew to loathe that house; **p. qn/qch pour** *(par méprise)* to mistake sb/sth for; *(volontairement)* to take sb/sth for, to consider sb/sth to be; **on me prend souvent pour ma sœur** I'm often mistaken for my sister; **je vous avais pris pour Robert** I thought you were Robert; **pour qui me prenez-vous?** what do you take me for?, who do you think I am?; **tu me prends pour ta bonne?** do you think I'm your maid?; **elle va me p. pour un idiot** she'll think I'm a fool; **p. qn/qch comme** to take sb/sth as; **p. qch comme excuse** to use *or* to take sth as an excuse; **p. un monument comme point de repère** to use a monument as a landmark; **à tout p.** all in all, by and large, all things considered; **à tout p., je préférerais le faire moi-même** all things considered I'd rather do it myself

4 *(traiter* ▸ *personne)* to handle, to deal with; **p. qn par la douceur** to use gentle persuasion on sb; **elle sait très bien p. les enfants** she knows how to handle children; *Mil & Fig* **p. l'ennemi de front/à revers** to tackle the enemy head on/from the rear

F. *ENREGISTRER* **1** *(consigner* ▸ *notes)* to take *or* to write down; *(*▸ *empreintes, mesures, température, tension)* to take; **je n'ai pas eu le temps de p. son numéro** I didn't have time to take (down) his/her number; **p. les dimensions d'une pièce** to measure a room

2 *Phot* **p. qn/qch (en photo)** to take a picture *or* photo *or* photograph of sb/sth; **ne prends pas la tour, elle est affreuse** don't take (a picture of) the tower, it's hideous

G. *DÉCIDER DE, ADOPTER* **1** *(s'octroyer* ▸ *vacances)* to take, to have; *(*▸ *bain, douche)* to have, to take; **p. un jour de congé** to take *or* to have the day off; **p. un congé maternité** to take maternity leave; **p. du repos** to rest, to have a rest; **p. du bon temps** to have fun *or* a good time; **p. le temps de faire qch** to take the time to do sth; **p. son temps** to take one's time; **p. un amant** to take a lover; **tu n'as pas le droit! – je le prends!** you've no right! – that's what you think!

2 *(s'engager dans* ▸ *mesure, risque)* to take; **p. une décision** *(gén)* to make a decision; *(après avoir hésité)* to make up one's mind, to come to a decision; **p. la décision de faire qch** to make up one's mind to do sth, to decide to do sth; **p. l'initiative** to take the initiative; **p. l'initiative de qch** to initiate sth; **p. l'initiative de faire qch** to take the initiative in doing sth, to take it upon oneself to do sth; **p. une (bonne) résolution** to make a (good) resolution; **p. de bonnes résolutions pour l'avenir** to resolve to do better in the future; **p. la résolution de faire qch** to resolve to do sth

3 *(choisir* ▸ *sujet d'examen, cadeau)* to take, to choose, to have; **j'ai pris le docteur Valiet comme médecin** I chose Dr Valiet to be *or* as my GP; **je prends la cravate rouge** I'll take *or* have the red tie; **qu'est-ce qu'on lui prend comme glace?** which ice cream shall we get him/her?; **c'est à p. ou à laisser** (you can) take it or leave it; **il y a à p. et à laisser dans son livre** his book is good in parts

4 *(se charger de* ▸ *poste)* to take, to accept; **p. ses fonctions** to start work; *Fam* **j'ai fini par p. des ménages** in the end I took on some cleaning jobs; **j'ai un appel pour toi, tu le prends?** I've got a call for you, will you take it?

5 *(adopter* ▸ *air)* to put on, to assume; *(*▸ *ton)* to assume; **elle a pris de grands airs pour me le dire** she told me very condescendingly

USAGE ABSOLU 1 *Cartes* **je prends** I'll try it; **j'ai pris à cœur** I went hearts

2 *Fam (subir)* **quand les deux frères font une bêtise, c'est toujours l'aîné qui prend** when the two brothers have been up to some mischief, it's always the eldest who gets the blame ▫ *or* gets it in the neck

VI 1 *(se fixer durablement* ▸ *végétal)* to take (root); *(*▸ *bouture, greffe, vaccin)* to take; *(*▸ *mode, slogan)* to catch on; **la peinture ne prend pas sur le plastique** the plastic won't take the paint; **ça ne prendra pas avec elle** *(mensonge)* it won't work with her, she won't be taken in; *Fam* **ça prend pas!** give me a break!, yeah right!, *Br* pull the other one!

2 *(durcir* ▸ *crème, ciment, colle)* to set; *(*▸ *lac, étang)* to freeze (over); *(*▸ *mayonnaise)* to thicken

3 *(passer)* **prends à gauche** *(tourne à gauche)* turn left; **tu peux p. par Le Mans** you can go via Le Mans; **p. à travers bois/champs** to cut through the woods/fields

4 *(commencer)* to start, to get going; **le feu a pris dans la grange** the fire started in the barn; **je n'arrive pas à faire p. le feu/les brindilles** I can't get the fire going/the twigs to catch; **le sapin prend bien** pine is easy to get going *or* to light

5 *Mus & Théât* **prenons avant la sixième mesure/à la scène 2** let's take it from just before bar six/from scene 2

• **prendre sur** VT IND **1** *(entamer)* to use (some of); **p. sur son capital pour payer qch** to use some of *or* to dig into one's capital to pay for sth; **je ne prendrai pas sur mon week-end pour finir le travail!** I'm not going to give up *or* to sacrifice part of my weekend to finish the job!; **après quelques jours sans nourriture, l'organisme prend sur ses réserves** after a few days without food, the body starts using up its reserves **2** *(locutions)* **p. sur soi** to grin and bear it; **p. sur soi de faire qch** to take (it) upon oneself to do sth

VPR se prendre 1 *(emploi passif)* **ces cachets se prennent avant les repas** these tablets should be taken before meals

2 *(emploi réciproque)* **ils se sont pris pour époux** they were united in matrimony

3 *(se coincer* ▸ *emploi passif)* to get caught *or* trapped; **le foulard s'est pris dans la portière** the scarf got caught *or* shut in the door

4 *(se coincer* ▸ *personne)* **attention, tu vas te p. les doigts dans la charnière!** careful, you'll trap your fingers *or* get your fingers caught in the hinge!; **se p. les pieds dans qch** to trip over sth

5 *Fam (choisir)* **se p. qch** to get sth for oneself; **prends-toi un gâteau** get yourself a cake

6 *(se laisser aller)* **se p. à qch** to get (drawn) into sth; **on se prend au charme de sa musique** you gradually succumb to the charm of his/her music; **se p. à faire qch** to find oneself starting to do sth; **se p. à rêver** to find oneself dreaming; **je me pris à l'aimer/le haïr** I found myself falling in love with him/starting to hate him

7 se p. d'amitié pour qn to feel a growing affection for sb

8 *(se considérer)* **elle se prend pour une artiste** she likes to think she's an artist; **il ne se prend pas pour rien** *ou* **pour n'importe qui** he thinks he's God's gift to humanity; **tu te prends pour qui pour me parler sur ce ton?** who do you think you are, talking to me like that?

9 s'en p. à qn/qch *(l'attaquer)* to attack sb/sth; *(le rendre responsable)* to put the blame on sb/sth; **pourquoi faut-il toujours que tu t'en prennes à moi?** why do you always take it out on me?; **l'équipe perd un match et l'on s'en prend tout de suite à l'entraîneur** the team loses a match and the coach automatically gets the blame; **ne t'en prends qu'à toi-même** you've only (got) yourself to blame; **s'en p. à une institution/un système** *(l'accuser)* to put the blame on an institution/a system; *(le critiquer)* to attack an institution/a system

10 *(locutions)* **comment pourrions-nous nous y p.?** how could we go about it?; **tu t'y prends un peu tard pour t'inscrire!** you've left it a bit late to enrol!; **il faut s'y p. deux mois à l'avance pour avoir des places** you have to book two months in advance to be sure of getting seats; **elle s'y est prise à trois fois pour faire démarrer la tondeuse** she made three attempts before the lawnmower would start; **s'y p. bien/mal avec qn** to handle sb the right/wrong way; **elle s'y prend bien** *ou* **sait s'y p. avec les enfants** she's good with children; **si tu t'y prends bien avec lui** if you get on the right side of him; **je n'arrive pas à repasser le col – c'est parce que tu t'y prends mal** I can't iron the collar properly – that's because you're going about it the wrong way *or* doing it wrong

---

preneur, -euse [prənœr, -øz] NM,F **1** *(acheteur)* buyer; *(d'un chèque, d'une lettre de change)* payee; **trouver p. pour qch** to find someone (willing) to buy sth, to find a buyer for sth; **si vous me le laissez à 20 euros, je suis p.** I'll buy it if you'll take 20 euros for it **2** *(locataire)* lessee, leaseholder **3** *(ravisseur)* **p. d'otages** hostage-taker

• **preneur de son, preneuse de son** NM,F sound engineer, sound technician

prenne *etc voir* **prendre**

prénom [prenɔ̃] NM first name, *Am* given name

prénommé, -e [prenɔme] ADJ **un garçon p. Julien** a boy called *or* named Julien; *aussi Hum* **la prénommée Maria** the said Maria

NM,F *Jur* above-named (person); **le p.** the above-named

prénommer [3] [prenɔme] VT to call, to name; **si c'est une fille, nous la prénommerons Léa** if it's a girl, we'll call *or* name her Léa

VPR se prénommer comment se prénomme-t-il? what's his first name?; **il se prénomme Robin** his first name is Robin

prénuptial, -e, -aux, -ales [prenypsjal, -o] ADJ premarital, antenuptial; **examen p.** premarital medical check

préoccupant, -e [preɔkypɑ̃, -ɑ̃t] ADJ worrying

préoccupation [preɔkypasjɔ̃] **NF 1** *(souci)* concern, worry; **le chômage reste notre p. première** unemployment remains our major cause for concern; **ceux pour qui l'argent n'est pas une p.** those who don't have to worry about money *or* who don't have money worries; **j'ai d'autres préoccupations** I have other things to worry about; **j'ai été un sujet de p. pour mes parents** I was a worry to my parents **2** *(priorité)* concern, preoccupation; **ma seule p. est de divertir le public** my only concern *or* sole preoccupation is to keep the audience entertained; **depuis qu'elle est partie, il n'a plus qu'une p., la retrouver** since she left his one thought is to find her again

préoccupé, -e [preɔkype] **ADJ** *(inquiet)* worried, preoccupied, concerned; **d'un ton p.** in a worried tone

préoccuper [3] [preɔkype] **VT 1** *(tracasser ▸ sujet: avenir, question)* to worry; **sa santé me préoccupe** I'm worried *or* anxious *or* concerned about his/her health; **son avenir professionnel n'a pas l'air de la p.** she doesn't seem to be concerned about her career, her career doesn't seem to worry her **2** *(obséder)* to preoccupy, to concern, to be of concern to; **l'environnement est un sujet qui nous préoccupe beaucoup** we are deeply concerned with environmental issues; **le foot est tout ce qui le préoccupe** football is all he thinks about; **il est trop préoccupé de sa petite personne** he's too wrapped up in himself

VPR se préoccuper se p. de to be concerned with, to care about; **se p. de l'avenir** to care about the future; **se p. de ses enfants** to worry about one's children; **il ne s'est pas beaucoup préoccupé de savoir si j'allais bien** he didn't bother himself much to find out if I was all right; **ne te préoccupe donc pas de ça!** don't you worry *or* bother about that!

préopératoire [preɔperatwar] **ADJ** preoperative, presurgical, *Fam* preop

prépa [prepa] **NF** *Fam Univ* = class preparing for the competitive entrance exam to a "grande école"; **faire une p., être en p.** = to be studying for the entrance exam to a "grande école"

pré-paiement [prepɛmɑ̃] *(pl* **pré-paiements)** **NM** prepayment

préparamétré, -e [preparametre] **ADJ** *Ordinat (logiciel)* preconfigured

préparateur, -trice [preparatœr, -tris] **NM,F 1** *Univ* = assistant to a professor of science **2** *Pharm* **p. en pharmacie** assistant to a dispensing *Br* chemist *or Am* pharmacist

préparatifs [preparatif] **NMPL** preparations; **p. de départ/guerre** preparations for leaving/war; **j'étais en pleins p. de départ quand…** I was in the middle of preparing *or* getting ready to leave when…

préparation [preparasjɔ̃] **NF 1** *(réalisation ▸ d'un plat, d'un médicament)* preparation; *(apprêt ▸ d'une peau, de la laine)* dressing; **les moules ne demandent pas une longue p.** mussels don't take long to prepare

2 *(organisation ▸ d'un voyage, d'une fête, d'un attentat)* preparation; **la randonnée avait fait l'objet d'une soigneuse p.** the ramble had been carefully thought out *or* prepared

3 *(entraînement ▸ pour un examen)* preparation; *(▸ pour une épreuve sportive)* training, preparation; **la p. d'un examen** preparing *or* working for an exam; **manquer de p.** to be insufficiently prepared; *Mil* **p. militaire** pre-call-up training

4 *(chose préparée)* preparation; **p. culinaire** dish; **p. pour gâteau/sauce** cake/sauce mix; **p. (pharmaceutique)** (pharmaceutical) preparation

5 *Scol* **faire une p. à une grande école** = to be studying for the entrance exam to a "grande école"

6 *Beaux-Arts* primer

• **en préparation ADV** being prepared, in hand; **avoir un livre/disque en p.** to have a book/record in the pipeline

• **sans préparation ADV** *(courir)* without preparation, cold; *(parler)* extempore, ad lib; **tu ne peux pas le lui dire sans p.** you can't tell him/her just like that

préparatoire [preparatwar] **ADJ travail p.** groundwork; **p. à** preparatory to, in preparation for

préparer [3] [prepare] **VT 1** *(réaliser ▸ plat, sandwich)* to prepare, to make; *(▸ médicament, cataplasme)* to prepare; **qu'est-ce que tu nous as préparé de bon?** what delicious dish have you cooked for us?; **plats tout préparés** precooked *or* ready-cooked meals

2 *(rendre prêt ▸ valise)* to pack; *(▸ repas, chambre, champ)* to prepare, to get ready; *(▸ poisson, poulet)* to prepare, to dress; *(▸ document)* to prepare, to draw up; *(▸ ordonnance)* to make up; **préparez la monnaie, s'il vous plaît** please have change ready; **poulet tout préparé** oven-ready *or* dressed chicken; *Fam* **on dirait qu'il nous prépare une rougeole** (it) looks like he's getting the measles; **p. le terrain (pour)** to prepare the ground *or* to lay the ground (for); *Fig* to pave the way (for)

3 *(organiser ▸ attentat, conférence)* to prepare, to organize; *(▸ vacances)* to plan, to arrange; *(▸ complot)* to prepare, to hatch; **p. un coup** to be hatching something, to be cooking something up; **je suis sûr qu'il nous prépare quelque chose** I'm sure he's up to something; **elle avait préparé sa réponse** she'd got her *or* an answer ready; **p. une surprise à qn** to have a surprise in store for sb

4 *(travailler à ▸ œuvre)* to be preparing, to be working on; *(▸ examen)* to be preparing for; *(▸ épreuve sportive)* to be in training for; *(▸ discours)* to prepare; *Fam* **tu as préparé quelque chose en géographie?** did you revise any geography?; **il prépare une grande école** he's studying for the entrance exam to a "grande école"

5 *(former ▸ élève)* to prepare; *(▸ athlète)* to train; **p. qn à qch** *(examen)* to prepare sb for sth; *(épreuve sportive)* to train sb for sth; **on les prépare intensivement à l'examen** they're being coached for the exam; **rien ne m'avait préparé à ce type de problème** nothing had prepared me for this kind of problem

6 *(habituer)* to accustom; **nous avons préparé les enfants à l'idée qu'ils vont changer d'école** we've got the children used to the idea of changing schools

VPR se préparer 1 *(s'apprêter)* to get ready; **le temps qu'elle se prépare, on aura raté la séance** by the time she's ready, we'll have missed the show; **se p. à qch/à faire qch** to prepare *or* to get ready for sth/to do sth; **se p. au combat** to prepare for action *or* combat; **nous nous préparions à répondre à ses critiques** we got ready to reply to his/her criticism

2 *(s'entraîner)* to train; **se p. pour Roland-Garros** to train for the French Open tennis tournament

3 *(être sur le point d'arriver)* **un orage se prépare** there's a storm brewing; **je sens qu'il se prépare quelque chose** I can feel there's something afoot *or* in the air

4 *(pour soi-même)* **se p. un café** to make oneself a coffee; **tu te prépares bien des ennuis/des désillusions** you're in for trouble/a disappointment

5 se p. à qch *(être disposé à)* to be ready *or* prepared for sth; **préparez-vous à vous faire tremper!** be ready *or* prepared to get soaked!; **je ne m'étais pas préparé à un tel accueil** I wasn't prepared for *or* I wasn't expecting such a welcome

6 se p. à faire qch *(être sur le point de)* to be about to do sth; **on se préparait à passer à table** we were about to sit down to eat

prépayé, -e [prepeje] **ADJ** prepaid

pré-planification [preplanifikasjɔ̃] **NF** preplanning

prépondérance [prepɔ̃derɑ̃s] **NF** predominance, primacy (**sur** over)

prépondérant, -e [prepɔ̃derɑ̃, -ɑ̃t] **ADJ** predominant; **jouer un rôle p.** to play a prominent part *or* role; **sa voix sera prépondérante** he/she will have the casting vote

préposé, -e [prepoze] **NM,F 1** *(employé)* **p. des douanes** customs official *or* officer; **p. à la caisse** cashier; **p. au vestiaire** cloakroom attendant **2** *Admin* **p. (des postes)** *Br* postman, *Am* mailman **3** *Jur* agent

préposer [3] [prepoze] **VT** *(affecter)* **p. qn à** to place *or* to put sb in charge of; **il a été préposé à l'accueil** he was put in charge of reception

prépositif, -ive [prepozitif, -iv] = **prépositionnel**

préposition [prepozisjɔ̃] **NF** preposition

prépositionnel, -elle [prepozisjɔnel] **ADJ** prepositional

prépositive [prepozitiv] *voir* **prépositif**

préproduction [preprɔdyksjɔ̃] **NF** *Cin & TV* preproduction

préprogrammé, -e [preprɔgrame] **ADJ** *Ordinat* preprogrammed

prépubère [prepybɛr] **ADJ** prepubescent

prépublication [prepyblikasjɔ̃] **NF** prepublication

prépuce [prepys] **NM** foreskin, *Spéc* prepuce

préraphaélisme [prerafaelism] **NM** *Beaux-Arts* Pre-Raphaelism

préraphaélite [prerafaelit] *Beaux-Arts* **ADJ** Pre-Raphaelite

NMF Pre-Raphaelite

prérentrée [prerɑ̃tre] **NF** *Scol* = start of the new school year for teachers (a few days before the pupils)

prérequis, -e [prerəki, -iz] *Belg* **ADJ** *(préalable ▸ travail, formation)* preparatory; *(requis ▸ connaissance)* required

NM *(condition préalable)* prerequisite, precondition; *(connaissance requise)* required knowledge

préretraite [prerətrɛt] **NF 1** *(allocation)* early retirement allowance **2** *(période)* early retirement; **partir en p.** to take early retirement; **être mis en p.** to be retired early; **elle est en p.** she's taken early retirement

préretraité, -e [prerətrete] **NM,F** = person who has taken or been given early retirement

prérogative [prerɔgativ] **NF** prerogative, privilege

préromantique [prerɔmɑ̃tik] **ADJ** pre-Romantic

NMF pre-Romantic *(poet or artist)*

préromantisme [prerɔmɑ̃tism] **NM** pre-Romanticism

PRÈS [prɛ] **ADV 1** *(dans l'espace)* near, close; **cent mètres plus p.** one hundred metres nearer *or* closer; **aussi p. que** as near *or* close as; **le bureau est tout p.** the office is very near *or* just around the corner

2 *(dans le temps)* near, close, soon; **Noël, c'est tout p. maintenant** it'll be Christmas very soon now, Christmas will be here very soon now

PRÉP ambassadeur p. le gouvernement français ambassador to France

• **à… près ADV c'est parfait, à un détail p.** it's perfect but for *or* except for one thing; **j'ai raté mon train à quelques secondes p.** I missed my train by a few seconds; **on n'est pas à cinq euros p.** we can spare five euros; **tu n'es plus à cinq minutes p.** another five minutes won't make much difference

• **à cela près que CONJ** except that; **tout s'est bien passé, à cela p. que j'ai perdu mon portefeuille** everything went well except that I lost my wallet

• **à peu de choses près ADV** more or less; **à peu de choses p., il y en a 50** there are 50 of them, more or less *or* give or take a few

• **à peu près ADV 1** *(environ)* about, around; **il habite à peu p. à dix kilomètres** he lives about *or* around ten kilometres away; **il est à peu p. cinq heures** it's about *or* around five o'clock; **on était à peu p. 50** there were about *or* around 50 of us **2** *(plus ou moins)* more or less; **il sait à peu p. comment y aller** he knows more or less *or* roughly how to get there

• **de près ADV** at close range *or* quarters; **elle y voit mal de p.** she can't see very well close up *or* at close range; **il est rasé de p.** he's clean-shaven; **surveiller qn de p.** to keep a close watch *or* eye on sb; **frôler qch de p.** to come within an inch of sth; **les explosions se sont suivies de très p.** the explosions took place within seconds of each other; **regarder qch de (très) p.** to look at sth very closely; *Fig* to look (very) closely at sth, to look carefully into sth; **avant de donner de l'argent pour la recherche, il faut y regarder de p.** before giving money away for research, you must look into it carefully; **étudions la question de plus p.** let's take a closer look at the problem; **de p. ou de loin** however *or* whichever way you look at it; **cela ressemble, de p. ou de loin, à une habile escroquerie** however *or* whichever way you look at it, it's a skilful piece of fraud; **tout ce qui touche, de p. ou de loin à...** everything (which is) even remotely connected with...

• **près de** PRÉP **1** *(dans l'espace)* near; **il habite p. de Paris/d'ici** he lives near Paris/here; **il vit p. de chez moi** he lives near me; **assieds-toi p. de lui** sit near him *or* next to him; *Naut* **naviguer p. du vent** to sail close to the wind; **vêtements p. du corps** close-fitting *or* tight-fitting clothes

2 *(affectivement, qualitativement)* close to; **il a toujours été p. de ses parents** he's always been close to his parents; **les premiers candidats sont très p. les uns des autres** there's very little difference between the first few candidates; **ce comportement est plus p. de la bêtise que de la méchanceté** this behaviour is more like *or* closer to stupidity than malice; **être p. de ses sous** *ou* **de son argent** to be tightfisted

3 *(dans le temps)* **Noël est trop p. du jour de l'an** Christmas is too close to New Year's Day; **on est p. des vacances** it's nearly the holidays; **il doit être p. de la retraite** he must be about to retire; **nous étions p. de partir** we were about to leave; **vous êtes p. d'avoir deviné** you've nearly guessed; **je ne suis pas p. d'oublier ça** I'm not about to *or* it'll be a long time before I forget that; **ils ne sont pas p. de me revoir dans leur restaurant!** I shan't visit their restaurant again in a hurry!

4 *(environ, presque)* nearly, almost; **cela fait p. d'un mois qu'il est absent** he's been gone for almost a month; **il est p. de midi** it's nearly midday; **on était p. de cinquante** there were almost *or* nearly fifty of us; **ça nous a coûté p. de 100 euros** it cost us nearly 100 euros

présage [prezaʒ] NM **1** *(signe)* omen, *Littéraire* portent; **heureux/mauvais p.** good/bad omen; **j'y ai vu le p. d'un avenir meilleur** I viewed it as a sign of better days to come **2** *(prédiction)* prediction; **tirer un p. de qch** to make a prediction on the basis of sth

présager [17] [prezaʒe] VT **1** *(être le signe de)* to be a sign of, *Littéraire* to portend; **cela ne présage rien de bon** that doesn't bode well **2** *(prévoir)* to predict; **je n'aurais pu p. qu'il en arriverait à cette extrémité** I would never have guessed that he would go so far; **laisser p. qch** to be a sign of sth

présalaire [presalɛr] NM = allowance paid to students

pré-salé [presale] *(pl* **prés-salés**) NM *(mouton)* salt-meadow sheep; *(viande)* salt-meadow *or* pré-salé lamb

presbyte [presbit] *Opt* ADJ *Br* longsighted, *Am* farsighted, *Spéc* presbyopic

NMF *Br* longsighted *or Am* farsighted person, *Spéc* presbyope

presbytère [presbiter] NM presbytery

presbytérianisme [presbiterjanism] NM Presbyterianism

presbytérien, -enne [presbiterjɛ̃, -ɛn] ADJ Presbyterian

NM,F Presbyterian

presbytie [presbisi] NF *Opt Br* longsightedness, *Am* farsightedness, *Spéc* presbyopia

prescience [presjɑ̃s] NF *(pressentiment)* foreknowledge, foresight, *Littéraire* prescience; **avoir la p. de qch** to have a premonition of sth

prescient, -e [presjɑ̃, -ɑ̃t] ADJ *Littéraire* prescient

préscolaire [preskɔlɛr] ADJ preschool *(avant n)*

préscolarisation [preskɔlarizasjɔ̃] NF preschool education

prescripteur, -trice [preskriptœr, -tris] NM,F prescriber; *Mktg* opinion leader

prescription [preskripsjɔ̃] NF **1** *Jur* prescription; **p. de la peine** lapse *or* lapsing of the sentence; **y a-t-il p. pour les crimes de guerre?** is there a statutory limitation relating to war crimes?; *Fig* **il y a p.** it's all in the past now; **p. acquisitive** positive *or* acquisitive prescription; **p. civile** prescription; **p. extinctive** negative prescription; **p. légale** statute of limitations **2** *(instruction)* **se conformer aux prescriptions** to conform to instructions *or* regulations; **les prescriptions de la morale** moral dictates **3** *Méd (ordonnance)* prescription; **il ne doit pas y avoir p. d'antibiotiques dans ce cas** antibiotics should not be prescribed in this case

prescriptrice [preskriptris] *voir* **prescripteur**

prescrire [99] [preskrir] VT **1** *(recommander)* to prescribe; **p. qch à qn** to prescribe sth for sb; **on lui a prescrit du repos** he/she was ordered to rest; **p. à qn de faire qch** to order sb to do sth **2** *(stipuler)* to prescribe, to stipulate; **les formalités que prescrit le règlement** the procedures stipulated in the regulations; **ce que l'honneur prescrit** the demands *or* dictates of honour **3** *Jur (propriété)* to obtain by prescription; *(sanction, peine)* to lapse; **il faut 20 ans pour p. la peine** the sentence only lapses after 20 years

VPR **se prescrire** *Jur (s'acquérir)* to be obtained by prescription; *(se périmer)* to lapse

prescrivait *etc voir* **prescrire**

préséance [preseɑ̃s] NF **1** *(priorité)* precedence, priority (**sur** over); **avoir la p. sur qn** to have precedence over sb **2** *(étiquette)* **la p. veut qu'on le serve avant vous** according to (the rules of) etiquette, he should be served before you

présélecteur [preselɛktœr] NM *Tech* preselector

présélection [preselɛksjɔ̃] NF **1** *(premier choix)* short-listing **2** *Aut* **boîte de vitesses à p.** preselector gearbox **3** *Rad* **poste avec/sans p.** radio with/without preset

présélectionner [3] [preselɛksjɔne] VT **1** *(faire un premier choix parmi)* to short-list **2** *(fixer à l'avance* ▸ *heure, programme)* to preset, to preselect

présence [prezɑ̃s] NF **1** *(fait d'être là)* presence; **si ma p. vous gêne, je peux partir** if my presence disturbs you, I can leave; **j'ignorais ta p.** I didn't know you were here; **je sentais une p. derrière moi** I could feel a presence behind me; **merci de nous avoir honorés de votre p.** thank you for honouring us with your presence; **cela s'est passé hors de ma p.** I wasn't present when it happened; **faire acte de p., faire de la p.** to put in an appearance; **réunion à neuf heures, p. obligatoire** meeting at nine o'clock, attendance compulsory; **p. assidue aux cours** regular attendance in class; **p. policière** police presence

2 *(existence)* presence; **la p. de sang dans les urines** the presence of blood in the urine; **expliquez-moi la p. de cette arme ici** explain to me how this weapon comes to be here

3 *Théât (personnalité)* presence; **avoir de la p.** to have great presence; **il n'a aucune p. sur scène** he has no stage presence whatsoever

4 *(influence)* presence; **la p. française en Afrique** the French presence in Africa

• **en présence** ADJ *(en opposition)* **les armées/équipes en p.** the opposing armies/teams; *Jur* **les parties en p.** the opposing parties, *Spéc* the litigants ADV **mettre deux personnes en p.** to bring two people together *or* face to face

• **en présence de** PRÉP **la lecture du testament s'est faite en p. de toute la famille** the will was read out in the presence of the entire family; **je ne parlerai qu'en p. de mon avocat** I refuse to talk unless my lawyer is present; **en ma p.** in my presence; **nous nous trouvons en p. d'un problème insoluble** we are faced with an insoluble problem

• **présence d'esprit** NF presence of mind; **conserver sa p. d'esprit** to keep one's presence of mind, to keep one's wits about one

présent, -e [prezɑ̃, -ɑ̃t] ADJ **1** *(dans le lieu dont on parle)* present; **les personnes ici présentes** the people here present; **qui était p. quand la bagarre a éclaté?** who was present when the fight broke out?; **le racisme est p. à tous les niveaux** racism can be found at all levels; **croyez bien que je suis p. en pensée** *ou* **par le cœur** I can assure you I am with you in spirit *or* that my thoughts are with you; **être p. à une conférence** to be present at *or* to attend a conference; *Mil* **être p. à l'appel** to be present at roll call; **Duval? – p.!** Duval? – here *or* present!; **avoir qch p. à l'esprit** to bear *or* to keep sth in mind; **je n'ai pas p. à l'esprit le terme exact qu'il a employé** I can't bring *or* call to mind the precise word he used; **des images que nous garderons longtemps présentes à l'esprit** images which will linger in our minds; **répondre p.** *Scol* to answer to one's name, to be present at roll call; *Fig* to rise to the challenge; **des centaines de jeunes ont répondu p. à l'appel du pape** hundreds of young people answered the Pope's call

2 *(actif)* **il a été très p. après la mort de mon mari** he was very supportive after my husband died; **les Français ne sont pas du tout présents dans le jeu** the French team is making no impact on the game at all; **on a rarement vu un chanteur aussi p. sur scène** seldom has one seen a singer with such stage presence

3 *(en cours)* **dans le cas p.** in the present case; **la présente convention** this agreement

NM,F **il y avait 20 présents à la réunion** 20 people were present at *or* attended the meeting

NM **1** *(moment)* present; **vivre dans le p.** to live in the present; **pour le p.** for the time being, for the moment

2 *Gram* present (tense); **au p.** in the present; **le p. historique** *ou* **de narration** the historical present; **p. de l'indicatif/du subjonctif** present indicative/subjunctive; **p. historique** historic present; **p. progressif** present progressive; **p. simple** simple present

3 *Littéraire (cadeau)* gift, present; **faire p. de qch à qn** to present sb with sth

• **présente** NF *Admin (lettre)* **la présente** the present (letter), this letter; **je vous informe par la présente que...** I hereby inform you that...; **je joins à la présente un chèque à votre nom** I herewith enclose a cheque payable to you

• **à présent** ADV now; **tu peux t'en aller à p.** you may go now; **je travaille à p. dans une laiterie** I'm working in a dairy at present

• **à présent que** CONJ now that

• **d'à présent** ADJ modern-day, present-day

présentable [prezɑ̃tabl] ADJ presentable; **ta tenue n'est pas p.** you're not fit to be seen in that outfit

présentateur, -trice [prezɑ̃tatœr, -tris] NM,F *Rad & TV (des programmes)* announcer, presenter; *(du journal)* newscaster, *Am* anchorman, *f* anchorwoman; *(de variétés)* host, *Br* compere; **p. de talk-show** *Br* chat show *or Am* talk show host; **p. de télévision** television presenter; **p. de (vidéo)clips** video jockey, VJ

présentation [prezɑ̃tasjɔ̃] NF **1** *(dans un groupe)* introduction; **faire les présentations** to do the introductions; **Robert, faites donc les présentations** *(entre plusieurs personnes)* Robert, could you introduce everybody?; **venez par ici, vous deux, je vais faire les présentations** come over here, you two, I want to introduce you; **maintenant que les présentations sont faites** now that everybody's been introduced

2 *Rad & TV (des informations)* presentation, reading; *(des variétés, d'un jeu)* hosting, *Br* compering; **assurer la p. d'une séquence** to present a news story

3 *Couture* fashion show; **aller à une p. de collection** *ou* **couture** *ou* **mode** to attend a fashion show

4 *(exposition)* presenting, showing; *Com (à un client potentiel)* presentation; **la p. des modèles a d'abord provoqué une vive controverse** there was fierce controversy when the models were first presented *or* unveiled

5 *(aspect formel* ▸ *d'un texte)* presentation; *(*▸ *d'une lettre)* layout; **bon devoir mais soignez davantage la p.** a good piece of work, but take more care with the presentation; **l'idée de départ est bonne mais la p. des arguments n'est pas convaincante** the original idea is good but the arguments are not presented in a convincing manner

6 *Com (emballage)* presentation, packaging

7 *Mktg (étalage)* display; **la p. des objets dans une vitrine** the presentation *or* display of items in a shop window; **p. sur le lieu de vente** point-of-sale display; **p. en masse** mass display; **p. du produit** product display; **p. au sol** floor display; **p. à la sortie** check-out display; **p. en vrac** dump display

8 *(allure)* **il a une mauvaise/bonne p.** he doesn't look/he looks very presentable; **recherche hôtesses, excellente p.** *(dans une annonce)* receptionists required, must be of smart appearance

9 *(d'un document, d'un laissez-passer)* showing; *(d'un compte, d'une facture)* presentation; **la p. de la facture a lieu un mois après** the bill is presented a month later; *Banque* **p. à l'encaissement** paying in, *Br* encashment; **p. au paiement** presentation for payment

10 *Obst* **p. par le sommet/siège** head/breech presentation

11 *Rel* **la P. du Seigneur/de la Vierge** the Presentation of Christ (in the Temple)/of the Virgin Mary • **sur présentation de** PRÉP on presentation of

présentatrice [prezɑ̃tatris] *voir* **présentateur**

présentement [prezɑ̃tmɑ̃] ADV at present, *Am* presently

> Il faut noter que le terme anglais britannique **presently** est un faux ami. Il signifie **bientôt** ou **peu de temps après**, selon le contexte.

PRÉSENTER [3] [prezɑ̃te]

VT
- to introduce **1, 7**
- to present **3–9, 11, 13**
- to submit **7**
- to explain **9**
- to have **11**
- to describe **2**
- to show **3, 11**
- to enter **8**
- to offer **10, 12**

VPR
- to introduce oneself **1**
- to look **4**
- to present **7**
- to appear **3**
- to arise **6**

VT **1** *(faire connaître)* to introduce; **je te présente ma sœur Blanche** this is *or* let me introduce my sister Blanche; **nous n'avons pas été présentés** we haven't been introduced; **on ne vous présente plus** *(personne célèbre)* you need no introduction from me

2 *(décrire)* to describe, to portray; **on me l'a présenté comme un homme de parole** he was described to me as a man of his word; **on vous présente souvent comme une mélomane** you're often spoken of *or* portrayed as a music lover

3 *(remettre ▸ ticket, papiers)* to present, to show; *(▸ facture, devis)* to present; **p. une traite à l'acceptation** to present a bill for acceptance; **p. un chèque à l'encaissement** to present a cheque for payment

4 *(montrer publiquement)* to present; **le nouveau musée sera présenté à la presse demain** the new museum will be presented *or* opened to the press tomorrow; **les Ballets de la Lune (vous) présentent...** the Moon Ballet Company presents...

5 *Com (conditionner)* to present, to package; **c'est aussi présenté en granulés** it also comes in granules; **bouteille/vitrine joliment présentée** attractively packaged bottle/dressed window

6 *Rad & TV (informations)* to present, to read; *(variétés, jeu)* to host, *Br* to compere; **les informations vous sont présentées par Claude Mart** the news is presented *or* read by Claude Mart; **l'émission de ce soir est présentée par Margot Collet** your host for tonight's programme is Margot Collet

7 *(soumettre ▸ démission)* to present, to submit, to hand in; *(▸ pétition)* to put in, to submit; *(▸ projet de loi)* to present, to introduce; **p. sa candidature à un poste** to apply for a position

8 *(dans un festival)* to present; *(dans un concours)* to enter; **pourquoi présentez-vous votre film hors festival?** why aren't you showing your film as part of the festival?; *Scol & Univ* **p. l'anglais à l'oral** to take English at the oral exam; **il a présenté un de ses élèves au Conservatoire** he has entered one of his pupils for the Conservatoire entrance exam; **p. un candidat** *(à un concours)* to enter a candidate; *Pol* to put up a candidate

9 *(expliquer ▸ dossier)* to present, to explain; *(▸ rapport)* to present, to bring in; **vous avez présenté votre cas de manière fort convaincante** you have set out *or* stated your case most convincingly; **présentez-leur la chose gentiment** put it to them nicely; **présentez vos objections** state your objections

10 *(dans des formules de politesse)* to offer; **p. ses condoléances à qn** to offer one's condolences to sb, to offer sb one's condolences; **je vous présente mes condoléances** please accept *or* I'd like to offer my condolences; **p. ses hommages à qn** to pay one's respects to sb; **p. ses excuses** to offer (one's) apologies; **p. ses félicitations à qn** to congratulate sb

11 *(comporter ▸ anomalie, particularité)* to have, to present; *(▸ symptômes, traces, signes)* to show; *(▸ difficulté, risque)* to involve; **la colonne vertébrale présente une déviation** the spine shows *or* presents curvature; **p. l'avantage de** to have the advantage of; **la cuisine est petite, mais elle présente l'avantage d'être équipée** the kitchen may be small, but it has the advantage of being fully equipped; **cette œuvre présente un intérêt particulier** this work is of particular interest; **les deux systèmes présentent peu de différences** the two systems present or display very few differences; **votre compte présente un découvert de 500 euros** your account shows a 500 euro overdraft *or* is overdrawn by 500 euros

12 *(offrir)* **p. sa main à qn** to hold out one's hand to sb; **p. des petits fours** to offer *or* to pass round petit fours

13 *Mil (armes)* to present

VI *Fam* **il présente bien, ton ami** your friend looks good; **le type présentait plutôt mal** the guy didn't look too presentable

VPR **se présenter 1** *(décliner son identité)* to introduce oneself

2 *(emploi passif)* **ça se présente sous forme de poudre ou de liquide** it comes as a powder or a liquid

3 *(se manifester)* to appear; **se p. au QG** to report to HQ; **aucun témoin ne s'est encore présenté** no witness has come forward as yet; **vous devez vous p. au tribunal à 14 heures** you are required to be in court at 2 p.m.; **elle s'est présentée à son entretien avec une heure de retard** she arrived one hour late for the interview; **se p. chez qn** to call on sb, to go to sb's house; **après cette soirée, il n'a pas osé se p. chez elle** after the party, he didn't dare show his face at her place; **il ne s'est présenté aucun acheteur/volontaire** no buyer/volunteer has come forward; **ne pas écrire, se p.** *(dans une petite annonce)* applicants should apply in person, no letters please

4 *(avoir telle tournure)* **les choses se présentent plutôt mal** things aren't looking too good; **ça se présente mal pour qu'on ait fini mardi** it doesn't look as if we'll have finished by Tuesday; **tout cela se présente fort bien** it all looks very promising; **l'affaire se présente sous un jour nouveau** the matter can be seen *or* appears in a new light

5 *(être candidat)* **se p. aux présidentielles** to run for president; **se p. à un examen** to take an exam; **se p. à un concours de beauté** to go in for *or* to enter a beauty contest; **se p. pour un poste** to apply for a job; **pour le moment, deux personnes se sont présentées** *(pour une offre d'emploi)* two people have applied so far

6 *(survenir)* to arise; **une image terrible se présenta à mon esprit** a ghastly vision came into *or* sprang into my mind; **la scène qui se présentait à nos yeux** the scene that met our eyes; **si l'occasion se présente** if an opportunity arises; **si une difficulté se présente** if any difficulty should arise; **elle a épousé le premier qui s'est présenté** she married the first man that came along; **j'attends que quelque chose d'intéressant se présente** I'm waiting for something interesting to turn up *or* to come my way

7 *Obst* to present; **le bébé se présente par le siège** the baby is in a breech position, it's a breech baby; **le bébé se présente par la tête** the baby's presentation is normal, the baby's in a head position

présentoir [prezɑ̃twar] NM *Mktg (étagère)* (display) shelf; *(support)* (display) stand, display unit; *(panier)* dump bin; **p. de caisse** check-out display; **p. au sol** floor display, floor stand

présérie [preseri] NF *Ind* test series, pilot series

préservateur, -trice [prezervatœr, -tris] ADJ *Vieilli* preservative; *(mesures)* preventive

NM *(dans la nourriture)* preservative

préservatif, -ive [prezervatif, -iv] ADJ *Littéraire* preventive, protective

NM condom, sheath; **p. féminin** female condom; *(diaphragme)* diaphragm

> Il faut noter que le terme anglais **preservative** est un faux ami. Il signifie **agent de conservation**.

préservation [prezervasjɔ̃] NF preservation, protection; **la p. de l'espèce/de la faune** the preservation of the species/of wildlife; **la p. de l'emploi** safeguarding jobs

préservative [prezervativ] *voir* **préservatif**

préservatrice [prezervatris] *voir* **préservateur**

préserver [3] [prezerve] VT **1** *(maintenir)* to preserve, to keep; **notre peuple tient à p. son identité culturelle** our people want to preserve their cultural identity; **pour p. l'intégrité de notre territoire** in order to retain our territorial integrity **2** *(protéger)* **p. de** to protect *or* to preserve from; **à p. de l'humidité/la chaleur** *(sur emballage)* to be kept in a dry/cool place; **Dieu** *ou* **le ciel me préserve de tomber jamais aussi bas!** God *or* Heaven forbid that I should ever fall so low!; **le ciel m'en préserve!** heaven forbid!

VPR **se préserver se p. de** to guard against; **pour se p. du froid** to guard against *or* to protect oneself from the cold

présidence [prezidɑ̃s] NF **1** *(fonction) & Pol* presidency; *Univ Br* vice-chancellorship, *Am* presidency; *(d'un homme) Com* chairmanship, directorship; *Admin* chairmanship; **une femme a été nommée à la p.** *Pol* a woman was made President; *Admin* a woman was appointed to the chair *or* made chairperson; **sous la p. de M. Fabre** under the chairmanship of Mr Fabre; *UE* **p. tournante** rotating presidency

2 *(durée ▸ prévue)* term of office; *(▸ effectuée)* period in office; **sa p. aura duré un an** he'll/she'll have been in office for a year

3 *(lieu)* presidential residence *or* palace

4 *(services)* presidential office; **vous avez la p. en ligne** you're through to the President's *or* the Presidential office; **à la p., on ne dit rien** presidential aides are keeping silent

président [prezidɑ̃] NM **1** *Pol* president; **p. de l'Assemblée nationale** President of the National Assembly; **p. de la Commission européenne** President of the European Commission; **p. élu** president elect; **le p. du Parlement européen** the President of the European Parliament; **le p. de la République française** the French President; **p. du Sénat** President of the Senate; **p. à vie** life president

2 *Admin* chairperson, chairman, *f* chairwoman; **p. d'honneur** honorary chairman *or* president

3 *Com* chairman, *f* chairwoman; **p.-directeur général** *Br* chairman and managing director, *Am* (president and) chief executive officer; **p. du conseil d'administration** Chairman of the Board

4 *Jur* **p. d'audience** presiding magistrate *or* judge; **p. du tribunal** presiding judge

5 *Univ Br* vice-chancellor, *Am* president; **p. du jury (d'examen)** chief examiner

6 *Sport* **p. d'un club de football** president of a football club; **p. du jury** chairman of the panel of judges

présidente [prezidɑ̃t] NF **1** *Pol (titulaire)* (woman) president; *Vieilli (épouse du président)* president's wife

2 *Admin* chairwoman; **p. d'honneur** honorary chairwoman *or* president

3 *Com (titulaire)* chairwoman; *Vieilli (épouse du président)* chairman's wife; **p.-directrice générale** *Br* chairwoman and managing director, *Am* (president and) chief executive officer; **p. du conseil d'administration** Chairwoman of the Board

4 *Jur* **p. d'audience** presiding magistrate; **p. du tribunal** presiding judge

5 *Univ* principal, *Br* vice-chancellor, *Am* president; **p. du jury (d'examen)** chief examiner

6 *Sport* **p. d'un club de football** president of a football club; **p. du jury** chairwoman of the panel of judges

présidentiable [prezidɑ̃sjabl] NMF would-be presidential candidate

présidentialisme [prezidɑ̃sjalism] NM presidential (government) system

présidentiel, -elle [prezidɑ̃sjel] ADJ **1** *(du président ▸ gén)* presidential, president's *(avant n)*; *(▸ élection)* presidential; **dans l'entourage p.** among the president's close associates **2** *(centralisé ▸ régime)* presidential

• **présidentielles** NFPL presidential election *or* elections

LES PRÉSIDENTIELLES

In France, since 1873, the president had been traditionally elected for a renewable seven-year term ("le septennat"). However, as a result of a referendum held in September 2000 the seven-year term of office was replaced in 2002 by a five-year term ("le quinquennat"). Candidates are usually nominated by the main political parties, but anyone who collects the requisite number of sponsors can run. If no candidate wins an outright majority in the first round of voting, a runoff between the two frontrunners is held two weeks later.

présider [3] [prezide] **VT** *(diriger ▸ séance)* to preside at *or* over; *(▸ réunion)* to chair; *(▸ œuvre de bienfaisance, commission)* to preside over, to be the president of; *(table)* to be at the head of

• **présider à VT IND p. aux destinées d'un pays** to rule over a country; **un réel esprit de coopération a présidé à nos entretiens** a genuine spirit of co-operation prevailed during our talks; **les règles qui président à cette cérémonie** the rules governing this ceremony

présomptif, -ive [prezɔ̃ptif, -iv] **ADJ** presumptive

présomption [prezɔ̃psjɔ̃] **NF 1** *(prétention)* presumption, presumptuousness **2** *(supposition)* presumption, assumption; **il s'agit là d'une simple p. de votre part** you're only assuming this (to be the case) **3** *Jur* presumption; **de fortes présomptions pèsent sur lui** he is under great suspicion; **p. d'innocence** presumption of innocence

présomptive [prezɔ̃ptiv] *voir* **présomptif**

présomptueux, -euse [prezɔ̃ptɥø, -øz] **ADJ** presumptuous

NM un jeune p. a presumptuous young man

présono [presɔno] **NF** *Fam TV & Rad* playback□

présonorisation [presɔnɔrizasjɔ̃] **NF** *TV & Rad* playback

presque [presk] **ADV 1** *(dans des phrases affirmatives)* almost, nearly; **les cerises sont p. mûres** the cherries are almost *or* nearly ripe; **l'espèce a p. entièrement disparu** the species is virtually *or* all but extinct; **l'ambulance est arrivée p. aussitôt** the ambulance arrived almost immediately *or* at once; **il est p. minuit** it's almost *or* nearly midnight; **de l'avis de p. tous les collègues,...** in the opinion of almost all of our colleagues...; **il termine p.** he's just finishing; **nous y sommes p.** we're almost there; **il a p. terminé** he has nearly *or* almost finished; **ça n'est pas sûr mais p.** it's not certain, but just about *or* but as good as; **c'est p. de l'inconscience!** it's little short of madness!

2 *(dans des phrases négatives)* hardly, scarcely; **ils ne se sont p. pas parlé** they hardly spoke to each other; **je n'avais p. pas mangé de la journée** I'd eaten next to *or* almost *or* virtually nothing all day; **tu fumes beaucoup en ce moment? – non, p. pas** do you smoke much at the moment? – no, hardly at all; **est-ce qu'il reste des gâteaux? – non, p. pas** are there any cakes left? – hardly any; **je ne dors p. plus** I hardly *or* scarcely get any sleep any more; **il n'y a p. plus de café** there's hardly any coffee left; **p. jamais** scarcely *or* hardly ever, almost never; **je n'ai p. rien fait de la journée** I've done virtually *or* almost nothing all day; *Fam* **c'est p. rien** it's hardly anything

3 *(quasi)* **la p. totalité des électeurs** almost *or* nearly all the voters

• **ou presque ADV c'est sûr, ou p.** it's almost *or* practically certain; **j'ai vu tout le monde ou p.** I saw everybody or almost *or* virtually everybody

presqu'île [preskil] **NF** peninsula

pressage [presaʒ] **NM 1** *(d'un vêtement, d'un tissu)* pressing; **p. à la vapeur** steam-pressing **2** *(d'un disque)* pressing

pressant, -e [presɑ̃, -ɑ̃t] **ADJ 1** *(urgent)* urgent; **un travail p.** an urgent piece of work **2** *(insistant ▸ question, invitation)* pressing, insistent; **elle se faisait de plus en plus pressante** she was becoming more and more insistent

press-book [presbuk] *(pl* **press-books)** **NM** portfolio

presse [pres] **NF 1** *(journaux, magazines etc)* **la p. (écrite)** the press, the papers; **que dit la p.?** what do the papers say?; **la grande p.** large-circulation newspapers and magazines; **p. de bas étage** popular press, gutter press, ≃ tabloids; **p. de charme** soft-porn magazines; **la p. du cœur** romantic fiction (magazines); **la p. féminine** women's magazines; **la p. financière** the financial press; **la p. généraliste** the general(-interest) press; **p. gratuite** free press; **la p. magazine** news magazines; **p. masculine** men's magazines; **p. musicale** music press; **la p. nationale** the national press; **la p. d'opinion** the quality newspapers; **p. people** the celebrity press; **p. périodique** periodical press; **la p. poubelle** the gutter press; **la p. professionnelle** the trade press; **p. de qualité** quality newspapers; **p. quotidienne** daily press; **p. régionale** regional press; **la p. à sensation** *ou* **à scandale** the popular press, ≃ the tabloids, *Péj* the gutter press; **la p. du soir** the evening newspapers; **la p. spécialisée** the specialist press; **la p. sportive** the sports press; **avoir bonne/mauvaise p.** to have a good/bad press; *Fig* to be well/badly thought of; **le nucléaire n'a pas très bonne p.** nuclear power has a bad image *or* press

2 *Typ* press; **sous p.** in the press; **être mis sous p.** to go to press; **au moment où nous mettons sous p.** at the time of going to press; **sortir de p.** to come out; *Typ* **p. d'imprimerie** printing press; **p. à retiration** perfecting machine; **p. à rogner** plough; **p. rotative** rotary press; **p. typographique** printing press *or* machine

3 *Agr, Tech & Tex* press; **p. hydraulique/mécanique** hydraulic/power press; **p. à main** *ou* **à serrer** hand *or* screw press; **p. monétaire** coining press

4 *(pour le vin)* winepress

5 *Littéraire (foule, bousculade)* press, throng; **au moment de Noël, il y a toujours p.** it's always busy at Christmas

6 *Can (urgence)* urgency; **il n'y a pas de p.!** there's no urgency!, there's no need to panic!

• **de presse ADJ 1** *(campagne, coupure, attaché)* press *(avant n)* **2** *(moment, période)* peak *(avant n)*; **nous avons des moments de p.** we get very busy at times

pressé, -e [prese] **ADJ 1** *(personne)* **être p.** to be pressed for time, to be in a hurry *or* rush; **je suis horriblement p.** I'm in an awful hurry *or* rush; **ils ne sont jamais pressés** they're never in a hurry; **tu n'as pas l'air p. de la revoir** you seem in no hurry *or* you don't seem eager to see her again; **je suis p. d'en finir** I'm anxious to get the whole thing over with

2 *(précipité ▸ démarche, geste)* hurried; **aller d'un pas p.** to walk hurriedly

3 *(urgent ▸ réparation, achat)* urgent; **si vous n'avez rien de plus p. à faire** if you've got nothing more urgent to do; **il n'a rien trouvé de plus p. que d'aller tout raconter à sa femme** he wasted no time in telling his wife the whole story; **le plus p., c'est de prévenir son mari** the first thing to do is to tell her husband

4 *(exprimé ▸ agrume)* freshly squeezed; **p. à froid** cold-pressed

presse-agrumes [presagrym] **NM INV** juicer, juice extractor

presse-ail [presaj] **NM INV** garlic press

presse-bouton [presbutɔ̃] **ADJ INV** *voir* **guerre**

presse-citron [pressitrɔ̃] *(pl* **inv** *ou* **presse-citrons) NM** lemon squeezer

presse-étoupe [presetup] *(pl* **inv** *ou* **presse-étoupes) NM** *Tech* stuffing box, packing box (and gland); **garniture de p.** packing

pressens *etc voir* **pressentir**

pressentiment [presɑ̃timɑ̃] **NM** premonition; **avoir le p. de.../que...** to have a feeling of.../that...; **avoir le p. de malheurs à venir** to have a premonition of disaster; **avoir le p. que la mort est proche** to have a feeling of impending death, to have a foreboding *or* premonition of death; **j'ai eu le curieux p. que je reviendrais ici un jour** I had the odd feeling *or* a hunch that I'd be back again some day

pressentir [37] [presɑ̃tir] **VT 1** *(prévoir ▸ gén)* to sense (in advance), to have a premonition of; *(▸ malheur)* to have a premonition *or* foreboding of; **p. un danger/des difficultés** to sense danger/trouble; **p. que...** to have a feeling *or* premonition that...; **son attitude me fait p. que...** I get the feeling *or* I can sense from his attitude that...; **rien ne laissait p. qu'elle allait démissionner** nothing indicated *or* suggested that she would resign **2** *(contacter)* to approach, to contact; **il a été pressenti pour jouer le Christ à l'écran** he's been approached about portraying Christ on the screen; **toutes les personnes pressenties** all the people who were contacted

presse-papiers [prespapje] **NM INV 1** *(objet lourd)* paperweight **2** *Ordinat* clipboard

presse-purée [prespyre] **NM INV** potato masher

presser [4] [prese] **VT 1** *(extraire le jus de)* to squeeze; **p. le raisin** to press grapes; *Fam* **p. le citron à qn, p. qn comme un citron** to exploit sb to the full□, to squeeze sb dry

2 *(faire se hâter)* to rush; **j'ai horreur qu'on me presse** I hate being rushed; **qu'est-ce qui te presse?** what's the hurry?, what's (all) the rush for?; **rien ne nous presse** we're not in any hurry *or* rush; **p. le pas** to speed up

3 *(serrer)* to squeeze; **elle pressait sa poupée dans ses bras** she was hugging her doll; **il pressait sur son cœur la photo de sa fille** he was clasping a picture of his daughter to his heart; **p. la main à qn** to squeeze sb's hand, to give sb's hand a squeeze; **nous étions pressés contre les barrières** we were pressed *or* crushed against the gates; **pressés les uns contre les autres** packed *or* squashed together

4 *(appuyer sur ▸ commutateur, bouton)* to press, to push

5 p. qn de faire qch *(l'inciter à faire)* to urge sb to do sth; **je le pressai de quitter le pays** I urged him to leave the country; **il m'a pressé de lui donner la combinaison du coffre** he pressured *or* pressurized me into giving him the combination of the safe

6 *(accabler, harceler)* **pressé par ses créanciers** pressed by his creditors; **p. qn de questions** to ply *or* to bombard sb with questions; **être pressé par le temps/l'argent** to be pressed for time/money

7 *Tech (disque, pli)* to press

VI le temps presse time is short; **l'affaire presse** it's an urgent matter; **rien ne presse, ça ne presse pas** there's no (need to) rush *or* hurry; **pressons!** come on, let's hurry up!

VPR se presser 1 *(se dépêcher)* to hurry; **il n'est que deux heures, il n'y a pas de raison de se p.** it's only two o'clock, there's no point in rushing *or* no need to hurry; **allons les enfants, pressons-nous un peu** come on children, get a move on; **faire qch sans se p.** to take one's time over doing sth; **répondre sans se p.** to answer deliberately *or* leisurely, to give an unhurried answer; **se p. de faire qch** to be in a hurry to do sth; **je ne me pressai pas de répondre** I was in no hurry to reply; **pressons-nous de rentrer** let's hurry back; **heureusement que tu les as fait se p. un peu ou on y serait encore!** thank goodness you hurried them up a bit, otherwise we'd still be there!

2 *(se serrer)* **il se pressait contre moi tant il avait peur** he was pressing up against me in fear; **on se pressait pour entrer** people were pushing to get in; **les badauds se pressaient autour de la victime** the onlookers crowded *or* clustered around the victim; **les mots se pressaient dans sa bouche** he/she couldn't get his/her words out (fast enough)

3 *Fam* **se p. le citron** to rack one's brains

presse-raquette [presraket] *(pl* **inv** *ou* **presse-raquettes) NM** racket press

pressing [presiŋ] **NM 1** *(repassage)* pressing; **p. à la vapeur** steam-pressing **2** *(boutique)* dry cleaner's **3** *Fam* **faire le p.** to put *or* to pile on the pressure

pression [presjɔ̃] **NF 1** *(action)* pressure; **une simple p. de la main suffit** you just have to press lightly; **exercer une p. sur qch, faire p. sur qch** to exert pressure on sth

2 *Phys* pressure; **la p. de l'eau** water pressure; *Aut* **p. des pneus** tyre pressure; **p. acoustique** sound pressure; *Méd* **p. artérielle** blood pressure; *Météo* **p. atmosphérique** atmospheric pressure; **zone de hautes/basses pressions** area of high/low pressure; **à haute/basse p.** high-/low-pressure; **mettre sous p.** to pressurize; **récipient/cabine sous p.** pressurized container/cabin; *Fig* **être sous p.** to be stressed *or* under pressure; **entre midi et deux heures, on est sous p.** we're always under pressure between twelve and two; **faire monter la p.** to pile on *or* increase the pressure; *Fam* **mettre la p. à qn** to pressurize sb□, to put pressure on sb□

3 *(contrainte morale)* pressure; **céder à la p. populaire/familiale** to give in to popular/family pressure; **faire p. sur qn** to put pressure on sb; **on a fait p. sur lui pour qu'il démissionne** they put pressure on him to resign, they pressured *or* pressurized him into resigning; **il faut exercer une p. sur la classe politique** we must put pressure on *or* bring pressure to bear on the political community; **il y a une forte p. sur le dollar/l'équipe belge** the dollar/the Belgian team is under heavy pressure; **sous la p. des événements, il dut démissionner** the pressure of events was such that he had to resign

4 *(bouton-pression) Br* press stud, *Am* snap (fastener)

5 *(bière)* draught (beer); **garçon, trois pressions!** waiter, *Br* three half pints of lager *or Am* three beers!

6 *Écon* **p. fiscale** tax burden; **p. inflationniste** inflationary pressure

• **à la pression** ADJ *(bière)* draught

pressoir [preswar] NM **1** *(appareil)* **p. (à vin)** winepress; **p. à cidre/huile** cider/oil press **2** *(lieu)* presshouse

pressurage [presyraʒ] NM *(du raisin)* pressing

pressurer [3] [presyre] VT **1** *(raisin)* to press; *(citron)* to squeeze **2** *Fig (exploiter)* to squeeze, to exploit

VPR **se pressurer** *Fam* **se p. le cerveau** to rack one's brains

pressurisation [presyrizasjɔ̃] NF pressurization

pressuriser [3] [presyrize] VT to pressurize

prestance [prestɑ̃s] NF **un jeune homme de belle/noble p.** a handsome/noble-looking young man; **il a de la p.** he is a fine figure of a man; **son costume anglais lui donne une certaine p.** his English suit gives him a certain air of elegance

prestataire [prestatɛr] NMF **1** *(bénéficiaire)* recipient *(of an allowance)*; **depuis la majorité de mes enfants, je ne suis plus p. des allocations familiales** since my children came of age, I have not been able to claim child benefit **2** *(fournisseur)* **p. de service** service provider

prestation [prestasjɔ̃] NF **1** *(allocation)* allowance, benefit; **verser les prestations** to pay out benefits; **recevoir des prestations** to receive benefits; **p. compensatoire** *(en cas de divorce)* compensation; **prestations familiales** family benefits *(such as child benefit, rent allowance etc)*; **p. d'invalidité** (industrial) disablement benefit; **prestations maladie** sickness benefit; *Mil* **p. en nature** benefit in kind; **prestations sociales** social security benefits; **p. de vieillesse** old-age pension

2 *Com* **p. de service** provision *or* delivery of a service; **p. de capitaux** provision of capital

3 *(d'un artiste, d'un sportif etc)* performance; **faire une bonne/mauvaise p.** to perform well/badly; **faire une bonne p. scénique/télévisuelle** to put on a good stage/television performance

4 *Jur & Hist* **p. de serment** taking the oath; **sa p. de serment aura lieu mardi** he/she will be sworn in on Tuesday

preste [prest] ADJ swift, nimble; **avoir la main p.** *(être adroit)* to have a light touch

prestement [prestəmɑ̃] ADV *(se faufiler)* swiftly, nimbly; *(travailler)* swiftly, quickly

prestidigitateur, -trice [prestidiʒitatœr, -tris] NM,F conjuror, magician

prestidigitation [prestidiʒitasjɔ̃] NF conjuring, *Sout* prestidigitation; **faire de la p.** *(en amateur)* to do conjuring (tricks); *(en professionnel)* to be a conjuror; *Fig* **c'est de la p.!** it's magic!

prestidigitatrice [prestidiʒitatris] *voir* **prestidigitateur**

prestige [prestiʒ] NM prestige; **le p. de l'uniforme** the glamour of the uniform

• **de prestige** ADJ *(politique, publicité, magazine)* prestige *(avant n)*; *(résidence)* luxury *(avant n)*

• **pour le prestige** ADV for the sake of prestige

prestigieux, -euse [prestiʒjø, -øz] ADJ **1** *(magnifique)* prestigious **2** *(renommé ▸ produit)* renowned, famous, world-famous

presto [presto] ADV **1** *Mus* presto **2** *Fam (vite)* at *or* on the double, double-quick

présumable [prezymabl] ADJ presumable; **il est p. que...** it is to be presumed that...

présumer [3] [prezyme] VT *(supposer)* to presume, to assume; **je présume que vous êtes sa sœur** I take it *or* presume you're his/her sister; **p. qn innocent** to presume sb (to be) innocent

• **présumer de** VT IND *(surestimer)* **j'ai un peu présumé de mes forces** I overdid things somewhat; **p. de qn** to rely on sb too much

présupposé [presypoze] NM presupposition

présupposer [3] [presypoze] VT to presuppose

présupposition [presypozisjɔ̃] NF presupposition

présure [prezyr] NF *Biol & Chim* **1** *(enzyme)* rennin **2** *(pour le fromage etc)* rennet

prêt¹ [prɛ] NM **1** *(action)* lending, loaning; **c'est seulement un p.** it's only a loan; **conditions de p.** lending conditions

2 *(bancaire)* loan; **solliciter un p.** to apply for a loan; **obtenir un p. d'une banque** to secure a bank loan; **accorder un p. à qn** to lend money to sb; **p. à court/moyen/long terme** short-/medium-/long-term loan; **p. d'accession à la propriété** home loan; **p. bancaire** bank loan; **p. à la consommation** consumer loan; **p. à la construction** building loan; **p. conventionné** = approved mortgage loan; **p. à découvert** overdraft loan; **p. de démarrage** start-up loan; **p. d'épargne-logement** home loan; **p. à fonds perdus** loan without security, unsecured loan; **p. sur gage** loan against security; **p. gagé** *ou* **garanti** guaranteed *or* secured loan, collateral loan; **p. d'honneur** loan on trust; **p. hypothécaire** *ou* **sur hypothèque** mortgage loan; **p. immobilier** home loan, ≃ mortgage; **p. à intérêt** loan at *or* with interest, interest-bearing loan; **p. sans intérêt** interest-free loan; **p. non-garanti** unsecured loan; **p. participatif** equity loan; **prêts aux particuliers** personal loans; **p. personnalisé** *ou* **personnel** personal loan; **p. relais** bridging loan; **p. à terme (fixe)** term loan; **p. sur titres** loan against securities; **p. à vue** loan at call, loan repayable on demand

3 *Mil* pay; **p. franc** (subsistence) allowance *(paid in money)*

4 *(dans une bibliothèque ▸ document)* loan, issue, book issued; *Fam* **allez aux prêts** go to the issuing desk

prêt², -e [prɛ, prɛt] ADJ **1** *(préparé)* ready; **le dîner/votre costume est p.** dinner/your suit is ready; **je suis p., on peut partir** I'm ready, we can go now; **mes valises sont prêtes** my bags are packed; **p. à l'emploi** ready for use; **p. à emporter** *Br* take-away *(avant n)*, *Am* take-out *(avant n)*; **poulet p. à cuire** *ou* **rôtir** oven-ready *or* dressed chicken; **être (fin) p. au départ** to be all set to go; **l'armée se tient prête à intervenir** the army is ready to step in *or* to intervene; **tout est (fin) p. pour la cérémonie** everything is ready for the ceremony; *Fam* **j'ai toujours une cassette de prête** I always have a tape ready **2** *(disposé)* **toujours p.** *(devise des scouts)* be prepared; **p. à faire qch** ready *or* willing to do sth; **ils ne sont pas prêts à vendre** they aren't ready *or* willing to sell; **être p. à tout** to be game for anything; **il est p. à tout (faire) pour réussir** he'd do anything *or* stop at nothing to succeed; **Paul est tout p. à te remplacer** Paul is ready and willing to stand in for you **3** *Littéraire (sur le point de)* **p. à faire qch** on the point of doing sth; **p. à mourir** at the point of death

prêt-à-boire [prɛtabwar] *(pl* **prêts-à-boire***)* NM ready-mixed alcoholic drink

prêt-à-porter [prɛtapɔrte] *(pl* **prêts-à-porter***)* NM ready-to-wear fashion; **une collection de p. féminin** a women's ready-to-wear show; **acheter du p.** to buy ready-to-wear *or Br* off-the-peg clothes

prêté [prete] NM *(locution)* **c'est un p. pour un rendu** it's tit for tat

prétendant, -e [pretɑ̃dɑ̃, -ɑ̃t] NM,F *(à un bien, à un titre)* claimant (à to); **p. au trône** pretender to the throne

NM **1** *Hum (soupirant)* suitor, wooer **2** *Mktg* challenger

prétendre [73] [pretɑ̃dr] VT **1** *(se vanter de)* to claim; **il prétend qu'il peut rester 10 minutes sans respirer** he claims he can stay 10 minutes without breathing; **je n'ai jamais prétendu détenir la clé de la sagesse** I never claimed to hold the key to wisdom **2** *(affirmer)* to claim, to say, to maintain; **il prétendait être un descendant de Napoléon** he claimed to be descended from Napoleon; **je ne prétends pas que ce soit** *ou* **que c'est de ta faute** I'm not saying *or* I don't say it's your fault; **on prétend que ...** people say that ..., it is said that ...; **on la prétend folle** she's said *or* alleged to be mad; **à ce qu'elle prétend, son mari est ambassadeur** according to her, her husband is an ambassador; **ce n'est pas le chef-d'œuvre qu'on prétend** it's not the masterpiece it's made out to be **3** *(avoir l'intention de)* to intend, to mean; **qui prétendez-vous choisir comme successeur?** whom do you intend to choose as your successor?; *Belg* **il ne prétend pas le faire** he doesn't intend to do it

• **prétendre à** VT IND **1** *(revendiquer)* to claim **2** *Littéraire (aspirer à)* to aspire to; **p. aux honneurs** to aspire to honours; **il prétend au titre de champion** he is aiming for the championship

VPR **se prétendre** *(se dire)* to claim to be; **il se prétend avocat/infirme** he claims to be a lawyer/disabled; *Fam* **et ça se prétend original en plus!** and what's more it claims to be original!

> Il faut noter que le verbe anglais **to pretend** est un faux ami. Il signifie **faire semblant**.

prétendu, -e [pretɑ̃dy] ADJ *(par soi-même)* so-called, self-styled; *(par autrui)* so-called, alleged; **le p. professeur était en fait un espion** the so-called professor was in fact a spy

NM,F *Vieilli (fiancé, fiancée)* betrothed, intended

prétendument [pretɑ̃dymɑ̃] ADV *(par soi-même)* supposedly; *(par autrui)* supposedly, allegedly; **cet individu p. architecte nous avait construit une horreur** this so-called architect built us a monstrosity

prête-nom [prɛtnɔ̃] *(pl* **prête-noms***)* NM **1** *(homme de paille)* figurehead, man of straw **2** *Fin (société)* nominee company

prétentaine [pretɑ̃tɛn] NF *Vieilli* **courir la p.** to chase (after) women

prétentieuse [pretɑ̃sjøz] *voir* **prétentieux**

prétentieusement [pretɑ̃sjøzmɑ̃] ADV pretentiously, self-importantly

prétentieux, -euse [pretɑ̃sjø, -øz] ADJ *(personne, style, remarque)* pretentious

NM,F conceited *or* self-important person, poseur; **un jeune p.** a conceited young man; **regarde-la, quelle prétentieuse!** look at her, she's so full of herself *or* she really fancies herself!

prétention [pretɑ̃sjɔ̃] NF **1** *(orgueil)* pretentiousness, conceit, self-conceit; **il est plein de p.** he's so conceited **2** *(ambition)* pretension, claim; **je n'ai pas la p. d'avoir été complet sur ce sujet** I don't claim to have fully covered the subject; **avoir une p. à la sagesse** to pretend to wisdom; **l'article a des prétentions littéraires** the article has literary pretensions

• **prétentions** NFPL **1** *(exigences)* claims; **avoir des prétentions sur un héritage/une propriété** to lay claim to an inheritance/a property; **renoncer à ses prétentions** to renounce one's claims **2** *(financières)* **prétentions (de salaire)** expected salary, target earnings; **vos prétentions sont trop élevées** you're asking for too high a salary; **envoyez une lettre spécifiant vos prétentions** send a letter specifying your salary expectations

• **sans prétention** ADJ unpretentious; **un homme sans p.** an unassuming *or* unpretentious man; **c'est un scénario sans p.** it's an unpretentious script; **un repas sans p.** a simple meal

prêter [4] [prete] VT **1** *(argent, bien)* to lend, to loan; **peux-tu me p. ta voiture?** can you lend me *or* can I borrow your car? **2** *(attribuer)* to attribute, to accord; **p. de l'importance à qch** to attach importance to sth; **on me prête des talents que je n'ai malheureusement pas** I am credited with skills that I unfortunately do not possess; **l'opposition vous prête l'intention d'organiser un coup d'État** the opposition claims *or* alleges that you intend to stage a coup; **ce sont les propos prêtés au sénateur** these are the words attributed to the senator **3** *(offrir)* to give; **p. asile à qn** to give *or* to offer sb shelter; **p. assistance** *ou* **secours à qn** to give *or* to lend assistance to sb; **p. attention à** to pay attention to; **ne pas p. attention à** to ignore; **p.**

l'oreille to listen; **p. une oreille attentive à qn** to listen attentively to sb; **p. une oreille distraite à qn** to listen to sb with only half an ear; **p. sa voix à** *(chanter)* to sing the part of; *(parler)* to speak the part of; *(soutenir)* to speak on behalf *or* in support of; **p. serment** to take the oath; *Pol* to be sworn in; **faire p. serment à qn** to put sb under oath; **p. son nom à une cause** to lend one's name to a cause; **p. le flanc à la critique** to lay oneself open to *or* to invite criticism; **p. le flanc à l'adversaire** to give the adversary an opening

USAGE ABSOLU la banque prête à 9 pour cent the bank lends at 9 percent; **p. sur gages** to lend (money) against security; *Prov* **on ne prête qu'aux riches** = people don't lend money to those who really need it; *Fig* = people are judged according to their reputation

VI *(tissu, cuir)* to give, to stretch

• **prêter à VT IND** *(donner lieu à)* to give rise to, to invite; **le texte prête à confusion** the text is open to misinterpretation; **il est d'une naïveté qui prête à rire** he is ridiculously naive

VPR se prêter 1 se p. à *(consentir à)* to lend oneself to; **se p. à un arrangement** to lend oneself to *or* to consent to an arrangement; **se p. au jeu** to enter into the spirit of the game **2 se p. à** *(être adapté à)* to be suitable for; **si le temps s'y prête** weather permitting; **les circonstances ne se prêtaient guère aux confidences** it was no time for confidences; **ma petite maison ne se prête pas à une grande réception** my little house is hardly the (ideal) place for a big party

prétérit [preterit] **NM** *Gram* preterite; **au p.** in the preterite

prétériter [3] [preterite] **VT** *Suisse (personne)* to wrong

pré-test [pretɛst] *(pl* **pré-tests)** **NM** *Mktg* pre-test; **p. publicitaire** copy test

pré-tester [3] [pretɛste] **VT** *Mktg* to pre-test

préteur [pretœr] **NM** *Antiq* praetor

prêteur, -euse [prɛtœr, -øz] **ADJ elle n'est pas prêteuse** she doesn't like lending, she's very possessive about her belongings

NM,F lender, moneylender; **p. sur gages** pawnbroker; **p. sur hypothèque** mortgagee; **p. sur titre** money broker

prétexte[1] [pretɛkst] **ADJ F** *Antiq (toge)* praetexta

NF *Antiq* toga praetexta

prétexte[2] [pretɛkst] **NM 1** *(excuse)* pretext, excuse; **trouver un bon p.** to come up with a good excuse; **un mauvais p.** a lame *or* feeble excuse; **servir de p. à qn** to provide sb with a pretext; **prendre p. de qch** to use sth as an excuse; **pour toi, tous les prétextes sont bons pour ne pas travailler** any excuse is good for avoiding work as far as you're concerned **2** *(occasion)* **pour toi, tout est p. à rire/au sarcasme** you find cause for laughter/sarcasm in everything

• **sous aucun prétexte ADV** on no account

• **sous prétexte de PRÉP il est sorti sous p. d'aller acheter du pain** he went out on the pretext of buying some bread

• **sous prétexte que CONJ sous p. qu'elle a été malade, on lui passe tout** just because she's been ill, she can get away with anything

prétexter [4] [pretɛkste] **VT** to give as a pretext, to use as an excuse; **j'ai prétexté un rendez-vous chez le dentiste** I used a dental appointment as an excuse; **p. que** to give as a pretext *or* an excuse that; **elle va sûrement p. qu'elle n'a pas trouvé de taxi** she'll certainly pretend *or* come up with the excuse that she couldn't find a taxi; **p. la fatigue** to plead fatigue

prétoire [pretwar] **NM 1** *Jur* court **2** *Antiq (tente, palais)* praetorium

Pretoria [pretɔrja] **NM** Pretoria

prétorien, -enne [pretɔrjɛ̃, -ɛn] **ADJ** *Antiq (d'un magistrat)* pretorian, praetorian; *(d'un garde)* praetorian

NM Praetorian Guard

prêtre [prɛtr] **NM** *Rel* priest; **les prêtres** the clergy; *aussi Fig* **grand p.** high priest

prêt-relais [prɛrəlɛ] *(pl* **prêts-relais)** **NM** *Br* bridging loan, *Am* bridge loan

prêtre-ouvrier [prɛtruvrije] *(pl* **prêtres-ouvriers)** **NM** worker-priest

prêtresse [pretrɛs] **NF** *Rel* priestess; *aussi Fig* **grande p.** high priestess

prêtrise [pretriz] **NF** priesthood; **recevoir la p.** to be ordained a priest

preums [prəms] *Fam* **ADJ** first[□]; **je suis p.!** I'm first!

NMF first[□]

preuve [prœv] **NF 1** *(indice)* proof, piece of evidence, evidence *(UNCOUNT)*; **avoir la p. que...** to have proof that...; **avez-vous des preuves de ce que vous avancez?** can you produce evidence of *or* can you prove what you're saying?; **avoir la p. que.../de...** to have proof that.../of...; **c'est à nous de fournir la p.** it's up to us to show proof, the onus of proof is on us; **p. d'amour** token of love; **p. par commune renommée** hearsay evidence; **p. par écrit** written evidence; **p. indiciaire** circumstantial evidence; **p. littérale** documentary evidence; **p. par ouï-dire** hearsay evidence; **p. recevable** admissible evidence; **p. tangible** hard evidence; **p. testimoniale** testimony

2 *(démonstration)* proof; **faire la p. de qch** to prove sth; **mon avocat fera la p. de mon innocence** my lawyer will prove that I'm innocent, my lawyer will prove my innocence; **ce n'est pas une p.** that proves nothing *or* doesn't prove anything; **la p. de son inexpérience, c'est qu'il n'a pas demandé de reçu** his not asking for a receipt goes to show *or* proves that he lacks experience; *Fam* **il n'est pas fiable, la p., il est déjà en retard** you can never rely on him, look, he's already late; **j'en veux pour p....** the proof of it is...; **faire p. d'un grand sang-froid** to show *or* to display great presence of mind; **c'est un produit qui a fait ses preuves** it's a tried and tested product; **la mission exige des gens ayant fait leurs preuves** the mission calls for experienced people; **il avait fait ses preuves dans le maquis** he'd won his spurs *or* proved himself in the Maquis

3 *Tech* = test measuring the alcohol content of a liquid

• **à preuve ADV** *Fam* **tout le monde peut devenir célèbre, à p. moi-même** anybody can become famous, take me for instance *or* just look at me; **le directeur est un incapable, à p. le déficit de la maison** the manager is incompetent, witness the firm's deficit

• **à preuve que CONJ** *Fam* which goes to show that; **il m'a trahi, à p. qu'on ne peut se fier à personne** he betrayed me, which (just) goes to show that you can't trust anybody

• **preuves en main ADV** with cast-iron proof available; **affirmer qch preuves en main** to back sth up with cast-iron evidence *or* proof

preux [prø] *Arch ou Littéraire* **ADJ M** valiant, gallant

NM valiant *or* gallant knight

prévalence [prevalɑ̃s] **NF** prevalence

prévaloir [61] [prevalwar] **VI** *(prédominer)* to prevail (**sur/contre** over *ou* against/against); **l'optimisme prévaut encore dans les milieux financiers** optimism still prevails in financial circles; **nous lutterons pour faire p. nos droits légitimes** we will fight for our legitimate rights; **faire p. son opinion** to win acceptance for one's opinion; **ce principe prévaut sur tous les autres** this principle takes precedence *or* prevails over all others; **rien ne prévalut contre son obstination** nothing could prevail against *or* overcome his/her obstinacy

VPR se prévaloir 1 se p. de *(profiter de)* to take advantage of; *(faire valoir ▸ droit)* to exercise; **elle se prévalait de son ancienneté pour imposer ses goûts** she took advantage of her seniority to impose her preferences **2 se p. de** *(se vanter de)* to boast of *or* about; **il se prévalait de ses origines aristocratiques** he boasted of *or* about his aristocratic background

prévaricateur, -trice [prevarikatœr, -tris] *Jur* **ADJ** corrupt

NM,F corrupt official

prévarication [prevarikasjɔ̃] **NF** *Jur (corruption)* breach of trust, corrupt practice

prévaricatrice [prevarikatris] *voir* **prévaricateur**

prévariquer [3] [prevarike] **VI** *Jur* to depart from justice

prévaudrai, prévaux *etc voir* **prévaloir**

prévenance [prevnɑ̃s] **NF** consideration, thoughtfulness; **être plein de p. à l'égard de qn** to show consideration for *or* to be considerate towards sb

prévenant, -e [prevnɑ̃, -ɑ̃t] **ADJ 1** *(personne)* considerate, thoughtful (**envers** towards); *(geste)* thoughtful; **des manières prévenantes** attentive manners **2** *Vieilli (engageant)* **un homme à l'air p.** a man of engaging appearance

prévenir [40] [prevnir] **VT 1** *(informer)* **p. qn (de qch)** to inform sb (about *or* of sth), to let sb know (about *or* of sth); **si tu m'avais prévenu, j'aurais préparé à dîner** if you'd let me know, I'd have prepared something for dinner; **je vais le p. que vous êtes ici** I'll tell him *or* let him know that you're here; **en cas d'accident, qui dois-je p.?** who should I inform *or* notify in case of an accident?; **p. la police** to call *or* to notify the police

2 *(mettre en garde)* to warn, to tell; **on m'avait prévenu de n'ouvrir à personne** I had been warned *or* told not to open to anybody; **tu es** *ou* **te voilà prévenu!** you've been warned!

3 *(empêcher ▸ maladie)* to prevent; *(▸ catastrophe)* to avert; *(▸ danger)* to ward *or* stave off; *Prov* **mieux vaut p. que guérir** prevention is better than cure

4 *(anticiper ▸ désir, besoin)* to anticipate; *(▸ accusation, critique)* to forestall

5 *(influencer)* **p. qn en faveur de** to predispose sb towards; **p. qn contre** to prejudice sb against

USAGE ABSOLU partir sans p. to leave without warning *or* notice

préventif, -ive [prevɑ̃tif, -iv] **ADJ** preventive, preventative; **mesures préventives** preventive *or* precautionary measures; **prenez ce médicament à titre p.** take this medicine as a precaution

• **préventive NF** custody *(pending trial)*; **faire de la préventive** to be remanded in custody; **ils ont fait trois mois de préventive** they were imprisoned without trial for three months

prévention [prevɑ̃sjɔ̃] **NF 1** *(ensemble de mesures)* prevention; **nous nous attachons à la p. des accidents** we endeavour to prevent accidents; **la p. routière** the road safety administration, *Br* ≃ the Royal Society for the Prevention of Accidents **2** *(parti pris ▸ positif)* predisposition, bias (**en faveur de** in favour of); *(▸ négatif)* prejudice, bias (**contre** against); **avoir des préventions à l'égard de** *ou* **contre qn** to be prejudiced *or* biased against sb; **toute innovation dans ce domaine se heurte aux préventions du public** any innovation in this domain meets with public resistance **3** *Jur* custody; **il a fait un an de p. avant d'être jugé** he was remanded in custody for one year before being tried

préventive [prevɑ̃tiv] *voir* **préventif**

préventivement [prevɑ̃tivmɑ̃] **ADV** *(comme précaution)* preventatively, as a precaution *or* preventive

préventorium [prevɑ̃tɔrjɔm] **NM** tuberculosis sanatorium, preventorium

prévenu, -e [prevny] **PP** *voir* **prévenir**

ADJ 1 *(partial)* biased (**en faveur de** *or* **pour/contre** in favour of/against) **2** *Jur (poursuivi judiciairement)* charged; **p. de meurtre** charged with murder

NM,F *(à un procès)* defendant; *(en prison)* prisoner

prévient, prévint *etc voir* **prévenir**

prévisibilité [previzibilite] **NF** foreseeability

prévisible [previzibl] **ADJ** foreseeable, predictable; **son échec était p.** it was to be expected that he'd/she'd fail; **c'était difficilement p.** it was hard to foresee

prévision [previzjɔ̃] **NF 1** *(gén pl) (calcul)* expectation; **le coût de la maison a dépassé nos prévisions** the house cost more than we expected; **selon nos prévisions** according to our forecast **2** *Écon (activité)* forecasting; *(résultat)* forecast; **p. de la base** grass-roots forecasting; **p. boursière** Stock Market forecast; **prévisions budgétaires** budget forecasts *or* estimates; **prévisions conjoncturelles** economic prospects; **p. de la demande** forecast of demand; **prévisions économiques** economic forecasts; **p. événementielle** hazard forecasting; **p. du marché** market forecasting; **prévisions qualitatives** qualitative fore-

casting; **prévisions quantitatives** quantitative forecasting; **p. de ventes** sales forecast; **p. des ventes et profits** sales and profit forecast **3** *Météo (technique)* (weather) forecasting; **prévisions météorologiques** *(bulletin)* weather forecast
• **en prévision de** PRÉP in anticipation of

prévisionnel, -elle [previzjɔnel] ADJ *(analyse, étude)* forward-looking; *(coût, budget)* estimated

pré-visionner **[3]** [previzjɔne] VT *TV & Cin* to preview

prévisionniste [previzjɔnist] NMF forecaster

prévisualisation [previzɥalizasjɔ̃] NF *Ordinat* print preview

prévoir **[63]** [prevwar] VT **1** *(prédire ▸ gén)* to foresee, to anticipate; *(▸ augmentation, baisse, ventes)* to forecast; *Météo* to forecast; **p. une augmentation du trafic** to anticipate *or* to expect an increase in traffic; **on ne peut pas toujours tout p.** you can't always think of everything in advance; *Fam* **alors ça, ça n'était pas prévu au programme** we weren't expecting that to happen□; *Fam* **heureusement qu'on avait prévu le coup!** luckily we had anticipated this!□; **et maintenant, le temps prévu pour demain** and now, tomorrow's weather; **rien ne laissait p. pareil accident** nothing indicated that such an accident could happen; **rien ne laissait p. qu'il nous quitterait si rapidement** we never expected him to pass away so soon; **tout laisse p. que...** everything points *or* all signs point to...

2 *(projeter)* to plan; **tout s'est passé comme prévu** everything went according to plan *or* smoothly; **on a dîné plus tôt que prévu** we had dinner earlier than planned; **tout est prévu pour les invités** everything has been laid on *or* arranged for the guests; **le repas est prévu pour 100 personnes** a meal for 100 people has been planned; **l'ouverture du centre commercial est prévue pour le mois prochain** the opening of the shopping *Br* centre *or Am* mall is scheduled for next month; **l'argent que nous avions prévu pour le voyage n'a pas suffi** the money we allowed for *or* budgeted for *or* set aside for the trip wasn't enough; **p. de faire qch** to plan to do sth; **j'ai prévu d'apporter des boissons chaudes pour tout le monde** I'm planning to bring hot drinks for everyone

3 *(emporter ▸ repas, imperméable)* to bring; **prévoyez des vêtements chauds** make sure you bring some warm clothes

4 *Jur* to provide for; **la loi n'a pas prévu un cas semblable** the law makes no provision for a case of this kind

prévôt [prevo] NM *Hist* provost

prévoyait *etc voir* **prévoir**

prévoyance [prevwajɑ̃s] NF foresight, foresightedness, forethought; **faire preuve de p.** to be provident; **elle a manqué de p. en achetant cette voiture** it was rather short-sighted *or* unwise of her to buy the car; **p. sociale** social security provisions

prévoyant, -e [prevwajɑ̃, -ɑ̃t] ADJ provident, prudent; **ses parents ont été prévoyants** his/her parents made provision for the future

prévu, -e [prevy] PP *voir* **prévoir**

priapisme [prijapism] NM *Méd* priapism

prie-Dieu [pridjø] NM INV prie-dieu, prayer stool

prier **[10]** [prije] VT **1** *(ciel, Dieu)* to pray to; **je prie Dieu (et tous ses saints) que...** I pray (to) God (and all his saints) that...

2 *(supplier)* to beg, to beseech; **je vous en prie, emmenez-moi** I beg you to take me with you; **je te prie de me pardonner** please forgive me; **les enfants, je vous en prie, ça suffit!** children, please, that's enough!; **il adore se faire p.** he loves to be coaxed; **elle ne s'est pas fait p. pour venir** she didn't need any persuasion to come along

3 *(enjoindre)* to request; **vous êtes priés d'arriver à l'heure** you're requested to arrive on time; **je te prie de ne pas t'occuper de ça!** I'd be obliged if you minded your own business!, kindly *or* please mind your own business!; **je vous prie de croire qu'il m'a écouté cette fois!** believe (you) me, he listened to me this time!

4 *(dans des formules de politesse)* **merci – je vous en prie** thank you – (please) don't mention it; **puis-je entrer? – je vous en prie** may I come in? – please do; **pourriez-vous m'indiquer où est le commissariat, je vous prie?** could you please tell me *or* would you be kind enough to tell me where the police station is?; **M. et Mme Lemet vous prient de bien vouloir assister au mariage de leur fille** *(sur une invitation)* Mr and Mrs Lemet request the pleasure of your company at their daughter's wedding; **je vous prie de croire à mes sentiments distingués** *ou* **les meilleurs** *(à quelqu'un dont on connaît le nom) Br* yours sincerely, *Am* sincerely (yours); *(à quelqu'un dont on ne connaît pas le nom) Br* yours faithfully, *Am* sincerely (yours)

5 *Littéraire (inviter)* **p. qn à qch** to ask *or* to invite sb for sth, *Littéraire* to request sb's presence at sth; **il nous a priés à déjeuner** he asked *or* invited us to lunch

VI to pray; **p. pour qn/qch** to pray for sb/sth

prière [prijɛr] NF **1** *Rel* prayer; **dire** *ou* **faire** *ou* **réciter ses prières** to pray, to say one's prayers; **être en p.** to be praying *or* at prayer; **pensez à moi dans vos prières** remember me in your prayers; **tu peux faire tes prières** *(menace)* say your prayers

2 *(requête)* request, plea, entreaty; **elle a fini par céder aux prières de ses enfants** she finally gave in to her children's pleas; **p. de ne pas ouvrir la fenêtre** *(sur panneau)* please keep the window closed; **p. de ne pas fumer** *(sur panneau)* no smoking (please) **3** *(utilisé dans la correspondance)* **p. de nous couvrir par chèque** kindly remit by cheque; **p. de faire suivre** please forward

prieur, -e [prijœr] NM prior
• **prieure** NF prioress

prieuré [prijœre] NM *(communauté)* priory; *(église)* priory (church)

prima donna [primadɔna] *(pl* **prime donne** [primedɔne]) NF prima donna

primage [primaʒ] NM *Tech* priming

primaire [primɛr] ADJ **1** *(premier ▸ d'une série)* primary; **élection p.** primary election; **école/enseignement p.** *Br* primary *or Am* elementary school/education

2 *(couleur)* primary

3 *(de base)* **connaissances primaires** basic knowledge

4 *(borné ▸ personne)* narrow (in outlook), unsophisticated; *(▸ attitude)* simplistic, unsophisticated; **faire de l'anticommunisme p.** to be a dyed-in-the-wool *or* an out-and-out anticommunist

NMF *(personne bornée)* person of narrow outlook; **ces gens sont des primaires, ils voteront pour n'importe quel démagogue** these people aren't very sophisticated, they'll vote for any rabble-rouser

NM **1** *Scol* **le p.** *Br* primary *or Am* elementary education; **être en p.** to be at *Br* primary *or Am* elementary school; **dans le p.** in *Br* primary *or Am* elementary schools **2** *Écon* **le p.** the primary sector

NF *Pol* primary (election); **les primaires** the primaries

primat [prima] NM **1** *Rel* primate **2** *Littéraire (supériorité)* sway, primacy

primate [primat] NM **1** *Zool* primate **2** *Fam (homme grossier)* ape, brute

primauté [primote] NF **1** *(supériorité)* primacy; **avoir la p.** to have priority, to come first; **avoir la p. sur** to have priority over; **donner la p. à la théorie sur la pratique** to accord more importance to theory than to practice **2** *Rel* primacy

prime [prim] ADJ **1** *Math* prime **2** *Littéraire (premier)* **dès sa p. enfance** *ou* **jeunesse** from his/her earliest childhood; **elle n'est plus vraiment dans sa p. jeunesse** she's not that young any more; **de p. saut** *(à la première impulsion)* on the first impulse; *(dès la première fois)* at the first attempt, at once

NF **1** *(gratification)* bonus; **p. d'ancienneté** = bonus for long service; **p. de départ** severance pay, golden handshake; **p. d'encouragement** incentive; **p. d'intéressement** incentive bonus; **p. d'objectif** incentive bonus; **p. de rendement** productivity bonus; *(pour mission réussie)* success fee

2 *(indemnisation ▸ par un organisme)* allowance; *(▸ par l'État)* subsidy; **p. pour l'emploi** = tax credit awarded to low wage-earners, as an incentive to continue working and not claim benefit instead; **p. de transport/déménagement** travel/relocation allowance; **p. de licenciement** redundancy payment; **p. de risque** danger money; **p. de vie chère** cost-of-living allowance

3 *(incitation)* subsidy; *Fig* **cette mesure est une p. à la délation** this measure will only encourage people to denounce others; **p. à l'exportation** export subsidy; **p. à l'investissement** investment subsidy; **p. au retour** repatriation allowance

4 *Fin (cotisation)* premium; *(indemnité)* indemnity; **p. d'assurance** insurance premium; **ils ne toucheront pas la p.** *(bonus)* they will not qualify for the no-claims bonus; **p. de renouvellement** renewal premium

5 *Bourse (taux)* option rate; *(somme)* option money; **faire p.** to stand at a premium; **lever la p.** to exercise *or* take up an option; **réponse des primes** declaration of options; **p. acheteur** buyer's option; **p. du change** agio; **p. de conversion** conversion premium; **p. d'émission** premium on option to buy shares; **p. de remboursement** premium on redemption, redemption fee; **p. de risque de marché** risk premium; **p. vendeur** seller's option

6 *Mktg (cadeau)* free gift, giveaway; **p. autopayante** self-liquidating premium; **p. contenant** container premium; **p. différée** on-pack offer; **p. directe** with-pack premium; **p. à l'échantillon** free sample; **p. produit en plus** bonus pack
• **de prime abord** ADV at first sight *or* glance
• **en prime** ADV as a bonus; **en p. vous recevrez trois tasses à café** as a bonus, you will get a free gift of three coffee cups; **non seulement il ne fait rien mais en p. il se plaint!** not only does he do nothing, but he complains as well!

primé, -e [prime] ADJ *(film, vin, fromage)* award-winning; *(animal)* prizewinning

prime donne [primedɔne] *voir* **prima donna**

primer **[3]** [prime] VT **1** *(récompenser ▸ animal, invention)* to award a prize to; **elle a été primée au concours du plus beau bébé** she won *or* was awarded a prize in the beautiful baby contest **2** *(prédominer sur)* to take precedence over

VI *(avoir l'avantage)* to take precedence; **pour lui, c'est l'intelligence qui prime** intelligence is what counts most for him; **ce qui prime chez lui, c'est l'honnêteté** honesty is his most outstanding quality; **p. sur** to take precedence over; **le salaire a primé sur tous les autres avantages** the salary took precedence over all the other advantages; **son dernier argument a primé sur tous les autres** his/her final argument won out over all the others

primerose [primroz] NF *Bot* hollyhock, rose mallow

primesautier, -ère [primsotje, -ɛr] ADJ **1** *(spontané)* impulsive, spontaneous **2** *(vif ▸ humeur)* jaunty

prime time [prajmtajm] NM *TV* prime time

primeur [primœr] NF *(exclusivité)* **notre chaîne a eu la p. de l'information** our channel was first with the news; **je vous réserve la p. de mon reportage** you'll be the first one to have *or* you'll have first refusal of my article; **merci de me donner la p.** thank you for letting me know first
• **primeurs** NFPL early fruit and vegetables

primevère [primvɛr] NF *Bot (sauvage)* primrose; *(cultivée)* primula; **p. officinale** cowslip

primipare [primipar] ADJ primiparous
NF primipara

primitif, -ive [primitif, -iv] ADJ **1** *(initial)* primitive, original; **voici notre projet dans sa forme primitive** here is our project in its original form; **le sens p. du mot a disparu** the original meaning of the word has disappeared; **l'homme p.** primitive *or* early man; **langage p.** primitive language; *Ling* **temps p.** basic tense; *Géol* **terrain p.** primeval *or* primitive formations

2 *(non industrialisé ▸ société)* primitive; **leur technologie est plus que primitive** their technology is definitely primitive *or* archaic; **la vie dans ces montagnes est restée très primitive** life in these mountains is still very primitive; *Fig* **ton installation électrique est plutôt primitive!** the wiring in your place is a bit primitive!

3 *(fruste ▸ personne)* primitive, unsophisticated; **il est gentil mais un peu p.** he's nice but a bit unsophisticated

4 *Beaux-Arts* primitive

5 *Opt* **couleurs primitives** major colours
NM,F 1 *(en anthropologie)* member of a primitive society, primitive **2** *Beaux-Arts* primitive (painter)

primitivement [primitivmɑ̃] **ADV** originally, in the first place

primitivisme [primitivism] **NM** *Beaux-Arts* primitivism

primo [primo] **ADV** *Fam* first of all, for starters; **p., je n'en ai pas envie, (et) secundo je n'ai pas le temps** first of all, I don't feel like it, (and) second, I haven't got the time

primo-accédant [primoaksedɑ̃] *(pl* **primo-accédants)** **NM** first-time buyer

primo-arrivant, primo-arrivante [primɔarivɑ̃, -ɑ̃t] *(mpl* **primo-arrivants,** *fpl* **primo-arrivantes)** **ADJ** recently immigrated
NM,F recent immigrant

primogéniture [primɔʒenityr] **NF** primogeniture

primo-infection [primoɛ̃fɛksjɔ̃] *(pl* **primo-infections)** **NF** primary infection

primordial, -e, -aux, -ales [primɔrdjal, -o] **ADJ 1** *(essentiel)* fundamental, essential; **d'une importance primordiale** of prime importance; **elle a eu un rôle p. dans les négociations** she played a crucial role in the negotiations; **il est p. que tu sois présent** it's essential for you to be there; **il est p. de leur faire parvenir de la nourriture** it's essential *or* vital to get food to them **2** *(originel ▸ élément, molécule)* primordial, primeval; **les instincts primordiaux de l'homme** man's primal instincts

prince [prɛ̃s] **NM 1** *(souverain, fils de roi)* prince; **le p. consort** the prince consort; **le p. héritier** the crown prince; **le p. régent** the Prince Regent; **le p. de Galles** the Prince of Wales; **le P. Charmant** Prince Charming; **les princes qui nous gouvernent** the powers that be; **être** *ou* **se montrer bon p.** to behave generously; **je suis bon p., je vous pardonne** I'll be magnanimous *or* generous and forgive you; **il a agi en p.** he behaved royally; **cet enfant est traité/vêtu comme un p.** that child is treated/dressed like a prince
2 *(personnage important)* prince; **le p. des enfers** *ou* **des ténèbres** Satan, the prince of darkness
3 *(sommité)* prince; **le p. des poètes** the prince of poets
4 *Fam (homme généreux)* real gem *or Br* gent; **merci, mon p.!** thanks, *Br* mate *or Am* buddy!

prince-de-galles [prɛ̃sdəgal] **ADJ INV** Prince-of-Wales check *(avant n)*
NM INV Prince-of-Wales check material

princeps [prɛ̃sɛps] **ADJ INV** **édition p.** first edition

princesse [prɛ̃sɛs] **NF 1** *(souveraine, fille de roi)* princess; **arrête de faire la p., tu veux!** stop giving yourself airs! **2** *(robe)* princess dress

princier, -ère [prɛ̃sje, -ɛr] **ADJ 1** *(du prince)* prince's *(avant n)*, royal; **dans la loge princière** in the royal box **2** *(luxueux ▸ don, somme)* princely

princièrement [prɛ̃sjɛrmɑ̃] **ADV** *(dîner, recevoir, être traité)* in grand style, royally; **nous avons été accueillis p.** we were given a (right) royal welcome

principal, -e, -aux, -ales [prɛ̃sipal, -o] **ADJ 1** *(essentiel)* main; **les principaux intéressés** the main parties involved; **la porte/l'entrée principale** the main gate/entrance **2** *Gram (verbe, proposition)* main **3** *(supérieur)* principal, chief
NM 1 *(essentiel)* **le p.** the main thing, most important thing; **le p., c'est que tu ne sois pas blessé** what is most important is that you're not hurt; **c'est fini, c'est le p.** it's over, that's the main thing **2** *Fin (capital)* principal; *(de l'impôt)* = original amount of tax payable before surcharges; **p. et intérêts** principal and interest **3** *Mus* principal
NM,F *Scol* (school) principal

principalement [prɛ̃sipalmɑ̃] **ADV** chiefly, mostly, principally

principauté [prɛ̃sipote] **NF** principalité

principe [prɛ̃sip] **NM 1** *(règle morale)* principle, rule of conduct; **j'ai des principes** I've got principles; **cela ne fait pas partie de mes principes** it's against my principles; **j'ai toujours eu pour p. d'agir honnêtement** I have always made it a principle to act with honesty; **c'est une question de p.** it's a matter of principle; **elle est sans principes** she has no principles
2 *(axiome)* principle, law, axiom; **posons comme p. que nous avons les crédits nécessaires** let us assume that we get the necessary credits; **un p. de base** a basic principle; *Compta* **p. de la partie double/simple** double-entry/single-entry method; **c'est le p. des vases communicants** it's the principle of communicating vessels; *Fig* there's been a knock-on effect
3 *(notion ▸ d'une science)* principle; **enseigner les principes de la biologie** to teach the basic principles of biology
4 *(fonctionnement)* principle; **le p. de la vente par correspondance, c'est...** the (basic) principle of mail-order selling is...
5 *(fondement)* principle, constituent; **votre déclaration contredit le p. même de notre Constitution** your statement goes against the very principle *or* basis of our Constitution; **le fromage est riche en principes nutritifs** cheese has a high nutritional value; **p. de précaution** precautionary principle
6 *(origine)* origin; **le p. de la vie** the origin of life; **remonter au p. des choses** to go back to first principles
7 *Chim (extrait)* principle; **p. actif** active principle *or* constituent
• **de principe** **ADJ** *(accord, approbation)* provisional
• **en principe** **ADV 1** *(en théorie)* in principle, in theory, theoretically; **en p., je devrais pouvoir venir** all being well, I should be able to come **2** *(d'habitude)* usually; **en p., nous descendons à l'hôtel** we usually stop at a hotel
• **par principe** **ADV** on principle; **il refuse de l'écouter par p.** he refuses to listen to him/her on principle
• **pour le principe** **ADV** on principle; **tu refuses de signer pour le p. ou pour des raisons personnelles?** are you refusing to sign for reasons of principle or for personal reasons?

printanier, -ère [prɛ̃tanje, -ɛr] **ADJ 1** *(du printemps)* spring *(avant n)*; **il fait un temps p.** it feels like spring, spring is in the air **2** *(gai et jeune ▸ tenue, couleur)* springlike **3** *Culin (potage, salade)* printanier *(garnished with early mixed vegetables, diced)*

printemps [prɛ̃tɑ̃] **NM 1** *(saison)* spring; **au p.** in (the) spring, in (the) springtime **2** *Littéraire (année)* summer; **une jeune fille de vingt p.** a young girl of twenty summers **3** *Littéraire (commencement)* spring; **au p. de la vie** in the springtime of life

prion [priɔ̃] **NM** *Biol* prion

prioritaire [prijɔritɛr] **ADJ 1** *Transp* priority *(avant n)*, having priority; **ce véhicule est p. lorsqu'il quitte son arrêt** this vehicle has (the) right of way *or* has priority when leaving a stop **2** *(usager, industrie)* priority *(avant n)*; **notre projet est p. sur tous les autres** our project has priority over all the others; **mon souci p., c'est de trouver un logement** my main *or* first problem is to find somewhere to live
NMF person with priority; **cette place est réservée aux prioritaires titulaires d'une carte** this seat is reserved for priority cardholders

priorité [prijɔrite] **NF 1** *(sur route)* right of way; **avoir la p.** to have the right of way; **tu as la p.** it's your right of way; **laisser la p. à une voiture** *Br* to give way *or Am* to yield to a car; **il y a p. à droite** *ou Belg* **de droite** you must *Br* give way to *or Am* yield to traffic coming from the right
2 *(en vertu d'un règlement)* priority; **les handicapés ont la p. pour monter à bord** disabled people are entitled to board first
3 *(antériorité)* priority, precedence
4 *(primauté)* priority; **donner** *ou* **accorder la p. à qch** to prioritize sth, to give priority to sth; **la p. sera donnée à la lutte contre le cancer** priority will be given to the fight against cancer; **ce dossier a la p. absolue** this file is top priority; **avoir la p. sur** to have *or* take priority *or* precedence over
5 *Bourse* **action de p.** *Br* preference share, *Am* preferred stock
• **en priorité, par priorité** **ADV** as a priority, as a matter of urgency; **nous discuterons en p. des droits de l'homme** we'll discuss human rights as a priority; **leur dossier sera traité en p.** their file will get priority treatment

pris, -e [pri, -iz] **PP** *voir* **prendre**
ADJ 1 *(occupé ▸ personne)* busy; *(siège, place)* taken; **je suis déjà p. ce jour-là** I've already got something on that day, that day's booked already; **aide-moi, tu vois bien que j'ai les mains prises** help me, can't you see my hands are full?
2 *Méd* **avoir le nez p.** to have a blocked nose; **avoir la gorge prise** to have a sore throat
3 *(crème, colle, ciment)* set; *(eau, rivière)* frozen
4 *(envahi)* **p. de pitié/peur** stricken by pity/fear; **p. de panique** panic-stricken; **p. de remords** smitten with remorse; **p. d'une violente douleur** seized with a terrible pain; **p. de boisson** under the influence of alcohol
• **prise** **NF 1** *(point de saisie)* grip, hold; *(en escalade)* hold; *(pour le pied)* foothold; **avoir prise sur qn** to have a hold over sb; **je n'ai aucune prise sur mes filles** I can't control my daughters at all; **les menaces n'ont aucune prise sur lui** threats have no effect *or* make no impression on him; **donner prise à la critique** *(personne)* to lay oneself open to attack; *(idée, réalisation)* to be open to attack; *aussi Fig* **lâcher prise** to let go
2 *(de judo, de lutte)* hold; **faire une prise de judo à qn** to use a judo throw on sb
3 *(absorption ▸ d'un médicament)* taking; **la prise du médicament doit se faire à heures régulières** the medication must be taken regularly
4 *(dose ▸ de tabac)* pinch; *(▸ de cocaïne)* snort
5 *(capture ▸ de contrebande, de drogue)* seizure, catch; *(dans un jeu)* capture; *Pêche* catch; *Mil* **la prise de la Bastille** the storming of the Bastille; **prises de guerre** spoils of war
6 *Élec* **prise (de courant), prise électrique** *(mâle)* plug; *(femelle)* socket; **prise murale** wall socket; **prise multiple** adaptor; **prise Péritel®** Scart plug; *(qui reçoit)* Scart socket; **prise de terre** *Br* earth, *Am* ground; **l'appareil n'a pas de prise de terre** the appliance is not *Br* earthed *or Am* grounded
7 *Tech* **prise d'air** *(ouverture)* air inlet; *(introduction d'air)* ventilation; **prise d'eau** water point; *Aut* **prise directe** direct drive; **prise de vapeur** steam outlet
8 *(durcissement ▸ du ciment, de la colle)* setting; *(▸ d'un fromage)* hardening
9 *Cin & TV* **prise longue** long take; **prise des marques** blocking; **prise panoramique** panning shot; **prise unique** single take
10 *(dans des expressions) Fin* **prise de bénéfices** profit-taking; **prise de conscience** realization; **ma première prise de conscience de la souffrance humaine** the first time I became aware of human suffering; **prise en considération** taking into account; **nous insistons sur la prise en considération des circonstances individuelles** we stress that personal circumstances must be taken into account; **prise de contact** meeting; **ce ne sont que les premières prises de contact entre nous** we're just meeting to get to know each other better; *Écon* **prise de contrôle** takeover; **prise de décision(s)** decision-making; **prise de notes** note-taking; **prise d'otages** hostage-taking; **encore trois prises de parole avant la fin de la session** three more speeches to go before the end of the session; *Écon* **prise de participation** *(dans une entreprise)* acquisition of an interest in a company; **prise de position** opinion, stand; *Bourse* position taking; **à l'origine, vos prises de position étaient moins libérales** originally, your position was less liberal *or* you took a less liberal stand; **prise de possession** *(d'un héritage)* acquisition; *(d'un territoire)* taking possession; **prise de pouvoir** *(légale)* (political) takeover; *(illégale)* seizure of power; *Fam* **prise de tête** hassle
• **aux prises avec** **PRÉP** grappling *or* battling with; **être aux prises avec qch** to be grappling *or* battling with sth; **je l'ai laissé aux prises avec un problème de géométrie** I left him grappling *or* wrestling with a geometry problem
• **en prise** **ADV** *Aut* in gear; **mets-toi en prise** put the car in *or* into gear **ADJ** *Fig* **être en prise (directe) avec la réalité** to have a good hold on *or* to have a firm grip on reality
• **prise à partie** **NF** *Jur* = civil action against a judge or magistrate
• **prise d'armes** **NF** (military) parade

• **prise de bec** NF row, squabble
• **prise de sang** NF blood test
• **prise de son** NF sound (recording); **la prise de son est de Raoul Fleck** sound (engineer), Raoul Fleck
• **prise de vues** NF *Cin & TV (technique)* shooting; *(cliché)* (camera) shot; *(de tournage)* take; **prise de vues: Jaroslaw Mitchell** camera: Jaroslaw Mitchell; **prise de vue aérienne** aerial shot; **prise de vue sur grue** crane shot; **prise de vue en mouvement** running shot; **prise de vue en travelling** travelling shot
• **prise en charge** NF **1** *(par la Sécurité sociale)* refunding *(of medical expenses through the social security system)* **2** *(par un taxi)* minimum (pick-up) charge **3** *Fin (de frais)* payment, covering

prisée [prize] NF *Jur* valuation

priser [3] [prize] VT **1** *Littéraire (estimer)* to prize, to value highly; **je ne prise guère sa compagnie** I don't particularly relish his/her company **2** *(tabac)* to take; *(cocaïne)* to snort
VI to take snuff

priseur, -euse [prizœr, -øz] NM,F *(de tabac)* snuff-taker

prismatique [prismatik] ADJ prismatic

prisme [prism] NM **1** *Phys* prism; **jumelles à p.** prismatic binoculars **2** *Fig* **tu vois toujours la réalité à travers un p.** you always distort reality

prison [prizɔ̃] NF **1** *(lieu)* prison, jail; **être/aller en p.** to be in/to go to prison *or* jail; **mettre qn en p.** to put sb in prison *or* jail; **sortir de p.** to get out (of prison *or* jail); **pour lui, la pension a été une véritable p.** boarding school was like a prison for him; **p. ouverte** open prison **2** *(peine)* imprisonment; **faire de la p.** to be in prison *or* jail, to serve time; **elle a fait deux ans de p.** she spent two years in prison *or* jail; **il a été condamné à cinq ans de p.** he was sentenced to five years in prison *or* jail; **il risque la p.** he risks going to prison *or* jail; **p. à vie** *ou* **à perpétuité** life sentence; **p. ferme** imprisonment **3** *Fig* prison; **son amour était une p.** I felt caged in by his/her love

prisonnier, -ère [prizɔnje, -ɛr] ADJ **1** *(séquestré)* captive; **plusieurs mineurs sont encore prisonniers au fond de la mine** several miners are still trapped at the bottom of the shaft; **je ne sortais pas et restais p. dans mon petit studio** I shut myself away in my little bedsit and never went out; **il gardait ma main prisonnière** he wouldn't let go of my hand **2** *Fig* **être p. de ses promesses** to be the prisoner of *or* to be trapped by one's promises; **être p. de ses principes** to be a slave to one's principles; **être p. de ses habitudes** to be a creature of habit
NM,F prisoner; **il a été fait p.** he was taken prisoner; **se constituer p.** to give oneself up, to turn oneself in; **les prisonniers sont montés sur le toit pour protester** the inmates staged a rooftop protest; **p. de guerre** prisoner of war, POW; **p. d'opinion** prisoner of conscience; **p. politique** political prisoner

Prisunic® [prizynik] NM = low-priced general goods store; *Péj* **il m'a donné un truc de P.** he gave me a real cheapo present

prit *etc voir* **prendre**

privatif, -ive [privatif, -iv] ADJ **1** *(privé)* private **2** *(réservé à une personne)* exclusive **3** *Ling (élément, préfixe)* privative
NM *Ling* privative prefix

privation [privasjɔ̃] NF *(perte)* loss, deprivation; **pour moi, arrêter de boire n'a pas été une p.** giving up drinking was no deprivation for me
• **privations** NFPL *(sacrifices)* hardship, hardships; **une vie de privations** a life of hardship; **les privations de la guerre** the hardships of war; **à force de privations** through constant sacrifice, by constantly doing without

privatique [privatik] NF stand-alone technology

privatisable [privatizabl] ADJ which can be privatized, privatizable

privatisation [privatizasjɔ̃] NF privatization, privatizing

privatiser [3] [privatize] VT to privatize
VPR **se privatiser** to go private

privative [privativ] *voir* **privatif**

privauté [privote] NF *(familiarité)* **p. de langage** crude *or* coarse language; **une telle p. de langage n'est pas de mise** there's no call for that sort of language
• **privautés** NFPL *(libertés déplacées)* liberties; **avoir** *ou* **se permettre des privautés avec qn** to take liberties with sb

privé, -e [prive] ADJ **1** *(personnel ▸ vie, propriété, correspondance)* private
2 *(non public ▸ visite, audience)* private
3 *(officieux)* unofficial; **nous avons appris sa démission de source privée** we've learned unofficially that he/she has resigned
4 *(non géré par l'État)* private
NM **1** *Ind* private sector; **travailler dans le p.** to work for the private sector *or* a private company; *Fam* **elle est médecin à l'hôpital mais elle fait aussi du p.** she works as a doctor in a hospital but she also has *or* takes private patients
2 *(enseignement privé)* private education; **elle a mis ses filles dans le p.** she sent her daughters to a private school
3 *(intimité)* private life; **dans le p.** in private life
4 *Fam (détective privé)* private eye, *Am* dick, shamus
• **en privé** ADV in private; **pourrais-je vous parler en p.?** could I talk to you privately *or* in private?; **intimidante en public, elle est pourtant charmante en p.** she may be intimidating in public, but in private life she's charming

priver [3] [prive] VT **1** *(démunir)* to deprive; **prenez mon écharpe, ça ne me prive guère** have my scarf, I won't miss *or* don't need it; **je ne vous en prive pas?** can you spare it?, I'm not depriving you, am I?; **ça la prive beaucoup de ne plus fumer** she misses smoking a lot; **être privé de** to be deprived of, to have no; **nous avons été privés de trains pendant quatre semaines à cause de la grève** we had no trains for four weeks because of the strike; **privé d'eau/d'air/de sommeil** deprived of water/air/sleep; **ce genre de situation me prive de tous mes moyens** I completely lose my head *or* I go completely to pieces in that kind of situation; **le cancer/la guerre m'a privé de mon meilleur ami** I lost my best friend to cancer/in the war, cancer/the war took my best friend (away) from me
2 *(comme sanction)* to deprive; **p. qn de qch** to make sb go *or* do without sth; **tu seras privé de dessert/télévision** no dessert/television for you; **il a été privé de sortie** he wasn't allowed to go out, he was grounded
VPR **se priver 1** *(faire des sacrifices)* **elle s'est privée pour leur payer des études** she made great sacrifices to pay for their education; **il n'aime pas se p.** he hates denying himself anything; **ne pas se p.** to deny oneself nothing; **un jour de congé supplémentaire, il ne se prive pas!** another day off, he certainly looks after himself!
2 se p. de *(renoncer à)* to deprive oneself of, to do without; **il se prive d'alcool** he cuts out alcohol, he goes without alcohol
3 *(se gêner)* **il ne s'est pas privé de se moquer de toi** he didn't hesitate to make fun of you; **je ne vais pas me p. de le lui dire!** I'll make no bones about telling him/her!; **tu peux te reposer cinq minutes, elle ne s'en est pas privée!** you can have a rest for five minutes, SHE did!

privilège [privilɛʒ] NM **1** *(avantage)* privilege; **le p. de l'âge** the prerogative of old age; **j'ai eu le p. de la voir sur scène** I was privileged (enough) to see her perform; **j'ai le triste p. de vous annoncer...** it is my sad duty to inform you...; **j'ai eu le triste p. de connaître cet individu** it was once my misfortune to be acquainted with this individual
2 *(exclusivité)* **l'homme a le p. de la parole** man is unique in being endowed with the power of speech
3 *(faveur)* privilege, favour; **accorder des privilèges à qn** to grant sb favours
4 *Fin & Jur* **p. de créancier** creditor's preferential claim; **p. fiscal** tax privilege; **p. général/spécial** general/particular lien

privilégié, -e [privileʒje] ADJ **1** *(avantagé)* privileged; **l'île jouit d'un climat p.** the island enjoys an excellent climate; **les classes privilégiées** the privileged classes; **la minorité privilégiée** the privileged few
2 *(choisi ▸ client, partenaire)* favoured; **avoir des relations privilégiées avec un pays** to have a special relationship with a country
3 *(préféré)* favourite, preferred; **le moyen d'expression p. de cet artiste** the artist's favourite *or* preferred means of expression, the means of expression favoured by the artist
4 *Fin (action) Br* preference *(avant n)*, *Am* preferred *(avant n)*; *Jur* **créancier p.** preferential creditor
NM,F privileged person; **quelques privilégiés ont assisté à la représentation** a privileged few attended the performance; **nous faisons partie des privilégiés** we are among the privileged

privilégier [9] [privileʒje] VT **1** *(préférer)* to privilege; **nous avons privilégié cette méthode pour l'enseignement de la langue** we've singled out this method for language teaching **2** *(avantager)* to favour; **les basketteurs adverses sont privilégiés par leur haute taille** the basketball players in the opposing team are helped by the fact that they're taller; **cette augmentation privilégie les hauts salaires** this increase is of particular benefit to high earners

prix [pri] NM **1** *(tarif fixe)* price, cost; **à moitié p.** half price; **six yaourts pour le p. de quatre** six yoghurts for the price of four; **ça coûte un p. fou** it costs a fortune *or* the earth; **mes bottes, dis un p. pour voir!** how much do you think my boots cost?; **le p. du voyage comprend le repas de midi** the cost of the trip includes lunch; **laissez-moi au moins régler le p. des places** let me at least pay for the tickets; **à bas** *ou* **vil p.** very cheaply; **acheter qch à bas p.** to buy sth at a low price *or* very cheaply; **j'ai acheté le lot à vil p.** I bought the lot for next to nothing; **à ce p.-là** at that price; **à ce p.-là, ce serait bête de se le refuser** at that price, it would be silly not to buy it; **dans mes p.** within my (price) range; **c'est tout à fait dans mes p.** it's well within what I can afford *or* within my price range; **ce n'est déjà plus tout à fait dans ses p.** that's already a little more than he/she wanted to spend; **le p. fort** *(maximal)* top *or* maximum price; *(excessif)* high price; **j'ai payé le p. fort pour ma promotion** I was promoted but I paid a high price for it *or* it cost me dear; **je l'ai acheté un bon p.** I bought it for a very reasonable price; **je l'ai vendu un bon p.** I got a good price for it; **on achète aujourd'hui ses esquisses à p. d'or** his sketches are now worth their weight in gold *or* now cost the earth; **je l'ai acheté à p. d'or** I paid a small fortune for it; *Fam* **au p. où sont les choses** *ou* **où est le beurre** seeing how expensive everything is[□]; **j'ai fini par trouver le cuir que je voulais mais j'ai dû y mettre le p.** I finally found the type of leather I was looking for, but I had to pay top price for it; *Fig* **elle a été reçue à son examen, mais il a fallu qu'elle y mette le p.** she passed her exam, but she really had to work hard for it; **mettre un p. à qch** to price sth, to put a price on sth; **p. d'acceptabilité** psychological price; **p. d'achat** purchase price; *Bourse* bid price; *Bourse* **p. acheteur** bid price; **p. affiché** sticker price, displayed price; **p. d'appel** loss leader price; **p. cassés** knockdown prices; **p. catalogue** catalogue price, list price; **p. (au) comptant** cash price; *Bourse* spot price; **p. conseillé** recommended retail price; **p. courant** going *or* market price; **p. coûtant** cost price; **à p. coûtant** at cost price; **acheter/vendre qch à p. coûtant** to buy/sell sth at cost (price); **p. demandé** asking price; **p. de demi-gros** trade price; **p. départ usine** price ex-works, factory price; **p. de détail** retail price; **p. directeur** price leader; *Bourse* **p. du disponible** spot price; *Bourse* **p. d'émission** *(d'actions)* issue price; **p. exceptionnel** bargain price; **p. à l'exportation, p. (à l') export** export price; **p. de fabrique** manufacturer's price; **p. facturé, p. de facture** invoiced price; **p. de faveur** preferential price; **p. fixe** fixed price; **p. forfaitaire, p. à forfait** fixed price, all-inclusive price; **p. de gros** wholesale price; **p. hors taxe(s)** price net of tax, price before tax; **p. à l'importation, p. (à l')import** import price; **p. imposé** fixed price; **p. indicatif** approximate price; **p. initial** basic price, prime cost, starting price; **p. au kilo** price per kilo; **p. de lancement** introductory price; **p. libre** deregulated price; **p. marchand** trade price; *Bourse* **p. du marché** market price; **p. marqué** marked price; **p. minimum rentable** break-even price; **p. de négociation** trade price; **p. net** net price; *(sur un menu)* price inclusive of service; **p. offert** offer price, selling price; **p. officiel** standard price; *Bourse* **p. de l'option** option price; **p. optimum** optimal price; *Mktg* **p. de pénétration** penetration price; **p. plafond** ceiling price; **p. plancher** floor price; **p. pratiqué** current price; **p. de prestige** premium price, prestige price; **p. promotionnel** promotional price; **p. psychologique** psychological price; **p. public** (normal) retail price; **p. de rabais** reduced price, discount price; **p. de rachat** redemption price; **p. recommandé** recommended retail price; **p. réduit** reduced price, discount price; **p. de revient** cost price; **p. seuil** floor price; **p. de solde** bargain price; **p. standard** standard price; **p. taxé** standard price; **p. taxe comprise** price inclusive of tax; **p. tout compris** *ou* **tous frais compris** *ou* **toutes taxes comprises** all-inclusive price; **p. de transport** freight price; **p. unique** flat price; **p. unitaire, p. à l'unité** unit price; **p. d'usine** factory price; **p. vendeur** offer price, selling price; **p. à la vente** sticker price, displayed price; **p. de vente** selling price

2 *(étiquette)* price (tag), price label; **il n'y avait pas de p. dessus** it wasn't priced, there was no price (tag) on it

3 *(barème convenu)* price; **votre p. sera le mien** name your price; **faire un p. (d'ami) à qn** to do a special deal for sb; **c'était la fin du marché, elle m'a fait un p. pour les deux cageots** the market was nearly over, so she let me have both boxes cheap; **mettre qch à p.** *(aux enchères)* to set *Br* a reserve *or Am* an upset price on sth; **les deux chandeliers mis à p.** the two chandeliers with *Br* a reserve *or Am* an upset price; *Fig* **sa tête a été mise à p.** there's a price on his/her head *or* a reward for his/her capture

4 *(valeur)* price, value; **le p. de la vie/liberté** the price of life/freedom; **j'ai pris conscience du p. de mon indépendance** I realized how valuable my independence was to me; **donner du p. à qch** to make sth worthwhile; **il donne** *ou* **attache plus de p. à sa famille depuis sa maladie** his family is more important to him since his illness; **ça n'a pas de p.** it's priceless, you can't put a price on it; **le sourire d'un enfant, ça n'a pas de p.** a child's smile is the most precious thing in the world

5 *(contrepartie)* **à ce p.** at that *or* such a price; **il fallait céder tous ses droits d'auteur, et à ce p. j'ai refusé** giving up the copyright was too high a price to pay, so I refused (to do it); **oui, mais à quel p.!** yes, but at what cost!

6 *(dans un concours commercial, un jeu)* prize; **premier/deuxième p.** first/second prize

7 *(dans un concours artistique, un festival)* prize, award; **elle a eu le p. de la meilleure interprétation** she got the award for best actress; *Sport* **le Grand P. (automobile)** the Grand Prix; **le p. Goncourt** = the most prestigious French annual literary prize; **le p. Nobel** the Nobel prize; **le p. Pulitzer** the Pulitzer prize

8 *(œuvre primée ▸ livre)* award-winning book *or* title; *(▸ disque)* award-winning record; *(▸ film)* award-winning movie *or Br* film

9 *(lauréat)* prizewinner; **nous recevons aujourd'hui le P. Nobel de la Paix** we welcome today the winner of the Nobel Peace prize; **p. de vertu** paragon of virtue

10 *Scol (distinction)* **jour de la distribution des p.** prize *or* prizegiving day; **p. de consolation** consolation prize; **p. d'excellence** first prize; **p. d'honneur** second prize

• **à aucun prix** ADV not at any price, not for all the world, on no account; **je ne quitterais le pays à aucun p.!** nothing would induce me to leave the country!

• **à n'importe quel prix** ADV at any price, no matter what (the cost); **il veut se faire un nom à n'importe quel p.** he'll stop at nothing to make a name for himself

• **à tout prix** ADV **1** *(obligatoirement)* at all costs; **tu dois à tout p. être rentré à minuit** you must be back by midnight at all costs **2** *(coûte que coûte)* at any cost, no matter what (the cost); **nous voulons un enfant à tout p.** we want a child no matter what (the cost)

• **au prix de** PRÉP at the cost of; **je ne veux pas du succès au p. de ma santé/notre amitié** I don't want success at the cost *or* expense of my health/our friendship; **collaborer avec eux au p. d'une trahison, jamais!** if collaborating with them means becoming a traitor, never!

• **de prix** ADJ *(bijou, objet)* valuable

• **pour prix de** PRÉP in return for

• **sans prix** ADJ invaluable, priceless; **l'estime de mes amis est sans p.** I value the esteem of my friends above all else

> Attention: ne pas confondre **price** et **prize** lorsque l'on traduit le terme **prix**. **Price** désigne une somme à payer, alors que **prize** désigne toujours une récompense.

prix-courant [prikurɑ̃] *(pl* **prix-courants)** NM *Com* price list, catalogue

pro [pro] *Fam (abrév* **professionnel)** ADJ **1** *(émission, film)* professional◻ **2** *Sport* professional◻; **il est joueur p. maintenant** he's turned pro

NMF pro; **c'est une vraie p.** she's a real pro; **passer p.** to turn pro; **ils ont fait un vrai travail de p.** they did a really professional job◻

proactif, -ive [prɔaktif, -iv] ADJ proactive

probabilité [prɔbabilite] NF **1** *(vraisemblance)* probability, likelihood; **selon toute p.** in all probability *or* likelihood **2** *(supposition)* probability; **je ne dis pas qu'il l'a volé, c'est une p.** I'm not saying he stole it, but it's probable *or* likely **3** *Math & Phys* probability

probable [prɔbabl] ADJ **1** *(vraisemblable)* likely, probable; **il est peu p. qu'elle soit sa sœur** it's not very likely that she's his/her sister **2** *(possible)* probable; **il est p. qu'elle viendra** she'll probably come; **est-il à Paris? – c'est p.** is he in Paris? – quite probably (he is); *Fam* **je parie qu'elle va refuser – p.!** I bet she'll say no – more than likely!

probablement [prɔbabləmɑ̃] ADV probably; **tu viendras demain? – très p.** will you come tomorrow? – very probably *or* quite likely; *Fam* **p. qu'il acceptera** he's likely to accept, he'll probably say yes

probant, -e [prɔbɑ̃, -ɑ̃t] ADJ **1** *(convaincant ▸ argument, fait, expérience)* convincing; **peu p.** unconvincing **2** *Jur (pièce)* probative

probation [prɔbasjɔ̃] NF *Jur* probation; **être en p.** to be on probation

probatoire [prɔbatwar] ADJ probationary; **période p.** trial period; *Jur* **délai p.** probation

probe [prɔb] ADJ *Littéraire* upright, endowed with integrity

probité [prɔbite] NF probity, integrity, uprightness

problématique [prɔblematik] ADJ problematic, problematical

NF *(problèmes)* set of problems *or* issues; *Phil* problematics

problématiquement [prɔblematikmɑ̃] ADV problematically

problème [prɔblɛm] NM **1** *Math* problem; **résoudre un p. d'algèbre** to solve an algebra *or* algebraic problem **2** *(difficulté)* problem, difficulty; **avoir des problèmes** to have problems; **ne t'inquiète pas, tu n'auras aucun p.** don't worry, you'll be all right; **tu n'auras aucun p. à la convaincre** you won't have any problem convincing her; **pas de p., viens quand tu veux** no problem, you can come whenever you want; *Fam* **tu pourras passer me prendre? – oui, sans p.** could you come and pick me up? – sure, no problem; **nous avons un gros p.** we have a major problem, we're in big trouble here; **un p. personnel** a personal matter; **il a toujours eu des problèmes d'argent** he always had money troubles *or* problems; *Fam* **dis donc, c'est ton p., pas le mien** listen, it's your problem, not mine; **avoir des problèmes psychologiques** to be psychologically disturbed **3** *(question)* problem, issue, question; **soulever un p.** to raise a question *or* an issue; *Fig* **faux p.** red herring; **nous discutons d'un faux p.** we're not discussing the real problem here

• **à problèmes** ADJ *(peau, cheveux)* problem *(avant n)*; *Fam* **ma cousine, c'est une femme à problèmes** my cousin's always got problems◻

procédé [prɔsede] NM **1** *(comportement)* conduct, behaviour; **vos procédés sont indignes** your behaviour is shameful; **je n'ai pas du tout apprécié son p.** I wasn't very impressed with what he/she did **2** *(technique)* process; **p. de fabrication** manufacturing process **3** *Péj (artifice)* **toute la pièce sent le p.** the whole play seems contrived

procéder [18] [prɔsede] VI **1** *(progresser)* to proceed; **p. par ordre** to take things in order; **procédons par ordre** let's do one thing at a time **2** *(se conduire)* to behave; **j'apprécie sa manière de p. avec nous** I like the way he deals with us

• **procéder à** VT IND **1** *(effectuer)* to conduct; **p. à une étude** to conduct a study; **p. à un examen approfondi de la situation** to examine the situation thoroughly; **p. à l'élection du bureau national du parti** to elect the national executive of the party **2** *Jur* **p. à l'arrestation d'un criminel** to arrest a criminal

• **procéder de** VT IND *Littéraire (provenir de)* to proceed from, to originate in; **tous ses problèmes procèdent d'une mauvaise administration** all his/her problems spring *or* derive from poor management

procédure [prɔsedyr] NF **1** *(démarche)* procedure, way to proceed; **nous suivrons la p. habituelle** we'll follow the usual procedure; **procédures de sécurité** safety procedures **2** *Jur (ensemble des règles)* procedure, practice; *(action)* proceedings; **engager** *ou* **entamer une p. contre qn** to start proceedings against sb; **p. civile** civil procedure; **p. de divorce** divorce proceedings; **p. de faillite** bankruptcy proceedings; **p. pénale** criminal procedure **3** *Ordinat* procedure; **p. de chargement** loading procedure

procédurier, -ère [prɔsedyrje, -ɛr] ADJ **1** *Péj (personne)* pettifogging, quibbling; **être p.** to be a pettifogger *or* a quibbler **2** *(action, démarche)* litigious; **formalités procédurières** procedural formalities, red tape

NM,F *Péj* pettifogger, quibbler

procès [prɔsɛ] NM **1** *Jur (pénal)* trial; *(civil)* lawsuit, legal proceedings; **p. civil** lawsuit; **p. criminel** (criminal) trial; **p. en diffamation** libel case, libel suit; **p. équitable** fair trial; **faire** *ou* **intenter un p. à qn** to institute legal proceedings against sb; **intenter un p. en divorce à qn** to institute divorce proceedings against sb; **entreprendre** *ou* **engager un p. contre qn** to take sb to court; **être en p. avec qn** to be involved in a lawsuit with sb; **il a gagné/perdu son p. contre nous** he won/lost his case against us; **un p. pour meurtre** a murder trial; *Fig* **sans autre forme de p.** without further ado; **renvoyé sans autre forme de p.** unceremoniously dismissed **2** *(critique)* **faire le p. de qn/qch** to put sb/sth on trial; **pas de p. d'intention, s'il vous plaît!** don't put words in my mouth, please!; **faire un mauvais p. à qn** to make groundless accusations against sb; **tu lui fais un mauvais p.** you're being unfair to him/her **3** *Anat* process

> Il faut noter que le nom anglais **process** est un faux ami. Il signifie le plus souvent **processus, procédé**.

processeur [prɔsesœr] NM *Ordinat* **1** *(organe)* (hardware) processor; *(unité centrale)* central processing unit **2** *(ensemble de programmes)* (language) processor; **p. entrée/sortie** input/output processor, I/O processor; **p. de données** data processor; **p. frontal/graphique/maître** front-end/display/master processor; **p. d'image tramée** raster image processor; **p. RISC** RISC processor

processif, -ive [prɔsesif, -iv] ADJ *Littéraire (procédurier)* pettifogging, quibbling

procession [prɔsesjɔ̃] NF *(cortège)* procession; **une p. de voitures** a motorcade; **s'avancer en p.** to march in procession

processionnaire [prɔsesjɔnɛr] *Entom* ADJ processionary

NF *(papillon)* processionary moth; *(chenille)* processionary caterpillar

processionnel, -elle [prɔsesjɔnɛl] ADJ processional

processive [prɔsesiv] *voir* **processif**

processus [prɔsesys] NM **1** *(méthode, démarche, évolution)* process; **le p. d'acquisition de la lecture** learning to read; **le p. de démocratisation est en marche** the democratization process is under way; *Mktg* **p. d'achat** purchasing process; *UE* **p. de convergence** convergence process; **p. déci-**

sionnel *ou* **de décision** decision-making process; **p. de diffusion** *ou* **de distribution** distribution process; **p. de fabrication** manufacturing process; **p. industriel** industrial processing; **p. de paix** peace process **2** *Méd* process; **p. pathologique** pathology

procès-verbal [prɔsɛvɛrbal] (*pl* **procès-verbaux** [-o]) **NM 1** *Jur (acte ▸ d'un magistrat)* (official) report, record; *(▸ d'un agent de police)* (police) report **2** *(pour une contravention)* parking ticket; **dresser un p. à qn** to give sb a parking ticket **3** *(résumé ▸ d'une réunion, d'une assemblée)* minutes; *(▸ d'un colloque)* proceedings; *(▸ d'un témoignage)* record; **tenir le p. des réunions** to keep the minutes of the meetings

prochain, -e [prɔʃɛ̃, -ɛn] **ADJ 1** *(dans le temps)* next; **je te verrai la semaine prochaine** I'll see you next week; **à samedi p.!** see you next Saturday!; **le mois p.** next month, this coming month; **ça sera pour une prochaine fois** we'll do it some other time; **la prochaine fois, fais attention** next time, be careful

2 *(dans l'espace)* next; **je descends au p. arrêt** I'm getting off at the next stop

3 *(imminent)* imminent, near; **dans un avenir p.** in the near future; **un jour p.** one day soon; **leur p. départ** their imminent departure

4 *(immédiat ▸ cause, pouvoir)* immediate

NM son p. one's fellow man; **aime ton p. comme toi-même** love your neighbour as yourself

• **prochaine NF** *Fam* **1** *(arrêt)* next stop; **je descends à la prochaine** I'm getting off at the next stop **2** *(locution)* **à la prochaine!** see you (soon)!, be seeing you!, *Am* so long!

prochainement [prɔʃɛnmɑ̃] **ADV** shortly, soon; **p. sur vos écrans** *(film)* coming soon

PROCHE [prɔʃ]

ADJ
- nearby **1**
- imminent **2**
- similar **5**
- near **1, 2**
- close **3, 4**

NM
- close relative

ADJ 1 *(avoisinant)* nearby; **elle entra dans une église p.** she went into a nearby church; **le bureau est tout p.** the office is close at hand *or* very near; **le village le plus p.** the nearest village

2 *(dans l'avenir)* near, imminent; *(dans le passé)* in the recent past; **dans un avenir p.** in the near future; **le dénouement est p.** the end is in sight; **Noël est p.** we're getting close to Christmas; **la fin du monde est p.** the end of the world is nigh; **la dernière guerre est encore p. de nous** the last war belongs to the not too distant past

3 *(cousin, parent)* close; **adresse de votre plus p. parent** address of your next of kin

4 *(intime)* close; **nous sommes plus proches depuis ce deuil** we've grown closer since we were bereaved; **l'un des proches conseillers du président** one of the president's trusted *or* close advisors

5 *(semblable)* similar

NM close relative *or* relation; **la mort d'un p.** the death of a loved one; **ses proches** his/her friends and relatives

• **de proche en proche ADV** *(petit à petit)* gradually, step by step

• **proche de PRÉP 1** *(dans l'espace)* near (to), close to, not far from

2 *(dans le temps)* close; **la guerre est encore p. de nous** the war is still close to us

3 *(en contact avec)* close to; **il est resté p. de son père** he remained close to his father; **être p. de la nature** to be close to *or* in touch with nature; **des sources proches de la Maison-Blanche** sources close to the White House

4 *(semblable à ▸ langage, espèce animale)* closely related to; *(▸ style, solution)* similar to; **la haine est p. de l'amour** hatred is akin to love; **portrait p. de la réalité** accurate *or* lifelike portrait; **une obsession p. de la névrose** an obsession verging on the neurotic

5 *(sans différence de rang, d'âge avec)* close to; **les candidats sont proches les uns des autres** there's little to choose between the candidates; **mes frères et moi sommes proches les uns des autres** my brothers and I are close together (in age)

Proche-Orient [prɔʃɔrjɑ̃] **NM le P.** the Middle East, the Near East

proche-oriental, -e [prɔʃɔrjɑ̃tal] (*mpl* **proche-orientaux** [-o], *fpl* **proche-orientales**) **ADJ** Middle-Eastern, Near-Eastern

proclamation [prɔklamasjɔ̃] **NF 1** *(annonce)* (official) announcement *or* statement; **p. du résultat des élections à 20 heures** the results of the election will be announced at 8 p.m. **2** *(texte)* proclamation

proclamer [3] [prɔklame] **VT 1** *(déclarer ▸ innocence, vérité)* to proclaim, to declare; **p. que...** to declare that...; **nous proclamons que la paix sera bientôt instaurée** we declare that we will soon be at peace; **elle est allée p. partout qu'il la battait** she went around telling everybody that he beat her **2** *(annoncer publiquement)* to publicly announce *or* state, to proclaim; **p. la république** to proclaim the republic; **p. le résultat des élections** to announce the results of the election

proclitique [prɔklitik] *Ling* **ADJ** proclitic
NM proclitic

proconsul [prɔkɔ̃syl] **NM** *Antiq* proconsul

proconsulaire [prɔkɔ̃sylɛr] **ADJ** *Antiq* proconsular

proconsulat [prɔkɔ̃syla] **NM** *Antiq* proconsulate

procréateur, -trice [prɔkreatœr, -tris] *Littéraire*
ADJ procreant, procreative
NM,F procreator

procréation [prɔkreasjɔ̃] **NF** procreation; **p. artificielle** artificial reproduction; **p. médicalement assistée** assisted conception

procréatique [prɔkreatik] **NF** *Biol* = field of study relating to the techniques of artificial reproduction

procréatrice [prɔkreatris] *voir* **procréateur**

procréer [15] [prɔkree] *Littéraire* **VT** to procreate
VI to procreate

procurateur [prɔkyratœr] **NM** *Hist* procurator

procuration [prɔkyrasjɔ̃] **NF 1** *Jur (pouvoir ▸ gén)* power *or* letter of attorney; *(▸ pour une élection)* proxy (form); **donner p. à qn** to authorize *or* to empower sb; **p. générale** full power of attorney **2** *Banque* mandate; **il a une p. sur mon compte** he has a mandate to operate my account

• **par procuration ADJ** *(vote)* proxy *(avant n)*
ADV 1 *(voter)* by proxy **2** *Fig* vicariously

procurer [3] [prɔkyre] **VT 1** *(fournir)* to provide; **p. de l'argent à qn** to provide sb with money, to obtain money for sb; **je lui ai procuré un emploi** I found him/her a job; **son travail lui procure d'importants revenus** his/her job provides him/her with *or* brings in a substantial income; **les places qu'il m'a procurées étaient excellentes** the seats he found *or* obtained for me were superb **2** *(apporter)* to bring; **la lecture me procure beaucoup de plaisir** reading brings me great pleasure

VPR se procurer to get, to obtain; **essaye de te p. son dernier livre** try to get his/her latest book; **il faut que je me procure un visa** I must get a visa

procureur [prɔkyrœr] **NM** *Jur* prosecutor; **p. général** = public prosecutor at the "Parquet", *Br* ≃ Director of Public Prosecutions, *Am* ≃ district attorney; **p. de la République** = public prosecutor at a "tribunal de grande instance", ≃ Attorney General

prodigalité [prɔdigalite] **NF 1** *(générosité)* extravagance, *Sout* prodigality, profligacy; **donner avec p.** to be extremely generous **2** *(dépenses)* extravagance, *Sout* prodigality; **connu pour ses prodigalités** well-known for his/her extravagance *or* for his/her extravagant spending habits **3** *Littéraire (surabondance)* (lavish) abundance, *Sout* prodigality

prodige [prɔdiʒ] **NM 1** *(miracle)* marvel, wonder; **faire des prodiges** to work wonders, to achieve miracles; **ton médicament a fait des prodiges** your medicine worked wonders; **tenir du p.** to be nothing short of miraculous *or* a miracle; **cela tient du p. que personne ne soit mort** it's nothing short of a miracle that nobody was killed; **un p. de...** a wonder of...; **cet appareil est un p. de la technique moderne** this machine is a wonder of modern technology **2** *(personne)* prodigy
ADJ musicien/enfant p. musical/child prodigy

prodigieuse [prɔdiʒjøz] *voir* **prodigieux**

prodigieusement [prɔdiʒjøzmɑ̃] **ADV 1** *(beaucoup)* enormously, tremendously; **je me suis p. amusé** I enjoyed myself tremendously; **il m'agace p.** he really gets on my nerves **2** *(magnifiquement)* fantastically, magnificently; **elle dessine p. bien** she draws fantastically well

prodigieux, -euse [prɔdiʒjø, -øz] **ADJ 1** *(extrême)* huge, tremendous; **avoir un succès p.** to be hugely successful; **être d'une bêtise prodigieuse** to be prodigiously stupid; **être d'une force prodigieuse** to be tremendously strong; **une quantité prodigieuse** a huge amount **2** *(peu commun)* prodigious, astounding, amazing **3** *Littéraire (miraculeux)* prodigious, miraculous; **guérison prodigieuse** miracle cure

prodigue [prɔdig] **ADJ 1** *(dépensier)* extravagant, *Sout* profligate **2** *Fig* **p. de** generous *or* overgenerous with; **elle n'est guère p. de détails** she doesn't go in much for detail; **tu es toujours p. de bons conseils** you're always full of good advice
NMF spender, spendthrift

prodiguer [3] [prɔdige] **VT 1** *(faire don de)* to be lavish with; **la nature nous prodigue ses bienfaits** nature is profuse *or* lavish in its bounty; **elle a prodigué des soins incessants à son fils** she lavished endless care on her son; **il lui prodiguait ses conseils** he was generous with his advice, he lavished advice on him/her **2** *(gaspiller)* to waste, to squander

prodrome [prɔdrom] **NM 1** *Méd* warning symptom, *Spéc* prodrome **2** *Littéraire (signe)* forerunner, early sign

producteur, -trice [prɔdyktœr, -tris] **ADJ** producing; **les pays producteurs de pétrole/de blé** oil-producing/wheat-growing countries; *Cin* **société productrice** production company

NM,F *Cin, Rad, Théât & TV (personne)* producer; **p. associé** associate producer, production associate; **p. de cinéma** movie *or Br* film producer; **p. délégué** executive producer; **p. de disques** record producer; **p. d'émissions de radio** radio producer; **p. exécutif** executive producer

NM *Agr & Écon* producer; *(société)* production company; **directement du p. au consommateur** directly from the producer to the consumer; **les producteurs de melons** melon growers *or* producers; **ce pays est le premier p. de composants électroniques du monde** this country is the world's largest producer of electronic components

productible [prɔdyktibl] **ADJ** *(marchandise)* producible

productif, -ive [prɔdyktif, -iv] **ADJ 1** *(travailleur)* productive; *(auteur)* prolific; **de manière productive** productively **2** *Fin* **p. d'intérêts** interest-bearing **3** *Agr & Mines* productive; **le sol est peu p.** the yield from the soil is poor

production [prɔdyksjɔ̃] **NF 1** *(activité économique)* **la p.** production; **la p. ne suit plus la consommation** supply is failing to keep up with demand; **à ce stade de la p., nous perdons de l'argent** at this stage of production, we're losing money

2 *(rendement) & Ind* output; *Agr* yield; **la p. a augmenté/diminué** *Ind* output has risen/dropped; *Agr* the yield is higher/lower; **l'usine a une p. de 10 000 voitures par an** the factory turns out *or* produces 10,000 cars a year

3 *(produits) & Agr* produce *(UNCOUNT)*, production *(UNCOUNT)*; *Ind* products, production; **productions maraîchères** *Br* market-garden *or Am* truck-garden produce; **le pays veut écouler sa p. de maïs** the country wants to sell off its maize crop *or* the maize it has produced; **p. excédentaire** surplus production; **p. vendue** sales

4 *(fabrication ▸ gén)* production, manufacturing; *(▸ d'électricité)* production, generation; **p. à la chaîne** production line system, mass production; **p. sur** *ou* **à la commande** production to order; **p. discontinue** production in batches; **p. juste à temps** just-in-time production; **p. manufacturée** secondary production; **p. de matières premières** primary production; **p. textile** textile manufacturing

5 *(d'une œuvre d'art ▸ action de créer)* production, creation; *Cin, Théât & TV* production

6 *(d'une œuvre d'art ▸ résultat créé)* *Cin* production, *Br* film, *Am* movie; *Rad* production, programme; *Théât* production, play; **la p. contemporaine** contemporary works; **la p. dramatique/romanesque du XVIIIème siècle** 18th-century plays/novels; **une importante p. littéraire** a large literary output

7 *(d'une œuvre d'art ▸ financement)* production; **assurer la p. de** to produce; **assistant/directeur de p.** production assistant/manager; **société de p.** production company

8 *(présentation ▸ d'un document etc)* presentation

9 *(fait d'occasionner)* production, producing, making; **la p. d'un son** making a sound

10 *Fin* **p. immobilisée** = fixed assets produced for use by the company

productique [prɔdyktik] **NF** industrial automation

productive [prɔdyktiv] *voir* **productif**

productivisme [prɔdyktivism] **NM** *Péj* obsession with productivity

productiviste [prɔdyktivist] **ADJ** *Péj* that emphasizes productivity to an obsessive degree

productivité [prɔdyktivite] **NF 1** *(fertilité ▸ d'un sol, d'une région)* productivity, productiveness **2** *(rendement)* productivity; **accroissement de la p.** increase in productivity; *Fin* **p. de l'impôt** (net) tax revenue

productrice [prɔdyktris] *voir* **producteur**

produire [98] [prɔdɥir] **VT 1** *(fabriquer ▸ bien de consommation)* to produce, to manufacture; *(▸ énergie, électricité)* to produce, to generate; *Agr (faire pousser)* to produce, to grow; **p. qch en masse** to mass-produce sth

2 *(fournir ▸ sujet: usine)* to produce; *(▸ sujet: sol)* to produce, to yield; *Fin (bénéfice)* to yield, to return

3 *(causer ▸ bruit, vapeur)* to produce, to make; *(▸ douleur, démangeaison)* to produce, to cause; *(▸ sensation)* to create, to generate; *(▸ changement)* to effect, to bring about; *(▸ résultat)* to produce; **la lumière produit une illusion spectaculaire** the light creates a spectacular illusion; **l'effet produit par son discours a été catastrophique** the effect of his/her speech was disastrous; **p. une impression favorable sur qn** to make a favourable impression on sb

4 *(créer ▸ sujet: artiste)* to produce; **il a produit quelques bons romans** he has written *or* produced a few good novels

5 *Cin, Rad, Théât & TV* to produce

6 *(engendrer)* to produce; **combien le XIXème siècle/Mexique a-t-il produit de romancières?** how many female novelists did the 19th century produce/has Mexico produced?

7 *(présenter ▸ passeport)* to produce, to show; *(▸ preuve)* to produce, *Sout* to adduce; *(▸ témoin)* to produce

USAGE ABSOLU *Écon* to produce, to be productive; **tes arbres ne produiront jamais** your trees will never bear fruit; **il produit beaucoup** *(écrivain)* he writes a lot; *(musicien)* he writes *or* composes a lot; *(cinéaste)* he makes a lot of movies *or Br* films

VPR se produire 1 *(événement)* to happen, to occur; **ça peut encore se p.** it may happen again; **il s'est produit un très grave accident près d'ici** there was a very serious accident near here **2** *(personne)* to appear, to give a performance; **se p. sur scène** to appear on stage; **se p. en public** to give a public performance

produit [prɔdɥi] **NM 1** *Ind* product, article; *Agr* product, produce *(UNCOUNT)*; **les produits de la terre** the produce of the land; **produits d'achat courant** convenience goods; **produits agricoles** agricultural produce; **produits alimentaires, produits d'alimentation** food products, foodstuffs; *Mktg* **p. d'appel** loss leader, traffic builder; **p. augmenté** augmented product; **p. de beauté** beauty product; **les produits de beauté** cosmetics, beauty products; **produits blancs** white goods; **produits bruns** brown goods; **p. brut** raw product; **produits chimiques** chemicals; **garanti sans produits chimiques** guaranteed no (chemical) additives; *Mktg* **p. ciblé** niche product; **p. colorant** colouring agent; **produits de consommation** consumables, consumable goods; **produits de consommation courante** consumer goods; **p. dérivé** by-product; *Mktg* **p. drapeau** own-brand product; **p. écologique** green product; *Mktg* **p. d'élite** premium product; **p. d'entretien** (household) cleaning product; **produits étrangers** foreign produce, foreign goods; **produits exotiques** exotic goods; **p. final** end product; **p. fini** finished product, end product; **p. générique** own-brand product; **produits de grande consommation** consumer products; **p. de haut niveau** high standard product; **p. d'imitation** imitative product; **produits de luxe** luxury goods *or* articles; **p. manufacturé** manufactured product; **produits manufacturés** manufactured goods *or* products; **produits maraîchers** *Br* market-garden *or Am* truck-farm produce; **produits de marque** branded *or* brand-name goods *or* products; **p. sans marque** unbranded product; *Mktg* **p. à marque du distributeur** own-brand product; **produits naturels** natural produce; *Mktg* **p. sans nom** no-name product; **p. novateur** innovative product; **produits d'origine nationale** domestic products; **p. ouvré** finished product, end product; **produits du pays** home produce; **produits périssables** perishable goods; **produits pharmaceutiques** drugs, pharmaceuticals; *Mktg* **p. de prestige** premium product; **produits "prêts-à-consommer"** convenience goods; **produits de second choix** seconds, rejects; **produits spécialisés** speciality goods; **p. de substitution** substitute; **p. substitut** substitute product; **p. de synthèse** synthetic product; *Mktg* **p. tactique** me-too product, follow-me product; **p. vert** green product

2 *(résultat)* product, outcome; **le p. d'une matinée de travail** the result *or* product of a morning's work; **c'est un pur p. de ton imagination** it's a complete figment of your imagination

3 *(bénéfice)* profit; **le p. de la vente** the profit made on the sale; *Com* **le p. de la journée** the day's takings *or* proceeds; **il vit du p. de ses terres** he lives off his land; **vivre du p. de son travail** to work for a living; **p. brut** gross proceeds, gross income; **produits d'exploitation** operating income, income from operations; **p. financier** *(recette)* interest received; **p. de l'impôt** tax revenue; **produits à recevoir** accrued income, accruals

4 *Fin* **p. financier** *(dispositif d'investissement)* financial product

5 *Écon* **le p. industriel** industrial earnings; **p. intérieur brut** gross (domestic) product; **p. intérieur net** net domestic product; **p. national brut/net** gross/net national product

6 *Chim & Math* product

proembryon [proɑ̃brijɔ̃] **NM** *Biol* proembryo

proéminence [prɔeminɑ̃s] **NF 1** *Littéraire (caractère)* prominence, conspicuousness **2** *(saillie)* protuberance; **la montagne présente une p. à gauche du pic** the mountain juts out *or* protrudes left of the peak

proéminent, -e [prɔeminɑ̃, -ɑ̃t] **ADJ** prominent

prof [prɔf] **NMF** *Fam (abrév* **professeur***)* **1** *Scol* teacher□ **2** *Univ (sans chaire) Br* ≃ lecturer□, *Am* ≃ instructor□; *(titulaire de chaire)* prof; **elle est p. de fac** ≃ she's a *Br* lecturer *or Am* instructor **3** *(hors d'un établissement scolaire)* teacher□, tutor□; **p. de piano** piano teacher

profanateur, -trice [prɔfanatœr, -tris] *Littéraire* **ADJ** blasphemous, sacrilegious

NM,F profaner

profanation [prɔfanasjɔ̃] **NF 1** *(sacrilège)* blasphemy, sacrilege, profanation; *(d'une sépulture)* desecration **2** *(avilissement)* defilement, debasement

profanatrice [prɔfanatris] *voir* **profanateur**

profane [prɔfan] **ADJ 1** *(ignorant)* uninitiated; **je suis p. en la matière** I know nothing about the subject **2** *(non religieux)* secular, non-religious

NMF 1 *(ignorant)* lay person, layman, *f* laywoman; **je n'ai jamais fait de ski, je suis un p.** I've never skied, I'm a complete beginner; **pour le p.** to the layman *or* uninitiated **2** *(non religieux)* lay person, non-initiate

profaner [3] [prɔfane] **VT 1** *(tombe, église, hostie)* to desecrate **2** *(dégrader ▸ justice, talent)* to debase, to defile, *Sout* to profane; *(▸ innocence)* to defile

profeciat, proféciat [prɔfesjat] **EXCLAM** *Belg* congratulations!; **souhaiter p. à qn** to congratulate sb

proférer [18] [prɔfere] **VT** *(insultes, menaces)* to utter; **p. des injures contre qn** to heap insults on sb

profès, -esse [prɔfɛ, -ɛs] *Rel* **ADJ** professed

NM,F professed monk, *f* professed nun

professer [4] [prɔfese] **VT 1** *Littéraire (opinion)* to profess; **il a toujours professé qu'il haïssait la religion** he has always professed hatred for *or* claimed that he hated religion **2** *Vieilli (enseigner)* to teach; **p. l'anglais/l'histoire à l'université** to teach English/history at university

professeur [prɔfesœr] **NM 1** *(du primaire, du secondaire)* teacher, schoolteacher; **p. des écoles** *Br* primary *or Am* elementary school teacher; **p. principal** *Br* ≃ form tutor, *Am* ≃ homeroom teacher

2 *(de l'enseignement supérieur ▸ assistant) Br* ≃ lecturer, *Am* ≃ instructor; *(▸ au grade supérieur)* professor; **elle est p. à l'université de Lyon** she teaches at Lyons University

3 *Can Univ* **p. adjoint** assistant professor; *Univ* **p. agrégé** associate professor; **p. titulaire** *Scol* staff teacher, member of (teaching) staff; *Univ Br* tenured lecturer, *Am* full professor

4 *Belg & Suisse Univ* **p. ordinaire** *Br* tenured lecturer, *Am* full professor; **p. extraordinaire** = lecturer with a reduced teaching schedule (because of other professional commitments)

5 *(hors d'un établissement scolaire)* teacher, tutor; **p. de piano** piano teacher

profession [prɔfesjɔ̃] **NF 1** *(métier)* occupation, job, profession; *(d'un commerçant, d'un artisan)* trade; *(d'un artiste, d'un industriel)* profession; **quelle est votre p.?** what is your occupation?, what do you do (for a living)?; **de p.** professional; **je suis mécanicien de p.** I'm a mechanic by trade; *Hum* **rebelle de p.** professional rebel; **p. libérale** (liberal) profession; **les professions libérales** *(métiers)* the professions; *(gens)* professional people

2 *(corporation ▸ de commerçants, d'artisans)* trade; *(▸ d'artistes, d'industriels)* profession

3 *(déclaration)* **faire p. de** to profess, to declare; **faire p. de libéralisme/socialisme** to declare oneself a liberal/socialist

4 *Rel* **p. de foi** profession of faith

• **sans profession** *Admin* **ADJ** unemployed

NMF unemployed; **les sans p.** the unemployed

professionnalisation [prɔfesjɔnalizasjɔ̃] **NF** *(d'une activité)* professionalization; *(d'un sportif)* turning professional

professionnaliser [3] [prɔfesjɔnalize] **VT** *(joueur, sportif)* **p. qn** to make sb into a professional

VPR se professionnaliser *(sportif)* to turn professional; *(sport)* to become professional *or* a professional sport

professionnalisme [prɔfesjɔnalism] **NM** professionalism

professionnel, -elle [prɔfesjɔnɛl] **ADJ 1** *(lié à une profession ▸ maladie, risque)* occupational; *(▸ enseignement)* vocational; **avoir des soucis professionnels** to have work problems; **aucun changement au niveau p.** nothing new on the job front; **je suis satisfait sur le plan p.** I'm satisfied with my job; **une vie professionnelle satisfaisante** a rewarding job **2** *(non amateur ▸ musicien, sportif)* professional **3** *(compétent)* professional, accomplished; **le jeu des jeunes acteurs était très p.** the young actors performed like real professionals

NM,F 1 *Sport* professional; **les professionnels de la boxe** professional boxers; **passer p.** to turn professional **2** *(personne expérimentée)* professional; **l'œuvre d'un p.** the work of a professional

professionnellement [prɔfesjɔnɛlmɑ̃] **ADV** professionally; **p., il a plutôt réussi** he did rather well in his professional life; **je n'ai affaire à elle que p.** I only have a professional relationship with her, my relations with her are strictly business

professoral, -e, -aux, -ales [prɔfesɔral, -o] **ADJ 1** *(de professeur)* professorial **2** *(pédant)* patronizing, lecturing

professorat [prɔfesɔra] **NM** teaching

profil [prɔfil] NM 1 *(côté du visage)* profile; **avoir un p. de médaille** to have very regular features
2 *(silhouette)* profile, outline; **on devinait le p. du volcan dans la brume** the volcano was silhouetted in the mist; *Fig* **adopter/garder un p. bas** to adopt/to keep a low profile
3 *(aptitude)* profile; **elle a le p. de l'emploi** she seems right for the job; **il a le p. idéal pour être président** he's ideal presidential material; **son p. de carrière** his/her career profile
4 *(description)* profile; *Mktg* **p. de la clientèle** customer profile; *Mktg* **p. du** *ou* **des consommateurs** consumer profile; **p. démographique** demographic profile; **p. d'entreprise** company profile; **p. du marché** market profile; **p. médical** medical history; *Banque* **p. patrimonial** personal assets profile; **p. de poste** job description; *Mktg* **p. de produit** product profile; *Psy & Mktg* **p. psychologique** psychological profile
5 *Géog* profile; **p. fluvial en long** long profile of a river; **p. fluvial en travers** river section
6 *Com* **le p. des ventes montre une augmentation** the sales outline *or* profile shows a definite increase
• **de profil** ADV in profile; **être de p.** to be in profile *or* side-on; **se mettre de p.** to turn to one side *(so that one's face is in profile)*; **mettez-vous de p. par rapport à la caméra** show your profile *or* stand side-on to the camera

profilage [prɔfilaʒ] NM 1 *Menuis* profiling, moulding; *Métal* shaping, forming; *Aut (d'une carrosserie)* streamlining **2** *(en criminologie)* criminal profiling **3** *Mktg* customer profiling

profilé, -e [prɔfile] ADJ *Menuis* profiled, moulded; *Métal* shaped, formed; *Aut (carrosserie)* streamlined
NM *Métal* section

profiler [3] [prɔfile] VT 1 *Menuis* to profile, to mould; *Métal* to shape, to form; *Aut (carrosserie)* to streamline
2 *(représenter de profil)* to draw in section
3 *Littéraire (laisser voir)* **les montagnes au loin profilaient leur silhouette** the mountains were silhouetted in the distance
4 *(en criminologie)* to profile
VPR **se profiler 1** *(se découper)* to stand out, to be silhouetted (**sur** *ou* **contre** against); **l'église se profile en haut de la colline** the church stands out on top of the hill **2** *(apparaître)* to emerge; **une solution se profile enfin** a solution is finally emerging; **des nuages noirs/des périodes difficiles se profilent à l'horizon** black clouds/difficult times are coming up on the horizon

profileur [prɔfilœr] NM (psychological) profiler

profit [prɔfi] NM 1 *(avantage)* profit, advantage; **tirer p. de ses lectures** to benefit from one's reading; **tirer p. de l'expérience des autres** to profit from other people's experience; **tirer p. d'une situation** to take advantage of *or* make the most of a situation; **j'ai lu ton livre avec p.** reading your book taught me a lot; **vous étudierez avec p. la préface** you will find it enlightening to study the preface; **mettre qch à p.** to take advantage of *or* to make the most of sth; **essayez de mettre à p. les connaissances acquises** try to make the most of what you already know; **faire son p. de qch** to profit by *or* from sth; *Fam* **ta veste t'aura fait du p.** you certainly got your money's worth out of that jacket; **il y a trouvé son p., sinon il ne l'aurait pas fait** he got something out of it otherwise he wouldn't have done it
2 *Com & Fin (bénéfice)* profit; **faire** *ou* **réaliser des profits** to make a profit; **vendre à p.** to sell at a profit; **le p. réalisé sur la vente de la propriété** the return on *or* the revenue from the sale of the property; **p. brut** gross profit; **p. espéré** anticipated profit; **profits exceptionnels** windfall profits; **profits de l'exercice** year's profits; **p. d'exploitation** operating profit; **p. net** net profit; **profits et pertes** profit and loss; **p. pur** pure profit; **p. réel** real profit; **il n'y a pas de petits profits** every little helps
• **au profit de** PRÉP *(organisation caritative, handicapés etc)* in aid of; **à son/mon seul p.** for his/her/my sole benefit; **il a été écarté de la direction au p. de son fils** he was replaced as manager by his son; **les socialistes perdront des voix au p. des communistes** votes will swing from the Socialists to the Communists, the Communists will pick up votes from the Socialists

profitabilité [prɔfitabilite] NF profitability

profitable [prɔfitabl] ADJ profitable; **ce séjour en Italie lui a été p.** the time he/she spent in Italy did him/her a lot of good

profitablement [prɔfitabləmɑ̃] ADV profitably

profiter [3] [prɔfite] VI *Fam* to thrive□, to do well□
• **profiter à** VT IND to benefit, to be beneficial to; **cet argent ne profite à personne** this money's not benefitting anyone; **les études ne t'ont guère profité** studying didn't do you much good; **il mange comme quatre mais ça ne lui profite guère!** he eats like a horse but it doesn't do him any good!
• **profiter de** VT IND 1 *(financièrement)* to profit from; **tous n'ont pas profité de l'expansion** not everybody gained by the expansion
2 *(jouir de)* to enjoy; **p. de sa retraite/de la vie** to enjoy *or* make the most of one's retirement/of life; *Fam* **vivement Noël que je puisse p. de mes petits-enfants!** I can't wait for Christmas so I can be with my grandchildren!
3 *(tirer parti de)* to take advantage of; **p. du soleil** to make the most of the sun; **il profite de ce qu'elle est absente** he's taking advantage of the fact that she's away; **p. de l'occasion** to make the most of *or* seize the opportunity; **p. de la situation** to take advantage of the situation; **profitesen, ça ne va pas durer!** make the most of it, it won't last!; **comme j'avais un deuxième billet, j'en ai fait p. ma copine** since I had a second ticket, I took my girlfriend along
4 *(exploiter)* to exploit, to take advantage of, to use; **tu profites de moi, c'est tout!** you're taking advantage of me *or* using me, that's all!

profiteroles [prɔfitrɔl] NFPL profiteroles; **p. au chocolat** chocolate profiteroles

profiteur, -euse [prɔfitœr, -øz] NM,F profiteer

profond, -e [prɔfɔ̃, -ɔ̃d] ADJ 1 *(enfoncé ▸ lac, racine, blessure)* deep; **peu p.** shallow; **p. de 10 mètres** 10 metres deep; **dans les couches profondes du sol** deep in *or* in the deepest layers of the earth; **des préjugés dont l'origine est profonde** deep-rooted *or* deep-seated prejudices; **la haine de l'ennemi est profonde** hatred of the enemy runs deep; **la France profonde** *(rurale)* provincial France; **l'Amérique/l'Angleterre profonde** *(d'un point de vue sociologique)* middle America/England; *(rurale)* provincial America/England
2 *(plongeant ▸ révérence, salut)* deep, low; *(▸ regard)* penetrating; *(▸ décolleté)* plunging
3 *(intense ▸ respiration)* deep; *(▸ soupir, sommeil)* deep, heavy; *(▸ silence)* profound, utter; *(▸ changement)* profound; *(▸ mépris, respect, amour, tristesse)* deep, profound; **dans une solitude profonde** in extreme isolation; **absorbé dans de profondes pensées** deep in thought; **de profonds bouleversements** profound changes; **cette expérience a laissé en elle des marques profondes** the experience marked her for life
4 *(grave ▸ voix)* deep
5 *(obscur)* deep, dark; **dans la nuit profonde** at dead of night
6 *(foncé ▸ couleur)* deep
7 *(sagace)* deep, profound; **avoir un esprit p.** to have profound insight; **elle leur reproche de ne pas être assez profonds** she reproaches them for their shallowness *or* with being shallow
8 *(véritable ▸ cause)* deep, underlying, primary; **je ne connais pas ses intentions profondes** I don't know what his/her intentions are deep down
ADV *(aller, creuser)* deep
NM **au plus p. de** in the depths of; **au plus p. de la terre** in the depths *or* bowels of the earth; **au plus p. de la nuit** at dead of night; **au plus p. de mon cœur** deep in my heart

profondément [prɔfɔ̃demɑ̃] ADV 1 *(creuser, enfouir)* deep; **il salua p. la foule** he greeted the crowd with a deep bow **2** *(respirer)* deeply; *(soupirer)* heavily, deeply; **dormir p.** to be sound asleep; **je dors très p.** I sleep very heavily; **p. endormi** sound *or* fast asleep **3** *(en intensif)* profoundly, deeply; **je suis p. choqué** I'm deeply shocked; **elle est p. convaincue de son bon droit** she's utterly convinced she's right; **je regrette p.!** I'm deeply sorry!

profondeur [prɔfɔ̃dœr] NF 1 *(dimension)* depth; **quelle est la p. du puits?** how deep is the well?; **un trou de trois mètres de p.** a hole three metres deep; **on s'est arrêtés à huit mètres de p.** we stopped eight metres down; **de grande p.** very deep; **de faible p.** shallow; **la faible p. de l'étang** the shallowness of the lake
2 *(intensité ▸ d'un sentiment)* depth, *Sout* profundity
3 *(perspicacité)* profoundness, profundity; **un film sans p.** a film with no depth, a shallow *or* superficial film; **sa p. d'esprit** his/her insight
4 *Opt & Phot* **p. de champ** depth of field; **p. de foyer** depth of focus
• **profondeurs** NFPL *Littéraire* depths
• **en profondeur** ADJ *(étude)* in-depth, thorough; **il nous faut des changements en p.** we need fundamental changes ADV *(creuser)* deep; **notre crème antirides agit en p.** our anti-wrinkle cream works deep into the skin; **il faut agir en p.** we need to make fundamental changes

pro forma [prɔfɔrma] ADJ **facture p.** pro forma invoice

profus, -e [prɔfy, -yz] ADJ profuse

profusément [prɔfyzemɑ̃] ADV profusely

profusion [prɔfyzjɔ̃] NF 1 *(abondance)* profusion, abundance; **avec une p. d'exemples** with abundant examples **2** *(excès)* excess; **avec une p. de détails** with too much detail
• **à profusion** ADV galore, plenty; **il y avait à boire et à manger à p.** there was food and drink galore, there was plenty to eat and drink

progéniture [prɔʒenityr] NF offspring, *Sout* progeny; *Hum* **que fais-tu de ta nombreuse p. le dimanche?** what do you do with your brood *or* all your offspring on Sundays?

progestatif, -ive [prɔʒestatif, -iv] *Physiol* ADJ *(hormones)* progestative; **corps p.** corpus luteum
NM progestin, progestogen

progestérone [prɔʒesterɔn] NF *Physiol* progesterone

progiciel [prɔʒisjɛl] NM *Ordinat* package; **p. de communication** comms package; **p. intégré** integrated package

prognathe [prɔgnat] ADJ prognathous, prognathic
NMF prognathous subject

programmable [prɔgramabl] ADJ programmable

programmateur, -trice [prɔgramatœr, -tris] NM,F *Rad & TV* programme planner; *Ordinat* programmer
NM *(d'une cuisinière)* programmer, autotimer; *(d'une machine à laver)* programme selector

programmation [prɔgramasjɔ̃] NF 1 *Rad & TV* programme planning; **un changement de p.** a change to the advertised *or* scheduled programme **2** *Ordinat* programming; **p. absolue/dynamique/linéaire** absolute/dynamic/linear programming; **p. orientée objet, p. par objets** object-oriented programming **3** *Écon* programming

programmatrice [prɔgramatris] *voir* **programmateur**

programme [prɔgram] NM 1 *(contenu ▸ d'une cérémonie, d'un spectacle)* programme; **qu'est-ce qu'il y a au p. ce soir à l'Opéra?** what's on tonight at the Opéra?; **il y a un bon p. ce soir à la télé** it's a good night on TV tonight
2 *(brochure ▸ d'un concert, d'une soirée)* programme; *(▸ de cinéma, de télévision)* listings, guide; **demandez le p.!** programmes on sale here!; **le p. de télévision est en page 4** the TV guide is on page 4
3 *(emploi du temps)* schedule, programme; **arrêter un p.** to draw up *or* arrange a programme; **notre p. est très chargé cette semaine** we have a busy schedule this week; **qu'avons-nous au p. aujourd'hui?** what's our schedule (for) today?, what's on the agenda for today?; **inscrire qch au p.** to schedule sth; *Mktg* **p. des annonces** advertising schedule; **p. de production** production programme *or* schedule; *Com* **p. des ventes** sales programme *or* schedule
4 *Scol (d'une année)* curriculum; *(dans une matière)* syllabus; **une question hors p.** a question not covered by the syllabus; **Shakespeare est** *ou*

figure au p. cette année Shakespeare is on this year's syllabus; **les auteurs au p.** the set authors; **le p. de première année** the first-year programme *or* syllabus

5 *Pol (plate-forme) Br* manifesto, *Am* platform; **p. commun** common *or* joint manifesto; **p. électoral** (election) platform; **p. de gouvernement** government manifesto

6 *(projet)* programme; **lancer un p. de réformes** to launch a package *or* programme of reforms; **le p. nucléaire** the nuclear programme; **quel est ton p. pour les vacances?** what have you got planned *or* arranged for the holidays?; *Fam* **ton voyage, c'est tout un p.!** this trip sounds like it's quite something!; *Hum* **je voudrais l'intéresser à l'actualité – tout un p.!** I'd like to get him/her interested in current affairs – that's a tall order!; **p. alimentaire mondial** world food programme; *Mktg* **p. d'amélioration de la qualité** quality improvement programme; **p. économique** economic programme *or* plan; **p. de fabrication** production programme *or* schedule; *Mktg* **p. de fidélisation** loyalty programme; **p. de formation** training programme; **p. d'investissement** investment programme; **p. de licenciement** planned redundancy scheme; *Mktg* **p. de stimulation** incentive scheme

7 *Ordinat* program; **p. objet/source** object/source program; **p. amorce** initial program loader, bootstrap; **p. antivirus** antivirus program; **p. d'assemblage** assembler; **p. de chargement** loader; **p. de commande d'impression** printer driver; **p. de commande de la souris** mouse driver; **p. de conversion** conversion program; **p. en cours d'exécution** active program; **p. de création de pages Web** web authoring program; **p. de dessin** drawing program, paint program; **p. de diagnostic** malfunction routine; **p. de gestion** driver; **p. d'installation** setup program, installer; **p. sentinelle** watchdog program; **p. de service** utility program; **p. de test** check program; **p. utilitaire** utility program; **p. virus** virus program

8 *Can Rad & TV (émission)* programme

programmer [3] [prɔgrame] **VT 1** *Cin, Rad, Théât & TV* to bill, to programme; **le débat n'a jamais été programmé** the debate was never shown *or* screened

2 *(planifier)* to plan

3 *Électron (appareil)* to set, to programme

4 *Ordinat* to program; **p. qch en assembleur** to program sth in assembly language

VI *Ordinat* to program

programmeur, -euse [prɔgramœr, -øz] **NM,F** *Ordinat* programmer

progrès [prɔgrɛ] **NM 1** *(amélioration)* progress *(UNCOUNT)*; *(avancée)* breakthrough, advance; **faire des p.** *(élève, malade, enquêteurs)* to make progress; **être en p.** to be making progress, to be improving; **il y a du p., continuez** that's better, keep it up; **le XXème siècle a connu de grands p. scientifiques** the 20th century witnessed some great scientific breakthroughs; **le p.** progress; *aussi Ironique* **tu vois, c'est ça le p.!** that's progress for you! **2** *(progression)* **les p. de** *(armée)* the progress *or* advance of; *(criminalité)* the upsurge *or* increase in; *(maladie)* the progress *or* progression of

progresser [4] [prɔgrese] **VI 1** *(s'améliorer ▸ élève)* to improve, to progress, to make progress; *(▸ projet)* to progress, to make progress; *(▸ enquête, enquêteur)* to make progress *or* headway; **vous avez bien progressé depuis le début de l'année** you've improved a lot *or* made great strides since the beginning of the year **2** *(gagner du terrain ▸ ennemi)* to advance, to gain ground; *(▸ marcheur)* to make progress; *(▸ maladie)* to progress; *(▸ inflation)* to creep up, to rise; **p. lentement/rapidement** to make slow/rapid progress; **la recherche scientifique progresse de jour en jour** scientific research is making progress every day

progressif, -ive [prɔgresif, -iv] **ADJ 1** *(graduel ▸ gén)* gradual, progressive; *(▸ taux)* graduated, increasing **2** *Ling* continuous, progressive **3** *Méd (maladie)* progressive

progression [prɔgresjɔ̃] **NF 1** *(avancée)* progress, advance; **l'ennemi a poursuivi sa p. vers l'intérieur des terres** the enemy advanced *or* progressed inland

2 *(développement ▸ d'une maladie, d'un parti politique)* progression, progress; *(▸ du racisme)* spread, development; *(▸ de la délinquance, du chômage)* rise (**de** in); *(▸ d'un secteur économique)* expansion; *Bourse (▸ des cours)* rise, improvement (**de** in); *(▸ dans une carrière)* progress, advancement; **notre chiffre d'affaires est en constante p.** our turnover is constantly increasing *or* improving

3 *Math* progression; **p. arithmétique** arithmetical progression

4 *Mus* progression; **p. harmonique** harmonic progression

progressiste [prɔgresist] **ADJ** *(politique, parti)* progressive

NMF progressive

progressive [prɔgresiv] *voir* **progressif**

progressivement [prɔgresivmɑ̃] **ADV** progressively, gradually

progressivité [prɔgresivite] **NF** progressiveness; *Fin* **p. de l'impôt** progressive increase in taxation

prohiber [3] [prɔibe] **VT** to prohibit, to ban

prohibitif, -ive [prɔibitif, -iv] **ADJ 1** *(prix, tarif)* prohibitive **2** *(loi)* prohibitory

prohibition [prɔibisjɔ̃] **NF 1** *(interdiction)* prohibition, ban; **la p. du port d'armes** the ban on carrying weapons; **p. d'entrée** *ou* **à l'importation** import ban; **p. de sortie** export ban **2** *Hist* **la P.** Prohibition

prohibitionnisme [prɔibisjɔnism] **NM** prohibitionism

prohibitionniste [prɔibisjɔnist] **ADJ** prohibitionist

NMF prohibitionist

prohibitive [prɔibitiv] *voir* **prohibitif**

proie [prwa] **NF 1** *(animal)* prey **2** *(victime)* prey; **il est une p. facile pour les cambrioleurs** he's easy prey for burglars; **être la p. de qn** to be the prey *or* victim of sb; **les enfants sont la p. de la publicité** children are the victims of advertising

• **en proie à PRÉP** in the grip of; **en p. au doute** racked with *or* beset by doubt; **être en p. à des hallucinations** to suffer from hallucinations

projecteur [prɔʒɛktœr] **NM 1** *(pour illuminer un spectacle)* spotlight; *(pour illuminer un édifice)* floodlight; *(pour surveiller)* searchlight; **éclairé par des projecteurs** floodlit; *Fig* **sous les projecteurs de l'actualité** in the spotlight; **p. ponctuel** spotlight **2** *(d'images)* projector; **p. de cinéma** cine-projector; **p. (de diapositives)** slide projector **3** *Aut* headlight; **p. halogène** halogen headlight

projectif, -ive [prɔʒɛktif, -iv] **ADJ** *Géom & Psy* projective

projectile [prɔʒɛktil] **NM 1** *Mil* projectile **2** *(objet lancé)* projectile, missile

projection [prɔʒɛksjɔ̃] **NF 1** *Cin & Phot (action)* projection; *(séance)* screening, showing; **ils durent interrompre la p.** they had to stop the film; **une p. de diapos** a slide show; **une conférence avec p.** a lecture (illustrated) with slides; **appareil de p.** projector; *Cin & TV* **p. frontale** front projection; **p. privée** private showing; *Cin & TV* **p. en transparence** rear projection

2 *(jet ▸ d'un liquide)* splashing; *(▸ de boue)* splashing, splattering; *(▸ de graisse)* spattering; **sali par des projections de boue** splattered *or* splashed with mud; *Géol* **projections volcaniques** ejecta, volcanic debris

3 *Psy* projection (**sur** onto); *Fam* **tu fais une p.** you're projecting

4 *Math* projection

5 *(prévision)* projection; **p. des ventes** sales projection

6 *(dans un récit, un film)* **p. en avant** flashforward

projectionniste [prɔʒɛksjɔnist] **NMF** projectionist

projective [prɔʒɛktiv] *voir* **projectif**

projet [prɔʒɛ] **NM 1** *(intention)* plan; **faire** *ou* **former le p. de faire qch** to plan to do sth; **j'ai fait le p. de me rendre en Italie** I'm planning on going to Italy; **faire des projets** to make plans; **faire des projets d'avenir** to plan *or* make plans for the future; **il a plusieurs projets de spectacle** he has plans for several new shows; **je n'ai pas de projets pour ce soir** I have no plans for tonight **2** *(esquisse)* plan, outline; **ma pièce n'est encore qu'à l'état de p.** my play is still only a draft *or* at the planning stage; *Jur* **p. d'accord/de contrat** draft agreement/contract; **p. de loi** bill **3** *(d'un bâtiment)* plan; *(d'une machine)* blueprint; **p. de construction** building project

• **en projet ADV qu'avez-vous en p. pour le printemps?** what are your plans for the spring?; **nous avons un nouveau modèle d'avion en p.** we're working on (the plans for) a new design of aircraft

projeter [27] [prɔʃte] **VT 1** *(prévoir)* to plan, to arrange; **j'ai projeté un voyage pour cet été** I've planned a trip for this summer; **je n'ai pas projeté de sortir ce soir** I haven't planned *or* arranged to go out tonight; **nous avons dû abandonner la promenade projetée** we had to abandon our plans for a walk

2 *(lancer ▸ gén)* to throw; *(▸ violemment)* to hurl; *(▸ liquide)* to splash; *(▸ boue)* to splatter, to splash; *(▸ graisse)* to spatter; **elle a été projetée hors de la voiture** she was thrown out of the car

3 *(faire apparaître ▸ ombre, lumière)* to project, to cast, to throw

4 *Cin & Phot (film, diapositives)* to show, to project

5 *Psy* to project; **p. ses fantasmes sur qn** to project one's fantasies onto sb

6 *Math* to project

7 *(voix)* to project

VPR se projeter 1 *(ombre)* to fall, to be cast; **son ombre se projetait sur l'écran** he was silhouetted against the screen **2** *Psy* **se p. sur qn** to project oneself onto sb

projeteur [prɔʃtœr] **NM 1** *(technicien)* design engineer **2** *(dessinateur)* industrial (design) draughtsman

projette *etc voir* **projeter**

projo [prɔʒo] **NM** *Fam* projector□

prolapsus [prɔlapsys] **NM** *Méd* prolapse

prolétaire [prɔletɛr] **ADJ 1** *Vieilli (masse, parti)* proletarian **2** *(quartier)* working-class

NMF proletarian, member of the proletariat

prolétariat [prɔletarja] **NM** proletariat

prolétarien, -enne [prɔletarjɛ̃, -ɛn] **ADJ** proletarian; **solidarité prolétarienne** solidarity of the working class

prolétarisation [prɔletarizasjɔ̃] **NF** proletarianization

prolétariser [3] [prɔletarize] **VT** to proletarianize, to make working-class

VPR se prolétariser to become proletarianized *or* working-class

prolifération [prɔliferasjɔ̃] **NF 1** *(gén)* proliferation, multiplication; **p. des armes** arms proliferation; **la p. des industries** the mushrooming of industry **2** *Biol & Nucl* proliferation

prolifère [prɔlifɛr] **ADJ** *Bot* proliferous

proliférer [18] [prɔlifere] **VI** to proliferate; **les insectes prolifèrent dans le marécage** insects proliferate in the swamp; **les affichages illégaux prolifèrent** flyposting is on the increase

prolifique [prɔlifik] **ADJ 1** *(fécond)* prolific **2** *Fig (auteur, peintre)* prolific, productive

prolixe [prɔliks] **ADJ 1** *(description, style)* wordy, verbose, *Sout* prolix **2** *(écrivain)* verbose, *Sout* prolix; **il n'est pas p.** *(bavard)* he's a man of few words

prolixement [prɔliksəmɑ̃] **ADV** at great length

prolixité [prɔliksite] **NF 1** *(d'un discours)* wordiness, verbosity **2** *(d'un auteur)* verbosity, prolixity

prolo [prɔlo] *Fam* **ADJ** plebby

NMF pleb, prole

prologue [prɔlɔg] **NM 1** *Littérature, Mus & Théât* prologue (**de** to) **2** *(début)* prologue, prelude, preamble; **en p. à la réunion** as a prologue *or* prelude *or* preamble to the meeting

prolongation [prɔlɔ̃gasjɔ̃] **NF 1** *(allongement)* extension **2** *Sport Br* extra time, *Am* overtime; **jouer les prolongations** to play *or* to go into *Br* extra time *or Am* overtime

> Do not confuse with **prolongement**, which conveys the idea of physical extension.

prolonge [prɔlɔ̃ʒ] NF *Mil* ammunition wagon; **p. d'artillerie** gun carriage

prolongé, -e [prɔlɔ̃ʒe] ADJ **1** *(long ▸ applaudissements, séjour, absence)* lengthy, prolonged **2** *(trop long)* protracted, prolonged; **attention à la station debout/assise prolongée** be careful not to spend too much time standing/sitting **3** *(attardé)* **un adolescent p.** an overgrown schoolboy

prolongement [prɔlɔ̃ʒmɑ̃] NM **1** *(extension ▸ d'une route)* continuation; *(▸ d'un mur, d'une voie ferrée, d'une période)* extension **2** *(suite)* outcome, consequence

• **prolongements** NMPL *(conséquences)* effects, consequences, repercussions; **les prolongements du scandale se font encore sentir** the effects of *or* ripples from the scandal can still be felt

• **dans le prolongement de** PRÉP **les deux rues sont dans le p. l'une de l'autre** the two streets are a continuation of each other; **je veux installer le frigidaire dans le p. de l'évier** I want the fridge in line with the sink; **c'est tout à fait dans le p. de mes préoccupations actuelles** that's along exactly the same lines as what I'm concerned with at the moment

> Do not confuse with **prolongation**, which only has to do with duration.

prolonger [17] [prɔlɔ̃ʒe] VT **1** *(dans le temps)* to extend, to prolong; **p. son séjour** to extend one's stay, to stay longer than planned; **p. un délai** to extend a deadline **2** *(dans l'espace)* to extend, to continue; **la route sera prolongée de deux kilomètres** the road will be made 2 km longer *or* will be extended by 2 km **3** *Mus (note)* to hold

VPR **se prolonger 1** *(dans le temps ▸ situation)* to persist, to go on; *(▸ effet)* to last; *(▸ réunion)* to be prolonged, to go on; **la guerre semble se p. indéfiniment** the war seems to be going on forever **2** *(dans l'espace)* to go on, to continue; **le sentier se prolonge dans la forêt** the path continues through the forest

promenade [prɔmnad] NF **1** *(à pied ▸ gén)* walk; *(▸ courte)* stroll; *(à bicyclette, à cheval)* ride; *(en voiture)* ride, drive; **faire une p.** *(à pied)* to go for a walk *or* stroll; *(à bicyclette, à cheval)* to go for a ride; **faire une p. en voiture** to go for a drive; **je lui ai fait faire une p.** I took him/her out for a walk; **l'heure de la p.** *(d'un détenu)* exercise time; **aller en Angleterre de nos jours, c'est presque devenu une p.** going to England nowadays is almost like going next door; *Fam* **ç'a été une vraie p.** *(victoire facile)* it was a real walkover **2** *(allée ▸ gén)* walk (way); *(en bord de mer)* promenade

• **en promenade** ADV *(à pied)* out walking, out for a walk; *(à bicyclette, à cheval)* out riding, out for a ride; *(en voiture)* out riding *or* driving, out for a ride *or* drive

promener [19] [prɔmne] VT **1** *(sortir ▸ à pied)* to take (out) for a walk *or* stroll; *(▸ en voiture)* to take (out) for a drive; **j'ai passé le week-end à p. un ami étranger dans Paris** I spent the weekend showing a foreign friend around Paris; **p. le chien** to walk the dog, to take the dog for a walk; **cela vous promènera un peu** it'll get you out (of the house) a bit; *Fam* **envoyer p. qn** *(l'éconduire)* to send sb packing, to tell sb where to go; *Fam* **tout envoyer p.** *Br* to chuck *or* to pack it all in, *Am* to chuck everything

2 *Fig (emmener ▸ personne)* **il m'a promené de bureau en bureau** he dragged me from office to office; **j'en ai assez d'être promené de poste en poste** I've had enough of being sent *or* shunted around from one job to another

3 *(mentir à)* **il m'a promené pendant trois semaines** he kept me hanging on for three weeks

4 *(déplacer)* **elle promène son regard sur la foule** her eyes scan the crowd; **p. ses doigts sur le piano** to run one's fingers over the keys

5 *(traîner)* **p. son ennui/désespoir** to go around looking bored/disconsolate

6 *(transporter)* to take around; **le roman nous promène dans la France du XIXème siècle** the novel takes us for a stroll round 19th-century France; **ses récits de voyage nous ont promenés dans le monde entier** his/her travel stories have taken us all around the world

VPR **se promener 1** *(à pied)* to go for a walk *or* stroll; *(en voiture)* to go for a drive; *(à bicyclette, à cheval)* to go for a ride; *(en bateau)* to go for a sail; **viens te p. avec moi** come for *or* on a walk with me; **emmener p. qn** to take sb (out) for a walk; *Fam* **va te p.!** (go) get lost!

2 *(mains, regard)* **ses doigts se promenaient sur le clavier** his/her fingers wandered over the keyboard

3 *Fam (traîner)* **j'en ai assez que tes affaires se promènent dans toute la maison!** I've had enough of your things lying about all over the house!; **où sont-elles encore allées se p., ces lunettes?** where have those glasses got to this time?

4 *Fam (éprouver de la facilité)* **il se promène en anglais** English is a walk in the park for him

promeneur, -euse [prɔmnœr, -øz] NM,F *(dans un parc, en ville)* stroller, walker; *(randonneur)* walker, rambler

promenoir [prɔmnwar] NM **1** *Théât* promenade **2** *(dans un parc)* covered walk

promesse [prɔmɛs] NF **1** *(engagement)* promise, assurance; **faire une p.** to (make a) promise; **faire des promesses** to make promises; **manquer à/tenir sa p.** to break/to keep one's promise; **je ne vous fais pas de p.** I won't promise anything; **rappelle-toi, j'ai ta p.** remember, you promised (me) *or* gave your word; **il m'a fait la p. de revenir** he promised me he would come back; **elle m'avait fait de grandes promesses** she promised me great things; **encore une p. en l'air** *ou* **d'ivrogne** *ou* **de Gascon!** promises, promises!; *Pol* **p. électorale** electoral promise; **p. de mariage** promise of marriage

2 *Com & Fin* commitment; **p. écrite** written promise, written undertaking; **p. d'achat/de vente** promise to buy/to sell; **p. unique de vente** unique selling point *or* proposition

3 *Mktg* claim; **p. mensongère** false claim

4 *Littéraire (espoir)* promise; **la p. d'une journée magnifique/d'un avenir meilleur** the promise of a beautiful day/of a better future

• **promesses** NFPL *(avenir)* promise; **un jeune joueur plein de promesses** a young player showing great promise, a very promising young player

promet *etc voir* **promettre**

Prométhée [prɔmete] NPR *Myth* Prometheus

prométhéen, -enne [prɔmeteɛ̃, -ɛn] ADJ Promethean

prometteur, -euse [prɔmetœr, -øz] ADJ **1** *(début, situation)* promising, encouraging; *(sourire)* full of promise; *aussi Ironique* **voilà qui est p.!** that's a good sign! **2** *(musicien, acteur)* promising, of promise

promettre [84] [prɔmɛtr] VT **1** *(jurer)* to promise; **je te l'ai promis** I promised (you); **je ne peux rien vous p.** I can't promise anything; **je te promets de ne pas lui en parler** I promise I won't say a word to him/her about it; **je te promets que je ne dirai rien** I promise (you) I won't say anything; **on nous a promis de l'aide** we were promised help; **p. une récompense** to offer a reward; **je te rembourserai, c'est promis** I'll pay you back, I promise

2 *(annoncer)* to promise; **la météo nous promet du beau temps pour toute la semaine** the weather forecast promises nice weather for the whole week; **tout cela ne promet rien de bon** it doesn't look *or* sound too good

3 *(destiner)* to destine; **il est promis à un grand avenir** he is destined for a great future, he has a great future ahead of him

4 *Fam (affirmer)* to assure; **je te promets qu'il s'en souviendra, de ce dîner!** I can assure you he'll remember that dinner!

VI **1** *(faire naître des espérances)* to promise; **un jeune auteur qui promet** a promising young author

2 *Fam (laisser présager des difficultés)* **ce gamin promet!** that kid's got a great future ahead of him!; *Ironique* **eh bien, ça promet!** that's a good start!; **eh bien, ça promet pour la fin de la semaine!** well then, it looks as if we're in for a great weekend!

VPR **se promettre 1** *(emploi réciproque)* **ils se sont promis de se revoir** they promised (each other) that they would meet again

2 *(espérer)* **se p. du bon temps** to look forward to enjoying oneself

3 *(se jurer à soi-même)* to swear, to promise (to) oneself; **je me suis bien promis de ne jamais recommencer** I swore never to do it again, I promised myself I would never do it again; **je me suis promis d'aller lui rendre visite un de ces jours** I mean to visit him/her one of these days

promeut, promeuvent *etc voir* **promouvoir**

promis, -e [prɔmi, -iz] ADJ promised

NM,F *Vieilli* betrothed

promiscuité [prɔmiskɥite] NF **1** *(voisinage)* overcrowding; **vivre dans la p.** to live in overcrowded conditions; **je ne supporte pas la p.** *(dans un hôpital etc)* I can't stand the lack of privacy; *(dans le métro)* I can't stand the overcrowding **2 p. sexuelle** (sexual) promiscuity

> Il faut noter que le terme anglais **promiscuity** est un faux ami. Il désigne uniquement **un changement fréquent de partenaires sexuels.**

promit *etc voir* **promettre**

promo [prɔmo] NF *Fam* **1** *Mil, Scol & Univ Br* year, *Am* class; **la p. 94** the class of '94 **2** *Com* promotion[□], promo; **en p.** on special offer

promontoire [prɔmɔ̃twar] NM *Géog* headland, promontory

promoteur, -trice [prɔmɔtœr, -tris] ADJ **société promotrice privée** development company

NM,F **1** *Littéraire (créateur)* promoter, instigator; **2** *Com* promoter **3** *Constr* **p. (immobilier)** property developer

promotion [prɔmosjɔ̃] NF **1** *(avancement)* promotion; **j'ai eu une p.** I've been promoted; **fêter la p. de qn** to celebrate sb's promotion; **p. au mérite/à l'ancienneté** promotion on merit/by seniority; **p. des cadres** executive promotion; **p. interne** internal promotion; **p. sociale** upward mobility

2 *Com & Mktg (publicité)* promotion; *(offre spéciale)* special offer, promotion; **faire une p. sur un produit** to promote a product; **faire la p. de qch** to promote sth; **la p. du jour** *(sur la vitrine d'un magasin, dans un marché)* today's special offer; **notre p. de la semaine** this week's special offer *or Am* special; **p. collective** tie-in promotion; **p. d'entreprises** corporate identity; **p. sur le lieu de vente** point-of-sale promotion, in-store promotion; **p. on-pack** on-pack promotion; **p. sur point d'achat** point-of-purchase promotion; **p. de prestige** prestige promotion; **p. spéciale** special promotion; **p. des ventes** sales promotion

3 *Mil, Scol & Univ Br* year, *Am* class; **ils étaient camarades de p.** they were in the same class *or* year; **le premier de sa p.** the first in his year

4 *Constr* **p. immobilière** property development

• **en promotion** ADJ *Com* on special offer, on promotion, *Am* on special

promotionnel, -elle [prɔmosjɔnɛl] ADJ *(brochure)* promotional; *(tarif)* special; *(budget)* promotional, publicity; **tarifs promotionnels sur ce voyage en Israël!** special offer on this trip to Israel!

promotrice [prɔmɔtris] *voir* **promoteur**

promouvoir [56] [prɔmuvwar] VT **1** *(faire monter en grade)* to promote; **il a été promu capitaine** he was promoted (to the rank of) captain **2** *(encourager ▸ réforme)* to advocate, to push for; *(▸ recherche, création d'entreprise)* to promote, to further **3** *Com (article)* to promote, to publicize

prompt, -e [prɔ̃, prɔ̃t] ADJ prompt, quick, swift; **p. à répondre** quick with an answer; **vous avez été trop p. à agir** you acted rashly; **p. à la colère** easily moved to anger; **avoir l'esprit p.** to be quick-witted; **avoir la repartie prompte** to have a ready wit, to always be ready with an answer

promptement [prɔ̃tmɑ̃] ADV quickly, swiftly; **répondre p.** to give a prompt reply

prompteur [prɔ̃ptœr] NM teleprompter, *Br* Autocue®; **p. déroulant** roller prompter

promptitude [prɔ̃tityd] NF quickness, swiftness

promu, -e [prɔmy] PP *voir* **promouvoir**

NM,F promoted person; **voici la liste des promus dans l'ordre de la Légion d'honneur** here is the list of those decorated with the Legion of Honour; *Univ* **les nouveaux promus** = this year's graduates of a "grande école"

promulgation [prɔmylgasjɔ̃] NF promulgation
promulguer [3] [prɔmylge] VT to promulgate
prône [pron] NM *Rel* (Sunday) sermon
prôner [3] [prone] VT *(patience, indulgence, tolérance)* to strongly recommend, to advocate, to urge; *(méthode)* to strongly recommend, to advocate
pronom [prɔnɔ̃] NM pronoun; **p. indéfini/interrogatif/personnel/relatif** indefinite/interrogative/personal/relative pronoun
pronominal, -e, -aux, -ales [prɔnɔminal, -o] ADJ *(adjectif, adverbe)* pronominal; *(verbe)* reflexive
NM reflexive verb
pronominalement [prɔnɔminalmɑ̃] ADV pronominally
prononçable [prɔnɔ̃sabl] ADJ pronounceable; **un nom qui n'est pas p.** an unpronounceable name
prononcé, -e [prɔnɔ̃se] ADJ *(traits)* strong; *(forme)* strong, definite; *(tendance)* marked; *(accent)* broad, pronounced, strong; **un accent peu p.** a faint *or* slight accent
NM *Jur* (announcement of) decision
prononcer [16] [prɔnɔ̃se] VT **1** *(dire ▸ parole)* to say, to utter; *(▸discours)* to make, to deliver; **sans p. un mot** without a word; **il a prononcé quelques mots sur la situation en Chine** he said a few words about the situation in China; **ne prononce plus jamais son nom** never mention his/her name again
2 *(proclamer ▸ jugement)* to pronounce; **p. un divorce** to issue a divorce decree, to pronounce a couple divorced; **p. la sentence** to pronounce *or* to pass sentence; **il a prononcé lui-même sa condamnation** he's condemned himself
3 *Rel* **p. ses vœux** to take one's vows
4 *(articuler ▸ mot, langue)* to pronounce; *(▸ phonème)* to articulate; **mal p. qch** to mispronounce sth
USAGE ABSOLU **apprendre à p.** to learn proper pronunciation; **il prononce mal** his pronunciation is poor; **c'est la mode chez certains acteurs de ne pas p. clairement** it is the fashion among certain actors to slur their speech
VI **1** *Jur* to deliver *or* to give a verdict (**sur** on) **2** *Vieilli ou Littéraire (choisir)* to pronounce; **p. en faveur de/contre** to pronounce in favour of/against
VPR **se prononcer 1** *(mot)* to be pronounced; **le "a" se prononce en ouvrant la bouche** "a" is pronounced by opening the mouth; **le deuxième "i" ne se prononce pas** the second "i" isn't sounded *or* is silent; **comment ça se prononce?** how do you say *or* pronounce it? **2** *(s'exprimer ▸ gén)* to give one's opinion; *(▸ juge)* to give a verdict; *(▸ médecin)* to give one's prognosis; **ils se sont prononcés pour/contre la peine de mort** they pronounced *or* declared themselves in favour of/against the death penalty; **ne se prononcent pas** *(dans un sondage)* don't knows
prononciation [prɔnɔ̃sjasjɔ̃] NF **1** *(d'un mot)* pronunciation; **un mot avec deux prononciations différentes** a word with two different pronunciations; **la p. du "th" anglais est difficile pour un Français** pronouncing the English "th" is difficult for a French person **2** *(d'une personne)* pronunciation; **elle a une bonne/mauvaise p. en allemand** her German pronunciation is good/bad **3** *(d'un jugement)* pronouncing; **j'attends la p. du divorce** I'm waiting for the divorce to be made final *or* to come through
pronostic [prɔnɔstik] NM **1** *Sport* forecast; *(pour les courses)* forecast, (racing) tip **2** *(conjecture)* forecast; **les pronostics économiques** economic forecasts; **p. du marché** market forecast **3** *Méd* prognosis
pronostiquer [3] [prɔnɔstike] VT **1** *(prévoir)* to forecast, *Sout* to prognosticate **2** *(être signe de)* to be a sign *or* forerunner of
pronostiqueur, -euse [prɔnɔstikœr, -øz] NM,F **1** *Écon* forecaster **2** *Sport* tipster
pronucléus [pronykleys] NM *Biol* pronucleus
pronunciamiento [prɔnunsjamjɛnto] NM *(gén)* military coup; *(en pays de langue espagnole)* pronunciamento
propagande [prɔpagɑ̃d] NF **1** *(politique)* propaganda; **p. électorale** electioneering **2** *(publicité)* publicity, plugging; **faire de la p. pour qn/qch** to advertise sb/sth; **tu me fais de la p.!** you're a good advert for my cause!
• **de propagande** ADJ *(film, journal)* propaganda *(avant n)*
propagandiste [prɔpagɑ̃dist] ADJ propagandist
NMF propagandist
propagateur, -trice [prɔpagatœr, -tris] NM,F *(de nouvelles)* propagator, spreader; *(d'idées)* disseminator
propagation [prɔpagasjɔ̃] NF **1** *Littéraire (reproduction)* propagation, spreading **2** *(diffusion ▸ d'un incendie, d'une doctrine, d'une rumeur)* spreading; **ils n'ont pu empêcher la p. de l'incendie** they couldn't stop the fire (from) spreading **3** *Élec & Phys* propagation; **p. guidée** guided (wave) propagation; **vitesse de p. d'une onde** velocity of propagation of a wave
propagatrice [prɔpagatris] *voir* **propagateur**
propager [17] [prɔpaʒe] VT **1** *(répandre ▸ foi, idées)* to propagate, to disseminate, to spread; *(▸ épidémie, feu, rumeur, mode)* to spread; **sa spécialité c'est de p. des rumeurs** he's/she's a specialist in spreading gossip **2** *Bot & Zool* to propagate
VPR **se propager 1** *(s'étendre ▸ nouvelle, épidémie etc)* to spread **2** *Phys (onde, son)* to be propagated **3** *(plante)* to propagate, to reproduce
propane [prɔpan] NM *Chim* propane
propanier [prɔpanje] NM propane tanker *or* carrier
propédeutique [prɔpedøtik] NF **1** *(enseignement préparatoire)* propaedeutics **2** *Anciennement Univ* = first year of university course
propène [prɔpɛn] = **propylène**
propension [prɔpɑ̃sjɔ̃] NF **1** *(tendance)* propensity (à to); **avoir une forte p. à qch/à faire qch** to have a strong tendency to do sth **2** *Écon* propensity; **p. à consommer/épargner** propensity to consume/to save
propergol [prɔpɛrgɔl] NM propellant
prophète [prɔfɛt] NM prophet; **p. de malheur** prophet of doom; **faux p.** false prophet
prophétie [prɔfesi] NF prophecy; **faire une p.** to prophesy
prophétique [prɔfetik] ADJ **1** *Rel* prophetic **2** *Fig (prémonitoire)* prophetic, premonitory; **il a eu une vue p. de la catastrophe** he had a premonition of the catastrophe
prophétiquement [prɔfetikmɑ̃] ADV prophetically
prophétiser [3] [prɔfetize] VT **1** *Rel* to prophesy **2** *Fig (prédire)* to foretell, to predict, to prophesy
VI *(prédire)* to make pompous predictions
prophylactique [prɔfilaktik] ADJ *(mesure)* prophylactic
prophylaxie [prɔfilaksi] NF prophylaxis
propice [prɔpis] ADJ **1** *(favorable ▸ temps, période, vent)* favourable; **les cieux n'ont pas l'air bien propices** the sky looks rather menacing; **l'automne est p. à la méditation** autumn is conducive to *or* is an appropriate time for meditation; **les festivals sont propices aux rencontres** festivals are good places to meet people; **si la fortune nous est p.** if Fortune smiles on us **2** *(opportun)* suitable; **peu p.** inauspicious; **au moment p.** at the right moment; **un endroit plus p.** a more suitable place
propitiation [prɔpisjasjɔ̃] NF *Rel* propitiation
propitiatoire [prɔpisjatwar] ADJ *Rel* propitiatory
proportion [prɔpɔrsjɔ̃] NF *(rapport)* proportion, ratio; **la p. d'alcool dans un vin** the percentage of alcohol in a wine, the alcohol content of a wine; **la p. des maisons individuelles est stationnaire** the proportion *or* comparative number of detached houses remains stable; **tu n'as pas respecté les proportions dans le dessin** your drawing isn't in proportion; **dans la** *ou* **une p. de 15 pour cent** in the ratio of 15 percent; **dans la** *ou* **une p. de cent contre un** in the ratio of a hundred to one; **dans la même p.** in equal proportions; **dans une juste p.** in the correct proportion; **hors de p. avec** out of proportion to; **sans p. avec** out of (all) proportion with
• **proportions** NFPL **1** *(importance)* (great) importance; **prendre des proportions énormes** to grow out of all proportion; **pourquoi un incident aussi minime a-t-il pris de telles proportions?** why was such a trivial incident blown out of all proportion?; **si les commandes diminuent dans de sérieuses proportions** if orders should decrease to any great extent **2** *(dimensions)* dimensions, size; **tout dépendra des proportions de l'armoire** it will all depend on the size of the wardrobe; **c'est la même chose, toutes proportions gardées** it's the same thing but on a different scale
• **à proportion** ADV proportionately, at the same rate; **tout augmente, et les salaires à p.** everything is going up, and salaries are keeping pace
• **à proportion de** PRÉP in proportion to
• **en proportion** ADJ in proportion; **il a de gros frais, mais son salaire est en p.** he has a lot of expenses, but he has a correspondingly high salary ADV proportionately, at the same rate; **vous serez récompensé en p.** you'll be rewarded accordingly
• **en proportion de** PRÉP in proportion to; **son succès est en p. de son talent** his/her success is proportional *or* in proportion to his/her talent
proportionnalité [prɔpɔrsjɔnalite] NF **1** *Math* proportionality
2 *(rapport)* balance, (good) proportions
3 *(répartition)* equal distribution
4 *Écon* **p. de l'impôt** fixed rate system of taxation
proportionné, -e [prɔpɔrsjɔne] ADJ **1** *(harmonieux)* **bien p.** well-proportioned; **mal p.** out of proportion **2** *(adapté)* **p. à** commensurate with, in proportion to, proportional to; **la cotisation est proportionnée à vos revenus** payment is commensurate with *or* proportional to your income
proportionnel, -elle [prɔpɔrsjɔnɛl] ADJ **1 p. à** *(en rapport avec)* proportional to, in proportion with, commensurate with; **ils gagnent un salaire p. à leur travail** they earn a salary in proportion to the work they do; **directement/inversement p. (à)** directly/inversely proportional (to) **2** *Com & Écon (droits, impôt)* ad valorem **3** *Math & Pol* proportional
• **proportionnelle** NF *Pol* **la proportionnelle** *(processus)* proportional system; *(résultat)* proportional representation; **être élu à la proportionnelle** to be elected by proportional representation
proportionnellement [prɔpɔrsjɔnɛlmɑ̃] ADV *(gén)* proportionately (**à** to); *Math & Écon* proportionally, in direct ratio (**à** to)
proportionner [3] [prɔpɔrsjɔne] VT to match; **il est juste de p. le délit et la sanction** the punishment must fit the crime; **il faudrait p. la note à l'effort fourni par l'élève** the mark should reflect *or* match the amount of effort put in by the pupil
propos [prɔpo] NM **1** *(sujet)* subject, topic; **à ce p.** in this respect *or* connection; **à ce p., que penses-tu de ma suggestion?** which reminds me, what do you think of my suggestion?; **c'est à quel p.?** what's it about?; **elle veut te voir – à quel p.?** she wants to see you – what about *or* what for? **2** *Littéraire (but)* intention, aim; **mon p. n'est pas de vous convaincre** my aim is not to convince you; **là n'est pas le/mon p.** that is not the/my point; **avoir le ferme p. de faire qch** to firmly intend to do sth, to have the firm intention of doing sth
NMPL *(paroles)* words, talk; **menus p.** small talk; **tenir des p. injurieux** to make offensive remarks; **les p. qu'ils échangèrent sont restés confidentiels** their talk *or* conversation has remained confidential; **ses p. étaient à peine audibles** his words could hardly be heard
• **à propos** ADJ appropriate; **elle n'a pas jugé à p. de nous le dire** she didn't think it appropriate to tell us ADV **1** *(opportunément)* at the right moment; **arriver** *ou* **tomber à p.** to occur at the right time; **répondre à p.** *(pertinemment)* to answer appropriately; *(au bon moment)* to answer at the right moment; **mal à p.** at the wrong moment; **tu ne pouvais pas tomber plus mal à p.** you couldn't have come at a worse time **2** *(au fait)* by the way, incidentally; **à p., as-tu reçu ma carte?** by the way *or* incidentally, did you get my postcard?
• **à propos de** PRÉP about, concerning, regarding; **j'ai quelques remarques à faire à p. de vo-**

tre devoir I have a few things to say to you about your homework; **dis donc, à p. d'argent** hey, (talking) about money *or* on the subject of money

• **à tout propos** ADV constantly, at the slightest provocation

• **de propos délibéré** ADV deliberately, on purpose

proposer [3] [prɔpoze] VT **1** *(suggérer)* to suggest; **qu'est-ce que tu proposes?** what would *or* do you suggest?; **je propose qu'on aille au cinéma** I suggest going to the cinema; **je vous propose de rester dîner** I suggest (that) you stay for dinner; **écoutez, voilà ce que je vous propose** listen, this is what I suggest; **l'agence nous a proposé un projet original** the agency submitted an original project to us; **proposez vos idées** put forward your ideas; **le chef vous propose sa quiche au saumon** the chef's suggestion *or* recommendation is the salmon quiche; **le cinéma le César vous propose cette semaine...** this week at le César:...; **"asseyons-nous", proposa-t-elle** "let's sit down," she said

2 *(offrir)* to offer; **il a proposé sa place à la vieille dame** he offered the old lady his seat; **p. ses services à qn** to offer *or* to volunteer one's services to sb; **elle m'a proposé de m'aider** she offered to help me

3 *(personne)* to recommend, to put forward; **p. la candidature de qn** to nominate sb

4 *Scol (sujet, exercice) Br* to set, *Am* to assign

5 *Admin & Pol* **p. une loi** to introduce a bill; **p. un ordre du jour** to move an agenda

VPR **se proposer 1** *(être volontaire)* to offer one's services; **se p. comme secrétaire** to offer to act as secretary, to offer one's services as secretary; **je me propose pour coller les enveloppes** I'm volunteering to stick the envelopes; **se p. pour un poste** to apply for a post **2 se p. de** *(avoir l'intention de)* to intend to; **ils se proposaient de passer ensemble une semaine tranquille** they intended to spend a quiet week together

> Il faut noter que le verbe anglais **to propose to somebody** signifie **demander quelqu'un en mariage.**

proposition [prɔpozisjɔ̃] NF **1** *(suggestion)* suggestion, proposal; **faire une p.** to make a suggestion *or* proposal; **quelqu'un a-t-il une autre p. à faire?** has anyone any other suggestions *or* anything else to suggest?; **vos propositions ne sont pas recevables** what you're suggesting *or* proposing is unacceptable; **faire une p. à qn** to make sb a proposition; **je vais te faire une p., partons dimanche!** I tell you what, why don't we leave on Sunday!

2 *(offre)* offer; **faire une p. à qn** to make sb an offer; **faire** *ou* **formuler une p.** to make a proposal; **refuser une p.** to turn down an offer; **j'ai déjà eu quelques propositions de tournage** I've already had one or two film offers; *Euph* **faire des propositions à qn** to proposition sb; **p. d'affaires** business proposition; **p. de paiement** payment proposal; **p. de prix** price proposal; **p. de rachat** offer to buy

3 *Phil & (en logique)* proposition

4 *(recommandation)* recommendation; **sur (la) p. du comité** on the committee's recommendation

5 *Pol* **mettre une p. aux voix** to put a motion to the vote; **la p. est votée** the motion is passed; **p. européenne** proposed European legislation; **p. de loi** *Br* private member's bill, *Am* private bill; **p. de réforme** reform proposal; **propositions de paix** peace proposals

6 *Gram* clause; **p. principale/subordonnée/relative** main/subordinate/relative clause; **p. circonstancielle de temps/lieu/but** adverbial clause of time/place/purpose

7 *Mktg* **p. unique de vente** unique selling proposition *or* point, USP

PROPRE [prɔpr]

ADJ	
• clean **A1**	• neat **A1, 4**
• toilet-trained **A2**	• honest **A3**
• non-polluting **A5**	• own **B1**
• proper **B2, 4, 5**	• specific **B3**
NM	
• cleanliness **1**	• tidiness **1**
• distinctive feature **2**	

ADJ **A. 1** *(nettoyé, lavé)* clean; *(rangé)* neat, tidy; **chez eux c'est bien p.** their house is neat and tidy; **gardez votre ville p.** *Br* don't drop litter!, *Am* don't litter!; *Péj* **p. sur lui** neat and proper; *Ironique* **nous voilà propres!** now we're in a fine mess!; **p. comme un sou neuf** spick and span, clean as a new pin

2 *Euph (éduqué ▸ bébé)* toilet-trained, potty-trained; *(▸ chiot) Br* house-trained, *Am* housebroken

3 *(honnête)* honest; **une affaire pas très p.** a shady business

4 *(bien exécuté ▸ travail)* neat, well done

5 *École* clean, non-polluting, non-pollutant

B. 1 *(avant le nom) (en intensif)* own; *(privé)* own, private; **ma p. maison/fille** my own house/daughter; **de sa p. main** personally; **de son p. chef** on his/her own initiative *or* authority; **les propres paroles du Prophète** the Prophet's very *or* own words

2 *(légitime)* proper, legitimate

3 *(caractéristique)* **p. à** specific *or* peculiar to; **pour des raisons qui lui sont propres** for reasons of his/her own; **sa méthode de travail lui est p.** he/she has his/her own particular way of working; **une habitude p. à notre génération** a habit peculiar to *or* specific to our generation

4 *(adapté)* proper; **le mot p.** the proper *or* correct term; **p. à** suited to, fit for, appropriate to; **p. à la consommation humaine** fit for human consumption; **mesures propres à stimuler la production** appropriate measures for boosting production

5 *Ling (nom)* proper; *(sens)* literal

6 *Ordinat* **erreur p.** inherent error

7 *Fin* **capitaux** *ou* **fonds propres** capital stock

NM **1** *(propreté)* cleanliness, tidiness; **sentir le p.** to smell clean; *Belg* **faire du p.** to spring-clean; *Fam Ironique* **c'est du p.!** *(gâchis)* what a mess!; *(action scandaleuse)* shame on you!

2 *(caractéristique)* peculiarity, distinctive feature; **la raison est le p. de l'homme** reason is unique to man

• **au propre** ADV **1** *(en version définitive)* **mettre qch au p.** to copy sth out neatly, to make a fair copy of sth **2** *Ling* literally

• **en propre** ADV by rights; **avoir en p.** to possess (by rights); **la fortune qu'il a en p.** his own fortune, the fortune that's his by rights

> Il faut noter que l'adjectif anglais **proper** est un faux ami. Il ne se rapporte jamais à la propreté.

propre-à-rien [prɔprarjɛ̃] *(pl* **propres-à-rien)** NMF good-for-nothing

proprement [prɔprəmɑ̃] ADV **1** *(sans salir ▸ gén)* cleanly, tidily; *(▸ écrire)* neatly; **l'hôtel est très p. tenu** the hotel is spotlessly clean; **habillé p.** neatly *or* tidily dressed; **manger p.** to eat without making a mess; **coupe ta viande p.!** cut your meat without making a mess!

2 *(absolument)* truly, totally, absolutely; **elle est p. insupportable!** she's absolutely unbearable!; **c'est p. scandaleux!** it's an absolute disgrace!

3 *(comme il faut)* well and truly; **il l'a p. ridiculisée** he made an absolute fool of her

4 *(spécifiquement)* specifically, strictly

5 *Littéraire (convenablement)* decently, properly, honourably

• **à proprement parler** ADV strictly speaking

• **proprement dit, proprement dite** ADJ actual; **la maison p. dite** the actual house, the house itself

> Il faut noter que l'adverbe anglais **properly** est un faux ami. Il signifie **correctement.**

propret, -ette [prɔprɛ, -ɛt] ADJ neat and tidy; **un petit jardin bien p.** a neat little garden

propreté [prɔprəte] NF **1** *(hygiène, soin)* cleanliness; *(des vêtements, de la vaisselle)* cleanness; *(d'une pièce, d'un travail)* neatness, tidiness; *(absence de saleté)* cleanness, cleanliness; *Euph* **l'apprentissage de la p.** *(chez l'enfant)* toilet-training, potty-training; **ils ne connaissent pas les règles élémentaires de p.** they don't know the basic rules of hygiene **2** *École* cleanness, absence of pollution

propriétaire [prɔprijetɛr] NMF **1** *(celui qui possède)* owner; **ils ont voulu être propriétaires** they wanted to own their (own) place; **devenir p. de qch** to acquire sth; **tous les propriétaires seront soumis à la taxe** all householders *or* homeowners will be liable to tax; **qui est le p. de cette valise?** to whom does this case belong?; **p. légitime** rightful *or* legal owner; **p. occupant** owner-occupier; **p. terrien** landowner **2** *(celui qui loue)* landlord, *f* landlady

propriété [prɔprijete] NF **1** *(chose possédée)* property; *(terres)* property, estate; **une très belle/une grande/une petite p.** an excellent/a large/a small property; **p. foncière/immobilière** landed/real estate; **p. de l'État** government *or* state property; **p. grevée d'hypothèques** encumbered estate; **p. en indivision** jointly-owned property; *Jur* **p. mobilière** personal property, movables; **p. privée** private (property); **p. privée, défense d'entrer** *(sur panneau)* private property, keep out

2 *(fait de posséder)* ownership

3 *Jur* ownership; **p. commune** joint ownership; **p. individuelle** personal *or* private property; **p. industrielle** patent rights; **p. intellectuelle** intellectual property; **p. littéraire et artistique** copyright

4 *(propriétaires)* property owners

5 *(qualité)* property, characteristic, feature; **la codéine a des propriétés antitussives** codeine suppresses coughing

6 *(exactitude ▸ d'un terme)* aptness, appropriateness; **sans p. dans les termes, pas de clarté** if the correct terms are not used, clarity is lost

> Il faut noter que le terme anglais **propriety** est un faux ami. Il signifie **bienséance.**

proprio [prɔprijo] NMF *Fam* landlord, *f* landlady□

propulser [3] [prɔpylse] VT **1** *Aut* to drive; *Astron* to propel; *Tech* to propel, to drive **2** *(pousser)* to push, to fling; *Fig* **elle s'est trouvée propulsée à la tête de l'entreprise** she suddenly found herself in charge of the business

VPR **se propulser** *Fam* to shoot; **il s'est propulsé dans le bureau du patron** he shot off to the boss's office

propulseur [prɔpylsœr] NM **1** *Tech & Naut (hélice)* (screw) propeller; *(moteur)* power unit; *(carburant)* propellant **2** *Astron* rocket engine

propulsif, -ive [prɔpylsif, -iv] ADJ propellant, propelling, propulsive; **roue propulsive** driving wheel

propulsion [prɔpylsjɔ̃] NF **1** *Aviat, Tech & Naut (phénomène)* propulsion, propelling force; *(résultat)* propulsion, propulsive motion, drive; **à p. atomique/nucléaire** atomic-powered/nuclear-powered **2** *Élec* **p. électrique** electric drive; **p. turbo-électrique** turbo-electric propulsion

propulsive [prɔpylsiv] *voir* **propulsif**

propylène [prɔpilɛn] NM *Chim* propylene, propene

prorata [prɔrata] NM INV proportion; **en respectant le p.** in due ratio

• **au prorata** ADV proportionally, pro rata

• **au prorata de** PRÉP in proportion to; **bénéfices au p. du nombre d'actions** profits shared out pro rata to (the number of) shares held

prorogatif, -ive [prɔrɔgatif, -iv] ADJ *Jur* prorogating

prorogation [prɔrɔgasjɔ̃] NF **1** *Admin & Jur (d'un délai)* extension; *(d'un visa, d'un contrat)* renewal **2** *Pol (suspension ▸ d'une assemblée)* adjournment, *Spéc* prorogation

prorogative [prɔrɔgativ] *voir* **prorogatif**

proroger [17] [prɔrɔʒe] VT **1** *Admin & Jur (délai, compétence)* to extend; *(traité, contrat, visa)* to renew; *(échéance)* to defer **2** *Pol (suspendre ▸ assemblée)* to adjourn, *Spéc* to prorogue

prosaïque [prozaik] ADJ mundane, pedestrian, prosaic; *Hum* **pour en revenir à des préoccupations plus prosaïques, qu'est-ce qu'on mange ce soir?** to get back to more mundane matters, what are we having for dinner?

prosaïquement [prozaikmɑ̃] ADV mundanely, prosaically

prosaïsme [prozaism] NM ordinariness, prosaicness; **quel p.!** how romantic!

prosateur, -trice [prozatœr, -tris] NM,F prose writer

proscenium [prɔsenjɔm] NM **1** *Théât* apron, proscenium **2** *Antiq* proscenium

proscription [prɔskripsjɔ̃] NF **1** *Hist (exil)* exiling, banishment **2** *(interdiction)* prohibition, banning, proscription

proscrire [99] [prɔskrir] VT **1** *(exiler)* to banish, to proscribe; **p. qn de la société** to ostracize sb **2** *(interdire ▸ gén)* to forbid; *(▸ par la loi)* to outlaw; *(déconseiller)* to advise against; **cet usage est à p.** this expression is to be avoided

proscrit, -e [prɔskri, -it] ADJ **1** *(exilé)* proscribed **2** *(interdit)* forbidden; **c'est un usage p.** *(déconseillé)* the expression is to be avoided; *(tabou)* the expression is taboo

NM,F outlaw

proscrivait *etc voir* **proscrire**

prose [proz] NF **1** *Littérature* prose **2** *Fam (style)* (writing) style **3** *Fam Hum (écrit)* work□; *Ironique* masterpiece; **vous, au fond de la classe, apportez-moi votre p.!** you there, in the back row, bring me over your masterpiece!

• **en prose** ADJ prose *(avant n)*; **texte en p.** prose text ADV **écrire en p.** to write (in) prose

prosélyte [prɔzelit] NMF proselyte; **l'idée a fait de nombreux prosélytes** there were many converts to the idea, many people espoused the idea

prosélytisme [prɔzelitism] NM proselytism, missionary zeal; **faire du p.** *Br* to proselytize, *Am* to proselyte

prosodie [prɔzɔdi] NF **1** *Littérature* prosody **2** *Mus* rules of musical arrangement

prosodique [prɔzɔdik] ADJ prosodic

prospect¹ [prɔspɛ] NM *Mktg* prospective customer, prospect; **prospects à forte potentialité** hot prospect pool

prospect² [prɔspekt] NM *Constr & Jur* minimum distance between buildings

prospecter [4] [prɔspekte] VT **1** *Mktg (région)* to comb; *(clientèle)* to canvass; *(marché)* to explore, to investigate **2** *Mines* to prospect; **p. une région pour trouver de l'or** to prospect an area for gold; **on prospecte la région pour trouver du pétrole** they're looking for oil in the area

USAGE ABSOLU *Mktg* to canvass customers; *Mines* to prospect

prospecteur, -trice [prɔspektœr, -tris] ADJ prospecting, investigating

NM,F **1** *Mktg* canvasser **2** *Mines* prospector

prospectif, -ive [prɔspektif, -iv] ADJ prospective

• **prospective** NF **1** *(dans l'administration, le management)* long-term planning; *Écon* (long-term) forecasting **2** *(science)* futurology

prospection [prɔspeksjɔ̃] NF **1** *Mines* prospecting; **p. minière/pétrolière** mining/oil exploration **2** *Mktg (de la clientèle)* canvassing, prospecting; *(des tendances, du marché)* exploring; **faire de la p.** to explore the market; **p. du marché** market exploration; **p. téléphonique** *ou* **par téléphone** telephone canvassing; **p. sur le terrain** field research

prospective [prɔspektiv] *voir* **prospectif**

prospectrice [prɔspektris] *voir* **prospecteur**

prospectus [prɔspektys] NM **1** *Com (de publicité)* leaflet; *(de plusieurs pages)* brochure; **il n'y a rien que des p. dans la boîte aux lettres** there's nothing but advertising leaflets in the letter box; **nous avons envoyé des p. à tous nos clients** we have sent a mailshot to *or* we have circularized all our customers; **p. de publicité directe** fly sheet **2** *Bourse* prospectus

prospère [prɔsper] ADJ **1** *(florissant ▸ ville, région, commerce)* flourishing, thriving; *(▸ santé)* glowing; **les affaires sont prospères** business is booming **2** *(riche)* prosperous

prospérer [18] [prɔspere] VI *(entreprise)* to flourish, to thrive; *(pays)* to prosper, to thrive, to do well; *(personne)* to fare well, to thrive; *(plante)* to thrive; **le tourisme a fait p. toute la région** tourism brought wealth to the whole area

prospérité [prɔsperite] NF prosperity, success; **une période de (grande) p.** a boom; **être en pleine p.** to be thriving; **(santé et) p. à tous!** here's to health and prosperity!

prostaglandine [prɔstaglɑ̃din] NF *Physiol* prostaglandin

prostate [prɔstat] NF *Anat* prostate (gland); **se faire opérer de la p.** to have a prostate operation; *Méd* **cancer de la p.** prostate cancer

prostatique [prɔstatik] *Méd* ADJ prostatic

NM prostate sufferer

prosternation [prɔstɛrnasjɔ̃] NF **1** *Rel* bowing-down, *Sout* prosternation **2** *Fig Littéraire (servilité)* toadying

prosternement [prɔstɛrnəmɑ̃] NM **1** *Rel* bowing-down, *Sout* prosternation **2** *Fig Littéraire (servilité)* toadying

prosterner [3] [prɔstɛrne] **se prosterner** VPR **1** *Rel* to bow down (**devant** before) **2** *Fig Littéraire* **se p. devant qn** to grovel to sb

prostitué, -e [prɔstitɥe] NM,F *(homme)* male prostitute; *(femme)* prostitute

prostituer [7] [prɔstitɥe] VT **1** *(personne)* to make a prostitute of, to prostitute **2** *Fig* **p. son talent** to sell *or* to prostitute one's talent

VPR **se prostituer** *aussi Fig* to prostitute oneself

prostitution [prɔstitysjɔ̃] NF *aussi Fig* prostitution

prostration [prɔstrasjɔ̃] NF **1** *Méd & Rel* prostration **2** *Écon* collapse, crash

prostré, -e [prɔstre] ADJ **1** *(accablé)* prostrate, despondent **2** *Méd* prostrate

protagoniste [prɔtagɔnist] NMF **1** *(principal participant)* protagonist **2** *Cin & Littérature* (chief) protagonist, main character

protal, -als [prɔtal] NM *Fam Br* headmaster□, head, *Am* principal□

prote [prɔt] NM *Vieilli* foreman *(in printing works)*

protecteur, -trice [prɔtɛktœr, -tris] ADJ **1** *(qui protège)* protective; **crème protectrice** barrier cream **2** *(condescendant)* patronizing **3** *Écon* protectionist

NM,F **1** *(gardien)* custodian, guardian, guarantor **2** *(mécène)* patron

NM *(d'une prostituée)* procurer

protection [prɔtɛksjɔ̃] NF **1** *(défense)* protection; **assurer la p. de qn** to protect sb; **demander la p. des services de police** to ask for police protection; **prendre qn sous sa p.** to take sb under one's wing; **ne t'inquiète pas, tu es sous ma p.** don't worry, I'll protect *or* shield you; *Mil* **p. aérienne** aerial protection; **p. civile** *(en temps de guerre)* civil defence; *(en temps de paix)* disaster management; **p. du consommateur** consumer protection; **p. diplomatique** diplomatic protection; **p. de l'emploi** personal security, job protection; **p. de l'enfance** child welfare; **p. de l'environnement** environmental protection, protection of the environment; **p. des espèces menacées** protection of endangered species; **p. fiscale** tax shield; **p. judiciaire** (court) supervision (of a minor), wardship; **p. de la nature** nature conservation *or* conservancy; **p. rapprochée** *(d'une personne)* police protection; **p. sociale** social welfare (system)

2 *(prévention)* protection, preservation, conservation; **c'est une bonne p. contre la rouille/les fraudes** it's a good protection against rust/fraud

3 *(soutien)* **solliciter la p. de qn** to ask for sb's support, to ask sb to use their influence on one's behalf; **par p.** through (personal) influence

4 *Beaux-Arts & Sport* patronage

5 *(serviette hygiénique)* **p. (féminine)** *Br* sanitary towel, *Am* sanitary napkin

6 *Ordinat* security; **p. contre la copie** copy protection; **p. contre l'écriture** *ou* **en écriture** write-protection; **p. de fichier** file protection, protected file access; **p. de l'information** data protection; **p. mémoire** protected location; **p. par mot de passe** password protection

• **de protection** ADJ protective, safety *(avant n)*; **gaine/vernis de p.** protective cover/varnish

protectionnisme [prɔtɛksjɔnism] NM protectionism

protectionniste [prɔtɛksjɔnist] ADJ protectionist

NMF protectionist

protectorat [prɔtɛktɔra] NM protectorate

protectrice [prɔtɛktris] *voir* **protecteur**

protégé, -e [prɔteʒe] ADJ **1** *École (espèce, zone)* protected

2 *Électron* protected

3 *Ordinat* **p. contre la copie** copy-protected; **p. contre l'écriture** *ou* **en écriture** write-protected; **p. par mot de passe** password-protected

4 *(relations sexuelles)* protected; **rapports non protégés** unprotected sex

NM,F protégé

protège-cahier [prɔtɛʒkaje] *(pl* **protège-cahiers)** NM exercise-book cover

protège-dents [prɔtɛʒdɑ̃] NM INV gum-shield

protéger [22] [prɔteʒe] VT **1** *(assurer ▸ la sécurité de)* to protect, to defend; *(▸ la santé, la survie de)* to protect, to look after; **p. qch contre le** *ou* **du froid** to protect *or* to insulate sth against the cold; **p. qch contre** *ou* **de la chaleur** to heat-proof sth, to protect sth against heat; **les arbres protègent la maison du vent** the trees shelter the house from the wind; **il fit p. sa fille par des gardes du corps** he employed bodyguards to protect his daughter; **c'est pour p. son frère qu'elle a dit cela** she said it in order to protect *or* to shield her brother

2 *Com & Écon* to protect; *Bourse (position)* to hedge; *Jur* **p. qch par un brevet** to patent sth

3 *(aider ▸ les arts)* to be a patron of; *(▸ le sport)* to encourage, to be a patron of; **on la protège en haut lieu** she has friends in high places

4 *(sujet: racketteur)* to protect

5 *Ordinat* **p. contre la copie** to copy-protect; **p. contre l'écriture** *ou* **en écriture** to write-protect; **p. par mot de passe** to password-protect

VPR **se protéger** to protect oneself; **protégez-vous contre la grippe** protect yourself against the flu; **se p. contre le** *ou* **du soleil** to shield oneself from the sun; **les jeunes sont encouragés à se p. lors de leurs relations sexuelles** young people are encouraged to protect themselves (by using a condom)

protège-slip [prɔtɛʒslip] *(pl* **protège-slips)** NM panty liner

protège-tibia [prɔtɛʒtibja] *(pl* **protège-tibias)** NM shin pad

protège-tympan [prɔtɛʒtɛ̃pɑ̃] *(pl* **protège-tympans)** NM INV earplug

protéiforme [prɔteifɔrm] ADJ multiform, *Littéraire* protean

protéine [prɔtein] NF protein; **protéines animales/végétales** animal/vegetable proteins

protéique [prɔteik] ADJ proteinaceous, protein *(avant n)*

protéomique [prɔteɔmik] *Biol & Chim* ADJ proteomic

NF proteomics *(singulier)*

protestable [prɔtestabl] ADJ *Banque* protestable; *Jur* which may be protested

protestant, -e [prɔtestɑ̃, -ɑ̃t] ADJ Protestant

NM,F Protestant

protestantisme [prɔtestɑ̃tism] NM *(doctrine)* Protestantism; *(ensemble des protestants)* Protestant churches, Protestant community

protestataire [prɔtestatɛr] ADJ *(délégué)* protesting; *(mesure)* protest *(avant n)*

NMF protester, protestor

protestation [prɔtestasjɔ̃] NF **1** *(mécontentement)* protest, discontent; **mouvement/manifestation de p.** protest rally/demonstration **2** *(opposition)* protest; **paroles/geste de p.** words/gesture of protest; **en signe de p.** as a protest; **sans p.** without protest **3** *Jur* protesting, protestation

• **protestations** NFPL *Littéraire (déclarations)* **protestations d'amitié** protestations *or* assurances of friendship; **faire à qn des protestations d'amour/de loyauté** to profess one's love/loyalty to sb

protester [3] [prɔteste] VI *(dire non)* to protest (**contre** against *ou* about); **je proteste!** I protest!, I object!; **elle a protesté auprès du directeur** she complained to the manager

VT **1** *Jur* to protest **2** *Vieilli (affirmer)* to protest, to declare; **je proteste avec la dernière énergie que je n'ai pas reçu votre convocation** I strongly protest that *or* I solemnly declare that I didn't receive your notification

protêt [prɔtɛ] NM *Jur* protest; **faire dresser un p.** to (make a) protest

prothèse [prɔtez] *Méd* NF **1** *(technique)* prosthetics *(UNCOUNT)*; **p. dentaire** prosthodontics *(singulier)* **2** *(dispositif)* prosthesis; **p. auditive** hearing aid; **p. dentaire totale** (set of) dentures; **p. dentaire fixe** bridge, *Spéc* fixed dental prosthesis

prothésiste [prɔtezist] **NMF** *Méd* prosthetist; **p. dentaire** prosthodontist, dental prosthetist

prothétique [prɔtetik] *Méd* **ADJ** prosthetic
NF prosthetics *(singulier)*

protide [prɔtid] **NM** protein

protocolaire [prɔtɔkɔlɛr] **ADJ** *(respectueux des usages)* formal; *(conforme à l'étiquette)* mindful of *or* conforming to etiquette; **le prince dans une attitude peu p.** the Prince in a relaxed pose

protocole [prɔtɔkɔl] **NM 1** *Jur & Pol* protocol; **p. d'accord** draft agreement; **le P. de Kyoto** the Kyoto Protocol
2 *Ordinat (gén)* protocol; *(de réseau)* frame format; *(de traitement)* procedure; **p. HTTP sécurisé** secure HTTP; **p. multivoiee** multi-channel protocol; **p. Internet** Internet protocol; **p. de téléchargement** download protocol; **p. de transfert anonyme** anonymous FTP; **p. de transfert de fichiers** file transfer protocol; **p. de transmission** transmission protocol; **p. univoie** single-channel protocol
3 *Typ* style sheet
4 *(cérémonial)* **le p.** protocole, etiquette; **le chef du p.** the chief of protocol; **le bain de foule n'était pas prévu par le p.** the walkabout was not part of the (prearranged) schedule
5 *Com* **p. d'achat et de vente** buy-sell agreement

protoétoile [prɔtɔetwal] **NF** *Astron* protostar

protohistoire [prɔtɔistwar] **NF** protohistory

proton [prɔtɔ̃] **NM** *Phys* proton

protoplasma [prɔtɔplasma], **protoplasme** [prɔtɔplasm] **NM** *Biol* protoplasm

prototype [prɔtɔtip] **NM 1** *Ind* prototype **2** *(archétype)* standard; **c'est le p. du vieil imprimeur** he's the archetypal old printer **3** *(comme adj; avec ou sans trait d'union)* prototype *(avant n)*

protoxyde [prɔtɔksid] **NM** *Chim* protoxide

protozoaire [prɔtɔzɔɛr] *Zool* **NM** protozoan, protozoon
ADJ protozoal, protozoic

protractile [prɔtraktil] **ADJ** protractile

protrusion [prɔtryzjɔ̃] **NF** protrusion

protubérance [prɔtyberɑ̃s] **NF 1** *(bosse)* bump; *(enflure)* bulge, *Spéc* protuberance **2** *Anat* protuberance

protubérant, -e [prɔtyberɑ̃, -ɑ̃t] **ADJ** *(muscle)* bulging; *(menton, front)* prominent; *(œil, ventre)* protruding, bulging

protuteur, -trice [prɔtytœr, -tris] **NM,F** *Jur* acting guardian

prou [pru] *voir* **peu**

proue [pru] **NF** *Naut* bow, bows, prow
• **en proue ADJ** projecting **ADV s'avancer en p.** to protrude

prouesse [pruɛs] **NF 1** *Littéraire (acte héroïque)* deed of valour **2** *(action remarquable)* exploit, feat; *Fig* **le convaincre a été une p.** convincing him was quite a feat; **faire des prouesses** *(briller)* to perform outstandingly; *(faire des efforts)* to do one's utmost; **j'ai fait des prouesses pour finir dans les délais** I did my utmost to finish on time; *Hum* **il n'a pas/je n'ai pas fait de prouesses** he/I didn't exactly shine

proustien, -enne [prustjɛ̃, -ɛn] **ADJ** Proustian

prout [prut] **NM** *Fam* **1** *(pet)* fart; **faire un p.** to fart, *Br* to let off, *Am* to lay one **2 p., ma chère!** *(pour singer un homosexuel)* ooh, ducky!

prout-prout [prutprut] **ADJ** *Fam* snobby, up oneself; **qu'est-ce qu'elle peut être p., sa gonzesse!** his girlfriend can be so up herself!

prouvable [pruvabl] **ADJ** provable; **ce n'est pas p.** it can't be proved; **facilement/difficilement p.** easy/difficult to prove

prouver [3] [pruve] **VT 1** *(faire la preuve de)* to prove; **cela n'est pas encore prouvé, cela reste à p.** it remains to be proved; **il n'est pas prouvé que...** there's no proof that...; **les faits ont prouvé qu'elle était bel et bien absente** the facts proved her to have indeed been absent; **p. qch à qn** to prove sth to sb, to give sb proof of sth; **prouve-moi le contraire!** give me proof of *or* to the contrary!; **il t'a menti – prouve-le-moi!** he lied to you – prove it!; **il m'a prouvé par A + B que j'avais tort** he demonstrated that I was wrong in a very logical way **2** *(mettre en évidence)* to show; **cela prouve bien que j'avais raison** it shows that I was right; **tous les tests ont prouvé la supériorité du nouveau système** all the tests showed *or* demonstrated the superiority of the new system; **son désintéressement n'est plus à p.** his/her impartiality is no longer open to question **3** *(témoigner)* to demonstrate; **p. à qn son amitié/sa reconnaissance** to demonstrate one's friendship/gratitude to sb, to give sb proof of one's friendship/gratitude
VPR se prouver se p. qch (à soi-même) to prove sth (to oneself); **que cherche-t-il à se p.?** what's he trying to prove (to himself)?

provenance [prɔvnɑ̃s] **NF** *(d'un mot)* origin; *(d'une rumeur)* source; **des marchandises de p. étrangère** imported goods; **des produits de p. anglaise** goods of English origin; **pays de p.** country of origin
• **en provenance de PRÉP** (coming) from; **le train en p. de Genève** the train from Geneva, the Geneva train; **les voyageurs en p. de Montréal** passengers (recently arrived) from Montreal

provençal, -e, -aux, -ales [prɔvɑ̃sal, -o] **ADJ** Provençal
NM *(dialecte)* Provençal
• **Provençal, -e, -aux, -ales NM,F** = inhabitant of or person from Provence
• **à la provençale ADJ** *Culin* à la provençale *(cooked with olive oil, garlic, tomatoes and chopped parsley)*

provende [prɔvɑ̃d] **NF** *Vieilli* provender

provenir [40] [prɔvnir] **provenir de VT IND 1** *(lieu)* to come from; **d'où provient cette statuette?** where does this statuette come from?; **des produits provenant du Japon** products from Japan **2** *(résulter de)* to arise *or* to result from, to arise out of

proverbe [prɔvɛrb] **NM** proverb, adage; **passer en p.** to become proverbial

proverbial, -e, -aux, -ales [prɔvɛrbjal, -o] **ADJ 1** *(de proverbe)* proverbial **2** *(connu)* well-known, proverbial; **au lycée, son talent d'imitateur est p.** he's become well-known throughout the school for his impersonations

proverbialement [prɔvɛrbjalmɑ̃] **ADV** proverbially

providence [prɔvidɑ̃s] **NF 1** *Rel* Providence **2** *(aubaine)* salvation, piece of luck **3** *(personne)* **tu es ma p.!** you're my saviour!; **vous rentrez à Nice en voiture? vous êtes ma p.!** you're driving back to Nice? you've saved my life!

providentiel, -elle [prɔvidɑ̃sjɛl] **ADJ** providential, miraculous; **c'est l'homme p.!** he's the man we need!; **sans cette grève providentielle, nous n'aurions jamais fait connaissance** if that strike hadn't happened at just the right time, we'd never have met

providentiellement [prɔvidɑ̃sjɛlmɑ̃] **ADV** providentially, miraculously

provient *etc voir* **provenir**

province [prɔvɛ̃s] **NF 1** *(régions en dehors de la capitale)* **la p.** *(en France)* provincial France; *(dans d'autres pays)* the provinces; **il doit bientôt partir en p.** he'll soon be leaving town; **un week-end en p.** a weekend out of town; **ils vivent en p.** they live in the provinces; **nous avons également des bureaux en p.** we also have provincial branches; **arriver** *ou* **débarquer tout droit de sa p.** to be fresh from the country *or* the provinces; **une petite ville de p.** a small country town; **Bordeaux est une grande ville de p.** Bordeaux is a major provincial town **2** *Belg & Can Admin* = administrative district similar to the French "département"; *Can* **la Belle P.** Quebec **3** *Hist* province
ADJ INV notre quartier est encore très p. there's still a small-town feeling to our area; **sa famille est restée un peu p.** his/her family's kept up a rather provincial way of life

provincial, -e, -aux, -ales [prɔvɛ̃sjal, -o] **ADJ 1** *(en dehors de Paris)* provincial; **la vie provinciale** provincial life, life in the provinces **2** *Belg & Can Admin* relating to a "province"; *Belg* **conseil p.** ≃ county council; *Belg* **conseiller p.** ≃ county councillor **3** *Péj (personne, comportement)* provincial, parochial
NM,F provincial

provincialisme [prɔvɛ̃sjalism] **NM 1** *Ling* provincialism **2** *Péj (étroitesse d'esprit)* small-town mentality, parochialism

provint *etc voir* **provenir**

provirus [provirys] **NM** *Biol* provirus

proviseur [prɔvizœr] **NM 1** *(directeur)* *Br* head teacher, headmaster, *f* headmistress, *Am* principal **2** *Belg (adjoint)* *Br* deputy head, *Am* vice principal

provision [prɔvizjɔ̃] **NF 1** *(réserve ▸ de bois, de nourriture)* stock, store, supply; *(▸ d'eau)* supply; **nos provisions d'eau/de bois** our water/wood supply; **avoir une bonne p. de chocolat/patience** to have a good supply of chocolate/plenty of patience; **faire p. de** *(nourriture, enveloppes)* to stock up with; *(bois de chauffage)* to build up a stock of; **les écureuils font p. de noix pour l'hiver** squirrels store up nuts for the winter; **faire des provisions** to stock up on food, to lay in stocks of food; **faire des provisions de qch** to stock up with sth
2 *(acompte)* advance *or* down payment; *Banque* (sufficient) funds; **je n'ai pas de p.** I don't have sufficient funds *or* enough money in my account; **manque de p.** *(sur chèque)* no funds; **verser une p.** *ou* **des provisions** to deposit funds; **faire p. pour une lettre de change** to provide for *or* to protect a bill of exchange
3 *(d'un bilan comptable)* provision; *(couverture)* cover; **p. pour amortissement, p. pour dépréciation** provision for depreciation, depreciation allowance; **p. pour risques et charges** contingency and loss provision
4 *(honoraires)* retainer
• **provisions NFPL** *(courses)* **provisions (de bouche)** shopping *(UNCOUNT)*, groceries; **qu'est-ce que tu as fait des provisions?** what have you done with the groceries?
• **à provisions ADJ** *(filet, sac)* shopping *(avant n)*; **armoire à provisions** store cupboard

provisionnel, -elle [prɔvizjɔnɛl] **ADJ** provisional

provisionnement [prɔvizjɔnmɑ̃] **NM** *Banque* funding

provisoire [prɔvizwar] **ADJ 1** *(momentané)* temporary, provisional; **c'est une solution p.** it's a temporary solution *or* a stopgap
2 *(précaire)* makeshift
3 *(intérimaire ▸ gouvernement)* provisional; *(▸ directeur)* acting
4 *Jur (jugement)* provisional, interlocutory; *(mise en liberté)* conditional
NM ça n'est que du p. it's only temporary, it's only for the time being; *Hum* **ces préfabriqués devaient être remplacés par des nouveaux bâtiments, c'est du p. qui dure** those prefabs were meant to be replaced by new buildings, unfortunately it's a case of a temporary solution becoming permanent; **il s'est installé dans le p.** he's got used to living on a day-to-day basis; **je ne veux plus vivre dans le p.** I'm tired of living in uncertainty

provisoirement [prɔvizwarmɑ̃] **ADV** temporarily, provisionally; **la piscine est p. fermée** the swimming-pool is temporarily closed; **je fais repeindre la chambre et, p., je couche dans le salon** I'm having the bedroom redecorated and I'm sleeping in the living room for the time being

provitamine [prɔvitamin] **NF** provitamin

provoc [prɔvɔk] **NF** *Fam* provocation[a]; **tu fais de la p. ou quoi?** are you trying to *Br* wind me up *or* *Am* tick me off?

provocant, -e [prɔvɔkɑ̃, -ɑ̃t] **ADJ 1** *(agressif)* aggressive, provocative; **sur un ton p.** provocatively; **de façon provocante** provocatively **2** *(osé)* blatant **3** *(aguicheur)* provocative

provocateur, -trice [prɔvɔkatœr, -tris] **ADJ** *(discours, propagande)* inflammatory; *(argument, propos)* provocative; **geste p.** offensive gesture
NM,F *Pol* provocateur

provocation [prɔvɔkasjɔ̃] **NF 1** *(stratégie)* provocation, incitement; *(acte)* provocation; **c'est de la p.!** it's an act of provocation!; **faire qch par p.** to do sth as an act of provocation; **se livrer à**

des provocations à l'égard de qn to provoke sb; **les provocations policières** police provocation; **il a dit ça par pure p.** he only said it to try and shock people **2** *Littéraire (séduction)* teasing, provocativeness

provocatrice [prɔvɔkatris] *voir* **provocateur**

provolone [prɔvɔlɔn] **NM** *(fromage)* provolone

provoquer [3] [prɔvɔke] **VT 1** *(défier)* to provoke, to push (to breaking point); *Fam* **arrête de me p.!** don't push me!; **c'est lui qui m'a provoqué!** he started it!; **p. le destin** to tempt fate; **p. qn en duel** to challenge sb to a duel

2 *(sexuellement)* to tease, arouse

3 *(occasionner ▸ maladie, sommeil)* to cause, to induce; *(▸ sentiment)* to arouse, to stir up, to give rise to; *(▸ réaction, explosion, changement)* to cause; *(▸ événement)* to cause, to be the cause of, to bring about; **ce médicament peut p. une légère somnolence** this medicine may cause drowsiness; **pouvant p. la mort** potentially fatal; **il ne se doutait pas qu'il allait p. sa jalousie** he didn't realize that he would make him/her jealous; **il disait cela pour p. les rires de ses camarades** he said that to make his schoolfriends laugh; **elle fit cette déclaration pour p. une nouvelle enquête** she made that statement so that there would be a new enquiry

4 *(inciter)* **p. les jeunes à la violence/au crime** to incite young people to violence/to crime

5 *Méd* **p. l'accouchement** to induce labour

proxénète [prɔksenɛt] **NMF** procurer, *f* procuress

proxénétisme [prɔksenetism] **NM** procuring

proximité [prɔksimite] **NF 1** *(dans l'espace)* closeness, nearness, proximity; **la p. du casino est une grande tentation** having the casino so close (by) is very tempting **2** *(dans le temps)* closeness, imminence; **la p. de Noël** Christmas being near; **la p. du départ les rend fébriles** the approaching departure is getting them excited

• **à proximité ADV** nearby, close at hand

• **à proximité de PRÉP** near, close to, not far from

• **de proximité ADJ 1** *Tech* proximity *(avant n)* **2** *(de quartier)* **commerces de p.** local shops; **emplois de p.** = employment in the community *(as a way of reducing unemployment)*; **des actions de p.** community work

proyer [prwaje] **NM** *Orn* bunting

Prozac® [prɔzak] **NM** *Pharm* Prozac®

prude [pryd] **ADJ** prudish, prim and proper; **et pourtant, je ne suis pas p.** and yet I'm not afraid to call a spade a spade

NMF prude, puritan; **ne fais pas la p.!** don't be so prudish!, don't be such a prude!

prudemment [prydamɑ̃] **ADV 1** *(avec précaution)* carefully, cautiously, prudently; **2** *(avec sagesse)* wisely, prudently

prudence [prydɑ̃s] **NF 1** *(précaution)* caution, carefulness; **elle conduit avec la plus grande p.** she's a very careful driver; *Prov* **p. est mère de sûreté** look before you leap **2** *(méfiance)* wariness, caginess; *(ruse)* cunning; **avoir la p. du serpent** to be a sly fox **3** *Vieilli (sagesse)* wisdom, good judgment, prudence

• **prudences NFPL** *Littéraire* wariness *(UNCOUNT)*, caginess *(UNCOUNT)*; **ses prudences en matière de musique contemporaine** his/her wariness of modern music

• **avec prudence ADV** *(avec attention)* cautiously, carefully

• **par prudence, par mesure de prudence ADV** as a precaution; **par p., je n'ai pas voulu lui en parler tout de suite** I thought it wiser not to speak of it to him/her right away

prudent, -e [prydɑ̃, -ɑ̃t] **ADJ 1** *(attentif)* careful, prudent; **tu peux lui confier tes enfants, elle est très prudente** you can safely leave your children with her, she's very sensible

2 *(mesuré)* discreet, circumspect, cautious; **une réponse prudente** a diplomatic *or* circumspect answer; **trop p.** overcautious

3 *(prévoyant ▸ gén)* judicious, wise; *(▸ décision)* wise, sensible; **un homme de loi p.** a wise lawyer; **tu sors sans écharpe, ce n'est pas p.** you're going out without a scarf, that's not very sensible; **ses parents s'étaient montrés prudents et avaient mis de l'argent de côté pour lui** his parents had looked ahead *or* had been provident and had put aside some money for him; **on n'est jamais trop p.** you can't be too careful

4 *(préférable)* advisable, better; **il serait p. de partir avant la nuit** it would be better for us to leave before nightfall

pruderie [prydri] **NF** prudishness, prudery

prud'homme [prydɔm] *Jur* **NM (conseiller) p.** member of an industrial tribunal

• **prud'hommes NMPL** *(tribunal)* **les prud'hommes, le conseil de prud'hommes** the industrial tribunal; **aller aux prud'hommes** to go before an industrial tribunal

pruine [prɥin] **NF** *(sur un fruit)* bloom

prune [pryn] **NF 1** *(fruit)* plum; **p. de Damas** damson

2 *(alcool)* plum brandy

3 *Fam (balle)* bullet[□], slug; *(coup)* clout, thump

4 *Fam (contravention)* fine[□]

5 *Fam (locutions)* **des prunes!** no way!, nothing doing!; **pour des prunes** for nothing[□]; **je suis allé en classe pour des prunes, le prof n'était pas là** I went to school for nothing, the teacher wasn't there

ADJ INV plum-coloured

> Il faut noter que le terme anglais **prune** est un faux ami. Il signifie **pruneau.**

pruneau, -x [pryno] **NM 1** *(fruit sec)* prune

2 *Suisse (prune)* red plum

3 *Fam Vieilli (personne hâlée)* **c'est un vrai p.** he's/she's as brown as a berry

4 *Fam (balle)* bullet[□], slug; **il s'est pris un p. dans le buffet** someone filled his belly with lead

prunelle [prynɛl] **NF 1** *Bot* sloe

2 *(alcool)* sloe gin

3 *Anat* pupil; **je tiens à ce livre comme à la p. de mes yeux** I wouldn't give this book up *or* away for the world

4 *(regard)* eye; *Fam* **jouer de la p.** to flutter one's eyelashes

prunellier [prynelje] **NM** sloe, blackthorn

prunier [prynje] **NM** plumtree

prunus [prynys] **NM** *Bot* prunus, Japanese flowering cherry

prurigineux, -euse [pryriʒinø, -øz] **ADJ** *Méd* pruritic

prurit [pryrit] **NM** *Méd* pruritus

Prusse [prys] **NF la P.** Prussia

Prusse-Orientale [prysɔrjɑ̃tal] **NF** *Hist* **la P.** East Prussia

prussiate [prysjat] **NM** *Vieilli* cyanide

prussien, -enne [prysjɛ̃, -ɛn] **ADJ** Prussian

• **Prussien, -enne NM,F** Prussian

prytanée [pritane] **NM le P. militaire de La Flèche** the La Flèche military academy *(free school for sons of members of the armed forces)*

PS[1] [peɛs] **NM** *(abrév* **parti socialiste**) = French socialist party

PS[2] [peɛs] **NM** *(abrév* **post-scriptum**) PS, ps

psallette [psalɛt] **NF** choir school

psalmiste [psalmist] **NM** psalmist

psalmodie [psalmɔdi] **NF 1** *Rel* psalmody, intoning **2** *Fig Littéraire* drone

psalmodier [9] [psalmɔdje] **VI 1** *Rel* to chant **2** *Fig Littéraire* to drone (on)

VT 1 *Rel* to chant **2** *Fig* to intone, to drone (out)

psaltérion [psalterjɔ̃] **NM** *Mus* psaltery

psaume [psom] **NM** psalm

psautier [psotje] **NM** psalter

PSC [peɛsse] **NM** *UE (abrév* **Pacte de stabilité et de croissance**) SGP

pseudo [psødo] **NM** *Fam (abrév* **pseudonyme**) pseudonym

pseudo- [psødo] **PRÉF** pseudo-, false; **méfie-toi de leur pseudo-contrat** beware of their so-called contract; **ses pseudo-excuses** his/her fake apologies; **des p.-intellectuels** pseudo-intellectuals; **le pseudo-démarcheur attaquait les vieilles dames** the bogus salesman preyed on old ladies

pseudomembrane [psødomɑ̃bran] **NF** *Méd* pseudomembrane, false membrane

pseudonyme [psødɔnim] **NM** *(nom d'emprunt ▸ gén)* assumed name; *(▸ d'un écrivain)* pen name, pseudonym; *(▸ d'acteur)* stage name; *(▸ de criminel)* alias; **prendre un p.** to adopt a pseudonym; **sous le p. de** under the pseudonym of

psi [psi] **NM** *(lettre grecque)* psi

psitt [psit] **EXCLAM** psst!, hey!

psittacose [psitakoz] **NF** psittacosis

psoriasis [psɔrjazis] **NM** psoriasis

pst [pst] = **psitt**

psy [psi] *Fam* **NMF** *(psychanalyste)* shrink

NF *(psychanalyse)* psychoanalysis[□]

psychanalyse [psikanaliz] **NF** *(discipline)* psychoanalysis; *(traitement)* analysis, psychoanalysis, therapy; **il fait une p.** he's in *or* undergoing (psycho)analysis, he's in therapy

psychanalyser [3] [psikanalize] **VT** to psychoanalyse, to analyse; **elle se fait p.** she's in *or* undergoing psychoanalysis, she's in therapy; **je me suis fait p. pendant cinq ans** I went to see an analyst *or* therapist for five years

psychanalyste [psikanalist] **NMF** analyst, psychoanalyst

psychanalytique [psikanalitik] **ADJ** analytical, psychoanalytical

psyché [psiʃe] **NF** *Psy* psyche

psychédélique [psikedelik] **ADJ** psychedelic

psychiatre [psikjatr] **NMF** psychiatrist

psychiatrie [psikjatri] **NF** psychiatry; **p. infantile** child psychiatry

psychiatrique [psikjatrik] **ADJ** psychiatric

psychique [psiʃik] **ADJ 1** *Méd (blocage)* mental; *(troubles)* mental, *Spéc* psychic; **les maux de tête peuvent être d'origine p.** headaches may be psychosomatic **2** *Fam (psychologique)* psychological; **je ne peux pas voir une souris sans défaillir, c'est p.** I feel faint whenever I see a mouse, I know it's all in the mind but I can't help it

NM *Fam* mind, psychological side; **chez lui, c'est le p. qui va mal** he's got a psychological problem

psychisme [psiʃism] **NM** psyche, mind; **son p. est perturbé** the balance of his/her mind is disturbed

psycho [psiko] **NF** *Fam (psychologie)* **il a fait (des études de) p.** he studied psychology[□]; **il t'a plu, le cours de p.?** did you like the psychology lecture?[□]

psychoactif, -ive [psikoaktif, -iv] **ADJ** psychoactive; **agent p.** psychoactive agent

psychodrame [psikɔdram] **NM 1** *(thérapie)* role-play techniques, psychodrama **2** *(séance)* (psychotherapeutic) role-play session **3** *Fig* **ma mère m'a fait un p. parce que j'ai oublié son anniversaire** my mum made a big scene because I forgot her birthday

psychographie [psikografi] **NF** psychographics *(singulier)*

psychographique [psikografik] **ADJ** psychographic

psycholinguistique [psikɔlɛ̃gɥistik] **ADJ** psycholinguistic

NF psycholinguistics *(singulier)*

psychologie [psikɔlɔʒi] **NF 1** *(étude)* psychology; **faire de** *ou* **étudier la p.** to do *or* to study psychology; **p. expérimentale/clinique/scolaire/sociale** experimental/clinical/educational/social psychology; **p. commerciale** psychology of marketing; **p. des consommateurs** consumer psychology; **p. des profondeurs** analytical psychology; **p. de la publicité** advertising psychology; **p. du travail** occupational psychology

2 *(intuition)* perception; **faire preuve de p.** to have good psychological insight, to be perceptive; **tu manques de p.** you're not very perceptive

3 *(mentalité)* psychology, mind; **la p. des citadins** the psychology *or* mind of the town-dweller; **il faut comprendre sa p.** you have to understand the way his/her mind works

4 *(dimension psychologique)* psychology; **la p. de son dernier film est tout à fait sommaire** the psychological content of his/her last movie *or Br* film leaves a lot to be desired

psychologique [psikɔlɔʒik] **ADJ 1** *(méthode, théorie)* psychological

2 *Méd (état, troubles)* psychological, mental; **son état p. n'était pas bon du tout** he/she wasn't in a good state of mind *or* frame of mind at all; **il suffit qu'elle parle à son médecin pour aller mieux, c'est p.** she only has to talk to her doctor to feel better, it's all in her mind

3 *(dimension)* psychological; **la vérité p. de ses personnages** his/her true-to-life characters

4 *(propice)* **le moment** *ou* **l'instant p.** the right *or* appropriate moment

psychologiquement [psikɔlɔʒikmɑ̃] **ADV** psychologically

psychologue [psikɔlɔg] **ADJ** insightful, perceptive

NMF psychologist; **p. scolaire** educational psychologist; **p. du travail** occupational psychologist

psychonévrose [psikonevroz] **NF** psychoneurosis

psychopathe [psikɔpat] **NMF** psychopath

psychopathie [psikɔpati] **NF** psychopathy, psychopathic personality

psychopathologie [psikɔpatɔlɔʒi] **NF** psychopathology

psychopédagogie [psikɔpedagɔʒi] **NF** educational psychology

psychopharmacologie [psikɔfarmakɔlɔʒi] **NF** psychopharmacology

psychophysiologie [psikɔfizjɔlɔʒi] **NF** psychophysiology

psychose [psikoz] **NF 1** *Psy* psychosis; **p. maniaco-dépressive** manic depression; **p. (traumatique) du soldat** combat stress **2** *(angoisse ▸ individuelle)* (obsessive) fear (**de** of); *(▸ collective)* fear; **il a la p. du cambriolage** he has an obsessive fear of being *Br* burgled *or Am* burglarized; **il règne ici une véritable p. de guerre** people here are in the grip of war hysteria

psychosociologie [psikɔsɔsjɔlɔʒi] **NF** psychosociology

psychosomatique [psikɔsɔmatik] **ADJ** *(médecine, trouble)* psychosomatic

NF psychosomatics *(singulier)*

psychotechnique [psikɔteknik] **ADJ** psychotechnical

NF psychotechnology

psychothérapeute [psikɔterapøt] **NMF** psychotherapist

psychothérapie [psikɔterapi] **NF** psychotherapy; **faire une p.** to be in therapy; **faire une p. de groupe** to go to *or* to do group therapy; **p. analytique** analytical (psycho)therapy

psychothérapique [psikɔterapik] **ADJ** psychotherapeutic

psychotique [psikɔtik] **ADJ** psychotic

NMF psychotic

psychotonique [psikɔtɔnik] **ADJ** mood-elevating, *Spéc* psychotonic

NM mood elevator, *Spéc* psychotonic (drug)

psychotrope [psikɔtrɔp] **ADJ** psychotropic, psychoactive

NM psychotropic (drug)

ptérodactyle [pterɔdaktil] **NM** pterodactyl

ptérosaurien [pterɔsɔrjɛ̃] **NM** pterosaur

Ptolémée [ptɔleme] **NPR** Ptolemy

ptomaïne [ptɔmain] **NF** *Biol* ptomaine

PTT [petete] **NFPL** *Anciennement (abrév* **Postes, Télécommunications et Télédiffusion**) = former French post office and telecommunications network

PU [pey] **NM** *Com (abrév* **prix unitaire**) unit price

pu [py] **PP** *voir* **pouvoir**[2]

puant, -e [pɥɑ̃, -ɑ̃t] **ADJ 1** *(nauséabond)* stinking, foul-smelling **2** *Fam (très vaniteux)* cocky; **il est vraiment p.!** he really thinks he's something special!

NM *Fam (fromage)* smelly cheese□

puanteur [pɥɑ̃tœr] **NF** foul smell, stench

pub[1] [pyb] **NF** *Fam* **1** *(publicité)* advertising□; **il travaille dans la p.** he's *or* he works in advertising; **faire de la p. pour qch** to advertise sth□; **un coup de p.** a plug; **ils ont fait un gros coup de p. autour de ce livre** they really hyped the book **2** *(annonce ▸ gén)* ad, advertisement□; *Rad & TV* commercial□

pub[2] [pœb] **NM** *(bar)* pub

pubère [pybɛr] **ADJ** pubescent; **il est p.** he's reached (the age of) puberty

puberté [pybɛrte] **NF** puberty

pubescent, -e [pybesɑ̃, -ɑ̃t] **ADJ** *Bot* pubescent, puberulent

pubien, -enne [pybjɛ̃, -ɛn] **ADJ** pubic

pubis [pybis] **NM** *(os)* pubis; *(bas-ventre)* pubis, *Spéc* pubes

publiable [pyblijabl] **ADJ** publishable; **ce n'est guère p.** it's hardly fit for publication *or* to be printed

public, -ique [pyblik] **ADJ 1** *(ouvert à tous)* public; **la séance est publique** it's an open session

2 *(connu)* public, well-known; **sa nomination a été rendue publique ce matin** his/her nomination was officially announced *or* was made public this morning; **l'homme p.** the man the public sees

3 *(de l'État)* public, state *(avant n)*

NM 1 *(population)* public; **le grand p.** the general public, the public at large

2 *(audience ▸ d'un spectacle)* public, audience; *(▸ d'un écrivain)* readership, readers; *(▸ d'un match)* spectators; *(▸ d'un produit, d'une publicité)* audience; **p. féminin/familial** female/family audience; **s'adresser à un vaste p./à un p. restreint** to address a vast/limited audience; **c'est un excellent livre, mais qui n'a pas encore trouvé son p.** although the book is excellent, it hasn't yet found the readership it deserves; **p. cible** target audience; **être bon p.** to be easy to please

3 *(secteur)* **le p.** the public sector

• **en public ADV** publicly, in public; **les livres ont été brûlés en p.** the books were publicly burnt; **cette émission a été enregistrée en p.** this programme was recorded before a live audience; **faire honte à qn en p.** to show sb up in public

• **grand public ADJ INV émission grand p.** programme designed to appeal to a wide audience; **film grand p.** blockbuster; **l'électronique grand p.** consumer electronics

publicain [pyblikɛ̃] **NM** *Antiq* tax gatherer; *Bible* publican

publication [pyblikasjɔ̃] **NF 1** *(d'un livre, d'un journal)* publication, publishing; **j'attends la p. pour consulter mon avocat** I'm waiting for publication *or* for the book to be published before I consult my lawyer; **interdire la p. de qch** to stop sth coming out *or* being published; **date de p.** publication date, date of publication; **p. assistée par ordinateur** desktop publishing **2** *Jur (d'un arrêté, d'une loi)* promulgation, publication **3** *(document)* publication, magazine; *Fin* **p. des comptes** disclosure (of accounts); **p. scientifique** scientific publication *or* journal; **p. spécialisée** specialist review

publiciste [pyblisist] **NMF 1** *Jur* specialist in public law **2** = **publicitaire**

publicitaire [pyblisitɛr] **ADJ** *(gén)* advertising *(avant n)*, promotional; *(vente)* promotional; **budget p.** advertising budget; **documents publicitaires** advertising *or* promotional material

NMF *(personne)* advertising man, *f* woman; **c'est un p./une p.** he's/she's in *or* he/she works in advertising

publicité [pyblisite] **NF 1** *(action commerciale, profession)* advertising; **être dans la p.** to be *or* to work in advertising; **faire de la p. pour qch** to advertise *or* to publicize sth; **en ce moment, ils font de la p. pour les banques** there are a lot of advertisements for banks at the moment; **passer une p. à la télévision** to advertise on TV; **p. audiovisuelle/par affichage** audiovisual/poster advertising; **p. agressive** hard sell; **p. de bouche à oreille** word-of-mouth advertising; **p. collective** group advertising; **p. comparative** comparative advertising; **p. concurrentielle** competitive advertising; **p. directe** direct advertising, direct mail advertising; **p. d'entreprise** corporate advertising; **p. extérieure** outdoor advertising; **p. guérilla** guerrilla advertising; **p. intensive** saturation advertising; **p. sur le lieu de vente** *(activité)* point-of-sale advertising; *(promotion)* point-of-sale promotion; **p. de marque** brand advertising; **p. média** media advertising; **p. mensongère** misleading advertising; **p. sur panneau** billboard advertising; **p. au point de vente** point-of-sale advertising; **p. de produit** product advertising; **p. par publipostage** direct mail advertising; **p. subliminale** subliminal advertising; **p. télévisée** television advertising; **p. par voie d'affiches** poster advertising

2 *(diffusion)* publicity; **ça ne peut que lui faire de la p.** it's bound to be publicity for him/her; **faire sa propre p.** to sell oneself; **il a fait de la p. pour toi, tu sais!** he gave you a good press, you know!; **faire de la p. pour qch** to publicize sth

3 *(annonce commerciale)* advertisement, advert; *Rad & TV* commercial; **passer une p. à la télévision** to advertise on TV; **p. mensongère** misleading advertisement; **p. télévisée** television advertisement

4 *(caractère public)* public nature; **la p. de cette déclaration ne lui laisse pas la possibilité de se rétracter** the fact that he/she made the statement publicly leaves him/her no room to retract; **la p. des débats parlementaires garantit-elle la démocratie?** is democracy safeguarded by the fact that debates in Parliament are (held in) public?

5 *Jur (en droit civil)* public announcement

publier [10] [pyblije] **VT 1** *(éditer ▸ auteur, texte)* to publish; **un article qui n'a jamais été publié** an unpublished article **2** *(rendre public ▸ communiqué)* to make public, to release; *(▸ brochure)* to publish, to issue, to release; *(▸ décret, loi)* to promulgate, to publish

publi-information [pybliɛ̃fɔrmasjɔ̃] *(pl* **publi-informations**) **NF** special advertising section, *Am* advertorial

publiphobe [pyblifɔb] **ADJ** anti-advertising

NMF = person who is against advertising

Publiphone® [pyblifɔn] **NM** cardphone

publipostage [pyblipɔstaʒ] **NM** mailshot, mailing; **faire un p.** to send a mailshot *or* mailing

publi-promotion [pybliprɔmosjɔ̃] *(pl* **publi-promotions**) **NF** promotional offer

publique [pyblik] *voir* **public**

publiquement [pyblikmɑ̃] **ADV** publicly, in public; **il s'est confessé p.** he admitted his fault in public; **sa mère lui a fait honte p.** his/her mother showed him/her up in front of everybody

publireportage [pybliгəpɔrtaʒ] **NM** special advertising section, *Am* advertorial

puce [pys] **NF 1** *Entom* flea; **ce nom m'a mis la p. à l'oreille** the name gave me a clue *or* set me thinking; *Fam* **il est excité comme une p.** he's so excited he can't sit still

2 *Fam (par affection)* **ma p.** sweetie; **tu veux quelque chose, ma p.?** do you want something, sweetie?; **où elle est, la petite p.?** where's my little girl then?

3 *Électron (composant)* chip; **p. à ADN** DNA chip; *TV* **p. antiviolence** V-chip; **p. logique** logic chip; **p. mémoire** memory chip; **p. de reconnaissance vocale** voice recognition chip

4 *Ordinat & Typ (symbole)* bullet (point)

ADJ INV *(couleur)* puce

• **puces NFPL 1** *(jeu)* **jeu de puces** tiddly-winks **2** *(marché)* flea market; **elle s'habille aux puces** she wears secondhand clothes

puceau, -elle [pyso, -ɛl] *Fam* **ADJ il est p.** he's a virgin□

NM,F virgin□

pucelage [pyslaʒ] **NM** *Fam* virginity□; **perdre son p.** to lose one's virginity

pucelle [pysel] *voir* **puceau**

puceron [pysrɔ̃] **NM** greenfly, aphid, plant louse

pucier [pysje] **NM** *très Fam (lit)* bed□, *Br* pit

pudding [pudiŋ] **NM 1** *(au pain rassis)* = bread pudding **2** *(anglais)* (plum) pudding, Christmas pudding

puddlage [pœdlaʒ] **NM** *Métal* puddling

puddler [3] [pœdle] **VT** *Métal* to puddle

pudeur [pydœr] **NF 1** *(décence)* modesty, decency, propriety; **avec p.** modestly; **par p., il n'a pas abordé le sujet** out of a sense of decency *or* propriety he did not mention the subject; **manquer de p.** to have no sense of decency; **fausse p.** false modesty **2** *(délicatesse)* tact, sense of propriety; **il aurait pu avoir la p. de se taire** he could have been tactful enough to keep quiet

pudibond, -e [pydibɔ̃, -ɔ̃d] **ADJ** prudish, prim

NM,F prude

> Do not confuse with **pudique**.

pudibonderie [pydibɔ̃dri] **NF** prudishness

pudicité [pydisite] **NF** *Littéraire* modesty

pudique [pydik] **ADJ 1** *(chaste)* chaste, modest **2** *(discret)* discreet

> Do not confuse with **pudibond**.

pudiquement [pydikmɑ̃] **ADV 1** *(avec pudeur)* modestly **2** *(avec tact)* discreetly

puer [7] [pɥe] **VI** to stink; **ça pue ici!** what a stink *or* stench!

VT 1 *(répandre ▸ odeur)* to stink of; **p. le vin/l'éther** to stink of wine/ether; **il pue l'ail à quinze pas!** he *or* his breath reeks of garlic!; *Fam* **tu pues des pieds** your feet stink; *très Fam* **il pue de la gueule** his breath stinks **2** *(laisser paraître ▸ défaut)* **p. la méchanceté/l'hypocrisie** to be oozing spitefulness/hypocrisy; **il pue l'arriviste** you can smell the social climber (in him) a mile off

puériculteur, -trice [pɥerikyltœr, -tris] **NM,F** nursery nurse

puériculture [pɥerikyltyr] **NF 1** *(gén)* child care *or* welfare **2** *Scol* nursery nursing

puéril, -e [pɥeril] **ADJ 1** *(enfantin)* childlike **2** *(immature, naïf)* childish, infantile, puerile

puérilement [pɥerilmɑ̃] **ADV** childishly

puérilité [pɥerilite] **NF** *(non-maturité)* childishness, puerility

• **puérilités NFPL** childish *or* petty trifles

puerpéral, -e, -aux, -ales [pɥerperal, -o] **ADJ** *Méd* puerperal

puffin [pyfɛ̃] **NM** *Orn* shearwater

pugilat [pyʒila] **NM 1** *(bagarre)* brawl, scuffle **2** *Antiq* boxing

pugiliste [pyʒilist] **NM 1** *Littéraire (boxeur)* pugilist **2** *Antiq* boxer

pugnace [pygnas] **ADJ** *Littéraire* **1** *(combatif)* belligerent **2** *(dans la discussion)* pugnacious

pugnacité [pygnasite] **NF** *Littéraire* **1** *(combativité)* belligerence **2** *(dans la discussion)* pugnacity

puîné, -e [pɥine] *Vieilli* **ADJ** *(de deux enfants)* younger; *(de plusieurs enfants)* youngest

NM,F *(de deux enfants)* younger child; *(de plusieurs enfants)* youngest child

puis[1] [pɥi] *voir* **pouvoir**[2]

puis[2] [pɥi] **ADV 1** *(indiquant la succession)* then; **il a regardé un moment, p. a semblé s'en désintéresser** he looked for a while, then seemed to lose interest; **prenez à gauche p. à droite** turn left then right **2** *(dans une énumération)* then; **elle a mangé une cerise, p. une autre, p. une troisième** she ate a cherry, then another, then another

• **et puis ADV 1** *(indiquant la succession)* **il a dîné rapidement et p. il s'est couché** he ate quickly and then he went to bed; **en tête du cortège, le ministre et p. les conseillers** at the head of the procession the minister followed by the counsellors; **et p. qu'est-ce qui s'est passé?** then what happened?, what happened then *or* next?; **et p. après?** *(pour solliciter la suite)* what then?, what happened next?; *(pour couper court)* it's none of your business!; *(exprimant l'indifférence)* so what!; **oui, je vais vendre ma voiture, et p. après?** yes, I'll sell my car, if it's any of your business!; **et p. c'est tout!, et p. voilà!** and that's all!, and that's that!, and that's all there is to it!; **tu n'iras pas, et p. c'est tout!** you're not going, and that's that!

2 *(dans une énumération)* **il y avait mes parents, mes frères et p. aussi mes cousins** there were my parents, my brothers and also my cousins

3 *(d'ailleurs)* **je n'ai pas envie de sortir, et p. il fait trop froid** I don't feel like going out, and anyway *or* and what's more it's too cold

puisage [pɥizaʒ] **NM** drawing (of water)

puisard [pɥizar] **NM 1** *(pour l'évacuation)* sump **2** *(pour l'épuration)* cesspool, drainage well

puisatier [pɥizatje] **NM 1** *(terrassier)* well sinker **2** *Mines* sumpman

puisement [pɥizmɑ̃] = **puisage**

puiser [3] [pɥize] **VT 1** *(eau)* to draw; **p. l'eau d'un puits/d'une citerne** to draw water from a well/a tank **2** *(extraire)* to get, to take, to derive; **où a-t-il puisé le courage de parler ainsi?** where did he get the nerve to say such things?; **p. sa force/son inspiration dans** to draw one's strength/one's inspiration from **3** *(prélever)* to draw, to take; **tu peux p. de l'argent sur mon compte si tu en as besoin** you can draw some money from my account if you need any

VI *(se servir)* to draw; **p. dans ses économies** to draw on *or* upon one's savings; **est-ce que je peux p. dans ta réserve de crayons?** can I dip into *or* help myself from your stock of pencils?; **p. dans son expérience** to draw on one's experience; **ils n'ont pas puisé dans la même documentation** they didn't use the same source material

puisque [pɥiskə] **CONJ 1** *(parce que)* since, because; **tu ne peux pas acheter de voiture, p. tu n'as pas d'argent** you can't buy a car because *or* since you don't have any money **2** *(étant donné que)* since; **je viendrai dîner, p. vous insistez** I will come to dinner, since you insist; **bon, p. tu le dis/y tiens** all right, if that's what you say/want; **p. c'est comme ça, je m'en vais!** if that's how it is, I'm leaving!; **puisqu'il en est ainsi** since that's the way things are; **ce chantage, puisqu'il faut l'appeler ainsi…** this blackmail, since there's no other word for it… **3** *(emploi exclamatif)* **mais p. je te dis que je ne veux pas!** but I'm telling you that I don't want to!; **p. je te dis que je vais le faire!** I've told you I'm going to do it!; **tu vas vraiment y aller? – p. je te le dis!** so are you really going? – isn't that what I said?

puissamment [pɥisamɑ̃] **ADV 1** *(avec efficacité)* greatly; **ils ont p. contribué à la victoire** their part in the victory was decisive; *Ironique* **p. raisonné!** brilliant thinking! **2** *(avec force)* powerfully, *Sout* mightily

puissance [pɥisɑ̃s] **NF 1** *(force physique ▸ d'une personne, d'une armée)* power, force, strength

2 *(pouvoir, autorité)* power

3 *(capacité)* power, capacity; **une grande p. de travail** a great capacity for work; **une grande p. de séduction** great powers of seduction

4 *(d'un appareil)* power, capacity, capability; **augmenter/diminuer la p.** to turn the volume up/down; *Aut* **p. effective** power output; *Mil* **p. de feu** fire power; *Aut* **p. administrative** *ou* **fiscale** engine rating; *Aut* **p. nominale/au frein** nominal/brake horsepower

5 *Com* power; **p. d'achat** buying *or* puchasing power; **p. publicitaire** *ou* **de vente** selling power

6 *Math* power; **six (à la) p. cinq** six to the power (of) five; *Fig* **c'est comme une étincelle, mais à la p. mille** it's like a spark, but a thousand times bigger

7 *Jur* authority; **p. paternelle** paternal authority

8 *Admin* **la p. publique** the authorities

9 *(pays puissant)* power; **p. économique** economic power; **p. mondiale** world power

• **puissances NFPL** powers; **les puissances des ténèbres** the powers of darkness; *Pol* **les grandes puissances** the great powers

• **en puissance ADJ** *(virtuel)* potential, prospective; **un candidat en p.** a potential candidate; **un client en p.** a prospective customer

puissant, -e [pɥisɑ̃, -ɑ̃t] **ADJ 1** *(efficace ▸ remède)* powerful, potent; *(▸ antidote, armée, moteur, ordinateur)* powerful; *(▸ membre, mouvement)* strong, powerful, *Littéraire* mighty; **une théorie qui soit assez puissante pour expliquer l'évolution** a theory powerful enough to explain evolution

2 *(intense ▸ odeur, voix)* strong, powerful

3 *(influent)* powerful, *Littéraire* mighty

4 *(profond)* powerful; **un p. instinct de conservation** a powerful instinct of self-preservation

5 *Fam (remarquable)* wicked, *Br* fab, *Am* awesome

• **puissants NMPL les puissants** the powerful

puisse *etc voir* **pouvoir**[2]

puits [pɥi] **NM 1** *(pour l'eau)* well; **p. à ciel ouvert** open well; **p. perdu** cesspool; **p. artésien** artesian well

2 *Pétr* **p. de pétrole** oil well

3 *Mines* shaft, pit

4 *Constr* **p. d'amarrage** *ou* **d'ancrage** anchor block (hole)

5 *Fig* **un p. de science** a walking encyclopedia, a fount of knowledge, a mine of information

6 *Géog* pothole

• **puits d'amour NM** *Culin* cream puff

pull [pyl] **NM** sweater, *Br* jumper

pullman [pulman] **NM 1** *Rail* Pullman® (car) **2** *(autocar)* luxury touring bus, *Br* luxury coach

pull-over [pylɔvɛr] *(pl* **pull-overs)** **NM** sweater, *Br* jumper

pullulation [pylylasjɔ̃] **NF** pullulation

pulluler [3] [pylyle] **VI 1** *(abonder)* to congregate, to swarm; **au lever du jour, les mouettes pullulent sur la falaise** seagulls congregate *or* swarm on the cliffs at dawn; **les marchands de chaussures pullulent dans ce coin de la ville** this part of town is full of *or* swarming with shoe shops; **des égouts où les rats pullulent** sewers overrun by rats **2** *(se multiplier)* to multiply, to proliferate; **les mauvaises herbes pullulaient dans le jardin** weeds were taking over the garden **3 p. de** *(fourmiller de)* to swarm *or* to be alive with; **la plage pullule de baigneurs** the beach is swarming with bathers; **ce texte pullule de fautes de frappe** this text is riddled with typing errors

pulmonaire [pylmɔnɛr] **ADJ 1** *Anat* pulmonary **2** *Anat & Méd* pulmonary, lung *(avant n)*

NF *Bot* lungwort

pulpe [pylp] **NF 1** *(de fruit)* pulp; **yaourt/boisson à la p. de fruit** yoghurt/drink with real fruit **2** *Anat* pulp; *(des doigts)* pad; **p. dentaire** tooth *or* dental pulp

pulpeux, -euse [pylpø, -øz] **ADJ 1** *Anat & Bot* pulpy **2** *(charnu ▸ lèvres, formes)* fleshy, voluptuous; **une blonde pulpeuse** a curvaceous blonde

pulsar [pylsar] **NM** *Astron* pulsar

pulsation [pylsasjɔ̃] **NF 1** *Anat (du cœur)* beat; *(du pouls)* pulsation; **pulsations cardiaques** heartbeats **2** *Phys* (mechanical) pulsation **3** *Mus* beat

pulser [3] [pylse] **VT** *(air)* to extract, to pump out

VI *Méd & Mus* to throb

pulsion [pylsjɔ̃] **NF 1** *(motivation)* impulse, unconscious motive **2** *Psy* drive, urge; **pulsions sexuelles** sexual desire, sexual urge; **p. de mort** death wish

pulsionnel, -elle [pylsjɔnɛl] **ADJ** drive *(avant n)*

pulsoréacteur [pylsɔreaktœr] **NM** pulse-jet (engine)

pulvérisable [pylverizabl] **ADJ 1** *(qui peut être réduit en poudre)* that can be crushed **2** *(liquide)* that can be sprayed

pulvérisateur [pylverizatœr] **NM 1** *(vaporisateur)* spray **2** *Agr* sprayer

pulvérisation [pylverizasjɔ̃] **NF 1** *(d'un liquide)* spraying **2** *(broyage)* pulverizing, crushing **3** *(de médicament)* **prendre un médicament en pulvérisations** to take a medicine in the form of a spray

pulvériser [3] [pylverize] **VT 1** *(broyer)* to pulverize, to crush **2** *Fig (détruire)* to demolish, to smash to pieces; **les bombes ont pulvérisé la ville** the bombs reduced the town to ashes *or* to a heap of rubble; **p. un record** to smash a record; *Fam* **je vais le p., ce type!** I'm going to flatten *or* make mincemeat out of the guy! **3** *(vaporiser)* to spray

pulvériseur [pylverizœr] **NM** disc harrow

pulvérulence [pylverylɑ̃s] **NF** powderiness, dustiness

pulvérulent, -e [pylverylɑ̃, -ɑ̃t] **ADJ** powdery, dusty

puma [pyma] **NM** puma, cougar, mountain lion

punaise [pynez] **NF 1** *Entom* bug; **p. des lits** bed bug; **p. des bois** *(pentatome)* forest bug

2 *(clou)* tack, *Br* drawing pin, *Am* thumbtack

3 *Fam (personne)* vixen

4 *Fam Péj* **p. de sacristie** sanctimonious person

EXCLAM *Fam Br* sugar!, *Am* shoot!

punaiser [4] [pyneze] **VT** to pin up, to put up with *Br* drawing pins *or Am* thumbtacks

punch[1] [pɔ̃ʃ] **NM** *(boisson)* punch

punch[2] [pœnʃ] **NM INV 1** *Fam (dynamisme)* pep, get-up-and-go; **avoir du p.** to be full of get-up-and-go; **une politique qui a du p.** a hard-hitting policy; **ça vous donnera du p. pour la suite!** it'll give you energy *or* set you up for what's to come! **2** *Sport (d'un boxeur)* **il a le p.** he's got a knock-out *or* devastating punch

punching-ball [pœnʃiŋbol] (*pl* **punching-balls**) NM punch *or* speed ball

punique [pynik] ADJ *(civilisation, guerre)* Punic
NM *(langue)* Punic

punir [32] [pynir] VT **1** *(élève, enfant)* to punish **2** *Jur* to punish, to penalize; **être puni par la loi** to be punished by law, to be prosecuted; **être puni de prison** to be sentenced to prison; **le kidnapping est puni de la prison à vie** kidnapping is punishable by life imprisonment; **tout abus sera puni** *(sur panneau)* penalty for improper use; **p. qn de qch** *(à cause de)* to punish sb for sth; **elle est bien punie de sa méchanceté** she's paying the price for her spitefulness; **me voilà puni de ma gourmandise!** it serves me right for being greedy!, that'll teach me to be greedy!; **se faire p.** to be punished; *Fam* **c'est le ciel** *ou* **le bon Dieu qui t'a puni** it serves you right

punissable [pynisabl] ADJ punishable, deserving (of) punishment; **p. de trois mois de prison** *(délit)* carrying a penalty of three months imprisonment; *(criminel)* liable to three months in jail

punitif, -ive [pynitif, -iv] ADJ *(expédition, mesures)* punitive; **en agissant ainsi, je n'ai pas d'intentions punitives** I do not intend this as punishment

punition [pynisjɔ̃] NF **1** *(sanction)* punishment; **donner une p. à un enfant** to punish a child; **en guise de p.** as (a) punishment; **il est en p.** he is being kept in detention; **p. corporelle** corporal punishment; **p. de Dieu** *ou* **du ciel** divine retribution **2** *Fam (défaite)* thrashing, hammering; **les Bordelais ont infligé une rude p. aux Parisiens** the Bordeaux team wiped the floor with *or* thrashed *or* hammered the Paris club **3** *(conséquence)* punishment, penalty; **la p. est lourde** it's a heavy price to pay
• **en punition de** PRÉP as a punishment for

punk [pœnk] ADJ INV punk
NMF punk

pupe [pyp] NF *Entom* pupa, chrysalis

pupillaire [pypilɛr] ADJ **1** *Jur* pupillary **2** *Anat* pupillary

pupillarité [pypilarite] NF *Jur* wardship

pupille[1] [pypij] NMF **1** *(en tutelle)* ward (of court) **2** *(orphelin)* orphan; **p. de l'État** child in care

pupille[2] [pypij] NF *Anat* pupil

pupillomètre [pypijɔmɛtr] NM pupilometer

pupilloscopie [pypijɔskɔpi] NF *Méd* skiascopy, sciascopy

pupitre [pypitr] NM **1** *Aviat & Ordinat* console; *(clavier)* keyboard; *Ordinat* **p. (de commande)** console (desk); **p. de mélange** *ou* **de mixage** mixing desk, mixing console, audio-mixer; *Ordinat* **p. de visualisation** visual display unit
2 *Mus (support ▸ sur pied)* music stand; *(▸ sur un instrument)* music rest; *(groupe)* section; **le p. des violons** the violin section, the violins
3 *(tablette de lecture)* (table) lectern
4 *Vieilli (bureau d'écolier)* desk

pupitreur, -euse [pypitrœr, -øz] NM,F console operator; *(claviste)* keyboarder

pur, -e [pyr] ADJ **1** *(non pollué ▸ eau)* pure, clear, uncontaminated; *(▸ air)* clean, pure, unpolluted; *(▸ ciel)* clear
2 *(sans mélange ▸ liquide)* undiluted; *(▸ whisky, gin etc)* straight, neat; *(▸ race)* pure; *(▸ bonheur, joie)* unalloyed, pure; *(▸ note, voyelle, couleur)* pure; **le cognac se boit p.** cognac should be taken straight *or* neat; **p. style dorique** pure Doric style; **pure laine (vierge)** pure (new) wool; **biscuits p. beurre** (100 percent) butter biscuits; **cheval p. sang** thoroughbred horse; **c'est un p. produit de la bourgeoisie** he's/she's a genuine middle-class product; *Euph* **ce n'est pas un p. esprit** he's/she's made of flesh and blood; **à l'état p.** pure, unalloyed, unadulterated; **p. et dur** *(fidèle)* strict; *(intransigeant)* hard-line; *Hum* **les amateurs de café purs et durs** serious *or* dedicated coffee drinkers; **c'est un socialiste p. jus** he's a socialist through and through
3 *(sans défaut)* faultless, perfect; **un style p.** an unaffected style; **elle parle un italien très p.** she speaks very refined *or* polished Italian
4 *(innocent)* pure, clean; **ses pensées sont pures** his/her thoughts are clean *or* pure; **une conscience pure** a clear conscience; **une jeune fille pure** an innocent young girl
5 *(théorique)* pure, theoretical; **sciences pures** pure science
6 *(en intensif)* sheer, utter, pure; **c'est de la folie pure!** it's sheer lunacy!; **par pure méchanceté** out of sheer malice; **p. et simple** pure and simple
7 *Fam (excellent)* wicked, cool, *Am* awesome
NM,F *Pol (fidèle)* dedicated follower; *(intransigeant)* hardliner

purée [pyre] NF **1** *Culin (de légumes)* purée; **p. de tomates/carottes** tomato/carrot purée; **p. (de pommes de terre)** mashed potatoes; **p. Mousseline** instant mashed potato; **réduire qch en p.** *Culin* to purée sth; *Fig* to smash sth to a pulp; **j'ai retrouvé mes coquillages en p. au fond du sac** my shells were all crushed at the bottom of the bag **2** *Fam (misère)* **être dans la p.** to be broke
EXCLAM *Fam (colère, agacement)* hell!, blast (it)!; *(surprise)* wow!
• **purée de pois** NF *Fam (brouillard)* pea souper

purement [pyrmɑ̃] ADV **1** *(uniquement)* purely, only, solely; **ses connaissances sont p. techniques** his/her knowledge is purely technical **2** *(entièrement)* purely, wholly; **p. et simplement** purely and simply; **le contrat est p. et simplement annulé** the contract is unconditionally cancelled; **non, c'est p. et simplement impossible!** no, it's quite simply out of the question!

pureté [pyrte] NF **1** *(propreté)* cleanness, purity; **la p. du ciel** the clearness of the sky
2 *Chim* purity
3 *(harmonie ▸ d'un contour)* neatness, purity; *(▸ d'une langue, d'un style)* purity, refinement; **la p. de ses traits** the perfection in his/her face *or* of his/her features
4 *(innocence)* purity, chastity; **je doute de la p. de ses intentions** I doubt whether his/her intentions are honourable

purgatif, -ive [pyrgatif, -iv] ADJ purgative
NM purgative

purgation [pyrgasjɔ̃] NF *Méd (remède)* purgative; *(processus)* purging, cleansing

purgative [pyrgativ] *voir* **purgatif**

purgatoire [pyrgatwar] NM *Rel & Fig* purgatory; **au p.** in purgatory

purge [pyrʒ] NF **1** *Tech (processus ▸ gén)* draining, bleeding; *(▸ d'un radiateur, des freins)* bleeding; *(dispositif)* bleed key; **robinet de p.** drain *or* bleed cock
2 *Méd* purge, purging
3 *Fig (au sein d'un groupe)* purge
4 *Jur* **p. d'hypothèque** redemption of mortgage

purgeoir [pyrʒwar] NM purifying tank, filtering tank

purger [17] [pyrʒe] VT **1** *Tech (radiateur, freins)* to bleed; *(réservoir)* to drain; *(tuyau à gaz)* to allow to blow off, to blow off
2 *Jur (peine)* to serve, **il a purgé six mois de prison** he served six months in prison; **p. sa peine** to serve one's sentence
3 *(dette)* to pay off; *(hypothèque)* to redeem
4 *Méd (personne)* to purge, to give a laxative to
5 *(débarrasser)* **le parti a été purgé de ses contestataires** the party has been purged of disloyal elements; **p. un quartier** to clean up an area
6 *(nettoyer, purifier)* **ils ont purgé le texte de toute allusion politique** they removed all political references from the text
VPR **se purger** to take a purgative

purgeur [pyrʒœr] NM *(vidange)* drain cock, bleed cock; *(trop-plein)* bleed tap

purifiant, -e [pyrifjɑ̃, -ɑ̃t] ADJ **1** *(crème, lotion)* cleansing, purifying **2** *(air)* healthy

purificateur, -trice [pyrifikatœr, -tris] ADJ purifying
NM **p. (d'air** *ou* **d'atmosphère)** (air) purifier

purification [pyrifikasjɔ̃] NF **1** *Chim* purifying; *Métal* refining; **p. de l'air/l'eau** air/water purifying **2** *Fig (de l'âme)* cleansing; **p. ethnique** ethnic cleansing

purificatrice [pyrifikatris] *voir* **purificateur**

purifier [9] [pyrifje] VT **1** *(nettoyer ▸ air)* to purify, to clear; *(▸ peau)* to cleanse
2 *(âme)* to cleanse
3 *(corriger ▸ langue, style)* to purify
4 *Chim (filtrer)* to purify, to decontaminate; **eau purifiée** purified *or* decontaminated water
5 *Métal* to refine
VPR **se purifier** *(devenir propre)* to become clean *or* pure; **plus on monte, plus l'air se purifie** the higher you go, the purer the air becomes

purin [pyrɛ̃] NM liquid manure, slurry

purisme [pyrism] NM *(gén) & Ling* purism

puriste [pyrist] ADJ purist
NMF purist

puritain, -e [pyritɛ̃, -ɛn] ADJ **1** *(strict)* puritan, puritanical **2** *Hist* Puritan
NM,F **1** *(personne stricte)* puritan **2** *Hist* **les puritains** the Puritans

puritanisme [pyritanism] NM **1** *(austérité)* puritanism, austerity **2** *Hist* Puritanism

purotin [pyrɔtɛ̃] NM *Fam Vieilli* hard-up person, person who is always broke

purpura [pyrpyra] NM *Méd* purpura

purpurin, -e [pyrpyrɛ̃, -in] ADJ *Littéraire* crimson, purpurine
• **purpurine** NF *Chim* purpurin

pur-sang [pyrsɑ̃] NM INV *Zool* thoroughbred

purulence [pyrylɑ̃s] NF purulence, purulency

purulent, -e [pyrylɑ̃, -ɑ̃t] ADJ *Méd (plaie)* suppurating; *(sinusite)* purulent

pus [py] NM *Méd* pus

push-pull [puʃpul] ADJ INV push-pull
NM INV push-pull

pusillanime [pyzilanim] ADJ *Littéraire* pusillanimous

pusillanimité [pyzilanimite] NF *Littéraire* pusillanimity

pustule [pystyl] NF **1** *Méd* pustule **2** *Bot & Zool* pustule

pustuleux, -euse [pystylø, -øz] ADJ *Méd* pustular, pustulous

put[1] *etc voir* **pouvoir**[2]

put[2] [put] NM *Bourse* put (option)

putain [pytɛ̃] *Vulg* NF *(prostituée)* whore, hooker; *(femme aux mœurs légères)* tart, slut, *Br* slag; **faire la p.** *(chercher à plaire)* to prostitute oneself◻; *(renoncer à ses principes)* to sell out
ADJ **il est très p.** he's a real bootlicker
EXCLAM fuck!, fucking hell!; **p., j'ai oublié mon parapluie!** shit, I've forgotten my umbrella!; **p. de bagnole/de temps!** (this) fucking car/weather!; **p. de merde!** oh, fuck!

putassier, -ère [pytasje, -ɛr] ADJ *Vulg* **1** *(vulgaire ▸ manières)* tarty **2** *(servile, obséquieux)* ingratiating◻

putatif, -ive [pytatif, -iv] ADJ **1** *Jur* putative **2** *(supposé)* assumed, supposed

pute [pyt] NF *Vulg* **1** *(prostituée)* whore; **fils de p.!** you son of a bitch!; **faire la p.** *(chercher à plaire)* to prostitute oneself◻ **2** *(femme facile)* tart, slut, *Br* slag **3** *(femme méprisable)* bitch

putois [pytwa] NM **1** *Zool* polecat **2** *(fourrure)* fitch, polecat fur

putréfaction [pytrefaksjɔ̃] NF putrefaction, decomposition; **matière en (état de) p.** putrefying matter

putréfier [9] [pytrefje] VT to putrefy, to rot
VPR **se putréfier** to putrefy, to rot, to become putrid

putrescence [pytresɑ̃s] NF putrescence

putrescent, -e [pytresɑ̃, -ɑ̃t] ADJ putrescent, rotting

putrescible [pytresibl] ADJ putrescible, putrefiable

putride [pytrid] ADJ **1** *(pourri ▸ viande, cadavre)* decomposed, putrid; *(▸ eau)* putrid, contaminated **2** *(nauséabond)* foul, putrid **3** *Littéraire (immoral ▸ lettre, pièce)* depraved

putridité [pytridite] NF *Littéraire* rottenness, putridness

putsch [putʃ] NM military coup, putsch

putschiste [putʃist] ADJ *(officiers)* involved in the putsch
NMF putschist, author of a military coup

puzzle [pœzl] NM **1** *(jeu de société)* (jigsaw) puzzle **2** *(énigme)* puzzle, puzzling question, riddle;

je commence à rassembler les morceaux du p. I'm beginning to fit the pieces of the puzzle together

PV [peve] **NM** *Fam* (*abrév* **procès-verbal**) (parking) ticket; **mettre un PV à qn** to give sb a ticket

PVC [pevese] **NM** (*abrév* **polyvinyl chloride**) PVC

PVD [pevede] **NM** (*abrév* **pays en voie de développement**) developing country

pygmée [pigme] **ADJ** Pygmy

NMF *Péj* **1** *Arch (nain)* pygmy, dwarf **2** *(personne insignifiante)* nobody, pygmy

• **Pygmée NMF** Pygmy

pyjama [piʒama] **NM un p.** (a pair of) pyjamas; **encore en p. à cette heure-ci?** you're still in your *or* wearing pyjamas at this time of day?; **j'y suis comme dans un p.** it's really comfortable

pylône [pilon] **NM 1** *(d'électricité, de téléphone)* pylon; *(pour fils télégraphiques)* lattice mast; **p. électrique** electricity pylon **2** *Archit* monumental column, pylon

pylore [pilɔr] **NM** *Anat* pylorus

pyorrhée [pjɔre] **NF** *Méd* pyorrhoea

pyramidal, -e, -aux, -ales [piramidal, -o] **ADJ 1** *Écon, Géom & Méd* pyramidal **2** *(objet)* pyramid-shaped; **forme pyramidale** pyramid shape

pyramide [piramid] **NF 1** *Archit & Géom* pyramid; **la P. du Louvre** = glass pyramid in the courtyard of the Louvre which acts as its main entrance

2 *(empilement)* **une p. de fruits** a pyramid of fruit; **entasser des oranges en p.** to pile up oranges in a pyramid; **p. humaine** human pyramid

3 *(en sociologie)* **p. des âges** population pyramid

4 *École* **p. alimentaire** food pyramid

5 *Fin* **p. des salaires** wage pyramid

pyrénéen, -enne [pireneɛ̃, -ɛn] **ADJ** Pyrenean

• **Pyrénéen, -enne NM,F** Pyrenean

Pyrénées [pirene] **NFPL les P.** the Pyrenees

pyrèthre [piretr] **NM** *Bot* feverfew, pyrethrum; **poudre de p.** insect powder

Pyrex® [pirɛks] **NM** Pyrex®; **plat en P.** Pyrex® dish

pyrexie [pirɛksi] **NF** *Méd* pyrexia

pyrite [pirit] **NF** *Minér* pyrite

pyrogravure [pirɔgravyr] **NF** *(procédé)* poker-work, *Spéc* pyrography; *(résultat)* pyrograph

pyrolyse [pirɔliz] **NF** pyrolysis

pyromane [pirɔman] **NMF** *Psy* pyromaniac; *Jur (incendiaire)* arsonist

pyromanie [pirɔmani] **NF** pyromania

pyromètre [pirɔmɛtr] **NM** pyrometer

pyrosis [pirɔzis] **NM** heartburn, *Spéc* pyrosis

pyrotechnie [pirɔtɛkni] **NF** pyrotechnics *(singulier)*, pyrotechny, fireworks

pyrotechnique [pirɔtɛknik] **ADJ** pyrotechnic, pyrotechnical; **un spectacle p.** a firework display

Pythagore [pitagɔr] **NPR** Pythagoras

pythagoricien, -enne [pitagɔrisjɛ̃, -ɛn] **ADJ** Pythagorean

NM,F Pythagorean

pythagorisme [pitagɔrism] **NM** *Phil* Pythagoreanism

python [pitɔ̃] **NM** *Zool* python

pyxide [piksid] **NF 1** *(boîte à couvercle)* pyxis **2** *Rel* pyx

Q, q [ky] **NM INV** *(lettre)* Q, q

Qatar [katar] **NM le Q.** Qatar, Katar; **vivre au Q.** to live in Qatar; **aller au Q.** to go to Qatar

QCM [kyseɛm] **NM** *(abrév* **questionnaire à choix multiple***)* multiple-choice questionnaire

QG [kyʒe] **NM** *(abrév* **quartier général***)* HQ

QI [kyi] **NM** *(abrév* **quotient intellectuel***)* IQ

quad [kwad] **NM 1** *(moto)* quad bike; *(sport)* quad biking; **faire du q.** to go quad biking **2** *(patin à roulettes)* quad (roller) skate

quadra [kwadra, kadra] *Fam (abrév* **quadragénaire***)* **ADJ** quadragenarian⊐; **être q.** to be in one's forties⊐

NMF *(personne)* person in his/her forties⊐; **c'est un q.** he's in his forties

quadragénaire [kwadraʒenɛr, kadraʒenɛr] **ADJ** quadragenarian; **être q.** to be in one's forties

NMF person in his/her forties, quadragenarian; **un sémillant q.** a dashing forty-year-old

quadrangulaire [kwadrɑ̃gylɛr, kadrɑ̃gylɛr] **ADJ** *(figure)* quadrangular, four-angled; *(tour, bâtiment)* four-sided

quadrant [kwadrɑ̃, kadrɑ̃] **NM** *Géom* quadrant

quadratique [kwadratik, kadratik] **ADJ 1** *Math* quadratic **2** *Minér* tetragonal

quadrature [kwadratyr, kadratyr] **NF 1** *Géom* quadrature, squaring; **c'est la q. du cercle** it's like trying to square a circle *or* to get a quart into a pint pot **2** *Astron* quadrature **3** *Math* integration

quadriceps [kwadriseps] **NM** *Anat* quadriceps

quadrichromie [kwadrikrɔmi, kadrikrɔmi] **NF** four-colour processing *or* printing

quadriennal, -e, -aux, -ales [kwadrijenal, -o, kadrijenal, -o] **ADJ** quadrennial, four-year *(avant n)*; **les jeux Olympiques sont quadriennaux** the Olympic Games take place every four years

quadrijumeaux [kwadriʒymo, kadriʒymo] **ADJ MPL** *Anat* **tubercules q.** quadrigeminal bodies, corpora quadrigemina

NMPL *Biol* quadruplets

quadrilatère [kwadrilatɛr, kadrilatɛr] **ADJ** *Géom* quadrilateral

NM *Géom & Mil* quadrilateral

quadrillage [kadrijaʒ] **NM 1** *(réseau)* grid; **q. des rues** grid arrangement *or* layout of streets

2 *(tracé)* grid *or* criss-cross pattern; *(sur une carte)* grid, graticule

3 *(division)* division; **q. administratif** division into administrative areas

4 *(contrôle)* surveillance; **la police a établi un q. du quartier** the police have the district under tight surveillance

quadrille [kadrij] **NM** quadrille; **le q. des lanciers** the lancers

quadrillé, -e [kadrije] **ADJ** squared, cross-ruled

quadriller [3] [kadrije] **VT 1** *(papier)* to criss-cross, to mark into squares **2** *(surveiller)* to put under tight surveillance; **la police quadrille le quartier** police presence is heavy in the district; **tout le quartier est quadrillé** the whole district is under tight surveillance **3** *(être réparti sur)* to be scattered about *or* dotted over

quadrimestriel, -elle [kadrimɛstrijɛl] **ADJ** four-monthly

NM = publication appearing every four months

quadrimoteur [kwadrimɔtœr, kadrimɔtœr] **ADJ M** four-engined

NM four-engined plane

quadriphonie [kwadrifɔni, kadrifɔni] **NF** quadraphony, quadraphonics *(singulier)*

quadriplégie [kwadripleʒi] **NF** *Méd* quadriplegia, tetraplegia

quadriréacteur [kwadrireaktœr, kadrireaktœr] **ADJ M** four-engined

NM four-engined plane *or* jet

quadrisyllabe [kwadrisilab] **NM** quadrisyllable, tetrasyllable

quadrisyllabique [kwadrisilabik] **ADJ** quadrisyllabic, tetrasyllabic

quadrumane [kwadryman, kadryman] *Zool* **ADJ** quadrumanous, four-handed

NM quadrumane; **les quadrumanes** the Quadrumana

quadrupède [kwadrypɛd, kadrypɛd] **ADJ** quadruped, quadrupedal, four-footed

NM quadruped

quadruple [kwadrypl, kadrypl] **ADJ 1** *(à quatre éléments)* quadruple; **en q. exemplaire** in quadruplicate **2** *Mus* **q. croche** *Br* hemidemisemiquaver, *Am* sixty-fourth note

NM quadruple; **le q. (de)** *(quantité, prix)* four times as much (as); *(nombre)* four times as many (as); **douze est le q. de trois** twelve is four times three; **j'ai gagné 100 euros et le vendeur le q.** I earned 100 euros and the seller four times that; **elle gagne le q. de ce que je gagne** she earns four times as much as I do

quadrupler [3] [kwadryple, kadryple] **VI** to increase fourfold, to quadruple; **ses revenus ont quadruplé depuis l'année dernière** his/her income has increased fourfold *or* quadrupled since last year, he/she earns four times more than he/she did last year

VT to increase fourfold, to quadruple

quadruplés, -ées [kwadryple, kadryple] **NM,F PL** quadruplets, quads

quai [ke] **NM 1** *(d'une gare)* platform; **le train est à q.** the train is in; **arrivée du train q. numéro 5** train arriving on platform 5; **accès aux quais** *(sur panneau)* to the trains

2 *Naut* quay, wharf; **arriver** *ou* **venir à q.** to berth; **le navire est à q.** the ship has berthed; *Com* **livrable à q.** *(marchandises)* ex-quay, ex-wharf; **droit de q.** wharfage; **q. de chargement** loading platform; **q. de déchargement** offloading platform; **q. d'embarquement** loading platform

3 *(berge)* bank, embankment; **sur les quais de la Seine** on the banks of the Seine

4 *(rue bordant un fleuve)* street; **prendre les quais** to drive along the river *(in a town)*; **le Q.** *(le Quai d'Orsay)* the (French) Foreign Ministry; *(le Quai des Orfèvres)* Police Headquarters *(in Paris)*

quaker, -eresse [kwekœr, kwekrɛs] **NM,F** Quaker, *f* Quakeress; **les quakers** the Quakers, the Society of Friends

quakerisme [kwekœrism] **NM** Quakerism

qualifiable [kalifjabl] **ADJ 1** *Sport (athlète, concurrent)* liable to qualify **2** *(descriptible)* **sa conduite n'est pas q.** his/her behaviour is indescribable

qualificatif, -ive [kalifikatif, -iv] **ADJ** qualifying

NM 1 *(mot)* term, word; **il n'y a pas de q. assez fort pour la décrire** there's no word strong enough to describe her **2** *Gram* qualifier, modifier

qualification [kalifikasjɔ̃] **NF 1** *(formation)* qualification, skill; **sans q.** unskilled; **il n'a pas les qualifications requises pour ce poste** he's not qualified *or* he hasn't got the right qualifications for this job; **q. professionnelle** professional qualifications

2 *Sport* preliminary, qualifying; **obtenir sa q.** to qualify; **leur q. est assurée** they are sure to qualify; **épreuves/match de q.** qualifying heats/match

3 *(appellation)* name; **la q. de faussaire paraît exagérée** the term forger seems a bit extreme

4 *Jur* legal definition

5 *Bourse* qualification *(by acquisition of shares)*

qualificative [kalifikativ] *voir* **qualificatif**

qualifié, -e [kalifje] **ADJ 1** *(compétent)* skilled, qualified; **elle est qualifiée pour remplir cette tâche** she's qualified to do this task; **je suis certainement q. pour en parler** I am certainly qualified to speak about it; **un professeur q.** a qualified teacher; **non q. pour** ineligible for **2** *Sport (choisi)* qualifying **3** *Jur* aggravated

qualifier [9] [kalifje] **VT 1** *(appeler)* **q. qn/qch de...** to describe sb/sth as...; **il qualifie tout le monde de snob** he calls *or* dubs everybody a snob

2 *(professionnellement)* to qualify; **son expérience la qualifie parfaitement pour ce poste** her experience qualifies her perfectly for this job

3 *Sport* to qualify

4 *Ling* to qualify, to modify

VPR se qualifier 1 se q. de... *(se dire)* to call oneself...; **elle se qualifie volontiers d'artiste** she likes to call herself an artist **2** *(être choisi)* to qualify; **se q. pour la finale** to qualify for *or* to get through to the final

qualitatif, -ive [kalitatif, -iv] **ADJ** qualitative; **d'un point de vue q.** from a qualitative point of view

qualité [kalite] **NF 1** *(côté positif* ▸ *d'une personne)* quality, virtue; *(*▸ *d'une chose)* good point, positive feature; **elle a beaucoup de qualités** she has many (good) qualities; **elle n'a pas que des qualités** she isn't all good; **les qualités et les défauts** good and bad qualities

2 *(propriété)* quality, property; **cette plante a des qualités laxatives** this plant has laxative properties

3 *(niveau)* quality, grade; **de q. inférieure, de mauvaise q.** low-quality, poor-quality; **de q. supérieure** good-quality, high-quality; **de bonne q.** quality, good-quality; **de première q.** *(gén)* top-quality, first-rate; *(viande)* prime; **un pneumologue de sa q. devrait le savoir** a lung specialist of his/her calibre should know; **q. de vie** quality of life; *Com* **q. totale** total quality management

4 *(statut)* position; *Jur* quality, capacity; **nom, prénom, âge et q.** name, first name, age and occupation; **avoir q. pour faire qch** *(être habilité)* to be entitled to do sth; *(être capable)* to be qualified to do sth; **qui a q. pour décider, ici?** who's entitled *or* empowered to decide around here?

5 *(valeur supérieure)* quality; **la q. et la quantité** quality and quantity; **la q. se paie** you get what you pay for

6 *Ordinat* **q. brouillon** draft quality; **q. courrier** (near) letter quality; **q. d'impression** print quality

• **qualités** NFPL *(mérites)* skills, qualities; **pensez-vous avoir les qualités requises?** do you think you've got the required skills?; **nous l'avons choisi pour ses qualités de gestionnaire** we chose him for his managerial skills
• **de qualité** ADJ **1** *(de luxe)* quality *(avant n)*, high-standard **2** *Vieilli (noble)* **gens de q.** gentlefolk, people of quality
• **en qualité de** PRÉP **en q. de tuteur, je peux intervenir** (in my capacity) as guardian, I can intervene; **en ma q. de chef de l'opposition, je...** as leader of the opposition, I...
• **ès qualités** ADV *Admin & Jur* in one's official capacity; **le ministre n'est pas intervenu ès qualités, mais à titre personnel** the minister intervened in a personal rather than an official capacity

QUAND [kɑ̃] CONJ **1** *(lorsque)* when; **q. tu le verras, demande-lui de me téléphoner** when you see him, ask him to ring me; **elle venait de partir q. il arriva** she had just left when he arrived; **q. je te disais qu'il serait en retard!** I TOLD you he'd be late!; **q. je pense à l'argent que j'ai dépensé!** when I think *or* to think of the money I spent!; *Fam* **q. il n'y en a plus il y en a encore** there's plenty more where that came from; *Prov* **q. le vin est tiré, il faut le boire** you've made your bed, now you must lie in it
2 *(alors que)* when; **pourquoi rester ici q. on pourrait partir en week-end?** why stay here when we could go away for the weekend?
3 *(introduisant une hypothèse)* even if; **q. il serait le plus riche des hommes, elle n'en voudrait pas** even if he were the richest man in the world, she wouldn't want to have anything to do with him
ADV when; **q. viendras-tu nous voir?** when will you come and visit us?; **je ne sais pas encore q. je pars** I don't know when I'm leaving yet; **depuis q. es-tu là?** how long have you been here?; **à q. le mariage?** when's the wedding?; **c'est pour q., ce mariage?** when is this wedding going to happen?; **jusqu'à q. restez-vous?** until when *or* how long are you staying?; *Fam* **q. est-ce que tu y vas?** when are you going there?
• **quand bien même** CONJ even if; **j'irai, q. bien même je devrais y aller à pied!** I'll go, even if I have to go on foot!
• **quand même** ADV **1** *(malgré tout)* all the same, even so; **c'était q. même bien** it was still good, it was good all the same; **je pense qu'il ne viendra pas, mais je l'inviterai q. même** I don't think he'll come but I'll invite him all the same **2** *(en intensif)* **tu pourrais faire attention q. même!** you really should be more careful!

quant [kɑ̃] **quant à** PRÉP as for *or* to; **q. aux photos, je ne les ai même jamais vues** as for the photographs, I never even saw them; **q. à la publication de l'ouvrage, elle devrait avoir lieu en juin** as for *or* regarding the publication of the work, it should take place in June; **je partage votre opinion q. à ses capacités** I share your opinion about his/her ability; **q. à moi** as for me, for my part, as far as I am concerned; **q. à ce que vous nous proposez...** as for your proposal...; **q. à le faire vraiment, c'est une autre histoire** as for actually doing it *or* as far as actually doing it is concerned, that's quite another matter

quant-à-soi [kɑ̃taswa] NM INV **rester** *ou* **se tenir sur son q.** to remain distant *or* aloof

quantième [kɑ̃tjɛm] NM day (and date) of the month; **la lettre ne spécifie pas le q. du mois pour la livraison** the letter doesn't specify what day of the month delivery is to be made

quantifiable [kɑ̃tifjabl] ADJ quantifiable

quantification [kɑ̃tifikasjɔ̃] NF **1** *(gén) & Phil* quantification **2** *Phys* quantization

quantifier [9] [kɑ̃tifje] VT **1** *(gén) & Phil* to quantify **2** *Phys* to quantize

quantique [kwɑ̃tik, kɑ̃tik] ADJ *(mécanique, nombre, théorie)* quantum
NF quantum mechanics *(singulier)*

quantitatif, -ive [kɑ̃titatif, -iv] ADJ quantitative; *Ling* **terme q.** quantifier

quantitativement [kɑ̃titativmɑ̃] ADV quantitatively

quantité [kɑ̃tite] NF **1** *(mesure)* amount, quantity; **quelle q. de lessive faut-il mettre?** how much detergent do you have to put in?; **de petites quantités de peinture/vitamines** small amounts of paint/doses of vitamins; **une q. de, des quantités de** lots of, a lot of, a great many; **il n'en reste pas des quantités** there aren't a lot left; **en grande/petite q.** in large/small quantities; **acheter qch en grande q.** to buy sth in bulk; *Fam* **une q. industrielle de** masses and masses of, heaps and heaps of; **en quantités industrielles** in industrial quantities
2 *Phys (grandeur)* quantity; **q. constante/variable** constant/variable quantity; **q. d'électricité** quantity *or* charge of electricity; **q. de mouvement** linear momentum
3 *Phil & Ling* quantity
4 *(locutions)* **tenir qn/qch pour q. négligeable** to disregard sb/sth; **traiter qn/qch comme une q. négligeable** to treat sb/sth as unworthy of consideration; **il considère mon avis comme q. négligeable** he doesn't care a jot for my opinion
• **en quantité** ADV **du vin/des prix en q.** lots of wine/prizes; **il y avait du saumon en q. dans le torrent** there was plenty of salmon in the stream
• **quantité de** DÉT a great many, lots of; **q. de femmes vous diront que...** a large number of women will tell you that...; **elle trouve q. de raisons pour ne pas le faire** she finds any number of *or* lots of reasons not to do it

quantum [kwɑ̃tɔm] (*pl* **quanta** [-ta]) NM **1** *Math & Phys* quantum; **théorie des quanta** quantum theory **2** *(montant)* amount; **q. des dommages et intérêts** sum of damages **3** *(proportion)* proportion, ratio

quarantaine [karɑ̃tɛn] NF **1** *(quantité)* **une q.** around *or* about forty, forty or so; **une q. de voitures** around *or* about forty cars; **elle a une q. d'années** she's around *or* about forty (years old) **2** *(âge)* **avoir la q.** to be around *or* about forty; **les problèmes typiques de la q.** the typical problems of the fortysomething generation; **quand on arrive à** *ou* **atteint la q.** when you hit forty **3** *Méd & Vét (isolement)* quarantine
• **en quarantaine** ADJ **1** *Méd & Vét* in quarantine **2** *Fig* excluded, ostracized ADV *Méd & Vét* **mettre en q.** to quarantine; *Fig* to ostracize, to exclude

quarante [karɑ̃t] ADJ **1** *(gén)* forty; **elle a q. de fièvre** she has a temperature of forty (degrees); **en q.** *(en 1940)* in 1940 **2** *(dans des séries)* fortieth; **page/numéro q.** page/number forty; *Can* **vieux comme l'an q.** ancient, as old as the hills
PRON forty
NM INV **1** *(gén)* forty; **les Q.** = the members of the "Académie française"
2 *(numéro d'ordre)* number forty
3 *(chiffre écrit)* forty
4 *(au tennis)* forty; **q. partout** deuce; *voir aussi* **cinquante**

quarantenaire [karɑ̃tnɛr] ADJ **1** *(qui dure quarante ans)* forty-year *(avant n)* **2** *Méd* quarantine *(avant n)*; *(maladie) Br* notifiable, *Am* quarantinable

quarantième [karɑ̃tjɛm] ADJ fortieth
NMF **1** *(personne)* fortieth **2** *(objet)* fortieth (one)
NM **1** *(partie)* fortieth **2** *Naut* **les quarantièmes rugissants** the roaring forties; *voir aussi* **cinquième**

quark [kwark] NM *Phys* quark

quart¹ [kar] NM **1** *(quatrième partie)* quarter; **5 est le q. de 20** 5 is a quarter of 20; **un q. de beurre** a quarter (of a pound) of butter; **un q. de la tarte** one quarter of the tart; **un kilo un q.** a kilo and a quarter, one and a quarter kilos; **un q. de cercle** *(gén)* a quarter (of a) circle; *Géom* a quadrant; **q. de finale** quarter final; **un q. de tour** a quarter turn; **démarrer** *ou* **partir au q. de tour** to start first go; *Fam* **le débat a démarré au q. de tour** the debate took off right away; *Fam* **il a réagi au q. de tour** he reacted straight away; *Fam* **elle a compris au q. de tour** she understood straight off *or* right away
2 *Mus* **q. de soupir** *Br* semiquaver rest, *Am* sixteenth rest; **q. de ton** quarter tone
3 *(quinze minutes) Br* quarter of an hour, *Am* quarter hour; **l'horloge sonne tous les quarts** the clock chimes on the quarter of every hour; **une heure et q., une heure un q.,** *Belg* **une heure q.** a quarter past *or Am* after one; **une heure moins le q.,** *Belg* **une heure moins q.** a quarter to *or Am* of one; *Fam* **viens au q.** get here at a quarter past; *Fam* **j'étais là à moins le q.** I was there at a quarter to
4 *(petite quantité)* fraction; **il dit cela mais il n'en pense pas le q.** that's what he says but he doesn't really mean it
5 *Naut (garde)* watch; *(aire de vent)* rhumb; **prendre le q.** to take the watch; **être de q.** to be on watch *or* duty; **officier de q.** officer of the watch; **homme de q.** watch keeper; **petit q.** dogwatch; **grand q.** six-hour (evening) watch
6 *(bouteille ou pichet)* quarter litre
7 *(gobelet)* (quarter litre) mug *or* beaker
8 *Fam* **q. de brie** *(nez)* beak, *Br* conk, hooter

quart², -e¹ [kar, kart] ADJ *Vieilli* fourth
NF **1** *Mus* fourth **2** *Escrime* quarte **3** *Cartes* quart

quarté [karte] NM *Courses de chevaux* = bet in which the punter predicts the first four horses to finish a race

quarteron, -onne [kartərɔ̃, -ɔn] NM,F *(métis)* quadroon
NM *Péj (petit nombre)* bunch, gang

quartette [kwartɛt] NM *Mus* quartet, quartette

quartier [kartje] NM **1** *(partie d'une ville)* district, area; *Admin* district; **le q. des affaires** the business district; **le q. juif** the Jewish quarter *or* area; **le q. chinois** Chinatown; **le q.** *(le voisinage)* the neighbourhood; **tout le q. en parle** the whole neighbourhood is talking about it; **je ne suis pas du q.** I'm not from around here; **demandez aux gens du q.** ask the locals *or* the local people; **q. commerçant** shopping area; **les beaux quartiers** the fashionable districts; **les bas quartiers** the less salubrious parts of town; **les quartiers nord de la ville** the north side of (the) town; **le Q. latin** the Latin Quarter *(area on the Left Bank of the Seine traditionally associated with students and artists)*
2 *Mil* quarters; *aussi Fig* **q. général** headquarters; **la bande a établi son q. général près de la gare** the gang set up its headquarters near the station; **grand q. général** General Headquarters; **quartiers d'hiver** winter quarters; *Fig* **prendre ses quartiers d'hiver à** to winter at *or* in; **avoir q. libre** *Mil* to be off duty; *Fig* to be free
3 *(partie d'une prison)* wing; **q. de haute sécurité** *ou* **de sécurité renforcée** high- *or* top-security wing
4 *(quart)* quarter; *(morceau)* portion, section; **un q. de pomme** a quarter of an apple; **un q. d'orange** an orange segment; **un q. de bœuf** a quarter of beef; **cinquième q.** offal
5 *Astron* quarter; **la Lune est dans son premier/dernier q.** the Moon is in its first/last quarter
6 quartiers de noblesse degree of noble descent; *Fig* **avoir ses quartiers de noblesse** to be well established
7 *(pitié)* mercy, quarter; *Vieilli* **demander q.** to ask for quarter; **l'armée victorieuse n'a pas fait de q.** the victorious army gave no quarter; **pas de q.!** no quarter!
8 *Belg (appartement)* furnished one-bedroom *Br* flat *or Am* apartment
• **de quartier** ADJ *(médecin, cinéma)* local

quartier-maître [kartjemɛtr] (*pl* **quartiers-maîtres**) NM *Naut* leading seaman

quartile [kwartil] NM *Math* quartile

quart-monde, quart monde [karmɔ̃d] (*pl* **quarts-mondes, quarts mondes**) NM **le q.** *(ensemble de pays)* the least developed countries, the Fourth World; *(dans un pays)* the poor

quartz [kwarts] NM quartz
• **à quartz** ADJ quartz *(avant n)*

quartzeux, -euse [kwartsø, -øz] ADJ quartz *(avant n)*

quartzite [kwartsit] NM *Minér* quartzite

quasar [kazar] NM *Astron* quasar

quasi [kazi] ADV = **quasiment**
NM chump end

quasi-collision [kazikɔlizjɔ̃] (*pl* **quasi-collisions**) NF **q. (aérienne)** air miss

quasi-contrat [kazikɔ̃tra] (*pl* **quasi-contrats**) NM *Jur* quasi-contract, implied contract

quasi-délit [kazideli] (*pl* **quasi-délits**) **NM** criminal negligence

quasiment [kazimɑ̃] **ADV** *Fam* almost, practically; **attends-moi, j'ai q. fini** wait for me, I've nearly finished; **c'est q. la même chose** it's more or less the same; **je n'ai q. rien senti** I hardly *or* barely *or* scarcely felt a thing

Quasimodo [kazimɔdo] **NF** *Rel* Quasimodo, Low Sunday
NPR Quasimodo, the hunchback of Notre-Dame

quaternaire [kwatɛrnɛr] **ADJ 1** *Géol* **ère q.** Quaternary era **2** *Chim & Math* quaternary
NM *Géol* Quaternary (period)

quatorze [katɔrz] **ADJ 1** *(gén)* fourteen **2** *(dans des séries)* fourteenth; **page/numéro q.** page/number fourteen; **le 14 juillet** Bastille Day; **en q.** during World War I; **la guerre de q.** World War I, the First World War; *Fam Hum* **c'est (re)parti comme en q.!** once more into the breach!
PRON fourteen
NM INV 1 *(gén)* fourteen **2** *(numéro d'ordre)* number fourteen **3** *(chiffre écrit)* fourteen; *voir aussi* **cinq**

quatorzième [katɔrzjɛm] **ADJ** fourteenth
NMF 1 *(personne)* fourteenth **2** *(objet)* fourteenth (one)
NM 1 *(partie)* fourteenth **2** *(arrondissement de Paris)* fourteenth (arrondissement)
NF *Mus* fourteenth; *voir aussi* **cinquième**

quatorzièmement [katɔrzjɛmmɑ̃] **ADV** in fourteenth place

quatrain [katrɛ̃] **NM** *Littérature* quatrain

quatre [katr] **ADJ 1** *(gén)* four; **les q. vertus cardinales** the cardinal virtues
2 *(dans des séries)* fourth; **page/numéro q.** page/number four
3 *Aut* **4L** Renault 4; **4 x 4** = **quatre-quatre**
4 *(locutions)* **il a fait les q. cents coups dans sa jeunesse** he sowed his wild oats when he was young; **il n'y est pas allé par q. chemins** he came straight to the point *or* didn't beat about the bush; **ils viennent des q. coins du monde** they come from the four corners of the world; **être tiré à q. épingles** to be immaculately dressed *or* dressed to the nines; *Fam* **les q. fers en l'air** flat on one's back; **il s'est retrouvé les q. fers en l'air** he fell flat on his back; *Fam* **ton q. heures** your afternoon snack; **un de ces q. matins**, *Fam* **un de ces q.** one of these days; **être enfermé entre q. murs** to be shut away indoors; *Fam* **être entre q. planches** to be six feet under; **ça ne vaut pas q. sous** it's not worth *Br* tuppence *or Am* a red cent; **une bague de q. sous** a cheap ring; **un hôtel de q. sous** a cut-price *or* low-rate hotel; **être logé aux q. vents** to live in a draughty old place; **dire ses q. vérités à qn** to tell sb a few home truths; **faire les q. volontés de qn** to pander to sb's every whim; **se mettre en q. pour qn** to go to no end of trouble *or* to bend over backwards for sb; **se mettre en q. pour faire qch** to go out of one's way to do sth
PRON four
NM INV 1 *(gén)* four
2 *(numéro d'ordre)* number four
3 *(chiffre écrit)* four
4 *(en aviron)* four; **q. de couple** quadruple; **q. de pointe avec barreur** coxed four; **q. de pointe sans barreur** coxless *or* straight four
• **à quatre mains** *Mus* **ADJ morceau à q. mains** piece for four hands **ADV jouer à q. mains** to play a duet
• **à quatre pattes ADV** on all fours; **marcher à q. pattes** to walk on all fours; **se mettre à q. pattes** to go down on all fours
• **comme quatre ADV boire/manger/parler comme q.** to eat/to drink/to talk a lot; *voir aussi* **cinq**

Quatre-Cantons [katrkɑ̃tɔ̃] **NMPL le lac des Q.** Lake Lucerne

quatre-cent-vingt-et-un [katrəsɑ̃vɛ̃teœ̃] **NM INV** = simple dice game usually played in cafés; the loser pays for a round of drinks

quatre-épices [katrepis] **NM INV** allspice

quatre-mâts [katrəma] **NM INV** four-master

quatre-quarts [katkar] **NM INV** ≃ pound cake *(without fruit)*

quatre-quatre [katkatr] **NM INV OU NF INV** four-wheel drive (vehicle), *Am* SUV

quatre-saisons [katrəsezɔ̃] **NF INV** *(légume)* second-crop *or* second-cropping vegetable; *(fruit)* second-crop *or* second-cropping fruit

quatre-vingt-dix [katrəvɛ̃dis] **ADJ 1** *(gén)* ninety **2** *(dans des séries)* ninetieth; **page/numéro q.** page/number ninety
PRON ninety
NM INV 1 *(gén)* ninety
2 *(numéro d'ordre)* number ninety
3 *(chiffre écrit)* ninety
4 *Fam (sur une voiture)* = sticker showing the maximum speed at which a new licence holder can drive a car; *voir aussi* **cinquante**

quatre-vingt-dixième [katrəvɛ̃dizjɛm] (*pl* **quatre-vingt-dixièmes**) **ADJ** ninetieth
NMF 1 *(personne)* ninetieth **2** *(objet)* ninetieth (one)
NM 1 *(partie)* ninetieth **2** *(étage)* *Br* ninetieth floor, *Am* ninety-first floor; *voir aussi* **cinquième**

quatre-vingtième [katrəvɛ̃tjɛm] (*pl* **quatre-vingtièmes**) **ADJ** eightieth
NMF 1 *(personne)* eightieth **2** *(objet)* eightieth (one)
NM eightieth; *voir aussi* **cinquième**

quatre-vingts [katrəvɛ̃] **ADJ 1** *(gén)* eighty; **q. personnes** eighty people; **quatre-vingt-deux** eighty-two **2** *(dans des séries)* eightieth; **page/numéro quatre-vingt** page/number eighty
PRON eighty
NM INV 1 *(gén)* eighty **2** *(numéro d'ordre)* number eighty **3** *(chiffre écrit)* eighty; *voir aussi* **cinquante**

quatrième [katrijɛm] **ADJ** fourth; **le q. âge** *(période)* advanced old age; *(groupe social)* very old people
NMF 1 *(personne)* fourth **2** *(objet)* fourth (one)
NM 1 *(partie)* fourth **2** *(étage)* *Br* fourth floor, *Am* fifth floor **3** *(arrondissement de Paris)* fourth (arrondissement)
NF 1 *Scol Br* ≃ third year, *Am* ≃ eighth grade **2** *Aut* fourth gear **3** *(en danse)* fourth position; *voir aussi* **cinquième**
• **en quatrième vitesse ADV** *Fam* in a hurry, at breakneck speed; **rapporte ce livre à la bibliothèque, et en q. vitesse!** take this book back to the library and be quick about it!; **j'ai bu mon café en q. vitesse** I drank my coffee in a rush

quatrièmement [katrijɛmmɑ̃] **ADV** fourthly, in fourth place

quattrocento [kwatrɔtʃento] **NM** *Beaux-Arts & Littérature* quattrocento

quatuor [kwatɥɔr] **NM 1** *Mus* quartet; **q. à cordes/vent** string/wind quartet **2** *Can Fam (groupe)* foursome

quat'zyeux [katzjø] **entre quat'zyeux ADV** *Fam* in private

QUE [kə]

> En anglais, le pronom relatif objet peut être omis. La conjonction **that** peut être omise après les verbes d'opinion, ainsi que **say**, **know** etc, p. ex. **je sais que c'est possible** I know (that) it's possible.

ADV 1 *(combien, comme)* **q. tu es naïf!** you're so naive!, aren't you naive!; **q. de bruit ici!** it's so noisy here!, what a lot of noise there is in here!; **q. d'assurance chez une femme si jeune!** so much self-confidence in such a young woman!; **q. de choses à faire dans une maison!** there are so many things to do in a house!; *Fam* **qu'est-ce q. tu es bête!** you're (ever) so stupid!; **qu'est-ce q. c'est bon!** it's delicious!, it's so good!; *Fam* **qu'est-ce qu'il m'a déçu!** he really disappointed me!
2 *(exprimant l'indignation)* **q. m'importent ses états d'âme!** what do I care about what he/she feels!
3 *(pourquoi)* why; **q. ne l'as-tu (pas) dit plus tôt!** why didn't you say so earlier?, I wish you had said so *or* that earlier!
PRON RELATIF 1 *(représente une personne)* who, that, *Sout* whom; **la fille qu'il a épousée** the girl (whom) he married; **sa sœur, q. je n'avais pas vue depuis dix ans, était là aussi** his/her sister, whom *or* who I hadn't seen for ten years, was there too; **le responsable q. j'ai vu** the official (whom *or* that) I saw; **la femme qu'elle était devenue** the woman (that) she'd become
2 *(représente un animal)* which, that; **les chenilles q. les enfants ont rapportées** the caterpillars (which *or* that) the children brought back
3 *(représente une chose, une idée)* which, that; **le contrat q. j'ai signé** the contract (which *or* that) I signed; **la chose la plus drôle q. j'aie jamais entendue** the funniest thing I've ever heard; **je ne suis pas la seule, q. je sache** I'm not the only one as far as I know
4 *(pour souligner une caractéristique)* **malheureux q. vous êtes!** you unfortunate man!; **fatiguée qu'elle était, elle continuait à l'aider** tired though *or* as she was, she carried on helping him/her; **de timide qu'il était, il est devenu expansif** once a shy man, he's now an extrovert; **en bon père/électricien qu'il était** being the good father/electrician he was; **bel exploit q. le sien!** what he's/she's done is quite a feat!; **drôles de gens q. ces gens-là!** strange people, those!
5 *(dans des expressions de temps, de durée)* **voici trois mois q. je ne joue plus** it's three months since I stopped playing, I haven't played for three months; **ça fait deux heures q. j'attends** I've been waiting for two hours; **un soir qu'il faisait très chaud** one very hot evening, one evening when the weather was very hot; **le temps q. tu te prépares, il sera trop tard** by the time you're ready it'll be too late; **il n'y a pas longtemps qu'elle l'a vendu** it wasn't long ago that she sold it; **il y a bien longtemps q. je le sais** I've known for a long time; **chaque fois q. je m'absente, il téléphone** every time I'm out he phones; *Littéraire* **du temps q. les bêtes parlaient** at the time when animals could speak
PRON INTERROGATIF 1 *(dans le discours direct)* what; **q. se passe-t-il?** what's happening?; **qu'y a-t-il?** what's the matter?; **q. dis-tu?** what are you saying?; **q. devient-elle?** what's become of her?; **qu'est-ce q. ça veut dire?** what does it mean?; **qu'est-ce qui t'arrive?** what's the matter with you?; **qu'est-ce q. la liberté?** what is freedom?
2 *(dans le discours indirect)* what; **je ne sais plus q. penser** I don't know what to think any more
CONJ 1 *(après des verbes déclaratifs ou des verbes d'évaluation)* that; **je sais q. je peux le faire** I know (that) I can do it; **crois-tu qu'il se serait excusé?** do you think he'd have apologized?; **il est possible q. je revienne** I may come back; **il est surprenant qu'elle n'ait pas téléphoné** it's strange (that) she hasn't phoned; **exigez qu'on vous indemnise** demand compensation *or* to be compensated; **je préférerais qu'on me laisse à l'écart de tout cela** I'd rather be left out of all this; **il dit qu'il était déçu** he said (that) he was disappointed
2 *(en début de proposition)* **q. leur fils ait fugué, cela ne devrait pas nous surprendre** the fact that their son ran away shouldn't come as a surprise to us; **q. vous ayez raison, c'est bien évident** it's quite obvious (that) you're right
3 *(et déjà)* than; **il n'a pas fini de lire un roman qu'il en commence un autre** no sooner has he finished one novel than he starts reading another
4 *(afin que)* so that; **approche-toi, q. je te voie mieux** come closer so that I can see you better
5 *Fam (tellement que)* **elle tousse q. ça réveille tout le monde** she coughs so much (that) she wakes everybody up; **il est têtu q. ça en devient un vrai problème** he's so stubborn (that) it's a real problem
6 *(suivi du subjonctif) (pour formuler un ordre, un souhait, une éventualité)* **qu'elle parle!** *(faites-la parler)* make her talk!; *(laissez-la parler)* let her speak!; **q. l'on apporte à boire!** bring some drinks!; **q. le bal commence!** let the dancing begin!; **eh bien, qu'il s'en aille s'il n'est pas content!** he can leave if he doesn't like it!; **q. Dieu nous pardonne** may God forgive us
7 *(dans une double hypothèse)* **il me l'interdirait q. je le ferais quand même** I would do it even if he forbade me to; **aurais-je le moyen d'y aller q. je n'en aurais pas envie** even had I the means of going, I still would not have the will
8 *(répète la conjonction précédente)* **quand je serai grande et q. j'aurai un métier** when I'm grown up and (I) have a job; **comme il l'aime/s'il l'aime et qu'elle l'aime...** as/if he loves her and she loves him...; **comme/puisque j'ai horreur de cuisiner et**

q. Pierre aussi... as/since I hate cooking and Pierre (does) too...

9 *(formule de présentation et d'insistance)* **je croyais l'affaire faite et voilà qu'elle n'est pas d'accord** I thought the deal was clinched and now I find she disagrees; **si je n'ai rien dit, c'est q. je craignais de te vexer** if I said nothing, it was because I was afraid of upsetting you; **q. oui!** oh yes indeed!; **q. non!** certainly not!; **tu n'iras pas – q. si!** you won't go – oh yes I will *or* I will too!; **tu ne le savais pas? – q. si!** didn't you know? – oh yes, I did!

10 *(dans une formule interrogative)* **est-ce q. tu viendras?** will you come?; *Fam* **comment qu'il a fait?** how did he manage?▫; *Fam* **où qu'elle est partie?** where did she go (to)?▫

11 *(suivi de "faire")* **je n'ai q. faire de vos souhaits** I don't want your good wishes

• **que... ou non** CONJ whether... or not; **q. tu me croies ou non** whether you believe me or not

• **que... (ou) que** CONJ whether... or; **q. je parte ou q. je reste** whether I go or (whether I) stay; **qu'il fasse beau, qu'il pleuve, je sors me promener** come rain or come shine, I go out for a walk

Québec [kebɛk] NM **1** *(province)* **le Q.** Quebec; **au Q.** in Quebec; **la province de** *ou* **du Q.** Quebec State **2** *(ville)* Quebec; **à Q.** in (the city of) Quebec

québécisme [kebesism] NM Quebec French word/phrase

québécité [kebesite] NF Quebec identity

québécois, -e [kebekwa, -az] ADJ from Quebec NM *Ling* Quebec French

• **Québécois, -e** NM,F Québecois, Quebecker

quel, -elle [kɛl] ADJ INTERROGATIF *(personne)* which; *(animal, chose)* which, what; **quelle actrice serait capable de jouer ce rôle?** which actress could play this part?; **de q. côté es-tu?** which *or* whose side are you on?; **de q. magasin parlez-vous?** which shop are you talking about?; **je ne sais quels sont ses projets** I don't know what his/her plans are; **quelle heure est-il?** what's the time?, what time is it?; **quelle sorte d'homme est-ce?** what kind of man is he?

ADJ EXCLAMATIF what; **q. dommage!** what a pity!, **q. idiot!** what a fool!; **q. sale temps!** what terrible weather!; **q. talent chez ce peintre!** what talent this painter has!, what a talented painter!; **quelle bêtise d'avoir oublié le tire-bouchon!** how stupid to have forgotten the corkscrew!; **il s'est exprimé en japonais, et avec quelle aisance!** he spoke in Japanese, and so fluently too!; **si tu savais à q. point il tient à cette montre** if you knew how fond he is of this watch; **quelle ne fut pas ma surprise (quand je le vis entrer)!** imagine my surprise (when I saw him come in)!

ADJ RELATIF *(en corrélation avec "que" ▸ personne)* whoever; *(▸ animal)* whichever; *(▸ chose)* whichever, whatever; **il a refusé de recevoir les nouveaux arrivants, quels qu'ils fussent** he refused to see the new arrivals, whoever they were; **les mammifères quels qu'ils soient** all mammals; **quelle que soit l'assurance que vous choisissiez...** whichever insurance policy you choose...; **quelle que soit mon affection pour elle** however great my affection for her, much as I love her; **il se baigne q. que soit le temps** he goes swimming whatever the weather

PRON INTERROGATIF which (one); **q. est le plus jeune des deux?** which one is the younger of the two?; **de tous vos matchs, q. fut le plus difficile?** of all the matches you've played, which (one) was the most difficult *or* which was the most difficult one?

quelconque [kɛlkɔ̃k] ADJ INDÉFINI **1** *(quel qu'il soit)* any, some or other; **si, pour une raison q., tu ne pouvais pas venir** if, for some reason or other *or* if, for any reason, you can't come; **s'il y a un problème q.** if there is any problem (whatever); **je trouverai bien une excuse q.** I'll find some excuse or other; **as-tu une q. idée du prix?** have you got any idea of the price? **2** *Math* any; **un quadrilatère q.** any quadrilateral figure

ADJ *(insignifiant, banal ▸ nourriture, visage)* ordinary, plain; *(▸ personne)* average, ordinary; *(▸ comédien, film, spectacle)* run-of-the-mill, second-rate, (pretty) average; *(▸ exécution, réalisation)* mediocre, lacklustre; **on ne peut pas lui donner un emploi q.** we can't give him/her an ordinary job *or Fam* any old job; **moi, je le trouve très q.** I don't think there's anything special about him

quelle [kɛl] *voir* **quel**

quelles [kɛl] *voir* **quel**

QUELQUE [kɛlkə] ADJ INDÉFINI **1** *(un peu de)* some; **j'ai eu q. peine à le reconnaître** I had some difficulty (in) recognizing him; **elle est bizarre depuis q. temps** she's been acting strangely for a time now *or* for some time now

2 *(n'importe quel)* some; **je trouverai bien q. prétexte** no doubt I'll think of some excuse (or other)

3 *(en corrélation avec "que")* **dans q. pays que tu sois** whichever *or* whatever country you may be in; **à q. heure que ce soit** whatever the time, at whatever time

ADV **1** *(approximativement)* around, about; **il y a q. quarante ans de cela** that was about forty years ago, that was forty or so years ago

2 *(en corrélation avec "que")* **nous y arriverons, q. difficile que ce soit** we will manage, however difficult it may be

• **quelques** ADJ INDÉFINI **1** *(sans déterminant)* a few, some; **quelques jours plus tard** a few days later; **amène quelques amis** bring some *or* a few friends along; **quelques dizaines de journalistes** a few dozen journalists; *Fam* **ça pèse deux kilos et quelques** it's a little *or* a bit over two kilos; *Fam* **il était 5 heures et quelques** it was just after 5 o'clock; *Fam* **50 euros et quelques** just over 50 euros **2** *(avec déterminant)* few; **les quelques millions de téléspectateurs qui nous regardent** the few million viewers watching us; **elle n'a laissé que ces quelques vêtements** she only left these few clothes

• **en quelque sorte** ADV **1** *(en un sens)* as it were, so to speak, in a manner of speaking; **c'est en q. sorte un cheval avec un buste d'homme** it is, as it were *or* so to speak, a horse with the head and shoulders of a man **2** *(en résumé)* in a nutshell, in fact; **tu veux, en q. sorte, refaire le monde** in a nutshell *or* in fact, you want to set the world to rights

• **quelque chose** PRON INDÉFINI **1** *(dans une affirmation)* something; **elle a q. chose aux poumons** she's got something wrong with her lungs; **q. chose me dit que...** something tells me that..., I've got the feeling that...; **ça m'a fait q. chose de le revoir 20 ans plus tard** it was really weird to see him 20 years later; **quand il est parti, ça m'a vraiment fait q. chose** when he left it really affected me; **q. chose de blanc/beau** something white/beautiful; **elle a fait q. chose de bien** she did a very good thing, she did something very good; **il trouvera encore q. chose de pire à faire** he'll find (still) worse to do *or* something even worse to do

2 *(dans une question, une négation, une hypothèse)* anything, something; **tu veux q. chose à manger?** do you want something *or* anything to eat?; **s'il m'arrivait q. chose...** if anything *or* something should happen to me...; **q. chose ne va pas?** is there anything wrong?, is there something wrong?, is anything the matter?; **ça te ferait vraiment q. chose si je partais?** would it really matter to you *or* would you feel anything if I left?; **tu n'as pas q. chose d'autre?** haven't you got something *or* anything else?

3 *Fam (dans une approximation)* **elle a q. chose comme 80 ans** she's about 80 *or* 80 or so; **c'était une Renault 5 ou q. chose comme ça** it was a Renault 5 or something (of the kind *or* like that); **elle est q. chose au parti socialiste** she's something in the Socialist Party; **Anne q. chose a téléphoné** Anne something *or* somebody phoned

4 *Fam (emploi expressif)* **il s'est viandé, q. chose de bien** he got smashed up something awful; **il lui a passé un savon, q. chose de bien** he gave him/her an almighty telling-off; **il tenait q. chose comme cuite!** he was totally plastered!; **c'est q. chose!** *(ton exaspéré)* that's a bit much!; *(ton admiratif)* that's quite something!; **je t'ai dit trois fois de ranger ta chambre, c'est q. chose!** I've told you three times to tidy up your room, for God's sake!

• **quelque part** ADV **1** *(dans un lieu)* somewhere; **tu vas q. part à Noël?** are you going anywhere (special) for Christmas? **2** *Fam Euph (au derrière)* **c'est mon pied q. part que tu veux?** do you want a kick up the backside?; **elle lui a foutu un coup de genou q. part** *(dans les testicules)* she kneed him in the you-know-where *or* where it hurts most

• **quelque part que** CONJ *Littéraire* **q. part qu'elle regardât** wherever she looked

quelquefois [kɛlkəfwa] ADV sometimes, from time to time; **je vais q. au concert** sometimes *or* from time to time I go to concerts; **q., je me demande si j'ai raison d'insister** sometimes I wonder if I'm right to insist

quelqu'un, -e [kɛlkœ̃, -yn] PRON INDÉFINI *Littéraire (l'un, l'une)* **q. de** one of; **quelqu'une de ces demoiselles va vous conduire** one of these young ladies will show you the way

• **quelqu'un** PRON INDÉFINI **1** *(dans une affirmation)* someone, somebody; **q. devra le faire!** someone *or* somebody will have to do it!; **q. te demande au téléphone** there's someone *or* somebody on the phone for you; **demande à q. du village** ask one of the villagers, ask someone *or* somebody from the village; **q. de frisé/barbu** someone *or* somebody with curly hair/a beard; **c'est q. de bien** he's/she's a nice person; **tu peux lui parler, c'est q. de sûr** you can talk to him/her, he's/she's a reliable person; **il faut q. de plus** one more (person) is needed; **c'est q.!** *(ton admiratif)* he's/she's quite somebody!; *Péj* **ce garçon, c'est q.!** that boy's a little horror!; **elle veut devenir q. (dans le monde de l'art)** she wants to become someone famous (in the world of art); *Péj* **il se prend pour** *ou* **se croit q.** he thinks he's really something, he thinks he's it **2** *(dans une question, une négation, une hypothèse)* anyone, anybody; **il y a q.?** is (there) anyone *or* anybody in?; **si q. me demande** if anyone *or* anybody asks for me; **y a-t-il eu q. de blessé?** was anyone *or* anybody hurt?; **q. parmi vous le connaît-il?** do any of you know him?

quels [kɛl] *voir* **quel**

quémander [3] [kemɑ̃de] VT *(aide, argent, nourriture)* to beg for; *(compliment)* to fish *or* to angle for; **q. qch auprès de qn** to beg for sth from sb

quémandeur, -euse [kemɑ̃dœr, -øz] NM,F *Littéraire (mendiant)* beggar

qu'en-dira-t-on [kɑ̃diratɔ̃] NM INV gossip; **elle a peur du q.** she's afraid of what people will say; **je me moque du q.** I don't care what people say

quenelle [kənɛl] NF *Culin* quenelle

quenotte [kənɔt] NF *Fam (dent d'un enfant)* tooth▫

quenouille [kənuj] NF **1** *Tex* distaff; *Fig* **tomber en q.** to fall to the distaff; *(échouer)* to go to rack and ruin **2** *(d'un lit)* bedpost

• **quenouilles** NFPL *Can Fam Péj* long skinny legs▫, matchstick legs

quéquette [kekɛt] NF *Fam Br* willy, *Am* peter

querelle [kərɛl] NF quarrel; *(verbale)* quarrel, argument; **avoir une q. avec qn** to have a quarrel *or* a row with sb; **ce n'est qu'une q. d'amoureux** it's only a lovers' tiff; **q. de famille** *(brouille)* family squabble; *(sérieuse)* family feud; **q. d'ivrognes** drunken brawl; **la q. déclenchée au sein du gouvernement** the row sparked off within the cabinet; **vaines querelles** pointless squabbles; **q. d'Allemand, mauvaise q.** quarrel for quarrelling's sake; **q. de personnes** ad personam quarrel

quereller [4] [kərele] VT *Vieilli* to reprimand

VPR **se quereller** to quarrel (with one another); **elles se querellent pour des riens** they quarrel *or* squabble over nothing; **se q. avec qn** to have an argument *or* to quarrel with sb

querelleur, -euse [kərɛlœr, -øz] ADJ quarrelsome, belligerent; **il est très q.** he's always picking fights *or* looking for arguments

NM,F quarrelsome person

quérir [kerir] VT *Littéraire (à l'infinitif seulement)* **envoyer** *ou* **faire q. qn** to summon sb; **le roi le fit q.** the king bade him come

qu'est-ce que [kɛskə], **qu'est-ce qui** [kɛski] *voir* **que** PRON INTERROGATIF

questeur [kɛstœr] NM **1** *Antiq* quaestor **2** *Pol* parliamentary administrator

question [kɛstjɔ̃] NF **1** *(interrogation)* question; **je ferme la porte à clé? – bien sûr, quelle q.!** shall I lock the door? – of course, what a question!; **y a-t-il des questions?** are there any questions?; **peut-on lui faire confiance, toute la q. est là** *ou* **voilà la q.!** can he/she be trusted, that's the question!; **poser une q. à qn** to ask sb a question; **c'est moi qui pose les questions!** I'm (the one) asking the questions!, I do the asking!; *Pol* **poser une q.** to table a question; **c'est une q. que je me pose depuis longtemps** that's something *or* a question I've been asking myself for a long time; **je commence à me poser des questions sur sa compétence** I'm beginning to have (my) doubts about *or* to wonder how competent he/she is; **se poser la q. de savoir si…** to ask oneself whether…; **q. à choix multiple** multiple-choice question; *Pol* **q. écrite/orale** written/oral question; **q. fermée** closed-ended *or* yes/no question; **q. ouverte** open-ended question; *Pol* **poser la q. de confiance** to ask for a vote of confidence; **q. piège** *(dans un jeu)* trick question; *(dans un interrogatoire)* loaded *or* leading question; **q. subsidiaire** *(dans un jeu)* tie-breaker

2 *(sujet)* question, topic; **j'en connais un bout sur la q.!** I know quite a bit about this (topic)!; **de quoi est-il q. dans ce paragraphe?** what is this paragraph about?; **il a beaucoup été q. d'échanges culturels à la réunion** during the meeting they talked a lot about cultural exchanges *or* the overriding topic was cultural exchanges; **dans notre prochaine émission, il sera q. de l'architecture romane** in our next programme, we will examine Roman architecture; **il n'est jamais q. de la répression dans son livre** repression is never mentioned in his/her book; *Fam* **prête-moi 100 euros – pas q.!** lend me 100 euros – no way *or Br* nothing doing!; **il n'en est pas q.!, c'est hors de q.!** it's out of the question!; **il n'est pas q.** *ou* **il est hors de q. que je le voie!** there's no way I'll see him!, there's no question of my seeing him!; *Fam* **q. salaire, je ne me plains pas** as far as the salary is concerned *or* salary-wise, I'm not complaining; *Fam* **q. soleil, on n'a pas été gâtés** we didn't see much in the way of sunshine

3 *(affaire, difficulté)* question, matter, point (at issue); **la q. du nucléaire** the nuclear energy question *or* issue; **là n'est pas la q.** that's not the point *or* the issue; **(une) q. de** a question of; **ce n'est plus qu'une q. de temps** it's only a question *or* matter of time; **c'est une q. d'habitude/de politesse** it's a question of habit/of politeness; **c'est une q. de vie ou de mort** it's a matter of life and death; **ils se sont disputés pour des questions d'argent** they had an argument over *or* about money; **je ne lis pas les critiques, q. de principe!** I don't read reviews on principle!; **ça c'est une autre q.!** that's another problem *or* story!

4 son talent ne fait pas (de) q. his/her talent is beyond (all) question *or* (any) doubt; **c'est son passé qui fait q.** what's doubtful is his/her past

5 *Hist* question; **mettre** *ou* **soumettre qn à la q.** to put sb to the question

• **en question** ADJ in question, concerned; **la personne en q. veut garder l'anonymat** the person in question wishes to remain anonymous ADV **mettre qch en q.** *(mettre en doute)* to call sth into question, to challenge *or* question sth; **mettez-vous mon honnêteté en q.?** are you questioning my honesty?; **remettre en q.** *(mettre en doute)* to (call into) question, to challenge; *(compromettre)* to call into question; **la moindre querelle et leur couple est remis en q.** the slightest argument and their relationship is put in jeopardy again; **se remettre en q.** to do some soul-searching

questionnaire [kestjɔnɛr] NM questionnaire; **q. à choix multiple** multiple-choice questionnaire

questionnement [kestjɔnəmɑ̃] NM questioning

questionner [3] [kestjɔne] VT *(interroger)* **q. qn** to question sb, to ask sb questions; **elle m'a questionné sur mon emploi du temps** she asked me questions about *or* questioned me on my timetable; **se faire q.** to be questioned

VPR **se questionner** to question each other

questionneur, -euse [kestjɔnœr, -øz] ADJ *(enfant, air)* inquisitive

NM,F *Littéraire* questioner

questure [kestyr] NF **1** *Antiq* quaestorship **2** *Pol* = treasury and administrative department of the French Parliament

quête [kɛt] NF **1** *(d'argent)* collection; **faire une q.** to collect money, to make a collection; **faire la q.** *(à l'église)* to take (the) collection; *(dans la rue)* to go round with the hat, to pass the hat round; **ils font la q. pour la fête de l'école** they're collecting money *or* making a collection for the school fête **2** *Littéraire (recherche)* quest (**de** for); **la q. du Graal** the Quest for the Holy Grail; **q. initiatique** journey of self-discovery **3** *Chasse* search

• **en quête de** PRÉP *Littéraire* in search *or* pursuit of, searching for; **le poète en q. de la beauté** the poet in search *or* pursuit of beauty; **se mettre en q. de** to go in search of; **elle est en q. d'un travail** she's job-hunting

quêter [4] [kete] VI *(à l'église)* to take (the) collection; *(parmi un groupe)* to collect money, to make a collection; *(dans la rue)* to pass the hat round, to go round with the hat

VT **1** *Littéraire (approbation, louanges)* to seek; *(compliments)* to fish for, to angle for **2** *Chasse (gibier)* to search

quêteur, -euse [ketœr, -øz] NM,F **1** *(personne qui fait la quête)* collector **2** *Can (mendiant)* beggar

quetsche [kwɛtʃ] NF **1** *Bot* quetsch (plum) **2** *(eau-de-vie)* quetsch brandy

queue [kø] NF **1** *Zool* tail; **q. de renard** fox's brush; *Aut* **faire une q. de poisson à qn** to cut in in front of sb; **leur relation a fini en q. de poisson** their relationship fizzled out; *Fam* **il est parti la q. basse** *ou* **entre les jambes** he left with his tail between his legs

2 *Bot (d'une cerise, d'une feuille)* stalk; *(d'une fleur)* stalk, stem; *Suisse Fam* **ne pas se prendre pour la q. de la poire** to think one is the bee's knees

3 *(extrémité ▸ d'une poêle, d'une casserole)* handle; *(▸ d'un avion, d'une comète, d'un cerf-volant)* tail; *(▸ d'une étoile filante)* trail; *(▸ d'un cortège)* back, tail (end); *(▸ d'un orage, d'un tourbillon)* tail (end); *(▸ d'une procession, d'un train)* rear; **les voitures de q.** the rear carriages; **être à la** *ou* **en q.** *(d'un cortège)* to be at the rear; **je monte toujours en q.** I always get on at the rear (of the train); *Sport* **il est en q. de peloton** he is at the back or rear of the bunch; *Fam* **il y en avait pas la q. d'un/d'une** there wasn't a single one[□], there wasn't one to be seen[□]; *Fam* **ce que tu dis n'a ni q. ni tête** you're making no sense at all, you're talking nonsense; *Fam* **la pièce n'avait ni q. ni tête** you couldn't make head or *or* nor tail of the play; *Fam* **une histoire sans q. ni tête** a shaggy-dog story

4 *(dans un classement)* bottom; **être à la q. de la classe/du championnat** to be at the bottom of the class/league

5 *(file d'attente) Br* queue, *Am* line; **faire la q.** *Br* to queue (up), *Am* to stand in line; **vous faites la q.?** *Br* are you queuing up?, *Am* are you in line?; **allez à la q.!** go to the back of the *Br* queue *or Am* line!

6 *Vulg (pénis)* cock, prick

7 *(au billard)* **q. (de billard)** (billiard) cue; **(faire une) fausse q.** (to) miscue

8 *Typ (d'une lettre)* stem, tail, *Spéc* descender; *(d'une note de musique)* stem

• **à la queue leu leu** ADV in single *or* Indian file

queue-d'aronde [kødarɔ̃d] *(pl* **queues-d'aronde)** NF *Menuis* dovetail; **assemblage à q.** dovetail(ed) joint

queue-de-cheval [kødʃəval] *(pl* **queues-de-cheval)** NF *(cheveux)* ponytail; **avoir une q.** to have a ponytail, to wear one's hair in a ponytail

queue-de-cochon [kødkɔʃɔ̃] *(pl* **queues-de-cochon)** NF **1** *(vrille)* auger **2** *(ornement)* wrought-iron twist

queue-de-morue [kødmɔry] *(pl* **queues-de-morue)** NF **1** *(habit)* tailcoat, *Fam* tails **2** *(brosse)* flat (paint) brush

queue-de-pie [kødpi] *(pl* **queues-de-pie)** NF tailcoat

queue-de-rat [kødra] *(pl* **queues-de-rat)** NF *Menuis* rat-tail file

queue-de-renard [kødrənar] *(pl* **queues-de-renard)** NF *Bot (amarante)* love-lies-bleeding; *(mélampyre)* cow-wheat; *(vulpin)* foxtail fescue

queuter [3] [køte] VI **1** *(au billard)* to hit through the ball **2** *très Fam (rater)* to screw up

VT *Vulg (forniquer avec)* to screw, to shaft

QUI [ki]

> En anglais, le pronom relatif objet peut être omis lorsque la préposition qui l'introduit est rejetée en fin de phrase, p. ex. **l'amie avec qui j'ai passé mes vacances** the friend (who) I spent my holiday with.

PRON RELATIF **1** *(représente une personne)* who, that; **il y a des gens q. aiment ça** there are people who like that; **toi q. connais le problème, tu pourras m'aider** you who *or* as you are acquainted with the problem, you can help me out; **c'est Pierre q. me l'a dit** Pierre told me, it was Pierre who told me

2 *(après une préposition)* whom, who; **la personne à q. je l'ai prêté** the person I lent it to *or Sout* to whom I lent it; **il ne peut résister à q. lui fait des compliments** he can't resist anyone who pays him compliments; **c'est à q. aura le dernier mot** each tries *or* they all try to have the last word; **c'était à q. crierait le plus fort** it was down to who could shout the loudest; **le collègue avec q. j'ai déjeuné** the colleague I had lunch with *or Sout* whom I had lunch with *or* with whom I had lunch; **les personnes au nom de q. ils ont agi** the people in whose name they acted; **l'homme en q. j'avais confiance** the man (whom) I trusted; **l'amie par q. j'ai eu cette adresse** the friend I got this address from *or Sout* from whom I got this address; **le couturier pour q. elle travaille** the designer she works for *or Sout* whom she works for *or* for whom she works; **c'est rebutant pour q. n'est pas habitué** it's disconcerting for somebody who isn't *or* for whoever isn't used to it; **la personne sans q. nous n'aurions jamais pu écrire ce livre** the person without whom this book would never have been written; **je ne sais plus sur q. compter** I don't know who *or Sout* whom to rely on any more; **à q. de droit…** to whom it may concern…

3 *(sans antécédent)* whoever, anyone (who); **vienne q. voudra** anyone who wants to can come; **emmenez q. vous voulez** take whoever you like with you; **faites-vous aider par q. vous voulez** get help from anyone *or* whoever you like; **q. tu sais, q. vous savez** you know who; **q. tu sais doit venir ce soir** you know who is coming tonight; **nous avons contacté q. vous savez** we contacted you know who *or Sout* whom; **c'est la responsabilité de q. vous savez** it's you know who's responsibility

4 *(représente un animal)* which, that; **les animaux q. parcourent la jungle** the animals which *or* that roam the jungle

5 *(représente une chose, une idée)* which, that; **le festival, q. débutera en mai** the festival, which will start in May; **donne-moi le magazine q. est sur la table** give me the magazine (that *or* which is) on the table; **elle veut une poupée q. marche** she wants a walking doll, she wants a doll that can walk; **l'année q. suivit son divorce** the year following *or* after his/her divorce; **la seule q. me plaise** the only one (that) I like

6 *(après des verbes de perception)* **je l'ai entendu q. se plaignait** I heard him moaning; **tu ne la vois pas q. descend?** can't you see her coming down?

7 *(formule de présentation)* **le voilà q. pleure, maintenant!** now he's crying!; **voilà q. ne m'aide pas beaucoup** that doesn't help me much; **voilà q. est bien** that is a good thing

8 *(en corrélation avec "que")* **q. que tu sois, q. que vous soyez** whoever you are *or Sout* you may be; **q. que ce soit** *(sujet)* whoever; *(objet)* anybody, anyone; **q. que ce soit téléphone, répondez que je suis absent** whoever phones, tell them I'm not here; **je défie q. que ce soit de faire mieux que je n'ai fait** I challenge anybody *or* anyone to improve on what I did

9 *(locutions)* **q. aime bien châtie bien** spare the rod and spoil the child; **q. a bu boira** a leopard never changes its spots; **q. ne dit mot consent** silence is consent; **q. sème le vent récolte la tempête** he who sows the wind shall reap the whirlwind; **q. vole un œuf vole un bœuf** he that will steal a penny will steal a pound

PRON INTERROGATIF **1** *(sujet ou attribut dans le dis-*

cours direct) who; **q. m'appelle?** who's calling (me)?; **q. sait?** who knows?; *Mil* **q. vive?, q. va là?** who goes there?; **q. suis-je?** who am I?; **q. est votre médecin?** who's your doctor?; **on me l'a donné – q. donc?** I was given it – by who? *or* who by? *or Sout* by whom?; **q. donc t'a frappé?** who hit you?; **q. est-ce q. en veut?** who wants some?; *Fam* **c'est q. qui** *ou* **qui c'est q. te l'a dit?** who told you?

2 *(objet dans le discours direct)* who, *Sout* whom; **q. cherchez-vous?** who are you looking for?; **c'est à q.?** whose is it?; **à q. le tour?** whose turn (is it)?; **à q. mens-tu?** who are you lying to?; **de q. parles-tu?** who *or Sout* whom are you talking about?; **chez q. dors-tu ce soir?** whose place are you staying at tonight?, who *or Sout* whom are you staying with tonight?; **vers q. me tourner?** to whom can I turn?, who *or* whom can I turn to?; **q. est-ce que tu connais ici?** who do you know around here?; **à q. est-ce que je dois de l'argent?** who do I owe money to?

3 *(sujet dans le discours indirect)* who; **je ne vois pas q. pourrait t'aider** I can't see who could *or* I can't think of anyone who could help you

4 *(objet dans le discours indirect)* who, *Sout* whom; **sais-tu q. j'ai rencontré ce matin?** do you know who I met this morning?; **je ne me souviens pas à q. je l'ai donné** I can't remember who I gave it to; **sais-tu à q. ça appartient?** do you know who it belongs to *or Sout* to whom it belongs?; **tu ne m'as pas dit pour q. tu travaillais** you haven't told me who you work/worked for

• **qui... qui** PRON INDÉFINI **ils étaient déguisés, q. en Pierrot, q. en bergère** they were in fancy dress, some as Pierrots, others as shepherdesses

quiche [kiʃ] NF quiche; **q. lorraine** quiche lorraine

quiconque [kikɔ̃k] PRON RELATIF INDÉFINI whoever, anyone *or* anybody who; **q. désobéira sera puni** whoever disobeys *or* anyone who *or* anybody who disobeys will be punished; *Bible* **q. frappera par l'épée périra par l'épée** he who lives by the sword shall die by the sword

PRON INDÉFINI anyone *or* anybody (else); **il connaît les volcans mieux que q.** he knows volcanoes better than anyone *or* anybody else

quid [kwid] PRON INTERROGATIF *Hum* **q. de...?** what about...?

quidam [kidam] NM *Hum* fellow, individual

qui est-ce que [kiɛskə], **qui est-ce qui** [kiɛski] *voir* **qui** PRON INTERROGATIF

quiet, -ète [kjɛ, kjɛt] ADJ *Littéraire* calm, tranquil

quiétisme [kjetism] NM quietism

quiétiste [kjetist] ADJ quietist

NMF quietist

quiétude [kjetyd] NF *Littéraire* **1** *(d'une demeure)* quiet, tranquillity, *Littéraire* quietude **2** *(d'esprit)* peace of mind; **elle attendait les résultats en toute q.** she was calmly waiting for the results

quignon [kiɲɔ̃] NM **q. (de pain)** *(morceau)* (crusty) chunk of bread; *(extrémité)* end crust (of the loaf)

quillard [kijar] NM *Fam Arg mil* = soldier about to be discharged or nearing the end of his national service

quille [kij] NF **1** *(jeu)* skittle, pin; **jouer aux quilles** to play ninepins *or* skittles

2 *Fam (jambe)* leg□, *esp Br* pin; **il ne tient pas sur ses quilles** he's shaky on his pins

3 *Fam Arg mil (fin du service)* discharge□, *Br* demob; *Fig* **vivement la q.!** I can't wait to get out of here!

4 *Naut* keel; **la q. en l'air** bottom up; **q. de roulis** bilge keel

quilleur, -euse [kijœr, -øz] NM,F *Can* bowler *(person)*

quillier [kije] NM set of skittles

quincaillerie [kɛ̃kajri] NF **1** *(articles, commerce)* hardware **2** *(boutique) Br* ironmonger's, *Am* hardware store **3** *Fam Péj (bijoux)* cheap costume jewellery□

quincaillier, -ère [kɛ̃kaje, -ɛr] NM,F hardware dealer, *Br* ironmonger

quinconce [kɛ̃kɔ̃s] NM quincunx; **en q.** arranged in a quincunx

quinine [kinin] NF *Pharm* quinine

quinqua [kɛ̃ka] *Fam (abrév* **quinquagénaire)** ADJ quinquagenarian□; **être q.** to be in one's fifties□

NMF person in his/her fifties□; **c'est un q.** he's in his fifties

quinquagénaire [kɛ̃kaʒenɛr] ADJ quinquagenarian; **être q.** to be in one's fifties

NMF person in his/her fifties, quinquagenarian; **un sémillant q.** a dashing fifty-year-old

Quinquagésime [kɛ̃kaʒezim] NF *Anciennement* Quinquagesima (Sunday)

quinquennal, -e, -aux, -ales [kɛ̃kenal, -o] ADJ *(plan)* five-year *(avant n)*; *(élection, foire)* five-yearly, quinquennial

quinquennat [kɛ̃kena] NM five-year period, quinquennium, lustrum

quinquet [kɛ̃kɛ] NM (Argand) oil lamp

• **quinquets** NMPL *Fam (yeux)* peepers, eyes□; **ouvrez/fermez les quinquets!** open/close your eyes!

quinquina [kɛ̃kina] NM **1** *Bot & Pharm* cinchona **2** *(boisson)* quinine tonic wine

quintal, -aux [kɛ̃tal, -o] NM (metric) quintal

quinte [kɛ̃t] NF **1** *Méd* **q. (de toux)** coughing fit, fit of coughing

2 *Mus* fifth; **q. juste** perfect fifth

3 *Cartes (gén)* quint; *(au poker)* straight; **q. flush** straight flush; **q. flush royale** royal flush

4 *Escrime* quinte

quintefeuille [kɛ̃tfœj] NF *Hér & Bot* cinquefoil

NM *Archit* cinquefoil

quintessence [kɛ̃tesɑ̃s] NF *Littéraire* quintessence; **la q. du romantisme** the epitome *or* quintessence *or* very essence of Romanticism

quintette [kɛ̃tɛt] NM quintet, quintette; **q. à cordes/vent** string/wind quintet

quinteux, -euse [kɛ̃tø, -øz] ADJ **1** *Méd (toux)* fitful **2** *Littéraire (acariâtre)* crotchety, testy **3** *(cheval)* restive

quintuple [kɛ̃typl] ADJ *(à cinq éléments)* quintuple, five-fold; **un q. meurtre** a quintuple murder

NM quintuple; **le q. (de)** *(quantité, prix)* five times as much (as); *(nombre)* five times as many (as); **vingt-cinq est le q. de cinq** twenty-five is five times five; **le q. de sa valeur** five times its value

quintupler [3] [kɛ̃typle] VI to increase fivefold, to quintuple; **la paix a fait q. le nombre des naissances** peace has multiplied the number of births by five

VT to increase fivefold, to quintuple

quintuplés, -ées [kɛ̃typle] NM,F PL quintuplets, *Br* quins, *Am* quints

quinzaine [kɛ̃zɛn] NF **1** *(durée)* **une q. (de jours)** two weeks, *Br* a fortnight; **venez me voir dans une q.** come and see me in a couple of weeks *or* in two weeks *or Br* in a fortnight's time

2 *(quantité)* **une q. de** about fifteen; **une q. de crayons** about fifteen pencils, fifteen pencils or so

3 *Com* **q. commerciale** two-week sale; *Cin* **Q. des réalisateurs** = competition forming part of the Cannes film festival which frequently gives awards to less mainstream films and less well-known directors

4 *(salaire)* two weeks' pay, *Br* a fortnight's pay

quinze [kɛ̃z] ADJ **1** *(gén)* fifteen; **q. jours** two weeks, a fortnight **2** *(dans des séries)* fifteenth; **page/numéro q.** page/number fifteen

PRON fifteen

NM INV **1** *(gén)* fifteen; **lundi en q.** two weeks from *or Br* a fortnight on Monday

2 *(numéro d'ordre)* number fifteen

3 *(chiffre écrit)* fifteen

4 *Sport* **le q. de France** the French Fifteen;

5 *Anciennement Pol & UE* **les Q.** = the fifteen member states of the European Union from 1995 to 2004 *voir aussi* **cinq**

quinzième [kɛ̃zjɛm] ADJ fifteenth

NMF **1** *(personne)* fifteenth **2** *(objet)* fifteenth (one)

NM **1** *(partie)* fifteenth **2** *(étage) Br* fifteenth floor, *Am* sixteenth floor **3** *(arrondissement de Paris)* fifteenth (arrondissement)

NF *Mus* fifteenth; *voir aussi* **cinquième**

quinzièmement [kɛ̃zjɛmmɑ̃] ADV in fifteenth place

quinzomadaire [kɛ̃zɔmadɛr] *FamJourn* ADJ bimonthly□, *Br* fortnightly□

NM *(gén)* bimonthly *or Br* fortnightly publication□

quiproquo [kiprɔko] NM *(sur l'identité d'une personne)* mistake; *(sur le sujet d'une conversation)* misunderstanding; **l'intrigue est fondée sur un q.** the plot revolves round a case of mistaken identity; **il y a q., nous ne parlons pas du même étudiant** there is a misunderstanding, we're not talking about the same student

quittance [kitɑ̃s] NF **q. de gaz/d'électricité** gas/electricity bill; **q. de loyer** rent receipt; **q. finale, q. libératoire** receipt in full; **q. pour solde** receipt in full; *Banque* **q. pour solde de tout compte** closing account balance

quittancer [16] [kitɑ̃se] VT to give a receipt for

quitte [kit] ADJ **1** *(libéré ▸ d'une dette, d'une obligation)* **être q. envers qn** to be even *or* quits *or* (all) square with sb; **être q. d'une dette** to be rid *or* clear of a debt; **donne-moi seulement 50 euros, tu es q. du reste** just give me 50 euros, let's not worry about the rest *or* I'll let you off the rest; **considérer** *ou* **estimer qn q. de** to consider sb to be rid *or* clear of; **vous êtes tenu q. de ce que vous me devez** consider your debt to me (to be) paid; **être q. envers la société** *(après une peine de prison)* to have paid one's debt to society; **je ne te tiens pas q. de ta promesse!** I don't consider that you have fulfilled your promise!

2 *(au même niveau)* **être quittes** to be quits *or* all square

3 en être q. pour qch *(s'en tirer avec quelque chose)* to get away with sth; **il en a été q. pour quelques égratignures/la peur** he got away with a few scratches/a bit of a fright

4 en être q. pour faire to have to do sth; **j'ai oublié mes papiers à la banque, j'en suis q. pour y retourner** I've left my papers at the bank, so I have to go back there now

5 q. ou double *(dans un jeu de hasard)* nothing *or Br* double or quits; *Fig* **c'est jouer à q. ou double** it's a big gamble *or* risk

6 *Belg* **être q. de qch** to be deprived of sth

• **quitte à** PRÉP **1** *(au risque de)* even if it means; **je lui dirai, q. à me faire renvoyer** I'll tell him/her, even if it means being fired **2** *(puisqu'il faut)* since it is necessary to; **q. à les inviter, autant le faire dans les règles** since we have to invite them, we may as well do things properly

QUITTER [3] [kite] VT **1** *(lieu)* to leave; *(ami, époux)* to leave, to split up with; *(emploi)* to leave, to quit, to give up; *(fonction, chambre d'hôtel)* to vacate; *(habitude)* to drop, to get rid of; **je quitte (le bureau) à 5 heures** I leave the office *or* I finish at 5 o'clock; *Naut* **q. le port** to leave port; **la voiture a quitté la route** the car came off *or* ran off *or* left the road; **il ne peut pas encore q. son lit** he can't leave his bed yet, he's still confined to bed; **elle ne quitte pratiquement pas son atelier** she hardly ever sets foot outside *or* leaves her workshop; **il faut que je te quitte** I must be going, I must go; **je ne te quitterai jamais** I'll never leave you; **il ne la quitta pas des yeux** *ou* **du regard** he never took his eyes off her, he watched her every move; **il suffit que je la quitte des yeux une seconde pour qu'elle fasse des bêtises** if I let her out of my sight *or* if I take my eyes off her for a second, she gets up to some mischief; **il a quitté les affaires/le théâtre** he retired from business/gave up the stage; **quel plaisir de tout q.!** how nice to get away from it all!; *Euph* **il nous a quittés hier** he passed away yesterday; *Euph* **elle a quitté ce monde** she has departed this world *or* this life

2 *(abandonner ▸ sujet: courage, force)* to leave, to desert, *Sout* to forsake; **son optimisme ne l'a jamais quitté** he remained optimistic throughout; **son bon sens semblait l'avoir quitté** he seemed to have taken leave of his senses; **c'est une idée qui ne me quitte pas** I can't get the idea out of my head

3 *(retirer ▸ habit)* to take off; **il ne quitte jamais son chapeau** he never takes his hat off, he always has his hat on; **tu vas adorer ce pull, tu ne le quitteras plus** you'll love this sweater, you won't want to take it off; **q. le deuil** to come out of mourning

4 *(au téléphone)* **ne quittez pas** hold on, hold the line

5 *Ordinat (base de données, programme)* to quit; **q. le système** to quit

VPR se quitter *(amis)* to part; *(amoureux)* to part, to break *or* to split up; **il est tard, nous devons nous q.** it's late, we have to say goodbye now; **depuis qu'ils se sont rencontrés, ils ne se quittent plus** ever since they met they have been inseparable

quitus [kitys] **NM** *Jur* (full) discharge, quietus; **donner q. à qn** to discharge sb

qui-vive [kiviv] **NM INV être sur le q.** *(soldat)* to be on the alert *or* the qui vive; *(animal)* to be on the alert; **je la sentais sur le q.** I felt she was on edge, I felt she was waiting for something to happen

QUOI [kwa] **PRON RELATIF** what, which; **c'est ce à q. je voulais en venir** that's what I was getting at; **c'est ce à q. je me suis intéressé** that's what I was interested in; **il a refusé, ce en q. il a eu raison** he refused, which was quite right of him; **on est allés au jardin, après q. il a fallu rentrer** we went to the garden, and then we had to come back in; **prends de q. boire/écrire/payer** get something to drink/to write/to pay with; **il y a de q. nourrir au moins dix personnes** there's enough to feed at least ten people; **il n'y a pas de q. se faire du souci** there's nothing to worry about; **il y a de q. être satisfait** there are good grounds for satisfaction; *Fam* **je suis en colère – il y a de q.!** I'm angry – it's no wonder! *or* with good reason!; **...sur q. il se lève et sort** ...whereupon he got up and left; **merci! – il n'y a pas de q.** thank you! – not at all *or* you're welcome *or* don't mention it

ADV INTERROGATIF 1 *(quelle chose)* what; **c'est q.?** what's that?; *Fam* **c'est q. ton nom?** what's your name?; *Fam* **tu fais q. ce soir?** what are you doing this evening?; **à q. penses-tu?** what are you thinking about?; **je me demande à q. ça sert/il pense** I wonder what it's for/what he's thinking about; **en q. puis-je vous être utile?** how can I help you?; **je voudrais parler au directeur – c'est pour q.?** I'd like to talk to the manager – what (is it) about?; **sur q. va-t-elle travailler?** what is she going to work on?; **elle ne sait plus q. lui dire** she doesn't know what to say to him/her any more; *Fam* **salut, alors q. de neuf?** hi, what have you been up to *or* what's new?; **q. de plus naturel?** what could be more natural?; **à q. bon?** what's the use?; **à q. bon l'attendre?** what's the use of waiting for him?; **q. encore?** what else?; *(ton irrité)* what is it now?

2 *Fam (pour faire répéter)* **q.?** what?; **q., qu'est-ce que tu dis?** what did you say?

3 *(emplois expressifs)* **eh bien q., qu'est-ce que tu as?** well, what's the matter with you?; **enfin q.,** *ou* **eh bien q., tu pourrais regarder où tu vas!** come on now, watch where you're going!; **de q.? tu n'es pas d'accord?** what's that, you don't agree?; **tu viens (oui) ou q.?** are you coming or not?; **décide-toi, q.!** well make up your mind!; **mais puisque je l'ai vue, q.!** but I saw her, I'm telling you!; **si je comprends bien, tu es fauché, q.!** if I've understood you, you're broke, aren't you?; **je vais lui acheter ce livre, pour lui faire un petit cadeau, q.** I'm going to buy him/her this book... you know, just as a little present

• **quoi que CONJ q. qu'il arrive** whatever happens; **q. qu'il en soit** be that as it may, however that may be; **q. qu'il dise** whatever he may say; **q. que vous en pensiez** whatever you may think of it; **je te défends de lui dire q. que ce soit!** I forbid you to tell him/her anything (whatsoever)!; **si je peux t'aider en q. que ce soit** if I can help you in any way

quoique [kwakə] **CONJ 1** *(bien que)* though, although; **quoiqu'il fût déjà minuit** though *or* although it was already midnight; **q. riche, il n'était guère généreux** although rich, he was hardly generous; **q. née en France, elle a passé sa vie en Angleterre** though *or* although born in France, she spent her life in England **2** *(introduisant une restriction)* **bien sûr 500 euros c'est cher, q. tu sais, ce n'est pas exagéré** of course 500 euros is a lot of money, although you know *or* but mind you it's not excessive; **je vous installerais bien dans cette chambre... q. vous seriez mieux dans celle qui donne sur la cour** I'd like to put you in this room... although you'd be better off in the one which overlooks the courtyard; **il a l'air compétent... q....** he seems competent... mind you...

quolibet [kɔlibɛ] **NM** gibe, jeer, taunt; **les enfants le poursuivaient de leurs quolibets** the children jeered at him *or* taunted him relentlessly

quorum [kwɔrɔm, kɔrɔm] **NM** quorum; **nous avons atteint le q.** we're quorate, we have a quorum

quota [kɔta] **NM** quota; **q. à l'exportation** *ou* **d'exportation** export quota; **q. à l'importation** *ou* **d'importation** import quota; **q. laitier** milk quota; *Can Fig* **avoir son q.** to be fed up

quote-part [kɔtpar] *(pl* **quotes-parts)** **NF** share; **q. des bénéfices** share in the profits

quotidien, -enne [kɔtidjɛ̃, -ɛn] **ADJ 1** *(de chaque jour* ▸ *entraînement, promenade, repas)* daily; *(*▸*préoccupations)* everyday; **leurs disputes étaient devenues presque quotidiennes** they'd got to the stage where they were arguing almost every day **2** *(routinier* ▸ *tâche)* run-of-the-mill, humdrum

NM daily (paper); **un grand q.** a (major) national daily; *Presse* **Le Q. de Paris** = daily Paris newspaper

• **au quotidien ADV** *Fam* on a day-to-day basis; **le cancer/le sida au q.** living with cancer/Aids (from day to day)

quotidiennement [kɔtidjɛnmɑ̃] **ADV** daily, every day

quotidienneté [kɔtidjɛnte] **NF** everyday nature; **la q. de leur existence** the routine of their everyday life

quotient [kɔsjɑ̃] **NM 1** *Math* quotient

2 *Psy* **q. intellectuel** intelligence quotient

3 *Jur* **q. électoral** electoral quota; **q. familial** dependants' allowance

4 *Physiol* **q. respiratoire** respiratory quotient

quotité [kɔtite] **NF 1** *Fin* quota; *Com* **q. imposable** taxable portion of income **2** *Jur* **q. disponible** disposable portion (of estate)

QWERTY [kwɛrti] **ADJ INV clavier Q.** Qwerty keyboard

r

R¹, r [ɛr] **NM INV** *(lettre)* R, r

R² [ɛr] *(abrév* **Renault***)* **une R19/21/25** a Renault 19/21/25

R³ *(abrév écrite* **rand***)* R

R., r. *(abrév écrite* **rue***)* St

> **PREFIX**
>
> **R-, RE-, RÉ-**
>
> • This prefix is often used to express REPETITION and as such it is very frequent.
>
> • When it is used with verbs it is mostly translated by using **again**, more rarely by using the prefix **re-**:
>
> **redire** to say again; **revoir** to see again; **redemander** to ask again; **remanger** to eat again; **repasser** to call again; **redonner** to give again (as in **redonne-moi ton numéro de téléphone**), **réélire** to re-elect; **relire** to reread; **réécrire** to rewrite
>
> • it can also be used with nouns:
>
> **réélection** re-election; **redéploiement** redeployment; **rediffusion** repeat
>
> In informal usage it is widely used, as in **rebonjour** (sometimes abbreviated to just **re**), meaning "hello again".
>
> It is also used in telegraphic style to indicate the repetition of an event:
>
> **le lendemain, re-pluie** the next day it rained again; **au retour, re-embouteillage** on the way back we were stuck in a traffic jam again; **pour le dîner, re-haricots** for dinner we had beans again.
>
> **Re-** can even be used more than once as a prefix:
>
> **on a crevé une fois à l'aller, on a recrevé au retour, et re-recrevé en allant au garage** we had a puncture on the way there, another one on the way back and yet another one when driving to the garage.
>
> • As in English, the prefix **re-** may signal a RETURN TO A PREVIOUS STATE that had been interrupted:
>
> **réarmer** to rearm; **rétablir** to re-establish; **reconstruire** to rebuild; **réchauffer** to reheat
>
> In other cases, English will use the adverb **back** instead of a prefix:
>
> **redescendre** to come back down; **revenir** to come back; **rallumer** to switch back on; **redonner** to give back (as in **redonne-moi le stylo que je t'ai prêté**).
>
> • Note that in many instances the prefix **re-** has lost its original meaning. Some words starting with **re-** have superseded the words they were derived from:
>
> **raffiner, refroidir, remplir.**
>
> Some words have different meanings depending on the meaning of the prefix **re-**. The verb **rechercher** is one of them:
>
> **la police recherche le prisonnier qui s'est évadé** the police are looking for the escaped prisoner; **il n'y a plus de lait, il faut que j'aille en rechercher** there's no milk left, I'll have to go and get some more

R&B [ɛrɛnbi] **NM** *Mus* R & B

rab [rab] *Fam* **NM** *(excédent)* leftovers◻, extra◻; **il y a du r. de poulet** there's some chicken left over; **qui veut du r.?** who wants seconds?; **faire du r.** *(au travail)* to put in a bit of overtime *or* a few extra hours; *(à l'armée)* to serve extra time; **j'ai eu deux heures de r. au lit** I had an extra two hours in bed
• **en rab ADJ il y a des patates en r.** there are some spuds left (over); **vous auriez pas un oreiller en r.?** do you have a spare pillow?◻

rabâchage [rabɑʃaʒ] **NM** *Fam* **son cours, c'est vraiment du r.** he's/she's always going over the same old things in class

rabâcher [3] [rabɑʃe] *Fam* **VT 1** *(conseils)* to keep (on) repeating◻; *(malheurs)* to keep harping on about; **tu n'arrêtes pas de r. la même chose** you're like a record that's got stuck, you do go on; **elle nous a rabâché qu'il fallait faire attention au verglas** she kept on at us about being careful of the ice; **des arguments rabâchés** the same old arguments; **le prof rabâche le même cours depuis dix ans** the teacher's been regurgitating *or* churning out the same old course for ten years **2** *(leçon)* to go over and over
VI to keep repeating oneself◻, to keep harping on

rabâcheur, -euse [rabɑʃœr, -øz] *Fam* **ADJ il est très r.** he's always repeating himself◻ *or* harping on about the same thing; **elle devient un peu rabâcheuse** she's starting to repeat herself◻
NM,F drone, bore

rabais [rabɛ] **NM** reduction, discount; **avec un r. de 15 pour cent, avec 15 pour cent de r.** with a 15 percent discount *or* reduction; **faire un r. de 10 pour cent sur le prix** to knock 10 percent off the price; **faire** *ou* **accorder un r. sur qch** to give a discount on sth; **il m'a fait un r. de 20 pour cent** he gave me 20 percent off *or* a 20 percent discount
• **au rabais ADJ** *(vente)* cut-price; *Péj (formation)* second-rate; *(travail)* underpaid **ADV acheter/vendre qch au r.** to buy/to sell sth at a reduced price *or* at a discount

rabaissement [rabɛsmɑ̃] **NM** *(de l'être humain)* debasement

rabaisser [4] [rabese] **VT 1** *(diminuer ▸ prétentions)* to moderate, to reduce; *(▸ niveau)* to lower; *(▸ orgueil)* to humble; *(▸ prix)* to reduce, to lower **2** *(dévaloriser ▸ mérites)* to devalue, to belittle; *(▸ personne)* to belittle, to run *or* to put down; **il prend un malin plaisir à la r. devant ses collègues** he takes a perverse pleasure in putting her down in front of his/her colleagues; **de tels actes rabaissent l'homme au niveau de l'animal** such actions reduce man to the level of an animal **3** *(voilette, jupe)* to pull (back) down
VPR se rabaisser 1 *(se dévaloriser)* to belittle oneself, to run *or* to put oneself down, to sell oneself short; **il est toujours en train de se r. devant ses collègues** he's always putting *or* running himself down in front of his colleagues **2** *(s'avilir)* to degrade oneself

rabane [raban] **NF** *(matière)* raffia fabric; *(tapis)* raffia mat

rabat [raba] *voir* **rabattre**
NM 1 *(d'un sac, d'une poche)* flap; *(de toge)* bands **2** *Chasse* beating, driving

rabat-joie [rabaʒwa] **ADJ INV ce qu'ils sont r.!** what a bunch of killjoys they are!
NMF INV killjoy, spoilsport

rabattable [rabatabl] **ADJ** *(siège)* folding

rabattage [rabataʒ] **NM** *Chasse* beating

rabatteur, -euse [rabatœr, -øz] **NM,F 1** *Chasse* beater **2** *Com* tout **3** *Pol* canvasser

rabattre [83] [rabatr] **VT 1** *(toit ouvrant, strapontin ▸ pour baisser)* to pull down; *(▸ pour lever)* to pull up; *(couvercle, siège des toilettes)* to close, to shut; *(chapeau)* to pull down; *(col, visière)* to turn down; **rabats le drap sur la couverture** fold the sheet back over the blanket; **rabattez le tissu avant de coudre** fold the material over before sewing; **les cheveux rabattus sur le front** hair brushed forward *or* down over the forehead; **une bourrasque rabattit le volet contre le mur** a gust of wind blew the shutter back against the wall; **le vent rabattait la pluie contre son visage** the wind was driving the rain against his/her face; **r. la balle** *(au tennis)* to smash the ball; **l'oiseau se posa et rabattit ses ailes** the bird landed and folded back its wings
2 *(ramener ▸ gibier)* to drive; **la police rabattait les manifestants vers ou sur la place** the police were driving the demonstrators (back) towards the square; *Fam* **r. des clients** *(racoler)* to tout for customers
3 *(déduire)* to take off, to deduct; **il a rabattu 5 pour cent sur le prix affiché** he took *or* knocked 5 percent off the marked price
4 *(diminuer)* **r. l'orgueil de qn** to humble sb; **en r.** *(modérer ses exigences)* to climb down, to lower one's sights
5 *Couture* to stitch down; **r. une couture** to fell a seam; **r. deux mailles** *(en tricot)* to decrease two stitches; **r. toutes les mailles** to cast off
6 *Hort* to cut (down), to prune away
VPR se rabattre 1 *(véhicule ▸ graduellement)* to move back into position; *(▸ brusquement)* to cut in; *(coureur)* to cut in *or* across; **le car s'est rabattu juste devant moi** the bus cut in just in front of me **2** *(se fermer ▸ volet)* to slam shut; *(▸ siège de voiture)* to fold down; *(▸ table)* to fold away **3 se r. sur** *(se contenter de)* to fall back on, to make do with; **il a dû se r. sur un emploi de veilleur de nuit** he had to make do with a night watchman's job

> Do not confuse with **rebattre**.

rabbin [rabɛ̃] **NM** rabbi; **grand r.** chief rabbi

rabbinique [rabinik] **ADJ** rabbinical, rabbinic

rabbinisme [rabinism] **NM** rabbinism

rabbiniste [rabinist] **NMF** rabbinist

rabelaisien, -enne [rablɛzjɛ̃, -ɛn] **ADJ** Rabelaisian

rabibochage [rabibɔʃaʒ] **NM** *Fam* patching up, repairing, mending; *Fig (entre amis)* making up, reconciliation

rabibocher [3] [rabibɔʃe] *Fam* **VT 1** *(réconcilier)* to patch things up between **2** *Vieilli (réparer)* to fix *or* to patch up
VPR se rabibocher to make up; **se r. avec qn** to patch things up with sb

rabiot [rabjo] = **rab**

rabioter [3] [rabjɔte] *Fam* **VT 1** *(obtenir en supplément)* to wangle; **elle a réussi à r. une semaine de congé de maladie** she managed to wangle a week's sick leave **2** *(s'octroyer)* **il m'a rabioté 5 euros sur la monnaie** he pocketed 5 euros when he gave me my change
VI to skimp; **ils rabiotent sur la nourriture** they skimp on the food

rabique [rabik] ADJ rabies *(avant n)*, rabic

rabistoquer [3] [rabistɔke] VT *Belg Fam (réparer)* to patch up; *(remonter le moral à)* to buck up

râble [rɑbl] NM *Zool* back, saddle; *Culin* **r. de lièvre** saddle of hare; *Fam* **tomber** *ou* **sauter sur le r. à qn** *(attaquer)* to lay into sb, to go for sb; *(critiquer)* to go for sb; *Fam* **je ne pouvais pas me douter de ce qui allait me tomber sur le r.** I didn't suspect what was waiting for me round the corner

râblé, -e [rɑble] ADJ **1** *(animal)* broad-backed **2** *(personne)* stocky

rabot [rabo] NM *Menuis* plane; **passer qch au r., donner un coup de r. à qch** to plane sth

rabotage [rabɔtaʒ], **rabotement** [rabɔtmɑ̃] NM planing (down)

raboter [3] [rabɔte] VT to plane (down)

raboteur [rabɔtœr] NM *(ouvrier)* planer

raboteux, -euse [rabɔtø, -øz] ADJ **1** *(sentier)* bumpy, rugged; *(plancher)* uneven, rough; *(bois)* knotty **2** *Littéraire (style)* rugged, unpolished, rough

• **raboteuse** NF *(outil)* planing machine, planer

rabougri, -e [rabugri] ADJ **1** *(plante)* shrivelled **2** *(personne)* shrivelled, wizened

rabougrir [32] [rabugrir] VT *(dessécher)* to shrivel (up); *(entraver la croissance de)* to stunt (the growth of)

VPR **se rabougrir 1** *(plante)* to shrivel (up) **2** *(personne)* to become wizened, to become shrivelled (with age)

rabouter [3] [rabute] VT *(tuyaux)* to join, to put end to end; *(cordes)* to tie together, to put end to end

rabrouer [6] [rabrue] VT to send packing; **se faire r. par qn** to feel the sharp end of sb's tongue

racaille [rakaj] NF **1** *Vieilli (populace)* rabble, riffraff **2** *Péj (voyous)* trash, *Br* yobs; **la r. de banlieue** *Br* ≃ council estate yobs, *Am* ≃ hoods from the projects **3** *Péj (voyou)* lout, *Br* yob

raccommodable [rakɔmɔdabl] ADJ mendable, repairable

raccommodage [rakɔmɔdaʒ] NM *(de linge, d'un filet)* mending, repairing; *(d'une chaussette)* darning, mending; **j'ai du r. à faire** I've got some mending to do

raccommodement [rakɔmɔdmɑ̃] NM *Fam* patching things up

raccommoder [3] [rakɔmɔde] VT **1** *(réparer ▸ linge, filet)* to repair, to mend; *(▸ chaussette)* to darn, to mend; **peux-tu r. mon pantalon/mes chaussettes?** can you mend my trousers/darn my socks? **2** *Fam (réconcilier)* to patch things up between; **je suis raccommodé avec elle** I've patched things up *or* made it up with her

VPR **se raccommoder** *Fam (se réconcilier)* to make it up, to patch things up (**avec** with)

raccommodeur, -euse [rakɔmɔdœr, -øz] NM,F mender

raccompagner [3] [rakɔ̃paɲe] VT **1** *(reconduire à la porte)* **r. qn** to show *or* to see sb out **2** *(accompagner)* **je vais te r. chez toi** *(à pied)* I'll walk *or* take you back home; *(en voiture)* I'll give you a *Br* lift *or Am* ride home, I'll drive *or* run you home; **tu me raccompagnes jusqu'au bout de la rue?** will you walk me *or* see me to the end of the street?; **r. qn à la gare/à l'aéroport** to see sb off at the station/airport; **fais-toi r.** get a *Br* lift *or Am* ride home

raccord [rakɔr] NM **1** *(en décoration)* join; **papier avec r.** wallpaper with pattern match; **compte 33 centimètres pour le r.** allow 33 centimetres for pattern match

2 *Cin (liaison de scènes)* continuity; *(plan)* link shot; **scène de r.** link scene; *Littérature* link

3 *(retouche)* touch-up; **la peinture de la cuisine a besoin de quelques raccords** the kitchen paintwork needs some touching up; *Fam* **elle s'est fait un petit r. devant la glace** she touched up her make-up in front of the mirror

4 *Tech (pour tuyaux différents)* adaptor; *(joint)* connector; **r. en T** T-union

raccordement [rakɔrdəmɑ̃] NM **1** *(opération de connexion) & Rail* linking, joining; *(travaux publics)* connecting, linking, joining; *Élec* joining, connecting; *Tél* **faire le r. (au réseau)** to connect the phone **2** *(voie ferrée)* junction **3** *Ordinat* link

raccorder [3] [rakɔrde] VT **1** *(route, chemin de fer)* to link up, to join up; **la ville nouvelle est raccordée à l'autoroute** the new town is linked up to the motorway *or* has a motorway link-up

2 *(morceaux cassés, papier peint)* to align, to join (up); *(bandes magnétiques)* to splice; **les motifs ne sont pas raccordés** the pattern doesn't line up

3 *Élec (au secteur)* to couple; *(à un circuit)* to join; **nous ne sommes toujours pas raccordés au réseau électrique** we still don't have mains electricity

4 *Tél* **r. qn au réseau** to connect (up) sb's phone

5 *Fig (indices, faits)* to link up, to connect

6 *Cin (scènes)* to link up

VPR **se raccorder 1 se r. à** *(route, voie ferrée)* to join up with **2 se r. à** *(être lié à)* to tie in with; **le dernier paragraphe ne se raccorde pas au reste** the last paragraph doesn't tie in with the rest **3** *Ordinat* **se r. à** to link up to

raccourci [rakursi] NM **1** *(trajet)* shortcut; **prendre un r.** to take a shortcut

2 *(énoncé)* **un r. saisissant** a pithy turn of phrase

3 *Beaux-Arts* foreshortening *(UNCOUNT)*

4 *Ordinat* **r. clavier** keyboard shortcut

• **en raccourci** ADV *(en résumé)* in brief, in a nutshell; *(en miniature)* on a small scale, in miniature

raccourcir [32] [rakursir] VT **1** *(vêtement, rideau)* to shorten, to take up; *(cheveux, barbe)* to trim; *(discours, texte, trajet, film)* to shorten; *(séjour)* to cut short; **j'ai raccourci la robe de 3 centimètres** I've shortened the dress by 3 centimetres, I've taken the dress up by 3 centimetres; **tu as trop raccourci les manches** you've made the sleeves too short; **le sentier raccourcit le trajet de deux kilomètres** the path shortens the trip by two kilometres; **elle a dû r. ses vacances d'une semaine** she had to come back from her holidays a week early **2** *Fam (décapiter)* **r. qn** to chop sb's head off

VI **1** *(en durée)* **les jours raccourcissent** the days are growing shorter *or* drawing in **2** *(en longueur)* **son tee-shirt a raccourci au lavage** his/her T-shirt has shrunk in the wash; **les manteaux vont r. à l'automne prochain** coats will be shorter next autumn **3** *(distance)* **ça raccourcit** it's shorter

VPR **se raccourcir** *(diminuer)* **les délais de livraison se sont considérablement raccourcis** delivery times have been considerably shortened *or* reduced

raccourcissement [rakursismɑ̃] NM *(des jours)* shortening, drawing in; *(d'un vêtement au lavage)* shrinking; *(des délais)* shortening, reducing; **on remarque un r. des jupes dans la collection automne-hiver** hemlines are higher in this year's autumn-winter collection

raccroc [rakro] **par raccroc** ADV by a stroke of good luck

raccrocher [3] [rakrɔʃe] VT **1** *(remettre en place ▸ habit, rideau)* to hang back up; *(▸ tableau)* to put back on the hook, to hang *or* to put back up; *(▸ téléphone)* to put down, to hang up; *Fam* **r. les gants** *(boxeur)* to hang up one's gloves; *Fam* **r. le client** *(prostituée)* to solicit[□], *Am* to hustle, to hook

2 *(relier ▸ wagons)* to couple, to hitch together; **la remorque a été mal raccrochée à la voiture** the trailer wasn't properly hitched up to the car; *Fig* **c'est la seule chose qui la raccroche à la vie** it's the only thing which keeps her going, it's her only lifeline

3 *(rattraper ▸ affaire)* to save at the last minute; **ils ont raccroché les négociations** they managed to rescue the negotiations at the last minute

4 *Fam (obtenir par chance ▸ commande)* to pull off, to bring off

VI **1** *(au téléphone)* to hang up, to put the receiver down; **elle m'a raccroché au nez** she hung up on me; **je n'ai pas envie de me faire r. au nez** I don't want to have the phone put down on me **2** *Fam (cesser une activité ▸ gén)* to pack it in, *Am* to hang it up; *(▸ boxeur)* to hang up one's gloves

VPR **se raccrocher 1 se r. à** *(se rattraper à)* to grab *or* to catch hold of; *Fig* **il n'a personne à qui se r.** he has nobody to turn to; *Fig* **il se raccrochait à cet espoir** he hung on to that hope **2 se r. à** *(être relié à)* to be linked *or* related to

race [ras] NF **1** *(d'un humain)* race; **la r. blanche/noire** the white/black race; **de r. blanche** white; **de r. noire** black; **il est de r. asiatique** he's of Asian origin

2 *(catégorie)* **il est de la r. des gens qui se plaignent tout le temps** he's one of those people who are always moaning; **elle est de la r. des gagnants** she's a born winner; *très Fam* **(quelle) sale r.!** (what) scum!

3 *(d'un animal)* breed; **la r. canine/féline/bovine/porcine** dogs/cats/cattle/pigs

4 *Littéraire (lignée)* line; **être de r. noble** to be of noble stock *or* blood

5 *(distinction)* **avoir de la r.** to have breeding

6 *très Fam* **ta r.!** *Br* piss off!, *Am* take a hike!; *Vulg* **enculé de ta r.!** you fucking prick!; *Vulg* **niquer sa r. à qn** to beat the shit out of sb

• **de race** ADJ *(chien, chat)* purebred, pedigree *(avant n)*; *(cheval)* thoroughbred; **avoir de la r.** *(chien, chat)* to be purebred; *(cheval)* to be a thoroughbred

racé, -e [rase] ADJ **1** *(chien, chat)* purebred, pedigree *(avant n)*; *(cheval)* thoroughbred **2** *(personne)* distinguished(-looking), tall and aristocratic-looking **3** *(voilier, voiture)* handsome

rachat [raʃa] NM **1** *(de ce qu'on avait vendu)* repurchase, buying back; *Jur* **avec faculté de r.** with option of repurchase

2 *Com (achat)* **nous vous proposons le r. de votre ancienne voiture!** we offer to take your old car as a trade-in *or Br* in part-exchange!

3 *Fin (d'actions, d'obligations)* buying up *or* in; *(d'une affaire)* takeover; *(d'une franchise, d'une rente)* redemption; *Bourse (d'actions)* buy-back, repurchase; *(de police d'assurance)* surrender; **r. d'entreprise financé par l'endettement** leveraged buy-out; **r. de l'entreprise par la direction** management buy-out; **r. d'entreprise par les salariés** staff *or* employee buy-out

4 *(de captifs)* **ils ont convenu du r. des captifs** they came to an agreement over the prisoners' ransom; **l'opposition a condamné le r. des otages** the opposition condemned the ransom being paid to free the hostages

5 *(des péchés)* redemption

rachetable [raʃtabl] ADJ **1** *Fam (remplaçable)* **un vase, c'est r.** a vase is replaceable **2** *Littéraire (dette, rente, péché)* redeemable

racheter [28] [raʃte] VT **1** *(en plus)* to buy some more (of); **rachète du pain** buy some more bread; **r. des actions** *(en supplément)* to buy some more shares; *(pour remplacer celles qu'on a vendues)* to buy back *or* to repurchase shares; **je vais r. un service à café** I'm going to buy another *or* a new coffee set

2 *(acheter ▸ gén)* to buy; *(▸ entreprise)* to take over; *Bourse (actions)* to repurchase, to buy back; **r. qch à qn** *(à un particulier)* to buy sth from sb; *Com* **on vous rachète vos anciens meubles** your old furniture taken *Br* in part-exchange *or Am* as a trade-in; *Fin* **j'ai racheté sa part/son affaire** I've bought him/her out (of the business)/bought him/her out

3 *(rente, cotisations, obligation)* to redeem

4 *(erreur, défaut)* to make up for, to compensate for; *(péché)* to atone for, *Sout* to expiate; *(vie dissolue)* to make amends for, to make up for; *(pécheur)* to redeem; **Jésus-Christ est mort pour r. les hommes** Christ died to redeem mankind; **il n'y en a pas un pour r. l'autre** one's as bad as the other; **l'humour ne rachète pas la lourdeur du style** the humour doesn't compensate for *or* make up for the clumsiness of the style

5 *Hist (soldat)* to buy out; *(prisonnier, esclave)* to ransom, to buy the freedom of

6 *Scol & Univ* **r. un candidat** to pass a candidate *(in spite of insufficient marks)*; **r. une (mauvaise) note** to make up for a (poor) grade

VPR **se racheter** *(gén)* to make amends, to redeem oneself; *(pécheur)* to redeem oneself; **que puis-je faire pour me r.?** what can I do to make up for it?, how can I redeem myself?; **ce n'est pas en m'offrant des fleurs que tu vas te r.!** it'll take more than flowers to bring me round!

racheteur [raʃtœr] NM purchaser

rachidien, -enne [raʃidjɛ̃, -ɛn] ADJ rachidian, rachidial

rachis [raʃis] NM *Anat, Bot & Orn* rachis; **r. cervical** cervical vertebrae; **r. lombaire** lumbar vertebrae

rachitique [raʃitik] ADJ **1** *Méd* suffering from rickets, *Spéc* rachitic **2** *(chétif ▸ plante)* stunted; *(▸ chien, personne)* puny, scrawny
NMF person suffering from rickets

rachitisme [raʃitism] NM *Méd* rickets *(singulier)*, *Spéc* rachitis

racho [raʃo] *Fam* ADJ *(personne, arbre)* weedy, scrawny; *(portion)* mean, stingy

racial, -e, -aux, -ales [rasjal, -o] ADJ racial, race *(avant n)*; **attiser la haine raciale** to stir up racial hatred; **émeute raciale** race riot

racine [rasin] NF **1** *Bot* root; **r. aérienne** aerial root; **r. pivotante** taproot; **racines alimentaires** root crops; **racines (comestibles)** root vegetables; **r. de gingembre** root ginger; **prendre r.** to take root; *Fam* **il prend r.** *(il s'installe)* he's getting a bit too comfortably settled[□]; *Fam* **tu vas prendre r.!** *(l'attente est longue)* you'll take root!
2 *Anat (d'un cheveu, d'un poil, d'une dent)* root; *(du nez)* base; *Fam* **se faire faire les racines** *(chez le coiffeur)* to have one's roots done
3 *Ling & Math* root; **r. carrée/cubique/énième** square/cube/nth root
4 *Ordinat* root directory
• **racines** NFPL *(origines)* roots; **elle a ses racines en Écosse** her roots are in Scotland; **je suis sans racines** I don't have any roots, I don't belong anywhere; **retrouver ses racines** to go back to one's roots; **cette croyance a ses racines dans le folklore breton** this belief is rooted in Breton folklore

raciner [3] [rasine] VT *(en reliure)* to tree-marble

racisme [rasism] NM racism, racial prejudice; **c'est du r. anti-vieux** that's ageism; **c'est du r. anti-jeunes** that's prejudice against young people

raciste [rasist] ADJ racist
NMF racist

racket [rakɛt] NM *(activité)* racketeering; *(contre protection)* (protection) racket; **la lutte contre le r. à l'école** the fight to stop schoolchildren being bullied into handing over their money or possessions

racketter [4] [rakete] VT to extort money from; **se faire r.** *(gén)* to be a victim of extortion; *(contre protection)* to pay protection money; **il est inadmissible que les enfants se fassent r. dans les écoles** it is unacceptable for schoolchildren to be bullied into handing over their money and possessions

racketteur, -euse [raketœr, -øz] NM,F racketeer

raclage [raklaʒ] NM scraping

raclée [rakle] NF *Fam* **1** *(coups)* thrashing, hiding; **flanquer une r. à qn** to give sb a good thrashing *or* hiding; **prendre** *ou* **recevoir une r.** to get a good thrashing *or* hiding **2** *(défaite)* thrashing, hammering; **mettre une r. à qn** to thrash sb; **il a pris une** *ou* **sa r. en finale** he got thrashed *or* hammered in the final

raclement [rakləmɑ̃] NM scraping (noise); **on entendit quelques raclements de gorge** some people could be heard clearing their throats

racler [3] [rakle] VT **1** *(frotter ▸ gén)* to scrape; *(▸ pour enlever)* to scrape off; **r. la semelle de ses souliers** to scrape the soles of one's shoes; **r. la peinture de la table** to scrape the paint off the table; **un petit vin blanc qui racle le gosier** a white wine that is rough on *or* that burns your throat; *Fig* **r. les fonds de tiroir** to scrape some money together **2** *Péj (instrument)* **r. du violon** to scrape away at the fiddle
VPR **se racler se r. la gorge** to clear one's throat

raclette [raklɛt] NF **1** *Culin (plat)* raclette, = Swiss speciality consisting of melted cheese prepared at the table using a special heater or grill, served with potatoes and cold meats; *(fromage)* raclette *(cheese)* **2** *(grattoir)* scraper **3** *(pour vitres)* squeegee

racloir [raklwar] NM **1** *Menuis* scraper plane **2** *Archéol* racloir, side scraper

raclure [raklyr] NF **1** *(résidu)* scraping **2** *très Fam (homme méprisable)* bastard, *Am* son-of-a-bitch; *(femme méprisable)* bitch

racolage [rakɔlaʒ] NM **1** *(par une prostituée)* soliciting; *(par un vendeur)* touting (for customers); *(par un militant)* canvassing; **faire du r.** *(prostituée)* to solicit; *(commerçant)* to tout (for customers); *(militant)* to canvass (support) **2** *Hist (de soldats)* press-ganging

racoler [3] [rakɔle] VT **1** *(clients ▸ sujet: prostituée)* to accost; *(▸ sujet: vendeur)* to tout for; *(électeurs)* to canvass **2** *Hist (soldat)* to press-gang
VI *(prostituée)* to solicit

racoleur, -euse [rakɔlœr, -øz] ADJ *(sourire)* enticing; *(affiche)* eye-catching; *(titre, journal)* sensationalist; *(campagne électorale)* vote-catching
NM,F *(politicien)* canvasser; *(commerçant)* tout
NM *Hist* crimp
• **racoleuse** NF *(prostituée)* prostitute *(soliciting on the street)*

racontable [rakɔ̃tabl] ADJ **ce n'est pas r. devant des enfants** I can't say it in front of children; **alors que s'est-il passé? – ce n'est pas r.!** so what happened? – it defies description!

racontar [rakɔ̃tar] NM *Fam* piece of gossip; **n'écoute pas les racontars** don't listen to gossip; **tout ça, c'est des racontars** that's just gossip *or* talk

raconter [3] [rakɔ̃te] VT **1** *(conte, histoire)* to tell; **la tapisserie de Bayeux raconte la conquête de l'Angleterre** the Bayeux tapestry tells (the story) of the conquest of England; **il a raconté l'histoire à son voisin** he told his neighbour the story, he told the story to his neighbour
2 *(événement, voyage)* to tell, to relate; **il a raconté l'accident à sa mère** he told his mother about the accident; **r. ses malheurs à qn** to tell sb all one's troubles, to pour one's heart out to sb; *Fam* **r. sa vie** to tell one's (whole) life story; *Fam* **nous raconte pas ta vie!** we don't want to hear your life story!
3 *(dire)* to tell; **ne crois pas tout ce qu'on raconte** don't believe everything people tell you; **on raconte beaucoup de choses sur lui** you hear all sorts of stories about him; **on m'avait raconté que vous étiez malade** I heard that you were ill; **on raconte qu'il a été marié plusieurs fois** people say he's been married several times; **à ce qu'on raconte, elle était la maîtresse du docteur** she was the doctor's mistress, at least that's what people say; **elle est allée tout lui r.** she went and told him/her everything; **mais enfin qu'est-ce que tu racontes?** what (on earth) are you on about?; **ne raconte pas de bêtises** don't be silly; **qu'est-ce que tu racontes (de beau)?** so, what's new?; *Fam* **je te raconte pas!** you can't imagine!; **on s'est pris une de ces cuites, je te raconte pas...** you can't imagine how plastered we got
USAGE ABSOLU **vite, raconte!** go on, *or* quick, tell me!; **r. bien/mal** to be a good/bad storyteller
VPR **se raconter 1** *(événement)* **des choses pareilles ne se racontent pas** such things are best left unsaid; **il faut l'avoir vécu, ça ne se raconte pas** I couldn't describe what it was like, you had to be there **2** *(parler de soi)* to talk about oneself **3** *Fam (à soi-même)* **se r. des histoires** to fool *or* to delude oneself[□]; **se la r.** to show off

raconteur, -euse [rakɔ̃tœr, -øz] NM,F storyteller

racornir [32] [rakɔrnir] VT **1** *(peau)* to toughen; *(cuir, parchemin)* to stiffen; *(cœur)* to harden **2** *(plante)* to shrivel up
VPR **se racornir 1** *(peau, viande)* to become tough; *(cuir, parchemin)* to stiffen, to become stiff **2** *(plante)* to shrivel up, to become shrivelled up **3** *(personne)* to become hardened *or* hardhearted

racornissement [rakɔrnismɑ̃] NM **1** *(de la peau)* toughening; *(du cuir, du parchemin)* stiffening; *(du cœur)* hardening **2** *(d'une plante)* shrivelling up

racrapoter [3] [rakrapɔte] **se racrapoter** VPR *Belg (confortablement)* to curl up; *(dans l'inconfort)* to huddle up; *Fig* to retreat into oneself

radar [radar] NM radar; **r. d'autoguidage** homing radar; **r. de navigation** navigation radar; **r. de veille** military surveillance radar; **écran/système r.** radar screen/system; **contrôle-r.** *(sur la route)* radar speed trap; *Fam* **marcher au r.** *(ne pas être bien réveillé)* to be on automatic pilot

radariste [radarist] NMF radar specialist *or* engineer

rade [rad] NF **1** *Naut (bassin)* (natural) harbour, *Spéc* roads, roadstead; **en r. de San Francisco** in San Francisco harbour; **mouiller en r. de Brest** to lie at anchor off Brest (harbour); **le navire a coulé en r. de Toulon** the ship sank off Toulon (harbour) **2** *Fam (locutions)* **laisser qn en r.** *(abandonner)* to leave sb stranded *or* in the lurch; **on est restés en r.** we were left stranded; **être en r.** *(en panne)* to have broken down[□] *or* conked out; **tomber en r.** *(en panne)* to break down[□], to conk out
NM *Fam (bar)* joint

radeau, -x [rado] NM raft; **r. de sauvetage** life raft; **r. pneumatique** inflatable raft

radial, -e, -aux, -ales [radjal, -o] ADJ *Math & Anat* radial
• **radiale** NF *(autoroute urbaine)* urban expressway *(leading out from the city centre)*

radian [radjɑ̃] NM radian

radiance [radjɑ̃s] NF *Vieilli* radiance

radiant, -e [radjɑ̃, -ɑ̃t] ADJ radiant
NM radiant

radiateur [radjatœr] NM *(à eau, d'un véhicule)* radiator; **r. à bain d'huile** oil-filled radiator; **r. à gaz** gas heater; **r. électrique** electric radiator *or* heater; **r. soufflant** fan heater

radiation [radjasjɔ̃] NF **1** *Biol & Phys* radiation **2** *(élimination ▸ d'un candidat, d'un médecin)* removal, striking off; *(▸ d'un avocat)* disbarment; *(▸ d'une dette)* cancellation; **ils ont demandé sa r. de l'ordre des médecins/du barreau** they asked that he/she should be struck off the medical register/that he/she should be disbarred from practising law

radical, -e, -aux, -ales [radikal, -o] ADJ **1** *(complet)* radical, drastic; **un changement r.** a drastic *or* radical change; **une réorganisation radicale** a thoroughgoing *or* root and branch reorganization
2 *(efficace)* **l'eucalyptus c'est r. contre le rhume** eucalyptus is just the thing for colds; *Fam* **il s'endort quand je mets la radio, c'est r.** he goes to sleep as soon as I put on the radio, it works like a dream
3 *Pol* radical
4 *Bot* radical, root *(avant n)*
5 *Ling* root *(avant n)*
NM,F *Pol* radical; **r. de gauche** member of the "Parti radical de gauche"
NM **1** *Ling* radical, stem **2** *Chim* radical; **radicaux libres** free radicals **3** *Math* radical (sign)

radicalement [radikalmɑ̃] ADV radically, completely; **r. faux** completely untrue; **il a r. changé** he's completely different, he's a different person

radicalisation [radikalizasjɔ̃] NF radicalization; **il est pour la r. des revendications** he wants the demands to be made more radical; **la r. du conflit** the heightening of the conflict

radicaliser [3] [radikalize] VT to radicalize, to make more radical
VPR **se radicaliser le mouvement étudiant s'est radicalisé** the student movement has become more radical

radicalisme [radikalism] NM radicalism

radical-socialisme [radikalsɔsjalism] *(pl* **radical-socialismes)** NM radical-socialism

radical-socialiste, radicale-socialiste [radikalsɔsjalist] *(mpl* **radicaux-socialistes** [radikososjalist], *fpl* **radicales-socialistes)** ADJ radical-socialist
NM,F radical-socialist

radicelle [radisɛl] NF rootlet, *Spéc* radicel

radicule [radikyl] NF radicle

radier[1] [radje] NM *Constr (dalle)* concrete slab; *(revêtement)* apron

radier[2] [9] [radje] VT *(éliminer ▸ candidat, médecin)* to strike off; *(▸ avocat)* to disbar; *(▸ dette)* to cancel; **elle a été radiée de l'ordre des médecins/du barreau** she was struck off the medical register/disbarred from practising law; *Bourse* **r. qch de la cote** *(société, actions)* to delist sth

radiesthésie [radjɛstezi] NF divination, divining

radiesthésiste [radjɛstezist] NMF diviner

radieux, -euse [radjø, -øz] ADJ *(matinée, temps)* glorious; *(soleil, beauté)* brilliant, radiant; *(vi-*

sage, personne) radiant, glowing (with happiness); **un sourire r.** a beaming smile

radin, -e [radɛ̃, -in] *Fam* **ADJ** tightfisted, stingy
NM,F skinflint, tightwad

radiner [3] [radine] **VI** *Fam (arriver)* to turn *or* to show *or* to roll up; **alors, tu radines?** are you coming then?
VPR se radiner *Fam* to turn *or* to show *or* to roll up; **allez, vite, radine-toi!** come on, get a move on!

radio [radjo] **NF 1** *(récepteur)* radio
2 *(diffusion)* **la r.** radio (broadcasting); **faire de la r.** to be *or* to work as a radio presenter; **à la r.** on the radio; **passer à la r.** *(personne)* to be on the radio; *(chanson)* to be played on the radio; *(jeu, concert)* to be broadcast (on the radio), *Am* to be radiocast
3 *(station)* radio station; **sur toutes les radios** on all stations; **écoutez r. TSW!** tune in to TSW!; **R. France** = state-owned radio broadcasting company; **R. France Internationale** = French overseas broadcasting service; **r. musicale** music station; **r. périphérique** = radio station broadcasting from outside national territory; **r. pirate** pirate radio station
4 *(radiotéléphonie)* radiotelephony
5 *Méd* X-ray (photograph); **passer une r.** *ou Fam* **à la r.** to have an X-ray (done), to be X-rayed; **faire une r. de qch** to X-ray sth
NM 1 *Vieilli (télégramme)* radio(gram) **2** *(opérateur)* radio operator
ADJ INV radio *(avant n)*; **message r.** radio message

radio(-)journal *(pl* **radio(-)journaux***)* **NM** *Rad* radio news, news bulletin

radioactif, -ive [radjɔaktif, -iv] **ADJ** radioactive

radioactivité [radjɔaktivite] **NF** radioactivity

radioalignement [radjɔaliɲmɑ̃] **NM** *(méthode)* radio navigation; *(dispositif)* radio direction finder

radioamateur [radjɔamatœr] **NM** radio ham

radioastronomie [radjɔastrɔnɔmi] **NF** radio astronomy

radiobalisage [radjɔbalizaʒ] **NM** radio beacon signalling

radiobalise [radjɔbaliz] **NF** radio beacon

radiocassette [radjɔkasɛt] **NM** radio cassette player

radiochimie [radjɔʃimi] **NF** radiochemistry

radiocommunication [radjɔkɔmynikasjɔ̃] **NF** radiocommunication

radiocompas [radjɔkɔ̃pa] **NM** radio compass

radioconducteur [radjɔkɔ̃dyktœr] **NM** *Phys* radioconductor

radiodermite [radjɔdɛrmit] **NF** *Méd* radiodermatitis

radiodiagnostic [radjɔdjagnɔstik] **NM** *Méd* X-ray diagnosis

radiodiffuser [3] [radjɔdifyze] **VT** to broadcast (on radio), *Am* to radiocast

radiodiffusion [radjɔdifyzjɔ̃] **NF** (radio) broadcasting

radioélectricien, -enne [radjɔelɛktrisjɛ̃, -ɛn] **NM,F** radio engineer

radiogénique [radjɔʒenik] **ADJ voix r.** good broadcasting voice; **elle est très r.** she's good radio material

radiogoniomètre [radjɔgɔnjɔmɛtr] **NM** (radio) direction finder, radiogoniometer

radiogoniométrie [radjɔgɔnjɔmetri] **NF** (radio) direction finding, radiogoniometry

radiogramme [radjɔgram] **NM** radiogram

radiographie [radjɔgrafi] **NF** *(technique)* radiography, X-ray photography; *(image)* X-ray

radiographier [9] [radjɔgrafje] **VT** to X-ray

radiographique [radjɔgrafik] **ADJ** *(technique)* radiographic; *(examen)* X-ray *(avant n)*

radioguidage [radjɔgidaʒ] **NM 1** *Aviat* radio direction finding, radio guidance; *(de missile)* homing **2** *Aut* traffic news

radioguidé, -e [radjɔgide] **ADJ** *(avion)* radio-controlled; *(projectile, missile)* guided

radiologie [radjɔlɔʒi] **NF** radiology

radiologique [radjɔlɔʒik] **ADJ** radiological; **examen r.** X-ray examination

radiologiste [radjɔlɔʒist], **radiologue** [radjɔlɔg] **NMF** radiologist

radiomètre [radjɔmɛtr] **NM** radiometer

radionavigant [radjɔnavigɑ̃] **NM** radio officer *or* operator

radionavigation [radjɔnavigasjɔ̃] **NF** radio navigation

radiophare [radjɔfar] **NM** radio beacon

radiophonie [radjɔfɔni] **NF** broadcasting, radiotelephony

radiophonique [radjɔfɔnik] **ADJ** *(émission, feuilleton)* radio *(avant n)*; *(studio)* broadcasting *(avant n)*

radiorepérage [radjɔrəperaʒ] **NM** radiolocation

radioreportage [radjɔrəpɔrtaʒ] **NM** *(émission)* (radio) report; *(commentaire)* (radio) commentary

radioreporter [radjɔrəpɔrtɛr] **NM** (radio) reporter *or* correspondent

radioréveil [radjɔrevɛj] **NM** radio alarm (clock)

radioscopie [radjɔskɔpi] **NF 1** *Méd* radioscopy **2** *(étude)* in-depth analysis

radioscopique [radjɔskɔpik] **ADJ** X-ray *(avant n)*

radiosondage [radjɔsɔ̃daʒ] **NM** radiosondage, radiosonde sounding

radiosonde [radjɔsɔ̃d] **NF** *Météo* radiosonde, radiometeorograph

radio-taxi [radjɔtaksi] *(pl* **radio-taxis***)* **NM** radio cab, radio-taxi

radiotechnique [radjɔtɛknik] **ADJ** radiotechnical
NF radiotechnics *(singulier)*, radio technology

radiotélégramme [radjɔtelegram] **NM** radiotelegram

radiotélégraphie [radjɔtelegrafi] **NF** radiotelegraphy, wireless telegraphy

radiotéléphone [radjɔtelefɔn] **NM** radiotelephone

radiotéléphonie [radjɔtelefɔni] **NF** radiotelephony, radiocommunication

radiotélescope [radjɔtelɛskɔp] **NM** radio telescope

radiotélévisé, -e [radjɔtelevize] **ADJ** broadcast simultaneously on radio and TV, simulcast

radiotélévision [radjɔtelevizjɔ̃] **NF** radio and television

radiothérapeute [radjɔterapøt] **NMF** radiotherapist

radiothérapie [radjɔterapi] **NF** radiotherapy

radis [radi] **NM 1** *Bot* radish; **r. noir** black radish **2** *Fam (sou)* **j'ai plus un r.** I haven't a bean *or Am* a red cent; **sans un r.** broke, *Br* skint

radium [radjɔm] **NM** *Chim* radium

radius [radjys] **NM** radius

radon [radɔ̃] **NM** *Chim* radon

radotage [radɔtaʒ] **NM** drivel

radoter [3] [radɔte] *Fam* **VI** *(se répéter)* to witter on; *(divaguer)* to ramble on; **excuse-moi si je radote, mais...** sorry to go on and on about it, but...; **là, il radote!** he's going soft in the head!
VT 1 *(raconter)* **qu'est-ce que tu radotes?** what are you drivelling *or Br* wittering on about? **2** *(répéter)* **il radote cent fois les mêmes histoires** he's always going on about the same old things

radoteur, -euse [radɔtœr, -øz] **NM,F** drivelling fool

radoub [radu] **NM 1** *(réparation)* repair, refitting; **le voilier est au r.** the yacht is being refitted **2** *(cale)* dry dock

radouber [3] [radube] **VT 1** *(bateau)* to repair, to refit **2** *(filet)* to mend

radoucir [32] [radusir] **VT 1** *(caractère)* to soften; *(personne)* to calm down, to mollify **2** *Météo* to make milder; **les chutes de neige ont radouci le temps** there's been a slight rise in temperature due to the snowfall
VPR se radoucir 1 *(voix)* to soften, to become gentler; *(personne)* to yield, to soften; **elle a fini par se r. devant leurs prières** her attitude softened *or* she relented in the face of their pleas **2** *(température)* to get milder; **le temps s'est radouci** the weather's milder

radoucissement [radusismɑ̃] **NM 1** *Météo* (slight) rise in temperature; **net r. des températures ce matin** a marked rise in temperature this morning **2** *(d'une personne)* softening

rafale [rafal] **NF 1** *Météo (de vent, de pluie* ▸ *gén)* gust; *(*▸ *en mer)* squall; *(de neige)* flurry; **le vent souffle en** *ou* **par rafales** it's blustery **2** *Mil* burst; **une r. de mitraillette** a burst of machine-gun fire **3** *Fig* burst; **par** *ou* **en rafales** intermittently

raffermir [32] [rafɛrmir] **VT 1** *(muscle, peau)* to tone *or* to firm up; *(chair)* to firm up, to make firm(er) **2** *(consolider)* to strengthen, to reinforce; **r. sa position** to consolidate one's position; **l'équipe gouvernementale est sortie raffermie du conflit** the government team came out of the conflict stronger
VPR se raffermir 1 *(muscle, peau)* to tone *or* to firm up; *(chair)* to firm up, to become firmer **2** *(se consolider)* to get stronger; **son autorité se raffermit** he/she is recovering *or* regaining his/her authority; **se r. dans ses intentions** to stiffen one's resolve **3** *Fin (monnaie, prix)* to strengthen

raffermissement [rafɛrmismɑ̃] **NM** *(de muscle, de la peau)* toning *or* firming up; *(de chair)* firming up; *(de la voix)* steadying; *(de l'autorité, du pouvoir)* strengthening, consolidation

raffinage [rafinaʒ] **NM** refining

raffiné, -e [rafine] **ADJ 1** *Ind* refined **2** *(élégant* ▸ *personne, style)* refined, sophisticated **3** *(*▸ *politesse)* extreme, exquisite; *(*▸ *goût)* refined, discriminating

raffinement [rafinmɑ̃] **NM 1** *(élégance* ▸ *d'une personne, d'un style)* refinement, sophistication
2 *(subtilité* ▸ *de la pensée)* subtlety; *(*▸ *du goût)* refinement
3 *(détail élégant)* subtlety, refinement
4 *(surenchère)* **avec un r. de cruauté** with exquisite *or* refined cruelty

raffiner [3] [rafine] **VT 1** *Ind* to refine **2** *(rendre plus délicat)* to polish, to refine
VI to be overparticular (**sur** about); **elle raffine beaucoup sur la toilette** she's overparticular about her appearance; **je n'ai pas eu le temps de r. sur les détails** I didn't have time to pay that much attention to the details

raffinerie [rafinri] **NF** refinery; **r. de pétrole/sucre** oil/sugar refinery

raffineur, -euse [rafinœr, -øz] **NM,F** *Pétr* refiner
NM (paper) refiner

raffoler [3] [rafɔle] **raffoler de VT IND** to be crazy *or* mad about; **il raffole de ses petits-enfants** he's mad about his grandchildren; **super, de la glace, j'en raffole!** ooh, ice cream, I LOVE ice cream!

raffut [rafy] **NM** *Fam* **1** *(bruit)* racket, din; **qu'est-ce que c'est que tout ce r.?** *(voix)* what's all this shouting about? **2** *(scandale)* **faire du r.** to cause a stink, to set tongues wagging

raffûter [3] [rafyte] **VT** *Sport* to hand off

rafistolage [rafistɔlaʒ] **NM** *Fam* patching up; **c'est le roi du r.** he's always making do; *Fig* **ces changements ne sont que du r.** these changes will do nothing more than patch things up, these are nothing more than cosmetic changes

rafistoler [3] [rafistɔle] **VT** *Fam* to patch up

rafle [rafl] **NF 1** *(arrestation)* raid; **une r. de police** a police raid; **la police a fait une r. dans le club** the police raided the club; *Hist* **la r. du Vel' d'Hiv** = the rounding up of Jews in the Paris Vélodrome d'Hiver in 1942 **2** *Fig* **il y a eu une r. sur le sucre en prévision de l'embargo** all the sugar available in the shops was snatched up in anticipation of the embargo; **les cambrioleurs ont fait une r. dans les bijouteries du quartier** the burglars made a clean sweep of *or* cleaned out all the *Br* jewellers' shops *or Am* jewelry stores in the area

rafler [3] [rafle] **VT** *Fam* **1** *(voler)* to swipe, *Br* to nick **2** *(saisir)* to grab; *Com* to buy up; **les clients ont tout raflé en moins de deux heures** the customers cleared the shelves in less than two hours; **les enfants ont tout raflé dans la cuisine** the children have made off with everything in the kitchen **3** *(remporter ▸ prix)* to walk off with; **le film a raflé toutes les récompenses** the film made a clean sweep of the awards

rafraîchir **[32]** [rafreʃir] **VT 1** *(refroidir)* to cool (down); **ces averses ont rafraîchi le temps** the weather's a bit cooler because of the showers; **un verre d'eau te rafraîchira** a glass of water will cool you down **2** *(remettre en état ▸ vêtement)* to smarten *or* to brighten up; *(▸ barbe)* to trim; *(▸ peintures, maquillage)* to freshen up; **à r.** *(logement)* needs some redecoration **3** *Fam Fig (raviver)* **r. la mémoire à qn** to refresh *or* to jog sb's memory; **je vais te r. les idées** *ou* **la mémoire, moi!** I'll refresh your memory for you!

USAGE ABSOLU je coupe ou je rafraîchis simplement? *(chez le coiffeur)* do you want me to cut it or just tidy it up *or* give it a trim?

VI 1 *Météo* to get cooler *or* colder; **le temps rafraîchit** it's getting colder **2** *Culin* to chill; **mettre qch à r.** to chill sth **3** *Ordinat* to refresh

VPR se rafraîchir 1 *(se refroidir)* to get colder **2** *(faire sa toilette)* to freshen up **3** *(boire)* to have a cool drink

rafraîchissant, -e [rafreʃisɑ̃, -ɑ̃t] **ADJ 1** *(froid)* cool, refreshing; *(tonique)* refreshing, invigorating; **une boisson rafraîchissante** a refreshing drink **2** *(charmant)* refreshing; **d'une simplicité/spontanéité rafraîchissante** refreshingly simple/spontaneous

rafraîchissement [rafreʃismɑ̃] **NM 1** *(refroidissement)* cooling; **net r. des températures sur tout le pays** temperatures are noticeably cooler throughout the country **2** *(boisson)* cool *or* cold drink **3** *Ordinat* refresh

raft [raft], **rafting** [raftiŋ] **NM** white-water rafting

raga [raga] **NM INV** *Mus* raga

ragaillardir **[32]** [ragajardir] **VT** to buck *or* to perk up; **ragaillardi par une nuit de sommeil** refreshed *or* reinvigorated after a good night's sleep

rage [raʒ] **NF 1** *Méd & Vét* **la r.** rabies; **r. de dents** (severe) toothache

2 *(colère ▸ d'adulte)* rage, fury; *(▸ d'enfant)* tantrum; **être fou de r.** to be absolutely furious; **mettre qn en r.** to infuriate sb; **elle est repartie la r. au cœur** she went off boiling *or* seething with rage; **j'ai accepté, mais la r. au cœur** I accepted, but actually I was furious about it

3 *(passion)* passion, mania (**de** for); **ils ont la r. du jeu** they're mad on gambling; **avoir la r. de vivre** to have an insatiable lust for life; **avoir la r. d'apprendre** to have a passionate desire to learn **4** *(locution)* **faire r.** *(incendie, ouragan)* to rage; *(mode)* to be all the rage

rageant, -e [raʒɑ̃, -ɑ̃t] **ADJ** *Fam* infuriating□

rager **[17]** [raʒe] **VI** to fume, to be furious; **je rage de la voir se pavaner** it makes me mad *or* it infuriates me to see her strutting about; **ça (vous) fait r.!** it's absolutely infuriating!; **ça me fait r. de voir tout cet argent dépensé pour rien** it makes my blood boil to see all that money just wasted

rageur, -euse [raʒœr, -øz] **ADJ 1** *(irrité ▸ ton)* angry, enraged; *(▸ geste, réponse)* bad-tempered, angry; **...dit-elle d'un ton r.** ...she said furiously; **"va au diable!" dit-il, r.** "go to hell!" he said furiously **2** *(coléreux)* hot-tempered

rageusement [raʒøzmɑ̃] **ADV** furiously, angrily

raglan [raglɑ̃] **ADJ INV** raglan; **des manches r.** raglan sleeves

NM raglan coat

ragondin [ragɔ̃dɛ̃] **NM 1** *Zool* coypu **2** *(fourrure)* nutria

ragot[1] [rago] **NM** piece of gossip; **des ragots** gossip

ragot[2], **-e** [rago, -ɔt] *Chasse & Zool* **ADJ F laie ragote** sow in its third year

NM boar in its third year

ragoût [ragu] **NM** stew, ragout

• **en ragoût ADJ** stewed; **faire qch en r.** to stew sth

ragoûtant, -e [ragutɑ̃, -ɑ̃t] **ADJ peu r.** *(mets)* unappetizing; *(personne)* unsavoury; *(lieu)* insalubrious

ragréer **[15]** [ragree] **VT** *Constr* to finish off

ragtime [ragtajm] **NM** *Mus* ragtime

rahat-loukoum [raatlukum] *(pl* **rahat-loukoums**), **rahat-lokoum** [raatlɔkum] *(pl* **rahat-lokoums**) **NM** piece of Turkish delight; **des rahat-loukoums** Turkish delight

rai [rɛ] **NM** *Littéraire (rayon)* **un r. de lumière** a shaft of light

raï [raj] **NM** *Mus* rai *(mixture of North African and Western music)*

raid [rɛd] **NM 1** *Mil* raid, surprise attack; **r. aérien** air raid **2** *Sport (avec des véhicules)* long-distance rally; *(à pied)* trek **3** *Bourse* raid; **lancer un r. contre** *ou* **sur** to mount a raid on

raide [rɛd] **ADJ 1** *(rigide ▸ baguette, étoffe)* stiff, rigid; *(tendu ▸ fil, ficelle)* taut, tight; *(droit)* straight; **avoir une jambe r.** to have a stiff leg; **assis tout r. sur un tabouret/dans son lit** sitting stiffly on a stool/bolt upright in his bed; **avoir les cheveux raides (comme des baguettes de tambour)** to have (poker-)straight hair; **se tenir r. comme un piquet** to stand as stiff as a pole *or* a poker

2 *(guindé ▸ personne, démarche)* stiff; *(▸ style, jeu de scène)* wooden; *(inébranlable ▸ personne, comportement)* rigid, inflexible; *Littéraire* **être r. comme la justice** to be totally unbending *or* inflexible

3 *(abrupt)* steep; **la côte est (en pente) r.** the hill climbs steeply; **la descente est en pente r.** *(piste de ski)* the slope is very steep; *(route)* the way down is very steep

4 *Fam (fort ▸ alcool)* rough

5 *Fam (osé ▸ détail, récit, scène)* risqué□; **le vieux canapé a dû en voir de raides** the old sofa has seen a thing or two

6 *Fam (surprenant)* **elle est r., celle-là!** that's a bit far-fetched *or* hard to swallow!; **elle m'en a dit de raides sur toi** *(méchancetés)* she told me some pretty nasty things about you

7 *Fam (désargenté)* broke, *Br* skint; **être r. comme un passe-lacet** to be flat broke *or* cleaned out

8 *Fam (drogué)* stoned, wasted; *(ivre)* plastered, *Br* legless

ADV 1 *(à pic)* steeply; **ça descend/monte r. derrière** the ground slopes steeply downwards/upwards **2** *Fam (en intensif)* **tomber r.** to fall to the ground; **r. mort** dead as a doornail, *Br* stone dead

raider [rɛdœr] **NM** raider

raideur [rɛdœr] **NF 1** *(d'une étoffe, d'une attitude)* stiffness; *(d'une baguette)* stiffness, rigidity; *(d'une corde)* tautness; *(des cheveux)* straightness; *(d'un style, d'un jeu de scène)* woodenness; *(du caractère)* inflexibility, rigidity; **elle répondit avec r.** she answered stiffly **2** *(d'un muscle)* stiffness; **avoir une r. dans l'épaule** to have a stiff shoulder **3** *(d'un sentier, d'une pente)* steepness

raidillon [rɛdijɔ̃] **NM** steep path *or* climb

raidir **[32]** [redir] **VT 1** *(tendre ▸ corde, câble)* to tighten, to pull tight *or* taut; **r. les bras/jambes** to brace one's arms/legs **2** *(faire perdre sa souplesse à ▸ tissu)* to stiffen

VPR se raidir 1 *(perdre sa souplesse)* to stiffen, to go stiff, to become stiffer **2** *(se tendre ▸ muscle, corps)* to tense (up), to stiffen; *(▸ cordage)* to tighten, to grow taut **3** *(rassembler sa volonté)* to steel *or* to brace oneself; **se r. contre l'adversité** to stand firm in the face of adversity

raidissement [redismɑ̃] **NM 1** *(physique)* tensing, stiffening **2** *(moral)* **face au r. des patrons** faced with the tougher line taken by the employers

raidisseur [redisœr] **NM 1** *(tendeur)* stretcher **2** *Aviat* stiffener, stringer **3** *Constr & Naut* stringer

raie [rɛ] *voir* **rayer**

NF 1 *(trait)* line; *(rayure)* stripe; *(griffure)* scratch, mark

2 *(dans les cheveux)* *Br* parting, *Am* part; **une r. sur le côté** a side *Br* parting *or Am* part; **se coiffer avec la r. à gauche/droite** to part one's hair on the left/right; **je ne porte pas de r.** I don't have a *Br* parting *or Am* part

3 *Anat* slit; **r. des fesses** cleft of the buttocks

4 *Agr* furrow

5 *Opt & Phys* line

6 *Ich* ray, skate; *Culin* skate

raifort [rɛfɔr] **NM** *Bot* horseradish; **sauce au r.** horseradish sauce

rail [raj] **NM 1** *(barre d'acier)* rail; **les rails** *(la voie)* the tracks, the rails; **poser des rails** to lay track; **sortir des rails** to leave the rails, to go *or* to come off the rails; *Fig* **remettre qn/qch sur les rails** to put sb/sth back on the rails; **elle a remis l'entreprise sur ses** *ou* **les rails** she put *or* set the firm (back) on the rails again

2 *(moyen de transport)* **le r.** rail; **transport par r.** rail transport

3 *(glissière)* track; **r. de sécurité** *(sur la route)* crash barrier

4 *Naut* shipping lane

5 *Fam Arg drogue (de cocaïne)* line; **se faire un r.** to do a line

railler **[3]** [raje] *Littéraire* **VT** to mock, to laugh *or* to scoff at; **il en a eu assez de se faire r. par tout le monde** he was fed up with everyone laughing at him

VI to jest

VPR se railler se r. de qn/qch to scoff at sb/sth

raillerie [rajri] **NF 1** *(attitude)* mocking, *Littéraire* raillery; *Vieilli* **il n'entend pas r. sur les choses religieuses** he will not have jokes made about religion **2** *(remarque)* jibe; **il décida d'ignorer leurs railleries** he decided to ignore their scoffing

railleur, -euse [rajœr, -øz] **ADJ** mocking, scoffing

NM,F mocker, scoffer; **faire taire les railleurs** to silence the scoffers

rainer **[4]** [rene] **VT** to groove

rainette[1] [renɛt] **NF** *Zool (grenouille)* tree frog

rainette[2] [renɛt] **NF** *Menuis* tracing iron

rainure [renyr] **NF 1** *(sillon)* groove; *(guide)* channel, slot; **les rainures du parquet** the gaps between the floorboards; **à rainures** grooved **2** *Anat* groove

rainurer **[3]** [renyre] **VT** to (cut a) groove (in)

raiponce [rɛpɔ̃s] **NF** *Bot* rampion

raisin [rɛzɛ̃] **NM 1** *(en grappes)* grapes; **acheter du r.** to buy grapes; **r. blanc/noir** white/black grapes; **r. de cuve/table** wine/eating grapes **2** *Culin* **raisins de Corinthe** currants; **raisins secs** raisins; **raisins de Smyrne** *Br* sultanas, *Am* golden raisins **3** *Bot* **r. de renard** herb Paris; **r. d'ours** bearberry

> Il faut noter que le terme anglais **raisin** est un faux ami. Il signifie **raisin sec**.

raisiné [rezine] **NM 1** *(confiture)* = fruit preserved in grape jelly **2** *Fam Arg crime (sang)* blood□, *Br* claret

raisinet [rezine] **NM** *Suisse* redcurrant

raison [rɛzɔ̃] **NF 1** *(motif)* reason; **il n'y a aucune r. pour que vous partiez** there's no reason for you to leave; **y a-t-il une r. de s'inquiéter?** is there any reason to worry?; **quelle est la r. de...?** what's the reason for...?; **la r. pour laquelle je vous écris** the reason (why *or* that) I'm writing to you; **la r. en est que...** the reason is (that)..., it's because...; **pour quelle r.?** why?; **pour des raisons familiales/personnelles** for family/personal reasons; **pour raisons de santé** for reasons of ill-health, for health reasons; **avoir de bonnes raisons** *ou* **des raisons (de faire qch)** to have good reasons (for doing sth); **avoir ses raisons** to have one's reasons; **avec r.** with good reason; **sans r.** for no reason (at all); **pour une r. ou pour une autre** for one reason or another; **pour la (bonne et) simple r. que** for the simple reason that; **elle n'est pas venue, pour la (bonne et) simple r. qu'elle était malade** the reason she didn't come was simply that she was ill; **ce n'est pas une r.!** that's no excuse!; **ce n'est pas une r. pour vous fâcher** that's no reason for you to get angry; **r. de vivre** reason to live; **cet enfant c'est sa r. de vivre** he/she lives for that child; **à plus forte r.** all the more so; **mais je suis malade! – r. de plus!** but I'm not feeling well! – all the more reason!; **r. de plus pour le faire** that's one more reason for doing so; *Fam* **qu'elle se débrouille toute seule, y a pas de r.!** there's no reason why she shouldn't sort it out for herself!; **se rendre aux raisons de qn** to yield to sb's arguments

2 *(lucidité)* **il n'a pas/plus toute sa r.** he's not/he's no longer in his right mind; **il n'a plus toute sa r. depuis la catastrophe** the disaster affected his mind; **perdre la r.** to lose one's mind; **recouvrer la r.** to recover one's faculties

3 *(bon sens)* reason; **agir contre toute r.** to behave quite unreasonably; **faire entendre r. à qn, ramener qn à la r.** to make sb see reason; **rappeler qn à la r.** to bring sb to his/her senses; **revenir à la r.** to come to one's senses; **plus que de r.** to excess, more than is reasonable; **elle boit plus que de r.** she drinks to excess *or* more than is good for her; **il faut r. garder** one must keep one's head

4 *(faculté de penser)* reason; **l'homme est un être doué de r.** man is a thinking being

5 *Math* proportion; **en r. inverse/directe (de)** in inverse/direct proportion (to)

6 *(locutions)* **avoir r.** to be right; **avoir (bien) r. de faire qch** to be (quite) right to do *or* justified in doing sth; **donner r. à qn** *(personne)* to agree that sb is right; *(événement)* to prove sb right; **se faire une r.** to resign oneself; **fais-toi une r., c'est trop tard** you'll just have to put up with *or* to accept the fact that it's too late; **avoir r. de qn/qch** to get the better of sb/sth, to overcome sb/sth; **le traitement a finalement eu r. de son eczéma** the treatment finally cured his/her eczema; **demander r. à qn (de)** to demand satisfaction from sb (for); *Prov* **la r. du plus fort est toujours la meilleure** might is right

• **à raison de** PRÉP at the rate of

• **comme de raison** ADV and rightly so

• **en raison de** PRÉP on account of, because of

• **raison commerciale** NF trademark

• **raison d'État** NF reasons of State, raison d'état

• **raison d'être** NF raison d'être; **sa présence n'a plus aucune r. d'être** there's no longer any reason for him/her to be here

• **raison sociale** NF corporate *or* company name

raisonnable [rɛzɔnabl] ADJ **1** *(sensé ▸ personne, solution, décision)* sensible; **sois r.!** be reasonable!; **tu n'es (vraiment) pas r. de boire autant** it's not sensible to drink so much; **ce n'est pas r. d'imposer une semaine de soixante heures à ses employés** it's unreasonable to expect one's employees to work a sixty-hour week; **je sais, je devrais être plus r.** I know, I should be more careful *or* sensible; **il devrait/tu devrais être plus r.** he/you should know better; *Hum* **est-ce bien r.?** is that wise?

2 *(normal, naturel)* reasonable; **il est r. de penser que...** it's reasonable to think that...

3 *(acceptable ▸ prix, heure, conditions)* reasonable; *(▸ salaire)* decent; **leurs exigences restent très raisonnables** they're very moderate in their demands

4 *(doué de raison)* rational

raisonnablement [rɛzɔnabləmɑ̃] ADV **1** *(de manière sensée)* sensibly, properly; **quand donc te conduiras-tu r.?** when are you going to behave sensibly *or* properly? **2** *(normalement)* reasonably; **elle peut r. espérer une augmentation** she can reasonably expect a pay rise **3** *(modérément)* in moderation; **vous pouvez boire, mais r.** you may drink, but in moderation

raisonné, -e [rɛzɔne] ADJ **1** *(analyse, projet, décision)* reasoned; **voilà qui est bien r.!** well worked out! **2** *(grammaire, méthode)* structured

raisonnement [rɛzɔnmɑ̃] NM **1** *(faculté, réflexion)* **le r.** reasoning; **r. par l'absurde** reductio ad absurdum **2** *(argumentation)* reasoning; **mon r. est le suivant** my reasoning is as follows; **son r. est assez convaincant** his/her arguments are quite convincing; **il ne faudra pas tenir ce r. avec lui** we mustn't use that argument with him; **ce n'est pas un r.!** you're wrong to think like that!

raisonner [3] [rɛzɔne] VI **1** *(penser)* to think; **r. avant d'agir** to think before doing something **2** *(enchaîner des arguments)* **non, là vous raisonnez mal!** no, your reasoning isn't sound there!; **r. par analogie** to use analogy as the basis of one's argument; **r. par induction/déduction** to use inductive/deductive reasoning **3** *(discuter)* **r. avec lui, c'est perdre son temps** it's a waste of time trying to reason with him

VT **1** *(faire appel à la raison de)* to reason with; **j'ai essayé de le r., rien à faire** I tried to reason with him *or* to make him see reason, but it was no use; **il faut absolument la r.** she must be made to see reason *or* sense **2** *(examiner)* to think out *or* through; **r. ses choix** to make reasoned choices

VPR **se raisonner 1** *(emploi réfléchi)* **raisonne-toi, essaie de manger moins** be reasonable and try not to eat so much **2** *(emploi passif)* **la passion ne se raisonne pas** there's no reasoning with passion, passion knows no reason

raisonneur, -euse [rɛzɔnœr, -øz] ADJ **1** *(discutailleur)* argumentative **2** *(qui pense)* reasoning, rational

NM,F **1** *(discutailleur)* arguer, quibbler **2** *(penseur)* reasoner

raja(h) [raʒa] NM rajah

rajeunir [32] [raʒœnir] VI **1** *(redevenir jeune)* to grow young again; **elle voudrait r.** she'd like to be younger; **je ne rajeunis pas** I'm not getting any younger **2** *(paraître plus jeune)* to look *or* to seem younger; **je le trouve rajeuni** he looks younger to me; **il a rajeuni de plusieurs années depuis son mariage** he looks years younger since he got married **3** *(retrouver de l'éclat ▸ façade)* to look like new

VT **1** *(rendre jeune)* **r. qn** to rejuvenate sb, to make sb younger; *Fig* to make sb look younger; **cette coiffure/robe la rajeunit** that hairstyle/dress makes her look younger; **il a perdu des kilos, ça le rajeunit** he's lost weight, it takes years off him; **r. le personnel d'une société** to bring new blood into a company

2 *(attribuer un âge moins avancé à)* **très aimable à vous, mais vous me rajeunissez!** that's very kind of you but you're making me younger than I am!; **vous me rajeunissez de cinq ans** I'm five years older than you said

3 *(faire se sentir plus jeune)* **ça me rajeunit!** it makes me feel younger!; **ça ne nous rajeunit pas!** it makes you realize how old we are!, it makes you feel your age!

4 *(moderniser ▸ mobilier, équipement)* to modernize; *(▸ robe, veste)* to update

VPR **se rajeunir 1** *(se faire paraître plus jeune)* to make oneself look younger **2** *(se dire plus jeune)* to lie about one's age, to make oneself out to be younger than one is; **elle se rajeunit de cinq ans** she claims to be five years younger than she really is

rajeunissant, -e [raʒœnisɑ̃, -ɑ̃t] ADJ rejuvenating

rajeunissement [raʒœnismɑ̃] NM **1** *Biol & Physiol* rejuvenation; **elle a fait une cure de r.** she went to a health farm **2** *(modernisation ▸ d'un équipement, d'une entreprise)* modernization **3** *(abaissement de l'âge)* **le r. de la population** the decreasing average age of the population; **il y a aujourd'hui un net r. des amateurs de musique classique** there has been a marked drop in the average age of classical music lovers

rajout [raʒu] NM **1** addition; **faire des rajouts à qch** to make additions to sth, to add things to sth **2** *(pour les cheveux)* **rajouts** extensions

rajouter [3] [raʒute] VT **1** *(ajouter)* to add (à to) **2** *(dire en plus)* to add (à to); **je n'ai rien à r.** I have nothing to add, I have nothing more to say; **r. que...** to add that... **3** *Fam (locution)* **en r.** to lay it on a bit thick; **je t'en prie, n'en rajoute pas!** oh, for God's sake, give it a rest!

rajustement [raʒystəmɑ̃] NM adjustment

rajuster [3] [raʒyste] VT **1** *(prix, salaires, vêtements)* to adjust; *(chignon)* to fix, to tidy **2** *(rectifier)* **r. le tir** to adjust *or* to correct one's aim

VPR **se rajuster** to tidy oneself up

râle [rɑl] NM **1** *(respiration)* rattle; **r. (d'agonie)** death rattle **2** *Méd* rale **3** *Orn* rail; **r. d'eau** water rail; **r. des genêts** corncrake

ralenti, -e [ralɑ̃ti] ADJ **depuis son infarctus, il mène une vie ralentie** since his coronary, he's been taking things easy

NM **1** *Cin* slow motion **2** *Aut & Tech* idling speed; **régler le r.** to adjust the idling speed

• **au ralenti** ADV **1** *Cin* **passer une scène au r.** to show a scene in slow motion **2** *(à vitesse réduite)* **avancer au r.** to move slowly forward; **tourner au r.** *(moteur)* to idle; **l'usine tourne au r.** the factory is running under capacity; **ils travaillent au r.** *(pour protester)* they're on *Br* a go-slow *or Am* a slowdown; *(par nécessité)* they're working at a slower pace

ralentir [32] [ralɑ̃tir] VI to slow down; **attention, r.** *(sur panneau)* reduce speed now; **r., travaux** *(sur panneau)* slow, roadworks ahead

VT **1** *(mouvement, effort)* to slow down; **r. sa course** *ou* **l'allure** to reduce speed, to slow down; **r. le pas** to slow down **2** *(processus)* to slow down

VPR **se ralentir** to slow down

ralentissement [ralɑ̃tismɑ̃] NM **1** *(décélération)* decrease in speed, slowing-down; **un r. de 10 kilomètres sur la N10** slow-moving traffic for 10 kilometres on the N10 **2** *(diminution)* reduction; **un r. des ventes** a fall-off in sales; **un r. des fonctions cérébrales** a reduction in brain activity; **un r. de l'économie** economic downturn; **le commerce entre les deux pays a connu un net r.** trade between the two countries has fallen off considerably

ralentisseur [ralɑ̃tisœr] NM **1** *(sur une route)* speed bump, *Br* sleeping policeman **2** *Aut & Tech* idler, speed reducer **3** *Phys* moderator

râler [3] [rɑle] VI **1** *(blessé)* to moan, to groan; *(agonisant)* to give a death rattle **2** *Fam (se plaindre)* to grumble, to moan; **mais qu'est-ce qu'elle a encore à r.?** what is she moaning about now?; **r. contre qch** to moan about sth; **juste pour la faire r.** just to make her mad **3** *(tigre)* to growl

râleur, -euse [rɑlœr, -øz] *Fam* ADJ bad-tempered❑, grumpy

NM,F grouch, moaner; **quel r.!** he never stops moaning!

ralliement [ralimɑ̃] NM **1** *(adhésion)* **lors de son r. à notre parti/notre cause** when he/she came over to our party/cause **2** *(rassemblement)* rally, gathering; **signe/cri de r.** rallying sign/cry; **point de r.** rallying point; **ce bar est un bon point de r.** the bar is a good meeting place

rallier [9] [ralje] VT **1** *(rejoindre ▸ groupe, poste)* to go back to

2 *(adhérer à)* to join

3 *(rassembler ▸ autour de soi, d'un projet)* to win over; *(▸ des troupes)* to gather together, to rally; **il a su r. la majorité des actionnaires à son projet** he managed to convince the majority of the shareholders that his project was a good idea; **r. tous les suffrages** to meet with general approval; **r. qn à sa cause** to win sb over

4 *Chasse (chiens)* to call in

5 *Naut* **r. le bord** to rejoin ship

VPR **se rallier 1** *(se joindre)* **il a fini par se r.** he ended up joining; **se r. à un parti** to join a party **2 se r. à un avis/un point de vue** *(se montrer favorable à)* to come round to an opinion/a point of view; **se r. à l'avis général** to come round to *or* to rally to the opinion of the majority

rallonge [ralɔ̃ʒ] NF **1** *(électrique)* extension (cable)

2 *(d'une table)* extension; *Can (d'un bâtiment) Br* extension, *Am* addition

3 *(tuyau)* extension tube *(of a vacuum cleaner)*

4 *Fam (délai)* extra time *(UNCOUNT)*; **une r. de quelques jours** a few extra days

5 *Fam (supplément)* extra money *(UNCOUNT)*; **il nous a donné une r. de 20 euros** he gave us an extra 20 euros; **r. budgétaire** addition to the budget

• **à rallonge(s)** ADJ **1 table à r.** *ou* **rallonges** extending table **2** *(week-end)* long *(avant n)*; *(histoire)* never-ending; *(nom)* double-barrelled

rallongement [ralɔ̃ʒmɑ̃] NM *(gén)* lengthening, extension; *(d'un vêtement)* letting down

rallonger [17] [ralɔ̃ʒe] VT **1** *(gén)* to extend; *(durée, liste)* to lengthen, to make longer, to extend; **r. un article de quelques lignes** to extend an article by a few lines **2** *(vêtement ▸ en défaisant l'ourlet)* to let down; *(▸ en ajoutant du tissu)* to make longer; **r. qch de dix centimètres** to make sth ten centimetres longer **3** *Fam (sujet: trajet, itinéraire)* **ça nous rallonge** it's taking us out of our way; **en passant par Lille, ça te rallonge d'une heure** if you go via Lille, it'll add an hour to your journey time

USAGE ABSOLU **ça rallonge de passer par Lille** it takes longer if you go via Lille

VI **les jours rallongent** the days are getting longer

rallumer [3] [ralyme] VT **1** *(feu)* to rekindle, to light again; *(lampe, télévision)* to put back on, to switch on again; *(électricité)* to turn on again; **r. une cigarette** *(éteinte)* to relight a cigarette; *(une autre)* to light up another cigarette **2** *(faire renaître ▸ haine, passion)* to rekindle; **cet événement a rallumé la guerre** this event sparked the war off again

USAGE ABSOLU *(lampe)* **rallume!** put the light back on!

VPR se rallumer 1 *(feu, incendie)* to flare up again; *(lampe, appareil)* to come back on **2** *(espoir)* to be revived; *(conflit)* to break out again; *(passion)* to flare up **3 elle se ralluma une énième cigarette** she lit yet another cigarette

rallye [rali] **NM 1** *(course)* **r. (automobile)** rally, car rally **2** *(soirée)* = exclusive upper-class ball for young people

RAM, Ram [ram] **NF** *Ordinat (abrév* **random access memory***)* RAM

ramadan [ramadã] **NM** *Rel* Ramadan, Ramadhan; **faire** *ou* **observer le r.** to observe Ramadan

ramage [ramaʒ] **NM** *Littéraire (d'un oiseau)* song
• **ramages NMPL** floral pattern

ramas [rama] **NM** *Vieilli ou Littéraire* raggle-taggle assortment, hotchpotch

ramassage [ramasaʒ] **NM 1** *(cueillette ▸ du bois, des fruits)* gathering; *(▸ des pommes de terre)* picking, digging up; *(▸ des champignons)* picking, gathering; **r. manuel** hand picking
2 *(collecte)* collection; **r. des ordures** *Br* rubbish *or Am* garbage collection
3 *(transport)* picking up; **r. scolaire** school bus service
4 *Bourse (d'actions)* buying up

ramasse [ramas] **NF** *Fam* **être à la r.** to be all at sea

ramassé, -e [ramase] **ADJ 1** *(trapu ▸ homme, corps)* stocky, squat; *(▸ bâtisse, forme)* squat **2** *(recroquevillé)* huddled; **un village r. autour de son église** a village huddled *or* clustering round its church **3** *(style)* terse

ramasse-miettes [ramasmjɛt] **NM INV** crumb sweeper

ramasse-monnaie [ramasmɔnɛ] **NM INV** change tray

ramasse-poussière, ramasse-poussières [ramaspusjɛr] *(pl* **ramasse-poussières***)* **NM** *Belg* dustpan

RAMASSER **[3]** [ramase]

VT	
• to pick up **1, 7**	• to pick **2**
• to gather **2, 3**	• to collect **3, 4**
• to condense **5**	• to buy up **6**
• to get **8**	• to catch **9**
VPR	
• to be picked (up) **1**	• to pick oneself up **2**
• to crouch **4**	• to come a cropper **5**

VT 1 *(objet à terre)* to pick up; *Fam* **ils ramassent des fraises à la pelle dans leur jardin** they get loads of strawberries from their garden; *Fam* **des mauvaises notes, il en a ramassé à la pelle cette année** he's been getting bad *Br* marks *or Am* grades by the dozen this year; *Fig* **r. qn dans le ruisseau** to pick sb up out of the gutter; *Fam* **il était à r. à la petite cuillère** *(épuisé)* he was all washed out; *(blessé)* you could have scraped him off the ground; **encore un pas et je serai bon à r. à la petite cuillère!** one more step and I'll fall to bits!
2 *(cueillir ▸ champignons)* to pick, to gather; *(▸ pommes de terre)* to dig; *(▸ marrons)* to gather
3 *(rassembler ▸ copies)* to collect, to take in; *(▸ cartes à jouer)* to gather up; *(▸ feuilles mortes)* to sweep up; *(▸ bois)* to gather; *Fam* **il a ramassé pas mal d'argent** he's picked up *or* made quite a bit of money; **r. ses forces** to gather one's strength; *Fam* **r. le paquet** to hit the jackpot
4 *(élèves, ouvriers)* to collect; **r. les ordures** to collect the *Br* rubbish *or Am* garbage
5 *(résumer)* to condense
6 *Bourse (actions)* to buy up
7 *Fam (trouver)* to pick up, to dig up
8 *Fam (recevoir)* to get[□]; **r. une gifle/un coup/un PV** to get a slap/a clout/a parking ticket
9 *Fam (attraper ▸ maladie)* to catch[□]
10 *Fam (arrêter)* to nab; **se faire r.** *(se faire emmener par la police)* to get picked up *or* nabbed *or Br* lifted; *(échouer)* to fail[□], *Br* to come a cropper

VPR se ramasser 1 *(emploi passif)* to be picked (up); *Fam* **les truffes se ramassent à la pelle dans cette région** there are loads of truffles around here
2 *Fam (se relever)* to pick oneself up[□]
3 *Fam (recevoir)* **se r. une gifle/un coup/un PV** to get a slap/a clout/a parking ticket
4 *(avant de bondir)* to crouch
5 *Fam (tomber)* to fall flat on one's face, to go flying; *(échouer)* to fail[□], *Br* to come a cropper

ramassette [ramasɛt] **NF** *Belg* dustpan

ramasseur, -euse [ramasœr, -øz] **NM,F** gatherer; **r./ramasseuse de balles** *(au tennis)* ball boy/girl; **r. de lait** milk collector
NM *Agr (machine)* pick-up

ramassis [ramasi] **NM** *Péj (d'objets)* jumble; *(de personnes)* bunch; *(d'idées)* collection, hotchpotch

ramassoire [ramaswar] **NF** *Suisse* dustpan

rambarde [rãbard] **NF** rail, guardrail

ramdam [ramdam] **NM** *Fam (vacarme)* racket, din; **faire du r.** to make a racket *or* a din

rame [ram] **NF 1** *(aviron)* oar; **nous avons rejoint le port à la r.** we rowed into port
2 *(de papier)* ream
3 *(train)* train; **r. de métro** *Br* underground *or Am* subway train
4 *(branche)* prop, stake; **haricots à rames** stick beans, *Br* runner beans, *Am* pole beans
5 ne pas *Fam* **en fiche** *ou très Fam* **en foutre une r.** to do zilch *or Br* bugger *or* sod all

rameau, -x [ramo] **NM 1** *(branche)* (small) branch; **r. d'olivier** olive branch **2** *Fig (division)* branch, subdivision **3** *Anat* ramification
• **Rameaux NMPL** *Rel* **les Rameaux, le dimanche des Rameaux** Palm Sunday

ramée [rame] **NF 1** *Littéraire (feuillage)* foliage **2** *(locution) Fam* **il n'en a pas fichu une r.** he hasn't done a stroke (of work)

ramener **[19]** [ramne] **VT 1** *(personne, véhicule ▸ au point de départ)* to take back; *(▸ à soi)* to bring back; **je vous ramène?** *(chez vous)* shall I give you a *Br* lift *or Am* ride home?; *(à votre point de départ)* shall I give you a *Br* lift *or Am* ride back?; **son chauffeur le ramène tous les soirs** his chauffeur drives him back every evening; **je te ramènerai la voiture lundi** I'll bring the car back on Monday; **r. les enfants à l'école** to take the children back to school; **il a fallu le r. à l'hôpital** he had to be taken back into hospital
2 *(rapporter)* **je te ramènerai un souvenir d'Italie** I'll bring you back a souvenir from Italy; **il faut que je ramène les clefs à l'agence** I've got to take the keys back to the estate agent
3 *(rétablir)* to bring back, to restore; **r. la paix** to restore peace; **r. l'espérance** to bring back *or* to revive hope
4 *(placer)* **elle ramena le châle sur ses épaules** she pulled the shawl around her shoulders; **r. ses cheveux en arrière** to draw one's hair back; **r. ses genoux sous son menton** to pull one's knees up under one's chin
5 *(faire revenir)* **l'été a ramené les visiteurs** the summer has brought back the tourists; **le film m'a ramené dix ans en arrière** the film took me back ten years; **ce qui nous ramène au problème de...** which brings us back to the problem of...; **r. la conversation à** *ou* **sur qch** to bring the conversation back (round) to sth; **r. qn à la vie** to bring sb back to life, to revive sb; **r. un malade à lui** to bring a patient round; **r. qn dans le rang** to pull sb back into line
6 *(réduire)* **ne ramenons pas son attitude à de la jalousie** let's not reduce his/her attitude to simple jealousy; **r. tout à soi** to bring everything back to *or* to relate everything to oneself
7 *(locution) Fam* **la r., r. sa fraise** *(vouloir s'imposer)* to stick one's oar in, to butt in; *(faire l'important)* to show off

VPR se ramener 1 *Fam (arriver)* to turn up, to show up; **ramène-toi en vitesse!** come on, hurry up! **2 se r. à** *(se réduire à)* to boil down to; **toute l'affaire se ramenait finalement à une querelle de famille** in the end the whole business boiled down to *or* was nothing more than a family quarrel

ramequin [ramkɛ̃] **NM 1** *(récipient)* ramekin (mould) **2** *(tartelette)* (small) cheese tart

ramer **[3]** [rame] **VI 1** *(pagayer)* to row; **r. en couple** to scull **2** *Fam (avoir des difficultés)* to have a hard time of it; **r. pour faire qch** to sweat blood *or* to bust a gut to do sth; **qu'est-ce qu'on a ramé pour trouver cet appartement!** it was such a hassle finding this *Br* flat *or Am* apartment!
VT 1 *Hort* to stick, to stake **2** *Fam* **ne pas en r. une** to do zilch *or Br* bugger all *or* sod all

rameur, -euse[1] [ramœr, -øz] **NM,F** rower, oarsman, *f* oarswoman; **r. de couple** sculler

rameux, -euse[2] [ramø, -øz] **ADJ** branching, *Spéc* ramose

rami [rami] **NM** *Cartes* rummy; **faire r.** to go rummy

ramie [rami] **NF** ramie

ramier [ramje] **ADJ M pigeon r.** ringdove, wood pigeon
NM *(pigeon)* ringdove, wood pigeon

ramification [ramifikasjɔ̃] **NF 1** *Bot* offshoot, *Spéc* ramification **2** *Anat* ramification; **ramifications nerveuses** nerve plexus **3** *(d'un fleuve)* ramification, distributary; *(d'une voie ferrée)* branch line; *(d'un réseau, d'une organisation)* branch; *(d'un complot)* ramification

ramifier **[9]** [ramifje] **se ramifier VPR 1** *Anat & Bot* to ramify, to divide **2** *(se subdiviser)* to split

ramille [ramij] **NF** twig, branchlet

ramolli, -e [ramɔli] **ADJ 1** *(beurre)* soft **2** *Fam (gâteux)* soft; **il est un peu r. du cerveau, il a le cerveau un peu r.** he's gone a bit soft (in the head) *or* soft-headed **3** *Fam (sans énergie)* **se sentir tout r.** to feel washed out
NM,F *Fam* **un vieux r.** an old dodderer

ramollir **[32]** [ramɔlir] **VT 1** *(rendre mou)* to soften **2** *(affaiblir)* to weaken
VI to go soft; **faire r. du beurre** to soften butter
VPR se ramollir 1 *(devenir mou)* to go soft **2** *Fam (perdre son tonus)* **depuis que j'ai arrêté le sport, je me suis ramolli** I've been out of condition since I stopped doing sport[□] **3** *Fam (devenir gâteux)* **son cerveau se ramollit** he's/she's going soft in the head

ramollissement [ramɔlismã] **NM** *(du beurre, de la cire)* softening; **r. cérébral** softening of the brain

ramollo [ramɔlo] *Fam* **ADJ 1** *(mou)* washed out, wiped; **se sentir tout r.** to feel like a wet rag **2** *(gâteux)* doddery
NMF wet rag *(person)*

ramon [ramɔ̃] **NM** *Belg* broom

ramonage [ramɔnaʒ] **NM 1** *(d'une cheminée)* chimney-sweeping; *(d'une machine)* cleaning; *(d'une pipe)* cleaning (out) **2** *Sport (en alpinisme)* chimneying

ramoner **[3]** [ramɔne] **VT 1** *(cheminée)* to sweep; *(machine)* to clean; *(pipe)* to clean (out) **2** *(en alpinisme)* to chimney
VI *(en alpinisme)* to (climb a) chimney

ramoneur [ramɔnœr] **NM** chimney sweep

rampant, -e [rãpã, -ãt] **ADJ 1** *Biol (animal)* creeping, crawling, *Spéc* reptant
2 *Bot* creeping; **plante rampante** creeper
3 *(évoluant lentement)* **inflation rampante** creeping inflation
4 *Péj (personne, caractère)* crawling, grovelling
5 *Hér* rampant
6 *Archit (arc)* rampant; *(pièce)* raked
NM *Archit* pitch

rampe [rãp] **NF 1** *(main courante)* handrail, banister; **r. (d'escalier)** banister; *Fam* **tiens bon la r.!** hang in there!, don't give in!; *Fam Euph* **lâcher la r.** *(mourir)* to croak, *Br* to kick the bucket
2 *(plan incliné)* ramp; **r. d'accès** approach ramp; **r. de chargement** loading ramp; *Astron* **r. de lancement** launch pad, launching pad
3 *(côte)* slope, incline
4 *Théât* footlights; **passer la r.** to get across to the audience; **il passe mal la r.** he doesn't come across well
5 *Aviat* **r. (de balisage)** marker *or* runway lights

rampement [rãpmã] **NM** creeping, crawling

ramper **[3]** [rãpe] **VI 1** *(lierre)* to creep; *(personne)* to crawl; *(serpent)* to slither, to crawl; **entrer/sortir en rampant** to crawl in/out **2** *(doute, inquiétude)* to lurk **3** *Fig (s'abaisser)* to grovel; **r. devant qn** to grovel before sb

rampon [rãpɔ̃] **NM** *Suisse* lamb's lettuce

ramponneau, -x [rãpɔno] **NM** *Fam (coup)* clout; **(se) prendre un r.** to get a clout

ramure [ramyr] NF **1** *Bot* **la r.** the branches, the tree tops **2** *(d'un cerf)* antlers

rancard [rɑ̃kar] NM **1** *Fam (rendez-vous ▸ gén)* appointment□; *(▸ amoureux)* date□; **j'ai r. avec lui à 15 heures** I'm meeting him at 3; **filer (un) r. à qn** to arrange to meet sb□; **on s'est filé (un) r. pour la semaine prochaine** we arranged to meet next week, we made a date for next week **2** *Fam Arg crime (renseignement)* info□ *(UNCOUNT)*, *Br* gen *(UNCOUNT)*; *(tuyau)* tip, tip-off

rancarder [3] [rɑ̃karde] *Fam Arg crime* VT *(renseigner)* to tip off; **r. qn sur qch** to give sb the low-down on sth

VPR **se rancarder** to get information□

rancart [rɑ̃kar] NM **1** = **rancard 2 mettre** *ou* **jeter qn au r.** to throw sb on the scrap heap; **mettre** *ou* **jeter qch au r.** *(objet)* to chuck sth out, *(projet)* to scrap sth

rance [rɑ̃s] ADJ *(beurre, huile)* rancid; *(noix)* stale

NM **odeur/goût de r.** rancid smell/taste; **avoir un goût de r.** to taste rancid; **sentir le r.** to smell rancid

ranch [rɑ̃tʃ] *(pl* **ranchs** *ou* **ranches)** NM ranch

rancir [32] [rɑ̃sir] VI **1** *(beurre, huile)* to go rancid; *(noix)* to go stale **2** *Fig Littéraire* to become stale

rancœur [rɑ̃kœr] NF resentment, rancour; **avoir de la r. envers qn** to feel resentful towards sb; **plein de r.** *(personne, ton)* resentful, bitter

rançon [rɑ̃sɔ̃] NF **1** *(somme d'argent)* ransom; *Arch ou Littéraire* **mettre qn à r.** to hold sb to ransom **2** *(contrepartie)* **c'est la r. de la gloire/du succès** that's the price of fame/success

rançonner [3] [rɑ̃sɔne] VT **1** *Littéraire (exiger une rançon de)* to hold to ransom **2** *(voler ▸ voyageur)* to hold up (and rob) **3** *Fam (exploiter)* to fleece, to swindle

rancune [rɑ̃kyn] NF grudge; **plein de r.** spiteful; **garder r. à qn, avoir de la r. contre qn** to bear *or* to harbour a grudge against sb; **elle garde r. à son frère de son refus** she has a grudge against her brother because of his refusal; **sans r.?** no hard feelings?; **sans r.!** no hard feelings!, let's shake hands and forget it!

rancunier, -ère [rɑ̃kynje, -ɛr] ADJ spiteful; **être r.** to bear grudges

NM,F spiteful person

randomisation [rɑ̃dɔmizasjɔ̃] NF randomization

randomiser [3] [rɑ̃dɔmize] VT to randomize

randonnée [rɑ̃dɔne] NF **1** *(promenade ▸ à pied sur le plat)* ramble, hike; *(▸ à pied en montagne)* trek; *(▸ à bicyclette)* ride; *(▸ à skis)* cross-country hike; *(▸ à cheval)* trek; **r. équestre** pony trek; **r. à pied** *ou* **pédestre** *(sur le plat)* ramble, hike; *(en montagne)* trek; **faire une r. (à pied** *ou* **pédestre)** *(sur le plat)* to go rambling *or* hiking; *(en montagne)* to go trekking; **faire une r. à bicyclette** to go for a bike ride; **faire une r. à skis** to go cross-country skiing; **faire une r. à cheval** to go pony-trekking **2** *(sport ▸ à pied sur le plat)* rambling, hiking; *(▸ à pied en montagne)* hill-walking, trekking; *(▸ à skis)* cross-country skiing; **la r. pédestre** *(sur le plat)* rambling, hiking; *(en montagne)* trekking; **grande r.** long-distance hiking; **faire de la r.** *(à pied sur le plat)* to go rambling *or* hiking; *(à pied en montagne)* to go hill-walking *or* trekking; *(à bicyclette)* to go cycling; *(à skis)* to go cross-country skiing; *(à cheval)* to go pony-trekking

randonneur, -euse [rɑ̃dɔnœr, -øz] NM,F *(à pied sur le plat)* rambler, hiker; *(à pied en montagne)* hill-walker; *(à bicyclette)* cyclist; *(à skis)* cross-country skier; *(à cheval)* pony-trekker

rang [rɑ̃] NM **1** *(rangée ▸ de personnes)* row, line; *(▸ de fauteuils)* row; *(▸ de crochet, de tricot)* row (of stitches); **sur un r.** in one row; **un collier à double r. de perles** a double string of pearls; **le premier/dernier r.** the front/back row; **on était au premier r.** we were in the front row

2 *(dans une hiérarchie)* rank; **cette entreprise occupe le premier r. mondial du marché des composants électroniques** this company is number one in the world in the electronic component market; **l'entreprise a été reléguée au cinquième r. pour la production d'appareils électroménagers** the company has slipped to fifth place in the white goods market; **ce problème devrait être au premier r. de nos préoccupations** this problem should be at the top of our list of priorities; **venir au deuxième/troisième r.** to rank second/third; **par r. d'âge** according to age; **par r. d'ancienneté** in order of seniority; **il a pris r. parmi les meilleurs** he ranks among the best; **de r. inférieur/supérieur** low-/high-ranking; **de premier r.** high-ranking, first-class, top-class; **de second r.** second-rate

3 *(condition sociale)* (social) standing; **le respect qui est dû à son r.** the respect which his/her position commands; **elle a épousé quelqu'un d'un r. plus élevé** she married above her station; **tenir son r.** to maintain one's position in society; **être digne de son r.** to be worthy of one's standing; **de haut r.** of high standing

4 *Mil* **le r.** the ranks; **les militaires du r.** the rank and file; **sortir du r.** to come up through the ranks; *Fig* to stand out; **rentrer dans le r.** to return to the ranks; *Fig* to give in, to submit

5 *Can* = group of farms in long strips of land, at right angles to a road or a river; *Fig* **les rangs** the countryside; **ils sont des rangs** they're from good country stock; *Péj* they're from the back of beyond

• **rangs** NMPL ranks; *Mil* **à vos rangs fixe!** fall in!; *Mil* **en rangs serrés** in close order; **être** *ou* **se mettre sur les rangs** to line up; **trois candidats sont sur les rangs** three candidates are lined up for *or* are in the running for the job; **servir dans les rangs d'une armée** to serve in the ranks of an army; **servir dans les rangs d'un parti/syndicat** to be a member *or* to serve in the ranks of a party/union; **rentrer dans les rangs** to fall in

• **au rang de** PRÉP **1** *(dans la catégorie de)* **une habitude élevée** *ou* **passée au r. de rite sacré** a habit which has been raised to the status of a sacred rite **2** *(au nombre de)* **mettre qn au r. de ses amis** to count sb among one's friends **3** *(à la fonction de)* **élever qn au r. de ministre** to raise *or* to promote sb to the rank of minister

• **en rang** ADV in a line *or* row; **entrez/sortez en r.** go in/out in single file; **se mettre en r.** to line up, to form a line; **en r. d'oignons** in a line *or* row

rangé, -e[1] [rɑ̃ʒe] ADJ **1** *(en ordre ▸ chambre, vêtements)* tidy **2** *(raisonnable ▸ personne)* steady, level-headed; *(▸ vie)* settled; **une jeune personne rangée** a very sober *or* well-behaved young person; **il mène une petite vie bien rangée** he leads a very settled existence **3** *Fam (assagi)* settled□; **être r. des voitures** to have settled down□; *(criminel)* to have gone straight

rangée[2] [rɑ̃ʒe] NF row

rangement [rɑ̃ʒmɑ̃] NM **1** *(mise en ordre ▸ d'une pièce)* tidying (up); **faire du r.** to tidy up; **avoir la manie du r.** to have a mania for tidiness, to be fanatically tidy

2 *(d'objets, de vêtements)* putting away

3 *(agencement)* arrangement, classification

4 *(meuble)* storage unit; *(cagibi)* storage room; *(espace)* storage space; **quelques solutions de r.** a few storage ideas; **cette cuisine manque de rangements** this kitchen lacks storage space

ranger[1] [rɑ̃dʒœr] NM *Mil* ranger

• **rangers** NMPL combat boots

ranger[2] [17] [rɑ̃ʒe] VT **1** *(mettre en ordre ▸ pièce)* to tidy (up)

2 *(mettre à sa place ▸ vêtement, objets)* to put away; *(▸ document)* to file away; **où range-t-on les photocopies?** where do you keep *or* file the photocopies?; **j'ai rangé la voiture au garage** I've put the car in the garage; **tout est si bien rangé!** everything is arranged so neatly *or* tidily!

3 *(classer)* to sort (out); **r. des dossiers par année** to file documents according to year; *Fig* **r. qn parmi** to rank sb amongst

4 *(mettre en rang ▸ troupes)* to draw up

VPR **se ranger 1** *(emploi passif)* **où se rangent les serviettes?** where do the towels go?, where are the towels kept?

2 *(s'écarter ▸ piéton)* to stand aside; *(▸ véhicule)* to pull over

3 *(se mettre en rang ▸ élèves, coureurs)* to line up; **rangez-vous deux par deux** get into rows of two, line up in twos

4 *(se placer)* **se r. du côté de qn** to side with sb; **se r. contre** to pull up next to; **la voiture se rangea le long du trottoir** the car pulled up beside the kerb

5 *Fam (s'assagir)* to settle down□; **se r. des voitures** to settle down; *(criminel)* to go straight

6 *Naut* **se r. à quai** to berth

7 se r. à *(adhérer à ▸ avis)* to go along with; *(▸ décision)* to abide by, to go along with; **se r. au choix de qn** to go along with sb's decision; **ils se sont finalement rangés à mon avis** they ended up coming round to my point of view

rani [rani] NF INV rani, ranee

ranimation [ranimasjɔ̃] NF resuscitation

ranimer [3] [ranime] VT **1** *(feu)* to rekindle, to relight **2** *(conversation)* to bring back to life; *(haine, passion, souvenir)* to rekindle, to revive; *(douleur)* to bring back; *(ville, industrie)* to revive, to put new life into; **r. le moral des troupes** to restore the morale of the troops; **r. le courage de qn** to put new heart into sb; **r. le débat** to revive the controversy **3** *(malade)* to revive, to bring round; *(après un arrêt cardiaque)* to resuscitate

VPR **se ranimer** *(conversation)* to pick up again; *(personne)* to come round; *(visage)* to light up; *(haine, passion)* to flare up again, to be rekindled

rap [rap] NM *Mus* rap

rapace [rapas] ADJ **1** *Orn* predatory **2** *Fig (avare)* grasping, avaricious

NM **1** *Orn* bird of prey **2** *Fig (avare)* vulture

rapacité [rapasite] NF *Littéraire* **1** *(avarice)* rapaciousness, rapacity; **avec r.** rapaciously **2** *(d'un animal)* rapacity

râpage [rɑpaʒ] NM *(du métal, du bois)* filing down

rapapilloter [3] [rapapijɔte] **se rapapilloter** VPR *Fam (se réconcilier)* to patch things up

rapatrié, -e [rapatrije] NM,F repatriate; **les rapatriés d'Algérie** = French settlers in Algeria who were repatriated as a result of Algerian independence in 1962

rapatriement [rapatrimɑ̃] NM repatriation; **r. sanitaire** repatriation for health reasons

rapatrier [10] [rapatrije] VT *(personnes, capitaux)* to repatriate; *(objets)* to send *or* to bring home; **son corps a été rapatrié le mois dernier** his/her body was sent home last month; **se faire r.** to be sent back to one's home country

râpe [rɑp] NF **1** *(de cuisine)* grater; **r. à fromage/muscade** cheese/nutmeg grater

2 *Tech (en outillage)* rasp *or* rough file

3 *Suisse Fam (avare)* skinflint

4 *Fam (guitare)* guitar□, axe

râpé, -e [rɑpe] ADJ **1** *(carotte, fromage etc)* grated **2** *(vêtement)* worn out, threadbare **3** *Fam (raté)* **c'est r.!** we've/you've/*etc* had it!; **c'est r. pour nos vacances en Australie!** bang goes our holiday in Australia!, that's our holiday in Australia out the window!

NM **1** *(fromage)* grated cheese **2** *(vin)* rape wine

râper [3] [rɑpe] VT **1** *(carotte, fromage etc)* to grate **2** *Tech* to file down **3** *Fig* **un vin qui râpe la gorge** a rough wine

rapetassage [raptasaʒ] NM *Fam* patching up, mending□

rapetasser [3] [raptase] VT *Fam* to patch up, to mend□

rapetissement [raptismɑ̃] NM **1** *(réduction)* **il observa le r. de l'image sur l'écran** he watched the picture get smaller and smaller on the screen **2** *Fig (fait de dévaloriser)* belittling

rapetisser [3] [raptise] VT **1** *(rendre plus petit)* to make smaller **2** *(faire paraître plus petit)* **r. qn/qch** to make sb/sth seem smaller; **la distance rapetisse les objets** distance makes things look smaller **3** *(dévaloriser)* to belittle

VI *(gén)* to get smaller; *(au lavage)* to shrink; **la piste rapetissait à vue d'œil** the runway grew rapidly smaller and smaller

VPR **se rapetisser** *(se dévaloriser)* **se r. aux yeux de qn** to belittle oneself in front of sb

râpeux, -euse [rɑpø, -øz] ADJ *(vin)* rough; *(voix)* rasping

raphia [rafja] NM **1** *Bot* raffia *or* raphia palm **2** *Tex* raffia, raphia

rapiat, -e [rapja, -at] *Fam* ADJ *(avare)* tight-fisted, stingy
NM,F skinflint, tightwad

rapide [rapid] ADJ **1** *(véhicule, sportif, cheval)* fast; *(courant)* fast-flowing; **r. comme l'éclair** quick as lightning; **r. comme une flèche** swift as an arrow
2 *(esprit, intelligence, travail)* quick; *(progrès, réaction, changement)* rapid; **c'est l'homme des décisions rapides** he's good at making quick decisions; **une réponse r.** a quick *or* speedy reply; **il n'a pas l'esprit très r.** he's a bit slow on the uptake; **être r. à la détente** to be quick off the mark
3 *(rythme)* quick, fast; **marcher d'un pas r.** to walk at a brisk *or* quick pace
4 *Tech* **acier r.** high-speed steel; **colle à prise r.** quick-setting adhesive; *Ordinat* **imprimante/lecteur r.** high-speed printer/drive
5 *(court, sommaire)* quick; **le chemin le plus r.** the shortest *or* quickest way; **c'est plus r. si tu passes par là** it's faster *or* quicker if you go that way; **un examen r. des dossiers** a quick *or* cursory glance through the documents; **jeter un coup d'œil r. sur qch** to have a quick glance at sth
6 *(hâtif ▸ jugement, décision)* hurried, hasty; **une visite r.** a hurried visit
7 *(facile ▸ recette)* quick
NMF *Fam (personne)* **c'est un r.** *(il comprend vite)* he's really quick on the uptake; *(il travaille vite)* he's a fast worker; **ce n'est pas un r.** *(il ne comprend pas vite)* he's a bit slow on the uptake; *(il ne travaille pas vite)* he's not a fast worker
NM **1** *(cours d'eau)* rapid **2** *(train)* express (train), fast train

rapidement [rapidmɑ̃] ADV **1** *(vite)* quickly, rapidly; **la situation se détériore r.** the situation is deteriorating rapidly; **il faut que je réponde r.** I must reply quickly **2** *(superficiellement)* briefly; **j'ai lu r. les journaux de ce matin** I had a quick look at *or* I briefly glanced at the morning papers

rapidité [rapidite] NF **1** *(vitesse ▸ d'une course, d'une attaque)* speed; *(▸ d'une réponse)* quickness; **avec r.** quickly, speedily, rapidly; **le chat a une r. de détente remarquable** the speed with which the cat is able to pounce is remarkable; **grâce à sa r. d'esprit** because of his/her quick mind, because of the speed with which he/she grasps things; **la r. avec laquelle elle faisait des progrès** the speed *or* rapidity with which she progressed; **avec la r. de l'éclair** in a flash, with lightning speed **2** *(du pouls)* rapidity **3** *Ordinat* **r. d'impression** print speed

rapido [rapido], **rapidos** [rapidos] ADV *Fam* quickly□; **boire un coup r.** to have a quick drink□ *or* a quick one

rapiècement [rapjɛsmɑ̃], **rapiéçage** [rapjesaʒ] NM **1** *(raccommodage)* patching (up) **2** *(pièce de tissu, de cuir)* patch

rapiécer [20] [rapjese] VT to patch up

rapière [rapjɛr] NF rapier

rapin [rapɛ̃] NM *Péj (peintre sans talent)* dauber

rapine [rapin] NF *Littéraire* **1** *(pillage)* pillage, plunder **2** *(butin)* plunder

raplapla [raplapla] ADJ INV *Fam* **1** *(fatigué)* washed out, wiped; **je me sens tout r. aujourd'hui** I don't have any go in me at all today **2** *(plat)* flat; **il est r., ton ballon!** your ball's as flat as a pancake!

rappareiller [4] [rapareje] VT to match up again

rappel [rapɛl] NM **1** *(remise en mémoire)* reminder; *(en publicité)* follow-up; **le r. de ces événements tragiques la bouleversait** she was deeply upset to be reminded of those tragic events; **commençons par un r. historique** let's start by recalling the historical background; **voici un r. des titres de l'actualité** here's a summary of today's news; **r.! défense de stationner** *(sur panneau)* no parking; **r.! défense de doubler** *(sur panneau) Br* no overtaking, *Am* no passing; **(lettre de) r.** (letter of) reminder; **r. à l'ordre** *(gén)* call to order; *Br Pol* ≃ naming; **il a fallu trois rappels à l'ordre pour qu'il se taise** he had to be called to order three times before he stopped talking
2 *(d'un ambassadeur, de produits défectueux)* recall; *Com (d'une somme avancée)* calling in; **r. sous les drapeaux** *(de réservistes)* (reservists') call-up *or* recall
3 *Théât* curtain call; *(à un concert)* encore; **il y a eu plusieurs rappels** *(au théâtre)* he/she/*etc* took several curtain calls *or* was called back several times; *(à un concert)* there were several encores
4 *(répétition ▸ dans un tableau, une toilette)* **r. de couleur** colour repeat
5 *Méd* booster; **ne pas oublier le r. l'an prochain** don't forget to renew the vaccination next year
6 *(arriéré)* **r. de salaire** back pay; **r. de cotisation** payment of contribution arrears
7 *Tél* **r. automatique** recall
8 *Tech (retour)* return; **ressort/vis de r.** return spring/screw
9 *Sport (en alpinisme ▸ activité)* abseiling, rappelling; *(▸ descente)* abseil, rappel; **descendre en r.** to rope *or* to abseil *or* to rappel down
10 *Ordinat* calling up

RAPPELER [24] [raple]

> **VT**
> • to remind **1** • to recall **2**
> • to call back **2, 3** • to phone back **3**
> • to call up **5**
> **VPR**
> • to remember **3**

VT **1** *(remettre en mémoire)* **r. qch à qn** to remind sb of sth; **rappelez-moi votre nom** what was your name again, please?; **rappelle-moi de lui écrire** remind me to write to him/her; **rappelle-moi que c'est son anniversaire** remind me it's his/her birthday; **il faut r. que...** it should be borne in mind *or* remembered that...; **les portes ferment à 8 heures, je vous le rappelle** let me remind you that the doors are closed at 8; **le premier mouvement n'est pas sans r. Brahms** the first movement is somewhat reminiscent of Brahms; **ça m'a rappelé mes vacances en Grèce** it reminded me of my holiday in Greece; **ça me rappelle quelque chose** that rings a bell; **numéro à r. dans toute correspondance** *(dans une lettre)* please quote this number in all correspondence
2 *(faire revenir ▸ personne)* to recall, to call back; *(▸ marchandises défectueuses)* to recall; **r. un ambassadeur** to recall an ambassador; *Mil* **r. des réservistes** to recall reservists; *Euph* **le Seigneur a rappelé à lui son serviteur** he has been called to a better *or* higher place; **l'acteur a été rappelé plusieurs fois** the actor had several curtain calls
3 *(au téléphone)* to call back, to phone *or Br* to ring back; **rappelez-moi plus tard** call me back later
4 *(faire écho à)* **son collier de turquoise rappelle la couleur de ses yeux** her turquoise necklace echoes the colour of her eyes; **les rideaux rappellent la couleur de la moquette** the curtains pick out the colour of the carpet
5 *Ordinat* to call up
6 *(locution)* **r. qn à la vie** to bring sb back to life
VPR **se rappeler 1** *(emploi réciproque)* **on se rappelle demain?** shall we talk again tomorrow?
2 *(emploi réfléchi)* **se r. au bon souvenir de qn** to send sb one's best regards
3 *(se souvenir de)* to remember; **tu te rappelles mon frère?** do you remember my brother?; **rappelle-toi que je t'attends!** remember *or* don't forget (that) I'm waiting for you!; **elle se rappelle avoir reçu une lettre** she remembers receiving a letter

> Attention: ne pas confondre les verbes **to remember** et **to remind** lorsque l'on traduit le verbe **rappeler. Se rappeler quelque chose** se traduit **to remember something,** alors que **rappeler quelque chose à quelqu'un** se dit **to remind somebody of something.**

rappeur, -euse [rapœr, -øz] NM,F rapper

rappliquer [3] [raplike] VI *Fam (arriver)* to turn up, to show up, to roll up; *(revenir)* to get back

RAPPORT [rapɔr]

> **NM**
> • report **1** • profit **2**
> • ratio **3** • connection **4**
> • link **4**
> **NMPL**
> • relationship

NM **1** *(compte rendu ▸ gén)* report; *Mil* briefing; **faire** *ou* **rédiger un r. (sur)** to make *or* to draw up a report (on); **soumettre un r. à qn** to submit a report to sb; **faire un r. sur les conditions de travail** to report on working conditions; **r. d'activité** progress report; **r. annuel** annual report; **r. commercial** market report; **r. détaillé** item-by-item report, full rundown; **r. d'expert** audit report; *Compta* **r. d'exploitation** operating statement; **r. financier** annual (financial) report *or* statement; **r. de gestion** management report; **r. périodique** progress report; **r. de police** police report; **r. de recherche** research paper
2 *(profit)* profit; **en r.** *(capital)* interest-bearing, productive; **il vit du r. de son capital** he lives on the income from his investments; **d'un bon r.** profitable; **d'un mauvais r.** unprofitable; **cette terre est d'un bon r.** this land gives a good yield; **r. annuel** annual return
3 *(proportion)* ratio; **dans le r. de 1 à 5** in a ratio of 1 to 5; **r. cours-bénéfice** price-earnings ratio; **r. coût-efficacité** cost-effectiveness; **r. coût-profit** cost-benefit ratio; **r. profit-ventes** profit-volume *or* profit-to-volume ratio; **r. qualité-prix** *(gén)* value for money; *Com* quality-price ratio; **c'est d'un bon r. qualité-prix** it's good value for money; **r. signal-bruit** signal-to-noise ratio
4 *(relation)* connection, link; **avoir r. à** to be connected with, to relate to; **n'avoir aucun r. avec qch** to have no connection with *or* to bear no relation to sth; **son dernier album n'a aucun r. avec les précédents** his/her latest record is nothing like his/her earlier ones; **c'est sans r. avec le sujet** that's beside the point, that's irrelevant; **je ne vois pas le r.** I don't see the connection; **où est le r.?** what's that got to do with it?; **mais ça n'a aucun r.!** but that's got nothing to do with it!; **cette décision n'est pas sans r. avec les récents événements** this decision isn't totally unconnected to recent events; **établir un r. entre deux événements** to establish a link *or* connection between two events; **le r. de forces entre les deux pays** the balance of power between the two countries; **il y a un r. de forces entre eux** they are always trying to see who can get the upper hand; **r. de causalité** causal relation
• **rapports** NMPL *(relations)* relationship, relations; **des rapports sociaux/culturels** social/cultural relations; **rapports entre l'Est et l'Ouest** East-West relations; **rapports patrons-syndicats** relations between the employers and the unions; **cesser tous rapports avec qn** to break off all relations with sb; **nous n'avons plus de rapports avec cette société** we no longer deal with that company; **entretenir de bons rapports avec qn** to be on good terms with sb; **rapports sexuels** (sexual) intercourse; **avoir des rapports (avec qn)** to have sex (with sb)
• **de rapport** *voir* **immeuble**
• **en rapport avec** PRÉP **1** *(qui correspond à)* in keeping with **2** *(en relation avec)* **mettre qn en r. avec qn** to put sb in touch with sb; **il les a mis en r. (l'un avec l'autre)** he put them in contact (with each other); **mettre qch en r. avec** to link sth to; **se mettre en r. avec qn** to get in touch *or* contact with sb; **être en r. avec qn** to be in touch with sb
• **par rapport à** PRÉP **1** *(en ce qui concerne)* regarding **2** *(comparativement à)* compared with, in comparison to; **on constate un retrait de l'euro par r. au dollar** the euro has dropped sharply against the dollar
• **par rapport que** PRÉP *Can Fam* because□
• **rapport à** PRÉP *Fam (en ce qui concerne)* about□; **r. à notre affaire, tu as du nouveau?** any news about our little business?
• **sous le rapport de** PRÉP as regards; **sous le r. des prix** as far as prices are concerned, as regards prices; **sous ce r.** in this respect
• **sous tous (les) rapports** ADV in every respect; **jeune homme bien sous tous rapports** *(petite annonce)* respectable young man

rapportage [rapɔrtaʒ] NM *Scol Fam* tale-telling, sneaking

rapporté, -e [rapɔrte] ADJ added on; **sans élément r.** plain; **poche rapportée** patch *or* sewn-on pocket; **poignée rapportée** detachable handle; **terre rapportée** made ground

rapporter **[3]** [rapɔrte] **VT 1** *(remettre à sa place)* to bring back; **tu rapporteras la clé** bring back the key

2 *(apporter avec soi)* to bring; *Chasse* to retrieve; **j'ai rapporté des fleurs du jardin** I brought some flowers in from the garden; **as-tu rapporté le journal?** did you get *or* buy the paper?; **le chien rapporte la balle** the dog brings back the ball; **je rapporte une impression favorable de cet entretien** I came away with a favourable impression of that meeting

3 *(apporter de nouveau ou en plus)* **rapporte-nous un peu plus de vin** bring us a little more wine

4 *(rendre)* to take back, to return; **pouvez-vous r. ces livres à la bibliothèque?** could you take these books back *or* return these books to the library?

5 *(ajouter)* to add; *Couture* to sew on; *Math* **r. un angle** to plot an angle

6 *(produire)* to produce, to yield; **r. des bénéfices** to yield a profit; **r. des intérêts** to yield interest; **le compte d'épargne vous rapporte 3,5 pour cent** the savings account has a yield of 3.5 percent *or* carries 3.5 percent interest; **sa boutique lui rapporte beaucoup d'argent** his/her shop brings in a lot of money; **et qu'est-ce que ça t'a rapporté en fin de compte?** what did you get out of it in the end?; **ça peut r. gros!** it could make you a lot of money!

7 *(répéter ▸ propos)* to tell, to say; **on m'a rapporté que les travaux n'étaient pas terminés** I was told that the work was not finished

8 *(faire le compte rendu de)* to report (on); *Pol* **r. les décisions d'une commission** to report on the decisions of a committee

9 *Admin & Jur (annuler)* to cancel, to revoke; **r. un projet de loi** to throw out a bill

10 r. qch à *(rattacher)* to relate sth to; **elle rapporte tout à elle** she always brings everything back to herself

11 *Compta (écriture)* to post

VI 1 *(être rentable)* to yield a profit; **c'est un métier qui rapporte** it's a profitable career; *Fam* **ça rapporte** it pays **2** *Chasse* to retrieve **3** *Fam (enfant)* to tell tales, to sneak

VPR se rapporter 1 se r. à *(avoir un lien avec)* to refer *or* to relate to; **l'affiche ne se rapporte pas au sujet de la pièce** the poster bears no relation to the play itself **2** *Gram* **se r. à** to relate to **3 s'en r. à** *(s'en remettre à)* to rely on; **je m'en rapporterai à votre expérience** I'll rely on *or* trust your experience

rapporteur, -euse [rapɔrtœr, -øz] **ADJ** telltale, *Br* sneaky

NM,F 1 *(personne indiscrète)* telltale, *Br* sneak, *Am* tattletale **2** *Admin & Pol (porte-parole)* reporter, recorder; **r. officiel** official recorder; **r. de la commission** = committee member who acts as spokesperson

NM *Géom* protractor

rapprendre [raprɑ̃dr] = **réapprendre**

rapproché, -e [raprɔʃe] **ADJ** *(dans l'espace, dans le temps)* close; *(yeux)* close-set; **des maisons très rapprochées** houses very close together; **j'ai trois réunions très rapprochées dans la journée** I've got three meetings one right after the other

rapprochement [raprɔʃmɑ̃] **NM 1** *(réconciliation ▸ entre groupes, personnes)* reconciliation, *Pol & Sout* rapprochement; **des tentatives de r.** attempts at reconciliation; **un r. israélo-palestinien** an Israeli-Palestinian rapprochement

2 *(comparaison)* link, connection; **elle fait un r. saisissant entre Mao et Jung** she draws a striking parallel between Mao and Jung; **tu n'avais pas fait le r.?** hadn't you made the connection?

3 *(convergence)* coming together; **on assiste à un r. des thèses des deux parties** the arguments of the two parties are coming closer together

4 *Compta* **r. bancaire** bank reconciliation

rapprocher **[3]** [raprɔʃe] **VT 1** *(approcher)* to bring closer *or* nearer; **il a rapproché son tabouret du piano** he brought *or* moved his stool closer to the piano; **rapprochez les deux toiles** bring the two canvases closer together; *Couture* **r. les morceaux bord à bord** to put the two pieces edge to edge; *Typ* **à r.** close up

2 *(dans le temps)* **chaque minute le rapprochait du moment fatidique** every minute brought the fateful moment closer

3 *(faire paraître proche)* to bring closer

4 r. qn *(de sa destination)* to take *or* to bring sb closer; **je te dépose à Concorde, ça te rapprochera** I'll drop you off at Concorde, that'll get you a bit closer to where you're going

5 *(affectivement)* to bring (closer) together; **cette naissance n'a pas suffi à les r.** that baby wasn't enough to bring them together; **ça m'a rapproché de mon père** it's brought me closer to my father, it's brought my father and me closer together

6 *(comparer)* to compare

VPR se rapprocher 1 *(emploi réciproque)* **les deux pays cherchent à se r.** the two countries are seeking a rapprochement

2 *(venir près)* to come close *or* closer; **la date du mariage/le vacarme des moteurs se rapproche** the wedding day/the roar of the engines is getting closer; **rapprochez-vous de moi** come closer (to me); **rapprochez-vous de l'estrade** move closer to the stage

3 se r. de *(se réconcilier avec)* to get *or* to become closer to; **j'ai essayé sans succès de me r. d'elle avant sa mort** I tried in vain to get closer to her before she died; **il se rapproche actuellement des catholiques** he's now moving closer to Catholicism

4 se r. de *(être comparable à)* to be similar to; **le style se rapproche du reggae** the style is similar to *or* resembles reggae

rapsodie [rapsɔdi] = **rhapsodie**

rapt [rapt] **NM** *(kidnapping)* abduction, kidnapping; **r. d'enfant** abduction of a child

râpure [rɑpyr] **NF** filings

raqué, -e [rake] **ADJ** *Can Fam (en panne, en ruine)* wrecked; *Fig (épuisé) Br* knackered, *Am* bushed

raquer **[3]** [rake] *Fam* **VT** to cough up, to fork out

VI to pay up, to cough up

raquette [rakɛt] **NF 1** *(de tennis)* racket; *(de ping-pong)* bat; *Fam* **c'est une bonne r.** *(joueur)* he's/she's a good tennis player[◻] **2** *(pour la neige)* snowshoe; **ils sont montés en raquettes** they snowshoed up

rare [rar] **ADJ 1** *(difficile à trouver)* rare, uncommon; **ce qui est r. est cher** anything that is in short supply is expensive; **l'amour vrai est un sentiment si r.** true love is such a rare feeling; **un musicien d'un r. talent** an exceptionally talented musician; **plantes/timbres rares** rare plants/stamps; **être d'une beauté r.** to be uncommonly beautiful

2 *(peu fréquent)* rare; **à de rares intervalles** at rare *or* infrequent intervals; **lors d'une de ses rares visites** on one of his/her rare *or* few visits; **tes visites sont trop rares** you don't visit us nearly often enough; **il est r. qu'elle veuille bien venir avec moi** she rarely *or* seldom agrees to come with me; **ça n'a rien de r.** there's nothing unusual about that; **il n'est pas r. de le voir ici** it's not uncommon *or* unusual to see him here; *Fam* **tu te fais r. ces derniers temps** you've become quite a stranger lately, where have you been hiding lately?; **c'est un mot r.** that's a rare word

3 *(peu nombreux)* few; **les rares électeurs qui ont voté pour lui** the few who voted for him; **les rares amis qu'elle s'est faits** the few friends she made; **rares sont ceux qui l'apprécient** not many people like him/her; **à de rares exceptions près** with only *or* apart from a few exceptions; **elle est une des rares personnes que je connaisse à aimer le jazz** she's one of the very few people I know who enjoys jazz; **les visiteurs se font rares** there are fewer and fewer visitors; **les bons pâtissiers se font rares** good pastry chefs are hard to find nowadays

4 *(peu abondant)* scarce; **la main-d'œuvre/l'argent était r.** there was a shortage of labour/money, labour/money was scarce; **les denrées de base se font rares** basic food items are becoming scarce

5 *(clairsemé)* thin, sparse; **il a le cheveu r.** his hair is thinning

6 *Phys (raréfié)* rare

raréfaction [rarefaksjɔ̃] **NF 1** *Phys (de l'air)* rarefaction **2** *(des denrées, de l'argent)* increasing scarcity

raréfier **[9]** [rarefje] **VT** *Phys (air)* to rarefy, to rarify

VPR se raréfier 1 *Phys (air)* to rarefy, to rarify **2** *(argent, denrées)* to become scarce; *(visites)* to become less frequent

rarement [rarmɑ̃] **ADV** rarely, seldom; **elle téléphone r., pour ne pas dire jamais** she seldom, if ever, calls

rareté [rarte] **NF 1** *(d'un fait, d'un phénomène)* rarity; *(d'un mot, d'une maladie)* rareness; *(de visites)* infrequency; *(d'une denrée)* scarcity **2** *(objet ▸ rare)* rarity, rare object; *(▸ bizarre)* curio

RAS [ɛraes] **ADV** *Fam (abrév* **rien à signaler)** nothing to report

ras[1] [ra] **NM** *(radeau)* raft

ras[2] [ras] **NM** *(titre éthiopien)* ras

ras[3]**, -e** [ra, raz] **ADJ 1** *(cheveux)* close-cropped, very short; *(tête)* close-cropped; *(barbe)* very short

2 *(végétation)* short; *(pelouse)* closely-mown

3 *(plein)* **mesure rase** full measure; **deux cuillerées rases de sucre** two level spoonfuls of sugar

4 *(locution)* **en rase campagne** in the open countryside; **la voiture est tombée en panne en rase campagne** the car broke down in the middle of nowhere

ADV 1 *(très court)* short; **avoir les ongles coupés r.** to keep one's nails cut short; **une haie taillée r.** a closely-clipped hedge **2** *Fam* **en avoir r. le bol** *ou* **la casquette** *ou Vulg* **le cul (de qch)** to have had it up to here (with sth), to be fed up (to the back teeth) (with sth); *Fam* **r. le bol!** enough is enough!

• **à ras ADV coupé à r.** cut short

• **à ras bord, à ras bords ADV** to the brim *or* top

• **à ras de PRÉP** level with; **à r. de terre** level with the ground

• **au ras de PRÉP au r. de l'eau** just above water level, level with the water; *Fam* **elle portait une minijupe qui lui arrivait au r. des fesses** she was wearing a mini-skirt which was more like a belt; *Fam* **ses remarques étaient au r. des pâquerettes** he/she came out with some very uninspired comments; *Fam* **le débat est au r. des pâquerettes** the discussion isn't exactly highbrow, the tone of the discussion is rather low

rasade [razad] **NF** *(dans un verre)* glassful; *(au goulot)* swig

rasage [razaʒ] **NM 1** *(de la barbe)* shaving **2** *Tex* shearing

rasant, -e [razɑ̃, -ɑ̃t] **ADJ 1** *(bas)* **un soleil r.** a low sun; **lumière rasante** oblique *or* low-angled light **2** *Mil* **tir r.** grazing fire **3** *Fam (assommant)* deadly dull; **c'était r.** it was a real drag

rascasse [raskas] **NF** *Ich* scorpion fish

rase-mottes [razmɔt] **NM INV 1** *Aviat* **voler en** *ou* **faire du r.** to hedgehop **2** *Péj* runt, shortie

raser **[3]** [raze] **VT 1** *(cheveux, poils)* to shave off; *(crâne, personne)* to shave; **mal rasé** ill-shaven; **être rasé de près** to be close-shaven; **se faire r.** *(la barbe)* to be given a shave

2 *(détruire)* to raze; **la vieille église a été rasée** the old church was razed to the ground

3 *(frôler ▸ sol, eau)* to skim; **la balle lui rasa l'épaule** the bullet grazed his/her shoulder; **r. les murs** to hug the walls

4 *Fam (lasser)* to bore[◻]; **tu nous rases!** you're boring us to tears!

VPR se raser 1 *(couper ses poils)* to shave; **se r. de près** to shave closely; **se r. les jambes** to shave one's legs; **se r. la barbe** to shave off one's beard **2** *Fam (s'ennuyer)* to be bored stiff *or* to tears; **qu'est-ce qu'on se rase ici!** it's deadly dull here!

• **à raser ADJ** shaving *(avant n)*; **mousse à r.** shaving foam

raseur, -euse [razœr, -øz] **NM,F** *Fam* bore, drag; **quel r.!** what a bore *or* drag!

rasibus [razibys] **ADV** *Fam* **1** *(court)* short[◻], very close[◻]; **il s'est fait couper les cheveux r.** he's been scalped **2** *(très près)* very close[◻]; **la balle est passée r.** the bullet whizzed past

rasif [razif] **NM** *Fam* razor; **ils se sont battus à coups de r.** they were going at each other with open razors

ras-le-bol [ralbɔl] **NM INV** *Fam* **il y a un r. général dans la population** people in general are sick and tired of *or* fed up with the way things are going

rasoir [razwar] **NM** razor; **r. électrique** (electric) shaver; **r. mécanique** *ou* **de sûreté** safety razor; **demander une coupe au r.** to ask for a razor cut; **coupé au r.** cut with a razor

ADJ *Fam* deadly dull; **ce qu'il peut être r.!** he's such a bore!

rassasiement [rasazimã] **NM** satisfaction

rassasier [9] [rasazje] **VT 1** *(faim)* to satisfy; **r. qn** to satisfy sb's hunger; **je suis rassasié** I'm full **2** *Fig* **alors, vous êtes rassasiés de plein air?** so, have you had your fill of fresh air?; **il n'est jamais rassasié de la voir** he never tires of seeing her

USAGE ABSOLU les fruits ne rassasient pas fruit isn't very filling *or* doesn't satisfy your hunger

VPR se rassasier 1 *(apaiser sa faim)* to eat one's fill; **se r. d'un plat** to eat one's fill of a dish **2** *(assouvir son désir)* **se r. de qch** to get one's fill of sth; **je ne me rassasie pas de cette vue/sa présence** I never tire of this view/his presence

rassemblement [rasãbləmã] **NM 1** *(réunion sur la voie publique* ▸ *gén)* gathering, group; *(*▸ *en politique)* rally; **disperser un r.** to break up *or* to disperse a gathering; **r. pour la paix** peace rally

2 *(dans un nom de parti)* party, union, alliance; **votez pour le R. écologiste** vote for the Green party; *Anciennement* **R. pour la République** = right-wing French political party

3 *(fait de se rassembler)* gathering; **tous les rassemblements sont strictement interdits** all rallies *or* gatherings are strictly forbidden; **vous devez empêcher le r. des élèves dans le hall** you must prevent the pupils from gathering in the hall

4 *(union)* union; **œuvrer au r. de la gauche** to work towards the union of the left

5 *Mil* **sonner le r.** to sound the assembly; **r.!** fall in!

6 *(de documents, d'outils)* collecting, assembling, gathering

7 *Ordinat (de données)* gathering

rassembler [3] [rasãble] **VT 1** *(objets, idées, preuves)* to collect, to gather; *(documents, outils)* to collect, to assemble, to gather; *Ordinat (données)* to gather; **elle rassembla tous les journaux de la semaine passée** she gathered together all the previous week's newspapers; **r. des preuves pour une inculpation** to gather *or* to collect evidence for a charge; **il a rassemblé des documents pour écrire une biographie** he has collected *or* assembled documents to write a biography; **j'eus à peine le temps de r. quelques affaires** I hardly had enough time to gather *or* to put a few things together; **r. ses forces** to gather *or* to muster one's strength; **r. ses esprits** to gather *or* to collect one's wits; **r. ses idées** to gather one's thoughts; **r. son courage** to summon up one's courage

2 *(personnes)* to gather together; *(troupes)* to assemble, to muster; *(animaux)* to round up; **puisque nous voici ici rassemblés** since we are (gathered) here together; **leur manifestation a rassemblé des milliers de personnes** their demonstration drew *or* attracted thousands of people; **ce qui nous rassemble ici ce soir, c'est la passion du théâtre** it is a passion for the theatre which has brought us here this evening

3 *Équitation* to collect

VPR se rassembler *(gén)* to gather together, to assemble; *(foule)* to collect, to gather; *(troupes)* to fall in, to muster, to assemble; **nous nous rassemblons tous les jeudis dans ce bar** we meet *or* get together in this bar every Thursday

rasseoir [65] [raswar] **VT 1** *(asseoir de nouveau)* **r. qn** *(qui était debout)* to sit sb down (again); **faire r. qn** to have sb sit down again **2** *(replacer)* to put back; **r. une statue sur son socle** to put a statue back on its plinth

VPR se rasseoir 1 *(personne)* to sit down again; **allez vous r.** go back to your seat, go and sit down again **2** *(liquide)* to settle

rasséréner [18] [raserene] *Littéraire* **VT r. qn** to put sb's mind at rest; **ses déclarations m'ont complètement rasséréné** what he/she said put my mind completely at rest

VPR se rasséréner to become calm *or* serene again

rasseyait, rassied *etc voir* **rasseoir**

rassir [32] [rasir] **VI** *(gâteau, pain)* to go stale; **faire r. du pain** to let bread go stale

VPR se rassir to go stale

rassis[1], -e[1] [rasi, -iz] **PP** *voir* **rasseoir**

rassis[2], -e[2] [rasi, -iz] **ADJ 1** *(gâteau, pain)* stale; *(viande)* properly hung **2** *Littéraire (calme)* calm, composed; *(pondéré)* balanced

rassoit *etc voir* **rasseoir**

rassortir [rasɔrtir] = **réassortir**

rassoyait *etc voir* **rasseoir**

rassurant, -e [rasyrã, -ãt] **ADJ 1** *(personne)* reassuring; **le président n'a pas été très r. dans ses dernières déclarations** the president's most recent statements were not very reassuring; **elle a été rassurante pour tout le monde** she comforted everybody **2** *(nouvelle, déclaration, ton, voix)* reassuring, comforting

rassurer [3] [rasyre] **VT** to reassure; **va vite r. ta mère** go and tell your mother she has nothing to worry about, go and set your mother's mind at ease; **je te rassure tout de suite, je ne vais pas te demander de le faire à ma place!** I can assure you, I won't ask you to do it for me!; **je n'étais pas très rassuré** I felt rather worried; **je ne suis pas très rassuré de la savoir seule** I have my worries about her being alone; **il n'a pas l'air très rassuré** he's not looking too happy; **ah, me voilà rassuré!** that's a relief!

VPR se rassurer 1 *(se raisonner)* to reassure oneself **2** *(cesser de s'inquiéter)* **rassure-toi** don't worry

rasta [rasta] *Fam* **ADJ INV** Rasta

NMF Rasta

rastaquouère [rastakwer] **NM** *Fam Vieilli* = racist term used with reference to wealthy foreigners

rat [ra] **NM 1** *(animal)* rat; **faire la chasse aux rats** to go ratting; **r. d'Amérique** muskrat, musquash; **r. des champs** field mouse; **r. d'eau** water vole *or* rat; **r. d'égout** common *or* brown *or* Norway *or* sewer rat; **r. gris** common *or* brown *or* Norway *or* sewer rat; **r. musqué** muskrat, musquash; **r. noir** black rat; **les rats quittent le navire** the rats are leaving the sinking ship; *très Fam* **être fait comme un r.** to have no escape, to be cornered; **vous êtes faits comme des rats!** you're caught like rats in a trap!; *très Fam* **s'emmerder** *ou* **se faire chier comme un r. mort** to be bored shitless

2 *Fig (personne)* **r. de bibliothèque** bookworm, *Am* library rat; **r. d'hôtel** hotel thief

3 petit r. de l'Opéra ballet student *(at the Opéra de Paris)*

4 *Fam Péj (avare)* skinflint, tightwad

5 *(par affection)* **mon (petit) r.** my darling

6 *Can Fam Péj (personne sournoise)* sly customer; *(non gréviste)* scab, strikebreaker□

ADJ M *Fam Péj* **1** *(avare)* stingy, tight-fisted; **il est tellement r.!** he's so stingy!, he's such a miser *or* skinflint! **2** *Can (sournois)* wily□, sly□

rata [rata] **NM** *Fam* food□, grub; **ne pas s'endormir sur le r.** not to fall asleep on the job

ratafia [ratafja] **NM** ratafia (liqueur)

ratage [rataʒ] **NM** failure; **un r. complet** a complete failure

rataplan [rataplã] **ONOMAT** rat-a-tat

ratatiné, -e [ratatine] **ADJ 1** *(fruit)* shrivelled (up) **2** *(visage)* wrinkled, wizened **3** *Fam (voiture, vélo)* smashed up; *(soufflé)* flat

ratatiner [3] [ratatine] **VT 1** *Fam (démolir)* **la voiture a été complètement ratatinée** the car was completely smashed up

2 *(flétrir)* **l'âge l'a complètement ratatiné** he has become wizened with age

3 *Fam (battre)* to thrash; **je me suis fait r. au tennis/aux échecs** I got thrashed at tennis/chess

4 *Fam (assassiner)* to do in; **il s'est fait r.** he got done in

VPR se ratatiner 1 *(se dessécher)* to shrivel; **son visage s'est ratatiné** his/her face has become all wizened **2** *(rapetisser)* to shrink; **elle se ratatine en vieillissant** she's shrinking with age **3** *Fam (s'écraser)* to crash□; **la voiture s'est ratatinée contre un mur** the car crashed *or* smashed into a wall

ratatouille [ratatuj] **NF** *Culin* **r. (niçoise)** ratatouille

rate [rat] **NF 1** *Zool* she-rat, female rat **2** *Anat* spleen; *Fam* **se dilater la r.** to be in stitches, to kill oneself (laughing), to split one's sides

raté, -e [rate] **ADJ 1** *(photo, sauce)* spoilt; *(coupe de cheveux)* disastrous; **il est complètement r., ce gâteau** this cake is a complete disaster **2** *(attentat)* failed; *(vie)* wasted; *(occasion)* missed; *(tentative)* failed, abortive, unsuccessful; **un musicien r.** a failed musician

NM,F failure, loser

NM 1 *(bruit)* misfiring *(UNCOUNT)*; **le moteur a des ratés** the engine is misfiring **2** *(difficulté)* hitch **3** *Mil* misfire

râteau, -x [rɑto] **NM 1** *(de jardin)* rake; **ramasser les feuilles mortes avec un r.** to rake up the dead leaves; **donner un coup de r. à l'allée** to give the path a rake; **r. faneur** tedder; **r. mécanique** raker

2 *(de croupier)* rake

3 *(de métier à tisser)* comb

4 *Fam (locution)* **se prendre un r.** to get turned down□ *or* knocked back *Br* to get a knockback

5 *Suisse Fam (avare)* miser, skinflint

râteler [24] [rɑtle] **VT** to rake up

râtelier [rɑtəlje] **NM 1** *(support)* rack; **r. à fusils/outils/pipes** gun/tool/pipe rack **2** *(mangeoire)* rack; *Fam* **manger à tous les râteliers** to have a finger in every pie **3** *Fam (dentier)* dentures□

rater [3] [rate] **VI 1** *Fam (échouer)* to fail; **je t'avais dit qu'elle serait en retard, et ça n'a pas raté!** I told you she'd be late, and sure enough she was!; **ça ne rate jamais** it never fails; **tais-toi, tu vas tout faire r.!** shut up or you'll ruin everything!

2 *Mil* **le coup a raté** the gun failed to go off

VT 1 *(but)* to miss; **elle a raté la marche** she missed the step; **j'ai raté ma chance** I missed my opportunity *or* chance; *Fam* **j'ai raté mon coup** I made a mess of it; *Fam* **s'il recommence, je te jure que je ne le raterai pas!** if he does it again, I swear I'll get him!; *Fam* **le coiffeur ne t'a pas raté, dis donc!** the hairdresser didn't mess about with you!

2 *(avion, rendez-vous, visiteur, occasion)* to miss; **je n'ai pas vu le concert – tu n'as rien raté/tu as raté quelque chose!** I didn't see the concert – you didn't miss anything!/you really missed something!; **c'est une émission à ne pas r.** this programme is a must *or* is unmissable; **tu vas nous faire r. la séance!** you're going to make us miss the movie *or Br* film!; *Fam* **tu n'en rates pas une!** you're always putting your foot in it!

3 *(ne pas réussir)* **il a complètement raté son oral** he made a complete mess of his oral; **j'ai encore raté mon permis de conduire** I've failed my driving test again; **il a raté son effet** he didn't achieve the desired effect; **il a raté sa sortie** his exit didn't quite come off; **il rate toujours les mayonnaises** his mayonnaise always goes wrong; **j'ai raté mon gâteau** I made a mess of the cake; **r. sa vie** to make a mess of one's life; **c'est raté, il ne reste plus de places** we've had it, there are no tickets left; **si tu voulais lui parler, c'est raté, il vient de partir** if you wanted to talk to him, you're too late, he's just gone

VPR se rater *Fam* **1** *(personnes)* to miss each other□; **on avait rendez-vous à l'Arc de Triomphe mais on s'est ratés** we were supposed to meet at the Arc de Triomphe but we missed each other

2 *(soi-même)* **il s'est coupé les cheveux lui-même, il s'est complètement raté!** he cut his hair himself and made a complete mess of it!; **elle est tombée de vélo, elle ne s'est pas ratée!** she really *or Br* didn't half hurt herself when she fell off her bike!; **elle s'est ratée pour la troisième fois** that's her third (unsuccessful) suicide attempt

ratiboiser [3] [ratibwaze] **VT** *Fam* **1** *(voler)* **r. qch à qn** to pinch *or Br* to nick sth from sb **2** *(ruiner)* to clean out; **je suis ratiboisé!** I'm cleaned out!; **on s'est fait r. au casino** we were cleaned out at the casino **3** *(cheveux)* **se faire r. (la colline)** to get scalped

ratiche [ratiʃ] **NF** *Fam* tooth□

raticide [ratisid] **NM** rat poison

ratier [ratje] **ADJ M** ratter

NM ratter

ratière [ratjer] **NF** *(piège)* rat trap

ratification [ratifikasjɔ̃] **NF** *Jur* ratification

ratifier [9] [ratifje] **VT 1** *Jur* to ratify; **ils ont fait r. le traité par le gouvernement** they put the treaty before Parliament for ratification **2** *Littéraire (confirmer)* to confirm

ratio [rasjo] NM ratio; **r. de capitalisation** p/e ratio, price/earnings ratio; **r. capital-travail** capital-labour ratio; **r. cours-bénéfices** price-earnings ratio; *Compta* **r. d'exploitation** performance ratio, operating ratio; *Compta* **r. de gestion** financial ratio; **r. de levier** leverage; *Compta* **r. de liquidité (générale)** liquidity ratio; *Compta* **r. de liquidité immédiate** quick ratio, acid test ratio; *Compta* **r. de solvabilité** solvency ratio; *Compta* **r. de trésorerie** cash ratio; **r. des ventes** sales ratio

ratiocination [rasjɔsinasjɔ̃] NF quibble; **ce sont des ratiocinations!** you're just splitting hairs!

ratiociner [3] [rasjɔsine] VI to quibble, to split hairs

ration [rasjɔ̃] NF **1** *(portion)* ration; **rations de guerre** war rations; *Fig* **il a eu sa r. de problèmes** he's had his share of problems; *Hum* **non merci, j'ai eu ma r.!** no thanks, I've had my fill (of it)! **2** *(quantité nécessaire)* daily intake; **r. alimentaire** food intake **3** *Mil* rations; **r. de combat** combat rations; **avoir une r. réduite** to be on short rations; **rations de survie** survival rations

rationalisation [rasjɔnalizasjɔ̃] NF rationalization; *Compta* **r. des choix budgétaires** planning-programming-budgeting system

rationaliser [3] [rasjɔnalize] VT to rationalize

rationalisme [rasjɔnalism] NM rationalism

rationaliste [rasjɔnalist] ADJ rationalist
NMF rationalist

rationalité [rasjɔnalite] NF rationality

rationnel, -elle [rasjɔnɛl] ADJ **1** *Math & Phil* rational **2** *(sensé)* rational; **il n'a pas une attitude très rationnelle** his attitude is not very rational **3** *Écon* **l'organisation rationnelle de l'industrie** the rationalization *or* streamlining of industry

rationnellement [rasjɔnɛlmɑ̃] ADV **1** *Math & Phil* rationally **2** *(avec bon sens)* rationally, sensibly, logically

rationnement [rasjɔnmɑ̃] NM rationing

rationner [3] [rasjɔne] VT **1** *(quelque chose)* to ration **2** *(quelqu'un)* to put on rations, to ration
VPR **se rationner** to ration oneself

ratissage [ratisaʒ] NM **1** *(nettoyage)* raking **2** *(fouille)* combing, thorough search

ratisser [3] [ratise] VT **1** *(gravier, allée)* to rake; *(feuilles, herbe coupée)* to rake up
2 *Fam (voler)* to pinch, *Br* to nick; **je me suis fait r. mon sac** I got my bag pinched *or Br* nicked
3 *(ruiner)* to clean out; **il s'est fait r. au poker** he got cleaned out playing poker
4 *(fouiller)* to comb
VI *Fam Fig* **r. large** to cast one's net wide

raton [ratɔ̃] NM **1** *(animal)* young rat; **r. laveur** raccoon **2** *(par affection)* **mon r.!** my darling! **3** *Vulg* = offensive term used to refer to North African Arabs

ratonnade [ratɔnad] NF = violent racist attack on North African Arab immigrants

ratoureux, -euse [raturø, -øz] *Can* ADJ wily, devious; **parfois le bonheur est un peu r.** sometimes happiness is not all it seems
NM,F shady customer

RATP [ɛratepe] NF *(abrév* **Régie autonome des transports parisiens***)* = Paris transport authority

rattachement [rataʃmɑ̃] NM *Admin & Pol* **le r. de la Savoie à la France** the incorporation of Savoy into France; **opérer le r. de territoires à la métropole** to bring territories under the jurisdiction of the home country; **demander son r. à un service** to ask to be attached to a department

rattacher [3] [rataʃe] VT **1** *(paquet)* to tie up again, to do up again; *(ceinture, lacet)* to do up again; *(cheveux en chignon)* to put up (again); *(cheveux en queue-de-cheval)* to tie back; *(chien)* to tie up again; *(plante grimpante)* to tie back **2** *Admin & Pol* **r. plusieurs services à une même direction** to bring several departments under the same management; **nous sommes rattachés à l'Hôpital Broussais** we're attached to the Broussais Hospital; **r. un territoire à un pays** to bring a territory under the jurisdiction of a country **3** *(lier ► idée)* **r. qch à** to connect *or* to link sth with, to relate sth to; **c'était la seule chose qui nous rattachait l'un à l'autre** it was the only thing that bound us together
VPR **se rattacher 1 se r. à** *(découler de)* to derive from; **des dialectes qui se rattachent à une langue** dialects which derive from the same language **2 se r. à** *(avoir un lien avec)* to be connected *or* linked with, to be related to; **voici le rapport et toutes les pièces qui s'y rattachent** here is the report and its related documents

rattachiste [rataʃist] *Belg* ADJ *(personne, politique)* = advocating the integration of French-speaking regions of Belgium into France
NMF = advocate of the integration of French-speaking regions of Belgium into France

rattrapage [ratrapaʒ] NM **1** *(au bac)* **être admis au r.** = to be allowed to sit further oral examinations to gain a pass mark in the "baccalauréat"; **l'oral de r.** = further oral examination to gain a pass mark in the "baccalauréat"
2 *(remise à niveau)* **r. scolaire** ≃ remedial teaching; **cours de r.** = extra class for pupils who need to catch up
3 *(d'une maille)* picking up
4 *Écon* **r. des salaires** wage adjustment

rattraper [3] [ratrape] VT **1** *(animal, prisonnier)* to recapture, to catch again
2 *(objet qui tombe)* to catch (hold of); **je l'ai rattrapé de justesse** I caught (hold of) it just in time; **r. la balle au vol/bond** to catch the ball in the air/on the bounce
3 *(quelqu'un parti plus tôt)* to catch up with; **passe devant, je te rattraperai** go on ahead, I'll catch up with you *or* catch you up
4 *(compenser)* **r. le temps perdu** *ou* **son retard** to make up for lost time; **il a rattrapé les cours manqués** he has caught up on the lessons he missed; **r. du sommeil** to catch up on one's sleep
5 *(erreur, maladresse)* to put right; *(situation, mayonnaise)* to salvage; **dis-moi comment r. le mal que je t'ai fait** tell me how I can make up for the hurt I've caused you
6 *(étudiant)* to let through
7 *(maille)* to pick up
VPR **se rattraper 1** *(emploi passif) Prov* **le temps perdu ne se rattrape jamais** = you can never make up for lost time
2 *(éviter la chute)* to catch oneself (in time); **heureusement il s'est rattrapé** luckily he managed to avoid falling; **se r. à qn/qch** to grab *or* to catch hold of sb/sth to stop oneself falling
3 *(avant de faire une erreur)* to stop oneself; **...mais je me suis rattrapé de justesse** ...but I caught *or* stopped myself just in time
4 *(compenser)* **j'ai l'intention de me r.!** I'm going to make up for it!; **la limonade est en promotion, mais ils se rattrapent sur le café** lemonade is on special offer, but they've put up the price of coffee to make up for it
5 *(élève)* to catch up

rature [ratyr] NF crossing out, deletion; **tu as fait trop de ratures** you've crossed too many things out; **sans ratures ni surcharges** *(dans un formulaire)* without deletions or alterations

raturer [3] [ratyre] VT to cross out, to delete; **les devoirs raturés ne seront pas corrigés** homework with too many crossings-out in it will not be marked

raucité [rosite] NF *Littéraire* **1** *(enrouement)* hoarseness; *(caractère voilé)* huskiness **2** *(d'un cri)* raucousness

raugmenter [rɔgmɑ̃te] VI *Fam (d'un prix)* to go up again

rauque [rok] ADJ **1** *(voix ► enrouée)* hoarse; *(► voilée)* husky **2** *(cri)* raucous **3** *Belg (personne ► enrouée)* hoarse

ravagé, -e [ravaʒe] ADJ **1** *(pays)* ravaged, devastated; *(personne ► par la fatigue)* haggard; *(► par le désespoir, le chagrin)* devastated, torn apart; *(► par la maladie, la douleur)* ravaged; **les traits ravagés par l'alcool** his/her features ravaged by alcohol **2** *Fam (fou)* crazy, nuts

ravager [17] [ravaʒe] VT *(région, ville)* to ravage, to lay waste, to devastate; *(récoltes)* to ravage, to devastate, to play havoc with; *(visage)* to ravage

ravages [ravaʒ] NMPL *(destruction)* devastation; **les r. du feu/de la tempête** the devastation *or* destruction caused by the fire/the storm; **les r. de la maladie/du temps** the ravages of disease/of time; **faire des r.** to wreak havoc; *Fig* **l'alcoolisme faisait des r.** alcoholism was rife; **notre cousin fait des r. (dans les cœurs)!** our cousin is a heart-breaker!

ravageur, -euse [ravaʒœr, -øz] ADJ **1** *(destructeur)* destructive, devastating; **des insectes ravageurs** insect pests; **les effets ravageurs du chômage** the devastating effects of unemployment **2** *(sourire)* devastating; *(humour)* scathing
NM,F ravager

ravalement [ravalmɑ̃] NM **1** *(d'une façade ► nettoyage)* cleaning; *(► recrépissage)* re-roughcasting **2** *Fam Fig* **se faire faire un r. (de façade)** *(opération)* to have a facelift□; *(maquillage)* to put on one's warpaint **3** *(d'un arbre)* pruning, cutting back

ravaler [3] [ravale] VT **1** *Constr* to redo; *Fam* **se faire r. la façade** *ou* **le portrait** to have a facelift□
2 *(salive)* to swallow; *(larmes)* to hold *or* to choke back; *(colère)* to stifle, to choke back; *(fierté)* to swallow; *Fam* **faire r. ses paroles à qn** to make sb eat his/her words
3 *(abaisser)* to lower; **de tels sentiments nous ravalent au niveau de la bête** such feelings lower *or* reduce us to the level of animals
4 *(arbre)* to prune, to cut back
VPR **se ravaler 1** *(s'abaisser)* to debase *or* to lower oneself; **se r. au rang de la brute** to be reduced to the level of animals **2** *Fam* **se r. la façade** *(se maquiller)* to slap some make-up on, to put on one's warpaint

ravaleur [ravalœr] NM cleaner, stone-cleaner

ravaudage [ravodaʒ] NM *Vieilli* **1** *(action ► de chaussettes)* darning; *(► de vêtements)* mending **2** *(résultat ► de chaussettes)* darn; *(► d'un vêtement)* mend

ravauder [3] [ravode] VT *Vieilli (chaussettes)* to darn; *(vêtements)* to mend
VI *Can* **1** *(errer)* to wander about; *(faire l'idiot)* to fool *or* to clown around **2** *Can (faire du bruit)* to make a racket

ravaudeur, -euse [ravodœr, -øz] NM,F *Vieilli (de chaussettes)* darner; *(de vêtements)* mender

rave[1] [rav] NF *(radis)* radish; *(navet)* turnip

rave[2] [rɛv] NF *(soirée)* rave

raveur, -euse [rɛvœr, -øz] NM,F raver

ravi, -e [ravi] ADJ delighted (**de qch** with sth); **il n'a pas eu l'air r.** he didn't look too pleased; **d'un air r.** delightedly; **je suis r. de vous voir** I'm delighted to see you; **r. (de faire votre connaissance)** (I'm) delighted *or* very pleased to meet you

ravier [ravje] NM hors-d'œuvres dish

ravigotant, -e [ravigɔtɑ̃, -ɑ̃t] ADJ *Fam (vent)* invigorating□, bracing□; *(soupe, vin)* warming□

ravigote [ravigɔt] *Culin* NF ravigote sauce *(vinaigrette with herbs and hard-boiled eggs)*
• **à la ravigote** ADJ with a ravigote sauce

ravigoter [3] [ravigɔte] VT *Fam* to buck up; **cette promenade/ce petit whisky m'a ravigotée** that walk/that little whisky bucked me up; **la voilà toute ravigotée** she's full of life again

ravin [ravɛ̃] NM gully, ravine

ravine [ravin] NF gully

ravinement [ravinmɑ̃] NM **1** *(action)* gullying **2** *(résultat)* **ravinements** gullies

raviner [3] [ravine] VT **1** *Géog* to gully **2** *Fig* to furrow; **un visage raviné** a deeply lined face

ravioli [ravjɔli] *(pl inv ou* **raviolis***)* NM piece of ravioli; **des raviolis** ravioli

ravir [82] [ravir] VT **1** *(enchanter)* to delight; **son dernier film ravira les amateurs d'humour noir** his/her latest movie *or Br* film will delight lovers of black humour; **cette naissance les a ravis** they were thrilled with the new baby **2** *Littéraire (enlever ► femme)* to ravish; *(► enfant)* to abduct; **r. qch à qn** to rob sb of sth; **il s'est fait r. la première place par un jeune inconnu** he was beaten to first place by a youngster nobody had heard of; **prématurément ravi à l'affection des siens** taken too early from (the bosom of) family and friends
• **à ravir** ADV *(merveilleusement)* **la robe lui va à r.** the dress looks lovely on her; **il dessine à r.** he draws beautifully; **elle est belle à r.** she's ravishing

raviser [3] [ravize] **se raviser** VPR to change one's mind, to have second thoughts

ravissant, -e [ravisɑ̃, -ɑ̃t] ADJ *(vêtement)* gorgeous, beautiful; *(endroit, maison)* delightful, beautiful; *(femme)* strikingly *or* ravishingly beautiful

ravissement [ravismɑ̃] NM **1** *(enchantement)* **c'est un véritable r. (pour les yeux)** it is an enchanting sight; **avec r.** *(écouter, contempler)* in delight, delightedly; **c'est ce que nous avons découvert avec r.** that's what we found out to our delight; **mettre** *ou* **plonger qn dans le r.** to send sb into raptures **2** *Littéraire (enlèvement* ▸ *d'une femme)* ravishment; *(*▸ *d'un enfant)* abduction **3** *Rel* rapture

ravisseur, -euse [ravisœr, -øz] ADJ *Entom* **patte ravisseuse** grasping tibia
NM,F kidnapper, *Sout* abductor

ravitaillement [ravitajmɑ̃] NM **1** *Mil & Naut* supplying; **assurer le r. de qn en munitions/carburant/vivres** to supply sb with ammunition/fuel/food; **le r. des grandes villes est l'un des problèmes majeurs en temps de guerre** maintaining supplies in large cities is one of the major problems in wartime; **bateau/véhicule de r.** supply ship/vehicle **2** *Aviat* refuelling; **r. en vol** in-flight *or* mid-air refuelling **3** *(denrées)* food supplies

ravitailler [3] [ravitaje] VT **1** *Mil* to supply; **r. un régiment en vivres** to supply a regiment with food, to supply food to a regiment **2** *Aviat & Naut* to refuel **3** *(famille, campement)* **r. qn en** to supply sb with, to give sb fresh supplies of
VPR **se ravitailler 1** *(en nourriture)* to get (fresh) supplies **2** *(en carburant)* to refuel

ravitailleur, -euse [ravitajœr, -øz] ADJ **avion r.** supply plane, (air) tanker; **véhicule/navire r.** supply vehicle/ship
NM,F *Mil* quartermaster; *Naut* supply officer
NM **1** *Aviat (avion)* tanker aircraft **2** *Mil* supply vehicle **3** *Naut (d'escadre, de sous-marin)* supply ship

ravivage [ravivaʒ] NM **1** *Métal (gén)* cleaning; *(à l'abrasif)* scouring; *(à l'acide)* pickling; *(au chalumeau)* burning off **2** *Tex (d'une couleur)* brightening up, reviving

raviver [3] [ravive] VT **1** *(feu)* to rekindle, to revive; *(couleur)* to brighten up **2** *(sensation, sentiment)* to rekindle, to revive; **r. le chagrin/la douleur de qn** to revive sb's feelings of grief/sorrow; **le procès va r. l'horreur/les souffrances de la guerre** the trial will bring back the horrors/sufferings of the war **3** *Métal (gén)* to clean; *(à l'abrasif)* to scour; *(à l'acide)* to pickle; *(au chalumeau)* to burn off
VPR **se raviver** *(sentiment)* to return; **sa haine se ravivait dès qu'il le voyait** every time he saw him, his hatred flared up again

ravoir [ravwar] *(à l'infinitif seulement)* VT **1** *(récupérer)* to get back **2** *(nettoyer)* **r. une chemise/casserole** to get a shirt/pan clean **3** *(maladie)* **je ne veux pas r. la grippe** I don't want to get flu again
VPR **se ravoir** *Belg (reprendre haleine)* to get one's breath back; *(retrouver ses esprits)* to come to one's senses

rayage [rejaʒ] NM **1** *(éraflement)* scratching **2** *(rature)* scoring **3** *(d'arme à feu)* rifling

rayé, -e [reje] ADJ **1** *(à raies* ▸ *papier)* lined, ruled; *(*▸ *vêtement)* striped; **tissu r. bleu et rouge** blue and red striped fabric, fabric with blue and red stripes **2** *(éraflé* ▸ *verre, disque, carrosserie)* scratched **3** *(arme à feu)* rifled

rayer [11] [reje] VT **1** *(abîmer)* to scratch
2 *(éliminer* ▸ *faute, coquille)* to cross *or* to score out; *(*▸ *clause, codicille)* to cancel; *(*▸ *médecin)* to strike off; *(*▸ *avocat)* to disbar; **on vous a rayé** *ou* **on a rayé votre nom de la liste** your name has been struck off *or* crossed off the list; **r. la mention inutile** *(dans un formulaire)* delete where inapplicable; **rayé de la carte** wiped off the face of the earth
3 *(fusil)* to rifle
4 *Mil* **r. qn des contrôles** to strike sb off the strength

rayon[1] [rejɔ̃] NM **1** *Opt & Phys* ray; **r. laser** laser beam; **r. lumineux** (light) ray; **r. vert** green flash
2 *(de lumière)* beam, shaft; *(du soleil)* ray; *Fig (d'espoir)* ray; **un r. de lune** a moonbeam; **un r. de soleil** a ray of sunshine, a sunbeam; *Météo* a brief sunny spell; *Fig* a ray of sunshine; **cet enfant est un peu notre r. de soleil** this child has brought a ray of sunshine into our life
3 *Math (vecteur)* radius vector; *(d'un cercle)* radius
4 *(de roue)* spoke
5 *(distance)* radius; **dans un r. de vingt kilomètres autour de** within (a radius of) twenty kilometres of
6 *Aut* **r. de braquage** turning circle
7 r. d'action range; **à grand r. d'action** long-range; *Fig* **étendre son r. d'action** to widen the scope of one's activities
• **rayons** NMPL **1** *Méd* radiation treatment *(UNCOUNT) (for cancer)*; *Fam* **on lui fait des rayons** he's/she's having radiotherapy *or* radiation treatment; **mal** *ou* **maladie des rayons** radiation sickness **2** *Phys* **rayons bêta** beta rays; **rayons gamma** gamma rays; **rayons infrarouges** infrared light; **rayons X** X-rays; **passer qch aux rayons X** to X-ray sth; **rayons ultraviolets** ultraviolet light

rayon[2] [rejɔ̃] NM **1** *(étagère* ▸ *gén)* shelf; *(*▸ *à livres)* shelf, bookshelf
2 *Com (dans un magasin)* department; **le r. des jouets/des surgelés** the toy/the frozen food department; **nous n'en avons plus en r.** we're out of stock
3 *Fam (domaine)* **il en connaît un r. en électricité** he really knows a thing or two about electricity; **c'est/c'est pas mon r.** that's/that's not my department
4 *Entom* comb; *(d'abeilles)* honeycomb

rayonnage [rejɔnaʒ] NM *(étagères)* shelving *(UNCOUNT)*, shelves; **sur les rayonnages** on the shelves

rayonnant, -e [rejɔnɑ̃, -ɑ̃t] ADJ **1** *(radieux)* radiant; **r. de joie** radiant with joy; **r. de santé** glowing *or* blooming with health **2** *Archit & Beaux-Arts* radiating; **gothique r.** High Gothic

rayonne [rejɔn] NF *Tex* rayon

rayonnement [rejɔnmɑ̃] NM **1** *(influence)* influence
2 *Littéraire (éclat)* radiance; **un r. émanait de tout son être** his/her entire being was radiant with joy
3 *(lumière* ▸ *d'une étoile, du feu)* radiance
4 *Phys* radiation

rayonner [3] [rejɔne] VI **1** *(personne, physionomie)* to be radiant; **r. de joie** to be radiant with joy; **r. de bonheur** to radiate happiness; **r. de santé** to be blooming with health; **son visage rayonnait/ses yeux rayonnaient d'allégresse** he/she was beaming/his/her eyes were shining with joy
2 *Littéraire (soleil)* to shine
3 *(circuler* ▸ *influence)* to spread; *(*▸ *touriste)* to tour around; *(*▸ *chaleur)* to radiate; **nos cars rayonnent dans toute la région** our coaches cover every corner of the region; **nous avons rayonné autour d'Avignon** we toured the region around Avignon
4 *(être disposé en rayons)* to radiate; **sept avenues rayonnent à partir de la place** seven avenues radiate (out) from the square

rayure [rejyr] NF **1** *(ligne)* line, stripe; *(du pelage)* stripe; **papier à rayures** lined *or* ruled paper; **tissu à rayures** striped fabric; **une chemise à rayures bleues** a blue-striped shirt; **un drapeau à rayures bleues** a flag with blue stripes **2** *(éraflure)* score, scratch **3** *(d'une arme à feu)* groove, rifling

raz [ra] NM **1** *(détroit)* strait *(run by fast tidal races, in Brittany)* **2** *(courant)* race

raz-de-marée, raz de marée [radmare] NM INV **1** *Géog* tidal wave, tsunami **2** *Fig (bouleversement)* tidal wave; **r. électoral** landslide victory

razzia [razja, radzja] NF **1** *Mil* foray, raid **2** *Fam Fig* raid; **faire une r. sur qch** to raid sth

R-C *(abrév écrite* **rez-de-chaussée)** *Br* ground floor, *Am* first floor

R-D [ɛrde] NM *Mktg (abrév* **recherche et développement)** R & D, R and D

RDA [ɛrdea] NF *Anciennement (abrév* **République démocratique allemande)** GDR

RDC [ɛrdese] NF *(abrév* **République démocratique du Congo)** **la R.** the DRC

RdC *(abrév écrite* **rez-de-chaussée)** *Br* ground floor, *Am* first floor

RDS [ɛrdeɛs] NM **1** *Fin (abrév* **remboursement de la dette sociale)** = contribution paid by every taxpayer towards the social security deficit **2** *Tech (abrév* **radio data system)** RDS

re- [rə] *voir* **r-**

ré [re] NM INV D; *(chanté)* re, ray

réa[1] [rea] NM pulley (wheel)

réa[2] [rea] NF *Fam (abrév* **réanimation)** **être en salle de r.** to be in intensive care[☐] *or Am* the ICU

réabonnement [reabɔnmɑ̃] NM *(au cinéma, au théâtre etc)* renewal of one's season ticket (**à** for); *(à une revue)* renewal of one's subscription (**à** to)

réabonner [3] [reabɔne] VT **r. qn au théâtre** to renew sb's season ticket for the theatre; **r. qn à une revue** to renew sb's subscription to a magazine
VPR **se réabonner** *(au cinéma, au théâtre etc)* to renew one's season ticket (**à** for); *(à une revue)* to renew one's subscription (**à** to)

réabsorber [3] [reapsɔrbe] VT to reabsorb

réabsorption [reapsɔrpsjɔ̃] NF reabsorption

réac [reak] *Fam Péj* ADJ reactionary[☐]
NMF reactionary[☐]

réaccoutumer [3] [reakutyme] VT to reaccustom; **r. qn à qch** to reaccustom sb to sth, to get sb used to sth again
VPR **se réaccoutumer se r. à qch** to reaccustom oneself to sth, to get used to sth again; **j'aurais du mal à me r.** I'd have trouble getting used to it again

réachat [reaʃa] NM *Com* rebuy, repurchase

réacheminement [reaʃəminmɑ̃] NM *(de marchandises)* rerouting; *(de message)* redirecting

réacheminer [3] [reaʃəmine] VT *(marchandises)* to reroute; *(message)* to redirect

réacheter [28] [reaʃte] VT *Com* to rebuy, to repurchase

réactance [reaktɑ̃s] NF reactance

réacteur [reaktœr] NM **1** *Aviat* jet (engine) **2** *Chim, Nucl & Phys* reactor; **r. nucléaire** nuclear reactor

réactif, -ive [reaktif, -iv] ADJ *Chim & Phys* reactive; **papier r.** reagent paper; **substance réactive** reactant
NM *Chim* reagent

réaction [reaksjɔ̃] NF **1** *(réponse)* reaction, response; *(des consommateurs)* feedback; **la nouvelle l'a laissée sans r.** she showed no reaction to the news; **elle eut une r. de peur/de colère** her reaction was one of fear/anger; **il a eu une r. très violente** he reacted very violently; **il n'a eu aucune r.** he didn't react at all; **avoir des réactions lentes** to be slow to react; **la voiture a de très bonnes réactions** the car responds well *or* handles well; **r. à un stimulus** stimulus response, response to a stimulus; **temps de r.** *Méd* reaction time; *Psy* latent period *or* time; **r. affective** emotional response; **r. auditive** response to auditory stimulus; **r. cutanée** skin *or Spéc* cutaneous reaction; **r. émotionnelle** emotional response; *Méd* **r. immunitaire** immune response, immunoreaction; **r. tactile** tactile response
2 *(riposte)* reaction; **en** *ou* **par r. contre** as a reaction against; **la décision a été prise en r. à...** the decision was taken in response to...
3 *Pol (mouvement)* reaction; *(personnes)* reactionaries; **gouvernement/vote de r.** reactionary government/vote
4 *Aviat, Astron, Chim & Phys* reaction; **propulsion par r. atomique** atomic-powered propulsion; **r. en chaîne** chain reaction; *Fig* chain reaction, domino effect
5 *Électron* **r. négative** negative feedback

réactionnaire [reaksjɔnɛr] ADJ reactionary
NMF reactionary

réactive [reaktiv] *voir* **réactif**

réactiver [3] [reaktive] VT **1** *(feu)* to rekindle; *(circulation sanguine)* to restore; *(système)* to reactivate; *(négociations)* to revive **2** *Chim* to reactivate

réactivité [reaktivite] NF **1** *Chim* reactivity **2** *Biol* reactivity, excitability

réactualisation [reaktɥalizasjɔ̃] NF **1** *(ajustement)* adapting, readjustment **2** *(modernisation)* updating, bringing up to date

réactualiser **[3]** [reaktɥalize] **VT 1** *(ajuster ▸ système)* to adapt, to readjust **2** *(moderniser)* to update, to bring up to date

réadaptation [readaptasjɔ̃] **NF 1** *(rééducation ▸ d'un invalide, d'un prisonnier)* rehabilitation; *(▸ d'un muscle)* re-education **2** *(réaccoutumance)* readjustment, readaptation (**à** to)

réadapter **[3]** [readapte] **VT** *(invalide, prisonnier)* to rehabilitate; *(muscle)* to re-educate

VPR se réadapter *(invalide, handicapé, exilé)* to readjust (**à** to); **après 20 ans d'exil, ils ont du mal à se r.** after 20 years in exile they're finding it hard to adjust *or* to readjust *or* to adapt

réadmettre **[84]** [readmɛtr] **VT** to readmit

réadmission [readmisjɔ̃] **NF** readmission, readmittance

réaffectation [reafɛktasjɔ̃] **NF 1** *(de ressources, de subventions)* reassignment, reallocation **2** *(d'un employé)* reassignment; **il a demandé sa r. à son poste initial** he asked to be reassigned to his original job **3** *Ordinat* reallocation

réaffecter **[4]** [reafɛkte] **VT 1** *(ressources, subventions)* to reassign, to reallocate **2** *(employé ▸ à une fonction)* to reassign; *(▸ à une région, à un pays)* to post back **3** *Ordinat* to reallocate

réafficher **[3]** [reafiʃe] **VT** *Ordinat* to redisplay

réaffirmer **[3]** [reafirme] **VT** to reaffirm, to reassert

réagir **[32]** [reaʒir] **VI 1** *Chim, Phot & Phys* to react **2** *(répondre)* to react; **il a bien/mal réagi à son départ** he reacted well/badly to his/her leaving; **il faut absolument r.** we really have to do something; **tu réagis trop violemment** you're overreacting; **et tu restes là sans r.!** how can you just sit there (and do nothing)?; **au moins ça l'a fait r.** at least it got a reaction from him/her

3 *Méd* to respond; **elle réagit bien au traitement** she's responding well to the treatment

4 *(avoir des répercussions)* **r. sur** to have an effect on, to affect

réajuster [reaʒyste] = **rajuster**

réal¹, -aux [real, -o] **NM** *(monnaie)* real

réal², -e, -aux, -ales [real, -o] **ADJ** *Hist* **galère réale** royal galley

réalésage [realezaʒ] **NM** *(action)* reboring; *(résultat)* rebore

réaléser **[18]** [realeze] **VT** to rebore

réalignement [realiɲəmɑ̃] **NM** realignment; **r. monétaire** realignment of currencies

réaligner **[3]** [realiɲe] **VT** to realign

réalisable [realizabl] **ADJ 1** *(projet)* feasible, workable; *(rêve)* attainable **2** *Fin* realizable

réalisateur, -trice [realizatœr, -tris] **NM,F 1** *Cin* director, film-maker **2** *Rad & TV* producer **3** *(maître d'œuvre)* **il a été le r. du projet** he was the one who brought the project to fruition

réalisation [realizasjɔ̃] **NF 1** *(d'un projet)* carrying out, execution; *(d'une œuvre d'art)* creation; *(d'un rêve)* fulfilment; *(d'un exploit)* achievement; **être en cours de r.** to be under way; **pour moi, c'est la r. d'un vieux rêve** for me it's an old dream come true

2 *(chose réalisée)* achievement; **le nouveau centre commercial est une r. remarquable** the new shopping centre is a major achievement; **l'une des dernières réalisations du grand architecte** one of the great architect's last works

3 *Jur (d'un contrat)* fulfilment; *Com (d'une vente)* clinching, closing; *Fin (liquidation)* realization

4 *Cin (mise en scène)* directing; *(film)* production, movie, *Br* film; **r. (de) George Cukor** *(dans un film)* directed by George Cukor; **beaucoup de comédiens se lancent dans la r. (de films)** many actors are taking up film directing; **la r. de ce film coûterait trop cher** it would cost too much to make this movie *or Br* film

5 *Rad & TV (processus)* production; *(enregistrement)* recording; **à la r., Fred X** sound engineer, Fred X

6 *Fin (d'actions)* selling out; *(d'un bénéfice)* making

réaliser **[3]** [realize] **VT 1** *(rendre réel ▸ projet)* to carry out; *(▸ rêve, ambition)* to fulfil, to realize; *(▸ espoir)* to realize

2 *(accomplir ▸ œuvre)* to complete, to carry out; *(▸ œuvre d'art)* to create; *(▸ exploit)* to achieve, to perform; **les efforts réalisés** the efforts that have been made

3 *Com (vente)* to make; *Fin (capital, valeurs)* to realize; *(bénéfice)* to make; *(actions)* to sell out; **r. des économies** to make savings; **r. un chiffre d'affaires de 10 millions d'euros** to have a turnover of 10 million euros, to have a 10 million-euro turnover

4 *Cin* to direct, to make

5 *Rad & TV* to produce

6 *(comprendre)* to realize; **as-tu réalisé que la situation est grave?** do you realize how serious the situation is?

USAGE ABSOLU je ne réalise pas encore it hasn't sunk in yet; **laisse-lui le temps de r.** give him/her time for it to sink in; **elle est encore sous le choc, mais quand elle va r.!** she's still in a state of shock, but wait till it hits her!

VPR se réaliser 1 *(s'accomplir ▸ projet)* to be carried out; *(▸ rêve, vœu)* to come true, to be fulfilled; *(▸ prédiction)* to come true **2** *(personne)* to fulfil oneself

réalisme [realism] **NM 1** *(gén)* realism; **faire preuve de r.** to be realistic; **r. politique** political realism *or* pragmatism **2** *Beaux-Arts & Littérature* realism

réaliste [realist] **ADJ 1** *(gén)* realistic **2** *Beaux-Arts & Littérature* realist

NMF realist

réalité [realite] **NF 1** *(existence)* reality; **douter de la r. d'un fait** to doubt the reality of a fact **2** *(univers réel)* **la r.** reality; **regarder la r. en face** to face up to reality; **la dure r. quotidienne** the harsh reality of everyday existence; **dans la r.** in real life; **quand la r. dépasse la fiction** when truth is stranger than fiction; *Ordinat* **r. virtuelle** virtual reality **3** *(fait)* fact; **n'en doutez pas, c'est une r.!** you'd better believe it, it's the truth!; **prendre conscience des réalités (de la vie)** to face facts; **les réalités de ce monde** the realities of this world; **elle n'a pas le sens des réalités** she has no sense of reality, she doesn't live in the real world

• **en réalité ADV 1** *(en fait)* in (actual) fact; **on m'en avait dit beaucoup de mal, mais en r. il est charmant** I'd heard a lot of bad things about him, but in (actual) fact he is charming **2** *(vraiment)* in real life; **à la scène, elle paraît plus jeune qu'elle n'est en r.** on stage, she looks younger than she is in real life

reality show [realitiʃo] **NM** *TV* reality show

realpolitik [realpɔlitik] **NF** realpolitik

réaménagement [reamenaʒmɑ̃] **NM 1** *(d'un bâtiment)* refitting *(UNCOUNT)* **2** *(d'un projet)* reorganization, replanning *(UNCOUNT)*; **r. urbain** urban redevelopment **3** *Fin (d'une dette)* rescheduling

réaménager **[17]** [reamenaʒe] **VT 1** *(espace, salle)* to refit, to refurbish **2** *(horaire)* to replan, to readjust; *(politique)* to reshape **3** *Fin (dette)* to reschedule

réamorcer **[16]** [reamɔrse] **VT 1** *(discussion)* to begin *or* to start again, to reinitiate **2** *Ordinat* to reboot

VPR se réamorcer *Ordinat* to reboot

réanimation [reanimasjɔ̃] **NF** *(action)* resuscitation; **service de r. (intensive)** intensive care unit; **admis en r.** *(service)* put in intensive care

réanimer **[3]** [reanime] **VT 1** *(malade)* to resuscitate **2** *(conversation, intérêt)* to revive

réapparaître **[91]** [reaparɛtr] **VI** *(aux être ou avoir) (gén)* to come back, to reappear, to appear again; *(douleur)* to come back, to recur, to return; *(thème, métaphore, motif)* to recur, to be repeated; **tous ces facteurs ont contribué à faire r. les conflits entre les ethnies** all of these factors have contributed to the resurgence of ethnic conflicts

réapparition [reaparisjɔ̃] **NF 1** *(du soleil, d'une personne)* reappearance; *(d'une douleur)* recurrence; *(du nationalisme, d'une maladie)* resurgence **2** *(d'une vedette)* comeback

réapparu, -e [reapary] **PP** *voir* **réapparaître**

réapproprier **[10]** [reaprɔprije] **se réapproprier VPR** to reclaim, to take back; **dans leur campagne ils veulent se r. le thème de la sécurité et du maintien de l'ordre** in their election campaign they want to reclaim the issue of law and order; **pour ce remake, le metteur en scène a réussi à se r. l'histoire** for this remake, the director managed to put his own stamp on the story

réapprovisionnement [reaprɔvizjɔnmɑ̃] **NM** *Com (d'un magasin)* restocking; *(d'un commerçant)* resupplying; **assurer le r. d'un magasin** to restock a *Br* shop *or Am* store

réapprovisionner **[3]** [reaprɔvizjɔne] **VT** *Com (magasin)* to restock (**en** with); *(commerçant)* to resupply (**en** with)

VPR se réapprovisionner *(magasin, commerçant)* to stock up again, to restock (**en** with); *(famille)* to replenish one's supplies (**en** of), to stock up (**en** on)

réargenter **[3]** [rearʒɑ̃te] **VT** to resilver

réarmement [rearməmɑ̃] **NM 1** *Mil* rearmament, rearming; *Pol* rearmament; **r. moral** moral rearmament

2 *Naut* refitting

3 *(d'arme à feu)* cocking

4 *(d'un appareil photo)* winding on, resetting

réarmer **[3]** [rearme] **VT 1** *Mil & Pol* to rearm

2 *Naut* to refit

3 *(arme à feu)* to cock

4 *(appareil photo)* to wind on, to reset

VI *(pays)* to rearm

réassort [reasɔr] **NM** new stock

réassortiment [reasɔrtimɑ̃] **NM 1** *Com (d'un magasin)* restocking; *(d'un stock)* renewing; *(de marchandises)* new stock, fresh supplies **2** *(de pièces d'un service)* matching (up); *(d'une soucoupe)* replacing

réassortir **[32]** [reasɔrtir] **VT 1** *Com (magasin)* to restock; *(stock)* to renew **2** *(tissu, parure de lit, etc)* to match

VPR se réassortir to replenish one's stock (**en** of)

réassurance [reasyrɑ̃s] **NF** reinsurance

réassurer **[3]** [reasyre] **VT** to reinsure

VPR se réassurer to reinsure

réassureur [reasyrœr] **NM** reinsurer

rebaptiser **[3]** [rəbatize] **VT** to rename

rébarbatif, -ive [rebarbatif, -iv] **ADJ 1** *(personne)* cantankerous, surly **2** *(sujet, tâche, idée)* daunting; *(style)* off-putting

rebat *etc voir* **rebattre**

rebâtir **[32]** [rəbatir] **VT** to rebuild

rebattre **[83]** [rəbatr] **VT 1** *(cartes)* to reshuffle **2** *(locution)* **elle m'a rebattu les oreilles de son divorce** she went on and on *or* she kept harping on about her divorce

> Do not confuse with **rabattre**.

rebattu, -e [rəbaty] **ADJ** *(éculé ▸ histoire, thème)* hackneyed, trite

rebelle [rəbɛl] **ADJ 1** *Pol* rebel *(avant n)*

2 *(indomptable ▸ cheval)* rebellious; *(▸ cœur, esprit)* rebellious, intractable; *(▸ enfant)* rebellious, wilful; *(▸ mèche)* unruly, wild

3 r. à *(réfractaire à)* impervious to; **r. à tout conseil** unwilling to heed advice, impervious to advice; **r. à toute discipline** unamenable to discipline

4 *(acné, fièvre)* stubborn, *Spéc* refractory

NMF rebel

rebeller **[4]** [rəbele] **se rebeller VPR** to rebel; **se r. contre** to rebel against; **la jeune génération de cinéastes qui se rebellent contre les conventions** the younger generation of film-makers who flout established conventions

rébellion [rebeljɔ̃] **NF 1** *(révolte)* rebellion; **entrer en r. (contre)** to rebel (against) **2** *(rebelles)* **la r.** the rebels

rebelote [rəbəlɔt] **NF** *Cartes* rebelote *(said when playing the second card of a pair of king and queen of trumps while playing belote)*

EXCLAM *Fam* here we go again!

rebeu [rəbø] **NM** *Fam (verlan de* **beur***)* = person born and living in France of North African immigrant parents

rebibes [rəbib] **NFPL** *Suisse (de fromage)* = thin slices of cheese; *(de viande)* = small pieces of cured meat

rebiffer **[3]** [rəbife] **se rebiffer VPR** *Fam* **quand je lui fais une remarque, il se rebiffe** when I say anything to him he reacts really badly *or* he immediately takes offence; **se r. contre qch** to kick out against sth

rebiquer [3] [rəbike] **VI** *Fam* to stick up

rebirth [ribœrs], **rebirthing** [ribœrsiŋ] **NM** *Psy* rebirthing

reblochon [rəblɔʃɔ̃] **NM** Reblochon (cheese)

reboire [108] [rəbwar] **VT** to drink again; **jamais je ne reboirai de ce vin** I'll never drink *or* touch that wine again
VI to drink again

reboisement [rəbwazmɑ̃] **NM** reafforestation

reboiser [3] [rəbwaze] **VT** to reafforest

rebond [rəbɔ̃] **NM 1** *(d'une balle)* bounce, rebound; **je l'ai attrapé au r.** I caught it on the rebound **2** *Fin (d'actions, de marché, de monnaie)* recovery

rebondi, -e [rəbɔ̃di] **ADJ** *(joue, face)* chubby, plump; *(formes)* well-rounded; **ventre r.** paunch; **une jeune fille aux formes rebondies** a curvaceous young woman; **à la poitrine rebondie** buxom

rebondir [32] [rəbɔ̃dir] **VI 1** *(balle, ballon)* to bounce
2 *(conversation, intrigue)* to get going *or* moving again; *(intérêt)* to revive, to be renewed; **faire r. qch** *(procès, scandale)* to give new impetus to sth
3 *(se remettre ▸ économie)* to recover, to pick up again; **il n'a jamais vraiment rebondi après cet échec** he never really recovered from that setback
4 *Can Fam (chèque)* to bounce

rebondissement [rəbɔ̃dismɑ̃] **NM 1** *(d'une balle)* bouncing **2** *(d'une affaire)* (new) development

rebord [rəbɔr] **NM** *(d'un fossé, d'une étagère, d'un puits)* edge; *(d'une assiette, d'un verre)* rim; *(d'une cheminée)* mantelpiece; *(d'une fenêtre)* (window) ledge *or* sill; **le savon est sur le r. de la baignoire** the soap is on the side *or* edge of the bath

reborder [3] [rəbɔrde] **VT 1** *(chapeau, vêtement)* to renew the edging on **2** *(enfant, drap)* to tuck in again

rébou [rebu] **ADJ INV** *Fam (verlan de* **bourré***) (ivre) Br* pissed, *Am* bombed

reboucher [3] [rəbuʃe] **VT 1** *(bouteille de vin)* to recork; *(flacon, carafe)* to restopper; *(tube de colle, de dentifrice)* to put the top back on; **r. après usage** *(sur emballage)* replace lid after use **2** *(évier)* to block again **3** *Constr (trou)* to fill, to plug; *(fissure)* to fill, to stop
VPR se reboucher *(évier)* to get blocked again

rebours [rəbur] **à rebours ADV 1** *(à l'envers ▸ compter, lire)* backwards; *(dans le mauvais sens)* the wrong way; **tu as compris à r.** you've got the wrong idea, *Br* you've got the wrong end of the stick; **il ne faut pas le prendre à r.!** you mustn't rub him up the wrong way!; **tu prends tout à r.!** you're always getting the wrong idea!, *Br* you're always getting the wrong end of the stick! **2** *Tex* against the nap *or* the pile
• **à rebours de PRÉP aller à r. de tout le monde** to go *or* to run counter to the general trend; **elle fait tout à r. de ce qu'on lui dit** she does the exact opposite of what people tell her

reboutement [rəbutmɑ̃] **NM** *Méd* bonesetting

rebouteur, -euse [rəbutœr, -øz], **rebouteux, -euse** [rəbutø, -øz] **NM,F** *Méd* bonesetter

reboutonner [3] [rəbutɔne] **VT** to button up again, to rebutton
VPR se reboutonner to do oneself up again

rebrancher [rəbrɑ̃ʃe] **VT** to reconnect

rebrousse-poil [rəbruspwal] **à rebrousse-poil ADV 1** *(brosser)* against the nap *or* the pile; **caresser un chat à r.** to stroke a cat the wrong way *or* against its fur **2** *(maladroitement)* the wrong way; **mieux vaut ne pas prendre le patron à r.** better not rub the boss up the wrong way

rebrousser [3] [rəbruse] **VT 1** *(cheveux)* to ruffle **2** *(poil)* to brush the wrong way; *Fam* **r. le poil à qn** to rub sb up the wrong way **3** *(locution)* **r. chemin** to turn back, to retrace one's steps

rebuffade [rəbyfad] **NF** rebuff; **essuyer une r.** to suffer a rebuff

rébus [rebys] **NM** rebus; *Fig* **ce texte est un r. pour moi** this text is a real puzzle for me

rebut [rəby] **NM 1** *(article défectueux)* second, reject
2 *(poubelle, casse)* **mettre** *ou* **jeter au r.** to throw away, to discard; **bon à mettre au r.** *(vêtement)* only fit to be thrown out; *(véhicule)* ready for the scrapheap
3 *Fig Littéraire* **le r. de la société** the dregs of society
4 *(envoi postal)* dead letter
• **de rebut ADJ 1** *(sans valeur)* **meubles de r.** unwanted furniture; **vêtements de r.** cast-offs **2** *(défectueux)* **marchandises de r.** seconds, rejects

rebutant, -e [rəbytɑ̃, -ɑ̃t] **ADJ 1** *(repoussant)* repulsive; **un visage r.** a repulsive face **2** *(décourageant ▸ style, vocabulaire)* unappealing, *esp Br* off-putting; *(▸ méthode, programme)* discouraging, *esp Br* off-putting; *(▸ tâche)* unpleasant

rebuter [3] [rəbyte] **VT 1** *(décourager)* to discourage, to put off; **ses façons ont de quoi vous r.** his/her manners are enough to put you off **2** *(dégoûter)* to put off; **cette nourriture rebuterait un homme affamé** even a starving man would be put off by that food **3** *(choquer)* **ses manières me rebutent** I find his/her behaviour quite shocking
VPR se rebuter *(se lasser)* **il était plein d'ardeur mais il s'est vite rebuté** he used to be very keen but he soon lost heart *or* his enthusiasm

recacheter [27] [rəkaʃte] **VT** to reseal

recadrage [rəkadraʒ] **NM** *Phot* cropping; *Cin* framing; *Fig* refocusing, reorientation

recadrer [3] [rəkadre] **VT** *Phot* to crop; *Cin* to frame; *Fig* to refocus, to reorientate

recalage [rəkalaʒ] **NM** *Fam (à un examen)* failing[□], *Am* flunking

recalcification [rəkalsifikasjɔ̃] **NF** recalcification

recalcifier [9] [rəkalsifje] **VT** to recalcify

récalcitrant, -e [rekalsitrɑ̃, -ɑ̃t] **ADJ** *(animal)* stubborn; *(personne)* recalcitrant, rebellious
NM,F recalcitrant

recalé, -e [rəkale] *Fam* **ADJ recalée en juin, j'ai réussi en septembre** I failed[□] *or Am* flunked in June but passed in September
NM,F failed candidate[□]; **il y a eu cinq recalés dans la classe** five people in the class have failed[□] *or Am* flunked

recaler [3] [rəkale] **VT** *Fam (candidat)* to fail[□], *Am* to flunk; **il s'est fait r. à l'examen pour la deuxième fois** he failed[□] *or Am* flunked the exam for the second time

recapitalisation [rəkapitalizasjɔ̃] **NF** *Fin* recapitalization

recapitaliser [3] [rəkapitalize] **VT** *Fin* to recapitalize

récapitulatif, -ive [rekapitylatif, -iv] **ADJ** *(note)* summarizing; *(tableau)* summary *(avant n)*
NM summary, recapitulation, résumé

récapitulation [rekapitylasjɔ̃] **NF** *(résumé)* summary, recapitulation, résumé; *(liste)* recapitulation, summary; **faire la r. de qch** to recap *or* to sum up sth

récapitulative [rekapitylativ] *voir* **récapitulatif**

récapituler [3] [rekapityle] **VT 1** *(résumer)* to summarize, to recapitulate **2** *(énumérer)* to go *or* to run over; **récapitulons vos arguments** let's run over *or* go over your arguments
USAGE ABSOLU to recap, to sum up; **alors, je récapitule...** so, I'll recap...

recaser [3] [rəkaze] *Fam* **VT** *(dans un emploi)* to find a new job for[□]
VPR se recaser *(retrouver un emploi)* to get fixed up with a new job; *(se remarier)* to get hitched again, to settle down again[□]

recel [rəsɛl] **NM** *Jur* **1** *(d'objets ▸ action)* receiving stolen goods; *(▸ résultat)* possession of stolen goods; **faire du r.** to deal in stolen goods; **condamné pour r. de bijoux volés** convicted for possession of stolen jewels **2** *(de personnes)* **r. de déserteur/malfaiteur** harbouring a deserter/a (known) criminal

receler [25] [rəsəle] **VT 1** *Jur (bijoux, trésor)* to receive; *(personne)* to harbour **2** *(mystère, ressources)* to hold; **la maison recèle un secret** the house holds a secret; **le sous-sol recèle beaucoup de pétrole** the subsoil holds a great deal of oil

receleur, -euse [rəsəlœr, -øz] **NM,F** *Jur* receiver (of stolen goods)

récemment [resamɑ̃] **ADV 1** *(dernièrement)* recently, not (very) long ago; **un journaliste r. rentré d'Afrique** a journalist just back from Africa; **ils ont emménagé r.** they moved in recently *or* not (very) long ago; **tout r. encore** just recently; **l'as-tu rencontrée r.?** have you met her lately? **2** *(nouvellement)* recently, newly; **membres r. inscrits** newly registered members

recensement [rəsɑ̃smɑ̃] **NM 1** *(inventaire ▸ gén)* count, inventory; *(▸ de population)* census; **faire un r.** to make a count *or* an inventory; **faire le r. de la population** to take a census of the population **2** *Pol* **r. des votes** registering *or* counting of the votes **3** *Mil (des futurs conscrits)* registering (for military service); *(des équipements)* inventorying

recenser [3] [rəsɑ̃se] **VT 1** *(population)* to take *or* to make a census of; *(objets)* to count, to make an inventory of; *(marchandises)* to inventory, to take stock of; **r. les marchandises en magasin** to do the stock-taking **2** *Pol (votes)* to count, to register **3** *Mil (futurs conscrits)* to register; *(équipements)* to inventory; **se faire r.** to register for military service

recenseur, -euse [rəsɑ̃sœr, -øz] **NM,F** census taker

récent, -e [resɑ̃, -ɑ̃t] **ADJ 1** *(événement)* recent; **leur mariage est tout r.** they've just *or* recently got married; **jusqu'à une date récente** until recently **2** *(bourgeois, immigré)* new

recentrage [rəsɑ̃traʒ] **NM 1** *Aut* recentring; *Tech* realigning **2** *Écon* streamlining, rationalization **3** *Pol* refocusing, redefinition

recentrer [3] [rəsɑ̃tre] **VT 1** *Aut* to recentre; *Tech* to realign
2 *Écon* to streamline, to rationalize
3 *Pol* to refocus, to redefine
4 *Sport* to cross again
VPR se recentrer to become refocused

récépissé [resepise] **NM** (acknowledgment of) receipt; **r. de dépôt** deposit receipt

réceptacle [reseptakl] **NM 1** *(réservoir)* container, vessel, receptacle **2** *Bot* receptacle

récepteur, -trice [reseptœr, -tris] **ADJ** *Rad, Tél & TV* receiving, receiver *(avant n)*
NM 1 *Électron* receiver
2 *Rad & TV* (receiving) set, receiver; **r. de radio** radio receiver; **r. de télévision** television receiver
3 *(téléphonique)* receiver; **décrocher le r.** to lift the receiver
4 *Méd* receptor; *(en neurologie)* receptor (molecule); **r. olfactif/auditif/tactile** olfactory/auditory/tactile receptor
5 *Ling* receiver

réceptif, -ive [reseptif, -iv] **ADJ 1** *(ouvert)* receptive; **r. à** open *or* receptive to **2** *Méd* susceptible (to infection)
NM *Mktg* **r. précoce** early adopter

réception [resepsjɔ̃] **NF 1** *(du courrier, d'une commande)* receipt; **dès r. de la présente** on receipt of this letter; **à payer à la r.** *Br* cash *or Am* collect on delivery; **acquitter** *ou* **payer à la r.** to pay on receipt *or* delivery; *Com* **r. définitive** final acceptance
2 *Rad & TV* reception; **ma télévision a une bonne/mauvaise r.** I get good/bad reception on my TV
3 *(accueil)* welcome, reception; **une r. chaleureuse** a warm welcome; **une r. glaciale** an icy reception; **faire une bonne r. à qn** to give sb a good reception *or* warm welcome, to receive *or* welcome sb warmly
4 *(fête, dîner)* party, reception
5 *(d'un hôtel, d'une société ▸ lieu)* reception area *or* desk; *(▸ personnel)* reception staff; **demandez à la r.** ask at reception
6 *(cérémonie d'admission)* admission; **discours de r.** induction speech
7 *Constr* **r. des travaux** acceptance (of work done)
8 *Sport (d'un sauteur)* landing; *(du ballon ▸ avec la main)* catch; **bonne r. de Pareta qui passe à Loval** *(avec le pied)* good control by Pareta who passes to Loval; **mauvaise r. de Petit** Petit miscontrols the pass

réceptionnaire [resepsjɔnɛr] NMF **1** *(dans un hôtel)* head of reception **2** *Com (de marchandises)* consignee **3** *Naut* receiving agent, receiver, consignee

réceptionner [3] [resepsjɔne] VT **1** *(marchandises)* to check and sign for, to take delivery of **2** *Sport (balle ▸ avec la main)* to catch; *(▸ avec le pied)* to control, to trap **3** *(recevoir)* to receive

réceptionniste [resepsjɔnist] NMF receptionist

réceptive [reseptiv] *voir* **réceptif**

réceptivité [reseptivite] NF **1** *(sensibilité)* receptiveness, responsiveness
2 *Méd* susceptibility (to infection)
3 *Psy* receptiveness
4 *Mktg* **r. des consommateurs** consumer acceptance

réceptrice [reseptris] *voir* **récepteur**

récessif, -ive [resesif, -iv] ADJ *Biol (gène)* recessive

récession [resesjɔ̃] NF **1** *(crise économique)* recession; **r. économique** economic recession **2** *Astron & Géog* receding *(UNCOUNT)*

récessive [resesiv] *voir* **récessif**

recette [rəsɛt] NF **1** *Com Br* takings, *Am* take; **on a fait une bonne/mauvaise r.** the *Br* takings *or Am* take were good/poor; **faire r.** *Com* to be profitable; *(film, pièce)* to be a (box-office) success, to be a hit at the box office; *(idée)* to catch on; *(mode)* to be all the rage; *(personne)* to be a great success, to be a hit; **r. annuelle** annual earnings; **r. brute** gross income *or* earnings; *Cin* **r. guichet** box-office receipts; **r. journalière** daily *Br* takings *or Am* take; **r. nette** net income *or* receipts; *Cin* **r. en salles** box-office receipts
2 *Jur & Fin (recouvrement)* collection; *(bureau)* tax (collector's) office; **faire la r. des contributions** to collect the contributions; **r. fiscale** *(administration)* revenue service, *Br* Inland Revenue, *Am* IRS; *(revenus)* tax revenue
3 *Culin* **r. (de cuisine)** recipe; **elle m'a donné la r. des crêpes** she gave me the recipe for pancakes; **livre de recettes** cookbook, *Br* cookery book
4 *Pharm* formula
5 *Fig (méthode)* **elle a une r. pour enlever les taches** she's got a foolproof method of getting rid of stains; **la r. du bonheur** the secret of *or* recipe for happiness
• **recettes** NFPL *(sommes touchées)* income *(UNCOUNT)*, receipts, incomings; **recettes et dépenses** *(gén)* income and expenses, incomings and outgoings; *(en comptabilité)* credit and debit; **recettes en devises** foreign currency earnings; **recettes de l'État** public revenue, state revenue; **recettes publiques** public revenue, statute income

recevable [rəsəvabl] ADJ **1** *(offre, excuse)* acceptable **2** *Jur (témoignage)* admissible; *(demande)* allowable; *(personne)* entitled; **témoignage non r.** inadmissible evidence; **être déclaré r. dans une demande** to be declared entitled to proceed with a claim **3** *(marchandises)* fit for acceptance

recevant, -e [rəsəvɑ̃, -ɑ̃t] ADJ *Can (personne)* hospitable, who likes to entertain

receveur, -euse [rəsəvœr, -øz] NM,F **1** *Transp* **r. (d'autobus)** (bus) conductor **2** *Admin* **r. (des postes)** postmaster, *f* postmistress; **r. (des impôts)** tax collector *or* officer; **r. des contributions** income tax collector; **r. des douanes** collector of customs; **r. des finances** district tax collector **3** *Méd* recipient

RECEVOIR [52] [rəsəvwar]

VT	
• to receive **1–3, 8, 10, 11**	• to get **1–3, 10**
• to welcome **4**	• to greet **4**
• to put up **4**	• to entertain **4**
• to admit **6**	• to see **5**
	• to pass **9**
VI	
• to entertain **1**	• to see clients/patients **2**
VPR	
• to visit each other **1**	• to land **2**

VT **1** *(courrier, commandes, coup de téléphone, compliments)* to receive, to get; *(salaire, somme)* to receive, to get, to be paid; *(cadeau)* to get, to receive, to be given; *(prix, titre)* to receive, to get, to be awarded; *(déposition, réclamation, ordre)* to receive; **nous n'avons toujours rien reçu** we still haven't received anything; **voilà longtemps que je n'ai pas reçu de ses nouvelles** it's a long time since I last heard from him/her; **nous avons bien reçu votre courrier du 12 mai** we acknowledge receipt *or* confirm receipt of your letter dated *Br* 12 May *or Am* May 12; **je reçois une livraison chaque semaine** I get weekly deliveries; **cette hypothèse n'a pas encore reçu de confirmation** that hypothesis has yet to be confirmed; **je n'ai de conseils à r. de personne!** I don't have to take advice from anybody!; **je n'ai pas l'habitude de r. des ordres** I'm not in the habit of taking orders; **veuillez r., Madame, l'expression de mes sentiments les meilleurs** *ou* **mes salutations distinguées** *(à quelqu'un dont on connaît le nom) Br* yours sincerely, *Am* sincerely (yours); *(à quelqu'un dont on ne connaît pas le nom) Br* yours faithfully, *Am* sincerely (yours)
2 *(attention)* to receive, to get; *(affection, soins)* to receive; *(éducation)* to get
3 *(subir ▸ coups)* to get, to receive; **r. un coup sur la tête** to receive a blow to *or* to get hit on the head; **elle a reçu plusieurs coups de couteau** she was stabbed several times; **la bouteille est tombée et c'est lui qui a tout reçu** the bottle fell over and it went all over him
4 *(chez soi ▸ accueillir)* to greet, to welcome; *(▸ inviter)* to entertain; *(▸ héberger)* to take in, to put up; **je reçois quelques amis lundi, serez-vous des nôtres?** I'm having a few friends round on Monday, will you join us?; **r. qn à dîner** *(avec simplicité)* to have sb round for dinner, to invite sb to dinner; *(solennellement)* to entertain sb to dinner; **ils m'ont reçu à bras ouverts** they welcomed me with open arms; **j'ai été très bien reçu** I was made (to feel) most welcome; **j'ai été mal reçu** I was made to feel unwelcome; **elle est reçue partout** she's welcomed in all circles; **ils ont reçu la visite de cambrioleurs** they were visited by burglars; **ils ont reçu la visite de la police** they received a visit from the police; **je reçois mes parents pour une semaine** I'm having my parents to stay for a week; **nous ne pouvons guère r. plus de deux personnes** we can hardly have more than two people
5 *(à son lieu de travail ▸ client, représentant)* to see; **crois-tu qu'elle va nous r.?** do you think she'll see us?; **ils furent reçus par le Pape** they had an audience with *or* were received by the Pope
6 *(dans un club, une société ▸ nouveau membre)* to admit; **Livot a été reçu à l'Académie française** Livot has been admitted to the Académie Française
7 *(abriter)* **l'école peut r. 800 élèves** the school can take up to 800 pupils; **l'hôtel peut r. 100 personnes** the hotel can accommodate 100 people; **le chalet peut r. six personnes** the chalet sleeps six (people); **ce port peut r. les gros pétroliers** the port can handle large oil tankers; **le stade peut r. jusqu'à 75000 personnes** the stadium can hold up to 75,000 people *or* has a capacity of 75,000
8 *(eaux de pluie)* to collect; *(lumière)* to receive
9 *(surtout au passif) (candidat)* to pass; **elle a été reçue à l'épreuve de français** she passed her French exam; **je ne suis pas reçu** I didn't pass
10 *Rad & TV* to receive, to get; **vous recevez la huitième chaîne?** do you get channel eight?
11 *Rel (sacrement, vœux)* to receive; *(confession)* to hear
12 *Fin* **à r.** *(effets, intérêts)* receivable

VI **1** *(donner une réception)* to entertain; **elle sait r.** she's a good hostess
2 *(avocat, conseiller)* to be available (to see clients); *(médecin)* to see patients; **le médecin reçoit/ne reçoit pas aujourd'hui** the doctor is/isn't seeing patients today

VPR **se recevoir 1** *(s'inviter)* to visit each other
2 *Sport* to land; **elle s'est mal reçue** she landed badly *or* awkwardly

rechange [rəʃɑ̃ʒ] NM **1** *Banque (d'un effet)* redraft **2** *(vêtements)* change of clothes, spare set of clothes
• **de rechange** ADJ **1** *(de secours ▸ pièce, vêtement)* spare; **elle n'avait même pas de linge de r.** she didn't even have a change of clothes **2** *(de remplacement ▸ solution, politique)* alternative

rechanger [17] [rəʃɑ̃ʒe] VT to change (again), to exchange (again)

rechanter [3] [rəʃɑ̃te] VT to sing again

rechapage [rəʃapaʒ] NM *Aut* retreading

rechaper [3] [rəʃape] VT *Aut* to retread; **pneus réchapés** retreads

réchapper [3] [reʃape] **réchapper à, réchapper de** VT IND *(maladi, accident)* to survive, to come through; **il ne réchappera pas à ce scandale** his reputation won't survive the scandal; **en r.** *(rester en vie)* to come through, to escape alive; **si j'en réchappe** if I come through this, if I survive

recharge [rəʃarʒ] NF **1** *(d'arme)* reload; *(de stylo, de briquet, de parfum)* refill; *(de téléphone portable)* top-up card **2** *(action) & Mil* reloading; *Élec* recharging; **mettre l'accumulateur en r.** to put the battery on charge

rechargeable [rəʃarʒabl] ADJ *(briquet, stylo, vaporisateur)* refillable; *(pile, batterie)* rechargeable

rechargement [rəʃarʒəmɑ̃] NM **1** *(d'une arme, d'un appareil photo)* reloading; *(d'une pile, d'une batterie)* recharging; *(d'un briquet, d'un stylo, d'un vaporisateur, d'un poêle à bois, à charbon)* refilling; *(d'un poêle à mazout)* refuelling **2** *(de voiture, de camion)* reloading

recharger [17] [rəʃarʒe] VT **1** *(réapprovisionner ▸ arme, appareil photo)* to reload; *(▸ pile, batterie)* to recharge; *(▸ briquet, stylo, vaporisateur, poêle à bois, à charbon)* to refill; *(▸ poêle à mazout)* to refuel; *Fam Fig* **r. ses accus** to recharge one's batteries; **r. un téléphone portable** *(recharger la batterie)* to charge (up) *or* recharge a *Br* mobile phone *or Am* cellphone; *(ajouter des unités) Br* to top up a mobile phone, *Am* to refill a cellphone **2** *(voiture, camion)* to reload; **il a fallu r. les bagages dans la voiture** we had to load the bags back into the car **3** *Ordinat* to reload

réchaud [reʃo] NM **1** *(de cuisson)* (portable) stove; **r. à alcool** spirit stove; **r. de camping** *(à gaz)* camping stove; *(à pétrole)* Primus® (stove); **r. à gaz** (portable) gas stove **2** *(chauffe-plats)* plate warmer, chafing dish

réchauffage [reʃofaʒ] NM reheating

réchauffé, -e [reʃofe] ADJ **1** *(nourriture)* reheated, warmed-up, heated-up **2** *Fig (plaisanterie)* stale
NM **ça a un goût de r.** it tastes like it's been reheated; *Fig Péj* **c'est du r.** that's old hat; **rien de nouveau dans le journal sur l'affaire, il n'y a que du r.** there's nothing new in the paper about the business, just a rehash of what's been said already

réchauffement [reʃofmɑ̃] NM warming up *(UNCOUNT)*; **r. de l'atmosphère, r. de la planète** *ou* **planétaire** global warming; **on annonce un léger r. pour le week-end** temperatures will rise slightly this weekend

réchauffer [3] [reʃofe] VT **1** *(nourriture)* to heat *or* to warm up (again); **je vais faire r. la soupe** I'll heat up the soup **2** *(personne, salle)* to warm up; **il frappait ses mains l'une contre l'autre pour les r.** he was clapping his hands together to warm them up; **tu as l'air** *ou* **tu es bien réchauffé!** don't you feel the cold? **3** *Fig (ambiance)* to warm up; *(ardeur)* to rekindle; **ça vous réchauffe le cœur de les voir** it warms (the cockles of) your heart to see them; **ses bonnes paroles m'avaient réchauffé le cœur** his/her kind words had warmed my heart
USAGE ABSOLU **ça réchauffe, hein?** it really warms you up *or* gives you a nice warm glow inside, doesn't it?
VPR **se réchauffer 1** *(emploi passif)* **un soufflé ne se réchauffe pas** you can't reheat a soufflé **2** *(personne)* to warm up; **je n'arrive pas à me r. aujourd'hui** I just can't get warm today; **alors, tu te réchauffes?** so, are you warming up a bit now?; **se r. les pieds/mains** to warm one's feet/hands (up) **3** *(pièce, sol, temps)* to warm up, to get warmer; **ça ne se réchauffe guère!** the weather isn't exactly getting warmer!

réchauffeur [reʃofœr] NM heater; **r. d'air/d'eau/d'huile** air/water/oil heater

rechausser [3] [rəʃose] VT **1** *(personne)* **r. qn** to put sb's shoes back on for him/her

2 *(skis)* to put on again
3 *Agr & Hort* to earth *or* to bank up
4 *Constr* to consolidate (the base of)
VPR **se rechausser** to put one's shoes back on

rêche [rɛʃ] ADJ **1** *(matière, vin)* rough; *(fruit)* bitter **2** *Fig (voix, ton)* harsh, rough

recherche [rəʃɛrʃ] NF **1** *(d'un objet, d'une personne, d'un emploi, de la vérité)* search (**de** for); *(du bonheur, de la gloire, du plaisir)* pursuit (**de** of); *(d'informations)* research (**de** into); **la r. d'un bon avocat m'a déjà pris deux mois** I've already spent two months looking for *or* searching for a good lawyer
2 *Ordinat* search, searching *(UNCOUNT)*; *(de données, d'un fichier)* retrieval; **faire une r.** to do a search; **r. arrière** backward search; **r. avant, r. vers le bas** forward search; **r. booléenne** Boolean search; **r. documentaire** information retrieval; **r. de données** data retrieval; **r. globale** global search; **r. et remplacement** search and replace; **r. vers le haut** backward search
3 *Jur* search; **action en r. de paternité** paternity proceedings *or Am* suit
4 *(prospection)* **r. minière** mining; **r. pétrolière** oil prospecting
5 *(en sciences, en art, en lettres)* **la r.** research; **le budget de la r.** the research budget; **la r. sur le cancer** cancer research; **bourse/travaux de r.** research grant/work; **faire de la r.** to do research; **elle fait de la r. en chimie** *(spécialiste)* she's a research chemist; *(étudiante)* she's a chemistry research student; **r. scientifique** scientific research
6 *Mktg* research; **r. ad hoc** ad hoc research; **recherches sur les besoins des consommateurs** consumer research; **r. commerciale** marketing research; **r. et développement** research and development; **r. documentaire** desk research; **recherches par panel** panel research; **r. sur les prix** pricing research; **r. de produits** product research; **r. par sondage** survey research; **recherches sur le terrain** field research
7 *(raffinement)* sophistication, refinement; *(affectation)* affectation, ostentatiousness; **vêtu avec r.** elegantly dressed; **s'habiller avec r.** to be a fastidious dresser; **s'exprimer avec r.** to be highly articulate; **sans r.** *(style)* simple, plain
• **recherches** NFPL **1** *(enquête)* search; **les recherches de la police pour rattraper le fuyard sont restées vaines** despite a police search, the runaway has not been found; **dans l'affaire Mennesson, la police continue les** *ou* **ses recherches** the police are continuing their enquiry into the Mennesson affair; **faire des recherches (sur qch)** *(gén)* to inquire (into sth) **2** *(travaux ▸ gén)* work, research; *(▸ de médecine)* research; **une équipe d'archéologues mène déjà des recherches sur le site** a team of archeologists is already working on *or* researching the site
• **à la recherche de** PRÉP in search of, looking *or* searching for; **être/partir/se mettre à la r. de** to be/to set off/to go in search of; **ils ont fait tout Paris à la r. d'un vase identique** they searched the whole of Paris for an identical vase; **nous sommes toujours à la r. d'un remède** we're still looking for a cure; **depuis combien de temps êtes-vous à la r. d'un emploi?** how long have you been looking for a job?; **une vie passée à la r. des plaisirs/de la fortune** a life spent in pursuit of pleasure/riches

recherché, -e [rəʃɛrʃe] ADJ **1** *(prisé ▸ mets)* choice *(avant n)*; *(▸ comédien)* in demand, much sought-after; *(▸ objet rare)* much sought-after; **ce style de fauteuil est très r.** there's a lot of demand for this type of chair **2** *(raffiné ▸ langage)* studied, recherché; *(▸ tenue)* elegant; *(▸ style)* ornate, elaborate; *Péj (affecté)* affected

rechercher [3] [rəʃɛrʃe] VT **1** *(document, objet)* to look *or* to search for; *(disparu)* to search for; *(assassin)* to look for; **r. un passage dans un livre** to try and find a passage in a book; *Tél* **nous recherchons votre correspondant** we're trying to connect you; **on recherche pour meurtre homme brun, 32 ans** wanted for murder: brown-haired, 32-year-old man; **la police recherche les témoins de l'accident** the police are appealing for anyone who witnessed the accident to come forward
2 *(dans une annonce)* **(on) recherche jeunes gens pour travail bien rémunéré** young people wanted for well-paid job
3 *(cause)* to look into, to investigate; **on recherche toujours la cause du sinistre** the cause of the fire is still being investigated
4 *(compliments, pouvoir, gloire)* to seek (out); *(sécurité, solitude)* to look for; *(fortune, plaisirs)* to be in search of; *(beauté, pureté)* to strive for, to aim at; **r. l'affection/la compagnie de qn** to seek out sb's affection/company
5 *(récupérer ▸ personne)* to collect, to fetch back (again); **je viendrai te r.** I'll come and fetch you; **j'ai laissé ma bicyclette chez Paul, il va falloir que j'aille la r.** I left my bike at Paul's place, I'll have to go and get it back
6 *(chercher à nouveau)* to search *or* to look for again
7 *(prendre à nouveau)* **va me r. du pain chez le boulanger/à la cuisine** go and get me some more bread from the baker's/kitchen
8 *Ordinat* to search; **r. et remplacer qch** to search and replace sth; **r. vers le bas/haut** to search forwards/backwards

rechigner [3] [rəʃiɲe] VI **1** *(montrer sa mauvaise humeur)* to grimace, to frown **2** *(protester)* to grumble; **fais-le sans r.** do it without making a fuss
• **rechigner à** VT IND **elle rechigne à faire cette vérification** she's reluctant to carry out this check; **r. à la tâche** *ou* **à l'ouvrage** to be unwilling to do it; **la vieille Marie, en voilà une qui ne rechignait pas à l'ouvrage!** old Marie didn't mind a bit of hard work!

rechute [rəʃyt] NF **1** *Méd* relapse; **avoir** *ou* **faire une r.** to (have a) relapse **2** *(d'une mauvaise habitude)* relapse **3** *Écon* **on craint une r. de l'activité économique** there are fears of a further slump

rechuter [3] [rəʃyte] VI **1** *Méd* to (have a) relapse **2** *(dans une mauvaise habitude)* to relapse

récidivant, -e [residivɑ̃, -ɑ̃t] ADJ recurring

récidive [residiv] NF **1** *Jur (après première condamnation)* second offence; *(après deuxième condamnation)* subsequent offence; **en cas de r.** in the event of a second *or* subsequent offence; **elle n'en est pas à sa première r.** this is the latest in a long line of offences, she has reoffended on more than one occasion; *Fig* **à la première r., je confisque ton vélo!** if you do that once more, I'll confiscate your bike! **2** *Méd* recurrence

récidiver [3] [residive] VI **1** *Jur (après première condamnation)* to commit a second offence; *(après deuxième condamnation)* to commit a subsequent offence **2** *(recommencer)* **il récidive dans ses plaintes** he keeps making the same complaints (over and over again) **3** *Méd* to recur, to be recurrent

récidiviste [residivist] ADJ reoffending, *Spéc* recidivist
NMF *(pour la première fois)* second offender, *Spéc* recidivist; *(de longue date)* persistent *or* habitual offender, *Spéc* recidivist

récif [resif] NM reef; **r. corallien** *ou* **de corail** coral reef

récipiendaire [resipjɑ̃dɛr] NMF **1** *(nouveau venu)* member elect **2** *(d'une médaille, d'un diplôme)* recipient

récipient [resipjɑ̃] NM container

> Il faut noter que le terme anglais **recipient** est un faux ami. Il signifie **destinataire** ou **bénéficiaire**.

réciprocité [resiprɔsite] NF reciprocity

réciproque [resiprɔk] ADJ **1** *(mutuel)* mutual; **je vous hais! – c'est r.!** I hate you! – I hate you too *or* the feeling's mutual!; **l'affection qu'elle portait au jeune homme n'était pas r.** her affection for the young man was not reciprocated *or* returned
2 *(bilatéral ▸ accord, convention)* reciprocal
3 *(en logique)* converse; **proposition r.** converse (proposition)
4 *Gram & Math* reciprocal
NF **1 la r.** *(l'inverse)* the reverse, the opposite; **pourtant la r. n'est pas vraie** though the reverse isn't true, but not vice versa; **je ne l'aime pas, et la r. est vraie** I don't like him/her and he/she doesn't like me either *or* and the feeling's mutual **2 la r.** *(la même chose)* the same; **ils vous ont invités, à vous de leur rendre la r.** they invited you, now it's up to you to do the same *or* to invite them in return; **elle m'a roulé, mais j'ai bien l'intention de lui rendre la r.** she conned me, but I fully intend to get even with her *or* to get my own back **3** *Math* reciprocal function

réciproquement [resiprɔkmɑ̃] ADV **1** *(mutuellement)* **ils ont le devoir de se protéger r.** it is their duty to protect each other *or* one another **2** *(inversement)* vice versa; **ce qui est blanc ici est noir là-bas et r.** what is white here is black over there and vice versa

réciproquer [3] [resiprɔke] *Belg* VI **je vous souhaite une bonne année! – je réciproque!** happy New Year! – same to you!
VT *(voeux)* to return

récit [resi] NM **1** *(histoire racontée)* story, tale, *Sout* narration; **il nous fit le r. de ses aventures** he gave us an account of his adventures; **faites le r. de vos dernières vacances** write an account of your last *Br* holiday *or Am* vacation; **nous avons tous frémi au r. de cette histoire** we all shivered when we heard the tale
2 *(exposé)* account; **le r. chronologique des faits** a chronological account of the facts; **un r. circonstancié** a blow-by-blow account
3 *Littérature & Théât* narrative; **r. de voyage** *(livre)* travel book
4 *Mus (dans un opéra)* recitative; *(solo)* solo; *(clavier d'orgue)* third manual, choir (organ)

récital, -als [resital] NM recital; **r. de piano** piano recital

récitant, -e [resitɑ̃, -ɑ̃t] ADJ *Mus* solo
NM,F *Cin & Théât* narrator; *Mus* soloist

récitatif [resitatif] NM recitative

récitation [resitasjɔ̃] NF **1** *(d'un texte)* recitation **2** *Scol (poème)* recitation piece; **on leur a fait apprendre une belle r.** they were given a beautiful poem to learn (by heart)

réciter [3] [resite] VT **1** *(dire par cœur ▸ leçon)* to repeat, to recite; *(▸ discours)* to give; *(▸ poème, prière)* to say, to recite; *(▸ formule)* to recite **2** *(dire sans sincérité)* **elle avait l'air de r. un texte** she sounded as if she was reading from a book; **le témoin a récité sa déposition** the witness reeled off his statement

reck [rɛk] NM *Suisse* **1** *Sport* horizontal bar **2** *(pente)* steep slope

réclamant, -e [reklamɑ̃, -ɑ̃t] NM,F *Jur* claimant

réclamation [reklamasjɔ̃] NF **1** *Admin (plainte)* complaint; **pour toute r., s'adresser au guichet 16** all complaints should be addressed *or* referred to desk 16; **faire une r.** to lodge a complaint; **service/bureau des réclamations** complaints department/office
2 *Jur (demande)* claim, demand; **faire une r.** to lodge a claim; **r. en dommages-intérêts** claim for damages; **r. d'indemnité** claim for compensation
3 *(récrimination)* complaining *(UNCOUNT)*; **les réclamations continuelles des enfants** the children's incessant complaining
4 *(dans le domaine fiscal)* tax adjustment claim

réclame [reklam] NF *Vieilli* **1 la r.** *(la publicité)* advertising *(UNCOUNT)*; **faire de la r. pour qch** to advertise sth; *Fig* **ça ne va pas lui faire de r.** it's not a very good advertisement for him/her **2** *(annonce, panneau)* advertisement; **j'ai vu la r. de cette voiture à la télé** I saw the commercial *or Br* advert for this car on TV; **r. lumineuse** illuminated sign
• **en réclame** ADJ on (special) offer; **article en r.** special offer; **le café est en r. cette semaine** there's a special offer on coffee *or* coffee's on special offer this week ADV at a discount

réclamer [3] [reklame] VT **1** *(argent, augmentation ▸ gén)* to ask for; *(▸ avec insistance)* to demand; *(attention, silence)* to call for, to demand; *(personne)* to ask *or* to clamour for; **l'enfant ne cesse de r. sa mère** the child is continually asking for his mother; **je réclame le silence!** silence, please!; **Monsieur le Président, je réclame la parole** Mr President, may I say something?; **elle me doit encore de l'argent mais je n'ose pas le lui r.** she still owes me money but I daren't ask for it back; **r. le secours de qn** to ask sb for assistance
2 *(revendiquer ▸ droit)* to claim; *(▸ somme due)* to put in for, to claim; **r. des dommages et intérêts** to claim compensation *or* damages; **r. sa part d'héritage** to claim one's share of the inheritance; **je**

ne fais que r. mon dû I am merely claiming what is mine

3 *(nécessiter ▸ précautions)* to call for; *(▸ soins)* to require; *(▸ explication)* to require, to demand; **la situation réclame des mesures d'exception** the situation calls for special measures

USAGE ABSOLU *Fam* **le bébé est toujours à r.** the baby's always wanting to be fed

VI 1 *(se plaindre)* to complain; **r. auprès de qn** to complain to sb

2 *(protester)* **r. contre qch** to cry out against sth

VPR se réclamer se r. de qn *(utiliser son nom)* to use sb's name; *(se prévaloir de lui)* to invoke sb's name; **les organisations se réclamant du marxisme** organizations calling *or* labelling themselves Marxist

> Il faut noter que le verbe anglais **to reclaim** est un faux ami. Il signifie **récupérer**.

reclassement [rəklasmɑ̃] **NM 1** *(de données ▸ alphabétiques)* reordering; *(▸ numériques)* reordering, resequencing

2 *(d'un dossier ▸ remise en place)* refiling; *(▸ nouveau classement)* reclassifying

3 *Admin (d'un fonctionnaire)* regrading

4 *(d'un chômeur)* placement; *(d'un handicapé, d'un ex-détenu)* rehabilitation

reclasser [3] [rəklase] **VT 1** *(par ordre alphabétique)* to reorder; *(par ordre numérique)* to reorder, to resequence

2 *(ranger)* to put back, to refile; *(réorganiser)* to reclassify, to reorganize

3 *Admin (salaires)* to restructure; *(fonctionnaire)* to regrade

4 *(chômeur)* to place; *(handicapé, ex-détenu)* to rehabilitate

reclus, -e [rəkly, -yz] **ADJ** solitary, secluded; **mener une vie recluse** to lead a secluded existence

NM,F recluse; **vivre en r.** to live like a hermit *or* recluse

réclusion [reklyzjɔ̃] **NF 1** *Littéraire (solitude)* reclusion, seclusion **2** *Jur* imprisonment; **r. criminelle** imprisonment with labour; **condamné à la r. criminelle à perpétuité** sentenced to life (imprisonment), given a life sentence

réclusionnaire [reklyzjɔnɛr] **NMF** prisoner

récognition [rekɔgnisjɔ̃] **NF** recognition

recoiffer [3] [rəkwafe] **VT r. ses cheveux** to do *or* to redo one's hair; **r. qn** *(le peigner)* to redo sb's hair, to do sb's hair (again); *(lui remettre un chapeau)* to put sb's hat back on

VPR se recoiffer 1 *(se peigner)* to do *or* to redo one's hair **2** *(remettre son chapeau)* to put one's hat back on

recoin [rəkwɛ̃] **NM 1** *(coin)* corner, nook; **elle a dû le cacher dans quelque r.** she must have hidden it in some corner or other; **une maison pleine de recoins** a rambling house, a house full of nooks and crannies; **chercher dans le moindre r.** *ou* **dans tous les (coins et) recoins** to search every nook and cranny **2** *Fig (partie secrète)* recess; **les recoins de l'inconscient** the (hidden) recesses of the unconscious

reçoit, reçoivent *etc voir* **recevoir**

récollection [rekɔlɛksjɔ̃] **NF** *Rel (recueillement)* meditation, recollection; *(retraite spirituelle)* retreat

recoller [3] [rəkɔle] **VT 1** *(objet brisé)* to stick *or* to glue back together; *(timbre)* to stick back on; *(enveloppe)* to stick back down, to restick; *(semelle)* to stick *or* to glue back on; **r. les morceaux** *(avec de la colle)* to stick *or* to glue the pieces back together (again); *(avec de l'adhésif)* to tape the pieces back together (again); *Fig* to patch things up **2** *(appuyer)* **il recolla son front à la vitre glacée** he pressed his forehead back against the frosted window pane **3** *Fam (redonner)* **on m'a recollé une amende** I've been landed with another fine; **on nous a recollé un prof nul** we've been landed with another useless teacher

• **recoller à VT IND** *Sport* **r. au peloton** to catch up with the bunch

VPR se recoller 1 *(emploi passif)* **ça se recolle très facilement** it can easily be stuck back together **2** *(se ressouder ▸ os)* to knit (together), to mend; *(▸ objet)* to stick (together) **3** *Fam Fig* **se r. avec qn** *(se réinstaller avec)* to move back in with sb□

récoltable [rekɔltabl] **ADJ** ready for harvesting

récoltant, -e [rekɔltɑ̃, -ɑ̃t] **ADJ propriétaire** *ou* **viticulteur r.** = winegrower who harvests his own grapes

NM,F grower

récolte [rekɔlt] **NF 1** *(des céréales)* harvesting *(UNCOUNT)*; *(des fruits, des légumes)* picking *(UNCOUNT)*; *(des pommes de terre)* lifting *(UNCOUNT)*; *(du miel)* gathering, collecting *(UNCOUNT)*; **ils ont déjà commencé à faire la r.** they've already started harvesting **2** *(quantité récoltée)* harvest; *(denrées récoltées)* crop; **la r. a été bonne cette année** the harvest *or* crop was good this year **3** *(de documents, d'informations)* gathering, collecting

récolter [3] [rekɔlte] **VT 1** *(céréales)* to harvest; *(légumes, fruits)* to pick; *(pommes de terre)* to lift; *(miel)* to collect, to gather; *Fig* **il récolte ce qu'il a semé** it's his own fault, he's reaping what he sowed **2** *(informations, argent)* to collect, to gather; **la police a pu r. quelques indices** the police were able to gather a few clues **3** *Fam (ennuis, maladie, etc)* to get; **tout ce que j'ai récolté, c'est un bon rhume** all I got (out of it) was a bad cold; **depuis qu'il a acheté cette maison, il n'a récolté que des ennuis** he's had nothing but trouble since he bought that house

recombinaison [rəkɔ̃binɛzɔ̃] **NF** *Biol & Chim* recombination

recombinant, -e [rəkɔ̃binɑ̃, -ɑ̃t] **ADJ** *Biol & Chim* recombinant

recommandable [rəkɔmɑ̃dabl] **ADJ** commendable; **r. à tous égards** *(personne)* highly respectable; **un individu/hôtel peu r.** a rather disreputable character/hotel; **le procédé est peu r.** that isn't a very commendable thing to do

recommandation [rəkɔmɑ̃dasjɔ̃] **NF 1** *(conseil)* advice, recommendation; **tout ira bien si tu suis mes recommandations** everything will be all right if you follow my advice; **faire qch sur la r. de qn** to do sth on sb's recommendation; **je lui ai fait mes dernières recommandations** I gave him/her some last-minute advice

2 *(appui)* recommendation, reference; **avez-vous des recommandations?** do you have references?; **je vous mets un mot de r. pour le spécialiste** I'll write you a referral for the specialist

3 *(d'un courrier ▸ sans avis de réception) Br* registering, *Am* certifying; *(▸ avec avis de réception)* recording

4 *Pol* **r. de l'ONU** UN recommendation

recommandé, -e [rəkɔmɑ̃de] **ADJ 1** *(conseillé)* advisable; **il est r. de...** it is advisable to...; **il est r. aux visiteurs de se munir de leurs passeports** visitors are advised to take their passports; **la réservation est fortement recommandée** you are strongly advised to book in advance **2** *(courrier ▸ avec avis de réception) Br* recorded, *Am* certified; *(▸ à valeur assurée)* registered

NM *(courrier ▸ avec avis de réception) Br* recorded *or Am* certified delivery item; *(▸ à valeur assurée)* registered item; **par courrier r.** by *Br* recorded delivery *or Am* certified mail; **en r.** *(avec avis de réception)* by *Br* recorded delivery *or Am* certified mail; *(à valeur assurée)* by registered *Br* post *or Am* mail

recommander [3] [rəkɔmɑ̃de] **VT 1** *(conseiller ▸ produit, personne)* to recommend; **cet hôtel est recommandé par tous les guides** this hotel is recommended in all the guidebooks; **je te recommande vivement mon médecin** I (can) heartily recommend my doctor to you

2 *(exhorter à)* to recommend, to advise; **je vous recommande la prudence** I recommend *or* I advise you to be cautious, I advise caution; **r. à qn de faire qch** to advise sb to do sth

3 *(confier)* **r. qn à qn** to place sb in sb's care; *Rel* **r. son âme à Dieu** to commend one's soul *or* oneself to God

4 *(courrier ▸ pour attester sa réception) Br* to record, *Am* to certify; *(▸ pour l'assurer)* to register

5 *(boisson)* **r. un café/whisky** to order another coffee/whisky

VPR se recommander 1 se r. à *(s'en remettre à)* to commend oneself to; **recommandons-nous à Dieu** let us commend our souls to God

2 se r. de qn *(postulant)* to give sb's name as a reference; **tu peux te r. de moi** *(à un postulant)* you can give my name as a referee

3 *Littéraire (montrer sa valeur)* **elle se recommande par son efficacité** her efficiency commends her *or* is a strong point in her favour

4 *Suisse (insister)* **se r. auprès de qn que...** to point out to sb that...; **je me recommande pour que vous fermiez bien la porte à la clé** I'd just like to remind you to make sure you lock the door

recommencement [rəkɔmɑ̃smɑ̃] **NM** resumption; **la vie est un éternel r.** every day is a new beginning; **l'histoire est un éternel r.** history is always repeating itself

recommencer [16] [rəkɔmɑ̃se] **VT 1** *(refaire ▸ dessin, lettre, travail etc)* to start *or* to begin again; *(▸ attaque)* to renew, to start again; *(▸ expérience)* to repeat; *(▸ erreur)* to repeat, to make again; **recommence ta phrase depuis le début** start your sentence again from the beginning; **ne recommence pas tes bêtises** don't start that nonsense again; **recommençons la scène 4** let's do scene 4 again; **si seulement on pouvait r. sa vie!** if only one could start one's life afresh *or* begin one's life all over again!; **tout est à r., il faut tout r.** we have to start *or* to begin all over again

2 *(reprendre ▸ histoire, conversation)* to resume, to carry on with; *(▸ lecture, travail)* to resume, to go back to; *(▸ campagne, lutte)* to resume, to take up again; **la vie est une lutte toujours recommencée** life is an ongoing *or* continuous struggle

USAGE ABSOLU ça fait trois fois que je recommence I've started this three times; **ne recommence pas!** don't do that again!; **le voilà qui recommence!** he's at it again!

VI 1 *(depuis le début)* to start *or* to begin again; *(après interruption)* to resume; **les cours ne recommencent qu'en octobre** term doesn't begin *or* start again until October; **tenez-vous tranquilles, ça ne va pas r. comme hier, non?** calm down, you're not going to start behaving like you did yesterday, are you?; **ça y est, ça recommence!** here we go again!

2 *(se remettre)* **r. à faire qch** to start doing *or* to do sth again; **elle a recommencé à danser deux mois après son accident** she started dancing again *or* she went back to dancing two months after her accident; **depuis quand a-t-il recommencé à boire?** when did he start drinking again?; **mon genou recommence à me faire mal** my knee's started aching again

3 *(tournure impersonnelle)* **il a recommencé à neiger dans la nuit** it started snowing again during the night; **il recommence à faire froid** it's beginning *or* starting to get cold again; **il recommence à y avoir des moustiques** the mosquitoes are back (again)

recommercialiser [3] [rəkɔmɛrsjalize] **VT** to re-market

récompense [rekɔ̃pɑ̃s] **NF 1** *(d'un acte)* reward, *Sout* recompense; **en r. de** as a reward *or* in return for; **en r.** *ou* **pour ta r., accepte ce cadeau** please accept this gift as a reward; *Fam Ironique* **il a trimé toute sa vie, et voilà sa r.!** he's slaved away all his life and that's all the thanks *or* the reward he gets!; **qu'il soit heureux, ce serait là ma plus belle r.** as long as he is happy, that will be ample recompense *or* reward for me; **la juste r. de ses crimes** just retribution for his/her crimes; **forte r.** *(petite annonce)* generous reward **2** *(prix)* award, prize; **la remise des récompenses** the presentation of awards

récompenser [3] [rekɔ̃pɑ̃se] **VT 1** *(pour un acte)* to reward, *Sout* to recompense (**de** for); **tu mérites d'être récompensé** you deserve a reward *or* to be rewarded; *Ironique* **voilà comment je suis récompensé de ma peine!** that's all the reward I get for my troubles! **2** *(primer)* to give an award *or* a prize to, to reward; **le scénario a été récompensé à Cannes** the script won an award at Cannes

recomposer [3] [rəkɔ̃poze] **VT 1** *(reconstituer)* to piece *or* to put together (again), to reconstruct

2 *Typ (page)* to reset; *(texte)* to rekey

3 *Chim & Ling* to recompose

4 *Tél* to redial, to dial again

recomposition [rəkɔ̃pozisjɔ̃] **NF 1** *(reconstitution)* reconstruction **2** *Typ (d'une page)* resetting; *(d'un texte)* rekeying **3** *Chim & Ling* recomposition

recompter [3] [rəkɔ̃te] **VT** to count again

réconciliation [rekɔ̃siljasjɔ̃] **NF 1** *(entente)* reconciliation **2** *Jur & Rel* reconciliation

réconcilier [9] [rekɔ̃silje] **VT 1** *(deux personnes)* to reconcile **2** *Fig (réunir, allier)* **r. qn avec** *(doctrine, religion)* to reconcile sb with; *(idée)* to reconcile sb to; **ça m'a réconcilié avec la vie** it renewed my appetite for life, it made life seem worth living again; **r. qch avec qch** to reconcile sth with sth; **il voulait r. classicisme et romantisme** he wanted to bridge the gap between classicism and romanticism **3** *Rel* to reconcile

VPR se réconcilier *(personnes)* to make up; *(pays)* to make peace; *Hum* **se r. sur l'oreiller** to make up in bed; **se r. avec soi-même** to come to terms with oneself

reconditionner [3] [rəkɔ̃disjɔne] **VT** *(marchandises)* to repackage

reconductible [rəkɔ̃dyktibl] **ADJ** *Jur* renewable

reconduction [rəkɔ̃dyksjɔ̃] **NF** *(d'un contrat, d'un budget)* renewal; *(de mesures, d'une politique)* continuation; *(d'un bail)* renewal, extension; **voter la r. de la grève** to vote for the continuation of the strike *or* for continued strike action

reconduire [98] [rəkɔ̃dɥir] **VT 1** *(accompagner)* **r. qn** *(chez lui)* to see sb home; *(vers la sortie)* to show sb to the door; **r. qn à pied/en voiture** to walk/to drive sb home **2** *(expulser)* to escort; **les terroristes ont été reconduits à la frontière sous bonne escorte** the terrorists were taken (back) to the border under police escort **3** *(renouveler ▸ contrat, budget, mandat)* to renew; *(▸ mesures, politique, grève)* to continue; *(▸ bail)* to renew, to extend

reconfiguration [rəkɔ̃figyrasjɔ̃] **NF 1** *(d'une société)* re-engineering **2** *Ordinat* reconfiguration

reconfigurer [3] [rəkɔ̃figyre] **VT 1** *(société)* to re-engineer **2** *Ordinat* to reconfigure

réconfort [rekɔ̃fɔr] **NM** comfort; **tu m'es d'un grand r.** you're a great comfort to me; **avoir besoin de r.** to need cheering up

réconfortant, -e [rekɔ̃fɔrtɑ̃, -ɑ̃t] **ADJ 1** *(moralement)* comforting, reassuring **2** *(physiquement)* fortifying, invigorating, stimulating

réconforter [3] [rekɔ̃fɔrte] **VT 1** *(moralement)* to comfort, to reassure; **tes bonnes paroles m'ont réconfortée** your kind words comforted me *or* gave me hope; **cela me réconforte de voir que je ne suis pas la seule** I'm glad to see I'm not the only one **2** *(physiquement)* **bois ça, ça va te r.** drink this, it'll make you feel better

VPR se réconforter 1 *(physiquement)* to make oneself feel better **2** *(moralement)* to cheer oneself up, to console oneself

reconnais *etc voir* **reconnaître**

reconnaissable [rəkɔnesabl] **ADJ** recognizable; **il était à peine r.** he was hardly recognizable *or* you could hardly recognize him; **r. entre tous** unmistakeable; **r. à** identifiable by

reconnaissait *etc voir* **reconnaître**

reconnaissance [rəkɔnesɑ̃s] **NF 1** *(gratitude)* gratitude; **avoir/éprouver de la r. envers qn** to be/to feel grateful to *or* towards sb; **je lui en ai une vive r.** I am most grateful to him/her; **témoigner de la r. à qn** to show gratitude to sb; **avec r.** gratefully, with gratitude; **en r. de votre dévouement** as a token of my/our/*etc* gratitude for your devotion; *Fam* **c'est la r. du ventre** that's cupboard love

2 *(exploration)* reconnaissance; **partir en r.** to go on reconnaissance; *Fig* **elle est partie en r.** *ou* **est allée faire une r. des lieux** she went to check the place out; **patrouille de r.** reconnaissance patrol; **vol de r.** reconnaissance flight

3 *(identification)* recognition

4 *(aveu)* admission; *Jur* **r. de culpabilité** guilty plea

5 *Pol (d'un gouvernement, d'un État, de l'indépendance)* recognition

6 *Jur (d'un droit)* recognition, acknowledgment; **r. de dette** acknowledgment of a debt, IOU; **r. d'enfant** legal recognition of a child

7 *(reçu)* **acte de r. (du mont-de-piété)** pawn ticket

8 *Ordinat* recognition; **r. optique des caractères** optical character recognition; **r. de la parole, r. vocale** speech recognition

reconnaissant, -e [rəkɔnesɑ̃, -ɑ̃t] **ADJ** grateful; **se montrer r.** to show one's gratitude; **je te suis r. de ta patience** I'm most grateful to you for your patience; **je vous en suis très r.** I'm very grateful, I'm in your debt; **je vous serais r. de me fournir ces renseignements dans les meilleurs délais** I would be (most) obliged *or* grateful if you would provide me with this information as soon as possible

reconnaître [91] [rəkɔnetr] **VT 1** *(air, personne, pas)* to recognize; **je t'ai reconnu à ta démarche** I recognized you *or* I could tell it was you by your walk; **je ne l'aurais pas reconnue, elle a vieilli de dix ans!** I wouldn't have known (it was) her, she looks ten years older!; **on ne le reconnaît plus** you wouldn't recognize *or* know him now; **je te reconnais bien (là)!** that's just like you!, that's you all over!; **il a été reconnu par plusieurs témoins** he was identified by several witnesses; **on reconnaît bien là la marque du génie** you can't fail to recognize the stamp of genius; **je reconnais bien là ta mauvaise foi!** that's just typical of your insincerity!

2 *(admettre ▸ torts)* to recognize, to acknowledge, to admit; *(▸ aptitude, talent, vérité)* to acknowledge, to recognize; **il faut au moins lui r. cette qualité** you have to say this for him/her; **l'accusé reconnaît-il les faits?** does the accused acknowledge the facts?; **il est difficile de lui faire r. ses erreurs** it's hard to get him/her to acknowledge he's/she's wrong; **sa prestation fut décevante, il faut bien le r.** it has to be admitted that his/her performance was disappointing; **elle est douée, il faut le r.!** she's clever, you've got to admit it *or* give her that!; **je reconnais que j'ai eu tort** I admit I was wrong; **elle refuse de r. qu'elle est malade** she won't admit *or* acknowledge that she's ill; **il n'a jamais reconnu avoir falsifié les documents** he never admitted to having falsified the documents

3 *Jur & Pol (État, chef de file)* to recognize; *(enfant)* to recognize legally; *(dette, document, signature)* to authenticate; **tous le reconnaissent comme leur maître** they all acknowledge him as their master; **être reconnu coupable** to be found guilty; **organisme reconnu d'utilité publique** officially approved organization; **je ne reconnais à personne le droit de me juger** nobody has the right to judge me

4 *(explorer)* **il envoya dix hommes r. le terrain** he ordered ten men to go and reconnoitre the ground; **l'équipe de tournage est allée r. les lieux** the film crew went to have a look round (the place)

VPR se reconnaître 1 *(emploi réfléchi) (physiquement, moralement)* to see oneself; **je me reconnais dans la réaction de ma sœur** I can see myself reacting in the same way as my sister; **je ne me reconnais pas dans votre description** I don't recognize myself in your description

2 *(emploi réciproque)* to recognize each other

3 *(emploi passif)* to be recognizable; **un poisson frais se reconnaît à l'odeur** you can tell a fresh fish by the smell

4 *(se retrouver)* **mets des étiquettes sur tes dossiers, sinon comment veux-tu qu'on s'y reconnaisse?** label your files, otherwise we'll get completely confused

5 *(s'avouer)* **se r. coupable** to admit *or* to confess one's guilt

reconnecter [3] [rəkɔnɛkte] **VT** to reconnect

VPR se reconnecter *Ordinat* to reconnect

reconquérir [39] [rəkɔ̃kerir] **VT 1** *(territoire, peuple)* to reconquer, to recapture **2** *(liberté, honneur, avantage)* to win back, to recover **3** *(personne, estime, amitié)* to win back

reconquête [rəkɔ̃kɛt] **NF 1** *(d'un territoire, d'un peuple)* reconquest, recapture **2** *(de la liberté, de l'honneur, d'un avantage)* winning back *(UNCOUNT)*, recovery

reconquiert *etc voir* **reconquérir**

reconquis, -e [rəkɔ̃ki, -iz] **PP** *voir* **reconquérir**

reconsidérer [18] [rəkɔ̃sidere] **VT** to reconsider

reconstituant, -e [rəkɔ̃stitɥɑ̃, -ɑ̃t] **ADJ** *(aliment, boisson)* fortifying; *(traitement)* restorative

NM restorative

reconstituer [7] [rəkɔ̃stitɥe] **VT 1** *(reformer ▸ groupe)* to bring together again, to reconstitute; *(▸ armée, gouvernement)* to reconstitute; *(▸ société, parti)* to revive; *(▸ capital)* to rebuild, to build up again; *(▸ fichier)* to recreate; **r. des stocks** to replenish stocks, to restock; **bois reconstitué** chipboard; **lait reconstitué** reconstituted milk **2** *(recréer ▸ objet archéologique)* to piece *or* to put back together; *(▸ histoire, meurtre)* to reconstruct; **ils ont reconstitué un décor d'époque** they created a period setting

reconstitution [rəkɔ̃stitysjɔ̃] **NF 1** *(d'un groupe)* reconstituting *(UNCOUNT)*, bringing together again *(UNCOUNT)*; *(d'une armée, d'un gouvernement)* reconstitution; *(d'une société, d'un parti)* revival; *(d'un capital)* rebuilding *(UNCOUNT)*, building up again; *(d'un fichier)* recreating *(UNCOUNT)* **2** *(d'un objet archéologique)* piecing together; *(d'une histoire, d'un meurtre)* reconstruction; **r. historique** *(spectacle)* historical reconstruction

reconstruction [rəkɔ̃stryksjɔ̃] **NF** reconstruction, rebuilding; **en r.** being rebuilt

reconstruire [98] [rəkɔ̃strɥir] **VT** *(bâtiment)* to reconstruct, to rebuild; *(fortune, réputation)* to rebuild, to build up again; **r. sa vie** to put one's life back together, to rebuild one's life

reconventionnel, -elle [rəkɔ̃vɑ̃sjɔnɛl] **ADJ** *Jur* **demande reconventionnelle** counterclaim

reconversion [rəkɔ̃vɛrsjɔ̃] **NF** *(d'une usine)* conversion (**en** into); *(d'un individu)* retraining; **r. économique** economic restructuring; **r. industrielle** industrial redeployment

reconvertir [32] [rəkɔ̃vɛrtir] **VT** *(usine)* to convert (**en** into)

VPR se reconvertir *(employé)* to retrain; **il s'est reconverti dans l'informatique** he retrained and went into IT; **l'entreprise s'est reconvertie dans le bâtiment** the company moved into construction

reconvocation [rəkɔ̃vɔkasjɔ̃] **NF** *Pol (du Parlement, d'un ministre)* recall

reconvoquer [3] [rəkɔ̃vɔke] **VT** *Pol (Parlement, ministre)* to recall

recopier [9] [rəkɔpje] **VT 1** *(mettre au propre)* to write up, to make *or* to take a fair copy of **2** *(copier à nouveau)* to copy again, to make another copy of

record [rəkɔr] **NM 1** *Sport & Fig* record; **battre un r. de vitesse** to break a speed record; **r. de hauteur/longueur** high/*Br* long *or Am* broad jump record; **le r. du monde** the world record; *Fam* **tu bats tous les records d'idiotie!** they don't come any more stupid than you!; *Fam* **ça bat tous les records** that beats everything *or* the lot **2** *(comme adj, avec ou sans trait d'union)* record *(avant n)*; **l'inflation a atteint le chiffre-r. de 200 pour cent** inflation has risen to a record *or* record-breaking 200 percent; **en un temps-r.** in record time

recorder [3] [rəkɔrde] **VT** *(raquette)* to restring

recordman [rəkɔrdman] *(pl* **recordmans** *ou* **recordmen** [-mɛn]*)* **NM** (men's) record holder; **le r. du 5000 mètres** the record holder for the (men's) 5,000 metres

recordwoman [rəkɔrdwuman] *(pl* **recordwomans** *ou* **recordwomen** [-mɛn]*)* **NF** (women's) record holder; **la r. du saut en hauteur** the record holder for the women's high jump

recoucher [3] [rəkuʃe] **VT** *(personne)* to put back to bed; *(objet)* to lay down again

VI *Fam* **r. avec qn** to sleep with sb again

VPR se recoucher to go back to bed

recoudre [86] [rəkudr] **VT 1** *(bouton, badge etc)* to sew on again; *(accroc, ourlet etc)* to sew up again **2** *Méd* to sew *or* to stitch up (again)

recoupement [rəkupmɑ̃] **NM 1** *(vérification)* crosschecking; **faire un r.** to crosscheck, to do a crosscheck **2** *Géom* resection

recouper [3] [rəkupe] **VT 1** *(couper à nouveau)* **r. de la viande** to cut *or* to carve some more meat; **je vous recoupe une tranche de gâteau?** shall I cut you another slice *or* piece of cake? **2** *Couture* to cut again, to recut **3** *(concorder avec)* to tally with, to match up with

VI *Cartes* to cut again

VPR se recouper 1 *(se blesser ▸ personne)* to cut oneself again **2** *(ensembles, routes)* to intersect **3** *(statistiques, témoignages)* to tally

recouponnement [rəkupɔnmɑ̃] NM *Bourse* renewal of coupons

recouponner [3] [rəkupɔne] VT *Bourse* to renew the coupons of

recourbé, -e [rəkurbe] ADJ *(gén)* bent, curved; *(cils)* curved; *(nez)* hooked

recourber [3] [rəkurbe] VT to bend, to curve
VPR **se recourber** to bend, to curve

recourir [45] [rəkurir] VT *Sport* to run again
VI **1** *Sport* to run *or* to race again **2** *Jur* to appeal (**contre** against)
• **recourir à** VT IND **1** *(personne)* **r. à qn** to appeal *or* to turn to sb; **en cas de désaccord, il faudra r. à un expert** in the event of a disagreement you will have to seek the help of an expert **2** *(objet, méthode etc)* **r. à qch** to resort to sth

recours [rəkur] NM **1** *(ressource)* recourse, resort; **c'est notre dernier r.** this is our last resort *or* the last course left open to us; **c'est sans r.** there's nothing we can do about it; **avoir r. à** *(moyen)* to resort to; *(personne)* to turn to; **nous n'aurons r. à l'expulsion qu'en dernière limite** we shall only resort to *or* have recourse to eviction if absolutely necessary **2** *Jur* appeal; **r. en cassation** appeal (to the appellate court); *Can* **r. collectif** class action; **r. en grâce** *(pour une remise de peine)* petition for pardon; *(pour une commutation de peine)* petition for clemency *or* remission; **r. gracieux** application for an ex gratia settlement
• **en dernier recours** ADV as a last resort

recouru, -e [rəkury] PP *voir* **recourir**

recousait *etc voir* **recoudre**

recouvert, -e [rəkuvɛr, -ɛrt] PP *voir* **recouvrir**

recouvrable [rəkuvrabl] ADJ *(dette, facture)* collectable, recoverable; *(impôt)* collectable

recouvrement [rəkuvrəmɑ̃] NM **1** *(récupération ▸ d'une somme)* collecting, collection; *(▸ de la santé)* recovering, recovery
2 *Fin (perception)* collection; *(d'une créance)* recovery; **l'impôt est mis en r. après le 31 octobre** payment of tax is due from *Br* 31 October *or Am* October 31; **modalités de r.** methods of payment
3 *(d'une surface)* covering (over)
4 *Constr & Menuis* lap
5 *Ordinat & Math* overlap
• **recouvrements** NMPL *(dettes)* outstanding debts

recouvrer [3] [rəkuvre] VT **1** *(récupérer ▸ santé, biens)* to recover; *(▸ liberté)* to regain; **elle n'a pas recouvré tous ses moyens** she hasn't recovered *or* regained the full use of her faculties; **il a recouvré l'usage de sa jambe** he has got back *or* recovered the use of his leg; **laissez-lui le temps de r. ses esprits** give him/her time to get his/her wits back **2** *Fin (percevoir)* to collect, to recover; **créances à r.** outstanding debts

recouvrir [34] [rəkuvrir] VT **1** *(couvrir)* to cover (**de** in *or* with); **r. un gâteau de chocolat** to coat a cake with chocolate; **ajouter suffisamment d'eau pour r. les légumes** add enough water to cover the vegetables **2** *(couvrir à nouveau ▸ personne)* to cover (up) again; *(▸ siège)* to re-cover, to reupholster; *(▸ livre)* to re-cover **3** *(englober)* to cover; **le mot ne recouvre pas les mêmes notions dans les deux langues** the word doesn't cover the same concepts in the two languages
VPR **se recouvrir 1** *(remettre des vêtements)* **recouvre-toi, le soleil s'est caché** cover yourself up again, the sun's gone in **2** *Météo* to get cloudy again **3** *(surface)* **se r. de moisissure** to become covered with *or* in mould; **la glace s'est recouverte de buée** the mirror steamed up

recracher [3] [rəkraʃe] VT **1** *(cracher)* to spit out (again); **r. un noyau** to spit out a stone **2** *Fam (cours, leçon)* to regurgitate
VI to spit again

récré [rekre] NF *Fam (dans le primaire) Br* playtime◻, *Am* recess◻; *(dans le secondaire) Br* break◻; *Am* recess◻

récréatif, -ive [rekreatif, -iv] ADJ recreational; **une journée récréative** a day of recreation *or* relaxation; **lecture récréative** light reading

récréation [rekreasjɔ̃] NF **1** *Scol (dans le primaire) Br* playtime, *Am* recess; *(dans le secondaire) Br* break, *Am* recess **2** *(délassement)* recreation, leisure activity; **le tricot/la télé, c'est ma r.** knitting/watching TV is how I relax, I relax by knitting/watching TV

récréative [rekreativ] *voir* **récréatif**

recréer [15] [rəkree] VT **1** *(suivant un modèle)* to recreate **2** *(créer)* to create; **il recrée un décor à son goût** he is creating a decor more to his liking

recrépir [32] [rəkrepir] VT *Constr* to roughcast

recrépissage [rəkrepisaʒ] NM resurfacing *or* redoing with roughcast

recreuser [5] [rəkrøze] VT *(creuser ▸ davantage)* to dig deeper; *(▸ un nouveau trou)* to dig again; *Fig (question)* to dig deeper *or* to go deeper into

récrier [10] [rekrije] **se récrier** VPR **1** *(protester)* to cry out, to protest (**contre** against) **2** *Littéraire (s'exclamer)* to cry out, to exclaim (**de** in)

récriminateur, -trice [rekriminatœr, -tris] ADJ recriminative, recriminatory

récrimination [rekriminasjɔ̃] NF recrimination, protest

récriminatrice [rekriminatris] *voir* **récriminateur**

récriminer [3] [rekrimine] VI *(critiquer)* to recriminate (**contre** against)

récrire [rekrir] = **réécrire**

récriture [rekrityr] = **réécriture**

recroquevillé, -e [rəkrɔkvije] ADJ **1** *(confortablement)* curled up; *(dans l'inconfort)* hunched *or* huddled up **2** *(feuille, pétale)* curled *or* shrivelled up

recroqueviller [3] [rəkrɔkvije] **se recroqueviller** VPR **1** *(confortablement)* to curl up; *(dans l'inconfort)* to hunch *or* to huddle up **2** *(feuille, pétale)* to shrivel *or* to curl (up)

recru, -e[1] [rəkry] ADJ *Littéraire* **être r. de fatigue** to be exhausted

recrudescence [rəkrydesɑ̃s] NF *(aggravation ▸ d'une maladie)* aggravation, worsening; *(▸ de la fièvre)* new bout; *(▸ d'une épidémie, d'un incendie)* fresh *or* new outbreak; *(▸ du froid)* new spell; *(▸ de la délinquance)* upsurge (**de** in *or* of); **la r. du terrorisme** the new wave *or* outbreak of terrorism; **la r. de la violence/des bombardements** the renewed violence/bombing; **nous nous attendons à une r. des pluies** we are expecting more frequent spells of rain

recrudescent, -e [rəkrydesɑ̃, -ɑ̃t] ADJ *Littéraire* increasing, mounting, *Sout* recrudescent

recrue[2] [rəkry] NF **1** *Mil* recruit **2** *Fig* recruit, new member; **faire de nouvelles recrues** to gain new recruits

recrutement [rəkrytmɑ̃] NM recruiting, recruitment *(UNCOUNT)*; **le r. du personnel s'effectue par concours** staff are recruited by competitive examination

recruter [3] [rəkryte] VT **1** *(engager)* to recruit; **l'entreprise recrute des ingénieurs en informatique** the firm is recruiting computer engineers **2** *Mil & Pol* to recruit, to enlist; **les membres du parti sont recrutés dans les milieux ouvriers** party members are recruited from the working classes
USAGE ABSOLU to recruit; **en ce moment, les sociétés d'informatique recrutent** computing companies are recruiting (new staff) at the moment
VPR **se recruter 1** *(être engagé)* to be recruited (**parmi** from among); **les ingénieurs se recrutent sur diplôme** engineers are recruited on the basis of their qualifications **2 se r. dans** *(provenir de)* to come from; **les futurs ministres se recrutent généralement dans les grandes écoles** future ministers generally come from the "grandes écoles"

recruteur, -euse [rəkrytœr, -øz] ADJ recruiting; **sergent r.** recruiting sergeant
NM,F recruiter

recta [rɛkta] ADV *Fam* **payer r.** to pay on the nail

rectal, -e, -aux, -ales [rɛktal, -o] ADJ *Anat* rectal

rectangle [rɛktɑ̃gl] NM **1** *(forme)* rectangle, oblong; *Ordinat* **r. de sélection** selection box **2** *Géom* rectangle
ADJ **triangle r.** right-angled triangle

rectangulaire [rɛktɑ̃gylɛr] ADJ **1** *(forme)* rectangular, oblong **2** *Géom* rectangular

recteur, -trice [rɛktœr, -tris] ADJ *Orn* **penne rectrice** tail feather
NM,F **1** *Scol & Univ (d'académie)* = chief administrative officer of an education authority, *Br* ≃ (Chief) Education Officer, *Am* ≃ Commissioner of the State Board of Education; *(d'une université catholique)* ≃ rector **2** *Belg Univ* principal, *Br* vice-chancellor, *Am* president
NM *Rel (d'un sanctuaire)* ≃ rector; *(en Bretagne)* priest, rector
• **rectrice** NF *Orn* rectrix

rectificateur [rɛktifikatœr] NM *Chim* rectifier

rectificatif, -ive [rɛktifikatif, -iv] ADJ correcting; **mention rectificative** correction
NM correction, rectification

rectification [rɛktifikasjɔ̃] NF **1** *(d'un document, d'un texte)* amendment, correction; *(d'un calcul)* correction, adjustment; *(d'une erreur)* rectification, correction; *(d'un compte, d'un instrument)* adjustment; *(d'une courbe, d'une frontière)* adjustment, rectification; *(d'un alignement)* straightening; **je voudrais faire** *ou* **apporter une r.** I'd like to make a correction; **apporter une r. à une déclaration** to correct a statement; *Journ* **droit de r.** ≃ right of reply **2** *Chim & Math* rectification

rectificative [rɛktifikativ] *voir* **rectificatif**

rectifier [9] [rɛktifje] VT **1** *(corriger ▸ document, texte)* to amend, to correct; *(▸ calcul)* to correct, to adjust; *(▸ erreur)* to rectify, to correct; *(ajuster ▸ compte, instrument)* to adjust; *(▸ courbe, frontière)* to adjust, to rectify; *(▸ alignement)* to straighten; **r. le tir** *Mil* to adjust the range; *Fig* to take a slightly different tack; **"il est banquier", rectifia-t-elle** "he's a banker," she corrected him/her/me/*etc* **2** *Chim & Math* to rectify **3** *Fam (tuer)* to bump off; **se faire r.** to get bumped off

rectiligne [rɛktiliɲ] ADJ *(droit)* straight; *Math* rectilinear

rectilinéaire [rɛktilineɛr] ADJ rectilinear

rectitude [rɛktityd] NF **1** *(droiture)* (moral) rectitude, uprightness; **agir avec r.** to behave correctly *or* with integrity **2** *Littéraire (exactitude ▸ d'un raisonnement)* correctness, soundness **3** *Littéraire (d'une ligne)* straightness

recto [rɛkto] NM front of a page, *Spéc* recto; **n'écrivez qu'au r.** write on this side only; **voir au r.** see over
• **recto verso** ADV on both sides

rectorat [rɛktɔra] NM **1** *Univ (d'une académie ▸ administration) Br* ≃ Education Office, *Am* ≃ State Board of Education; *(▸ bâtiment) Br* ≃ Education offices, *Am* ≃ Board of Education offices **2** *(chez les jésuites)* rectorship

rectrice [rɛktris] *voir* **recteur**

rectum [rɛktɔm] NM *Anat* rectum

reçu, -e [rəsy] PP *voir* **recevoir**
ADJ *(usages)* accepted, recognized; *(opinion)* received
NM,F *(candidat)* successful candidate; **il n'y a que dix reçus** only ten people passed
NM *(quittance)* receipt; *Can* **r. de caisse** (till) receipt; **r. libératoire** receipt in full discharge

recueil [rəkœj] NM *(de chansons, de recettes)* collection; *(de poèmes)* collection, selection, anthology; *(de lois)* compendium, body; **r. de morceaux choisis** selection, anthology; *Ordinat* **r. de données** data collection

recueillement [rəkœjmɑ̃] NM contemplation, meditation; **écouter qch avec r.** to listen reverently to sth

recueillera *etc voir* **recueillir**

recueilli, -e [rəkœji] ADJ contemplative, meditative; **un public très r.** a very attentive audience; **un visage r.** a composed expression

recueillir [41] [rəkœjir] VT **1** *(récolter ▸ miel, pollen)* to gather, to collect; *(▸ eaux de pluie)* to collect; *(▸ votes, suffrages)* to win; *Fig* **r. le fruit de son travail** to reap the fruit of one's labour **2** *(renseignements)* to collect, to obtain; *(déposition)* to take; *(argent, fonds)* to collect; **propos recueillis par Daniel Renault** *(dans un article de journal)* (story by) Daniel Renault **3** *(héberger ▸ personne)* to take in; **r. un oiseau tombé du nid** to take care of a bird which has fallen from its nest
VPR **se recueillir** *(penser)* to spend some moments in silence; *(prier)* to pray; **le chef de l'État s'est recueilli devant le cénotaphe** the head of state reflected a while in front of the cenotaph;

aller se r. sur la tombe de qn to spend some moments in silence at sb's graveside

recuire [98] [rəkɥir] **VT 1** *Culin (à l'eau, à la poêle)* to cook longer; *(au four)* to cook longer in the oven **2** *(métal, verre)* to anneal

VI faire r. un rôti to recook a joint; **faire r. un gâteau** to rebake a cake

recuit [rəkɥi] **NM** *(du métal, du verre)* annealing

recul [rəkyl] **NM 1** *(mouvement ▸ gén)* backward movement; *(▸ d'un glacier, d'une armée)* retreat; *(▸ d'un fusil)* recoil, kick; *(▸ d'un canon)* recoil; **il eut un mouvement de r.** he stepped back; *(brusquement)* he recoiled

2 *(distance)* **as-tu assez de r. pour juger du tableau/prendre la photo?** are you far enough away to judge the painting/to take the photograph?; **on n'a pas assez de r. pour admirer le bâtiment** *(dans une rue étroite)* you can't get back far enough to admire the building

3 *(réflexion)* **avec le r.** retrospectively, with (the benefit of) hindsight; **prendre du r. par rapport à un événement** to stand back (in order) to assess an event; **je manque de r. pour juger** I'm too closely involved *or* too close to be able to judge; **nous n'avons pas assez de r. pour juger des effets à long terme** it's too early *or* not enough time has passed to assess what long-term effects there might be

4 *(baisse)* fall, drop, decline; **le r. de la mortalité** the downturn *or* decline in the death rate; **le r. de l'industrie textile** the decline of the textile industry; **le r. du yen par rapport au dollar** the fall of the yen against the dollar

reculade [rəkylad] **NF** *(d'une armée)* retreat; *(politique)* climbdown

reculé, -e [rəkyle] **ADJ 1** *(dans l'espace)* remote, far-off; **ils habitent dans un coin r.** they live in an out-of-the-way place **2** *(dans le temps)* remote, far-off, distant; **les temps les plus reculés** the distant past

reculer [3] [rəkyle] **VT 1** *(dans l'espace)* to push *or* to move back; **r. une clôture d'un mètre** to move a fence back by one metre **2** *(dans le temps ▸ rendez-vous)* to delay, to postpone, to defer; *(▸ date)* to postpone, to put back; *(▸ décision)* to defer, to postpone, to put off; **r. la date de son départ** to postpone one's departure

VI 1 *(aller en arrière ▸ à pied)* to step *or* to go *or* to move back; *(▸ en voiture)* to reverse, to move back; **recule d'un pas!** take one step backwards!; **reculez ou je tire!** get back or I'll shoot!; **mets le frein à main, la voiture recule!** put the handbrake on, the car is rolling backwards!; **il a heurté le mur en reculant** he backed *or* reversed into the wall; **faire r. un cheval** to back a horse; **la police a fait r. la foule** the police moved the crowd back

2 *(céder du terrain ▸ falaise, forêt, eaux)* to recede; *Mil* to fall back, to retreat; *Fig* **faire r. les frontières de la science** to push *or* to roll back the frontiers of science

3 *(renoncer)* to retreat, to shrink (back), to draw back; **il est trop tard pour r.** it's too late to draw back *or* to pull out; **il n'est pas homme à r. devant les difficultés** he is not the kind of man to shrink back in the face of difficulties; **il ne recule devant rien** nothing daunts him; **r. devant l'ennemi** to retreat in the face of the enemy; **r. devant le danger** to retreat in the face of danger; **cela en a fait r. plus d'un** that's put off *or* daunted more than one person; **c'est r. pour mieux sauter** that's just putting off the inevitable

4 *(faiblir ▸ cours, valeur)* to fall, to weaken; *(▸ épidémie, criminalité, mortalité)* to recede; **le yen recule par rapport au dollar** the yen is losing ground *or* falling against the dollar; **faire r. la pauvreté** to reduce (the level of) poverty

5 *(avoir un mouvement de recul)* to recoil

VPR se reculer *Fam* to step *or* to move back; **recule-toi!** get back!

reculons [rəkylɔ̃] **à reculons ADV 1** *(en marche arrière)* backwards; **marcher** *ou* **aller à r.** to walk backwards; **sortir à r.** to back out; *Hum* **avancer à r.** to be getting nowhere **2** *(avec réticence)* under protest

récup [rekyp] **NF** *Fam* **1 de la r.** *(des matériaux de récupération)* scrap **2** *Pol (récupération idéologique)* hijacking□, takeover□

récupérable [rekyperabl] **ADJ 1** *(objet)* salvageable, worth rescuing; **vêtements récupérables** (still) serviceable clothes

2 *(personne)* redeemable; **les récidivistes sont-ils récupérables?** can persistent offenders be reeducated?

3 *(temps)* recoverable; **ces heures supplémentaires sont récupérables** time off will be given in lieu of overtime worked

4 *Fin (TVA)* reclaimable

récupérateur, -trice [rekyperatœr, -tris] **ADJ 1** *(qui recycle)* **industrie récupératrice** = industry based on reclaimed or recycled materials **2** *(qui repose)* **sommeil r.** refreshing *or* restorative sleep

NM,F = industrialist or builder working with reclaimed materials

NM *Tech* recuperator; **r. de chaleur** heat economizer

récupération [rekyperasjɔ̃] **NF 1** *(après séparation, perte)* recovery

2 *Écol* recycling, reclaiming; **matériau de r.** scrap *(UNCOUNT)*

3 *(de sportif)* recovery

4 *Pol* hijacking, takeover; **il y a eu r. du mouvement par les extrémistes** the movement has been hijacked *or* taken over by extremists

5 *(au travail)* making up; **quand je fais des heures supplémentaires, j'ai des jours de r.** when I work overtime, I get time off in exchange *or* in lieu

6 *Ordinat (d'un fichier, de données)* retrieval, recovery

7 *Fin (d'une dette)* recovery; *(de TVA)* reclaiming; *(des débours)* recoupment

récupérer [18] [rekypere] **VT 1** *(retrouver ▸ gén)* to get back; *(▸ bagages)* to retrieve, to reclaim; **elle est passée r. ses affaires** she dropped by to pick up her things; **je passe te r. en voiture** I'll come and pick you up; **je n'ai jamais pu r. mon livre** I never managed to get my book back; **j'ai récupéré l'usage de ma main gauche** I recovered the use of my left hand; **tout a brûlé, ils n'ont rien pu r.** everything was destroyed by the fire, they didn't manage to salvage anything

2 *(pour utiliser ▸ chiffons, papier, verre, ferraille)* to salvage; *(▸ chaleur, énergie)* to save; **j'ai récupéré des chaises dont personne ne voulait** I've rescued some chairs no one wanted; **je ne jette rien, je récupère tout** I don't throw anything away, I save everything

3 *(jour de congé)* to make up for, to compensate for; **on récupère ce jour férié vendredi prochain** we are making up for this public holiday by working next Friday; **les jours fériés travaillés seront récupérés** employees will be allowed time off in lieu of public holidays worked

4 *Pol* to hijack, to take over; **le mouvement a été récupéré par le gouvernement** the movement has been hijacked by the government for its own ends

5 *Ordinat (fichier, données)* to retrieve, to recover

6 *Fin (dette)* to recover; *(TVA)* to reclaim; **r. ses débours** to recoup one's expenditure

VI *(se remettre)* to recover, to recuperate; **j'ai besoin de r.** *(de prendre des vacances)* I need to get my breath back, I need to relax

récurage [rekyraʒ] **NM** *(de casserole, d'évier)* scouring; *(avec une brosse)* scrubbing

récurer [3] [rekyre] **VT** *(casserole, évier)* to scour; *(avec une brosse)* to scrub

récurrence [rekyrɑ̃s] **NF** recurrence

récurrent, -e [rekyrɑ̃, -ɑ̃t] **ADJ 1** *(thème, son, mot)* recurrent, recurring

2 *Méd (fièvre)* recurrent, relapsing

3 *Anat* **nerf r.** nervus laryngeus recurrens

4 *Ordinat & Math* **suite** *ou* **série récurrente** recursion series

5 *Écon* **coûts récurrents** recurrent *or* running costs

récusable [rekyzabl] **ADJ** *Jur (témoignage)* challengeable, *Sout* impugnable; *(juré, témoin)* challengeable; **c'est une affirmation r.** that statement is open to challenge

récusation [rekyzasjɔ̃] **NF** *(d'une thèse, d'un témoin)* challenging

récuser [3] [rekyze] **VT** *(thèse)* to challenge; *Jur (juge, juré, expert)* to challenge, to take exception to, to object to; *(décision, témoignage)* to challenge, *Sout* to impugn

VPR se récuser 1 *(lors d'un procès)* to declare oneself incompetent **2** *(lors d'une entrevue, d'un débat)* to refuse to give an opinion, to decline to (make any) comment

reçut *etc voir* **recevoir**

recyclabilité [rəsiklabilite] **NF** recyclability

recyclable [rəsiklabl] **ADJ** recyclable

recyclage [rəsiklaʒ] **NM 1** *Ind* recycling; *Aut* **r. des gaz d'échappement** exhaust gas recirculation **2** *(perfectionnement)* refresher course; *(reconversion)* retraining **3** *(stage)* retraining course

recycler [3] [rəsikle] **VT 1** *Ind* to recycle; **papier recyclé** recycled paper **2** *(perfectionner)* to send on a refresher course; *(reconvertir)* to retrain

VPR se recycler *(pour se perfectionner)* to go on a refresher course; *(pour se reconvertir)* to retrain; **se r. dans la comptabilité** to retrain as an accountant

recycleur [rəsiklœr] **NM 1** *(industriel du recyclage)* recycling company **2** *(appareil pour recycler l'eau)* water recycler

rédacteur, -trice [redaktœr, -tris] **NM,F 1** *(auteur ▸ d'un livre)* writer; *(▸ d'un guide)* compiler; **les rédacteurs de l'encyclopédie** the contributors to the encyclopedia; **le r. du contrat n'a pas prévu cela** the person who drew up the contract didn't foresee this **2** *Journ* writer, contributor; **r. associé** associate editor; **r. en chef** *(d'une revue)* (chief) editor; *(du journal télévisé)* television news editor; **r. en chef technique** production editor; **r. publicitaire** copywriter; **r. sportif** sports editor

rédaction [redaksjɔ̃] **NF 1** *(écriture)* writing; *(d'un guide, d'un dictionnaire)* compiling; **il vient d'achever la r. de son roman** he's just finished writing his novel; **la r. de la thèse a pris moins de temps que la recherche** writing up the thesis took less time than researching it; **la r. d'un projet de loi/d'un contrat d'assurance** the drafting of a bill/of an insurance contract

2 *Journ (lieu)* editorial office; *TV* newsdesk, newsroom; *(équipe)* editorial staff; **la r. est en grève** the editorial staff is *or* are on strike

3 *Scol (composition)* ≃ essay

4 *(dans l'édition)* **r. électronique** online publishing; **r. publicitaire** copywriting

rédactionnel, -elle [redaksjɔnel] **ADJ** editorial

rédactrice [redaktris] *voir* **rédacteur**

reddition [redisjɔ̃] **NF 1** *Mil* surrender **2** *Fin & Jur* rendering

redécoupage [rədekupaʒ] **NM** *Pol* **r. électoral** redrawing of electoral *or* constituency boundaries; **procéder à** *ou* **effectuer un r. électoral** to redraw the electoral boundaries

redécouverte [rədekuvɛrt] **NF** rediscovery

redécouvrir [34] [rədekuvrir] **VT** to rediscover

redéfinir [32] [rədefinir] **VT** to redefine; **r. la politique du logement** to lay down new housing policy guidelines

redemander [3] [rədəmɑ̃de] **VT 1** *(demander à nouveau)* to ask again; **je lui ai redemandé son nom** I asked him/her his/her name again; **je lui ai redemandé de fermer la porte** I asked him/her again to close the door **2** *(demander davantage)* to ask for more; **il a redemandé de la soupe** he asked for some more soup; *Fig* **tout le monde en redemande** everybody is clamouring *or* keeps asking for more, they can't get enough of it **3** *(après un prêt)* to ask for; **redemande ton vélo dès que tu en as besoin** ask for your bike back as soon as you need it

redémarrage [rədemaraʒ] **NM 1** *(d'une machine)* starting up again *(UNCOUNT)*; *Ordinat* reboot, restart; **r. à chaud** warm boot, warm start **2** *(économique)* recovery, upturn

redémarrer [3] [rədemare] **VI 1** *(moteur)* to start up again **2** *(processus)* to get going *or* to take off again; **l'économie redémarre** the economy is looking up again; **les cours redémarrent fin octobre** classes start again at the end of October **3** *Ordinat* to reboot

rédempteur, -trice [redɑ̃ptœr, -tris] **ADJ** redeeming, *Sout* redemptive

NM,F redeemer; **le R.** the Redeemer

rédemption [redɑ̃psjɔ̃] **NF** *Rel* **la R.** Redemption

rédemptrice [redɑ̃ptris] *voir* **rédempteur**

redéploiement [rədeplwamɑ̃] NM **1** *Mil* redeployment **2** *Écon* reorganization, restructuring

redéployer [13] [rədeplwaje] VT **1** *Mil* to redeploy **2** *Écon* to reorganize, to restructure

VPR **se redéployer 1** *Mil* to redeploy **2** *Écon* to reorganize its operations

redescendre [73] [rədesɑ̃dr] VT **1** *(colline, montagne etc ▸ en voiture)* to drive (back) down; *(▸ à pied)* to walk (back) down; *(sujet: alpiniste)* to climb back down **2** *(apporter ▸ du point de vue de quelqu'un qui est en haut)* to take down again, to take back down; *(▸ du point de vue de quelqu'un qui est en bas)* to bring down again, to bring back down; **je redescendrai les cartons plus tard** *(je suis en haut)* I'll take the cardboard boxes back down later; *(je suis en bas)* I'll bring the cardboard boxes back down later

VI *(aux être)* **1** *(descendre ▸ du point de vue de quelqu'un qui est en haut)* to go down again, to go back down; *(▸ du point de vue de quelqu'un qui est en bas)* to come down again, to come back down; *(alpiniste)* to climb back down; **quand tu redescendras, veux-tu...?** *(nous sommes en haut)* when you go down again *or* go back down, will you...?; *(je suis à l'étage inférieur)* when you come down again *or* come back down, will you ...?; **la température/le niveau de l'eau redescend** the temperature/the water level is falling (again); **je suis redescendu en chasse-neige** I snowploughed (back) down **2** *(descendre à nouveau ▸ du point de vue de quelqu'un qui est en haut)* to go down again; *(▸ du point de vue de quelqu'un qui est en bas)* to come down again; **r. de voiture** to get out of the car again

redevable [rədəvabl] ADJ **1** *Fin* **être r. d'une somme d'argent à qn** to owe sb a sum of money; **être r. de l'impôt** to be liable to tax **2** *Fig (moralement)* **être r. de qch à qn** to be indebted to sb for sth; **je lui suis r. de ma promotion** I owe him/her my promotion, I owe it to him/her that I was promoted

redevait *etc voir* **redevoir**

redevance [rədəvɑ̃s] NF **1** *TV* licence fee; *Tél* rental charge **2** *Com & Fin (pour un service)* dues, fees; *(royalties)* royalties **3** *Hist* tax

redevenir [40] [rədəvnir] VI *(aux être)* to become again; **le ciel redevient nuageux** the sky is clouding over again; **r. amis** to become friends again; **r. silencieux** to fall silent again; **j'ai l'impression d'être redevenu moi-même** I feel like my old self again

redevoir [53] [rədəvwar] VT *(aux temps simples seulement)* **il redoit cinquante mille euros** he still owes fifty thousand euros

rédhibition [redibisjɔ̃] NF *Jur* = cancellation of sale due to a latent defect

rédhibitoire [redibitwar] ADJ **1** *Jur* **vice r.** latent defect **2** *Fig (insurmontable)* **le prix est élevé mais pas r.** the price is high but not prohibitive; **une mauvaise note à l'écrit, c'est r.** a bad mark in the written exam is enough to fail the candidate; **dans ce métier, être petit est r.** being small is a bar to entering this profession

rediffuser [3] [rədifyze] VT to repeat, to rebroadcast; **nous rediffuserons ces images** we'll be showing these scenes again, we'll be rebroadcasting these scenes

rediffusion [rədifyzjɔ̃] NF repeating, rebroadcasting; *(programme rediffusé)* repeat

rédiger [17] [rediʒe] VT *(manifeste, contrat)* to write, to draw up; *(thèse, rapport)* to write up; *(ordonnance)* to write out; *(lettre)* to write, to compose; *(article)* to write; *(guide, manuel)* to write, to compile; **il a rédigé sa lettre en termes énergiques** he wrote a strongly worded letter

USAGE ABSOLU **il rédige bien** he writes well

redimensionnable [rədimɑ̃sjɔnabl] ADJ *Ordinat (fenêtre)* resizable

redimensionnement [rədimɑ̃sjɔnmɑ̃] NM *Ordinat (d'une fenêtre)* resizing

redimensionner [3] [rədimɑ̃sjɔne] VT *Ordinat (fenêtre)* to resize

redingote [rədɛ̃gɔt] NF **1** *(de femme)* tailored *or* fitted coat **2** *(d'homme)* frock coat

redire [102] [rədir] VT **1** *(répéter)* to say again, to repeat; *(rabâcher)* to keep saying, to repeat; **je tiens à vous r. combien j'ai été heureux de vous voir** I'd like to say again how happy I was to see you; **redites lentement les mots après moi** repeat slowly after me; **et que je n'aie pas à te le r.!** and I don't want to have to tell you again!; **on le lui a dit et redit** he's/she's been told again and again; **elle a redit la même chose tout au long de son discours** throughout her speech she repeated the same thing **2** *(rapporter)* to (go and) tell, to repeat; **surtout, n'allez pas le lui r.** whatever you do, don't go and tell him/her **3** *(locutions)* **quelque chose/rien à r.** something/nothing to object to; **elle ne voit rien à r. aux nouvelles mesures** she can't see anything wrong with *or* she has no objections to the new measures; **trouver à r. (à)** to find fault (with); **l'organisation était parfaite, je n'y ai pas trouvé à r.** the organization was perfect, there was nothing I could find fault with *or* I had no complaint to make

redirection [rədirɛksjɔ̃] NF *Tél* **r. d'appel** call forwarding, call redirection

rediriger [rədiriʒe] VT *Tél* to redirect

rediscuter [3] [rədiskyte] VT to discuss again, to have further discussion(s) about

• **rediscuter de** VT IND to talk about *or* to discuss again

redisons *etc voir* **redire**

redistribuer [7] [rədistribɥe] VT *(cartes)* to deal again; *(fortune)* to redistribute; *(emplois)* to reallocate; **r. les rôles** to recast the show; *Fig* to reallocate the tasks

redistribution [rədistribysjɔ̃] NF *(des revenus, des terres, des richesses)* redistribution

redites [rədit] *voir* **redire**

redoit, redoivent *etc voir* **redevoir**

redondance [rədɔ̃dɑ̃s] NF **1** *(répétition)* redundancy; **de nombreuses redondances** a lot of redundancy **2** *Ordinat, Ling & Tél* redundancy

redondant, -e [rədɔ̃dɑ̃, -ɑ̃t] ADJ **1** *(mot)* redundant, superfluous; *(style)* redundant, verbose, wordy **2** *Ordinat, Ling & Tél* redundant

redonner [3] [rədɔne] VT **1** *(donner de nouveau)* to give again; **j'ai redonné les chaussures au cordonnier** I took the shoes back *or* returned the shoes to the cobbler's; **elle lui a redonné un coup de pied** she kicked him/her again; **cette promenade m'a redonné faim** that walk has made me hungry again

2 *(donner davantage de)* to give more of; **redonnez-lui du sirop** give him/her some more cough mixture; **r. à manger/de l'argent/du travail à qn** to give sb some more food/money/work

3 *(rendre)* to give back; **ce médicament va vous r. des forces** the medicine will give you back your strength; **r. de l'appétit à qn** to restore sb's appetite, to give sb back his/her appetite; **ça m'a redonné confiance/courage** it restored my confidence/my courage; **ça m'a redonné envie de voyager** it made me want to travel again

4 *Théât* to stage again

• **redonner dans** VT IND to lapse *or* to fall back into

redorer [3] [rədɔre] VT **1** *Tech* to regild **2** *(société, image)* to repackage

redormir [36] [rədɔrmir] VI *(plus longtemps)* to sleep some more; *(à nouveau)* to sleep again; **je n'ai pas pu r.** I couldn't get back to sleep

redoublant, -e [rədublɑ̃, -ɑ̃t] NM,F *Br* pupil repeating a year, *Am* student repeating a grade

redoublé, -e [rəduble] ADJ **1** *(lettre)* double **2** *(intensifié)* **faire des efforts redoublés** to redouble one's efforts; **frapper à coups redoublés** *(à la porte)* to knock even harder

redoublement [rədubləmɑ̃] NM **1** *Scol* repeating a *Br* year *or Am* grade **2** *Ling* reduplication **3** *(accroissement)* increase, intensification; **seul un r. d'efforts lui permettra de réussir** he/she will only succeed if he/she works much harder; **avec un r. de zèle** with renewed *or* redoubled zeal

redoubler [3] [rəduble] VT **1** *(rendre double)* **r. une consonne** to double a consonant **2** *Scol* **r. une classe** to repeat a *Br* year *or Am* grade **3** *(augmenter ▸ sentiment, chagrin)* to add to; **r. ses efforts** to redouble one's efforts

USAGE ABSOLU to repeat a *Br* year *or Am* class; **ils l'ont fait r.** they made him/her do the year again

VI *(froid, tempête)* to increase, to intensify

• **redoubler de** VT IND to increase in; **les coups redoublèrent de violence** the blows rained down more heavily; **r. d'efforts** to redouble one's efforts; **r. de patience** to be doubly *or* extra patient

redoutable [rədutabl] ADJ **1** *(dangereux ▸ personne, adversaire)* formidable; *(▸ ennemi)* fearsome, formidable; *(▸ maladie)* dreadful; **la compagnie d'assurances a des enquêteurs redoutables** the insurance company has very able investigators; **elle a un revers r.** she has a lethal backhand **2** *(effrayant ▸ aspect, réputation)* awesome, fearsome, awe-inspiring

redoute [rədut] NF *(fortification)* redoubt

redouter [3] [rədute] VT to dread; **un professeur redouté de tous les élèves** a much-dreaded teacher; **il redoute de te rencontrer** he dreads meeting you; **elle redoute que tu (ne) lui en parles** she's terrified that you'll mention it to him/her

redoux [rədu] NM milder spell of weather *(during winter)*

redresse [rədrɛs] **à la redresse** ADJ *Fam* **un type à la r.** a tough guy

redressement [rədrɛsmɑ̃] NM **1** *(du corps, d'une barre)* straightening up; *(de la tête)* lifting up, raising

2 *(d'un véhicule)* **son pneu a explosé juste après un r. dans un virage** his/her tyre burst just after he/she straightened up coming out of a bend

3 *Com & Écon* recovery; **plan de r.** recovery programme; **r. économique** economic recovery

4 *Compta* adjustment; **r. financier** gearing adjustment; *Admin* **r. fiscal, r. d'impôt** tax adjustment

5 *Jur* **r. judiciaire** receivership; **être mis en r. judiciaire** to go into receivership

6 *Électron* rectification

redresser [4] [rədrese] VT **1** *(arbre, poteau)* to straighten (up), to set upright; *(véhicule, volant)* to straighten (up); *(bateau)* to right; *(avion)* to right, to straighten up, to lift the nose of; **r. la tête** *(la lever)* to lift up one's head; *(avec fierté)* to hold one's head up high; **r. les épaules** to straighten one's shoulders

2 *(corriger ▸ courbure)* to put right, to straighten out; *(▸ anomalie)* to rectify, to put right; *(▸ situation)* to sort out, to put right, to put back on an even keel; *(▸ compte)* to adjust

3 *(entreprise)* to put back on its feet; **pour r. l'économie** in order to bring about an economic recovery

4 *Électron* to rectify

USAGE ABSOLU *Aut* to straighten up, to recover; **il n'a pas redressé assez vite à la sortie du virage** he didn't straighten up quickly enough after he came out of the bend

VPR **se redresser 1** *(personne assise)* to sit up straight; *(personne allongée)* to sit up; *(personne voûtée ou penchée)* to straighten up; *(avec fierté)* to draw oneself up, to hold one's head up **2** *Fig (remonter)* to recover; **les résultats se redressent depuis mai** output figures have been looking up *or* have been recovering since May; **la situation se redresse un peu** the situation is on the mend; **le dollar se redressait nettement jeudi matin** the dollar made a marked recovery on Thursday morning

redresseur, -euse [rədrɛsœr, -øz] ADJ *Élec* rectifying

NM **1** *Élec* rectifier **2** *(personne)* **r. de torts** righter of wrongs

redû, -ue [rədy] PP *voir* **redevoir**

NM *Fin* balance due, amount owed

réduc [redyk] NF *Fam (réduction)* discount ▫

réducteur, -trice [redyktœr, -tris] ADJ **1** *(limitatif)* simplistic **2** *Tech* reduction *(avant n)* **3** *Chim* reducing

NM **1** *Tech* reduction gear **2** *Chim* reducer, reductant, reducing agent

réductible [redyktibl] ADJ **1** *(dépenses, dimensions)* which can be reduced; *(théorie)* which can be reduced *or* simplified **2** *Chim, Math & Méd* reducible

réduction [redyksjɔ̃] NF **1** *(remise)* discount, rebate; **accorder** *ou* **faire une r. de cinq euros sur le**

prix total to give a five-euro discount on the overall cost; **faire une r. à qn** to give sb a reduction

2 *(baisse)* reduction, cut (**de** in); *Fin (du capital)* writing down; **ils nous ont imposé une r. des dépenses/salaires** they've cut our expenditure/ wages; **r. de capacité** *ou* **d'effectifs** staff cuts, downsizing; **r. des prix** price reduction; **la r. du temps de travail** = reduction of the working week in France from 39 to 35 hours, introduced by the government of Lionel Jospin in 1998 and phased in from 2000 onwards; **ils ont promis une r. des impôts** they promised to reduce *or* to lower taxes

3 *(copie plus petite ▸ d'une œuvre)* (scale) model

4 *Biol, Chim & Métal* reduction

5 *Méd* setting, reducing; **la r. d'une fracture** setting a broken bone

6 *Math, Mus & Phil* reduction

7 *Jur* **r. de peine** mitigation (of sentence); **il a eu une r. de peine** he got his sentence cut *or* reduced

• **en réduction** ADJ scaled-down

réductrice [redyktris] *voir* **réducteur**

réduire [98] [redɥir] VT **1** *(restreindre ▸ consommation)* to reduce, to cut down on; *(▸ inflation, chômage)* to reduce, to bring down, to lower; *(▸ dépenses, effectifs)* to reduce, to cut back on; *(▸ distance)* to reduce, to decrease; *(▸ chauffage)* to lower, to turn down; *Fin (▸ capital)* to write down; **réduis la flamme** turn down the gas; **il a réduit le prix de dix pour cent** he cut *or* reduced the price by ten percent; **j'ai réduit mon budget vêtements à 50 euros par mois/mon texte à trois pages** I've cut down my spending on clothes to 50 euros a month/my text to three pages; **ils ont réduit le temps d'attente de deux jours** they've cut *or* they've shortened the waiting time by two days; **r. qch de moitié** to cut sth by half, to halve sth

2 *(rapetisser ▸ photo)* to reduce; *(▸ schéma)* to scale down; *(▸ texte)* to shorten, to cut (**de** by); *Ordinat (▸ fenêtre)* to minimize

3 *(changer)* **r. qch à l'essentiel** to boil sth down; **il a réussi à r. à néant le travail de dix années** he managed to reduce ten years' work to nothing; **r. qch en miettes** to smash sth to bits *or* pieces; **r. qch en cendres** to reduce sth to ashes; **r. qch à sa plus simple expression** to reduce sth to its simplest expression

4 *(forcer)* **r. qn à** to reduce sb to; **r. la presse/l'opposition au silence** to silence the press/the opposition; **r. à la clandestinité** to drive underground; **r. qn au désespoir** to drive sb to despair; **en être réduit au suicide** to be driven to suicide; **r. qn à faire qch** to force *or* to compel *or* to drive sb to do sth; **j'en suis réduit à mendier** I'm reduced to begging

5 *(vaincre)* to quell, to subdue, to crush; **r. les poches de résistance** to crush the last pockets of resistance

6 *Chim & Culin* to reduce

7 *Méd* to set, to reduce

8 *Math & Mus* to reduce

9 *Suisse (ranger)* to put away

VI *Culin* to reduce; **faire r.** to reduce

VPR **se réduire 1** *(économiser)* to cut down **2 se r. à** *(consister en)* to amount to; **la rencontre s'est réduite à un échange poli** the meeting amounted to nothing more than a polite exchange of views; **son influence se réduit à peu de chose** his/ her influence amounts to very little

réduit, -e [redɥi, -it] ADJ **1** *(échelle, format etc)* scaled-down, small-scale **2** *(taille)* small; *(tarif)* reduced, cut; **à vitesse réduite** at reduced *or* low speed; **billet à prix r.** cheap *or* cut-price ticket; **voyager à prix r.** to travel at reduced rates; **la fréquentation est réduite l'hiver** attendance is lower in the winter **3** *(peu nombreux ▸ débouchés)* limited, restricted

NM **1** *Péj (logement)* cubbyhole **2** *(recoin)* recess; *(placard)* cupboard

réduplication [redyplikasjɔ̃] NF *Ling* reduplication

rééchelonnement [reeʃlɔnmɑ̃] NM *(d'une dette)* rescheduling

rééchelonner [3] [reeʃəlɔne] VT *(dette)* to reschedule

réécrire [99] [reekrir] VT to rewrite; **r. l'histoire** to rewrite history

VI **r. à qn** to write to sb again, to send sb another letter

réécriture [reekrityr] NF rewriting

réédification [reedifikasjɔ̃] NF reconstruction, re-erection

réédifier [9] [reedifje] VT to reconstruct, to re-erect

rééditer [3] [reedite] VT **1** *Typ* to republish **2** *Fam (refaire)* to repeat

réédition [reedisjɔ̃] NF **1** *Typ (nouvelle édition)* new edition; *(action de rééditer)* republishing, republication **2** *Fam (répétition)* repeat, repetition

rééducation [reedykasjɔ̃] NF **1** *Méd (d'un membre)* re-education; *(d'un malade)* rehabilitation, re-education; **faire de la r.** to undergo *Br* physiotherapy *or Am* physical therapy; **r. motrice** motor re-education; **r. de la parole** speech therapy **2** *(morale)* re-education; *Jur (d'un délinquant)* rehabilitation

rééduquer [3] [reedyke] VT **1** *Méd (malade)* to give *Br* physiotherapy *or Am* physical therapy to; *(membre)* to re-educate **2** *(délinquant)* to rehabilitate

réel, -elle [reɛl] ADJ **1** *(concret ▸ gén)* real; *(▸ date)* effective; *(▸ résultats, fait)* actual; **besoins réels** genuine needs; **dans la vie réelle, c'est différent** it's different in real life; **en termes réels** in real terms **2** *(avant le nom) (appréciable)* genuine, real; **une réelle amélioration** real *or* genuine progress; **elle a fait preuve d'un r. talent** she's shown true *or* genuine talent; **prendre un r. plaisir à faire qch** to take real *or* great pleasure in doing sth

NM **le r.** reality, the real

réélection [reelɛksjɔ̃] NF re-election

rééligible [reeliʒibl] ADJ re-eligible; **ils sont/ne sont pas rééligibles** they are/aren't entitled to stand for election again

réélire [106] [reelir] VT to re-elect

réellement [reɛlmɑ̃] ADV really; **ces faits ont r. eu lieu** these events really did take place

réélu, -e [reely] PP *voir* **réélire**

réembaucher [3] [reɑ̃boʃe] VT to take back on, to take on again, to re-employ; **sa société l'a réembauché** his company took him on again; **il a réussi à se faire r.** he managed to get another job (in the same company)

VI to hire again; **l'entreprise réembauche** the company is taking people on again

réémetteur [reemetœr] NM relay transmitter

réemploi [reɑ̃plwa] = **remploi**

réemployer [reɑ̃plwaje] = **remployer**

réemprunter [reɑ̃prœ̃te] = **remprunter**

réenregistrable [reɑ̃rəʒistrabl] ADJ rerecordable

rééquilibrage [reekilibraʒ] NM *(de roues)* balancing; *(du budget)* rebalancing

rééquilibrer [3] [reekilibre] VT *(roues)* to balance; *(budget)* to rebalance, to balance again; *(situation)* to restabilize

réescompte [reeskɔ̃t] NM rediscount

réescompter [3] [reeskɔ̃te] VT to rediscount

réessayer [11] [reeseje] VT *(voiture, produit, méthode)* to try again; *(vêtement)* to try on again

réévaluation [reevalɥasjɔ̃] NF *(d'une devise, d'une monnaie)* revaluation; *(d'un budget, d'un salaire ▸ gén)* reappraisal, reassessment; *(▸ à la hausse)* upgrade, upgrading; *(▸ à la baisse)* downgrade, downgrading

réévaluer [7] [reevalɥe] VT **1** *(devise, monnaie)* to revalue; *(budget, salaire)* to reappraise; *(à la hausse)* to upgrade; *(à la baisse)* to downgrade **2** *(qualité, travail)* to reassess, to reevaluate

réexamen [reɛgzamɛ̃] NM *(d'une politique, d'une situation)* re-examination, reassessment; *(d'une décision)* reconsideration; *(d'un dossier, d'une question)* re-examination

réexaminer [3] [reɛgzamine] VT *(politique, situation)* to re-examine, to reassess; *(décision)* to reconsider; *(dossier, question)* to re-examine, to examine again

réexpédier [9] [reɛkspedje] VT **1** *(courrier ▸ à l'expéditeur)* to return (to sender), to send back; *(▸ au destinataire)* to forward **2** *Fam (personne)* to throw out; **je l'ai réexpédié vite fait** I got rid of him in no time

réexpédition [reɛkspedisjɔ̃] NF *(à l'expéditeur)* sending back, returning (to sender); *(au destinataire)* forwarding, redirecting; **service de r. du courrier** mail-forwarding *or* mail-redirecting service

réexportation [reɛkspɔrtasjɔ̃] NF *(activité)* re-exportation; *(produit)* re-export

réexporter [3] [reɛkspɔrte] VT to re-export

réfaction [refaksjɔ̃] NF *Com* reimbursement, allowance

refaire [109] [rəfɛr] VT **1** *(à nouveau ▸ travail, traduction etc)* to redo, to do again; *(▸ voyage)* to make again; **tout est à r.** everything will have to be done (all over) again; **r. une opération pour la vérifier** to do a calculation again to check it; **r. un pansement** to redo a bandage; **r. une piqûre à qn** to give sb another injection; **r. le numéro** *(de téléphone)* to redial; **r. ses lacets** to tie one's laces again; **quand pourras-tu r. du sport?** when will you be able to start doing sport again?; **j'ai dû r. du riz** I had to make (some) more rice; **il a refait le dessin en tenant compte de nos remarques** he redid the drawing taking our comments into account; **nous avons refait à pied les 20 kilomètres qui nous séparaient du village** we walked the 20 kilometres back to the village; **tu ne vas pas me r. une scène!** you're not going to start again!; *Fig* **vous ne la referez pas** you won't change her; **r. le monde** to put *or* to set the world to rights; **r. sa vie** to start a new life, to make a fresh start (in life); **r. sa vie avec qn** to make *or* to start a new life with sb; **si c'était à r., je ne l'épouserais pas** if I could start all over again, I wouldn't marry him/her; **si c'était à r.? – je suis prêt à recommencer** and if you had to do it all again? – I would do the same thing

2 *(réparer)* to redo; **r. la toiture** to redo the roof; **r. la peinture** redo the paintwork; **ils refont la route** they are resurfacing the road; **le moteur a été complètement refait à neuf** the engine has had a complete overhaul; *Méd* **se faire r. le nez** to have a nose job

3 *Fam (berner)* to do, to have, to con; **j'ai été refait!** I've been done *or* had *or* conned!; **il m'a refait de dix euros** he did me out of ten euros

V IMPERSONNEL **il refait soleil/froid** it's sunny/ cold again

VPR **se refaire 1** *(se changer)* **on ne se refait pas** you can't change the way you are

2 *Fam (financièrement)* to recoup one's losses; **j'ai besoin de me r.** I need to get hold of some more cash

3 se r. une tasse de thé to make oneself another cup of tea; **se r. une beauté** to powder one's nose; **se r. une santé** to recuperate

4 se r. à qch to get used to sth again; **il a du mal à se r. à la vie urbaine** he's finding it hard getting used to city life again *or* getting reaccustomed to city life

réfection [refɛksjɔ̃] NF *(gén)* redoing; *(d'une pièce)* redecorating; *(d'une maison)* redoing, doing up; *(d'une route)* repairs; **pendant les travaux de r.** *(d'une maison)* while the house is being done up; *(d'une route)* during repairs to the road

réfectoire [refɛktwar] NM *(dans une communauté)* refectory; *Scol* dining hall, canteen; *Univ* (dining) hall, *Br* refectory

refera *etc voir* **refaire**

référé [refere] NM *Jur (procédure)* summary proceedings; *(arrêt)* summary judgement; *(ordonnance)* temporary injunction; **assigner qn en r.** to bring *or* to institute summary proceedings against sb, to apply for a summary judgement to be granted against sb

référence [referɑ̃s] NF **1** *(renvoi)* reference

2 *Admin & Com* reference number; **r. à rappeler dans toute correspondance** *(correspondance administrative)* reference number to be quoted in all correspondence

3 *(base d'évaluation)* reference; **le film a été primé à Cannes mais ce n'est pas une r.** the movie *or Br* film won a prize at Cannes but that's no recommendation; **ton ami n'est pas une r.** your friend is nothing to go by; **faire r. à** to refer to, to make (a) reference to; **la biographie fait plusieurs**

fois r. à son éthylisme the biography makes several references to his/her alcoholism; dans ce passage il fait r. à Platon in this passage he is referring to Plato; servir de r. (pour) to be a benchmark (for)
4 *Ling* reference
• **références** NFPL *(pour un emploi ▸ témoignages)* references, credentials; *(▸document)* reference letter, testimonial; **sérieuses références exigées** *(petite annonce)* good references required
• **de référence** ADJ reference *(avant n)*; **ouvrage/livre de r.** reference work/book; *Fin* **année de r.** base year

référencé, -e [referɑ̃se] ADJ **être r.** to have a reference number; **votre lettre référencée 450/198** your letter reference number 450/198

référencer [16] [referɑ̃se] VT *Com* 1 *(produit)* to list 2 *Ordinat* to reference

référendaire [referɑ̃dɛr] ADJ referendum *(avant n)*; **conseiller r.** ≃ public auditor

référendum [referɛ̃dɔm] NM referendum; **les Norvégiens ont décidé par r. de ne pas entrer dans l'Union européenne** the Norwegians have voted in a referendum *or* by referendum not to join the European Union

référent [referɑ̃] NM referent

référer [18] [refere] **référer à** VT IND *Ling* to refer to
• **en référer à** VT IND to refer back to; **il ne peut rien décider sans en r. à son supérieur** he can't decide anything without referring back to his boss
VPR **se référer** 1 **se r. à** *(se rapporter à)* to refer to; **l'article se réfère à l'affaire Dreyfus** the article refers to the Dreyfus affair; **nous nous référons à la définition ci-dessus** the reader is referred to the above definition; **tout ce qui ne se réfère pas directement à notre affaire** anything that is not directly connected with *or* related to our business 2 **se r. à** *ou* **s'en r. à qn, se r. à** *ou* **s'en r. à l'avis de qn** *(s'en remettre à)* to leave it up to sb to decide

refermable [rəfɛrmabl] ADJ recloseable, resealable

refermer [3] [rəfɛrme] VT to close, to shut
VPR **se refermer** *(porte)* to close, to shut; *(blessure)* to close *or* to heal up; *(piège)* to snap shut; **la porte s'est refermée sur mes doigts** the door closed on my fingers; *Fig* **le piège se referme sur l'espion** the net is closing in around the spy

refiler [3] [rəfile] VT *Fam* 1 *(donner)* to give[□]; **il m'a refilé sa grippe/son vieux blouson** he gave me the flu/his old jacket; **ils vont nous r. les enfants pour le week-end** they're palming the kids off on us *or* dumping the kids on us for the weekend 2 *(locution)* **r. le bébé à qn** to unload a problem onto sb, to pass the buck onto sb

refinancement [rəfinɑ̃smɑ̃] NM refinancing

refinancer [16] [rəfinɑ̃se] VT to refinance

refit *etc voir* **refaire**

réfléchi, -e [refleʃi] ADJ 1 *(caractère, personne)* reflective, thoughtful; *(action, opinion)* deliberate, considered; **une analyse réfléchie** a thoughtful *or* well thought-out analysis; **un enfant très r. pour son âge** a child who thinks very seriously for his age 2 *Ling* reflexive

réfléchir [32] [refleʃir] VT 1 *Phot & Phys* to reflect 2 *(s'aviser)* **il réfléchit que son argent ne suffirait pas** it occurred to him that he wouldn't have enough money
VI to think, to reflect; **as-tu bien réfléchi?** have you thought about it carefully?; **je n'ai pas eu le temps de r.** I haven't had a chance to reflect; **laisse-moi le temps de r.** give me time to think; **parler sans r.** to speak without thinking; **il fallait r. avant de parler!** you should have thought before you spoke!; **j'ai longuement réfléchi** I gave it a lot of thought; **quand on voit comment ça se passe, ça fait r.** when you see what's happening, it makes you think; **tes mésaventures m'ont donné à r.** your mishaps have given me food for thought; **r. à qch** to think about sth, to reflect on sth, to consider sth; **réfléchissez à ma proposition** do think about my offer; **as-tu réfléchi aux conséquences de ton départ?** have you thought about *or* considered the consequences of your going?; **j'ai beaucoup réfléchi au problème** I've given the problem a great deal of thought; **tout bien réfléchi** all things considered, after careful consideration; **c'est tout réfléchi** it's all settled, my mind's made up
VPR **se réfléchir** *(lumière, son)* to be reflected

réfléchissant, -e [refleʃisɑ̃, -ɑ̃t] ADJ *Phys* reflecting

réflecteur, -trice [reflɛktœr, -tris] ADJ reflecting
NM 1 *Astron* reflector, reflecting telescope 2 *Phys & Aut* reflector

réflectif, -ive [reflɛktif, -iv] ADJ *Physiol* reflexive

réflectorisé, -e [reflɛktɔrize] ADJ reflective

réflectrice [reflɛktris] *voir* **réflecteur**

reflet [rəflɛ] NM 1 *(lumière)* reflection, glint, light; **les reflets du soleil sur l'eau** the reflection of the sun on the water 2 *(couleur ▸ gén)* tinge, glint, highlight; *(▸ de la soie)* sheen, shimmer; **des cheveux châtains avec des reflets dorés** brown hair with tints of gold; **se faire faire des reflets** to have highlights put in; **avoir des reflets changeants** to shimmer 3 *(image)* reflection; **on voit le r. du flash dans la fenêtre** you can see the reflection of the flash on the windowpane; **ses lettres sont le r. de son caractère** his/her letters reflect *or* mirror his/her character

refléter [18] [rəflete] VT 1 *(renvoyer ▸ lumière)* to reflect; *(▸ image)* to reflect, to mirror 2 *(représenter)* to reflect, to mirror; **son air perplexe reflétait son trouble intérieur** his/her puzzled look indicated *or* betrayed his/her inner turmoil; **ce qu'il dit ne reflète pas ce qu'il pense/mon opinion** his words are not a fair reflection of what he thinks/of my opinion
VPR **se refléter** 1 *(lumière, rayon)* to be reflected 2 *(se manifester)* to be reflected; **son éducation religieuse se reflète dans sa manière de vivre** his/her religious education is reflected in the way he/she lives; **le bonheur se reflète sur son visage** you can see the happiness in his/her face

refleurir [32] [rəflœrir] VI 1 *(plante)* to flower again, to blossom again 2 *Fig Littéraire* to blossom *or* to flourish again

reflex [reflɛks] ADJ INV reflex *(avant n)*
NM INV reflex (camera)

réflexe [reflɛks] NM 1 *Biol & Physiol* reflex (action); **avoir de bons réflexes** to have good reflexes; **r. inné** instinctive reflex; **r. rotulien** knee reflex *or* jerk 2 *(réaction)* reaction; **il a eu/n'a pas eu le r. de tirer le signal d'alarme** he instinctively pulled/he didn't think to pull the alarm; **son premier r. a été d'appeler à l'aide** his/her immediate reaction was to call for help; **c'est devenu un r.** it's become automatic
ADJ reflex *(avant n)*

réflexif, -ive [reflɛksif, -iv] ADJ *Math & Phil* reflexive

réflexion [reflɛksjɔ̃] NF 1 *(méditation)* thought; **après mûre r.** after careful consideration, after much thought; **leur proposition demande r.** their offer will need thinking over; **donner matière à r.** to provide food for thought; **s'absorber dans ses réflexions** to be deep *or* lost in thought; **r. faite, à la r.** *(finalement)* on reflection; *(quand on change d'avis)* on further consideration, on second thoughts
2 *(discernement)* **son rapport manque de r.** his/her report hasn't been properly thought out *or* through
3 *(remarque)* remark, comment; **faire des réflexions à qn** to make remarks to sb; **elle ne supporte pas qu'on lui fasse la moindre r.** she can't stand the slightest criticism; **elle a fait d'amères réflexions sur son passé** she commented bitterly on her past life; **sa r. ne m'a pas plu** I didn't like his/her remark *or* what he/she said
4 *(de la lumière)* reflection

réflexive [reflɛksiv] *voir* **réflexif**

refluer [7] [rəflye] VI 1 *(liquide)* to flow back; *(marée)* to ebb; *(foule, public)* to surge back; **faire r. les manifestants** to push back the demonstrators; *Fin* **faire r. le dollar/yen** to keep down the value of the dollar/yen 2 *Fig Littéraire (pensée, souvenir)* to come flooding *or* rushing back

reflux [rəfly] NM 1 *(de la marée)* ebb 2 *(d'une foule)* backward surge 3 *Méd* reflux

refondateur, -trice [rəfɔ̃datœr, -tris] ADJ reformative
NM,F reformer, reinventor

refondation [rəfɔ̃dasjɔ̃] NF *(d'un parti politique)* radical reform

refondatrice [rəfɔ̃datris] *voir* **refondateur**

refonder [3] [rəfɔ̃de] VT *(parti politique)* to radically reform

refondre [75] [rəfɔ̃dr] VT 1 *(métal)* to remelt, to melt down again; *(cloche)* to recast; *(monnaie)* to recoin, to remint 2 *Fig (remanier)* to recast, to reshape, to refashion; **r. un projet de loi** to redraft *or* to recast a bill; **la troisième édition a été entièrement refondue** the third edition has been entirely revised
VI *(neige, glace)* to melt again

refont [rəfɔ̃] *voir* **refaire**

refonte [rəfɔ̃t] NF 1 *Métal (nouvelle fonte)* remelting; *(nouvelle coulée)* recasting; *(de la monnaie)* recoinage 2 *Fig (remaniement)* recasting, reshaping, refashioning; *(d'un texte)* rewriting, revision

réformable [refɔrmabl] ADJ 1 *Mil* = liable for exemption from military service 2 *(modifiable)* reformable, capable of being modified

reformatage [rəfɔrmataʒ] NM *Ordinat* reformatting

reformater [3] [rəfɔrmate] VT *Ordinat* to reformat

réformateur, -trice [refɔrmatœr, -tris] ADJ reforming; **idées réformatrices** ideas of reform
NM,F reformer

réformation [refɔrmasjɔ̃] NF 1 *Littéraire (action)* reform, reformation 2 *Vieilli Rel* **la R.** the Reformation 3 *Jur* reversal

réformatrice [refɔrmatris] *voir* **réformateur**

réforme [refɔrm] NF 1 *(modification)* reform; *Pol* **r. constitutionnelle** constitutional reform; **r. électorale** electoral reform; **r. monétaire** monetary reform; **réformes sociales** social reforms; **la r. de l'orthographe** = attempt by the "Académie française" to simplify spelling rules 2 *Mil (de matériel)* scrapping; *(d'un soldat)* discharge; *(d'un appelé)* declaration of unfitness for service; **r. temporaire** deferment; **commission de r.** ≃ Army Medical Board 3 *Rel* **la R.** the Reformation

réformé, -e [refɔrme] ADJ *(religion, Église)* Reformed, Protestant
NM,F *(calviniste)* Protestant
NM *Mil (recrue)* = conscript declared unfit for service; *(soldat)* discharged soldier

reformer [3] [rəfɔrme] VT to re-form, to form again; **r. un groupe** to bring a group back together; **r. les rangs** to fall into line again
VPR **se reformer** to re-form, to form again; **la fissure se reforme tous les hivers** the crack reappears every winter; **l'association va se r. autour d'une nouvelle équipe** the association will be set up again *or* re-formed around a new team

Do not confuse with **réformer**.

réformer [3] [refɔrme] VT 1 *(modifier)* to reform
2 *Littéraire (supprimer)* to put an end to
3 *Mil (recrue)* to declare unfit for service; *(soldat)* to discharge; *(tank, arme)* to scrap; **se faire r.** to be exempted from military service; **être réformé P4** to be discharged for reasons of mental health
4 *Jur (décision)* to reverse

Do not confuse with **reformer**.

réformisme [refɔrmism] NM reformism

réformiste [refɔrmist] ADJ reformist
NMF reformist

reformulation [rəfɔrmylasjɔ̃] NF rewording

reformuler [3] [rəfɔrmyle] VT to rephrase, to reword; **je ne comprends pas votre question, pouvez-vous la r.?** I don't understand your question, could you rephrase it?

refoulé, -e [rəfule] ADJ *(instinct, sentiment)* repressed; *(ambition)* frustrated; *(personne)* inhibited
NM,F inhibited person
NM *Psy* **le r.** repressed content; **retour du r.** return of the repressed

refoulement [rəfulmɑ̃] **NM 1** *(d'assaillants)* driving *or* pushing back; *(d'immigrants)* turning back *or* away **2** *Psy* repression

refouler [3] [rəfule] **VT 1** *(assaillants)* to drive *or* to push back, to repulse; *(immigrants)* to turn back *or* away; **les forces de police ont refoulé les manifestants hors de la place** the police drove the demonstrators out of the square; **on nous a refoulés à l'entrée** we got turned away at the door; **ils se sont fait r. à la frontière** they were turned back at the border

2 *(liquide)* to force to flow back; *(courant)* to stem; *(air)* to pump out

3 *(retenir)* **r. ses larmes** to hold *or* to choke back one's tears; **r. sa colère** to keep one's anger in check

4 *Psy* to repress

5 *Rail* to back

VI 1 *(mal fonctionner)* **l'égout refoule** a stench is coming up from the sewer; **la cheminée refoule** the fire is blowing back **2** *Vulg (sentir mauvais)* to stink▫, *Br* to pong

réfractaire [refrakter] **ADJ 1** *(matériau)* refractory, heat-resistant **2** *(personne)* **r. à** resistant *or* unamenable to; **être r. à l'autorité** to reject authority; **je suis r. aux mathématiques** I'm incapable of understanding mathematics, mathematics is a closed book to me; **r. aux charmes de la nature** impervious to nature's charms **3** *Méd & Tech* refractory

NM 1 *Mil* defaulter **2** *Hist* = French citizen refusing to work in Germany during World War II

réfracter [3] [refrakte] **VT** to refract

VPR se réfracter to be refracted

réfracteur, -trice [refraktœr, -tris] **ADJ** refracting

NM refracting telescope, refractor

réfraction [refraksjɔ̃] **NF** refraction; **indice de r.** refractive index

réfractrice [refraktris] *voir* **réfracteur**

refrain [rəfrɛ̃] **NM 1** *(d'une chanson, d'un poème)* chorus, refrain; *(chanson)* tune, song; **reprendre le r. en chœur** to sing the chorus; **chanter de vieux refrains** to sing old songs *or* tunes; **r. publicitaire** (advertising) jingle **2** *Péj (sujet)* **change de r.** can't you talk about something else?; **avec toi c'est toujours le même r.** it's always the same old story with you

réfrangible [refrɑ̃ʒibl] **ADJ** refrangible

refrapper [3] [rəfrape] **VT** *Ordinat* to rekey

refréner [rəfrene], **réfréner [18]** [refrene] **VT** to hold back, to hold in check, to curb; **r. sa colère** to stifle one's anger

réfrigérant, -e [refriʒerɑ̃, -ɑ̃t] **ADJ 1** *(liquide)* cooling *(avant n)*, *Spéc* refrigerant; **mélange r.** refrigerant **2** *Fig (comportement, individu)* frosty, icy

NM *Ind (appareil)* cooler

réfrigérateur [refriʒeratœr] **NM** refrigerator, *Br* fridge, *Am* icebox; **conserver au r.** keep refrigerated; *Fig* **mettre qn au r.** to sideline sb; *Fig* **mettre un projet au r.** to shelve a plan, to put a plan on ice *or* in cold storage

réfrigération [refriʒerasjɔ̃] **NF** refrigeration; **appareils de r.** refrigeration appliances

réfrigéré, -e [refriʒere] **ADJ 1** *(personne)* frozen **2** *(véhicule)* refrigerated

réfrigérer [18] [refriʒere] **VT 1** *(denrée)* to cool, to refrigerate; *Fam* **je suis réfrigérée!** I'm freezing! **2** *Fig* **son abord glacial m'a réfrigéré** his/her icy manner cut me dead

réfringence [refrɛ̃ʒɑ̃s] **NF** refringence, refringency

réfringent, -e [refrɛ̃ʒɑ̃, -ɑ̃t] **ADJ** refringent

refroidir [32] [rəfrwadir] **VT 1** *Tech (moteur, fluide)* to cool; *(métal)* to quench **2** *Fig (personne)* to cool (down); *(sentiment, enthousiasme)* to dampen, to put a damper on; **cet échec l'a refroidi** this failure has dampened his enthusiasm **3** *Fam (assassiner)* to bump off

VI 1 *(devenir froid)* to get cold; *(devenir moins chaud)* to cool down; **faites r. pendant deux heures au réfrigérateur** cool *or* leave to cool in the refrigerator for two hours; **viens manger, le potage va r.!** come and eat, the soup's getting cold!; **ne laisse pas r. ton thé** don't let your tea get cold; **le temps a refroidi** *(légèrement)* it *or* the weather has got cooler; *(sensiblement)* it *or* the weather has got colder **2** *Fam Fig* **laisser r. qch** to leave *or* to keep *or* to put sth on ice **3** *(à cache-cache)* **tu refroidis!** you're getting colder!

VPR se refroidir 1 *(devenir froid)* to get cold; *(devenir moins chaud)* to cool down; **le temps va se r.** *(légèrement)* it's going to get cooler; *(sensiblement)* it's going to get cold *or* colder **2** *(diminuer)* to cool off; **sa passion s'est refroidie** his/her passion has cooled **3** *(prendre froid)* to catch a chill

refroidissement [rəfrwadismɑ̃] **NM 1** *Tech (de l'eau, d'un moteur)* cooling; *(du métal)* quenching; **à r. par circulation d'eau** water-cooled; **à r. par ventilation** air-cooled; **plaque/tour de r.** cooling plate/tower

2 *(du temps)* drop in temperature

3 *(rhume)* chill

4 *Fig (dans une relation)* cooling (off); **il y a eu un net r. dans leurs relations** there's been a definite cooling off in their relationship

refroidisseur [rəfrwadisœr] **NM** *Tech* cooler

refuge [rəfyʒ] **NM 1** *(abri)* refuge; **servir de r. à qn** to offer refuge to sb, to provide a roof for sb; **chercher/trouver r. dans une grange** to seek/to find shelter in a barn; **donner r. à** to give shelter to, to shelter

2 *(en montagne)* (mountain) refuge

3 *(réconfort)* haven; **chercher r. dans les livres** to seek refuge in books; **ce quartier est le r. des artistes** this area is a haven for artists

4 *(dans une rue)* refuge, (traffic) island

réfugié, -e [refyʒje] **NM,F** refugee; **r. politique** political refugee

réfugier [9] [refyʒje] **se réfugier VPR 1** *(s'abriter)* to take refuge *or* shelter; **ils se sont réfugiés dans une grotte** they took refuge in a cave; **ils se sont réfugiés sous un arbre** they sheltered under a tree **2** *Fig* **elle se réfugie dans ses livres** she takes refuge in her books

refus [rəfy] **NM** *(réponse négative)* refusal, rebuff; *(rejet ▸ d'une proposition, d'un candidat, d'un manuscrit)* rejection; **s'exposer à un r.** to run the risk of a refusal *or* of being turned down; **opposer un r. à qn** to turn sb down; **opposer un r. catégorique à qn** to give an outright refusal to sb; *Fam* **ce n'est pas de r.!** I wouldn't say no!, I don't mind if I do!; **r. d'acceptation** non-acceptance; **r. de coopérer** non-cooperation; **r. d'obéissance** refusal to comply; **r. d'obtempérer** obstruction; **r. de paiement** non-payment; **r. de priorité** refusal to give way

> Il faut noter que le terme anglais **refuse** est un faux ami. Il signifie **ordures.**

refuser [3] [rəfyze] **VT 1** *(don)* to refuse to accept; *(livraison)* to reject; *(offre, proposition)* to turn down, to refuse; *(invitation)* to turn down, to decline; *(candidat)* to turn down; *(chèque)* to bounce; **r. une marchandise pour non-conformité** to refuse to accept an unfit *or* a faulty product; **je suis obligé de r. du travail** I have to turn jobs down *or* to refuse work; **le restaurant refuse du monde tous les soirs** the restaurant turns people away every evening; **être refusé** *(à un examen)* to fail

2 *(autorisation)* to refuse, to turn down; *(service)* to refuse, to deny; **je lui ai refusé l'accès au jardin** I denied him/her access to the garden; **r. sa porte à qn** to refuse to see sb; **r. de faire qch** to refuse to do sth; **il refuse de sortir de sa chambre** he refuses to leave his room; **r. de payer une somme** to withhold a sum of money; **il ne peut rien lui r.** he can refuse him/her nothing; **comment peux-tu lui r. ça?** how can you deny him/her that?; **on leur a refusé l'entrée du château** they weren't allowed in the castle; **il s'est vu r. l'autorisation** he was refused *or* denied permission

3 *(objet)* **le tiroir refuse de s'ouvrir** the drawer refuses to *or* won't open

4 *(maladie, responsabilité)* to refuse, to reject; **je refusais tout à fait cette idée** I wouldn't accept that idea at all; **r. le combat** to refuse battle *or* to fight; **r. de lutter contre la maladie/d'utiliser la force** to refuse to combat illness/to use force; **r. les responsabilités** to shun responsibilities, to refuse to take on responsibilities

VPR se refuser 1 *(emploi passif)* **une telle offre ne se refuse pas** such an offer is not to be refused *or* can't be turned down; **un séjour au bord de la mer, ça ne se refuse pas** a stay at the seaside, you can't say no to that **2** *(à soi-même)* to deny oneself; *Fam* **des vacances au Brésil, on ne se refuse rien!** a holiday in Brazil, you're certainly spoiling yourself! **3 se r. à faire qch** to refuse to do sth; **je me refuse à croire de pareilles sornettes!** I refuse to believe such twaddle!; **l'avocat se refuse à tout commentaire** the lawyer is refusing to make any comment *or* is declining to comment; **se r. à l'évidence** to shut one's eyes to the facts

réfutable [refytabl] **ADJ** refutable; **des arguments qui ne sont pas réfutables** arguments which cannot be refuted

réfutation [refytasjɔ̃] **NF** refutation

réfuter [3] [refyte] **VT 1** *(en prouvant)* to refute, to disprove **2** *(contredire)* to contradict

refuznik [rəfyznik] **NMF** refusnik, refusenik

regagner [3] [rəgaɲe] **VT 1** *(gagner ▸ à nouveau)* to win back, to regain; *(▸ après une perte)* to win back; **le dollar regagne quelques centimes sur le marché des changes** the dollar has regained a few cents on the foreign exchange market; **r. la confiance de ses électeurs** to win back the voters' trust; **r. le temps perdu** to make up for lost time; **r. du terrain** to recover lost ground **2** *(retourner à)* to go back *or* to return to; **r. la ville/la France** to return to (the) town/to France; **il a regagné la côte à la nage** he swam (back) to the shore; **r. sa place** to get back to one's seat *or* place

regain [rəgɛ̃] **NM 1** *(retour, accroissement)* renewal, revival; **un r. de vie** a new lease of life; **un r. d'énergie** fresh energy; **un r. d'espoir** renewed hope; **on constate un r. d'activité sur les marchés boursiers** we can see renewed activity *or* a renewal of activity on the Stock Market **2** *Agr* aftermath

régal, -als [regal] **NM 1** *(délice)* delight, treat; **ce repas est un vrai r.** this meal is a real treat **2** *(plaisir)* delight; **c'est un vrai r. de l'écouter** it's a treat *or* a pleasure to listen to him/her; **c'est un r. pour les yeux** it's a sight for sore eyes

régalade [regalad] **NF boire à la r.** = to drink without letting the bottle touch one's lips

régale [regal] **ADJ F** *Chim* **eau r.** aqua regia

régaler [3] [regale] **VT 1** *(offrir à manger, à boire à)* to treat; **r. ses amis d'un excellent vin** to treat one's friends to an excellent wine **2** *Fig* to regale; **elle régalait ses collègues d'anecdotes croustillantes** she regaled her colleagues with *or* treated her colleagues to spicy anecdotes

USAGE ABSOLU *Fam* **aujourd'hui, c'est moi qui régale** today it's on me *or* I'm treating you *or* it's my treat

VPR se régaler 1 *(en mangeant)* **je me suis régalé** it was a real treat, I really enjoyed it **2** *Fig* **je me régale à l'écouter** it's a real treat for me to listen to him/her; **elle se régale avec ses petits-enfants** she's having the time of her life with her grandchildren

regard [rəgar] **NM 1** *(expression)* look, expression; **son r. était haineux** he/she had a look of hatred in his/her eye *or* eyes, his/her eyes were full of hatred; **il a un r. doux/torve** he has a gentle/menacing look in his eyes; **un r. vitreux** a glassy stare; **un r. concupiscent** a leer; **un r. méfiant** a suspicious look

2 *(coup d'œil)* look, glance, gaze; **mon r. s'arrêta sur une fleur** my eyes fell on a flower; **attirer les regards** to be the centre of attention; **nos regards se croisèrent** our eyes met; **je sentis son r. se poser sur moi** I felt him/her looking at me, I felt his/her gaze on me; **il a détourné le r.** he averted his gaze, he looked away; **ils échangèrent un r. de connivence** they exchanged knowing *or* conspiring looks; **un r. qui en disait long** an eloquent look; **chercher du r.** to look (around) for; **interroger qn du r.** to give sb a questioning look; **jeter** *ou* **lancer un r. à qn** to glance *or* to cast a glance at sb; **caché aux regards du public** out of the public eye; **loin des regards curieux** far from prying eyes; **sous les regards de la foule** while the crowd looked on; **elle attire tous les regards** everyone turns to look at her; *Fig* **porter un r. nouveau sur qn/qch** to look at sb/sth in a new light; **couver qn/**

qch du r. to stare at sb/sth with greedy eyes; *Hum* **suivez mon r.** mentioning no names

3 *(d'égout)* manhole; *(de four)* peephole

4 *(contrôle)* **droit de r.** right of inspection; **je demande un droit de r. sur tous les textes qui sortent de ce bureau** I demand the right to check all texts leaving this office

• **au regard de** PRÉP **1** *(aux termes de)* in the eyes of; **mes papiers sont en règle au r. de la loi** my papers are in order from a legal point of view **2** *(en comparaison avec)* in comparison with, compared to; **ce n'est pas grand-chose au r. de ce que je dois au percepteur** that's not much compared to what I owe the *Br* taxman *or Am* IRS

• **en regard** ADV **un texte latin avec la traduction en r.** a Latin text with a translation on the opposite page

• **en regard de** PRÉP **1** *(face à)* **en r. de la colonne des chiffres** facing *or* opposite the column of figures **2** *(en comparaison avec)* compared with

> Il faut noter que le terme anglais **regard** est un faux ami. Il ne correspond jamais au français **regard**.

regardant, -e [rəgardɑ̃, -ɑ̃t] ADJ **1** *(avare)* sparing, grudging, *Euph* careful with money **2** *(pointilleux)* demanding; **elle n'est pas très regardante sur la propreté** she's not very particular when it comes to cleanliness

REGARDER [3] [rəgarde]

VT	
• to look at **1, 2, 5**	• to see **1**
• to watch **1**	• to look up **3**
• to concern **4**	• to regard **5**
VI	
• to look **1**	• to face **2**

VT **1** *(voir)* to look at, to see; *(observer)* to watch, to see; **r. qch rapidement** to glance at sth; **r. qch fixement** to stare at sth; **r. qch longuement** to gaze at sth; **regarde s'il arrive** see if he's coming; **si tu veux t'instruire, regarde-le faire** if you want to learn something, watch how he does it; **il n'aime pas qu'on le regarde manger** he doesn't like people watching him eat; **as-tu regardé le match?** did you watch *or* see the match?; *Fam* **regarde voir dans la chambre** go and look *or* have a look in the bedroom; *Fam* **regarde voir si ton petit frère dort** look *or* check and see if your little brother is sleeping, will you?; *Fam* **regarde-moi ça!** just look at that!; *Fam* **regarde-moi ce travail!** just look at this mess!; *Fam* **tu ne m'as pas regardé!** what do you take me for?, who do you think I am?

2 *(examiner ▸ moteur, blessure)* to look at, to check; *(▸ notes, travail)* to look over *or* through; **as-tu eu le temps de r. le dossier?** did you have time to look at the file?

3 *(vérifier)* to look up; **regarde son prénom dans le dictionnaire** look up his/her first name in the dictionary; **tu regardes constamment la pendule!** you're always looking at *or* watching the clock!; *Fam* **non mais, tu as regardé l'heure?** *(il est tard)* have you seen the time?, do you realize what time it is?; **je vais r. quelle heure il est** *ou* **l'heure** I'm going to see *or* to check what time it is

4 *(concerner)* to concern; **ceci ne regarde que toi et moi** this is (just) between you and me; **ça ne te regarde pas!** that's *or* it's none of your business!; **cette affaire ne me regarde plus** this affair is no longer any concern *or* business of mine; **en quoi est-ce que ça me regarde?** what's that got to do with me?

5 *(considérer ▸ sujet, situation)* to look at, to view; **un projet que l'on regardait alors avec suspicion** a project which was regarded *or* viewed with suspicion at the time; **il regarde avec envie la réussite de son frère** he casts an envious eye upon his brother's success, he looks upon his brother's success with envy; **ne r. que** *(ne penser qu'à)* to be concerned only with, to think only about; **il ne regarde que ses intérêts** he thinks only about his own interests; **r. qn comme** to consider sb as, to regard sb as, to look upon sb as; **je l'ai toujours regardé comme un frère** I've always looked upon him as a brother; **on le regarde comme un futur champion** he is seen *or* regarded as a future champion; **r. qch comme** to regard sth as, to look upon sth as, to think of sth as

USAGE ABSOLU **regarde à la lettre D** look through the D's, look at the letter D

VI **1** *(personne)* to look; **nous avons regardé partout** we looked *or* searched everywhere; **tu ne sais pas r.** you should learn to use your eyes; **ne reste pas là à r., fais quelque chose!** don't just stand there (staring), do something!

2 *(bâtiment, pièce)* **r. à l'ouest** to face West; **le balcon regarde vers la mer** the balcony looks out over *or* faces the sea

• **regarder à** VT IND **1** *(morale, principes)* to think of *or* about, to take into account; *(apparence, détail)* to pay attention to; **nous regardons d'abord au bien-être de nos patients** we are primarily concerned with the welfare of our patients; **regarde à ne pas faire d'erreur** watch you don't make a mistake; **r. à la dépense** to be careful with one's money; **ne regardons pas à la dépense!** let's not think about the money!; **acheter sans r. à la dépense** to buy things regardless of the expense; **y r. à deux** *ou* **à plusieurs fois avant de faire qch** to think twice before doing sth; **à y bien r., à y r. de plus près** when you think it over, on thinking it over **2** *Belg (veiller sur)* to look after

• **regarder après** = **regarder à 2**

• **regarder de** VT IND *Belg* **r. de faire qch** to make sure *or* to take care to do sth

VPR **se regarder 1** *(emploi réfléchi) aussi Fig* to look at oneself; **se r. dans un miroir** to look at oneself in a mirror; *Fam* **tu ne t'es pas regardé!** you should take a (good) look at yourself! **2** *(emploi réciproque) (personnes)* to look at each other *or* at one another; *(bâtiments)* to be opposite one another, to face each other; **elles se regardaient dans les yeux** they were looking *or* staring into each other's eyes **3** *(emploi passif) (spectacle)* **ça se regarde volontiers** it's quite enjoyable to watch

> Il faut noter que le verbe anglais **to regard** est un faux ami. Il ne signifie jamais **regarder**.

regarnir [32] [rəgarnir] VT *(rayons, garde-manger)* to restock, to refill, to stock up again; *(maison)* to refurnish

régate [regat] NF *Naut* regatta; **faire une r.** to sail in a regatta

régater [3] [regate] VI **1** *Naut* to race *or* to sail in a regatta; **r. avec qn** to race sb in a regatta **2** *Suisse (être à la hauteur)* to measure up, to match up

régatier [regatje] NM entrant *or* competitor in a regatta

regel [rəʒɛl] NM renewed frost

regeler [25] [rəʒəle] VT to freeze again

VI to freeze again

V IMPERSONNEL **il regèle** it's freezing again

régence [reʒɑ̃s] NF regency

• **Régence** NF **la R.** the Regency of Philippe II *(in France)* ADJ INV *(style)* (French) Regency; **un fauteuil R.** a Regency armchair

régénérateur, -trice [reʒeneratœr, -tris] ADJ regenerative; *Rel* **eau régénératrice** baptismal water

NM regenerator

régénération [reʒenerasjɔ̃] NF regeneration

régénératrice [reʒeneratris] *voir* **régénérateur**

régénérer [18] [reʒenere] VT **1** *Biol & Chim* to regenerate **2** *(rénover)* to regenerate, to restore; **je me sens régénéré après cette douche** I feel refreshed *or* revived after that shower

VPR **se régénérer** *Biol & Chim* to regenerate (itself)

régent, -e [reʒɑ̃, -ɑ̃t] ADJ **reine régente** Queen Regent; **prince r.** Prince Regent

NM,F **1** *Pol* regent **2** *Belg* = qualified secondary school teacher

régenter [3] [reʒɑ̃te] VT to rule over, to run; **il veut tout r.** he wants to run everything *or* the show; **il veut r. tout le monde** he wants everybody to be at his beck and call

reggae [rege] NM *Mus* reggae

régicide [reʒisid] ADJ regicidal

NMF *(personne)* regicide

NM *(acte)* regicide

régie [reʒi] NF **1** *(d'une entreprise publique ▸ par l'État)* state control; *(▸ par le département)* local government control; *(▸ par la commune)* local authority control; **(société en) r.** *(par l'État)* state-controlled corporation; *(par le département)* local government controlled company; *(par la commune)* ≃ local authority controlled company; **il travaille à la r. municipale des eaux** he works for the local water board; *Hist* **la R.** = collection of taxes by state functionaries, *Br* ≃ Customs and Excise; *Can* **R. des Loyers** rental board

2 *(pièce ▸ dans un studio de télévision ou de radio)* control room; *(▸ dans un théâtre)* lighting box; *(équipe)* production team

3 *Mktg* **r. publicitaire** advertising sales agency

4 *Fin* excise

regimber [3] [rəʒɛ̃be] VI **1** *(cheval)* to rear up, to jib **2** *(personne)* to grumble, to complain; **faire qch sans r.** to do sth without grumbling *or* complaining; **inutile de r.** it's no use grumbling *or* complaining

régime [reʒim] NM **1** *Pol (système)* regime, (system of) government; *(gouvernement)* regime; **r. militaire/parlementaire/totalitaire** military/parliamentary/totalitarian regime; **la chute du r.** the fall of the regime *or* the government; **sous le r. de Pompidou/Clinton** during the Pompidou/Clinton administration

2 *Admin & Jur (système)* system, scheme; *(règlement)* rules, regulations; **le r. des visites à l'hôpital** hospital visiting hours and conditions; **r. de Sécurité sociale** = subdivision of the French social security system applying to certain professional groups; **être marié sous le r. de la communauté/de la séparation de biens** to have opted for a marriage based on joint ownership of property/on separate ownership of property; **r. d'assurance vieillesse** old-age pension fund *or* scheme; **r. complémentaire** additional retirement cover; **r. douanier** customs regulations; **r. fiscal** tax regime *or* system; *Fin* **r. du forfait** standard assessment system, fixed-rate tax assessment system; **le r. général de la Sécurité sociale** the social security system; **r. légal** statutory regime; **r. pénitentiaire** prison system; **r. de retraite** retirement scheme; **r. de retraite des artisans, commerçants et professions libérales** self-employed pension; **r. de retraite par capitalisation** funded pension scheme; **le r. du travail** the organization of labour

3 *Écon* **r. préférentiel** special arrangements

4 *(alimentaire)* diet; **faire un r.**, *Belg* **faire r.** to go on a diet; **être au r.** to be on a diet, to be dieting; **se mettre au r.** to go on a diet; **r. alimentaire** diet; **r. amaigrissant** *Br* slimming *or Am* reducing diet; **r. grossissant** fattening diet; *Fam Hum* **je suis au r. sec** I'm on an alcohol-free diet□; **r. sans sel** salt-free diet

5 *Ind & Tech* engine speed; **fonctionner à plein r.** *(usine)* to work to full capacity; **travailler à plein r.** *(personne)* to work flat out; **à ce r. vous ne tiendrez pas longtemps** at this rate you won't last long; **r. de croisière** economic *or* cruising speed

6 *Géog (d'un cours d'eau)* rate of flow, regimen; **r. des pluies** rainfall pattern

7 *Ling* **r. direct/indirect** direct/indirect object; **cas r.** objective case

8 *Phys* regimen, flow rate

9 *Bot (de bananes)* hand, stem, bunch; *(de dattes)* bunch, cluster

régiment [reʒimɑ̃] NM **1** *Mil (unité)* regiment; **r. d'infanterie** infantry regiment **2** *Vieilli (service militaire)* **faire son r. dans l'infanterie** *Br* ≃ to do one's military service in the infantry, *Am* ≃ to be drafted into the infantry; **un de mes camarades de r.** a friend from my military service days **3** *Fam (grand nombre)* **il a tout un r. de cousins** he's got a whole army of cousins; **il y en a pour un r.** there's enough for a whole army

régimentaire [reʒimɑ̃tɛr] ADJ *Mil* regimental

région [reʒjɔ̃] NF **1** *Géog* region, area; **les régions tempérées/polaires** the temperate/polar regions; **la Sologne est une r. marécageuse** the Sologne is a marshy area *or* region; **dans la r. de Nantes** in the Nantes area, in the region of Nantes; **les habitants de Paris et sa r.** the inhabitants of Paris and the surrounding region *or* area; **le nouveau médecin n'est pas de la r.** the new doctor isn't from the area *or* from around here; **si jamais tu passes dans la r....** if you're ever in the area...; **la r. parisienne** the Paris area, the area around Paris 2 *Anat* r. cervicale/lombaire cervical/lumbar region; une douleur dans la r. du foie a pain somewhere around *or* near the liver

• **Région** NF *Admin* region *(French administrative area made up of several departments)*; je suis financé par la R. I get funding from the region

régional, -e, -aux, -ales [reʒjɔnal, -o] ADJ 1 *(de la région)* regional; *(de la localité)* local 2 *(sur le plan international)* local, regional; un conflit r. a regional conflict

• **régionale** NF *Belg (fédération)* = regionally-based organization; *(amicale d'étudiants)* = regionally-based students' association

régionalisation [reʒjɔnalizasjɔ̃] NF regionalization

régionaliser [3] [reʒjɔnalize] VT to regionalize

régionalisme [reʒjɔnalism] NM regionalism

régionaliste [reʒjɔnalist] ADJ regionalist

NMF *(gén) & Pol* regionalist; *(écrivain)* regional writer

régir [32] [reʒir] VT 1 *(déterminer)* to govern 2 *Vieilli (domaine)* to manage

régisseur, -euse [reʒisœr, -øz] NM,F 1 *(d'un domaine)* steward 2 *Cin & TV* assistant director; *Théât* stage manager; r. de plateau floor manager 3 *Écon* comptroller

registre [rəʒistr] NM 1 *Admin & Jur* register; *(de comptes)* account book; noter qch dans un r. to write sth down in *or* to enter sth into a register; signer le r. *(d'un hôtel)* to sign the register; s'inscrire au r. du commerce to register one's company; r. de l'état civil ≃ register of births, marriages and deaths; R. du commerce et des sociétés the Registrar of companies; *Compta* r. de comptabilité account book, ledger; r. foncier land register

2 *Mus (d'un orgue)* stop; *(d'une voix)* range, register; avoir un r. étendu to have a wide range; un r. aigu/grave a high/low pitch

3 *Ling* register, level of language

4 *(style)* tone, style; le livre est écrit dans un r. plaisant the book is written in a humorous style

5 *Ordinat* register

réglable [reglabl] ADJ 1 *(adaptable)* adjustable; le dossier est r. en hauteur the height of the seat is adjustable 2 *(payable)* payable

réglage [reglaʒ] NM 1 *(mise au point)* adjustment, regulation; procéder au r. des phares to adjust the headlights; r. d'un thermostat thermostat setting

2 *Aut, Rad & TV* tuning; r. du contraste/de la luminosité de l'écran contrast/brightness control; *Phot* le r. de l'appareil est automatique the camera is fully automatic

3 *Mil* r. du tir range finding *or* adjustment

4 *(du papier)* ruling

règle [rɛgl] NF 1 *(instrument)* ruler, rule; r. à calcul slide rule; r. graduée ruler 2 *(principe, code)* rule; c'est la r. that's the rule; se plier à une r. to abide by a rule; les règles de la politesse exigent que... courtesy demands that...; enfreindre la r. to break the rule *or* rules; j'ai pour r. de me coucher de bonne heure I make it a rule to go to bed early; il est de r. de porter une cravate ici it's customary to wear a tie here; les règles de base en grammaire the basic rules of grammar; règles d'exploitation operating regulations; la r. du jeu the rules of the game; respecter la r. du jeu to play by the rules; r. d'or golden rule; règles de sécurité safety regulations; r. de trois rule of three; dans les règles (de l'art) according to the (rule) book, by the book

• **règles** NFPL *Physiol (en général)* periods; *(d'un cycle)* period; avoir ses règles to be menstruating, to have one's period; je n'ai plus de *ou* mes règles depuis trois mois I haven't had a period for three months; avoir des règles douloureuses to have painful periods, *Br* to suffer from period pain *or* pains, *Am* to suffer from menstrual cramps

• **en règle** ADJ être en r. *(document)* to be in order; *(personne)* to have one's papers in order, to be in possession of valid papers; se mettre en r. to sort out one's situation; une bataille en r. a battle according to the rules; recevoir un avertissement en r. to be given an official warning; tenir sa comptabilité en r. to keep one's accounts in order

• **en règle générale** ADV generally, as a (general) rule

réglé, -e [regle] ADJ 1 *(organisé)* regular, well-ordered; une vie bien réglée a well-ordered existence 2 *(rayé ou quadrillé)* papier r. ruled *or* lined paper; c'est r. comme du papier à musique it's as regular as clockwork

• **réglée** ADJ F *(jeune fille)* depuis combien de temps êtes-vous réglée? how long have you been having your periods?; est-elle réglée? has she started her periods (yet)?

règlement [rɛgləmɑ̃] NM 1 *Admin* regulation, rules; observer le r. to abide by the rules; d'après le r., il est interdit de... it's against the regulations to...; le r. a été affiché dans chaque classe the rules have been pinned up in each classroom; r. intérieur *(d'une école)* school rules; *(d'un bureau)* company *or* staff regulations; r. sanitaire health regulations 2 *(d'un compte)* settlement; *(d'une facture)* payment, settlement; en r. de votre compte in settlement of your account; faire un r. par chèque to pay by cheque; r. à la commande cash with order; pour r. de tout compte in full settlement; r. par carte de crédit/au comptant payment by credit card/in cash; r. en espèces cash payment *or* settlement; r. en nature settlement in kind 3 *(résolution)* settlement, settling; r. de compte *ou* comptes settling of scores; il y a eu des règlements de comptes some old scores were settled; *Jur* r. à l'amiable amicable settlement; *(sans procès)* out-of-court settlement; r. de gré à gré amicable settlement, settlement by negotiation; *Jur* r. judiciaire compulsory liquidation, *Br* winding-up; se mettre en r. judiciaire to go into liquidation *or* receivership

réglementaire [rɛgləmɑ̃tɛr] ADJ 1 *(conforme)* regulation *(avant n)*; longueur/uniforme r. regulation length/uniform; modèle de chaudière r. approved *or* standard type of boiler; il a passé l'âge r. he's above the statutory age limit; le score était de 0–0 à l'issue du temps r. *(au foot)* the score was 0–0 after ninety minutes; ce n'est pas r. it's against the rules 2 *Jur* pouvoir r. statutory *or* regulative power 3 *Admin (décision)* statutory; dispositions réglementaires regulations

réglementariste [rɛgləmɑ̃tarist] ADJ *(attitude, professeur etc)* pernickety, nit-picking; un fonctionnaire r. a civil servant who goes by the book

N nit-picker, pernickety person

réglementation [rɛgləmɑ̃tasjɔ̃] NF 1 *(mesures)* regulations; la r. du travail labour regulations *or* legislation 2 *(limitation)* control, regulation; la r. des prix price regulation

réglementer [3] [rɛgləmɑ̃te] VT to regulate, to control; la vente des boissons alcoolisées est très réglementée the sale of alcoholic drinks is under strict control *or* is strictly controlled

régler [18] [regle] VT 1 *(résoudre ▸ litige)* to settle, to resolve; *(▸ problème)* to solve, to iron out, to sort out; alors c'est réglé, nous irons au bord de la mer it's settled then, we'll go to the seaside; c'est une affaire réglée it is (all) settled now

2 *(payer ▸ achat)* to pay (for); *(▸ facture, mensualité)* to pay, to settle; *(▸ compte)* to settle; *(▸ épicier, femme de ménage, loyer)* to pay; *(▸ créancier)* to settle up with; mon salaire ne m'a pas été réglé my salary hasn't been paid (in); r. l'addition to pay *or* to settle the bill; r. qch en espèces to pay cash for sth; r. qch par chèque/par carte de crédit to pay for sth by cheque/by credit card; je peux vous r. par chèque? will you take a cheque?, can I pay by cheque?; r. ses comptes (avec qn) to settle up (with sb); *Fig* to settle (one's) scores (with sb); r. quelques comptes to settle a few scores; j'ai un compte à r. avec toi I've got a bone to pick with you; *Fam* r. son compte à qn *(se venger de lui)* to get even with sb; *(le tuer)* to take care of sb

3 *(volume, allumage, phare etc)* to adjust; *(vitesse, thermostat)* to set; *(température)* to regulate; *(circulation)* to control; *(moteur)* to tune; j'ai réglé mon réveil sur sept heures/le four à 200° I've set my alarm for seven o'clock/the oven at 200°; comment r. la radio sur France-Musique? how do you tune in to France-Musique?; *Sport* r. l'allure to set the pace; r. qch sur *(accorder par rapport à)* to set sth by; r. sa montre sur l'horloge parlante to set one's watch by the speaking clock; r. son rythme sur celui du soleil to model one's rhythm of life on the movement of the sun; r. son allure sur celle de qn to adjust one's pace to that of sb

4 *(déterminer)* to decide (on), to settle; quelques détails à r. a few details to be settled

5 *(papier)* to rule

6 *Jur (résoudre)* to settle; r. qch à l'amiable to settle sth amicably; *(sans procès)* to settle sth out of court

VPR se régler 1 *(mécanisme)* to be set *or* regulated; *(luminosité, phare)* to be adjusted; *(récepteur)* to be tuned 2 *(se résoudre)* to be settled; ça s'est réglé à l'amiable it was settled amicably 3 se r. sur *(imiter)* to model oneself on, to follow (the example of); elle a tendance à se r. sur (l'exemple de) sa mère she has a tendency to model herself on her mother

réglette [reglɛt] NF 1 *(petite règle)* short ruler, straightedge 2 *Ordinat (pour un clavier)* template

réglisse [reglis] NF liquorice; bâton de r. stick of liquorice; bonbon à la r. liquorice-flavoured *Br* sweet *or Am* candy

réglo [reglo] *Fam* ADJ INV *(personne)* straight, on the level; *(opération, transaction)* legit, kosher; un type r. an OK *or Am* a regular guy; elle a été très r. she played by the rules; il n'a pas été très r. avec moi he didn't treat me right; il trempe toujours dans des affaires pas très r. he's always mixed up in some kind of shady business

ADV by the book, fair and square; il a intérêt à jouer r. he'd better play fair; on fait ça r., hein? we'll do it by the book, OK?

réglure [reglyr] NF ruling

régnant, -e [reɲɑ̃, -ɑ̃t] ADJ 1 *(qui règne)* reigning 2 *(qui prédomine)* prevailing, reigning, dominant; la mode régnante prevailing fashion

règne [rɛɲ] NM 1 *(gouvernement)* reign; sous le r. de Catherine II in the reign of Catherine II 2 *(domination ▸ de la bêtise, de la justice)* rule, reign; c'est le r. de l'argent/de la technologie money/technology reigns supreme 3 *Biol* r. animal/végétal animal/plant kingdom

régner [8] [reɲe] VI 1 *(gouverner)* to reign, to rule; r. sur un pays to reign over *or* to rule (over) a country 2 *(dominer ▸ idée)* to predominate, to prevail; *(▸ ordre, silence)* to reign, to prevail; la suspicion qui règne au bureau the climate of suspicion in the office *or* which pervades the office; r. sur to rule over; r. en maître (sur) to rule supreme (over); *Littéraire* elle règne dans mon cœur she reigns in my heart; faire r. la paix to keep the peace; faire r. le silence to keep everybody quiet; faire r. l'ordre to keep things under control; un dictateur qui a fait r. la terreur a dictator who established a reign of terror; *Ironique* la confiance règne! there's trust *or* confidence for you! 3 *(tournure impersonnelle)* il règne enfin une paix profonde a great peace reigns at last; il règne dans la famille une atmosphère de haine an atmosphere of hatred reigns in the family

regonfler [3] [rəgɔ̃fle] VT 1 *(gonfler de nouveau ▸ ballon, bouée)* to blow up (again), to reinflate; *(▸ matelas pneumatique)* to pump up (again), to reinflate; *Fam* son séjour à la mer l'a regonflée à bloc her stay at the seaside has bucked her up (no end); *Fam* je suis regonflé à bloc! I'm back on form! 2 *(gonfler davantage ▸ pneus)* to put more air in *or* into

VI *(gén) & Méd* to swell (up) again

regorger [17] [rəgɔrʒe] VI *Littéraire (liquide)* to overflow

• **regorger de** VT IND to overflow with, to abound in; la terre regorge d'eau the ground is waterlogged; les cafés regorgent de clients the cafés are packed with customers; la ville regorge de musées the town has an abundance of museums

régresser [4] [regrese] VI 1 *(baisser ▸ chiffre, population)* to drop; *(▸ douleur)* to improve; le chiffre d'affaires a régressé there has been a drop in turnover

2 *(décliner ▸ civilisation)* to regress; *(▸ industrie)* to be in decline; j'ai régressé en maths my maths has deteriorated

3 *(s'atténuer)* la maladie a régressé the patient's condition has improved

4 *Biol & Psy* to regress

régressif, -ive [regresif, -iv] **ADJ** *(gén)* regressive; *(impôt)* degressive; *Biol* **forme régressive** throwback

régression [regresjɔ̃] **NF 1** *(recul)* decline, decrease, regression; **être en r.** *(épidémie)* to be on the decline, to be losing ground; *(chômage, production)* to be on the decline, to be declining; **r. sociale** downward mobility **2** *Psy & Biol* regression

régressive [regresiv] *voir* **régressif**

regret [rəgrɛ] **NM 1** *(remords)* regret; **elle m'a fait part de ses regrets** she expressed her regret to me; **je n'ai aucun r.** I have no regrets; **je n'ai qu'un r., c'est d'avoir dû lui mentir** my only regret is that I had to lie to him/her; **tu l'achètes, pas de regrets?** so you're buying it, no regrets?; **sans un r.** without a single regret; **tous mes regrets** I'm terribly *or* awfully sorry; **regrets éternels** *(faire-part de décès)* deeply regretted, greatly lamented **2** *(tristesse)* regret; **je vous quitte avec beaucoup de r.** I leave you with great regret, I'm very sorry I have to leave you; **nous nous en sommes séparés avec r.** we were sorry to part with it; **nous sommes au** *ou* **nous avons le r. de vous annoncer que...** we are sorry *or* we regret to have to inform you that...; **à mon grand r.** (much) to my regret

• **à regret ADV** *(partir, sévir)* regretfully, with regret; **il s'éloigna comme à r.** he walked away with apparent reluctance

regrettable [rəgretabl] **ADJ** regrettable, unfortunate; **il est r. que tu n'aies pas été informée à temps** it is unfortunate *or* a pity (that) you were not informed in time

regretter [4] [rəgrete] **VT 1** *(éprouver de la nostalgie pour ▸ personne, pays)* to miss; *(▸ jeunesse, passé)* to be nostalgic for; **il sera regretté de tous** he'll be greatly *or* sorely missed; **son regretté mari** her late lamented husband **2** *(se repentir de)* to be sorry about, to regret; **tu n'as rien à r.** you've got nothing to feel sorry about *or* to regret; **je ne regrette pas le temps passé là-dessus/l'argent que ça m'a coûté** I'm not sorry I spent time/money on it; **il me ferait presque r. ma gentillesse** I'm almost sorry I was so kind to him; **je ne regrette rien** I've no regrets; **je saurai te faire r. ta plaisanterie** I'll make you sorry for that joke; **tu ne le regretteras pas!** you won't regret it!, you won't be sorry!; **vous le regretterez!** you'll regret it!, you'll be sorry!, you'll rue the day!; **je regrette qu'elle soit partie si tôt** I'm sorry that she left so early, I wish she hadn't left so early

USAGE ABSOLU pouvez-vous venir? – non, je regrette will you be able to come? – no, I'm afraid not *or* – sorry, no; **ah non! je regrette! j'étais là avant toi!** I'm sorry but I was here first!

• **regretter de VT IND 1** *(se reprocher de)* **tu ne regretteras pas de m'avoir écouté** you won't be sorry you listened to me, you won't regret having listened to me **2** *(dans des expressions de politesse)* **nous regrettons de ne pouvoir donner suite à votre appel** *(au téléphone)* we regret *or* we are sorry we are unable to connect you; **je regrette de devoir vous annoncer que...** I regret to inform you that...

regrèvement [rəgrɛvmɑ̃] **NM** *Fin* tax increase

regrimper [3] [rəgrɛ̃pe] **VT** to climb (up) again

VI 1 *(sur une montagne, sur un arbre)* to climb (up) again **2** *(augmenter ▸ température, taux)* to go up *or* to rise again

regrossir [32] [rəgrosir] **VI** to put on weight again

regroupement [rəgrupmɑ̃] **NM 1** *(d'animaux, d'enfants)* rounding up, round-up; *(de troupes)* gathering together, rallying; *(d'une équipe, d'un parti)* regrouping; **le r. des différentes tendances politiques** the rallying (together) of various shades of political opinion; **r. familial** = policy of authorizing the families of immigrant workers in possession of long-term work permits to join their relatives in France **2** *(de sociétés, de services)* merger, amalgamation **3** *(de comptes)* consolidation

regrouper [3] [rəgrupe] **VT 1** *(rassembler ▸ animaux, enfants)* to round up, to gather together; *(▸ troupes)* to gather together, to rally; *(▸ équipe, parti)* to regroup

2 *(unir ▸ sociétés, services)* to merge, to amalgamate; **regroupons le parti autour d'une idée-force** let us unite the party around a key idea

3 *(contenir)* to contain; **le centre culturel regroupe sous un même toit un cinéma et un théâtre** the arts centre accommodates *or* has a cinema and a theatre (under the same roof)

4 *(comptes)* to consolidate

VPR se regrouper *(institutions)* to group together; *(foule)* to gather; *(équipe, parti, troupes)* to regroup; **les sociétés se sont regroupées pour mieux faire face à la concurrence** the companies have joined forces to deal more effectively with the competition; **les manifestants se regroupent devant la mairie** demonstrators are gathering *or* assembling in front of the town hall

régularisation [regylarizasjɔ̃] **NF 1** *(d'une situation)* straightening out, regularization **2** *Fin (d'un compte, des stocks, des charges)* adjustment

régulariser [3] [regylarize] **VT 1** *(rendre légal)* to regularize; **il a fait r. son permis de séjour** he got his residence permit sorted out *or* put in order; **r. sa situation** to have one's papers sorted out *or* put in order; *Hum (se marier)* to tie the knot **2** *(rendre régulier)* to regulate **3** *Fin (compte, stocks, charge)* to adjust

régularité [regylarite] **NF 1** *(dans le temps)* regularity, steadiness; **la r. des battements de son cœur** the regularity of his/her heartbeat; **faire preuve de r.** *(dans son travail)* to be reliable; **les factures tombent avec r.** there's a steady flow of bills to pay; **les lettres me parvenaient sans aucune r.** letters would reach me fairly erratically

2 *(dans l'espace ▸ de la dentition)* evenness; *(▸ d'une surface)* smoothness; *(▸ de plantations)* straightness

3 *(en valeur, en intensité)* consistency; **travailler avec r.** to work steadily

4 *(légalité)* lawfulness, legality

régulateur, -trice [regylatœr, -tris] **ADJ** regulating, control *(avant n)*

NM *(dispositif, horloge)* regulator; **r. de tension** voltage smoother; **r. de vitesse** cruise control

régulation [regylasjɔ̃] **NF 1** *(contrôle)* control, regulation; *(réglage)* regulation, correction; **r. de la circulation** traffic control; *Fin* **la r. du marché des changes** foreign exchange control; **r. des naissances** birth control **2** *Biol* regulation; **r. thermique** (body) temperature control

régulatrice [regylatris] *voir* **régulateur**

régulier, -ère [regylje, -ɛr] **ADJ 1** *(fixe, permanent)* regular; **des revenus réguliers** a regular *or* steady income; **manger à heures régulières** to eat regularly *or* at regular times; **de façon régulière** on a regular basis; **liaisons régulières** *(en avion)* regular flights; **les vols réguliers** scheduled flights; **armée régulière** regular army; **troupes régulières** regular troops, regulars

2 *(dans l'espace ▸ gén)* regular, even; *(▸ plantations)* evenly distributed; **des espacements réguliers** regular intervals; **une écriture régulière** regular *or* neat handwriting

3 *(uniforme ▸ montée, déclin)* steady; *(▸ distribution)* even; **être r. dans son travail** to be a steady worker; **c'est un élève r.** he's a consistent pupil

4 *(harmonieux ▸ traits)* regular

5 *(conforme à la règle ▸ transaction)* legitimate; *(▸ procédure)* correct, fair; *(conforme à la loi)* legal; *Sport* permissible; **c'est un procédé pas très r.** that's not quite above board; **le coup n'était pas r.** it was a bit of a dirty trick, it was a low blow; **être en situation régulière** to be in line with the law

6 *Fam (honnête)* on the level, straight; **ils sont réguliers en affaires** they're straight *or* honest in business; **il n'a pas été très r. avec moi** he didn't play fair with me, he wasn't straight *or* on the level with me

7 *Bot, Géom, Ling & Zool* regular

8 *Rel (clergé, abbé)* regular

NM *Mil & Rel* regular

• **régulière NF** *Fam Hum (épouse)* old lady, *Br* missus; *(maîtresse)* mistress[□], *Br* bit on the side

• **à la régulière ADV** *Fam* fair and square, above board; **ça a été fait à la régulière** it was all (done) above board, there was nothing shady about it

régulièrement [regyljɛrmɑ̃] **ADV 1** *(dans l'espace ▸ disposer)* evenly, regularly, uniformly; **les arbres sont plantés r.** the trees are evenly *or* regularly spaced

2 *(dans le temps ▸ progresser)* steadily; *(▸ mettre à jour, rendre visite)* regularly; **donne de tes nouvelles r.** write often *or* regularly *or* on a regular basis; **elle avait r. de bonnes notes** she got consistently good *Br* marks *or Am* grades; **je la vois assez r.** I see her quite regularly *or* quite frequently

3 *(selon la règle)* lawfully; **assemblée élue r.** lawfully *or* properly elected assembly

4 *Fam (normalement)* in principle, normally; **r., c'est lui qui devrait gagner** ordinarily *or* in principle, he should win

régurgitation [regyrʒitasjɔ̃] **NF** regurgitation

régurgiter [3] [regyrʒite] **VT** to regurgitate

réhabilitation [reabilitasjɔ̃] **NF 1** *Jur* rehabilitation; **obtenir la r. de qn** to clear sb's name; **r. judiciaire** judicial discharge **2** *(d'une personne)* rehabilitation, clearing the name of **3** *(d'un quartier)* rehabilitation

réhabilité, -e [reabilite] **ADJ** rehabilitated; *Fin* discharged

NM,F *Jur* rehabilitated person; *Fin* discharged bankrupt

réhabiliter [3] [reabilite] **VT 1** *Jur (condamné)* to rehabilitate; *(failli)* to discharge; **r. la mémoire de qn** to clear sb's name; **r. qn dans ses fonctions** to reinstate sb **2** *(revaloriser ▸ profession)* to rehabilitate, to restore to favour; *(▸ quartier)* to rehabilitate

VPR se réhabiliter to rehabilitate oneself, to restore one's reputation

réhabituer [7] [reabitɥe] **VT r. qn à qch/à faire qch** to get sb used to sth again/to doing sth again

VPR se réhabituer se r. à to get used to again; **j'ai eu du mal à me r. à la vie à Paris** I had a hard time getting used to life in Paris again *or* getting reaccustomed to life in Paris; **se r. à faire qch** to get back into the habit of doing sth, to get used to doing sth again

rehaussement [rəosmɑ̃] **NM** *(d'un mur, d'un plafond)* raising

rehausser [3] [rəose] **VT 1** *(surélever ▸ plafond)* to raise; *(▸ mur)* to make higher **2** *(faire ressortir ▸ goût)* to bring out; *(▸ beauté, couleur)* to emphasize, to enhance; **du velours noir rehaussé de broderies** black velvet set off by embroidery **3** *(revaloriser)* to enhance, to increase; **une nouvelle victoire pour r. le prestige de l'équipe** a further victory which will increase *or* enhance the team's prestige

rehausseur [rəosœr] *Aut* **ADJ M** *(siège)* booster *(avant n)*

NM booster seat

rehaut [rəo] **NM** *Beaux-Arts* highlight

réhydratation [reidratasjɔ̃] **NF** moisturizing, *Spéc* rehydration

reiki [reki] **NM** reiki

réimperméabiliser [3] [reɛ̃pɛrmeabilize] **VT** to re-proof

réimplantation [reɛ̃plɑ̃tasjɔ̃] **NF 1** *Méd* reimplantation **2** *(d'une industrie, d'une usine)* re-establishment; *(d'une tribu)* resettling

réimplanter [3] [reɛ̃plɑ̃te] **VT 1** *Méd* to reimplant **2** *(industrie, usine)* to set up again, to re-establish; *(tribu)* to resettle

réimportation [reɛ̃pɔrtasjɔ̃] **NF** *(activité)* reimportation, reimporting; *(produit)* reimport

réimporter [3] [reɛ̃pɔrte] **VT** to reimport

réimposer [3] [reɛ̃poze] **VT 1** *(taxer à nouveau)* to tax again **2** *Typ* to reimpose

réimposition [reɛ̃pozisjɔ̃] **NF 1** *(taxe)* further taxation **2** *Typ* reimposition

réimpression [reɛ̃presjɔ̃] **NF** *(processus)* reprinting; *(résultat)* reprint; **en cours de r.** *(sur catalogue)* being reprinted, new edition pending; **ce livre est en cours de r.** this book is being reprinted

réimprimer [3] [reɛ̃prime] **VT** to reprint

Reims [rɛ̃s] **NM** Reims, Rheims

rein [rɛ̃] **NM** *Anat* kidney; **r. artificiel** artificial kidney, kidney machine; **coup de r.** heave

• **reins NMPL** *(dos)* back; *Littéraire (taille)* waist; **avoir mal aux reins** to have (a) backache; **avoir mal dans le bas des** *ou* **au creux des reins** to have a pain in the small of one's back; **les cheveux lui tombaient jusqu'aux reins** her hair went down to the small of her back; **donner un coup de reins** to heave; *Fig* to pull oneself together; *Fam* **avoir les**

reins solides to have good financial backing□; *Fam* **je lui briserai** *ou* **casserai les reins** I'll break him/her

réincarcération [reẽkarserasjɔ̃] **NF** reimprisonment; **après sa r.** after he/she was sent back to jail

réincarcérer [18] [reẽkarsere] **VT r. qn** to send sb back to jail, to reimprison sb

réincarnation [reẽkarnasjɔ̃] **NF** reincarnation

réincarner [3] [reẽkarne] **se réincarner VPR** to be reincarnated (**en** as)

reine [rɛn] **NF 1** *(femme du roi)* queen (consort); *(souveraine)* queen; **la r. Anne** Queen Anne; **la r. mère** the Queen Mother; **la r. de Suède/des Pays-Bas** the Queen of Sweden/of the Netherlands

2 *Cartes & Échecs* queen; *Cartes* **la r. de cœur/pique** the queen of hearts/spades

3 *Fig* queen; **la r. de la soirée** the belle of the ball, the star of the party; **tu es vraiment la r. des imbéciles** you're the most stupid woman I've ever come across; **r. de beauté** beauty queen; *Vieilli* **la petite r.** the bicycle

4 *Entom* queen; **la r. des abeilles/termites** the queen bee/termite

5 *Hort* **r. des reinettes** rennet *(apple)*

6 *Suisse (vache)* **r. (à cornes)** = champion Hérens cow of a herd that has won a cowfighting competition; **r. (à lait)** best milker

reine-claude [rɛnklod] *(pl* **reines-claudes)** **NF** (Reine Claude) greengage

reine-des-prés [rɛndepre] *(pl* **reines-des-prés)** **NF** *Bot* meadowsweet *(UNCOUNT)*

reine-marguerite [rɛnmargərit] *(pl* **reines-marguerites)** **NF** *Bot* (China *or* annual) aster

reinette [rɛnɛt] **NF** ≃ pippin; **r. grise** russet *(apple)*

réinfecter [4] [reẽfɛkte] **VT** to reinfect

VPR se réinfecter to become reinfected

réinfection [reẽfɛksjɔ̃] **NF** reinfection

réinitialisation [reinisjalizasjɔ̃] **NF** *Ordinat* reset; *(de la mémoire)* reinitialization

réinitialiser [3] [reinisjalize] **VT** *Ordinat* to reset; *(mémoire)* to reinitialize

réinscriptible [reẽskriptibl] **ADJ** *Ordinat (support)* rewritable

réinscription [reẽskripsjɔ̃] **NF** reregistration

réinscrire [99] [reẽskrir] **VT** *(étudiant)* to reregister, to re-enrol; *(électeur)* to reregister; *(sur un agenda)* to put down again

VPR se réinscrire to reregister, to re-enrol; **je me suis réinscrit au cours de poterie** I put my name down for *or* I joined the pottery class again; **se r. au chômage** to reregister as unemployed

réinsérer [18] [reɛ̃sere] **VT 1** *(paragraphe, bloc)* to reinsert **2** *(détenu, drogué)* to rehabilitate, to reintegrate (**dans** into *or* in)

VPR se réinsérer to rehabilitate oneself, to become rehabilitated *or* reintegrated

réinsertion [reɛ̃sɛrsjɔ̃] **NF 1** *(d'un paragraphe, d'un bloc)* reinsertion **2** *(d'un détenu, d'un drogué)* rehabilitation; **r. professionnelle** = getting back into the job market; **la r. sociale** social rehabilitation, reintegration into society

réinstallation [reɛ̃stalasjɔ̃] **NF** relocation; *Ordinat* reinstallation; **notre r. en Europe a été facile** settling in Europe again *or* moving back to Europe was easy

réinstaller [3] [reɛ̃stale] **VT 1** *(chauffage, électricité, téléphone)* to reinstall, to put back; *Ordinat* to reinstall **2** *(déplacer)* to move; *(remettre au même endroit)* to move back

VPR se réinstaller 1 *(déménager)* to move; *(revenir au même endroit)* to go back, to settle again; **il s'est réinstallé dans son ancien bureau** he's gone *or* moved back to his old office **2** *(se rasseoir)* to settle (back) down in one's seat

réintégration [reɛ̃tegrasjɔ̃] **NF 1** *(d'un fonctionnaire)* reinstatement; *(dans un parti)* readmission

2 *(d'un évadé)* reimprisonment

3 *(recouvrement d'un droit)* reintegration

4 *Jur* **r. du domicile conjugal** return to the marital home

réintégrer [18] [reɛ̃tegre] **VT 1** *(fonctionnaire)* to reinstate; *(membre d'un parti)* to readmit; **il a été réintégré dans l'Administration** he was reinstated in the Civil Service **2** *(regagner)* to go back *or* to return to; *Jur* **r. le domicile conjugal** to return to the marital home

réintroduction [reɛ̃trɔdyksjɔ̃] **NF** reintroduction

réintroduire [98] [reɛ̃trɔdɥir] **VT r. qch** *(dans un texte)* to reintroduce sth, to put sth back in; *(projet de loi)* to put up again, to reintroduce

réinvestir [32] [reɛ̃vɛstir] **VT** to reinvest

réitératif, -ive [reiteratif, -iv] **ADJ** reiterative

réitération [reiterasjɔ̃] **NF** reiteration

réitérative [reiterativ] *voir* **réitératif**

réitérer [18] [reitere] **VT** *(interdiction, demande)* to reiterate, to repeat

rejaillir [32] [rəʒajir] **VI 1** *(gicler ▸ gén)* to splash (back); *(▸ violemment)* to spurt (up) **2** *(se répercuter)* **r. sur** to reflect on *or* upon

rejaillissement [rəʒajismɑ̃] **NM** *Littéraire* **1** *(d'une fontaine)* splashing up **2** *Fig (retombées)* repercussion, reflection

rejet [rəʒɛ] **NM 1** *(physique)* throwing back *or* up, driving back; **rejets toxiques** toxic waste

2 *(refus)* rejection; *Jur (d'une réclamation, d'un appel)* dismissal; **elle a été très déçue par le r. de son manuscrit/de son offre** she was very disappointed when her manuscript/her offer was turned down; **ne lui parle pas de sport, il fait un r.** don't talk to him about sport, he can't stand it; **les enfants handicapés sont parfois victimes d'un phénomène de r. à l'école** disabled children are sometimes rejected by other children at school

3 *Littérature (enjambement)* run-on; *Gram* **il y a r. du verbe à la fin de la proposition subordonnée** the verb is put *or* goes at the end of the subordinate clause

4 *Méd (d'une greffe)* rejection

5 *Géol* throw; **r. horizontal** heave

6 *Bot* shoot

7 *Ordinat* ignore (character)

rejeter [27] [rəʒte] **VT 1** *(relancer)* to throw back; *(violemment)* to hurl back; **il rejeta son chapeau en arrière** he tilted his hat back; **elle rejeta ses cheveux en arrière** she tossed her hair back; **r. la tête en arrière** to throw one's head back; **r. un verbe en fin de phrase** to put a verb at the end of a sentence

2 *(repousser ▸ ennemi)* to drive *or* to push back; *(bannir)* to reject, to cast out, to expel; **r. une armée au-delà des frontières** to drive an army back over the border; **elle a été rejetée par sa famille** her family rejected *or* disowned her; **la société les rejette** society rejects them *or* casts them out; **se faire r.** to be rejected

3 *(rendre ▸ nourriture)* to spew out, to throw up, to reject; *(▸ déchets)* to throw out, to expel; **son estomac rejette tout ce qu'elle absorbe** she can't keep anything down; **r. de la bile/du sang** to throw up *or* to bring up bile/blood; **la mer a rejeté plusieurs épaves** several wrecks were washed up *or* cast up by the sea

4 *(refuser ▸ gén)* to reject, to turn down; *(▸ projet de loi)* to throw out; *Jur (▸ réclamation, appel)* to dismiss; **r. une offre/une demande** to reject an offer/a request; **ne rejette pas d'emblée cette idée/hypothèse** don't dismiss this idea/hypothesis out of hand

5 *(déplacer)* **r. la faute/la responsabilité sur qn** to shift the blame/responsibility on to sb

6 *Méd (greffe)* to reject

VPR se rejeter 1 se r. en arrière to jump backwards **2** *(se renvoyer)* **ils se rejettent mutuellement la responsabilité de l'accident** they blame each other for the accident

rejeton [rəʒtɔ̃] **NM 1** *Péj ou Hum (enfant)* kid; **que fais-tu de tes rejetons cet été?** what will you do with your offspring *or* kids this summer? **2** *Bot* offshoot, shoot

rejette *etc voir* **rejeter**

rejoindre [82] [rəʒwɛ̃dr] **VT 1** *(retrouver)* to meet (up with), to join; *(avec effort)* to catch up with; **tu me rejoins au café en bas?** can you meet (up with) me in the café downstairs?; **je viendrai vous r. dans le Midi dès que je pourrai** I'll come and meet up with you *or* join you in the Midi as soon as I can; **il est parti r. sa femme** he went to meet up with *or* join *or* rejoin his wife; **il a rejoint le gros du peloton** he's caught up with the pack

2 *(retourner à)* to get back *or* to return to; **l'ambassadeur a rejoint son poste à Moscou** the ambassador has returned to his post in Moscow; **le nageur eut du mal à r. le rivage** the swimmer had difficulty reaching the shore; **il a reçu l'ordre de r. son régiment** he was ordered to rejoin his regiment

3 *(aboutir à)* to join *or* to meet (up with); **le chemin rejoint la route à la hauteur de la borne** the path meets *or* joins (up with) the road at the milestone

4 *(être d'accord avec) (ressembler à)* to be along the same lines as; **ses propos rejoignent les miens** he/she echoes what I say; **cela rejoint ce que je disais tout à l'heure** that fits in with what I was saying just now

5 *Pol (adhérer à)* to join; **elle a fini par r. l'opposition** she ended up joining the opposition

VPR se rejoindre 1 *(se réunir)* to meet again *or* up; **nous nous rejoindrons à Marseille** we'll meet up in Marseilles **2** *(rivières, routes, lignes)* to join (up), to meet (up) **3** *(concorder)* **nos opinions se rejoignent entièrement** our views concur perfectly, we are in total agreement; **nous avons voulu faire se r. différents témoignages** we aimed to bring together different accounts

rejouer [6] [rəʒwe] **VT 1** *(refaire ▸ jeu)* to play again; *(▸ match)* to replay, to play again; **r. le même cheval** to bet on the same horse again; **elle a rejoué toute sa fortune sur le 7** she gambled her whole fortune on the 7 again; *Cartes* **tu devrais r. atout** you should lead trumps again **2** *(pièce de théâtre)* to perform again; *(morceau)* to play again; **il leur a fait r. la scène au moins 50 fois** he made them go through the scene at least 50 times

VI *(en sport, aux cartes etc)* to play again; *(au casino)* to start gambling again

réjoui, -e [reʒwi] **ADJ** joyful, happy, pleased; **avoir** *ou* **prendre un air r.** to look cheerful; **je voyais à sa mine réjouie que les nouvelles étaient bonnes** I could see from the joyful expression on his/her face *or* from his/her joyful expression that it was good news

réjouir [32] [reʒwir] **VT** to delight; **la nouvelle a réjoui tout le monde** everyone was delighted at the news; **ça ne me réjouit guère d'y aller** I'm not particularly keen on *or* thrilled at going; **ça lui a réjoui le cœur** it gladdened his/her heart

VPR se réjouir to be delighted (**de qch** at sth); **je me réjouis de vous accueillir chez moi** I'm delighted to welcome you to my home; **se r. du malheur des autres** to gloat over other people's misfortunes; **je me réjouis de votre succès** I'm glad to hear of your success; **je me réjouis à la pensée de les retrouver** I'm thrilled *or* delighted at the idea of meeting them again; **je m'en réjouis d'avance** I'm really looking forward to it; *Suisse* **se r. de qch/de faire qch** to look forward to sth/to doing sth

réjouissance [reʒwisɑ̃s] **NF** *(gaieté)* rejoicing

• **réjouissances NFPL** *(fête)* festivities; **réjouissances publiques** public festivities; *Hum* **quel est le programme des réjouissances?** what exciting things lie in store for us today?

réjouissant, -e [reʒwisɑ̃, -ɑ̃t] **ADJ** *(spectacle)* delightful; *(nouvelles)* joyful; **peu r.** rather grim; *Ironique* **c'est r.!** that's just great!; **je ne vois pas ce que tu trouves de si r. à cette histoire** I don't see what you find so funny *or* amusing about this story

relâche [rəlaʃ] **NF 1** *(pause)* respite, rest; **accordons-nous un peu de r.** let's rest a while *or* take a short break **2** *Cin & Théât (fermeture)* **le dimanche est notre jour de r.** there is no performance on Sundays; **nous ferons r. en août** no performances in August; **r. le mardi** *(salle de spectacle)* no performance on Tuesdays **3** *Naut* **le navire a fait r. à Nice** the boat called in at Nice; **(port de) r.** port of call

• **sans relâche ADV** without respite, continuously; **travailler sans r.** to work continuously *or* without respite; **il écrit sans r. jusqu'à l'aube** he writes without letting up *or* without any break till dawn

relâché, -e [rəlaʃe] **ADJ 1** *(négligé ▸ discipline, effort)* lax, loose; *(▸ style)* flowing, *Péj* loose **2** *(détendu ▸ muscle, corde)* lax, relaxed

relâchement [rəlaʃmɑ̃] **NM 1** *(laisser-aller)* laxity, loosening; *(de la discipline)* relaxation; *(des efforts)* let-up; *(de l'attention)* wavering; **il y a du r. dans votre travail** you're letting your work slide; **le r. des mœurs** the laxity of *or* decline in moral standards **2** *Méd (de l'intestin)* loosening; *(d'un muscle)* relaxation **3** *(d'une corde, d'un lien)* loosening, slackening

relâcher **[3]** [rəlaʃe] **VT 1** *(libérer ▸ animal)* to free; *(▸ prisonnier)* to release, to set free; **les otages ont été relâchés** the hostages have been released *or* set free; **il a relâché l'oiseau** he let the bird go, he freed the bird; **le ministre l'a fait r. immédiatement** the minister arranged for his immediate release **2** *(diminuer)* to relax, to slacken; **r. son attention** to let one's attention wander; **ne relâchons pas nos efforts** we must not relax *or* slacken our efforts **3** *(détendre ▸ câble, corde)* to loosen, to slacken; *(▸ muscle)* to relax; **elle a relâché son étreinte** she relaxed *or* loosened her grip

VI *Naut* to put into port

VPR se relâcher 1 *(muscle)* to relax, to loosen; *(câble, corde)* to loosen, to slacken; *(étreinte)* to relax, to loosen **2** *(devenir moins rigoureux ▸ personne, mœurs, discipline)* to become lax *or* laxer; **se r. dans son travail** to become lax about one's work; **elle se relâche en tout** she's letting things slide; **son attention se relâche** his/her attention is flagging

relaie *etc voir* **relayer**

relais [rəlɛ] **NM 1** *(succession)* shift; **passer le r. à qn** to hand over to sb; **il est temps que je passe le r.** it's time I handed over (control); **prendre le r. (de qn)** to take over (from sb); **j'ai commencé le travail, tu n'as plus qu'à prendre le r.** I started the work, just carry on *or* take over

2 *(intermédiaire)* **le graphiste sert de r. entre le client et l'imprimeur** the graphic artist is the link between the customer and the printer

3 *Sport* relay; **courir le r. 4 x 400 mètres** to run the 4 x 400 metres relay

4 *Hist (lieu)* coaching inn; *(chevaux)* relay

5 *(auberge)* inn; **r. autoroutier** *Br* motorway café, *Am* truck stop

6 *(comme adj; avec ou sans trait d'union) Élec (appareil, station)* relay *(avant n)*; *(processus)* relaying

7 *Tél* **r. hertzien** radio relay; **r. de télévision** television relay station

8 *Banque* **(crédit) r.** bridging loan

relais-bébé **NM INV** baby changing room *(in shopping centre etc)*

relance [rəlɑ̃s] **NF 1** *(nouvelle impulsion)* revival, boost

2 *Écon* **il y a une r. de la production sidérurgique** steel production is being boosted *or* increased; **politique de r.** reflationary policy; **r. économique** reflation, economic revival

3 *Admin & Com (d'un client)* follow-up; **des relances téléphoniques** follow-up calls; **lettre de r.** follow-up letter

4 *Mktg (d'un produit, d'une marque, d'une entreprise)* relaunch

5 *Cartes* raise; **faire une r.** to raise (the stakes); **limiter la r.** to limit the raise

relancement [rəlɑ̃smɑ̃] **NM** *Mktg (d'un produit)* relaunch

relancer **[16]** [rəlɑ̃se] **VT 1** *(donner un nouvel essor à ▸ gén)* to relaunch, to revive; *(▸ ventes)* to boost; *(▸ produit)* to relaunch; **r. l'économie d'un pays** to give a boost to *or* to boost *or* to reflate a country's economy

2 *(solliciter à nouveau ▸ client)* to follow up; *Fig* to chase after, *Br* to chase up; **il faudra le r. pour obtenir un rendez-vous** you'll have to chase after him *or Br* to chase him up if you want an appointment; **c'est à lui de r. ses clients** it's his job to follow up on *or Br* to chase up his clients; **je l'ai relancée plusieurs fois pour qu'elle vienne dîner à la maison** I pestered her several times to come to dinner; **arrête de me r.!** stop badgering me!; **elle s'est déjà fait r. trois fois par la banque** she's already had three reminders from her bank

3 *(jeter ▸ à nouveau)* to throw again; *(▸ pour rendre)* to throw back

4 *(faire redémarrer ▸ moteur)* to restart; *Ordinat (▸ programme)* to rerun; *(▸ logiciel)* to restart

VI *Cartes* to raise (the bid) (**de** by)

VPR se relancer se r. dans le tissage to take up weaving again; **se r. dans de longues explications** to re-embark on a long explanation

relaps, -e [rəlaps] **ADJ** relapsed

NM,F *Rel* relapsed person, backslider

relater **[3]** [rəlate] **VT** *(raconter)* to relate, to recount; **les faits ont été relatés dans la presse** the facts were reported *or* detailed in the papers

relatif, -ive [rəlatif, -iv] **ADJ 1** *(gén) & Gram & Math* relative; **donner une valeur relative** to give a relative value; **comparer les mérites relatifs de...** to compare the relative merits of...; **tout est r.** it's all relative

2 r. à *(concernant)* relating to, concerning

3 *(approximatif)* **les élèves sont rentrés dans un ordre r.** the pupils went back inside in a more or less orderly fashion; **un confort très r.** very limited comfort; **nous avons goûté un repos tout r.** we enjoyed a rest of sorts; **un isolement r.** relative *or* comparative isolation

4 *Mus* relative

NM *Gram* relative pronoun

• **relative NF** *Gram* relative clause

relation [rəlasjɔ̃] **NF 1** *(corrélation)* relationship, connection; **r. de cause à effet** relation *or* relationship of cause and effect; **mettre deux questions en r. l'une avec l'autre, faire la r. entre deux questions** to make the connection between *or* to connect two questions; **c'est sans r. avec..., il n'y a aucune r. avec...** there's no connection with..., it's nothing to do with...

2 *(rapport)* relationship; **nouer des relations professionnelles** to form professional contacts; **nos relations sont purement professionnelles** our relationship is purely professional; **les relations sino-japonaises** relations between China and Japan, Sino-Japanese relations; **nos relations sont assez tendues** relations between us are rather strained; **avoir** *ou* **entretenir des relations avec qn** to be in touch with sb; **entretenir des relations de bon voisinage avec qn** to be on good terms with sb; **avoir de bonnes/mauvaises relations avec qn** to be on good/bad terms with sb; **être en r. avec qn** to be in touch *or* in communication with sb; **nous sommes en r. d'affaires depuis des années** we've had business dealings *or* a business relationship for years; **en excellentes/mauvaises relations avec ses collègues** on excellent/bad terms with one's colleagues; **entrer en r. avec qn** *(le contacter)* to get in touch *or* to make contact with sb; **mettre qn en r. avec un ami/une organisation** to put sb in touch with a friend/an organization; **r. (amoureuse)** love affair; **avoir une r. (amoureuse) avec qn** to have a relationship with sb; *Mktg* **relations clientèle** customer relations; **relations diplomatiques** diplomatic relations *or* links; **relations extérieures** foreign affairs; **relations humaines** *(gén)* dealings between people; *(en sociologie)* human relations; **relations presse** press relations; **relations publiques** public relations; **relations sexuelles** sexual relations *or* intercourse; **relations sexuelles avant le mariage** sex before marriage, permarital sex

3 *(connaissance)* acquaintance; **une r. d'affaires** a business acquaintance *or* connection; **c'est une r. de travail** he's a colleague; **avoir de nombreuses relations** to know a lot of people; **utilise tes relations** use your connections; **j'ai trouvé à me loger par relations** I found a place to live through knowing the right people *or* through the grapevine

4 *Math* relation; **r. de Chasles** Chasles relation

5 *(compte rendu)* relation, narration; **sa r. des faits** his/her account of the story; **faire la r. de qch** to give an account of sth

relationnel, -elle [rəlasjɔnɛl] **ADJ 1** *Psy* relationship *(avant n)*; **avoir des difficultés relationnelles** to have trouble relating to people **2** *Ling* relational, relation *(avant n)*

relative [rəlativ] *voir* **relatif**

relativement [rəlativmɑ̃] **ADV 1** *(passablement)* relatively, comparatively, reasonably **2** *(de façon relative)* relatively, *Sout* contingently

• **relativement à PRÉP 1** *(par rapport à)* compared to, in relation to **2** *(concernant)* concerning; **entendre un témoin r. à une affaire** to hear a witness in relation to a case

relativiser **[3]** [rəlativize] **VT r. qch** to consider sth in context, *Spéc* to relativize sth

USAGE ABSOLU il faut r., ça pourrait être pire you've got to keep things in perspective, it could be worse

relativisme [rəlativism] **NM** *Phil* relativism

relativiste [rəlativist] **ADJ 1** *Phys* relativistic **2** *Phil* relativist, relativistic

NMF *Phil* relativist

relativité [rəlativite] **NF 1** *(gén)* relativity; **la r. des connaissances humaines** the relative nature *or* relativeness of human knowledge **2** *Phys* relativity; **(théorie de) la r.** (theory of) relativity

relaver **[3]** [rəlave] **VT 1** *(laver de nouveau)* to wash again, to rewash **2** *Belg & Suisse (vaisselle)* to wash

relax [rəlaks] **ADJ INV 1** *Fam (personne, ambiance)* easy-going, laid-back; *(activité, vacances)* relaxing; **c'est une fille plutôt r.** she's an easy-going sort of girl; **r. Max!** *(locution)* chill out! **2 fauteuil r.** reclining chair

ADV *Fam* **on va réviser, mais r., OK?** we'll do some revision, but we'll take it easy, OK?

relaxant, -e [rəlaksɑ̃, -ɑ̃t] **ADJ** relaxing, soothing

relaxation [rəlaksasjɔ̃] **NF 1** *(détente)* relaxation, relaxing; **faire de la r.** to do relaxation exercises **2** *Phys & Psy* relaxation

relaxe [rəlaks] **ADJ = relax ADJ 1**

NF *Jur* discharge, release

relaxer **[3]** [rəlakse] **VT 1** *(relâcher ▸ muscle)* to relax **2** *(détendre)* to relax; **ce bain m'a bien relaxé** I feel really relaxed after my bath **3** *Jur (prisonnier)* to discharge, to release

VPR se relaxer to relax

relayer **[11]** [rəleje] **VT 1** *(suppléer)* to relieve, to take over from

2 *(transmettre ▸ information)* to relay, to transmit

3 *Rad & TV* to relay

4 *Sport* to take over, to take the baton

VI *Arch* to relay, to change horses

VPR se relayer to take turns (**pour faire qch** doing sth); *Sport* to take over from each other; **se r. au volant** to take turns at the wheel

relayeur, -euse [rəlɛjœr, -øz] **NM,F** *Sport* relay runner

relecture [rəlɛktyr] **NF une r. de sa lettre m'a donné l'impression que quelque chose n'allait pas** a closer (second) reading of his/her letter gave me the impression something was wrong; **la r. du manuscrit a pris une heure** it took an hour to reread the manuscript; **à la r., j'ai trouvé que...** on reading it again *or* when I reread it, I found that...; **le metteur en scène nous propose une véritable r. de la pièce** the director gives us a totally new interpretation to the play; *Typ* **r. d'épreuves** proofreading

relégation [rəlegasjɔ̃] **NF 1** *Sport* relegation **2** *Jur* relegation **3** *Hist* banishment

reléguer **[18]** [rəlege] **VT 1** *(cantonner)* to relegate; **r. au second plan** to put in the background; **r. un tableau au grenier** to relegate *or* consign a picture to the attic; *Sport* **leur équipe a été reléguée en deuxième division cette année** their team was relegated to the second division this year **2** *Jur* to relegate **3** *Hist* to banish

relent [rəlɑ̃] **NM 1** *(gén pl) (mauvaise odeur)* stink *(UNCOUNT)*, stench *(UNCOUNT)*; **des relents de tabac froid** a stench of stale tobacco; *Fig* **un r. de scandale entoure ce politicien** there is a whiff of scandal about this politician **2** *(trace)* residue, hint, trace

relevable [rəlvabl] **ADJ** *(siège, appuie-tête)* (vertically) adjustable; *(accoudoir)* folding; **siège à dossier r.** reclinable seat

relevage [rəlvaʒ] **NM** *Tech* lifting

relevailles [rəlvaj] **NFPL** *Rel* churching

relève [rəlɛv] **NF 1** *(manœuvre)* relieving, changing; **prendre la r. (de qn)** to take over (from sb); **la r. de la garde** the changing of the guard **2** *(groupe)* replacement, stand-in; **la r.** *(au travail)* the relief team; *Mil* the relief troops; *(garde)* the relief guard

relevé, -e [rəlve] **ADJ 1** *(redressé ▸ col, nez)* turned-up; **ses manches étaient relevées jusqu'au coude** his/her sleeves were rolled up to the elbows; **elle portait un chapeau à bords relevés** she wore a hat with a turned-up brim **2** *Culin (assaisonné)* seasoned, well-seasoned; *(pimenté)* spicy, hot; **je n'aime pas trop les plats relevés** I don't like spicy food much **3** *(distingué)* elevated, refined

NM 1 *(de recettes, de dépenses)* summary, statement; *(de gaz, d'électricité)* reading; *(de noms)* list; **faire le r. du gaz** to read the gas meter; *Banque* **r. de compte** bank statement; **r. de factures** statement of invoices; **r. de fin de mois** monthly *or* end-of-month statement; **r. d'identité bancaire** = document giving details of one's bank account; *Banque* **r. d'identité postal** = document giving details of one's post office account; *Banque* **r. mensuel** monthly statement; *Scol* **r. de notes** examination results; **r. de température** temperature recording

2 *(en topographie)* survey; **faire le r. d'un terrain** to plot a piece of land

3 *Archit* layout

4 *(en danse)* relevé

> **RELEVÉ D'IDENTITÉ BANCAIRE**
>
> An "RIB" is a small slip of paper with all of a person's bank details. Employers, utility companies and other financial institutions may ask for one to effect standing orders.

relèvement [rəlɛvmɑ̃] **NM 1** *(rétablissement)* recovery, restoring; **contribuer au r. d'un pays/d'une économie** to help a country/an economy recover; **mesures prises pour favoriser le r. d'une société** measures adopted to help put a company back on its feet *or* to help a company recover

2 *(fait d'augmenter)* raising; *(résultat)* increase, rise; **le r. des impôts/des salaires** tax/salary increase

3 *(reconstruction)* re-erecting, rebuilding

4 *(rehaussement)* raising, increase; **le r. du niveau des eaux** the rise in the water level

RELEVER [19] [rəlve]

- to stand up again **1**
- to raise **2, 3**
- to increase **3**
- to enhance **6**
- to notice **8**
- to take down **9**
- to pick up **1, 4, 11**
- to put up **2, 3**
- to re-erect **5**
- to season **7**
- to record **9**
- to relieve **10**

VT 1 *(redresser ▸ lampe, statue)* to stand up again; *(▸ chaise)* to pick up; *(▸ tête)* to lift up again; **ils m'ont relevé** *(debout)* they helped me (back) to my feet; *(assis)* they sat me up *or* helped me to sit up

2 *(remonter ▸ store)* to raise; *(▸ cheveux)* to put up; *(▸ col, visière)* to turn up; *(▸ pantalon, manches)* to roll up; *(▸ rideaux)* to tie back; *(▸ strapontin)* to tie up

3 *(augmenter ▸ prix, salaires)* to increase, to raise, to put up; *(▸ notes)* to put up, to raise; **ils ont relevé les notes d'un point** they put up *or* raised the *Br* marks *or Am* grades by one point

4 *(ramasser, recueillir)* to pick up; *Scol* **r. les copies** to collect the papers

5 *(remettre en état ▸ mur)* to rebuild, to re-erect; *(▸ pylône)* to re-erect, to put up again; **r. des ruines** *(ville)* to reconstruct *or* to rebuild a ruined city; *(maison)* to rebuild a ruined house; *Fig* **c'est lui qui a relevé la nation** he's the one who put the country back on its feet (again) *or* got the country going again; **r. l'économie** to rebuild the economy; **r. le moral des troupes** to boost the troops' morale

6 *(mettre en valeur)* to enhance

7 *Culin* to season, to spice up; **relevez l'assaisonnement** make the seasoning more spicy

8 *(remarquer)* to notice; **r. des fautes** to notice *or* to pick out mistakes; **elle n'a pas relevé l'allusion** *(elle n'a pas réagi)* she didn't pick up the hint; *(elle l'a sciemment ignorée)* she pretended not to notice the hint

9 *(enregistrer ▸ empreinte digitale)* to record; *(▸ cote, mesure)* to take down, to plot; *(▸ informations)* to take *or* to note down; *(▸ plan)* to sketch; **on a relevé des traces de boue sur ses chaussures** traces of mud were found *or* discovered on his/her shoes; *Fam* **r. l'eau** *ou* **le compteur d'eau** to read the water meter; *Fam* **r. le gaz** *ou* **le compteur du gaz** to read the gas meter; **les faits relevés ne plaident pas en ta faveur** the facts as they have been recorded do not help your case; *Météo* **températures relevées à 16 heures** temperatures recorded at 4 p.m.

10 *(relayer ▸ garde)* to relieve; *(▸ coéquipier)* to take over from; **r. qn de ses fonctions** to relieve sb of his/her duties

11 *(en tricot)* to pick up

USAGE ABSOLU *(remarquer)* **ce ne sont que des ragots, il vaut mieux ne pas r.** it's just gossip, (best) ignore it; **je ne relèverai pas!** I'll ignore that!

• **relever de VT IND 1** *(être de la compétence de ▸ juridiction)* to fall *or* to come under; *(▸ spécialiste)* to be a matter for; *(▸ magistrat)* to come under the jurisdiction of; **cela relève des tribunaux/de la psychiatrie** it's a matter for the courts/the psychiatrists **2** *(tenir de)* **cela relève du miracle** it's truly miraculous **3** *(se rétablir de)* **r. de couches** to come out of confinement; **elle relève d'une grippe** she is recovering from flu

VPR se relever 1 *(être inclinable)* to lift up

2 *(se remettre ▸ debout)* to get *or* to stand up again; *(▸ assis)* to sit up again; **il l'aida à se r.** he helped him/her to his/her feet again; **se r. la nuit** to get up in the night; **je ne veux pas avoir à me r.!** I don't want to have to get up (again)!

3 *(remonter)* **les commissures de ses lèvres se relevèrent** the corners of his/her mouth curled up

4 *Fig* **se r. de** to recover from, to get over; **le parti se relève de ses cendres** *ou* **ruines** the party is rising from the ashes; **je ne m'en relèverai/ils ne s'en relèveront pas** I'll/they'll never get over it

releveur, -euse [rəlvœr, -øz] **ADJ** *Anat* **muscle r.** levator muscle

NM,F *(employé)* meter reader

NM *Anat* levator

relief [rəljɛf] **NM 1** *Beaux-Arts, Géog & Opt* relief; **la région a un r. accidenté** the area is hilly **2** *(contraste)* relief, highlight; **donner du r. à qch** to highlight sth; **sans r.** *(paysage, style)* flat; **son discours manquait de r.** his speech was a rather lacklustre affair **3** *Ordinat* highlight; **mettre en r.** to highlight

• **reliefs NMPL** *Littéraire* **les reliefs** *(d'un repas)* the remnants *or* leftovers

• **en relief ADJ** *Beaux-Arts & Typ* relief *(avant n)*, raised; **cinéma/photographie en r.** stereoscopic cinema/photography; **impression en r.** relief printing; **lettres en r.** embossed letters; **motif en r.** raised design, design in relief **ADV** *(en valeur)* **mettre qch en r.** to bring sth out; *Ordinat* to highlight sth; **le jus de citron met en r. le goût des fraises** lemon juice brings out *or* accentuates the taste of strawberries; **mets ce paragraphe en r. en faisant des marges plus larges** make this paragraph stand out by making the margins wider

> Il faut noter que le nom anglais **relief** signifie le plus souvent **soulagement** ou **aide**, selon le contexte.

relier [9] [rəlje] **VT 1** *(faire communiquer)* to link up, to link (together), to connect; **les deux pièces sont reliées par un long couloir** the two rooms are linked (together) *or* connected by a long corridor; **un vol quotidien relie Paris à Lourdes** a daily flight links Paris to Lourdes; **la route qui relie Bruxelles à Ostende** the road running from *or* linking Brussels to Ostend; **le cordon ombilical relie la mère à l'enfant** the umbilical cord attaches *or* connects the mother to the baby **2** *(mettre en rapport)* to connect, to link (together), to relate; **les deux paragraphes ne sont pas reliés** there is no link *or* connection between the two paragraphs; **vos idées sont bien/mal reliées entre elles** your ideas are well/badly linked together **3** *(livre)* to bind; **relié en cuir** leather-bound; **relié toile** cloth-bound

relieur, -euse [rəljœr, -øz] **NM,F** bookbinder

religieuse [rəliʒjøz] *voir* **religieux**

religieusement [rəliʒjøzmɑ̃] **ADV 1** *(pieusement)* religiously; **se marier r.** to get married in church **2** *(soigneusement)* religiously, rigorously, scrupulously; *(avec vénération)* reverently, devoutly; **il lit 'L'Humanité' r. tous les jours** he reads 'L'Humanité' religiously every day

religieux, -euse [rəliʒjø, -øz] **ADJ 1** *(cérémonie, éducation, ordre, art)* religious; *(mariage, école)* church *(avant n)* **2** *(personne)* religious; **il n'a jamais été très r.** he was never very religious **3** *(empreint de gravité)* religious; **un silence r. se fit dans la salle** a reverent silence fell on the room; **elle nettoyait les cuivres avec un soin r.** she cleaned the brasses with almost religious care, she took an almost religious care over the brasses

NM member of a religious order

• **religieuse NF 1** *Rel* nun **2** *Culin* cream puff; **religieuse au chocolat/au café** chocolate/coffee cream puff **3** *Suisse Culin (de raclette)* = crusty burnt edges of a raclette cheese casing; *(de fondue)* = burnt cheese at the bottom of a fondue dish

religion [rəliʒjɔ̃] **NF 1** *(croyance)* religion; **l'histoire de la r.** the history of religion; **la r. juive** the Jewish religion *or* faith; **être sans** *ou* **n'avoir pas de r.** to have no religion, to be of no religious faith; **se convertir à la r. catholique/musulmane** to be converted to Catholicism/Islam; **le football est une r. pour certains** football is a religion with some people, some people make a religion out of football; **entrer en r.** to join a religious order; **la r. est l'opium du peuple** religion is the opium of the people **2** *(piété)* religious faith; *Littéraire* **avoir de la r.** to be religious *or* devout; **connu pour sa r.** well-known for the strength of his religious faith; *Arch* **se faire une r. de qch** to be obsessed with sth

religiosité [rəliʒjozite] **NF** religiosity, religiousness

reliquaire [rəlikɛr] **NM** reliquary

reliquat [rəlika] **NM** *(d'une somme)* remainder, balance; *(d'un compte)* balance; **après apurement des comptes, il n'y a plus aucun r.** after balancing the accounts, there is nothing left over *or* there is no surplus

relique [rəlik] **NF** *Rel & Fig* relic; **conserver qch comme une r.** to treasure sth

relire [106] [rəlir] **VT** *(lire à nouveau)* to read again, to reread; *(pour corriger ▸ épreuves)* to read; *(▸ texte, lettre)* to read over

VPR se relire to read (over) what one has written; **j'ai du mal à me r.** I have difficulty reading my own writing

reliure [rəljyr] **NF 1** *(technique)* binding, bookbinding; **atelier de r.** bindery **2** *(couverture)* binding; **r. pleine** full binding; **r. pleine toile** cloth binding; **r. sans couture** perfect binding; **r. à spirale** spiral binding

relocalisation [rəlɔkalizasjɔ̃] **NF** relocation

relogement [rəlɔʒmɑ̃] **NM** rehousing

reloger [17] [rəlɔʒe] **VT** to rehouse

relookage [rəlukaʒ] **NM** makeover, new look

relooker [3] [rəluke] *Fam* **VT** to revamp

VPR se relooker to change one's image[□], to give oneself a makeover

relouer [6] [rəlwe] **VT** *(sujet: propriétaire)* to rent out again, to relet; *(sujet: locataire)* to rent again; **nous relouons chaque année le même appartement** we rent *or* take the same *Br* flat *or Am* apartment every year

relu, -e [rəly] **PP** *voir* **relire**

réluctance [relyktɑ̃s] **NF** *Phys* reluctance

reluire [97] [rəlɥir] **VI** *(casque, casserole, parquet)* to gleam, to shine; *(pavé mouillé)* to glisten; **faire r. ses cuivres** to do *or* to polish the brasses

reluisant, -e [rəlɥizɑ̃, -ɑ̃t] **ADJ 1** *Fam (gén nég)* **peu** *ou* **pas r.** *(médiocre)* shabby; **un individu peu r.** an unsavoury character; **notre avenir n'apparaît guère r.** our future hardly looks bright **2** *(brillant)* shining, shiny, gleaming

reluisent *etc voir* **reluire**

reluquer [3] [rəlyke] **VT** *Fam (personne)* to eye up, to check out, *Am* to scope (out); *(objet, fortune)* to have one's eye on, to covet[□]; **se faire r.** to be *or* to get stared at

relutif, -ive [rəlytif, -iv] **ADJ** *Fin* **avoir un effet r.** to strengthen the equity capital of a company

relution [rəlysjɔ̃] **NF** *Fin* strengthening of equity capital

relutive [rəlytiv] *voir* **relutif**

rem [rem] NM *Nucl (abrév* **roentgen equivalent man)** rem

remâcher [3] [rəmaʃe] VT **1** *(mâcher de nouveau)* to chew again; *(sujet: ruminant)* to ruminate **2** *(ressasser)* to brood over

remailler [3] [rəmaje] VT *(filet)* to mend; *(bas, chaussette)* to darn

remake [rimɛk] NM *Cin* remake; **faire un r.** to do a remake

rémanence [remanɑ̃s] NF **1** *Phys* remanence, retentivity **2** *Physiol (durabilité)* persistence **3** *Opt* after-image

rémanent, -e [remanɑ̃, -ɑ̃t] ADJ **1** *Phys (aimantation)* remanent, retentive; *(magnétisme)* residual **2** *(gén) & Chim* persistent; **image rémanente** after-image

remanger [17] [rəmɑ̃ʒe] VT *(manger à nouveau)* to have *or* to eat again; *(manger davantage de)* to have *or* to eat some more

VI to eat again

remaniement [rəmanimɑ̃] NM **1** *(d'un projet de loi)* redrafting, amending, altering; *(d'un discours)* revision, altering; *(d'un programme)* modification; **procéder au r. d'un projet de loi** to redraft *or* amend *or* alter a bill **2** *(d'un gouvernement, d'un ministère)* reshuffle; **r. ministériel** cabinet reshuffle

remanier [9] [rəmanje] VT **1** *(texte, discours)* to revise; *(projet de loi)* to amend, to redraft, to alter; *(programme)* to modify **2** *(gouvernement, ministère)* to reshuffle; **l'équipe a été complètement remaniée** the team was completely reshuffled

remaquiller [3] [rəmakije] VT to make up again

VPR **se remaquiller** *(entièrement)* to reapply one's make-up; *(partiellement)* to touch up one's make-up

remarcher [3] [rəmarʃe] VI **1** *(accidenté, handicapé)* to walk again **2** *(mécanisme, méthode)* to work again; **ça a l'air de bien r. entre eux** they seem to be getting on again

remariage [rəmarjaʒ] NM remarriage

remarier [9] [rəmarje] VT to remarry; **finalement, il a réussi à r. son fils** he eventually managed to marry off his son again

VPR **se remarier** to get married *or* to marry again, to remarry; **se r. avec qn** to remarry sb

remarquable [rəmarkabl] ADJ **1** *(marquant)* striking, notable, noteworthy; **un événement r.** a noteworthy event; **de façon r.** remarkably **2** *(émérite)* remarkable, outstanding, exceptional; **un travail r.** a remarkable *or* an outstanding piece of work; **d'un courage r.** remarkably brave **3** *(particulier)* conspicuous, prominent; **la girafe est r. par la longueur de son cou** the giraffe is notable for its long neck

remarquablement [rəmarkabləmɑ̃] ADV remarkably, strikingly, outstandingly; **elle joue r. du violon** she plays the violin outstandingly well

remarque [rəmark] NF **1** *(opinion exprimée)* remark, comment; *(critique)* (critical) remark; **je l'ai trouvée insolente et je lui en ai fait la r.** I thought she was insolent and (I) told her so; **tu sais, je m'en étais fait la r.** it had crossed my mind, you know; **j'en ai assez de tes remarques** I've had enough of your remarks *or* criticism; **cette r. t'était destinée** that remark was aimed at you, that was a dig at you; **faire une r. à qn sur qch** to pass a remark to sb about sth **2** *(commentaire écrit)* note; **j'ai ajouté quelques remarques grammaticales en fin de chapitre** I have added a few grammatical notes at the end of the chapter

remarqué, -e [rəmarke] ADJ conspicuous, noticeable, striking; **il a fait une intervention très remarquée** the speech he made attracted a great deal of attention; **une entrée remarquée** a conspicuous entrance

remarquer [3] [rəmarke] VT **1** *(constater)* to notice; **je n'ai même pas remarqué que tu étais parti** I didn't even notice you had left; **je remarque que personne n'en a parlé** I notice *or* note that no one has spoken about it; **faire r. qch à qn** to point sth out to sb, to call sb's attention to sth; **on m'a fait r. que…** it's been pointed out to me *or* it's been drawn to my attention that…; **puis-je vous faire r. que nous sommes en retard?** may I point out to you that we're late?; **je te ferai r. qu'il est déjà minuit** look, it's already midnight; **remarque, je m'en moque éperdument** mind you, I really couldn't care less

2 *(distinguer)* to catch sight of, to notice; **il l'avait déjà remarquée la semaine précédente** he'd already noticed *or* spotted her the week before; **il est entré sans que je le remarque** he came in without me noticing (him); **elle a été remarquée par un metteur en scène** she attracted the attention of a producer; **se faire r.** to draw attention to oneself; **elle partit sans se faire r.** she left unnoticed *or* without drawing attention to herself

3 *(dire)* to remark; **"il ne viendra pas", remarqua-t-il** "he won't come," he remarked

4 *(marquer de nouveau ▸ date, adresse)* to write *or* to note down again; *(▸ linge)* to tag *or* to mark again

VPR **se remarquer** *(être visible)* to be noticed, to show; **le défaut du tissu se remarque à peine** the flaw in the material is scarcely noticeable *or* hardly shows; **ça ne se remarquera pas** it won't show, it won't be noticed

> Il faut noter que le verbe anglais **to remark** est un faux ami. Il ne signifie jamais **s'apercevoir de**; il signifie uniquement **faire remarquer**.

remastériser [3] [rəmasterize] VT to remaster

remballage [rɑ̃balaʒ] NM *(d'affaires personnelles, de marchandises)* packing up again; *(d'un paquet)* rewrapping

remballer [3] [rɑ̃bale] VT **1** *(affaires personnelles, marchandises)* to pack up again; *(paquet)* to wrap (up) again, to rewrap **2** *Fam Fig* **tu peux r. tes compliments** you can keep your compliments to yourself

rembarquement [rɑ̃barkəmɑ̃] NM *(de produits)* reloading; *(de passagers)* re-embarkation

rembarquer [3] [rɑ̃barke] VT *(produits)* to reload; *(passagers)* to re-embark

VI *(passagers)* to re-embark

VPR **se rembarquer 1** *(passagers)* to re-embark **2** *Fig* **se r. dans qch** to get involved in sth again; **tu ne vas pas te r. dans une histoire pareille** you're not going to get mixed up in a mess like that again

rembarrer [3] [rɑ̃bare] VT *Fam* **r. qn** to tell sb where to go *or* where to get off; **je me suis fait (drôlement) r.!** I was told (in no uncertain terms) where to get off!

remblai [rɑ̃blɛ] NM **1** *(action ▸ de talus)* embanking, banking (up); *(▸ de fossé)* backfilling **2** *Rail & Constr (talus)* embankment; **route en r.** (em)banked road **3** *(terre rapportée)* **(terre de) r.** *(pour chemin de fer, route)* ballast; *(pour excavation)* backfill

remblaie *etc voir* **remblayer**

remblayage [rɑ̃blɛjaʒ] NM *(de talus)* embanking, banking (up); *(de fossé)* backfilling

remblayer [11] [rɑ̃bleje] VT *Constr* to bank up; **r. un fossé** to fill up a ditch

rembobiner [3] [rɑ̃bɔbine] VT *(film, bande magnétique)* to rewind, to spool back

VPR **se rembobiner** to rewind

remboîtage [rɑ̃bwataʒ], **remboîtement** [rɑ̃bwatmɑ̃] NM **1** *Méd (d'une articulation, d'un os)* repositioning, resetting **2** *Typ (d'un livre)* recasing

remboîter [3] [rɑ̃bwate] VT **1** *Méd (articulation, os)* to reposition, to reset **2** *(pièces, tuyaux)* to fit together again **3** *Typ (livre)* to recase

rembourrage [rɑ̃buraʒ] NM *(d'un coussin, d'un vêtement)* padding; *(d'un siège)* stuffing

rembourrer [3] [rɑ̃bure] VT *(coussin, vêtement)* to pad; *(siège)* to stuff; *Fam* **il est plutôt bien rembourré** he's a bit podgy *or* a bit on the plump side; *Hum* **rembourré avec des noyaux de pêches** as hard as bricks

remboursable [rɑ̃bursabl] ADJ *(billet, frais)* refundable; *(prêt)* repayable; *Fin (rente, obligation)* redeemable; **non r.** non-redeemable

remboursement [rɑ̃bursəmɑ̃] NM *(d'un billet, d'un achat)* refund; *(d'un prêt)* repayment, settlement; *(d'une dépense)* reimbursement; *Fin (d'une rente, d'une obligation)* redemption; **le r. de ses dettes lui a pris deux ans** it took him/her two years to pay off his/her debts; **j'ai obtenu le r. de mes frais de déplacement** I got my travelling expenses reimbursed *or* refunded *or* paid; **envoi** *ou* **expédition contre r.** cash on delivery; **r. anticipé** early repayment; **r. des droits de douane** customs drawback

rembourser [3] [rɑ̃burse] VT *(argent)* to pay back *or* off, to repay; *(dépense, achat)* to reimburse, to refund; *(personne)* to pay back, to reimburse; *(prêt)* to repay; *Fin (rente, obligation)* to redeem; **les billets non utilisés seront remboursés** unused tickets will be reimbursed *or* refunded; **frais de port remboursés** postage refunded; **r. qn de qch** to reimburse *or* refund sb for sth; **est-ce que tu peux me r.?** can you pay me back?; **se faire r.** to get a refund; **tu t'es fait r. pour ton trajet en taxi?** did they reimburse you for your taxi journey?; **ce médicament n'est remboursé qu'à 40 pour cent (par la Sécurité sociale)** only 40 percent of the price of this drug is refunded (by the Health Service)

VPR **se rembourser** to get one's money back; **elle s'est remboursée dans la caisse** she paid herself back out of the till

rembrunir [32] [rɑ̃brynir] **se rembrunir** VPR **1** *Littéraire (s'assombrir)* to darken, to cloud (over) **2** *(se renfrogner)* to darken; **son visage s'est rembruni à l'annonce de la nouvelle** his/her face darkened when he/she heard the news

remède [rəmɛd] NM **1** *(solution)* remedy, cure; **trouver un r. au désespoir/à l'inflation** to find a cure for despair/for inflation; *Fig* **le chômage est-il sans r.?** is there no cure for *or* no answer to unemployment?; **porter r. à qch** to cure *or* to find a cure for sth **2** *(thérapeutique)* cure, remedy; **un r. contre le cancer/le SIDA** a cure for cancer/for Aids; *Fig* **le r. est pire que le mal** the cure is worse than the disease; *Fam* **c'est un (vrai) r. contre l'amour** he's/she's a real turn-off **3** *Vieilli (médicament)* remedy; **un r. de bonne femme** a traditional *or* an old-fashioned remedy; **un r. de cheval** a drastic remedy; *Prov* **aux grands maux les grands remèdes** desperate times call for desperate measures

remédier [9] [rəmedje] **remédier à** VT IND **1** *(maladie)* to cure; *(douleur)* to alleviate, to relieve **2** *(problème)* to remedy, to find a remedy *or* solution for; *(manque)* to remedy; *(défaut)* to make up for, to compensate for; *(erreur)* to put right; **nous ne savons pas comment r. à la situation** we don't know how to remedy the situation

remembrement [rəmɑ̃brəmɑ̃] NM land consolidation *or* reallotment

remembrer [3] [rəmɑ̃bre] VT to redistribute *or* to reallot

remémorer [3] [rəmemɔre] *Littéraire* VT **r. qch à qn** to remind sb of sth, to bring sth to sb's mind

VPR **se remémorer** to recollect, to recall, to remember

remerciement [rəmɛrsimɑ̃] NM **1** *(action)* thanks, thanking; **une lettre de r.** a letter of thanks, a thank-you letter; **un geste/un mot de r.** a gesture/a word of thanks **2** *(parole)* thanks; **remerciements** *(dans un livre)* acknowledgements; **je crois que j'ai droit à un r.** *ou* **des remerciements** I think I deserve a thank you; **(je vous adresse) tous mes remerciements pour ce que vous avez fait** (I) thank you for what you did; **il a balbutié quelques remerciements et s'est enfui** he stammered out a few words of thanks and ran off; **avec mes remerciements** with (many) thanks

remercier [9] [rəmɛrsje] VT **1** *(témoigner sa gratitude à)* to thank (**de** *ou* **pour** for); **je te remercie** thank you; **comment vous r. pour ce que vous avez fait?** I don't know how to thank you for what you did; **tu peux r. le Ciel!** you can count yourself lucky!; **elle nous a remerciés par un superbe bouquet de fleurs** she thanked us with a beautiful bouquet of flowers; **il me remercia d'un sourire** he smiled his thanks, he thanked me with a smile; **je te remercie de m'avoir aidé** thank you for helping me *or* for your help; **et c'est comme ça que tu me remercies!** and that's all the thanks I get!

2 *(pour décliner une offre)* **encore un peu de thé? – je vous remercie** would you like some more tea? – no, thank you; **je te remercie mais je n'ai que faire de ton aide** I can do without your help, thanks all the same; *Ironique* **je te remercie du conseil** thanks for the advice

3 *Euph (licencier)* to let go; **ils ont décidé de la r.** they decided to let her go *or* to dispense with her services

réméré [remere] **NM** *Jur* repurchase (clause)

remettant [rəmetɑ̃] **NM** *Fin* remitter

remetteur, -euse [rəmetœr, -øz] **ADJ** *(banque)* remitting

NM,F remitter

REMETTRE [84] [rəmɛtr]

VT	
• to put back **1**	• to put **1**
• to add **4**	• to put on again **5**
• to hand over **7**	• to give **7**
• to hand in **7**	• to place **8**
• to give back **9**	• to put off **10**
• to remember **12**	• to remit **13**
VPR	
• to recover **4**	• to start again **5**
• to rely on **6**	

VT 1 *(replacer ▸ gén)* to put back; *(▸ horizontalement)* to lay, to put; **remets le livre où tu l'as trouvé** put the book back where you found it; **remets les cartes face dessous** lay *or* place the cards face down again; **r. qch à plat** to lay sth flat again *or* back (down) flat; **l'oiseau remit sa tête sous son aile** the bird put *or* tucked its head back under its wing; **r. qn debout** to stand sb up again *or* sb back up; **je l'ai remis en pension** I sent him back to boarding school; *Fig* **r. qn sur la voie** to put sb back on the right track; *Fig* **r. qn sur le droit chemin** to set sb on the straight and narrow again; **r. qch à cuire** to put sth back on to cook; **r. qch à sécher/tremper** to put sth back up to dry/back in to soak

2 *(remplacer)* **il faut simplement lui r. des piles** you just have to put new batteries in (it); **faire r. un verre à ses lunettes** to have a lens replaced *or* to have a new lens put in one's glasses

3 *(rétablir dans un état)* **r. qch en marche** to get sth going again; **r. qch en état** to repair sth; **r. qch à neuf** to restore sth; **r. une pendule à l'heure** to set a clock right (again); **ces mots me remirent en confiance** those words restored my faith; *Fam* **elle a remis la pagaille dans toute la maison** she plunged the whole household into chaos again

4 *(rajouter)* to add; **remets un peu de sel** put in a bit more salt, add some (more) salt; *Fam* **en r.** *(exagérer)* to overstate one's case◻; *Fam* **il est assez puni comme ça, n'en remets pas** he's been punished enough already, no need to rub it in

5 *(vêtements, chaussures)* to put on again, to put back on; **remets tes skis/ta casquette** put your skis/cap back on

6 *(recommencer)* **la balle est à r.** *(au tennis)* play a let; *Fam* **voilà qu'elle remet ça!** there she goes again!, she's at it again!; *Fam* **tu ne vas pas r. ça avec ma mère!** don't you start going on about my mother again!; *Fam* **les voilà qui remettent ça avec leur grève!** here they go striking again!; *Fam* **allez, on remet ça!** *(au café)* come on, let's have another round *or* another one!; *Fam* **remettez-nous ça!** same again, please!; *Belg Fam* **r. le couvert** to start again◻

7 *(donner ▸ colis, lettre, message)* to deliver, to hand over; *(▸ objet, dossier à régler, rançon)* to hand over, to give; *(▸ dossier d'inscription, dissertation)* to hand *or* to give in; *(▸ pétition, rapport)* to present, to hand in; *(▸ démission)* to hand in, to tender; *(▸ médaille, récompense)* to present, to give; **on nous a remis 10 euros à chacun** we were each given 10 euros; **r. qn aux autorités** to hand *or* to turn sb over to the authorities; **on lui a remis le prix Nobel** he/she was presented with *or* awarded the Nobel prize

8 *(confier)* to place; **r. son sort/sa vie entre les mains de qn** to place one's fate/life in sb's hands; **r. son âme à Dieu** to commit one's soul to God, to place one's soul in God's keeping

9 *(rendre ▸ copies)* to hand *or* to give back; *(▸ clés)* to hand back, to return; **l'enfant a été remis à sa famille** the child was returned to his family

10 *(ajourner ▸ entrevue)* to put off, to postpone, *Br* to put back; *(▸ décision)* to put off, to defer; **la réunion a été remise à lundi** the meeting has been put off *or* postponed until Monday; **r. qch à plus tard** to put sth off until later

11 *Méd (replacer ▸ articulation, os)* to put back in place; **sa cheville n'est pas vraiment encore remise** his/her ankle isn't reset yet

12 *Fam (reconnaître ▸ personne)* to remember◻; **je ne la remets pas** I don't remember her, I can't place her

13 *(faire grâce de ▸ peine de prison)* to remit; *(pardonner ▸ péché)* to forgive, *Sout* to remit; *(▸ offense)* to forgive, to pardon; **r. une dette à qn** to let sb off a debt

14 *Belg (vomir)* to vomit

15 *Belg (rendre ▸ monnaie)* **il m'a remis trois euros** he gave me three euros change

16 *Belg & Suisse (céder)* to sell; **ils ont remis leur boutique** they gave up *or* sold their shop

• **remettre à VT IND** *Belg (identifier avec)* to identify with; *(associer à)* to associate with

VPR se remettre 1 *(se livrer)* **se r. à la police** to give oneself up to the police; **se r. entre les mains de qn** to put *or* to place oneself in sb's hands

2 *Vieilli* **se r. qn** *(reconnaître)* to remember *or* to place sb

3 *(se replacer ▸ dans une position, dans un état)* **se r. au lit** to go back to bed; **se r. debout** to stand up again, to get back up; **se r. en route** to get started *or* going again; **tu ne vas pas te r. en colère!** don't go getting angry again!; **se r. avec qn** *(se réconcilier)* to make it up with sb; *(se réinstaller)* to go *or* to be back with sb again

4 *(guérir)* to recover, to get better; **elle se remettra, ne t'inquiète pas** *(d'un choc)* she'll get over it, don't worry; *(d'une dépression)* she'll pull out of it, don't worry; **se r. de qch** to get over sth; **se r. d'un accident** to recover from *or* to get over an accident; **il ne s'est pas encore complètement remis de son opération** he's not fully recovered from his operation yet; **allons, remets-toi!** come on, pull yourself together *or* get a grip on yourself!; **je ne m'en remets pas** I can't get over it; **elle va s'en r.** she'll get over it

5 **se r. à qch/à faire qch** *(reprendre, recommencer à)* to start *or* to take up sth/doing sth again; **il s'est remis à fumer** he started smoking again; **je me suis remis à l'espagnol** I've taken up Spanish again; **la pluie se remet à tomber, il se remet à pleuvoir** the rain's starting again, it's started raining again; **le temps se remet au beau** it's brightening up; **le temps se remet à la neige** it looks like snow again

6 **s'en r. à** *(se fier à)* to rely on, to leave it (up) to; **tu peux t'en r. à moi** you can rely on me *or* leave it (up) to me; **je m'en remets à lui pour tout ce qui concerne le financement du projet** I'm leaving the financial arrangements of the plan to him *or* in his hands; **s'en r. à la décision de qn** to leave it (up) to sb to decide; **s'en r. au bon sens de qn** to rely on sb's common sense

remeubler [5] [rəmœble] **VT** *(de nouveau)* to refurnish; *(avec de nouveaux meubles)* to put new furniture in *or* into

VPR se remeubler to refurnish one's house/flat

remilitarisation [rəmilitarizasjɔ̃] **NF** remilitarization

remilitariser [3] [rəmilitarize] **VT** to remilitarize

VPR se remilitariser to become remilitarized

réminiscence [reminisɑ̃s] **NF 1** *(souvenir)* reminiscence, recollection; **quelques réminiscences de ce qu'elle avait appris à l'école** a few vague memories of what she'd learned at school; **des réminiscences de mon enfance** reminiscences *or* recollections of my childhood **2** *(influence)* overtone; **il y a des réminiscences de Mahler dans ce morceau** there are some echoes of Mahler in this piece, this piece is reminiscent of Mahler **3** *Phil & Psy* reminiscence

remis, -e [rəmi, -iz] **PP** *voir* **remettre**

ADJ être r. to be well again; **une semaine de repos et me voilà r.** a week's rest and I'm back on my feet (again); **être r. de** to have recovered from, to have got over; **il n'est pas encore r. de sa frayeur/son cauchemar** he hasn't yet got over his fright/nightmare

• **remise NF 1** *(dans un état antérieur)* **la remise en place des meubles/en ordre des documents nous a pris du temps** putting all the furniture back into place/sorting out the papers again took us some time; **remise en cause** *ou* **question** calling into question; **ses remises en question continuelles** his/her constant doubts *or* questioning; **remise en état** *(d'une maison)* restoration; **remise en jeu** *ou* **en touche** *(au hockey)* push-in; *(au rugby)* line-out; *(au foot)* throw-in; **la remise en marche du moteur** restarting the engine; **remise à neuf** restoration; **il a besoin d'une remise à niveau** he needs a refresher course; *Ordinat* **remise à zéro** *(effacement)* core flush; *(réinitialisation)* resetting; *Aut* **la remise à zéro du compteur kilométrique a été faite récemment** the mileometer has recently been put back to zero

2 *(livraison)* delivery; **remise d'une lettre/d'un paquet en mains propres** personal delivery of a letter/package; **la remise des clés sera faite par l'agence** the agency will be responsible for handing over the keys; *Scol* **remise des prix** prize-giving

3 *Com (réduction)* discount, reduction, *Spéc* remittance; **une remise de 15 pour cent** a 15 percent discount, 15 percent off; **faire une remise sur qch** to allow a discount on sth; **faire une remise à qn** to give sb a discount; **remise de caisse** cash discount; **remise de fidélité** customer loyalty discount; **remise sur marchandises** trade discount; **remise promotionnelle** promotional discount; **remise quantitative** *ou* **pour quantité** *ou* **sur la quantité** bulk *or* quantity discount; **remise saisonnière** seasonal discount; **remise d'usage** trade discount

4 *(d'effet, de chèque)* remittance; **faire une remise de fonds à qn** to send sb a remittance, to remit funds to sb; **faire une remise de chèque** to pay in a cheque; **remise d'effets** remittance of bills; **remise de fonds** remittance of funds; **remise à vue** demand deposit

5 *Fin (d'un impôt)* allowance

6 *Jur* remission; **faire remise d'une dette** to discharge a debt; **faire remise d'une amende** to remit *or* to reduce a fine; **remise de peine** reduction of (the) sentence

7 *(ajournement)* putting off, postponement; **la remise à huitaine de l'ouverture du procès** the postponement *or Sout* deferment of the opening of the trial for a week

8 *(resserre)* shed

9 *Aut* **voiture de grande remise** chauffeur-driven hire limousine

remiser [3] [rəmize] **VT** *(ranger)* to store away, to put away

VI *(parier à nouveau)* to place another bet

remisier [rəmizje] **NM** *Bourse* intermediate broker

rémissible [remisibl] **ADJ** *Littéraire (crime, faute, péché)* remissible, subject to remission

rémission [remisjɔ̃] **NF 1** *Rel (de péché)* remission **2** *Jur (de peine)* remission **3** *Méd (d'une maladie)* remission; *(de la douleur, de la fièvre)* abatement; **la r. fut de courte durée** the remission didn't last; **être en r.** to be in remission

• **sans rémission ADJ** *(implacable)* merciless, pitiless **ADV 1** *(sans pardon possible)* mercilessly, without mercy **2** *(sans relâche)* unremittingly, relentlessly

remit *etc voir* **remettre**

rémittent, -e [remitɑ̃, -ɑ̃t] **ADJ** *Méd (fièvre, mal)* remittent

remix [rəmiks] **NM** *Mus* remix

remixer [3] [rəmikse] **VT** *Mus* to remix

remmailler [rɑ̃maje] = **remailler**

remmener [19] [rɑ̃mne] **VT** *(au point de départ)* to take back; *(à soi)* to bring back; **je te remmènerai chez toi en voiture** I'll drive you back home; **nous l'avons remmené au zoo** we took him to the zoo again *or* back to the zoo

remodelage [rəmɔdlaʒ] **NM 1** *(d'une silhouette, des traits)* remodelling **2** *(d'un quartier)* replanning; *(d'une institution)* reorganization; *(d'un projet)* redesigning, revising

remodeler [25] [rəmɔdle] **VT 1** *(silhouette, traits)* to remodel **2** *(quartier)* to replan; *(institution)* to reorganize; *(projet)* to redesign, to revise

rémois, -e [remwa, -az] **ADJ** of/from Rheims *or* Reims

• **Rémois, -e NM,F** = inhabitant of or person from Rheims

remontage [rəmɔ̃taʒ] **NM 1** *(d'une pendule)* winding up, rewinding **2** *(d'une étagère, d'un mécanisme)* reassembly, reassembling

remontant, -e [rəmɔ̃tɑ̃, -ɑ̃t] **ADJ 1** *Bot (fraisier)* double-cropping, *Spéc* remontant; *(rosier)* remontant **2** *(fortifiant)* invigorating
NM tonic

remonte [rəmɔ̃t] **NF 1** *Mil* remount **2** *Naut* sailing upstream *or* upriver **3** *(d'un poisson qui fraie)* run

remonte-pente [rəmɔ̃tpɑ̃t] *(pl* **remonte-pentes)** **NM** ski tow, T-bar

remonter [3] [rəmɔ̃te] **VT 1** *(côte, étage)* to go *or* to climb back up; **r. l'escalier** to go *or* to climb back up the stairs
2 *(porter à nouveau)* to take back up; **r. une valise au grenier** to take a suitcase back up to the attic
3 *(parcourir ▸ en voiture, en bateau etc)* to go up; **r. le Nil** to sail up the Nile; **les saumons remontent le fleuve** the salmon are swimming upstream; **r. la rue** to go *or* to walk back up the street; **en remontant le cours des siècles** *ou* **du temps** going back several centuries
4 *(relever ▸ chaussette)* to pull up; *(▸ manche)* to roll up; *(▸ col, visière)* to raise, to turn up; *(▸ robe)* to raise, to lift; *(▸ store)* to pull up, to raise; **r. qch** to put sth higher up, to raise sth; **remonte ton pantalon** pull your *Br* trousers *or Am* pants up; **elle a remonté la vitre** she wound the window up
5 *(augmenter ▸ salaire, notation)* to increase, to raise, to put up; **tous les résultats des examens ont été remontés de deux points** all exam results have been put up *or* raised by two marks
6 *(assembler à nouveau ▸ moteur, kit)* to reassemble, to put back together (again); *(▸ étagère)* to put back up; *Cin (▸ film)* to re-edit
7 *Com (rouvrir)* to set up again; **à sa sortie de prison, il a remonté une petite affaire de plomberie** when he came out of prison he started up another small plumbing business
8 *(faire prospérer à nouveau)* **il a su r. l'entreprise** he managed to set *or* to put the business back on its feet; **elle a remonté la scierie après la mort de son père** she got the sawmill going again after her father died
9 *(renouveler)* to restock, to stock up again; **r. sa cave** to stock up one's cellar again, to restock one's cellar; **il faut que je remonte ma garde-robe pour l'hiver** I must buy myself some new clothes *or* a new wardrobe for the winter
10 *(mécanisme, montre)* to wind (up)
11 *(ragaillardir ▸ physiquement)* to pick up; *(▸ moralement)* to cheer up; *Fam* **prends un whisky, ça te remontera** have a whisky, it'll perk you up; **r. le moral à qn** to cheer sb up
12 *Théât* to stage again, to put on (the stage) again; **une pièce oubliée que personne n'avait jamais remontée** a forgotten play which had never been revived
VI *(surtout aux être)* **1** *(monter de nouveau)* to go back up, to go up again; **l'enfant remonta dans la brouette/sur l'escabeau** the child got back into the wheelbarrow/up onto the stool; **remonte dans ta chambre** go back up to your room; **r. au troisième étage** to go back up to the third floor; **r. à Paris** to go back to Paris
2 *Transp* **r. dans** *(bateau, bus, train)* to get back onto; *(voiture)* to get back into; **r. à cheval** *(se remettre en selle)* to remount; *(refaire de l'équitation)* to take up riding again
3 *(s'élever ▸ route)* to go back up, to go up again; **le sentier remonte jusqu'à la villa** the path goes up to the villa; **la rivière a remonté cette nuit** *(a un niveau supérieur)* the level of the river rose again last night; **la mer remonte** the tide's coming in (again); **le baromètre remonte** the barometer is rising; **le prix du sucre a remonté** *(après une baisse)* the price of sugar has gone back up again; **sa fièvre remonte de plus belle** his/her temperature is going up even higher; **tu remontes dans mon estime** you've gone up in my esteem; *Fig* **sa cote remonte** he's/she's becoming more popular; *Fig* **ses actions remontent** things are looking up *or* picking up for him/her
4 *(jupe)* to ride up, to go up
5 *(faire surface ▸ mauvaise odeur)* to come back up; **r. à la surface** *(noyé)* to float back (up) to the surface; *(plongeur)* to resurface; *(scandale)* to re-emerge, to resurface; **un sentiment de culpabilité remontait à sa conscience de temps en temps** a guilty feeling would well up in him/her from time to time
6 *(retourner vers l'origine)* **r. dans le temps** to go back in time; **il avait beau r. dans ses souvenirs, il ne la reconnaissait pas** however far back he tried to remember, he couldn't place her; **il est remonté très loin dans l'histoire de sa famille** he delved back a long way into his family history; **si l'on remonte encore plus loin dans le passé** looking *or* going back even further into the past; **r. à** *(se reporter à)* to go back to, to return to; **r. à la cause première/à l'origine de qch** to go back to the primary cause/the origins of sth; **le renseignement qui nous a permis de r. jusqu'à vous** the piece of information which enabled us to trace you; **r. à** *(dater de)* to go *or* to date back to; **ça remonte à loin maintenant** it happened a long time *or* years *or* ages ago; **leur brouille remonte à loin** their quarrel is of long standing, they quarrelled a long time ago; **cela remonte à plusieurs mois** this goes *or* dates back several months; **cela remonte à 1958** this goes *or* dates back to 1958; **les recherches font r. sa famille à 1518** research shows that his/her family goes back to 1518; **on fait généralement r. la crise à 1910** the crisis is generally believed to have started in 1910
7 *Naut* **r. au vent** to tack into the wind
VPR se remonter 1 *(emploi passif)* **ces montres ne se remontent pas** these watches don't have to be wound up; **ça se remonte avec une clé** you wind it up with a key **2** *(emploi réfléchi) (physiquement)* to recover one's strength; *(moralement)* to cheer oneself up; **elle dit qu'elle boit pour se r.** she says she drinks to cheer herself up *or* to make herself feel better; **il s'est bien remonté depuis hier** he's cheered up a lot since yesterday; **se r. le moral** to cheer oneself up **3** *Fam* **se r. en** *(se réapprovisionner en)* to replenish one's stock of[□]; **il s'est remonté en cravates/en chaussettes** he's replenished his stock of ties/socks

remontoir [rəmɔ̃twar] **NM** *(d'une montre)* winder

remontrance [rəmɔ̃trɑ̃s] **NF** *(gén pl) (reproche)* remonstrance, reproof; **faire des remontrances à qn** to reprimand *or* to admonish sb

remontrer [3] [rəmɔ̃tre] **VT 1** *(montrer de nouveau)* to show again; **tu peux me r. ton livre?** can you show me your book again?; **j'aimerais que tu me remontres comment tu as fait** I'd like you to show me again *or* once more how you did it **2** *Littéraire (faute, tort)* to point out **3** *(locutions)* **crois-tu vraiment pouvoir m'en r.?** do you really think you have anything to teach me?; **il veut toujours en r. à tout le monde** he's always trying to show off to people; **il en remontrerait à ses professeurs** he could teach *or* show his teachers a thing or two
VPR se remontrer to show up again; **et ne t'avise pas de te r. ici!** and don't ever show your face (around) here again!

rémora [remɔra] **NM** *Ich* remora, sharksucker

remordre [76] [rəmɔrdr] **VT** to bite again
• **remordre à VT IND** *(se remettre à)* **elle ne veut plus r. à l'informatique** she doesn't want to have anything more to do with computers

remords [rəmɔr] **NM 1** *(repentir)* remorse; **avoir des r.** to be full of remorse; **j'ai des r. de l'avoir laissé partir à pied** I feel bad about leaving him to walk; **je n'ai aucun r.!** I'm not the slightest bit sorry!; **des r. de conscience** twinges of conscience; **être bourrelé de** *ou* **torturé par le r.** to be stricken with remorse; **elle est rongée par le r.** she is consumed with remorse; **il a été pris de r.** his conscience got the better of him; **sans aucun r.** without a qualm, without any compunction, without (the slightest) remorse **2** *(regret)* **tu ne veux vraiment pas l'acheter, c'est sans r.?** you're sure you won't regret not buying it?

remorquage [rəmɔrkaʒ] **NM** towing

remorque [rəmɔrk] **NF 1** *(traction ▸ d'une voiture)* towing; *(▸ d'un navire)* tugging, towing; **câble de r.** towline, towrope; **prendre une voiture en r.** to tow a car; **être en r.** to be *Br* on tow *or Am* in tow; **véhicule accidenté en r.** *Br* on tow, *Am* in tow **2** *(véhicule)* trailer **3** *Fig* **être à la r. de qn** to tag (along) behind sb; **il est toujours à la r.** he always lags behind

remorquer [3] [rəmɔrke] **VT 1** *(voiture)* to tow; *(navire)* to tug, to tow; *(masse)* to haul; **se faire r. jusqu'au garage** to get a tow to the garage **2** *Fam (traîner ▸ enfant, famille)* to drag along

remorqueur, -euse [rəmɔrkœr, -øz] **ADJ** *(avion, bateau, train)* towing
NM *Naut* towboat, tug

rémoulade [remulad] **NF** *Culin* rémoulade (sauce)

remoulage [rəmulaʒ] **NM 1** *(du café)* regrinding **2** *(en meunerie ▸ action)* remilling; *(▸ résultat)* middlings

rémouleur [remulœr] **NM** (itinerant) knife grinder

remous [rəmu] **NM 1** *(tourbillon)* swirl, eddy; *(derrière un bateau)* wash, backwash; **r. d'air** eddy **2** *(mouvement)* ripple, stir; **un r. parcourut la foule** a ripple *or* stir went through the crowd **3** *(réaction)* stir, flurry; **l'article va sûrement provoquer quelques r. dans la classe politique** the article will doubtless cause a stir *or* raise a few eyebrows in the political world; **sa nomination n'a pas provoqué de r.** his/her appointment didn't cause a stir

rempaillage [rɑ̃pajaʒ] **NM** *(d'une chaise)* reseating (with rushes), rushing

rempailler [3] [rɑ̃paje] **VT** *(chaise)* to reseat (with rushes)

rempailleur, -euse [rɑ̃pajœr, -øz] **NM,F** chair-rusher

rempaqueter [27] [rɑ̃pakte] **VT** to wrap (up) again, to rewrap

rempart [rɑ̃par] **NM 1** *(enceinte)* rampart, bulwark; **les remparts** *(d'une ville)* ramparts, city walls **2** *Fig Littéraire* bulwark, bastion; **elle lui fit un r. de son corps** she shielded him/her with her body; **le r. de nos libertés** the bulwark *or* bastion of our liberties

rempiéter [18] [rɑ̃pjete] **VT** *Constr* to underpin

rempiler [3] [rɑ̃pile] **VT** to pile (up) again
VI *Fam Arg mil* to re-enlist[□], to sign up again[□], *Am* to re-up; **il a rempilé pour cinq ans** he signed up for five more years

remplaçable [rɑ̃plasabl] **ADJ** replaceable; **difficilement r.** hard to replace

remplaçant, -e [rɑ̃plasɑ̃, -ɑ̃t] **NM,F 1** *(gén)* replacement, stand-in; *Univ Br* supply *or Am* substitute teacher; *(d'un médecin, d'un dentiste)* replacement, *Br* locum **2** *Sport* reserve; *(au cours du match)* substitute **3** *Mus, Théât & TV* understudy

remplacement [rɑ̃plasmɑ̃] **NM 1** *(substitution)* replacement; **le juge a procédé au r. de deux jurés** the judge has replaced two members of the jury; **le r. des pneus va me coûter cher** it's going to cost me a lot to replace the tyres; **en r. de** in place of, as a replacement *or* substitute for **2** *(suppléance)* **je ne trouve que des remplacements** I can only find work standing in *or* covering for other people; **faire un r.** to stand in, to fill in; **faire des remplacements** *(gén)* to do temporary replacement work; *(comme secrétaire)* to do temporary secretarial work; *(comme enseignant)* to work as a *Br* supply *or Am* substitute teacher
• **de remplacement ADJ un avion arrive avec du matériel de r.** a plane is arriving with replacement equipment *or* with spares; **produit de r.** substitute product; **solution de r.** alternative *or* fallback (solution)

remplacer [16] [rɑ̃plase] **VT 1** *(renouveler ▸ pièce usagée)* to replace, to change; **r. une tuile cassée/un fusible** to replace a broken tile/a fuse
2 *(mettre à la place de)* to replace (**par** with); **nous avons remplacé les vieux bâtiments par un grand jardin** we have made a big garden where the old buildings used to be; **remplacez les adjectifs par d'autres expressions** replace the adjectives with other phrases
3 *(prendre la place de)* to replace, to take the place of; **dans de nombreuses tâches, la machine remplace maintenant l'homme** for a lot of tasks, machines are now taking over from men; **le pétrole a remplacé le charbon** oil has taken the place of coal
4 *(suppléer)* to stand in *or* to substitute for; **tu dois absolument trouver quelqu'un pour le r.** you must find someone to replace him; **rien ne peut r. une mère** there is no substitute for a mother; **personne ne peut la r.** she's irreplaceable; **si vous ne pouvez pas venir, faites-vous r.** if you can't come, get someone to stand in for you; **il l'a rem-**

placé deux fois comme capitaine de l'équipe nationale he's stood in for him twice as captain of his country's team; on l'a remplacé pendant la seconde mi-temps he was taken off *or* substituted during the second half; tu as l'air épuisé, je vais te r. you look exhausted, I'll take over from you; je me suis fait r. par un collègue pendant mon absence I got a colleague to replace me while I was away

VPR se remplacer to be replaced; cette pièce se remplace facilement the part is easy to replace *or* easily replaced; une sœur, ça ne se remplace pas there's no substitute for a sister; une secrétaire comme ça, ça ne se remplace pas you won't find another secretary like her

remplage [rɑ̃plaʒ] NM *Archit (d'une fenêtre gothique)* tracery

rempli, -e [rɑ̃pli] ADJ j'ai eu une journée bien remplie I've had a very full *or* busy day; un emploi du temps très *ou* bien r. a very busy schedule; *Fam* j'ai le ventre bien r., ça va mieux! I feel a lot better for that meal!

NM *Couture* tuck

remplir [32] [rɑ̃plir] VT 1 *(emplir)* to fill; remplissez votre casserole d'eau fill your saucepan with water; le vase est rempli à ras bord the vase is full to the brim; la foule a rapidement rempli la rue the crowd quickly filled the street; cela a rempli ma journée it took up my whole day; on ne remplit plus les salles avec des comédies comedies don't pull audiences *or* aren't box-office hits any more; la cave est remplie de bons vins the cellar is filled *or* stocked with good wines; elle a déjà rempli dix pages she has already written *or* filled ten pages

2 *(compléter ▸ questionnaire, dossier)* to fill in *or* out; *(▸ chèque)* to fill *or* to make out

3 *(combler ▸ trou)* to fill in

4 *(accomplir ▸ engagement, rôle)* to fulfil; *(▸ fonction, mission)* to carry out; dès que j'aurai rempli mes obligations, je vous rejoindrai as soon as I've fulfilled my obligations I'll join you

5 *(satisfaire ▸ condition)* to fulfil, to satisfy, to meet

6 *(d'émotion)* r. qn de joie/d'espoir to fill sb with joy/with hope; être rempli de soi-même/de son importance to be full of oneself/of one's own importance

VPR se remplir 1 to fill (up); le ciel s'est rapidement rempli de nuages noirs the sky quickly filled with dark clouds; ses yeux se remplirent de larmes his/her eyes filled with tears; le fossé s'est rempli d'eau en quelques minutes the ditch filled (up) with water within a few minutes 2 *Fam* se r. l'estomac *ou* la panse to stuff oneself *or* one's face; se r. les poches to line one's pockets

remplissage [rɑ̃plisaʒ] NM 1 *(d'une fosse, d'un récipient)* filling (up) 2 *Fig (d'un texte)* padding; faire du r. to pad 3 *Constr* studwork

remploi [rɑ̃plwa] NM 1 *(d'un travailleur)* re-employment 2 *(d'une machine, de matériaux)* reuse 3 *Fin* reinvestment

remployer [13] [rɑ̃plwaje] VT 1 *(travailleur)* to take on again, to re-employ 2 *(machine, matériaux)* to reuse, to use again 3 *Fin* to reinvest

remplumer [3] [rɑ̃plyme] se remplumer VPR 1 *(d'un oiseau)* to get new feathers *or* new plumage 2 *Fam (physiquement)* to put a bit of weight back on□ 3 *Fam (financièrement)* to improve one's cash flow□, to get back on one's feet

rempocher [3] [rɑ̃pɔʃe] VT to pocket again, to put back in one's pocket

remporter [3] [rɑ̃pɔrte] VT 1 *(reprendre)* to take back; n'oublie pas de r. ton livre don't forget to take your book with you 2 *(obtenir)* to win, to get; r. un prix to carry off *or* to win a prize; r. un succès to be successful 3 *Sport* to win

rempotage [rɑ̃pɔtaʒ] NM *(d'une plante)* repotting

rempoter [3] [rɑ̃pɔte] VT *(plante)* to repot

remprunter [3] [rɑ̃prœ̃te] VT 1 *(emprunter ▸ de nouveau)* to borrow again; *(▸ en supplément)* to borrow more 2 *(route)* r. le même chemin to take the same road again

remuant, -e [rəmɥɑ̃, -ɑ̃t] ADJ 1 *(agité)* restless, fidgety; que cet enfant est r.! that child never sits still! 2 *(entreprenant)* energetic, active, lively; *Euph* son parti trouve qu'il est un peu trop r. his party finds him somewhat over-enthusiastic

remue-ménage [rəmymenaʒ] NM INV 1 *(d'objets)* jumble, disorder; il a fallu tout déménager, tu aurais vu le r. dans le bureau hier we had to move out all the furniture, you should've seen the mess *or* shambles in the office yesterday 2 *(agitation bruyante)* commotion, hurly-burly, rumpus; les gens du dessus font leur r. habituel the people upstairs are making their usual rumpus; *Fig* la nouvelle de sa démission a fait un de ces r.! the news of his/her resignation caused quite a commotion *or* stir

remue-méninges [rəmymenɛ̃ʒ] NM INV *Offic* brainstorming; un r. a brainstorming session

remuement [rəmymɑ̃] NM *Littéraire* movement, moving, stirring

remuer [7] [rəmɥe] VT 1 *(agiter ▸ tête, jambes)* to move; *(▸ oreilles)* to waggle; r. les lèvres to move one's lips; r. les bras to wave one's arms (about); la brise remue les branches/les herbes the breeze is stirring the branches/the grass; le chien remuait la queue the dog was wagging its tail

2 *(déplacer ▸ objet)* to move, to shift

3 *(retourner ▸ cendres)* to poke; *(▸ terre, compost)* to turn over; *(▸ salade)* to toss; *(▸ boisson, préparation)* to stir; remuez délicatement le chocolat et les blancs d'œufs gently fold the chocolate into the egg whites; r. des fortunes *ou* de grosses sommes to handle huge amounts of money; *Fam* r. l'or à la pelle to be rolling in money; r. ciel et terre to move heaven and earth, to leave no stone unturned

4 *(ressasser)* to stir up, to brood over; à quoi bon r. le passé? what's the good of stirring up *or* raking over the past?; r. des souvenirs to turn *or* to go over memories

5 *(troubler)* to move; être (tout)/profondément remué to be (very)/deeply moved; ton histoire m'a remué your story moved me

VI 1 *(s'agiter ▸ nez, oreille)* to twitch; la queue du chien/du chat/du cheval remuait the dog was wagging/the cat was flicking/the horse was flicking its tail 2 *(personne, animal ▸ bouger)* to move; *(▸ gigoter)* to fidget; *Fam* les gosses, ça remue tout le temps kids can't stop fidgeting *or* never keep still 3 *Fig* to get restless; les mineurs commencent à r. the miners are getting restless

VPR se remuer 1 *(bouger)* to move; j'ai besoin de me r. un peu I need to get some exercise 2 *(se démener)* to put oneself out; il a fallu que je me remue pour t'inscrire I had to go to a lot of trouble to get you on the course; *Fam* remue-toi un peu! *(agis)* get a move on!, shift yourself!, *Br* get up off your backside!

rémunérateur, -trice [remyneratœr, -tris] ADJ *(investissement)* remunerative; *(emploi)* lucrative, well-paid

rémunération [remynerasjɔ̃] NF remuneration, payment (de for); *(salaire)* pay; r. du capital interest on capital; r. de départ starting salary

rémunératoire [remyneratwar] ADJ *Jur* remunerative; legs r. legacy in consideration of service rendered

rémunératrice [remyneratris] *voir* rémunérateur

rémunérer [18] [remynere] VT *(personne)* to remunerate, to pay; *(travail, services)* to pay for; travail bien/mal rémunéré well-paid/badly-paid work; avoir un emploi rémunéré to be gainfully employed, to be in gainful employment; vous êtes-vous fait r. pour ce travail? did you get paid for this job?

renâcler [3] [rənakle] VI 1 *(cheval)* to snort 2 *(personne)* to grumble, to moan; *Fig* il a un peu renâclé he dragged his feet a bit; il a accepté en renâclant he reluctantly accepted; r. à faire qch to be (very) loath *or* reluctant to do sth; r. à la besogne to be workshy

renais, renaissait *etc voir* renaître

renaissance [rənɛsɑ̃s] NF 1 *(réincarnation)* rebirth 2 *(renouveau)* revival, rebirth

renaissant, -e [rənɛsɑ̃, -ɑ̃t] ADJ *(intérêt, enthousiasme)* renewed; *(passion)* reawakening; *(douleur)* recurring; *(économie)* reviving; leur amour r. their rekindled love; sans cesse r. *(espoir)* ever renewed; *(problème)* ever recurring

renaître [92] [rənɛtr] VI *(inusité aux temps composés)* 1 *(naître de nouveau ▸ gén)* to come back to life, to come to life again; *(▸ végétation)* to spring up again; se sentir r. to feel like a new person; *Rel* r. par le baptême/la pénitence to be born again through baptism/repentance; *Littéraire* r. à la vie to come alive again; *Littéraire* r. à l'espoir/l'amour to find new hope/a new love; *Fig* r. de ses cendres to rise from the ashes 2 *(revenir ▸ jour)* to dawn; *(▸ courage, économie)* to revive, to recover; *(▸ lettres, arts)* to revive; *(▸ bonheur, espoir)* to return; faire r. le passé/un antagonisme to revive the past/an antagonism; faire r. les espérances de qn to revive sb's hopes, to get sb's hopes up again; faire r. la confiance to restore confidence; l'espoir renaît dans l'équipe/le village the team/the village has found fresh hope; l'espoir *ou* l'espérance renaît toujours hope springs eternal

rénal, -e, -aux, -ales [renal, -o] ADJ *Anat* kidney *(avant n)*, *Spéc* renal

renaquit *etc voir* renaître

renard [rənar] NM 1 *Zool* fox; r. argenté/bleu silver/blue fox; r. polaire Arctic fox; r. roux common *or* red fox

2 *(fourrure)* fox fur

3 *Fig* vieux r. (sly) old fox, cunning old devil; c'est un fin r. he's as sly as a fox

4 *Tech (brèche)* breach, leakage

renarde [rənard] NF *Zool* vixen

renardeau, -x [rənardo] NM fox cub

renardière [rənardjɛr] NF 1 *(tanière)* fox's earth *or* den 2 *Can (élevage)* fox farm

renauder [3] [rənode] VI *Fam Vieilli* to whinge, to moan and groan

rencaissage [rɑ̃kɛsaʒ] NM *(d'une plante)* reboxing

rencaissement [rɑ̃kɛsmɑ̃] NM *Fin* cashing (in) again

rencaisser [4] [rɑ̃kese] VT 1 *(plante)* to rebox 2 *Fin (toucher)* to cash again; *(remettre en caisse)* to put back in the till

rencard [rɑ̃kar] = rancard

rencarder [rɑ̃karde] = rancarder

renchérir [32] [rɑ̃ʃerir] VI 1 *(devenir plus cher)* to become more expensive, to go up 2 *(faire une surenchère)* to make a higher bid, to bid higher

VT *(rendre plus cher)* la crise a renchéri les produits courants the crisis has pushed up the price of everyday goods

USAGE ABSOLU "un homme fort aimable", renchérit-elle "a most likable man," she added

• **renchérir sur** VT IND 1 *(personne)* to outbid; *(enchère)* to bid higher than 2 *(en actes ou en paroles)* to go further than, to outdo; il renchérit toujours sur ce que dit sa femme he always goes further *or* one better than his wife

renchérissement [rɑ̃ʃerismɑ̃] NM increase, rise; un r. des produits laitiers an increase *or* a rise in the price of dairy products

rencogner [3] [rɑ̃kɔɲe] VT *Fam* to corner

VPR se rencogner to huddle up

rencontre [rɑ̃kɔ̃tr] NF 1 *(entrevue)* meeting, encounter; c'était une r. tout à fait inattendue it was a completely unexpected encounter; faire la r. de qn to meet sb; faire une r. to meet someone; faire une mauvaise r. to have an unpleasant encounter; faire de mauvaises rencontres to meet the wrong kind of people; aller *ou* marcher à la r. de qn to go to meet sb; je pars à sa r. I'm going to go and meet him/her; rencontres en ligne on-line dating

2 *(conférence)* meeting, conference; une r. internationale sur l'énergie nucléaire an international meeting *or* conference on nuclear energy; r. au sommet summit meeting

3 *Sport* match, game, *Br* fixture; *(en boxe)* fight; une r. d'athlétisme an athletics meeting

4 *(combat)* engagement, encounter; *(duel)* duel

5 *(jonction ▸ de deux fleuves)* confluence; *(▸ de deux routes)* junction; *(collision ▸ de deux voitures)* collision

rencontrer [3] [rɑ̃kɔ̃tre] VT 1 *(croiser)* to meet, *Sout* to encounter; *(faire la connaissance de)* to meet; je l'ai rencontré (par hasard) au marché I met him (by chance) *or* bumped into him at the market; **je lui ai fait r. quelqu'un qui peut l'aider professionnellement** I've put him/her in touch with somebody who can offer him/her professional help; **c'est moi qui lui ai fait r. son mari** I was the one who introduced her to her future husband

2 *(avoir une réunion avec)* to meet, to have a meeting with; **il ne peut pas vous r. avant lundi** he can't meet you before Monday

3 *(affronter)* to meet; *Sport* to play against, to meet

4 *(heurter)* to strike, to hit; *(entrer en contact avec)* to meet; **la fourche rencontra une grosse pierre** the fork struck *or* hit a big stone; **r. les yeux de qn** to meet sb's eyes; **sa main rencontra quelque chose de froid** his/her hand came up against *or* met something cold

5 *(trouver ▸ thème, plante, arbre)* to come across, to encounter; *(▸ opposition, difficulté, obstacle)* to encounter, to meet with, to come *or* run up against; **r. l'assentiment de tous** to meet with everyone's approval; **sans r. la moindre résistance** without meeting with *or* experiencing the least resistance; **c'est un écrivain comme on n'en rencontre plus guère** he's the sort of writer you hardly ever come across nowadays; **r. l'amour/Dieu** to find love/God

6 *Belg (argument, objection)* to counter; *(besoin, exigence)* to meet, to satisfy

VPR se rencontrer 1 *(se trouver en présence)* to meet; **c'est elle qui les a fait se r.** she arranged for them to meet; **où vous êtes-vous rencontrés?** where did you meet?; **comme on se rencontre!** (it's a) small world!

2 *Sport* to play (against), to meet

3 *(se rejoindre ▸ fleuves)* to meet, to join; *(▸ routes)* to meet, to merge; *(se heurter)* to collide, to run into each other; **leurs yeux** *ou* **regards se sont rencontrés** their eyes met

4 *(être d'accord ▸ personnes)* to agree

5 *(emploi passif)* **un homme intègre, ça ne se rencontre pas souvent** it's not often you come across *or* meet an honest man

rendement [rɑ̃dmɑ̃] **NM 1** *(production)* output; **travailler à plein r.** *(usine)* to work at full capacity; **r. à l'heure, r. horaire** output per hour; **r. optimal** *ou* **maximum** maximum *or* peak output

2 *(rentabilité ▸ gén)* productivity; *(▸ d'un ordinateur)* throughput; **le r. de cette machine est supérieur** this machine is more productive

3 *(efficacité)* efficiency; **mon r. s'en est trouvé affecté** it's affected my efficiency; **r. effectif** performance rating

4 *Agr* yield; **le r. de ces champs est faible** those fields give a low yield; **une terre sans aucun r.** a land that yields no return

5 *Fin* yield, return; **à haut/bas r.** high-/low-yield; **r. annuel** annual return; **r. brut** gross yield *or* return; **r. moyen** average yield; **r. net** net return; **r. réel** inflation-adjusted yield

6 *Élec & Phys* efficiency

rendez-vous [rɑ̃devu] **NM INV 1** *(rencontre ▸ gén)* appointment; *(▸ d'amoureux)* date; **prendre r. avec qn/un r. chez le coiffeur** to make an appointment with sb/at the hairdresser's; **j'ai r. chez le médecin** I have an appointment with the doctor; **donner r. à qn** to arrange to meet sb; **se donner r.** to arrange to meet; **avez-vous r.?** do you have an appointment?; **le réceptionniste m'a pris r. pour 11 heures** the receptionist made an appointment for me for 11 o'clock; **être en r.** to be in a meeting; **lieu de r.: devant l'église** meet in front of the church; **r. chez mes parents à 10 heures** let's meet at 10 o'clock at my parents' (house); **un r. manqué** a missed meeting; *Fig* **le soleil était au r.** the sun was shining; **r. d'affaires** business meeting *or* appointment; **r. citoyen** = name sometimes given to the "journée d'appel de préparation à la défense" **2** *(endroit)* meeting place; **j'étais le premier au r.** I was the first one to turn up *or* to arrive; **ici, c'est le r. des étudiants** this is a student haunt; **r. de chasse** *(lieu de rassemblement)* meet; *(bâtiment)* hunting lodge **3** *(personne)* **votre r. est arrivé** your client/patient/*etc* is here

rendormir [36] [rɑ̃dɔrmir] **VT** to put *or* to send back to sleep

VPR se rendormir to go back to sleep, to fall asleep again; **je n'arrive pas à me r.** I can't get back to sleep

RENDRE [73] [rɑ̃dr]

VT	
• to give back **1**	• to return **1, 2, 10**
• to make **3**	• to portray **5**
• to render **5**	• to give out **7**
• to vomit **8**	• to pronounce **10**
• to yield **11**	
VI	
• to be productive **1**	• to be effective **2**
• to vomit **3**	
VPR	
• to surrender **1**	• to make oneself **2**
• to go **3**	• to give in **1, 4**

VT 1 *(restituer ▸ objet prêté, volé ou donné)* to give back, to return; *(▸ objet défectueux)* to take back, to return; *(▸ somme)* to pay back; *(▸ réponse)* to give; **il est venu r. la chaise** he brought the chair back; **donne-moi dix euros, je te les rendrai demain** give me ten euros, I'll pay you back *or* I'll give it back to you tomorrow; **r. un devoir** *(sujet: élève)* to hand *or* to give in a piece of work; *(sujet: professeur)* to hand *or* to give back a piece of work; **l'enfant a été rendu à sa famille** the child was handed back *or* returned to his family; **r. un otage** to return *or* to hand over a hostage

2 *(donner en retour)* to return; **r. un baiser à qn** to kiss sb back; **r. le bien pour le mal/coup pour coup** to return good for evil/blow for blow; **rends-moi trois euros** give me three euros back *or* three euros change; **elle m'a rendu deux euros de trop** she gave me back two euros too much; **r. la monnaie (sur)** to give change (out of *or* from); **elle me méprise, mais je le lui rends bien** she despises me, but the feeling's mutual

3 *(suivi d'un adj) (faire devenir)* to make; **r. qch public** to make sth public; **la nouvelle n'a pas encore été rendue publique** the news hasn't been made public *or* been released yet; **r. qn aveugle** to make sb (go) blind, to blind sb; *Fig* to blind sb; **r. qn célèbre** to make sb famous; **r. qn fou** to drive *or* to make sb mad; **r. qn heureux/idiot/malade** to make sb happy/stupid/ill; **rien que de penser aux examens, ça me rend malade** just thinking about the exams makes me (feel) ill; **r. qn responsable** to make *or* to hold sb responsible; **r. qn sourd** to make sb (go) deaf; **l'absence de ponctuation rend le texte incompréhensible** the lack of punctuation makes the text incomprehensible; **ils veulent r. la Loire navigable** they want to make the river Loire navigable

4 *(faire recouvrer)* **r. l'ouïe/la santé/la vue à qn** to restore sb's hearing/health/sight, to give sb back his/her hearing/health/sight; **tu m'as rendu l'espoir** you've given me new hope; **r. son honneur à qn** to restore sb's honour; **r. sa forme à un chapeau** to pull a hat back into shape; **Brillax rend à vos sols l'éclat du neuf!** Brillax puts the shine back into your floors!

5 *(exprimer ▸ personnalité)* to portray, to capture; *(▸ nuances, pensée)* to convey, *Sout* to render; **la traduction rend bien sa pensée** the translation successfully conveys *or Sout* renders his/her thought; **voyons comment il a rendu cette scène à l'écran** *(metteur en scène)* let's see how he transferred this scene to the screen; **l'enregistrement ne rend pas la qualité de sa voix** the recording doesn't do justice to the quality of his/her voice

6 *(produire)* **r. un son métallique/cristallin** to sound metallic/like glass; **ici le mur rend un son creux** the wall sounds hollow here; **ça ne rend rien** *ou* **pas grand-chose** *(décor, couleurs)* it doesn't look much; **les photos n'ont pas rendu grand-chose** the pictures didn't come out very well; **mes recherches n'ont encore rien rendu** my research hasn't come up with anything yet *or* hasn't produced any results yet

7 *Culin* to give out; **quand les champignons ont rendu toute leur eau** when the mushrooms have released all their juices

8 *(vomir ▸ repas)* to vomit, to bring up; **il a tout rendu** he's brought everything back up

9 *Sport* **r. du poids** to have a weight handicap; **r. 150 mètres** to have a 150 metres handicap; **r. cinq kilos** to give *or* to carry five kilos

10 *(prononcer ▸ jugement, arrêt)* to pronounce; *(▸ verdict)* to deliver, to return; **r. une sentence** to pass *or* to pronounce sentence

11 *Agr & Hort (produire)* to yield, to have a yield of; **cette terre rend peu de blé à l'hectare** ≃ this land doesn't yield much wheat per acre; **ce blé rend beaucoup de farine** this wheat has a high flour yield

VI 1 *Agr & Hort* to be productive; **les vignes ont bien rendu** the vineyards have given a good yield *or* have produced well; **cette terre ne rend pas** this land is unproductive *or* yields no return; **le verger rend peu** the orchard is not very productive

2 *(ressortir)* to be effective; **ce tapis rend très bien/ne rend pas très bien avec les rideaux** this carpet looks really good/doesn't look much with the curtains

3 *(vomir)* to vomit, to be sick; **j'ai envie de r.** I want to be *or* I feel sick

VPR se rendre 1 *(criminel)* to give oneself up, to surrender; *(ville)* to surrender; **se r. à la police** to give oneself up to the police; **rendez-vous!** give yourself up!, surrender!; *Fig* **il a fini par se r.** he finally gave in

2 *(suivi d'un adj) (devenir)* to make oneself; **elle sait se r. indispensable** she knows how to make herself indispensable; **rends-toi utile!** make yourself useful!; **tu vas te r. malade** you'll make yourself ill; **ne te rends pas malade pour ça!** it's not worth making yourself ill about *or* over it!

3 *(aller)* to go; **je me rends à l'école à pied/à vélo/en voiture** I walk/ride (my bike)/drive to school, I go to school on foot/by bike/by car; **il s'y rend en train** he goes *or* gets *or* travels there by train; **je me rendais chez elle quand je l'ai vue** I was going to *or* I was on my way to her place when I saw her; **les pompiers se sont rendus sur les lieux** the fire brigade went to *or* arrived on the scene

4 se r. à *(accepter)* to yield to; **se r. à l'avis de ses supérieurs** to bow to the opinion of one's superiors; **se r. à la raison** to give in to reason; **il ne s'est pas rendu à leurs raisons** he didn't give in to their arguments; **se r. à l'évidence** *(être lucide)* to face facts; *(reconnaître les faits)* to acknowledge *or* to recognize the facts; **se r. aux prières de qn** to give way *or* to yield to sb's entreaties

rendu, -e [rɑ̃dy] **ADJ 1** *(arrivé)* **nous/vous voilà rendus** here we/you are; **tu seras plus vite r. par le train** you'll get there quicker by train; *Can* **r. à la porte, il a changé d'idée** having got as far as the door, he changed his mind

2 *(harassé)* exhausted, worn *or* tired out

3 *Com* **r. droits acquittés/non acquittés** delivery duty paid/unpaid; **r. à domicile** delivered to your door; **r. franco à bord** (delivered) free on board, f.o.b.; **r. frontière** delivered at frontier

4 *Can (devenu)* **et la voilà rendue maîtresse d'école!** and now she's become a schoolteacher!

NM 1 *Com* returned article, return; **faire un r.** to return *or* exchange an article **2** *Beaux-Arts & Ordinat* rendering

rêne [rɛn] **NF** *(courroie)* rein; *Fig* **lâcher les rênes** to let go; *Fig* **prendre les rênes** to take over the reins; *Fig* **c'est lui qui tient les rênes** he's the one who's really in charge

renégat, -e [rənega, -at] **NM,F** renegade

renégociation [rənegɔsjasjɔ̃] **NF** *(d'un contrat)* renegotiation; *(d'une dette)* rescheduling

renégocier [9] [rənegɔsje] **VT** *(contrat)* to renegotiate; *(dette)* to reschedule

reneiger [23] [rəneʒe] **V IMPERSONNEL** to snow again; **il reneige** it's snowing again

renfermé, -e [rɑ̃fɛrme] **ADJ** uncommunicative, withdrawn, silent; **elle est du genre r.** she's the uncommunicative type

NM une odeur de r. a stale *or* musty smell; **ça sent le r. ici** it smells musty in here

renfermer [3] [rɑ̃fɛrme] **VT 1** *(contenir)* to hold, to contain; **son histoire renferme une part de vérité** there's some truth in what he/she says **2** *(enfermer de nouveau)* to shut up again **3** *Vieilli (ranger)* to put away

VPR se renfermer to withdraw (into oneself)

renfiler [3] [rɑ̃file] **VT** *(aiguille)* to rethread, to thread again; *(perles)* to restring; *(vêtement)* to slip back into

renflé, -e [rɑ̃fle] ADJ *(colonne, forme)* bulging, bulbous

renflement [rɑ̃fləmɑ̃] NM *(d'une colonne, d'un vase)* bulge; **la poche forme un r. à hauteur de la hanche** the pocket bulges (out) at the hip

renfler [3] [rɑ̃fle] VT **le pigeon renfla ses plumes** the pigeon fluffed up its feathers

VPR **se renfler** to bulge out

renflouage [rɑ̃fluaʒ], **renflouement** [rɑ̃flumɑ̃] NM **1** *Naut (d'un bateau échoué)* refloating, floating off; *(d'un bateau coulé)* raising **2** *Écon (d'une entreprise, d'un projet)* bailing out, refloating

renflouer [6] [rɑ̃flue] VT **1** *Naut (bateau échoué)* to refloat, to float off; *(bateau coulé)* to raise **2** *Écon (entreprise, projet)* to bail out; **r. les caisses de l'État** to swell the government's coffers; **ça va r. nos finances** that will bail us out

renfoncement [rɑ̃fɔ̃smɑ̃] NM **1** *(dans un mur)* recess, hollow; **r. d'une porte** doorway **2** *Typ* indentation

renfoncer [16] [rɑ̃fɔ̃se] VT **1** *(bouchon)* to push further in; *(clou)* to knock further in; *(chapeau)* to pull down; *Fig* **je voulais lui r. ses paroles dans la gorge** I wanted to shove the words down his/her throat **2** *Typ* to indent

renforcement [rɑ̃fɔrsəmɑ̃] NM **1** *(consolidation ▸ d'une poutre, d'un mur)* reinforcement; *(▸ des pouvoirs, d'une équipe)* strengthening **2** *Phot* intensification

renforcer [16] [rɑ̃fɔrse] VT **1** *Constr & Couture* to reinforce

2 *(augmenter ▸ effectif, service d'ordre)* to reinforce, to strengthen; **le candidat choisi viendra r. notre équipe de chercheurs** the ideal candidate will join our team of researchers; **le dispositif de sécurité a été renforcé** security has been increased *or* tightened up

3 *(affermir ▸ conviction)* to reinforce, to strengthen, to intensify; *(▸ craintes)* to heighten; *(▸ impression)* to strengthen, to heighten; **sa méchanceté a renforcé ma détermination** his/her nastiness made me all the more *or* even more determined; **il m'a renforcé dans mon opinion** he confirmed me in my belief

4 *(mettre en relief)* to set off, to enhance; **utilisez un adverbe pour r. l'adjectif** use an adverb to reinforce *or* underline the adjective

5 *Scol* **suivre des cours d'anglais renforcé** to do extra English

VPR **se renforcer** *(devenir plus fort ▸ pouvoir)* to be consolidated, to increase; *(▸ conviction, sentiment)* to grow stronger; *(▸ tendance)* to increase; **sa popularité s'est beaucoup renforcée** his/her popularity has greatly increased *or* has grown considerably

renfort [rɑ̃fɔr] NM **1** *(aide)* reinforcement; **demander du r.** *(gén)* to ask for help; *(sujet: policiers, pompiers)* to ask for backup; **nous avons reçu le r. de bénévoles** we were aided by volunteers, we had backup from a team of volunteers; *Hum* **j'ai besoin de r. pour faire la cuisine** I need some extra pairs of hands to help me do the cooking; **il amène toujours sa sœur en r.** he always brings his sister along to back him up; **des troupes furent envoyées en r.** troops were sent in as reinforcements **2** *(pièce de tissu)* lining; **collant avec renforts aux talons/à l'entrejambe** tights with reinforced heels/gusset **3** *Tech* reinforcement

• **renforts** NMPL *Mil (soldats)* reinforcements; *(matériel)* (fresh) supplies

• **à grand renfort de** PRÉP with a lot of, with much/many; **ils ont fait sortir tout le monde à grand r. de hurlements** they got everyone out with much yelling (and shouting); **il s'expliquait à grand r. de gestes** he expressed himself with the help of a great many gestures; **son nouveau film, dont la sortie a été annoncée à grand r. de publicité** his/her much publicized new movie *or Br* film

• **de renfort** ADJ reinforcement *(avant n)*

renfrogné, -e [rɑ̃frɔɲe] ADJ *(air, visage)* sullen, dour; *(personne)* sulky, dour; **il est toujours r.** he's always sulking

renfrogner [3] [rɑ̃frɔɲe] **se renfrogner** VPR to scowl, to frown; **elle se renfrognait quand on parlait de lui** she became sullen whenever his name was mentioned

rengagé [rɑ̃gaʒe] NM *Mil* re-enlisted man

rengagement [rɑ̃gaʒmɑ̃] NM *(d'un soldat)* re-enlistment; *(d'un combat)* re-engagement; *(d'argent)* reinvestment; **la banque a annoncé son r.** *(employé)* the bank announced it was taking him/her on again

rengager [17] [rɑ̃gaʒe] VT *(combat)* to re-engage; *(conversation)* to start again, to take up again; *(employé)* to re-engage, to take on again; *(argent)* to reinvest, to plough back

VI *Mil* to re-enlist

VPR **se rengager** *Mil* to re-enlist, to join up again

rengaine [rɑ̃gɛn] NF **1** *(refrain)* (old) tune, (old) song **2** *Fig* **avec eux, c'est toujours la même r.** they never change their tune, with them it's always the same (old) story

rengainer [4] [rɑ̃gene] VT **1** *(arme)* **r. un revolver** to put a revolver back in its holster; **r. une épée** to put a sword back in its sheath **2** *Fig* to hold back, to contain; **tu peux r. tes compliments** you can keep your compliments to yourself

rengorger [17] [rɑ̃gɔrʒe] **se rengorger** VPR **1** *(volatile)* to puff out its throat **2** *(personne)* to puff oneself up; **il se rengorge quand on lui parle de sa pièce** he puffs up with pride when you talk to him about his play

reniement [rənimɑ̃] NM *(d'une promesse)* breaking; *(de sa famille, de ses racines)* disowning, *Sout* repudiation; *(de sa religion, d'un principe, de ses convictions)* renouncing, abandonment; *Rel (du Christ)* denial

renier [9] [rənje] VT *(promesse)* to break; *(famille, racines)* to disown, *Sout* to repudiate; *(religion, principe, convictions)* to renounce, to abandon; **il a renié ses engagements** he's reneged on *or* broken his promises; **Pierre a renié Jésus par trois fois** Peter denied Christ three times

VPR **se renier** to retract

reniflard [rəniflar] NM *Aut* breather

reniflement [rəniflәmɑ̃] NM *(action ▸ en pleurant)* sniffing, sniffling; *(▸ à cause d'un rhume)* snuffling; *(bruit)* sniff, sniffle, snuffle; **reniflements** snivelling

renifler [3] [rənifle] VT **1** *(humer)* to sniff at; **r. le bouquet d'un vin** to smell a wine's bouquet; **il renifla la bonne odeur qui s'échappait de la cuisine** his nose picked up the lovely smell coming from the kitchen **2** *(aspirer par le nez ▸ tabac, cocaïne)* to sniff **3** *Fam Fig* to sniff out; **r. une histoire louche** to smell a rat; **il sait r. une bonne affaire** he's got a (good) nose for a bargain, he's good at sniffing out bargains

VI **1** *(en pleurant)* to sniffle; *(à cause d'un rhume)* to snuffle, to sniff; **arrête de r.** stop sniffling *or* snuffling **2** *Fam (sentir mauvais)* to stink, *Br* to pong, to niff

renifleur, -euse [rəniflœr, -øz] ADJ **avion r.** sniffer plane

NM,F *Fam* sniffer, sniffler, snuffler

renipper [3] [rənipe] *Can* VT *(rénover ▸ maison, pièce)* to do up, to renovate

VPR **se renipper** to smarten oneself up, to smarten up one's appearance

renne [rɛn] NM *Zool* reindeer

renom [rənɔ̃] NM **1** *(notoriété)* fame, renown; **il doit son r. à son invention** he became famous thanks to his invention **2** *Littéraire (réputation)* reputation; **votre attitude est préjudiciable à votre r.** your attitude is detrimental to your reputation

• **de renom, en renom** ADJ famous, renowned; **un musicien de (grand) r.** a musician of high renown *or* repute; **une école en r.** a famous *or* renowned school

renommé, -e [rənɔme] ADJ *(célèbre)* famous, renowned, celebrated; **elle est renommée pour ses omelettes** she's famous for her omelettes

• **renommée** NF *(notoriété)* fame, repute; **un musicien de renommée internationale** a world-famous musician, a musician of international repute; **ce vin est digne de sa renommée** this wine is worthy of its reputation

renommer [3] [rənɔme] VT **1** *(à un poste)* to re-appoint, to renominate **2** *Ordinat* to rename

renonce [rənɔ̃s] NF *Cartes* renounce, inability to follow suit; **je fais une r.** I can't follow suit; **avoir une r. à cœur** to be short of hearts; **faire une fausse r.** to revoke

renoncement [rənɔ̃smɑ̃] NM renunciation; **vivre dans le r.** to live a life of renunciation *or* abnegation

renoncer [16] [rənɔ̃se] VI *Cartes* to renounce, to fail to follow suit; *(faire une fausse renonce)* to revoke

VT **1** *Belg (bail)* to cancel **2** *Arch (renier ▸ personne)* to disown

USAGE ABSOLU **je renonce!** I give up!; **je ne renoncerai jamais** I'll never give up

• **renoncer à** VT IND *(gén)* to renounce, to give up; *(projet, métier)* to give up, to abandon; *(habitude)* to give up; *(pouvoir, couronne)* to relinquish; *(droit)* to waive, to relinquish; *(vacances)* to sacrifice, to forgo; **il a renoncé au trône** he renounced *or* gave up the throne; **elle ne veut à aucun prix r. à son indépendance** nothing would make her give up her independence; **r. au tabac** to give up smoking; *Rel* **r. au monde** to renounce the world; **r. à faire qch** *(en cours de route)* to give up doing sth; *(avant d'avoir commencé)* to give up the idea of doing sth; **je renonce à la convaincre** I've given up trying to convince her

renonciation [rənɔ̃sjasjɔ̃] NF **1** *(à la couronne, à sa carrière, à la violence)* renunciation (**à** of); *(à un projet)* abandonment (**à** of); *(à un droit)* waiver, waiving (**à** of) **2** *Jur* release

renonciatrice [rənɔ̃sjatris] *voir* **renonciateur**

renoncule [rənɔ̃kyl] NF *Bot* buttercup, *Spéc* ranunculus; **fausse r.** lesser celandine

renouée [rənwe] NF *Bot* knotgrass

renouer [6] [rənwe] VT **1** *(rattacher ▸ ruban, lacet)* to retie, to tie (up) again; *(cravate)* to reknot, to tie again **2** *(reprendre ▸ discussion, relations)* to resume, to renew; **r. une liaison** to rekindle *or* to revive an old affair

VI to get back together again; **j'ai renoué avec mes vieux amis** I've taken up with my old friends again; **r. avec la tradition/l'usage** to revive traditions/customs; **r. avec le succès** to enjoy renewed success

renouveau, -x [rənuvo] NM **1** *(renaissance)* revival; **connaître un r.** to undergo a revival **2** *(recrudescence)* **un r. de succès** renewed success **3** *Littéraire (retour du printemps)* springtime, springtide

renouvelable [rənuvlabl] ADJ **1** *(offre)* repeatable; *(permis, bail, abonnement)* renewable; **l'offre ne sera pas r.** it's an unrepeatable offer; **l'abonnement n'est pas r. par téléphone** the subscription cannot be renewed by phone; *Écol* **énergie r.** renewable energy; **non r.** non-renewable **2** *Admin & Pol* **le comité est r. tous les ans** the committee must *Br* stand *or Am* run for office each year; **mon mandat est r.** I am eligible to *Br* stand *or Am* run (for office) again

renouveler [24] [rənuvle] VT **1** *(prolonger ▸ abonnement, passeport, contrat)* to renew; **le crédit a été renouvelé pour six mois** the credit arrangement was extended for a further six months

2 *(répéter)* to renew, to repeat; **r. un exploit/une tentative** to repeat a feat/an attempt; **r. une promesse/une plainte** to repeat a promise/a complaint; *Rel* **r. ses vœux** to renew one's vows; **je vous renouvelle mes félicitations** I congratulate you once more *or* again; **il faudra r. votre candidature** you'll have to apply again *or* to reapply; **avec une ardeur renouvelée** with renewed vigour; **j'ai préféré ne pas r. l'expérience** I chose not to repeat the experience

3 *(changer)* to renew, to change; *(▸ commande, achat)* to repeat; **r. l'eau d'un aquarium** to change the water in an aquarium; **r. l'air d'une pièce** to let some fresh air into a room; **elle a renouvelé son stock de confitures** she renewed *or* replenished her stock of jams; **r. sa garde-robe** to get *or* to buy some new clothes; **il nous revient avec un répertoire entièrement renouvelé** he's back with an entirely new repertoire; **elle a renouvelé le genre policier** she gave the detective story a new lease of life; **une découverte qui renouvelle totalement notre conception du temps** a discovery which radically alters our conception of time

4 *(réélire ▸ groupe, assemblée)* to re-elect

VPR **se renouveler 1** *(se reformer ▸ épiderme)* to be renewed

2 *(se reproduire)* to recur, to occur again and again; **les appels anonymes se sont renouvelés pendant un mois** the anonymous phone calls persisted for a month; **je te promets que cela ne se renouvellera pas** I promise you it won't happen again
3 *(changer de style)* to change one's style; **c'est un bon acteur mais il ne se renouvelle pas assez** he's a good actor but he doesn't vary his roles enough
4 *(groupe, assemblée)* to be re-elected *or* replaced

renouvellement [rənuvɛlmɑ̃] **NM 1** *(reconduction* ▸ *d'un abonnement, d'un passeport, d'un contrat)* renewal
2 *(répétition)* repetition, recurrence
3 *(changement)* **procéder au r. d'une équipe** to change the line-up of a team; **procéder au r. de sa garde-robe** to get *or* to buy some new clothes; **la marée assure le r. de l'eau dans les viviers** the water in the tanks is changed by the action of the tide; **ce produit active le r. cellulaire** this product encourages the cells to renew themselves; **dans la mode actuelle, il n'y a aucun r.** there are no new ideas in (the world of) fashion today
4 *Rel* confirmation; **faire son r.** to be confirmed
5 *Com (de marchandises)* restocking, reordering; *(de matériel)* replacement; **r. du personnel** staff turnover; **r. de stock** restocking
6 *Fin (d'un crédit)* extension

renouvellerai *etc voir* **renouveler**

rénovateur, -trice [renɔvatœr, -tris] **ADJ** reformist, reforming
NM,F reformer; **les grands rénovateurs de la science** the people who revolutionized *or* radically transformed science
NM *(pour nettoyer)* restorer

rénovation [renɔvasjɔ̃] **NF 1** *(d'un meuble, d'un immeuble)* renovation; *(d'un quartier)* redevelopment, renovation; **la maison est en r.** the house is being done up *or* is having a complete facelift; **r. urbaine** urban renewal **2** *Fig (rajeunissement* ▸ *d'une méthode)* updating; *(*▸ *d'une institution)* updating, reform

rénovatrice [renɔvatris] *voir* **rénovateur**

rénover [3] [renɔve] **VT 1** *(remettre à neuf* ▸ *meuble)* to restore, to renovate; *(*▸ *immeuble)* to renovate, to do up; *(*▸ *quartier)* to redevelop, to renovate; *(*▸ *salle de bains)* to modernize; **toute la façade ouest a été rénovée** the whole of the west front has been done up *or* has been given a facelift **2** *(rajeunir* ▸ *méthode)* to update; **r. les institutions politiques** to reform political institutions

renseignement [rɑ̃sɛɲəmɑ̃] **NM 1** *(information)* piece of information, information *(UNCOUNT)*; **un précieux r.** an invaluable piece of information, some invaluable information; **de précieux renseignements** (some) invaluable information; **pour tout r., veuillez appeler ce numéro** for information *or* if you have any queries, please call this number; **demander un r.** *ou* **des renseignements à qn** to ask sb for information; **prendre des renseignements sur qn/qch** to make enquiries about sb/sth; **renseignements pris, elle était la seule héritière** after making some enquiries it turned out (that) she was the sole heir; **tu n'obtiendras aucun r.** you won't get any information; *aussi Ironique* **merci pour le r.** thanks for letting me know; **aller aux renseignements** to go and (see what one can) find out **2** *Fam (surveillance)* **être/travailler dans le r.** to be/to work in intelligence❐
• **renseignements NMPL 1** *Admin (service)* enquiries (department); *(réception)* information *or* enquiries (desk); *Tél* **appeler les renseignements** to phone *Br* directory enquiries *or Am* information **2** *(espionnage)* intelligence; **agent/services de renseignements** intelligence agent/services; **elle travaille pour les services de renseignements** she works in intelligence; **les Renseignements généraux** = the secret intelligence branch of the French police force, *Br* ≃ the Special Branch, *Am* ≃ the FBI

renseigner [4] [rɑ̃seɲe] **VT 1** *(mettre au courant* ▸ *étranger, journaliste)* to give information to, to inform; *(*▸ *automobiliste)* to give directions to; **elle vous renseignera sur les prix** she'll tell you the prices, she'll give you more information about the prices; **pardon, Monsieur, pouvez-vous me r.?** excuse me, sir, could you help me, please?; **r. qn sur qn/qch** to tell sb about sb/sth; **bien/mal renseigné** well-informed/misinformed; **on vous a mal renseigné** you have been misinformed; **l'office du tourisme nous a très bien/très mal renseignés** the tourist board gave us excellent information/totally the wrong information
2 *(donner des indices à)* **ça ne me renseigne pas sur ses motivations** that doesn't tell me anything about his/her motives; **seule sa biographie peut nous r. sur son passé militaire** only his/her biography can tell us something of *or* about his/her military career; *Ironique* **nous voilà bien renseignés!** that doesn't get us very far!, that doesn't give us much to go on!
3 *Belg (indiquer)* **pouvez-vous me r. le chemin?** could you show me the way?; **pouvez-vous me r. un livre?** *(conseiller)* could you recommend me a book?
VPR se renseigner to make enquiries; **se r. sur qn/qch** to find out about sb/sth; **il aurait fallu se r. sur son compte** you should have made (some) enquiries about him/her; **essaie de te r. pour savoir combien coûterait un billet** try to find out how much a ticket would cost; **renseignez-vous auprès de votre agence de voyages** ask your travel agent for further information

rentabilisation [rɑ̃tabilizasjɔ̃] **NF la r. de l'affaire prendra peu de temps** it will not be long before the business becomes profitable *or* starts to make a profit

rentabiliser [3] [rɑ̃tabilize] **VT** *(affaire)* to make profitable; *(investissement)* to obtain a return on

rentabilité [rɑ̃tabilite] **NF** profitability, cost-effectiveness (**de** of); *(d'une affaire)* profitability; *(d'un investissement)* rate of return; *(des ventes)* return (**de** on); **taux de r.** rate of profit; **r. nette d'exploitation** net operating profit

rentable [rɑ̃tabl] **ADJ** profitable, cost-effective; **l'opération s'est avérée r.** the operation turned out to be profitable *or* has paid off; **si je les vends moins cher, ce n'est plus r.** if I sell them any cheaper, I no longer make a profit *or* any money; **c'est plus r. d'acheter que de louer en ce moment** you're better off buying than renting at the moment

rente [rɑ̃t] **NF 1** *(revenu)* private income; **avoir des rentes** to have a private income, to have independent means; **vivre de ses rentes** to live on *or* off one's private income
2 *(pension)* pension, annuity, *Spéc* rente; **servir une r. à qn** to pay sb an allowance; **r. foncière** ground rent; **r. viagère** life annuity
3 *Écon* rent
4 *Bourse* (government) bond; **r. annuelle** annuity; **r. à paiement différé** deferred annuity; **r. de situation** guaranteed income

rentier, -ère [rɑ̃tje, -ɛr] **NM,F** person of private means; **mener une vie de r.** to live a life of ease; **petit r.** person with a small private income; **r. viager** life annuitant

rentrant, -e [rɑ̃trɑ̃, -ɑ̃t] **ADJ 1** *Aviat* **train d'atterrissage r.** retractable undercarriage **2** *Ordinat* re-entrant

rentré, -e¹ [rɑ̃tre] **ADJ 1** *(refoulé)* suppressed **2** *(creux* ▸ *joues)* hollow, sunken; *(*▸ *yeux)* sunken, deep-set
NM *Couture* turn in

rentre-dedans [rɑ̃tdədɑ̃] **NM INV** *Fam* **faire du r. à qn** to come on to sb, *Br* to chat sb up, *Am* to hit on sb

rentrée² [rɑ̃tre] **NF 1** *Scol* **r. (scolaire** *ou* **des classes)** start of the (new) academic year; **la r. des élèves/des professeurs** the day the pupils/teachers go back; **depuis la r. de Noël/Pâques** since the spring/summer term began, since the Christmas/Easter break; **la r. est fixée au 6 septembre** school starts again *or* schools reopen on 6 September; **j'irai le mardi de la r.** I'll go on the first Tuesday of the (new) term; **c'est quand, la r., chez vous?** when do you go back? *(to school, college etc)*; **on se revoit à la r.!** see you next term!, see you after the holidays!; **les vitrines de la r.** back-to-school window displays
2 *(au Parlement)* reopening (of Parliament), new (parliamentary) session; **à la prochaine r. parlementaire** at the beginning of the new parliamentary session; **faire sa r. politique** *(après les vacances)* to start the new political season *(after the summer)*; *(après une absence)* to make one's (political) comeback
3 *(saison artistique)* **la r. musicale/théâtrale** the new musical/theatrical season *(after the summer break)*; **la r. littéraire** the autumn's new books; **le disque sortira à la r.** the record will be released in the *Br* autumn *or Am* fall
4 *(retour* ▸ *des vacances d'été)* (beginning of the) *Br* autumn *or Am* fall; *(*▸ *de congé ou de week-end)* return to work; *Transp* city-bound traffic; **la r. a été dure** it was hard to get back to work after the summer *Br* holidays *or Am* vacation; **r. sociale** = return to work after the summer holidays
5 *(d'argent)* receipt; **j'attends une r. d'argent** I'm expecting some money
6 *Astron* **r. (atmosphérique)** re-entry (into the atmosphere)
7 *Cartes* pick-up
8 *Agr (des foins)* bringing *or* taking in
• **rentrées NFPL** *Fin* income, money coming in; **avoir des rentrées (d'argent) régulières** to have a regular income *or* money coming in regularly; **rentrées de caisse** cash receipts; **rentrées fiscales** tax receipts *or* revenue; *Compta* **rentrées et sorties de caisse** cash receipts and payments

> **LA RENTRÉE**
>
> The time of the year when children go back to school – in September – has considerable cultural significance in France. Coming after the long summer break, or "grandes vacances", it is the time when academic, political, social and commercial activity begins again in earnest.

RENTRER [3] [rɑ̃tre]

VI	
• to go in **1**	• to come in **1, 6**
• to fit in **1**	• to be part of **2**
• to return **4**	• to come/go home **4**
• to go back **5**	• to start again **5**
• to sink in **7**	
VT	
• to bring in **1**	• to put in **2**
• to hold back **3**	• to input **4**

VI *(aux être)* **1** *(personne* ▸ *vue de l'intérieur)* to come in; *(*▸ *vue de l'extérieur)* to go in; *(chose)* to go in; *(s'emboîter)* to go in, to fit in; **une souris essayait de r. dans le placard** a mouse was trying to get into the cupboard; **fais r. le chien** bring the dog back inside; **impossible de faire r. ce clou dans le mur** I can't get this nail to go into the wall; **la clé ne rentre pas dans la serrure** the key won't go into the keyhole; **tu n'arriveras pas à tout faire r. dans cette valise** you'll never fit everything in this case; **c'est par là que l'eau rentre** that's where the water is coming *or* getting in; **les rallonges rentrent sous la table** the leaves fit in under the table; **r. dans** *(poteau)* to crash into; *(véhicule)* to collide with; **les deux voitures sont rentrées l'une dans l'autre** the two cars crashed into each other; **je lui suis rentré dedans** *(en voiture)* I drove straight *or* right into him/her; *Fam* **il n'a pas arrêté de me r. dedans** *(verbalement)* he was constantly knocking me *or Br* having a go at me
2 *(faire partie de)* to be part of, to be included in; **la mesure en question ne rentre pas dans le cadre de la réforme** the measure under discussion is not part of the reform; **cela ne rentre pas dans mes attributions** that is not part of my duties
3 *(pour travailler)* **r. dans les affaires/la police** to go into business/join the police; **il est rentré dans la société grâce à son oncle** he got a job with the company thanks to his uncle
4 *(retourner* ▸ *gén)* to return, to come *or* to get back; *(revenir chez soi)* to come *or* to get (back) home; *(aller chez soi)* to go (back) *or* to return home; **nous rentrerons dimanche** we'll come *or* be back home on Sunday; **les enfants, rentrez!** children, get *or* come back in!; **il n'est pas encore rentré de (faire) ses commissions** he hasn't got back from shopping yet; **je ne rentrerai pas dîner** I won't be home for dinner; **je rentre chez moi pour déjeuner** *(tous les jours)* I have lunch at home; **je suis inquiète, elle n'est pas rentrée hier soir** I'm worried, she didn't come home last night; **il est rentré à cinq heures** he got in at five

o'clock; **je vous laisse, il faut que je rentre** I've got to leave you now, I must get (back) home; **en rentrant de l'école** on the way home *or* back from school; **le bateau n'est pas rentré au port** the boat hasn't come (back) in

5 *(reprendre ses occupations ▸ lycéen)* to go back to school, to start school again; *(▸ étudiant)* to go back, to start the new term; *(▸ parlementaire)* to start the new session, to return to take one's seat; *(▸ Parlement)* to reopen, to reassemble

6 *(être perçu ▸ argent)* to come in; **faire r. l'argent/les devises** to bring in money/foreign currency; **faire r. l'impôt/les cotisations** to collect taxes/dues

7 *Fam (explication, idée, connaissances)* to sink in; **ça rentre, l'informatique?** are you getting the hang of computing?; **le russe, ça rentre tout seul avec Sophie!** *(elle apprend bien)* Sophie is having no trouble picking up Russian!; *(elle enseigne bien)* Sophie makes learning Russian easy!; **je le lui ai expliqué dix fois, mais ça n'est toujours pas rentré** I've told him/her ten times but it hasn't gone *or* sunk in yet; **faire r. qch dans la tête de qn** to get sth into sb's head, to drum sth into sb; **tu ne lui feras jamais r. dans la tête que c'est impossible!** you'll never get it into his/her head *or* convince him/her that it's impossible!

8 *Sport* **r. dans la mêlée** to scrum down; *Ftbl* **faire r. le ballon dans les buts** to get the ball into the back of the net; **faire r. une bille** *(en billard)* to pot a ball

VT *(aux avoir)* **1** *(mettre à l'abri ▸ linge, moisson)* to bring in, to get in; *(▸ bétail)* to bring in, to take in; *(▸ véhicule)* to put away; *(▸ chaise)* to carry in, to take in; **il faut r. les plantes avant les grands froids** we must bring the plants in before it gets really cold; **rentre ta moto au garage** put your motorbike (away) in the garage; **r. les foins** to bring in the hay

2 *(mettre ▸ gén)* to put in; *(faire disparaître ▸ antenne)* to put down; *(▸ train d'atterrissage)* to raise, to retract; *(▸ griffes)* to draw in, to retract; **r. une clé dans une serrure** to put a key in a lock; **r. son chemisier dans sa jupe** to tuck one's blouse into one's skirt; **rentre ton ventre!** pull your stomach in!; **r. la tête dans les épaules** to hunch (up) one's shoulders; **avec la tête rentrée dans les épaules** with hunched shoulders

3 *(réprimer ▸ colère)* to hold back, to suppress; **r. ses larmes/son humiliation** to swallow one's tears/humiliation

4 *Ordinat* to input, to key in

5 *Typ* **r. une ligne** to indent a line

• **rentrer dans VT IND** *(recouvrer)* to recover; **r. dans son argent/ses dépenses** to recover one's money/expenses, to get one's money/expenses back; **r. dans ses fonds** to recoup (one's) costs; **r. dans ses droits** to recover one's rights; **r. dans la légalité** *(sujet: criminel)* to reform; *(sujet: opération, manœuvre)* to become legal

• **rentrer en VT IND r. en grâce auprès de qn** to get back into sb's good graces *or* good books; **r. en faveur auprès de qn** to regain favour with sb; **r. en possession de** to regain possession of

VPR se rentrer 1 *(emploi passif)* **les foins ne se rentrent pas avant juillet** the hay isn't brought in until July; **les rallonges se rentrent sous la table** the extension leaves fit in under the table **2** *Fam* **se r. dedans** *(se heurter)* they smashed *or* banged into one another; *(se disputer)* they laid into one another

renuméroter [3] [rənymerɔte] **VT** *Tech* to renumber, to reserialize

renversant, -e [rɑ̃vɛrsɑ̃, -ɑ̃t] **ADJ** *(nouvelle)* astounding, amazing, staggering; *(personne)* amazing, incredible; **elle est d'une bêtise renversante** she is incredibly stupid

renverse [rɑ̃vɛrs] **NF** *Naut (du vent)* change; *(du courant)* turn (of tide)

• **à la renverse ADV tomber** *ou* **partir à la r.** *(sur le dos)* to fall flat on one's back; **j'ai failli tomber à la r.** I almost fell over backwards; *Fig* **il y a de quoi tomber à la r.** it's amazing *or* staggering

renversé, -e [rɑ̃vɛrse] **ADJ 1** *(image)* reverse *(avant n)*, reversed, inverted; *(objet)* upside down, overturned **2** *(penché ▸ écriture)* backhanded, that slopes backwards; **le corps r. en arrière** with the body leaning *or* tilted back **3** *(stupéfait)* **être r.** to be staggered

NM *Suisse* milky coffee

renversement [rɑ̃vɛrsəmɑ̃] **NM 1** *(inversion ▸ d'une image)* inversion

2 *(changement)* **r. des alliances** reversal *or* switch of alliances; **ils ont attendu le r. de la marée** they waited for the tide to turn; **r. des rôles** role reversal; **r. de situation** reversal of the situation; **r. de tendance** shift *or* swing (in the opposite direction)

3 *(chute ▸ d'un régime, d'un gouvernement)* overthrow

4 *(inclinaison ▸ du buste, de la tête)* tipping *or* tilting back

5 *Mus* inversion

renverser [3] [rɑ̃vɛrse] **VT 1** *(répandre ▸ liquide)* to spill; *(faire tomber ▸ bouteille, casserole)* to spill, to knock over, to upset; *(▸ table, voiture)* to overturn; *(▸ bateau)* to capsize, to overturn; *(retourner exprès)* to turn upside down; **r. qch d'un coup de pied** to kick sth over

2 *(faire tomber ▸ personne)* to knock down; **être renversé par qn** to be knocked down *or* run over by sb; **se faire r. par une voiture** to get *or* be knocked over by a car

3 *(inverser)* to reverse; **r. l'ordre des mots** to reverse the word order; *Math* **r. une fraction** to invert a fraction; **le Suédois renversa la situation au cours du troisième set** the Swedish player managed to turn the situation round during the third set; **r. les rôles** to reverse the roles; **r. la vapeur** to reverse engines; *Fig* to change direction

4 *(détruire ▸ obstacle)* to overcome; *(▸ valeurs)* to overthrow; *(▸ régime)* to overthrow, to topple; **le président a été renversé** the President was thrown out of *or* removed from office; **r. un gouvernement** *(par la force)* to overthrow *or* to topple a government; *(par un vote)* to bring down *or* to topple a government

5 *(incliner en arrière)* to tilt *or* to tip back

6 *(stupéfier)* to amaze, to astound; **la nouvelle de leur divorce m'a renversé** I was completely taken aback *or* amazed when I heard they'd got divorced

VPR se renverser 1 *(bouteille)* to fall over; *(liquide)* to spill; *(véhicule)* to overturn; *(bateau)* to overturn, to capsize **2** *(personne)* to lean over backwards

renvoi [rɑ̃vwa] **NM 1** *(d'un colis, de marchandises ▸ gén)* return, sending back; *(▸ par avion)* flying back; *(▸ par bateau)* shipping back; **r. à l'expéditeur** *(sur enveloppe, sur colis)* return to sender

2 *Tél* **r. automatique d'appels** call forwarding

3 *Sport (d'une balle ▸ gén)* sending back; *(▸ à la main)* throwing back; *(▸ au pied)* kicking back; *(▸ au tennis)* return

4 *(congédiement ▸ d'un employé)* dismissal, *Br* sacking; *(▸ d'un élève)* expulsion; **demander le r. d'un élève/d'un employé** to ask for a pupil to be expelled/an employee to be dismissed; **au bout de trois avertissements, c'est le r. définitif** *(d'un employé)* after three warnings it's the sack; *(d'un élève)* after three warnings it's expulsion

5 *(ajournement)* postponement; **le tribunal décida le r. du procès à huitaine** the court decided to put off *or* to adjourn the trial for a week

6 *(transfert)* transfer; **ordonnance de r. aux assises** order of transfer to the High Court; **après le r. du texte en commission** after the text was sent to a committee

7 *(référence)* cross-reference; *(note au bas du texte)* footnote; **faire un r. à** to make a cross-reference to, to cross-refer to

8 *(éructation)* belch, burp; **avoir un r.** to belch, to burp

9 *Jur* amendment; **demande de r.** application for removal of action; **r. préjudiciel** preliminary ruling

10 *Tech* **levier de r.** reversing lever; **poulie de r.** return pulley

renvoyé [rɑ̃vwaje] **NM** *Jur* **r. des fins de la poursuite** acquittal

renvoyer [30] [rɑ̃vwaje] **VT 1** *(colis, formulaire, personne)* to send back; *(marchandises)* to return, to send back; *(cadeau)* to return, to give back; *(importun)* to send away; *(soldat, troupes)* to discharge; **r. qch à l'expéditeur** to return sth to sender; **on les a renvoyés chez eux** they were sent (back) home *or* discharged; **je le renvoie chez sa mère demain** I'm sending him back *or* off to his mother's tomorrow

2 *(lancer de nouveau ▸ ballon)* to send back, to return; **j'étais renvoyé de vendeur en vendeur** I was being passed *or* shunted around from one salesman to the next; **r. la balle à qn** *Sport* to throw *or* to pass the ball back to sb; *Ftbl* to kick *or* to pass the ball back to sb; *(au tennis)* to return to sb; *Fig* to answer sb tit for tat; *Fig* **savoir r. la balle** to give as good as one gets; **r. l'ascenseur à qn** to send the *Br* lift *or Am* elevator back to sb; *Fig* to return sb's favour

3 *(congédier ▸ employé)* to dismiss; *(▸ élève)* to expel; **tu vas te faire r.** *(de ton travail)* you're going to lose your job; *(de ton lycée)* you're going to get yourself expelled

4 *(différer)* to postpone, to put off; *Jur* to adjourn; **r. une affaire à huitaine** to adjourn a case for a week; **la réunion est renvoyée à mardi prochain** the meeting has been put off until *or* put back to next Tuesday

5 *(transférer ▸ affaire)* to refer; **l'affaire a été renvoyée en cour d'assises** the matter has been referred to the High Court; **r. qn en cour d'assises** to send sb before the High Court

6 *(faire se reporter)* to refer; **les numéros renvoient aux notes de fin de chapitre** the numbers refer to notes at the end of each chapter; **cet article renvoie à un autre** *(dans un dictionnaire)* this entry is cross-referred to another

7 *(réverbérer ▸ chaleur, lumière)* to reflect; *(▸ son)* to throw back, to echo; **la glace lui renvoyait son image** he/she saw his/her reflection in the mirror

VI *Can* to vomit, to throw up

VPR se renvoyer *(locution)* **on peut se r. la balle comme ça longtemps!** we could go on forever blaming each other like this!; **dans cette affaire d'évasion, les autorités françaises et suisses se renvoient la balle** in this escape business, the French and Swiss authorities are trying to make each other carry the can

réoccupation [reɔkypasjɔ̃] **NF** *(action militante)* reoccupation; *(réinstallation)* moving (back) in again; **nous envisageons la r. immédiate du bâtiment** *(pour y vivre)* we expect people to move straight back into the building

réoccuper [3] [reɔkype] **VT** *(usine, lieu public)* to reoccupy; *(habitation)* to move back into; *(emploi)* to take up again

réorganisateur, -trice [reɔrganizatœr, -tris] **ADJ** reorganizing

NM,F reorganizer

réorganisation [reɔrganizasjɔ̃] **NF** reorganization

réorganisatrice [reɔrganizatris] *voir* **réorganisateur**

réorganiser [3] [reɔrganize] **VT** to reorganize

VPR se réorganiser to reorganize oneself, to get reorganized

réorientation [reɔrjɑ̃tasjɔ̃] **NF 1** *Pol* redirecting **2** *Univ* changing to a different course

réorienter [3] [reɔrjɑ̃te] **VT 1** *Pol* to reorientate, to redirect **2** *Univ* to put onto a different course

réouverture [reuvɛrtyr] **NF 1** *(d'un magasin, d'un guichet, d'un musée, d'une route, d'un col)* reopening; **r. du cabinet médical à 14 heures** the *Br* surgery *or Am* doctor's office reopens at 2 p.m. **2** *(reprise ▸ d'un débat)* resumption; *Bourse* **à la r. des marchés ce matin** when trading resumed this morning

repaie *etc voir* **repayer**

repaire [rəpɛr] **NM 1** *(d'animaux)* den, lair **2** *(d'individus)* den, haunt; **un r. d'espions/de malfaiteurs** a den of spies/of criminals

repaître [91] [rəpɛtr] **VT** *Littéraire (nourrir)* to feed; **r. ses yeux de qch** to feast one's eyes on sth

VPR se repaître 1 *Littéraire* **se r. de** *(manger)* to feed on **2** *Fig (savourer)* **se r. de bandes dessinées** to feast on comic strips; **se r. de chimères** to indulge in vain imaginings; **se r. de sang** to wallow in blood

répandre [74] [repɑ̃dr] **VT 1** *(renverser accidentellement ▸ liquide, sel)* to spill; *(verser ▸ sable, sciure)* to spread, to sprinkle, to scatter; **r. des larmes** to shed tears; **r. le sang** to spill *or* to shed blood

2 *(propager ▸ rumeur, terreur, usage)* to spread

3 *(dégager ▸ odeur)* to give off; *(▸ lumière)* to

shed, to give out; (▸*chaleur, fumée)* to give out *or* off; **ce poêle répand une douce chaleur dans la maison** the stove spreads a gentle warmth throughout the house

4 *(dispenser* ▸ *bienfaits)* to pour out, to spread (around); **cette nouvelle répandit la tristesse dans la ville** the news cast a gloom over *or* spread gloom throughout the town; **cette nouvelle répandit le bonheur dans toute la maison** the news brought a general air of happiness to the house

VPR se répandre 1 *(eau, vin)* to spill; **les eaux se sont répandues dans toute la ville** the water spread throughout the town; *Fig* **les supporters se sont répandus sur le terrain** the fans spilled (out) *or* poured onto the field

2 *(se propager* ▸ *nouvelle, mode, coutume)* to spread, to become widespread; **l'usage de la carte de crédit s'est répandu parmi les jeunes** credit card use has become widespread among young people; **se r. comme une traînée de poudre** to spread like wildfire

3 *(se dégager* ▸ *odeur)* to spread, to be given off; **la fumée se répandit dans la carlingue** smoke spread through the cabin; **il se répandit une odeur de brûlé** the smell of burning filled the air

4 *(prodiguer)* **se r. en compliments** to be full of compliments; **se r. en excuses** to apologize profusely; **se r. en invectives contre qn** to heap abuse on sb; **se r. en louanges sur qn** to heap praise on sb; **inutile de se r. en commentaires là-dessus** no need to keep on (making comments) about it

répandu, -e [repɑ̃dy] **ADJ** widespread; **un préjugé (très) r.** a very widespread *or* widely held prejudice; **une vue (très) répandue** a commonly held *or* widely found view; **la technique n'est pas encore très répandue ici** the technique isn't widely used here yet

réparable [reparabl] **ADJ 1** *(appareil)* repairable; **j'espère que c'est r.** I hope it can be mended *or* repaired, I hope it's not beyond repair; **c'est facilement/difficilement r.** it's easy/difficult to repair **2** *(erreur, perte)* reparable; **une maladresse difficilement r.** a blunder which will be hard to correct *or* to put right

reparaître [91] [rəparɛtr] **VI 1** *(journal, revue)* to be out again, to be published again **2 = réapparaître**

réparateur, -trice [reparatœr, -tris] **ADJ un sommeil r.** restorative *or* refreshing sleep

NM,F repairer, repairman, *f* repairwoman

réparation [reparasjɔ̃] **NF 1** *(processus)* repairing, fixing, mending; *(résultat)* repair; **pendant les réparations** during (the) repairs; **les réparations de l'appartement/de la toiture** the repairs to the flat/the roof; **toutes les réparations sont à la charge du locataire** the tenant is liable for all repair work *or* all repairs; **atelier/service de r.** repair shop/department

2 *(compensation)* redress, compensation; **en r. des dégâts occasionnés** in compensation for *or* to make up for the damage caused; **en r. d'un tort** to make up for *or Sout* in atonement for a wrong; *Littéraire* **demander/obtenir r.** to demand/to obtain redress; **demander/obtenir r. par les armes** to demand/to obtain satisfaction by a duel

3 *Jur* damages, compensation; **r. civile** compensation; **r. légale** legal redress

4 *(correction* ▸ *d'une négligence)* correction; (▸ *d'une omission)* rectification

• **réparations NFPL** *Hist* **les réparations** (war) reparations

• **de réparation ADJ** *Sport* penalty *(avant n)*; **surface de r.** penalty area; **point de r.** penalty spot; **coup de pied de r.** penalty (kick)

• **en réparation ADJ** under repair, being repaired

réparatrice [reparatris] *voir* **réparateur**

réparer [3] [repare] **VT 1** *(appareil, chaussure)* to repair, to mend; *(maison)* to repair; *(défaut de construction)* to repair, to make good; *(meuble, porcelaine)* to restore; **faire r. qch** to get sth repaired *or* put right; **donner ses chaussures à r.** to take one's shoes to the mender's

2 *(compenser* ▸ *gén)* to make up for, to compensate for; (▸ *pertes)* to repair, to make good; **il est encore temps de r. le mal qui a été fait** there's still time to make up for *or* to undo the harm that's been done; **r. les dégâts** to repair the damage; *Fig* to pick up the pieces

3 *(corriger* ▸ *omission)* to rectify, to repair; (▸ *négligence, erreur)* to correct, to rectify

4 *(santé, forces)* to restore

USAGE ABSOLU aujourd'hui, les gens ne réparent plus, ils jettent people today don't mend things, they just throw them away

VPR se réparer to mend; **ça ne se répare pas** it can't be mended

reparler [3] [rəparle] **VT** *(langue)* to speak again; **ce voyage m'a donné l'occasion de r. arabe** this trip gave me the opportunity to speak Arabic again

VI to speak again; **il a reparlé de son roman** he talked about his novel again; **retenez bien son nom, c'est un chanteur dont on reparlera** remember this singer's name, you'll be hearing more of him; **je laisse là les Incas, nous allons en r.** I won't say any more about the Incas now, we'll come back to them later; **il n'en a plus reparlé** he never mentioned it again; **r. à qn (de qch)** to speak to sb (about sth) again; **elle ne lui a pas reparlé depuis** she hasn't spoken (another word) to him/her since; **si je vous surprends à r. ensemble...** if I catch you two talking again...

VPR se reparler *(se réconcilier)* to be back on speaking terms; **nous ne nous sommes pas reparlé depuis** we haven't spoken to one another since

repars *etc voir* **repartir**

repartie [rəparti], **répartie** [reparti] **NF** *(réplique)* retort, repartee; **avoir de la r., avoir l'esprit de r., avoir la r. prompte** to have a good sense of repartee

repartir[1] **[43]** [rəpartir] **VT** *aux avoir Littéraire (répliquer)* to retort, to reply, to rejoin; **on me repartit que le maître serait bientôt de retour** I received the reply that the master would soon be back

> Do not confuse with **répartir**.

repartir[2] **[43]** [rəpartir] **VI** *(aux être)* **1** *(se remettre en chemin)* to start *or* to set off again; *(se remettre à fonctionner* ▸ *machine)* to start (up) again; **quand repars-tu?** when are you off *or* leaving again?; **je repars pour Paris** I'm off to Paris again; **l'économie est bien repartie** the economy has picked up again; **votre carrière semble être bien repartie** your career seems to have taken off well again; **c'est reparti, encore une hausse de l'électricité!** here we go again, another rise in the price of electricity!; **r. à l'assaut** *ou* **à l'attaque** *Mil* to mount a fresh assault; *Fig* to try again; **r. à zéro** to start again from scratch, to go back to square one; **r. du bon pied** to make a fresh start; **il est reparti d'un éclat de rire** he burst out laughing again **2** *Hort* to start growing *or* to sprout again

> Do not confuse with **répartir**.

répartir [32] [repartir] **VT 1** *(distribuer* ▸ *encouragements, sanctions)* to give; (▸ *héritage, travail)* to share out, to divide up (**entre** among); (▸ *tâches, responsabilités)* to allocate, to apportion; (▸ *frais, risques)* to share; (▸ *soldats, policiers)* to deploy, to spread out; (▸ *poids, chaleur, ventilation)* to distribute; **les bénéfices seront répartis entre les actionnaires** profits will be shared out *or* distributed among the shareholders; **le tout, c'est de bien r. les livres dans les cartons** the important thing is for the books to be evenly *or* properly distributed in the boxes; **répartissez les enfants en trois groupes** get *or* split up the children into three groups

2 *(étaler* ▸ *confiture, cirage)* to spread

3 *(dans le temps)* **r. des remboursements** to pay back in instalments; **r. des paiements** to spread out the payments

4 *Ordinat* **être réparti** to be distributed *(over a network)*

VPR se répartir 1 *(se diviser)* to split, to divide (up); **répartissez-vous en deux équipes** get yourselves *or* split into two teams; **les dépenses se répartissent en trois catégories** expenditure falls under three headings **2** *(partager)* **se r. le travail/les responsabilités** to share out the work/the responsibility

> Do not confuse with **repartir**.

répartiteur, -trice [repartitœr, -tris] **NM,F 1** *(personne)* distributor **2** *Aut* proportioner

répartition [repartisjɔ̃] **NF 1** *(partage* ▸ *de l'impôt, des bénéfices)* distribution; (▸ *d'un butin)* sharing out, dividing up; (▸ *d'allocations, de prestations)* allotment, sharing out; *Bourse (de titres)* allotment, allocation; **comment se fera la r. des frais?** how will the expenses be shared out?; **comment se fera la r. des tâches?** how will the tasks be shared out *or* allocated?; **la r. des portefeuilles ministériels** the distribution of ministerial posts; **la r. des richesses est très inégale** the distribution of wealth is very unequal; *Bourse* **première et unique r.** first and final dividend; *Bourse* **dernière r.** final dividend; **r. des actifs** asset allocation; **r. des risques** risk spreading; *Pol* **r. des votes** voting pattern

2 *(agencement* ▸ *dans un appartement)* layout

3 *(étalement* ▸ *dans l'espace)* distribution; (▸ *dans le temps)* spreading

4 *Écon* assessment

répartitrice [repartitris] *voir* **répartiteur**

reparu, -e [rəpary] **PP** *voir* **reparaître**

repas [rəpa] **NM 1** *(gén)* meal; *(d'un nourrisson, d'un animal) Br* feed, *Am* feeding; **faire un bon r.** to have a square *or* good meal; **faire quatre r. par jour** to have four meals a day, to eat four times a day; **prendre ses r. à la cantine** *(de l'école)* to have school lunches *or Br* dinners; *(de l'usine)* to eat in the (works) canteen; **à l'heure** *ou* **aux heures des r.** at mealtimes; **r. d'affaires** business lunch; **r. à la carte** à la carte meal; **r. chaud** hot meal; **r. livrés à domicile** meals on wheels; **r. de midi** lunch, *Br* midday *or Am* noon meal; **r. de noces** wedding meal; **r. du soir** dinner, evening meal **2** *(comme adj; avec ou sans trait d'union)* **plateau-r.** lunch *or* dinner tray; **ticket-r.** *Br* luncheon voucher, *Am* meal ticket

repassage [rəpasaʒ] **NM 1** *(du linge)* ironing; **faire du r.** to do some ironing **2** *(aiguisage* ▸ *gén)* sharpening; (▸ *avec une pierre)* whetting

repasser [3] [rəpase] **VI 1** *(passer à nouveau dans un lieu)* to go (back) again; **elle repassera** she'll drop by again; **je suis repassé la voir à l'hôpital** I went to see her in the hospital again; **je ne suis jamais plus repassé dans cette rue** I never again went down *or* visited that street; **si tu repasses à Berlin, fais-moi signe** if you're in *or* passing through Berlin again, let me know; **r. par le même chemin** to go back the way one came; **faire r. le fromage** to pass the cheese round again; **r. sur un dessin** to go over a drawing again, to go back over a drawing; **j'ai horreur qu'on repasse derrière moi** I hate to have people go over what I've done; **la livre est repassé au-dessous des deux dollars** the pound has fallen *or* dropped below two dollars again; *Fam* **il peut toujours r.** he hasn't a hope, he's got another think coming **2** *Cin & TV* to be on *or* to be shown again

VT 1 *(défriper)* to iron; **r. les plis** to iron out the creases

2 *(aiguiser* ▸ *gén)* to sharpen; (▸ *avec une pierre)* to whet

3 *(réviser) Scol* **r. ses leçons/le programme de physique** to go over one's homework/the physics course; *Compta* **r. des comptes** to re-examine a set of accounts

4 *Fam (donner)* **elle m'a repassé sa tunique** she let me have her smock

5 *(traverser à nouveau)* **r. un fleuve** to go back across a river, to cross a river again

6 *(subir à nouveau)* **r. un examen** to take an exam again, *Br* to resit an exam; **je dois r. l'allemand/le permis demain** I have to retake German/my driving test tomorrow; **r. une échographie** to go for another ultrasound scan

7 *(à nouveau)* to pass again; **repasse-moi la confiture** pass me (over) the jam again; **voulez-vous r. la salade?** would you hand *or* pass the salad round again?; **repasse-moi mon mouchoir** hand me back my handkerchief

8 *(remettre)* **r. une couche de vernis** to put on another coat of varnish; **r. un manteau** *(le réessayer)* to try a coat on again; **r. un poisson sur le gril** to put a fish back on the grill, to give a fish a bit more time on the grill; **repasse-moi la diapo 3** show me slide 3 again

9 *(au téléphone)* **je te repasse Paul** I'll put Paul on again, I'll hand you back to Paul; **repassez-moi le standard** put me through to the switchboard again

VPR se repasser to iron; **le voile ne se repasse pas** *(ne doit pas être repassé)* the veil mustn't be ironed; *(n'a pas besoin de repassage)* the veil doesn't need ironing

repasseur, -euse [rəpasœr, -øz] **NM,F 1** *(de linge)* ironer **2** *(rémouleur)* knife-grinder, knife-sharpener

• **repasseuse NF** *(machine)* ironing machine

repayer **[11]** [rəpeje] **VT** *(payer à nouveau)* to pay again; *(payer en plus)* to pay more for; **je lui ai repayé un café** I bought him/her another coffee; **si l'on veut visiter la maison des reptiles, il faut r.** if you wish to visit the reptile house, you have to pay extra

repêchage [rəpɛʃaʒ] **NM 1** *(d'un objet)* fishing out; *(d'un corps)* recovery **2** *Univ (d'un candidat)* letting through; **épreuve de r.** resit **3** *Sport* repechage

repêcher **[4]** [rəpeʃe] **VT 1** *(noyé)* to fish out, to recover; **r. un corps/une voiture dans le fleuve** to fish a body/a car out of the river **2** *Univ* to let through; **j'ai été repêché à l'oral** I passed on my oral **3** *Sport* to let through on the repechage

repeindre **[81]** [rəpɛ̃dr] **VT** to repaint, to paint again

repeint [rəpɛ̃] **NM** *Beaux-Arts* touched-up area

repens *etc voir* **repentir**[2]

repenser **[3]** [rəpɑ̃se] **VT** to reconsider, to rethink; **l'entrepôt a été entièrement repensé** the layout of the warehouse has been completely redesigned; **il faudra r. notre stratégie** we'll have to rethink our strategy

• **repenser à VT IND** to think about again; **en y repensant** thinking back on it all; **je n'ai plus jamais repensé à elle** I never thought of her again *or* gave her another thought; **ah mais oui, j'y repense, elle t'a appelé ce matin** oh yes, now I come to think of it, she phoned you this morning; **tout à coup, ça m'a fait r. à ce qu'il avait dit** suddenly it made me think of what he had said

repentant, -e [rəpɑ̃tɑ̃, -ɑ̃t] **ADJ** repentant, penitent

repenti, -e [rəpɑ̃ti] **ADJ** repentant, penitent; **alcoolique/fumeur r.** reformed alcoholic/smoker; *Vieilli* **fille repentie** reformed prostitute

NM,F *(ancien terroriste)* = former terrorist who now collaborates with the police

repentir[1] [rəpɑ̃tir] **NM 1** *(remords)* remorse; **verser des larmes de r.** to shed tears of remorse *or* regret

2 *Rel* repentance; **mener une vie de r.** to live a life of repentance *or* penance

3 *(correction)* alteration

4 *Beaux-Arts* reworking, retouching

repentir[2] **[37]** [rəpɑ̃tir] **se repentir VPR 1** to repent **2 se r. de qch** to regret, to be sorry for sth; **elle se repent d'avoir été trop sévère** she's sorry for having been too harsh; **j'ai refusé son offre et je m'en suis amèrement repenti** I turned down his/her offer and I've lived to rue the day *or* I bitterly regret it; **se r. d'une faute/d'avoir péché** to repent of a fault/of having sinned; **elle s'en repentira** she'll be sorry, she'll rue the day

repérage [rəperaʒ] **NM 1** *(localisation)* spotting, pinpointing

2 *Mil* location

3 *Cin* **être en r.** to be looking for locations *or* choosing settings

4 *Typ* registry, laying

répercussion [reperkysjɔ̃] **NF 1** *(conséquence)* repercussion, consequence (**sur** on) **2** *(renvoi ▸ d'un son)* repercussion, echo **3** *Fin* **le coût final est aggravé par la r. de l'impôt** the final cost is increased because taxes levied are passed on (to the buyer)

répercuter **[3]** [reperkyte] **VT 1** *(renvoyer ▸ son)* to echo, to reflect **2** *Fin* to pass on; **r. l'impôt sur le prix de revient** to pass a tax on in the selling price; **r. l'augmentation des salaires sur les prix** to pass the wage increase on to prices **3** *(transmettre ▸ ordre)* to pass on *or* along

VPR se répercuter 1 *(bruit)* to echo **2 se r. sur** to have an effect on *or* upon, to affect; **les problèmes familiaux se répercutent sur le travail scolaire** family problems have repercussions on *or* affect children's performances at school

repère [rəpɛr] **NM 1** *(marque)* line, mark; *(indice ▸ matériel)* landmark; *(▸ qui permet de juger)* benchmark, reference mark; **verser le liquide jusqu'au r.** pour in the liquid until it reaches the mark; **point de r.** landmark **2** *Tech* (index) mark; **r. de montage** assembly *or* match mark **3** *(référence)* reference point, landmark; **la date de son mariage me sert de r.** I use the date of his/her wedding as a reference point *or* to help me remember; *Fig* **j'ai l'impression de n'avoir plus aucun (point de) r.** I've lost my bearings

repérer **[18]** [rəpere] **VT 1** *(indiquer par un repère)* to mark; *Tech* to mark out *or* off

2 *(localiser)* to locate, to pinpoint; **r. d'abord l'église sur la carte** first locate the church on the map

3 *(remarquer)* to spot, to pick out, to notice; **je l'avais repéré au premier rang** I'd noticed *or* spotted him in the first row; **tu vas nous faire r. avec tes éternuements** you'll get us caught *or* spotted with your sneezing

4 *(dénicher)* to discover; **j'ai repéré un très bon petit restaurant** I've discovered a really nice little restaurant

VPR se repérer 1 *(déterminer sa position)* to find *or* to get one's bearings; **on n'arrive jamais à se r. dans un aéroport** you can never find your way about *or* around in an airport **2** *Fig* **beaucoup de jeunes ont du mal à se r. dans la jungle universitaire** many young people find it difficult to get *or* to find their bearings in the jungle of university life; **je n'arrive plus à me r. dans ses mensonges** I don't know where I am any more with all those lies he/she tells

répertoire [repɛrtwar] **NM 1** *(liste)* index, list; **r. alphabétique/thématique** alphabetical/thematic index

2 *(livre)* notebook, book; **ils notent le vocabulaire dans un r.** they write down the vocabulary in a notebook; **r. d'adresses** address book; **r. à onglets** thumb-index notebook *or* book; **r. des rues** street index

3 *Mus & (en danse)* repertoire; *Théât* repertoire, repertory; *Fig (de plaisanteries, d'injures, etc)* repertoire; **jouer une pièce du r.** *(acteur)* to be in rep; *(théâtre)* to put on a play from the repertoire *or* a stock play; *Fig* **tu devrais ajouter ça à ton r.** that could be another string to your bow

4 *Ordinat* directory; **r. central** *ou* **principal** main directory

répertorier **[9]** [repɛrtɔrje] **VT 1** *(inventorier)* to index, to list **2** *(inscrire dans une liste)* to list; **répertorié par adresses/professions** listed under addresses/professions

répéter **[18]** [repete] **VT 1** *(dire encore)* to repeat; **je t'ai répété cent fois de ne pas le faire** I've told you a hundred times not to do it; **je vous répète que ce n'est pas possible!** it's not possible, I tell you!, I repeat, it's not possible!; **je ne veux pas avoir à le r.** I don't want to have to say it again *or* to repeat it; **elle ne se l'est pas fait r. (deux fois)** she didn't need telling twice

2 *(raconter ▸ fait)* to repeat; *(▸ histoire)* to retell, to relate; **répète-moi exactement ce qu'il a dit** tell me (again) exactly what he said; **ne lui répète pas** don't tell him/her, don't repeat this to him/her; **ne va pas le r. (à tout le monde)** don't go telling everybody

3 *(recommencer)* to repeat, to do again; **des tentatives répétées de chantage** repeated attempts to blackmail people

4 *(mémoriser ▸ leçon)* to go over, to practise; *(▸ morceau de musique)* to practise; *(▸ pièce, film)* to rehearse; **répétons la séquence une dernière fois** let's run through the sequence one more time; **faire r. son rôle à qn** to help sb rehearse his/her lines, to go over sb's lines with him/her; **faire r. ses leçons à un enfant** to go over a child's lessons with him/her

5 *(reproduire ▸ motif)* to repeat, to duplicate; *(▸ refrain)* to repeat

USAGE ABSOLU répétez après moi repeat after me; **répète un peu pour voir?** let's hear you repeat that (if you dare)!; **on ne répète pas demain** *(au cinéma, au théâtre)* there's no rehearsal tomorrow

VPR se répéter 1 *(redire la même chose)* to repeat oneself; **au risque de me r.** at the risk of repeating myself; **depuis son premier roman, elle se répète** since her first novel, she's just been rewriting the same thing **2** *(se reproduire ▸ situation, événement)* to recur, to reoccur, to be repeated; *(▸ motif)* to be repeated; **et que ça ne se répète plus!** don't let it happen again!; **l'histoire se répète** history repeats itself

répététrice [repetitris] *voir* **répétiteur**

répéteur [repetœr] **NM** *Élec* repeater

répétiteur, -trice [repetitœr, -tris] **NM,F** *Vieilli* coach *(at home or in school)*

répétitif, -ive [repetitif, -iv] **ADJ** repetitive, repetitious

répétition [repetisjɔ̃] **NF 1** *(d'un mot, d'un geste)* repetition **2** *(d'un événement)* repetition **3** *(séance de travail)* rehearsal; **être en r.** to be rehearsing; **r. générale** dress rehearsal; **r. technique** technical run, technical walk-through

• **à répétition ADJ 1** *(en armurerie, en horlogerie)* repeater *(avant n)* **2** *Fam (renouvelé)* **il fait des bêtises à r.** he keeps doing stupid things; **des laryngites à r.** repeated bouts of laryngitis

répétitive [repetitiv] *voir* **répétitif**

repeuplement [rəpœpləmɑ̃] **NM** *(par des hommes)* repopulation; *(par des animaux)* restocking; *(par des plantes)* replantation, replanting *(UNCOUNT)*; *(d'une forêt)* replanting

repeupler **[5]** [rəpœple] **VT** *(pays, secteur)* to repopulate; *(étang)* to restock; *(forêt)* to replant

VPR se repeupler cette région commence à se r. people are starting to move back to the area; **la rivière se repeuple** life is coming back to the river

repiquage [rəpikaʒ] **NM 1** *Agr & Hort* planting *or* bedding out

2 *(sur bande)* rerecording, taping; *(sur disque)* transfer

3 *Couture* restitching

4 *(de la chaussée)* repaving

5 *Phot* touching up

repiquer **[3]** [rəpike] **VT 1** *Agr & Hort* to plant *or* to pick *or* to bed out

2 *Fam (attraper de nouveau)* to catch *or* to nab again; **et que je ne te repique pas à faire ça!** don't let me catch you doing that again!

3 *(enregistrer ▸ sur cassette)* to rerecord, to tape; *(▸ sur disque)* to transfer

4 *Couture* to restitch

5 *Fam Arg scol (classe)* to repeat ◻

6 *(repaver)* to repave

7 *Phot* to touch up

VI 1 *Fam (recommencer)* to start again ◻; **r. à un plat** to have a second helping ◻; **r. au truc** to be at it again **2** *Fam Arg scol (redoubler une classe)* to repeat a *Br* year *or Am* grade ◻

répit [repi] **NM** respite, rest; **un moment de r.** a breathing space; **mes enfants ne me laissent pas un instant de r.** my children never give me a minute's rest; **s'accorder quelques minutes de r.** to give oneself a few minutes' rest; **la douleur ne lui laisse aucun r.** he/she is in constant pain, he/she has no respite from the pain

• **sans répit ADV** *(lutter)* tirelessly; *(poursuivre, interroger)* relentlessly, without respite

replacement [rəplasmɑ̃] **NM 1** *(remise en place)* replacing, putting back **2** *(de capitaux)* reinvestment **3** *(de personnes)* **des mesures pour permettre le r. des licenciés** steps to find new employment for workers made redundant

replacer **[16]** [rəplase] **VT 1** *(remettre)* to replace, to put back; **r. les événements dans leur contexte** to put events into their context

2 *Fam (réutiliser)* to put in again ◻; **elle est bonne, celle-là, je la replacerai!** that's a good one, I must remember it *or* use it myself sometime! ◻

3 *(capitaux)* to reinvest

4 *(trouver un nouvel emploi pour)* to find a new position for

5 *Can (reconnaître)* to recognize; **je ne l'avais pas vue depuis si longtemps que je n'arrivais pas à la r.** it was so long since I'd seen her that I couldn't place her

VPR se replacer 1 *(se remettre en place)* to take up one's position again **2** *(domestique)* to find (oneself) a new job **3** *(dans une situation déterminée)* to imagine oneself, to visualize oneself; **il faut se r. dans les conditions de l'examen pour comprendre son échec** you have to imagine yourself in the exam situation to understand why he/she failed

replanter **[3]** [rəplɑ̃te] **VT** to replant; **r. une forêt en sapins** to replant a forest with firs

replat [rəpla] **NM** *Géog* sloping ledge, shoulder

replâtrage [rəplatraʒ] **NM 1** *Constr* replastering **2** *Fam Fig (réconciliation)* patching-up; *(réarrangement)* tinkering

replâtrer **[3]** [rəplatre] **VT 1** *Constr* to replaster **2** *Fam Fig* to patch up

replet, -ète [rəplɛ, -ɛt] **ADJ** *(personne)* plump, podgy, portly; *(visage)* plump, chubby; *(ventre)* full, rounded; **un petit garçon au visage r.** a chubby-faced little boy

réplétion [replesjɔ̃] **NF** *Physiol* repletion

repleuvoir **[68]** [rəplœvwar] **V IMPERSONNEL** **il repleut** it's (started) raining again

repli [rəpli] **NM 1** *(pli ▸ du terrain)* fold; *(▸ de l'intestin)* coil; *(courbe ▸ d'une rivière)* bend, meander

2 *Mil* withdrawal, falling back *(UNCOUNT)*; **solution** *ou* **stratégie de r.** fallback option; *Mil & Mktg* **r. stratégique** strategic withdrawal

3 *Fig Littéraire (recoin)* recess; **les sombres replis de l'âme** the dark recesses *or* reaches of the soul

4 *(baisse)* fall, drop; **on note un léger r. de la livre sterling** sterling has fallen slightly *or* has eased (back); **la livre est en r. de 0,15 pour cent** the pound is down 0.15 percent

5 *(introversion)* **un r. sur soi** a turning in on oneself

repliable [rəplijabl] **ADJ** folding

repliement [rəplimɑ̃] **NM** *(introversion)* withdrawal; **r. sur soi-même** withdrawal (into oneself), turning in on oneself, self-absorption

replier **[10]** [rəplije] **VT 1** *(plier ▸ journal)* to fold up again; *(▸ bord, coin)* to turn *or* fold down; *(▸ couteau)* to fold, to close; **replie le bas de ton pantalon** turn up the bottom of your *Br* trousers *or Am* pants **2** *(ramener ▸ ailes)* to fold; *(▸ jambes)* to tuck under **3** *Mil (troupes)* to withdraw; **r. les populations civiles** to move the civilian population back

VPR se replier 1 *(emploi passif)* to fold back; **la lame se replie dans le manche** the blade folds back into the handle **2** *Mil* to withdraw, to fall back; *Bourse (monnaie)* to fall back **3** *(emploi réfléchi)* **se r. sur soi-même** to withdraw into oneself, to turn in on oneself; **il est trop replié sur lui-même** he's too much of an introvert

réplique [replik] **NF 1** *(réponse)* reply, retort, *Sout* rejoinder; **la r. ne s'est pas fait attendre** his/her/*etc* reply wasn't long in coming; **ce gamin a la r. facile** this kid is always ready with *or* is never short of an answer; **je cite toujours la r. de de Gaulle le jour où...** I like to quote the reply made by de Gaulle when...; **avoir le sens de la r.** to be always ready with an answer; **argument sans r.** irrefutable *or* unanswerable argument; **quand elle a décidé quelque chose, c'est sans r.** when she's made up her mind about something, she's quite adamant!; **obéissez, et pas de r.!** do as you're told and no argument!; **un échange de répliques assez vives** a rather lively exchange **2** *(dans une pièce, dans un film)* line, cue; **manquer sa r.** to miss one's cue; **oublier sa r.** to forget one's lines; **donner la r. à un acteur** *(en répétition)* to give an actor his cues; *(dans une distribution)* to play opposite an actor **3** *(reproduction)* replica, studio copy; **il est la r. vivante de son père** he's the spitting image of *or* a dead ringer for his father; **réaliser la r. de qch** to design a replica of sth

répliquer **[3]** [replike] **VT** *(répondre)* to reply, to retort

• **répliquer à** **VT IND 1** *(répondre à ▸ remarque, insulte)* to reply to; **r. à une critique** to reply to *or* to answer criticism; **r. à qn** to answer sb back **2** *(contre-attaquer)* to respond to; **la France a répliqué à cette déclaration en rappelant son ambassadeur** France has responded to this declaration by recalling her ambassador

USAGE ABSOLU monte te coucher et ne réplique pas! go upstairs to bed and no argument!; **le pays a été attaqué et a répliqué immédiatement** the country was attacked and immediately retaliated; **il répliqua par un coup de pied** he answered with a kick

VPR se répliquer *Biol* to replicate

replonger **[17]** [rəplɔ̃ʒe] **VT 1** *(plonger à nouveau)* to dip back; **l'enfant replongea ses doigts dans la confiture** the child plunged *or* stuck his/her fingers back into the jam **2** *Fig (faire sombrer à nouveau)* to plunge back, to push back; **le film m'a replongé dans le Paris de mon enfance** the film takes me right back to the Paris of my childhood

VI 1 *(plonger à nouveau)* to dive again **2** *Fam Fig (reprendre une habitude)* to be at it again; **r. dans l'alcoolisme/la délinquance** to relapse into drinking/delinquency; **r. dans la dépression** to sink back *or* to relapse into depression; **un rien peut faire r. un alcoolique** it doesn't take much to push an alcoholic back into his old ways **3 se r. dans** to go back to; **se r. dans son travail** to immerse oneself in work again, to go back to one's work; **se r. dans ses recherches** to get involved in one's research again

replu [rəply] **PP** *voir* **repleuvoir**

repolir **[32]** [rəpɔlir] **VT** to polish up again

répondant, -e [repɔ̃dɑ̃, -ɑ̃t] **NM,F 1** *(garant)* guarantor, surety; **être le r. de qn** *(financièrement)* to stand surety for sb, to be sb's guarantor; *(moralement)* to answer *or* to vouch for sb **2** *(d'un questionnaire)* respondent

NM avoir du r. *(avoir des économies)* to have plenty of cash stashed away; *(avoir de la repartie)* to have quick repartee, to be quick at repartee

répondeur, -euse [repɔ̃dœr, -øz] **ADJ** *(insolent)* who answers back; **il est déjà r. à son âge** *Br* he's got a lot of cheek *or Am* he's very sassy for his age

NM r. (téléphonique) (telephone) answering machine; **r. enregistreur** answering machine; **r. interrogeable à distance** remote-control answering machine

RÉPONDRE **[75]** [repɔ̃dr]

VT
- to answer **1, 3, 4**
- to reply **1, 3**
- to answer back **2**
- to write back **3**
- to respond **5**

VT
- to answer **1, 2**
- to reply **1, 2**
- to write back **2**

VI 1 *(répliquer)* to answer, to reply; **réponds quand je t'appelle!** answer (me) when I call you!; **ma sœur a répondu pour moi** my sister answered for me *or* in my place; **bien répondu!** well said *or* spoken!; **répondez par oui ou par non** answer *or* say yes or no; **il n'a répondu que par des grognements** his only answer *or* reply was a series of grunts; **elle répondit en riant** she answered *or* replied with a laugh; **r. par un clin d'œil/hochement de tête** to wink/to nod in reply; **r. par l'affirmative/la négative** to answer in the affirmative/negative; **r. à qn/qch** to answer sb/sth; **vous ne répondez pas à ma question** you haven't answered my question

2 *(être insolent)* to answer back; **r. à ses parents/professeurs** to answer one's parents/teachers back

3 *(à une lettre)* to answer, to reply, to write back; **r. par écrit** to answer *or* to reply in writing; **il faut leur r. par écrit** you must give them a written answer *or* reply; **je n'ai jamais répondu** I never wrote back *or* answered *or* replied; **il ne m'a pas encore répondu** he hasn't written back to me yet, I still haven't had a reply from him; **répondez au questionnaire suivant** answer the following questions, fill in the following questionnaire; **je réponds toujours aux vœux qu'on m'envoie** I always reply to any messages of goodwill that people send me; **r. à une invitation** *(dire qu'on l'a reçue)* to reply to *or* to answer an invitation; **je suis ravi que vous ayez pu r. à mon invitation** *(que vous soyez venu)* I'm delighted that you were able to accept my invitation

4 *(à la porte, au téléphone)* to answer; **ne réponds pas!** don't answer!; **je vais r.** *(à la porte)* I'll go; *(au téléphone)* I'll answer it, I'll get it; **ça ne répond pas** nobody's answering, there's no answer; **r. au téléphone** to answer the phone *or* telephone

5 *(réagir ▸ véhicule, personne, cheval)* to respond (à to); **les gens répondent par milliers** people are responding in their thousands; **le public répond mal** there is a low level of public response; **les freins répondent bien** the brakes respond well; **son organisme ne répond plus au traitement** his/her body isn't responding to treatment any more; **r. à l'amitié de qn** to respond to *or* to return sb's friendship; **elle répondit à son accueil par un sourire glacial** she responded to *or* met his/her welcome with an icy smile; **r. à un coup** *ou* **à une attaque** to fight back, to retaliate; **r. à une accusation/critique** to counter an accusation/a criticism; **r. à la force par la force** to meet *or* to answer force with force

VT 1 *(gén)* to answer, to reply; *(après une attaque)* to retort; **r. (que) oui/non** to say yes/no in reply, to answer yes/no; **"à trois heures et demie", répondit-elle** "at half past three," she answered *or* replied; **qu'as-tu répondu?** what did you say?, what was your answer?; **je n'ai rien trouvé à r.** I could find no answer *or* reply; **est-ce qu'elle a répondu quelque chose?** did she give any answer?, did she say anything in reply?; **si on me demande pourquoi, je répondrai ceci** if I'm asked the reason why, this is what I'll say *or* answer; **elle m'a répondu de le faire moi-même** she told me to do it myself; **que r. à cela?** there's no answer to that (, is there?); **il répondit ne pas s'en soucier** he answered *or* replied that he did not care about it

2 *(par lettre)* to answer, to reply (in writing *or* by letter); **r. que...** to write (back) that...

3 *Rel* **r. la messe** to give the responses (at Mass)

• **répondre à** **VT IND 1** *(satisfaire ▸ besoin, demande)* to answer, to meet; *(▸ attente, espoir)* to come *or* to live up to, to fulfil; *(correspondre à ▸ norme)* to meet; *(▸ condition)* to fulfil; *(▸ description, signalement)* to answer, to fit; **les dédommagements ne répondent pas à l'attente des sinistrés** the amount offered in compensation falls short of the victims' expectations **2** *(s'harmoniser avec)* to match; **au bleu du ciel répond le bleu de la mer** the blue of the sky matches the blue of the sea **3 r. au nom de** *(s'appeler)* to answer to the name (of)

• **répondre de** **VT IND 1** *(cautionner ▸ filleul, protégé)* to answer for; **r. de l'exactitude de qch/de l'intégrité de qn** to vouch for the accuracy of sth/sb's integrity; **je réponds de lui comme de moi-même** I can fully vouch for him; **je ne réponds plus de rien** I am no longer responsible for anything **2** *(assurer)* **je vous en réponds que cela ne se renouvellera pas!** I guarantee (you) it won't happen again! **3** *(expliquer)* to answer *or* to account for, to be accountable for; **je n'ai pas à r. de mes décisions** I do not have to account for my decisions; **les ministres répondent de leurs actes devant le Parlement** ministers are accountable for their actions before Parliament; *Jur* **r. d'un crime** to answer for a crime

VPR se répondre *(instruments de musique)* to answer each other; *(sculptures, tableaux)* to match each other; *(couleurs, formes, sons)* to harmonize

> Il faut noter que le verbe anglais **to respond** est un faux ami. Il signifie le plus souvent **réagir**.

répons [repɔ̃] **NM** *Rel* response

réponse [repɔ̃s] **NF 1** *(réplique)* answer, reply; **elle a toujours r. à tout** *(elle sait tout)* she has an answer for everything; *(elle a de la repartie)* she's never at a loss for *or* she's always ready with an answer; **elle fait toujours les questions et les réponses** she does all the talking; **pour toute r., elle me claqua la porte au nez** her only reply was to slam the door in my face; **une r. de Normand** an evasive answer; **c'est la r. du berger à la bergère** it's tit for tat

2 *(à un courrier)* reply, answer, response; *(à une demande)* reply, response; *(à une offre d'emploi)* reply; **en r. à votre courrier du 2 mai** in reply *or* response to your letter dated *Am* May 2 *or Br* 2 May; **leur lettre est restée sans r.** their letter remained *or* was left unanswered; **leur demande est restée sans r.** there was no reply *or* response to their request; **j'ai sonné plusieurs fois, mais pas de r.** I've rung several times, but there's no answer; **r. par retour du courrier** reply by return of post; **je lui ai donné une r. positive** *(à son offre)* I accepted his/her offer; *(à sa candidature)* I told him/her his/her application had been successful; **je lui ai donné une r. négative** I turned him/her down; **r. payée** reply paid

3 *(réaction)* response; **la r. du gouvernement fut d'imposer le couvre-feu** the government's response was to impose a curfew

4 *(solution)* answer; **je n'ai pas la r. (à ton problème)** I don't have the answer (to your problem), I don't know what the answer (to your problem) is; **la r. à la question numéro 5 est fausse** the answer to number 5 is wrong

5 *Tech* response; **temps de r. d'un appareil** response time of a device

6 *(comme adj; avec ou sans trait d'union)* **bulletin-r.** reply slip; **coupon-r.** reply coupon

repopulation [rəpɔpylasjɔ̃] **NF** repopulation

report [rəpɔr] **NM 1** *(renvoi à plus tard)* postponement, deferment

2 *Compta* carrying forward *or* over; *(en haut du page)* (balance) brought forward; **faire le r. d'une somme** to carry forward *or* over an amount; **r. de l'exercice précédent** carried forward from the previous financial year; **r. à l'exercice suivant** carried forward to the next financial year; **r. à nouveau** balance (carried forward); *(en haut de colonne)* brought forward; *(en bas de colonne)* carried forward

3 *(transfert ▸ de corrections)* transfer; **r. des voix** transfer of votes

4 *Phot* transfer

> Il faut noter que le nom anglais **report** est un faux ami. Il signifie **rapport**.

reportage [rəpɔrtaʒ] **NM 1** *(récit, émission)* report; **r. filmé/télévisé/photo** film/television/photo report; **r. en direct** live coverage; **r. en exclusivité** scoop, exclusive (report); **faire un r. sur qch** to do a report on sth; **j'ai fait mon premier grand r. pour 'Nice-Matin'** I covered my first big story for 'Nice-Matin'; **r. publicitaire** special advertising feature, *Am* advertorial **2** *(métier)* (news) reporting, reportage; **faire du r.** to be a news reporter; **r. télévisé** television reporting

reporté, -e [rəpɔrte] **NM,F** *Bourse (d'actions)* giver

reporter¹ [rəpɔrtɛr] **NM** *Rad, TV & Journ* (news) reporter; **grand r.** international reporter; **r. photographe** photojournalist; **r. sportif** sports reporter

reporter² **[3]** [rəpɔrte] **VT 1** *(rapporter)* to take back

2 *(transcrire ▸ note, insertion)* to transfer, to copy out; *Compta* to carry forward; *Compta* **solde à r.** balance (to be) carried forward; *Compta* **tu dois r. le total à la page suivante** you must carry the total forward to the next page

3 *(retarder ▸ conférence, rendez-vous)* to postpone, to put off; *(▸ annonce, verdict)* to put off, to defer; *(▸ date)* to defer, *esp Br* to put back; **r. qch à une prochaine fois** to put sth off until another time

4 *(faire revenir en arrière)* to take back; **ces photos me reportent à l'été 43** these photographs take me back to the summer of '43

5 *(transférer)* to shift, to transfer; **elle a reporté ses notes dans son cahier bleu** she copied out her notes into her blue notebook; **les votes ont été reportés sur le candidat communiste** the votes were transferred to the communist candidate; **il a reporté toute son amertume sur sa fille** he's transferred *or* shifted all his bitterness onto his daughter

VPR se reporter 1 se r. à *(se référer à)* to turn *or* to refer to, to see; **reportez-vous à notre dernier numéro** see our last issue **2 se r. à** *(revenir en arrière)* to look *or* think back to, to cast one's mind back to; **se r. au passé** to look back *or* think back to the past **3 se r. sur** *(se transférer sur)* to be transferred to; **tout son amour s'est reporté sur sa fille** all his/her love was switched to his/her daughter

> Il faut noter que le verbe anglais **to report** est un faux ami. Il ne correspond jamais au verbe français **reporter**.

reporter-cameraman [rəpɔrtɛrkameraman] *(pl* **reporters-cameramans** *ou* **reporters-cameramen** [-mɛn]) **NM** television news reporter

reporteur [rəpɔrtœr] **NM 1** *Bourse (d'actions)* taker (of stock) **2** *Journ* **r. d'images** television news reporter

repos [rəpo] **NM 1** *(détente)* rest; **prendre quelques jours de r.** to take *or* to have a few days' rest; **un moment de r.** a short rest; **trois jours de r. complet** three days of complete rest; **j'ai besoin d'un peu de r.** I need a bit of a rest, I need to rest a little; **mon médecin m'a conseillé le r.** my doctor has advised me to rest; **ces enfants ne lui laissent aucun r.** those children give him/her no rest

2 *(période d'inactivité)* rest (period), time off; **trois jours de r., un r. de trois jours** three days off; **après un mois de r.** after a month's rest; **le dimanche est mon seul jour de r.** Sunday is my only day off *or* day of rest; **r. compensateur** ≃ time off in lieu; **r. dominical** Sunday rest; **r. hebdomadaire** weekly time off

3 *Littéraire (tranquillité ▸ de la nature)* peace and quiet; *(▸ intérieure)* peace of mind; **trouver le r.** to relax; **troubler le r. de qn** to disturb sb; **je n'aurai pas de r. tant que...** I won't rest as long as...

4 *Littéraire (sommeil)* sleep, rest; **respecte le r. des autres** let other people sleep (in peace); **r. éternel** eternal rest

5 *Mil* **r.!** at ease!

• **au repos ADJ** *(moteur, animal)* at rest; *(volcan)* dormant, inactive; *(muscle, corps)* relaxed **ADV 1** *Agr* **laisser un champ au r.** to let a field lie fallow **2** *Mil* **mettre la troupe au r.** to order the troops to stand at ease

• **de tout repos ADJ le voyage n'était pas de tout r.** it wasn't exactly a restful journey

• **en repos ADJ 1** *(inactif)* **l'imagination de l'artiste ne reste jamais en r.** an artist's imagination never rests *or* is never at rest **2** *(serein)* **elle a la conscience en r.** she has an easy *or* a clear conscience

reposant, -e [rəpozɑ̃, -ɑ̃t] **ADJ** *(vacances)* relaxing; *(ambiance, lumière, musique)* soothing

reposé, -e [rəpoze] **ADJ** fresh, rested; **on repartira quand tu seras bien r.** we'll set off again once you've had a good rest; **tu as l'air r.** you look rested

repose-bras [rəpozbra] **NM INV** armrest

repose-pieds [rəpozpje] **NM INV** footrest

repose-poignets [rəpozpwaɲɛ] **NM INV** wrist rest

REPOSER **[3]** [rəpoze]

VT	
• to ask again **1**	• to put down **2**
• to rest **3**	
VI	
• to rest **1–3**	• to lie **1, 3**
VPR	
• to rest **1**	• to rely on **2**

VT 1 *(question)* to ask again, to repeat; *(problème)* to raise again, to bring up again

2 *(objet)* to put down (again) *or* back down; **on a dû faire r. de la moquette** we had to have the carpet relaid

3 *(personne, corps, esprit)* to rest; **r. ses jambes** to rest one's legs; **ça le repose de tous ses soucis** it gives him a rest from all his worries

4 *Mil* **reposez armes!** order arms!

VI 1 *(être placé)* to rest, to lie; **sa tête reposait sur l'oreiller** his/her head rested *or* lay on the pillow

2 *Littéraire (dormir)* to sleep; *(être allongé)* to rest, to be lying down; *(être enterré)* to rest, to be buried; **r. sur son lit de mort** to be lying on one's deathbed; **elle repose non loin de son village natal** she rests *or* she's buried not far from her native village; **ici reposent les victimes de la guerre** here lie the victims of the war

3 *(être posé)* to rest, to lie, to stand; **l'épave reposait par 100 mètres de fond** the wreck lay 100 metres down

4 *(liquide, mélange)* **laissez le vin r.** leave the wine to settle, let the wine stand; **laissez r. la pâte/colle** leave the dough to stand/glue to set

5 *Agr* **laisser la terre r.** to let the land lie fallow

• **reposer sur VT IND 1** *(être posé sur)* to rest on, to lie on, to stand on; *Constr* to be built *or* to rest on **2** *(être fondé sur ▸ sujet: témoignage, conception)* to rest on; **sur quelles preuves repose votre affirmation?** what evidence do you have to support your assertion?, on what evidence do you base your assertion?; **l'ordre social repose sur la famille** social order hinges *or* is based on the family

VPR se reposer 1 *(se détendre)* to rest; **va te r. une heure** go and rest *or* go take a rest for an hour; **se r. des fatigues de la journée** to rest after a tiring day; *Fig* **se r. sur ses lauriers** to rest on one's laurels **2 se r. sur** *(s'en remettre à)* to rely on; **le Président se repose trop sur ses conseillers** the President relies *or* depends too much on his advisers; **je me repose sur elle pour les histoires d'argent** I rely on her as far as money matters are concerned

repose-tête [rəpoztɛt] **NM INV** headrest

repositionnement [rəpozisjɔnmɑ̃] **NM** *Com (d'un produit)* repositioning

repositionner **[3]** [rəpozisjɔne] **VT 1** *(remettre en position)* to reposition **2** *Com (produit)* to reposition

VPR se repositionner *Com* **se r. sur le marché** to reposition oneself in the market; **se r. à la baisse** to move downmarket; **se r. à la hausse** to move upmarket

reposoir [rəpozwar] **NM** *(dans une église)* altar of repose; *(dans une maison)* (temporary) altar

repourvoir **[64]** [rəpurvwar] **VT** *Suisse (poste)* to fill

repoussage [rəpusaʒ] **NM 1** *Beaux-Arts* repoussé (work) *(UNCOUNT)*, chasing *(UNCOUNT)*, embossing *(UNCOUNT)*; *(travail du cuir)* embossing *(UNCOUNT)* **2** *Métal* repoussé

repoussant, -e [rəpusɑ̃, -ɑ̃t] **ADJ** repulsive, repellent; **être d'une laideur repoussante** to be repulsively *or* horribly ugly

repousse [rəpus] **NF** new growth; **des pilules qui facilitent la r. des cheveux** hair-restoring pills

repoussé [rəpuse] **ADJ M** repoussé *(avant n)*

NM *(technique ▸ gén)* repoussé (work); *(▸ au marteau)* chasing; *(relief)* repoussé

repousse-peaux [rəpuspo] **NM INV** cuticle remover

repousser **[3]** [rəpuse] **VT 1** *(faire reculer ▸ manifestants)* to push *or* to drive back; *(▸ agresseur)* to drive off, to beat off, to repel; *(▸ attaque)* to drive back, to repel; **r. les frontières de l'imaginaire/l'horreur** to push back the frontiers of imagination/horror

2 *(écarter)* to push aside *or* away; **elle repoussa violemment l'assiette** she pushed the plate away violently; **r. qn d'un geste brusque** to push *or* to shove sb out of the way roughly

3 *(refuser ▸ offre, mesure, demande en mariage)* to turn down, to reject; *(▸ solution, thèse)* to reject, to dismiss, to rule out; *(▸ tentation, idées noires)* to resist, to reject, to drive away; **r. un projet de loi** to throw out *or* to reject a bill; **r. les avances de qn** to reject sb's advances

4 *(mendiant)* to turn away; *(prétendant)* to reject

5 *(dégoûter)* to repel, to put off; **il me repousse** he repels me

6 *(retarder ▸ conférence, travail)* to postpone, to put off; *(▸ date)* to defer, *Br* to put back; *(▸ décision, jugement)* to defer; **repoussé au 26 juin** postponed until *Br* 26 June *or Am* June 26

7 *Tech (cuir)* to emboss; *(métal)* to chase, to work in repoussé

VI *(barbe, plante)* to grow again *or* back; **elle se laisse r. les cheveux** she's letting her hair grow again

repoussoir [rəpuswar] **NM 1** *(faire-valoir)* foil; **servir de r. à (la beauté de) qn** to act as a foil to sb's beauty

2 *(laideron)* ugly duckling; **sa sœur est un véritable r.** his/her sister's really ugly

3 *Constr (ciseau)* drift (chisel)

4 *(spatule de manucure)* orange stick

répréhensible [repreɑ̃sibl] **ADJ** reprehensible, blameworthy; **un acte r.** a reprehensible *or* an objectionable deed; **je ne vois pas ce que ma conduite a de r.** I don't see what's reproachable about my behaviour

REPRENDRE [79] [rəprɑ̃dr]

VT
- to pick up again **1**
- to take hold of again **3**
- to get back **4**
- to collect **4**
- to have back **5**
- to have more **7**
- to restart **8**
- to repeat **9**
- to carry on **10**
- to rework **13**
- to repair **15**
- to catch **17**
- to take over **19**
- to recapture **2**
- to pick up **4**
- to take back **4, 5, 11**
- to go back to **6**
- to resume **8**
- to take up again **8**
- to take up **12**
- to alter **14**
- to reprimand **16**
- to return **18**

VI
- to improve **1**
- to pick up **1**
- to start again **2, 3**
- to recover **1**
- to resume **2**

VPR
- to pull oneself together **1**
- to recover **2**
- to start again **4**
- to settle down **1**
- to correct oneself **3**

VT 1 *(saisir à nouveau ▸ objet)* to pick up again, to take again; **r. les rênes** *Équitation* to take in the reins; *Fig* to resume control

2 *Mil (s'emparer à nouveau de ▸ position, ville)* to retake, to recapture; *(▸ prisonnier)* to recapture, to catch again

3 *(sujet: maladie, doutes)* to take hold of again; **quand la douleur me reprend** when the pain comes back; **l'angoisse me reprit** anxiety took hold of me again; **ça y est, ça le reprend!** there he goes again!

4 *(aller rechercher ▸ personne)* to pick up; *(▸ objet)* to get back, to collect; *(remporter)* to take back; **je (te) reprendrai mon écharpe demain** I'll get my scarf back (from you) tomorrow; **ils reprennent aux uns ce qu'ils donnent aux autres** they take away from some in order to give to others; **tu peux r. ton parapluie, je n'en ai plus besoin** I don't need your umbrella any more, you can take it back; **je te reprendrai à la sortie de l'école** I'll pick you up *or* I'll collect you *or* I'll come and fetch you after school; **vous pouvez (passer) r. votre montre demain** you can come (by) and collect *or* pick up your watch tomorrow

5 *(réengager ▸ employé)* to take back, to have back; *(réadmettre ▸ élève)* to take back, to have back

6 *(retrouver ▸ un état antérieur)* to go back to; **elle a repris son nom de jeune fille** she went back to her maiden name; **il a repris sa bonhomie coutumière** he has recovered his usual good spirits; **je n'arrivais plus à r. ma respiration** I couldn't get my breath back; **r. son sang-froid** to calm down; **r. courage** to regain *or* to recover courage; **si tu le fais sécher à plat, il reprendra sa forme** if you dry it flat, it'll regain its shape *or* it'll get its shape back

7 *(se resservir)* **reprends un biscuit** have another biscuit; **reprenez-en (un peu)** have some more *or* a little more; **son ragoût était tellement bon que j'en ai repris deux fois** his/her stew was so good that I had three helpings; **votre poulet était bon la dernière fois, je vais en r.** your chicken was good last time, I'll have some again *or* more

8 *(recommencer, se remettre à ▸ recherche, combat)* to resume; *(▸ projet)* to take up again; *(▸ enquête)* to restart, to reopen; *(▸ lecture)* to go back to, to resume; *(▸ hostilités)* to resume, to reopen; *(▸ discussion, voyage)* to resume, to carry on (with), to continue; *Ordinat (programme)* to restart; **r. ses études** to take up one's studies again, to resume one's studies; **je reprends l'école le 15 septembre** I start school again *or* I go back to school on *Br* 15 September *or Am* September 15; **r. le travail** *(après des vacances)* to go back to work, to start work again; *(après une pause)* to get back to work, to start work again; *(après une grève)* to go back to work; **r. contact avec qn** to get in touch with sb again; **r. la plume/la caméra/le pinceau** to take up one's pen/movie camera/brush once more; **r. la route** *ou* **son chemin** to set off again, to resume one's journey; **elle a repris le volant après quelques heures** she took the wheel again after a few hours; **je reprends des antibiotiques depuis une semaine** I've been taking antibiotics again for a week; **r. la mer** *(sujet: marin)* to go back to sea; *(sujet: navire)* to (set) sail again

9 *(répéter ▸ texte)* to read again; *(▸ argument, passage musical)* to repeat; *(▸ refrain)* to take up; *(récapituler ▸ faits)* to go over again; *TV* to repeat; *Cin* to rerun; *Théât* to revive, to put on again, to put back on the stage; **il reprend toujours les mêmes thèmes** he always repeats the same themes, *Péj* he always harps on the same themes; **elle leur a fait r. en chœur les trois dernières mesures** she made them repeat the last three bars in chorus; **on reprend tout depuis le** *ou* **au début** *(on recommence)* let's start (all over) again from the beginning; **reprends la lecture depuis le début du paragraphe** start reading again from the beginning of the paragraph; **un sujet repris par tous vos hebdomadaires** an issue taken up by all your weeklies; **quand j'ai repris le rôle de Tosca** *(que j'avais déjà chanté)* when I took on the part of Tosca again; *(que je n'avais jamais chanté)* when I took on *or* over the part of Tosca

10 *(dire)* to go on, to carry on; **"et lui?" reprit-elle** "what about him?" she went on

11 *Com (article refusé)* to take back; **les vêtements ne sont ni repris ni échangés** clothes cannot be returned or exchanged; **ils m'ont repris ma voiture pour 1000 euros** I traded my car in for 1,000 euros

12 *(adopter ▸ idée, programme politique)* to take up; **r. à son compte les idées de qn** to take up sb's ideas

13 *(modifier ▸ texte)* to rework, to go over again; *(▸ peinture)* to touch up; **il a fallu tout r.** it all had to be gone over *or* done again; **c'était parfait, je n'ai rien eu à r.** it was perfect, I didn't have to make a single correction *or* alteration; **il faudra r. le projet de fond en comble** the plan has to be completely reviewed

14 *Couture (gén)* to alter; *(rétrécir)* to take in; **je vais r. le pantalon à la taille** I'll take in the *Br* trousers *or Am* pants at the waist; **r. une maille** *(en tricot)* to pick up a stitch

15 *Constr* to repair; *Tech (pièce)* to rework, to machine

16 *(réprimander)* to pull up, to pick up, *Sout* to reprimand; *(corriger)* to correct, to pull up; **j'ai été obligé de la r. en public** I had to put her straight in front of everybody

17 *(surprendre)* **r. qn à voler/fumer** to catch sb stealing/smoking again; **que je ne t'y reprenne plus!** don't let me catch you at it again!; **on ne m'y reprendra plus!** that's the last time you'll catch me doing that!

18 *Sport* to return; **r. la balle en revers** to take *or* to return the ball on one's backhand

19 *Fin (acheter ▸ entreprise)* to take over, to buy out; *(prendre à son compte ▸ cabinet, boutique)* to take over

VI 1 *(s'améliorer ▸ affaires)* to improve, to recover, to pick up, to look up; *Bourse* to rally; *(repousser ▸ plante)* to pick up, to recover; *Bourse* **les cours ont repris** the market rallied; **les affaires reprennent** business is picking *or* looking up

2 *(recommencer ▸ lutte)* to start (up) again, to resume; *(▸ pluie, vacarme)* to start (up) again; *(▸ cours, école)* to start again, to resume; *(▸ feu)* to rekindle; *(▸ fièvre, douleur)* to return, to start again; **je n'arrive pas à faire r. le feu** I can't get the fire going again; **l'incendie a repris au dernier étage** the fire has started again on the top floor; **la tempête reprit de plus belle** the storm started again with renewed ferocity; **le froid a repris** the cold weather has set in again *or* has returned

3 *(retourner au travail ▸ employé)* to start again; **je reprends à 2 heures** I'm back (at work) at 2, I start again at 2

VPR se reprendre 1 *(recouvrer ses esprits)* to get a grip on oneself, to pull oneself together; *(retrouver son calme)* to settle down

2 *Sport (au cours d'un match)* to recover, to rally; **après un mauvais début de saison, il s'est très bien repris** he started the season badly but has come back strongly *or* has staged a good comeback

3 *(se ressaisir ▸ après une erreur)* to correct oneself; **se r. à temps** *(avant une bévue)* to stop oneself in time

4 se r. à faire qch to start doing sth again; **elle se reprit à divaguer** she started rambling again; **je m'y suis reprise à trois fois** I had to start again three times *or* to make three attempts

repreneur [rəprənœr] **NM** *Écon* buyer; **les repreneurs de la chaîne** the people who bought up *or* acquired the channel

reprennent, reprenons *etc voir* **reprendre**

représailles [rəprezaj] **NFPL** reprisals, retaliation *(UNCOUNT)*; **exercer des r. contre** *ou* **envers qn** to take reprisals against sb; **en (guise de)** *ou* **par r. contre** in retaliation for, as a reprisal for

représentable [rəprezɑ̃tabl] **ADJ** representable

représentant, -e [rəprezɑ̃tɑ̃, -ɑ̃t] **NM,F 1** *Pol* (elected) representative; **les représentants du peuple** the people's representatives

2 *(porte-parole)* representative; **un des derniers représentants de la Nouvelle Vague** one of the last representatives of New Wave cinema

3 *(délégué)* delegate, representative; **le r. de la France à l'ONU** France's *or* the French representative at the UN; **où sont les représentants des élèves?** where are the class *or* student delegates?; **r. du personnel** staff delegate *or* representative; **r. syndical** union representative, *esp Br* shop steward

4 *Com* representative, agent; **je suis r. en électroménager** I'm a representative for an electrical appliances company; **notre r. au Japon** our agent in Japan; **r. (de commerce), r. commercial** (sales) representative; **r. exclusif** sole agent; **r. du personnel** staff representative

représentatif, -ive [rəprezɑ̃tatif, -iv] **ADJ** representative; **voilà des photos, mais elles ne sont pas très représentatives** here are some photos but they don't really give you the right idea; **être r. de qn/qch** to be representative of sb/sth; **c'est assez r. de la mentalité des jeunes** it's fairly typical of the way young people think

représentation [rəprezɑ̃tasjɔ̃] **NF 1** *(image)* representation, illustration

2 *Théât* performance; **r. en matinée** matinee (performance); **r. en soirée** evening performance

3 *(évocation)* description, portrayal; **une r. féroce des milieux d'affaires** a vitriolic portrayal of the business world

4 *(matérialisation par un signe)* representing *(UNCOUNT)*; **l'écriture est un système de r. de la langue** writing is a way of representing language

5 *Admin & Pol* representation; **assurer la r. d'un pays** to represent a country, to act as a country's representative; **r. proportionnelle** proportional representation

6 *Jur* **r. en justice** legal representation

7 *Com* (sales) representation; *(agence)* agency; **avoir une r. à l'étranger** to have an office abroad; **faire de la r., être dans la r.** to be a (sales) representative; **r. exclusive** sole agency; **avoir la r. exclusive de** to be sole agents for

8 *Psy* representation

9 *Beaux-Arts* representation

• **en représentation ADJ 1** *(personne)* **il est toujours en r.** he's always trying to project a certain image of himself **2** *(pièce de théâtre)* in performance

représentative [rəprezɑ̃tativ] *voir* **représentatif**

représentativité [rəprezɑ̃tativite] **NF** representativeness; **quelle est la r. de cet exemple?** how representative *or* typical is this example?

représenter [3] [rəprezɑ̃te] **VT 1** *(montrer)* to depict, to show, to represent; **le tableau représente une femme assise** the picture shows a seated woman; **je ne vois pas ce que cette sculpture est censée r.** I can't see what this sculpture is supposed to be *or* to represent

2 *(incarner)* to represent; *(symboliser)* to represent, to stand for; **elle représentait pour lui l'idéal féminin** she represented *or* symbolized *or* embodied the feminine ideal for him; **tu ne représentes plus rien pour moi** you don't mean anything to me any more; **chaque signe repré-**

sente un son each sign stands for *or* represents a sound

3 *(constituer)* to account for, to make up, to represent; **les produits de luxe représentent 60 pour cent de nos exportations** luxury items account for *or* make up *or* represent 60 percent of our exports; **le loyer représente un tiers de mon salaire** the rent amounts *or* comes to one third of my salary; **les immigrés représentent dix pour cent de l'échantillon** immigrants account for *or* make up *or* represent ten percent of the sample; **cela représente 200 heures de travail** 200 hours of work went into this, this represents 200 hours' work

4 *Théât (faire jouer)* to stage, to put on; *(jouer)* to play, to perform

5 *(être le représentant de)* to represent; **120 athlètes représentent la France aux jeux Olympiques** 120 athletes are representing France in the Olympic Games; **le maire s'est fait r. par son adjoint** the mayor was represented by his deputy, the mayor sent his deputy to represent him

6 *Com (agir au nom de)* to represent, to be a representative for

VPR se représenter 1 *(à une élection)* to *Br* stand *or Am* run (for election) again; *(à un examen)* to take *or Br* to sit an examination again **2** *(se manifester à nouveau ▸ problème)* to crop *or* to come up again; **une occasion qui ne se représentera sans doute jamais** an opportunity which doubtless will never again present itself; **la même pensée se représenta à mon esprit** the same thought crossed my mind once more **3** *(imaginer)* to imagine, to picture; **j'essaie de me la r. avec 20 ans de moins** I try to imagine *or* picture her (as she was) 20 years ago; **le métier d'actrice n'est pas comme je me l'étais représenté** being an actress isn't what I imagined *or* thought it would be; **représentez-vous le scandale que c'était à l'époque!** just imagine *or* think how scandalous it was in those days!

répressif, -ive [represif, -iv] **ADJ** repressive

répression [represjɔ̃] **NF 1** *(punition)* **ils exigent une r. plus sévère des actes terroristes** they are demanding a crackdown on terrorist activities; **mesures de r. de la fraude fiscale** measures to suppress tax evasion; **r. des fraudes** *(service gouvernemental)* consumer protection office **2** *(étouffement ▸ d'une révolte)* suppression, repression

répressive [represiv] *voir* **répressif**

réprimande [reprimɑ̃d] **NF** *(semonce ▸ amicale)* scolding, rebuke; *(▸ par un supérieur hiérarchique)* reprimand; **faire** *ou* **adresser une r. à qn** to rebuke *or* to reprimand sb; **sur un ton de r.** in a reproving tone (of voice), in a tone of rebuke

réprimander [3] [reprimɑ̃de] **VT** *(gronder)* to reprimand, to rebuke; **il s'est fait r.** *(par son père)* he was told off; *(par son patron)* he was given a reprimand

réprimer [3] [reprime] **VT 1** *(étouffer ▸ rébellion)* to suppress, to quell, to put down **2** *(punir ▸ délit, vandalisme)* to punish; **r. le banditisme/terrorisme** to crack down on crime/terrorism **3** *(sourire, colère)* to suppress; *(larmes)* to hold *or* to choke back; *(bâillement)* to stifle; *(juron)* to suppress, to smother; **des rires réprimés** repressed *or* stifled laughter

reprint [rəprint] **NM** *(livre)* reprint; *(réimpression)* reprinting

repris, -e [rəpri, -iz] **PP** *voir* **reprendre**

NM r. de justice ex-convict

• **reprise NF 1** *(d'une activité, d'un dialogue)* resumption; *Com (des affaires)* recovery, upturn; *Ordinat (d'un programme)* restart; **reprise des hostilités hier sur le front oriental** hostilities resumed on the eastern front yesterday; **la reprise du travail a été votée à la majorité** the majority voted in favour of going back *or* returning to work; *Com* **une reprise des affaires** an upturn *or* a recovery in business activity; **reprise (économique)** (economic) recovery

2 *Rad & TV* repeat, rerun; *Cin* rerun, reshowing; *Théât* revival, reprise; *Mus (d'un passage)* repeat, reprise; **une reprise d'une chanson des Beatles** a cover (version) of a Beatles song

3 *(rachat)* **deux hommes sont candidats à la reprise de la chaîne** two men have put in an offer to take over *or* to buy out the channel; **reprise de l'entreprise par ses salariés** employee *or* staff buy-out

4 *Com (de marchandises invendues, d'articles en solde)* taking back, return; **nous ne faisons pas de reprise** goods cannot be returned; **il m'offre une reprise de 500 euros pour ma vieille voiture** he'll give me 500 euros as a trade-in *or Br* in part exchange for my old car

5 *(entre locataires)* = payment made to an outgoing tenant (when renting property)

6 *Aut* speeding up, acceleration; **une voiture qui a de bonnes reprises** a car with good acceleration

7 *Sport (à la boxe)* round; *Escrime* bout; *Équitation (leçon)* riding lesson; *(cavaliers)* riding team; **reprise de volée** *(au tennis)* return volley; *Ftbl* **à la reprise, la Corée menait 2 à 0** Korea was leading 2–0 when the game resumed after half-time *or* at the start of the second half

8 *Couture (dans la maille)* darn; *(dans le tissu)* mend; **faire une reprise à une chemise** to mend a shirt

9 *Compta* **reprises sur provisions** recovery of provisions, write-back of provisions

10 *Hort* regrowth

• **reprises NFPL à diverses/multiples reprises** on several/numerous occasions; **à maintes reprises** on several *or* many occasions; **à trois ou quatre reprises** three or four times, on three or four occasions

reprisage [rəprizaʒ] **NM** *Couture (d'une chaussette, d'une moufle)* darning, mending; *(d'un vêtement)* mending

reprise [rəpriz] *voir* **repris**

repriser [3] [rəprize] **VT** *Couture (raccommoder ▸ chaussette, moufle)* to darn, to mend; *(▸ pantalon)* to mend

reprit *etc voir* **reprendre**

réprobateur, -trice [reprɔbatœr, -tris] **ADJ** reproving, reproachful; **jeter un regard r. à qn** to give sb a reproving look, to look at sb reprovingly *or* reproachfully; **..., dit-elle d'un ton r.** ..., she said reproachfully *or* in a reproving tone

réprobation [reprɔbasjɔ̃] **NF 1** *(blâme)* disapproval, censure, *Sout* reprobation; **soulever la r. générale** to give rise to general reprobation, to be unanimously reproved; **encourir la r. générale** to meet with general disapproval **2** *Rel* reprobation

réprobatrice [reprɔbatris] *voir* **réprobateur**

reproche [rəprɔʃ] **NM 1** *(blâme)* reproach; **accabler qn de reproches** to heap reproaches on sb; **faire un r. à qn** to reproach sb; **les reproches qu'on lui fait sont injustifiés** the reproaches levelled *or* directed at him/her are unjustified; **il y avait un léger r. dans sa voix/remarque** there was a hint of reproach in his/her voice/remark; **regarder qn d'un air plein de r.** to look at sb reproachfully; **d'un ton de r.** in a tone of reproach *or* reproachful tone; **faire r. à qn de qch** to upbraid sb for sth **2** *(critique)* **le seul r. que je ferais à la pièce, c'est sa longueur** the only thing I'd say against the play *or* my only criticism of the play is that it's too long **3** *Jur* **r. de témoin** barring of a witness

• **sans reproche ADJ** *(parfait)* above *or* beyond reproach, irreproachable; *(qui n'a pas commis d'erreur)* blameless **ADV soit dit sans r., tu n'aurais pas dû y aller** I don't mean to blame *or* to reproach you, but you shouldn't have gone

reprocher [3] [rəprɔʃe] **VT 1 r. qch à qn** *(erreur, faute)* to blame *or* to reproach sb for sth; **je lui reproche son manque de ponctualité** what I don't like about him/her is his/her lack of punctuality; **on ne peut pas r. au gouvernement son laxisme** you can't criticize the government for being too soft; **je ne vous reproche rien** I'm not blaming you for anything; **il n'y a absolument rien à lui r.** he's/she's totally blameless; **r. à qn de faire qch** to blame sb for doing sth; **il lui a toujours reproché de l'avoir quitté** he always blamed her for leaving him; **il s'est fait r. un certain laisser-aller dans le service** he was accused of a certain slackness in his department **2 r. qch à qch** *(défaut)* to criticize sth for sth; **ce que je reproche à ce beaujolais, c'est sa verdeur** the criticism I would make of this Beaujolais is that it's too young; **je n'ai rien à r. à son interprétation** in my view his/her interpretation is faultless, I can't find fault with his/her interpretation; **qu'est-ce que vous reprochez à ce livre?** what have you got against the book?; **r. à qch d'être...** to criticize sth for being...; **on a reproché à ma thèse d'être trop courte** my thesis was criticized for being too short **3** *Jur (témoin)* to bar

VPR se reprocher n'avoir rien à se r. to have nothing to feel guilty about, to have nothing with which to reproach oneself; **tu n'as pas à te r. son départ** you shouldn't blame yourself for his/her departure; **je me reproche de lui avoir fait confiance** I blame myself for trusting him/her

reproducteur, -trice [rəprɔdyktœr, -tris] **ADJ** *(organe, cellule)* reproductive; **cheval r.** stud-horse, stallion; **poule reproductrice** breeder hen

NM,F *(poule)* breeder; *(cheval)* stud

NM *Tech* template

reproductibilité [rəprɔdyktibilite] **NF** reproducibility, repeatability

reproductible [rəprɔdyktibl] **ADJ** reproducible, repeatable

reproductif, -ive [rəprɔdyktif, -iv] **ADJ** reproductive

reproduction [rəprɔdyksjɔ̃] **NF 1** *Biol & Bot* reproduction; *Agr* breeding; **cycle/organes de la r.** reproductive cycle/organs; **l'époque de la r.** the breeding season; **r. asexuée** asexual reproduction; **r. sexuée** sexual reproduction

2 *(restitution)* reproduction, reproducing; **cela se prête bien à la r.** it reproduces well; **techniques de r. des sons** sound reproduction techniques

3 *Typ (nouvelle publication)* reprinting, reissuing; *(technique)* reproduction, duplication; **droits de r.** reproduction rights; **tous droits de r. réservés pour tous pays** all rights of reproduction reserved for all countries; **r. interdite** *(sur vidéocassette, disque)* all rights reserved

4 *(réplique)* reproduction, copy; **la qualité des reproductions dans un ouvrage d'art** the quality of the reproduction *or* reproductions in an art book; **une r. du 'Baiser' de Rodin/de 'Guernica'** a copy of Rodin's 'Kiss'/of 'Guernica'; **une r. en couleur(s)** a colour print

5 *(département)* reprographic department; **les documents sont partis à la r.** the documents have gone off to repro

reproductive [rəprɔdyktiv] *voir* **reproductif**

reproductrice [rəprɔdyktris] *voir* **reproducteur**

reproduire [98] [rəprɔdɥir] **VT 1** *(faire un autre exemplaire de ▸ gén)* to copy; *(▸ clé)* to cut; **r. une médaille par moulage** to copy a medal by taking a mould of it; **ce tableau a été reproduit à des milliers d'exemplaires** thousands of reproductions have been made of this picture

2 *(renouveler)* to repeat; **tu as reproduit les mêmes erreurs** you've made the same mistakes as before

3 *(imiter)* to reproduce, to copy; **les enfants reproduisent les attitudes des adultes** children copy *or* mimic adult attitudes

4 *(représenter)* to show, to depict, to portray; **la tapisserie reproduit une scène de chasse** the tapestry depicts a hunting scene

5 *(restituer ▸ son)* to reproduce

6 *Typ (republier ▸ texte)* to reissue; *(▸ livre)* to reprint; *(photocopier)* to photocopy; *(reprographier)* to duplicate, to reproduce; *(polycopier)* to duplicate

7 *Hort* to reproduce, to breed; **plantes reproduites en serre** plants propagated in a greenhouse

VPR se reproduire 1 *Biol & Bot* to reproduce, to breed **2** *(se renouveler)* to recur; **ces tendances se reproduisent de génération en génération** these trends recur *or* are repeated with each successive generation; **et que cela ne se reproduise plus!** don't let it happen again!

reprogrammable [rəprɔgramabl] **ADJ** *Ordinat (touche)* reprogrammable

reprogrammer [3] [rəprɔgrame] **VT 1** *Cin & TV* to reschedule **2** *Ordinat* to reprogram

reprographie [rəprɔgrafi] **NF** reprography, repro

reprographier [9] [rəprɔgrafje] **VT** *(polycopier)* to duplicate; *(photocopier)* to photocopy

réprouvé, -e [repruve] **ADJ** *Rel* reprobate
NM,F 1 *Rel* reprobate **2** *(personne rejetée)* **vivre en r.** to live as an outcast

réprouver [3] [repruve] **VT 1** *(attitude, pratique)* to condemn, to disapprove of; **r. l'attitude de qn** to reprove *or* to condemn sb's attitude; **nous réprouvons l'usage qui a été fait de cet argent** we disapprove of *or* condemn the way this money has been used; **des pratiques/tendances que la morale réprouve** morally unacceptable practices/tendencies **2** *Rel* to reprobate, to damn

reps [rɛps] **NM** *Tex* rep, repp

reptation [rɛptasjɔ̃] **NF** crawling, *Spéc* reptation

reptile [rɛptil] **ADJ** reptile, reptant
NM reptile

repu, -e [rəpy] **PP** *voir* **repaître**
ADJ *Sout (rassasié)* sated, satiated; **être r.** to be full (up), to have eaten one's fill; **je suis r. de films policiers** I've had my fill of detective films

républicain, -e [repyblikɛ̃, -ɛn] **ADJ** *(esprit, système)* republican
NM,F *(gén)* republican; *(aux États-Unis, en Irlande)* Republican; *Hist* **Républicains indépendants** Independent Republicans *(conservative Gaullist party founded in the early 1960s)*

républicanisme [repyblikanism] **NM** republicanism

république [repyblik] **NF 1** *(régime politique)* republic; **vivre en r.** to live in a republic; *Fam* **je fais ce que je veux, on est en r., non?** I'll do as I like, it's a free country, isn't it? **2** *(État)* Republic; **la R. arabe unie** the United Arab Republic; *Péj* **r. bananière** banana republic; *Anciennement* **la R. démocratique allemande** the German Democratic Republic; **la R. démocratique du Congo** the Democratic Republic of Congo; **la R. dominicaine** the Dominican Republic; *Anciennement* **la R. fédérale d'Allemagne** the Federal Republic of Germany; **la R. française** the French Republic; **la R. d'Irlande** the Irish Republic, the Republic of Ireland; **la R. populaire de Chine** the People's Republic of China; **la R. tchèque** the Czech Republic; **la r. une et indivisible** = Jacobin concept of a unified state which is one of the basic principles of the French Republic; *Hist* **la R. de Weimar** the Weimar Republic **3** *(confrérie)* **dans la r. des lettres** in the literary world, in the world of letters

> **RÉPUBLIQUE**
>
> The concept of the "République" has been the keystone of the political system in France since the French Revolution. The proclamation of the First Republic (1792–1804) was marked by the dissolution of the monarchy. The Second Republic (1848–52) was established after the revolution of 1848 and the abdication of King Louis-Philippe. The Third Republic (1870–1940) was created after the Franco-Prussian War. It collapsed in 1940 when France was occupied by Germany, and was replaced by the Vichy regime. The Fourth Republic (1946–58) was established in 1946 but was plagued by instability. In October 1958 de Gaulle called a referendum as a result of which, in January 1959, he created the current Fifth Republic, whose constitution provides for a much stronger executive government.

répudiation [repydjasjɔ̃] **NF 1** *(d'une épouse)* repudiation, disowning **2** *(d'une nationalité, d'un héritage)* renunciation, relinquishment; *(d'un principe, d'un devoir)* renunciation, renouncement

répudier [9] [repydje] **VT 1** *(renvoyer ▸ épouse)* to repudiate, to disown; **se faire r.** to be rejected **2** *(renoncer à ▸ nationalité, héritage)* to renounce, to relinquish; *(▸ principe, devoir)* to renounce; **r. ses anciennes convictions** to go back on *or* to renounce one's former beliefs

répugnance [repyɲɑ̃s] **NF 1** *(dégoût)* repugnance (**pour** for), loathing (**pour** of *or* for), disgust; **avoir de la r. pour qn/qch** to loathe sb/sth **2** *(mauvaise volonté)* reluctance; **éprouver une certaine r. à faire qch** to be somewhat reluctant *or* loath to do sth; **je m'attelai à la tâche avec r.** I set about the task reluctantly *or* unwillingly; **la r. du syndicat à relancer le dialogue** the union's reluctance to resume talks

répugnant, -e [repyɲɑ̃, -ɑ̃t] **ADJ 1** *(physiquement)* repugnant, loathsome, disgusting; **avoir un physique r.** to be repulsive; **odeur répugnante** disgusting smell; **tâche répugnante** revolting task; **une chambre d'une saleté répugnante** a revoltingly *or* disgustingly filthy room **2** *(moralement ▸ individu, crime)* repugnant; *(▸ livre, image)* disgusting, revolting; **il s'est conduit de façon répugnante avec ses employés** he behaved disgracefully *or* abominably towards his employees

répugner [3] [repyɲe] **VT** *Littéraire (personne)* to be repugnant to
• répugner à VT IND 1 *(être peu disposé à)* **r. à faire qch** to be reluctant *or* loath to do sth **2** *(dégoûter)* **r. à qn** to repel sb, to be repugnant to sb; **tout ce qui est tâche domestique me répugne** I can't bear anything to do with housework; **ça ne te répugne pas, l'idée de manger des escargots?** doesn't the idea of eating snails disgust you *or* put you off?; **tout en cet homme me répugne** I loathe everything about that man, everything about that man is repulsive (to me) **3** *(tournure impersonnelle)* **il me répugne de travailler avec lui** I hate *or* loathe working with him

répulsif, -ive [repylsif, -iv] **ADJ 1** *Phys* repulsive **2** *Littéraire (répugnant)* repulsive, repugnant, repellent

répulsion [repylsjɔ̃] **NF 1** *(dégoût)* repulsion, repugnance; **éprouver de la r. pour qch** to feel repulsion for sth, to find sth repugnant; **leurs méthodes m'inspirent une grande r.** I find their methods repugnant **2** *Phys* repulsion

répulsive [repylsiv] *voir* **répulsif**

réputation [repytasjɔ̃] **NF 1** *(renommée)* reputation, repute; **avoir (une) bonne/mauvaise r.** to have a good/bad reputation; **jouir d'une bonne r.** to have *or* to enjoy a good reputation; **se faire une r.** to make a reputation *or* name for oneself; **un hôtel de bonne/mauvaise r.** a hotel of good/ill repute; *Fam* **il n'a pas volé sa r. de frimeur** they don't call him a show-off for nothing; **elle a la r. de noter sévèrement** she has a reputation *or* she's well-known for being a tough *Br* marker *or Am* grader; **marque de r. mondiale** *ou* **internationale** world-famous brand, brand of international repute; **c'est ce qui a fait sa r.** that's what made their name, that's how they made their name; *Fam* **tu me fais une sale r.** you're giving me a bad name▫; **leur r. n'est plus à faire** their reputation is well-established; **connaître qn de r.** to know sb by repute *or* reputation **2** *(honorabilité)* reputation, good name; **je suis prêt à mettre ma r. en jeu** I'm willing to stake my reputation on it; **porter atteinte à la r. de qn** to damage *or* to blacken sb's good name

réputé, -e [repyte] **ADJ 1** *(illustre ▸ orchestre, restaurant)* famous, renowned; **l'un des musiciens les plus réputés de son temps** one of the most famous musicians of his day; **des vins très réputés** wines of great repute; **un écrivain pas très r.** a little-known writer; **elle est réputée pour ses colères** she's famous *or* renowned for her fits of rage; **il est r. pour être un avocat efficace** he has the reputation of being *or* he's reputed to be a good lawyer **2** *(considéré comme)* reputed; **elle est réputée intelligente** she has a reputation for intelligence, she's reputed to be intelligent; **il est r. ne rien ignorer de cette science** he is reputed *or* said to know everything about the science

requérant, -e [rəkerɑ̃, -ɑ̃t] *Jur* **ADJ** claiming; **la partie requérante** the claimant, the petitioner
NM,F claimant, petitioner

requérir [39] [rəkerir] **VT 1** *(solliciter ▸ aide, présence)* to request; *(nécessiter)* to call for, to require; **ce travail requiert beaucoup d'attention** the work requires *or* demands great concentration; **r. les civils** to call upon civilian help **2** *Jur* to call for, to demand; **le juge a requis une peine de deux ans de prison** the judge recommended a two-year prison sentence **3** *(sommer)* **r. qn de faire qch** to request that sb do sth

requête [rəkɛt] **NF 1** *(demande)* request, petition; **adresser une r. à qn** to make a request to sb, *Sout* to petition sb; **à la** *ou* **sur la r. de qn** at sb's request *or* behest; **elle est venue à ma r.** she came at my request **2** *Jur* petition; **adresser une r. au tribunal** to petition the court, to apply for legal remedy; **r. en cassation** application for appeal; **r. conjointe** joint petition **3** *Ordinat* query

requiem [rekɥijɛm] **NM INV** *Rel & Mus* requiem

requiert *etc voir* **requérir**

requin [rəkɛ̃] **NM 1** *Ich* shark; **r. bleu** blue shark; **(grand) r. blanc** (great) white shark **2** *(personne)* shark; *Fin* **r. (de la finance)** shark, raider

requin-marteau [rəkɛ̃marto] *(pl* **requins-marteaux)** **NM** *Ich* hammerhead (shark)

requinquer [3] [rəkɛ̃ke] *Fam* **VT** *(redonner des forces à)* to pep up, to buck up; **le voilà requinqué** he's (back to) his old self again
VPR se requinquer to recover▫, to perk up; **il a eu du mal à se r.** it took him a while to recover *or* to get back to his old self again

requis, -e [rəki, -iz] **PP** *voir* **requérir**
ADJ 1 *(prescrit)* required, requisite; **remplir les conditions requises** to meet the required *or* prescribed conditions; **les conditions requises sont simples** the requirements are simple; **avoir l'âge r.** to meet the age requirements; **avoir les qualifications requises** to have the requisite *or* necessary qualifications **2** *(réquisitionné)* commandeered, requisitioned; **fonctionnaire r.** commandeered civil servant; **gréviste r.** requisitioned striker
NM commandeered civilian; **les r. du travail (obligatoire)** labour conscripts

réquisition [rekizisjɔ̃] **NF 1** *Mil & Fig* requisition, requisitioning, commandeering; **on a annoncé la r. des ouvriers grévistes** it has been announced that the striking workers are to be requisitioned; **il y a eu r. de tous les véhicules par l'armée** the army has requisitioned *or* commandeered all vehicles **2** *Jur* **r. d'audience** petition to the court **3** *Fin* **r. de paiement** demand for payment
• réquisitions NFPL *Jur (conclusions)* closing speech (for the prosecution); *(réquisitoire)* charge

réquisitionner [3] [rekizisjɔne] **VT 1** *(matériel, troupe, employé)* to requisition, to commandeer **2** *Hum (faire appel à)* **r. qn pour faire qch** to rope sb into doing sth; **elle nous a réquisitionnés pour faire la vaisselle** she requisitioned us to do the washing-up, she dragooned us into doing the washing-up

réquisitoire [rekizitwar] **NM 1** *Jur (dans un procès)* prosecutor's arraignment *or* speech *or* charge **2** *Fig* indictment (**contre** of); **ces résultats constituent un véritable r. contre la politique du gouvernement** these results are an indictment of the government's policy

requit *etc voir* **requérir**

RER [ɛrəɛr] **NM** *Rail (abrév* **Réseau express régional)** = Paris metropolitan and regional rail system

RES [ɛrəɛs] **NM** *Fin (abrév* **rachat de l'entreprise par ses salariés)** employee buy-out

RESA [reza] **NF** *(abrév* **réservation)** = TGV seat reservation ticket

résa [reza] **NF** *(abrév* **réservation)** reservation, booking

resaler [3] [rəsale] **VT** to put more salt in, to add more salt to

resalir [32] [rəsalir] **VT** to make dirty again; **j'ai resali le tailleur que je viens de faire nettoyer** I've just got my suit back from the cleaners and I've got it dirty again; **évitez de r. des assiettes** try not to dirty any more plates
VPR se resalir to get oneself dirty again

rescapé, -e [rɛskape] **ADJ** surviving
NM,F 1 *(d'un accident, d'un désastre)* survivor; **les rescapés de la catastrophe** the survivors of the catastrophe **2** *Fig* **les quelques rescapés du Tour de France** the few remaining participants in the Tour de France

rescinder [3] [rəsɛ̃de] **VT** to rescind

rescision [resizjɔ̃] **NF** *Jur* rescission

rescousse [rɛskus] **à la rescousse ADV aller/venir à la r. de qn** to go/to come to sb's rescue; **arriver à la r.** to come to the rescue; **nous avons appelé quelques amis à la r.** we called on a few friends for help

réseau, -x [rezo] **NM 1** *(de fils, de veines)* network; *Mil* **r. de barbelés** barbed wire entanglement

2 *Transp* network; **r. aérien/ferroviaire/routier** air/rail/road network; **r. urbain** city bus network; **R. express régional** = Paris metropolitan and regional rail system

3 *Tél & TV* network; **r. câblé** cable network; *Rad* **r. hertzien** radio relay network; **r. satellitaire** satellite network; **r. satellite** satellite network; **r. de télécommunications** telecommunications network; **r. de téléphonie mobile** *Br* mobile phone *or Am* cellphone network; **r. téléphonique** telephone network; **r. de télévision** television network; **r. télévisuel** television network

4 *(organisation)* network; **développer un r. commercial** to develop *or* to expand a sales network; **r. de distribution** distribution network; **r. d'espionnage** spy ring, network of spies; **r. de trafiquants de drogue** drug ring; **r. de vente** sales network

5 *Littéraire* network, web; **je suis pris dans un r. de contraintes** I'm caught in a network *or* web of constraints

6 *Élec* grid; **r. bouclé** ring main

7 *Géog* **r. fluvial** river system

8 *Ordinat* network; **mettre en r.** to network; **r. analogique** analogue network; **r. en anneau** ring network; **r. de communication de données** datacomms network; **r. à commutation par paquets** packet-switching network; **r. de données** data network; **r. en étoile/maillé** star/mesh network; **r. informatique** computer network; **r. à large bande** broadband network; **r. local** local-area network, LAN; **r. longue distance** wide-area network, WAN; **r. national d'interconnexion** backbone; **r. numérique** digital network; **r. numérique à intégration de services** integrated services digital network; **r. de télématique** datacomms network; **r. d'utilisateurs** user network

réséda [rezeda] **ADJ INV** *(couleur)* reseda

NM 1 *Bot* reseda; **r. des teinturiers** weld, dyer's rocket **2** *Hort* mignonette **3** *(couleur)* reseda

réservataire [rezervater] **ADJ** *Jur* **elle est r. pour un tiers** a third of the legacy devolves to her by law; **héritier r.** heir who cannot be totally disinherited

NMF heir who cannot be totally disinherited

réservation [rezervasjɔ̃] **NF 1** *(d'un billet, d'une chambre, d'une table)* reservation, booking; **faire une r.** *(à l'hôtel)* to make a reservation; *(au restaurant)* to reserve a table; **faut-il faire une r.?** is it necessary to reserve *or* to book?; **la r. est obligatoire** reservations are necessary; **souhaitez-vous un billet avec ou sans r.?** do you wish to reserve a seat with your ticket or not? **2** *Jur* reservation

réserve [rezɛrv] **NF 1** *(stock)* reserve, stock; **nous ne disposons pas d'une r. suffisante d'eau potable** we do not have sufficient reserves of drinking water; **une r. d'argent** some money put by; **faire des réserves de** to lay in supplies *or* provisions of; *Écon* **r. légale** reserve assets; **r. liquide** liquid assets, cash reserve; **r. métallique** bullion reserve; **r. occulte** secret reserve; **r. de prévoyance** contingency reserve; **r. statutaire** statutory reserve

2 *(réticence)* reservation; **permettez-moi de formuler quelques réserves** I have some reservations which I should like to express; **avoir des réserves au sujet d'un projet** to have (some) reservations about a project; **faire** *ou* **émettre des réserves** to express reservations

3 *(modestie, retenue)* reserve; **une jeune femme pleine de r.** a very reserved young woman; **elle est** *ou* **demeure** *ou* **se tient sur la r.** she's being *or* remaining reserved (about it); **il a accueilli mon frère avec une grande r.** he welcomed my brother with great restraint

4 *(en anthropologie)* reservation; *École* reserve, sanctuary; **r. de chasse/pêche** hunting/fishing preserve; *Can* **r. faunique** wildlife reserve; *Can* **r. indienne** Indian reservation; **r. naturelle** nature reserve; **r. ornithologique** *ou* **d'oiseaux** bird sanctuary

5 *(resserre ▸ dans un magasin)* storeroom; *(collections réservées ▸ dans un musée, dans une bibliothèque)* reserve collection

6 *Jur (clause)* reservation; *Jur* **sous toutes réserves** without prejudice; **sous r. de la signature du contrat** subject to contract

7 *Mil* **la r.** the reserve

• **réserves NFPL 1** *Fin* reserves; **réserves bancaires** bank reserves; **réserves de change** monetary reserves; **réserves en espèces** cash reserves; **réserves monétaires/de devises** monetary/currency reserves; **réserves monétaires internationales** international monetary reserves; **réserves obligatoires** statutory reserves **2** *(naturelles)* reserves; *Mines* **les réserves de charbon d'un pays** *(gisements)* a country's coal reserves; *(stocks)* a country's coal stocks; **réserves mondiales** *(de matières premières)* world reserves

• **de réserve ADJ 1** *(conservé pour plus tard)* reserve *(avant n)*; **nous avons un stock de r.** we have a reserve supply **2** *Fin* **monnaie de r.** reserve currency **3** *Mil* **officier de r.** officer of the reserve; **régiment de r.** reserve regiment

• **en réserve ADV 1** *(de côté)* in reserve; **avoir de la nourriture en r.** to have food put by, to have food in reserve; **mettre de la nourriture en r.** to put food aside; **je tiens en r. quelques bouteilles pour notre anniversaire** I've put a few bottles aside *or* to one side for our anniversary **2** *Com* in stock; **avoir qch en r.** to have sth in stock; **nous avons du papier en r. pour un mois** we have one month's supply *or* stock of paper in reserve

• **sans réserve ADJ** *(admiration)* unreserved; *(dévotion)* unreserved, unstinting; *(approbation)* unreserved, unqualified **ADV** without reservation, unreservedly

• **sous réserve de PRÉP** subject to; **sous r. de vérification** subject to verification, pending checks; **le départ aura lieu à 8 heures sous r. d'annulation** departure, subject to cancellation, will be at 8 o'clock

• **sous toute réserve ADV** with all proper reserves; **attention, c'est sous toute r.!** there's no guarantee as to the accuracy of this!; **la nouvelle a été publiée sous toute r.** the news was published with no guarantee as to its accuracy

réservé, -e [rezɛrve] **ADJ 1** *(non public)* **chasse réservée** *(sur panneau)* private hunting; *Euph* **quartier r.** red-light district

2 *(retenu)* reserved, *Br* booked; **désolé Monsieur, cette table est réservée** I'm sorry, sir, this table is reserved; **r.** *(table dans un restaurant)* reserved

3 *(distant)* reserved; **une jeune fille très réservée** a very reserved young girl; **il a toujours eu une attitude très réservée à mon égard** he was always very reserved towards me

4 *Jur* reserved

réserver [3] [rezɛrve] **VT 1** *(retenir à l'avance)* to reserve, to book; **on vous a réservé une chambre** a room has been reserved for you; **je vous ai réservé une place sur le prochain vol** I've booked *or* reserved a seat for you *or* I've booked you on the next flight; **r. une place de concert** to book *or* to reserve a ticket for a concert; **nous réservons toujours cette table à nos meilleurs clients** we always reserve this table for our best customers

2 *(conserver ▸ gén)* to reserve, to keep; *(▸ pour un usage particulier)* to save, to keep, to set *or* to put aside; **il a réservé une partie de sa maison pour peindre** he keeps *or* he's set aside part of his house to paint in; **il a promis de nous r. une partie de sa récolte** he promised to put aside *or* to keep part of his crop for us; **r. le meilleur pour la fin** to keep *or* to save the best till last; **r. sa réponse** to delay one's answer; **r. son opinion** to reserve one's opinion; **r. son jugement** to reserve judgement; **être réservé à qn** to be reserved for sb; **un privilège/sport réservé aux gens riches** a privilege/sport enjoyed solely by rich people; **toilettes réservées aux handicapés** toilets (reserved) for the disabled; **emplacements réservés aux médecins** parking (reserved) for doctors only

3 *(destiner)* to reserve, to have in store; **r. une surprise à qn** to have a surprise (in store) for sb; **r. un accueil glacial/chaleureux à qn** to reserve an icy/a warm welcome for sb; **que nous réserve l'avenir?** what does the future have in store for us?; **nous ignorons le sort qui lui sera réservé** we do not know what fate has in store for him/her

USAGE ABSOLU Mesdames, bonsoir, avez-vous réservé? good evening, ladies, do you have a reservation *or Br* have you booked?; **j'ai réservé au nom de Roux** I have a reservation in the name of Roux; **pour r., appeler...** for reservations, call...

VPR se réserver 1 *(par prudence)* to hold back; **je me réserve pour le fromage** I'm keeping some room *or* saving myself for the cheese

2 *Sport & Fig* to save one's strength; **je me réserve pour le match de ce soir** I'm saving my strength for this evening's match

3 se r. qch to reserve *or* to keep sth (for oneself); **je me suis réservé le blanc du poulet/la chambre du haut** I've saved the chicken breast/I've kept the top bedroom for myself; **se r. un droit de regard sur** to retain the right to inspect sth; **se r. le droit de faire qch** to reserve the right to do sth

réserviste [rezɛrvist] **NM** *Mil* reservist

réservoir [rezɛrvwar] **NM 1** *(d'essence, de mazout)* tank; *Aut* (fuel *or Br* petrol) tank; *(d'eau)* (water) tank; *(des W-C)* cistern; **r. d'eau chaude** hot water tank; *Aut* **r. de liquide de frein** brake fluid reservoir; *Com* **r. de main-d'œuvre** labour pool; *Fig* **un r. de jeunes talents** a breeding ground for young talent **2** *(étang, lac)* reservoir; *(pour poissons)* fish pond

résidant, -e [rezidɑ̃, -ɑ̃t] **ADJ** resident

NM,F resident

résidence [rezidɑ̃s] **NF 1** *(domicile)* residence; **établir sa r. à Nice** to take up residence in Nice; **avoir sa r. à Lyon** to be resident *or* to live in Lyons; **r. d'été** summer quarters; **r. officielle** official residence; **r. principale/secondaire** main/second home

2 *(bâtiment) Br* block of (luxury) flats, *Am* (luxury) apartment block; **r. hôtelière** apartment hotel; **r. médicalisée** nursing home; *Univ* **r. universitaire** *Br* hall of residence, *Am* dormitory

3 *(maison)* residential property

4 *Jur* residence; **assigner qn à r.** to put sb under house arrest; **être en r. surveillée** to be under house arrest

résident, -e [rezidɑ̃, -ɑ̃t] **NM,F 1** resident, (foreign) national; **tous les résidents français de Londres** all French nationals living in London **2** *Belg* **second r.** weekender, holiday resident

ADJ *Ordinat* resident

résidentiel, -elle [rezidɑ̃sjɛl] **ADJ** residential

résider [3] [rezide] **VI 1** *(habiter)* **r. à** to live in, *Sout* to reside; **r. à l'étranger/à Genève** to live abroad/in Geneva **2** *Fig* **r. dans** to lie in; **sa force réside dans son influence sur l'armée** his/her strength lies in *or* is based on his/her influence over the army; **c'est là que réside tout l'intérêt du film** that is where the strength of the film lies

résidu [rezidy] **NM** *(portion restante)* residue

• **résidus NMPL** *(détritus)* residue, remnants; *Nucl* **résidus de fission** radioactive waste; **résidus de raffinage** waste oil

résiduaire [rezidɥɛr] **ADJ** residuary

résiduel, -elle [rezidɥɛl] **ADJ 1** *(qui constitue un résidu ▸ huile, matière)* residual **2** *(persistant ▸ chômage)* residual; **fatigue résiduelle** constant tiredness **3** *Géog* **relief r.** residual relief

résignation [reziɲasjɔ̃] **NF 1** *(acceptation)* resignation, resignedness; **accepter son destin avec r.** to accept one's fate resignedly *or* with resignation **2** *Jur* abandonment (of a right)

> Il faut noter que le terme anglais **resignation** signifie également **démission**.

résigné, -e [reziɲe] **ADJ** resigned (à to); **prendre un air r.** to look resigned; **parler d'un ton r.** to speak in a resigned *or* philosophical tone of voice; **je suis r.** I've resigned myself

NM,F resigned person; **les résignés** people who have accepted their fate

résigner [3] [reziɲe] **VT** *(se démettre de)* to resign, to relinquish

VPR se résigner 1 *(se soumettre)* **il n'a jamais voulu se r.** he would never give up *or* in, he would never submit; **il faut se r.** you must resign yourself to it *or* accept it **2 se r. à** *(accepter)* to resign oneself to; **il s'est résigné à vivre dans la pauvreté** he has resigned himself to living in poverty; **se r. à une perte** to resign oneself to a loss

résiliable [reziljabl] **ADJ** *Jur (bail, contrat, marché)* cancellable, terminable, voidable; **non r.** indefeasible

résiliation [reziljasjɔ̃] **NF** *Jur (d'un bail, d'un contrat, d'un marché ▸ en cours)* cancellation, avoidance; *(▸ arrivant à expiration)* termination

résilience [reziljɑ̃s] NF resilience

résilient, -e [reziljɑ̃, -ɑ̃t] ADJ resilient

résilier [9] [rezilje] VT *(bail, contrat, marché ▸ en cours)* to cancel; *(▸ arrivant à expiration)* to terminate

résille [rezij] NF 1 *(à cheveux)* hairnet 2 *(d'un vitrail)* cames, leading, leads

résine [rezin] NF *Bot & Tech* resin; **r. époxyde** *ou* **epoxy** epoxy resin; **r. synthétique** synthetic resin

résiné, -e [rezine] ADJ resinated

NM resinated wine

résiner [3] [rezine] VT 1 *(enduire)* to resin 2 *(gemmer)* to tap

résineux, -euse [rezinø, -øz] ADJ 1 *(essence, odeur)* resinous 2 *(arbre, bois)* resiniferous, coniferous

NM conifer

résistance [rezistɑ̃s] NF 1 *(combativité)* resistance (**à** to); **la r. de l'armée** resistance by the troops, the troops' resistance; **n'offrir aucune r.** to put up *or* to offer no resistance; **elle a opposé une r. farouche à ses agresseurs** she put up a fierce resistance to her attackers; **il s'est laissé emmener sans r.** he let himself be taken away quietly *or* without resistance; **je sens une r. de sa part quand j'essaie de lui en parler** I can feel a reluctance on his/her part to talk about it

2 *(rébellion)* resistance; **r. active/passive** active/passive resistance; **faire de la r. passive** to engage in passive resistance; *Hist* **la R.** the (French) Resistance; **il est entré dans la R. dès 1940** he joined the Resistance as early as 1940

3 *(obstacle)* resistance; **son projet n'a pas rencontré de r.** his/her project met no opposition *or* was unopposed; **venir à bout de toutes les résistances** to overcome all obstacles *or* all resistance

4 *(robustesse)* resistance, stamina; **elle a survécu grâce à sa r. exceptionnelle** she survived thanks to her great powers of resistance; **r. à la fatigue/au froid** resistance to tiredness/cold; **les limites de la r. humaine** the limits of human resistance *or* endurance

5 *Tech (solidité)* resistance, strength; *(propriété physique)* resistance; **r. aux chocs** resilience; **r. à la traction/à la flexion** tensile/bending strength; **la r. d'un pont/d'une poutre** the resistance of a bridge/beam; **r. des matériaux** strength of materials; **acier à haute r.** high-resistance *or* high-tensile steel; **r. de l'air** air resistance

6 *Élec* resistance; *(dispositif chauffant)* element; *(conducteur)* resistor

résistant, -e [rezistɑ̃, -ɑ̃t] ADJ 1 *(personne)* resistant, tough; *(plante)* hardy; *(emballage)* resistant, strong, solid; *(couleur)* fast; **c'est une enfant peu résistante** she's not a very strong child; **nos soldats sont résistants, bien entraînés** our soldiers are tough and well-trained 2 *Élec & Phys* resistant; **r. au froid/gel** cold/frost resistant; **r. aux chocs** shockproof; **r. à la chaleur** heatproof, heat-resistant

NM,F freedom fighter; *Hist (en France)* (French) Resistance fighter

résister [3] [reziste] **résister à** VT IND 1 *(agresseur, attaque)* to resist, to hold out against; *(autorité)* to resist, to stand up to; *(gendarme, huissier)* to put up resistance to; *(pression)* to resist; **il a résisté aux officiers venus l'arrêter** he resisted arrest; **il n'a pas pu r. au courant** he couldn't fight against the current; **j'ai toujours résisté à ses caprices** I've always stood up to *or* opposed his/her whims; **je ne peux pas lui r., il est si gentil** I can't resist him, he's so nice

2 *(fatigue, faim)* to withstand, to put up with; *(maladie, épidémie)* to overcome; *(solitude, douleur)* to stand, to withstand; **r. à la tentation** to resist temptation; **r. à ses désirs/penchants** to fight against one's desires/inclinations

3 *(à l'usure, à l'action des éléments)* to withstand, to resist, to be proof against; **qui résiste au feu** fireproof; **qui résiste à la chaleur** heatproof; **qui résiste aux chocs** shockproof; **r. au temps** to stand the test of time; **couleurs qui résistent au lavage** fast colours

4 *(sujet: livre, projet)* to stand up to; **r. à l'analyse/l'examen** to stand up to analysis/investigation; **son œuvre ne résistera pas à la critique** his/her work won't stand up to criticism

USAGE ABSOLU **toute la famille a résisté** *(a fait partie de la Résistance)* the whole family fought in the Resistance; **je n'ai pas pu r., je les ai achetés** I couldn't resist them so I bought them; **la serrure résiste** the lock is sticking; **la toiture/théière n'a pas résisté** the roof/teapot didn't stand up to the shock

résistivité [rezistivite] NF *Élec* resistivity, specific resistance

resituer [7] [rəsitɥe] VT to place (**dans** in); **il faut r. cet événement dans son contexte** the event needs to be placed *or* put into context

résolu, -e [rezɔly] PP *voir* **résoudre**

ADJ 1 *(personne)* resolute, determined; **d'un air r.** determinedly, with an air of determination, resolutely; **je suis r. à ne pas céder** I'm determined not to give in 2 *(attitude)* **une foi résolue en l'avenir** an unshakeable faith in the future

résoluble [rezɔlybl] ADJ 1 *(question, situation)* soluble, solvable 2 *Jur (bail, contrat)* annullable, cancellable

résolument [rezɔlymɑ̃] ADV 1 *(fermement)* resolutely, firmly, determinedly; **je m'oppose r. à cette décision** I'm strongly *or* firmly opposed to this decision 2 *(vaillamment)* resolutely, steadfastly, unwaveringly

résolut *etc voir* **résoudre**

résolution [rezɔlysjɔ̃] NF 1 *(décision)* resolution; **prendre une r.** to make a resolution; **prendre la r. de faire qch** to make up one's mind *or* to resolve to do sth; **sa r. est prise** his/her mind is made up; **bonnes résolutions** *(gén)* good intentions; *(du nouvel an)* NewYear resolutions

2 *(détermination)* determination, resolve, single-mindedness; **avec r.** resolutely, determinedly; **elle a fait preuve de beaucoup de r.** she showed great determination *or* resolution *or* resolve

3 *(solution)* solution, resolution; **la r. d'une énigme/d'un problème** the solution to an enigma/a problem

4 *Pol* resolution; **prendre une r.** to pass a resolution; **la r. a été votée à l'unanimité par l'Assemblée** the resolution was unanimously adopted by the Assembly

5 *Jur (d'un contrat)* annulment, cancellation

6 *Ordinat & TV (d'un écran)* resolution; **mauvaise/bonne r.** poor/high resolution; **écran à haute r.** high-resolution screen

7 *Méd* resolution; **r. des membres** muscular relaxation

8 *Opt* **pouvoir de r.** resolving power

résolutoire [rezɔlytwar] ADJ *Jur* resolutive

résolvait *etc voir* **résoudre**

résonance [rezɔnɑ̃s] NF 1 *(gén) & Phys & Tél* resonance; *Fig* **avoir une r.** *ou* **des résonances (dans)** to find an echo (in); **sa déclaration a eu quelque r. dans la classe politique** his/her statement found an echo *or* had a certain effect amongst politicians; **ces images éveillèrent en lui une étrange r.** these pictures touched a chord deep within him/her; **r. magnétique** magnetic resonance; **r. magnétique nucléaire** nuclear magnetic resonance 2 *Littéraire (tonalité)* connotation, colouring *(UNCOUNT)*; **un poème de Donne aux résonances très modernes** a poem by Donne with very modern overtones; **ce mot prend une r. toute particulière dans ce contexte** in this context, the word has particular connotations

résonant, -e [rezɔnɑ̃, -ɑ̃t] = **résonnant**

résonateur [rezɔnatœr] NM *Phys* resonator

résonnant, -e [rezɔnɑ̃, -ɑ̃t] ADJ *(gén) & Phys* resonant; **r. de cris** resounding *or* echoing with cries

resonner [3] [rəsɔne] VT *Belg (rappeler au téléphone)* to call *or* phone back, *Br* to ring back

résonner [3] [rezɔne] VI 1 *(sonner)* to resonate, to resound; **sa voix résonnait dans les hauts-parleurs** his/her voice blared out *or* boomed out over the loudspeakers 2 *(renvoyer le son)* to resound, to be resonant; **ça résonne!** there's an echo, it echoes!; **la halle résonnait des cris des vendeurs** the hall resounded *or* echoed *or* reverberated with the cries of the traders

résorber [3] [rezɔrbe] VT 1 *(éliminer ▸ chômage, inflation, déficit)* to reduce, to bring down, to curb; *(▸ dettes)* to wipe out, to clear; *(▸ excédent)* to absorb 2 *Méd* to resorb

VPR **se résorber** 1 *(chômage, inflation, déficit)* to be reduced; *(excédent)* to be absorbed; **la crise ne va pas se r. toute seule** the crisis isn't going to just disappear 2 *Méd* to be resorbed

résorption [rezɔrpsjɔ̃] NF 1 *(de l'inflation, du chômage, d'un déficit)* curbing, reduction; *(de dettes)* clearing, wiping out 2 *Méd* resorption

résoudre [88] [rezudr] VT 1 *(querelle, conflit)* to settle, to resolve; *(crise)* to solve, to resolve; *(énigme, mystère)* to solve; *(difficulté)* to resolve, to sort out; *(problème)* to solve, to resolve; **le problème a été résolu en cinq minutes/après des années** the problem was solved in five minutes/was resolved over the years; **non résolu** unresolved

2 *Math* to resolve; **r. une équation** to solve an equation

3 *(décider)* to decide (on); **r. de faire qch** to decide to do sth

4 *(entraîner)* **r. qn à faire qch** to induce *or* to move sb to do sth

5 *Chim, Méd & Mus* to resolve (**en** into)

6 *Jur (bail, contrat)* to annul, to avoid

VPR **se résoudre** 1 *Méd* to resolve; **la tumeur s'est résolue lentement** the tumour slowly resolved itself

2 **se r. à faire qch** *(se résigner à)* to resign *or* reconcile oneself to doing sth; **il faudra te r. à voir tout le monde** you'll just have to see everyone whether you like it or not; **je ne peux m'y r.** I can't bring myself to do it

3 **se r. à** *(consister en)* to amount to, to result in; **son aide se résout à peu de chose** his/her help amounts to little (in the end)

4 *Chim* **se r. à** to resolve itself (**en** into)

respect [rɛspɛ] NM *(estime)* respect (**pour** for); **avec r.** with respect, respectfully; **faire qch par r. pour qn** to do sth out of respect *or* regard for sb; **r. de soi** self-respect; **elle m'inspire beaucoup de r.** I have a great deal of respect for her; **élevé dans le r. des traditions** brought up to respect traditions; **avoir du r. pour qn** to respect sb, to have respect for sb; **avoir le r. des lois/des convenances** to respect *or* have respect for *or* have regard for the law/the conventions; **manquer de r. à qn** to be disrespectful to sb; **marquer son r. à qn** to show respect to sb; **avec (tout)** *ou* **sauf le r. que je vous dois** with all due respect; **sauf votre r.** with respect; **tenir qn en r.** to keep sb at bay *or* at a (respectful) distance; **il nous tenait en r. avec un couteau** he kept us back *or* at bay with a knife

• **respects** NMPL respects, regards; **présenter ses respects à qn** to present one's respects to sb; **mes respects à madame votre mère** please give my respects to your mother

respectabilité [rɛspɛktabilite] NF respectability

respectable [rɛspɛktabl] ADJ 1 *(estimable)* respectable, deserving of respect; *Hum* respectable 2 *(important)* respectable; **un nombre r. de manifestants** a respectable *or* fair number of demonstrators; *Sport* **avec une avance r.** with an impressive lead

respecter [4] [rɛspɛkte] VT 1 *(honorer ▸ personne)* to respect, to have *or* to show respect for; **dans le pays, tout le monde le respecte** everyone respects him in our country; **il a un nom respecté dans notre ville** his name is held in respect in our city; **elle sait se faire r.** she commands respect; **il faut savoir se faire r. dans son travail** you have to earn people's respect at work; **il n'a pas su se faire r.** he was unable to gain respect

2 *(se conformer à)* to respect, to keep to; **si les formes sont respectées, vous obtiendrez ce que vous voulez** if the conventions are adhered to *or* respected, you'll get what you want; **r. les dernières volontés de qn** to abide by sb's last wishes; **r. les délais de livraison** to meet delivery schedules; **r. l'ordre alphabétique** to keep to alphabetical order; **r. la parole donnée** to keep one's word; **vous n'avez pas respecté la priorité** *(sur la route)* you didn't *Br* give way *or Am* yield; **faire r. la loi** to enforce the law

3 *(ne pas porter atteinte à)* to show respect for; **les jeunes d'aujourd'hui ne respectent plus rien** today's young people do not show any respect for

anything; **r. la tranquillité/le repos de qn** to respect sb's need for peace and quiet/rest; *Vieilli* **r. une femme** to respect a woman's honour

VPR se respecter 1 *(soi-même)* to respect oneself; **elle ne se respecte plus** she's lost all her self-respect; **comme tout enseignant qui se respecte** like any self-respecting teacher

2 *(mutuellement)* to respect each other

respectif, -ive [rɛspɛktif, -iv] **ADJ** respective

respectivement [rɛspɛktivmɑ̃] **ADV** respectively; **Paul et Jean sont âgés r. de trois et cinq ans** Paul and Jean are three and five years old respectively

respectueuse [rɛspɛktɥøz] *voir* **respectueux**

respectueusement [rɛspɛktɥøzmɑ̃] **ADV** respectfully, with respect

respectueux, -euse [rɛspɛktɥø, -øz] **ADJ 1** *(personne)* respectful; **se montrer r. envers qn** to be respectful to sb; **être r. de** to be respectful of; **r. des lois** law-abiding **2** *(lettre, salut)* respectful; **prendre un ton r. pour parler à qn** to adopt a respectful tone towards sb; *Fig* **se tenir à distance respectueuse** to keep a respectful distance **3** *(dans des formules de politesse)* **je vous prie d'agréer mes respectueuses salutations** *(à quelqu'un dont on connaît le nom)* *Br* yours sincerely, *Am* sincerely (yours); *(à quelqu'un dont on ne connaît pas le nom)* *Br* yours faithfully, *Am* sincerely (yours)

respirable [rɛspirabl] **ADJ 1** *(qu'on peut respirer)* breathable; **l'air est difficilement r. ici** it's hard to breathe in here **2** *Fig (supportable)* **l'ambiance du bureau est à peine r.** the atmosphere at the office is almost unbearable

respirant, -e [rɛspirɑ̃, -ɑ̃t] **ADJ** *(tissu, textile)* breathable

respirateur [rɛspiratœr] **NM 1** *(masque)* gas mask, respirator **2** *Méd (poumon d'acier)* iron lung; *(à insufflation)* positive pressure respirator; **r. artificiel** respirator, ventilator

respiration [rɛspirasjɔ̃] **NF 1** *Physiol (action)* breathing, *Spéc* respiration; *(résultat)* breath; **reprendre sa r.** to get one's breath back; **retenir sa r.** to hold one's breath; **avoir la r. difficile** *ou* **des difficultés de r.** to have trouble *or* difficulty breathing; *aussi Fig* **j'en ai eu la r. coupée** it took my breath away; *Méd* **r. artificielle** artificial respiration; **pratiquer la r. artificielle sur qn** to give sb artificial respiration; *Méd* **r. assistée** assisted respiration; *Méd* **r. contrôlée** controlled respiration **2** *(de plante)* respiration **3** *Mus* phrasing

respiratoire [rɛspiratwar] **ADJ** *(organe)* respiratory; *(appareil, exercice, problème)* breathing *(avant n)*; *Méd* **défaillance r.** respiratory failure; *Méd* **difficultés respiratoires** breathing difficulties; *Bot* **quotient r.** respiratory quotient; *Méd* **troubles respiratoires** breathing *or* respiratory problems; *Anat* **voies respiratoires** respiratory tract

respirer [3] [rɛspire] **VI 1** *Physiol* to breathe; **ça l'empêche de r.** it prevents him/her from breathing; **il a du mal à r., il respire avec difficulté** he has difficulty breathing, he's breathing with difficulty; **r. par la bouche/le nez** to breathe through one's mouth/nose; **respirez à fond, expirez!** breathe in, and (breathe) out!

2 *(plante, peau, vin)* to breathe

3 *(être rassuré)* to breathe again; **il est sauf, je respire** he's safe, I can breathe again; **ouf, je respire!** phew, thank goodness for that!

4 *(faire une pause)* **du calme, laissez-moi r.!** give me a break!; **on n'a jamais cinq minutes pour r.** you can't even take a breather for five minutes

VT 1 *Physiol* to breathe (in), *Spéc* to inhale; *(sentir ▸ fleur, parfum)* to smell **2** *(exprimer)* to radiate, to exude; **elle respire la santé** she radiates good health; **il respire le bonheur** he's the very picture of happiness; **la maison respire la douceur de vivre** the whole house is bathed in *or* alive with the joy of living

resplendir [32] [rɛsplɑ̃dir] **VI** *Littéraire* **1** *(étinceler ▸ casque, chaussure)* to gleam, to shine; **r. de propreté** to be spotlessly clean; **la mer resplendit au soleil** the sea is glinting in the sun **2** *(s'épanouir)* **son visage resplendit de bonheur** his/her face is shining *or* radiant with happiness; **les jeunes mariés resplendissent de joie** the newlyweds are radiant with joy

resplendissant, -e [rɛsplɑ̃disɑ̃, -ɑ̃t] **ADJ 1** *(éclatant ▸ meuble, parquet)* shining; *(▸ casserole, émail)* gleaming; *(▸ soleil, temps)* glorious **2** *(radieux)* resplendent, radiant; **tu as une mine resplendissante** you look radiant; **r. de santé** radiant *or* blooming with health; **r. de joie** radiant with joy; **une femme d'une beauté resplendissante** a radiantly beautiful woman

responsabiliser [3] [rɛspɔ̃sabilize] **VT 1** *(donner des responsabilités à)* **tu ne le responsabilises pas assez** you don't give him enough responsibility **2** *(rendre conscient de ses responsabilités)* **r. qn** to make sb aware of their responsibilities

responsabilité [rɛspɔ̃sabilite] **NF 1** *(obligation morale)* responsibility (**de** for); **nous déclinons toute r. en cas de vol** we take no responsibility in the event of theft; **c'est une grosse r.!** it's a big responsibility!; **prends tes responsabilités!** face up to your responsibilities!; **fuir les responsabilités** to evade *or* avoid responsibility; **faire porter la r. de qch à qn** to hold sb responsible for sth; **ils ont une r. morale vis-à-vis de nous** they have a moral obligation towards us; **assumer entièrement la r. de qch** to take on *or* to shoulder the entire responsibility for sth; **faire qch sous sa propre r.** to do sth on one's own responsibility

2 *(charge administrative)* function, position; **des responsabilités gouvernementales/ministérielles** a post in the government/cabinet; **il a accepté de nouvelles responsabilités au sein de notre compagnie** he took on new responsibilities within our company; **démis de ses responsabilités** relieved of his responsibilities *or* position; **avoir un poste à responsabilités** to have a responsible job; **elle a la r. du département publicité** she's in charge of the advertising department

3 *Jur* liability, responsibility (**de** for); *(acte moral)* responsibility; **r. civile** *(d'un individu)* civil liability, strict liability; *(d'une société)* business liability; **être assuré r. civile** to have personal liability insurance; **r. collective** collective responsibility; **r. contractuelle/délictuelle** contractual/negligent liability; **r. de l'employeur** employer's liability; **r. (sociale) de l'entreprise** corporate responsibility; **r. du fabricant** manufacturer's liability; **r. illimitée** unlimited liability; **r. limitée** limited liability; **r. pénale** legal responsibility; **r. au tiers** third-party liability

responsable [rɛspɔ̃sabl] **ADJ 1** *(garant)* responsible (**de** for); **les parents sont légalement responsables de leurs enfants** parents are legally responsible for their children; *Jur* **il n'est pas r. de ses actes** he cannot be held responsible for his (own) actions

2 *(chargé)* in charge (**de** of), responsible (**de** for); **il est r. du service après-vente** he's in charge of the after-sales department

3 *(à l'origine)* responsible (**de** for); **tenir qn/qch pour r. de qch** to hold sb/sth responsible for sth; **il est r. de l'accident** he is responsible for (causing) the accident

4 *Jur* liable; **r. civilement** liable in civil law

5 *Pol* **le ministre est r. devant le Parlement** the Minister is responsible *or* answerable *or* accountable to Parliament

6 *(réfléchi)* responsible; **ce n'est pas très r. de sa part** that isn't very responsible of him/her; **elle s'est toujours comportée en personne r.** she has always acted responsibly

NMF 1 *(coupable)* person responsible *or* to blame (**de** for); **qui est le r. de l'accident?** who's responsible for the accident?; **nous retrouverons les responsables** we will find the people *or* those responsible; **il n'y a jamais de responsables!** nobody is ever to blame! **2** *(dirigeant ▸ politique)* leader; *(▸ d'une société)* manager; *(▸ d'un service)* head; **parler avec les responsables politiques** to speak with the political leaders; **réunion avec les responsables syndicaux** meeting with the union representatives *or* officials; **je veux parler au r.** I want to speak to the person in charge; **r. de** *ou* **du budget** account executive; **r. commercial** business manager; **r. des comptes-clients** account handler; **r. (du) marketing** marketing manager; **r. politique** political leader; **r. produit** product manager; **r. syndical** union official

resquillage [rɛskijaʒ] **NM** *Fam (sans payer)* sneaking in; *(dans l'autobus, dans le métro etc)* fare-dodging; *(sans attendre son tour)* *Br* queue-jumping, *Am* line-jumping

resquiller [3] [rɛskije] *Fam* **VI** *(ne pas payer)* to sneak in; *(dans l'autobus, dans le métro etc)* to dodge the fare; *(ne pas attendre son tour)* to push in, *Br* to jump the queue, *Am* to cut in the line

VT to fiddle, to wangle; **r. une place pour le concert** to fiddle *or* to wangle oneself a seat for the concert

resquilleur, -euse [rɛskijœr, -øz] **NM,F** *Fam (qui ne paie pas)* = person who sneaks in without paying; *(dans l'autobus, dans le métro etc)* fare-dodger; *(qui n'attend pas son tour)* *Br* queue-jumper, *Am* line-jumper

ressac [rəsak] **NM** backwash *(of a wave)*

ressaisir [32] [rəsezir] **VT 1** *(agripper de nouveau)* to catch *or* to grab again, to seize again; **le chien ressaisit sa proie** the dog got hold of *or* caught his prey again; *Fig* **la peur l'a ressaisi** fear gripped him again **2** *(occasion)* to seize again **3** *Ordinat* to rekey

VPR se ressaisir *(se calmer)* to pull oneself together; **ressaisis-toi!** pull yourself together!, get a hold of *or* a grip on yourself!; **il s'est ressaisi et a finalement gagné le deuxième set** he recovered *or* rallied and finally won the second set; **heureusement, elle s'est ressaisie au second trimestre** luckily, she improved *or* made more of an effort in the second term

ressasser [3] [rəsase] **VT 1** *(répéter)* to go *or* to harp on about; **r. les exploits de sa jeunesse** to go *or* to harp on about one's youthful exploits; **les mêmes histoires ressassées l'amusent toujours** he's/she's still amused by the same worn-out old stories **2** *(repenser à)* to turn over in one's mind

ressaut [rəso] **NM 1** *Géog* rise; *(en alpinisme)* step, projection **2** *Constr (en saillie)* step; *(en recul)* offset; **faire r.** to jut out

ressauter [3] [rəsote] **VT** *(barrière)* to jump again **VI** to jump again

ressayage [resejaʒ] = **réessayage**

ressayer [reseje] = **réessayer**

ressemblance [rəsɑ̃blɑ̃s] **NF 1** *(entre êtres humains)* likeness, resemblance; **la r. entre la mère et la fille est étonnante** mother and daughter look amazingly alike; **il y a une r. entre les deux cousins** the two cousins look alike; **il y a quelques ressemblances entre eux** they resemble each other in a few respects, there are a few points of similarity *or* likeness between them **2** *(entre choses)* similarity; **il existe une certaine r. entre les deux livres** both books are somehow similar; **il n'y a aucune r. entre ta situation et la mienne** there's no similarity *or* comparison between your situation and mine

ressemblant, -e [rəsɑ̃blɑ̃, -ɑ̃t] **ADJ** *(photo, portrait)* true to life, lifelike; **ta photo n'est pas très ressemblante** your photo doesn't look like you; **elle est très ressemblante sur le dessin** the drawing really looks like her

ressembler [3] [rəsɑ̃ble] **ressembler à VT IND 1** *(avoir la même apparence que)* to resemble, to look like; **il ressemble à sa mère** he looks like his mother, *Sout* he favours his mother; **elle me ressemble un peu** she looks a bit like me; **ça ne ressemble en rien à une maison** that doesn't look like a house at all; **la moustache le fait r. à son père** his moustache makes him look like his father; **à quoi ressemble-t-elle?** what's she like?, what does she look like? **2** *(avoir la même nature que)* to resemble, to be like; **il a toujours cherché à r. à son père** he always tried to be like his father; **je n'ai rien qui ressemble à une tenue de soirée** I have nothing that you could even vaguely call evening wear **3** *Fam (locutions)* **ça ne ressemble à rien** *(ça ne veut rien dire)* it makes no sense at all; *(c'est laid)* it looks like nothing on earth; **à quoi ça ressemble de quitter la réunion sans même s'excuser?** what's the idea *or* meaning of leaving the meeting without even apologizing?; **cela ne me/te/leur ressemble pas** that's not like me/you/them; **ça lui ressemble bien d'oublier mon anniversaire** it's just like him/her to forget my birthday

VPR se ressembler 1 *(emploi réciproque)* to look

alike, to resemble each other; **ils se ressemblent** they look alike *or* like each other; **tous les amoureux se ressemblent** all lovers are alike, lovers are all alike; **se r. comme deux gouttes d'eau** to be like two peas (in a pod); *Prov* **qui se ressemble s'assemble** birds of a feather flock together **2** *(emploi réfléchi)* **depuis sa maladie, il ne se ressemble plus** he's not been himself since his illness

ressemelage [rəsəmlaʒ] **NM** *(action)* soling, resoling; *(nouvelle semelle)* new sole

ressemeler [24] [rəsəmle] **VT** to sole, to resole

ressens *etc voir* **ressentir**

ressentiment [rəsɑ̃timɑ̃] **NM** resentment, ill will; **éprouver du r. à l'égard de qn** to feel resentment against sb, to feel resentful towards sb; **je n'ai aucun r. à ton égard** I don't bear you any resentment *or* ill will; **c'est un homme aigri, plein de r.** he's embittered and full of resentment

ressentir [37] [rəsɑ̃tir] **VT 1** *(éprouver ▸ bienfait, douleur, haine)* to feel; **j'ai ressenti la même impression que vous quand je l'ai vu** I felt the same way you did *or* I had the same feeling as you when I saw him; **je ne ressens aucune tendresse pour elle** I don't feel any affection for her **2** *(être affecté par)* to feel, to be affected by; **il a ressenti très vivement la perte de son père** he was deeply affected by his father's death; **j'ai ressenti ses propos comme une véritable insulte** I felt *or* was extremely insulted by his/her remarks

VPR se ressentir 1 se r. de to feel the effect of; **je me ressens encore des suites de mon accident** I still feel *or* I'm still suffering from the effects of my accident; **la production a été accélérée et la qualité s'en ressent** they've speeded up production at the expense of quality; **elle est inquiète et son travail s'en ressent** she's worried and it shows in her work **2** *Fam* **s'en r. pour** to feel fit for, to feel up to

> Il faut noter que le verbe anglais **to resent** est un faux ami. Il signifie **ne pas aimer du tout**.

resserre [rəsɛr] **NF** *(à outils)* shed, outhouse; *(à produits)* storeroom; *(à provisions)* store cupboard, larder

resserrement [rəsɛrmɑ̃] **NM 1** *(d'une route ▸ contraction)* narrowing; *(▸ passage étroit)* narrow part; **il y a un r. de la route après le pont** the road narrows after the bridge

2 *(d'un nœud, d'un boulon)* tightening

3 *(limitation)* tightening; *Écon* **r. du crédit** credit squeeze, credit crunch

4 *(renforcement ▸ d'un lien affectif, d'une amitié)* strengthening; *(▸ de la discipline)* tightening (up)

5 *(des pores)* closing

resserrer [4] [rəsere] **VT 1** *(nœud, boulon ▸ serrer de nouveau)* to retighten, to tighten again; *(▸ serrer davantage)* to tighten up; **resserre-le** tighten it (up)

2 *(renforcer ▸ lien affectif, amitié)* to strengthen; *(▸ discipline)* to tighten (up)

3 *(fermer)* to close (up); **pour r. les pores** to close *or* to tighten the pores

4 *(diminuer ▸ texte, exposé)* to condense, to compress

VPR se resserrer 1 *(devenir plus étroit)* to narrow; **la route se resserre après le village** the road narrows past the village **2** *(se refermer ▸ nœud, boulon)* to tighten; *Fig* **les mailles du filet se resserrent** the police are closing in **3** *(devenir plus fort)* **nos relations se sont resserrées depuis l'année dernière** we have become closer (to each other) *or* our relationship has grown stronger since last year

resservir [38] [rəsɛrvir] **VT 1** *(de nouveau)* to serve again; **elle nous a resservi les pâtes d'hier en gratin** she served up yesterday's pasta in a bake **2** *(davantage)* to serve (out) some more *or* another helping; **donne-moi ton assiette, je vais te r.** give me your plate, I'll give you another helping **3** *Fam (répéter)* **il nous ressert la même excuse tous les ans** he comes out with *or* he trots out the same (old) excuse every year

VI 1 *(être utile)* **j'ai une vieille robe longue qui pourra bien r. pour l'occasion** I have an old full-length dress which would do for this occasion; **garde-le, ça pourra toujours r.** keep it, it might come in handy *or* useful again (one day) **2** *Mil & (au tennis)* to serve again

VPR se resservir 1 *(reprendre à manger)* to help oneself to some more *or* to a second helping; **ressers-toi** help yourself to (some) more; **puis-je me r.?** may I help myself to some more *or* take a second helping?; **resservez-vous du riz** help yourself to *or* have some more rice *or* another helping of rice **2 se r. de** *(réutiliser)* to use again

ressors *etc voir* **ressortir**[1]

ressort [rəsɔr] **NM 1** *(mécanisme)* spring; **faire r.** to act as a spring; **actionné** *ou* **mû par r.** spring-driven; **r. à boudin** coil spring; **r. hélicoïdal/spiral** helical/spiral spring; **r. à lames** leaf *or* coach spring; **r. de montre** watch spring, hairspring; **r. de sommier** bedspring

2 *(force morale)* spirit, drive; **manquer de r.** to lack drive

3 *(mobile)* motivation; **les ressorts de l'âme humaine** the deepest motivations of the human soul *or* spirit

4 *(propriété)* springiness, *Spéc* elasticity

5 *(compétence)* **les problèmes qui sont de mon r.** problems I am qualified to deal with; **ce n'est pas de mon/ton r.** it is not my/your responsibility

6 *Jur* jurisdiction; **cette affaire est du r. de la cour** this case is *or* falls within the competence of the court; **juger une affaire en premier/dernier r.** to judge a case in the first instance/in a court of last resort

• **à ressort(s) ADJ** spring-loaded; **matelas à ressorts** spring mattress

• **en dernier ressort ADV** as a last resort

ressortir[1] **[43]** [rəsɔrtir] **VT** *(aux avoir)* **1** *(vêtement, ustensile)* to take out again **2** *(film)* to rerelease, to bring out again; *(pièce de théâtre)* to rerun **3** *Fam (répéter)* to trot out again; **tu ne vas pas r. cette vieille histoire?** you're not going to come out with that old story again, are you?

VI *(aux être)* **1** *(sortir à nouveau ▸ vu de l'intérieur)* to go out again, to leave again; *(▸ vu de l'extérieur)* to come out again; *(sortir ▸ vu de l'intérieur)* to go out, to leave; *(▸ vu de l'extérieur)* to come out; **je n'ai pas envie de r., il fait trop froid** I don't feel like going out again, it's too cold; **il n'est pas encore ressorti de chez le médecin** he hasn't left the doctor's yet

2 *(se détacher)* to stand out (**sur** against); **le rouge ressortira mieux** red will stand out better; **le foulard qu'elle porte fait r. ses yeux bleus** the scarf she's wearing brings out the blue of her eyes; **faire r. les avantages d'une solution** to stress *or* to highlight the advantages of a solution; **ce rapport fait r. un certain nombre de problèmes importants** the report brings out a number of important points

3 *(réapparaître)* **la pointe est ressortie de l'autre côté du mur** the tip came through the other side of the wall; **la balle est ressortie par l'épaule** the bullet came out *or* exited through the shoulder

4 *(film)* to show again, to be rereleased; **ses films viennent de r. à Paris** his/her movies *or Br* films have just started showing again in Paris *or* have just been rereleased in Paris

5 *(chiffre, carte)* to come up again

• **ressortir de VT IND** to emerge *or* to flow from; **il ressort de votre analyse que les affaires vont bien** according to your analysis, business is good; **il ressort de tout cela qu'il a menti** the upshot of all this is that he's been lying

ressortir[2] **[32]** [rəsɔrtir] **ressortir à VT IND 1** *Jur* to come under the jurisdiction of **2** *Littéraire (relever de)* to pertain to; **pareil sujet ressortit au roman plutôt qu'à l'essai** such a subject pertains to the novel rather than to the essay (genre)

ressortissant, -e [rəsɔrtisɑ̃, -ɑ̃t] **NM,F** *(d'un pays)* national; **r. d'un pays de l'Union européenne** EU national

ressouder [3] [rəsude] **VT 1** *(tuyau)* to resolder, to reweld, to weld together again **2** *Fig (alliance, couple)* to bring *or* to get together again, to reunite

VPR se ressouder *(os, fracture)* to knit (again)

ressource [rəsurs] **NF 1** *(secours)* recourse, resort; **tu es mon unique r.** you're the only person who can help me *or* my only hope; **elle n'a eu d'autre r. que la mendicité** there was no other course (of action) open *or* left to her but to become a beggar; **être à bout de ressources** to have exhausted all one's possibilities; **en dernière r.** as a last resort

2 *(présence d'esprit)* **un homme/une femme de r.** *ou* **ressources** a resourceful man/woman

3 *(endurance, courage)* **avoir de la r.** to have strength in reserve

4 *Aviat* flattening out, pull-out

• **ressources NFPL 1** *(fonds)* funds, resources, income; **25 ans et sans ressources** 25 years old and no visible means of support; **ressources d'appoint** additional sources of income; **ressources de l'État** government resources; **ressources financières** financial resources; **ressources fiscales** tax resources; **ressources personnelles** private means **2** *(réserves)* resources; **ressources humaines** human resources, personnel; **ressources naturelles/minières d'un pays** natural/mineral resources of a country; **des ressources en hommes** manpower resources **3** *(moyens)* resources, possibilities; **nous mobilisons toutes nos ressources pour retrouver les marins disparus** we're mobilizing all our resources *or* all the means at our disposal to find the missing sailors; **toutes les ressources de notre langue** all the possibilities *or* resources of our language

ressourcer [16] [rəsurse] **se ressourcer VPR 1** *(retourner aux sources)* to go back to one's roots **2** *(reprendre des forces)* to recharge one's batteries

ressurgir [32] [rəsyrʒir] **VI 1** *(source)* to reappear **2** *(problème)* to reoccur; **faire r. de vieux souvenirs** to bring back old memories

ressusciter [3] [resysite] **VT** *(aux avoir)* **1** *Rel* to resurrect, to raise from the dead; **le Christ ressuscitera les morts** Christ will raise the dead to life **2** *(ranimer)* to resuscitate; *Méd* to bring back to life, to revive; **vos piqûres m'ont littéralement ressuscité** those injections you gave me literally brought me back to life; *Hum* **un whisky à r. les morts** whisky strong enough to bring the dead back to life; **tes larmes ne vont pas le r.** crying won't bring him back (to life); **r. une mode** to bring back a fashion **3** *Littéraire (faire ressurgir ▸ tradition)* to revive, to resurrect; **r. le passé** to summon up *or* to revive the past

VI 1 *(aux être) Rel* to rise again *or* from the dead; **le Christ est ressuscité (d'entre les morts)** Christ has risen (from the dead) **2** *(aux avoir) (revivre ▸ sentiment, nature)* to come back to life, to revive

> Il faut noter que le verbe anglais **to resuscitate** est un faux ami et ne correspond jamais au français **ressusciter**. Il signifie le plus souvent **ranimer**.

restant, -e [rɛstɑ̃, -ɑ̃t] **ADJ** remaining; **les cinq euros restants** the remaining five euros, the five euros remaining *or* left (over); **ils se sont partagé les chocolats restants** they shared the chocolates that were left

NM *(reste)* rest, remainder; **dépenser le r. de son argent** to spend the rest of one's money *or* one's remaining money; **un r. de tissu** a leftover piece of material; **pour le r. de mes/leurs/***etc* **jours** until my/their/*etc* dying day; *Com* **r. en caisse** cash surplus

• **restants NMPL** *Can (de nourriture)* leftovers

restau [rɛsto] **NM** *Fam* restaurant[□]

restaurant [rɛstɔrɑ̃] **NM** restaurant; **manger au r.** to eat out; **ce soir, on dîne au r.** we're eating out tonight; **ils vont souvent au r.** they often eat out; **r. d'entreprise** (staff) canteen; **r. gastronomique** gourmet restaurant; **r. routier** *Br* transport café, *Am* truck stop; **r. universitaire** university canteen *or* cafeteria *or* refectory

restaurateur, -trice [rɛstɔratœr, -tris] **NM,F 1** *(d'œuvres d'art)* restorer **2** *(qui tient un restaurant)* restaurant owner, *Sout* restaurateur **3** *Littéraire (d'un régime, d'une monarchie etc)* restorer

restauration [rɛstɔrasjɔ̃] **NF 1** *(d'œuvres d'art)* restoration; **la r. des vitraux a pris plusieurs années** it took several years to restore the stained-glass windows

2 *(rétablissement)* restoration; *Hist* **la R.** = the restoration of the Bourbon monarchy in France, from 1815 to 1830

3 *(hôtellerie)* catering; **dans la r.** in the restaurant trade *or* the catering business; **la r. collective** institutional catering; **la r. rapide** the fast-food business

4 *Ordinat* restore

restauratrice [rɛstɔratris] *voir* **restaurateur**

restaurer [3] [rɛstɔre] **VT 1** *(édifice, œuvre d'art)* to restore **2** *Littéraire (rétablir ▸ discipline, autorité)* to restore, to re-establish; **r. la paix** to restore peace **3** *Littéraire (nourrir)* to feed

VPR se restaurer to have something to eat; **nous nous arrêterons vers midi pour nous r. un peu** we'll stop around noon to have a bite to eat

restau-U [rɛstoy] *(pl* **restaus-U***)* **NM** *Fam* university canteen *or* cafeteria *or* refectory□

reste [rɛst] **NM 1** *(suite, fin)* rest; **puis-je vous payer le r. à la fin du mois?** can I pay you the rest at the end of the month?; **il a dormi le r. de la journée** he slept for the rest of the day; **le r. du temps** the rest of the time; **le r. de ta vie** the rest of your life; **si vous êtes sages, je vous raconterai le r. demain** if you're good, I'll tell you the rest of the story tomorrow; **pour le r., quant au r.** as for the rest; **et (tout) le r.!** and so on (and so forth)!; **tout le r. n'est que littérature/qu'illusion** everything else is just insignificant/an illusion; **sans attendre** *ou* **demander son r.** without (any) further ado; **elle s'est enfuie sans demander son r.** she left without further ado; **j'irai encaisser le chèque sans attendre mon r.** I'll go and cash in the cheque and have done with it; **être** *ou* **demeurer en r.** to be outdone, to be at a loss

2 *(résidu ▸ de nourriture)* food left over, leftovers (of food); *(▸ de boisson)* drink left over; *(▸ de tissu, de papier)* remnant, scrap; **il y avait un r. de beurre/lait** there was a bit of butter/milk left (over); **accommoder un r. de viande** to use up the leftover meat; **un r. de courage/d'espoir** some remnants of courage/hope; **un r. de sa gloire passée** a vestige *or* remnant of his/her past glory

3 *Math* remainder; **le r. égale cinq** the remainder is five

• **restes NMPL 1** *(d'un repas)* leftovers; **on mangera les restes ce soir** we'll have the leftovers tonight; *Fig* **je ne veux pas de ses restes!** I don't want his/her leftovers! **2** *(vestiges)* remains **3** *(ossements)* (last) remains **4** *Fam (locution)* **elle a de beaux restes** she's still beautiful despite her age□

• **au reste** = **du reste**

• **de reste ADJ** surplus *(avant n)*, spare; **vous auriez du pain de r.?** do you have any bread left (over)?, do you have any bread to spare?; **passez me voir demain, j'aurai du temps de r.** come and see me tomorrow, I'll have some spare time; **il a de la patience de r.** he has patience to spare

• **du reste ADV** besides, furthermore, moreover; **inutile de discuter, du r., ça ne dépend pas de moi** there's no point in arguing and, besides, it's not up to me to decide; **du r., je ne suis pas d'accord avec toi** what's more, I don't agree with you

RESTER [3] [rɛste]

• to stay **1**	• to remain **1, 2**
• to be left **2**	• to live **4**
• to die **5**	• to endure **6**

VI 1 *(dans un lieu, une situation)* to stay, to remain; **c'est mieux si la voiture reste au garage** it's better if the car stays in the garage; **malgré mes efforts, la tache est restée** despite my efforts, the stain wouldn't come out; **ceci doit r. entre nous** this is strictly between me and you, this is for our ears only; **restez donc à déjeuner/dîner** do stay for lunch/dinner; **je ne reste pas** I'm not staying *or* stopping; *Fig* **savoir r. à sa place** to know one's place; **r. debout/assis** to remain standing/seated; **elle est restée debout toute la nuit** she stayed up all night; **r. paralysé** to be left paralysed; **r. fidèle à qn** to be *or* to stay faithful to sb; **r. en fonction** to remain in office; **r. dans l'ignorance** to remain in ignorance; **r. célibataire** to remain single; **r. sans rien faire** to sit around doing nothing; **elle ne reste pas en place** she never keeps still; **tu veux bien r. tranquille!** will you keep still!; **r. en contact avec qn** to keep *or* to stay in touch with sb; **je reste sur une impression désagréable** I'm left with an unpleasant impression; **je n'aime pas r. sur un échec** I don't like to stop at failure; **r. dans les mémoires** *ou* **les annales** to go down in history; **nous en sommes restés à la page 160** we left off at *or* got as far as page 160; **nous en resterons à cet accord** we will limit ourselves to *or* go no further than this agreement; **restons-en là!** let's leave it at that!; *Fam* **r. en rade** *ou* **en carafe** to be left high and dry *or* stranded; **ça m'est resté sur le cœur** it still rankles with *or* galls me; **j'y suis, j'y reste!** here I am and here I stay!

2 *(subsister)* to be left; **r. sans résultat** to remain ineffective; **c'est tout ce qui me reste** that's all I have left; **cette mauvaise habitude lui est restée** he/she still has that bad habit; **restent les deux dernières questions à traiter** the last two questions still have to be dealt with; **reste à savoir qui ira** there still remains the problem of deciding who is to go

3 *(tournure impersonnelle)* **il nous reste un peu de pain et de fromage** we have a little bit of bread and cheese left; **il me reste la moitié à payer** I (still) have half of it to pay; **il nous reste de quoi vivre** we have enough left to live on; **lisez beaucoup, il en restera toujours quelque chose** do a lot of reading, there will always be something to show for it *or* there's always something to be got out of it; **cinq ôté de quinze, il reste dix** five (taken away) from fifteen leaves ten; **il reste encore à examiner les points a et c** points a and c still remain to be examined; **il ne reste plus rien à faire** there's nothing left to be done; **il reste à faire l'ourlet** the hem is all that remains *or* that's left to be done; **il reste encore 12 kilomètres à faire** there's still 12 kilometres to go; **il reste que le problème de succession n'est pas réglé** the fact remains that the problem of the inheritance hasn't been solved; **il n'en reste pas moins que vous avez tort** you are nevertheless wrong

4 *Can & (en Afrique francophone) (habiter)* to live

5 *Euph (mourir)* to meet one's end; **il est resté sur le champ de bataille** he died on the battlefield; *Fam* **y r.** to kick the bucket

6 *(durer)* to live on, to endure; **son souvenir restera** his/her memory will live on

7 *Belg* **r. faire qch** to go on *or* continue doing sth

VT *Can Fam* **être resté** to be *Br* knackered *or Am* bushed

restituable [rɛstitɥabl] **ADJ** *(somme)* repayable

restituer [7] [rɛstitɥe] **VT 1** *(rendre ▸ bien)* to return, to restore; *(▸ argent)* to refund, to return; **r. qch à qn** to return sth to sb; **elle dut r. les fonds détournés** she had to pay back *or* to return the embezzled funds **2** *(reconstituer ▸ œuvre endommagée)* to restore, to reconstruct; *(▸ ambiance)* to reconstitute, to render; **r. fidèlement les sons/les couleurs** to reproduce sounds/colours faithfully

restitution [rɛstitysjɔ̃] **NF 1** *(d'un bien)* return, restitution; *(d'argent)* refund; **r. d'impôts** tax refund; *Jur* **r. d'indu** return of payment made in error **2** *(d'une œuvre endommagée)* restoration; *(d'une ambiance)* reconstitution; *(d'un son, d'une couleur)* reproduction

resto [rɛsto] **NM** *Fam* restaurant□; **les restos du cœur** = charity food distribution centres

restoroute [rɛstɔrut] **NM** *(sur autoroute)* ≃ *Br* motorway *or Am* freeway restaurant; *(sur route)* roadside restaurant

resto-U [rɛstoy] *(pl* **restos-U***)* = **restau-U**

restreindre [81] [rɛstrɛ̃dr] **VT** *(ambition, dépense)* to restrict, to limit, to curb; *(sorties, achats)* to cut back (on), to restrict, to limit; *(consommation)* to cut down; *(budget)* to restrict; *(autorité, pouvoir)* to limit, to restrict; **r. les libertés** to restrict liberties; **en raison de son âge, il a dû r. ses activités** he had to limit his activities because of his age; **elle a dû r. ses recherches à un domaine précis** she had to limit her research to a precise field

VPR se restreindre 1 *(se rationner)* to cut down; **tu ne sais pas te r.** you don't know when to stop **2** *(diminuer)* **le champ d'activités de l'entreprise s'est restreint** the company's activities have become more limited; **son cercle d'amis s'est restreint** his/her circle of friends has got smaller

restreint, -e [rɛstrɛ̃, -ɛ̃t] **ADJ 1** *(réduit)* limited; **l'espace est r.** there's not much room; **édition à tirage r.** limited edition **2** *(limité)* restricted (à to); **une offre restreinte aux abonnés** an offer restricted to subscribers; **la distribution de ces produits est restreinte à Paris et à sa région** these products are sold exclusively in the Paris area

restrictif, -ive [rɛstriktif, -iv] **ADJ** restrictive

restriction [rɛstriksjɔ̃] **NF 1** *(réserve)* reservation; **émettre quelques restrictions à l'égard d'un projet** to express some reservations about a project; **r. mentale** mental reservation **2** *(limitation)* restriction, limitation; **r. de la concurrence** anti-competitive practices; **r. de crédit** restriction on credit, credit squeeze **3** *Ordinat* **r. d'accès** access restriction

• **restrictions NFPL** restrictions; **les restrictions en temps de guerre** wartime restrictions *or* austerity; **restrictions budgétaires** budget restrictions; **restrictions salariales, restrictions des salaires** wage restraint

• **sans restriction ADV** *(entièrement)* **je vous approuve sans r.** you have my unreserved approval

restrictive [rɛstriktiv] *voir* **restrictif**

restructuration [rəstryktyrasjɔ̃] **NF 1** *(d'un quartier, d'une ville)* redevelopment **2** *(d'une société, d'un service)* restructuring, reorganization **3** *(de dette)* rescheduling

restructurer [3] [rəstryktyre] **VT** *(société, service)* to restructure, to reorganize

VPR se restructurer to be restructured

resucée [rəsyse] **NF** *Fam* **1** *(quantité supplémentaire)* **une r.** some more□; **t'en prendras bien une petite r.?** will you have some more? **2** *(répétition)* rehash; **ils ne montrent que des resucées à la télévision** all they ever show on TV is (old) repeats

résultant, -e [rezyltɑ̃, -ɑ̃t] **ADJ** resulting

• **résultante NF 1** *(résultat)* result, outcome **2** *Math & Phys* resultant

résultat [rezylta] **NM 1** *(réalisation positive)* result; **on arrive à d'excellents résultats avec ce médicament** we're getting excellent results with this drug; **sans r.** *(action)* fruitless; **j'ai essayé de le lui faire comprendre, sans r.** I tried unsuccessfully to make him/her understand; **ne donner aucun r.** to have no effect; **il n'y a pas que le r. qui compte** the (end) result is not the only important thing

2 *(aboutissement)* result, outcome; **le r. final** the end result; **voici le r. de nombreuses années de recherche** this is the result of several years of research; **son attitude a eu pour r. de rapprocher le frère et la sœur** his/her attitude led to *or* resulted in closer ties between brother and sister; **ça a eu pour r. de le mettre en colère** it made him angry, he got angry as a result

3 *Fam (introduisant une conclusion)* **il a voulu trop en faire, r., il est malade** he tried to do too much and sure enough he fell ill; **r., je n'ai toujours pas compris** so I'm still none the wiser; **r. des courses...** the upshot was..., as a result...; **r. des courses, on s'est retrouvés au poste** the whole thing ended up with us in the police station

4 *Math* result; **j'ai le même r. que toi** I get the same result as you

5 *Pol & Sport* result; **r. partiel** by-election result; **le r. des courses** *Sport* the racing results; *Fig* the outcome (of the situation); **r.** *ou* **résultats des courses: il a été licencié** as a result he was dismissed, the upshot of it all was that he was dismissed

6 *Compta* profit; **dégager un r.** to make a profit; **r. brut** gross return; **r. courant** profit before tax and extraordinary items; **r. exceptionnel** extraordinary profit or loss; **r. de l'exercice** profit or loss for the financial year, statement of income; **r. d'exploitation** operating profit or loss; **r. final** final statement; **r. financier** financial profit or loss; **r. net** net profit; **r. de la période** profit or loss for the financial period; **résultats prévisionnels** earnings forecast

• **résultats NMPL** *Fin, Pol & Sport* results; *Com* performance; *Scol* results, *Br* marks, *Am* grades; *Mktg* **résultats antérieurs** past performance; **les résultats de l'exercice en cours sont mauvais** the results are poor for the current (financial) year; **les résultats du Loto** the winning lottery numbers

résulter [3] [rezylte] **résulter de VT IND** to result *or* to ensue from; **il est difficile de dire ce qui en résultera** at the moment it's difficult to say what the result *or* outcome will be; **je ne sais pas ce qui en résultera** I don't know what the end result will be *or* what's going to come out of this; **le travail/souci qui en résulte** the ensuing work/worry; **il résulte de l'enquête que...** the result of the investigation shows that..., it has emerged from the investigation that...; **il en a résulté que...** the result *or* the outcome was that...

résumé [rezyme] NM **1** *(sommaire)* summary, résumé; **faites un r. du passage suivant** write a summary *or* a précis of the following passage; **r. des épisodes précédents** the story so far **2** *(bref exposé)* summary; **faites-nous le r. de la situation** sum up *or* summarize the situation for us **3** *(ouvrage)* summary, précis

• **en résumé** ADV *(en conclusion)* to sum up; *(en bref)* in short, in brief, briefly; **en r., nous ne sommes d'accord sur aucun des points soulevés** in short, we do not agree on any of the points raised

résumer [3] [rezyme] VT **1** *(récapituler)* to summarize, to sum up; **je vais vous r. notre conversation** let me summarize our conversation; **voici le problème résumé en quelques chiffres** here is the problem summed up in a few figures; **résume-lui l'histoire en quelques mots** sum up the story for him/her in a few words; **voilà toute l'affaire résumée en un mot** that's the whole thing in a nutshell; **pour r. les faits** to sum up **2** *(symboliser)* to typify, to symbolize; **ce cas résume tous les autres du même genre** this case sums up all others of the same type

VPR **se résumer 1** *(récapituler)* to sum up; **pour me r., je dirai que nous devons être vigilants** to sum up, I would say that we must be vigilant **2 se r. à** to come down to; **cela se résume à peu de chose** it doesn't amount to much

> Il faut noter que le verbe anglais **to resume** est un faux ami. Il signifie **reprendre, recommencer.**

résurgence [rezyrʒɑ̃s] NF **1** *Géog* resurgence **2** *(réapparition)* resurgence, revival

résurgent, -e [rezyrʒɑ̃, -ɑ̃t] ADJ resurgent

resurgir [rəsyrʒir] = **ressurgir**

résurrection [rezyrɛksjɔ̃] NF **1** *Rel* resurrection; **la R. (du Christ)** the Resurrection (of Christ) **2** *(renaissance)* revival **3** *(guérison)* **depuis qu'il sait que sa fille est saine et sauve, c'est une véritable r.!** now he knows his daughter is safe, he's made a miraculous recovery!

retable [rətabl] NM *(sur l'autel)* retable; *(derrière l'autel)* reredos

rétablir [32] [retablir] VT **1** *(établir de nouveau)* to restore; **le courant a été rétabli dans l'après-midi** the power was reconnected *or* restored in the afternoon; **r. le calme/l'ordre/une vieille coutume** to restore calm/order/an old custom; **r. l'équilibre** to redress the balance; **nous prendrons les mesures nécessaires pour r. la situation** we'll take the measures required to restore the situation to normal; **r. un texte** to restore a text *(to its original form)*; **r. qn dans son emploi** to reinstate sb; **elle a été rétablie dans tous ses droits** all her rights were restored **2** *(guérir)* **r. qn** to restore sb to health; **son séjour l'a complètement rétabli** his holiday brought about his complete recovery **3** *(rectifier)* to re-establish; **rétablissons les faits** let's re-establish the facts, let's get down to what really happened

VPR **se rétablir 1** *(guérir)* to recover; **elle est partie se r. à la campagne** she went to the country to recuperate *or* to recover **2** *(revenir ▸ ordre, calme)* to be restored; *(▸ silence)* to return **3** *Sport* to pull oneself up

rétablissement [retablismɑ̃] NM **1** *(de l'ordre, des communications)* restoration; **le r. du courant prendra deux heures** it will be two hours before the power comes back on; **nous souhaitons tous le r. de la paix** we all want peace to be restored

2 *(d'un fonctionnaire)* reinstatement

3 *(guérison)* recovery; **nous vous souhaitons un prompt r.** we wish you a speedy recovery

4 *Sport* **faire un r. à la barre fixe** to do a pull-up on the horizontal bar

rétamage [retamaʒ] NM retinning

rétamé, -e [retame] ADJ **1** *(étamé de nouveau)* retinned **2** *Fam (épuisé) Br* knackered, *Am* bushed

rétamer [3] [retame] VT **1** *(étamer de nouveau)* to retin

2 *Fam (battre au jeu)* to clean out; **je me suis fait r. au casino** I got cleaned out at the casino

3 *Fam (épuiser)* to wear out, *Br* to knacker

4 *Fam (refuser ▸ candidat)* to fail□, *Am* to flunk; **je me suis fait r. en anglais** I failed *or Am* flunked my English exam

VPR **se rétamer** *Fam* **1** *(tomber)* to go flying, to take a tumble **2** *(échouer)* to fail□, *Am* to flunk; **je me suis rétamé à l'oral** I messed up *or Am* flunked my oral

rétameur [retamœr] NM tinker, tinsmith

retapage [rətapaʒ] NM *Fam (d'un lit)* straightening□, making□; *(d'une maison, d'une voiture)* doing up

retape [rətap] NF *Fam* **1** *(racolage)* **faire (de) la r.** *Br* to be on the game, *Am* to hustle **2** *(publicité)* loud advertising□, hyping (up), plugging; **faire de la r. pour** to plug

retaper [3] [rətape] VT **1** *Fam (lit)* to straighten□, to make□

2 *Fam (maison, voiture)* to do up

3 *Fam (malade)* to buck up; **mon séjour à la montagne m'a retapé** my stay in the mountains set me back on my feet again

4 *(lettre, texte)* to retype, to type again

VPR **se retaper** *Fam* **1** *(physiquement)* to get back on one's feet again; **elle a grand besoin de se r.** she badly needs to recharge her batteries **2** *(refaire)* **j'ai dû me r. la lecture du rapport** I had to read through the blasted report again; **on se retape une belote?** how about another game of belote?; **je me retaperais bien une petite bière** I wouldn't mind another beer, I wouldn't say no to another beer

retapisser [3] [rətapise] VT **1** *(pièce, mur ▸ avec du papier peint)* to repaper; *(▸ avec du tissu)* to hang with new material; *(fauteuil)* to recover **2** *Fam Arg crime (reconnaître)* to clock

retard [rətar] NM **1** *(manque de ponctualité)* lateness; *(temps écoulé)* delay; **il ne s'est même pas excusé pour son r.** he didn't even apologize for being late; **mon r. est dû à...** I'm late because of...; **avoir du r.** to be late; **j'avais plus d'une heure de r.** I was more than an hour late; **prendre du r.** *(sujet: personne)* to fall behind; *(sujet: train)* to be running late; **l'avion Londres–Paris est annoncé avec deux heures de r.** a two-hour delay is expected on the London to Paris flight; **son bébé est né avec cinq jours de r.** her baby was born five days late; **rapportez vos livres sans r.** return your books without delay; **r. de paiement** delay in payment, late payment

2 *(intervalle de temps, distance)* **il a un tour de r. sur son principal adversaire** he's a lap behind his main opponent; **le peloton est arrivé avec cinq minutes de r. sur le vainqueur** the pack arrived five minutes after *or* behind the winner

3 *(d'une horloge)* **ma montre a plusieurs minutes de r.** my watch is several minutes slow

4 *(d'un élève)* backwardness; **il a du r. en allemand** he's behind in German; **il doit combler son r. en physique** he's got to catch up in physics; **r. mental** backwardness; **r. scolaire** learning difficulties

5 *(handicap)* **nous avons comblé notre r. industriel en quelques années** we caught up on *or* we closed the gap in our industrial development in a few years; **nous avons des années de r. (sur eux)** we're years behind (them)

6 *Tech* **r. à l'allumage** retarded ignition

ADJ INV *Pharm* delayed(-action) *(avant n)*; **insuline/pénicilline r.** slow-release insulin/penicillin

• **en retard** ADJ **je suis en r. pour la réunion** I'm late for the meeting; **j'ai des lettres/du tricot en r.** I'm behind with my mail/knitting; **un élève en r. sur les autres** a pupil lagging behind the others; **un élève en r. dans ses études** a pupil who is behind in his studies; **elle est très en r. pour son âge** *Psy* she's rather immature *or* slow for her age; *Scol* she's rather behind for her age; **paiement en r.** *(qui n'est pas fait)* arrears, overdue payment; *(qui est fait)* late payment; **il est en r. dans ses paiements** he's behind *or* in arrears with (his) payments; **un pays en r. sur les autres** a backward country, a country lagging behind the others; **être en r. sur son époque** *ou* **son temps** to be behind the times ADV late; **arriver en r.** to arrive late; **elle s'est mise en r.** she made herself late; **nous avons rendu nos épreuves en r.** we were late handing in our tests

retardataire [rətardatɛr] ADJ **1** *(qui n'est pas à l'heure)* late; *(qui a été retardé)* delayed **2** *(désuet)* obsolete, old-fashioned; **vous avez vraiment des méthodes retardataires** your methods are completely obsolete *or* outdated

NMF latecomer

retardateur, -trice [rətardatœr, -tris] ADJ retarding; *Mil* **action retardatrice** delaying tactics

NM **1** *Chim* retarder, negative catalyst **2** *Phot* (camera) self-timer

retardé, -e [rətarde] ADJ *Fam (arriéré)* retarded, backward, *Péj* slow

NM,F **r. (mental)** (mentally) retarded person

retardement [rətardəmɑ̃] **à retardement** ADJ *(mécanisme)* delayed-action *(avant n)*

ADV **comprendre à r.** to understand after the event

retarder [3] [rətarde] VT **1** *(ralentir ▸ visiteur, passager)* to delay, to make late; *(entraver ▸ enquête, progrès, travaux)* to delay, to hamper, to slow down; **la pluie/grève m'a retardé** the rain/strike made me late; **les problèmes financiers l'ont retardé dans ses études** financial problems slowed him down *or* hampered him in his studies

2 *(ajourner)* to postpone, to put back; **nous avons dû r. la date d'ouverture du congrès** we had to put back the date for *or* postpone the start of the congress; **l'intervention du Président a été retardée d'une heure** the President's address has been moved back one hour; **elle retarde par tous les moyens le moment de le rencontrer** she's using every opportunity to put off *or* to postpone *or* to delay meeting him

3 *(montre)* to put back; **j'ai retardé la pendule de quelques minutes** I put the clock back a few minutes

VI **1** *(montre)* to be slow; **la pendule retarde** the clock is slow; **mon réveil retarde de cinq minutes** my alarm (clock) is five minutes slow

2 *Fam (personne)* to be out of touch; **r. sur son temps** *ou* **son siècle** to be behind the times; **il retarde de 20 ans sur notre époque** *ou* **temps** he's 20 years behind the times; **r. (d'un métro)** to be out of touch

VPR **se retarder** to make oneself late; **ne te retarde pas pour ça** don't let this hold you up *or* delay you

retâter [3] [rətate] VT *(étoffe)* to feel again

• **retâter de** VT IND *Fam* **il n'a pas envie de r. de la prison** he doesn't want to sample the delights of prison life again

reteindre [81] [rətɛ̃dr] VT to dye again, to redye

retéléphoner [rətelefɔne] VI to call *or Br* to ring back *or* again; **r. à qn** to call *or Br* to ring sb (up) again, to call *or Br* to ring sb back

VPR **se retéléphoner** to call each other again, to speak to each other on the phone again; **on se retéléphone demain, d'accord?** talk to you again tomorrow, OK?

retendre [73] [rətɑ̃dr] VT **1** *(corde, câble)* to retighten, to tauten (again); *(ressort)* to reset; *(corde de raquette)* to tauten (again) **2** *(piège)* to reset

RETENIR [40] [rətənir]

VT	
• to hold **1**	• to hold back **2, 3**
• to book **4**	• to remember **5**
• to retain **6, 8**	• to deduct **7**
• to carry **9**	
VPR	
• to restrain onself **1**	• to hold on **2, 3**

VT **1** *(immobiliser)* to hold, to keep; **retiens le chien, il va sauter!** hold the dog back, it's going to jump!; **j'ai retenu la chaise juste à temps** I caught the chair just in time; **le mur est retenu par un échafaudage** the wall is held up by scaffolding; **r. l'attention de qn** to hold sb's attention; **votre CV a retenu toute mon attention** I studied your *Br* CV *or Am* résumé with great interest; **r. qn prisonnier** to hold sb prisoner; **r. qn en otage** to hold sb hostage; **r. qn à dîner** to invite sb for dinner; **je ne vous retiens pas, je sais que vous êtes pressé** I won't keep you, I know you're in a hurry

2 *(empêcher d'agir)* to hold back; **quand il est en colère, personne ne peut le r.** when he's angry, there's no holding him *or* nobody can stop him;

Fam **je ne sais pas ce qui me retient de l'envoyer promener** I don't know what's stopping *or* keeping me from telling him/her to go to hell; *Fam* **retiens-moi ou je fais un malheur** hold me back or I'll do something desperate
3 *(refouler ▸ émotion)* to curb, to hold in check, to hold back; *(▸ larmes, sourire)* to hold back; *(▸ cri)* to stifle; **elle ne pouvait r. ses larmes/un sourire** she couldn't hold back her tears/a smile; **r. un geste d'impatience** to hold back *or* to check a gesture of impatience; **r. son souffle** *ou* **sa respiration** to hold one's breath
4 *(réserver)* to book, to reserve; **r. une chambre dans un hôtel** to book a room in a hotel; **retiens la date du 20 juin pour notre réunion** keep 20 June free for our meeting
5 *(se rappeler)* to remember; **r. qch** to remember *or* to recall sth; **et surtout, retiens bien ce qu'on t'a dit** and above all, remember *or* don't forget what you've been told; *Fam* **je te retiens, toi et tes soi-disant bonnes idées!** I'll remember you and your so-called good ideas!
6 *(candidature, suggestion)* to retain, to accept; **r. une accusation contre qn** to uphold a charge against sb
7 *(décompter)* to deduct, to keep back; **j'ai retenu 50 euros sur votre salaire** I've deducted 50 euros from your salary; **sommes retenues à la base** *ou* **source** sums deducted at source
8 *(conserver ▸ chaleur)* to keep in, to retain, to conserve; *(▸ eau)* to retain; *(▸ lumière)* to reflect; **un filtre retient les impuretés** a filter retains the impurities
9 *Math* to carry; **je pose 5 et je retiens 4** I put down 5 and carry 4
10 *Can* **r. de qn** to look like sb; **elle retient de sa mère** she looks like her mother
VPR se retenir 1 *(se contrôler)* to restrain oneself; **se r. de pleurer** to stop oneself crying
2 *Fam Euph* to hold on; **il n'a pas pu se r.** he couldn't wait (to go to the toilet)
3 *(s'agripper)* to hold on; **retiens-toi à la branche** hold on to the branch

rétenteur, -trice [retɑ̃tœr, -tris] **ADJ** *(force)* retaining; *Anat* **muscle r.** retentor (muscle)

rétention [retɑ̃sjɔ̃] **NF 1** *Méd* retention; **faire de la r. d'urines/d'eau** to suffer from urine/water retention
2 *(refus de communiquer)* **faire de la r. d'information** to hold back *or* to withhold information
3 *Jur* **droit de r.** lien; **r. administrative** = detention of illegal immigrants or of asylum seekers due to be deported
4 r. du personnel staff retention

retentir [32] [rətɑ̃tir] **VI 1** *(résonner ▸ gén)* to resound, to ring, to echo; *(▸ Klaxon®)* to sound, to honk; *(▸ tonnerre, canon)* to crash; *(▸ alarme)* to ring, to sound; *(▸ coup de feu, cri)* to ring out; **de bruyants applaudissements retentirent dans la salle** the auditorium resounded with deafening applause, loud applause rang out *or* burst forth in the auditorium; **la voix des enfants retentissait dans l'escalier** the children's voices rang out *or* echoed in the stairway; **l'explosion a retenti dans toute la ville** the explosion was heard right across the city; **la maison retentit du bruit des ouvriers** the house is filled with the noise of the workers; **faire r. qch** *(instrument de musique)* to blow sth **2** *(avoir des répercussions)* **r. sur** to have an effect on; **l'accident de sa femme a retenti sur son moral** his wife's accident shook him a great deal

retentissant, -e [rətɑ̃tisɑ̃, -ɑ̃t] **ADJ 1** *(éclatant ▸ cri, bruit, gifle)* resounding, ringing; *(▸ voix)* ringing; *(▸ sonnerie)* loud **2** *(remarquable)* tremendous; **un succès r.** a resounding success; *Fam* **un bide r.** a resounding flop

retentissement [rətɑ̃tismɑ̃] **NM 1** *(contrecoup)* repercussion; **ça n'a aucun r. sur notre pouvoir d'achat** it doesn't affect our purchasing power in any way **2** *(impact)* effect, impact; **le r. dans l'opinion publique a été considérable/nul** there was considerable/no effect on public opinion; **cette déclaration devrait avoir un certain r.** this statement should create quite a stir **3** *Littéraire (bruit)* ringing, resounding

rétentrice [retɑ̃tris] *voir* **rétenteur**

retenu, -e [rətəny] **PP** *voir* **retenir**
ADJ *(discret ▸ personne)* subdued; **s'exprimer de façon retenue** to express oneself in restrained terms, to be restrained
• **retenue NF 1** *(déduction)* deduction; **opérer une retenue de 9 pour cent sur les salaires** to deduct *or* to stop 9 percent from salaries; **faire une r. de 5 pour cent sur les salaires** to deduct *or* withhold 5 percent from salaries; **on a fait une retenue de 50 euros sur son salaire** 50 euros have been docked from his/her wages; **moins 5,6 pour cent en retenues diverses** less 5.6 percent in deductions *or Br* stoppages; **retenue à la source** payment (of income tax) at source, *Br* ≃ PAYE, *Am* ≃ pay as you go
2 *(réserve)* reserve, self-control, restraint; **s'exprimer sans retenue** to express oneself without restraint, to speak freely; **se confier à qn sans retenue** to confide in sb unreservedly *or* freely; **rire sans retenue** to laugh uproariously *or* uncontrollably; **c'est une jeune femme pleine de retenue** she's a very reserved *or* reticent young woman; **un peu de retenue!** show some restraint!, keep a hold of yourself!
3 *Transp (ralentissement)* tailback
4 *Scol (punition)* detention; **mettre qn en retenue** to keep sb in after school, to put sb in detention; **j'ai quatre heures de retenue la semaine prochaine** I've got four hours' detention next week
5 *Math* **reporter la retenue** to carry over; **la retenue, c'est combien?** how much is there to carry over?
6 *(d'eau)* damming up *(UNCOUNT)*; **lac de retenue** impoundment, dam reservoir; **retenue d'eau** volume of water *(in dam)*

réticence [retisɑ̃s] **NF 1** *(hésitation)* reluctance, reticence; **avec quelque r.** with some reticence *or* reservations; **avoir des réticences (sur qch)** to feel reticent *or* to have reservations (about sth); **j'ai remarqué un peu de r. dans son accord** I noticed he/she agreed somewhat reluctantly; **après bien des réticences, il a dit oui** after much hesitation he said yes; **parler avec r.** to speak reticently **2** *(omission)* omission

réticent, -e [retisɑ̃, -ɑ̃t] **ADJ** *(hésitant)* reticent, reluctant, reserved; **je suis un peu r. à l'égard de votre proposition** I feel slightly reluctant about your proposal; **se montrer r.** to seem rather doubtful; **se montrer r. à faire qch** to be hesitant about doing sth, to be reluctant *or* unwilling to do sth

> Il faut noter que l'adjectif anglais **reticent** est un faux ami. Il signifie **réservé, discret**.

réticulaire [retikylɛr] **ADJ** reticular

réticule [retikyl] **NM 1** *(sac)* reticule **2** *Opt* reticle

réticulé, -e [retikyle] **ADJ 1** *Archit* reticulated, reticular **2** *Anat & Bot* reticulate

retient *etc voir* **retenir**

rétif, -ive [retif, -iv] **ADJ 1** *(cheval)* stubborn **2** *(enfant)* restive, fractious, *Sout* recalcitrant

rétine [retin] **NF** retina; *Méd* **r. décollée** detached retina

rétinien, -enne [retinjɛ̃, -ɛn] **ADJ** retinal

retint *etc voir* **retenir**

retirable [rətirabl] **NM** withdrawable, that may be withdrawn *or* removed

retirage [rətiraʒ] **NM** *(processus)* reprinting; *(résultat)* reprint; **je voudrais faire un r. de ces photos** I'd like prints of these photos

retiré, -e [rətire] **ADJ 1** *(isolé)* remote, secluded, out-of-the-way; **ils cherchent une maison retirée** they're looking for a secluded house; **elle habite un quartier r.** she lives in an out-of-the-way neighbourhood **2** *(solitaire)* secluded; **mener une vie retirée à la campagne** to live a secluded life in the country; **vivre r. du monde** to live in seclusion **3** *(à la retraite)* retired

RETIRER [3] [rətire]

VT	
• to take off **1**	• to remove **1, 3**
• to take away **1, 4, 5**	• to take out **3, 6**
• to withdraw **4, 6**	• to collect **6**
• to get **7**	• to fire again **8**
• to reprint **9**	

VI	
• to fire again **1**	• to shoot again **2**
VPR	
• to withdraw **1, 2**	• to retire **2**
• to recede **3**	• to vanish **4**

VT 1 *(ôter)* to take off *or* away, to remove; **retire tes gants** take off your gloves; **il aida l'enfant à r. son manteau** he helped the child off with his coat
2 *(ramener à soi)* **retire ta main** take your hand away; **retire tes jambes** move your legs back
3 *(faire sortir)* to take out, to remove; **on a retiré de nombreux corps du bâtiment** a large number of bodies were removed from *or* taken out of the building; **elle a été obligée de r. son fils de l'école** she had to remove her son from the school
4 *(annuler ▸ droit)* to take away; *(▸ plainte, offre)* to withdraw; *(▸ accusation)* to take back; **r. sa candidature** to withdraw one's candidature, to stand down; **d'accord, je retire tout ce que j'ai dit sur lui** OK, I take back all I said about him; **r. un magazine de la circulation** to withdraw a magazine (from circulation); **la pièce a été retirée de l'affiche après une semaine** the play came off *or* closed after a week
5 *(confisquer)* **r. qch à qn** to take sth away from sb; **retire-lui le verre des mains** take the glass away from him/her; **on lui a retiré la garde des enfants** he/she lost custody of the children; **on lui a retiré son permis de conduire** he's/she's been banned from driving; **r. sa confiance à qn** to no longer trust sb
6 *(récupérer ▸ argent)* to withdraw, to take out, to draw; *(▸ bagage, ticket)* to pick up, to collect; **j'ai retiré un peu d'argent de mon compte** I drew *or* withdrew some money from my bank account; **retire 80 euros, ça suffira** take *or* get 80 euros out, that will be enough
7 *(obtenir)* to gain, to get; **r. un bénéfice important d'une affaire** to make a large profit out of a deal; **je n'ai retiré que des désagréments de cet emploi** I got nothing but trouble from that job
8 *(coup de feu)* to fire again
9 *Typ* to reprint; **r. une photo** to make a new *or* fresh print (from a photo)
VI 1 *(refaire feu)* to fire again
2 *Sport* to shoot again
VPR se retirer 1 *(s'éloigner)* to withdraw; **il est tard, je vais me r.** it's late, I'm going to retire *or* to withdraw; **ils se sont retirés discrètement pour pouvoir parler entre eux** they withdrew discreetly so that they could talk together; **se r. de** to withdraw from; **se r. de la politique/compétition** to withdraw from politics/the competition; **se r. de la vie active** to retire; *Hum* **se r. dans ses appartements** to retire *or* to withdraw to one's room
2 *(s'établir)* to retire; *(se cloîtrer)* to retire, to withdraw; **il s'est retiré dans le Midi** he retired to the South of France; **se r. du monde** to cut oneself off from the world
3 *(mer)* to recede, to ebb; *(inondations)* to recede

rétive [retiv] *voir* **rétif**

retombée [rətɔ̃be] **NF** *Littéraire (déclin)* **la r. de l'enthousiasme populaire** the decline in popular enthusiasm
• **retombées NFPL 1 retombées radioactives** radioactive fallout **2** *Fig (répercussions)* repercussions, effects; **les retombées d'une campagne publicitaire** the results of an advertising campaign; **la grève aura des retombées sur les prix** the strike will have repercussions *or* a knock-on effect on prices; **les retombées du scandale/de l'affaire** the fallout from *or* the repercussions of the scandal/affair

retomber [3] [rətɔ̃be] **VI** *(aux être)* **1** *(bouteille, balai)* to fall over again; *(mur, livres empilés)* to fall down again *or* back down; *(ivrogne, bambin)* to fall over *or* down again; **se laisser r. par terre/sur une chaise** to fall *or* to drop back onto the ground/onto a chair; **se laisser r. sur son lit** to flop *or* to fall back onto one's bed; **r. de cheval** to fall off a horse again; **faire r. qch** to drop sth again; **le savon est retombé dans l'eau** the soap has fallen into the water again
2 *(atterrir ▸ chat, sauteur, parachutiste, missile)* to land; *(▸ balle)* to come (back) down; *(redescen-*

dre ▸ couvercle, rideau de fer, clapet) to close; *(▸ soufflé, mousse)* to collapse; **laissez r. votre main droite** let your right hand come down *or* drop down; *Fig* **r. sur ses pattes** to land on one's feet

3 *(devenir moins fort ▸ fièvre, prix)* to drop; *(▸ agitation)* to fall, to tail off, to die away; *(▸ enthousiasme)* to fall, to wane; **le dollar est retombé** the dollar has fallen *or* dropped again

4 *(dans un état, une habitude)* to fall back, *Sout* to lapse; **r. dans la pénurie/l'ennui** to fall back into poverty/boredom; **r. dans les mêmes erreurs** to make the same mistakes again; **r. en enfance** to lapse into one's second childhood

5 *Météo (vent)* to fall (again), to drop, to die down; *(brume)* to disappear, to be dispelled; *(tournure impersonnelle)* **il retombe de la pluie/neige/grêle** it's raining/snowing/hailing again

6 *(pendre ▸ drapé, guirlande, ourlet)* to hang; **les fleurs retombent en lourdes grappes** the flowers are hanging in heavy clusters

7 *(redevenir)* **r. amoureux** to fall in love again; **r. d'accord** to come to *or* to reach an agreement again; **r. enceinte** to get pregnant again; **r. malade** to become *or* to fall ill again

• **retomber sur** VT IND **1** *(rejaillir)* **la responsabilité retombe sur moi** the blame for it falls on me; **tous les torts sont retombés sur elle** she had to bear the brunt of all the blame; *Fam* **un de ces jours ça va te r. sur le nez!** one of these days you'll get your comeuppance *or* what's coming to you!

2 *Fam (rencontrer à nouveau)* **r. sur qn** to bump into *or* to come across sb again; **r. sur qch** to come across sth again; **je suis retombé sur le même prof/sujet à l'oral** I got the same examiner/question for the oral exam; **en tournant à droite, vous retombez sur l'avenue** if you turn right you're back on the avenue again

retordre [76] [ʀətɔʀdʀ] VT *Tex* to twist

rétorquer [3] [ʀetɔʀke] VT **1** *(répliquer)* to retort; **il a rétorqué que ça ne me regardait pas** he retorted *or* rejoined that it was none of my business; **"certainement pas!" rétorqua-t-elle vivement** "certainly not!" she snapped back *or* replied indignantly **2** *Arch ou Littéraire (accusation)* to cast back, to hurl back; **r. un argument contre qn** to turn sb's argument against him/her

retors, -e [ʀətɔʀ, -ɔʀs] ADJ **1** *(machiavélique)* crafty, tricky; **méfie-toi, il est r.** be careful, he's a wily customer *or* he knows all the tricks of the trade **2** *Tex* **fil r.** twisted *or* warp yarn

rétorsion [ʀetɔʀsjɔ̃] NF **1** *(représailles)* retaliation; **mesures de r.** retaliatory measures **2** *Jur* retortion

retouche [ʀətuʃ] NF **1** *(correction)* alteration; **faire des retouches à un texte** to make alterations to a text; **je dois apporter quelques retouches à mon texte** I need to make a few alterations to my text

2 *Beaux-Arts (action)* retouching *(UNCOUNT)*; *(résultat)* retouch; **je veux faire des retouches à cette sculpture avant de l'exposer** I want to work a little more on this sculpture before exhibiting it

3 *Couture* alteration; **faire des retouches à un vêtement** to make alterations to a garment; **il faudra faire une r. dans le dos** it will have to be altered at the back

4 *Phot* touching up *(UNCOUNT)*

5 *Ordinat* **r. d'images** photo editing

retoucher [3] [ʀətuʃe] VT *(modifier ▸ texte, vêtement)* to alter; *(▸ œuvre)* to retouch; *(▸ photo)* to retouch, to touch up

• **retoucher à** VT IND *(se remettre à)* to go back to; **et depuis, tu n'as plus jamais retouché à une cigarette?** and since then you haven't touched a *or* another cigarette?; **il n'a plus jamais retouché à son piano** he never touched *or* played his piano again

retoucheur, -euse [ʀətuʃœʀ, -øz] NM,F **1** *Couture* alterer **2** *Phot* retoucher

RETOUR [ʀətuʀ] NM **1** *(chez soi, au point de départ)* return; **à ton r.** when you get back; **à son r. de l'hôpital nous l'inviterons au restaurant** when he/she gets out of hospital we'll take him/her out for a meal; **à son r. de l'usine il prenait le temps de lire le journal** when he got back from the factory he would take the time to read the newspaper; **nous comptons sur ton r. pour Noël** we expect you back (home) for Christmas; **après dix années d'exil, c'est le r. au pays** after a ten-year exile he's/she's coming home; **partir sans espoir de r.** to leave without any hope of returning; **r. à un stade antérieur** reverting *or* returning to an earlier stage; **sur le chemin** *ou* **la route du r.** on the way back; **voyage/vol de r.** return journey *or* trip/flight; **r. à la nature/au calme** return to nature/a state of calm; **r. à la normale** return to normal; **r. aux sources** return to one's roots; **c'est un r. aux sources qu'il fait en se rendant à Varsovie** he's going back to his roots on this trip to Warsaw; **r. à la terre** return to the land; **être sur le r.** to be about to return, to be on the point of returning; *Fig* to be past one's prime; **ils doivent être sur le r. à présent** they must be on their way back now; **un don Juan sur le r.** an ageing Don Juan; **une beauté sur le r.** a fading beauty

2 *(nouvelle apparition ▸ d'une célébrité)* return, reappearance; *(récurrence ▸ d'une mode, d'un thème)* return, recurrence; **on note un r. des jupes longues** long skirts are back (in fashion)

3 *(mouvement inverse)* **faire un r. sur soi-même** to review one's past life; **r. de bâton** kickback; **r. (de) chariot** carriage return; *Tech & Fig* **r. de flamme** backfire; **r. offensif** renewed outbreak; **r. rapide** *(d'une cassette)* rewind; *Élec* **r. par la terre** *Br* earthing, *Am* grounding; **r. à la case départ** *(dans un jeu)* back to the start; *Fig* back to square one *or* to the drawing board; **par un juste r. des choses il a été licencié** he was sacked, which seemed fair enough under the circumstances

4 *(réexpédition)* return; **r. à l'envoyeur** *ou* **à l'expéditeur** return to sender; **par r. du courrier** by return of post

5 *Transp (trajet)* return (journey), journey back; **combien coûte le r.?** how much is the return fare?

6 *(sur un clavier)* return; **touche r.** return key; **appuyez sur la touche r.** press return; **r. arrière** backspace; **r. à la ligne automatique** word wrap; **r. à la ligne forcé** hard return

7 *(au tennis)* return; **r. de service** return of serve, service return

8 *Ordinat* **r. (d'information)** (information) feedback

9 *Fin (amortissement)* return; *(effet)* dishonoured bill, bill returned dishonoured; purchase return; **r. sans frais** return free of charge; **r. sur investissements** return on investments; **r. sur ventes** return on sales

10 *Com (de marchandises)* return; **marchandises de r., retours** returns; **vendu avec possibilité de r.** sold on a sale or return basis

ADJ INV *Sport* **match r.** return match

• **retours** NMPL *(de vacances)* return traffic *(from weekends etc)*; **il y a beaucoup de retours ce soir** many people are driving back to the city tonight

• **de retour** ADV back; **je serai de r. demain** I'll be back tomorrow; **les hirondelles sont de r.** the swallows are back (again) *or* with us again; **de r. chez lui, il réfléchit** (once he was) back home, he thought it over

• **de retour de** PRÉP back from; **de r. de Rio, je tentai de la voir** on my return from Rio, I tried to see her

• **en retour** ADV in return

• **sans retour** ADV *Littéraire (pour toujours)* forever, irrevocably

• **retour d'âge** NM change of life

• **retour de manivelle** NM **1** *Tech* kickback **2** *(choc en retour)* backlash; *(conséquence néfaste)* backlash, repercussion

• **retour en arrière** NM **1** *Cin & Littérature* flashback; **faire un r. en arrière** to flash back **2** *Fig (régression)* step backwards

retourne [ʀətuʀn] NF **1** *Cartes* **la r. est à cœur** hearts are trumps **2** *Fam* **les avoir à la r.** to be bone idle

retournement [ʀətuʀnəmɑ̃] NM *(revirement)* **un r. de situation** a turnaround *or* a reversal (of the situation)

RETOURNER [3] [ʀətuʀne]

VT
- to turn round **1, 3**
- to send back **2**
- to turn over **3**
- to toss **4**
- to turn upside down **5**

VI
- to return
- to go back

VPR
- to turn round **1**
- to turn over **2, 3**
- to overturn **3**
- to sort things out **4**
- to change completely **5**

VT *(aux avoir)* **1** *(orienter dans le sens contraire)* to turn round *or* around; *(renverser ▸ situation)* to reverse, to turn inside out *or* back to front; **retourne le plan** turn the map round *or* around *or* the other way round; **r. une arme contre** *ou* **sur qn** to turn a weapon on sb; **je lui ai retourné son** *ou* **le compliment** I returned the compliment

2 *(renvoyer ▸ colis, lettre)* to send back

3 *(mettre à l'envers ▸ literie)* to turn round *or* around; *(▸ carte à jouer)* to turn up; *(▸ champ, paille)* to turn over; *(▸ verre)* to turn upside down; *(▸ grillade)* to turn over; *(▸ gant, poche)* to turn inside out; **il a retourné la photo contre le mur** he turned the photo against the wall; *Fig* **r. sa veste** to sell out; **il te retournera comme une crêpe** *ou* **un gant** he'll twist you round his little finger

4 *(mélanger ▸ salade)* to toss

5 *(fouiller ▸ maison, pièce)* to turn upside down

6 *(examiner ▸ pensée)* **tourner et r. une idée dans sa tête** to mull over an idea (in one's head)

7 *Fam (émouvoir)* **j'en suis encore tout retourné!** I'm still reeling from the shock!

VI *(aux être)* **1** *(aller à nouveau)* to return, to go again *or* back; **jamais je ne retournerai là-bas** I will never go there again *or* go back there; **je n'y étais pas retourné depuis des années** I had not been back there for years; **si tu étais à ma place, tu retournerais le voir?** if you were me, would you (ever) go and see him again?; **je retournai la voir une dernière fois** I paid her one *or* my last visit; **la pièce m'a tellement plu que je suis retourné la voir** I liked the play so much that I went (back) to see it again

2 *(revenir)* to go back, to return; **r. chez soi** to go (back) home; **r. à sa place** *(sur son siège)* to go back to one's seat

V IMPERSONNEL **peut-on savoir de quoi il retourne?** what is it all about?, what exactly is going on?

• **retourner à** VT IND *(reprendre, retrouver)* to return to, to go back to; **r. à l'ouvrage** to go back to work; **r. à un stade antérieur** to revert to an earlier stage; *Fig* **r. à ses premières amours** to go back to one's first loves

VPR **se retourner 1** *(tourner la tête)* to turn round; **partir sans se r.** to leave without looking back; **tout le monde se retournait sur eux** everybody turned round to look at them

2 *(se mettre sur l'autre face)* to turn over; **se r. sur le dos/ventre** to turn over on one's back/stomach; **je me suis retourné dans mon lit toute la nuit** I tossed and turned all night; **elle doit se r. dans sa tombe** she must be turning in her grave

3 *(se renverser ▸ auto, tracteur)* to overturn, to turn over

4 *(réagir)* to sort things out; **ils ne me laissent pas le temps de me r.** *(de décider)* they won't give me time to make a decision; *(de me reprendre)* they won't give me time to sort things out

5 *(situation)* to be reversed, to change completely; **le lendemain, la situation s'était retournée** the following day, the situation had changed beyond recognition

6 **s'en r.** *(partir)* to depart, to leave; *(rentrer)* to make one's way back

7 **se r. un ongle/doigt** to twist a nail/finger

8 **se r. contre qn** *(agir contre)* to turn against sb; **tout cela finira par se r. contre toi** all this will eventually backfire on you

9 *Belg (locution)* **ne pas se r. après** *ou* **pour** *ou* **sur qch** not to pay attention to sth, not to care about sth

retracer [16] [ʀətʀase] VT **1** *(relater)* to relate *or Sout* to recount, to tell of; **retraçons les faits** let's go back over the facts **2** *(dessiner à nouveau ▸ trait, cercle)* to draw again, to redraw; *(▸ sentier)* to mark out again

rétractable [ʀetʀaktabl] ADJ **1** *Jur* retractable, revocable **2** *(emballage)* **film r.** shrink wrap **3** *(pointe)* retractable; **stylo à pointe r.** propelling pen

rétractation [retraktasjɔ̃] NF *(d'un aveu, d'un témoignage)* withdrawal, retraction, *Sout* retractation

rétracter [3] [retrakte] VT 1 *Zool (griffes)* to retract, to draw back; *(cornes)* to retract, to draw in 2 *(aveu, témoignage)* to retract, to withdraw

VPR **se rétracter** 1 *(griffes)* to draw back, *Spéc* to retract 2 *(témoin)* to retract, *Sout* to recant; **il lui a fallu se r.** he/she had to withdraw his/her statement

rétracteur [retraktœr] ADJ M **muscle r.** retractor (muscle)

rétractile [retraktil] ADJ retractile

rétraction [retraksjɔ̃] NF retraction

retrait [rətrɛ] NM 1 *(annulation ▸ d'une licence)* cancelling; *(▸ d'un mot d'ordre)* calling off; **un r. de l'ordre de grève est hors de question** calling off the strike is out of the question; *Jur* **r. d'autorité parentale** withdrawal of parental authority; **r. de candidature** *(par un prestataire)* withdrawal of application; *(par un député)* standing down, withdrawal; **r. de permis (de conduire)** revocation of *Br* driving licence *or Am* driver's license

2 *Banque (d'un effet)* withdrawal; *(de monnaies)* withdrawal from circulation, calling in; **faire un r.** to withdraw money; **je veux faire un r. de 200 euros** I want to take out *or* to withdraw 200 euros; **r. automatique** automated withdrawal; **r. d'espèces** cash withdrawal

3 *(récupération)* **le r. des billets/bagages se fera dès onze heures** tickets/luggage may be collected from eleven o'clock onwards; **r. des bagages** *(dans un aéroport)* baggage reclaim

4 *(départ ▸ d'un joueur, du contingent)* withdrawal

5 *(recul ▸ des eaux d'inondation)* subsiding, receding; *(▸ de la marée)* ebbing; *(▸ des glaces)* retreat

6 *Jur (d'un acte administratif)* revocation; *(d'un acte de vente)* redemption; **r. successoral** redemption of an estate

7 *Tech* shrinkage

• **en retrait** ADV set back; **en r. par rapport au mur** *(clôture)* set back from the wall; *(étagère)* recessed; *Typ* **mettre en r.** to indent; **rester en r.** to stand back; *Fig* to remain in the background; **vivre en r.** to lead a quiet life

• **en retrait de** PRÉP 1 *(en arrière de)* set back from; **la maison est en r. de la route** the house is set back from the road 2 *(en dessous de)* below, beneath; **son offre est en r. de ce qu'il avait laissé entendre** his offer doesn't come up to what he'd led us to expect

retraite [rətrɛt] NF 1 *Admin (pension)* pension; **toucher** *ou* **percevoir sa r.** to get *or* to draw one's pension; **r. par capitalisation** self-funded pension scheme; **r. complémentaire** supplementary pension; **r. minimum** guaranteed minimum pension; **r. par répartition** contributory pension scheme

2 *(cessation d'activité)* retirement; **il est à la** *ou* **en r.** *(gén)* he has retired; *(officier)* he is on the retired list; **un médecin/policier à la r.** a retired doctor/police officer; **un militaire à la** *ou* **en r.** an army pensioner; **prendre sa r.** to retire; **mettre qn à la r.** to make sb take retirement, to retire sb; **être mis à la r.** to be made to take retirement, to be retired; **l'âge de la r.** retirement age; **r. anticipée** early retirement; **prendre sa r. anticipée** to take early retirement; **r. forcée** compulsory retirement; **r. d'office** compulsory retirement

3 *Chasse & Mil* retreat; **sonner la r.** to sound the retreat

4 *Rel* retreat; **suivre** *ou* **faire une r.** to go on a retreat

5 *Littéraire (cachette ▸ gén)* hiding place, refuge, shelter; *(▸ de voleurs)* hideout

6 *Constr* tapering, offsetting

retraité, -e [rətrete] ADJ *(qui est à la retraite ▸ gén)* retired; *(▸ officier)* on the retired list

NM,F *Admin* pensioner; *(personne ne travaillant plus)* retired person; **les retraités** retired people, senior citizens

retraitement [rətrɛtmɑ̃] NM *Ind & Nucl* reprocessing; **centre** *ou* **usine de r. (des déchets nucléaires)** (nuclear) reprocessing plant

retraiter [4] [rətrete] VT *Ind & Nucl* to reprocess

retranchement [rətrɑ̃ʃmɑ̃] NM *Mil* retrenchment, entrenchment; *Fig* **pousser** *ou* **forcer qn dans ses derniers retranchements** to force sb to the wall

retrancher [3] [rətrɑ̃ʃe] VT 1 *Math* to subtract; **r. 10 de 20** to take 10 away from 20, to subtract 10 from 20 2 *(enlever)* to remove, to excise; **r. un passage d'un livre** to remove *or* to excise a passage from a book 3 *(déduire ▸ pour des raisons administratives)* to deduct (**de** from); *(▸ par sanction)* to deduct, to dock (**de** from)

VPR **se retrancher** 1 *(se protéger)* **se r. derrière** *(se cacher)* to hide behind; *(se réfugier)* to take refuge behind; **se r. dans le silence** *ou* **le mutisme** to take refuge in silence; **ils se sont retranchés derrière la raison d'État/les statistiques** they hid behind the public interest/statistics; **se r. sur ses positions** to remain entrenched in one's position 2 *Mil* to entrench oneself

retranscription [rətrɑ̃skripsjɔ̃] NF 1 *(processus)* retranscription 2 *(résultat)* new transcript

retranscrire [99] [rətrɑ̃skrir] VT to retranscribe

retransmettre [84] [rətrɑ̃smɛtr] VT 1 *Rad* to broadcast; *TV* to broadcast, to screen, to show; **concert retransmis en direct** live concert; **r. une émission en direct/différé** to broadcast a programme live/a recorded programme 2 *(ordre, information)* to pass on, to relay

retransmission [rətrɑ̃smisjɔ̃] NF *Rad* broadcast; *TV* broadcast, screening, showing; **la r. du match est prévue pour 14h45** *(à la télévision)* the match will be shown *or* broadcast at 2.45 p.m.; *(à la radio)* the match will be broadcast at 2.45 p.m.; **r. en direct/différé** live/prerecorded broadcast; **r. par satellite** satellite broadcast; *(action)* satellite broadcasting

retransmit *etc voir* **retransmettre**

retravailler [3] [rətravaje] VT *(texte, mouvement de gym)* to work on again; *(argile, pâte)* to work again; **votre thèse a besoin d'être retravaillée** your thesis needs reworking

VI to (start) work again

rétréci [retresi] ADJ 1 *(vêtement)* shrunken 2 *(route etc)* narrow

rétrécir [32] [retresir] VT 1 *(tissu, vêtement ▸ au lavage)* to shrink; *Couture* **r. une jupe** to take in a skirt 2 *(route)* to narrow

VI *(tissu, vêtement)* to shrink; **r. au lavage** to shrink in the wash

VPR **se rétrécir** *(allée, goulot)* to narrow, to get narrower; *(cercle, diaphragme)* to contract, to get smaller; *(budget)* to shrink, to dwindle

rétrécissement [retresismɑ̃] NM 1 *(d'un couloir, d'un diaphragme)* narrowing *(UNCOUNT)*; **r. de la chaussée** bottleneck 2 *Méd* stricture 3 *(d'un tissu, d'un vêtement)* shrinkage

retrempe [rətrɑ̃p] NF *Métal* requenching

retremper [3] [rətrɑ̃pe] VT 1 *Métal* to requench 2 *(doigt)* to dip again; *(linge)* to soak again

VPR **se retremper** 1 *(dans l'eau)* to have another dip 2 **se r. dans** *(un milieu, un sujet)* to go back into; *Littéraire* **se r. aux sources** to go back to basics

rétribuer [7] [retribɥe] VT *(employé)* to pay, to remunerate; *(travail, service rendu)* to pay for; **travail rétribué** paid work

rétribution [retribysjɔ̃] NF 1 *(salaire)* remuneration, salary 2 *(récompense)* recompense, reward

> Il faut noter que le terme anglais **retribution** est un faux ami. Il signifie **châtiment**.

retriever [retrivœr] NM retriever

rétro[1] [retro] ADJ INV retro; **mode r.** retro fashion

NM 1 *(style)* **le r.** retro style 2 *(au billard)* screw shot

ADV **s'habiller r.** to wear retro clothes; **leur appartement est meublé r.** their *Br* flat *or Am* apartment is furnished in retro style

rétro[2] [retro] NM *Fam* rearview mirror

rétroactif, -ive [retroaktif, -iv] ADJ retroactive; **avec effet r. au 1er janvier** backdated to 1 January; **la loi a été votée, avec effet r. à dater de mars** the bill was passed, retroactive *or* retrospective to March

rétroaction [retroaksjɔ̃] NF 1 *(action en retour)* retrospective *or* retroactive effect, retroaction 2 *Biol* feedback

rétroactive [retroaktiv] *voir* **rétroactif**

rétroactivement [retroaktivmɑ̃] ADV retrospectively, retroactively, with retrospective *or* retroactive effect

rétroactivité [retroaktivite] NF retroactivity; *Jur* retrospectiveness

rétrocéder [18] [retrosede] VT 1 *(rendre)* to cede back, to retrocede 2 *(revendre)* to resell

rétrocession [retrosesjɔ̃] NF *Jur* retrocedence, retrocession

rétroéclairage [retroeklεraʒ] NM *Ordinat* backlight

rétroéclairé, -e [retroeklere] ADJ *Ordinat* backlit

rétroflexe [retroflɛks] *Ling* ADJ retroflex

NF retroflex consonant

rétrofusée [retrofyze] NF *Aviat & Astron* retrorocket

rétrogradation [retrogradasjɔ̃] NF 1 *Admin* demotion, downgrading; *Mil* demotion

2 *Aut Br* changing down *or Am* shifting down (to a lower gear)

3 *Astron* retrogradation, retrograde motion

4 *Littéraire (dans un développement)* regression, retrogression

rétrograde [retrograd] ADJ 1 *(passéiste ▸ esprit)* reactionary, backward; *(▸ mesure, politique)* reactionary, backward-looking, *Sout* retrograde

2 *(de recul ▸ mouvement)* backward, *Sout* retrograde

3 *Astron, Géol, Méd & Mus* retrograde

4 *(en billard)* **effet r.** screw

rétrograder [3] [retrograde] VT *(fonctionnaire)* to downgrade, to demote; *(officier)* to demote; **il a été rétrogradé** he was demoted

VI 1 *Aut Br* to change down, *Am* to shift down 2 *(dans une hiérarchie)* to move down; *Sport* **il a rétrogradé en cinquième position** he's fallen back to fifth place 3 *Astron* to retrograde

rétrogression [retrogresjɔ̃] NF retrogression

rétropédalage [retropedalaʒ] NM *Cyclisme* backpedalling

rétropédaler [3] [retropedale] VI *Cyclisme* to back-pedal

rétroplanning [retroplaniŋ] NM reverse planning

rétroprojecteur [retroproʒεktœr] NM overhead projector

rétroprojection [retroproʒεksjɔ̃] NF *Cin & TV* back projection

rétropropulsion [retropropylsjɔ̃] NF reverse thrust

rétrospectif, -ive [retrospεktif, -iv] ADJ *(étude)* retrospective

• **rétrospective** NF 1 *Beaux-Arts* retrospective; *Cin* season, retrospective; **une rétrospective Richard Burton** a Richard Burton season; **une rétrospective de l'année 1944** a look back at the events of 1944 2 *Fin* review

rétrospectivement [retrospεktivmɑ̃] ADV 1 *(à la réflexion)* looking back; **r., je me rends compte que j'ai eu tort** looking back, I realize I was wrong 2 *(après coup)* in retrospect; **tout est devenu clair r.** it all became clear in retrospect

retroussé, -e [rətruse] ADJ 1 *(jupe)* bunched *or* pulled up; *(manches, pantalon)* rolled *or* turned up 2 *(nez)* turned up 3 *(babines)* curled up; *(moustache)* curled *or* twisted up

retroussement [rətrusmɑ̃] NM *(d'une jupe)* bunching *or* pulling up; *(d'un pantalon)* rolling *or* turning up; *(de manches)* rolling up; **avec un r. des lèvres** with a curl of the lip

retrousser [3] [rətruse] VT 1 *(jupe)* to bunch *or* to pull up; *(pantalon)* to roll *or* to turn up; *(manches)* to roll up; *aussi Fig* **il va falloir r. nos manches** we'll have to roll our sleeves up 2 *(babines)* to curl up; *(moustache)* to curl *or* to twist up

VPR **se retrousser** 1 to pull *or* to hitch up one's skirt/trousers/*etc*; **j'ai dû me r. jusqu'aux genoux pour ne pas mouiller ma robe** I had to pull my dress up around my knees to stop it getting wet 2 *(bords, feuille)* to curl up

retroussis [rətrusi] **NM** *(revers)* lapel; *(d'un uniforme)* lappet; **chapeau à r.** cocked hat; **bottes à r.** topboots

retrouvable [rətruvabl] **ADJ** recoverable, retrievable; **facilement r.** easy to find

retrouvailles [rətruvaj] **NFPL 1** *(après une querelle)* getting back on friendly terms again; *(après une absence)* reunion, getting together again **2** *(retour ▸ dans un lieu)* rediscovery, return; *(▸ à un travail)* return; **mes r. avec le train-train quotidien** getting back into my daily routine

RETROUVER **[3]** [rətruve]

> **VT**
> • to find **1, 2** • to meet up with **2**
> • to come across **2** • to remember **3**
> • to uncover **4** • to get back **5**
> • to recognize **6**
> **VPR**
> • to meet **1, 3** • to get together **2**
> • to find oneself back **4** • to end up **5**
> • to find one's way **6** • to go back to one's roots **7**

VT 1 *(clés, lunettes)* to find (again); **a-t-elle retrouvé sa clé?** *(elle-même)* did she find her key?; *(grâce à autrui)* did she get her key back?; **elle n'a toujours pas retrouvé de travail** she still hasn't found any work; **r. un poste** to find a (new) job; **r. son (ancien) poste** to get one's (old) job back; **r. son chemin** to find one's way (again); **là vous retrouvez la Nationale** that's where you join up with the main road; **r. la trace de qch** to find trace of sth; **on n'a rien retrouvé après l'explosion** there was nothing left after the blast; **r. tout propre/sens dessus dessous** to find everything clean/upside down; **r. qn affaibli/changé** to find sb weaker/a different person

2 *(ami, parent)* to be reunited with, to meet up with (again); *(voleur)* to catch up with (again), to find; *(revoir par hasard)* to come across (again), to run into again; *(rejoindre)* to meet up with again; **et que je ne vous retrouve pas ici!** don't let me catch you (around) here again!; **celle-là, je la retrouverai** I'll get even with her (one day); **retrouve-moi en bas** meet me downstairs

3 *(se rappeler)* to remember, *Sout* to recall; **ça y est, j'ai retrouvé le mot!** that's it, the word's come back to me now!

4 *(redécouvrir ▸ secret, parchemin, formule)* to uncover

5 *(jouir à nouveau de)* **nous avons retrouvé notre petite plage/maison** here we are back on our little beach/in our little house; **r. son calme** to regain one's composure; **r. l'appétit/ses forces/sa santé** to get one's appetite/strength/health back; **r. la forme** to get fit again, to be back on form; **r. la foi** to find (one's) faith again; **r. la mémoire** to get one's memory back again; **r. le sommeil** to go back to sleep; **il a retrouvé le sourire** he's smiling again now, he's found his smile again; **le bonheur/l'amour retrouvé** new-found happiness/love

6 *(reconnaître)* to recognize, to trace; **on retrouve dans le premier mouvement des accents mozartiens** the influence of Mozart is recognizable *or* noticeable in the first movement; **on retrouve les mêmes propriétés dans les polymères** the same properties are to be found in polymers; **je n'ai pas retrouvé la jeune fille gaie d'autrefois** she's not the happy young girl I used to know; **enfin, je te retrouve!** I'm glad to see you're back to your old self again!

VPR se retrouver 1 *(avoir rendez-vous)* to meet (one another); **on se retrouve demain** see you tomorrow; **retrouvons-nous sous l'horloge** let's meet under the clock

2 *(se réunir)* to get together; **ils aiment se r. entre eux** they like to get together; **on se retrouve entre gourmets/jeunes au Cheval Blanc** food-lovers/young people get together at the Cheval Blanc

3 *(se rencontrer à nouveau)* to meet again; *Fam* **on se retrouvera, mon bonhomme!** I'll get even with you, chum!; **comme on se retrouve!** fancy meeting you here!, well, well, well, look who's here!

4 *(être de nouveau)* to find oneself back (again); **se r. dans la même situation (qu'avant)** to find oneself back in the same situation (as before)

5 *(par hasard)* to end up; **je me suis retrouvé de l'autre côté de la frontière** I ended up on the other side of the border; **à 40 ans, il s'est retrouvé veuf** he (suddenly) found himself a widower at 40; **tu vas te r. à l'hôpital** you'll end up in hospital

6 *(se repérer)* to find one's way; **je ne m'y retrouve plus dans tous ces formulaires à remplir** I can't make head or tail of all these forms to fill in; **s'y r.** *(résoudre un problème)* to sort things out; *(faire un bénéfice)* to make a profit

7 *(se ressourcer)* to find oneself again, to go back to one's roots

rétroversion [retrɔversjɔ̃] **NF** *Méd* retroversion

rétrovirus [retrɔvirys] **NM** *Méd* retrovirus

rétroviseur [retrɔvizœr] **NM** *Aut* **r. (central)** (rear-view) mirror; **r. extérieur** wing mirror; **r. latéral** *Br* wing mirror, *Am* side-view mirror

rets [re] **NM 1** *(gén pl) Littéraire (piège)* snare; *Fig* **attraper** *ou* **prendre qn dans ses r.** to ensnare sb; *Fig* **tomber dans les r. de qn** to be caught in sb's trap **2** *(filet ▸ de chasse)* net, snare; *(▸ de pêche)* (fishing) net

reuch [rœʃ] **ADJ INV** *Fam (verlan de* **cher***)* expensive☐, pricey

reuf [rœf] **NM** *Fam (verlan de* **frère***)* brother☐, bro

reum [rœm] **NF** *Fam (verlan de* **mère***)* old lady, *Br* old dear

réunification [reynifikasjɔ̃] **NF** reunification

réunifier **[9]** [reynifje] **VT** to reunify, to reunite

Réunion [reynjɔ̃] **NF (l'île de) la R.** Réunion

réunion [reynjɔ̃] **NF 1** *(rassemblement)* gathering, get-together; **r. de famille** family reunion *or* gathering; **c'est l'occasion d'une r. familiale** it's an opportunity to bring the family together; **droit de r.** right of assembly

2 *(fête)* gathering, party; **j'organise une petite r. entre amis** I'm having a small party for my friends, I'm entertaining a few friends

3 *(retrouvailles)* reunion; **r. d'anciens élèves** reunion of former pupils

4 *(congrès)* meeting; *(séance)* session, sitting; **dites que je suis en r.** say that I'm at *or* in a meeting; **r. d'actionnaires** shareholders' meeting; **r. préparatoire** briefing; **r. publique** public *or* open meeting; **r. au sommet** summit (meeting *or* conference)

5 *(regroupement ▸ de faits, de preuves)* bringing together, assembling, gathering; *(▸ de sociétés, de services)* merging; *(▸ d'États)* union; **la r. de ces territoires à la France a eu lieu en 1823** these territories were united with France in 1823

6 *Sport* meeting; **r. (sportive)** sports meeting, sporting event

7 *Math* union

réunionnais, -e [reynjɔnɛ, -ɛz] **ADJ** of/from Réunion

• **Réunionnais, -e NM,F** = inhabitant of or person from Réunion

réunionnite [reynjɔnit] **NF** *Fam* meeting mania

réunir **[32]** [reynir] **VT 1** *(relier ▸ pôles, tuyaux)* to join (together); *(▸ brins, câbles)* to tie together

2 *(mettre ensemble ▸ objets)* to collect together; *(▸ bétail)* to round up; **le spectacle réunit ses meilleures chansons** the show is a collection of his/her greatest hits; **r. qch à qch** *(province)* to join sth to sth; **propriétés réunies au domaine royal en 1823** land acquired by the Crown in 1823

3 *(combiner ▸ goûts, couleurs)* to combine; *(▸ qualités)* to have; *(conditions requises)* to meet, to satisfy

4 *(recueillir ▸ statistiques, propositions, informations)* to put *or* to collect together; *(▸ preuves)* to put together; *(▸ fonds)* to raise

5 *(personnes ▸ rassembler)* to bring together; *(▸ après une séparation)* to reunite; **nous sommes enfin réunis!** *(après rendez-vous manqué)* here we are together at last!, we found each other at last!; *(après querelle)* we're back together again!; **le séminaire réunira des chercheurs émérites** some highly talented researchers will be attending the conference; **réunissez les élèves par groupes de dix** gather *or* put the pupils into groups of ten

VPR se réunir 1 *(se retrouver ensemble ▸ amis)* to meet, to get together; **l'assemblée se réunit une fois par semaine** the assembly meets once a week **2** *(fusionner)* to unite, to join (together)

réussi, -e [reysi] **ADJ** successful; **ton tricot/soufflé est très r.** your sweater/soufflé is a real success; **ce fut un retour r.** the homecoming was a success; *Ironique* **comme fête, c'était r.!** call that a party!; *Ironique* **ah c'est r., la voilà en larmes!** well done *or* very clever, she's in tears now!

réussir **[32]** [reysir] **VT** *(manœuvre, œuvre, recette)* to make a success of, to carry off; *(exercice)* to succeed in doing; *(examen)* to pass; **il a réussi son saut périlleux/sa nature morte** his somersault/still life was a success; **elle réussit bien les omelettes** she makes very good omelettes; *Fam* **j'ai bien réussi mon coup** it worked out (well) for me, I managed to pull it off; *Ironique* **ah bravo, tu as bien réussi ton coup!** well done!, very clever!; **r. sa vie** to make a success of one's life; **r. son effet** to achieve the desired effect; **avec ce concert, il réussit un tour de force** his concert is a great achievement

VI 1 *(dans la vie, à l'école)* to do well, to be successful; **je veux r.** I want to succeed *or* to be a success *or* to be successful; **il a réussi dans la vie** he's done well in life, he's a successful man; **un jeune acteur qui va r.** an up-and-coming young actor; **une femme d'affaires qui a réussi** a successful businesswoman; **r. à un examen** to pass an exam; **nous sommes ravis d'apprendre que vous avez réussi** we're delighted to hear of your success

2 *(affaire, entreprise)* to succeed, to be a success; **l'opération n'a pas vraiment réussi** the operation wasn't really a success

3 *(parvenir)* **r. à faire qch** to manage to do sth, to succeed in doing sth; **j'ai réussi à le réparer/à me couper** I managed to mend it/to cut myself; **je n'ai pas réussi à la convaincre** I didn't manage *or* I failed to persuade her

4 *(convenir)* **r. à qn** *(climat, nourriture)* to agree with sb, to do sb good; **le café lui réussit/ne lui réussit pas** coffee agrees/doesn't agree with him/her; **on dirait que ça te réussit, le mariage!** being married seems to suit you!; **tout lui réussit** he's/she's successful in everything he/she does, everything he/she does turns out well; **rien ne lui réussit** he/she can't do anything right

réussite [reysit] **NF 1** *(succès)* success; **c'est une r.!** it's a (real) success!; **son premier album est une r.** his/her first album is a success; **à quoi attribuez-vous votre r.?** what is the secret of your success?; **fêter sa r. à un examen** to celebrate passing an exam *or* getting through an exam; **r. (sociale)** (social) success **2** *Cartes* patience; **faire une r.** to have a game of patience

réutilisation [reytilizasjɔ̃] **NF** reuse

réutiliser **[3]** [reytilize] **VT** to reuse, to use again

revaccination [rəvaksinasjɔ̃] **NF** revaccination

revacciner **[3]** [rəvaksine] **VT** to revaccinate

revaloir **[60]** [rəvalwar] **VT je te revaudrai ça** *(en remerciant)* I'll repay you some day; *(en menaçant)* I'll get even with you for that, I'll pay you back for that

revalorisation [rəvalɔrizasjɔ̃] **NF 1** *(d'une monnaie)* revaluation **2** *(des salaires, des retraites)* raising, revaluation, increment **3** *(d'une théorie, d'une profession)* upgrading, reassertion

revaloriser **[3]** [rəvalɔrize] **VT 1** *(monnaie)* to revaluate **2** *(salaires, retraites)* to raise, to revalue **3** *(théorie, profession)* to improve the status *or* prestige *or* standing of, to upgrade

revanchard, -e [rəvɑ̃ʃar, -ard] *Péj* **ADJ** *(attitude, politique)* of revenge, revengeful, *Sout* revanchard; *(personne)* revengeful, set on revenge, *Sout* revanchist

NM,F revanchist

revanche [rəvɑ̃ʃ] **NF 1** *(sur un ennemi)* revenge; **prendre sa r. (sur qn)** to take *or* to get one's revenge (on sb) **2** *Sport & (dans un jeu)* return game; **donner sa r. à qn** to give sb his/her revenge

• **en revanche ADV** on the other hand

revanchisme [rəvɑ̃ʃism] **NM** revanchism, spirit of revenge

revanchiste [rəvɑ̃ʃist] **ADJ & NMF** revanchist

rêvasser **[3]** [rɛvase] **VI** to daydream, to dream away, to muse

rêvasserie [rɛvasri] **NF** daydream; **des rêvasseries sans fin** endless musing *or* daydreaming

rêvasseur, -euse [rɛvasœr, -øz] **ADJ** dreamlike, dreamy
NM,F daydreamer

revaudra *etc voir* **revaloir**

rêve [rɛv] **NM 1** *(d'un dormeur)* dream; **un mauvais r.** a nightmare, a bad dream; **faire un r.** to have a dream; **je l'ai vu en r.** I saw him in my *or* in a dream; **comme dans un r.** as if in a dream; **bonne nuit, fais de beaux rêves!** good night, sweet dreams!; *Psy* **le r.** dreams, dreaming
2 *(d'un utopiste)* dream, fantasy, pipe dream; **mon r., ce serait d'aller au Japon** my dream is to go to Japan, I dream of going to Japan; **tout ça, ce sont des rêves** that's all (just) fantasy *or* cloud-cuckoo-land; **rêves de gloire/célébrité** dreams of glory/fame; **un r. devenu réalité** a dream come true; **dans mes rêves les plus fous** in my wildest dreams *or* imaginings; **perdu dans son r.** *ou* **ses rêves** lost in his/her dream world; **un r. éveillé** a waking dream
3 *Fam* **le r.** *(l'idéal)* the ideal thing; **c'est/ce n'est pas le r.** it's/it isn't ideal; **c'est le r. pour un pique-nique, ici!** this place is just perfect for a picnic!; **ce n'est pas le r. mais il faudra faire avec** it's not exactly what I'd/we'd/*etc* dreamt of but it'll have to do
• **de mes rêves, de ses rêves** *etc* **ADJ** of my/his/her/*etc* dreams; **la maison de leurs rêves** the house of their dreams, their dream house; **la femme de ses rêves** the woman of his dreams, his dream woman
• **de rêve ADJ** ideal, perfect; **une vie de r.** a sublime *or* an ideal existence; **un mariage de r.** a perfect marriage; **il fait un temps de r.** the weather is perfect

rêvé, -e [rɛve] **ADJ** perfect, ideal; **c'est l'endroit r. pour camper** this is the ideal place *or* just the place to camp

revêche [rəvɛʃ] **ADJ** *(personne)* surly, cantankerous, tetchy; *(voix, air)* surly, grumpy

revécu, -e [rəveky] **PP** *voir* **revivre**

réveil [revɛj] **NM 1** *(après le sommeil)* waking (up), *Littéraire* awakening; **je déteste l'heure du r.** I hate waking up *or* having to wake up (in the morning); **j'attendrai ton r. pour partir** I'll wait until you've woken up *or* until you're awake before I leave; **j'ai des réveils difficiles** *ou* **le r. difficile** I find it hard to wake up; **à mon r. il était là** when I woke up he was there
2 *(prise de conscience)* awakening
3 *Mil* reveille; **r. au clairon** (bugle) reveille; *Fig* **j'ai eu droit à un r. en fanfare, ce matin!** I was treated to a very noisy awakening this morning!
4 *(de la mémoire, de la nature)* reawakening; *(d'une douleur)* return, new onset; *(d'un volcan)* (new) stirring, fresh eruption
5 *(pendule)* alarm (clock); **j'ai mis le r. (à 7 heures)** I've set the alarm (for 7 o'clock); **r. téléphonique** wake-up service; **r. de voyage** travelling alarm clock

réveillé, -e [reveje] **ADJ** awake; **je suis mal r.** I'm still half asleep

réveille-matin [revɛjmatɛ̃] **NM INV** *Vieilli* alarm (clock)

réveiller [4] [reveje] **VT 1** *(tirer ▸ du sommeil, de l'évanouissement)* to wake (up); *(▸ d'une réflexion, d'une rêverie)* to rouse, to stir; **il faut que l'on se fasse r. à 7 heures si on ne veut pas rater l'avion** we need to make sure somebody wakes us up at 7 a.m. if we don't want to miss the plane; **un bruit/une explosion à r. les morts** a noise/an explosion loud enough to wake the dead; **r. les consciences** to stir people's consciences **2** *(faire renaître ▸ enthousiasme, rancœur, souvenirs)* to reawaken, to revive
VPR se réveiller 1 *(sortir ▸ du sommeil, de l'évanouissement)* to wake (up), to awake *or* to awaken; *(▸ d'une réflexion, de la torpeur)* to wake up, to stir *or* to rouse oneself; **se r. en retard** to oversleep; **se r. en sursaut** to wake up with a start; **il faut vous r.!** you'd better pull yourself together!; **le pays est en train de se r.** the country is beginning to stir itself *or* shake itself *or* waken up **2** *(se ranimer ▸ passion, souvenir)* to revive, to be stirred up *or* aroused (again); *(▸ volcan)* to stir *or* to erupt again; *(▸ nature)* to revive; *(▸ maladie, douleur)* to start up again, to return

réveillon [revɛjɔ̃] **NM** = family meal eaten on Christmas Eve or New Year's Eve; **r. (de Noël)** *(fête)* Christmas Eve party; *(repas)* Christmas Eve supper; **r. (de la Saint-Sylvestre** *ou* **du jour de l'an)** *(fête)* New Year's Eve party; *(repas)* New Year's Eve supper

> **RÉVEILLONS**
>
> Christmas is traditionally a family celebration. In Catholic families, the "crèche", or miniature nativity scene, is decorated and everyone goes on Christmas Eve to midnight mass, after which the long and copious Christmas dinner is served: this includes oysters and, for dessert, the traditional "bûche de Noël" or yule log. The presents under the Christmas tree are opened either on Christmas Eve or on Christmas Day morning. The "réveillon de la Saint-Sylvestre" on New Year's Eve is usually celebrated among friends, either at home or in a restaurant. Champagne is drunk at midnight and everybody embraces and wishes each other a happy New Year. New Year greeting cards can, in theory, be sent up until the end of January.

réveillonner [3] [revɛjɔne] **VI** *(faire une fête ▸ à Noël)* to have a Christmas Eve party; *(▸ pour la Saint-Sylvestre)* to have a New Year's Eve party; *(faire un repas ▸ à Noël)* to have a Christmas Eve supper; *(▸ pour la Saint-Sylvestre)* to have a New Year's Eve supper; **nous avons trop bien réveillonné** we had too much to eat and drink *(on Christmas Eve or New Year's Eve)*

révélateur, -trice [revelatœr, -tris] **ADJ** *(détail)* revealing, indicative, significant; *(lapsus, sourire)* revealing, telltale; **une interview révélatrice** a revealing interview; **les chiffres sont révélateurs** the figures speak volumes; **ce sondage est très r. de la tendance actuelle** this poll tells us *or* reveals a lot about the current trend; **c'est tout à fait r. de notre époque** it says a lot about our times; **c'est r. de son manque de confiance en lui** it reveals *or* shows his lack of confidence
NM,F revealer
NM 1 *(indice)* telltale sign **2** *Phot* developer

révélation [revelasjɔ̃] **NF 1** *(information)* revelation, disclosure; **faire des révélations à la presse/police** to give the press a scoop/the police important information
2 *(personne)* revelation; **il pourrait bien être la r. musicale de l'année** he could well turn out to be this year's musical revelation *or* discovery
3 *(prise de conscience)* revelation; **ce voyage en Égypte a été une r.** that trip to Egypt was an eye-opener *or* a revelation; **avoir une r.** to have a brainwave
4 *(divulgation)* disclosure, revealing; **la r. d'un complot** the revealing *or* uncovering of a plot
5 *Rel* revelation

révélatrice [revelatris] *voir* **révélateur**

révélé, -e [revele] **ADJ** *(religion)* revealed

révéler [18] [revele] **VT 1** *(secret, information, intention)* to reveal, to disclose; *(état de fait)* to reveal, to bring to light; *(vérité)* to reveal, to tell; **j'ai des choses importantes à r. à la police** I have important information to give to the police; **elle a révélé mon secret** *(intentionnellement)* she revealed my secret; *(involontairement)* she gave away my secret; **le nom de la victime n'a toujours pas été révélé** the victim's name has still not been disclosed *or* released; **il refuse de r. son identité** he's refusing to disclose his identity *or* to say who he is; *Journ* **r. ses sources** to reveal one's sources
2 *(montrer ▸ don, qualité, anomalie)* to reveal, to show; **ce comportement révèle une nature violente** this behaviour reveals a violent temperament; **la mauvaise gestion révélée par ces chiffres** the bad management brought to light *or* evidenced by these results; *Méd* **une grosseur que les radios n'avaient pas révélée** a growth which hadn't shown up on the X-rays; **l'actrice révèle dans cette scène un talent prometteur** the actress shows promising talent in this scene
3 *(faire connaître)* **r. qn** to make sb famous; **révélé par un important metteur en scène** discovered by an important director; **dans l'album qui l'a révélé (au public)** on the album which brought him fame
4 *Phot* to develop
VPR se révéler 1 *(s'avérer)* **se r. coûteux/utile** to prove (to be) expensive/useful; **il s'est révélé d'un égoïsme effrayant** he proved to be dreadfully selfish; **l'expérience ne s'est pas révélée concluante** the experiment wasn't conclusive *or* turned out to be inconclusive; **elle se révéla piètre vendeuse** she turned out *or* proved to be a poor sales assistant; **il s'est révélé être un escroc** he turned out to be a crook **2** *(se faire connaître)* to be revealed *or* discovered, to come to light; **tu t'es révélé sous ton vrai jour** you've shown yourself in your true colours; **elle s'est révélée (au grand public) dans 'Carmen'** she had her first big success in 'Carmen'

revenant, -e [rəvnɑ̃, -ɑ̃t] **NM,F** *Fam Hum* **tiens, un r.!** hello, stranger!, long time no see!
NM *(fantôme)* ghost, spirit; **une histoire de revenants** a ghost story

revendable [rəvɑ̃dabl] **ADJ** resaleable

revendeur, -euse [rəvɑ̃dœr, -øz] **NM,F 1** *(détaillant)* retailer, dealer; **vous trouverez le dernier modèle chez votre r. habituel** you'll find the latest model at your local dealer **2** *(de billets, de tickets) Br* tout, *Am* scalper; *(d'articles d'occasion)* second-hand dealer; **r. de drogue** drug dealer; **r. de voitures** second-hand car dealer

revendicateur, -trice [rəvɑ̃dikatœr, -tris] **ADJ** **des discours revendicateurs** speeches setting out demands *or* claims
NM,F les revendicateurs demandaient une augmentation de salaire the claimants *or* protestors were pushing for a wage increase

revendicatif, -ive [rəvɑ̃dikatif, -iv] **ADJ** protest *(avant n)*; **un mouvement r.** a protest movement; **journée revendicative** day of action *or* protest

revendication [rəvɑ̃dikasjɔ̃] **NF 1** *(réclamation)* demand; **journée de r.** day of action *or* protest; **revendications salariales** wage demands *or* claims; **revendications syndicales** union demands **2** *Jur* claim; **mener une action en r. contre qn** to set up *or* to lodge a claim against sb

revendicative [rəvɑ̃dikativ] *voir* **revendicatif**

revendicatrice [rəvɑ̃dikatris] *voir* **revendicateur**

revendiquer [3] [rəvɑ̃dike] **VT 1** *(réclamer ▸ dû, droit, part d'héritage)* to claim; *(▸ hausse de salaire)* to demand; **il revendique le droit de s'exprimer librement** he claims the right of free speech **2** *(assumer)* to lay claim to, to claim; **r. la responsabilité de qch** to claim responsibility for sth; **l'attentat n'a pas été revendiqué** nobody has claimed responsibility for the attack; **il n'a jamais revendiqué cette paternité** he never claimed this child as his
• **se revendiquer VPR il se revendique comme anarchiste** he's a staunch anarchist

revendre [73] [rəvɑ̃dr] **VT 1** *(vendre ▸ gén)* to sell; *(sujet: détaillant)* to retail; *Bourse (titres)* to sell out; **revends ta voiture, si tu as besoin d'argent** if you need money sell your car **2** *Fam (locutions)* **des crayons, j'en ai à r.** I've got loads of pencils; **elle a du talent/de l'ambition à r.** she's got masses of talent/ambition; **avoir de l'énergie à r.** to be bubbling over with energy
VPR se revendre ce genre d'appareil ne se revend pas facilement this sort of equipment isn't easy to resell; **dans cinq ans, cette maison se revendra beaucoup plus cher** in five years this house will be worth far more than it is now

revenez-y [rəvnezi] **NM INV** *Fam (locution)* **ce vin a un petit goût de r.!** this wine is rather moreish!

REVENIR [40] [rəvnir]

> • to come back **1-3** • to return **1, 2**
> • to recur **2** • to reappear **2**
> • to crop up again **2**

VI 1 *(venir à nouveau ▸ gén)* to come back; *(▸ chez soi)* to come back, to come (back) home, to return home; *(▸ au point de départ)* to return, to come *or* to get back; **pouvez-vous r. plus tard?** could you come back later?; **une fois revenue chez elle** once she'd got (back) *or* returned home; **je suis revenue de Rome hier** I came *or* I got back from Rome yesterday; **passe me voir en revenant du bureau** call in to see me on your way back *or* home from the office; **je reviens (tout de suite)** I'll be (right) back; **les gens sont revenus à leur place** people are back in *or* have returned to their seats; **il n'est pas encore revenu de faire ses commissions** he hasn't come *or* got back from the shops yet; **je suis revenu déçu de la visite** I came back disappointed after the visit; **le boomerang revient vers celui qui l'a lancé** boomerangs return to the thrower; **la lettre m'est revenue** the letter was returned to me; **ça ne sert à rien de pleurer, ça ne va pas le faire r.!** it's no use crying, it's not going to bring him back!; **r. à qn** *(renouer le contact avec)* to come back to sb; **enfin tu me reviens!** at last, you've come back to me!; **d'où nous revenez-vous?** and where have you been?; **nous aimons r. ici** we like coming (back) here; **je ne reviendrai jamais chez ce coiffeur** I'll never come back to this hairdresser again; **je suis très satisfait de mes achats, je reviendrai** I'm very pleased with what I've bought, I'll be back; **r. en arrière** *(dans le temps)* to go back (in time); *(dans l'espace)* to retrace one's steps, to go back; **r. au point de départ** to go back to the starting point; *Fig* to be back to square one

2 *(se manifester à nouveau ▸ doute, inquiétude)* to return, to come back; *(▸ calme, paix)* to return, to be restored; *(▸ symptôme)* to recur, to return, to reappear; *(▸ problème)* to crop up *or* to arise again; *(▸ occasion)* to crop up again; *(▸ thème, rime)* to recur, to reappear; *(▸ célébration)* to come round again; *(▸ saison)* to return, to come back; *(▸ soleil)* to come out again, to reappear; **le temps des fêtes est revenu** the festive season is with us again *or* has come round again; **la question qui revient le plus fréquemment dans les entretiens** the most commonly asked question *or* the question that crops up most often in interviews; **la question revient toujours sur le tapis** that question always comes up for discussion; **c'est un thème qui revient toujours dans ses romans** it's a recurring theme in his/her novels; **c'est une erreur qui revient souvent dans vos devoirs** you often make this mistake in your homework; **ses crises reviennent de plus en plus souvent** his/her fits are becoming more and more frequent; **j'ai désherbé, mais les orties reviennent de plus belle** I've weeded, but the nettles are even worse than before

3 *Sport (dans une course)* to come back, to catch up; **le peloton est en train de r. sur les échappés** the pack is catching up with *or* gaining on the breakaway group; **et voici Bapow qui revient pour prendre la troisième place!** and it's Bapow who comes back to take the third place!

4 *(coûter)* **r. cher** to be expensive; **elle a dû te r. cher, ta petite sortie!** your little night out must have cost you a lot!; **r. à** to cost, to amount to, to come to; **le voyage nous est revenu à 300 euros** the trip cost us 300 euros; **le tout ne reviendra pas à plus de 100 euros** it won't come to *or* cost any more than 100 euros for everything

5 *Culin* **faire r.** to brown; **une fois les oignons revenus** once the onions have browned *or* are brown

• **revenir à VT IND 1** *(équivaloir à)* to come down to, to amount to; **cela reviendrait à une rupture de contrat** that would amount to *or* mean a breach of contract; **cela revient toujours à une question de relations** it always boils *or* comes down to having the right connections; **ce qui revient à dire que...** which amounts to saying that...; **ça revient au même!** it amounts to *or* comes to the same thing!; **pour moi, ça revient au même, il faudra que j'y aille** it's all the same to me, I'll have to go anyway

2 *(reprendre ▸ mode, procédé, thème)* to go back to, to revert to, to return to; **le gouvernement veut r. à la liberté des prix** the government wants to return to price deregulation; **on revient aux** *ou* **à la mode des cheveux courts** short hair is coming back *or* on its way back; **r. à une plus juste vision des choses** to come round to a more balanced view of things; **r. à de meilleures dispositions** *ou* **à de meilleurs sentiments** to return to a better frame of mind; **on (en) revient à des formes d'énergie naturelles** natural sources of energy are coming back into use, we're reverting to natural sources of energy; **mais revenons** *ou* **revenons-en à cette affaire** but let's get *or* come back to this matter; **bon, pour (en) r. à notre histoire...** right, to get back to *or* to go on with our story...; **j'en** *ou* **je reviens à ma question, où étiez-vous hier?** I'm asking you again, where were you yesterday?; **et si nous (en) revenions à vous, M. Lebrun?** now what about you, Mr Lebrun?; **voilà 20 euros, et n'y reviens plus!** here's 20 euros, and don't ask me again!; **il n'y a pas** *ou* **plus à y r.!** and that's final *or* that's that!; **r. à soi** to come to, to come round

3 *(sujet: part, récompense)* to go *or* to fall to, to devolve on; *(sujet: droit, tâche)* to fall to; **à chacun ce qui lui revient** to each his due; **avec les honneurs qui lui reviennent** with the honours (which are) due to him/her; **ses terrains sont revenus à l'État** his/her lands passed *or* went to the State; **il devrait encore me r. 20 euros** I should still get 20 euros; **ce titre lui revient de droit** this title is his/hers by right; **tout le mérite t'en revient** the credit is all yours, you get all the credit for it; **la décision nous revient, il nous revient de décider** it's for us *or* up to us to decide

4 *(sujet: faculté, souvenir)* to come back to; **l'appétit lui revient** he's/she's recovering his/her appetite *or* getting his/her appetite back; **la mémoire lui revient** his/her memory is coming back; **son nom ne me revient pas (à la mémoire)** his/her name escapes me *or* has slipped my mind; **attends, ça me revient!** wait, I've got it now *or* it's coming back to me now!; **ça me revient seulement maintenant, ils ont divorcé** I've just remembered, they got divorced; **tu ne te souviens pas de cet article? – si, ça me revient maintenant!** don't you remember that article? – yes, I'm with you now *or* it's coming back to me now!

5 *(tournure impersonnelle)* **il m'est revenu que...** word has got back to me *or* has reached me that...

6 *Fam (plaire à)* **ses manières ne me reviennent pas** his/her manners aren't to my liking; **elle a une tête qui ne me revient pas** I don't really like the look of her

• **revenir de VT IND 1** *(émotion, maladie)* to get over, to recover from; *(évanouissement)* to come round from, to come to after; **alors, tu es revenu de ta grande frayeur?** so,are you less frightened now *or* have you got over the fright now?; *Euph* **elle revient de loin!** *(elle a failli mourir)* it was touch and go (for her)!; *(elle a eu de graves ennuis)* she's had a close shave!; **je n'en reviens pas!** I can't get over it!; **je n'en reviens pas qu'il ait dit ça!** it's amazing he should say that!, I can't get over him saying that!; **quand je vais te le raconter, tu n'en reviendras pas** when I tell you the story you won't believe your ears **2** *(idée, préjugé)* to put *or* to cast aside, to throw over; *(illusion)* to shake off; *(principe)* to give up, to leave behind; **r. de ses erreurs** to realize *or* to recognize one's mistakes; *Fam* **moi, l'homéopathie, j'en suis revenu!** as far as I'm concerned, I've done *or* I'm through with homeopathy!; *Fam* **ce type-là, j'en suis bien revenue!** I couldn't care less about that guy now!; **il est revenu de tout** he's seen it all (before) **3 s'en r.** to be on one's way back; **nous nous en revenions tranquillement lorsque...** we were slowly making our way home when...

• **revenir sur VT IND 1** *(question)* to go back over, to hark back to; **elle ne peut s'empêcher de r. sur cette triste affaire** she can't help going *or* mulling over that sad business; **la question est réglée, ne revenons pas dessus** the matter's settled, let's not go back over it again **2** *(décision, déclaration, promesse)* to go back on; **ma décision est prise, je ne reviendrai pas dessus** my mind is made up and I'm not going to change it; **r. sur sa parole** *ou* **sur la parole donnée** to go back on one's word, to break one's promise **3** *Belg (locution)* **ne pas r. sur** not to remember

---

revente [rəvɑ̃t] **NF** resale; *Bourse (de titres)* selling out

revenu[1] [rəvəny] **NM 1** *(rétribution ▸ d'une personne)* income *(UNCOUNT)*; **elle a de gros/petits revenus** she has a large/small income; **sans revenus** without any income; **revenus accessoires** incidental income; **revenus actuels** current earnings *or* income; **r. annuel** annual income; **r. brut** gross income; **r. cumulé** cumulative revenue; **r. disponible** disposable income; **r. fixe** fixed income; **r. foncier** income from real estate; **r. par habitant** *ou* **par tête** per capita income; **r. imposable** taxable income; **r. minimum d'insertion** = minimum welfare payment paid to people with no other source of income, *Br* income support, *Am* welfare; **r. net** net income; **revenus salariaux, r. du travail** earned income **2** *(recettes ▸ de l'État)* revenue; *Écon* **r. national brut/net** gross/net national income; **revenus de l'exportation** export revenue, export earnings; **revenus publics** *ou* **de l'État** public revenue **3** *(intérêt)* income, return; *(dividende ▸ d'une action)* yield (**de** on); **un investissement produisant un r. de 7 pour cent** an investment with a 7 percent rate of return; *Bourse* **r.** *ou* **revenus obligataire(s), r.** *ou* **revenus des obligations** income from bonds

revenu[2], **-e** [rəvəny] **PP** *voir* **revenir**

rêver [4] [rɛve] **VI 1** *(en dormant)* to dream (**de** of); **r. tout haut** to talk in one's sleep; **elle rêve (tout) éveillée** she's a daydreamer, she's lost in a dream *or* daydream; **c'est ce qu'il m'a dit, je n'ai pas rêvé!** that's what he said, I didn't dream it up *or* imagine it!; **toi ici? (dites moi que) je rêve!** you here? I must be dreaming!; **r. de** to dream of; **j'ai rêvé d'un monstre** I dreamed of *or* had a dream about a monster; **on croit r.!** *(ton irrité)* is this a joke?; **elle en rêve la nuit** she dreams about it at night; *Fig* she's obsessed by it

2 *(divaguer)* to be imagining things, to be in cloud-cuckoo-land; **dis-moi aussi que je rêve!** go ahead, tell me I'm imagining things!; **toi, gagner ta vie tout seul, non mais tu rêves!** you, earn your own living? you must be joking!; **ça fait r.!** that's the stuff that dreams are made of!; **13 pour cent d'intérêt, ça fait r., hein?** 13 percent interest, isn't that just great?; **des plages/salaires à faire r.** dream beaches/wages; **(quand on voit) des paysages comme ça, ça fait r.** scenery like that is just out of this world; **des mots qui font r.** words that fire the imagination; **on peut toujours r.** there's no harm in dreaming!, there's no harm in a little fantasizing!; **faut pas r.!** let's not get carried away!; **la semaine de 25 heures? faut pas r.!** the 25-hour week? that'll be the day!

3 *(rêvasser)* to dream, to daydream; **r. à** to dream of, *Sout* to muse over; **j'étais en train de r. à ma jeunesse** I was lost in thoughts of my youth

VT 1 *(sujet: dormeur)* to dream; **vous l'avez rêvé!** you must have imagined *or* dreamt it!, you must have been dreaming!; **r. que...** to dream that...

2 *(souhaiter)* to dream of; **on ne saurait r. (une) occasion plus propice** you couldn't wish for a more appropriate occasion; **je n'ai jamais rêvé mariage/fortune!** I've never dreamed of marriage/being wealthy!

3 *(inventer de toutes pièces)* to dream up; **il a dû r. toute cette histoire** he must have dreamt up the whole story

• **rêver de VT IND** *(espérer)* to dream of; **j'avais tellement rêvé de ton retour** I so longed for your return; **l'homme dont toutes les femmes rêvent** the man every woman dreams about *or* desires; **je n'avais jamais osé r. d'un bonheur pareil!** I'd never have dared dream of such happiness!; **r. de faire qch** to be longing to do sth

réverbération [reverberasjɔ̃] **NF** *(de la chaleur, de la lumière)* reflection; *(du son)* reverberation; **à cause de la r. du soleil sur la neige** because of the glare of the sun on the snow

réverbère [reverbɛr] **NM 1** *(lampe)* streetlamp, streetlight; *(poteau)* lamppost **2** *(réflecteur)* reflector

réverbérer [18] [reverbere] **VT** *(chaleur, lumière)* to reflect; *(son)* to reverberate, to send back

reverdir [32] [rəverdir] **VI** to grow *or* to turn green again

VT le printemps reverdit les champs spring makes the fields green again

révérence [reverɑ̃s] **NF 1** *Littéraire (déférence)* reverence; **traiter qn avec r.** to treat sb with reverence *or* reverently; *Vieilli* **r. parler** saving your reverence, begging your pardon **2** *(salut ▸ d'homme)* bow; *(▸ de femme)* curtsy; **faire la r. à qn** *(sujet: homme)* to bow to sb; *(sujet: femme)* to curtsy to sb; **tirer sa r. à qn** to walk out on sb; **je vous tire ma r.** I'm off; **tirer sa r. à qch** to bow out of sth **3** *Rel* **Votre R.** Your Reverence

révérencieux, -euse [reverɑ̃sjø, -øz] ADJ *Littéraire* reverent

révérend, -e [reverɑ̃, -ɑ̃d] ADJ reverend; **la révérende mère supérieure** the Reverend Mother (Superior); **le r. père Thomas** (the) Reverend FatherThomas

NM reverend; **oui, mon r.** yes, Reverend

révérer [18] [revere] VT to revere, *Sout* to reverence; **il révère son frère** he's devoted to *or* he reveres his brother

rêverie [rɛvri] NF **1** *(réflexion)* daydreaming *(UNCOUNT)*, reverie; **plongé dans mes/ses/***etc* **rêveries** *ou* **ma/sa/***etc* **r.** deep in thought **2** *(chimère)* dream, daydream, delusion

revernir [32] [rəvɛrnir] VT to revarnish

reverra *etc voir* **revoir**[2]

revers [rəvɛr] NM **1** *(d'une blouse, d'un veston)* lapel; *(d'un pantalon) Br* turn-up, *Am* cuff; *(d'une manche)* (turned-back) cuff; *(d'un uniforme)* facing; **peignoir à r. de soie** dressing gown with silk lapels; **col/bottes à r.** turned-down collar/boots **2** *(d'une feuille, d'un tissu, d'un tableau, de la main)* back; *(d'une médaille, d'une pièce)* reverse (side); **essuyant d'un r. de main la sueur qui coulait de son front** wiping the sweat from his/her forehead with the back of his/her hand; *Fig* **le r. de la médaille** the other side of the coin

3 *(échec, défaite)* setback; **essuyer un r.** to suffer a setback; **r. de fortune** reverse of fortune, setback (in one's fortunes)

4 *(au tennis)* backhand (shot); **faire un r.** to play a backhand shot; **jouer en r.** to play backhand

• **à revers** ADV *Mil* from *or* in the rear

reversement [rəvɛrsəmɑ̃] NM *Fin* transfer

reverser [3] [rəvɛrse] VT **1** *(verser ► de nouveau)* to pour again, to pour (out) more (of); *(► dans le récipient d'origine)* to pour back; **je vous reverse un verre?** shall I pour you another glass? **2** *Fin (reporter)* to transfer; **r. des intérêts sur un compte** to pay interest on an account; **la prime d'assurance vous sera intégralement reversée au bout d'un an** the total premium will be paid back to you after one year

réverser [3] [reverse] VT *Typ (texte)* to reverse out

réversibilité [reversibilite] NF **1** *(d'un processus)* reversibility **2** *Jur (d'un bien, d'une pension)* revertibility

réversible [reversibl] ADJ **1** *(vêtement)* reversible **2** *Jur (bien, pension)* revertible

réversion [reversjɔ̃] NF *Biol & Jur* reversion

revêtement [rəvɛtmɑ̃] NM **1** *(intérieur ► peinture)* covering; *(► enduit)* coating; *(extérieur ► gén)* facing; *(► crépi)* rendering; **r. de sol** flooring; **r. mural** wall covering **2** *Constr (d'une voie)* surface (material); **refaire le r. d'une route** to resurface a road **3** *Tech (d'un câble électrique)* housing, sheathing; *(d'un pneu)* casing; *(d'un conduit)* lining

revêtir [44] [rəvetir] VT **1** *Sout (endosser)* to don; **r. ses plus beaux atours** to array oneself in *or* to don one's finest attire

2 *Sout (habiller)* **r. qn de** to dress *or* to array sb in, to clothe sb in *or* with; **on l'avait revêtue d'une lourde cape** she had been arrayed *or* garbed in a heavy cloak; **un mur revêtu de lierre** an ivy-clad wall; *Fig* **r. qn d'une dignité/d'une autorité** to invest sb with a dignity/an authority

3 *(importance, signification)* to take on, to assume; *(forme)* to appear in, to take on, to assume; **ses propos revêtent un caractère dangereux** there's something dangerous in what he/she says; **Merlin revêtit l'aspect d'une souris** Merlin took on *or* assumed the appearance of a mouse

4 *Archit & Constr (rue ► asphalter)* to surface; *(► paver)* to pave; **r. une surface de** to cover a surface with; **des murs revêtus de boiseries** panelled walls

5 *Jur* **r. un contrat de signatures** to append signatures to a contract; **laissez-passer revêtu du tampon obligatoire** authorization bearing the regulation stamp

VPR **se revêtir** *Sout* **se r. de** *(endosser)* to don

reveulent *voir* **revouloir**

rêveur, -euse [rɛvœr, -øz] ADJ **1** *(distrait)* dreamy; **avoir un caractère r.** to be a daydreamer; **d'un air r.** dreamily; **d'un ton r.** dreamily **2** *(perplexe)* **laisser qn r.** to leave sb baffled *or* in a state of bafflement; **cette dernière phrase me laissa r.** these last words puzzled *or* baffled me; **ça laisse r.!** it makes you wonder!

NM,F dreamer, daydreamer

rêveusement [rɛvøzmɑ̃] ADV dreamily; **regarder r. par la fenêtre** to gaze absent-mindedly out of the window

reveut, reveux *voir* **revouloir**

revient[1] *etc voir* **revenir**

revient[2] [rəvjɛ̃] NM *voir* **prix**

revigorant, -e [rəvigɔrɑ̃, -ɑ̃t] ADJ *(gén)* invigorating; *(vent, promenade)* bracing; *(bain)* invigorating, refreshing; *(boisson, aliment)* reviving, refreshing

revigorer [3] [rəvigɔre] VT **1** *(stimuler ► sujet: vent, promenade)* to invigorate; *(► sujet: bain)* to invigorate, to refresh; *(► sujet: boisson, aliment)* to revive, to refresh; **une petite promenade pour vous r.?** how about a bracing little walk? **2** *(relancer ► économie)* to boost, to give a boost to; **les subventions ont revigoré l'entreprise** the subsidies gave the company a new lease of life

revint *etc voir* **revenir**

revirement [rəvirmɑ̃] NM *(changement ► d'avis)* about-face, change of mind; *(► de situation)* turnaround, about-face, sudden turn; **un r. dans l'opinion publique** a complete swing *or* turnaround in public opinion; **un r. de la tendance sur le marché des valeurs** a sudden reversal of stock market trends

révisable [revizabl] ADJ **1** *(gén)* revisable **2** *Jur* reviewable

réviser [3] [revize] VT **1** *Scol & Univ, Br* to revise, to go over (again), *Am* to review

2 *(réévaluer ► jugement, situation)* to review, to re-examine, to reappraise; *(► contrat, salaire)* to review; **r. à la baisse/hausse** to downgrade/upgrade, to scale down/up; **il a fallu r. à la baisse les prévisions pour l'an prochain** the projected figures for next year have had to be scaled down

3 *Jur (jugement)* to review; **r. un procès** to reopen a trial; **r. le procès de qn** to retry sb

4 *(voiture)* to service; *(machine)* to overhaul; **faire r. une voiture** to have a car serviced; **faire r. les freins** to have the brakes checked

5 *(clause)* to revise; *(liste électorale)* to update, to revise; *(manuscrit)* to check, to go over; *(épreuves)* to revise, *Spéc* to line edit

USAGE ABSOLU *Scol & Univ* **on a passé le week-end à r.** we spent the weekend *Br* revising *or* doing revision work *or Am* studying; **je ne peux pas venir, je révise pour l'exam de linguistique** I can't come, I'm *Br* revising *or Am* studying for the linguistics exam

réviseur, -euse [revizœr, -øz] NM,F **1** *Écon* **r. comptable** auditor; **r. externe/interne** external/internal auditor; *Belg* **r. d'entreprises** auditor **2** *(d'épreuves ► gén)* reviser, checker; *(► correcteur)* proofreader; **il est traducteur-r.** he translates and edits, he's a translator and editor

révision [revizjɔ̃] NF **1** *Scol & Univ* revision *(UNCOUNT)*, revising *(UNCOUNT)*; **faire des révisions** to revise; **où en es-tu de tes révisions?** how much have you revised so far?

2 *(d'une clause)* revision; *(d'une liste électorale)* updating, revision; *(d'un manuscrit)* checking; *(d'épreuves)* checking, revising

3 *(d'une voiture)* service; *(d'une machine)* overhaul, overhauling; **la r. des 5000 km** the 5,000 km service

4 *(réévaluation ► d'un jugement, d'une situation)* reappraisal, review; *(► d'un contrat)* revision; *(► d'un salaire)* review; **la r. à la baisse/hausse des prévisions** the downgrading/upgrading of the forecast figures; **les prix peuvent faire l'objet d'une r.** prices are subject to review

5 *Jur (d'un procès)* rehearing; *(d'un jugement)* reviewing

révisionnisme [revizjɔnism] NM revisionism

révisionniste [revizjɔnist] ADJ revisionist

NMF revisionist

revisiter [3] [rəvizite] VT **1** *(visiter à nouveau)* to revisit **2** *(voir sous un jour nouveau)* to reinterpret; **Racine revisité par le célèbre metteur en scène** a new angle *or* a new take on Racine by the famous director

revisser [3] [rəvise] VT to screw back again

revit 1 *voir* **revivre 2** *voir* **revoir**[2]

revitalisant, -e [rəvitalizɑ̃, -ɑ̃t] ADJ revitalizing

revitalisation [rəvitalizasjɔ̃] NF revitalization

revitaliser [3] [rəvitalize] VT **1** *(ranimer ► économie)* to revitalize **2** *(régénérer ► peau)* to revitalize

revival, -als [rivajvœl, rəvival] NM revival

revivifier [9] [rəvivifje] VT **1** *(personne)* to revitalize **2** *Littéraire (souvenir)* to bring back to life, to revive

revivre [90] [rəvivr] VI **1** *(renaître)* to come alive (again); **les examens sont terminés, je revis!** the exams are over, I can breathe again *or* what a weight off my mind!; **quel calme, je me sens r.!** how quiet it is around here, I feel like a new person!

2 *(nature, campagne)* to come alive again

3 *(personne ou animal mort)* to come back to life; **r. dans** *ou* **par qn** to live again in *or* through sb

4 *(redevenir actuel)* **faire r. la tradition** to restore *or* to revive tradition; **faire r. les années de guerre** to bring back the war years

VT **1** *(se souvenir de)* to relive, to live *or* to go through (again); **toutes les nuits je revis l'accident** I relive the accident every night **2** *(vivre à nouveau)* to relive; **avec lui, elle revit un grand amour** with him, she's reliving a grand passion

révocabilité [revɔkabilite] NF **1** *Admin (d'un fonctionnaire)* dismissibility **2** *Jur (d'un acte juridique)* revocability **3** *Pol (d'un élu)* recallability

révocable [revɔkabl] ADJ **1** *Admin (fonctionnaire)* dismissible **2** *Jur (acte juridique)* revocable, subject to repeal **3** *Pol (élu)* recallable, subject to recall

révocation [revɔkasjɔ̃] NF **1** *Admin (d'un fonctionnaire)* dismissal; *(d'un dirigeant)* removal **2** *Jur (d'un acte juridique)* repeal, revocation; *(d'un testament)* revocation; *(d'un ordre)* rescinding; **la r. de l'édit de Nantes** the revocation of the Edict of Nantes **3** *Pol (d'un élu)* removal, recall

révocatoire [revɔkatwar] ADJ revocatory

revoici [rəvwasi] PRÉP **me r.!** here I am again!, it's me again!; **nous r. à Paris** here we are in Paris again *or* back in Paris; **la r. qui pleure** she's crying again

revoilà [rəvwala] PRÉP **r. le printemps!** it looks like spring's here again!; **enfin, te r.!** you're back at last!; **les r.!** there they are again!; **nous r. à Paris** here we are in Paris again *or* back in Paris; **la r. qui pleure** she's crying again; **nous y r., je m'y attendais!** here we go again! I just knew it

revoir[1] [rəvwar] NM *Littéraire* **le charme du r.** the delights of meeting again

• **au revoir** EXCLAM goodbye! NM goodbye; **ce n'est qu'un au r.** we'll meet again

revoir[2] **[62]** [rəvwar] VT **1** *(rencontrer à nouveau)* to see *or* to meet again; **il y a longtemps que tu le revois?** is it a long time since you started seeing him again?; **tu ne croyais pas me r. de sitôt, hein?** you didn't expect to see me again so soon, did you?; **et que je ne te revoie plus ici, compris?** and don't let me see *or* catch you around here again, is that clear?

2 *(retourner à)* to see again, to go back to; **c'est bon de r. son pays** it's good to be back in *or* to see one's country (again); **elle ne devait plus r. sa terre natale** she was never to see her native land again

3 *(examiner à nouveau ► images)* to see again, to have another look at; *(► exposition, spectacle)* to see again; *(► dossier)* to re-examine, to look at again; *(► vidéocassette)* to watch again; **c'est un documentaire qu'il faut r.** the documentary is well worth seeing a second time; **je l'ai revu trois fois à la télévision** I've seen it three times on television

4 *(assister de nouveau à ► incident)* to see *or* to witness again; **nous ne voulons plus jamais r. ces scènes sur nos écrans** we never want to witness *or* to see such scenes on our screens again

5 *(par l'imagination)* **je nous revois encore, autour du feu de camp** I can still see *or* picture us around the campfire; **je la revois petite** I can see her in my mind's eye when she was little; **quand je revois ces moments de bonheur** when I think back to those happy times

6 *(vérifier ▸ installation, mécanisme, moteur)* to check, to look at again

7 *(réexaminer ▸ texte)* to re-examine, to revise; *(▸ épreuves)* to read; *(▸ comptes)* to go over *or* look over again; *(▸opinion)* to modify, to revise; **je voudrais r. quelques points avec toi** I'd like to go over a few points with you; **la première partie de ta thèse est à r.** the first part of your thesis will have to be gone over again *or* revised; **édition revue et corrigée** *(dans un livre)* revised edition; **r. à la hausse/baisse** to revise upwards/downwards

8 *Scol & Univ (cours)* to go over (again), *Br* to revise, *Am* to review; **revoyez les racines carrées pour demain** go over the section on square roots for tomorrow; **tu ferais bien de r. ta physique!** *(réviser)* you'd better *Br* revise *or Am* review your physics!; *(réapprendre)* you'd better study *or* learn your physics again!

VPR se revoir 1 *(emploi réciproque)* to meet again, to see each other again; **nous reverrons-nous?** will we see each other *or* meet again? **2** *(emploi réfléchi)* to see *or* to picture oneself again; **je me revois enfant, chez ma grand-mère** I can still see myself as a child at my grandmother's

révoltant, -e [revɔltɑ̃, -ɑ̃t] **ADJ** *(violence, lâcheté, injustice)* appalling, shocking; *(grossièreté)* revolting, outrageous, scandalous; **il est d'un égoïsme r.** he's horribly self-centred

révolte [revɔlt] **NF 1** *(sédition)* revolt, rebellion; *(dans une prison)* riot; **la r. fut durement réprimée** the revolt was harshly repressed **2** *(insoumission)* rebellion, revolt; **être en r. contre qn** to be in revolt against sb; **elle est en r. contre ses parents** she's rebelling against her parents; **esprit de r.** spirit of revolt *or* rebellion **3** *(réprobation)* outrage; **nous manifestons notre r. contre la vivisection** we're expressing our outrage against vivisection

révolté, -e [revɔlte] **ADJ 1** *(rebelle)* rebellious, rebel *(avant n)*; **r. contre** in revolt against **2** *(indigné)* outraged **3** *Mil* mutinous

NM,F 1 *(gén)* rebel **2** *Mil* rebel, mutineer

révolter [3] [revɔlte] **VT** *(scandaliser)* to appal, to revolt, to shock; **ça ne te révolte pas, toi?** don't you think that's disgusting *or* revolting *or* shocking?; **révolté par la misère/tant de violence** outraged by poverty/at so much violence

VPR se révolter 1 *(gén)* to revolt; **les mineurs se révoltent contre leurs syndicats** the miners are revolting *or* are in revolt against their unions; **adolescent, il s'est révolté contre ses parents** he rebelled against his parents when he was a teenager **2** *(marin, soldat)* to mutiny

révolu, -e [revɔly] **ADJ 1** *Littéraire (d'autrefois)* **aux jours révolus de ma jeunesse** in the bygone days of my youth; **en des temps révolus** in days gone by **2** *(fini)* past; **l'époque des hippies est révolue** the hippie era is over **3** *Admin* **âgé de 18 ans révolus** over 18 (years of age); **au bout de trois années révolues** after three full years

révolution [revɔlysjɔ̃] **NF 1** *Pol & Hist* revolution; **faire la r.** to have a revolution; **la r. industrielle** the Industrial Revolution; **une r. de palais** a palace coup *or* revolution; **la première/seconde r. d'Angleterre** the English/Glorious Revolution; **la R. culturelle** *(en Chine)* the Cultural Revolution; **la R. (française)** the French Revolution; **la r. d'octobre** the October Revolution; *Can* **la R. tranquille** the Quiet Revolution *(period of social, political and economic change in Quebec in the 1960s)*; **r. verte** green revolution

2 *(changement)* revolution; **une r. dans** a revolution in; **faire** *ou* **causer une r. dans qch** to revolutionize sth

3 *(agitation)* turmoil; **tout le service est en r.** the whole department is in turmoil; **tous ces cambriolages ont mis la ville en r.** the town is up in arms *or* in uproar because of all these burglaries

4 *Astron & Math* revolution

révolutionnaire [revɔlysjɔnɛr] **ADJ** *Pol, Hist & Fig* revolutionary; **une découverte r.** a revolutionary discovery

NMF 1 *Pol & Hist* revolutionary; *Fig* innovator

révolutionnarisme [revɔlysjɔnarism] **NM** revolutionism

révolutionner [3] [revɔlysjɔne] **VT 1** *(système, domaine)* to revolutionize; *(vie)* to change radically **2** *Fam (bouleverser ▸ personne)* to upset (deeply)[□]; *(▸ village, service)* to cause a stir in; **cette nouvelle l'a révolutionnée** the news made a deep impression on her

revolver [revɔlvɛr] **NM** revolver; **un coup de r.** a gunshot

révoquer [3] [revɔke] **VT 1** *Admin (fonctionnaire)* to dismiss; *(dirigeant)* to remove (from office) **2** *Jur (acte juridique)* to revoke, to repeal; *(testament, contrat)* to revoke; *(ordre)* to revoke, to rescind **3** *Pol (élu)* to recall **4** *Littéraire* **r. qch en doute** to call sth into question

revoter [3] [rəvɔte] **VI** to vote again

VT *(personne, parti)* to vote for again; *(loi)* to pass *or* adopt again

revouloir [57] [rəvulwar] **VT** *Fam (davantage de)* to want some more; *(de nouveau)* to want again; **j'en reveux!** I want some more!

revoyait *etc voir* **revoir²**

revoyure [rəvwajyr] **NF** *Fam* **à la r.!** see you (around)!

revu, -e¹ [rəvy] **PP** *voir* **revoir²**

revue² [rəvy] **NF 1** *(publication ▸ gén)* magazine; *(▸ spécialisée)* review, journal; **r. de linguistique** review of linguistics; **r. littéraire** literary journal; **r. de mode** fashion magazine; **r. scientifique** science journal; **r. spécialisée** trade paper, journal, review

2 *(de music-hall)* variety show; *(de chansonniers)* revue

3 *Mil (inspection)* inspection, review; *(défilé)* review, march-past; **la r. du 14 juillet** the 14 July (military) parade; **passer en r.** *(troupes)* to hold a review of, to review; *(uniformes)* to inspect

4 *(inventaire)* **faire la r. de qch, passer qch en r.** *(vêtements, documents)* to go *or* to look through sth; *(solutions)* to go over sth in one's mind, to review sth

• **revue de presse NF** review of the press *or* of what the papers say

révulsé, -e [revylse] **ADJ** *(traits, visage)* contorted; **r. de douleur** *(visage)* contorted with pain; **les yeux révulsés** with one's eyes rolled upwards

révulser [3] [revylse] **VT 1** *(dégoûter)* to revolt, to fill with loathing, to disgust **2** *(crisper)* to contort **3** *Méd* to counter-irritate

VPR se révulser *(traits, visage)* to contort, to become contorted; *(yeux)* to roll upwards

révulsif, -ive [revylsif, -iv] *Méd* **ADJ** revulsant

NM revulsant, revulsive

révulsion [revylsjɔ̃] **NF 1** *Méd* revulsion, counter-irritation **2** *(dégoût)* revulsion, loathing; **éprouver de la r. pour** to be repelled by

révulsive [revylsiv] *voir* **révulsif**

rewriter¹ [rirajtœr] **NM** rewriter

rewriter² [3] [rirajte] **VT** to rewrite

rewriting [rirajtiŋ] **NM** rewriting

Reykjavik [rɛkjavik] **NM** Reykjavik

rez-de-chaussée [redʃose] **NM INV** *Br* ground floor, *Am* first floor; **au r.** on the *Br* ground *or Am* first floor; **habiter un r.** to live in a *Br* ground floor flat *or Am* first floor apartment

rez-de-jardin [redʒardɛ̃] **NM INV** ground *or* garden level; **pièces en r.** ground-level rooms; **appartement en r.** garden *Br* flat *or Am* apartment

RF *(abrév écrite* **République française**) French Republic

RFA [ɛrɛfa] **NF** *Anciennement (abrév* **République fédérale d'Allemagne**) FRG, West Germany

RG [ɛrʒe] **NMPL** *(abrév* **Renseignements généraux**) = secret intelligence branch of the French police, *Br* ≃ Special Branch, *Am* ≃ the FBI

Rh *Physiol (abrév écrite* **Rhésus**) Rh

rhabillage [rabijaʒ] **NM 1** *(d'une montre)* overhaul **2** *(d'une personne)* **le r. des enfants après la gymnastique prend beaucoup de temps** the children take a long time getting dressed again after gym

rhabiller [3] [rabije] **VT 1** *(habiller à nouveau)* to dress again; *(acheter de nouveaux vêtements pour)* to buy new clothes for; **rhabille-le, il va prendre froid** put his clothes back on, he'll catch cold

2 *Archit* to revamp, to refurbish; **on a rhabillé tout le foyer du théâtre** the entire foyer of the theatre has been refurbished

3 *Fig (idée rebattue)* to give a new look to

4 *Tech (montre)* to overhaul

VPR se rhabiller 1 *(s'habiller à nouveau)* to put one's clothes back on, to dress *or* to get dressed again **2** *Fam (locution)* **tu peux aller te/il peut aller se r.!** you can/he can forget it!

rhabilleur, -euse [rabijœr, -øz] **NM,F** *(de montres)* repairer

rhapsode [rapsɔd] **NM** *Antiq* rhapsode, rhapsodist

rhapsodie [rapsɔdi] **NF** *Mus* rhapsody

rhénan, -e [renɑ̃, -an] **ADJ 1** *(du Rhin)* of the Rhine, Rhenish; **le pays r.** the Rhineland **2** *(de la Rhénanie)* of the Rhineland

Rhénanie [renani] **NF la R.** the Rhineland

rhénium [renjɔm] **NM** *Chim* rhenium

rhéostat [reɔsta] **NM** *Élec* rheostat

Rhésus [rezys] **NM** *Physiol (système sanguin)* **facteur R.** rhesus *or* Rh factor; **R. positif/négatif** rhesus positive/negative

rhésus [rezys] **NM** *Zool* rhesus monkey

rhéteur [retœr] **NM 1** *Antiq* rhetor **2** *Littéraire* rhetorician

rhétoricien, -enne [retɔrisjɛ̃, -ɛn] **NM,F 1** *(spécialiste)* rhetorician **2** *Belg Scol Br* ≃ lower sixth-former, *Am* ≃ student in eleventh grade, junior

rhétorique [retɔrik] **ADJ** rhetoric, rhetorical

NF 1 *(art)* rhetoric; **figure de r.** figure of speech **2** *Péj (affectation)* **ce n'est que de la r.** it's just rhetoric *or* posturing **3** *Belg Scol Br* ≃ lower sixth form, *Am* ≃ eleventh grade

rhéto-roman, -e [retɔrɔmɑ̃, -an] *(mpl* **rhéto-romans**, *fpl* **rhéto-romanes**) *Ling* **ADJ** Rhaeto-Romance *(avant n)*

NM Rhaeto-Romance

Rhin [rɛ̃] **NM le R.** the Rhine

rhinite [rinit] **NF** *Méd* rhinitis

rhinocéros [rinɔserɔs] **NM** *Zool* rhinoceros, rhino; **r. blanc** white *or* square-lipped rhinoceros; **r. noir** black *or* hook-lipped rhinoceros

rhinologie [rinɔlɔʒi] **NF** *Méd* rhinology

rhino-pharyngé, -e [rinɔfarɛ̃ʒe] *(mpl* **rhino-pharyngés**, *fpl* **rhino-pharyngées**) **ADJ** rhinopharyngal, rhinopharyngeal

rhino-pharyngite [rinɔfarɛ̃ʒit] *(pl* **rhino-pharyngites**) **NF** *Méd* inflammation of the nasal passages, *Spéc* rhinopharyngitis

rhino-pharynx [rinɔfarɛ̃ks] **NM INV** rhinopharynx

rhinoplastie [rinɔplasti] **NF** *Méd* rhinoplasty

rhinoscopie [rinɔskɔpi] **NF** *Méd* rhinoscopy

rhizome [rizom] **NM** rhizome

rhodanien, -enne [rɔdanjɛ̃, -ɛn] **ADJ** *(du Rhône)* from the Rhône; **le couloir r.** the Rhône corridor

Rhodes [rɔd] **NF** *(ville)* Rhodes

NFPL *(en Suisse)* **les R.-Extérieures** (Appenzell) Ausserrhoden; **les R.-Intérieures** (Appenzell) Innerrhoden

Rhodésie [rɔdezi] **NF** *Anciennement* **la R.** Rhodesia; **la R. du Nord** Northern Rhodesia; **la R. du Sud** Southern Rhodesia

rhodésien, -enne [rɔdezjɛ̃, -ɛn] *Anciennement* **ADJ** Rhodesian

• **Rhodésien, -enne NM,F** Rhodesian

rhodium [rɔdjɔm] **NM** *Chim* rhodium

rhododendron [rɔdɔdɛ̃drɔ̃] **NM** rhododendron

rhombique [rɔ̃bik] **ADJ** rhombic

rhomboïdal, -e, -aux, -ales [rɔ̃bɔidal, -o] **ADJ** rhomboid, rhomboidal

rhomboïde [rɔ̃bɔid] **NM 1** *Géom* rhomboid **2** *Anat* rhomboideus

Rhône [ron] **NM 1** *(fleuve)* **le R.** the (River) Rhône **2** *(département)* **le R.** the Rhône

rhubarbe [rybarb] NF rhubarb; **confiture/tarte à la r.** rhubarb jam/tart

rhum [rɔm] NM rum; **au r.** *(dessert)* rum-flavoured; *(boisson)* rum-based; **r. blanc** white rum

rhumatisant, -e [rymatizɑ̃, -ɑ̃t] ADJ rheumatic NM,F rheumatic

rhumatismal, -e, -aux, -ales [rymatismal, -o] ADJ rheumatic

rhumatisme [rymatism] NM rheumatism *(UNCOUNT)*; **mes rhumatismes me font souffrir** my rheumatism is playing up; **avoir un r.** *ou* **des rhumatismes au genou** to have rheumatism in one's knee; **r. articulaire aigu** rheumatic fever

rhumatoïde [rymatɔid] ADJ rheumatoid

rhumatologie [rymatɔlɔʒi] NF rheumatology

rhumatologue [rymatɔlɔg] NMF rheumatologist

rhume [rym] NM cold; **avoir un r.** to have a cold; *Fam* **je tiens un bon r.!** I've got a nasty cold!; **un gros r.** a bad *or* heavy cold; **tu vas attraper un r.** you're going to catch (a) cold; **r. de cerveau** head cold; **r. des foins** hay fever

rhumerie [rɔmri] NF rum distillery

rhytidectomie [ritidɛktɔmi] NM *Méd* facelift, *Spéc* rhytidectomy

ri [ri] PP *voir* **rire**

ria [rija] NF *Géol* ria

riad [rijad] NM riad *(traditional Moroccan house with enclosed garden)*

riant, -e [rijɑ̃, -ɑ̃t] ADJ **1** *(visage, yeux)* smiling **2** *(nature, paysage)* pleasant

RIB [rib] NM *(abrév* **relevé d'identité bancaire***)* = document giving details of one's bank account

ribambelle [ribɑ̃bɛl] NF **1** *(d'enfants)* flock, swarm; *(de noms)* string, torrent; *Fam* **suivi d'une r. de gamins** followed by a long string of *or* a swarm of kids; **une r. de jurons** a flood *or* torrent of oaths **2** *(papier découpé)* paper dolls

• **en ribambelle** ADV **les enfants sortent de l'école en r.** the children stream out of the school

ribaud, -e [ribo, -od] *Arch ou Littéraire* ADJ ribald NM,F **un r.** a ribald fellow; **une ribaude** a brazen wench

riboflavine [riboflavin] NF *Biol* riboflavin, riboflavine

ribonucléique [ribonykleik] ADJ *Biol & Chim* ribonucleic

ribote [ribɔt] NF *Vieilli ou Littéraire* high living; **en r.** *(ivre)* drunk; **faire r.** *(s'enivrer)* to go drinking

ribouldingue [ribuldɛ̃g] NF *Fam Vieilli* **une sacrée r.** a real shindig; **faire la r.** to go on a spree *or* binge

ricain, -e [rikɛ̃, -ɛn] *Fam* ADJ Yank, *Br* Yankee

• **Ricain, -e** NM,F Yank, *Br* Yankee, = pejorative or humorous term used with reference to Americans

ricanement [rikanmɑ̃] NM *(rire ► méchant)* snigger; *(► nerveux, bête)* giggle; **ricanements** *(méchants)* sniggering; *(nerveux, bêtes)* giggling

ricaner [3] [rikane] VI *(rire ► méchamment)* to snigger; *(► nerveusement, bêtement)* to giggle

ricaneur, -euse [rikanœr, -øz] ADJ *(riant ► méchamment)* sniggering; *(► bêtement)* giggling NM,F *(méchant)* sniggerer; *(bête)* giggler

Richard [riʃar] NPR **R. Cœur de Lion** Richard the Lion-Heart, Richard Cœur de Lion

richard, -e [riʃar, -ard] NM,F *Fam Péj* moneybags, *Br* nob

RICHE [riʃ]

ADJ
- rich **1, 3–5**
- wealthy **1**
- lavish **2**
- lush **3**
- fertile **3**
- full **5**

NMF
- rich person

ADJ **1** *(fortuné ► famille, personne)* rich, wealthy, well-off; *(► nation)* rich, wealthy; **une r. héritière** a wealthy heiress; **ils ont l'air r.** they look wealthy; **on n'est pas bien r. chez nous** we're not very well-off; **je te paie le restaurant, aujourd'hui, je suis r.** I'll treat you to a meal, I'm feeling rich today; **je suis plus r. de 500 euros maintenant** I'm 500 euros better off *or* richer now; **être r. comme Crésus** *ou* **à millions** to be as rich as Croesus *or* Midas

2 *(avant le nom) (demeure, décor)* lavish, sumptuous, luxurious; *(étoffe, enluminure)* magnificent, splendid; **un r. cadre doré** a heavy gilt frame

3 *(végétation)* lush, luxuriant, profuse; *(terre)* fertile, rich; *(aliment, vie)* rich; **un sol r.** a rich soil; **ce qu'il vous faut, c'est une alimentation r.** what you need is a nutritious diet; **le gâteau est un peu trop r.** the cake is a little too rich; **la ville a une histoire très r.** the town has had a very varied history; **vous y trouverez une documentation très r. sur Proust** you'll find a wide range of documents on Proust there; *Fam ou Ironique* **c'est une r. idée que tu as eue là** that's a wonderful *or* great idea you've just had

4 *(complexe)* rich; **des tons riches** rich hues; **elle a un vocabulaire/une langue r.** she has a rich vocabulary/a tremendous command of the language; **une imagination r.** a fertile imagination

5 r. en *(vitamines, minerais)* rich in; *(événements)* full of; **r. en lipides** with a high lipid content; **régime r. en calcium** calcium-rich diet; **texte r. en superlatifs** text overflowing with superlatives; **la journée fut r. en émotions** the day was packed full of excitement; **la journée fut r. en rebondissements** spectacular things happened all day

6 *(qualités, possibilités)* **un livre r. d'enseignements** a very informative book; **son premier roman est r. de promesses** his/her first novel is full of promise *or* shows great promise

NMF rich person; **les riches** the rich, the wealthy; **voiture de r.** rich man's car

ADV *Fam* **ça fait r.** it looks posh

richelieu [riʃəljø] *(pl inv ou* **richelieus***)* NM lace-up shoe

richement [riʃmɑ̃] ADV **1** *(luxueusement)* richly, handsomely; **cette pièce est r. meublée** this room is richly *or* handsomely furnished **2** *(abondamment)* lavishly, sumptuously, richly; **r. illustré** lavishly illustrated **3** *(de manière à rendre riche)* **il a r. marié sa fille** *ou* **marié sa fille r.** he married his daughter into a wealthy family

richesse [riʃɛs] NF **1** *(fortune ► d'une personne)* wealth; *(► d'une région, d'une nation)* wealth, affluence, prosperity; **vivre dans la r.** to be wealthy; **ses livres sont sa seule r.** his/her books are all he/she has; **le tourisme est la seule r. de la région** tourism is the region's only resource *or* only source of income; **ces traditions ancestrales font la r. de ce peuple** these ancestral traditions make up the rich cultural heritage of this people

2 *(d'un décor)* luxuriousness, lavishness, sumptuousness; *(d'un tissu)* beauty, splendour

3 *(luxuriance ► de la végétation)* richness, lushness, profuseness, luxuriance; **la r. du sous-sol** the wealth of (underground) mineral deposits; **la r. en fer d'un légume** the high iron content of a vegetable; **notre r. en matières premières** our wealth of raw materials

4 *(complexité ► du vocabulaire, de la langue)* richness; *(► de l'imagination)* creativeness, inventiveness; *(► d'une description)* detailed nature; **la r. culturelle de notre capitale** the cultural wealth of our capital city

5 *(réconfort)* blessing; **avoir un ami fidèle est une grande r.** to have a faithful friend is to be rich indeed

• **richesses** NFPL *(biens, capital)* riches, wealth *(UNCOUNT)*; *(articles de valeur)* treasures, wealth; *(ressources)* resources; **richesses minières/naturelles** mining/natural resources; **les richesses que recèle ce site archéologique** the treasures contained in this archeological site

richissime [riʃisim] ADJ *Fam* fantastically wealthy, loaded

ricin [risɛ̃] NM *Bot* castor-oil plant, *Spéc* ricinus

ricocher [3] [rikɔʃe] VI **1** *(caillou)* to ricochet, to bounce, to glance (**sur** off); **les enfants font r. des pierres sur l'eau** the children are skimming stones across the water *or* are playing ducks and drakes **2** *(balle)* to ricochet (**sur** off)

ricochet [rikɔʃɛ] NM **1** *(d'un caillou)* bounce, rebound; **faire des ricochets (sur l'eau)** to skim pebbles, to play ducks and drakes; **j'ai fait trois ricochets!** I made the pebble bounce three times!; *Fig* **par r.** indirectly; **les épargnants ont perdu de l'argent par r.** savers lost money as an indirect consequence; *Fig* **ces mesures feront r.** these measures will have a knock-on effect **2** *(d'une balle)* ricochet

ric-rac [rikrak] ADV *Fam* **1** *(très exactement)* **il nous a payés r.** he paid us right down to the last *Br* penny *or Am* cent **2** *(de justesse)* **avec mon petit salaire, à la fin du mois c'est r.** on my salary, money gets a bit tight at the end of the month; **il a réussi l'examen r.** he only just scraped through the exam; **c'était r.** it was touch and go, it was a close thing

rictus [riktys] NM grimace, *Sout* rictus; **un affreux r. déformait son visage** his/her face was twisted into a hideous grimace; **il eut un horrible r.** a hideous grimace passed across his face

ride [rid] NF **1** *(d'un visage)* line, wrinkle; *(sur un fruit)* wrinkle; **creusé de rides** furrowed with wrinkles; **prendre des rides** to age; *Fig* **le documentaire n'a pas pris une r.** the documentary hasn't dated in the slightest **2** *(sur l'eau, sur le sable)* ripple, ridge

ridé, -e [ride] ADJ *(visage)* wrinkled, lined; *(pomme)* wrinkled; **un front r.** a deeply lined forehead; **r. comme une vieille pomme** wrinkled like a prune

rideau, -x [rido] NM **1** *(en décoration intérieure)* curtain, *Am* drape; **fermé par un r.** curtained off; **mettre des rideaux aux fenêtres** to put curtains up; **tirer** *ou* **ouvrir les rideaux** to draw *or* to open the curtains; **tirer** *ou* **fermer les rideaux** to draw *or* to close the curtains; **r. de douche** shower curtain; **doubles rideaux** thick curtains; **rideaux bonne femme** tieback curtains; *Fig* **tirer le r. sur qch** to draw a veil over sth; *Belg Fig Hum* **le r. de betteraves** = the linguistic frontier between Flemish and French speakers in Belgium

2 *Théât* curtain; **r.!** curtain!

3 *(écran)* screen, curtain; **r. de bambou** bamboo curtain; **r. de cyprès** screen of cypress trees; *Mil* **r. de feu** covering fire; **r. de fumée** smokescreen; **r. de pluie** sheet of rain; *Mil* **r. de troupes** screen of troops

4 *(d'un bureau)* roll-top; **classeur à r.** tambour-door filing cabinet, roll-shutter cabinet

5 *TV* **r. de fond** sky cloth

• **rideau de fer** NM **1** *(d'un magasin)* (metal) shutter **2** *Théât* safety curtain **3** *Hist & Pol* Iron Curtain

ridelle [ridɛl] NF *(d'un camion)* side panel

rider [3] [ride] VT **1** *(peau, front)* to wrinkle, to line, to furrow; *(fruit)* to wrinkle, to shrivel **2** *(eau, sable)* to ripple, to ruffle the surface of

VPR **se rider 1** *(visage, peau)* to become wrinkled; *(fruit)* to shrivel, to go wrinkly **2** *(eau)* to ripple, to become rippled

ridicule [ridikyl] ADJ **1** *(risible ► personne)* ridiculous, laughable; *(► tenue)* ridiculous, ludicrous; **se sentir r.** to feel ridiculous; **se rendre r.** to make a fool of oneself, to make oneself look ridiculous; **tu es r. avec cette perruque** you look ridiculous with that wig on **2** *(absurde)* ridiculous, ludicrous, preposterous; **c'est r. d'avoir peur de l'avion** it's ridiculous to be afraid of flying **3** *(dérisoire)* ridiculous, laughable, derisory; **un salaire r.** *(trop bas)* a ridiculously low salary

NM **1** *(ce qui rend ridicule)* ridicule; **craindre le r.** to fear ridicule; **se couvrir de r.** to make oneself a laughing stock, to make a complete fool of oneself; **couvrir qn de r.** to heap ridicule on sb; **tourner qn/qch en r.** to ridicule sb/sth, to hold sb/sth up to ridicule; **s'exposer au r.** to lay oneself open to ridicule; **tomber** *ou* **donner dans le r.** to become ridiculous; **le r. ne tue pas** ridicule never did anyone any real harm **2** *(absurdité ► d'une situation)* ridiculousness; **c'est d'un r. (achevé** *ou* **fini)!** it's utterly ridiculous!, it's a farce!

• **ridicules** NMPL *Littéraire (traits absurdes)* ridiculous ways

ridiculement [ridikylmɑ̃] ADV **1** *(dérisoirement)* ridiculously, ludicrously; **r. petit/bas/grand** ridiculously small/low/big **2** *(risiblement)* ridiculously, laughably

ridiculiser [3] [ridikylize] VT to ridicule, to hold up to ridicule

VPR **se ridiculiser** to make oneself (look) ridiculous, to make a fool of oneself

ridule [ridyl] **NF** small wrinkle

RIEN [rjɛ̃]

- nothing **1, 2**
- anything **3**
- love **5**

PRON INDÉFINI 1 *(nulle chose)* nothing; **créer qch à partir de r.** to create something out of nothing; **faire qch à partir de r.** to do sth from scratch; **passer son temps à r. faire** to spend one's time doing nothing; **la tisane, r. de tel pour dormir!** there's nothing like herbal tea to help you sleep!; **r. de tel qu'un bon (roman) policier** there's nothing like a good detective story; **r. de cassé/grave, j'espère?** nothing broken/serious, I hope?; **r. d'autre** nothing else; **r. de nouveau** no new developments; **r. de plus** nothing else *or* more; **j'ai fait mon devoir, r. de plus** I've done my duty, nothing more; **r. de moins** nothing less; **il veut le poste de directeur, r. de moins** he wants the post of director, nothing less *or* no less; **qu'est-ce qui ne va pas? – r.!** what's wrong? – nothing!; **à quoi tu penses? – à r.!** what are you thinking about? – nothing!; **qu'est-ce que tu lui laisses? – r. de r.!** what are you leaving him/her? – not a thing!; **r. du tout** nothing at all; **je vous remercie – de r.!** thanks – you're welcome *or* not at all *or* don't mention it!; *Péj* **une fille de r.** a worthless girl; **une affaire de r. du tout** a trifling *or* trivial matter; **une égratignure de r. du tout** a little scratch; **c'est ça ou r.** take it or leave it; **c'est tout ou r.** it's all or nothing; **avec lui c'est toujours tout ou r.** with him it's always all or nothing; **r. à dire, c'est parfait!** what can I say, it's perfect!; **r. à faire, la voiture ne veut pas démarrer** it's no good, the car (just) won't start; *Douanes* **r. à déclarer** nothing to declare; **j'en ai r.** *Fam* **à faire** *ou très Fam* **à foutre** I don't give a damn *or* a toss; **faire semblant de r.** to pretend that nothing happened

2 *(en corrélation avec "ne")* **r. n'est plus beau que...** there's nothing more beautiful than...; **r. ne la fatigue** nothing tires her *or* makes her tired; **plus r. n'a d'importance** nothing matters any more; **r. de grave n'est arrivé** nothing serious happened; **r. n'y a fait, elle a refusé** (there was) nothing doing, she said no; **ce n'est r., ça va guérir** it's nothing, it'll get better; **ce n'est pas r.** it's no small thing *or* matter; **repeindre la cuisine, ce n'est pas r.** redecorating the kitchen is no small thing *or* no easy task; **ce n'est r. en comparaison de** *ou* **à côté de...** it's nothing compared to...; **je croyais avoir perdu, il n'en est r.** I thought I'd lost, but not at all *or* quite the contrary; **ils se disaient mariés, en fait il n'en est r.** they claimed they were married but they're nothing of the sort; **sans elle il n'est r.** without her he's nothing; **je ne suis r. sans mes livres** I'm lost without my books; **il n'est (plus) r. pour moi** he's *or* he means nothing to me (any more); **et moi alors, je ne suis r. (dans tout ça)?** and what about me (in all this), don't I count for anything *or* don't I matter?; **je ne comprends r.** I don't understand anything; **je n'ai r. compris** I haven't understood anything, I've understood nothing; **je ne me souviens de r.** I remember nothing, I don't remember anything; **on ne voit r. avec cette fumée** you can't see anything *or* a thing with all this smoke; **ce soupçon ne repose sur r.** the suspicion is without foundation *or* based on nothing; **il n'y a r. entre nous** there is nothing between us; **cela** *ou* **ça ne fait r.** it doesn't matter; **ça ne (te) fait r. si je te dépose en dernier?** would you mind if I dropped you off last?, is it OK with you if I drop you off last?; **dis-lui – je n'en ferai r.** tell him/her – I shall do nothing of the sort; **ça n'a r. à voir** it's got nothing to do with it; **ça n'a r. à voir avec toi** it's got nothing to do with you, it doesn't concern you; **Paul et Fred n'ont r. à voir l'un avec l'autre** there's no connection between Paul and Fred; **je n'ai r. contre lui** I have nothing against him, I don't have anything against him; **elle veut déménager, je n'ai r. contre** she wants to move, I've got nothing against it; **ne t'inquiète pas, tu n'y es pour r.** don't worry, it's not your fault; **ça n'a r. d'un chef-d'œuvre** it's far from being a masterpiece; **il n'a r. du séducteur** there's nothing of the lady-killer about him; **il n'y a r. de moins sûr** nothing could be less certain; **r. de moins que** nothing less than; **ils ne veulent r. de moins que sa démission** they want nothing less than his/her resignation; **je ne méprise r. tant que le mensonge** I despise nothing so much as lying; **elle n'aime r. tant qu'à rester à lire sur le balcon** she likes nothing better than sitting reading on the balcony; **elle n'a r. fait que ce qu'on lui a demandé** she only did what she was asked to do; **il n'y a plus r. à faire** there's nothing more to be done; **pour ne r. vous cacher...** to be completely open with you...; **elle n'avait jamais r. vu de semblable** she had never seen such a thing *or* anything like it; **je ne sais r. de r.** I don't know a thing; **r. ne sert de courir (il faut partir à point)** slow and steady wins the race

3 *(quelque chose)* anything; **y a-t-il r. que je puisse faire?** is there nothing I can do?; **y a-t-il eu jamais r. de plus beau?** was there ever anything more beautiful?; **j'ai compris avant qu'il dise r.** I understood before he said anything; **on ne peut pas vivre sans r. faire** you can't live without doing anything; **appelle-moi avant de r. faire** call me before you do *or* before doing anything

4 r. ne va plus *(dans un jeu)* rien ne va plus

5 *(au tennis)* love; **r. partout** love all; **40 à r.** 40 love

6 *(locutions)* **elle est r. moins que décidée à le poursuivre en justice** *(bel et bien)* she's well and truly determined to take him to court; **elle est r. moins que sotte** *(nullement)* she is far from stupid

ADV *Fam (très)* very□; **ils sont r. riches** *Br* they really are rolling in it, *Am* they sure as hell are rich

NM 1 *(néant)* **le r.** nothingness

2 *(chose sans importance)* **un r.** the merest trifle *or* slightest thing; **un r. la met en colère** the slightest thing *or* every little thing makes her angry; **un r. l'habille** he/she looks good in anything; **on se faisait gronder pour un r.** we used to be scolded for the slightest thing; **il se fâche pour un r.** he loses his temper over the slightest little thing

3 un r. de *(très peu de)* a touch of; **un r. de cannelle** a touch *or* hint of cinnamon; **un r. de canard/vin** a taste of duck/wine; **un r. de frivolité** a touch *or* tinge *or* hint of frivolity; **en un r. de temps** in (next to) no time

• **en rien ADV ça ne me dérange en r.** that doesn't bother me at all *or* in the least; **il ne ressemble en r. à son père** he looks nothing like his father; **ça n'a en r. affecté ma décision** it hasn't influenced my decision at all *or* in the least *or* in any way

• **pour rien ADV ne le dérange pas pour r.** don't disturb him for no reason; **il est venu pour r.** he came for nothing; **j'ai acheté ça pour r. chez un brocanteur** I bought it for next to nothing in a second-hand shop; **pour deux/trois fois r.** for next to nothing

• **rien du tout NMF un/une r. du tout** a nobody

• **rien que ADV r. que pour toi** just *or* only for you; **r. que cette fois** just this once; **r. qu'une fois** just *or* only once; **viens, r. qu'un jour** do come, (even) if only for a day; **r. que le billet coûte une fortune** the ticket alone costs a fortune; **r. que d'y penser, j'ai des frissons** the mere thought of it *or* just thinking about it makes me shiver; **la vérité, r. que la vérité** the truth and nothing but the truth; *Ironique* **r. que ça?** is that all?

• **un rien ADV** a touch, a shade, a tiny bit; **sa robe est un r. trop étroite** her dress is a touch *or* a shade *or* a tiny bit too tight; **c'est un r. trop sucré pour moi** it's a shade *or* a tiny bit too sweet for me

riesling [rislin] **NM** Riesling

rieur, -euse [rijœr, -øz] **ADJ** *(enfant)* cheery, cheerful; *(visage, regard)* laughing

NM,F laugher; **les rieurs** those who laugh; **avoir les rieurs de son côté** to have laughter on one's side

rififi [rififi] **NM** *Fam (bagarre)* trouble, *Br* aggro; **il va y avoir du r.** there's going to be trouble *or Br* aggro

riflard [riflar] **NM** *Fam Vieilli (parapluie)* umbrella□, *Br* brolly

riflette [riflɛt] **NF** *Fam Vieilli (guerre)* war□; *(zone des combats)* front□; **partir pour la r.** to go off to war *or* to the front□

rift [rift] **NM** *Géol* rift valley

Riga [riga] **NM** Riga

rigide [riʒid] **ADJ 1** *(solide* ▸ *gén)* rigid; *(*▸ *couverture de livre)* stiff **2** *(intransigeant)* rigid, inflexible, unbending **3** *(austère, strict)* rigid, strict; **une éducation r.** a strict upbringing

rigidement [riʒidmɑ̃] **ADV** rigidly, inflexibly, strictly

rigidifier **[9]** [riʒidifje] **VT** to rigidify, to stiffen

rigidité [riʒidite] **NF 1** *(raideur)* rigidity, stiffness; **r. cadavérique** rigor mortis **2** *(caractère strict)* strictness, inflexibility

rigolade [rigɔlad] **NF** *Fam* **1** *(amusement)* fun□; **prendre qch à la r.** *(avec humour)* to see the funny side of sth, to treat sth as a joke; *(avec légèreté)* not to take sth too seriously□; **chez eux, l'ambiance n'est pas/est franchement à la r.** it isn't exactly/it's a laugh a minute round their place; **la vie n'est qu'une vaste r.** life is one big joke *or* farce; **élever quatre enfants, ce n'est pas une (partie de) r.** raising four children is no laughing matter; **soulever des poids est une r. pour elle** lifting weights is child's play for her; **c'est de la r.!** *(ce n'est pas sérieux)* it's a joke!; *(c'est sans importance)* it's nothing!; *(c'est très facile)* it's a piece of cake!; **c'est pas de la r.!** it's no picnic! **2** *(fou rire)* fit of laughter□; **ah, la r.!, quelle r.!** what a hoot *or* scream!

rigolard, -e [rigɔlar, -ard] *Fam* **ADJ** *(personne)* fond of a joke *or* a laugh□; **il a toujours un air r.** he's always got a grin on his face, something always seems to be amusing him

NM,F c'est un r. he likes a good laugh

rigole [rigɔl] **NF 1** *(filet d'eau)* rivulet, rill **2** *(conduit)* trench, channel; *(fossé)* ditch

rigoler **[3]** [rigɔle] **VI** *Fam* **1** *(rire)* to laugh□; **moi, il ne me fait pas r. du tout** I don't find him funny *or* he doesn't make me laugh at all; *Ironique* **tu me fais r. avec tes remords!** you, sorry? don't make me laugh! **2** *(plaisanter)* to joke□; **il a dit ça pour r.** he said that in jest, he meant it as a joke; **histoire de r., pour r.** for a laugh, for fun; **tu rigoles!** you're joking *or* kidding!; **il ne faut pas r. avec le fisc** you shouldn't mess about with the *Br* taxman *or Am* IRS; **ils rigolent pas avec la sécurité dans cet aéroport** they don't mess about *or* take any chances with security at this airport **3** *(s'amuser)* to have fun□; **on a bien rigolé cette année-là** we had some good laughs *or* great fun that year; **avec lui comme prof, tu ne vas pas r. tous les jours** it won't be much fun for you having him as a teacher

rigolo, -ote [rigɔlo, -ɔt] *Fam* **ADJ 1** *(amusant)* funny□; **ce serait r. que tu aies des jumeaux** wouldn't it be funny if you had twins; **c'est pas r. de bosser avec lui** working with him is no joke **2** *(étrange)* funny□, odd□; **c'est r., mais est-ce pratique?** it's certainly funny, but is it useful?

NM,F 1 *(rieur)* hoot, scream; **c'est une rigolote** she's a hoot **2** *(incompétent)* joker, clown, *Péj* comedian; **c'est un (petit) r.** he's a real comedian; **qui est le petit r. qui a débranché la prise?** what joker pulled the plug out?

rigorisme [rigɔrism] **NM** rigorism

rigoriste [rigɔrist] **ADJ** rigid, rigoristic

NMF rigorist

rigoureuse [rigurøz] *voir* **rigoureux**

rigoureusement [rigurøzmɑ̃] **ADV 1** *(scrupuleusement)* rigorously; **suivre r. les consignes** to follow the instructions to the letter **2** *(complètement)* **r. interdit** strictly forbidden; **les deux portraits sont r. identiques** the two portraits are exactly the same *or* absolutely identical; **c'est r. vrai** it's perfectly true **3** *(sévèrement)* harshly, severely

rigoureux, -euse [rigurø, -øz] **ADJ 1** *(scrupuleux* ▸ *analyse, définition, entraînement)* rigorous; *(*▸ *contrôle)* strict, stringent; *(*▸ *raisonnement)* careful; *(*▸ *description)* minute, precise; *(*▸ *discipline)* strict; **observer une rigoureuse neutralité** to remain strictly neutral; **soyez plus r. dans votre travail** be more thorough in your work **2** *(sévère* ▸ *personne)* severe, strict; *(*▸ *sanction)* harsh, severe; *(*▸ *discipline)* severe; *(*▸ *principe)* strict **3** *(rude* ▸ *climat)* harsh; *(*▸ *hiver)* hard, harsh

rigueur [rigœr] **NF 1** *(sévérité)* harshness, severity, rigour; **traiter qn avec r.** to be extremely strict with sb, to treat sb harshly; **tenir r. à qn de qch** to hold sth against sb

2 *(austérité* ▸ *d'une gestion)* austerity, stringency; *(*▸ *d'une morale)* rigour, strictness, sternness; **politique de r.** austerity (measures)

3 *(âpreté ▸ d'un climat, d'une existence)* rigour, harshness, toughness; **l'hiver a été d'une r. exceptionnelle** the winter has been exceptionally harsh

4 *(précision ▸ d'un calcul)* exactness, precision; *(▸ d'une analyse, d'une logique, d'un esprit)* rigour; **il manque de r. dans son analyse** he's not rigorous enough in his analysis; **r. professionnelle** professionalism

• **rigueurs** NFPL *Littéraire* rigours; **les rigueurs de l'hiver/de la vie carcérale** the rigours of winter/of prison life

• **à la rigueur** ADV **1** *(peut-être)* **il a bu deux verres à la r., mais pas plus** he may possibly have had two drinks but no more **2** *(s'il le faut)* at a pinch, if need be; **à la r., on pourrait y aller à pied** at a pinch *or* if need be *or* if the worst comes to the worst we could walk there

• **de rigueur** ADJ **la ponctualité est de r.** punctuality is insisted upon, *Sout* it's de rigueur to be on time; **tenue de soirée de r.** *(sur carton d'invitation, dans un restaurant)* dress formal; **délai de r.** deadline

rillettes [rijɛt] NFPL *Culin* rillettes *(potted meat)*

rimailler [3] [rimaje] VI *Fam Vieilli Péj* to write poetry of a sort, to dabble in writing poetry

rimailleur, -euse [rimajœr, -øz] NM,F *Fam Vieilli Péj* rhymester, versifier, poetaster

rimbaldien, -enne [rɛ̃baldjɛ̃, -ɛn] ADJ **la poésie rimbaldienne** Rimbaud's poetry, the poetry of Rimbaud; **avoir des accents rimbaldiens** *(écrit)* to be reminiscent of Rimbaud, to have Rimbaud-like overtones

rime [rim] NF **1** *Littérature* rhyme; **créer un mot pour la r.** to coin a word for the sake of rhyme; **rimes croisées** *ou* **alternées** alternate rhymes; **rimes embrassées** abba rhyme scheme; **r. interne** internal rhyme; **r. masculine/féminine** masculine/feminine rhyme; **r. pauvre** poor rhyme; **rimes plates** rhyming couplets; **r. riche** rich *or* perfect rhyme **2** *(locution)* **sans r. ni raison** *(partir, décider)* without rhyme or reason; **il me tenait des propos sans r. ni raison** what he was telling me had neither rhyme nor reason to it, there was neither rhyme nor reason in what he was telling me

rimer [3] [rime] VT to versify, to put into verse; **poésie rimée** rhyming verse

VI **1** *Littéraire (faire de la poésie)* to write poetry *or* verse **2** *(finir par le même son)* to rhyme (**avec** with); **les premier et dernier vers riment** the first and last lines rhyme **3** *(équivaloir à)* **pour beaucoup de gens bonheur rime avec argent** many people equate happiness with money; **amour ne rime pas toujours avec fidélité** love and fidelity don't aways go together *or* hand in hand

• **rimer à** VT IND **à quoi rime cette scène de jalousie?** what's the meaning of this jealous outburst?; **tout cela ne rime à rien** none of this makes any sense, there's no sense in any of this; **ça ne rime à rien de le gronder** there's absolutely no point in telling him off, it makes absolutely no sense to tell him off

rimeur, -euse [rimœr, -øz] NM,F *Péj* versifier, rhymester, poetaster

Rimmel® [rimɛl] NM mascara

rinçage [rɛ̃saʒ] NM **1** *(au cours d'une lessive)* rinse, rinsing; **produit de r.** *(pour lave-vaisselle)* rinsing agent *or* aid **2** *(pour les cheveux)* (colour) rinse

rince-bouteilles [rɛ̃sbutɛj] NM INV bottle-washing machine

rince-doigts [rɛ̃sdwa] NM INV finger bowl

rincée [rɛ̃se] NF *Fam* **1** *Vieilli (défaite)* licking, hammering, thrashing; *(coups)* thrashing; **prendre une r.** *(défaite)* to get hammered *or* licked *or* thrashed; *(coups)* to get thrashed **2** *(averse)* downpour[□]; **prendre une r.** to get caught in a downpour

rincer [16] [rɛ̃se] VT **1** *(passer à l'eau)* to rinse; **r. qch abondamment** to rinse sth thoroughly, to give sth a thorough rinse **2** *Fam (mouiller)* **se faire r.** to get caught in a downpour[□] **3** *Fam (ruiner)* **il s'est fait r. au jeu** he got cleaned out at the gambling table

VI *Fam (offrir à boire)* to buy the drinks[□]; **c'est moi qui rince!** I'm buying the drinks!, the drinks are on me!; **c'est le patron qui rince!** the drinks are on the house!

VPR **se rincer se r. la bouche/les mains** to rinse one's mouth (out)/one's hands; *Fam* **se r. le bec** *ou* **la dalle** *ou* **le gosier** *(boire)* to wet one's whistle; *Fam* **se r. l'œil** *(regarder)* to get an eyeful; **alors, on se rince l'œil?** seen enough, have you?

rincette [rɛ̃sɛt] NF *Fam (eau-de-vie)* nip of brandy[□], brandy chaser[□] *(after coffee)*

rinceur, -euse [rɛ̃sœr, -øz] ADJ *(dispositif)* rinsing

• **rinceuse** NF *(machine)* bottle-washing machine

ring [riŋ] NM **1** *(estrade)* (boxing) ring; **monter sur le r.** *(au début d'un combat)* to get into the ring; **quand il est monté sur le r.** *(quand il a débuté)* when he took up boxing; **une légende du r.** a boxing legend, a legend of the ring **2** *Belg (rocade)* ring road

ringard[1] [rɛ̃gar] NM *Métal* rabble

ringard[2], -e [rɛ̃gar, -ard] *Fam Péj* ADJ *(démodé ▸ gén)* corny, *Br* naff; *(▸ chanson)* corny, cheesy; *(▸ décor)* tacky, *Br* naff; **elle est ringarde** she's such a geek

NM,F *(individu démodé)* geek, nerd, *Br* anorak

ringardisation [rɛ̃gardizasjɔ̃] NF *Fam* going out of fashion[□]; **cette station balnéaire est en voie de r.** the seaside resort is on its way down *or* is not as fashionable as it used to be[□]

ringardise [rɛ̃gardiz] NF *Fam* tackiness, *Br* naffness; **la déco était d'une r., je te dis pas!** the decor was unbelievably tacky *or Br* naff!

ringardiser [3] [rɛ̃gardize] *Fam* VT to put out of fashion[□]

VPR **se ringardiser** to go out of fashion[□]

ringardissime [rɛ̃gardisim] ADJ *Fam* incredibly tacky *or Br* naff

ringuette [rɛ̃gɛt] NF ringette *(women's sport similar to ice hockey)*

RIP [rip, ɛripe] NM *Banque* (*abrév* **relevé d'identité postale**) = document giving details of one's post office account

ripage [ripaʒ] NM *Constr* scraping

ripaille [ripaj] NF *Fam Vieilli* feast[□]; **faire r.** to have a feast

ripailler [3] [ripaje] VI *Fam Vieilli* to have a feast[□]

ripailleur, -euse [ripajœr, -øz] *Fam Vieilli* NM,F reveller[□]

ADJ revelling[□], feasting[□]

ripaton [ripatɔ̃] NM *Fam* foot[□]; **attention les ripatons!** mind your feet!

riper [3] [ripe] VT **1** *Constr* to scrape **2** *(faire glisser ▸ chargement)* to slide along

VI **1** *(glisser)* to slip **2** *Fam (s'en aller)* to beat it, to push off

Ripolin® [ripɔlɛ̃] NM enamel paint, Ripolin®

ripoliner [3] [ripɔline] VT to paint *(with enamel paint)*; **murs ripolinés** walls painted with enamel paint *or* with Ripolin®

riposte [ripɔst] NF **1** *(réplique)* retort, riposte; **avoir la r. rapide** to be good at repartee

2 *(réaction)* reaction; **quand on l'attaque, la r. ne se fait pas attendre** when he's/she's attacked, he/she doesn't take long to react

3 *Mil (contre-attaque)* counterattack, reprisal

4 *Escrime* riposte

riposter [3] [ripɔste] VI **1** *(rétorquer)* to answer back

2 *(réagir)* to respond; **il a riposté à son insulte par une gifle** he countered his/her insult with a slap; **ils ont riposté par une rafale de mitraillette** they responded with a burst of machine-gun fire; **nous riposterons immédiatement** we will take immediate retaliatory action

3 *(contre-attaquer)* to counterattack; **r. à un assaut** to counterattack; **r. à une agression** to counter an aggression

4 *Escrime* to riposte

VT **elle riposta que ça ne le regardait pas** she retorted that it was none of his business; **"pas question", riposta-t-il** "no way," he snarled *or* snapped

ripou, -x *ou* **-s** [ripu] *Fam (verlan de* **pourri***)* ADJ *(personne)* corrupt[□]; **des flics ripoux** *Br* bent *or Am* bad cops

NM *Br* bent *or Am* bad cop; **ce flic est un r.** he's *Br* a bent *or Am* a bad cop

riquiqui [rikiki] ADJ INV *Fam* **1** *(minuscule)* teeny-weeny; **une portion r.** a minute *or* minuscule helping; **une natte r.** a dinky little plait **2** *(étriqué ▸ mobilier)* shabby, grotty; *(▸ vêtement)* skimpy; **ça fait r.** *(mesquin)* it looks a bit stingy *or* mean

rire [95] [rir] VI **1** *(de joie)* to laugh; **ta lettre nous a beaucoup fait r.** your letter made us all laugh a lot; **ça ne me fait pas r.** that's not funny; **fais-moi r.** make me laugh, say *or* do something funny; **"c'est vrai", dit-il en riant** "that's true," he laughed *or* he said with a laugh; **sa gêne/tenue prêtait à r.** his/her embarrassment/outfit was really funny; **r. bêtement** to giggle, to titter; **r. de bon cœur** to laugh heartily; **r. bruyamment** to guffaw; **il n'y a pas de quoi r.** this is no joke *or* no laughing matter; **il vaut mieux en r.** it's best to laugh, you might as well laugh; **il vaut mieux en r. qu'en pleurer** you have to laugh or else you cry; **je n'en pouvais plus de r.** I was helpless with laughter; *Fam* **j'étais morte de r.** I nearly died laughing, I was doubled up with laughter; *Fam* **c'est à mourir** *ou* **crever de r.** it's a hoot *or* a scream; **r. aux éclats** *ou* **à gorge déployée** to howl with laughter; **il m'a fait r. aux larmes avec ses histoires** his jokes made me laugh until I cried; **r. du bout des dents** *ou* **des lèvres** to force a laugh; **r. dans sa barbe** *ou* **sous cape** to laugh up one's sleeve, to laugh to oneself; **r. au nez** *ou* **à la barbe de qn** to laugh in sb's face; *Fam* **r. comme un bossu** *ou* **une baleine** to laugh oneself silly, *Br* to laugh like a drain; **se tenir les côtes** *ou* **se tordre de r.** to split one's sides (with laughter), to be in stitches; **r. jaune** to give a hollow laugh; *Ironique* **tu me fais r., laisse-moi r., ne me fais pas r.!** don't make me laugh!; **tu me fais r. toi, avec tes principes** you don't really think I take your so-called principles seriously, do you?; *Can Fam* **il fait froid pour pas en r. aujourd'hui!** it's freezing *or Br* baltic today!; *Can Fam* **il y avait du monde en pas pour r. à la manifestation** there were quite a few *or* quite a lot of people at the demonstration[□]; *Prov* **rira bien qui rira le dernier** he who laughs last laughs *Br* longest *or Am* best

2 *Fam (plaisanter)* to joke; **j'ai dit ça pour r.** *ou* **pour de r.** I (only) said it in jest, I was only joking; **c'était pour r.** it was only for fun; **je te le disais en riant** it was a joke, I was pulling your leg; **tu veux r.!** you must be joking!, you've got to be kidding!; **sans r., tu comptes y aller?** joking apart *or* aside, do you intend to go?

3 *(se distraire)* to have fun; **qu'est-ce qu'on a pu r. pendant ses cours!** we had such fun in his/her lessons!

4 *Littéraire (yeux)* to shine *or* to sparkle (with laughter); *(visage)* to beam (with happiness)

NM laugh, laughter *(UNCOUNT)*; **j'adore son r.** I love his/her laugh *or* the way he/she laughs; **le r. est une bonne thérapie** laughter is the best medicine; **j'entends des rires** I hear laughter *or* people laughing; **gros r.** guffaw; **il eut un gros r.** he roared with laughter; **r. gras** coarse laugh, cackle; **r. moqueur** sneer; **un petit r. sot** a silly giggle; **un petit r. méchant** a wicked little laugh, a snigger; *Rad & TV* **rires préenregistrés** *ou Fam* **en boîte** prerecorded *or* canned laughter

• **rire de** VT IND *(se moquer de)* to laugh at; **un jour nous rirons de tout cela** we'll have a good laugh over all this some day

VPR **se rire 1 se r. de** *(conseil, doute)* to laugh off, to make fun of; *(danger, maladie, difficultés)* to make light of **2** *Littéraire* **se r. de** *(se moquer de)* to laugh *or* to scoff at

ris [ri] NM **1** *Culin* sweetbread; **r. de veau** calf sweetbreads **2** *Naut* reef; **prendre/larguer un r.** to take in/to shake out a reef **3** *Arch (rire)* laughter

risée [rize] NF **1** *(moquerie)* mockery, ridicule; **être un objet de r.** to be a laughing stock; **devenir la r. du village/de la presse** to become the laughing stock of the village/the butt of the press's jokes; **tu t'exposerais à la r. de tout le monde** you'd lay yourself open to public ridicule **2** *(brise)* flurry (of wind)

risette[1] [rizɛt] NF *Fam* **1** *(sourire d'enfant)* **allez, fais r. à mamie** come on, give grandma a nice little smile **2** *(flagornerie)* **faire r.** *ou* **des risettes à qn** *Br* to smarm up *or Am* to play up to sb

risette[2] [rizɛt] NF *Suisse* **brosse à r.** stiff brush

risible [rizibl] ADJ **1** *(amusant)* funny, comical; **la situation n'avait rien de r.** the situation was not at all funny, there was nothing to laugh at in the situation **2** *(ridicule)* ridiculous, laughable

risotto [rizɔto] NM *Culin* risotto

risque [risk] NM **1** *(danger)* risk, hazard, danger; **il y a un r. de contagion/d'explosion** there's a risk of contamination/of an explosion; **est-ce qu'il y a un r. que cela se reproduise?** is there any risk of that happening again?; **au r. de te décevoir/de le faire souffrir** at the risk of disappointing you/of hurting him; **r. professionnel** occupational hazard; **à r.** *(groupe, comportement, pratique)* high-risk; **à mes/tes risques et périls** at my/your own risk; **ce sont les risques du métier** it's an occupational hazard **2** *(initiative hasardeuse)* risk, chance; **il y a une part de r.** there's an element of risk; **cela n'est pas sans r.** it is not without its risks *or* dangers; **prendre un r.** to run a risk, to take a chance; **ne prenez pas de risques inutiles** don't take any unnecessary risks *or* chances; **courir le r. de se faire prendre** to run the risk of getting caught; **j'ai toujours gagné en ne prenant pas de risques** I've always won by playing safe; **avoir le goût du r., aimer le r.** to enjoy taking chances; **r. calculé** calculated risk **3** *(préjudice)* risk; *Fin* **r. de change** foreign exchange risk; *Fin* **r. de contrepartie** credit risk; **r. d'incendie** fire hazard *or* risk; **r. de marché** market risk; *Fin* **capitaux à risques** risk *or* venture capital; *Assur* **souscrire un r.** to underwrite a risk

risqué, -e [riske] ADJ **1** *(dangereux)* risky, dangerous; **c'est une entreprise risquée** it's a risky business **2** *(osé)* risqué, racy

risque-pays [riskəpei] NM *Pol* country risk

risquer [3] [riske] VT **1** *(engager ▸ fortune, crédibilité)* to risk; **r. sa vie** *ou Fam* **sa peau** to risk one's life *or* neck; *Fam* **r. le paquet** to chance one's arm, to stake one's all; **on risque le coup?** shall we have a shot at it?, shall we chance it?; *Prov* **qui ne risque rien n'a rien** nothing ventured nothing gained **2** *(s'exposer à)* to risk; **elle risque la mort/la paralysie** she runs the risk of dying/of being left paralysed; **on ne risque rien à essayer** we can always try; **tu ne risques rien avec ce masque/avec moi à tes côtés** you'll be safe with this mask/with me beside you; **tu peux laisser ça dehors, ça ne risque rien** you can leave it outside, it'll be safe; **après tout, qu'est-ce que tu risques?** what have you got to lose, after all? **3** *(oser)* to venture; **r. une comparaison** to risk drawing a comparison, to venture a comparison; *Fam* **r. un regard** *ou* **un œil** to venture a look *or* a peep; *Fam* **r. le nez dehors** to poke one's nose outside

• **risquer de** VT IND to risk; **ton idée risque de ne pas marcher** there's a chance your idea mightn't work; **ça risque d'être long** this might take a long time; **il risque de se faire mal** he might hurt himself; **ils risquent d'être renvoyés** they run the risk of being sacked; **le plafond risquait de s'écrouler d'une minute à l'autre** the ceiling was likely to collapse at any minute; **ne m'attends pas, je risque d'être en retard** don't wait for me, I'm likely to be late *or* the chances are I'll be late; *Hum* **je ne risque pas de me remarier!** (there's) no danger of my getting married again!; **ça ne risque pas!** no chance!

VPR **se risquer se r. dehors** to venture outside; **se r. à faire qch** to venture *or* to dare to do sth; **je ne m'y risquerais pas si j'étais toi** I wouldn't take a chance on it if I were you; **se r. dans qch** *(entreprise, aventure)* to get involved in sth

risque-tout [riskətu] ADJ INV **il est très r.** he's a daredevil

NMF INV daredevil

rissole [risɔl] NF *Culin* rissole

rissoler [3] [risɔle] *Culin* VT to brown; **pommes rissolées** sauté *or* sautéed potatoes

VI **faire r.** to brown

ristourne [risturn] NF **1** *(réduction)* discount, reduction; **faire une r. à qn** to give sb a discount; **j'ai eu une r. de 20 pour cent sur la moto** I got a 20 percent discount on the motorbike; **r. de fidélité** customer loyalty discount; **r. de prime** premium discount **2** *(remboursement)* refund, reimbursement **3** *Com (versement)* bonus

ristourner [3] [risturne] VT **1** *(faire une ristourne de)* to give a discount of; **il nous a ristourné 20 pour cent du prix** he gave us a 20 percent discount *or* 20 percent off **2** *(rembourser)* to refund, to give a refund of

USAGE ABSOLU *Com* **r. à qn** to give a bonus to sb

ristrette [ristrɛt], **ristretto** [ristreto] NM *Suisse* very strong black coffee

rital, -e, -als, -ales [rital] *Fam* ADJ = racist term used to refer to an Italian

NM,F *Br* Eyetie, *Am* Macaroni, = racist term used to refer to an Italian

Ritaline® [ritalin] NF *Pharm* Ritalin®

rite [rit] NM **1** *Rel* rite; **rites d'initiation** initiation rites; **r. de passage** rite of passage **2** *(coutume)* ritual

ritournelle [riturnɛl] NF **1** *Fam (histoire)* **avec lui c'est toujours la même r.** he's always giving us the same old story **2** *Mus* ritornello

ritualiser [3] [ritɥalize] VT to ritualize

ritualisme [ritɥalism] NM ritualism

ritualiste [ritɥalist] ADJ ritualistic

NMF ritualist

rituel, -elle [ritɥɛl] ADJ **1** *(réglé par un rite)* ritual **2** *(habituel)* ritual, usual, customary

NM *(rite)* ritual; **r. d'initiation** initiation rite(s) *or* ritual

rituellement [ritɥɛlmɑ̃] ADV **1** *(selon un rite)* ritually **2** *(invariablement)* without fail, religiously; **ils y vont r. chaque année** they go without fail *or* religiously every year

rivage [rivaʒ] NM *(littoral)* shore; *Littéraire* **de lointains rivages** distant shores

> Do not confuse with **rive**.

rival, -e, -aux, -ales [rival, -o] ADJ *(antagonique)* rival *(avant n)*

NM,F **1** *(adversaire)* rival, opponent; **r. politique** political rival *or* opponent **2** *(concurrent)* rival; **elle n'a pas eu de rivale en son temps** she was unrivalled in her day

• **sans rival** ADJ unrivalled

rivaliser [3] [rivalize] VI to compete (**avec** with); **nos vins peuvent r. avec les meilleurs crus français** our wines can compare with *or* hold their own against *or* rival French vintages; **elles rivalisent d'élégance** they are trying to outdo each other in elegance

rivalité [rivalite] NF *(gén)* rivalry; *(en affaires)* competition; **des rivalités d'intérêts** conflicting interests

rive [riv] NF *(bord ▸ d'un lac, d'une mer)* shore; *(▸ d'une rivière)* bank; **r. droite/gauche** *(gén)* right/left bank; **mode/intellectuels r. gauche** *(à Paris)* Left Bank fashion/intellectuals *(in Paris)*

> Do not confuse with **rivage**.

> **RIVE DROITE, RIVE GAUCHE**
>
> The Right (north) Bank of the Seine is traditionally associated with business and trade, and has a reputation for being more conservative than the Left Bank. The Left (south) Bank includes districts traditionally favoured by artists, students and intellectuals, and has a reputation for being Bohemian and unconventional.

river [3] [rive] VT **1** *(joindre ▸ plaques)* to rivet; *(▸ clou)* to clinch; *Fam* **r. son clou à qn** to shut sb up **2** *Fig (fixer)* to rivet; **il avait les yeux rivés sur elle** he couldn't take his eyes off her; **être rivé à la télévision/à son travail** to be glued to the television/chained to one's work; **rester rivé sur place** to be riveted *or* rooted to the spot; **ils étaient rivés au sol par une force invisible** an invisible force held *or* pinned them to the ground

riverain, -e [rivrɛ̃, -ɛn] ADJ *(d'un lac)* lakeside, waterside; *(d'une rivière)* riverside, waterside, *Sout* riparian; **les restaurants riverains de la Seine** the restaurants along the banks of the Seine; **les maisons riveraines de la grande route** the houses stretching along *or* bordering the main road

NM,F *(qui vit au bord ▸ d'un lac)* lakeside resident; *(▸ d'une rivière)* riverside resident; **les riverains du parc s'opposent au concert** residents living near the park are against the concert; **interdit sauf aux riverains** *(sur panneau)* residents only, no entry except for access

rivet [rivɛ] NM rivet

rivetage [rivtaʒ] NM riveting

riveter [27] [rivte] VT to rivet

riveteuse [rivtøz] NF riveting machine

rivière [rivjɛr] NF **1** *Géog* river; **remonter/descendre une r.** to go up/down a river; **pêche en r.** river fishing **2** *(collier)* **r. de diamants** (diamond) rivière **3** *Équitation* water jump

rivoir [rivwar] NM *(marteau)* riveting hammer; *(machine)* riveting machine

rivure [rivyr] NF **1** *(tête de rivet)* rivet head **2** *(opération)* riveting

rixe [riks] NF brawl, scuffle

riz [ri] NM rice; **r. blanc** white rice; **r. complet** brown rice; **r. court/long** short-grain/long-grain rice; **r. au lait** rice pudding; **r. pilaf/cantonnais/créole** pilaff/Cantonese/Creole rice; **r. rond** pudding rice; **r. sauvage** wild rice

rizette [rizɛt] = **risette**

riziculteur, -trice [rizikyltœr, -tris] NM,F rice grower

riziculture [rizikyltyr] NF *(processus)* rice-growing; *(secteur)* rice production

rizière [rizjɛr] NF rice field, paddyfield

riz-pain-sel [ripɛ̃sɛl] NM INV *Fam Arg mil Br* quartermaster, *Am* commissary

RMI [ɛremi] NM *(abrév* **revenu minimum d'insertion***)* = minimum welfare payment paid to people with no other source of income, *Br* income support, *Am* welfare

RMIste [ɛremist] NMF = person receiving the "RMI"

RMN [ɛremɛn] NF *(abrév* **résonance magnétique nucléaire***)* NMR

RN [ɛrɛn] NF *(abrév* **route nationale***)* *Br* ≃ A-road, *Am* ≃ state highway

R'n'B [ɛrɛnbi] NM *Mus* R & B

RNIS [ɛrɛnis] NM *Ordinat (abrév* **réseau numérique à intégration de services***)* ISDN; **envoyer qch par R.** to ISDN sth, to send sth by ISDN

roaming [romiŋ] NM *Ordinat & Tél* roaming

robe [rɔb] NF **1** dress; **je me mets en r. ou en jupe?** shall I wear a dress or a skirt?; **r. de bal** ballgown; **r. de baptême** christening robe; **r. de chambre** *Br* dressing gown, *Am* bathrobe; **pomme de terre en r. de chambre** baked *or* jacket potato; **r.-chasuble** pinafore dress; **r. de grossesse** maternity dress; **r. d'intérieur** housecoat; **r. de mariée** wedding dress, bridal gown; **r. de plage** sundress; **r. du soir** evening dress

2 *(tenue ▸ d'un professeur)* gown; *(▸ d'un cardinal, d'un magistrat)* robe; **les gens de r., la r.** the legal profession; *Can Rel* **prendre la r.** to take the habit, to take holy orders

3 *(pelage)* coat

4 *(enveloppe ▸ d'un fruit)* skin; *(▸ d'une plante)* husk

5 *(en œnologie)* colour *(general aspect of wine in terms of colour and clarity)*

> Il faut noter que le terme anglais **robe** ne désigne jamais un vêtement de femme.

robe-pull [rɔbpyl] *(pl* **robes-pulls***)* NF sweater dress

roberts [rɔber] NMPL *Fam* tits, boobs

robin [rɔbɛ̃] NM *Péj Littéraire* lawyer, gownsman

robinet [rɔbinɛ] NM *(à eau, à gaz)* *Br* tap, *Am* faucet; *(de tonneau)* spigot; **ouvrir/fermer le r.** to turn the *Br* tap *or Am* faucet on/off; **r. d'eau chaude/froide** hot/cold water *Br* tap *or Am* faucet; **r. d'arrivée d'eau** stopcock; **r. mélangeur/mitigeur** *Br* mixer tap, *Am* mixing faucet

robinetterie [rɔbinɛtri] NF **1** *(dispositif)* plumbing **2** *(usine)* *Br* tap *or Am* faucet factory; *(commerce)* *Br* tap *or Am* faucet trade

robineux [rɔbinø] NM *Can Fam* tramp, *Am* hobo

robot [rɔbo] NM robot; **comme un r.** robot-like, like an automaton; **r. ménager** *ou* **de cuisine** food processor

robotique [rɔbɔtik] ADJ robotic

NF robotics *(singulier)*

robotisation [rɔbɔtizasjɔ̃] **NF** robotizing; *(d'un atelier, d'une usine)* automation

robotiser **[3]** [rɔbɔtize] **VT 1** *(atelier, usine, travail)* to automate, to robotize **2** *(personne)* to robotize

robre [rɔbr] **NM** *Cartes (au whist, au bridge)* rubber

robusta [rɔbysta] **NM** robusta (coffee)

robuste [rɔbyst] **ADJ 1** *(personne)* robust, sturdy, strong; **des jambes robustes** sturdy legs
2 *(santé)* sound; *(appétit)* robust, healthy; **doté d'une r. constitution** blessed with a robust *or* sound constitution
3 *(arbre, plante)* hardy
4 *(meuble, voiture, moteur)* sturdy, robust
5 *(conviction)* firm, strong

robustesse [rɔbystɛs] **NF 1** *(d'une personne)* robustness **2** *(d'un arbre, d'une plante)* hardiness **3** *(d'un meuble, d'une voiture, d'un moteur)* sturdiness, robustness

ROC [erose] **NF** *Ordinat (abrév* **reconnaissance optique des caractères***)* OCR

roc [rɔk] **NM** *(pierre)* rock; **dur** *ou* **ferme comme un r.** solid *or* firm as a rock; *Fig* **Jules, c'est un r.** Jules is as solid as a rock

rocade [rɔkad] **NF 1** *Constr* bypass **2** *Mil* communications line

rocaille [rɔkaj] **NF 1** *(pierraille)* loose stones; *(terrain)* stony ground **2** *(jardin)* rock garden, rockery **3** *(style)* rocaille

rocailleux, -euse [rɔkajø, -øz] **ADJ 1** *(terrain)* rocky, stony **2** *(voix)* gravelly **3** *(style)* rough, rugged

rocambole [rɔkɑ̃bɔl] **NF** *Bot* rocambole, sand leek, giant *or* elephant garlic

rocambolesque [rɔkɑ̃bɔlɛsk] **ADJ** *(aventures)* fantastic; *(histoire)* incredible; **le scénario est r.** the script is all thrills and spills

roche [rɔʃ] **NF 1** *Géol* rock; **roches ignées/métamorphiques/sédimentaires** igneous/metamorphic/sedimentary rocks; **r. mère** parent rock **2** *(pierre)* rock, boulder; **sculpté à même la r.** *ou* **dans la r.** *(bas-relief)* carved in the rock; *(statue)* carved out of the rock; **le sentier serpentait à travers les éboulis de roches** the path wound its way across a scree of boulders

rocher[1] [rɔʃe] **NM 1** *Géol* rock; **grimper/pousser à flanc de r.** to climb up/to grow on the rock face; **côte hérissée de rochers** rocky coast; **r. branlant** rocking *or* logan stone; **le R.** = the town of Monaco; **le r. de Gibraltar** the Rock of Gibraltar
2 *Sport* **faire du r.** to go rock-climbing
3 *Anat* petrous bone
4 *(en chocolat)* rocher *(rock-shaped chocolate)*

rocher[2] **[3]** [rɔʃe] **VI 1** *Métal* to spit **2** *(bière)* to froth

rochet [rɔʃɛ] **NM 1** *Tex* spool **2** *Tech* **roue à r.** ratchet wheel

rocheux, -euse [rɔʃø, -øz] **ADJ** *(paysage, région)* rocky

rock [rɔk] *Mus* **ADJ INV** rock
NM *(musique)* rock (music); *(danse)* rock (and roll), jive; **danser le r.** to jive, to rock (and roll); **un groupe/chanteur de r.** a rock group/singer; **r. alternatif** alternative rock; **r. progressif** prog rock

rocker [rɔkœr] **NM 1** *(artiste)* rock singer *or* musician **2** *Fam (fan)* rocker

rocking-chair [rɔkiŋtʃɛr] *(pl* **rocking-chairs***)* **NM** rocking chair

rockumentaire [rɔkymɑ̃tɛr] **NM** *Cin* rockumentary

rococo [rɔkoko] **ADJ INV 1** *Beaux-Arts* rococo **2** *Péj (tarabiscoté)* over-ornate, rococo; *(démodé)* antiquated, rococo
NM *Beaux-Arts* rococo

rodage [rɔdaʒ] **NM 1** *(d'un moteur, d'une voiture)* *Br* running in, *Am* breaking in; **tant que la voiture est en r.** while the car is being *Br* run in *or Am* broken in **2** *Fig (mise au point)* **le r. de ce service va prendre plusieurs mois** it'll take several months to get this new service running smoothly **3** *Tech* grinding

rodéo [rɔdeo] **NM 1** *(à cheval)* rodeo; **faire du r.** *(métier)* to be a rodeo rider; **r. mécanique** bucking bronco **2** *Fam (en voiture)* **les policiers et les gangsters ont fait un r. dans le quartier** the police and the gangsters had a high-speed car chase through the streets□; **ils font du r. en voitures volées** they go joyriding

roder **[3]** [rɔde] **VT 1** *(moteur, voiture)* *Br* to run in, *Am* to break in **2** *Fig (mettre au point)* **r. un service/une équipe** to get a department/a team up and running; **r. un spectacle** to get a show into its stride; **il est rodé maintenant** he knows the ropes now; **tout est bien rodé** everything is running smoothly **3** *Tech (surface)* to grind

rôder **[3]** [rode] **VI** *(traîner ▸ sans but)* to hang around, to roam *or* to loiter about; *(▸ avec une mauvaise intention)* to lurk *or* to skulk around; **r. dans les rues** to prowl about *or* hang about the streets; **il rôdait autour de la banque** he was lurking *or* loitering around the bank

rôdeur, -euse [rodœr, -øz] **NM,F** prowler

rodomontade [rɔdɔmɔ̃tad] **NF** *Littéraire* bragging *(UNCOUNT)*, swaggering *(UNCOUNT)*; **il est connu pour ses rodomontades** he's notorious for being a braggart; **faire des rodomontades** to brag, to bluster

rœsti [røʃti] **NMPL** *Suisse Culin* roesti, potato pancake

rogations [rɔgasjɔ̃] **NFPL** *Rel* rogations

rogatoire [rɔgatwar] **ADJ** *Jur* rogatory

rognage [rɔɲaʒ] **NM** *(action ▸ du cuir, du métal)* paring; *(▸ du papier)* trimming; *Ordinat (d'image)* cropping

rogne [rɔɲ] **NF** *Fam* anger□, rage□; **être/se mettre en r. (contre qn)** to be/go mad *or* crazy (with/at sb); **mettre qn en r.** to make sb hopping mad

rogner **[3]** [rɔɲe] **VT 1** *(couper ▸ métal)* to pare, to clip; *(▸ cuir)* to pare, to trim; *(▸ papier)* to trim; *(▸ livre)* to guillotine, to trim; *Ordinat (image)* to crop; **r. les griffes à un oiseau** to clip *or* to pare a bird's claws **2** *(réduire ▸ budget, salaire)* to cut (back)
• **rogner sur VT IND** to cut back *or* down on; **r. sur la nourriture** to cut back *or* to skimp on food

rognon [rɔɲɔ̃] **NM** *Culin* kidney

rognonner **[3]** [rɔɲɔne] **VI** *Fam Vieilli* to grumble, to grouse

rognures [rɔɲyr] **NFPL** *(de métal, de carton, d'étoffe)* clippings, trimmings; *(d'ongles)* clippings, parings; *(de viande)* scraps, offcuts

rogomme [rɔgɔm] **NM** *Fam* **voix de r.** hoarse *or* gruff voice□

rogue [rɔg] **ADJ** *(arrogant)* arrogant, haughty

roi [rwa] **NM 1** *(monarque)* king; **le r. Louis XIII** (King) Louis XIII; **r. de droit divin** king by divine right; **le R. des rois** the King of Kings; *Bible* **les Rois mages** the Magi, the Three Wise Men; *Rel* **les Rois** *(Épiphanie)* Twelfth Night; **tirer les Rois** to eat "galette des Rois"; **digne d'un r.** fit for a king; **être heureux comme un r.** to be as happy as a king *or Br* a sandboy; **vivre comme un r.** to live like a king *or* a lord; **le r. n'est pas son cousin** he's terribly stuck-up; **le r. est mort, vive le r.!** the King is dead, long live the King! **2** *Fig* **le r. des animaux** the king of beasts; **les rois du pétrole** the oil tycoons *or* magnates; **le r. du surgelé** the leading name in frozen food, the frozen food king; *Hum* **c'est le r. de la resquille** he's a champion *Br* queue-jumper *or Am* line-jumper; **tu es vraiment le r. de la gaffe!** you're an expert at putting your foot in it!; **c'est vraiment le r. des imbéciles** he's a prize idiot; *très Fam* **c'est le r. des cons** he's a complete prick **3** *Cartes* king; **r. de carreau/pique** king of diamonds/spades

> **TIRER LES ROIS**
>
> The French traditionally celebrate Epiphany with a round, almond-flavoured pastry ("la galette des Rois") containing a small porcelain figurine ("la fève" – originally a dried bean). The pastry is shared out and the person who finds the "fève" is appointed "king" or "queen" and given a cardboard crown to wear. This tradition is called "tirer les Rois".

roide [rwad], **roideur** [rwadœr], **roidir** [rwadir] *Arch* = **raide, raideur, raidir**

roille [rɔj] **NF** *Suisse Fam* downpour□; **pleuvoir à la r.** to pour down, *Br* to chuck it down

roiller **[3]** [rɔje] **V IMPERSONNEL** *Suisse Fam* to pee down, *Br* to chuck it down

Roi-Soleil [rwasɔlɛj] **NM** *Hist* **le R.** the Sun King *(Louis XIV)*

roitelet [rwatlɛ] **NM 1** *Péj (roi)* kinglet **2** *Orn* wren, *Am* winter wren; **r. huppé** goldcrest

rôle [rol] **NM 1** *Cin, Théât & TV* role, part; **apprendre son r.** to learn one's part *or* lines; **il joue le r. d'un espion** he plays (the part of) a spy; **distribuer les rôles** to do the casting, to cast; **il a toujours des rôles de névropathe** he's always cast as a neurotic, he always gets to play neurotics; **avec Jean Dumay dans le r. du Grand Inquisiteur** starring Jean Dumay as the Inquisitor General; **r. de composition** character part *or* role; **r. muet** non-speaking part; **r. parlant** speaking part, speaking role; **r. principal** leading role, starring role, lead; **r. secondaire** supporting role; **r. sérieux** straight part; **petit r.** walk-on part; **premier r.** *(acteur)* leading actor, *f* actress; *(personnage)* lead; **avoir le premier r.** *ou* **le r. principal** to have the starring role, to play the leading role; *Fig* to be the star of the show; **second r.** secondary *or* supporting role; **jouer les seconds rôles (auprès de qn)** to play second fiddle (to sb); **meilleur second r. masculin/féminin** best supporting actor/actress; **jeu de r.** role play; **avoir le beau r.** to have it *or* things easy
2 *(fonction)* role; **jouer un r. important dans qch** to play an important part in sth; **cet élément ne joue qu'un r. secondaire dans le processus** this factor plays a secondary role in the process; **le r. du cœur dans la circulation du sang** the role *or* the part played by the heart in blood circulation; **le r. de l'exécutif** the role *or* function of the executive; **il prend très à cœur son r. de père** he takes his role as father *or* his paternal duties very seriously; **les femmes n'ont pas toujours un r. facile** a woman's role is not always easy, women do not always have it easy; **ce n'est pas mon r. de m'occuper de ça** it's not my job *or* it's not up to me to do it
3 *(liste)* roll; *Naut* **r. d'équipage** muster roll, crew list

rôle-titre [roltitr] *(pl* **rôles-titres***)* **NM** *Cin & Théât* title role

roller [rɔlœr] **NM** rollerblading; **faire du r.** to go rollerblading; **r. in-line** in-line skating; **faire du r. in-line** to go in-line skating
• **rollers NMPL** rollerblades; **rollers in-line** in-line skates

rolleur, -euse [rɔlœr, -øz] **NM,F** rollerblader
NM rollerblading; **faire du r.** to go rollerblading
• **rolleurs NMPL** rollerblades

rollier [rɔlje] **NM** *Orn* roller

rollmops [rɔlmɔps] **NM** *Culin* rollmop (herring)

roll on-roll off [rɔlɔnrɔlɔf] **ADJ INV** *(navire)* roll-on-roll-off, ro-ro
NM INV *(navire)* roll-on-roll-off ship, ro-ro ship

ROM [rɔm] **NF** *Ordinat (abrév* **read only memory***)* ROM, Rom

romain, -e [rɔmɛ̃, -ɛn] **ADJ 1** Roman; **l'Église romaine** the Church of Rome **2** *Belg Pol* Christian Socialist
• **Romain, -e NM,F** Roman
NM *Typ* roman
• **romaine NF 1** *(salade)* *Br* cos lettuce, *Am* romaine (lettuce) **2** *(balance)* steelyard **3** *Fam (locution)* **être bon comme la romaine** *(bienveillant)* to be too kind-hearted for one's own good

roman[1] [rɔmɑ̃] **NM 1** *Littérature* novel; **il n'écrit que des romans** he only writes novels *or* fiction; **on dirait un mauvais r.** it sounds like something out of a cheap novel; **sa vie est un vrai r.** you could write a book about his/her life; **r. d'apprentissage** Bildungsroman; **r. d'aventures/d'amour** adventure/love story; **r. de cape et d'épée** swashbuckling tale; **r. de chevalerie** tale of chivalry; **r. à clef** roman à clef; **r. d'épouvante** horror novel; **r. d'espionnage** spy story; *Péj* **r. de gare** airport *or Am* dime novel; **r. historique** historical novel; **r. de mœurs** social novel; **r. noir** thriller; **r. policier** detective story *or* novel; **r. de science-fiction** science-fiction *or* sci-fi novel; **r. à thèse** roman à thèse, novel of ideas **2** *(genre médiéval)* romance

roman², -e [rɔmɑ̃, -an] ADJ **1** *Ling* Romance *(avant n)* **2** *Archit* Romanesque; *(en Angleterre* ▸ *architecture, style)* Norman; *(*▸ *portail)* Romanesque

NM **1** *(langue)* Romance **2** *Archit* **le r.** Romanesque architecture; *(en Angleterre)* Norman architecture, the Norman style

> Il faut noter que le terme anglais **Roman** est un faux ami. Il signifie **romain**.

romance [rɔmɑ̃s] NF *(poème, musique)* romance; *(chanson sentimentale)* sentimental love song *or* ballad

romancer [16] [rɔmɑ̃se] VT *(histoire)* to novelize; **r. une biographie** to write a biography in the form of a novel

VI *Fig* **avoir tendance à r.** to have a tendency to embroider the facts

romanche [rɔmɑ̃ʃ] ADJ Romansh

NM Romansh

romancier, -ère [rɔmɑ̃sje, -ɛr] *Littérature* NM,F novelist, novel *or* fiction writer

romand, -e [rɔmɑ̃, -ɑ̃d] ADJ of French-speaking Switzerland

• **Romand, -e** NM,F French-speaking Swiss; **les Romands** the French-speaking Swiss

romanesque [rɔmanɛsk] ADJ **1** *Littérature (héros, personnage)* fictional, in a novel; *(technique, style)* novelistic; **l'œuvre r. de Sartre** Sartre's fiction *or* novels **2** *Fig (aventure)* fantastic(al), fabulous; *(imagination, amour)* romantic

NM *Littérature* **les règles du r.** the rules of fiction writing

> Do not confuse with **romantique**.

roman-feuilleton [rɔmɑ̃fœjtɔ̃] *(pl* **romans-feuilletons)** NM *Littérature* serialized novel, serial; **sa vie est un vrai r.** his/her life is a real adventure story

roman-fleuve [rɔmɑ̃flœv] *(pl* **romans-fleuves)** NM *Littérature* roman-fleuve, saga; **il m'a écrit un r.** the letter he sent me was one long *or* endless saga

romanichel, -elle [rɔmaniʃɛl] NM,F *Péj* **1** *(Tsigane)* Romany, gipsy **2** *(nomade)* gipsy

romaniser [3] [rɔmanize] VT to romanize

romaniste [rɔmanist] NMF **1** *Rel* Romanist **2** *Ling* specialist in Romance languages **3** *Beaux-Arts & Jur* romanist

romano [rɔmano] NMF *Fam* gippo, = offensive term used to refer to a gipsy

roman-photo [rɔmɑ̃fɔto] *(pl* **romans-photos)** NM photo novel, photo romance

romantique [rɔmɑ̃tik] ADJ **1** *Beaux-Arts, Littérature & Mus* Romantic **2** *(sentimental)* romantic

NMF **1** *Beaux-Arts, Littérature & Mus* Romantic; **les romantiques** the Romantics **2** *(sentimental)* romantic

> Do not confuse with **romanesque**.

romantisme [rɔmɑ̃tism] NM **1** *Beaux-Arts, Littérature & Mus* Romanticism **2** *(sentimentalisme)* romanticism; **ça ne manque pas de r.** it's quite romantic

romarin [rɔmarɛ̃] NM rosemary

rombière [rɔ̃bjɛr] NF *Fam* **une vieille r.** a stuck-up old cow

Rome [rɔm] NF Rome; **la R. antique** Ancient Rome

rompre [78] [rɔ̃pr] VT **1** *(mettre fin à* ▸ *jeûne, silence, contrat)* to break; *(*▸ *fiançailles, relations)* to break off; *(*▸ *marché)* to call off; *(*▸ *équilibre)* to upset; **le charme est rompu** the spell is broken; *Hum* **désolé de r. ce doux entretien** sorry to break in on your tête-à-tête; **r. les chiens** to call off the hounds; *Fig* to change the subject

2 *(briser)* to break; **le fleuve a rompu ses digues** the river has burst its banks; *Littéraire* **r. ses chaînes** *ou* **fers** to break one's chains; *Naut* **r. les amarres** to break (free from) the moorings; **r. le pain** to break bread; *Littéraire* **r. le pain avec qn** to break bread with sb; *Fig* **r. des lances contre qn** to cross swords with sb

3 *(accoutumer)* to break in; **r. qn à qch** to break sb in to sth; **r. qn à une discipline** to initiate sb into *or* to train sb in a discipline; **sa vie à la ferme l'a rompu aux travaux pénibles** life on the farm has inured him to hard labour

4 *Mil* to break; **r. les rangs** to break ranks; **rompez (les rangs)!** dismiss!, fall out!

VI **1** *(se séparer)* to break up; **r. avec** to break with; **r. avec ses amis/son milieu** to break with one's friends/one's milieu; **r. avec l'étiquette/la tradition** to break with etiquette/tradition; **r. avec une habitude** to break (oneself of) a habit **2** *(se briser* ▸ *corde, branche)* to break, to snap; *(*▸ *digue)* to break, to burst **3** *Sport (reculer)* to break

VPR **se rompre 1** *(se briser* ▸ *branche)* to break *or* to snap (off); *(*▸ *corde)* to break *or* to snap; *(*▸ *digue)* to burst, to break; *(*▸ *vaisseau sanguin)* to rupture **2 se r. les os** *ou* **le cou** to break one's neck

rompu, -e [rɔ̃py] ADJ **1** *(épuisé)* **r. (de fatigue)** tired out, worn out, exhausted; **r. de travail** worn out *or* tired out by work; **j'ai les jambes rompues** my legs are giving way under me **2** *(habitué)* **r. aux affaires/à la diplomatie** experienced in business/in diplomacy; **il est r. à ce genre d'exercice** he's accustomed *or* used to this kind of exercise; **r. aux rigueurs de** accustomed *or* inured to the rigours of

romsteck [rɔmstɛk] NM *(partie du bœuf)* rumpsteak; *(morceau coupé)* slice of rumpsteak

ronce [rɔ̃s] NF **1** *Bot* blackberry bush; **les ronces** *(buissons)* the brambles; **r. artificielle** barbed wire **2** *(nœud dans le bois)* burr, *Spéc* swirl; **r. de noyer** burr walnut

ronceraie [rɔ̃srɛ] NF bramble patch, brambles

ronchon, -onne [rɔ̃ʃɔ̃, -ɔn] *Fam* ADJ crotchety, grumpy, grouchy

NM,F grumbler, grouse, *Am* grouch

ronchonnement [rɔ̃ʃɔnmɑ̃] NM *Fam* grousing *(UNCOUNT)*, grouching *(UNCOUNT)*, griping *(UNCOUNT)*

ronchonner [3] [rɔ̃ʃɔne] VI *Fam* to grouse, to gripe, to grouch (**après** at)

ronchonneur, -euse [rɔ̃ʃɔnœr, -øz] = **ronchon**

roncier [rɔ̃sje] NM *Bot* bramble (bush)

roncière [rɔ̃sjɛr] NF = **roncier**

rond, -e¹ [rɔ̃, rɔ̃d] ADJ **1** *(circulaire)* round, circular; **faire** *ou* **ouvrir des yeux ronds** to stare in disbelief

2 *(bien en chair)* round, full, plump; **des seins ronds** full breasts; **un ventre r.** a rounded belly; **un visage tout r.** a round face, *Péj* a moon face; **un petit homme r.** a *Br* podgy *or Am* pudgy little man

3 *Fam (ivre)* wasted, loaded; **il était complètement r.** he was totally wasted; **r. comme une queue de pelle** *ou* **comme un boudin** *Br* as pissed as a newt, *Am* stewed to the gills

4 *(franc)* straightforward, straight; **il est r. en affaires** he's very direct *or* straightforward *or* up front when it comes to business

5 *(chiffre, somme)* round

NM **1** *(cercle)* circle, ring; **faire des ronds de fumée** to blow *or* to make smoke rings; **faire des ronds dans l'eau** to make rings in the water; *Fig* to fritter away one's time

2 *(anneau)* ring; **r. de serviette** napkin ring; *Ftbl* **r. central** centre circle

3 *Fam (sou)* **je n'ai plus un r.** I'm flat broke, *Br* I'm skint; **je n'ai pas un r. sur moi** I don't have a *Br* penny *or Am* cent on me

4 *(en danse)* **r. de jambe** rond de jambe; *Fig* **faire des ronds de jambe** to bow and scrape

ADV *Fam (locutions)* **qu'est-ce qui ne tourne pas r.?** what's the matter?ᵒ, what's the problem?ᵒ; **ça ne tourne pas r.** things aren't going (very) wellᵒ; **ne pas tourner r.** *(machine)* to be on the blink; *(personne)* to be not all there, to have a screw *or Br* a slate loose; **tout r.** *(en entier* ▸ *avaler)* wholeᵒ; *(exactement)* exactlyᵒ; **tu me dois 20 euros tout r.** you owe me exactly 20 euros

• **en rond** ADV *(se placer, s'asseoir)* in a circle; *(danser)* in a ring; *aussi Fig* **tourner en r.** *(ne pas parvenir à une solution)* to go round (and round) in circles; *(ne pas savoir quoi faire)* to hang around aimlessly

rond-de-cuir [rɔ̃dkɥir] *(pl* **ronds-de-cuir)** NM *Péj* penpusher

ronde² [rɔ̃d] NF **1** *(inspection* ▸ *d'un vigile)* round, rounds, patrol; *(*▸ *d'un soldat)* patrol; *(*▸ *d'un policier)* beat, round, rounds; **faire sa r.** *(sujet: veilleur)* to make one's round *or* rounds; *(sujet: policier)* to be on patrol *or* on the beat

2 *(mouvement circulaire)* circling, turning; **nous regardions la r. incessante des voitures** we were watching the cars go round and round

3 *Mus Br* semibreve, *Am* whole note

4 *(danse)* round (dance), ronde; **faire la r.** to dance round in a circle *or* ring

5 *(écriture)* round hand

• **à la ronde** ADV **il n'y a pas une seule maison à 20 kilomètres à la r.** there's no house within 20 kilometres, there's no house within *or* in a 20-kilometre radius; **(faire) passer le vin à la r.** to pass the wine round, to hand round the wine; **répétez-le à la r.** go round and tell everybody

rondeau, -x [rɔ̃do] NM **1** *Littérature* rondeau **2** *Mus* rondo

ronde-bosse [rɔ̃dbɔs] *(pl* **rondes-bosses)** NF sculpture in the round; **en r.** in the round

rondelet, -ette [rɔ̃dlɛ, -ɛt] ADJ *Fam* **1** *(potelé)* chubby, plump, plumpish **2** *(important)* **une somme rondelette** a tidy *or* nice little sum

rondelle [rɔ̃dɛl] NF **1** *(de salami, de citron)* slice; **couper qch en rondelles** to slice sth, to cut sth into slices **2** *Tech* disc; *(d'un écrou)* washer **3** *(au hockey)* puck

rondement [rɔ̃dmɑ̃] ADV **1** *(promptement)* briskly, promptly, quickly and efficiently; **des négociations r. menées** competently conducted negotiations **2** *(franchement)* frankly, outspokenly; **il me l'a dit r.** he told me straight out

rondeur [rɔ̃dœr] NF **1** *(forme* ▸ *d'un visage, d'un bras)* roundness, plumpness, chubbiness; *(*▸ *d'un sein)* fullness; *(*▸ *d'une épaule)* roundness **2** *(franchise)* frankness; **avec r.** frankly

• **rondeurs** NFPL *Euph* curves; **une jeune femme tout en rondeurs** a curvaceous young woman

rondin [rɔ̃dɛ̃] NM *(bois)* round billet, log; **cabane en rondins** log cabin

rondo [rɔ̃do] NM *Mus* rondo

rondouillard, -e [rɔ̃dujar, -ard] ADJ *Fam* tubby, *Br* podgy, *Am* pudgy

rond-point [rɔ̃pwɛ̃] *(pl* **ronds-points)** NM *Br* roundabout, *Am* traffic circle

Ronéo® [rɔneo] NF Roneo®

ronflant, -e [rɔ̃flɑ̃, -ɑ̃t] ADJ **1** *(moteur)* purring, throbbing; *(feu)* roaring **2** *Péj (discours)* bombastic, high-flown; *(titre)* grand-sounding; *(promesses)* grand

ronflement [rɔ̃fləmɑ̃] NM **1** *(d'un dormeur)* snore, snoring *(UNCOUNT)* **2** *(bruit* ▸ *sourd)* humming *(UNCOUNT)*, droning *(UNCOUNT)*; *(*▸ *fort)* roar, roaring *(UNCOUNT)*, throbbing *(UNCOUNT)*

ronfler [3] [rɔ̃fle] VI **1** *(en dormant)* to snore **2** *(vrombir* ▸ *doucement)* to drone, to hum; *(*▸ *fort)* to roar, to throb; **faire r. le moteur** to rev up the engine

ronflette [rɔ̃flɛt] NF *Fam* snooze; **piquer une r.** to have a nap *or* a snooze

ronfleur, -euse [rɔ̃flœr, -øz] NM,F snorer

NM *Élec & Tél* buzzer

ronger [17] [rɔ̃ʒe] VT **1** *(mordiller)* to gnaw (away) at, to eat into; **r. un os** to gnaw at a bone; **rongé par les vers/mites** worm-/moth-eaten; *Fig* **r. son frein** to champ at the bit **2** *(corroder* ▸ *sujet: mer)* to wear away; *(*▸ *sujet: acide, rouille)* to eat into; **rongé par la rouille** eaten away with rust, rusted away; **être rongé par la maladie** to be wasted by disease; **le mal qui ronge la société** the evil that eats away at society; **être rongé par les soucis** to be careworn

VPR **se ronger se r. les ongles** to bite one's nails

rongeur, -euse [rɔ̃ʒœr, -øz] *Zool* ADJ *(mammifère)* rodent-like

NM *Zool* rodent

ronron [rɔ̃rɔ̃] NM **1** *(d'un chat)* purr, purring *(UNCOUNT)*; **faire r.** to purr **2** *(d'une machine)* whirr, hum **3** *(routine)* routine; **le r. de la vie quotidienne** the daily routine

ronronnement [rɔ̃rɔnmɑ̃] NM **1** *(d'un chat)* purr, purring *(UNCOUNT)* **2** *(d'une machine)* whirr, hum, whirring *(UNCOUNT)*, humming *(UNCOUNT)*; *(d'un bon moteur)* purr, purring

(UNCOUNT); *(d'un avion)* drone, droning *(UNCOUNT)*

ronronner [3] [rɔ̃rɔne] VI **1** *(chat)* to purr; **r. de plaisir** to purr with pleasure **2** *(machine)* to whirr, to hum; *(bon moteur)* to purr; *(avion)* to drone

roque [rɔk] NM *Échecs* castling; **petit/grand r.** king's/queen's side castling

roquefort [rɔkfɔr] NM Roquefort (cheese)

roquer [3] [rɔke] VI **1** *Échecs* to castle **2** *(au croquet)* to croquet the ball

roquet [rɔkɛ] NM **1** *(chien)* yappy *or* noisy dog; **sale r.!** damn *or Br* bloody animal! **2** *Fam Péj (personne)* pest; **espèce de petit r.!** you little pest!

roquette [rɔkɛt] NF **1** *(projectile)* rocket; **r. antichar** anti-tank rocket **2** *Bot Br* rocket, *Am* arugula

rorqual, -als [rɔrkwal] NM *Zool* rorqual; **grand r.** blue whale; **petit r.** minke (whale); **r. commun** fin whale

rosace [rozas] NF *Archit (moulure)* (ceiling) rose; *(vitrail)* rose window, rosace; *(figure)* rosette

rosacé, -e [rozase] ADJ **1** *Bot* rose-like, *Spéc* rosaceous **2** *Méd* **acné rosacée** acne rosacea

rosaire [rozɛr] NM **1** *(chapelet)* rosary; **égrener un r.** to count *or Br* to tell one's beads **2** *(prières)* **dire** *ou* **réciter son r.** to recite the rosary

rosâtre [rozatr] ADJ pinkish, *Littéraire* roseate

Rosbif [rɔzbif] NMF *Fam (Britannique)* Brit, = pejorative or humorous term used with reference to British people

rosbif [rɔzbif] NM *(cru)* roasting beef *(UNCOUNT)*, joint *or* piece of beef *(for roasting)*; *(cuit)* roast beef *(UNCOUNT)*, joint of roast beef

rose [roz] ADJ **1** *(gén)* pink; *(teint, joue)* rosy; **r. bonbon/saumon** candy/salmon pink; **r. fluo** fluorescent *or* dayglo pink

2 *(agréable)* **la vie d'un athlète n'est pas toujours r.** an athlete's life isn't all roses; **ce n'est pas (tout) r.** it isn't exactly a bed of roses

3 *(érotique)* erotic, soft-porn *(avant n)*

4 *Pol* left-wing *(relating to the French Socialist Party)*

NF **1** *Bot* rose; **r. blanche/rouge** white/red rose; **r. de Damas** damask rose; **r. de Jéricho** rose of Jericho, resurrection plant; **r. trémière** rose mallow, *Br* hollyhock; **teint de r.** rosy complexion; *Fam Euph* **ça ne sent pas la r. ici** it stinks a bit, *Br* it's a bit whiffy; *Fam* **envoyer qn sur les roses** to send sb packing, to tell sb where to go *or* where to get off; *Prov* **il n'y a pas de r. sans épines** there's no rose without a thorn **2** *Archit* rose window, rosace **3** *(en joaillerie)* **(diamant en) r.** rose (diamond)

NM **1** *(couleur)* pink; **r. nacré** oyster pink **2** *(locution)* **voir la vie** *ou* **tout en r.** to see things through rose-tinted *Br* spectacles *or Am* glasses

• **rose des sables, rose du désert** NF gypsum flower

• **rose des vents** NF wind rose

rosé, -e[1] [roze] ADJ **1** *(teinte)* pinkish, rosy **2** *(vin)* rosé

NM rosé (wine)

roseau, -x [rozo] NM *Bot* reed; **le r. plie mais ne rompt pas** the reed bends but does not break

rose-croix [rozkrwa] NM INV Rosicrucian; **les r.** the Rosicrucians

NF **la r.** Rosicrucianism

rosée[2] [roze] NF dew; *Phys* **point de r.** dew point

roselet [rozlɛ] NM *(fourrure)* ermine

roselier, -ère [rozəlje, -jɛr] ADJ **marais r.** reed marsh

NF **roselière** reed bed

roséole [rozeɔl] NF *Méd* roseola

roser [3] [roze] VT *Littéraire* **r. qch** to make *or* turn sth pink

roseraie [rozrɛ] NF rose garden, rosery, rosarium

Rosette [rozɛt] NPR Rosetta; **la pierre de R.** the Rosetta stone

rosette [rozɛt] NF **1** *(nœud)* bow; **faire une r.** to tie a bow **2** *(cocarde)* rosette; **avoir/recevoir la r.** *(de la Légion d'honneur)* to have been awarded/be awarded the Legion of Honour **3** *Culin* **r. (de Lyon)** = broad type of salami

rosicrucien, -enne [rozikrysjɛ̃, -ɛn] ADJ Rosicrucian

NM,F Rosicrucian

rosier [rozje] NM *Bot* rosebush, rose tree; **r. grimpant/nain** climbing/dwarf rose; **r. sauvage** wild dog *or* rose

rosière [rozjɛr] NF = young girl traditionally awarded a crown of roses and a prize for virgin purity

rosiériste [rozjerist] NMF rose grower, rosarian

rosir [32] [rozir] VT to give a pink hue to; **l'air de la montagne avait rosi ses joues** the mountain air had tinged *or* suffused his/her cheeks with pink

VI *(ciel)* to turn pink; *(personne)* to go pink

rosse [rɔs] *Fam* ADJ *(chanson, portrait)* nasty[❑], vicious[❑]; *(conduite)* rotten, lousy, horrid[❑]; *(personne)* nasty[❑], horrid[❑], catty; **être r. envers** *ou* **avec qn** to be horrid *or* nasty to sb; **un professeur r.** a hard[❑] *or* tough[❑] teacher

NF **1** *(personne)* rotten beast, *Br* rotter **2** *Vieilli (cheval)* nag, jade

rossée [rɔse] NF *Fam* hiding, thrashing; **flanquer une r. à qn** to give sb a good hiding *or* thrashing

rosser [3] [rɔse] VT *Fam* **1** *(frapper)* to thrash; **se faire r.** to get thrashed **2** *(vaincre)* to thrash, to hammer; **se faire r.** to get thrashed, to get hammered

rosserie [rɔsri] NF *Fam* **1** *(remarque)* nasty remark[❑]; *(acte)* dirty trick; **dire des rosseries sur qn** to say nasty[❑] *or* rotten things about sb **2** *(caractère)* nastiness[❑], rottenness; **il/elle est d'une r.!** he's/she's rotten *or Br* a rotter!

rossignol [rɔsiɲɔl] NM **1** *Orn* nightingale **2** *(clef)* picklock, skeleton key **3** *Fam (objet démodé)* piece of junk; **on t'a refilé un r.** they've sold you a dud *or* a piece of junk

rossinante [rɔsinɑ̃t] NF *Littéraire (cheval)* scrag, nag

rostre [rɔstr] NM *Antiq & Zool* rostrum

rot[1] [rɔt] NM *Bot* rot

rot[2] [ro] NM *(renvoi)* belch, burp; **faire** *ou* **lâcher un r.** to (let out a) belch *or* burp; **il a fait son r.?** *(bébé)* has he burped?; **faire faire son r. à un bébé** to burp a baby

rôt [ro] NM *Arch (rôti)* roast

rotatif, -ive [rɔtatif, -iv] ADJ *(mouvement)* rotary, rotating; *(moteur, pompe)* rotary

• **rotative** NF *Typ* (rotary) press; *Fig* **faire tourner** *ou* **marcher les rotatives** to give the newspapers something to write about

rotation [rɔtasjɔ̃] NF **1** *(mouvement) & Géom* rotation; *(sur un axe)* spinning; *Sport* turn, turning *(UNCOUNT)*; **angle/sens/vitesse de r.** angle/direction/speed of rotation; **mouvement de r.** rotational *or Spéc* rotary motion; **masse en r.** rotating mass; **effectuer une r.** to rotate, to spin round

2 *(renouvellement)* turnover; **r. des stocks/du personnel** inventory/staff turnover; **le délai de r. des stocks est de quatre mois** stocks are turned round every four months

3 *Fin* turnover; **r. des capitaux** turnover of capital; *Bourse* **r. de portefeuille** churning

4 *Agr* **la r. des cultures** crop rotation

rotative [rɔtativ] *voir* **rotatif**

rotatoire [rɔtatwar] ADJ **1** *(mouvement)* rotatory, rotary **2** *Chim* **pouvoir r.** rotatory power

rote[1] [rɔt] NF *Cathol (tribunal)* Rota

rote[2] [rɔt] NF *Belg Fam* anger[❑], rage[❑]; **être/se mettre en r. (contre qn)** to be/to go mad *or* crazy (at sb); **mettre qn en r.** to make sb hopping mad

roter [3] [rɔte] VI to belch, to burp

roteuse [rɔtøz] NF *Fam (bouteille de champagne)* bottle of bubbly *or Br* champers

rôti [roti] NM *(viande ▸ crue)* joint *(of meat for roasting)*; *(▸ cuite)* joint, roast; **r. de porc** *(cru)* joint *or* piece of pork for roasting; *(cuit)* piece of roast pork

rôtie [roti] NF *(pain grillé)* slice of toast

rotin [rɔtɛ̃] NM **1** *Bot (tige)* rattan; **chaise en r.** rattan chair **2** *Fam (sou)* **il n'a plus un r.** he's totally broke *or Br* skint

rôtir [32] [rotir] VT **1** *(cuire)* to roast; **faire r. une viande** to roast a piece of meat; **dinde rôtie** roast turkey; **quand la viande est bien rôtie** when the meat is done to a turn **2** *Fam (dessécher ▸ terre)* to parch; *(▸ plantes)* to dry up, to parch; **le soleil me rôtissait le dos** my back was getting roasted by the sun

VI *(cuire)* to roast; **mettre une oie à r.** to roast a goose; *Fam* **baisse le thermostat, on va r.** turn down the thermostat or we'll roast

VPR **se rôtir** *Fam* **se r. au soleil** to bask *or* to fry in the sun

rôtissage [rotisaʒ] NM *Culin* roasting

rôtisserie [rotisri] NF **1** *(restaurant)* grillroom, steakhouse, rotisserie **2** *(magasin)* rotisserie *(shop selling roast meat)*

rôtisseur, -euse [rotisœr, -øz] NM,F **1** *(restaurateur)* grillroom *or* steakhouse owner; *(cuisinier)* roaster (chef) **2** *(vendeur)* seller of roast meat

rôtissoire [rotiswar] NF *(appareil)* roaster; *(broche)* (roasting) spit, rotisserie

rotogravure [rɔtɔgravyr] NF rotogravure

rotonde [rɔtɔ̃d] NF **1** *Archit* rotunda; **disposition en r.** circular layout **2** *(dans les autobus)* semicircular bench seat *(at rear)* **3** *Rail* (circular) engine shed, roundhouse

rotondité [rɔtɔ̃dite] NF **1** *(forme sphérique)* rotundity, roundness **2** *(corpulence)* plumpness, rotundity; *Hum* **rotondités** *(de femme)* curves

rotor [rɔtɔr] NM rotor; *(d'un hélicoptère)* rotor arm

rottweiler, rottweiller [rɔtvajlœr] NM *(chien)* Rottweiler

rotule [rɔtyl] NF **1** *Anat* kneecap, *Spéc* patella; *Fam* **être sur les rotules** to be wiped (out) *or Br* knackered; *Fam* **mettre qn sur les rotules** to wipe sb out, *Br* to knacker sb **2** *Tech* ball-and-socket joint; **à r.** ball-and-socket *(avant n)*

rotulien, -enne [rɔtyljɛ̃, -ɛn] ADJ *Anat* patellar

roture [rɔtyr] NF *Littéraire* commonalty; **elle a épousé quelqu'un de la r.** she married a commoner

roturier, -ère [rɔtyrje, -ɛr] ADJ *Hist (non noble)* common; **être d'origine roturière** to be of common birth *or* stock

NM,F *Hist* commoner, plebeian

rouage [rwaʒ] NM **1** *Tech* moving part, movement; *(engrenage)* cogwheel; **les rouages d'une horloge** the works *or* movement of a clock **2** *Fig* cog; **il n'était qu'un r. dans la vaste machine politique** he was only a cog in the huge political machine; **les rouages de la justice** the wheels of justice; **une organisation aux rouages bien huilés** a smooth-running organization, an organization that runs like clockwork

rouan, -anne [rwɑ̃, -an] ADJ roan

NM roan (horse)

roubignoles [rubiɲɔl] NF *Vulg (testicules)* balls, *Br* bollocks

roublard, -e [rublar, -ard] *Fam* ADJ *(rusé)* sly[❑], wily[❑], crafty[❑]

NM,F dodger; **c'est un fin r.** he's a sly (old) fox *or* devil, he's an artful dodger

roublardise [rublardiz] NF *Fam* **1** *(habileté)* slyness[❑], craftiness[❑], wiliness[❑] **2** *(manœuvre)* clever *or* crafty trick, dodge

rouble [rubl] NM rouble

roucoulade [rukulad] NF **1** *(d'un pigeon)* (billing and) cooing *(UNCOUNT)* **2** *(des amoureux)* billing and cooing *(UNCOUNT)*

roucoulement [rukulmɑ̃] NM **1** *(du pigeon)* (billing and) cooing *(UNCOUNT)* **2** *(des amoureux)* billing and cooing

roucouler [3] [rukule] VI **1** *(pigeon)* to (bill and) coo **2** *(amoureux)* to bill and coo, to whisper sweet nothings

VT **1** *(sujet: amoureux)* to coo **2** *Péj (sujet: chanteur)* to croon

roudoudou [rududu] NM *Fam Br* hard sweet, *Am* candy *(licked out of a small round box or shell)*

roue [ru] NF **1** *Transp* wheel; **véhicule à deux/trois roues** two-wheeled/three-wheeled vehicle; **r. directrice** guiding *or* leading wheel; **r. motrice** drive *or* driving wheel; **r. de secours** spare (wheel); **pousser à la r.** to give a helping hand; **je voudrais les empêcher de s'engager dans l'armée mais leur père pousse à la r.** I'd like to stop them joining up but their father is egging them on

2 *Tech (cog or gear)* wheel; **r. crantée** toothed wheel; **r. dentée** cog (wheel), toothed wheel; **r. à godets** bucket wheel; **r. hydraulique** water-wheel; **r. libre** freewheel; **j'ai descendu la côte en r. libre** I freewheeled down the hill

3 *(objet circulaire)* wheel; **une r. de gruyère** a large round Gruyère cheese; **la grande r.** the Ferris wheel, *Br* the big wheel; **la r. de la Fortune** the wheel of Fortune; **la r. tourne** the wheel of Fortune is turning; **faire la r.** *(paon)* to spread *or* to fan its tail; *(gymnaste)* to do a cartwheel; *(séducteur)* to strut about

4 *Hist* **(le supplice de) la r.** the wheel

5 *Naut* **r. à aubes** *ou* **à palettes** paddle wheel; **r. du gouvernail** helm

6 *(locution)* **être la cinquième r. du carrosse** to feel utterly superfluous, to feel like a fifth wheel

roué, -e [rwe] **ADJ** sly, tricky, wily

NM,F sly fox

rouelle [rwɛl] **NF 1** *Culin* **r. (de veau)** thick round of veal **2** *(rondelle)* (round) slice

rouennais, -e [rwanɛ, -ɛz] **ADJ** of/from Rouen

• **Rouennais, -e NM,F** = inhabitant of or person from Rouen

rouer [6] [rwe] **VT 1** *Hist* **r. qn** to break sb on the wheel **2** *(locution)* **r. qn de coups** to pummel sb

rouerie [ruri] **NF** *Littéraire* **1** *(caractère)* cunning, foxiness, wiliness **2** *(manœuvre)* sly *or* cunning trick

rouet [rwɛ] **NM 1** *(pour filer)* spinning wheel **2** *Tech (de poulie)* sheave; *(de serrure)* ward

rouf [ruf] **NM** *Naut* deckhouse

rouge [ruʒ] **ADJ 1** *(gén)* red; **être r.** *(après un effort)* to be flushed, to be red in the face; **être r. de plaisir/de colère** to be flushed with pleasure/anger; **être r. de honte** to be red in the face (with shame), to be red-faced; **r. brique** brick-red; **r. sang** blood-red; **r. vermillon** vermilion; **être r. comme un coq** *ou* **un coquelicot** *ou* **une écrevisse** *ou* **une pivoine** *ou* **une tomate** to be as red as a lobster *or Br* a beetroot; **quand il est arrivé il était tout r. tellement il avait couru** when he arrived he was all red in the face *or* his face was all flushed from having run so much; **la mer R.** the Red Sea; **la place R.** Red Square

2 *(pelage, cheveux)* red, ginger, *Péj* carroty

3 *Métal* red-hot

4 *Péj (communiste)* red

NMF *Péj (communiste)* Red

NM 1 *(couleur)* red; **le r. lui monta au visage** he/she went red in the face, his/her face went red; **r. cerise** cherry red

2 *Transp* **le feu est passé au r.** the lights turned to *or* went red; **la voiture est passée au r.** the car went through a red light

3 *Fam (vin)* red wine▫; **bouteille de r.** a bottle of red; **un coup de r.** a glass of red wine▫; **du gros r.** cheap red wine▫; **du gros r. qui tache** (red) plonk

4 *(cosmétique)* **r. (à joues)** blusher, rouge

5 *Métal* **porté au r.** red-hot; **portez le métal au r.** heat the metal until it's red-hot

6 *Banque* red; **je suis dans le r.** I'm in the red *or* overdrawn; **sortir du r.** *(cesser d'être en déficit)* to get out of the red, to clear one's overdraft

ADV 1 *Péj Pol* **voter r.** to vote communist **2** *(locution)* **voir r.** to see red

• **rouge à lèvres NM** lipstick

rougeâtre [ruʒatr] **ADJ** reddish, reddy

rougeaud, -e [ruʒo, -od] **ADJ** red-faced, ruddy, ruddy-cheeked

NM,F red-faced *or* ruddy *or* ruddy-cheeked person

rouge-gorge [ruʒgɔrʒ] *(pl* **rouges-gorges***)* **NM** *Orn* robin

rougeoiement [ruʒwamɑ̃] **NM** reddish glow

rougeole [ruʒɔl] **NF** measles *(singulier)*; **avoir la r.** to have (the) measles

rougeoleux, -euse [ruʒɔlø, -øz] **ADJ** *(enfant)* suffering from measles

NM,F person with measles

rougeoyant, -e [ruʒwajɑ̃, -ɑ̃t] **ADJ** glowing (red); **lueur rougeoyante** flush of red, red glow

rougeoyer [13] [ruʒwaje] **VI 1** *(briller)* to glow (red) **2** *(devenir rouge)* to turn red, to redden, to take on a reddish hue

rouge-queue [ruʒkø] *(pl* **rouges-queues***)* **NM** *Orn* redstart

rouget [ruʒɛ] **NM** *Ich* **r. barbet** *ou* **de vase** red mullet; red gurnard; **r. de roche** surmullet

rougeur [ruʒœr] **NF 1** *(couleur ▸ du ciel)* redness, glow; *(▸ des joues)* redness, ruddiness **2** *(rougissement)* flush, blush; **sa r. l'a trahie** her blush gave her away **3** *Méd* red patch *or* blotch

rougir [32] [ruʒir] **VT 1** *(colorer en rouge)* **r. son eau** to put a drop of (red) wine in one's water; **des yeux rougis par les larmes/la poussière** eyes red with weeping/with the dust **2** *Métal* to heat to red heat *or* until red-hot **3** *Fig Littéraire* **mes mains sont rougies de (son) sang** my hands are stained with (his/her) blood

VI 1 *(chose, personne ▸ gén)* to go *or* to turn red; *(personne ▸ de gêne)* to blush; *(▸ d'excitation)* to flush; **les pommes/mes joues rougissent** the apples/my cheeks are turning red; **r. de plaisir/colère** to flush with pleasure/anger; **r. de honte** to blush with shame; **"je vous aime", dit-il en rougissant** "I love you," he said, blushing *or* with a blush; **je me sentais r.** I could feel myself going red (in the face); **faire r. qn** to make sb blush; *Hum* **arrête, tu vas me faire r.** spare my blushes, please; **r. jusqu'au blanc des yeux** *ou* **jusqu'aux oreilles** to blush to the roots of one's hair **2** *Fig* **r. de qn/qch** *(avoir honte de)* to be ashamed of sb/sth; **tu n'as pas/il n'y a pas à en r.** there's nothing for you/nothing to be ashamed of; **ne r. de rien** to be shameless **3** *Métal* to become red-hot

rougissant, -e [ruʒisɑ̃, -ɑ̃t] **ADJ** reddening; *(de gêne)* blushing; *(d'excitation)* flushing

rougissement [ruʒismɑ̃] **NM** reddening; *(de gêne)* blushing; *(d'excitation)* flushing

rouille [ruj] **NF 1** *(corrosion d'un métal)* rust; **traiter une surface contre la r.** to rustproof a surface **2** *Bot & Agr* **r. blanche** white rust; **r. du blé** wheat rust; **r. des feuilles** leaf mould; **r. noire des céréales** stem rust **3** *Culin* rouille sauce *(spicy sauce made with hot red peppers and garlic)*

ADJ INV rust, rust-coloured

rouillé, -e [ruje] **ADJ 1** *(grille, clef)* rusty, rusted; **la serrure est complètement rouillée** the lock is rusted up **2** *Fig (muscles)* stiff; **être r.** *(physiquement ▸ gén)* to feel stiff; *(▸ athlète)* to be out of practice; *(intellectuellement)* to feel a bit rusty **3** *Bot (blé)* affected by rust, rusted; *(feuille)* mouldy

rouiller [3] [ruje] **VT 1** *(métal)* to rust **2** *(intellect, mémoire)* to make rusty

VI to rust, to go rusty

VPR se rouiller 1 *(métal, outil, machine)* to rust up, to get rusty **2** *(intellect, mémoire)* to become *or* to get rusty **3** *(muscle)* to grow *or* to get stiff; *(athlète)* to get out of practice

rouillure [rujyr] **NF 1** *Chim* rustiness **2** *Bot* rust, rusting *(UNCOUNT)*

roulade [rulad] **NF 1** *Mus* roulade, run

2 *(d'un oiseau)* trill

3 *Culin* rolled meat, roulade; **r. de bœuf** rolled (piece of) beef, beef roulade

4 *(culbute)* roll; **r. avant/arrière** forward/backward roll; **faire des roulades** to do rolls

roulage [rulaʒ] **NM 1** *Agr & Métal* rolling

2 *(transport)* haulage; **entreprise de r.** carrier, haulier, *Am* hauler

3 *Naut* **manutention par r.** roll-on-roll-off

4 *Belg (circulation)* traffic; **accident de r.** traffic accident

roulant, -e [rulɑ̃, -ɑ̃t] **ADJ 1** *(surface)* moving; *(meuble)* on wheels **2** *Rail* **matériel r.** rolling stock; **personnel r.** train crews **3** *Fin (capital, fonds)* working

• **roulante NF** field *or* mobile kitchen

roulé, -e [rule] **ADJ 1** *Couture* rolled

2 *Ling* **r r.** rolled *or* trilled r

3 *Culin (gâteau, viande)* rolled

4 *Fam (locution)* **elle est bien roulée** she's curvy

NM *(gâteau)* Swiss roll; *(viande)* = meat in a roll of puff pastry; **r. au chocolat** chocolate Swiss roll

rouleau, -x [rulo] **NM 1** *(de papier, de tissu, de pellicule)* roll; *(de fil)* coil; **r. de papier hygiénique** roll of toilet paper, *Br* toilet roll; **r. de parchemin** roll *or* scroll of parchment; **r. de pièces** roll of coins; **r. de réglisse** liquorice roll

2 *(outil ▸ de peintre, de jardinier, de relieur)* roller; *(cylindre ▸ de machine à écrire)* barrel, platen; **r. imprimeur** *ou* **encreur** (press) cylinder; **r. à pâtisserie**, *Can & Suisse* **r. à pâte** rolling pin

3 *(bigoudi)* roller, curler

4 *Culin* **r. de printemps** spring roll

5 *Sport (en saut en hauteur)* roll; **sauter en r.** to do a roll; **r. costal** western roll; **r. dorsal** Fosbury flop; **r. ventral** straddle

6 *(vague)* roller

7 *Constr* roller; **r. compresseur** *(à gazole)* roadroller; *(à vapeur)* steamroller; *Fig* steamroller; **le r. compresseur de la mondialisation** the steamroller of globalization

roulé-boulé [rulebule] *(pl* **roulés-boulés***)* **NM** *(culbute)* roll; **faire des roulés-boulés** to roll

roulement [rulmɑ̃] **NM 1** *(mouvement)* **un r. d'yeux** a roll of the eyes; **un r. de hanches** a swing of the hips

2 *(grondement)* rumble, rumbling *(UNCOUNT)*; **le r. du tonnerre** the rumble *or* roll *or* peal of thunder; **un r. de tonnerre** a roll *or* rumble of thunder, a thunderclap; **le r. des canons** the rumble *or* roar of the cannons; **r. de tambour** drum roll

3 *(tour de rôle)* rotation; **établir un r.** to set up *Br* a rota *or Am* a rotation system; **par r.** in rotation

4 *Tech (mécanisme)* bearing; **r. à billes/à rouleaux/à aiguilles** ball/roller/needle bearings

5 *Fin* **r. des capitaux** circulation of capital

ROULER [3] [rule]

VT	
• to roll **1–3, 6–8**	• to roll up **2**
• to diddle, to swindle **4**	• to sway **5**
• to roll out **6**	
VI	
• to go **1**	• to drive **1**
• to roll **2–4**	• to take turns **5**

VT 1 *(faire tourner)* to roll; **r. les yeux** to roll one's eyes; **r. de sombres pensées** to turn dark thoughts over in one's mind; *très Fam* **r. une pelle** *ou* **une galoche** *ou* **un pallot** *ou* **un patin à qn** to French-kiss sb, *Br* to snog sb; *Fig* **r. qn dans la farine** to pull the wool over sb's eyes

2 *(poster, tapis, bas de pantalon)* to roll up; *(corde, câble)* to roll up, to wind up; *(cigarette)* to roll; **aide-moi à r. la laine en pelote** help me to wind the wool up into a ball; **r. un blessé dans une couverture** to wrap an injured person in a blanket

3 *(déplacer ▸ Caddie®)* to push (along); *(▸ balle, tronc, fût)* to roll (along); **il a roulé le rocher jusqu'en bas de la colline** he rolled the rock right down the hill; *Vieilli* **r. carrosse** to have an expensive lifestyle; *Fam* **j'ai roulé ma bosse** I've been around, I've seen it all

4 *Fam (escroquer ▸ lors d'un paiement)* to diddle; *(▸ dans une affaire)* to swindle▫; **elle m'a roulé de cinq euros** she diddled *or* did me out of five euros; **se faire r.** to be conned *or* had; **ce n'est pas du cuir, je me suis fait r.** it's not genuine leather, I've been done *or* had

5 *(balancer)* **r. des** *ou* **les épaules** to sway one's shoulders; **r. des** *ou* **les hanches** to swing one's hips; *Fam* **r. des mécaniques** to walk with a swagger; *Fig* to come *or* to play the hard guy

6 *(aplatir ▸ gazon, court de tennis)* to roll; *Culin (pâte)* to roll out

7 *Ling* **r. les r** to roll one's r's

VI 1 *(véhicule)* to go, to run; *(conducteur)* to drive; **une voiture qui a peu/beaucoup roulé** a car with a low/high mileage; **et ta Renault, elle roule toujours?** is your Renault still going *or* running?; **la moto roulait au milieu de la route** the motorbike was going *or* driving down the middle of the road; **à quelle vitesse rouliez-vous?** what speed were you travelling at?, what speed were you doing?, how fast were you going?; **j'ai beaucoup roulé quand j'étais jeune** I did a lot of driving when I was young; **seulement deux heures? tu as bien roulé!** only two hours? you've made good time!; **r. au pas** to go at a walking pace, to crawl along; **roule moins vite** slow down, drive more slowly; **elle roule en Jaguar** she drives (around in) a Jaguar; **r. à moto/à bicyclette** to ride a motorbike/a bicycle; **ça roule mal/bien dans Anvers** there's a lot of traffic/there's no traffic through Antwerp

2 *(balle, dé, rocher)* to roll; **ses billes allèrent r. dans le caniveau** his/her marbles rolled down into the gutter; **des larmes roulaient sur sa joue** tears were rolling down his/her cheeks; **faire r.** *(balle)* to roll; *(chariot)* to wheel (along); *(roue)* to roll along; **il a roulé jusqu'en bas du champ** he rolled *or* tumbled down to the bottom of the field; *Fam* **r. sous la table** to end up (dead drunk) under the table

3 *Naut* to roll

4 *(gronder ▸ tonnerre)* to roll, to rumble; *(▸ tambour)* to roll

5 *(se succéder)* to take turns; **nous ferons r. les équipes dès janvier** as from January, we'll start the teams off on *Br* a rota system *or Am* rotation

6 *(argent)* to circulate; **il sait faire r. l'argent** he knows how to make money work

7 r. sur *(conversation)* to be centred upon; **la conversation a d'abord roulé sur la politique** we started off talking about politics

8 *Fam (locutions) (aller bien)* **ça roule** things are fine, everything's OK; **salut! ça roule?** hi, how are things?; **r. sur l'or** to be rolling in money *or* in it; **mon salaire est correct, mais je ne roule pas sur l'or** I've got a decent salary, but I'm not exactly well-off *or* rolling in it

VPR **se rouler 1** *(se vautrer)* **se r. par terre** *(de douleur)* to be doubled up with pain; *(de rire)* to be doubled up with laughter; **c'était à se r. par terre** *(de rire)* it was hysterically funny

2 *très Fam* **se r. une pelle** *Br* to snog, *Am* to make out; *Fam* **s'en r. une** to roll a smoke *or Br* a fag; *Fam* **se r. les pouces, se les r.** to twiddle one's thumbs

roulette [rulɛt] NF **1** *(roue ▸ libre)* wheel; *(▸ sur pivot)* caster, castor; **à roulettes** *(libres)* with wheels; *(sur pivot)* on casters *or* castors; *Fam* **marcher** *ou* **aller comme sur des roulettes** *(opération)* to go off without a hitch; *(organisation, projet)* to go like clockwork; *Fam* **et ton entrevue? – ça a marché comme sur des roulettes** what about your interview? – it all went off very smoothly *or* without a hitch **2** *(ustensile ▸ de relieur)* fillet (wheel); *(▸ de graveur)* roulette; *Couture* tracing wheel; **r. de dentiste** dentist's drill; **r. à pâte** pastry cutting wheel **3** *(jeu)* roulette; *(roue)* roulette wheel; **r. russe** Russian roulette; *aussi Fig* **jouer à la r. russe** to play Russian roulette; **c'est un peu la r. russe, ta proposition** your proposal is a bit dicey *or* is pretty much of a gamble

rouleur [rulœr] NM *Cyclisme* flat racer; **c'est un bon r.** he's good on the flat

roulier [rulje] NM **1** *Hist* cart driver **2** *Naut* roll-on-roll-off ship

rouli-roulant [rulirulɑ̃] *(pl* **roulis-roulants***)* NM *Can* skateboard

roulis [ruli] NM *Aviat & Naut* roll, rolling; **il y a du r.** the ship is rolling; **coup de r.** strong roll; **il y eut un grand coup de r.** the ship started to roll violently

roulotte [rulɔt] NF **1** *(tirée par des chevaux)* horse-drawn caravan **2** *(caravane)* caravan, mobile home

roulotté, -e [rulɔte] *Couture* ADJ *(ourlet)* rolled
NM rolled hem

roulottier [rulɔtje] NM *Fam (voleur)* = thief who robs parked cars

roulure [rulyr] NF *très Fam Péj* **1** *(prostituée)* hooker, whore **2** *(homme méprisable)* bastard, *Am* son-of-a-bitch; *(femme méprisable)* bitch

roumain, -e [rumɛ̃, -ɛn] ADJ Rumanian, Ro(u)manian
NM *(langue)* Romanian
• **Roumain, -e** NM,F Rumanian, Ro(u)manian

Roumanie [rumani] NF **la R.** Romania, Ro(u)mania

round [rawnd, rund] NM *(à la boxe, dans un débat)* round

roupettes [rupɛt] NFPL *très Fam (testicules)* nuts, balls

roupie [rupi] NF **1** *(monnaie)* rupee **2** *(locutions)* **c'est de la r. de sansonnet** that's (worthless) rubbish; **ce n'est pas de la r. de sansonnet** it's not to be sniffed at

roupiller [3] [rupije] VI *Fam (dormir)* to sleep□, *Br* to kip; *(faire un somme)* to get some shut-eye, *Br* to have a kip

roupillon [rupijɔ̃] NM *Fam* snooze, nap, *Br* kip; **faire** *ou* **piquer un r.** to have a snooze *or* a nap *or Br* a kip

rouquin, -e [rukɛ̃, -in] *Fam* ADJ *(personne)* red-haired□, ginger-haired; *(chevelure)* red□, ginger, *Péj* carroty; **elle est rouquine** she has red□ *or* ginger *or Péj* carroty hair
NM,F redhead
NM *(vin)* red wine□

rouscailler [3] [ruskaje] VI *très Fam* to whinge, to moan (and groan)

rouspétance [ruspetɑ̃s] NF *Fam* moaning (and groaning), grumbling; **pas de r.!** I don't want to hear any moaning (and groaning) *or* grumbling!

rouspéter [18] [ruspete] VI *Fam* to moan (and groan), to grumble (**contre** about)

rouspéteur, -euse [ruspetœr, -øz] *Fam* ADJ grumpy, grouchy
NM,F moaner, grumbler

roussâtre [rusatr] ADJ reddish

rousse [rus] *voir* **roux**

rousserolle [rusrɔl] NF *Orn* reed warbler

roussette [rusɛt] NF **1** *Ich* spotted dogfish; *Culin* rock salmon **2** *Zool (chauve-souris)* flying fox **3** *Zool (grenouille)* common frog

rousseur [rusœr] NF *(teinte)* redness, gingery colour
• **rousseurs** NFPL *(sur le papier)* foxing

roussi [rusi] NM **ça sent le r.** something's burning; *Fam Fig* there's trouble ahead *or* brewing; **il a démissionné quand ça a commencé à sentir le r.** he resigned when things started going wrong

roussin[1] [rusɛ̃] NM *Hist (cheval)* charger

roussin[2] [rusɛ̃] NM *Fam Vieilli (policier)* policeman□; *(espion)* police spy□

roussir [32] [rusir] VT **1** *(rendre roux)* **r. qch** to turn sth brown **2** *(brûler)* to scorch, to singe; **la gelée a roussi l'herbe** the grass has turned brown with the frost
VI **1** *(feuillage, arbre)* to turn brown *or* russet **2** *Culin* **faire r. qch** to brown sth

rouste [rust] NF *Fam* thrashing, hammering; **flanquer une r. à qn** to give sb a thrashing *or* a hammering

roustons [rustɔ̃] NMPL *très Fam (testicules)* balls, nuts

routage [rutaʒ] NM **1** *(de courrier)* sorting and mailing **2** *Naut* routing; **assurer le r. d'un navire** to plot the course of a ship

routard, -e [rutar, -ard] NM,F *Fam* backpacker□

ROUTE [rut]

- road **1, 2, 5**
- way **3–5**
- path **5**
- route **3**
- journey **4**

NF **1** *(voie de circulation)* road; **les petites routes (de campagne)** small country roads; **c'est la r. de Genève** it's the road to Geneva; **sur r., la voiture consomme moins** when cruising *or* on the open road, the car's fuel consumption is lower; **il va y avoir du monde sur la r.** *ou* **les routes** there'll be a lot of cars on the roads *or* a lot of traffic; **je n'aime pas le savoir sur la r.** I don't like the idea of him driving; **tenir la r.** *(sujet: voiture)* to hold the road; *Fig* **cette politique ne tient pas la r.** there's no mileage in that policy; **r. départementale** secondary road; **r. nationale** major road, *Br* trunk road; **r. de montagne** mountain road

2 *(moyen de transport)* **par la r.** by road; **les accidents de la r.** road accidents; **les victimes de la r.** road casualties

3 *(itinéraire)* way; **chercher sa r.** to try and find one's way; **c'est sur ma r.** it's on my way; **faire r. vers** *(sujet: bateau)* to be headed for, to be en route for, to steer a course for; *(sujet: voiture, avion)* to head for *or* towards; *(sujet: personne)* to be on one's way to, to head for; **en r. pour** *ou* **vers** bound for; **faisant r. vers** *(sujet: bateau, avion)* bound for, heading for, on its way to; *(sujet: personne)* on one's way to, heading for; **prendre la r. des vacances/du soleil** to set off on holiday/to the south; **r. aérienne** air route; **r. commerciale** commercial route, trade route; **la r. des épices** the spice trail *or* route; **la r. des Indes** the road to India; **r. maritime** shipping *or* sea route; **la r. de la soie** the silk road; **la R. des Vins** = tourist trail passing through wine country; **faire fausse r.** *(sujet: conducteur)* to go the wrong way, to take the wrong road; *Fig (dans un raisonnement)* to be on the wrong track

4 *(trajet)* journey; **j'ai fait la r. à pied** I did the journey on foot; **il y a six heures de r.** *(en voiture)* it's a six-hour drive *or* ride *or* journey; *(à bicyclette)* it's a six-hour ride *or* journey; **il y a une bonne heure de r.** it takes at least an hour to get there; **(faites) bonne r.!** have a good *or* safe journey!; **faire r. avec qn** to travel with sb; **faire de la r.** to do a lot of driving *or* mileage; **j'ai dû perdre ma montre en r.** I must have lost my watch on the way; **prendre la** *ou* **se mettre en r.** to set off, to get going; **reprendre la r., se remettre en r.** to set off again, to resume one's journey; **allez, en r.!** come on, let's go!

5 *Fig (voie)* road, way, path; **la r. du succès** the road to success; **la r. est toute tracée pour lui** the path is all laid out for him

6 mettre en r. *(appareil, véhicule)* to start (up); *(projet)* to set in motion, to get started *or* under way; **se mettre en r.** *(machine)* to start (up); *Fam* **j'ai du mal à me mettre en r. le matin** I find it hard to get started *or* going in the morning

> Il faut noter que le terme anglais **route** signifie **itinéraire, parcours.**

router [3] [rute] VT **1** *(courrier)* to sort and mail **2** *Naut (navire)* to plot a course for, to route

routeur, -euse [rutœr, -øz] NM,F **1** *Typ* sorting-and-mailing clerk **2** *Naut* route planner
NM *Ordinat* router

routier, -ère [rutje, -ɛr] ADJ road *(avant n)*
NM **1** *(chauffeur)* (long-distance) *Br* lorry *or Am* truck driver; *Fig* **c'est un vieux r. du journalisme** he's a veteran journalist **2** *Fam (restaurant) Br* transport café, *Am* truck-stop **3** *Sport (cycliste)* road racer *or* rider
• **routière** NF *Aut* touring car

routine [rutin] NF **1** *(habitude)* routine; **la r. quotidienne** the daily routine *or Péj* grind; **se laisser enfermer dans la r.** to get into a rut; **sortir de la r.** to get out of a rut **2** *Ordinat* routine
• **de routine** ADJ *(contrôle, visite)* routine *(avant n)*

routinier, -ère [rutinje, -ɛr] ADJ *(tâche, corvée)* routine *(avant n)*, *Péj* humdrum; *(vérification, méthode)* routine *(avant n)*; **être r.** *(personne)* to be a creature of habit, to like one's routine; **de façon routinière** routinely
NM,F **c'est un r.** he's a creature of habit, he likes his routine

rouvert, -e [ruvɛr, -ɛrt] PP *voir* **rouvrir**

rouvrir [34] [ruvrir] VT **1** *(livre, hôtel, débat, dossier)* to reopen **2** *Fig (raviver)* **r. une blessure** *ou* **plaie** to open an old wound
VI *(magasin)* to reopen, to open again
VPR **se rouvrir** *(porte, fenêtre)* to reopen; *(blessure)* to reopen, to open up again

roux, rousse [ru, rus] ADJ *(feuillage, fourrure)* reddish-brown, russet; *(chevelure, moustache)* red, ginger; *(vache)* brown; **une petite fille rousse** a little girl with red hair, a little redhead
NM,F redhead
• **rousse** NF *Fam Arg crime Vieilli* **la rousse** *(la police)* the fuzz, *Br* the Old Bill
NM **1** *(teinte ▸ d'un feuillage)* reddish-brown (colour), russet; *(▸ d'une chevelure, d'une moustache)* reddish *or* gingery colour **2** *Culin* roux

royal, -e, -aux, -ales [rwajal, -o] ADJ **1** *Hist & Pol (puissance)* royal, regal; *(bijoux, insignes, appartements, palais, académie)* royal; **la famille royale** *(en Grande-Bretagne)* the Royal Family; *(ailleurs)* the royal family; **prince r.** crown prince, heir apparent

2 *(somptueux ▸ cadeau)* magnificent, princely; *(▸ pourboire)* lavish; *(▸ salaire)* princely; *(▸ accueil)* royal; **un train de vie r.** a sumptuous lifestyle

3 *(extrême ▸ mépris)* total; *Fam* **il m'a fichu une paix royale** he left me in total peace

4 *Cartes* **quinte royale** royal flush

• **à la royale** ADJ *Culin* **lièvre à la royale** hare royale

royalement [rwajalmɑ̃] ADV **1** *(avec magnificence)* royally, regally; **ils nous ont reçus r.** they treated us like royalty; **il l'a r. payé** he paid him a princely sum **2** *Fam (complètement)* totally; **je m'en fiche** *ou* **moque r.!** I really couldn't care less!, I don't give a damn!

royalisme [rwajalism] NM royalism

royaliste [rwajalist] ADJ royalist; **il ne faut pas être plus r. que le roi** one mustn't try to out-Herod Herod *or* to be more Catholic than the Pope
NMF royalist

royalties [rwajalti] NFPL royalties *(for landowner or owner of patent)*

royaume [rwajom] NM **1** *Hist & Pol* kingdom
2 *Rel* **le r. céleste** *ou* **des cieux** the kingdom of Heaven; *Littéraire* **le r. des morts** the kingdom of the dead
3 *Fig (domaine)* realm; **le r. de l'imagination** the realm of the imagination; **mon atelier, c'est mon r.** my workshop is my private world *or* domain; **le r. éternel** the hereafter; **le r. des ombres** the netherworld
4 *(locutions)* **je ne le ferais pas/je n'en voudrais pas pour un r.** I wouldn't do it/have it for all the tea in China; *Prov* **au r. des aveugles, les borgnes sont rois** in the kingdom of the blind the one-eyed man is king

Royaume-Uni [rwajomyni] NM **le R. (de Grande-Bretagne et d'Irlande du Nord)** the United Kingdom (of Great Britain and Northern Ireland), the UK

royauté [rwajote] NF **1** *(monarchie)* monarchy **2** *(rang)* royalty, kingship; **il aspirait à la r.** he had designs on the throne

RP [erpe] NFPL *(abrév* **relations publiques***)* PR

RPR [erpeer] NM *Anciennement Pol (abrév* **Rassemblement pour la République***)* = right-wing French political party

RSS [ereses] NM *Ordinat (abrév* **Really Simple Syndication***)* RSS

RSVP *(abrév écrite* **répondez s'il vous plaît***)* RSVP

RTL [erteel] NF *(abrév* **Radio-télévision Luxembourg***)* = private broadcasting network based in Luxembourg

RTT [ertete] NF *(abrév* **réduction du temps de travail***)* = reduction of the working week in France from 39 to 35 hours, introduced by the government of Lionel Jospin in 1998 and phased in from 2000 onwards; **être en R.** to have time off *(because one has accumulated annual leave through the "RTT" system)*

RU [ry] NM *Fam (abrév* **restaurant universitaire***)* university cafeteria *or Br* canteen *or* refectory

ruade [ryad] NF kick; **lancer** *ou* **décocher une r. à** to kick *or* to lash out at

Ruanda [rwɑ̃da] = **Rwanda**

ruandais, -e [rwɑ̃dɛ, -ɛz] = **rwandais**

ruban [rybɑ̃] NM **1** *(ornement)* ribbon; *(liseré)* ribbon, tape; *(bolduc)* tape; *(sur chapeau)* band; **le r. rouge** the ribbon of the "Légion d'honneur"
2 *(de cassette)* tape; *(de machine à écrire)* ribbon; **r. adhésif** adhesive tape; **r. correcteur** correction tape; **r. isolant** insulating tape; **r. magnétique** magnetic *or* recording tape; *Ordinat* **r. perforé** perforated tape
4 *(en gymnastique rythmique)* ribbon

rubané, -e [rybane] ADJ *Géol* ribbon *(avant n)*, banded

rubaner [3] [rybane] VT *Vieilli* to decorate *or* adorn with ribbons

rubanerie [rybanri] NF *(fabrication)* ribbon manufacture; *(commerce)* ribbon trade

rubato [rubato] *Mus* ADV rubato
NM rubato

rubéole [rybeɔl] NF German measles *(UNCOUNT)*, *Spéc* rubella

rubican [rybikɑ̃] ADJ M roan

rubicond, -e [rybikɔ̃, -ɔ̃d] ADJ *Littéraire* rubicund, ruddy, rosy-cheeked

rubidium [rybidjɔm] NM *Chim* rubidium

rubis [rybi] NM **1** *(pierre précieuse)* ruby **2** *(d'une montre)* jewel, ruby

rubricard, -e [rybrikar, -ard] NM,F *Journ* columnist

rubrique [rybrik] NF **1** *(dans la presse* ▸ *article)* column; *(*▸*page)* page; *(*▸*cahier)* section; **la r. littéraire** the book column/page/section; **r. mondaine** society column; **la r. nécrologique** the obituaries; **r. pratique** advice column; **elle tient la r. cinéma** *(critiques)* she writes the movie *or Br* film reviews **2** *(catégorie)* heading; **la somme se trouve dans** *ou* **sous la r. frais généraux** the sum comes under the heading of overheads *or* is entered as an overhead **3** *(d'un dictionnaire)* field label

ruche [ryʃ] NF **1** *(abri* ▸ *en bois)* beehive; *(*▸ *en paille)* beehive, *Spéc* skep; *(colonie d'abeilles)* hive; *Fam* **se piquer la r.** *(s'enivrer)* to get wasted *or Br* pissed **2** *Fig* hive of activity **3** *Couture* ruche, rouche

ruché [ryʃe] NM *Couture* ruche, rouche; **des ruchés** ruching

ruchée [ryʃe] NF hive

rucher [ryʃe] NM apiary

rude [ryd] ADJ **1** *(rugueux* ▸ *surface, vin, peau)* rough; *(*▸ *toile)* rough, coarse; *(*▸ *brosse)* stiff, hard; *(*▸*voix)* gruff; *(*▸*son)* rough, harsh
2 *(*▸ *manières, paysan)* rough, uncouth, unrefined; *(*▸*traits)* rugged
3 *(difficile* ▸ *climat, hiver)* harsh, severe; *(*▸*conditions, concurrent)* tough; *(*▸ *concurrence)* severe, tough; *(*▸*vie, tâche)* hard, tough; *(*▸*métier)* demanding; *(*▸ *côte)* hard, stiff; **être mis à r. épreuve** *(personne)* to be severely tested, to be put through the mill; *(vêtement, matériel)* to get a lot of wear and tear; **ma patience a été mise à r. épreuve** it was a severe strain on my patience
4 *(sévère* ▸ *ton, voix)* rough, harsh, hard; *(*▸*personne)* harsh, hard, severe
5 *Fam (important, remarquable)* **avoir un r. appétit** to have a hearty appetite; **un r. gaillard** a hearty fellow; **ça a été un r. coup pour lui** it was a hard blow for him

> Il faut noter que le terme anglais **rude** est un faux ami. Il signifie **grossier**.

rudement [rydmɑ̃] ADV **1** *Fam (diablement)* **c'est r. bon/beau** it's really good/lovely; **c'est r. cher** it's incredibly *or* awfully expensive; **il est r. plus intelligent que son frère** he's a damn sight more intelligent than his brother; **elle est r. culottée!** she's got some gall *or Br* cheek!; **ça m'a fait r. mal!** it hurt like hell! **2** *(sans ménagement)* roughly, harshly; **tu lui parles trop r.** you talk to him/her too roughly **3** *(brutalement)* hard; **il a frappé à la porte r.** he banged hard on the door

rudesse [rydɛs] NF **1** *(rugosité* ▸ *d'une surface, d'un vin, de la peau)* roughness; *(*▸ *d'une toile)* roughness, coarseness; *(*▸ *d'une voix)* gruffness; *(*▸*d'un son)* roughness, harshness
2 *(rusticité* ▸ *des manières, d'un paysan)* roughness, uncouthness; *(*▸*des traits)* ruggedness
3 *(sévérité* ▸ *d'un ton, d'une voix)* roughness, harshness, hardness; *(*▸ *d'un maître)* severity, harshness; **traiter qn avec r.** to treat sb brusquely
4 *(dureté* ▸ *d'un climat, d'un hiver)* hardness, harshness, severity; *(*▸*d'une concurrence, d'une tâche)* toughness

rudiment [rydimɑ̃] NM *Biol* rudiment; **un r. de queue** a rudimentary tail
• **rudiments** NMPL *(d'un art, d'une science)* basics, rudiments; **tu apprendras vite les rudiments** you'll soon learn the basics; **apprendre les rudiments de la grammaire** to learn some basic grammar, to get a basic (working) knowledge of grammar; **je n'ai que des rudiments d'informatique** I have only a rudimentary knowledge of computing; **avoir des rudiments de chinois** to speak basic Chinese

rudimentaire [rydimɑ̃tɛr] ADJ **1** *(élémentaire)* rudimentary, basic; **des notions rudimentaires d'informatique** basic notions of computing
2 *(commençant)* rudimentary, undeveloped; **cette technique est encore r.** the technique is still in its infancy
3 *(succinct)* basic; **des informations trop rudimentaires** inadequate information
4 *Biol* rudimentary

rudoie *etc voir* **rudoyer**

rudoyer [13] [rydwaje] VT to treat harshly; **il les a un peu rudoyés** he was a bit harsh with them

rue [ry] NF street; **de la r., des rues** street *(avant n)*; **toute la r. en parle** the whole street *or* neighbourhood is talking about it; **r. pavée** paved street *(with small, flat paving stones)*; **r. piétonnière** *ou* **piétonne** pedestrian street; **r. principale** main street; **r. à sens unique** one-way street; **la grande r.** the main *or Br* high street; **les petites rues** the side streets; **être/se retrouver à la r.** to be/find oneself on the streets; **tu sais que tu n'es pas à la r., tu peux compter sur nous** you know we'll always put you up; **mettre** *ou* **jeter qn à la r.** to turn *or* to put sb out into the street; *Belg* **à r.** *(fenêtre)* looking out over the street; *(façade)* facing the street

ruée [rɥe] NF rush; **il y a eu une r. vers le buffet** everybody made a mad dash for the buffet; **il y a eu une r. sur les tickets de loterie** there's been a big run on lottery tickets; **dès que les portes se sont ouvertes, ç'a été la r.** the minute the doors opened, there was a mad rush; *Hist* **la r. vers l'or** the gold rush

ruelle [rɥɛl] NF **1** *(voie)* lane, narrow street, alley **2** *(de lit)* space between bed and wall

ruer [7] [rɥe] VI **1** *(animal)* to kick (out) **2** *Fam (locution)* **r. dans les brancards** *(verbalement)* to kick up a fuss; *(par ses actions)* to kick *or* to lash out
VPR **se ruer se r. sur qn** *(gén)* to rush at sb; *(agressivement)* to hurl *or* to throw oneself at sb; **se r. vers la sortie** to dash *or* to rush towards the exit; **ils se sont tous rués sur le buffet** they made a mad dash for the buffet; **dès qu'une chambre se libère, tout le monde se rue dessus** as soon as a room becomes vacant, everybody pounces on it; **on se rue pour aller voir son dernier film** people are flocking to see his/her latest movie *or Br* film; **se r. à l'attaque** to charge into the attack

ruffian, rufian [ryfjɑ̃] NM **1** *Arch (souteneur)* whoremonger **2** *(aventurier)* adventurer

rugby [rygbi] NM rugby (football); **r. à quinze** Rugby Union; **r. à treize** Rugby League

rugbyman [rygbiman] *(pl* **rugbymen** [-mɛn]) NM rugby player

rugir [32] [ryʒir] VI **1** *(fauve)* to roar **2** *(personne)* to bellow, to howl (**de** with) **3** *(moteur)* to roar; *(vent)* to howl
VT *(insultes, menaces)* to bellow out, to roar out

rugissant, -e [ryʒisɑ̃, -ɑ̃t] ADJ **1** *(fauve, moteur)* roaring **2** *Littéraire (flots)* roaring; *(vent, tempête)* roaring, howling

rugissement [ryʒismɑ̃] NM **1** *(d'un lion, d'un moteur)* roar, roaring **2** *Littéraire (des flots)* roar, roaring; *(du vent, de la tempête)* roar, roaring, howling **3** *(d'une personne)* roar; **r. de fureur** roar of fury, howl of rage; **r. de douleur** howl of pain; **pousser des rugissements de colère** to roar *or* howl with anger

rugosité [rygozite] NF *(d'une écorce, d'un plancher, de la peau)* roughness; *(d'une toile)* roughness, coarseness
• **rugosités** NFPL bumps, rough patches; **de petites rugosités sur la main** little rough patches (of skin) on the hand

rugueux, -euse [rygø, -øz] ADJ *(écorce, plancher, peau)* rough; *(toile)* rough, coarse

Ruhr [rur] NF **la R.** the Ruhr

ruine [rɥin] NF **1** *(faillite financière)* ruin; **le jeu a causé sa r.** gambling ruined him/her *or* caused his/her ruin; **aller** *ou* **courir à la r.** to head for ruin; **être au bord de la r.** to be on the verge of ruin *or* bankruptcy
2 *Fam (dépense exorbitante)* ruinous expense; **20 euros, ce n'est pas la r.!** 20 euros won't break *or* ruin you!; **l'entretien du bateau est une r.** maintaining the boat is ruinously expensive
3 *(bâtiment délabré)* ruin
4 *(personne usée)* wreck
5 *(destruction* ▸ *d'une institution)* downfall, ruin; *Fig* ruin; **il veut ma r.** he wants to ruin *or* finish me; **le scandale fut la r. de sa carrière politique** the scandal ruined his/her political career
• **ruines** NFPL ruins; **les ruines d'un vieux château** the ruins *or* remains of an old castle
• **en ruine** ADJ ruined; **un château en r.** a ruined castle; **la ferme est en r.** the farmhouse is in ruins
ADV in ruins; **tomber en r.** to go to ruin

ruiner [3] [rɥine] VT **1** *(financièrement)* to ruin, to cause the ruin of, *Sout* to bring ruin upon; **ça ne va pas te r.!** it won't break *or* ruin you!; **tu vas me r.!** you'll be the ruin *or* the ruination of me! **2** *Littéraire (endommager ▸ architecture, cultures)* to ruin, to destroy; *(▸ espérances)* to ruin, to dash; *(▸ carrière, santé)* to ruin, to wreck

VPR **se ruiner 1** *(perdre sa fortune)* to ruin *or* to bankrupt oneself; *(dépenser beaucoup)* to spend a fortune; **il s'est ruiné aux courses** he ruined *or* bankrupted himself at the races; **je me ruine à te payer des études** I'm bleeding myself white *or* ruining myself paying for your studies; **je ne me suis pas ruiné** I didn't spend much; **elle se ruine en vêtements/livres** she spends a fortune on clothes/books **2 se r. la santé/la vue** to ruin one's health/eyesight

ruineux, -euse [rɥinø, -øz] ADJ extravagantly expensive, ruinous; **20 euros, ce n'est pas r.** 20 euros is hardly extravagant

ruisseau, -x [rɥiso] NM **1** *(cours d'eau)* brook, stream

2 *Littéraire (torrent)* stream; **ruisseaux de larmes** floods of tears; **il coulait des ruisseaux de lave/de boue** the lava/mud was flowing in streams; *Prov* **les petits ruisseaux font les grandes rivières** tall oaks from little acorns grow

3 *(rigole)* gutter

4 *Péj (caniveau)* gutter; **rouler dans le r.** to end up in the gutter; **tirer qn du r.** to pull *or* to drag sb out of the gutter

ruisselant, -e [rɥislɑ̃, -ɑ̃t] ADJ **1** *(inondé)* **r. (d'eau)** *(imperméable, personne)* dripping (wet); *(paroi)* streaming *or* running with water; **le visage r. de sueur** his/her face streaming *or* dripping with sweat; **une pièce ruisselante de lumière** a room bathed in *or* flooded with light **2** *(qui ne cesse de couler)* **eaux ruisselantes** running waters

ruisseler [24] [rɥisle] VI *(couler ▸ eau, sang, sueur)* to stream, to drip; **la sueur ruisselait sur son front** his/her brow was streaming *or* dripping with sweat; *Fig* **la lumière ruisselait par la fenêtre** light flooded in through the window

• **ruisseler de** VT IND *(être inondé de)* to stream with; **r. de sang/sueur** to stream with blood/sweat; **les murs ruisselaient d'humidité** the walls were streaming *or* oozing with damp; **ses joues ruisselaient de larmes** tears were streaming down his/her cheeks, his/her cheeks were streaming with tears; *Fig* **le palais ruisselait de lumière** the palace was bathed in *or* flooded with *or* awash with light

ruisselet [rɥislɛ] NM *Littéraire* little stream, brook

ruisselle *etc voir* **ruisseler**

ruissellement [rɥisɛlmɑ̃] NM **1** *(écoulement)* **le r. de la pluie sur les vitres** the rain streaming *or* running down the window panes; *Littéraire* **r. de lumière** stream of light **2** *Géol* **r. pluvial, eaux de r.** (immediate) runoff

rumba [rumba] NF rumba

rumen [rymɛn] NM *Zool* rumen

rumeur [rymœr] NF **1** *(information)* rumour; **il y a des rumeurs de guerre** there's talk of war; **selon certaines rumeurs, le réacteur fuirait toujours** rumour has it *or* it's rumoured that the reactor is still leaking; **j'ai entendu des rumeurs selon lesquelles…** I've heard rumours *or* whispers *or* a whisper that…

2 *(bruit ▸ d'un stade, d'une classe)* hubbub, hum; *(▸ de l'océan)* murmur; *(▸ de la circulation)* rumbling, hum; **la r. lointaine de la ville/de l'usine** the distant sound of the city/the factory

3 *(manifestation)* **r. de mécontentement** rumblings of discontent

4 *(opinion)* **la r. publique le tient pour coupable** rumour has it that he is guilty; **victime de la r. publique, elle dut quitter la ville** a victim of local gossip, she had to leave town

ruminant [ryminɑ̃] NM *Zool* ruminant

rumination [ryminasjɔ̃] NF *Zool* rumination

ruminer [3] [rymine] VI *Zool* to chew the cud, *Spéc* to ruminate

VT **1** *(ressasser ▸ idée)* to ponder, to chew over; *(▸ malheurs)* to brood over; *(▸ vengeance)* to ponder **2** *Zool* to ruminate

rumsteck [rɔmstɛk] = **romsteck**

runabout [rœnəbawt] NM *Naut* runabout

rune [ryn] NF rune

runique [rynik] ADJ runic

rupestre [rypɛstr] ADJ **1** *Archéol & Beaux-Arts (dessin)* rock *(avant n)*; *(peinture)* cave *(avant n)* **2** *Bot* rock *(avant n)*, *Spéc* rupestrine

rupin, -e [rypɛ̃, -in] *Fam* ADJ *(quartier)* plush, *Br* posh; *(intérieur)* ritzy, *Br* posh; *(personne)* loaded, *Br* rolling in it

NM,F moneybags; **c'est des rupins** they're rolling in money *or Br* rolling in it; **les rupins** the rich

rupiner [rypine] VI *Arg* **r. à un examen** to do well in an exam

rupteur [ryptœr] NM **1** *Élec (d'une bobine)* circuit breaker **2** *Aut* **r. (d'allumage)** (contact) breaker

rupture [ryptyr] NF **1** *(d'une corde, d'une poutre etc)* breaking; *(d'un barrage)* bursting

2 *Méd (dans une membrane)* breaking, tearing, splitting; *(dans un vaisseau)* bursting; **il y a eu r. du ligament** the ligament tore; **r. d'anévrysme** aneurysmal rupture

3 *Tech* **r. de circuit** circuit break

4 *(cessation ▸ de négociations, de fiançailles)* breaking off; *(▸ de relations diplomatiques)* severance, breaking off; **la r. des pourparlers était inévitable** the talks were bound to break down; **une r. avec le passé** a break with the past

5 *(dans un couple)* break-up; **scène de r.** break-up scene; **leur couple semble toujours au bord de la r.** they always seem on the verge of splitting *or* breaking up

6 *(changement)* break; **r. de ton** sudden change in *or* of tone

7 *Com* **être en r. de stock** to be out of stock

8 *Jur* **r. de ban** illegal return (from banishment); *Fig* **être en r. de ban avec son milieu/sa famille** to be at odds with one's environment/one's family; **r. de contrat/garantie** breach of contract/guarantee; **r. abusive (de contrat)** ≃ illegal dismissal

9 *Ind* **r. de charge** break of load, transshipment

• **en rupture avec** PRÉP **être en r. avec le parti** to be at odds with the party; **ils se sont mariés à la mairie, en r. avec la tradition** in a break with tradition, they got married at the town hall

> Il faut noter que le nom anglais **rupture** signifie également **hernie**.

rural, -e, -aux, -ales [ryral, -o] ADJ *(droit, population)* rural; *(vie, paysage)* country *(avant n)*, rural; *(chemin)* country *(avant n)*; **en milieu r.** in rural areas

NM,F country person; **les ruraux** country people, countryfolk

NM *Suisse* farm building

ruse [ryz] NF **1** *(trait de caractère)* cunning, craftiness, slyness; **s'approprier qch par (la) r.** to obtain sth through *or* by trickery; **elle a dû recourir à la r. pour s'échapper** she had to resort to cunning to escape **2** *(procédé)* trick, ruse, wile; **r. de guerre** tactics, stratagem; *Fig* good trick

• **ruses** NFPL *Belg* trouble *(UNCOUNT)*

rusé, -e [ryze] ADJ *(personne)* crafty, sly, wily; *(air, regard)* sly; **il est r. comme un renard** he's as sly *or* cunning *or* wily as a fox

NM,F **tu es une petite rusée!** you're a crafty one *or* a sly one, my girl!

ruser [3] [ryze] VI to use cunning *or* trickery *or* guile; **il va falloir r.!** we'll have to be clever!; **r. avec qn** to outsmart sb; **r. avec qch** to get round sth by using cunning

rush [rœʃ] (*pl* **rushs** *ou* **rushes**) NM **1** *(ruée)* rush, stampede **2** *Sport (effort soudain)* spurt

rushes [rœʃ] NMPL *Cin* rushes

russe [rys] ADJ Russian

NM *(langue)* Russian

• **Russe** NMF Russian; **R. blanc** White Russian

Russie [rysi] NF **la R.** Russia; **la R. soviétique** Soviet Russia

russification [rysifikasjɔ̃] NF Russification, Russianization

russifier [9] [rysifje] VT to Russianize, to Russify

rustaud, -e [rysto, -od] *Péj* ADJ yokelish

NM,F yokel, (country) bumpkin

rusticité [rystisite] NF **1** *(d'un comportement, d'une personne)* uncouthness, boorishness **2** *(d'un mobilier)* rusticity **3** *Agr* hardiness

Rustine® [rystin] NF = (bicycle tyre) rubber repair patch

rustique [rystik] ADJ **1** *(de la campagne ▸ vie)* rustic, rural **2** *(meubles)* rustic; *(poterie)* rusticated

NM **le r.** *(style)* rustic style; *(mobilier)* rustic furniture

rustre [rystr] ADJ boorish, uncouth

NMF boor, lout

rut [ryt] NM *Zool (de mâle)* rut; *(de femelle)* heat; **au moment du r.** during the rutting season; **être en r.** *(mâle)* to (be in) rut; *(femelle)* to be *Br* on *or Am* in heat

rutabaga [rytabaga] NM swede, *Am* rutabaga, *Scot* turnip

ruthénium [rytenjɔm] NM *Chim* ruthenium

rutilance [rytilɑ̃s] NF gleam, shine; *(rouge)* red glow

rutilant, -e [rytilɑ̃, -ɑ̃t] ADJ **1** *(propre ▸ carrosserie, armure)* gleaming, shining **2** *Littéraire (rouge ▸ cuivre)* rutilant; *(▸ visage)* ruddy

rutilement [rytilmɑ̃] NM gleam, shine; *(rouge)* red glow

rutiler [3] [rytile] VI **1** *(étinceler)* to gleam, to shine **2** *Littéraire (d'un éclat rouge)* to glow red

Rwanda [rwɑ̃da] NM **le R.** Rwanda

rwandais, -e [rwɑ̃dɛ, -ɛz] ADJ Rwandan

• **Rwandais, -e** NM,F Rwandan

rythme [ritm] NM **1** *Mus* rhythm; **ils dansaient sur/à un r. endiablé** they were dancing to/at a furious rhythm; **avoir le sens du r.** *(sujet: personne)* to have rhythm; **avoir le r. dans la peau** to have a natural sense of rhythm, to have rhythm; **marquer le r.** to mark time; **suivre le r.** to follow the beat

2 *Cin, Théât & Littérature* rhythm; **le spectacle/film manque de r.** the show is a bit slow-moving *or* lacks pace

3 *(allure ▸ d'une production)* rate; *(▸ des battements du cœur)* rate, speed; *(▸ de vie)* tempo, pace; **il te faudra changer de r. quand tu auras des enfants** once you have children, you'll have to change pace *or* slow down a bit; **travailler à un r. soutenu** to work at a sustained pace; **au r. auquel il écrit ses romans** at the rate at which he writes novels; **à ce r.-là** at that rate; **ils avaient du mal à suivre le r.** they had trouble keeping up the pace; **les rythmes scolaires** = the way in which the school year is organized; **r. de travail** work rate

4 *(succession ▸ de marées, de saisons)* rhythm

5 *Anat & Biol* **r. biologique** biorhythm; **r. cardiaque** heartbeat, *Spéc* cardiac rhythm; **r. respiratoire** breathing rate

• **au rythme de** PRÉP **1** *(au son de)* to the rhythm of; **ils défilaient au r. d'une marche militaire** they paraded to the rhythm of a military march **2** *(à la cadence de)* at the rate of; **au r. d'un milliard d'habitants en plus par décennie** at the rate of an extra one billion inhabitants per decade

rythmé, -e [ritme] ADJ *(musique)* rhythmic, rhythmical; *(prose)* rhythmical; **musique très rythmée** music with a good rhythm *or* beat

rythmer [3] [ritme] VT **1** *(mouvements de danse, texte)* to put rhythm into, to give rhythm to; **r. une chanson** to mark time to a song; **je n'ai pas pu m'empêcher de r. la chanson du pied** I couldn't help tapping my foot to the song **2** *(ponctuer)* **ces événements ont rythmé sa vie** these events gave a certain rhythm to *or* punctuated his/her life

rythmique [ritmik] ADJ rhythmic, rhythmical

NF *Littérature* rhythmics *(UNCOUNT)*

S

S¹, s [ɛs] **NM INV 1** *(lettre)* S, s **2** *(forme)* S-shape; **faire des S** to zigzag; **à cet endroit, la route fait un S** at this point, there's a double bend *or* an S bend in the road

• **en S ADJ** *(crochet)* S-shaped; *(route, sentier)* winding, zigzagging

S² *(abrév écrite* **Sud***)* S

SA [ɛsa] **NF** *(abrév* **Société Anonyme***)* *Br* ≃ plc, *Am* ≃ Corp.; **une SA** a limited company

sa [sa] *voir* **son³**

Saba [saba] **NPR** Sheba

sabayon [sabajɔ̃] **NM** *(entremets)* zabaglione; *(sauce)* sabayon sauce

sabbat [saba] **NM 1** *Rel* Sabbath; **le jour du s.** the Sabbath **2** *(de sorcières)* witches' sabbath

sabbatique [sabatik] **ADJ 1** *Rel* sabbatical **2** *Univ* sabbatical; **une année s.** a sabbatical year, a year's sabbatical; **être en congé s.** to be on sabbatical

Sabin, -e [sabɛ̃, -in] **NM,F** Sabine

sabir [sabir] **NM 1** *Ling* lingua franca **2** *Fam (jargon)* gobbledegook, mumbo-jumbo; **dans leur s.** in their lingo

sablage [sablaʒ] **NM 1** *(en travaux publics)* gritting **2** *Constr* sandblasting

sable [sabl] **NM 1** *Géol* sand; **s. fin** fine sand; **s. de construction** coarse sand; *Fam Fig* **être sur le s.** *(sans argent)* to be broke *or Br* skint; *(sans emploi)* to be out of a job; **ils m'ont mis sur le s.** *(ruiné)* they've ruined *or* bankrupted me **2** *Métal* (moulding) sand; **s. de fer** fine iron filings; *Constr* **s. liant** *ou* **mordant** sharp sand **3** *Hér* sable

ADJ INV sand-coloured, sandy

• **sables NMPL les sables (du désert)** the desert sands; **sables mouvants** quicksand *(UNCOUNT)*

• **de sable ADJ** *(château)* sand *(avant n)*; *(dune)* sand *(avant n)*, sandy; *(fond)* sandy

sablé, -e [sable] **ADJ** *(allée)* sandy

NM shortbread (*Br* biscuit *or Am* cookie), piece of shortbread

sabler [3] [sable] **VT 1** *(route)* to grit **2** *(mur)* to sandblast **3** *(locution)* **s. le champagne** to crack open a bottle of champagne

sableux, -euse [sablø, -øz] **ADJ 1** *(mêlé de sable* ▸ *eau, terrain)* sandy; *(*▸ *champignons, moules)* gritty **2** *(rugueux* ▸ *pâte)* grainy

• **sableuse NF 1** *(en travaux publics)* sander, sandspreader **2** *Constr* sandblaster

sablier, -ère [sablije, -ɛr] **ADJ** *(industrie, commerce)* sand *(avant n)*

NM 1 *(gén)* hourglass, sand glass; *(de cuisine)* egg timer **2** *(pour sécher l'encre)* sandbox

• **sablière NF 1** *(lieu)* sand quarry, sandpit **2** *(de locomotive)* sandbox

sablonneux, -euse [sablɔnø, -øz] **ADJ** sandy

sablonnière [sablɔnjɛr] **NF** sand quarry, sandpit

sabord [sabɔr] **NM** scuttle, porthole; **s. de charge** cargo door

sabordage [sabɔrdaʒ], **sabordement** [sabɔrdəmɑ̃] **NM** *Naut & Fig* scuttling

saborder [3] [sabɔrde] **VT 1** *Naut* to scuttle, to sink **2** *(stopper* ▸ *entreprise, journal)* to scuttle, to sink, to wind up **3** *(faire échouer* ▸ *plans, recherche)* to scuttle, to put paid to, *Br* to scupper

VPR se saborder 1 *(équipage)* to scuttle one's ship **2** *(entreprise)* to fold, to close down; *(parti)* to wind (oneself) up

sabot [sabo] **NM 1** *(soulier)* clog, sabot; *Fam* **je te vois venir avec tes gros sabots** I know what you're after, I can see you coming a mile off; *Fam* **elle danse comme un s.** she's got two left feet; *Fam* **je chante comme un s.** I can't sing to save my life

2 *Zool* hoof; **animaux à sabots** hoofed animals

3 *Fam Péj (instrument, machine)* pile of junk

4 *Cartes* shoe

5 *Tech* **s. d'arrêt** chock; **s. de Denver** *Br* wheel clamp, *Am* Denver boot; **mettre le s. de Denver à une voiture** *Br* to clamp *or Am* to (Denver) boot a car; *Rail* **s. d'enrayage** skidpan; **s. de frein** brake shoe *or* block

6 *(d'un meuble)* metal shoe

7 *(jouet)* whipping top

sabotage [sabɔtaʒ] **NM 1** *(destruction* ▸ *de matériel)* sabotage; *Fig* **le s. d'un plan de paix** the sabotage *or* sabotaging of a peace plan **2** *(acte)* **un s.** an act *or* a piece of sabotage **3** *(travail bâclé)* botched work

sabot-de-Vénus [sabodvenys] *(pl* **sabots-de-Vénus***)* **NM** *Bot* lady's slipper

saboter [3] [sabɔte] **VT 1** *(détruire, empêcher volontairement)* to sabotage; **des manifestants sont venus s. l'émission** demonstrators came to sabotage *or* to disrupt the programme **2** *(bâcler)* to bungle

USAGE ABSOLU tu sabotes! you're making a mess of the whole thing!

saboteur, -euse [sabɔtœr, -øz] **NM,F 1** *(destructeur)* saboteur **2** *(mauvais travailleur)* bungler

sabre [sabr] **NM** *(épée)* sabre; **tirer son s.** to draw one's sword; **s. d'abattis** machete; **s. d'abordage** cutlass; **s. de cavalerie** cavalry sabre; **s. au clair** with drawn sword; **le s. et le goupillon** the Army and the Church

sabrer [3] [sabre] **VT 1** *(texte)* to make drastic cuts in; *(paragraphe, phrases, passage)* to cut

2 *Fam (critiquer* ▸ *auteur, pièce, film)* to savage, to rubbish

3 *Fam (étudiant* ▸ *noter sévèrement)* to give a lousy *Br* mark *or Am* grade to; *(*▸ *recaler)* to fail□, *Am* to flunk; *(employé* ▸ *renvoyer)* to fire, *Br* to sack, *Am* to can; **se faire s.** to get the chop *or* the boot *or Br* the sack

4 *(marquer vigoureusement)* to slash; *Fig* **la toile avait été sabrée à coups de crayon** great pencil slashes marked the canvas

5 *(bâcler)* to botch, to bungle

6 *(ouvrir)* **s. le champagne** to crack open a bottle of champagne *(originally, using a sabre)*

USAGE ABSOLU je vais devoir s. I'll have to do some drastic editing

sabreur [sabrœr] **NM 1** *Escrime* fencer **2** *Mil* sabreur

sac [sak] **NM 1** *(contenant* ▸ *petit, léger)* bag; *(*▸ *grand, solide)* sack; **s. à bandoulière** shoulder bag; **s. de billes** bag of marbles; **s. de couchage** sleeping bag; **s. à dos** rucksack, knapsack; *Aut* **s. gonflable** airbag®; **s. à main** *(à poignée)* *Br* handbag, *Am* purse; *(à bandoulière)* shoulder bag; **s. de marin** kitbag; *Mil* **s. à munitions** cartridge pouch; **s. à ouvrage** workbag, sewing bag; **s. à pain** bread bag *(made of cloth)*; **s. en papier** paper bag; **s. de plage** beach bag; **s. (en) plastique** *(petit)* plastic bag; *(solide et grand)* *Br* plastic carrier (bag), *Am* large plastic bag; **s. à pommes de terre** potato sack; **s. à poussière** *(d'un aspirateur)* dust bag; **s. à provisions** shopping bag; **s. de sable** *Mil* sandbag; *Sport* punchbag; **s. seau** bucket bag; *Fam* **s. à viande** inner sheet□ *(of a sleeping bag)*; **s. de voyage** overnight *or* travelling bag; **je ne prendrai pas de valise, juste un s.** I won't pack a suitcase, just an overnight bag

2 *(contenu* ▸ *petit, moyen)* bag, bagful; *(*▸ *grand)* sack, sackful

3 *Anat & Bot* sac; **s. lacrymal** lacrymal sac

4 *Rel* **le s. et la cendre** sackcloth and ashes

5 *(pillage)* sack, pillage; **mettre qch à s.** *(ville, région)* to ransack *or* to plunder *or* to pillage sth; *(maison)* to ransack sth

6 *(locutions)* *Fam* **méfie-toi, c'est un s. de nœuds, leur affaire** be careful, that business of theirs is a real hornets' nest; *Fam* **voyons un peu ce s. d'embrouilles!** let's try and sort out this muddle!; **s. à malices** bag of tricks; *Fam* **c'est un s. d'os** he's/she's all skin and bone *or* a bag of bones; *Fam* **s. à puces** *(chien)* fleabag; *Fam* **s. à vin** drunk, lush; **être fagoté** *ou* **ficelé comme un s.** to look like a feather bed tied in the middle; *Fam* **ça y est, l'affaire est** *ou* **c'est dans le s.!** it's as good as done!, it's in the bag!; **ils sont tous à mettre dans le même s.** they're all as bad as each other; **attention, ne mettons pas racisme et sexisme dans le même s.!** let's not lump racism and sexism together!; *Fam Vieilli* **avoir le (gros) s.** to be loaded, to be rolling in it; *Fam Vieilli* **épouser le (gros) s.** to marry (into) money

saccade [sakad] **NF** jerk, jolt, (sudden) start; **après quelques saccades, le moteur s'arrêta** the engine jolted to a halt

• **par saccades ADV** jerkingly, joltingly, in fits and starts; **la voiture avançait par saccades** the car was lurching *or* jerking forward; **elle parlait par saccades** she spoke haltingly *or* in a disjointed manner

saccadé, -e [sakade] **ADJ** *(pas)* jerky; *(mouvement)* disjointed; *(voix)* halting; *(respiration)* irregular

saccader [3] [sakade] **VT** *Équitation (rênes)* to jerk

saccage [sakaʒ] **NM** (wanton) destruction; **quel s.!** what a mess!

saccager [17] [sakaʒe] **VT 1** *(dévaster* ▸ *maison, parc)* to wreck, to wreak havoc in, to devastate; *(*▸ *matériel, livres)* to wreck, to ruin; *(*▸ *cultures)* to lay waste, to devastate; **le village a été saccagé par l'inondation** the village was devastated by the flood; **les cambrioleurs ont (tout) saccagé (dans) le salon** the burglars wrecked (everything in) the living room **2** *(piller* ▸ *ville, région)* to lay waste, to sack

saccageur, -euse [sakaʒœr, -øz] **NM,F** vandal

saccharin, -e [sakarɛ̃, -in] **ADJ** sugar *(avant n)*, saccharine

• **saccharine NF** saccharin

saccharose [sakaroz] **NM** *Chim* saccharose

sacerdoce [sasɛrdɔs] **NM 1** *Rel* priesthood **2** *(vocation)* vocation, calling; **l'enseignement est un s.** teaching is a real vocation *or* calling

sacerdotal, -e, -aux, -ales [sasɛrdɔtal, -o] **ADJ** priestly, sacerdotal

sachant *voir* **savoir**

sachem [saʃɛm] **NM** sachem

sachet [saʃɛ] **NM 1** *(petit sac)* (small) bag; **s. de lavande** lavender bag *or* sachet; **s. pour garniture périodique** sanitary disposal bag **2** *(dose ► de soupe, d'entremets)* packet, sachet; *(► d'herbes aromatiques)* sachet; **un s. d'aspirine** a dose of aspirin; **un s. de thé** a teabag; **du thé en sachets** teabags; **soupe en sachets** packet soup **3** *Belg (sac)* bag; **s. poubelle** binbag, *Br* dustbin *or Am* garbage can liner

sachet-cuisson [saʃɛkɥisɔ̃] *(pl* **sachets-cuissons***)* **NM en s.** boil-in-the-bag

sacoche [sakɔʃ] **NF 1** *(besace ► du facteur)* bag, mailbag, *Br* postbag; **s. à outils** toolbag

2 *(de vélo)* saddlebag, *Br* pannier

3 *(d'encaisseur)* money bag

4 *Belg & Can (sac à main) Br* handbag, *Am* purse

sac-poubelle [sakpubɛl] *(pl* **sacs-poubelle***)* **NM** *Br* dustbin liner, binbag, *Am* garbage can liner, garbage bag

sacquer [3] [sake] *Fam* **VT 1** *(employé)* **s. qn** to fire sb, *Br* to sack *or Am* to can sb; **se faire s.** to get fired, to get the *Br* sack *or Am* ax **2** *(étudiant)* to mark strictly❑; **je me suis encore fait s. par le prof!** I got another rotten *Br* mark *or Am* grade from the teacher! **3** *(locution)* **il ne peut pas la s.** he can't stand (the sight of) her

USAGE ABSOLU le prof de maths saque vachement the *Br* maths *or Am* math teacher is a really tough *Br* marker *or Am* grader

sacral, -e, -aux, -ales [sakral, -o] **ADJ** sacred

sacraliser [3] [sakralize] **VT** to regard as sacred

sacramentel, -elle [sakramɑ̃tɛl] **ADJ 1** *Rel* sacramental **2** *Fig Littéraire (moment, paroles)* ritual, sacramental

sacrant, -e [sakrɑ̃, -ɑ̃t] **ADJ** *Can Fam* **1** *(fâcheux)* annoying❑, bothersome; **cet accident est bien s.!** this accident is a real pain! **2 au plus s.** as quickly as possible❑

sacre [sakr] **NM 1** *(d'un empereur)* coronation and anointment; *(d'un évêque)* consecration; **recevoir le prix Goncourt, c'est le s. pour un écrivain** being awarded the prix Goncourt is the crowning achievement of a writer's career **2** *Can (juron)* swear word, expletive *(usually the name of a religious object)*

sacré, -e [sakre] **ADJ 1** *Rel (édifice)* sacred, holy; *(art, textes, musique)* sacred, religious; *(animal)* sacred; **dans l'enceinte sacrée** within the place of worship

2 *(devoir, promesse)* sacred, sacrosanct; *(droit)* sacred, hallowed; **sa voiture, c'est s.!** his/her car is sacred!; **rien de plus s. que sa promenade après le repas** his/her after-dinner walk is sacrosanct

3 *(avant le nom) Fam (en intensif)* **j'ai un s. mal de dents!** I've got raging toothache!; **j'ai un s. boulot en ce moment!** I've got a hell of a lot of work on at the moment!; **il a un s. culot!** he's got a lot of nerve!; **elle a eu une sacrée vie** she's had quite a life; **c'est un s. cuisinier, ton mari!** your husband is a damn good cook *or* a terrific cook!; *aussi Ironique* **s. Marcel, toujours le mot pour rire!** good old Marcel, never a dull moment with him!; **s. farceur!** you old devil!; **c'est un s. veinard** he's a lucky *or Br* jammy devil; **t'as eu une sacrée veine!** you were damn lucky!; *très Fam* **un s. con** a total *Br* arsehole *or Am* asshole; *très Fam* **un s. fouteur de merde** a hell of a shit-stirrer; **c'est un s. numéro** he's quite a character *or* case!; **cette sacrée bagnole est encore en panne** the damn *or Br* bloody car's broken down again

4 *(avant le nom) Fam (satané)* damned, blasted; **s. nom de nom!** damn and blast it!; **s. nom de Dieu!** bloody hell!; **s. nom d'un chien!** *Br* damn it!, *Am* goddamn!

NM le s. the sacred

Sacré-Cœur [sakrekœr] **NM 1** *(édifice)* **le S., la basilique du S.** Sacré-Cœur **2** *(fête)* **le S., la fête du S.** the (Feast of the) Sacred Heart

sacredieu [sakrədjø] **EXCLAM** *Vieilli & Hum* hell's bells!

sacrement [sakrəmɑ̃] **NM** sacrament; **les derniers sacrements** the last rites

sacrément [sakremɑ̃] **ADV** *très Fam* damn, *Br* bloody; **il s'est s. foutu de notre gueule** he made a total damn *or Br* bloody fool of us; **il est s. radin, celui-là!** he's so damn *or Br* bloody tight!

sacrer [3] [sakre] **VT 1** *(empereur)* to crown and anoint; *(évêque)* to consecrate; **s. qn roi/empereur** to crown sb king/emperor

2 *(nommer, instituer)* to consecrate; **on l'a sacré meilleur acteur du siècle** he was acclaimed *or* hailed as the greatest actor of the century; **il a été sacré champion de France en 2003** he was crowned French champion in 2003

3 *Can Fam (donner)* to give❑; **s. une claque à qn** to slap sb, to give sb a slap

4 *Can Fam (mettre)* to chuck; **s. qn dehors** to chuck sb out

5 *Can Fam* **s. le** *ou* **son camp** *(s'en aller)* to beat it, *Br* to bugger off

VI *Can & Vieilli* to swear, to curse

sacrifiable [sakrifjabl] **ADJ** expendable

sacrificateur, -trice [sakrifikatœr, -tris] **NM,F** *Antiq* sacrificer; **le grand s.** the (Jewish) High Priest

sacrifice [sakrifis] **NM 1** *Rel* sacrifice, offering; **offrir qch en s. à Dieu** to offer sth as a sacrifice to God, to sacrifice sth to God; **offrir qn en s. aux divinités** to sacrifice sb to the gods **2** *(effort, compromis)* sacrifice; **je n'ai pas le goût du s.** I have no desire to sacrifice myself; **faire des sacrifices/un s.** to make sacrifices/a sacrifice; **elle a fait de grands sacrifices pour monter la pièce/pour ses enfants** she's sacrificed a lot to put on the play/for her children; **faire le s. de sa vie pour qn** to lay down *or* to sacrifice one's life for sb

• au sacrifice de PRÉP at the cost of; **au s. de sa vie** at the cost of his/her own life

sacrifié, -e [sakrifje] **ADJ** sacrificed, lost; *(prix)* rock-bottom; *(article)* at a rock-bottom price; **prix sacrifiés!** *(sur panneau)* rock-bottom prices!; **la génération sacrifiée** the lost generation

NM,F (sacrificial) victim

sacrifier [9] [sakrifje] **VT 1** *Rel* to sacrifice; *Fig* **c'est toute une génération qui a été sacrifiée** a whole generation was sacrificed **2** *(renoncer à ► carrière, santé)* to sacrifice (**à** for *or* to); *(► loisirs)* to give up (**à** for *or* to); **s. sa vie** to make the ultimate sacrifice; **s. sa vie à une cause** to devote one's (entire) life to a cause; **il a sacrifié sa vie pour sa patrie** he sacrificed *or* laid down his life for his country; **s. ses amis à sa carrière** to sacrifice one's friends to one's career **3** *Com (articles)* to sell at rock-bottom prices; **je les sacrifie, Mesdames!** ladies, I'm giving them away!

• sacrifier à VT IND 1 *Rel* to sacrifice to; **s. aux idoles** to sacrifice to idols **2** *(se conformer à)* to conform to; **s. à la mode** to conform to *or* to go along with (the dictates of) fashion; **à Noël, sacrifiez à la tradition** keep tradition alive at Christmas

VPR se sacrifier to sacrifice oneself; **se s. pour son pays** to sacrifice oneself for one's country; **se s. pour la bonne cause** to sacrifice oneself in a good cause; *Fam Hum* **il reste des frites – allez, je me sacrifie!** there are some chips left over – oh well, I'll force them down!

sacrilège [sakrilɛʒ] **ADJ** sacrilegious

NMF profaner

NM 1 *Rel* sacrilege, profanation **2** *Fig (crime)* sacrilege, crime; **ce serait un s. de retoucher la photo** it would be criminal *or* a sacrilege to touch up the photograph; *Hum* **je mets toujours un peu d'eau dans mon vin – s.!** I always put a drop of water in my wine – that's sacrilege!

sacristain [sakristɛ̃] **NM 1** *Rel (catholique)* sacristan; *(protestant)* sexton **2** *Culin* = small puff pastry cake in the shape of a paper twist

sacristi [sakristi] **EXCLAM** *Vieilli (exprimant l'étonnement)* (good) heavens!; *(exprimant la colère)* for heaven's sake!

sacristie [sakristi] **NF** *(d'une église catholique)* sacristy; *(d'une église protestante)* vestry

sacro-saint, -e [sakrɔsɛ̃, -ɛ̃t] *(mpl* **sacro-saints**, *fpl* **sacro-saintes***)* **ADJ 1** *Vieilli* sacrosanct **2** *Fam (intouchable)* sacred, sacrosanct

sacrum [sakrɔm] **NM** sacrum

sadique [sadik] **ADJ** sadistic

NMF sadist

sadisme [sadism] **NM** sadism

sado-maso [sadomazo] *(pl* **sado-masos***)* *Fam (abrév* **sadomasochiste***)* **ADJ** SM, S & M; **il a des tendances sado-masos** he's into S & M, he has S & M tendencies

NMF sadomasochist❑; **c'est un s.** he's into S & M

sadomasochisme [sadɔmazɔʃism] **NM** sadomasochism

sadomasochiste [sadɔmazɔʃist] **ADJ** sadomasochistic

NMF sadomasochist

safari [safari] **NM** safari; **faire un s.** to go on (a) safari

safari-photo [safarifɔto] *(pl* **safaris-photos***)* **NM** photographic *or* camera safari

safran [safrɑ̃] **NM 1** *Bot & Culin* saffron **2** *Naut* rudder blade

ADJ INV saffron *(avant n)*, saffron-yellow

safrané, -e [safrane] **ADJ 1** *(teinte)* saffron *(avant n)*, saffron-yellow **2** *Culin* saffron-flavoured

safraner [3] [safrane] **VT** *Culin* to flavour with saffron, to saffron

saga [saga] **NF** *Littérature* saga

sagace [sagas] **ADJ** sharp, acute, *Sout* sagacious

sagacité [sagasite] **NF** judiciousness, wisdom, *Sout* sagacity; **avec s.** shrewdly, judiciously; **pour une fois, il a fait preuve de s.** for once, he behaved shrewdly

sagaie [sagɛ] **NF** assagai, assegai

sage [saʒ] **ADJ 1** *(tranquille, obéissant)* good, well-behaved; **sois s., Paul!** *(recommandation)* be a good boy, Paul!; *(remontrance)* behave yourself, Paul!; **les enfants ont été sages** the children behaved themselves; **l'école l'a rendu plus s.** school has quietened him down; **être s. comme une image** to be as good as gold

2 *(sensé, raisonnable ► personne)* wise, sensible; *(► avis, conduite, décision)* wise, sensible, reasonable; **une politique peu s.** an unwise policy, not a very sensible policy; **le plus s. serait de...** the most sensible thing (to do) would be...

3 *(sobre ► tenue)* modest, sober; *(► robe)* demure; *(► vie sentimentale)* quiet; *(► film, livre)* restrained, understated; *(► goûts)* tame, *Péj* unadventurous; **elle était habillée de façon très s.** she was very soberly dressed

4 *Euph Vieilli (chaste)* **elle est s.** she's a good girl

NM 1 *(personne)* wise person; **un vieux s.** a wise old man **2** *Pol* **une commission de sages** an advisory committee **3** *Antiq* sage

sage-femme [saʒfam] *(pl* **sages-femmes***)* **NF** midwife; **un homme s.** a male midwife

sagement [saʒmɑ̃] **ADV 1** *(tranquillement)* quietly, nicely; **attends-moi s. ici, Marie** wait for me here like a good girl, Marie; **il est en train de dessiner bien s.** he's drawing nice and quietly **2** *(raisonnablement)* wisely, sensibly **3** *(pudiquement)* **elle baissa s. les yeux** she modestly lowered her eyes

sagesse [saʒɛs] **NF 1** *(discernement ► d'une personne)* good sense, insight, wisdom; *(► d'une décision, d'une suggestion)* good sense, wisdom; **la s. voudrait que tu refuses** you'd be better advised *or* it'd be wiser to refuse; **elle a eu la s. de ne pas en parler** she was wise *or* sensible enough not to mention it; **agir avec s.** to act wisely *or* sensibly; **plein de s.** *(remarque)* very sensible; *(décision)* very sensible *or* wise

2 *(obéissance)* good behaviour; **elle n'a pas été d'une grande s. aujourd'hui!** she wasn't particularly well behaved today!

3 *(sobriété ► d'une toilette, d'un livre)* soberness, tameness; *(► d'une vie sentimentale)* quietness; **la trop grande s. de leur projet leur fera du tort** the lack of ambition of their project will work against them

4 *Euph (chasteté)* proper behaviour

Sagittaire [saʒitɛr] **NM** *Astron & Astrol* Sagittarius; **être S.** to be Sagittarius *or* a Sagittarian

sagou [sagu] **NM** sago

sagouin, -e [sagwɛ̃, -in] **NM,F** *Fam (personne ► malpropre)* filthy pig; *(► incompétente)* slob; **travailler comme un s.** to be a sloppy worker; **manger comme un s.** to eat like a pig

NM *Zool* marmoset, sagouin

Sahara [saara] **NM le (désert du) S.** the Sahara (desert); **au S.** in the Sahara

saharien, -enne [saarjɛ̃, -ɛn] **ADJ** *(gén)* Saharan; *(troupes)* desert *(avant n)*; *Fig (température)* scorching, sizzling

• **Saharien, -enne NM,F** Saharan

• **saharienne NF** *(veste)* safari jacket

Sahel [saɛl] **NM le S.** the Sahel

sahib [saib] **NM** sahib

sahraoui, -e [sarawi] **ADJ** Sahrawi, from Western Sahara, of Western Sahara

• **Sahraoui, -e NM,F** Sahrawi, Western Saharan

saignant, -e [sɛɲɑ̃, -ɑ̃t] **ADJ 1** *Culin (steak)* rare **2** *(blessure)* bleeding

saignée [seɲe] **NF 1** *Méd* bleeding *(UNCOUNT)*, bloodletting *(UNCOUNT)*; **faire une s. à qn** to bleed sb, to let sb's blood

2 *(pertes humaines)* **la terrible s. de la Première Guerre mondiale** the terrible slaughter of the First World War

3 *Anat* **à la s. du bras** at the crook of the arm

4 *(dépenses)* drain; **des saignées dans le budget** drains on the budget

5 *(entaille)* notch; *Constr (dans un mur, pour un tuyau, pour un câble)* hole; **faire une s. sur un pin** to tap a pine tree

6 *(rigole)* (surface) drainage channel

saignement [sɛɲmɑ̃] **NM** bleeding; **s. de nez** nosebleed

saigner [4] [seɲe] **VI 1** *(plaie, blessé)* to bleed; **je saigne du nez** my nose is bleeding, I've got a nosebleed; **il saigne de la bouche** *(coupure superficielle)* his mouth is bleeding; *(hémorragie interne)* he's bleeding from the mouth; *Fig* **c'est une plaie qui saigne encore** it's an open wound, it still rankles **2** *Fig Littéraire* **son cœur saigne à cette pensée** his/her heart bleeds at the thought

VT 1 *(malade, animal)* to bleed; *(cochon)* to stick

2 *(faire payer ▸ contribuable)* to bleed, to fleece; *(épuiser ▸ pays)* to drain the resources of, to drain *or* to suck the lifeblood from; **s. qn à blanc** to bleed sb dry, to clean sb out

3 *Fam (tuer à l'arme blanche)* to stab to death ☐

4 *(arbre)* to tap

5 *(fossé)* to cut

VI *Fam* **ça va s.** there's going to be trouble; **c'est France–All Blacks aujourd'hui, ça va s.!** France are playing the All Blacks today, the fur's going to fly!

VPR se saigner se s. pour qn to work one's fingers to the bone for sb; **se s. aux quatre veines pour qn** to bleed oneself dry for sb

saigneur [sɛɲœr] **NM** slaughterer, slaughterman

saillant, -e [sajɑ̃, -ɑ̃t] **ADJ 1** *(en relief ▸ veines)* prominent; *(▸ os, tendon, menton)* protruding; *(▸ muscle, yeux)* bulging, protruding; *(▸ corniche, rocher)* projecting; **avoir les pommettes saillantes** to have prominent *or* high cheekbones **2** *(remarquable ▸ trait, fait)* salient, outstanding; **l'ouvrage est plein de traits saillants** the work is full of striking features; **les faits saillants de l'année** the highlights of the year

NM 1 *(de fortification)* salient **2** *(angle)* salient angle

saillie [saji] **NF 1** *(d'un mur, d'une montagne)* ledge; *(d'un os)* protuberance; **faire s., être en s.** *(balcon, roche)* to jut out, to project; **une des briques faisait s.** one of the bricks was jutting *or* sticking out

2 *Constr* projection

3 *Littéraire (trait d'esprit)* sally, witticism, flash of wit

4 *Zool* covering, serving

saillir¹ [32] [sajir] **VT** *Zool* to cover, to serve

saillir² [50] [sajir] **VI** *(rocher, poutre)* to project, to jut out; *(menton)* to protrude; *(os)* to protrude, to stick out; *(yeux)* to bulge, to protrude; *(muscle, veine)* to stand out, to bulge; **l'effort faisait s. les veines de son cou** the veins on his/her neck were swelling *or* bulging with the strain

sain, -e [sɛ̃, sɛn] **ADJ 1** *(robuste ▸ enfant)* healthy, robust; *(▸ cheveux, peau)* healthy; *(▸ dent)* sound, healthy; **des dents très saines** teeth in perfect condition, healthy teeth; **être s. d'esprit** to be sane; **s. de corps et d'esprit** sound in mind and body; **un esprit s. dans un corps s.** a healthy mind in a healthy body

2 *(en bon état ▸ charpente, fondations, structure)* sound; *(▸ situation financière, entreprise, gestion)* sound, healthy; *(▸ viande)* good; **ne gardez que les parties saines de l'ananas** keep only the unblemished parts of the pineapple; **la gestion de l'entreprise n'était pas saine** the company was mismanaged

3 *(salutaire ▸ alimentation, mode de vie)* wholesome, healthy; *(▸ air, climat)* healthy, invigorating; **tu ne devrais pas rester enfermé toute la journée, ce n'est pas s.** you shouldn't stay in all day long, it's not good for you *or* it's unhealthy

4 *(irréprochable ▸ opinion)* sane, sound; *(▸ lectures)* wholesome; **son rapport avec sa fille n'a jamais été très s.** his/her relationship with his/her daughter was never very healthy

5 *Naut* safe

• **sain et sauf, saine et sauve ADJ** safe and sound, unhurt, unharmed

saindoux [sɛ̃du] **NM** lard

sainement [sɛnmɑ̃] **ADV 1** *(hygiéniquement)* healthily; **se nourrir s.** to eat wholesome *or* healthy food; **vivre s.** to lead a healthy life **2** *(sagement)* soundly; **juger s. (de)** to make a sound judgment (on)

saint, -e [sɛ̃, sɛ̃t] **ADJ 1** *(après le nom) (sacré ▸ lieu, livre, image, guerre)* holy; **la semaine sainte** Holy Week; **les Saintes Écritures** the Scriptures; **la Sainte Église** the Holy Church; **leur s. patron** their patron saint; **le s. sacrement** the sacrament of Holy Communion, the Eucharist; *Fam* **elle le promène comme le s. sacrement** she shows it off as if it was the crown jewels; **le s. suaire (de Turin)** the Turin Shroud; **la Sainte Vierge** the Blessed Virgin; **une petite sainte vierge en ivoire** an ivory miniature of the Blessed Virgin

2 *(canonisé)* Saint; **s. André** Saint Andrew; **sainte Catherine** Saint Catherine; **s. Nicolas** Saint Nicholas

3 *(avant le nom) (exemplaire)* holy; **sa mère était une sainte femme** his/her mother was a real saint; **être saisi** *ou* **pris d'une sainte colère/indignation** to be seething with righteous anger/indignation

4 *(en intensif)* **toute la sainte journée** the whole blessed day; **j'ai une sainte horreur des araignées** I have a real horror of spiders

NM,F 1 *Rel* saint; **le s. du jour** the Saint of the day; **les saints du dernier jour** the Latter-Day Saints, the Mormons; **il lasserait la patience d'un s.** he'd try the patience of a saint; **je ne sais (plus) à quel s. me vouer** I don't know which way to turn (any more) **2** *Fig* saint; **vous êtes une sainte** you're a saint; **les promoteurs ne sont pas des petits saints** property developers are no angels; *Fam* **arrête de faire ton petit s.** stop being such a prig!

NM *Rel* **le s. des saints** the Holy of Holies; *Fig* the inner sanctum

• **Saint, -e ADJ** *(avec trait d'union) (dans des noms de lieux, de fêtes)* **c'est la S.-Marc aujourd'hui** it's Saint Mark's day today, it's the feast of Saint Mark today; **ils vont à la messe à S.-Augustin** they attend Mass at Saint Augustine's (church)

saint-bernard [sɛ̃bɛrnar] **NM INV 1** *Zool* Saint Bernard (dog) **2** *Hum (personne généreuse)* **c'est un vrai s.** he's a good Samaritan

Saint-Cyr [sɛ̃sir] **NM** Saint-Cyr military academy

saint-cyrien, -enne [sɛ̃sirjɛ̃, -ɛn] *(mpl* **saint-cyriens,** *fpl* **saint-cyriennes) NM,F** *(élève)* = cadet training at the Saint-Cyr military academy

Sainte-Hélène [sɛ̃telɛn] **NF** St Helena; **à S.** on St Helena

Saint-Elme [sɛ̃tɛlm] **NM feu S.** corposant, Saint-Elmo's fire

Sainte-Lucie [sɛ̃tlysi] **NF** St Lucia; **à S.** in St Lucia

saintement [sɛ̃tmɑ̃] **ADV vivre s.** to lead a saintly life; **mourir s.** to die a saintly death

sainte-nitouche [sɛ̃tnituʃ] *(pl* **saintes-nitouches) NF** *Péj* goody-two-shoes; **avec ses airs de s.** looking as though butter wouldn't melt in his/her mouth

Saint-Esprit [sɛ̃tɛspri] **NM le S.** the Holy Spirit *or* Ghost

sainteté [sɛ̃tte] **NF 1** *(d'une personne)* saintliness, godliness; *(d'une action, d'une vie)* saintliness; *(d'un édifice, des Écritures, de la Vierge)* holiness, sanctity; *(du mariage)* sanctity **2** *(titre)* **Sa S. (le pape)** His Holiness (the Pope)

saint-frusquin [sɛ̃fryskɛ̃] **NM INV** *Fam* **tout le s.** the whole caboodle

Saint-Glinglin [sɛ̃glɛ̃glɛ̃] **NF** *Fam* **attendre jusqu'à la S.** to wait forever *or* until doomsday; **c'est maintenant qu'il faut le faire, pas à la S.** it has to be done now, not whenever

Saint-Graal [sɛ̃gral] **NM le S.** the (Holy) Grail

saint-honoré [sɛ̃tɔnɔre] **NM INV** = gateau consisting of a layer of caramel-covered profiteroles on top of a layer of pastry

Saint-Jean [sɛ̃ʒɑ̃] **NF la S.** Midsummer's Day; *Can* **la S.-Baptiste** = the Quebec national day

saint-marcellin [sɛ̃marsəlɛ̃] **NM INV** = small round cheese produced in the Lyons area

Saint-Marin [sɛ̃marɛ̃] **NM** San Marino

Saint-Martin [sɛ̃martɛ̃] **NM** *Suisse* = holiday held in the canton of Jura around 11 November

Saint-Michel [sɛ̃miʃɛl] **NF la S.** Michaelmas

saint-nectaire [sɛ̃nɛktɛr] **NM INV** Saint Nectaire *(cheese)*

Saint-Office [sɛ̃tɔfis] **NM** *Hist* **le S.** the Holy Office

Saint-Père [sɛ̃pɛr] *(pl* **Saints-Pères) NM** Holy Father

Saint-Pétersbourg [sɛ̃petɛrsbur] **NM** St Petersburg

saint-pierre [sɛ̃pjɛr] **NM INV** *Ich* John Dory

Saint-Pierre-et-Miquelon [sɛ̃pjɛremiklɔ̃] **NM** St Pierre and Miquelon

Saint-Sépulcre [sɛ̃sepylkr] **NM le S.** the Holy Sepulchre

Saint-Siège [sɛ̃sjɛʒ] **NM le S.** the Holy See

Saint-Sylvestre [sɛ̃silvɛstr] **NF la S.** = New Year's Eve; **le réveillon de la S.** = New Year's Eve dinner and party

saisi, -e [sezi] **NM,F** *Jur* distrainee

• **saisie NF 1** *Ordinat* keyboarding, keying; **saisie de données** data capture, keyboarding; **saisie automatique/manuelle** automatic/manual input **2** *Typ (clavetage)* keyboarding **3** *Jur (d'une propriété, d'un bien mobilier)* seizure, distraint, distress; *(de produits d'une infraction)* seizure, confiscation; *(d'un bien pour non-paiement des traites)* repossession; **saisie conservatoire** sequestration *or* seizure of goods *(to prevent sale)*; **saisie immobilière** seizure of property; **saisie mobilière** seizure *or* distraint of goods; **faire** *ou* **opérer une saisie** to levy a distress **4** *Naut* seizure, embargo

saisie-attribution [seziatribysjɔ̃] *(pl* **saisies-attributions) NF** *Jur* garnishment

saisie-contrefaçon [sezikɔ̃trəfasɔ̃] *(pl* **saisies-contrefaçons) NF** *Jur* = seizure of counterfeit goods

saisie-vente [sezivɑ̃t] *(pl* **saisies-ventes) NF** *Jur* = seizure of movable goods for sale

saisine [sezin] **NF** *Jur (d'un héritier)* seisin; **la s. d'un tribunal** the referral of a case to a court

saisir [32] [sezir] **VT 1** *(avec brusquerie)* to grab (hold of), to seize, to grasp; *(pour porter, déplacer)* to catch (hold of), to take hold of, to grip; *(pour s'approprier)* to snatch; **s. qch au vol** to catch sth in mid-air; **s. un outil par le manche** to take (hold of) a tool by the handle; **s. qn aux épaules** to grab *or* to grip sb by the shoulders; **il m'a saisi par la manche** he grabbed me by the sleeve; **elle saisit ma main** she gripped my hand

2 *(mettre à profit)* to seize, to grab; **s. le moment propice** to choose the right moment; **s. l'occasion de faire qch** to seize *or* to grasp the opportunity to do sth; **s. sa chance** to seize an opportunity; **je n'ai pas su s. ma chance** I missed (out on) my chance, I didn't seize the opportunity; **à s.** *(achat)* a real bargain

3 *(envahir ▸ sujet: colère, terreur, dégoût)* to take hold of, to seize, to grip; **elle a été saisie d'un malaise, un malaise l'a saisie** she suddenly felt faint; **saisi d'étonnement** startled, staggered; **saisie de terreur** terror-stricken; **elle fut saisie de panique** she suddenly panicked; **le froid me saisit** the cold hit me

4 *(impressionner)* to strike, to stun; **la ressem-**

blance entre les deux frères nous a saisis we were struck by the resemblance between the two brothers; **quand j'ai vu le mort, je suis resté saisi** when I saw the dead man, I was (quite) overcome

5 *(percevoir ▸ bribes de conversation, mot)* to catch, to get; **je n'ai pas bien saisi son nom** I didn't quite catch his/her name

6 *(comprendre ▸ explications, sens d'une phrase)* to understand, to get, to grasp; **elle a tout de suite saisi de quoi il s'agissait** she immediately grasped *or* got what it was about; **s. la nuance** to see the difference; **as-tu saisi l'allusion?** did you get the hint?

7 *Jur (débiteur, biens)* to seize, to levy distress (upon); *(navire)* to seize, to attach; *(articles prohibés)* to seize, to confiscate; *(tribunal)* to submit *or* to refer a case to; **s. un tribunal d'une affaire** to refer a matter to a court, to lay a matter before a court; **la juridiction compétente a été saisie** the case was referred to the appropriate jurisdiction; **l'huissier a fait s. tous ses biens** the bailiff ordered all his/her goods to be seized

8 *Ordinat* to capture; **s. des données (sur clavier)** to keyboard data

9 *Culin* to seal, to sear

10 *Naut (arrimer)* to stow, to secure

USAGE ABSOLU *(comprendre)* **je ne saisis pas bien** I don't quite get it; **il saisit vite** he's quick (on the uptake); **alors, tu saisis?** do you get it?

VPR se saisir 1 se s. de *(prendre)* to grab (hold of), to grip, to seize; **se s. du pouvoir/d'une ville** to seize power/a town **2 se s. de** *(étudier)* to examine; **le conseil doit se s. du dossier** the council will put the file on its agenda

saisissable [sezisabl] **ADJ 1** *Jur* distrainable **2** *(perceptible)* perceptible

saisissant, -e [sezisɑ̃, -ɑ̃t] **ADJ 1** *(vif ▸ froid)* biting, piercing **2** *(surprenant ▸ ressemblance)* striking; *(▸ récit, spectacle)* gripping; *(▸ contraste)* startling **3** *Jur (qui opère ou fait opérer une saisie)* seizing

NM,F *(opérant une saisie)* distrainer, distrainor

saisissement [sezismɑ̃] **NM 1** *(émotion)* shock, rush of emotion; *(surprise)* astonishment, amazement; **pâle de s.** pale with emotion; **je suis resté muet de s. devant tant de beauté** I was dumbfounded by so much beauty **2** *(sensation de froid)* sudden chill; **il éprouva un s. au contact de l'eau glacée** he shivered as he entered the icy water

saison [sezɔ̃] **NF 1** *(période de l'année)* season; **en cette s.** at this time of (the) year; **en toutes saisons** all year round; **la s. n'est pas très avancée cette année** the season's a bit late this year; **la belle s.** *(printemps)* the spring months; *(été)* the summer months; **la mauvaise s., la s. froide** the winter months; **à la belle/mauvaise s.** when the weather turns warm/cold; *Littéraire* **la nouvelle s.** springtime; **la s. sèche** the dry season; **la s. des pluies** the rainy season, the rains

2 *(pour certains travaux, certains produits)* **ce n'est pas encore la s. des jonquilles** the daffodils aren't out yet; **ce n'est pas encore la s. des aubergines** aubergines aren't in season yet; **des fraises! mais ce n'est pas la s.!** strawberries! but it isn't the season for them!; **la s. des cerises** the cherry season; **la s. des vendanges** grape-harvesting time; **la s. des amours** the mating season; **la s. de la chasse** *(à courre)* the hunting season; *(à tir)* the shooting season; **la s. de la pêche** the fishing season

3 *(temps d'activité périodique)* season; **la s. théâtrale** the theatre season; **la s. touristique** the tourist season; **une s. sportive** a season; **il a fait deux saisons à Nice** *(footballeur)* he played two seasons for Nice; **faire les saisons** *(barman, femme de chambre)* to do seasonal work

4 *Com* season; **les restaurateurs ont fait une bonne s.** restaurant owners had a good season; **ici la s. commence en juin** the season starts in June here; **en s.** during the season; **en basse** *ou* **en morte s.** off season; **en haute s.** during the high season; **la pleine s.** the busy season; **en pleine s.** at the height of the season; **moyenne s.** shoulder period; **s. creuse** off season, slack season

5 *(cure)* season; **le médecin lui a recommandé une s. dans une station thermale** the doctor recommended that he/she spend a season at a spa

6 *Littéraire (âge de la vie)* age, time of life

• **de saison ADJ 1** *(adapté à la saison)* seasonal; **ce n'est pas un temps de s.** this weather's unusual for the time of the year; **être de s.** *(fruit)* to be in season; *(vêtement)* to be seasonable **2** *(opportun)* timely; **tes critiques ne sont pas de s.** this is not the time or place for your criticism

saisonnier, -ère [sɛzɔnje, -ɛr] **ADJ** seasonal, seasonable; **nous avons un temps bien s.** this is just the (right) sort of weather for the time of year

NM *(employé)* seasonal worker; **les saisonniers** seasonal staff

sait *etc voir* **savoir**

sajou [saʒu] **NM** *Zool* capuchin monkey, sapajou

saké [sake] **NM** sake

saki [saki] **NM** *Zool* saki

salade [salad] **NF 1** *Bot* **s. (verte)** lettuce; **une s.** a (head of) lettuce

2 *Culin* salad; **s. de concombre/de haricots** cucumber/bean salad; **champignons/haricots verts en s.** mushroom/green bean salad; *Belg* **s. de blé** lamb's lettuce, corn salad; **s. composée** mixed salad; **s. de fruits** fruit salad; **s. grecque** Greek salad; **s. niçoise** salade niçoise, niçoise salad; **s. russe** Russian salad; **s. verte** green salad

3 *Fam (situation embrouillée)* muddle, mess; **quelle s.!** what a muddle *or* mess!

4 *Fam* **vendre sa s.** to make a pitch□, to try to sell an idea□

• **salades NFPL** *Fam (mensonges)* tall stories, fibs; **raconter des salades** to tell fibs *or Br* porkies

saladier [saladje] **NM 1** *(récipient)* (salad) bowl **2** *(contenu)* **un s. de haricots** a bowlful of beans

salage [salaʒ] **NM** *Culin & (en travaux publics)* salting

salaire [salɛr] **NM 1** *Écon (gén)* pay; *(d'un ouvrier ▸ journalier, hebdomadaire)* wages, pay; *(d'un cadre supérieur)* salary; **un s. de famine** starvation wages; **s. à la tâche** *ou* **aux pièces** pay for piece work, piece rate; **s. après impôts** after-tax salary; **s. de base** basic salary *or* pay; **s. brut** gross pay; **s. de départ, s. d'embauche** starting salary; **s. fixe** fixed salary; **s. hebdomadaire** weekly pay *or* wage; **s. horaire** hourly wage; **s. indexé** index-linked pay; **s. indirect** fringe benefits; **s. mensuel** monthly pay; **s. au mérite** performance-related pay; **s. minimal** minimum wage; **s. minimum** minimum wage; **s. minimum interprofessionnel de croissance** = index-linked guaranteed minimum wage; **s. net** take-home pay, net salary; **s. nominal** nominal wage; **s. plafonné** wage ceiling; **s. réel** actual wage; **à s. unique** single-income **2** *Fig (dédommagement)* reward (**de** for); *(punition)* retribution (**de** for); **nous touchons maintenant le s. des années d'inflation** this is the price we have to pay for years of inflation

salaison [salɛzɔ̃] **NF** *(opération)* salting

• **salaisons NFPL** *(gén)* salted foods; *(viande, charcuterie)* salt *or* salted meat

salamalecs [salamalɛk] **NMPL** *Fam* bowing and scraping; **faire des s. à qn** to kowtow to sb, to bow and scrape before sb

salamandre [salamɑ̃dr] **NF** *Zool* salamander

salami [salami] **NM** salami

salant [salɑ̃] **ADJ M** salt *(avant n)*

NM salt marsh

salarial, -e, -aux, -ales [salarjal, -o] **ADJ** *(politique, revendications)* pay *(avant n)*, wage *(avant n)*, salary *(avant n)*; **revenus salariaux** income from salaries

salariat [salarja] **NM 1** *(personnes)* wage earners **2** *(mode de rémunération ▸ à la semaine)* (weekly) wages; *(▸ au mois)* (monthly) salary **3** *(état)* **le s. ne lui convient pas** being an employee doesn't suit him/her

salarié, -e [salarje] **ADJ 1** *(travailleur ▸ au mois)* salaried; *(▸ à la semaine)* wage-earning; **êtes-vous s.?** *(non chômeur)* are you in paid employment?; *(non libéral)* are you paid a salary? **2** *(travail)* paid; *(emploi, poste)* salaried

NM,F *(au mois)* salaried employee; *(à la semaine)* wage-earner; **les salariés** the employees; **les salariés de ce pays** this country's workforce

salarier **[9]** [salarje] **VT** to put on one's salaried staff *or* on the payroll; **je voudrais me faire s.** I'd like to get a permanent (salaried) job

salaud [salo] *très Fam* **NM** bastard; **c'est un beau s.** he's a real bastard; **je pars à Tahiti – ben mon s.!** I'm off to Tahiti – you lucky bastard *or Br* sod!

ADJ M un mec s. a bastard; **c'est s. de faire/de dire ça** that's a really shitty thing to do/to say; **il a été s. avec elle** he's been a real bastard to her

sale [sal] **ADJ 1** *(malpropre)* dirty; **blanc s.** dirty white; **elle est s. dans son travail** she's messy in her work, she's a messy worker; **il est s. comme un cochon** *ou* **un peigne** *ou* **un porc** he's filthy dirty

2 *(salissant)* dirty; **un travail s.** dirty work

3 *(obscène)* filthy, dirty

4 *(avant le nom) Fam (mauvais, désagréable)* nasty, rotten; **c'est une s. affaire** it's a nasty business; **c'est un s. boulot** it's a rotten *or* a lousy job; **faire le s. boulot** to do the dirty work; **elle a un s. caractère** she has a filthy temper; **quel s. temps!** what rotten *or* foul weather!; **il m'a joué un s. tour** he played a dirty trick on me; **s. bête** *(insecte)* nasty creature, *Hum* creepy crawly; *(personne)* nasty character *or* piece of work; *très Fam* **avoir une s. tête** *ou* **gueule** *(à faire peur)* to look evil, to be nasty-looking; **il a une s. tête ce matin** *(malade)* he looks under the weather *or Br* off-colour this morning; *(renfrogné)* he's got a face like a thundercloud this morning; **quand je vais lui dire, il va faire une s. tête** he's not going to be very pleased when I tell him; **s. fasciste!** dirty Fascist!

5 *Fam* **pas s.** *(appréciable)* pretty good, not bad

NMF *(personne)* dirty person

NM *Fam* **au s.** in *or* with the dirty washing□; **ton pantalon est au s.** your trousers are with the dirty washing

salé, -e[1] [sale] **ADJ 1** *Culin (beurre, cacahuètes, gâteaux secs)* salted; *(non sucré ▸ mets)* savoury; *(▸ goût)* salty; *(conservé dans le sel ▸ morue, porc)* salt *(avant n)*, salted; **ta soupe est trop salée** your soup's too salty

2 *(lac)* salt *(avant n)*; **eau salée** salt water

3 *Fam (exagéré ▸ condamnation)* stiff, heavy; *(▸ addition)* steep, stiff; **on a eu une addition salée** the bill was a bit steep

4 *Fam (osé ▸ histoire, plaisanterie)* steamy, X-rated **NM 1 le s.** *(non sucré)* savoury food; *(avec adjonction de sel)* salty food; **il vaut mieux manger le s. avant le sucré** it's better to eat savoury dishes before sweet ones **2** *Culin* salt pork; **petit s.** salted (flank end of) belly pork

ADV je ne mange pas très s. I don't like too much salt in my food; **je mange s.** I like my food well salted

salement [salmɑ̃] **ADV 1** *(malproprement)* dirtily; **qu'il mange s.!** he's such a messy eater! **2** *Fam (beaucoup)* badly□; *(très) Br* dead, *Am* real; **s. blessé** badly injured; **il a s. vieilli** he's really aged□

saler **[3]** [sale] **VT 1** *Culin (assaisonner)* to salt, to add salt to; *(en saumure)* to pickle, to salt (down)

2 *(chaussée)* to salt

3 *Fam (inculpé)* to throw the book at

4 *Fam (facture)* to inflate□; **c'était bon, mais ils ont salé l'addition!** it was good but the bill was a bit steep!; **je me suis fait s.!** I paid through the nose!, I've been stung *or* fleeced!

USAGE ABSOLU *Culin* **je ne sale presque pas** I hardly use any salt

saleté [salte] **NF 1** *(manque de propreté)* dirtiness; **les rues sont d'une s. incroyable** the streets are incredibly dirty *or* filthy

2 *(tache, crasse)* speck *or* piece of dirt; **il y a des petites saletés dans l'eau** there's some dirt in the water; **tu as une s. sur ta veste** you've got some dirt on your jacket; **faire des saletés** to make a mess; **ne rentre pas avec tes bottes, tu vas faire des saletés** don't come in with your boots on, you'll get dirt everywhere

3 *Fam (chose de mauvaise qualité) Br* rubbish, *Am* trash; **c'est de la s.** it's *Br* rubbish *or Am* trash; **c'est de la vraie s., ces chaussures en plastique** these plastic shoes are total *Br* rubbish *or Am* trash; **à la récréation, ils ne mangent que des saletés** all they eat at break is junk food

4 *(chose nuisible)* foul thing, nuisance; **le liseron, c'est de la s., ça étouffe toutes les fleurs** bindweed is a damned nuisance, it chokes all the flowers; **je dois prendre cette s. avant chaque repas!** I have to take this horrible stuff before every meal!; **quelle s., cette grippe!** this flu is a real pain *or* nuisance!

5 *très Fam (en injure)* **s.!** *(à un homme)* swine!, bastard!; *(à une femme)* bitch!, *Br* cow!; **c'est une vraie s.** *(homme)* he's a real bastard; *(femme)* she's a real bitch; **s. de chien!** damned *or Br* bloody dog!; **quelle s. de temps!** what foul *or* lousy weather!; **cette s. de voiture ne veut pas démarrer** the damned *or Br* bloody car won't start

6 *(calomnie)* (piece of) dirt; **tu as encore raconté des saletés sur mon compte** you've been spreading filthy rumours about me again

7 *(acte)* dirty *or* filthy trick; **il m'a fait une s.** he played a dirty trick on me

• **saletés** NFPL *(grossièretés)* dirt, filth, smut; **raconter des saletés** to say dirty things; *Euph* **les chiens font leurs saletés dans les jardins publics** dogs do their business in the parks

saleur, -euse [salœr, -øz] NM,F *Culin* salter

• **saleuse** NF *(en travaux publics)* salt spreader

salicoque [salikɔk] NF *(en Normandie)* prawn

salicorne [salikɔrn] NF *Bot* glasswort

salicylate [salisilat] NM *Chim* salicylate

salicylique [salisilik] ADJ *Chim* salicylic

salière [saljɛr] NF **1** saltcellar, *Am* salt shaker **2** *Fam (d'une personne maigre)* saltcellar

saligaud, -e [saligo, -od] NM,F *très Fam* **1** *(homme méprisable)* swine, bastard; *(femme méprisable)* bitch, *Br* cow **2** *Vieilli (homme sale)* filthy pig; *(femme sale)* slut

salin, -e [salɛ̃, -in] ADJ saline

NM **1** *Géog* salt marsh **2** *Chim* saline

• **saline** NF **1** *(établissement)* saltworks *(singulier)* **2** *(marais)* salt marsh

salinage [salinaʒ] NM **1** *(établissement)* saltworks *(singulier)* **2** *(concentration)* concentrating of the brine

salinier, -ère [salinje, -ɛr] ADJ salt *(avant n)*, salt-producing

NM,F salt producer

salinité [salinite] NF **1** *(degré)* (degree of) salinity **2** *(fait d'être salé)* salinity

salique [salik] ADJ *Hist* salic

salir [32] [salir] VT **1** *(eau, surface)* to (make) dirty; *(vêtements)* to (make) dirty, to mess up, to soil; **tu as sali beaucoup de vaisselle** you've dirtied a lot of dishes; *Euph* **s. ses draps** *ou* **son lit** to soil one's bed; **je ne veux pas te faire s. d'autres draps, nous dormirons dans ceux-là** I don't want to make more dirty washing for you, we'll sleep on these sheets **2** *(honneur, amitié)* to besmirch; *(réputation, nom)* to besmirch, to sully; **ils cherchent à s. le leader de l'opposition** they're trying to sully *or* to smear the reputation of the leader of the opposition

VPR **se salir 1** *(emploi réfléchi)* to get dirty, to dirty oneself; *Fig* to lose one's reputation; *aussi Fig* **se s. les mains** to get one's hands dirty; **c'est lui qui décide des licenciements, à moi de me s. les mains** he decides who'll get fired and I do the dirty work **2** *(emploi passif)* to get dirty; **ne prends pas un manteau beige, ça se salit vite** don't buy a beige coat, it shows the dirt *or* it gets dirty very quickly

salissant, -e [salisɑ̃, -ɑ̃t] ADJ **1** *(qui se salit)* **être s.** to show the dirt; **c'est une teinte salissante** this shade shows the dirt **2** *(qui salit ▸ travail)* dirty, messy

salissure [salisyr] NF *(restée en surface)* speck of dirt; *(ayant pénétré le tissu)* dirty mark, stain; **le papier peint est couvert de salissures** the wallpaper's stained all over

salivaire [salivɛr] ADJ salivary

salivation [salivasjɔ̃] NF salivation

salive [saliv] NF **1** *Physiol* saliva, spit **2** *Fam (locutions)* **gaspiller sa s.** to waste one's breath; **n'usez pas** *ou* **ne gaspillez pas** *ou* **épargnez votre s.** save *or* don't waste your breath; **avant d'obtenir les subventions, j'ai dû dépenser** *ou* **user beaucoup de s.** before getting the subsidies, I had to do a lot of (fast) talking; **avaler** *ou* **ravaler sa s.** *(se taire)* to keep quiet

saliver [3] [salive] VI **1** *Physiol* to salivate **2** *(avoir l'eau à la bouche)* **le menu me fait s.** the menu is making my mouth water; **le chien salivait devant sa pâtée** the dog was drooling *or* dribbling at the sight of his food **3** *Fam (d'envie)* to drool; **il salivait devant les voitures de sport** he was drooling over the sports cars; **il me fait s. en me parlant de ses vacances aux Caraïbes** he makes me green with envy talking about his holidays in the Caribbean

salle [sal] NF **1** *(dans une habitation privée)* room; **s. de bains** *(lieu)* bathroom; *(mobilier)* bathroom suite; **s. d'eau** shower room; **s. de jeu** *(d'une maison) Br* playroom, *Am* rumpus room; *(d'un casino)* gaming room; **s. à manger** *(lieu)* dining room; *(mobilier)* dining room suite; **s. de séjour** living room

2 *(dans un édifice public)* hall, room; *(dans un musée)* room, gallery; **s. d'accueil (de la clientèle)** reception room; **s. d'attente** waiting room; **s. d'audience** courtroom; **s. de bal** ballroom; **s. des banquets** banqueting hall; *Bourse* **s. des changes** dealing room; **s. de classe** classroom; **s. des coffres** strongroom; **s. des commandes** control room; *Typ* **s. de composition** composing room; **s. de concert** concert hall, auditorium; **s. de conférences** *Univ* lecture *Br* theatre *or Am* hall; *(pour colloques)* conference room; *TV* **s. de contrôle de production** production control room; **s. de démonstration** showroom; *TV* **s. de détente** *(pour invités)* green room; **s. d'embarquement** departure lounge; **s. d'études** *Br* prep room, *Am* study hall; **s. d'exposition** showroom; *(pour une foire)* exhibition hall; **s. des fêtes** village hall; **s. de garde** (hospital) staffroom; *TV* **s. de maquillage** make-up room; *Bourse* **s. des marchés** trading floor; *Cin* **s. de montage** cutting room; **s. paroissiale** church hall; **s. des pas perdus** *Rail* (station) concourse; *(au tribunal)* waiting room *or* hall; **s. des professeurs** *Scol* (school) staffroom; *Univ Br* staff common room, *Am* professors' lounge; **s. de projection** projection room; **s. de réanimation** resuscitation unit; **s. de rédaction** *(d'un journal)* newsroom; **s. de restaurant** (restaurant) dining room; **s. de réception** *(dans un hôtel)* function room; *(dans un palais)* stateroom; **s. de réunion** boardroom, meeting room; **s. de shoot** *(pour les drogués)* injection room; **s. de spectacle** auditorium; **s. de travail** workroom; **s. du trône** stateroom, throne room; **s. des tortures** torture chamber; **s. des ventes** *Br* auction room, *Am* auction gallery

3 *(dans un hôpital) Br* ward, *Am* room; **s. d'opération** operating *Br* theatre *or Am* room; **s. des urgences** *Br* emergency ward, *Am* emergency room

4 *Cin & Théât (lieu)* theatre, auditorium; *(spectateurs)* audience; **faire s. comble** to pack the house; **le cinéma a cinq salles** it's a five-screen *Br* cinema *or Am* movie theater; **sa dernière production sort en s. en septembre** his/her latest production will be released *or* out in September; **dans les salles d'art et d'essai** *ou* **les petites salles** in arthouse *Br* cinemas *or Am* movie theaters; **dans les salles obscures** in the *Br* cinemas *or Am* movie theaters; **s. de cinéma** theatre, auditorium

5 *Sport* **athlétisme en s.** indoor athletics; **jouer en s.** to play indoors

salmigondis [salmigɔ̃di] NM mish-mash, *Br* hotchpotch, *Am* hodgepodge

salmis [salmi] NM salmi, salmis *(game part-cooked by roasting then stewed in a wine sauce)*

salmonelle [salmɔnɛl] NF *Biol* salmonella

salmonellose [salmɔneloz] NF *Méd* salmonellosis

salmoniculteur, -trice [salmɔnikyltœr, -tris] NM,F salmon farmer

salmoniculture [salmɔnikyltyr] NF salmon farming

saloir [salwar] NM **1** *(récipient)* salting *or* brine tub **2** *(pièce)* salting room **3** *Vieilli (salière)* salt pot

Salomon [salɔmɔ̃] NPR *Bible* (King) Solomon

NFPL *Géog* **les îles S.** the Solomon Islands

salon [salɔ̃] NM **1** *(chez un particulier ▸ pièce)* living *or* sitting room, *Br* lounge; *(▸ meubles)* living-room suite; **s. en cuir** leather suite; **grand s.** drawing room; **s. de jardin** garden set; **s. de réception** reception room

2 *(dans un hôtel, un aéroport)* lounge; *(pour réceptions, pour fêtes)* function room; *(d'un paquebot)* saloon, lounge; **s. d'attente** waiting room; **s. classe affaires** *(dans un aéroport)* business lounge

3 *(boutique)* **s. de beauté** beauty parlour *or* salon; **s. de coiffure** hairdressing salon; **s. de manucure** nail salon, nail bar; **s. de thé** tearoom; **s. d'essayage** fitting room, changing room

4 *Com (exposition)* exhibition, trade fair; **S. de l'Automobile** Car *or Br* Motor *or Am* Automobile Show; **S. du Livre** = annual book fair in Paris; **S. nautique** *ou* **de la navigation** Boat Show; **s. professionnel** trade show *or* fair

5 *Ordinat* **s. (de bavardage)** chat room

6 *Beaux-Arts* salon

7 *Littérature* salon; **tenir s.** to hold a salon; *Fig* **alors, mesdemoiselles, on fait** *ou* **tient s.?** having an important discussion, are we, ladies?; **conversation de s.** idle chatter

salonnier [salɔnje] NM *Journ* society columnist

saloon [salun] NM saloon *(bar in the Wild West)*

salop [salo] NM *très Fam Vieilli* bastard, *Am* son-of-a-bitch

salopard [salɔpar] NM *très Fam* bastard, *Am* son-of-a-bitch

salope [salɔp] *Vulg* NF **1** *(femme méprisable)* bitch, *Br* cow; *(femme aux mœurs légères)* tart, slut, *Br* slapper **2** *(homme méprisable)* bastard, *Am* son-of-a-bitch; **c'est vraiment une s., ce type!** he's a real bastard, that guy!

ADJ F **tu as été s. avec moi** you were a bitch to me

saloper [3] [salɔpe] VT *très Fam* **1** *(salir)* to dirty[□], to mess up **2** *(mal exécuter)* to make a dog's breakfast *or Br* a pig's ear of

saloperie [salɔpri] NF *très Fam* **1** *(marchandise de mauvaise qualité)* garbage, junk, *Br* rubbish

2 *(chose désagréable, nuisible)* **c'est de la s. à poser, ce papier peint** this wallpaper's a real pain to put on; **quelles saloperies, ces taupes!** these moles are a damn nuisance!; **le chien a avalé une s.** the dog has eaten something nasty; **c'est une vraie s., ce nouveau virus** this new virus is really nasty; **s. de neige!** damn *or Br* bloody snow!; **s. de voiture, elle ne veut pas démarrer!** the damn *or Br* bloody car won't start!

3 *(chose sale)* **tu as une s. sur ta manche** you've got a dirty mark on your sleeve; **il y avait toutes sortes de saloperies par terre** there was a load of crud *or Br* muck on the floor

4 *(calomnie)* nasty *or* bitchy remark; *(action méprisable)* nasty *or* dirty trick; **faire une s. à qn** to play a dirty *or* a nasty trick on sb

• **saloperies** NFPL **1** *(grossièretés)* filthy language *(UNCOUNT)*; **dire des saloperies** to use filthy language **2** *(calomnies)* nasty *or* bitchy remarks; **elle a encore dit des saloperies sur moi** she made some more bitchy remarks about me **3** *(aliments malsains)* junk (food), garbage, *Br* rubbish; **il bouffe que des saloperies** he eats nothing but garbage *or* junk *or Br* rubbish

salopette [salɔpɛt] NF *(de ville) Br* dungarees, *Am* overalls; *(de ski)* salopette; *(d'un ouvrier) Br* overalls, *Am* overall

salpêtre [salpɛtr] NM saltpetre

salpêtrer [4] [salpetre] VT **1** *(champ)* to treat with saltpetre **2** *(humidité)* to treat with saltpetre **3** *(murs)* to rot

salpicon [salpikɔ̃] NM *Culin* salpicon *(diced meat, poultry, vegetables etc in sauce, used as a filling for vol-au-vents etc)*

salpingite [salpɛ̃ʒit] NF *Méd* salpingitis

salsa [salsa] NF **1** *(musique, danse)* salsa **2** *Culin* **s. mexicaine** salsa

salsepareille [salsəparɛj] NF sarsaparilla

salsifis [salsifi] NM salsify

saltimbanque [saltɛ̃bɑ̃k] NMF **1** *(acrobate)* acrobat **2** *(professionnel du spectacle)* entertainer

salto [salto] NM *Sport (en gymnastique)* salto

salubre [salybr] ADJ **1** *(climat)* salubrious, hygienic, wholesome; *(logement)* salubrious **2** *Fig (mesures)* salubrious, hygienic

salubrité [salybrite] NF **1** *(d'un local)* salubrity; *(d'un climat)* salubriousness, salubrity, healthiness **2** *Jur* **s. publique** public health

saluer [7] [salɥe] VT **1** *(dire bonjour à)* to say hello to, to greet; *(dire au revoir à)* to say goodbye to; *(faire signe à ▸ de la main)* to wave at; *(▸ de la tête)* to nod to; **il est passé sans me s.** he walked past me without saying hello; **l'acteur salue le public** the actor bows to the audience *or* takes his bow; **il m'a demandé de vous s.** he asked me to give you his regards; **comment doit-on s. le pape?** how should one address the Pope?; **s. qn bien bas** to take one's hat off to sb; *Hum* **au revoir, mes amis, je vous salue bien bas** goodbye, my friends, and a very good day to you

2 *Mil* to salute

3 *Rel* **je vous salue Marie** Hail Mary

4 *(accueillir)* to greet; **je voudrais tout d'abord s. tous ceux qui nous ont aidés à préparer cette conférence** first of all I'd like to welcome all those who have helped us prepare this conference; **son film a été unanimement salué par la presse** his/her movie *or Br* film was unanimously acclaimed by the press; **sa suggestion fut saluée par des cris de joie** his/her suggestion was greeted with cheers; **des protestations ont salué sa nomination** his/her appointment met with protests

5 *(rendre hommage à ▸ courage, génie)* to salute, to pay homage *or* tribute to; *(reconnaître en tant que)* to hail; **on a salué en elle le chef de file du mouvement** she was hailed as the leader of the movement; **je salue en lui notre sauveur** I salute him as our saviour

VI *Naut* **s. du pavillon** *ou* **des pavillons** to dip a flag (in salute)

VPR se saluer *(se dire bonjour)* to say hello

salure [salyr] **NF** *(état)* saltiness; *(teneur en sel)* salinity

salut [saly] **NM 1** *(marque de politesse)* **faire un s. de la main à qn** to wave to sb; **faire un s. de la tête à qn** to nod to sb; **il lui retourna son s.** *(en paroles)* he returned his/her greeting; *(de la main)* he waved back at him/her; **répondre au s. de qn** to return sb's greeting

2 *Mil* salute; **faire le s. militaire** to (give the military) salute; **s. au drapeau** saluting the colours

3 *(survie ▸ d'une personne, d'un pays)* salvation, safety; *(▸ d'une entreprise, d'une institution)* salvation; **je dois mon s. à son arrivée** I was saved by his/her arrival, his/her arrival was my salvation; **chercher/trouver le s. dans la fuite** to seek/to find safety in flight

4 *Littéraire (sauveur)* saviour

5 *Rel (rédemption)* salvation; **prions pour le s. de son âme** let us pray for the salvation of his/her soul

6 *Naut (du pavillon)* dipping the flag

EXCLAM *Fam (en arrivant)* hi *or* hello (there)!; *(en partant)* bye!, see you!; **s. la compagnie!** *(en partant)* bye, everybody!

salutaire [salytɛr] **ADJ 1** *(physiquement ▸ air)* healthy; *(▸ remède)* beneficial; *(▸ exercice, repos)* salutary, beneficial; **cette semaine dans les Alpes m'a été s.** that week in the Alps did my health a power of good **2** *(moralement ▸ conseil, épreuve)* salutary; *(▸ lecture, effet)* beneficial

salutations [salytasjɔ̃] **NFPL** greetings; **elle t'envoie ses s.** she sends you her regards, she sends her regards to you; **je vous prie d'agréer, Monsieur, mes s. distinguées** *(à quelqu'un dont on connaît le nom) Br* yours sincerely, *Am* sincerely (yours); *(à quelqu'un dont on ne connaît pas le nom) Br* yours faithfully, *Am* sincerely (yours)

salutiste [salytist] **ADJ** Salvationist

NMF Salvationist

Salvador [salvadɔr] **NM le S.** El Salvador

salvadorien, -enne [salvadɔrjɛ̃, -ɛn] **ADJ** Salvadorian, Salvadorean

• **Salvadorien, -enne NM,F** Salvadorian, Salvadorean

salvateur, -trice [salvatœr, -tris] **ADJ** *Littéraire* saving *(avant n)*; **la mort salvatrice** the blessed release of death

salve [salv] **NF 1** *Mil* salvo, volley; **tirer une s. (d'honneur)** to fire a salute **2** *Fig* **s. d'applaudissements** round *or* burst of applause

samare [samar] **NF** *Bot* samara, key *or* winged seed

samaritain, -e [samaritɛ̃, -ɛn] **ADJ** Samaritan

NM *Suisse (secouriste)* qualified first-aider

• **Samaritain, -e NM,F** Samaritan; **le bon S.** the good Samaritan; *Fig* **faire le bon S., jouer les bons Samaritains** to be a Good Samaritan; **les Samaritains** the Samaritans

samba [sɑ̃ba] **NF** samba

samedi [samdi] **NM** Saturday; **S. saint** Holy *or* Easter Saturday; *voir aussi* **mardi**

samizdat [samizdat] **NM** samizdat

Samoa [samɔa] **NFPL** *Géog* **les S. occidentales/orientales** Western/Eastern Samoa

samossa [samɔsa] **NM** *Culin* samosa

samouraï [samuraj] **NM** samurai

samovar [samɔvar] **NM** samovar

sampan, sampang [sɑ̃pɑ̃] **NM** sampan

sampler[1] [sɑ̃plœr] **NM** *Mus* sampler

sampler[2] **[3]** [sɑ̃ple] **VT** *Mus* to sample

SAMR [ɛsaɛmɛr] **NM** *Méd (abrév* **staphylococcus aureus méticillino-résistant)** MRSA

SAMU, Samu [samy] **NM** *(abrév* **Service d'aide médicale d'urgence)** = French ambulance and emergency service, *Br* ≃ ambulance service, *Am* ≃ Paramedics; **appelez le S.!** call an ambulance!; **le S. social** = mobile medical and support service for homeless people

samurai [samuraj] = **samouraï**

sana [sana] **NM** *Fam (abrév* **sanatorium)** *Br* sanatorium▫, *Am* sanitarium▫

sanatorium [sanatɔrjɔm] **NM** *Br* sanatorium, *Am* sanitarium

sanctificateur, -trice [sɑ̃ktifikatœr, -tris] **ADJ** sanctifying

NM,F sanctifier; **le S.** the Holy Ghost

sanctification [sɑ̃ktifikasjɔ̃] **NF** sanctification

sanctificatrice [sɑ̃ktifikatris] *voir* **sanctificateur**

sanctifier [9] [sɑ̃ktifje] **VT 1** *Rel (rendre sacré)* to sanctify; *(célébrer)* to hallow; **que Ton nom soit sanctifié** hallowed be thy name **2** *Fig (patrie, valeurs)* to hold sacred

sanction [sɑ̃ksjɔ̃] **NF 1** *(mesure répressive)* sanction; **imposer des sanctions à** to apply sanctions against, to impose sanctions on; **lever des sanctions (prises) contre** to raise (the) sanctions against; **prendre des sanctions contre** to take sanctions against; **s. administrative** administrative sanction; **sanctions diplomatiques/économiques** diplomatic/economic sanctions; **sanctions ciblées** smart sanctions

2 *Scol & Sport* punishment, disciplinary action *(UNCOUNT)*; **prendre des sanctions contre un élève** to punish a pupil; **prendre des sanctions contre un sportif** to take disciplinary action against an athlete

3 *Jur* sanction, penalty; **s. pénale** penal sanction

4 *(approbation)* sanction, ratification; **l'expression a reçu la s. de l'usage** the expression has become generally accepted

5 *(conséquence)* result, outcome; **c'est la s. du succès** that's the price of success

sanctionner [3] [sɑ̃ksjɔne] **VT 1** *(punir ▸ délit, élève)* to punish; *(▸ sportif, haut fonctionnaire)* to take disciplinary action against; *(▸ pays)* to impose sanctions on; **il s'est fait s. pour sa grossièreté envers l'arbitre** he was penalized for being rude to the umpire **2** *(ratifier ▸ loi)* to sanction, to ratify; *(▸ décision)* to sanction, to agree with; **sa théorie a été sanctionnée par le temps** time has proved his/her theory to be correct; **sanctionné par l'usage** generally accepted

sanctuaire [sɑ̃ktɥɛr] **NM 1** *Rel* sanctuary

2 *(asile)* sanctuary; **l'île est un s. pour les oiseaux** the island is a favourite haunt for birds

3 *(foyer, centre vital)* hub, centre

4 *Littéraire (tréfonds)* innermost part; **dans le s. de mon cœur** in my innermost being

5 *Pol* territory under the nuclear umbrella

sanctuariser [3] [sɑ̃ktɥarize] **VT** *(nature)* to preserve, to protect; *(territoire)* to protect, to safeguard; *(lieu, établissement)* to make secure; *(budget, fonds, crédits)* to ring-fence

sanctus [sɑ̃ktus] **NM** *Rel & Mus* Sanctus

sandale [sɑ̃dal] **NF** sandal

sandalette [sɑ̃dalɛt] **NF** (light) sandal

Sandow® [sɑ̃do] **NM 1** *(tendeur)* elastic luggage strap **2** *Sport (en gymnastique)* chest expander

sandre [sɑ̃dr] **NM** *Ich* zander, pikeperch

sandwich [sɑ̃dwitʃ] *(pl* **sandwichs** *ou* **sandwiches) NM 1** *(gén)* sandwich; **s. au fromage** cheese sandwich; *Fam* **prendre qn en s.** to sandwich sb; *Fam* **j'étais pris en s. entre eux** I was sandwiched between them **2** *Belg (pain au lait)* finger roll *(made with milk)*; **s. garni** sandwich

sandwicherie [sɑ̃dwiʃəri, sɑ̃dwitʃəri] **NF** sandwich bar

sang [sɑ̃] **NM 1** *Biol* blood; **à s. froid/chaud** cold-/warm-blooded; **fais un garrot pour arrêter le s.** make a tourniquet to stop the bleeding; **ça se transmet par le s.** it's transmitted in the blood; **du s. à la une** gory front-page news; **s. artériel/veineux** arterial/venous blood; **donner son s.** *(pour transfusion)* to give blood; *Fig* **avoir du s. sur les mains** to have blood on one's hands; **répandre** *ou* **verser** *ou* **faire couler le s.** to shed *or* to spill blood; **noyer une révolte dans le s.** to put down a revolt ruthlessly; **être en s., nager** *ou* **baigner dans son s.** to be covered in blood; **se mordre les lèvres jusqu'au s.** to bite one's lips until one draws blood; **il m'a griffé jusqu'au s.** he scratched me and drew blood; *Fig* **avoir du s. dans les veines** to have courage *or* guts; *Fam* **ne pas avoir de s. dans les veines, avoir du s. de poulet** *ou* **de navet** to have no guts, to be a complete wimp; *Fig* **avoir le s. chaud** *(colérique)* to be *or* to have a short fuse; *(impétueux)* to be hot-headed; *(sensuel)* to be hot-blooded; **avoir la chanson dans le s.** to be a born singer; **il a ça dans le s.** it's in his blood; **mon s. s'est glacé** *ou* **figé dans mes veines** my blood ran cold; **le s. lui est monté au visage** *ou* **à la tête** the blood rushed to his/her cheeks; *Fig* **mon s. n'a fait qu'un tour** *(d'effroi)* my heart missed *or* skipped a beat; *(de rage)* I saw red; *Fig* **se faire du mauvais s.** to worry; **se faire un s. d'encre, se manger** *ou* **se ronger les sangs** to worry oneself sick, to be worried stiff, to fret; **je me fais du mauvais s. pour lui** I'm worried sick about him; **ça m'a tourné le s.** *ou* **les sangs** it gave me quite a turn; *Fig* **du s. frais** *ou* **nouveau** *ou* **neuf** *(personnes)* new blood; *(argent)* new *or* fresh money

2 *Littéraire (vie)* (life)blood; **donner son s. pour son pays** to shed one's blood *or* to sacrifice one's life for one's country; **payer de son s.** to pay with one's life

3 *(race, extraction)* blood; **épouser qn de son s.** to marry a blood relative; **nous ne sommes pas du même s.** we're not of the same flesh and blood; **les liens du s.** blood ties; **de s. royal** of royal blood; **s. noble** noble *or* blue blood; **avoir du s. noble** to be of noble blood; **s. bleu** blue blood; **lorsque l'on a du s. bleu dans les veines...** when one is blue-blooded...; *Prov* **bon s. ne saurait mentir** blood is thicker than water

4 *Fam (locution)* **bon s. (de bonsoir)!** *(exprimant la surprise) Br* blimey!, *Am* gee (whiz)!; *(exprimant la colère)* blast it!, hell!

• **au sang ADJ** *Culin (canard)* = served with a sauce incorporating its own blood

• **de sang ADJ** *(cheval)* blood *(avant n)*

• **du sang ADJ** *(princier)* of the blood (royal)

sang-froid [sɑ̃frwa] **NM INV** composure, calm, sang-froid; **garder** *ou* **conserver son s.** to stay calm, to keep one's cool; **perdre son s.** to lose one's self-control *or* one's cool

• **de sang-froid ADV** in cold blood, cold-bloodedly; **tuer qn de s.** to kill sb in cold blood *or* cold-bloodedly; **commis de s.** cold-blooded

sanglant, -e [sɑ̃glɑ̃, -ɑ̃t] **ADJ 1** *(blessure, bataille, règne)* bloody; *(bras, mains)* covered in blood, bloody; *(linge)* bloody, blood-soaked; *(spectacle)* gory **2** *(blessant ▸ critiques)* scathing; *(▸ reproches)* bitter; *(▸ affront)* cruel **3** *Littéraire (couleur de sang)* blood-red

sangle [sɑ̃gl] **NF** *(lanière ▸ gén)* strap; *(▸ d'un lit, d'une chaise)* webbing; *(▸ d'un cheval)* girth

sangler [3] [sɑ̃gle] **VT 1** *(cheval)* to girth **2** *(paquet, valise)* to strap up **3** *Fig (serrer)* **sanglée dans son corset** tightly corseted; **sanglé dans son uniforme** buttoned up tight in his uniform

VPR se sangler *(dans un vêtement très étroit)* to do oneself up tight

sanglier [sɑ̃glije] **NM** *Zool* (wild) boar

sanglot [sɑ̃glo] **NM 1** *(hoquet, pleurs)* sob; **"non", dit-il dans un s.** "no," he sobbed; **avec des sanglots dans la voix** with a sob in one's voice; **il pleurait à**

gros sanglots he was sobbing his heart out **2** *Littéraire (bruit plaintif)* lamentation; **les sanglots du vent** the moaning of the wind

sangloter [3] [sɑ̃glɔte] VI **1** *(pleurer)* to sob; **elle s'endormit en sanglotant** she cried herself to sleep **2** *Littéraire (océan, vent)* to sob, to sigh; *(accordéon)* to sigh

sang-mêlé [sɑ̃mele] NMF INV *Vieilli* half-caste

sangria [sɑ̃grija] NF sangria

sangsue [sɑ̃sy] NF **1** *Zool* leech **2** *Fam (importun)* leech; **son frère est une véritable s.!** his/her brother sticks *or* clings to you like a leech!

sanguin, -e [sɑ̃gɛ̃, -in] ADJ **1** *(groupe, plasma, transfusion, vaisseau)* blood *(avant n)*; *(système)* circulatory **2** *(rouge ▸ visage, teint)* ruddy **3** *(humeur, tempérament)* sanguine

NM,F fiery person

• **sanguine** NF **1** *Beaux-Arts (crayon)* red chalk, sanguine; *(dessin)* red chalk drawing, sanguine **2** *Géol* red haematite **3** *(orange)* blood orange

> Il faut noter que l'adjectif anglais **sanguine** est un faux ami. Il signifie **optimiste**.
> Do not confuse with **sanguinaire**.

sanguinaire [sɑ̃ginɛr] ADJ **1** *(assoiffé de sang)* bloodthirsty **2** *Littéraire (féroce ▸ bataille, conquête)* bloody, sanguinary

> Do not confuse with **sanguin**.

sanguinolent, -e [sɑ̃ginɔlɑ̃, -ɑ̃t] ADJ **1** *(sécrétion)* spotted *or* streaked with blood; *(linge, pansement)* soiled *or* tinged with blood; *(plaie)* oozing blood; *(personne)* covered in blood, blood-streaked **2** *Littéraire (rouge ▸ lèvres)* blood-red

sanie [sani] NF *Vieilli Méd* pus and blood, *Spéc* sanies

sanitaire [sanitɛr] ADJ **1** *Admin & Méd (conditions)* sanitary, health *(avant n)*; *(règlement, mesures)* health *(avant n)*; *(personnel)* medical, health *(avant n)* **2** *Constr* sanitary, plumbing *(UNCOUNT)*; **l'équipement s.** the plumbing; **système s.** sanitation (system)

NM *(installations)* plumbing (for bathroom and toilet)

• **sanitaires** NMPL (bathroom and) toilet; **les sanitaires du camp sont tout à fait insuffisants** the sanitary arrangements in the camp are totally inadequate

SANS [sɑ̃] PRÉP **1** *(indiquant l'absence, la privation, l'exclusion)* without; **il est parti s. argent** he left without any money; **avec ou s. sucre?** with or without sugar?; **avec de la glace ou s.?** with or without ice?; **j'ai trouvé s. problème** I found it without any difficulty *or* with no difficulty; **je voudrais te parler s. témoins** I'd like to speak to you alone; **son comportement est s. reproche** his/her behaviour is beyond reproach; **être s. scrupules** to have no scruples, to be unscrupulous; **tu as oublié le rendez-vous? tu es s. excuse!** you forgot the appointment? that's unforgivable!; **homme s. cœur/s. pitié** heartless/pitiless man; **couple s. enfants** childless couple; **s. additif** additive-free; **essence s. plomb** unleaded *or* lead-free petrol; **bonbons s. sucre** sugar-free sweets; **régime s. sel** salt-free diet; **marcher s. but** to walk aimlessly; **s. commentaire!** no comment!; **la chambre fait 40 euros, s. le petit déjeuner** the room costs 40 euros, breakfast not included *or* exclusive of breakfast; **nous y sommes arrivés s. difficultés** *ou* **mal** we managed it without any difficulty; **il n'est pas s. charme** he's not without charm, he's not lacking in charm; **très** *Fam* **être s. un** to be broke *or Br* skint

2 *(exprimant la condition)* but for; **s. toi, je ne l'aurais jamais fait** if it hadn't been for you *or* but for you, I would never have done it; **s. la pluie, tout aurait été parfait** had it not been raining *or* but for the rain, everything would have been perfect

3 *(avec un infinitif)* without; **elle a réussi s. travailler beaucoup** she passed without doing much work; **s. être vu** without being seen; **partons s. plus attendre** come on, let's not wait any more; **s. plus attendre, je passe la parole à M. Blais** without further ado, I'll hand you over to Mr Blais; **tu n'es pas s. savoir qu'il est amoureux d'elle** you must be aware that he's in love with her; **je ne suis pas s. avoir de craintes** I am somewhat anxious; **il est responsable s. l'être tout à fait** it's his responsibility, but only to a certain extent; **je comprends s. comprendre** I understand, but only up to a point

ADV without; **il faudra faire s.!** we'll have to go without!; **passe-moi mon manteau, je ne peux pas sortir s.** hand me my coat, I can't go out without it; **c'est un jour s.!** *(tout va mal)* it's one of those days!

• **non sans** PRÉP not without; **on est arrivés non s. peine** we got there, not without difficulty; **non s. protester** not without protesting; **je suis parti non s. leur dire ma façon de penser** I didn't leave without telling them what I thought

• **sans cela, sans ça** CONJ *Fam* otherwise❑; **je serai absente; s. cela, j'aurais accepté votre invitation** I won't be here, otherwise I would have accepted your invitation

• **sans que** CONJ **ils ont réglé le problème s. que nous ayons à intervenir** they dealt with the problem without us having to intervene

• **sans quoi** CONJ **soyez ponctuels, s. quoi vous ne pourrez pas vous inscrire** be sure to be on time, otherwise you won't be able to register

sans-abri [sɑ̃zabri] NMF INV homeless person; **les s.** the homeless

sans-cœur [sɑ̃kœr] ADJ INV heartless

NMF INV heartless person

sanscrit, -e [sɑ̃skri, -it] = **sanskrit**

sans-culotte [sɑ̃kylɔt] *(pl* **sans-culottes**) NM sans-culotte; *Hist* **les sans-culottes** the sans-culottes

sans-dessein [sɑ̃desɛ̃] *Can Fam Péj* ADJ INV clueless, gormless

NMF INV clueless *or* gormless person

sans-emploi [sɑ̃zɑ̃plwa] NMF INV unemployed *or* jobless person; **les s.** the unemployed

sans-façon [sɑ̃fasɔ̃] NM INV *Littéraire* casualness, offhandedness

sans-faute [sɑ̃fot] NM INV **faire un s.** *Sport* to do *or* to have a clear round; *Scol* not to make a single mistake; **pour l'instant, c'est un s.!** *(dans un jeu)* so far so good!

sans-fil [sɑ̃fil] ADJ INV *Ordinat & Tel* wireless

NM INV cordless telephone

sans-gêne [sɑ̃ʒɛn] ADJ INV *(personne)* inconsiderate; *(manières)* bad; **qu'est-ce qu'il est s.!** he's got no consideration!

NM INV lack of consideration

NMF INV inconsiderate person; **en voilà une s.!** she's got no consideration!

sanskrit, -e [sɑ̃skri, -it] ADJ Sanskrit

NM *(langue)* Sanskrit

sans-le-sou [sɑ̃lsu] NMF INV *Fam* pauper❑, penniless person❑; **les s.** the have-nots❑

sans-logis [sɑ̃lɔʒi] NMF INV homeless person; **les s.** the homeless

sansonnet [sɑ̃sɔnɛ] NM *Orn* starling

sans-papiers [sɑ̃papje] NMF INV illegal immigrant

sans-parti [sɑ̃parti] NMF INV *Pol (gén)* independent member *(of an assembly or a Parliament)*; *(dans un système de parti unique)* non-party member

sans-patrie [sɑ̃patri] NMF INV stateless person

sans-souci [sɑ̃susi] ADJ INV carefree, happy-go-lucky

NMF INV *Littéraire* happy-go-lucky person

santal, -als [sɑ̃tal] NM *Bot* sandal; **bois de s.** sandalwood

santé [sɑ̃te] NF **1** *(de l'esprit, d'une économie, d'une entreprise)* health, soundness; *(d'une personne, d'une plante)* health; **avoir une bonne/mauvaise s.** to be healthy/unhealthy; *Fam* **comment va la s.?** how are you keeping?; **c'est bon/mauvais pour la s.** it's good/bad for your health *or* for you; **en bonne s.** *(personne)* healthy, in good health; *(plante)* healthy; *(économie)* healthy, sound; *(monnaie)* strong; **je vous espère en bonne s.** I hope you're quite well, I hope you're in good health; **meilleure s.!** hope you're better soon *or* you get well soon!; **en mauvaise s.** *(animal, personne)* in bad *or* poor health; *(plante)* unhealthy; *(économie, monnaie)* weak; **le bon air lui a rendu** *ou* **redonné la s.** the fresh air has restored him/her to health; **état de s.** health; **s. mentale** mental health; *Fam* **avoir la s.** *(être infatigable)* to be a bundle of energy; **avoir une s. de fer** to have an iron constitution, to be (as) strong as a horse; **avoir une petite s., ne pas avoir de s.** to be very delicate; *Fam* **avoir de la s.** *(avoir de l'audace)* to have a nerve *or Br* a brass neck

2 *Admin* **la s. publique** public health; **services de s.** health services

3 *Naut* **la s.** the quarantine service

4 *Mil* **service de s. des armées** medical corps

EXCLAM **1** *Fam (en trinquant)* cheers! **2** *Suisse (à vos souhaits)* bless you!

• **à la santé de** PRÉP *(en portant un toast)* **à votre/ta s.!** cheers!, your (good) health!; **à la s. de ma femme!** (here's) to my wife!; **buvons à la s. des mariés!** let's drink to the bride and groom!

santiags [sɑ̃tjag] NFPL *Fam* cowboy boots❑

santon [sɑ̃tɔ̃] NM crib *or* manger figurine *(in Provence)*

saoudien, -enne [saudjɛ̃, -ɛn] ADJ Saudi (Arabian)

• **Saoudien, -enne** NM,F Saudi (Arabian)

saoul, -e [su, sul] = **soûl**

saoulard, -e [sular, -ard] = **soûlard, -e**

saouler [sule] = **soûler**

sapajou [sapaʒu] NM *Zool* capuchin monkey, sapajou

sape [sap] NF **1** *Mil & (en travaux publics) (travaux)* sapping; *(tranchée)* sap **2** *Fig* **travail de s.** (insidious) undermining; **par un patient travail de s., ils ont fini par avoir raison de lui** they chipped away at him until he gave in **3** *(outil)* mattock

• **sapes** NFPL *Fam* clothes❑, *Br* gear, clobber

saper [3] [sape] VT **1** *Mil & (en travaux publics)* to sap **2** *(nuire à)* to sap, to undermine; **ce travail lui a sapé la santé** this work undermined his/her health; **s. le moral à qn** to get sb down **3** *Fam (habiller)* to dress❑; **il est toujours bien sapé** he's always really smartly dressed

VPR **se saper** *Fam (s'habiller)* to get dressed❑; *(s'habiller chic)* to get all dressed up; **elle aime bien se s. pour sortir** she likes to get all dressed up to go out; **il sait pas se s.** he's got no dress sense

saperlipopette [sapɛrlipɔpɛt] EXCLAM *Arch ou Hum* gad(zooks)!, strewth!

sapeur-pompier [sapœrpɔ̃pje] *(pl* **sapeurs-pompiers**) NM *Br* fireman, *Am* firefighter; **les sapeurs-pompiers** *Br* the fire brigade, *Am* the fire department

saphique [safik] ADJ Sapphic

saphir [safir] ADJ INV *Littéraire* sapphire *(avant n)*

NM **1** *(pierre précieuse)* sapphire **2** *Littéraire (bleu)* sapphire

saphisme [safism] NM *Littéraire* sapphism, lesbianism

sapin [sapɛ̃] NM **1** *(arbre)* fir (tree); **s. de Noël** Christmas tree **2** *(bois)* fir, deal; **en s.** fir *(avant n)*, deal *(avant n)* **3** *Fam Hum* **ça sent le s.** he's/she's/*etc* on his/her/*etc* last legs; **une toux qui sent le s.** a graveyard cough, a death-rattle of a cough

sapine [sapin] NF **1** *(planche)* fir plank **2** *Constr* jib crane

sapinière [sapinjer] NF **1** *(plantation)* fir plantation **2** *(forêt)* fir forest

saponaire [sapɔnɛr] NF *Bot* soapwort

saponifiant, -e [sapɔnifjɑ̃, -ɑ̃t] *Chim* ADJ saponifying

NM saponifier, saponifying agent

saponification [sapɔnifikasjɔ̃] NF *Chim* saponification

saponifier [9] [sapɔnifje] VT *Chim* to saponify

sapristi [sapristi] EXCLAM *Vieilli (exprimant l'étonnement)* heavens!; *(exprimant la colère)* for heaven's sake!

saprophage [saprɔfaʒ] *Biol* ADJ saprophagous

NM *(insecte)* saprophagous insect

saprophyte [saprɔfit] *Biol* ADJ saprophytic

NM saprophyte

saquer [sake] = **sacquer**

sarabande [sarabɑ̃d] NF 1 *Mus & (danse)* saraband 2 *Fam (tapage)* racket, *Br* row; **les enfants font la s.** the children are making a racket 3 *(ribambelle)* string, succession

Sarajevo [sarajevo] NM Sarajevo

sarbacane [sarbakan] NF *(arme)* blowpipe; *(jouet)* peashooter

sarcasme [sarkasm] NM 1 *(ironie)* sarcasm; **tu n'arriveras à rien par le s.** being sarcastic won't get you anywhere 2 *(remarque)* sarcastic remark

sarcastique [sarkastik] ADJ sarcastic; **d'un ton s.** sarcastically

sarcastiquement [sarkastikmɑ̃] ADV sarcastically

sarcelle [sarsɛl] NF *Orn* **s. (d'hiver)** teal

sarclage [sarklaʒ] NM weeding

sarcler [3] [sarkle] VT 1 *(mauvaises herbes ▸ à la main)* to pull up; *(▸ avec une houe)* to hoe 2 *(betteraves, champ ▸ à la main)* to weed; *(▸ avec une houe)* to hoe

sarclette [sarklɛt] NF (weeding) hoe

sarcloir [sarklwar] NM (Dutch) hoe, spud

sarcome [sarkom] NM *Méd* sarcoma

sarcophage [sarkɔfaʒ] NM 1 *(cercueil)* sarcophagus 2 *Entom* fleshfly

Sardaigne [sardɛɲ] NF **la S.** Sardinia

sarde [sard] ADJ Sardinian

NM *(langue)* Sardinian

• **Sarde** NMF Sardinian

sardine [sardin] NF 1 *Ich* sardine; **sardines à l'huile/à la tomate** sardines in oil/in tomato sauce 2 *très Fam Arg mil* stripe▫ 3 *(de tente)* tent peg

sardinerie [sardinri] NF sardine cannery

sardinier, -ère [sardinje, -ɛr] NM,F 1 *(pêcheur)* sardine fisher 2 *(ouvrier)* sardine canner

NM 1 *(bateau)* sardine boat *or* fisher 2 *(filet)* sardine net

sardonique [sardɔnik] ADJ sardonic

sardonyx [sardɔniks] NF *Minér* sardonyx

sargasse [sargas] NF *Bot* sargasso, gulfweed

sari [sari] NM sari, saree

sarigue [sarig] NF *Zool* possum, opossum

sarin [sarɛ̃] NM sarin

SARL, Sarl [ɛsaɛrɛl] NF *(abrév* **société à responsabilité limitée***)* limited liability company; **Balacor S.** *Br* ≃ Balacor Ltd, *Am* ≃ Balacor Inc

sarment [sarmɑ̃] NM *(tige)* twining *or* climbing stem, bine; **s. de vigne** vine shoot

sarmenteux, -euse [sarmɑ̃tø, -øz] ADJ climbing *(avant n)*, sarmentous

sarong [sarɔ̃g] NM sarong

saroual, -als [sarwal], **sarouel** [sarwɛl] NM = baggy trousers traditionally worn in North Africa

sarrasin[1] [sarazɛ̃] NM *Bot* buckwheat

sarrasin[2]**, -e**[1] [sarazɛ̃, -in] ADJ Saracen

• **Sarrasin, -e** NM,F Saracen

sarrasine[2] [sarazin] NF *(d'un château fort)* portcullis

sarrau, -s [saro] NM smock

Sarre [sar] NF 1 *(région)* **la S.** Saarland, the Saar 2 *(rivière)* **la S.** the (River) Saar

sarriette [sarjɛt] NF *Bot & Culin* savory

sarrois, -e [sarwa, -az] ADJ of/from the Saar

• **Sarrois, -e** NM,F = inhabitant of or person from the Saar

sas [sas] NM 1 *(pièce étanche ▸ de sous-marin, d'engin spatial)* airlock; *(d'une banque)* security (double) door 2 *(d'écluse)* lock (chamber); *(entre deux écluses)* airlock 3 *(crible)* sieve, screen

sassafras [sasafra] NM sassafras

sassage [sasaʒ] NM *(de farine, de plâtre)* sifting, sieving

sasser[1] **[3]** [sase] VT *(farine, plâtre)* to sift, to sieve; *Littéraire* **s. (et ressasser)** *(preuves)* to sift, to scrutinize; *(le pour et le contre)* to examine minutely; *(sujet)* to go over again and again

sasser[2] **[3]** [sase] VT *Naut (bateau)* to lock, to sluice

Satan [satɑ̃] NPR Satan

satané, -e [satane] ADJ *(avant le nom) Fam* 1 *(détestable)* **faites donc taire ce s. gosse!** shut that blasted kid up!; **s. temps!** what rotten weather! 2 *(en intensif)* **c'est un s. menteur** he's an out-and-out liar

satanique [satanik] ADJ 1 *(de Satan)* satanic 2 *(démoniaque, pervers)* fiendish, diabolical, satanic; **avoir l'œil s.** to have an evil glint in one's eye

satanisme [satanism] NM 1 *(culte)* satanism 2 *(méchanceté)* fiendishness, evil

sataniste [satanist] ADJ satanist

NMF satanist

satellisation [satelizasjɔ̃] NF 1 *Astron (d'une fusée)* putting *or* launching into orbit; **programme de s.** space programme 2 *(d'une nation, d'une ville, d'une organisation)* satellization

satelliser [3] [satelize] VT 1 *Astron (fusée)* to put into orbit 2 *(nation, ville, organisation)* to satellize

VPR **se satelliser** 1 *Astron (fusée)* to go into orbit 2 *(nation, ville, organisation)* to become a satellite

satellitaire [sateliter] ADJ satellite *(avant n)*

satellite [satelit] NM 1 *Astron & Tél* satellite; **en direct par s.** live via satellite; **s. artificiel/météorologique/de télécommunications** artificial/meteorological/telecommunications satellite; **s. espion** spy satellite; **s. géostationnaire** geostationary satellite; **s. lunaire/terrestre** moon-orbiting/earth-orbiting satellite; **s. d'observation** observation satellite; **s. de radiodiffusion** broadcast satellite; **s. de reconnaissance** reconnaissance satellite; **s. de télédétection** spy satellite; **s. de télédiffusion** broadcast satellite; **s. de télédiffusion directe** direct-broadcast satellite; **s. de télévision** television satellite; **transmission par s.** satellite transmission; **émission retransmise par s.** satellite broadcast 2 *Pol (personne, pays, ville)* satellite; **les satellites du bloc socialiste** the satellite countries of the socialist bloc 3 *(d'une aérogare)* satellite

ADJ 1 *(ville, pays)* satellite *(avant n)*; **ordinateur s.** satellite computer 2 *Anat* **veines satellites** companion veins

satiété [sasjete] NF satiety; **manger à s.** to eat one's fill; **redire qch jusqu'à s.** to repeat sth ad nauseam

satin [satɛ̃] NM 1 *Tex* satin; **de s.** satin *(avant n)*; *Fig* **une peau de s.** a satin-smooth skin 2 *(douceur ▸ gén)* softness, silkiness; *(▸ de la peau)* silky softness

satiné, -e [satine] ADJ *(tissu, reflets)* satiny, satin *(avant n)*; *(papier)* calendered; *(peau)* satin *(avant n)*, satin-smooth; **un fini s.** a satin finish; **peinture satinée** satin-finish paint

NM *(d'une peinture, d'un papier, d'un tissu)* satin finish; **la lumière mettait en valeur le s. de sa peau** the light showed off his/her satin complexion

satiner [3] [satine] VT *(tissu)* to give a satin finish to, to put a satin finish on; *(papier)* to calender; *(peau)* to make smooth

satinette [satinɛt] NF *(en coton)* sateen; *(en soie et coton)* (silk and cotton) satinet

satire [satir] NF 1 *Littérature* satire 2 *(critique)* satire, spoof; **faire la s. de son époque** to satirize one's times; **sa s. du Premier ministre est excellente** his/her take-off of the Prime Minister is excellent

satirique [satirik] ADJ satirical

NMF satirist

satiriquement [satirikmɑ̃] ADV satirically

satiriser [3] [satirize] VT to satirize

satiriste [satirist] NMF satirist

satisfaction [satisfaksjɔ̃] NF 1 *(plaisir)* satisfaction, gratification; **éprouver de la s./une grande s. à faire qch** to feel satisfaction/great satisfaction in doing sth; **il a la s. d'être utile** he has the satisfaction of being useful; **donner (entière** *ou* **toute) s. à qn** *(personne)* to give sb (complete) satisfaction; *(travail)* to give sb a lot of (job) satisfaction; **mon travail me donne peu de s.** my work is not very satisfying *or* fulfilling; **à ma grande s.** to my great satisfaction, to my gratification; **le problème fut résolu à la s. générale** the problem was solved to everybody's satisfaction; **je constate/je vois avec s. que...** I am pleased to note/to see that...; **s. de la clientèle** customer satisfaction; **s. du consommateur** consumer satisfaction 2 *(sujet de contentement)* source *or* cause for satisfaction; **j'ai eu une grande s. aujourd'hui** something really good happened today; **mon travail m'apporte de nombreuses satisfactions** my job gives me great satisfaction; **mon fils m'apporte de nombreuses satisfactions** my son is a great source of pride to me; **s. professionnelle** job satisfaction; **avoir des satisfactions professionnelles/financières** to be rewarded professionally/financially

3 *(assouvissement ▸ d'un désir)* satisfaction, gratification, fulfilment; *(▸ d'ambitions, d'un besoin)* satisfying, fulfilment; *(▸ de la faim)* satisfying; *(▸ de la soif)* quenching; **c'est pour elle une s. d'amour-propre** it flatters her self-esteem

4 *(gain de cause)* satisfaction; **accorder** *ou* **donner s. à qn** to give sb satisfaction; **obtenir s.** to obtain satisfaction

5 *(réparation)* satisfaction; **exiger/obtenir s. (de qch)** to demand/to obtain satisfaction (for sth); **obtenir s. d'un affront** to obtain satisfaction for an affront

satisfaire [109] [satisfɛr] VT 1 *(contenter ▸ sujet: résultat, travail)* to satisfy, to give satisfaction to; *(▸ sujet: explication)* to satisfy; *(sexuellement)* to satisfy; **rien ne le satisfait** nothing satisfies him, he's never satisfied; **elle est difficile à s.** she's hard to please; **votre rapport ne me satisfait pas du tout** I'm not satisfied at all with your report, I don't find your report at all satisfactory; **ce que j'ai me satisfait pleinement** I'm quite content with what I've got; **j'espère que cet arrangement vous satisfera** I hope (that) you'll find this arrangement satisfactory *or* to your satisfaction 2 *(répondre à ▸ attente)* to come *or* to live up to; *(▸ désir)* to satisfy, to fulfil; *(▸ besoin)* to satisfy, to answer; *(▸ curiosité)* to satisfy; *(▸ demande)* to meet, to satisfy, to cope with, to keep up with; *(▸ faim)* to satisfy; *(▸ soif)* to quench; **il reste des revendications non satisfaites** there are still a few demands which haven't been met; *Euph* **s. un besoin naturel** to answer a call of nature

• **satisfaire à** VT IND *(conditions)* to meet, to satisfy, to fulfil; *(besoin, exigences)* to meet, to fulfil; *(désir)* to satisfy, to gratify; *(attente)* to live *or* to come up to; *(promesse)* to fulfil, to keep; *(goût)* to satisfy; *(norme)* to comply with, to satisfy

VPR **se satisfaire** 1 *(sexuellement)* to have one's pleasure 2 *(uriner)* to relieve oneself 3 **se s. de** to be satisfied *or* content with; **tu te satisfais de peu!** it doesn't take much to make you happy!; **il ne se satisfait pas de promesses** he's not content with promises, promises aren't good enough for him

satisfaisant, -e [satisfəzɑ̃, -ɑ̃t] ADJ 1 *(convenable ▸ réponse, travail, devoir scolaire)* satisfactory; **de manière satisfaisante** satisfactorily; **en quantité satisfaisante** in sufficient quantities; **ce n'est pas une excuse satisfaisante** it's not a good enough excuse; **peu s.** *(résultat, travail)* unsatisfactory, poor; **cette solution n'était satisfaisante pour personne** this solution pleased nobody 2 *(gratifiant ▸ métier, occupation)* satisfying

> Attention: ne pas confondre **satisfying** et **satisfactory** lorsqu'on traduit **satisfaisant**.

satisfaisons *etc voir* **satisfaire**

satisfait, -e [satisfɛ, -ɛt] PP *voir* **satisfaire**

ADJ *(air, personne, regard)* satisfied, happy; **être s. de qn** to be satisfied *or* happy with sb; **es-tu s. de ta secrétaire?** are you satisfied *or* happy with your secretary?; **j'espère que vous en serez entièrement s.** *(appareil ménager, ordinateur etc)* I trust it will give you complete satisfaction; **s. ou remboursé** *(sur un produit)* satisfaction or your money back, money-back guarantee; **être s. de soi** *ou* **de soi-même** to be satisfied with oneself, to be self-satisfied; **être s. de** *(arrangement, résultat)* to be satisfied with, to be happy with *or* about; *(voiture, service)* to be satisfied with; **je suis très s. de ma prestation** I'm quite satisfied *or* pleased with my performance; **elle est partie maintenant, tu es s.?** now she's gone, are you satisfied?

satisfecit [satisfesit] NM INV 1 *Scol* star, credit 2 *(approbation)* full credit; **décerner un s. à qn pour avoir fait qch** to congratulate sb for having done sth

satisfera *etc voir* **satisfaire**

satisfont *voir* **satisfaire**

saton [satɔ̃] NM *Fam* **coup de s.** kick⁻, boot; **donner des coups de s. à qn/dans qch** to boot sb/sth, to give sb/sth a kicking

satonner [3] [satɔne] VT *Fam* **s. qn/qch** to boot sb/sth, to give sb/sth a kicking

saturable [satyrabl] ADJ saturable

saturant, -e [satyrɑ̃, -ɑ̃t] ADJ saturating, saturant
NM saturant

saturateur [satyratœr] NM **1** *Chim* saturator, saturater **2** *(pour radiateur)* humidifier

saturation [satyrasjɔ̃] NF **1** *Biol & Phys* saturation **2** *TV* chroma; *TV & Rad* **s. acoustique** popping **3** *Fig (d'une autoroute, d'un aéroport)* saturation, paralysis, gridlocking; *(d'un circuit de communication)* saturation, overloading; *(d'un marché)* saturation (point); **arriver** *ou* **parvenir à s.** to reach saturation point

saturé, -e [satyre] ADJ **1** *Biol & Phys* saturated **2** *(rassasié, écœuré)* **s. de** sated with; **des enfants saturés de télévision** children who have watched too much television; **ah non, assez de pub, j'en suis s.!** no more ads, I'm sick of them! **3** *(engorgé ▸ autoroute, aéroport)* saturated, paralysed, gridlocked; *(▸ circuit de communication)* saturated, overloaded; *(▸ marché)* saturated

saturer [3] [satyre] VT **1** *Biol & Phys* to saturate; **s. qch de** to saturate sth with **2** *(surcharger, remplir en excès)* to saturate; **s. un marché de produits agricoles** to saturate a market with agricultural products; **nous sommes saturés de publicité** we're swamped with advertising; **le professeur nous sature de travail** the teacher is overloading us with work; **être saturé de travail** to be up to one's eyes in work; **les appels de nos téléspectateurs ont saturé le standard** our viewers' calls have jammed the switchboards; **saturé d'eau/de sang** saturated with water/with blood; **le jardin est saturé d'eau** the garden is waterlogged *or* saturated with water

VI *Fam* **1** *(marché)* to become saturated; *(lignes téléphoniques)* to overload; **ça sature** *(sonorisation)* we're getting distortion **2** *(personne)* **je sature** I've had enough, I've had it up to here

saturnales [satyrnal] NFPL *Littéraire (débauche)* saturnalia, (wild) orgies

Saturne [satyrn] NF *Astron* Saturn
NPR *Myth* Saturn

saturnie [satyrni] NF *Entom* emperor moth

saturnien, -enne [satyrnjɛ̃, -ɛn] ADJ *Littéraire (morose)* saturnine

saturnin, -e [satyrnɛ̃, -in] ADJ **1** *Chim* lead *(avant n)* **2** *Méd* saturnine

saturnisme [satyrnism] NM *Méd* (chronic) lead poisoning, *Spéc* saturnism

satyre [satir] NM **1** *Myth & Entom* satyr **2** *(homme lubrique)* lech

satyrique [satirik] ADJ satyric, satyrical

sauce [sos] NF **1** *Culin* sauce; *(de salade)* salad dressing; *(vinaigrette)* French dressing, vinaigrette; *(jus de viande)* gravy; **s. à la moutarde/aux câpres** mustard/caper sauce; **s. béarnaise/hollandaise** béarnaise/hollandaise sauce; **s. béchamel** béchamel *or* white sauce; **s. de soja** soy sauce; **s. tartare** tartare sauce; **pâtes à la s. tomate** pasta with tomato sauce; *Fam* **mettre** *ou* **servir qch à toutes les sauces** to make sth fit every occasion; *Fam* **une expression qui a été mise à toutes les sauces** a hackneyed phrase⁻; *Fam* **je me demande à quelle s. nous allons être mangés** I wonder what lies in store for us⁻ *or* what they're going to do to us; *Prov* **la s. fait passer le poisson** a spoonful of sugar helps the medicine go down; *Fam* **allonger** *ou* **rallonger la s.** *(à l'écrit)* to waffle on

2 *Fam (pluie)* rain⁻; **prendre** *ou* **recevoir la s.** to get drenched *or* soaked (to the skin)

3 *Fam (courant électrique)* juice; **il n'y a pas assez de s.** there's not enough juice *or* power; *Fam* **mettre la s.** to pull out all the stops, to go all out

4 *Beaux-Arts* soft black crayon

• **en sauce** ADJ served in a sauce

saucée [sose] NF *Fam* downpour; **prendre** *ou* **recevoir la s.** to get drenched *or* soaked (to the skin); **il va y avoir une s.** it's going to bucket down

saucer [16] [sose] VT **1** *Vieilli (tremper)* **s. son pain** to dip one's bread in sauce **2** *(essuyer ▸ assiette)* to wipe (off) **3** *Fam (locution)* **se faire s.** to get drenched *or* soaked (to the skin)

saucier [sosje] NM sauce chef

saucière [sosjɛr] NF *(pour sauce)* sauce boat; *(pour jus)* gravy boat

sauciflard [sosiflar] NM *Fam* (dried) sausage⁻

saucisse [sosis] NF **1** *Culin* sausage; **s. de Francfort** frankfurter; **s. de Strasbourg** knackwurst; **s. de Toulouse** = type of pork sausage

2 *Fam Arg mil (ballon captif)* barrage balloon⁻

3 *Fam (personne)* **grande s.** beanpole; **espèce de grande s.!** you great lump!, you numbskull!

4 *Fam Hum* **s. à pattes** *(chien)* sausage dog

saucisson [sosisɔ̃] NM **1** *Culin* **s. (sec)** (dry) sausage; **s. à l'ail** garlic sausage; **s. pur porc** 100 percent pork sausage **2** *(pain)* sausage-shaped loaf **3** *Fam Hum* **s. à pattes** *(chien)* sausage dog

saucissonnage [sosisɔnaʒ] NM *Fam* dividing up⁻

saucissonner [3] [sosisɔne] *Fam* VI to picnic⁻, to have a snack⁻

VT **1** *(attacher ▸ personne)* to tie up⁻; **ils ont saucissonné le gardien sur la chaise** they trussed up the caretaker and tied him to a chair; *Fig* **saucissonnée dans son collant/dans sa robe** bulging out of her tights/dress **2** *(diviser)* **le film a été saucissonné** the movie *or Br* film was divided up into episodes; **un film saucissonné par des publicités** a movie *or Br* film with frequent commercial breaks

saucissonneur, -euse [sosisɔnœr, -øz] NM,F *Fam* picnicker

sauf[1] [sof] PRÉP **1** *(à part)* except, apart from, *Sout* save; **tout le monde s. Paul** everyone except (for) *or* apart from Paul; **j'ai voyagé partout en Allemagne, s. en Bavière** I've been everywhere in Germany except (for) Bavaria; **il a pensé à tout, s. à ça** he thought of everything except that; **il sait tout faire s. cuisiner** he can do everything except *or* but cook; **il s'arrête toujours ici s. s'il n'a pas le temps** he always stops here except if *or* unless he's in a hurry **2** *(à moins de)* unless; **s. avis contraire** unless otherwise instructed; **s. indications contraires** unless otherwise stated; **s. erreur ou omission** errors and omissions excepted

• **sauf à** PRÉP *Littéraire* **il a pris cette décision, s. à changer plus tard** he took this decision, but reserved the right to change it later

• **sauf que** CONJ except (for the fact) that, apart from the fact that; **il n'a pas changé, s. que ses cheveux ont blanchi** he hasn't changed, except (for the fact) that he has gone grey

sauf[2]**, sauve** [sof, sov] ADJ **1** *(indemne ▸ personne)* safe, unhurt, unharmed **2** *Fig (intact)* **au moins, les apparences sont sauves** at least appearances have been kept up *or* saved; **sa réputation est sauve** his/her reputation is intact *or* saved

sauf-conduit [sofkɔ̃dɥi] *(pl* **sauf-conduits***)* NM safe-conduct

sauge [soʒ] NF *Bot & Culin* salvia

saugrenu, -e [sogrəny] ADJ absurd, ridiculous

saule [sol] NM willow; **s. pleureur** weeping willow

saumâtre [somɑtr] ADJ **1** *(salé)* brackish, briny **2** *Fam (désagréable)* bitter⁻, nasty⁻; **il l'a trouvée s.!** he didn't appreciate it at all, he wasn't amused *or* impressed

saumon [somɔ̃] NM **1** *Ich* salmon; *Culin* **s. fumé** *Br* smoked salmon, *Am* lox **2** *(couleur)* salmon, salmon-pink
ADJ INV salmon, salmon-pink

saumoné, -e [somɔne] ADJ *(couleur)* salmon, salmon-pink

saumure [somyr] NF brine; **conserver du poisson/des cornichons dans la s.** to pickle fish/gherkins (in brine)

saumurer [3] [somyre] VT to pickle (in brine)

sauna [sona] NM sauna

saupiquet [sopike] NM *Culin (au lapin, au lièvre, au canard)* = type of spicy stew made from rabbit, hare or duck; *(au jambon)* = fried ham served with a spicy sauce

saupoudrage [sopudraʒ] NM **1** *Culin* sprinkling, dusting **2** *Fin & Pol (de crédits)* = allocation of small amounts of funding to various beneficiaries

saupoudrer [3] [sopudre] VT **1** *Culin* to dust, to sprinkle (**de** with) **2** *Fin & Pol* **s. des crédits** = to allocate small amounts of funding to various beneficiaries **3** *Fig Littéraire (parsemer)* to scatter, to sprinkle (**de** with); **s. un discours de citations** to pepper a speech with quotations

VPR **se saupoudrer se s. les mains de talc** to dust one's hands with talcum powder

saupoudreuse [sopudrøz] NF sprinkler

saur [sɔr] *voir* **hareng**

saura *etc voir* **savoir**

saurer [3] [sɔre] VT *(harengs)* to kipper, to smoke; *(jambon)* to smoke, to cure

saurien [sɔrjɛ̃] *Zool* NM saurian

saut [so] NM **1** *Sport* jump; **le s.** jumping; **championnat/épreuves de s.** jumping championship/events; **s. en hauteur/en longueur** high/*Br* long *or Am* broad jump; **s. de l'ange** *Br* swallow *or Am* swan dive; **s. de carpe** jack-knife dive; *Fig* **faire des sauts de carpe** to bounce around; **s. carpé** pike; **s. en chute libre** free-fall jump; **s. en ciseaux** scissors jump; **s. à la corde** skipping; **s. à l'élastique** bungee jumping; **s. de haies** hurdling; **s. d'obstacles** showjumping; **s. en parachute** *(discipline)* parachuting, skydiving; *(épreuve)* parachute jump; **faire du s. en parachute** to go parachuting *or* skydiving; **s. à la perche** *(discipline)* pole vaulting; *(épreuve)* pole vault; **s. périlleux** somersault; **s. à pieds joints** standing jump; **s. à skis** *(discipline)* ski-jumping; *(épreuve)* (ski-)jump

2 *(bond)* jump, leap; **faire un s.** to jump, to leap, to take a leap; **se lever d'un s.** to leap *or* to jump to one's feet; **s. de puce** step; **au s. du lit** *(en se levant)* on *or* upon getting up; *(tôt)* first thing in the morning

3 *(chute)* drop; **elle a fait un s. de cinq mètres dans le vide** she fell *or* plunged five metres into the void

4 *(brève visite)* flying visit; **elle a fait un s. chez nous hier** she dropped by (our house) yesterday; **je ne fais qu'un s.** *(quelques instants)* I'm only passing, I'm not staying; *(quelques heures)* I'm only on a flying visit; **fais un s. chez le boucher** pop over *or* along to the butcher's

5 *Fig (changement brusque)* leap; **faire un s. dans l'inconnu** to take a leap in the dark; **faire un s. dans le passé** to go back into the past; **le grand s.** *(la mort)* the big sleep; **faire le s.** to take the plunge

6 *Géog* falls, waterfall

7 *Ordinat & Math* jump

8 *Typ* **s. de ligne** line break; **s. de ligne manuel** hard return; **s. de page** page break

9 *Cin & TV* **s. en avant** flash forward; **faire un s. en avant** to flash forward; *Cin & TV* **s. de montage** jump cut

• **sauts** NMPL *(en danse)* jumps

saut-de-lit [sodli] *(pl* **sauts-de-lit***)* NM dressing gown, light robe

saut-de-loup [sodlu] *(pl* **sauts-de-loup***)* NM haha

saut-de-mouton [sodmutɔ̃] *(pl* **sauts-de-mouton***)* NM *Br* flyover, *Am* overpass

saute [sot] NF **1** *Météo* **s. de vent** shift (of the wind); **s. de température** sudden change in temperature **2** *Fig* **s. d'humeur** mood swing

sauté, -e [sote] ADJ *(pommes de terre, viande)* sautéed, sauté
NM sauté

saute-mouton [sotmutɔ̃] NM INV leapfrog; **jouer à s.** to play leapfrog; **il jouait à s. par-dessus les tréteaux** he was leapfrogging over the trestles

SAUTER [3] [sote]

VI	
• to jump **1–3, 6**	• to leap **1**
• to blow up **4**	• to come off **5**
• to flicker **7**	• to snap **7**
• to fall **8**	
VT	
• to jump over **1**	• to leave out **2**

VI 1 *(bondir ▸ personne)* to jump, to spring up; *(▸ chat)* to jump, to leap; *(▸ oiseau, insecte)* to hop; *(▸ grenouille, saumon)* to leap; *(▸ balle)* to bounce; **s. dans une tranchée/dans un puits** to jump into a trench/down a well; **s. d'une branche/d'une falaise** to leap off a branch/a cliff; **s. par-dessus une corde/un ruisseau** to leap over a rope/across a stream; **il faut s. pour atteindre l'étagère** you've got to jump up to reach the shelf; **s. par la fenêtre** to jump out of the window; **quand je pense que je la faisais s. sur mes genoux il n'y a pas si longtemps** when I think that not so long ago, I was bouncing *or* dandling her on my knee; *Fig* **s. de joie** to jump for joy; *Fam* **s. au plafond, s. en l'air** *(de colère)* to hit the roof; *(de joie)* to be thrilled to bits, to jump for joy; **s. comme un cabri** to frolic

2 *Sport & (jeux)* **s. à cloche-pied** to hop; **s. à la corde** *Br* to skip (with a rope), *Am* to skip *or* to jump rope; **s. en parachute** to (parachute) jump, to parachute; **s. en hauteur/en longueur** to do the high jump/the *Br* long *or Am* broad jump; **s. à la perche** to pole-vault; **s. à skis** to ski-jump

3 *(se ruer)* to jump, to pounce; **s. (à bas) du lit** to jump *or* to spring out of bed; **s. dans un taxi** to jump *or* to leap into a taxi; **il sauta sur le malheureux passant** he pounced on the wretched passer-by; *Fam* **s. sur l'occasion** to jump at the chance; **c'est une excellente occasion, je saute dessus** it's a great opportunity, I'll grab it; **se faire s. dessus** to be jumped on; **s. à la gorge** *ou* **au collet de qn** to jump down sb's throat; *Fam* **va te laver les mains, et que ça saute!** go and wash your hands and jump to it *or* make it snappy!; **ça saute aux yeux** it's plain for all to see *or* as the nose on your face

4 *(exploser)* to blow up, to explode, to go off; **faire s. un pont/un char** to blow up a bridge/a tank; **faire s. une mine** to explode a mine; *Élec* **les plombs ont sauté** the fuses have blown; *Élec* **faire s. les plombs** to blow the fuses; **la lampe/le circuit a sauté** *Br* the lamp/the circuit has fused, *Am* the lamp fuze/the circuit has blown

5 *(être projeté)* **les boutons ont sauté** the buttons flew off *or* popped off; **faire s. le bouchon d'une bouteille** to pop a cork; *Fam* **se faire s. la cervelle** *ou* **le caisson** to blow one's brains out; *aussi Fig* **faire s. la banque** to break the bank

6 *(changer sans transition)* to jump

7 *(cesser de fonctionner ▸ chaîne, courroie)* to come off; *(▸ image de télévision)* to flicker; *(▸ serrure)* to snap; *Ordinat (▸ réseau)* to crash

8 *Fam (être renvoyé)* to fall; **le gouvernement a sauté** the government has fallen; **le ministre a sauté** the minister got fired *or Br* got the sack

9 *Culin* **faire s. des pommes de terre** to sauté potatoes; **faire s. des crêpes** to toss pancakes

VT 1 *(obstacle)* to jump *or* to leap over; *Fig* **s. le pas** to take the plunge

2 *(omettre)* to skip, to leave out; **s. une ligne** to leave a line

3 *Vulg (sexuellement)* **s. qn** to screw *or Br* to shag sb; **se faire s.** to get laid

4 *très Fam (locution)* **la s.** *(se passer de manger)* to skip a meal; *(avoir faim)* to be starving

sauterelle [sotʀɛl] **NF 1** *Entom* grasshopper; *(criquet)* locust **2** *Fam (fille, femme)* chick, *Br* bird; **grande s.** beanpole

sauterie [sotʀi] **NF** *Hum* party◻, do, get-together

saute-ruisseau [sotʀɥiso] **NM INV** *Vieilli* errand boy

sauteur, -euse [sotœʀ, -øz] **ADJ** jumping, hopping

NM,F *Sport* jumper; **s. en hauteur/en longueur** high/*Br* long *or Am* broad jumper; **s. à la perche** pole-vaulter

NM *Fam (homme sans sérieux)* unreliable sort

• **sauteuse NF 1** *Culin* high-sided *Br* frying pan *or Am* fry pan **2** *Menuis* jigsaw, scroll saw

sautillant, -e [sotijɑ̃, -ɑ̃t] **ADJ 1** *(démarche, oiseau)* hopping, skipping; **d'un pas s.** with a dancing step **2** *Fig (style)* light; *(refrain)* gay, bouncy

sautillement [sotijmɑ̃] **NM 1** *(petit saut)* hop, skip, skipping *(UNCOUNT)* **2** *(changement constant)* jumping around, chopping and changing

sautiller [3] [sotije] **VI 1** *(faire de petits sauts)* to hop, to skip; **marcher en sautillant** to skip along; **s. sur un pied** to hop **2** *(papillonner)* to flit; **sa pensée sautille sans cesse** his/her mind flits from one thing to another

sautoir [sotwaʀ] **NM 1** *(bijou)* chain; **en s.** on a chain; **s. de perles** string of pearls **2** *Sport* long-jump area **3** *Culin* high-sided frying pan

sauvage [sovaʒ] **ADJ 1** *Zool (non domestique)* wild; *(non apprivoisé)* untamed; **il est redevenu s.** *(chat)* he's gone feral *or* wild; *(jeune fauve)* he's gone back to the wild; **à l'état s.** wild

2 *(non cultivé)* wild; **le jardin est redevenu s. depuis leur départ** since they left the garden has become overgrown

3 *(peu fréquenté ▸ lieu)* wild, remote

4 *(réservé, timide)* shy; *(peu sociable)* unsociable

5 *Vieilli & (en anthropologie)* savage, uncivilized; **retourner à la vie s.** to go back to the wild

6 *(barbare ▸ personne, geste, violence)* savage, brutal; *(▸ mœurs)* uncivilized

7 *(illégal ▸ camping, vente)* unauthorized; *(▸ urbanisation)* unplanned; *(▸ immigration)* illegal

NMF 1 *Vieilli & (en anthropologie)* savage; **le bon s.** the noble savage **2** *(personne fruste, grossière)* boor, brute; **il se conduit comme un s.** he's a real brute; *Fam* **on n'est pas des sauvages!** we're not savages! **3** *(personne farouche)* unsociable person, recluse

sauvagement [sovaʒmɑ̃] **ADV** savagely, viciously

sauvageon, -onne [sovaʒɔ̃, -ɔn] **NM,F** wild child

NM *(arbre)* wildling

sauvagerie [sovaʒʀi] **NF 1** *(méchanceté)* viciousness, brutality **2** *(misanthropie)* unsociability

sauvagin, -e [sovaʒɛ̃, -in] **ADJ** *Chasse (odeur, goût)* gamey

• **sauvagine NF 1** *Chasse* wildfowl *(UNCOUNT)*; **chasse à la sauvagine** wildfowling **2** *(fourrure)* common pelts, fur skins

sauve [sov] *voir* **sauf²**

sauvegarde [sovgaʀd] **NF 1** *(protection)* safeguard, safeguarding *(UNCOUNT)*; **s. des ressources naturelles** conservation of natural resources; **sous la s. de qn** under sb's protection **2** *(sécurité)* safety **3** *Ordinat* backup; **faire une s.** to save; **faire la s. d'un fichier** to save a file; **s. automatique** autosave, automatic backup; **s. rapide** fast save

sauvegarder [3] [sovgaʀde] **VT 1** *(protéger ▸ bien)* to safeguard, to watch over; *(▸ honneur, réputation)* to protect **2** *Ordinat* to save, to back up; **s. un fichier sur disquette** to save a file to disk; **s. automatiquement** to autosave

sauve-qui-peut [sovkipø] **NM INV** stampede

sauver [3] [sove] **VT 1** *(personne ▸ gén)* to save, to rescue (**de** from); *(▸ dans un accident, dans une catastrophe)* to rescue; **s. la vie à qn** to save sb's life; **s. qn de la noyade/de la faillite** to rescue sb from drowning/from bankruptcy; *Fig* **tu me sauves!** you're a lifesaver!; **être sauvé** *(sain et sauf)* to be safe; *(par quelqu'un)* to have been saved *or* rescued; **ils ont atteint la côte, ils sont sauvés!** they've reached the shore, they're safe!; **le malade est sauvé** the patient is out of danger; *Fig* **tout est prêt pour la kermesse demain, nous sommes sauvés!** everything is ready for tomorrow's fete, we're home free *or Br* home and dry; *Fam* **s. sa peau** to save one's skin *or* hide

2 *(protéger)* **s. les apparences** to keep up appearances; **s. la face** to save face; **s. la situation** to save *or* to retrieve the situation; **la musique sauve le film** the music saves the movie *or Br* film; **ce qui le sauve, c'est que…** his saving grace is that…; *Fam* **je lui ai sauvé la mise** I've got him/her out of trouble, I've bailed him/her out

3 *(préserver)* to salvage, to save; **on n'a pu s. qu'un morceau du toit** only part of the roof survived *or* could be salvaged; *Fam* **s. les meubles** to salvage something from the situation

4 *Rel* to save

VPR se sauver 1 *Rel* to be saved

2 *(animal)* to escape (**de** from); *(pensionnaire)* to run away (**de** from); *(prisonnier)* to escape, to break out (**de** from); *(matelot)* to jump ship; **se s. à toutes jambes** to take to one's heels (and run)

3 *Fam (lait)* to boil over◻

4 *Fam (s'en aller)* to leave, *Am* to split; **sauve-toi!** run along now!; **bon, je me sauve!** right, I'm off *or* on my way!

• **sauve qui peut EXCLAM** run for your life!, every man for himself!

sauvetage [sovtaʒ] **NM 1** *(d'un accidenté)* rescue; **opérer** *ou* **effectuer le s. d'un équipage** to rescue a crew; **mission de s.** rescue mission; *Fig* **s. d'une entreprise** financial rescue of a company; **s. aérien/en montagne/en mer** air/mountain/sea rescue; **s. aérien en mer** air-sea rescue **2** *Naut (de l'équipage)* life saving, sea rescue; *(de la cargaison)* salvage

• **de sauvetage ADJ** life *(avant n)*

sauveteur [sovtœʀ] **NM** rescuer

sauvette [sovɛt] **à la sauvette ADJ marchand** *ou* **vendeur à la s.** (illicit) street peddler *or* hawker

ADV 1 *(illégalement)* **vendre qch à la s.** to hawk *or* to peddle sth (without authorization) **2** *(discrètement)* stealthily

sauveur [sovœʀ] **NM 1** *(bienfaiteur)* saviour; *Hum* **tu es mon s.!** you've saved my life! **2** *Rel* **le S.** Our Saviour

ADJ M saving *(avant n)*

SAV [ɛsave] **NM** *(abrév* **service après-vente***)* after-sales service

savamment [savamɑ̃] **ADV 1** *(avec érudition)* learnedly; **elle expose s. ses connaissances** she presents her knowledge in a learned manner **2** *(habilement)* cleverly, cunningly **3** *(par expérience)* **j'en parle s.** I know what I'm talking about, I have first-hand experience (in this matter)

savane [savan] **NF 1** *(dans les pays chauds)* bush, savanna, savannah **2** *Can (marécage)* bog

savant, -e [savɑ̃, -ɑ̃t] **ADJ 1** *(érudit ▸ livre, moine, société)* learned; *(▸ traduction, conversation)* scholarly; *(▸ mot, terme)* specialist, technical; **être s. en peinture/en grec** to be well-versed in painting/in Greek; **c'est trop s. pour lui!** that's (totally) beyond his grasp!; **faire de savants calculs** to work things out in complex detail **2** *(habile)* skilful, clever; **un s. édifice de paquets de lessive** a cleverly constructed tower of soap powder packs **3** *(dressé ▸ chien, puce)* performing

NM,F *(lettré)* scholar

NM *(scientifique)* scientist

savarin [savaʀɛ̃] **NM** savarin (cake)

savate [savat] **NF 1** *(chaussure)* worn-out (old) shoe; *(pantoufle)* old slipper; *Fam* **comme une s.** appallingly badly; **il chante comme une s.** he can't sing to save his life; *Fam* **traîner la s.** *(être sans le sou)* to be completely broke; *(être oisif)* to hang around, to bum around **2** *Sport* **la s.** kick boxing **3** *Tech* sole (plate)

savater [3] [savate] **VT** *Fam* to kick◻, to boot

saveur [savœʀ] **NF 1** *(goût)* savour, flavour; **ce fruit est sans s.** this fruit is tasteless *or* has no flavour; **pleine de s.** tasty; **quelle s.!** very tasty! **2** *(trait particulier)* fragrance, savour; **il y a toute la s. de l'Italie dans son accent** there is all the flavour of Italy in his accent **3** *(piment ▸ d'une remarque, d'un récit)* spice, pungency; **la s. du péché** the sweet taste of sin

Savoie [savwa] **NF la S.** Savoy, Savoie

SAVOIR [59] [savwaʀ]

NM
- knowledge

VT
- to know **1–3, 5, 7, 8, 10**
- to be aware of **7**
- to know how to **6**

USAGE ABSOLU
- to know

VPR
- to become known **1**

ADV
- namely

NM knowledge; **un homme d'un grand s.** a very knowledgeable *or* learned man; **savoirs comportementaux** soft skills

VT 1 *(connaître ▸ donnée, réponse, situation)* to know; **nous ne savons toujours pas le nom du vainqueur** we still don't know the winner's name; **que savez-vous de lui?** what do you know about *or* of him?; **tu sais la nouvelle?** have you heard the news?; **on le savait malade** we knew *or* we were aware (that) he was ill; *Littéraire* **je lui savais une grande fortune** I knew him/her to be wealthy; **je ne te savais pas si susceptible** I didn't know *or* I didn't realize *or* I never thought you were so touchy; **je ne sais rien de plus apaisant que la musique** I don't know anything more soothing than music

2 *(être informé de)* **comment sais-tu que j'habite ici?** how do you know I live here?; **que va-t-il arriver àTintin? pour le s., lisez notre prochain numéro!** what's in store forTintin? find out in our next issue!; **c'est toujours bon à s.** it's (always) worth knowing; *Fam* **je sais des choses...** *(sur un ton taquin)* I know a thing or two; **c'est sa maîtresse – tu en sais des choses!** she's his mistress – you seem well informed!; **je sais ce que j'ai vu** I know what I saw; **je n'en sais pas plus que toi** I don't know any more than you do; **ce n'est pas elle qui l'a dénoncé – qu'en savez-vous?** she wasn't the one who turned him in – what do you know about it *or* how do you know?; **je n'en sais rien du tout** I don't know anything about it, I haven't got a clue; **après tout, tu n'en sais rien!** after all, what do YOU know about it!; **il est venu ici, mais personne n'en a rien su** he came here, but nobody found out about it; **chercher à en s. davantage** to try and find out more; **en s. long sur qn/qch** to know a great deal about sb/sth; **en s. quelque chose** to have some knowledge (of a subject); **oh oui ça fait mal, j'en sais quelque chose!** yes, it's very painful, I can tell you!; **il n'aime pas les cafardeurs – tu dois en s. quelque chose!** he doesn't like sneaks – you'd know all about that!; **pour ce que j'en sais** for all I know; **je sais à quoi m'en tenir sur lui** I know what kind of (a) person he is; **je ne sais pas si elle a eu mon message** I don't know whether she got my message; **sais-tu où/pourquoi il est parti?** do you know where/why he went?; **je crois s. qu'ils ont annulé la conférence** I have reason *or* I'm led to believe that they called off the conference; **tout le monde sait que...** it's a well-known fact *or* everybody knows that...; **je ne sais combien, on ne sait combien** *(d'argent)* who knows how much; **il y a je ne sais combien de temps** a very long time ago; **je ne sais comment, on ne sait comment** God knows how; **je ne sais où, on ne sait où** God knows where; **je ne sais pourquoi, on ne sait pourquoi** God *or* who knows why; **sans (trop) s. pourquoi** *(agir, parler)* without really knowing why; *(marcher)* aimlessly; **sans trop s. quoi faire** *(attendre, marcher)* aimlessly; **je ne sais quel/quelle...** some... or other; **retenu par je ne sais quelle affaire** held up by some business or other; **je ne sais qui, on ne sait qui** somebody or other; **il y a je ne sais quoi de bizarre chez lui** there's something a bit weird about him; **il vendait des tapis, des bracelets et que sais-je encore** he was selling carpets, bracelets and goodness *or* God knows what else; *Sout ou Hum* **je ne sache pas qu'on ait modifié le calendrier, on n'a pas modifié le calendrier, que je sache** the calendar hasn't been altered that I know of *or* as far as I know; **a-t-elle la permission? – pas que je sache** has she got permission? – not to my knowledge *or* not as far as I know; **va s. ce qui lui a pris!** who knows what possessed him/her?; **pourquoi est-elle partie? – allez s.?** why did she leave? – who knows?

3 *(être convaincu de)* to know, to be certain *or* sure; **je savais bien que ça ne marcherait pas!** I knew it wouldn't work!; **je ne sais pas si ça en vaut la peine** I don't know if it's worth it; **je n'en sais trop rien** I'm not too sure, I don't really know

4 *(apprendre)* **s. qch par qn** to hear sth from sb; **je l'ai su par son frère** I heard it from his/her brother; **on a fini par s. qu'un des ministres était compromis** it finally leaked out that one of the ministers was compromised; **faire s. qch à qn** to inform sb *or* to let sb know of sth; **si elle arrive, faites-le moi s.** if she comes, let me know

5 *(se rappeler)* to know, to remember; **je ne sais plus la fin de l'histoire** I can't remember the end of the story; **est-ce que tu sais ton rôle?** *Théât* do you know your lines?; *Fig* do you know what you're supposed to do?

6 *(pouvoir)* to know how to, to be able to; **s. faire qch** to know how to *or* to be able to do sth; **tu sais plonger/conduire?** can you dive/drive?; **elle ne sait ni lire ni écrire** she can't read or write; **j'ai su danser le charleston** I used to know how to *or* I used to be able to dance the charleston; **elle sait (parler) cinq langues** she can speak *or* she knows five languages; **il ne sait pas/il sait bien faire la cuisine** he's a bad/good cook; **si je sais bien compter/lire** if I count/read right; **quand on lui a demandé qui était président à l'époque, il n'a pas su répondre** when asked who was President at the time, he didn't know (what the answer was); **je ne sais pas mentir** I can't (tell a) lie; **il sait se contenter de peu** he can make do with very little; **je n'ai pas su la réconforter** I wasn't able to comfort her; **il faut s. écouter le patient** you have to be able to listen to your patient; **je sais être discret** I can be *or* I know when to be discreet; **elle ne sait pas se reposer** *(elle travaille trop)* she doesn't know when to stop; **il a su rester jeune/modeste** he's managed to remain young/modest; **s. s'y prendre avec les enfants** to know how to handle children, to be good with children; **laisse-moi découper le poulet, tu ne sais pas y faire** let me carve the chicken, you don't know how to do it; **s. y faire avec qn** to know how to handle sb; **elle sait y faire avec le patron!** she knows how to get round *or* to handle the boss!; **il sait y faire avec les filles!** he knows how to get his (own) way with girls!; **je ne saurais te le dire** I couldn't tell you; **on ne saurait être plus aimable/déplaisant** you couldn't be nicer/more unpleasant

7 *(être conscient de)* to know, to be aware of; **si tu savais combien j'ai souffert!** if you knew how much I've suffered!; **je sais que c'est un escroc** I know he's a crook; **sachez-le bien** make no *or* let there be no mistake about this; **il faut s. que le parti n'a pas toujours suivi Staline** you've got to remember that the party didn't always toe the Stalinist line; **sache qu'en fait, c'était son idée** you should know that in fact, it was his/her idea; **sachez que je le fais bénévolement** for your information, I do it for nothing; **elle ne sait plus ce qu'elle fait ni ce qu'elle dit** *(à cause d'un choc, de la vieillesse)* she's become confused; *(sous l'effet de la colère)* she's beside herself (with anger); **il est tellement soûl qu'il ne sait plus ce qu'il dit** he's so drunk he doesn't know what he's saying; **je sais ce que je dis** I know what I'm saying; **elle sait ce qu'elle veut** she knows (exactly) what she wants; **tu ne sais pas ce que tu rates** you don't know what you're missing; **tu ne sais pas ce que tu dis** you don't know what you're talking about; **il faudrait s. ce que tu dis!** make up your mind!; **laisse-la, elle sait ce qu'elle fait** let her be, she knows what she's doing

8 *(imaginer)* **ne (plus) s. que** *ou* **quoi faire** to be at a loss as to what to do, not to know what to do; **elle ne savait que faire pour le rassurer** she didn't know what to do to reassure him; **je ne sais (plus) que faire avec ma fille** I just don't know what to do with my daughter; **il ne sait plus quoi faire pour se rendre intéressant** he'd stop at nothing *or* there's nothing he wouldn't do to attract attention to himself; *Fam* **je ne savais plus où me mettre** *ou* **me fourrer** *(de honte)* I didn't know where to put myself

9 *Belg* **il ne sait pas venir demain** he can't make it tomorrow; **je ne sais pas l'attraper** I can't reach it; **ses résultats ne sont pas brillants, savez-vous?** *(n'est-ce pas)* his/her results aren't very good, are they *or* am I right?

10 *(pour prendre l'interlocuteur à témoin)* **ce n'est pas toujours facile, tu sais!** it's not always easy, you know!; **tu sais, je ne crois pas à ses promesses** to tell you the truth, I don't believe in his/her promises; *Fam* **tu sais que tu commences à m'énerver?** you're getting on my nerves, you know that *or* d'you know that?

USAGE ABSOLU ceux qui savent informed people *or* sources; **oui, oui, je sais!** yes, yes, I'm aware of that *or* I know *or* I realize!; *Fam* **où est-elle? – est-ce que je sais, moi?** where is she? – don't ask me *or* how should I know?; **si j'avais su, je ne t'aurais rien dit** if I'd known, I wouldn't have said a word (to you); **comment s.?** how can you tell *or* know?; **qui sait?** who knows?; **peut-être guérira-t-il, qui sait?** he might recover, who knows? *or* you never can tell!; **on ne sait jamais, sait-on jamais** you never know; **faudrait s.!** make up your mind!

ADV namely, specifically, i.e.; **le personnel se compose de 200 hommes, s. 160 employés et 40 cadres** the staff is made up of 200 people: 160 employees and 40 executives

VPR se savoir 1 *(emploi passif)* *(nouvelle)* to become known; **tout se sait dans le village** news travels fast in the village; **ça finira par se s.** people are bound to find out; *Fam* **cela** *ou* **ça se saurait s'il était si doué que ça** if he was that good, you'd know about it

2 *(personne)* **il se sait malade** he knows he's ill

• **à savoir ADV** namely, that is, i.e.; **son principal prédateur, à s. le renard** its most important predator, namely the fox

• **à savoir que CONJ** meaning *or Sout* to the effect that; **il nous a donné sa réponse, à s. qu'il accepte** he's given us his answer, that is, he accepts *or* to the effect that he accepts

• **savoir si CONJ** *Fam* but who knows whether; **elle a bien affirmé que oui, s. si elle était réellement informée** she did say yes, but who knows whether *or* but it remains to be seen whether she really knew what she was talking about

---

savoir-faire [savwarfɛr] **NM INV** know-how

savoir-vivre [savwarvivr] **NM INV** good manners, breeding; **avoir du s.** to have (good) manners; **manquer de s.** to have no manners; **manque de s.** bad manners, ill-breeding; **quel manque de s.!** how rude!

savon [savɔ̃] **NM** soap; **un (morceau de) s.** a bar of soap; **s. à barbe** shaving soap; **s. doux** mild soap; **s. liquide** liquid soap; **s. de Marseille** household soap *(traditionally used for both for washing and for laundry)*; **s. en paillettes** soap flakes; **s. en poudre** soap powder; *Fam* **passer un s. à qn** to give sb a roasting, to bawl sb out; *Fam* **se faire passer** *ou* **prendre un s.** to get a roasting, to get bawled out; *Fam* **tu vas encore recevoir** *ou* **te faire passer un s.!** you'll get it in the neck again!

savonnage [savɔnaʒ] **NM** *(de linge)* washing (with soap)

savonner **[3]** [savɔne] **VT 1** *(linge, surface)* to soap; *Littéraire* **la pente savonnée** the slippery slope; *Fig* **s. la planche à qn** to make things difficult for sb **2** *(barbe)* to lather; **s. le dos à qn** to soap sb's back **3** *Fam (locution)* **s. la tête à qn** to give sb the rough edge of one's tongue

VPR se savonner to soap oneself (down); **se s. le visage/les mains** to soap (up) one's face/one's hands

savonnerie [savɔnri] **NF 1** *(usine)* soap factory **2** *(fabrication)* soap manufacture

savonnette [savɔnɛt] **NF** *(savon)* (small) bar of soap, bar of toilet soap

savonneux, -euse [savɔnø, -øz] **ADJ** soapy

savourer **[3]** [savure] **VT 1** *(vin, mets, repas)* to enjoy, to savour **2** *Fig (moment, repos etc)* to relish, to savour; **elle savoure sa vengeance** she's savouring her vengeance

savoureuse [savurøz] *voir* **savoureux**

savoureusement [savurøzmɑ̃] **ADV 1** *(préparé)* tastily **2** *(raconté)* with relish

savoureux, -euse [savurø, -øz] **ADJ 1** *(succulent)* tasty, flavoursome, full of flavour **2** *Fig (anecdote, détails)* juicy; *(plaisanterie)* good

savoyard, -e [savwajar, -ard] **ADJ** of/from Savoie

• **Savoyard, -e NM,F** = inhabitant of or person from Savoie

Saxe [saks] **NF la S.** Saxony; **la Basse-S.** Lower Saxony

saxe [saks] **NM 1** *(matière)* Dresden china *(UNCOUNT)* **2** *(objet)* piece of Dresden china

saxhorn [saksɔrn] **NM** saxhorn; **s. basse** euphonium

saxifrage [saksifraʒ] **NF** *Bot* saxifrage

saxo [sakso] **NM** *Fam* **1** *(abrév* **saxophone***)* sax **2** *(abrév* **saxophoniste***)* sax (player)

saxon, -onne [saksɔ̃, -ɔn] **ADJ** Saxon

NM *(langue)* Saxon

• **Saxon, -onne NM,F** Saxon

saxophone [saksɔfɔn] **NM** saxophone

saxophoniste [saksɔfɔnist] **NMF** saxophone player, saxophonist

saynète [sɛnɛt] **NF** playlet, sketch

SBF [ɛsbeɛf] **NF** *(abrév* **Société des bourses françaises***)* = company which runs the Paris Stock Exchange, *Br* ≃ LSE, *Am* ≃ NYSE; **le S.120** = broad-based French stock exchange index

sbire [sbir] **NM** henchman

SBS [ɛsbeɛs] **NF** *Méd* (*abrév* **syndrome du bébé secoué**) SBS

SCA [ɛsseɑ] **NF** *Com* (*abrév* **société en commandite par actions**) partnership limited by shares

scabieux, -euse [skabjø, -øz] **ADJ** *Méd* scabious
• **scabieuse NF** *Bot* scabious

scabreux, -euse [skabrø, -øz] **ADJ 1** (*indécent*) obscene **2** *Littéraire* (*dangereux*) risky, tricky

scalaire [skalɛr] **ADJ** *Math* scalar
NM 1 *Math* scalar **2** *Ich* angelfish

scalène [skalɛn] **ADJ 1** *Anat* scalene **2** *Math* scalene
NM *Anat* scalenus (muscle)

scalp [skalp] **NM 1** (*chevelure*) scalp **2** (*action*) scalping (*UNCOUNT*)

scalpel [skalpɛl] **NM** scalpel

scalper [3] [skalpe] **VT** to scalp; **se faire s.** to get scalped

scandale [skɑ̃dal] **NM 1** (*indignation*) scandal; **au grand s. de...** to the indignation of...; **faire s.** to cause a scandal **2** (*scène*) scene, fuss; **il va encore faire (tout) un s.** he's going to make a (tremendous) fuss again **3** (*honte*) **c'est un s.!** (it's) outrageous!, it's an outrage!
• **à scandale ADJ** (*journal, presse*) sensationalist

scandaleuse [skɑ̃daløz] *voir* **scandaleux**

scandaleusement [skɑ̃daløzmɑ̃] **ADV** scandalously, outrageously

scandaleux, -euse [skɑ̃dalø, -øz] **ADJ** (*attitude, mensonge*) disgraceful, outrageous, shocking; (*article, photo*) sensational, scandalous; (*prix*) outrageous, shocking; **les loyers ont atteint des prix s.** rents have reached outrageously high levels

scandaliser [3] [skɑ̃dalize] **VT** to shock, to outrage; **elle a scandalisé tout le monde par sa grossièreté** she shocked everyone with her vulgarity; **son cynisme a scandalisé la classe politique** his/her cynicism scandalized the politicians
VPR se scandaliser se s. de qch to be shocked *or* scandalized by sth; **elle ne se scandalise de rien** nothing shocks her, she's unshockable

scander [3] [skɑ̃de] **VT 1** *Littérature* to scan **2** (*slogan*) to chant; (*mots, phrases, phrase musicale*) to stress

scandinave [skɑ̃dinav] **ADJ** Scandinavian
NM (*langue*) Scandinavian, Northern Germanic
• **Scandinave NMF** Scandinavian

Scandinavie [skɑ̃dinavi] **NF la S.** Scandinavia

scandium [skɑ̃djɔm] **NM** *Chim* scandium

scanner[1] [skanɛr] **NM 1** *Ordinat* scanner; **insérer qch par s., capturer qch au s.** to scan sth in; **s. à main** hand-held scanner; **s. optique** optical scanner; **s. à plat** flatbed scanner **2** *Méd* scanner; **passer au s.** (*sujet: personne*) to have a scan (done)

scanner[2] **[3]** [skane] **VT** to scan

scannérisation [skanerizasjɔ̃] **NF** scanning

scanneur [skanœr] = **scanner**[1]

scanographie [skanɔgrafi] **NF 1** (*technique*) scanning (*UNCOUNT*) **2** (*image*) scan, scanner image

scansion [skɑ̃sjɔ̃] **NF** *Littérature* scanning (*UNCOUNT*), scansion

scaphandre [skafɑ̃dr] **NM 1** *Naut* diving suit; **s. autonome** aqualung **2** *Astron* spacesuit

scaphandrier [skafɑ̃drije] **NM** *Naut* (deep-sea) diver

scaphoïde [skafɔid] *Anat* **ADJ** scaphoid, boat-shaped
NM scaphoid

scapulaire [skapylɛr] *Anat* **ADJ** scapular
NM scapular

scarabée [skarabe] **NM 1** *Entom* scarab (beetle) **2** *Archéol* scarab

scare [skar] **NM** *Ich* parrot fish, scar

scarificateur [skarifikatœr] **NM 1** *Méd* scarificator **2** *Agr & Hort* scarifier

scarifier [9] [skarifje] **VT** to scarify

scarlatine [skarlatin] **NF** *Méd* scarlet fever, *Spéc* scarlatina

scarole [skarɔl] **NF** endive (*broad-leaved variety*)

scat [skat] **NM** *Mus* scat

scato [skato] **ADJ** *Fam* (*blague*) disgusting[□]; **humour s.** toilet humour

scatologie [skatɔlɔʒi] **NF** scatology

scatologique [skatɔlɔʒik] **ADJ** (*goûts, écrit*) scatological; (*humour*) lavatorial

scatophage [skatɔfaʒ] **ADJ** scatophagous

sceau, -x [so] **NM 1** (*cachet*) seal; **apposer *ou* mettre son s. sur un document** to affix one's seal on *or* to a document; **sous le s. du secret** under the seal of secrecy **2** *Littéraire* (*empreinte*) mark; **le s. du génie** the mark *or* the stamp of genius

sceau-de-Salomon [sodəsalɔmɔ̃] (*pl* **sceaux-de-Salomon**) **NM** *Bot* Solomon's seal

scélérat, -e [selera, -at] *Littéraire* **ADJ** heinous, villainous
NM,F villain, scoundrel, rogue

scellé [sele] **NM** seal; **mettre *ou* apposer/lever les scellés** to put on/to remove the seals; **mettre *ou* apposer les scellés sur qch** to seal sth off
• **sous scellés ADV** under seal

scellement [sɛlmɑ̃] **NM** embedding, sealing

sceller [4] [sele] **VT 1** (*officialiser* ▸ *acte, document*) to seal; **s. un pacte** to set the seal on an agreement **2** (*fermer*) to put seals on, to seal up **3** (*fixer*) to fix, to set, to embed; **une fenêtre aux barreaux solidement scellés** a heavily barred window; **s. une couronne sur une dent** to crown a tooth

scénarimage [senarimaʒ] **NM** *Offic* storyboard

scénario [senarjo] (*pl* **scénarios *ou* scenarii** [senarii]) **NM 1** *Cin* (*histoire, trame*) screenplay, scenario; (*texte*) (shooting) script, scenario; *Fig* **tout s'est déroulé selon le s. prévu** everything went as scheduled *or* according to plan; **s. d'auteur** writer's script; *Cin* **s. dialogué** continuity script; *TV & Cin* **s.-maquette** storyboard; *Cin* **s. de répétition** rehearsal script; *Fig* **elle a encore perdu ses clés, c'est décidément un s. à répétition!** she's lost her keys again, she's making a habit of it *or* it's becoming a habit with her!; **un s. catastrophe** a nightmare scenario
2 *Théât* scenario
3 (*d'une bande dessinée*) story, storyboard, scenario
4 *Écon* (*cas de figure*) case, scenario

scénarisation [senarizasjɔ̃] **NF 1** (*écriture de scénario*) scriptwriting **2** (*adaptation*) screen adaptation

scénariser [3] [senarize] **VT 1** (*écrire le scénario de*) to script, to write the screenplay for **2** (*adapter pour l'écran*) to adapt for the screen

scénariste [senarist] **NMF** scriptwriter; **s. de réécriture** script editor

scène [sɛn] **NF 1** (*plateau d'un théâtre, d'un cabaret etc*) stage; **être en s.** (*acteur*) to be on (stage); **monter sur s.** to go on the stage; **sortir de s.** to come off stage, to exit; **Arlequin sort de s.** exit Harlequin; **il sera sur la s. du Palladium à partir du 3 mars** (*chanteur, comique*) he'll be appearing at the Palladium from 3 March onwards; **scènes nationales** national stages; **s. tournante** revolving stage; **entrer en s.** to come on stage; *Fig* to come *or* to step in; **le Duc entre en s.** enter the Duke; *Fig* **c'est là que tu entres en s.** that's where you come in
2 (*art dramatique*) **la s.** the stage; **il a beaucoup écrit pour la s.** he's written a lot of plays *or* pieces for the stage; **quitter la s.** to retire from the stage *or* from acting; **adapter un livre pour la s.** to adapt a book for the stage *or* the theatre; **porter qch à la s.** to adapt sth for the stage; **mettre 'Phèdre' en s.** (*monter la pièce*) to stage 'Phèdre'; (*diriger les acteurs*) to direct 'Phèdre'; **la façon dont il met Polonius en s.** the way he directs Polonius; *Fig* **l'écrivain met en s. deux personnages hauts en couleur** the writer portrays two colourful characters
3 *Cin & Théât* (*séquence*) scene; **la première s.** the first *or* the opening scene; **la s. finale** the last *or* the closing scene; **acte II, s. trois** act two, scene three; **dans la s. d'amour/du balcon** in the love/balcony scene; **s. de foule** crowd scene; **s. de poursuite** chase scene; **la s. se passe à Montréal** the action takes place in *or* the scene is set in Montreal; *Fig Hum* **jouer la grande s. du II** to make a big scene
4 (*décor*) scene; **la s. représente une clairière** the scene represents a clearing
5 (*moment, événement*) scene; **ce fut une s. déchirante** it was a heartbreaking scene; **une s. de la vie quotidienne** a scene of everyday life; **imagine la s.!** imagine *or* picture the scene!, just imagine *or* picture it!
6 (*dispute*) scene; **faire une s.** to make a scene; **il m'a fait une s.** he made a scene; **s. de ménage** row
7 *Beaux-Arts* scene; **le tableau représente une s. de chasse** the painting represents a hunting scene; **s. de genre** genre painting
8 (*univers*) scene; **la s. internationale/politique** the international/political scene

scène-raccord [senrakɔr] (*pl* **scènes-raccords**) **NF** *Cin & TV* link scene

scénique [senik] **ADJ** (*éclairage, décor*) stage (*avant n*); **l'art s.** stage design

scéniquement [senikmɑ̃] **ADV** theatrically

scénographe [senɔgraf] **NMF** *Théât* **1** (*qui aménage la scène*) stage designer **2** (*peintre*) scenographer

scénographie [senɔgrafi] **NF** *Théât* **1** (*aménagement de la scène*) stage design **2** (*peinture*) scenography

scepticisme [sɛptisism] **NM** scepticism; **avec s.** sceptically

sceptique [sɛptik] **ADJ** (*incrédule*) sceptical
NMF (*personne qui doute*) sceptic; *Phil* Sceptic

sceptiquement [sɛptikmɑ̃] **ADV** sceptically

sceptre [sɛptr] **NM 1** (*d'un roi*) sceptre **2** *Littéraire* (*autorité*) authority, royalty; **un s. de fer** a rod of iron

schako [ʃako] **NM** shako

scheik [ʃɛk] **NM** sheik

schelem [ʃlɛm] **NM** *Cartes & Sport* slam; **grand s.** grand slam; **petit s.** small *or* little slam

schéma [ʃema] **NM 1** *Tech* diagram; (*dessin*) sketch; **faire un s.** to make *or* to draw a diagram; **comme le montre le s.** as shown in the diagram
2 *Admin & Jur* **s. directeur** urban development plan
3 (*aperçu*) (broad) outline
4 (*système*) pattern
5 *Ordinat* **s. de clavier** keyboard map

schématique [ʃematik] **ADJ 1** *Tech* diagrammatical, schematic **2** (*simplificateur*) schematic, simplified; **trop s.** oversimplified, simplistic

schématiquement [ʃematikmɑ̃] **ADV 1** *Tech* diagrammatically, schematically **2** (*en simplifiant*) **décrire un projet/une opération s.** to give the basic outline of a project/an operation; **s., voici comment nous allons nous y prendre** in broad outline, this is how we're planning to handle it

schématisation [ʃematizasjɔ̃] **NF 1** *Tech* schematization, presenting as a diagram **2** (*simplification*) simplification, simplifying (*UNCOUNT*); *Péj* oversimplification

schématiser [3] [ʃematize] **VT 1** *Tech* to schematize, to present in diagram form **2** (*simplifier*) to simplify; *Péj* to oversimplify
USAGE ABSOLU il schématise à l'extrême he's being much too oversimplistic

schématisme [ʃematism] **NM 1** *Phil* schema **2** (*simplification*) simplification

schème [ʃɛm] **NM 1** *Phil & Psy* schema **2** *Beaux-Arts* scheme

scherzando [skɛrtsando, skɛrdzɑ̃do] **ADV** *Mus* scherzando

scherzo [skɛrdzo] *Mus* **NM** scherzo
ADV scherzando

schilling [ʃiliŋ] **NM** *Anciennement* schilling

schismatique [ʃismatik] **ADJ** schismatic
NMF schismatic

schisme [ʃism] **NM** schism, split; **faire s.** to break away

schiste [ʃist] **NM** *Minér* schist

schisteux, -euse [ʃistø, -øz] **ADJ** schistose, schistous

schistosomiase [ʃistɔzɔmjaz] NF *Méd* schistosomiasis
schizogamie [skizɔgami] NF *Biol* schizogamy
schizoïde [skizɔid] *Psy* ADJ schizoid
NMF schizoid
schizoïdie [skizɔidi] NF *Psy* schizoidism
schizophrène [skizɔfrɛn] ADJ schizophrenic
NMF schizophrenic
schizophrénie [skizɔfreni] NF schizophrenia
schizophrénique [skizɔfrenik] ADJ schizophrenic
schizothymie [skizɔtimi] NF *Psy* schizothymia
schizothymique [skizɔtimik] *Psy* ADJ schizothymic
NMF schizothyme
schlague [ʃlag] NF **1** *Hist* flogging **2** *Fam (autorité brutale)* **elle mène son monde à la s.** she rules everybody with a rod of iron□
schlass[1] [ʃlas] NM *très Fam (couteau)* knife□, blade, *Am* shiv
schlass[2], **schlasse** [ʃlas] ADJ *très Fam (ivre)* smashed, wasted; *(fatigué) Br* knackered, *Am* beat
schlinguer [ʃlɛ̃ge] = **chlinguer**
schlittage [ʃlitaʒ] NM transporting by sledge
schlitte [ʃlit] NF sledge *(for transporting lumber)*
schlitter **[3]** [ʃlite] VT to transport by sledge
schlof [ʃlɔf] NM *Fam* bed□, *Br* pit; **se mettre au s.** to hit *Br* the sack *or Am* the hay
schmilblick [ʃmilblik] NM *Fam* **faire avancer le s.** to make progress□, to get somewhere; **tout ça, ça fait pas avancer le s.** that's not getting us any further forward
schnaps [ʃnaps] NM schnapps
schnauzer [ʃnozer, ʃnawzœr] NM *(chien)* schnauzer
schnock, schnoque [ʃnɔk] *très Fam* ADJ INV *(cinglé)* nuts, loopy
NM *(imbécile)* halfwit, dope; **un vieux s.** an old fogey, an old codger; **espèce de vieux s.!** you old fogey *or* codger!; **alors, tu viens, du s.?** are you coming, dumbo?
schnorchel, schnorkel [ʃnɔrkɛl] NM snorkel
schnouf, schnouffe [ʃnuf] NF *Fam Arg drogue (héroïne)* junk; *(cocaïne)* snow, charlie, coke
schofar [ʃɔfar] NM *Rel* schofar
schuss [ʃus] NM schuss; **descendre en s.** to schuss down
ADV **descendre tout s.** to schuss down
Schweppes® [ʃwɛps] NM tonic (water)
SCI [ɛssei] NF **1** *(abrév* **société civile immobilière***)* property investment partnership **2** *Écon (abrév* **société de commerce international***)* international trading corporation
sciage [sjaʒ] NM sawing; **(bois de) s.** sawn timber
sciatique [sjatik] ADJ *Anat* sciatic
NF *Méd* sciatica
scie [si] NF **1** *Tech* saw; **s. à bois** wood saw; **s. à chaîne** chainsaw; **s. à chantourner** fretsaw; **s. circulaire** *Br* circular saw, *Am* buzz saw; **s. électrique** power saw; **s. mécanique** *ou* **à main** hand saw; **s. à métaux** hacksaw; **s. à ruban** bandsaw, ribbon saw; **s. sabre** *ou* **sauteuse** jigsaw, scroll saw
2 *Mus* **s. musicale** musical saw
3 *Fam (chanson)* song played to death; *(message)* message repeated again and again□
4 *Fam Péj (personne ou chose ennuyeuse)* bore, drag
sciemment [sjamɑ̃] ADV **1** *(consciemment)* knowingly **2** *(délibérément)* deliberately, on purpose
science [sjɑ̃s] NF **1** *(connaissances)* **la s.** science; **dans l'état actuel de la s.** in the current state of (our) knowledge
2 *(gén pl) (domaine spécifique)* science; **les sciences appliquées/physiques** the applied/physical sciences; **s. dure/molle** hard/soft science; **les sciences économiques** economics; **les sciences exactes** the exact sciences; **les sciences expérimentales** experimental science; **les sciences humaines** *(gén)* human sciences, the social sciences; *Univ* ≃ Arts; **les sciences mathématiques, la s. mathématique** mathematics, the mathematical sciences; **les sciences naturelles** *(gén)* the natural sciences; *Scol* biology; **la s. occulte, les sciences occultes** the occult (sciences); **les sciences politiques** politics, political sciences; *Univ* **les sciences sociales** social studies; *Scol* **les sciences de la vie** the life sciences
3 *(technique)* science, art; *(habileté)* skill; **la s. militaire** *ou* **de la guerre** the art *or* the science of war; **sa s. des effets dramatiques** his/her skill in producing dramatic effects
4 *(érudition)* knowledge; **il croit avoir la s. infuse** he thinks he's a fount of knowledge; **je n'ai pas la s. infuse!** I don't know everything!; **il faut toujours qu'il étale sa s.** he's always trying to impress everybody with his knowledge
• **sciences** NFPL *Univ (par opposition aux lettres)* science, sciences; **être bon en sciences** to be good at science *or* at sciences
• **de science certaine** ADV *Littéraire* **savoir qch de s. certaine** to know sth for certain *or* for a fact
science-fiction [sjɑ̃sfiksjɔ̃] *(pl* **sciences-fictions***)* NF science fiction; **livre/film de s.** science-fiction book/film
Sciences-Po [sjɑ̃spo] NF = "grande école" for political science
scientificité [sjɑ̃tifisite] NF scientificity, scientific quality
scientifique [sjɑ̃tifik] ADJ scientific; **de manière s.** scientifically
NMF **1** *(savant)* scientist **2** *(personne douée pour les sciences)* **ce n'est pas un s.** he's not very scientifically-minded
scientifiquement [sjɑ̃tifikmɑ̃] ADV scientifically
scientisme [sjɑ̃tism] NM **1** *Phil* scientism **2** *Rel* Christian Science
scientiste [sjɑ̃tist] ADJ *Phil & Rel* scientistic
NMF **1** *Phil* proponent of scientism **2** *Rel* (Christian) Scientist
scientologie [sjɑ̃tɔlɔʒi] NF Scientology
scientologue [sjɑ̃tɔlɔg] NMF Scientologist
scier **[9]** [sje] VT **1** *(couper)* to saw; **s. une planche en deux** to saw through a plank, to saw a plank in two; **s. la branche d'un arbre** to saw a branch off a tree; **s. un tronc en rondins** to saw up a tree trunk (into logs); *Suisse Fam* **s. du bois** to snore like a pig **2** *(blesser)* to cut into; **la ficelle du paquet me scie les doigts** the string around the parcel is cutting into my fingers **3** *Fam (surprendre)* to amaze□, to flabbergast; **ça m'a scié d'apprendre que...** I was flabbergasted *or Br* gobsmacked to find out that...
scierie [siri] NF sawmill
scieur [sjœr] NM **1** *(ouvrier)* sawyer; **s. de long** pit sawyer; *Can Fig Péj* **s. de bois** drudge **2** *(patron)* sawmill owner
scieuse [sjøz] NF *(machine)* mechanical saw
scille [sil] NF *Bot* scilla
scinder **[3]** [sɛ̃de] VT *(gén)* to divide, to split (up) (**en** into); *(société)* to break up, to split; **s. qch en deux** to divide *or* to split sth (up) into two
VPR **se scinder** to split (**en** into); **le parti s'est scindé en deux tendances** the party split into two
scinque [sɛ̃k] NM *Zool* skink
scintigramme [sɛ̃tigram] NM *Méd* scintigram
scintigraphie [sɛ̃tigrafi] NF *Méd* scintigraphy
scintillant, -e [sɛ̃tijɑ̃, -ɑ̃t] ADJ *(yeux)* sparkling, twinkling; *(bijoux, reflet)* glittering, sparkling, scintillating; *(étoile)* twinkling
NM tinsel decoration(s)
scintillation [sɛ̃tijasjɔ̃] NF *(éclat lumineux)* scintillation
scintillement [sɛ̃tijmɑ̃] NM **1** *(des yeux)* sparkling *(UNCOUNT)*, twinkling *(UNCOUNT)*; *(d'une lumière, de bijoux, de l'eau, d'un reflet)* glittering *(UNCOUNT)*, scintillating *(UNCOUNT)*; *(d'une étoile)* twinkling *(UNCOUNT)* **2** *Cin & TV* flicker, flickering, shimmer
scintiller **[3]** [sɛ̃tije] VI *(yeux)* to sparkle, to twinkle; *(lumière, bijoux, eau, reflet)* to sparkle, to glitter; *(étoile)* to twinkle
scion [sjɔ̃] NM **1** *Bot (pousse)* (year's) shoot; *(à greffer)* scion **2** *Pêche* tip (of rod)
scirpe [sirp] NM *Bot* club rush, bulrush
scission [sisjɔ̃] NF **1** *Pol & Rel* scission, split, rent; **faire s.** to split off, to secede **2** *Biol & Phys* fission, splitting **3** *(d'une société)* demerger; *Fin* **s. d'actifs** divestment of assets, hive-off of assets
scissionniste [sisjɔnist] ADJ secessionist
NMF secessionist
scissipare [sisipar] ADJ *Biol* fissiparous
scissiparité [sisiparite] NF *Biol* fissiparousness, scissiparity, schizogenesis
scissure [sisyr] NF *Anat (du cerveau)* fissure, sulcus; *(du foie)* scissura, scissure
sciure [sjyr] NF **s. (de bois)** sawdust; **s. de marbre** marble dust
scléral, -e, -aux, -ales [skleral, -o] ADJ *Anat* sclerotic
scléreux, -euse [sklerø, -øz] ADJ **1** *Méd* sclerous **2** *Bot* sclerotic
sclérodermie [sklerɔdɛrmi] NF *Méd* scleroderma
sclérogène [sklerɔʒɛn] ADJ *Méd* sclerogenic
scléroprotéine [sklerɔprɔtein] NF *Biol & Chim* scleroprotein
sclérosant, -e [sklerozɑ̃, -ɑ̃t] ADJ **1** *Méd* sclerosing, sclerosis-causing **2** *Fig* paralysing; *(mode de vie, travail)* mind-numbing
sclérose [skleroz] NF **1** *Méd* sclerosis; **s. en plaques** multiple sclerosis, MS **2** *Fig* ossification
sclérosé, -e [skleroze] ADJ **1** *Méd* sclerotic **2** *Fig* antiquated, ossified; **avoir l'esprit s.** to have become set in one's ways
NM,F *Méd* sclerosis sufferer
scléroser **[3]** [skleroze] VT **1** *Méd* to cause sclerosis of; **molécule qui sclérose les tissus** tissue-sclerosing molecule **2** *Fig (système)* to ossify, to paralyse; *(esprit)* to make rigid; **le parti a été sclérosé par des années d'inactivité** years of inertia have brought the party to a political standstill
VPR **se scléroser 1** *Méd* to sclerose **2** *Fig (se figer)* to ossify, to become paralysed; **se s. dans ses habitudes** to become set in one's ways
sclérotique [sklerɔtik] NF sclerotic, sclera
scolaire [skɔlɛr] ADJ **1** *(de l'école)* school *(avant n)*; *(du cursus)* school *(avant n)*, academic; **le milieu s.** the school environment; **niveau/succès s.** academic standard/achievement; **2** *Péj (écriture, raisonnement)* dry, scholastic; **il est très s.** his work is very unoriginal; **à l'université, il faut être moins s. et organiser soi-même son travail** university students shouldn't expect to be spoonfed like schoolchildren
NMF *(enfant)* schoolchild
scolairement [skɔlɛrmɑ̃] ADV *Péj (réciter)* mechanically; *(écrire)* in a dry *or* scholastic way
scolarisable [skɔlarizabl] ADJ **population s.** school-age population
scolarisation [skɔlarizasjɔ̃] NF **1** *Admin & Jur* school attendance, schooling; **la s. est obligatoire à partir de six ans** (attendance at) school is compulsory from the age of six; **je suis pour la s. des enfants à partir de l'âge de cinq ans** I'm in favour of children going to *or* starting school at the age of five; **taux de s.** percentage of children in full-time education **2** *(d'une région, d'un pays)* school-building programme
scolariser **[3]** [skɔlarize] VT **1** *(enfant)* to send to school, to provide with formal education; **l'enfant est-il déjà scolarisé?** is the child already at school *or* attending school? **2** *(région, pays)* to equip with schools
scolarité [skɔlarite] NF **1** *Admin & Jur* school attendance, schooling; **la s. est gratuite et obligatoire** schooling is free and compulsory; **la s. a tendance à se prolonger** pupils are tending to leave school later, the school-leaving age is rising **2** *(études)* school career; *(période)* schooldays; **j'ai eu une s. difficile** I had a difficult time at school
scolasticat [skɔlastika] NM **1** *(bâtiment)* theological college **2** *(études)* theological course
scolastique [skɔlastik] ADJ **1** *Hist* scholastic **2** *(formaliste)* scholastic, *Péj* pedantic
NF *Phil & Rel* scholasticism
NM **1** *Hist* Scholastic, Schoolman **2** *Rel* theology student
scoliaste [skɔljast] NM scholiast

scoliose [skɔljoz] **NF** *Méd* scoliosis, lateral curvature of the spine

scolopendre [skɔlɔpɑ̃dr] **NF 1** *Bot* hart's-tongue, *Spéc* scolopendrium **2** *Entom* scolopendra

sconse [skɔ̃s] **NM** *Zool* skunk

scoop [skup] **NM 1** *(exclusivité)* scoop; **faire un s.** to get a scoop **2** *Fam Fig* **j'ai un s.!** I've got some hot news!; **ce n'est pas vraiment un s.!** it's not exactly headline news!

scooter [skutœr] **NM** (motor) scooter; **s. des mers** jet ski; **s. des neiges** snowmobile, skidoo

scootériste [skuterist] **NMF** scooter rider

scopie [skɔpi] **NF** *Fam* X-ray

scopolamine [skɔpɔlamin] **NF** *Pharm* scopolamine, hyoscine

scorbut [skɔrbyt] **NM** *Méd* scurvy

scorbutique [skɔrbytik] *Méd* **ADJ** scorbutic
NMF scurvy sufferer

score [skɔr] **NM 1** *Sport* score; **où en est** *ou* **quel est le s.?** what's the score? **2** *(résultat)* **faire un bon s. aux élections** to get a good result in the election **3** *Mktg* score; **s. d'agrément** approval rating *or* score; **s. d'attribution** attribution score; **s. de mémorisation** recall score; **s. de reconnaissance** recognition score

scoriacé, -e [skɔrjase] **ADJ** scoriaceous

scorie [skɔri] **NF 1** *Métal* **s., scories** slag; *(laitier)* cinders; *(de fer)* (iron) dross **2** *Géol* **scories (volcaniques)** scoria **3** *Fig Littéraire* **scories** *(déchet)* waste, dregs

scorpène [skɔrpɛn] **NF** *Ich* scorpion fish

scorpion [skɔrpjɔ̃] **NM** *Entom* scorpion; **s. d'eau** water scorpion; *Ich* **s. de mer** sea scorpion

scorsonère [skɔrsɔnɛr] **NF 1** *Bot* scorzonera **2** *Culin* black salsify

scotch [skɔtʃ] (*pl* **scotchs** *ou* **scotches**) **NM** *(whisky)* Scotch (whisky)

Scotch® [skɔtʃ] **NM** adhesive tape, *Br* Sellotape®, *Am* Scotch tape

scotché, -e [skɔtʃe] **ADJ 1** *(collé)* taped, *Br* sellotaped, *Am* scotchtaped; *Fam Fig* **être s. devant la télé** to be glued to the TV **2** *Fam (stupéfait)* **je suis resté s.** I was staggered *or Br* gobsmacked

scotcher [3] [skɔtʃe] **VT 1** *(coller)* to tape, *Br* to sellotape, *Am* to scotchtape **2** *Fam (stupéfaire)* to flabbergast, to knock sideways; **ça m'a vraiment scotché!** I was staggered *or Br* gobsmacked!

scotch-terrier [skɔtʃterje] (*pl* **scotch-terriers**) **NM** Scottish terrier, Scottie

scottish-terrier [skɔtiʃterje] (*pl* **scottish-terriers**) **NM** Scottish terrier, Scottie

scoumoune [ʃkumun] **NF** *très Fam* rotten luck; **avoir la s.** to be jinxed

scout, -e [skut] **ADJ 1** *(relatif au scoutisme)* scout *(avant n)*; **camp/mouvement s.** scout camp/movement **2** *Fig* boy scout *(avant n)*; **il a un petit côté s.** he's a boy scout at heart
NM,F *(personne)* (Boy) Scout, *f Br* (Girl) Guide, *Am* Girl Scout; **des scouts** (a troop of) Boy Scouts; **des scoutes** (a troop of) *Br* Girl Guides *or Am* Girl Scouts; **s., toujours prêt!** *(devise des scouts)* be prepared!; *Hum* always at your service!

scoutisme [skutism] **NM 1** *(activité)* scouting **2** *(association ▸ pour garçons)* Boy Scout movement; *(▸ pour filles) Br* Girl Guide *or Am* Girl Scoutmovement

SCPI [ɛssepei] **NF** *(abrév* **Société civile de placement immobilier***)* = company which owns and manages rented accommodation

Scrabble® [skrabl] **NM** Scrabble®

scratch [skratʃ] **ADJ INV** *Sport (course, joueur)* scratch *(avant n)*
NM 1 *Sport (course)* scratch race **2** *Mus (en rap)* scratching; **faire un s.** to scratch **3** *(fermeture velcro)* Velcro®

scratcher [3] [skratʃe] **VT** *Sport* to scratch, to withdraw
VI *Mus* to scratch
VPR se scratcher *Fam* to go off the road; **il s'est scratché avec la moto de son frère** he went off the road on his brother's motorbike

scratching [skratʃiŋ] **NM** *Mus* scratching

scribe [skrib] **NM 1** *Antiq & Rel* scribe **2** *(écrivain public)* copyist, public writer **3** *Péj Vieilli (gratte-papier)* pen-pusher

scribouillard, -e [skribujar, -ard] **NM,F** *Fam Péj* pen-pusher

script [skript] **NM 1** *(écriture)* script; **écrire en s.** to write in block letters, to print (in block letters) **2** *Cin & Rad* script **3** *Bourse* scrip

scripte [skript] **NMF** continuity man, *f* girl

script-girl [skriptgœrl] (*pl* **script-girls**) **NF** continuity girl

scriptural, -e, -aux, -ales [skriptyral, -o] **ADJ 1** *(relatif à l'écriture)* written **2** *Fin* cashless

scrofulaire [skrɔfylɛr] **NF** *Bot* figwort, *Spéc* scrophularia; **s. noueuse** common figwort

scrofule [skrɔfyl] **NF** *Méd* scrofula

scrofuleux, -euse [skrɔfylø, -øz] *Méd* **ADJ** scrofulous
NM,F scrofulous person

scrotum [skrɔtɔm] **NM** *Anat* scrotum

scrupule [skrypyl] **NM 1** *(cas de conscience)* scruple, qualm (of conscience); **avoir des scrupules** to have scruples; **elle n'a aucun s.** she has no scruples; *Fam* **ce ne sont pas les scrupules qui l'étouffent** he's completely unscrupulous; **se faire s. de qch** to have scruples *or* qualms about doing sth; **il ne s'est pas embarrassé de scrupules pour le renvoyer** he didn't have any scruples about firing him; **avoir s. à faire qch** to have scruples *or* qualms about doing sth; **je n'aurai aucun s. à le lui dire** I'll have no scruples *or* qualms about telling him/her so; **n'ayez aucun s. à faire appel à moi** don't hesitate to ask for my help **2** *(minutie)* punctiliousness; **exact jusqu'au s.** scrupulously *or* punctiliously exact
• **sans scrupules ADJ** *(individu)* unscrupulous, unprincipled, without scruples

scrupuleuse [skrypyløz] *voir* **scrupuleux**

scrupuleusement [skrypyløzmɑ̃] **ADV** scrupulously, punctiliously

scrupuleux, -euse [skrypylø, -øz] **ADJ 1** *(honnête)* scrupulous, scrupulously honest; **peu s.** unscrupulous; **d'une honnêteté scrupuleuse** scrupulously honest **2** *(minutieux)* scrupulous, meticulous

scrutateur, -trice [skrytatœr, -tris] **ADJ** searching *(avant n)*; **d'un air s.** searchingly
NM,F *Admin Br* scrutineer, *Am* teller

scruter [3] [skryte] **VT 1** *(pour comprendre)* to scrutinize, to examine; **s. qn du regard** to give sb a searching look; **il scruta son visage** he searched his/her face **2** *(en parcourant des yeux)* to scan, to search

scrutin [skrytɛ̃] **NM 1** *(façon d'élire)* vote, voting *(UNCOUNT)*, ballot; **procéder au s.** to take a ballot; **dépouiller le s.** to count the votes; **s. d'arrondissement** district election system; **s. à deux tours** second ballot; **s. de liste** list system; **s. majoritaire** election on a majority basis, *Br* first-past-the-post election; **s. majoritaire plurinominal** first-past-the-post system *(voting for as many candidates/parties as there are seats)*; **s. majoritaire uninominal** first-past-the-post system *(voting for a single candidate)*; **s. plurinominal** = voting for more than one candidate; **s. proportionnel** *ou* **à la proportionnelle** (voting using the system of) proportional representation; **s. secret** secret ballot; **voter au s. secret** to have a secret ballot; **s. uninominal** voting for a single candidate **2** *(fait de voter)* ballot; **par (voie de) s.** by ballot; **s. de ballottage** second ballot, *Am* runoff election **3** *(consultation électorale)* election

SCS [ɛsseɛs] **NF** *(abrév* **société en commandite simple***)* limited partnership

SCSI [ɛseɛsi] **NF** *(abrév* **small computer systems interface***)* SCSI

SCT [ɛssete] **NM** *Méd (abrév* **syndrome du choc toxique***)* TSS

scull [skyl, skœl] **NM** *Sport* scull

sculpter [3] [skylte] **VT 1** *(pierre, marbre)* to sculpt; **s. qch dans le marbre** to sculpt sth out of marble; **escalier sculpté** sculptured staircase **2** *(bois)* to carve; *(bâton)* to scrimshaw **3** *Fig (façonner)* to sculpt, to carve, to fashion
USAGE ABSOLU *(faire de la sculpture)* to sculpt

sculpteur, -trice [skyltœr, -tris] **NM,F** sculptor; **femme s.** sculptor, sculptress; **s. sur bois** woodcarver

sculptural, -e, -aux, -ales [skyltyral, -o] **ADJ 1** *(relatif à la sculpture)* sculptural **2** *(beauté, formes)* statuesque

sculpture [skyltyr] **NF 1** *(art)* sculpture *(UNCOUNT)*, sculpting *(UNCOUNT)*; **faire de la s.** to sculpt; **il fait de la s.** he's a sculptor; **s. sur bois** woodcarving **2** *(œuvre)* sculpture, piece of sculpture

scutellaire [skytelɛr] **NF** *Bot* skullcap, *Spéc* scutellaria

scythe [sit] **ADJ** Scythian
• **Scythe NMF** Scythian

Scythie [siti] **NF** *Géog* **la S.** Scythia

SDF [ɛsdeɛf] **NMF INV** *(abrév* **sans domicile fixe***)* homeless person; **les S.** the homeless

SDN [ɛsdeɛn] **NF** *(abrév* **Société des Nations***)* **la S.** the League of Nations

SE [sə]

> s' is used before a word beginning with a vowel or h mute.

PRON PERSONNEL 1 *(avec un verbe pronominal réfléchi)* **se salir** to get dirty; **s'exprimer** to express oneself; **elle se coiffe** she's doing her hair; **le chat s'est brûlé** the cat burnt itself; **elles s'en sont persuadées** they've convinced themselves of it; **il s'écoute parler** he listens to his own voice; **il s'est acheté une voiture** he bought himself a car; **il s'attribuera tout le mérite de l'affaire** he'll take all the credit for it
2 *(se substituant à l'adjectif possessif)* **elle se lave les mains** she's washing her hands; **il s'est fracturé deux côtes** he broke two ribs; **se mordre la langue** to bite one's tongue
3 *(avec un verbe pronominal réciproque)* **pour s'aider, ils partagent le travail** to help each other *or* one another, they share the work; **ils ne se supportent pas** they can't stand each other *or* one another; **ils s'aiment profondément** they love each other deeply; **elles se sont envoyé des lettres** they sent letters to each other, they exchanged letters
4 *(avec un verbe pronominal passif)* **cette décision s'est prise sans moi** this decision has been taken without me; **ce modèle se vend bien** this model sells well; **ça se mange?** can you eat it?; **ça se mange froid** you eat it cold; **ça se trouve où?** where can you find that?
5 *(avec un verbe pronominal intransitif)* **ils s'en vont** they're leaving; **elle s'est évanouie** she fainted; **ils s'en sont emparés** they grabbed *or* snatched it; **il se sentit défaillir** he felt himself becoming faint; **ils s'y voient contraints** they find themselves forced to do it; **il se laisse convaincre trop facilement** he is too easily persuaded; *Fam* **il s'est fait avoir!** he's been had!; **il se croyait lundi** he thought it was Monday today; **elle se croyait en sécurité** she thought she was safe; **elle se sait perdue** she knows (that) she's incurable; **il se dit médecin** he claims to be a doctor
6 *(dans des tournures impersonnelles)* **il s'en est vendu plusieurs millions d'exemplaires** several million copies have been sold; **il se fait tard** it's getting late; **il s'est mis à neiger** it started to snow; **il se peut qu'ils arrivent plus tôt** it's possible that they'll arrive earlier, they might arrive earlier; **il s'est glissé une erreur dans la dernière page** a mistake slipped into the last page
7 *Fam (emploi expressif)* **il se fait 5000 euros par mois** he's got 5,000 euros coming in per month; **elle se l'est écouté au moins 30 fois, ce disque** she listened to this record at least 30 times

séance [seɑ̃s] **NF 1** *(réunion)* session; **être en s.** *(comité, Parlement)* to be sitting *or* in session; *(tribunal)* to be in session; **lever la s.** *(groupe de travail)* to close the meeting; *(comité)* to end *or* to close the session; *(Parlement)* to adjourn; **la s. est levée!** *(au tribunal)* the court will adjourn!; *Fam* **on lève la s.?** *(après une période de travail)* shall we call it a day?; **suspendre la s.** *(au Parlement, au tribunal)* to adjourn; **je déclare la s. ouverte** I declare the meeting open; **la s. est ouverte!** *(au tribunal)* this court is now in session!; **en s. publique** *(au tribunal)* in open court; **s. de**

concertation *(au Parlement)* policy meeting; *Mktg* **s. de créativité** brainstorming session; **s. d'information** briefing (session); **s. plénière** *(au Parlement)* plenary (session); **s. publique** *(au Parlement)* public sitting

2 *Bourse* **ce fut une bonne/mauvaise s. aujourd'hui à la Bourse** it was a good/a bad day today on the Stock Exchange; **en début/en fin de s., les actions Roman étaient à 40 euros** the Roman shares opened/closed at 40 euros; **s. de clôture** closing session; **s. d'ouverture** opening session

3 *(période ▸ d'entraînement, de traitement)* session; **s. de photo** photocall, photo opportunity; **s. de projection** slide show; **s. de rééducation** session of physiotherapy; **s. de spiritisme** seance; **s. de travail** working session

4 *Cin* showing; **s. à 19h10, film à 19h30** programme 7.10, film starts 7.30; **je vais à la s. de 20 heures** I'm going to the 8 o'clock showing; **s. privée** private showing

5 *Fam (crise)* scene, fuss, tantrum; **il nous a fait une de ces séances!** he made such a scene!; **il nous a fait une s. de larmes** he turned on the waterworks

• **séance tenante** ADV forthwith, right away, without further ado

• **à la séance** ADJ *TV (film, programme)* pay-per-view

séancier [seɑ̃sje] NM *(parlementaire)* parliamentary reporter

séant, -e [seɑ̃, -ɑ̃t] ADJ **1** *Littéraire (convenable)* becoming, seemly; **il n'est pas s. de partir sans un mot de remerciement** it's not done to leave without a word of thanks **2** *Arch (flatteur)* becoming (**à** to)

NM *(postérieur)* **se mettre sur son s.** to sit up; **tomber sur son s.** to fall on one's behind

seau, -x [so] NM **1** *(récipient)* bucket, pail; **s. à champagne** champagne bucket; **s. à charbon** coal scuttle; **s. d'enfant** child's bucket; **s. à glace** *Br* ice bucket, *Am* ice-pail **2** *(contenu)* bucketful

• **à seaux** ADV *Fam* **il pleut à seaux, la pluie tombe à seaux** it's pouring *or Br* bucketing down

sébacé, -e [sebase] ADJ *Méd* sebaceous

sébile [sebil] NF *Littéraire* begging bowl

séborrhée [sebɔre] NF *Méd* seborrhoea

sébum [sebɔm] NM sebum

SEC, SÈCHE[1] [sɛk, sɛʃ]

ADJ	
• dry **1, 3–5**	• dried **2**
• neat **2**	• curt **4**
ADV	
• dry **1**	• hard **2**

ADJ **1** *(air, bois, endroit, vêtement etc)* dry; **il fait un froid s.** it's cold and dry, the air is crisp and cold; **avoir l'œil s.** *ou* **les yeux secs** *Méd* to have dry eyes; *Fig* to be dry-eyed

2 *(légume, fruit)* dried; *(alcool)* neat

3 *(non gras ▸ cheveux, peau, mine de crayon)* dry; *(maigre ▸ personne)* lean; *Fam* **être s. comme un coup de trique** to be all skin and bone *or* as thin as a rake

4 *(désagréable ▸ ton, voix, explication, remarque)* dry; **d'un ton s.** curtly *or* tersely; **un bruit s.** a snap, a crack; **ouvrir/fermer qch avec un bruit s.** to snap sth open/shut; **d'un coup s.** smartly, sharply; **casser qch d'un coup s.** to snap sth; **retire le sparadrap d'un coup s.** pull the sticking plaster off smartly; *Fam* **l'avoir s.** *(être déçu)* to be miffed

5 *(champagne, vin)* dry

ADV **1** *Météo* **il fera s. toute la semaine** the weather *or* it will be dry for the whole week

2 *(brusquement)* hard; **démarrer s.** *(conducteur)* to shoot off at top speed; *(course)* to get a flying start; **il a pris son virage assez s.** he took the bend rather sharply

3 *Fam (beaucoup)* a lot[▫]; **il boit s.** he can really knock it back; **ils ont dérouillé s. pendant la guerre** they went through total hell during the war

• **à sec** ADJ **1** *(cours d'eau, source etc)* dry, dried-up; *(réservoir)* empty **2** *Fam (sans argent ▸ personne)* broke, *Br* skint; *(▸ caisse)* empty[▫] **3** *Constr* **maçonnerie à s.** dry-stone (work) ADV **1** *(sans eau)* **on met la piscine à s. chaque hiver** the pool's drained (off) every winter; **le soleil a mis le marais à s.** the sun has dried up the marsh **2** *Fam (financièrement)* **mettre une entreprise à s.** to ruin a company

• **au sec** ADV **garder** *ou* **tenir qch au s.** to keep sth in a dry place, to keep sth dry; **rester au s.** to stay dry

sécable [sekabl] ADJ **1** *Pharm* breakable, divisible **2** *Géom* divisible

SECAM, Secam [sekam] *TV (abrév* **séquentiel couleur à mémoire)** ADJ INV SECAM

NM INV SECAM

sécant, -e [sekɑ̃, -ɑ̃t] ADJ intersecting, secant

• **sécante** NF secant

sécateur [sekatœr] NM **un s.** *(pour les fleurs)* (a pair of) secateurs; *(pour les haies)* pruning shears

sécession [sesesjɔ̃] NF secession; **faire s.** to secede

sécessionniste [sesesjɔnist] ADJ secessionist

NMF secessionist

séchage [seʃaʒ] NM **1** *(du linge, des cheveux, du foin)* drying **2** *(du bois)* seasoning

sèche[2] [sɛʃ] ADJ F *voir* **sec**

NF *Fam (cigarette)* smoke, *Br* fag, *Am* cig

sèche-cheveux [sɛʃʃəvø] NM INV hairdryer

sèche-linge [sɛʃlɛ̃ʒ] NM INV *(à tambour)* tumble-drier; *(placard)* airing cupboard

sèche-mains [sɛʃmɛ̃] NM INV hand-dryer

sèchement [sɛʃmɑ̃] ADV **1** *(durement ▸ parler, répondre)* dryly, curtly, tersely; **"ne comptez pas sur moi", répondit-elle s.** "don't count on me," she snapped back **2** *(brusquement ▸ taper)* sharply **3** *(sans fioritures)* dryly; **il expose toujours ses arguments un peu s.** he always sets out his arguments rather unimaginatively

sécher [18] [seʃe] VT **1** *(gén)* to dry; *(avec un torchon, avec une éponge)* to wipe dry; **sèche tes larmes** *ou* **tes yeux** dry your tears *or* your eyes; **s. les larmes** *ou* **les pleurs de qn** to console sb

2 *(vêtement)* to dry; **ne pas s. en machine** *(sur étiquette de vêtement)* do not tumble-dry

3 *(sujet: chaleur, soleil ▸ terrain, plante)* to dry up; *(déshydrater ▸ fruits)* to dry (up); **le vent sèche la peau** wind dries (out) the skin; **figues séchées au soleil** sun-dried figs

4 *Fam Arg scol (cours) Br* to bunk off, *Am* to skip

5 *Fam (boire)* to knock back

VI **1** *(surface)* to dry (off); *(linge)* to dry; *(éponge)* to dry (out); *(sol, puits)* to dry up; *(cours d'eau)* to dry up, to run dry

2 faire s. du linge to leave clothes to dry; **mettre le linge à s.** to put the washing out to dry; **faire s. sans essorer** *(sur l'étiquette d'un vêtement)* do not spin dry; **laisser s. les peintures** to leave the paintwork to dry

3 *(plante)* to dry up *or* out; *(bois)* to dry out; *(fruits, viande)* to dry; **faire s. du bois** to season wood; **s. sur pied** *(plante)* to wilt, to wither; *Fam* **on a séché sur pied tout l'été** we've been bored out of our minds all summer; *Littéraire* **s. d'impatience/d'ennui** to be consumed with impatience/with boredom

4 *Fam Arg scol (ne pas aller en classe) Br* to bunk off, *Am* to play hookey

5 *Fam (ne pas connaître la réponse)* to be completely stumped; **j'ai séché en physique/sur la deuxième question** the physics exam/the second question had me completely stumped

VPR **se sécher** to dry oneself; **se s. avec une serviette/au soleil** to dry oneself with a towel/in the sun; **se s. les mains/les cheveux** to dry one's hands/hair

sécheresse, sècheresse [sɛʃrɛs] NF **1** *(d'un climat, d'un terrain, d'un style)* dryness; *(d'un trait)* dryness, harshness; *(d'une réplique, d'un ton)* abruptness, curtness; **répondre avec s.** to answer curtly *or* abruptly *or* tersely; **montrer une grande s. de cœur** to show great heartlessness **2** *Météo* drought; **pendant la** *ou* **les mois de s.** during the dry months

sécherie, sècherie [sɛʃri] NF **1** *(lieu)* drying room; *(d'une machine)* dryer; *(industrie)* drying plant **2** *Typ* dry end

sécheur [seʃœr] NM *(à tabac)* dryer

séchoir [seʃwar] NM **1** *Agr & Tech (salle)* drying room; *(hangar)* drying shed; *(râtelier)* drying rack **2** *(à usage domestique)* dryer; **s. à cheveux** hairdryer; **s. à linge** *(à tambour)* tumble-drier; *(pliant)* clotheshorse **3** *Typ* **s. à plat** sheet dryer

second, -e[1] [səgɔ̃, -ɔ̃d] ADJ **1** *(dans l'espace, dans le temps)* second; **pour la seconde fois** for the second time; **en s. lieu** secondly, in the second place

2 *(dans une hiérarchie)* second; *(éclairagiste, maquilleur)* assistant *(avant n)*; **la seconde ville de France** France's second city; *Com* **s. associé** junior partner; *Transp* **seconde classe** second class; *Bourse* **s. marché** unlisted securities market, secondary market; *Littéraire* **sans s., à nul autre s.** *(sans pareil)* second to none, unparalleled; *Jur* **s. original** = second original copy of a document; *Cin* **s. rôle** secondary *or* supporting role; **meilleur s. rôle masculin/féminin** best supporting actor/actress

3 *(autre ▸ chance, jeunesse, vie)* second; **l'Angleterre, c'est une seconde patrie pour elle** England's a second home for her; **c'est une seconde nature chez lui** it's second nature to him; **seconde vue** clairvoyance, second sight; **être doué de seconde vue** to be clairvoyant, to have second sight

NM,F **1** *(dans l'espace, dans le temps)* second; **je lis le premier paragraphe, et toi le s.** I read the first paragraph, and you the second one *or* the next one **2** *(dans une hiérarchie)* second; **la seconde de ses filles** his/her second daughter; **mon s.** *(enfant)* my second child; **arriver (le) s.** *(dans une course, à une élection)* to come second

NM **1** *(assistant ▸ d'un directeur)* right arm; *(▸ dans un duel)* second; *Naut* first mate; *Mil* second in command; **s. de cuisine** senior sous chef; *TV & Cin* **s. assistant** best boy **2** *(dans une charade)* **mon s. est...** my second is... **3** *(étage) Br* second floor, *Am* third floor

• **seconde** NF **1** *Aut* second gear; **passe en seconde** change into *or* to second gear

2 *Transp (classe)* second class; **(billet de) seconde** second-class ticket; **les secondes, les wagons de seconde** second-class carriages; **voyager en seconde** to travel second class

3 *Scol Br* ≃ fifth year, *Am* ≃ tenth grade

4 *(en danse)* second position

5 *Mus* second; **seconde majeure/mineure** major/minor second

• **secondes** NFPL *Typ* second proofs

• **en second** ADJ **capitaine en s.** first mate ADV second, secondly; **passer en s.** to be second

secondaire [səgɔ̃dɛr] ADJ **1** *(question, personnage, route)* secondary; **c'est s.** it's of secondary importance *or* of minor interest; *Théât & Littérature* **intrigue s.** subplot **2** *Scol* secondary **3** *Géol* **ère s.** Mesozoic era

NM **1** *Géol* **le s.** the Mesozoic

2 *Scol* **le s.** *Br* secondary *or Am* high school *(UNCOUNT)*

3 *Élec* secondary winding; *Rad (du transformateur)* secondary

4 *Écon* **le s.** secondary production

secondairement [səgɔ̃dɛrmɑ̃] ADV secondarily

seconde[2] [səgɔ̃d] NF **1** *(division horaire)* second; **s. intercalaire** leap second **2** *(court instant)* **(attendez) une s.!** just a second!; **j'en ai pour une s.** I'll only be a second *or* a moment; **je reviens dans une s.** I'll be back in a second, I'll be right back; **une s. d'inattention** a momentary lapse in concentration; **à une s. près, je ratais le train** I was within a second of missing the train; **à la s.** instantly, there and then; **avec lui, il faut que ce soit fait à la s.** he wants things done instantly

secondement [səgɔ̃dmɑ̃] ADV second, secondly

seconder [3] [səgɔ̃de] VT **1** *(assister)* to assist, to back up **2** *(action, dessein)* to second

secoué, -e [skwe] ADJ *Fam (fou)* off one's nut *or* rocker

secouement [səkumɑ̃] NM *Littéraire* shaking

secouer [6] [səkwe] VT **1** *(arbre, bouteille, personne)* to shake; *(tapis, vêtement)* to shake (out); *(coussin, oreiller)* to plump up, to shake up; **la tempête secouait le bateau** the storm was buffeting the boat; **nous avons été secoués pendant la traversée/le vol** we were shaken about during the crossing/the flight, we had a rough crossing/flight; **l'explosion secoua l'immeuble**

the explosion shook *or* rocked the building; **de violents spasmes secouaient son corps tout entier** violent spasms shook his/her whole body; **s. la tête** *(acquiescer)* to nod one's head; *(refuser)* to shake one's head; *Fam* **s. qn comme un prunier** to shake sb like a rag doll; *Fig* **s. le cocotier** to get rid of the dead wood

2 *(se débarrasser de ▸ poussière, sable, miettes)* to shake off; *Fig (▸ paresse, torpeur etc)* to shake off; **s. le joug de l'oppresseur** to shake off the yoke of the oppressor; *Fam* **s. les puces à qn** *(le gronder) Br* to tick sb off, *Am* to chew sb out

3 *Fam (houspiller ▸ personne)* to shake up; **il a besoin d'être secoué pour travailler** he needs a good shake before he gets down to work

4 *(bouleverser ▸ personne)* to shake up, to give a jolt *or* a shock to; **la nouvelle l'a beaucoup secoué** the news really shook him up

5 *très Fam* **j'en ai rien à s.** I don't give a damn *or Br* toss

USAGE ABSOLU ça secoue *(en avion, en train)* it's bumpy; *(en bateau)* it's rough

VPR se secouer *Fam* to shake oneself up, to snap out of it; **il serait grand temps de te s.!** it's high time you pulled yourself together!

secourable [səkurabl] **ADJ** helpful; **peu s.** unhelpful

secourir [45] [səkurir] **VT 1** *(blessé)* to help; *(personne en danger)* to rescue **2** *(pauvre, affligé)* to aid, to help **3** *Littéraire (misères)* to relieve, to ease

secourisme [səkurism] **NM** first aid

secouriste [səkurist] **NMF 1** *(d'une organisation)* first-aid worker **2** *(personne qualifiée)* qualified first-aider

secourra *etc voir* **secourir**

secours [səkur] **NM 1** *(assistance)* help, assistance, aid; **appeler** *ou* **crier au s.** to call out for help; **au s.!** help!; **appeler à son s.** *(blessé, entreprise)* to call upon sb for help, to call sb to the rescue; **allez chercher du s.!** go and get (some) help!; **porter** *ou* **prêter s. à qn** to give sb assistance; **porter s. à un blessé** to give first aid to an injured person; **personne ne s'est arrêté pour me porter s.** nobody stopped to (come and) help me; **aller** *ou* **se porter au s. de qn** to go to sb's assistance; **venir au s. de qn** to come to sb's aid; **venir au s. d'une entreprise** to rescue a company; **société de s. mutuels** friendly *or Am* benefit society

2 *(sauvetage)* aid, assistance; **le** *ou* **les s. aux brûlés** aid *or* assistance for burn victims; **envoyer des s. à qn** to send relief to sb; **les s. ne sont pas encore arrivés** aid *or* help hasn't arrived yet; **le s. en montagne/en mer** sea/mountain rescue; **le** *ou* **les s. d'urgence** emergency aid

3 *(appui)* help; **être d'un grand s. à qn** to be of great help to sb; **la calculette ne m'a pas été d'un grand s.** the calculator was of (very) little help *or* use to me; **avec le s. du dictionnaire, je devrais me débrouiller** with the help *or* with the aid of the dictionary, I should be able to get by

NMPL *Mil (troupes)* relief troops, relieving force

• **de secours ADJ** *(équipement, éclairage, porte, sortie)* emergency *(avant n)*; *(équipe, poste)* rescue *(avant n)*; *(locomotive, train)* relief *(avant n)*; *Ordinat (copie, fichier, disquette)* backup

secouru, -e [səkury] **PP** *voir* **secourir**

secousse [səkus] **NF 1** *(saccade)* jerk, jolt; **elle se dégagea d'une s.** she shook *or* jerked herself free; **elle réussit à déplacer la malle par secousses** she managed to jerk the trunk along; **le train avançait par secousses** the train jolted forwards; **s. (électrique)** electric shock **2** *Fig (bouleversement)* jolt, shock, upset **3** *Géol* **s. (sismique** *ou* **tellurique)** (earth) tremor

secret, -ète [səkrɛ, -ɛt] **ADJ 1** *(inconnu ▸ accord, code, document etc)* secret; **cela n'a rien de s.** it's no secret; **garder** *ou* **tenir qch s.** to keep sth secret

2 *(caché ▸ escalier, passage, vie)* secret

3 *(intime ▸ ambition, désir, espoir, pensée)* secret, innermost

4 *(personne)* secretive, reserved

NM 1 *(confidence)* secret; **c'est un s.!** it's a secret!; **ce n'est un s. pour personne** it's no secret, everybody knows about it; **elle n'en fait pas un s.** she makes no secret of the fact; **confier un s. à qn** to let sb into a secret; **être dans le s.** to be in on the secret; **mettre qn dans le s.** to let sb in on the secret; **ne pas avoir de secrets pour qn** *(sujet: personne)* to have no secrets from sb; *(sujet: question, machine)* to hold no secret for sb; **faire un s. de tout** to be secretive about everything; **s. d'État** state secret; *Fig* **ce n'est pas un s. d'État!** it's not a state secret!; **être dans le s. des dieux** to have privileged information

2 *(mystère ▸ d'un endroit, d'une discipline)* secret; **les secrets du cœur/de la nature** secrets of the heart/of nature

3 *(recette)* secret, recipe; **le s. du bonheur** the secret of *or* the recipe for happiness; **ses secrets de beauté** his/her beauty secrets *or* tips; **trouver le s. pour faire qch** to find the knack of doing sth; *Com* **s. de fabrication** *ou* **de fabrique** trade secret

4 *(discrétion)* secrecy *(UNCOUNT)*; **exiger/promettre le s. (absolu)** to demand/to promise (absolute) secrecy; **je vous demande le s. sur cette affaire** I want you to keep silent about this matter; **s. bancaire** banking secrecy; **s. professionnel** professional confidentiality; *Journ* obligation to respect the confidentiality of sources; **enfreindre le s. professionnel** to commit a breach of confidentiality; *Journ* to betray a confidential source

5 *Rel* **le s. de la confession** the seal of confession

• **secrète NF 1 la secrète** *(police)* the secret police **2** *Rel (oraison)* secret

• **à secret ADJ** *(cadenas)* combination *(avant n)*; *(tiroir)* with a secret lock; *(meuble)* with secret drawers

• **au secret ADV être au s.** to be (detained) in solitary confinement; **mettre qn au s.** to detain sb in solitary confinement

• **en secret ADV 1** *(écrire, économiser)* in secret, secretly **2** *(croire, espérer)* secretly, privately

secrétaire [səkretɛr] **NMF 1** *(dans une entreprise)* secretary; **s. bilingue/trilingue** bilingual/trilingual secretary; **s. du conseil d'administration** secretary to the Board of Directors; **s. de direction** executive secretary, personal assistant; **s. d'édition** *(dans l'édition)* assistant editor; *Journ* subeditor; **s. général** *(dans une entreprise)* company secretary; *(d'un syndicat)* general secretary; **s. juridique** legal secretary; **s. médical** medical secretary; **s. particulier** private secretary; *Cin & TV* **s. de plateau** script supervisor; **s. de production** production secretary; **s. de rédaction** *(dans l'édition)* desk *or* assistant editor; *Presse* subeditor; **s. de séance** meetings secretary **2** *Pol* **s. d'ambassade** secretary; **s. général** *(auprès d'un ministre)* ≃ permanent secretary; *(dans un parti)* general secretary; **s. général de l'ONU** Secretary-General of the UN; **s. général de l'Assemblée** ≃ Clerk of the House; **s. général du Sénat** ≃ Clerk of the House; **s. d'État** *(en France)* ≃ Junior Minister; *(en Grande-Bretagne)* Secretary of State; *(aux États-Unis)* State Secretary; **s. d'État à la santé/aux transports** *(en France)* ≃ Junior Minister for Health/Transport; *(en Grande-Bretagne)* Secretary of State for Health/Transport; **s. perpétuel** Permanent Secretary *(of a learned society)* **3** *Admin* **s. d'administration** *(fonctionnaire)* administrative officer, administrator; **s. de mairie** ≃ chief executive

NM 1 *(meuble)* writing desk, *Sout* secrétaire **2** *Orn* secretary bird

secrétariat [səkretarja] **NM 1** *(fonction)* secretaryship; **pendant son s.** during his/her term of office as secretary; **s. de rédaction** *(dans l'édition)* desk *or* assistant editorship; *Journ* post of subeditor

2 *(employés)* secretarial staff; **le budget du s.** budgeting for secretarial services; **faire partie du s.** to be a member of the secretariat

3 *(bureau)* secretariat; **aller au s.** to go to the secretariat *or* secretary's office; *Journ* **s. de rédaction** copy desk

4 *(tâches administratives)* secretarial *or* administrative work; **apprendre le s.** to do a secretarial course

5 *Pol* **s. d'État** *(fonction en France)* post of Junior Minister; *(ministère français)* Junior Minister's Office; *(fonction en Grande-Bretagne)* post of Secretary of State; *(ministère britannique)* Secretary of State's Office; *(fonction aux États-Unis)* post of State Secretary; **s. général de l'ONU** UN Secretary-Generalship

secrètement [səkretmɑ̃] **ADV 1** *(en cachette)* secretly, in secret; **elle avait vendu ses bijoux s.** she had secretly sold her jewels **2** *(intérieurement)* secretly; **je souhaite s. qu'il échoue** I secretly hope that he'll fail

sécréter [18] [sekrete] **VT 1** *Biol & Physiol* to secrete **2** *Fig (ennui)* to exude, to ooze; *(passion, désir)* to cause, to release

sécréteur, -euse *ou* **-trice** [sekretœr, -øz,-tris] **ADJ** *Biol & Physiol* secretory

sécrétion [sekresjɔ̃] **NF** *Biol & Physiol* secretion; **glande à s. externe/interne** exocrine/endocrine gland

sécrétoire [sekretwar] **ADJ** *Biol & Physiol* secretory

sectaire [sɛktɛr] **ADJ** sectarian

NMF sectarian

> Il faut noter qu'en anglais britannique, le terme **sectarian** fait le plus souvent référence à l'hostilité et à l'intolérance qui caractérisent les relations entre catholiques et protestants en Irlande du Nord et en Écosse.

sectarisme [sɛktarism] **NM** sectarianism

> Il faut noter qu'en anglais britannique, le terme **sectarianism** fait le plus souvent référence à l'hostilité et à l'intolérance qui caractérisent les relations entre catholiques et protestants en Irlande du Nord et en Écosse.

secte [sɛkt] **NF** sect

secteur [sɛktœr] **NM 1** *Écon* sector; **s. d'activité** area of activity; **s. d'affaires** business sector; **s. de croissance** growth sector; **s. économique** economic sector; **s. en expansion** growth sector; **s. de la grande distribution** mass distribution sector; **s. industriel** branch *or* sector of industry; **s. primaire** primary sector; **s. privé** private sector *or* enterprise; **s. privé à but non lucratif** private non-profit-making sector; **s. public** public sector; **s. sanitaire** health sector; **s. secondaire** secondary sector; **s. des services** service sector; **s. tertiaire** tertiary sector

2 *(zone d'action ▸ d'un policier) Br* beat, *Am* patch; *(▸ d'un représentant)* area, patch; *(▸ de l'urbanisme)* district, area; *Mil & Naut* sector; *Admin* = local area covered by the French health and social services department; **le s. français de Berlin** the French sector of Berlin; **s. sauvegardé** area of listed buildings, buildings zoned for preservation; **s. de vente** sales area, sales territory

3 *Fam (quartier)* **c'est dans le s.** it's around here□; **ça fait longtemps que je ne l'ai pas vu dans le s.** I haven't seen him around here for ages□; **changer de s.** to make oneself scarce; **tu ferais mieux de changer de s.** *(partir)* you'd better make yourself scarce

4 *Fam (domaine)* **ce n'est pas mon s.** that's not my line

5 *Élec* **le s.** the mains (supply); **branché sur le s.** plugged into the mains; **ça se branche sur le s.** it runs off the mains

6 *Math & Astron* sector; **s. sphérique** sector of a sphere

7 *Ordinat* sector; **s. endommagé** bad sector; **s. d'initialisation** boot sector

8 *Aut* **s. de direction** steering sector

section [sɛksjɔ̃] **NF 1** *(d'une autoroute, d'une rivière)* section, stretch; *(de ligne de bus, de tramway)* fare stage; *(d'un livre)* part, section; *(d'une bibliothèque)* section; *(d'un service)* branch, division, department

2 *Univ (département)* department

3 *Scol* = one of the groups into which "baccalauréat" students are divided, depending on their chosen area of specialization, *Br* ≃ stream, *Am* ≃ track; **s. économique/scientifique/littéraire** ≃ economics/science/arts *Br* stream *or Am* track; **au lycée, j'étais en s. économique** my main subject at school was economics

4 *(d'un parti)* local branch; **s. syndicale** = local branch of a union; *(dans l'industrie de la presse et du livre)* (union) chapel

5 *Math & Géom* section; **un câble de 12 mm de s.** a

12 mm (section) cable; **dessiner la s. de qch** to draw the section of sth *or* sth in section; **s. conique/plane** conic/plane section; **point de s.** point of intersection
6 *Nucl* **s. efficace** cross section
7 *(coupure)* cutting *(UNCOUNT)*, severing *(UNCOUNT)*; *Méd* amputation
8 *Biol (groupe, coupe)* section
9 *Élec* **s. morte** dummy coil
10 *Mil* section; **s. de bombardiers** bomber flight
11 *Mus* **s. rythmique** rhythm section
12 *Pol* **s. électorale** ward

sectionnement [sɛksjɔnmɑ̃] **NM 1** *(coupure)* cutting *(UNCOUNT)*, severing *(UNCOUNT)* **2** *(division)* division into sections **3** *Élec* sectioning (and isolation)

sectionner **[3]** [sɛksjɔne] **VT 1** *(tendon, câble, ligne)* to sever, to cut; *Méd* to amputate; **la lame avait sectionné le ligament** the blade had cut through the ligament **2** *(diviser)* to section, to divide *or* to split (into sections)
VPR se sectionner *(être coupé)* to be severed

sectionneur [sɛksjɔnœr] **NM** section switch

sectoriel, -elle [sɛktɔrjɛl] **ADJ** sector-based; **revendications sectorielles** sector-based demands; **l'application sectorielle d'une mesure** the application of a measure to a certain sector (only)

sectorisation [sɛktɔrizasjɔ̃] **NF** *(gén)* sectorization, division into sectors; *(des services de santé)* = division into areas of responsibility for health and social services

sectoriser **[3]** [sɛktɔrize] **VT** *(gén)* to sector, to divide into areas *or* sectors; *(services de santé)* to divide into areas of health and social services responsibility

Sécu [seky] **NF** *Fam Admin (abrév* **Sécurité sociale)** *(système) Br* ≃ Social Security, *Am* ≃ welfare; *(organisme de remboursement) Br* ≃ DWP, *Am* ≃ Social Security

séculaire [sekylɛr] **ADJ 1** *(vieux ▸ tradition)* age-old; *(▸ arbre)* ancient
2 *(de cent ans)* a hundred years old; **un arbre plusieurs fois s.** a tree several hundred years old
3 *(qui a lieu tous les cent ans)* centennial; **année s.** last year of the century
4 *Astron* secular

> Do not confuse with **séculier.**

sécularisation [sekylarizasjɔ̃] **NF** secularization, secularizing *(UNCOUNT)*

séculariser **[3]** [sekylarize] **VT** to secularize

sécularité [sekylarite] **NF** secularity

séculier, -ère [sekylje, -ɛr] **ADJ** secular
NM secular

> Do not confuse with **séculaire.**

secundo [səgɔ̃do] **ADV** in the second place, second, secondly

sécurisant, -e [sekyrizɑ̃, -ɑ̃t] **ADJ 1** *(qui rassure)* reassuring **2** *Psy* security *(avant n)*

sécuriser **[3]** [sekyrize] **VT 1** *(rassurer)* **s. qn** to make sb feel secure *or* safe, to reassure sb, to give sb a feeling of security **2** *(stabiliser)* to (make) secure; **des mesures visant à s. l'emploi** employment-conserving measures **3** *Fin* **s. un financement** to guarantee a loan; **s. un paiement** *(sur l'Internet)* to guarantee *or* to ensure the security of a transaction

Securit® [sekyrit] **NM (verre) S.** Triplex® glass

sécuritaire [sekyritɛr] **ADJ programme s.** security-conscious programme; **mesures sécuritaires** drastic security measures; **idéologie s.** law-and-order ideology

sécurité [sekyrite] **NF 1** *(protection d'une personne ▸ physique)* safety, security; *(▸ matérielle, affective etc)* security; **assurer la s. de qn** to ensure sb's safety; **veiller à la s. de qn** to make sure sb is safe; **l'installation offre une s. totale** the plant is completely safe; **un bon contrat d'assurance, c'est une s.** a good insurance policy makes you feel safe *or* puts your mind at rest *or* gives you peace of mind; **s. active** active security; **s. affective** emotional security; **s. civile** civil defence; *Ordinat* **s. des données** data security; **la s. de l'emploi** job security; **s. juridique** legal security; **s. matérielle** financial security; **s. nationale/internationale** national/international security; **s. passive** passive security; **s. préventive** preventive security; **s. publique** public safety; **s. routière** road safety **2** *(surveillance ▸ de bâtiments, d'installations)* security **3** *(dispositif ▸ gén)* safety catch; *(▸ d'un tank, d'un navire)* safety catch *or* mechanism; **une porte munie d'une s. enfants** a door with a childproof lock
• **de sécurité ADJ** *(dispositif, mesure, règles)* safety *(avant n)*; *(services)* security *(avant n)*
• **en sécurité ADJ** safe; **être/se sentir en s.** to be/ to feel safe **ADV** in a safe place; **mettre qch en s. dans un coffre** to keep sth in a safe
• **en toute sécurité ADV** in complete safety
• **Sécurité sociale NF** *Admin (système)* = French social security system providing public health benefits, pensions, maternity leave etc, *Br* ≃ Social Security, *Am* ≃ welfare; *(organisme de remboursement) Br* ≃ DWP, *Am* ≃ Social Security

> Attention: ne pas confondre **security** et **safety** lorsqu'on traduit **sécurité**.

> **SÉCURITÉ SOCIALE**
>
> The "Sécu", as it is popularly known, was created in 1945 and provides services such as public health benefits, pensions and maternity benefit. These benefits are paid for by obligatory insurance contributions ("cotisations") made by employers ("cotisations patronales") and employees ("cotisations salariales"). Many French people have complementary health insurance provided by a "mutuelle" which guarantees payment of all or part of the expenses not covered by the "Sécurité sociale".

sédatif, -ive [sedatif, -iv] **ADJ** sedative
NM sedative

sédation [sedasjɔ̃] **NF** sedation, sedating *(UNCOUNT)*

sédative [sedativ] *voir* **sédatif**

sédentaire [sedɑ̃tɛr] **ADJ 1** *(travail, habitude)* sedentary; *(employé)* desk-bound **2** *(population)* settled, non-nomad, sedentary; *(oiseau)* non-migrant; *(troupes)* garrison(ed)
NMF *(personne)* sedentary person

sédentairement [sedɑ̃tɛrmɑ̃] **ADV vivre s.** to live a sedentary life

sédentarisation [sedɑ̃tarizasjɔ̃] **NF la s. d'une population** a people's adoption of a sedentary lifestyle

sédentariser **[3]** [sedɑ̃tarize] **VT** *(tribu)* to make sedentary, to settle
VPR se sédentariser to become sedentary, to settle

sédentarité [sedɑ̃tarite] **NF** sedentary lifestyle

sédiment [sedimɑ̃] **NM 1** *Géol* sediment, deposit **2** *Méd & (en œnologie)* sediment

sédimentaire [sedimɑ̃tɛr] **ADJ** sedimentary

sédimentation [sedimɑ̃tasjɔ̃] **NF** sedimentation

séditieux, -euse [sedisjø, -øz] **ADJ 1** *(propos, écrit)* seditious **2** *(troupe, armée)* insurrectionary, insurgent
NM,F insurgent, rebel

sédition [sedisjɔ̃] **NF** rebellion, revolt, sedition

séducteur, -trice [sedyktœr, -tris] **ADJ** *(personne, sourire etc)* seductive
NM,F seducer, *f* seductress; **c'est un grand s.** he's a real charmer; **c'est une grande séductrice** she's a real seductress

séduction [sedyksjɔ̃] **NF 1** *(charme ▸ d'une personne)* charm; *(▸ d'une musique, d'un tableau)* appeal, captivating power; *Mktg (▸ d'un produit)* appeal; **elle ne manque pas de s.** she's very seductive; *Mktg* **s. du client** customer appeal
2 *(action)* seduction; **pouvoir de s.** powers of seduction; **exercer une s. mystérieuse/irrésistible sur qn** to exercise a mysterious/an irresistible attraction over sb
3 *Jur* **s. de mineur** corruption of a minor
4 *(d'une chose)* attraction, attractiveness; **le pouvoir de s. de l'argent** the seductive power of money

séductrice [sedyktris] *voir* **séducteur**

séduire **[98]** [sedɥir] **VT 1** *(charmer ▸ sujet: personne)* to attract, to charm; *(▸ sujet: beauté, gentillesse, sourire)* to win over; *(▸ sujet: livre, tableau)* to appeal to; **la ferme m'a tout de suite séduit** I immediately fell in love with the farmhouse
2 *(tenter ▸ sujet: idée, projet, style de vie)* to appeal to, to be tempting to; **sa proposition ne me séduit pas beaucoup** his/her proposal doesn't tempt me *or* appeal to me very much; **j'ai été séduite du premier coup** it took my fancy *or* attracted me *or* appealed to me right away
3 *(tromper ▸ sujet: politicien, promesses, publicité)* to lure, to seduce; **j'ai envie de me laisser s.** I'm very *or* sorely tempted; **ne vous laissez pas s. par leurs beaux discours!** don't let yourselves be led astray by their fine words!
4 *(attirer ▸ client)* to attract
5 *(sexuellement)* to seduce
USAGE ABSOLU *(charmer)* **il aime s.** he's a real charmer; **le secret pour s., c'est de ne pas trop en faire** the secret of seduction is not to overdo it

> Il faut noter que le verbe anglais **to seduce** ne signifie pas **charmer.**

séduisant, -e [sedɥizɑ̃, -ɑ̃t] **ADJ 1** *(charmant ▸ personne)* attractive; *(▸ beauté)* seductive, enticing; *(▸ sourire, parfum, mode etc)* appealing, seductive; **de manière séduisante** seductively **2** *(alléchant ▸ offre, idée, projet)* attractive, appealing

séduisit *etc voir* **séduire**

séduit, -e [sedɥi, -it] **PP** *voir* **séduire**

séfarade [sefarad] **ADJ** Sephardic
NMF Sephardi; **les séfarades** the Sephardim

segment [sɛgmɑ̃] **NM 1** *Anat & Math* segment
2 *Tech* ring; **s. de piston** piston ring; *Aut* **s. de frein** (segmental) brake shoe; *Aut* **s. primaire** primary *or* leading shoe; *Aut* **s. secondaire** secondary shoe, trailing shoe
3 *Mktg* segment; **s. démographique** demographic segment; **s. de marché** market segment
4 *Ordinat* segment; **s. de programme** program segment

segmentation [sɛgmɑ̃tasjɔ̃] **NF 1** *Biol & Physiol* segmentation **2** *Ordinat* segmentation **3** *Mktg* segmentation; **s. comportementale** behaviour segmentation; **s. démographique** demographic segmentation; **s. du marché** market segmentation; **s. stratégique** strategic segmentation; **s. par styles de vie** lifestyle segmentation

segmenter **[3]** [sɛgmɑ̃te] **VT** *(diviser)* to segment
VPR se segmenter to segment, to break into segments

ségrégation [segregasjɔ̃] **NF 1** *(discrimination)* segregation; **une s. au niveau des salaires** a discriminatory wage policy; **s. raciale/sociale** racial/social segregation **2** *Biol, Métal & Tech* segregation

ségrégationnisme [segregasjɔnism] **NM** racial segregation

ségrégationniste [segregasjɔnist] **ADJ** *(personne)* segregationist; *(politique)* segregationist, discriminatory
NMF segregationist

séguedille [segədij], **seguidilla** [segidija] **NF** seguidilla

seiche [sɛʃ] **NF** *Zool (mollusque)* cuttlefish

séide [seid] **NM** *Littéraire (partisan)* zealot, fanatically dedicated henchman

seigle [sɛgl] **NM** rye

seigneur [sɛɲœr] **NM 1** *Hist* feudal lord *or* overlord
2 *(maître)* lord; **le s. du château** the lord of the manor; *aussi Hum* **le s. de ces lieux** the lord of the manor; *Hum* **mon s. et maître** my lord and master; **agir en grand s.** to play the fine gentleman; **vivre en grand s.** to live like a lord; **comme un s., en grand s.** *(avec luxe)* like a lord; *(avec noblesse)* nobly; **être grand s., faire le grand s.** to spend money like water *or* as if there were no tomorrow; *Prov* **à tout s. tout honneur** give honour where honour is due

3 *(magnat)* tycoon, baron; **les seigneurs de l'industrie** captains of industry; **les seigneurs de la guerre** the war lords

4 *Rel* **le S.** the Lord; **Notre-S. Jésus-Christ** Our Lord Jesus Christ; *Littéraire* **S. (Dieu)!** Good Lord!; **le jour du S.** the Lord's Day

seigneurial, -e, -aux, -ales [sɛɲœrjal, -o] **ADJ 1** *Hist* seigniorial, seigneurial **2** *Littéraire (digne d'un seigneur)* stately, lordly

seigneurie [sɛɲœri] **NF 1** *Hist (propriété)* seigneury, lord's domain *or* estate; *(pouvoir, droits)* seigneury **2** *(titre)* **Votre S.** Your Lordship; *Hum* **Sa S.** his lordship **3** *Belg (maison de retraite)* retirement home, old people's home

sein [sɛ̃] **NM 1** *(partie du corps)* breast; **elle se promène les seins nus** she walks about topless; **le s.** *(pour allaiter)* the breast; **donner le s. à** to breast-feed; **être nourri au s.** to be breast-fed; **prendre le s.** to take the breast; *Méd* **cancer du s.** breast cancer

2 *Littéraire (ventre)* womb; **porter un enfant dans son s.** to carry a child in one's womb

3 *Littéraire (buste)* bosom; **serrer qn/qch contre son s.** to press sb/sth against one's bosom; **s'épancher dans le s. d'une amie** *(auprès de)* to open one's heart to a friend; **le s. de l'Église** the bosom of the Church

4 *Littéraire (centre)* **le s. de la terre** the bowels of the earth; **dans le s. de** *(au centre de)* in *or* at the heart of, in the bosom of

• **au sein de PRÉP** within; **au s. du parti** within the party; **au s. de la famille** in the bosom *or* midst of the family

Seine [sɛn] **NF la S.** the (River) Seine

seine [sɛn] **NF** *Pêche* seine

seing [sɛ̃] **NM** *(signature)* signature

• **sous seing privé ADJ acte sous s. privé** private agreement, simple contract

séisme [seism] **NM 1** *Géol* earthquake, *Spéc* seism **2** *Fig Littéraire (bouleversement)* upheaval

séismique [seismik] **ADJ** seismic

seize [sɛz] **ADJ 1** *(gén)* sixteen **2** *(dans des séries)* sixteenth; **page/numéro s.** page/number sixteen

PRON sixteen

NM INV 1 *(gén)* sixteen **2** *(numéro d'ordre)* number sixteen **3** *(chiffre écrit)* sixteen; *voir aussi* **cinq**

seizième [sezjɛm] **ADJ** sixteenth

NMF 1 *(personne)* sixteenth **2** *(objet)* sixteenth (one)

NM 1 *(partie)* sixteenth **2** *(étage) Br* sixteenth floor, *Am* seventeenth floor **3** *(arrondissement de Paris)* sixteenth (arrondissement)

NF *Mus* sixteenth; *voir aussi* **cinquième**

• **seizièmes NMPL** *Sport* **les seizièmes de finale** the first round *(of a four-round knockout competition)*, the second round *(of a five-round knockout competition)*

> **SEIZIÈME**
>
> This term often refers to the upper-class social background, lifestyle, way of dressing etc associated with the sixteenth arrondissement in Paris: "elle est très seizième".

séjour [seʒur] **NM 1** *(durée)* stay, sojourn; *Littéraire* delay; **il a fait un s. de deux mois à la mer** he spent two months at the seaside; **je te souhaite un bon s. à Venise** I hope you have a nice time *or* I hope you enjoy your stay in Venice; **il a fait plusieurs séjours en hôpital psychiatrique** he's been in a psychiatric hospital several times; *Fam Fig* **il a fait un s. à l'ombre** he's been inside, he's done time **un s. linguistique** a language-learning trip **2** *(pièce)* **(salle de) s.** living *or* sitting room, *Br* lounge **3** *Littéraire (habitation)* abode, dwelling place

séjourner **[3]** [seʒurne] **VI 1** *(habiter)* to stay, to sojourn; **s. à l'hôtel/chez un ami** to stay at a hotel/with a friend **2** *(eau, neige, brouillard)* to lie

sel [sɛl] **NM 1** *Culin* salt; **mettre du s. dans une sauce** to add salt to a sauce; **vous devriez supprimer le s.** you should cut out salt altogether; **gros s.** coarse salt; **s. de céleri** celery salt; **s. de cuisine** kitchen salt; **s. de table, s. fin** table salt; **s. marin** *ou* **de mer** sea salt

2 *Chim* salt

3 *Géol* salt; **s. gemme** rock salt; *Bible & Littéraire* **le s. de la terre** the salt of the earth

4 *Pharm* salt; **s. d'Epsom** *ou* **d'Angleterre** Epsom salts; **s. de Vichy** sodium bicarbonate

5 *(piquant)* wit *(UNCOUNT)*; **une remarque pleine de s.** a witty remark; **la situation ne manque pas de s.!** the situation is not without a certain piquancy!

• **sels NMPL** *Pharm* (smelling) salts; **respirer des sels** to smell salts; **sels de bain** bath salts

• **sans sel ADJ** *(régime, biscotte)* salt-free; *(beurre)* unsalted

sélect, -e [selɛkt] **ADJ** *Fam* select, high-class

sélecteur [selɛktœr] **NM 1** *Rad & Tél* selector; **s. de programmes** programme selector **2** *Tech* gear shift; *(d'une moto)* (foot) gearshift control **3** *Ordinat* chooser

sélectif, -ive [selɛktif, -iv] **ADJ 1** *(mémoire, herbicide, poste de radio)* selective **2** *Ordinat* **en mode s.** in veto mode

sélection [selɛksjɔ̃] **NF 1** *(fait de choisir)* selection; **opérer une s. parmi 200 candidats** to make a selection *or* to choose from 200 candidates; **épreuve de s.** selection trial; *Univ* **s. à l'entrée** selective *Br* entry *or Am* admission; *Mktg* **s. au hasard** random selection; **s. professionnelle** professional recruitment

2 *(échantillon)* selection, choice; **une s. de fromages** a choice of cheeses, a cheese selection

3 *Sport (choix)* selection; *(équipe)* team, squad; **match de s.** trial game; **Sandy Campbell a 51 sélections en équipe nationale** Sandy Campbell has been capped 51 times, Sandy Campbell has 51 caps

4 *Biol* **s. naturelle** natural selection; **s. artificielle** artificial selection

5 *Bourse* **s. d'actions** sharepicking; **s. de titres** stockpicking; **s. de portefeuille** portfolio selection

sélectionné, -e [selɛksjɔne] **ADJ** *(choisi)* selected; **s. pour les jeux Olympiques** selected for the Olympics; **s. en équipe nationale** capped; **des vins sélectionnés** selected *or* choice wines

NM,F 1 *(candidat)* selected candidate *or* contestant **2** *Sport* selected player

sélectionner **[3]** [selɛksjɔne] **VT 1** *(gén)* to select **2** *Ordinat (texte)* to block, to select; **s. qch par défaut** to default to sth

USAGE ABSOLU ils sélectionnent à l'entrée they have a selection process for admission

sélectionneur, -euse [selɛksjɔnœr, -øz] **NM,F** *Sport* selector

sélective [selɛtiv] *voir* **sélectif**

sélectivement [selɛktivmɑ̃] **ADV** selectively

sélectivité [selɛktivite] **NF** *Élec, Opt & Rad* selectivity

sélénieux [selenjø] **ADJ M** selenious

sélénite[1] [selenit] **ADJ** of the moon

NMF *(habitant de la Lune)* moon-dweller

sélénite[2] [selenit] **NM** *Chim* selenite

sélénium [selenjɔm] **NM** *Chim* selenium

sélénographie [selenɔgrafi] **NF** selenography

sélénographique [selenɔgrafik] **ADJ** selenographic

self [sɛlf] **NF** *Élec* self inductance

NM *Psy* self

NM INV *Fam (restaurant)* self-service (restaurant)[□], cafeteria[□]

self-control [sɛlfkɔ̃trol] *(pl* **self-controls)** **NM** self-control, self-command

self-défense [sɛlfdefɑ̃s] **NF** self-defence

self-inductance [sɛlfɛ̃dyktɑ̃s] *(pl* **self-inductances)** **NF** self-inductance

self-induction [sɛlfɛ̃dyksjɔ̃] *(pl* **self-inductions)** **NF** self-induction

self-made-man [sɛlfmɛdman] *(pl* **self-made-men** [-mɛn]) **NM** self-made man

self-média [sɛlfmedja] **NM** self-media

self-service [sɛlfsɛrvis] *(pl* **self-services)** **NM 1** *(restaurant)* self-service (restaurant), cafeteria **2** *(service)* self-service; **les pompes à essence sont en s.** the *Br* petrol *or Am* gas pumps are self-service

selle [sɛl] **NF 1** *(de cheval)* saddle; **monter sans s.** to ride bareback; **monter en s.** to mount, to get into the saddle; **aider qn à monter en s.** to help sb into the saddle; *aussi Fig* **être bien en s.** to be firmly in the saddle; *aussi Fig* **mettre qn en s.** to give sb a leg up; *Fig* **remettre qn en s.** to put sb back on the rails; **se mettre en s.** to mount, to get into the saddle; *Fig* to get down to the job; *aussi Fig* **se remettre en s.** to get back in *or* into the saddle

2 *(de bicyclette)* saddle

3 *Culin* saddle; **s. de mouton/de chevreuil** saddle of mutton/of venison

4 *(escabeau de sculpteur)* turntable

5 *Méd* **aller à la s.** to have a bowel movement; **allez-vous à la s. régulièrement?** are you regular?

• **selles NFPL** *(excréments)* faeces, stools

seller **[4]** [sele] **VT** to saddle (up)

sellerie [sɛlri] **NF 1** *(équipement)* saddlery; *(pour voitures)* upholstery **2** *(lieu)* saddle room, tack-room **3** *(commerce)* saddlery trade

sellette [sɛlɛt] **NF 1** *Hist (siège)* (high) stand *or* table; *Fig* **mettre qn sur la s.** to put sb in the hot seat; *Fig* **être sur la s.** *(critiqué)* to be in the hot seat, to come under fire; *(examiné)* to be undergoing reappraisal

2 *Constr* slung cradle

3 *(pour sculpteur)* turntable

4 *(de cheval de trait)* saddle

5 *Aut* fifth wheel

sellier [selje] **NM** *(fabricant, marchand)* saddler; **façon s.** hand-stitched

selon [səlɔ̃] **PRÉP 1** *(conformément à)* in accordance with; **agir s. les vœux de qn** to act in accordance with sb's wishes; **agir s. les règles** to act *or* to go by the rules; **s. toute apparence** by *or* from *or* to all appearances; **s. toute vraisemblance** in all probability **2** *(en fonction de)* according to; **dépenser s. ses moyens** to spend according to one's means; **s. le cas** as the case may be; **s. les circonstances** depending on the circumstances; **ils varient s. les saisons** they vary from season to season; *Fam* **on se reverra? – c'est s.!** will we see each other again? – it all depends!; **elle y allait à pied ou en voiture, c'était s.** she went on foot or used the car, depending **3** *(d'après)* according to; **s. les experts** according to the experts; **s. moi/vous** in my/your opinion, to my/your mind; **s. vos propres termes** in your own words; **s. l'expression consacrée** as the hallowed expression has it

• **selon que CONJ s. qu'on est étudiant ou non** depending on whether one is a student or not

Seltz [sɛls] **NPR eau de S.** soda water, *Am* club soda

SEM [sɛm] **NF** *Écon (abrév* **société d'économie mixte)** = company financed by state and private capital

semailles [səmaj] **NFPL 1** *(action)* sowing **2** *(graines)* seeds **3** *(période)* sowing season; **les s. d'automne** autumn sowing

semaine [səmɛn] **NF 1** *(sept jours)* week; **toutes les semaines** *(nettoyer, recevoir)* every *or* each week; *(publier, payer)* weekly, on a weekly basis; **deux visites par s.** two visits a week *or* per week; **dans une s.** in a week's time; **je serai de retour dans une s.** I'll be back in a week *or* in a week's time; **une s. de vacances** a week's holiday; **faire des semaines de 50 heures** to work a 50-hour week; **qui est de s.?** who's on duty this week?; **officier de s.** duty officer for the week; **la s. anglaise** the five-day (working) week; **faire la s. anglaise** to work a five-day week; **la s. de 35 heures** the 35-hour working week; **il te remboursera la s. des quatre jeudis** he'll never pay you back in a month of Sundays

2 *Rel* week; **la s. sainte** Holy Week; **la s. pascale** Easter week

3 *Com* **la promotion de la s.** this week's special offer; **la s. de la photo** photography week; **s. commerciale** week-long promotion *or* sale; *Hum* **c'est sa s. de bonté** he's/she's been overcome by a fit of generosity

4 *(salaire)* week's pay *or* wages; **je lui donne dix euros pour sa s.** *(argent de poche)* I give him/her ten euros a week pocket money

5 *(bracelet)* seven-band bangle; *(bague)* seven-band ring

• **à la petite semaine** *Fam* **ADJ** *(politique)* short-sighted, day-to-day **ADV prêter à la petite s.** to make short-term loans *(with high interest)*; **vivre à la petite s.** to live from day to day *or* from hand to mouth
• **à la semaine ADV** *(payer)* weekly, on a weekly basis, by the week
• **en semaine ADV** during the week, on weekdays, on a weekday

semainier, -ère [səmenje, -ɛr] **NM,F** *(personne)* worker on duty for the week
NM 1 *(calendrier)* page-a-week diary **2** *(meuble)* semainier *(seven-drawer chest)* **3** *Ind* weekly time sheet

sémantème [semɑ̃tɛm] **NM** *Ling* semanteme

sémanticien, -enne [semɑ̃tisjɛ̃, -ɛn] **NM,F** semanticist

sémantique [semɑ̃tik] **ADJ** semantic
NF semantics *(singulier)*

sémaphore [semafɔr] **NM 1** *Rail* semaphore signal **2** *Naut (poste)* signal station

semblable [sɑ̃blabl] **ADJ 1** *(comparable)* similar; **un cas s.** a similar case; **ils sont semblables** they are similar *or* alike; **s. à** similar to, like **2** *(tel)* **je n'ai rien dit de s.** I said nothing of the sort *or* no such thing; **je n'avais jamais rien vu de s.** I had never seen anything like it; **de semblables projets/propos** such plans/remarks, plans/remarks like that **3** *Géom & Math* similar
NMF *(avec possessif)* **1** *(être humain)* **vous et vos semblables** you and your kind; **il n'a pas son s. dans l'art occidental** there's no-one like him in western art **2** *(animal)* related species

semblant [sɑ̃blɑ̃] **NM 1** *(apparence)* **un s. d'intérêt/d'affection** a semblance of interest/affection; **offrir un s. de résistance** to put on a show of *or* to put up a token resistance **2 faire s.** *(feindre)* to pretend; **il ne dort pas, il fait s.** he's not asleep, he's just pretending; **ne fais pas s. d'avoir oublié** don't pretend to have forgotten *or* (that) you've forgotten; **ne faire s. de rien** to pretend not to notice

sembler **[3]** [sɑ̃ble] **VI** to seem, to appear; **son histoire semble (être) vraie** his/her story seems *or* appears to be true; **tu sembles préoccupé** you look *or* seem worried; **ça peut s. drôle à certains** this may seem *or* sound funny to some
V IMPERSONNEL 1 il semble que… *(on dirait que)* it seems…; **il semble qu'il y a** *ou* **ait eu un malentendu** it seems that *or* it looks as if there's been a misunderstanding, there seems to have been a misunderstanding; **il semblait pourtant que tout allait bien** and yet everything seemed to be all right; **il semblerait qu'il ait décidé de démissionner** reports claim *or* it has been reported that he intends to resign **2** *(pour exprimer l'opinion)* **cela ne te semble-t-il pas injuste?** don't you find this unfair?, doesn't this strike you as being unfair?; **c'est bien ce qu'il m'a semblé** I thought as much; **il ne me semblait pas te l'avoir dit** I didn't think I'd told you about it; **il était, me semblait-il, au courant de tout** it seemed *or* appeared to me that he was aware of everything; **il me semble qu'on s'est déjà vus** I think we've met before; **je vous l'ai déjà dit, il me semble** *ou* **me semble-t-il** I'm sure I've already told you that; **faites comme bon vous semble** do as you think fit *or* best, do as you please; **il le fera si bon lui semble** he'll do it if he wants to; **je sors quand/avec qui bon me semble** I go out whenever/with whoever I please
• **à ce qu'il semble, semble-t-il ADV** seemingly, apparently

sème [sɛm] **NM** *Ling* seme

semelle [səmɛl] **NF 1** *(d'une chaussure, d'un ski)* sole; **bottes à semelles fines/épaisses** thin-soled/thick-soled boots; **chaussures à semelles compensées** platform shoes; **s. intérieure** insole, inner sole
2 *Fam (viande dure)* **c'est de la s., ce steak!** this steak is like (shoe) leather *or Br* is as tough as old boots!
3 *Constr (de plancher)* sill *or* sole plate; *(de poutre)* flange; *(de toiture)* inferior (roof) purlin; *(d'une marche)* tread
4 *Tech (d'une machine, d'un tour)* bedplate
5 *Naut* **s. de dérive** leeboard
6 *(locutions)* **ne la lâchez** *ou* **quittez pas d'une s.** don't let her out of your sight; **on n'a pas avancé** *ou* **bougé d'une s.** we haven't moved an inch, we haven't made any progress whatsoever

semence [səmɑ̃s] **NF 1** *(graine)* seed; **pomme de terre/blé de s.** seed potato/corn
2 *Littéraire (germe)* **les semences d'une révolte** the seeds of a revolt
3 *Littéraire (sperme)* semen, seed
4 *(en joaillerie)* **s. de perles** seed pearls; **s. de diamants** diamond sparks
5 *(clou)* tack; **s. de tapissier** upholstery tack

semer **[19]** [səme] **VT 1** *Agr & Hort* to sow
2 *Fig (disperser* ▸ *fleurs, paillettes)* to scatter, to strew; **semé de** scattered *or* strewn with; **parcours semé d'embûches** course littered with obstacles; **il sème ses affaires partout** he leaves his things everywhere
3 *Fam (laisser tomber)* to drop[□]
4 *(distancer)* to lose, to shake off; **s. le peloton** to leave the pack behind
5 *(propager)* to bring; **s. le désordre** *ou* **la pagaille** to wreak havoc; **s. la terreur/la mort** to bring terror/death; **s. le doute dans l'esprit de qn** to sow *or* to plant a seed of doubt in sb's mind
USAGE ABSOLU *Agr & Hort* **s. à la volée** to sow broadcast; **s. en ligne** to drill

semestre [səmɛstr] **NM 1** *(dans l'année civile)* half-year, six-month period; **pour le premier s.** for the first half of the year *or* six months of the year **2** *Univ* half-year, semester **3** *(rente)* half-yearly pension; *(intérêt)* half-yearly interest

semestriel, -elle [səmɛstrijɛl] **ADJ 1** *(dans l'année civile)* half-yearly **2** *Univ* semestral

semestriellement [səmɛstrijɛlmɑ̃] **ADV 1** *(dans l'année civile)* half-yearly, every six months **2** *Univ* per *or* every semester

semeur, -euse [səmœr, -øz] **NM,F 1** *Agr* sower **2** *Fig (propagateur)* **s. de trouble** troublemaker; **s. de discorde** sower of discord
• **Semeuse NF** *(sur les pièces)* = symbol of the French Republic on stamps and coins

semi- [səmi] **PRÉF** semi-

semi-automatique [səmiotɔmatik] *(pl* **semi-automatiques)** **ADJ** semiautomatic

semi-auxiliaire [səmiɔksiljɛr] *(pl* **semi-auxiliaires)** *Gram* **ADJ** semiauxiliary
NM semiauxiliary verb

semi-chenillé, -e [səmiʃənije] *(mpl* **semi-chenillés,** *fpl* **semi-chenillées)** **ADJ** half-tracked
NM half-track

semi-circulaire [səmisirkylɛr] *(pl* **semi-circulaires)** **ADJ** semicircular

semi-conducteur, -trice [səmikɔ̃dyktœr, -tris] *(mpl* **semi-conducteurs,** *fpl* **semi-conductrices)** **ADJ** semiconducting
NM semiconductor

semi-conserve [səmikɔ̃sɛrv] *(pl* **semi-conserves)** **NF** = foodstuff which has a limited life and must be refrigerated

semi-consonne [səmikɔ̃sɔn] *(pl* **semi-consonnes)** **NF** *Ling* semiconsonant, semivowel

semi-fini, -e [səmifini] *(mpl* **semi-finis,** *fpl* **semi-finies)** **ADJ** semi-finished, semi-manufactured

semi-grossiste [səmigrosist] *(pl* **semi-grossistes)** **NMF** = wholesaler who also deals in retail

semi-liberté [səmilibɛrte] **NF** *Jur* temporary release *(from prison)*; **être en s.** to be out on temporary release

sémillant, -e [semijɑ̃, -ɑ̃t] **ADJ** sprightly, spirited

semi-lunaire [səmilynɛr] *(pl* **semi-lunaires)** **ADJ** half-moon shaped, semilunar

semi-mensuel, -elle [səmimɑ̃sɥɛl] *(mpl* **semi-mensuels,** *fpl* **semi-mensuelles)** **ADJ** bi-monthly, *Br* fortnightly

semi-métal [səmimetal] *(pl* **semi-métaux** [-o]) **NM** *Chim* metalloid

séminaire [seminɛr] **NM 1** *(réunion)* seminar, workshop **2** *Rel* seminary; **grand s.** seminary; **petit s.** Roman Catholic boys' school *(staffed by priests)*

séminal, -e, -aux, -ales [seminal, -o] **ADJ** seminal

séminariste [seminarist] **NM** seminarist, *Am* seminarian

semi-nomade [səminɔmad] *(pl* **semi-nomades)** **ADJ** seminomadic
NMF seminomad

semi-nomadisme [səminɔmadism] **NM** seminomadism

semi-occlusif, -ive [səmiɔklyzif, -iv] *(mpl* **semi-occlusifs,** *fpl* **semi-occlusives)** **ADJ 1** *Méd (pansement)* semi-occlusive **2** *Ling (consonne)* semi-occlusive

semi-officiel, -elle [səmiɔfisjɛl] *(pl* **semi-officels,** *fpl* **semi-officielles)** **ADJ** semiofficial

sémiologie [semjɔlɔʒi] **NF** semiology, semeiology

sémiologique [semjɔlɔʒik] **ADJ** semiological, semeiological

sémiologue [semjɔlɔg] **NMF** semiologist

sémiotique [semjɔtik] **ADJ** semiotic
NF semiotics *(singulier)*

semi-ouvré, -e [səmiuvre] *(mpl* **semi-ouvrés,** *fpl* **semi-ouvrées)** **ADJ** semimanufactured, semifinished

semi-perméable [səmipɛrmeabl] *(pl* **semi-perméables)** **ADJ** semipermeable

semi-précieux, -euse [səmipresjø, -øz] *(mpl* **semi-précieux,** *fpl* **semi-précieuses)** **ADJ** semi-precious

semi-présidentiel, -elle [səmiprezidɑ̃sjɛl] *(mpl* **semi-présidentiels,** *fpl* **semi-présidentielles)** **ADJ** *Pol* semi-presidential

semi-produit [səmiprɔdɥi] *(pl* **semi-produits)** **NM** semi-finished product

semi-professionnel, -elle [səmiprɔfesjɔnɛl] *(mpl* **semi-professionnels,** *fpl* **semi-professionnelles)** **ADJ** semiprofessional

semi-public, -ique [səmipyblik] *(mpl* **semi-publics,** *fpl* **semi-publiques)** **ADJ** semipublic

sémique [semik] **ADJ** semic

semi-remorque [səmirəmɔrk] *(pl* **semi-remorques)** **NF** semitrailer
NM *Br* articulated lorry, *Am* trailer truck

semi-rigide [səmiriʒid] *(pl* **semi-rigides)** **ADJ** semirigid

semis [səmi] **NM 1** *(action)* sowing
2 *(terrain)* seedbed
3 *(jeune plante)* seedling
4 *Fig* **c'était un tissu à fond blanc avec un s. de petites fleurs bleues** the material had a pattern of small blue flowers on a white background

sémite [semit] **ADJ** Semitic
• **Sémite NMF** Semite

sémitique [semitik] **ADJ** Semitic

sémitisant, -e [semitizɑ̃, -ɑ̃t] **NM,F** Semitist

sémitisme [semitism] **NM** *(études)* Semitics *(singulier)*; *(phénomène)* Semitism

semi-ton [səmitɔ̃] *(pl* **semi-tons)** **NM** *Mus* semitone

semi-voyelle [səmivwajɛl] *(pl* **semi-voyelles)** **NF** *Ling* semivowel, semiconsonant

semoir [səmwar] **NM 1** *(panier)* seed-bag **2** *(machine)* sower, seeder

semonce [səmɔ̃s] **NF 1** *(réprimande)* reprimand, rebuke **2** *Naut (navire)* order to stop; *Naut & Fig* **coup de s.** warning shot

semoule [səmul] **NF** semolina; **s. blanche** *ou* **de riz** rice flour; **s. de maïs** cornflour; **s. de blé dur** durum wheat flour

sempiternel, -elle [sɑ̃pitɛrnɛl] **ADJ** neverending, endless

sempiternellement [sɑ̃pitɛrnɛlmɑ̃] **ADV** eternally, forever

sénat [sena] **NM 1** *(assemblée)* senate; **le S.** the (French) Senate **2** *(lieu)* senate (house)

> **SÉNAT**
>
> The Sénat is the upper house of the French Parliament. Its members are elected for a nine-year mandate by the Deputies of the "Assemblée nationale" and certain other government officals. The President of the Senate may deputize for the President of the Republic in the case of incapacity or death. The powers of the Senate are almost as extensive as those of the "Assemblée nationale", although the latter is empowered to override the decisions of the Senate in cases where the two houses disagree.

sénateur [senatœr] **NM** senator
sénatorial, -e, -aux, -ales [senatɔrjal, -o] **ADJ** senatorial, senate *(avant n)*
• **sénatoriales** **NFPL** senatorial elections
séné [sene] **NM** *Bot & Pharm* senna
sénéchal, -aux [seneʃal, -o] **NM** *Hist* seneschal
sénéchaussée [seneʃose] **NF** *Hist (juridiction)* seneschalsy; *(tribunal)* seneschal's court
séneçon [sensɔ̃] **NM** *Bot* groundsel
Sénégal [senegal] **NM le S.** Senegal
sénégalais, -e [senegalɛ, -ɛz] **ADJ** Senegalese
• **Sénégalais, -e** **NM,F** Senegalese; **les S.** the Senegalese
Sénèque [senɛk] **NPR** Seneca
sénescence [senesɑ̃s] **NF** senescence
sénescent, -e [senesɑ̃, -ɑ̃t] **ADJ** senescent
sénevé [senve] **NM** *Bot* (wild) mustard, charlock; *(graine)* mustard seed
sénile [senil] **ADJ** senile
sénilité [senilite] **NF** senility
senior [senjɔr] *Sport* **ADJ** senior
NMF senior
senne [sen] **NF** *Pêche* seine
señorita [seɲɔrita] **NM** *(cigare)* = French-made cigarillo

SENS [sɑ̃s]

NM	
• sense **1, 2, 4**	• meaning **4**
• direction **5**	• line **6**
NMPL	
• senses	

voir **sentir**
NM 1 *Physiol* sense; **le s. du toucher** the sense of touch; **sixième s.** sixth sense; **reprendre ses s.** to come to; *Fig* to come to one's senses
2 *(instinct)* sense; **s. moral/pratique** moral/practical sense; **avoir le s. pratique** to be practical; **avoir le s. de la nuance** to be subtle; **avoir le s. de l'humour** to have a (good) sense of humour; **avoir le s. de l'orientation** to have a good sense of direction; **avoir le s. des affaires** to have a good head for business; **ne pas avoir le s. des réalités** to have no grasp of reality; **avoir le s. du rythme** to have natural rhythm; **bon s., s. commun** common sense; **plein de bon s.** very sensible; **manquer de bon s.** to lack common sense; **gros bon s.** horse sense, (sound) common sense; **avec son gros bon s., il avait tout de suite vu que...** he had the good sense to see straight away that...; **ça tombe sous le s.** it's obvious, it stands to reason
3 *(opinion)* **à mon/son s.** according to me/him/her; **à mon s., c'est impossible** as I see it *or* to my mind, it's impossible
4 *(signification ▸ d'un mot, d'une phrase)* meaning, sense; *(▸ d'une allégorie, d'un symbole)* meaning; *Ling* **le s.** meaning *(UNCOUNT)*, signification; **quel est le s. de ce mot?** what does this word mean?; **ce que tu dis n'a pas de s.** *(c'est inintelligible ou déraisonnable)* what you're saying doesn't make sense; **lourd** *ou* **chargé de s.** meaningful; **vide de s.** meaningless; **au s. propre/figuré** in the literal/figurative sense; **au s. strict** strictly speaking; **le s. caché des choses** the hidden meaning of things; **chercher/trouver un s. à la vie** to look for/to find a meaning to life
5 *(direction)* direction; **dans tous les s.** in all directions, all over the place; *Fig* **chercher dans tous les s.** to look everywhere; **arrête de t'agiter dans tous les s.!** keep still for a minute!; **en s. inverse** the other way round *or* around; **le train qui venait en s. inverse** the oncoming train; **pose l'équerre dans ce s.-là/dans l'autre s.** lay the set square down this way/the other way round; **scier une planche dans le s. de la largeur/la longueur** to saw a board widthwise/lengthwise; **dans le s. nord-sud/est-ouest** in a southerly/westerly direction; **installer qch dans le bon s.** to fix sth the right way up; **fais demi-tour, on va dans le mauvais s.!** turn round, we're going the wrong way *or* in the wrong direction!; **il n'y a plus de trains dans le s. Paris–Lyon** there are no more trains from Paris to Lyons; **la circulation est bloquée dans le s. Paris–province** traffic leaving Paris is at a standstill; **dans le s. de la marche** facing the front *(of a vehicle)*; **dans le s. contraire de la marche** facing the rear *(of a vehicle)*; **dans le s. du courant** with the current; **dans le s. des aiguilles d'une montre** clockwise; **dans le s. inverse des aiguilles d'une montre** *Br* anticlockwise, *Am* counterclockwise; **dans le s. du bois** with the grain (of the wood); **dans le s. du tissu** along the weave (of the cloth); *Transp* **s. giratoire** *Br* roundabout, *Am* traffic circle; **s. interdit** *(panneau)* no-entry sign; *(rue)* one-way street; **être** *ou* **rouler en s. interdit** to be going the wrong way up/down a one-way street; **(rue à) s. unique** one-way street; *Fig* **à s. unique** *(amour)* unrequited; *(décision)* unilateral, one-sided
6 *Fig (orientation)* line; **nous agirons dans le même s.** we'll move along the same lines, we'll take the same sort of action; **des mesures allant dans le s. d'une plus grande justice** measures directed at greater justice; **nous avons publié une brochure dans ce s.** we have published a brochure along those (same) lines *or* to that effect; **leur politique ne va pas dans le bon s.** their policy's going down the wrong road
NMPL *(sensualité)* (carnal) senses; **pour le plaisir des s.** for the gratification of the senses
• **dans le sens où** **CONJ** in the sense that, in so far as
• **dans un certain sens** **ADV** in a way, in a sense, as it were
• **en ce sens que** **CONJ** in the sense that, in so far as
• **sens dessus dessous** **ADV** upside down; **la maison était s. dessus dessous** *(en désordre)* the house was all topsy-turvy
• **sens devant derrière** **ADV** back to front, the wrong way round

sensas, sensass [sɑ̃sas] **ADJ INV** *Fam* sensational, terrific, *Br* fab
sensation [sɑ̃sasjɔ̃] **NF 1** *(impression)* sensation, feeling; **s. de fraîcheur** feeling of freshness, fresh sensation; **j'avais la s. qu'on reculait** I had the feeling we were going backwards; **privé de s.** numb, insensate; **les amateurs de sensations fortes** people who like thrills, *Fam* adrenaline junkies **2** *(impact)* **faire s.** to cause a stir *or* a sensation **3** *Physiol* sensation
• **à sensation** **ADJ** *(roman, titre)* sensational; **un reportage à s.** a shock *or* a sensation-seeking report
sensationnel, -elle [sɑ̃sasjɔnel] **ADJ 1** *(spectaculaire ▸ révélation, image)* sensational **2** *Fam (remarquable)* sensational, terrific, *Br* fab
NM le s. the sensational; **un journal qui donne dans le s.** a sensationalist newspaper
sensé, -e [sɑ̃se] **ADJ** sensible, well-advised, wise; **dire des choses sensées** to talk sense; **ce qu'il a dit n'est pas très s.** what he said doesn't make much sense
senseur [sɑ̃sœr] **NM** *Tech* sensor
sensibilisateur, -trice [sɑ̃sibilizatœr, -tris] **ADJ 1** *Chim* sensitizing **2 une campagne sensibilisatrice** an awareness campaign
NM *Phot* sensitizer
• **sensibilisatrice** **NF** *Biol* sensitizer
sensibilisation [sɑ̃sibilizasjɔ̃] **NF 1** *(prise de conscience)* awareness; **il y a une grande s. des jeunes aux dangers du tabagisme** young people are aware of the dangers of smoking; **la s. de l'opinion publique à l'environnement** raising public awareness of the environment; **campagne de s.** awareness campaign **2** *Méd & Phot* sensitization
sensibilisatrice [sɑ̃sibilizatris] *voir* **sensibilisateur**
sensibiliser [3] [sɑ̃sibilize] **VT 1** *(gén)* **s. qn à qch** to make sb conscious *or* aware of sth; **il faudrait essayer de s. l'opinion** we'll have to try and make people aware **2** *Méd & Phot* to sensitize
VPR se sensibiliser se s. à qch to become aware of sth
sensibilité [sɑ̃sibilite] **NF 1** *(physique)* sensitiveness, sensitivity; **s. à la douleur/au soleil** sensitivity to pain/to the sun
2 *(intellectuelle)* sensibility; *(émotive)* sensitivity; **avoir une s. littéraire** to have a literary sensibility; **elle est d'une s. maladive** she's painfully *or* excruciatingly sensitive; **tu manques totalement de s.** you're utterly insensitive; *Mktg* **s. compétitive** competitive awareness; *Mktg* **s. aux marques** brand sensitivity; *Mktg* **s. aux prix** price sensitivity
3 *Écon* **la s. du marché des changes** the sensitivity of the foreign exchange market
4 *Phot, Physiol & Rad* sensitivity
sensible [sɑ̃sibl] **ADJ 1** *(physiquement, émotivement)* sensitive; **avoir l'ouïe s.** to have sensitive hearing; **s. à** sensitive to; **trop s.** oversensitive; **être s. au froid** to be sensitive to *or* to feel the cold; **être s. aux souffrances d'autrui** to be sensitive to other people's sufferings; **cet enfant est très s. à la musique** this child has a great feeling for music; **s. à la beauté de qn** susceptible to sb's beauty; **nous avons été très sensibles à son geste** we really appreciated what he/she did; **c'est une nature s.** he's/she's the sensitive kind, he's/she's easily affected by things; **personnes sensibles s'abstenir** not recommended for people of a nervous disposition; *Mktg* **s. aux marques** brand-sensitive; *Mktg* **s. aux prix** price-sensitive
2 *(délicat ▸ peau, gencive)* sensitive; *(▸ endroit douloureux)* tender; **s. au toucher** tender *or* painful to the touch; **être s. du dos/des oreilles** to be prone to backaches/to earache
3 *(qui réagit ▸ balance, microphone)* sensitive, responsive; *(▸ direction de voiture)* responsive
4 *(phénomène ▸ perceptible)* perceptible; *(▸ notable)* noticeable, marked, *Sout* sensible; **s. à l'ouïe** perceptible to the ear; **la crise est le plus s. dans le Nord** the crisis is most acutely felt in the North; **il n'y a pas eu de progrès s.** there's been no appreciable *or* noticeable progress; **d'une manière s.** noticeably
5 *Phil* sensory; **un être s.** a sentient being; **le monde s.** the world as perceived by the senses
6 *Mus (note)* leading
7 *Phot* sensitive; **papier s. à la lumière** light-sensitive paper
NMF c'est un grand s. he's very sensitive
NF *Mus* leading note, subtonic

> Il faut noter que l'adjectif anglais **sensible** est un faux ami. Il signifie **sensé**.

sensiblement [sɑ̃sibləmɑ̃] **ADV 1** *(beaucoup)* appreciably, noticeably, markedly **2** *(à peu près)* about, approximately, more or less, roughly
sensiblerie [sɑ̃sibləri] **NF** oversensitiveness, squeamishness
sensitif, -ive [sɑ̃sitif, -iv] **ADJ 1** *Anat* sensory **2** *(hypersensible)* oversensitive
NM,F *(hypersensible)* **c'est un s.** he's oversensitive
• **sensitive** **NF** *Bot* sensitive plant
sensoriel, -elle [sɑ̃sɔrjel] **ADJ** *(organe, appareil)* sense *(avant n)*; *(nerf, cortex)* sensory
sensorimoteur, -trice [sɑ̃sɔrimɔtœr, -tris] **ADJ** sensorimotor, sensomotor
sensualisme [sɑ̃sɥalism] **NM** *Phil* sensualism
sensualiste [sɑ̃sɥalist] *Phil* **ADJ** sensual
NMF sensualist
sensualité [sɑ̃sɥalite] **NF** sensuality
sensuel, -elle [sɑ̃sɥel] **ADJ 1** *(plaisir, personne)* sensual, sybaritic **2** *(lèvres, voix)* sensuous; *(musique)* sensual
NM,F sensualist, sybarite
sentant [sɑ̃tɑ̃] **ADJ** sentient
sente [sɑ̃t] **NF** *Littéraire* path, footpath, track
sentence [sɑ̃tɑ̃s] **NF 1** *(jugement)* sentence, verdict; **prononcer une s.** to pass *or* to give *or* to pronounce sentence **2** *(maxime)* maxim, saying
sentencieuse [sɑ̃tɑ̃sjøz] *voir* **sententieux**
sentencieusement [sɑ̃tɑ̃sjøzmɑ̃] **ADV** sententiously, moralistically
sentencieux, -euse [sɑ̃tɑ̃sjø, -øz] **ADJ** sententious, moralistic, moralizing
senteur, -euse [sɑ̃tœr] **ADJ** *Can Péj (indiscret)* nosy, prying
NF *Littéraire* fragrance, scent, aroma
senti, -e [sɑ̃ti] **ADJ bien s.** *(lecture, interprétation)* appropriate, *Sout* apposite; **c'était une repartie bien sentie** it was a retort that struck home; **une vérité bien sentie** a home truth
NM *Phil* sense datum
sentier [sɑ̃tje] **NM 1** *(allée)* path, footpath **2** *Sport* **s. de grande randonnée** long-distance hiking

path **3** *Fig Littéraire* path, way; **être sur le s. de la guerre** to be on the warpath; **suivre les sentiers battus** to keep to well-trodden paths; **sortir des sentiers battus** to get *or* to wander off the beaten track

sentiment [sɑ̃timɑ̃] **NM 1** *(émotion)* feeling; **un s. de honte** a feeling of shame; **ses sentiments vis-à-vis de moi** his/her feelings towards me; **je ne doute pas de ses sentiments pour moi** I have no doubt that he/she loves me; **prendre qn par les sentiments** to appeal to sb's feelings; *Hum* **si tu me prends par les sentiments!** if you go for the heartstrings!

2 *(sensibilité)* feeling *(UNCOUNT)*; **le s. religieux** religious feeling *or* fervour; **chanter avec s.** to sing with feeling; **avoir le s. du tragique** to have a feeling for tragedy; **avoir le s. de la beauté** to have a sense of the aesthetic

3 *(sensiblerie)* (silly) sentimentalism; **ce n'est pas le moment de faire du s.** this is no time to get sentimental; **en affaires, je ne fais jamais de s.** I don't let emotions get in the way of business; *Fam* **avoir qn au s.** to get around sb; **n'essaie pas de m'avoir** *ou* **de me la faire au s.** don't try to get around me by appealing to my better nature

4 *(opinion)* feeling, opinion; **quel est votre s. sur la question?** what is your feeling about the matter?; **si vous voulez savoir mon s.** if you want to know what I think *or* feel; **j'ai ce s.-là aussi** my feelings exactly

5 *(conscience)* **avoir le/un s. de** to have the/a feeling of; **avoir le s. de sa solitude** to have a feeling of loneliness; **il avait le s. de sa mort prochaine** he sensed he would die soon; **j'ai le s. très net de m'être trompé** I have a distinct feeling that I've made a mistake

• **sentiments NMPL 1** *(disposition)* **faire appel aux bons sentiments de qn** to appeal to sb's better *or* finer feelings; **ramener qn à de meilleurs sentiments** to bring sb round to a more generous point of view; **revenir à de meilleurs sentiments** to be in a better frame of mind **2** *(dans la correspondance)* **veuillez agréer l'expression de mes sentiments distingués** *(à quelqu'un dont on connaît le nom) Br* yours sincerely, *Am* sincerely (yours); *(à quelqu'un dont on ne connaît pas le nom) Br* yours faithfully, *Am* sincerely (yours); **nos sentiments les meilleurs** kindest regards

sentimental, -e, -aux, -ales [sɑ̃timɑ̃tal,-o] **ADJ 1** *(affectif)* sentimental; **valeur sentimentale** sentimental value; **vie sentimentale** love life; **la pièce ne compte que pour l'intrigue sentimentale** the play is only saved by its love interest **2** *Péj* sentimental, mawkish

NM,F c'est un grand s. he's a great romantic; **je ne suis pas une sentimentale** I'm not given to sentimentality

sentimentalement [sɑ̃timɑ̃talmɑ̃] **ADV** sentimentally; *Péj* mawkishly

sentimentalisme [sɑ̃timɑ̃talism] **NM** *Péj* sentimentality, mawkishness; **faire du s.** to be overly sentimental

sentimentaliste [sɑ̃timɑ̃talist] **ADJ** sentimentalist

NMF sentimentalist

sentimentalité [sɑ̃timɑ̃talite] **NF** *Péj* sentimentality, mawkishness

sentine [sɑ̃tin] **NF 1** *Naut* bilge **2** *Littéraire (cloaque)* pigsty; **s. de tous les vices** sink of iniquity

sentinelle [sɑ̃tinɛl] **NF** *Mil* sentinel, sentry; **en s.** on guard; **être en s.** to stand sentinel *or* sentry, to be on sentry duty; **les cambrioleurs ont mis un homme en s. à la sortie de la banque** the robbers have put a lookout in front of the bank

SENTIR **[37]** [sɑ̃tir]

VT	
• to smell **A1**	• to taste **A2**
• to feel **A3–6**	• to sense **A4**
• to be aware of **A4**	• to have a feel for **A8**
• to smell of **B1**	• to smack of **B3**
VI	
• to smell **1, 2**	
VPR	
• to show **2**	• to feel **3, 4**

VT A. *AVOIR UNE IMPRESSION DE* **1** *(par l'odorat)* to smell; **je ne sens rien** I can't smell anything; *Fam* **sens-moi cette soupe!** just smell this soup!□; **je sens une odeur de gaz** I can smell gas

2 *(par le goût)* to taste; **tu sens le goût du romarin?** can you taste the rosemary?

3 *(par le toucher)* to feel; **s. un caillou dans sa chaussure** to feel a stone in one's shoe; **je n'ai rien senti!** I didn't feel a thing!; **je ne sens plus mon nez** *(de froid)* my nose has gone numb; **je ne sens plus ma main** *(d'ankylose)* my hand's gone numb *or* dead; **je ne sens plus mes jambes** *(de fatigue)* my legs are killing me; *Fam* **quand je monte l'escalier, je sens mon genou** *(douleur ancienne)* my knee plays up when I walk up the stairs; **elle commence à s. son âge** she's starting to feel her age; **s. son visage s'empourprer** to feel oneself blushing; **il sentit les larmes lui monter aux yeux** he could feel tears coming to his eyes; **elle sentait le sommeil la gagner** she felt sleepier and sleepier; **je sentais battre mon cœur** I could feel my heart beating; **je n'ai pas senti l'après-midi/les années passer** the afternoon/years just flashed by; **j'ai senti qu'on essayait de mettre la main dans ma poche** I was aware *or* I felt that someone was trying to reach into my pocket; *Fam* **je l'ai sentie passer** *(douleur, claque, facture)* I knew all about it!; *Fam* **je l'ai sentie passer, la piqûre!** I really felt that jab!; **vous allez la s. passer, l'amende!** you'll certainly know all about it when you get the fine!; **c'est lui qui a payé le repas, il a dû le s. passer!** he paid for the meal, it must have cost him an arm and a leg!

4 *(avoir l'intuition de ▸ mépris, présence, réticence)* to feel, to sense, to be aware of; *(▸danger, menace)* to be aware *or* conscious of, to sense; **on ne m'a pas dit qu'il était mort, mais je l'ai senti** I wasn't told he was dead but I sensed it *or* I had a feeling he was; **tu ne sens pas ta force** you don't know your own strength; *Fam* **ça devait arriver, je le sentais venir de loin** I could see it coming a mile off; **ils n'ont pas senti venir le danger** they didn't smell *or* sense (the) danger; **elle sentait le pouvoir lui échapper** she could feel (that) power was slipping away from her; **je le sentais résolu** I could feel *or* tell he was determined; **je sens bien qu'il m'envie** I can feel *or* tell that he envies me; **j'ai senti qu'on me suivait** I felt *or* sensed (that) I was being followed; **sens-tu à quel point il t'aime?** do you realize how much he loves you?; **faire s. qch à qn** to make sb aware of sth, to show sb sth; **il m'a fait s. que j'étais de trop** he made me understand *or* he hinted that I was in the way; *Fam* **elle nous le fait s. qu'elle est le chef!** she makes sure we know who's boss!; **les conséquences de votre décision se feront s. tôt ou tard** the implications of your decision will be felt sooner or later; *Fam Hum* **tu fais comme tu sens, coco!** just do your own thing, pal!

5 *(éprouver ▸ joie, chagrin, remords)* to feel; **je ne sens rien pour lui** I feel nothing for him

6 *(apprécier ▸ art, musique)* to feel, to have a feeling for

7 *Fam (être convaincu par)* **je ne la sens pas pour le rôle** my feeling is that she's not right for the part; **je ne le sens pas, ton projet** I'm not convinced by your plan

8 *(maîtriser ▸ instrument, outil)* to have a feel for; *(▸ rôle, mouvement à exécuter)* to feel at ease with; **s. sa monture** to feel good in the saddle; **je ne sentais pas bien mon service aujourd'hui** *(au tennis)* my service wasn't up to scratch today; **tu ne pourras pas sculpter tant que tu ne sentiras pas la pierre** you won't become a sculptor until you have the right feeling for stone; **cet acteur n'est pas convaincant, il ne sent pas son texte** this actor isn't very convincing, he doesn't get inside the role

9 *Fam (tolérer)* **je ne peux pas la s.** I can't stand *or Br* stick her; **je le sens pas bien, ce mec-là** there's something about that guy I don't like; **je ne peux pas s. ses blagues sexistes** I can't stomach *or* I just can't take his/her sexist jokes

B. *EXHALER, DONNER UNE IMPRESSION* **1** *(dégager ▸ odeur, parfum)* to smell of, to give off a smell of; **qu'est-ce que ça sent?** what's that smell?; **s. le gaz** to smell of gas; **ça sent le poisson** it smells fishy *or* of fish; **les roses ne sentent rien** the roses don't smell of anything; **ça sent bon le lilas, ici** there's a nice smell of lilac in here

2 *(annoncer)* **ça sent l'automne** there's a hint *or* a trace of autumn in the air; **ça sent la pluie/la neige** it feels like rain/snow; **ça sentait la mutinerie** there was mutiny in the air; **ses propositions sentent le traquenard** there's something a bit suspect about his/her proposals; **se faire s.** *(devenir perceptible)* to be felt, to become obvious; **la fatigue se fait s. chez les concurrents** the contestants are showing signs of tiredness; **l'hiver commence à se faire s.** the first signs of winter are appearing

3 *(laisser deviner)* to smack of, to savour of; **son livre sent la morale catholique** his/her book smacks of Catholic morality; **son interprétation/son style sent un peu trop le travail** his/her performance/style is rather too laborious; *Fam* **il sent le policier à des kilomètres** you can tell he's a policeman a mile off; **son accent sentait bon le terroir** he/she had a wonderful rural *or* country accent

VI 1 *(avoir une odeur)* to smell; **le fromage sent fort** the cheese smells strong; **ça sent bon** *(fleur, parfum)* it smells nice; *(nourriture)* it smells good *or* nice; **ça sent mauvais** it doesn't smell very nice; *Fam Fig* **ça commence à s. mauvais, filons!** things are beginning to turn nasty, let's get out of here!

2 *(puer)* to smell, to stink, to reek; **la viande commence à s.** the meat is starting to smell; **il sent des pieds** his feet smell, he's got smelly feet

3 *Can (être indiscret)* to snoop, to stick one's nose into other people's business

VPR se sentir 1 *(se supporter) Fam* **ils ne peuvent pas se s.** they can't stand *or Br* stick each other

2 *(être perceptible)* to show; **lorsqu'elle est déprimée, cela se sent dans ses lettres** when she's depressed, you can sense it *or* it shows in her letters; **il ne l'aime pas – ça se sent** he doesn't like him/her – you can tell (he doesn't) *or* it shows

3 *(suivi d'un adjectif ou d'un infinitif)* to feel; **se s. fatigué** to feel tired; **est-ce que tu te sens visé?** do you feel this was meant for you?; **se s. en sécurité/en danger** to feel safe/threatened; **je me sentais glisser** I could feel myself slipping; **se s. mal** *(s'évanouir)* to feel faint; *(être indisposé)* to feel ill; **se s. bien** to feel good *or* all right; **se s. mieux** to feel better; **je ne m'en sens pas capable** I don't feel up to it *or* equal to it; *Fam* **non mais, tu te sens bien?** have you gone mad?; *Hum* **ne plus se s.** *(se comporter de façon étrange)* to have taken leave of one's senses; *Fam* **ne plus se s. (pisser)** *(être vaniteux)* to be too big for one's *Br* boots *or Am* britches; *Fam* **elle ne se sent plus depuis qu'elle a eu le rôle** she's been really full of it since she landed the part; *Fam* **du caviar? tu te sens plus, toi!** caviar? hey, steady on!; **ne plus se s. de joie** to be bursting *or* beside oneself with joy

4 *Fam* **se s. de faire qch** *(avoir le courage)* to feel up to doing sth; **tu te sens d'y aller?** do you feel up to going?; **je ne me sens pas de le lui dire** I don't feel like telling him/her; **te sens-tu le cœur d'y aller?** do you feel up to going?

seoir **[67]** [swar] **seoir à VT IND** *Littéraire* **1** *(aller à)* to become, to suit; **le noir ne te sied pas** black doesn't become you **2** *(convenir à)* to suit; **cet air de gravité seyait à sa personne** this solemn air suited him/her

V IMPERSONNEL *Littéraire* **il sied de** *(il convient de)* it is right *or* proper to; **il sied d'envoyer un mot de remerciement** it is proper *or* fitting to send a note of thanks; **il sied à qn de...** it is proper for sb to..., *Sout* it behoves sb to...; **il ne vous sied pas** *ou* **il vous sied mal de protester** it ill becomes *or* befits you to complain; **comme il sied** as is proper *or* fitting

Séoul [seul] **NM** Seoul

sépale [sepal] **NM** *Bot* sepal

séparable [separabl] **ADJ s. de** separable from; **l'intelligence n'est pas s. de la sensibilité** intelligence cannot be separated from the emotions; **deux théories difficilement séparables** two theories which are difficult to separate

séparateur, -trice [separatœr, -tris] **ADJ** separating, separative; *Opt* **pouvoir s.** resolving power

NM 1 *Élec & Tech* separator; *TV* **s. de faisceau** beam splitter **2** *Ordinat* separator

séparation [separasjɔ̃] **NF 1** *(éloignement)* separation, parting; **elle n'a pas supporté la s. d'avec ses enfants** she couldn't bear to be parted *or* separated from her children

2 *(rupture)* break-up, split-up; **leur s. est imminente** they are on the brink of splitting up *or* breaking up
3 *Jur* separation (agreement); **s. amiable** *ou* **de fait** voluntary separation; **s. de corps** legal separation
4 *Pol* **la s. des pouvoirs** the separation of powers; **la s. de l'Église et de l'État** the separation of Church and State
5 *(cloison)* partition, division; **mur de s.** dividing wall
6 *Ordinat* **s. automatique des pages** automatic pagination
7 *Typ* **s. des couleurs** colour separation; **s. quadrichromique** four-colour separation

séparatisme [separatism] NM separatism

séparatiste [separatist] ADJ separatist
NMF separatist

séparatrice [separatris] *voir* **séparateur**

séparé, -e [separe] ADJ **1** *(éléments, problèmes, courrier)* separate **2** *(époux)* separated; **nous sommes séparés depuis un an** we've been separated for a year; **il vit s. de sa femme** he's separated (from his wife)

séparément [separemɑ̃] ADV separately; **vivre s.** to live apart *or* separately; **c'est un problème à traiter s.** this problem must be dealt with separately

séparer [3] [separe] VT **1** *(isoler)* to separate (**de** from); **s. des gaz/des isotopes** to separate gases/isotopes; **s. le blanc et le jaune d'un œuf** to separate the yolk and *or* from the white; *Bible & Fig* **s. le bon grain de l'ivraie** to separate the wheat from the chaff
2 *(éloigner ▸ gens)* to part, to separate, to pull apart; **rien ne peut nous s.** nothing can come between us; **des milliers de kilomètres nous séparent** we are thousands of miles apart, we are separated by thousands of miles; **jusqu'à ce que la mort nous sépare** till death do us part; **séparez-les, ils vont se tuer!** you have to separate them or they'll kill each other!; **on les a séparés de leur père** they were separated from *or* taken away from their father
3 *(différencier)* **s. l'amour et l'amitié amoureuse** to distinguish between love and a loving friendship; **leurs opinions politiques les séparent** their political opinions divide them; **tout les sépare** they're worlds apart, they have nothing in common
4 *(diviser ▸ gén)* to separate, to divide; (▸ *cheveux)* to part; **la piste de ski est séparée en deux** the ski slope is divided into two; **le Nord est séparé du Sud** *ou* **le Nord et le Sud sont séparés par un désert** the North is separated from the South by a desert; **deux heures/cinq kilomètres nous séparaient de la frontière** we were two hours/five kilometres away from the border
VPR **se séparer 1** *(se quitter ▸ amis, parents)* to part; (▸ *époux, amants)* to break up; **les Beatles se sont séparés en 1970** the Beatles split up *or* broke up in 1970; **nous devons nous s. maintenant** we'll have to say goodbye now; **on se sépara sur le pas de la porte** we parted on the doorstep
2 *(bifurquer)* to divide, to branch (off); **le fleuve se sépare en plusieurs bras** the river divides *or* splits into several channels; **c'est ici que nos chemins se séparent** this is where we go our separate ways
3 se s. de *(se priver de)* to part with; **j'ai dû me s. de mes disques de jazz/de mon jardinier** I had to part with my jazz records/let my gardener go; **je ne me sépare jamais de mon plan de Paris** I'm never without my street map of Paris; **il ne se sépare pas si facilement de son argent** he and his money are not so easily parted
4 se s. de *(quitter)* to separate from

sépia [sepja] ADJ INV sepia, sepia-coloured
NF **1** *Ich* cuttlefish ink **2** *Beaux-Arts (couleur)* sepia; *(dessin)* sepia (drawing)

sept [set] ADJ **1** *(gén)* seven; **les S. Merveilles du monde** the Seven Wonders of the World **2** *(dans des séries)* seventh; **page/numéro s.** page/number seven **3** *Cartes* **le jeu des s. familles** Happy Families
PRON seven
NM INV **1** *(gén)* seven
2 *(numéro d'ordre)* number seven
3 *(chiffre écrit)* seven
4 *Cartes* seven

septain [setɛ̃] NM *Littérature* seven-line stanza

septantaine [septɑ̃tɛn] NF *Belg & Suisse* **1** *(quantité)* **une s.** around *or* about seventy, seventy or so; **une s. de voitures** around *or* about seventy cars; **elle a une s. d'années** she's around *or* about seventy (years old) **2** *(âge)* **avoir la s.** to be around *or* about seventy; **quand on arrive à la s.** when you hit seventy

septante [septɑ̃t] *Belg & Suisse* ADJ **1** *(gén)* seventy **2** *(dans des séries)* seventieth; **page/numéro s.** page/number seventy
PRON seventy
NM INV **1** *(gén)* seventy **2** *(numéro d'ordre)* number seventy **3** *(chiffre écrit)* seventy; *voir aussi* **cinquante**

septantième [septɑ̃tjem] *Belg & Suisse* ADJ seventieth
NMF **1** *(personne)* seventieth **2** *(objet)* seventieth (one)
NM **1** *(partie)* seventieth **2** *(étage) Br* seventieth floor, *Am* seventy-first floor; *voir aussi* **cinquième**

septembre [septɑ̃br] NM September; *voir aussi* **mars**

septennal, -e, -aux, -ales [septenal, -o] ADJ **1** *(qui a lieu tous les sept ans)* septennial **2** *(qui dure sept ans)* septennial, seven-year *(avant n)*

septennat [septena] NM **1** *Pol* (seven-year) term of office **2** *(période)* seven-year period

septentrion [septɑ̃trijɔ̃] NM *Arch ou Littéraire* septentrion

septentrional, -e, -aux, -ales [septɑ̃trijɔnal, -o] ADJ septentrional, northern

septicémie [septisemi] NF *Méd* blood poisoning, *Spéc* septicaemia

septicémique [septisemik] ADJ *Méd* septicaemic

septième [setjem] ADJ seventh; **le s. art** cinema, the seventh art; **être au s. ciel** to be in seventh heaven
NMF **1** *(personne)* seventh **2** *(objet)* seventh (one)
NM **1** *(partie)* seventh **2** *(étage) Br* seventh floor, *Am* eighth floor **3** *(arrondissement de Paris)* seventh (arrondissement)
NF **1** *Anciennement Scol Br* = last year of primary school, *Am* ≃ fifth grade **2** *Mus* seventh; *voir aussi* **cinquième**

septièmement [setjemmɑ̃] ADV seventhly, in seventh place

septique [septik] ADJ septic

septuagénaire [septɥaʒenɛr] ADJ septuagenarian; **être s.** to be in one's seventies
NMF person in his/her seventies

septuagésime [septɥaʒezim] NF *Rel* Septuagesima

septum [sɛptɔm] NM **1** *Anat* septum **2** *(diaphragme)* membrane

septuor [septɥɔr] NM septet, septette

septuple [septyp] ADJ septuple, sevenfold
NM septuple

septupler [3] [septyple] VT **s. qch** to increase sth sevenfold, to septuple sth
VI to increase sevenfold, to septuple

sépulcral, -e, -aux, -ales [sepylkral, -o] ADJ *Littéraire* sepulchral; **un silence s.** the silence of the grave

sépulcre [sepylkr] NM *Littéraire* sepulchre

sépulture [sepyltyr] NF **1** *(lieu)* burial place **2** *Littéraire (enterrement)* burial, sepulture; **être privé de s.** to be refused burial

séquelle [sekel] NF *(d'une maladie)* after-effect
• **séquelles** NFPL *(d'un bombardement, d'une guerre)* aftermath

séquençage [sekɑ̃saʒ] NM *Biol & Chim* sequencing

séquence [sekɑ̃s] NF **1** *Cin, Géol, Mus & Rel* sequence; *Cin* **s. d'archives** stock scene; *Cin* **s. filmique** film sequence; *Cin* **s. onirique** dream sequence **2** *Cartes* **s. de cartes** run, sequence of cards **3** *Ordinat* sequence; **s. d'appel** call sequence; **s. de caractères** character string, sequence of characters; **s. de commandes** command sequence

séquencer [16] [sekɑ̃se] VT *Biol* to sequence

séquenceur [sekɑ̃sœr] NM *Ordinat* sequencer

séquentiel, -elle [sekɑ̃sjɛl] ADJ **1** *(ordonné)* sequential **2** *Ordinat (accès)* sequential, serial; *(traitement)* sequential

séquestration [sekestrasjɔ̃] NF *Jur (d'une personne)* illegal confinement *or* restraint; *(de biens)* sequestration (order)

séquestre [sekestr] NM **1** *Jur (saisie)* sequestration; *Naut* embargo **2** *(personne)* sequestrator
• **sous séquestre** ADJ *(biens)* sequestrated
ADV **mettre** *ou* **placer des biens sous s.** to sequestrate property

séquestrer [3] [sekestre] VT **1** *(personne)* **s. qn** to keep sb locked up; *Jur* to confine sb illegally **2** *Jur (biens)* to sequestrate; *(navire)* to lay an embargo upon

séquoia [sekɔja] NM *Bot* sequoia

sera *etc voir* **être**[1]

sérac [serak] NM *Géog & Culin* serac

sérail [seraj] NM **1** *(harem)* seraglio, harem **2** *(palais d'un sultan)* seraglio; *Fig* **fils de ministre, il a été élevé** *ou* **nourri dans le s. (politique)** as a cabinet minister's son, he grew up in a political atmosphere; **c'est un homme du s.** *(homme politique)* he's an establishment figure *or* an insider; *(commercial)* he's a company *or* an organization man

séraphin [serafɛ̃] NM seraph

séraphique [serafik] ADJ seraphic, seraphical

serbe [sɛrb] ADJ Serbian
NM *(langue)* Serb
• **Serbe** NMF Serb

Serbie [sɛrbi] NF **la S.** Serbia

serbo-croate [sɛrbɔkrɔat] *(pl* **serbo-croates)** ADJ Serbo-Croat, Serbo-Croatian
NM *(langue)* Serbo-Croat, Serbo-Croatian

Sercq [sɛrk] NF (isle of) Sark

séré [sere] NM *Suisse* fromage frais

serein, -e [sɔrɛ̃, -ɛn] ADJ **1** *(esprit, visage)* serene, peaceful **2** *Littéraire (eau, ciel)* serene, clear, tranquil **3** *(jugement)* unbiased, dispassionate; *(réflexion)* undisturbed, unclouded
NM *Littéraire* evening dew

sereinement [sɔrɛnmɑ̃] ADV **1** *(tranquillement)* serenely, peacefully **2** *(impartialement)* dispassionately

sérénade [serenad] NF **1** *Mus* serenade; *(concert)* serenade; **donner la s. à qn** to serenade sb **2** *Fam (tapage)* racket; **le bébé nous a fait une drôle de s. toute la nuit** the baby screamed at the top of his lungs the whole night

sérénissime [serenisim] ADJ **la S. République** La Serenissima, the Venetian Republic

sérénité [serenite] NF **1** *(d'une personne)* serenity, peacefulness; *(d'un jugement)* dispassionateness; *(des pensées)* clarity; **il envisage avec s. l'approche de la vieillesse** he has a serene attitude towards growing old **2** *Littéraire (du ciel)* serenity, tranquillity, clarity

séreux, -euse [serø, -øz] ADJ *Physiol* serous
• **séreuse** NF *Anat* serous membrane

serf, serve [sɛrf, sɛrv] ADJ **1** *Littéraire (soumis)* serflike, servile **2** *Hist* **la condition serve** serfdom
NM,F *Hist* serf

serfouette [sɛrfwɛt] NF *Agr* hoe-fork

serge [sɛrʒ] NF *Tex* serge

sergent [sɛrʒɑ̃] NM **1** *Mil* sergeant; **s. fourrier** quartermaster sergeant; **s. instructeur** drill sergeant; **s. recruteur** recruiting sergeant **2** *Vieilli (agent de police)* **s. de ville** police officer, *esp Br* police constable **3** *Tech* cramp, clamp

sergent-chef [sɛrʒɑ̃ʃɛf] *(pl* **sergents-chefs)** NM *(dans l'armée de terre) Br* ≃ staff sergeant, *Am* ≃ master sergeant; *(dans l'armée de l'air) Br* ≃ flight sergeant, *Am* ≃ master sergeant

séricicole [serisikɔl] ADJ silkworm-breeding *(avant n)*

sériciculteur, -trice [serisikyltœr, -tris] NM,F silkworm breeder

sériciculture [serisikyltyr] NF silkworm breeding

série [seri] **NF 1** *(suite ▸ de questions, de changements, de conférences)* series *(singulier)*; *(▸ d'attentats)* series, spate, string; *(▸ d'échecs)* series, run, string; *(▸ de tests)* series, battery
2 *(ensemble ▸ de clefs, de mouchoirs)* set; *(▸ de poupées russes, de tables gigognes)* nest; *Com & Ind* (production) batch; **elle en a toute une s.** she has a whole collection of them; **s. limitée** limited run; **s. de prix** rates, list of charges
3 *(catégorie)* class, category; **classé dans la s. des récidivistes/des chefs-d'œuvre** belonging to the class of recidivists/of masterpieces; *Hum* **dans la s. "scandales de l'été", tu connais la dernière?** have you heard the latest in the series of summer scandals?
4 *TV* **s. dramatique** drama series; **s. policière** crime series; **s. (télévisée)** television series
5 *(au lycée)* = one of the groups into which baccalaureat students are divided, depending on their chosen area of specialization, *Br* ≃ stream, *Am* ≃ track
6 *Sport (classement)* series; *(épreuve)* qualifying heat *or* round; *(au billard)* break
7 *Géol, Chim, Math, Mus & Nucl* series *(singulier)*
ADJ INV *Ordinat* serial
• **de série ADJ 1** *Ind* mass-produced **2** *Com (numéro)* serial *(avant n)* **3** *Aut (modèle)* production *(avant n)*
• **en série ADJ 1** *Ind (fabrication)* mass *(avant n)* **2** *Élec (couplage, enroulement)* series *(avant n)* **ADV 1** *Ind* **fabriquer qch en s.** to mass-produce sth **2** *Élec* **monté en s.** connected in series **3** *(à la file)* one after the other; **en ce moment, les malheurs arrivent en s.** it's just one disaster after another at the moment
• **série B NF (film de) s. B** B-movie
• **série noire NF 1** *Littérature* crime thriller; **c'est un vrai personnage de s. noire** he's/she's like something out of a detective novel **2** *Fig* catalogue of disasters

sériel, -elle [serjɛl] **ADJ** serial; **musique sérielle** serial music

sérier [9] [serje] **VT** to arrange, to classify, to grade; **commençons par s. les problèmes** let's prioritize our problems

sérieuse [serjøz] *voir* **sérieux**

sérieusement [serjøzmɑ̃] **ADV 1** *(consciencieusement)* seriously; **as-tu étudié la question s.?** have you looked at the matter thoroughly?
2 *(sans plaisanter)* seriously, in earnest; **je pense me présenter aux élections – s.?** I think I'll stand in the election – seriously *or* really?
3 *(gravement)* seriously, gravely
4 *(vraiment)* seriously, really; **ça commençait à bouchonner s.** traffic was really building up; **il en a s. besoin** he's seriously in need of it

sérieux, -euse [serjø, -øz] **ADJ 1** *(grave ▸ ton, visage)* serious, solemn; **s. comme un pape** as solemn as a judge; **vous n'êtes pas s.!** you can't be serious!, you must be joking!
2 *(important ▸ lecture, discussion)* serious; **on a discuté de choses sérieuses** we had a serious discussion; **entre elle et moi, c'est s.** we have a serious relationship
3 *(consciencieux ▸ employé)* serious, responsible; *(▸ élève)* conscientious, serious; *(▸ travail)* conscientious; **c'est du travail s.** it's good work; **être s. dans son travail** to be serious about one's work, to take one's work seriously; **être s. pour son âge** to be serious for one's age; **ça ne fait pas très s.** it won't make a very good impression; **arriver au bureau à midi, ça ne fait pas très s.** turning up at the office just before lunchtime isn't very responsible
4 *(digne de foi ▸ partenaire, offre, candidature, revue)* serious, reliable, dependable; *(▸ analyse, enquête)* serious, thorough, in-depth; **peu s.** *(personne)* unreliable
5 *(dangereux ▸ situation, maladie)* grave, serious; *(▸ blessure)* severe
6 *(sincère, vrai)* serious; **pas s. s'abstenir** no time-wasters; **c'est s., tu pars?** it's true that you're leaving?; **c'est s., cette histoire d'augmentation?** is this talk about getting a *Br* rise *or Am* raise serious?
7 *(avant le nom) (important ▸ effort)* real; *(▸ dégâts, difficultés)* serious; *(▸ risques)* great, considerable; *(▸ somme d'argent)* sizeable; **il a de sérieuses chances de gagner** he stands a good chance of winning; **de s. progrès techniques** considerable technical advances; **ils ont une sérieuse avance sur nous** they are well ahead of us
NM 1 *(gravité ▸ d'une personne)* seriousness; *(▸ d'une situation)* gravity; **garder son s.** to keep a straight face **2** *(application)* seriousness, serious-mindedness; **elle fait son travail avec s.** she's serious about her work; **manque de s.** unreliability **3** *(fiabilité ▸ d'une intention)* seriousness, earnestness; *(▸ d'une source de renseignements)* reliability, dependability **ADV** *Fam (sérieusement)* seriously[□]; **ils se sont foutus sur la gueule s.** they seriously went for each other; **s.?** seriously?
• **au sérieux ADV prendre qn/qch au s.** to take sb/sth seriously; **se prendre (trop) au s.** to take oneself (too) seriously

serif [serif] **NM** *Typ* serif

sérigraphie [serigrafi] **NF 1** *(procédé)* silk-screen *or* screen process printing **2** *(ouvrage)* silk-screen print

sérigraphié, -e [serigrafje] **ADJ** silk-screen printed

serin, -e [sərɛ̃, -in] **NM,F 1** *Orn* canary **2** *Fam (personne)* nitwit
ADJ *Fam (personne)* silly[□], idiotic[□]
ADJ M INV *(couleur)* **jaune s.** bright *or* canary yellow

seriner [3] [sərine] **VT 1** *Fam (répéter)* **s. qch à qn** to drill *or* to drum sth into sb; **il m'a seriné ça toute la soirée** he kept banging on about it all evening; **s. à qn que…** to tell sb time after time that…[□] **2** *(instruire)* **s. un oiseau** to teach a bird to sing *(using a bird-organ)*

seringue [sərɛ̃g] **NF 1** *Méd* needle, syringe; **s. hypodermique** hypodermic needle *or* syringe; **s. à injections** hypodermic needle *or* syringe; **s. jetable** disposable syringe
2 *Hort* garden syringe, (garden) pump spray
3 *Culin* syringe
4 *Aut* **s. de graissage** grease gun

serment [sɛrmɑ̃] **NM 1** *(parole solennelle)* oath; **témoigner sous s.** to testify under oath; **déclaration sous s.** sworn statement, statement under oath; **déclarer sous la foi du s.** to declare on *or* upon oath; **faire un s. sur l'honneur** to pledge one's word of honour; **s. d'allégeance** oath of allegiance; *Méd* **s. d'Hippocrate** Hippocratic oath; **s. judiciaire** oath *or* affirmation *(in a court of law)*; **s. politique** oath of allegiance; **s. professionnel** *(des magistrats, des policiers etc)* oath of office
2 *(promesse)* pledge; **serments d'amour** pledges *or* vows of love; **on a fait le s. de ne pas se quitter** we've pledged *or* sworn never to part; **j'ai fait le s. de ne rien dire** I'm pledged *or* sworn to secrecy; **s. d'ivrogne** *ou* **de joueur** vain promise; *Fam* **tout ça, c'est des serments d'ivrogne!** I'll believe that when I see it!

sermon [sɛrmɔ̃] **NM 1** *Rel* sermon; **faire un s.** to deliver *or* to preach a sermon **2** *Fig Péj* lecture; **épargne-moi tes sermons** spare me the lecture

sermonner [3] [sɛrmɔne] **VT** *(morigéner)* to lecture, to sermonize, to preach at

sermonneur, -euse [sɛrmɔnœr, -øz] **ADJ** sermonizing, lecturing
NM,F sermonizer

séroconversion [serokɔ̃vɛrsjɔ̃] **NF** *Méd* seroconversion

sérodiagnostic [serodjagnɔstik] **NM** *Méd* serodiagnosis, serum diagnosis

sérogroupe [serogrup] **NM** *Méd* serogroup

sérologie [serɔlɔʒi] **NF** *Méd (science)* serology; **faire une s.** to be screened for antibodies

séronégatif, -ive [serɔnegatif, -iv] *Méd* **ADJ** *(gén)* seronegative; *(HIV)* HIV negative
NM,F HIV-negative person

séronégativité [serɔnegativite] **NF** *Méd (gén)* seronegativity; *(HIV)* HIV-negative status; **prouver sa s.** to prove that one is HIV negative

séropo [seropo] *Fam Méd* **ADJ** HIV positive[□]
NMF HIV-positive person[□]

séropositif, -ive [serɔpozitif, -iv] *Méd* **ADJ** *(gén)* seropositive; *(HIV)* HIV positive
NM,F HIV-positive person

séropositivité [serɔpozitivite] **NF** *Méd (gén)* seropositivity; *(HIV)* HIV infection; **il a été renvoyé à cause de sa s.** he was dismissed for being HIV positive

sérosité [serozite] **NF** *Physiol* serous fluid

sérotype [serɔtip] **NM** *Méd* serotype

serpe [sɛrp] **NF** bill, billhook; **un visage taillé à la s.** *ou* **à coups de s.** a rough-hewn face

serpent [sɛrpɑ̃] **NM 1** *Zool* snake; **avec la ruse du s.** with fox's cunning; **s. d'eau** water snake; **s. à lunettes** Indian cobra; **s. marin** sea snake; **s. de mer** *Myth* sea monster *or* serpent; *Presse* silly-season story; **le vieux s. de mer de la nationalisation** the old chestnut of nationalization; *Antiq* **s. à sonnette** rattlesnake; **c'est (comme) le s. qui se mord la queue** it's a vicious circle
2 *Littéraire (personne)* viper; **réchauffer un s. dans son sein** to nourish a viper in one's bosom
3 *(forme sinueuse)* **s. de fumée** ribbon of smoke; **le long s. des véhicules sur la route** the long trail of vehicles winding up the road
4 *Fin* **s. monétaire** currency snake; **le s. monétaire européen** the European currency snake

serpentaire [sɛrpɑ̃tɛr] **NM** *Orn* secretary bird
NF *Bot* snakeroot

serpenteau, -x [sɛrpɑ̃to] **NM 1** *Zool* young snake **2** *(feu d'artifice)* serpent

serpenter [3] [sɛrpɑ̃te] **VI** *(courant, route etc)* to wind along, to meander

serpentin, -e [sɛrpɑ̃tɛ̃, -in] **ADJ** *Littéraire* twisting, winding, sinuous
NM 1 *(de papier)* (paper) streamer **2** *Phys* coil

serpette [sɛrpɛt] **NF** pruning hook *or* knife

serpillière [sɛrpijɛr] **NF** *(torchon)* floorcloth; **il faudrait passer la s. dans la cuisine** the kitchen floor needs cleaning

serpolet [sɛrpɔlɛ] **NM** *Bot & Culin* wild thyme

serrage [seraʒ] **NM** *(d'une vis)* screwing down, tightening; *(d'un joint)* clamping

serre [sɛr] **NF 1** *Hort & Agr (en verre)* greenhouse, *Br* glasshouse; *(en plastique)* greenhouse; **cultures en** *ou* **de s.** greenhouse plants; **légumes poussés en** *ou* **sous s.** vegetables grown under glass; *Fig* **ils élèvent leurs enfants en** *ou* **sous s.** they wrap their children in cotton wool; **s. chaude** hothouse; *École* **effet de s.** greenhouse effect; **gaz à effet de s.** greenhouse gas **2** *Orn* claw, talon **3** *Tech (d'une substance)* pressing, squeezing

serré, -e [sere] **ADJ 1** *(nœud, ceinture, vêtement)* tight; **s. à la taille** *(volontairement)* fitted at the waist, tight-waisted
2 *(contracté)* **les lèvres/les dents serrées** with set lips/clenched teeth; **la gorge serrée** with a lump in one's throat; **c'est le cœur s. que j'y repense** when I think of it, it gives me a lump in my throat
3 *(dense ▸ style)* tight, concise; *(▸ réseau)* dense; *(▸ débat)* closely-conducted, closely-argued; *(▸ écriture)* cramped; *(▸ pluie)* teeming; **deux pages d'une écriture serrée** two closely written pages
4 *(délimité ▸ emploi du temps)* tight, busy; *(▸ budget)* tight
5 *(café)* strong
6 *Sport (arrivée, peloton)* close; *(match)* tight, close-fought
ADV écrire s. to have cramped handwriting; **jouer s.** to play a tight game

serre-fils [sɛrfil] **NM INV** *(vis)* binding screw; *(pince)* wire grip

serre-frein [sɛrfrɛ̃] *(pl* **serre-freins***)* **NM** *Rail* brakeman

serre-joint [sɛrʒwɛ̃] *(pl* **serre-joints***)* **NM** (builder's) clamp

serre-livres [sɛrlivr] **NM INV** bookend

serrement [sɛrmɑ̃] **NM s. de cœur** pang, tug at the heartstrings; **avoir un s. de cœur** to feel a pang *or* a tug at the heartstrings; **s. de main** handshake

serre-patte [sɛrpat] *(pl* **serre-pattes***)* **NM** *Fam* sergeant[□]

SERRER [4] [sere]

VT
• to hold tight **1** • to be too tight for **2**
• to tighten **3** • to clench **4**
• to put away **8** • to arrest **9**
VPR
• to squeeze up **1**

VT **1** *(presser)* to hold tight; **il serrait la clé dans sa main** he was holding the key tight *or* he was clutching the key in his hand; **serre-moi fort dans tes bras** hold me tight in your arms; **s. qch contre son cœur** to clasp sth to one's breast; **s. qn contre son cœur** to clasp sb to one's bosom; **s. qn à la gorge** to grab sb by the throat; *Fam* **s. le kiki à qn** to try to strangle sb; *Fam* **s. la main** *ou* **la pince à qn** to shake hands with sb, to shake sb's hand
2 *(sujet: vêtement, chaussure)* to be too tight for; **le col me serre un peu** the collar is a bit tight; **ton jean te serre trop aux cuisses** your jeans are too tight round the thighs
3 *(bien fermer ▸ nœud, lacets)* to tighten, to pull tight; *(▸ joint)* to clamp; *(▸ écrou)* to tighten (up); *(▸ frein à main)* to put on tight; *Fam* **s. la vis à qn** to crack down (hard) on sb
4 *(contracter)* to clench; **s. les lèvres** to set *or* to tighten one's lips; **s. les dents** to clench *or* to grit one's teeth; **en serrant les poings** clenching one's fists; *Fig* barely containing one's anger; **des images qui vous serrent le cœur** heart-rending images; **avoir la gorge serrée par l'émotion/le chagrin** to be choked with emotion/grief; *Fam* **s. les fesses** to have the jitters
5 *(rapprocher)* **en les serrant bien, une boîte suffira** if we pack them in tight, one box will do; *Typ* **s. une ligne** to close up a line; *Fig* **s. les rangs** to close ranks; *Sport* **s. le jeu** to play a tight game; **être serrés comme des sardines** *ou* **des harengs** to be squashed up like sardines
6 *(suivre) Aut* **s. le trottoir** to hug the kerb; **s. qn de près** to follow close behind sb, to follow sb closely; *Fig* **s. une femme de près** to be all over a woman; **s. un problème de plus près** to study a problem more closely
7 *Naut* **s. la côte** to hug the coast; **s. le vent** to sail close to *or* to hug the wind
8 *(enfermer, ranger)* to put away; **serrez bien vos bijoux** put your jewellery away in a safe place
9 *Fam (arrêter) Br* to nick, to lift, *Am* to bust
VI *Aut* **s. à droite/à gauche** to keep to the right/left
VPR **se serrer 1** *(se rapprocher)* to squeeze up; **si on se serre un peu, on pourra tous entrer** if we squeeze up a bit, we can all get in; **se s. contre qn** *(par affection)* to cuddle *or* to snuggle up to sb; *(pour se protéger)* to huddle up against sb; **se s. les uns contre les autres** to huddle together; **se s. contre un mur** to hug a wall
2 *(se contracter)* **je sentais ma gorge se s.** I could feel a lump in my throat; **mon cœur se serra en les voyant** my heart sank when I saw them
3 *(pour se saluer)* **se s. la main** to shake hands

serre-tête [sertɛt] NM INV **1** *(accessoire)* headband, hairband **2** *Sport (d'athlète)* headband; *(de rugbyman)* scrum cap **3** *(d'aviateur)* helmet

serriculture [serikyltyr] NF hothouse growing

serrure [seryr] NF lock; **laisser la clef dans la s.** to leave the key in the lock *or* in the door; **s. à carte perforée** card-operated lock; **s. à combinaison** combination lock; **s. électronique** electronic lock; **s. encastrée** mortise lock; **s. magnétique** magnetic lock; **s. à pompe** high security spring lock *(with pump action mechanism)*; *Aut* **s. de sécurité** childproof lock; **s. de sûreté** safety lock

serrurerie [seryrri] NF **1** *(métier)* locksmithing, locksmithery **2** *(magasin)* locksmith's *Br* (shop) *or Am* store **3** *(ferronnerie)* ironwork; **grosse s.** heavy ironwork; **s. d'art** decorative ironwork

serrurier [seryrje] NM **1** *(qui pose des serrures)* locksmith **2** *(en ferronnerie)* iron manufacturer

sert *etc voir* **servir**

sertir [32] [sertir] VT **1** *(pierre précieuse)* to set; **couronne sertie de diamants** crown set with diamonds **2** *Métal (tôles)* to crimp over; *(rivet)* to clinch; *(cartouche, boîte de conserve)* to crimp

sertissage [sertisaʒ] NM **1** *(d'une pierre précieuse)* setting **2** *Métal (de tôles)* crimping together; *(d'un rivet)* clinching; *(d'une cartouche, d'une boîte de conserve)* crimping

sertisseur, -euse [sertisœr, -øz] NM,F **1** *(en joaillerie)* (jewel) setter **2** *Métal* crimper
NM *(appareil)* closing *or* sealing *or* double seaming machine

sertissure [sertisyr] NF **1** *(sertissage)* setting **2** *(partie du chaton)* setting

sérum [serɔm] NM **1** *Physiol* **s. (sanguin)** (blood) serum **2** *Pharm* serum; **s. antivenimeux** antivenin serum; **s. physiologique** saline; **s. de vérité** truth drug **3** *(du lait)* whey

servage [servaʒ] NM **1** *Hist* serfdom **2** *Littéraire (esclavage)* bondage, thraldom

serval, -als [serval] NM *Zool* serval (cat)

servant [servɑ̃] ADJ M *Rel* **frère s.** lay brother *(with domestic tasks)*
NM **1** *Rel* **s. (de messe)** server **2** *Mil* **s. (de canon)** gunner

servante [servɑ̃t] NF **1** *(domestique)* servant, maidservant; *Littéraire Ironique* **(je suis votre) s.** I would rather not *or* no, thank you **2** *Menuis* vice; **s. d'établi** bench vice **3** *(table)* serving table, *Br* dumbwaiter

serve [serv] *voir* **serf**

serveur, -euse [servœr, -øz] NM,F **1** *(de restaurant)* waiter, *f* waitress; *(de bar)* barman, *f* barmaid **2** *Sport* server **3** *Cartes* dealer
NM *Ordinat* server; **(centre) s.** information retrieval centre; **s. de données** on-line data service; **s. de fichiers** file server; **s. FTP** FTP server; **s. mandataire** proxy server; **s. Minitel®** Minitel® service provider; **s. de réseau** network server; **s. sécurisé** secure server; **s. télématique** bulletin board (system); **s. Web** Web server

serviabilité [servjabilite] NF helpfulness, obligingness, willingness to help

serviable [servjabl] ADJ helpful, obliging, willing to help

SERVICE [servis]

NM	
• duty **1, 8**	• service **2, 3, 7, 8, 10–13**
• sitting **4**	• favour **5**
• department **6**	• servicing **9**
• set **12**	
NMPL	
• services **1–3**	

NM **1** *(travail)* duty, shift; **mon s. commence à 18 heures** I go on duty *or* I start my shift *or* I start work at 6 p.m.; **l'alcool est interdit pendant le s.** drinking is forbidden while on duty; **il n'a pu assurer son s.** he wasn't able to go to work; **qui est de s. ce soir?** who's on duty tonight?; **les pompiers de service** the *Br* firemen *or Am* firefighters on duty; *Fam Fig* **le plaisantin/le râleur de service** the resident joker/grouch; **s. de jour/de nuit** day/night duty; **il n'est pas de s.** he's off-duty; **elle a 22 ans de s. dans l'entreprise** she's been with the company for 22 years; **finir son s.** to come off duty; **prendre son s.** to go on *or* to report for duty; **il ne plaisante pas avec le s.** he sticks to the rule book; **reprendre du s.** to be employed for a supplementary period; *Fam Hum* **mon vieux manteau a repris du s.** my old coat has been saved from the bin
2 *(pour la collectivité)* service, serving; **le s. de l'État** public service, the service of the state; **ses états de s.** his/her service record
3 *(pour un client, pour un maître)* service; **prendre qn à son s.** to take sb into service; **elle a deux ans de s. comme femme de chambre** she's been in service for two years as a chambermaid; **à votre s.** at your service; **elle a passé sa vie au s. des autres** she spent her life helping others; **il a mis son savoir-faire au s. de la société** he put his expertise at the disposal of the company; **je ne suis pas à ton s.!** I'm not your slave!; **qu'y a-t-il pour votre s.?** what can I do for you?; **entrons ici, le s. est rapide** let's go here, the service is quick; **le s. laissait plutôt à désirer** the service left a lot to be desired; **demander 15 pour cent pour le s.** to impose a 15 percent service charge; **s. compris/non compris** *(dans un restaurant)* service included/not included; **prends ces cacahuètes et fais le s.** take these peanuts and hand them round; **après dix ans de bons et loyaux services** after ten years of good and faithful service; **s. après-vente** *(prestation)* after-sales service; **s. d'assistance** *(téléphonique)* help desk, help line; **s. clientèle** *ou* **clients** *(prestation)* customer service; **s. consommateurs** *(prestation)* customer service; **s. de livraison** delivery service; **s. de messageries** courier service; *Mktg* **s. perçu** perceived service; *Mktg* **s. premier** premium service; **s. de relation clientèle** customer service; **escalier/porte/entrée de s.** service staircase/door/entrance
4 *(série de repas)* sitting; **premier/deuxième s.** first/second sitting
5 *(aide)* favour; **puis-je te demander un petit/un grand s.?** could I ask you to do me a small/a big favour?; **rendre un s. à qn** *(sujet: personne)* to help sb out, to do sb a favour; **elle n'aime pas rendre s.** she's not very helpful; **tu m'as bien rendu s.** you were a great help to me; **tu m'as bien rendu s. en me le prêtant** you did me a great favour by lending it to me; **rendre un mauvais s. à qn** to do sb a disservice; **te faire tous tes devoirs, c'est un mauvais s. à te rendre!** it won't do you any good if I do all your homework for you!; **le congélateur me rend de grands services** I find the freezer very useful; **ton dictionnaire m'a bien rendu s.** your dictionary was very useful; **ça peut encore/toujours rendre s.** it can still/it'll always come in handy
6 *(département ▸ d'une entreprise, d'un hôpital)* department; **s. des achats** purchasing department; **s. d'action commerciale** marketing department; **s. après-vente** after-sales department; **s. clientèle** *ou* **clients** customer service department; **s. des commandes** order department; **s. commercial** sales department; **s. commercial export** export department; **les services commerciaux** the sales department *or* division; **s. de (la) comptabilité** accounts department; **s. consommateurs** customer service department; **s. du contentieux** *(département)* legal department; *(personnes)* legal experts; **s. contrôle qualité, s. de contrôle de qualité** quality control department; **s. du courrier** mail room; **s. d'études** research department; **s. d'étude marketing** market research department; **s. des expéditions** dispatch department; **s. export** *ou* **des exportations** export department; **s. du feu** *Br* fire brigade, *Am* fire department; **s. informatique** computer *or* IT department; **s. juridique** legal department; **s. du marketing** marketing department; **S. médical d'urgence et de réanimation** = French ambulance and emergency unit; **s. du personnel** personnel department *or* division; **s. de presse** *(département)* press office; *(personnes)* press officers, press office staff; **je les ai eus par le s. de presse** *(livres)* I got them free as review copies; *(places de spectacle)* they're complimentary tickets I got for reviewing purposes; **s. de publicité** advertising *or* publicity department; **s. de relation clientèle** customer service department; **S. régional de la police judiciaire** = regional crime unit; **s. de relation clientèle** customer service department; **s. des renseignements** information office; **s. des urgences** *Br* casualty *or* A&E department, *Am* emergency room; **s. des ventes** sales department; **s. vente-marketing** sales and marketing department
7 *Transp* service; **le s. de nuit des autobus** the night bus service; **s. d'été/d'hiver** summer/winter timetable; **s. non assuré le dimanche** no service on Sundays, no Sunday service; **le s. a été interrompu** the service has been suspended; *Tél* **services voix et données** rich voice
8 *Mil* **s. actif** active service; **s. civil** = community work done by conscientious objectors instead of military service; **s. militaire** *ou* **national** military service; **faire son s. (militaire)** to do one's military service; **bon pour le s.** fit for military duties; *Fig Hum* **allez, bon/bons pour le s.!** it'll/they'll do!; **en s. commandé** on an official assignment; **tué en s. commandé** killed in action *or* whilst on active duty; **le s. de santé** the (army) medical corps; **le s. des transmissions** signals
9 *Fin* servicing; **s. de la dette extérieure** servicing the foreign debt; **assurer le s. de la dette** to service the debt
10 *Rel* **s. (divin)** service; **s. funèbre** funeral service
11 *Admin* **s. des douanes** customs service; **s. postal** *ou* **des postes** postal service(s); **s. public** public service; *(gaz, eau, électricité) Br* public utility, *Am* utility; **le s. public de l'audiovisuel** the publicly-owned channels *(on French television)*
12 *(assortiment ▸ de linge, de vaisselle)* set; **un s. (de table) de 20 pièces** a 20-piece dinner set *or* service; **acheter un s. de six couverts en argent** to buy a six-place canteen of silver cutlery; **s. à**

café/à thé coffee/tea set; *Fam Hum* **s. trois pièces** *(sexe de l'homme)* wedding tackle

13 *Sport* serve, service; **avoir un bon/mauvais s.** to have a good/poor serve, to serve well/badly; **Pichot au s.!, s. Pichot!** Pichot to serve!; **prendre le s. de qn** to break sb's serve

14 *(d'un étalon)* serving, mating

EXCLAM *Suisse (je vous en prie)* don't mention it!, you're welcome!

• **services NMPL 1** *Écon (secteur)* services, service industries, tertiary sector; **biens et services** goods and services; **services aux entreprises, services du secteur tertiaire** business services **2** *(collaboration)* services; **se passer des services de qn** to do without sb's help; *Euph (le licencier)* to dispense with sb's services; **offrir ses services à qn** to offer one's services to sb, to offer to help sb out **3** *Pol* **services de renseignements** intelligence services; **services secrets** *ou* **spéciaux** secret service **4** *Suisse (couverts)* knives and forks *(for laying at table)*

• **en service ADJ** in service, in use **ADV mettre un appareil en s.** to put a machine into service; **cet hélicoptère/cette presse entrera en s. en mai** this helicopter will be put into service/this press will come on stream in May

• **service d'ordre NM 1** *(système)* policing; **assurer le s. d'ordre dans un périmètre** to police a perimeter; **mettre en place un s. d'ordre dans un quartier** to establish a strong police presence in an area **2** *(gendarmes)* police (contingent); *(syndiqués, manifestants)* stewards

> **SERVICE MILITAIRE**
>
> Military service (for a period of ten months) used to be compulsory for French men aged between 18 and 26 unless they were declared unfit for service ("réformé"). As an alternative to military duty, some chose to work overseas, often in developing countries, as part of a voluntary aid scheme known as "la coopération". However, a reform was introduced in order to gradually abolish military service and move towards an exclusively professional army. This process was completed in 2001, putting an end to compulsory military service in France.

serviette [sɛrvjɛt] **NF 1** *(linge)* **s. de bain** bath towel; **s. hygiénique** sanitary *Br* towel *or Am* napkin; **s. en papier** paper napkin; **s. de plage** beach towel; **s. (de table)** table napkin; **s. (de toilette)** towel; *(pour s'essuyer les mains)* (hand) towel **2** *(cartable)* briefcase

serviette-éponge [sɛrvjɛtepɔ̃ʒ] *(pl* **serviettes-éponges) NF** (terry) towel

servile [sɛrvil] **ADJ 1** *(personne, esprit, attitude)* servile, subservient, *Sout* sycophantic; *(manières)* servile, cringing, fawning **2** *(imitation, traduction)* slavish

servilement [sɛrvilmɑ̃] **ADV 1** *(bassement)* obsequiously, subserviently **2** *(sans originalité)* slavishly

servilité [sɛrvilite] **NF 1** *(bassesse)* obsequiousness, subservience **2** *(manque d'originalité)* slavishness

SERVIR **[38]** [sɛrvir]

> **VT**
> • to serve **1, 2, 4, 5, 7–9**
> • to pay (out) **6**
> • to give **3**
> • to work to the advantage of **5**
>
> **USAGE ABSOLU**
> • to serve
>
> **VI**
> • to serve **3, 4**
> • to be useful **1**
>
> **VPR**
> • to help oneself **1**
> • to use **4**
> • to be served **3**

VT 1 *(dans un magasin)* to serve; **on vous sert?** *(dans un café, dans une boutique)* are you being served?; **s. qn de** *ou* **en qch** to serve sb with sth, to serve sth to sb; **c'est difficile de se faire s. ici** it's difficult to get served here; **il y a une cliente, allez la s.** here comes a customer, go and see *or* attend to her; *Fig* **tu voulais du changement, tu es** *ou* **te voilà servi!** you wanted some changes, now you've got more than you bargained for *or* now how do you like it?; **s. qn en qch** *(approvisionner)* to supply sb with sth; **c'est toujours lui qui me sert en huîtres** I always get my oysters from him

2 *(donner ▸ boisson, mets)* to serve; *(dans le verre)* to pour (out); *(dans l'assiette)* to dish out *or* up, to serve up; **sers le café** pour the coffee; **puis-je te s. du poulet?** can I serve you some chicken?; **le dîner est servi!** dinner's ready *or* served!; **Monsieur est servi** *(au dîner)* dinner is served, Sir; **une collation sera servie dans le hall** light refreshments will be served in the hall; **s. qch à qn** to serve sb with *or* to help sb to sth; **sers-moi à boire** give *or* pour me a drink; **faites-vous s. à boire** get the waiter to bring you a drink; **on nous a servi le petit déjeuner dans la chambre** our breakfast was brought up to *or* served in our room

3 *Fam (raconter)* to give[a]; **si tu avais entendu les injures qu'il nous a servies!** you should have heard the way he insulted us!; **si tu n'as que cette excuse à lui s., tu ferais mieux de ne rien dire** if that's the only excuse you can give him/her *or* come up with, you'd better keep quiet; **ils nous servent toujours les mêmes histoires aux informations** they always dish out the same old stories on the news

4 *(travailler pour ▸ famille)* to be in service with; *(▸ communauté, pays, parti)* to serve; *(▸ justice)* to be at the service of; *(▸ patrie, cause)* to serve; **à la fin de la guerre, la grande bourgeoisie dut renoncer à se faire s.** by the end of the war the upper classes had to give up having servants; **j'aime bien me faire s.** I like to be waited on; **vous avez bien/mal servi votre entreprise** you have served your company well/haven't given your company good service; **s. l'intérêt public** *(sujet: loi, mesure)* to be in the public interest; *(sujet: personne)* to serve the public interest; **s. l'État** *Pol* to serve the state; *(être fonctionnaire)* to be employed by the state; **s. Dieu** to serve God, to be a servant of God; *Hum* **Charles Albert, pour vous s.** Charles Albert, at your service; *Prov* **on n'est jamais si bien servi que par soi-même** if you want something done, do it yourself

5 *(aider ▸ sujet: circonstances)* to be of service to, to be *or* to work to the advantage of; **s. les ambitions de qn** to serve *or* to aid *or* to further sb's ambitions; **le mauvais temps l'a servi** the bad weather served him well *or* worked to his advantage *or* was on his side; **si la chance nous sert, nous réussirons** if our luck is in *or* if luck is on our side, we'll succeed; **sa mémoire la sert beaucoup** her memory's a great help to her; *Fam* **finalement, son culot ne l'a pas servi** his cheek didn't get him anywhere in the end

6 *(payer ▸ pension, rente)* to pay (out); **s. les intérêts d'une dette** to service a debt

7 *Sport* to serve; **s. une deuxième balle** to serve a second ball, to second-serve; **s. un ace** to serve an ace

8 *Rel* **s. la messe** to serve mass

9 *Cartes (cartes)* to deal (out); *(joueur)* to serve, to deal to; **c'est à toi de s.** it's your turn to deal

10 *Vét & Zool (saillir)* to cover, to serve

11 *Suisse (utiliser)* to use; **c'est un manteau que je ne sers plus** I don't wear this coat any more

USAGE ABSOLU nous ne servons plus après 23 heures we don't take orders after 11 p.m., last orders are at 11 p.m.; **servez chaud** serve hot; **(à) s. frais/frappé** *(sur emballage)* serve cool/chilled

VI 1 *(être utile ▸ outil, vêtement, appareil)* to be useful *or* of use, to come in handy; **garde la malle, ça peut toujours s.** keep the trunk, you might need it *or* it might come in handy one day; **le radiateur électrique peut encore s.** the electric heater can still be of use; **ça me servira pour ranger mes lettres** I can use it to put my letters in; **il a servi, ce manteau!** I got a lot of use *or* wear out of this coat!; **cet argument a beaucoup servi** this argument has been put forward many times; **cela fait longtemps que cette gare ne sert plus** this station has been out of use *or* been disused for a long time; **ça n'a jamais servi** it's never been used

2 *(travailler)* **elle sert au château depuis 40 ans** she's worked as a servant *or* been in service at the castle for 40 years; **s. comme cuisinière/comme jardinier** to be in service as a cook/a gardener; **s. dans un café/dans un restaurant** *(homme)* to be a waiter in a café/restaurant; *(femme)* to be a waitress in a café/restaurant

3 *Mil* to serve; **être fier de s.** to be proud to serve (one's country); **s. dans l'artillerie** to serve in the artillery; **il a servi sous MacArthur/sous la République** he served under MacArthur/the Republic

4 *Sport* to serve; **à toi de s.!** your serve *or* service!; **elle sert bien** *(gén)* she has a good service *or* serve; *(dans ce match)* she's serving well; **à Dancy de s.** Dancy to serve

• **servir à VT IND 1** *(être destiné à)* to be used for; **ça sert à quoi, cette machine?** what's this machine (used) for?; **le sonar sert à repérer les bateaux** the sonar is used to locate ships

2 *(avoir pour conséquence)* **ça ne sert à rien de lui en parler** it's useless *or* of no use talking to him/her about it; **ne pleure pas, ça ne sert à rien** don't cry, it won't make any difference; **crier ne sert à rien** there's no point in shouting; *Fam* **à quoi ça sert que je parle si personne ne m'écoute?** what's the point *or* the use of me talking if nobody listens?; **tu vois bien que ça a servi à quelque chose de faire une pétition!** as you see, getting up a petition did serve some purpose!; **ça n'a servi qu'à le rendre encore plus furieux** it only served to make him *or* it only made him even more furious

3 *(être utile à)* **merci, ça m'a beaucoup servi** thanks, it was really useful; **ma connaissance du russe m'a servi dans mon métier** my knowledge of Russian helped me in my job; **les circonstances m'ont beaucoup servi** the circumstances were in my favour; **ce recoin sert la nuit aux clochards du quartier** this corner is used at night by the local tramps; **ça me servira à couper la pâte** I'll use it to cut the dough

• **servir de VT IND** *(sujet: article, appareil)* to be used as; *(sujet: personne)* to act as, to be; **le coffre me sert aussi de table** I also use the trunk as a table; **un vieux sac lui servait de manteau** he/she was wearing an old sack as a coat; **le proverbe qui sert d'exergue au chapitre** the proverb which heads the chapter; **je lui ai servi d'interprète** I acted as *or* was his/her interpreter; **il lui a servi de père** he was like a father to him/her

VPR se servir 1 *(emploi réfléchi) (à table, dans un magasin)* to help oneself; **servez-vous de** *ou* **en légumes** help yourself to vegetables; **je me suis servi un verre de lait** I poured myself a glass of milk; **sers-toi!** help yourself!; *Euph* **il s'est servi dans la caisse** he helped himself to (the money in) the till; **je l'ai surpris à se s. dans la caisse** I caught him with his fingers in the till

2 *(s'approvisionner)* **je me sers chez le boucher de l'avenue** I buy my meat at the butcher's on the avenue; **où te sers-tu en fromage?** where do you shop for *or* buy your cheese?

3 *Culin (emploi passif)* to be served; **ça se sert chaud ou froid** it can be served *or* you can serve it either hot or cold; **le vin rouge se sert chambré** red wine should be served at room temperature

4 se s. de qch to use sth; **il ne peut plus se s. de son bras droit** he can't use his right arm anymore; **c'est une arme dont on ne se sert plus** it's a weapon which is no longer used *or* in use; **quand tu auras fini de te s. du sèche-cheveux** when you've finished using *or* with the hairdryer; **je ne sais pas me s. de la machine à coudre** I don't know how to work *or* to use the sewing machine; **elle se sert toujours des mêmes arguments** she always uses the same old arguments; **se s. de qch comme qch** to use sth as sth; **il s'est servi de sa grippe comme prétexte** he used flu as an excuse; *Hum* **tu te sers de ta raquette comme d'une poêle à frire!** you hold *or* you handle your racket like a *Br* frying pan *or Am* fry pan!; **se s. de qn** to make use of *or* to use sb; **on s'est servi de vous (comme appât)!** you've been used (as bait)!

serviteur [sɛrvitœr] **NM** (male) servant; *Arch* **votre très humble s.** *(dans une lettre)* your obedient servant; *Hum* **votre (humble) s.!** at your service!; *Littéraire Ironique* **(je suis votre) s.** I would rather not *or* no, thank you; **si vous n'êtes pas satisfait, adressez-vous à votre s.!** if you're not happy, please complain to yours truly!

servitude [sɛrvityd] **NF 1** *(soumission)* servitude **2** *(contrainte)* constraint; **se plier aux servitudes**

de la mode to be a slave to fashion **3** *Jur* easement; **s. de passage** right of way

servocommande [sɛrvɔkɔmɑ̃d] **NF** servocontrol, power-assisted control, *Am* power booster

servodirection [sɛrvɔdirɛksjɔ̃] **NF** *Aut* servo steering, power steering

servofrein [sɛrvɔfrɛ̃] **NM** *Aut* servo brake, servo-assisted brake

servomécanisme [sɛrvɔmekanism] **NM** servomechanism, servosystem

servomoteur [sɛrvɔmɔtœr] **NM** servomotor

ses [se] *voir* **son**[3]

sésame [sezam] **NM 1** *Bot & Culin* sesame; **graine de s.** sesame seed; **huile de s.** sesame oil **2** *(locutions)* **S., ouvre-toi!** open, Sesame!; **le s. (ouvre-toi) de la réussite** the key to success

session [sesjɔ̃] **NF 1** *(réunion ▸ d'une assemblée)* session, sitting; **la s. de printemps du Parlement** Parliament's spring session **2** *Univ* exam period; **il a été collé à la s. de juin** he failed the June exams; **elle a eu son DEUG à la deuxième s.** she passed her DEUG in the repeat examinations *or Br* the resits; **la s. de repêchage** *ou* **de rattrapage** the repeat examinations, *Br* the resits

sesterce [sɛstɛrs] **NM** *Antiq* sestertius, sesterce

set [sɛt] **NM 1** *(objet)* **s. (de table)** *(individuel)* table mat; *(ensemble)* set of table mats **2** *Sport* set; **gagner en deux sets** to win in two sets; **balle de s.** set point **3** *Can (meubles)* **s. de chambre** bedroom suite; **s. de cuisine** set of kitchen furniture **s. de table** *(mobilier)* dining-room suite; *(pour mettre sous une assiette)* table mat

SET® [ɛsəte] **NF** *Ordinat (abrév* **secure electronic transaction**) SET®

sétacé, -e [setase] **ADJ** *Biol* setaceous

setter [setɛr] **NM** *(chien)* setter; **s. anglais/irlandais** English/Irish *or* red setter

seuil [sœj] **NM 1** *(dalle)* doorstep; *(entrée)* doorway, threshold; **franchir le s.** to cross the threshold; **sur le s.** in the doorway

2 *(début)* threshold, brink; **être au s. d'une ère nouvelle** to be on the brink of a new era; **être au s. de la mort** to be on the verge of death

3 *(limite)* threshold; **la population a atteint le s. critique d'un milliard** population has reached the critical level *or* threshold of one billion; *Écon* **le s. de pauvreté** the poverty line

4 *Psy* threshold

5 *Physiol* **s. absolu/différentiel** absolute/difference threshold; **s. de sensibilité** threshold of sensitivity *or* of response

6 *Bourse* **s. d'annonce obligatoire** disclosure threshold; **s. d'imposition** tax threshold; *Com* **s. de prix** price threshold; **s. de rentabilité/de saturation** break-even/saturation point; **atteindre le s. de rentabilité** to break even

7 *Géog* sill

SEUL, SEULE [sœl]

> **ADJ**
> - alone **1, 3, 5**
> - lonely **2**
> - mere **7**
> - on one's own **1, 3**
> - only **4, 6**
>
> **NM,F**
> - only one

ADJ 1 *(sans compagnie)* alone, on one's own; **s. au monde** *ou* **sur la terre** (all) alone in the world; **laissons-le s.** let's leave him alone *or* on his own *or* by himself; **il n'est bien que s.** he prefers his own company; **enfin seuls!** alone at last!; **nous nous sommes retrouvés seuls** we found ourselves alone (together *or* with each other); **s. à s.** *(en privé)* in private, privately; **je voudrais te parler s. à s.** I'd like to talk to you in private; **se retrouver s. à s. avec qn** to find oneself alone with sb; **elle vit seule avec sa mère** she lives alone with her mother; **un homme s. a peu de chances de réussir** *(sans aucune aide)* it's unlikely that anybody could succeed on their own; **je dois d'abord y aller seule, tu entreras après** I must go in alone *or* on my own first and then you can come in; **agir s.** to act alone *or* on one's own; **tu seras s. à défendre le budget** you'll be the only one speaking for the budget; **prends donc un verre, je n'aime pas boire s.** have a drink, I don't like drinking on my own; **elle parle toute seule** she's talking to herself; **il a bâti sa maison tout s.** he built his house all by himself; **leur entrevue ne s'est pas passée toute seule!** their meeting didn't go smoothly!; **le dîner ne se préparera pas tout s.!** dinner isn't going to make itself!; *Fam* **laisse des pommes de terre, t'es pas tout s.!** leave some potatoes, you're not the only one eating!

2 *(abandonné, esseulé)* lonely, *Am* lonesome; **se sentir s.** to feel lonely

3 *(sans partenaire, non marié)* alone, on one's own; **un homme s.** *(non accompagné)* a man on his own; *(célibataire)* a single man, a bachelor; **elle est seule avec trois enfants** she's bringing up three children on her own; **les personnes seules ne toucheront pas l'allocation** single *or* unmarried people will not be eligible for the allowance

4 *(avant le nom) (unique)* only, single, sole; **une seule pensée l'obsédait** he/she was obsessed by one idea (and one idea alone) *or* by one sole idea; **c'est l'homme d'une seule passion** he's a man with one overriding *or* ruling passion; **c'est l'homme d'une seule femme** he's a one-woman man; **une seule erreur et tout est à refaire** a single *or* one mistake and you have to start all over again; **un s. mot et tu es mort** one word and you're dead; **je n'ai été en retard qu'une seule fois** I was late only once; **pas un s..../pas une seule...** not one..., not a single...; **pas un s. élève ne l'a oublié** not one pupil has forgotten him; **un s. et même.../une seule et même...** one and the same...; **il s'agit d'une seule et même personne** they are one and the same person; **un s. et unique.../une seule et unique...** only one (and one only)...; **vous avez droit à un s. et unique essai** you may have only one attempt; **le s. et unique exemplaire** the one and only copy; **le s. problème** *ou* **la seule chose, c'est que...** the only problem *or* thing is that...; **la seule fois que je l'ai vue** the only *or* one time I saw her; **c'est la seule possibilité** it's the only possibility, there's no other possibility; **mon s. passe-temps** my only *or* sole *or* one hobby

5 *(sans autre chose)* **le numéro s.** *ou* **le s. numéro permet de retrouver le dossier** the number alone is enough to trace the file; **le vase s. vaut combien?** how much is it for just the vase?; **la propriété à elle seule leur donne de quoi vivre** the property alone brings in enough for them to live on

6 *(comme adverbe)* only; **s. Pierre a refusé** only Pierre refused, Pierre was the only one to refuse; **seuls les nouveaux n'ont pas été interrogés** only the newcomers weren't questioned

7 *(avant le nom) (simple)* mere; **la seule évocation de la scène lui donnait des frissons** the mere mention of *or* merely talking about the scene gave him/her goose pimples

NM,F 1 *(personne)* only one (person); **tu es la seule à qui je puisse me confier** you're the only one I can confide in; **je te crois mais je dois être la seule!** I believe you, thousands wouldn't!; *Fam* **tu voudrais t'arrêter de travailler? t'es pas le s.!** you'd like to stop work? you're not the only one!; *Littéraire* **tout dépend des caprices d'un s.** everything hinges on one person's whims; **pas un s. (de ses camarades) n'était prêt à l'épauler** not a single one (of his/her friends) was prepared to help him/her; **pas un s. n'a survécu** not one (of them) lived

2 *(animal, objet)* only one; **prends le chaton noir, c'est le s. qui me reste** have the black kitten, it's the only one I've got left

> Attention: ne pas confondre **alone** et **lonely** lorsqu'on traduit **seul**. Contrairement à l'adjectif **alone**, **lonely** suggère toujours un sentiment de solitude. Par ailleurs **alone** est toujours utilisé comme attribut.

seulement [sœlmɑ̃] **ADV 1** *(uniquement)* only; **il y avait s. deux personnes** there were only two people; **j'ai dit ça s. pour rire** I only meant it as a joke; **elle m'a donné s. les plus mûres** she gave me only *or* she only gave me the ripest ones; **il ne s'agit pas s. d'argent** it's not only *or* just a question of money; **non s.... mais aussi..., non s.... mais encore...** not only... but also...; **nous voulons conquérir non s. le marché européen, mais aussi** *ou* **encore des parts du marché mondial** we want not only to capture the European market, but also part of the world market (too); **non s.... mais en plus...** not only... but also...; **non s. il refuse de travailler, mais en plus il distrait les autres** not only does he refuse to do any work, but he also distracts the others

2 *(dans le temps)* **il arrive s. ce soir** he won't arrive before this evening; **il est arrivé s. ce matin** he only arrived this morning; **je viens s. de finir** I've only just finished; **et c'est s. maintenant que tu me le dis!** and you're only telling me about it now!

3 *(même)* even; **il est parti sans s. dire au revoir à ses hôtes** he left without even saying goodbye to his hosts

4 *(mais)* only, but; **je viendrais bien, s....** I'd like to come but... *or* only...; **je veux y aller, s. voilà, avec qui?** I'd love to go, but *or* only the problem is who with?

5 *Fam (pour renforcer)* **essaie s.!** just (you) try!

6 *Belg & Suisse (pour atténuer un impératif)* **faites s.** please do; **entrez s.** please, come in; **restez s.** why don't you stay

sève [sɛv] **NF 1** *Bot* sap; **sans s.** sapless **2** *(énergie)* **la s. de la jeunesse** the vigour of youth

sévère [sever] **ADJ 1** *(strict ▸ personne, caractère, règlement)* strict, severe

2 *(dur ▸ critique, verdict)* severe, harsh; **ne sois pas trop s. avec lui** don't be too hard on him

3 *(austère ▸ visage)* stern; *(▸ style, uniforme)* severe, austere, unadorned

4 *(important ▸ pertes, dégâts)* severe

ADV *Fam (gravement)* something rotten; **je déprime s. en ce moment** I'm depressed something rotten at the moment

sévèrement [severmɑ̃] **ADV 1** *(strictement)* strictly, severely **2** *(durement)* severely, harshly **3** *(gravement)* severely, seriously

sévérité [severite] **NF 1** *(d'une personne, d'un caractère, d'un règlement)* strictness, severity **2** *(d'une critique, d'un verdict)* severity, harshness **3** *(d'un visage)* sternness; *(d'un style, d'un uniforme)* severity, austerity

sévices [sevis] **NMPL être victime de s.** to suffer cruelty, to be ill-treated; **faire subir des s. à qn** to ill-treat sb; **s. sexuels** sexual abuse

Séville [sevij] **NM** Seville

sévir [32] [sevir] **VI 1** *(personne)* **si tu continues à tricher, je vais devoir s.** if you keep on cheating, I'll have to do something about it; **s. contre la fraude fiscale** to deal ruthlessly with tax evasion **2** *(fléau, épidémie)* to rage, to be rampant *or* rife, to reign supreme; *(vandales)* to wreak havoc; **la crise qui sévit actuellement** the present crisis; *Hum* **Morin ne sévira pas longtemps comme directeur à la comptabilité** Morin won't reign long as head of accounts; **c'est une idée qui sévit encore dans les milieux économiques** unfortunately the idea still has currency among economists

sevrage [səvraʒ] **NM 1** *(d'un bébé)* weaning **2** *(d'un drogué)* coming off (drugs) **3** *Hort* separation

sevrer [19] [səvre] **VT 1** *(bébé)* to wean

2 *(drogué)* **s. qn** to get sb off drugs

3 *Fig* **s. qn de qch** to deprive sb of sth; **nous avons été sevrés de musique/de liberté** we were deprived of music/of freedom

4 *Hort* to separate *(a layer)*

sèvres [sɛvr] **NM 1** *(matière)* Sèvres (china); **un service de s.** a Sèvres china service **2** *(objet)* piece of Sèvres china

sexage [sɛksaʒ] **NM** *(des poussins)* sexing

sexagénaire [sɛksaʒenɛr] **ADJ** sexagenarian; **être s.** to be in one's sixties

NMF person in his/her sixties

sex-appeal [sɛksapil] *(pl* **sex-appeals**) **NM** sex appeal; **avoir du s.** to be sexy, to have sex appeal

sexe [sɛks] **NM 1** *(caractéristique)* sex; **enfant du s. masculin/féminin** male/female child; **le s. opposé** the opposite sex; **changer de s.** to have a sex change; **le beau s.** the fair *or* the gentle sex; **le s. fort/faible** the stronger/weaker sex **2** *(parties sexuelles)* sex (organs), genitals **3 le s.** *(sexualité)* sex; **il ne pense qu'au s.** all he ever thinks about is sex

sexisme [sɛksism] **NM 1** *(idéologie)* sexism **2** *(politique)* sexual discrimination

sexiste [sɛksist] **ADJ** sexist

NMF sexist

sexologie [sɛksɔlɔʒi] **NF** sexology
sexologue [sɛksɔlɔg] **NMF** sexologist
sexothérapeute [sɛksoterapøt] **NMF** sex therapist
sex-shop [sɛksʃɔp] (*pl* **sex-shops**) **NM** sex shop
sextant [sɛkstɑ̃] **NM** sextant
sextuor [sɛkstɥɔr] **NM** sextet, sextette
sextuple [sɛkstypl] **ADJ** sextuple, six-fold
NM sextuple; **le s. (de)** *(quantité, prix)* six times as much (as); *(nombre)* six times as many (as); **le s. de sa valeur** six times its value; **120 est le s. de 20** 120 is six times 20
sextupler **[3]** [sɛkstyple] **VT s. qch** to sextuple sth, to increase sth sixfold
VI to sextuple, to increase sixfold
sextuplés, -ées [sɛkstyple] **NM,F PL** sextuplets
sexualisation [sɛksɥalizasjɔ̃] **NF** sexualization
sexualiser **[3]** [sɛksɥalize] **VT** to sexualize
sexualité [sɛksɥalite] **NF** sexuality
sexué, -e [sɛksɥe] **ADJ** *(animal)* sexed; *(reproduction)* sexual
sexuel, -elle [sɛksɥɛl] **ADJ** *(comportement)* sexual; *(organes, éducation, hormone)* sex *(avant n)*; **l'acte s.** the sex *or* the sexual act
sexuellement [sɛksɥɛlmɑ̃] **ADV** sexually; **maladie s. transmissible** sexually transmitted disease
sexy [sɛksi] **ADJ INV** *Fam* sexy
seyait *etc voir* **seoir**
seyant, -e [sɛjɑ̃, -ɑ̃t] **ADJ** becoming; **peu s.** unbecoming; **sa nouvelle coiffure est peu seyante** his/her new hairstyle doesn't suit him/her
Seychelles [sɛʃɛl] **NFPL les (îles) S.** the Seychelles
SF [ɛsɛf] **NF** *Fam (abrév* **science fiction**) sci-fi, SF
SGAO [ɛsʒeao] **NM** *Ordinat (abrév* **système de gestion assisté par ordinateur**) computer-assisted management system
SGBD [ɛsʒebede] **NM** *Ordinat (abrév* **système de gestion de base de données**) DBMS
SGBDR [ɛsʒedebeɛr] **NM** *Ordinat (abrév* **système de gestion de bases de données relationnelles**) RDBMS
shah [ʃa] **NM** shah, Shah
shake-hand [ʃɛkɑ̃d] **NM INV** *Arch & Hum* handshake
shaker [ʃɛkœr] **NM** (cocktail) shaker
shakespearien, -enne [ʃɛkspirjɛ̃, -ɛn] **ADJ** Shakespearean, Shakespearian
shako [ʃako] **NM** shako
shampoing [ʃɑ̃pwɛ̃] **NM 1** *(produit)* shampoo; **s. pour cheveux secs/gras** shampoo for dry/greasy hair; **s. antipelliculaire** anti-dandruff shampoo; **s. sec** dry shampoo; **s. traitant** medicated shampoo; **s. pour moquettes** carpet shampoo **2** *(lavage)* shampoo; **se faire un s.** to shampoo *or* to wash one's hair; **faire un s. à qn** to shampoo sb('s hair), to wash sb's hair
shampooiner **[3]** [ʃɑ̃pwine] **VT** to shampoo
shampooineur, -euse [ʃɑ̃pwinœr, -øz] **NM,F 1** *(personne)* shampooer **2** *(machine)* carpet cleaner *or* shampooer
shampouing [ʃɑ̃pwɛ̃] = **shampoing**
shampouiner [ʃɑ̃pwine] = **shampooiner**
shampouineur, -euse [ʃɑ̃pwinœr, -øz] = **shampooineur**
shantoung, shantung [ʃɑ̃tuŋ] **NM** *Tex* shantung (silk)
shareware [ʃɛrwɛr] **NM** *Ordinat* shareware
sharia [ʃarja] = **charia**
sheik [ʃɛk] **NM** sheik
shekel [ʃekɛl] **NM** *(monnaie)* shekel
shérif [ʃerif] **NM 1** *(aux États-Unis)* sheriff **2** *(en Grande-Bretagne)* sheriff *(representative of the Crown)*
sherpa [ʃɛrpa] **NM** *(guide)* sherpa
• **Sherpas** **NMPL** *(peuple)* Sherpas
sherry [ʃeri] (*pl* **sherrys** *ou* **sherries**) **NM** sherry
shetland [ʃɛtlɑ̃d] **NM 1** *Tex* Shetland (wool) **2** *(pullover)* Shetland jumper **3** *Zool* Shetland pony
shilling [ʃiliŋ] **NM** shilling
shimmy [ʃimi] **NM** *Aut* shimmy
shinto [ʃinto], **shintoïsme** [ʃintɔism] **NM** Shinto, Shintoism
shintoïste [ʃintɔist] **ADJ** Shintoist
NMF Shintoist
shipchandler [ʃipʃɑ̃dlœr] **NM** ship chandler
shit [ʃit] **NM** *Fam Arg drogue* hash
shocking [ʃɔkiŋ] **ADJ INV** *Hum* shocking
shogoun [ʃɔgun] **NM** shogun
shoot [ʃut] **NM 1** *Sport* shot **2** *très Fam Arg drogue (injection de drogue)* fix, shot; **se faire un s.** to shoot up, to jack up
shooter **[3]** [ʃute] **VI** *Sport* to shoot
VT *Sport* **s. un penalty** to take a penalty
VPR se shooter *très Fam Arg drogue (drogué)* to shoot up, to jack up; **se s. à l'héroïne** to shoot *or* to mainline heroin; *Hum* **il se shoote au café** he has to have his fix of coffee
shopping [ʃɔpiŋ] **NM** shopping; **faire du s.** to go shopping; **je fais toujours mon s. chez eux** I always shop there
short [ʃɔrt] **NM** (pair of) shorts; **être en s.** to be in *or* wearing shorts
show [ʃo] **NM 1** *(spectacle)* show; **s. aérien** air show **2** *(d'un homme politique)* performance; **le s. télévisé du Premier ministre** the Prime Minister's TV performance
show-biz [ʃobiz] **NM INV** *Fam* showbiz
show-business [ʃobiznɛs] **NM INV** show business
showroom [ʃorum] **NM** showroom
shrapnel, shrapnell [ʃrapnɛl] **NM** shrapnel
shunt [ʃœt] **NM 1** *Élec* shunt; **moteur s.** shunt motor **2** *Méd* shunt
shunter **[3]** [ʃœte] **VT 1** *Élec* to shunt **2** *Fam Fig (court-circuiter* ▸ *personne)* to bypass
si[1] [si] **NM INV** *Mus* B; *(chanté)* si, ti

SI[2] [si]

ADV
- so **1**
- however **2**
- yes **4**
- such **1**
- as **3**

CONJ
- if **1, 2, 5–10**
- what about **3**
- when **9**
- what if **4**
- whether **6**

ADV 1 *(tellement* ▸ *avec un adjectif attribut, un adverbe, un nom)* so; (▸ *avec un adjectif épithète)* such; **elle est si belle** she's so beautiful; **il est si mignon!** he's (ever) so sweet!; **ce n'est pas si facile que ça** it isn't as easy as (all) that; **elle est si femme** she's so womanly; **je la vois si peu** I see so little of her, I see her so rarely; **ça fait si mal!** it hurts so much!; **elle a de si beaux cheveux!** she has such beautiful hair!; *Ironique* **il est prétentieux – oh, si peu!** he's pretentious – oh isn't he just *or* I don't know what you mean!; **si... que...** so… that…; **c'est si petit qu'on ne peut le voir à l'œil nu** it's so small that it can't be seen with the naked eye
2 *(exprimant la concession)* however; **si aimable soit-il...** however nice he may be...; **si occupé soit-il, il n'en reste pas moins aimable** however busy he is, he's always friendly; **si vous le vexez si peu que ce soit, il fond en larmes** if you upset him even the slightest bit, he bursts into tears
3 *(dans une comparaison)* **si... que...** as… as…; **elle n'est pas si blonde que sa sœur** she's not as blonde as her sister; **il n'est pas si bête qu'il en a l'air** he's not as stupid as he seems
4 *(en réponse affirmative)* yes; **ce n'est pas fermé? – si** isn't it closed? – yes (it is); **tu ne me crois pas? – si(, je te crois)** don't you believe me? – yes (I do); **ça n'a pas d'importance – si, ça en a!** it doesn't matter – it DOES *or* yes it does!; **tu n'aimes pas ça? – si, si!** don't you like that? – oh yes I DO!; **je ne veux pas que tu me rembourses – si, si, voici ce que je te dois** I don't want you to pay me back – no, I insist, here's what I owe you; **si, si, acceptez!** DO accept!, oh but you MUST accept!; **je te dérange, si, si, je le vois bien!** I'm disturbing you, don't say I'm not, I can tell!; **tu ne l'as pas jeté tout de même? – eh si!** you didn't throw it away, did you? – yes I did!; **je n'y arriverai jamais – mais si!** I'll never manage – of course you will!; **le spectacle n'est pas gratuit – il paraît que si** the show isn't free – apparently it is; **vous n'allez pas me disqualifier? – que si!** you're not going to disqualify me, are you? – oh yes we are!; *Littéraire* **ne voyez-vous pas un moyen de parvenir à vos fins? – si fait!** can you not see a way whereby you might succeed? – indeed I can!
CONJ 1 *(exprimant une condition)* if; **si tu veux, on y va** we'll go if you want; **si vous approchez, je crie** if you come near me I'll scream; **si je m'en sors, je te revaudrai ça** if I get out of this, I'll repay you for it; **si tu ne réfléchis pas par toi-même et si** *ou* **que tu crois tout ce qu'on te dit...** if you don't think for yourself and you believe everything people tell you...; **je ne lui dirai que si tu es d'accord** I'll tell him/her only if you agree, I won't tell him/her unless you agree; **s'ils ont quelque chose à dire, qu'ils le disent** if they have something to say, let them say it; **si tu oses...!** *(ton menaçant)* don't you dare!; **avez-vous des enfants? si oui, remplissez le cadre ci-dessous** do you have any children? if yes, fill in the box below
2 *(exprimant une hypothèse)* if; **si tu venais de bonne heure, on pourrait finir avant midi** if you came early we would be able to finish before midday; **s'il m'arrivait quelque chose, prévenez John** should anything happen to me *or* if anything should happen to me, call John; **si j'avais le temps, je viendrais volontiers avec vous** if I had the time I'd love to come with you; **ah toi, si je ne me retenais pas...!** I just count yourself lucky I'm restraining myself!; **si l'on croyait tout ce qu'on lit dans les journaux!** if we believed everything we read in the papers!; **si j'avais su, je me serais méfié** if I had known *or* had I known, I would have been more cautious; **s'il avait vécu** *ou Littéraire* **s'il eut vécu de notre temps, il eût été sénateur** if he had lived in our time, he would have been a senator
3 *(exprimant une éventualité)* what if; **et si tu te trompais?** what if you were wrong?
4 *(exprimant une suggestion)* what about; **et si on jouait aux cartes?** what about playing cards?
5 *(exprimant un souhait, un regret)* **ah, si j'étais plus jeune!** I wish *or* if only I were younger!; **si ça pouvait marcher!** if only it worked!; **si seulement il avait accepté!** if only he'd accepted!
6 *(dans l'interrogation indirecte)* if, whether; **dites-moi si vous venez** tell me if *or* whether you're coming; *Littéraire* **est-ce bien lui? ou si mes yeux me trompent!** is it he, or do my eyes deceive me?
7 *(introduisant une complétive)* if, that; **je dois vérifier si tout est en ordre** I must check if *or* whether *or* that everything is in order; **ne sois pas surprise s'il a échoué** don't be surprised that *or* if he failed
8 *(introduisant une explication)* if; **si quelqu'un a le droit de se plaindre, c'est bien moi!** if anyone has reason to complain, it's me!; *Fam* **c'est de ta faute si ça a raté** it's your fault if it didn't work; **si ça ne répond pas, c'est qu'il n'est pas là** if there's no answer, it's because he's not there
9 *(exprimant la répétition)* if, when; **si l'on excite le nerf, le muscle se contracte** if *or* when the nerve is stimulated, the muscle contracts; **si je prends une initiative, elle la désapprouve** whenever *or* every time I take the initiative, she disapproves (of it)
10 *(exprimant la concession, l'opposition)* **comment faire des économies si je gagne le salaire minimum?** how can I save if I'm only earning the minimum wage?; **si elle fut exigeante avec nous, elle l'était encore plus avec elle-même** if she was demanding with us, she was still more so with herself; **si son premier roman a été un succès, le second a été éreinté par la critique** though his/her first novel was a success, the second was slated by the critics
11 *(emploi exclamatif)* **tu penses s'il était déçu/heureux!** you can imagine how disappointed/happy he was!; **tu as l'intention de continuer? – si j'ai l'intention de continuer? bien sûr!** do you intend to go on? – of course I do *or* I certainly do *or* I do indeed!; **si ce n'est pas mignon à cet âge-là!** aren't they cute at that age!; **si je m'attendais à te voir ici!** well, I (certainly) didn't expect to meet you here!, fancy meeting you here!
NM INV *Prov* **avec des si, on mettrait Paris en bou-**

teille if ifs and ands were pots and pans, there'd be no trade for tinkers

• **si bien que** CONJ *(de telle sorte que)* so; **il ne sait pas lire une carte, si bien qu'on s'est perdus** he can't read a map, and so we got lost

• **si ce n'est** PRÉP **1** *(pour rectifier)* if not; **ça a duré une bonne heure, si ce n'est deux** it lasted at least an hour, if not two **2** *(excepté)* apart from, except; **tout vous convient?– oui, si ce n'est le prix** is everything to your satisfaction? – yes, apart from *or* except the price; **si ce n'était sa timidité, c'est un garçon très agréable** he's a nice young man, if a little shy

• **si ce n'est que** CONJ apart from the fact that, except (for the fact) that; **il n'a pas de régime, si ce n'est qu'il ne doit pas boire d'alcool** he has no special diet, except that he mustn't drink alcohol

• **si tant est que** CONJ provided that; **on se retrouvera à 18 heures, si tant est que l'avion arrive à l'heure** we'll meet at 6 p.m. provided (that) *or* if the plane arrives on time; **essaie, si tant est que tu en as le courage** try, if you've got the courage (that is); **si tant est qu'il nous ait** *ou* **a vus** if he saw us at all

---

Siam [sjam] NM **le S.** Siam; **au S.** in Siam

siamois, -e [sjamwa, -az] ADJ **1** *Géog* Siamese **2** *Méd* Siamese; **frères s.** (male) Siamese twins; **sœurs siamoises** (female) Siamese twins

NM **1** *(langue)* Siamese **2** *(chat)* Siamese (cat)

• **Siamois, -e** NM,F Siamese; **les S.** the Siamese

siau [sjo] NM *Can Fam* bucket[□], pail[□]

Sibérie [siberi] NF **la S.** Siberia

sibérien, -enne [siberjɛ̃, -ɛn] ADJ Siberian; **il fait un froid s.** it's bitterly cold

• **Sibérien, -enne** NM,F Siberian

sibilance [sibilɑ̃s] NF *Méd* **s. respiratoire** wheezing

sibilant, -e [sibilɑ̃, -ɑ̃t] ADJ sibilant, hissing

sibylle [sibil] NF sibyl

sibyllin, -e [sibilɛ̃, -in] ADJ **1** *Littéraire (mystérieux)* enigmatic, cryptic **2** *Myth* sibylic, sibyllic **3** *Antiq* **livres sibyllins** Sibylline Books; **oracles sibyllins** Sibylline Prophecies

sic [sik] ADV sic

SICAF, Sicaf [sikaf] NF *Bourse & Fin (abrév* **société d'investissement à capital fixe***)* closed-end investment company

SICAV, Sicav [sikav] NF *Bourse & Fin (abrév* **société d'investissement à capital variable***)* **1** *(société)* OEIC, *Br* ≃ unit trust, *Am* ≃ mutual fund; **S. actions** equity-based unit trust; **S. éthique** ethical investment fund; **S. monétaire** money-based unit trust; **S. obligataire** bond-based unit trust **2** *(action)* = share in an open-ended investment trust

siccatif, -ive [sikatif, -iv] ADJ siccative

NM (paint) dryer, siccative

Sicile [sisil] NF **la S.** Sicily

sicilien, -enne [sisiljɛ̃, -ɛn] ADJ Sicilian

NM *(langue)* Sicilian

• **Sicilien, -enne** NM,F Sicilian

SIDA, Sida [sida] NM *Méd (abrév* **syndrome immuno-déficitaire acquis***)* Aids, AIDS; **S. déclaré** full-blown Aids

sidatique [sidatik] *Péj* = **sidéen**

side-car [sidkar, sajdkar] *(pl* **side-cars***)* NM **1** *(habitacle)* sidecar **2** *(moto)* motorbike and sidecar

sidéen, -enne [sideɛ̃, -ɛn] ADJ suffering from Aids

NM,F Aids sufferer

sidéral, -e, -aux, -ales [sideral, -o] ADJ sidereal

sidérant, -e [siderɑ̃, -ɑ̃t] ADJ *Fam* staggering, mind-blowing

sidéré, -e [sidere] ADJ *Fam (abasourdi)* flabbergasted, staggered

sidérer [18] [sidere] VT **1** *Fam (abasourdir)* to stagger; **j'ai été sidéré d'apprendre cela** I was staggered to hear that **2** *Méd* to siderate

sidérose [sideroz] NF **1** *Minér* siderite **2** *Méd* siderosis

sidérurgie [sideryrʒi] NF **1** *(technique)* (iron and) steel metallurgy **2** *(industrie)* (iron and) steel industry

sidérurgique [sideryrʒik] ADJ (iron and) steel *(avant n)*; **usine s.** steelworks, steel factory

sidérurgiste [sideryrʒist] NMF **1** *(ouvrier)* steel worker **2** *(industriel)* steelworks owner

siècle [sjɛkl] NM **1** *(cent ans)* century; **l'église a plus de quatre siècles** the church is more than four centuries old; **au début du s.** at the turn of the century; **au IIème s. avant/après J.-C.** in the 2nd century BC/AD; **les écrivains du seizième s.** sixteenth-century writers **2** *(époque)* age; **vivre avec son s.** to keep up with the times; **c'est un homme de son s./d'un autre s.** he's a man of his time(s)/he belongs to another age *or* another century; *Fam* **ça fait des siècles que je ne suis pas allé à la patinoire** I haven't been to the ice rink for ages; **l'affaire du s.** the bargain of the century; **le s. des Lumières** the Enlightenment, the Age of Reason; **de s. en s.** through *or* down the ages **3** *Rel* **le s.** worldly life, the world; **vivre dans le s.** to live in the world; **abandonner le s.** to leave one's worldly life behind; **pour les siècles des siècles** for ever and ever

sied *etc voir* **seoir**

siège [sjɛʒ] NM **1** *(chaise ▸ gén)* seat; *(▸ de cocher)* box; **prenez donc un s.** (do) take a seat, do sit down; **une chaise à s. en cuir** a leather-seated chair; **le s. des W-C** the toilet seat; *Aut* **s. avant/arrière/baquet** front/back/bucket seat; *Aut* **s. basculant** tilting seat; *Aviat* **s. éjectable** ejector seat; **s. inclinable** reclining seat; **s. du passager** passenger seat; *Aut* **s. rehausseur** child booster seat; **s. de voiture pour bébé** baby car seat

2 *Pol* seat; **perdre/gagner des sièges** to lose/to win seats; **s. parlementaire** seat in Parliament; **s. vacant** *ou* **à pourvoir** vacant seat

3 *(centre ▸ gén)* seat; *(▸ d'un parti)* headquarters; **le s. du gouvernement** the seat of government; **s. administratif** administrative headquarters; *Com* **s. d'exploitation** (company) works; **s. social** registered *or* head office; **la société a son s. (social) à Nanterre** the company's head office is in Nanterre

4 *Mil* siege; **faire le s. d'une ville, mettre le s. devant une ville** to lay siege to *or* to besiege a town; **lever le s.** to raise a siege; *Fig (partir)* to make tracks

5 *Méd* **l'enfant s'est présenté par le s.** it was a breech birth

6 *Jur* **le s.** the bench

7 *Rel* **s. épiscopal** (episcopal) see

8 *Tech (d'une valve)* seating

siéger [22] [sjeʒe] VI **1** *(député)* to sit; **s. au Parlement** to have a seat *or* to sit in Parliament; **s. au tribunal** to be on the bench; **s. à un comité/au conseil d'administration** to sit on a committee/ on the board

2 *(assemblée ▸ tenir séance)* to be in session

3 *(avoir son siège)* to be based; **l'UNESCO siège à Paris** UNESCO's headquarters are in Paris

4 *(se trouver)* to be located; **chercher où siège la difficulté/l'infection** to seek to locate the difficulty/the infection

sien [sjɛ̃] *(f* **sienne** [sjɛn], *mpl* **siens** [sjɛ̃], *fpl* **siennes** [sjɛn]) ADJ **il a fait sienne cette maxime** he made this maxim his own; *Littéraire* **une sienne cousine** a cousin of his/hers

• **le sien** *(f* **la sienne**, *mpl* **les siens**, *fpl* **les siennes***)* PRON *(possesseur masculin)* his; *(possesseur féminin)* hers; *(en insistant)* his/her own; *(en se référant à un objet, à un animal)* its; **j'ai pris ma voiture et lui la sienne** I took my car and he took his; **elle n'en a pas besoin, elle a le s.** she doesn't need it, she has her own; **chacun doit acheter la sienne** everyone must buy their own; **elle a pris une valise qui n'était pas la sienne** she took a suitcase that wasn't hers *or* that didn't belong to her; **les deux siens** his/her two, the two *or* both of his/ hers; *Fam* **le s. de bébé est plus intelligent!** his/her baby is more intelligent![□]; *Fam* **à la sienne!** *(en buvant)* let's drink to him/her!; **y mettre du s.** *(faire un effort)* to make an effort; *(être compréhensif)* to be understanding

• **les siens** NMPL one's family and friends; **Jacques a encore fait des siennes** Jacques has (gone and) done it again; **ma voiture ne cesse de faire des siennes!** my car's always playing up!

Sienne [sjɛn] NM Siena

siéra *etc voir* **seoir**

sierra [sjera] NF sierra; **la s. Nevada** the Sierra Nevada

Sierra Leone [sjeraleɔn] NF *Géog* **la S.** Sierra Leone

sieste [sjɛst] NF *(repos)* (afternoon) nap *or* rest; **faire la s.** to have *or* to take a nap (in the afternoon); **faire une petite s.** to have a little nap; **l'heure de la s. en Espagne** siesta time in Spain

sieur [sjœr] NM **1** *Jur* **le s. Roux** Mr Roux **2** *Fam Hum* **le s. Dupond** old Dupond

sifflant, -e [siflɑ̃, -ɑ̃t] ADJ **1** *(respiration)* hissing, whistling, wheezing **2** *Ling* sibilant

• **sifflante** NF **1** *Rad* sibilance **2** *Ling* sibilant

sifflard [siflar] NM *Fam* (dried) sausage[□]

sifflement [sifləmɑ̃] NM **1** *(action ▸ gén)* whistling *(UNCOUNT)*; *(▸ d'un serpent, de la vapeur)* hiss, hissing *(UNCOUNT)*; *(▸ d'un fouet)* swish, swishing *(UNCOUNT)*; *(▸ d'un asthmatique)* wheezing *(UNCOUNT)*; **entendre le s. du vent dans les arbres** to hear the wind whistling through the trees; **les sifflements du public mécontent** the hissing *or* the booing of the angry crowd; **elle ignora les sifflements admiratifs des maçons** she ignored the builders' wolf whistles **2** *(bruit)* whistle; **s. d'oreilles** ringing in the ears

siffler [3] [sifle] VI **1** *(serpent)* to hiss; *(oiseau)* to whistle; *Fig* **s. comme un merle** *ou* **comme un pinson** to sing like a lark

2 *(personne)* to whistle; *(gendarme, arbitre)* to blow one's whistle

3 *(respirer difficilement)* to wheeze

4 *(vent, train, bouilloire)* to whistle; **les balles sifflaient de tous côtés** bullets were whistling all around us

VT **1** *(chanson)* to whistle

2 *(chien, personne, taxi)* to whistle for; **s. les filles** to (wolf-)whistle at girls; *Fam* **je me suis fait s. (par la police)** I've been pulled up (by the police)

3 *(sujet: gendarme)* to blow one's whistle at; *(sujet: arbitre)* to whistle for; **s. la mi-temps** to blow the half-time whistle, to blow the whistle for half-time; **s. un penalty** to blow the whistle for a penalty

4 *(orateur, pièce)* to hiss, to boo, to catcall

5 *Fam (boire)* to sink, to down, to knock back

VPR **se siffler il s'est sifflé un litre de rouge à lui tout seul** he sank *or* downed *or* knocked back a litre of red wine on his own

sifflet [siflɛ] NM **1** *(instrument)* whistle; *Naut* pipe; **donner un coup de s.** to (blow the) whistle; **démarrez au coup de s.** start when you hear the whistle *or* when the whistle blows; *Sport* **donner le coup de s. final** to blow the final whistle; *Naut* **s. de brume** fog whistle; **s. à vapeur** steam whistle **2** *(sifflement)* whistle; **sifflets** *(huées)* hisses, catcalls; **quitter la scène sous les sifflets** to be booed off the stage

siffleur, -euse [siflœr, -øz] ADJ *(oiseau)* whistling; *(serpent)* hissing

NM,F *(à un spectacle)* catcaller, heckler

NM *Orn* wigeon, widgeon

siffleux [siflø] NM *Can (marmotte)* groundhog, woodchuck

sifflotement [siflɔtmɑ̃] NM whistling *(UNCOUNT)*

siffloter [3] [siflɔte] VT **s. qch** *(doucement)* to whistle sth to oneself; *(gaiement)* to whistle sth happily

VI *(doucement)* to whistle to oneself; *(gaiement)* to whistle away happily

sigillaire [siʒilɛr] ADJ **anneau s.** signet ring

sigillé, -e [siʒile] ADJ *Archéol* sigillate, sigillated

sigisbée [siʒizbe] NM *Littéraire* escort; **ses sigisbées** her gallant retinue

sigle [sigl] NM abbreviation, initials; *(acronyme)* acronym

sigma [sigma] NM **1** *(lettre)* sigma **2** *Chim* sigma bond

signal, -aux [siɲal, -o] NM **1** *(signe)* **au s., tous se levèrent** on the given signal *or* when the signal was given they all stood up; **donner le s. du départ** to give the signal for departure; *Sport* to give the starting signal; **envoyer un s. de détresse** to send out a distress signal *or* an SOS

2 *(annonce)* signal; **cette loi a été le s. d'un changement de politique** this law signalled *or* was the signal for a shift in policy

3 *(dispositif)* signal; **s. d'alarme/d'incendie** alarm/fire signal; **actionner le s. d'alarme** to pull the alarm cord; **s. d'alerte** warning (signal); **s. d'appel** *Tél* call waiting; *Tech* call *or* calling signal; **s. d'arrêt** stop sign; **s. audio** audio signal; **s. d'avertissement** *ou* **avertisseur** warning signal; **s. codé** coded signal; **s. de danger** warning sign; *Rad & TV* **s. de départ** in-cue; **s. de détresse** distress *or* SOS signal; *Rad & Tél* **s. horaire** time signal; *TV* **s. d'image** picture signal; **s. lumineux** light signal; **signaux lumineux** traffic lights; **s. optique** visible *or* visual signal; **s. radiophonique** radio signal; **signaux routiers** road signs; **s. son** audio signal; **s. sonore** tone, beep; *(pour avertir)* warning beep; *Rad & TV* **s. de sortie** out-cue; **s. stéréo** stereo signal

4 *Naut* signal; **s. à bras** hand signal; **s. de brume** fog signal; **signaux de port** port *or* harbour signals

5 *Rail* signal; **s. à l'arrêt** signal at danger; **s. d'arrêt** danger signal; **s. avancé** *ou* **à distance** distant signal; **s. de chemin de fer** railway *or Am* railroad signal; **s. d'entrée** home signal; **s. fermé/ouvert** on/off signal

6 *Ordinat & Tél* signal; **s. analogique/numérique** analog/digital signal; *Ordinat* **s. d'invitation à transmettre** proceed-to-send *or Am* start-dialing signal

7 *Écon* **s. du marché** market indicator

signalé, -e [siɲale] **ADJ** *Littéraire (remarquable)* signal, notable

signalement [siɲalmɑ̃] **NM 1** description, particulars; **donner le s. de son agresseur** to describe one's attacker **2** *Jur* reporting

signaler **[3]** [siɲale] **VT 1** *(faire remarquer ▸ faute, détail)* to point out, to indicate, to draw attention to; *(▸ événement important)* to draw attention to; *(▸ accident, cambriolage)* to report; *(▸ changement d'adresse)* to notify; **la serrure est cassée, il faudra le s.** the lock's broken, we'll have to report it; **je l'ai signalé au directeur** I mentioned it to the manager; **s. qch à la police** to report sth to the police; **on signale des secousses telluriques dans la région** there are reports of earth tremors in the area; *TV & Rad* **on me signale que le ministre est à présent en ligne** I'm being told that the minister is now on air; **rien à s.** nothing to report; **à s. encore, une exposition à Beaubourg** another event worth mentioning is an exhibition at Beaubourg; **permettez-moi de vous s. qu'il est interdit de...** allow me to draw your attention to the fact that *or* to point out that it's forbidden to...; **il est déjà onze heures, je te signale!** for your information, it's already eleven o'clock!; **son ouvrage n'est signalé nulle part dans votre thèse** his/her book is not mentioned anywhere in your thesis; **c'est lui qui m'a signalé ce CD** he was the one who told me about this CD

2 *(sujet: drapeau)* to signal; *(sujet: sonnerie)* to signal; *(sujet: panneau indicateur)* to signpost, to point to; **passage à niveau non signalé** unmarked level crossing; **le village n'est même pas signalé au croisement** the village is not even signposted *or* there's not even a signpost for the village at the junction; **la chapelle n'est pas signalée sur le plan** the chapel isn't indicated *or* marked on the map; **il n'a pas signalé qu'il tournait** he didn't signal *or* indicate that he was turning

3 *(dénoter)* to indicate, to be the sign of; **c'est le symptôme qui nous signale la présence du virus** this symptom tells us that the virus is present

4 *Ordinat (marquer)* to flag up

VPR se signaler 1 se s. à l'attention de qn to draw sb's attention to oneself; **je me permets de me s. à votre attention** I would like to draw your attention to my case **2** *(se distinguer)* **le mâle se signale par son long bec** the male is recognizable by its long beak; **elle ne s'est jamais signalée par quoi que ce soit** she's never done anything remarkable; **elle se signale surtout par son absence** she's remarkable mostly by her absence

signalétique [siɲaletik] **ADJ** *(plaque)* descriptive, identification *(avant n)*

NF 1 *(étude des signaux)* signaletics *(singulier)* **2** *(signalisation)* signals

signaleur [siɲalœr] **NM 1** *Mil* signaller **2** *Rail* signalman

signalisation [siɲalizasjɔ̃] **NF 1** *(matériel ▸ ferroviaire)* signals; **s. aérienne** markings and beacons; *Rail* **s. automatique** automatic signalling; **s. maritime** naval signalling; **s. routière** *(sur la chaussée)* (road) markings; *(panneaux et feux)* road signs and traffic lights **2** *(aménagement)* **faire la s. d'une section de route** to mark out and signpost a stretch of road; **faire la s. d'une section de voie ferrée** to put signals along a stretch of railway line; **faire la s. d'une piste aérienne** to mark out a runway

signaliser **[3]** [siɲalize] **VT** *(route)* to provide with roadsigns and markings; *(voie ferrée)* to equip with signals; *(piste d'aéroport)* to provide with markings and beacons; **bien/mal signalisé** *(route)* been well/badly signposted

signataire [siɲatɛr] **ADJ** signatory

NMF signatory

signature [siɲatyr] **NF 1** *(signe)* signature; **elle a apposé sa s. au bas de la lettre** she signed the letter at the bottom of the page; **il ne manque plus que votre s. sur le contrat** it only remains for you to sign *or Sout* to put your signature to the contract; *Jur* **avoir la s.** to be an authorized signatory *(on behalf of a company)*; **pour s.** *(sur lettre)* for signature; **s. collective** joint signature; **s. électronique** *ou* **numérique** e-signature, digital signature; **s. sociale** signature of the company

2 *(marque distinctive)* signature; **cet attentat à la bombe porte leur s.** this bomb attack bears their mark *or* their imprint

3 *(artiste)* **les plus grandes signatures de la mode sont représentées dans le défilé** the biggest names in fashion are represented on the catwalk

4 *(acte)* signing; **vous serez payé à la s. du contrat** you'll be paid once the contract has been signed

5 *Typ* signature

6 *Mktg* **s. musicale publicitaire** (advertising) jingle

SIGNE [siɲ]

- sign **1, 2, 4, 6**
- gesture **1**
- mark **3, 5**

NM 1 *(geste)* sign, gesture; **parler par signes** to communicate by sign language *or* by signs; **faire un s. à qn** to make a sign *or* to signal to sb; **faire un s. de tête à qn** *(affirmatif)* to nod to sb; *(négatif)* to shake one's head at sb; **faire un s. de la main à qn** *(pour saluer, pour attirer l'attention)* to wave to sb; **agiter la main en s. d'adieu** to wave goodbye; **elle me fit approcher d'un s. du doigt** she beckoned to me to come nearer; **faire s. à qn** to signal to sb; **il m'a fait s. d'entrer** he beckoned me in; **il m'a fait s. de sortir** he signalled to me to go out; **le douanier nous a fait s. de passer** the customs officer waved us through; **fais-lui s. de se taire** signal (to) him/her to be quiet; **faire s. que oui** to nod (in agreement); **faire s. que non** *(de la tête)* to shake one's head (in refusal); *(du doigt)* to shake one's finger; *Fig* **quand vous serez à Paris, faites-moi s.** when you're in Paris, let me know; *Rel* **s. de la croix** sign of the cross; **faire un s. de croix** *ou* **le s. de la croix** to cross oneself, to make the sign of the cross

2 *(indication)* sign; **c'est un s.** *(mauvais)* that's ominous; *(bon)* that's a good sign; **c'est s. de pluie/de beau temps** it's a sign of rain/of good weather; **c'est s. que...** it's a sign that...; **il ne nous a pas téléphoné, c'est s. que tout va bien** he hasn't phoned us, it means *or* it's a sign that everything's all right; **c'est s. qu'il est coupable** it shows *or* it's a sign that he's guilty; **c'est bon s.** it's a good sign, *Sout* it augurs well; **c'est mauvais s.** it's a bad sign, it's ominous; **il n'y a aucun s. d'amélioration** there's no sign of (any) improvement; **un s. des temps** a sign of the times; **il n'a pas donné s. de vie depuis janvier** there's been no sign of him since January; **donner des signes d'impatience** to give *or* to show signs of impatience; **la voiture donne des signes de fatigue** the car is beginning to show its age; **s. annonciateur** *ou* **avant-coureur** *ou* **précurseur** forerunner, portent

3 *(marque)* mark; *Admin* **signes particuliers** distinguishing marks; **signes particuliers: néant** *(sur carte d'identité, sur passeport)* distinguishing marks: none

4 *Ling, Math, Méd & Mus* sign; **s. d'égalité** *ou* **d'équivalence** equals sign; **s. moins/plus** minus/plus sign

5 *Typ* **s. de correction** proofreading mark *or* symbol; **s. d'insertion** insert mark; **s. de paragraphe** section mark; **s. de ponctuation** punctuation mark

6 *Astrol* **s. (du zodiaque)** sign (of the zodiac); **tu es de quel s.?** what sign are you?; **s. d'air/de terre/d'eau/de feu** air/earth/water/fire sign

• **en signe de** **PRÉP** as a sign *or* as a mark of; **en s. de respect** as a sign *or* as a mark of respect

• **sous le signe de** **PRÉP 1** *Astrol* under the sign of; **né sous le s. du Cancer** born under the sign of Cancer **2** *Fig* **la réunion s'est tenue sous le s. de la bonne humeur** the atmosphere at the meeting was good-humoured

signer **[3]** [siɲe] **VT 1** *(chèque, formulaire, lettre)* to sign; *(pétition)* to sign, to put one's name to; **s. son nom** to sign one's name; **c'est écrit "je reviens" et c'est signé Paul** it says "I'll be back" and it's signed Paul; **elle signe toujours "Julie B"** she always signs herself "Julie B"; **s. ici** (please) sign here; *Fig* **s. son arrêt de mort** to sign one's (own) death warrant

2 *(laisser sa marque personnelle sur)* to sign, to put one's signature to; **une veste signée Prada** a jacket by Prada, a Prada jacket; **en étranglant sa victime, il a signé son crime** by strangling his victim, he put his signature to the crime; **c'est signé!** no prizes for guessing who did that!; *Fam* **cette pagaille, c'est signé Maud!** this mess has Maud written all over it!

3 *(officialiser ▸ contrat, traité)* to sign; **nous allons s. un accord commercial avec Dandy** we're going to sign a commercial agreement with Dandy; *Ftbl* **il a signé un contrat de deux ans avec Marseille** he's signed up with Marseilles for two years

4 *(être l'auteur de ▸ argenterie)* to hallmark; *(▸ pièce, film, chanson)* to write, to be the author of; *(▸ tableau)* to sign; *(▸ ligne de vêtements)* to design; **elle a signé les meilleures chansons de l'époque** she wrote all the best songs of that era; **il a signé ses derniers tableaux d'un pseudonyme** he signed his latest pictures with a pseudonym

5 *(dédicacer ▸ livre)* to sign copies of; **elle signera son livre demain** she will be signing copies of her book tomorrow

VI 1 *(tracer un signe)* to sign; **s. d'une croix/de son sang** to sign with a cross/in one's blood; **s. de son nom** to sign one's name **2** *(établir un acte officiel)* to sign; **nous signons demain pour la maison** we're signing (the papers) for the house tomorrow **3** *(s'exprimer par le langage des signes)* to sign

VPR se signer to cross oneself, to make the sign of the cross

signet [siɲɛ] **NM** *(d'un livre, sur une page Web)* bookmark; *Ordinat* **créer un s. sur une page** to bookmark a page

signifiant [siɲifjɑ̃] **ADJ** *Littéraire (plein de sens)* meaningful

NM *Ling* **le s.** the signifier

significatif, -ive [siɲifikatif, -iv] **ADJ 1** *(riche de sens ▸ remarque, geste, symbole)* significant; *(▸ regard)* significant, meaningful; **de façon significative** significantly **2** *(révélateur)* **s. de** revealing *or* suggestive of; **c'est très s. de son caractère/de ses goûts** it says a lot about his/her character/taste **3** *(important ▸ écart, différence, changement)* significant

signification [siɲifikasjɔ̃] **NF 1** *(sens ▸ d'un terme, d'une phrase, d'un symbole)* meaning, *Sout* signification; *(▸ d'une action)* meaning; **lourd de s.** pregnant with meaning

2 *(importance ▸ d'un événement, d'une déclaration)* import, significance; **des changements sans s.** inconsequential changes; **c'est une mesure sans s. pour la suite du travail** this measure has no significance for the rest of the work

3 *Jur* (official) notification; **s. à domicile** service to an address

4 *Ling* **la s.** signifying, the signifying processes

significative [siɲifikativ] *voir* **significatif**

signifié [siɲifje] **NM** *Ling* **le s.** the signified

signifier [9] [siɲifje] **VT 1** *(avoir tel sens ▸ sujet: mot, symbole)* to mean, to signify; **que signifie ce dicton?** what does this saying mean?; **les statistiques ne signifient rien pour moi** figures don't mean anything *or* a thing to me
2 *(indiquer ▸ sujet: mimique, geste, acte)* to mean; **que signifie ce sourire?** what does that smile mean?; **il y a peu d'espoir de le retrouver, mais cela ne signifie pas que l'on va abandonner** there's little hope of finding him, but it doesn't mean *or* imply that we're giving up; **il ne m'a pas encore téléphoné – cela ne signifie rien** he hasn't phoned me yet – that doesn't mean anything
3 *(pour exprimer l'irritation)* **que signifie ceci?** what's the meaning of this?; **ils donnent de l'argent d'une main et le reprennent de l'autre, qu'est-ce que ça signifie?** what do they think they're doing giving out money with one hand and taking it back with the other?
4 *(être le signe avant-coureur de)* to mean; **les brumes matinales signifient que l'automne approche** the morning mists mean that autumn will soon be here; **cela signifierait sa ruine** that would spell ruin for him/her
5 *(impliquer)* to mean, to imply; **sa promotion signifie un surcroît de travail pour moi** his/her promotion means more work for me
6 *(notifier)* to make known, to express; **s. ses intentions à qn** to make one's intentions known *or* to state one's intentions to sb; **il m'a signifié son départ** he has informed me that he is leaving; **il lui a signifié que…** he informed him/her that…; **j'ai écrit au ministre pour lui s. mon indignation** I've written to the Minister to express my indignation; **s. son congé à qn** to give sb his/her notice, *Sout* to give sb notice of dismissal
7 *Jur (jugement)* to notify; **s. à qn que…** to serve notice on *or* upon sb that…

signofile, signofil [siɲofil] **NM** *Suisse Aut (lampe) Br* indicator, *Am* turn signal; **mettre son s. (à droite/gauche)** *Br* to indicate (to the right/left), *Am* to put on one's turn signal (to turn right/left)

sikh [sik] **ADJ** Sikh
NM Sikh

silence [silɑ̃s] **NM 1** *(absence de bruit)* silence; **un peu de s., s'il vous plaît!** *(avant un discours)* (be) quiet please!; *(dans une bibliothèque, dans une salle d'étude)* quiet *or* silence, please!; **mais papa… – s.!** but Daddy… – (be) quiet *or* not another word (out of you)!; **demander** *ou* **réclamer le s.** to call for silence; **à son arrivée, tout le monde fit s.** there was a hush *or* everyone fell silent when he/she arrived; **garder le s.** to keep silent *or* quiet; **faire** *ou* **obtenir le s.** to make everyone keep quiet; *Cin* **s. on tourne!** quiet on the set, action!; **dans le s. de la nuit** in the still *or* in the silence of the night; **il régnait un s. de mort** it was as quiet *or* silent as the grave; **s. radio** radio silence; *Fam* **j'ai reçu quelques cartes postales peu après son départ, mais depuis, c'est le s. radio** I got a few postcards shortly after he/she left, but since then there's been total silence *or* I haven't heard a word
2 *(secret)* **acheter le s. de qn** to buy sb's silence; **garder le s. sur qch** to keep quiet about sth; **gardez le s. là-dessus** keep this very quiet; **imposer le s. à qn** to shut sb up; **passer qch sous s.** to pass over sth in silence, to keep quiet about sth
3 *(lacune)* **le s. de la loi en la matière** the absence of legislation regarding this matter
4 *(pause)* silence; **une lettre vint enfin rompre son s.** a letter came, thus breaking his/her silence; **après 15 ans de s., elle publia un roman** after a 15-year silence *or* break, she published a novel; **son récit était entrecoupé de nombreux silences** his/her story was interrupted by numerous pauses
5 *Mus* rest
6 *Biol & Méd* **mise sous s. des gènes** gene silencing
• **en silence ADV** *(se regarder)* in silence, silently; *(se déplacer)* silently, noiselessly; *(souffrir)* in silence, uncomplainingly

silencieuse [silɑ̃sjøz] *voir* **silencieux**

silencieusement [silɑ̃sjøzmɑ̃] **ADV** *(se regarder)* silently, in silence; *(se déplacer)* in silence, noiselessly; *(souffrir)* in silence, uncomplainingly

silencieux, -euse [silɑ̃sjø, -øz] **ADJ 1** *(où règne le calme ▸ trajet, repas, salle)* quiet, silent; **le reste de la soirée fut s.** the rest of the evening passed in silence **2** *(qui ne fait pas de bruit ▸ pendule, voiture)* quiet, noiseless; *(▸ mouvement)* noiseless; *(▸ pas)* silent **3** *(qui ne parle pas)* silent, quiet; *(taciturne)* quiet, silent, *Péj* uncommunicative; **la majorité silencieuse** the silent majority
NM 1 *(arme)* silencer **2** *Aut Br* silencer, *Am* muffler **3** *Rad & Tél (pour supprimer les bruits de fond)* squelch

Silène [silɛn] **NPR** *Myth* Silenus

silène [silɛn] **NM** *Bot* campion

siler [3] [sile] **VI** *Can* **1** *(siffler)* to whistle; *Fig* **j'ai les oreilles qui me silent** my ears are ringing **2** *(gémir)* to whine **3** *(respirer avec difficulté)* to wheeze

Silésie [silezi] **NF la S.** Silesia

silex [silɛks] **NM 1** *Géol* flint, flintstone **2** *Archéol (outil, arme)* flint

silhouette [silwɛt] **NF 1** *(ligne générale ▸ du corps)* figure; *(▸ d'un véhicule)* lines; **elle a une jolie s.** she's got a nice *or* a good figure
2 *(contours)* silhouette, outline; *(forme indistincte)* (vague) form *or* shape; **leurs silhouettes se détachaient sur le soleil couchant** they were silhouetted against the sunset
3 *Mil* **s. de tir** figure *or* silhouette target
4 *Beaux-Arts* silhouette

silhouetter [4] [silwete] **VT** *Beaux-Arts (dessiner les contours de)* to outline; *(découper dans du papier)* to silhouette
VPR se silhouetter *Littéraire* **se s. sur** to stand out *or* to be silhouetted against

silicate [silikat] **NM** *Chim* silicate

silice [silis] **NF** *Chim* silica; **verre de s., s. fondue** *ou* **vitreuse** silica glass

siliceux, -euse [silisø, -øz] **ADJ** *Chim* siliceous

silicium [silisjɔm] **NM** *Chim* silicon

silicone [silikɔn] **NF** *Chim* silicone
NM *(pour la cosmétologie, pour les prothèses)* silicone

siliconer [3] [silikɔne] **VT 1** *(matériau)* to coat with silicone **2** *(poitrine)* **un mannequin siliconé** a model with silicone implants; **elle a la poitrine siliconée** she has silicone implants

silicose [silikoz] **NF** *Méd* silicosis

silicosé, -e [silikoze] *Méd* **ADJ** silicotic
NM,F silicosis sufferer

silique [silik] **NF** *Bot* siliqua, silique

sillage [sijaʒ] **NM 1** *(d'une personne, d'un véhicule, d'un navire)* wake; **il y avait toujours deux ou trois gamins dans son s.** he/she always had two or three kids following him/her around; **les troupes n'avaient laissé que désolation dans leur s.** the troops had left total devastation in their wake; **cette mesure entraîne dans son s. une refonte de nos structures hospitalières** this decision brings with it *or* entails a restructuring of our hospital system; *aussi Fig* **marcher dans le s. de qn** to follow in sb's footsteps *or* in sb's wake **2** *Aviat (trace)* (vapour) trail; *(remous)* wake; **effet de s.** wake effect

sillon [sijɔ̃] **NM 1** *Agr (de gros labours)* furrow; *(petite rigole)* drill; *Littéraire* **sillons** *(champs)* fields, country; *Fig* **creuser** *ou* **tracer son s.** to plough one's furrow
2 *Littéraire (ride)* furrow
3 *(d'un disque)* groove
4 *(traînée)* **s. de lumière/de feu** *(d'une fusée)* streak of light/of fire
5 *Anat (du cerveau)* fissure, sulcus

sillonner [3] [sijɔne] **VT 1** *(parcourir ▸ sujet: canaux, voies)* to cross, to criss-cross; **des éclairs sillonnaient le ciel** flashes of lightning were streaking the sky; **j'ai sillonné la Bretagne** I've visited every corner of *or* I've travelled the length and breadth of Brittany; **il sillonnait les mers depuis 20 ans** he'd been sailing the seas for 20 years; **pays sillonné de rivières** country criss-crossed by rivers **2** *(marquer)* to furrow, to groove; **visage sillonné de rides** furrowed *or* deeply lined face; **les torrents sillonnent le flanc de la montagne** the mountainside is grooved *or* scored by rushing streams **3** *Agr* to furrow

silo [silo] **NM 1** *Agr* silo; **mettre en s.** to silo; **s. à blé** grain silo; **s. à ciment** cement silo **2** *Mil* **s. (de lancement)** (launching) silo

silotage [silɔtaʒ] **NM** ensilage

silure [silyr] **NM** *Ich* silurid

silurien, -enne [silyrjɛ̃, -ɛn] **ADJ** Silurian
NM Silurian

SIM [esiɛm] **NM 1** *voir* **carte 2** *Mktg (abrév* **système d'information marketing)** MIS

simagrées [simagre] **NFPL faire des s.** *(minauder)* to simper; *(faire des chichis)* to put on airs; **arrête tes s. et prends-le!** stop pretending you don't want it!

simien, -enne [simjɛ̃, -ɛn] *Zool* **ADJ** simian
NM simian, ape

simiesque [simjɛsk] **ADJ** monkey-like, ape-like, *Spéc* simian

similaire [similɛr] **ADJ** similar (**à** to)

similairement [similɛrmɑ̃] **ADV** similarly

similarité [similarite] **NF** similarity, likeness

simili [simili] **PRÉF** imitation, artificial; **s. marbre** imitation marble
NM *(imitation)* **c'est du s.** it's artificial *or* an imitation; **bijoux en s.** imitation *or* costume jewellery

similicuir [similikɥir] **NM** imitation leather, leatherette

similigravure [similigravyr] **NF 1** *(procédé)* half-tone process **2** *(cliché)* half-tone engraving

similitude [similityd] **NF 1** *(d'idées, de style)* similarity, *Sout* similitude; *(de personnes)* similarity, likeness; **leur s.** the likeness between them **2** *Math* similarity

simoniaque [simɔnjak] *Rel* **ADJ** simoniacal
NM simoniac, simonist

simonie [simɔni] **NF** *Rel* simony

simoun [simun] **NM** simoon

simple [sɛ̃pl] **ADJ 1** *(facile ▸ exercice, système)* simple, straightforward, easy; **c'est très s. à utiliser** it's very easy *or* simple to use; **ce n'est pas s. d'élever des enfants!** bringing up children isn't easy!; **c'est bien s., il accepte ou on part** it's quite simple, either he accepts or we go; **c'est s. comme bonjour** it's as easy as ABC *or* as pie
2 *(avant le nom) (avec une valeur restrictive)* mere, simple; **c'est une s. question d'argent** it's simply *or* only a matter of money; **pour la s. raison que…** for the simple reason that…; **réduit à sa plus s. expression** reduced to its simplest form; **il a été arrêté sur un s. soupçon** he was arrested on mere suspicion; **vous aurez une démonstration gratuite sur s. appel** simply phone this number for a free demonstration; **ce n'est qu'une s. formalité** it's merely a *or* it's a mere formality; **d'un s. bond, il franchit le fossé** with one leap, he was on the other side of the ditch; **ce n'est qu'un s. employé de bureau** he's just an ordinary office worker; **un s. particulier** an ordinary citizen; **s. soldat** private (soldier); **s. matelot** ordinary seaman
3 *(non raffiné ▸ gens)* unaffected, uncomplicated; *(▸ objets, nourriture, goûts)* plain, simple; *Hum* **elle est apparue dans le plus s. appareil** she appeared in her birthday suit
4 *(ingénu)* simple, simple-minded
5 *(non composé ▸ mot, élément, fleur, fracture)* simple; *(▸ chaînette, nœud)* single; **un cornet s. ou double?** *(de glace)* one scoop or two?
NM 1 *(ce qui est facile)* **aller du s. au complexe** to progress from the simple to the complex **2** *(proportion)* **augmenter du s. au double** to double; **les prix varient du s. au double** prices can double; **passer du s. au triple** to triple **3** *Sport* singles; **jouer en s.** to play a singles match; **s. messieurs/dames** men's/ladies' singles
• **simples NMPL** medicinal herbs *or* plants
• **simple d'esprit NM** simpleton, halfwit **ADJ il est un peu s. d'esprit** he's a bit simple

simplement [sɛ̃pləmɑ̃] **ADV 1** *(seulement)* simply, merely, just; **je te demande s. de me dire la vérité** I'm simply *or* just asking you to tell me the truth **2** *(sans apprêt ▸ parler)* unaffectedly, simply; *(▸ s'habiller)* simply, plainly; *(▸ vivre)* simply; **elle nous a reçus très s.** she received us simply *or* without ceremony; **nous avons déjeuné très s.** we had a very simple *or* plain lunch **3** *(clairement)* **expliquer qch s.** to explain sth in simple *or* straightforward terms

simplet, -ette [sɛ̃plɛ, -ɛt] **ADJ 1** *(personne ▸ peu intelligente)* simple, simple-minded; *(▸ ingénue)* naive; **elle est un peu simplette** she's a bit simple **2** *(sans finesse ▸ jugement, réponse, scénario)* simplistic, black-and-white

simplex [sɛ̃plɛks] **NM** *Ordinat & Tél* simplex

simplicité [sɛ̃plisite] **NF 1** *(facilité)* simplicity, straightforwardness; **l'exercice est d'une s. enfantine** the exercise is child's play; **l'opération est d'une grande s.** the operation is very straightforward; **cette machine est la s. même** this machine is simplicity itself

2 *(de vêtements, d'un décor, d'un repas)* plainness, simplicity; **avec s.** simply, plainly

3 *(naturel)* unaffectedness, lack of affectation; **j'aimais sa s.** his/her lack of affectation appealed to me; **elle manque de s.** she is pretentious *or* affected

4 *(naïveté)* naivety; **il fallait être d'une grande s. pour y croire** you would have to have been very naive to believe it

• **en toute simplicité ADV nous avons dîné en toute s.** we had a very simple dinner; **elle l'a avoué en toute s.** she admitted it without making a big thing of it

simplifiable [sɛ̃plifjabl] **ADJ 1** *Math* reducible **2** *(procédé)* which can be simplified *or* made simpler

simplificateur, -trice [sɛ̃plifikatœr, -tris] **ADJ** simplifying

simplification [sɛ̃plifikasjɔ̃] **NF 1** *Math* reduction **2** *(d'un système)* simplification, simplifying

simplificatrice [sɛ̃plifikatris] *voir* **simplificateur**

simplifier [9] [sɛ̃plifje] **VT 1** *(procédé)* to simplify; *(explication)* to simplify, to make simpler; **en simplifiant le texte à outrance** *ou* **à l'excès** by over-simplifying the text; **cela me simplifie la vie** that simplifies my life, that makes life *or* things easier for me **2** *Math (fraction)* to reduce, to simplify; *(équation)* to simplify

VPR se simplifier 1 to become simplified *or* simpler; **avec l'automatisation, les procédés de fabrication se simplifient** automation has simplified manufacturing processes **2** to simplify; **elle se simplifie l'existence en refusant de prendre des responsabilités** she makes her life simpler by refusing to take any responsibility

simplisme [sɛ̃plism] **NM** simplism

simplissime [sɛ̃plisim] **ADJ** dead easy

simpliste [sɛ̃plist] **ADJ** *(théorie, explication)* simplistic, oversimple; *(esprit)* simplistic, superficial

NMF simplistic person

simulacre [simylakr] **NM 1** *(par jeu, comme méthode)* imitation **2** *(pour tromper)* **un s. de négociations** mock *or* sham negotiations; **un s. de résistance** a (poor) show of resistance; **ce n'était qu'un s. de procès** it was a mockery of a trial

simulateur, -trice [simylatœr, -tris] **NM,F 1** *(imitateur)* simulator; *Hum* **s., va!** you're such a fraud! **2** *(faux malade)* malingerer

NM *Aviat, Ordinat & Mil* simulator; **s. de réalité virtuelle** virtual reality simulator; **s. de vol** flight simulator

simulation [simylasjɔ̃] **NF 1** *(d'un sentiment)* feigning, faking, simulation; *(d'une maladie)* malingering **2** *(de bataille, de vol etc)* simulation; **s. d'entretien d'embauche** practice job interview; **s. sur ordinateur** computer simulation **3** *Jur* non-disclosure *or* concealment of contract

simulatrice [simylatris] *voir* **simulateur**

simulcasting [simylkastiŋ] **NM** *Rad & TV* simulcasting

simulé, -e [simyle] **ADJ 1** *(pitié, douleur)* faked, feigned **2** *Aviat, Ordinat & Mil* simulated **3** *Jur* **acte s.** bogus deed *(concealing a contract)*

simuler [3] [simyle] **VT 1** *(feindre ▸ douleur, ivresse, folie)* to feign; **s. l'innocence** to put on an air *or* a show of innocence; **s. la folie** to pretend to be mad, to feign madness; **s. la maladie** *(appelé, employé)* to malinger; *(enfant)* to pretend to be ill; **l'animal simule la mort** the animal is playing dead

2 *(imiter)* **la porte simule un rideau** the door is made to look like a curtain

3 *Mil & Tech* to simulate

4 *Jur (acte)* to deceive *(by nondisclosure of a contract)*

USAGE ABSOLU *(feindre)* **je ne pense pas qu'elle simule** I don't think she's pretending

simultané, -e [simyltane] **ADJ** simultaneous

simultanéité [simyltaneite] **NF** simultaneity, simultaneousness

simultanément [simyltanemɑ̃] **ADV** simultaneously

Sinaï [sinaj] **NM le S.** Sinai; **le mont S.** Mount Sinai

sinapisé, -e [sinapize] **ADJ bain/cataplasme s.** mustard bath/poultice *or* plaster

sinapisme [sinapism] **NM** sinapism, mustard plaster

sincère [sɛ̃sɛr] **ADJ 1** *(amitié, chagrin, remords)* sincere, genuine, true; *(personne)* sincere, genuine; *(réponse)* honest, sincere; **tu n'es pas s. quand tu dis cela** you're being insincere in saying that; **être s. avec soi-même** to be honest with oneself **2** *(dans les formules de politesse)* **nos vœux les plus sincères** our very best wishes; **je vous présente mes sincères condoléances** please accept my sincere *or* heartfelt condolences; **veuillez agréer mes sincères salutations** *(à quelqu'un dont on connaît le nom) Br* yours sincerely, *Am* sincerely (yours); *(à quelqu'un dont on ne connaît pas le nom) Br* yours faithfully, *Am* sincerely (yours) **3** *Jur (acte)* genuine, authentic

sincèrement [sɛ̃sɛrmɑ̃] **ADV 1** *(avec sincérité)* sincerely, genuinely, truly **2** *(à vrai dire)* honestly, frankly; **s., ça ne valait pas le coup** to tell you the truth, it wasn't worth it

sincérité [sɛ̃serite] **NF 1** *(franchise)* sincerity; **je ne remets pas en cause sa s.** I'm not saying he/she wasn't sincere *or* genuine; **en toute s.** in all sincerity, to be quite honest; **manque de s.** lack of sincerity, disingenuousness **2** *(authenticité ▸ d'une amitié, de remords)* genuineness; *(▸ d'une réponse)* honesty **3** *(absence de truquage ▸ d'une élection, d'un document)* honesty, genuineness

sinécure [sinekyr] **NF** sinecure; *Fam* **ce n'est pas une s.** it's no picnic

sine die [sinedje] **ADV remettre qch s.** to postpone sth indefinitely

sine qua non [sinekwanɔn] **ADJ INV condition s.** essential condition; **c'est la condition s. de ma participation** it's an essential condition if I am to take part at all

Singapour [sɛ̃gapur] **NF** Singapore

singapourien, -enne [sɛ̃gapurjɛ̃, -ɛn] **ADJ** Singaporean

• **Singapourien, -enne NM,F** Singaporean

singe [sɛ̃ʒ] **NM 1** *Zool (à longue queue)* monkey; *(sans queue)* ape; **les grands singes** the (great) apes; **s. araignée** spider monkey; **s. capucin** capuchin monkey; **s. hurleur** howler monkey; **s. rhésus** rhesus monkey; **le s. imite l'homme!** copycat!

2 *(imitateur)* mimic; **quel s.!** isn't he a little comic!; **faire le s.** *(faire des grimaces)* to make faces; *(faire des pitreries)* to clown *or* to monkey around

3 *très Fam (chef)* boss[□]

4 *très Fam (bœuf en conserve)* corned beef[□]

singer [17] [sɛ̃ʒe] **VT 1** *(personne)* to ape, to mimic **2** *(manières distinguées, passion)* to feign, to fake

singerie [sɛ̃ʒri] **NF** *(section d'un zoo)* monkey *or* ape house

• **singeries NFPL** *(tours et grimaces)* clowning; *(d'un clown)* antics; *Péj (manières affectées)* affectedness, airs and graces; **faire des singeries** to clown *or* to monkey around

single [siŋgəl] **NM 1** *(disque)* single

2 *Rail* single sleeper

3 *Sport* singles (game)

4 *(dans un hôtel)* single (room)

singulariser [3] [sɛ̃gylarize] **VT s. qn** to make sb conspicuous, to set sb apart; **s. qn de** to set sb apart from, to make sb stand out from

VPR se singulariser 1 *(se faire remarquer)* to make oneself conspicuous; **il faut toujours que tu te singularises!** you always have to be different from everyone else, don't you? **2** *(être remarquable)* **il s'est singularisé par son courage** he distinguished himself by his courage

singularité [sɛ̃gylarite] **NF 1** *(étrangeté ▸ d'un comportement, d'idées, d'une tenue)* oddness, strangeness

2 *(trait distinctif ▸ d'une personne)* peculiarity; *(▸ d'un système)* distinctive feature, peculiarity; **c'est une des singularités de son caractère** it's one of the strange *or* odd things about him/her; **la boîte présentait cette s. de s'ouvrir par l'arrière** the box was unusual in that it opened at the back

3 *Littéraire (unicité)* uniqueness

4 *Math & Phys* singularity

singulier, -ère [sɛ̃gylje, -ɛr] **ADJ 1** *(étrange ▸ comportement, idées)* odd, strange, *Sout* singular

2 *(remarquable ▸ courage, beauté)* remarkable, rare, unique

3 *Ling* singular

4 *(d'un seul)* singular, single

NM *Gram* singular; **au s.** in the singular

singulièrement [sɛ̃gyljɛrmɑ̃] **ADV 1** *(beaucoup)* very much; **il m'a s. déçu** I was extremely disappointed in him; **s. réussi** hugely successful **2** *(étrangement)* oddly, strangely, *Sout* singularly **3** *(notamment)* especially, particularly

sinistre [sinistr] **ADJ 1** *(inquiétant ▸ lieu, bruit)* sinister; *(▸ personnage)* sinister, evil-looking; **c'est s. ici!** it's spooky here! **2** *(triste ▸ personne, soirée)* dismal, grim; *(▸ paysage)* bleak **3** *(avant le nom) (en intensif)* **c'est un s. imbécile/une s. canaille** he's a total idiot/crook

NM 1 *(incendie)* fire, blaze; *(inondation, séisme)* disaster **2** *Assur* **déclarer un s.** to put in a claim; **évaluer un s.** to estimate a claim

sinistré, -e [sinistre] **ADJ** *(bâtiment, village, quartier ▸ gén)* damaged, stricken; *(▸ brûlé)* burnt-out; *(▸ bombardé)* bombed-out; *(▸ inondé)* flooded; **la ville est sinistrée** *(après un tremblement de terre)* the town has been devastated by the earthquake; **les personnes sinistrées** the disaster victims; *(après des inondations)* the flood victims; **population sinistrée** stricken population; *Admin* **région** *ou* **zone (déclarée) sinistrée** disaster area

NM,F disaster victim

sinistrement [sinistrəmɑ̃] **ADV** sinisterly, in a sinister way

sinistrose [sinistroz] **NF 1** *Psy* post-traumatic stress disorder **2** *Fam* (systematic) pessimism[□]; **le pays est en proie à la s.** the country's morale is very low

sinologue [sinɔlɔg] **NMF** specialist in Chinese studies, sinologist

sinon [sinɔ̃] **CONJ 1** *(sans cela)* otherwise, or else; **un jus d'orange, s. rien** an orange juice, otherwise nothing; **je ne peux pas me joindre à vous, s. je l'aurais fait avec plaisir** I can't join you, much as I would have liked to; **j'essaierai d'être à l'heure, s. partez sans moi** I'll try to be on time, but if I'm not go without me; **tiens-toi tranquille, s. je me fâche** keep still, or else *or* otherwise I'll get angry; **tais-toi, s....!** be quiet or else...! **2** *(si ce n'est)* if not; **elle était, s. jolie, du moins gracieuse** she was, if not pretty, at least graceful; **faites-le, s. avec plaisir, du moins de meilleure grâce** if you can't do it with pleasure, at least do it with better grace; **elle l'a, s. aimé, du moins apprécié** although *or* if she didn't like it she did at least appreciate it **3** *(excepté)* except, other than; **que faire, s. attendre?** what can we do other than *or* except wait?

• **sinon que CONJ** except that; **je ne sais rien, s. qu'il est parti** all I know is that he's left

sinoque [sinɔk] *Fam* **ADJ** crazy, nuts

NMF nutcase, *Br* nutter

sinuer [7] [sinye] **VI** *Littéraire* to wind

sinueux, -euse [sinyø, -øz] **ADJ 1** *(tracé, chemin)* winding, sinuous; *(fleuve)* winding, meandering **2** *(pensée)* convoluted, tortuous

sinuosité [sinyozite] **NF 1** *(fait d'être courbé ▸ d'un tracé, d'un chemin)* winding; *(▸ d'une rivière)* winding, meandering **2** *(courbe ▸ d'un tracé)* curve; *(▸ d'un chemin)* curve, bend; *(▸ d'une rivière)* meander

• **sinuosités NFPL** *Fig (d'un raisonnement)* tortuousness, convolutions

sinus [sinys] **NM 1** *Anat* sinus **2** *Math* sine

sinusite [sinyzit] **NF** *Méd* sinusitis; **avoir une s.** to have sinusitis

sinusoïdal, -e, -aux, -ales [sinyzɔidal,-o] **ADJ** sinusoidal

sinusoïde [sinyzɔid] **NM** *Anat* sinusoid
NF *Math* sine curve

Sion [sjɔ̃] **NF** Zion, Sion

sionisme [sjɔnism] **NM** Zionism

sioniste [sjɔnist] **ADJ** Zionist
NMF Zionist

sioux [sju] **ADJ 1** *(amérindien)* Sioux **2** *Fam (astucieux)* sharp
NM *(langue)* Sioux
• **Sioux NMF** Sioux; **les S.** the Sioux (Indians)

siphon [sifɔ̃] **NM 1** *Méd, Phys, Géol & Zool* siphon **2** *(d'appareils sanitaires)* trap, U-bend **3** *(carafe) Br* soda siphon, *Am* siphon bottle

siphonné, -e [sifɔne] **ADJ** *Fam (fou)* crazy, nuts

siphonner [3] [sifɔne] **VT** to siphon; **s. de l'eau/un réservoir** to siphon off water/a reservoir

sire [sir] **NM** *(seigneur)* lord; **un triste s.** a dubious character
• **Sire NM** *(à un roi)* Your Majesty, *Arch* Sire; *(à un empereur)* Your Imperial Majesty, *Arch* Sire

sirène [sirɛn] **NF 1** *(des pompiers, d'une voiture de police, d'une ambulance, d'une usine)* siren; *(d'un navire)* siren, (fog) horn; **s. d'alarme** *(d'incendie)* fire alarm; *(en temps de guerre)* air-raid siren **2** *(femme séduisante) & Myth* siren

SIRET [siret] **NM n° S.** company registration number

sirocco [sirɔko] **NM** sirocco

sirop [siro] **NM 1** *Culin (concentré)* syrup, cordial; *(dilué)* (fruit) cordial *or* drink; **s. d'érable** maple syrup; **s. de fraise/de menthe** strawberry/mint cordial; **s. d'orgeat** barley water; **s. de sucre** golden syrup **2** *Pharm* syrup; **s. pour** *ou* **contre la toux** cough mixture *or* syrup **3** *Fig Péj* mawkishness, schmaltz; **son film, c'est du s.** his/her movie *or Br* film is pure schmaltz

siroter [3] [sirɔte] **VT** to sip, to take sips of
VI *Fam* to booze; **il sirote bien** he likes a drop of the hard stuff

sirupeux, -euse [sirypø, -øz] **ADJ 1** *(visqueux et sucré)* syrupy **2** *Péj (sentiment)* schmaltzy, syrupy

sis, -e [si, siz] **ADJ** *Jur* **s. à** located *or* situated at; **maison sise rue Saint-Honoré** house located *or* situated in the Rue Saint-Honoré

sisal, -als [sizal] **NM** *Bot* sisal

sismal, -e, -aux, -ales [sismal, -o] **ADJ** seismic

sismicité [sismisite] **NF** seismicity

sismique [sismik] **ADJ** seismic

sismogramme [sismɔgram] **NM** seismogram

sismographe [sismɔgraf] **NM** seismograph

sismographie [sismɔgrafi] **NF** seismography

sismologie [sismɔlɔʒi] **NF** seismology

sismomètre [sismɔmɛtr] **NM** seismometer

Sisyphe [sizif] **NPR** *Myth* Sisyphus; **un travail de S.** a never-ending task

sitar [sitar] **NM** *Mus* sitar

sitcom [sitkɔm] **NM OU NF** *TV* sitcom

site [sit] **NM 1** *(panorama)* beauty spot; **il y a plusieurs sites touristiques par ici** there are several tourist spots *or* places of interest for tourists round here; *Admin* **s. classé** conservation area, *Br* ≃ National Trust area; **s. historique** historical site
2 *(environnement)* setting
3 *(emplacement)* site, siting; **le choix du s. de la centrale a posé problème** the siting of the power station has caused problems; **s. archéologique** *(gén)* archeological site; *(en cours d'excavation)* archeological dig
4 *Chim & Écon* site; *Mktg* **s. témoin** test site
5 *Ordinat* site; **s. de bavardage** chat room; **s. FTP** FTP site; **s. marchand** e-commerce site; **s. miroir** mirror site; **s. de réseaux sociaux** social networking site; **s. Web** Web site
6 *Transp* **s. propre** bus lane
• **de site ADJ** *Mil* **angle/ligne de s.** angle/line of sight

sit-in [sitin] **NM INV** sit-in; **faire un s.** to stage a sit-in

sitôt [sito] **ADV 1** *(avec une participiale)* **s. le dîner fini, il partit** as soon as dinner was over, he left; **s. dit, s. fait** no sooner said than done **2** *Littéraire (aussitôt)* immediately; **s. après l'orage** immediately after the storm; **s. après la gare** just *or* immediately past the station **3** *Littéraire (si rapidement)* **une rose épanouie et s. fanée** a rose in full bloom and yet so quick to wither
PRÉP *Littéraire* **s. son élection...** as soon as he/she was elected..., no sooner was he/she elected...
• **pas de sitôt ADV on ne se reverra pas de s.** we won't be seeing each other again for a while; **je n'y retournerai pas de s.!** I won't go back there *or* you won't catch me going back there in a hurry!; **la société idéale n'existera pas de s.** the ideal society is a long way off
• **sitôt que CONJ** *Littéraire* as soon as; **s. qu'il la vit, il se mit à rire** as soon as he saw her he started to laugh

sittelle [sitɛl] **NF** *Orn* nuthatch

situation [sitɥasjɔ̃] **NF 1** *(circonstances)* situation, position; **s. économique/politique** economic/political situation; **quelle est votre s. financière exacte?** what is your precise *or* exact financial position?; **ma s. financière n'est pas brillante!** my financial situation is *or* my finances are none too healthy!; **se trouver dans une s. délicate** to find oneself in an awkward situation *or* position; *Vieilli Euph* **elle est dans une s. intéressante** *(enceinte)* she's in an interesting condition; **tu vois un peu la s.!** do you get the picture?; **c'est l'homme de la s.** he's the right man for the job; *Admin* **s. de famille** marital status; **s. gagnant-gagnant** win-win situation
2 *(emploi rémunéré)* job; **chercher/trouver une s.** to look for/to find a job; **avoir une bonne s.** *(être bien payé)* to have a well-paid job; *(être puissant)* to have a high-powered job; **elle s'est fait une belle s.** she worked her way up to a very good position; **être sans s.** to have no job; **s. sociale** *(d'une personne)* social position, standing in society
3 *(lieu)* situation, position, location; **le manoir jouit d'une magnifique s.** the manor house is beautifully situated
4 *Fin (d'une société)* report of assets; **s. en banque** financial position *or* situation; **s. de caisse** cash statement; **s. de compte** account position *or* balance; **s. financière** financial situation *or* position; **s. nette** net assets, net worth; **s. de trésorerie** cash budget
5 *Littérature & Théât* situation; **comique de s.** situation comedy
• **en situation ADV** in real life; **voyons comment elle va aborder les choses en s.** let's see how she gets on in real life *or* when faced with the real thing; **mettre qn en s.** to give sb experience of a real-life situation
• **en situation de PRÉP être en s. de faire qch** to be in a position to do sth; **je ne suis pas en s. de décider** I'm not in a position to decide

situé, -e [sitɥe] **ADJ maison bien/mal située** well-/poorly-situated house

situer [7] [sitɥe] **VT 1** *(dans l'espace, dans le temps ▸ gén)* to place; *(▸ roman, film etc)* to set; **je connais la ville mais je ne saurais pas la s.** I know the name of the town but I wouldn't be able to place it *or* to say where it is; **à quelle époque situez-vous l'action de votre roman?** in what period have you set your novel?; **on situe l'apparition de l'écriture à cette époque** writing is believed to have appeared during this period; **je n'arrive pas à le s.** I'm afraid I can't place him **2** *(classer)* to place, to situate; **il est difficile de le s. dans l'architecture/dans la politique française** it's difficult to know where to place him in French architecture/politics; **je situerais plutôt ce groupe dans le courant trip-hop** I would describe the band as being more trip-hop **3** *Fam (cerner ▸ personne)* to define[□]; **on a du mal à la s.** it's difficult to know what makes her tick
VPR se situer 1 *(prendre position)* **se s. par rapport à qn/qch** to place oneself in relation to sb/sth; **où vous situez-vous dans ce conflit?** where do you stand in this conflict? **2** *(gén)* to be situated *or* located; *(scène, action)* to take place; **leur groupe se situe très à gauche** their group is on the far left; **l'augmentation se situera aux alentours de 3 pour cent** the increase will be in the region of 3 percent

six [sis] **ADJ 1** *(gén)* six; *Sport* **les S. Jours** the Six Day Race **2** *(dans des séries)* sixth; **page/numéro s.** page/number six
PRON six
NM INV 1 *(gén)* six
2 *(numéro d'ordre)* number six
3 *(chiffre écrit)* six
4 *Cartes* six; *voir aussi* **cinq**

sixain [sizɛ̃] **NM 1** *Littérature* six-line stanza, *Spéc* hexastich **2** *Cartes* set of six packs *or Am* decks of cards

six-huit [sisɥit] **NM INV** *Mus* six-eight time

sixième [sizjɛm] **ADJ** sixth
NMF 1 *(personne)* sixth **2** *(objet)* sixth (one)
NM 1 *(partie)* sixth **2** *(étage) Br* sixth floor, *Am* seventh floor **3** *(arrondissement de Paris)* sixth (arrondissement)
NF 1 *Scol Br* ≃ first year, *Am* ≃ sixth grade **2** *Mus* sixth; *voir aussi* **cinquième**

sixièmement [sizjɛmmɑ̃] **ADV** sixthly, in sixth place

six-quatre-deux [siskatdø] **à la six-quatre-deux ADV** *Fam* **faire qch à la s.** to do sth any old how; **une dissertation faite à la s.** a slapdash *or* rushed essay

sixte [sikst] **NF 1** *Mus* sixth **2** *Escrime* sixte

Sixtine [sikstin] **NF la chapelle S.** the Sistine Chapel

sizain [sizɛ̃] = **sixain**

Skaï® [skaj] **NM** imitation leather, Leatherette®

skateboard [skɛtbɔrd] **NM** skateboard; **faire du s.** to skateboard, to go skateboarding

skatepark [skɛtpark] **NM** skatepark

skeleton [skəlɛtɔn] **NM** *(luge, sport)* skeleton

sketch [skɛtʃ] *(pl* **sketches) NM** sketch

ski [ski] **NM 1** *Sport (activité)* skiing; **faire du s.** to go skiing; **s. alpin/nordique** Alpine/Nordic skiing; **s. artistique** freestyle skiing; **s. de descente** downhill skiing; **s. de fond** cross-country skiing; **s. nautique** water-skiing; **faire du s. nautique** to water-ski; **s. de randonnée** ski-touring; **s. sauvage** *ou* **hors piste** off-piste skiing **2** *(planche)* ski; **skis compacts** *ou* **courts** short skis; **skis paraboliques** parabolic skis, carving skis **3** *Aviat* landing skid
• **de ski ADJ** *(chaussures, lunettes, station)* ski *(avant n)*; *(vacances, séjour)* skiing *(avant n)*

skiable [skjabl] **ADJ** skiable; **la piste noire n'est plus s.** it's now impossible to ski down *or* to use the black run

ski-bob [skibɔb] *(pl* **ski-bobs) NM** skibob; **faire du s.** to go skibobbing

skier [10] [skje] **VI** to ski; **je vais s. tous les dimanches** I go skiing every Sunday

skieur, -euse [skjœr, -øz] **NM,F** skier; **s. de fond** cross-country skier; **s. nautique** water-skier

skiff [skif] **NM** skiff; *(en aviron)* single scull

skinhead [skinɛd] **NM** skinhead

skip [skip] **NM** *Ind* skip

skipper [skipœr] **NM** *Naut* skipper

Skype® [skajp] **NM** *Ordinat & Tél* Skype®

skyscraper [skajskrɛpœr] **NM** *Mktg* skyscraper ad

slalom [slalɔm] **NM 1** *Sport (course)* slalom; **descendre une piste en s.** to slalom down a slope; **s. spécial/géant** special/giant slalom **2** *Fam (zigzags)* zigzagging[□]; **faire du s. entre** to zigzag between *or* to weave in and out of; **la moto faisait du s. entre les voitures** the motorbike was dodging in and out among the cars *or* weaving in and out of the traffic

slalomer [3] [slalɔme] **VI 1** *Sport* to slalom **2** *Fam (zigzaguer)* **s. entre** to zigzag[□] *or* to weave in and out of; **il est dangereux de s. entre les voitures** weaving in and out of the traffic is dangerous

slalomeur, -euse [slalɔmœr, -øz] **NM,F** slalom skier

slam [slam] **NM 1** *(concours de poésie)* poetry slam **2** *(fait de se faire porter par la foule)* crowd surfing

slave [slav] **ADJ** Slavonic, *Am* Slavic
NM *(langue)* Slavonic, Slavic
• **Slave NMF** Slav

slavisant, -e [slavizɑ̃, -ɑ̃t] **NM,F** Slavicist, Slavist

sleeping [slipiŋ] NM *Vieilli* sleeping car

slibard [slibar] NM *très Fam Br* boxers, *Am* shorts, skivvies

slip [slip] NM **1** *(d'homme)* (pair of) (under)pants, *Am* shorts; *(de femme) Br* pants, *Am* panties; **où est mon s.?** where are my pants?; **s. de bain** *(d'homme)* bathing *or* swimming trunks; **s. kangourou** Y-fronts **2** *Naut* slip, slipway

Il faut noter que le terme anglais **slip** est un faux ami; il ne signifie jamais **culotte**.

sloche [slɔʃ] NF *Can Joual* slush

slogan [slɔgɑ̃] NM slogan; **s. publicitaire** advertising slogan

sloop [slup] NM *Naut* sloop

sloughi [slugi] NM saluki

slovaque [slɔvak] ADJ Slovak, Slovakian
NM *(langue)* Slovak
• **Slovaque** NMF Slovak, Slovakian

Slovaquie [slɔvaki] NF **la S.** Slovakia

slovène [slɔvɛn] ADJ Slovene, Slovenian
NM *(langue)* Slovene
• **Slovène** NMF Slovene, Slovenian

Slovénie [slɔveni] NF **la S.** Slovenia

slow [slo] NM **1** *(gén)* slow number; **le s. de l'été** the slow number everyone's dancing to this summer; **danser un s. avec qn** to slow dance with sb **2** *(fox-trot)* slow fox trot

SM [ɛsɛm] NM *(abrév* **sado-masochisme***)* S&M

smala, smalah [smala] NF **1** *(d'un chef arabe)* retinue **2** *Fam (famille)* tribe

smart [smart] ADJ INV *Fam Vieilli* chic, smart

smash [smaʃ] *(pl* **smashs** *ou* **smashes***)* NM *Sport* smash; **faire un s.** to smash (the ball)

smasher [3] [smaʃe] *Sport* VI to smash
VT to smash

SME [ɛsɛmə] NM *Écon (abrév* **Système monétaire européen***)* EMS

smectique [smɛktik] ADJ *Chim & Phys* smectic; **argile s.** fuller's earth

SMI [ɛsɛmi] NM *(abrév* **Système monétaire international***) Écon* IMS

SMIC, Smic [smik] NM *(abrév* **salaire minimum interprofessionnel de croissance***)* = index-linked guaranteed minimum wage

smicard, -e [smikar, -ard] NM,F *Fam* minimum-wage earner▫; **les smicards** people earning *or* on the minimum wage▫

smiley [smajli] NM *Ordinat* smiley, emoticon

smocks [smɔk] NMPL smocking

smog [smɔg] NM smog

smoking [smɔkiŋ] NM *Br* dinner suit, *Am* tuxedo; **(veste de) s.** *Br* dinner jacket, *Am* tuxedo

SMS [ɛsɛmɛs] NM *Tél (abrév* **short message service***)* SMS

smurf [smœrf] NM breakdancing; **faire du s.** to breakdance

snack [snak] NM **1** *(restaurant)* snack bar, self-service restaurant, cafeteria **2** *(collation)* snack

snack-bar [snakbar] *(pl* **snack-bars***)* NM snack bar, self-service restaurant, cafeteria

SNC[1] [ɛsɛnse] NF *Écon (abrév* **société en nom collectif***)* general partnership

SNC[2] *(abrév écrite* **service non compris***)* service not included

SNCB [ɛsɛnsebe] NF *Belg (abrév* **Société nationale des chemins de fer belges***)* = Belgian national railway company

SNCF [ɛsɛnseɛf] NF *(abrév* **Société nationale des chemins de fer français***)* = French national railway company; **la S. est en grève** there's a (French) rail strike; **il travaille à la S.** he works for the (French) *Br* railways *or Am* railroads

sniff [snif] EXCLAM *(bruit de pleurs)* boo hoo!
NM *très Fam Arg drogue (de cocaïne)* snort

sniffer [3] [snife] *très Fam Arg drogue* VI to snort
VT *(cocaïne)* to snort; *(colle)* to sniff▫

snob [snɔb] ADJ snobbish, snobby; **elle est un peu s.** she's a bit of a snob
NMF snob

snober [3] [snɔbe] VT *(personne)* to snub; *(chose)* to turn one's nose up at; **certains libraires snobent les bandes dessinées** some booksellers think it beneath them to stock comics

snobinard, -e [snɔbinar, -ard] *Fam* ADJ stuck-up, snobby
NM,F snob▫

snobisme [snɔbism] NM snobbery, snobbishness; **il joue au golf par s.** he plays golf out of snobbery; **du s. à rebours** inverted snobbery

snowboard [snobɔrd] NM *(sport)* snowboarding; *(planche)* snowboard

snow-boot [snobut] *(pl* **snow-boots***)* NM snow boot

snowpark [snopark] NM snowpark

sobre [sɔbr] ADJ **1** *(personne ▸ tempérante)* sober, temperate, *Sout* abstemious; *(▸ non ivre)* sober; **être s. comme un chameau** to be as sober as a judge **2** *(modéré, discret ▸ architecture, tenue, style)* sober, restrained; *(▸ vêtement)* simple; **elle est toujours s. dans ses déclarations** she always speaks with restraint

sobrement [sɔbrəmɑ̃] ADV **1** *(avec modération)* temperately, soberly **2** *(avec discrétion, avec retenue)* soberly

sobriété [sɔbrijete] NF **1** *(tempérance)* soberness, temperance **2** *(discrétion, retenue)* soberness; **il mit de la s. dans ses félicitations** he was restrained in his congratulations **3** *(dépouillement ▸ d'un style, d'un décor)* bareness

sobriquet [sɔbrikɛ] NM nickname; **un petit s. affectueux** a pet name

soc [sɔk] NM ploughshare

sociabilité [sɔsjabilite] NF sociableness, sociability

sociable [sɔsjabl] ADJ **1** *(individu, tempérament)* sociable, gregarious; **j'ai été un enfant très s.** I was a very outgoing child **2** *(vivant en société)* social

social, -e, -aux, -ales [sɔsjal, -o] ADJ **1** *(réformes, problèmes, ordre, politique)* social; **c'est une menace sociale** it represents a threat to society
2 *Admin* social *(avant n)*, welfare *(avant n)*; **avantages sociaux** welfare benefits; **logements sociaux** public housing; **services sociaux** social services
3 *Zool* social; **l'homme est un animal s.** man is a social animal
4 *Jur* company *(avant n)*; **un associé peut être tenu responsable des dettes sociales** a partner may be liable for company debts
NM **le nouveau gouvernement s'intéresse beaucoup au s.** the new government takes a strong interest in social issues; **travailler dans le s.** to work in the social sector; *Fam Fig* **je ne suis pas là pour faire du s.** that's not my problem

social-chrétien, sociale-chrétienne [sɔsjalkretjɛ̃, -ɛn] *(mpl* **sociaux-chrétiens** [sɔsjokretjɛ̃], *fpl* **sociales-chrétiennes***) Belg* ADJ Christian Socialist
NM,F Christian Socialist

social-démocrate, sociale-démocrate [sɔsjaldemɔkrat] *(mpl* **sociaux-démocrates** [sɔsjodemɔkrat], *fpl* **sociales-démocrates***)* ADJ social democratic
NMF *(gén)* social democrat; *(adhérent d'un parti)* Social Democrat

social-démocratie [sɔsjaldemɔkrasi] *(pl* **social-démocraties***)* NF social democracy

socialement [sɔsjalmɑ̃] ADV socially

socialisant, -e [sɔsjalizɑ̃, -ɑ̃t] ADJ **1** *Pol* left-leaning, with left-wing tendencies **2** *(préoccupé de justice sociale)* socialistic
NM,F **1** *Pol* socialist sympathizer **2** *(contestataire social)* advocate of social equality

socialisation [sɔsjalizasjɔ̃] NF **1** *Écon* collectivization **2** *Pol* **depuis la s. du pays** since the country went socialist **3** *Psy* socialization

socialiser [3] [sɔsjalize] VT **1** *Écon* to collectivize **2** *Psy* to socialize

socialisme [sɔsjalism] NM socialism; **s. chrétien** Christian socialism; **s. d'État** State socialism

socialiste [sɔsjalist] ADJ socialist
NMF socialist

social-révolutionnaire, sociale-révolutionnaire [sɔsjalrevɔlysjɔnɛr] *(mpl* **sociaux-révolutionnaires** [sɔsjorevɔlysjɔnɛr], *fpl* **sociales-révolutionnaires***)* ADJ social-revolutionary
NM,F social-revolutionary

sociétaire [sɔsjetɛr] NMF **1** *(d'une association)* member **2** *Fin (d'une société anonyme) Br* shareholder, *Am* stockholder

société [sɔsjete] NF **1** *(communauté)* society; **la s.** society; **problème de s.** social problem; **vivre en s.** to live in society; **les insectes qui vivent en s.** social insects; **la s. d'abondance/de consommation** the affluent/consumer society
2 *Littéraire (présence)* company, society; **rechercher la s. de qn** to seek (out) sb's company
3 *Fam (personnes réunies)* company, gathering
4 *(catégorie de gens)* society; **cela ne se fait pas dans la bonne s.** it's not done in polite society; **la haute s.** high society
5 *(association ▸ de gens de lettres, de savants)* society; *(▸ de sportifs)* club; **s. littéraire/savante** literary/learned society; **s. secrète** secret society; **la S. des Nations** the League of Nations; **la S. protectrice des animaux**, *Br* ≃ RSPCA, *Am* ≃ ASPCA
6 *Com, Jur & Écon (entreprise)* company, firm; **le matériel appartient à la s.** the equipment belongs to the firm *or* to the company; **la S. Martin** Martin's; **s. par actions** joint-stock company, *Am* incorporated company; **s. affiliée** affiliated company, *Am* affiliate; **s. anonyme** (public) limited company; **s. d'assurance** insurance company; **s. de Bourse** stockbroker, stockbroking firm; **s. de capital-risque** venture capital company; **s. à capital variable** company with variable capital; **s. de capitaux (à responsabilité limitée)** limited liability company; **s. civile immobilière** property investment partnership; **S. civile de placement immobilier** = company which owns and manages rented accommodation; **s. civile professionnelle** professional *or* non-trading partnership; **s. en commandite** limited partnership; **s. en commandite par actions** partnership limited by shares; **s. en commandite simple** ≃ general partnership; **s. de commerce international** international trading corporation; **s. commerciale** company, firm; **s. de conseil en investissement** investment consultancy; **s. cotée en Bourse** listed company; **s. cotée à la Cote officielle** quoted company; **s. de crédit immobilier** *Br* ≃ building society, *Am* ≃ savings and loan association; **s. d'économie mixte** government-controlled corporation; **s. d'État** state-owned *or* public company; **s. d'études** research company; **s. d'exploitation en commun** joint venture; **s. de fait** de facto partnership; **s. familiale** family business; **s. fictive** dummy company; **S. française d'enquêtes par sondages** = French market research company; **s. de gestion** holding company; **s. immobilière** real-estate company; **s. d'investissement à capital fixe** closed-end investment company; **s. d'investissement à capital variable** open-ended investment trust, *Br* ≃ unit trust, *Am* ≃ mutual fund; **s. de location de voitures** *Br* car hire company, *Am* car rental company; **s. mère** parent company; **s. multinationale** multinational company *or* corporation, multinational; **s. nationale** state-owned *or* public company; *Rail* **S. nationale des chemins de fer français** = French national railway company; **s. en nom collectif** general partnership; **s. en participation** joint venture; **s. de personnes** partnership; *Belg* **s. de personnes à responsabilité limitée** limited liability company; **s. de placement** investment trust; **s. à portefeuille** holding company; **s. de prévoyance** provident society; **s. à responsabilité limitée** ≃ limited liability company; **s. de services** service company; **s. sœur** sister company; **s. de transport** carrier, transport firm; **s. unipersonnelle** single-person company; **s. d'utilité publique** *Br* public utility company, *Am* utility; **s. de vente par correspondance** mail-order company *or* firm
7 *Banque* **s. financière/de crédit** finance/credit company
8 *Jur* **s. d'acquêts** joint (matrimonial) assets
9 *Ordinat* **s. de services et d'ingénierie informatique** services and software organization

société-écran [sɔsjeteekrɑ̃] *(pl* **sociétés-écrans***)* NF shield company

socio- [sɔsjɔ] PRÉF socio-

socio [sɔsjo] **NF** *Fam* (*abrév* **sociologie**) sociology□

socioculturel, -elle [sɔsjɔkyltyrɛl] **ADJ** *(tendances, étude, groupe)* sociocultural; **centre s.** social and cultural centre

sociodrame [sɔsjɔdram] **NM** sociodrama

socio-économique [sɔsjɔekɔnɔmik] *(pl* **socio-économiques)** **ADJ** socioeconomic

socio-éducatif, -ive [sɔsjɔedykatif, -iv] *(mpl* **socio-éducatifs**, *fpl* **socio-éducatives)** **ADJ** socio-educational

sociogramme [sɔsjɔgram] **NM** sociogram

sociolinguistique [sɔsjɔlɛ̃gɥistik] **ADJ** sociolinguistic
NF sociolinguistics *(singulier)*

sociologie [sɔsjɔlɔʒi] **NF** sociology; **s. religieuse** sociology of religion

sociologique [sɔsjɔlɔʒik] **ADJ** sociological

sociologiquement [sɔsjɔlɔʒikmɑ̃] **ADV** sociologically

sociologue [sɔsjɔlɔg] **NMF** sociologist

socioprofessionnel, -elle [sɔsjɔprɔfesjɔnɛl] **ADJ** socio-professional

socio-style [sɔsjɔstil] *(pl* **socio-styles)** **NM** *Mktg* lifestyle group

socle [sɔkl] **NM 1** *Archit (piédestal)* pedestal, base; *(stylobate)* stylobate
2 *(d'un vase, d'une lampe, d'un moniteur)* base; *(d'un appareil)* stand; **s. orientable** *ou* **pivotant** *(d'un moniteur)* swivel base
3 *Constr (d'un bâtiment)* plinth, socle; *(d'un mur)* footing; **s. de béton** base course, (concrete) sole
4 *Géol* shelf
5 *Menuis (de chambranle)* skirting, capping; *(de marche)* string, stairstring

socque [sɔk] **NM 1** *Antiq* sock **2** *(chaussure)* clog

socquette [sɔkɛt] **NF** ankle sock, *Am* bobby sock

Socrate [sɔkrat] **NPR** Socrates

socratique [sɔkratik] **ADJ** Socratic

soda [sɔda] **NM 1** *(boisson gazeuse)* fizzy drink, *Am* soda; **s. à l'orange** orangeade, *Am* orange soda **2** *(eau de Seltz)* soda (water); **whisky s.** whisky and soda

sodique [sɔdik] **ADJ** sodic, sodium *(avant n)*

sodium [sɔdjɔm] **NM** sodium

Sodome [sɔdɔm] **NF** *Bible* Sodom; **S. et Gomorrhe** Sodom and Gomorrah

sodomie [sɔdɔmi] **NF** sodomy, buggery

sodomiser [3] [sɔdɔmize] **VT** to sodomize, to bugger

sodomite [sɔdɔmit] **NM** sodomite

sœur [sœr] **NF 1** *(parente)* sister; **ma grande/petite s.** my big/little sister; **ma s. aînée/cadette** my elder *or* older/younger sister; **s. de lait/de sang** foster/blood sister; *très Fam* **et ta s.!** mind your own damn business!; *Fig* **l'envie et la calomnie sont sœurs** envy and slander are sisters **2** *Rel* sister, nun; **chez les sœurs** with the nuns, in a convent; **bien, ma s.** very well, sister; *Fam* **bonne s.** nun□

sœurette [sœrɛt] **NF** *Fam* (little) sister□; **ça va, s.?** alright, sis?

sofa [sɔfa] **NM** sofa

soffite [sɔfit] **NM** *Archit* soffit

Sofia [sɔfja] **NM** Sofia

SOFRES, Sofres [sɔfrɛs] **NF** (*abrév* **Société française d'enquêtes par sondages**) **la S.** = French market research company

soft[1] [sɔft] **NM INV** *Fam* software□

soft[2] [sɔft] *Fam* **ADJ INV** *(ambiance, atmosphère, approche)* non-violent, calm; *(pornographie)* soft(core); *(film, roman)* soft-porn
NM soft porn

software [sɔftwɛr] **NM** software

soi [swa] **PRON 1** *(représentant un sujet indéterminé)* oneself; **n'aimer que s.** to love only oneself; **être content de s.** to be pleased with oneself; **il ne faut pas penser qu'à s.** one shouldn't think only of oneself; **marmonner qch pour s. seul** to mumble sth to oneself *or* under one's breath; **quand on marche, il faut regarder devant s.** you must keep looking in front of you when you walk; **ne pas regarder derrière s.** not to look back; **avoir de l'argent/ses papiers sur s.** to have some money/one's papers on one; **prendre sur s.** to get a grip on oneself **2** *(représentant un sujet déterminé ▸ homme)* himself; *(▸ femme)* herself; *(▸ être inanimé)* itself; **on ne pouvait lui reprocher de ne penser qu'à s.** he/she couldn't be blamed for thinking only of himself/herself **3** *(locutions)* **en s.** in itself, *Sout* per se; **ce geste en s. n'est pas condamnable** the gesture is not blameworthy in itself; **cela va de s.** of course, that goes without saying; **il va de s. que…** it goes without saying that…
NM *Phil* **le s.** the self; *Psy* the id

soi-disant [swadizɑ̃] **ADJ INV 1** *(qu'on prétend tel ▸ liberté, gratuité)* so-called; *(▸ coupable, responsable)* alleged **2** *(qui se prétend tel ▸ aristocrate)* self-styled; *(▸ ami, héritier, génie)* so-called; **ce s. plombier était en fait un espion** the so-called plumber turned out to be a spy
ADV *Fam (à ce qu'on prétend)* supposedly□, allegedly□; **tu étais s. absent!** you were supposed to be out!□; **elle est sortie, s. pour acheter du fromage** she went out, supposedly to get some cheese□ *or* to get some cheese, or so she said□
• **soi-disant que** **CONJ** *Fam* apparently□; **s. qu'il ne nous aurait pas vus!** he didn't see us, or so he said!□

soie [swa] **NF 1** *Tex* silk; **s. grège/naturelle/sauvage** raw/natural/wild silk; **s. moirée** watered silk; *Fig* **dormir** *ou* **vivre dans la s.** to live in the lap of luxury **2** *Zool (de sanglier, de chenille)* bristle; *(de bivalves)* byssus; **blaireau en soies de sanglier** bristle shaving brush **3** *(d'un couteau, d'une épée)* tang
• **de soie** **ADJ** *(étoffe, tapis)* silk *(avant n)*; *(peau)* silky

soierie [swari] **NF 1** *(étoffe)* silk **2** *(activité)* silk trade

soif [swaf] **NF 1** *(envie de boire)* thirst; **avoir s.** to be thirsty; **avoir grand s.** to be parched; **ça m'a donné s.** it made me thirsty; *Fam* **il fait s.** I'd kill for a drink, *Br* I could murder a drink; **jusqu'à plus s.** *(boire)* till one's thirst is quenched; *Fig* to one's heart's content; *Fig* **rester sur sa s.** to remain unsatisfied **2** *Fig (désir)* **s. de pouvoir/de richesses** craving for power/for wealth; **s. de connaissances** thirst for knowledge; **avoir s. de sang** to thirst for blood

soiffard, -e [swafar, -ard] *Fam* **ADJ** *(personne)* boozy
NM,F boozer, alky

soignant, -e [swaɲɑ̃, -ɑ̃t] **ADJ personnel s.** nursing staff

soigné, -e [swaɲe] **ADJ 1** *(propre ▸ apparence, personne)* neat, tidy, well-groomed; *(▸ vêtements)* neat; *(▸ ongles)* well-kept; *(▸ mains)* well-cared for; **être très s. de sa personne** to be very well-groomed; **peu s.** *(apparence, personne, tenue)* untidy; *(coiffure)* unkempt; **très peu s.** slovenly **2** *(fait avec soin ▸ décoration)* carefully done; *(▸ style)* polished; *(▸ écriture, coiffure)* neat, tidy; *(▸ travail)* neat, careful; *(▸ dîner)* carefully prepared; *(▸ jardin)* neat, well-kept; **peu s.** *(jardin)* badly kept; *(dîner)* carelessly put together; *(écriture)* untidy; *(travail)* careless, shoddy **3** *Fam (en intensif)* **j'ai un mal de tête s.!** I've got a splitting headache!; **le devoir de chimie était s.!** the chemistry paper was a real stinker!; **l'addition était soignée** the *Br* bill *or Am* check was a bit steep

soigner [3] [swaɲe] **VT 1** *(malade)* to treat, to nurse, to look after; *(maladie)* to treat; **il ne veut pas se faire s.** he refuses (any) treatment; **ils m'ont soigné aux antibiotiques** they treated me with antibiotics; **je n'arrive pas à s. mon rhume** I can't get rid of my cold; *Fam* **il faut te faire s.!** you need (to get) your head examined!
2 *(bien traiter ▸ ami, animal, plantes)* to look after, to take care of; *(▸ jardin)* to look after; *Fam* **elle soigne son petit mari** she takes good care of *or* she looks after her hubby
3 *(être attentif à ▸ apparence, tenue, présentation, prononciation)* to take care *or* trouble over; *(▸ écriture, style)* to polish (up); *(▸ image de marque)* to take good care of, to nurse; *(▸ repas)* to prepare carefully, to take trouble over (the preparation of); **s. le moindre détail** to take care over every detail
4 *Fam (exagérer)* **ils ont soigné l'addition!** the *Br* bill's *or Am* check's a bit steep!
• **se soigner** **VPR 1** *(prendre des médicaments)* **tu devrais te s.** you should take something for it; **il se soigne à l'homéopathie** he relies on homeopathic treatment when he's ill; *Hum* **je suis timide mais je me soigne!** I'm shy but I'm doing my best to overcome it! **2** *(pouvoir être soigné)* to be susceptible to treatment; **ça se soigne bien** it can be easily treated; **ça se soigne difficilement** it's difficult to treat (it); *Fam Hum* **ça se soigne, tu sais!** they have a cure for that these days, you know!

soigneur [swaɲœr] **NM** *(d'un boxeur)* second; *(d'un cycliste)* trainer; *(d'une équipe de football, de rugby) Br* physiotherapist, *Am* physical therapist

soigneuse [swaɲøz] *voir* **soigneux**

soigneusement [swaɲøzmɑ̃] **ADV** *(écrire, plier)* neatly, carefully; *(rincer, laver)* carefully; **elle ferma très s. la porte** she closed the door very carefully *or* with great care; **sa chambre est toujours rangée très s.** his/her room is always very neat (and tidy)

soigneux, -euse [swaɲø, -øz] **ADJ 1** *(propre et ordonné)* tidy; **il n'est pas du tout s. dans son travail** he's quite untidy *or* messy in his work; **tu n'es pas assez s. de tes habits** you're not careful enough with *or* you don't take enough care of your clothes **2** *(consciencieux ▸ employé)* meticulous; *(▸ recherches, travail)* careful, meticulous; **elle est très soigneuse dans ce qu'elle fait** she's very careful in what she does, she takes great care over her work **3** *(soucieux)* **s. de sa réputation** mindful of his reputation

soi-même [swamɛm] **PRON** oneself; **être/rester s.** to be/to remain oneself; **il faut tout faire s. ici** you have to do everything yourself around here; **faire qch de s.** to do sth spontaneously; **par s.** by oneself, on one's own; **se replier sur s.** to withdraw into oneself

SOIN [swɛ̃]

NM	
• care **1, 2**	• concern **2**
• neatness **3**	• task **4**
NMPL	
• care **1, 2**	• treatment **1**
• attention **2**	

NM 1 *(attention)* care; **avoir** *ou* **prendre (bien) s. de qch** to take (good) care of sth; **prendre s. de qn** to look after *or* to take care of sb; **avoir** *ou* **prendre s. de faire qch** to take care to do *or* to make a point of doing sth; **prends s. de fermer toutes les portes à clé** take care to *or* make sure that you lock all the doors; **elle a bien pris s. de lui cacher son identité** she took great care to conceal *or* went to a great deal of trouble concealing her identity from him/her; **avec s.** carefully, with care; **être sans s. (dans son travail)** to be careless (in one's work); **faire qch sans s.** to do sth carelessly; **manque de s.** carelessness
2 *(souci)* care, concern; **mon premier s. fut de tout ranger** my first concern *or* the first thing I did was to put everything back into place
3 *(propreté)* neatness; **avoir beaucoup de s.** to be very tidy *or* orderly; **elle n'a aucun s.** she's totally untidy *or* messy; **avec s.** neatly, tidily; **sa maison est toujours rangée avec s.** his/her house is always very neat *or* tidy; **être sans s.** to be untidy; **il a peint le cadre sans aucun s.** he made a mess of painting the frame
4 *(responsabilité)* task; **je te laisse le s. de la convaincre** I'm leaving it (up) to you to convince her; **confier à qn le s. de faire qch** to entrust sb with the task of doing sth; **il lui a confié le s. de gérer son garage** he entrusted him/her with running his garage
• **soins** **NMPL 1** *(prodigués à une personne ▸ de routine)* care; *(▸ médicaments)* treatment; **cela ne requiert pas de soins particuliers** it doesn't require any special medical attention *or* care; **donner** *ou* **dispenser des soins à** *(médicaux)* to give medical care to; **premiers soins, soins d'urgence** first aid; **soins de beauté** skin care *(for the face)*; **soins du corps** skin care *(for the body)*; **soins dentaires** dental treatment *or* care; **soins intensifs** intensive care; **soins (médicaux)** medical care *or*

treatment; **soins post-hospitaliers** follow-up care; **soins prolongés** extended care; **soins du visage** skin care *(for the face)* **2** *(attention)* care, attention; **nous apporterons tous nos soins au règlement de cette affaire** we'll do our utmost to settle this matter; **confier qn aux (bons) soins de qn** to leave sb in the care of sb; **aux bons soins de** *(dans le courrier)* care of; *Fam* **sa grand-mère est aux petits soins pour lui** his grandmother waits on him hand and foot

soir [swar] **NM 1** *(fin du jour)* evening; *(début de la nuit)* night; **les soirs d'été** summer evenings; **le s. tombe** night is falling, the evening is drawing in; **le s. de ses vingt ans** on the evening of her twentieth birthday; *Littéraire* **au s. de sa vie** in the evening of his/her life **2** *(dans des expressions de temps)* **ce s.** tonight, this evening; **à ce s.!** see you tonight *or* this evening!; **lundi s.** Monday evening *or* night; **hier s.** yesterday evening, last night; **le onze au s.** on the eleventh in the evening, on the evening of the eleventh; **le s.** in the evening, in the evenings; **tous les soirs, chaque s.** every evening; **vers six heures du s.** around six (o'clock) in the evening, around six p.m.; **à dix heures du s.** at ten (o'clock) at night, at ten p.m.

• **du soir ADJ 1** *(journal)* evening *(avant n)*; *(prière)* night *(avant n)* **2** *Fam (personne)* **il est du s.** he's a night owl

soirée [sware] **NF 1** *(fin de la journée)* evening; **les longues soirées d'hiver** the long winter evenings; **viens dans la s.** *(aujourd'hui)* come this evening; *(un jour quelconque)* come in the evening; *Fam* **on s'est fait une s. télévision/théâtre** we spent the evening in front of the television/at the theatre; **bonne s.!** have a nice evening!, enjoy your evening! **2** *(fête, réunion)* party; **s. dansante** (evening) dance; **s. de gala** gala evening; **s. musicale** musical evening **3** *Cin & Théât* evening performance; **projeter un film en s.** to show a movie *or Br* film in the evening, to have an evening showing of a film; **elle n'a pas joué en s.** she didn't play in the evening performance

sois *etc voir* **être**[1]

soit CONJ [swa] **1** *(c'est-à-dire)* that is to say; **il a perdu toute sa fortune, s. plusieurs millions d'euros** he has lost his entire fortune, that is to say several million euros **2** *(introduisant une hypothèse)* **s. une droite AB** let AB be a line, given a line AB

ADV [swat] **s., j'accepte vos conditions** very well then, I accept your conditions; **tu préfères cela? eh bien s.!** all right *or* very well then, if that's what you prefer!

• **soit que... ou que... CONJ** either... or...; **s. que le train ait eu du retard ou qu'il y ait eu des embouteillages, ils arrivèrent après minuit** either the train was late or they were held up in traffic, but they arrived after midnight

• **soit que..., soit que... CONJ** either... or...; **s. que vous veniez chez moi, s. que j'aille chez vous, nous nous retrouverons demain** either you come to my place or I'll go to yours, but we'll meet up tomorrow

• **soit... soit... CONJ** either... or...; **s. toi, s. moi** either you or me; **j'ai cet article s. en rouge, s. en bleu, s. en vert** I have this item (either) in red, blue or green; **c'est s. l'un, s. l'autre** it's (either) one or the other

soixantaine [swasɑ̃tɛn] **NF 1** *(quantité)* **une s.** around *or* about sixty, sixty or so; **une s. de voitures** around *or* about sixty cars **2** *(âge)* **avoir la s.** to be around *or* about sixty; **quand on arrive à la s.** when you hit sixty

soixante [swasɑ̃t] **ADJ 1** *(gén)* sixty **2** *(dans des séries)* sixtieth; **page/numéro s.** page/number sixty

PRON sixty

NM INV 1 *(gén)* sixty **2** *(numéro d'ordre)* number sixty **3** *(chiffre écrit)* sixty; *voir aussi* **cinquante**

soixante-dix [swasɑ̃tdis] **ADJ INV 1** *(gén)* seventy **2** *(dans des séries)* seventieth; **page/numéro s.** page/number seventy

PRON INV seventy

NM INV 1 *(gén)* seventy **2** *(numéro d'ordre)* number seventy **3** *(chiffre écrit)* seventy; *voir aussi* **cinquante**

soixante-dixième [swasɑ̃tdizjɛm] *(pl* **soixante-dixièmes) ADJ** seventieth

NMF 1 *(personne)* seventieth **2** *(objet)* seventieth (one)

NM 1 *(partie)* seventieth **2** *(étage) Br* seventieth floor, *Am* seventy-first floor; *voir aussi* **cinquième**

soixante-huitard, -e [swasɑ̃tɥitar, -ard] *(mpl* **soixante-huitards,** *fpl* **soixante-huitardes) ADJ** *(réforme)* = brought about by the students' revolt of 1968; *(tendance)* anti-establishment

NM,F veteran of the 1968 students' revolt

soixante-neuf [swasɑ̃tnœf] **NM INV** *Fam (position sexuelle)* sixty-nine

soixantième [swasɑ̃tjɛm] **ADJ** sixtieth

NMF 1 *(personne)* sixtieth **2** *(objet)* sixtieth (one)

NM 1 *(partie)* sixtieth **2** *(étage) Br* sixtieth floor, *Am* sixty-first floor; *voir aussi* **cinquième**

soja [sɔʒa] **NM** soya; **lait de s.** soya milk

sol [sɔl] **NM INV** *Mus* G; *(chanté)* sol, so, soh

NM 1 *Agr & Hort (terre)* soil; **s. calcaire** chalky soil

2 *(surface ▸ de la Terre)* ground; *(▸ d'une planète)* surface; **l'avion s'est écrasé au s.** the plane crashed

3 *(surface aménagée ▸ à l'intérieur)* floor; **le s. du hangar** the floor of the shed; **pour l'entretien des sols** for cleaning floors

4 *Littéraire (patrie)* soil; **sur le s. américain** on American soil; **son s. natal** his/her native soil

5 *Géol* soil, *Spéc* solum

6 *Chim* sol

• **au sol ADJ 1** *Sport (exercice)* floor *(avant n)* **2** *Aviat (vitesse, ravitaillement, personnel)* ground *(avant n)*

> Attention: ne pas confondre **floor** et **ground** lorsqu'on traduit **sol. Floor** désigne toujours le sol à l'intérieur d'un bâtiment, alors que **ground** s'utilise uniquement pour l'extérieur.

sol-air [sɔlɛr] **ADJ INV** ground-to-air; **S. Missile** surface-to-air missile, SAM

solaire [sɔlɛr] **ADJ 1** *Astron* solar; **le rayonnement s.** the Sun's radiation

2 *(qui utilise le soleil ▸ capteur, four)* solar; *(▸ habitat)* solar, solar-heated

3 *(qui protège du soleil)* sun *(avant n)*; **crème/huile s.** suntan cream/oil

4 *Anat* **plexus s.** solar plexus

NM *École* **le s.** solar energy

solarisation [sɔlarizasjɔ̃] **NF** solarization

solariser **[3]** [sɔlarize] *Phot* **VT** to solarize

VPR se solariser to solarize

solarium [sɔlarjɔm] **NM** solarium

soldat [sɔlda] **NM 1** *Mil* soldier; *(grade)* private; **s. Dubois!** Private Dubois!; **se faire s.** to go into *or* to join the army; **simple s., s. de deuxième classe** *(dans l'armée de terre)* private; *(dans l'armée de l'air) Br* aircraftman, *Am* airman basic; **s. de première classe** *(dans l'armée de terre) Br* ≃ lance corporal, *Am* ≃ private first class; **le S. inconnu** the Unknown Soldier *or* Warrior **2** *(jeu)* **(petits) soldats de plomb** tin *or* lead *or* toy soldiers; **jouer aux petits soldats** to play with toy soldiers; *Fam* **jouer au petit s.** to swagger **3** *Entom* soldier (ant)

soldate [sɔldat] **NF** *Fam* woman soldier[□], servicewoman[□]

soldatesque [sɔldatɛsk] *Littéraire* **ADJ des manières soldatesques** rough soldierly manners

NF *Péj* **la s.** army rabble

solde[1] [sɔld] **NF 1** *Mil* pay **2** *(en Afrique francophone) (salaire)* salary, wages

• **à la solde de PRÉP** *Péj* in the pay of; **il était à la s. de l'ennemi** he was in the pay of the enemy; **avoir qn à sa s.** to be sb's paymaster

solde[2] [sɔld] **NM 1** *Fin (d'un compte)* (bank) balance; *(à payer)* outstanding balance; **pour s. de tout compte** in full settlement; **régler le s.** to pay the balance; **s. actif** credit balance; **s. bancaire, s. en banque** bank balance; **s. bénéficiaire** credit balance; **s. en caisse** cash balance; **s. commercial** balance of trade; **s. créditeur** credit balance; **s. cumulé** cumulative balance; **s. débiteur** *ou* **déficitaire** debit balance, balance owed; **s. à découvert** outstanding balance; **s. disponible** available balance; **s. de dividende** final dividend; **s. dû** balance due; **s. de fin de mois** end-of-month balance; *Compta* **s. à nouveau** balance brought forward; *Compta* **s. nul** nil balance; **s. d'ouverture** opening balance; **s. passif** debit balance; *Compta* **s. reporté** balance brought forward; **s. à reporter** balance carried forward; **s. de trésorerie** cash balance **2** *Com (vente)* sale; *(marchandise)* sale item *or* article; **en s.** *(marchandise) Br* in the sale, *Am* on sale; **acheter** *ou* **avoir qch en s.** to buy *or* to get sth *Br* in the sale *or Am* on sale; **le bonnet était en s.** the hat was reduced; **mettre** *ou* **vendre qch en s.** to sell sth off; **s. de fermeture** closing-down sale; **s. de fin de saison** end-of-season sale

• **soldes NMPL** *(période)* sale, sales; **au moment des soldes** during the sales, when the sales are on; **faire les soldes** to go round the sales; **ils font des soldes toute l'année** they have sales *or* a sale on all year round

solder **[3]** [sɔlde] **VT 1** *Com (stock)* to sell off, to discount; **toutes nos chemises sont soldées** all our shirts are at a reduced *or* at sale price; **elle me l'a soldé pour 30 euros** she knocked the price down to 30 euros, she let me have it for 30 euros **2** *(dette)* to settle; **s. l'arriéré** to make up back payments **3** *Banque (compte)* to close

USAGE ABSOLU *Com* **on solde!** the sales are on!, there's a sale on!

VPR se solder 1 se s. par *(se terminer par)* to result in; **se s. par un échec** to result in failure, to come to nothing; **leurs cinq derniers matchs se sont soldés par une défaite** their last five matches ended in defeat **2** *Com, Écon & Fin* **se s. par un excédent/un déficit de qch** to show a surplus/a deficit of sth

soldeur, -euse [sɔldœr, -øz] **NM,F** discount trader

sole [sɔl] **NF 1** *(d'un four)* hearth

2 *Agr* break (field)

3 *Mines* sill, sole

4 *(d'un cheval)* sole

5 *Tech* sole piece

6 *Constr* (trowel) throw

7 *Naut (d'un navire)* flat bottom

8 *Ich* sole

solécisme [sɔlesism] **NM** *Gram* solecism

soleil [sɔlɛj] **NM 1** *(étoile qui éclaire la Terre)* **le S.** the Sun; **se lever avec le s.** to be up with the lark; **le s. levant/couchant** the rising/setting sun; **au s. levant/couchant** at sunrise/sunset; **le s. de minuit** the midnight sun; **il n'y a rien de nouveau sous le s.** there is nothing new under the sun; *Prov* **le s. brille pour tout le monde** = the sun shines for everyone

2 *(étoile quelconque)* sun

3 *(chaleur)* sun, sunshine; *(clarté)* sun, sunlight, sunshine; **quelques brèves apparitions du s.** some sunny spells; **il y a** *ou* **il fait du s.** the sun is shining, it's sunny; **une journée sans s.** a day with no sunshine; **un s. de plomb** a blazing sun; **ma chambre manque de s.** my room doesn't get enough sun *or* sunlight; **on a le s. sur le balcon jusqu'à midi** the balcony gets the sun until noon; **au s.** in the sun; *Fig* **avoir des biens** *ou* **du bien au s.** to own property; **tu es en plein s.** you're right in the sun; **prendre le s.** to sunbathe

4 *Bot* sunflower

5 *Sport* (backward) grand circle

6 *(feu d'artifice)* Catherine wheel

7 *Hér* sol

solennel, -elle [sɔlanɛl] **ADJ 1** *(obsèques, honneurs, silence)* solemn; **prendre des airs solennels** to adopt a solemn air **2** *(déclaration, occasion, personne, ton)* solemn, formal **3** *Jur (contrat)* solemn

solennellement [sɔlanɛlmɑ̃] **ADV 1** *(en grande pompe)* formally, ceremoniously **2** *(cérémonieusement)* solemnly, in a solemn voice **3** *(officiellement)* solemnly; **je le jure s.** I solemnly swear

solenniser **[3]** [sɔlanize] **VT** to solemnize

solennité [sɔlanite] **NF 1** *(d'une réception)* solemnity **2** *(d'un ton, d'une personne)* solemnity, formality; **avec s.** solemnly **3** *(fête)* solemn ceremony *or* celebration

solénoïde [sɔlenɔid] **NM** solenoid

Solex® [sɔlɛks] **NM** ≃ moped

solfatare [sɔlfatar] **NF** solfatara

solfège [sɔlfɛʒ] **NM 1** *(notation)* music theory; *(déchiffrage)* sight-reading; **faire du s.** to study music theory; **s. chanté** sol-fa **2** *(manuel)* music primer

solfier **[9]** [sɔlfje] **VT** to sol-fa

solidaire [sɔlidɛr] **ADJ 1** *(personnes)* **être solidaires** *(les uns des autres)* to stand *or* to stick together; *(l'un de l'autre)* to show solidarity with each other; **nous sommes solidaires de nos camarades** we support *or* we stand by our comrades
2 *(reliés ▸ processus, pièces mécaniques)* interdependent; **être s. de** to interact with; **une roue s. d'une autre** a wheel integral with another
3 *(interdépendants)* interdependent; **ces deux questions sont solidaires (l'une de l'autre)** these two questions are interdependent
4 *Jur (responsabilité)* joint and several; *(personnes)* jointly liable; **obligation s.** obligation binding on all parties

solidairement [sɔlidɛrmɑ̃] **ADV 1** *(conjointement)* jointly, in solidarity with each other
2 *Fig* **les processus fonctionnent s.** the processes are interdependent
3 *Tech (par engrenage)* in a mesh; *(directement)* locked (together)
4 *Jur* jointly and severally

solidariser [3] [sɔlidarize] **VT 1** *(faire partager les mêmes intérêts)* to unify, to bring together **2** *(relier ▸ processus)* to make interdependent **3** *Tech (par engrenage)* to mesh; *(directement)* to lock (together), to interlock
VPR se solidariser se s. (avec) to make common cause (with), to show solidarity (with)

solidarité [sɔlidarite] **NF 1** *(entre personnes)* solidarity; **par s. avec** out of fellow-feeling for, in order to show solidarity with; **s. ministérielle** ministerial responsibility
2 *(de processus)* interdependence
3 *Tech (engrenage)* meshing; *(entraînement)* locking, interlocking
4 *Jur* joint and several liability

SOLIDE [sɔlid]

ADJ
- solid **1, 2, 4, 5, 7**
- strong **1, 2**
- firm **2**
- resistant **6**
- sturdy **1, 3**
- sound **2, 3**
- substantial **4**

NM
- solid ground **2**
- solid **4**
- solid food **3**

ADJ 1 *(résistant ▸ meubles, matériel)* solid, sturdy, strong; *(▸ papier)* tough, strong; *(▸ vêtements)* hard-wearing; *(▸ bâtiment)* solid, strong; *(▸ verrou, nœud)* secure; **peu s.** *(chaise, pont)* rickety; **attention, cette chaise n'est pas très s.** careful, that chair's not very safe
2 *(établi, stable ▸ formation, culture, technique)* sound; *(▸ entreprise)* well-established; *(▸ institution, argument, preuves)* solid, sound; *(▸ garanties)* solid, reliable; *(▸ professionnalisme, réputation)* solid; *(▸ bases)* solid, sound, firm; *(▸ amitié)* firm, strong; *(▸ foi)* firm, staunch; *(▸ principes, qualités)* staunch, sound, sterling *(avant n)*; *(▸ liens)* strong, close; *(▸ monnaie)* strong, firm; **j'ai de solides raisons de croire que...** I have good reasons for believing that...; **ça ne repose sur rien de s.** there is no sound *or* no solid basis for that
3 *(robuste ▸ personne, membre)* sturdy, robust; *(▸ santé)* sound; **avoir une s. constitution** to have a strong constitution; **le poulain n'est pas encore très s. sur ses pattes** the foal isn't very steady on its legs yet; **le cœur n'est plus très s.** the heart's getting weaker; **la tête n'est plus très s.** his/her mind's going; **être encore s. comme un roc** to be still hale and hearty
4 *(avant le nom) Fam (substantiel)* substantial[□], solid[□]; **un s. petit déjeuner** a substantial *or* solid breakfast; **avoir une s. avance sur ses concurrents** to enjoy a secure *or* comfortable lead over one's rivals[□]; **avoir un s. appétit** *ou* **coup de fourchette** to have a hearty appetite[□]
5 *(non liquide ▸ aliments, corps, état)* solid; **la lave devient s. en refroidissant** lava solidifies *or* hardens as it cools down; **elle ne peut rien manger de s.** she can't eat solid foods *or* solids
6 *Tex (tissu)* resistant; *(teinture)* fast
7 *Math* solid
NM 1 *(ce qui est robuste)* **les voitures suédoises, c'est du s.** Swedish cars are built to last; *Fam* **son dernier argument, c'est du s.!** his/her last argument is rock solid!
2 *(sol ferme)* solid ground
3 *(aliments solides)* solids, solid food
4 *Math & Phys* solid; **s. de révolution** solid of revolution

solidement [sɔlidmɑ̃] **ADV 1** *(fortement)* securely, firmly; **attache-le s. à cet arbre** tie it securely to this tree; **un homme s. bâti** a solidly *or* a sturdily built man **2** *(profondément)* firmly; **c'est une croyance s. ancrée** it's a deeply-rooted *or* a deep-seated belief **3** *Fam (en intensif)* seriously; **je l'ai s. grondé** I gave him a good talking-to

solidification [sɔlidifikasjɔ̃] **NF** solidification

solidifier [9] [sɔlidifje] **VT** to solidify, to harden
VPR se solidifier to solidify, to harden

solidité [sɔlidite] **NF 1** *(d'un meuble)* solidity, sturdiness; *(d'un vêtement)* sturdiness, durability; *(d'un bâtiment)* solidity; **c'est d'une s. à toute épreuve** it stands up to anything
2 *(d'une institution, de principes, d'arguments)* solidity, soundness; *(d'une amitié)* firmness, strength; *(d'une équipe)* reliability; *(d'une monnaie)* strength
3 *(force d'une personne)* sturdiness, robustness
4 *Tex (d'un tissu)* resistance; *(d'une teinture)* colourfastness

soliloque [sɔlilɔk] **NM** soliloquy

soliloquer [3] [sɔlilɔke] **VI** to soliloquize

solin [sɔlɛ̃] **NM** *Constr (espace)* space between joists; *(enduit)* plaster filling

solipsisme [sɔlipsism] **NM** *Phil* solipsism

soliste [sɔlist] **NMF** soloist

solitaire [sɔlitɛr] **ADJ 1** *(personne, existence, activité)* solitary, lonely
2 *(isolé ▸ île, quartier, retraite)* solitary, lone; **passer des vacances solitaires** to spend one's holidays on one's own
3 *Archit (colonne)* isolated
4 *Bot & Zool* solitary; **ver s.** tapeworm
NMF *(misanthrope)* loner
NM 1 *(anachorète)* hermit, recluse **2** *(jeu, diamant)* solitaire **3** *Zool (sanglier)* solitary boar
• **en solitaire ADJ** *(course, vol)* solo *(avant n)*; *(navigation)* single-handed **ADV** *(vivre, travailler)* on one's own; *(naviguer)* single-handed; **il vit en s. dans sa vieille maison** he lives on his own in his old house

solitairement [sɔlitɛrmɑ̃] **ADV se promener s.** to walk alone; **vivre s.** to lead a solitary life

solitude [sɔlityd] **NF 1** *(d'une personne ▸ momentanée)* solitude; *(▸ habituelle)* loneliness; **rechercher la s.** to seek solitude; **la s. lui pèse** solitude weighs heavily upon him/her; **j'aime la s.** I like to be alone *or* on my own; **vivre dans la s.** to live alone *or* on one's own; **la s. à deux** the loneliness of a couple *(when the two stop communicating with each other)* **2** *(d'une forêt, d'un paysage)* loneliness, solitude **3** *Littéraire (lieu solitaire)* **les grandes solitudes désertiques** the vast lonely expanses of the desert

solive [sɔliv] **NF** *Constr* joist

sollicitation [sɔlisitasjɔ̃] **NF 1** *(requête)* request, entreaty; **j'ai fini par céder à leurs sollicitations** I ended up giving in to their requests
2 *(tentation)* temptation
3 *(poussée, traction)* **les freins répondent à la moindre s.** the brakes are extremely responsive
4 *Constr* stress

solliciter [3] [sɔlisite] **VT 1** *(requérir ▸ entrevue)* to request, to solicit, *Sout* to beg the favour of; *(▸ aide, conseils)* to solicit, to seek (urgently); *(▸ emploi)* to apply for; *(▸ voix)* to canvass for; **s. qch de qn** to request sth from sb; **je me permets de s. votre bienveillance** may I appeal to your kindness
2 *(mettre en éveil ▸ curiosité, attention)* to arouse; *(▸ élève)* to spur *or* to urge on
3 *(texte)* to overinterpret
4 *(faire appel à)* to approach, to appeal to; **être très sollicité** to be (very much) in demand; **on m'a déjà sollicité pour une séance de pose** I've already been approached for a photocall; **s. qn de faire qch** to appeal to sb to do sth
5 *(faire fonctionner ▸ mécanisme)* to put a strain on; **dès que les freins sont sollicités** as soon as you touch the brakes
6 *Équitation (cheval)* to spur *or* to urge on

solliciteur, -euse [sɔlisitœr, -øz] **NM,F** *(quémandeur)* suppliant, supplicant

sollicitude [sɔlisityd] **NF** *(intérêt ▸ affectueux)* (excessive) care, *Sout* solicitude; *(▸ soucieux)* concern, *Sout* solicitude; **être plein de s. envers qn** to be very attentive to *or* towards sb

solo [sɔlo] *(pl* **solos** *ou* **soli** [-li]) **NM 1** *Mus* solo; **s. de piano** piano solo; **elle chante en s.** she sings solo **2** *Théât (spectacle ▸ d'homme)* one-man show; *(▸ de femme)* one-woman show
NMF *(pl* **solos)** *(célibataire)* single person; **les solos** singles
ADJ INV solo *(avant n)*; **album s.** solo album; *Théât* **spectacle s.** *(d'homme)* one-man show; *(de femme)* one-woman show

sol-sol [sɔlsɔl] **ADJ INV** *(missile)* ground-to-ground

solstice [sɔlstis] **NM** solstice; **s. d'été/d'hiver** summer/winter solstice

solubiliser [3] [sɔlybilize] **VT** to solubilize, to make soluble

solubilité [sɔlybilite] **NF** solubility

soluble [sɔlybl] **ADJ 1** *Chim* soluble; **s. dans l'eau** water-soluble **2** *(problème)* solvable, soluble

soluté [sɔlyte] **NM** *Chim* solute; **s. physiologique** saline solution, (artificial) serum

solution [sɔlysjɔ̃] **NF 1** *(résolution, clé)* solution, answer (**de** to); *Scol* **la s. d'un exercice** the solution *or* the answer to an exercise; **l'envoyer en prison ne serait pas une s.** sending him/her to prison wouldn't solve anything *or* wouldn't be a solution; **une s. de facilité** an easy way out; **s. de principe** standard solution
2 *(terme ▸ d'une crise)* resolution, settling; *(▸ d'une situation complexe)* resolution
3 *Hist* **la s. finale** the Final Solution
4 *Math* solution
5 *Méd* **s. de continuité** solution of continuity; *Fig* **sans s. de continuité** without interruption
6 *Chim & Pharm* solution; **en s.** dissolved, in (a) solution; *Phot* **s. de fixage** fixing solution; **s. de rinçage** wetting solution

solutionner [3] [sɔlysjɔne] **VT** to solve, to resolve

solvabilité [sɔlvabilite] **NF** solvency; **degré de s.** credit rating

solvable [sɔlvabl] **ADJ** solvent

> Il faut noter que l'adjectif anglais **solvable** est un faux ami. Il signifie **soluble, résoluble**.

solvant [sɔlvɑ̃] **NM** *Chim* solvent

soma [sɔma] **NM** *Biol* soma

somali, -e [sɔmali] **ADJ** Somalian, Somali
NM *(langue)* Somali
• **Somali, -e NM,F** Somali; **les Somalis** the Somalis *or* Somali

Somalie [sɔmali] **NF 1 la S.** *(république)* Somalia **2** *(bassin)* Somaliland; *Hist* **la S. britannique/italienne** British/Italian Somaliland

somalien, -enne [sɔmaljɛ̃, -ɛn] **ADJ** Somalian, Somali
NM *(langue)* Somali
• **Somalien, -enne NM,F** Somali; **les Somaliens** the Somalis *or* Somali

somatique [sɔmatik] **ADJ** somatic

somatisation [sɔmatizasjɔ̃] **NF** somatization

somatiser [3] [sɔmatize] **VT** *Psy* to somatize
USAGE ABSOLU mais non, tu n'es pas malade, tu somatises you're not really ill, it's all in your head

somatologie [sɔmatɔlɔʒi] **NF** somatology

sombre [sɔ̃br] **ADJ 1** *(pièce, ruelle, couleur, robe)* dark; **il fait très s.** it's very dark **2** *(personne, pensées, caractère, humeur, regard)* gloomy, melancholy, sombre; *(avenir, perspectives)* gloomy; **les jours les plus sombres de notre histoire** the darkest days of our history **3** *(avant le nom) Fam (en intensif)* **c'est une s. crapule/un s. crétin** he's the scum of the earth/a total idiot; **ils se sont fâchés pour une s. histoire d'argent** they quarrelled over some sordid little business of money; **un s. individu** an unsavoury character

sombrement [sɔ̃brəmɑ̃] **ADV** gloomily, sombrely; **"rien", fit-il s.** "nothing," he said gloomily

sombrer [3] [sɔ̃bre] **VI 1** *(bateau)* to sink, to founder **2** *(être anéanti ▸ civilisation)* to fall, to decline, to collapse; (▸ *entreprise*) to go bankrupt, to fail, to collapse; (▸ *projet*) to collapse, to fail; (▸ *espoir*) to fade, to be dashed; **sa raison a sombré** he/she lost his/her reason **3 s. dans** *(s'abandonner à)* to sink into; **s. dans le désespoir/la folie/l'alcoolisme** to sink into despair/insanity/alcoholism

sombrero [sɔ̃brero] **NM** sombrero

sommaire [sɔmɛr] **ADJ 1** *(succinct)* brief, succinct

2 *(rudimentaire ▸ réparation)* makeshift; (▸ *repas*) scanty; **il n'a reçu qu'une éducation s.** his education was rudimentary, to say the least

3 *(superficiel ▸ analyse)* summary, basic, superficial; (▸ *examen*) cursory, perfunctory; **faire une toilette s.** to have a quick wash

4 *(expéditif ▸ procès, exécution)* summary

NM *(d'un magazine)* summary; *(d'un livre)* summary, synopsis; **au s. de notre journal ce soir** our main news stories tonight

sommairement [sɔmɛrmɑ̃] **ADV 1** *(brièvement)* briefly **2** *(rudimentairement)* basically; **leur appartement est très s. meublé** their *Br* flat *or Am* apartment is very sparsely furnished *or* very basic **3** *(expéditivement)* summarily; **les prisonniers ont été s. exécutés** the prisoners were summarily executed

sommation [sɔmasjɔ̃] **NF 1** *Mil (avant de tirer)* warning, challenge; **faire une s.** to challenge; **tirer sans s.** to fire without warning

2 *Jur* notice, demand; **avoir s. de payer une dette** to receive notice *or* a demand to pay a debt; **s. de se présenter au tribunal** summons to appear (in court)

3 *(requête)* demand

4 *Math* summation

5 *Physiol* convergence

somme[1] [sɔm] **NM** nap; **faire un (petit) s.** to have a nap

somme[2] [sɔm] **NF 1** *Fin* **s. (d'argent)** sum *or* amount (of money); **pour la s. de 50 euros** for (the sum of) 50 euros; **j'ai dépensé des sommes folles** I spent huge amounts of money; **c'est une s.!** that's a lot of money!; **s. due** amount *or* total due; **s. forfaitaire** lump sum; **s. nette** net amount; *Compta* **sommes payables** sums payable; **s. totale** total amount, sum total

2 *Math* sum; **la s. totale** the grand total; **faire une s.** to add up (figures); **faire la s. de 15 et de 16** to add (up) 15 and 16; **s. algébrique** algebraic sum

3 *(quantité)* amount; **s. de travail/d'énergie** amount of work/of energy; **ça représente une s. de sacrifices/d'efforts importante** it means great sacrifices/a lot of effort

4 *(œuvre)* general survey

• **en somme ADV 1** *(en bref)* in short; **en s., tu refuses** in short, your answer is no **2** *(en définitive)* all in all; **c'est assez simple en s.** all in all, it's quite easy

• **somme toute ADV** all things considered, when all is said and done

sommeil [sɔmɛj] **NM 1** *(repos)* sleep; **je manque de s.** I haven't been getting enough sleep; **il cherchait le s.** he was trying to sleep; **j'en perds le s.** I'm losing sleep over it; **j'ai le s. léger/profond** I'm a light/a heavy sleeper; **une nuit sans s.** a sleepless night, a night without sleep; **avoir s.** to be *or* to feel sleepy; **tomber de s.** to be ready to drop, to be falling asleep (on one's feet); **s. lent/paradoxal** NREM/REM sleep; **s. partagé** co-sleeping; **le premier s.** the first hours of sleep; *Littéraire* **le s. éternel, le dernier s.** eternal rest; **dormir d'un s. de plomb** *(d'habitude)* to be a heavy sleeper, to sleep like a log; *(ponctuellement)* to be sleeping like a log *or* fast asleep **2** *Fig (inactivité)* inactivity, lethargy, sluggishness

• **en sommeil ADJ** *(volcan, économie)* inactive, dormant **ADV rester en s.** to remain dormant *or* inactive; **laisser une affaire en s.** to put a matter on the back burner

sommeiller [4] [sɔmeje] **VI 1** *(personne)* to doze **2** *(affaire, passion, volcan)* to lie dormant

sommelier, -ère [sɔməlje, -ɛr] **NM,F 1** *(caviste)* cellarman; *(qui sert les vins)* sommelier, wine waiter, *f* wine waitress **2** *Suisse (serveur)* waiter, *f* waitress

sommellerie [sɔmɛlri] **NF 1** *(métier)* sommelier's *or* wine waiter's job **2** *(cave)* wine cellar

sommer [3] [sɔme] **VT 1** *Jur* **s. qn de faire qch** to summon sb to do sth

2 *(ordonner à)* **s. qn de faire qch** to order sb to do sth

3 *Archit* to crown, to top

4 *Math* to add up

sommes *voir* **être**[1]

sommet [sɔmɛ] **NM 1** *(plus haut point ▸ d'un mont)* summit, highest point, top; (▸ *d'un bâtiment, d'un arbre)* top

2 *(partie supérieure ▸ d'un arbre, d'une colline)* crown; (▸ *d'une montagne)* top, summit; (▸ *d'une vague)* crest; (▸ *de la tête)* crown, *Spéc* vertex; *Méd* **présentation d'un bébé par le s.** head presentation of a baby

3 *(degré suprême ▸ d'une hiérarchie)* summit, top; (▸ *d'une carrière)* top, summit, *Sout* acme; **une décision prise au s.** a decision taken from the top; **le s. de la perfection** the acme of perfection; **le s. de la gloire** the height *or* pinnacle of fame

4 *Élec* node

5 *Math (d'un angle, d'une hyperbole)* vertex

6 *Pol* summit (meeting); **rencontre au s.** summit meeting

sommier [sɔmje] **NM 1** *(de lit)* (bed) base; **s. à lattes** slatted base; **s. métallique** wire mattress

2 *Archit (d'une voûte ▸ poutre)* springer, skewback; (▸ *pierre)* impost; *(d'un clocher)* stock

3 *Constr (d'une porte)* lintel; *(d'une grille)* crossbar

4 *Mus (d'un orgue)* windchest; *(d'un piano)* frame

5 *(de comptabilité)* register, ledger

sommité [sɔmite] **NF 1** *(personnage)* authority; **les sommités de la médecine** leading medical experts; **sommités du monde de l'art** leading figures *or* lights in the art world; **ce n'est pas une s.!** he's no genius! **2** *Bot* head

somnambule [sɔmnɑ̃byl] **ADJ être s.** to sleepwalk, to be a sleepwalker *or Spéc* somnambulist

NMF sleepwalker, *Spéc* somnambulist; **parler comme un s.** to speak like a zombie

somnambulisme [sɔmnɑ̃bylism] **NM** sleepwalking, *Spéc* somnambulism

somnifère [sɔmnifɛr] *Pharm* **ADJ** soporific, sleep-inducing

NM *(substance)* soporific; *(comprimé)* sleeping pill *or* tablet

somnolence [sɔmnɔlɑ̃s] **NF 1** *(d'une personne)* drowsiness, sleepiness, *Sout* somnolence; **la chaleur nous plonge dans un état de s.** the heat makes us drowsy *or* lethargic **2** *(d'une économie)* lethargy, sluggishness

somnolent, -e [sɔmnɔlɑ̃, -ɑ̃t] **ADJ 1** *(personne)* drowsy, sleepy, *Sout* somnolent **2** *(village)* sleepy; *(voix)* droning; *(esprit)* dull, lethargic, apathetic; *(économie)* lethargic, sluggish; *(faculté intellectuelle)* dormant

somnoler [3] [sɔmnɔle] **VI 1** *(personne)* to doze **2** *(ville)* to be sleepy; *(économie)* to be lethargic *or* in the doldrums; *(faculté intellectuelle)* to lie dormant, to slumber

somptuaire [sɔ̃ptɥɛr] **ADJ 1** *(dépenses)* extravagant **2** *Beaux-Arts* **arts somptuaires** decorative arts **3** *Antiq & Hist* sumptuary

somptueuse [sɔ̃ptɥøz] *voir* **somptueux**

somptueusement [sɔ̃ptɥøzmɑ̃] **ADV** *(décorer, illustrer)* sumptuously, lavishly, richly; *(vêtir)* sumptuously, magnificently

somptueux, -euse [sɔ̃ptɥø, -øz] **ADJ 1** *(luxueux ▸ vêtements, cadeau)* sumptuous, splendid; (▸ *décor, salon, palais)* magnificent, splendid **2** *(superbe ▸ banquet)* sumptuous, lavish; (▸ *illustration)* lavish; **la pièce a une somptueuse distribution** the play has a glittering cast

somptuosité [sɔ̃ptɥozite] **NF** *Littéraire (d'une toilette)* sumptuousness, magnificence; *(d'un décor, d'une pièce, d'illustrations)* sumptuousness, splendour, lavishness

son[1] [sɔ̃] **NM 1** *Ling, Mus & Phys* sound; **un s. étouffé** a muffled sound; **un s. sourd** a thump, a thud; **un s. strident** *(de Klaxon®, de trompette)* a blast; **émettre un s.** to give out a sound; **le mur rend un s. creux** the wall has a hollow sound; **le s. du tambour/de la trompette** the beat of the drum/blare of the trumpet; **danser au s. de l'accordéon** to dance to the music *or* to the sound *or* to the sounds of the accordeon; *Fig* **c'est un autre s. de cloche** that's (quite) another story; **j'ai entendu plusieurs sons de cloche** I've heard several variants *or* versions of that story; **annoncer qch à s. de trompe** to trumpet sth abroad; **(spectacle) s. et lumière** son et lumière **2** *(volume)* sound, volume; **baisser/monter le s.** to turn the sound up/down; **le niveau du s.** the sound level; **on a le s. mais pas l'image** we've got sound but no picture; *Cin* **le s. était épouvantable** the soundtrack was terrible **s. numérique/stéréo** digital/stereo sound; **s. 3D** surround sound

son[2] [sɔ̃] **NM** *Agr* bran; **s. d'avoine** oat bran; **flocons de s.** bran flakes; **pain au s.** bran loaf

son[3]**, sa, ses** [sɔ̃, sa, se]

> **sa** becomes **son** before a word beginning with a vowel or mute h.

ADJ POSSESSIF 1 *(d'un homme)* his; *(d'une femme)* her; *(d'une chose)* its; *(d'un bateau, d'une nation)* its, her; **s. frère et sa sœur, ses frère et sœur** his/her brother and sister; **il a mis s. chapeau et ses gants** he put on his hat and (his) gloves; **un de ses amis** a friend of his/hers, one of his/her friends; **donne-lui s. biberon** give him/her his/her bottle; **le bébé, dès ses premiers contacts avec le monde** the baby, from its first experience of the world; **la police est à sa recherche** the police are looking for him/her/it; **s. propre fils** his/her own son; *Fam* **dans sa maison à lui** in HIS house, in his own house; *Fam* **s. imbécile de frère** his/her idiot of a brother

2 *(d'un sujet indéfini)* **il faut faire ses preuves** you have to show your mettle, *Sout* one has to show one's mettle; **tout le monde a ses problèmes** we all have our problems; **chacun a pris s. sac** everybody took their bags; **ici, on passe s. temps à bavarder** everybody spends their time chatting here; **en Alsace, on prend s. café en même temps que le dessert** in Alsace, they have their coffee along with their dessert

3 *(dans des titres)* **S. Altesse Royale** His/Her Royal Highness; **Sa Majesté** His/Her Majesty

4 *(d'une abstraction)* **avant de prendre une décision, il faut penser à ses conséquences** before taking a decision, you must think about the consequences (of it); **dans cette affaire, tout a s. importance** in this affair everything is of importance

5 *(emploi expressif)* **ça a s. charme** it's got its own charm *or* a certain charm; *Fam* **il fait s. intéressant** he's trying to draw attention to himself; *Fam* **elle fait sa timide** she's being all shy; *Fam* **il va encore piquer sa colère!** he's going to have another one of his outbursts!; *Fam* **il a réussi à avoir s. samedi** he managed to get Saturday off

sonal, -als [sɔnal] **NM** *Offic* jingle

sonar [sɔnar] **NM** sonar

sonate [sɔnat] **NF** sonata; **s. pour violon** violin sonata

sonatine [sɔnatin] **NF** sonatina

sondage [sɔ̃daʒ] **NM 1** *(enquête)* poll, survey; *(activité)* sampling; **faire un s. (sur qch)** to carry out a poll *or* a survey (on sth); **faire un s. auprès d'un groupe** to poll a group, to carry out a survey among a group; **j'ai fait un petit s. parmi mes amis** I sounded out some of my friends; **s. aléatoire** random sampling; **s. d'opinion** opinion poll; **s. par quotas** quota sampling; **s. par téléphone** telephone interviewing

2 *(d'un terrain)* sampling, sounding

3 *Méd* probe, probing; **s. vésical** urethral catheterization

4 *Mines & Pétr (processus)* boring; *(puits)* bore hole

5 *Naut* sounding; **faire des sondages** to take soundings

6 *Géol* **s. sismique** sonoprobing

Sonde [sɔ̃d] *voir* **archipel**

sonde [sɔ̃d] **NF 1** *Astron & Météo* sonde; **s. aérienne** balloon sonde; *Astron* **s. spatiale** (space) probe

2 *Naut* **(ligne de) s.** lead (line), sounding line; **être sur les sondes** to be on soundings; **naviguer**

à la s. to navigate by soundings
3 *Méd* probe, sound; **s. (d'alimentation)** feeding tube; **nourri à la s.** tube-fed; **s. (creuse)** catheter, can(n)ula; **s. œsophagienne** oesophageal probe, probang
4 *Com (pour les liquides, le beurre, le fromage)* taster; *(pour les grains)* sampler
5 *Tech* **s. thermométrique** thermometer probe
6 *Pétr* drill

sondé, -e [sɔ̃de] **NM,F** *Mktg* respondent, person polled

sonder **[3]** [sɔ̃de] **VT 1** *(personne ▸ gén)* to sound out; *(▸ dans une enquête)* to poll; **je vais tâcher de la s. là-dessus** I'll try and sound her out on that; **nous n'avons sondé que des étudiants** we polled students only; **s. l'opinion** to carry out *or* conduct an opinion poll
2 *Naut* to sound; **s. la côte** to take soundings along the coast
3 *Météo* to probe; **s. l'atmosphère** to make soundings in the atmosphere
4 *Méd (plaie)* to probe; *(malade, vessie)* to catheterize
5 *Pétr* to bore, to drill; *Fig* **s. le terrain** to test the ground *or* the waters
6 *(fromage, liquides)* to taste; *(grains)* to sample
7 *(intentions)* to sound out; **s. l'âme/le cœur de qn** to try to penetrate sb's soul/sb's heart

sondeur, -euse [sɔ̃dœr, -øz] **NM,F** *(pour une enquête)* pollster
NM 1 *Naut* depth finder, sounder **2** *Météo* **s. acoustique** echo sounder **3** *Géol* probe
• **sondeuse** **NF** *Pétr* boring *or* drilling machine

songe [sɔ̃ʒ] **NM** *Littéraire* **1** *(rêve)* dream; **faire un s.** to have a dream; **voir qn/qch en s.** to see sb/sth in one's dreams **2** *(chimère)* dream, daydream, illusion

songé, -e [sɔ̃ʒe] **ADJ** *Can Fam (réfléchi)* reflective, thoughtful; **il est très s. comme garçon** he's the sort of boy who thinks about things very deeply

songe-creux [sɔ̃ʒkrø] **NM INV** *Littéraire* dreamer, daydreamer; **air de s.** dreamy look

songer **[17]** [sɔ̃ʒe] **VT** to muse, to reflect, to think; **il est charmant, songeait-elle** he's charming, she mused *or* reflected; **comment aurais-je pu s. qu'ils nous trahiraient?** how could I have imagined that they'd betray us?
VI *(rêver)* to dream
• **songer à VT IND 1** *(penser à)* to think about; *(se souvenant)* to muse over, to think back to; **à quoi songes-tu?** what are you thinking about?, what's on your mind?; **je songeais aux Noëls passés** I was musing over *or* thinking back to Christmases past
2 *(prendre en considération ▸ carrière, personne)* to think of, to have regard for; **songe un peu plus aux autres!** be a bit more considerate (of others)!
3 *(envisager)* to contemplate, to think of; **voyons, vous n'y songez pas!** come now, you can't mean it *or* be serious!; **il ne faut pas y s.** that's quite out of the question; **songez donc!** just think!, just imagine!; **il songe sérieusement à se remarier** he's seriously considering *or* contemplating remarriage; **il ne songe qu'à gagner de l'argent** making money is all he thinks about
4 *(s'occuper de)* to remember; **as-tu songé aux réservations?** did you remember to make reservations?
5 *(réfléchir à ▸ offre, suggestion)* to think over, to consider

songerie [sɔ̃ʒri] **NF** *Littéraire* daydreaming

songeur, -euse [sɔ̃ʒœr, -øz] **ADJ** *(rêveur)* dreamy; *(pensif)* pensive, thoughtful; **d'un air s.** dreamily; **ça laisse s.** it makes you wonder

sonique [sɔnik] **ADJ** sonic; **gong s.** supersonic boom *or* bang, sonic boom

sonnaille [sɔnaj] **NF 1** *(pour le bétail)* cowbell **2** *(bruit)* jangling

sonnant, -e [sɔnɑ̃, -ɑ̃t] **ADJ** sharp; **à trois heures sonnantes** at three (o'clock) sharp, at three on the dot, at the stroke of three (o'clock)

sonné, -e [sɔne] **ADJ 1** *(annoncé par la cloche)* gone, past; **il est midi s.** it's past *or Br* gone twelve
2 *Fam (révolu)* **elle a la cinquantaine bien sonnée** she's on the wrong side of fifty
3 *Fam (fou)* crazy, nuts
4 *Fam (assommé)* groggy; **un boxeur s.** a punch-drunk boxer

sonner **[3]** [sɔne] **VI 1** *(téléphone, cloche)* to ring; *(minuterie, réveil)* to go off; *(carillon, pendule)* to chime; *(glas, tocsin)* to toll, to sound; **la cloche n'a pas encore sonné** *(à l'école)* the bell hasn't gone *or* rung yet; **j'ai mis le réveil à s. à huit heures** I've set the alarm for eight o'clock
2 *(avoir un son ▸ instrument en cuivre)* to sound; *(▸ clefs, pièces métalliques)* to jingle, to jangle; *(▸ pièces de monnaie)* to jingle, to chink; *(▸ enclume, marteau)* to ring, to resound; *(▸ rire)* to ring, to peal (out); *(▸ voix)* to resound, to ring; **s. du clairon/du cor** to sound the bugle/the horn; **s. bien/mal** to sound good/bad; **l'italien sonne bien à l'oreille** Italian is a pleasant-sounding language; **s. clair** *(monnaie)* to ring true; *(marteau)* to give *or* to have a clear ring; **s. creux** to sound hollow, to give a hollow sound; *Fig* to have a hollow ring; **s. faux** to ring false; *Fig* not to ring true
3 *(heure)* to strike; **quatre heures ont sonné** it has struck four o'clock, four o'clock has struck; *Fig* **l'heure de la vengeance a sonné** the time for revenge has come
4 *(à la porte)* to ring; **on a sonné** there's someone at the door; **s. chez qn** to ring sb's doorbell
5 *(accentuer)* **faire s. une consonne** to sound a consonant; **"pour la gloire", dit-il en faisant s. le dernier mot** "for glory," he said, making the last word ring out; **faire s. ses bottes sur le parquet** to stamp one's boots on the floor
VT 1 *(cloche)* to ring, to chime; *(glas, toscin)* to sound, to toll; *Fam* **s. les cloches à qn** to bawl sb out, to give sb what-for; **tu vas te faire s. les cloches!** you'll catch it!
2 *(pour faire venir ▸ infirmière, valet)* to ring for; *Fam* **toi, on t'a pas sonné!** nobody asked you!
3 *(pour annoncer ▸ messe, vêpres)* to ring (the bells) for; *Mil (▸ charge, retraite, rassemblement)* to sound; **sonnez le dîner** ring the bell for dinner, ring the dinner-bell
4 *(sujet: horloge)* to strike; **la pendule vient de s. deux heures** the clock has just struck two
5 *Fam (assommer)* to knock out, to stun; *(abasourdir)* to stun, to stagger, to knock (out); **ça l'a sonné!** he was reeling under the shock!
6 *Tech (sonder ▸ installation, monnaie)* to sound
7 *Belg (appeler)* to telephone, to call

sonnerie [sɔnri] **NF 1** *(son)* ring; **la s. du téléphone/du réveil la fit sursauter** the telephone/the alarm clock gave her a start; **s. de clairon** bugle call
2 *(mélodie)* ringtone; **télécharger des sonneries** *(sur un téléphone portable)* to download ringtones; **s. hi-fi** realtone; **s. polyphonique** polyphonic ringtone
3 *Mil* call
4 *(cloches)* (set of) bells *or* chimes
5 *(mécanisme ▸ d'un réveil)* alarm, bell; *(▸ d'une pendule)* chimes; *(▸ d'une sonnette)* bell
6 *(alarme)* alarm (bell)

sonnet [sɔnɛ] **NM** sonnet

sonnette [sɔnɛt] **NF 1** *(avertisseur)* bell; **s. d'alarme** alarm bell; **tirer la s. d'alarme** *Rail* to pull the communication cord; *Fig* to sound the alarm **2** *(son)* **(coup de) s.** ring; **personne ne répondit à mon coup de s.** no one answered the bell; **as-tu entendu la s.?** did you hear the bell? **3** *(en travaux publics)* pile-driver

sonneur [sɔnœr] **NM 1** *(de cloches)* bellringer; **dormir comme un s.** to sleep like a log **2** *Mus* player **3** *Tech* pile-driver operator

sono [sɔno] **NF** *Fam (abrév* **sonorisation***)* *(d'un groupe, d'une discothèque)* sound system[□], sound; *(d'une salle de conférences)* public-address system[□], PA (system)[□]

sonore [sɔnɔr] **ADJ 1** *(signal)* acoustic, sound *(avant n)*; *(onde, effets, niveau)* sound *(avant n)*
2 *(bruyant ▸ rire, voix)* loud, ringing, resounding; *(▸ claque, baiser)* loud, resounding
3 *(résonnant ▸ escalier, voûte)* echoing; **le vestibule est s.** sound reverberates *or* echoes in the hall
4 *Ling (phonème)* voiced; **le "d" est s.** the "d" is voiced
NF *Ling* voiced consonant

> Il faut noter que l'adjectif anglais **sonorous** signifie souvent **grandiloquent**.

sonorisation [sɔnɔrizasjɔ̃] **NF 1** *(d'un lieu ▸ action)* wiring for sound
2 *(équipement ▸ d'une salle de conférences)* public-address system, PA system; *(▸ d'une discothèque)* sound system
3 *Cin (d'un film)* dubbing
4 *Ling* voicing

sonoriser **[3]** [sɔnɔrize] **VT 1** *(salle de conférences)* to fit with a public-address *or* PA system; *(discothèque)* to fit with a sound system **2** *Cin (film)* to dub, to add the soundtrack to **3** *Ling* to voice

sonorité [sɔnɔrite] **NF 1** *(d'un instrument de musique)* tone; *(de la voix)* tone, *Sout* sonority; *(d'une langue)* sonority **2** *(résonance ▸ de l'air)* resonance, *Sout* sonority; *(▸ d'une pièce)* acoustics *(singulier)*; *(▸ d'un lieu)* sonority **3** *Ling* voicing

sonothèque [sɔnɔtɛk] **NF** sound (effects) library

Sonotone® [sɔnɔtɔn] **NM** miniature hearing aid

sont *voir* **être**[1]

Sopalin® [sɔpalɛ̃] **NM** kitchen paper

sophisme [sɔfism] **NM** sophism

sophiste [sɔfist] **NMF 1** *(raisonneur)* sophist **2** *Antiq* Sophist

sophistication [sɔfistikasjɔ̃] **NF 1** *(raffinement)* refinement, sophistication
2 *(affectation)* affectation, sophistication
3 *(complexité technique)* sophistication, complexity
4 *Vieilli (action de frelater)* adulteration

sophistique [sɔfistik] **ADJ** sophistic
NF sophistry

sophistiqué, -e [sɔfistike] **ADJ 1** *(raffiné)* sophisticated, refined
2 *(affecté)* affected, sophisticated
3 *(complexe)* complex, sophisticated
4 *Vieilli (frelaté)* adulterated

Sophocle [sɔfɔkl] **NPR** Sophocles

sophrologie [sɔfrɔlɔʒi] **NF** sophrology *(form of autogenic relaxation)*

sophrologue [sɔfrɔlɔg] **NMF** sophrologist

soporifique [sɔpɔrifik] **ADJ 1** *Pharm* soporific **2** *(ennuyeux)* boring, soporific
NM *Vieilli* soporific; **ce livre est un vrai s.** this book is terribly boring

soprane [sɔpran] **NMF** soprano

sopraniste [sɔpranist] **NM** male soprano

soprano [sɔprano] *(pl* **sopranos** *ou* **soprani** [-ni]) **NM** *(voix ▸ de femme)* soprano; *(▸ d'enfant)* soprano, treble
NMF soprano

sorbe [sɔrb] **NF** sorb (apple)

sorbet [sɔrbɛ] **NM** *Br* sorbet, *Am* sherbet; **s. au cassis** blackcurrant *Br* sorbet *or Am* sherbet

sorbetière [sɔrbətjɛr] **NF** *(de glacier)* ice-cream churn; *(de ménage)* ice-cream maker

sorbier [sɔrbje] **NM** *Bot* sorb, service tree; **s. des oiseleurs** *ou* **des oiseaux** rowan tree, mountain ash

sorbique [sɔrbik] **ADJ** *Chim* sorbic

sorbonnard, -e [sɔrbɔnar, -ard] *Fam* **ADJ** *(esprit)* niggling, pedantic
NM,F *(professeur)* Sorbonne academic[□]; *(étudiant)* Sorbonne student[□]

Sorbonne [sɔrbɔn] **NF la S.** the Sorbonne

sorcellerie [sɔrsɛlri] **NF 1** *(pratique)* sorcery, witchcraft **2** *Fam (effet surprenant)* magic; **c'est de la s.!** it's magic!

sorcier, -ère [sɔrsje, -ɛr] **NM,F 1** *(magicien)* wizard, *f* witch; *Fam* **il ne faut pas être (grand) s. pour comprendre cela** you don't need to be a genius to understand that; *Can Fam* **être en s.** to be fuming, to be hopping mad **2** *(en anthropologie)* sorcerer, *f* sorceress
• **sorcier ADJ M** *Fam* **ce n'est pourtant pas s.** it's not exactly rocket science
• **sorcière NF** *(mégère)* witch, harpy

sordide [sɔrdid] **ADJ 1** *(misérable ▸ vêtements)* filthy; *(▸ pièce, quartier)* squalid, sordid **2** *(vil ▸ égoïsme)* petty; *(▸ crime)* foul, vile **3** *(mesquin ▸ motif)* squalid, sordid

sordidement [sɔrdidmɑ̃] **ADV** *(agir)* sordidly; **vivre s.** to live in squalor

sordidité [sɔrdidite] **NF** *Littéraire* sordidness

sorgho [sɔrgo] **NM** sorghum

Sorlingues [sɔrlɛ̃g] **NFPL les (îles) S.** the Scilly Isles

sornettes [sɔrnɛt] **NFPL** balderdash *(UNCOUNT)*, twaddle *(UNCOUNT)*; **débiter** *ou* **raconter des sornettess** to talk nonsense

sors *etc voir* **sortir**[2]

sort [sɔr] **NM 1** *(condition)* fate, lot; **être content de son s.** to be happy with one's lot; **des mesures ont été prises pour améliorer le s. des immigrés** steps were taken to improve the lot *or* the status of immigrants; **tu m'abandonnes à mon triste s.!** you've left me to my fate!; *Fam* **faire un s. à** *(plat)* to make short work of, to polish off; *(bouteille)* to polish off, to drink up

2 *(destin)* fate, destiny; **mon s. est entre vos mains** my future depends on you, *Sout* my fate is in your hands; **toutes les demandes d'emploi subissent le même s.** all letters of application meet with the same fate *or* receive the same treatment

3 *(puissance surnaturelle)* **le s.** Fate, Fortune, Destiny; **le s. lui fut enfin favorable** Fate *or* Fortune smiled upon him/her at last; **je me demande ce que le s. nous réserve** I wonder what fate has in store for us; **mais le s. en a décidé autrement** but fate decided otherwise; **le mauvais s.** misfortune; **le s. en est jeté** the die is cast

4 *(sortilège ▸ gén)* spell; *(▸ défavorable)* curse; **jeter un s. à qn** to cast a spell on sb

sortable [sɔrtabl] **ADJ tu n'es vraiment pas s.!** I can't take you anywhere!

sortant, -e [sɔrtɑ̃, -ɑ̃t] **ADJ 1** *Pol* outgoing; **le maire s.** the outgoing mayor **2** *(au jeu)* **les numéros sortants** the numbers chosen **3** *Ordinat* output *(avant n)*

NM,F 1 *Pol* incumbent **2** *(personne qui sort)* **on contrôle également les sortants** those leaving are also screened

sorte [sɔrt] **NF 1** *(genre)* sort, kind, type; **pour moi, il y a deux sortes de gens** in my opinion, there are two kinds *or* sorts *or* types of people; **toutes sortes de** all kinds *or* sorts of; **des gens de toute s.** *ou* **toutes sortes** all sorts *or* kinds of people **2** *(pour exprimer une approximation)* **une s. de** a sort *or* a kind of; **c'est une s. de gelée** it's a sort of jelly **3** *Typ* sort

• **de la sorte ADV** that way; **comment osez-vous me traiter de la s.?** how dare you treat me in that way *or* like that!; **je n'ai rien dit/rien fait de la s.** I said/did no such thing, I said/did nothing of the kind *or* sort

• **de sorte à CONJ** in order to, so as to

• **de (telle) sorte que CONJ 1** *(suivi du subjonctif) (de manière à ce que)* so that, in such a way that; **disposez vos plantes de (telle) s. qu'elles reçoivent beaucoup de lumière** arrange your plants so that they receive maximum light **2** *(suivi de l'indicatif) (si bien que)* so that; **elle m'a montré la ville, de (telle) s. que le temps a passé très vite** she showed me round the town, so the time just flew by

• **en aucune sorte ADV** *Littéraire* not in the least; **en avez-vous parlé à quelqu'un? – en aucune s.** did you tell anyone? – not at all *or* by no means

• **en quelque sorte ADV** as it were, in a way, somewhat; **immobile, pétrifié en quelque s.** motionless, as it were paralysed; **alors, on repart à zéro? – oui, en quelque s.** so, we're back to square one? – yes, in a manner of speaking

• **en sorte de CONJ** so as to; **fais en s. d'arriver à l'heure** try to be there on time

• **en sorte que CONJ 1 faites en s. que tout soit prêt à temps** see to it that everything is ready in time **2** *Littéraire* = **de (telle) sorte que**

sorteur, -euse[1] [sɔrtœr, -øz] *Belg* **ADJ ils sont très sorteurs** they like to party *or* to live it up

NM,F reveller, partygoer

NM *(videur)* bouncer

sorteux, -euse[2] [sɔrtø, -øz] *Can Fam* **ADJ** sociable▫, who likes going out▫

NM,F sociable person▫

SORTIE [sɔrti]

- exit **1, 6, 7**
- outing **4, 12**
- sortie **5**
- export **8**
- release **9**
- output **10**
- end **3**
- evening out **4**
- entrance **6**
- outgoing **8**
- launch **9**

NF 1 *(action) & Théât* exit; **sa s. fut très remarquée** his/her exit *or* departure did not go unnoticed; *Théât* **faire sa s.** to leave the stage, to exit; **faire une fausse s.** to make as if to leave

2 *(moment)* **à ma s. de prison/d'hôpital** on my release from prison/discharge from hospital; **les journalistes l'ont assaillie dès sa s. de l'hôtel** the journalists thronged round her as soon as she came out of the hotel; **retrouvons-nous à la s. du travail** let's meet after work; **il s'est retourné à la s. du virage** he rolled (his car) over just after *or* as he came out of the bend

3 *(fin)* end; **à la s. de l'hiver** when winter was (nearly) over; **à ma s. de l'école** *(à la fin de mes études)* when I left school

4 *(excursion, promenade)* outing; *(soirée en ville)* evening *or* night out; **on a organisé une petite s. en famille/à vélo** we've organized a little family outing/cycle ride; **priver qn de s.** to confine sb to quarters, *Fam* to ground sb; **ils m'ont privé de s. trois dimanches de suite** they kept me in for three Sundays in a row, *Fam* I was grounded for three Sundays in a row; **s. scolaire** school outing

5 *Aviat & Mil* sortie; **s. offensive** sally

6 *(porte, issue ▸ d'une école, d'une usine)* entrance, gates; *(▸ d'une salle de spectacles)* exit, way out; **par ici la s.!** this way out, please!; **attends-moi à la s.** wait for me outside; **gagner la s.** to reach the exit; **le supermarché se trouve à la s. de la ville** the supermarket is on the outskirts of the town; **s. de secours** emergency exit; **s. des artistes** stage door

7 *(sur route)* exit; **j'ai raté la s.** I've missed the exit

8 *Banque & Écon (de produits, de devises)* export; *(de capital)* outflow; *(sujet de dépense)* item of expenditure; *(dépense)* outgoing

9 *(d'un disque, d'un film)* release; *(d'un roman)* publication; *(d'un modèle)* launch; **au moment de sa s. dans les salles parisiennes** when released in Parisian cinemas

10 *Ordinat (de données)* output, readout; *(option sur programme)* exit; **s. sur imprimante** printout; **s. papier** output

11 *Sport* **s. en touche** going out of play *or* into touch; **il y a s. en touche!** the ball's gone into touch!; **faire une s.** *(gardien de but)* to come out of goal, to leave the goalmouth; *(en gymnastique)* to exit

12 *(d'un cheval)* outing

13 *Fam (remarque)* quip, sally; *(emportement)* outburst; **elle a parfois de ces sorties!** you don't know what she's going to come out with next!

14 *(d'eau, de gaz)* outflow, outlet

15 *Beaux-Arts (gravure)* fading, tailing off

• **de sortie ADJ c'est son jour de s.** *(domestique)* it's his/her day off; **la cuisinière est de s. le lundi** Monday is the cook's day off; *Fam* **je suis de s. demain** *(au restaurant, au spectacle)* I'm going out tomorrow

• **sorties NFPL** *Fin* outgoings; **sorties de fonds** expenses, outgoings

sortie-de-bain [sɔrtidbɛ̃] *(pl* **sorties-de-bain***)* **NF** bathrobe

sortie-de-bal [sɔrtidbal] *(pl* **sorties-de-bal***)* **NF** evening wrap, opera cloak

sortilège [sɔrtilɛʒ] **NM** charm, spell

sortir[1] [sɔrtir] *Littéraire* **NM** *(fin)* **dès le s. de l'enfance, il dut apprendre à se défendre** he was barely out of his childhood when he had to learn to fend for himself

• **au sortir de PRÉP 1** *(dans le temps)* at the end of; **au s. de l'hiver** as winter draws to a close; **au s. de la guerre** at the end of the war **2** *(dans l'espace)* **je vis la cabane au s. du bois** as I was coming out of the woods, I saw the hut

SORTIR[2] **[32]** [sɔrtir]

VI
- to go out **1, 3, 13**
- to come through **4**
- to come up **4, 8**
- to exit **11, 14**
- to come out **1, 5, 7, 10**
- to get out **6**

VT
- to take out **1, 3, 4**
- to bring out **2, 6**
- to say **7**
- to put out **2**
- to throw out **5**

VPR
- to get out of

VI *(aux être)* **1** *(quitter un lieu ▸ vu de l'intérieur)* to go out; *(▸ vu de l'extérieur)* to come out; **ne sors pas sans manteau** don't go out without a coat (on); **il vient de s.** *(d'ici)* he's just gone out; **s. par la fenêtre** to get out *or* to leave by the window; **sors!** get out (of here)!; **Madame, je peux s.?** please Miss, may I leave the room?; **le médecin lui a dit de ne pas s.** the doctor told him/her to stay indoors *or* not to go out; **vivement que je puisse s.!** I can't wait to get out!; **elle est sortie déjeuner/se promener** she's gone (out) for lunch/for a walk; **si elle se présente, dites-lui que je suis sorti** if she calls, tell her I'm out *or* I've gone out *or* I'm not in; **il était si mauvais que le public est sorti** he was so bad that the audience walked out (on him); **s. d'une pièce** to leave a room; **les gens sortaient du théâtre** people were coming out of *or* leaving the theatre; **s. d'une voiture** to get out of a car; **je l'ai vu qui sortait de l'hôpital/l'école vers seize heures** I saw him coming out of the hospital/school at about four p.m.; **fais s. ce chien de la voiture** get that dog out of the car; **faites-les s.!** send them out!; **il faisait s. des lapins de son chapeau** he pulled rabbits out of his hat; **sors de ta cachette!** come out wherever you are!; **s. de l'eau** to emerge from the water; **sors de l'eau!** get out of the water!; **s. du lit/du bain** to get out of bed/of the bath; **alors que l'express sortait de la gare** as the express train was pulling out of *or* leaving the station; **il est sorti de sa vie** he's out of his/her life; *Fam* **ça me sort par les yeux** I'm sick and tired of it, I've had it up to here; *Fam* **d'où tu sors?** where have you been?, what planet have you been on?

2 *(marquant la fin d'une activité, d'une période)* **s. de table** to leave the table; **elle sort de l'hôpital demain** she's getting out of hospital tomorrow; **laisser qn s. de l'hôpital** to let sb out of *or* to discharge sb from hospital; **s. de l'école/du bureau** *(finir sa journée)* to finish school/work; **à quelle heure sors-tu?** *(du bureau, du lycée)* what time do you finish?; **s. de prison** to come out of *or* to be released from prison

3 *(pour se distraire)* **je sors très peu** I hardly ever go out; **ils sortent au restaurant tous les soirs** they eat out every night; **s. avec qn** to go out with sb; *Fam* **je ne sors plus avec lui** I'm not going out with him *or* I'm not seeing him any more; *Fam* **ils sortent ensemble depuis trois ans** they've been going out together for three years

4 *(apparaître ▸ dent, bouton)* to come through; *(▸ pousse)* to come up, to peep through; **l'antenne sort quand on appuie sur le bouton** the *Br* aerial *or Am* antenna comes out when you press the button

5 *(se répandre)* to come out; **le son sort par là** the sound comes out here; **c'est pour que la fumée sorte** it's to let the smoke out *or* for the smoke to escape

6 *(s'échapper)* to get out; **des pensionnaires réussissaient parfois à s.** some boarders would manage to get out *or* to escape from time to time; **aucun dossier ne doit s. de l'ambassade** no file may be taken out of *or* leave the embassy; **faire s. qn/des marchandises d'un pays** to smuggle sb/goods out of a country; **je vais te confier quelque chose mais cela ne doit pas s. d'ici** I'm going to tell you something, but it mustn't go any further than these four walls

7 *(être mis en vente ▸ disque, film)* to be released, to come out; *(▸ livre)* to be published, to come out; **s. sur le marché** *(produit)* to come onto the market; **le film sortira (sur les écrans) en septembre** the film will be released *or* will be out in September; **à l'heure où les journaux sortent** when the papers come off the presses; **ça vient de s.!** it's just (come) out!, it's (brand) new!

8 *(être révélé au public ▸ sujet d'examen)* to come up; *(▸numéro de loterie)* to be drawn; *(▸numéro à la roulette)* to turn *or* to come up; *(▸tarif, barême)* to be out

9 *(être promulgué)* **la loi a été votée mais le décret d'application ne sortira qu'en septembre** the bill has been passed, but it won't become law until September

10 *Fam (être dit)* to come out; **il fallait que ça sorte!** it had to come out *or* to be said!; **c'est sorti comme ça, je n'ai pas pu m'en empêcher** I just came out with it *or* blurted it out, I couldn't help myself

11 *Ordinat* **s. (d'un système)** to exit (from a system); **s. d'un programme** to exit a program

12 *Naut & Aviat* **s. du port** to leave harbour; **s. en mer** to put out to sea; **aujourd'hui, les avions/les bateaux ne sont pas sortis** the planes were grounded/the boats stayed in port today

13 *Sport (balle)* to go out; **la balle est sortie (du court)** the ball was out; **le ballon est sorti en corner/en touche** the ball went out for a corner/ went into touch; **on a fait s. le joueur (du terrain)** *(pour faute)* the player was sent off; *(il est blessé)* the player had to go off because of injury

14 *Théât* **le roi sort** exit the King; **les sorcières sortent** exeunt (the) witches

VT *(aux avoir)* **1** *(mener dehors ▸ pour se promener, se divertir)* to take out; **sors le chien** take the dog out (for a walk); **il faut s. les chiens régulièrement** dogs have to be walked regularly; **viens avec nous au concert, ça te sortira** come with us to the concert, it'll get you out (of the house)

2 *(mettre dehors ▸ vu de l'intérieur)* to put out *or* outside; *(▸ vu de l'extérieur)* to bring out *or* outside; **s. la poubelle** to take out *Br* the rubbish *or Am* the trash

3 *(présenter ▸ crayon, outil)* to take out; *(▸pistolet)* to pull out; *(▸papiers d'identité)* to produce; **on va bientôt pouvoir s. les vêtements d'été** we'll soon be able to get out our summer clothes; **l'escargot sort ses cornes** the snail is putting out its horns

4 *(extraire)* **s. qch de qch** to take *or* to get sth out of sth; **sors un verre du placard** get a glass out of *or* from the cupboard; **il a sorti quelque chose de sa poche** he drew *or* took *or* got something out of his pocket; **sors les mains de tes poches!** take *or* get your hands out of your pockets!; **des mesures ont été prises pour s. le pays de la crise** measures have been taken to get the countryout of *or* to rescue the country from the present crisis; **s. qn de qch** to get *or* to pull sb out of sth; **ils ont sorti les blessés des décombres** they pulled the injured out of the rubble; **s. qn du sommeil** to wake sb; **j'ai eu du mal à le s. de son lit** *(le faire lever)* I had trouble getting him out of bed; **je vais te s. d'affaire** *ou* **de là** I'll get you out of it

5 *Fam (expulser)* to get *or* to throw out; **sortez-le ou je fais un malheur!** get him out of here before I do something I'll regret!; **elle a sorti la Suédoise en trois sets** she disposed of *or* beat the Swedish player in three sets

6 *(mettre sur le marché)* to launch, to bring out; **s. un disque/un film** *(auteur)* to bring out a record/a movie *or Br* film; *(distributeur)* to release a record/a movie *or Br* film; **s. un livre** to bring out *or* to publish a book

7 *Fam (dire)* to say▫, to come out with; **elle n'a sorti que des banalités** she just came out with a load of clichés; **il m'a sorti que j'étais trop vieille!** he told me I was too old, just like that!

8 *(roue, train d'atterrissage)* to drop; *(volet)* to raise

• **sortir de VT IND 1** *(emplacement, position)* to come out of, to come off; **la porte coulissante est sortie de la rainure** the sliding door has come out of the groove; **s. des rails** to go off *or* to jump the rails; **s. de la piste** *(voiture)* to come off *or* to leave the track; *(skieur)* to come off the piste; **ça m'était complètement sorti de la tête** *ou* **de l'esprit** it had gone right out of my head *or* mind

2 *(venir récemment de)* to have (just) come from *or* left; **elle sort de chez moi** she's just left my place; **je sortais de chez le coiffeur** I was just coming out of the hairdresser's; **il sort de son examen** he has just got out of his exam; **je sors d'une grippe** I'm just recovering from a bout of flu; *Fam* **s. de faire qch** to have just done sth▫; *Fam* **je sors de lui parler** I was just this minute talking to him/her

3 *(venir à bout de)* to come out of; **nous avons eu une période difficile mais heureusement nous en sortons** we've had a difficult time but fortunately we're now emerging from it *or* we're seeing the end of it now; *Fam* **est-ce qu'on va enfin en s.?** when are we going to see an end to all this?

4 *(se tirer de, se dégager de)* **elle est sortie indemne de l'accident** she came out of the accident unscathed; **elle est sortie première de sa promotion** she came out first in her class; **qui sortira victorieux de ce match?** who will win this match?; **s. de sa rêverie** to emerge from one's reverie; **lorsqu'on sort de l'adolescence pour entrer dans l'âge adulte** when one leaves adolescence (behind) to become an adult

5 *(se départir de)* **il est sorti de sa réserve après quelques verres de vin** he opened up *or* he loosened up after a few glasses of wine; **elle est sortie de son silence pour écrire son second roman** she broke her silence to write her second novel

6 *(s'écarter de)* **attention à ne pas s. du sujet!** be careful not to get off *or* to stray from the subject!; **cela sort de mes compétences** that's not my field; **s. de l'ordinaire** to be out of the ordinary; **il n'y a pas à s. de là** *(c'est inévitable)* there's no way round it, there's no getting away from it

7 *(être issu de)* **s. d'une bonne famille** to come from *or* to be of a good family; **pour ceux qui sortent des grandes écoles** for those who have studied at *or* are the products of the "grandes écoles"; **il ne faut pas être sorti de Polytechnique pour savoir ça** you don't need a PhD to know that; **mais d'où sors-tu?** *(tu es mal élevé)* where did you learn such manners?, where were you brought up?; *(tu ne connais rien)* where have you been?, what planet have you been on?

8 *(être produit par)* to come from; **la veste sortait de chez un grand couturier** the jacket was made by a famous designer; **mes personnages sortent tout droit de mon imagination** my characters are straight out of my imagination

9 *(tournure impersonnelle) (résulter de)* **il ne sortira rien de bon de toutes leurs manigances** no good will come of all their schemes; **il n'est rien sorti de son interrogatoire** his/her interrogation revealed nothing

VPR se sortir j'ai du mal à me s. du lit le matin I find it difficult to get out of bed in the morning; **se s. d'une situation embarrassante** to get (oneself) out of *or Sout* to extricate oneself from an embarrassing situation; *Fam* **aide-moi à finir, je ne m'en sortirai jamais seul!** give me a hand, I'll never get this finished on my own; **donne-lui une fourchette, il ne s'en sort pas avec des baguettes** give him a fork, he can't manage with chopsticks; **tu t'en es très bien sorti** you did very well; **la voiture a fait un tonneau mais il s'en est sorti sans une égratignure** his car turned right over but he escaped without a scratch; **il s'en est finalement sorti** *(il a survécu)* he pulled through in the end; *(il a réussi)* he won through in the end; **s'en s. à peu près** *(financièrement)* to get by; **s'en s. très bien** to manage very well; **malgré les allocations, on ne s'en sort pas** in spite of the allowance, we're not making ends meet; *Fam* **s'en s. pour** *(avoir à payer)* to be stung for

---

SOS [ɛsoɛs] **NM 1** *(signal de détresse)* SOS; **lancer un S.** to put *or* to send out an SOS **2** *(dans des noms de sociétés)* **S.-Amitié** = charity providing support for people in despair, ≃ the Samaritans; **S. médecins/dépannage** emergency medical/repair service; **S.-Racisme** = voluntary organization set up to combat racism in French society

sosie [sɔzi] **NM** double, doppelganger; **c'est ton s.!** he's/she's the spitting image of you!

sot, -otte [so, sɔt] **ADJ 1** *(idiot)* stupid; **il n'est pas s.** he's no fool **2** *Littéraire (embarrassé)* dumbfounded **3** *Belg (fou)* mad, crazy

NM,F 1 *(idiot)* fool, idiot **2** *Belg (fou)* madman, *f* madwoman

> Il faut noter que le nom anglais **sot** est un faux ami. Il signifie **ivrogne**.

sotie [sɔti] **NF** *Littérature* medieval farce

sot-l'y-laisse [solilɛs] **NM INV** oyster *(in poultry)*

sotte [sɔt] *voir* **sot**

sottement [sɔtmɑ̃] **ADV** foolishly, stupidly

sottise [sɔtiz] **NF 1** *(caractère)* stupidity, silliness; **a-t-on idée d'une pareille s.!** how can anyone be so silly? **2** *(acte)* stupid *or* foolish action; **arrête de faire des sottises** *(à un enfant)* stop messing about; **je viens de faire une grosse s.** I've just done something very stupid *or* silly **3** *(parole)* stupid remark; **ne dis pas de sottises** don't talk nonsense; **ai-je dit une s.?** have I said something stupid?

• **sottises NFPL** *Vieilli (injures)* insults; **elle m'a dit des sottises** she insulted me

sottisier [sɔtizje] **NM** collection of howlers

sou [su] **NM 1** *Hist (sol)* sol, sou; *(cinq centimes)* five centimes; **cent sous** five francs

2 *Fam (argent)* penny, *Am* cent; **tu n'auras pas un s.!** you won't get a *Br* penny *or Am* cent!; *Fam* **ça ne vaut pas un s.** it's not worth *Br* tuppence *or Am* a red cent; **économiser s. à** *ou* **par s.** to save every spare penny; **il a dépensé jusqu'à son dernier s.** he's spent every last *Br* penny *or Am* cent he had; **ils n'ont pas le s.** they haven't got a penny (to their name); **être sans le s.** to be broke; **je suis sans un s.** I haven't got any money (on me); **un s. est un s.** a penny saved is a penny gained

3 *(locutions) Fam* **elle n'a pas deux sous de jugeote** she hasn't an ounce of sense; **elle n'est pas méfiante pour un s.** *ou* **deux sous** she's not in the least suspicious▫; **être propre comme un s. neuf** to be as clean as a new pin

4 *Can (cent)* cent *(of a dollar)*; **un cinq sous** a nickel; **un dix sous** a dime

• **sous NMPL** *Fam (argent)* cash; **c'est une affaire de gros sous** there's a lot of cash involved; **des sous, toujours des sous!** money for this, money for that!

souahéli, -e [swaheli] **ADJ** Swahili

NM *(langue)* Swahili

• **Souahéli, -e NM,F** Swahili; **les S.** the Swahilis *or* Swahili

soubassement [subasmɑ̃] **NM 1** *Archit & Constr* foundation

2 *Géol* bedrock

3 *(base ▸ d'une théorie)* basis, underpinnings

4 *Can (sous-sol)* basement

soubresaut [subrəso] **NM 1** *(secousse)* jerk, jolt **2** *(haut-le-corps)* shudder; **avoir un s.** to shudder **3** *(saccade)* **les derniers soubresauts de la bataille** the last throes of the battle

soubrette [subrɛt] **NF 1** *Théât* soubrette, maid; **jouer les soubrettes** to play minor roles **2** *Littéraire (servante)* lady's maid

souçaille [susaj] **NM** *Fam (souci)* worry▫; **no s.!** *Br* no worries!, *Am* no sweat!

souche [suʃ] **NF 1** *Bot (d'un arbre en terre)* stock, bole; *(d'un arbre coupé)* stump; *(d'une vigne)* stock; **ne reste pas là planté comme une s.!** don't just stand there like *Br* a lemon *or Am* a turkey!

2 *(d'un carnet)* stub, counterfoil

3 *(origine)* descent, stock; **de s. paysanne** of peasant stock; **mot de s. saxonne** word with a Saxon root *or* of Saxon origin; **faire s.** *(ancêtre)* to found *or* to start a line

4 *Fam (crétin)* idiot, dumbo

5 *Constr* base; **s. de cheminée** chimney stack

6 *Biol* strain

7 *Jur* stock

8 *Belg (ticket de caisse, reçu)* receipt

• **de souche ADJ ils sont français de s.** they're of French extraction *or* origin

• **de vieille souche ADJ** of old stock

souci [susi] **NM 1** *(inquiétude)* worry; **se faire du s.** to worry, to fret; **se faire du s. pour qn/qch** to worry *or* to be worried about sb/sth; **elle n'a pas le moindre s. à se faire quant à son avenir** she needn't worry in the slightest about her future; **ne te fais donc pas tant de s.!** don't worry so much!; **donner du s. à qn** to worry sb; **mon fils me donne bien du s.!** my son is a great worry to me

2 *(préoccupation)* worry; **avoir des soucis** to have worries; **cet enfant est un perpétuel s.** this child is a perpetual (source of) worry; **c'est un s. de moins!** that's one thing less to worry about!; **des soucis d'argent/de santé** money/health worries;

c'est le dernier *ou* **le cadet de mes soucis!** that's the least of my worries!; *Fam* **il n'y a pas de soucis!** *Br* no worries!, *Am* no sweat!

3 *(soin)* concern; **avoir le s. de la vérité/de l'exactitude** to be meticulously truthful/accurate; **avoir le s. de bien faire** to be concerned *or* to care about doing things well

4 *Bot* marigold

• **dans le souci de** CONJ **je l'ai fait dans le s. de t'aider** I was (only) trying to help you when I did it
• **dans un souci de** PRÉP **je me suis limité à deux auteurs dans un s. de clarté** I limited myself to two authors in order to keep things clear
• **sans souci** ADJ *(vie, personne ▸ insouciant)* carefree; **être sans s.** *(sans tracas)* to be free of worries ADV **vivre sans s.** *(de façon insouciante)* to live a carefree life; *(sans tracas)* to live a life free of worries

soucier [9] [susje] VT *Arch (causer de l'inquiétude à)* to trouble, to worry
VPR **se soucier 1 se s. de** *(s'inquiéter de)* to worry about; *(s'intéresser à)* to care about; **pars en vacances et ne te soucie de rien** go on holiday and don't worry about a thing; *Fam* **il s'en soucie comme de sa première chemise** *ou* **de l'an quarante** he doesn't give a damn about it **2** *Littéraire* **je ne me soucie pas qu'il vienne** I am not anxious that he should come

soucieux, -euse [susjø, -øz] ADJ **1** *(inquiet)* worried, preoccupied; **elle m'a regardé d'un air s.** she looked at me worriedly **2 s. de** *(attaché à)* concerned about, mindful of; **peu s. de la rencontrer** unconcerned about meeting her; **elle a toujours été soucieuse de ne pas les décevoir** she has always been anxious not to let them down; **elle était soucieuse que tout se passe bien** she was anxious that everything should go well

soucoupe [sukup] NF saucer; **s. volante** flying saucer; **faire des yeux comme des soucoupes** to have eyes like saucers

soudage [sudaʒ] NM **s. à l'arc** arc welding; **s. autogène** welding; **s. hétérogène** soldering

soudain, -e [sudɛ̃, -ɛn] ADJ sudden, unexpected
ADV all of a sudden, suddenly; **s. la porte s'ouvrit** all of a sudden *or* suddenly, the door opened

soudainement [sudɛnmɑ̃] ADV suddenly, all of a sudden; **pourquoi est-il parti si s.?** why did he leave so hurriedly?

soudaineté [sudɛnte] NF suddenness; **la s. de son départ** his/her hurried *or* sudden departure

Soudan [sudɑ̃] NM **le S.** (the) Sudan

soudanais, -e [sudanɛ, -ɛz], **soudanien, -enne** [sudanjɛ̃, -ɛn] ADJ Sudanese
• **Soudanais, -e, Soudanien, -enne** NM,F Sudanese (person); **les S.** the Sudanese

soudant, -e [sudɑ̃, -ɑ̃t] ADJ welding *(avant n)*

soudard [sudar] NM **1** *Hist* ill-disciplined soldier **2** *Littéraire (individu grossier et brutal)* brute **3** *Belg (soldat)* soldier; *(conscrit)* conscript

soude [sud] NF **1** *Chim* soda; **s. caustique** caustic soda **2** *Bot* barilla

souder [3] [sude] VT **1** *Tech (par soudure ▸ autogène)* to weld; *(▸ hétérogène)* to solder; **s. à l'arc** to arc-weld; **s. au cuivre** *ou* **au laiton** to braze; **s. à l'étain** to soft-solder; **s. par points** to spot-weld **2** *(unir)* to bring together, to unite; **le malheur les avait soudés** misfortune had united them
VPR **se souder 1** *(vertèbres, mots)* to become fused **2** *(s'unir ▸ personnes, groupe)* to unite

soudeur, -euse [sudœr, -øz] NM,F *(par soudure ▸ hétérogène)* solderer; *(▸ autogène)* welder; **s. au chalumeau** lamp *or* torch welder
• **soudeuse** NF *(machine)* welder, welding machine

soudoyer [13] [sudwaje] VT **1** *(acheter)* to bribe; **s. qn pour qu'il fasse qch** to bribe sb into doing sth; **se faire s.** to be bribed **2** *Arch (mercenaire)* to pay

soudure [sudyr] NF **1** *(soudage ▸ autogène)* welding; *(▸ hétérogène)* soldering; **s. au cuivre** *ou* **au laiton** brazing; **s. à l'étain** soft-soldering; **s. par points** spot weld

2 *(résultat ▸ autogène)* weld; *(▸ hétérogène)* soldered joint

3 *(jonction)* join; **ça s'est cassé à (l'endroit de) la s.** it broke along the join; *Fig* **assurer** *ou* **faire la s. (entre)** to bridge the gap (between)

4 *(alliage ▸ autogène)* weld; *(▸ hétérogène)* solder

5 *Anat & Bot* suture

souffert, -e [sufɛr, -ɛrt] PP *voir* **souffrir**

soufflage [suflaʒ] NM **1** *(modelage ▸ du verre)* blowing; *(▸ des polymères)* inflation **2** *Naut* sheathing **3** *Métal* blow

soufflant, -e [suflɑ̃, -ɑ̃t] ADJ **1** *(appareil)* **machine soufflante** blowing *or* blast engine; **radiateur s.** fan heater **2** *Fam (étonnant)* amazing
NM *très Fam (pistolet)* gun[□]
• **soufflante** NF **1** *(dans un haut fourneau)* blower **2** *(dans un turboréacteur)* turbofan

soufflard [suflar] NM *Géol* fumarole (jet)

souffle [sufl] NM **1** *(air expiré ▸ par une personne)* blow; **elle dit oui dans un s.** she breathed her assent; *Littéraire* **dernier s.** last breath; **jusqu'à mon dernier s.** as long as I live and breathe, to my dying day

2 *(respiration)* breath; *(rythme respiratoire)* breathing; **je sentis un s. sur ma nuque** I felt a breath on my neck; **il a éteint toutes les bougies d'un s.** he blew out all the candles in one go; **exhaler son dernier s.** to breathe one's last; **avoir du s.** to have a lot of breath; **avoir le s. court, manquer de s.** to be short of breath; **être à bout de s., n'avoir plus de s.** *(haletant)* to be out of breath; *Fig* **l'entreprise est à bout de s.** the company is on its last legs; **reprendre son s.** to get one's breath *or* wind back; *aussi Fig* **retenir son s.** to hold one's breath; **trouver un deuxième** *ou* **un second s.** to get *or* to find one's second wind; *Fig* to get a new lease of life

3 *(courant d'air)* **s. d'air** *ou* **de vent** breath of air; **il n'y a pas un s. de vent** there isn't a breath of air, the air is completely still

4 *Littéraire (force)* breath, spirit; **un s. épique traverse le poème** the poem is imbued with an epic spirit; **le s. vital** the breath of life

5 *(d'une explosion)* blast; **le magasin a été détruit par le s.** the *Br* shop *or Am* store was destroyed by the blast

6 *Méd* murmur; **s. au cœur** heart murmur

7 *Zool (d'un cétacé)* blow

soufflé, -e [sufle] ADJ **1** *Tech* blown

2 *Fam (étonné)* amazed

3 *Culin* soufflé *(avant n)*; **pommes de terre soufflées** soufflé potatoes

4 *(boursouflé ▸ visage, main)* puffy, swollen
NM **1** *Culin* soufflé; **s. au fromage** cheese soufflé **2** *Tech* blowing

soufflement [sufləmɑ̃] NM *Littéraire* blowing

SOUFFLER [3] [sufle]

VI	
• to breathe out **1**	• to blow **2, 3, 6**
• to get one's breath back **4**	• to have a break **5**
VT	
• to blow out **1**	• to whisper **3, 4**
• to stagger **5**	• to blow up **8**
• to blow **9**	
USAGE ABSOLU	
• to whisper	

VI **1** *(expirer ▸ personne)* to breathe out; **inspirez, soufflez!** breathe in, breathe out!; **soufflez dans le ballon** *(Alcootest®)* blow into the bag; **ils m'ont fait s. dans le ballon** they gave me a breath test; **s. dans un cor/dans un trombone** to blow (into) a horn/a trombone; **il soufflait sur ses mains** he was blowing on his hands; **souffle sur ton potage si c'est trop chaud** blow on your soup if it's too hot; **s. sur le feu** to blow on the fire; *Fig* to add fuel to the flames; *Fam* **s. dans les bronches à qn** to bawl sb out

2 *Météo (vent)* to blow; **le vent soufflera sur tout le pays** it will be windy all over the country; **le vent soufflait en rafales** there were gusts of wind, the wind was gusting; **le vent souffle à plus de 120 km/h par endroits** there are gusts of wind reaching 120 km/h in places

3 *(respirer avec difficulté)* to blow, to puff, to breathe hard; **suant et soufflant** puffing and blowing; *Fam* **s. comme un bœuf** *ou* **une locomotive** *ou* **un phoque** to wheeze like a pair of old bagpipes

4 *(retrouver sa respiration ▸ personne)* to get one's breath back; *(▸ cheval)* to get its breath back; **souffle un peu, avant de soulever l'armoire** get your breath back before you move the cupboard; **laisser s. son cheval** to blow *or* to wind one's horse

5 *(se reposer)* to have a break *or* a breather; **ça fait trois semaines que je travaille sans arrêt, j'ai besoin de s. un peu** I've been working for three weeks non-stop, I need a break *or* a breather; **au bureau, on n'a pas le temps de s.!** it's all go at the office!; **tu ne prends donc jamais le temps de s.?** don't you ever let up *or* give yourself a break?

6 *Zool (cétacé)* to blow
VT **1** *(bougie)* to blow out; **elle a soufflé toutes les bougies d'un seul coup** she blew all the candles out in one go

2 *(exhaler)* **va s. ta fumée de cigarette ailleurs** go and blow your smoke elsewhere; *Fig* **s. le chaud et le froid** to blow hot and cold

3 *(murmurer ▸ mot, réponse)* to whisper; *Théât* to prompt; **s. qch à qn** to whisper sth to sb; **ne pas s. mot (de qch)** not to breathe a word (about sth)

4 *(suggérer ▸ idée, conseil)* to whisper, to suggest; **et qui t'a soufflé cette brillante idée?** who did you get that bright idea from?

5 *Fam (époustoufler ▸ sujet: événement, personne)* to stagger; **son insolence m'a vraiment soufflé!** I was quite staggered at his/her rudeness!

6 *Fam (dérober)* **s. qch à qn** to pinch sth from sb; **je me suis fait s. ma place** someone's pinched my seat

7 *(dans un jeu ▸ pion)* to huff; **s. n'est pas jouer!** to huff doesn't count as a move!

8 *(sujet: bombe, explosion)* to blow up; **l'explosion a soufflé la toiture** the blast blew the roof off

9 *Métal & Tech* to blow
USAGE ABSOLU *(murmurer)* **on ne souffle pas!** no whispering!, don't whisper (the answer)!

soufflerie [sufləri] NF **1** *Aviat* wind tunnel; **en s.** in a wind tunnel **2** *Ind* blower; *(d'une forge)* bellows **3** *Mus (d'un orgue)* bellows

soufflet [suflɛ] NM **1** *(instrument)* (pair of) bellows; **s. de forge** (forge *or* blacksmith's) bellows
2 *(d'un cartable)* extendible pocket
3 *Littéraire (gifle)* slap; *(affront)* snub
4 *Couture* (pocket) gusset
5 *Phot* bellows
6 *Rail* (wagon) communication bellows
7 *Mus (d'un orgue)* bellows

souffleter [27] [suflǝte] VT *Littéraire (gifler)* to slap in the face; *(insulter)* to insult

soufflette [suflɛt] NF *Belg (ampoule)* blister; *(boursouflure)* swelling

souffleur, -euse [suflœr, -øz] NM,F **1** *Théât* prompter **2** *Tech* **s. de verre** glassblower
• **souffleuse** NF **1** *Agr* blower container **2** *Can* **souffleuse (à neige)** snowblower, snow thrower, snow sweeper

soufflure [suflyr] NF **1** *Métal (à la surface)* blister; *(à l'intérieur)* blowhole **2** *(dans un enduit, dans une peinture)* blister **3** *(dans le verre)* blister, bubble

souffrance [sufrɑ̃s] NF **1** *(fait de souffrir)* suffering **2** *(mal ▸ physique)* pain; *(▸ psychologique)* pain, torment; **mettre fin aux souffrances de qn** to put an end to sb's suffering
• **en souffrance** ADV *(dossier)* pending; *(factures)* overdue, outstanding; *(colis)* held up in transit, awaiting delivery; **être** *ou* **rester en s.** to be held up

souffrant, -e [sufrɑ̃, -ɑ̃t] ADJ **1** *(malade)* **être s.** to be unwell **2** *(malheureux)* suffering; **l'humanité souffrante** the downtrodden masses

souffre-douleur [sufrədulœr] NM INV scapegoat; **à l'école, c'était toujours lui le s.** at school, he was always the one who got bullied

souffreteux, -euse [sufrətø, -øz] ADJ **1** *(malingre)* sickly, *Péj* puny; **un enfant s.** a sickly *or* a delicate child **2** *(maladif ▸ air)* sickly; **une mine souffreteuse** an unhealthy *or* a sickly complexion **3** *(rabougri ▸ plante)* stunted, scrubby

souffrir [34] [sufrir] VT **1** *(endurer ▸ épreuves)* to endure, to suffer; **si tu avais souffert ce que j'ai souffert!** if you'd suffered as much as I have!, if you had gone through what I have!; **s. le martyre** to go through *or* to suffer agonies

2 *Littéraire (tolérer)* **elle ne souffre pas qu'on la critique** she can't stand *or* take criticism; **je ne peux pas s. cet homme** I can't bear *or* stand that man **3** *Littéraire (admettre ► sujet: personne)* to allow, to tolerate; *(► sujet: règlement)* to allow (for), to admit of; **souffrez au moins que je vous accompagne** at least allow me to accompany you; **cette règle ne souffre aucune exception** the rule admits of no exception

4 *Fam (supporter)* **elle ne peut pas le s.** she can't stand him

USAGE ABSOLU les récoltes n'ont pas trop souffert the crops didn't suffer too much *or* weren't too badly damaged; **c'est le sud du pays qui a le plus souffert** the southern part of the country was the worst hit

VI 1 *(avoir mal)* to be in pain, to suffer; **tu souffres?** are you in pain?, does it hurt?; **souffre-t-il beaucoup?** is he in much pain?, is he suffering a lot?; **où souffrez-vous?** where is the pain?, where does it hurt?; **elle a beaucoup souffert lors de son accouchement** she had a very painful delivery; **s. en silence** to suffer in silence; **il est mort sans s.** he felt no pain when he died; *Hum* **il faut s. pour être belle!** one must suffer to be beautiful!; **faire s. qn** to cause pain to sb, to hurt sb; **mon dos me fait s. ces temps-ci** my back's been hurting (me) lately **2** *(moralement)* to suffer; **elle l'a fait terriblement s.** she's caused him/her a lot of pain **3** *Fam (peiner)* to toil, to have a hard time (of it); **notre équipe a souffert pendant la première mi-temps** our team had a rough time *or* was put through the mill during the first half

• **souffrir de VT IND** *(avoir mal à cause de)* **s. de la hanche** to have trouble with one's hip; **pour tous les gens qui souffrent du diabète/du dos** for all diabetes sufferers/people with back problems; **s. de la faim/de la soif** to suffer from hunger/thirst; **s. de la chaleur** *(être très sensible à)* to suffer in the heat; *(être atteint par)* to suffer from the heat; **s. de la solitude** to feel lonely; **ils souffrent de son indifférence** they're hurt by his/her indifference; **elle souffre de le savoir si loin** it pains her to know he's so far away; **sa renommée a souffert du scandale** his/her reputation suffered from the scandal

VPR se souffrir *Littéraire* **ils ne peuvent pas se s.** they can't stand *or* bear each other

soufi [sufi] **NM** *Rel* Sufi

soufisme [sufism] **NM** *Rel* Sufism

soufrage [sufraʒ] **NM 1** *(des allumettes)* sulphuring **2** *Agr & Tex* sulphuration

soufre [sufr] **NM 1** *Chim* sulphur **2** *(locution)* **sentir le s.** to be highly unorthodox

ADJ INV sulphur (yellow)

soufrer [3] [sufre] **VT 1** *(allumettes)* to sulphur **2** *Agr* to (treat *or* spray with) sulphur **3** *Tex* to sulphurate

souhait [swɛ] **NM** wish; **faire un s.** to make a wish; **tous nos souhaits de bonheur** all our best wishes for your future happiness; **envoyer ses souhaits de bonne année** to send New Year greetings; **à tes souhaits!, à vos souhaits!** bless you! *(after a sneeze)*

• **à souhait ADV** *Littéraire* extremely well, perfectly; **tout marche à s.** everything's going well *or* perfectly; **rôti à s.** cooked to perfection, done to a turn

souhaitable [swetabl] **ADJ** desirable; **ce n'est guère s.** this is not to be desired; **il serait s. que vous n'en parliez à personne** it would be better if you didn't mention this to anybody

souhaiter [4] [swete] **VT 1** *(espérer)* to wish *or* to hope for; **il ne reviendra plus – souhaitons-le!** he won't come back – let's hope not!; **ce n'est pas à s.!** it's not something we would wish for!; **s. la ruine/le bonheur de qn** to wish for sb's ruin/happiness; **s. que...** to hope that...; **souhaitons que tout aille bien** let's hope everything goes all right; **il est à s. que...** it's to be hoped that... **2** *(formuler un vœu de)* to wish; **en vous souhaitant un prompt rétablissement/un bon anniversaire** wishing you a swift recovery/a happy birthday; **nous vous souhaitons un joyeux Noël** with our best wishes for a happy Christmas; **s. sa fête/son anniversaire à qn** to wish sb a happy saint's day/a happy birthday; **je te souhaite beaucoup de réussite/d'être heureux** I wish you every success/happiness; **je vous souhaite de réussir** I hope you will succeed; **souhaite-moi bonne chance!** wish me luck!; **je ne leur ai pas encore souhaité la bonne année** *(par écrit)* I haven't sent them my wishes for the New Year yet; *(oralement)* I haven't wished them a happy New Year yet; **je vous souhaite bonne nuit** I'll say good night to you; **je ne le souhaite à personne** I wouldn't wish that on anyone; *Fam Ironique* **je te souhaite bien du plaisir!** best of luck to you! **3** *(désirer)* to wish; **je souhaite qu'on me tienne au courant** I wish to be kept informed; **je souhaiterais parler au responsable** I'd like to speak to the person in charge; **je souhaiterais pouvoir t'aider** I wish I could help (you), I'd like to be able to help (you)

VPR se souhaiter nous nous sommes souhaité la bonne année we wished each other a happy New Year

souiller [3] [suje] **VT** *Littéraire* **1** *(maculer)* to soil; **des vêtements souillés de boue** mudstained clothes **2** *(polluer)* to contaminate, to pollute, to taint **3** *(entacher ► réputation)* to ruin, to sully, to tarnish; *(► innocence)* to defile, to taint

souillon [sujɔ̃] **NMF** *(homme)* slob; *(femme)* slob, slut; *(servante)* slovenly maid

souillure [sujyr] **NF 1** *Littéraire (tache)* stain **2** *Littéraire (flétrissure)* blemish, taint; **la s. du péché** the stain of sin

souk [suk] **NM 1** *(marché)* souk **2** *Fam (désordre)* shambles; **c'est le s. dans sa piaule!** his/her room's an absolute bombsite *or* pigsty!; **foutre le s. (dans)** to make a mess (of)□; **il fout le s. en classe** he creates havoc in the classroom□

soul [sul, sol] *Mus* **ADJ INV** soul *(avant n)*

NM *(jazz)* hard bop

NF *(pop)* soul (music)

soûl, -e [su, sul] **ADJ 1** *(ivre)* drunk; *Fam* **s. comme une bourrique** *ou* **un cochon** *ou* **un Polonais** *Br* (as) drunk as a lord, *Am* stewed to the gills **2** *Fig Littéraire* **s. de** *(rassasié de)* sated with; *(étourdi par)* drunk *or* intoxicated with

NM tout son s. to one's heart's content; **manger/boire tout son s.** to eat/to drink one's fill *or* to one's heart's content; **dormir tout son s.** to sleep as much as one wants

soulagement [sulaʒmɑ̃] **NM** relief, *Sout* solace; **éprouver un sentiment de s.** to feel relieved; **c'est un s. de le savoir sain et sauf** it's a relief to know he's safe and sound

soulager [17] [sulaʒe] **VT 1** *(personne ► physiquement)* to relieve, to bring relief to; **les comprimés ne me soulagent plus** the pills don't bring me relief any more; **cela devrait vous s. de votre mal de tête** this should relieve *or* help your headache

2 *(personne ► moralement)* to relieve, to soothe; **pleure, ça te soulagera** have a good cry, you'll feel better afterwards; **je suis soulagé de l'apprendre** I'm relieved to hear it; **si ça peut te s., sache que je suis dans la même situation** if it makes you feel any better, I'm in the same situation; **s. la conscience de qn** to ease sb's conscience

3 *(diminuer ► misère, souffrances)* to relieve; *(► douleur)* to relieve, to soothe

4 *(décharger)* to relieve; **mon collègue me soulage parfois d'une partie de mon travail** my colleague sometimes relieves me of part of my work; *Hum* **s. qn de son portefeuille** to relieve sb of his/her *Br* wallet *or Am* billfold

5 *Constr (étayer)* to shore up

6 *Naut (ancre)* to weigh

VPR se soulager 1 *(d'une charge de travail)* to lessen the strain on oneself; **prends un collaborateur pour te s.** take somebody on to take some of the pressure of work off you

2 *(moralement)* to get *or* to find relief, to take comfort; **il m'arrive de crier pour me s.** sometimes I shout to let *or* to blow off steam

3 *Fam (uriner, déféquer)* to relieve oneself

4 *très Fam (se masturber)* to give oneself relief

soûlant, -e [sulɑ̃, -ɑ̃t] **ADJ** *Fam* exhausting□, *Br* knackering; **elle parle, elle parle, c'en est s.!** she goes on and on, it makes your head spin!

soûlard, -e [sular, -ard], **soûlaud, -e** [sulo, -od] **NM,F** *Fam* boozer, alky; **c'est une vieille soûlarde** she's an old soak

soûler [3] [sule] **VT 1** *Fam (rendre ivre)* **s. qn** to get sb drunk□ **2** *(étourdir)* to make dizzy *or* giddy; **tu me soûles, avec tes questions!** you're making me dizzy with all these questions!

VPR se soûler 1 *Fam (s'enivrer)* to get drunk□; *très Fam* **se s. la gueule** *Br* to get pissed, *Am* to tie one on **2** *Fig (s'étourdir)* **se s. de** to get intoxicated with; **il se soûle de paroles** he talks so much that it goes to his head

soûlerie [sulri] **NF** *Fam* **1** *(beuverie)* bender, drinking session□ **2** *(ivresse)* drunkenness□

soulèvement [sulɛvmɑ̃] **NM 1** *(mouvement)* lifting; **déclenché par le s. du clapet** triggered by the lifting of the valve **2** *(insurrection)* uprising **3** *Géol* **s. de terrain** upheaval *or* uplift (of the ground)

soulever [19] [sulve] **VT 1** *(pour porter, pour élever ► charge, personne debout)* to lift (up); *(► couvercle, loquet, voile)* to lift; *(► capot)* to lift, to open; *(► personne allongée)* to raise (up); *(► chapeau)* to raise; *(► voiture)* to lift; *(► voiture sur cric)* to jack up; *(► avec effort)* to heave; **de gros sanglots soulevaient sa poitrine** his/her chest was heaving with sobs; **le vent m'a presque soulevée de terre!** the wind nearly lifted me off the ground *or* off my feet!

2 *(remuer ► poussière, sable)* to raise; **le vent soulevait les feuilles mortes** the wind was stirring up dead leaves

3 *(provoquer ► protestations, tollé)* to raise; *(► enthousiasme, émotion)* to arouse; *(► difficulté)* to bring up, to raise; **son imitation souleva une tempête de rires** his/her impersonation caused gales of laughter; **sa déclaration souleva un tonnerre d'applaudissements** his/her announcement met with thunderous applause

4 *(poser ► question, objection)* to raise, to bring up; **je voudrais s. le point suivant** I'd like to raise the following point

5 *(pousser à se révolter ► population)* to stir up; **ils ont tout fait pour s. le peuple contre la monarchie** they did everything they could to stir up the people against the monarchy

6 *(retourner)* **ça m'a soulevé le cœur** it turned my stomach, it made me sick; **une puanteur à vous s. le cœur** a sickening stench

7 *très Fam (prendre ► chose)* to pinch; *(► mari, maîtresse)* to steal

VPR se soulever 1 *(se redresser)* to lift *or* to raise oneself up; **il l'aida à se s.** he helped him/her to sit up **2** *(mer)* to swell (up), to heave; *(poitrine)* to heave; **sa jupe se soulevait au moindre souffle de vent** the slighest puff of wind blew her skirt up **3** *(peuple)* to rise up, to revolt

soulier [sulje] **NM 1** *(chaussure)* shoe **2** *Fam (locution)* **être dans ses petits souliers** to feel (very) small

soulignage [suliɲaʒ], **soulignement** [suliɲəmɑ̃] **NM** underlining

souligner [3] [suliɲe] **VT 1** *(mettre un trait sous)* to underline **2** *(accentuer)* to enhance, to emphasize; **s. son regard d'un trait de khôl** to enhance *or* to emphasize one's eyes with a touch of kohl; **une robe qui souligne la taille** a dress which emphasizes the waist **volant souligné d'un liseré bleu** flounce trimmed with blue ribbon **3** *(faire remarquer)* to emphasize, to stress; **je souligne que je n'y suis pour rien** let me stress that I have nothing to do with it; **soulignons que l'auteur a lui-même connu la prison** let's note *or* let's not forget that the author himself spent some time in prison

soûlographie [sulɔgrafi] **NF** *Fam (ivrognerie)* drunkenness□

soûlon [sulɔ̃] **NM** *Suisse & Can Fam* lush, soak

soûlot, -e [sulo, -ɔt] = **soûlard**

soumettre [84] [sumetr] **VT 1** *(se rendre maître de ► nation)* to subjugate; *(► mutins)* to take control of, to subdue, to bring to heel; *(► passion)* to control, to tame **2** *(à une épreuve, à un règlement)* **s. qn à** to subject sb to; **s. qn à sa volonté** to subject *or* to bend sb to one's will; **être soumis à des règles strictes** to be bound by strict rules; **s. qch à un examen** to subject sth to an examination; **s. un malade à un régime strict** to put a patient on a strict diet; **s. qn/qch à l'impôt** to subject sb/sth to tax **3** *(présenter ► loi, suggestion, texte)* to submit; **je lui soumettrai votre demande** I'll refer your request to him/her; **je voulais d'abord le s. à votre approbation** I wanted to submit it for your approval first; **s. une lettre à la signature** to present a letter for signature

VPR se soumettre to give in, to submit, to yield; **les rebelles ont fini par se s.** the rebels finally gave in; **se s. à** *(se plier à)* to submit *or* to subject oneself to; *(s'en remettre à)* to abide by; **se s. à la décision de qn** to abide by sb's decision

soumis, -e [sumi, -iz] **ADJ 1** *(docile)* submissive, obedient, dutiful **2** *(astreint)* subject (**à** to); **s. à l'impôt sur le revenu** liable to income tax

soumission [sumisjõ] **NF 1** *(obéissance ▸ à un pouvoir)* submission, submitting; *(▸ à une autorité)* acquiescence, acquiescing; **faire acte de s.** to submit; **il exigeait une totale s. au règlement** he demanded rigid adherence to the rules **2** *(asservissement)* submissiveness; **vivre dans la s.** to live a submissive life, to live one's life in a state of submission **3** *Com* tender; **par (voie de) s.** by tender; **faire une s. pour un travail** to tender for a piece of work

soumissionnaire [sumisjɔnɛr] **NMF** tenderer

soumissionner **[3]** [sumisjɔne] **VT** to bid *or* to tender for

soumit *etc voir* **soumettre**

soundcheck [saundtʃɛk] **NM** *Mus* sound check

soupape [supap] **NF 1** *Aut & Tech* valve; **s. d'admission** inlet valve; **s. d'échappement** exhaust *or* outlet valve; *aussi Fig* **s. de sécurité** *ou* **de sûreté** safety valve; **soupapes en tête** overhead valves
2 *(bonde)* plug
3 *Élec* valve, tube
4 *Mus* pallet

soupçon [supsõ] **NM 1** *(suspicion)* suspicion; **de graves soupçons pèsent sur lui** grave suspicions hang over him; **éveiller les soupçons** to arouse *or* to excite suspicion; **avoir des soupçons sur qn/qch** to be suspicious of sb/sth; **j'ai eu des soupçons dès le début** I suspected something from the beginning; **être à l'abri** *ou* **au-dessus de tout s.** to be free from *or* above all suspicion **2** *(idée, pressentiment)* suspicion, inkling; **je n'en avais pas le moindre s.** I didn't have the slightest suspicion, I never suspected it for a moment **3** *(petite quantité)* **un s. de crème** a touch *or* a dash of cream; **un s. d'ironie** a touch *or* a hint of irony; **un s. de rhum** a dash *or* a (tiny) drop of rum

soupçonnable [supsɔnabl] **ADJ** open to suspicion, suspicious

soupçonner **[3]** [supsɔne] **VT 1** *(suspecter)* to suspect; **s. qn de meurtre/de trahison** to suspect sb of murder/of treason; **soupçonné d'avoir fait de l'espionnage** suspected of having been a spy *or* of espionage
2 *(pressentir ▸ piège)* to suspect; **comment pouvais-je s. qu'il ferait une fugue?** how could I possibly have foreseen *or* predicted that he'd run away?
3 *(douter de)* to doubt; **il n'y a aucune raison de s. sa bonne foi** there's no reason to doubt his/her good faith
4 *(imaginer)* to imagine, to suspect

soupçonneuse [supsɔnøz] *voir* **soupçonneux**

soupçonneusement [supsɔnøzmã] **ADV** suspiciously, with suspicion

soupçonneux, -euse [supsɔnø, -øz] **ADJ** suspicious; **d'un air s.** suspiciously

soupe [sup] **NF 1** *Culin* soup; **s. aux choux/à l'oignon** cabbage/onion soup; **s. au lait** bread and milk; *Fig* **elle est très s. au lait** she flies off the handle easily; *Fam* **faire la s. à la grimace** to sulk[□], to be in a huff; **il est rentré tard hier soir et a eu droit à la s. à la grimace** he got home late last night, so now he's in the doghouse; *Fig* **aller à la s.** to have an eye to the main chance; *Fam* **par ici la bonne s.!** that's the way to make money! **2** *Fam (repas)* grub, nosh; **s. populaire** soup kitchen; **à la s.!** grub's up!, come and get it! **3** *Fam (neige)* slushy snow

soupente [supãt] **NF 1** *(dans un grenier)* loft; *(sous un escalier) esp Br* cupboard, *Am* closet *(under the stairs)* **2** *Tech (barre de soutien)* supporting bar

souper[1] [supe] **NM 1** *Vieilli ou Can, Belg, Suisse & (en français régional) (dîner)* dinner, supper **2** *(après le spectacle)* (late) supper

souper[2] **[3]** [supe] **VI 1** *Vieilli ou Can, Belg, Suisse & (en français régional) (dîner)* to have dinner; **s. de qch** to dine on sth **2** *(après le spectacle)* to have a late supper *(after a show)* **3** *Fam* **en avoir soupé de qch** to have had enough of sth, to be fed up (to the back teeth) of sth

soupeser **[19]** [supəze] **VT 1** *(en soulevant)* to feel the weight of, to weigh in one's hand *or* hands **2** *(juger)* to weigh up

soupière [supjɛr] **NF** (soup) tureen

soupir [supir] **NM 1** *(expiration)* sigh; **un gros s.** a heavy *or* a deep sigh; **s. de soulagement** sigh of relief; **pousser des soupirs** to sigh; **"oui", murmura-t-elle dans un s.** "yes," she sighed; *Littéraire* **dernier s.** last breath; **rendre le dernier s.** to breathe one's last **2** *Mus Br* crotchet rest, *Am* quarter *or* quarter-note rest
• **soupirs NMPL** *Littéraire (désirs)* **l'objet de mes soupirs** the one I yearn for

soupirail, -aux [supiraj, -o] **NM** *(d'une cave)* (cellar) ventilator; *(d'une pièce)* basement window

soupirant [supirã] **NM** suitor

soupiraux [supiro] *voir* **soupirail**

soupirer **[3]** [supire] **VI** *(pousser un soupir)* to sigh; **s. d'aise** to sigh with contentment; **"eh oui", dit-il en soupirant** "I'm afraid so," he sighed
VT *(dire)* to sigh; **"c'est impossible", soupira-t-elle** "it's impossible," she sighed
• **soupirer après VT IND** *Littéraire* to long *or* to sigh *or* to yearn for
• **soupirer pour VT IND** *Littéraire (être amoureux de)* to sigh for

souple [supl] **ADJ 1** *(lame)* flexible, pliable, supple; *(branche)* supple; *(plastique)* non-rigid
2 *(malléable)* **argile s.** plastic clay
3 *(agile ▸ athlète, danseur, corps)* supple; *(▸ démarche)* fluid, flowing
4 *(doux ▸ cuir, peau, brosse à dents)* soft; **pour rendre votre linge plus s.** to make your washing softer; **une voiture dotée d'une suspension s.** a car with smooth suspension
5 *(aménageable)* flexible, adaptable; **la réglementation/l'horaire est s.** the rules/the hours are flexible
6 *(qui sait s'adapter)* flexible, adaptable
7 *(docile)* docile, obedient
8 *(écriture, style)* flowing
9 *(en œnologie)* smooth
10 *Aut (moteur)* flexible

souplesse [suplɛs] **NF 1** *(d'une personne, d'un félin, d'un corps)* suppleness; *(d'une démarche)* suppleness, springiness; **admirez la s. du trait chez Degas** observe the easy flow of Degas' lines
2 *(douceur ▸ d'un cuir, d'un tissu)* softness; *(▸ de la peau)* smoothness
3 *(malléabilité ▸ d'une matière)* flexibility, pliability
4 *(d'un horaire, d'une méthode, d'une personne)* flexibility, adaptability; **s. d'esprit** *(agilité)* nimble-mindeness; *(adaptabilité)* versatility; *Péj (servilité)* servility
• **en souplesse ADV** smoothly; **retomber en s. sur ses jambes** *(après une chute)* to land nimbly on one's feet; *(en gymnastique)* to make a smooth landing; **une transition en s.** a smooth transition

souquenille [suknij] **NF** *Vieilli* smock

souquer **[3]** [suke] **VT 1** *(amarrage)* to pull taut **2** *(bateau)* to push to its limits
VI to pull at the oars, to stretch out; **s. ferme** to pull hard at the oars

source [surs] **NF 1** *(point d'eau)* spring; **la s. est tarie** the spring has dried up; **s. chaude** *ou* **thermale** hot spring
2 *(origine)* spring, source; **où la Seine prend-elle sa s.?** where is the source of the Seine?, where does the Seine originate?; **remonter jusqu'à la s.** *(d'un fleuve)* to go upriver until one finds the source; *(d'une habitude, d'un problème)* to go back to the root; **à la s.** *(au commencement)* at the source, in the beginning; **retenir les impôts à la s.** to deduct tax at source; **il nous faut aller à la s. (même) du mal** we must go to the very root *or* heart of the trouble
3 *(cause)* source; **une s. de revenus** a source of income; **cette maison n'a été qu'une s. d'ennuis** this house has been nothing but trouble; **être s. de qch** to give rise to sth; **cette formulation peut être s. de malentendus** the way it's worded could give rise to misinterpretations
4 *Presse* **tenir ses renseignements de bonne s.** *ou* **de s. sûre** *ou* **de s. bien informée** to have information on good authority; **nous savons de s. sûre que…** we have it on good authority that…, we are reliably informed that…; **de s. officielle/officieuse, on apprend que…** official/unofficial sources reveal that…; **citer ses sources** to cite one's sources
5 *Astron* **s. de rayonnement** radiation source
6 *Élec* **s. de courant** power supply
7 *Ordinat* source; **s. de données** data source
8 *Ling (comme adj)* source *(avant n)*
9 *Nucl* **s. radioactive** radioactive source
10 *Phys* **s. lumineuse** *ou* **de lumière** light source; **s. de chaleur/d'énergie** source of heat/energy, heat/energy source
11 *Pétr* oil deposit
12 *Jur* **s. du droit** source of law

sourcer **[16]** [surse] **VT 1** *(citation)* to source, to acknowledge the source of **2** *Journ (information)* to check the source of

sourcier, -ère [sursje, -ɛr] **NM,F** dowser, water-diviner

sourcil [sursi] **NM** eyebrow; **il a des sourcils bien fournis** he's beetle-browed

sourcilier, -ère [sursilje, -ɛr] **ADJ** superciliary

sourciller **[3]** [sursije] **VI** to frown; **sans s.** without batting an eyelid *or* turning a hair; **elle n'a pas sourcillé** she didn't bat an eyelid *or* turn a hair

sourcilleux, -euse [sursijø, -øz] **ADJ 1** *(pointilleux)* pernickety, finicky **2** *Littéraire (hautain)* haughty, supercilious

sourd, -e [sur, surd] **ADJ 1** *(personne)* deaf; **être s. de naissance** to be born deaf; **s. de l'oreille gauche** deaf in the left ear; **arrête de crier, je ne suis pas s.!** stop shouting, I'm not deaf *or* I can hear (you)!; **grand-père devient s./est un peu s.** grandpa is losing his hearing/is a bit deaf; **faire la sourde oreille** to pretend not to hear; *Fam* **être s. comme un pot** to be as deaf as a post
2 *(indifférent)* **le gouvernement est resté s. à leurs revendications** the government turned a deaf ear to their demands
3 *(atténué ▸ son, voix)* muffled, muted; **il y eut trois coups sourds à la porte** there were three muffled knocks on the door; **la poire tomba avec un bruit s.** the pear fell with a (dull) thud
4 *(mal défini ▸ douleur, teinte)* dull; *(▸ sentiment)* muted, subdued; **j'éprouvais une sourde inquiétude** I felt vaguely worried
5 *(clandestin)* hidden, secret
6 *(en acoustique)* **chambre** *ou* **salle sourde** dead room
7 *Ling* unvoiced, voiceless
NM,F deaf person; **les sourds** the deaf; **c'est comme si on parlait à un s.** it's like talking to a brick wall; **crier comme un s.** to scream *or* to shout at the top of one's voice; **frapper comme un s.** to bang with all one's might
• **sourde NF** *Ling* unvoiced *or* voiceless consonant

sourdement [surdəmã] **ADV** *Littéraire* **1** *(sans bruit)* dully, with a muffled noise **2** *(secrètement)* secretly; **intriguer s.** to engage in silent intrigue

sourdine [surdin] **NF** *Mus (d'une trompette, d'un violon)* mute; *(d'un piano)* soft pedal; *Fig* **mettre une s. à qch** *(critiques, démonstrations de joie)* to tone sth down; *Fig* **mettre la s.** to tone it down
• **en sourdine ADJ** muted **ADV 1** *Mus (jouer)* quietly, softly; *Fam Fig* **mets-la en s.!** put a sock in it! **2** *(en secret)* quietly, on the quiet

sourdingue [surdɛ̃g] *Fam* **ADJ** cloth-eared
NMF cloth-ears

sourd-muet, sourde-muette [surmɥɛ, surdmɥɛt] *(mpl* **sourds-muets**, *fpl* **sourdes-muettes)**
ADJ deaf and dumb
NM,F deaf-mute, deaf-and-dumb person

sourdre **[73]** [surdr] **VI** *Littéraire* **1** *(liquide)* to rise (up) **2** *(idée, sentiment)* to well up; **que verra-t-on s. de ces événements?** what will arise from these events?

souri [suri] **PP** *voir* **sourire**[2]

souriant, -e [surjã, -ãt] **ADJ 1** *(regard, visage)* smiling, beaming; *(personne)* cheerful **2** *(agréable ▸ paysage)* pleasant, welcoming; *(▸ pensée)* agreeable; **un avenir s.** a bright future

souriceau, -x [suriso] **NM** baby mouse

souricière [surisjɛr] **NF 1** *(ratière)* mousetrap **2** *(piège)* trap; **dresser une s.** to set a trap; **se jeter dans la s.** to fall into a trap

sourire¹ [surir] **NM** smile; **elle esquissa un s.** she smiled faintly; **il entra, le s. aux lèvres** he came in with a smile (on his lips *or* face); **avec un grand** *ou* **large s.** beaming, with a broad smile; **faire un s. à qn** to smile at sb; **fais-moi un petit s.** give me a smile!; **avoir le s.** to have a smile on one's face; **elle n'a pas le s. aujourd'hui** she doesn't look very happy today; **il a pris la nouvelle avec le s.** he took the news cheerfully; **il faut savoir garder le s.** you have to learn to keep smiling

sourire² **[95]** [surir] **VI** to smile; **souriez!** *(pour une photo)* smile!; **je vais lui faire passer l'envie de s.!** I'll knock *or* wipe the smile off his/her face!; **la remarque peut faire s.** this remark may bring a smile to your face *or* make you smile; **quand tu vois la manière dont ils agissent, ça fait s.** it is rather amusing to see the way they behave; **s. à qn** to smile at sb, to give sb a smile

• **sourire à VT IND 1** *(être favorable à)* to smile on; **la fortune lui sourit enfin** fortune is smiling on him/her at last **2** *(plaire à ▸ sujet: idée, perspective)* to appeal to

• **sourire de VT IND** *(se moquer de)* to smile *or* to laugh at; **il souriait de mon entêtement** my stubbornness made him smile

souris [suri] **NF 1** *Zool* mouse; *Fig* **j'aurais aimé être une petite s.!** I'd like to have been a fly on the wall!

2 *très Fam (femme)* chick, *Br* bird

3 *Culin (de gigot)* knuckle-joint

4 *Ordinat* mouse; **s. à infrarouge** infrared mouse; **s. optique** optical mouse; **s. sans fil** cordless *or* wireless mouse; **s. tactile** touchpad mouse; **s. à trois boutons** three-button mouse

ADJ INV mousy, mouse-coloured

• **souris d'hôtel NF** (female) hotel thief

sournois, -e [surnwa, -az] **ADJ 1** *(personne, regard)* cunning, shifty, sly **2** *(attaque, procédé)* underhand **3** *(douleur)* dull, gnawing

NM,F sly person

sournoisement [surnwazmɑ̃] **ADV** slyly

sournoiserie [surnwazri] **NF 1** *(caractère)* shiftiness, slyness, underhand manner **2** *(acte)* sly piece of work; *(parole)* sly remark

SOUS [su]

• under **1, 2, 5, 8**	• underneath **1**
• beneath **1, 2**	• behind **2**
• during **3**	• within **4**

PRÉP 1 *(dans l'espace)* under, underneath, beneath; **le plancher grinçait s. ses pieds** the floor creaked beneath *or* under his/her feet; **son journal s. le bras** (with) his/her newspaper under his/her arm; **être s. la douche** to be in the *or* having a shower; **se promener s. la pluie** to walk in the rain; **un paysage s. la neige** a snow-covered landscape; **Londres s. les bombes** London during the air raids; **nager s. l'eau** to swim underwater; **s. terre** underground, below ground; **assis s. le parasol** sitting under *or* underneath *or* beneath the parasol; **il venait chanter s. sa fenêtre** he'd come and sing under his/her window; *Fam* **enlève ça de s. la table** get it out from under the table; **s. l'Équateur** at the Equator; **s. les tropiques** in the Tropics; **ça s'est passé s. nos yeux** it took place before our very eyes; **les expressions figées sont données s. le premier mot** set phrases are given under the first word

2 *Fig (derrière)* behind, under, beneath; **il cache beaucoup de bienveillance s. des airs indifférents** he hides a lot of goodwill behind a cold exterior; **s. des dehors taciturnes** behind a stern exterior; **s. son air calme...** beneath his/her calm appearance...

3 *(à l'époque de)* **s. Louis XV** during the reign of *or* under Louis XV; **s. sa présidence/son ministère** under his/her presidency/ministry; **s. la Commune** during *or* at the time of the Paris Commune

4 *(dans un délai de)* within; **s. huitaine/quinzaine** within a week/two weeks *or Br* a fortnight

5 *(marquant un rapport de dépendance)* under; **s. ses ordres** under his/her command; **il est placé s. ma responsabilité** I'm in charge of him; **s. caution** on bail; **s. serment** under oath; **s. surveillance** under surveillance; **tomber s. le coup de la loi** to be within the law

6 *Méd* **être s. anesthésie** to be under anaesthetic; **être s. antibiotiques/s. perfusion** to be on antibiotics/a drip

7 *(marquant la manière)* **emballé s. vide** vacuum-packed; **s. verre** under glass; **s. pli scellé** in a sealed envelope; **elle a acheté le billet s. un faux nom** she bought the ticket under an assumed name; **vu s. cet angle** seen from this angle; **vu s. cet éclairage nouveau** considered in this new light; **parfait s. tous rapports** perfect in every respect

8 *(avec une valeur causale)* under; **s. la torture** under torture; **s. le coup du choc...** with the shock...; **s. le coup de l'émotion** in the grip of the emotion; **s. l'influence de l'alcool** under the influence of alcohol; **s. le poids de** under the weight of; **s. la pression des événements** under the pressure of events

> PREFIX
>
> **SOUS-**
>
> This is a very productive prefix in French.
>
> • When added to nouns, **sous-** can convey the idea of a LOWER POSITION IN SPACE. Its English equivalent is often *under-* or *sub-*, eg:
>
> **sous-sol** subsoil/cellar/basement; **sous-marin** submarine; **sous-bois** undergrowth; **sous-vêtement** piece of underwear, undergarment
>
> • When added to nouns or verbs, **sous-** can suggest a relation of SUBORDINATION. Although the translation can vary, several job titles in English include the prefix *sub-* or *under-*, eg:
>
> **sous-directeur** assistant manager/deputy head; **sous-lieutenant** second lieutenant/sublieutenant; **sous-préfet** subprefect; **sous-secrétaire d'État** undersecretary of State; **sous-traitant** subcontractor; **sous-traiter** to subcontract
>
> • **Sous-** is also used to prefix nouns to convey an idea of SUBDIVISION. The usual English equivalent in this case is *sub-*, eg:
>
> **sous-continent** subcontinent; **sous-catégorie** subcategory; **sous-ensemble** subset; **sous-ordre** suborder
>
> • **Sous-** is particularly productive when describing INSUFFICIENCY OR POOR QUALITY. The idea of insufficiency is usually conveyed by the prefix *under-* in English, whereas *sub-* tends to be used more pejoratively to imply poor quality. The more established variations on this theme are prefixed nouns, verbs or adjectives, but it is also possible to use **sous-** before a proper noun when referring to a work of art, a book, a film, etc which is deemed to be a pale imitation of a better author's work, or even to a person considered a *second-rate...*, eg:
>
> **sous-peuplement** underpopulation; **sous-peuplé** underpopulated; **sous-utiliser** to underuse, to underutilize; **sous-exploiter** to underexploit; **sous-payé** underpaid; **sous-humanité** subhumanity; **une sous-merde** a nobody, a non-entity; **il fait du sous-Picasso** he paints like a second-rate Picasso; **un sous-Marlon Brando** a second-rate Marlon Brando

sous-affréter **[18]** [suzafrete] **VT** *Transp* to subcharter

sous-alimentation [suzalimɑ̃tasjɔ̃] **NF** malnutrition, undernourishment

sous-alimenté, -e [suzalimɑ̃te] *(mpl* **sous-alimentés,** *fpl* **sous-alimentées) ADJ** undernourished, underfed; **des enfants sous-alimentés** children suffering from malnutrition

sous-bail [subaj] *(pl* **sous-baux) NM** sublease

sous-bibliothécaire [subibliɔtekɛr] *(pl* **sous-bibliothécaires) NMF** sub-librarian, assistant librarian

sous-bock [subɔk] *(pl* **sous-bocks) NM** beer mat

sous-bois [subwa] **NM INV 1** *(végétation)* undergrowth, underwood; **se promener dans les s.** to walk in the undergrowth **2** *Beaux-Arts* picture of a forest interior

sous-brigadier [subrigadje] *(pl* **sous-brigadiers) NM** deputy sergeant

sous-calibré, -e [sukalibre] *(mpl* **sous-calibrés,** *fpl* **sous-calibrées) ADJ** undersize, undersized

sous-capitalisation [sukapitalizasjɔ̃] **NF** *Écon* under-capitalization, underfunding

sous-capitalisé, -e [sukapitalize] *(mpl* **sous-capitalisés,** *fpl* **sous-capitalisées) ADJ** *Écon* under-capitalized, underfunded

sous-chaîne [suʃɛn] *(pl* **sous-chaînes) NF** *Ordinat* substring

sous-chef [suʃɛf] *(pl* **sous-chefs) NM 1** *(gén)* second-in-command

2 *(de bureau)* deputy chief clerk

3 *(dans un restaurant)* sous-chef, underchef

4 *Rail* **s. de gare** assistant station master

sous-chemise [suʃmiz] *(pl* **sous-chemises) NF** folder

sous-classe [suklas] *(pl* **sous-classes) NF** subclass

sous-comité [sukɔmite] *(pl* **sous-comités) NM** subcommittee

sous-commission [sukɔmisjɔ̃] *(pl* **sous-commissions) NF** subcommittee

sous-compte [sukɔ̃t] *(pl* **sous-comptes) NM** subaccount

sous-consommation [sukɔ̃sɔmasjɔ̃] **NF** underconsumption, underconsuming *(UNCOUNT)*

sous-continent [sukɔ̃tinɑ̃] *(pl* **sous-continents) NM** subcontinent; **le s. indien** the Indian subcontinent

sous-contractant, -e [sukɔ̃traktɑ̃, -ɑ̃t] *(mpl* **sous-contractants,** *fpl* **sous-contractantes) NM,F** subcontractor

sous-contrat [sukɔ̃tra] *(pl* **sous-contrats) NM** subcontract

souscoté, -e [sukɔte] **ADJ** *Fin (action, marché, monnaie)* undervalued

sous-couche [sukuʃ] *(pl* **sous-couches) NF 1** *(de peinture, de vernis)* undercoat

2 *Géol* underlayer

3 *Nucl* subshell

4 *Phot* subbing, substratum

souscripteur [suskriptœr] **NM 1** *Fin (d'un emprunt)* subscriber **2** *(d'une assurance)* policy holder **3** *(d'une publication)* subscriber

souscription [suskripsjɔ̃] **NF 1** *(engagement)* subscription, subscribing *(UNCOUNT)*

2 *(somme)* subscription; **lancer** *ou* **ouvrir une s.** to start a fund; **verser une s.** to pay a subscription

3 *(signature)* signing *(UNCOUNT)*

4 *Fin* application, subscription

5 *(d'une police d'assurance)* taking out

• **en souscription ADV publier une revue en s.** to publish a journal on a subscription basis; **uniquement en s.** available to subscribers only

souscrire **[99]** [suskrir] **VT 1** *Jur (signer ▸ acte)* to sign, to put one's signature to, *Sout* to subscribe; *(▸ billet, chèque)* to draw, to sign **2** *(abonnement, police d'assurance)* to take out **3** *Fin (actions)* to apply for

• **souscrire à VT IND 1** *(approuver)* to approve, to subscribe to, to go along with; **je souscris entièrement à ce qui vient d'être dit** I go along totally with what's just been said **2** *(sujet: lecteur)* to take out a subscription to **3** *Fin (emprunt)* to subscribe to; *(actions)* to apply for

USAGE ABSOLU pour combien souscrivez-vous? how much will you subscribe?; **s. pour 50 euros** to subscribe 50 euros

sous-culture [sukyltyr] *(pl* **sous-cultures) NF** subculture

sous-cutané, -e [sukytane] *(mpl* **sous-cutanés,** *fpl* **sous-cutanées) ADJ** subcutaneous

sous-développé, -e [sudevlɔpe] *(mpl* **sous-développés,** *fpl* **sous-développées) ADJ 1** *(pays, région)* underdeveloped **2** *(usine)* underequipped

sous-développement [sudevlɔpmɑ̃] *(pl* **sous-développements) NM** underdevelopment

sous-diacre [sudjakr] *(pl* **sous-diacres) NM** subdeacon

sous-directeur, -trice [sudirɛktœr, -tris] (*mpl* **sous-directeurs**, *fpl* **sous-directrices**) NM,F **1** *(de société)* assistant manager **2** *(d'une école) Br* deputy head, *Am* assistant principal

sous-diviser [3] [sudivize] VT to subdivide

sous-division [sudivizjɔ̃] (*pl* **sous-divisions**) NF subdivision

sous-document [sudɔkymɑ̃] (*pl* **sous-documents**) NM *Ordinat* subdocument

sous-dominant, -e [sudɔminɑ̃, -ɑ̃t] (*mpl* **sous-dominants**, *fpl* **sous-dominantes**) ADJ *Biol* subdominant

• **sous-dominante** NF *Mus* subdominant

sous-dossier [sudosje] (*pl* **sous-dossiers**) NM *Ordinat* subfolder

sous-embranchement [suzɑ̃brɑ̃ʃmɑ̃] (*pl* **sous-embranchements**) NM *Biol* sub-branch

sous-emploi [suzɑ̃plwa] (*pl* **sous-emplois**) NM underemployment

sous-employé, -e [suzɑ̃plwaje] (*mpl* **sous-employés**, *fpl* **sous-employées**) ADJ *(travailleur)* underemployed; *(appareil)* underused

sous-ensemble [suzɑ̃sɑ̃bl] (*pl* **sous-ensembles**) NM subset

sous-entendre [73] [suzɑ̃tɑ̃dr] VT to imply; **que sous-entendez-vous par là?** what are you hinting *or* driving at?, what are you trying to imply?; **sous-entendu, je m'en moque!** meaning I don't care!

sous-entendu [suzɑ̃tɑ̃dy] (*pl* **sous-entendus**) NM innuendo, hint, insinuation; **en fixant sur moi un regard lourd de sous-entendus** giving me a meaningful look

sous-entrepreneur [suzɑ̃trəprənœr] (*pl* **sous-entrepreneurs**) NM subcontractor

sous-équipé, -e [suzekipe] (*mpl* **sous-équipés**, *fpl* **sous-équipées**) ADJ underequipped

sous-équipement [suzekipmɑ̃] (*pl* **sous-équipements**) NM underequipment

sous-espace [suzespas] (*pl* **sous-espaces**) NM *Math* subspace

sous-espèce [suzespes] (*pl* **sous-espèces**) NF subspecies

sous-estimation [suzestimasjɔ̃] (*pl* **sous-estimations**) NF **1** *(jugement)* underestimation, underestimating, underrating **2** *Fin (d'un revenu)* underestimation, underassessment; *(d'un bien)* undervaluation

sous-estimer [3] [suzestime] VT **1** *(qualité, bien)* to underestimate, to underrate **2** *Fin* to undervalue

VPR **se sous-estimer** to underestimate oneself

sous-évaluation [suzevalɥasjɔ̃] (*pl* **sous-évaluations**) NF undervaluation

sous-évaluer [7] [suzevalɥe] VT to undervalue

sous-exposé, -e [suzekspoze] (*mpl* **sous-exposés**, *fpl* **sous-exposées**) ADJ *Phot* underexposed

sous-exposer [3] [suzekspoze] VT *Phot* to underexpose

sous-exposition [suzekspozisjɔ̃] (*pl* **sous-expositions**) NF *Phot* underexposure

sous-famille [sufamij] (*pl* **sous-familles**) NF subfamily

sous-fifre [sufifr] (*pl* **sous-fifres**) NM *Fam* underling[□], minion[□]

sous-garde [sugard] (*pl* **sous-gardes**) NF gunlock

sous-genre [suʒɑ̃r] (*pl* **sous-genres**) NM subgenus

sous-gouverneur [suguvɛrnœr] (*pl* **sous-gouverneurs**) NM deputy governor, vice-governor

sous-groupe [sugrup] (*pl* **sous-groupes**) NM subgroup

sous-homme [suzɔm] (*pl* **sous-hommes**) NM *Péj* subhuman

sous-humanité [suzymanite] NF *Péj* subhumanity

sous-ingénieur [suzɛ̃ʒenjœr] (*pl* **sous-ingénieurs**) NM *Ind etc* assistant engineer

sous-inspecteur, -trice [suzɛ̃spɛktœr, -tris] (*mpl* **sous-inspecteurs**, *fpl* **sous-inspectrices**) NM,F assistant inspector

sous-jacent, -e [suʒasɑ̃, -ɑ̃t] (*mpl* **sous-jacents**, *fpl* **sous-jacentes**) ADJ **1** *(caché)* underlying; **l'urbanisation et les problèmes sous-jacents** urbanization and its underlying problems **2** *Géol* subjacent

Sous-le-Vent [sulәvɑ̃] NFPL **les îles S.** *(en Polynésie)* the Leeward Islands, the Western Society Islands; *(aux Antilles)* the Netherlands (and Venezuelan) Antilles

sous-lieutenant [suljøtnɑ̃] (*pl* **sous-lieutenants**) NM *(dans l'armée de terre)* ≃ second lieutenant; *(dans l'armée de l'air) Br* ≃ pilot officer, *Am* ≃ second lieutenant; *(dans la marine) Br* ≃ sub-lieutenant, *Am* ≃ lieutenant junior grade

sous-locataire [sulɔkatɛr] (*pl* **sous-locataires**) NMF subtenant

sous-location [sulɔkasjɔ̃] (*pl* **sous-locations**) NF **1** *(action ▸ par le propriétaire)* subletting; *(▸ par le locataire)* subrenting **2** *(bail)* subtenancy

sous-louer [6] [sulwe] VT *(sujet: propriétaire)* to sublet; *(sujet: locataire)* to subrent

sous-main [sumɛ̃] NM INV **1** *(buvard)* desk blotter **2** *(carton, plastique)* pad

• **en sous-main** ADV secretly; **il y a eu des tractations en s.** some underhand deals were struck

sous-maître, -maîtresse [sumetr, -metres] (*mpl* **sous-maîtres**, *fpl* **sous-maîtresses**) *Arch* NM,F *Scol* teacher's assistant

• **sous-maîtresse** NF brothel-keeper's assistant

sous-marché [sumarʃe] (*pl* **sous-marchés**) NM sub-market

sous-marin, -e [sumarɛ̃, -in] (*mpl* **sous-marins**, *fpl* **sous-marines**) ADJ *(câble, plante)* submarine, underwater; *(navigation)* submarine; *(courant)* submarine, undersea; *(photographie)* underwater, undersea

NM **1** *Naut* submarine; **s. nucléaire** nuclear(-powered) submarine; **s. de poche** pocket submarine **2** *Fam (espion)* mole **3** *Fam (véhicule de surveillance)* = converted van used for police surveillance

sous-marinier [sumarinje] (*pl* **sous-mariniers**) NM submariner

sous-marque [sumark] (*pl* **sous-marques**) NF sub-brand

sous-maxillaire [sumaksilɛr] (*pl* **sous-maxillaires**) ADJ *Anat* submaxillary

sous-menu [sumәny] (*pl* **sous-menus**) NM *Ordinat* submenu

sous-merde [sumɛrd] (*pl* **sous-merdes**) NF *très Fam* nobody[□], non-entity[□]; **traiter qn comme une s.** to treat sb like shit

sous-ministre [suministr] (*pl* **sous-ministres**) NM *Can Br* undersecretary (of state), *Am* deputy minister

sous-multiple [sumyltipl] (*pl* **sous-multiples**) NM submultiple

sous-munitions [sumynisjɔ̃] NFPL *Mil* submunition

sous-nappe [sunap] (*pl* **sous-nappes**) NF undercloth

sous-nutrition [sunytrisjɔ̃] NF malnutrition

sous-œuvre [suzœvr] **en sous-œuvre** ADV **reprendre un bâtiment en s.** to underpin a building; **reprise en s.** underpinning

sous-off [suzɔf] (*pl* **sous-offs**) NM *Fam Arg mil (abrév* **sous-officier***)* non-commissioned officer[□]

sous-officier [suzɔfisje] (*pl* **sous-officiers**) NM non-commissioned officer

sous-ordre [suzɔrdr] (*pl* **sous-ordres**) NM **1** *Biol* suborder **2** *(subordonné)* subordinate, underling, minion

• **en sous-ordre** ADJ *(opposant, créancier)* subsidiary

sous-palan [supalɑ̃] **en sous-palan** ADV *Com* ready for delivery

sous-payer [11] [supeje] VT to underpay

sous-peuplé, -e [supœple] (*mpl* **sous-peuplés**, *fpl* **sous-peuplées**) ADJ underpopulated

sous-peuplement [supœplәmɑ̃] NM underpopulation

sous-pied [supje] (*pl* **sous-pieds**) NM stirrup *(on trousers)*

sous-plat [supla] (*pl* **sous-plats**) NM *Belg* table mat

sous-préfectoral, -e [suprefɛktɔral] (*mpl* **sous-préfectoraux** [-o], *fpl* **sous-préfectorales**) ADJ subprefectorial

sous-préfecture [suprefɛktyr] (*pl* **sous-préfectures**) NF subprefecture

sous-préfet [suprefɛ] (*pl* **sous-préfets**) NM subprefect

sous-préfète [suprefɛt] (*pl* **sous-préfètes**) NF **1** *(fonctionnaire)* (female) subprefect **2** *(épouse)* subprefect's wife

sous-production [suprɔdyksjɔ̃] (*pl* **sous-productions**) NF underproduction

sous-produit [suprɔdɥi] (*pl* **sous-produits**) NM **1** *Ind & Com* by-product **2** *(ersatz)* poor imitation, (inferior) derivative

sous-programme [suprɔgram] (*pl* **sous-programmes**) NM *Ordinat* subroutine, subprogram; **s. ouvert** open subroutine *or* subprogram

sous-prolétaire [suprɔletɛr] (*pl* **sous-prolétaires**) NMF member of the urban underclass

sous-prolétariat [suprɔletarja] NM urban underclass

sous-pull [supyl] (*pl* **sous-pulls**) NM thin poloneck sweater

sous-refroidissement [surәfrwadismɑ̃] NM *Phys* supercooling

sous-répertoire [surepɛrtwar] (*pl* **sous-répertoires**) NM *Ordinat* subdirectory

sous-représentation [surәprezɑ̃tasjɔ̃] NF *Pol* under-representation

sous-représenté, -e [surәprezɑ̃te] (*mpl* **sous-représentés**, *fpl* **sous-représentées**) ADJ *Pol* underrepresented

soussaille [susaj] = **souçaille**

sous-secrétaire [susәkretɛr] (*pl* **sous-secrétaires**) NM **s. (d'État)** undersecretary (of State), junior minister

sous-secrétariat [susәkretarja] (*pl* **sous-secrétariat**) NM **1** *(bureau)* undersecretary's office **2** *(poste)* undersecretaryship

sous-section [suseksjɔ̃] (*pl* **sous-sections**) NF *(au Conseil d'État)* section; **sous-sections réunies** combined sections

sous-seing [susɛ̃] NM INV *Jur* private agreement *or* contract

soussigné, -e [susiɲe] ADJ undersigned; **je s. Robert Brand, déclare avoir pris connaissance de l'article 4** I, the undersigned Robert Brand, declare that I have read clause 4

NM,F **le s. déclare/les soussignés déclarent que...** the undersigned declares/declare that...

sous-sol [susɔl] (*pl* **sous-sols**) NM **1** *Géol* subsoil **2** *(d'une maison)* cellar; *(d'un magasin)* basement, lower ground floor

sous-station [sustasjɔ̃] (*pl* **sous-stations**) NF *Élec* substation

sous-système [susistem] (*pl* **sous-systèmes**) NM subsystem

sous-tasse [sutas] (*pl* **sous-tasses**) NF saucer

sous-tendre [73] [sutɑ̃dr] VT **1** *Géom* to subtend **2** *(être à la base de)* to underlie, to underpin

sous-tension [sutɑ̃sjɔ̃] (*pl* **sous-tensions**) NF undervoltage

sous-titrage [sutitraʒ] (*pl* **sous-titrages**) NM subtitling; **le s. est excellent** the subtitles are very good

sous-titre [sutitr] (*pl* **sous-titres**) NM **1** *Presse* subtitle, subheading, subhead **2** *Cin* subtitle

sous-titrer [3] [sutitre] VT **1** *(article de journal)* to subtitle, to subhead; *(livre)* to subtitle **2** *(film)* to subtitle

sous-titreur [sutitrœr] (*pl* **sous-titreurs**) NM subtitler

sous-total [sutɔtal] (*pl* **sous-totaux** [-to]) NM subtotal

soustractif, -ive [sustraktif, -iv] **ADJ** subtractive

soustraction [sustraksjɔ̃] **NF 1** *Math* subtraction; **il ne sait pas encore faire les soustractions** he can't subtract yet **2** *Jur (vol)* removal, removing *(UNCOUNT)*, *Sout* purloining *(UNCOUNT)*; **s. de documents** abstraction of documents

soustractive [sustraktiv] *voir* **soustractif**

soustraire [112] [sustrɛr] **VT 1** *Math* to subtract, to take away; **s. 10 de 30** to take 10 away from 30 **2** *(enlever)* **s. qn/qch à** to take sb/sth away from; **s. qn à la justice** to shield sb from justice, to protect sb from the law **3** *(subtiliser)* to remove; **s. un dossier aux archives** to remove a file from the archives

VPR se soustraire se s. à l'impôt/à une obligation to evade tax/an obligation; **se s. à la justice** to escape the law

sous-traitance [sutretɑ̃s] *(pl* **sous-traitances)** **NF** subcontracting; **donner un travail en s.** to subcontract a job; **faire de la s.** to subcontract; **je fais ce travail en s.** I'm on this job as subcontractor

sous-traitant, -e [sutretɑ̃, -ɑ̃t] *(mpl* **sous-traitants**, *fpl* **sous-traitantes)** **ADJ** subcontracting

NM subcontractor; **donner un travail à un s.** to farm out a piece of work

sous-traiter [4] [sutrete] **VT s. un travail** *(entrepreneur principal)* to subcontract a job, to contract a job out; *(sous-entrepreneur)* to contract into *or* to subcontract a job

soustrayait *etc voir* **soustraire**

sous-utiliser [3] [suzytilize] **VT** to underuse, to underutilize

sous-variété [suvarjete] *(pl* **sous-variétés)** **NF** *Biol & Math* subvariety

sous-ventrière [suvɑ̃trijɛr] *(pl* **sous-ventrières)** **NF** girth *(for a horse)*; *Fam Fig* **manger à s'en faire péter la s.** to pig out, to stuff oneself

sous-verre [suvɛr] *(pl* **sous-verres)** **NM INV** *(pour encadrer)* glass mount; *(photo, image)* photograph *or* picture mounted under glass

NM *Belg (dessous-de-verre)* coaster

sous-vêtement [suvɛtmɑ̃] *(pl* **sous-vêtements)** **NM** piece of underwear, undergarment; **en sous-vêtements** in one's underwear *or* underclothes

sous-virage [suviraʒ] *(pl* **sous-virages)** **NM** *Aut* understeer

sous-virer [3] [suvire] **VI** *Aut* to understeer

sous-vireur, -euse [suvirœr, -øz] *(mpl* **sous-vireurs**, *fpl* **sous-vireuses)** **ADJ** *Aut* which understeers

soutache [sutaʃ] **NF** *Couture* braid

soutacher [3] [sutaʃe] **VT** *Couture* to braid

soutane [sutan] **NF** cassock; **porter (la) s.** to be in Holy Orders; **prendre la s.** to enter the Church, to take (Holy) Orders; *Fam* **la s.** *(prêtres)* men of the cloth

soute [sut] **NF** hold; **s. à bagages** luggage hold; *Aviat* **s. à bombes** bomb bay; **s. à charbon** coal bunker, *Br* coal hole; **s. à essence** fuel bunker; **s. à mazout** oil tank; **s. à munitions** magazine; **s. à voiles** sail locker

• **soutes NFPL** *(combustible)* fuel oil

soutenable [sutnabl] **ADJ 1** *(défendable)* defensible, tenable **2** *(supportable)* bearable

soutenance [sutnɑ̃s] **NF** *Univ* **s. (de thèse)** = oral examination for thesis, *Br* viva

soutènement [sutɛnmɑ̃] **NM 1** *Constr* support **2** *Mines* timbering

• **de soutènement ADJ** support *(avant n)*, supporting

souteneur [sutnœr] **NM 1** *(proxénète)* pimp **2** *Littéraire (d'une cause, d'une idée)* defender, upholder

SOUTENIR [40] [sutnir]

VT	
• to hold up **1**	• to support **1–4, 6**
• to uphold **4**	• to assert **5**
• to withstand **6**	• to keep up **7**
• to sustain **7, 8**	
VPR	
• to stand by each other **1**	• to hold oneself up **2**
	• to be kept up **3**

VT 1 *(maintenir ▸ sujet: pilier, poutre)* to hold up, to support; *(▸ sujet: attelle, gaine, soutien-gorge)* to support; **il lui tendit la main pour la s.** he gave her his hand for support; **un médicament pour s. le cœur** a drug to sustain the heart *or* to keep the heart going

2 *(réconforter)* to support, to give (moral) support to; **sa présence m'a beaucoup soutenue dans cette épreuve** his/her presence was a great comfort to me in this ordeal

3 *(être partisan de ▸ candidature, cause, politique etc)* to support, to back (up), to stand by; **nous vous soutiendrons!** we'll be right up there with *or* we'll stand by you!; **tu soutiens toujours ta fille contre moi!** you always stand up for *or* you're always siding with your daughter against me!; **s. une équipe** to be a fan of *or* to support a team

4 *(faire valoir ▸ droits)* to uphold, to defend; *(▸ argument, théorie)* to uphold, to support

5 *(affirmer)* to assert, to claim; **il soutient que tu mens** he keeps saying that you're a liar; *Fam* **elle m'a soutenu mordicus qu'il était venu ici** she swore blind *or* she insisted that he'd been here

6 *(résister à ▸ attaque)* to withstand; *(▸ regard)* to bear, to support; **ils ont soutenu l'assaut des produits japonais** they were able to bear the onslaught of Japanese products; **s. la comparaison avec** to stand *or* to bear comparison with; *Mil* **s. un siège** to last out *or* to withstand a siege

7 *(prolonger ▸ attention, discussion, suspense etc)* to keep up, to sustain; *(▸ réputation)* to maintain, to keep up

8 *Mus (note)* to sustain, to hold

9 *Univ* **s. sa thèse** to defend one's thesis, *Br* to take one's viva

VPR se soutenir 1 *(personnes)* to stand by each other, to stick together

2 *(se tenir)* to hold oneself up, to support oneself; **le vieillard n'arrivait plus à se s. sur ses jambes** the old man's legs could no longer support *or* carry him; **elle se soutenait avec peine** she could hardly stay upright

3 *(se prolonger ▸ attention, intérêt, suspense)* to be kept up *or* maintained

soutenu, -e [sutny] **ADJ 1** *(intense ▸ couleur)* intense, deep; *(▸ note de musique)* sustained; *(▸ attention, effort)* unfailing, sustained, unremitting; *(▸ rythme)* steady, sustained **2** *Ling* formal; **en langue soutenue** in formal speech

souterrain, -e [suterɛ̃, -ɛn] **ADJ 1** *(sous la terre)* underground, subterranean; **câble s.** underground cable; **des eaux souterraines** ground water **2** *(dissimulé)* hidden, secret **3** *Mines* deep, underground

NM 1 *(galerie)* underground *or* subterranean passage **2** *(en ville)* *Br* subway, *Am* underpass

soutien [sutjɛ̃] **NM 1** *(soubassement)* supporting structure, support

2 *(aide)* support; **apporter son s. à qn** to support sb, to back sb up; **s. financier** financial backing; **mesures de s. à l'économie** measures to bolster the economy

3 *(défenseur)* supporter; **c'est l'un des plus sûrs soutiens du gouvernement** he's one of the mainstays of the government

4 *Scol* **cours de s.** remedial class

5 *Jur* **s. de famille** (main) wage earner; **être s. de famille** to have dependents *(and receive special treatment as regards French National Service)*

6 *Écon* **s. des prix** price support; *Mktg* **s. commercial** sales support

7 *Mil* support; **unité de s.** support unit

soutien-gorge [sutjɛ̃gɔrʒ] *(pl* **soutiens-gorge)** **NM** bra; **s. d'allaitement** nursing bra

soutient *etc voir* **soutenir**

soutier [sutje] **NM 1** *Naut* stoker **2** *Fig (personne qui occupe une fonction ingrate)* toiler

soutif [sutif] **NM** *Fam* bra

soutint *etc voir* **soutenir**

soutirage [sutiraʒ] **NM 1** *(action)* decanting, decantation **2** *(vin)* decanted wine

soutirer [3] [sutire] **VT 1** *(vin)* to draw off, to decant **2** *(extorquer)* **s. qch à qn** to get sth from *or* out of sb; **s. une promesse à qn** to extract a promise from sb; **s. des renseignements à qn** to get *or* to squeeze some information out of sb; **il s'est fait s. pas mal d'argent par ses petits-enfants** his grandchildren managed to squeeze a lot of money out of him

souvenance [suvnɑ̃s] **NF** *Littéraire* **à ma s.** as far as I can recall *or* recollect; **je n'ai pas s. de cela** I don't recall this, I have no recollection of this

souvenir¹ [suvnir] **NM 1** *(impression)* memory, recollection; **l'été 1999 m'a laissé un s. impérissable** the summer of 1999 has left me with lasting memories; **votre opération ne sera bientôt plus qu'un mauvais s.** your operation will soon be nothing but a bad memory; **je garde un excellent s. de ce voyage** I have excellent memories of that trip; **n'avoir aucun s. de** to have no remembrance *or* recollection of; **elle n'en a qu'un vague s.** she has only a dim *or* vague recollection of it; **mes souvenirs d'enfance** my childhood memories; **j'ai le s. d'un homme grand et fort** I remember a tall strong man

2 *(dans des formules de politesse)* **avec mon affectueux s.** yours (ever); **mes meilleurs souvenirs à votre sœur** (my) kindest regards to your sister; **meilleurs souvenirs de Rome** greetings from Rome

3 *(objet ▸ donné par une personne)* keepsake; *(▸ rappelant une occasion)* memento; *(▸ pour touristes)* souvenir; **cette broche est un s. de ma grand-mère** this brooch is a keepsake from my grandmother; **s. de Lourdes** souvenir of Lourdes

4 *(comme adj; avec ou sans trait d'union)* souvenir *(avant n)*; **poser pour la photo-s.** to pose for a commemorative photograph

• **en souvenir de PRÉP** *(afin de se remémorer)* **prenez ce livre en s. de cet été/de moi** take this book as a souvenir of this summer/as something to remember me by

> Il faut noter que le terme anglais **souvenir** ne s'applique qu'à un objet.

souvenir² [40] [suvnir] **V IMPERSONNEL** *Littéraire* **il me souvient un détail/de l'avoir aperçu** I remember a detail/having seen him; **du plus loin qu'il m'en souvienne** as far back as I can remember

VPR se souvenir se s. de *(date, événement)* to remember, to recollect, to recall; *(personne, lieu)* to remember; **on se souviendra d'elle comme d'une grande essayiste** she'll be remembered as a great essay-writer; **je ne me souviens jamais de son adresse** I keep forgetting *or* I can never remember his/her address; **je ne me souviens pas de l'avoir lu** I can't remember *or* I don't recall *or* I don't recollect having read it; *Fam Ironique* **je m'en souviendrai, de ses week-ends reposants à la campagne!** I won't forget his/her restful weekends in the countryside in a hurry!; **je ne veux pas te le prêter – je m'en souviendrai!** I don't want you to borrow it – I'll remember that!

USAGE ABSOLU mais si, souviens-toi, elle était toujours au premier rang come on, you must remember her, she was always sitting in the front row

souvent [suvɑ̃] **ADV** often; **il va s. au théâtre** he often goes to the theatre; **on se voit de moins en moins s.** we see less and less of each other; **pas** *ou* **peu s.** not often, seldom; **il ne vient pas s. nous voir** he doesn't often come and see us, he seldom comes to see us; **le plus s., c'est elle qui conduit** most often *or* more often than not *or* usually, she's the one who does the driving; **c'est (bien) s. ce qui arrive si l'on va trop vite** it's what (very) often happens when you go too fast; **plus s. qu'à son tour** far too often

souvenu, -e [suvny] **PP** *voir* **souvenir²**

souverain, -e [suvrɛ̃, -ɛn] **ADJ 1** *(efficace ▸ remède)* excellent, sovereign

2 *Pol (pouvoir, peuple)* sovereign; *Jur (tribunal)* supreme; **la Chambre est souveraine** the House is a sovereign authority

3 *(suprême)* supreme; **avoir un s. mépris pour qch** to utterly despise sth

4 *Phil* **le s. bien** the sovereign good

5 *Rel* **le s. pontife** the Pope, the Supreme Pontiff

NM,F monarch, sovereign; **notre souveraine** our Sovereign; **s. absolu** absolute monarch

NM *(monnaie)* sovereign (coin)

souverainement [suvrɛnmɑ̃] **ADV 1** *(suprêmement)* utterly, totally, intensely **2** *(sans appel)* with sovereign power

souveraineté [suvrɛnte] **NF** sovereignty

souverainisme [suvʀenism] **NM 1** *(doctrine des défenseurs d'une Europe des nations)* (European) sovereignism *or* pro-sovereignty **2** *Can (doctrine des partisans d'un Québec indépendant)* (Quebec) separatism

souverainiste [suvʀenist] **ADJ 1** *(favorable à une Europe des nations)* (European) sovereignist *or* pro-sovereignty **2** *Can (favorable à l'indépendance du Québec)* (Quebec) separatist

NMF 1 *(personne favorable à une Europe des nations)* (European) sovereignist **2** *Can (personne favorable à l'indépendance du Québec)* (Quebec) separatist

souvient *etc voir* **souvenir**[2]

souvint *etc voir* **souvenir**[2]

soviet [sɔvjɛt] **NM** *(assemblée)* soviet; **le S. Suprême** the Supreme Soviet

soviétique [sɔvjetik] **ADJ** Soviet

• **Soviétique NMF** Soviet

soviétisation [sɔvjetizasjɔ̃] **NF** sovietization, sovietizing *(UNCOUNT)*

soviétiser [3] [sɔvjetize] **VT** to sovietize

soviétologue [sɔvjetɔlɔg] **NMF** Sovietologist

soyeux, -euse [swajø, -øz] **ADJ** silky

NM *(dans la région de Lyon) (fabricant)* silk manufacturer; *(négociant)* silk merchant

soyons *voir* **être**[1]

SPA [ɛspea] **NF** *(abrév* **Société protectrice des animaux***)* = society for the protection of animals, *Br* ≃ RSPCA, *Am* ≃ ASPCA

spa [spa] **NM 1** *(bain à remous bouillonnant)* spa bath **2** *(centre d'hydrothérapie)* (health) spa

spacieuse [spasjøz] *voir* **spacieux**

spacieusement [spasjøzmɑ̃] **ADV ils sont très s. installés** they've got a very roomy *or* spacious place

spacieux, -euse [spasjø, -øz] **ADJ** spacious, roomy

spadassin [spadasɛ̃] **NM 1** *Arch* swordsman **2** *Littéraire (tueur)* (hired) killer; **un mafioso et ses spadassins** a Mafia boss and his hit men

spadice [spadis] **NM** *Bot* spadix

spaetzli [ʃpetsli] **NM** *Suisse Culin* = small strips of pasta often served with game

spaghetti [spageti] *(pl* **inv** *ou* **spaghettis***)* **NM des s., des spaghettis** spaghetti; **un s.** a strand of spaghetti; **spaghettis bolognaise/carbonara** spaghetti bolognese/carbonara

spahi [spai] **NM** spahi *(native member of the Algerian, Moroccan or Tunisian cavalry in the French army)*

spalax [spalaks] **NM** *Zool* mole rat

spam [spam] **NM** *Ordinat* spam e-mail

spammer [3] [spame] **VT** *Ordinat* to spam

spammeur [spamœr] **NM** *Ordinat* spammer

spamming [spamiŋ] **NM** *Ordinat* spamming

sparadrap [sparadra] **NM** *Br* (sticking) plaster, *Am* Band-Aid

sparages [sparaʒ] **NM** *Can Fam* big *or* expansive gestures□; **il parlait en faisant de grands s.** he gestured expansively as he spoke□

spart [spart] **NM** *Bot* esparto (grass)

Sparte [spart] **NF** Sparta

sparte [spart] = **spart**

spartiate [sparsjat] **ADJ 1** *(de Sparte)* Spartan **2** *Fig (austère)* spartan, ascetic

• **Spartiate NMF** Spartan

• **spartiates NFPL** *(sandales)* (Roman) sandals

• **à la spartiate ADV** austerely; **élever ses enfants à la s.** to give one's children a spartan upbringing

spasme [spasm] **NM** spasm

spasmodique [spasmɔdik] **ADJ** spasmodic, spastic

spasmodiquement [spasmɔdikmɑ̃] **ADV** spasmodically

spasmophilie [spasmɔfili] **NF** *Méd* spasmophilia

spastique [spastik] **ADJ** spastic, spasmodic

spath [spat] **NM** *Minér* spar; **s. fluor** fluor spar, fluorspar, fluorite

spatial, -e, -aux, -ales [spasjal, -o] **ADJ 1** *(de l'espace)* spatial; *Math* **coordonnées spatiales** spatial coordinates **2** *Astron & Mil* space *(avant n)*

NM space industry

spatialisation [spasjalizasjɔ̃] **NF 1** *(du temps, des sons)* spatialization **2** *(d'un engin)* sending into space

spatialiser [3] [spasjalize] **VT** *(lancer dans l'espace)* to send into space

spationaute [spasjɔnot] **NMF** spaceman, *f* spacewoman

spationef [spasjɔnɛf] **NM** spaceship

spatio-temporel, -elle [spasjɔtɑ̃pɔrɛl] *(mpl* **spatio-temporels**, *fpl* **spatio-temporelles***)* **ADJ** spatiotemporal

spatule [spatyl] **NF 1** *Culin* spatula

2 *(d'un ski)* tip

3 *Beaux-Arts* (pallet) knife

4 *Constr* jointer

5 *Ich* paddlefish

6 *Orn* spoonbill

spatulé, -e [spatyle] **ADJ** spatulate

speaker, speakerine [spikœr, spikrin] **NM,F** announcer

NM *Pol (en Grande-Bretagne, aux États-Unis)* **le s.** the Speaker

spécial, -e, -aux, -ales [spesjal, -o] **ADJ 1** *(d'une catégorie particulière)* special, particular, specific, distinctive; **une clef spéciale** a special key; **des caractéristiques spéciales** distinctive features; **savon s. peaux grasses** soap for greasy skin

2 *(exceptionnel ▸ gén)* special, extraordinary, exceptional; *(▸ numéro, édition)* special; **rien de s.** nothing special

3 *(bizarre)* peculiar, odd; **ils ont une mentalité spéciale** they're a bit eccentric *or* strange; **ce livre est s., on aime ou on n'aime pas** this book is very particular, either you like it or you don't; **toi, t'es s.!** you're a bit weird!

4 *Écon* **commerce s.** import-export trade (balance)

5 *Sport (slalom)* special

NM *Fam* (special) slalom□

• **spéciale NF 1** *Scol* = second year of a two year entrance course for a "grande école" **2** *(huître)* = type of cultivated oyster **3** *Sport* (short) off-road rally

> Il faut noter qu'en anglais l'adjectif **special** ne s'emploie jamais à propos de quelque chose d'inhabituel ou d'étrange.

spécialement [spesjalmɑ̃] **ADV 1** *(à une fin particulière)* specially, especially; **je me suis fait faire un costume s. pour le mariage** I had a suit made specially for the wedding; **parlez-nous de l'Italie et (plus) s. de Florence** tell us about Italy, especially Florence **2** *(très)* particularly, especially; **ça n'a pas été s. drôle** it wasn't particularly *or* especially amusing; **tu veux lui parler? – pas s.** do you want to talk to him/her? – not particularly *or* especially

spécialisation [spesjalizasjɔ̃] **NF** specialization, specializing

spécialisé, -e [spesjalize] **ADJ** *(gén)* specialized; *(école, hôpital)* special; *Ordinat* dedicated, special-purpose; **des chercheurs spécialisés dans l'intelligence artificielle** researchers specializing in artificial intelligence

spécialiser [3] [spesjalize] **VT 1** *(étudiant, travailleur)* to turn *or* to make into a specialist; **nous spécialisons des biochimistes** we train specialists in biochemistry **2** *(usine, activité)* to make more specialized

VPR se spécialiser to specialize; *Scol* **quatorze ans, c'est trop tôt pour se s.** fourteen is too young to start specializing in certain subjects; **se s. dans la dermatologie** to specialize in dermatology

spécialiste [spesjalist] **NMF 1** *(gén) & Méd* specialist; **un s. en maladies respiratoires** a specialist in respiratory illnesses; **c'est un s. du marketing** he's an expert in marketing **2** *Fam (habitué)* **c'est un s. des gaffes** he's an expert at putting his foot in it

ADJ 1 *(médecin)* specialist **2** *Fam (habitué)* **elle est s. de ce genre de gaffes** she's an expert at putting her foot in it like that

spécialité [spesjalite] **NF 1** *Culin* speciality; **spécialités de la région** local specialities *or* products; **fais-nous une de tes spécialités** cook us one of your special recipes *or* dishes; **la s. du chef** *(sur la carte d'un restaurant)* (the) chef's speciality

2 *Pharm* **s. pharmaceutique** branded pharmaceutical *or* (patented) pharmaceutical product

3 *Scol & Univ* field, area; **s. médicale** area of medicine; **quelle est votre s.?** what area do you specialize in?; **ma s., c'est la botanique** I specialize in botany; **le meilleur dans** *ou* **de sa s.** the best in his field

4 *(manie, habitude)* **le vin, c'est sa s.** he's/she's the wine expert; **encore en retard? c'est ta s., ma parole!** late again? you seem to be making a habit of it!

spécieuse [spesjøz] *voir* **spécieux**

spécieusement [spesjøzmɑ̃] **ADV** speciously, fallaciously

spécieux, -euse [spesjø, -øz] **ADJ** specious, fallacious

spécification [spesifikasjɔ̃] **NF** specification; **sans s. de** without specifying, without mention of; **une réunion a été décidée sans s. d'heure ni de lieu** a meeting was arranged, but the time and place were not specified; **s. de la fonction** job specification

spécificité [spesifisite] **NF** distinctiveness, distinctive nature; **s. culturelle** cultural specificity; **ce type d'institution est une s. française** this kind of institution is a specifically French phenomenon *or* is a distinctive feature of France

spécifier [9] [spesifje] **VT** to specify, to state, to indicate; **s. les conditions d'un prêt** to specify *or* to indicate the conditions of a loan; **je lui ai bien spécifié l'heure du rendez-vous** I made sure I told him/her the time of the appointment

spécifique [spesifik] **ADJ** specific

spécifiquement [spesifikmɑ̃] **ADV** specifically

spécimen [spesimɛn] **NM 1** *(exemple)* specimen, example; **s. de signature** specimen signature **2** *Typ* specimen; **s. (gratuit)** *(d'un livre)* desk copy **3** *Fam (individu bizarre) Br* queer fish, *Am* odd duck; **méfie-toi, c'est un drôle de s.!** be careful, he's a *Br* queer fish *or Am* an odd duck!

spectacle [spɛktakl] **NM 1** *(représentation)* show; **aller au s.** to go to (see) a show; **faire un s.** to do a show; **monter un s.** to put on a show; **le s.** *(activité)* showbusiness; **s. solo** one-man show; **s. de variétés** variety show; **le s. continue** the show must go on **2** *(ce qui se présente au regard)* sight, scene; **le s. qui s'offrait à nous** the sight before our eyes; **sur le port nous attendait un s. affligeant** on the quayside, a heart-breaking scene met our eyes; **elle présentait un bien triste/curieux s.** she looked a rather sorry/odd sight; **au s. de sa mère blessée, il s'évanouit** at the sight of *or* on seeing his injured mother, he fainted

• **à grand spectacle ADJ film à grand s.** epic

• **en spectacle ADV on nous les donne en s.** they are paraded in front of us; **se donner** *ou* **s'offrir en s.** to make an exhibition *or* a spectacle of oneself

spectaculaire [spɛktakylɛr] **ADJ 1** *(exceptionnel, frappant)* spectacular, impressive; **de manière s.** dramatically; **elle a fait une chute s.** she had a spectacular fall **2** *(notable)* spectacular; **des progrès spectaculaires** spectacular progress

spectateur, -trice [spɛktatœr, -tris] **NM,F 1** *(au théâtre, au cinéma)* spectator, member of the audience; *Sport* spectator; **les spectateurs** *(au théâtre, au cinéma)* the audience; *Sport* the crowd; **plusieurs spectateurs ont quitté la salle** several people in *or* members of the audience walked out **2** *(d'un accident, d'un événement)* spectator, witness; **les spectateurs finirent par se disperser** the crowd eventually began to disperse **3** *(simple observateur)* onlooker; **il a participé à nos réunions en s.** he just came to our meetings as an onlooker

spectral, -e, -aux, -ales [spɛktral, -o] **ADJ 1** *Littéraire (fantomatique)* ghostly, ghostlike, spectral **2** *Phys* spectral; **analyse spectrale** spectrum *or* spectroscopic analysis

spectre [spɛktr] **NM 1** *(fantôme)* ghost, phantom, spectre

2 *Fam (personne maigre)* ghostly figure, apparition

3 *(représentation effrayante)* **le s. de la famine** the spectre of famine; **agiter le s. de la révolution** to invoke the spectre of rebellion

4 *Chim, Élec & Phys* spectrum; **s. solaire** solar spectrum

5 *Pharm (d'un antibiotique)* spectrum

spectrogramme [spɛktrɔgram] **NM** spectrogram

spectrographe [spɛktrɔgraf] **NM** spectrograph

spectromètre [spɛktrɔmɛtr] **NM** spectrometer

spectrométrie [spɛktrɔmetri] **NF** spectrometry

spectroscope [spɛktrɔskɔp] **NM** spectroscope

spectroscopie [spɛktrɔskɔpi] **NF** spectroscopy

spéculaire [spekylɛr] **ADJ 1** *(minéral)* specular **2** *(produit par un miroir ► image, écriture)* mirror *(avant n)*

spéculateur, -trice [spekylatœr, -tris] **NM,F** speculator; **s. à la baisse** bear; **s. à la hausse** bull

spéculatif, -ive [spekylatif, -iv] **ADJ** speculative

spéculation [spekylasjɔ̃] **NF** speculation; **s. à la baisse/hausse** bear/bull operations; **s. immobilière** property speculation

spéculative [spekylativ] *voir* **spéculatif**

spéculatrice [spekylatris] *voir* **spéculateur**

spéculer [3] [spekyle] **VI 1** *Bourse* to speculate; **s. à la baisse** to go a bear, to speculate for a fall *or* on a falling market; **s. à la hausse** to go a bull, to speculate for a rise *or* on a rising market; **s. en Bourse** to speculate on the stock exchange; **s. sur l'or** to speculate in gold **2** *Littéraire (méditer)* to speculate

• **spéculer sur VT IND** *(compter sur)* to count *or* to bank *or* to rely on; **le gouvernement spécule sur une hausse de la natalité** the government is banking *or* relying on a rise in the birthrate

spéculum [spekylɔm] **NM** *Méd* speculum

speech [spitʃ] *(pl* **speechs** *ou* **speeches)** **NM** *Fam* (short) speech□; **il nous a refait son s. sur l'importance des bonnes manières** he made the same old speech about the importance of good manners

speed [spid] *Fam* **ADJ** *(nerveux)* hyper

NM *(amphétamines)* speed

speedé, -e [spide] **ADJ** *Fam* **1** *(nerveux)* hyper **2** *(drogué aux amphétamines)* **être s.** to be speeding

speeder [3] [spide] **VI** *Fam* **1** *(être sous l'effet d'amphétamines)* to be speeding **2** *(se dépêcher)* to get a move on, *Am* to get it in gear

spéléologie [speleɔlɔʒi] **NF** *(science et étude)* speleology; *(sport) Br* potholing, *Am* spelunking

spéléologique [speleɔlɔʒik] **ADJ** speleologic

spéléologue [speleɔlɔg] **NMF** *(savant, chercheur)* speleologist; *(sportif) Br* potholer, *Am* spelunker

spencer [spensœr] **NM** *(veste ► d'homme)* monkey jacket; *Mil* mess jacket; *(► de femme)* spencer

spermaceti [spɛrmaseti] **NM** spermaceti, sperm oil

spermatique [spɛrmatik] **ADJ** *(du sperme)* spermatic

spermatogenèse [spɛrmatɔʒenɛz] **NF** spermatogenesis

spermatozoïde [spɛrmatɔzɔid] **NM 1** *Biol* sperm (cell), spermatozoon **2** *Bot* spermatozoid

sperme [spɛrm] **NM** sperm

spermicide [spɛrmisid] **ADJ** spermicidal

NM spermicide

spermophile [spɛrmɔfil] **NM** *Zool* ground squirrel, *Spéc* spermophile

sphaigne [sfɛɲ] **NF** *Bot* sphagnum (moss), peat moss

sphénoïde [sfenɔid] *Anat* **ADJ** sphenoid

NM sphenoid, sphenoidal bone

sphère [sfɛr] **NF 1** *Astron & Géom* sphere; **s. céleste** celestial sphere; **s. terrestre** globe **2** *(zone)* field, area, sphere; **nous n'évoluons pas dans les mêmes sphères** we don't move in the same circles; **s. d'activité** field *or* sphere of activity; **s. d'influence** sphere of influence; *Littéraire* **les hautes sphères** the higher realms

sphéricité [sferisite] **NF** sphericity

sphérique [sferik] **ADJ** spherical, spheric

sphéroïde [sferɔid] **NM** spheroid

sphéromètre [sferɔmɛtr] **NM** *Phys* spherometer

sphincter [sfɛ̃ktɛr] **NM** *Anat* sphincter

sphinx [sfɛ̃ks] **NM 1** *Beaux-Arts & Myth* sphinx; **le S.** the Sphinx **2** *(personne énigmatique)* sphinx; **son impassibilité de s. me déroutait** his/her sphinx-like inscrutability disconcerted me **3** *Entom* hawkmoth

sphygmomanomètre [sfigmɔmanɔmɛtr] **NM** *Méd* sphygmomanometer

SPI [ɛspei] **NMPL** *(abrév* **Secrétariats professionnels internationaux)** ITS

spi [spi] **NM** *Naut* spinnaker, balloon sail

spic [spik] **NM** *Bot* spike lavender

spider [spidɛr] **NM** *Aut Br* dickey (seat), *Am* rumble seat

spin [spin] **NM** *Phys* spin

spina-bifida [spinabifida] **NM INV** spina bifida

spinal, -e, -aux, -ales [spinal, -o] **ADJ** spinal

spinelle [spinɛl] **NM** *Minér* spinel

spinnaker [spinekɔr] **NM** *Naut* spinnaker, balloon sail

spiral, -e, -aux, -ales [spiral, -o] **ADJ** spiral, helical

NM *(ressort)* spiral, spring; *(d'une montre)* hairspring

• **spirale NF 1** *(circonvolution)* spiral; **des spirales de fumée** coils of smoke **2** *(hausse rapide)* spiral; **la spirale inflationniste** the inflationary spiral; **la spirale des prix et des salaires** the wage-price spiral **3** *Journ* **spirale du silence** spiral of silence

• **à spirale ADJ** *(cahier)* spiral, spiralbound

• **en spirale ADJ** *(escalier, descente)* spiral **ADV** in a spiral, spirally; **s'élever/retomber en spirale** to spiral upwards/downwards

spirant, -e [spirɑ̃, -ɑ̃t] *Ling* **ADJ** spirant

• **spirante NF** spirant

spire [spir] **NF** *(d'un coquillage)* whorl; *(d'une spirale, d'une hélice)* turn, spire

spirée [spire] **NF** *Bot* spiraea

spirille [spirij] **NM** spirillum

spirite [spirit] **ADJ** spiritualistic

NMF spiritualist

spiritisme [spiritism] **NM** spiritualism, spiritism

spiritualiser [3] [spiritɥalize] **VT** to give a spiritual dimension to, to spiritualize

spiritualisme [spiritɥalism] **NM** spiritualism

spiritualiste [spiritɥalist] **ADJ** spiritualistic

NMF spiritualist

spiritualité [spiritɥalite] **NF** spirituality

spirituel, -elle [spiritɥɛl] **ADJ 1** *Phil* spiritual; **la nature spirituelle de l'âme** the spiritual nature of the soul

2 *(non physique)* spiritual; **père s.** spiritual father

3 *(plein d'esprit)* witty; **elle est très spirituelle** she's very witty; **une repartie spirituelle** a witty reply; **comme c'est s.!** how clever!

4 *Rel* spiritual; **chef/pouvoir s.** spiritual head/ power; **concert s.** concert of sacred music

NM *Rel* **1** *Hist (Franciscain dissident)* spiritual **2 le s.** things spiritual; **le s. et le temporel** the spiritual and the temporal

spirituellement [spiritɥɛlmɑ̃] **ADV 1** *Phil & Rel* spiritually **2** *(brillamment)* wittily

spiritueux, -euse [spiritɥø, -øz] **ADJ** *(boisson)* strong, *Spéc* spirituous

NM spirit; **vins et s.** wines and spirits

spiroïdal, -e, -aux, -ales [spirɔidal, -o] **ADJ** spiroid; **fracture spiroïdale** spiral fracture

spitant, -e [spitɑ̃, -ɑ̃t] **ADJ** *Belg* **1** *(personne)* lively **2** *(gazeux)* **eau spitante** carbonated water

spleen [splin] **NM** *Littéraire* spleen, melancholy; **avoir le s.** to be melancholic

spleenétique [splinetik] **ADJ** *Littéraire* splenetic, melancholy

splendeur [splɑ̃dœr] **NF 1** *(somptuosité)* magnificence, splendour

2 *(merveille)* **son collier est une s.** her necklace is splendid *or* magnificent; **les splendeurs des églises baroques** the magnificence of baroque churches

3 *(prospérité, gloire)* grandeur, splendour; *Littéraire* **Rome, au temps de sa s.** Rome at her apogee; *Hum* **voilà le macho dans toute sa s.** that's macho man in all his glory

4 *Littéraire (du soleil)* brilliance, splendour

splendide [splɑ̃did] **ADJ 1** *(somptueux ► décor, fête, repas)* splendid, magnificent **2** *(beau ► gén)* magnificent, wonderful, splendid; *(► journée, temps)* splendid; **une s. créature entra** a gorgeous *or* magnificent creature entered; **tu es s. aujourd'hui** you look wonderful today **3** *(rayonnant ► soleil)* radiant

splendidement [splɑ̃didmɑ̃] **ADV** splendidly, magnificently

splénectomie [splenɛktɔmi] **NF** *Méd* splenectomy

splénique [splenik] **ADJ** *Méd* splenic

spoiler [spɔjlœr] **NM** *Aut & Aviat* spoiler

spoliateur, -trice [spɔljatœr, -tris] *Littéraire* **ADJ** spoliatory, despoiling

NM,F spoliator, despoiler

spoliation [spɔljasjɔ̃] **NF** *Littéraire* spoliation, despoilment

spoliatrice [spɔljatris] *voir* **spoliateur**

spolier [9] [spɔlje] **VT** *Littéraire* to spoliate, to despoil; **spoliés de leurs droits/possessions** stripped of their rights/possessions

spondée [spɔ̃de] **NM** *Ling* spondee

spondylarthrite [spɔ̃dilartrit] **NF** *Méd* spondylarthritis; **s. ankylosante** ankylosing spondylitis

spondylite [spɔ̃dilit] **NF** *Méd* spondylitis

spongieux, -euse [spɔ̃ʒjø, -øz] **ADJ 1** *Anat* spongy **2** *(sol, matière)* spongy, sponge-like

sponsor [spɔ̃sɔr, spɔnsɔr] **NM** sponsor

sponsoring [spɔ̃sɔriŋ, spɔnsɔriŋ], **sponsorat** [spɔ̃sɔra, spɔnsɔra] **NM** sponsorship

sponsorisation [spɔ̃sɔrizasjɔ̃] **NF** sponsoring

sponsoriser [3] [spɔ̃sɔrize] **VT** to sponsor

spontané, -e [spɔ̃tane] **ADJ** spontaneous; *(aveux)* unprompted

spontanéité [spɔ̃taneite] **NF** spontaneity, spontaneousness

spontanément [spɔ̃tanemɑ̃] **ADV** spontaneously; **elle a avoué s.** she owned up of her own accord

sporadique [spɔradik] **ADJ** *(attaque, effort)* sporadic, occasional; *(symptôme, crise)* sporadic, isolated; *(averse)* scattered

sporadiquement [spɔradikmɑ̃] **ADV** sporadically

sporange [spɔrɑ̃ʒ] **NM** *Bot* sporangium

spore [spɔr] **NF** *Biol* spore

sport [spɔr] **ADJ INV 1** *(pratique, de détente)* casual; **manteau/chaussures s.** casual coat/ shoes **2** *Vieilli (fair-play)* sporting

ADV habillé s. casually dressed

NM 1 *(ensemble d'activités, exercice physique)* sport; *(activité de compétition)* (competitive) sport; **faire du s.** to do *Br* sport *or Am* sports; **un peu de s. te ferait du bien** some physical exercise would do you good; **il y a trop de s. à la télé** there's too much sport on TV; **sports aquatiques** water sports; **s. cérébral** *ou* **intellectuel** brainteasers; *Fam Hum* **s. en chambre** *(rapports sexuels)* bedroom sports; **s. de combat** combat sport; **s. de contact** contact sport; **s. équestre** equestrian sport, equestrianism; **sports d'équipe** team sports; **sports d'hiver** winter sports; **aller aux sports d'hiver** to go skiing, to go on a winter sports *Br* holiday *or Am* vacation; **s. individuel** individual sport; **sports nautiques** water sports; **la page des sports** the sports page **2** *Fam (locutions)* **c'est du s. de faire démarrer la tondeuse!** getting the mower started is no picnic *or* is the devil's own job!; **il va y avoir du s.!** now we're going to see some fun!; **faire qch pour le s.** to do sth for the fun *or* the hell of it

• **de sport ADJ** *(terrain, vêtement, voiture)* sports *(avant n)*

sportif, -ive [spɔrtif, -iv] **ADJ 1** *(association, club, magazine, reportage)* sports *(avant n)*; **reporter s.** sports reporter, sportscaster

2 *(événement, exploit)* sporting

3 *(personne ► qui aime le sport)* sporty; **elle est très sportive** she does a lot of sport; **je ne suis**

pas très s. I'm not very sporty; **avoir une allure sportive** to look athletic
4 *(loyal ▸ public)* sporting, fair; *(▸ attitude, geste)* sporting, sportsmanlike; **avoir l'esprit s.** to show sportsmanship
NM,F sportsman, *f* sportswoman; *Hum* **c'est un s. en chambre** he's an armchair sportsman

sportivement [spɔrtivmɑ̃] **ADV** sportingly; **il a pris les choses très s.** he was very sporting about things

sportivité [spɔrtivite] **NF** *(d'une personne)* sportsmanship; **le match a manqué de s.** it wasn't a very sporting match

sportswear [spɔrtswɛr], **sportwear** [spɔrtwɛr] **NM** sportswear, casual wear

sporuler **[3]** [spɔryle] **VI** *Biol* to sporulate

spot [spɔt] **NM 1** *(projecteur, petite lampe)* spotlight; **s. à pince** clip lamp
2 *Phys* light spot
3 *Électron* spot
4 *(publicité)* **s. publicitaire** advert, commercial; **s. télé** *ou* **TV** TV advert, TV commercial

spouler **[3]** [spule] **VT** *Ordinat* to spool

spouleur [spulœr] **NM** *Ordinat* spooler

Spoutnik [sputnik] **NM** Sputnik

sprat [sprat] **NM** *Ich* sprat

spray [sprɛ] **NM** spray; **parfum/peinture en s.** spray *or* spray-on perfume/paint

spread [sprɛd] **NM** *Bourse* spread

springbok [spriŋbɔk] **NM 1** *Zool* springbok, springbuck **2** *Sport* **les Springboks** the Springboks

springer [springœr, springɛr] **NM** springer (spaniel)

sprint [sprint] **NM** *Sport (course)* sprint (race); *(pointe de vitesse ▸ gén)* spurt; *(▸ en fin de parcours)* final spurt *or* sprint; **elle m'a battu au s.** she beat me in the final sprint; **il est bon au s.** he's got a good sprint finish; *Fam* **j'ai dû piquer un s. pour avoir mon train** I had to sprint to catch my train

sprinter[1] [sprintœr] **NM** sprinter

sprinter[2] **[3]** [sprinte] **VI** to sprint; *(en fin de parcours)* to put on a spurt

squale [skwal] **NM** shark

squame [skwam] **NF** *Méd* scale, *Spéc* squama

squameux, -euse [skwamø, -øz] **ADJ** *Méd* scaly, *Spéc* squamous

square [skwar] **NM 1** *(jardin)* (small) public garden *or* gardens **2** *(place)* square; **il habite s. Blériot** he lives in Blériot Square

squash [skwaʃ] **NM** squash; **jouer au s.** to play squash

squat [skwat] **NM** *(habitation)* squat

squatter[1] [skwatœr] **NM** squatter

squatter[2] **[3]** [skwate] **VT 1** *(bâtiment)* to squat in **2** *Fam (monopoliser)* to take over, to hog; **il squatte toujours la télécommande quand on regarde la télé** he always hogs the remote control when we're watching TV; **arrête de s. le joint, fais tourner!** stop bogarting that joint, pass it round!
VI to squat; **ça fait trois semaines qu'il squatte chez moi** he's been squatting *or* camping out at mine for three weeks now

squatteur, -euse [skwatœr, -øz] **NM,F** squatter

squaw [skwo] **NF** squaw

squeeze [skwiz] **NM** *Cartes (au bridge)* squeeze

squelette [skəlɛt] **NM 1** *Anat* skeleton; **c'est un s. ambulant** he's nothing but skin and bone, he's a walking skeleton
2 *(d'un discours)* skeleton, broad outline
3 *Chim* skeleton
4 *Constr & Naut* carcass, skeleton

squelettique [skəletik] **ADJ 1** *(animal, enfant)* skeleton-like, skeletal; *(plante)* stunted; **elle a des jambes squelettiques** she's got legs like matchsticks; **il est devenu s.** he's become emaciated **2** *(troupes)* decimated; *(équipe)* skeleton *(avant n)* **3** *Anat* skeletal

squille [skij] **NF** *Zool* squilla

SR [esɛr] **NM** *Journ (abrév* **secrétaire de rédaction***)* subeditor

SRAS [sras] **NM** *Méd (abrév* **syndrome respiratoire aigu sévère***)* SARS

Sri Lanka [srilɑ̃ka] **NM le S.** Sri Lanka

sri lankais, -e [srilɑ̃kɛ, -ɛz] **ADJ** Sri Lankan
• **Sri Lankais, -e NM,F** Sri Lankan

SRPJ [ɛsɛrpeʒi] **NM** *(abrév* **Service régional de la police judiciaire***)* = French regional crime unit

SS [ɛsɛs] *Hist (abrév* **Schutzstaffel***)* **NF** SS
NM un SS a member of the SS; **les SS** the SS

SSR [ɛsɛsɛr] **NF** *Suisse TV (abrév* **Société suisse de Radiodiffusion et de Télévision***)* = French-speaking Swiss broadcasting company

St *(abrév écrite* **saint***)* St., St

stabilisant, -e [stabilizɑ̃, -ɑ̃t] **ADJ** stabilizing
NM stabilizing agent, stabilizer

stabilisateur, -trice [stabilizatœr, -tris] **ADJ** stabilizing
NM 1 *(de vélo)* stabilizer
2 *Aviat (horizontal)* tail plane, *Am* horizontal stabilizer; *(vertical)* fin, *Am* vertical stabilizer
3 *Aut* antiroll *or* torsion bar
4 *Chim* stabilizer
5 *Élec* **s. de tension** voltage regulator *or* stabilizer

stabilisation [stabilizasjɔ̃] **NF 1** *Aviat & Astron* stabilization, stabilizing *(UNCOUNT)*
2 *Chim* stabilization
3 *Écon* supporting *(UNCOUNT)*
4 *Métal & (en travaux publics)* stabilizing *(UNCOUNT)*

stabilisatrice [stabilizatris] *voir* **stabilisateur**

stabiliser **[3]** [stabilize] **VT 1** *(échafaudage ▸ donner un équilibre à)* to stabilize; *(▸ maintenir en place)* to hold steady
2 *(consolider ▸ situation)* to stabilize, to normalize
3 *(personne)* **son mariage va le s.** marriage will make him settle down
4 *(monnaie, devise, prix)* to stabilize
5 *(malade, maladie)* to stabilize
VPR se stabiliser 1 *(monnaie, prix, ventes)* to stabilize, to level out; *(situation)* to stabilize; *(objet)* to steady; *(athlète)* to regain one's balance; **la situation militaire semble se s.** the military situation seems to be stabilizing **2** *(personne)* to settle down

stabilité [stabilite] **NF 1** *(d'un véhicule, d'un échafaudage, d'une structure)* steadiness, stability
2 *(d'une monnaie, d'un marché, des prix) & Pol* stability
3 *(psychologique)* stability
4 *Chim, Météo & Phys* stability

stable [stabl] **ADJ 1** *(qui ne bouge pas ▸ véhicule, échafaudage, structure)* steady, stable; **la table n'est pas très s.** the table's a bit unsteady *or* wobbly
2 *(constant ▸ marché, emploi)* stable, steady; *(▸ monnaie, prix, ventes)* steady; *(▸ situation politique)* stable; **l'état du malade est s.** the patient's condition is stable
3 *(psychologiquement)* stable
4 *Chim, Météo & Phys* stable

stabulation [stabylasjɔ̃] **NF 1** *(entretien)* stalling (of cattle) **2** *(bâtiment)* stalls

staccato [stakato] *Mus* **ADV** staccato
NM staccato

stade [stad] **NM 1** *Sport* stadium
2 *(étape, phase)* stage; **à ce s. de l'enquête** at this stage of the investigation; **j'en suis arrivé au s. où…** I've reached the stage where…
3 *Antiq* stadium
4 *Psy* stage; **le s. anal/oral/génital** the anal/oral/genital stage

stadier, -ère [stadje, -ɛr] **NM,F** steward *(at sports stadium)*

staff [staf] **NM 1** *Constr* staff **2** *(personnel)* staff

stage [staʒ] **NM 1** *(cours)* training course; *(sur le temps de travail)* in-service training; *(expérience professionnelle) Br* work placement, *Am* internship; **un s. de trois mois** a three-month *Br* work placement *or Am* internship; **faire un s.** *(cours)* to go on a training course; *(expérience professionnelle)* to go on *Br* a work placement *or Am* an internship; **être en s.** *(cours)* to be on a course; *(expérience professionnelle)* to be on *Br* a work placement *or Am* an internship; **s. en entreprise** *Br* work experience *or* placement, *Am* internship; **s. de formation** training course; **s. pédagogique** teaching practice; **s. de perfectionnement** advanced training course **2 faire un s. de plongée** *(cours)* to have scuba diving lessons; *(vacances)* to go on a scuba diving holiday; **faire un s. d'espagnol/de traitement de texte** to go on a Spanish/word-processing course

> Il faut noter que le terme anglais **stage** est un faux ami.

stagflation [stagflasjɔ̃] **NF** stagflation

stagiaire [staʒjɛr] **ADJ** *(en entreprise, dans l'armée)* trainee *(avant n)*; *(avocat)* pupil *(avant n)*; *(journaliste)* cub *(avant n)*; **un instituteur s.** a student teacher
NMF *Br* = person on work experience or a work placement, *Am* intern; **il est s.** *Br* he's doing work experience *or* a work placement, *Am* he's an intern; **un s. en comptabilité** a trainee accountant *(gaining work experience)*

stagnant, -e [stagnɑ̃, -ɑ̃t] **ADJ 1** *(eau)* stagnant **2** *(affaires)* sluggish

stagnation [stagnasjɔ̃] **NF** stagnation, stagnating

stagner **[3]** [stagne] **VI 1** *(liquide)* to stagnate; **des bancs de brume stagnaient dans la vallée** patches of mist were lying in the valley **2** *(économie, affaires)* to stagnate, to be sluggish **3** *(personne)* to stagnate, to get into a rut; **s. dans son ignorance** to be bogged down in one's own ignorance

stakhanovisme [stakanɔvism] **NM** Stakhanovism

stalactite [stalaktit] **NF** stalactite

stalag [stalag] **NM** stalag

stalagmite [stalagmit] **NF** stalagmite

stalinien, -enne [stalinjɛ̃, -ɛn] **ADJ** Stalinist
NM,F Stalinist

stalinisme [stalinism] **NM** Stalinism

stalle [stal] **NF** *(de cheval, d'église)* stall

stance [stɑ̃s] *Littérature* **NF** stanza
• **stances NFPL** = lyrical poem composed of stanzas

stand [stɑ̃d] **NM 1** *(d'exposition)* stand; *(de fête foraine, de kermesse)* stall; **s. d'exposition** exhibition stand
2 *Mil & (loisir)* **s. (de tir)** (shooting) range
3 *Sport* **s. (de ravitaillement)** pit
4 *(de machine à écrire, de calculatrice)* stand, rest

standard [stɑ̃dar] **ADJ 1** *(normalisé ▸ modèle, pièce, prix, taille)* standard *(avant n)* **2** *(non original ▸ discours, goûts)* commonplace, unoriginal, standard **3** *Ling* standard
NM 1 *Com & Ind* standard **2** *Écon* **s. de vie** living standard **3** *Tél* switchboard

standardisation [stɑ̃dardizasjɔ̃] **NF** standardization, standardizing

standardiser **[3]** [stɑ̃dardize] **VT** *(normaliser, uniformiser)* to standardize

standardiste [stɑ̃dardist] **NMF** (switchboard) operator

stand-by [stɑ̃dbaj] **ADJ INV 1** *Aviat (billet, passager, siège)* standby *(avant n)* **2** *Fin* standby *(avant n)*; **crédit s.** standby credit
NM INV (ticket/passager en) s. standby (ticket/passenger)

standing [stɑ̃diŋ] **NM 1** *(d'une personne ▸ position sociale)* social status *or* standing; *(▸ réputation)* (good) reputation, standing **2** *(confort)* **appartement (de) grand s.** luxury *Br* flat *or Am* apartment

standiste [stɑ̃dist] **NMF** stand designer

staphylocoque [stafilɔkɔk] **NM** staphylococcus

star [star] **NF 1** *Cin* (film) star; *Mus & Théât* star; **en une semaine, elle était devenue une s.** within a week, she'd risen to stardom
2 *(du monde politique, sportif)* star
3 *(favorite)* number one; **la s. des routières de la décennie** the top touring car of the decade
4 *Mktg (produit)* star

stariser **[3]** [starize] **VT** to make a star of, to bring to stardom

starlette [starlɛt] **NF** starlet

star-system [starsistɛm] (*pl* **star-systems**) **NM** *Cin, Mus & Théât* star system

starter [startɛr] **NM 1** *Aut* choke; **mettre le s.** to pull the choke out; **enlever le s.** to push in the choke; **j'ai roulé avec le s.** I drove with the choke out **2** *Sport* starter; **les chevaux sont sous les ordres du s.** the horses are under starter's orders

> Il faut noter que le terme anglais **starter** est un faux ami: il ne désigne jamais le dispositif servant à faciliter le démarrage d'un moteur.

starting-block [startiŋblɔk] (*pl* **starting-blocks**) **NM** starting block

starting-gate [startiŋget] (*pl* **starting-gates**) **NM OU NF** starting gate

start-up [startœp] (*pl* **start-ups**) **NF** start-up

stase [staz] **NF** *Méd* stasis

station [stasjɔ̃] **NF 1** *Transp* **s. d'autobus** bus stop; **s. de métro** *Br* underground *or Am* subway station; **s. de taxis** taxi *Br* rank *or Am* stand
2 *(centre)* **s. d'épuration** sewage treatment plant; **s. de lavage** carwash; **s. météorologique** weather station; **s. de pompage** *(de pétrole)* pumping station
3 *Rad, TV & Tél* station; **s. de base** base station; **s. d'écoute** monitoring station; **s. émettrice** broadcasting station, transmitting station; **s. d'émission** broadcasting station, transmitting station; **s. généraliste** general-interest station; **s. musicale** music station; **s. périphérique** private radio station; **s. de radio** radio station; **s. satellite** satellite station, outstation; **s. de télévision** television station; **s. terrestre** ground *or* earth station
4 *(lieu de séjour)* resort; **s. d'altitude** mountain resort; **s. balnéaire** seaside resort; **s. de ski** *ou* **de sports d'hiver** ski resort; **s. thermale** (thermal) spa; **s. verte** = rural tourist centre
5 *Ordinat (d'un réseau)* station, node; **s. d'accueil** docking station; **s. de travail** workstation
6 *(position)* posture; **s. verticale** upright position; **la s. debout est déconseillée** standing is not advisable
7 *(pause)* stop; **faire de longues stations devant les magasins** to stop for long periods in front of shops
8 *Astron (d'une planète)* stationary point
9 *Astron (engin spatial)* **s. orbitale/spatiale** orbital/space station
10 *Belg (gare)* station

stationnaire [stasjɔnɛr] **ADJ 1** *Math & Biol* stationary; *Astron* **théorie de l'état** *ou* **de l'Univers s.** steady-state theory **2** *Méd (état)* stable **3** *Phys (phénomène)* stable; *(onde)* stationary, standing; *(état)* stationary
NM *Naut* station ship

stationnement [stasjɔnmɑ̃] **NM 1** *(arrêt)* parking; **s. bilatéral** parking on both sides of the road; **s. en double file** double-parking; **s. unilatéral** parking on one side (only); **s. payant** parking fee payable; **s. interdit** *(sur panneau ▸ gén)* no parking; *(▸ devant une gare)* no waiting; **s. gênant** *(sur panneau)* ≃ restricted parking **2** *Can (parc de stationnement) Br* car park, *Am* parking lot
• **en stationnement ADJ 1** *(véhicule)* parked **2** *Mil* stationed

stationner [3] [stasjɔne] **VI 1** *(véhicule)* to be parked; **une voiture stationnait en double file** a car was double-parked **2** *Mil* **les troupes stationnées en Allemagne** troops stationed in Germany **3** *(rester sur place ▸ personne)* to stay, to remain; **ne pas s. devant la sortie** *(sur panneau)* keep exit clear; **défense de s.** *(sur panneau ▸ gén)* no parking; *(▸ devant une gare)* no waiting

station-service [stasjɔ̃sɛrvis] (*pl* **stations-service**) **NF** service station, *Br* petrol *or Am* gas station

station-sol [stasjɔ̃sɔl] (*pl* **stations-sol**) **NF** *Rad* ground station

statique [statik] **ADJ 1** *(immobile)* static **2** *(inchangé)* static, unimaginative; **une politique s.** an unimaginative policy **3** *Élec* static
NF statics *(singulier)*

statiquement [statikmɑ̃] **ADV** statically

statisticien, -enne [statistisjɛ̃, -ɛn] **NM,F** statistician

statistique [statistik] **ADJ** statistical
NF 1 *(étude)* statistics *(singulier)* **2** *(donnée)* statistic; **des statistiques** statistics, a set of figures; **statistiques démographiques** demographics

statistiquement [statistikmɑ̃] **ADV** statistically

stator [statɔr] **NM** stator

statoréacteur [statɔreaktœr] **NM** *Aviat* ramjet (engine)

statuaire [statɥɛr] **ADJ** statuary
NMF sculptor, *f* sculptress
NF statuary

statue [staty] **NF** *Beaux-Arts* statue; **la s. de la Liberté** the Statue of Liberty; **s. en pied** *ou* **pédestre** standing *or* pedestrian statue; *Fig* **s. de sel** pillar of salt; **la réponse de son père l'a changée en s. de sel** her father's reply rooted her to the spot

statuer [7] [statɥe] **VT** to rule; **le tribunal a statué qu'il y avait eu faute** the court ruled that misconduct had taken place
• **statuer sur VT IND s. sur un litige** to rule on a lawsuit; **la cour n'a pas statué sur le fond** the court pronounced no judgement *or* gave no ruling on the merits of the case

statuette [statɥɛt] **NF** statuette

statufier [9] [statyfje] **VT 1** *(représenter en statue)* to erect a statue of *or* to **2** *(faire un éloge excessif de)* to lionize **3** *Littéraire (pétrifier)* to petrify; **statufié par la peur** transfixed with fear, petrified

statu quo [statykwo] **NM INV** status quo

stature [statyr] **NF 1** *(carrure)* stature; **de haute s.** very tall **2** *(envergure)* stature, calibre; **son frère est d'une autre s.** his/her brother is in a different league (altogether)

statut [staty] **NM** *(état)* status; **mon s. de femme mariée** my status as a married woman; **avoir le s. de cadre/de fonctionnaire** to have executive/civil servant status; **s. juridique** *ou* **légal** legal status; **s. social** social status; **il réclame le s. de réfugié politique** he is asking for political refugee status
• **statuts NMPL** *(règlements)* statutes, articles of association, *Am* bylaws; **statuts et règlements** rules and regulations

statutaire [statytɛr] **ADJ 1** *(conforme aux statuts)* statutory **2** *(désigné par les statuts ▸ gérant)* registered

statutairement [statytɛrmɑ̃] **ADV** statutorily

stayer [stɛjœr] **NM** *Cyclisme (derrière une moto)* long-distance cyclist; *Courses de chevaux* stayer

Sté *(abrév écrite* **société***)* Co; **S. Leroux** Leroux

steak [stɛk] **NM** steak; **s. frites** steak and chips; **un s. haché** a burger, a hamburger, *Br* a beefburger; **s. au poivre** pepper steak; **s. tartare** steak tartare

stéarine [stearin] **NF** *Chim* stearin

stéarique [stearik] **ADJ** *Chim* stearic

stéatite [steatit] **NF** *Minér* steatite, soapstone

stéatopyge [steatɔpiʒ] **ADJ** steatopygic

stéatose [steatoz] **NF** *Méd* steatosis

steeple [stipl], **steeple-chase** [stipəltʃɛz] (*pl* **steeple-chases**) **NM** steeplechase

stéganographie [steganɔgrafi] **NF** *Tech* steganography

stèle [stɛl] **NF** stele

stellage [stelaʒ] **NM** *Bourse* put and call option, double option

stellaire [stelɛr] **ADJ 1** *Astron* stellar **2** *Anat (ganglion)* stellate
NF *Bot* stitchwort, starwort

stem, stemm [stɛm] **NM** *Ski* stem (turn)

stencil [stɛnsil] **NM** stencil

sténo [steno] **NMF** shorthand note-taker, *Am* stenographer
NF shorthand; **prendre une lettre en s.** to take down a letter in shorthand

sténodactylo [stenɔdaktilo] **NMF** *(personne) Br* shorthand typist, *Am* stenographer
NF *(activité) Br* shorthand typing, *Am* stenography

sténodactylographie [stenɔdaktilɔgrafi] **NF** *Br* shorthand typing, *Am* stenography

sténographe [stenɔgraf] **NMF** shorthand note-taker, *Am* stenographer; **s. judiciaire** court reporter

sténographie [stenɔgrafi] **NF** shorthand

sténographier [9] [stenɔgrafje] **VT** to take down in shorthand; **notes sténographiées** shorthand notes, notes in shorthand

sténographique [stenɔgrafik] **ADJ** shorthand *(avant n)*

sténopé [stenɔpe] **NM** *Phot* pinhole

sténotype [stenɔtip] **NF** Stenotype®

sténotyper [3] [stenɔtipe] **VT** to take down on a Stenotype®

sténotypie [stenɔtipi] **NF** stenotypy

sténotypiste [stenɔtipist] **NMF** stenotypist

stentor [stɑ̃tɔr] **NM** *Zool* stentor

step [stɛp] **NM** step (aerobics)

stéphanois, -e [stefanwa, -az] **ADJ** of/from Saint-Étienne
• **Stéphanois, -e NM,F** = inhabitant of or person from Saint-Étienne

steppe [stɛp] **NF** steppe

stercoraire [stɛrkɔrɛr] **ADJ** *Méd* stercoraceous
NM 1 *Entom* dung beetle **2** *Orn* skua

stère [stɛr] **NM** stere *(cubic metre of wood)*

stéréo [stereo] **ADJ INV** stereo
NF 1 *(procédé)* stereo **2** *Fam (récepteur)* stereo
• **en stéréo ADJ** stereo *(avant n)* **ADV** in stereo

stéréogramme [stereɔgram] **NM** stereogram

stéréographie [stereɔgrafi] **NF** stereography

stéréométrie [stereɔmetri] **NF** stereometry

stéréophonie [stereɔfɔni] **NF** stereophony
• **en stéréophonie ADJ** stereo *(avant n)* **ADV** in stereo, in stereophonic sound

stéréophonique [stereɔfɔnik] **ADJ** stereophonic

stéréoscope [stereɔskɔp] **NM** stereoscope

stéréoscopie [stereɔskɔpi] **NF** stereoscopy

stéréoscopique [stereɔskɔpik] **ADJ** stereoscopic

stéréotype [stereɔtip] **NM 1** *(formule banale)* stereotype, cliché **2** *Typ* stereotype

stéréotypé, -e [stereɔtipe] **ADJ** *(comportement)* stereotyped; *(tournure)* clichéd, hackneyed

stéréotypie [stereɔtipi] **NF** stereotypy

stérile [steril] **ADJ 1** *(femme)* infertile, sterile, barren; *(homme)* sterile; *(mariage)* childless; *(sol)* barren; *(végétal)* sterile
2 *(improductif ▸ artiste)* unproductive; *(▸ imagination)* barren, infertile; *(▸ hypothèse)* unproductive, vain; *(▸ rêve)* vain, hopeless; *(▸ discussion, effort)* vain, fruitless
3 *Méd (aseptique)* sterile, sterilized
4 *Mines & Minér* dead
NM *Mines & Minér* dead ground
• **stériles NMPL** *Géol* deads, waste rock

stérilement [sterilmɑ̃] **ADV** *Littéraire (vainement)* fruitlessly

stérilet [sterile] **NM** *Méd* IUD, coil; **se faire poser/enlever un s.** to have a coil put in/taken out

stérilisant, -e [sterilizɑ̃, -ɑ̃t] **ADJ 1** *(procédure, technique)* sterilizing **2** *(idéologie, mode de vie)* numbing, brain-numbing
NM sterilant

stérilisateur [sterilizatœr] **NM** sterilizer

stérilisation [sterilizasjɔ̃] **NF 1** *(action de rendre infécond)* sterilization **2** *(désinfection)* sterilization **3** *Littéraire (de la créativité)* stifling

stériliser [3] [sterilize] **VT 1** *(rendre infécond)* to sterilize **2** *(rendre aseptique)* to sterilize **3** *(appauvrir, tuer ▸ créativité)* to stifle

stérilité [sterilite] **NF 1** *(d'une femme)* sterility, infertility, barrenness; *(d'un homme)* infertility, sterility; *(d'un sol)* barrenness **2** *Méd (asepsie)* sterility **3** *(de l'imagination)* barrenness; *(d'une discussion, d'efforts)* fruitlessness, futility

sterling [stɛrliŋ] **ADJ INV** sterling
NM INV sterling

sterne [stɛrn] **NF** *Orn* tern

sternum [stɛrnɔm] **NM 1** *Anat* breastbone, *Spéc* sternum **2** *Orn* sternum

sternutatoire [sternytatwar] **ADJ** sternutatory; **poudre s.** sneezing powder

stéroïde [steroid] *Pharm* **ADJ** steroidal

NM steroid; **stéroïdes anabolisants** anabolic steroids

stérol [sterol] **NM** *Chim* sterol

stertoreux, -euse [stertorø, -øz] **ADJ** *Méd* stertorous

stéthoscope [stetoskop] **NM** *Méd* stethoscope

steward [stiwart] **NM** *(à bord d'un avion, d'un paquebot)* steward

stick [stik] **NM 1** *(de colle)* stick; **déodorant en s.** stick deodorant **2** *Sport (au hockey)* (hockey) stick; *(de cavalier)* (riding) stick; *(de parachutistes)* stick **3** *Fam Arg drogue (de marijuana)* (thin) joint *or Br* spliff

stigmate [stigmat] **NM 1** *Méd* mark, *Spéc* stigma

2 *(marque)* **porter les stigmates de la débauche/de la guerre** to bear the signs of debauchery/the cruel marks of war

3 *Hist (châtiment)* brand

4 *Bot (tache)* eyespot, stigma

5 *Entom* (respiratory) stigma

• **stigmates NMPL** *Rel* stigmata

stigmatisation [stigmatizasjõ] **NF** stigmatization, stigmatizing

stigmatisé, -e [stigmatize] *Rel* **ADJ** stigmatized

NM,F stigmatized person

stigmatiser [3] [stigmatize] **VT 1** *(dénoncer)* to stigmatize, to condemn, to pillory **2** *Littéraire (marquer ▸ condamné)* to brand, to stigmatize

stimulant, -e [stimylã, -ãt] **ADJ 1** *(fortifiant ▸ climat)* bracing, stimulating; *(▸ boisson)* stimulant *(avant n)* **2** *(encourageant ▸ résultat, paroles)* encouraging

NM 1 *(remontant, tonique)* stimulant **2** *(pour relancer)* stimulus, spur **3** *(pour encourager)* incentive

stimulateur, -trice [stimylatœr, -tris] **ADJ** stimulative

NM *Méd* stimulator; **s. (cardiaque)** pacemaker

stimulation [stimylasjõ] **NF 1** *Chim, Physiol & Psy* stimulation, stimulus; **stimulations sensorielles** sensory stimulation *or* stimuli **2** *(d'une fonction organique)* stimulation; **pour la s. de leur appétit** to stimulate *or* to whet their appetite **3** *(incitation)* stimulus; *(encouragement)* incentive; **s. financière** cash incentive

stimulatrice [stimylatris] *voir* **stimulateur**

stimuler [3] [stimyle] **VT 1** *(activer ▸ fonction organique)* to stimulate; **s. l'appétit** to stimulate *or* to whet the appetite

2 *(enflammer ▸ sentiment, imagination)* to stimulate

3 *(encourager ▸ personne)* to encourage, to motivate; **s. les élèves par des récompenses** to motivate pupils by a system of rewards; **il faut sans arrêt le s.** you have to keep prodding him

4 *(intensifier ▸ activité)* to stimulate

stimulus [stimylys] *(pl* **inv** *ou* **stimuli** [-li]) **NM** stimulus

stipendié, -e [stipãdje] **ADJ** *Littéraire Péj* venal, corrupt

stipendier [9] [stipãdje] **VT** *Littéraire Péj (mercenaire, tueur)* to hire; *(homme politique, fonctionnaire)* to bribe, to buy

stipulation [stipylasjõ] **NF 1** *(spécification)* stipulation, stipulating **2** *Jur* stipulation; **s. pour autrui** third-party provision; **s. particulière** special provision

stipuler [3] [stipyle] **VT 1** *Jur* to stipulate **2** *(spécifier)* to stipulate, to specify; **la circulaire stipule que l'augmentation sera appliquée à partir du mois prochain** the circular stipulates that the *Br* rise *or Am* raise will be applicable as from next month; **j'avais bien stipulé que j'en voulais deux** I'd made it clear I wanted two of them

stochastique [stokastik] **ADJ** *Math* stochastic

stock [stok] **NM 1** *Com* stock; *Écon* stock, supply; *Compta* **stocks** stock, *Am* inventory; **dans la limite des stocks disponibles** while stocks last, subject to availability; **constituer des stocks** to build up stocks; **épuiser les stocks** to deplete *or* exhaust stocks; **s. d'alerte** minimum stock level; **stocks excédentaires** surplus stock; **s. existant** stock in hand; **s. final** closing stock; **s. d'or** *(d'une banque d'État)* gold reserve; **s. d'ouverture** opening stock; **stocks de réserve** stockpile; **s. de sécurité** safety stock; **s. stratégique** perpetual inventory; **s. tampon** buffer stock **2** *(réserve personnelle)* stock, collection, supply; **tu peux prendre des confitures, j'en ai tout un s.** you can take some jam, I've got plenty of it *or* a whole stock of it; **faire des stocks (de)** to stock up (on) **3** *Biol* stock

• **en stock ADJ** *(marchandise)* in stock **ADV avoir qch en s.** to have sth in stock; **nous n'avons plus de shampooing en s.** we're out of shampoo, *Com* shampoo is out of stock

stockage [stokaʒ] **NM 1** *(constitution d'un stock ▸ gén)* stocking (up); *(▸ en grande quantité)* stockpiling, building up of stocks

2 *(conservation ▸ d'énergie, d'informations, de liquides, d'armes)* storage

3 *Tech* storage; **s. dynamique** flow storage

4 *Ordinat* storage; **s. de données** data storage

stock-car [stokkar] *(pl* **stock-cars**) **NM** *(voiture)* stock car; *(course)* stock car racing; **faire du s.** to go stock car racing

stocker [3] [stoke] **VT 1** *(s'approvisionner en)* to stock up on; *(avoir ▸ en réserve)* to (keep in) stock; *(▸ en grande quantité)* to stockpile **2** *Ordinat* to store

stockfish [stokfiʃ] **NM INV** stockfish

Stockholm [stokolm] **NM** Stockholm

stockiste [stokist] **NMF** *Com* stockist, *Am* dealer; *Aut* dealer, agent

stoeffer[1] [stufər] **NM** *Belg* show-off

stoeffer[2] **[3]** [stufe] **VI** *Belg* to show off

stoïcien, -enne [stoisjẽ, -ɛn] **ADJ 1** *Phil* Stoic **2** *Littéraire (impassible)* stoic, stoical

NM,F *Phil* Stoic

stoïcisme [stoisism] **NM 1** *(impassibilité)* stoicism **2** *Phil* Stoicism

stoïque [stoik] **ADJ** stoical

NMF stoic

stoïquement [stoikmã] **ADV** stoically

stolon [stolõ] **NM 1** *Bot* runner, *Spéc* stolon **2** *Zool* stolon

stomacal, -e, -aux, -ales [stomakal, -o] **ADJ** stomach *(avant n)*, gastric

stomachique [stomaʃik] **ADJ** stomachic, stomachical

stomatite [stomatit] **NF** *Méd* stomatitis

stomatologie [stomatoloʒi] **NF** stomatology

stomatologiste [stomatoloʒist], **stomatologue** [stomatolog] **NMF** stomatologist

stomie [stomi] **NF** *Méd* ostomy

stop [stop] **NM 1** *(panneau)* stop sign

2 *(lumière)* brake light, stoplight

3 *Fam (auto-stop)* hitching, hitchhiking; **faire du s.** to hitch, to thumb *Br* a lift *or Am* ride; **je suis descendu à Nice en s.** I hitched to Nice

4 *(dans un télégramme)* stop

EXCLAM stop!; **j'ai dit s.!** I said that's enough!; **tu me diras s. – s.!** *(en versant à boire)* say when – when!

stoppage [stopaʒ] **NM** *Tex* invisible mending

stopper [3] [stope] **VT 1** *(train, voiture)* to stop, to bring to a halt; *(engin, maladie)* to stop; *(développement, processus, production)* to stop, to halt; *(pratique)* to put a stop to, to stop **2** *Tex* to mend *(using invisible mending)*

VI *(marcheur, véhicule, machine, processus, production)* to stop, to come to a halt *or* standstill

stoppeur, -euse [stopœr, -øz] **NM,F 1** *Fam (en voiture)* hitcher, hitchhiker **2** *Ftbl* stopper, centre back **3** *Tex* invisible mender

store [stor] **NM** *(intérieur)* blind; *(extérieur ▸ d'un magasin)* awning; **s. vénitien** Venetian blind

story-board [storibord] *(pl* **story-boards**) **NM** *TV & Cin* storyboard

strabisme [strabism] **NM** *Opt* squint, *Spéc* strabismus; **elle a un léger s.** she has a slight squint; **s. convergent** esotropia, convergent strabismus; **s. divergent** exotropia, divergent strabismus

stradivarius [stradivarjys] **NM** Stradivarius

strangulation [strãgylasjõ] **NF** strangulation, strangling *(UNCOUNT)*; **il est mort par s.** he died by strangulation, he was strangled to death

strapontin [strapõtẽ] **NM 1** *(siège)* jump *or* folding seat **2** *(locutions)* **avoir un s.** to hold a minor position; **elle n'a obtenu qu'un s. au conseil** she was given only minor responsibilities on the board

strapping [strapiŋ] **NM** *Méd* strapping

stras [stras] = **strass**

strasbourgeois, -e [strazburʒwa, -az] **ADJ** of/from Strasbourg

• **Strasbourgeois, -e NM,F** = inhabitant of or person from Strasbourg

strass [stras] **NM** paste *(UNCOUNT)*, strass; **en s.** *(bijou)* paste

stratagème [strataʒɛm] **NM** stratagem, ruse

strate [strat] **NF 1** *Géol* stratum **2** *(niveau)* layer; **les strates de la personnalité** the layers *or* strata of the personality **3** *Bot* zone

stratège [stratɛʒ] **NM** *Mil* strategist; *Fig* **un fin s.** a cunning strategist

stratégie [strateʒi] **NF** strategy; **s. commerciale** business strategy; **s. de croissance** growth strategy; **s. de l'entreprise** corporate strategy; **s. marketing** game plan, marketing strategy; **s. de pénétration** market penetration strategy; **s. de positionnement** positioning strategy; **s. publicitaire** advertising strategy

stratégique [strateʒik] **ADJ** *Mil* strategic, strategical; *Fig* **un repli s.** a strategic retreat

stratégiquement [strateʒikmã] **ADV** strategically

stratification [stratifikasjõ] **NF** stratification, stratifying *(UNCOUNT)*; **la s. sociale** social stratification

stratifié, -e [stratifje] **ADJ** *(roches, société)* stratified; *Tech (papier, tissu)* laminated

NM laminate

stratifier [9] [stratifje] **VT** to stratify

strato-cumulus [stratokymylys] **NM INV** stratocumulus

stratosphère [stratosfer] **NF** stratosphere

stratosphérique [stratosferik] **ADJ** stratospheric

stratus [stratys] **NM** stratus

streamé, -e [strime] **ADJ** *Ordinat* streamed

streamer [strimœr] **NM** *Ordinat* tape streamer

streaming [strimiŋ] **NM** *Ordinat* streaming

streptocoque [streptokok] **NM** streptococcus

streptomycine [streptomisin] **NF** streptomycin

stress [strɛs] **NM** stress; **les maladies liées au s.** stress-related illnesses

stressant, -e [strɛsã, -ãt] **ADJ** stressful, stress-inducing

stresser [4] [strese] **VT** to put under stress; **elle me stresse** I find her very stressful

VPR se stresser to get stressed

Stretch® [strɛtʃ] **ADJ INV** stretch *(avant n)*, stretchy; **une jupe en S.** a stretch skirt

NM stretch material

striation [strijasjõ] **NF** striation

strict, -e [strikt] **ADJ 1** *(astreignant, précis ▸ contrôle, ordre, règle, principe)* strict; **la loi est très stricte à ce sujet** the law's very strict on that

2 *(minimal)* strict; **le s. nécessaire** *ou* **minimum** the bare minimum; **faire le s. minimum** to do only what is strictly necessary; **les obsèques seront célébrées dans la plus stricte intimité** the funeral will take place strictly in private

3 *(sévère ▸ éducation, personne)* strict; *(▸ discipline)* strict, rigorous; **ils sont très stricts sur la politesse** they're very strict about politeness

4 *(austère ▸ intérieur, vêtement, coiffure)* severe, austere

5 *(rigoureux, absolu)* strict, absolute; **c'est ton droit le plus s.** it's your lawful right; **c'est la stricte vérité!** it's absolutely true!

strictement [striktəmã] **ADV 1** *(rigoureusement)* strictly, scrupulously; **vous devez observer s. le règlement** you must obey the rules to the letter **2** *(absolument)* strictly, absolutely; **c'est s. confidentiel** it's strictly *or* highly confidential **3** *(sobrement)* severely

striction [striksjõ] **NF 1** *Méd* stricture **2** *Métal* contraction, necking (down)

stricto sensu [striktosɛ̃sy] ADV strictly speaking, *Sout* stricto sensu

strident, -e [stridɑ̃, -ɑ̃t] ADJ *(son, voix)* strident, shrill, piercing

stridulation [stridylɑsjɔ̃] NF stridulation, stridulating

strie [stri] NF **1** *(sillon)* (thin) groove, *Spéc* stria
2 *(ligne de couleur)* streak
3 *Archit* stria, fillet
4 *Géol & Minér* stria

strié, -e [strije] ADJ **1** *(cannelé ▸ roche, tige)* striated **2** *(veiné ▸ étoffe, marbre)* streaked **3** *Anat* striated

strier [10] [strije] VT **1** *(creuser)* to striate, to groove **2** *(veiner)* to streak; **strié de bleu** streaked with blue

strike [strajk] NM *(au bowling)* strike; **faire un s.** to get a strike

string [striŋ] NM G-string

strioscopie [strijɔskɔpi] NF schlieren photography

stripping [stripiŋ] NM *Méd & Pétr* stripping

strip-tease [striptiz] (*pl* **strip-teases**) NM striptease act; **faire un s.** to do a strip-tease

strip-teaseur, -euse [striptizœr, øz] (*mpl* **strip-teaseurs**, *fpl* **strip-teaseuses**) NM,F *(homme)* male stripper; *(femme)* stripper

striure [strijyr] NF striation

stroboscope [strɔbɔskɔp] NM stroboscope, strobe (light)

stroboscopique [strɔbɔskɔpik] ADJ stroboscopic

strombolien, -enne [strɔ̃bɔljɛ̃, -ɛn] ADJ Strombolian

strontium [strɔ̃sjɔm] NM *Chim* strontium

strophe [strɔf] NF **1** *(d'un poème)* stanza **2** *(de tragédie grecque)* strophe

structural, -e, -aux, -ales [stryktyral, -o] ADJ structural

structuralisme [stryktyralism] NM structuralism

structuraliste [stryktyralist] ADJ structuralist
NMF structuralist

structurant, -e [stryktyrɑ̃, -ɑ̃t] ADJ structuring

structuration [stryktyrɑsjɔ̃] NF *(action)* structuring; *(résultat)* structure

structure [stryktyr] NF **1** *(organisation ▸ d'un service, d'une société, d'un texte)* structure; **votre devoir manque de s.** your essay is badly organized *or* structured; **réformes de s.** structural reforms; **s. de l'entreprise** corporate *or* company structure; **s. hiérarchique** line organization
2 *(institution)* system, organization; **structures administratives/politiques** administrative/political structures
3 *(ensemble de services)* facility; **structures d'accueil** reception facilities *(for recently arrived tourists, refugees etc)*
4 *Constr* building, structure
5 *Ling* structure; **s. profonde/superficielle** deep/surface structure
6 *Ordinat* structure; **s. en anneau/étoile** ring/star structure; **s. arborescente** directory *or* tree structure; **s. de fichier** file structure

structuré, -e [stryktyre] ADJ structured, organized

structurel, -elle [stryktyrɛl] ADJ structural

structurellement [stryktyrɛlmɑ̃] ADV structurally

structurer [3] [stryktyre] VT to structure, to organize; **c'est une ébauche de scénario qu'il faudrait s.** it's the idea for a scenario which needs to be given some shape
VPR **se structurer** to take shape

strume [strym] NF *Vieilli Méd* struma, goitre

strychnine [striknin] NF strychnine

stuc [styk] NM stucco
• **en stuc** ADJ stucco *(avant n)*

stucage [stykaʒ] NM stucco work

stucateur [stykatœr] NM stucco worker

studieuse [stydjøz] *voir* **studieux**

studieusement [stydjøzmɑ̃] ADV studiously

studieux, -euse [stydjø, -øz] ADJ **1** *(appliqué ▸ élève)* hard-working, studious **2** *(consacré à l'étude)* **une soirée studieuse** an evening of study, a studious evening; **une retraite studieuse** *(endroit)* a place of study

studio [stydjo] NM **1** *(appartement) Br* studio flat, *Am* studio apartment
2 *Cin, TV, Mus & Rad* studio; **s. de cinéma** film studio; **s. de doublage** dubbing suite; **s. d'enregistrement** recording studio; **s. de télévision** television studio
3 *(atelier ▸ de peintre, de photographe)* studio; **s. de danse** dance studio
4 *Belg (chambre dans un hôtel de passe)* = room rented out by prostitutes; *(hôtel de passe)* = hotel used for prostitution
• **en studio** ADV **tourné en s.** shot in studio; **scène tournée en s.** studio scene

stupéfaction [stypefaksjɔ̃] NF amazement, astonishment, stupefaction; **je constate avec s. que…** I am amazed to note that…; **à ma (grande) s.** to my utter amazement

stupéfait, -e [stypefɛ, -ɛt] ADJ *(personne)* astounded, amazed, stupefied; **je suis s. de voir qu'il est revenu** I'm amazed to see he came back

stupéfiant, -e [stypefjɑ̃, -ɑ̃t] ADJ **1** *(nouvelle, réaction)* amazing, astounding, stupefying **2** *Pharm* narcotic
NM *(drogue)* drug, narcotic

stupéfier [9] [stypefje] VT **1** *(abasourdir)* to amaze, to astound, to stun; **sa décision a stupéfié sa famille** his/her family was stunned by his/her decision **2** *Littéraire (sujet: froid, peur)* to stupefy

stupeur [stypœr] NF **1** *(ahurissement)* amazement, astonishment; **le public était plongé dans la s.** the audience was dumbfounded *or* stunned; **je constate avec s. que…** I am amazed to note that… **2** *Méd & Psy* stupor

stupide [stypid] ADJ **1** *(inintelligent ▸ personne, jeu, initiative, réponse, suggestion)* stupid, silly, foolish; *(▸ raisonnement)* stupid **2** *(absurde ▸ accident, mort)* stupid; **ce serait trop s. de rater le début** it'd be stupid *or* a shame to miss the beginning **3** *(ahuri)* stunned, dumbfounded; **je restai s. devant son aveu** his/her confession left me speechless

stupidement [stypidmɑ̃] ADV stupidly, foolishly; **rire s.** to give a stupid laugh; **mourir s.** to die a stupid death

stupidité [stypidite] NF **1** *(d'une action, d'une personne, d'un propos)* stupidity, foolishness **2** *(acte)* piece of foolish behaviour **3** *(parole)* stupid *or* foolish remark; **arrête de dire des stupidités!** stop talking nonsense!; **répondre par une s.** to give a stupid answer

stupre [stypr] NM *Littéraire* depravity

stups [styp] NMPL *Fam* **la brigade des s., les s.** the Drug Squad

stuquer [3] [styke] VT to stucco

St-Vincent-et-les-Grenadines [sɛ̃vɛ̃sɑ̃elegrənadin] N St Vincent and the Grenadines

style [stil] NM **1** *(d'un écrivain, d'un journal)* style; **dans un s. très pompeux** in a highly pompous *or* bombastic style; **c'est écrit dans le plus pur s. administratif/journalistique** it's written in purest bureaucratic jargon/journalese; **en s. télégraphique** in a telegraphic style; **s. maison** *(dans l'édition, le journalisme)* house style
2 *(d'un artiste, d'un sportif)* style; **son s. de jeu** his (particular) way of playing, his style; **ce skieur a un beau s.** this skier has (a) good style
3 *Beaux-Arts* style; **un opéra (de) s. italien** an opera in the Italian style; **s. gothique/Régence** Gothic/Regency style
4 *(genre, ordre d'idée)* style; **dis-leur que tu vas réfléchir, ou quelque chose dans** *ou* **de ce s.** tell them you'll think about it, or something along those lines *or* in that vein; **une veste un peu dans le s. de la tienne** a jacket the same sort of style as yours
5 *Fam (manière d'agir)* style; **tu aurais pu l'avoir dénoncé – ce n'est pas mon s.** you could have informed on him – it's not my style *or* that's not the sort of thing I'd do; **serait-il parti sans nous prévenir? – ce n'est pas son s.** he may have gone without telling us – it's not like him; **ça serait bien son s.!** that would be just like him/her *or* just his/her style!
6 *(élégance)* style, class; **avoir du s.** to have style; **elle a beaucoup de s.** she's very stylish *or* chic; **elle s'habille avec beaucoup de s.** she dresses very stylishly
7 *Bot & Zool* style
8 *(d'un cadran solaire)* style, gnomon; *(d'un cylindre enregistreur)* needle, stylus; *Antiq & Hist (poinçon)* style, stylus
9 *Zool (d'une antenne)* style, seta
10 s. de vie lifestyle
11 *Ling* **s. direct/indirect** direct/indirect speech; **s. indirect libre** free indirect speech
• **de style** ADJ *(meuble, objet)* period *(avant n)*; **un fauteuil de s.** a period chair

stylé, -e [stile] ADJ *(personnel)* well-trained

styler [3] [stile] VT to train

stylet [stilɛ] NM **1** *Méd* stilet, stylet **2** *(dague)* stiletto **3** *Zool* stylet

stylicien, -enne [stilisjɛ̃,- ɛn] NM,F designer

stylique [stilik] NF design

stylisation [stilizɑsjɔ̃] NF stylization

styliser [3] [stilize] VT to stylize; **oiseau stylisé** stylized (drawing of a) bird

stylisme [stilism] NM **1** *(de mode)* fashion design; *(dans l'industrie)* industrial design **2** *(en littérature)* attention to style

styliste [stilist] NMF **1** *(de mode, dans l'industrie)* designer **2** *(auteur)* stylist

stylisticien, -enne [stilistisjɛ̃, -ɛn] NM,F expert in stylistics

stylistique [stilistik] ADJ stylistic
NF stylistics *(singulier)*

stylite [stilit] NM *Rel* stylite

stylo [stilo] NM pen; **s. (à bille)** ballpoint (pen), *Br* Biro®; **s. à encre/cartouche** fountain/cartridge pen; **s. correcteur** eraser pen; *Ordinat* **s. optique** light pen

stylo-feutre [stiloføtr] (*pl* **stylos-feutres**) NM felt-tip pen

stylographe [stilɔgraf] NM *Vieilli* fountain pen

Stylomine® [stilɔmin] NM propelling pencil

styrax [stiraks] NM *Bot* storax, styrax

styrène [stirɛn] NM *Chim* styrene

Styx [stiks] NM **le S.** the Styx

su, -e [sy] PP *voir* **savoir**
NM **au su de qn** to the knowledge of sb; **au vu et au su de tout le monde** in front of everybody, quite openly

suage [sɥaʒ] NM sweating, oozing

suaire [sɥɛr] NM shroud

suant, -e [sɥɑ̃, -ɑ̃t] ADJ **1** *Fam (ennuyeux)* dull[□], boring[□]; *(énervant)* annoying[□]; **ce que tu peux être s.!** you're a pain (in the neck)! **2** *(en sueur)* sweaty

suave [sɥav] ADJ *(manières, ton)* suave, sophisticated; *(senteur)* sweet; *(teintes)* subdued, mellow; *Hum* **de sa voix s.** in his suave voice, in dulcet tones

> Il faut noter que le terme anglais **suave** ne se rapporte pas aux sens et a le plus souvent une connotation péjorative.

suavement [sɥavmɑ̃] ADV suavely, smoothly

suavité [sɥavite] NF *(de manières, d'un ton)* suaveness, suavity, smoothness; *(d'une musique, de senteurs)* sweetness; *(de teintes)* mellowness

subaigu, -ë [sybegy] ADJ *Méd* subacute

subalpin, -e [sybalpɛ̃, -in] ADJ subalpine

subalterne [sybaltɛrn] ADJ **1** *(position)* secondary; **un rôle s.** a secondary *or* minor role **2** *(personne)* subordinate, junior *(avant n)*; **j'ai eu affaire à un fonctionnaire s.** I saw a junior clerk
NMF subordinate, subaltern; *Péj* underling; *Mil* subaltern (officer)

subaquatique [sybakwatik] ADJ subaquatic

subatomique [sybatɔmik] ADJ subatomic

subconscience [sybkɔ̃sjɑ̃s] NF subconsciousness

subconscient, -e [sybkɔ̃sjɑ̃, -ɑ̃t] ADJ subconscious
NM subconscious

subdiviser [3] [sybdivize] VT to subdivide
VPR **se subdiviser se s. (en)** to subdivide (into)

subdivision [sybdivizjɔ̃] NF 1 *(processus)* subdivision, subdividing 2 *(catégorie)* subdivision

subéquatorial, -e, -aux, -ales [sybekwatɔrjal, -o] ADJ subequatorial

subéreux, -euse [syberø, -øz] ADJ *Bot* cork *(avant n)*, *Spéc* subereous

subir [32] [sybir] VT 1 *(dommages, pertes)* to suffer, to sustain; *(conséquences, défaite)* to suffer; *(attaque, humiliation, insultes, sévices)* to be subjected to, to suffer; **la maison a subi quelques dégâts pendant les orages** the house sustained some storm damage; **faire s. une punition à qn** to inflict a punishment on sb; **faire s. une torture à qn** to subject sb to torture; **après tout ce qu'elle m'a fait s.** after all she inflicted on me *or* made me go through; **il lui a fait s. les pires humiliations** he made him/her suffer *or* endure the most terrible humiliations 2 *(situation, personne)* to put up with; **s. l'influence de qn** to be under sb's influence; **il a l'air de s. le match** he looks as though he's just letting the match go on around him 3 *(opération, transformation)* to undergo

subit, -e [sybi, -it] ADJ sudden

subitement [sybitmɑ̃] ADV suddenly, all of a sudden

subito [sybito] ADV 1 *Fam (tout à coup)* suddenly❑, all of a sudden❑ 2 *(locutions)* **s. presto** *Mus* subito presto; *Fam (tout de suite)* at once❑, immediately❑; **va me chercher le journal, allez, s. presto!** go and get me the paper, and make it snappy!

subjectif, -ive [sybʒɛktif, -iv] ADJ subjective

subjectivement [sybʒɛktivmɑ̃] ADV subjectively

subjectivisme [sybʒɛktivism] NM subjectivism

subjectivité [sybʒɛktivite] NF subjectivity, subjectiveness

subjonctif, -ive [sybʒɔ̃ktif, -iv] ADJ subjunctive
NM subjunctive; **au s.** in the subjunctive

subjuguer [3] [sybʒyge] VT 1 *(sujet: discours, lecture)* to enthral, to captivate; *(sujet: beauté, charme, regard)* to enthral, to beguile; *(sujet: éloquence)* to enthral; **elle le subjuguait** she held him spellbound; **je restai subjugué devant tant de grâce** I was enthralled by so much grace 2 *Vieilli Littéraire (asservir ▸ esprits, peuple)* to subjugate

sublimation [syblimasjɔ̃] NF 1 *(élévation morale)* sublimation, sublimating 2 *Chim & Psy* sublimation

sublimatoire [syblimatwar] ADJ sublimatory

sublime [syblim] ADJ 1 *(noble, grand)* sublime, elevated; **une beauté s.** sublime beauty 2 *(exceptionnel, parfait)* sublime, wonderful, magnificent; **tu as été s.** you were magnificent; **un repas s.** a wonderful meal; **un tableau s.** a sublime painting
NM **le s.** the sublime

sublimé, -e [syblime] ADJ sublimated
NM *Chim* sublimate

sublimement [syblimmɑ̃] ADV sublimely

sublimer [3] [syblime] VT 1 *Psy* to sublimate 2 *Chim* to sublimate, to sublime

subliminal, -e, -aux, -ales [sybliminal,-o], **subliminaire** [sybliminer] ADJ subliminal

sublimité [syblimite] NF *Littéraire* sublimeness

sublingual, -e, -aux, -ales [syblɛ̃gwal,-o] ADJ *Anat* sublingual; **comprimé s.** tablet to be placed under the tongue

submerger [17] [sybmɛrʒe] VT 1 *(inonder)* to flood, to submerge; **des villages entiers sont submergés** entire villages have been flooded *or* are under water 2 *(envahir ▸ sujet: angoisse, joie)* to overcome, to overwhelm; *(▸ sujet: réclamations)* to inundate, to swamp; *(▸ sujet: dettes)* to overwhelm, to swamp; **notre standard est submergé d'appels** our switchboard's swamped with *or* jammed by calls; **je suis submergé de travail** I'm snowed under with work; **se laisser s.** to allow oneself to be overcome 3 *(écraser ▸ défenseur)* to overwhelm, to overrun; **le service d'ordre fut rapidement submergé par les manifestants** the police were soon unable to contain the demonstrators

submersible [sybmɛrsibl] ADJ 1 *(bateau, moteur)* submersible 2 *Bot (plante)* submersed
NM submersible

submersion [sybmɛrsjɔ̃] NF *Littéraire* submersion, submerging; **mort par s.** death by drowning

submillimétrique [sybmilimetrik] ADJ submillimetric

subodorer [3] [sybɔdɔre] VT *Hum (danger)* to smell, to sense; **je subodore un canular** I can smell a hoax

subordination [sybɔrdinasjɔ̃] NF 1 *(dans une hiérarchie)* subordination, subordinating; **il a refusé sa s. au directeur commercial** he refused to work under the sales manager 2 *Gram* subordination; **complément/conjonction de s.** subordinating complement/conjunction

subordonnant [sybɔrdɔnɑ̃] *Gram* ADJ subordinating
NM subordinating word

subordonné, -e [sybɔrdɔne] ADJ 1 *(subalterne)* subordinate 2 *Gram* subordinate, dependent
NM,F *(subalterne)* subordinate, subaltern
• **subordonnée** NF *Gram* subordinate *or* dependent clause

subordonner [3] [sybɔrdɔne] VT 1 *(hiérarchiquement)* **s. qn à** to subordinate sb to; **les statuts subordonnent le directeur au conseil d'administration** the director is answerable to the board
2 *(faire dépendre)* **s. qch à** to subordinate sth to, to make sth dependent on; **il fallait tout s. à ses désirs** his/her wishes had to come before everything else; **l'admission est subordonnée à l'obtention de la moyenne au concours** admission is subject to passing the entrance exam
3 *(faire passer après)* **s. qch à** to subordinate sth to; **je ne subordonnerai jamais mes devoirs de père à ma carrière** I'll never allow my career to come before my duties as a father
4 *Ling (proposition)* to subordinate

subornation [sybɔrnasjɔ̃] NF subornation

suborner [3] [sybɔrne] VT 1 *Jur (témoin)* to suborn 2 *Vieilli (avec des pots-de-vin)* to bribe 3 *Littéraire (jeune fille)* to seduce

suborneur, -euse [sybɔrnœr, -øz] NM,F *Jur* suborner
NM *Littéraire (séducteur)* seducer

subprimes [sybprim] NFPL *Fin* subprime loans

subreptice [sybrɛptis] ADJ 1 *Littéraire (manœuvre)* surreptitious, stealthy 2 *Jur* **acte s.** subreption

subrepticement [sybrɛptismɑ̃] ADV *Littéraire* surreptitiously, stealthily

subrogation [sybrɔgasjɔ̃] NF subrogation, subrogating *(UNCOUNT)*

subrogé, -e [sybrɔʒe] ADJ 1 *(remplaçant)* surrogate 2 *Jur* **s. tuteur** deputy *or* surrogate guardian
NM,F *Jur* surrogate, deputy

subroger [17] [sybrɔʒe] VT to subrogate

subséquemment [sypsekamɑ̃] ADV subsequently, later on

subséquent, -e [sypsekɑ̃, -ɑ̃t] ADJ 1 *Littéraire (qui suit)* subsequent 2 *Géog* **affluent s.** subsequent stream

subside [sypsid] NM *(de l'État)* grant, subsidy; **il vivait des subsides de ses parents** he lived on the allowance he received from his parents

subsidence [sypsidɑ̃s, sybzidɑ̃s] NF *Géol* subsidence

subsidiaire [sybzidjɛr] ADJ *(motif, ressources)* subsidiary, additional

subsidiairement [sypzidjɛrmɑ̃] ADV subsidiarily; **s. à** in addition to

subsidiarité [sybzidjarite] NF subsidiarity

subsistance [sybzistɑ̃s] NF 1 *(existence matérielle)* subsistence; **pourvoir à la s. de qn** to support *or* to maintain *or* to keep sb; **elle arrive tout juste à assurer sa s.** she has just manages to survive, she has just enough to keep body and soul together; **moyen de s.** means of support 2 *Mil* **mise en s.** secondment

subsistant, -e [sybzistɑ̃, -ɑ̃t] ADJ remaining, subsisting
NM,F *(assuré social)* transferred (benefit) claimant
NM *Mil (soldat)* seconded soldier; *(officier)* seconded officer

subsister [3] [sybziste] VI 1 *(demeurer ▸ doute, espoir, rancœur, traces)* to remain, to subsist; *(▸ tradition)* to live on; **plus rien ne subsiste de ces magnifiques monuments** nothing is left *or* remains of those magnificent buildings 2 *(survivre)* to survive; **ces nomades trouvent à peine de quoi s. dans le désert** these nomads can barely eke out an existence in the desert; **je n'ai que 50 euros par semaine pour s.** I only have 50 euros a week to live on

subsonique [sypsɔnik] ADJ subsonic

substance [sypstɑ̃s] NF 1 *(matière)* substance; **plaie avec perte de s.** wound with loss of tissue; **s. active** active ingredient; **s. biodégradable/solide/liquide** biodegradable/solid/liquid substance; **s. organique/vivante** organic/living matter; **s. alimentaire** food; *Anat* **s. blanche/grise** white/grey matter
2 *(essentiel ▸ d'un texte)* substance, gist; *(▸ d'une idéologie)* substance; **je ne peux pas traduire toute la lettre – donne-nous-en juste la s.** I can't translate the whole letter – just give us the gist of it; **en s.** in substance; **c'est, en s., ce qu'elle m'a raconté** that's the gist of what she told me
3 *(profondeur, signification)* substance; **quelques exemples auraient donné un peu plus de s. à votre exposé** a few examples would have given more substance to your talk; **des mots vides de toute s.** words empty of substance, meaningless words
4 *Phil & Rel* substance; *(matérialité)* substance, reality; **des créatures sans s.** insubstantial *or* ghostly beings

substantialité [sypstɑ̃sjalite] NF *Phil* substantiality, substantialness

substantiel, -elle [sypstɑ̃sjɛl] ADJ 1 *(nourriture, repas)* substantial, filling 2 *(argument)* substantial, sound; **je cherche des lectures un peu plus substantielles** I'm looking for books with a bit more substance (to them) 3 *(avantage, différence)* substantial, significant, important; *(somme)* substantial, considerable

substantiellement [sypstɑ̃sjelmɑ̃] ADV substantially

substantif, -ive [sypstɑ̃tif, -iv] ADJ substantive
NM noun, *Spéc* substantive

substantifique [sypstɑ̃tifik] ADJ F **la s. moelle** the pith, the very substance

substantive [sypstɑ̃tiv] *voir* **substantif**

substantivement [sypstɑ̃tivmɑ̃] ADV as a noun, *Spéc* substantively

substantiver [3] [sypstɑ̃tive] VT to turn into a noun *or Spéc* substantive

substituer [7] [sypstitɥe] VT 1 **s. qch à qch** to substitute sth for sth, to replace sth by sth 2 *Chim* to substitute 3 *Jur* **s. un héritier** to appoint an heir in succession to another *or* failing another; **s. un héritage** to entail an estate
VPR **se substituer se s. à** *(pour aider, représenter)* to substitute for, to stand in for, to replace; *(de façon déloyale)* to substitute oneself for; **personne ne peut se s. à la mère** no one can take the place of the mother

substitut [sypstity] NM 1 *(produit, personne)* substitute (**de** for) 2 *Jur* deputy *or* assistant public prosecutor 3 *Psy* surrogate

substitution [sypstitysjɔ̃] NF 1 *(d'objets, de personnes)* substitution; **il y a eu s. de documents** documents have been substituted; **il y a eu s. d'enfant** the babies were switched round; *Jur* **s. de motifs** substitution of motives 2 *Chim, Ling & Math* substitution
• **de substitution** ADJ *(réaction)* substitution *(avant n)*; *(père, mère)* surrogate; **produit de s.** substitute

substrat [sypstra] NM 1 *Chim & Électron* substrate 2 *Géol, Ling & Phil* substratum

subterfuge [sypterfyʒ] NM piece of subterfuge, ruse, trick; **user de subterfuges** to resort to subterfuge

subtil, -e [syptil] ADJ 1 *(argument, esprit, raisonnement, personne)* subtle, discerning; **ses plaisanteries ne sont pas très subtiles** his/her jokes aren't very subtle *or* are a bit heavy-handed
2 *(allusion, différence)* subtle; *(nuance, distinction)* subtle, fine, nice

3 *(arôme, goût, parfum)* subtle, delicate
4 *Arch (fluide)* tenuous, thin

subtilement [syptilmɑ̃] **ADV** subtly

subtiliser [3] [syptilize] **VT 1** *(voler)* to steal, to spirit away; *Hum* **ils lui ont subtilisé sa montre** they relieved him/her of his/her watch **2** *Arch (raffiner)* to refine
VI *Littéraire Péj (être trop subtil)* to subtilize

subtilité [syptilite] **NF 1** *(d'un raisonnement, d'un parfum, d'une nuance)* subtlety, subtleness, delicacy; **les subtilités de la langue** the subtleties of the language **2** *(argutie)* hairsplitting; **je ne comprends rien à ces subtilités** all these fine distinctions are beyond me

subtropical, -e, -aux, -ales [syptrɔpikal, -o] **ADJ** subtropical

suburbain, -e [sybyrbɛ̃, -ɛn] **ADJ** suburban

subvenir [40] [sybvənir] **subvenir à VT IND** *(besoins)* to provide for; *(dépenses)* to meet

subvention [sybvɑ̃sjɔ̃] **NF** subsidy; **subventions en capital** capital grants; **notre troupe reçoit une s. de la mairie** our company gets a subsidy from *or* is subsidized by the city council; **s. d'État** government subsidy; **s. d'exploitation** operating subsidy; **s. à l'exportation** export subsidy; **s. de fonctionnement** operational subsidy

subventionné, -e [sybvɑ̃sjɔne] **ADJ** *(cinéma, théâtre, recherches)* subsidized

subventionner [3] [sybvɑ̃sjɔne] **VT** *(entreprise, théâtre)* to subsidize, to grant funds to; *(recherche)* to subsidize, to grant funds towards

subvenu, -e [sybvəny] **PP** *voir* **subvenir**

subversif, -ive [sybvɛrsif, -iv] **ADJ** subversive

subversion [sybvɛrsjɔ̃] **NF** subversion, subverting *(UNCOUNT)*

subversive [sypvɛrsiv] *voir* **subversif**

subversivement [sybvɛrsivmɑ̃] **ADV** subversively

subvertir [32] [sybvɛrtir] **VT** *Littéraire* to overthrow, to subvert

subvient *etc voir* **subvenir**

subvint *etc voir* **subvenir**

suc [syk] **NM 1** *Physiol* juice; **sucs gastriques** gastric juices **2** *Bot* sap **3** *Littéraire* **le s. de la science** the essence of scientific knowledge

succédané [syksedane] **NM 1** *(ersatz)* substitute; **un s. de café** coffee substitute, ersatz coffee **2** *(personne ou chose de second ordre)* **un s. de Rembrandt** a second-rate Rembrandt **3** *Pharm* substitute, *Spéc* succedaneum

succéder [18] [syksede] **succéder à VT IND 1** *(remplacer dans une fonction)* to succeed, to take over from; **qui lui succédera?** who will take over from him/her?, who will be his/her successor?; **tous ceux qui lui ont succédé** all his/her successors, all those who came after him/her; **s. à qn sur le trône** to succeed sb to the throne **2** *(suivre)* to follow; **les pleurs avaient succédé aux rires** laughter had given way to tears; **puis les défaites succédèrent aux victoires** after the victories came defeats; **le désert succéda à la steppe** the steppe gave way to desert **3** *Jur (hériter de ▸ personne)* to inherit from; *Arch* **s. au trône** to succeed to the throne; *Arch* **s. à une fortune** to inherit a fortune
VPR se succéder 1 *(se suivre)* to follow each other; **les crises se succèdent** it's just one crisis after another; **les hypothèses les plus folles se succédaient dans ma tête** the wildest suppositions ran through my head **2** *(alterner)* **les Ravit se sont succédé à la tête de l'entreprise depuis 50 ans** the Ravit family has been running the company for 50 years

succès [syksɛ] **NM 1** *(heureux résultat, réussite personnelle)* success; **être couronné de s.** to be crowned with success, to be successful; **cette voix qui a fait le s. de Maria Petit** the voice which has made Maria Petit so successful
2 *(exploit, performance)* success, achievement; *(en amour)* conquest; **l'opération est un s. total** the operation is a complete success; **leurs nombreux s. en coupe d'Europe** their many victories in the European Cup
3 *(approbation ▸ du public)* success, popularity; *(▸ d'un groupe)* success; **remporter un immense s.** to achieve great success; **avoir du s.** *(œuvre, artiste)* to be successful; *(suggestion)* to be very well received; **avoir un s. fou** *(artiste, film)* to be hugely successful; **sa pièce a eu beaucoup de s. auprès des critiques** his/her play was acclaimed by the critics; **il a beaucoup de s. auprès des femmes/jeunes** he's very popular with women/young people; **je n'ai pas eu de s. avec ma proposition** I was unsuccessful *or* had no success with my proposal; **eh bien, il a du s., mon soufflé!** well, I see you like my soufflé *or* my soufflé appears to be a success!
4 *(chanson)* hit; *(film, pièce)* (box-office) hit *or* success; *(livre)* success, bestseller; **s. d'estime** succès d'estime; **l'ouvrage a été un s. d'estime** the book was well-received by the critics (but not by the public); **s. de librairie** bestseller; **un gros s.** *(film)* a big success; *(livre)* a best-seller; *(disque)* a hit
• **à succès ADJ** *(auteur, chanteur)* popular; **chanson à s.** hit record *or* song; **romancier à s.** popular *or* best-selling novelist
• **avec succès ADV** successfully, with success; **il a tenté avec s. d'escalader la face nord** he was successful in his attempt to climb the north face; **passer un examen avec s.** to pass an exam
• **sans succès ADV** *(essayer)* unsuccessfully, without (any) success; **elle s'est présentée plusieurs fois sans s. à ce poste** she made several unsuccessful applications for this job

successeur [syksesœr] **NM 1** *(remplaçant)* successor **2** *Jur* heir **3** *Math* successor

successif, -ive [syksesif, -iv] **ADJ** successive

succession [syksesjɔ̃] **NF 1** *Jur (héritage)* succession, inheritance; *(biens)* estate; **liquider une s.** to settle a succession; **elle a laissé une s. énorme** she left a large estate; **s. vacante** estate in abeyance **2** *(remplacement)* succession; **prendre la s. d'un directeur** to take over from *or* to succeed a manager **3** *(suite ▸ gén)* succession, series *(singulier)*; *(▸ de visiteurs, d'admirateurs)* stream, succession; **la s. des événements est difficile à suivre** the succession of events is difficult to follow

successive [syksesiv] *voir* **successif**

successivement [syksesivmɑ̃] **ADV** successively, one after the other

succinct, -e [syksɛ̃, -ɛ̃t] **ADJ 1** *(bref, concis)* brief, concise, succinct **2** *(laconique)* brief, laconic; **soyez s., nous n'avons pas beaucoup de temps** be brief, we haven't much time **3** *(sommaire)* **un repas s.** a light meal

succinctement [syksɛ̃tmɑ̃] **ADV 1** *(brièvement)* briefly, succinctly; **résumer s. une discussion** to sum up a discussion briefly **2** *(sommairement)* frugally; **déjeuner s.** to have a light lunch

succion [sy(k)sjɔ̃] **NF 1** *(aspiration)* suction; **des bruits de s.** sucking noises **2** *Bot & Tech* suction

succomber [3] [sykɔ̃be] **VI 1** *(décéder)* to die, *Sout* to succumb **2** *(céder ▸ personne)* to succumb; **s. sous un fardeau** to collapse under a burden; **l'entreprise a succombé sous la concurrence** the company couldn't hold out against the competition; **le nounours était si adorable, j'ai succombé** the teddy bear was so cute I couldn't resist it; **s. à** *(désir, tentation)* to yield to, *Sout* to succumb to; *(désespoir, émotion)* to give way to, *Sout* to succumb to; *(fatigue, sommeil)* to succumb to; *(blessures)* to die from, *Sout* to succumb to; **j'ai succombé à ses charmes** I fell (a) victim *or* I succumbed to his/her charms

succube [sykyb] **NM** succubus

succulence [sykylɑ̃s] **NF** *Littéraire* succulence, succulency

succulent, -e [sykylɑ̃, -ɑ̃t] **ADJ 1** *(savoureux ▸ mets, viande)* succulent; *Fig* **son autobiographie est remplie d'anecdotes succulentes** his/her autobiography is full of juicy anecdotes **2** *Bot* **plante succulente** succulent

succursale [sykyrsal] **NF 1** *Com* branch **2** *Rel* succursal church

sucer [16] [syse] **VT 1** *(liquide)* to suck; *(bonbon, glace, sucette)* to eat, to suck; **pastilles à s.** lozenges to be sucked
2 *(doigt, stylo)* to suck (on); **s. son pouce** to suck one's thumb; *Fam* **s. la pomme** *ou* **la poire à qn** *Br* to snog sb, *Am* to make out with sb
3 *Vulg* **s. qn** *(pratiquer la fellation sur)* to go down on sb, to suck sb off; *(pratiquer le cunnilingus sur)* to go down on sb, to give sb head
4 *Fam (boisson)* to knock back; **il ne suce pas que de la glace** *ou* **des glaçons** he drinks like a fish
VPR se sucer 1 se s. les doigts to suck one's fingers **2** *très Fam (l'un l'autre)* **se s. la pomme** *ou* **la poire** *Br* to snog, *Am* to make out **3** *(emploi passif)* **ces cachets se sucent** these tablets are (meant) to be sucked

sucette [sysɛt] **NF 1** *(friandise)* lollipop, *Br* lolly; *Fam* **partir en s.** to go down the tubes *or* pan **2** *(tétine) Br* dummy, *Am* pacifier

suceur, -euse [sysœr, -øz] **ADJ** sucking
NM,F *Littéraire* **s. de sang** bloodsucker
NM 1 *(d'aspirateur)* nozzle **2** *Entom* sucking insect **3** *très Fam (flatteur) Br* arse-licker, *Am* ass-licker
• **suceuse NF** *Agr* suction dredger

suçon [sysɔ̃] **NM** *Br* lovebite, *Am* hickey; **faire un s. à qn** to give sb a *Br* lovebite *or Am* hickey

suçoter [3] [sysɔte] **VT** to suck (slowly); **il suçotait sa pipe** he was sucking at his pipe

sucrage [sykraʒ] **NM 1** *(gén)* sugaring **2** *(en œnologie)* chaptalization

sucrant, -e [sykrɑ̃, -ɑ̃t] **ADJ** sweetening; **agent s.** sweetener

sucrase [sykraz] **NF** sucrase, invertase

sucre [sykr] **NM 1** *(produit de consommation)* sugar; **enrobé de s.** sugar-coated; **je prends toujours mon thé sans s.** I don't take sugar in my tea; **confiture sans s.** sugar-free jam; **s. de betterave** beet sugar; **s. brun** brown sugar; **s. candi** candy sugar; **s. de canne** cane sugar; **s. cristallisé** (coarse) granulated sugar; **s. d'érable** maple sugar; *Belg* **s. fin** (fine) caster sugar; **s. glace,** *Belg* **s. impalpable** *Br* icing sugar, *Am* confectioner's *or* powdered sugar; **s. en morceaux** lump *or* cube sugar; **s. d'orge** *(produit)* barley sugar; *(bâton)* stick of barley sugar; *Can* **s. du pays** maple sugar; **s. en poudre** (fine) caster sugar; **s. roux** brown sugar; **s. semoule** (fine) caster sugar; *Belg* **s. ultrafin** (fine) caster sugar; **s. vanillé** vanilla sugar
2 *(sucreries)* **évitez le s.** avoid sugar *or* sweet things
3 *(morceau)* sugar lump *or* cube; **tu prends ton café avec un ou deux sucres?** do you take your coffee with one or two sugars?
4 *Biol, Chim & Méd* sugar; **s. d'amidon** starch sugar
5 *(comme adj)* **il est tout s. tout miel** he's all sweetness and light
6 *Can (bonbon)* **s. à la crème** maple fudge
• **au sucre ADJ** *(fruits, crêpes)* (sprinkled) with sugar
• **en sucre ADJ 1** *(confiserie, décoration)* sugar *(avant n)*, made with sugar **2** *Fam Fig* **mon bébé en s.** my sweetie pie

sucré, -e [sykre] **ADJ 1** *(naturellement)* sweet; *(artificiellement)* sweetened; **mon thé est trop s.** my tea is too sweet, there's too much sugar in my tea; **je n'aime pas le café s.** I don't like sugar in my coffee; **un verre d'eau sucrée** a glass of sugar water; **non s.** unsweetened **2** *(doucereux ▸ paroles)* sugary, sweet, honeyed; *(▸ voix)* suave, sugary
NM,F faire le s./la sucrée to go all coy
NM le s. sweet things; **j'ai envie de s.** I'd like something sweet to eat; **c'est une sauce qui combine le s. et le salé** it's a sauce which is sweet and savoury at the same time; **aimer le s.** to have a sweet tooth

sucrer [3] [sykre] **VT 1** *(avec du sucre ▸ café, thé)* to sugar, to put sugar in; *(▸ vin)* to add sugar to, to chaptalize; *(▸ fruits)* to sprinkle with sugar; **sucrez à volonté** add sugar to taste; **je ne sucre jamais mon thé** I never put sugar in my tea; *Fam* **s. les fraises** *(trembler)* to have shaky hands; *(être gâteux)* to be doddery **2** *(avec une matière sucrante)* to sweeten; **il sucre son lait avec du miel** he sweetens his milk with honey **3** *très Fam (supprimer ▸ permis, licence)* to take away□; *(▸ permission, prime)* to cancel□; *(▸ argent de poche)* to stop□
VI le miel sucre moins que le sucre sugar is a better sweetener than honey
VPR se sucrer *Fam* **1** *(prendre du sucre)* to help oneself to sugar□ **2** *(s'octroyer un bénéfice)* to line one's pockets

sucrerie [sykrəri] **NF 1** *(friandise)* sweet thing, sweetmeat; **elle adore les sucreries** she loves sweet things, she has a sweet tooth
2 *(raffinerie)* sugar refinery; *(usine)* sugar house
3 *Can (forêt d'érables)* maple plantation
4 *(en Afrique francophone) (boisson)* soft drink

Sucrette® [sykrɛt] **NF** (artificial) sweetener

sucrier, -ère [sykrije, -ɛr] **ADJ** *(industrie, betterave)* sugar *(avant n)*; *(région)* sugar-producing
NM 1 *(pot)* sugar basin *or* bowl; **s. verseur** sugar shaker **2** *(producteur)* sugar producer

sud [syd] **NM INV 1** *(point cardinal)* south; **au s.** in the south; **où est le s.?** which way is south?; **la partie la plus au s. de l'île** the southernmost part of the island; **le vent vient du s.** it's a south *or* southerly wind, the wind is coming from the south; **un vent du s.** a southerly wind; **le vent du s.** the south wind; **aller au** *ou* **vers le s.** to go south *or* southwards; **les trains qui vont vers le s.** trains going south, southbound trains; **rouler vers le s.** to drive south *or* southwards; **aller droit vers le s.** to head due south; **la cuisine est plein s.** *ou* **exposée au s.** the kitchen faces due south *or Sout* has a southerly aspect **2** *(partie d'un pays, d'un continent)* south, southern area *or* regions; *(partie d'une ville)* south; **le s. de l'Italie** southern Italy, the south of Italy; **elle habite dans le S.** she lives in the South; **il habite dans le s. de Paris** he lives in the south of Paris; **elle est du S.** she's from the south
ADJ INV south *(avant n)*, southern; (▸ *côte, face*) south; (▸ *banlieue, partie, région*) southern; **la façade s. d'un immeuble** the south-facing wall of a building; **la chambre est côté s.** the bedroom faces south; **dans la partie s. de la France** in the South of France, in southern France; **suivre la direction s.** to head *or* to go southward
• **Sud ADJ INV** South; **le Pacifique S.** the South Pacific **NM** *Géog* **le S.** the South
• **au sud de PRÉP** (to the) south of; **il habite au s. de Paris** he lives to the south of Paris

sud-africain, -e [sydafrikɛ̃, -ɛn] *(mpl* **sud-africains,** *fpl* **sud-africaines)** **ADJ** South African
• **Sud-Africain, -e NM,F** South African

sud-américain, -e [sydamerikɛ̃, -ɛn] *(mpl* **sud-américains,** *fpl* **sud-américaines)** **ADJ** South American
• **Sud-Américain, -e NM,F** South American

sudation [sydasjɔ̃] **NF** sweating, *Spéc* sudation

sud-coréen, -enne [sydkɔreɛ̃, -ɛn] *(mpl* **sud-coréens,** *fpl* **sud-coréennes)** **ADJ** South Korean
• **Sud-Coréen, -enne NM,F** South Korean

sud-est [sydɛst] **ADJ INV** south-east *(avant n)*
NM INV 1 *(point cardinal)* south-east; **au s. de Lyon** south-east of Lyons; **vent de s.** south-east *or* south-easterly wind **2** *Géog* **le S. asiatique** South East Asia

sudiste [sydist] *Hist* **ADJ** Confederate
NMF Confederate

sudoku [sudoku] **NM** sudoku

sudorifère [sydɔrifɛr] **ADJ** sudoriferous; **glande s.** sweat gland

sudorifique [sydɔrifik] **ADJ** sudorific
NM sudorific

sudoripare [sydɔripar] = **sudorifère**

sud-ouest [sydwɛst] **ADJ INV** south-west *(avant n)*
NM INV south-west; **au s. de Tokyo** south-west of Tokyo; **vent de s.** south-west *or* south-westerly wind
• **Sud-Ouest NM** *Hist* **le S. africain** South West Africa

sud-sud-est [sydsydɛst] **ADJ INV** south-south-east *(avant n)*
NM INV south-south-east

sud-sud-ouest [sydsydwɛst] **ADJ INV** south-south-west *(avant n)*
NM INV south-south-west

sud-vietnamien, -enne [sydvjɛtnamjɛ̃,-ɛn] *(mpl* **sud-vietnamiens,** *fpl* **sud-vietnamiennes)** **ADJ** South Vietnamese
NM,F South Vietnamese

Suède [sɥɛd] **NF la S.** Sweden

suédé, -e [sɥede] **ADJ** imitation suede
NM suede cloth, imitation suede

suédine [sɥedin] **NF** suedette

suédois, -e [sɥedwa, -az] **ADJ** Swedish
NM *(langue)* Swedish
• **Suédois, -e NM,F** Swede; **les S.** the Swedish

suée [sɥe] **NF** *Fam (transpiration)* sweat▫; **attraper** *ou* **prendre une (bonne) s.** *(en faisant un effort)* to work up quite a sweat; **j'en ai encore des suées** I still break out in a cold sweat when I think about it

suer [7] [sɥe] **VI 1** *(transpirer* ▸ *personne)* to sweat, to get sweaty; **s. à grosses gouttes** to be pouring with sweat, to be sweating profusely
2 *(bois, plâtres)* to ooze, to sweat; *Culin* **faire s. des oignons** to sweat onions
3 *Fam (fournir un gros effort)* to slave (away), *Br* to slog; **j'en ai sué pour faire démarrer la tondeuse!** I had the devil's own job trying to get the mower started!; *Fam* **faire s. le burnous** to be a real slave-driver
4 *Fam (locutions)* **faire s. qn** *(l'embêter)* to bug sb, *Br* to get up sb's nose; **il nous fait s.!** he's a pain in the neck!; **ça me ferait s. de devoir y retourner** I'd hate to have to go back there; **elle m'a fait s. toute la matinée pour que je joue avec elle** she pestered me all morning to play with her; **se faire s.** *(s'ennuyer)* to get bored stiff *or* to death
VT 1 *(sueur)* to sweat; **s. sang et eau** *(faire de grands efforts)* to sweat blood **2** *(humidité)* to ooze **3** *Littéraire (laisser paraître* ▸ *bêtise, ennui, égoïsme)* to exude, to reek of

sueur [sɥœr] **NF 1** *(transpiration)* sweat; **sa chemise était mouillée par la s.** his/her shirt was sweaty *or* was damp with sweat; **être en s.** to be in a sweat, to be sweating; **j'en ai eu des sueurs froides** I was in a cold sweat; **donner des sueurs froides à qn** to put sb in a cold sweat **2** *(effort intense)* sweat; **vivre de la s. du peuple** to live off the sweat of the people; **à la s. de son front** by the sweat of one's brow

Suez [sɥez] **NM** Suez

suffire [100] [syfir] **VI 1** *(en quantité)* to be enough, to be sufficient, *Sout* to suffice; **quelques gouttes suffisent** a few drops are enough *or* sufficient; **deux bouteilles pour cinq, ça ne suffira pas** two bottles for five people won't be enough; **une cuillerée, ça te suffit?** is one spoonful enough for you?; **mon salaire ne nous suffit plus** we can no longer survive on my salary; **une heure me suffira pour tout ranger** one hour will be enough for me to put everything away; **je ne lui rendrai plus service, cette expérience m'a suffi** I won't help him/her again, I've learned my lesson; **il faut doubler l'effectif – le budget n'y suffira jamais** the staff has to be doubled – the budget won't cover it **2** *(en qualité)* to be (good) enough; **ma parole devrait vous s.** my word should be good enough for you; **l'amitié ne lui suffisait pas** he/she wanted more than friendship; **s. aux besoins de qn** to meet sb's needs **3** *(tournure impersonnelle)* **je n'avais jamais volé – il suffit d'une fois!** I've never stolen before – once is enough!; **il suffit d'une heure pour tout nettoyer** it only takes an hour to clean everything; **il suffit d'une erreur pour que tout soit à recommencer** one single mistake means starting all over again; **il a suffi de quelques mots pour le persuader** a few words were enough to persuade him; **il suffirait de peu pour que le régime s'écroule** it wouldn't take much to bring down the regime; **il suffit de l'écouter parler deux minutes pour saisir sa personnalité** you only have to listen to him/her for two minutes to know what sort of person he/she is; **s'il suffisait de travailler pour réussir!** if only work was enough to guarantee success!; **il suffit qu'on me dise ce que je dois faire** I just have *or* need to be told what to do; **il suffisait que tu passes un coup de téléphone** all you had to do was phone; **il suffit que je tourne le dos pour qu'elle fasse des bêtises** I only have to turn my back and she's up to some mischief; *Fam* **ça suffit!** (that's) enough!; **ça suffit comme ça!** that's enough now!
VPR se suffire 1 *(emploi réciproque)* **ils se suffisent l'un à l'autre** they've got each other and that's all they need **2 se s. à soi-même** *(matériellement)* to be self-sufficient; *(moralement)* to be quite happy with one's own company

suffisamment [syfizamɑ̃] **ADV** sufficiently, enough; **le travail n'est pas s. rémunéré** the work isn't sufficiently well paid, the pay isn't adequate; **je t'ai s. prévenu** I've warned you often enough; **s. de** enough; **il n'y a pas s. de couverts pour tout le monde** there aren't enough places set for all these people

suffisance [syfizɑ̃s] **NF 1** *(vanité)* self-importance, conceit; **c'est un homme plein de s.** he's very self-important **2** *Littéraire* **avoir sa s. de qch, avoir qch à s.** to have plenty of sth; **manger à sa s.** to eat one's fill; **de l'argent en s.** plenty of *or* sufficient money

suffisant, -e [syfizɑ̃, -ɑ̃t] **ADJ 1** *(en quantité)* sufficient; **ma retraite est suffisante pour deux** my pension's sufficient *or* enough for two; **trois bouteilles pour cinq, c'est amplement s.** three bottles for five, that's plenty *or* that's quite enough **2** *(en qualité)* sufficient, good enough; **des excuses ne seront pas suffisantes, il veut un démenti** apologies won't be sufficient *or* won't do, he wants a denial; **tes résultats à l'école sont tout juste suffisants** your school results are just about satisfactory; **c'est une raison suffisante pour qu'il accepte** it's a good enough reason *or* it's reason enough to make him accept **3** *(arrogant* ▸ *air, personne)* self-important, conceited; **d'un air s.** smugly
NM,F faire le s. to give oneself airs

suffisons *etc voir* **suffire**

suffixe [syfiks] **NM** suffix

suffixer [3] [syfikse] **VT** to suffix; **mot suffixé** word with a *or* that has a suffix

suffocant, -e [syfɔkɑ̃, -ɑ̃t] **ADJ 1** *(atmosphère, chaleur, odeur)* suffocating, stifling **2** *(ahurissant)* astounding, staggering, stunning

suffocation [syfɔkasjɔ̃] **NF** suffocation; **j'ai des suffocations** I feel as if I am choking

suffoquer [3] [syfɔke] **VI** *(étouffer)* to suffocate, to choke; **on suffoque ici!** it's stifling in here!; **s. de colère** to be choking with anger; **s. de joie** to be overcome with happiness
VT 1 *(sujet: atmosphère, fumée, odeur)* to suffocate, to choke; **la chaleur nous suffoquait** the heat was suffocating, it was stiflingly hot; **le fou rire la suffoquait** she was choking with laughter
2 *(causer une vive émotion à)* to choke; **la colère le suffoquait** he was choking with anger
3 *(ahurir* ▸ *sujet: attitude, prix)* to stagger, to stun, to confound; **ma réponse l'avait suffoqué** my answer left him speechless *or* fairly took his breath away
4 *Arch (tuer)* to suffocate

suffragant [syfragɑ̃] *Rel* **ADJ M** suffragan
NM suffragan (bishop)

suffrage [syfraʒ] **NM 1** *Pol (système)* suffrage; *Hist* **s. censitaire** suffrage with property qualification *or* for householders (only); **s. restreint** restricted suffrage; **s. universel (direct/indirect)** (direct/indirect) universal suffrage; **être élu au s. direct/indirect** to be elected by direct/indirect suffrage **2** *(voix)* vote; **obtenir beaucoup/peu de suffrages** to poll heavily/badly; **c'est leur parti qui a eu le plus de suffrages** their party headed the poll **3** *Littéraire (approbation)* approval, approbation; **avoir le s. de qn** to win sb's approval; **sa dernière pièce a remporté tous les suffrages** his last play was an unqualified success

suffragette [syfraʒɛt] **NF** suffragette

suffusion [syfyzjɔ̃] **NF** *Méd* suffusion

suggérer [18] [sygʒere] **VT 1** *(conseiller, proposer* ▸ *acte)* to suggest; (▸ *nom, solution)* to suggest, to put forward, to propose; **nous lui avons suggéré de renoncer** we suggested he/she should give up; **je suggère que nous partions tout de suite** I suggest that we go right away **2** *(évoquer)* to suggest, to evoke; **que vous suggèrent ces images?** what do these pictures suggest to you?

suggestibilité [sygʒɛstibilite] **NF** suggestibility

suggestible [sygʒɛstibl] **ADJ** suggestible

suggestif, -ive [sygʒɛstif, -iv] **ADJ 1** *(évocateur)* suggestive, evocative; **de façon suggestive** suggestively **2** *(érotique* ▸ *pose)* suggestive, provocative; *(décolleté)* revealing, plunging

suggestion [sygʒɛstjɔ̃] **NF 1** *(conseil, proposition)* suggestion; **faire une s.** to make a suggestion **2** *Psy* suggestion **3** *(influence)* suggestion, incitement; *Littéraire* **les suggestions du démon** the suggestions of the Evil One

suggestionner [3] [sygʒɛstjɔne] **VT s. qn** to put an idea/ideas into sb's head; **elle s'est laissé s. par lui** she allowed him to put ideas into her head

suggestive [sydʒɛstiv] *voir* **suggestif**

suicidaire [sɥisidɛr] **ADJ 1** *(instinct, personne, tendance)* suicidal **2** *(qui conduit à l'échec)* suicidal; **de si gros investissements, ce serait s.!** such large investments would be suicidal *or* courting disaster!

NMF suicidal person, potential suicide

suicide [sɥisid] **NM 1** *(mort)* suicide; **faire une tentative de s.** to try to commit suicide, to attempt suicide; **s. assisté** assisted suicide **2** *(désastre)* suicide; **ce serait un s. politique** it would be political suicide; *Fig* **n'y va pas, c'est du s.!** don't go, it would be madness *or* it's suicide!

ADJ INV suicide *(avant n)*; **une mission s.** a suicide mission

suicidé, -e [sɥiside] **ADJ** who has committed suicide

NM,F suicide

suicider [3] [sɥiside] **se suicider VPR 1** *(se tuer)* to commit suicide, to kill oneself; **tenter de se s.** to attempt suicide, to try to commit suicide **2** *Fig (causer sa propre perte)* to commit suicide

suie [sɥi] **NF** soot; **être couvert** *ou* **noir de s.** to be all sooty *or* black with soot

suif [sɥif] **NM 1** *(de bétail)* fat; *Culin* suet; *(pour chandelles)* tallow **2** *Fam (bagarre)* **chercher du s. à qn** to try to pick a fight with sb; **faire du s.** to kick up a fuss; **il va y avoir du s.** there's going to be a scrap

suiffer [3] [sɥife] **VT** *(cuir)* to tallow; *(gond)* to grease

sui generis [sɥiʒeneris] **ADJ INV** sui generis, unique; *Euph* **une odeur s.** a rather distinctive smell

suint [sɥɛ̃] **NM** suint

suintant, -e [sɥɛ̃tɑ̃, -ɑ̃t] **ADJ** *(gén)* sweating, oozing; *(plaie)* running, weeping; **des murs suintants** damp walls

suintement [sɥɛ̃tmɑ̃] **NM 1** *(écoulement ▸ gén)* sweating *(UNCOUNT)*, oozing *(UNCOUNT)*; *(▸ de blessure)* running *(UNCOUNT)*, weeping *(UNCOUNT)* **2** *Pétr* oozing (forth) *(UNCOUNT)*

suinter [3] [sɥɛ̃te] **VI 1** *(s'écouler)* to ooze, to seep; **l'humidité suinte des murailles** the walls are dripping with moisture **2** *(laisser échapper un liquide ▸ plaie)* to weep; **ce mur suinte** this wall is running with moisture **3** *Littéraire (se manifester)* to ooze; **l'ennui suinte dans cette petite ville** this little town has a pervasive atmosphere of boredom

VT *Littéraire (l'ennui, la haine)* to ooze

suis 1 *voir* **être**[1] **2** *voir* **suivre**

Suisse [sɥis] **NF la S.** Switzerland; **la S. allemande** *ou* **alémanique/romande** the German-speaking/French-speaking part of Switzerland

suisse [sɥis] **ADJ** Swiss; **s. allemand/romand** Swiss German/French

NM 1 *(au Vatican)* Swiss guard **2** *(bedeau)* beadle **3** *Can* chipmunk

• **Suisse NMF** Swiss (person); **S. allemand/romand** German-speaking/French-speaking Swiss; **les Suisses** the Swiss

• **en suisse ADV boire/manger en s.** to drink/to eat on one's own

Suissesse [sɥisɛs] **NF** Swiss woman

suit *etc voir* **suivre**

SUITE [sɥit]

• continuation **1**	• sequel **1**
• follow-up **1**	• series **2**
• retinue **3**	• suite **4**
• consequence **5**	• coherence **6**

NF 1 *(prolongation ▸ gén)* continuation; *(▸ d'un film, d'un roman)* sequel; *(▸ d'une émission)* follow-up; **elle a écrit une s. à 'Autant en emporte le vent'** she wrote a sequel to 'Gone with the Wind'; **s. page 17** continued on page 17; **la s. au prochain numéro** to be continued (in our next issue); **ceci n'est qu'un préambule, lis la s.** *(le reste)* this is just a preamble, read what comes afterwards; **s. et fin** final instalment; **apportez-moi la s.** *(pendant un repas)* bring me the next course; **écoute la s.** *(du discours)* listen to what comes next; *(de mon histoire)* listen to what happened next; **je n'ai pas pu entendre la s.** I couldn't hear the rest; **attendons la s. des événements** let's wait to see what happens next; **faire s. à** to follow; **de violents orages ont fait s. à la sécheresse** the drought was followed by violent storms; **prendre la s. de qn** to take over from sb, to succeed sb

2 *(série)* series, succession; **une s. de malheurs** a run *or* series of misfortunes

3 *(cortège)* retinue

4 *(dans un hôtel)* suite; **la s. présidentielle/royale** the presidential/royal suite

5 *(répercussion)* consequence; **la s. logique/naturelle de mon adhésion au parti** the logical/natural consequence of my joining the party; **donner s. à qch** *(lettre, réclamation)* to follow sth up; *(commande)* to deal with sth; *(projet)* to carry on with sth; **avoir des suites** to have repercussions; **elle est morte des suites de ses blessures** she died as a result of her injuries

6 *(lien logique)* coherence; **ses propos n'avaient guère de s.** what he/she said wasn't very logical; **avoir de la s. dans les idées** to be coherent *or* consistent; *Hum* **tu as de la s. dans les idées!** you certainly know what you want!

7 *Jur* pursuit; **droit de s.** *(d'un belligérant)* right of (hot) pursuit; *(d'un créancier)* right to follow property

8 *Ling & Math* sequence

9 *Mus* suite

• **à la suite ADV 1** *(en succession)* one after the other; **nous avons fait plusieurs voyages à la s.** we made several trips one after the other **2** *(après)* **un nom avec plusieurs chiffres inscrits à la s.** a name followed by a string of numbers

• **à la suite de PRÉP 1** *(derrière ▸ dans l'espace)* behind; *(▸ dans un écrit)* after; **il entra et nous à sa s.** he went in and we followed; **cinq chambres les unes à la s. des autres** five rooms in a row **2** *(à cause de)* following; **à la s. de son discours télévisé, sa cote a remonté** following his/her speech on TV, his/her popularity rating went up

• **de suite ADV 1** *Fam (immédiatement)* straightaway, right away; **il revient de s.** he'll be right back **2** *(à la file)* in a row, one after the other, in succession; **il a mangé dix œufs durs de s.** he ate ten hard-boiled eggs in a row; **elle est restée de garde 48 heures de s.** she was on duty for 48 hours solid; **on n'a pas eu d'électricité pendant cinq jours de s.** we didn't have any electricity for five whole days *or* five days running

• **par la suite ADV** *(dans le passé)* afterwards, later; *(dans le futur)* later; **il se l'est beaucoup reproché par la s.** he very much blamed himself for it afterwards *or* later; **ils se sont mariés par la s.** they eventually got married

• **par suite ADV** therefore

• **par suite de PRÉP** due to, owing to; **par s. d'un arrêt de travail des techniciens** due to industrial action by technical staff

• **sans suite ADJ 1** *(incohérent)* disconnected; **il tenait des propos sans s.** his talk was incoherent **2** *Com (article)* discontinued

• **suite à PRÉP** *Admin* **s. à votre lettre** further to *or* in response to *or* with reference to your letter; **s. à votre appel téléphonique** further to your phone call

suivait *etc voir* **suivre**

suivant[1] [sɥivɑ̃] **PRÉP 1** *(d'après)* according to; **s. son habitude, elle s'est levée très tôt** as is her habit *or Sout* wont, she got up very early; **s. leurs indications, ça devrait être à gauche** according to their directions, it should be on the left; **s. vos instructions** *(dans une lettre)* as per your instructions **2** *(en fonction de)* according to, depending on; **vous donnerez s. vos possibilités** you'll give according to your means; **s. votre âge/vos besoins** depending on your age/your needs; **cela varie s. le jour/la température** it varies from day to day/with the temperature **3** *(le long de)* **découper s. le pointillé** cut along the dotted line

• **en suivant ADV** *Belg (d'affilée ▸ gén)* in a row; *(▸ dans le temps)* at a stretch

• **suivant que CONJ** according to whether; **s. que vous parlez avec l'un ou l'autre** according to which one you talk to

suivant[2]**, -e** [sɥivɑ̃, ɑ̃t] **ADJ 1** *(qui vient après ▸ chapitre, mois, semaine)* following, next; *(▸ échelon, train)* next; **les trois jours suivants** the next three days; **quel est le chiffre s.?** what's the next number?, what number comes next? **2** *(pour introduire)* following; **il m'a raconté l'histoire suivante** he told me the following story; **procédez de la manière suivante** follow these instructions

NM,F 1 *(dans une succession)* next one; **(au) s., s'il vous plaît** next, please; **son premier roman, et même les suivants** his/her first novel and even the following ones *or* the ones that followed; **pas mardi prochain mais le s.** not this coming Tuesday but the next one *or* the one after; **voir page 6 et suivantes** see page 6 and following *or Sout* et seq **2** *(pour introduire)* **la raison est la suivante** here is why; **les résultats sont les suivants** here are the results, the results are as follows **3** *Mktg* follower; *(sur le marché)* market follower; **s. immédiat** early follower

NM *(membre d'une escorte)* attendant

• **suivante NF** *Théât* lady's maid

suiveur, -euse [sɥivœr, -øz] **ADJ voiture suiveuse** = car following a cycle race

NM 1 *(de femmes ▸ gén)* skirt-chaser; *(▸ en voiture)* kerb-crawler

2 *Mktg* follower; *(sur le marché)* market follower

3 *Sport* **les suiveurs** = officials and back-up squads following a cycle race

4 *(inconditionnel, imitateur)* slave, uncritical follower

suivi, -e [sɥivi] **PP** *voir* **suivre**

ADJ 1 *(ininterrompu ▸ effort)* sustained, consistent; *(▸ correspondance)* regular; *(▸ qualité)* consistent; *(▸ activité)* steady; *Com (▸ demande)* steady, persistent; **nous avons eu une correspondance très suivie pendant des années** we wrote to each other very regularly for years; *Com* **article s.** stock item **2** *(logique ▸ propos, raisonnement)* coherent; *(▸ politique)* consistent **3** *(qui a la faveur du public)* **mode/émission très suivie** very popular fashion/programme; **conférence peu/très suivie** poorly attended/well-attended conference; **la grève a été peu/très suivie** there was little/a lot of support for the strike

NM *(d'un cas, d'un dossier)* follow-up; **assurer le s. de qch** *(cas, dossier)* to follow sth through; *(commande)* to deal with sth; *Com (article)* to continue to stock sth; **je m'occuperai personnellement du s. de votre dossier** I'll deal with your case personally; *Jur* **s. socio-judiciaire** = social and judicial supervision of sex offenders following release from custody

suivisme [sɥivism] **NM** *(attitude d'imitation servile)* herd instinct

SUIVRE [89] [sɥivr]

VT	
• to follow **A1–3, B1, 4, C1, 3**	• to come after **A2, 3**
• to walk/drive/sail along **B2**	• to undergo **B3**
• to keep up (with) **C1**	• to comply with **B4**
• to deal with **C4**	• to pay attention to **C2**
• to follow the progress of **C4**	
USAGE ABSOLU	
• to follow suit **4**	
VI	
• to follow **2, 3**	• to keep up (with) **1**
VPR	
• to follow one another **1**	• to be in the right order **2**
• to be coherent **4**	

VT A. *DANS L'ESPACE, LE TEMPS* **1** *(pour escorter, espionner, rattraper)* to follow; **les enfants suivaient leurs parents en courant** the children were running behind their parents; **suivez-moi** follow me; **suivez le guide** this way (for the guided tour), please; **ils sont entrés, suivis de leur chien** they came in followed by their dog; **la police les a suivis sur plusieurs kilomètres** the police chased them for several kilometres; **il l'a fait s. par un détective privé** he had him/her followed by a private detective; **s. qn de près** *(gén)* to follow close behind sb; *(pour le protéger)* to stick close to sb; **le coureur anglais, suivi de très près par le Belge** the English runner, with the Belgian close on his heels; **s. la piste de qn** to follow sb's trail; **s. qn à la trace** to follow sb's tracks; **s. qn comme son ombre** to follow sb like a shadow; **s. qn des yeux** *ou* **du regard** to follow sb with one's eyes; **il suivait des yeux ses moindres gestes** he was watching his/her every move; **certaines personnes, suivez mon regard, n'ont pas fait leur travail** certain people, who shall be *or* remain nameless, haven't done their work

2 *(se dérouler après)* to follow (on from), to come after; **la réunion sera suivie d'une collation** refreshments will be served after the meeting; **pendant l'heure qui a suivi** during the hour that followed; **le jour qui suivit** (the) next day, the following day; **il suit de votre déclaration que le témoin ment** it follows from your statement that the witness is lying

3 *(être placé après)* to follow, to come after; **votre nom suit le mien sur la liste** your name is right after mine on the list; **les conjonctions toujours suivies du subjonctif** the conjunctions always followed by *or* that always govern the subjunctive; **dans les pages qui suivent** in the following pages

B. *ADOPTER, OBÉIR À* **1** *(emprunter ▸ itinéraire, rue)* to follow; **en suivant un long couloir, on arrive au cloître** at the end of a long corridor, one comes to the cloister; **il vous suffit de s. la grande avenue** just follow the main avenue

2 *(longer ▸ à pied)* to walk along; *(▸ en voiture)* to drive along; *(▸ en bateau)* to sail along; **la route suit la rivière sur plusieurs kilomètres** the road runs along *or* follows (the course of) the river for several kilometres; **découper en suivant les pointillés** cut along the dotted line

3 *(se soumettre à ▸ traitement)* to undergo; **s. des cours de cuisine** to attend a cookery course; **s. un régime** to be on a diet

4 *(se conformer à ▸ conseil, personne, instructions)* to follow; *(▸ règlement)* to comply with; **vous n'avez qu'à s. les panneaux** just follow the signs; **son exemple n'est pas à s.** he's/she's not a good example; **je préfère s. mon idée** I prefer to do it my way; *Fam* **s. le mouvement** to go with the flow

5 *Cartes* **je suis** I'm in

6 *Com (stocker)* to stock; *(produire)* to produce

C. 1 *(observer ▸ carrière, progrès, feuilleton)* to follow; *(▸ actualité)* to keep up with; **il suit le feuilleton à la radio tous les jours** he tunes in to the serial every day; **je ne suis pas les sports** I don't follow sport

2 *(se concentrer sur ▸ exposé, messe)* to listen to, to pay attention to; **maintenant, suivez-moi bien** now, listen to me carefully *or* pay close attention; **suis bien mes gestes** watch my gestures closely

3 *(comprendre ▸ explications, raisonnement)* to follow; **il est difficile parfois de le s. dans ses divagations** it's sometimes difficult to follow his train of thought; **je ne te suis plus** I'm not with you any more, I don't follow you

4 *(s'occuper de ▸ dossier, commande)* to deal with; *(▸ élève, patient)* to follow the progress of; **je suis suivie par un très bon médecin** I'm with *or* under a very good doctor

USAGE ABSOLU 1 *(être derrière)* **ils ne suivent plus** they're not behind us any more

2 *(prêter attention)* **encore un qui ne suivait pas!** *(distrait)* so, someone else wasn't paying attention!; **je vais s. avec Pierre** *(sur son livre)* I'll share Pierre's book

3 *(garder le rythme)* **marche moins vite, je ne peux pas s.** slow down, I can't keep up

4 *(faire la même chose)* to follow suit

VI 1 *Scol (assimiler le programme)* to keep up; **il a du mal à s. en physique** he's having difficulty keeping up in physics; **elle suit très bien en classe** *ou* **à l'école** she keeps up well with her schoolwork

2 *(être acheminé après)* **les bagages vont s.** luggage follows; **lettre suit** *(correspondance administrative)* will write soon, letter follows; **faire s.** *(lettre)* to forward, to send on; *(sur enveloppe ou colis)* please forward; **faire s. son courrier** to have one's mail forwarded

3 *(être ci-après)* to follow; **sont reçus les candidats dont les noms suivent** the names of the successful candidates are as follows; **procéder comme suit** proceed as follows

VPR se suivre 1 *(être l'un derrière l'autre ▸ personnes, lettres)* to follow one another; **par temps de brouillard, ne vous suivez pas de trop près** in foggy conditions, keep your distance (from other vehicles); **les trois coureurs se suivent de très près** the three runners are very close behind one another *or* are tightly bunched

2 *(être dans l'ordre ▸ pages)* to be in the right order, to follow on from one another

3 *(se succéder dans le temps) Prov* **les jours se suivent et ne se ressemblent pas** every day is a new dawn

4 *(s'enchaîner logiquement ▸ raisonnement)* to be coherent

• **à suivre ADJ c'est une affaire à s.** it's something we should keep an eye on **ADV** *(dans une série télévisée)* to be continued

sujet, -ette [syʒɛ, -ɛt] **ADJ 1 s. à** *(susceptible de ▸ migraine, attaques)* subject to; **s. au mal de mer** liable to become seasick, prone to seasickness; **s. à des crises de larmes** liable to burst into tears; **nous sommes tous sujets à l'erreur** anyone can make a mistake; **nos prix sont sujets à révision** our prices are subject to revision **2 s. à caution** *(franchise, honnêteté, moralité)* questionable; **leurs informations sont sujettes à caution** their information should be taken warily **3** *Littéraire (assujetti)* subjugated, enslaved; **peuple s. de Rome** people subject to Rome

NM,F *(citoyen)* subject

NM 1 *(thème ▸ d'une discussion)* subject, topic; *(▸ d'une pièce, d'un roman, d'un exposé, d'une recherche)* subject; **le s. de notre débat ce soir est...** the question we'll be debating tonight is...; **quel est le s. du livre?** what's the book about?; **je tiens le s. d'une pièce** I have an idea *or* a subject for a play; **s. de conversation** topic (of conversation); **changeons de s.** let's change the subject; **s. de plainte** grievance; **c'est devenu un s. de plaisanterie** it has become a standing joke; **s. d'examen** examination question

2 *(motif)* **s. de** cause of, ground for, grounds for; **ils ont de nombreux sujets de discorde** they have many reasons to disagree; **leur salaire est leur principal s. de mécontentement** the main cause of their dissatisfaction is their salary; **sa santé est devenue un gros s. de préoccupation** his/her condition is now giving serious grounds for concern *or* has become a great source of anxiety; **tu n'as pas s. de te plaindre** you have no cause *or* grounds for complaint

3 *Beaux-Arts & Mus* subject

4 *(individu)* **mauvais s.** bad lot, ne'er-do-well; **brillant s.** *(élève)* brilliant pupil

5 *(figurine)* figurine; **des petits sujets en porcelaine** little china figures *or* figurines

6 *Gram (fonction)* subject; *Ling* **le s. parlant** the speaker

7 *Méd, Phil & Psy* subject; **s. d'expérience** experimental subject

8 *Jur* **s. de droit** possessor of a right

9 *Hort* stock

• **au sujet de PRÉP** about, concerning; **c'est au s. de Martha?** is it about Martha?; **j'aimerais vous faire remarquer, à ce s., que...** concerning this matter, I'd like to point out to you that...; **je voudrais parler au directeur – c'est à quel s.?** I'd like to talk to the manager – what is it about?

sujétion [syʒesjɔ̃] **NF 1** *Pol (d'un peuple)* subjection, enslavement (**à** to); **vivre dans la s.** to live in subjection; **tenir en s.** to hold *or* to have in one's power **2** *(à une règle)* subjection, subjecting *(UNCOUNT)* (**à** to); **une habitude devient vite une s.** we soon become slaves to a habit **3** *(contrainte)* constraint; **c'est une vraie s. d'avoir des animaux domestiques** having pets is a real tie

sulfamide [sylfamid] **NM** *Pharm* sulphonamide

sulfatage [sylfataʒ] **NM** *Agr* copper sulphate treatment

sulfate [sylfat] **NM** *Chim* sulphate

sulfaté, -e [sylfate] **ADJ 1** *Chim* sulphated, sulphate *(avant n)* **2** *Agr* treated with copper sulphate

sulfater [3] [sylfate] **VT 1** *Agr* to treat with copper sulphate **2** *Élec* to sulphate

sulfateur, -euse [sylfatœr, -øz] **NM,F** *Agr* = person who treats vines with copper sulphate

• **sulfateuse NF 1** *Agr* copper sulphate sprayer **2** *très Fam (mitrailleuse)* submachine *or* machine gun, *Br* typewriter

sulfhydrique [sylfidrik] **ADJ M** *Chim* **acide s.** hydrogen sulphide

sulfite [sylfit] **NM** *Chim* sulphite

sulfurage [sylfyraʒ] **NM** *Agr* sulphuration

sulfuration [sylfyrasjɔ̃] **NF** *Chim* sulphuration

sulfure [sylfyr] **NM** *Chim* sulphide; **s. de fer** iron pyrites

sulfuré, -e [sylfyre] **ADJ** *Chim* sulphuretted; **hydrogène s.** hydrogen sulphide

sulfurer [3] [sylfyre] **VT 1** *Chim* to sulphuret, to sulphurate **2** *Agr* to treat with sulphide

sulfureux, -euse [sylfyrø, -øz] **ADJ 1** *Chim* sulphurous; *(eau, source)* sulphur *(avant n)* **2** *Fig (charme)* fiendish, infernal; *(écrit, discours, thèse)* heretical, subversive; **il a toujours eu une réputation sulfureuse** there's always been a whiff of scandal *or* of sulphur about him

sulfurique [sylfyrik] **ADJ** *Chim* sulphuric

sulfurisé, -e [sylfyrize] **ADJ** *Chim* sulphurized; **papier s.** *Br* greaseproof *or Spéc* sulphurized paper, *Am* sulfurized paper

sulky [sylki] **NM** sulky

sultan [syltɑ̃] **NM** sultan

sultanat [syltana] **NM** sultanate

sultane [syltan] **NF 1** *(titre)* sultana, sultaness **2** *(canapé)* sultana

sumac [symak] **NM** *Bot* sumach (tree)

sumérien, -enne [symerjɛ̃, -ɛn] **ADJ** Sumerian

NM *(langue)* Sumerian

• **Sumérien, -enne NM,F** Sumerian

summum [sɔmɔm] **NM 1** *(d'une carrière)* peak, *Sout* zenith; *(d'une civilisation)* highest point; *(de l'élégance, du luxe, de l'arrogance)* height; **au s. de sa puissance** at the peak of its power; **elle était au s. de son art quand elle peignit ce tableau** her talent was at its peak *or* height when she painted this picture **2** *Fam (locution)* **c'est le s.!** *(on ne peut faire mieux)* it's the tops!; *(on ne peut faire pire)* it's the pits!

sumo [symo, sumo] **NM** sumo (wrestling); **lutteur de s.** sumo wrestler

sunlight [sœnlajt] **NM** *Cin* (artificial) sunlight

sunnite [synit] **ADJ** Sunni

NMF Sunnit, Sunnite

sup [syp] **ADJ INV** *Fam* **faire des heures s.** to work overtime

super [sypɛr] *Fam* **ADJ INV** great, terrific, fantastic; **ce serait s. si tu pouvais venir!** it'd be great if you could come!; **s. mardi** super Tuesday, = the first Tuesday in March, the most important day for primary elections in the United States

ADV *(compliqué, bon, cher, propre, gentil) Br* dead, *Am* real; **un bouquin s. chiant** a *Br* dead *or Am* real boring book; **elle est s. organisée** she's incredibly well-organized; **on s'est s. bien marrés** we had a great time

EXCLAM great!, terrific!

NM *(essence) Br* four-star (petrol), *Am* premium

NF *Belg (essence) Br* four-star (petrol), *Am* premium

super- [sypɛr] **PRÉF 1** *(en intensif)* super; **des collants super-fins** extra-sheer tights; **super-rapide** superfast **2** *Fam (exceptionnel)* super; **super-flic** supercop; **une super-voiture** a supercar; **un super-cerveau** a superbrain

super-8 [sypɛrɥit] **ADJ** *Cin & TV* Super 8

superaliment [syperalimɑ̃] **NM** superfood

superbe [sypɛrb] **ADJ 1** *(magnifique ▸ yeux, bijou, ville)* superb, beautiful, magnificent; *(▸ bébé, femme)* beautiful, gorgeous; *(▸ homme)* good-looking, handsome; *(▸ voix)* superb, beautiful; *(▸ journée)* glorious, beautiful; *(▸ temps)* wonderful; **tu as une mine s. aujourd'hui** you look radiant today; **il a fait un temps s.** the weather was wonderful **2 s. de** *(sublime)* superbly; **il a été s. de cynisme/d'indifférence** he was superbly cynical/indifferent **3** *Littéraire (altier ▸ air)* haughty

NF *Littéraire* haughtiness

superbement [syperbəmɑ̃] ADV **1** *(splendidement)* superbly, magnificently, beautifully **2** *Littéraire (arrogamment)* arrogantly, haughtily

superbénéfice [syperbenefis] NM excess profit, surplus profit

supercagnotte [syperkaɲɔt] NF superjackpot *(in the "Loto")*

supercar [syperkar] NF supercar

supercarburant [syperkarbyrɑ̃] NM *Br* fourstar *or* high-octane petrol, *Am* premium

supercherie [syperʃəri] NF hoax

superdividende [syperdividɑ̃d] NM *Fin* surplus dividend

supérette [syperɛt] NF mini-market, *Am* superette

superfétation [syperfetasjɔ̃] NF *Littéraire* superfluity, redundancy, supererogation; **ce serait une s. de...** it would be superfluous *or* supererogatory to...

superfétatoire [syperfetatwar] ADJ *Littéraire* superfluous, unnecessary, redundant

superficialité [syperfisjalite] NF superficiality

superficie [syperfisi] NF **1** *(d'un champ)* acreage, area; *(d'une maison)* surface area, floor space; **l'entrepôt fait 3000m² de s.** the warehouse has a surface area of 3,000m² **2** *Littéraire (apparence)* superficial *or* external appearance; **s'arrêter à la s. des choses** to do no more than skim the surface of things; **il ne connaît le problème qu'en s.** he has only a superficial knowledge of the problem **3** *Agr* **s. agricole utile** *ou* **utilisée** utilized agricultural area

superficiel, -elle [syperfisjɛl] ADJ **1** *(brûlure)* superficial, surface *(avant n)*; *Géog* **eau superficielle** surface water **2** *(connaissances, personne)* shallow, insubstantial; *(étude, travail)* superficial, perfunctory; *(contrôle)* superficial, cursory

superficiellement [syperfisjɛlmɑ̃] ADV **1** *(blesser)* superficially **2** *(inspecter, corriger)* cursorily, superficially; **répondre s.** to give a superficial answer

superfin, -e [syperfɛ̃, -in] ADJ *(produit)* top-quality, of superior quality; *(qualité)* superior

superflu, -e [syperfly] ADJ **1** *(non nécessaire ▸ biens, excuse, recommandation)* superfluous, unnecessary **2** *(en trop ▸ détails, exemple)* redundant, superfluous; **un grand lessivage ne serait pas s.** a good scrub wouldn't do any harm *or* wouldn't go amiss; **pour vous débarrasser de vos kilos/poils superflus** to get rid of that excess weight/unwanted hair

NM **le s.** = that which is superfluous; **se passer du s.** to do without non-essentials

superfluité [syperflyite] NF *Littéraire* superfluity

super-g [syperʒe] NM INV *Ski* super-g

super-géant [syperʒeɑ̃] *(pl* **super-géants***)* NM *Ski* super-giant (slalom)

supergéante [syperʒeɑ̃t] NF *Astron* supergiant

supergrand [sypergrɑ̃] NM *Fam* superpower

super-huit [syperɥit] ADJ INV super eight

NM INV *(format)* super eight; *(caméra)* super-eight (film) camera

supérieur, -e [syperjœr] ADJ **1** *(plus haut que le reste ▸ étagère, étage)* upper, top; *(▸ ligne)* top; *(juste au-dessus ▸ étagère, ligne)* above; **le bord s. droit de la page** the top right-hand corner of the page; **le cours s. d'un fleuve** the upper reaches of a river; **la partie supérieure de l'immeuble** the top *or* upper part of the building; **les jouets sont à l'étage s.** toys are on the next floor *or* the floor above

2 *(quantitativement ▸ efficacité)* higher, greater (**à** than); *(▸ prix, rendement, vitesse)* higher (**à** than); *(▸ volume)* bigger, greater (**à** than); **j'ai fait une offre supérieure** I bid more *or* made a higher bid; **troupes supérieures en nombre** troops superior in number; **leurs joueurs se retrouvent maintenant supérieurs en nombre** their players now outnumber the opposition; **donne-moi un chiffre s. à huit** give me a number higher than eight; **taux légèrement s. à huit pour cent** rate slightly over eight percent; **une note supérieure à 10** a mark above 10; **d'une longueur/largeur supérieure à...** longer/wider than...; **il est d'une taille supérieure à la moyenne** he's taller than average

3 *(au sommet de la hiérarchie ▸ échelons)* upper, topmost; *(▸ classes sociales)* upper; *(▸ enseignement)* higher; *(juste au-dessus ▸ niveau)* next; *(▸ grade, rang)* senior; **les autorités supérieures** the powers above; *Scol* **passer dans la classe supérieure** to move up one class

4 *(dans une échelle de valeurs ▸ intelligence, esprit, être)* superior; *(▸ intérêts)* higher; *(▸ produit, marchandises)* of superior quality, top-quality; **de qualité supérieure** of superior quality, top-quality; **intelligence supérieure à la moyenne** above-average intelligence; **leur lessive est-elle vraiment supérieure à toutes les autres?** is their washing powder really better than all the others?; *Sport* **il est techniquement s. au Suédois** his technique is superior to *or* better than that of the Swedish player; **il se croit s. à tout le monde** he thinks he's above everyone else, he thinks he's superior; **se montrer s. aux événements** to rise above events

5 *(hautain ▸ air, ton)* superior; **ne prends pas cet air s.!** don't look so superior!

6 *Anat (membre, mâchoire)* upper

7 *Astron (planète)* superior

8 *Biol (animal, espèce, végétal)* higher

9 *Géog (en amont)* upper

10 *Math* superior; **s. ou égal à** superior or equal to, greater than or equal to

11 *Rel* **le Père s.** the father superior; **la Mère supérieure** the mother superior

NM,F *(dans une hiérarchie)* **s. (hiérarchique)** superior

NM *Univ* **le s.** higher education

• **Supérieur, -e** NM,F *Rel* father, *f* mother superior ADJ **le lac S.** Lake Superior

supérieurement [syperjœrmɑ̃] ADV exceptionally; **elle est s. douée** she's exceptionally gifted

supériorité [syperjɔrite] NF **1** *(en qualité)* superiority; **ils vantent la s. des transports en commun** they praise the superiority of public transport; **c'est indubitablement une s. que vous avez sur elle** that's definitely one area where you're better than she is **2** *(en quantité)* superiority; **s. militaire** military superiority; **s. numérique** superiority in numbers **3** *(arrogance)* patronizing attitude, superiority; **un air de s.** a superior air

superlatif, -ive [syperlatif, -iv] ADJ superlative

NM *Ling* superlative; **s. relatif/absolu** relative/absolute superlative

• **au superlatif** ADV **1** *Ling* in the superlative **2** *(très)* extremely; **il est paresseux au s.** he's extremely lazy

superlativement [syperlativmɑ̃] ADV *Fam Vieilli* superlatively

superléger [syperleʒe] NM *Boxe* light welterweight

superlourd [syperlur] NM *Boxe* super heavyweight

superman [syperman] *(pl* **supermans** *ou* **supermen** [-mɛn]*)* NM *Fam* superman; **jouer les supermen** to play at being superman

supermarché [sypermarʃe] NM supermarket

supernova [sypernɔva] *(pl* **-ae***)* NF *Astron* supernova

superordinateur [syperɔrdinatœr] NM supercomputer

superpétrolier [syperpetrɔlje] NM supertanker

superphosphate [syperfɔsfat] NM superphosphate

superposable [syperpozabl] ADJ **1** *Géom* superposable **2** *(chaise, lit)* stacking *(avant n)*

superposé, -e [syperpoze] ADJ *(images)* superimposed; **des couches superposées de chocolat et de chantilly** layers of chocolate and whipped cream one on top of the other; **lits superposés** bunk beds, bunks

superposer [3] [syperpoze] VT **1** *(meubles)* to stack (up); *(images, couleurs)* to superimpose (**à** on *or* upon) **2** *Géom* to superpose **3** *Ordinat* **s. une écriture** to overwrite

VPR **se superposer 1** *(emploi passif) (étagères)* to stack; **les plateaux se superposent facilement** the trays are easy to stack **2** *(se mêler ▸ images, couleurs, sons)* to be superimposed; **leurs deux visages se superposent dans ma mémoire** their two faces have become indistinguishable in my memory **3** *Géom* to be superposed

superposition [syperpozisjɔ̃] NF **1** *(d'étagères, de plats)* stacking

2 *Géom* superposition

3 *(d'images, de couleurs, de sons)* superimposition, superimposing *(UNCOUNT)*

4 *Géol* **principe de s.** principle of superposition

superproduction [syperprɔdyksjɔ̃] NF *Cin* big-budget movie *or Br* film

superprofit [syperprɔfi] NM enormous profit

superpuissance [syperpɥisɑ̃s] NF superpower

supersonique [sypersɔnik] ADJ supersonic

NM supersonic aircraft

superstar [syperstar] NF superstar

superstitieuse [syperstisjøz] *voir* **superstitieux**

superstitieusement [syperstisjøzmɑ̃] ADV superstitiously

superstitieux, -euse [syperstisjø, -øz] ADJ superstitious

NM,F superstitious person

superstition [syperstisjɔ̃] NF superstition; **j'évite les échelles par pure s.** I walk round ladders simply because I'm superstitious; **avoir la s. du passé** to be excessively attached to the past

superstrat [syperstra] NM *Ling* superstratum

superstructure [syperstryktyr] NF superstructure

supertanker [sypertɑ̃kœr] NM supertanker

superviser [3] [sypervize] VT to supervise, to oversee

superviseur [sypervizœr] NM **1** *(personne)* supervisor **2** *Ordinat* supervisor, scheduler

supervision [sypervizjɔ̃] NF supervision; **être sous la s. de qn** to be supervised by sb, to be under sb's supervision

superwoman [syperwuman] *(pl* **superwomans***)* NF *Fam* superwoman

supin [sypɛ̃] NM *Ling* supine

supplanter [3] [syplɑ̃te] VT **1** *(rival)* to supplant, to displace, to supersede; **un autre l'avait supplanté dans son cœur** another man had supplanted him in his/her affections; **il s'est fait s. à la tête de la société** he was replaced at the head of the company **2** *(machine, système)* to supplant, to take over from; **la machine va-t-elle s. l'homme?** will machines take the place of people?

suppléance [sypleɑ̃s] NF **1** *Scol (poste de remplaçant) Br* supply post, *Am* substitute post; *(poste d'adjoint)* assistantship; *(activité ▸ de remplaçant) Br* supply *or Am* substitute teaching; *(▸ d'adjoint)* assistantship; **assurer la s. de qn** *(le remplacer)* to deputize for sb; *(l'assister)* to assist sb **2** *Jur & Pol* deputy **3** *Ling* suppletion

suppléant, -e [sypleɑ̃, -ɑ̃t] ADJ **1** *Scol (remplaçant) Br* supply *(avant n)*, *Am* substitute *(avant n)*; *(adjoint)* assistant *(avant n)*

2 *(médecin)* locum *(avant n)*

3 *Jur & Pol* deputy *(avant n)*

4 *Gram (verbe, terme)* substitute *(avant n)*

NM,F **1** *Scol (remplaçant) Br* supply teacher, *Am* substitute teacher; *(adjoint)* assistant teacher **2** *(médecin)* locum **3** *Jur & Pol* deputy

suppléer [15] [syplee] VT **1** *Littéraire (remédier à ▸ manque)* to make up for, to compensate for; *(▸ lacune)* to fill in

2 *Littéraire (ajouter ▸ réponse manquante)* to provide, to supply

3 *(compléter)* to complement, to supplement; **là où l'intelligence artificielle peut s. l'intelligence humaine** the areas where artificial intelligence can take over from human intelligence; **s. qch par** to complete sth with

4 *Scol (remplacer)* to replace, to stand in for

5 *Jur & Pol (remplacer)* to deputize for

• **suppléer à** VT IND **1** *(remédier à ▸ insuffisance)* to make up for, to compensate for **2** *(remplacer ▸ sujet: personne)* to replace

supplément [syplemɑ̃] NM **1** *(coût)* extra *or* additional charge; **ils demandent un s. de huit euros pour le vin** they charge eight euros extra for wine; **payer un s.** to pay extra; **s. chambre individuelle** single room supplement

2 *Rail* supplement; **s. couchette** sleeper charge; **un train à s.** a train with a fare surcharge *or* supplement
3 *(de nourriture)* extra portion; *Fin (de crédits)* additional facility; **un s. d'informations** additional *or* further information; **s. d'enquête** further investigation; **le juge a demandé un s. d'enquête** the judge asked that the investigation be pursued further; **un s. d'âme** a little extra
4 *(à un livre, un journal)* supplement; **le s. du dimanche** the Sunday supplement; **s. détachable** pullout
5 *Jur* **s. de revenu familial** ≃ family income supplement
6 *Math* supplement
• **en supplément** ADV extra; **c'est en s.** it comes as an extra, it's an extra; **menu 15 euros, boisson en s.** set menu 15 euros, drinks extra

supplémentaire [syplemɑ̃tɛr] ADJ **1** *(crédit, dépense)* additional, supplementary, extra; **un délai s.** an extension (of deadline); **nous attendons des informations supplémentaires** we are awaiting further information
2 *Rail (train)* relief *(avant n)*
3 *Math* supplementary
4 *Mus* **lignes supplémentaires** ledger *or* added lines

supplémentation [syplemɑ̃tasjɔ̃] NF **s.** *ou* **s. nutritionnelle** nutritional supplementation, taking nutritional supplements

supplétif, -ive [sypletif, -iv] ADJ **1** *(gén)* auxiliary, additional
2 *Jur (loi)* supplementary
3 *Mil* auxiliary
4 *Ling* suppletive
NM *Mil* auxiliary

suppliant, -e [syplijɑ̃, -ɑ̃t] ADJ begging, imploring, beseeching; **d'un air s.** pleadingly; **d'un ton s.** imploringly, pleadingly
NM,F supplicant

supplication [syplikasjɔ̃] NF **1** *(demande)* entreaty, *Sout* supplication; **malgré toutes mes supplications** despite all my pleading **2** *Rel* supplication

supplice [syplis] NM **1** *Hist* torture; **conduire un prisonnier au s.** to take a prisoner to his place of execution; **s. chinois** Chinese water torture; *Fig* extreme torment; **subir le s. de la roue** to be broken on the wheel; **le s. de Tantale** the punishment of Tantalus; **le dernier s.** *(la peine de mort)* execution **2** *(douleur physique)* agony, torture; *(douleur morale)* torture, torment, agony; **ce mal de tête est un vrai s.** this headache is absolute agony; **la conversation était devenue un s.** the conversation had become sheer torture; **être au s.** to be in agonies; **je suis au s., quand rentrera-t-il?** this is sheer torture, when will he be back?; **mettre qn au s.** to torture sb **3** *Rel* **les supplices éternels** the torments of the damned

supplicié, -e [syplisje] NM,F *(personne ▸ qui a subi la peine de mort)* execution victim; *(▸ qui a été torturée)* torture victim

supplicier [9] [syplisje] VT *Littéraire* **1** *(exécuter)* to execute; *(torturer)* to torture **2** *(tourmenter)* to torment, to rack, to plague; **les remords la suppliciaient** she was racked by remorse

supplier [10] [syplije] VT to beg, to implore, to beseech; **s. qn (à genoux) de faire qch** to beg sb (on bended knee) to do sth; **épargnez-le, je vous en supplie** spare him, I beg you *or Sout* I beseech you

> Il faut noter que le verbe anglais **to supply** est un faux ami. Il signifie **fournir**.

supplique [syplik] NF *Jur & Rel* petition; **présenter une s. à qn** to petition sb

support [sypɔr] NM **1** *(de colonne, de meuble)* base, support; *(de statuette)* stand, pedestal; *(pour un échafaudage)* support; *(pour outils)* rest; *(pour une lampe, un tube à essai)* stand; **s. mural** wall bracket; **s. de tasse** *(dans une voiture)* cup holder
2 *(de communication)* medium; **supports audiovisuels** audiovisual aids, audiovisuals; **s. publicitaire** publicity *or* advertising medium; **supports visuels** visual aids, visuals
3 *(en acoustique)* **s. magnétique** magnetic tape
4 *Culin* base
5 *Hér* supporter
6 *Typ* support; **s. d'impression** = material on which printing is done
7 *Ordinat* medium; **s. de données** data carrier; **s. d'information** data support; **sur s. papier** hard copy; **s. de sortie** output medium; **s. de stockage** storage medium; **s. technique** technical support
8 *Math & Phot* support

supportable [sypɔrtabl] ADJ **1** *(douleur)* bearable; **il fait froid, mais c'est s.** it's cold but not unbearably so **2** *(conduite, personne)* tolerable; **tu n'es plus s.!** I can't take any more of this from you!

supporter[1] [sypɔrtɛr] NM *Sport* supporter

SUPPORTER[2] [3] [sypɔrte]

VT	
• to support **1, 8**	• to hold up **1**
• to assume **2**	• to bear **2, 5, 6**
• to be subject to **3**	• to withstand **4**
• to put up with **5**	• to stand **6**
VPR	
• to bear each other **2**	• to be bearable **3**

VT **1** *(servir d'assise à)* to support, to hold up; **cinq piliers supportent la voûte** the roof is held up by five pillars
2 *(assumer ▸ responsabilité, obligation)* to assume; *(prendre en charge ▸ dépense)* to bear; **l'acheteur supporte les frais** the fees are borne by the purchaser
3 *(être assujetti à ▸ impôt)* to be subject to; **les articles de luxe supportent de lourdes taxes** luxury goods are subject to heavy taxes
4 *(résister à)* to stand up to, to withstand; **la porcelaine fine ne supporte pas la chaleur excessive** fine china will not withstand excessive heat; **des plantes qui supportent pas le froid** plants that do well in the cold; **leur nouvelle voiture supporte la comparaison avec la concurrence** their new car will bear *or* stand comparison with anything produced by their competitors; **elle a bien supporté la route** *(personne)* she came through the journey all right; *(voiture)* it stood up to the journey all right; **bien s. une opération** to come through an operation in good shape; **mal s. une opération** to have trouble recovering from an operation; **je ne supporte pas l'alcool/la pilule** drink/the pill doesn't agree with me; **on supporterait bien une petite laine** it's cold enough to wear a jumper
5 *(subir sans faillir ▸ épreuve, privation)* to bear, to endure, to put up with; *(▸ insulte, menace)* to bear; **elle supporte tout de lui** she puts up with anything from him; **elle supporte mal la douleur** she can't cope with pain, she has a low pain threshold; **comment s. tant de misère/d'ineptie?** how can one possibly put up with such poverty/nonsense?
6 *(tolérer, accepter)* to bear, to stand; **je ne supporte pas la fumée** I can't bear *or* stand cigarette smoke; **je ne supporte pas de perdre** I can't stand losing; **décidément, je ne la supporte pas!** I just can't stand her!; **il faudra le s. encore deux jours** we'll have to put up with him for two more days; **j'arrive tout juste à les s.** I can just about tolerate them
7 *(en Afrique francophone) (personne, famille)* to support
8 *Sport (encourager)* to support
VPR **se supporter 1** *(emploi réfléchi)* **je ne me supporte plus en blonde/en noir** blonde hair/black just isn't right for me any more
2 *(emploi réciproque)* to bear *or* to stand each other
3 *(emploi passif)* to be bearable; **le froid sec se supporte plus facilement** when it's cold and dry, it's more bearable

supporteur, -trice [sypɔrtœr, -tris] NM,F supporter

supposé, -e [sypoze] ADJ **1** *(faux ▸ testament)* false, forged; *(▸ nom)* assumed
2 *(admis)* **la vitesse est supposée constante** the speed is assumed to be constant
3 *(présumé ▸ vainqueur)* supposed, presumed; *(▸ père)* putative; *(▸ dimension)* estimated; **l'auteur s. du pamphlet** the supposed author of the pamphlet; **le nombre s. des victimes** the presumed number of casualties
4 *Can (censé)* supposed to
• **supposé que** CONJ supposing (that), assuming that

supposer [3] [sypoze] VT **1** *(conjecturer, imaginer)* to suppose, to assume; **je suppose qu'il t'a emprunté de l'argent** I suppose *or* I assume he borrowed money from you; **je suppose que tu n'es pas prêt** I take it *or* I suppose you're not ready; **on le suppose à Paris, on suppose qu'il est à Paris** he is supposed to be in Paris; **cela laisse s. que...** this suggests that...; **tout laisse s. qu'il avait été contacté par la CIA** everything points to his having been contacted by the CIA; **en supposant que tu échoues** suppose (that) *or* supposing (that) *or* let's suppose (that) you fail; **à s. que** assuming that, supposing
2 *(estimer, penser)* **et tu la supposes assez bête pour se laisser faire?** so you think she's stupid enough to let it happen?; **vous lui supposez une grandeur d'âme qu'il n'a pas** you credit him with a magnanimity he doesn't possess
3 *(impliquer)* to imply, to require, to presuppose; **une mission qui suppose de la discrétion** an assignment where discretion is required *or* is a must; **cela suppose la connaissance des mathématiques** it presupposes a knowledge of mathematics
4 *Jur (imposteur)* to put forward; *(faux testament)* to present

supposition [sypozisjɔ̃] NF supposition, assumption; **des suppositions gratuites** mere *or* gratuitous suppositions; **je n'en suis pas sûr, c'est une s.** I'm not sure, I'm only assuming; **faire des suppositions** to speculate; *Fam* **une s. qu'elle dise la vérité** supposing (that) she's telling the truth□

suppositoire [sypozitwar] NM suppository

suppôt [sypo] NM *Littéraire* henchman; **s. de Satan** *ou* **du diable** fiend

suppression [sypresjɔ̃] NF **1** *(abrogation)* abolition; *(annulation ▸ d'un service d'autobus, d'un train)* cancellation; **la s. de la peine de mort** the abolition of the death penalty
2 *(dans un texte)* deletion
3 *(élimination)* elimination; **s. de la douleur par piqûres** elimination of pain by injections
4 *(assassinat)* elimination, liquidation
5 *Écon* **il y a eu beaucoup de suppressions d'emploi dans la région** there were many job losses in the area

supprimable [syprimabl] ADJ that can be got rid of

supprimer [3] [syprime] VT **1** *(faire cesser ▸ cause, effet)* to do away with; *(▸ habitude, obstacle)* to get rid of; *(▸ pauvreté, racisme)* to put an end to, to do away with; *(▸ douleur)* to kill, to stop; *(▸ fatigue)* to eliminate
2 *(démolir ▸ mur, quartier)* to knock *or* to pull down, to demolish
3 *(annuler ▸ loi)* to repeal, to annul; *(▸ projet)* to do away with; *(▸ service d'autobus, train)* to cancel; *(▸ allocation, prime)* to withdraw, to stop; *(▸ concurrence)* to cut out
4 *(retirer)* **s. des emplois** to axe jobs; **on va te s. ton permis de conduire** they'll take away your *Br* driving licence *or Am* driver's license; **vous devez s. le sucre de votre alimentation** you must cut sugar out of your diet; **ils vont s. des trains dans les zones rurales** train services will be cut in rural areas
5 *(enlever ▸ opération, séquence)* to cut (out), to take out; *(▸ mot, passage)* to delete; **s. les intermédiaires** to cut out the middlemen
6 *(tuer)* to do away with; **il s'est fait s. par la mafia** the mafia did away with him
VPR **se supprimer** to take one's own life

> Il faut noter que le verbe anglais **to suppress** est un faux ami. Il signifie le plus souvent **réprimer** ou **interdire**.

suppurant, -e [sypyrɑ̃, -ɑ̃t] ADJ suppurating

suppuration [sypyrasjɔ̃] NF suppuration

suppurer [3] [sypyre] VI to suppurate

supputation [sypytasjɔ̃] NF calculation, estimation

supputer [3] [sypyte] VT *(quantité)* to estimate; *(possibilités)* to assess; **s. ses chances** to calculate one's chances

supra [sypra] ADV supra; **voir s.** supra, see above

supraconducteur, -trice [syprakɔ̃dyktœr, -tris] **ADJ** superconductive
NM superconductor

supraconductivité [syprakɔ̃dyktivite] **NF** supraconductivity

supraconductrice [syprakɔ̃dyktris] *voir* **supraconducteur**

supraliminaire [sypraliminɛr] **ADJ** supraliminal

supranational, -e, -aux, -ales [sypranasjɔnal, -o] **ADJ** supranational

supranationalisme [sypranasjɔnalism] **NM** supranationalism

supranationalité [sypranasjɔnalite] **NF** supranationality

supraterrestre [sypratɛrɛstr] **ADJ** superterrestrial

suprématie [sypremasi] **NF** supremacy

suprême [syprɛm] **ADJ 1** *(supérieur)* supreme; **le pouvoir s.** the supreme power; *Rel* **l'Être s.** the Supreme Being

2 *(extrême ▸ importance, bonheur, plaisir)* extreme, supreme; *(▸ ignorance)* utter, blissful, sublime; *(▸ mépris)* sublime; **au s. degré** to the highest *or* greatest degree

3 *(dernier)* supreme, final; **dans un s. effort** in a final attempt; **à l'heure** *ou* **au moment s.** at the hour of reckoning, at the moment of truth

4 *Culin* supreme

NM *Culin* suprême; **s. de volaille** chicken suprême

suprêmement [syprɛmmɑ̃] **ADV** supremely

SUR¹ [syr]

- on **1, 10, 11**
- on top of **1**
- in **1**
- towards **4**
- after **7**
- out of **12**
- over **1, 3, 13**
- against **1**
- for **3**
- around **4**
- upon **7**
- by **12**

PRÉP 1 *(dans l'espace ▸ dessus)* on; *(▸ par-dessus)* over; *(▸ au sommet de)* on top of; *(▸ contre)* against; **s. la table** on the table; **étendu s. le lit/le sol** lying on the bed/the floor; **dormir s. le dos** to sleep on one's back; **elle avait des bleus s. tout le visage** she had bruises all over her face, her face was covered in bruises; **s. la place du village** on the village green; **s. le continent** on the continent; **il a jeté ses affaires s. le lit** he threw his things onto the bed; **monter s. un escabeau** to climb (up) a stepladder; **monter s. un manège/une bicyclette** to get on a roundabout/bicycle; **mets un châle s. tes épaules** put a shawl round *or* over your shoulders; **versez le rhum s. le gâteau** pour the rum over the cake; *Fam* **retire tes pieds de s. la chaise** take your feet off the chair; **jeter une passerelle s. une rivière** to build a footbridge over *or* across a river; **demain, du soleil s. le nord** tomorrow there will be sunshine in the north; **ouragan s. la ville** hurricane over the city; **une chambre avec vue s. la mer** a room with a view of *or* over the sea; **des fenêtres qui donnent s. la rue** windows giving onto *or* overlooking the street; **s. pilotis** on stilts; **s. la pile de livres** on (top of) the pile of books; **s. la colline** on the top of the hill; **s. la cime de l'arbre** at the top of the tree; **je lui ai mis les mains s. les yeux** I put my hands over his/her eyes; **mettre un doigt s. sa bouche** to put a finger to one's lips; **il y a des graffiti partout s. le mur** there's graffiti all over the wall; **la peinture est appliquée directement s. le plâtre** the paint is applied directly onto the plaster; **sa silhouette se détachait s. le ciel** he/she was silhouetted against the sky; **j'ai toujours mon agenda s. moi** I always have my diary with *or* on me; **je n'ai pas d'argent s. moi** I haven't got any money on me; **s'appuyer s. un mur** to lean against a wall; **il y avait un monde fou, on était tous les uns s. les autres** there was a huge crowd, we were all crushed up together *or* one on top of the other; **vivre les uns s. les autres** to live in overcrowded conditions *or* on top of one another; **je l'ai lu s. le journal** I read it in the paper; **s. la photo** in the photo; **les données sont s. disquette** the data is on disk; **la ville n'est pas s. la carte** the town isn't on the map; **la clef est s. la porte** the key's in the door; **je n'ai plus d'argent s. mon compte** I haven't any money left in my account; *Beaux-Arts* **sculpture s. bois** wood carving; *Beaux-Arts* **sculpture s. marbre** marble sculpture; **il est s. le chantier** he's on the (building) site; **je cherche un logement s. Paris** I'm looking for somewhere to live in Paris

2 *(indiquant la direction)* **s. votre gauche, le Panthéon** on *or* to your left, the Pantheon; **en allant s. Rennes** going towards Rennes; **ils avançaient s. Moscou** they were advancing towards *or* on Moscow; **obliquer s. la droite** to turn *or* to bear right; **diriger son regard s. qn** to look in sb's direction; **tirer s. qn** to shoot at sb; **les policiers se sont jetés s. eux** the police charged (at) them; **le malheur s'est abattu s. cette famille** unhappiness has fallen upon this family; **la porte s'est refermée s. elle** the door closed behind *or* after her

3 *(indiquant une distance)* over, for; **virages s. 3 km** *(sur panneau)* bends for 3 km; **il est le plus rapide s. 400 mètres** he's the fastest over 400 metres; **la foire s'étend s. 3000m²** the fair covers 3,000m²; **s. toute la longueur du parcours** over the whole *or* entire length of the course

4 *(dans le temps ▸ indiquant l'approximation)* towards, around; **s. les 4 heures, quelqu'un a téléphoné** (at) around 4, somebody phoned; **s. le soir, un orage éclata** a thunderstorm broke towards evening

5 *(indiquant la proximité)* **s. le moment** *ou* **le coup, j'étais étonné** at the time *or* at first, I was surprised; **être s. le départ** to be about to leave; **il va s. ses 40 ans** he's approaching *or* nearly 40

6 *(indiquant la durée)* **c'est un contrat s. cinq ans** it's a five-year contract, the contract runs for five years; **les versements sont étalés s. plusieurs mois** the instalments are spread over several months

7 *(indiquant la répétition)* after, upon; **il commet gaffe s. gaffe** he makes blunder after *or* upon blunder; **je lui ai envoyé lettre s. lettre** I sent him/her letter after *or* upon letter; **elle écrit roman s. roman** she writes one novel after another

8 *(indiquant la cause)* **condamné s. faux témoignage** condemned on false evidence; **juger qn s. ses propos/son apparence** to judge sb by his/her words/appearance; **j'ai agi s. vos ordres** I acted on your orders; **il est venu s. votre invitation** he came at your invitation

9 *(indiquant la manière, l'état, la situation)* **jurer qch s. la Bible** to swear sth on the Bible; **prendre modèle s. qn** to model oneself on sb; **faire pression s. qn** to put pressure on sb; **avoir un effet s. qn/qch** to have an effect on sb/sth; **s. la base de 1000 euros par mois** on the basis of 1,000 euros per month; **danser s. un air connu** to dance to a well-known tune; *Mus* **s. le mode majeur/mineur** in the major/minor key; **c'est s. France Inter** it's on France Inter

10 *(indiquant le moyen)* **vivre s. ses économies/un héritage** to live off one's savings/a legacy; **je n'aime pas choisir s. catalogue** I don't like choosing from a catalogue; **ça s'ouvre s. simple pression** you open it just by pressing it; **vous obtiendrez le renseignement s. (un) simple coup de téléphone** just phone for information; **fait s. traitement de texte** done on a word-processor; **le film se termine s. une vue du Lido** the film ends with *or* on a view of the Lido

11 *(indiquant le domaine, le sujet)* **on a un dossier s. lui** we've got a file on him; **je sais peu de choses s. elle** I don't know much about her; **s. ce point, nous sommes d'accord** we agree on that point; **travailler s. qch** to work on sth; **30 personnes sont s. le projet** there are 30 people on *or* involved in the project; **faire des recherches s. qch** to do some research into sth; **un essai s. la métaphysique** an essay on metaphysics; **un poème s. la solitude** a poem about solitude; **questionner qn s. ses projets** to ask sb about his/her plans; **elle s'est expliquée s. ses choix politiques** she explained her political choices; **médite s. ce qu'elle t'a dit** think about what she told you; **s'apitoyer s. soi-même** to feel sorry for oneself; **il y a des réductions s. les meubles** there are discounts on furniture; **impôt s. le tabac/l'alcool** tax on tobacco/alcohol; **je prends une commission de 12 pour cent s. les ventes** I take a 12 percent commission on sales; **prélever un pourcentage s. une somme** to deduct a percentage from a sum; **les cotisations sont prises s. le salaire** contributions are deducted from one's salary

12 *(indiquant ▸ une proportion)* out of; *(▸ une mesure)* by; **un homme s. deux** one man in two, every second man; **un jour s. deux** every other day; **un lundi s. trois** every third Monday; **s. 100 candidats, 15 ont été retenus** 15 out of 100 candidates were shortlisted; **99 fois s. 100** 99 times out of 100; **tu as une chance s. deux de gagner** you've got a fifty-fifty chance of winning; **5 mètres s. 3** 5 metres by 3; *Math* **12 s. 3 égale 4** 12 divided by *or* over 3 equals 4; **noter s. 20** to mark out of 20; **j'ai eu 12 s. 20** I got 12 out of 20; **faire une enquête s. 1000 personnes** to do a survey of *or* involving 1,000 people

13 *(indiquant une relation de supériorité)* over; **régner s. un pays** to rule over a country; **avoir de l'autorité s. qn** to have authority over sb; **son emprise s. moi** his/her influence over me; **c'est une victoire s. la maladie** it's a victory over illness; **l'emporter s. qn** to defeat sb; **son pouvoir s'exerce s. tous** he/she has power over everybody

SUR- PREFIX

This prefix has two main uses, one of which is still generating new coinages today.

• **Sur-** can mean HIGHER or ABOVE when coupled with a noun or a verb. The word *over*, used as an adverb or a prefix, often features in the English translation, eg:

surchemise overshirt; **surtitre** strapline/surtitle; **surligner** to highlight (with a fluorescent pen); **surligneur** highlighter (pen); **survoler** to fly over; **surnager** to float; **surplomber** to overhang

• **Sur-** can suggest SUPERIORITY or EXCESS when added to nouns, verbs or adjectives. The English translation usually includes an equivalent prefix *(over-, super-)* or expression of abundance, eg:

surhomme superman; **surhumain** superhuman; **surabondance** overabundance, profusion, wealth; **des... en surnombre** too many...; **suralimenté(e)** overfed/supercharged; **surcharger** to overload/to overburden; **surchauffé(e)** overheated

The use of **sur-** in connection with the idea of excess has been quite productive in recent years, mostly in media-speak, which is often the way in which new coinages enter the language, eg:

aujourd'hui les gens sont surinformés today people are bombarded with too much information; **la surmédicalisation de la grossesse** excessive medical intervention during pregnancy; **surbooking, surréservation** overbooking, double booking; **être surlooké(e)** to be a fashion victim; **surjouer** to overact, to ham

sur², -e [syr] **ADJ** sour

SÛR, -E [syr] **ADJ 1** *(certain, convaincu)* sure, certain; **j'en suis tout à fait s., j'en suis s. et certain** I'm absolutely sure, I'm positive; **c'est s. et certain** it's a hundred percent sure; **j'en étais s.!** I knew it!; **n'en sois pas si s.** don't be so sure; **il l'a oublié, c'est s.** he has forgotten it, that's for certain *or* sure; **c'est s. qu'il pleuvra** it's bound to rain; **c'est s. qu'ils ne viendront pas** it's certain that they won't come; **une chose est sûre** one thing's for sure; **tu viendras? – ce n'est pas s.** are you coming? – I don't know for sure; **être s. de son fait** to be positive; **elle est sûre de réussir** she's sure she'll succeed; **je suis s. d'avoir raison** I'm sure I'm right; **je ne suis pas s. d'avoir gardé un double** *(d'un document)* I'm not sure (whether) I kept a copy

2 *(confiant)* sure, confident; **être s. de qn** to have (every) confidence in sb; **le général n'était plus s. de ses hommes** the general had lost confidence in his men; **être s. de soi** *(en général)* to be self-assured *or* self-confident; *(sur un point particulier)* to be confident; **être s. de son coup** to be sure of success

3 *(fiable ▸ personne, ami)* trustworthy, reliable; *(▸ données, mémoire, raisonnement)* reliable, sound; *(▸ alarme, investissement)* safe; *(▸ goût)* reliable; **avoir la main sûre** to have a steady hand;

avoir le pied s. to be surefooted; **avoir l'oreille sûre** to have a keen ear; **le temps n'est pas s.** the weather is unreliable

4 *(sans danger)* safe; **l'avion est plus s. que la voiture** flying is safer than travelling by car; **des rues peu sûres** unsafe streets; **le plus s. est de…** the safest thing is to…; **appelle-moi, c'est plus s.!** call me, just to be on the safe side!

ADV *Fam* **s. qu'il va gagner!** he's bound to win!; *Fam* **il va accepter – pas s.!** he'll accept – don't count on it!

• **à coup sûr ADV** definitely, no doubt; **elle sera à coup s. en retard** she's sure to be late

• **pour sûr ADV** *Fam* for sure

---

surabondance [syrabɔ̃dɑ̃s] **NF** overabundance, profusion, wealth; *(de marchandises)* surfeit, glut; **une s. de** a wealth of; **une s. de céréales** an overabundance of cereals

surabondant, -e [syrabɔ̃dɑ̃, -ɑ̃t] **ADJ** overabundant, profuse

surabonder [3] [syrabɔ̃de] **VI les minéraux surabondent dans la région** the region is rich in minerals; **les activités culturelles surabondent dans cette ville** the town offers a wide range of cultural activities; **les campeurs surabondent dans la région** the area is overrun with campers

• **surabonder de, surabonder en VT IND** to abound with *or* in

suraccumulation [syrakymylɑsjɔ̃] **NF** overaccumulation

suractivé, -e [syraktive] **ADJ** superactivated

suractivité [syraktivite] **NF** overactivity

surah [syra] **NM** syrah

suraigu, -ë [syregy] **ADJ 1** *(voix, son)* very shrill **2** *(douleur)* intense, acute

surajouter [3] [syraʒute] **VT** to add

VPR se surajouter to come on top (**à** of)

suralimentation [syralimɑ̃tɑsjɔ̃] **NF 1** *(d'une personne ▸ consommation excessive)* overeating; *(▸ par quelqu'un d'autre)* overfeeding; *(d'un animal)* overfeeding **2** *Tech* boosting, supercharging **3** *Méd* superalimentation

suralimenté, -e [syralimɑ̃te] **ADJ 1** *(personne, animal)* overfed **2** *Tech (moteur)* supercharged

suralimenter [3] [syralimɑ̃te] **VT 1** *(personne, animal)* to overfeed **2** *Tech (moteur)* to supercharge

suranné, -e [syrane] **ADJ 1** *(style, idées)* old-fashioned, outmoded; **une mode surannée** an outdated fashion **2** *Arch (qui a expiré)* expired

surarmement [syrarməmɑ̃] **NM** stockpiling of weapons

surbaissé, -e [syrbese] **ADJ 1** *(plafond)* lowered; *(arc, voûte)* surbased **2** *Aut* **voiture (à carrosserie) surbaissée** underslung *or* low-slung car

surbaissement [syrbesmɑ̃] **NM** *Archit* surbasement

surbaisser [4] [syrbese] **VT 1** *(plafond)* to lower; *(arc, voûte)* to surbase **2** *Aut* to undersling

surbooker [3] [syrbuke] **VT** to overbook

surbooking [syrbukiŋ] **NM** overbooking, double-booking

surboum [syrbum] **NF** *Vieilli* party *(for teenagers)*

surbrillance [syrbrijɑ̃s] **NF** highlighting; **apparaître en s.** to be highlighted

surcapacité [syrkapasite] **NF** overcapacity

surcapitalisation [syrkapitalizɑsjɔ̃] **NF** overcapitalization, overcapitalizing *(UNCOUNT)*

surcapitaliser [3] [syrkapitalize] **VT** to overcapitalize

VI to overcapitalize

surcharge [syrʃarʒ] **NF 1** *(excédent de poids)* overload, overloading; **s. de bagages** excess luggage; **la s. de la voiture est à l'origine de l'accident** the accident occurred because the car was overloaded; *Méd* **s. pondérale** excess weight

2 *(excès)* overabundance, surfeit; **s. de travail** extra work; **les parents se plaignent de la s. des programmes scolaires** parents are complaining that the school curriculum is overloaded

3 *(sur un mot)* alteration

4 *(sur un timbre)* surcharge, overprint

5 *Constr (d'un enduit)* overthick coat; *(ornementation)* frills, over-embellishment

6 *Élec* overload

7 *(d'un cheval de course)* (weight) handicap

• **en surcharge ADJ** excess *(avant n)*, extra *(avant n)* **ADV prendre des passagers en s.** to take on excess passengers

surcharger [17] [syrʃarʒe] **VT 1** *(véhicule)* to overload

2 *(accabler)* to overburden (**de** with); **surchargé de travail** overworked

3 *(alourdir)* to weigh down

4 *(raturer)* to alter

5 *(marché)* to glut, to overload

6 *(timbre)* to surcharge, to overprint

surchauffe [syrʃof] **NF 1** *Phys* superheating **2** *(d'un moteur, d'un appareil)* overheating **3** *Écon* overheating **4** *Métal (technique)* superheating; *(défaut)* overheating

surchauffer [3] [syrʃofe] **VT 1** *(pièce, appareil)* to overheat **2** *Phys* to superheat

surchoix [syrʃwa] **ADJ** *(produit)* top-quality *(avant n)*

NM top quality

surclassement [syrklasmɑ̃] **NM** *Transp* upgrade

surclasser [3] [syrklase] **VT 1** *(surpasser)* to outclass **2** *Transp* to upgrade

surcompensation [syrkɔ̃pɑ̃sɑsjɔ̃] **NF** overcompensation

surcomposé, -e [syrkɔ̃poze] **ADJ** *Gram* = which uses an auxiliary twice

surcompression [syrkɔ̃presjɔ̃] **NF** *(procédé)* supercharging; *(état)* supercharge

surcomprimer [3] [syrkɔ̃prime] **VT** to supercharge

surconsommation [syrkɔ̃sɔmɑsjɔ̃] **NF** overconsumption, excess *or* excessive consumption

surcontrer [3] [syrkɔ̃tre] **VT** *Cartes* to redouble

surcoté, -e [syrkɔte] **ADJ** *(action, marché, monnaie)* overvalued

surcouper [3] [syrkupe] **VT** *Cartes* to overtrump

surcoût [syrku] **NM** *(supplément prévu)* surcharge, overcharge; *(dépense)* overspend, overexpenditure

surcroît [syrkrwa] **NM un s. de travail** extra *or* additional work

• **de surcroît ADV** moreover, what's more; **il est beau, et intelligent de s.** he's handsome, and moreover *or* what's more, he's bright

• **en surcroît ADV** *(en plus)* in addition; **venir** *ou* **être donné en s.** to come on top

• **par surcroît = de surcroît**

surdéveloppé, -e [syrdevlɔpe] **ADJ** *Écon (très développé)* highly developed; *(excessivement développé)* overdeveloped

surdéveloppement [syrdevlɔpmɑ̃] **NM** *Écon (haut niveau)* high state of development; *(excès)* overdevelopment

surdimensionné, -e [syrdimɑ̃sjɔne] **ADJ** oversized

surdi-mutité [syrdimytite] **NF** deaf-muteness, deaf-mutism

surdiplômé, -e [syrdiplome] **ADJ** overqualified

surdité [syrdite] **NF** deafness; **s. de perception/transmission** perceptive/conductive deafness; **s. verbale** word-deafness

surdon [syrdɔ̃] **NM 1** *(compensation)* = compensation allowable to purchaser for damage to goods **2** *(droit)* = right to non-acceptance of damaged goods

surdosage [syrdozaʒ] **NM** overdosage, overdosing

surdose [syrdoz] **NF** overdose

surdoué, -e [syrdwe] **ADJ** gifted, *Spéc* hyperintelligent

NM,F gifted *or Spéc* hyperintelligent child

sureau, -x [syro] **NM** *Bot* elder, elderberry tree

sureffectif [syrefektif] **NM** overstaffing; **être en s.** to be overstaffed

surélévation [syrelevɑsjɔ̃] **NF** *Constr (action)* heightening; *(état)* additional *or* extra height

surélevé, -e [syrelve] **ADJ 1** *(voie ferrée)* elevated **2** *Archit (arche, rez-de-chaussée etc)* raised

surélever [19] [syrelve] **VT** *Constr (mur)* to heighten, to raise; **s. un immeuble de deux étages** to add two floors to a building; **on a surélevé la voie ferrée** the railway has been raised above ground level

suremballage [syrɑ̃balaʒ] **NM 1** *(excès d'emballage)* over-packaging **2** *(emballage extérieur)* outer packaging

sûrement [syrmɑ̃] **ADV 1** *(en sécurité)* safely

2 *(efficacement)* efficiently, with a sure hand; **conduire s. ses affaires** to run one's affairs with a sure hand

3 *(certainement)* certainly, surely; **ce que tu as dit l'a condamné plus s. que s'il avait été pris sur le fait** what you said condemned him even more surely than if he'd been caught red-handed; **il sera s. en retard** he's bound to *or* sure to be late; **ils ont s. été pris dans les embouteillages** they must have been caught in the traffic; **oui, s., il vaudrait mieux le prévenir** yes, no doubt, it would be better to warn him

4 *(oui)* certainly; **s. pas!** certainly not!

surémission [syremisjɔ̃] **NF** overissue

suremploi [syrɑ̃plwa] **NM** overemployment

surenchère [syrɑ̃ʃɛr] **NF 1** *(prix)* higher bid, overbid; **faire une s.** to make a higher bid; **faire une s. sur qn** to bid higher than sb **2** *Fig* **la s. électorale** exaggerated political promises *(during an election campaign)*; **la s. publicitaire/médiatique** advertising/media overkill; **une s. de violence** an increase in violence; **faire de la s.** to go one better

surenchérir [32] [syrɑ̃ʃerir] **VI 1** *(offrir de payer plus)* to overbid, to raise one's bid, to make a higher bid; **si personne ne vient s.** if nobody makes a higher bid; **s. sur qn** to bid higher than sb **2** *Fig* **s. sur** to go one better than; **s. sur une offre** to make a better offer

surenchérisseur, -euse [syrɑ̃ʃerisœr, -øz] **NM,F** higher bidder

surencombré, -e [syrɑ̃kɔ̃bre] **ADJ 1** *(rue, ville, port)* (severely) congested (**de** with) **2** *(établissement)* overcrowded

surencombrement [syrɑ̃kɔ̃brəmɑ̃] **NM 1** *(d'une ville, des routes)* (severe) congestion **2** *(d'un établissement)* overcrowding

surendetté, -e [syrɑ̃dete] **ADJ** heavily in debt

surendettement [syrɑ̃dɛtmɑ̃] **NM** excessive debt

surentraînement [syrɑ̃trɛnmɑ̃] **NM** overtraining

surentraîner [4] [syrɑ̃trene] **VT** to overtrain

suréquipement [syrekipmɑ̃] **NM** *(action)* overequipping; *(état)* overequipment; *(excès)* excess equipment

suréquiper [3] [syrekipe] **VT** to overequip

surestarie [syrɛstari] **NF** *Naut* demurrage

surestimation [syrɛstimɑsjɔ̃] **NF 1** *(action)* overestimation; *Com* overvaluing **2** *(résultat)* overestimate; *Com* overvaluation

surestimer [3] [syrɛstime] **VT 1** *Com (objet)* to overvalue **2** *(valeur, difficultés, personne)* to overestimate

VPR se surestimer to think too highly of oneself

suret, -ette [syrɛ, -ɛt] **ADJ** sourish, slightly tart; **un petit vin s.** a wine with a hint of tartness

sûreté [syrte] **NF 1** *(sécurité)* safety; **la s. de l'État** state security; **s. nucléaire** nuclear safety; **s. publique** public safety; **par mesure de s.** as a precaution

2 *(fiabilité ▸ de la mémoire, d'une méthode, d'un diagnostic, des freins)* reliability; *(▸ de la main)* sureness, steadiness; *(▸ de la vision, du goût, du jugement)* soundness; *(▸ d'une serrure)* security

3 *(système de protection)* safety device; **équiper sa porte d'une s.** to fit one's door with a security system

4 *Jur* **s. personnelle** guarantee, surety; **s. individuelle** (rights of) personal security *(against arbitrary detention)*; **s. réelle** (valuable) security; **la S. (nationale)** = the French criminal investigation department, *Br* ≃ CID, *Am* ≃ FBI

• **de sûreté ADJ** *(épingle, serrure etc)* safety *(avant n)*

• **en sûreté ADJ être en s.** to be safe *or* out of

harm's way **ADV mettre qch en s.** to put sth in a safe place *or* away for safekeeping

surévaluation [syrevalɥasjɔ̃] **NF** overvaluation, overestimation

surévaluer [7] [syrevalɥe] **VT 1** *(donner une valeur supérieure à)* to overvalue **2** *(accorder une importance excessive à)* to overestimate

surexcitable [syrɛksitabl] **ADJ 1** *(gén)* overexcitable **2** *Psy* hyperexcitable

surexcitation [syrɛksitasjɔ̃] **NF** overexcitement

surexciter [3] [syrɛksite] **VT 1** *(personne)* to overexcite **2** *(imagination, sentiment, faculté)* to overexcite, to overstimulate, to inflame

surexploitation [syrɛksplwatasjɔ̃] **NF 1** *(d'une terre, de ressources)* overexploitation **2** *(de la main-d'œuvre)* exploitation

surexploiter [3] [syrɛksplwate] **VT 1** *(terre, ressources)* to overexploit **2** *(ouvrier)* to exploit **3** *(idée)* to overuse

surexposer [3] [syrɛkspoze] **VT** to overexpose

surexposition [syrɛkspozisjɔ̃] **NF** overexposure

surf [sœrf] **NM 1** *(planche)* surfboard **2** *(sport)* surfing; **faire du s.** to go surfing; **s. des neiges** snowboarding; **faire du s. des neiges** to snowboard, to go snowboarding

surface [syrfas] **NF 1** *(aire)* (surface) area; **calculer la s. d'une pièce** to calculate the (surface) area of a room; **quelle est la s. de l'entrepôt?** how big is the warehouse?; *Ordinat* **s. d'affichage** display area; *Jur* **s. corrigée** surface area *(used in the evaluation of a reasonable rent)*; *Mktg* **s. d'exposition** display space; **s. au sol** floor space; **s. de travail** work surface; **s. utile** floor space; **s. de vente** sales area;

2 *(partie extérieure)* surface, outside; **la s. de la Terre** the Earth's surface; **une peau se forme à la s. du lait** skin forms on the surface *or* on top of the milk; **remonter à la s., faire s.** *(sous-marin, nageur)* to surface; **refaire s., revenir à la s.** *(après évanouissement)* to come to *or* round; *(après anesthésie)* to come out of anaesthetic, to come round; *(après une dépression)* to pull out of it; *(après une absence)* to reappear; **le corps du mineur a été remonté à la s.** the miner's body was brought up to the surface

3 *(apparence)* surface, (outward) appearance; **la s. des choses** the surface of things; **il reste à la s. des choses** he doesn't go into things in any depth

4 *Fam (position sociale)* status❑; **avoir de la s.** to be influential

5 *Aviat* **s. portante** *Br* aerofoil, *Am* airfoil

6 *Élec* **s. d'onde** wavefront

7 *Géog, Ling & Math* surface

8 *Phot* **s. sensible** sensitized surface

9 *Sport* **s. de réparation** penalty area

10 *Tech* **s. de chauffe** heating surface

11 *Fin* **s. financière** financial standing

• **de surface ADJ 1** *Naut & Phys* surface *(avant n)* **2** *(amabilité, regrets)* superficial

• **en surface ADV 1** *(à l'extérieur)* on the surface **2** *(superficiellement)* on the face of things, superficially

surfaceuse [syrfasøz] **NF** surfacer

surfacturation [syrfaktyrasjɔ̃] **NF** overbilling, overcharging

surfacturer [3] [syrfaktyre] **VT** to overbill, to overcharge

surfaire [109] [syrfɛr] **VT** *Littéraire* **1** *(marchandise)* to overprice **2** *(ouvrage, talent)* to overrate, to overvalue

surfait, -e [syrfɛ, -ɛt] **ADJ 1** *(auteur, œuvre)* overrated; *(réputation)* inflated **2** *(surévalué)* overvalued; **leurs prix sont surfaits** their prices are too high

surfer [3] [sœrfe] **VI** to surf; **s. sur Internet** to surf the net *or* the Internet

surfeur, -euse [sœrfœr, -øz] **NM,F** surfer; **s. des neiges** snowboarder

surfilage [syrfilaʒ] **NM** *Couture* whipping

surfiler [3] [syrfile] **VT 1** *Couture* to whip, to whip-stitch **2** *Tex (fil)* to give an extra twist to

surfin, -e [syrfɛ̃, -in] **ADJ** *(produit)* top-quality, of superior quality; *(qualité)* superior

surfréquentation [syrfrekɑ̃tasjɔ̃] **NF** *(d'un lieu)* overvisiting; **les problèmes de pollution sont dus à la s. touristique** the pollution problems are caused by too many tourists

surfréquenté, -e [syrfrekɑ̃te] **ADJ** *(lieu touristique)* attracting too many visitors

surgé [syrʒe] **NMF** *Fam Arg scol* head supervisor❑ *(person in charge of school discipline)*

surgélateur [syrʒelatœr] **NM** (industrial) deep freeze *or* freezer

surgélation [syrʒelasjɔ̃] **NF** (industrial) deep-freezing

surgelé, -e [syrʒəle] **ADJ** frozen, deep-frozen

NM j'ai acheté du s. pour ce soir I've bought a frozen dinner for tonight; **surgelés** frozen food

surgeler [25] [syrʒəle] **VT** to deep-freeze *(industrially)*

surgénérateur, -trice [syrʒeneratœr, -tris] *Nucl* **ADJ** fast breeder *(avant n)*

NM breeder reactor

surgeon [syrʒɔ̃] **NM** *Bot* sucker

surgir [32] [syrʒir] **VI 1** *(personne, animal, objet)* to appear *or* to materialize suddenly, to loom up; *(hors du sol et rapidement)* to shoot *or* to spring up; **des gens, surgis d'on ne sait où** people who had sprung from nowhere; **l'eau surgit du sol entre deux rochers** the water springs *or* gushes out of the ground between two rocks **2** *(conflit)* to arise; *(difficultés)* to crop up, to arise; **la situation a fait s. un certain nombre de problèmes annexes** the situation gave rise to a number of related problems

surgissement [syrʒismɑ̃] **NM** *Littéraire* sudden appearance, looming up; *(hors du sol et rapide)* shooting *or* springing up

surhaussé, -e [syrose] **ADJ** *Constr* stilted

surhaussement [syrosmɑ̃] **NM** *Constr* raising

surhausser [3] [syrose] **VT** *Constr* to raise

surhomme [syrɔm] **NM 1** *(gén)* superman **2** *Phil* übermensch, superman

surhumain, -e [syrymɛ̃, -ɛn] **ADJ** superhuman; **ce qu'on me demande est s.** I'm being asked to do something beyond human endurance

surimi [syrimi] **NM** surimi

surimposer [3] [syrɛ̃poze] **VT** *Fin* to overtax

surimposition [syrɛ̃pozisjɔ̃] **NF 1** *Fin* overtaxation **2** *Géog* superimposition

surimpression [syrɛ̃presjɔ̃] **NF** superimposition; **les deux images sont en s.** the two pictures are superimposed

surimprimer [3] [syrɛ̃prime] **VT** *Ordinat* to overprint

surin [syrɛ̃] **NM 1** *Bot* young appletree stock **2** *Fam Arg crime (couteau)* knife❑, blade

Surinam, Suriname [syrinam] **NM le S.** Surinam, Suriname

suriner [3] [syrine] **VT** *Fam Arg crime (blesser avec un couteau)* to knife❑, to cut; *(tuer avec un couteau)* to stab to death❑

surinfection [syrɛ̃fɛksjɔ̃] **NF** *Méd* secondary infection

surinformation [syrɛ̃fɔrmasjɔ̃] **NF** information overload

surinformé, -e [syrɛ̃fɔrme] **ADJ les gens sont surinformés** people are bombarded with too much information

surintendance [syrɛ̃tɑ̃dɑ̃s] **NF** superintendency

surintendant, -e [syrɛ̃tɑ̃dɑ̃, -ɑ̃t] **NM,F** (in-house) social worker

NM *Hist* **s. général des finances** ≃ Lord High Treasurer

• **surintendante NF** *Hist* First Lady-in-Waiting

surinvestissement [syrɛ̃vɛstismɑ̃] **NM** *Fin & Psy* overinvestment

surir [32] [syrir] **VI** to (become *or* turn) sour

surjet [syrʒɛ] **NM** *(point)* overcast stitch; *(couture)* overcast seam

surjeter [27] [syrʒəte] **VT** to overcast

surjouer [6] [syrʒwe] **VT** *(rôle)* to overact

VI to overact

sur-le-champ [syrləʃɑ̃] **ADV** immediately, at once, straightaway

surlendemain [syrlɑ̃dmɛ̃] **NM le s. de la fête** two days after the party; **il m'a appelé le lendemain, et le s.** he called me the next day, and the day after; **et le s., j'étais à Paris** and two days later, I was in Paris

surligner [3] [syrliɲe] **VT** to highlight *(with a fluorescent pen)*

surligneur [syrliɲœr] **NM** highlighter

surlouer [6] [syrlwe] **VT** *(donner ou prendre en location)* to rent at an unreasonable *or* excessive price

surmarquage [syrmarkaʒ] **NM** overpricing, overcharging

surmarquer [3] [syrmarke] **VT** to overprice

surmédiatisation [syrmedjatizasjɔ̃] **NF** excessive media coverage

surmédiatiser [3] [syrmedjatize] **VT** to give excessive media coverage to

surmédicalisation [syrmedikalizasjɔ̃] **NF** excessive medical intervention

surmédicaliser [3] [syrmedikalize] **VT** to overmedicalize

surmenage [syrmənaʒ] **NM** *(nerveux)* overstrain, overexertion; *(au travail)* overwork, overworking; **souffrir de s.** to be overworked, to suffer from overwork; **s. intellectuel** mental strain

surmené, -e [syrməne] **ADJ** *(nerveusement)* in a state of nervous exhaustion; *(par le travail)* overworked

NM,F *(nerveusement)* person suffering from nervous exhaustion; *(par le travail)* overworked person

surmener [19] [syrməne] **VT 1** *(bête de somme, cheval)* to overwork, to drive too hard **2** *(personne ▸ physiquement)* to overwork; *(▸ nerveusement)* to overtax

VPR se surmener to overtax oneself, to overdo it

surmoi [syrmwa] **NM INV** *Psy* superego

surmontable [syrmɔ̃tabl] **ADJ** surmountable, which can be overcome, *Sout* superable

surmonter [3] [syrmɔ̃te] **VT 1** *(être situé sur)* to surmount, to top; **un dôme surmonte l'édifice** the building is crowned by a dome; **une colonne surmontée d'une croix** a column surmounted *or* topped by a cross **2** *(triompher de ▸ difficulté)* to get over, to surmount, to overcome; *(▸ peur, émotion)* to overcome, to get the better of, to master; *(▸ fatigue)* to overcome; *Littéraire* **s. ses ennemis** to overcome one's enemies

VPR se surmonter to master *or* control one's feelings

surmortalité [syrmɔrtalite] **NF** comparatively high death rate

surmultiplication [syrmyltiplikasjɔ̃] **NF** overdrive (device)

surmultiplié, -e [syrmyltiplije] **ADJ vitesse surmultipliée** overdrive

• **surmultipliée NF** overdrive

surnager [17] [syrnaʒe] **VI 1** *(flotter)* to float **2** *(subsister ▸ ouvrage)* to remain; *(▸ souvenir)* to linger on

surnatalité [syrnatalite] **NF** comparatively high birth rate

surnaturel, -elle [syrnatyrel] **ADJ 1** *(d'un autre monde)* supernatural **2** *(fabuleux, prodigieux)* uncanny; **le clair de lune donnait au paysage une beauté surnaturelle** the landscape was uncannily beautiful in the moonlight **3** *(divin)* spiritual; **la vie surnaturelle** the spiritual life

NM le s. the supernatural

surnom [syrnɔ̃] **NM 1** *(appellation)* nickname; **on lui a donné le s. de Rick** he was given the nickname of Rick, he was nicknamed Rick; **Cœur de Lion était le s. du roi Richard** King Richard was known as the Lionheart **2** *Antiq* agnomen

> Il faut noter que le terme anglais **surname** est un faux ami. Il signifie **nom de famille.**

surnombre [syrnɔ̃br] **NM** excessive numbers

• **en surnombre ADJ** redundant, excess *(avant n)*; **des ouvriers en s.** too many workers; **nous étions en s.** there were too many of us

surnommer [3] [syrnɔme] **VT** to nickname; **elles l'ont surnommé "le Tombeur"** they nicknamed him "The Ladykiller"; **dans sa famille, on la surnomme "Rosita"** her family's pet name for her is "Rosita"; **ce n'est pas pour rien qu'il se fait s. "l'homme invisible"!** they don't call him "the invisible man" for nothing!

surnuméraire [syrnymerɛr] **ADJ** supernumerary
NMF supernumerary

surocclusion [syrɔklyzjɔ̃] **NF** overbite

suroffre [syrɔfr] **NF 1** *(offre plus avantageuse)* higher bid *or* offer **2** *Écon* oversupply

suroît [syrwa] **NM 1** *(vent)* southwester, southwesterly **2** *(chapeau)* sou'wester

suroxygéner [18] [syrɔksiʒene] **VT** *Chim* to hyperoxygenate

surpaie *etc voir* **surpayer**

surpasser [3] [syrpɑse] **VT 1** *(surclasser)* to surpass, to outdo; **il a surpassé ses concurrents** he outdid his competitors; **s. qn en habileté** to be more skilful than sb **2** *(aller au-delà de)* to surpass, to go beyond; **leur enthousiasme surpasse toutes mes espérances** their enthusiasm is beyond all my expectations, they're far more enthusiastic than I expected
VPR se surpasser to excel oneself; **quel gâteau, tu t'es surpassé!** what a cake, you've really surpassed *or* excelled yourself!

surpaye [syrpɛj] **NF** overpayment

surpayé, -e [syrpeje] **ADJ** overpaid

surpayer [11] [syrpeje] **VT 1** *(employé)* to overpay **2** *(marchandise)* to be overcharged for

surpeuplé, -e [syrpœple] **ADJ** *(pays, région)* overpopulated; *(bar, plage)* overcrowded

surpeuplement [syrpœpləmɑ̃] **NM** *(d'un pays, d'une région)* overpopulation; *(d'un bar, d'une plage)* overcrowding

surplace [syrplas] **NM faire du s.** *(à vélo)* to do a track stand; *(en voiture)* to be stuck; *Fig* **l'économie fait du s.** the economy is marking time *or* treading water; **en allemand, je fais du s.** I'm not getting anywhere with German

surplis [syrpli] **NM** surplice

surplomb [syrplɔ̃] **NM** overhang
• **en surplomb ADJ** overhanging

surplombant, -e [syrplɔ̃bɑ̃, -ɑ̃t] **ADJ** overhanging

surplomber [3] [syrplɔ̃be] **VT** to overhang; **des falaises qui surplombent la mer** overhanging cliffs; **de chez elle on surplombe tout Paris** from her window you have a bird's-eye view of the whole of Paris
VI to overhang

surplus [syrply] **NM 1** *(excédent)* surplus, extra; **le s. de la récolte** the surplus crop
2 *(supplément ▸ à une quantité)* supplement; *(▸ à un prix)* surcharge; **vous paierez le s. le mois prochain** you'll pay the extra next month
3 *Écon (stock excédentaire)* surplus (stock); *(gain)* surplus; **s. d'importation** import surplus; *Fin* **s. monétaire** monetary surplus
4 *(boutique)* (army) surplus (store); **les s. américains** US army surplus
5 *(revenu)* disposable income
• **au surplus ADV** moreover, what's more

surpopulation [syrpɔpylasjɔ̃] **NF** overpopulation

surpositionnement [syrpozisjɔnmɑ̃] **NM** *Mktg* over-positioning

surprenait *etc voir* **surprendre**

surprenant, -e [syrprənɑ̃, -ɑ̃t] **ADJ 1** *(inattendu, étonnant)* surprising; **ça n'a rien de s.** that's hardly surprising **2** *(exceptionnel)* astonishing, amazing; **un film s. de lyrisme** an astonishingly lyrical film

surprendre [79] [syrprɑ̃dr] **VT 1** *(dans un acte délictueux)* **s. qn** to catch sb in the act; **on l'a surprise à falsifier la comptabilité** she was caught (in the act of) falsifying the accounts
2 *(prendre au dépourvu)* **ils sont venus nous s. à la maison** they paid us a surprise visit at home; **ils réussirent à s. la sentinelle** they managed to take the sentry by surprise; **s. qn au saut du lit** to catch sb when he/she has just got up; **la mort l'a surpris dans son sommeil** he died in his sleep; **se laisser s. par** *(orage)* to get caught in; *(marée)* to get caught by; *(crépuscule)* to be overtaken by
3 *(conversation)* to overhear; *(secret)* to find out; **j'ai surpris leur regard entendu** I happened to see the knowing look they gave each other
4 *(déconcerter)* to surprise; **être surpris de qch** to be surprised at sth; **ça a l'air de vous s.** you seem surprised; **cela ne surprendra personne** this will come as a surprise to nobody; **là, vous me surprenez!** well, you astound me!
5 *Littéraire (tromper)* **s. la confiance de qn** to violate sb's trust; **votre bonne foi a été surprise** your good faith was taken advantage of
VPR se surprendre se s. à faire qch to find *or* to catch oneself doing sth; **je me surprends à en douter** I catch myself having doubts about it

surpression [syrpresjɔ̃] **NF** very high pressure

surprime [syrprim] **NF** extra *or* additional premium

surpris, -e [syrpri, -iz] **PP** *voir* **surprendre**
ADJ 1 *(pris au dépourvu)* surprised; **l'ennemi, s., n'opposa aucune résistance** caught off their guard, the enemy put up no resistance **2** *(déconcerté)* surprised; **en apercevant son père, elle parut extrêmement surprise** when she saw her father, she looked extremely surprised; **je suis s. de son absence/de ne pas la voir/qu'elle ne réponde pas** I'm surprised (that) she's not here/not to see her/(that) she doesn't reply; **être agréablement/désagréablement s.** to be pleasantly/unpleasantly surprised; **je serais bien s. si elle ne demandait pas une augmentation** I'd be surprised if she didn't ask for a *Br* rise *or Am* raise; **quand on m'a dit que ma fille se mariait, j'ai été le premier s.** when I heard that my daughter was getting married, it came as a real surprise **3** *(vu, entendu par hasard)* **quelques mots s. entre deux portes** a snatch of overheard conversation
• **surprise NF 1** *(étonnement, stupéfaction)* surprise; **cette information causa une grande surprise** this information was received with amazement *or* caused much surprise; **à la grande surprise de** to the great surprise of; **à la grande surprise de toute la famille, il s'est marié** to his family's great surprise, he got married; **à ma grande surprise** to my great surprise, much to my surprise; **à la surprise générale** to everybody's surprise; **regarder qn avec surprise** to look at sb in surprise; **on va de surprise en surprise avec eux** with them it's just one surprise after another
2 *(événement inattendu)* surprise; **quelle (bonne) surprise!** what a (nice *or* pleasant) surprise!; **avoir une surprise** to be surprised; **tout le monde a eu la surprise d'avoir une prime** everyone was surprised to get a bonus; **faire une surprise à qn** to spring a surprise on sb; **ne lui dis pas, je veux lui faire la surprise** don't tell him/her, I want it to be a surprise; **on a souvent de mauvaises surprises avec lui** you often have unpleasant surprises with him; **attaque surprise** surprise attack; **visite surprise** surprise *or* unexpected visit
3 *(cadeau)* surprise; *(pour les enfants)* lucky bag; **j'ai une petite surprise pour toi** I brought you a little surprise
4 *Mil* surprise
• **par surprise ADV** *Mil* **prendre une ville par surprise** to take a town by surprise
• **sans surprise(s) ADJ ce fut un voyage sans surprise** it was an uneventful trip; **son père est sans surprise** his/her father is very predictable

surprise-partie [syrprizparti] *(pl* **surprises-parties)** **NF** *Vieilli* party

surprit *etc voir* **surprendre**

surprix [syrpri] **NM** excess price

surproducteur, -trice [syrprɔdyktœr, -tris] **ADJ** overproducing

surproduction [syrprɔdyksjɔ̃] **NF** overproduction

surproductrice [syrprɔdyktris] *voir* **surproducteur**

surproduire [98] [syrprɔdɥir] **VT** to overproduce

surprofit [syrprɔfi] **NM** abnormally high profit

surprotection [syrprɔtɛksjɔ̃] **NF** *(d'un enfant)* overprotection, coddling

surpuissant, -e [syrpɥisɑ̃, -ɑ̃t] **ADJ 1** *Tech* ultra-powerful **2** *(personne)* too powerful

surqualifié, -e [syrkalifje] **ADJ** overqualified

surréaction [syrreaksjɔ̃] **NF** *Écon* overshooting

surréalisme [syrrealism] **NM** surrealism

surréaliste [syrrealist] **ADJ 1** *Beaux-Arts & Littérature* surrealist **2** *(magique)* surreal
NMF surrealist

surréel [syrreel] **ADJ** surreal, surrealistic
NM le s. the surreal

surrégénérateur, -trice [syrreʒeneratœr, -tris] **ADJ** fast breeder *(avant n)*
NM breeder reactor

sur-régime [syrreʒim] **NM** *Aut* overspeeding

surrénal, -e, -aux, -ales [syrrenal, -o] **ADJ** suprarenal, adrenal
• **surrénale NF** suprarenal *or* adrenal gland

surreprésentation [syrrəprezɑ̃tasjɔ̃] **NF** over-representation; **la s. des jeunes dans les accidents de la route** the higher proportion of young people involved in road accidents

surreprésenté, -e [syrrəprezɑ̃te] **ADJ** over-represented; **les jeunes sont surreprésentés parmi les victimes de la route** proportionally more young people are injured or killed in road accidents

surréservation [syrrezɛrvɑsjɔ̃] **NF** overbooking

sursalaire [syrsalɛr] **NM** bonus

sursaturation [syrsatyrasjɔ̃] **NF 1** *Écon* oversaturation **2** *Phys* supersaturation

sursaturé, -e [syrsatyre] **ADJ 1** *Géol* oversaturated **2** *Fam* **s. de** *(information, sensations)* flooded with

sursaturer [3] [syrsatyre] **VT 1** *Écon* to oversaturate **2** *Phys* to supersaturate

sursaut [syrso] **NM 1** *(tressaillement)* start, jump; **elle eut un s. de peur** she jumped in alarm **2** *(regain subit)* burst; **un s. d'énergie** a burst of energy
• **en sursaut ADV** *(brusquement)* with a start; **elle se réveilla en s.** she woke up with a start

sursauter [3] [syrsote] **VI** to start, to jump; **faire s. qn** to give sb a start, to make sb start *or* jump

surseoir [66] [syrswar] **surseoir à VT IND 1** *Littéraire (différer ▸ publication, décision)* to postpone, to defer **2** *Jur* **s. à statuer, s. à un jugement** to defer a judgment; **s. à une exécution** to stay an execution

sursis [syrsi] **PP** *voir* **surseoir**
NM 1 *(délai)* reprieve, extension; **ils bénéficient d'un s. pour payer leurs dettes** they've been granted an extension of the time limit for paying their debts **2** *Jur* reprieve; **bénéficier d'un s.** to be granted *or* given a reprieve; **s. avec mise à l'épreuve** ≃ probation order; **s. probatoire** probation order; **s. simple** ≃ conditional discharge **3** *(ajournement)* deferment, extension; **s. à exécution** stay of execution; **s. à statuer** stay of proceedings; *Mil* **s. d'incorporation** deferment *or* deferral of call-up
• **avec sursis ADJ** suspended; **il est condamné à (une peine de) cinq ans avec s.** he's been given a five-year suspended (prison) sentence
• **en sursis ADJ 1** *Jur* in remission **2** *(en attente)* **c'est un mort en s.** he's living on borrowed time

sursitaire [syrsitɛr] *Mil* **ADJ** provisionally exempted
NM provisionally exempted conscript

sursoit *etc voir* **surseoir**

sursouscription [syrsuskripsjɔ̃] **NF** *Fin* oversubscription

sursouscrire [99] [syrsuscrir] **VT** *Fin* to oversubscribe

sursouscrit, -e [syrsuskri, -it] **ADJ** *Fin* oversubscribed

sursoyait *etc voir* **surseoir**

surtaux [syrto] **NM** excessively high rate

surtaxe [syrtaks] **NF 1** *(taxe supplémentaire)* surcharge; **s. à l'importation** import surcharge **2** *(taxe excessive)* excessive tax

surtaxer [3] [syrtakse] **VT** *(frapper d'une taxe ▸ supplémentaire)* to surcharge; *(▸ excessive)* to overcharge

surtension [syrtɑ̃sjɔ̃] **NF** (voltage) overload, overvoltage

surtitre [syrtitr] **NM 1** *Journ* strapline **2** *(traduction)* surtitle

surtout[1] [syrtu] **ADV 1** *(avant tout, par-dessus tout)* above all; *(plus particulièrement)* particularly, especially; **il leur faut naturellement de l'argent, mais s. de l'aide** they obviously need money, but above all *or* but most important of all, they need help; **il y avait s. des touristes dans la salle** most of the audience were tourists; **elle aime s. l'art moderne** she particularly likes modern art; **j'adore la viande, s. bien cuite** I love meat, especially when it's well done; **ils sont pingres, s. lui!** they're tight-fisted, especially him!; **il est agréable s. quand il a besoin d'aide!** he's very nice, especially when he needs help! **2** *(renforçant un conseil, un ordre)* **s., téléphonez-moi dès que vous serez arrivé** you MUST call me as soon as you get there; **s., pas de panique!** whatever you do, don't panic!; **ne faites s. pas de bruit** don't you make ANY noise; **je vais lui dire – s. pas!** I'll tell her – you'll do nothing of the sort!

• **surtout que CONJ** *Fam* especially as; **il ne devrait pas fumer, s. qu'il a les poumons fragiles** he shouldn't smoke, especially as he has weak lungs

surtout[2] [syrtu] **NM 1** *(décor de table)* centrepiece, epergne **2** *Vieilli* overcoat

survaleur [syrvalœr] **NF** *Compta* goodwill

survalorisation [syrvalɔrizasjɔ̃] **NF 1** *(d'un prix, d'une somme, d'un bien)* overvaluation **2** *(d'une qualité, d'une idée)* overemphasis; *(d'une personne)* overestimation

survaloriser [syrvalɔrize] **VT 1** *(bien)* to overvalue **2** *(idée, qualité)* to attach too much importance to, to overemphasize; *(personne)* to overestimate

survécu, -e [syrveky] **PP** *voir* **survivre**

surveillance [syrvɛjɑ̃s] **NF 1** *(contrôle ▸ de travaux)* supervision, overseeing; *(▸ médical)* monitoring; *(▸ des prix)* monitoring; **c'est Jane qui est chargée de la s. des enfants ce matin** Jane's looking after the children this morning; **exercer une s. discrète sur** to keep a discreet watch on; **déjouer la s. de qn** to give sb the slip; **chargé de la s. des travaux/de l'examen** responsible for overseeing the work/*Br* invigilating *or Am* proctoring the examination; **s. électronique** electronic surveillance **2** *Admin & Jur* surveillance; **s. légale** sequestration (by the courts); **s. de la pêche** fisheries protection service; **s. du territoire** counter-espionage *or* counterintelligence section

• **de surveillance ADJ 1** *(service, salle)* security *(avant n)*; *(avion, équipe)* surveillance *(avant n)*; *(appareil)* supervisory; *(caméra)* surveillance *(avant n)*, closed-circuit *(avant n)* **2** *Méd* monitoring

• **en surveillance ADV le malade est en s. à l'hôpital** the patient is under observation in hospital

• **sans surveillance ADV** unattended, unsupervised

• **sous la surveillance de PRÉP** under the surveillance of, under observation by; **sous la s. de la police** under police surveillance

• **sous surveillance ADV 1** *(par la police)* under surveillance; **placer qch sous s.** to put sth under surveillance; **banque sous s. électronique** bank under electronic surveillance **2** *Méd* under observation

surveillant, -e [syrvɛjɑ̃, -ɑ̃t] **NM,F 1** *(de prison)* prison guard; *(d'hôpital)* supervisor; *(de magasin)* store detective; *(de chantier)* supervisor, overseer **2** *Scol* monitor; *(d'examen) Br* invigilator, *Am* proctor; **s. d'internat** boarders' supervisor; *Vieilli* **s. général** head supervisor *(person in charge of school discipline)*

> Il faut noter que le terme anglais **surveyor** est un faux ami. Il signifie le plus souvent **expert** ou **géomètre**.

surveiller [4] [syrveje] **VT 1** *(épier)* to watch; **s. un prisonnier** to guard a prisoner; **il fait s. sa femme par un détective privé** he's having his wife watched by a private detective; **le commissaire faisait s. l'entrepôt** the superintendent placed the warehouse under surveillance; **on nous surveille** we're being watched

2 *(contrôler ▸ travaux, ouvriers, études)* to oversee, to surpervise; *(▸ cuisson)* to watch; *(▸ examen) Br* to invigilate, *Am* to proctor; *(▸ prix)* to monitor; **vous devriez s. les fréquentations de vos enfants** you should keep an eye on the company your children keep; **voilà ce qui arrive aux adolescents que leurs parents ne surveillent pas** that's what happens to unsupervised adolescents

3 *(observer)* to watch, to keep watch on *or* over; **s. un territoire** to keep watch over a territory; **l'ambassade est surveillée de près** *(gén)* the embassy is closely watched; *(exceptionnellement)* the embassy is under strict surveillance; **la situation est à s. de près** the situation should be very closely monitored

4 *(veiller sur ▸ bébé, bagages)* to watch, to keep an eye on; **s. un malade** *(personne)* to watch over a patient; *(avec une machine)* to monitor a patient; **vas-y, je surveille tes affaires** go ahead, I'll keep an eye on your things; **j'aurais dû le s. davantage** I should have kept a closer watch on him

5 *(prendre soin de ▸ santé, ligne)* to watch; **s. son langage** to watch *or* to mind one's language

USAGE ABSOLU to keep watch; **je surveille, vous pouvez y aller** go ahead, I'm keeping watch

VPR se surveiller 1 *(se contrôler)* to be careful what one does; **dans ce pays, il faut sans cesse se s.** you have to be very careful in this country **2** *(se restreindre)* to watch oneself, to keep a watch on oneself; **tu as grossi, tu devrais te s.** you've put on weight, you should watch yourself

> Il faut noter que le verbe anglais **to survey** est un faux ami. Il ne signifie jamais **surveiller**.

survenance [syrvənɑ̃s] **NF** *Jur* unexpected arrival *or* appearance; **s. d'enfant** unforeseen childbirth

survendre [73] [syrvɑ̃dr] **VT** *Com* to overcharge for

survenir [40] [syrvənir] **VI 1** *(problème, complication)* to arise, to crop up; *(événement, incident)* to happen, to occur, to take place **2** *Littéraire (personne)* to appear *or* to arrive unexpectedly

V IMPERSONNEL s'il ne survient pas de complications if no complications arise; *Littéraire* **s'il survient un visiteur** if a visitor happens to come

survenu, -e [syrvəny] **PP** *voir* **survenir**

• **survenue NF** *Littéraire* **1** *(d'une personne)* unexpected arrival *or* appearance **2** *(d'une complication)* appearance

survêt [syrvet] **NM** *Fam* tracksuit

survêtement [syrvɛtmɑ̃] **NM** tracksuit

survie [syrvi] **NF 1** *(continuation de la vie)* survival; **quelques jours de s.** a few more days to live; **donner à un malade quelques mois de s.** to prolong a patient's life for a few more months; **la s. d'une tradition** the continuance *or* survival of a tradition; **nous luttons pour la s. de notre entreprise** we are fighting for the survival of our company; **équipement de s.** *(d'astronaute)* life support equipment

2 *(au-delà de la mort)* afterlife

3 *Jur* **droits** *ou* **gains de s.** (stipulated *or* contractual) rights of survivorship

4 *École* survival

survient *etc voir* **survenir**

survint *etc voir* **survenir**

survirage [syrviraʒ] **NM** *Aut* oversteer

survirer [3] [syrvire] **VI** *Aut* to oversteer

survireur, -euse [syrvirœr, -øz] **ADJ** *Aut* that tends to oversteer

survit *etc voir* **survivre**

survitaminé, -e [syrvitamine] **ADJ** *Fam* hyper

survivance [syrvivɑ̃s] **NF 1** *(d'une coutume)* trace, survival; **c'est une s. des rites païens** it's a relic *or* a survival from pagan rites **2** *Littéraire (survie)* survival; **s. de l'âme** the survival of the soul after death **3** *Ling* archaicism

survivant, -e [syrvivɑ̃, -ɑ̃t] **ADJ** *(conjoint, coutume)* surviving *(avant n)*

NM,F survivor; **c'est le seul s.** he is the sole survivor

survivre [90] [syrvivr] **VI 1** *(réchapper)* to survive, to live on; **ceux qui ont survécu** those who survived, the survivors **2** *(continuer à exister)* to survive; **une coutume qui a survécu à travers les siècles** a custom that has survived *or* endured through the ages; **dans le monde des affaires, il faut lutter pour s.** in business, it's a struggle for survival; **s. à** *(accident)* to survive; *(personne)* to survive, to outlive; **elle a survécu à tous ses enfants** she has survived *or* outlived all her children; **je ne veux pas lui s.** I don't want to live on after his/her death; **la statue a survécu aux bombardements** the statue has survived the bombing

VPR se survivre 1 *(artiste, célébrité)* to outlive one's fame *or* success **2** *Littéraire* **se s. dans qn/qch** to live through sb/sth; **se s. dans ses enfants** to live on through one's children

survol [syrvɔl] **NM 1** *Aviat* **l'Espagne a refusé le s. de son territoire** Spain refused to allow the aircraft to fly over *or* to overfly its territory **2** *(d'un texte)* skimming through; *(d'une question)* skimming over; **un s. du roman montre que...** a quick look at the novel shows that...

survoler [3] [syrvɔle] **VT 1** *Aviat* to overfly, to fly over **2** *(texte)* to skim through; *(question)* to skim over; **vous ne faites que s. la question** your treatment of the question is (too) cursory *or* superficial **3** *Ordinat* to browse through

survoltage [syrvɔltaʒ] **NM** (voltage) overload, overvoltage

survolté, -e [syrvɔlte] **ADJ** *Fam (surexcité)* hyper, worked up

survolteur [syrvɔltœr] **NM** *Élec (transformateur)* booster, step-up transformer

sus [sy(s)] **ADV** *Littéraire* **courir s. à qn** to give chase to sb

EXCLAM *Arch* **s., mes amis!** come, my friends!; **s. à l'ennemi!** have at them!

• **en sus ADV** in addition

• **en sus de PRÉP** in addition to

susceptibilité [sysɛptibilite] **NF 1** *(sensibilité)* touchiness, sensitiveness; **il est d'une grande s.** he's very touchy *or* sensitive; **blesser la s. de qn** to hurt sb's feelings; **ménager la s. de qn** to humour sb **2** *Phys* **s. magnétique** magnetic susceptibility

susceptible [sysɛptibl] **ADJ 1** *(sensible)* touchy, oversensitive, thin-skinned; **trop s.** oversensitive; **ne sois pas si s.** don't be so touchy *or* ready to take offence **2** *(exprime la possibilité)* **ce cheval est s. de gagner** that horse is capable of winning; **votre offre est s. de m'intéresser** I might be interested in your offer; **une situation s. de se produire** a situation likely to occur; **projet s. d'être amélioré** project open to improvement

susciter [3] [sysite] **VT 1** *(envie, jalousie, haine, intérêt, sympathie)* to arouse; *(mécontentement, incompréhension, étonnement)* to cause, to give rise to; *(problèmes)* to give rise to, to create **2** *(déclencher ▸ révolte)* to stir up; *(▸ dispute)* to provoke; *(▸ malveillance)* to incite

suscription [syskripsjɔ̃] **NF 1** *(adresse)* address, *Sout* superscription **2** *(sur un acte diplomatique)* superscription **3** *Jur* **acte de s.** (testamentary) superscription

sus-dénommé, -e [sysdenɔme] *(mpl* **sus-dénommés**, *fpl* **sus-dénommées)** *Jur* **ADJ** above-named, aforenamed

NM,F above-named, aforenamed

susdit, -e [sysdi, -it] *(mpl* **susdits**, *fpl* **susdites)** *Jur* **ADJ** aforesaid

NM,F aforesaid

sus-dominante [sysdɔminɑ̃t] *(pl* **sus-dominantes)** **NF** *Mus* submediant, sixth

susmentionné, -e [sysmɑ̃sjɔne] **ADJ** *Jur* above-mentioned, aforementioned

susnommé, -e [sysnɔme] *Jur* **ADJ** above-named, aforenamed

NM,F above-named, aforenamed

suspect, -e [syspɛ, -ɛkt] **ADJ 1** *(attitude, objet)* suspicious, suspect; *(aliment)* suspect; **un individu s.** a suspicious-looking person; **se rendre s. à qn** to arouse sb's suspicions; **cela m'est s.** it looks suspicious *or* suspect to me, I don't like the look of it

2 *(dont on peut douter)* **je trouve ses progrès soudains très suspects** I'm rather suspicious of his/her sudden progress

3 *(suspecté)* **être s. de qch** to be suspected *or* under suspicion of sth

4 *(susceptible)* **elle était peu suspecte de sympathie envers le terrorisme** she was hardly likely to approve of terrorism

NM,F suspect

suspecter **[4]** [syspɛkte] **VT 1** *(soupçonner)* to suspect (**de qch/de faire qch** of sth/of doing sth); **on le suspecte d'avoir commis un meurtre** he's suspected of murder, he's under suspicion of murder; **je le suspecte de ne pas me dire la vérité** I suspect he's not telling me the truth, I suspect him of not telling me the truth; **je suspecte un mauvais coup** I suspect there's some foul play going on **2** *(douter de)* to doubt, to have doubts about; **je suspecte la véracité de son témoignage** I doubt the truth of his testimony; **s. la sincérité de qn** to doubt sb's sincerity

suspendre **[73]** [syspɑ̃dr] **VT 1** *(accrocher ▸ lustre, vêtement)* to hang; **suspends ta veste à la patère** hang your jacket (up) on the hook; **suspendu dans le vide** hanging *or* suspended in mid-air

2 *Fig* **être suspendu à** *(dépendre de)* to depend *or* to be dependent on; **l'avenir de l'entreprise est suspendu à votre décision** the future of the firm depends entirely on your decision, your decision holds the key to the future of the firm

3 *(interrompre ▸ hostilités, paiements)* to suspend; *(▸ négociations)* to break off; *(▸ séance, audience)* to adjourn; *(▸ récit)* to interrupt; **la séance est suspendue** we will now adjourn; *Banque* **s. le paiement d'un chèque** to stop a cheque; *Ordinat* **s. l'exécution d'un programme** to abort a program

4 *(différer ▸ décision)* to defer, to postpone; **s. son jugement** to suspend *or* to reserve judgment

5 *(interdire ▸ émission, journal)* to ban; *(révoquer ▸ fonctionnaire, prêtre, juge)* to suspend; **l'administration l'a suspendu** he's been suspended

VPR se suspendre to hang (**à/par** from/by)

suspendu, -e [syspɑ̃dy] **ADJ 1** *Constr* hanging *(avant n)*

2 *(en travaux publics ▸ pont)* suspension *(avant n)*

3 *Aut* **voiture bien/mal suspendue** car with good/bad suspension

4 *Bot* suspended

5 *Géog* **vallée suspendue** hanging valley

suspens [syspɑ̃] **ADJ M** *Rel* suspended

• **en suspens ADJ 1** *(affaire, dossier)* pending, unfinished; *(problème, question)* unresolved; *(lecteur)* uncertain **2** *(flocons, planeur)* suspended, hanging **ADV tenir qn en s.** to keep sb in suspense; **laisser un dossier en s.** to keep a file pending; **laisser une question en s.** to leave a question unanswered *or* unresolved

suspense[1] [syspɑ̃s] **NF** *Rel* suspension

suspense[2] [syspens] **NM** suspense; **il y a un s. terrible dans le livre** the book's full of suspense; **prolonger le s.** to prolong the suspense; **ne fais pas durer le s., raconte-nous la fin!** the suspense is killing us, do tell us the ending!

• **à suspense ADJ** suspense *(avant n)*; **film à s.** thriller; **roman à s.** thriller, suspense story

suspensif, -ive [syspɑ̃sif, -iv] **ADJ** *Jur* suspensive

suspension [syspɑ̃sjɔ̃] **NF 1** *(d'un objet)* hanging

2 *(interruption)* suspension; *Mil* **s. d'armes** suspension of hostilities; *Jur* **s. d'audience** adjournment (of hearing); *Ordinat* **s. d'exécution** *(d'un programme)* abort; *Jur* **s. d'instance** deferment of proceedings; **s. de paiement** suspension *or* withholding of payment; *Jur* **s. de peine** ≃ deferred sentence; **s. provisoire des poursuites** suspension of proceedings; **demander une s. de séance** to ask for an adjournment

3 *Admin (sanction)* suspension; **s. de permis de conduire** suspension of *Br* driving licence *or Am* driver's license; **sous peine d'un an de s. du permis de conduire** the penalty being a one-year driving ban

4 *Aut* suspension; **s. hydraulique** hydraulic suspension; **s. hydropneumatique** hydropneumatic suspension; **s. à roues indépendantes** independent suspension

5 *Chim, Géog, Mus & Rail* suspension; *Méd* **s. buvable** oral suspension

6 *Typ* **points de s.** suspension points

7 *Mines* **s. dense** dense *or* heavy medium

8 *(luminaire)* ceiling light fitting

• **en suspension ADJ 1** *(poussière)* hanging; **en s. dans l'air** hanging in the air **2** *Chim* in suspension

suspensive [syspɑ̃siv] *voir* **suspensif**

suspicieux, -euse [syspisjø, -øz] **ADJ** *Littéraire* suspicious, suspecting

suspicion [syspisjɔ̃] **NF 1** *(défiance)* suspicion, suspiciousness; *Littéraire* **avoir de la s. à l'égard de qn** to have one's suspicions about sb; **jeter la s. sur qn** to cast suspicion on sb **2** *Jur (supposition d'un délit)* suspicion; **s. de fraude** suspicion of fraud; **s. légitime** = reasonable suspicion that a fair trial will not be given

sustentation [systɑ̃tɑsjɔ̃] **NF 1** *Aviat* lift **2** *Phys* sustentation; **base** *ou* **polygone de s.** basis of support

sustenter **[3]** [systɑ̃te] **VT 1** *Vieilli (nourrir ▸ personne)* to sustain **2** *Aviat* to lift

VPR se sustenter *Hum* to feed, to take sustenance; **nous nous sustentions de quelques morceaux de pain** we fed on a few pieces of bread

sus-tonique [systɔnik] *(pl* **sus-toniques)** **NF** *Mus* supertonic

susurrement [sysyrmɑ̃] **NM** *Littéraire* susurration, whispering; *(du vent)* whispering; *(de la mer)* murmuring; *(des arbres)* rustling

susurrer **[3]** [sysyre] *Littéraire* **VT** *(chuchoter)* to whisper; **s. des mots doux à l'oreille de qn** to whisper sweet nothings in sb's ear

VI 1 *(bruire ▸ vent)* to whisper; *(▸ mer)* to murmur; *(▸ arbres)* to rustle **2** *(chuchoter)* to whisper

sut *etc voir* **savoir**

suture [sytyr] **NF 1** *Bot, Géol & Zool* suture **2** *Anat & Méd* suture; **point de s.** stitch; **on lui a fait cinq points de s.** he/she had five stitches (put in)

suturer **[3]** [sytyre] **VT** *Méd* to stitch up, *Spéc* to suture

suzerain, -e [syzrɛ̃, -ɛn] **ADJ** suzerain

NM,F suzerain, (feudal) overlord

suzeraineté [syzrɛnte] **NF** suzerainty

svastika [svastika] **NM** swastika

svelte [svɛlt] **ADJ** *(bras, jambes)* slender; *(personne)* slender, svelte

sveltesse [svɛltɛs] **NF** *Littéraire* svelteness, slenderness, slimness

SVP [ɛsvepe] *(abrév* **s'il vous plaît)** please

swahili, -e [swaili] **ADJ** Swahili

NM *(langue)* Swahili

• **Swahili, -e NM,F** Swahili; **les S.** the Swahilis *or* Swahili

swap [swap] **NM** *Bourse* swap; *Fin* **s. d'actifs** asset swap; *Fin* **s. de change** exchange rate swap; *Bourse* **s. vanilla** vanilla swap

Swaziland [swazilɑ̃d] **NM le S.** Swaziland; **vivre au S.** to live in Swaziland; **aller au S.** to go to Swaziland

sweater [swetœr] **NM** sweater

sweat-shirt [switʃœrt] *(pl* **sweat-shirts)** **NM** sweatshirt

sweepstake [swipstɛk] **NM** sweepstake

swing [swiŋ] **NM 1** *Mus (rythme)* swing, swinging; *(style)* swing **2** *Sport* swing

swinguer **[3]** [swiŋge] **VI** to swing; **quel orchestre, ça swingue!** that band really swings!

sybarite [sibarit] **ADJ** *Littéraire* sybaritic

NMF *Littéraire (hédoniste)* hedonist, sybarite, pleasure-seeker

• **Sybarite NMF** *Antiq* Sybarite

sybaritique [sibaritik] **ADJ** *Littéraire* sybaritic

sybaritisme [sibaritism] **NM** *Littéraire* sybaritism

sycomore [sikɔmɔr] **NM** sycamore

sycophante [sikɔfɑ̃t] **NM 1** *Littéraire (dénonciateur)* informer; *(calomniateur)* scandal-monger **2** *Antiq* sycophant

syllabaire [silabɛr] **NM 1** *(livre)* (syllabic) spelling-book **2** *Ling* syllabary

syllabe [silab] **NF 1** *Ling* syllable; **s. ouverte/fermée** open/closed syllable **2** *(parole)* **elle n'a pas prononcé une s.** she never opened her mouth; **je n'ai pas pu lui arracher une seule s.** I couldn't get a single word out of him/her

syllabique [silabik] **ADJ** syllabic

syllogisme [silɔʒism] **NM** syllogism

syllogistique [silɔʒistik] **ADJ** syllogistic, syllogistical

NF syllogistic, syllogistics *(singulier)*

sylphe [silf] **NM** *Myth* sylph

sylvestre [silvɛstr] **ADJ** *Littéraire* sylvan, forest *(avant n)*

sylvicole [silvikɔl] **ADJ** forestry *(avant n)*, *Spéc* silvicultural

sylviculteur, -trice [silvikyltœr, -tris] **NM,F** forester, *Spéc* silviculturist

sylviculture [silvikyltyr] **NF** forestry, *Spéc* silviculture

symbiose [sɛ̃bjoz] **NF** *Biol & Fig* symbiosis

• **en symbiose ADV** symbiotically, in symbiosis; *Fig* **ils vivent en s.** they're inseparable; **vivre en s. avec la nature** to live in harmony with nature

symbole [sɛ̃bɔl] **NM 1** *(signe)* symbol; **le drapeau est le s. de la nation** the flag is the symbol of the nation

2 *(personnification)* symbol, embodiment; **il est le s. du respect filial** he's the embodiment of filial duty, he's filial duty personified

3 *Rel* **S.** Creed; **le S. des Apôtres/de Nicée** the Apostles'/Nicene Creed

4 *Chim, Ordinat & Math* symbol

symbolique [sɛ̃bɔlik] **ADJ 1** *(fait avec des symboles)* symbolic; **langage/logique s.** symbolic language/logic; **écriture s.** writing in symbols **2** *(sans valeur réelle)* token, nominal; **une somme s.** a nominal amount; **un geste s.** a symbolic *or* token gesture

NM le s. the symbolic

NF 1 *(ensemble des symboles)* symbolic system, symbolism **2** *(étude des symboles)* interpretation of symbols, symbology

symboliquement [sɛ̃bɔlikmɑ̃] **ADV** symbolically; **on leur a donné s. un euro à chacun** they each got a token one-euro piece

symbolisation [sɛ̃bɔlizasjɔ̃] **NF 1** *(mise en symboles)* symbolization **2** *Math* symbolization

symboliser **[3]** [sɛ̃bɔlize] **VT** to symbolize; **on symbolise la justice par une balance** justice is symbolized by a pair of scales

symbolisme [sɛ̃bɔlism] **NM 1** *(système)* symbolism **2** *Beaux-Arts & Littérature* Symbolism

symboliste [sɛ̃bɔlist] **ADJ 1** *(relatif aux symboles)* symbolistic **2** *Beaux-Arts & Littérature* Symbolist

NMF Symbolist

symétrie [simetri] **NF 1** *(gén)* symmetry; **son visage manque de s.** his/her face lacks symmetry **2** *Géom* **s. de révolution/d'axes** rotational/axial symmetry; **s. à droite/gauche** right/left inverse

symétrique [simetrik] **ADJ 1** *(gén)* symmetrical; **une rangée s. de l'autre** one row symmetrical to the other **2** *Géom* symmetrical; *Math* symmetric **3** *Électron (circuit)* balanced

NM *(point)* symmetrical point; *(élément)* symmetrical element

NF *(figure)* symmetrical figure; **x est une s. de y** x and y are symmetrical

symétriquement [simetrikmɑ̃] **ADV** symmetrically

sympa [sɛ̃pa] **ADJ** *Fam* nice[□]; **merci, c'était une soirée super s.** thank you, that was a really great evening

sympathectomie [sɛ̃patɛktɔmi], **sympathicectomie** [sɛ̃patisɛktɔmi] **NF** *Méd* sympathectomy

sympathie [sɛ̃pati] **NF 1** *(cordialité)* friendship, fellow feeling; **il y a une grande s. entre eux** they get on very well; **être en s. avec qn** to be on friendly terms with sb

2 *(penchant)* liking; **éprouver de la s. pour qn** to like sb, to have a liking for sb; **je n'ai aucune s. pour lui** I don't like him at all, I have no liking for him at all; **inspirer la s.** to be likeable

3 *(bienveillance)* sympathy *(UNCOUNT)*; **témoigner de la s. à qn** to be friendly towards sb; **croyez à notre s.** our deepest sympathy; **recevoir des témoignages de s.** to receive expressions of sympathy

4 *(pour une idée)* sympathy; **je n'ai pas beaucoup de s. pour ce genre d'attitude** I don't have much time for that kind of attitude

5 *Méd* sympathy

• **sympathies** **NFPL** *(tendances)* sympathies; **ses sympathies vont vers les républicains** his sympathies are *or* lie with the Republicans

> Il faut noter que le terme anglais **sympathy** est un faux ami. Il signifie **compassion**.

sympathique [sɛ̃patik] **ADJ 1** *(personne)* nice, pleasant; **elle m'est très s.** I like her very much **2** *(visage)* friendly; *(idée)* good; *(lieu)* pleasant, nice; *(plat)* appetizing; *(ambiance, soirée, spectacle)* pleasant; *(attitude)* kind, friendly; **ce n'est pas très s. de sa part** that's not very nice of him/her; **il est bien s., ce petit vin/fromage!** nice little wine/cheese, this! **3** *Physiol* sympathetic

NM *Anat* sympathetic nervous system

> Il faut noter que le terme anglais **sympathetic** est un faux ami. Il signifie **compréhensif, compatissant**.

sympathiquement [sɛ̃patikmɑ̃] **ADV** nicely, in a kindly way

sympathisant, -e [sɛ̃patizɑ̃, -ɑ̃t] **ADJ** sympathizing

NM,F sympathizer; **un s. du New Labour** a New Labour sympathizer

sympathiser **[3]** [sɛ̃patize] **VI 1** *(s'entendre)* **s. avec** *esp Br* to get on with, *esp Am* to get along with; **il n'a pas sympathisé avec les autres enfants** he didn't get on with the other children; **nous avons tout de suite sympathisé** we took to *or* liked each other right away **2** *Pol* **elle sympathise avec les communistes** she's a communist sympathizer

> Il faut noter que le verbe anglais **to sympathize** est un faux ami. Il signifie **compatir, se montrer solidaire**.

symphonie [sɛ̃fɔni] **NF 1** *Mus* symphony; **les symphonies de Mozart** Mozart's symphonies; **s. concertante** sinfonia concertante **2** *Littéraire (harmonie)* symphony; **le paysage offrait toute une s. de verts** the countryside was a harmonious blend of greens

symphonique [sɛ̃fɔnik] **ADJ** *(œuvre, poème)* symphonic; *(orchestre)* symphony *(avant n)*

symphoniste [sɛ̃fɔnist] **NMF 1** *(auteur)* symphonist **2** *(musicien)* orchestral player, symphonist

symphyse [sɛ̃fiz] **NF 1** *Anat* symphysis; **s. mentonnière** symphisis mandibulae **2** *Méd* **s. cardiaque** cardiac symphisis; **s. pleurale** adherent pleura

symposium [sɛ̃pozjɔm] **NM** *(colloque)* symposium

symptomatique [sɛ̃ptɔmatik] **ADJ 1** *Méd* symptomatic **2** *(caractéristique)* symptomatic, indicative (**de** of); **c'est s. de leurs relations** it's symptomatic of *or* it tells you something about their relationship

symptomatiquement [sɛ̃ptɔmatikmɑ̃] **ADV** symptomatically

symptomatologie [sɛ̃ptɔmatɔlɔʒi] **NF** symptomatology

symptôme [sɛ̃ptom] **NM 1** *Méd* symptom; **quand avez-vous ressenti les premiers symptômes?** when did you first notice the symptoms? **2** *(signe)* symptom, sign; **les premiers symptômes de qch** the forerunners *or* first signs of sth

synagogue [sinagɔg] **NF** synagogue

synapse [sinaps] **NF 1** *Anat* synapse **2** *Biol* synapsis

synchrone [sɛ̃kron] **ADJ** synchronous (**avec** with)

synchronie [sɛ̃krɔni] **NF** synchrony

synchronique [sɛ̃krɔnik] **ADJ** synchronic

synchronisateur [sɛ̃krɔnizatœr] **NM** synchronizer

synchronisation [sɛ̃krɔnizasjɔ̃] **NF** synchronization

synchronisé, -e [sɛ̃krɔnize] **ADJ** synchronized

synchroniser **[3]** [sɛ̃krɔnize] **VT** to synchronize (**avec** with)

synchroniseur [sɛ̃krɔnizœr] **NM 1** *Aut* synchromesh (device) **2** *Cin, Élec & Phot* synchronizer **3** *École* biorhythm trigger *or* signal

synchronisme [sɛ̃krɔnism] **NM** synchronism

synchrotron [sɛ̃krɔtrɔ̃] **NM** *Phys* synchrotron

synclinal, -e, -aux, -ales [sɛ̃klinal, -o] **ADJ** synclinal

NM syncline

syncope [sɛ̃kɔp] **NF 1** *Méd* faint, blackout, *Spéc* syncope; **tomber en s., avoir une s.** to faint **2** *Ling* syncope **3** *Mus* syncopation

syncopé, -e [sɛ̃kɔpe] **ADJ** syncopated

syncrétisme [sɛ̃kretism] **NM** syncretism

syndic [sɛ̃dik] **NM 1** *Admin* **s. (d'immeuble)** managing agent

2 *Anciennement Jur* **s. (de faillite)** (official) receiver *(before 1985)*

3 *Hist* syndic

4 *Bourse* president

5 *Suisse (président de commune)* = high-ranking civic official, similar to a mayor, in certain Swiss cantons

> **SYNDIC**
>
> A "syndic" is an administrative body which represents the interests of the owners of all the flats in a building, collectively known as the "syndicat de copropriété". The role of the "syndic" is to ensure the upkeep of the building and to organize meetings during which a vote is taken on any repairs, improvements etc that are deemed necessary. The services of the "syndic" are paid for by the owners of the flats.

syndical, -e, -aux, -ales [sɛ̃dikal, -o] **ADJ 1** *Pol (Br* trade *or Am* labor) union *(avant n)* **2** *Admin* management *(avant n)*; **droit s.** right of association

syndicalisation [sɛ̃dikalizasjɔ̃] **NF** unionization; **le taux de s. dans l'industrie est en chute libre depuis 20 ans** union membership in this industry has been plummeting for the last 20 years

syndicaliser **[3]** [sɛ̃dikalize] **VT** to unionize

syndicalisme [sɛ̃dikalism] **NM 1** *(mouvement) (Br* trade *or Am* labor) unionism

2 *(ensemble des syndicats) (Br* trade *or Am* labor) unions

3 *(action)* union activities; **faire du s.** to be active in a union

4 *(doctrine)* unionism

syndicaliste [sɛ̃dikalist] **ADJ 1** *(mouvement) (Br* trade *or Am* labor) union *(avant n)* **2** *(doctrine)* unionist

NMF *(Br* trade *or Am* labor) unionist

syndicat [sɛ̃dika] **NM 1** *Pol (travailleurs) (Br* trade *or Am* labor) union; **se former** *ou* **se regrouper en s.** to form a union; **s. ouvrier** *(Br* trade *or Am* labor) union; **s. patronal** employers' confederation *or* association; **s. professionnel** trade *or* professional association, trade body; **s. des typographes** print union **2** *Jur (association)* association; **s. de communes** association of communes; **s. intercommunal à vocation multiple** = group of local authorities pooling public services; **s. interdépartemental** association of regional administrators; **s. de copropriétaires** co-owners' association **3** *Fin* **s. d'émission/de garantie** issuing/underwriting syndicate; **s. d'enchères** tender pool; **s. financier** financial syndicate; **s. de prise ferme** underwriting syndicate

• **syndicat d'initiative** **NM** tourist (information) office

syndicataire [sɛ̃dikatɛr] **ADJ 1** *(d'un syndicat de copropriétaires)* = of a co-owners' association **2** *Fin* syndicate *(avant n)*

NMF 1 *(copropriétaire)* member of a co-owners' association **2** *Fin* underwriter

syndiqué, -e [sɛ̃dike] **ADJ 1** *(membre d'un syndicat financier)* belonging to a syndicate **2** *(membre d'un syndicat de travailleurs)* belonging to a *(Br* trade *or Am* labor) union; **être s.** to be a member of a *(Br* trade *or Am* labor) union

NM,F *(Br* trade *or Am* labor) union member

syndiquer **[3]** [sɛ̃dike] **VT** to unionize, to organize; **s. les travailleurs d'un atelier** to organize the workers in a workshop

VPR se syndiquer 1 *(se constituer en syndicat)* to form a *(Br* trade *or Am* labor) union **2** *(adhérer à un syndicat)* to join a *(Br* trade *or Am* labor) union

syndrome [sɛ̃drom] **NM** *Méd* syndrome; **s. d'alcoolisme fœtal** foetal alcohol syndrome, FAS; **s. d'Asperger** Asperger's syndrome; **s. du bébé secoué** shaken baby syndrome; *Fam* **s. de la blouse blanche** white coat syndrome; **s. cervical traumatique** whiplash injury; **s. du choc toxique** toxic shock syndrome; **s. du côlon irritable** irritable bowel syndrome, IBS; **s. de Cushing** Cushing's syndrome; **s. de Down** Down's syndrome; **s. d'enfermement** locked-in syndrome; **s. de fatigue chronique** chronic fatigue syndrome; **s. des faux souvenirs** false memory syndrome; **s. de Gilles de la Tourette** Tourette's syndrome; **s. de Guillain-Barré** Guillain-Barré syndrome; **s. immunodéficitaire acquis** acquired immunodeficiency syndrome, Aids; **s. inflammatoire pelvien** pelvic inflammatory disease, PID; **s. métabolique** metabolic syndrome; **s. des ovaires polykystiques** polycystic ovary syndrome; **s. postviral** postviral syndrome; **s. prémenstruel** premenstrual tension *or* syndrome; **s. du QT long** long QT syndrome; **s. respiratoire aigu sévère** severe acute respiratory syndrome; **s. de Stockholm** Stockholm syndrome; **s. de stress post-traumatique** post-traumatic stress disorder; **s. d'Usher, s. de Usher** Usher syndrome

synectique [sinɛktik] **NF** synectics *(singulier)*

synérèse [sinerɛz] **NF** *Chim & Ling* synaeresis

synergiciel [sinɛrʒisjɛl] **NM** *Ordinat* groupware

synergie [sinɛrʒi] **NF** synergy, synergism

synergisme [sinɛrʒism] **NM** synergism

synesthésie [sinɛstezi] **NF** synaesthesia

syngnathe [sɛ̃gnat] **NM** *Ich* pipefish

synode [sinɔd] **NM** *Rel* synod

synodique [sinɔdik] **ADJ** *Astron & Rel* synodic

NM *Rel* synodal

synonyme [sinɔnim] **ADJ** synonymous (**de** with)

NM synonym; **cherchez un s. de "beau"** find another word *or* a synonym for "beautiful"

synonymie [sinɔnimi] **NF** synonymy

synopse [sinɔps] **NF** synoptic table of the Gospels

synopsis [sinɔpsis] **NF** *(bref aperçu)* synopsis

NM *Cin* synopsis

synoptique [sinɔptik] **ADJ** synoptic, synoptical; **les Évangiles synoptiques** the Synoptic Gospels

• **synoptiques** **NMPL** **les synoptiques** the Synoptic Gospels

synovial, -e, -aux, -ales [sinɔvjal, -o] *Anat* **ADJ** synovial

• **synoviale** **NF** synovium, synovial membrane

synovie [sinɔvi] **NF** *Physiol* synovia, synovial fluid

synovite [sinɔvit] **NF** *Méd* synovitis

syntacticien, -enne [sɛ̃taktisjɛ̃, -ɛn] **NM,F** *Ling* syntactician

syntactique [sɛ̃taktik] **ADJ** *Chim & Ling* syntactic

syntagmatique [sɛ̃tagmatik] *Ling* **ADJ** syntagmatic

NF syntagmatic analysis, syntagmatics *(singulier)*

syntagme [sɛ̃tagm] **NM** phrase, *Spéc* syntagm; **s. nominal/verbal/adjectival** noun/verb/adjectival phrase

syntaxe [sɛ̃taks] **NF** *Ordinat & Ling* syntax

syntaxique [sɛ̃taksik] **ADJ 1** *Ling* syntactic **2** *Ordinat* syntax *(avant n)*

synthèse [sɛ̃tez] **NF 1** *(structuration de connaissances)* synthesis; **faire la s. d'un récit** to summarize the main elements of a story

2 *(exposé, ouvrage)* summary, résumé; **écrire une s. sur l'histoire de l'après-guerre** to write a brief history of the post-war years

3 *Biol, Chim & Phil* synthesis

4 *Ordinat* synthesis; **s. des images** image synthesis; **s. de la parole** speech synthesis

• **de synthèse** **ADJ 1** *(non analytique)* **avoir l'esprit de s.** to be able to see the overall picture **2** *(fibre, parole)* synthetic

synthétique [sɛ̃tetik] **ADJ 1** *(raisonnement, approche)* all-encompassing; *(bilan)* summary; **une vue s. des choses** an overall *or* all-encompassing view of things; **avoir un esprit s.** to be able to see the overall picture **2** *Chim (fibre)* synthetic, man-made, artificial **3** *Ling & Phil* synthetic
NM *(matière)* synthetic *or* man-made fibres

synthétiquement [sɛ̃tetikmɑ̃] **ADV** synthetically

synthétiser [3] [sɛ̃tetize] **VT 1** *(idées, résultats, relevés)* to synthesize, to bring together **2** *Biol & Chim* to synthesize

synthétiseur [sɛ̃tetizœr] **NM** synthesizer; **s. de paroles** speech *or* voice synthesizer

syntonisation [sɛ̃tɔnizasjɔ̃] **NF** *Rad* syntonization

syntoniser [3] [sɛ̃tɔnize] **VT** *Rad* to syntonize

syntoniseur [sɛ̃tɔnizœr] **NM** tuner

syphilis [sifilis] **NF** syphilis

syphilitique [sifilitik] **ADJ** syphilitic
NMF syphilitic

Syrie [siri] **NF la S.** Syria

syrien, -enne [sirjɛ̃, -ɛn] **ADJ** Syrian
NM *(langue)* Syrian
• **Syrien, -enne NM,F** Syrian

syringe [sirɛ̃ʒ] **NF** *Archéol* rock-cut tomb

sysop [sizɔp] **NM** *Ordinat (abrév* **Systems Operator**) SYSOP

systématique [sistematik] **ADJ 1** *(méthodique)* methodical, orderly, systematic; **de façon s.** systematically
2 *(invariable ▸ réaction)* automatic, invariable; *(▸ refus)* automatic; **c'est s., quand je dis oui, il dit non** when I say yes, he invariably *or* automatically says no; **je le fais parfois mais ce n'est pas s.** I do it sometimes but not as a matter of course *or* not automatically
3 *(inconditionnel ▸ soutien)* unconditional, solid
4 *Méd* systemic
NF *Biol & Phys* systematics *(singulier)*

systématiquement [sistematikmɑ̃] **ADV** systematically

systématisation [sistematizasjɔ̃] **NF** systematization

systématiser [3] [sistematize] **VT** *(organiser en système)* to systemize, to systematize
USAGE ABSOLU *(être de parti pris)* to systemize, to systematize; **il a trop tendance à s.** he's too inclined to reduce everything to a system; **il ne faut pas s.** we mustn't generalize

système [sistɛm] **NM 1** *(structure)* system; **s. philosophique** philosophical system; **le s. éducatif/de santé français** the French educational system/health services; **s. scolaire** school system; **s. de production** system of production; **s. de valeurs** system of values; **il refuse d'entrer dans le s.** he refuses to be part of the system; **avoir l'esprit de s.** to have a systematic mind; **s. bancaire** bank *or* banking system; *Banque* **s. de compensation** clearing system; **s. comptable** accounting system; *Compta* **s. de contrôle de stocks** stock control system; **s. de direction** management system; *Com* **s. de distribution** distribution system; *Fin* **s. fiscal** tax system; **s. d'information marketing** marketing information system; *Com* **s. d'inventaire** inventory method; *Jur* **s. du juge unique** single judge system; *Écon* **s. monétaire européen** European Monetary System; **s. de participation aux bénéfices** profit-sharing scheme; **s. de retraite** pension scheme; **s. de retraite par répartition** contributory pension plan; **s. solaire** solar system
2 *(méthode)* way, means; **il faut trouver un s. pour sortir de là** we've got to find a way of getting out of here; **je connais un bon s. pour faire fortune** I know a good way of making a fortune; **il a trouvé le s. pour ne pas être dérangé** he's found a way to avoid being disturbed; **s. D** resourcefulness[◻]; **recourir au s. D** to use one's wits
3 *(appareillage)* system; **s. de chauffage/d'éclairage** heating/lighting system; **s. de fermeture/de freinage** locking/braking system; **s. de navigation** navigation system
4 *(réseau ▸ de routes, de canaux)* system, network
5 *Anat & Méd* system; **s. nerveux/digestif/immunitaire** nervous/digestive/immune system; **s. nerveux central** central nervous system; **s. osseux** bone structure; **s. pileux** hair *(on body and head)*; **s. végétatif** vegetative system
6 *(armement)* **s. d'arme** weapon *or* weapons system
7 *Constr* **s. de construction** system
8 *Géol* system
9 *Ordinat* system; **s. expert** expert system; **s. d'exploitation** operating system; **s. d'exploitation de** *ou* **à disques** disk operating system; **s. d'exploitation réseau** network operating system; **s. de gestion de bases de données** database management system; **s. de gestion de fichiers** file management system; **s. d'information** information system; **s. informatique** computer system; **s. informatisé** computerized information system; **s. multi-utilisateur** multi-user system; **s. de sauvegarde sur bande** tape backup system; **s. de secours** backup system; **s. serveur** host system; **s. à tour** tower system; **s. de traitement de l'information** data processing system
10 *Math* **s. décimal** decimal system; **s. d'équations** simultaneous equations
11 *Météo* **s. nuageux** cloud system
12 *Phys* **s. international d'unités** SI unit; **s. métrique** metric system
13 *Fam (locution)* **taper sur le s. à qn** to get on sb's nerves *or Br* wick
• **par système ADV** as a matter of principle

systémique [sistemik] **ADJ** systemic
NF systems analysis

systole [sistɔl] **NF** *Physiol* systole

syzygie [siziʒi] **NF** *Astron* syzygy; **les marées de s.** the spring tides

t

T¹, t¹ [te] **NM INV 1** *(lettre)* T, t; **T comme Thérèse** ≃ T for Tommy **2** *(forme)* T (shape)

• **en T ADJ** T-shaped **ADV mettre les bureaux en T** to arrange the desks so that they form a T

T² 1 *(abrév écrite* **tesla)** T **2** *(abrév écrite* **téra)** T

t² *(abrév écrite* **tonne)** t.

t' [t] *voir* **te, tu**

T9 [tenœf] **NM** *Tél* T9, predictive text (input)

ta [ta] *voir* **ton³**

tabac [taba] **ADJ INV** *(couleur)* buff

NM 1 *Bot* tobacco plant

2 *(produit)* tobacco; **le t. peut provoquer le cancer** smoking can cause cancer; **campagne contre le t.** anti-smoking campaign; **t. blond/brun** mild/dark tobacco; **t. à chiquer** *ou* **à mâcher** chewing tobacco; **t. à priser, t. râpé** snuff

3 *(magasin) Br* tobacconist's, *Am* tobacco store *(which also sells stamps, phonecards and lottery tickets)*

4 *Hist & Admin* **les Tabacs** the Tobacco Department

5 *Météo* **coup de t.** squall, gale

6 *Fam (locutions)* **faire un t.** to be a big hit; **passer qn à t.** to beat sb up, to give sb a hammering; **passage à t.** beating (up), hammering; **c'est le même t.** it's the same difference, it amounts to the same thing; **c'est toujours le même t.** it's always the same old thing *or* story

• **du même tabac ADJ** *Fam* of the same kind□; **ils sont du même t.** they're tarred with the same brush; **il doit avoir eu des ennuis avec la police ou quelque chose du même t.** he must have had some trouble with the police, or something (like that)

tabacologie [tabakɔlɔʒi] **NF** = study of smoking addiction and prevention

tabagie [tabaʒi] **NF 1** *Fam (lieu enfumé)* **c'est une vraie t. ici** you can't see for smoke around here **2** *Can (magasin) Br* tobacconist's, *Am* tobacco store

tabagique [tabaʒik] **ADJ** tobacco *(avant n)*, nicotine-related

NMF chain-smoker

tabagisme [tabaʒism] **NM** tobacco addiction, *Spéc* nicotinism; **t. passif** passive smoking; **lutter contre le t.** to campaign against smoking

tabard [tabar] **NM** *Hist* tabard

tabassée [tabase] **NF** *Fam* beating, hammering

tabasser **[3]** [tabase] *Fam* **VT t. qn** to beat sb up, to give sb a hammering; **se faire t.** to be *or* to get beaten up

VPR se tabasser to beat each other up

tabatière [tabatjɛr] **NF 1** *(boîte)* snuffbox **2** *Constr* skylight (opening), roof light

tabellion [tabeljɔ̃] **NM** *Littéraire Péj (notaire)* lawyer

tabernacle NM [tabɛrnakl] *Naut & Rel* tabernacle

EXCLAM [tabɛrnak] *Can Vulg* fucking hell!

tablar, tablard [tablar] **NM** *Suisse* shelf

tablature [tablatyr] **NF** tablature

table [tabl] **NF 1** *(pour les repas)* table; **dresser** *ou* **mettre la t.** to lay *or* to set the table; **débarrasser** *ou* **desservir la t.** to clear the table; **sortir** *ou* **se lever de t.** to leave the table; **qui sera mon voisin de t.?** who will I be sitting next to (for the meal)?; **retenir une t. (pour quatre personnes)** to book *or* to reserve a table (for four people); **une t. de six couverts** a table set for six; **propos de t.** table talk; **t. d'hôte** table d'hôte; **faire t. d'hôte** = to provide a meal where all paying guests eat at the same table; **tenir t. ouverte** to keep open house

2 *(nourriture)* **la t.** food; **avoir une bonne t.** to keep a good table; **sa t. et sa cave sont bonnes** he/she serves good food and wine; **aimer la t.** to enjoy *or* to like good food

3 *(tablée)* table, tableful; **présider la t.** to preside over the guests *(at a meal)*

4 *(meuble à usages divers)* table; **t. de chevet** *ou* **de nuit** bedside table; **t. de cuisine/de salle à manger** kitchen/dining-room table; **t. anglaise** gateleg table; **t. basse** coffee table; **t. de billard** billiard table; **t. de cuisson** hob; **t. à découper** carving table; **t. à dessin** drawing board; **t. de jeu** card table; **t. à langer** baby-changing table; **t. de lecture** turntable; **t. de mixage** *TV* mixing console; *Rad* sound mixer; **t. de montage** *Typ & Phot* light table; *Cin* cutting table; *TV* editing desk *or* table; **t. des négociations** negotiating table; **s'asseoir à la t. des négociations** to get round the negotiating table; **t. d'opération** operating table; **t. d'orientation** panoramic table, viewpoint indicator; **t. à ouvrage** work table; **t. de ping-pong** table-tennis table; **t. à rallonges** extending table; **t. à repasser** ironing board; *Littérature* **la T. ronde** the Round Table; *aussi Fig* **t. ronde** round table; *(débat)* debate; **t. roulante** *ou* **à roulettes** *Br* trolley, *Am* tea wagon; **t. de toilette** washstand; **t. tournante** = table used for séances; **faire tourner les tables** to hold a séance; **t. de travail** work table; **t. à volets** drop-leaf table; **tables gigognes** nest of tables

5 *(liste, recueil)* table; **t. de logarithmes/mortalité/multiplication** log/mortality/multiplication table; **t. des matières** (table of) contents, contents page; *Écon* **t. des parités** parity table; *Phil* **t. de vérité** truth table; *Bible* **les Tables de la Loi** the Tables of the Law; *Phil* **t. rase** tabula rasa; *Fig* **faire t. rase** to wipe the slate clean, to make a fresh start; *Fig* **faire t. rase de qch** to make a clean sweep of sth; *Fig* **faire t. rase du passé** to wipe the slate clean; *Assur* **t. de survie** mortality table

6 *Astron* **t. de lancement** launch pad, launching pad *or* platform

7 *Constr (plaque)* panel; *(panneau)* panel, table; *Tech (de marteau, de valve)* face; *(de poutre métallique)* flange

8 *(de pierre)* slab; *(d'un dolmen)* cap stone

9 *Tél* switchboard

10 *Électron* table, board

11 *Ordinat* table; **t. traçante** plotter; **t. de corrélation/correspondance/décision** correlation/function/decision table; **t. des fichiers** file allocation table, FAT; **t. de recherche** *ou* **de référence** look-up table; **t. de vérité** truth table; **t. à digitaliser** digitizing pad

12 *(en joaillerie)* table; **diamant en t.** table (diamond)

13 *Mus (d'un violon)* sounding board, belly; **t. d'harmonie** soundboard

14 *Rail* **t. de roulement** running *or* rail surface; *(d'un rail)* tread

15 *Rel* **t. d'autel** (altar) table; **la t. de communion, la sainte t.** the communion *or* the Lord's table

• **à table ADV** at table; **passer à** *ou* **se mettre à t.** to sit down to a meal; **nous pouvons passer à t.** the meal is ready now; **être à t.** to be at (the) table *or* at dinner/lunch/*etc*; **je te rappelle plus tard, je suis à t.** I'll call you later, I'm eating; *très Fam Arg crime* **se mettre** *ou* **passer à t.** *(parler)* to spill the beans **EXCLAM** it's ready!

• **table d'écoute NF** wiretapping set *or* equipment; **elle est sur t. d'écoute** her phone is tapped; **mettre qn sur t. d'écoute** to tap sb's phone

TABLEAU, -X [tablo]

• board **1–3**	• painting **4**
• picture **4–6**	• scene **5, 18**
• table **7, 8, 12, 14**	• chart **7**
• list **8**	• statement **9**

NM 1 *Scol* board, blackboard; **aller au t.** to go up to the board *or* to the front of the class; **t. noir** blackboard; **t. blanc** whiteboard

2 *(support mural)* rack, board; **t. pour fusibles** fuseboard

3 *(panneau d'information)* board; **t. d'affichage** *Br* notice *or Am* bulletin board; **t. des arrivées/départs** arrivals/departures board; **t. des publications de mariage** = board where banns are posted

4 *Beaux-Arts* painting, picture; **un t. de Goya** a painting by Goya; **un t. ancien** an old master

5 *Fig (spectacle)* scene, picture; **ils formaient un t. touchant** they were a touching sight; *Fam* **tu imagines le t.!** you can picture *or* imagine the scene!; *Fam* **je vois d'ici le t.!** I can just picture it!; *Fam* **vieux t.** *(vieille coquette)* (painted) old hag

6 *Fig (description)* picture; **vous nous faites un t. très alarmant de la situation** you've painted an alarming picture of the situation; **pour achever le t.** to cap it all

7 *(diagramme)* table; *(graphique)* chart; **mettre qch sous forme de t.** to tabulate sth; **tableaux d'activité économique** economic activity tables; **t. d'avancement de commandes** order flowchart; *Gram* **t. de conjugaison** conjugation table; **t. de conversion** conversion table; **t. des réservations** reservations chart; *Com* **t. de service** rota; **t. synoptique** synopsis, summary

8 *(liste ▸ gén)* list, table; *(▸ d'une profession)* roll; **t. des avocats** roll of lawyers; **être rayé** *ou* **se faire rayer du t.** to be struck off the rolls; **se faire inscrire au t.** *(avocat)* to be called to the bar; **t. d'avancement** promotions roster *or* list; *Chim* **t. des éléments** periodic table; **t. de gonflage** tyre-pressure table; *Scol* **t. d'honneur** board of honour; **t. horaire** *(des trains)* timetable; *Chim* **t. de Mendeleïev** periodic table

9 *Compta* **t. d'amortissement** depreciation schedule; **t. comptable** (financial) statement; **t. des emplois et ressources de fonds** statement of sources and applications of funds; **t. de financement** statement of sources and uses of funds, cashflow statement; *(planning)* finance plan; **t. de roulement** statement of changes in working capital

10 *Constr* reveal

11 *Élec* **t. de commande** *(d'appareil électroménager)* control panel, panel of switches; *Élec & Tél* **t. commutateur** switchboard, distribution board *or* panel; **t. de contrôle** control board; **t. de distri-**

bution distribution board *or* switchboard; **t. d'éclairage** lighting panel; **t. de manœuvre** instrument board *or* panel
12 *Typ* table
13 *Ordinat* array; **t. de connexions** plugboard
14 *Math* table
15 *Méd* **t. clinique** overall clinical picture
16 *Naut* transom
17 *Pharm* (French) drugs classification; **t. A** toxic drugs (list); **t. B** narcotics (list); **t. C** dangerous drugs (list)
18 *Théât* scene; **premier t. du troisième acte** act three, scene one; **t. de service** *(répétitions)* rehearsal roster; *(représentations)* performances roster; **t. vivant** tableau vivant
19 *(locutions)* **gagner sur les deux/tous les tableaux** to win on both/all counts; **perdre sur tous les tableaux** to lose on all counts; **jouer** *ou* **miser sur plusieurs tableaux** to hedge one's bets
• **tableau de bord** NM **1** *Aut* dashboard **2** *Aviat & Naut* instrument panel **3** *Écon* (list of) indicators; *Com* management control data **4** *Ordinat* control panel; **t. de connexions** plugboard
• **tableau de chasse** NM **1** *Chasse* bag **2** *Aviat* list of kills **3** *Fig (conquêtes amoureuses)* conquests; **tu pourras la mettre à ton t. de chasse!** that's another notch on your gun!

tableautin [tablotɛ̃] NM *(peinture)* small painting

tablée [table] NF table; **toute la t. s'est levée** the whole table *or* company stood up; **une t. de jeunes** a tableful *or* party of youngsters; **une joyeuse t.** a merry gathering (around a table)

tabler [3] [table] **tabler sur** VT IND to bank *or* to count on

tablette [tablɛt] NF **1** *(petite planche)* shelf; *(dans un avion)* table; *Aut* **t. arrière** rear parcel shelf, back shelf; **t. à coulisse** *(d'un bureau)* pull-out flap; **t. de piano** music rest
2 *Culin (de chewing-gum)* stick; *(de chocolat)* bar; *Fam Hum* **avoir les abdos en t. de chocolat** to have a six-pack
3 *Constr (de cheminée)* mantelpiece; *(d'une maçonnerie)* coping; **t. de fenêtre** windowsill
4 *Ordinat* **t. graphique** graphics tablet
5 *Pharm* tablet
6 *Élec* **t. à bornes** terminal plate
• **tablettes** NFPL *Antiq* tablets; *Fig* **je vais l'inscrire** *ou* **le noter dans mes tablettes** I'll make a note of it

tabletter [3] [tablete] VT *Can* **1** *(ne pas tenir compte de)* to ignore, to leave aside **2** *Fam (employé)* to sideline

tableur [tablœr] NM *Ordinat* spreadsheet; **t. de graphiques** graphics spreadsheet

tablier [tablije] NM **1** *(de cuisine)* apron; *(blouse) Br* overall, *Am* work coat; *(d'enfant)* smock; **rendre son t.** *(démissionner)* to hand in one's resignation; *(domestique)* to give notice; *Fig* to give up, to throw in the towel
2 *(rideau ▸ de cheminée)* register; *(▸ d'un magasin)* shutter
3 *(de pont)* roadway
4 *Aut (d'une voiture)* cowl; *(d'un scooter)* footrest; *Mil (d'avant-train)* footboard; **t. de pare-chocs** bumper apron
5 *Rail* foot plate
6 *Tech (de machine-outil, de tour)* apron; *(de laminoir)* table; *(de forge)* hearth; *Ind* **t. sans fin** apron feed

tabloïd, tabloïde [tablɔid] NM **1** *(journal)* tabloid **2** *Pharm* tablet
ADJ **format t.** tabloid format

tabou, -e [tabu] ADJ taboo; **c'est un sujet t.** that's taboo, that's a taboo subject
NM taboo; **ce sont des tabous** these are taboo subjects

taboulé [tabule] NM tabbouleh

tabouret [taburɛ] NM **1** *(siège)* stool; **t. de bar/cuisine/piano** bar/kitchen/piano stool; **t. à traire** milking stool **2** *(pour les pieds)* foot stool

tabulaire [tabylɛr] ADJ tabular

tabulateur [tabylatœr] NM tabulator; **régler les tabulateurs** to set tabs (à at)

tabulation [tabylasjɔ̃] NF **1** *(positionnement)* tabulation **2** *(taquets)* tabs; **poser des tabulations dans** to tab

tabulatrice [tabylatris] NF tabulator

tabuler [3] [tabyle] VT to tabulate, to tab

tac [tak] ONOMAT *(bruit sec)* tap, rat-a-tat; **et t.!** so there!
NM *(locutions)* **du t. au t.** tit for tat; **répondre du t. au t.** to answer tit for tat; **je lui ai répondu du t. au t. que...** I retorted quick as a flash that..., I came back quick as lightning that...

tacet [tasɛt] NM *Mus* tacet

tache [taʃ] NF **1** *(marque)* stain; **t. d'encre** ink-stain; *Psy* inkblot; **t. de graisse** grease stain *or* mark; **t. de sang** bloodstain; **t. de suie** fleck of soot, smut; **t. de vin** wine stain; **faire une t./des taches** to make a mess; **tu as fait une t. à ta chemise** you've got a stain on your shirt; **je me suis fait une t.** I've stained my clothes; **la t. ne partira pas** the stain won't come out; *Fam* **faire t.** *(jurer)* to stand *or* stick out like a sore thumb; **faire t. d'huile** to spread
2 *(partie colorée)* patch, spot; *(de couleur, de lumière)* splash; **des taches bleues dans un ciel gris** patches of blue in a grey sky; **t. de lumière** *Théât & Cin* hot spot; *TV* shading
3 *(sur un fruit)* mark, blemish; *(dans une pierre précieuse)* flaw, blemish
4 *(sur la peau)* mark, spot; **la rougeole donne des taches rouges sur la peau** measles causes the skin to come out in red spots; **t. de rousseur** *ou* **de son** freckle; **t. de vin** strawberry mark *(birthmark)*
5 *Fig (souillure morale)* blot, stain, blemish; **cette fraude est une t. à sa réputation** this fraud has stained his/her reputation
6 *Astron* **t. solaire** sunspot
7 *Méd (sur une radiographie)* opacity; *(coloration anormale)* spot; **t. de Mariotte** blind *or* Mariotte's spot
8 *Zool* patch, spot, mark; **chien blanc à taches feu** white dog with reddish markings *or* patches *or* spots
9 *Fam (personne)* nonentity, loser, no-hoper; **quelle t. ce mec-là!** what a total non-entity *or* loser *or* no-hoper that guy is!
• **sans tache** ADJ **1** *(fruit)* unblemished **2** *Fig (réputation)* spotless

tâche [taʃ] NF **1** *(travail)* task, job; **remplir une t.** to fulfil a task; **tâches ménagères** housework **2** *(mission, rôle)* task, mission; **la t. des scientifiques d'aujourd'hui** the mission of today's scientists; *Littéraire* **prendre à t. de faire qch** to undertake to do sth **3** *Ordinat* task; **t. d'arrière-plan** *ou* **de fond** background task *or* job
• **à la tâche** ADJ *Ind* **travail à la t.** piece-work ADV *Ind* **travailler à la t.** to be on piecework; **il est à la t.** he's a pieceworker; *Fam* **on n'est pas à la t.!** what's the rush?

taché, -e [taʃe] ADJ **1** *(vêtement, tissu)* stained; **t. d'encre/de sang/de graisse** ink-/blood-/grease-stained **2** *(fruit)* bruised **3** *(animal)* spotted; **un chien à la robe noire tachée de blanc** a dog with a black coat with white markings

tachéomètre [takeɔmɛtr] NM *Géog* tacheometer, tachymeter

tachéométrie [takeɔmetri] NF *Géog* tacheometry, tachymetry

tacher [3] [taʃe] VT **1** *(salir ▸ vêtement, tapis)* to stain; **t. de sang/chocolat** to stain with blood/chocolate **2** *Fig (ternir ▸ réputation, nom, honneur)* to stain
VI *(encre, sauce, vin)* to stain
VPR **se tacher 1** *(emploi réfléchi)* to get oneself dirty, to stain one's clothes **2** *(emploi passif) (tissu)* to stain; *(bois, peinture, moquette)* to mark; *(fruit)* to become marked; **le noir ne se tache pas** black doesn't show the dirt

tâcher [3] [taʃe] VT **t. que...** to make sure that...; **tâche qu'elle ne l'apprenne pas** make sure she doesn't hear about it
• **tâcher de** VT IND to try to; **tâchez de ne pas oublier** try not to forget

tâcheron [taʃrɔ̃] NM **1** *(petit entrepreneur)* jobber; *(ouvrier agricole)* hired hand **2** *Péj (travailleur)* drudge, workhorse; *(écrivaillon)* hack; **j'en ai assez de faire ce métier de t.!** I've had enough of this drudgery *or* skivvying!

tacheté, -e [taʃte] ADJ *(papier, plumage)* speckled, mottled; *(chat)* tabby; **une robe blanche tachetée de vert** a white dress spotted with green

tacheter [27] [taʃte] VT to spot, to speckle, to fleck

tacheture [taʃtyr] NF spot, speckle

tachisme [taʃism] NM *Beaux-Arts* tachism, tachisme

tachiste [taʃist] *Beaux-Arts* ADJ tachist, tachiste
NMF tachist, tachiste

Tachkent [taʃkent] NM Tashkent

tachycardie [takikardi] NF *Méd* tachycardia

tachygraphe [takigraf] NM tachograph

tachymètre [takimɛtr] NM tachometer; *Aut* speedometer

Tacite [tasit] NPR Tacitus

tacite [tasit] ADJ tacit; **c'était un aveu t.** it was a tacit admission; **(par) t. reconduction** (by) tacit agreement to renew

tacitement [tasitmɑ̃] ADV tacitly

taciturne [tasityrn] ADJ taciturn

tacle [takl] NM *Ftbl* tackle; **t. glissé** sliding tackle; **faire un t. à qn** to tackle sb

tacler [3] [takle] VT *Ftbl* to tackle

tacot [tako] NM *Fam* **1** *(vieille voiture)* (old) heap, *Br* banger **2** *(taxi)* taxi[❑], cab, *Am* hack

tact [takt] NM **1** *Vieilli Physiol* (sense of) touch **2** *(délicatesse)* tact, delicacy; **être plein de t.** to be very tactful; **avoir du t.** to be tactful; **manquer de t.** to be tactless; **manque de t.** tactlessness; **avec t.** tactfully; **sans t.** tactlessly

tacticien, -enne [taktisjɛ̃, -ɛn] NM,F **1** *Mil* (military) tactician **2** *Fig (stratège)* strategist

tactile [taktil] ADJ tactile

tactique [taktik] ADJ tactical
NF **1** *Mil* tactics *(singulier)* **2** *(moyens)* tactics; **t. commerciale** marketing tactics; **je vais devoir changer de t.** I'm going to have to change my tactics; **ce n'est pas la meilleure t. pour le convaincre** it's not the best way of convincing him

tadjik [tadʒik] ADJ Tadzhiki
NM *(langue)* Tadzhiki
• **Tadjik** NMF Tadzhik; **les T.** the Tadzhik

Tadjikie [tadʒiki] NF = **Tadjikistan**

Tadjikistan [tadʒikistɑ̃] NM **le T.** Tadzhikistan

tadorne [tadɔrn] NM *Orn* sheldrake; **t. de Belon** shelduck

tænia [tenja] = **ténia**

taf [taf] NM *Fam (travail)* work[❑]; *(emploi)* job[❑]

taffe [taf] NF *Fam (de cigarette)* drag

taffer [3] [tafe] VI *Fam (travailler)* to work[❑]

taffetas [tafta] NM **1** *Tex* taffeta; **une robe en** *ou* **de t.** a taffeta dress **2** *Pharm* **t. gommé** *ou* **anglais** adhesive bandage

tafiard, -e [tafjar, -ard], **tafieux, -euse** [tafjø, -øz] *Belg* ADJ boastful
NM,F boaster

tag [tag] NM tag *(piece of graffiti)*

Tage [taʒ] NM **le T.** the (River) Tagus

tagine [taʒin] = **tajine**

tagliatelle [tagljatɛl, taljatɛl] *(pl* **inv** *ou* **tagliatelles)** NF piece of tagliatelle; **des t.** *ou* **tagliatelles** tagliatelle

taguer [3] [tage] VT to cover in graffiti[❑]

tagueur, -euse [tagœr, -øz] NM,F graffiti artist[❑], tagger

Tahiti [taiti] NF Tahiti; **à T.** in Tahiti

tahitien, -enne [taisjɛ̃, -ɛn] ADJ Tahitian
NM *(langue)* Tahitian
• **Tahitien, -enne** NM,F Tahitian

taïaut [tajo] EXCLAM *Chasse* tally-ho!

taie [tɛ] NF **1** *(enveloppe)* **t. d'oreiller** pillowcase, pillow slip; **t. de traversin** bolster case **2** *Méd* leucoma; *Fig Littéraire* **avoir une t. sur l'œil** to be blinkered, to have tunnel vision

taïga [tajga] NF taiga

taillable [tajabl] ADJ **1** *Hist* subject to tallage **2** *(locution)* **être t. et corvéable à merci** *(sujet à l'im-*

pôt) to be subject to tallage; *(soumis à des travaux)* to be a drudge

taillade [tajad] NF *(estafilade)* slash, gash; **se faire une t. au doigt** to gash one's finger

tailladé, -e [tajade] ADJ *Couture* slashed

taillader [3] [tajade] VT to gash *or* to slash (through)

VPR **se taillader se t. le doigt/le menton** to gash one's finger/chin; **se t. les poignets** *ou* **les veines** to slash one's wrists

taillandier [tajɑ̃dje] NM edge-tool maker

taillaule [tajol] NF *Suisse* = sweet pastry roll

taille [taj] NF **1** *(hauteur ▸ d'une personne, d'un animal)* height; **une femme de haute t.** a tall woman; **un homme de petite t.** a short man; **un enfant de t. moyenne** a child of average height; **ils ont à peu près la même t.** they're about the same height; **de la t. de** as big as, the size of; **atteindre sa t. adulte** to reach one's full height

2 *(grandeur ▸ d'un endroit, d'un objet)* size; **une pièce de t. moyenne** an average-sized room; **une lettre de la t. d'une affiche** a letter the size of a poster, a poster-sized letter; **des avocats de la t. du poing** avocados the size of your fist; **il te faudrait un plat d'une t. plus grande** you need a larger (-sized) dish

3 *(importance)* size; **une erreur de cette t. est impardonnable** a mistake of this magnitude is unforgivable

4 *(de vêtement)* size; **quelle est votre t.?, quelle t. faites-vous?** what size are you *or* do you take?; **ce n'est pas ma t.** it's not my size; **deux tailles au-dessus/en dessous** two sizes bigger/smaller; **avez-vous la t. au-dessus/en dessous?** do you have the next size up/down?; **donnez-moi la t. en dessous/au-dessus** give me one size down/up; **les grandes/petites tailles** the large/small sizes; **pour les grandes tailles** outsize; **elles font toutes deux la même t.** they both wear the same size; **t. XL** size XL; **t. unique** one size; **je n'ai plus votre t.** I'm out of your size; **elle a la t. mannequin** she's got a real model's figure

5 *(partie du corps)* waist; **avoir la t. longue/courte** to be long-/short-waisted; **avoir la t. fine** to be slim-waisted *or* slender-waisted; **sa robe est serrée/trop serrée à la t.** her dress is fitted/too tight at the waist; **avoir une t. de guêpe** *ou* **de nymphe** to have an hourglass figure; **avoir la t. bien prise** to have a nice *or* good figure; **prendre qn par la t.** *(d'un bras)* to put an arm round sb's waist; *(des deux mains)* to take sb by the waist, to seize sb round the waist

6 *(partie d'un vêtement)* waist; **robe à t. haute/basse** high-/low-waisted dress; **un jean (à) t. basse** low-waisted *or* low-rise *or Br* hipster *or Am* hip-hugger jeans

7 *Ordinat* **t. de disque dur** hard disk size; **t. de champ** field size; **t. (de) mémoire** storage capacity

8 *Typ* **t. de corps** body size; **t. de fonte** font size; **t. des caractères** typesize

9 *Hort (d'un arbre ▸ gén)* pruning; *(▸ importante)* cutting back; *(▸ légère)* trimming; *(d'une haie)* trimming, clipping; *(de la vigne)* pruning

10 *(tranchant)* edge; **frapper de t.** to strike *or* to slash with the edge of one's sword

11 *Beaux-Arts (du bois, du marbre)* carving; *(en gravure)* etching

12 *Constr (à la carrière)* hewing, cutting; *(sur le chantier)* dressing

13 *Hist (impôt)* taille, tallage

14 *Ind (d'un engrenage)* milling, cutting; **t. bâtarde/croisée/simple** bastard/crosscut/float cut

15 *(en joaillerie)* cutting; **t. à angles** step-cut

• **à la taille de** PRÉP in keeping with; **ses moyens ne sont pas à la t. de ses ambitions** his/her ambitions far exceed his/her means

• **à ma/sa/leur/***etc* **taille** ADV *(de même envergure)* **trouver un adversaire à sa t.** to meet one's match

• **de taille** ADJ **1** *(énorme)* huge, great; **le risque est de t.** the risk is considerable; **une fraude de t.** a major fraud; **un mensonge de t.** a whopper; **une surprise de t.** a huge surprise **2** *(capable)* **être de t.** to measure up; **face à un adversaire comme lui, tu n'es pas de t.** you're no match for an opponent like him; **de t. à** capable of, able to; **elle n'est pas de t. à se défendre** she's not capable of defending herself; **il n'est pas de t. à être chef** he's not cut out to be a leader, he's not the stuff that leaders are made of; **je ne suis pas de t. à vous prouver le contraire** I'm not in a position to prove you wrong; **il n'est pas de t. à lutter contre vous** he is no match for you, he stands no chance against you; **rien à craindre, il n'est pas de t.** there's nothing to be afraid of, he's not up to it

taillé, -e [taje] ADJ **1** *(coupé ▸ arbre)* trimmed, pruned; *(▸ haie)* trimmed, clipped; *(▸ cristal)* cut; *(▸ crayon)* sharpened; *(▸ barbe, moustache, ongles)* trimmed; **bien/mal t.** *(haie, barbe, moustache, ongles)* neatly/badly trimmed; *(crayon)* sharp/blunt; *(costume)* well/badly cut **un crayon t. en pointe** a sharp pencil; **une barbe taillée en pointe** a goatee (beard); **avoir les cheveux taillés en brosse** to have a brush cut; **t. dans le roc** carved out of the rock **2** *(bâti)* **un homme bien t.** a well-built man **3** *Fig (apte à)* **t. pour** cut out for; **tu n'es pas t. pour ce métier** you're not cut out for this job; **être t. pour faire qch** to be cut out to do sth

taille-crayon [tajkrejɔ̃] *(pl inv ou* **taille-crayons**) NM pencil sharpener

taille-douce [tajdus] *(pl* **tailles-douces**) NF intaglio; **gravure** *ou* **impression en t.** copper-plate engraving

tailler [3] [taje] VT **1** *(ciseler ▸ pierre)* to cut, *Sout* to hew; *(▸ verre)* to engrave; *(▸ bois, marbre)* to carve; *(▸ diamant)* to cut; *Fig* **t. en pièces une armée** to cut an army to pieces; *Fig* **la critique l'a taillé en pièces** the reviewers made mincemeat out of him; *Fam* **t. la route** *(parcourir beaucoup de chemin)* to eat up the miles; *(partir)* to beat it

2 *(couper ▸ barbe, moustache)* to trim; *(▸ crayon)* to sharpen; *(▸ bifteck)* to cut; *Fam* **t. une bavette** to have a chat *or Br* a chinwag

3 *(façonner)* to cut, *Sout* to hew; **il a taillé un escalier dans la pente** he cut some steps into the hillside

4 *Couture (vêtement)* to cut (out); **t. une jupe dans du velours** to cut a skirt out of a piece of velvet; *Fam* **t. une veste** *ou* **un costard à qn** to badmouth sb, *Br* to slag sb off; *Fam* **il a failli se faire t. un short en traversant la rue** he almost got run over crossing the street[▫]

5 *Hort (arbre)* to prune, to cut back; *(haie)* to trim, to clip; *(vigne)* to prune

VI **1** *(inciser)* to cut; **t. dans les chairs avec un scalpel** to cut into the flesh with a scalpel **2** *(vêtement)* **cette robe taille grand/petit** this dress *Br* is cut *or Am* runs large/small

VPR **se tailler 1** *Fam (partir)* to beat it; **allez, on se taille!** come on, let's beat it!; **2** *(se couper)* **se t. la barbe** to trim one's beard **3** *(se faire)* **se t. un chemin à travers les ronces** to hack one's way through the brambles; **se t. un chemin à travers la foule** to force one's way through the crowd; **se t. un (beau) succès** to be a great success

tailleur [tajœr] NM **1** *(couturier)* tailor; **t. pour dames** ladies' tailor **2** *(ouvrier ▸ de diamants, de pierres, de marbre)* cutter; **t. de verre** glass engraver **3** *(vêtement)* (lady's) suit; **un t. sur mesure** a tailor-made suit

• **en tailleur** ADV cross-legged; **s'asseoir en t.** to sit cross-legged

tailleur-pantalon [tajœrpɑ̃talɔ̃] *(pl* **tailleurs-pantalons**) NM *Br* trouser suit, *Am* pantsuit

taillis [taji] NM coppice, copse, thicket; **dans les t.** in the copse *or* coppice

ADJ **bois t.** copsewood, brushwood

tain [tɛ̃] NM **1** *(pour miroir)* silvering; **refaire le t. d'une glace** to resilver a mirror; **glace** *ou* **miroir sans t.** two-way mirror **2** *Métal (bain)* tin bath

taire [111] [tɛr] VT **1** *(passer sous silence ▸ raisons)* not to mention, to say nothing about; *(▸ information)* to hush up; *(▸ plan, projet)* to keep secret, to say nothing about, to keep quiet about; **une personne dont je tairai le nom** a person who shall remain nameless; **il a préféré t. ses projets** he preferred to keep his plans secret; **t. qch à qn** to keep *or* hide *or* conceal sth from sb **2 faire t. qn** *(adversaire)* to silence sb, to force sb to be quiet; **faire t. la critique** to silence the critics; **faites t. les enfants** make the children be quiet; **mais faites-le t.!** somebody shut him up, for goodness' sake!; **faire t. qch** to stifle sth; **faire t. sa conscience** to stifle one's conscience; **fais t. tes scrupules** forget your scruples

VPR **se taire 1** *(être silencieux)* to be quiet *or* silent; *(cesser de parler)* to stop talking, to fall silent; *(décider de ne rien dire)* to keep quiet *or* silent; **tais-toi!** be quiet!; *Hum* **elle a perdu une occasion de se t.** she would have done better to say nothing *or* to keep her mouth shut **2** *(cesser de s'exprimer)* to fall silent; **l'opposition s'est tue** the opposition has gone very quiet **3** *Littéraire (cesser de faire du bruit)* to fall *or* to become silent; *(bruit)* to stop, to cease

taiseux, -euse [tezø, -øz] *Belg* ADJ taciturn

NM,F taciturn person

taisons *etc voir* **taire**

Taïwan [tajwan] NF Taiwan

taïwanais, -e [tajwanɛ, -ɛz] ADJ Taiwanese

• **Taïwanais, -e** NM,F Taiwanese; **les T.** the Taiwanese

tajine [taʒin] NM *Culin* tagine, tajine

take-off [tekɔf] NM INV *Écon* takeoff

talbin [talbɛ̃] NM *Fam (billet de banque) Br* note[▫], *Am* greenback

talc [talk] NM *Minér* talc; *(produit)* talcum powder, talc

talé, -e [tale] ADJ *(fruit)* bruised

taleggio [taledʒjo] NM *(fromage)* taleggio

talent[1] [talɑ̃] NM **1** *(capacité artistique)* **le t.** talent; **avoir du t.** to have talent, to be talented **2** *(don, aptitude particulière)* talent, skill, gift; **son t. de pianiste** his/her talent as a pianist; **exploiter ses talents de cuisinier** to make use of one's talents as a cook; **votre fille a vraiment tous les talents** your daughter is extremely talented; *Fam* **montrer ses talents à qn** to show sb what one can do **3** *(personne)* talent; **il est à la recherche de jeunes/nouveaux talents** he's looking for young/fresh talent; **faire appel à tous les talents** to call in the best talent *or* brains

• **de talent** ADJ talented; **un jeune écrivain de t.** a talented young writer

• **sans talent** ADJ untalented; **chanteur sans t.** untalented singer

talent[2] [talɑ̃] NM *Hist (unité de poids, monnaie)* talent

talentueuse [talɑ̃tɥøz] *voir* **talentueux**

talentueusement [talɑ̃tɥøzmɑ̃] ADV with talent

talentueux, -euse [talɑ̃tɥø, -øz] ADJ talented, gifted

taler [3] [tale] VT to bruise

talet, taleth [talɛt] NM *Rel* tallith

talion [taljɔ̃] NM talion; *Hist* **la loi du t.** lex talionis, an eye for an eye (and a tooth for a tooth); **appliquer la loi du t.** to demand an eye for an eye; *Fig* **dans ce cas-là, c'est la loi du t.** in that case, it's an eye for an eye (and a tooth for a tooth)

talisman [talismɑ̃] NM **1** *(amulette)* talisman **2** *Littéraire (sortilège)* spell, charm

talitre [talitr] NM *Zool* sand flea, sandhopper

talkie-walkie [tɔkiwɔki] *(pl* **talkies-walkies**) NM walkie-talkie

talk-show [tɔkʃo] *(pl* **talk-shows**) NM talk-show

Tallinn [talin] NM Tallinn

Talmud [talmyd] NM **le T.** the Talmud

talmudique [talmydik] ADJ Talmudic

talmudiste [talmydist] NMF Talmudist

taloche [talɔʃ] NF **1** *Constr* float **2** *Fam (gifle)* clout, cuff; **filer** *ou* **flanquer une t. à qn** to clout sb

talocher [3] [talɔʃe] VT *Fam* **t. qn** to clout *or* to cuff sb

talon [talɔ̃] NM **1** *Anat* heel; **son t. d'Achille** his Achilles' heel; **donner du t. à son cheval** to give one's horse the spur; **être** *ou* **marcher sur les talons de qn** to follow close on sb's heels; **montrer** *ou* **tourner les talons** *(s'enfuir)* to show a clean pair of heels; **tourner les talons** *(faire demi-tour)* to turn on one's heel

2 *(d'une chaussure)* heel; **talons aiguilles** spike *or Br* stiletto heels; **(chaussures à) talons aiguilles** spike heels, *Br* stilettos; **talons bottiers** medium heels; **talons compensés** built-up heels; **(chaussures à) talons hauts** high-heeled shoes; **porter des talons hauts** *ou* **des hauts talons** to wear high heels; **(chaussures à) talons plats** flat-heeled shoes, flats; **porter des talons plats** to wear flat heels

3 *(d'une chaussette)* heel
4 *(d'un fromage, d'un jambon)* heel
5 *(d'un chèque)* stub, counterfoil; *(d'un carnet à souches)* counterfoil; **t. à retourner** reply slip; **t. et volant** *(de chèque)* counterfoil and leaf
6 *(de queue de billard)* butt; *(de lame d'épée, de baïonnette, de palan, d'essieu)* shoulder
7 *Archit (moulure)* talon *or* ogee moulding
8 *Cartes* stock, talon
9 *Mus* heel, nut
10 *Tech (de quille, de serrure, de ski)* heel

talonnage [talɔnaʒ] **NM 1** *Sport* heeling *(UNCOUNT)*; **faire un t.** to heel (the ball) **2** *Naut* touching *(UNCOUNT)*

talonnement [talɔnmɑ̃] **NM** *(de cheval)* spurring on; *Fig (harcèlement)* hounding

talonner [3] [talɔne] **VT 1** *(poursuivre)* **t. qn** to follow on sb's heels; **le coureur marocain, talonné par l'Anglais** the Moroccan runner, with the Englishman close on his heels
2 *(harceler ▸ sujet: créancier)* to hound; *(▸ sujet: gêneur)* to pester; **le directeur me talonne pour que je remette mon rapport** the manager's after me to get my report in; **se faire t. par le fisc** to have the *Br* tax man *or Am* IRS breathing down one's neck
3 *(tourmenter ▸ sujet: faim)* to gnaw at; **être talonné par la mort** to be pursued by death
4 *(cheval)* to spur on
5 *Sport* to heel, to hook
VI 1 *Naut (navire)* to touch the bottom **2** *Sport* to heel

talonnette [talɔnɛt] **NF 1** *(d'une chaussure)* counter; *(à l'intérieur de la chaussure)* heel pad **2** *(d'un pantalon)* binding strip

talonneur [talɔnœr] **NM** *(au rugby)* hooker

talquer [3] [talke] **VT** to put talcum powder *or* talc on

talure [talyr] **NF** bruise

talus [taly] **NM 1** *(d'un chemin)* (side) slope; **en t.** sloping; **couper** *ou* **tailler qch en t.** to cut sth at an angle; **la voiture est tombée dans le t.** the car fell down the slope **2** *(d'une voie ferrée, d'un canal)* embankment **3** *Géol* **t. d'éboulis** scree, talus

talweg [talvɛg] **NM** *Géol & Météo* talweg, thalweg

tamanoir [tamanwar] **NM** *Zool* (great) anteater

tamarin [tamarɛ̃] **NM 1** *Zool* tamarin **2** *Bot (tamarinier, fruit du tamarinier)* tamarind **3** *Bot (tamaris)* tamarisk

tamarinier [tamarinje] **NM** *Bot* tamarind (tree)

tamaris [tamaris], **tamarix** [tamariks] **NM** *Bot* tamarisk

tambouille [tɑ̃buj] **NF** *Fam* **1** *(cuisine)* cooking□; **faire la t.** to do the cooking **2** *(nourriture)* food□, grub; **on s'est fait une bonne petite t.** we made ourselves some great grub

tambour [tɑ̃bur] **NM 1** *Mus (instrument)* drum; **jouer du t.** to play the drum; **t. de basque** tambourine; *Fig* **sans t. ni trompette** discreetly, unobtrusively; *Fig* **t. battant** briskly; **elle a mené l'affaire t. battant** she didn't waste any time getting it done
2 *(son)* drumbeat
3 *(joueur)* drummer; **les tambours battent la retraite** the drummers are beating the retreat; *Hist* **t. de ville** town crier
4 *Archit, Aut & Électron* drum; *Élec (d'une bobine)* cylinder; **t. de frein** brake drum
5 *Constr (sas)* tambour (door); *(tourniquet)* revolving door; *(d'église)* vestibule
6 *Couture (à broder)* tambour, hoop
7 *Tech (de lave-linge)* drum

tambourin [tɑ̃burɛ̃] **NM** *(de basque)* tambourine; *(provençal)* = small drum used in Provençal folk music

tambourinage [tɑ̃burinaʒ] **NM** drumming

tambourinaire [tɑ̃burinɛr] **NM 1** *(musicien)* "tambourin" player **2** *Hist (annonceur)* town crier

tambourinement [tɑ̃burinmɑ̃] **NM** drumming

tambouriner [3] [tɑ̃burine] **VI** *(frapper)* to drum (on); *(avec les doigts)* to drum one's fingers; **la grêle tambourinait à la fenêtre** hailstones were drumming on *or* beating against the window pane
VT 1 *Mus (air, cadence)* to drum (out); *(avec les doigts)* to tap out **2** *Hist (proclamer)* to announce; *Fig Vieilli* to shout from the rooftops

tambour-major [tɑ̃burmaʒɔr] *(pl* **tambours-majors)** **NM** drum major

Tamerlan [tamɛrlɑ̃] **NPR T. le Grand** Tamerlane *or* Tamburlaine the Great

tamil, -e [tamil] **ADJ** Tamil
NM *(langue)* Tamil
• **Tamil, -e NM,F** Tamil; **les Tamils** the Tamils *or* Tamil

tamis [tami] **NM 1** *(à farine)* sieve; *(en fil de soie, de coton)* tammy (cloth), tamis; **passer au t.** *(farine, sucre)* to sieve; *Fig (dossier, témoignage)* to go through with a fine-tooth comb **2** *Constr (à sable)* sifter, *Spéc* riddle; **passer au t.** *(sable)* to sift

tamisage [tamizaʒ] **NM** *(de farine, de sucre)* sieving; *(de sable)* sifting, *Spéc* riddling

Tamise [tamiz] **NF la T.** the Thames

tamiser [3] [tamize] **VT 1** *(farine, sucre)* to sieve **2** *(éclairage)* to subdue; *(lumière naturelle)* to filter **3** *Constr (sable)* to sift, *Spéc* to riddle

tamoul, -e [tamul] **ADJ** Tamil
NM *(langue)* Tamil
• **Tamoul, -e NM,F** Tamil; **les Tamouls** the Tamils *or* Tamil

tampon [tɑ̃pɔ̃] **NM 1** *(pour absorber)* wad
2 *(pour imprégner)* pad; **t. encreur** ink pad
3 *(pour nettoyer)* pad; **t. à récurer** scouring pad, scourer
4 *(pour obturer)* plug, bung; *(d'un tonneau)* bung; **il a bouché la fissure avec un t. de papier** he stopped up the crack with a wad of paper
5 *(plaque gravée)* rubber stamp; *(oblitération)* stamp; **le t. de la poste** the postmark; **t. dateur** date stamp
6 *Fig* buffer; **il sert de t. entre la direction et le personnel** he acts as a buffer between the management and the staff
7 *Constr (dalle)* cover; *(cheville)* wall plug; **t. d'égout** manhole cover
8 *Méd & Pharm (pour nettoyer)* swab; *(pour boucher)* pad, plug; **t. (périodique** *ou* **hygiénique)** tampon
9 *(comme adj) Pol* **État/zone t.** buffer state/zone; *Chim* **substance t.** buffer

tampon-buvard [tɑ̃pɔ̃byvar] *(pl* **tampons-buvards)** **NM** blotter

tamponnage [tɑ̃pɔnaʒ] **NM 1** *Méd* dabbing **2** *Ch* neutralizing

tamponne [tɑ̃pɔn] **NF** *Belg Fam* (drinking) binge; **prendre une t.** to get plastered

tamponnement [tɑ̃pɔnmɑ̃] **NM 1** *(accident)* collision **2** *Méd* tamponage **3** *(obturation)* plugging

tamponner [3] [tɑ̃pɔne] **VT 1** *(document, passeport)* to stamp; *(lettre timbrée)* to postmark; **faire t. un document** to have a document stamped
2 *(télescoper)* to collide with, to hit, to bump into; *(violemment)* to crash into
3 *(sécher ▸ front, lèvres, yeux)* to dab (at)
4 *(enduire ▸ meuble)* to dab
5 *Chim* to buffer
6 *Constr (mur)* to plug
7 *Méd (plaie)* to tampon, to plug
8 *Vieilli (boucher)* to plug, to stop (up)
VPR se tamponner 1 *(emploi réciproque)* to collide, to bump into one another; **ils se sont tamponnés** they collided **2** *(emploi réfléchi)* **se t. le front** to mop one's brow; **se t. les yeux** to dab one's eyes; *très Fam* **je m'en tamponne (le coquillard)!** I don't give a damn! **3** *Belg Fam* to get plastered

tamponneur, -euse [tɑ̃pɔnœr, -øz] **ADJ** colliding; **le train t.** the train which crashed into the back of the other one

tamponnoir [tɑ̃pɔnwar] **NM** pin *or* wall bit

tam-tam [tamtam] *(pl* **tam-tams)** **NM 1** *Mus (d'Afrique)* tom-tom; *(gong)* tam-tam **2** *Fam (publicité tapageuse)* hype; *(vacarme)* fuss, to-do; **faire du t. autour de qch** to make a great fuss *or* to-do about sth

tan [tɑ̃] **NM** tanbark

tancer [16] [tɑ̃se] **VT** *Littéraire* to scold; **t. vertement qn** to berate sb

tanche [tɑ̃ʃ] **NF 1** *Ich* tench **2** *Fam Br* pillock, plonker, *Am* meathead

tandem [tɑ̃dɛm] **NM 1** *(vélo)* tandem **2** *(couple)* duo, pair; **le t. qu'ils forment est redoutable** together, they make a formidable pair
• **en tandem ADJ** *(attelage)* tandem *(avant n)*; *Tech* **cylindres en t.** tandem cylinders **ADV** *(agir, travailler)* in tandem, as a pair; **chevaux attelés en t.** horses driven tandem

tandis que [tɑ̃dikə]

tandis qu' is used before a word beginning with a vowel or h mute.

CONJ 1 *(pendant que)* while, *Sout* whilst; *(au même moment que)* as; **le téléphone sonna tandis qu'il ouvrait la porte** the phone rang as he opened the door **2** *(alors que)* whereas

tangage [tɑ̃gaʒ] **NM** *Aviat & Naut* pitching; **il y avait du t.** the boat was pitching

tangara [tɑ̃gara] **NM** *Orn* tanager; **t. rouge** scarlet tanager

tangence [tɑ̃ʒɑ̃s] **NF** tangency; **point de t.** point of contact *or Spéc* tangency

tangent, -e [tɑ̃ʒɑ̃, -ɑ̃t] **ADJ 1** *Géom & Math* tangent, tangential; **t. à** at a tangent to **2** *Fam (limite ▸ cas, candidat)* borderline; **je ne l'ai pas renvoyé, mais c'était t.** I didn't fire him but it was touch and go *or* it was a close thing
• **tangente NF 1** *Géom & Math* tangent **2** *Fam (locution)* **prendre la tangente** *(se sauver)* to slip off *or* away, to make oneself scarce; *(esquiver une question)* to dodge the issue

tangentiel, -elle [tɑ̃ʒɑ̃sjɛl] **ADJ** tangential

tangentiellement [tɑ̃ʒɑ̃sjɛlmɑ̃] **ADV** tangentially

Tanger [tɑ̃ʒe] **NM** Tangier, Tangiers

tangible [tɑ̃ʒibl] **ADJ 1** *(palpable)* tangible, *Sout* palpable; **la réalité t.** tangible reality **2** *(évident)* tangible, real

tangiblement [tɑ̃ʒibləmɑ̃] **ADV** *Littéraire* tangibly, palpably

tango¹ [tɑ̃go] **ADJ INV** *(couleur)* bright orange

tango² [tɑ̃go] **NM** *(danse)* tango; **danser le t.** to tango

tango³ [tɑ̃go] *(boisson)* = cocktail consisting of beer and grenadine

tangon [tɑ̃gɔ̃] **NM** *Naut (mobile)* swinging boom; *(de spi)* spinnaker boom

tanguer [3] [tɑ̃ge] **VI 1** *Naut* to pitch; **la tempête faisait t. le navire** the storm was tossing the boat around, the boat was tossed about in the storm **2** *Fam (tituber)* to reel, to sway **3** *Fam (vaciller ▸ décor)* to spin; **tout tanguait autour d'elle, elle sentit qu'elle allait s'évanouir** everything around her was spinning and she felt she was going to faint

tanière [tanjɛr] **NF 1** *(d'un animal)* den, lair **2** *(habitation)* retreat; **il ne sort jamais de sa t.** he never leaves his den **3** *(habitation sordide)* hovel

tanin [tanɛ̃] **NM** tannin

tank [tɑ̃k] **NM** *Ind, Mil & Hum (voiture)* tank

tanker¹ [tɑ̃kœr] **NM** *Naut* tanker

tanker² [3] [tɑ̃ke] **VI** *Can Joual (faire le plein)* to tank up; *Fig (boire beaucoup)* to knock it back

tankini [tɑ̃kini] **NM** *(maillot)* tankini

tankiste [tɑ̃kist] **NM** *Mil* soldier with a tank unit

tannage [tanaʒ] **NM** tanning

tannant, -e [tanɑ̃, -ɑ̃t] **ADJ 1** *(produit)* tanning **2** *Can Fam (remuant)* boisterous□ **3** *Fam (importun)* annoying□; *(énervant)* maddening□; **ce que tu peux être t. avec tes questions!** you're a real pain with all these questions!
NM,F *Can Fam (enfant turbulent)* little devil, scamp
• **tannante NF** *Can Fam* **une tannante de tempête** a hell of a storm; **j'ai attrapé une tannante de grippe** I've caught an awful dose of (the) flu

tanne [tan] **NF 1** *(sur le cuir)* spot **2** *(sur le visage)* blackhead

tanné, -e [tane] **ADJ 1** *(traité ▸ peaux, cuir)* tanned **2** *(hâlé ▸ peau)* weathered, weather-beaten **3** *Can Fam* **être t.** *(en avoir assez)* to be fed up; **je suis tannée à faire le ménage** I'm fed up *or* I've had it up to here doing housework; **être t. de qn/qch** to be sick of sb/sth
NM 1 *(couleur)* tan (colour) **2 gants en t.** tan *or* tanned leather gloves

• **tannée** NF *très Fam (correction, défaite)* thrashing; **prendre une tannée** to get a thrashing; **il a pris** *ou* **s'est ramassé une tannée aux présidentielles** he got well and truly thrashed in the presidential election

tanner [3] [tane] VT 1 *(traiter ▸ peaux, cuir)* to tan
2 *(hâler ▸ peau)* to tan
3 *Fam (harceler)* to pester, to badger; **son fils le tanne pour avoir une moto** his/her son keeps pestering him for a motorbike
4 *très Fam* **t. (le cuir à) un enfant** to thrash a child, to tan a child's hide; **il s'est fait t. le cuir par des voleurs** he was beaten up by thieves

tannerie [tanri] NF 1 *(établissement)* tannery 2 *(industrie, opérations)* tanning

tanneur, -euse [tanœr, -øz] NM,F tanner

tannin [tanɛ̃] = **tanin**

tannique [tanik] ADJ tannic

tanrec [tɑ̃rɛk] NM *Zool* tenrec

tan-sad [tɑ̃sad] *(pl* **tan-sads***)* NM pillion(-seat)

TANT [tɑ̃] ADV 1 *(avec un verbe) (tellement, à tel point)* so much; **il l'aime t.** he loves her so much; **ne fume pas t.!** don't smoke so much!; **j'en ai t. rêvé** I've dreamt about it so much *or* often; **ce n'est pas la peine de t. vous presser** you needn't be in such a hurry
2 *(avec un verbe, en corrélation avec "que")* **j'ai t. crié que je suis enroué** I shouted so much that I've lost my voice; **ils ont t. fait qu'ils ont obtenu tout ce qu'ils voulaient** they worked so hard that they ended up getting everything they wanted; **t. était grande sa discrétion que...** so great was his/her discretion that...; *Prov* **t. va la cruche à l'eau qu'à la fin elle se casse** the pitcher will go to the well once too often
3 *(avec un participe passé)* **le jour t. attendu arriva enfin** the long-awaited day arrived at last
4 *(introduisant la cause)* so, to such a degree; **les plantes ont gelé t. il a fait froid** it was so cold the plants froze; **il ne peut pas se lever t. il est malade** he's too ill to get up
5 *(exprimant une quantité imprécise)* so much; **ce sera t. par mois** that will be so much per month; **il gagne t. de l'heure** he earns so much per hour
6 *(introduisant une comparaison)* **le spectacle peut plaire t. aux enfants qu'aux parents** the show is aimed at children as well as adults; **pour des raisons t. économiques que politiques** for economic as well as political reasons; **elle n'est pas t. sotte que naïve** she's not so much stupid as naive; **t. aux Indes qu'ailleurs** both in India and elsewhere; **t. pour vous que pour moi** for your sake as much as mine, for you as much as for me; **il est sévère t. avec ses enfants qu'avec ses élèves** he is as strict with his children as he is with his pupils; **je suis à l'aise t. avec lui qu'avec elle** I get on with him AND with her
7 *(locutions)* **une maison de banlieue comme il y en a t.** one of those suburban houses that you come across so often; *Fam* **tu m'en diras t.!** you don't say!
NM **suite à votre lettre du t.** with reference to your letter of such and such a date; **vous serez payé le t. de chaque mois** you'll be paid on such and such a date every month
• **en tant que** CONJ 1 *(en qualité de)* as; **en t. que directeur, la décision vous revient** as director, the decision is yours 2 *(dans la mesure où)* as long as; **il ne s'intéresse à nous qu'en t. que nous lui rendons service** he's only interested in us as long as *or* while we can be of use to him; **l'homme en t. qu'il diffère des animaux** man, as distinct from animals
• **tant bien que mal** ADV after a fashion; **je l'ai repassé t. bien que mal** I've ironed it after a fashion *or* as best I could; **le moteur est reparti, t. bien que mal** somehow, the engine started up again
• **tant de** DÉT 1 *(tellement de ▸ suivi d'un nom non comptable)* so much, such; *(▸ suivi d'un nom comptable)* so many; **t. de bonheur** such *or* so much happiness; **elle s'est donné t. de mal** she went to such (a lot of) *or* so much trouble; **t. de gens** so many people; **t. de fois** so many times, so often 2 *(en corrélation avec "que")* **elle a t. de travail qu'elle n'a même plus le temps de faire les courses** she has so much work that she doesn't even have the time to go shopping any more; **vous m'avez reçu avec t. de générosité que je ne sais quoi dire** you've made me so welcome that I'm lost for words; **t. d'années ont passé que j'ai oublié** it was so many years ago that I've forgotten 3 *(exprimant une quantité imprécise)* **il y a t. de lignes par page** there are so many lines to a page; **t. de centimètres** so many centimetres; **t. de grammes** so many grammes
• **tant et plus** ADV 1 *(à maintes reprises)* over and over again, time and time again; **j'ai insisté t. et plus** I insisted over and over again *or* time and time again; **ils tiraient t. et plus** they were pulling for all they were worth 2 *(nombreux)* **il a des amis t. et plus** he has plenty of friends
• **tant et plus de** DÉT **il a t. et plus d'argent** he has any amount of money
• **tant et si bien que** CONJ so much so that...; **t. et si bien que je ne lui parle plus** so much so that we're no longer on speaking terms; **ils ont fait t. et si bien qu'ils ont réussi** they worked so hard that they succeeded
• **tant et tant que** CONJ **j'ai crié t. et t. qu'il est parti** I shouted so much that he went (away); **on a attendu t. et t. que...** we waited so long that...
• **tant il est vrai que** CONJ **il s'en remettra, t. il est vrai que le temps guérit tout** he'll get over it, for it's true that time is a great healer
• **tant mieux** ADV good, fine, so much the better; **vous n'avez rien à payer – t. mieux!** you don't have anything to pay – good *or* fine!; **il est parti et c'est t. mieux** he's left and just as well *or* and a good thing too; **t. mieux pour lui** good for him
• **tant pis** ADV never mind, too bad; **il n'est pas là – t. pis!** he isn't in – never mind!; **je reste, t. pis s'il n'est pas content** I'm staying, too bad if he doesn't like it; **t. pis pour lui** too bad (for him)
• **tant que** CONJ 1 *(autant que)* as *or* so much as; **elle ne travaille pas t. que les autres** she doesn't work as much *or* as hard as the others; **j'ai couru t. que j'ai pu** I ran as hard as I could; **n'aimer rien t. que...** to like nothing more than...; **elle gagne plus de 3000 euros par mois – t. que ça!** she earns over 3,000 euros a month – as much as that *or* that much!; **il y en a déjà plus de cent – t. que ça?** there are already more than a hundred (of them) – as many as that *or* that many?; **tu l'aimes t. que ça?** do you love him/her that much?; **ça fait mal! – t. que ça?** it hurts! – that much?; **il y a 15 ans – t. que ça?** that was 15 years ago – that long ago?; **il peut espérer gagner dans les 5000 euros – non, pas t. que ça** he can expect to earn about 5,000 euros – no, not as much as that *or* not that much; **il souffre? – non, pas t. que ça** is he in pain? – no, not really; **il en faudra combien, une centaine? – pas t. que ça** how many (of them) will we need, about a hundred? – no, not as many as that *or* not that many; **elle est jolie – pas t. que ça** she's pretty – not really; **tous t. que nous sommes** all of us, every single *or* last one of us; *Fam* **il pleut t. que ça peut** it's raining like anything
2 *(aussi longtemps que)* as long as; *(pendant que)* while; **t. que je vivrai** as long as I live; **tu peux rester t. que tu veux** you can stay as long as you like; **rien ne peut être décidé t. qu'il n'a pas donné son avis** nothing can be decided until (such time as) he makes his opinion known; **t. qu'il y aura des hommes** as long as there are men; **t. que j'y pense, as-tu reçu ma carte?** while I think of it *or* before I forget, did you get my card?; **pourquoi pas un château avec piscine t. que tu y es!** why not a castle with a swimming pool while you're at it!; **t. qu'il y a de la vie, il y a de l'espoir** where there's life there's hope; *Fam* **t. que ce n'est pas grave!** as long as it's not serious!
3 *(quelque)* however; **t. aimable qu'il soit** however pleasant he may be
4 *Belg* **t. que maintenant** up to now, until now, till now
• **tant qu'à** CONJ 1 *(quitte à)* **t. qu'à partir, autant partir tout de suite** if I/you/*etc* must go, I/you/*etc* might as well do it right away; **t. qu'à m'expatrier, j'aime mieux que ce soit dans un beau pays** if I have to go and live abroad, I'd rather go somewhere nice; **t. qu'à faire** *ou Can* **t. qu'à y être, je préférerais du poisson** I'd rather have fish if I have the choice; **t. qu'à faire** *ou Can* **t. qu'à y être, sortons maintenant** we might as well go out now 2 *Can Fam (quant à)* as for[□]; **t. qu'à moi/lui** as for me/him 3 *Belg* **t. qu'à présent** up to now, until now, till now
• **tant s'en faut** ADV far from it
• **tant soit peu** ADV **s'il est t. soit peu intelligent, il comprendra** if he is even the slightest bit intelligent, he'll understand
• **un tant soit peu** ADV a little, somewhat; **si tu étais un t. soit peu observateur** if you were the least bit observant; **si elle avait un t. soit peu de bon sens** if she had the slightest bit of common sense

Tantale [tɑ̃tal] NPR *Myth* Tantalus

tantale [tɑ̃tal] NM *Chim* tantalum

tante [tɑ̃t] NF 1 *(dans une famille)* aunt; **t. Marie** Aunt Marie 2 *très Fam (mont-de-piété)* **chez ma t.** at my uncle's, at the pawnshop[□] 3 *très Fam (homosexuel)* fairy, = offensive term used to refer to a male homosexual

tantième [tɑ̃tjɛm] ADJ **la t. partie des bénéfices** so much of the profits
NM *(part proportionnelle)* proportion; *(quote-part de bénéfice)* director's fee *or* percentage

tantine [tɑ̃tin] NF *Fam* aunty

tantinet [tɑ̃tinɛ] NM tiny bit; **un t. stupide** a tiny bit stupid; **un t. plus long** a tiny bit *or* a shade *or* a fraction longer

tantôt [tɑ̃to] ADV 1 *Fam (cet après-midi)* this afternoon[□]; **je dois le voir t.** I have to see him this afternoon
2 *Belg & (régional) (plus tard)* later; **à t.** see you later
3 *Belg & (régional) (plus tôt)* earlier; **je l'ai vu t.** I saw him earlier
4 *Vieilli (régional) (bientôt)* soon, presently; **voici t. deux mois qu'il est parti** it will soon be two months since he left
• **tantôt..., tantôt...** sometimes..., sometimes...; **nous passons le week-end t. chez mes parents, t. chez les siens** sometimes we spend the weekend with my parents, sometimes with his/hers; **t. triste, t. gai** now sad, now happy

tantouse, tantouze [tɑ̃tuz] NF *très Fam* fairy, = offensive term used to refer to a male homosexual

tantrique [tɑ̃trik] ADJ Tantric

tantrisme [tɑ̃trism] NM Tantrism

Tanzanie [tɑ̃zani] NF **la T.** Tanzania

tanzanien, -enne [tɑ̃zanjɛ̃, -ɛn] ADJ Tanzanian
• **Tanzanien, -enne** NM,F Tanzanian

TAO [teao] NF *(abrév* **traduction assistée par ordinateur***)* CAT

tao [tao] NM Tao

taoïsme [taɔism] NM Taoism

taoïste [taɔist] ADJ Taoist
NMF Taoist

taon [tɑ̃] NM *Entom* horsefly

tapage [tapaʒ] NM 1 *(bruit)* din, racket; **faire du t.** to make a racket 2 *(scandale)* scandal, fuss; **ça a fait tout un t.** there was quite a fuss about it; **faire du t. autour de qch** to make a great fuss *or* a song and dance about sth 3 *Jur* **t. nocturne** breach of the peace *(at night)*

tapageur, -euse [tapaʒœr, -øz] ADJ 1 *(bruyant)* noisy, rowdy 2 *(voyant ▸ vêtement, couleur)* loud, flashy; *(▸ publicité)* obtrusive 3 *(dont on parle beaucoup)* **une liaison tapageuse** a much talked-about affair

tapageusement [tapaʒøzmɑ̃] ADV flashily, showily

tapant, -e [tapɑ̃, -ɑ̃t] ADJ **je serai là à dix heures tapantes** I'll be there at ten o'clock sharp *or* on the dot; **il est rentré à minuit t.** he came home on the stroke of midnight

tape [tap] NF 1 *(pour punir)* (little) slap, tap; **je lui ai donné une petite t. sur les fesses** I gave him/her a little smack *or* slap on the bottom 2 *(amicale)* pat; **donner une petite t. sur le dos/bras de qn** to pat sb's back/arm 3 *(pour attirer l'attention)* tap; **donner une petite t. sur l'épaule de qn** to tap sb's shoulder

tapé, -e [tape] ADJ 1 *Fam (fou)* nuts, crackers
2 *(fruit ▸ abîmé)* bruised; *(▸ séché)* dried
3 *Fam (juste et vigoureux ▸ réplique)* smart; **ça, c'est une réponse bien tapée!** that's really hit the nail on the head!
4 *Fam (marqué par l'âge ▸ visage)* aged[□]
• **tapée** NF *Fam (multitude)* **une tapée** *ou* **des ta-**

pées de... masses *or* heaps *or* loads of...; **une tapée de dossiers** heaps of files; **il y avait une tapée de photographes** there was a swarm of photographers

tape-à-l'œil [tapalœj] *Fam* **ADJ INV** *(couleur, bijoux, toilette)* flashy, showy

NM INV c'est du t. *(objets, toilette)* it's all show; **il aime le t.** he likes showy things

tape-cul *(pl* **tape-culs**), **tapecul** [tapky] **NM 1** *(tilbury)* gig

2 *Fam Équitation* **faire du t.** to do a sitting trot

3 *Fam (voiture)* boneshaker

4 *Fam (balançoire) Br* seesaw[□], *Am* teeter-totter[□]

5 *(voile)* jigger; *(mât)* jigger mast

tapée [tape] *voir* **tapé**

TAPER[1] [3] [tape]

VT	
• to hit **1**	• to tap **2**
• to hammer **2**	• to bang **2**
• to knock **3**	• to type **4**
• to key **5**	• to dial **6**
• to thump out **7**	
VI	
• to bang **1**	• to hit **1, 2**
• to type **3**	• to beat down **4**
VPR	
• to hit each other **1**	• to bang **2**

VT 1 *(personne ▸ gén)* to hit; *(▸ gifler)* to smack; **arrête ou je te tape!** stop or I'll smack you!

2 *(marteler ▸ doucement)* to tap; *(▸ fort)* to hammer, to bang; **elle tapait rageusement le sol avec son pied** she was stamping her foot angrily; *Fam* **t. le carton** to play cards[□], to have a game of cards[□]

3 *(heurter)* **t. un coup à une porte** to knock once on a door; **il est venu t. plusieurs coups sur ma vitre** he came and knocked (several times) on my window

4 *(dactylographier)* to type; **t. un document à la machine** to type (out) a document; **un devoir tapé à la machine** a typed *or* typewritten piece of homework; **t. 40 mots à la minute** to type 40 words per minute

5 *Ordinat* to key; **tapez entrée ou retour** select enter or return; **t. qch sur ordinateur** to key sth (on the computer)

6 *Tél (code)* to dial; **tapez le 36 15** dial 36 15

7 *Fam (jouer ▸ air de musique)* to thump *or* to hammer out; **il tapait une valse sur le piano** he was hammering out a waltz on the piano

8 *Fam* **t. qch à qn** *(emprunter ▸ objet)* to borrow sth from sb[□]; *(▸ argent)* to bum *or* cadge sth off sb, to hit *or Br* tap sb for sth; **il est encore venu me t.** he came to scrounge off me again; **il m'a tapé de 50 euros** he bummed *or* cadged 50 euros off me

9 *Fam (atteindre)* **t. le cent/le deux cents** to hit a hundred/two hundred (kilometres an hour)

VI 1 *(donner un coup à quelque chose)* **t. sur** *(clavier)* to bang *or* to thump away at; *(clou, pieu)* to hit; *(avec un marteau)* to hammer (away at); **elle a tapé (du poing) sur la table** she banged *or* thumped her fist on the table; *Fam Mil* **t. sur un objectif** to strafe a target; **t. à la porte** to bang on the door; **t. au carreau** to knock on *or* at the window; **t. au plafond** *(avec un balai etc)* to bang *or* to knock on the ceiling; **t. dans une balle** *(lui donner un coup)* to kick a ball; *(s'amuser avec)* to kick a ball around; **t. avec un marteau (contre le mur)** to hammer (the wall); **t. à côté** to miss the target; *Fig* **alors là, tu as tapé à côté** you're way off beam, *Am* you're way out in left field; **la bôme est venu t. contre le mât** the boom hit the *or* banged into the mast; **t. du pied** *ou* **des pieds** to stamp one's foot *or* feet; **t. des mains** to clap one's hands

2 *(battre, frapper)* **t. sur qn** *(une fois)* to hit sb; *(à coups répétés)* to beat sb up; **c'est un bon boxeur et il tape dur** he's a good boxer and he hits hard *or* packs a powerful punch; *Fam* **t. sur le ventre à qn** to give sb a dig in the ribs *(as a mark of familiarity)*; *Fam* **t. sur la gueule à qn** to belt sb; **se faire t. sur les doigts** to get rapped over the knuckles; *Fam* **elle lui a tapé dans l'œil** he/she was really taken with her, he/she took quite a shine to her

3 *(dactylographier)* **t. (à la machine)** to type; **t. au toucher** to touch-type; **il tape bien/mal** he types well/badly, he's a good/bad typist; **tape sur cette touche** *(de machine à écrire, d'ordinateur)* press *or* hit this key

4 *Fam (soleil)* to beat down; **le soleil tapait** the sun was beating down; **ça tape** *(il fait chaud)* it's scorching; **le vin rouge m'a tapé sur la tête** the red wine knocked me out

5 *Fam (critiquer)* **t. sur** *(personne, film)* to run down, to knock; **elle s'est fait t. dessus dans la presse** *ou* **par les journaux** the newspapers really slated her

6 *Fam* **t. sur un piano** *(mal jouer)* to bash away *or* to thump away on a piano

7 *Fam (puiser)* **t. dans** *(réserves, économies)* to dig into; *(tiroir-caisse)* to help oneself from; *(nourriture)* to help oneself to, to dig into; **voilà la viande, tapez dedans!** here's the meat, dig *or esp Br* tuck in!; **elle ne pouvait pas s'empêcher de t. dans la caisse** she couldn't keep her fingers out of the till

8 *très Fam (sentir mauvais)* to reek, to stink; **ça tape dans ta chambre!** your room stinks!

VPR se taper 1 *(emploi réciproque)* to hit each other; **ils ont fini par se t. dessus** eventually they came to blows; *très Fam* **se t. sur le ventre** *(être en bonnes relations)* to be very close[□]; **lui et le ministre se tapent sur le ventre** he and the minister are great buddies

2 *(se cogner)* **se t. le front** to bang one's forehead; **se t. la tête contre qch** to bang one's head against sth

3 *Fam (consommer ▸ dîner, petits fours)* to guzzle, *Br* to scoff; *(▸ boisson)* to sink, to lower; **je me taperais bien une bière** I'd kill for *or Br* I could murder a beer

4 *très Fam (sexuellement)* to screw, *Br* to shag

5 *Fam (subir ▸ corvée, travail, gêneur)* to get stuck *or Br* landed *or* lumbered with; **je me suis tapé les cinq étages à pied** I had to walk up the five floors[□]; **on s'est tapé les embouteillages** we got stuck in the traffic jams[□]; **il a fallu que je me tape tout Proust pour l'examen** I had to devour the entire works of Proust for the exam

6 *très Fam (s'en moquer)* **elle s'en tape** she doesn't give a shit *or Br* a toss *or Am* a rat's ass; **si tu savais comme je m'en tape!** I don't give a shit!

7 *(locutions) Fam* **se t. (sur) les cuisses** *(de satisfaction, de rire)* to slap one's thighs; *très Fam* **tu peux (toujours) te t.!** you can whistle for it!; **c'était à se t.** *Fam* **le derrière** *ou très Fam* **le cul par terre** it was hysterical *or* side-splitting; *Fam* **c'est à se t. la tête contre les murs** it's enough to drive you crazy; *Fam* **se t. la cloche** to pig out, *Br* to have a blow-out

taper[2] [3] [tape] **VT** *Tech & Naut (boucher ▸ trou)* to plug, to stop up

tapette [tapet] **NF 1** *(petite tape)* pat, tap

2 *(piège à souris)* mousetrap

3 *Fam (bagou)* **il a une bonne** *ou* **fière t.** he's a real chatterbox!, can HE talk!

4 *très Fam (homosexuel)* fairy = offensive term used to refer to a male homosexual

5 *(contre les mouches)* flyswatter; *(pour les tapis)* carpet beater

6 *(petit marteau)* mallet

tapeur, -euse [tapœr, -øz] **NM,F** *Fam* sponger, scrounger

tapin [tapɛ̃] **NM** *très Fam* **faire le t.** *(se prostituer)* to walk the streets, *Br* to be on the game

tapiner [3] [tapine] **VI** *très Fam* to walk the streets, *Br* to be on the game

tapineur, -euse [tapinœr, -øz] **NM,F** *très Fam* streetwalker

tapinois [tapinwa] **en tapinois ADV** *(entrer, se glisser)* sneakily, furtively; **s'approcher en t.** to creep up

tapioca [tapjɔka] **NM** tapioca

tapir[1] [tapir] **NM** *Zool* tapir

tapir[2] [32] [tapir] **se tapir VPR 1** *(se baisser)* to crouch (down); *(se dissimuler ▸ par peur)* to hide; *(▸ en embuscade)* to lurk; **il se tapit derrière un buisson et l'attendit** he lay in wait for her behind a bush **2** *(se retirer)* to hide away

tapis [tapi] **NM 1** *(recouvrant le sol)* carpet; *(de petite taille)* rug; *(pour la gymnastique)* mat; **recouvrir le plancher d'un t.** to carpet the floor; **t. chinois/persan** Chinese/Persian carpet; **t. de bain, t. de salle de bains** bath mat; **t. de haute laine** deep-pile carpet; **t. de laine rase** short-pile carpet; **t. d'Orient** oriental carpet; **t. de prière** prayer mat; *aussi Fig* **t. rouge** red carpet; *Fig* **dérouler le t. rouge pour qn** to roll out the red carpet for sb, to give sb the red carpet treatment; **t. de selle** saddlecloth; **t. de sol** *(sol de tente)* ground sheet; *(petit matelas)* sleeping mat *(underneath sleeping bag)*; *(pour la gymnastique)* floor mat; *Ordinat* **t. de souris** mouse mat; **t. volant** flying *or* magic carpet; **t. de yoga** yoga mat; *Fig* **se prendre les pieds dans le t.** to get into a mess

2 *(recouvrant un meuble)* cloth, cover; *(de billard, d'une table de jeu)* cloth, baize; **t. de table** table cover; **t. vert** *(table de jeu)* green baize; *(de conférence)* baize; **T. Vert** = game of chance organized by the French national lottery; *Fig* **le t. brûle** *ou* **crie** there's a stake missing

3 *Littéraire (couche ▸ de feuilles, de neige)* carpet; **un t. d'aiguilles de pin/de fleurs** a carpet of pine needles/of flowers

4 *Sport (dans une salle de sport)* mat; *(à la boxe)* canvas; **aller au t.** *(boxeur)* to be knocked down; **envoyer son adversaire au t.** to floor one's opponent; *Fig* **une entreprise mise au t. par la concurrence** a company knocked for six *or* KO'd by the competition; **il est resté au t.** he stayed down, he didn't get up

5 *Tech* **t. roulant** *(pour piétons)* travelator, moving *Br* pavement *or Am* sidewalk; *(pour marchandises, pour bagages)* conveyor belt; **t. transporteur** *(pour bagages, pièces de montage)* conveyor (belt); **t. de livraison des bagages** baggage carousel *or* conveyor (belt)

6 *Belg* **t. plain** carpet

• **sur le tapis ADV 1** *(dans un jeu)* on the table; **il y avait plus de 1000 euros sur le t.** there were more than 1,000 euros on the table **2** *Fig* **mettre qch sur le t.** to bring sth up for consideration *or* for discussion; **l'affaire est de nouveau sur le t.** the matter is being discussed again; **à quoi bon remettre toutes nos vieilles querelles sur le t.?** what's the use of bringing up *or* raking over all our old quarrels again?

tapis-brosse [tapibrɔs] *(pl* **tapis-brosses) NM** doormat

tapisser [3] [tapise] **VT 1** *(mur ▸ avec du papier peint)* to wallpaper; *(▸ avec du tissu)* to hang with material; *(▸ avec des tentures)* to hang with *Br* curtains *or Am* drapes; *(fauteuil)* to upholster; *(étagères)* to cover; **mur tapissé d'affiches** wall covered *or* plastered with posters; **les murs sont tapissés de jaune** the walls are papered in yellow

2 *(l'intérieur d'une armoire)* to line *or* to cover (**de** with); *Culin (garnir)* to line; **tapissez votre moule de papier d'aluminium** line your *Br* tin *or Am* pan with foil

3 *Littéraire (sujet: bruyère, neige ▸ sol)* to carpet; *(sujet: lierre ▸ mur)* to cover; **le trèfle tapissait le champ** the field was carpeted with clover; **un banc tapissé de mousse/neige** a moss-/snow-covered bench

4 *Anat & Bot* to line

tapisserie [tapisri] **NF 1** *(art, panneau)* tapestry; **la t. de Bayeux** *ou* **de la reine Mathilde** the Bayeux tapestry; *Hum* **faire t.** *(dans une réunion)* to be left out; *(au bal)* to be a wallflower

2 *(petit ouvrage)* tapestry; **faire de la t.** to do tapestry *or* tapestry-work; **chaise en t.** chair upholstered with tapestry, tapestry chair

3 *(papier peint)* wallpaper *(UNCOUNT)*; **refaire les tapisseries d'une chambre** to repaper a bedroom

4 *(métier)* tapestry-making

tapissier, -ère [tapisje, -ɛr] **NM,F 1** *(fabricant)* tapestry-maker **2** *(vendeur)* upholsterer **3** *(décorateur)* interior decorator

tapocher [3] [tapɔʃe] **VT** *Can Fam (frapper)* to thump; *(battre)* to hammer

tapon [tapɔ̃] **NM** *Vieilli (bouchon)* plug, bung; **rouler qch en t.** to roll sth into a ball

tapotement [tapɔtmɑ̃] **NM** *(avec les doigts)* tapping; *(avec la main)* patting; *(au piano)* plonking

tapoter [3] [tapɔte] **VT 1** *(dos, joue)* to pat; *(surface)* to tap; **elle lui a tapoté amicalement la joue** she gave his/her cheek a friendly pat **2** *(air de musique)* to bang out

VI 1 *(tambouriner)* to tap; *(en signe d'énervement)* to drum **2** *(jouer médiocrement)* **il tapotait sur le**

vieux piano he was banging out a tune on the old piano

tapuscrit [tapyskri] NM typescript

taquet [takɛ] NM 1 *(cale ▸ de meuble, de porte)* wedge; **t. de sûreté** safety stop
2 *Constr (coin en bois)* (wood) angle block; *(d'une porte)* catch
3 *(d'arpenteur) & Agr* (small) picket, peg
4 *Naut* **t. (de tournage)** (belaying) cleat; *(en aviron)* button, collar
5 *Tech (d'une machine à écrire, d'un ordinateur)* tabulator stop; **poser un t. (de tabulateur)** to set a tab *or* a tabulator stop

taquin, -e [takɛ̃, -in] ADJ teasing; **d'un air t.** teasingly, playfully; **il est un peu t. par moments** he's a bit of a tease sometimes; **elle est très taquine** she's a great one for teasing
NM,F *(personne)* teaser, tease

taquiner [3] [takine] VT 1 *(faire enrager)* to tease
2 *(être légèrement douloureux)* to bother; **j'ai une dent qui me taquine** one of my teeth is bothering me *or* giving me a bit of bother 3 *Fam (locutions)* **t. le piano/violon** to play the piano/violin a bit; **t. le goujon** to do a bit of fishing
VPR **se taquiner** to tease each other

taquinerie [takinri] NF 1 *(action)* teasing; **il m'a dit que j'étais gros – c'était par t.** he said I was fat – he was just teasing (you) 2 *(parole)* **cesse tes taquineries** stop teasing

tarabiscoté, -e [tarabiskɔte] ADJ 1 *(bijou)* overornate 2 *(style, phrases)* fussy, affected 3 *(explication, récit)* complicated, involved, convoluted

tarabuster [3] [tarabyste] VT 1 *(houspiller ▸ personne)* to pester, to badger 2 *(tracasser)* to bother

tarage [taraʒ] NM *Com* taring

tarama [tarama] NM taramasalata

taratata [taratata] EXCLAM *Fam (pour exprimer la méfiance, l'incrédulité)* nonsense!, *Br* rubbish!

taraud [taro] NM *(pour filetage)* tap, screw tap

taraudage [tarodaʒ] NM 1 *(action)* tapping 2 *(trou)* female thread

tarauder [3] [tarode] VT 1 *Tech (acier)* to tap, to thread 2 *Fig Littéraire (obséder ▸ personne)* to gnaw at

taraudeuse [tarodøz] NF tapping machine, tapper

tarbouch, tarbouche [tarbuʃ] NM tarboosh

tard [tar] ADV 1 *(à la fin de la journée, d'une période)* late; **il est t.** it's late; **il se fait t.** it's getting late; **t. dans la matinée/l'après-midi** late in the morning/afternoon 2 *(après le moment fixé ou opportun)* late; **j'ai déjeuné t. aujourd'hui** I had a late lunch *or* had lunch late today; **les magasins restent ouverts t.** the shops stay open late *or* keep late opening hours; **il est un peu t. pour changer d'avis** it's a little late to change your mind; **tu arrives bien t. aujourd'hui** you're very late today; **c'est trop t.** it's too late; **se marier t.** to marry late (in life) 3 **plus t.** *(après un certain temps)* later (on); **il est arrivé encore plus t. que moi** he came in even later than I did; **nous parlions de lui pas plus t. que ce matin** we were talking about him only *or* just this morning; **je le ferai et pas plus t. que ce soir** I'll do it this very evening; **pas plus t. qu'hier** as recently as yesterday, only yesterday; **deux minutes plus t. et je manquais le bateau** another two minutes and I would have missed the boat; **remettre qch à plus t.** to put sth off until later
• **au plus tard** ADV at the latest; **donnez-moi votre réponse lundi au plus t.** give me your answer on Monday at the latest
• **sur le tard** ADV late (on) in life

tarder [3] [tarde] VI 1 *(être lent à se décider ▸ personne)* to delay; **je n'aurais pas dû tant t.** I shouldn't have left it so late *or* have put it off so long 2 *(être long à venir ▸ événement)* to be a long time coming, to take a long time to come; **leur décision n'a pas tardé** their decision wasn't long (in) coming, they didn't take long to decide; **ça ne tardera plus maintenant** it won't be long now; **cela n'a pas tardé** it wasn't long (in) coming; **et cela n'a pas tardé, il s'est cassé la cheville** and as expected, he duly broke his ankle; **tu vas recevoir une gifle, cela ne va pas t.** you're going to get smacked before long *or* in a minute or two; **la réponse tardait à venir** the answer took a long time to come; **aujourd'hui, le soleil tarde à se montrer** it's taking a long time for the sun to come out today; **un conflit ne tardera pas à éclater entre les deux pays** it won't be long before the two countries enter into conflict 3 *(mettre du temps ▸ personne)* **t. en chemin** to loiter on the way; **elle devrait être rentrée, elle ne va pas t.** she should be back by now, she won't be long; **pourquoi tarde-t-il?** why is he (taking) so long?; **nous ne tarderons pas à le savoir** we'll soon know; **elle n'a pas tardé à se rendre compte que…** it didn't take her long to realize that…, she soon realized that…; **t. à faire qch** to take a long time doing sth; **il a trop tardé à donner son accord** he waited too long before giving his approval
V IMPERSONNEL **il lui tarde de partir** he/she is longing to get away; **il nous tarde tant que tu reviennes** we long so much for you to return; **il me tarde que tu sois grand/aies 18 ans** I can't wait until you're grown up/18
• **sans (plus) tarder** ADV without delay; **partons sans plus t.** let's leave without further delay

tardif, -ive [tardif, -iv] ADJ 1 *(arrivée, fruit, récolte)* late; *(remords, excuses)* tardy, belated 2 *(heure)* late, *Sout* advanced; **à cette heure tardive** at this late hour

tardivement [tardivmɑ̃] ADV 1 *(à une heure tardive)* late 2 *(trop tard)* belatedly, tardily 3 *(se marier, s'établir)* late in life

tare [tar] NF 1 *(défectuosité ▸ physique)* (physical) defect; *(▸ psychique)* abnormality
2 *Fig* defect, flaw; *Hum* **ça n'est pas une t.!** it's not a crime!
3 *Com (perte de valeur)* loss, shrinkage
4 *(d'une balance, d'un poids brut, d'un prix)* tare; **faire la t.** to allow for the tare

taré, -e [tare] ADJ 1 *(gâté ▸ fruit)* imperfect
2 *(atteint d'une tare)* abnormal
3 *(corrompu)* corrupt; **un politicien t.** a corrupt politician
4 *Fam (fou)* crazy; *(imbécile) Br* thick, *Am* dumb
5 *Vét* unsound
NM,F 1 *Méd* imbecile 2 *(vicieux)* pervert 3 *Fam (fou)* nutcase, headcase; *(imbécile)* moron, idiot

tarentelle [tarɑ̃tɛl] NF tarantella

tarentule [tarɑ̃tyl] NF (European) tarantula

tarer [3] [tare] VT *Com* to tare

targette [tarʒɛt] NF small bolt
• **targettes** NFPL *Fam* 1 *(pieds)* feet◻, *Br* plates, *Am* dogs 2 *(chaussures)* shoes◻

targuer [3] [targe] **se targuer** VPR **se t. de qch/de faire qch** *(se vanter de)* to boast about sth/doing sth; *(s'enorgueillir de)* to pride oneself on sth/doing sth; **il se targue de connaître plusieurs langues** he boasts that he knows several languages; **un risque que je me targue d'avoir pris** a risk I'm proud to have taken *or* I pride myself on having taken

targui, -e [targi] ADJ Tuareg
• **Targui, -e** NM,F Tuareg

tarière [tarjɛr] NF 1 *Agr* drill; *Mines* borer 2 *Entom* terebra, ovipositor 3 *Menuis* (centre) auger

tarif [tarif] NM 1 *(liste de prix)* price list; *(barème)* rate, rates; **t. douanier** customs rate; **t. lettres** letter rate; **tarifs postaux** postal *or* postage rates; **t. progressif** increasing rate; **il est payé au t. syndical** he's paid the union rate; **t. horaire** hourly rate
2 *(prix pratiqué)* rate; *(d'un billet d'avion ou de train)* fare; **tarifs aériens/ferroviaires** air/rail fares; **quel est votre t.?, quels sont vos tarifs?** *(femme de ménage, baby-sitter, mécanicien, professeur particulier)* how much do you charge?; *(conseiller, avocat)* what fee do you charge?, what are your fees?; **quel est le t. courant pour une traduction?** what's the usual *or* going rate for translation?; **t. normal** standard rate; **t. heures creuses/pleines** *(gaz, électricité)* off-peak/full tariff rate; **à plein t.** *Transp* full-fare; *(au cinéma, au musée)* full-price; **billet (à) plein t.** full-fare ticket; **payer plein t.** *(passagers)* to pay full fare; *(pour marchandises)* to pay the full rate; **à t. réduit** *Transp* reduced-fare; *(au cinéma, au musée)* reduced-price; **t. réduit le lundi** reduced price on Mondays; **t. réduit pour étudiants** *(au cinéma, au musée)* student discount; **t. d'abonnement** *(gén)* subscription charge; *(au gaz, à l'électricité)* standing charge; *Tél* rental; **t. affaires** business rate; *(transport)* business fare; **t. APEX** APEX fare; **t. de base** basic rate; **t. des chambres** room rate; **t. en chambre double** *(dans un hôtel)* double occupancy rate; *Aviat* **t. commun** common rated fare, joint fare; **t. couplage** *(en publicité)* combination rate; **t. du distributeur** dealer list price; *Com* **t. d'entrée** import list; **t. étudiant** student rate; *(d'un voyage)* student fare; **t. excursion** excursion fare, APEX fare; **t. export** export tariff; **t. famille** family rate; *(d'un voyage)* family fare; *Mktg* **t. des insertions** advertising rates; **t. jeunes** youth fare; **t. journalier** daily *or* day rate; **t. minimum** minimum charge; **t. promotionnel** promotional rate; *(d'un voyage)* promotional fare; **t. de la publicité** advertising rates; **t. de référence** basing fare; **t. des salaires** salary scale; **t. social** reduced train fare for the general public; **t. société** commercial *or* corporate rate; **t. standby** standby fare; **t. d'urgence** = first-class rate; **t. uniforme** flat rate
3 *Fam (sanction)* fine, penalty; **100 euros d'amende? – c'est le t.!** a 100-euro fine? – that's how much it is!; **dix jours de prison, c'est le t.** ten days in the cooler is what it's usually worth *or* what you usually get

tarifaire [tarifɛr] ADJ *(disposition, réforme)* tariff *(avant n)*; *Com* **politique t.** pricing policy

tarifer [3] [tarife] VT *(marchandises)* to fix the price of

tarification [tarifikasjɔ̃] NF pricing; **t. au coût-plus-marge** mark-up pricing; **t. différentielle** differential pricing; **t. discriminatoire** discriminatory pricing; **t. en fonction de la valeur perçue** perceived value pricing; **t. géographique** geographical pricing; **t. de pénétration du marché** market penetration pricing

tarin [tarɛ̃] NM 1 *Orn* **t. (des aulnes)** siskin 2 *Fam (nez) Br* hooter, conk, *Am* schnozzle

tarir [32] [tarir] VI 1 *(cesser de couler)* to dry up, to run dry; **le puits de pétrole a tari** the oil well has run dry 2 *(pleurs)* to dry (up) 3 *Fig (s'épuiser ▸ conversation)* to dry up; *(▸ enthousiasme, inspiration)* to dry up, to run dry; **la discussion n'a pas tari pendant deux heures** the discussion has been flowing freely for two hours; **une fois lancé sur ce sujet, il ne tarit pas** once he's started on the subject he never shuts up *or* stops; **ne pas t. d'éloges sur qn** to be full of praise for sb; **elle ne tarissait pas de détails** she gave a wealth of detail; **il ne tarit pas sur le sujet** he never stops talking *or* shuts up about the subject
VT 1 *(assécher ▸ puits, source)* to dry up 2 *(faire cesser ▸ pleurs)* to dry 3 *Fig (épuiser ▸ fortune, inspiration)* to dry up; **son imagination est tarie** his/her imagination has dried up
VPR **se tarir** 1 *(mare, puits)* to dry up; *(rivière)* to run dry; **son lait s'est tari** her milk dried up 2 *Fig (inspiration, enthousiasme, fortune)* to dry up, to peter out

tarissement [tarismɑ̃] NM 1 *(d'une source, d'un puits)* drying up 2 *Fig (d'une conversation, de l'imagination)* running dry, drying up

tarlatane [tarlatan] NF tarlatan

tarlouze, tarlouse [tarluz] NF *Vulg Br* poof, *Am* fag

tarmacadam [tarmakadam] NM tarmacadam

tarot [taro] NM 1 *Cartes (carte, jeu)* tarot; **jouer au t.** to play tarot; **faire un t.** *ou* **une partie de t.** to have a game of tarot 2 *(cartomancie)* Tarot, tarot

tarse [tars] NM tarsus

tarsien, -enne [tarsjɛ̃, -ɛn] ADJ tarsal

tartan [tartɑ̃] NM tartan

tartane [tartan] NF *Naut* tartan, tartane, tartana

tartare [tartar] ADJ 1 *Hist* Tatar, Tartar 2 *Culin* tartar, tartare
NM *Culin* steak tartare
• **Tartare** NMF *Hist* Tartar

tarte [tart] NF 1 *Culin* tart; **t. aux pommes** apple tart *or* pie; **t. Tatin** tarte Tatin, = caramelized apples covered in shortcrust pastry and turned out upside down; **t. à la crème** *Culin* custard pie *or* tart; *Fig (cliché)* stock reply, cliché 2 *très Fam (gifle)* clout, wallop; **flanquer une t. à qn** to clout *or* to wallop sb 3 *Fam (locutions)* **c'est pas de la t.** *(c'est difficile)* it's no walkover, it's no picnic

ADJ *Fam* **1** *(ridicule ▸ personne) Br* plain-looking, plain, *Am* homely; *(▸ chapeau, robe)* stupid-looking, *Br* naff **2** *(stupide) Br* daft, *Am* dumb

tartelette [tartəlɛt] **NF** tartlet

Tartempion [tartɑ̃pjɔ̃] **NPR** *Fam* thingy, what's-his-name, *f* what's-her-name

tartiflette [tartiflɛt] **NF** *Culin* = Savoyard dish of potatoes and melted reblochon cheese

tartignol, tartignolle [tartiɲɔl] **ADJ** *Fam* tacky, *Br* naff

tartine [tartin] **NF 1** *Culin* slice of bread; **t. grillée** slice *or* piece of toast; **une t. de beurre/confiture** *ou Belg* **au beurre/à la confiture** a slice of bread and butter/jam; **faire des tartines** to butter (some) bread **2** *Fam Fig (tirade)* long-winded speech; *(article de journal, lettre)* screed; **en mettre une t.** *ou* **des tartines** to write screeds, to waffle on **3** *Fam (pied)* foot□, *Br* plate, *Am* dog; *(chaussure)* shoe□

tartiner [3] [tartine] **VT 1** *Culin* to spread; **t. du pain de** *ou* **avec du beurre** to butter bread, to spread bread with butter **2** *Fam (enduire en grande quantité)* **t. qn/qch de qch** to cover sb/sth in sth□ **3** *Fam Fig (écrire)* to churn out; **il a fallu qu'elle (en) tartine des pages et des pages** she had to write page after page

VPR se tartiner *Fam* **se t. de qch** to cover oneself in sth□

tartir [32] [tartir] **VI** *très Fam* **se faire t.** to be bored shitless

tartre [tartr] **NM 1** *(dans une bouilloire, une machine à laver)* fur, scale

2 *(des dents, du vin)* tartar

3 *(sur un tonneau)* tartar, argol

4 *Chim* **crème de t.** cream of tartar

tartrique [tartrik] **ADJ** *Chim* tartaric

tartufe [tartyf] = **tartuffe**

tartuferie [tartyfri] = **tartufferie**

tartuffe [tartyf] **ADJ** *Littéraire (hypocrite)* **il est un peu t.** he's a bit of a hypocrite *or* Tartuffe

NM hypocrite, Tartuffe

tartufferie [tartyfri] **NF 1** *(caractère)* hypocrisy **2** *(parole, acte)* piece of hypocrisy

tas [tɑ] **NM 1** *(amoncellement ▸ de dossiers, de vêtements)* heap, pile; *(▸ de sable, de cailloux)* heap; *(▸ de planches, de foin)* stack; **mettre en t.** *(feuilles, objets)* to pile *or* to heap up; **t. de fumier** dung heap; **t. d'ordures** *Br* rubbish *or Am* garbage heap; *Mines* **t. de déblais** dump; *Fam* **son vieux t. de boue** *ou* **ferraille** his/her rusty old heap; *Fam Péj* **un gros t.** *(gros individu mou)* a big fat lump; *(grosse fille laide)* a fat cow

2 *Fam* **un t.** *ou* **des t. de** *(un grand nombre de, une grande quantité de)* loads of, tons of; **un t. de mensonges** a pack of lies; **tout un t. de gens** a whole gang (of people), a whole load of people; **elle a fait un t. de choses dans sa vie** she has done masses of things in her life; **il y a des t. de vieilleries à la cave** there are piles of old things in the cellar; **il y en a des t. (et des t.)** there are heaps *or* masses of them; **t. de paresseux/menteurs!** you bunch of lazybones/liars!, *Br* you lazy/lying lot!

3 *Constr* constructed fabric; *(construction)* building under construction; *(chantier)* building site

• **dans le tas ADV** *Fam* **1** *(dans un ensemble)* **il y aura bien quelqu'un dans le t. qui pourra me renseigner** there must be someone around who can tell me; **dans le t., il doit y en avoir un ou deux que tu connais** there must be one or two out of that lot that you know **2** *(au hasard)* **la police a tiré/tapé dans le t.** the police fired into the crowd/hit out at random

• **sur le tas** *Fam* **ADJ 1** *(formation)* on-the-job **2** *Constr* on-site **ADV 1** *(se former)* on the job; **il a appris son métier sur le t.** he learned his trade as he went along **2** *Constr (tailler)* on site

Tasmanie [tasmani] **NF la T.** Tasmania

tasmanien, -enne [tasmanjɛ̃, -ɛn] **ADJ** Tasmanian

• **Tasmanien, -enne NM,F** Tasmanian

tassage [tɑsaʒ] **NM** *Sport* boxing in, crowding

tasse [tɑs] **NF 1** *(récipient)* cup; **t. à café** coffee cup; **t. à thé** teacup **2** *(contenu)* cup, cupful; **t. de café/thé** cup of coffee/tea; **ajouter deux tasses de farine** add two cupfuls of flour; **voulez-vous une t. de thé?** would you like a cup of tea?; *Fig* **ce n'est pas ma t. de thé** it's not my cup of tea; *Fam* **boire la t.** *(avaler de l'eau)* to get a mouthful of water

• **tasses NFPL** *Fam (urinoirs)* street urinals□

tassé, -e [tɑse] **ADJ 1** *(serrés ▸ voyageurs)* packed *or* crammed in **2** *(ratatiné, voûté ▸ personne)* wizened

• **bien tassé, -e ADJ** *Fam* **1** *(café)* strong; *(scotch, pastis)* stiff; *(verre)* full (to the brim) **2** *(dépassé ▸ âge)* **elle a 60 ans bien tassés** she's 60 if she's a day **3** *(féroce ▸ remarque)* well-chosen□; **il lui a envoyé quelques remarques bien tassées** he came out with a few well-chosen remarks **4** *(grave ▸ maladie)* nasty; **je tenais une grippe bien tassée** I had a nasty bout of flu

tasseau, -x [tɑso] **NM** *Menuis (de lattis)* brace, strut; *(de tiroir)* batten, strip

tassement [tɑsmɑ̃] **NM 1** *(affaissement ▸ de neige, de terre)* packing down

2 *(récession)* slight drop, downturn (**de** in)

3 *Bourse* easing, falling back

4 *Constr* subsidence

5 *Méd* **t. de vertèbres** spinal compression

tasser [3] [tɑse] **VT 1** *(neige, terre)* to pack down, to tamp down

2 *(entasser)* to cram, to squeeze (**dans** into); **tasse les vêtements dans le sac** press the clothes down in the bag

3 *(faire paraître plus petit)* to shrink; **cette robe la tasse** that dress makes her look dumpy

4 *Sport* to box in, to crowd

VI *Hort* to thicken

VPR se tasser 1 *(s'effondrer ▸ fondations, terrain)* to subside

2 *(se voûter ▸ personne)* to shrink

3 *(s'entasser ▸ voyageurs, spectateurs)* to cram, to squeeze up; **tout le monde s'est tassé dans la salle à manger** everybody crammed into the dining room

4 *Fam (s'arranger ▸ situation)* to settle down

5 *(ralentir ▸ demande, vente)* to fall, to drop; *(▸ production)* to slow down

taste-vin [tastəvɛ̃] **NM INV** *(tasse)* taster (cup), tastevin

tata [tata] **NF 1** *(en langage enfantin ▸ tante)* aunty, auntie; **T. Jacqueline** aunty *or* auntie Jacqueline **2** *très Fam (homosexuel)* queer, fairy, = offensive term used to refer to a male homosexual

tatami [tatami] **NM** tatami

tatane [tatan] **NF** *Fam* shoe□

tataner [3] [tatane] **VT** *Fam* **t. qn/qch** to give sb/sth a kicking

tatar, -e [tatar] **ADJ** Tatar, Tartar

NM *(langue)* Tatar, Tartar

• **Tatar, -e NM,F** Tatar, Tartar

tâter [3] [tɑte] **VT 1** *(fruit, membre, tissu)* to feel; **t. la porte pour trouver la poignée** to feel for the door handle; **elle avançait en tâtant les objets de la chambre** she was groping her way across the room **2** *Fig (sonder)* **t. le terrain** to see how the land lies; **tâte le terrain avant de leur faire une proposition** put some feelers out before making them an offer **3** *(tester ▸ personne)* to sound out; **t. l'opinion** to sound out attitudes, to put out feelers

• **tâter de VT IND 1** *Hum (nourriture, vin)* to try, to taste **2** *(faire l'expérience de)* **elle a déjà tâté de la prison** she's already had a taste of prison; **il a tâté de plusieurs métiers** he's tried his hand at several jobs; *Littéraire* **t. du chagrin/dégoût** to experience sorrow/disgust

VPR se tâter 1 *(après un accident)* to feel oneself; **se t. la jambe/le bras** to feel one's leg/one's arm **2** *Fam (être indécis)* to be *Br* in *or Am* of two minds

tâte-vin [tɑtvɛ̃] **NM INV** *(tasse)* taster (cup), tastevin

tatie [tati] **NF** *Fam* aunty, auntie; **T. Sonia** aunty *or* auntie Sonia

tatillon, -onne [tatijɔ̃, ɔn] *Fam* **ADJ** *(vétilleux)* pernickety, finicky, fussy

NM,F *(personne)* nitpicker, fusspot

tâtonnant, -e [tɑtɔnɑ̃, -ɑ̃t] **ADJ 1** *(personne)* groping **2** *Fig (style)* hesitant; **nos recherches sont encore tâtonnantes** we're still proceeding by trial and error

tâtonnement [tɑtɔnmɑ̃] **NM avancer par tâtonnements** to grope one's way along; *Fig* to proceed by trial and error; *Fig* **nous n'en sommes encore qu'aux tâtonnements** we're still trying to find our way; *Fig* **les tâtonnements de la science/recherche** the tentative progress of science/research

tâtonner [3] [tɑtɔne] **VI 1** *(pour marcher)* to grope *or* to feel one's way (along); *(à la recherche de quelque chose)* to grope about *or* around; **t. pour retrouver la porte** to grope about for the door; **se diriger en tâtonnant vers qch** to grope *or* feel one's way towards sth **2** *Fig (hésiter)* to grope around; *(expérimenter)* to proceed by trial and error

tâtons [tɑtɔ̃] **à tâtons ADV 1** *(à l'aveuglette)* **avancer/entrer/sortir à t.** to grope *or* to feel one's way along/in/out; **elle chercha l'interrupteur à t.** she felt *or* groped around for the switch **2** *Fig* **c'est un domaine nouveau, nous devons avancer à t.** it's a new field, we have to feel our way (along)

tatou [tatu] **NM** armadillo

tatouage [tatwaʒ] **NM 1** *(action)* tattooing **2** *(dessin, numéro d'identification)* tattoo

tatouer [6] [tatwe] **VT** to tattoo; **se faire t.** to get a tattoo *or* tattooed; **se faire t. le bras** to have one's arm tattooed; **faire t. un chien/chat** to have a dog/cat tattooed *(for identification)*

tatoueur [tatwœr] **NM** tattoo artist, tattooist

tau [to] **NM INV** *(lettre grecque)* tau

taud [to] **NM** *Naut* (rain) awning

taudis [todi] **NM** slum, hovel; *Fig* dump; **c'est un vrai t. chez lui!** his place is a real dump *or* pigsty!

taulard, -e [tolar, -ard] **NM,F** *très Fam Arg crime* jailbird

taule [tol] *Fam* **NF 1** *(prison)* clink, slammer, *Br* nick; **sortir de t.** to come out of the clink *or* the slammer *or Br* the nick; **faire de la t.** to do time *or* a stretch; **elle a fait un an de t.** she did a one-year stretch (inside) **2** *(lieu de travail)* workplace□ **3** *(chambre)* room□

• **en taule ADV** inside; **je ne veux pas me retrouver en t.** I don't want to wind up inside

taulier, -ère [tolje, -ɛr] **NM,F** *Fam* **1** *(d'un hôtel)* boss **2** *(logeur)* landlord□, *f* landlady□

taupe [top] **NF 1** *Zool (mammifère)* mole; *(poisson)* porbeagle; *Fam* **vieille t.** old hag *or* bat

2 *(fourrure)* moleskin

3 *très Fam Arg scol* = second year of a two-year entrance course for the Science sections of the "grandes écoles"

4 *très Fam Arg mil* sapper

5 *Fam (agent secret)* mole

tauper [3] [tope] **VT** *Suisse Fam* **t. qch à qn** *(emprunter)* to bum *or* to cadge sth from sb; *(soustraire indûment)* to do *or* to con sb out of sth

taupier [topje] **NM** mole catcher

taupin [topɛ̃] **NM 1** *très Fam Arg scol* = pupil preparing for entry to the Science sections of the "grandes écoles" **2** *très Fam Arg mil Arch* sapper

taupinière [topinjɛr], **taupinée** [topine] **NF** molehill

taureau, -x [toro] **NM** bull; **t. de combat** fighting bull; **il a un cou de t.** he's got a neck like a bull; **son frère a une force de t.** his/her brother is as strong as an ox; *Fam* **prendre le t. par les cornes** to take the bull by the horns

taurillon [torijɔ̃] **NM** bull calf

taurin, -e [torɛ̃, -in] **ADJ** bullfighting; **jeux taurins** bullfights

• **taurine NF** *Biol & Chim* taurine

tauromachie [torɔmaʃi] **NF** bullfighting, *Spéc* tauromachy

tauromachique [torɔmaʃik] **ADJ** bullfighting, *Spéc* tauromachian

tautologie [totɔlɔʒi] **NF** tautology

tautologique [totɔlɔʒik] **ADJ** tautological

taux [to] **NM 1** *(tarif)* rate

2 *(proportion)* rate; *Scol* **t. d'absentéisme** truancy rate; **t. d'audience** *ou* **d'écoute** *TV* ratings, viewing figures; *Rad* ratings; **t. d'échec/de réussite** failure/success rate; **t. de fécondité** reproduction *or* fertility rate; **t. de fréquentation** attendance rate; *(de chambres d'hôtel)* sleeper occupancy; **t. de mortalité/natalité** death/birth rate; **t. de participation** *(d'élection)* (voter) turnout; **t. de scolari-**

sation = percentage of children attending school

3 *Aut* **t. de compression** compression ratio

4 *Fin, Banque & Com* rate; **à quel t. prêtent-ils?** what is their lending rate?; **à t. fixe** fixed-rate; **emprunter à un t. de 7 pour cent** to borrow at 7 percent (interest); **t. d'accroissement** rate of increase *or* of growth; **t. d'activité** participation rate; **t. actuariel annuel** annual equivalent rate, AER; **t. annualisé** annual percentage rate, APR; **t. de l'argent au jour le jour** overnight rate; **t. d'attribution** attribution rate; **t. de base bancaire** bank base lending rate; **t. de change** exchange rate; **t. de change à l'achat** bank buying rate; **t. de change à la vente** bank selling rate; **t. de change en cours** current rate of exchange; **t. de change flottant** floating exchange rate; **t. de conversion** conversion rate; **t. court** short-term rate; **t. de couverture** coverage rate; **t. de crédit** lending rate; **t. de croissance** growth rate; **t. directeur** intervention rate; **t. d'échange** rate of exchange, exchange rate; **t. effectif global** annual percentage rate, APR; **t. d'emprunt** borrowing rate; **t. d'épargne** savings rate; **t. d'escompte** discount rate; **t. hypothécaire** mortgage rate; **t. d'imposition** tax rate, rate of taxation; **t. d'inflation** inflation rate, rate of inflation; **t. interbancaire offert à Paris** Paris Inter-Bank Offer Rate; **t. d'intérêt** interest rate, rate of interest; **t. d'intérêt à court terme/à long terme** short-term/long-term interest rate; **t. linéaire** straight-line rate; *Banque* **t. Lombard** Lombard rate; **t. long** long-term rate; **t. long obligataire** long-term bond rate; **t. du marché monétaire** money market rate; *Bourse* **t. de marge** *ou* **de marque** mark-up (percentage); *Mktg* **t. de mémorisation** recall rate; *Mktg* **t. de notoriété** *(d'un produit)* awareness rating; *Mktg* **t. de pénétration** *(d'un marché)* penetration rate, rate of penetration; **t. plafonné** cap; *Can Banque* **t. préférentiel** prime rate; *Banque* **t. de prêt** lending rate; **t. de prévalence** prevalence rate; **t. privé** market rate; **t. proportionnel** *(d'un crédit)* proportional interest rate; *Mktg* **t. de réachat** rebuy *or* repurchase rate; *Fin* **t. réduit** reduced rate; *Banque* **t. de référence** reference *or* benchmark rate; **t. de refus** refusal rate; **t. de renouvellement** rate of renewal; **t. de rentabilité** rate of return; **t. de répétition** frequency rate; **t. de réponse** response rate; *Fin* **t. des repos** repo rate; *Com* **t. de rotation** *(des stocks)* turnover rate; **t. de TVA** VAT rate, rate of VAT; **t. uniforme** uniform *or* flat rate; *Fin* **t. d'usure** penal rate

5 *Compta* **t. d'actualisation** net present value rate, NPV rate; **t. d'amortissement** rate of depreciation, depreciation rate; **t. de capitalisation** price/earnings ratio, p/e ratio

6 *Ind* **t. horaire** hourly rate; *Tech & Ind* **t. de rendement** coefficient of efficiency, utilization factor

7 *Méd (d'albumine, de cholestérol)* level; **t. d'invalidité** degree of disability

8 *Ordinat* ratio, rate; **t. d'actualisation** refresh rate; **t. de cliquage** *(sur Internet)* click rate; **t. de compression** compression rate; **t. de rafraîchissement** refresh rate; **t. de transfert** transfer rate

tavelé, -e [tavle] ADJ **1** *(fruit)* marked **2** *(peau)* spotted, speckled (**de** with)

taveler [24] [tavle] VT **1** *(fruit)* to mark **2** *(peau)* to speckle (**de** with)

VPR **se taveler** *(fruit)* to become marked

tavelure [tavlyr] NF **1** *(d'un fruit)* mark **2** *(sur la peau)* speckle, (old-age) freckle **3** *Agr (maladie)* scab

taverne [tavɛrn] NF **1** *Hist* inn, public house **2** *Can (bistrot)* beer parlour, tavern **3** *(restaurant)* restaurant

tavernier, -ère [tavɛrnje, -ɛr] NM,F *Hist* innkeeper

taxable [taksabl] ADJ *Écon* taxable, liable to duty

taxateur, -trice [taksatœr, -tris] ADJ *(fonctionnaire)* taxing; *(juge)* assessing

NM taxer, assessor

taxation [taksasjɔ̃] NF **1** *Fin* taxation, taxing (UNCOUNT); **t. d'office** estimation of tax *(in the case of failure to file a tax return)*; *Com* **t. au poids** tax on weight; **t. différentielle** differential taxation; **t. à la valeur** tax on value **2** *Jur (réglementation* ▸ *des prix)* statutory price fixing; *(*▸ *des salaires)* statutory wage fixing; *(*▸ *des dépens)* assessment **3** *Tél* **zone de t.** charging area; *Ordinat* **période de t.** charging period

taxatrice [taksatris] *voir* **taxateur**

taxe [taks] NF **1** *Fin & Admin* tax; **toutes taxes comprises** inclusive of tax; **hors taxes** exclusive of tax; **t. à l'achat** purchase tax; **t. d'aéroport** airport tax; **t. d'apprentissage** = tax paid by businesses to fund training programmes; **t. d'atterrissage** airport landing tax; **t. sur le chiffre d'affaires** sales *or* turnover tax; **t. de départ** *(à l'aéroport)* departure tax; **t. de douane** customs duty; **t. écologique** ecotax; **t. d'entrée** *(à l'aéroport)* entry tax; **t. à l'exportation** export tax; **t. foncière** property tax; **t. forfaitaire** flat rate; **t. d'habitation** = tax paid on residence, *Br* ≃ council tax; **t. à l'importation** import tax; **t. locale** *(pour une entreprise)* uniform business *Br* rate *or Am* tax; *(pour un particulier)* local (property) tax; **t. de luxe** tax on luxury goods, luxury tax; **t. parafiscale** additional levy; **t. de port** harbour dues; **t. professionnelle** = tax paid by businesses and self-employed people; **t. régionale** local tax; **t. de séjour** visitor's *or* tourist tax; **t. supplémentaire** surcharge; **t. Tobin** Tobin tax; **t. à la** *ou* **sur valeur ajoutée** *Br* value-added tax, *Am* sales tax **2** *Jur (des dépens)* assessment **3** *(prix fixé)* controlled price; **vendre des marchandises à la t.** to sell goods at the controlled price

taxer [3] [takse] VT **1** *Écon & Fin* to tax; **t. les livres à 10 pour cent** to tax books at 10 percent, to put a 10 percent tax on books

2 *Jur* **t. les dépens** to fix *or* to assess *or* to tax costs

3 *Tél (appel)* to charge for

4 *(accuser)* **t. qn de** to accuse sb of, *Sout* to tax sb with; **vous m'avez taxé d'hypocrisie** you accused me of being a hypocrite

5 *(qualifier)* **on l'a taxé d'opportuniste** he's been called an opportunist; **une politique que je taxerais de rétrograde** a policy I would describe as backward-looking; **se faire t. d'égoïste** to be accused of selfishness *or* being selfish, to be called selfish

6 *Fam (emprunter)* to scrounge, to sponge, to bum; **il m'a taxé une cigarette** he scrounged a cigarette off me

7 *Fam (voler)* to pinch, *Br* to nick; **je me suis fait t. mon blouson en cuir par une bande de skins** I got my leather jacket pinched *or Br* nicked by a bunch of skinheads

taxi [taksi] NM **1** *(voiture)* taxi, cab; **prendre un t.** to take a taxi *or* a cab **2** *Fam (conducteur)* taxi *or* cab driver; **faire le t.** to be a taxi *or* cab driver

taxidermie [taksidɛrmi] NF taxidermy

taxidermiste [taksidɛrmist] NMF taxidermist

taxi-girl [taksigœrl] *(pl* **taxi-girls***)* NF taxi-dancer, hostess *(hired for dancing)*

taximètre [taksimɛtr] NM taximeter

taxinomie [taksinɔmi] NF taxonomy

taxinomique [taksinɔmik] ADJ taxonomic

Taxiphone® [taksifɔn] NM *Vieilli* public phone, pay-phone

taxiway [taksiwɛ] NM taxiway, taxi strip *or* track

taxonomie [taksɔnɔmi] NF taxonomy

taylorisation [telɔrizasjɔ̃] NF Taylorization

tayloriser [3] [telɔrize] VT to Taylorize

taylorisme [telɔrism] NM Taylorism

TBF [tebeɛf] NM *Banque (abrév* **transferts Banque de France***)* = French automated clearing system

Tbilissi [tbilisi] NM Tbilisi

TCA [tesea] NF *Fin (abrév* **taxe sur le chiffre d'affaires***)* sales *or* turnover tax

Tchad [tʃad] NM **le T.** Chad; **le lac T.** Lake Chad

tchadien, -enne [tʃadjɛ̃, -ɛn] ADJ Chadian

NM *(langue)* Chadic

• **Tchadien, -enne** NM,F Chadian

tchador [tʃadɔr] NM chador, chuddar

tchadri [tʃadri] NM chadri, burka

tchao [tʃao] = **ciao**

tchatche [tʃatʃ] NF *Fam* **avoir la t.** to have the gift of the gab; **tout ça c'est de la t.** that's just a lot of talk

tchatcher [3] [tʃatʃe] VI *Fam* to chat

tchatcheur, -euse [tʃatʃœr, -øz] NM,F *Fam* smooth talker

tchater [3] [tʃate] VI *Fam* to chat online

tchécoslovaque [tʃekɔslɔvak] *Anciennement* ADJ Czechoslovakian, Czechoslovak

• **Tchécoslovaque** NMF Czechoslovakian, Czechoslovak

Tchécoslovaquie [tʃekɔslɔvaki] NF *Anciennement* **la T.** Czechoslovakia

tchèque [tʃɛk] ADJ Czech

NM *(langue)* Czech

• **Tchèque** NMF Czech

tchétchène [tʃetʃɛn] ADJ Chechen

• **Tchétchène** NMF Chechen

Tchétchénie [tʃetʃeni] NF **la T.** Chechenya

tchi [tʃi] **que tchi** ADV *Fam* zilch, sweet FA; **il y comprend que t.** he doesn't understand a damn *or Br* bloody thing

tchin-tchin [tʃintʃin] EXCLAM *Fam* cheers!

TCI [tesei] NM *Com (abrév* **terme commercial international***)* incoterm

TD [tede] NMPL *Univ (abrév* **travaux dirigés***)* seminars

> **TD**
>
> In French universities, teaching is divided into the formal "cours magistraux" (lectures in a lecture theatre) and "travaux dirigés", colloquially referred to as "TD", classes consisting of smaller groups in which students are expected to contribute.

te [tə]

> **t'** is used before a word beginning with a vowel or h mute.

PRON **1** *(avec un verbe pronominal)* **tu te lèves tard** you get up late; **tu te fatigues** you're tiring yourself; **tu vas te faire mal** you'll hurt yourself; **arrête de te ronger les ongles** stop biting your nails; **à quelle heure t'es-tu levé?** what time did you get up (at)?; **tu te dépêches un peu?** hurry up, will you?; **tu te prends pour qui?** who do you think you are?; **va-t'en** go away

2 *(complément)* you; **je te crois** I believe you; **elle t'a envoyé un colis** she's sent you a parcel; **je te l'ai donné** I gave you it, I gave it to you; **le film t'a-t-il plu?** did you like the movie *or Br* film?; **elle t'est devenue indispensable** she has become indispensable to you; *Fam* **il te court après** he's after you; **ne te laisse pas faire** don't let yourself be pushed around

3 *Fam (emploi expressif)* **je te l'ai envoyé balader, celui-là!** I sent HIM packing!; **je vais te le mater, celui-là!** I'll sort HIM out!; **je vais te lui dire ce que je pense!** I'm going to give HIM/HER a piece of my mind!; **et je te range, et je te fais la cuisine** and I tidy up AND I do the cooking

4 *(en s'adressant à Dieu)* You, Thee

té [te] NM **1** *(équerre)* T-square **2** *Menuis* tee

• **en té** ADJ T-shaped; **règle en té** T-rule

teaser [tizœr] NM teaser *(in advertising)*

teasing [tiziŋ] NM *Mktg* teaser advertising

tec [tɛk] NF INV *(abrév* **tonne d'équivalent charbon***)* TCE

technicien, -enne [tɛknisjɛ̃, -ɛn] ADJ *(esprit, civilisation)* technically-oriented

NM,F *(en entreprise)* technician, engineer; **il est t. en informatique** he's a computer technician; *Cin & TV* **t. en chef** key grip; **t. du froid** refrigeration engineer; **t. de laboratoire** laboratory technician; **t. de maintenance** maintenance *or* service engineer; **t. de surface** cleaner

technicité [tɛknisite] NF **1** *(d'un mot, d'un texte)* technical nature *or* quality, *Sout* technicality **2** *(avance technologique)* technological sophistication; **matériel d'une haute t.** hi-tech equipment **3** *(savoir-faire)* skill

technico-commercial, -e [tɛknikokɔmɛrsjal] *(mpl* **technico-commerciaux** [-o], *fpl* **technico-commerciales***)* ADJ **notre personnel t.** our technical sales staff; **agent t.** sales technician, sales engineer; **service t.** technical sales (department)

NM,F sales technician, sales engineer

Technicolor® [teknikɔlɔr] **NM** Technicolor®; **en T.** Technicolor® *(avant n)*

technique [teknik] **ADJ** technical; **incident t.** technical hitch; **les progrès techniques en informatique** technical advances in computer science **le sens t. d'un mot** the technical sense *or* meaning of a word

NM *Scol* **le t.** vocational education; **élèves du t.** pupils taking technical subjects; **professeurs du t.** teachers of technical subjects

NF 1 *(d'un art, d'un métier)* technique; **la t. de l'aquarelle** the technique of watercolour painting

2 *(savoir-faire)* technique; **un très jeune joueur de tennis qui doit améliorer sa t.** a very young tennis player who has to improve his technique; **ce pianiste a une bonne t./manque de t.** this pianist has good technique/lacks technique; **t. de vente** sales technique

3 *(méthode)* technique; **c'est toute une t. d'ouvrir les huîtres** there's quite an art to opening oysters; **répondre à une question par une autre question, c'est sa t.** answering a question by another question is his/her speciality; **ce n'est pas la bonne t.** that's not the right way to go about it; **avec lui, j'ai ma t.** I have my own way of dealing with him; *Fam* **tu n'as pas la t.!** you haven't got the knack!; *Méd* **t. Alexander** Alexander technique; **techniques commerciales** marketing techniques

4 *(de production)* technique; **t. de pointe** state-of-the-art technique

5 *(applications de la science)* **la t.** applied science

techniquement [teknikmɑ̃] **ADV** technically; **t. faisable** technically feasible

techno [tekno] **ADJ** techno

NF techno

technocrate [teknɔkrat] **NMF** technocrat

technocratie [teknɔkrasi] **NF** technocracy

technocratique [teknɔkratik] **ADJ** technocratic

technologie [teknɔlɔʒi] **NF 1** *Scol* technology, applied science **2** *(technique)* technology; **de haute t.** high tech; **la t. de l'informatique** computer technology; **t. de substitution** alternative technology; **technologies avancées** advanced technology, high technology; **nouvelles technologies** new technologies **3** *(théorie)* technology, technological theory, technologies

technologique [teknɔlɔʒik] **ADJ** technological

technologue [teknɔlɔg], **technologiste** [teknɔlɔʒist] **NMF** technologist

teck [tek] **NM** teak

• **en teck ADJ** teak *(avant n)*

teckel [tekel] **NM** dachshund; **t. à poil ras/long** short-haired/long-haired dachshund

tectonique [tektɔnik] **ADJ** tectonic

NF tectonics *(singulier)*; **t. des plaques** plate tectonics

teddy-bear [tediber] *(pl* **teddy-bears***)* **NM 1** *Vieilli (ours)* teddy bear **2** *(fourrure synthétique)* plush

Te Deum [tedeɔm] **NM INV** Te Deum

tee [ti] **NM** *Golf* tee; **poser la balle sur le t.** to tee up; **partir du t.** to tee off

teenager [tinedʒœr] **NMF** teenager; **vêtements pour teenagers** teenage clothes

tee-shirt [tiʃœrt] *(pl* **tee-shirts***)* **NM** tee-shirt, T-shirt

Téflon® [teflɔ̃] **NM** Teflon®; **poêle en T.** Teflon® frying pan

téflonisé, -e [teflɔnize] **ADJ** Teflon® *(avant n)*

TEG [teəʒe] **NM** *Fin (abrév* **taux effectif global***)* APR

tégument [tegymɑ̃] **NM** *Bot & Zool* tegument, integument

Téhéran [teerɑ̃] **NM** Tehran, Teheran

teignait *etc voir* **teindre**

teigne [tɛɲ] **NF 1** *Entom* moth, *Spéc* tineid

2 *Méd* ringworm, *Spéc* tinea

3 *Bot* burdock

4 *Fam (homme)* louse; *(femme)* vixen[□]; **être mauvais** *ou* **méchant comme une t.** *Br* to be a nasty piece of work, *Am* to be real ornery

teigneux, -euse [tɛɲø, -øz] **ADJ 1** *Méd* suffering from ringworm **2** *Fam (hargneux)* nasty[□], *Am* ornery

NM,F 1 *Méd* ringworm sufferer **2** *Fam (homme)* bastard; *(femme)* bitch, *Br* cow

teindre [81] [tɛ̃dr] **VT 1** *(soumettre à la teinture)* to dye; **t. qch en rouge** to dye sth red; **se faire t. les cheveux** to have one's hair dyed **2** *Littéraire (colorer)* to tint; **la lumière du soleil teignait la mer en vert émeraude** the sunlight turned the sea emerald green

VPR se teindre 1 *(emploi passif)* **c'est une étoffe qui se teint facilement** it's a material which is easy to dye

2 *(emploi réfléchi)* **se t. (les cheveux)** to dye one's hair; **se t. les cheveux en roux** to dye one's hair red

3 *Littéraire (se colorer)* **la neige se teignit du sang des soldats blessés** the snow turned red with the blood of the wounded soldiers

4 *Fig Littéraire* **se t. de** *(se mêler de)* to be tinged with

teint [tɛ̃] **NM** *(habituel)* complexion; *(momentané)* colour, colouring; **avoir le t. pâle/jaune/mat** to have a pale/sallow/matt complexion; **avoir un t. de rose** to have a rosy complexion; **un homme au t. jaune** a man with a sallow complexion

• **bon teint ADJ INV 1** *Tex* colour-fast **2** *Fig (pur)* staunch; **des royalistes bon t.** staunch *or* dyed-in-the-wool royalists

• **grand teint ADJ INV** *(couleur)* fast; *(tissu)* colour-fast

> Do not confuse with **teinte**.

teinte [tɛ̃t] **NF 1** *(couleur franche)* colour; *(ton)* shade, tint, hue; **une t. grise** a greyish tinge; **plusieurs teintes de bleu** several shades of blue **2** *Fig (petit quantité ▸ de libéralisme, de sadisme)* tinge; *(▸ d'ironie, de mépris)* hint

> Do not confuse with **teint**.

teinter [3] [tɛ̃te] **VT 1** *(verre)* to tint, to stain; *(lunettes, papier)* to tint; *(boiseries)* to stain **2** *(colorer)* to tint; **le soleil couchant teintait le lac de rose** the setting sun gave the lake a pinkish tinge **3** *Fig (mêler)* to tinge; **son amitié était teintée de pitié** his/her friendship was tinged with pity

VPR se teinter 1 *(se colorer)* **se t. d'ocre/de rose** to take on an ochre/a pink tinge *or* hue **2** *Fig* **se t. de** *(être nuancé de)* to be tinged with; *(se nuancer de)* to become tinged with

teinture [tɛ̃tyr] **NF 1** *(action)* dyeing; **se faire faire une t.** to have one's hair dyed

2 *(produit)* dye; **un tissu qui prend bien la t.** a material that dyes well

3 *Pharm* tincture; **t. d'arnica** (tincture of) arnica; **t. d'iode** (tincture of) iodine

4 *Fig Littéraire (connaissance superficielle)* smattering; **elle a une t. d'histoire** she has a vague knowledge of history

teinturerie [tɛ̃tyrri] **NF 1** *(activité)* dyeing **2** *(boutique)* dry cleaner's

teinturier, -ère [tɛ̃tyrje, -ɛr] **NM,F 1** *(qui nettoie)* dry cleaner **2** *(qui colore)* dyer

tek [tek] = **teck**

TEL, TELLE [tel]

> **ADJ INDÉFINI**
> • such and such **A1**
> • like **A4, B2**
> • such as **B2**
> • such **A2, 3, 5, B3**
> • so **A5, B3**
>
> **PRON INDÉFINI**
> • so-and-so **2**

ADJ INDÉFINI A. *EMPLOYÉ SEUL* **1** *(avec une valeur indéterminée)* **t. jour, t. endroit, à telle heure** on such and such a day, at such and such a place, at such and such a time; **il m'a demandé de lui acheter t. et t. livres** he asked me to buy him such and such books; **pourrais-tu me conseiller t. ou t. plat?** could you recommend any particular dish?; **selon que telle ou telle méthode est choisie** depending on whether this or that method is chosen; **cela peut se produire dans telle ou telle circonstance** it can happen under certain circumstances

2 *(semblable)* such; **je n'ai rien dit de t.** I never said such a thing, I said nothing of the sort; **un t. homme peut être dangereux** a man like that can be dangerous; **tu ne retrouveras jamais une telle occasion** you'll never have such an opportunity *or* an opportunity like that again; **pourquoi un t. aveu?** why this confession?; **comme t./telle** as such; **il était médecin et comme t., il avait des passe-droits** he was a doctor and as such he enjoyed special rights and privileges; **il n'est pas avare, mais il passe pour t.** he's not mean, but people think he is; **elle est médecin, en tant que telle elle saura te conseiller** she's a doctor, as such she'll be able to advise you

3 *(ainsi)* **telle fut l'histoire qu'il nous raconta** such was the story he told us; **t. fut son langage** those were his/her words; *Hum* **pourquoi ça? – parce que t. est mon bon plaisir!** and why is that? – because I say so!

4 *(introduisant un exemple, une énumération, une comparaison)* like; **des métaux tels le cuivre et le fer** metals such as copper and iron; **elle a filé t. l'éclair** she shot off like a bolt of lightning; **il allait et venait telle une bête en cage** he paced to and fro like a caged animal; **il pleurait, t. un enfant** he was crying like a child; *Prov* **t. père, t. fils** like father, like son; *Ordinat* **t. écran-t. écrit** WYSIWYG

5 *(en intensif)* such; **c'est un t. honneur pour nous...** it is such an honour for us...; **une telle gentillesse est rare** such kindness is rare; **c'est un t. pianiste!** he's such a wonderful pianist!; **elle est d'une telle générosité!** she's so generous!; **c'est d'un t. ennui!** it's so boring!

B. *EN CORRÉLATION AVEC "QUE"* **1** *(introduisant une comparaison)* **il est t. que je l'ai toujours connu** he's just the same as when I knew him; **un homme t. que lui** a man like him; **la maison était telle qu'il l'avait décrite** the house was exactly how he had described it; **la clause telle qu'elle est** the clause as it stands; **voir les hommes/les choses tels qu'ils/telles qu'elles sont** to see men/things as they are; **telle que je la connais, elle va être en retard** knowing her, she's bound to be late; **telle que vous me voyez, je reviens de chez lui** I've just been to see him this very minute; *Fam* **tu prends le lot t. que** take the batch as it is; *Fam* **il me l'a dit t. que!** he told me just like that!

2 *(introduisant un exemple ou une énumération)* **t. que** such as, like; **les fauves, tels que le lion et le tigre** big cats like *or* such as lions and tigers; **un philosophe t. que Descartes** a philosopher such as *or* like Descartes

3 *(avec une valeur intensive)* **son bonheur était t. qu'il ne pouvait y croire** he was so happy that he could hardly believe it; **la douleur fut telle que je faillis m'évanouir** the pain was so bad that I nearly fainted; **il a fait un t. bruit qu'il a réveillé toute la maisonnée** he made such a noise *or* so much noise that he woke the whole house up; **elle n'en a pas un besoin t. qu'il faille le lui rendre aujourd'hui** she doesn't need it so badly that we have to give it back to her today; **(il n'y a) rien de t. qu'un bon cigare** there's nothing like *or* you can't beat a good cigar; **il n'est rien de t. que d'être jeune** there's nothing like being young

PRON INDÉFINI 1 *(désignant des personnes ou des choses non précisées)* **t. ou t. vous dira que...** some people will tell you that...; **telle ou telle de ses idées aurait pu prévaloir** one or other of his/her ideas might have prevailed; **c'est en manœuvrant t. et t. qu'il a réussi à se faire élire** he managed to get himself elected by manipulating various people; *Prov* **t. est pris qui croyait prendre** it's the biter bitten

2 *(en remplacement d'un nom propre)* **a-t-il rencontré Un t.?** did he meet so-and-so?; **Une telle m'a dit que...** so-and-so told me that...

• **tel quel, telle quelle ADJ tout est resté t. quel depuis son départ** everything is just as he/she left it; **il me l'a rendu t. quel** that's how he gave it back to me; **tu peux manger les huîtres telles quelles ou avec du citron** you can eat oysters on their own or with lemon

télé [tele] *Fam* **NF** *(poste, émissions)* TV, *Br* telly; **regarder la t.** to watch TV *or Br* the telly; **travailler à la t.** to work in TV; **passer à la t.** *(personne)* to be *or* to appear on TV *or Br* the telly; **c'est passé à la t.** it was on TV *or Br* the telly; **il n'y a rien ce soir à la t.** there's nothing on TV *or Br* the telly tonight

• **de télé ADJ** *(chaîne, émission)* TV *(avant n)*

téléachat [teleaʃa] **NM 1** *(d'articles présentés à la télévision)* teleshopping *(where articles are offered on television and ordered by telephone or Minitel®)* **2** *(par l'Internet)* on-line shopping; **ce**

nouveau logiciel améliore la sécurité des téléachats this new software makes on-line shopping *or* on-line transactions safer

téléacheteur, -euse [teleaʃtœr, -øz] **NM,F** television shopper *(who orders articles offered on television by telephone or Minitel®)*

téléacteur, -trice [teleaktœr, -tris] **NM,F** telesalesperson

téléassistance [teleasistɑ̃s] **NF** *Ordinat* remote help

téléavertisseur [teleavertisœr] **NM** *Can* pager

télébenne [teleben] **NF** cable car

téléboutique [telebutik] **NF 1** *(agence téléphonique) Br* telephone shop, *Am* telephone store **2** *(ensemble de cabines téléphoniques)* = public telephone centre for making low-cost international calls

télécabine [telekabin] **NF 1** *(cabine)* cable car; **les skieurs montent en t.** skiers go up in a cable car **2** *(installation)* cableway

Télécarte® [telekart] **NF** phonecard

téléchargeable [teleʃarʒabl] **ADJ** *Ordinat* downloadable

téléchargement [teleʃarʒəmɑ̃] **NM** *Ordinat* downloading

télécharger [17] [teleʃarʒe] **VT** *Ordinat* to download; *(vers un gros ordinateur)* to upload

télécinéma [telesinema] **NM 1** *(procédé)* telecine **2** *(appareil)* telecamera

télécommande [telekɔmɑ̃d] **NF 1** *(procédé, appareil)* remote control; **t. à infrarouge** infra-red remote control; **t. universelle** universal remote control **2** *(par radio)* radio-control **3** *Ordinat* telecommand

télécommander [3] [telekɔmɑ̃de] **VT 1** *(engin, mise à feu, télévision)* to operate by remote control **2** *Fig (ordonner de loin)* to mastermind, to manipulate; **ces mouvements ont été télécommandés depuis l'Europe** these movements have been masterminded from Europe

télécommunication [telekɔmynikasjɔ̃] **NF** telecommunication; **les télécommunications** telecommunications

téléconférence [telekɔ̃ferɑ̃s] **NF 1** *(procédé)* teleconferencing **2** *(conférence)* teleconference

téléconseil [telekɔ̃sej] **NM** teleconsulting

téléconseiller, -ère [telekɔ̃seje, -jer] **NM,F** teleconsultant

télécopie [telekɔpi] **NF** fax; **envoyer qch par t.** to fax sth; **t. sur papier ordinaire** plain paper fax

télécopieur [telekɔpjœr] **NM** fax (machine), *Spéc* facsimile machine

télécran [telekrɑ̃] **NM** large-sized television screen

tel écran-tel écrit [telekrɑ̃telekri] **ADJ INV** *Ordinat* WYSIWYG

télédéclaration [teledeklarasjɔ̃] **NF** online tax return *(or other administrative forms)*

télédémarchage [teledemarʃaʒ] **NM** *Mktg* telephone canvassing *or* prospecting

télédépannage [teledepanaʒ] **NM** *Ordinat* remote troubleshooting

télédétection [teledetɛksjɔ̃] **NF** remote sensing; **satellite de t.** spy satellite

télédiffuser [3] [teledifyze] **VT** to broadcast (on television), to televise

télédiffuseur [teledifyzœr] **NM** television broadcaster

télédiffusion [teledifyzjɔ̃] **NF** televising, (television) broadcasting; **t. directe par satellite** direct broadcasting by satellite; **T. de France** = French broadcasting authority

télédistribution [teledistribysjɔ̃] **NF** cable television

téléécriture [teleekrityr] **NF** telewriting

téléenseignement, télé-enseignement [teleɑ̃sɛɲmɑ̃] *(pl* **télé-enseignements)** **NM** distance learning

Téléfax® [telefaks] **NM** fax (machine)

téléférique [teleferik] = **téléphérique**

téléfilm [telefilm] **NM** TV movie, movie made for television

télégénique [teleʒenik] **ADJ** telegenic; **être t.** to look good on television

télégestion [teleʒestjɔ̃] **NF** teleprocessing, telecomputing

télégramme [telegram] **NM** telegram, cable; **envoyer un t. à qn** to send a telegram to sb; **t. téléphoné** = telegram delivered over the phone, *Br* ≃ Telemessage®

télégraphe [telegraf] **NM** telegraph

télégraphie [telegrafi] **NF** telegraphy; **t. optique** visual signalling; *Vieilli* **t. sans fil** *(appareil)* wireless; *(procédé)* wireless telegraphy

télégraphier [9] [telegrafje] **VT** to cable, to telegraph; **t. qch à qn** to cable sb sth

télégraphique [telegrafik] **ADJ 1** *Tél (poteau)* telegraph *(avant n)*; *(message)* telegraphic; **dépêche t.** telegram **2** *Fig* **(en) langage** *ou* **style t.** (in) telegraphic language *or* style

télégraphiquement [telegrafikmɑ̃] **ADV** by telegram, by cable, by wire

télégraphiste [telegrafist] **NMF** *(technicien)* telegrapher, telegraphist; *Vieilli* **(petit) t.** *(porteur de dépêches)* telegraph boy

téléguidage [telegidaʒ] **NM** radio control

téléguidé, -e [telegide] **ADJ 1** *(piloté à distance* ▸ *avion)* radio-controlled; **engin t.** guided missile **2** *Fig (manipulé)* manipulated; **sa décision était téléguidée** his/her decision was dictated by outside forces

téléguider [3] [telegide] **VT 1** *Tech (maquette)* to control by radio **2** *Fig (inspirer)* to manipulate; **c'est lui qui a téléguidé la campagne de presse** he's the one who masterminded the press campaign from behind the scenes

téléimpression [teleɛ̃presjɔ̃] **NF** teleprinting

téléimprimeur [teleɛ̃primœr] **NM** teleprinter

téléinformatique [teleɛ̃fɔrmatik] **NF** teleprocessing

téléjournal, -aux [teleʒurnal, -o] **NM** *Can* television news

téléjournaliste [teleʒurnalist] **NMF** television journalist

télékinésie [telekinezi] **NF** telekinesis

télémaintenance [telemɛ̃tnɑ̃s] **NF** remote maintenance; *Astron* housekeeping; *Ordinat* remote access

télémanipulateur [telemanipylatœr] **NM** remote manipulator

Télémaque [telemak] **NPR** *Myth* Telemachus

télémarché [telemarʃe] **NM** telemarket

télémark [telemark] **NM** *Vieilli Ski* telemark

télémarketing [telemarkɔtiŋ] **NM** telemarketing

télématique [telematik] **ADJ** telematic; **par voie t.** using data comms (technology)

NF data communications, telematics *(singulier)*

télémédecine [telemedsin] **NF** telemedicine, remote medicine

télémessage [telemesaʒ] **NM** *Tél* text message

télémessagerie [telemesaʒri] **NF** electronic messaging

télémesure [telemɔzyr] **NF** telemetry, telemetering

télémètre [telemɛtr] **NM** telemeter; *Mil & Phot* rangefinder

télémétrie [telemetri] **NF** telemetry; *Mil & Phot* range finding

téléobjectif [teleɔbʒɛktif] **NM** telephoto (lens), long lens; **photographie au t.** telephotography

téléologie [teleɔlɔʒi] **NF** *Phil* teleology

téléologique [teleɔlɔʒik] **ADJ** teleological

téléopérateur, -trice [teleɔperatœr, -tris] **NM,F** telesales operator

téléostéen [teleɔsteɛ̃] *Ich* **NM** teleost

• **téléostéens NMPL** Teleostei

télépaiement [telepemɑ̃] **NM** online payment

télépathe [telepat] **ADJ** telepathic; *Hum* **je ne suis pas t.!** I'm not psychic!

NMF telepathist, telepath

télépathie [telepati] **NF** telepathy; **communiquer par t.** to communicate via telepathy

télépathique [telepatik] **ADJ** telepathic

télépayer [telepeje] **VI** to pay online, to make an online payment

VT to pay online

télépéage [telepeaʒ] **NM** = toll system using electronic tagging of cars

téléphage [telefaʒ] **NM** couch potato

téléphérage [telefera ʒ] **NM** *Tech* telpherage, overhead cable transport

téléphérique [teleferik] **ADJ** *Tech (câble)* telpher

NM *(dispositif, cabine)* cable car

téléphone [telefɔn] **NM 1** *(instrument)* phone, telephone; **appeler qn au t.** to (tele)phone sb, to call sb; **t. bâtiment-terre** ship to shore (tele) phone; **t. à carte** cardphone; **t. cellulaire** cellular phone; **t. de courtoisie** courtesy phone; **t. intelligent** smart phone; **t. intérieur** internal telephone; **t. Internet** Internet telephone; **t. mobile** *Br* mobile phone, *Am* cellphone; **t. à pièces** payphone, coin-operated telephone; **t. portable** *ou* **portatif** *Br* mobile phone, *Am* cellphone; **t. public** public telephone, payphone; **le t. rouge** *(entre présidents)* the hot line; **t. sans fil** cordless telephone; **t. à touches** touch-tone telephone; **t. de voiture** carphone; **t. WAP** WAP phone

2 *(installation)* phone, telephone; **il a/n'a pas le t.** *Br* he's/he isn't on the phone, *Am* he has a/has no phone; **j'ai demandé à avoir le t.** I asked to have a phone put in

3 *(service)* **le t. marche plutôt mal chez nous** we have a rather bad telephone service

4 *Fam (numéro)* (phone) number; **donne-moi ton t.** give me your phone number

• **au téléphone ADV parler à qn au t.** to speak to sb on the phone; **je suis au t.** I'm on the phone; **je l'ai eu au t.** I talked to him on the phone; **je ne peux pas te le dire au t.** I can't tell you over the phone

• **de téléphone ADJ** *(facture, numéro)* phone *(avant n)*, telephone *(avant n)*; **coup de t.** (tele) phone call; **donner** *ou* **passer un coup de t.** to make a phone call; **passer un coup de t. à qn** to phone sb, to give sb a call

• **par téléphone ADV il a réservé par t.** he phoned (in) his booking; **commander qch par t.** to order sth by phone

• **téléphone arabe NM** grapevine; **j'ai appris par le t. arabe qu'il était rentré** I heard on the grapevine that he was back

téléphoner [3] [telefɔne] **VI** to make a phone call; **puis-je t.?** can I make a phone call?, may I use the phone?; **combien est-ce que ça coûte pour t. en Angleterre?** how much does it cost to call England?; **je passe tout mon temps à t.** I spend all my time on the phone; **t. à qn** to phone sb, to call sb

VT to phone; **je te téléphonerai tes résultats** I'll call and let you know your results, I'll call you with your results; **t. à qn de venir** to (tele)phone for sb

VPR se téléphoner to call each other; **on se téléphone, d'accord?** I'll talk to you later, OK?

téléphonie [telefɔni] **NF** telephony; **t. sans fil** wireless telephony; **la t. mobile** *ou* **portable** the mobile phone sector; **t. sur l'Internet** Internet telephony

téléphonique [telefɔnik] **ADJ** *(message, ligne, réseau)* telephone *(avant n)*, phone *(avant n)*; **commande t.** order by telephone, telephone order; **nous avons eu un entretien t.** we had a discussion over the phone

téléphoniste [telefɔnist] **NMF** *Br* telephonist, *Am* (telephone) operator

téléphotographie [telefɔtɔgrafi] **NF 1** *Tél* phototelegraphy **2** *Phot* telephotography; *(cliché)* telephotograph

téléportation [telepɔrtasjɔ̃] **NF** teleportation

téléporter [3] [telepɔrter] **VT** to teleport

télé-poubelle [telepubel] *(pl* **télé-poubelles)** **NF** *Fam* trash television

téléprompteur [teleprɔ̃ptœr] **NM** Teleprompter®, *Br* Autocue®

téléprospecteur, -trice [teleprɔspɛktœr, -tris] **NM,F** telesalesperson

téléprospection [teleprɔspɛksjɔ̃] **NF** telemarketing, teleprospecting

téléprospectrice [teleprɔspɛktris] *voir* **télé-prospecteur**

téléréalité [telerealite] **NF** reality TV

téléreportage [telerəpɔrtaʒ] **NM 1** *(émission)* television report **2** *(activité)* television reporting

téléréunion [telereynjɔ̃] **NF** teleconference

télescopage [teleskɔpaʒ] **NM 1** *(de véhicules)* collision; *(de trains etc)* telescoping; **t. (en série)** *(de véhicules)* pile-up **2** *Fig (d'idées, de souvenirs)* intermingling **3** *Ling* telescoping, blending

télescope [teleskɔp] **NM** telescope; **t. électronique** electron telescope

télescoper [3] [teleskɔpe] **VT** *(véhicule)* to collide with, to crash into; *(train)* to crash into

VPR se télescoper 1 *(véhicules, trains)* to concertina **2** *Fig (idées, souvenirs)* to intermingle

télescopique [teleskɔpik] **ADJ** *(antenne, volant)* telescopic

téléscripteur [teleskriptœr] **NM** teleprinter; *Bourse* ticker tape

télésecrétariat [telesəkretarja] **NM** remote secretarial services

téléservice [teleservis] **NM 1** *Ordinat* on-line service **2** *(fourni par un télétravailleur)* teleservicing

télésiège [telesjɛʒ] **NM** chair *or* ski lift

téléski [teleski] **NM** drag lift, ski tow

télésouffleur [telesuflœr] **NM** Teleprompter®, *Br* Autocue®

téléspectateur, -trice [telespektatœr,-tris] **NM, F** television *or* TV viewer

télésurveillance [telesyrvɛjɑ̃s] **NF** (security) telemonitoring

Télétel® [teletel] **NM** = computerized information network available through Minitel®

Télétex® [teleteks] **NM** teletex

télétexte [teletɛkst] **NM** teletext

téléthon [teletɔ̃] **NM** telethon

télétraitement [teletrɛtmɑ̃] **NM** teleprocessing

télétransmission [teletrɑ̃smisjɔ̃] **NF** *(gén)* remote transmission; *(de données informatiques)* teletransmission

télétravail, -aux [teletravaj, -o] **NM** teleworking, telecommuting

télétravailler [teletravaje] **VI** to telework, to telecommute

télétravailleur, -euse [teletravajœr, -øz] **NM,F** teleworker

Télétype® [teletip] **NM** Teletype

télévangéliste [televɑ̃ʒelist] **NMF** televangelist

télévendeur, -euse [televɑ̃dœr, -øz] **NM,F** = specialist in selling goods on shopping channels

télévente [televɑ̃t] **NF** = selling goods on shopping channels *(where articles are offered on television and ordered by telephone or Minitel®)*

télé-vérité [televerite] **NF** *TV* reality TV

téléviser [3] [televize] **VT** to broadcast on television, to televise

téléviseur [televizœr] **NM** television *or* TV (set); **t. couleur** colour television (set); **t. à écran plat** flat-screen television (set); **t. grand écran** wide-screen television (set); **t. numérique** digital television (set)

télévision [televizjɔ̃] **NF 1** *(entreprise, système)* television; **il regarde trop la t.** he watches too much television; **la t. à accès conditionnel** conditional access television; **t. câblée** *ou* **par câble** cable television; **t. à la carte** pay-per-view television; **t. en circuit fermé** closed-circuit television; **t. (en) couleur** colour television; **t. haute définition** high-definition TV, hi-def TV; **t. hertzienne** terrestrial television; **t. interactive** interactive television; **t. locale** local television; **t. du matin** breakfast television; **t. numérique** digital television; **t. numérique par satellite** digital satellite television; **t. numérique terrestre** digital terrestrial television; **t. ouverte** access broadcasting; **la t. à péage** pay-TV, pay television; **t. à plasma** plasma television; **t. par satellite** satellite television; **t. scolaire** schools *or* educational television, television for schools; **t. de service public** public television **2** *(appareil)* television; **regarder la t.** to watch television

• **à la télévision ADV** on television *or* TV; **passer à la t.** to go on television; **travailler à la t.** to work in television

télévisuel, -elle [televizɥɛl] **ADJ** televisual

télex [telɛks] **NM** telex; **envoyer un t.** to (send a) telex; **envoyer qch par t.** to telex sth

télexer [4] [telɛkse] **VT** to telex

télexiste [telɛksist] **NMF** telex operator

tellement [telmɑ̃] **ADV 1** *(avec un adverbe, un adjectif) (si)* so; **c'est t. loin** it's so far; **elle en parle t. souvent** she talks about it so often; **je n'ai pas t. mal** it doesn't hurt that *or* so much; **il est t. têtu** he's so stubborn; **c'est t. facile** it's so (very) easy; **ce serait t. plus simple** it would be so much simpler; **c'est t. mieux comme ça** it's so much better like that; **ce ne sera pas t. pire** it won't be so much worse; **ce n'est pas t. beau** it's not all that beautiful

2 *(avec un verbe)* **il l'aime t.** he loves her so much; **j'ai t. pleuré!** I cried so much!

3 *(en corrélation avec "que")* **il est t. sourd qu'il faut crier** he is so deaf that you have to shout; **j'en ai t. rêvé que j'ai l'impression d'y être déjà allée** I've dreamt about it so much *or* so often that I feel I've been there already; **il en sait déjà t. que...** he knows so much about it that...; **elle n'est pas t. malade qu'elle ne puisse se lever** she's not so ill that she can't get up

4 *(introduisant la cause)* **j'ai mal aux yeux t. j'ai lu** my eyes hurt from reading so much; **elle ne peut pas se lever t. elle est malade** she can't get up, she is so ill

5 *Fam (locutions)* **pas t.** not really; **je n'aime pas t. me presser** I don't really like to hurry; **ça te plaît? – pas t.** do you like it? – not very much *or* not really; **je n'ai pas t. envie de le revoir** I'm not all that keen on seeing him again; **je n'aime plus t. ça** I don't really like that any more

• **tellement de DÉT 1** *(nombre)* so many; *(quantité)* so much; **j'ai t. de travail/de soucis en ce moment** I've got so much work/so many worries at the moment; **j'ai t. de choses à faire!** I've got so many things *or* so much to do!; **des jeunes au chômage, comme on en voit t. dans la rue** young people on the dole such as you often come across on the street **2** *(en corrélation avec "que")* **il y avait t. de bruit que l'on ne s'entendait plus** there was so much noise that we could no longer hear ourselves speak; **il y a t. d'hôtels que je ne sais lequel choisir** there are so many hotels that I don't know which one to choose

tellure [telyr] **NM** *Chim* tellurium

tellurique [telyrik] **ADJ** telluric

téloche [telɔʃ] **NF** *Fam* TV, *Br* telly

tel-tel [teltel] **ADJ INV** *Ordinat* WYSIWYG

téméraire [temerer] **ADJ** *(personne, entreprise)* rash, reckless; *(jugement, déclaration)* rash

témérairement [temerɛrmɑ̃] **ADV** rashly, recklessly

témérité [temerite] **NF** rashness, recklessness

témoignage [temwaɲaʒ] **NM 1** *Jur (action de témoigner)* testimony, evidence; **porter t.** to give evidence; **porter t. en faveur de qn** to give evidence *or* to testify on sb's behalf; *Fig* **ce livre se contente de porter t. sur l'époque** the book is content to describe the era; **porter t. de qch** to bear witness to sth; **rendre t. de qch** to give evidence about sth; **les témoignages ont duré toute la journée** the hearing went on all day; **faux t.** perjury, false evidence, false witness; **faire un faux t.** to commit perjury, to give false evidence; **rendre t. à qch** *(rendre hommage)* to pay tribute to *or* to salute *or Sout* to hail sth; **rendre t. à qn** *(témoigner publiquement en sa faveur)* to testify in sb's favour; **la presse unanime a rendu t. au Premier ministre** all the newspapers came out in support of the Prime Minister

2 *(contenu des déclarations)* deposition, (piece of) evidence; **d'après** *ou* **selon son t.** according to his/her statement; **un t. de bonne conduite** a statement of (good) character, a character reference; *Fig* **t. des sens** evidence of the senses

3 *(preuve)* gesture, expression, token; **un t. d'amitié** a token of friendship; **en t. de qch** as a token *or* sign of sth

4 *(récit ▸ d'un participant, d'un observateur)* (eyewitness) account; **des témoignages sur les conditions de vie des paysans** accounts of the living conditions of peasants

5 *Mktg (publicité)* testimonial advertising

témoigner [3] [temwaɲe] **VI** *Jur* to testify, to give evidence; **t. en faveur de/contre l'accusé** to give evidence for/against the defendant; **t. par oral/écrit** to give oral/written evidence

VT 1 *Jur (certifier)* **t. que...** to testify that...; **j'irai t. que je ne l'ai pas vu ce soir-là** I'll go and testify that I didn't see him that night **2** *(montrer ▸ sympathie, dégoût, goût)* to show; *(▸ intérêt)* to show, *Sout* to evince; **il ne m'a témoigné que du mépris** he showed me nothing but contempt; **sa réaction témoigne qu'il s'y attendait** his reaction shows *or* is proof that he was expecting it

• **témoigner de VT IND 1** *Jur* to testify to; **je suis prêt à t. de son innocence** I'm ready to testify *or* to swear to his/her innocence **2** *(indiquer ▸ bonté, générosité, intérêt)* to show, to indicate; **cela témoigne de leur intérêt pour les problèmes sociaux** this shows their interest in social problems; **sa réponse témoigne d'une grande maturité** his/her answer shows great maturity **3** *(prouver)* to show, to bear witness *or* to testify to, *Sout* to attest

témoin [temwɛ̃] **NM 1** *Jur (qui fait une déposition)* witness; **citer qn comme t.** to call sb as a witness; **être entendu comme t.** to be a witness; **le t. est à vous** your witness; **t. assisté** = material witness who benefits from legal representation like the defendant, but who has not been formally charged; **t. à charge/décharge** witness for the prosecution/defence; **t. de fait** material witness; **t. instrumentaire** witness to a deed; **t. de moralité** character reference; **t. oculaire** eyewitness; **faux t.** perjurer

2 *(à un mariage, à la signature d'un contrat)* witness; *(à un duel)* second; **il était t. au mariage de sa sœur** he was a witness at his sister's wedding; **devant témoins** before witnesses

3 *(spectateur)* witness, eyewitness; **faire qch devant t.** to do sth before a witness; **l'accident s'est passé sans témoins** there were no witnesses to the accident; **ils se sont vus sans témoins** they saw each other in private, there were no witnesses present when they saw each other; **être t. de qch** to be witness to *or* to witness sth; **j'ai été un t. involontaire de leur dispute** I was an unwitting witness to their quarrel; **j'en suis t.** I'm a witness; **mes yeux en sont témoins** I saw it with my own eyes; **prendre qn à t.** to call upon sb as a witness; **Dieu/le ciel m'est t. que j'ai tout fait pour l'en empêcher** as God/heaven is my witness, I did all I could to stop him

4 *(preuve)* witness; **les témoins d'une civilisation perdue** the evidence of a lost civilization; **... t. les coups que j'ai reçus...** witness the blows which I received

5 *(borne)* boundary mark

6 *Constr* (plaster) telltale

7 *Aut* **t. d'allumage** ignition light

8 *Rel* **T. de Jéhovah** Jehovah's Witness

9 *Sport* baton; **passer le t.** to hand over *or* to pass the baton

10 *Can Ordinat* cookie

11 *(comme adj)* **appartement t.** *Br* show flat, *Am* model apartment; **groupe/sujet t.** control group/subject; **voici les bilans de quatre entreprises témoins** here are the balance sheets from four sample companies

tempe [tɑ̃p] **NF** temple; **ses tempes commencent à grisonner** he's/she's going grey at the temples

TEMPÉ [teəempe] **NM** *Bourse (abrév* **taux moyen pondéré en euros)** EONIA

tempera [tɑ̃pera] *Beaux-Arts* **NF** tempera

• **à tempera, à la tempera ADJ** *(peinture)* tempera *(avant n)* **ADV** *(peindre)* in tempera

tempérage [tɑ̃peraʒ] **NM** *(de chocolat)* tempering

tempérament [tɑ̃peramɑ̃] **NM 1** *(caractère)* temperament, disposition, nature; **ce n'est pas dans mon t.** it's not like me, it's not in my nature; **il est d'un t. plutôt instable** he's got a rather unstable character; **elle est violente de t., elle a un t. violent** she is of *or* has a violent disposition; **elle a un t. d'artiste** she has an artistic temperament, she's of an artistic disposition

2 *(disposition physique)* temperament, constitution; *Fam* **s'abîmer** *ou* **s'esquinter** *ou très Fam* **se crever le t. à faire qch** to wreck one's health doing sth

3 *Fam (sensualité)* sexual nature□; **être d'un t. fougueux/exigeant** to be an ardent/a demanding lover□; *Euph* **il a du t.!** he's hot-blooded!

4 *Fam (forte personnalité)* strong-willed person□; **avoir du t.** to have character

5 *Arch (modération)* moderation, restraint

6 *Com* **vente** *ou* **achat à t.** hire purchase, *Am* installment plan; **acheter qch à t.** to buy sth on hire purchase *or Am* on the installment plan

• **par tempérament** ADV naturally, by nature

tempérance [tɑ̃perɑ̃s] NF **1** *Rel* temperance **2** *(sobriété)* temperance, moderation; **société de t.** temperance society

tempérant, -e [tɑ̃perɑ̃, -ɑ̃t] ADJ temperate, sober

NM,F temperate person

température [tɑ̃peratyr] NF **1** *Méd & Physiol* temperature; **t. du corps humain** temperature of the human body, blood heat; *Fam* **avoir** *ou* **faire de la t.** to have a temperature; **prendre la t. de** *(patient)* to take the temperature of; *Fig (assemblée, public)* to gauge (the feelings of); **la méthode des températures** *(de contraception)* the rhythm method

2 *Météo* temperature; **il y eut une brusque chute de la t.** *ou* **des températures** there was a sudden drop in temperature; **on a atteint des températures de -17°C/40°C** temperatures went down to -17°C/reached 40°C

3 *(d'une pièce, d'une serre, d'un bain)* temperature

4 *Phys* temperature; **t. d'ébullition** boiling point

tempéré, -e [tɑ̃pere] ADJ **1** *Géog (climat, région)* temperate **2** *Mus (gamme)* tempered

tempérer [18] [tɑ̃pere] VT **1** *Littéraire (température excessive)* to temper, to ease **2** *(atténuer* ► *colère)* to soften, to appease; *(*► *ardeurs, passion, sévérité)* to soften, to temper; *(*► *enthousiasme)* to moderate **3** *(chocolat)* to temper

VPR **se tempérer 1** *(se modérer)* to restrain oneself **2 se t. de** *(être mêlé de)* to be softened *or* tempered with; **sa colère se tempérait d'un peu de pitié** a hint of pity softened his/her anger

tempête [tɑ̃pɛt] NF **1** *Météo* storm, *Littéraire* tempest; **le vent souffle en t.** it's blowing a gale, a gale force wind is blowing; **t.** *(sur un baromètre)* stormy; **t. de neige** snowstorm; **t. de sable** sandstorm **2** *Fig (troubles)* storm; **son livre a provoqué une véritable t. dans les milieux politiques** his/her book caused quite a stir in political circles; **nous avons traversé la t.** we've managed to weather the storm; **une t. dans un verre d'eau** *Br* a storm in a teacup, *Am* a tempest in a teapot **3** *Fig (déferlement)* wave, tempest, storm; **t. d'applaudissements/de critiques/de protestations** storm of applause/criticism/protest; **nous avons eu droit à une t. d'insultes** insults rained down on us

tempêter [4] [tɑ̃pete] VI to rage, to rant (and rave); **ils ne cessent de t. contre les syndicats** they're always railing against the unions

tempétueux, -euse [tɑ̃petɥø, -øz] ADJ *Littéraire* **1** *(côte, mer)* tempestuous, stormy; *(courant)* turbulent **2** *Fig (amour, passion)* tempestuous, stormy; *(accueil)* boisterous, tempestuous; *(vie)* turbulent, stormy

temple [tɑ̃pl] NM **1** *Rel (gén)* temple; *(chez les protestants)* church; **le T.** *(ordre)* the Order of the Temple, the Knights Templar **2** *Fig (haut lieu)* temple; **le t. de la mode/musique** the mecca of fashion/music

templier [tɑ̃plije] NM *Hist* (Knight) Templar

tempo [tɛmpo] NM **1** *Mus* tempo **2** *Fig (rythme* ► *d'un film, d'un roman)* tempo, pace; *(*► *de la vie)* pace

temporaire [tɑ̃pɔrɛr] ADJ **1** *(provisoire)* temporary; **c'est une employée t.** she's a temporary worker **2** *Mus* **valeur t. d'une note** time value of a note

temporairement [tɑ̃pɔrɛrmɑ̃] ADV temporarily

temporal, -e, -aux, -ales [tɑ̃pɔral, -o] *Anat* ADJ temporal

NM temporal bone

temporalité [tɑ̃pɔralite] NF *Littéraire* temporality, temporalness

temporel, -elle [tɑ̃pɔrɛl] ADJ **1** *Rel (autorité, pouvoir)* temporal; *(bonheur)* temporal, earthly; *(biens)* worldly, temporal **2** *(qui concerne le temps)* time **3** *Ling* temporal

temporellement [tɑ̃pɔrɛlmɑ̃] ADV temporally

temporisateur, -trice [tɑ̃pɔrizatœr, -tris] ADJ *(politique, tendance)* delaying, *Sout* temporizing; *(stratégie, tactique)* delaying

NM,F *Sout* temporizer; **c'est un t.** *(qui attend pour agir)* he doesn't make hasty decisions; *(qui fait traîner les choses)* he's always stalling *or* playing for time

NM **1** *Ordinat* timer **2** *Élec* (automatic) time switch

temporisation [tɑ̃pɔrizasjɔ̃] NF **1** *(fait de retarder)* delaying tactics, *Sout* temporization **2** *Élec* delay time

temporisatrice [tɑ̃pɔrizatris] *voir* **temporisateur**

temporiser [3] [tɑ̃pɔrize] VI to use delaying tactics, *Sout* to temporize

TEMPS [tɑ̃]

> **NM**
> • weather **A** • season **B7** • stage **B8** • stroke **B12**
> • time **B1–7, B9, 10, 15, 16, 18** • tense **B11** • beat **B13**
> **NMPL**
> • times

NM **A.** *CLIMAT* weather; **le t. s'améliorera lundi** there will be an improvement in the weather on Monday; **quel t. fait-il à Nîmes?** what's the weather like in Nîmes?; **avec le t. qu'il fait, par ce t.** in this weather; **si le t. le permet** weather permitting; **demain, le t. sera variable** tomorrow, the weather will be changeable *or* unsettled; **il fait beau/mauvais t.** the weather's fine/bad; **il fait un t. gris** it's overcast, the weather's gloomy *or Br* dull; **par beau t.** *ou* **par t. clair, on voit la côte anglaise** when it's fine *or* on a clear day, you can see the English coast; **par t. humide** in wet weather; **par t. de pluie/neige/brouillard** in wet/snowy/foggy weather; **par t. froid** in cold weather, when it's cold; **par gros t.** in rough weather at sea, in rough seas; **par tous les t.** in all weathers

B. *DURÉE* **1** *(écoulement des jours)* **le t.** time; **la fuite** *ou* **course du t.** the passing of time; **comme le t. passe!, comme** *ou* **que le t. passe vite!** how time flies!; *Prov* **le t., c'est de l'argent** time is money; **le T.** Old Father Time

2 *(durée indéterminée)* time *(UNCOUNT)*; **c'est du t. perdu** it's a waste of time; **nous avons gâché un t. précieux** we've wasted a lot of precious time; **mettre du t. à faire qch** to take time to do sth; **mettre du t. à se décider** to take a long time deciding *or* to decide; **je passe mon t. à lire** I spend (all) my time reading; **pour passer le t.** to while away *or* to pass the time; **prendre du t.** to take time; **cela ne m'a pas pris beaucoup de t. pour apprendre la chanson** it didn't take me long to learn the song; **chercher une maison prend beaucoup de t.** househunting is very time-consuming; **cela ne prendra pas beaucoup de t.** it won't take long **pour passer le t.** to pass the time, to while away the time; **trouver le t. long,** *Belg* **avoir le t. long** to feel time dragging by; **je commençais à trouver le t. long** *(d'impatience)* I was growing impatient *or* restless; *(d'ennui)* I was getting bored; **un (certain) t., quelque t.** for a while, for a time; **après quelque t., au bout d'un certain t.** after a time; **pendant ce t.** meanwhile, in the meantime; **il y a peu de t.** not long ago, a little while ago, a short time ago; **peu de t. après** shortly *or* a short time *or* not long after; **d'ici quelque t.** soon, shortly, in a short while; **au bout de très peu de t.** in a very short space of time; **tout le t.** all the time; **il est tout le t. en train de se plaindre** he is constantly *or* he keeps complaining; **c'est ce que je lui dis tout le t.** that's what I keep telling him/her; *Belg* **tout un t.** quite a while, quite a long time; *Belg* **un petit t.** (for) a while

3 *(durée nécessaire)* time; **va chercher du lait, le t. que je fasse du thé** go and get some milk while I make some tea; **le t. de faire qch** (the) time to do sth; **je voudrais prendre un peu de t. pour y réfléchir** I'd like to have some time to think about it; **elle a pris/trouvé le t. de nous l'expliquer** she took/found the time to explain it to us; **donner à qn le t. de faire qch** to give sb time to do sth; **(donnez-moi) le t. de signer** *ou* **que je signe et je suis à vous** just give me time *or* a minute to sign this and I'll be with you; **laissez-lui le t. de répondre/de réfléchir** give him/her time to answer/to think; **le t. d'enfiler un manteau et j'arrive** just let me put on a coat and I'll be with you; **juste le t. de les entendre** just long enough to hear them; **avoir le t. de faire qch** to have (the) time to do sth; **nous n'avons pas le t. à présent** we don't have time *or* there's no time now; **je n'ai même pas eu le t. de lui dire au revoir** I didn't even have time to say goodbye to him/her; **auras-tu le t. de venir me chercher?** will you have time to come and collect me?; **elle voudrait venir te voir mais elle n'a pas le t.** she'd like to come and see you but she hasn't got (the) time; **fais-le quand tu en auras le t.** do it at your leisure *or* when you've got (the) time; **prendre (tout) son t.** to take one's time; **je dois étudier le dossier – prenez votre t.** I have to take a close look at the file – take your time (over it); *Ironique* **surtout prends ton t.!** take your time, won't you?, don't hurry, will you?; **prendre le t. de faire qch** to take the time to do sth; **prends le t. de manger** take the time to eat; **il faut prendre le t. de vivre** you should take time to enjoy life; *Culin* **t. de cuisson/préparation** cooking/preparation time; **un t. partiel** a part-time job; **un t. plein** *ou* **plein t.** a full-time job; **être** *ou* **travailler à t. partiel** to work part-time, to have a part-time job; **être** *ou* **travailler à plein t.** *ou* **à t. plein** to work full-time, to have a full-time job; **travailler à t. complet** to work full-time; **faire un trois quarts (de) t.** ≃ to work 30 hours per week; *Mktg* **t. d'accès au marché** time to market; *Phot* **t. de pose** exposure time; *Belg* **t. de midi** lunchtime; **t. de repos** break; *Psy* **t. de réaction** response latency, reaction time; **le t. de la réflexion** time to think; *Astron* **le t. de révolution d'une planète** the period of a planet's orbit; **diminuer le t. de travail** to shorten working hours

4 *(loisir)* time; **maintenant qu'elle est à la retraite, elle ne sait plus quoi faire de son t.** now that she's retired, she doesn't know how to fill her time; **les enfants prennent tout mon t.** the children take up all my time; **pour aller à la pêche, il trouve toujours le t.!** he can always find time to go fishing!; **avoir du t.** *ou* **le t.** to have time; **je n'ai pas beaucoup de/j'ai besoin d'un peu plus de t.** I haven't got much/I need a bit more time; **mon train est à 7 heures, j'ai grandement** *ou* **tout le t.** my train is at 7, I've plenty of time (to spare); **avoir tout son t.** to have all the time in the world; **avoir du t. devant soi** to have time to spare *or* on one's hands; **t. libre** free time

5 *(moment favorable)* **il est (grand) t.!** it's high time!, it's about time!; **la voilà – il était t.!** here she is – it's about time *or* and about time too!; **il était t., le bol allait tomber** that was close, the bowl was about to fall; **il n'est plus t.** time's run out, it's too late; **je voulais tout recopier mais il n'est plus t.** I wanted to write it all out again but there's no time for that now; **cours vite prendre ton train, il n'est que t.** run and catch your train, there's not much time; **il est t. de...** now's the time for...; *Belg* **il devient t. de faire qch** it's time to do sth; **il est t. d'y penser** now's the time to think about it; **il n'est plus t. de discuter, il faut agir** the time for discussion is past *or* enough talking, we must act; **il est t. que tu t'inscrives** you'd better enrol soon, it's time you enrolled; **le t. est venu de nous ressaisir** it's time *or* the time has come for us to pull ourselves together; **le t. était venu pour moi de partir** the time had come for me to *or* it was time for me to leave

6 *(époque déterminée)* time; **le t. n'est plus aux querelles** we should put quarrels behind us, the time for quarrelling is past; **ce fut un grand homme dans son t.** he was a great man in his day *or* time; **elle a eu son t. de beauté** she was a beauty in her day; **du t.** *ou* **au t. de Napoléon** in Napoleon's time; **du t. de ma jeunesse, du t. où j'étais jeune** when I was young, in my youth; **il fut un t. où...** there was a time when...; **le t. n'est plus où...** gone are the days when...; **la plus grande découverte de notre t.** the biggest discovery of our time; **être en avance/en retard sur son t.** to be ahead of/behind one's time; **aller** *ou* **marcher avec son t.** to keep up *or* to move with the times; **être de son t., vivre avec son t.** to move with the times; **tu es bien de ton t., toi!** you really are a child of the times!; **il n'était pas de son t.** *(en retard)* he was out of step with his time; *(en avance)* he was ahead of his time; **dans mon jeune t.** when I was young, in my younger days; **un t.** for a (short) while; **j'ai cru, un t., que...** I thought, for a while, that...; **il y a un t. pour tout** there's a time for everything; **n'avoir** *ou* **ne durer qu'un t.** to last but a short time; **elle est fidèle – ça n'aura** *ou* **ne durera qu'un t.** she's faithful – it won't last; **cela ne durera qu'un t.** it won't last for ever; **un tel chagrin n'aura qu'un t.** such sorrow can't last (for ever); **tout n'a qu'un t.** everything must come to an end; **faire son t.** to do *or* to serve one's time; *(détenu)* to serve one's sentence; *Fam* **la cafetière/mon manteau a fait son t.** the coffee machine's/my coat's seen better days; **des idées qui ont fait leur t.** outmoded ideas; **les diligences ont fait leur t.** the days of stagecoaches are gone; **en t. normal** *ou* **ordinaire** usually, in normal circumstances; **en t. opportun** at an appropriate time, *Sout* in due season; **en t. voulu** in good time; **en t. utile** in due time *or* course; **en son t.** in due course; **chaque chose en son t.** there's a right time for everything; **le bon vieux t.** the good old days; **dans le t.** in the old days; *Arch* **au t. jadis** in times past, in days gone by, in bygone days; **de tout t.** always

7 *(saison, période de l'année)* time, season; **le t. des moissons** harvest (time); **le t. des cerises/pêches** the cherry/peach season

8 *(phase ▸ d'une action, d'un mouvement)* stage; **dans un premier t.** first; **dans un deuxième t.** secondly; **dans un troisième t.** thirdly

9 *Astron* **t. astronomique/sidéral** astronomical/sidereal time; **t. absolu** absolute time; **t. solaire** solar time, Greenwich MeanTime

10 *Jur* **t. civil/légal** civil/standard time

11 *Ling* tense; **t. composé/simple/du passé** compound/simple/past tense; **t. primitifs** *(d'un verbe)* principal parts

12 *Tech* stroke; **moteur à quatre t.** four-stroke engine; *Aut* **t. compression** *(d'un moteur)* compression stroke; *Aut* **t. détente** *(d'un moteur)* power stroke; *Aut* **t. explosion** *(d'un moteur)* power stroke; **t. de fonctionnement** *(d'une machine)* running time; **t. d'immobilisation** *(d'une machine)* down time; *Aut* **t. d'immobilité du piston** piston dwell; **t. mort** *(d'une machine)* idle time *or* period, down time; *Aviat* **t. mort au sol** turn-round time; **t. moteur** engine *or* power *or* working stroke; *Ind* **étude des t. et ordonnancements** time and motion study; *Élec & Électron* **t. d'ouverture** on period; **t. moyen entre deux pannes** *(d'une machine)* mean time between failures, MTBF; *Aut* **t. de réaction** thinking distance; **t. à vide** *(d'une machine)* offload period

13 *Mus* beat; **valse à trois t.** waltz in three-four time

14 *Rel* **le t. de l'avent/du carême** (the season of) Advent/Lent; **le t. pascal** Easter time, Eastertide

15 *Sport (d'une course)* time; *Escrime (durée ▸ d'une action)* time, temps; *(▸ d'un combat)* bout; **quel est son t. sur 100 mètres?** what's his/her time over 100 metres?; **elle a fait le meilleur t. aux essais** hers was the best time *or* she was the fastest in the trials

16 *Ordinat* **base de t.** time base; **t. d'accès** access time; **t. d'accès disque** disk access time; **t. d'adressage** address speed; **t. d'amorçage** start-up time; **t. d'attente** wait state; **t. critique** critical time; **en t. différé** off-line; **t. écoulé** elapsed time; **t. d'exécution** execution *or* execute time; **t. de libération** clearing time; **t. machine** machine time; **t. de montée** rise time; **t. partagé** time sharing; **t. réel** real time; **horloge t. réel** real-time clock; **travailler en t. réel** to work in real time; **t. de réponse** response time; **t. de retournement** turn-around time; **t. de sortie** output time; **t. total** elapsed time; **t. de traitement** processing time

17 *Com* **t. de cycle** business cycle

18 *Psy* **t. de latence** latent time

NMPL *(époque)* times, days; **les t. sont durs** *ou* **difficiles!** times are hard!; **les t. modernes/préhistoriques** modern/prehistoric times; **les t. anciens** ancient times *or* days; **signe des t.** sign of the times; **par les t. qui courent** in this day and age, these days, nowadays; **en d'autres t., je n'aurais pas hésité** once upon a time I wouldn't have hesitated; **ces t.-ci** these days

• **à temps ADV** in time; **je n'arriverai/je ne finirai jamais à t.!** I'll never make it/I'll never finish in time!

• **à temps perdu ADV** in one's spare time, in a spare moment

• **au même temps** = **en même temps**

• **au même temps que** = **en même temps que**

• **au temps de PRÉP** in *or* at the time of, in the days of; **au t. de Voltaire** in Voltaire's time *or* day

• **au temps jadis ADV** in times past, in the old days

• **au temps où, au temps que CONJ** in the days when, at the time when

• **avec le temps ADV** with the passing of time; **avec le t., tout s'arrange** time is a great healer

• **ces temps-ci ADV** these days, lately; **il était malade ces t.-ci** he's been ill lately

• **dans ce temps-là** = **en ce temps-là**

• **dans le même temps** = **en même temps**

• **dans le même temps que** = **en même temps que**

• **dans le temps ADV** before, in the old days

• **dans les temps ADV** on time; **vous devez finir dans les t.** you must finish on time

• **de temps à autre, de temps en temps ADV** from time to time, occasionally, (every) now and then

• **de temps immémorial ADV** from time immemorial

• **du temps de PRÉP du t. de Louis XIV** in the days of Louis the 14th; **du t. de notre père, tu n'aurais pas osé** when our father was (still) alive, you wouldn't have dared; **de mon t., ça n'existait pas** when I was young *or* in my day, there was no such thing

• **du temps où, du temps que** = **au temps où**

• **en ce temps-là ADV** at that time, then

• **en même temps ADV** at the same time; **en même t. mère et sœur** both mother and sister, mother and sister at the same time

• **en même temps que CONJ** at the same time as

• **en temps de PRÉP en t. de crise** in a crisis, at a time of crisis; **en t. de guerre/paix** in wartime/peacetime; **en t. de prospérité/récession** in times of prosperity/recession

• **en temps et lieu ADV** in due course *or* time, at the proper time and place

• **en un temps où CONJ** at a time when

• **par les temps qui courent ADV** *Fam* (things being as they are) these days *or* nowadays

• **tout le temps ADV** all the time, always; **elle est tout le t. là** she's always there, she's there all the time; **ne me harcèle pas tout le t.!** don't keep on pestering me!

• **temps fort NM** *Mus* strong beat; *Fig* high point, highlight; **les t. forts de l'actualité/de l'année 2005** the main points of the news/the main events of 2005; **un des t. forts du festival** one of the high points *or* highlights of the festival; **ce fut un des t. forts de ma vie/de la représentation** it was one of the high points of my life/of the performance

• **temps mort NM 1** *Sport (au basket-ball et au volley-ball)* time-out **2** *Fig* lull, slack period; **pendant les t. morts** *(dans une période de travail)* when things are quiet; *(dans une conversation)* lull, pause **3** *Phys* time-out (interval)

tenable [tənabl] **ADJ 1** *(supportable)* bearable; **la situation n'est plus t., il faut agir** the situation's become untenable *or* unbearable, we must take action; **la chaleur/le froid est à peine t.** the heat/the cold is hardly bearable **2** *Mil (position)* tenable, defensible

tenace [tənas] **ADJ 1** *(obstiné ▸ travailleur)* tenacious, obstinate; *(▸ chercheur)* tenacious, dogged; *(▸ ennemi)* relentless; *(▸ résistance, volonté)* tenacious; *(▸ refus)* dogged; *(▸ vendeur)* tenacious, insistent; **tu es t. toi!** you don't give up easily! **2** *(durable ▸ fièvre, grippe, toux)* persistent, stubborn; *(▸ douleur, souvenir, parfum)* persistent, lingering; *(▸ tache)* stubborn; *(▸ couleur)* fast; *(▸ préjugé, impression, superstition)* deep-rooted, stubborn, tenacious; *(▸ espoir)* stubborn, tenacious **3** *(qui adhère fortement ▸ colle)* strong; *(▸ plante, lierre)* clinging

tenacement [tənasmɑ̃] **ADV** tenaciously, persistently, stubbornly, doggedly

ténacité [tenasite] **NF 1** *(d'une personne, d'une volonté)* tenacity, tenaciousness; **avec t.** doggedly **2** *(d'une fièvre, d'une toux, d'une odeur, d'une douleur, d'un souvenir)* persistence; *(d'une tache)* stubbornness; *(d'un préjugé, d'une superstition)* deep-rootedness, persistence

tenaille [tənaj] **NF 1** *(de charpentier, de menuisier)* pincers; *(de cordonnier)* pincers, nippers; *(de forgeron)* tongs; **t. à vis** hand vice **2** *(fortification)* tenaille

• **en tenaille, en tenailles ADV prendre qn en t.** *ou* **tenailles** to catch *or* to trap sb in a pincer movement

tenailler [3] [tənaje] **VT 1** *(faim, soif)* to gnaw; *(doute, inquiétude, remords)* to gnaw (at), to rack, to torment; *(douleur)* to grip; **tenaillé par la faim** to be racked with hunger; **être tenaillé par le remords** to be tormented by remorse; **être tenaillé par la douleur** to be gripped with pain **2** *Hist* to torture

tenancier, -ère [tənɑ̃sje, -ɛr] **NM,F 1** *(d'un café, d'un hôtel, d'une maison de jeu)* manager; *(d'une maison close)* keeper **2** *(fermier)* tenant farmer **3** *Hist* (feudal) tenant

tenant, -e [tənɑ̃, -ɑ̃t] **ADJ chemise à col t.** shirt with a collar attached

NM,F *Sport* **t. (du titre)** holder, titleholder

NM 1 *(d'une doctrine, d'une idéologie, d'un principe)* supporter, upholder **2** *Hér* supporter

• **tenants NMPL** *(d'une terre)* adjacent parts, *Jur* abuttals; **les tenants et les aboutissants** *(d'une affaire)* the ins and outs, the full details

• **d'un (seul) tenant ADJ** all in one block

tendance [tɑ̃dɑ̃s] **NF 1** *(disposition, propension)* tendency, propensity, leaning; **avoir t. à** to tend to, to have a tendency to; **avoir (une) t. à la paresse/l'embonpoint** to be inclined *or* to tend to be lazy/to put on weight; **elle a t. à se laisser aller** she has a tendency *or* she's inclined to let herself go; **avoir t. à s'enrhumer facilement** to be prone to catching colds

2 *(orientation, évolution ▸ gén)* trend; *(▸ d'un créateur)* leanings; *(▸ d'un livre, d'un discours)* drift, tenor; **les nouvelles tendances de l'art/la mode** the new trends in art/fashion

3 *(position, opinion)* allegiance, leaning, sympathy; **un parti de t. libérale** a party with liberal tendencies; **des partis de toutes tendances étaient représentés** the whole spectrum of political opinion was represented; **à quelle t. appartiens-tu?** what are your political leanings?, where do your (political) sympathies lie?

4 *Bourse & Écon* trend; **une t. baissière** *ou* **à la baisse** a downward trend, a downswing; *Bourse* a bearish tendency; **tendances conjoncturelles** economic trends; **tendances de la consommation** consumer trends; **t. de croissance** growth trend; **t. de l'économie, t. économique** economic trend; **une t. haussière** *ou* **à la hausse** an upward trend, an upswing; *Bourse* a bullish tendency; **t. inflationniste** inflationary trend; **t. du marché** market trend

5 *(comme adj) Fam (à la mode)* trendy

tendanceur [tɑ̃dɑ̃sœr] **NM** *Mktg* trendspotter

tendancieuse [tɑ̃dɑ̃sjøz] *voir* **tendancieux**

tendancieusement [tɑ̃dɑ̃sjøzmɑ̃] **ADV** tendentiously, tendenciously

tendancieux, -euse [tɑ̃dɑ̃sjø, -øz] **ADJ** *(film, récit, interprétation)* tendentious, tendencious; *(question)* loaded

tender [tɑ̃dɛr] **NM** *Pétr & Rail* tender

tendeur [tɑ̃dœr] **NM 1** *(pour tendre ▸ câble)* tensioner; *(▸ toile de tente)* guy rope; *(▸ chaîne de bicyclette)* chain adjuster; *(de machine à coudre)* tension (device); *(pour chaussure)* shoe tree; *Aut* **t. de courroie** belt tensioner; **t. de sangle** belt tensioner; **t. à vis** turnbuckle **2** *(courroie élastique)* bungee (cord); *(pour porte-bagages)* luggage strap

tendineux, -euse [tɑ̃dinø, -øz] **ADJ 1** *Anat* tendinous **2** *(viande)* stringy

tendinite [tɑ̃dinit] **NF** *Méd* tendinitis

tendon [tɑ̃dɔ̃] **NM** tendon, sinew; **t. d'Achille** Achilles' tendon

tendre¹ [tɑ̃dr] **ADJ 1** *(aimant ▸ personne, regard, geste)* loving, gentle, tender; *(▸ voix)* gentle; *(▸ yeux)* gentle, loving; *(affectueux ▸ lettre)* loving, affectionate; **il n'a jamais un geste t. envers sa femme** he never shows his wife any affection; **elle n'est pas t. avec lui** she's hard on him; **les critiques n'ont pas été tendres pour son film** the reviewers were very hard on his/her movie *or Br* film; **dire à qn des mots tendres** to say tender *or* loving things to sb; **avoir le cœur t.** to be soft-hearted; **il a le vin t.** drink makes him sentimental

2 *(moelleux ▸ viande, légumes)* tender; **t. comme la rosée** (as) fresh as the morning dew

3 *(mou ▸ roche, mine de crayon, métal)* soft; **bois t.** softwood

4 *Littéraire (délicat ▸ feuillage, bourgeons)* tender, delicate; *(▸ herbe)* soft; **de tendres boutons de rose** tender rosebuds

5 *(doux ▸ teinte)* soft, delicate; **un tissu rose/vert t.** a soft pink/green material

6 *(jeune)* early; **nos tendres années** our early years; **âge t., t. enfance** early childhood; **dès sa plus t. enfance** since his/her earliest childhood

NMF soft-hearted person; **c'est un t.** he's soft-hearted

NM 1 *Arch* **avoir un t. pour qn** to have a soft spot for sb **2** *Culin* **t. de tranche** topside (of beef)

TENDRE² **[73]** [tɑ̃dr]

VT	
• to tighten **1**	• to tauten **1**
• to stretch **1**	• to hang **2**
• to cover **3**	• to tense **4**
• to stretch out **4**	• to hold out **4, 5**
• to offer **5**	
VPR	
• to tighten **1**	• to tauten **1**
• to stretch out **2**	• to become strained **3**

VT 1 *(étirer ▸ câble, corde de raquette, de violon)* to tighten, to tauten; *(▸ élastique, ressort)* to stretch; *(▸ corde d'arc)* to draw back; *(▸ arc)* to bend; *(▸ arbalète)* to arm; *(▸ peau d'un tambour)* to pull, to stretch

2 *(disposer ▸ hamac, fil à linge, tapisserie)* to hang; *(▸ voile)* to spread; *(▸ collet, souricière)* to set (à for); **ils ont tendu une corde en travers de la route** they stretched *or* tied a rope across the road; **t. des lignes** to put out (fishing) lines; **t. une embuscade** *ou* **un piège à qn** to set an ambush *or* a trap for sb; **t. ses filets** to set one's nets; *Fig* to set a trap

3 *(revêtir ▸ mur)* to cover; **les murs étaient tendus de papier peint à fleurs** there was flowered paper on the walls

4 *(allonger ▸ muscles)* to tense; *(▸ bras, jambe)* to stretch out, to hold out; **t. le cou** to crane *or* to stretch one's neck; **il tendit un doigt accusateur vers l'enfant** he pointed an accusing finger at the child; **elle tendit son front/sa joue à sa mère pour qu'elle l'embrasse** she offered her forehead/her cheek for her mother to kiss; **t. les bras** *(en signe de bienvenue)* to stretch one's arms wide, to throw one's arms out; **t. les bras vers qn** to stretch out one's arms towards sb; **t. la main** *(pour recevoir quelque chose)* to hold out one's hand; *(mendier)* to beg; **t. la main à qn** *(pour dire bonjour)* to hold out one's hand to sb; *(pour aider)* to offer a helping hand to sb; *(pour se réconcilier)* to extend a *or* the hand of friendship to sb; **t. l'autre joue** to turn the other cheek

5 *(offrir)* to offer; *(présenter)* to hold out; **t. qch à qn** *(offrir)* to offer sth to sb *or* sb sth; *(présenter)* to hold sth out to sb; **il lui tendit la boîte de chocolats/un miroir** he offered him/her the box of chocolates/held out the mirror to him/her

• **tendre à VT IND 1** *(avoir tendance à)* **c'est une pratique qui tend à disparaître** it's a custom which is dying out; **les douleurs tendent à disparaître** the pain is starting to go

2 *(contribuer à)* **cela tendrait à prouver que j'ai raison** this would seem to prove that I'm right

3 *(viser à)* **t. à la perfection** to aim for perfection; **t. à un idéal** to aim at an ideal

4 *(arriver à)* **t. à sa fin** to near an end; **la période de crise tend à sa fin** the end of the crisis is in sight, the crisis is nearing its end

• **tendre vers VT IND 1** *(viser à)* **t. vers la perfection** to aim for perfection, to strive towards perfection **2** *(approcher de)* **le rythme de la production tend vers son maximum** maximum output is close to being reached **3** *Math* **t. vers zéro/l'infini** to tend to zero/infinity

VPR se tendre 1 *(courroie, câble)* to tighten (up), to become taut, to tauten **2** *(main)* to stretch out **3** *Fig (atmosphère, relations)* to become strained

tendrement [tɑ̃drəmɑ̃] **ADV** *(embrasser, regarder, sourire)* tenderly, lovingly; **ils s'aiment t.** they love each other dearly

tendresse [tɑ̃drɛs] **NF 1** *(attachement ▸ d'un amant)* tenderness; *(▸ d'un parent)* affection, tenderness; **t. maternelle** maternal affection *or* love; **avec t.** tenderly; **aimer qn avec t.** to feel great affection for sb; **avoir de la t. pour qn** to feel affection for sb **2** *(inclination, penchant)* **je n'ai aucune t. pour les menteurs** I have no love for liars, I don't think much of liars; **avoir des tendresses royalistes** to have royalist sympathies

• **tendresses NFPL** *(témoignages d'affection)* **se dire des tendresses** to exchange sweet nothings; **je vous envoie mille tendresses ainsi qu'aux enfants** much love to you and to the children

tendreté [tɑ̃drəte] **NF** *(d'un légume, d'une viande)* tenderness

tendron [tɑ̃drɔ̃] **NM 1** *Culin* **t. de veau** middle-cut breast of veal **2** *Bot* shoot **3** *Fam (jeune fille)* **un t.** a slip of a girl

tendu, -e [tɑ̃dy] **PP** *voir* **tendre**

ADJ 1 *(personne, situation, atmosphère, climat politique)* tense; **elle est très tendue nerveusement** she's very tense, she's under a lot of strain

2 *(partie du corps, muscle)* tensed up; *(visage)* strained; **avoir les nerfs tendus** *(habituellement)* to be tense; *(momentanément)* to be tense *or* on edge

3 *(étiré ▸ corde, courroie)* tight, taut; *(▸ corde d'arc)* drawn; *(▸ arc)* drawn, bent; *(▸ voile, peau de tambour)* stretched; *Sport (tir)* straight; **la chaîne est mal tendue** *ou* **n'est pas assez tendue** the chain isn't tight enough *or* is a bit slack; *Bourse* **prix tendus** hard *or* firm prices

4 *(allongé)* **avancer le doigt t./le poing t./les bras tendus** to advance with pointed finger/raised fist/outstretched arms; **il est venu la main tendue** he came with his hand held out

5 *Ling* tense

6 *(tapissé)* **t. de** *(tapisseries, tissu)* hung with; *(papier peint)* covered with

ténèbres [tenɛbr] **NFPL 1** *(nuit, obscurité)* darkness *(UNCOUNT)*, dark *(UNCOUNT)*; **être plongé dans les t.** to be in total darkness; **les t. de la nuit** the darkness of the night **2** *Fig (de l'ignorance, de l'inconscient)* depths; **les t. de la superstition** the dark age of superstition

ténébreux, -euse [tenebrø, -øz] **ADJ** *Littéraire* **1** *(forêt, maison, pièce)* dark, gloomy, *Littéraire* tenebrous; *(recoin, cachot)* dark, murky

2 *(inquiétant ▸ intrigue, complot)* dark; *(▸ époque, affaire, situation)* obscure, murky; **de t. projets** devious plans

3 *(incompréhensible)* mysterious, unfathomable; **le t. langage de la loi** the obscure language of the legal profession

4 *(personne, caractère)* melancholic, *Littéraire* saturnine

NM,F 1 *Littéraire (personne mélancolique)* melancholic **2** *Hum* **un beau t.** a tall, dark, handsome stranger

teneur¹ [tənœr] **NF 1** *(contenu ▸ d'un document)* content; *(▸ d'un traité)* terms; **je vais vous résumer la t. de ses propos** I'll give you the general tenor *or* gist of what he/she said; **la t. du marché** the market trend *or* maker **2** *Chim* content; **t. en eau/fer** water/iron content; **t. en alcool** alcohol content, alcoholic strength **3** *Mines* content, grade, tenor; **t. en carbone** percentage of carbon, carbon content

teneur², -euse [tənœr, -øz] **NM,F 1** *Com* **t. de livres** bookkeeper **2** *Typ* **t. de copie** copyholder **3** *Bourse* **t. de marché** market maker

ténia [tenja] **NM** tapeworm, *Spéc* taenia

TENIR **[40]** [tənir]

VT	
• to hold **A, B1, 2,** **D1, 3, E2, G**	• to keep **B1, 3, C5, D2**
	• to get **C1**
• to have caught **C2**	• to have **C3, D3–5**
• to control **D1**	• to run **D2**
• to give **D4**	• to play **D5**
• to take up **E1, F2**	• to take **F1**
• to keep to **F2**	• to consider **G**
VI	
• to hold **1, 4**	• to last **2, 3**
• to hold out **2, 3**	• to stand **4**
• to fit **5**	
VPR	
• to take place **2**	• to hold on **4**
• to stand **5**	• to sit **5**
• to behave **6**	• to hold together **7**

VT A. *AVOIR DANS LES MAINS* **1** *(retenir)* to hold; **t. la main de qn** to hold sb's hand; **il tenait sa casquette sous le bras** he was holding his cap under his arm; **tiens mon sac deux minutes** can you hold my bag for a moment?; **tiens bien le livre** hold on tight to the book

2 *(manier)* to hold; **tu tiens mal ta raquette/ton arc** you're not holding your racket/your bow properly; **apprendre à t. le ciseau** to learn the correct way to hold a chisel; **tenez la lime horizontale** hold the file flat *or* horizontal *or* horizontally; **tenez la bouteille verticale** hold the bottle upright *or* vertical *or* vertically

B. *CONSERVER* **1** *(maintenir ▸ dans une position)* to hold, to keep; *(▸ dans un état)* to keep; **enlève les vis qui tiennent le panneau** undo the screws which hold the panel in place; **l'amarre qui tient le bateau** the cable tying up the boat; **tiens-lui la porte, il est chargé** hold the door open for him, he's got his hands full; **il tenait les yeux baissés** he kept his eyes lowered; **tenez-lui la tête hors de l'eau** hold his/her head above the water; **t. les fenêtres fermées/ouvertes** to keep the windows shut/open; **elle tient ses chiens attachés** she keeps her dogs tied up; **t. chaud** to keep warm; **je veux une robe qui tienne chaud** I'd like a warm dress; **t. un plat au chaud** to keep a dish hot; **tenez le bois au sec** keep the wood in a dry place; **t. une chambre en ordre** to keep a room tidy; **tenez-le prêt (à partir)** make sure he's ready (to leave); **ils tiennent le pont sous le feu de leurs mitraillettes** they're keeping the bridge under machine-gun fire

2 *(garder ▸ note)* to hold; **t. l'accord** to stay in tune; **tenez votre droite** *(panneau sur la route)* keep (to the) right; *(sur un escalator)* keep to the right

3 *Vieilli (conserver ▸ dans un lieu)* to keep; **où tenait-il les bijoux?** where did he keep the jewels?; **dans nos nouveaux locaux, nous tenons une plus grande sélection d'articles** we keep a larger selection of goods on our new premises

4 *Belg (collectionner)* to collect

C. *POSSÉDER* **1** *(avoir reçu)* **t. qch de qn** *(par hérédité)* to get sth from sb; **je tiens mes yeux bleus de mon père** I get my blue eyes from my father; **une passion pour les affaires qu'elle tient de famille** a taste for business which she inherited from her family; **les propriétés que je tenais de ma mère** *(par héritage)* the properties I'd inherited from my mother

2 *(avoir capturé)* to have caught, to have got hold of; *(avoir à sa merci)* to have got; **nous tenons son chien, qu'il vienne le chercher** we've got his dog, let him come and fetch it; **je tiens une truite!** I've caught *or* I've got a trout!; **c'est un cul-de-sac, nous le tenons** it's a dead end, he's trapped *or* we've got him; **ah, ah, petit coquin, je te tiens!** got you, you little devil!; **la police tient un des coupables** the police have caught one of the culprits; **vous avez trouvé un nouveau collaborateur? – oui, je tiens mon homme** have you found a new assistant? – yes, I've found the very man; **elle m'a tenu une heure avec ses histoires de divorce** I had to listen to her going on about her divorce for a whole hour

3 *(détenir ▸ indice, information, preuve)* to have; *(▸ contrat)* to have, to have won; *(▸ réponse, solution)* to have found *or* got; **ça y est, je tiens la solution!** hurrah, I've found *or* got the answer!; **je tiens enfin l'édition originale** I've finally got my hands on the original edition; **t. qch de** *(l'apprendre)* to have (got) sth from; *(le tirer de)* to derive sth from; **il a eu des troubles psychologiques – de qui tenez-vous cela?** he's had psychological problems – who told you that?; **nous tenons de source sûre/soviétique que...** we have it on good authority/we hear from Soviet sources that...; **je tiens mon autorité de l'État** I derive my power from the State; *Fam* **qu'est-ce que je tiens comme rhume!** I've got a horrible *or Br* stinking cold!; *Fam* **elle en tient une couche!** *Br* she's as thick as two short planks!, *Am* she's got rocks in her head!; *Fam* **il en tient une bonne ce soir** he's three sheets to the wind *or Br* he's had a skinful tonight; *Fam* **t. une bonne cuite** *(être ivre)* to be totally wasted *or Br* legless

4 *(transmettre)* **nous vous ferons t. une copie des documents** we will make sure you receive a copy of the documents; **faites-le-lui t. en mains propres** make sure it's handed to him/her personally

5 *Belg (élever ▸ volaille, animaux)* to keep

D. *CONTRÔLER, AVOIR LA RESPONSABILITÉ DE* **1** *(avoir prise sur, dominer)* to hold; *Mil* to control; *(avoir de l'autorité sur ▸ classe, élève)* to (keep under) control; **quand la colère le tient, il peut être dangereux** he can be dangerous when he's angry; **la jalousie le tenait** jealousy had him in its grip, he was gripped by jealousy; **ce rhume me tient depuis deux semaines** I've had this cold for two weeks; **les Anglais tenaient la mer** the English ruled the seas; **quand Noël approche, on ne peut plus les t.** when Christmas is near, you just can't control them

2 *(diriger, s'occuper de ▸ commerce, maison, hôtel)* to run; *(▸ comptabilité, registre)* to keep; **t. la caisse** to be at the cash desk, to be the cashier; **t. les livres** to keep the books; **je tiens la maison pendant son absence** I look after *or* I mind the house while he's/she's away; **elle tient la rubrique artistique à 'Madame'** she has a regular arts column in 'Madame'; **le soir, il tenait le bar** at night he used to serve behind the bar; *Sport & (dans un jeu)* **t. la marque** to keep score

3 *(donner ▸ assemblée, conférence, séance)* to hold, to have; **elle va t. une conférence de presse** she is going to hold *or* to have a press conference; **le tribunal tiendra audience dans le nouveau bâtiment** the court hearings will be held in the new building

4 *(prononcer ▸ discours)* to give; *(▸ raisonnement)* to have; *(▸ langage)* to use; **elle m'a tenu tout un discours sur la ponctualité** she gave me a lecture about being on time; **il me tint à peu près ce langage** here's roughly what he said to me; **t. des propos désobligeants/élogieux** to make offensive/appreciative remarks

5 *Théât (rôle)* to play, to have; **t. des emplois secondaires** to play minor parts; *Fig* **t. un rôle dans** to play a part in; **il a bien tenu son rôle de fils** he acted as a son should

6 *Équitation (cheval)* to keep in hand; **t. un cheval serré** to keep a tight rein on a horse; **t. un cheval court** to ride a horse on a short rein

E. *EXPRIME UNE MESURE* **1** *(occuper)* to take up, to occupy; **le fauteuil tient trop de place** the armchair takes up too much room; **la barricade tenait toute la rue** the barricade took up the whole width of the street; **t. une place importante** to have *or* to hold an important place

2 *(contenir)* to hold; **le réservoir ne tient pas plus de 40 litres** the tank doesn't hold more than 40 litres

F. *ÊTRE CONSTANT DANS* **1** *(résister à)* (to be able) to take; **il tient l'alcool** he can hold *or esp Br* take his drink; **je ne tiens pas le vin** wine doesn't agree with me; *Fam* **t. le coup** *(assemblage, vêtements)* to hold out; *(digue)* to hold (out); *(personne)* (to be able) to take it; **le soir, je ne tiens pas le coup** I can't take late nights; **elle travaillait trop et n'a pas tenu le coup longtemps** she was overworked and couldn't cope *or* take it for long; **sa foi l'a aidé à t. le coup** his faith helped him to keep going; **t. la mer** to keep the sea (well); **t. la route** *(véhicule)* to hold the road well, *Br* to have good road-holding; *Fig* **ton raisonnement ne tient pas la route** your argument doesn't stand up to scrutiny

2 *(respecter ▸ promesse)* to keep to, to stand by, to uphold; *(s'engager dans ▸ pari)* to take up; **t. (sa) parole** to keep one's word; **t. une promesse** to keep *or* to fulfil a promise; **je tiens la gageure** *ou* **le pari!** I'll take up the challenge!; **tenu!, je tiens!** *(dans un jeu)* you're on!

G. *CONSIDÉRER* to hold, to consider; **je tiens que les romanciers sont les historiens du présent** it is my belief *or* I hold that novelists are the chroniclers of our time; **t. qn/qch pour** to consider sb/sth to be, to look upon sb/sth as; **on la tenait pour une divinité** she was considered to be *or* as a deity

VI 1 *(rester en position ▸ attache)* to hold; *(▸ chignon)* to stay up, to hold; *(▸ bouton, trombone)* to stay on; *(▸ empilement, tas)* to stay up; **t. en place** to stay in place; **mets du gel, tes cheveux tiendront mieux** use gel, your hair'll hold its shape better; **la porte du placard ne tient pas fermée** the cupboard door won't stay shut; **tout ça tient avec de la colle** all this is held together with glue; **le porridge vous tient au corps** *ou* **à l'estomac** porridge keeps you going; **faire t. qch avec de la colle/des clous** to glue/to nail sth into position; **t. à** *(être fixé à)* to be fixed on *or* to; *(être contigu à)* to be next to; **assurez-vous que les ventouses tiennent bien au mur** make sure that the suction pads are securely fixed to the wall; **les bureaux tenant à l'atelier** the offices next to *or* adjoining the workshop; **il ne tient pas encore bien sur sa bicyclette/ses skis/ses jambes** he's not very steady on his bike/his skis/his legs yet; **je ne tiens plus sur mes jambes** *(de fatigue)* I can hardly stand; **cet enfant ne tient pas sur sa chaise** this child can't sit still *or* is always fidgeting in his chair; **elle ne tient pas en place** she can't sit still

2 *(résister ▸ union)* to last, to hold out; *(▸ chaise, vêtements)* to hold *or* to last out; *(▸ digue)* to hold out; *(▸ personne)* to hold *or* to last out; **leur mariage n'a pas tenu deux ans** their marriage didn't even last two years; **ce manteau a bien tenu** that coat lasted well; **je ne tiens plus au soleil, je rentre** I can't stand the sun any more, I'm going in; **je ne tiendrais pas longtemps sous la torture** I wouldn't hold out very long under torture; **on peut t. plusieurs jours sans manger** you can survive several days without eating; **le cœur ne tiendra pas** his/her/*etc* heart won't take it; **il n'a pas tenu longtemps au gouvernement** he didn't stay *or* last long in office; **tes arguments ne tiendront pas longtemps face à la réalité** your arguments won't hold water for very long in a real-life situation; **t. bon** *ou* **ferme** *(s'agripper)* to hold firm *or* tight; *(ne pas céder)* to hold out; **tenez bon, les secours arrivent** hold *or* hang on, help's on its way; **il me refusait une augmentation, mais j'ai tenu bon** he wouldn't give me a *Br* rise *or Am* raise but I held out *or* stood my ground; **la défense lyonnaise tient bon** the Lyons defence is holding fast *or* is standing firm; **le dollar tient toujours bon** the dollar is still holding firm; **n'y tenant plus, je l'appelai au téléphone** unable to stand it any longer, I phoned him/her; **ça sent si bon le chocolat, je ne vais pas pouvoir y t.** there's such a gorgeous smell of chocolate, I just won't be able to resist it; **c'est à n'y pas t.!** *(mauvaise odeur, mauvaise ambiance)* it's unbearable *or* intolerable!

3 *(durer, ne pas s'altérer ▸ fleurs)* to keep, to last; *(▸ tissu)* to last (well); *(▸ beau temps)* to last, to hold out; *(▸ bronzage)* to last; *(▸ neige)* to settle, to stay; **aucun parfum ne tient sur moi** perfumes don't last on me; **pour que votre rouge à lèvres tienne plus longtemps** so that your lipstick stays on longer

4 *(être valable, être d'actualité ▸ offre, pari, rendez-vous)* to stand; *(▸ promesse)* to hold; **l'invitation tient pour samedi** the invitation for Saturday is still on *or* still stands; **ça tient toujours pour demain?** is it still on for tomorrow?

5 *(pouvoir être logé)* to fit; **une fois plié, le sac tient dans la poche** when folded up, the bag fits in your pocket; **il ne tiendra pas sur cette chaise** he'll never fit in *or* get into that chair; **le compte rendu tient en une page** the report takes up one page; **t. en hauteur/largeur (dans)** to fit vertically/widthwise (in); **quatre enfants peuvent t. sur la banquette arrière** four children can fit on the back seat; **on ne tiendra jamais à 30 dans ton salon** you'll never get 30 people into your living-room; **on n'arrivera jamais à tout faire t. dans cette valise** we'll never get everything into this suitcase; **son histoire tient en peu de mots** his/her story can be summed up in a few words

6 *(locutions) Fam* **en t. pour qn** to have a crush on sb; *Fam* **en t. pour qch** *(aimer)* to be hooked on sth; *(ne considérer que)* to stick to sth; **il en tient pour la varappe** he's really hooked on *or* mad about rock climbing; *Prov* **un tiens vaut mieux que deux tu l'auras** a bird in the hand is worth two in the bush

7 tiens, tenez *(en donnant quelque chose)* here; **tiens, reprends ta bague** here, have your ring back; **tu me passes le sel? – tiens** can you pass me the salt? – here you are

8 tiens, tenez *(pour attirer l'attention, pour insister)* listen, look; **tenez, je vais tout vous raconter** look *or* listen, I'll tell you everything; **tiens, rends-toi utile** here, make yourself useful; **tenez, je ne vous ferai même pas payer l'électricité** look, I won't even charge you for the electricity; **s'il est intéressé par le salaire? tiens, bien sûr que oui!** is he interested in the salary? you bet he is!

9 tiens, tenez *(exprime la surprise, l'incrédulité)* **tiens, Bruno! que fais-tu ici?** (hello) Bruno, what are you doing here?; **tiens, je n'aurais jamais cru ça de lui** well, well, I'd never have expected it of him; **tiens, c'est bizarre** hmm, that's strange; **tiens, tiens, ça serait bien dans son style** hmm, that's just the sort of thing he'd/she'd do; *Fam Ironique* **elle a refusé? tiens donc!** she said no? you amaze me! *or* surprise, surprise!

• **tenir à VT IND 1** *(être attaché à ▸ personne)* to care for, to be very fond of; *(▸ objet)* to be attached to; *(▸ réputation)* to care about; *(▸ indépendance, liberté)* to value; **je tiens énormément à sa confiance** I set great store by *or* I greatly value his/her trust; **si tu tiens à la vie...** if you value your life...

2 *(vouloir)* **t. à faire qch** to be eager to do *or* to be keen on doing sth; **il tenait tellement à monter cette pièce** he was so keen on the idea of staging this play; **tu veux lui parler? – je n'y tiens pas vraiment** would you like to talk to him/her? – not really *or* not particularly; **je tiens à ce qu'ils aient une bonne éducation** I'm determined that they should have a good education; **je ne tiens pas à ce qu'on me reconnaisse** I don't want to be recognized; **tiens-tu à ce que cela se sache?** do you really want it to become known?

3 *(résulter de)* to stem *or* to result from, to be due to, to be caused by; **à quoi tient son charisme?** what's the secret of his/her charisma?; **sa défaite aux élections a tenu à trois voix** he/she was defeated in the election by just three votes; **le bonheur tient parfois à peu de chose** sometimes it's the little things that give people the most happiness; *Fam* **à quoi ça tient?** what's the reason for it?, what's it due to?; **qu'à cela ne tienne** never mind, *Hum* fear not; **vous n'avez pas votre voiture? qu'à cela ne tienne, je vais vous reconduire** you haven't got your car? never mind, I'll give you a lift

4 *(tournure impersonnelle) (être du ressort de)* **il ne tient qu'à toi de mettre fin à ce désordre** it's entirely up to you to sort out this shambles; **il ne tient qu'à vous de choisir** the choice rests *or* lies with you, it's entirely up to you; **il tenait à lui seul que ma nomination fût effective** it was entirely up to him to validate my appointment; **s'il ne tenait qu'à moi** if it was up to me *or* my decision; **il a tenu à peu de chose que je ne rate mon train** I very nearly missed my train

• **tenir de VT IND 1** *(ressembler à)* to take after; **elle tient de moi** she takes after me; **ce chien tient à la fois de l'épagneul et du setter** this dog is a cross between a spaniel and a setter; **elle est vraiment têtue/douée – elle a de qui t.!** she's so stubborn/gifted – it runs in the family! **2** *(relever de)* **sa guérison tient du miracle** his/her recovery is something of a miracle; **ça tient de l'exploit** it's something of *or* quite a feat; **des propos qui tiennent de l'injure** remarks verging on the insulting; **le paysage tenait de la féerie** the scenery was like something out of a fairytale

VPR se tenir 1 *(emploi réciproque)* **ils marchaient en se tenant la main** they were walking hand in hand; **ils se tenaient par le cou/la taille** they had their arms round each other's shoulders/waists

2 *(se dérouler* ▸ *conférence)* to be held, to take place; *(▸ festival, foire)* to take place; **la réunion se tiendra dans la salle de bal** the meeting will be held in the ballroom; **le festival se tient en plusieurs endroits** there are several venues for the festival

3 se t. la tête à deux mains to hold *or* to clutch one's head in one's hands

4 *(se retenir)* to hold on (tight); **tenez-vous bien, on démarre!** hold on tight *or* fast, here we go!; **se t. à** to hold on to; *(fortement)* to cling to, to clutch, to grip; **tiens-toi à la rampe pour descendre** hold on to the rail on the way down

5 *(se trouver* ▸ *en position debout)* to stand, to be standing; *(▸en position assise)* to sit, to be sitting *or* seated; **il se tenait sur le seuil/dans l'embrasure de la porte** he was standing on the doorstep/in the doorway; **se t. (légèrement) en retrait** to stand back (slightly); **se t. debout** to be standing (up); **se t. droit** *(debout)* to stand up straight; *(assis)* to sit up straight; **tiens-toi droit** straighten up; **tenez-vous droits!** *(à des personnes assises)* sit up straight *or* properly!; *(à des personnes debout)* stand up straight!; **tiens-toi mieux sur ta chaise** sit properly on your chair; **c'est parce que tu te tiens mal que tu as mal au dos** you get backaches because of bad posture; **se t. aux aguets** to be on the lookout, to watch out; **se t. coi** to remain silent; **se t. immobile** to remain *or* to be still

6 *(se conduire)* to behave; **elle ne sait pas se t. quand il y a des invités** she doesn't know how to behave when there are guests; **bien se t.** to behave oneself; **mal se t.** to behave badly

7 *(être cohérent)* to hold together, to stand up; *(coïncider* ▸ *indices, événements)* to hang together, to be linked; **se t. (bien)** *(argumentation, intrigue)* to hold together, to stand up; *(raisonnement)* to hold water, to hold together; **l'intrigue du roman ne se tient pas** the plot doesn't stand up *or* hang together; **je voudrais trouver un alibi qui se tienne** I'm looking for a plausible excuse

8 *(se considérer)* **je ne me tiens pas encore pour battu** I don't reckon I'm *or* I don't consider myself defeated yet; **se t. pour satisfait** to feel satisfied; **je ne me tiens pas pour un génie** I don't regard myself as *or* think of myself as *or* consider myself a genius

9 *(locutions)* **tenez-vous-en aux ordres** confine yourself to carrying out orders; **d'abord ingénieur puis directrice d'usine, elle ne s'en est pas tenue là** she started out as an engineer, then became a factory manager, but she didn't stop there; **tenons-nous-en là pour aujourd'hui** let's leave it at that for today, let's call it a day; **je ne m'en tiendrai pas à ses excuses** I won't be content with a mere apology from him/her; **ne pas se t. de** *(joie, impatience)* to be beside oneself with; **on ne se tenait plus de rire** we were in absolute fits (of laughter); **ils ont détourné, tiens-toi bien, 10 millions d'euros!** they embezzled, wait for it, 10 million euros!

10 *(locutions)* **je ne supporterai pas tes insolences, tiens-toi-le pour dit!** I'll say this only once, I won't put up with your rudeness!; **on lui a ordonné de ne plus revenir et il semble qu'il se le soit tenu pour dit** he was told never to come back and he seems to have got the message

tennis [tenis] **NM 1** *(activité)* tennis; **jouer au t.** to play tennis; **t. sur gazon** lawn tennis; **t. en salle** indoor tennis; **t. de table** table tennis **2** *(court)* (tennis) court

NMPL OU NFPL *(chaussures* ▸ *pour le tennis)* tennis shoes; *(▸ pour la marche) Br* trainers, *Am* sneakers

tennisman [tenisman] *(pl* **tennismans** *ou* **tennismen** [-men]) **NM** (male) tennis player

tenon [tənɔ̃] **NM 1** *Tech* tenon **2** *(d'une couronne dentaire)* pivot

• **à tenon ADJ assemblage à t.** tenon joint **ADV assembler à t.** to tenon

ténor [tenɔr] **NM 1** *Mus* tenor **2** *Fig (vedette)* big name; **tous les (grands) ténors de la politique seront là** all the big political names will be there

ADJ *Mus* **saxophone t.** tenor saxophone

tenseur [tɑ̃sœr] **ADJ M** *Anat* tensor

NM 1 *Anat & Math* tensor **2** = **tendeur**

tensif, -ive [tɑ̃sif, -iv] **ADJ** *Méd* tensive

tensioactif, -ive [tɑ̃sjɔaktif, -iv] *Chim* **ADJ** surface-active, surfactant

NM surface-active *or* wetting agent, surfactant

tension [tɑ̃sjɔ̃] **NF 1** *(étirement)* tension, tightness; *Tech* **t. de courroie** belt tension; *Tech* **t. de cisaillement** shear stress; *Tech* **t. de rupture** breaking strain *or* stress

2 *(état psychique)* **t. (nerveuse)** tension, strain, nervous stress; **elle est dans un tel état de t. qu'un rien la met en colère** she's so tense that the slightest thing makes her lose her temper

3 *Fig (désaccord, conflit, difficulté)* tension; **la t. monte entre les deux pays** tension is mounting between the two countries

4 *Fig (effort intellectuel intense)* **t. d'esprit** mental effort; **t. intellectuelle** mental stress

5 *Élec* voltage, tension; **t. de coupure/grille** cut-off/grid voltage; **t. de 2000 volts** tension of 2,000 volts; **t. nulle** zero voltage *or* potential; **basse/haute t.** low/high voltage; **danger, haute t.** *(sur panneau)* beware, high voltage; **sans t.** dead

6 *Méd* **t. artérielle** *ou* **vasculaire** blood pressure; **prendre la t. de qn** to check sb's blood pressure; *Fam* **avoir** *ou* **faire de la t.** to have high blood pressure▫; *Fam* **avoir deux de t.** to be all sluggish

7 *Ling* tenseness

8 *Phys (d'un liquide)* tension; *(d'un gaz)* pressure; **t. superficielle** surface tension

• **à basse tension ADJ** *Élec* low-voltage, low-tension

• **à haute tension ADJ** *Élec* high-voltage, high-tension; **câbles à haute t.** high-tension cables

• **sous tension ADJ 1** *Élec (fil)* live; **être sous t.** to be switched on, to be powered up; **mettre sous t.** *(circuit)* to apply the voltage to, to switch on; *(appareil)* to switch on **2** *(nerveux)* tense, under stress; **tout le monde était sous t.** everybody was under stress **ADV mettre un appareil sous t.** to switch on an appliance

tensive [tɑ̃siv] *voir* **tensif**

tensoriel, -elle [tɑ̃sɔrjel] **ADJ calcul t.** tensor calculus

tentaculaire [tɑ̃takylɛr] **ADJ 1** *Zool* tentacular **2** *Fig (ville)* sprawling; *(industrie, structure)* gigantic; *(organisme)* octopus-like; **une entreprise t.** a massive *or* gigantic organization

tentacule [tɑ̃takyl] **NM** *Zool* tentacle

tentant, -e [tɑ̃tɑ̃, -ɑ̃t] **ADJ** *(nourriture)* tempting; *(projet, pari, idée)* tempting; *(offre, suggestion)* tempting, attractive

tentateur, -trice [tɑ̃tatœr, -tris] **ADJ** *(propos)* tempting; *(sourire, charme)* alluring

NM tempter; *Rel* **le T.** the Tempter

• **tentatrice NF** temptress

tentation [tɑ̃tasjɔ̃] **NF 1** *(attrait, désir)* temptation; **céder** *ou* **succomber à la t.** to yield to temptation; **ne cède pas à la t. de l'humilier en public** don't give in to temptation and humiliate him/her in public; **avoir** *ou* **éprouver la t. de faire qch** to be tempted to do sth; **et si vous aviez la t. de nous rejoindre...** and if you felt tempted to join us... **2** *Rel* **induire qn en t.** to lead sb into temptation

tentative [tɑ̃tativ] **NF 1** *(essai)* attempt; **faire une t.** to make an attempt; **une t. d'évasion** an escape attempt, an attempted escape; **une t. de suicide** a suicide attempt, an attempted suicide; **faire une t. de suicide** *ou Fam* **une t.** to try to commit suicide; **faire une nouvelle t. de suicide** to make another suicide attempt; **faire une t. de conciliation** to make an attempt at reconciliation, to attempt reconciliation **2** *Jur* **t. d'assassinat** *ou* **de meurtre** attempted murder; **il a été accusé de t. d'assassinat** he has been charged with attempted murder

tentatrice [tɑ̃tatris] *voir* **tentateur**

tente [tɑ̃t] **NF 1** *(de camping)* tent; *(à une garden-party)* marquee; **monter une t.** to put up *or* to pitch a tent; **coucher sous la t.** to sleep under canvas; **t. conique** bell tent; **t. igloo** igloo tent

2 *(chapiteau de cirque)* (circus) tent; **la grande t.** the big top

3 *Méd* **t. à oxygène** oxygen tent

4 *Naut* awning

tenter [3] [tɑ̃te] **VT 1** *(risquer, essayer)* to try, to attempt; **t. d'inutiles efforts pour...** to make useless attempts to...; **t. une expédition de secours** to mount a rescue attempt; **t. une ascension difficile** to attempt a difficult climb; **je vais tout t. pour la convaincre** I'll try everything to convince her; **t. le tout pour le tout** to go for broke; **c'est une expérience à t.** it's worth having a go *or* giving it a try; **t. de faire qch** to try *or* to attempt *or Sout* to endeavour to do sth; **t. de se suicider** to attempt (to commit) suicide, to try to commit suicide, to make a suicide attempt **2** *(soumettre à une tentation)* to tempt; **le serpent tenta Ève** the serpent tempted Eve; **le gâteau me tentait** the cake looked very tempting; **cela m'a toujours tenté de partir là-bas** I've always been tempted to go there; **se laisser t.** to give in to temptation; **j'ai envie de me laisser t.** *(accepter)* I'm tempted to say yes; *(faire quelque chose)* I'm tempted to do it; **laisse-toi t.** be a devil; **il te propose une sortie, laisse-toi t.** he's offering to take you out, so why not accept?; **être tenté de faire qch** to be tempted *or* to feel inclined to do sth; **je suis tenté de tout abandonner** I feel like dropping the whole thing; **je serais tenté de croire qu'il est responsable, lui aussi** I'm tempted to believe that he is responsible too; **t. (la) fortune** *ou* **la chance** *ou* **le sort, t. sa chance** to try one's luck; *Fam* **t. le coup** to give it a try *or* go, to have a try *or* go; *Fig* **t. le diable** to tempt fate; *Fig* **t. la Providence** to tempt Providence

tenture [tɑ̃tyr] **NF 1** *(tapisserie)* hanging; *(ensemble de tapisseries)* hangings; **t. murale** wall-covering

2 *(rideaux) Br* curtain, *Am* drape

3 *Belg (double rideau)* (thick) *Br* curtain *or Am* drape

4 *(pour un service funèbre)* funeral hanging

tenu, -e[1] [təny] **PP** *voir* **tenir**

ADJ 1 bien t. *(maison, cahier de devoirs, registres, comptes etc)* well kept, tidy; *(jardin)* neat, trim; *(enfant)* neatly turned out; **mal t.** *(enfant, jardin etc)* neglected, uncared for; *(maison, cahier de devoirs, registres, comptes etc)* badly kept, untidy

2 *(astreint)* **être t. de faire qch** to be obliged to do sth; **les passants sont tenus de marcher sur le trottoir** pedestrians must walk on the pavement; **le médecin est t. au secret professionnel** doctors are bound by professional confidentiality; **nous sommes tenus à la discrétion** we're obliged to be very discreet; **être t. de faire qch** to have to do sth; **je me sens t. de la prévenir** I feel morally obliged *or* duty-bound to warn her

3 *(pari)* **t.!** done!, you're on!

4 *Bourse (actions)* firm

5 *Mus* sustained, held

NM *Ftbl & Boxe* holding

ténu, -e [teny] **ADJ 1** *(mince* ▸ *fil, pointe)* fine, slender; *(▸ voix, air, brume)* thin; *(▸ espoir)* slender, slight, slim **2** *(subtil* ▸ *raison, distinction)* tenuous; *(▸ nuance)* subtle, fine; *(▸ lien)* tenuous

TENUE[2] [təny]

• holding **A3, 7, 8**	• running **A2**
• firmness **A4**	• posture **B1**
• behaviour **B2**	• appearance **B3**
• clothes, outfit **B4**	• quality **B5**

NF A. 1 *(d'une séance, d'un rassemblement)* **ils ont interdit la t. de la réunion dans nos locaux** they banned the meeting from being held on our premises; **pendant la t. du concile** while the council was in session

2 *(gestion* ▸ *d'une maison, d'un établissement)* running; **je ne peux pas m'occuper en plus de la t. de la maison** I can't look after the running of the house as well; **l'école est réputée pour sa t.** the school is renowned for being well-run

3 *Aut* **t. de route** road holding; **avoir une bonne t. de route** to have good road-holding; **avoir une mauvaise t. de route** to have poor road holding

4 *Bourse (fermeté)* firmness; **la bonne/mauvaise t. des valeurs** the strong/poor performance of the stock market

5 *Compta* **t. de caisse** petty cash management; *Compta* **t. des comptes, t. des livres** bookkeeping

6 *Équitation (d'un cheval)* stamina

7 *Mus* holding

8 *Naut (qualité de mouillage)* hold, holding

9 *Ling* tenseness

B. 1 *(attitude corporelle)* posture, position; **trop d'élèves ont une mauvaise t. lorsqu'ils écrivent** too many pupils adopt a bad posture when writing

2 *(comportement, conduite)* behaviour; **manquer totalement de t.** to behave appallingly; **voyons, un peu de t.!** come now, behave yourself!

3 *(aspect extérieur d'une personne)* appearance; **sa t. négligée/stricte** his/her slovenly/austere appearance; **ils exigent de leurs employés une t. correcte** they require their employees to be smartly dressed

4 *(habits ▸ gén)* clothes, outfit, dress; *(▸ de policier, de militaire, de pompier)* uniform; **une t. de sport** sports gear *or* kit; **dans ma t. de travail** in my work clothes; **t. correcte exigée** *(à l'entrée d'un restaurant)* dress code; **t. de cérémonie, grande t.** full-dress *or* dress uniform; **t. de soirée** evening dress

5 *(rigueur intellectuelle)* quality; **un roman d'une haute t.** a fine novel; **un magazine d'une haute t.** a quality magazine

6 *Équitation (d'un cavalier)* seat

7 *Tex* firmness

• **en grande tenue** ADJ *Mil* in full-dress *or* dress uniform; **officiers en grande t.** officers in dress uniform

• **en petite tenue** ADJ scantily dressed *or* clad, in one's underwear; **se promener en petite t.** to walk around with hardly a stitch on

• **en tenue** ADJ *(militaire, policier)* uniformed; **ce jour-là, je n'étais pas en t.** *(militaire)* I was in civilian clothes that day; *(policier)* I was in plain clothes that day

• **en tenue légère** = **en petite tenue**

---

ténuité [tenɥite] NF *Littéraire* **1** *(minceur)* slenderness, thinness **2** *(subtilité)* tenuousness

tenure [tənyr] NF *Hist (système)* tenure; *(terre)* holding

TEP [teəpe] NM *Com (abrév* **terminal électronique de paiement***)* electronic payment terminal, PDQ
NF *Méd (abrév* **tomographie à émission de positrons***)* PET

tep [tɛp] NF INV *(abrév* **tonne d'équivalent pétrole***)* TOE

tequila [tekila] NF tequila

TER [teəɛr] NM *Transp (abrév* **transport express régional***)* = French regional network of trains and coaches

ter [tɛr] ADV **1** *(dans des numéros de rue)* ≃ b **2** *(à répéter trois fois)* three times; *Mus* ter

téraoctet [teraɔktɛ] NM *Ordinat* terabyte

tératogène [teratɔʒɛn] ADJ *Méd* teratogenic

tératologie [teratɔlɔʒi] NF *Méd & Biol* teratology

terbium [tɛrbjɔm] NM *Chim* terbium

tercet [tɛrsɛ] NM *Littérature* tercet

térébenthine [terebɑ̃tin] NF turpentine

térébinthe [terebɛ̃t] NM *Bot* terebinth, turpentine tree

térébrant, -e [terebrɑ̃, -ɑ̃t] ADJ **1** *(insecte)* boring, *Spéc* terebrant **2** *Méd (douleur)* piercing; *(ulcération)* deep

Tergal® [tɛrgal] NM *Tex Br* Terylene®, *Am* Dacron®

tergiversations [tɛrʒivɛrsasjɔ̃] NFPL prevarication; **après bien des t.** after a lot of prevarication; **cessez vos t.** stop prevaricating

tergiverser [3] [tɛrʒivɛrse] VI to prevaricate

termaillage [tɛrmajaʒ] NM *Écon* leads and lags

terme [tɛrm] NM **1** *(dans l'espace)* end, *Sout* term; **le t. de la course est une île du Pacifique** the race ends on the shores of a Pacific island

2 *(dans le temps)* end, *Sout* term; **parvenir** *ou* **toucher à son t.** *(aventure, relation)* to reach its conclusion *or Sout* term; **sa convalescence touche à son t.** his/her convalescence will soon be over; **la restructuration doit aller jusqu'à son t.** the restructuring must be carried through to its conclusion; **quel est le t. de leur mandat?** when does their mandate end?; **mettre un t. à qch** to put an end to sth; **mets un t. à tes récriminations** stop complaining

3 *(date butoir)* term, deadline; **passé ce t., vous devrez payer des intérêts** after that date, interest becomes due; **t. de livraison** delivery deadline

4 *(échéance d'un loyer)* date for payment of rent; *(montant du loyer)* rent; **l'augmentation prendra effet au t. de janvier** the increase applies to rent paid as from January; **avoir plusieurs termes de retard** to be several months behind (with one's rent); **t. de bail** term of lease

5 *(date d'un accouchement)* **le t. est prévu pour le 16 juin** the baby is due on 16 June; **elle a dépassé le t. de deux semaines** she is (two weeks) overdue

6 *(versement)* instalment; **payable en deux termes** payable in two instalments

7 *Banque & Bourse* date for payment; *Compta* **t. de liquidation** account *or* settlement period

8 *Jur* term; **t. de rigueur** latest due date; **t. de grâce** days of grace; **demander un t. de grâce** *(délai)* to ask for time to pay; **t. de préavis** notice period

9 *(mot)* term, word; **employer le t. propre** to use the right word; **ce furent ses propres termes** those were his/her very words; **en termes simples** in plain *or* simple terms; **il commenta la pièce en termes peu flatteurs** he commented on the play in rather unflattering terms; **parler de qn en bons/mauvais termes** to speak well/ill of sb; **je ne me suis pas exprimé en ces termes** that's not (quite) what I said; **puis, elle s'exprima en ces termes** then she said this; **il ne l'a pas dit en ces termes mais...** he didn't put it in quite those terms *or* words but...; **en d'autres termes** in other words; **t. argotique** slang expression; **termes commerciaux** commercial terms; **termes commerciaux internationaux** incoterms; **un t. de médecine/droit** a medical/legal term; **t. de métier** professional *or* technical term; **t. technique** technical term

10 *Beaux-Arts, Phil & Math* term

• **termes** NMPL **1** *(sens littéral d'un écrit)* wording *(UNCOUNT)*, terms; **les termes de la loi sont indiscutables** the wording of the law leaves no room for doubt **2** *(relations)* terms; **être en bons/mauvais termes avec qn** to be on friendly/bad terms with sb; **en quels termes êtes-vous?** what kind of terms are you on?; **en quels termes l'a-t-il quittée?** what terms were they on when he left her? **3** *(conditions ▸ d'un contrat)* terms, terms and conditions; **termes de paiement** terms of payment; *Écon* **termes de l'échange** commodity terms of trade

• **à court terme** ADJ *(prêt, projet)* short-term; *(prévisions)* short-term, short-range; *Fin (factures)* short-dated ADV in the short term *or* run

• **à long terme** ADJ *(prêt, projet)* long-term; *(prévisions)* long-term, long-range; *Fin (factures)* long-dated ADV in the long term *or* run; **il faut prévoir à long t.** you have to look to the long term

• **à terme** ADJ **1** *Banque* **compte à t.** = deposit account requiring notice for withdrawals, *Am* time deposit; **compte à t. de 30 jours** 30-days account; **assurance à t.** term insurance; **à t. fixe** fixed-term **2** *Bourse* **marché à t.** forward market; *(change)* futures market; **opérations à t.** forward transactions; **valeurs à t.** securities dealt in for the account ADV **1** *(à la fin)* to the end, to its conclusion; **arriver à t.** *(délai)* to expire; *(travail)* to reach completion; *(paiement)* to fall due; **conduire** *ou* **mener à t. une entreprise** to bring an undertaking to a successful conclusion, to carry an undertaking through successfully **2** *(tôt ou tard)* sooner or later, in the end, in the long run; **leur politique est condamnée à t.** their policy is doomed to failure in the long run **3** *Com (à la date prévue)* on credit **4** *Fin* **acheter à t.** to buy forward; **vendre à t.** to sell forward **5** *Méd* at term; **bébé né à t.** baby born at full term; **être à t.** *(femme enceinte)* to have reached term

• **au terme de** PRÉP *(à la fin de)* at the end of, in the final stage of; **parvenir au t. de son existence/aventure** to reach the end of one's life/adventure

• **aux termes de** PRÉP *(selon)* under the terms of; **aux termes de la loi/du traité** under the terms of the law/of the treaty

• **avant terme** ADV prematurely; **bébé né avant t.** premature baby; **il est né six semaines avant t.** he was six weeks premature

terminaison [tɛrminɛzɔ̃] NF **1** *(dénouement, fin)* end; **la t. de difficiles négociations** the end of difficult negotiations

2 *Jur (action ▸ de procès)* termination

3 *Anat* **terminaisons nerveuses** nerve endings

4 *Ling* ending; **mot à t. en "al"** word ending in "al"

terminal, -e, -aux, -ales [tɛrminal, -o] ADJ **1** *(qui forme l'extrémité)* terminal

2 *(final)* last, final

3 *Méd (phase, malade)* terminal; **cancer en phase terminale** terminal cancer; **être en phase terminale** *(malade)* to be terminally ill

4 *Scol* **classe terminale** *Br* ≃ final year, upper sixth (form), *Am* ≃ senior year, twelfth grade
NM **1** *Ordinat* terminal; **t. de consultation** look-up terminal; **t. distant** remote terminal; **t. éloigné** remote terminal; **t. graphique** graphic terminal, graphic display device; **t. intelligent** smart terminal, remote station; *Com* **t. de paiement électronique** electronic payment terminal, PDQ, pinpad; *Com* **t. de paiement en ligne** on-line terminal; **t. passif** dumb terminal; **t. de pilotage** control terminal; **t. point de vente** point-of-sale terminal **2** *Pétr* **t. pétrolier** oil terminal **3** *Transp* terminal; **t. d'aérogare** air terminal; **t. maritime** shipping terminal; **t. urbain** *(d'une ligne aérienne)* city terminal

• **terminale** NF *Scol Br* ≃ final year, upper sixth (form), *Am* ≃ senior year, twelfth grade; **élève de terminale** *Br* ≃ upper sixth former, *Am* ≃ twelfth grader

terminateur [tɛrminatœr] NM *Astron* terminator

terminer [3] [tɛrmine] VT **1** *(mener à sa fin ▸ repas, tâche, lecture, lettre)* to finish (off), to end; *(travail)* to complete, to finish (off); **c'est terminé, rendez vos copies** time's up, hand in your papers

2 *(stopper ▸ séance, débat)* to end, to close, to bring to an end *or* a close

3 *(être le dernier élément de)* to end; **le volume qui termine la série comprend un index** the last volume in the series includes an index

4 *(finir ▸ plat, boisson)* to finish (off), to eat up

5 *Tél* **t. une session** to log off, to log out

USAGE ABSOLU *(finir)* **j'ai presque terminé** I've nearly finished; **pour t., je remercie tous les participants** finally, let me thank all those who took part; *Rad* **terminé!** out!

• **(en) terminer avec** VT IND to finish with; **je termine avec M. Dubois et je suis à vous** I'll just finish with Mr Dubois and then I'll be with you; **il faut en t. avec cette histoire** we have to put an end to this

VPR **se terminer** **1** *(arriver à sa fin ▸ durée, période, saison)* to draw to a close; **la chanson/guerre vient de se t.** the song/war has just finished **2** *(se conclure ▸ soirée, film etc)* to end (**par** with); *(▸ rue, mot)* to end (**par** in); **se t. bien/mal** *(film, histoire)* to have a happy/an unhappy ending; *(équipée, menée)* to turn out well/disastrously; **comment tout cela va-t-il se t.?** where's it all going to end?; **leur aventure s'est terminée au poste** the whole affair ended up with them being taken to the police station; **se t. en** to end in; **se t. en pointe/spirale/v** to end in a point/spiral/v; **ça s'est terminé en drame** it ended in tragedy; **l'histoire se termine par la mort du héros** the story ends with the death of the hero

terminologie [tɛrminɔlɔʒi] NF terminology

terminologue [tɛrminɔlɔg] NMF terminologist

terminus [tɛrminys] NM terminus; **t.! tout le monde descend!** last stop! all change!
ADJ INV **gare t.** terminus

termite [tɛrmit] NM *Entom* termite; *Fig* **faire un travail de t.** to work secretly and destructively

termitière [tɛrmitjɛr] NF termite mound, *Spéc* termitarium

ternaire [tɛrnɛr] ADJ ternary; *Mus* **mesure t.** triple time

terne [tɛrn] ADJ **1** *(sans éclat ▸ cheveux, regard)* dull; *(▸ teint)* sallow **2** *(ennuyeux)* dull, drab, dreary; *(voix)* dull, flat; **il a eu une vie bien t.** he led a very dull *or* dreary life; **son style est t.** his/her style is dull *or* lacklustre **3** *(inintéressant)* dull; **un élève t.** a slow pupil; **une intelligence t.** a slow mind

ternir [32] [tɛrnir] VT **1** *(métal, argenterie)* to tarnish; *(glace)* to dull **2** *Fig (honneur, réputation, mémoire)* to tarnish, to stain, to smear; *(souvenir, beauté)* to cloud, to dull; **un amour que les ans n'ont pu t.** a love undimmed by the passing years
VPR **se ternir** **1** *(métal)* to tarnish; *(miroir)* to dull **2** *Fig (honneur, réputation)* to become tarnished *or* stained; *(beauté, nouveauté)* to fade; *(souvenir)* to fade, to grow dim

ternissure [ternisyr] **NF 1** *(condition)* tarnish, tarnished appearance **2** *(tache)* tarnished *or* dull spot

terrafungine [terafɔ̃ʒin] **NF** *Pharm* oxytetracycline, Terramycin®

TERRAIN [terɛ̃]

- soil **A1, 2**
- (plot of) land **B1, 2**
- field **B3, 4, C1**
- ground **A1, 3, B3, 5, C3, 4**

NM A. *SOL, TERRE* **1** *Géol* soil, ground; **terrains alluviaux** alluvial land; **terrains calcaires** limestone soil *or* areas; **t. sédimentaire/volcanique** sedimentary/volcanic formations

2 *Agr* soil; **t. argileux/fertile** clayey/fertile soil; **t. gras/humide/sec** sticky/damp/dry soil; **t. meuble** loose soil

3 *(relief)* ground, terrain; **t. accidenté** uneven terrain; **t. en pente** sloping ground

B. *LIEU À USAGE SPÉCIFIQUE* **1** *Constr* piece *or* plot of land; **le t. coûte cher à Genève** land is expensive in Geneva; **t. à bâtir** development land *(UNCOUNT)*, building plot; **t. loti** developed site; **t. vague** piece of waste ground *or* land, *Am* empty lot

2 *Agr* land; **t. cultivé/en friche** cultivated/uncultivated land

3 *Sport & (loisirs) (lieu du jeu)* field, *Br* pitch; *(moitié défendue par une équipe)* half; *(installations)* ground; **t. d'aventure** adventure playground; **t. de boules** = ground for playing boules; **t. de camping** campsite, campground; **t. de football/rugby** football/rugby field *or Br* pitch; **t. de golf** golf course *or* links; **t. de jeux** playground; **t. de sports** sports field *or* ground

4 *Aviat* field; **t. (d'aviation)** airfield; **t. d'atterrissage** landing field

5 *Mil* ground; *(d'une bataille)* battleground; *(d'une guerre)* war *or* combat zone; **t. d'exercice** *ou* **militaire** training ground; **t. miné** minefield; **l'armée occupe le t. conquis** the army is occupying the captured territory; **la prochaine offensive nous permettra de gagner du t.** the next offensive will enable us to gain ground

6 *(lieu d'un duel)* duelling place

C. *SENS ABSTRAIT* **1** *(lieux d'étude)* field; **vous n'êtes pas allé sur le t., vous ne savez pas de quoi vous parlez** you've not been in the field *or* you've no practical experience, you don't know what you're talking about; **un homme de t.** a man with practical experience

2 *(domaine de connaissances)* **être sur son t.** to be on familiar ground; **ils discutent de chiffres et je ne peux pas les suivre sur ce t.** they're discussing figures, so I'm out of my depth; **situons la discussion sur le t. juridique/psychologique** let's discuss this from the legal/psychological angle

3 *(ensemble de circonstances)* **elle connaît le t., laissons-la décider** she knows the situation, let her decide; **sonde le t. avant d'agir** see how the land lies before making a move; **je ne te suis pas sur ce t.** I'm not with you there; **être en t. neutre/sur un t. glissant** to be on neutral/on a dangerous ground; **être sur un t. mouvant** to be on shaky ground; **trouver un t. d'entente** to find common ground; **t. brûlant** dangerous ground; **perdre/gagner du t.** *(monnaie, entreprise)* to lose/to gain ground; **l'entreprise regagne du t. sur le marché français** the company is making up lost ground on the French market

4 *Méd* ground; **l'enfant présente un t. favorable aux angines** the child is susceptible to throat infections

terrarium [terarjɔm] **NM** terrarium

terrasse [teras] **NF 1** *(balcon)* balcony; *(entre maison et jardin)* terrace, (raised) patio; *(sur le toit)* (roof) terrace

2 *(d'un café, d'un restaurant)* **être assis à la t.** to sit outside; **elle attendait à la t. d'un café** she was waiting at a table outside a café

3 *(d'un jardin, d'un parc)* terrace, terraced garden

4 *(d'une pierre, d'un marbre)* terrace

• **en terrasse ADJ 1** *Agr* terrace *(avant n)*; **jardin en t.** terraced garden; **cultures en terrasses** terrace cultivation **2** *(à l'extérieur d'un café)* outside; **les clients en t.** the customers sitting outside; **prix des consommations en t.** price of drinks served outside **ADV** *(consommer)* outside; **nous prendrons le café en t.** we'll have our coffee at one of the outside tables

terrassement [terasmɑ̃] **NM 1** *(action)* excavation **2** *(remblai)* earthwork, excavation

• **de terrassement ADJ** *(travail)* excavation *(avant n)*; *(engin)* earth-moving; *(outil)* digging *(avant n)*

terrasser [3] [terase] **VT 1** *(jeter à terre, renverser)* to bring *or* to strike down; **on y voit un homme terrassant un taureau** it shows a man striking down a bull

2 *(foudroyer)* to strike down; *(sujet: maladie)* to lay low; **être terrassé par une crise cardiaque** to be struck down by a heart attack

3 *(atterrer, accabler)* to crush, to shatter; **l'annonce de leur mort l'a terrassé** he was shattered by the news of their death; **terrassé par le chagrin** prostrate *or* overcome with grief

4 *Agr (vignoble)* to work the soil of

terrassier [terasje] **NM** workman *(employed for excavation work)*

TERRE [ter]

NM

- Earth **A1**
- ground **B1, 8**
- country **B4**
- soil **B6, C1**
- earth **A2, B8, C**
- land **B2–6**
- estate **B5**
- clay **C2**

NMPL

- estate

NF A. *GLOBE* **1** *(planète)* **la T.** the Earth; **sciences de la T.** earth sciences

2 *(monde terrestre)* earth; **le bonheur existe-t-il sur la t.?** is there such a thing as happiness on this earth *or* in this world?; **si je suis encore sur cette t.** if I am still alive; **sur le point de quitter cette t.** about to give up the ghost

B. *SOL* **1** *(surface du sol)* ground; **j'avais l'impression que la t. se dérobait sous moi** I felt as if the ground was giving way beneath me; **la neige couvrait la t.** the ground was covered in snow; **elle souleva l'enfant de t.** she picked the child up (from the ground); **t. battue** *(dans une habitation)* earth *or* hard-earth *or* mud floor; *(dans une cour)* bare ground; *(sur un court de tennis)* clay (surface); **mettre qn plus bas que t.** *(en actes)* to treat sb like dirt; *(en paroles)* to tear sb to shreds

2 *(élément opposé à la mer)* land *(UNCOUNT)*; **on les transporte par voie de t.** they are transported overland *or* by land; **nous sommes en vue de la t.** we are in sight of land; **nous avons navigué sans nous éloigner des terres** we sailed close to the coast; *Naut* **t.!** land ahoy!; **prendre t.** to make land; **sur la t. ferme** on dry land, on terra firma

3 *(région du monde)* land; **les terres arctiques** the Arctic regions; **les terres australes** the Southern lands; **il reste des terres inexplorées** there are still some unexplored regions

4 *(pays)* land, country; **la t. de France** French soil; **(la) t. Adélie** Adelie Land; **la t. d'Arnhem** Arnhem Land; **la t. de Baffin** Baffin Island; **t. d'accueil** host country; **t. d'exil** place of exile; **t. natale** native land *or* country; **la T. promise** the Promised Land; **la T. sainte** the Holy Land

5 *(terrain)* land *(UNCOUNT)*, estate; **acheter une t.** to buy a piece of land

6 *(symbole de la vie rurale)* **la t.** the land, the soil; **homme de la t.** man of the soil; **revenir à/quitter la t.** to return to/to leave the land

7 *Beaux-Arts* **ligne de t.** ground line

8 *Élec Br* earth, *Am* ground; **mettre** *ou* **relier qch à la t.** *Br* to earth *or Am* to ground sth

C. *MATIÈRE* **1** *(substance ▸ gén)* earth, soil; **ne joue pas avec la t.** don't play in the dirt; **l'odeur de la t. fraîchement retournée** the smell of freshly-dug earth *or* soil; **mettre** *ou* **porter qn en t.** to bury sb; **t. à vigne/à blé** soil suitable for wine-growing/for wheat; **t. arable** farmland; **t. de bruyère** peaty soil; **t. grasse** heavy *or* clayey soil; **t. noire** chernozem, black earth; **t. végétale** topsoil; **t. vierge** virgin soil

2 *(matière première)* clay, earth; **t. cuite** earthenware; **en t. cuite** earthenware *(avant n)*; **des terres cuites** earthenware *(UNCOUNT)*; **t. à foulon** fuller's earth; **t. glaise** (brick) clay, *Br* brickearth; **t. de pipe** pipeclay; **t. rouge** terracotta

3 *(pigment)* **t. d'ombre** terra ombra, raw umber; *Chim* **terres rares** rare earths; **t. de Sienne** sienna; **t. verte** green earth, terra verde

• **terres NFPL** *(domaine, propriété)* estate, estates; **vivre sur/de ses terres** to live on/off one's estates

• **à terre ADV 1** *(sur le sol)* on the ground; **poser un fardeau à t.** to put a load down (on the ground); **frapper qn à t.** to strike sb when he's down **2** *Naut* on land; **descendre à t.** to land; **vous pourrez rester à t. deux heures** you may stay ashore for two hours **3** *Can Fam (déprimé)* down, depressed; **être à t.** to be *or* feel down

• **en pleine terre ADV** *Agr* in the open, in open ground

• **par terre ADJ** *(ruiné, anéanti)* spoilt, wrecked; **avec la pluie, notre promenade est par t.** the rain has ruined our plans for a walk *or* put paid to our walk **ADV** *(sur le plancher)* on the floor; *(sur le sol)* on the ground; **pose-le par t.** put it (down) on the floor; **tomber par t.** to fall down; *Fam* **j'ai lavé par t.** I've washed the floor

• **sous terre ADV 1** *(sous le sol)* underground **2** *(locutions)* **j'aurais voulu être à cent pieds sous t.** *ou* **rentrer sous t.** I wished the earth would swallow me up; **je l'ai fait rentrer sous t.** I made him eat humble pie

• **sur terre ADV 1** *(ici-bas)* on (this) earth; **pourquoi sommes-nous sur t.?** why were we put on this earth? **2** *(locutions)* **revenir** *ou* **redescendre sur t.** to come back to earth (with a bump)

terreau, -x [tero] **NM** compost *(UNCOUNT)*

terre-neuvas [ternœva] **NM INV** = **terre-neuvier**

Terre-Neuve [ternœv] **NF** Newfoundland; **à T.** in Newfoundland

terre-neuve [ternœv] **NM INV** *(chien)* Newfoundland

terre-neuvien, -enne [ternœvjɛ̃, -ɛn] *(mpl* **terre-neuviens,** *fpl* **terre-neuviennes) ADJ** of/from Newfoundland

• **Terre-Neuvien, -enne NM,F** Newfoundlander

terre-neuvier [ternœvje] *(pl* **terre-neuviers) NM 1** *(navire)* fishing boat (from Newfoundland) **2** *(marin)* fisherman (from Newfoundland)

terre-plein [terplɛ̃] *(pl* **terre-pleins) NM 1** *(sur route)* **t. central** *Br* central reservation, *Am* center divider strip; **t. circulaire** *(dans un rond-point)* central island **2** *Constr* earth platform

terrer [4] [tere] **VT 1** *Agr & Hort (arbre, plante)* to earth up; *(recouvrir de terre)* to cover over with soil; *(semis)* to earth over **2** *Tex* to full

VPR se terrer 1 *(se mettre à l'abri, se cacher)* to go to ground *or* to earth, to lie low; *(se retirer du monde)* to hide away; **être terré dans** to have gone to earth in, to be holed up in **2** *(dans un terrier)* to go to ground *or* to earth, to burrow; **être terré dans** to have gone to earth in

terrestre [terestr] **ADJ 1** *(qui appartient à notre planète)* earth *(avant n)*, earthly, terrestrial; **la croûte** *ou* **l'écorce t.** the Earth's crust

2 *(qui se passe sur la terre)* earthly, terrestrial; **durant notre vie t.** during our life on earth

3 *(vivant sur la terre ferme)* land *(avant n)*; **animaux/plantes terrestres** land animals/plants

4 *(établi au sol ▸ transport)* land *(avant n)*; *Mil* **effectifs terrestres** land forces

5 *(d'ici-bas ▸ joie, plaisir)* worldly, earthly

terreur [terœr] **NF 1** *(effroi)* terror, dread; **être fou de t.** to be wild with fear; **être glacé de t.** to be terror-stricken; **vivre dans la t.** to be terrified *or* in (a state of) terror; **vivre dans la t. de qch** to live in dread of sth; **avoir la t. de faire qch** to have a terror of doing sth

2 *(terrorisme)* **la t.** terror (tactics); *Hist* **la T.** the (Reign of) Terror; **gouverner par la t.** to rule by terror; **faire régner la t.** to instil terror; **un régime de t.** a reign of terror

3 *(voyou ▸ d'une ville, d'une école)* terror; **jouer les terreurs** to act the bully

4 *(personne ou chose effrayante)* **le patron est sa t.** he's/she's terrified of the boss

5 *Psy* **terreurs nocturnes** night terrors

terreux, -euse [terø, -øz] **ADJ 1** *(couvert de terre ▸ chaussure, vêtement)* muddy; *(▸ mains)* dirty; *(▸ légume)* caked with soil; *(▸ laitue)* gritty **2** *(brun ▸*

couleur, teint, ciel) muddy; **avoir le visage t.** to be ashen faced **3** *(qui rappelle la terre ▸ odeur, goût)* earthy

terrible [teribl] **ADJ 1** *(affreux ▸ nouvelle, accident, catastrophe)* terrible, dreadful; **ce n'est qu'une coupure, rien de (bien) t.** it's just a cut, nothing serious *or* major

2 *(insupportable ▸ chaleur, douleur)* terrible, unbearable; *(▸déception, conditions de vie)* terrible; **elle est t. avec sa façon de bouder sans raison** it's awful the way she sulks for no reason; **ces enfants sont terribles** those children are little terrors

3 *(en intensif ▸ bruit, vent, orage)* terrific, tremendous; **elle a eu une chance t.** she's been incredibly lucky

4 *(terrifiant ▸ colère, cri, rage)* terrible; **il est t. quand il s'énerve** he's awful *or* terrible when he loses his temper

5 *(pitoyable)* terrible, awful, dreadful; **le plus t., c'est de savoir que...** the worst thing *or* part of it is knowing that...

6 *Fam (fantastique)* terrific, great; **t.!** great!, smashing!; **pas t.** nothing special

ADV *Fam (très bien)* great; **son nouveau spectacle marche t.** his/her new show is going great; **ça ne va pas t.** things aren't too great

terriblement [teribləmɑ̃] **ADV** terribly, dreadfully

terrien, -enne [terjɛ̃, -ɛn] **ADJ 1** *(qui possède des terres)* landowning; **noblesse terrienne** landed aristocracy; **propriétaire t.** landowner **2** *(rural)* rural; **les habitudes terriennes** rural customs **3** *(de la Terre)* of the Earth

NM,F 1 *(habitant de la Terre)* inhabitant of the Earth; *(dans un récit de science-fiction)* earthling **2** *(paysan)* countryman **3** *(opposé au marin)* landsman, *Péj* landlubber

terrier[1] [terje] **NM** *(abri ▸ d'un lapin)* (rabbit) hole *or* burrow; *(▸d'un renard)* earth, hole, foxhole; *(▸d'un blaireau)* set; *(▸d'une taupe)* hole

terrier[2] [terje] **NM** *(chien)* terrier

terrifiant, -e [terifjɑ̃, -ɑ̃t] **ADJ 1** *(effrayant)* terrifying **2** *Fam (extraordinaire)* amazing, incredible

terrifier [9] [terifje] **VT** to terrify

terril [teril] **NM** slag heap

terrine [terin] **NF 1** *(récipient)* terrine dish **2** *Culin* terrine; **t. de lapin** rabbit terrine *or* pâté

terrir [32] [terir] **VI** *Pêche* **poissons qui terrissent** fish living in coastal waters

territoire [teritwar] **NM 1** *Géog* territory; **sur le t. français** on French territory; **en t. ennemi** in enemy territory; **le T. du Nord** Northern Territory; *Can* **les Territoires du Nord-Ouest** Northwest Territories; *Pol* **les territoires occupés** the occupied territories

2 *Admin* area; **territoires d'outre-mer** (French) overseas territories

3 *(de juge, d'évêque)* jurisdiction

4 *Zool* territory; **les animaux marquent leur t.** animals mark (out) their territory

5 *(secteur, fief)* territory

6 *Com & Mktg (d'un représentant)* territory; **t. exclusif** exclusive territory; **t. de vente** sales territory

territorial, -e, -aux, -ales [teritɔrjal, -o] **ADJ** territorial

NM *Mil* territorial

• **territoriale NF** *Mil* territorial army

territorialité [teritɔrjalite] **NF** *Jur* territoriality

terroir [terwar] **NM 1** *Agr* soil; **goût de t.** *(d'un vin)* tang of the soil, native tang **2** *(région agricole)* region **3** *(campagne, ruralité)* country; **il a gardé l'accent du t.** he has kept his rural accent; *Fig* **ses livres ont un goût de t.** his/her books are evocative of rural *or* country life

terrorisant, -e [terɔrizɑ̃, -ɑ̃t] **ADJ** terrorizing

terroriser [3] [terɔrize] **VT 1** *(martyriser)* to terrorize **2** *(épouvanter)* to terrify

terrorisme [terɔrism] **NM** terrorism; **t. écologique** eco-terrorism

terroriste [terɔrist] **ADJ** terrorist

NMF terrorist

tertiaire[1] [tersjer] **ADJ 1** *Chim & Méd* tertiary; *Géol* **ère t.** Tertiary era **2** *Admin & Écon* **secteur t.** tertiary sector, service industries

NM 1 *Géol* **le t.** the Tertiary era **2** *Admin & Écon* **le t.** the tertiary sector

tertiaire[2] [tersjer] **NMF** *Rel* tertiary

tertiairisation [tersjerizasjɔ̃], **tertiarisation** [tersjarizasjɔ̃] **NF** *Écon* expansion of the tertiary sector; **la t. de l'économie** the tertiarization of the economy

tertio [tersjo] **ADV** third, thirdly; **t., je n'ai pas le temps** thirdly, I haven't got time

tertre [tertr] **NM 1** *(monticule)* hillock, mound **2** *(sépulture)* **t. (funéraire)** burial mound

tes [te] *voir* **ton**[3]

tessiture [tesityr] **NF** tessitura; *(d'un instrument)* range

tesson [tesɔ̃] **NM** *(de verre, de poterie)* shard; **un mur hérissé de tessons de bouteille** a wall with broken glass all along the top

test[1] [test] **NM 1** *(essai individuel)* test; *(procédé)* testing; **soumettre qn à un t., faire passer un t. à qn** to give sb a test; **t. d'aptitude professionnelle** aptitude test; *Aut* **t. de choc** impact test; **t. comparatif** comparative test; **t. de conformité** compliance test; **t. d'hypothèse** statistical test; *Aut* **t. de roulage** road testing; **un t. de roulage** a road test; **t. à sec** dry run; **t. statistique** statistical test; **t. technique** engineering test; *Aut* **t. de tonneaux** rollover test

2 *(épreuve)* test; **sa réponse sera un t. de sa bonne volonté** his/her answer will be a test of his/her goodwill

3 *Ordinat* test

4 *Méd* test; **t. allergologique** allergy test; **t. cutané** cutaneous reaction test; **t. de dépistage du SIDA** Aids test; **t. de grossesse** pregnancy test

5 *Psy* test; **t. psychométrique** psychometric test; **t. de Rorschach** Rorschach *or* ink blot test

6 *Sport (test-match)* (rugby) test (match)

7 *Mktg* test; **tests** *(procédure)* testing; **t. auprès des consommateurs** consumer test; **t. aveugle** blind test; **t. de la bande dessinée** *ou* **de la bulle** balloon test; **t. comparatif** comparison test; **t. de concept** concept test; **t. d'enquête** enquiry test; **t. de frustration** balloon test; **t. du lendemain** (day-after) recall test; **t. de marché** market test; *(d'un produit)* test marketing, market test; **t. de média** media test; **t. de mémoire** *ou* **de mémorisation** memory *or* recall test; **t. monadique** monadic test; **t. de performance** performance test; **t. de performance du produit** product performance test; **t. sur place** field test; **t. de préférence** preference test; **t. de produit** product test; **t. de rappel** recall test; **t. de reconnaissance** recognition test; **t. de support** media test; **t. de vente** market test

8 *(comme adj; avec ou sans trait d'union)* test *(avant n)*; **population t.** test population; **région t.** test region; *Mktg* **ville-t.** test city

test[2] [test] **NM** *Zool* test

Testament [testamɑ̃] **NM** *Bible* **Ancien/Nouveau T.** Old/New Testament

testament [testamɑ̃] **NM 1** *Jur* will, testament; **faire son t.** to make one's will; **léguer qch à qn par t.** to leave sth to sb in one's will; **ceci est mon t.** this is my last will and testament; **elle l'a mis** *ou* **couché sur son t.** she put him in her will; **t. de vie** living will **2** *(ultime message d'un artiste)* legacy

testamentaire [testamɑ̃ter] **ADJ** testamental

testateur, -trice [testatœr, -tris] **NM,F** testator, *f* testatrix

tester[1] **[3]** [teste] **VT 1** *(déterminer les aptitudes de ▸ élèves)* to test **2** *(vérifier le fonctionnement de ▸ appareil, produit)* to test; *Mktg* to test, to test-market; **t. qch sur le marché** to test-market sth; **t. un questionnaire** to pilot a questionnaire; **testé en laboratoire** laboratory-tested **3** *(mettre à l'épreuve)* to put to the test

tester[2] **[3]** [teste] **VI** *Jur* to make out one's will

testiculaire [testikyler] **ADJ** testicular

testicule [testikyl] **NM** testicle, *Spéc* testis

testimonial, -e, -aux, -ales [testimɔnjal, -o] **ADJ** testimonial

testostérone [testɔsterɔn] **NF** testosterone

têt [tɛ] **NM t. à gaz** beehive shelf; **t. à rôtir** roasting crucible

tétanie [tetani] **NF** *Méd* tetany; **avoir une crise de t.** to go into spasms

tétanique [tetanik] **ADJ** tetanic; **malade t.** person with tetanus

NMF person with tetanus

tétaniser [3] [tetanize] **VT 1** *Méd* to tetanize **2** *Fig* **être tétanisé de peur/de froid** to be petrified/frozen stiff; **la vue des rats l'a tétanisée** she was petrified by the sight of the rats

tétanos [tetanos] **NM** lockjaw, *Spéc* tetanus; *(contraction de muscle)* tetanus

têtard [tetar] **NM 1** *Zool* tadpole **2** *Hort* pollard **3** *Fam (enfant)* kid, brat

TÊTE [tɛt]

• head **A1, 2, 4, 5, B, C2–4, D4, 5, 7–11**	• face **A3**
• person **C1**	• mind **B1**
• top **D1, 4**	• leader **C3**
	• front end **D2**

NF A. *PARTIE DU CORPS* **1** *Anat* head; **dresser** *ou* **redresser la t.** to raise one's head; **la t. haute** with (one's) head held high; **marcher la t. haute** to walk with (one's) head held high; **la t. la première** head first; **de la t. aux pieds** from head to foot *or* toe; **avoir mal à la t.** to have a headache; **avoir la t. lourde** to feel fuzzy, *Br* to have a thick head; **j'ai la t. qui tourne** *(malaise)* my head is spinning; **la t. me tourne** *(panique)* I'm in a spin; **ne tourne pas la t., elle nous regarde** don't look round, she's watching us; **dès qu'il m'a vu, il a tourné la t.** as soon as he saw me, he looked away; **tenir t. à qn** to stand up to sb; *Fam* **en avoir par-dessus la t.** to be sick (and tired) of it; **avoir la t. sur les épaules** to have a good head on one's shoulders; *Fam* **faire une (grosse) t.** *ou* **une t. au carré à qn** to smash sb's face in; **j'en donnerais** *ou* **j'en mettrais ma t. à couper** I'd stake my life on it; *Fam* **tomber sur la t.** to go off one's rocker, to lose it; *Fam* **non mais t'es tombé sur la t. ou quoi?** you must be out of your mind!; *Fam* **ça va pas la t.?** are you mad?; **il ne réfléchit jamais, il fonce t. baissée** he always charges in *or* ahead without thinking; *Fig* **se cogner** *ou* **se taper la t. contre les murs** to bang one's head against a (brick) wall; **se jeter à la t. de qn** to throw oneself at sb

2 *(en référence à la chevelure, à la coiffure)* **se laver la t.** to wash one's hair; **t. nue** bareheaded; **nos chères têtes blondes** *(les enfants)* our little darlings; *Hist* **têtes rondes** Roundheads

3 *(visage, expression)* face; **avoir une bonne t.** to look like a nice person; **ne fais pas cette t.!** don't make *or Br* pull such a long face!; **tu en fais une t.!** what's that look for?; **il a fait une de ces têtes quand je lui ai dit!** you should have seen his face when I told him!; **elle ne savait plus quelle t. faire** she didn't know how to react; **il a une t. à se faire rouler** he looks like he could be conned easily; **jeter** *ou* **lancer qch à la t. de qn** to throw sth in sb's face; *Fam* **il a** *ou* **c'est une t. à claques** he's got a face you want to slap; *très Fam* **t. de con, t. de nœud** dickhead; **faire la t.** to sulk; **faire la t. à qn** to ignore sb; **avec lui, c'est à la t. du client** *(restaurant)* he charges what he feels like; *(professeur)* he gives you a good *Br* mark *or Am* grade if he likes your face

4 *(mesure)* head; **il a une t. de plus que son frère** he's a head taller than his brother; **le favori a été battu d'une courte t.** the favourite was beaten by a short head

5 *Culin* head; **de la t. de veau** calf's head; *Belg* **t. pressée** *(fromage de tête) Br* pork brawn, *Am* headcheese

6 *Sport* header; **faire une t.** to head the ball

7 *Zool* **t. de lion** lionhead

B. *SIÈGE DE LA PENSÉE* **1** *(siège des pensées, de l'imagination, de la mémoire)* mind, head; **il a la t. bourrée de chiffres/dates** his head is stuffed with figures/dates; **il a des rêves plein la t.** he's a dreamer; **une drôle d'idée m'est passée par la t.** a strange idea came into my head; **se mettre qch dans la t.** to get sth into one's head; **se mettre dans la t. que...** to get it into one's head that...; **se mettre dans la t.** *ou* **en t. de faire qch** to make up one's mind to do sth; **elle s'est mis en t. de terminer son livre avant l'automne** she's made up her mind to finish her book before the autumn; **une t. bien faite** a good mind; *Fam* **être une t.** to be brainy, to have brains; *Fam* **avoir** *ou* **attraper la grosse t.** to have a big head, to be big-headed; **avoir toute sa t.** to have all one's faculties; **faire**

sa mauvaise t. to dig one's heels in; *Fam* **ce qu'il a dans la t. il ne l'a pas aux pieds** *ou* **aux talons** when he's made up his mind he wants something there's no stopping him; **avoir la t. chaude, avoir la t. près du bonnet** to be quick-tempered; **monter la t. à qn** to give sb big ideas; **monter à la t. de qn** *(succès)* to go to sb's head; *(chagrin)* to unbalance sb; **se monter la t.** to get carried away; **tourner la t. à qn** to turn sb's head; *Fam* **prendre la t. à qn** *Br* to get up sb's nose, to get on sb's wick, *Am* to tick sb off; *Fam* **prise de t.** pain (in the neck); **avoir la t. vide/dure** to be empty-headed/stubborn; **il est t. en l'air** he's got his head in the clouds; **excuse-moi, j'avais la t. ailleurs** sorry, I was thinking about something else *or* I was miles away; **il n'a pas de t.** *(il est étourdi)* he's scatterbrained *or* a scatterbrain; **ça m'est sorti de la t.** I forgot, it slipped my mind; **il ne sait plus où donner de la t.** he doesn't know whether he's coming or going; **n'en faire qu'à sa t.** to do exactly as one pleases; **je le lirai à t. reposée** I'll take the time to read it in a quiet moment; *Can* **être une t. de Papineau** to be extremely bright

2 *(sang-froid, présence d'esprit)* head; **elle a gardé toute sa t. devant le danger** she kept her head in the face of danger; **avoir** *ou* **garder la t. froide** to keep a cool head

C. *PERSONNE, ANIMAL* **1** *(individu)* person; **plusieurs têtes connues** several familiar faces; **prendre une assurance sur la t. de qn** to take out an insurance policy on sb; *Fam* **être une t. de lard** *ou* **de mule** *ou* **de pioche** to be as stubborn as a mule, to be pig-headed; **t. de linotte** *ou* **d'oiseau** *ou* **sans cervelle** scatterbrain; **t. de cochon** bloody-minded individual; **t. couronnée** crowned head; **forte t.** rebel; *Fam* **une grosse t.** a brain; *Fam* **petite t.** pinhead; *Fam* **avoir ses têtes** to have one's favourites

2 *(vie d'une personne)* head, neck; **jouer** *ou* **risquer sa t.** to risk one's skin; **sauver sa t.** to save one's skin *or* neck

3 *(meneur, leader)* head, leader; **il est la t. du mouvement** he's the leader of the movement; **les têtes pensantes du comité** the brains of the committee

4 *(animal d'un troupeau)* head *inv*; **50 têtes de bétail** 50 head of cattle

D. *PARTIE HAUTE, PARTIE AVANT, DÉBUT* **1** *(faîte)* top; **la t. d'un arbre** a treetop; **la t. d'un mât** the top of a mast

2 *(partie avant)* front end; **la t. du train** the front of the train; **t. de lit** bedhead; **prendre la t. du défilé** to head *or* to lead the march; **prendre la t.** *(marcher au premier rang)* to take the lead; *(commander, diriger)* to take over; **elle prendra la t. de l'entreprise** she'll take over the (running of the) firm; **t. de ligne** *(gén)* terminus, end of the line; *Rail* railhead

3 *(début)* **faites ressortir les têtes de chapitres** make the chapter headings stand out

4 *(dans un classement)* top, head; **les dix élèves qui forment la t. de la classe** the ten best pupils in the class; **t. d'affiche** top of the bill; **être en t. d'affiche** to top the bill; *Pol* **t. de liste** *Br* leading candidate, *Am* head of the ticket; *Sport* **t. de série** seeded player; **t. de série numéro 8** number 8 seed

5 *(extrémité ▸ d'un objet, d'un organe)* head; *(▸ d'un os)* head, caput; **la t. d'un clou** the head of a nail; **t. d'ail** head of garlic; **t. de bielle** big end; **t. de cylindre** cylinder head; **t. d'épingle** pinhead

6 *Can* **t. d'oreiller** pillow case

7 *(en audiovisuel)* head; **t. d'enregistrement** recording head; **t. de lecture** head

8 *Typ* head, top

9 *Ordinat* head; **t. de lecture-écriture** read-write head; **t. d'impression** print head

10 *Mil* head; **t. de pont** *(sur rivière)* bridgehead; *(sur plage)* beachhead

11 *Nucl* head; **t. chercheuse** homing device; **t. nucléaire** warhead

12 *Pétr* **t. d'injection** swivel; **t. de puits** well head

13 *Mktg* **t. de gondole** aisle end display, gondola end

• **à la tête de** PRÉP **1** *(en possession de)* **elle s'est trouvée à la t. d'une grosse fortune** she found herself in possession of a great fortune **2** *(au premier rang de)* at the head *or* front of; **à la t. du cortège** at the head of the procession **3** *(à la direction de)* in charge of, at the head of; **être à la t. d'une société** to head a company

• **de tête** ADJ **1** *(femme, homme)* able **2** *(convoi, voiture)* front *(avant n)* **3** *Typ* head *(avant n)* ADV *(calculer)* in one's head; **de t., je dirais que ça fait 600** working it out in my head, I'd say it comes to 600; **de t., je dirais que nous étions 20** at a guess I'd say there were 20 of us

• **en tête** ADV **1** *(devant)* **monter en t.** to go to the front; **être en t.** *(gén)* to be at the front; *(dans une course, une compétition)* to (be in the) lead **2** *(à l'esprit)* **avoir qch en t.** to have sth in mind; **j'ai encore en t. le souvenir de notre dernière rencontre** I can still remember our last meeting

• **en tête à tête** ADV alone together; **nous avons passé deux heures en t. à t.** we spent two hours alone together; **dîner en t. à t. avec qn** to have a quiet dinner (alone) with sb

• **en tête de** PRÉP **1** *(au début de)* at the beginning *or* start of; **tous les mots placés en t. de phrase** the first word of every sentence **2** *(à l'avant de)* at the head *or* front of **3** *(au premier rang de)* at the top of; **en t. du palmarès** at the top of the hit-parade; **en t. des sondages** leading the polls

• **par tête** ADV per head, a head, apiece; *Fin* per capita; **ça coûtera 40 euros par t.** it'll cost 40 euros a head *or* per head *or* apiece

• **par tête de pipe** *Fam* = **par tête**

• **sur la tête de** PRÉP **1** *(sur la personne de)* **le mécontentement populaire s'est répercuté sur la t. du Premier ministre** popular discontent turned towards the Prime Minister **2** *(au nom de)* in the name of; **il a mis tous ses biens sur la t. de sa femme** he's put all his possessions in his wife's name **3** *(en prêtant serment)* **je le jure sur la t. de mes enfants** I swear on my mother's grave

• **tête brûlée** NF hothead

• **tête croche** NF *Can* stubborn person, diehard

• **tête de mort** NF **1** *(crâne)* skull **2** *(emblème)* death's head, skull and crossbones

• **tête de nègre** = **tête-de-nègre** NF

• **tête de Turc** NF whipping boy, scapegoat

tête-à-queue [tɛtakø] NM INV **1** *(de voiture)* (180°) spin; **faire un t.** to spin round, to spin 180° **2** *(de cheval)* (sudden) turn; **faire un t.** to whip round

tête-à-tête [tɛtatɛt] NM INV **1** *(réunion)* tête-à-tête, private talk; **avoir un t. avec qn** to have a tête-à-tête with sb **2** *(sofa)* tête-à-tête, vis-à-vis **3** *(service ▸ à thé)* tea set for two; *(▸ à café)* coffee set for two

tête-bêche [tɛtbɛʃ] ADV *(lits, personnes)* head to foot *or* to tail; **dormir t.** to sleep head to foot; **ranger des bouteilles t.** to store bottles alternate ways up

tête-de-loup [tɛtdəlu] *(pl* **têtes-de-loup**) NF ceiling brush

tête-de-nègre [tɛtdənɛgr] *(pl* **têtes-de-nègre**) ADJ INV dark brown, chocolate-brown
NM INV *(couleur)* dark brown
NF *Culin* chocolate-coated meringue

tétée [tete] NF **1** *(action de téter)* feeding, breast-feeding **2** *(repas)* *Br* feed, *Am* feeding; **l'heure de la t.** *Br* feeding time, *Am* nursing time; **pendant les tétées** during feeds, while feeding; **donner la t. à un enfant** to feed a child

téter [18] [tete] VT **1** *(sein, biberon)* to suck (at); **t. sa mère** to suck (at) one's mother's breast, to feed *or* to breast-feed from one's mother **2** *(crayon, pipe)* to suck on; *(pouce)* to suck
USAGE ABSOLU **donner à t. à un enfant** to feed *or* suckle a child; **il tète encore** he's still being breast-fed, *Am* he's still nursing
VI *Fam (boire avec excès)* to knock it back, to drink like a fish

têtière [tɛtjɛr] NF **1** *(d'un fauteuil, d'un sofa)* antimacassar **2** *(d'un cheval)* headstall, crownpiece

tétine [tetin] NF **1** *Zool (mamelle)* teat **2** *(d'un biberon)* *Br* teat, *Am* nipple **3** *(sucette)* *Br* dummy, *Am* pacifier

téton [tetɔ̃] NM **1** *Fam (sein)* tit, boob **2** *Tech* stud, nipple; **t. de positionnement** spigot, dowel; **t. de purge** bleed nipple

tétrachlorure [tetraklɔryr] NM tetrachloride; **t. de carbone** carbon tetrachloride

tétracycline [tetrasiklin] NF *Chim* tetracycline

tétraèdre [tetraɛdr] NM tetrahedron

tétraédrique [tetraedrik] ADJ tetrahedral

tétralogie [tetralɔʒi] NF *Littérature, Théât & Mus* tetralogy

tétramètre [tetramɛtr] NM *Littérature* tetrameter

tétraplégie [tetrapleʒi] NF quadriplegia, tetraplegia

tétraplégique [tetrapleʒik] ADJ quadriplegic, tetraplegic
NMF quadriplegic

tétrapode [tetrapɔd] *Zool* ADJ tetrapod
NM tetrapod

tétrarque [tetrark] NM *Antiq* tetrarch

tétras [tetra] NM *Orn* grouse; **grand t.** capercaillie

tétrasyllabe [tetrasilab] *Littérature* ADJ tetrasyllabic
NM tetrasyllable

têtu, -e [tety] ADJ stubborn, obstinate; **il a un air t.** he has a stubborn look about him; **t. comme une mule** *ou* **un âne** *ou* **une bourrique** stubborn as a mule
NM *Tech* sledgehammer

teuf [tœf] NF *Fam (verlan de* **fête**) party

teufer [3] [tœfe] VI *Fam (verlan de* **fêter**) *(faire la fête)* to party

teufeur [tœfœr] NM *Fam* **1** *(dans une soirée)* party animal **2** *(dans une rave)* raver

teuf-teuf [tœftœf] *(pl* **teufs-teufs**) *Fam* NM *(train)* choo-choo train
NM OU NF *(vieille voiture)* jalopy, *Br* old banger
ONOMAT *(bruit du train)* puff-puff, choo-choo

> **-TEUR, -TEUSE/-TRICE** SUFFIX
>
> The suffix **-teur**, **-teuse** or **-teur**, **-trice** appears in adjectives and nouns derived from a verb and gives the idea of a person WHO PERFORMS THE ACTION described by the verb. It mostly refers to occupations or social activities, as well as character traits. The English suffixes *-er* and *-or* are common equivalents, eg:
>
> **un acheteur, une acheteuse** a buyer; **un éditeur, une éditrice** a publisher/an editor; **un lecteur, une lectrice** a reader; **un conducteur, une conductrice** a driver; **un menteur, une menteuse** a liar; **elle est très rouspéteuse** she's very grumpy
>
> The recent trend for systematically feminizing names of occupations has highlighted the difficulty in deciding between the **-teuse** and **-trice** forms when trying to come up with a new feminine equivalent. The general rule is to use **-trice** in most cases. However, **-teuse** is to be used
>
> (i) when there is a verb which is directly linked to the noun from a semantic point of view and which has a **-t-** in its ending, and/or
>
> (ii) when there is no correlated noun ending in **-tion**, **-ture** or **-torat**
>
> A few examples of newly feminized names of occupations following this model are:
>
> **ajusteuse** (masc. *ajusteur*) fitter; **apparitrice** (masc. *appariteur*) usher/porter; **arpentrice** (masc. *arpenteur*) (land) surveyor; **metteuse en scène** (masc. *metteur en scène*) director; **reportrice** (masc. *reporter*) reporter

teuton, -onne [tøtɔ̃, -ɔn] ADJ Teutonic
• **Teuton, -onne** NM,F **1** *Hist* Teuton **2** *Fam (Allemand)* Jerry, = offensive term used to refer to a German

teutonique [tøtɔnik] ADJ Teutonic; **les chevaliers teutoniques** the Teutonic knights

tévé [teve] NF *Fam* TV, *Br* telly

texan, -e [tɛksɑ̃, -an] ADJ Texan
• **Texan, -e** NM,F Texan

tex-mex [tɛksmɛks] *Culin* ADJ INV Tex-Mex
NM INV *(restaurant)* Tex-Mex

texte [tɛkst] NM **1** *(écrit)* text; **reportez-vous au t. original** consult the original; **ce n'était pas dans le t.** it was not in the text *or* in the original

2 *(œuvre littéraire)* text; **les grands textes classiques** the great classical texts *or* works

3 *(extrait d'une œuvre)* passage; **textes choisis** selected passages

4 *Mus (paroles d'une chanson)* lyrics; *(d'une pièce de théâtre)* script; *(d'un acteur)* lines; **un jeune chanteur qui écrit lui-même ses textes** a young singer who writes his own lyrics; **apprendre/savoir son t.** to learn/to know one's lines

5 *Jur (teneur d'une loi, d'un traité)* text, terms, wording; *(la loi elle-même)* law, act; *(le traité lui-même)* treaty; **selon le t. de la loi/du traité** according to the terms of the law/treaty; **le t. est paru au Journal officiel** the act was published in the official gazette

6 *Typ (opposé aux marges, aux illustrations)* text; **il y a trop de t. et pas assez de photos** there's too much text and not enough pictures; **gravure hors t.** plate, full-page engraving

7 *Ling (corpus, énoncé)* text

8 *Littérature* text, work; **t. de présentation** introduction

9 *Scol & Univ (sujet de devoir)* question *(for work in class or homework)*; **je vais vous lire le t. de la dissertation** I'll give you the essay question; **t. libre** free composition; **vous avez t. libre pour la rédaction** you can write about anything you like

10 *Mktg* **t. publicitaire** advertising copy

• **dans le texte** ADV in the original; **lire Platon dans le t.** to read Plato in the original

texteur [tɛkstœr] NM *Ordinat* word *or* text processor

textile [tɛkstil] ADJ textile

NM **1** *(tissu)* fabric, material; **les textiles synthétiques** *ou* **artificiels** synthetic *or* man-made fabrics, synthetics **2** *(industrie)* **le t., les textiles** the textile industry

texto[1] [tɛksto] ADV *Fam* word for word□, verbatim□; **il m'a dit t.: fous le camp** get the hell out of here, those were his exact *or* very words

texto[2] [tɛksto] NM *Tél* text (message)

textuel, -elle [tɛkstɥɛl] ADJ **1** *(conforme ▸ à ce qui est écrit)* literal, word-for-word; *(▸ à ce qui a été dit)* verbatim **2** *Littérature* textual; **analyse textuelle** textual analysis

ADV *Fam* quote unquote; **elle m'a dit qu'elle s'en fichait, t.!** she told me she didn't care, those were her exact *or* very words!

textuellement [tɛkstɥɛlmɑ̃] ADV word for word; **je reprends t. ses mots** those were his exact *or* very words

texture [tɛkstyr] NF **1** *(d'un bois, de la peau)* texture **2** *Géol, Métal & Tex* texture **3** *Littéraire (structure)* structure

texturer [3] [tɛkstyre] VT *Tex* to texturize

TF1 [teɛfɛ̃] NF *TV (abrév* **Télévision Française 1***)* = French independent television company

TGB [teʒebe] NF *(abrév* **très grande bibliothèque***)* = the new French national library in the Tolbiac area of Paris

TGV [teʒeve] NM *Rail (abrév* **train à grande vitesse***)* = French high-speed train

Thada [tada] NM *Méd (abrév* **trouble d'hyperactivité avec déficit de l'attention***)* ADHD

thaï, -e [taj] ADJ Thai

NM *(langue)* Thai

• **Thaï, -e** NM,F Thai

thaïlandais, -e [tajlɑ̃dɛ, -ɛz] ADJ Thai

• **Thaïlandais, -e** NM,F Thai

Thaïlande [tajlɑ̃d] NF **la T.** Thailand

thalamus [talamys] NM *Anat* thalamus

thalassémie [talasemi] NF *Méd* thalassaemia

thalassothérapie [talasɔterapi] NF seawater therapy, thalassotherapy

thalidomide [talidɔmid] NF thalidomide

thalle [tal] NM thallus

thallium [taljɔm] NM *Chim* thallium

thalweg [talvɛg] NM *Arch* talweg, thalweg

thatchérien, -enne [tatʃerjɛ̃, -ɛn] ADJ Thatcherite

NM,F Thatcherite

thatchérisme [tatʃerism] NM Thatcherism

thaumaturge [tomatyrʒ] NMF thaumaturge, thaumaturgist

thé [te] NM **1** *(boisson)* tea; **faire du t.** to make (some) tea; **prendre le t.** to have tea; **boire du t.** to drink tea; **t. blanc** white tea; **t. de Chine/Ceylan** China/Ceylon tea; **t. (au) citron** tea with lemon, *Br* lemon tea; **t. glacé** iced tea; **t. au lait** tea with milk; **t. à la menthe** mint tea; **t. nature** tea without milk; **t. noir** black (leaf) tea; **t. vert** green tea

2 *(feuilles)* tea, tea leaves

3 *(réception)* tea party; *(repas)* (afternoon) tea; **t. dansant** tea dance, thé dansant; **inviter qn pour le t.** to invite sb to *or* for tea

4 *Bot* tea, tea plant; **arbre à t.** tea tree

5 *Belg & Suisse (infusion)* herbal tea

théâtral, -e, -aux, -ales [teatral, -o] ADJ **1** *(relatif au théâtre)* theatrical, stage *(avant n)*, theatre *(avant n)*; **une représentation théâtrale** a theatrical production **2** *(scénique)* stage *(avant n)*; **l'adaptation théâtrale du roman** the stage adaptation of the novel **3** *(spectaculaire ▸ geste, action)* dramatic, theatrical; **faire une entrée théâtrale** to make a dramatic *or* grand entrance; **avec de grands gestes théâtraux** with a lot of histrionics *or* drama

théâtralement [teatralmɑ̃] ADV *(avec affectation)* theatrically

théâtraliser [3] [teatralize] VT to theatricalize

théâtralité [teatralite] NF *Littérature* stageworthiness

théâtre [teatr] NM **A. 1** *(édifice ▸ gén)* theatre, *Antiq* amphitheatre; **aller au t.** to go to the theatre; **t. d'eau** ornamental fountains; **t. lyrique** opera house; **t. d'ombres** shadow theatre; **t. en rond** theatre-in-the-round; **t. de verdure** open-air theatre

2 *(compagnie théâtrale)* theatre company; **t. municipal** local theatre; **t. national** national theatre

3 *(art, profession)* drama, theatre; **elle veut faire du t.** she wants to go on the stage *or* to become an actress *or* to act; **t. filmé** film of a play

4 *(genre)* drama, theatre; **le t. dans le t.** a play within a play; **le t. de l'absurde** the theatre of the absurd; **le t. de boulevard** mainstream popular theatre *(as first played in theatres on the Paris boulevards)*; **t. musical** musicals; **le t. de rue** street theatre

5 *(œuvres d'un auteur)* works, plays; **le t. complet d'Anouilh** the complete plays *or* dramatic works of Anouilh

6 *(attitude pleine d'outrance)* histrionics; **tout ça c'est du t.** it's all just histrionics *or* a show; **le voilà qui fait son t.** there he goes, putting on his usual act

B. 1 *(lieu d'un événement)* scene; **le t. du crime** the scene of the crime; **notre région a été le t. de nombreuses mutations** our part of the country has seen a lot of changes **2** *Mil* **t. d'opérations** *ou* **des opérations** the theatre of operations

• **de théâtre** ADJ *(critique, troupe)* drama *(avant n)*, theatre *(avant n)*; *(cours)* drama *(avant n)*; *(agence)* booking *(avant n)*; *(jumelles)* opera *(avant n)*; *(accessoire, décor)* stage *(avant n)*; **une femme de t.** a woman of the stage *or* theatre; **écrivain de t.** playwright; **metteur en scène de t.** (stage) director

théâtreux, -euse [teatrø, -øz] NM,F *Péj ou Hum* luvvie, thespian

thébaïde [tebaid] NF *Littéraire* solitary retreat

théier, -ère [teje, -ɛr] ADJ tea *(avant n)*; **la production théière** tea production

NM tea plant

• **théière** NF teapot

théine [tein] NF theine

théisme [teism] NM **1** *(consommation excessive)* excessive tea drinking; *(empoisonnement)* tea poisoning **2** *Rel* theism

théiste [teist] ADJ theist, theistic

NMF theist

thématique [tematik] ADJ thematic; **index/catalogue t.** subject index/catalogue

NF **1** *Littérature* themes; **la t. de Kafka** themes in Kafka **2** *Mus* themes

thème [tɛm] NM **1** *(sujet)* theme; **choisissons un t. de discussion** let's choose a subject for discussion; **sur le t. de** on the theme of

2 *Scol (traduction)* translation into a foreign language, prose; **faire du t.** to translate into a foreign language

3 *Beaux-Arts, Littérature & Mus* theme

4 *Ling* stem, theme

5 *Astrol* **t. astral** birth chart; **faire son t. à qn** to draw up sb's birth chart

théocratie [teɔkrasi] NF theocracy

théocratique [teɔkratik] ADJ theocratic

théodicée [teɔdise] NF *Phil* theodicy

théodolite [teɔdɔlit] NM theodolite

théogonie [teɔgɔni] NF theogony

théologal, -e, -aux, -ales [teɔlɔgal, -o] ADJ theological; **les trois vertus théologales** the three theological virtues

théologie [teɔlɔʒi] NF theology; **docteur en t.** doctor of divinity, DD; **faire sa t.** to study theology, to be a divinity student

théologien, -enne [teɔlɔʒjɛ̃, -ɛn] NM,F theologian

théologique [teɔlɔʒik] ADJ theological

théologiquement [teɔlɔʒikmɑ̃] ADV theologically

théorbe [teɔrb] NM *Mus* theorbo

théorème [teɔrɛm] NM theorem; **le t. de Pythagore** Pythagoras' theorem; **le t. de Newton** the binomial theorem

théorétique [teɔretik] *Phil* ADJ theoretical

NF theoretics *(singulier)*

théoricien, -enne [teɔrisjɛ̃, -ɛn] NM,F **1** *(philosophe, chercheur etc)* theorist, theoretician **2** *(adepte ▸ d'une doctrine)* theorist

théorie[1] [teɔri] NF **1** *(en science)* theory; **t. des ensembles** set theory; *Math* **t. des catastrophes** catastrophe theory; **t.** *Math & Ordinat* **t. des probabilités** theory of probability; **la t. de la relativité** the theory of relativity

2 *(ensemble de concepts)* theory; **la t. du surréalisme** the theory of surrealism

3 *(ensemble des règles)* theory; **avant de commencer le piano, il faut faire un peu de t.** before playing the piano you have to study a bit of theory; **il possède bien la t. des échecs** he has a good theoretical knowledge of chess

4 *(opinion)* theory; **bâtir une t.** to construct a theory

5 *(connaissance spéculative)* theory; **tout cela, c'est de la t.** this is all purely theoretical

6 *Mktg* **t. des jeux** game theory; **t. des prix** price theory; **t. quantitative** quantity theory

7 *Mil* theoretical instruction

• **en théorie** ADV in theory, theoretically

théorie[2] [teɔri] NF *Littéraire (défilé)* procession

théorique [teɔrik] ADJ theoretical; *Fin* **profits théoriques** paper profits

théoriquement [teɔrikmɑ̃] ADV theoretically, in theory

théoriser [3] [teɔrize] VT to theorize

VI to theorize, to speculate

théosophe [teɔzɔf] NMF theosophist

théosophie [teɔzɔfi] NF theosophy

thérapeute [terapøt] NMF **1** *(spécialiste des traitements)* therapist **2** *Littéraire (médecin)* doctor, physician **3** *(psychothérapeute)* therapist

thérapeutique [terapøtik] ADJ therapeutic; **les avancées thérapeutiques sont remarquables dans ce domaine** remarkable medical advances have been made in this field; **acte t.** invasive treatment; **aléa t.** risk attached to treatment; **accident t.** accident in the course of treatment

NF **1** *(traitement)* therapy, (course of) treatment **2** *(discipline médicale)* therapeutics *(singulier)*

thérapie [terapi] NF **1** *(traitement)* therapy, treatment; *Méd* **t. par électrochocs** electroconvulsive therapy **2** *Psy* therapy; **commencer une t.** to start a course of therapy, to start therapy; **être en t.** to be in therapy; **t. cognitive** cognitive therapy; **t. génique** gene therapy; **t. de groupe** group therapy; **t. primale** primal scream therapy

thermal, -e, -aux, -ales [tɛrmal, -o] ADJ *(eau)* thermal; *(source)* thermal, hot; **ville thermale** spa town

thermalisme [tɛrmalism] NM **1** *(science)* balneology **2** *(thérapie)* hydrotherapy, water cures

thermes [tɛrm] NMPL **1** *(établissement de cure)* thermal baths **2** *Antiq* thermae

thermicien, -enne [tɛrmisjɛ̃, -ɛn] NM,F heat engineer

thermidor [tɛrmidɔr] **NM** = 11th month of the French Revolutionary calendar (from 19 July to 17 August)

thermie [tɛrmi] **NF** *(ancienne unité de mesure)* 10^6 calories

thermique [tɛrmik] **ADJ** *(réacteur, équilibre, signature, papier)* thermal; *(énergie)* thermic; *(moteur, écran, traitement)* heat *(avant n)*
NF heat sciences
NM thermal

thermistance [tɛrmistɑ̃s] **NF** *Élec* thermistor

thermisteur [tɛrmistœr], **thermistor** [tɛrmistɔr] **NM** *Élec* thermistor

thermobarique [tɛrmɔbarik] **ADJ** *(bombe)* thermobaric

thermocautère [tɛrmɔkotɛr] **NM** thermocautery

thermochimie [tɛrmɔʃimi] **NF** thermochemistry

thermocollage [tɛrmɔkɔlaʒ] **NM** *Tech* heat sealing

thermoconduction [tɛrmɔkɔ̃dyksjɔ̃] **NM** *Phys* heat conduction

thermocontact [tɛrmɔkɔ̃takt] **NM** *Élec* thermal *or* temperature switch

thermocouple [tɛrmɔkupl] **NM** thermocouple

thermodynamique [tɛrmɔdinamik] **ADJ** thermodynamic
NF thermodynamics *(singulier)*

thermoélectricité [tɛrmɔelɛktrisite] **NF** thermoelectricity

thermoélectrique [tɛrmɔelɛktrik] **ADJ** thermoelectric; **couple t.** thermoelectric couple; **pile t.** thermopile; **pince t.** thermocouple

thermoélectronique [tɛrmɔelɛktrɔnik] **ADJ** thermoelectronic

thermoformage [tɛrmɔfɔrmaʒ] **NM** thermoforming

thermogène [tɛrmɔʒɛn] **ADJ** thermogenous, thermogenetic

thermographe [tɛrmɔgraf] **NM** *Phys* thermograph

thermomagnétisme [tɛrmɔmaɲetism] **NM** *Phys* thermomagnetism

thermomètre [tɛrmɔmɛtr] **NM 1** *(appareil)* thermometer; **le t. indique 5°** the thermometer stands at *or* registers 5°; **le t. monte/descend** the temperature (on the thermometer) is rising/falling; **t. médical** clinical thermometer; **t. à mercure** mercury thermometer; **t. à maximum et minimum** maximum and minimum thermometer **2** *Fig (indice)* barometer, gauge

thermométrie [tɛrmɔmetri] **NF** thermometry

thermométrique [tɛrmɔmetrik] **ADJ** thermometric

thermonucléaire [tɛrmɔnykleɛr] **ADJ** thermonuclear

thermopile [tɛrmɔpil] **NF** *Élec* thermopile

thermoplastique [tɛrmɔplastik] **ADJ** thermoplastic

thermoplongeur [tɛrmɔplɔ̃ʒœr] **NM** portable immersion heater

thermopompe [tɛrmɔpɔ̃p] **NF** heat pump

thermopropulsion [tɛrmɔprɔpylsjɔ̃] **NF** thermopropulsion

thermorégulateur, -trice [tɛrmɔregylatœr, -tris] **ADJ** thermoregulator

thermorégulation [tɛrmɔregylasjɔ̃] **NF** thermoregulation

thermorégulatrice [tɛrmɔregylatris] *voir* **thermorégulateur**

thermorésistant, -e [tɛrmɔrezistɑ̃, -ɑ̃t] **ADJ** heat-resistant, thermoresistant

Thermos® [tɛrmos] **NM OU NF** Thermos

thermoscope [tɛrmɔskɔp] **NM** thermoscope

thermosphère [tɛrmɔsfɛr] **NF** thermosphere

thermostat [tɛrmɔsta] **NM** thermostat; **t. 7** *(dans recette)* gas mark 7; **réglage par t.** thermostatic control

thermothérapie [tɛrmɔterapi] **NF** *Méd* deep-heat treatment, *Spéc* thermotherapy

thésard, -e [tezar, -ard] **NM,F** *Fam* research student[□], PhD student[□]

thésaurisation [tezɔrizasjɔ̃] **NF** *(gén)* & *Écon* hoarding

thésauriser [3] [tezɔrize] **VI** to hoard money
VT to hoard (up)

thésauriseur, -euse [tezɔrizœr, -øz] **ADJ** hoarding
NM,F hoarder

thésaurus, thesaurus [tezɔrys] **NM 1** *(lexique)* lexicon **2** *(outil de classement)* thesaurus

thèse [tɛz] **NF 1** *Scol* thesis; **t. de doctorat d'État** ≃ PhD, *Br* ≃ doctoral thesis, *Am* ≃ doctoral *or* PhD dissertation; **t. de troisième cycle** *(en lettres) Br* ≃ MA, *Am* ≃ master's thesis; *(en sciences) Br* ≃ MSc, *Am* ≃ master's thesis **2** *(théorie)* argument, thesis, theory; **t., antithèse, synthèse** thesis, antithesis, synthesis; **il défend la t. suivante:...** he argues that...
• **à thèse ADJ pièce à t.** problem play, drama of ideas; **roman à t.** novel of ideas

Thésée [teze] **NPR** *Myth* Theseus

Thessalonique [tesalɔnik] **NF** Thessalonika

thiamine [tjamin] **NF** thiamin

thibaude [tibod] **NF** carpet underlay felt

thiosulfate [tjɔsylfat] **NM** *Chim* thiosulphate

thio-urée [tjɔyre] *(pl* **thio-urées***)* **NF** *Chim* thiourea

thixotropie [tiksɔtrɔpi] **NF** *Chim* thixotropy

thomas [tɔma] **NM** *Fam Vieilli (pot de chambre)* chamberpot[□], *Br* jerry

thomisme [tɔmism] **NM** Thomism

thomiste [tɔmist] **ADJ** Thomistic, Thomistical
NMF Thomist

thon [tɔ̃] **NM 1** *(poisson)* tuna, *Br* tunny; *Culin* tuna (fish); *Culin* **t. à l'huile** tuna in oil; *Culin* **t. au naturel** tuna in brine **2** *Fam (femme laide)* dog, *Br* boot, *Am* beast

thonaire [tɔnɛr] **NM** *Pêche* tuna *or Br* tunny net

thonier [tɔnje] **NM** tuna *or Br* tunny boat

Thora [tɔra] = **Tora**

thoracique [tɔrasik] **ADJ** thoracic

thorax [tɔraks] **NM** *Anat* thorax

thorium [tɔrjɔm] **NM** *Chim* thorium

thoron [tɔrɔ̃] **NM** *Chim* thoron

Thrace [tras] **NF la T.** Thrace

thrène [trɛn] **NM** *Antiq* threnody

thriller [srilœr, trilœr] **NM** thriller

thrips [trips] **NM** *Entom* thrips, *Spéc* thysanopter

thrombine [trɔ̃bin] **NF** *Biol & Chim* thrombin

thrombose [trɔ̃boz] **NF** *Méd* thrombosis; **t. veineuse profonde** deep-vein thrombosis

THS [teaʃɛs] **NM** *Méd (abrév* **traitement hormonal substitutif***)* HRT

thulium [tyljɔm] **NM** *Chim* thulium

thune [tyn] **NF** *Fam* **1** *Vieilli* five-franc coin **2** *Suisse* Swiss five-franc coin **3** *(argent)* cash, *Br* dosh, *Am* bucks; **je n'avais pas une t.** I was broke, I didn't have a bean; **gagner de la t.** *ou* **des thunes** to be raking it in, to be making megabucks

thuriféraire [tyriferɛr] **NM 1** *Rel* thurifer **2** *Littéraire* flatterer, sycophant

thuya [tyja] **NM** *Bot* thuja; **t. occidental** white cedar

thylacine [tilasin] **NM** *Zool* Tasmanian wolf, *Spéc* thylacine

thym [tɛ̃] **NM** thyme

thymus [timys] **NM** thymus

thyristor [tiristɔr] **NM** *Élec* thyristor

thyroïde [tirɔid] **ADJ** thyroid
NF thyroid (gland)

thyroïdectomie [tirɔidɛktɔmi] **NF** *Méd* thyroidectomy

thyroïdien, -enne [tirɔidjɛ̃, -ɛn] **ADJ** thyroid *(avant n)*

thyroïdisme [tirɔidism] **NM** *Méd* thyroidism

thyroïdite [tirɔidit] **NF** *Méd* thyroiditis

thyrotoxicose [tirɔtɔksikoz] **NF** *Méd* Graves' disease

thyrse [tirs] **NM** *Myth & Bot* thyrsus

tiare [tjar] **NF 1** *(coiffure)* tiara **2** *(dignité papale)* **la t.** the Papal tiara; **coiffer la t.** to become Pope

Tibère [tibɛr] **NPR** Tiberius

Tibet [tibɛ] **NM le T.** Tibet

tibétain, -e [tibetɛ̃, -ɛn] **ADJ** Tibetan
NM *(langue)* Tibetan
• **Tibétain, -e NM,F** Tibetan

TIBEUR *Fin (abrév écrite* **taux interbancaire européen***)* EURIBOR

tibia [tibja] **NM 1** *Anat (os)* shinbone, *Spéc* tibia; *(devant de la jambe)* shin; **donner à qn un coup de pied dans les tibias** to kick sb in the shins **2** *Zool* tibia

tibial, -e, -aux, -ales [tibjal, -o] **ADJ** *Anat* tibial

Tibre [tibr] **NM le T.** the (River) Tiber

tic [tik] **NM 1** *(au visage)* tic, (nervous) twitch; **il a un t.** he has a twitch *or* a tic, his face twitches; **t. nerveux** nervous tic *or* twitch; **t. douloureux** facial neuralgia, *Spéc* tic douloureux
2 *(manie gestuelle)* (nervous) tic, twitch; *Fam* **il est bourré de tics** he's got a lot of nervous tics
3 *(répétition stéréotypée)* habit; **il a un t., il répète toujours le dernier mot de ses phrases** he has a habit of always repeating the last word of his sentences; **un t. de langage** a (speech) mannerism, a verbal tic
4 *Vét (avec déglutition d'air)* wind-sucking

ticket [tikɛ] **NM 1** *(de bus, de métro)* ticket; *(de vestiaire, de consigne)* slip, ticket; **t. de caisse** *Br* till receipt, *Am* sales slip; **t. de quai** platform ticket
2 *(coupon ▸ de rationnement, de pain)* coupon
3 *Anciennement Fam (dix francs)* ten-franc note[□]; **cette montre m'a coûté 100 tickets** this watch set me back a thousand francs
4 *Pol (aux États-Unis)* ticket
5 *Fam (locution)* **avoir un** *ou* **le t. (avec qn)** to have made a hit (with sb); **tu as le t.** *Br* he/she fancies you, *Am* he/she has a crush on you; **il a un t. avec elle** *Br* she fancies him, *Am* she has a crush on him
• **ticket modérateur NM** *(pour la Sécurité sociale)* = proportion of medical expenses payable by the patient

ticket-repas [tikɛrəpa] *(pl* **tickets-repas***)* **NM** = voucher given to employees to cover part of luncheon expenses, *Br* ≃ luncheon voucher, *Am* ≃ meal ticket

Ticket-Restaurant® [tikɛrɛstɔrɑ̃] *(pl* **Tickets-Restaurant***)* **NM** = voucher given to employees to cover part of luncheon expenses, *Br* ≃ luncheon voucher, *Am* ≃ meal ticket

tic-tac [tiktak] **NM INV** *(d'une pendule, d'une bombe)* ticking *(UNCOUNT)*, tick-tock; **faire t.** to tick (away), to go tick-tock
ONOMAT tick-tock

tictaquer [3] [tiktake] **VI** *(horloge)* to tick (away), to go tick-tock

tie-break [tajbrɛk] *(pl* **tie-breaks***)* **NM** tie break

tiédasse [tjedas] **ADJ** lukewarm, tepid

tiède [tjɛd] **ADJ 1** *(ni chaud ni froid)* lukewarm, warm, tepid; **un vent t. et agréable** a nice warm breeze; **salade t.** warm salad
2 *(pas suffisamment chaud)* lukewarm, not hot enough; **le thé va être t., bois-le vite** drink your tea before it gets cold *or* while it's hot
3 *Fig (peu enthousiaste ▸ accueil, réaction)* lukewarm, unenthusiastic, half-hearted; *(▸ sentiment, foi, défenseur)* half-hearted; **les syndicalistes sont tièdes** the union members lack conviction *or* are apathetic
4 *(avant le nom) (doux, calme)* pleasant, sweet
NMF *Fam (indifférent, mou)* wimp
ADV je préfère boire/manger t. I don't like drinking/eating very hot things; **il fait t. aujourd'hui** it's mild *or* warm today
NF *Suisse* heatwave

tièdement [tjɛdmɑ̃] **ADV** *(accueillir)* coolly, unenthusiastically; *(soutenir)* half-heartedly

tiédeur [tjedœr] **NF 1** *(d'un liquide)* lukewarmness; *(d'un solide)* warmth; *(de l'air)* mildness **2** *Fig (d'un accueil)* lukewarmness, coolness; *(d'un sentiment, d'un défenseur)* half-heartedness; **avec t.** half-heartedly, without any great enthusiasm; **la t. de ses paroles** his/her unenthusiastic *or* half-hearted words **3** *(agréable douceur)* warmth

tiédir [32] [tjedir] **VI 1** *(se refroidir ▸ boisson, métal, air)* to cool (down); **laisser t. le gâteau/lait** leave the cake/milk to cool down **2** *(se réchauffer)* to grow warmer; **faire t. du lait** to warm up some milk **3** *Fig (faiblir ▸ conviction, sentiment)* to wane, to weaken, to cool

VT 1 *(refroidir légèrement)* to cool (down); **le vent du soir a tiédi l'air** the evening breeze has cooled the air **2** *(réchauffer légèrement)* to warm (up)

tiédissement [tjedismɑ̃] **NM 1** *(refroidissement)* cooling (down *or* off) **2** *(réchauffement)* warming (up)

tien [tjɛ̃] *(f* **tienne** [tjɛn], *mpl* **tiens** [tjɛ̃], *fpl* **tiennes** [tjɛn]) **ADJ** *Littéraire* yours; *Vieilli* **un t. cousin** a cousin of yours; **tu feras tiens ses principes** you will adopt his/her principles as your own; **feras-tu tiennes les félicitations qu'ils m'adressent?** will you join them in congratulating me?

• **le tien** *(f* **la tienne**, *mpl* **les tiens**, *fpl* **les tiennes**) **PRON** yours; *Rel & Arch* thine; **prends ma voiture, si la tienne est au garage** use my car, if yours is at the garage; **il n'a qu'à prendre la tienne** he can just take yours; **il ressemble au t.** it looks like yours; **tu veux bien me donner du t.?** can I have some of yours?; **de toutes ces solutions, tu préfères la tienne?** out of those possible solutions, do you prefer your own?; **tu n'en as pas besoin, tu as le t.** you don't need it, you've got your own; **je n'en ai pas besoin, j'ai le t.** I don't need it, I've got yours; **mes enfants sont plus âgés que les tiens** my children are older than yours (are); **ce parapluie n'est pas le t.** this is not your umbrella, this umbrella is not yours *or* doesn't belong to you; **les deux tiens** your two, the two *or* both of yours; *(en insistant)* your own two; **tu lui as laissé deux des tiens** you gave him/her two of yours; *Fam* **le t. de bébé est plus intelligent** your baby is more intelligent□

NM le t. *(ce qui t'appartient)* yours; **ne cherchons pas à distinguer le t. du mien** let's not waste time arguing about who owns what; **ici, il n'y a pas de t. et de mien** it's share and share alike here; *Fam* **à la tienne!** *(à ta santé)* good health!, cheers!; *(bon courage)* all the best!; **mets-y du t.** *(fais un effort)* make an effort; *(sois compréhensif)* try to be understanding; *Fam* **tu as encore fait des tiennes!** you've (gone and) done it again!

NMPL les tiens *(ta famille)* your family, *Am* your folks; *(tes partisans)* your followers; *(tes coéquipiers)* your team-mates

tient *etc voir* **tenir**

tierce [tjɛrs] *voir* **tiers²**

tiercé¹, -e [tjɛrse] **ADJ 1** *Agr* third ploughed **2** *Hér* tierced, en tierce **3** *Littérature* **rimes tiercées** terza rima

tiercé² [tjɛrse] **ADJ M pari t.** triple forecast

NM triple forecast; **jouer au t.** = to put money on horses; **gagner le t. (dans l'ordre/le désordre)** to win on three horses (with the right placings/without the right placings); **toucher un gros t.** = to win a lot of money on the horses; **le t. gagnant** the first three horses

tiercelet [tjɛrsəle] **NM** *Orn* tercel, tiercel

tiercer [16] [tjɛrse] **VT** *Agr* to plough for the third time

tiers¹ [tjɛr] **NM 1** *(partie d'un tout divisé en trois)* third; **elle en a lu un t.** she's a third of the way through (reading it); **tu as droit aux deux t. de la somme** you're entitled to two thirds of the sum; **cinq est le t. de quinze** five is a third of fifteen, five goes into fifteen three times; **la maison était brûlée aux deux t.** two thirds of the house had been destroyed by fire; **une remise d'un t. (du prix)** a discount of a third, a third off

2 *(troisième personne)* third person; *(personne étrangère à un groupe)* stranger, outsider, third party; *Fam* **le t. et le quart** everybody, anybody; *Fam* **il se fiche** *ou* **se moque du t. comme du quart** he couldn't care less

3 *Jur* third party; **les dommages causés à un t.** third party damages; **t. détenteur** third-party holder; **t. possesseur** third-party owner; **t. saisi** garnishee

4 *Com* **t. bénéficiaire** *(d'un chèque, d'un effet)* beneficiary; **t. porteur** *(d'un effet de commerce)* second endorser; *(d'un effet)* holder in due course

5 *Fin* **t. provisionnel** = thrice-yearly income tax payment based on estimated tax due for the previous year

6 *Hist* **le t.** the Third Estate

7 *(pour la Sécurité sociale)* **t. payant** = system by which a proportion of the fee for medical treatment is paid directly to the hospital, doctor or pharmacist by the patient's insurer

• **au tiers ADJ** *Jur* third-party *(avant n)*; **assurance au t.** third-party insurance

• **en tiers ADV** *(en tant qu'étranger à un groupe)* as an outsider; **assister en t. à un entretien** to attend an interview as an outside observer

tiers², tierce [tjɛr, tjɛrs] **ADJ 1** *(étranger à un groupe)* third; **tierce personne** third party

2 *UE* **pays t.** third *or* non-EU country; **produits t.** non-community products

3 *Jur* **tierce collision** third-party *(avant n)*

4 *Hist* **le t. état** the Third Estate

5 *Ordinat* **tierce partie de confiance** trusted third party

• **tierce NF 1** *Cartes* tierce **2** *Escrime & Hér* tierce **3** *Typ* press proof **4** *Mus* third; **tierce majeure/mineure** major/minor third **5** *Astron & Math* = sixtieth part of a second **6** *Rel* terce, tierce

tiers-arbitre [tjɛrarbitr] *(pl* **tiers-arbitres**) **NM** *Jur* (independent) arbitrator

tiers-monde [tjɛrmɔ̃d] *(pl* **tiers-mondes**) **NM** Third World; **les pays du t.** Third World countries

tiers-mondiste [tjɛrmɔ̃dist] *(pl* **tiers-mondistes**) **ADJ 1** *(du tiers-mondisme)* pro-Third World **2** *(du tiers-monde)* Third World *(avant n)*

NMF 1 *(spécialiste du tiers-monde)* Third World expert **2** *(idéologue du tiers-mondisme)* Third Worldist

TIF [tif] **NM** *(abrév* **transport international ferroviaire**) international rail transport

tifoso [tifozo] *(pl* **tifosi** [-zi]) **NM** fan

tifs, tiffes [tif] **NMPL** *Fam* hair□

TIG [teiʒe] **NM** *Jur (abrév* **travail d'intérêt général**) ≃ community service

tige [tiʒ] **NF 1** *Bot (d'une feuille)* stem, stalk; *(de blé, de maïs)* stalk; *(d'une fleur)* stem; **tulipe à longue t.** long-stemmed tulip; **rosier sur t.** standard rose; **arbre de haute/basse t.** tall/half standard

2 *(axe ▸ d'une épingle, d'une aiguille, d'un clou, d'un candélabre, d'une flèche)* shaft; *(▸ d'un cadran solaire)* finger, pointer; *(▸ d'un guéridon)* pedestal; **une t. de bois** a wooden shaft, a dowel; **une t. de fer** an iron rod

3 *Fam (cigarette) Br* fag, *Am* cig

4 *(d'une chaussure)* upper; **bottes à tiges** top boots; **bottes à t. basse** ankle boots

5 *Fig Littéraire (origine d'une famille)* stock, line; **faire t.** to found a line

6 *Archit (de colonne)* shaft

7 *Aut* rod; *(sur le volant)* stalk; **t. de crémaillère** rack link; *(de la direction)* control rod; **t. de culbuteur/piston** push/piston rod; **t. de frein** brake rod; **t. de jauge** dipstick; **t. (de maintien) de capot** *Br* bonnet strut, *Am* hood strut; **t. de poussée** thrust pin, pushrod; **t. poussoir** pushrod; **t. à vis du frein** brake screw

8 *Pétr* **t. de forage** drill pipe

9 *Tech (d'une valve)* stem; *(d'une pompe, d'un piston, d'un paratonnerre)* rod; *(d'un rivet, d'une clé, d'une ancre, d'une lettre)* shank; *Mus (d'un archet)* stick; *Typ* **t. à caractères** type bar

tiglon [tiglɔ̃] = **tigron**

tignasse [tiɲas] **NF** *Fam* **1** *(chevelure mal peignée)* mop *or* mane (of hair) **2** *(chevelure)* hair□; **il l'a attrapée par la t.** he grabbed (hold of) her by the hair

Tigre [tigr] **NM** *Géog* **le T.** the (River) Tigris

tigre [tigr] **NM 1** *Zool* tiger; **t. du Bengale** Bengal tiger; **t. royal** Bengal tiger **2** *Littéraire (homme cruel)* **c'est un vrai t.** he's a real ogre; **t. de papier** paper tiger

tigré, -e [tigre] **ADJ** *(pelage)* striped, streaked; *(chat)* tabby *(avant n)*, tiger *(avant n)*

tigresse [tigrɛs] **NF 1** *Zool* tigress **2** *Littéraire (femme très jalouse)* tigress; **jalouse comme une t.** madly *or* wildly jealous

tigron [tigrɔ̃] **NM** tigon, tiglon

Tiki [tiki] **NM** Tiki

tiki [tiki] **NM** tiki *(statue representing a Polynesian god)*; **t. bar** tiki bar *(Polynesian-themed bar)*

tilbury [tilbyri] **NM** tilbury

tilde [tild, tilde] **NM** *(en espagnol)* tilde; *(en phonétique, pour remplacer un mot)* swung dash

tillac [tijak] **NM** *Naut & Hist* upper deck

tilleul [tijœl] **NM 1** *Bot* lime (tree) **2** *(feuilles séchées)* lime blossom *(UNCOUNT)*; *(infusion)* lime *or* lime-blossom tea **3** *(bois)* limewood; **en t.** *(coffret, boîte)* limewood

ADJ INV (vert) t. lime green

tilsit [tilsit] **NM** *Suisse* = hard cheese from the canton of Saint-Gall

tilt [tilt] **NM 1** *(dans un jeu)* tilt signal **2** *Fam (locutions)* **le mot a fait t.** *(je me suis souvenu)* the word rang a bell; **et soudain, ça a fait t.** *(j'ai compris)* and suddenly it clicked *or* the penny dropped

timbale [tɛ̃bal] **NF 1** *(gobelet)* (metal) cup; **t. en argent** *(donnée aux enfants baptisés)* silver christening cup **2** *Culin (moule)* timbale mould; *(préparation)* timbale; **t. de saumon** salmon timbale **3** *Mus* kettledrum; **une paire de timbales** timpani, a set of kettledrums; **les timbales** *(d'un orchestre)* the timpani

timbalier [tɛ̃balje] **NM** timpanist

timbrage [tɛ̃braʒ] **NM 1** *(action de timbrer)* stamping **2** *(procédé d'impression)* embossing

timbre¹ [tɛ̃br] **NM 1** *(pour lettre)* stamp; **mettre un t. sur une lettre** to stamp a letter, to put a stamp on a letter; **t. de collection** collector's stamp

2 *(vignette ▸ au profit d'une œuvre)* sticker *(given in exchange for a donation to charity)*; *(▸ attestant un paiement)* stamp *(certifying receipt of payment)*

3 *(sceau, marque)* stamp; **apposer son t. sur un document** to put one's stamp on *or* to rubber-stamp a document

4 *(instrument marqueur)* stamp; **t. dateur** date stamp; **t. en caoutchouc** rubber stamp; **t. sec** embossing stamp

5 *Jur* **t. fiscal** tax stamp

6 *Méd* patch; **t. tuberculinique** tuberculosis patch

> **TIMBRE FISCAL**
>
> These stamps are sold at most tobacconists' and are used to pay fees due for obtaining official documents, such as identity papers, vehicle documents and legal certificates.

timbre² [tɛ̃br] **NM 1** *(qualité sonore ▸ d'un instrument)* tone, timbre, colour; *(▸ d'une voix)* tone, resonance; **un beau t. de voix** beautiful mellow tones, a beautiful rich voice; **"ce n'est pas moi", dit-elle d'une voix sans t.** "it wasn't me," she said tonelessly **2** *(sonnette)* bell; *(de porte)* doorbell; **t. de bicyclette** bicycle bell; *Fam Arch* **avoir le t. fêlé** to be cracked *or* daft, to have a screw loose **3** *Mus (instrument)* (small) bell; *(de tambour)* snare

timbré, -e [tɛ̃bre] **ADJ 1** *Fam (fou)* nuts, crazy **2** *(document, enveloppe)* stamped; **une enveloppe timbrée portant vos nom et adresse** a stamped addressed envelope; **une lettre timbrée de Paris** a letter with a Paris postmark, a letter postmarked Paris **3** *(d'une bonne sonorité)* **une voix joliment** *ou* **agréablement timbrée** a pleasant voice; **de sa voix bien timbrée** in his/her mellow *or* rich tones

timbre-poste [tɛ̃brəpɔst] *(pl* **timbres-poste**) **NM** (postage) stamp

timbre-prime [tɛ̃brəprim] *(pl* **timbres-primes**) **NM** trading (discount) stamp

timbre-quittance [tɛ̃brəkitɑ̃s] *(pl* **timbres-quittances**) **NM** receipt stamp

timbrer [3] [tɛ̃bre] **VT 1** *(lettre, colis)* to stamp, to stick *or* to put a stamp on; **je n'ai pas assez timbré la lettre** I didn't put enough stamps *or* I put insufficient postage on the letter **2** *Jur (document)* to stamp, to put a stamp on, to affix a stamp to

VI *Suisse (au chômage)* to sign on

timbre-taxe [tɛ̃brətaks] *(pl* **timbres-taxe**) **NM** postage-due stamp

timide [timid] **ADJ 1** *(embarrassé ▸ sourire, air, regard)* timid, shy; *(▸ personne)* bashful, diffident;

il est t. avec les femmes he's shy of *or* he shrinks away from women; **faussement t.** coy **2** *(faible)* slight; *(critique)* hesitant; **une t. amélioration du dollar** a slight improvement in the position of the dollar;

NMF shy person; **c'est un grand t.** he's very shy

timidement [timidmɑ̃] **ADV 1** *(avec embarras)* timidly, shyly, diffidently; *(gauchement)* self-consciously, bashfully **2** *(de façon peu perceptible)* slightly; **le dollar remonte t.** the dollar is rising slightly

timidité [timidite] **NF 1** *(manque d'assurance)* timidity, shyness, diffidence; *(gaucherie)* self-consciousness, bashfulness **2** *(d'un projet, d'une réforme)* feebleness, half-heartedness

timing [tajmiŋ] **NM** timing *(of a technical process)*

timon [timɔ̃] **NM 1** *Agr (d'une charrette)* shaft; *(d'une charrue)* (draught) beam **2** *Aut* trailing arm **3** *Vieilli Naut* tiller

timonerie [timɔnri] **NF 1** *Naut (abri)* wheelhouse; *(service)* wheelhouse, steering; *(personnel)* wheelhouse crew; **kiosque de t.** wheelhouse, pilot house **2** *Aut* steering and braking gear

timonier [timɔnje] **NM 1** *Naut* helmsman; *(aux signaux)* signalman, wheelhorse, wheeler **2** *Agr* wheelhorse, wheeler

Timor [timɔr] **NM le T.** Timor; **le T. Oriental** East Timor

timorais, -e [timɔrɛ, -ɛz] **ADJ** Timorese
• **Timorais, -e NM,F** Timorese; **les T.** the Timorese

timoré, -e [timɔre] **ADJ** timorous, fearful; *Rel & Littéraire (conscience)* overscrupulous

NM,F timorous *or* fearful person

tinctorial, -e, -aux, -ales [tɛ̃ktɔrjal, -o] **ADJ** tinctorial, dye *(avant n)*

tinette [tinɛt] **NF** *(récipient)* mobile latrine
• **tinettes NFPL** *Fam (toilettes) Br* lav, *Am* john

tint *etc voir* **tenir**

tintamarre [tɛ̃tamar] **NM** *(vacarme)* racket, din; **faire du t.** to make a din *or* racket; *Fig* **on a fait du t. autour de son livre** there was a lot of hooha *or* a big to-do about his/her book

tintement [tɛ̃tmɑ̃] **NM 1** *(d'une cloche, d'une sonnette)* ringing *(UNCOUNT)*; *(d'un lustre)* tinkling *(UNCOUNT)*; *(de grelots, de clefs, de pièces de monnaie)* jingle, jingling *(UNCOUNT)*; *(de verres, de bouteilles)* chink, clink, clinking *(UNCOUNT)* **2** *Méd* **t. d'oreilles** ringing in the ears, *Spéc* tinnitus; **avoir des tintements d'oreilles** to have a ringing *or* buzzing (noise) in one's ears

tinter [3] [tɛ̃te] **VI 1** *(sonner lentement)* to ring (out), to peal; **minuit tinte au clocher** the church bell is ringing midnight **2** *(produire des sons clairs)* to tinkle, to jingle; **les verres tintaient sur le plateau** the glasses were clinking on the tray; **le lustre en cristal tintait doucement** the crystal chandelier was tinkling softly; **faire t. des pièces de monnaie** to jingle coins **3** *(oreilles)* to ring, to buzz; **les oreilles me tintaient** my ears were ringing *or* buzzing; *Fig* **les oreilles doivent lui t.** his/her ears must be burning

VT 1 *(sonner ▸ cloche)* to chime **2** *(coup)* **la cloche du village tintait les coups de midi** the church bell was striking twelve **3** *(annoncer ▸ glas, messe)* to toll the bell for; **t. le tocsin** to sound the tocsin

tintin [tɛ̃tɛ̃] **EXCLAM** *Fam* no way(, José)!, no chance!, nothing doing!; **les cadres ont eu une augmentation, et nous t.!** the management got a *Br* rise *or Am* raise, but we got zilch!; **faire t.** to go without

tintinnabuler [3] [tɛ̃tinabyle] **VI** *Littéraire* to tinkle, to jingle, to tintinnabulate

Tintoret [tɛ̃tɔrɛ] **NPR le T.** Tintoretto

tintouin [tɛ̃twɛ̃] **NM** *Fam* **1** *(inquiétude, souci)* grief, hassle; **se faire du t.** to get all worked up **2** *(vacarme)* racket, din **3** *(locution)* **sa canne à pêche, ses bottes, son chapeau et tout le t.** his/her fishing rod, boots, hat and all the rest of it

TIOP [tjɔp] **NM** *Banque (abrév* **taux interbancaire offert à Paris**) PIBOR

TIP [tip] **NM** *Banque (abrév* **titre interbancaire de paiement**) = payment slip for bills

tiper [3] [tipe] **VT** *Suisse (achat)* to ring up

tipi [tipi] **NM** tepee, teepee

TIPP [teipepe] **NF** *(abrév* **taxe intérieure sur les produits pétroliers**) domestic tax on petroleum products

tipper [tipe] = **tiper**

tip-top [tiptɔp] **ADJ INV 1** *(excellent)* first-rate **2** *Suisse (impeccable)* immaculate

tipule [tipyl] **NF** *Entom* crane fly

tique [tik] **NF** tick; **collier anti-tiques** tick collar

tiquer [3] [tike] **VI 1** *Fam (réagir)* to wince ▫; **il n'a pas tiqué** he didn't turn a hair *or* bat an eyelid; **t. sur qch** to baulk at sth **2** *Vét* to wind-suck

tiqueté, -e [tikte] **ADJ** speckled, mottled, dotted

TIR [teiɛr, tir] **NM** *Transp (abrév* **transport international routier**) TIR

tir [tir] **NM 1** *Mil (action de lancer au moyen d'une arme)* shooting, firing; *(projectiles envoyés)* fire; **les tirs cessèrent** the firing stopped; **un t. bien/mal ajusté** a well-aimed/badly-aimed launch *or* shot; **un t. intense/nourri/sporadique** heavy/sustained/sporadic fire; **il a un t. précis** he's a good shot *or* marksman; **il a un t. rapide** he shoots quickly; **allonger/raccourcir le t.** to increase/reduce the range; **adresse** *ou* **habileté au t.** marksmanship; *Fig* **rectifier le t.** to change one's angle of attack, to change one's approach to a problem; **t. d'accompagnement** cover (fire); **tirs amis** friendly fire; **t. d'artillerie** artillery fire; **t. automatique** automatic fire; **arme à t. automatique** automatic weapon; **t. de barrage** barrage fire; **t. de batterie** battery fire; **t. au but** precision firing; **t. courbe** high-angle fire; **t. direct/indirect** direct/indirect fire; **tirs fratricides** friendly fire; **t. par rafales** firing in bursts; **t. rasant/plongeant** raking/downward fire

2 *(endroit ▸ pour l'entraînement)* rifle *or* shooting range; **t. (forain)** shooting gallery

3 *Mines & (en travaux publics)* blasting

4 *Sport* **le t.** *(discipline olympique)* shooting; **t. à l'arbalète** crossbow archery; **t. à l'arc** archery; **t. à la carabine** *ou* **au fusil** rifle-shooting; **t. aux pigeons (d'argile)** clay pigeon shooting; **t. au pistolet** pistol-shooting

5 *Chasse* **chasse à t.** shooting

6 *Ftbl* shot; **faire un t. du pied gauche** to shoot with the left foot; **t. (au but)** shot at goal; *(penalty)* penalty; **les tirs au but, l'épreuve** *ou* **la séance des tirs au but** the penalty shootout

7 *(aux boules)* throw; **apprendre la technique du t.** to learn how to throw

8 *(au basket-ball)* shot; **t. en suspension** jump shot

• **de tir ADJ** *(concours, champion)* shooting; *(position, vitesse)* firing; **angle/ligne de t.** angle/line of fire

tirade [tirad] **NF 1** *Cin & Théât* monologue, speech **2** *Péj (discours)* speech, tirade

tirage [tiraʒ] **NM 1** *Typ (action)* printing; *(ensemble d'exemplaires)* print run, impression; *(d'une gravure, d'un enregistrement)* edition; **un t. de 50 000 exemplaires** a print run of 50,000; **un mille de t.** a (print) run of a thousand; **écrivain qui fait de gros tirages** bestselling author; **édition à t. limité** limited edition; **t. héliographique** arc print; **t. de luxe** de luxe edition; **t. numéroté** numbered edition; **t. à part** offprint

2 *Presse (action)* printing, running; *(exemplaires mis en vente)* circulation; **un t. de 50 000** circulation figures *or* a circulation of 50,000; **le t. a baissé** circulation is down *or* has fallen *or* has dropped; **à fort** *ou* **grand t.** with large circulation figures; **la presse à grand t.** the popular press

3 *Ordinat (sur imprimante)* printout

4 *Phot (action)* printing; *(copies)* prints; **deux tirages sur papier brillant** two sets of prints on gloss paper

5 *Banque* drawing; *(d'un prêt)* drawdown; **t. en blanc** *ou* **en l'air** drawing of a dud cheque, *Spéc* kiting; *Écon* **droits de t. spéciaux** special drawing rights; *Compta* **tirages annuels** annual drawings

6 *(d'une carte)* taking, picking; *(d'une tombola)* draw; **t. au sort** drawing of lots; **procéder à un t. au sort** to draw lots; **nous t'avons désigné par t. au sort** we drew lots and your name came up; *Sport* **on connaît maintenant le t. au sort des demi-finales** we now have the results of the draw for the semifinals

7 *(d'une cheminée, d'un poêle)* draught; **le t. est bon/mauvais** it draws well/doesn't draw well; **t. renversé** *ou* **inverti** back draught; *Aut* **carburateur à t. en bas** down-draught carburettor

8 *(action de ▸ traîner)* dragging; *(▸ haler)* hauling

9 *Métal* drawing

10 *(de rochers)* quarrying, extraction; **t. à la poudre** blasting

11 *Cin* copying; **t. en surimpression** overprint

12 *(d'un disque)* pressing

13 *Fam (locution)* **il y a du t. entre eux** there's some friction between them

tiraillement [tirajmɑ̃] **NM 1** *(sur une corde)* tugging, pulling **2** *(d'estomac)* gnawing pain; *(de la peau, d'un muscle)* tightness; **sentir les tiraillements de la faim** to feel pangs of hunger; **avoir des tiraillements d'estomac** to have gnawing pains in one's stomach *or* pangs of hunger

• **tiraillements NMPL** *(conflit)* struggle, conflict; **il y a des tiraillements dans la famille/le syndicat** there is friction within the family/the union

tirailler [3] [tiraje] **VT 1** *(tirer sur)* to tug at, to pull on, to give little pulls on **2** *(faire souffrir légèrement)* to prick; **la faim lui tiraillait l'estomac** he/she felt pangs of hunger **3** *(solliciter)* to dog, to plague; **être tiraillé entre ses parents** to be torn between one's parents

VI 1 *(avec une arme)* to fire at random; **on entendait t. dans les bois** random fire could be heard in the woods, people could be heard firing away in the woods **2** *(peau)* to feel tight; **j'ai la peau qui (me) tiraille** my skin feels tight

tiraillerie [tirajri] **NF 1** *Mil* wild firing **2** *(friction)* wrangling, friction

tirailleur [tirajœr] **NM 1** *(éclaireur)* scout **2** *Hist & Mil* skirmisher; **les tirailleurs algériens/sénégalais** the Algerian/Senegalese (Infantry) corps

• **en tirailleurs ADV** *(avancer)* in skirmishing order

Tirana [tirana] **NM** Tirana, Tiranë

tirant [tirɑ̃] **NM 1** *Naut* **t. d'eau** draught; **avoir cinq pieds de t. d'eau** to draw five feet (of water); **barque à faible t. d'eau** shallow draught barge; **échelle de t. d'eau** draught marks *or* numbers

2 *(d'une botte)* (boot) strap; *(d'une chaussure)* (heel) strap

3 *(d'une bourse)* purse string

4 *Constr (entrait)* tie beam; *(fer plat)* rod

5 *Tech* stay, brace; **t. de frein** brake rod

6 *(en travaux publics)* **t. d'air** (maximum) headroom

tire [tir] **NF 1** *très Fam (voiture)* car ▫, *Br* motor **2** *Can (friandise)* maple toffee *or Am* taffy; **t. d'érable** maple candy

tiré, -e [tire] **ADJ 1** *(fatigué et amaigri ▸ visage)* drawn, pinched; **avoir les traits tirés** to look drawn

2 *(tendu)* **broderie à fils tirés** drawn-thread work; **aux cheveux tirés** with one's hair drawn *or* pulled back

3 *Banque* **chèque t. sur qn** cheque drawn on sb

4 *(locution)* **t. par les cheveux** contrived, far-fetched

NM 1 *Banque* drawee **2** *Presse* **t. à part** off-print

• **tirée NF** *Fam* **1** *(trajet)* haul, trek; **ça fait une tirée d'ici à là-bas** it's a bit of a haul *or* trek from here **2 une tirée de qch** *(grande quantité)* loads of sth

tire-au-cul [tiroky] **NM INV** *très Fam Br* skiver, *Am* goldbrick

tire-au-flanc [tiroflɑ̃] **NM INV** *Fam Br* skiver, *Am* goldbrick

tire-botte [tirbɔt] *(pl* **tire-bottes**) **NM 1** *(pour mettre)* boot hook **2** *(pour enlever)* bootjack

tire-bouchon [tirbuʃɔ̃] *(pl* **tire-bouchons**) **NM** corkscrew

• **en tire-bouchon ADJ** corkscrew *(avant n)*; **un cochon à la queue en t.** a pig with a corkscrew tail

tire-bouchonner [3] [tirbuʃɔne] **VT** *(mèche)* to twiddle *or* to twist (round and round); *(fil de fer)* to twist

VI to twist round and round; *(pantalon)* to be crumpled

tire-bouton [tirbutɔ̃] *(pl* **tire-boutons**) **NM** *Vieilli* buttonhook

tire-clou [tirklu] *(pl* **tire-clous**) **NM** nail puller

tire-d'aile [tirdɛl] **à tire-d'aile** ADV **1** *(en volant)* **s'envoler à t.** to fly swiftly away **2** *Fig (à toute vitesse)* **partir** *ou* **s'éloigner à t.** to fly off

tire-fesses [tirfɛs] NM INV *Fam* ski tow, T-bar; **monter en t.** to go up by the T-bar, to take the T-bar up

tire-jus [tirʒy] NM INV *très Fam* snotrag

tire-laine [tirlɛn] NM INV *Littéraire Vieilli* highwayman

tire-lait [tirlɛ] NM INV breast-pump

tire-larigot [tirlarigo] **à tire-larigot** ADV *Fam* **boire à t.** to drink like a fish; **il y en a à t.** there's loads *or* tons of them

tire-ligne [tirliɲ] *(pl* **tire-lignes)** NM drawing pen

tirelire [tirlir] NF **1** *(boîte)* moneybox; *(en forme de cochon)* piggy bank; *Fig* **casser sa t.** to break into one's piggy bank **2** *très Fam (estomac)* belly, gut **3** *Fam (tête)* head[□], nut, *Br* bonce; *(visage)* face[□], mug

tire-moelle [tirmwal] NM INV *très Fam* snotrag

tire-pognon [tirpɔɲɔ̃] *(pl* **tire-pognons)** NM *Fam Vieilli* one-arm(ed) bandit, fruit machine

TIRER [3] [tire]

VT	
• to pull **A1-3, B1**	• to drag **A1**
• to draw **A1, 4, B1, 8, E1**	• to fire **C1**
• to set off **C2**	• to shoot **C3**
• to throw **C4**	• to print **E2, 3**
VI	
• to pull **4, 7**	• to get out of **4**
• to draw **5, 6**	• to fire **1**
• to shoot **1–3**	
VPR	
• to get going **2**	• to draw to a close **3**

VT **A.** *DÉPLACER* **1** *(traîner ▸ avec ou sans effort)* to pull, to drag; *(▸ en remorquant)* to draw, to tow; **tire la table au milieu de la pièce** pull the table out to the centre of the room; **un cheval tirait la péniche le long du canal** a horse was towing *or* pulling the barge along the canal; **tiré par un cheval** horse-drawn; **tiré par des bœufs** ox-drawn; **t. qn par le bras/les cheveux/les pieds** to drag sb by the arm/hair/feet

2 *(amener à soi)* to pull; *(étirer ▸ vers le haut)* to pull (up); *(▸ vers le bas)* to pull (down); **je sentis que quelqu'un tirait ma veste** I felt a tug at my jacket; **elle me tira doucement par la manche** she tugged *or* pulled at my sleeve; **tirez doucement le levier de vitesse** pull the gear lever gently (back); **t. les cheveux à qn** to pull sb's hair; **t. ses cheveux en arrière** to draw *or* to pull one's hair back; **tire bien le drap** stretch the sheet (taut); **t. un fil** *(accidentellement)* to pull a thread; *(pour faire un jour)* to draw a thread; **t. la couverture à soi** *(s'attribuer le mérite)* to take all the credit; *(s'attribuer le profit)* to take the lion's share; *Can* **t. la pipe à qn** to pull sb's leg, to tease sb

3 *(pour actionner ▸ cordon d'appel, élastique)* to pull; *(▸ tiroir)* to pull (open *or* out); **t. les rideaux** to pull *or* to draw the curtains; **t. un verrou** *(pour ouvrir)* to slide a bolt open; *(pour fermer)* to slide a bolt to, to shoot a bolt; **t. la chasse d'eau** to flush the toilet

4 *Naut* to draw; **t. cinq mètres** to draw five metres of water

B. *EXTRAIRE, OBTENIR* **1** *(faire sortir)* **t. qch de** to pull *or* to draw sth out of; **t. un revolver de son sac** to pull a gun out of one's bag; **t. de l'eau d'un puits** to draw water (out of a well); **t. le vin/cidre (du tonneau)** to draw wine/cider (off from the barrel); **t. qn de** *(le faire sortir de)* to get sb out of; **t. qn d'un asile/de prison** to get sb out of an asylum/prison; **t. qn d'une voiture en feu** to drag *or* to pull sb out of a blazing car; **va le t. du lit** go and get *or* drag him out of bed; *Fig* **t. qn d'un cauchemar** to rouse sb from a nightmare; **t. qn du sommeil** to wake sb up; **t. qn du coma** to pull sb out of a coma; **t. qn de sa rêverie** to rouse sb from his/her daydream; **t. qn de son silence** to draw sb out (of his/her silence); **t. qn d'une situation difficile** to get sb out of a difficult situation; **tire-moi de là** help me out

2 *(fabriquer)* **t. qch de** to derive *or* to get *or* to make sth from; **les produits que l'on tire du pétrole** oil-based products; **t. des sons d'un instrument** to get *or* to draw sounds from an instrument; **t. un film d'une pièce de théâtre** to adapt a play for the screen; **photos tirées d'un film** movie stills

3 *(percevoir ▸ argent)* **elle tire sa fortune de ses terres** she makes her money from her land; **elle savait ce qu'on peut t. d'un placement judicieux** she knew what could be gained from a wise investment; **il a bien tiré cinq millions de la vente de la maison** he must have made at least five million from the sale of the house; **tu ne tireras pas grand-chose de ta vieille montre** you won't get much (money) for your old watch

4 *(retirer ▸ chèque, argent liquide)* to draw; **t. de l'argent d'un compte** to draw money out of *or* to withdraw money from an account

5 *(extraire, dégager)* **t. la morale/un enseignement de qch** to learn a lesson from sth; **ce vers est tiré d'un poème de Villon** this line is (taken) from a poem by Villon; **ce que j'ai tiré de ce livre/cet article** what I got out of this book/article; **t. sa force de sa foi** to derive *or* to draw one's strength from one's faith; **ce roman tire son titre d'une chanson populaire** the title of this novel is taken from a popular song; **les mots que le français a tirés du latin** French words taken from Latin; **t. satisfaction de qch** to derive satisfaction from sth; **t. vanité de qch** to be proud of sth; **t. fierté de qch** to pride oneself on *or* in sth; **t. vengeance de qch** to avenge sth

6 *(obtenir, soutirer)* **t. de l'argent de qn** to extract money from sb, to get money out of sb; **la police n'a rien pu t. de lui** the police couldn't get anything out of him; **tu auras du mal à lui t. des excuses** you'll be hard pressed to get an apology out of him/her; **tu auras du mal à lui t. des remerciements** you'll get no thanks from him/her; **j'ai réussi à lui t. un sourire** I managed to get a smile out of him/her; **t. des larmes à qn** to make sb cry; *Fam* **t. les vers du nez à qn** to worm *or* drag it out of sb; *Fam* **on n'en tirera jamais rien, de ce gosse** *(il n'est bon à rien)* we'll never make anything out of this kid; *(il ne parlera pas)* we'll never get this kid to talk, we'll never get anything out of this kid; **je n'ai pas pu en t. davantage** I couldn't get any more out of him/her

7 *Fam (voler)* **je me suis fait t. mon portefeuille au cinéma!** somebody pinched *or Br* nicked my wallet at the *Br* cinema *or Am* movie theater!

8 *(billet, numéro)* to draw, to pick; *(loterie)* to draw, to carry out the draw for; *(carte)* to draw, to take; **tirez une carte postale au hasard** pick any postcard; **le gagnant sera tiré au sort** there will be a draw to decide the winner

C. *PROJETER* **1** *Mil (coup de fusil, missile)* to fire; *(balle, flèche)* to shoot; **t. un coup de feu** to fire a shot; **ils tiraient les passants comme des lapins** they were picking off passers-by one by one

2 *(feu d'artifice)* to set off; **ce soir, on tirera un feu d'artifice** there will be a fireworks display tonight

3 *Chasse (lapin, faisan)* to shoot; **t. un animal** to shoot an animal

4 *(à la pétanque ▸ boule en main)* to throw; *(▸ boule placée)* to knock out; *Ftbl* to take; *(au tennis ▸ passing-shot, volée)* to hit; *(en haltérophilie)* to lift; **t. un corner** to take a corner; **t. un coup franc** to take a free kick; **le penalty va être tiré par le capitaine** the penalty will be taken by the captain; *Escrime* **t. des armes** to fence

5 *Vulg (posséder sexuellement)* to screw, *Br* to shag; **t. un coup** to get laid, to have a screw *or Br* a shag

D. *PASSER Fam* to spend[□] **il est en train de t. dix piges pour vol à main armée** he's doing a ten-year stretch for armed robbery; **encore deux mois à t. avant les vacances** another two months to get through before the *Br* holidays *or Am* vacation

E. *TRACER, IMPRIMER* **1** *(dessiner ▸ ligne)* to draw; *(▸ plan)* to draw up; **tirez deux traits sous les verbes** underline the verbs twice

2 *Phot* to print

3 *Typ (livre)* to print; *(estampe, lithographie)* to print, to draw; *(tract)* to print, to run; *(gravure)* to strike, to pull, to print; **t. un tract à 5000 exemplaires** to print 5,000 copies of a tract; **ce magazine est tiré à plus de 200 000 exemplaires** this magazine has a print run *or* a circulation of 200,000; **"bon à t."** "passed for press"; **un bon à t.** *(épreuve)* a press proof; **signer le bon à t.** to pass for press

4 *Belg (locution)* **tu es assez grand, tu tires ton plan** you're old enough to look after yourself

VI **1** *Mil (faire feu)* to fire, to shoot; **ne tirez pas, je me rends!** don't shoot, I surrender!; **ne tirez plus!** hold your fire!, stop shooting!; **tirez dans les jambes** shoot at *or* aim at the legs; **il tire mal** he's a bad shot; **t. à la cible** to aim *or* to shoot at the target; **t. à balles/à blanc** to fire bullets/blanks; **t. en l'air/à vue** to shoot in the air/on sight; **t. sur qn** to take a shot *or* to shoot *or* to fire at sb; **ils ont l'ordre de t. sur tout ce qui bouge** they've been ordered to shoot *or* to fire at anything that moves; **on m'a tiré dessus** I was fired *or* shot at; **cette carabine tire juste** this rifle shoots straight

2 *Sport* **t. à l'arc/l'arbalète** *(activité sportive)* to do archery/crossbow archery; *(action ponctuelle)* to shoot a bow/crossbow; **t. à la carabine/au pistolet** *(activité sportive)* to do rifle/pistol shooting; *(action ponctuelle)* to shoot with a rifle/pistol

3 *Ftbl & Golf* to shoot; *Escrime* to fence; **il a tiré dans le mur/petit filet** he sent the ball against the wall/into the side netting

4 *(exercer une traction)* to pull; **à mon signal, tirez tous dans le même sens** when I give the signal, all pull in the same direction; **tire!** pull!, heave!; *Fam* **ça tire dans les genoux à la montée** going up is tough on the knees; *Fam* **elle tire bien, ta voiture!** it runs well, your car!; **la moto tire à droite** the motorbike pulls to the right; **la direction tire d'un côté** the steering pulls to one side; **t. sur un câble** to pull *or* to heave on a cable; **t. sur un levier** to pull (back) a lever; **t. sur les rênes** to pull on the reins; **ne tire pas sur ton gilet** don't pull your cardigan out of shape; **ne tire pas (sur la laisse), Rex!** stop pulling (on your lead), Rex!; *Fig* **t. sur** *(délais, budget)* to stretch; **elle tire un peu sur sa permission de minuit** she's stretching it a bit with her midnight curfew; **t. sur la ficelle** to go a bit far; *Suisse* **t. sur la même corde** to pull together

5 *(aspirer ▸ fumeur)* **t. sur une pipe** to draw on *or* to pull at a pipe; **t. sur une cigarette** to puff at *or* to draw on a cigarette

6 *(avoir un bon tirage ▸ cheminée, poêle)* **t. (bien)** to draw (well); **la cheminée/pipe tire mal** the fireplace/pipe doesn't draw properly

7 *(peau)* to feel tight; *(points de suture)* to pull; *Fam* **ma peau me tire** my skin feels tight; **aïe, ça tire!** ouch, it's pulling!

8 *(dans un jeu)* **t. au sort** to draw *or* to cast lots

9 *Typ* **t. à 50 000 exemplaires** to have a circulation of *or* to have a (print) run of 50,000 (copies); **à combien le journal tire-t-il?** what are the paper's circulation figures?

10 *Suisse (thé)* to brew

11 *Belg & Suisse (locution)* **ça tire** there's a draught

12 *Banque* **t. à découvert** to overdraw; **t. à vue** to draw at sight

• **tirer à** VT IND **1** *Presse* **t. à la ligne** to pad out an article *(because it is being paid by the line)* **2** *Naut* **t. au large** to make for the open sea **3** *Fam* **t. au flanc** *ou* **cul** to shirk, *Br* to skive **4** *(locution)* **t. à sa fin** to come to an end

• **tirer sur** VT IND *(couleur)* to verge *or* to border on; **ses cheveux tirent sur le roux** his/her hair is reddish *or* almost red

VPR **se tirer 1** *(emploi passif)* **le store se tire avec un cordon** the blind pulls down with a cord

2 *Fam (partir, quitter un endroit)* to hit the road, to get going; *(s'enfuir)* to beat it; **s'il n'est pas là dans cinq minutes, je me tire** if he's not here in five minutes I'm off *or* I'm out of here; **tire-toi!** *(ton menaçant)* beat it!; **on se tire, voilà les flics!** it's the cops, let's get out of here!

3 *Fam (toucher à sa fin ▸ emprisonnement, service militaire)* to draw to a close[□]; **plus qu'une semaine, ça se tire quand même!** only a week to go, it's nearly over!

4 se t. de *(se sortir de)* to get out of; **il s'est bien/mal tiré de l'entrevue** he did well/badly at the interview

5 *Fam* **s'en t.** *(s'en sortir)* **avec son culot, elle s'en tirera toujours** with her cheek, she'll always come out on top; **si tu ne m'avais pas aidé à finir la maquette, je ne m'en serais jamais tiré** if you hadn't given me a hand with the model, I'd never have managed; **on n'avait qu'un seul salaire, mais on s'en est tirés** we had just the one salary, but we got by *or* scraped by; **rien à faire, je ne m'en tire**

pas! *(financièrement)* it's impossible, I just can't make ends meet!; **il y a peu de chances qu'il s'en tire** *(qu'il survive)* the odds are against him pulling through; **je m'en suis tiré avec une suspension de permis** I got away with my licence being suspended; **tu ne t'en tireras pas avec de simples excuses** *(être quitte)* you won't get away *or* off with just a few words of apology; **je m'en suis tiré avec** *ou* **pour 500 euros de réparations** I had to cough up *or* fork out 500 euros for the repairs; **on n'a encaissé qu'un seul but, on ne s'en est pas trop mal tirés** they scored only one goal against us, we didn't do too badly

tiret [tirɛ] **NM 1** *Typ (de dialogue)* dash; *(en fin de ligne)* rule; **t. cadratin** em dash; **t. demi-cadratin** en dash; **t. de fin de ligne** line-end hyphen **2** *(trait d'union)* hyphen; *Ordinat & Typ* **t. conditionnel/insécable** soft/hard hyphen

tirette [tirɛt] **NF 1** *Vieilli (cordon ▸ de sonnette)* bellpull; *(▸ de stores)* cord; *(▸ de rideaux)* draw string

2 *Tech* pull handle, pull knob; *(d'un fourneau)* flue damper; *Aut* (pull-out) knob; *Élec* pull knob

3 *(d'un meuble)* (sliding) leaf; *(d'un bureau)* pull-out shelf

4 *Belg (fermeture Éclair®) Br* zip, *Am* zipper

tireur, -euse [tirœr, -øz] **NM,F 1** *(criminel, terroriste)* gunman; *(de la police)* marksman; **bon/mauvais t.** good/bad shot; **t. isolé** *ou* **embusqué** sniper; **t. d'élite** sharpshooter

2 *(aux boules)* thrower

3 *Banque* drawer

4 *Escrime* fencer

5 *Ftbl* shooter

6 *Phot* printer

7 t. de cartes, tireuse de cartes fortune-teller *(who reads cards)*

• **tireuse NF 1** *Phot (machine)* printer **2** *(pour le vin)* bottle-filling machine

tiroir [tirwar] **NM 1** *(de meuble)* drawer

2 *Rail* siding

3 *Tech* slide valve; **t. rond** *ou* **à pistons** piston valve

4 *Fam (ventre)* stomach◻, belly

• **à tiroirs ADJ 1** *(à épisodes)* **roman/comédie à tiroirs** episodic novel/play **2** *Fam (à rallonge)* **un nom à tiroirs** a double-barrelled name

tiroir-caisse [tirwarkɛs] *(pl* **tiroirs-caisses***)* **NM** till

tisane [tizan] **NF 1** *(infusion)* herb tea, herbal tea **2** *très Fam (raclée, volée)* thrashing, hiding

tisanière [tizanjɛr] **NF** teapot *(for herbal tea)*

tison [tizɔ̃] **NM** brand

tisonné, -e [tizɔne] **ADJ** *(robe d'un cheval)* with black spots

tisonner [3] [tizɔne] **VT** to poke

tisonnier [tizɔnje] **NM** poker; **donner un coup de t. dans le feu** to give the fire a poke

tissage [tisaʒ] **NM 1** *(procédé)* weaving; *(entrecroisement de fils)* weave; **un t. serré/lâche** a close/loose weave; **t. à la main** *ou* **à bras** handloom weaving; **t. mécanique** power-loom weaving **2** *(bâtiment)* cloth mill

tisser [3] [tise] **VT 1** *Tex (laine, coton, tissu)* to weave; **t. le lin/une nappe** to weave linen/a tablecloth **2** *(toile d'araignée)* to spin **3** *Fig (élaborer)* to weave, to construct

VPR se tisser *Fig (lien, intrigue)* to be woven

tisserand, -e [tisrɑ̃, -ɑ̃d] **NM,F** weaver

tisserin [tisrɛ̃] **NM 1** *(artisan)* weaver **2** *Orn* weaverbird

tisseur, -euse [tisœr, -øz] **NM,F 1** *(artisan)* weaver **2** *(industriel)* mill owner

tissu [tisy] **NM 1** *Tex* fabric, material, cloth; **une longueur de t.** a length of fabric; **du t. d'ameublement** furnishing fabric *or* material; **t. matelassé** quilted material; **t. métallique** wire gauze

2 *Fig (enchevêtrement)* **un t. de mensonges** a pack *or Sout* tissue of lies; **un t. d'absurdités** one absurdity after another; **c'est un t. d'incohérences** it's full of inconsistencies

3 *(en sociologie)* fabric, make-up; **le t. culturel de la nation** the cultural make-up *or* fabric of our country; **le t. social** the social fabric; **le t. urbain** the urban infrastructure

4 *Biol* tissue; **t. conjonctif** connective tissue; **t. musculaire** muscle tissue

5 *Bot* tissue

• **de tissu, en tissu ADJ** fabric *(avant n)*, cloth *(avant n)*

> Il faut noter que le terme anglais **tissue** ne signifie jamais **textile**. Il signifie souvent **mouchoir en papier.**

tissu-éponge [tisyepɔ̃ʒ] *(pl* **tissus-éponges***)* **NM** terry, terry-towelling, *Am* terry cloth; **en t.** terry *(avant n)*, terry-towelling *(avant n)*, *Am* terry cloth; **peignoir en t.** towelling robe; **serviette en t.** terry towel

tissulaire [tisylɛr] **ADJ** tissual, tissue *(avant n)*

Titan [titɑ̃] **NM 1** *Astron* Titan **2** *Mil* **(missile) T.** Titan missile

NMPL *Myth* **les Titans** the Titans

titane [titan] **NM** titanium

titanesque [titanesk] **ADJ** *Littéraire (force)* massive, superhuman; *(travail)* Herculean; *(ouvrage)* monumental

titanique[1] [titanik] = **titanesque**

titanique[2] [titanik] **ADJ** *Chim* titanic

titi [titi] *Fam* **NM t. parisien** Parisian street urchin◻

• **en titi** *Can* **ADJ être en t.** to be fuming, to be hopping mad **ADV** damn, *Br* bloody; **il fait froid en t.** it's damn *or Br* bloody cold

Titien [tisjɛ̃] **NPR (le) T.** Titian

titillation [titijasjɔ̃] **NF 1** *(léger chatouillement)* tickling, tickle **2** *Fig (excitation de l'esprit)* titillation

titiller [3] [titije] **VT 1** *(chatouiller agréablement)* to tickle **2** *Fig (exciter légèrement)* to titillate **3** *(énerver)* to pester, to aggravate

titisme [titism] **NM** Titoism

titiste [titist] **ADJ** Titoist

NMF Titoist

titrage [titraʒ] **NM 1** *(d'un film)* titling; *Journ* **t. à cheval** spread head

2 *Chim* titration, titrating

3 *Mines (d'un minerai)* assaying

4 *(d'un alcool, d'un vin)* determination of the strength

titraille [titraj] **NF** *Journ* coverline

TITRE [titr]

- title **A1, 2, B1, 3, C5**
- track **A4**
- credentials **C1**
- certificate **C4**
- headline **A3**
- qualification **B2**
- security **C3, 4**

NM A. 1 *(d'un roman, d'un poème)* title; *(d'un chapitre)* title, heading

2 *Typ* **t. courant** running title; **faux t.** half-title; **grand t.** full title; **(page de) t.** title page

3 *Journ* headline; **t. sur cinq colonnes à la une** five-column front-page headline; **les gros titres** the main headlines; **faire les gros titres des quotidiens** to hit *or* to make the front page of the daily newspapers

4 *(chanson, morceau)* track; **le CD comporte onze titres** there are eleven tracks on the CD

B. 1 *(désignation d'un rang, d'une dignité)* title; **le t. de roi/d'empereur** the title of king/emperor; **porter un t.** to have a title, to be titled; **porter le t. de duc** to have the title of duke; *Fig* **il revendique le t. de libérateur** he insists on being called a liberator; **un t. de noblesse** *ou* **nobiliaire** a title; **avoir des titres de noblesse** to be titled

2 *(nom de charge, de grade)* qualification; **conférer le t. de docteur à qn** to confer the title of doctor on *or* upon sb

3 *Sport* title; **mettre son t. en jeu** to risk one's title; **le boxeur défendra son t.** the boxer will defend his title; **disputer le t. de champion du monde à qn** *(boxeur)* to fight sb for the world championship title

C. 1 *(certificat)* credentials; **il a produit des titres authentiques** he produced genuine credentials; **voici les titres à présenter à l'appui de votre demande** the following documents must accompany your application; **t. de pension** pension book; **t. de permission** (leave) pass; **t. de transport** ticket

2 *Fig* **il s'est acquis des titres de reconnaissance du peuple** he won the people's gratitude; **son t. de gloire est d'avoir introduit l'informatique dans l'entreprise** his/her proudest achievement is to have computerized the company

3 *Banque* (transferable) security; **avance sur titres** advance on *or* against securities; **t. universel de paiement** universal payment order; **t. de crédit** proof of credit; **titres déposés en nantissement** securities lodged as collateral

4 *Bourse (certificat)* certificate; *(valeur)* security; **les titres** securities, bonds; **t. d'action** share certificate; **t. nominatif** registered bond; **titres en portefeuille** securities (in portfolio); **t. au porteur** *(action)* bearer share; *(obligation)* floater *or* bearer security; **t. de rente** government bond; **titres à terme** futures

5 *Jur* title; **t. exécutoire** writ of execution; **t. de propriété** title deed, document of title; **t. putatif** putative deed; **juste t.** good title

D. 1 *(en joaillerie)* fineness, *Spéc* titre

2 *Pharm* titre

3 *Tex* count

E. *(locutions)* **à t. amical** as a friend; **consulter qn à t. d'ami** to consult sb as a friend; **demander une somme à t. d'avance** to ask for some money by way of an advance; **à t. consultatif** in an advisory capacity; **à t. d'essai** on a trial basis; **à t. exceptionnel** exceptionally; **à t. d'exemple** by way of an example, as an example; **à t. privé/professionnel** in a private/professional capacity; **décoration attribuée à t. posthume** posthumous award; **à t. provisoire** on a provisional basis; **présidence accordée à t. honorifique** honorary title of president; **à t. gracieux** free of charge, without charge; **à t. onéreux** for a fee *or* consideration; **à t. de journaliste, vous pourrez entrer** you will be allowed in because you are from the press; **à t. indicatif** for information only; **à quel t.?** *(en vertu de quel droit)* in what capacity?; *(pour quelle raison)* on what grounds?; **à quel t. lui fais-tu ces reproches?** on what grounds do you criticize him/her?

• **à aucun titre ADV** on no account; **il n'est à aucun t. mon ami** he is no friend of mine

• **à ce titre ADV** *(pour cette raison)* for this reason, on this account; **l'accord est signé et à ce t. je suis satisfait** the agreement has been signed and for this reason I am satisfied

• **à de nombreux titres, à divers titres ADV** for several reasons, on more than one account; **je me félicite à plus d'un t. du résultat de ces négociations** I have more than one reason to be pleased with the outcome of these negotiations

• **à juste titre ADV** *(préférer)* understandably, rightly; *(croire)* correctly, justly, rightly; **elle s'est emportée, (et) à juste t.** she lost her temper and understandably *or* rightly so

• **à plus d'un titre** = **à de nombreux titres**

• **au même titre ADV** for the same reasons; **elle a obtenu une prime, j'en réclame une au même t.** she got a bonus, I think I should have one too for the same reasons

• **au même titre que CONJ** for the same reasons as

• **en titre ADJ 1** *Admin* titular **2** *(officiel ▸ fournisseur, marchand)* usual, appointed; **le fournisseur en t. de la cour de Hollande** the official *or* appointed supplier to the Dutch Court

titré, -e [titre] **ADJ 1** *(anobli)* titled **2** *Pharm (liqueur, solution)* standard *(avant n)*

titrer [3] [titre] **VT 1** *Presse* **t. qch** to run sth as a headline

2 *Pharm* to titrate

3 *Mines* to assay

4 *(alcool, vin)* to determine the strength of

5 *Tex & Tech (coton, fil de fer)* to size, to number

titreur, -euse [titrœr, -øz] **NM,F** *Journ* headline writer

• **titreuse NF 1** *Cin (appareil)* titler **2** *Typ (pour gros titres)* headliner

titrisation [titrizasjɔ̃] **NF** *Banque* securitization

titubant, -e [titybɑ̃, -ɑ̃t] **ADJ** *(démarche)* unsteady, weaving, wobbly; **un ivrogne t.** a drunkard staggering about

tituber [3] [titybe] **VI** *(ivrogne)* to stagger *or* to reel (along); *(malade)* to stagger (along); **marcher/entrer/sortir en titubant** to stagger *or* to lurch along/in/out

titulaire [tityler] **ADJ 1** *(enseignant)* tenured; *(évêque)* titular; **être t.** *(professeur d'université)* to have tenure; *(sportif)* to be under contract; **devenir t.** to get tenure **2** *(détenteur)* **être t. de** *(permis, document, passeport)* to hold **3** *Jur* **être t. d'un droit** to be entitled to a right

NMF 1 *Admin & Rel* incumbent

2 *(détenteur ▸ d'un permis)* holder; *(▸ d'un passeport)* bearer, holder; **t. d'action** shareholder

3 *Jur* **le t. d'un droit** the person entitled to a right

4 *Sport* player under contract, team member

titularisation [titylarizasjɔ̃] **NF la t. de qn** *(gén)* giving a permanent contract to sb; *(professeur d'université)* granting tenure to sb; *(enseignant)* appointing sb to a permanent post; *(sportif)* giving a contract to sb, signing sb up (as a full member of the team)

titulariser [3] [titylarize] **VT** *(gén)* to give a permanent contract to; *(professeur d'université)* to grant tenure to; *(enseignant)* to appoint to a permanent post; *(sportif)* to give a contract to, to sign up (as a full member of the team)

TJJ [teʒiʒi] **NM** *Fin (abrév* **taux d'argent au jour le jour***)* overnight *or* call rate

TMT [teemte] **NM** *(abrév* **technology, media and telecommunications***)* TMT

TNT [teente] **NM** *Chim (abrév* **trinitrotoluène***)* TNT

NF *TV (abrév* **télévision numérique terrestre***)* digital television, DTT

toast [tost] **NM 1** *(en buvant)* toast; **t. de bienvenue** welcome toast; **porter un t. à qn** to drink (a toast) to sb, to toast sb **2** *(pain grillé)* piece of toast; **des toasts** toast, toasted bread; **des toasts au saumon** salmon canapés

toasteur [tostœr] **NM** toaster

toboggan [tɔbɔgɑ̃] **NM 1** *(glissière ▸ dans un terrain de jeu)* slide; *(▸ dans l'eau)* chute, flume; *(▸ pour marchandises)* chute; **tu veux faire du t.?** do you want to go on the slide?; **t. de secours** escape chute **2** *(luge)* toboggan; **faire du t.** to go tobogganing **3** *Can (traîneau)* toboggan

• **Toboggan®** **NM** *(pont) Br* flyover, *Am* overpass

> Il faut noter que le terme anglais **toboggan** est un faux ami. Il signifie **luge**.

toc [tɔk] **NM** *Fam (imitation sans valeur ▸ d'un matériau)* fake□, worthless imitation□; *(▸ d'un bijou)* fake□; **en t.** fake□, imitation□; **sa bague, c'est du t.** his/her ring is fake□

ADJ INV *Fam* **1** *(faux)* trashy, tacky, *Br* rubbishy; **ça fait t.** it looks tacky **2 être un peu t. t.** *(fou)* to be a bit crazy *or* cracked

EXCLAM 1 *(coups à la porte)* **t. t.!** knock knock! **2** *Fam (après une remarque)* **et t.!** so there!, put that in your pipe and smoke it!; **et t., bien fait pour toi/lui/eux!** and (it) serves you/him/them right!

tocante [tɔkɑ̃t] **NF** *Fam* watch□

tocard, -e [tɔkar, -ard] *Fam* **ADJ** *(tableau, décor)* tacky, *Br* naff

NM,F *(personne)* dead loss, (born) loser

NM *(cheval de course)* mediocre racehorse

toccata [tɔkata] **NF** *Mus* toccata

tocsin [tɔksɛ̃] **NM** alarm bell, *Sout* tocsin; **sonner le t.** to ring the alarm, *Sout* to sound the tocsin

toge [tɔʒ] **NF 1** *Antiq* toga; **t. prétexte/virile** toga praetexta/virilis **2** *(de magistrat)* gown

Togo [tɔgo] **NM le T.** Togo

togolais, -e [tɔgɔlɛ, -ez] **ADJ** Togolese

• **Togolais, -e** **NM,F** Togolese; **les T.** the Togolese

tohu-bohu [tɔybɔy] **NM INV 1** *(désordre et confusion)* confusion, chaos **2** *(bruit ▸ de voitures, d'enfants)* racket, din; *(▸ d'un marché, d'une gare)* hustle and bustle; *(▸ d'une foule)* hubbub; *(▸ d'une foire)* hurly-burly

toi [twa] **PRON 1** *(après un impératif)* **dis-t. bien que...** bear in mind that...; **réveille-t.!** wake up!; **habille-t.!** get dressed!; **rappelle-t.!** remember!; **assieds-t.!** sit down!; **dis-le-lui, t.** YOU tell him/her

2 *(sujet)* you; **moi, je reste, et t., tu pars** I'll stay and you go; **qui va le faire? – t.** who's going to do it? – you (are); **t. parti, il ne restera personne** when you're gone there'll be nobody left; **tu en veux, t.?** do you want some?; **qu'est-ce que tu en sais, t.?** what do YOU know about it?; **tu t'amuses, t., au moins** at least YOU'RE having fun; **et t. qui lui faisais confiance!** and you trusted him/her!; **t. et moi** you and I; **t. et moi, nous irons ensemble** you and I will go together; **t. seul peux la convaincre** you're the only one who can persuade her

3 *(avec un présentatif)* you; **c'est t.?** is it you?; **je veux que ce soit t. qui y ailles** I want it to be you who goes; **c'est t. qui le dis!** that's what YOU say!; **ah c'est bien t., ça!** that's typical of you!, that's just like you!

4 *(complément)* you; **il vous a invités, Pierre et t.** he's invited you and Pierre; **t., je te connais!** I know you!

5 *(après une préposition)* **avec/sans/pour/etc t.** with/without/for/*etc* you; **c'est à t. qu'on l'a demandé** you were the one who was asked, YOU were asked; **qui te l'a dit, à t.?** who told YOU about it?; **à t., je peux le dire** I can tell YOU; *Fam* **un ami à t.** a friend of yours; **c'est à t.?** is this yours?; **ce livre est à t.** this book is yours *or* belongs to you; **à t. de jouer!** your turn!; **il est plus âgé que t.** he is older than you; **il n'aime que t.** he loves only you

6 *(pronom réfléchi)* yourself; **alors, tu es content de t.?** I hope you're pleased with yourself, then!

toile [twal] **NF 1** *Tex (matériau brut)* canvas, (plain) cloth; **t. de coton/lin** cotton/linen cloth; **t. d'amiante** asbestos; **t. à bâches** tarpaulin; **t. de Jouy** toile de Jouy; **t. de jute** gunny, (jute) hessian; **t. à matelas** ticking; **t. à sac** sackcloth, sacking; **t. de tente** canvas; **t. à voiles** sailcloth; **grosse t.** rough *or* coarse canvas

2 *(tissu apprêté)* cloth; **t. cirée** waxcloth; **nappe en t. cirée** waxed tablecloth; **t. émeri** emery cloth; **t. métallique** wire gauze; **t. de tente** tent canvas

3 *Fam (film)* **se payer** *ou* **se faire une t.** to go to the movies *or Br* the pictures

4 *Beaux-Arts (vierge)* canvas; *(peinte)* canvas, painting; **quelques toiles du jeune peintre** some paintings by the young artist

5 *Naut (ensemble des voiles d'un navire)* sails; **réduire la t.** to take in sail

6 *Théât* (painted) curtain; *aussi Fig* **t. de fond** backdrop; *Fig* **avec la guerre en t. de fond** with the war as a backdrop, against the backdrop of the war

7 *Zool* web; **t. d'araignée** cobweb, spider's web

8 *Ordinat* **la T.** the Web

• **toiles** **NFPL** *Fam (draps de lit)* sheets□; **se mettre dans les toiles** to hit the sack *or* the hay

• **de toile, en toile** **ADJ** *(robe, pantalon)* cotton *(avant n)*; *(sac)* canvas *(avant n)*; **reliure en t.** cloth binding

toilerie [twalri] **NF 1** *(atelier)* canvas mill **2** *(commerce)* canvas trade; *(fabrication)* canvas manufacturing, canvas making

toilettage [twaletaʒ] **NM** *(d'un chat, d'un chien)* grooming

toilette [twalɛt] **NF 1** *(soins de propreté)* washing, *Sout* toilet; **faire sa t.** to have a wash, to get washed; **faire une t. rapide** to have a quick wash; **faire une t. de chat** to have a catlick, to have a lick and a promise; **être à sa t.** *(se laver)* to be having a wash, to be getting washed; *Fam Vieilli (s'apprêter)* to be making one's toilet; **faire la t. d'un malade** to wash a sick person; **faire la t. d'un mort** to lay out a corpse; **produits pour la t. de bébé** baby care products; **articles** *ou* **produits de t.** toiletries

2 *(lustrage du pelage, des plumes)* grooming; **le chat fait sa t.** the cat's washing *or* grooming itself

3 *(tenue vestimentaire)* clothes, outfit, *Sout* toilette; **changer de t.** to change (one's outfit *or* clothes); **elle est en grande t.** she is (dressed) in all her finery

4 *(table)* dressing-table; *(avec vasque)* washstand

5 *Tech* reed packaging

6 *Culin* veal caul

7 *Belg & Can* = **toilettes**

• **toilettes** **NFPL** *(chez un particulier) Br* toilet, *Am* bathroom; *(dans un café)* toilet, *Br* toilets, *Am* restroom; **toilettes publiques** *Br* toilets, *Am* restroom; **aller aux toilettes** to go to the toilet

toiletter [4] [twalete] **VT 1** *(chien, chat)* to groom; **je fais t. le chien une fois par mois** I take the dog to be groomed once a month **2** *Fam (modifier légèrement ▸ texte)* to amend□, to doctor

toi-même [twamem] **PRON** yourself; **tu l'as vu t.** you saw it yourself; **il faut que tu le comprennes de t.** you must understand it (for) yourself; *Fam* **imbécile t.!** same to you!, look who's talking!; **menteur – t.!** liar – liar yourself!

toise [twaz] **NF 1** *(règle graduée)* height gauge; **passer qn à la t.** to measure sb's height **2** *Arch* = former French unit of measurement equal to 1.949 metres

toiser [3] [twaze] **VT 1** *(regarder)* **t. qn** to look sb up and down, to eye sb from head to foot **2** *Vieilli (personne)* to measure sb's height

VPR se toiser *(se regarder)* to look each other up and down, to take each other's measure

toison [twazɔ̃] **NF 1** *Zool* fleece; *(de lion, de cheval)* mane

2 *(chevelure)* mane

3 *Fam (poils)* bushy (tuft of) hair

4 *Myth* **la T. d'or** the Golden Fleece

toit [twa] **NM 1** *Archit & Constr* roof; **habiter sous les toits** *(dans une chambre)* to live in an attic room *or* in a garret; *(dans un appartement)* to live in a *Br* top-floor flat *or Am* top-story apartment with a sloping ceiling; **t. plat/en pente** flat/sloping roof; **t. de chaume** thatched roof; **une maison au t. de chaume** a thatched cottage; **t. en terrasse** terrace roof; **t. vert** green roof; **double t.** *(de tente)* flysheet; **le t. du monde** the Roof of the World **2** *Fig (demeure)* roof; **avoir un t.** to have a roof over one's head; **chercher un t.** to look for somewhere to live; **se retrouver sans t.** to find oneself without a roof over one's head; **sous le t. de qn** under sb's roof, in sb's house; **accueillir qn sous son t.** to take sb in; **vivre sous le même t.** to live under the same roof **3** *Aut* **t. ouvrant** sunroof; **t. ouvrant coulissant** sliding sunroof; **une voiture à t. ouvrant** a car with a sunroof

toiture [twatyr] **NF** *(ensemble des matériaux)* roofing; *(couverture)* roof; **toute la t. du manoir** all the roofs of the manor house; **refaire la t.** to repair the roof

tokai, tokay [tɔke] **NM** *(vin)* Tokay

Tokyo [tɔkjo] **NM** Tokyo

tôlard, -e [tolar, -ard] = **taulard**

tôle[1] [tol] **NF 1** *Métal (non découpée)* sheet metal; *(feuille)* metal sheet; **t. d'acier/d'aluminium** sheet steel/aluminium; **t. galvanisée/laminée** galvanized/laminated iron; **t. ondulée** corrugated iron; **toit en t. ondulée** corrugated iron roof; **t. froissée** crumpled metal **2** *Fam (mauvais revêtement de route)* uneven surface

tôle[2] [tol] = **taule**

Tolède [tɔlɛd] **NM** Toledo

tôlée [tole] *Ski* **ADJ F neige t.** crusted snow

NF crusted snow

tolérable [tɔlerabl] **ADJ** *(bruit, chaleur, douleur)* bearable, tolerable; **ça n'est pas t.** that is intolerable *or* cannot be tolerated; **son impertinence n'est plus t.** his/her impertinence can no longer be tolerated

NM à la limite du t. barely *or* scarcely tolerable

tolérance [tɔlerɑ̃s] **NF 1** *(à l'égard d'une personne)* tolerance; **faire preuve de t. (à l'égard de qn)** to be tolerant (with *or* towards sb); **manquer de t.** to lack tolerance, to be intolerant

2 *(à l'égard d'un règlement)* tolerance, latitude; **ce n'est pas un droit, c'est une simple t.** this is not a right, it is merely something which is tolerated; **t. zéro (vis-à-vis de qch)** zero tolerance (towards *or* regarding sth)

3 *Bot & Physiol* tolerance; **t. au bruit/à la chaleur/à une drogue** tolerance to noise/to heat/to a drug; **t. immunitaire** immunological tolerance

4 *(à la douane)* **t. (permise)** allowance; **il y a une t. d'un litre d'alcool par personne** each person is allowed to bring in a litre of spirits free of duty

5 *Tech* tolerance; **t. de fonctionnement** operational tolerance; **t. sur l'épaisseur/la longueur** thickness/length margin

6 *Rel* toleration

tolérant, -e [tɔlerɑ̃, -ɑ̃t] **ADJ 1** *(non sectaire)* tolerant, broad-minded **2** *(indulgent)* lenient, indulgent, easy-going; **une mère trop tolérante** an overindulgent *or* excessively lenient mother

tolérer [18] [tɔlere] **VT 1** *(permettre ▸ infraction)* to tolerate, to allow; **nous tolérons un petit excédent**

de bagages we allow a small amount of excess luggage **2** *(admettre ▸ attitude, personne)* to tolerate, to put up with; **je ne tolérerai pas son insolence** I won't stand for *or* put up with *or* tolerate his/her rudeness; **je ne tolère pas qu'on me parle sur ce ton!** I won't tolerate being spoken to like that!; **le directeur ne tolère pas les retards** the manager will not have people arriving late; **ici, on la tolère, c'est tout** we put up with her and that's about all **3** *(supporter ▸ médicament, traitement)* to tolerate; **son foie ne tolère plus l'alcool** his/her liver can no longer tolerate alcohol; **les femmes enceintes tolèrent bien ce médicament** pregnant women can take this drug without adverse effects

VPR se tolérer *(l'un l'autre)* to put up with *or* tolerate each other

tôlerie [tolri] **NF 1** *(fabrique)* sheet-metal workshop; *Aut* body shop

2 *(technique)* sheet-metal manufacture

3 *(commerce)* sheet-metal trade

4 *(d'un véhicule)* panels, bodywork; *(d'un réservoir)* plates, (steel) cladding

tôlier, -ère [tolje, -ɛr] **NM,F** = **taulier**

NM *Ind* **1** *(marchand)* sheet-iron merchant **2** *(ouvrier)* sheet-metal worker; *Aut* panel beater

tollé [tɔle] **NM** general outcry; **soulever un t. général** to provoke a general outcry

Tolstoï [tɔlstɔj] **NPR Léon T.** Leon Tolstoy

toluène [tɔlɥɛn] **NM** *Chim* toluene

TOM [tɔm] **NM INV** *Admin (abrév* **territoire d'outre-mer)** French overseas territory

tomahawk [tɔmaok] **NM** tomahawk

tomaison [tɔmɛzɔ̃] **NF** *Typ* volume numbering

tomate [tɔmat] **NF 1** *Bot (plante)* tomato (plant); *(fruit)* tomato; **t. cerise** cherry tomato; *Culin* **tomates farcies** stuffed tomatoes; *Fig* **envoyer des tomates (pourries) à qn** *(conspuer)* to boo sb **2** *Fam (boisson)* = pastis with grenadine

• **à la tomate ADJ** tomato-flavoured

tombal, -e, -als *ou* **-aux, -ales** [tɔ̃bal, -o] **ADJ** funerary, tomb *(avant n)*, tombstone *(avant n)*; **inscription tombale** funerary *or* tomb *or* tombstone inscription

tombant, -e [tɔ̃bɑ̃, -ɑ̃t] **ADJ 1** *(oreille, moustache)* drooping; *(seins, fesses)* sagging; *(épaules)* sloping; *(tentures)* hanging; **des yeux aux paupières tombantes** hooded eyes **2** *(jour)* failing, dwindling

tombe [tɔ̃b] **NF** *(fosse)* grave; *(dalle)* tombstone; *(monument)* tomb; **aller sur la t. de qn** *(pour se recueillir)* to visit sb's grave; **prier sur la t. de qn** to pray at sb's grave(side); **muet** *ou* **silencieux comme une t.** as silent *or* quiet as the grave; **suivre qn dans la t.** to follow sb to the grave; **avoir un pied dans la t.** to have one foot in the grave

> Do not confuse with **tombeau**.

tombé [tɔ̃be] **NM 1** *(en danse)* tombé **2** *Sport* fall; **coup de pied t.** drop kick

tombeau, -x [tɔ̃bo] **NM 1** *(sépulcre)* grave, tomb; **suivre qn au t.** to follow sb to the grave; **descendre au t.** to go to one's grave; **conduire** *ou* **mettre qn au t.** to entomb sb, to commit sb to the grave; *Fig (causer sa mort)* to send sb to his/her grave; **mise au t.** entombment

2 *Fig Littéraire (endroit)* morgue; *(fin)* death, end; **la guerre fut le t. de la dictature** the war spelt the end for the dictatorship

3 *(personne discrète)* **parle sans crainte, c'est un t.** you can speak freely, he's/she's the soul of discretion

4 *(locution)* **à t. ouvert** at breakneck speed

> Do not confuse with **tombe**.

tombée [tɔ̃be] **NF à la t. du jour** *ou* **de la nuit** at nightfall *or* dusk

TOMBER[1] [3] [tɔ̃be]

VI	
• to fall **A1, 3, 5–7, 9, 10**	• to get nabbed **A2**
• to fall off/out **A4**	• to die **A3**
• to droop **A5**	• to hang **A5**
• to disappear **A8**	• to drop **A7**
• to come out **B3**	• to fall on **B1**

VT	
• to defeat **1**	• to pick up **2**
• to take off **3**	

VI *(aux être)* **A.** *CHANGER DE NIVEAU* **1** *(personne)* to fall (down); *(meuble, pile de livres)* to fall over, to topple over; *(cloison)* to fall down, to collapse; *(avion, bombe, projectile)* to fall; **j'ai buté contre la racine et je suis tombé** I tripped over the root and fell; **t. par terre** to fall on the floor, to fall down; **t. à plat ventre** to fall flat on one's face; **t. dans l'eau** to fall into the water; **t. dans un fauteuil** to fall *or* to collapse into an armchair; **t. de fatigue** to be ready to drop (from exhaustion); **t. de sommeil** to be asleep on one's feet; **la tuile tomba à ses pieds** the tile fell at his/her feet; **t. d'un échafaudage** to fall off some scaffolding; **t. dans l'escalier** to fall down the stairs; **t. dans un ravin** to fall into a ravine; **t. de cheval** to fall off *or* from a horse; **t. de moto** to fall off a motorbike; **t. d'un arbre** to fall out of a tree *or* from a tree; **ne monte pas à l'échelle, tu vas t.** don't go up the ladder, you'll fall off; **faire t. qn** *(en lui faisant un croche-pied)* to trip sb up; *(en le bousculant)* to knock *or* to push sb over; **le vent a fait t. des arbres** the wind blew some trees over *or* down; **faire t. qch** *(en poussant)* to push sth over; *(en renversant)* to knock sth over; *(en lâchant)* to drop sth; *(en donnant un coup de pied)* to kick sth over; **j'ai fait t. mes lunettes** I've dropped my glasses; **le vent a fait t. mon chapeau** the wind blew my hat off; *Fig* **tu es tombé bien bas** you've sunk very low; **es-tu tombé si bas que tu réclames cet argent?** have you really sunk so low as to ask for this money back?

2 *Fam (être arrêté)* to get nabbed *or Br* lifted *or* nicked

3 *(mourir)* to fall, to die; **t. sur le champ de bataille** to fall on the battlefield; **ceux qui sont tombés au champ d'honneur** those killed in action; **ceux qui sont tombés pour la France** those who died for France

4 *(se détacher ▸ feuille, pétale, fruit)* to fall off, to drop off; *(▸ cheveu, dent)* to fall out, to come out; **ne ramasse pas les cerises qui sont tombées** don't pick the cherries which are on the ground; **on a le droit de prendre les pommes qui sont tombées** we're allowed to collect windfalls; **une boule est tombée du sapin de Noël** a bauble has come *or* fallen off the Christmas tree

5 *(pendre ▸ cheveux, tentures)* to fall, to hang; *(▸ moustaches)* to droop; *(▸ seins)* to sag, to droop; **ses longs cheveux lui tombaient dans le dos** his/her long hair hung down his/her back; **une mèche lui tombait sur un œil** a lock of hair hung over one eye; **il a les épaules qui tombent** he's got sloping shoulders; **bien t.** *(vêtement)* to hang well *or* nicely; **la robe tombe bien sur toi** the dress hangs well *or* nicely on you

6 *(s'abattre, descendre ▸ rayon de soleil, nuit)* to fall; *(▸ brouillard, gifle, coup)* to come down; **la neige/pluie tombait** it was snowing/raining; **quand la pluie aura fini de t.** when it stops raining, when the rain has stopped; *Fam* **qu'est-ce qu'il est tombé hier soir!** it was absolutely pouring *or Br* bucketing down *or* chucking it down last night!; **il tombera de la neige sur l'Est** there will be snow in the east; **il tombe quelques gouttes** it's spitting; **il tombe de gros flocons** big flakes are falling; **il tombe de la grêle** it's hailing; *Fam* **toi, tu as ta paie qui tombe tous les mois** you have a regular salary coming in (every month); *Fam* **il lui tombe au moins 4000 euros par mois** he has at least 4,000 euros coming in every month; *Fam* **ça va t.!** *(il va pleuvoir)* it's going to pour (with rain)!; *(il va y avoir des coups)* you're/we're/*etc* going to get it!; *Fam* **son père s'est mis en colère et c'est tombé!** his/her father got angry and *Br* he/she didn't half cop it *or Am* he/she caught hell!; **des têtes vont t.!** heads will roll!

7 *(diminuer ▸ prix, température, voix, ton)* to fall, to drop; *(▸ fréquentation)* to drop (off); *(▸ fièvre)* to drop; *(▸ colère)* to die down, to subside; *(▸ inquiétude)* to melt away, to vanish; *(▸ enthousiasme, agitation, intérêt)* to fall away, to fade away, to subside; *(▸ tempête)* to subside, to abate, to die away; *(▸ vent)* to drop, to fall, to die down; *(▸ jour)* to draw to a close; **la température est tombée de 10 degrés** the temperature has dropped *or* fallen (by) 10 degrees; **sa cote de popularité est tombée très bas/à 28 pour cent** his/her popularity rating has plummeted/has dropped to 28 percent; **faire t. la fièvre** to bring down *or* to reduce the fever

8 *(disparaître ▸ obstacle)* to disappear, to vanish; *(▸ objection, soupçon)* to vanish, to fade; **sa joie tomba brusquement** his/her happiness suddenly vanished *or* evaporated

9 *(s'effondrer ▸ cité)* to fall; *(▸ dictature, gouvernement, empire)* to fall, to be brought down, to be toppled; *(▸ record)* to be broken; *(▸ concurrent)* to go out, to be defeated; *(▸ plan, projet)* to fall through; **les candidats de droite sont tombés au premier tour** the right-wing candidates were eliminated in the first round; **le chef du gang est tombé hier** the ringleader was arrested yesterday; **le dernier joueur français est tombé en quart de finale** the last French player was knocked out in the quarter final; **faire t.** *(cité)* to bring down; *(gouvernement)* to bring down, to topple; *(record)* to break; *(concurrent)* to defeat

10 *(devenir)* **t. amoureux,** to fall in love; **t. enceinte** to become pregnant; **t. malade** to become *or* to fall ill; *Fam* **t. (raide) mort** to drop dead, to fall down dead

11 *Cartes* **tous les atouts sont tombés** all the trumps have been played; **le roi n'est pas encore tombé** the king hasn't been played yet; **faire t. la dame** to make one's opponent to play the queen

B. *SE PRODUIRE, ARRIVER* **1** *(événement)* to fall on, to be on; **mon anniversaire tombe un dimanche** my birthday is *or* falls on a Sunday; **t. juste** *(calcul)* to work out exactly; **bien t.** to come at the right moment *or* at a convenient time; **l'héritage n'aurait pas pu mieux t.!** the legacy couldn't have come at a better moment *or* more convenient time!; **mal t.** to come at the wrong moment *or* at an inconvenient time; **cette grossesse tombe vraiment mal** this pregnancy has come at a very inconvenient time

2 *(personne)* **je tombe toujours aux heures de fermeture** I always get there when it's closed; **on est tombés en plein pendant la grève des trains** we got there right in the middle of the rail strike; **t. juste** *(deviner)* to guess right; **bien t.** *(opportunément)* to turn up at the right moment; *(avoir de la chance)* to be lucky *or* in luck; **ah, vous tombez bien, je voulais justement vous parler** ah, you've come at just the right moment, I wanted to speak to you; **tu ne pouvais pas mieux t.!** you couldn't have come at a better time!; **il est excellent, ce melon, je suis bien tombé** this melon's excellent, I was lucky; **elle est bien tombée avec Hugo, c'est le mari parfait** she was lucky to meet Hugo, he's the perfect husband; **mal t.** *(inopportunément)* to turn up at the wrong moment; *(ne pas avoir de chance)* to be unlucky *or* out of luck; **tu tombes mal, on doit partir cet après-midi** you've picked a bad time, we're leaving this afternoon; **il ne pouvait pas plus mal t.** he couldn't have picked a worse time; **travailler pour Fanget? tu aurais pu plus mal t.** working for Fanget? it could have been a lot worse; **tu tombes à point!** you've timed it perfectly!, perfect timing!

3 *(nouvelles)* to be out, to come out; **les dernières nouvelles qui viennent de t. font état de 143 victimes** news just out *or* released puts the number of victims at 143; **à 20 heures, la nouvelle est tombée** the news came through at 8 p.m.

VT *(aux avoir)* **1** *(triompher de ▸ candidat, challenger)* to defeat

2 *Fam (séduire)* to pick up, *Br* to pull; **il les tombe toutes** he's got them falling at his feet

3 *Fam (enlever)* to take off[□]; **il a tombé la veste** he took his jacket off

• **tomber dans VT IND** *(se laisser aller à ▸ découragement, désespoir)* to sink into, to lapse into; **elle tombe souvent dans la vulgarité** she often lapses into vulgarity; **comment en parler sans t. dans le jargon scientifique?** how can we talk about it without lapsing into scientific jargon?; **sans t. dans l'excès inverse** without going to the other extreme; **des traditions qui tombent dans l'oubli** traditions which are falling into oblivion; **t. dans la dépression** to become depressed; **t. dans l'erreur** to commit an error; *Fam Fig* **t. dans les pommes** to pass out[□], to keel over

• **tomber en VT IND t. en lambeaux** to fall to bits *or* pieces; **t. en ruine** to go to rack and ruin; **t. en morceaux** to fall to pieces

• **tomber sur** VT IND *Fam* **1** *(trouver par hasard ▸ personne)* to come across, to run *or* to bump into; *(▸ objet perdu, trouvaille)* to come across *or* upon, to stumble across; **je suis tombé sur ton article dans le journal** I came across your article in the newspaper; **je suis tombé sur une arête** I bit on a fishbone; **on a tiré au sort et c'est tombé sur elle** lots were drawn and her name came up

2 *(avoir affaire à ▸ examinateur, sujet d'examen)* to get; **quand j'ai téléphoné, je suis tombé sur sa mère/un répondeur** when I phoned, it was his/her mother who answered (me)/I got an answering machine

3 *(assaillir ▸ personne)* to set about, to go for; **il tombe sur les nouveaux pour la moindre erreur** he comes down on the newcomers (like a ton of bricks) if they make the slightest mistake; **il a fallu que ça tombe sur moi!** it had to be me!

4 *(se porter sur ▸ regard, soupçon)* to fall on; *(▸ conversation)* to turn to; **les soupçons sont tombés sur la nièce** suspicion fell on the niece; **la conversation est tombée sur la religion** the conversation turned to religion; **mes yeux sont tombés sur un objet qui brillait** my eyes fell on a shiny object

---

tomber² [tɔ̃be] NM *Littéraire* **au t. du jour** *ou* **de la nuit** at nightfall *or* dusk

tombereau, -x [tɔ̃bro] NM **1** *(benne)* dumper, dump truck; **t. à ordures** *Br* bin lorry, dustcart, *Am* garbage truck **2** *(contenu)* truckload; *Fig* **des tombereaux de** masses of **3** *Rail* = high-sided open wagon

tombeur [tɔ̃bœr] NM *Fam* **1** *(séducteur)* womanizer **2** *Sport* **le t. du champion d'Europe** the man who defeated the European champion

tombola [tɔ̃bɔla] NF raffle, tombola

Tombouctou [tɔ̃buktu] NM Timbuktu

tome [tɔm] NM *(section d'un ouvrage)* part; *(volume entier)* volume

NF = **tomme**

tomme [tɔm] NF Tomme (cheese)

tomographie [tɔmɔgrafi] NF *Méd & Géol* tomography

tom-pouce [tɔmpus] NM INV **1** *Fam (nain)* dwarf, midget **2** *(petit parapluie)* stumpy umbrella

ton¹ [tɔ̃] NM **A. 1** *(qualité de la voix)* tone; **t. monocorde** drone; **sur un t. monocorde** monotonously

2 *(hauteur de la voix)* pitch (of voice); **t. nasillard** twang

3 *(intonation)* tone, intonation; **t. arrogant/amical/implorant** arrogant/friendly/pleading tone; **le t. des entretiens est resté cordial** the atmosphere of the talks remained cordial; **d'un t. sec** curtly; **hausser le t.** to up the tone; **pas la peine de prendre un t. ironique/méchant pour me répondre!** there's no need to be so ironic/spiteful when you answer me!; **ne me parle pas sur ce t.!** don't speak to me like that *or* in that tone of voice!; **ne le prends pas sur ce t.!** don't take it like that!

4 *(style ▸ d'une lettre, d'une œuvre artistique)* tone, tenor; **le t. de ses plaisanteries ne me plaît guère** I don't much like the tone of his/her jokes; **le t. général de la pièce est assez optimiste** the overall tone of the play is fairly optimistic

5 *(manière de se comporter)* **un t. provincial** a small-town flavour; **le bon t.** good form; **de bon t.** the thing to do

6 *Ling (en phonétique)* tone, pitch; *(dans une langue tonale)* pitch; **les langues à t.** tonal languages

B. 1 *(tonalité)* tone **2** *Mus (d'une voix, d'un instrument)* tone; *(tube)* crook, shank; *(mode musical)* key; **le t. d'une sonate** the tone of a sonata; **prendre le t.** to tune (up); **baisser/élever le t. en chantant** to lower/to raise the pitch while singing; **le t. majeur/mineur** major/minor key; **donner le t.** *Mus* to give the chord; *Fig* to set the tone; **elle a très vite donné le t. de la conversation** she quickly set the tone of the conversation

C. 1 *(couleur)* tone, shade; **dans les tons verts** in shades *or* tones of green; **être dans le même t. que** to tone in with **2** *Beaux-Arts* shade; **les tons chauds/froids** warm/cool tones

• **dans le ton** ADV **tu crois que je serai dans le t.?** do you think I'll fit in?; **se mettre dans le t. de qn** to take on sb's ways

• **de bon ton** ADJ in good taste; **il est de bon t. de mépriser l'argent** it's quite the thing *or* good form to despise money; **il est de bon t. de se moquer de l'astrologie** making fun of astrology is what's expected

• **sur le ton de** PRÉP **sur le t. de la conversation** conversationally, in a conversational tone; **sur le t. de la plaisanterie** jokingly, in jest, in a joking tone

• **sur tous les tons** ADV in every possible way; **on nous répète sur tous les tons que...** we're being told over and over again that..., it's being drummed into us that...

• **ton sur ton** ADJ *(en camaïeu)* in matching tones *or* shades

ton², ta, tes [tɔ̃, ta, te]

> **ta** becomes **ton** before a word beginning with a vowel or h mute.

ADJ POSSESSIF **1** *(indiquant la possession)* your; **t. ami/amie** your friend; **t. oncle et ta tante** your aunt and (your) uncle; **t. père et ta mère,** *Littéraire* **tes père et mère** your father and mother; **tes frères et sœurs** your brothers and sisters; **j'ai mis t. chapeau et tes gants** I put on your hat and (your) gloves; **un de tes amis** one of your friends, a friend of yours; **un professeur de tes amis** a teacher friend of yours **2** *Fam (emploi expressif)* **eh bien regarde-la, t. émission!** all right then, watch your (damned) programme!; **arrête de faire t. intéressant!** stop trying to draw attention to yourself!; **il pleut souvent dans ta Bretagne!** it rains a lot in your beloved Brittany!; **tu auras ta chambre à toi** you'll have your own room; **t. imbécile de frère** your idiot of a brother; **t. artiste de mari** your artist husband; **alors, je peux le rencontrer, t. artiste?** so, can I meet this artist of yours?; **alors, tu l'as eu, t. vendredi?** so you managed to get Friday off, then? **3** *Rel & Arch* Thy

> **SUFFIX**
>
> **-TON**
>
> This is an ARGOT suffix, that is one that was used in the language of the underworld. Although this type of slang is now largely outdated, some of its words are still in use today. This is the case for several words ending in **-ton**, eg:
>
> **biffeton, bifton** (from *billet*) note/ticket; *fiston* (from *fils*) son, sonny; **frometon** (from *fromage*) cheese; **mecton** (from *mec*, itself a slang word) guy, bloke; **cureton** (from *curé*) priest

tonal, -e, -als, -ales [tɔnal] ADJ **1** *Ling* pitch *(avant n)* **2** *Mus* tonal

tonalité [tɔnalite] NF **1** *Beaux-Arts & Phot* tonality

2 *Mus (organisation)* tonality; *(d'un morceau)* key; **j'aime la t. de cet instrument/de sa voix** I like the way the instrument/his/her voice sounds, I like the timbre of the instrument/his/her voice

3 *(atmosphère)* tone; **le film prend vite une t. tragique** the movie soon becomes tragic in tone

4 *(d'une radio)* tone

5 *Tél* **t. (continue** *ou* **d'invitation à numéroter)** dial *or Br* dialling tone; **attendez d'avoir la t.** wait for the dial *or Br* dialling tone; **t. d'appel** ringing tone

tondeur, -euse [tɔ̃dœr, -øz] NM,F shearer; **t. de moutons** sheepshearer

• **tondeuse** NF **1** *Hort* **tondeuse (à gazon)** (lawn) mower; **tondeuse électrique/à main** *ou* **mécanique** electric/hand mower; **passer la tondeuse à gazon** to mow the lawn, to give the lawn a mow **2** *(de coiffeur)* (pair of) clippers **3** *(pour moutons)* (pair of) sheep shears **4** *Tex* (pair of) shears

tondre [75] [tɔ̃dr] VT **1** *(cheveux ▸ couper très court)* to crop; *(▸ raser)* to shave off; *(laine de mouton)* to shear (off)

2 *(mouton)* to shear; *(chien)* to clip; **t. un caniche** to clip a poodle; **t. qn** to shave sb's head

3 *(pelouse)* to mow, to cut; *(haie)* to clip

4 *Tex* to shear, to crop

5 *Fam (dépouiller, voler)* to fleece; *(exploiter)* to fleece, to take to the cleaners; **t. qn** *(au jeu)* to clean sb out; **ils se sont laissé t. sans protester** they got taken to the cleaners and they didn't say a word; *Fig* **il tondrait un œuf** he's a real skinflint *or Am* tightwad

tondu, -e [tɔ̃dy] ADJ **1** *(cheveux ▸ coupés très court)* closely cropped; **avoir le crâne t.** *ou* **les cheveux tondus** *(être rasé)* to have a shaven head **2** *(mouton)* shorn; *(chien)* clipped **3** *(pelouse)* mowed, mown; *(haie)* clipped

NM,F *(personne ▸ aux cheveux coupés très court)* = person with close-cropped hair; *(▸ aux cheveux rasés)* = person with a shaven head

toner [tɔnɛr] NM toner

tong [tɔ̃g] NF *Br* flip-flop, *Am* thong

Tonga [tɔ̃ga] NFPL **les (îles) T.** Tonga

tonicité [tɔnisite] NF **1** *Physiol* muscle tone, *Spéc* tonicity **2** *(de l'air, de la mer)* tonic *or* bracing effect

tonifiant, -e [tɔnifjɑ̃, -ɑ̃t] ADJ *(air, climat)* bracing, invigorating; *(promenade)* invigorating; *(crème, exercice, massage)* tonic, toning

tonifier [9] [tɔnifje] VT *(corps, peau)* to tone up; *(cheveux)* to give new life to; *(esprit)* to stimulate; **une marche au grand air tonifie l'organisme** a walk in the open air does wonders for the constitution

tonique [tɔnik] ADJ **1** *(air, climat)* bracing; *(médicament)* tonic, fortifying; *(lotion)* toning, tonic; *(boisson)* tonic; *(activité)* stimulating, invigorating **2** *Physiol* tonic **3** *Ling (syllabe)* tonic, stressed

NM **1** *Méd* tonic **2** *(lotion)* toner

NF *Mus* tonic, keynote

tonitruant, -e [tɔnitryɑ̃, -ɑ̃t] ADJ thundering, resounding; **..., dit-il d'une voix tonitruante** ..., he thundered

tonitruer [3] [tɔnitrye] VI to thunder, to resound

Tonkin [tɔ̃kɛ̃] NM *Anciennement* **le T.** Tonkin

tonnage [tɔnaʒ] NM **1** *(d'un bateau)* tonnage; **t. brut/net** gross/net tonnage **2** *(d'un port)* tonnage **3 (droit de) t.** (duty based on) tonnage

tonnant, -e [tɔnɑ̃, -ɑ̃t] ADJ *(voix)* thundering; **voix tonnante** thunderous voice

tonne [tɔn] NF **1** *(unité de masse)* ton, tonne; **un bateau de mille tonnes** a thousand-ton ship; **un (camion de) deux tonnes** a two-ton *Br* lorry *or Am* truck; **t. d'équivalent charbon** tonne of coal equivalent; **t. d'équivalent pétrole** ton oil equivalent **2** *Fam* **des tonnes** *(beaucoup)* tons, heaps, loads; **j'ai des tonnes de choses à vous raconter** I've tons *or* loads of things to tell you; **en faire des tonnes** *(en rajouter)* to lay it on (really) thick **3** *Agr (réservoir)* tank; *(grand tonneau)* large cask *or* barrel; *(son contenu)* cask, barrel

tonneau, -x [tɔno] NM **1** *(contenant pour liquide)* cask, barrel; **vin au t.** wine from the barrel *or* cask; **mettre du vin en t.** to pour wine in *or* into barrels; **t. d'arrosage** water cart; **c'est le t. des Danaïdes** *(travail interminable)* it's an endless task; *(gouffre financier)* it's a bottomless pit; **le t. de Diogène** Diogenes' tub

2 *(quantité de liquide)* caskful, barrelful

3 *(accident)* somersault; **faire un t.** to roll over, to somersault; **la voiture a fait quatre tonneaux** the car rolled over *or* turned over four times

4 *Aviat* roll; **faire un t.** to do a barrel roll

5 *Naut* ton; **t. d'affrètement** measurement ton

• **du même tonneau** ADJ *Fam* of the same ilk

tonnelet [tɔnlɛ] NM keg, small cask

tonnelier [tɔnəlje] NM cooper

tonnelle [tɔnɛl] NF **1** *(abri)* bower, arbour; *Littéraire* **déjeuner sous la t.** to lunch al fresco **2** *Archit* barrel *or* tunnel vault

tonnellerie [tɔnɛlri] NF *(fabrication)* cooperage

tonner [3] [tɔne] VI *(artillerie)* to thunder, to roar, to boom; **on entendait t. les canons** you could hear the thunder *or* roar of the cannons

V IMPERSONNEL **il tonne** it's thundering; **il a tonné plusieurs fois aujourd'hui** it's been thundering quite a bit today

• **tonner contre** VT IND *(sujet: personne)* to fulminate against

tonnerre [tɔnɛr] NM **1** *(bruit de la foudre)* thunder; **le t. gronda dans le lointain** there was a rumble of thunder in the distance; **une voix de t.** a thunderous voice; **un bruit** *ou* **fracas de t.** a racket, a din; **coup de t.** thunderclap; *Fig* bombshell; *Fig* **ses révélations ont eu l'effet d'un coup de t. dans l'assemblée** the meeting was thunderstruck by his/her revelations **2** *Fig (tumulte soudain)* storm, tumult, commotion; **un t. d'applaudissements** thunderous applause

EXCLAM *Fam* **t. (de Dieu)!** hell and damnation!; **t.**

de Brest!, mille tonnerres! hang *or* damn it all! • **du tonnerre (de Dieu)** *Fam Vieilli* ADJ *(voiture, fille, repas, spectacle)* terrific, fantastic; **un solo de batterie du t.** a really mean drum solo ADV tremendously *or* terrifically well; **ça a marché du t.** it went like a dream

tonsure [tɔ̃syr] NF **1** *Rel (partie rasée)* tonsure; *(cérémonie)* tonsuring; **porter la t.** to be tonsured **2** *Fam (calvitie)* bald patch; **il commence à avoir une petite t.** he's going a bit thin on top

tonsuré [tɔ̃syre] ADJ M tonsured

NM *Péj (moine)* monk, cleric

tonsurer [3] [tɔ̃syre] VT to tonsure

tonte [tɔ̃t] NF **1** *(de moutons ▸ activité)* shearing; *(▸ époque)* shearing time **2** *(laine tondue)* fleece **3** *(d'une pelouse)* mowing

tontine [tɔ̃tin] NF **1** *Jur* tontine **2** *Hort* = covering placed around soil ball of plant

tonton [tɔ̃tɔ̃] NM **1** *Fam (oncle)* uncle▫; **T. Jules** Uncle Jules **2** *Hist* **t. macoute** Tonton Macoute, Haitian secret policeman *(under the Duvalier regime)*

• **Tonton** NPR = one of the nicknames of François Mitterrand

tonus [tɔnys] NM **1** *Fig (dynamisme)* dynamism, energy; **avoir du t.** to be full of energy **2** *Physiol* tonus; **t. musculaire** muscle tone

top [tɔp] NM **1** *(signal sonore)* pip, beep; **au quatrième t., il sera exactement une heure** at the fourth stroke, it will be one o'clock precisely **2** *(dans une course)* **t., partez!** ready, steady, go!; **donner le t. de départ** to give the starting signal **3** *Fam* **c'est le t. (du t.)!** it's the best of stuff!, *Br* it's the business!

ADJ INV *Fam* great, *Br* fab, *Am* awesome

topaze [tɔpaz] NF topaz; **couleur t.** topaz

toper [3] [tɔpe] VI *Fam* **tope là!** it's a deal!, you're on!

topette [tɔpɛt] NF small bottle

topinambour [tɔpinɑ̃bur] NM Jerusalem artichoke

topique [tɔpik] ADJ **1** *(argument)* relevant; *(remarque)* pertinent, relevant **2** *Pharm* topical

NM **1** *Ling* topic **2** *Pharm* topical remedy

NF *Phil* topics *(singulier)*

top-modèle [tɔpmɔdɛl] *(pl* **top-modèles***)* NM top model, supermodel

top niveau [tɔpnivo] *(pl* **top niveaux***)* NM *Fam* **elle est au t.** *(sportive)* she's a top-level sportswoman; *(cadre)* she's a top-flight executive

topo [tɔpo] NM *Fam (discours)* lecture▫; *(exposé)* rundown; **faire un t. à qn sur qch** to give sb the rundown on sth, *Am* to hip sb to sth; **c'est toujours le même t.!** it's always the same old story!; **tu vois (d'ici) le t.!** (you) see what I mean?

topographe [tɔpɔgraf] NMF topographer

topographie [tɔpɔgrafi] NF **1** *(technique, relief)* topography **2** *(représentation)* map, plan

topographique [tɔpɔgrafik] ADJ topographic, topographical

topologie [tɔpɔlɔʒi] NF topology

topologique [tɔpɔlɔʒik] ADJ topologic(al)

toponyme [tɔpɔnim] NM place name, *Spéc* toponym

toponymie [tɔpɔnimi] NF toponymy

toponymique [tɔpɔnimik] ADJ toponymical

top secret [tɔpsəkrɛ] ADJ INV top secret, highly confidential

toquade [tɔkad] NF *Fam* **1** *(lubie)* fad, whim; **les casquettes, c'est sa dernière t.!** baseball caps are his/her latest fad!; **ça lui passera, ce n'est qu'une t.** he'll/she'll get over it, it's just a passing fancy **2** *(engouement)* crush; **avoir une t. pour qn** to have a crush on sb

toquante [tɔkɑ̃t] = **tocante**

toquard, -e [tɔkar, -ard] = **tocard**

toque [tɔk] NF **1** *(de femme)* pill-box hat, toque; **t. de fourrure** (pill-box shaped) fur hat **2** *(de liftier, de jockey, de magistrat)* cap; **t. (blanche) de cuisinier** chef's hat **3** *(cuisinier dans un restaurant)* chef

toqué, -e [tɔke] *Fam* ADJ **1** *(cinglé)* crazy, nuts **2** **être t. de qn** *(passionné de)* to be mad *or* nuts about sb

NM,F *(fou)* headcase, *Br* nutter, *Am* wacko

toquer [3] [tɔke] **toquer à** VT IND *Vieilli* **t. à la porte** to tap on *or* to knock on the door

VPR **se toquer** *Fam* **se t. de qn** to become besotted with sb; **se t. de qch** to have a sudden passion for sth

Tora, Torah [tɔra] NF *Rel* Torah

torche [tɔrʃ] NF **1** *(bâton résineux)* torch; **à la lumière des torches** by torchlight; **elle n'était plus qu'une t. vivante** she'd become a human torch, her whole body was ablaze

2 *Élec & Tech* **t. électrique** flashlight, *Br* (electric) torch; **t. de soudage** soldering torch

3 *Aviat* **le parachute s'est mis en t.** the parachute didn't open properly

4 *Pétr* flare

torché, -e [tɔrʃe] ADJ *Fam* **1 bien t.** *(réponse, devoir, travail)* well put-together **2** *(bâclé ▸ travail)* botched

torche-cul [tɔrʃky] NM INV *très Fam* **1** *(papier) Br* bog roll, *Am* TP **2** *(texte)* trash, *Br* rubbish **3** *(journal)* rag

torchée [tɔrʃe] NF *Fam (correction)* thrashing, hammering; **filer une t. à qn** to thrash *or* hammer sb

torcher [3] [tɔrʃe] VT **1** *Fam (essuyer ▸ plat, casserole)* to wipe clean

2 *Fam (vider entièrement)* **ils avaient torché leurs assiettes** they'd scraped their plates clean

3 *très Fam (nettoyer ▸ fesses)* to wipe; *Vulg* **t. (le cul de) qn** to wipe sb's *Br* arse *or Am* ass

4 *Fam (bâcler ▸ lettre, exposé)* to knock off, to dash off; *(▸ réparation)* to make a pig's ear of, to botch

5 *Constr* to cob

VPR **se torcher** *très Fam* **1** *(se nettoyer)* **se t. (le derrière)**, *Vulg* **se t. le cul** to wipe one's *Br* arse *or Am* ass; **je m'en torche (de tes problèmes)!** I don't give a shit (about your problems)! **2** *(s'enivrer)* to get shit-faced *or Br* pissed

torchère [tɔrʃɛr] NF **1** *Pétr* flare stack **2** *(candélabre)* candle-stand, torchère

torchis [tɔrʃi] NM *Constr* cob

torchon [tɔrʃɔ̃] NM **1** *(pour essuyer)* **t. (à vaisselle)** dish towel, *Br* tea towel; **donner un coup de t. à qch** *(verre, table)* to give sth a wipe; *Fam* **coup de t.** *(querelle)* dust-up; *(épuration)* shake-up; *Fam* **le t. brûle** *(dans un parti, un gouvernement, une entreprise)* tempers are getting frayed; *(dans un couple, entre des collègues, des amis)* there's a bit of friction between them

2 *Fam (écrit mal présenté)* mess; *(devoir scolaire)* dog's breakfast *or* dinner; **qu'est-ce que c'est que ce t.?** do you call that mess homework?

3 *Fam (mauvais journal)* rag

4 *Belg (serpillière)* floorcloth

tordant, -e [tɔrdɑ̃, -ɑ̃t] ADJ *Fam (amusant)* hysterical, side-splitting; **elle est tordante, ta fille** your daughter's a scream *or* riot *or* hoot

tord-boyaux [tɔrbwajo] NM INV *Fam* rotgut, *Am* alky

tordre [76] [tɔrdr] VT **1** *(déformer ▸ en courbant, en pliant)* to bend; *(▸ en vrillant)* to twist; **tu as tordu le clou en tapant de travers** you've bent the nail by not hitting it straight

2 *(linge mouillé)* to wring (out)

3 *(membre)* to twist; **t. le bras à qn** to twist sb's arm; **t. le cou à une volaille** to wring a bird's neck; *Fam* **je vais lui t. le cou!** I'm going to wring his neck!; **t. l'estomac à qn** *(sujet: peur)* to churn up sb's insides; *Fam* **t. les boyaux à qn** *(sujet: alcool)* to rot sb's insides

4 *(défigurer)* **les traits tordus par la douleur** his/her features twisted *or* his/her face contorted with pain

5 *Tex* to twist

VPR **se tordre 1** *(ver)* to twist; *(pare-chocs)* to buckle; **se t. de douleur** to be doubled up with pain; **se t. (de rire)** to be in stitches, to kill oneself (laughing), to be doubled up (with laughter); **c'était à se t. de rire, il y avait de quoi se t.** it was a scream, it was hilarious **2 se t. la cheville** to sprain *or* to twist one's ankle; **se t. le pied** to sprain *or* to twist one's foot; **se t. les mains (de désespoir)** to wring one's hands (in despair)

tordu, -e [tɔrdy] ADJ **1** *(déformé ▸ bouche)* twisted; *(▸ doigt)* crooked; **un vieil homme tout t.** a crooked old man; **avoir les jambes tordues** to have crooked legs

2 *(plié, recourbé ▸ clef)* bent; *(▸ roue de vélo, pare-chocs)* buckled; *(vrillé)* twisted

3 *Fam (extravagant ▸ idée, logique)* twisted, weird; *(▸ esprit)* twisted, warped; **tu es complètement t.!** you're off your head!; **c'est un plan t.** it's a crazy idea

4 *Fam (vicieux)* **coup t.** *(acte malveillant)* mean *or* nasty *or* dirty trick; **c'est la spécialiste des coups tordus** she's always playing dirty tricks on people

NM,F *Fam (personne bizarre ou folle)* nutcase, headcase

tore [tɔr] NM **1** *Archit & Math* torus **2** *Ordinat* **t. magnétique** magnetic core

toréador [tɔreadɔr] NM *Vieilli* toreador, torero

toréer [15] [tɔree] VI *(professionnel)* to be a bullfighter; **il doit t. demain** he'll be bullfighting tomorrow

torero [tɔrero] NM bullfighter, torero

torgnole [tɔrɲɔl] NF *très Fam* clout, wallop; **je vais lui filer** *ou* **flanquer une t.** I'll clout *or* wallop *or* land him/her one

toril [tɔril] NM toril, bull pen

tornade [tɔrnad] NF *Météo* tornado; *Fig* **entrer comme une t.** to come in like a whirlwind

toron [tɔrɔ̃] NM strand

torpédo [tɔrpedo] NF *Aut Br* open tourer, *Am* open touring car

torpeur [tɔrpœr] NF torpor; **sortir de sa t.** to shake oneself up, to rouse oneself; **tirer qn de sa t.** to shake sb out of his/her torpor, to rouse sb

torpide [tɔrpid] ADJ *Littéraire* torpid

torpillage [tɔrpijaʒ] NM **1** *Mil* torpedoing **2** *Fig (sabotage)* sabotage, *Br* scuppering; **le t. de la négociation** the wrecking of the negotiations

torpille [tɔrpij] NF **1** *Mil (projectile sous-marin)* torpedo; **t. aérienne** aerial torpedo **2** *Ich* torpedo (ray), electric ray

torpiller [3] [tɔrpije] VT **1** *Mil* to torpedo **2** *(projet)* to torpedo, to scupper

torpilleur [tɔrpijœr] NM torpedo boat

torréfacteur [tɔrefaktœr] NM **1** *(machine ▸ pour le café)* roaster, coffee-roaster; *(▸ pour le tabac)* (tobacco) toaster **2** *(commerçant)* coffee merchant

torréfaction [tɔrefaksjɔ̃] NF *(du café, du cacao)* roasting; *(du tabac)* toasting

torréfier [9] [tɔrefje] VT *(café, cacao)* to roast; *(tabac)* to toast; **grains torréfiés** roasted beans

torrent [tɔrɑ̃] NM **1** *(ruisseau de montagne)* torrent, (fast) mountain stream **2** *(écoulement abondant)* torrent, stream; **un t. de lave** a torrent *or* stream of lava; **un t. de boue** a torrent of mud; **des torrents de larmes** floods of tears; **un t. d'injures** a stream *or* torrent of abuse; **des torrents de lumière** a flood of light; **des torrents de musique jaillissaient des haut-parleurs** loud music was booming from the loudspeakers

• **à torrents** ADV **il pleut à torrents** it's pouring down

torrentiel, -elle [tɔrɑ̃sjɛl] ADJ **1** *(d'un torrent ▸ eau, allure)* torrential **2** *(très abondant)* **des pluies torrentielles** torrential rain

torride [tɔrid] ADJ **1** *(chaleur, après-midi)* torrid, scorching; *(soleil)* scorching; *(été)* scorching (hot); *(région, climat)* torrid; **il fait une chaleur t.** it's scorching **2** *(érotisme)* torrid

tors, -e[1] [tɔr, tɔrs] ADJ **1** *(laine, soie)* twisted **2** *(colonne)* wreathed; *(pied de meuble)* twisted **3** *(membre)* crooked, bent

NM *Tex* twist

torsade [tɔrsad] NF **1** *(de cordes)* twist; **t. de cheveux** twist *or* coil of hair; **cheveux en torsades** braided *or* twisted hair **2** *(en tricot)* (point) **t.** cable stitch **3** *Archit* cabling, cable moulding

• **à torsades** ADJ **1** *Archit* cabled **2** *(vêtement)* **pull à torsades** cablestitch sweater

torsadé, -e [tɔrsade] **ADJ 1** *(cheveux)* coiled
2 *Archit* **colonne torsadée** cabled column
3 *Élec* **paire torsadée** twisted pair; **raccord t.** twist joint
4 *Biol & Chim* stranded

torsader [3] [tɔrsade] **VT** *(fil)* to twist; *(cheveux)* to twist, to coil

torse² [tɔrs] **ADJ F** *voir* **tors**
NM 1 *Anat* trunk, torso; **se mettre t. nu** to strip to the waist; **il était t. nu** he was bare-chested **2** *Beaux-Arts* torso

torseur [tɔrsœr] **NM** torque

torsion [tɔrsjɔ̃] **NF 1** *(d'un cordage, d'un bras)* twisting **2** *Math, Phys & Tech* torsion **3** *Tex* twist (level)

tort [tɔr] **NM 1** *(sans article)* **avoir t.** *(se tromper)* to be wrong; **tu as t. de ne pas la prendre au sérieux** you're making a mistake in not taking her seriously, you're wrong not to take her seriously; **tu n'avais pas tout à fait t. de te méfier** you weren't entirely wrong to be suspicious; **il n'est pas d'accord, et il n'a pas t.** he doesn't agree and he's right (not to); **donner t. à qn** *(rendre quelqu'un responsable)* to blame sb, to lay the blame on sb; *(désapprouver)* to disagree with sb; **elle me donne toujours t. contre son fils** she always sides with her son against me; **les faits lui ont donné t.** events proved him/her (to be) wrong *or* showed that he/she was (in the) wrong
2 *(défaut, travers)* fault, shortcoming; **je reconnais mes torts** I admit I was wrong; **c'est son seul t.** it's his/her only fault; **elle a le t. d'être trop franche** the trouble *or* problem with her is (that) she's too direct; **c'est un t. de le lui avoir dit** it was wrong *or* a mistake to tell him/her; **avoir le t. de** to make the mistake of; **il a eu le t. de lui faire confiance** he made the mistake of trusting him/her
3 *(dommage)* wrong; **réparer le t. qu'on a causé** to right the wrong one has caused, to make good the wrong one has done; **faire du t. à qn** to do harm to sb, to wrong sb, to harm sb; **ça lui a fait beaucoup de t.** that did him/her a lot of harm; **cette loi a fait beaucoup de t. aux petits épargnants** this law penalized the small saver heavily; **faire du t. à une cause** *(personne)* to harm a cause; *(initiative)* to be detrimental to a cause
4 *(part de responsabilité)* fault; **avoir tous les torts** *(gén)* to be entirely to blame; *(dans un accident)* to be fully responsible; *(dans un divorce)* to be the guilty party; *Jur* **prononcer un jugement au t. d'une des parties** to find against one of the parties
• **à tort ADV 1** *(faussement)* wrongly, mistakenly; **croire/affirmer qch à t.** to believe/to state sth wrongly **2** *(injustement)* wrongly; **condamner qn à t.** to blame sb wrongly
• **à tort ou à raison ADV** rightly or wrongly
• **à tort et à travers ADV tu parles à t. et à travers** you're talking nonsense; **elle dépense son argent à t. et à travers** she spends money like water
• **dans mon/son/***etc* **tort ADV être dans son t.** to be in the wrong; **se mettre dans son t.** to put oneself in the wrong; **en ne la prévenant pas, tu t'es mis dans ton t.** you put yourself in the wrong by not warning her
• **en tort ADV** in the wrong; **dans cet accident, c'est lui qui est en t.** he is to blame for the accident

torticolis [tɔrtikɔli] **NM** stiff neck, *Spéc* torticollis; **avoir un t.** to have a stiff neck

tortillard [tɔrtijar] **NM** *Fam* slow (local) train◻

tortillement [tɔrtijmɑ̃] **NM** *(d'un ver)* wriggling (UNCOUNT), squirming (UNCOUNT); *(des hanches)* wiggling (UNCOUNT)

tortiller [3] [tɔrtije] **VT 1** *(mèche, mouchoir, fil, papier, ruban)* to twist; *(doigts)* to twiddle; *(moustache)* to twirl **2** *(fesses)* to wiggle
VI 1 *(onduler)* **t. des fesses/hanches** to wiggle one's bottom/hips; **marcher en tortillant du postérieur** to walk with a wiggle **2** *très Fam* **y a pas à t.**, *Vulg* **y a pas à t. du cul pour chier droit** there's no getting away from it, there are no two ways about it
VPR se tortiller *(ver)* to wriggle, to squirm; *(personne ▸ par gêne, de douleur)* to squirm; *(▸ d'impatience)* to fidget, to wriggle; *(▸ en dansant)* to wriggle about; **se t. sur sa chaise comme un ver** to wriggle in one's chair like a worm

tortillon [tɔrtijɔ̃] **NM 1** *(de papier)* twist; **des tortillons de pâte à choux** choux pastry twists **2** *Beaux-Arts (estompe)* tortillon, stump

tortionnaire [tɔrsjɔnɛr] **ADJ policier t.** police torturer
NMF torturer

tortue [tɔrty] **NF 1** *Zool (reptile)* tortoise; **t. d'eau douce** terrapin; **t. géante** giant tortoise; **t. marine** sea turtle; **t. terrestre** tortoise; **t. verte** green turtle
2 *Entom* tortoiseshell (butterfly)
3 *Fam (traînard) Br* slowcoach, *Am* slowpoke; **avancer comme une t.** to go at a snail's pace, to crawl along
4 *Antiq & Mil* testudo

tortueuse [tɔrtɥøz] *voir* **tortueux**

tortueusement [tɔrtɥøzmɑ̃] **ADV 1** *(en lacets)* tortuously **2** *(se conduire, manœuvrer)* deviously

tortueux, -euse [tɔrtɥø, -øz] **ADJ 1** *(en lacets ▸ sentier)* winding, *Sout* tortuous; *(▸ ruisseau)* meandering, winding **2** *(compliqué ▸ raisonnement, esprit)* tortuous; *(▸ style)* convoluted, involved; *(retors ▸ moyens)* devious, crooked

torturant, -e [tɔrtyrɑ̃, -ɑ̃t] **ADJ** *(pensée)* tormenting, agonising

torture [tɔrtyr] **NF 1** *(supplice infligé)* torture; **instrument de t.** instrument of torture **2** *Fig (souffrance)* torture, torment; **l'attente des résultats fut pour lui une véritable t.** he suffered agonies waiting for the results
• **à la torture ADV être à la t.** to suffer agonies; **mettre qn à la t.** to put sb through hell
• **sous la torture ADV** under torture; **elle n'a pas parlé, même sous la t.** she refused to talk, even under torture

torturer [3] [tɔrtyre] **VT 1** *(supplicier ▸ sujet: bourreau)* to torture **2** *Fig (tourmenter ▸ sujet: angoisse, faim)* to torture, to torment, to rack; *(▸ sujet: personne)* to put through torture, to torture; **la jalousie le torturait** he was tortured by jealousy; **torturé par sa conscience** tormented by his conscience
VPR se torturer to torture oneself, to worry oneself sick; **ne te torture pas, ce n'est pas ta faute** don't torture yourself, it isn't your fault; **ne te torture pas l'esprit!** don't rack your brains (too much)!

torve [tɔrv] **ADJ il m'a lancé un regard t.** he shot me a murderous sideways look

toscan, -e [tɔskɑ̃, -an] **ADJ** Tuscan
NM *(dialecte)* Tuscan
• **Toscan, -e NM,F** Tuscan

Toscane [tɔskan] **NF la T.** Tuscany

tôt [to] **ADV 1** *(de bonne heure)* early; **se lever t.** *(ponctuellement)* to get up early; *(habituellement)* to be an early riser; **elle part t. le matin** she leaves early in the morning; **je prendrai l'avion t. demain** I'll catch an early plane tomorrow *or* a plane early tomorrow; **se coucher t.** to go to bed early
2 *(au début d'une période)* **t. dans l'après-midi** early in the afternoon, in the early afternoon; **t. dans la saison/le mois** early in the season/month
3 *(avant le moment prévu ou habituel)* soon; **il est trop t. pour le dire** it's too early *or* soon to say that; **arrive suffisamment t. ou il n'y aura pas de place** be there in good time or there won't be any seats left; **il fallait y penser plus t.** you should have thought about it earlier *or* before; **je suis arrivée plus t. que toi** I arrived earlier than you; **plus tôt que prévu** earlier than expected; **ce n'est pas trop t.!** at last!, (it's) about time too!
4 *(rapidement)* soon; **je ne m'attendais pas à le revoir si t.** I didn't expect to see him again so soon; **le plus t. possible** as early *or* as soon as possible; **le plus t. sera le mieux** the sooner, the better; **plus t. tu commenceras plus vite tu auras fini** the sooner you begin the sooner you'll finish; **je n'avais pas plus t. raccroché qu'il me rappela** no sooner had I put the receiver down than he phoned me back; **avoir t. fait de** to be quick to; **ils eurent t. fait de s'emparer du sac** they lost no time in seizing the bag; **je n'y retournerai pas de si t.!** I won't go back there in a hurry!; **on ne le reverra pas de si t.** *(il est parti fâché, ruiné etc)* we won't see him again in a hurry
• **au plus tôt ADV 1** *(rapidement)* as soon as possible; **partez au plus t.** leave as soon as possible *or* as soon as you can **2** *(pas avant)* at the earliest; **samedi au plus t.** on Saturday at the earliest, no earlier than Saturday
• **tôt ou tard ADV** sooner or later

total, -e, -aux, -ales [tɔtal, -o] **ADJ 1** *(entier ▸ liberté, obscurité)* total, complete; *(▸ grève, guerre)* all-out; **un silence t.** complete *or* total *or* absolute silence; **j'ai une confiance totale en elle** I trust her totally *or* implicitly; **la surprise fut totale** we/they were completely taken aback
2 *(généralisé ▸ destruction, échec)* total, utter, complete
3 *(global ▸ hauteur, poids, dépenses)* total; **somme totale** total (amount)
4 *Astron (éclipse)* total
ADV *Fam* **t., j'ai perdu mon boulot/il a fallu que je recommence** the upshot is, I lost my job/I had to start again; **et t. on l'a renvoyé** and, to cut a long story short, he got the sack; **tu voulais jouer les femmes indépendantes, et t., tu es toute seule, maintenant** you wanted to be independent and look where it's got you, you're all alone now
NM total (amount); **le t. s'élève à 130 euros** the total comes to 130 euros; **faire le t.** to work out the total; **fais le t. de ce que je te dois** work out everything I owe you; **t. à payer** total payable
• **totale NF** *Fam* **1** *Méd* (total) hysterectomy◻ **2** *(ensemble)* **on a eu droit à la totale, verglas, embouteillages, barrages de routiers** black ice, traffic jams, lorry drivers' road blocks, you name it, we had it; **quand il m'a demandée en mariage, il m'a fait la totale** when he proposed to me, he really went all out
• **au total ADV 1** *(addition faite)* in total; **au t., il vous revient 2000 euros** in total you are entitled to 2,000 euros **2** *(tout bien considéré)* all in all, all things (being) considered, on the whole

totalement [tɔtalmɑ̃] **ADV** *(ignorant, libre, ruiné)* totally, completely; *(détruit)* utterly; **il est t. incapable de gagner sa vie** he is totally *or* quite incapable of earning a living

totalisateur, -trice [tɔtalizatœr, -tris] **ADJ** totalizing; *(machine)* adding
NM 1 *(appareil)* adding machine, totalizer; *Ordinat* accumulator; *Aut* **t. kilométrique journalier** trip recorder **2** *(au turf)* totalizator

totalisation [tɔtalizasjɔ̃] **NF** adding up, addition, totalizing

totalisatrice [tɔtalizatris] *voir* **totalisateur**

totaliser [3] [tɔtalize] **VT 1** *(dépenses, recettes)* to add up, to total up, to reckon up, to totalize **2** *(atteindre le total de)* to have a total of, to total; **il totalise 15 victoires** he has won a total of 15 times; **qui totalise le plus grand nombre de points?** who has the highest score?

totalitaire [tɔtalitɛr] **ADJ** totalitarian

totalitarisme [tɔtalitarism] **NM** totalitarianism

totalité [tɔtalite] **NF 1** *(ensemble)* **la t. des marchandises** all the goods; **la presque t. des tableaux** almost all the paintings; **l'entreprise exporte la t. de sa production** the company exports its entire production; **les marchandises seront livrées dans leur t. avant le 20 décembre** all the goods will be delivered before 20 December **2** *(intégralité)* whole; **la t. de la somme** the whole (of the) sum; **elle dit ne pas pouvoir payer la t. de son loyer** she says she can't pay all her rent **3** *Phil* totality, wholeness
• **en totalité ADV** in full; **somme remboursée en t.** sum paid back in full

totem [tɔtɛm] **NM** totem

totémique [tɔtemik] **ADJ** totemic; **mât** *ou* **poteau t.** totem (pole)

totémisme [tɔtemism] **NM** totemism

toto [toto] **NM** *Fam (pou)* louse◻, *Am* cootie

toton [tɔtɔ̃] **NM** teetotum

touareg, -ègue [twarɛg] **ADJ** Tuareg
NM *(langue)* Tuareg
• **Touareg, -ègue NM,F** Tuareg; **les Touaregs** *ou* **T.** the Tuaregs *or* Tuareg

toubib [tubib] **NM** *Fam* doctor◻, doc

toucan [tukɑ̃] **NM** *Orn* toucan

touchant¹ [tuʃɑ̃] **PRÉP** *Littéraire (concernant)* concerning, about

touchant[2], **-e** [tuʃɑ̃, -ɑ̃t] **ADJ** *(émouvant)* touching, moving

TOUCHE [tuʃ]

- key **A1, 3, 4**
- button **A1**
- touch **C1–3**
- stroke **C1**
- look **C4**
- touchline **D1**

NF A. 1 *(gén)* key; *(d'un téléviseur)* button; *(d'un téléphone)* key, button

2 *Élec (plot de contact)* contact

3 *Mus (de clavier)* key; *(d'instrument à cordes)* fingerboard, fretboard

4 *Ordinat & (d'une machine à écrire)* key; **t. d'échappement** escape key; **t. d'effacement** delete key; **t. d'espacement arrière** backspace (key); **t. majuscule** shift key; **t. retour** return *or* enter key

B. 1 *Escrime* hit

2 *(en joaillerie)* touch

3 *Pêche* bite; **j'ai eu des touches mais je n'ai rien pris** I've had some bites but I haven't caught anything

4 *Fam (personne séduite)* **avoir une t. avec qn** to be in with sb; **je crois que j'ai fait une t.** I think I'm in there

C. 1 *(coup de pinceau)* touch, (brush) stroke; **en quelques touches** using just a few brush strokes; **mettre la t. finale à qch** to put the finishing touches to sth

2 *(cachet, style)* touch; **il était loin d'avoir la t. d'un Dickens** he lacked the Dickens touch

3 *(trace)* note, touch; **une t. de couleur** a touch of colour; **une t. de cynisme** a touch *or* tinge *or* hint of cynicism

4 *Fam (apparence)* look❑; **il a la t. d'un ancien militaire** he looks like an ex-army man, he has the look of an ex-army man (about him); **ton prof a une drôle de t.!** your teacher looks a bit weird!

D. *Sport* **1** *(ligne)* touchline

2 *(remise en jeu ▸ au rugby)* line-out; *(▸ au football)* throw-in; **il y a t.** *(sortie de ballon)* the ball is out; **jouer la t.** to play for time *(by putting the ball into touch)*

• **en touche ADV** *Sport* into touch; **envoyer le ballon en t.** to kick the ball into touch; **il a mis le ballon en t.** he kicked the ball into touch; **ils ne prennent aucune balle en t.** they never win a line-out

• **sur la touche ADV** *Sport* **rester sur la t.** to stay on the bench; *Fam Fig* **être** *ou* **rester sur la t.** to be left out; **quand il a eu 50 ans, ils l'ont mis sur la t.** when he was 50, they put him out to grass *or* they threw him on the scrap heap

touche-à-tout [tuʃatu] *Fam* **ADJ INV il est t.** *(enfant)* he's into everything

NMF INV 1 *(importun)* meddler; **c'est un t.** *(adulte)* he can't keep his hands off anything; *(enfant)* he's into everything **2** *(dilettante)* dabbler, Jack-of-all-trades (and master of none); **il écrit, il peint, c'est un peu un t.** he writes, he paints, he does a bit of everything

touche-pipi [tuʃpipi] **NM INV** *Fam* **jouer à t.** to play at doctors and nurses

toucher[1] [tuʃe] **NM 1** *(sens)* (sense of) touch; *(palpation)* touch

2 *(sensation)* feel; **le t. rugueux de l'écorce** the rough feel of bark

3 *(gén) & Mus (manière de toucher)* touch; **avoir un t. délicat/vigoureux** to have a light/energetic touch

4 *Méd* examination, *Spéc* (digital) palpation; **t. buccal/rectal/vaginal** oral/rectal/vaginal examination

5 *Sport* touch; **il a un bon t. de balle** he's got a nice touch

• **au toucher ADV** to the touch *or* feel; **doux/rude au t.** soft/rough to the touch; **c'est facile à reconnaître au t.** it's easy to tell what it is by touching it *or* by the feel of it

TOUCHER[2] **[3]** [tuʃe]

VT

- to touch **A1, 2, 6, B1, 2, 5, 6**
- to feel **A1**
- to reach **A3**
- to contact **A3**
- to hit **B3, 4**
- to examine **A4**
- to concern **B4**
- to affect **B4, 5**
- to receive **B7**
- to be adjacent (to) **C1**

VPR

- to touch **1**
- to be in contact **1**

VT A. 1 *(pour caresser, saisir)* to touch; *(pour examiner)* to feel; **tu m'as fait mal – je t'ai à peine touché** you hurt me – I hardly touched you; **ne touchez pas les fruits!** don't touch *or* handle the fruit!; **ne me touche pas!** get your hands off me!, don't touch me!; **t. qch du pied** to touch sth with one's foot; **prière de ne pas t.** *(dans un magasin)* please do not touch; *Fam* **pas touche!** hands off!; **touchez avec les yeux!** don't touch, just look!

2 *(entrer en contact avec)* to touch; **il a touché le filet avec sa raquette** he touched the net with his racket, his racket touched *or* hit the net; **sa robe touchait presque le sol** her dress reached almost to the ground; **au moment où la navette spatiale touche le sol** when the space shuttle touches down *or* lands

3 *Fam (joindre ▸ sujet: personne)* to contact, to reach, to get in touch with; *(▸ sujet: lettre)* to reach; **où peut-on vous t. en cas d'urgence?** where can you be contacted *or* reached in an emergency?

4 *Méd* to examine, *Spéc* to palpate

5 *Naut (port)* to put in at, to call at; *(rochers, fonds)* to hit, to strike; **nous toucherons Marseille lundi** we'll put in at *or* reach Marseilles on Monday

6 *(en joaillerie)* to touch

B. 1 *(se servir de ▸ accessoire, instrument)* to touch; **il n'a pratiquement pas touché le ballon pendant la première mi-temps** he hardly touched the ball during the first half; **cela fait des années que je n'ai pas touché une guitare** I haven't touched a guitar for years; *Fam* **son service est si puissant que je ne touche pas une balle** his/her serve is so powerful I can't get anywhere near the ball

2 *(consommer)* to touch; **il n'a même pas touché son repas/la bouteille** he never even touched his meal/the bottle

3 *(blesser)* to hit; **la balle l'a touché à la jambe** the bullet hit him in the leg; *Escrime* **touché!** touché!; *Fig* **t. juste** to hit the target

4 *(atteindre ▸ sujet: mesure)* to concern, to affect, to apply to; *(▸ sujet: crise, krach boursier, famine)* to affect, to hit; *(▸ sujet: incendie, épidémie)* to spread to; **la marée noire a touché tout le littoral** the oil slick spread all along the coast; **les personnes touchées par l'impôt sur les grandes fortunes** people in the top tax bracket

5 *(émouvoir ▸ sujet: film, geste, gentillesse, spectacle)* to move, to touch; *(affecter ▸ sujet: décès)* to affect, to shake; *(▸ sujet: critique, propos désobligeants)* to affect, to have an effect on; **vos compliments me touchent beaucoup** I'm very touched by your kind words; **elle a été très touchée par sa disparition** she was badly shaken by his/her death

6 *Fam (s'en prendre à ▸ personne)* to touch; **c'est le plus gros notable du pays, on ne peut pas le t.** he's the most important public figure in the region, we can't touch him

7 *(percevoir ▸ allocation, honoraires, pension, salaire)* to receive, to get, to draw; *(▸ indemnité, ration)* to receive, to get; *(▸ chèque)* to cash (in); **combien touches-tu par an?** how much do you get a year?, what's your yearly salary?; **les saisonniers ne touchent presque rien** seasonal workers don't get paid much; **elle touche 100 000 euros par an** she earns 100,000 euros a year; *Fam* **t. gros** to line one's pockets, to make a packet; **touchez-vous les allocations familiales?** do you get child benefit?; **t. le tiercé** to win the "tiercé"; **t. le chômage** *Br* to be on the dole, *Am* to be on welfare

C. 1 *(être contigu à)* to join onto, *Sout* to adjoin, to be adjacent to; **ma maison touche la sienne** my house is adjacent to his/hers

2 *(concerner)* **il s'occupe de tout ce qui touche le financement** he deals with all matters connected with financing *or* with all finance-related matters

VI 1 *Naut* to touch bottom

2 *Pêche* to bite

3 *très Fam (exceller)* to be brilliant **(en/à** at); **elle touche en informatique!** she's a wizard at *or* she knows a thing or two about computers!

4 *Fam (recevoir de l'argent)* to collect

5 *(locution)* **touchez là!** it's a deal!, (let's) shake on it!

• **toucher à VT IND 1** *(porter la main sur ▸ objet)* to touch; **évitez de t. aux fruits** try not to handle the fruit; **que je ne te reprenne pas à t. aux allumettes!** don't let me catch you playing with matches again!

2 *Fam (frapper ▸ adversaire, élève)* to touch, to lay hands *or* a finger on; **si tu touches à un seul cheveu de sa tête…!** if you so much as lay a finger on him/her…!

3 *(porter atteinte à)* to interfere with, to harm, to touch; **ne touchez pas aux parcs nationaux!** hands off the national parks!

4 *(modifier ▸ appareil, documents, législation)* to tamper *or* to interfere with; **quelqu'un a dû t. aux freins** someone must have tampered with the brakes; **ton dessin est parfait, n'y touche plus** your drawing is perfect, leave it as it is

5 *(utiliser ▸ aliment, instrument)* to touch; *(▸ somme d'argent)* to touch, to break into; **je n'ai jamais touché à la drogue** I've never touched drugs; **tu n'as pas touché à ton repas/assiette?** you haven't touched your meal/what was on your plate, have you?; **cela fait longtemps que je n'ai pas touché à un piano** I haven't touched a piano for a long time; **t. à tout** to fiddle with *or* to touch everything; *Fig* to dabble (in everything); **je touche un peu à tout** *(artisan)* I'm a Jack-of-all-trades, I do a little bit of everything; *(artiste)* I'm a man of many parts

6 *(être proche de ▸ sujet: pays, champ)* to border (upon), *Sout* to adjoin; *(▸ sujet: maison, salle)* to join on to, *Sout* to adjoin; **notre propriété touche aux salines** our property borders on the salt marsh; *Fig* **t. à la perfection** to be close to perfection

7 *(concerner, se rapporter à ▸ activité, sujet)* to have to do with, to concern; **les questions touchant à l'environnement** issues related to the environment, environment-related issues

8 *(aborder ▸ sujet, question)* to bring up, to come onto, to broach; **vous venez de t. au point essentiel du débat** you've put your finger on the key issue in the debate

9 *(atteindre ▸ un point dans l'espace, dans le temps)* to reach; **nous touchons au terme du voyage** we've reached the end of our trip; **notre séjour touche à sa fin** our stay is nearing its end

VPR se toucher 1 *(être en contact)* to touch, to be in contact; *(entrer en contact)* to touch, to come into contact; *(jardins, communes)* to touch, to be adjacent (to each other), *Sout* to adjoin each other; **à l'endroit où les deux lignes se touchent** where the two lines meet **2** *très Fam Euph (se masturber)* to play with oneself

touche-touche [tuʃtuʃ] **à touche-touche ADV** *Fam* **être à t.** to be nose to tail *or* bumper to bumper

touée [twe] **NF** *Naut* **1** *(câble)* warp, (warping) cable **2** *(longueur)* scope

touer [6] [twe] **VT** *Naut* to chain-tow

toueur [twœr] **NM** *Naut* tug *(using chain-towing)*

touffe [tuf] **NF 1** *(de cheveux, de poils)* tuft **2** *(d'arbustes)* clump, cluster **3** *(de fleurs)* clump; **t. d'herbe** tussock

touffeur [tufœr] **NF** *Littéraire* sultry *or* sweltering heat

touffu, -e [tufy] **ADJ 1** *(bois, feuillage, haie)* thick, dense; *(barbe, sourcils)* thick, bushy; *(arbre)* thickly covered, with dense foliage **2** *Fig (texte)* dense

touillage [tujaʒ] **NM** *Fam (d'une sauce)* stirring❑; *(d'une salade)* tossing❑

touiller [3] [tuje] **VT** *Fam (sauce, soupe)* to stir❑; *(salade)* to toss❑

toujours [tuʒur] **ADV 1** *(exprimant la continuité dans le temps)* always; **je l'ai t. dit/cru** I've always said/thought so; **elle regrettera t. d'avoir dit non** she will always regret having said no; **ça ne durera pas t.** it won't last forever; **ils n'ont pas t. été aussi riches** they haven't always been so rich; **depuis t.** always; **je t'aime depuis t.** I've always loved you; *Fam* **il est t. à se plaindre** he's always *or* he never stops complaining; **la t. charmante Sophie** the ever charming Sophie; **t. plus haut, t. plus**

vite, t. plus loin ever higher, ever faster, ever farther; **ils sont t. plus exigeants** they are more and more demanding

2 *(marquant la fréquence, la répétition)* always; **elle est t. en retard** she is always late; **c'est t. moi qu'on punit** I'm always the one who gets punished; **cette expérience ne réussit pas t.** this experiment is not always successful; **on a presque t. habité la même ville** we have almost always lived in the same town

3 *(encore)* still; **tu travailles t.?** are you still working?; **tu écris t. des poèmes?** do you still write poems?; **il fait t. aussi chaud** it is as hot as ever; *Ironique* **tu es t. aussi serviable!** you're just *or* still as helpful as ever(, I see)!; **t. pas** still not; **je ne suis t. pas satisfait** I'm still not satisfied; **elle n'a t. pas téléphoné** she hasn't phoned yet, she still hasn't phoned; **alors, il est rentré? – t. pas** he's back then? – not yet

4 *(dans des emplois expressifs)* **on peut t. lui demander** we can always ask him/her; **tu peux t. essayer** you can always try, you might as well try; **entrez t. mais je ne vous promets rien** come in anyway, but I'm not promising anything; **prends-le, tu peux t. en avoir besoin** take it, you may *or* might need it (some day); **ça peut t. servir** it might come in handy *or* useful; **c'est t. mieux que rien** still, it's better than nothing; **c'est t. ça (de pris)** (at any rate) it's better than nothing, at least it's something; **on trouvera t. un moyen** we're sure *or* bound to find a way; **tu peux t. pleurer, je ne céderai pas** (you can) cry as much as you like, I won't give in; **tu lui fais confiance? – pas dans le travail, t.!** do you trust him/her? – not when it comes to work, anyway!

• **comme toujours** ADV as always, as ever; **il a été charmant, comme t.** he was charming as always; **comme t., il est en retard** as always *or* as ever, he's late

• **de toujours** ADJ **une amitié de t.** a lifelong friendship; **ces coutumes sont de t.** these customs date from time immemorial

• **pour toujours** ADV for ever; **tu me le donnes pour t.?** can I keep it for ever *or* for good?; *Littéraire* **adieu pour t.!** farewell for ever!

• **toujours est-il que** CONJ the fact remains that; **j'ignore pourquoi elle a refusé, t. est-il que le projet tombe à l'eau** I don't know why she refused, but the fact remains that the plan has had to be abandoned

> Attention: ne pas confondre **still** et **always** lorsqu'on traduit **toujours**. **Still** exprime l'idée de continuité, alors que **always** exprime l'idée de répétition.

toulousain, -e [tuluzɛ̃, -ɛn] ADJ of/from Toulouse

• **Toulousain, -e** NM,F = inhabitant of or person from Toulouse

oundra [tundra] NF tundra

oupet [tupɛ] NM **1** *Fam (audace)* nerve, *Br* cheek; **avoir du t.** to have a nerve *or Br* a cheek; **elle a un sacré t.!, elle ne manque pas de t.!** she's got some nerve *or Br* cheek!; **il a eu le t. de...** he had the nerve *or Br* cheek to... **2** *(de cheveux)* tuft of hair, *Br* quiff; **faux t.** toupee, hairpiece **3** *Zool* *(d'un cheval)* forelock

oupie [tupi] NF **1** *(jeu)* (spinning) top; **t. à musique** humming top; **tourner comme une t.** to spin like a top

2 *(de meuble)* moulded foot *(Louis XVI style)*

3 *Menuis* spindle moulder

4 *(en plomberie)* turnpin, reamer

5 *Fam* **une vieille t.** *(harpie)* an old crone *or* bag

ur[1] [tur] NF **1** *Archit & Constr* tower; *Bible* **la t. de abel** the Tower of Babel; **le palais de l'Unesco est ne vraie t. de Babel** you can hear a real mixture languages at UNESCO headquarters; *Aviat* **t. contrôle** control tower; **la t. Eiffel** the Eiffel ower; **t. de guet** observation tower; *Fig* **t. ivoire** ivory tower; *Fig* **s'enfermer dans une t. ivoire** to remain aloof; **t. de lancement** launch wer; **la t. de Londres** the Tower of London; **t. observation** watchtower, observation tower; **la penchée) de Pise** the Leaning Tower of Pisa; *Ind* **de refroidissement** *ou* **de réfrigération** cooling wer

(immeuble) high-rise building; **t. d'habitation** tower *or* high-rise block; **t. de bureaux** office (tower) block

3 *Échecs* castle, rook

4 *Pétr* **t. de forage** drilling rig; **t. de sondage** derrick, rig

5 *Ordinat* tower

TOUR[2] [tur]

• girth **A1**	• circumference **A1**
• measurement **A2**	• tour **A4**
• walk **A5**	• drive **A5**
• ride **A5**	• turn **B1, D1, E1**
• round **B2**	• trick **C1–2**
• expression **D2**	• revolution **E1, 2**
• lathe **E5**	

NM **A.** *CERCLE* **1** *(circonférence ▸ d'un fût, d'un arbre)* girth; *(▸ d'un objet, d'une étendue)* circumference; **le t. du lac est planté d'arbres** trees have been planted all round *or* around the lake

2 *(mensuration)* **t. de taille/hanches** waist/hip measurement; **elle fait 55 cm de t. de taille** her waist (measurement) is 55 cm; **prends ton t. de taille** measure (round) your waist; **quel est votre t. de taille/hanches?** what size waist/hips are you?; **t. de cou** collar size; **il fait (un) 42 de t. de cou** he takes a size 42 collar; **t. de poitrine** *(d'une femme)* bust measurement *or* size; *(d'un homme)* chest measurement *or* size; **t. de tête** head measurement

3 *(parure)* **t. de cou** *(collier)* choker; *(en fourrure)* fur collar; **t. de lit** (bed) valance

4 *(circuit)* tour, circuit; **faire le t. d'un parc** to go round a park; **nous avons fait le t. du vieux quartier** we went round the old part of the town; **faire le t. du monde** to go round the world; **faire le t. du monde en auto-stop/voilier** to hitch-hike/to sail round the world; **t. de circuit** lap; **le T. de France** *(cycliste)* the Tour de France; *(des compagnons)* the Tour de France *(carried out by an apprentice to become a journeyman)*; **t. d'honneur** lap of honour; **t. d'horizon** overview; **faire un t. d'horizon** to take stock; **t. de piste** *(en athlétisme)* lap; *Équitation* round; **faire un t. de piste** *(en athlétisme)* to run a lap; **on a fait le t. du propriétaire** we went *or* looked round the property; **fais-moi faire le t. du propriétaire** show me round your property; *Fam* **j'ai fait le t. du cadran** I slept round the clock; *Fig* **l'anecdote a fait le t. des bureaux** the story went round the offices *or* did the rounds of the offices; **faire le t. d'une question** to consider a problem from all angles

5 *(promenade ▸ à pied)* walk, stroll; *(▸ en voiture)* drive, ride; *(▸ à bicyclette, à cheval, en hélicoptère)* ride; *(court voyage)* trip, outing; **faire un t.** *(à pied)* to go for a walk; *(en voiture)* to go for a drive *or* ride; *(à vélo)* to go for a ride; **faire un t. en ville** to go into town; **je vais faire un petit t. près de la rivière** I'm going for a short walk near the river; **nous irons faire un t. dans les Pyrénées** we'll go for a trip in the Pyrenees

B. *PÉRIODE, ÉTAPE* **1** *(moment dans une succession)* turn; *(dans un jeu ▸ gén)* turn, go; *Échecs* move; **c'est (à) ton t.** *(gén)* it's your turn *or* go; *Échecs* it's your move; **à qui le t.?** whose turn is it?, who's next?; **chacun son t.** everyone will have his turn; **prendre le t. de qn** to take sb's turn; **laisser passer son t.** to miss one's turn; **attendre son t.** to wait one's turn; **c'est à ton t. de mettre la table** it's your turn to lay *or* to set the table; **t. de garde** *(d'un médecin)* spell *or* turn of duty; *Pol* **t. de scrutin** ballot; **au premier t.** in the first ballot *or* round

2 *Sport (série de matches)* round; **le second t. de la coupe d'Europe** the second round of the European Cup

C. *ACTION HABILE OU MALICIEUSE* **1** *(stratagème)* trick; **elle prépare un mauvais t.** she's up to some mischief; **jouer un t. à qn** to play a trick on sb; **jouer un sale** *ou* **mauvais t. à qn** to play a nasty *or* dirty trick on sb; **ça va te jouer des tours!** you'll be sorry for it!, it'll catch up with you (one day)!; **ma mémoire/vue me joue des tours** my memory/sight is playing tricks on me; **et le t. est joué!** and there you have it!; **avoir plus d'un t. dans son sac** to have more than one trick up one's sleeve

2 *(numéro, technique)* **t. d'adresse** skilful trick, feat of skill; **t. de cartes** card trick; **t. de passe-passe** sleight of hand; **t. de prestidigitation** conjuring trick

D. *ASPECT* **1** *(orientation)* turn; **cette affaire prend un très mauvais t.** this business is going very wrong; **je n'aime pas le t. qu'a pris la situation** I don't like the turn the situation has taken *or* the way the situation is developing; **la manifestation prit un t. tragique** the demonstration took a tragic turn; **t. d'esprit** turn *or* cast of mind

2 *Ling (expression)* expression, phrase; *(en syntaxe)* construction; **un t. de phrase maladroit** an awkward turn of phrase

E. *ROTATION* **1** *(d'une roue, d'un cylindre)* turn, revolution; *(d'un outil)* turn; *Astron* revolution; **la Terre fait un t. sur elle-même en 24 heures** the Earth completes a revolution in 24 hours *or* revolves on its axis once every 24 hours; **faire un t./trois tours sur soi-même** to spin round once/three times (on oneself); **donner deux tours de clef** to give a key two turns, to turn a key twice; **n'oublie pas de donner un t. de clef (à la porte)** don't forget to lock the door; **t. de manège** ride on a merry-go-round *or Br* a roundabout; **t. de vis** (turn of the) screw; **il suffit de donner un seul t. de vis** all it needs is one turn of the screw

2 *Aut* revolution, rev

3 *Méd* **attraper** *ou* **se donner un t. de reins** to put one's back out, to rick one's back

4 *Culin* folding *(UNCOUNT)*; **donner trois tours à la pâte** fold the pastry over three times

5 *Tech* lathe; **t. de potier** potter's wheel; *Fig* **fait au t.** beautifully made

6 *(disque)* **un 33 tours** an LP; **un 45 tours** a single, a 45

• **à tour de bras** ADV *(frapper)* with all one's strength *or* might

• **à tour de rôle** ADV in turn; **ils président la réunion à t. de rôle** they chair the meeting in turn *or* turns, they take turns at chairing the meeting; **on peut le faire à t. de rôle si tu veux** we can take (it in) turns if you like

• **tour à tour** ADV alternately, by turns; **t. à t. charmant et odieux** alternately *or* by turns charming and obnoxious

• **tour de chant** NM (song) recital; **au programme de mon t. de chant ce soir** among the songs I'm going to sing tonight

• **tour de force** NM tour de force, (amazing) feat

• **tour de main** NM **1** *(savoir-faire)* knack; **avoir/prendre le t. de main** to have/to pick up the knack; **c'est un t. (de main) à prendre** it's just a knack one has to pick up **2** *(locution)* **en un t. de main** in no time (at all), in the twinkling of an eye

• **tour de table** NM **1** *Fin (réunion)* = meeting of shareholders or investors to decide a course of action; *(ensemble de partenaires)* pool, backers; **deux nouveaux actionnaires sont entrés dans le t. de table du groupe** two new shareholders have joined the group's pool **2** *(débat)* **faisons un t. de table** I'd like each of you in turn to give his or her comments; **réunir un t. de table** to organize a brainstorming session

> **TOUR DE FRANCE**
>
> This world-famous annual cycle race starts in a different town each year, but the home stretch is always the Champs-Élysées in Paris. The widespread excitement caused by the race, along with the heroic status of many "coureurs cyclistes", reflects the continuing fondness of the French for cycling in general.

tourangeau, -elle [turɑ̃ʒo, -ɛl] ADJ **1** *(de Touraine)* of/from the Touraine **2** *(de Tours)* of/from Tours

• **Tourangeau, -elle** NM,F **1** *(de Touraine)* = inhabitant of or person from the Touraine **2** *(de Tours)* = inhabitant of or person from Tours

tourbe [turb] NF *(matière)* peat, turf

tourbeux, -euse [turbø, -øz] ADJ *(sol)* peat *(avant n)*, peaty, boggy

tourbière [turbjɛr] NF peat bog

tourbillon [turbijɔ̃] NM **1** *Météo (vent tournoyant)* whirlwind, vortex

2 *(masse d'air, de particules)* **t. de poussière/sable** eddy of dust/sand; **t. de fumée** twist *or* coil *or* eddy of smoke; **t. de feuilles** flutter of whirling leaves; **t. de neige** snow flurry

3 *(dans l'eau* ▸ *important)* whirlpool; *(*▸ *petit)* swirl; **l'eau faisait des tourbillons** the water was eddying *or* swirling

4 *(rotation rapide)* whirling, spinning; **les tourbillons de la valse** the whirling motion of a waltz

5 *Littéraire (vertige, griserie)* whirl; **le t. de la vie moderne** the whirl of modern life; **un t. de plaisirs** a giddy round of pleasures; **emporté par un t. de souvenirs** carried away by a rush of memories

6 *Tech & Phys* vortex

• **en tourbillons ADV monter/descendre en tourbillons** to swirl up/down

tourbillonnant, -e [turbijɔnɑ̃, -ɑ̃t] **ADJ** *(vent, poussière)* whirling; *(feuilles, flocons)* swirling, whirling, fluttering

tourbillonnement [turbijɔnmɑ̃] **NM** *(de feuilles, de flocons)* whirling, swirling

tourbillonner **[3]** [turbijɔne] **VI 1** *(eau, rivière)* to swirl, to make eddies; **l'eau tourbillonnait autour des piles du pont** the water swirled around the bridge supports **2** *(tournoyer* ▸ *flocons, feuilles, sable)* to whirl, to swirl, to flutter; *(*▸ *fumée)* to whirl, to eddy; *(*▸ *danseur, patineur)* to spin *or* to whirl *or* to twirl (round); **le vent faisait t. les feuilles mortes** the dead leaves were fluttering in the wind **3** *(défiler rapidement* ▸ *pensées)* **les idées tourbillonnaient dans sa tête** ideas were whirling *or* dancing around in his/her head

tourelle [turɛl] **NF 1** *Archit* turret, tourelle; **à tourelles** turreted

2 *Mil (abri)* (gun) turret; *(d'un bateau)* conning tower

3 *Cin* (lens) turret

4 *Tech (d'un tour)* turret

tourière [turjɛr] **ADJ F sœur t.** = sister responsible for a convent's external relations

NF = sister responsible for a convent's external relations

tourillon [turijɔ̃] **NM 1** *Tech (d'une pièce)* pivot, trunnion; *(d'axe)* journal; *(axe)* (wheel) spindle **2** *(d'un canon)* trunnion **3** *Menuis* (fixing) dowel

tourisme [turism] **NM 1** *(fait de voyager)* touring; **faire du t.** *(dans un pays)* to go touring; *(dans une ville)* to go sightseeing; **t. d'affaires** business tourism; **t. agricole** agricultural tourism, agritourism; **t. de masse** mass tourism; **t. sexuel** sex tourism; **t. vert** green tourism **2** *(commerce)* **le t.** tourism, the tourist industry; **notre région vit du t.** we are a tourist area **3** *Aut* **(voiture) grand t.** tourer, touring car

• **de tourisme ADJ 1** *(agence)* travel *(avant n)* **2** *(à usage personnel* ▸ *avion, voiture)* private

touriste [turist] **NMF 1** *(gén)* tourist; *(pour la journée)* day-tripper; **il y a trop de touristes ici** there are too many tourists around here; **t. sexuel** sex tourist **2** *Fam Péj (dilettante, amateur)* (outside) observer; **faire qch en t.** to do sth amateurishly; **vous allez participer au débat? – non, je suis là en t.** are you going to take part in the discussion? – no, I'm just watching *or* just an observer *or* just sitting in

ADJ *Naut & Aviat* **classe t.** tourist class

touristique [turistik] **ADJ 1** *(pour le tourisme* ▸ *brochure, guide)* tourist *(avant n)*; **route t.** scenic route; **pendant la saison t.** in season, during the tourist season **2** *(qui attire les touristes)* tourist *(avant n)*; **c'est un village très t.** this village is very popular with tourists *or* is a very popular spot; **cette ville est beaucoup trop t. à mon goût** there are too many tourists in this town for my taste

tourmaline [turmalin] **NF** tourmaline

tourment [turmɑ̃] **NM 1** *Littéraire (physique)* intense suffering, agony; **les tourments de la maladie** the torments *or* throes of illness **2** *(moral)* agony, torment; **en proie aux tourments de la création** in the throes of creation; **endurer mille tourments** to go through torment, to suffer agonies; **mon fils me donne bien du t.** my son's giving me a lot of worry

tourmente [turmɑ̃t] **NF** *Littéraire* **1** *(tempête)* tempest, storm **2** *Fig (bouleversements)* turmoil

tourmenté, -e [turmɑ̃te] **ADJ 1** *(angoissé* ▸ *personne)* tormented, troubled, anguished; *(*▸ *conscience)* tormented, troubled

2 *(visage)* tormented; **un regard t.** a haunted *or* tormented look

3 *(agité* ▸ *époque)* troubled; **la période tourmentée des guerres de Religion** the troubled period of the Wars of Religion; **une époque tourmentée de ma vie** a turbulent time in my life

4 *(accidenté* ▸ *paysage, côte)* wild, rugged, craggy; *(changeant* ▸ *ciel)* changing, shifting; **un paysage d'orage sous un ciel t.** a stormy landscape under a shifting sky

5 *Littérature & Beaux-Arts* tortuous; **un bâtiment aux sculptures tourmentées** a building with contorted *or* convoluted sculptures

6 *Météo & Naut* **mer tourmentée** rough *or* heavy sea

tourmenter **[3]** [turmɑ̃te] **VT 1** *(martyriser* ▸ *animal, personne)* to torment, to ill-treat; **veux-tu cesser de t. cette pauvre bête!** will you stop tormenting *or* baiting that poor animal!

2 *(harceler)* to harass; **tourmenté par ses héritiers** plagued *or* harassed by his heirs

3 *(sujet: faim, soif, douleur)* to torment, to plague, to rack; *(sujet: incertitude, remords)* to torment, to haunt, to rack; *(sujet: jalousie)* to plague, to torment; *(sujet: obsession)* to torment, to haunt; **ses rhumatismes le tourmentent** he's plagued by rheumatism; **les souvenirs le tourmentent** he's tormented by his memories; **le remords/la douleur le tourmente** he's racked with remorse/pain

4 *Littérature & Beaux-Arts (style)* to overelaborate

VPR se tourmenter *(s'inquiéter)* to worry oneself, to fret, to be anxious; **ne vous tourmentez pas!** don't worry!; **ne vous tourmentez pas, nous la raccompagnerons** there's no need to be anxious, we'll take her home

tourmentin [turmɑ̃tɛ̃] **NM 1** *Naut* storm jib **2** *Orn* storm petrel

tournage [turnaʒ] **NM 1** *Cin* shooting, filming; **sur le t.** during filming; **sur les lieux du t.** on the set; **le t. de son nouveau film commence la semaine prochaine** shooting starts on his/her new movie next week **2** *Tech* turning **3** *Rail* turntabling

tournailler **[3]** [turnaje] **VI** *Fam* to wander round and round; **t. autour de** to hang *or* to prowl around; **les gamins tournaillaient devant l'entrée du bar** the kids were loitering outside the bar

tournant[1] [turnɑ̃] **NM 1** *(virage)* bend, turn; **une série de tournants dangereux** a series of dangerous bends; **la voiture s'est renversée dans un t.** the car overturned on a bend **2** *Fig* turning point, watershed; **le t. du match** the turning point in *or* the decisive moment of the match; **elle est à un t. de sa carrière** she is at a turning point in her career; **marquer un t.** to indicate *or* to mark a change of direction; **cette décision constitue un t. décisif** this decision marked a turning point *or* a watershed; **prendre le** *ou* **un t.** to adapt to changing circumstances; *Fam* **attendre qn au t.** to be waiting for a chance to get even with sb, to have it in for sb; *Fam* **avoir** *ou* **attraper qn au t.** to get one's own back on sb, to get even with sb

tournant[2]**, -e** [turnɑ̃, -ɑ̃t] **ADJ 1** *(dispositif, siège)* swivel *(avant n)*, swivelling; *(pont)* swing **2** *(scène)* revolving; *(escalier, route)* winding

• **tournante NF** *Fam (viol collectif)* gang rape

tourné, -e[1] [turne] **ADJ 1** *(façonné au tour)* turned; **un pied de lampe en bois t.** a hand-turned wooden lamp base **2** *Culin (altéré* ▸ *produits laitiers)* sour, curdled; *(*▸ *vin)* sour; **ce lait est t.** this milk is *Br* off *or Am* bad **3** *(locutions)* **bien t.** *(taille)* neat; *(lettre, réponse)* well-phrased; **mal t.** *(lettre, réponse)* badly phrased; **avoir l'esprit mal t.** to have a dirty mind

tournebouler [turnəbule] **VT** *Fam* **t. qn** *(le bouleverser)* to upset sb

tournebroche [turnəbrɔʃ] **NM** *(gén)* roasting jack *or* spit; *(d'un four)* rotisserie; **canard/agneau au t.** spit-roasted duck/lamb

tourne-disque [turnədisk] *(pl* **tourne-disques)** **NM** record player

tournedos [turnədo] **NM** tournedos

tournée[2] [turne] **ADJ F** *voir* **tourné**

NF 1 *(d'un facteur, d'un commerçant)* round; **faire sa t.** *(facteur, livreur)* to do *or* to make one's round; **faire une t. électorale** *(candidat, député)* to canvass one's constituency; *(dans une élection présidentielle)* to go on the campaign trail; **t. de conférences** lecture tour; **t. d'inspection** tour of inspection; *Fam* **faire la t. des popotes** to go on a tour of inspection[□]

2 *(d'un artiste, d'une troupe)* tour; **faire une t.** to go on tour; **il achèvera sa t. à Biarritz** his tour will finish (up) in Biarritz; **faire une t. en Europe** to go on a European tour

3 *(visite)* **faire la t. des galeries** to do the rounds of *or* to go round the art galleries; **faire la t. des grands ducs** to go out on the town

4 *Fam (au bar)* round; **t. générale!** drinks all round!; **c'est ma t.** it's my round; **c'est la t. du patron** drinks are on the house

5 *Fam (volée de coups)* hiding

• **en tournée ADV être en t.** *(facteur, représentant)* to be off on one's rounds; *(chanteur)* to be on tour

tournemain [turnəmɛ̃] **en un tournemain ADV** in no time at all

TOURNER **[3]** [turne]

VI
- to turn **A1, B1, 2**
- to spin (round) **A1**
- to rotate **A1, B3**
- to turn out **B4**
- to go round **A1, 2, C1**
- to tour **A3**
- to go bad **B6**

VT
- to turn **A1, 3, C1, 2**
- to turn over **A4**
- to phrase **C2**
- to stir **A2**
- to shoot **B**

VPR
- to turn round **1**
- to turn **2**

VI A. *DÉCRIRE DES CERCLES* **1** *(se mouvoir autour d'un axe* ▸ *girouette)* to turn, to revolve; *(*▸ *disque)* to revolve, to spin; *(*▸ *aiguille de montre, manège)* to turn, to go round; *(*▸ *objet suspendu, rouet, toupie)* to spin (round); *(*▸ *aile de moulin)* to turn *or* to spin round; *(*▸ *clef, pédale, poignée)* to turn; *(*▸ *hélice, roue, tour)* to spin, to rotate; **t. sur soi-même** to turn round; *(vite)* to spin (round and round); **la Terre tourne sur elle-même** the Earth spins on its axis; **je voyais tout t.** everything was spinning *or* swimming; **faire t.** *(pièce de monnaie, manège, roue)* to spin; *(clef)* to turn; **le croupier fit t. la roulette** the croupier spun the roulette wheel; **ça me fait t. la tête** it makes my head spin; *Fam* **t. de l'œil** to pass out[□], to keel over

2 *(se déplacer en cercle* ▸ *personne)* to go round; *(*▸ *oiseau)* to fly *or* to wheel round, to circle (round); *(*▸ *insecte)* to fly *or* to buzz round; *(*▸ *avion)* to fly round (in circles), to circle (round) *(*▸ *astre, satellite)* to revolve, to go round; **les pri[sonniers] tournaient dans la cour** the prisoners were walking round (and round) the yard; **l'avion a tourné plusieurs fois au-dessus de la piste** the plane circled the runway several times; **j'a[i] tourné dix minutes avant de trouver à me garer** [I] drove round (and round) for ten minutes before I found a parking space

3 *Fam (être en tournée* ▸ *chanteur)* to (be on) tour[□]

B. *CHANGER D'ORIENTATION, D'ÉTAT* **1** *(change[r] de direction* ▸ *vent)* to turn, to veer, to shift; *(*▸ *personne)* to turn (off); *(*▸ *véhicule)* to turn (off) to make a turn; *(*▸ *route)* to turn, to bend; **le ve[nt] a tourné** there was a change in the wind, th[e] wind turned; **tournez à droite** turn (off to th[e]) right; **la rue tourne légèrement après le parc** th[e] road turns *or* bends slightly beyond the par[k] **tourne dans l'allée** turn into the drive; **la chan[ce]** *ou* **la fortune a tourné (pour eux)** their luck h[as] changed

2 *(faire demi-tour)* to turn (round)

3 *Fam (se succéder* ▸ *équipes)* to rotate[□]

4 *(évoluer)* to go, to turn out; **la course aur[ait] tourné autrement si...** the race would've ha[d a] different outcome if...; **attends de voir comm[ent] les choses vont t.** wait and see how things tu[rn] out *or* go; **bien t.** *(situation, personne)* to turn [out] well *or* satisfactorily; **mal t.** *(initiative, plaisan[te]rie)* to turn out badly, to go wrong; **tout ça va [mal] t.!** no good will come of (all) that!; **la conver[sa]tion a très mal tourné** the discussion took a v[ery] nasty turn; **un jeune qui a mal tourné** a youngs[ter] who turned out badly *or* went off the rails

5 *Fam (devenir)* **t. homo/hippie** to become ga[y/] hippy[□]

6 *(s'altérer ▸ lait)* to turn (sour), to go *Br* off *or Am* bad; *(▸ viande)* to go bad *or Br* off; *(▸ crème, mayonnaise)* to curdle; **faire t. du lait/une mayonnaise** to curdle milk/mayonnaise

C. *MARCHER, RÉUSSIR* **1** *(fonctionner ▸ compteur)* to go round; *(▸ taximètre)* to tick away; *(▸ programme informatique)* to run; **le moteur tourne** the engine's running *or* going; **faire t. un moteur (à plein régime)** to run an engine (at full throttle); **l'heure** *ou* **la pendule tourne** time passes; **l'heure tourne et vous ne faites rien** time's marching on and you're not doing anything; **l'usine tourne à plein (rendement)** the factory's working at full capacity; **faire t. une entreprise** *(directeur)* to run a business; **ce sont les commandes étrangères qui font t. l'entreprise** orders from abroad keep the business going; *Ordinat* **je ne peux pas sauvegarder pendant que mon programme tourne** I can't save while my program's running

2 *(réussir ▸ affaire, entreprise, économie)* to be running well; *Fam* **alors, les affaires, ça tourne?** so, how's business (going)?; *Fam* **ça ne tourne pas très bien entre eux** it's not going too well between them

VT A. *FAIRE CHANGER D'ORIENTATION* **1** *(faire pivoter ▸ bouton, clé, poignée, volant)* to turn; **tourne le bouton jusqu'au 7** turn the knob to 7; **il faut t. le couvercle pour ouvrir le bocal** it's a jar with a twist-off top

2 *(mélanger ▸ sauce, café)* to (give a) stir; *(▸ salade)* to toss; **ajoutez la farine tout en tournant** add the flour while stirring

3 *(diriger ▸ antenne, visage, yeux)* to turn; **t. qch vers la droite/gauche** to turn sth to the right/left; **tourne la télévision vers moi** turn the set towards me; **t. son regard** *ou* **les yeux vers** to turn one's eyes *or* to look towards; **t. ses pensées vers** to turn one's thoughts to *or* towards; **t. son attention vers** to focus one's attention on

4 *(retourner ▸ carte)* to turn over *or* up; *(▸ page)* to turn (over); *(▸ brochette, grillade)* to give a turn, to turn (over); **tournez la page, s'il vous plaît** please turn (over) the page; **t. qch contre un mur** to turn sth to face a wall; **t. et retourner, t. dans tous les sens** *(boîte, gadget)* to turn over and over; *(problème)* to turn over and over (in one's mind), to mull over; *Sport* **t. la mêlée** to wheel the scrum (round)

5 *(contourner ▸ cap)* to round; *(▸ coin de rue)* to turn; *(▸ ennemi)* to get round; *Fig* **t. la difficulté/le règlement/la loi** to get round the problem/regulations/law

6 *(locution)* **t. le cœur à qn** to nauseate sb, to turn sb's stomach

B. *Cin & TV* **t. un film** *(cinéaste)* to shoot *or* to make a movie *or Br* film; *(acteur)* to make a movie *or* to make a movie *or Br* film; **t. une scène** *(cinéaste)* to shoot *or* to film a scene; *(acteur)* to play *or* to act a scene; **la dramatique a été tournée au Kenya/en studio/en extérieur** the TV play was shot in Kenya/in the studio/on location

C. *METTRE EN FORME* **1** *Menuis & Métal* to turn; **t. le bois** to work wood on the lathe, to turn wood

2 *(formuler ▸ compliment)* to turn; *(▸ critique)* to phrase, to express; **je ne sais pas comment t. cela** I don't know how to put it; **sa demande était bien tournée** his/her request was well phrased

3 *(transformer)* **elle tourne tout au tragique** she's always making a drama out of everything; **t. qch à son avantage/désavantage** to turn sth to one's advantage/disadvantage; **t. qn/qch en ridicule** to ridicule sb/sth, to make fun of sb/sth

USAGE ABSOLU elle a tourné plusieurs fois avec Pasolini she played in several of Pasolini's movies *or Br* films; **silence, on tourne!** quiet please, action!

tourner à VT IND t. à la catastrophe to take a disastrous turn; **t. au ridicule** to become ridiculous; **ça tourne à la farce!** it's turning into a farce!; **le temps tourne à la pluie/neige** it looks like rain/snow; **le ciel commençait à t. au rouge** the sky was beginning to turn red

tourner autour de VT IND 1 *(axe)* to move *or* to turn round; **les planètes qui tournent autour du soleil** the planets revolving round the Sun; **l'escalier tourne autour de l'ascenseur** the staircase spirals *or* winds round the lift

2 *(rôder)* **t. autour de qn** *(gén)* to hang *or* to hover round sb; *(pour le courtiser)* to hang round sb; **les enfants tournaient autour du magasin depuis un moment** *(par désœuvrement)* the children had been hanging around outside the shop for a while; *(avec de mauvaises intentions)* the children had been loitering outside the shop for a while

3 *(valoir environ)* to be around *or* about, to be in the region of; **les réparations devraient t. autour de 80 euros** the repairs should cost around *or* should cost about *or* should be in the region of 80 euros

4 *(concerner ▸ sujet: conversation)* to revolve round, to centre on, to focus on; *(▸ sujet: enquête policière)* to centre on; **tout le poème tourne autour de ce souvenir** the whole poem revolves round this memory

VPR se tourner 1 *(faire un demi-tour)* to turn round; **tourne-toi, je me déshabille** turn round *or* turn your back, I'm getting undressed

2 *(changer de position)* to turn; **tourne-toi sur le ventre** turn over onto your belly; *Fig* **de quelque côté qu'on se tourne** wherever you turn; **je ne sais plus de quel côté me t.** I don't know which way to turn any more

3 *Fam* **se t. les pouces, se les t.** to twiddle one's thumbs

4 se t. vers *(s'orienter vers)* to turn towards; **tous les regards se tournèrent vers elle** all eyes turned to look at her

5 *Fig* **se t. vers qn/Dieu** to turn to sb/God; **se t. vers la religion** to turn to religion

tournesol [turnəsɔl] **NM 1** *Bot* sunflower; **graine de t.** sunflower seed **2** *Chim (colorant)* litmus; **(papier de) t.** litmus (paper)

tourneur, -euse [turnœr, -øz] **NM,F** turner; **t. sur bois/métal** wood/metal turner

tournevis [turnəvis] **NM** screwdriver; **t. cruciforme** Phillips screwdriver®; **t. d'électricien** electrician's screwdriver

tournicoter [3] [turnikɔte] **VI** *Fam* to wander around aimlessly; **t. autour de qn** *(courtiser quelqu'un)* to hang around sb; **une idée qui me tournicote dans la tête** an idea that keeps running through my mind

tourniquet [turnike] **NM 1** *(à l'entrée d'un établissement)* turnstile; *(porte à tambour)* revolving door

2 *(présentoir)* revolving stand, spinner

3 *(pour arroser)* rotary sprinkler

4 *Méd* tourniquet

5 *(de volet)* (shutter) fastener

6 *Naut* roller

7 *Arg mil* **passer au t.** to be court-martialled

tournis [turni] **NM 1** *Vét* gid, sturdy, *Spéc* coenuriasis **2** *(locutions)* **avoir le t.** to feel giddy *or* dizzy; **donner le t. à qn** to make sb (feel) giddy

tournoi [turnwa] **NM 1** *Sport & (jeux)* tournament; **t. de tennis de table** table tennis tournament; **t. open** open (tournament); **T. des Six Nations** Six Nations Tournament **2** *Hist* tournament, tourney **3** *Littéraire (compétition)* challenge; **t. d'éloquence** contest of eloquence

tournoiement [turnwamɑ̃] **NM** *(de feuilles, de papiers)* whirling, swirling; *(de l'eau)* eddying, swirling; *(d'un danseur)* twirling, swirling, whirling

tournoyant, -e [turnwajɑ̃, -ɑ̃t] **ADJ** *(feuilles, fumée, flocons)* whirling, swirling; *(eau)* eddying, swirling; *(oiseau)* wheeling; *(danseur)* swirling, twirling, whirling

tournoyer [13] [turnwaje] **VI** *(feuilles, fumée, flocons)* to whirl, to swirl; *(eau)* to eddy, to swirl; *(oiseau)* to wheel *or* to circle round; *(danseur)* to swirl *or* to twirl *or* to whirl (round); **le radeau tournoyait dans les rapides** the raft was tossed round (and round) in the rapids; **descendre en tournoyant** to come whirling down; **faire t. qch** to whirl *or* to swing sth

tournure [turnyr] **NF 1** *(allure, aspect)* demeanour; **elle avait une t. un peu gauche** she was of a somewhat awkward demeanour **2** *(évolution, tendance)* trend, tendency; **d'après la t. que prend la situation** from the way the situation is developing *or* going; **prendre t.** to take shape; **les choses prennent (une) meilleure/une mauvaise t.** things are taking a turn for the better/the worse; **t. d'esprit** turn *or* cast of mind **3** *Ling (expression)* turn of phrase, expression; *(en syntaxe)* form, construction; **t. de phrase** turn of phrase; **t. impersonnelle/interrogative** impersonal/interrogative form

tour-opérateur [turɔperatœr] *(pl* **tour-opérateurs) NM** tour operator

tourte [turt] **NF 1** *(tarte)* pie; **t. aux poires/épinards** pear/spinach pie **2** *(pain rond)* round loaf

tourteau, -x [turto] **NM 1** *(crabe)* edible crab **2** *Agr* oil-cake, cattle cake **3** *Culin* **t. fromagé** ≃ baked cheesecake

tourtereau, -x [turtəro] **NM** *Orn* young turtle-dove

• **tourtereaux NMPL** *Hum* lovebirds; **où sont les tourtereaux?** *(à un mariage)* where's the happy couple?

tourterelle [turtərɛl] **NF** *Orn* turtledove

tourtière [turtjɛr] **NF** *(plat)* pie dish *or* plate

tous ADJ [tu] *voir* **tout**

PRON [tus] *voir* **tout**

Toussaint [tusɛ̃] **NF** *Rel* **(le jour de) la T.** All Saints' Day; **la veille de la T.** Hallowe'en; **un temps de T.** miserable weather

> **TOUSSAINT**
>
> All Saints' Day is a public holiday in France. It is the traditional occasion for a visit to the cemetery to lay flowers (usually chrysanthemums) on the graves of family and loved ones.

tousser [3] [tuse] **VI 1** *Méd* to cough; **tu tousses?** do you have a cough?; **je tousse beaucoup/un peu** I have a bad/slight cough; **il toussa pour m'avertir** he coughed *or* gave a cough to warn me **2** *(moteur)* to splutter; **le moteur toussa plusieurs fois puis démarra** the engine spluttered several times then came to life

tousseur, -euse [tusœr, -øz] **NM,F** *Fam* cougher

toussotement [tusɔtmɑ̃] **NM** (slight) coughing *(UNCOUNT)*, (slight) cough

toussoter [3] [tusɔte] **VI 1** *Méd* to have a bit of a cough *or* a slight cough **2** *(pour prévenir)* to give a little *or* a discreet cough

TOUT, -E [tu, tut]

> **ADJ**
> • all (the) **1, 2** • the whole (of the) **1**
> • completely **5** • only **6**
> • everything **7**
>
> **ADJ INDÉFINI**
> • any **A** • all (the) **A, B1**
> • every **A, B4**
>
> **PRON INDÉFINI**
> • everything **A** • anything **A**
> • all (the) **A, B1–3**
>
> **ADV**
> • very **1** • completely **1**
> • right **2**
>
> **NM**
> • whole **1**

> When **tous** is a pronoun, it is pronounced [tus].

(pl **tous, toutes) ADJ 1** *(entier)* all (the), the whole (of the); **toute la nuit** all night; **elle a parcouru toute la distance en deux heures** she covered the full distance in two hours; **pendant t. le concert** throughout the concert, during the whole concert; **il a plu toute la journée** it rained all day long; **t. le village/pays** the whole village/country; **toute une journée** a whole day; **t. ceci/cela** all (of) this/that; **toute cette histoire** this whole story; **t. ce travail pour rien!** all this work for nothing!; **j'ai t. mon temps** I've plenty of time *or* all the time in the world; **t. mon courage/enthousiasme a disparu** all my courage/enthusiasm has gone; **toute ma fortune** my whole fortune; **il doit venir avec toute sa famille** he's supposed to be coming with his whole family; **ils se sont aimés toute leur vie** they loved each other all their lives; **avec lui, c'est t. l'un ou t. l'autre** with him, it's all or nothing

2 *(devant un nom propre)* all; **t. Vienne l'acclamait** he/she was the toast of all Vienna; **j'ai visité t. Paris en huit jours** I saw all *or* the whole of Paris in a week; **il a lu t. Racine** he's read the whole *or*

the complete works of Racine; **il a lu t. 'les Misérables'** he's read the whole of 'Les Misérables'

3 *(devant un nom sans article)* **on a t. intérêt à y aller** it's in our every interest to go; **c'est en toute liberté que j'ai choisi** I made the choice completely of my own free will; **rouler à toute vitesse** to drive at full *or* top speed; **en toute franchise/simplicité** in all sincerity/simplicity; **c'est de toute beauté** it's extremely beautiful

4 *(avec une valeur emphatique)* **c'est toute une affaire!** it's quite a to-do!; **c'est toute une expédition pour y aller!** getting there involves quite a trek!; **c'est t. un travail de le nourrir!** feeding him's quite a job!

5 *(comme adv) (entièrement)* completely; **elle était toute à son travail** she was completely absorbed in her work; **elle était toute de bleu vêtue** she was dressed completely in blue

6 *(unique, seul)* only; **c'est t. l'effet que ça te fait?** is that all it means to you?; **pour t. remerciement on m'a renvoyé** by way of thanks I got fired; **pour toute indemnité, j'ai reçu 100 euros** 100 euros was the only compensation I got; **pour toute famille il n'avait qu'une cousine éloignée** one distant cousin was all the family he had

7 *(suivi d'une relative)* **t. ce qu'on dit** everything people say; **il représente t. ce que je déteste** he embodies all the things *or* everything I hate; **t. ce que l'entreprise compte de personnel qualifié** the company's entire qualified workforce; **ils s'amusaient t. ce qu'ils savaient** they were having a whale of a time; **ses enfants sont t. ce qu'il y a de bien élevés** his children are very well-behaved *or* are models of good behaviour; **ce projet est t. ce qu'il y a de plus sérieux** this project couldn't be more serious

ADJ INDÉFINI A. *AU SINGULIER (chaque, n'importe quel)* any, all, every; **t. citoyen a des droits** every citizen has rights, all citizens have rights; **toute personne ayant vu l'accident** anyone who witnessed the accident; **t. changement les inquiète** the slightest change worries them; **toute faute sera pénalisée** all mistakes will be penalized without exception; **pour t. renseignement, écrivez-nous** for further information, write to us; **pour éviter t. tracas** to avoid any worries; **à t. âge** at any age; **à toute heure** at any hour, at any time; **sandwiches à toute heure** sandwiches available at all times; **de t. temps** since time immemorial, from the beginning of time; **t. autre que lui aurait refusé** anyone other than him *or* anybody else would have refused

B. *AU PLURIEL* **1** *(exprimant la totalité)* all; **tous les hommes** all men, the whole of mankind; **tous les gens** everybody, everyone; **je veux tous les détails** I want all the details *or* the full details; **nous avons essayé tous les traitements** we've tried all the treatments *or* every (single) treatment available; **tous ceux-ci/ceux-là** all (of) these/those

2 *(devant un numéral)* **ils viennent tous les deux** both of them *or* the two of them are coming; **quand nous sommes tous les deux** when we're on our own, when there's just the two of us; **ils nous ont invitées toutes les quatre** they've invited the *or* all four of us; **toutes deux iront** both of them will go; **nous avons tous deux les mêmes goûts** we both have the same tastes

3 *(devant un nom sans article)* **ils étaient 1500, toutes disciplines confondues** there were 1,500 of them, taking all disciplines; **champion toutes catégories** overall champion; **il roulait tous feux éteints** he was driving with his lights off; **il est mon préféré à tous égards** I like him best in every respect

4 *(exprimant la périodicité)* every; **tous les jours** every day; **tous les lundis** every Monday; **le magazine paraît toutes les semaines/tous les mois** the magazine comes out every week/every month; **toutes les deux semaines** every other week, every second week, every two weeks; **à prendre toutes les quatre heures** *(sur médicament)* to be taken every four hours *or* at four-hourly intervals; **toutes les fois qu'on s'est rencontrés** every time we've met; **tous les 100 mètres** every 100 metres

PRON INDÉFINI A. *AU SINGULIER* everything, all; *(n'importe quoi)* anything; **j'ai t. jeté** I threw everything away; **il se plaint toujours de t.** he's always complaining about everything; **il me dit t.** he tells me everything, he has no secrets from me; **dis-moi t.** tell me all about it; *Fam* **t'as t. compris!** that's it!, that's right!; **c'est t. dire** that says it all; **elle est bonne en t.** she's good at everything, she's a good all-rounder; **il mange de t.** he eats anything; **capable de t.** capable of anything; **c'est t.** that's all; **ce sera t.?** *(dans un magasin)* will that be all?, anything else?; **ce n'est pas t.** that's not all; **il a du culot! – attendez, ce n'est pas t.!** he's got some nerve! – wait, there's more to come *or* that's not all!; **ce n'est pas t. de faire des enfants, il faut les élever ensuite** having children is one thing, but then you've got to bring them up; **être t. pour qn** to be everything for sb, to mean everything to sb; *Fam* **et t. et t.** and all that (sort of thing); **elle t'envoie ses amitiés et t. et t.** she sends her regards and all that sort of thing; **il y avait des bougies, de la musique et t. et t.** there were candles, music and all that sort of thing *or* and the whole works; **on aura t. vu!** now I've *or* we've seen everything!; **t. est là** *(objets)* that's everything; *(problème)* that's the whole point *or* the crux of the matter; **vous serez remboursé t. ou partie** you'll get all or part of your money back; **t. ou rien** all or nothing; **avec toi c'est t. ou rien** with you, it's all or nothing *or* one extreme or the other; **c'est t. sauf du foie gras** it's anything but foie gras; **il est t. sauf un génie** he's far from being a genius; **t. bien considéré, t. bien réfléchi** all things considered; **t. bien pesé** after weighing up the pros and the cons; **il a t. de l'escroc** he's your typical crook; **il a t. de son père** he's the spitting image of his father

B. *AU PLURIEL* **1** *(désignant ce dont on a parlé)* **il y a plusieurs points de vue, tous sont intéressants** there are several points of view, they are all interesting; **j'adore les prunes – prends-les toutes** I love plums – take them all *or* all of them

2 *(avec une valeur récapitulative)* all; **Jean, Pierre, Jacques, tous voulaient la voir** Jean, Pierre, Jacques, they all wanted to see her; *Fam* **c'est tous feignants et compagnie!** they're just a bunch of idlers!

3 *(tout le monde)* **vous m'entendez tous?** can you all hear me?; **écoutez-moi tous!** listen to me, all of you!; **des émissions pour tous** programmes suitable for all (audiences); **tous ensemble** all together; **tous tant** *ou* **autant que nous sommes** all of us, every (single) one of us

ADV

> The adverb agrees in gender and number before a feminine noun beginning with a consonant or aspirate h.

1 *(entièrement, tout à fait)* very, completely; **ils étaient t. seuls** they were quite *or* completely alone; **la ville t. entière** the whole town; **t. neuf** brand new; **t. nu** stark naked; **un t. jeune homme** a very young man; **elle était t. émue** she was very moved; **sa chevelure était toute hérissée** his/her hair was all messy; **elle est rentrée toute contente** she came back very happy; **ses t. premiers mots** his/her very first words; **les t. premiers temps** at the very beginning; **une robe t. en dentelle** a dress made entirely of lace; **être t. en sueur** to be all sweaty; **le jardin est t. en longueur** the garden is just one long strip; **un de nos t. meilleurs acteurs** one of our very best actors; **j'étais t. gêné** I was most *or* very embarrassed; **t. mouillé** wet *or* soaked through, drenched; **t. simplement/autrement** quite simply/differently; **il est toute bonté/générosité** he is goodness/generosity itself; **ça, c'est t. lui!** that's typical of him *or* just like him!

2 *(en intensif)* **t. en haut/bas** right at the top/bottom; **t. au début** right at the beginning; **c'est t. près** it's very close; **il roulait t. doucement** he was driving very *or* extremely slowly; **t. à côté de moi** right next to me; **c'est t. près d'ici** it's very close to here, it's a stone's throw (away) from here; **t. contre le mur** right up against the wall; **c'est t. le contraire!** it's quite the opposite!

3 *(déjà)* **t. prêt** *ou* **préparé** ready-made; **t. bébé, elle dansait déjà** even as a baby, she was already dancing; **on verra – c'est t. vu!** we'll see – it's already decided!

4 *(avec un gérondif) (indiquant la simultanéité)* **on mangera t. en marchant** we'll eat while we're walking; **t. en tricotant** while knitting

5 *(avec un gérondif) (indiquant la concession)* **t. en avouant son ignorance dans ce domaine, il continuait à me contredire** although he'd confessed his ignorance in that field, he kept on contradicting me

NM 1 *(ensemble)* whole; **former un t.** to make up a whole; **je vous vends le t. pour 50 euros** you can have the whole lot for 50 euros; **versez le t. dans un bol** put the whole mixture into a bowl; **mon t. est un instrument de musique** *(dans une charade)* my whole *or* all is a musical instrument

2 le t. *(l'essentiel)* the main *or* the most important thing; **le t./c'est de ne pas bafouiller** the most important thing is not to stutter; *Fam* **ce n'est pas le t., mais je dois partir** that's all very well, but I've got to go now; **ce n'est pas le t. de critiquer, il faut pouvoir proposer autre chose** it's not enough to criticize, you've got to be able to suggest something else; **jouer** *ou* **risquer le t. pour le t.** to risk (one's) all; **tenter le t. pour le t.** to make a (final) desperate attempt *or* a last-ditch effort; **s'engager dans le t. nucléaire** to go all-nuclear; **la politique du t. ou rien** an all-or-nothing policy; **changer du t. au t.** to change completely

• **du tout** **ADV** not at all; **je vous dérange? – du t., du t.!** am I disturbing you? – not at all *or* not in the least!; **elle finissait son café sans du t. se soucier de notre présence** she was finishing her coffee without paying any attention to us at all *or* whatsoever

• **en tout** **ADV 1** *(au total)* in total, in all; **cela fait 95 euros en t.** that comes to 95 euros in all *or* in total **2** *(exactement)* exactly, entirely; **la copie est conforme en t. à l'original** the copy matches the original exactly

• **en tout et pour tout** **ADV** (all) in all; **en t. et pour t., nous avons dépensé 600 euros** all in all, we've spent 600 euros

• **tout à coup** **ADV** all of a sudden, suddenly

• **tout à fait** **ADV 1** *(complètement)* quite, fully, absolutely; **en es-tu t. à fait conscient?** are you fully aware of it?; **je vous comprends t. à fait** I understand you perfectly well; **ce n'est pas t. à fait exact** it's not quite correct; **n'ai-je pas raison? – t. à fait!** am I right? – absolutely! **2** *(exactement)* exactly; **c'est t. à fait ce que je cherche** it's exactly what I've been looking for **3** *(oui)* certainly; **vous faites les retouches? – t. à fait** do you do alterations? – certainly (we do)

• **tout de même** **ADV 1** *(malgré tout)* all the same, even so; **j'irai t. de même** all the same, I'll still go **2** *(en intensif)* **t. de même, tu exagères!** steady on!, that's a bit much!

• **tout de suite** **ADV 1** *(dans le temps)* straight away, right away, at once; **apporte du pain – t. de suite!** bring some bread – right away! **2** *(dans l'espace)* immediately; **tournez à gauche t. de suite après le pont** turn left immediately after the bridge

• **tout... que** **CONJ** **t. directeur qu'il est** *ou* **qu'i[l] soit,...** although he's the boss,..., I don't care i[f] he is the boss,...; **toute enthousiaste qu'elle soit elle n'en devra pas moins attendre** however enthusiastic she is, she'll still have to wait

---

tout-à-l'égout [tutalegu] **NM INV** main c[...] mains drainage, main sewer; **avoir le t.** to b[e] connected to the main sewer

Toutankhamon [tutɑ̃kamɔ̃] **NPR** Tutankha[-]men, Tutankhamun

toutefois [tutfwa] **ADV** however, neverthele[ss] **t., j'ai omis** *ou* **j'ai t. omis un détail important** I hav[e] however *or* nevertheless omitted an importa[nt] detail; **je lui parlerai, si t. il veut bien me recev[oir]** I'll talk to him, that is, if he'll see me

toute-puissance [tutpɥisɑ̃s] **NF INV** omnip[o-]tence, all-powerful influence; *Fig (d'un dés[ir])* overwhelming nature

toute-puissante [tutpɥisɑ̃t] *voir* **tou[t-] puissant**

toutes-boîtes [tutbwat] **NM INV** *Belg* free p[a-]per, freesheet

toutim, toutime [tutim] **NM** *Fam* **et tout le t.** t[he] works, the whole enchilada, *Br* the full mont[y]

toutou [tutu] **NM** *Fam* **1** *(chien)* doggy, doggi[e] *(personne docile)* lapdog; **filer** *ou* **obéir com[me] un (petit) t.** to be a lapdog

Tout-Paris [tupari] NM INV le T. the Parisian smart set; le T. y était everyone who's anyone in Paris was there

tout-petit [tupəti] (*pl* tout-petits) NM (*qui ne marche pas*) infant; (*qui marche*) toddler; un livre/une émission pour les tout-petits a book/a programme for the very young

tout-puissant, toute-puissante [tupɥisɑ̃, tutpɥisɑ̃t] (*mpl* tout-puissants, *fpl* toutes-puissantes) ADJ 1 (*influent*) omnipotent, all-powerful; *Fig* (*désir*) overwhelming 2 *Rel* almighty

• **le Tout-Puissant** NM the Almighty

tout-terrain [tuterɛ̃] ADJ INV cross-country (*avant n*), off-road (*avant n*)

NM INV off-road driving

NM OU NF INV off-road vehicle, off-roader

tout-va [tuva] **à tout va** ADV like mad, like nobody's business; le gouvernement privatise à t. the government are privatizing things like nobody's business

ADJ galore; pour attirer le client, le magasin proposait des réductions à t. the shop was offering discounts galore to attract customers

tout-venant [tuvnɑ̃] NM INV 1 (*choses*) everyday things; (*personnes*) ordinary people; des places d'opéra qui ne sont pas pour le t. opera tickets that are beyond the means of ordinary people 2 *Minér* ungraded product; (*houille*) unsorted coal

toux [tu] NF cough; t. grasse/nerveuse/sèche loose/nervous/dry cough

township [tawnʃip] NM OU NF township

toxémie [tɔksemi] NF *Méd* toxaemia

toxicité [tɔksisite] NF toxicity; coefficient de t. toxicity rating

toxico [tɔksiko] NMF *Fam* junkie, addict

toxicodépendance [tɔksikodepɑ̃dɑ̃s] NF drug dependence *or* dependency

toxicologie [tɔksikɔlɔʒi] NF toxicology

toxicologique [tɔksikɔlɔʒik] ADJ toxicological

toxicologue [tɔksikɔlɔg] NMF toxicologist

toxicomane [tɔksikɔman] ADJ drug-addicted

NMF drug addict

toxicomanie [tɔksikɔmani] NF drug addiction

toxicomanogène [tɔksikɔmanɔʒɛn] ADJ *Méd* addictive

toxicose [tɔksikoz] NF *Méd* toxicosis

toxine [tɔksin] NF toxin

toxique [tɔksik] ADJ toxic, poisonous

NM poison, toxin

toxoplasmose [tɔksɔplasmoz] NF *Méd* toxoplasmosis

TP [tepe] NMPL 1 *Scol & Univ* (*abrév* travaux pratiques) avoir un TP de chimie to have a practical chemistry lesson *or* a chemistry lab; être en TP to be in the lab 2 (*abrév* travaux publics) civil engineering

NM *Fin* (*abrév* Trésor public) le TP *Br* ≃ the Treasury, *Am* ≃ the Treasury Department

TPC [tepese] NF *Ordinat* (*abrév* tierce partie de confiance) TTP

TPE [tepeə] NF *Écon* (*abrév* très petite entreprise) very small business (*employing fewer than 20 people*)

NM *Com* (*abrév* terminal de paiement électronique) PDQ, electronic payment terminal, pinpad

TPIR [tepeiɛr] NM *Jur* (*abrév* Tribunal pénal international pour le Rwanda) ICTR

TPIY [tepeiigrek] NM *Jur* (*abrév* Tribunal pénal international pour l'ex-Yougoslavie) ICTY

tpm [tepeɛm] NMPL *Tech* (*abrév* tours par minute) rpm

traboule [trabul] NF (*à Lyon*) alleyway

trac[1] [trak] NM *Fam* (*devant un public*) stage fright; (*à un examen*) exam nerves; avoir le t. to have the jitters; il a le t. avant d'entrer en scène he gets very nervous before going on stage; j'avais le t. avant mon entretien I had butterflies before the interview

trac[2] [trak] **tout à trac** ADV *Vieilli* out of the blue, just like that; elle a dit ça tout à t. she just came out with it, she blurted it out all of a sudden

traçage [trasaʒ] NM 1 (*d'un trait, d'une figure*) drawing; (*d'une inscription*) writing *or* tracing (out); (*d'une route*) laying out; (*d'un itinéraire*) plotting (out) 2 *Mines* horizontal working 3 *Tech* marking, scribing

traçant, -e [trasɑ̃, -ɑ̃t] ADJ 1 *Mil* (*projectile*) tracer (*avant n*) 2 *Bot* running, creeping

tracas [traka] NM 1 (*soucis*) worry, upset; cette affaire lui cause bien du t. this business is causing him/her a lot of worry *or* upset 2 (*efforts*) trouble, bother; tu t'es donné bien du t. you've gone to a great deal of trouble *or* bother; ne te donne pas tant de t. don't go to such trouble *or* bother

NMPL (*soucis matériels ou financiers*) troubles; tous les t. engendrés par le chômage all the worries caused by being unemployed

tracasser [3] [trakase] VT (*sujet: situation*) to worry, to bother; (*sujet: enfant*) to worry; son état de santé actuel me tracasse I'm worried about the current state of his/her health

VPR se tracasser to worry (pour qch about sth); ne te tracasse plus pour cela don't give it another thought

tracasserie [trakasri] NF (*souvent pl*) petty annoyance; faire face à des tracasseries administratives to put up with a lot of frustrating red tape; être en butte aux tracasseries de la police to be subjected to police harassment

tracassier, -ère [trakasje, -ɛr] ADJ (*administration, fonctionnaire*) pettifogging; (*personne*) nit-picking

NM,F nitpicker

trace [tras] NF 1 (*empreinte* ▸ *d'un animal*) track, trail, spoor; (▸ *d'un fugitif*) trail; des traces de pas footprints, footmarks; des traces de pneus tyre *or* wheel marks; retrouver la t. de qn to pick up the trail of sb; perdre la t. de qn to lose trace *or* track of sb; *Fig* suivre la t. *ou* les traces de qn, marcher sur les traces de qn to follow in sb's footsteps

2 (*d'un coup, d'une maladie*) mark; une t. de brûlure/piqûre a burn/needle mark; il portait des traces de coups his body showed signs of having been beaten; elle a quelques traces de varicelle she's got some chickenpox scars

3 (*marque, indice*) trace, smear; il y a des traces de doigts sur la vitre there are fingermarks on the window pane; des traces de peinture paint marks; des traces de sang sur le sol traces of blood on the ground; toute t. de cet événement semble avoir été effacée all traces of the event seem to have been wiped out; disparaître sans laisser de t. to disappear without trace; pas la moindre t. d'effraction no sign *or* evidence *or* trace of a break-in; on ne trouve pas t. de votre dossier your file cannot be traced, there's no trace of your file

4 (*quantité infime*) trace; on a retrouvé des traces d'arsenic dans le thé traces of arsenic have been found in the tea; elle parle sans la moindre t. d'accent she speaks without the slightest trace *or* hint of an accent

5 (*vestige*) trace; on y a retrouvé les traces d'une civilisation très ancienne traces of a very ancient civilization have been discovered there

6 (*marque psychique*) mark; cela a laissé en elle des traces profondes it affected her deeply *or* made a profound impression on her; une telle épreuve laisse forcément des traces such an ordeal is bound to take its toll

7 (*comme adj*) *Chim* élément t. trace element

8 *Sport* trail; faire la t. to break a trail; t. directe direct descent

• **à la trace** ADV (*d'après les empreintes*) suivre à la t. (*fuyard, gibier*) to track (down); il était blessé, ils l'ont suivi à la t. he was wounded and they followed his trail

• **sur la trace de** PRÉP (*à la recherche de*) on the trail of *or* track of; ils sont sur la t. du bandit they are on the bandit's trail; ils sont sur la t. d'un manuscript they're tracking down a manuscript

tracé [trase] NM 1 (*représentation* ▸ *d'une ville, d'un réseau*) layout, plan; faire le t. d'une route to lay out *or* to plan a road (*on paper*)

2 (*chemin suivi* ▸ *par un fleuve*) course; (▸ *par une voie*) route; suivre le t. du fleuve to follow the river

3 (*ligne* ▸ *dans un graphique*) line; (▸ *dans un dessin*) stroke, line; (*contour* ▸ *d'un littoral*) outline

4 (*en travaux publics*) tracing, marking out (*on site*)

tracer [16] [trase] VT 1 (*trait, cercle, motif*) to draw; t. une circonférence/ligne to draw a circumference/line; *Fig* vous nous tracez un tableau pessimiste de l'avenir you're painting a less than rosy picture of our future

2 (*inscription, lettre, mot*) to write; à cinq ans, ils ont encore du mal à t. les chiffres et les lettres at five years old they still have difficulty forming numbers and letters

3 (*marquer l'emplacement de* ▸ *itinéraire*) to trace, to plot; (▸ *chemin, terrain*) to mark *or* to stake *or* to lay out; (▸ *sillon*) to mark out; (▸ *chemin dans la jungle*) to open up; t. une route à travers la brousse to plot the course of a road through the bush; t. les lignes d'un court de tennis to mark out a tennis court

4 *Fig* (*indiquer*) to map out, to plot; sa voie est toute tracée his/her career is mapped out (for him/her); t. les grandes lignes de qch to outline sth, to indicate the general outlines of sth

5 *Math* (*courbe*) to plot; t. le graphe d'une fonction to plot the graph of a (mathematical) function

6 *Tech* to mark, to scribe

VI 1 *Fam* (*aller très vite*) to belt along, to bomb along; (*déguerpir*) to beat it, *Br* to clear off; elle trace, ta bagnole! your car goes like a bomb! 2 *Bot* (*racine*) to run out, to creep

traceur, -euse [trasœr, -øz] ADJ *Phys* tracer (*avant n*)

NM,F *Tech* scriber

NM 1 *Chim, Nucl & Phys* tracer 2 (*pour dessins*) tracer; (*d'un appareil enregistreur*) pen 3 *Ordinat* t. (de courbes) graph plotter

trachéal, -e, -aux, -ales [trakeal, -o] ADJ tracheal

trachée [traʃe] NF 1 *Anat* windpipe, *Spéc* trachea 2 *Zool* trachea 3 *Bot* tracheary elements, trachea

trachée-artère [traʃearter] (*pl* trachées-artères) NF *Anat* trachea

trachéite [trakeit] NF *Méd* tracheitis

trachéo-bronchite [trakeobrɔ̃ʃit] (*pl* trachéo-bronchites) NF *Méd* tracheobronchitis

trachéotomie [trakeɔtɔmi] NF *Méd* tracheotomy

trachome [trakom] NM *Méd* trachoma

traçoir [traswar] NM scriber, tracing awl

tract [trakt] NM pamphlet, leaflet, tract; distribuer des tracts (à) to leaflet

tractable [traktabl] ADJ towable

tractations [traktasjɔ̃] NFPL *Péj* dealings, negotiations; des t. eurent lieu et l'affaire fut étouffée negotiations took place and the whole business was hushed up

tracté, -e [trakte] ADJ motor-drawn

tracter [3] [trakte] VT to tow, to pull

VI *Fam* to leaflet

tracteur, -trice [traktœr, -tris] ADJ *Aut* towing (*avant n*)

NM 1 *Agr* tractor 2 *Aut* t. routier tractor; t. et semi-remorque articulated vehicle 3 (*d'imprimante*) t. de papier paper tractor; t. à picots tractor drive

traction [traksjɔ̃] NF 1 (*mode de déplacement*) traction, haulage

2 *Aut* t. avant/arrière (*système*) front-wheel/rear-wheel drive; une t. avant = old front-wheel drive Citroën model

3 *Méd* traction

4 *Phys* traction; force de t. tractive force; t. magnétique magnetic pull

5 *Rail* (*force*) traction; la t. = department dealing with the maintenance and driving of engines

6 *Sport* (*sur une barre, aux anneaux*) pull-up; (*au sol*) push-up, *Br* press-up; faire des tractions (*en tirant*) to do pull-ups; (*en poussant*) to do push-ups *or Br* press-ups

tractopelle [traktɔpɛl] NF backhoe loader

tractus [traktys] NM *Anat* tract, tractus; t. digestif digestive tract

trader [trɛdœr] NM **t. fou** *ou* **fraudeur** rogue trader

tradition [tradisjɔ̃] NF **1** *(ensemble des coutumes)* tradition; **la t. veut que l'on attende minuit** tradition dictates that we wait till midnight; **la t. veut qu'elle soit née ici** tradition has it that she was born here; **selon la t. bretonne** according to Breton tradition; **dans la plus pure t. française** in true French tradition; **t. populaire** folk tradition

2 *(usage)* tradition, custom; **dans notre famille, c'est une t.** it's a family tradition; **il existe une longue t. de liens culturels entre ces pays** there is a long history of cultural links between the countries

3 *Jur* tradition, transfer

4 *Rel* **la T.** Tradition

• **de tradition** ADJ traditional; **un peuple de t. orthodoxe** a traditional Orthodox people; **il est de t. de/que...** it's a tradition to/that...

traditionalisme [tradisjɔnalism] NM **1** *(gén)* traditionalism **2** *Rel* Traditionalism

traditionaliste [tradisjɔnalist] ADJ traditionalist

NMF traditionalist

traditionnel, -elle [tradisjɔnɛl] ADJ **1** *(fondé sur la tradition)* traditional; **une interprétation traditionnelle d'un texte** a conventional interpretation of a text **2** *(passé dans les habitudes)* usual, traditional; **la date traditionnelle de la remise des prix** the traditional *or* usual date for the prize-giving; **le t. baiser de la mariée** the time-honoured tradition of kissing the bride

traditionnellement [tradisjɔnɛlmɑ̃] ADV **1** *(selon la tradition)* traditionally; **se marier t.** to have a traditional wedding **2** *(comme d'habitude)* as usual, as always; **un secteur industriel t. déficitaire** an industrial sector which usually *or* traditionally runs at a loss

traducteur, -trice [tradyktœr, -tris] NM,F translator

NM **1** *Tech* transducer **2** *Ordinat* translator

• **traductrice** NF translating *or* translation machine

traduction [tradyksjɔ̃] NF **1** *(processus)* translating, translation; **son roman perd beaucoup à la t.** his/her novel loses a lot in translation; **c'est un mot qui a plusieurs traductions** it's a word which can be translated in several different ways; **t. de l'espagnol en allemand** translation from Spanish into German; **t. automatique** automatic translation; **t. littérale** literal *or* word-for-word translation; **t. simultanée** simultaneous translation **2** *(texte)* translation; **acheter une t. de 'Guerre et Paix'** to buy a translation of 'War and Peace' **3** *(transposition)* expression; **la t. musicale de sa passion** the expression of his/her passion in music, the musical expression of his/her passion

traductrice [tradyktris] *voir* **traducteur**

traduire [98] [tradɥir] VT **1** *(écrivain, roman, terme)* to translate (**de/en** from/into); **livre traduit de l'anglais** book translated from (the) English; **t. qch du russe en chinois** to translate sth from Russian *or* out of Russian into Chinese; **la première phrase est mal traduite** the first sentence is mistranslated *or* badly translated; **elle est peu traduite en Europe** very few of her works are translated in Europe

2 *(exprimer* ► *pensée, sentiment)* to express, to reflect, to convey; *(*► *colère, peur)* to reveal, to indicate; **cette réaction traduit une grande sensibilité** this reaction is indicative of *or* points to great sensitivity; **ce genre de comportement traduit un manque d'affection** this kind of behaviour is symptomatic of *or* a sign of a lack of affection

3 *Jur* **t. qn en justice** to bring sb before the courts, to prosecute sb

4 *Ordinat (carte)* to interpret

VI *Ling* to translate (**de/vers** from/into); **t. mot à mot** to translate word for word

VPR **se traduire 1** *(emploi passif)* to be translated; **la phrase peut se t. de différentes façons** the sentence can be translated *or* rendered in different ways

2 se t. par *(avoir pour résultat)* to result in; **le ralentissement de l'activité économique s'est traduit par de nombreux licenciements** the slowdown in economic activity resulted in numerous redundancies; **la sécheresse s'est traduite par une baisse de la production agricole** agricultural production fell as a result of the drought

3 se t. par *(être exprimé par)* to be expressed in; **son émotion se traduisit par des larmes** his/her emotion was expressed in tears

traduisible [tradɥizibl] ADJ **1** *(mot, expression, texte)* translatable; **difficilement t.** difficult to translate; **ce proverbe n'est pas t.** this proverb cannot be translated *or* is untranslatable **2** *Jur* **t. en justice** liable to prosecution

traduisons *etc voir* **traduire**

traduit, -e [tradɥi, -it] PP *voir* **traduire**

Trafalgar [trafalgar] NM *Fig* **coup de T.** underhand trick

trafic [trafik] NM **1** *(commerce illicite)* traffic, trafficking; **t. d'armes** arms dealing, gunrunning; **le t. de drogue** *ou* **de stupéfiants** drug trafficking; **faire du t. de drogue** to be involved in drug trafficking; *Fig* **faire t. de son corps** *ou* **de ses charmes** to sell one's body

2 *Fam (manigance)* fishy business; **il y a un drôle de t. dans cette boutique** there's something very odd *or* funny going on in that shop

3 *Jur* **t. d'influence** influence peddling; **il a obtenu ce marché grâce à un véritable t. d'influence** he landed the deal thanks to a fair amount of string-pulling

4 *Transp (circulation)* traffic; **t. aérien/ferroviaire/maritime/portuaire/routier** air/rail/sea/port/road traffic; **t. de voyageurs** passenger traffic; **le t. est dense/fluide sur l'autoroute** traffic is heavy/light on the motorway

5 *Électron* traffic; *Ordinat* **t. de réseau** network traffic

6 *Vieilli (commerce)* trading, trade

traficoter [3] [trafikɔte] *Fam Péj* VI to be on the fiddle; **il traficote** he's a small-time crook, he's into petty dealing

VT *(manigancer)* to be up to; **qu'est-ce que tu traficotes dans ma chambre?** what do you think you're up to in my room?

trafiquant, -e [trafikɑ̃, -ɑ̃t] NM,F dealer, trafficker; **t. de drogue** drug dealer *or* trafficker; **t. d'armes** gunrunner, arms dealer

trafiquer [3] [trafike] VI *(faire du commerce illicite)* to traffic; **il a fait fortune en trafiquant pendant la guerre** he made a fortune on the black market during the war

VT *Fam* **1** *(falsifier, altérer* ► *comptabilité, résultats électoraux)* to fiddle, to doctor[□]; *(*► *vin)* to adulterate[□]; *(*► *compteur électrique, freins)* to tamper with[□]; *(*► *compteur kilométrique)* to rig; *(moteur de voiture, Mobylette®)* to tinker with **2** *Fam (manigancer)* to be up to; **qu'est-ce que tu trafiques là-dedans?** what are you doing *or* what are you up to in there?; **je me demande ce qu'ils trafiquent** I wonder what they're up to

tragédie [traʒedi] NF **1** *Littérature* tragedy; **les tragédies d'Euripide** the tragedies of Euripides **2** *Théât* tragedy; **c'est dans la t. qu'elle a atteint au sublime** she gave her finest performances in tragic roles **3** *Fig (événement funeste)* tragedy, disaster, calamity; **la manifestation a tourné à la t.** the demonstration had a tragic outcome; **c'est une véritable t.** it's a real tragedy, it's really tragic

tragédien, -enne [traʒedjɛ̃, -ɛn] NM,F tragedian, *f* tragedienne, tragic actor, *f* actress

tragi-comédie [traʒikɔmedi] *(pl* **tragi-comédies)** NF **1** *Littérature* tragicomedy **2** *Fig* tragicomic saga; **leur liaison est une perpétuelle t.** their love affair is one long series of ups and downs

tragi-comique [traʒikɔmik] *(pl* **tragi-comiques)** ADJ *Littérature & Fig* tragicomic; **un incident t.** an incident that inspires both laughter and tears *or* that makes you laugh and cry

NM *Littérature* **le t.** the tragicomic

tragique [traʒik] ADJ **1** *Littérature* tragic; **un auteur t.** a tragic author, an author of tragedies, a tragedian **2** *Fig (dramatique)* tragic; **un sort t.** a tragic destiny; **elle a eu une fin t.** she came to a sad *or* tragic end; **ce qu'il y avait de vraiment t., c'est que...** what was really tragic *or* the real tragedy was that... **3** *Fig (angoissé* ► *regard)* anguished

NM **1** *Littérature* **le t.** tragedy, tragic art **2** *(auteur de tragédies)* tragic author, tragedian; **les tragiques grecs** the Greek tragedians **3** *Fig* tragedy; **le t. de sa situation** the tragic side *or* the tragedy of his/her situation; **prendre qch au t.** to make a tragedy out of sth; **elle ne prend jamais rien au t.** she never looks on the dark side of things, she never makes a drama out of things; **tourner au t.** to take a tragic turn, to go tragically wrong

tragiquement [traʒikmɑ̃] ADV tragically; **finir t.** to end tragically *or* in tragedy

trahir [32] [trair] VT **1** *(son camp)* to betray; **il a trahi son pays** he was a traitor to *or* he betrayed his country

2 *(renier* ► *idéal, foi)* to betray; **elle a trahi la cause de notre parti** she has betrayed the ideals of our party

3 *Littéraire (tromper* ► *ami, amant)* **t. qn** to deceive sb, to be unfaithful to sb

4 *(manquer à)* to break, to go against; **t. sa promesse/ses engagements** to break one's promise/one's commitments

5 *(décevoir)* to betray; **t. les intérêts de qn** to betray sb's interests; **les résultats ont trahi nos espoirs** the results failed to live up to our hopes *or* betrayed our hopes

6 *(dénaturer* ► *pensée)* to misinterpret, to distort, to do an injustice to; *(*► *en traduisant)* to give a false rendering of; **je ne crois pas t. votre pensée en disant cela** I don't think I'm misinterpreting your ideas by saying that; **mes paroles ont trahi ma pensée** my words failed to express my true thoughts

7 *(faire défaut à* ► *sujet: forces, mémoire)* to fail; **si ma mémoire ne me trahit pas** if my memory serves me right; **mes yeux m'auraient-ils trahi?** could my eyes have deceived me?

8 *(révéler)* to betray, to give away; **je faillis t. mes sentiments** I almost revealed my feelings; **t. un secret** to give away a secret

9 *(démasquer)* to give away; **les empreintes qu'ils ont laissées les ont trahis** the fingerprints they left gave them away

10 *(exprimer)* to betray; **elle s'efforçait de sourire pour ne pas t. son inquiétude** she did her best to smile so as not to betray her anxiety; **un léger tremblement trahissait sa nervosité** a slight tremble betrayed his/her nervousness

USAGE ABSOLU **ceux qui trahissent** *(patrie)* traitors, those who betray their country

VPR **se trahir 1** *(se révéler)* **l'angoisse se trahissait dans sa voix** his/her voice betrayed his/her anxiety **2** *(se faire découvrir)* to give oneself away; **il s'est trahi en faisant du bruit** he gave himself away by making a noise

trahison [traizɔ̃] NF **1** *Jur* treason; *Mil & Pol* **haute t.** high treason **2** *(déloyauté)* betrayal, treachery; **une t.** a betrayal, an act of treachery; **c'est (une) pure t. de ta part de ne pas l'avoir soutenu** you have totally betrayed him by not supporting him; **je l'ai vécu comme une t.** I took it as a betrayal **3** *(infidélité)* infidelity, unfaithfulness; **elle me soupçonne des pires trahisons** she thinks I'm always being unfaithful to her

traille [traj] NF **1** *(câble)* ferry cable **2** *(bac)* ferry

TRAIN [trɛ̃]

- train **A1–3, 9, 12, 14**
- set **A4, 11**
- pace **B1**
- backside **C2**
- rail **A2**
- stream **A10**
- quarters **C1**

NM **A. 1** *(convoi)* train; **j'irai t'attendre au t.** I'll wait for you at the station; **le t. de 9h40** the 9.40 train; **je prends le t. à Arpajon** I catch the train at Arpajon; **être dans le t.** to be on the train; **attention, un t. peut en cacher un autre** *(sur panneau)* beware of oncoming trains; **t. autocouchette** car-sleeper train; **t. de banlieue** suburban *or* commuter train; **t. direct** non-stop *or* through train; **t. électrique** *(jeu)* train set; **t. express** express train; **t. à grande vitesse** high-speed train; **t. de marchandises** freight *or* *Br* goods train; **t. omnibus** slow *or* local train; **ce t. est omnibus entre Paris et Vierzon** this train stops *or* calls at all stations between Paris and Vierzon; **t. pendulaire** tilting train; **t. postal** mail train; **t. rapide** fast train; **t. supplémentaire** relief train; **t. de voyageurs** passenger train; *Fig* **prendre le t. en marche** to climb onto *or* to jump on the bandwagon

2 *(moyen de transport)* **le t.** rail (transport), train;

j'irai par le *ou* **en t.** I'll go (there) by train; **j'aime (prendre) le t.** I like rail travel *or* travelling by train

3 *(file de véhicules)* **t. routier** convoy (of *Br* articulated lorries *or Am* semitrailers); **t. de flottage** timber raft; **t. de péniches** train *or* string of barges

4 *(ensemble, série)* set, batch; **t. de réformes** set of reforms; **t. de mesures économiques/fiscales** set of economic/tax measures

5 *Aviat* **t. d'atterrissage** landing gear, undercarriage

6 *Agr* **t. de bois** logging raft

7 *Astron* **t. spatial** space train

8 *Aut* **t. avant/arrière** front/rear wheel-axle unit; **t. de pneus** set of tyres

9 *Mil* **t. de combat** (combat *or* unit) train; **t. régimentaire** supply train; **t. sanitaire** hospital train

10 *Ordinat (de travaux)* stream

11 *Tech* **t. baladeur** sliding gear; **t. d'engrenages** gear train *or* set; **t. de roulement** set of bearings

12 *Métal* **t. de laminoirs** (mill) train

13 *Pétr* **t. de forage** *ou* **de sonde** (set of) drilling pipes

14 *Phys* **t. d'ondes** wave train

B.1 *(allure)* pace; **accélérer le t.** *(marcheur, animal)* to quicken the pace; *(véhicule)* to speed up; **au t. où vont les choses** the way things are going, at this rate; **aller à fond de t.** *ou* **à un t. d'enfer** to speed *or* to race along; **nous sommes rentrés à un t. d'enfer** we sped *or* raced home; **aller à un t. de sénateur** to have a stately gait; **aller bon t.** *(en marchant)* to walk at a brisk pace; **les négociations ont été menées bon t.** the negotiations made good progress; **aller son petit t.** *(marcher)* to jog along; *(agir posément)* to do things at one's own pace; **aller son t.** to carry on (as normal)

2 *(manière de vivre)* **t. de vie** lifestyle, standard of living; **t. de maison** (retinue of) servants; **mener grand t.** to live in grand style; **on menait grand t. chez les Duparc** the Duparcs had a lavish lifestyle *or* lived like kings

3 *Sport (dans une course ▸ de personnes, de chevaux)* pacemaker; **mener le t.** to set the pace

C.1 *Zool* quarters; **t. avant** *ou* **de devant** forequarters; **t. arrière** *ou* **de derrière** hindquarters

2 *Fam (fesses)* backside; **il nous faisait avancer à coups de pied dans le t.** he pushed us on with the occasional kick up the backside; **courir** *ou* **filer au t. de qn** *(suivre partout)* to stick to sb like glue; *(prendre en filature)* to tail *or* to shadow sb

• **en train** ADJ **1** *(en cours)* **être en t.** *(ouvrage, travaux)* to be under way; **j'ai un tricot en t.** I'm knitting something **2** *(personne)* **être en t.** *(plein d'allant)* to be full of energy; *(de bonne humeur)* to be in good spirits *or* in a good mood; **je ne me sens pas vraiment en t. en ce moment** I don't feel my usual perky self, I'm not feeling especially perky at the moment ADV **1** *(en route)* **mettre un projet en t.** to get a project started *or* under way; **se mettre en t.** to warm up **2** *(en forme)* **le repas m'avait mis en t.** the meal had put me in good spirits

• **en train de** PRÉP **être en t. de faire qch** to be (busy) doing sth; **il est toujours en t. de taquiner sa sœur** he's always teasing his sister; **l'opinion publique est en t. d'évoluer** public opinion is changing

traînailler [3] [trenɑje] VI *Fam* **1** *(être lent)* to dawdle **2** *(perdre son temps)* to hang about, *Br* to faff about

traînant, -e [trenɑ̃, -ɑ̃t] ADJ **1** *(lent ▸ élocution, voix)* drawling, lazy; *(▸démarche, pas)* shuffling, dragging; **"je m'en moque," dit-elle d'une voix traînante** "I don't care," she drawled **2** *(qui traîne à terre)* trailing; **une robe traînante** a dress that trails along the floor

traînard, -e [trenar, -ard] NM,F *Fam* **1** *(lambin) Br* slowcoach, *Am* slowpoke **2** *(dans une marche)* straggler

traînasser [3] [trenase] VI *Fam* **1** *(errer paresseusement)* to loaf *or* to hang about; **elle est toujours à t. dans les rues** she's always hanging around the streets **2** *(être lent)* to dawdle, to drag one's feet; *(n'avoir aucune énergie)* to drag oneself around **3** *(lambiner dans son travail)* to fall behind

train-couchettes [trɛ̃kuʃɛt] NM INV *Rail* sleeper

traîne [tren] NF **1** *(bas d'un vêtement)* train

2 *Météo* **ciel de t.** cloudy sky *(after a storm)*

3 *Naut* tow; **à la t.** in tow

4 *Pêche* dragnet; **pêche à la t.** trolling

5 *Can (traîneau)* sleigh

6 *Mktg* **longue t.** long tail

• **à la traîne** ADJ **être** *ou* **rester à la t.** *(coureur, pays, élève)* to lag *or* to drag behind

traîneau, -x [treno] NM **1** *(tiré par des chevaux)* sleigh; *(tiré par des chiens) Br* sledge, *Am* sled **2** *Pêche* dragnet

traînée [trene] NF **1** *(trace ▸ au sol, sur un mur)* trail, streak; *(▸ dans le ciel)* trail; **une t. de sang/peinture** a streak of blood/paint; **une t. de fumée** a trail of smoke; **l'escargot a laissé une t. visqueuse derrière lui** the snail has left a slimy trail behind it; **se propager** *ou* **se répandre comme une t. de poudre** to spread like wildfire

2 *très Fam Péj (femme)* tart, *Br* slapper, scrubber

3 *Aviat* **t. de condensation** (vapour) trail

4 *Phys (force)* drag

traîne-misère [trenmizer] NMF INV *Fam* down-and-out

TRAÎNER [4] [trene]

VT	
• to pull **1**	• to drag **1–3**
VI	
• to drag **1, 5**	• to lie around **2**
• to dawdle **3**	• to hang around **4**
VPR	
• to crawl (along) **1, 4**	• to drag on **3**

VT **1** *(tirer ▸ gén)* to pull; *(▸ avec effort)* to drag, to haul; *(▸ wagon)* to pull, to haul; **elle descendait les escaliers en traînant le sac derrière elle** she was dragging the sack down the stairs (behind her); **elle traînait cinq enfants derrière elle** she was trailing *or* dragging five children after her; **t. qn par les pieds** to drag sb (along) by the feet; **t. les pieds** to shuffle along, to drag one's feet; *Fig* to drag one's feet; *Fam* **t. la jambe** *ou* **patte** to hobble *or* to limp along; *Fig* **t. qn dans la boue** *ou* **la fange** to drag sb's name through the mud; *Fig* **t. un boulet** to have a millstone round one's neck; *Fam* **t. ses guêtres** *ou* **ses bottes** to loaf *or* to hang about

2 *(emmener ▸ personne réticente)* to drag along; *(▸personne non désirée)* to trail, to drag about; **t. qn chez le dentiste** to drag sb along to the dentist's; **j'ai dû le t. au concert** I had to drag him with me to the concert

3 *(garder avec soi ▸ fétiche, jouet)* to drag around; **elle traîne son nounours partout** she never goes anywhere without her teddy bear

4 *(avoir)* **t. son ennui** to be constantly bored; **t. un rhume** to have a nagging cold; **ça fait des semaines que je traîne cette angine** this sore throat has been with *or* plaguing me for weeks; **toute ma jeunesse, j'ai traîné ce sentiment de culpabilité** throughout my youth I carried around this sense of guilt

VI **1** *(pendre ▸ rideaux, nappe)* **t. (par terre)** to drag on the floor *or* ground

2 *Fam (ne pas être rangé ▸ documents, vêtements)* to lie around, to be scattered around; **tes vêtements traînent partout dans la maison** your clothes are scattered all over the house; **laisser t. qch** to leave sth lying around

3 *(s'attarder, flâner)* to dawdle; *(rester en arrière)* to lag *or* to drag behind; **ne traîne pas, Mamie nous attend** stop dawdling *or* do hurry up, Grandma's expecting us; **t. en chemin** *ou* **en route** to dawdle on the way; *Fam* **j'aime bien t. sur les quais** I like strolling along the banks of the river; *Fam* **on a traîné dans les musées toute la journée** we've been wandering around the museums all day long

4 *Péj (errer)* to hang about *or* around; **t. dans la rue** to hang *or* knock around the streets; **il traîne dans tous les bistrots** he hangs around in all the bars; **des chiens traînent dans le village** dogs roam around the village; *Fam* **fais attention, il y a toujours des flics qui traînent par ici** be careful, there are always cops hanging around here; **elle attrape toutes les maladies qui traînent** she catches every bug that's going around

5 *Fam Péj (s'éterniser ▸ affaire, conversation, procédure)* to drag on; *(▸maladie)* to linger *or* to drag on; **t. en longueur** *(discours, négociations)* to drag on; **les choses commencent à t. en longueur!** things are beginning to drag on!; **ça n'a pas traîné!** it didn't take long!, it wasn't long coming!; **déjà mariés? vous n'avez pas traîné!** married already? you didn't hang around, did you?; **faire t. des pourparlers/un procès** to drag out negotiations/a trial

6 *(ralentir ▸ voix)* to drawl (out); **elle a la voix qui traîne** she drawls

VPR **se traîner 1** *(blessé)* to crawl; **se t. par terre** to crawl on the floor *or* ground; **il se traîna jusqu'au fossé** he dragged himself *or* crawled to the ditch; *Fig* **je me suis traînée jusque chez le docteur** I dragged myself to the doctor's

2 *(manquer d'énergie)* **depuis la mort de son mari, elle se traîne** she's been moping around the place since her husband died

3 *(aller lentement ▸ conversation, soirée)* to drag on; **les journées se traînent** the days are dragging (by), the days are passing slowly

4 *Fam (conducteur, véhicule)* to crawl along, to go at a crawl; **on se traîne!** we're just crawling along!

5 *Fam (subir)* **je me suis traîné cette sale grippe tout l'hiver** I've had this rotten cold hanging around all winter; **je me suis traîné ces vieilles chaussures tout l'hiver** I've had to wear *or* put up with these old shoes all winter

traîne-savates [trensavat] NMF INV *Fam Br* dosser, *Am* bum

training [treniŋ] NM **1** *(chaussure)* sports shoe, trainer; *(survêtement)* tracksuit **2** *Sport (entraînement)* training

train-train, traintrain [trɛ̃trɛ̃] NM INV *Fam* routine[□]; **il est venu interrompre mon t.** he came and disrupted my (daily) routine; **le t. quotidien** the daily grind

traire [112] [trɛr] VT *(vache)* to milk; *(lait)* to draw; **machine à t.** milking machine

TRAIT [trɛ]

NM	
• line **1**	• feature **2**
• act **3**	• shaft **4–6**
NMPL	
• features	

NM **1** *(ligne)* line; *(en Morse)* dash; *Typ* **t. de soulignement** underscore; *Typ* **t. d'union** hyphen; **d'un t. de plume** with a stroke of the pen; **tirer** *ou* **tracer un t. (à la règle)** to draw a line (with a ruler); *Fig* **tirer un t. sur ses vacances** to say goodbye to one's holidays, to kiss one's holidays goodbye; *Fig* **cela fait longtemps que j'ai tiré un t. sur notre relation** I gave up all hope for our relationship long ago; *Fig* **tirer un t. sur le passé** to turn over a new leaf, to make a complete break with the past; *Fig* **tirons un t. sur cette dispute** let's forget this argument, let's put this argument behind us; **allez, on tire un t. là-dessus** come on, let's forgive and forget

2 *(marque distinctive ▸ d'un système, d'une œuvre, d'un style)* (characteristic) feature; **t. de caractère** (character) trait; *Biol* **t. génétique** genetic trait; **c'est l'un de ses traits distinctifs** it's one of his/her peculiarities *or* distinctive traits; **les grands traits de qch** the main features of sth

3 *(acte)* **t. de bravoure** act of bravery, brave deed; **t. d'esprit** witticism, flash of wit; **t. de générosité** act of generosity; **t. de génie** stroke of genius

4 *(de lumière)* beam, shaft

5 *Littéraire (projectile)* shaft, spear; **partir** *ou* **filer comme un t.** to set off like a shot

6 *Fig (repartie)* shaft; **un t. mordant** a sarcastic remark; **t. satirique** shaft of satire; **t. railleur** taunt, gibe; **envoyer** *ou* **lancer un t. à qn** to get a dig in at sb

7 *Mus (psaume)* tract; *(passage)* virtuosic passage

8 *Échecs* **avoir le t.** to have first move

9 *(locution)* **avoir t. à** *(avoir un rapport avec)* to have to do *or* to be connected with; **tout ce qui a t. à la psychanalyse** everything connected *or* to do with psychoanalysis; **ayant t. à** regarding, concerning

• **traits** NMPL *(du visage)* features; **il a des traits**

fins/grossiers he has delicate/coarse features; **avoir les traits réguliers** to have classical good looks; **avoir les traits tirés** to look drawn; *Fig* **on l'a présenté sous les traits d'un maniaque** he was portrayed as a maniac

• **à grands traits** ADV *(dessiner, esquisser)* roughly, in broad outline; **voici l'intrigue, résumée à grands traits** here's a broad *or* rough outline of the plot

• **à longs traits** ADV *(boire)* in long draughts

• **de trait** ADJ *(bête, cheval)* draught *(avant n)*

• **d'un (seul) trait** ADV *(avaler)* in one gulp, in one go; *(réciter)* (all) in one breath; *(lire)* without stopping, at a single sitting; *(dormir)* uninterruptedly

• **trait d'union** NM hyphen; *Fig* link; **ce mot prend un t. d'union** this word is hyphenated, this is a hyphenated word; **mettre un t. d'union à un mot** to hyphenate a word; *Fig* **servir de t. d'union entre** to bridge the gap between, to link

• **trait pour trait** ADV *(exactement)* exactly; **c'est sa mère t. pour t.** she's the spitting image of her mother

traitable [tretabl] ADJ **1** *(sujet, question)* treatable; *(problème)* manageable; **la question n'est pas t. en une demi-heure** the question cannot be dealt with in half an hour **2** *Littéraire (accommodant)* amenable, helpful

traitant, -e [tretɑ̃, -ɑ̃t] ADJ *(shampooing)* medicated

traite [trɛt] NF **1** *Com, Fin & Jur* draft, bill; *(lettre de change)* bill of exchange; **tirer une t. sur** to draw a bill *or* draft on; **t. bancaire** bank draft, banker's draft

2 *(versement)* instalment, payment; **on n'arrive plus à payer les traites de la maison** we can't pay the mortgage (on the house) any longer

3 *(commerce, trafic)* **t. d'êtres humains** people smuggling; **la t. des Noirs** the slave trade; **la t. des Blanches** the white slave trade

4 *Agr (action)* milking *(UNCOUNT)*; *(lait)* milk (yield); **t. manuelle** hand milking; **t. mécanique** machine milking

5 *(chemin)* stretch; **j'ai fait une longue t.** I've come a long way

6 *Can* **payer la t.** *(gén)* to pay for everybody, to treat everybody; *(dans un bar)* to buy a round

• **de traite** ADJ *(poste, salle)* milking *(avant n)*

• **d'une (seule) traite, tout d'une traite** ADV *(voyager)* in one go, without stopping; *(avaler)* at one go, in one gulp; *(lire, réciter)* in one stretch *or* breath; *(dormir)* uninterruptedly; *(travailler)* without interruption, at a stretch; **faire le chemin d'une t.** to do the journey non-stop *or* without stopping

traité [trete] NM **1** *(accord)* treaty; **t. d'adhésion** membership treaty; **t. de Maastricht** Maastricht Treaty; **t. de non-prolifération nucléaire** Nuclear Non-Proliferation Treaty; **t. de paix** peace treaty; **le t. de Rome** the Treaty of Rome **2** *(ouvrage)* treatise; **t. de philosophie sur** philosophical treatise on *or* upon

traitement [tretmɑ̃] NM **1** *Méd & Pharm* treatment; **un bon t. contre les poux** a cure for lice; **prescrire un t.** to prescribe treatment; **donner un t. à qn** to prescribe (a treatment) for sb; **suivre le t. d'un médecin** to follow the treatment prescribed by a doctor; **t. par la chaleur** heat treatment; **t. chirurgical** surgery; **t. par électrochocs** electroconvulsive therapy; **un t. homéopathique** a course of homeopathic treatment; **t. hormonal substitutif** hormone replacement therapy

2 *(d'un fonctionnaire)* salary, wage, wages; **t. de base** basic pay *or* salary

3 *(façon d'agir envers quelqu'un)* treatment *(UNCOUNT)*; **mauvais traitements** ill-treatment *(UNCOUNT)*; **faire subir de mauvais traitements à qn** to ill-treat sb; **t. de choc** shock treatment; **t. de faveur** special *or* preferential treatment; **avoir un** *ou* **bénéficier d'un t. de faveur** to enjoy preferential treatment

4 *Ordinat* processing; **t. par lots** batch processing; **t. à distance** teleprocessing; **t. de données** data processing, DP; **t. d'images** image processing; **t. de l'information** *ou* **des informations** data processing, DP, information processing; **t. électronique de l'information** electronic data processing, EDP; **t. de texte** word processing; *(logiciel)* word-processing package; *(machine)* word processor

5 *Ind* treatment, processing; **le t. des matières premières/des aliments** the processing of raw materials/of foodstuffs; **le t. des récoltes** the treating of crops; *(par avion)* the spraying of crops; *Com* **t. des commandes** order processing; **capacité de t.** processing *or* handling capacity

6 *(d'un problème, d'une question)* treatment, presentation; **le t. de l'information dans la presse** the way the news is presented in the press

• **en traitement, sous traitement** ADJ under treatment; **être en** *ou* **sous t.** to be being treated *or* having treatment *or* under treatment

traiter [4] [trete] VT **1** *(se comporter avec)* to treat; **t. qn avec égard** to treat sb with consideration, to show consideration to sb; **t. qn avec douceur** to treat *or* handle sb gently; **t. qn avec condescendance** to be condescending towards sb, to patronize sb; **t. qn en ami/enfant** to treat sb like *or* as a friend/a child; *Fam* **il me traite comme un ami/gamin** he treats me like a friend/kid; **bien t. qn** to treat sb well; **mal t. qn** to treat sb badly, to ill-treat sb; **t. qn d'égal à égal** to treat sb as an equal; **ils sont tous traités de la même façon** they're all treated equally, they all get the same treatment; **nous avons été très bien traités** we were very well looked after, we had very good service; **je ne supporterai pas de me faire t. comme cela!** I won't take being treated like this!, I won't take this treatment!

2 *Fam (insulter)* to bad-mouth, *Br* to slag off; **t. qn d'imbécile** to call sb an idiot; **se faire t. de menteur** to be called a liar; **t. qn de tous les noms** to call sb all the names under the sun

3 *(soigner* ▸ *patient, maladie)* to treat; **se faire t. pour** to undergo treatment *or* to be treated for; **je le traite à l'aspirine** *(patient)* I prescribe him aspirin; *(mal)* I treat it with aspirin, I use aspirin for it

4 *Ind* to treat, to process; *(aliments, minerai, matière première)* to process; *(bois)* to treat

5 *Agr (récoltes, cultures)* to treat, to spray; **oranges non traitées** unsprayed oranges

6 *Com (affaire, demande, dossier)* to deal with, to handle; *(marché)* to negotiate

7 *(étudier* ▸ *thème)* to treat, to deal with; **vous ne traitez pas le sujet** you're not addressing the question

8 *Ordinat (données, texte, images)* to process; **t. qch par lots** to batch-process sth; **données non traitées** raw data

• **traiter avec** VT IND to negotiate *or* to deal with; **nous ne traiterons pas avec des terroristes** we won't bargain *or* negotiate with terrorists

• **traiter de** VT IND *(sujet: roman, film, thèse)* to deal with, to be about; *(sujet: auteur)* to deal with

VPR **se traiter 1** *(maladie)* **ça se traite aux antibiotiques** it can be treated with antibiotics; **cela se traite très bien, maintenant** it can be treated now, there's treatment for it now **2** *(affaire)* to be dealt with; **l'affaire s'est traitée assez rapidement** the matter was dealt with quite quickly **3** *(emploi réciproque) (personne)* **ils se traitaient de menteurs** they were calling each other liars

traiteur [tretœr] NM *(qui livre)* caterer; **chez le t.** *(magasin)* at the delicatessen

traître, -esse [trɛtr, -ɛs] ADJ **1** *(déloyal* ▸ *personne)* traitorous, treacherous; **être t. à sa patrie** to be a traitor to *or* to betray one's country

2 *(trompeur* ▸ *visage, sourire)* deceptive; *(*▸ *paroles)* treacherous

3 *(dangereux* ▸ *escalier, crevasse, virage)* dangerous, treacherous; *(*▸ *soleil)* treacherous, strong; *(*▸ *vin)* deceptively strong; **il est t., ce petit vin de pays!** this local wine is stronger than you'd think!

4 *(locution)* **pas un t. mot** not a single word; **elle n'a pas dit un t. mot** she didn't breathe *or* say a (single) word; **je n'ai pas compris un t. mot de ce qu'il a dit** I didn't understand a single word of what he said

NM,F **1** *(gén) & Pol* traitor, *f* traitress; *Hum* **ah, le t., il ne nous a rien dit!** the sly devil, he didn't tell us! **2** *Théât* villain

• **en traître** ADV **prendre qn en t.** to play an underhand trick on sb; **agir en t.** to act treacherously

traîtreusement [trɛtrøzmɑ̃] ADV treacherously, traitorously, *Sout* perfidiously

traîtrise [tretriz] NF **1** *(caractère)* treacherousness, treachery **2** *(acte* ▸ *perfide)* (piece of) treachery; *(*▸ *déloyal)* betrayal

trajectoire [traʒɛktwar] NF **1** *(d'une balle, d'un missile)* trajectory, path; *(d'une planète, d'un avion)* path; **t. de vol** flight path **2** *(carrière professionnelle)* career path

trajet [traʒɛ] NM **1** *(chemin parcouru)* distance; *(voyage)* journey; *(d'un car, d'un autobus)* route; **je fais tous les jours le t. Paris-Gif** I commute everyday between Paris and Gif; **il y a bien deux heures de t.** it takes a good two hours; **elle a deux heures de t. pour aller au bureau** she has a two hour journey to the office; **il a fait le t. en huit heures** he covered the distance in eight hours; **j'ai fait une partie du t. en avion** I flew part of the way; **j'ai dû faire le t. à pied** I had to walk all the way; **faire le t. en voiture** to do the journey by car; **un t. en voiture/autobus** a car/bus journey or ride; **t. par mer** crossing

2 *Anat* course

3 *(d'un projectile)* path

4 *Élec (d'un courant)* path

tralala [tralala] *Fam* NM fuss[□], frills; **pas besoin de tant de t.** no need to make so much fuss; **se marier en grand t.** to get married with all the works *or* trimmings; **(et) tout le t.** the (full works, *Br* the full monty; **il y avait des petits fours, du champagne, tout le t.!** there were petit fours, champagne, the (whole) works!

EXCLAM **c'est moi qui l'ai eu, t.!** ha-ha, I got it!

tram [tram] NM **1** *(moyen de transport) Br* tram *Am* streetcar **2** *(véhicule) Br* tram, tramcar, *Am* streetcar

tramage [tramaʒ] NM weaving

tramail [tramaj] NM *Pêche* trammel (net)

trame [tram] NF **1** *Tex (base)* weft, woof; *(fil)* weft weft thread

2 *Fig (d'un livre, d'un film)* thread, basic outline *or* framework; **la t. du récit** the storyline

3 *Archit & Typ* screen; **t. optique** half-tone screen

4 *TV (lignes)* raster; *(ensemble)* field; *(pour lignes paires et impaires)* frame; **t. double** frame

tramer [3] [trame] VT **1** *(conspiration)* to hatch *(soulèvement)* to plot; *Fig* **elle trame quelque chose!** she's plotting something! **2** *Tex* to weave **3** *Typ & Phot* to screen; **t. un cliché** to take a negative through a screen

VPR **se tramer** to be afoot; **un complot se tramait contre l'empereur** a plot was being hatched against the emperor; **qu'est-ce qui se trame** what's going on?; **il se trame quelque chose** something's afoot

traminot [tramino] NM *Br* tram *or Am* streetcar worker

tramontane [tramɔ̃tan] NF *(vent)* **la t.** the tramontana

tramp [trɑ̃p] NM tramp (steamer)

trampoline [trɑ̃pɔlin] NM **1** *(appareil)* trampoline **2** *(sport)* trampolining; **faire du t.** to do trampolining

tram-train [tramtrɛ̃] *(pl* **trams-trains***)* NM *Trans* tram-train *(tram which can run on railways as well as traditional tramways)*

tramway [tramwɛ] NM **1** *(moyen de transport)* tramway (system) **2** *(véhicule) Br* tram, tramcar *Am* streetcar

tranchant, -e [trɑ̃ʃɑ̃, -ɑ̃t] ADJ **1** *(lame)* sharp keen, cutting; *(outil)* cutting; *(bord)* sharp, cutting **2** *Fig (personne, réponse, ton)* curt, sharp

NM **1** *(d'une lame)* sharp *or* cutting edge; *(d'un cale)* thin end; **le t. de la main** the edge of the hand **2** *(d'apiculteur)* hive tool **3** *(de tanneur)* fleshing knife, flesher

tranche [trɑ̃ʃ] NF **1** *(de pain, de viande, de pastèque)* slice; **t. de bacon** *(à frire)* rasher (of bacon); **t. de saumon** *(darne)* salmon steak; *(fumée)* slice *or* leaf of (smoked) salmon; **une t. fine** a sliver, a thin slice; *Culin* **t. napolitaine** Neapolitan ice cream; *Fig* **une t. de vie** a slice of life; *Fam* **s'en payer une t.** to have a ball *or Am* a blast

2 *(en boucherie)* **la t. (grasse)** top rump; **t. au petit os** *Br* middle of silverside; **morceau coupé dans la t.** = piece of topside

3 *(subdivision* ▸ *d'un programme de construction)* stage, phase; *Admin* **t. horaire** period of time;

d'âge age bracket; *(dans une étude de marché)* age group; **t. de salaires/de revenus** salary/income bracket; **elle est dans la t. des 50 000 euros par an** she's in the 50,000 (euros a year) bracket; **t. d'imposition** tax bracket
4 *Bourse & Fin (d'actions)* block, tranche; *(d'emprunt)* instalment; *(d'assistance financière internationale)* tranche; **t. d'émission** *(de loterie)* issue
5 *Élec (unité de production)* tranche
6 *Rail* portion
7 *Rad & TV* slot; **t. horaire** (time) slot
8 *(outil)* chisel
9 *(de marbre)* slab
10 *(bord ▸ d'un livre)* edge; *(▸ d'une médaille, d'une pièce)* edge, rim; **doré sur t.** gilt-edged
11 *Tech (coupe)* section; **t. verticale** vertical section
12 *Ordinat* wafer; **microprocesseur en tranches** bit slice microprocessor
• **en tranches** ADJ *(pain, saucisson)* sliced ADV **débiter** *ou* **couper qch en tranches** to slice sth (up), to cut sth into slices; **je vous le coupe en tranches?** would you like it sliced?

tranché, -e [trɑ̃ʃe] ADJ **1** *(sans nuances ▸ couleurs)* distinct, clear, sharply contrasted **2** *(distinct ▸ catégories)* distinct; *(▸ caractères)* distinct, well-defined, clear-cut **3** *(péremptoire ▸ position)* clear-cut, uncompromising, unequivocal
• **tranchée** NF **1** *Mil & (en travaux publics)* trench; *Agr* drain; **creuser une tranchée** to (dig a) trench; **il était dans les tranchées pendant la guerre** he fought in the trenches **2** *(en forêt)* cutting *(UNCOUNT)*; *(pare-feu)* firebreak
• **tranchées** NFPL *Méd* colic *(UNCOUNT)*, gripe *(UNCOUNT)*, gripes; **tranchées utérines** afterpains

tranchefile [trɑ̃ʃfil] NF *(en reliure)* headband

trancher [3] [trɑ̃ʃe] VT **1** *(couper ▸ pain, jambon)* to slice, to cut; **t. la gorge à qn** to cut *or* to slit sb's throat; **t. la tête à qn** to cut off *or* chop off sb's head; **la hache lui a tranché le doigt** the axe sliced *or* chopped his/her finger off, the axe severed his/her finger **2** *(différend)* to settle; *(difficulté)* to solve; *(question)* to decide; **je ne peux pas t. ce problème** I can't be the judge in this matter **3** *(discussion)* to bring to a sudden end, to cut short
VI *(décider)* to make *or* to take a decision, to decide; **qui va t.?** who's going to decide?; **t. dans le vif** to take drastic action
• **trancher avec, trancher sur** VT IND *(sujet: couleur)* to stand out against, to contrast sharply with; *(sujet: attitude)* to be in sharp contrast *or* to contrast strongly with; **sa déclaration tranche avec les propos apaisants du gouvernement** his/her remarks are in sharp contrast to the pacifying words of the government
VPR **se trancher se t. le doigt/la main** to chop one's finger/hand off

tranchet [trɑ̃ʃɛ] NM **1** *(de cordonnier)* leather *or* skiving knife; **t. à parer** paring knife **2** *(de forgeron)* hardy; *(de serrurier)* anvil cutter

trancheuse [trɑ̃ʃøz] NF **1** *(à jambon, à pain)* slicer **2** *Menuis* veneer saw **3** *(en travaux publics)* trench excavator, trencher, ditcher

tranchoir [trɑ̃ʃwar] NM *(planche)* chopping board

tranquille [trɑ̃kil] ADJ **1** *(sans agitation ▸ quartier, rue)* quiet; *(▸ campagne)* quiet, peaceful, tranquil; *(▸ soirée)* calm, quiet, peaceful; *(▸ sommeil, vie)* peaceful, tranquil; *(▸ air, eau, mer)* still, quiet, tranquil; **je cherche un endroit t. où je pourrai travailler** I'm looking for a quiet place where I'll be able to work; **aller** *ou* **marcher d'un pas t.** to stroll unhurriedly; *Fig* **vous pouvez dormir t.** you can sleep in peace, you can rest easy
2 *(en paix)* **on ne peut même plus être t. chez soi!** you can't even get peace and quiet at home any more!; **allons dans mon bureau, nous y serons plus tranquilles pour discuter** let's go into my office, we can talk there without being disturbed; **laisser qn t.** to leave sb alone *or* in peace; **laisse-le t. avec tes problèmes!** stop bothering him with your problems!; **laisse-moi t., je suis assez grand pour ouvrir la boîte tout seul!** leave me alone, I'm old enough to open the can on my own!; *Fam* **laisser qch t.** *(ne pas y toucher)* to leave sth alone; **laisse ma maquette t.!** hands off my model!, leave my model alone!
3 *(calme, sage)* quiet; **se tenir** *ou* **rester t.** to keep quiet *or* still; *(ne pas se faire remarquer)* to keep a low profile; **il n'y a que la télé pour les faire tenir tranquilles** TV's the only thing that keeps them quiet
4 *(serein ▸ personne, foi)* calm, serene; **t. comme Baptiste** perfectly calm
5 *(rassuré)* **soyez t.** don't worry, set your mind at rest *or* at ease; **sois t., elle va bien** don't worry *or* set your mind at rest, she's all right; **fais-le maintenant, comme ça tu seras t.** do it now, that way you won't have to worry about it; **je serais plus t. s'il n'était pas seul** I'd feel easier in my mind knowing that he wasn't on his own; **je ne suis pas** *ou* **ne me sens pas t. quand il est sur les routes** I worry when he's on the road; **je ne suis pas t. dans cette grande maison** I get nervous in this big house
6 *(sûr)* **tu peux être t. (que)...** you can rest assured (that)...; **ils n'auront pas mon argent, sois t.!** they won't get my money, that's for sure!

tranquillement [trɑ̃kilmɑ̃] ADV **1** *(calmement ▸ dormir, jouer)* quietly, peacefully; *(▸ répondre, regarder)* calmly, quietly **2** *(sans se presser ▸ marcher, travailler)* unhurriedly; **on est allés t. jusqu'à l'église avec grand-mère** we walked slowly to the church with grandma

tranquillisant, -e [trɑ̃kilizɑ̃, -ɑ̃t] ADJ *(paroles, voix, présence)* soothing, reassuring; *Pharm* **avoir un effet t.** to act as a sedative
NM *Pharm* tranquillizer; *Fam* **bourré de tranquillisants** doped up to the eyeballs (with tranquillizers)

tranquilliser [3] [trɑ̃kilize] VT **t. qn** to set sb's mind at rest, to reassure sb
VPR **se tranquilliser** to stop worrying, to be reassured; **tranquillise-toi, je ne rentrerai pas en autostop** don't worry, I won't hitch-hike home

tranquillité [trɑ̃kilite] NF **1** *(calme ▸ d'un lieu)* quietness, peacefulness, *Sout* tranquillity; *(▸ d'une personne)* peace, *Sout* tranquillity; *(▸ de sommeil)* peacefulness; **les enfants ne me laissent pas un seul moment de t.** the children don't give me a single moment's peace; **elle a besoin d'une parfaite t. pour écrire** she needs (complete) peace and quiet to write; **troubler la t. publique** *Br* to cause a breach of the peace, *Am* to disturb the peace **2** *(sérénité)* **t. d'esprit** peace of mind
• **en toute tranquillité** ADV *(sereinement)* with complete peace of mind

tranquillos [trɑ̃kilos] ADV *Fam (tranquillement)* **vas-y t., inutile de faire des excès de vitesse** take your time, there's no need to break the speed limit; **ils étaient dans le canapé en train de siroter mon whisky, t.** they were on the sofa sipping away at my whisky, without a care in the world

transaction [trɑ̃zaksjɔ̃] NF **1** *Bourse, Com & Écon* transaction, deal; **transactions** transactions, dealings; **transactions bancaires** bank transactions; **transactions boursières** Stock Exchange transactions; **transactions commerciales** business transactions **2** *Jur* (formal) settlement, compromise **3** *Ordinat* transaction

transactionnel, -elle [trɑ̃zaksjɔnɛl] ADJ **1** *Jur (formule, règlement)* compromise *(avant n)*; **solution transactionnelle** compromise **2** *Psy* transactional

transafricain, -e [trɑ̃zafrikɛ̃, -ɛn] ADJ transafrican, cross-Africa

transalpin, -e [trɑ̃zalpɛ̃, -in] ADJ **1** *(au-delà des Alpes)* transalpine **2** *(italien)* Italian

transaméricain, -e [trɑ̃zamerikɛ̃, -ɛn] ADJ transamerican

transat [trɑ̃zat] NM *Fam* deckchair[□]
NF *Sport* transatlantic race; **la t. en solitaire** the single-handed transatlantic race

transatlantique [trɑ̃zatlɑ̃tik] ADJ transatlantic
NM **1** *Naut* (transatlantic) liner **2** *(chaise longue)* deckchair
NF *Sport* transatlantic race

transbahuter [3] [trɑ̃sbayte] *Fam* VT to shift, to hump, to lug; **les bagages ont été transbahutés dans une autre voiture** the luggage was shoved into another car
VPR **se transbahuter** to shift oneself

transbordement [trɑ̃sbɔrdəmɑ̃] NM *(de marchandises)* transshipment; *Rail* transfer; *(de voyageurs)* transferring *(of passengers to another vessel or vehicle)*

transborder [3] [trɑ̃sbɔrde] VT *(marchandises)* to transship, to transfer; *(voyageurs)* to transfer

transbordeur [trɑ̃sbɔrdœr] NM *(navire)* transporter bridge
ADJ M **pont t.** transporter bridge

transcanadien, -enne [trɑ̃skanadjɛ̃, -ɛn] ADJ trans-Canadian, trans-Canada *(avant n)*
• **Transcanadienne** NF **la Transcanadienne** *(autoroute)* the Trans-Canada Highway

Transcaucasie [trɑ̃skokazi] NF **la T.** Transcaucasia

transcendance [trɑ̃sɑ̃dɑ̃s] NF **1** *Phil* transcendence, transcendency **2** *Math* transcendence

transcendant, -e [trɑ̃sɑ̃dɑ̃, -ɑ̃t] ADJ **1** *Fam (génial)* brilliant; **ce n'est pas t.!** *(livre, film)* it's not exactly brilliant!; **il n'est pas t.!** he's no genius! **2** *Math & Phil* transcendental

transcendantal, -e, -aux, -ales [trɑ̃sɑ̃dɑ̃tal, -o] ADJ transcendental

transcendantalisme [trɑ̃sɑ̃dɑ̃talism] NM transcendentalism

transcender [3] [trɑ̃sɑ̃de] VT to transcend
VPR **se transcender** to transcend oneself

transcodage [trɑ̃skɔdaʒ] NM *(gén)* transcoding, code translation; *Ordinat* compiling; *TV* transcoding, standards conversion

transcoder [3] [trɑ̃skɔde] VT *(gén)* to transcode; *Ordinat* to compile; *TV* to transcode

transcodeur [trɑ̃skɔdœr] NM *(gén)* transcoder; *Ordinat* compiler; *TV* transcoder, standards converter

transconteneur [trɑ̃skɔ̃tənœr] NM transcontainer; *(navire)* transcontainer ship

transcontinental, -e, -aux, -ales [trɑ̃skɔ̃tinɑ̃tal, -o] ADJ transcontinental

transcriptase [trɑ̃skriptaz] NF *Biol* **t. inverse** *ou* **reverse** reverse transcriptase

transcripteur [trɑ̃skriptœr] NM transcriber

transcription [trɑ̃skripsjɔ̃] NF **1** *(fait d'écrire ▸ gén)* transcription, transcribing, noting (down); *(▸ des notes)* copying out (in longhand); *(▸ un document officiel)* recording
2 *(copie)* copy, transcript; *(document officiel)* record; **t. à l'état civil** = certified copy of registry office document
3 *Ling & Mus (gén)* transcribing, transcription; *(translittération)* transliteration; **t. phonétique** phonetic transcription; **faire une t. phonétique** to transcribe a word into phonetic symbols
4 *Biol* **t. génétique** (genetic) transcription

transcrire [99] [trɑ̃skrir] VT **1** *(conversation)* to transcribe, to note *or* to take down; *(notes)* to copy *or* to write out (in longhand); *(dans un registre)* to record; *Jur (divorce)* to register; *Com* to post; **je transcris tout ce que vous dites** I'm taking down everything you're saying **2** *Ling (dans un autre alphabet)* to transcribe, to transliterate; **t. un livre en braille** to copy a book into Braille; **t. un mot d'un alphabet dans un autre** to transliterate a word; **t. un nom russe/chinois en caractères romains** to Romanize a Russian/Chinese name **3** *Mus* to transcribe

transculturel, -elle [trɑ̃skyltyrɛl] ADJ transcultural, cross-cultural

transcutané, -e [trɑ̃skytane] ADJ transcutaneous

transdermique [trɑ̃sdɛrmik] ADJ transdermal; **timbre t.** skin patch, transdermal patch

transdisciplinaire [trɑ̃sdisipliner] ADJ interdisciplinary

transducteur [trɑ̃sdyktœr] NM transducer

transe [trɑ̃s] NF **1** *(état d'hypnose)* trance **2** *(exaltation)* trance, exaltation
• **transes** NFPL **1** *(mouvements)* convulsions; **être pris de transes** to go into convulsions **2** *Vieilli ou Littéraire (anxiété)* fear; **être dans les transes** to be sick with worry, to be out of one's mind with anxiety
• **en transe** ADJ **être en t.** to be in a trance; *Fig* to be beside oneself ADV **entrer en t.** *(médium)* to go *or* to fall into a trance; *Fig Hum* to get all worked up; **faire entrer qn en t.** to put sb into a trance

transept [trɑ̃sɛpt] NM transept

transférable [trɑ̃sferabl] **ADJ** transferable

transfèrement [trɑ̃sfɛrmɑ̃] **NM** transfer, transferring; **t. cellulaire** transfer by police van

transférer [18] [trɑ̃sfere] **VT 1** *(prisonnier, sportif)* to transfer; *(diplomate)* to transfer, to move; *(évêque)* to translate; **t. qn de... à...** to transfer sb from... to...; **être transféré** *(sportif)* to be transferred; *(diplomate)* to move, to be moved

2 *(magasin, siège social)* to transfer, to move; *(fonds)* to transfer; *(reliques)* to translate; **il a transféré son argent sur un compte suisse** he's transferred *or* switched his money to a Swiss account; **succursale transférée au n° 42** *(sur écriteau)* our branch is now at no. 42

3 *Ordinat (information)* to transfer

4 *Jur (droits)* to transfer, to convey (**à** to); *(propriété ▸ gén)* to transfer, to convey (**à** to); *(▸ par legs)* to demise (**à** to); *(pouvoirs)* to transfer, to pass on (**à** to)

5 *Psy* **t. qch sur qn** to transfer sth onto sb

6 *Beaux-Arts* **t. un motif sur** to transfer a design on *or* onto; **t. un motif au pochoir** to stencil a motif

transfériste [trɑ̃sferist] **NMF** tour rep *(responsible for greeting tourists at the airport and coordinating travel to their destination)*

transfert [trɑ̃sfɛr] **NM 1** *(gén) & Com* transfer; *(de population)* resettlement (**dans** in); **t. d'actions** transfer of shares; **t. de capitaux** transfer of capital, capital transfer; **t. de devises** currency transfer; **t. de fonds** transfer of funds; **t. de fonds électronique, t. électronique de fonds** electronic funds transfer, EFT

2 *Rel (d'un évêque, de reliques)* translation

3 *Ordinat* transfer; **t. de données** data transfer; **t. de fichiers** file transfer

4 *Jur (de propriété)* transfer, conveyance; *(de droits, de pouvoirs)* transfer; **t. par legs** demise

5 *Psy* transference; **elle fait un t. sur toi** she's using you as the object of her transference

6 *Tél* **t. d'appel** call diversion

transfiguration [trɑ̃sfigyrasjɔ̃] **NF 1** *(changement profond)* transfiguration **2** *Rel* **la T.** the Transfiguration

transfigurer [3] [trɑ̃sfigyre] **VT** to transfigure

transfo [trɑ̃sfo] **NM** *Fam Élec* adapter[□], adaptor[□]

transformable [trɑ̃sfɔrmabl] **ADJ 1** *(modifiable)* changeable, alterable; **des décors transformables** flexible sets **2** *Sport* convertible

transformateur, -trice [trɑ̃sfɔrmatœr, -tris] **ADJ** *(influence)* transforming; *(station)* transformer *(avant n)*

NM *Élec* transformer; *(prise)* adapter, adaptor

transformation [trɑ̃sfɔrmasjɔ̃] **NF 1** *(d'une personnalité, d'un environnement)* transformation; *(d'une matière première, d'énergie)* conversion; *(d'une maison, d'un vêtement)* change, alteration; **subir une t.** *(personne)* to undergo a transformation; *(matière première)* to be converted

2 *(résultat d'un changement)* transformation, alteration, change; **nous avons fait des transformations dans la maison** *(travaux)* we've made some alterations to the house; *(décor, ameublement)* we've made some changes in the house

3 *(au rugby)* conversion; **réussir une t.** to make a conversion

4 *Ling & Math* transformation

transformatrice [trɑ̃sfɔrmatris] *voir* **transformateur**

transformer [3] [trɑ̃sfɔrme] **VT 1** *(faire changer ▸ bâtiment, personnalité, institution, paysage)* to transform, to change, to alter; *(▸ matière première)* to transform, to convert; *(▸ vêtement)* to make over, to alter; **sa maternité l'a complètement transformée** motherhood has completely transformed her; **t. une pièce en bureau** to convert a room into an office; **la sorcière l'a transformé en souris** the witch turned him into a mouse

2 *Ling & Math* to transform

3 *(au rugby)* to convert

4 *Électron* to transform, to map

VPR se transformer *(quartier, personnalité, paysage, institution)* to be transformed, to change; **l'environnement se transforme lentement/rapidement** the environment is changing slowly/rapidly; **se t. en** to turn into; **elle se transforma en cygne** she turned *or* changed into a swan; **ce voyage se transformait en cauchemar** the trip was turning into a nightmare

transformisme [trɑ̃sfɔrmism] **NM** transformism

transformiste [trɑ̃sfɔrmist] **ADJ** *(évolutionniste)* transformist *(avant n)*

NMF *(évolutionniste)* transformist

NM *(travesti)* drag artist; **spectacle de transformistes** drag show

transfrontalier, -ère [trɑ̃sfrɔ̃talje, -ɛr] **ADJ** cross-border *(avant n)*

transfuge [trɑ̃sfyʒ] **NMF** *Mil & Pol* renegade, turncoat; *(qui change de camp)* defector

transfusé, -e [trɑ̃sfyze] **ADJ sang t.** transfused blood

NM,F = person receiving/having received a (blood) transfusion; **le nombre des transfusés** the number of people receiving (blood) transfusions

transfuser [3] [trɑ̃sfyze] **VT 1** *Méd (sang)* to transfuse; *(malade)* to give a (blood) transfusion to, to transfuse; **elle se fait t. régulièrement à cause de sa maladie** she has regular blood transfusions because of her illness **2** *Littéraire (sentiment)* to instil, to communicate, to pass on

transfusion [trɑ̃sfyzjɔ̃] **NF t. sanguine** *ou* **de sang** blood transfusion; **centre de t. sanguine** blood transfusion centre; **faire une t. à qn** to give sb a (blood) transfusion

transgène [trɑ̃sʒɛn] **NM** *Biol* transgene

transgenèse [trɑ̃sʒənɛz], **transgénose** [trɑ̃sʒenoz] **NF** *Biol* transgenosis

transgénique [trɑ̃sʒenik] **ADJ** transgenic

transgresser [4] [trɑ̃sgrese] **VT** *(règle)* to break, *Sout* to infringe, to contravene; *(ordre)* to disobey, to go against; **t. la loi** to break the law; **t. les interdits** to break the taboos

transgresseur [trɑ̃sgresœr] **NM** *Littéraire* transgressor, contravenor (**de** of)

transgressif, -ive [trɑ̃sgresif, -iv] **ADJ** boundary-breaking, controversial

transgression [trɑ̃sgresjɔ̃] **NF 1** *(d'une règle, d'une loi)* infringement, contravention, breaking; *(d'un ordre)* disobeying **2** *Géol* transgression

transgressive [trɑ̃sgresif] *voir* **transgressif**

transhumance [trɑ̃zymɑ̃s] **NF** *(de troupeaux)* seasonal migration, *Spéc* transhumance; **au moment de la t.** when the herds are moved to the grazing grounds

transhumant, -e [trɑ̃zymɑ̃, -ɑ̃t] **ADJ** transhumant

transhumer [3] [trɑ̃zyme] **VI** *(vers les pâturages)* to move up to (summer) grazing grounds; *(vers la vallée)* to move down to the wintering grounds

VT 1 *(troupeaux)* to move **2** *Hort* to transplant

transi, -e [trɑ̃zi] **ADJ être t. (de froid)** to be chilled to the bone *or* to the marrow; **être t. de peur** to be paralysed *or* transfixed by fear

transiger [17] [trɑ̃ziʒe] **VI** *(composer)* to (come to a) compromise; **il n'a pas voulu t.** he refused all compromise; **t. avec qn** to seek a compromise *or* to bargain with sb; **nous ne transigerons pas avec les terroristes** we will not bargain with the terrorists; **t. avec sa conscience** to make a deal with one's conscience; **je ne transigerai pas avec le règlement** I refuse to compromise *or* I am intransigent when it comes to the rules; **t. sur ses principes** to compromise one's principles

Transilien® [trɑ̃siljɛ̃] **NM** *(abrév* **transport francilien***)* = Paris suburban train network

transir [32] [trɑ̃zir] **VT** *Littéraire (sujet: peur)* to paralyse; **le froid m'avait transi** the cold had gone right through me

transistor [trɑ̃zistɔr] **NM 1** *Rad* transistor (radio) **2** *Électron* transistor

• **à transistors ADJ** transistorized

transistoriser [3] [trɑ̃zistɔrize] **VT** *Électron* to transistorize

transit [trɑ̃zit] **NM 1** *Com (de marchandises, de touristes)* transit; **t. communautaire** Community transit; **t. douanier** Customs transit **2** *Physiol* **t. intestinal** intestinal transit; **favorise le t. intestinal** *(sur emballage)* relieves constipation

• **de transit ADJ** transit *(avant n)*; **salle de t.** *(dans un aéroport)* transit lounge; **marchandises de t.** goods for transit; **maison de t.** forwarding agency

• **en transit ADJ** in transit, transitting; **passagers en t.** *(dans un aéroport)* passengers in transit, transfer passengers

transitaire [trɑ̃zitɛr] **ADJ** *(commerce, port)* transit *(avant n)*; **pays t.** country of transit

NM forwarding agent; **t. aéroportuaire** airfreight forwarder; **t. portuaire** maritime freight forwarder

transiter [3] [trɑ̃zite] **VT** *(marchandises)* to forward

VI 1 *(voyageurs, marchandises)* **t. par** to pass through; **t. par Anchorage** to transit *or* to go via Anchorage; **ces dossiers transitent par mon service** those files come through my department **2** *Ordinat (signaux)* to flow

transitif, -ive [trɑ̃zitif, -iv] **ADJ** transitive

NM *Ling* transitive verb

transition [trɑ̃zisjɔ̃] **NF 1** *(entre deux états)* transition **2** *(entre deux paragraphes, deux scènes)* transition, link; *TV & Rad* **t. musicale** segue **3** *(entre deux gouvernements)* interim; **assurer la t.** to make sure there is no hiatus, to make sure there is a seamless transition

• **de transition ADJ 1** *(administration, gouvernement)* interim *(avant n)*; **période** *ou* **phase de t.** period of transition, transition *or* transitional period **2** *Aviat & Chim* transition *(avant n)*

• **sans transition ADV** without transition; **le journaliste est passé sans t. de l'accident d'avion à la météo** the newsreader went from the plane crash to the weather forecast without any transition *or* a break; **sans t., nous passons aux nouvelles sportives** and now for something completely different, over to the sports news; **elle passait sans t. de l'enthousiasme à la fureur** her mood used to change *or* to switch abruptly from enthusiasm to rage

transitive [trɑ̃zitiv] *voir* **transitif**

transitivement [trɑ̃zitivmɑ̃] **ADV** transitively

transitivité [trɑ̃zitivite] **NF** transitivity

transitoire [trɑ̃zitwar] **ADJ 1** *(administration, dispositions, régime)* interim *(avant n)*, transitional; *(mesure)* transitional, temporary; *(charge)* temporary **2** *(situation)* transitory, transient

Transjordanie [trɑ̃sʒɔrdani] **NF** *Hist* **la T.** Transjordan

translation [trɑ̃slasjɔ̃] **NF 1** *Rel (de cendres, de reliques)* translation; *(d'une fête)* transfer

2 *Jur (d'une juridiction, d'un dignitaire)* transfer; *(de propriété)* conveyance, transfer

3 *Ordinat* **t. dynamique** dynamic relocation

4 *Math & Phys* translation; **mouvement de t.** translating movement

5 *Tél (de message)* retransmission, relaying

translittération [trɑ̃sliterasjɔ̃] **NF** transliteration; *(en braille)* copying

translittérer [18] [trɑ̃slitere] **VT** to transliterate; *(en braille)* to copy

translucide [trɑ̃slysid] **ADJ** translucent

translucidité [trɑ̃slysidite] **NF** translucence, translucency

transmanche [trɑ̃smɑ̃ʃ] **ADJ INV** cross-Channel

transmet *etc voir* **transmettre**

transmetteur [trɑ̃smɛtœr] **NM 1** *Tél, Ordinat & Biol* transmitter

2 *Naut* **t. d'ordres** telegraph, transmitter

3 *Mil* ≃ soldier in the Signals Corps

4 *Méd (d'une maladie, d'un virus)* carrier

transmettre [84] [trɑ̃smɛtr] **VT 1** *Tél* to transmit

2 *Rad & TV (émission)* to transmit, to relay, to broadcast; *(information)* to send, to transmit

3 *Phys* to transmit; **t. un mouvement à qch** to set sth in motion

4 *(de la main à la main)* to hand (on), to pass on; **transmettez-lui ce colis** give him/her this parcel

5 *(de génération en génération ▸ gén)* to pass on to, to hand down; *(▸ recette, don)* to hand on; *(▸ connaissances)* to hand on, to pass on

6 *(communiquer ▸ information, ordre, remerciement)* to pass on, *Sout* to convey; *(▸ pli)* to send on, to forward; *(▸ secret)* to pass on; **transmette**

mes amitiés à votre frère *(à l'oral)* please remember me to your brother; *(dans une lettre)* please send my regards to your brother; **qui vous a transmis la nouvelle?** who gave *or* told you the news?, who passed the news on to you?

7 *(faire partager ▸ goût, émotion)* to pass on, to put over; **il m'a transmis son enthousiasme pour l'art abstrait** he communicated his enthusiasm for abstract art to me

8 *Méd* to transmit, to pass on

9 *Jur (propriété)* to pass on, to transfer; *(pouvoirs)* to pass on, to hand over, to transfer; *(actions)* to assign; **t. ses pouvoirs à qn** to hand over to sb

USAGE ABSOLU *(communiquer)* **laissez-moi un message et je transmettrai** leave me a message and I'll pass it on; **écrire au journal, qui transmettra** write care of the newspaper

VPR **se transmettre** to be transmitted; *(message, maladie)* to be passed on; *(coutume)* to be handed down, to be passed on; **le virus se transmet par contact/par la salive** the virus is transmitted by (direct) contact/through saliva; **la vibration se transmet à la membrane** the vibration spreads *or* is transmitted to the membrane; **le savoir se transmet de la mère à la fille** knowledge is handed down *or* passed on from mother to daughter

transmigration [trɑ̃smigrasjɔ̃] NF *(réincarnation)* transmigration

transmigrer [3] [trɑ̃smigre] VI *(âme)* to transmigrate

transmis, -e [trɑ̃smi, -iz] PP *voir* **transmettre**

transmissible [trɑ̃smisibl] ADJ **1** *Méd* transmittable, transmissible; **sexuellement t.** sexually transmitted; **c'est t. par contact/par la salive** it can be transmitted by (direct) contact/through saliva **2** *Jur (biens, droit)* transferable, transmissible; *Fin* **t. par endossement** transferable by endorsement

transmission [trɑ̃smisjɔ̃] NF **1** *Aut & Tech (pièces)* **organes de t.** transmission (system); *Aut* **t. automatique** automatic transmission; *Aut* **t. manuelle** manual transmission

2 *Phys (de chaleur, de son)* transmission

3 *Tél* transmission; *Rad & TV (d'une émission)* transmission, relaying, broadcasting; **erreur de t.** *(d'un message)* error in transmission; *Rad & TV* **t. différée** *ou* **en différé** recorded broadcast *or* programme; **t. directe** *ou* **en direct** live broadcast *or* programme; *Rad & TV* **t. par satellite** satellite broadcast

4 *Méd* passing on, transmission, transmitting; *Biol (de caractères génétiques)* transmission, handing on

5 *(d'une information, d'un ordre)* passing on, conveying; *(d'un secret)* passing on; *(d'une lettre)* forwarding, sending on; **t. de pensée** telepathy, thought transference; **c'est de la t. de pensée!** we/they/*etc* can read each other's minds!

6 *(d'une tradition)* handing down *or* on; *(du savoir)* handing on, passing on

7 *(legs ▸ d'un bijou, d'une histoire)* handing down, passing on; *(▸ d'un état d'esprit)* passing on

8 *Jur (de pouvoirs, de biens)* transfer; *(d'actions)* assignment; **t. de données** data transmission *or* transfer; *Admin* **t. des pouvoirs** *(d'un ministre à un autre, d'un président à un autre)* handover

9 *Ordinat* transmission; **t. de données** data transmission *or* transfer; **voie de t.** transmission channel

• **transmissions** NFPL *Mil* **les transmissions** ≃ the Signals Corps; **centre de transmissions** signal centre

transmit *etc voir* **transmettre**

transmuer [7] [trɑ̃smɥe] VT to transmute; **t. qch en** to transmute sth into

VPR **se transmuer** to be transmuted

transmutation [trɑ̃smytasjɔ̃] NF transmutation (**en** into)

transmuter [3] [trɑ̃smyte] VT to transmute; **t. qch en** to transmute sth into

VPR **se transmuter** to be transmuted

transnational, -e, -aux, -ales [trɑ̃snasjɔnal, -o] ADJ transnational

transpalette [trɑ̃spalɛt] NM pallet truck, stacker

transparaître [91] [trɑ̃sparɛtr] VI *(lumière, couleur, sentiment)* to show *or* to filter through; **son visage ne laissa rien t.** he/she remained impassive, his/her face showed no emotion; **l'auteur laisse t. son désenchantement** the author allows his/her disenchantment to show *or* to filter through

transparence [trɑ̃sparɑ̃s] NF **1** *(propriété ▸ d'une porcelaine, d'une surface)* transparence, transparency; *(▸ d'une peau)* clearness, transparence, transparency; *(▸ d'un regard, d'un liquide)* transparency, clearness; **regarder qch par t.** to look at sth against the light; **on peut le lire par t.** you can read it by holding it up to the light; **on voit son soutien-gorge par t.** her bra is showing through

2 *Fig (caractère d'évidence ▸ d'un dessein, d'une personnalité)* transparency, obviousness

3 *Fig (caractère public ▸ de transactions, d'une comptabilité)* public accountability; *(d'un parti politique)* transparency, openness

4 *Jur* **t. fiscale** open taxation

5 *Cin* back projection

transparent, -e [trɑ̃sparɑ̃, -ɑ̃t] ADJ **1** *(translucide ▸ porcelaine, papier, surface)* transparent; *(▸ regard, eau)* transparent, limpid; *(▸ vêtement)* transparent, see-through; **ta robe est très transparente** your dress is very transparent *or* see-through

2 *(lumineux, clair ▸ peau)* transparent, clear

3 *Fig (évident ▸ dessein, motif)* obvious, transparent

4 *Fig (public ▸ comptabilité, transaction)* open

NM **1** *(de projection)* transparency, OHP slide **2** *(pour écrire droit)* ruled sheet

transparu [trɑ̃spary] PP *voir* **transparaître**

transpercer [16] [trɑ̃spɛrse] VT **1** *(sujet: flèche, épée)* to pierce (through), to transfix; *(sujet: balle)* to go through, to pierce; **t. qn d'un coup d'épée** to run sb through with a sword; **il a eu le pied transpercé par la flèche** the arrow went (right) through his foot; **la balle l'a transpercé** the bullet went right through him/it **2** *(pénétrer ▸ sujet: pluie)* to get through; **un froid qui transperce** piercing cold; **la pluie a transpercé ses vêtements** the rain went *or* soaked right through his/her clothes

transpirant, -e [trɑ̃spirɑ̃, -ɑ̃t] ADJ perspiring, sweating

transpiration [trɑ̃spirasjɔ̃] NF **1** *Physiol (sudation)* perspiration; *(sueur)* perspiration, sweat; **humide de t.** *(vêtement)* sweaty **2** *Bot* transpiration

transpirer [3] [trɑ̃spire] VI **1** *Physiol* to perspire, to sweat; **t. des mains/pieds** to have sweaty hands/feet; **je transpirais à grosses gouttes** great drops *or* beads of sweat were rolling off my forehead

2 *Fig (faire des efforts)* to sweat blood, to be hard at it; *Fam* **t. sur qch** to sweat over sth

3 *Fig (être divulgué)* to leak out, to come to light; **la nouvelle a transpiré** the news has got *or* leaked out

4 *Bot* to transpire

> Il faut noter que le verbe anglais **to transpire** ne signifie jamais **suer**.

transplant [trɑ̃splɑ̃] NM *(avant l'opération)* organ for transplant; *(après l'opération)* transplant, transplanted organ

transplantable [trɑ̃splɑ̃tabl] ADJ transplantable

transplantation [trɑ̃splɑ̃tasjɔ̃] NF **1** *Méd (d'un organe ▸ méthode)* transplantation; *(▸ opération)* transplant; **t. cardiaque/rénale/hépatique** heart/kidney/liver transplant; **t. embryonnaire** surgical transplantation of an embryo **2** *Agr & Hort* transplantation, transplanting **3** *(déplacement ▸ de personnes)* moving, resettling; *(▸ d'animaux)* transplantation

transplanté, -e [trɑ̃splɑ̃te] NM,F receiver *(of a transplant)*; **les transplantés du cœur/du foie** people who have had heart/liver transplants; **le nombre des transplantés** the number of people receiving transplants

transplanter [3] [trɑ̃splɑ̃te] VT **1** *Méd (organe)* to transplant; *(embryon)* to implant; **t. un cœur/un rein** to perform a heart/a kidney transplant (operation); **un malade transplanté** a transplant patient **2** *Agr & Hort* to transplant **3** *(populations)* to move, to transplant, to uproot

transplantoir [trɑ̃splɑ̃twar] NM trowel

transpolaire [trɑ̃spɔlɛr] ADJ transpolar

transpondeur [trɑ̃spɔ̃dœr] NM *Tél* transponder

transport [trɑ̃spɔr] NM **1** *(acheminement ▸ de personnes, de marchandises) Br* transport, *Am* transportation; *(▸ d'énergie)* conveyance, conveying; **assurer le t. des blessés** to be responsible for transporting the wounded; **abîmé pendant le t.** damaged in transit; **t. aérien, t. par air** *ou* **avion** air transport, airfreight; **t. par chemin de fer** rail transport; **le t. civil aérien** civil aviation; **t. ferroviaire** rail transport; **t. fluvial** inland waterway transport; **t. international routier** TIR; **t. de marchandises** transport of goods; **t. maritime** *ou* **par mer** shipping; **t. par route** road transport *or* haulage; **t. terrestre** land transport; *Mil* **t. de troupes** *(acheminement)* troop transportation; *(navire, avion)* (troop) carrier, troop transport

2 *Littéraire (émotion)* transport, burst; **t. de joie** transport *or* burst of joy; **t. d'enthousiasme** burst *or* gush of enthusiasm; **t. de colère** burst *or* outburst of anger; **dans un t. d'admiration, elle me dit...** fairly carried away *or* transported with admiration, she said to me...; *Littéraire ou Hum* **transports amoureux** amorous transports

3 *Jur (cession)* **t.(-cession)** *(de biens, de droits)* transfer, conveyance; **t. sur les lieux, t. de justice** visit to the scene of the accident *or* crime

• **transports** NMPL *Admin* transport network; **les transports (publics** *ou* **en commun)** public transport *(UNCOUNT)*; **je passe beaucoup de temps dans les transports pour aller au travail** I spend a lot of time commuting; **prendre les transports en commun** to use public transport; **les transports routiers** road transport, road haulage; **les transports urbains** the urban transport system

• **de transport** ADJ *Br* transport *(avant n)*, *Am* transportation *(avant n)*

transportable [trɑ̃spɔrtabl] ADJ *(denrées)* transportable; *(blessé)* fit to be moved; **elle n'est pas t.** she's not fit to be moved, she can't be moved

transportation [trɑ̃spɔrtasjɔ̃] NF *Hist* transportation

transporté, -e [trɑ̃spɔrte] ADJ *Fig* carried away, transported; **t. de joie** beside oneself with joy, transported with joy

NM,F *Hist* transported convict, transport

transporter [3] [trɑ̃spɔrte] VT **1** *(faire changer d'endroit ▸ cargaison, passager, troupes)* to carry, to transport, *Sout* to convey; *(▸ blessé)* to move; **t. une caisse à la cave** to move a crate to the cellar; **t. des vivres par avion/par bateau** to fly/to ship food supplies; **t. qch par avion** to airfreight sth, to transport sth by air; **le camion transporte des explosifs** the truck is carrying explosives; **t. qn à l'hôpital** to take sb to hospital; **t. qn d'urgence à l'hôpital** to rush sb to hospital; **les personnes transportées** *(passagers)* passengers

2 *Fig (par l'imaginaire)* to take; **le premier acte nous transporte en Géorgie/au XVIIème siècle** the first act takes us to Georgia/takes us back to the 17th century

3 *(porter)* to carry; **les alluvions transportées par le fleuve** the sediment carried (along) by the river

4 *Phys* to convey

5 *Littéraire (enthousiasmer)* to carry away, to send into raptures; **cette bonne nouvelle l'a transporté** he was overjoyed by the good news; **je me sentais transporté par la musique** the music sent me into raptures; **être transporté de joie** to be overjoyed *or* in transports of delight

6 *Hist (condamné)* to transport

VPR **se transporter 1** *(se déplacer)* to move **2** *Fig (en imagination)* to imagine oneself; **se t. (par la pensée) dans un pays lointain** to let one's imagination carry one to a distant country; **transportez-vous maintenant au Moyen Âge** now let your imagination take you back to the Middle Ages

3 *Jur* **se t. sur les lieux** to visit the scene of the accident *or* crime

transporteur, -euse [trɑ̃spɔrtœr, -øz] **ADJ** carrying *(avant n)*; **benne transporteuse** skip; **hélice/courroie transporteuse** spiral/belt conveyor

NM 1 *(entreprise)* haulage contractor, *Br* haulier, *Am* hauler; *(en langage juridique)* carrier; **t. routier** road haulage contractor, road *Br* haulier *or Am* hauler

2 *(outil)* conveyor; **(chariot) t.** travelling crane *or* platform; **t. élévateur** elevator

3 *Naut* **t. de vrac** bulk carrier

4 *Pétr* **t. de gaz** gas transporter (ship)

transposable [trɑ̃spozabl] **ADJ** transposable; **difficilement t.** difficult to transpose; **t. à l'écran** that can be adapted for the screen

transposer [3] [trɑ̃spoze] **VT 1** *(intervertir ▸ mots)* to switch (round), to transpose **2** *(adapter)* **t. un sujet antique à l'époque moderne** to adapt an ancient subject to a contemporary setting; **t. un roman à l'écran/à la scène** to adapt a novel for the screen/for the stage **3** *Mus* to transpose

transposition [trɑ̃spozisjɔ̃] **NF 1** *(commutation)* transposition **2** *(adaptation)* adaptation; **t. d'un roman à l'écran/à la scène** screen/stage adaptation **3** *Mus* transposition

transpyrénéen, -enne [trɑ̃spireneɛ̃, -ɛn] **ADJ 1** *(qui traverse)* trans-Pyrenean **2** *(venant de l'autre côté)* from across the Pyrenees

transsaharien, -enne [trɑ̃ssaarjɛ̃, -ɛn] **ADJ** trans-Saharan

transsexualisme [trɑ̃ssɛksɥalism] **NM** transsexualism

transsexuel, -elle [trɑ̃ssɛksɥɛl] **ADJ** transsexual

transsibérien, -enne [trɑ̃ssiberjɛ̃, -ɛn] **ADJ** trans-Siberian

NM le T. the Trans-Siberian (Railway)

transsubstantiation [trɑ̃ssypstɑ̃sjasjɔ̃] **NF** *Rel* transubstantiation

Transvaal [trɑ̃sval] **NM le T.** the Transvaal; **au T.** in the Transvaal

transvasement [trɑ̃svazmɑ̃] **NM** *(d'un liquide)* decanting

transvaser [3] [trɑ̃svaze] **VT** to decant; **transvasez le bouillon dans un verre gradué** pour the stock into a measuring jug

transversal, -e, -aux, -ales [trɑ̃sversal, -o] **ADJ** *(coupe, fil, poutre, trait)* cross *(avant n)*, transverse, transversal; *(onde, axe, moteur)* transverse; *(voie)* which runs *or* cuts across; **rue transversale** side road; *Constr* **mur t.** partition (wall); *Anat* **muscle t.** transverse (muscle); *Naut* **soutes transversales** cross bunkers; *Géog* **vallée transversale** transverse valley

• **transversale NF 1** *Ftbl (barre)* crossbar; *(passe)* cross **2** *Géom* transversal **3** *(route)* cross-country *Br* trunk road *or Am* highway **4** *Rail (entre régions)* cross-country line; *(de ville à ville) Br* intercity *or Am* interurban line

transversalement [trɑ̃sversalmɑ̃] **ADV** transversally, across

transverse [trɑ̃svɛrs] **ADJ** *Anat & Géom* transverse

transvestisme [trɑ̃svɛstism] **NM** transvestism

transvider [3] [trɑ̃svide] **VT** to decant; **t. qch dans qch** to pour sth into sth, to transfer sth to sth

Transylvanie [trɑ̃silvani] **NF la T.** Transylvania

trapèze [trapɛz] **NM 1** *Géom Br* trapezium, *Am* trapezoid; **t. rectangle** right-angled trapezium **2** *Anat (muscle)* trapezius **3** *(activité)* trapeze; **faire du t.** to perform on the trapeze; **t. volant** flying trapeze

ADJ 1 *Anat* **muscle t.** trapezius; **os t.** trapezium **2** *(jupe, robe)* A-line

trapéziste [trapezist] **NMF** trapezist, trapeze artist

trapézoïdal, -e, -aux, -ales [trapezɔidal, -o] **ADJ** trapezoidal

trapézoïde [trapezɔid] **ADJ** trapezoid *(avant n)*

NM trapezoid (bone)

Trappe [trap] **NF 1** *(abbaye)* Trappist monastery **2** *(ordre)* **la T.** the Trappist order

trappe [trap] **NF 1** *(piège)* trap **2** *(sur le sol ▸ porte)* trap door; *(▸ ouverture)* hatch; *(d'une scène de théâtre)* trap opening; *(pour parachutiste)* exit door; *Tech* hatch; **passer à la t.** to be whisked away (without trace); **t. de visite** inspection hatch; *Aut* **t. à essence** petrol tank flap

trappeur [trapœr] **NM** trapper

trappiste [trapist] **NM** *(moine)* Trappist monk

NF *Belg (bière)* beer *(made by Trappist monks)*

trapu, -e [trapy] **ADJ 1** *(personne)* stocky, thickset

2 *(bâtiment)* squat

3 *Fam (difficile ▸ devoir, exercice)* tough, tricky; **l'examen était vraiment t.!** the exam was a real stinker!

4 *Fam (savant)* brainy; **il est t. en chimie** he's brilliant at chemistry

traquenard [traknar] **NM** *(machination)* snare, trap; **tomber dans un t.** to fall into a trap

traquer [3] [trake] **VT 1** *(criminel, fuyard)* to track *or* to hunt down; *(vedette)* to hound; *(erreur)* to track down; **en le traquant, ils ont découvert où il habitait** they tracked him down to his home; **se faire t.** to be tracked down *or* hunted down **2** *Chasse (rechercher)* to track down; *(rabattre)* to drive; **animal traqué** hunted animal

traquet [trakɛ] **NM 1** *(battant)* (mill) clapper *or* clack **2** *Orn* **t. (motteux)** wheatear; **t. (pâtre)** stonechat; **t. oreillard** black-eared wheatear

traqueur, -euse [trakœr, -øz] **NM,F** *Chasse* beater, driver

trash [traʃ] *Fam* **ADJ INV** *(musique, film, esthétique)* trash

NM *(style)* trash

trauma [troma] **NM** trauma

traumatique [tromatik] **ADJ** traumatic

traumatisant, -e [tromatizɑ̃, -ɑ̃t] **ADJ** traumatic

traumatiser [3] [tromatize] **VT** to traumatize; *Fam* **il ne faut pas que ça te traumatise** you mustn't let it traumatize you, you mustn't be traumatized by it

traumatisme [tromatism] **NM** trauma, traumatism; **t. crânien** cranial trauma

traumatologie [tromatɔlɔʒi] **NF** traumatology

traumatologiste [tromatɔlɔʒist] **NMF** traumatologist

travail¹, -s [travaj] **NM** *Vét* trave

TRAVAIL², -AUX [travaj, -o]

NM	
• work **A1, 2, 4, 5, 10–12, B2, C**	• job **A3, 7**
	• working **A6**
• labour **A8, 10**	• action **A9**
• piece **B1**	• workplace **C**
NMPL	
• work **1–3**	• working **1**

NM A. *ACTION* **1** *(occupation)* **le t.** work; **le t. de bureau** office work; **le t. de jour/nuit** day/night work; **t. à la chaîne** assembly-line work; **je finis le t. à cinq heures** I stop *or* finish work at five; **un t. de longue haleine** a long-term project; **le t. scolaire/universitaire** school/academic work; **le t. posté** *ou* **par roulement** shift work; *Jur* **t. d'intérêt général** community service; **le t. manuel** manual work *or* labour; **le t. au noir** *(occasionnel)* undeclared casual work, moonlighting; *(comme pratique généralisée)* the black economy; **t. à la pièce** piecework; **le t. saisonnier** seasonal work; **le t. salarié** paid work; **le t. temporaire** *(gén)* temporary work; *(dans un bureau)* temping; **t. à plein temps** full-time work; **t. à temps partiel** part-time work; **t. d'équipe** teamwork

2 *(tâches imposées)* work; **avoir beaucoup de t.** to have a lot of work; **donner du t. à qn** to give sb (some) work to do; **leur professeur leur donne trop de t.** their teacher gives *or* sets them too much work *or* homework

3 *(tâche déterminée)* job; **faire un t. de recherche/traduction** to do a piece of research/a translation; **c'est un t. de bagnard** *ou* **forçat** it's backbreaking work *or* a back-breaking job; **c'est un t. de bénédictin** it's painstaking work; **c'est un t. de fourmi** it's a painstaking task; **c'est un t. de Romain** *ou* **de Titan** it's a colossal job

4 *(efforts)* (hard) work; **c'est du t. d'élever cinq enfants!** bringing up five children is a lot of (hard) work!; **tout ce t. pour rien!** all this (hard) work for nothing!; **c'est tout un t., de vous réunir tous les huit!** it's quite a job, getting the eight of you together!

5 *(exécution)* work; **admirez le t. du pinceau** admire the brushwork; **regarde-moi ce t.!** just look at this mess!; **je ne retrouve pas une seule disquette, qu'est-ce que c'est que ce t.?** I can't find a single floppy disk, what's going on here?; *Fam* **et voilà le t.!** and that's all there is to it!, *Br* and Bob's your uncle!

6 *(façonnage)* working; **t. du bois** woodwork; **t. du métal** metalwork; **t. au tour** lathework

7 *(poste)* job, occupation, post; *(responsabilité)* job; **chercher du** *ou* **un t.** to be job-hunting, to be looking for a job; **un t. à mi-temps/plein temps** a part-time/full-time job; **sans t.** unemployed jobless, out of work; **le suivi des commandes c'est son t.** following up orders is his/her job; **je n'aurais pas à m'en occuper si tu faisais ton t.** I wouldn't have to worry about it if you did your job (properly)

8 *(dans le système capitaliste)* labour; **le t. et le capital** labour and capital

9 *(contrainte exercée ▸ par la chaleur, l'érosion)* action

10 *Physiol (accouchement)* labour; *(activité)* work; **le t. n'est pas commencé/est commencé** the patient has not yet gone/has gone into labour **réduire le t. du cœur/des reins** to lighten the strain on the heart/on the kidneys

11 *Tech & Phys* work; **l'unité de t. est le joule** the joule is the unit of work; **évaluer le t. d'une machine** to measure the work done by a machine

12 *Psy* work, working through; **t. de deuil** grieving process; **t. du rêve** dreamwork

B. *RÉSULTAT, EFFET* **1** *(écrit)* piece; **il a publié un t. très intéressant sur Proust** he published a very interesting piece on Proust

2 *(transformation ▸ gén)* work; *(modification interne ▸ dans le bois)* warping; *(▸ dans le fromage)* maturing; *(▸ dans le vin)* working

C. *LIEU D'ACTIVITÉ PROFESSIONNELLE* work workplace; **aller à son t.** to go to (one's) work; **je te téléphone du t.** I'm phoning you from work

• **travaux NMPL 1** *(tâches)* work, working; **faire faire des travaux** to have some work carried out *or* done; **ils font des travaux après le pont** there are roadworks after the bridge; **nous sommes en travaux à la maison** we're having some work done on the house, we've got (the) workmen in; **fermé pendant les travaux** *(sur la vitrine d'un magasin)* closed for refurbishment *or* alterations; **travaux** *(sur panneau) Br* roadworks ahead, *Am* roadwork ahead; **attention, travaux** *(sur panneau)* caution, work in progress; **travaux domestiques** *ou* **ménagers** housework; *Couture* **travaux d'aiguille** needlework; **travaux de construction** building work; **travaux d'entretien** maintenance work **travaux forcés** hard labour; **travaux d'Hercule** *Myth* labours of Hercules; *Fig* herculean tasks **travaux manuels** *(gén)* arts and crafts; *Scol* handicraft; **travaux d'utilité collective** ≃ YTS; **grands travaux** large-scale public works; **les Travaux publics** civil engineering

2 *(d'une commission)* work; **nous publierons le résultat de nos travaux** we'll publish our findings **l'Assemblée nationale reprendra ses travaux le mois prochain** the new session of the National Assembly begins next month

3 *Univ* **travaux universitaires** academic research; **travaux dirigés** tutorial, seminar; **travaux pratiques** *(gén)* practical work; *(en laboratoire)* lab work; **on nous l'a donné à faire en travaux pratiques** we had to do it for our practical

4 *Jur* **travaux préparatoires** *(à un projet de loi)* preliminary documents

• **au travail ADV 1** *(en activité)* at work, working **se mettre au t.** to get down *or* to set to work; **se remettre au t.** to start work again, to get down to one's work again; **allez, au t.!** come on, get to work! **2** *(sur le lieu d'activité)* at work, in the work place; **je vous donne mon numéro au t.** I'll give you my work number

• **de travail ADJ 1** *(horaire, séance)* working *(avant n)*; *(vêtement, camarade, permis)* work *(avant n)*; **mes instruments de t.** the tools of my trade; **contrat de t.** employment contract **2** *(d'ac-*

:ouchement ▸ période) labour (avant n); (▸ salle) abour (avant n), delivery (avant n)

• **du travail** ADJ (accident, sociologie, législa-ion) industrial; **conflit du t.** employment dis-)ute; **droit du t.** employment law

• **en travail** ADV Physiol (d'accouchement) in la-)our

ravaillé, -e [travaje] ADJ **1** (de travail) **jours tra-vaillés** (number of) days worked; **heures tra-vaillées** (number of) hours worked **2** (élaboré ▸ 'tyle) polished; (▸ façade, meuble) finely or elab-orately worked; (▸ fer) wrought **3** (préoccupé) **être t. par qch** to be tormented by sth

ravailler [3] [travaje] VI **1** (être actif) to work; **tu as le temps de t. avant dîner** you've got time to do some work or to get some work done before din-ner; **elle travaille beaucoup trop!** she's working (herself) too hard!; **t. dur** to work hard; **elle tra-vaille vite** she's a fast worker; **le maçon a bien tra-vaillé** the bricklayer made a good job of it; **t. 40 heures par semaine** to work a 40-hour week; **une femme qui travaille** a working woman; **j'y travaille** I'm working on it; **t. sur ordinateur** to work on a computer; **t. comme un bœuf** ou **forçat** to slave away, to work like a Trojan; Fam **t. du chapeau** to have a screw loose

2 (avoir une profession) to work; **vous travaillez?** do you work?, do you have a job?; **où travailles-tu?** where do you work?; **j'ai arrêté de t. à 55 ans** I stopped work or retired at 55; **t. pour payer ses études** to work one's way or to put oneself through college/university; **aller t.** to go to work; **t. en free-lance** to do freelance work, to be a freelancer; **t. en indépendant** to be self-em-ployed; **t. en usine** to work in a factory; **t. dans un bureau** to work in an office; **t. dans le privé** to work in the private sector; **elle travaille dans l'in-formatique** she works with computers; **elle tra-vaille dans la maroquinerie** she's in the leather trade; **les enfants travaillaient dans les mines dès l'âge de six ans** children were put to work in the mines at the age of six; **t. comme chauffeur de taxi** to work as a taxi driver; **t. à son compte** to have one's own business; **t. pour qn/une société** (être employé par) to work for sb/a company; **j'ai travaillé pour le roi de Prusse!** I got nothing what-soever for it!; **t. au ralenti** to go slow

3 (faire des affaires) to do (good) business; **en-treprise qui travaille bien/mal/à perte** thriving/ stagnating/lossmaking firm

4 (pratiquer son activité ▸ artiste, athlète) to prac-tise, to train; (▸ boxeur) to work out, to train; **faire t. ses jambes** to make one's legs work, to ex-ercise one's legs; **faire t. une machine** to work or run a machine; **fais t. ton imagination** use your imagination; **c'est ton imagination qui travaille** your imagination's working overtime, you're imagining things; Fig **faire t. son argent** to make one's money work

5 (changer de forme, de nature ▸ armature, pou-tre) to warp; (▸ fondations, vin) to work; (▸ mur) to crack; (▸ navire, câble) to strain

6 (œuvrer) **t. à** (succès) to work or to strive for; **t. à la perte de qn** ou **à perdre qn** to try to ruin sb; **t. contre/pour** to work against/for; **le temps tra-vaille contre/pour nous** time is working against us/is on our side

VT **1** (façonner ▸ bois, bronze, glaise) to work; Culin (mélange, sauce) to stir; Culin **t. la pâte** to knead or to work the dough; (peintre) to work the paste; **t. la terre** to work or Sout to till the land; **t. une balle** (au tennis) to put spin on a ball

2 (perfectionner ▸ discours, style) to work on, to polish up, to hone; (▸ concerto, scène) to work on, to rehearse; Sport (▸ mouvement) to practise, to work on; (étudier ▸ matière scolaire) to work at or on, to go over; (▸ texte, auteur) to study; **cet élève devra t. la trigonométrie** this pupil should work (harder) at trigonometry; **tu ferais mieux d'aller t. ton piano** you'd be better to go and do your pi-ano practice; **travaillez votre revers** work on your backhand

3 (préoccuper) to worry; **ça m'a travaillé toute la journée** it's been preying on my mind all day; **ça me travaille de le savoir malheureux** it worries me to know that he's unhappy; **l'idée de la mort le travaillait** (the idea of) death haunted him; **être travaillé par le remords/l'angoisse** to be torment-ed by remorse/anxiety

4 (tenter d'influencer) to work on; **t. les délégués pour les convaincre** to work on or to lobby the delegates in order to persuade them

5 Équitation to work

6 Pêche to work, to play

7 Boxe **t. qn au corps** to punch sb around the body

travailleur, -euse [travajœr, -øz] ADJ hard-working, industrious

NM,F **1** (exerçant un métier) worker; **t. intellectuel** white-collar worker; **t. manuel** manual or esp Am blue-collar worker; **les travailleurs** (gén) working people, the workers; (ouvriers) labour (UN-COUNT); (prolétariat) the working classes; **t. agricole** agricultural or farm worker; **t. à domicile** outworker, homeworker; **t. immigré** migrant worker; **travailleurs immigrés** immigrant workers or labour; **t. indépendant** self-employed person, freelance worker; **t. au noir** = worker in the black economy; **t. occasionnel** casual worker; **t. posté** shift worker; **t. saisonnier** seasonal worker; **t. à plein temps/à mi-temps** full-time/part-time worker **2** Admin **t. social** social worker; **tra-vailleuse familiale** home help **3** (personne labo-rieuse) hard worker; **c'est un gros t.** he's very hardworking

• **travailleuse** NF work table (for needlework)

travaillisme [travajism] NM Labour doctrine or philosophy

travailliste [travajist] ADJ Labour (avant n); **être t.** to be a member of the Labour Party or party; **le parti t.** the Labour Party or party

NMF member of the Labour Party; **les travaillis-tes se sont opposés à cette mesure** Labour op-posed the move

travée [trave] NF **1** (rangée de sièges, de personnes assises) row **2** Archit & Constr (d'une voûte, d'une nef) bay; (solivage) girder; (d'un pont) span **3** Aviat (d'aile) rib

traveller's cheque, traveller's check [tra-vlœrʃɛk, travlœrstʃɛk] (pl **traveller's cheques** ou **checks**) NM Br traveller's cheque, Am traveler's check

travelling [travliŋ] NM Cin **1** (déplacement ▸ gén) tracking; (▸ sur plate-forme) dollying; **faire un t.** (caméra, cameraman) to track; (sur plate-forme) to dolly; **t. avant/arrière/latéral** tracking in/out/ sideways; (sur plate-forme) dollying in/out/side-ways **2** (plate-forme) dolly, travelling platform **3** (prise de vue) tracking shot

travelo [travlo] NM très Fam drag queen, Br tran-ny; **habillé en t.** in drag

travers [travɛr] NM **1** (défaut) fault, shortcoming, failing; **elle tombait dans les mêmes t. que ses pré-décesseurs** she displayed the same shortcom-ings as his/her predecessors; **un petit t.** a minor fault; **tous les t. de son père** all the short-comings of her father's character; Arch **t. (d'es-prit)** eccentricity

2 (largeur) breadth

3 Naut **par le t.** abeam, on the beam; **collision par le t.** collision broadside on

4 (viande) **t. (de porc)** spare rib

• **à travers** PRÉP through, across; **à t. la fenêtre/ le plancher/les barreaux** through the window/the floor/the bars; **à t. la forêt** across or through the forest; **à t. la foule** through the crowd; **à t. les âges** throughout the centuries; **à t. les siècles** down (through) the centuries; **on voit à t. sa robe** you can see through her dress; **il jeta les livres à t. la chambre** he flung the books across the room; **prendre** ou **passer à t. champs** to go through the fields or across country; **couper à t. bois** to cut across or through the woods; Pêche & Fig **passer à t. les mailles du filet** to slip through the net

• **au travers** ADV **elle n'a pas réussi à passer au t.** she didn't manage to escape; **si tu crois passer au t., tu te trompes!** if you think you're going to get away with it you're mistaken

• **au travers de** PRÉP **1** (en franchissant) through **2** (par l'intermédiaire de) through, by means of; **son idée se comprend mieux au t. de cette comparaison** his/her idea is easier to un-derstand by means of this comparison

• **de travers** ADJ crooked; Naut **vent de t.** wind on the beam ADV **1** (en biais ▸ couper) askew, aslant; (▸ accrocher) askew; **votre chapeau est de t.** your hat is (on) crooked; **il a la bouche/le nez de t.** he's got a crooked mouth/nose; très Fam **elle a la gueule de t.** her face is all twisted; **j'ai avalé de t.** it went down the wrong way; **mar-cher de t.** (ivrogne) to stagger or to totter along **2** (mal) **tu fais tout de t.!** you do everything wrong!; **comprendre de t.** to misunderstand; **elle comprend tout de t.!** she gets everything wrong!, she always gets the wrong end of the stick!; **re-garder qn de t.** to give sb a funny look; **tout va** ou **marche de t.** everything's going wrong; **répondre de t.** to give the wrong answer; **il prend tout ce qu'on lui dit de t.** he takes everything the wrong way

• **en travers** ADV **1** (en largeur) sideways, across, crosswise; **autobus avec places disposées en t.** bus with seats arranged crosswise; **le wa-gon s'est mis en t.** the carriage ended up side-ways (across the tracks); **la remorque du camion s'est mise en t.** the truck jack-knifed **2** Naut abeam

• **en travers de** PRÉP across; **l'arbre était tombé en t. du chemin** the tree had fallen across the path; Fig **s'il se met en t. de mon chemin** ou **de ma route** if he stands in my way; Naut **en t. (du na-vire)** athwart (ships)

traversable [traversabl] ADJ which can be crossed; **la rivière est t.** (à gué) the river is ford-able; (en bateau) the river can be crossed by boat

traverse [travers] NF **1** Rail Br sleeper, Am cross-tie **2** Constr (de charpente) crossbeam, cross-piece; (entre deux montants) (cross) strut; (d'échelle) rung; **(barre de) t.** crossbar, cross-piece

traversée [traverse] NF **1** (d'une route, d'un pont, d'une frontière, d'un cours d'eau, d'une mer) cross-ing; (d'une agglomération, d'un pays) going or getting through, going or getting across; **com-bien de temps dure la t.?** how long is the crossing or does it take to get across?; **en 1927, Lindbergh effectuait la première traversée de l'Atlantique sans escale entre New York et Paris** in 1927 Lind-bergh was the first man to fly non-stop across the Atlantic from New York to Paris; **ils ont fait la t. en yacht jusqu'à Cherbourg** they sailed across or went over to Cherbourg in a yacht; **faire une bonne t.** to have a good crossing; **faire la t. de Douvres à Calais** to cross from Dover to Calais; **la t. de l'Atlantique en solitaire** crossing the Atlan-tic single-handed; Fig **après une longue t. du dé-sert...** (politicien) after a long time spent in the political wilderness...; (écrivain, artiste) after a long lean spell or period...; (entreprise, secteur) after a long period in the doldrums...; **il a fait sa t. du désert** (politicien) he spent his period in the political wilderness **2** (en alpinisme ▸ épreuve) through route; (▸ passage) traverse; Ski tra-verse; **faire une t.** to traverse **3** Rail crossing point

traverser [3] [traverse] VT **1** (parcourir ▸ mer, pièce, route) to go across, to cross, Sout to tra-verse; (▸ pont) to go over, to go across; (▸ tunnel, forêt) to go through, to pass through; (▸ ville, ré-gion, pays) to go through, to pass through, to cross; **t. qch à la nage/à cheval/en voiture/en ba-teau/en avion** to swim/to ride/to drive/to sail/ to fly across sth; **t. l'Europe en vélo** to cross or go across Europe on a bike, to bike across Europe; **t. une rivière à gué** to ford a river; **t. une pièce en courant/en sautillant** to run/to skip through a room; **aider qn à t. la route** to help sb across the road; **faire t. une vieille dame** to help an old lady across the road; **tu m'as fait t. Paris pour ça?** you mean you made me come from the other side of Paris for this?; **t. la foule** to make one's way or pass through the crowd

2 (s'étirer d'un côté à l'autre de ▸ sujet: voie) to cross, to run across, to go across; (▸ sujet: pont) to cross, to span; (▸ sujet: tunnel) to cross, to run under, to go under; **pont/route qui traverse la ri-vière** bridge/road that crosses or goes across the river

3 (vivre ▸ époque) to live through, to go through; (▸ difficultés) to go through; **t. les siècles** to come down through the ages; **son divorce lui a fait t. une période difficile** he/she went through a diffi-cult period because of the divorce

4 (transpercer ▸ sujet: épée) to run through, to pierce; (▸ sujet: balle) to go through; (▸ sujet: pluie, froid) to come through, to go through; **la**

balle lui traversa le bras the bullet went through *or* pierced his/her arm; **pour empêcher la pluie de t. la toile** to stop the rain soaking through the canvas; **t. l'esprit** *(idée, doute)* to cross one's mind; **une image me traversa l'esprit** an image passed *or* flashed through my mind

traversier, -ère [traversje, -ɛr] ADJ **rue traversière** cross street
NM *Can* ferry

traversin [traversɛ̃] NM **1** *(oreiller)* bolster **2** *Naut* crosstree

travesti, -e [travesti] ADJ **1** *(pour tromper)* in disguise, disguised; *(pour s'amuser)* dressed up (in fancy dress) **2** *Théât (comédien)* playing a female part; **rôle t.** = female part played by a man **3** *(vérité)* distorted; *(propos)* twisted, misrepresented
NM **1** *Théât* actor playing a female part; *(dans un cabaret)* female impersonator, drag artist; *(rôle)* female part (for an actor); **numéro** *ou* **spectacle de t.** drag act **2** *(homosexuel)* transvestite **3** *(vêtement ▸ d'homosexuel)* drag *(UNCOUNT)*; *(▸ de bal)* fancy dress *(UNCOUNT)*

travestir [32] [travestir] VT **1** *(pour une fête)* to dress up; *(comédien)* to cast in a female part; **t. qn en** to dress sb up as **2** *(pensées)* to misrepresent; *(vérité)* to distort; *(propos)* to twist **3** *Littérature (pièce, poème)* to parody, to burlesque; *(auteur)* to parody
VPR **se travestir 1** *(homme)* to dress as a woman, to put on drag; *(femme)* to dress as a man **2** *(pour une fête)* to dress up (in fancy dress), to put fancy dress on; **se t. en punk** to dress up as a punk

travestisme [travestism] NM transvestism

travestissement [travestismɑ̃] NM **1** *(pour une fête ▸ action)* dressing up, wearing fancy dress; *(▸ déguisement)* disguise; *Théât* **rôle à travestissements** quick-change part **2** *Psy* cross-dressing **3** *(de propos, de la vérité)* twisting, distortion, distorting; *(de pensées)* misrepresentation

traviole [travjɔl] **de traviole** *Fam* ADJ *(tableau)* lopsided, skew-whiff; *(dents)* crooked[□]
ADV **1** *(en biais)* **marcher de t.** *(ivrogne)* to be staggering all over the place; **j'écris de t.** my handwriting's all crooked; **tu as mis ton chapeau de t.** you've put your hat on crooked **2** *(mal)* **il fait tout de t.** he can't do anything right; **tout va de t.** everything's going wrong[□]; **tu comprends toujours tout de t.** you always get hold of the wrong end of the stick

trayait *etc voir* **traire**

trayeur, -euse [trejœr, -øz] NM,F milker, *Am* milkman, *f* milkwoman
• **trayeuse** NF milking machine

trayon [trejɔ̃] NM teat

trébuchant, -e [trebyʃɑ̃, -ɑ̃t] ADJ *(ivrogne, allure)* staggering, stumbling; *(diction)* stumbling, halting

trébucher [3] [trebyʃe] VI **1** *(perdre l'équilibre)* to stumble, to stagger; **t. sur une pierre** to stumble on a stone; **t. contre une marche** to trip over a step; **faire t. qn** to trip sb up **2** *(achopper)* to stumble; **t. sur un mot** to stumble over a word **3** *(balance)* to turn

trébuchet [trebyʃɛ] NM **1** *(piège)* bird trap **2** *(petite balance)* assay balance

tréfiler [3] [trefile] VT to wiredraw, to draw *(a wire)*

trèfle [trɛfl] NM **1** *Bot* clover, trefoil; **t. blanc** white *or* Dutch clover; **t. rouge** red clover; **t. à quatre feuilles** four-leaf clover
2 *Cartes* **du t.** clubs; **la dame de t.** the queen of clubs; **jouer à** *ou* **du t.** to play clubs
3 *Archit & Hér* trefoil
4 *(en travaux publics)* **carrefour en t.** cloverleaf (junction)
5 *(emblème irlandais)* shamrock
6 *Fam (argent)* cash, *Br* dosh, *Am* bucks

tréfonds [trefɔ̃] NM *Littéraire (partie profonde)* **être ému jusqu'au t. de son être** to be moved to the depths of one's soul; **atteint jusqu'au t.** very deeply hurt; **dans le t. de son âme** in the (innermost) depths of his/her soul; **au t. de mon cœur** in my heart of hearts

treillage [trejaʒ] NM *Hort* **1** *(assemblage)* trellis *or* lattice (work); *(d'une vigne)* wire trellis **2** *(clôture)* trellis fencing; **t. métallique** *ou* **en fil de fer** wire fencing

treillager [17] [trejaʒe] VT *(plante, vigne)* to trellis; *(fenêtre)* to lattice; **fenêtre treillagée** lattice window

treille [trej] NF **1** *(vigne)* climbing vine **2** *(tonnelle)* arbour

treillis [treji] NM **1** *Tex* canvas **2** *Mil* (usual) outfit **3** *(en lattes)* trellis; *(en fer)* wire-mesh

treize [trɛz] ADJ **1** *(gén)* thirteen; **acheter/vendre des huîtres t. à la douzaine** to buy/to sell thirteen oysters for the price of twelve; **il y en a t. à la douzaine** it's a baker's dozen; *Fig Péj* **des informaticiens, il y en a t. à la douzaine** computer scientists are *Br* ten a penny *or Am* a dime a dozen **2** *(dans des séries)* thirteenth; **page/numéro t.** page/number thirteen
PRON thirteen
NM INV **1** *(gén)* thirteen; **le t. porte malheur** thirteen is unlucky *or* is an unlucky number **2** *(numéro d'ordre)* number thirteen **3** *(chiffre écrit)* thirteen; *voir aussi* **cinq**

treizième [trezjɛm] ADJ thirteenth; **t. mois** = extra month's salary paid as an annual bonus
NMF **1** *(personne)* thirteenth **2** *(objet)* thirteenth (one)
NM **1** *(partie)* thirteenth **2** *(étage) Br* thirteenth floor, *Am* fourteenth floor; *voir aussi* **cinquième**

treizièmement [trezjɛmmɑ̃] ADV in thirteenth place

trek [trɛk], **trekking** [trekiŋ] NM trekking *(UNCOUNT)*; **faire un t.** to go on a trek; **faire du t. en Inde** to go trekking in India

tréma [trema] NM diaeresis; **e t.** e (with) diaeresis

tremblant, -e [trɑ̃blɑ̃, -ɑ̃t] ADJ **1** *(qui tremble ▸ flamme)* trembling, flickering; *(▸ feuilles)* fluttering, quivering; *(▸ main, jambes)* shaking, trembling, wobbly; *(▸ lèvres)* trembling, quivering; *(▸ voix)* tremulous, quavering, shaky; **t. de peur** trembling *or* shaking *or* shuddering with fear; **t. de froid** trembling *or* shivering with cold; **écrire d'une main tremblante** to write shakily; **répondre d'une voix tremblante** to answer tremulously **2** *(peu solide ▸ pont, chaise etc)* shaky, wobbly
• **tremblante** NF *Vét* **la tremblante du mouton** scrapie

tremble [trɑ̃bl] NM *Bot* aspen

tremblé, -e [trɑ̃ble] ADJ **1** *(écriture)* shaky, wobbly; *(trait)* wobbly, wavy **2** *Mus* **sons tremblés** quavering **3** *Typ* **filet t.** wavy rule
NM *Typ* wavy rule

tremblement [trɑ̃bləmɑ̃] NM **1** *(d'une personne ▸ de froid)* shiver; *(▸ de fièvre)* shivering *(UNCOUNT)*; *(▸ de peur)* tremor, shudder; **être pris de tremblements** to start to shake; **son corps était secoué** *ou* **parcouru de tremblements** his/her whole body was shaking *or* trembling
2 *(de la main)* shaking *(UNCOUNT)*, trembling *(UNCOUNT)*, tremor; *(de la voix)* trembling *(UNCOUNT)*, quavering *(UNCOUNT)*, tremor; *(des paupières)* twitch, twitching *(UNCOUNT)*; *(des lèvres)* trembling, tremble; **avoir des tremblements** to shake; **avec un t. dans la voix** with a tremor in his/her voice, in a tremulous voice; *Fam* **et tout le t.** the (full) works, *Br* the full monty; *Fam* **l'église, la robe blanche et tout le t.** the church, the white dress, the whole works
3 *(du feuillage)* trembling *(UNCOUNT)*, fluttering *(UNCOUNT)*; *(d'une lueur, d'une flamme)* trembling *(UNCOUNT)*, flickering *(UNCOUNT)*
4 *(d'un édifice)* trembling *(UNCOUNT)*, shaking *(UNCOUNT)*; *(d'une cloison, de vitres)* shaking *(UNCOUNT)*, rattling *(UNCOUNT)*
• **tremblement de terre** NM earthquake

trembler [3] [trɑ̃ble] VI **1** *(personne)* **t. de peur** to tremble *or* to shake with fear; **t. de froid** to shiver *or* to tremble with cold; **t. de rage** to tremble *or* to quiver with anger; **t. de tout son corps** *ou* **de tous ses membres** to be shaking *or* to be trembling all over, to be all of a tremble; **t. comme une feuille** to be shaking like a leaf
2 *(main, jambes)* to shake, to tremble; *(voix)* to tremble, to shake, to quaver; *(menton, lèvres)* to tremble, to quiver; *(paupière)* to twitch; **j'ai la main/voix qui tremble** my hand/voice is trembling
3 *(feuillage)* to tremble, to quiver, to flutte *(flamme, lueur)* to flicker; *(gelée)* to wobble
4 *(édifice, mur)* to shake; *(cloison, vitre)* to shake to rattle; *(terre)* to quake, to shake; **faire t. les vitres** to make the windows shake *or* rattle; **les trains font t. la maison** the trains are shaking th house; **la terre a tremblé** there's been an earth quake *or* an earth tremor; **il sentait le sol t. sous ses pas** he felt the ground tremble *or* shake be neath him
5 *(avoir peur)* to tremble (with fear); **t. devant qn/qch** to stand in fear of sb/sth, to be terrifie of sb/sth; **t. pour (la vie de) qn** to fear for sb *or* sb life; **t. à la pensée de/que** *(de crainte)* to tremble a the thought of/that; *(d'horreur)* to shiver at th thought of/that; **je tremble de le rencontrer** tremble *or* I am terrified at the thought of mee ing him; **il tremblait d'apprendre la vérité** h feared the truth, he was afraid to learn the trut

trembleur [trɑ̃blœr] NM *Élec* trembler; *Tél* buzz er

tremblotant, -e [trɑ̃blɔtɑ̃, -ɑ̃t] ADJ *(personne* trembling (slightly); *(corps)* quivering, shive ing; *(main)* shaking, trembling; *(voix)* trem lous, quavering, shaking; *(lueur)* flickering trembling

tremblote [trɑ̃blɔt] NF *Fam* **avoir la t.** *(de peur)* t have the jitters; *(de froid, à cause de la fièvre)* t have the shivers; *(à cause d'une maladie)* to hav the shakes; *(vieillard)* to be shaky

tremblotement [trɑ̃blɔtmɑ̃] NM **1** *(d'une pe sonne ▸ gén)* shaking *(UNCOUNT)*; *(▸ de fièvr de froid)* shivering *(UNCOUNT)*; *(▸ de peur)* shi ering *(UNCOUNT)*, shuddering *(UNCOUNT* **être pris de tremblotements** to start to shake *(d'une main)* (faint) shaking *or* trembling; *(d'un voix)* slight tremor, slight quavering *(UN COUNT)*; *(d'une lueur)* flickering *(UNCOUNT)*

trembloter [3] [trɑ̃blɔte] VI *(gén)* to trembl *(vieillard, main)* to shake; *(voix)* to quave *(lueur)* to flicker; *(de froid)* to shiver; *(de peur)* t shudder (with fear); **j'ai les mains qui trembloten** my hands are shaky

trémie [tremi] NF **1** *(pour les raisins, les bette ves)* hopper; *(pour le blé)* tank; *(pour les volaille* feed hopper
2 *Constr (pour béton)* trémie; **t. d'ascenseur** *Br* li *or Am* elevator shaft; **t. de cheminée** hearth ca ity; **t. d'escalier** stairwell
3 *(de sel)* pyramid salt formation
4 *(accès à un tunnel)* mouth, well, entrance

trémière [tremjer] *voir* **rose**

trémolo [tremolo] NM **1** *Mus* tremolo **2** *(d'un o gue)* tremolo stop **3** *Fig (de la voix)* **avec des tr molos dans la voix** with a tremor in his/her voic

trémoussement [tremusmɑ̃] NM jigging u and down *(UNCOUNT)*; *(en se dandinant)* wi gling *(UNCOUNT)*

trémousser [3] [tremuse] **se trémousser** VPR *(e fant)* to jig up and down; *(pour séduire)* to wiggl **elle marchait en se trémoussant** she wiggled h hips as she walked; **arrête de te t. sur ta chai** stop wriggling round *or* fidgeting on your cha

trempage [trɑ̃paʒ] NM **1** *(de l'orge, de vêtement* soaking **2** *Typ* damping, wetting

trempe [trɑ̃p] NF **1** *(caractère)* **une femme de sa** a woman with such moral fibre; **son frère e d'une autre t.** his/her brother is cast in a diffe ent mould
2 *Fam (correction)* thrashing, pasting; **recevo une bonne t.** to get a good thrashing *or* pastin **si tu continues, je vais te filer une t.** if you do stop, you'll get a thrashing
3 *(immersion)* soaking, steeping; **mettre qch e t.** to put sth in to soak
4 *Métal (traitement)* quenching; *(résultat)* te per; **de bonne t.** well-tempered; **acier/atelier de** hardening steel/plant; **bain de t.** hardening quenching bath
ADJ *Can, Suisse & (régional en France) (personn vêtements)* soaked, drenched; *(chaussures, ja din)* waterlogged; **t. de sueur** soaked with swea

trempé, -e [trɑ̃pe] ADJ **1** *(personne, vêtement* soaked, drenched; *(chaussures, jardin)* wate logged; **t. de sueur** soaked with sweat; **t. de la mes** *(mouchoir)* tear-stained; **être tout t.** to b soaked *or* wet through, to be soaking wet; *Fa*

tre t. jusqu'aux os *ou* comme une soupe to be oaked to the skin, to be wet through
2 *(vin, lait)* watered-down
3 *(énergique)* **avoir le caractère bien t.** to be resilient
4 *Métal* hardened, tempered
5 *(verre)* toughened

'emper [3] [trɑ̃pe] **VT 1** *(plonger ▸ chiffon)* to dip, o soak; *(▸ sucre, tartine, pain)* to dip, to dunk; *(▸ 'nge, vaisselle)* to soak; *(▸ écrevisses, moules, escargots)* to plunge; **t. sa plume dans l'encrier** to dip one's pen in the ink; **t. les mains dans l'eau** to dabble one's hands in the water; **je n'ai fait que t. mes lèvres dans le champagne** I just had a taste *or* took a sip of the champagne; **je n'ai fait que t. mes pieds dans l'eau** I only dipped my feet in the water; *Typ* **t. le papier** to wet *or* damp the paper
2 *Vieilli* **t. la soupe** *(la verser)* to pour soup over bread
3 *(mouiller)* **j'ai trempé ma chemise tellement je transpirais** I sweated so much (that) my shirt got soaked; **tu as trempé la nappe!** you've made the tablecloth (all) wet!; **se faire t. (par la pluie)** to get soaked
4 *Métal* to quench; *(fonte de fer)* to chill; **t. par induction** to induction harden
5 *Littéraire (affermir ▸ personnalité, caractère)* to steel, to toughen, to harden; **cela va lui t. le caractère** this'll toughen him/her up
VI *(vêtement, vaisselle, lentilles)* to soak; **mettre le linge à t.** to put the washing to soak; **faire t. les haricots** to soak beans, to leave beans to soak; **les clichés trempent dans un bain spécial** the photographs (are left to) soak in a special solution; **attention, tes manches trempent dans la soupe** careful, you've got your sleeves in the soup

tremper dans VT IND *Fam (être impliqué dans)* to be mixed up in; **elle a trempé dans une affaire sordide** she was involved in some sordid business

VPR se tremper 1 *(se baigner)* to have a quick dip **2** *(baigner)* to soak; **elle s'est trempé les pieds dans une bassine d'eau** she soaked her feet in a bowl of water **3** *(mouiller)* **il s'est trempé les pieds en marchant dans l'eau** he stepped into a puddle and got his feet wet

'empette [trɑ̃pɛt] **NF** *Fam* **faire t.** *(se baigner)* to have a (quick) dip; **les enfants font t. dans le bassin** the children are splashing about in the pool

'emplin [trɑ̃plɛ̃] **NM 1** *Sport (de gymnastique)* springboard; *(de plongeon)* diving board, springboard; *(de ski nautique, de planche à roulettes)* ramp; **t. de ski** ski jump; *(de ski nautique)* ski ramp **2** *Fig (impulsion initiale)* springboard, stepping stone, launching pad; **servir de t. à qn** to be a springboard for sb; **cet opéra a servi de t. à sa carrière** the opera was a springboard for his/her career *or* launched his/her career

'émulation [tremylasjɔ̃] **NF** *Méd* tremor

'ench-coat [trɛnʃkot] *(pl* **trench-coats**), **trench** [trɛnʃ] *(pl* **trenchs**) **NM** trench coat

'entaine [trɑ̃tɛn] **NF 1** *(quantité)* **une t.** around *or* about thirty, thirty or so; **une t. de voitures** around *or* about thirty cars; **elle a une t. d'années** she's around *or* about thirty (years old) **2** *(âge)* **avoir la t.** to be around *or* about thirty; **quand on arrive à** *ou* **atteint la t.** when you hit thirty

'ente [trɑ̃t] **ADJ 1** *(gén)* thirty **2** *(dans des séries)* thirtieth; **page/numéro t.** page/number thirty **3** *(au tennis)* **t. à** thirty all
PRON thirty
NM INV 1 *(gén)* thirty **2** *(numéro d'ordre)* number thirty **3** *(chiffre écrit)* thirty; *voir aussi* **cinquante**

LES TRENTE-CINQ HEURES

In an attempt to create new jobs and reduce the relatively high unemployment rate in France, the socialist government of Prime Minister Lionel Jospin (1997–2002) decided to phase in a reduction of the average working week from 39 to 35 hours (see entry "RTT"). There was a great deal of flexibility in the implementation of the law and many exemptions were allowed, especially for small and medium-sized companies. In many cases, the shift to the 35-hour week was negotiated at company level between management and trade unions. Initially, employers were very hostile to the idea but the fact that by way of compensation their national insurance contributions were significantly reduced brought most of them round. Overall, results have been mixed, with not as many new jobs being created as first expected. Some people feel the law has made their situation worse, as they have to do the same amount of work in fewer hours, while many others enjoy the extra leisure time. The centre-right government elected in 2002 has been moving towards introducing even more flexibility to the law.

trente-et-un [trɑ̃teœ̃] **ADJ** thirty-one
NM INV thirty-one; *Fam* **être sur son t.** to be dressed up to the nines; **se mettre sur son t.** to get all dressed up

trentenaire [trɑ̃tnɛr] **ADJ 1** *(qui dure trente ans)* thirty-year *(avant n)* **2** *(personne)* in his/her thirties, thirtysomething; *(bâtiment)* over thirty years old
NMF person in his/her thirties, thirtysomething

trente-six [trɑ̃tsis] **ADJ 1** *(gén)* thirty-six **2** *Fam (pour exprimer la multitude)* umpteen, dozens of; **il y en a pas t.** there aren't that many of them; **des raisons, je pourrais t'en citer t.** I could give you umpteen reasons; **il y a pas t. solutions** there's no getting away from it, there are no two ways about it; **j'ai t. mille choses à faire** I've a hundred and one things to do; **voir t. chandelles** to see stars
NM INV thirty-six; *Fam* **tous les t. du mois** once in a blue moon

trente-sixième [trɑ̃tsizjɛm] *(pl* **trente-sixièmes**) **ADJ 1** *(gén)* thirty-sixth **2** *Fam (locution)* **être au t. dessous** to be in a tight spot

trentième [trɑ̃tjɛm] **ADJ** thirtieth
NMF 1 *(personne)* thirtieth **2** *(objet)* thirtieth (one)
NM 1 *(partie)* thirtieth **2** *(étage) Br* thirtieth floor, *Am* thirty-first floor; *voir aussi* **cinquième**

trépan [trepɑ̃] **NM 1** *Méd* trephine **2** *Pétr & Tech* trepan

trépanation [trepanasjɔ̃] **NF** *Méd & Tech* trephination, trepanning

trépaner [3] [trepane] **VT** *Méd & Tech* to trephine, to trepan

trépas [trepa] **NM** *Littéraire* **le t.** death

trépassé, -e [trepase] **NM,F 1** *Littéraire* deceased; **les trépassés** the departed, *Sout* the dead **2** *Rel* **le jour** *ou* **la fête des Trépassés** All Souls' Day

trépasser [3] [trepase] **VI** *Littéraire* to depart this life, *Euph* to pass away

Il faut noter que le verbe anglais **to trespass** est un faux ami. Il ne signifie jamais **mourir.**

trépidant, -e [trepidɑ̃, -ɑ̃t] **ADJ 1** *(animé ▸ époque)* frantic, hectic; *(▸ vie)* hectic; *(▸ danse, rythme)* wild, frenzied **2** *(véhicule)* vibrating, throbbing

trépidation [trepidasjɔ̃] **NF 1** *(d'un moteur)* vibration **2** *Méd* tremor **3** *(agitation)* bustle, whirl

trépider [3] [trepide] **VI** *(moteur)* to vibrate, to throb; *(surface)* to vibrate

trépied [trepje] **NM 1** *(support ▸ d'appareil photo)* tripod; *(▸ pour cuisiner)* trivet **2** *(tabouret)* three-legged stool

trépignement [trepiɲmɑ̃] **NM** stamping (of feet)

trépigner [3] [trepiɲe] **VI** to stamp one's feet; **t. de colère** to stamp one's feet in anger; **t. d'impatience** to be hopping up and down with impatience; *Fig* **il trépignait à l'idée de partir** he was itching to start

trépointe [trepwɛ̃t] **NF** *(de chaussure)* welt

tréponème [trepɔnɛm] **NM** *Biol* treponema; **t. pâle** Treponema pallidum

très [trɛ] **ADV 1** *(avec un adjectif, un adverbe, une préposition)* very; **c'est t. bon** it's very good; **il est t. connu** he is very well known; **elle est t. estimée** she is greatly *or* highly respected; **elle est t. aimée** she is much *or* greatly liked; **il est t. snob** he's a real snob; **la soirée fut t. réussie** the evening was very successful *or* a huge success; **une entreprise t. compétitive** a highly competitive company; **un auteur t. lu** a very popular author; **t. peu utilisé** rarely used; **t. bien, je m'en vais** all right (then) *or* very well (then) *or* OK (then), I'm going; **vivre t. au-dessus de ses moyens** to live way beyond one's means; **il est t. enfant** he's such a child; **nous sommes tous t. famille** we're all very much into family life; **ce sont des gens t. comme il faut** they are very *or* highly respectable people; **faire des heures supplémentaires? t. peu pour moi!** me, do overtime? not likely!
2 *(dans des locutions verbales)* **avoir t. peur/faim** to be very frightened/hungry; **avoir t. envie de faire qch** to really feel like doing sth; **j'ai t. envie de sortir** I really feel like going out, I would really like to go out, I would love to go out; **j'ai t. envie de lui dire ses quatre vérités** I very much want to tell him/her a few home truths
3 *(employé seul, en réponse)* very; **fatigué? – oui, t.** tired? – yes, very; **il y a longtemps qu'il est parti? – non, pas t.** has he been gone long? – no, not very

trésor [trezɔr] **NM 1** *(objets précieux, argent)* treasure *(UNCOUNT)*; **trouver un t.** to find treasure; **t. de guerre** war chest
2 *Jur* treasure trove
3 *(chose précieuse)* treasure; **son grenier est plein de trésors** his/her attic is full of treasures *or* is a real treasure-house; **les trésors du Prado** the treasures of the Prado
4 *(d'une cathédrale)* (collection of) relics and ornaments; *(lieu)* treasure-house, treasury
5 *Archéol (d'un sanctuaire)* treasure, treasury
6 *(gén pl) (grande quantité)* **ce livre est un t. d'informations** this book is a treasure-trove *or* a mine of information, this book contains a wealth of information; **des trésors de bienfaits/de patience** a wealth of good/patience
7 *Fam (terme d'affection)* **mon (petit) t.** my treasure *or* darling *or* pet; **tu es un t.** you're a treasure *or* a darling *or* an angel
8 *Fin* **le T. (public)** *(service) Br* ≃ the Treasury, *Am* ≃ the Treasury Department; *(moyens financiers)* state finances
9 *Hist* exchequer

trésorerie [trezɔrri] **NF 1** *(argent ▸ gén)* treasury, finances; *(▸ d'une entreprise)* liquid assets; *(▸ d'une personne)* budget; **ses problèmes de t.** his/her cash (flow) problems
2 *(gestion)* accounts
3 *(bureaux ▸ gouvernementaux)* public revenue office; *(▸ privés)* accounts department; *Fin* **T. générale** paymaster's office
4 *(fonction ▸ gén)* treasurership; *(▸ d'un trésorier-payeur)* paymastership

trésorier, -ère [trezɔrje, -ɛr] **NM,F 1** *Admin* treasurer **2** *Mil* paymaster

tressage [trɛsaʒ] **NM** *(de rotin)* weaving; *(de cheveux)* plaiting, braiding

tressaillement [tresajmɑ̃] **NM** *(de joie)* thrill; *(de plaisir)* quiver; *(de peur)* shudder, quiver, quivering *(UNCOUNT)*; *(de surprise)* start, jump; *(de douleur)* wince

tressaillir [47] [tresajir] **VI 1** *(personne, animal ▸ de surprise, de peur)* to (give a) start; *(▸ de douleur)* to flinch, to wince; *(▸ de plaisir)* to quiver; **t. de joie** to thrill **2** *Littéraire (feuillage)* **un souffle soudain vint faire t. les peupliers** a sudden breeze set the leaves of the poplars rustling

tressautement [tresotmɑ̃] **NM 1** *(sursaut)* start, jump **2** *(secousse)* jolting *(UNCOUNT)*; **les tressautements du vieux tramway** the jolting *or Br* juddering of the old tram

tressauter [3] [tresote] **VI 1** *(sursauter)* to jump, to start **2** *(être cahoté ▸ passager)* to be tossed about; **les cahots du chemin faisaient t. les voyageurs** the passengers were thrown *or* jolted around by the bumps in the road

tresse [trɛs] **NF 1** *(de cheveux, de fils)* plait, *esp Am* braid; **se faire des tresses** to plait *or esp Am* braid one's hair; **porter des tresses** to have (one's hair in) plaits *or esp Am* braids **2** *Archit* strapwork *(UNCOUNT)* **3** *Élec* braid, braiding *(UNCOUNT)*; **fil conducteur sous t.** braided conductor wire

tresser [4] [trese] **VT** *(cheveux, rubans, fils)* to plait, to braid; *(paille, osier)* to plait; *(corbeille)* to weave; *(câble)* to twist; *(guirlande)* to wreathe;

Fig **t. des couronnes à qn** to praise sb to the skies; **je ne veux pas lui t. des couronnes, mais…** I don't want to praise him/her unduly, but…

tréteau, -x [treto] NM trestle; **table à tréteaux** trestle table; *Vieilli Fig* **monter sur les tréteaux** to become an actor, to tread the boards

treuil [trœj] NM winch, windlass; *(d'ascenseur)* winding gear *(UNCOUNT)*; **t. à chaîne** chain hoist

treuillage [trœjaʒ] NM winching

treuiller [5] [trœje] VT to winch; **t. une charge** *(vers le haut)* to winch up a load; *(vers le bas)* to winch down a load

trêve [trɛv] NF **1** *Mil* truce; *Hist* **la t. de Dieu** the Truce of God **2** *Fig (repos)* rest, break; **mes rhumatismes ne me laissent aucune t.** my rheumatism gives me no respite; **elle s'est accordée une t. dans la rédaction de sa thèse** she took a break from writing her thesis; **faire t. à** to suspend; **la t. des confiseurs** = the lull in political activities between Christmas and the New Year in France; **c'est la t. des confiseurs** it's the seasonal truce in political activity

• **sans trêve** ADV unceasingly, without respite, never-endingly

• **trêve de** ADJ enough; **t. de bavardages!** we must stop chatting!, enough of this chatting!; **allez, t. de plaisanteries, où est la clef?** come on, stop messing about, where's the key?

Trèves [trɛv] NM Trier

tri [tri] NM **1** *(de fiches)* sorting out, sorting, classifying; *(de renseignements)* sorting out, selecting; *(de candidats)* selection; *(de propositions)* screening; **faire le t. dans qch** to sort sth out; **faire du t. dans ses vêtements/papiers** to sort through *or* go through one's clothes/papers; **il faut faire le t. dans ce qu'il dit** you have to sift out the truth in what he says; **il va falloir faire le t.** we'll have to sort through them **2** *(de lettres)* sorting; **t. postal** mail sorting; **bureau de t.** *(de la Poste)* sorting office; **le (service du) t.** *(d'une entreprise)* the mail room **3** *Ordinat* sort; **effectuer un t.** to do a sort; **t. alphabétique** alphabetic sort, alpha sort; **t. en ordre croissant/décroissant** ascending/reverse *or* descending sort

triacide [triasid] NM *Chim* triacid

triade [trijad] NF *(groupe de trois)* triad

triage [trijaʒ] NM **1** *(pour répartir)* sorting (out); **t. à la main** hand sorting; **nous devons faire un t. à la main** we have to sort them by hand
2 *(pour choisir)* grading, selecting, sifting
3 *Mines* picking *(UNCOUNT)*
4 *(en papeterie)* assorting, sorting
5 *Rail* marshalling *(UNCOUNT)*

trial, -als [trijal] NM (motorbike) trial *or* trials
NF trial motorbike

triangle [trijɑ̃gl] NM **1** *Géom* triangle; **triangles semblables** similar triangles
2 *Géog* **le t. des Bermudes** the Bermuda Triangle; **le T. d'or** the Golden Triangle
3 *Mus* triangle
4 *Aut* **t. de présignalisation** hazard warning triangle; **t. de sécurité** warning triangle
• **en triangle** ADV in a triangle; **le jardin se termine en t.** the garden ends in a triangle

triangulaire [trijɑ̃gylɛr] ADJ **1** *(gén) & Géom* triangular; *(tissu, salle)* triangular, triangular-shaped **2** *(à trois éléments)* triangular; **élection t.** three-cornered election; *Hist* **commerce t.** triangular trade
NF *Pol* three-cornered contest *or* fight

triangulation [trijɑ̃gylasjɔ̃] NF triangulation, triangulating

trianguler [3] [trijɑ̃gyle] VT *(en arpentage)* to triangulate

trias [trijas] NM *Géol* **le t.** the Triassic *or* Trias

triasique [trijazik] ADJ *Géol* Triassic

triathlon [trijatlɔ̃] NM triathlon

triathlonien, -enne [trijatlɔnjɛ̃, -ɛn] NM,F triathlete

triatomique [triatɔmik] ADJ *Chim* triatomic

tribal, -e, -aux *ou* **-als, -ales** [tribal, -o] ADJ tribal

tribalisme [tribalism] NM tribalism

tri-bande [tribɑ̃d] ADJ *Tél* tri-band

triboélectricité [tribɔelɛktrisite] NF *Phys* triboelectricity

tribord [tribɔr] NM *Naut* starboard; **à t.** (to) starboard, on the starboard side

tribu [triby] NF **1** *Antiq & (en anthropologie)* tribe **2** *Fam (groupe nombreux)* **toute la t.** *(famille)* the entire clan; *(amis)* the (whole) crowd *or* gang

tribulations [tribylasjɔ̃] NFPL (trials and) tribulations; **après toutes ces t.** after all these trials and tribulations; **tu n'es pas au bout de tes t.!** you're not out of the woods yet!

tribun [tribœ̃] NM **1** *(orateur)* eloquent (public) speaker **2** *Antiq* tribune
• **de tribun** ADJ *(éloquence)* spellbinding; **il a un talent de t.** he's very good at public speaking

tribunal, -aux [tribynal, -o] NM **1** *Jur (édifice)* court, courthouse; *(magistrats)* court, bench; **en plein t.** in open court; **porter une affaire devant le t.** *ou* **les tribunaux** to take a matter to court *or* before the Courts; **comparaître devant le t.** to appear before the Court; **traîner qn devant les tribunaux** to take sb to court; **t. administratif** = court which deals with internal French civil service matters; **t. de commerce** *(pour litiges)* commercial court; *(pour liquidations)* bankruptcy court; **T. des conflits** = tribunal which settles jurisdictional disputes between the civil and administrative courts; **t. correctionnel** criminal court; **t. de droit commun** court of general jurisdiction; **t. pour enfants** juvenile court; **t. d'exception** special court *(with limited jurisdiction)*; **t. de grande instance** = court of first instance in civil and criminal matters; **t. d'instance** = lowest-level court in French legal system, having limited jurisdiction; **t. de police** = name given to a "tribunal d'instance" when a criminal case is being heard; *UE* **T. de première instance** European Court of First Instance; **t. révolutionnaire** revolutionary tribunal **2** *Mil* **t. militaire** court martial; **traduire qn devant le t. militaire** to court-martial sb; **passer devant le t. militaire** to be court-martialled **3** *Fig Littéraire* tribunal; **le t. de l'histoire jugera** History will judge

tribune [tribyn] NF **1** *(places ▸ assises)* grandstand, stand; *(▸ debout dans un stade de football) Br* terraces, *Am* bleachers; **t. d'honneur** VIP stand; **t. de la presse** press gallery; **t. du public** public gallery
2 *(estrade)* rostrum, platform, *Sout* tribune; **monter à la t.** *(gén)* to go to the rostrum; *(au Parlement)* to address the House
3 *(lieu de discussions)* forum; **notre émission offre une t. aux écologistes** our programme provides a platform for the Green Party; **à la t. de ce soir, le racisme** racism is the subject of our discussion tonight
4 *Journ* **t. libre** *(colonne)* opinion column; *(page)* opinions page; **s'exprimer dans les tribunes d'une émission de radio** to put one's point of view in an open radio programme
5 *Archit* gallery, tribune
6 *Mus* **t. d'orgues** organ loft

tribut [triby] NM **1** *Littéraire* tribute; **payer t. à la nature** to pay one's debt to nature; **le pays a payé un lourd t. à la guerre** the war cost the country dearly; **la population a payé un lourd t. à l'épidémie** the epidemic took a heavy toll of the population **2** *Hist* tribute

tributaire [tribytɛr] ADJ **1** *(dépendant)* **t. de** reliant *or* dependent on; **comme elle ne peut pas sortir de chez elle, elle est t. de ses voisins** she relies on her neighbours as she's housebound **2** *Géog* **être t. de** to be a tributary of, to flow into **3** *Hist* tributary
NM *Géog* tributary

tric [trik] = **trick**

tricard, -e [trikar, -ard] *Fam Arg crime* ADJ = prohibited from entering a certain area
NM,F = ex-convict prohibited from entering a certain area

tricentenaire [trisɑ̃tnɛr] ADJ three-hundred-year-old *(avant n)*
NM tercentenary

tricéphale [trisefal] ADJ three-headed

triceps [trisɛps] NM *Anat* triceps (muscle)

triche [triʃ] NF *Fam* **c'est le roi de la t.** he's a total cheat; **c'est de la t.!** that's cheating!

tricher [3] [triʃe] VI to cheat; **il triche** he's cheating, he's not playing by the rules; **t. aux cartes/à un examen** to cheat at cards/in an exam; **t. sur** to cheat on; **t. sur le poids** to give short weight; **t. sur les prix** to overcharge; **il triche sur son âge** he lies about his age; **on ne peut pas t. avec la maladie** you can't fool around with illness; **je n'aime pas t. avec les gens** I don't like being dishonest with people

tricherie [triʃri] NF cheating *(UNCOUNT)*; **j'en ai assez de toutes tes tricheries!** I've had enough of your cheating!

tricheur, -euse [triʃœr, -øz] NM,F *(au jeu, aux examens, en amour)* cheat; *(en affaires)* trickster, con man

trichloréthylène [triklɔretilɛn] NM *Chim* trichlorethylene, trichloroethylene

trichrome [trikrom] ADJ three-colour, *Spéc* trichromatic

trichromie [trikromi] NF **1** *Typ* three-colour printing, *Spéc* trichromatism **2** *Tex* trichrome printing **3** *TV* three-colour process

trick [trik] NM *(au bridge)* odd trick

tricolore [trikɔlɔr] ADJ **1** *(à trois couleurs)* three-coloured **2** *(aux couleurs françaises)* red, white and blue **3** *(français)* French; **l'équipe t.** the French team
NMF French player; **les tricolores** the French (team)

tricorne [trikɔrn] NM tricorn, cocked hat

tricorps [trikɔr] *Aut* ADJ notchback *(avant n)*
NM notchback vehicle

tricot [triko] NM **1** *(technique)* knitting *(UNCOUNT)*; **apprendre le t.** to learn to knit; **faire du t.** to knit, to do some knitting; **commencer/finir un t.** to cast on/off; **t. plat** flat knitting; **t. rond** circular knitting
2 *(étoffe)* knitted *or* worsted fabric
3 *(ouvrage)* knitting *(UNCOUNT)*; *Com* knitwear *(UNCOUNT)*; **j'ai commencé un t.** I've started to knit something; **où ai-je mis mon t.?** where did I put my knitting?
4 *(vêtement ▸ gén)* knitted garment; *(▸ pull)* pullover, sweater; *(▸ gilet)* cardigan; **t. de corps** *ou* **de peau** *Br* vest, *Am* undershirt
• **en tricot** ADJ *(cravate, bonnet)* knitted

tricotage [trikɔtaʒ] NM knitting

tricoter [3] [trikɔte] VT **1** *(laine, maille)* to knit *(vêtement)* to knit (up); **je lui tricote des gants** I'm knitting him/her some gloves; **tricoté (à la) main** hand-knitted **2** *Fig (mettre en forme, élaborer)* to work out; **l'auteur a tricoté une intrigue très intéressante** the author has woven a very interesting plot
VI **1** *Tex* to knit; **apprendre à t.** to learn to knit; **t. à la machine/main** to machine-/hand-knit **2** *Fam (s'activer ▸ coureur)* to scramble; *(▸ danseur, cheval)* to prance; *(▸ cycliste)* to pedal hard; **t. des jambes** *ou* **des gambettes** *(marcher vite)* to leg it, to belt along; *(pédaler)* to pedal like mad to go *Br* like the clappers *or Am* like sixty
• **à tricoter** ADJ *(aiguille, laine, machine)* knitting *(avant n)*

tricoteur, -euse [trikɔtœr, -øz] NM,F knitter
NM knitting worker
• **tricoteuse** NF **1** *(machine à tricoter)* knitting machine **2** *(table à ouvrage)* small worktable

trictrac [triktrak] NM *(jeu)* tric-trac, trick-track *(game similar to backgammon)*; *(partie)* game of tric-trac *or* trick-track; *(damier)* tric-trac or trick-track board

tricycle [trisikl] NM tricycle; **faire du t.** to go tricycling

trident [tridɑ̃] NM **1** *Pêche* three-pronged fish spear, trident **2** *Agr* three-pronged (pitch)fork **3** *Géom & Myth* trident

tridimensionnel, -elle [tridimɑ̃sjɔnɛl] ADJ *(gén) & Chim* three-dimensional

trièdre [triɛdr] *Géom* ADJ trihedral
NM trihedron, trihedral

triennal, -e, -aux, -ales [trijenal, -o] ADJ *(ayant lieu tous les trois ans)* three-yearly, *Sout* triennial **2** *(qui dure trois ans)* three-year *(avant n)*, three-year-long *(avant n)*, *Sout* triennial; **comité t.** committee appointed for three years **3** *A…* three-yearly

triennat [triena] **NM** three-year mandate *or* period of office

trier [10] [trije] **VT 1** *(sortir d'un lot ▸ fruits)* to pick (out); *(▸ photos, candidats)* to select; **triez les plus beaux fruits** pick out the best fruit; **triez les grains pour en extraire les cailloux** separate the grit from the grain; **ses amis sont triés sur le volet** his/her friends are hand-picked

2 *(répartir par catégories ▸ lettres)* to sort (out); *(▸ vêtements)* to sort *or* go through; *(▸ œufs)* to grade; *(▸ lentilles)* to pick over

3 *Rail (wagons)* to marshal

4 *Ordinat* to sort; **t. par ordre alphabétique** to sort in alphabetical order, to alphasort

VPR se trier *Ordinat* to sort

trière [trijɛr] **NF** *Antiq* trireme

trieur, -euse [trijœr, -øz] **NM,F** sorter, grader

NM 1 *Agr* sorting *or* grading machine **2** *Mines* picker (machine); **t. magnétique** magnetic separator

• **trieuse NF** *(machine)* sorter, sorting machine; *Ordinat* sorter; *(logiciel)* sort program

trieur-calibreur [trijœrkalibrœr] *(pl* **trieurs-calibreurs) NM** *Ind* grading machine

trieuse [trijøz] *voir* **trieur**

trifolié, -e [trifɔlje] **ADJ** *Bot* three-leafed, *Spéc* trifoliate, trifoliated

trifouiller [3] [trifuje] *Fam* **VT 1** *(fouiller)* to rummage through **2** *(toucher à)* to fiddle with, to tinker with

VI qu'est-ce que tu trifouilles? what are you up to?; **je ne sais pas ce que j'ai trifouillé mais ça ne marche plus** I don't know what I've done but it's not working

• **trifouiller dans VT IND 1** *(fouiller dans ▸ papiers, vêtements)* to rummage around in **2** *(tripoter ▸ moteur)* to tinker with

Trifouillis-les-Oies [trifujilezwa] **N** *Fam* = fictional name for the archetypal isolated village; **il vit à T.** he lives in the back of beyond

triglycéride [trigliserid] **NM** *Chim* triglyceride

trigo [trigo] **NF** *Fam Math (abrév* **trigonométrie)** trig, trigonometry▫

trigonométrie [trigɔnɔmetri] **NF** *Math* trigonometry

trigonométrique [trigɔnɔmetrik] **ADJ** *Math* trigonometric, trigonometrical

trijumeau, -x [triʒymo] *Anat* **ADJ M** trigeminal

NM trigeminal nerve

trilatéral, -e, -aux, -ales [trilateral, -o] **ADJ** *Géom* trilateral, three-sided

trilingue [trilɛ̃g] **ADJ** trilingual

NMF trilingual person

trille [trij] **NM** trill; **les trilles des oiseaux** the trilling of the birds; **faire des trilles** to trill

triller [3] [trije] **VT** to trill

VI to trill

trillion [triljɔ̃] **NM** *(10^18) Br* trillion, *Am* quintillion

trilobé, -e [trilɔbe] **ADJ 1** *Archit* trefoil *(avant n)* **2** *Bot* trilobate

trilobite [trilɔbit] *Zool* **NM** trilobite

• **trilobites NMPL les t.** the Trilobita

trilogie [trilɔʒi] **NF 1** *(groupe de trois)* triad **2** *Antiq & Littérature* trilogy; **le roman est une t.** the novel is a trilogy

trimaran [trimarɑ̃] **NM** *Naut* trimaran

trimarder [3] [trimarde] **VI** *Fam Vieilli* to be on the road

trimardeur, -euse [trimardœr, -øz] **NM,F** *Fam Vieilli* tramp, *Am* hobo

trimbalage [trɛ̃balaʒ], **trimbalement** [trɛ̃balmɑ̃] **NM** *Fam* lugging *or* dragging *or* carting around; **le t. du matériel a duré toute la nuit** it took all night to shift the equipment

trimbaler [3] [trɛ̃bale] *Fam* **VT 1** *(porter)* to hump, to lug around; **il trimbale sa famille partout où il va** he has his family in tow everywhere he goes **2** *(emmener)* to take▫; **elle trimbale son fils partout** she trails her son around *or* drags her son with her everywhere she goes; **le pauvre gosse s'est fait t. toute la journée de musée en musée** the poor kid was dragged about from museum to museum all day long **3** *(locution)* **qu'est-ce qu'il trimbale!** what a total halfwit!

VPR se trimbaler 1 *(aller et venir)* to trail around; **t'as pas honte de te t. en short?** I don't know how you can prance about in your shorts like that **2** *(se déplacer)* to go▫; **elle se trimbale toujours avec son frère** she drags that brother of hers around with her everywhere

trimballage [trɛ̃balaʒ] = **trimbalage**

trimballement [trɛ̃balmɑ̃] = **trimbalement**

trimballer [trɛ̃bale] = **trimbaler**

trimer [3] [trime] **VI** *Fam* to slave away; **il a trimé toute sa vie** he's spent his entire life slaving away *or* working his fingers to the bone; **faire t. qn** to keep sb hard at it, to keep sb's nose to the grindstone

trimestre [trimestr] **NM 1** *Scol & Univ* term; **premier t.** autumn term; **deuxième t.** spring term; **troisième t.** summer term **2** *(trois mois)* quarter; **payer tous les trimestres** *ou* **par t.** to pay on a quarterly basis **3** *(somme payée ou reçue)* quarterly instalment; *(salaire)* quarter's salary; *(loyer)* quarter's rent; *Scol (frais)* term fees; *(d'une assurance, une bourse)* quarterly instalment *or* payment

trimestriel, -elle [trimestrijel] **ADJ 1** *Scol (bulletin)* end-of-term *(avant n)*; *(réunion)* termly **2** *(réunion, magazine, loyer)* quarterly; **fonction trimestrielle** position lasting for three months

trimestriellement [trimestrijelmɑ̃] **ADV 1** *Scol & Univ* once a term, on a termly basis **2** *(payer, publier)* quarterly, on a quarterly basis, every three months

trimoteur [trimɔtœr] **ADJ M** three-engined

NM three-engined aircraft

tringle [trɛ̃gl] **NF 1** *(pour pendre)* rail; **t. à rideaux** curtain rail

2 *(pour tenir)* rod; **t. de tapis d'escalier** stair rod; **t. à rideau** curtain rod

3 *Tech* control rod

4 *(d'une crémone)* rod

5 *Archit* square moulding

tringler [3] [trɛ̃gle] **VT 1** *Tech (avec une ficelle crayeuse)* to mark with a line **2** *Vulg* to screw; **se faire t.** to get laid

trinitaire [trinitɛr] **ADJ** *Rel* Trinitarian

Trinité [trinite] **NF (l'île de) la T.** Trinidad

trinité [trinite] **NF** *Littéraire (trois éléments)* trinity

• **Trinité NF** *Rel* **la (sainte) T.** the (Holy) Trinity; **la (fête de la) T.** Trinity Sunday; **à la T.** on Trinity Sunday

Trinité-et-Tobago [triniteetɔbago] **NF** Trinidad and Tobago

trinitrotoluène [trinitrɔtɔlyɛn] **NM** *Chim* TNT, trinitrotoluene

trinôme [trinom] *Math* **ADJ** trinomial

NM trinomial

trinquer [3] [trɛ̃ke] **VI 1** *(choquer les verres)* to clink glasses; **t. à qn/qch** to drink (a toast) to sb/sth; **t. à la santé de qn** to drink a toast to sb; **trinquons!** let's drink to that! **2** *Fam (subir un dommage)* to be the one who suffers▫, to pay the price; **c'est ma voiture qui a trinqué** my car got the worst of it; **c'est lui qui va t.** he'll be the one who suffers; **les parents divorcent, les enfants trinquent** when the parents get a divorce, it's the children that suffer **3** *Fam (boire avec excès)* to booze; **on a trinqué ensemble** we had a few drinks together

trinquet [trɛ̃kɛ] **NM** *Naut* foremast

trinquette [trɛ̃kɛt] **NF** *Naut* forestaysail

trio [trijo] **NM 1** *(trois personnes)* trio, threesome; **notre t. n'en eut pas pour longtemps à résoudre le mystère** our three heroes solved the mystery in no time **2** *Mus* trio

triode [trijɔd] *Électron* **ADJ** triode *(avant n)*

NF triode

triolet [trijɔlɛ] **NM** *Mus & Littérature* triolet

triomphal, -e, -aux, -ales [trijɔ̃fal, -o] **ADJ** *(entrée, accueil)* triumphant; *(victoire, succès)* resounding; *(élection)* resoundingly successful; *(arc, procession)* triumphal; *(geste)* triumphant, of triumph

triomphalement [trijɔ̃falmɑ̃] **ADV** *(sourire, dire)* triumphantly; *(traiter, recevoir)* in triumph; **être accueilli t.** to be received in triumph *or* triumphantly; **descendre t. les Champs-Élysées** to parade down the Champs-Élysées in triumph

triomphalisme [trijɔ̃falism] **NM** triumphalism; **dans un moment de t.** in a moment of self-congratulation; **sans faire de t., il me semble que…** while I don't want to crow, it seems to me that…

triomphaliste [trijɔ̃falist] **ADJ** *(discours, vainqueur)* self-congratulatory, gloating; *(attitude)* overconfident

NMF crower

triomphant, -e [trijɔ̃fɑ̃, -ɑ̃t] **ADJ** triumphant; **un sourire t.** a triumphant smile; **d'un ton t.** triumphantly; **il est sorti t. de l'épreuve** he came out the winner; **il est arrivé t., avec la preuve qu'il avait raison** he came back cock-a-hoop with the proof that he was right

triomphateur, -trice [trijɔ̃fatœr, -tris] **ADJ** triumphant

NM,F winner, victor

NM *Antiq* conquering hero

triomphe [trijɔ̃f] **NM 1** *(d'une armée, d'un groupe)* triumph, victory; *(d'un artiste, d'une idée)* triumph; **remporter un t.** *(chose)* to be a resounding success; *(personne)* to be hugely successful; **la pièce a fait un t. à Paris** the play was a great *or* a triumphant success in Paris; **c'est le t. de la démocratie/de la bêtise** it's a triumph for democracy/of stupidity **2** *(jubilation)* triumph; **son t. fut de courte durée** his/her triumph was short-lived; **avoir le t. modeste** to be modest in victory; **pousser un cri de t.** to give a shout of triumph, to shout triumphantly **3** *(ovation)* **faire un t. à qn** to give sb a triumphant welcome; **ils m'ont fait un t. à la fin de mon discours** they gave me a standing ovation at the end of my speech; **porter qn en t.** to carry sb in triumph *or* shoulder-high

triompher [3] [trijɔ̃fe] **VI 1** *(armée)* to triumph; *(parti)* to win (decisively)

2 *(idée)* to triumph, to prevail; *(bêtise, corruption, racisme)* to be rife; **son point de vue a fini par t.** his/her point of view finally won the day *or* prevailed; **la vérité finit toujours par t.** truth will prevail; **faire t. une idée** to win recognition for an idea

3 *(artiste)* to be a great success; **elle triomphe dans le rôle d'Orlando** she's a great success in the role of Orlando; **il triomphe à l'Apollo tous les soirs** he's playing to packed houses at the Apollo every night

4 *(jubiler)* to gloat; **elle triomphe maintenant que tu es parti!** she's gloating now that you've gone!; **gardons-nous de t. trop vite** let's not celebrate too quickly

5 *Antiq* to triumph

• **triompher de VT IND** *(ennemi, rival)* to triumph over, to beat; *(malaise, obstacle)* to triumph over, to overcome; **sa persévérance l'a fait t. de toutes ces épreuves** his/her perseverance helped him/her through all these ordeals

trioxyde [triɔksid] **NM** *Chim* trioxide

trip [trip] **NM 1** *Fam Arg drogue* trip; **être en plein t.** to be on a trip, to be tripping; **faire un t.** to trip; **faire un mauvais t.** to have a bad trip; *Fig* to have a rough time **2** *Fam (centre d'intérêt)* kick **3** *Fam (locutions)* **il est en plein t. écolo en ce moment** he's on some environmental kick at the moment; **c'est vraiment pas mon t., ce genre de truc** I'm not really into that kind of thing, it's not my scene, that kind of thing

tripaille [tripaj] **NF** *Fam* innards, guts

triparti, -e [triparti] **ADJ** *(traité)* tripartite; *(négociations)* three-way; *(alliance électorale)* three-party *(avant n)*

tripartisme [tripartism] **NM** three-party government

tripartite [tripartit] **ADJ** *(traité)* tripartite; *(négociations)* three-way; *(alliance électorale)* three-party *(avant n)*

tripatouillage [tripatujaʒ] **NM** *Fam* **1** *(malaxage)* messing around **2** *(truquage ▸ d'un document)* tampering (**de** with); *(▸ des chiffres, des résultats)* fixing (**de** of); **t. des comptes** cooking the books; **il y a eu t. des résultats** the results were a fix

tripatouiller [3] [tripatuje] *Fam* **VT 1** *(truquer ▸ document)* to tamper with; *(▸ chiffres, résultats)* to fix; **t. les comptes** to cook the books; **t. les sta-**

tistiques to massage the figures **2** *(modifier ▸ textes)* to alter□ **3** *(toucher ▸ personne)* to paw, to feel up; *(▸ cheveux)* to play *or* fiddle with; *(▸ bouton)* to pick at; *(▸ nourriture)* to play with

VI les enfants adorent t. dans le sable children love messing around in the sand

tripatouilleur, -euse [tripatujœr, -øz] **NM,F** *Fam* **c'est un t.** *(mauvais bricoleur)* he's a botcher; *(mauvais écrivain)* he's a hack, he just cobbles other people's ideas together

triper [3] [tripe] **VI** *Fam* to trip *(after taking drugs)*

triperie [tripri] **NF 1** *(boutique)* tripe and offal shop **2** *(activité)* tripe (and offal) trade **3** *(abats)* offal *(UNCOUNT)*

tripes [trip] **NFPL 1** *Culin* **des t.** tripe; **t. à la mode de Caen** tripe à la mode de Caen *(tripe braised with onions, carrots and cider)* **2** *Fam (entrailles)* guts, insides **3** *Fam Fig* **une histoire qui vous prend aux t.** a story that gets you in the guts *or* right there; **la peur m'a pris aux t.** I was petrified with fear; **ce film m'a remué les t.** that movie really got me going; **jouer avec ses t.** to give it one's all; **dans ce film, elle joue vraiment avec ses t.** she gives a powerful performance in this movie□; **parler avec ses t.** to speak from the heart□ *Fam* **rendre tripes et boyaux** to be as sick as a dog

tripette [tripɛt] **NF** *Fam* **ça ne vaut pas t.** it's a load of tripe *or* dross, *Am* it's not worth diddly

triphasé, -e [trifaze] *Élec* **ADJ** three-phase

NM three-phase current; **installation en t.** three-phase wiring

triphtongue [triftɔ̃g] **NF** *Ling* triphthong

tripier, -ère [tripje, -ɛr] **NM,F** tripe (and offal) butcher

triplace [triplas] **ADJ** three-seater *(avant n)*

NM *Aviat* three-seater (plane)

triplan [triplɑ̃] **NM** *Aviat* triplane

triple [tripl] **ADJ 1** *(à trois éléments)* triple; **une t. semelle** a three-layer sole; **un t. menton** a triple chin; **un t. rang de perles** three rows *or* a triple row of pearls; **en t. exemplaire** in triplicate; **t. saut** triple jump; **t. saut périlleux** triple somersault; *Hist* **la T. Alliance** the Triple Alliance; *Hist* **la T. Entente** the Triple Entente

2 *(trois fois plus grand)* treble, triple; **ton jardin est t. du mien** your garden is treble the size of mine; **une t. dose** three times the usual amount

3 *Fam (en intensif)* **un t. sot** a prize idiot; **t. imbécile!** you stupid idiot!; **t. buse!** you stupid nit!

4 *Mus* **t. croche** *Br* demi-semiquaver, *Am* thirty-second note

NM le t. (de) *(quantité, prix)* three times as much (as); *(nombre)* three times as many (as); **neuf est le t. de trois** nine is three times three; **il fait le t. de travail** he does three times as much work; **le t. de poids/longueur** three times as heavy/long; **ça a pris le t. de temps** it took three times as long; **on a payé le t.** we paid three times that amount

• en triple ADV *(copier, signer)* in triplicate

triplé, -e [triple] **NM,F** triplet; **des triplées** (girl) triplets

NM 1 *(aux courses)* treble, = bet on the first three horses in a race; **gagner le t.** to win a treble **2** *(d'un athlète)* triple win; *(d'une équipe)* hat trick; **faire** *ou* **réussir le t.** *(athlète)* to come first in three events; *(footballeur)* to score a hat trick

triplement[1] [tripləmɑ̃] **ADV** in three ways, on three counts; **t. déçu** disappointed on three counts

triplement[2] [tripləmɑ̃] **NM** trebling, tripling; **le t. de mes ressources** the threefold increase in *or* the trebling of my income

tripler [3] [triple] **VT 1** *(dépenses, dose)* to treble, to triple **2** *Scol* **t. une classe** to repeat a *Br* year *or Am* class for a second time, to do a *Br* year *or Am* class for a third time

VI to treble, to triple; **la population a triplé** the population has tripled *or* has increased threefold

triplette [triplɛt] **NF 1** *(d'hommes)* three-man team; *(de femmes)* three-woman team; *(mixte)* three-person team **2** *(aux boules)* threesome

Triplex® [triplɛks] **NM** Triplex® (glass)

tripode [tripɔd] **ADJ 1** *Naut* tripod *(avant n)* **2** *(meuble)* three-legged, *Spéc* tripod *(avant n)*

NM automatic ticket barrier *(in Paris métro)*

Tripoli [tripɔli] **NM** Tripoli

triporteur [tripɔrtœr] **NM** delivery tricycle

tripot [tripo] **NM** *Péj* **1** *(lieu mal famé)* dive, sleazy joint **2** *(maison de jeu)* gambling den

tripotage [tripɔtaʒ] **NM** *Fam* **1** *(de fruits)* handling *(UNCOUNT)*; *(d'une breloque)* fiddling *(UNCOUNT)* **2** *(attouchements)* fondling *(UNCOUNT)*, groping *(UNCOUNT)* **3** *(pratique louche)* scam, *Br* fiddle; **le t. électoral est monnaie courante** election rigging is common; **tripotages** *(magouilles)* scheming *(UNCOUNT)*, dirty tricks, skulduggery *(UNCOUNT)*

tripotée [tripɔte] **NF** *Fam* **1** *(grand nombre)* **une t. de** tons of, loads of; **ils ont toute une t. d'enfants** they've got loads of kids **2** *(correction, défaite)* thrashing, hammering; **filer une t. à qn** to thrash *or* to hammer sb, to give sb a thrashing *or* a hammering; **prendre une t.** to get thrashed *or* hammered

tripoter [3] [tripɔte] **VT** *Fam* **1** *(toucher distraitement ▸ crayon, cheveux)* to twiddle, to play *or* to fiddle with **2** *(palper ▸ fruit, objet)* to handle, to finger; **arrête de t. tes boutons** stop touching *or* keep your hands off your spots **3** *(personne)* to feel up, to grope

VI *Fam* **1** *(fouiller)* to rummage *or* to root around, to root about; **t. dans les affaires de qn** to rummage *or* root about in sb's things **2** *(en affaires)* to be up to some funny *or Br* dodgy business; **t. dans qch** to be mixed up *or* involved in sth□; **t. dans la caisse** to tamper with the cash

VPR se tripoter *très Fam* **1** *(se masturber)* to play with oneself **2** *(deux personnes)* to paw *or* to grope each other, to feel each other up **3** *(toucher)* **se t. le nez/le menton** to fiddle with one's nose/chin

tripoteur, -euse [tripɔtœr, -øz] **NM,F** *Fam* **1** *(qui trafique)* shady dealer, crook **2** *(qui caresse)* fondler, groper

ADJ *(mains)* groping; **avoir les mains tripoteuses** to be a bit of a groper

triptyque [triptik] **NM 1** *Beaux-Arts, Littérature & Mus* triptych **2** *Aut & Admin* triptyque

trique [trik] **NF 1** *(bâton)* cudgel; **des coups de t.** cudgel blows; **donner des coups de t. à qn** to thrash sb; *Fig* **mener qn à la t.** to rule sb with a rod of iron; *Fig* **mener son monde à la t.** to rule with a rod of iron, to rule by fear **2** *Vulg (érection)* hard-on, boner; **avoir la t.** to have a hard-on *or* a boner

triquer [3] [trike] **VI** *Vulg* to have a hard-on *or* a boner

trirème [trirɛm] **NF** *Antiq* trireme

trisaïeul, -e [trizajœl] **NM,F** great-great-grandfather, *f* great-great-grandmother; **trisaïeuls** great-great-grandparents

trisannuel, -elle [trizanɥɛl] **ADJ 1** *(qui a lieu tous les trois ans)* three-yearly, *Sout* triennial **2** *(qui dure trois ans)* three-year-long *(avant n)*, *Sout* triennial

trisection [trisɛksjɔ̃] **NF** trisection

trisomie [trizɔmi] **NF** *Méd* trisomy; **t. 18** Edwards' syndrome; **t. 21** Down's syndrome, trisomy 21; **enfant atteint de t. 21** child with Down's syndrome

trisomique [trizɔmik] *Méd* **ADJ enfant t.** Down's syndrome child; **être t.** to have Down's syndrome

NMF child with Down's syndrome

trisser [3] [trise] *Fam* **VI** to hightail it, to scoot, *Am* to split

VPR se trisser to hightail it, to scoot, *Am* to split

triste [trist] **ADJ 1** *(déprimé ▸ personne)* sad; *(▸ sourire, visage)* sad, unhappy, sorrowful; *(▸ mine, air)* sad, forlorn; **d'un air t.** bleakly; **ne prends pas cet air t.** don't look so glum; **être tout t.** to be (very) dejected *or* in low spirits; **je fus (bien) t. d'apprendre que...** I was (very) sorry to hear that...; **un clown t.** a sad-looking clown; **t. comme un bonnet de nuit** as miserable as sin; **t. comme la mort** utterly dejected; *Littéraire* **faire t. figure** *ou* **mine** to look pitiful; **faire t. figure** *ou* **mine à qn** to give sb a cold reception

2 *(pénible)* sad, unhappy; **son t. sort** his/her sad *or* unhappy fate

3 *(attristant)* sad; **un film t.** a sad film; **c'est t. à dire** it's sad to say; **t. comme un lendemain de fête** a real anticlimax

4 *Fam* **c'est pas t.!** what a hoot *or* laugh!; **il est pas t., avec sa chemise à fleurs** he's a scream in his flowery shirt; **il est pas t., son frère!** his/her brother is quite a character!

5 *(terne ▸ couleur)* drab, dull; *(morne ▸ rue, saison)* bleak; *(▸ campagne)* bleak, depressing; *(▸ vie, pièce)* dreary, dismal, depressing; **être t. à mourir** *(gens, ambiance, lieu)* to be thoroughly depressing *or* dreary; **une ville t. à pleurer** a dreadfully bleak town

6 *(avant le nom) (déplorable)* deplorable, sorry, sad; **elle était dans un t. état** she was in a sorry state; **nous vivons une bien t. époque** we're living through pretty grim times; **c'est la t. réalité** that's the way things are; **c'est une t. affaire** it's a sorry *or* bad business; **c'est tout de même t.!** it's pretty pathetic!; **c'est quand même t. de voir ça dans notre pays!** it's dreadful to see that type of thing in our own country!

7 *Péj (méprisable ▸ repas, excuse)* poor, sorry, wretched; *(▸ morceau de pain)* sad- *or* sorry-looking; **un t. sire** an unsavoury character

NMF *(personne sombre)* gloomy *or* miserable person; **ce n'est pas un t.!** he's a lot of fun!

tristement [tristəmɑ̃] **ADV 1** *(en étant triste)* sadly **2** *(de façon terne)* drearily; **la maison est t. décorée** the house is decorated in a dreary *or* depressing fashion **3** *(de manière pénible)* sadly, regrettably; **faire t. défaut** to be sadly lacking; **t. célèbre** notorious

tristesse [tristɛs] **NF 1** *(sentiment)* sadness; **sourire avec t.** to smile sadly; **un sourire plein de t.** a very sad smile; **ressentir une grande t.** to feel very sad; **dans un moment de t.** in a moment of sadness; **c'est avec t. que je quitte ce pays** I am very sorry to be leaving this country; **quelle t. de voir une telle déchéance!** how sad to see such decrepitude! **2** *(d'un livre, d'une vie)* sadness; **la t. du paysage** the bleakness of the landscape; **la t. de son regard** the sad look *or* expression in his/her eyes **3** *(manque de vitalité)* dreariness, dullness; **ma vie est d'une grande t.** my life is very dreary

tristounet, -ette [tristunɛ, -ɛt] **ADJ** *Fam* **1** *(triste)* sad□; **il est un peu t. aujourd'hui** he's a bit low today; **une petite figure tristounette** a sad little face **2** *(qui rend triste)* gloomy□, dreary□, depressing□ **3** *(terne)* dull□; **un peu t. comme pull** that sweater is a bit drab

trisyllabe [trisilab] **ADJ** trisyllabic

NM trisyllable

trisyllabique [trisilabik] **ADJ** trisyllabic

trithérapie [triterapi] **NF** *Méd* combination therapy

tritium [tritjɔm] **NM** *Chim* tritium

triton [tritɔ̃] **NM 1** *Zool (amphibien)* newt, *Spéc* triton; *(gastropode)* triton, Triton's shell **2** *Mus* tritone **3** *Phys* triton

trituration [trityrasjɔ̃] **NF** grinding up, *Spéc* trituration

triturer [3] [trityre] **VT 1** *(pétrir ▸ bras, corps, pâte)* to knead **2** *(manipuler ▸ gants, breloque)* to fiddle with **3** *Pharm (médicament)* to crush, to grind, *Spéc* to triturate

VPR se triturer *Fam* **se t. les méninges** *ou* **la cervelle** to rack one's brains

triumvir [trijɔmvir] **NM** triumvir

triumvirat [trijɔmvira] **NM 1** *(groupe)* triumvirate, troika **2** *Antiq* triumvirate

trivalent, -e [trivalɑ̃, -ɑ̃t] **ADJ** trivalent

trivalve [trivalv] **ADJ** trivalvular, trivalve *(avant n)*

trivial, -e, -aux, -ales [trivjal, -o] **ADJ 1** *(grossier)* crude, offensive **2** *(banal)* trivial, trite; **un détail t.** a minor detail; **une remarque triviale** a commonplace, a mundane remark **3** *Math* trivial

> Il faut noter que l'adjectif anglais **trivial** est un faux ami. Il signifie **anodin, insignifiant**.

trivialement [trivjalmɑ̃] **ADV 1** *(vulgairement)* crudely, coarsely **2** *(banalement)* trivially, tritely

trivialité [trivjalite] **NF 1** *(caractère vulgaire)* crudeness, coarseness **2** *(parole vulgaire)* crude remark; *(expression)* vulgar *or* coarse expression **3** *(caractère banal)* triviality, banality; **des idées d'une t. affligeante** incredibly trivial *or* banal ideas

roc [trɔk] **NM 1** *(système économique)* barter; **(économie de) t.** barter economy; **faire du t.** to barter **2** *(échange)* swap; **je ne l'ai pas acheté, j'ai fait le t. avec quelqu'un** I didn't buy it, I bartered for it *or* I did a swap

rochaïque [trɔkaik] **ADJ** *Littérature* trochaic

rochée [trɔʃe] **NM** *Littérature* trochee

roène [trɔɛn] **NM** *Bot* privet

roglodyte [trɔglɔdit] **NM 1** *(en anthropologie)* cave dweller, *Spéc* troglodyte **2** *Orn* wren; **t. familier** house wren

roglodytique [trɔglɔditik] **ADJ** *(population)* cave-dwelling, *Spéc* troglodytic; **habitations troglodytiques** cave dwellings

rogne [trɔɲ] **NF** *Fam* face□, mug; **il avait une t. d'ivrogne** he had the look of a wino about him

rognon [trɔɲɔ̃] **NM 1** *(de pomme)* core; *(de chou, salade etc)* stalk; *très Fam* **il t'exploitera jusqu'au t.** he'll bleed you dry; *très Fam* **on s'est fait avoir jusqu'au t.** we were well and truly ripped off **2** *Fam (terme d'affection)* sweetie

ADJ *(invariable en genre) Fam* cute; **elles sont vraiment trognons** they're so cute

roie [trwa] **NF** Troy; **le cheval/la guerre de T.** the Trojan Horse/War

roïka [trɔika] **NF 1** *(traîneau)* troika **2** *(trois personnes)* troika; **la t. qui dirige maintenant le journal** the newspaper's new management trio

rois [trwa] **ADJ 1** *(gén)* three; *Théât* **frapper les t. coups** = to announce the beginning of a theatre performance by knocking three times; **maquette en t. dimensions** three-dimensional model; *Mus* **à t. temps** in triple *or* three-four time; **les t. quarts du temps** most of the time; **les t. Grâces** the (three) Graces; *Anciennement Mil* **les t. jours** *(à l'armée)* = in France, induction course preceding military service (now lasting one day); *Fam* **haut comme t. pommes** knee-high to a grasshopper **2** *(dans des séries)* third; **page/numéro t.** page/number three **3** *(exprimant une approximation)* **dans t. minutes** in a couple of minutes; **il n'a pas dit t. mots** he hardly said a word; **deux ou t., t. ou quatre** a few, a handful; **prends t. ou quatre prunes** take a few plums

PRON three

NM INV 1 *(gén)* three

2 *(numéro d'ordre)* number three

3 *(chiffre écrit)* three

4 *Cartes* three; *voir aussi* **cinq**

G [trwaʒe] **NF** *Ordinat & Tél (abrév* **troisième génération)** 3G

rois-huit [trwaɥit] **NM INV** *Mus* three-eight (time)

NMPL *Ind* **les t.** = shift system based on three eight-hour shifts; **faire les t.** to work in shifts of eight hours

roisième [trwazjɛm] **ADJ** third; *Cin* **t. dimension** third dimension; *Ordinat & Tél* **t. génération** third generation, 3G; *Gram* **la t. personne du singulier/pluriel** the third person singular/plural; **il était le t. larron dans cette affaire** he took advantage of the quarrel the other two were having; **de t. ordre** third-rate

NMF 1 *(personne)* third **2** *(objet)* third (one)

NM 1 *(partie)* third **2** *(étage) Br* third floor, *Am* fourth floor **3** *(arrondissement de Paris)* third (arrondissement)

NF 1 *Scol Br* $\simeq$ fourth year, *Am* $\simeq$ ninth grade

2 *Aut* third gear

3 *Mus* third

4 *(en danse)* third position

5 *(édition)* **t. de couverture** inside back cover; *voir aussi* **cinquième**

roisièmement [trwazjɛmmɑ̃] **ADV** thirdly, in third place

rois-mâts [trwama] **NM INV** *Naut* three-master

rois-pièces [trwapjɛs] **NM INV 1** *(appartement)* three-room(ed) *Br* flat or *Am* apartment; **t. cuisine** *Br* three-room flat with kitchen, *Am* three and a half **2** *(costume)* three-piece suit

rois-quarts [trwakar] **ADJ INV** three-quarter

NM INV 1 *(manteau)* three-quarter (length) coat **2** *Sport* three-quarter; **t. aile/centre** wing/centre (three-quarter); **la ligne des t.** the three-quarter line **3** *Mus (violon)* three-quarter violin

trois-quatre [trwakatr] **NM INV** *Mus* three-four time

troll [trɔl] **NM 1** *Myth* troll **2** *Fam Ordinat (message, personne)* troll

troller [trɔle] **VI** *Fam Ordinat* to troll

trolley [trɔlɛ] **NM 1** *Transp* trolleybus **2** *(chariot)* truck *(on cableway)* **3** *Élec* trolley; **perche de t.** trolley pole

trolleybus [trɔlɛbys] **NM** *Transp* trolleybus

trombe [trɔ̃b] **NF** *Météo (sur mer)* waterspout; *(sur terre)* whirlwind; **t. d'eau** downpour; **sous des trombes d'eau** in the torrential rain; **il pleuvait des trombes** it was pouring down

• **en trombe ADV** *Fam* briskly and noisily□; **elle entra en t.** she burst in; **la voiture passa en t.** the car shot past; **partir en t.** to shoot off

trombine [trɔ̃bin] **NF** *Fam (visage)* mug; *(physionomie)* look□; **si tu avais vu sa t.!** you should have seen his/her face!□

trombinoscope [trɔ̃binɔskɔp] **NM** *Fam* rogues' gallery

tromblon [trɔ̃blɔ̃] **NM 1** *(fusil)* blunderbuss **2** *(cylindre)* grenade sleeve

trombone [trɔ̃bɔn] **NM 1** *Mus (instrument)* trombone; *(musicien)* trombonist, trombone (player); **t. à coulisse/pistons** slide/valve trombone **2** *(agrafe)* paper clip

trompe [trɔ̃p] **NF 1** *Zool (d'éléphant)* trunk, *Spéc* proboscis; *(de papillon)* proboscis; *(de tapir)* snout, *Spéc* proboscis

2 *Mus* horn; *Naut* **t. de brume** foghorn; *Chasse* **t. de chasse** (French) hunting horn; *Chasse* **sonner de la t.** to sound the horn; *Fig* **publier qch à son de t.** to trumpet sth abroad

3 *Aut (avertisseur)* horn

4 *Anat* **t. d'Eustache** Eustachian tube; **t. utérine** *ou* **de Fallope** Fallopian tube

5 *Archit* squinch

6 *Tech* **t. à eau** water pump

trompe-la-mort [trɔ̃plamɔr] **NMF INV** daredevil

trompe-l'œil [trɔ̃plœj] **NM INV 1** *Beaux-Arts (style)* trompe l'œil **2** *Fig (faux-semblant)* window dressing; **son discours antiraciste n'était qu'un t.** his antiracist speech was mere window-dressing

• **en trompe-l'œil** *Beaux-Arts* **ADJ peinture en t.** trompe l'œil painting **ADV peindre en t.** to do a trompe l'œil painting, to use trompe l'œil techniques

tromper [3] [trɔ̃pe] **VT 1** *(conjoint)* to be unfaithful to, to cheat on, *Sout* to deceive, to betray; **il trompe sa femme avec sa secrétaire** he's having an affair with his secretary

2 *(donner le change à)* to fool, to trick, to deceive; **elle nous a trompés avec son doux sourire** she fooled us with her sweet smile; **cela ne trompe personne** nobody's taken in, nobody's fooled; **avec ses airs affables, il trompe bien son monde** everybody is taken in by his kindly manner

3 *(induire en erreur)* to mislead; **t. qn sur qn/qch** to deceive *or* mislead sb about sb/sth; **t. qn sur ses intentions** to mislead sb as to one's intentions; **mon instinct ne me trompe jamais** my instincts never let me down *or* fail me; **ne te laisse pas t. par les apparences** don't be taken in by appearances; **c'est ce qui nous a trompés** that's what misled *or* fooled *or* deceived us

4 *(échapper à)* **t. la vigilance de qn** to elude sb; **tu ne pourras pas t. la vigilance du percepteur** you won't hoodwink *or* outwit the *Br* taxman *or Am* IRS; **t. l'ennui** to stave off boredom; **pour t. le temps** to pass the time, to kill time

5 *(apaiser ▸ faim)* to appease

6 *Littéraire (décevoir)* **t. l'espoir de qn** to disappoint sb; **je ne voulais pas t. son attente** I didn't want to disappoint him/her

USAGE ABSOLU c'est un signe qui ne trompe pas it's a sure sign; **il a rougi, cela ne trompe pas!** his blushing said it all!

VPR se tromper 1 *(commettre une erreur)* to make a mistake; **je dois me t.** I must be mistaken, I must be wrong; **j'ai dû me t.** I must have made a mistake; **si je ne me trompe** if I'm not mistaken; **je ne m'étais pas trompé de beaucoup** I wasn't far wrong *or* far off; **c'est justement ce en quoi tu te trompes** that's just where you're wrong; **tout le monde peut se t.** anybody can make a mistake, we all make mistakes; **se t. dans une addition/dictée** to get a sum/dictation wrong; **je me suis trompé de trois euros** I was three euros *Br* out *or Am* off; **vous m'avez fait me t.** you made me make a mistake

2 *(prendre une chose pour une autre)* **se t. de jour** to get the day wrong; **se t. de bus** to get on the wrong bus; **se t. d'adresse** to get the wrong address; *Fam Fig* **si c'est un complice que tu cherches, tu te trompes d'adresse** if it's an accomplice you want, you've come to the wrong address; **je me suis trompé de direction/de maison** I went the wrong way/to the wrong house; **vous devez vous t. de numéro** *(au téléphone)* you must have the wrong number; **elle ressemble à sa sœur à s'y t.** you can't tell her and her sister apart

3 *(s'illusionner)* to make a mistake, to be wrong; **je le croyais intelligent mais je me suis trompé** I thought he was intelligent, but I was wrong; **se t. sur les motifs de qn** to misunderstand sb's motives; **que l'on ne s'y trompe pas** let there be no misunderstanding about that; **au fond, elle était malheureuse et ses amis ne s'y trompaient pas** deep down she was unhappy and her friends could tell

tromperie [trɔ̃pri] **NF** *(supercherie)* deception; **il y a t. sur la marchandise** this isn't what it was said to be; **j'en ai assez de tes tromperies** I've had enough of your deceit *or* deceitfulness

trompeter [27] [trɔ̃pete] **VT** *(fait)* to trumpet, to shout from the rooftops

VI *Vieilli (musicien)* to play the trumpet, to trumpet; *(aigle)* to scream

trompette [trɔ̃pɛt] **NF 1** *(instrument)* trumpet; **t. basse** bass trumpet; **t. bouchée** muted trumpet; **t. de cavalerie** bugle; *Bible* **les trompettes de Jéricho** the trumpets of Jericho; **la t. du Jugement dernier** (the sound of) the Last Judgment; **t. à pistons** valve trumpet; *Littéraire* **les trompettes de la Renommée** the trumpet blast of Fame; **t. simple** bugle **2** *Ich* **t. de mer** trumpet fish

NM *(musicien ▸ gén)* trumpet player, trumpet, trumpeter; *Mil* trumpeter

• **en trompette ADJ** *(nez)* turned up, upturned; **avoir le nez en t.** to have a turned up *or* an upturned nose

trompette-des-morts [trɔ̃pɛtdemɔr] *(pl* **trompettes-des-morts), trompette-de-la-mort** [trɔ̃pɛtdəlamɔr] *(pl* **trompettes-de-la-mort) NF** *Bot* horn of plenty

trompettiste [trɔ̃pɛtist] **NMF** trumpet player, trumpet, trumpeter

trompeur, -euse [trɔ̃pœr, -øz] **ADJ 1** *(personne)* lying, deceitful **2** *(signe, air, apparence)* deceptive, misleading; *(publicité)* misleading; **le vent faiblit mais c'est t.** the wind's dropping but you can't rely on that

NM,F deceiver; *Prov* **à t., t. et demi** it's the biter bit

trompeusement [trɔ̃pøzmɑ̃] **ADV** *(en apparence)* deceptively; *(traîtreusement)* deceitfully

tronc [trɔ̃] **NM 1** *Bot* trunk

2 *Anat (d'un être humain)* trunk, torso; *(d'un animal)* trunk, barrel; *(d'un nerf, d'une artère)* trunk, *Spéc* truncus

3 *(boîte pour collectes)* offertory box; **t. des pauvres** alms box

4 *Géom* **t. de cône/pyramide** truncated cone/pyramid

5 *Fam* **se casser le t.** to strain oneself; **il ne s'est pas cassé le t.** he didn't kill himself, he didn't overexert himself□

6 *(comme adj; avec ou sans trait d'union)* limbless; **homme-/femme-t.** armless and legless man/woman

• **tronc commun NM** *(d'une famille)* common stock, ancestry; *Scol* compulsory subjects, core curriculum

troncature [trɔ̃katyr] **NF** *Minér, Ordinat, Math & (gén)* truncation

tronche [trɔ̃ʃ] **NF** *Fam* **1** *(visage)* face□, mug; *(expression)* look□; **il a une sale t.** he's an ugly-looking customer; **il a une t. qui ne me revient pas** I don't like the look of him; **il a une drôle de t.** he looks really odd, he's really odd-looking; **il se l'est pris en plein dans la t.** he got it smack in the face; **t'en fais une t., qu'est-ce qu'il t'arrive?** you look really down, what's up?; **t'aurais vu la t. qu'il faisait!** you should have seen the look on his face!ᵔ; **faire la t.** *(bouder)* to sulkᵔ, to be in a huff **2** *(personne intelligente)* brain, brainy person; **ce mec-là, c'est une t.!** that guy's a real brain *or* so brainy!

troncher [3] [trɔ̃ʃe] VT *Vulg* to screw, *Br* to shag

tronçon [trɔ̃sɔ̃] NM **1** *(morceau coupé)* segment, section; *(de mât, de lance, d'épée)* (broken) stump; **un tuyau divisé en tronçons** a pipe divided into segments
2 *Transp (de voie)* section; *(de route)* section, stretch
3 *(d'un texte)* part, section
4 *Archit* frustum
5 *Menuis* log, block

tronconique [trɔ̃kɔnik] ADJ truncated

tronçonnage [trɔ̃sɔnaʒ], **tronçonnement** [trɔ̃sɔnmɑ̃] NM **1** *Menuis* sawing *or* chopping (into sections) **2** *Métal* sectioning

tronçonner [3] [trɔ̃sɔne] VT to cut *or* to chop (into sections); **t. un arbre** to saw a tree (into sections)

tronçonneuse [trɔ̃sɔnøz] NF motor saw; **t. à chaîne** chain saw

trône [tron] NM **1** *(siège, pouvoir)* throne; **monter sur le t.** to ascend *or* to come to the throne; **placer** *ou* **mettre qn sur le t.** to put sb on the throne **2** *Fam Hum* **être sur le t.** *(aux toilettes)* to be on the throne
• **trônes** NMPL *Rel* thrones

trôner [3] [trone] VI **1** *(personne)* to sit enthroned *or* in state **2** *(bouquet, œuvre d'art)* to sit prominently *or* imposingly; **son portrait trônait dans le salon** his/her portrait was displayed in a prominent position in the drawing room; **son diplôme trône sur la cheminée** his/her diploma occupies a place of honour on the mantelpiece **3** *Péj (faire l'important)* to lord it

tronqué, -e [trɔ̃ke] ADJ *(colonne, pyramide)* truncated; *(mât)* stub *(avant n)*; *(texte)* cut, truncated; *(citation)* shortened, truncated

tronquer [3] [trɔ̃ke] VT **1** *(phrase, récit)* to shorten; *(citation)* to shorten, to truncate **2** *(pilier, statue)* to truncate

TROP [tro] ADV **1** *(excessivement ▸ devant un adjectif, un adverbe)* too; **c'est t. difficile** it's too difficult; **il est t. gros** he's overweight *or* too fat; **un plat t. riche** an excessively rich dish; **de la viande t. cuite** overcooked meat; **être t. attaché à qn** to be too attached to sb, to be overfond of sb; **être t. habillé** *(porter trop de vêtements)* to have too many clothes on; *(porter des vêtements trop chic)* to be overdressed; **et en plus, c'est moi qui paye, c'est t. fort!** and what's more I'm the one who's paying, it really is too much!; **il habite t. loin** he lives too far away; **elle sort t. peu** she doesn't go out enough; **son t. peu de confiance en elle lui nuit** her lack of self-confidence works against her
2 *(excessivement ▸ avec un verbe)* too much; **boire t., t. boire** to drink to excess *or* too much; **manger t., t. manger** to overeat, to eat too much; **tu manges (beaucoup) t.** you eat (far) too much; **on a t. chargé la voiture** we've overloaded the car; **j'en ai déjà t. dit, j'en ai déjà dit t.** I've already said too much; **je ne l'ai que t. dit** I've said it time and time again; **cela n'a que t. duré** it's been going on far too long; **je ne la connais que t.** I know her all *or* only too well; **il ne le sait que t.** he knows (it) only too well; **on ne saurait t. le répéter** it cannot be repeated too often; **ne fais pas t. le difficile** don't be too awkward
3 *(en corrélation avec "pour")* **tu es t. intelligent pour croire cela** you're too intelligent to believe that; **le trou était t. étroit pour qu'un rat entrât par là** the hole was too narrow for a rat to get in by; **elle est t. belle pour toi** she's too beautiful for you; **ne soulève pas l'armoire, c'est t. lourd pour toi tout seul** don't (try to) lift the cupboard, it's too heavy for you on your own; **il est t. fier pour accepter** he's too proud to accept; **c'est t. beau pour être vrai** it's too good to be true; **il a t. tardé à répondre pour qu'elle lui écrive encore** he has taken too long in replying for her to write to him again; **c'est t. important pour que vous ne vous en occupiez pas vous-même** it's too important for you not to deal with it yourself
4 *(emploi nominal) (quantité)* too much; *(nombre)* too many; **ne demande pas t.** don't ask for too much; **prends la dernière part – non, c'est t.** have the last slice – no, it's too much; **je dépense t.** I'm overspending, I'm spending too much; **c'est t.!, c'en est t.!** that's it!, I've had enough!; **t. c'est t.!** enough is enough!; **je sors, t. c'est t.!** I'm leaving, I've had enough!
5 *(très, beaucoup)* so; **ce bébé est t. mignon!** this baby is so cute!; **il est t. drôle!** he's so funny!; **c'était t. drôle** it was too funny for words *or* just too funny; **c'est t. bête!** how stupid!; **vous êtes t. aimable** how very kind of you, you're very *or* too kind; *Fam* **j'étais t. dégoûté** I was so bummed *or Br* gutted; *Fam* **il est t. mortel, son plan** his/her plan's so *or* too brilliant; *Fam* **j'étais t. mort de rire** I was absolutely killing myself
6 *(dans des phrases négatives)* **il n'est pas t. content** he's not too *or* very happy; **je ne sais t.** I'm not sure; **je ne sais t. que dire/penser** I hardly know *or* I don't quite know what to say/think; **je n'aime pas t. le chocolat** I don't like chocolate very *or* that much, I'm not very *or* that keen on chocolate; **on ne se voit plus t.** we don't see much of each other any more; **je ne me sens pas t. à l'aise** I'm not overly comfortable, I'm none too comfortable; **sans t. savoir pourquoi** without really knowing why; **ça va? – pas t. mal** how are things? – not bad at all *or* not too bad; **ça te plaît? – pas t.** do you like it? – not (very) much
ADJ INV *Fam (incroyable)* too much, unreal; **il est t., lui!** he really is too much!
• **de trop** ADV **j'ai payé cinq euros de t.** I paid five euros too much; **il y a une assiette de t.** there's one plate too many; **c'est une fois de t.** that's once too often; **votre remarque était de t.** that remark of yours was uncalled for; **je suis de t., peut-être?** are you telling me I'm in the way *or* not wanted?; **se sentir de t.** to feel that one is in the way; *Fam* **tu fumes/bois de t.** you smoke/drink too muchᵔ; *Fam* **travailler de t.** to work too hard *or* too muchᵔ, to overworkᵔ; *Fam* **deux jours ne seront pas de t. pour tout terminer** two days should just about be enough to finish everything
• **en trop** ADV **j'ai une carte en t.** I have one card too many; **tu as des vêtements en t. à me donner?** have you got any spare clothes to give me?; **j'ai payé cinq euros en t.** I paid five euros too much; **il y a de l'argent en t.** there's too much money; **il y a un verre en t.** there's a *or* one glass too many
• **par trop** ADV *Littéraire* much too, far too; **il est par t. méfiant** he's much *or* far too distrustful; **c'est par t. injuste** it's simply too unfair (for words)
• **trop de** DÉT **1** *(suivi d'un nom non comptable)* too much; *(suivi d'un nom comptable)* too many; **ils ont t. d'argent** they've got too much money; **j'ai acheté t. de lait** I've bought too much milk; **il y a beaucoup t. de monde** there are far too many people; **tu veux des bonbons? – non, merci, j'en ai déjà t. mangé** do you want some sweets? – no thanks, I've already eaten too many; **je n'aurai pas t. d'une heure pour le faire** it will take me a good hour; **nous ne serons pas t. de cinq pour soulever le piano** it'll take at least five of us to lift the piano
2 *(en corrélation avec "pour")* **il a t. d'expérience pour se tromper** he is too experienced to make a mistake; **j'ai t. de soucis pour me charger des vôtres** I've too many worries of my own to deal with yours
3 *(comme nom)* **le t. d'énergie des enfants** the children's excess *or* surplus energy
4 *(locution)* **en faire t.** *(travailler)* to overdo things; *(pour plaire)* to overdo it

trope [trɔp] NM trope

trophée [trɔfe] NM trophy

tropical, -e, -aux, -ales [trɔpikal, -o] ADJ tropical

tropique [trɔpik] ADJ tropical
NM *Astron & Géog* tropic; **le t. du Cancer/Capricorne** the tropic of Cancer/Capricorn
• **tropiques** NMPL *Géog* **les tropiques** the tropics; **sous les tropiques** in the tropics

tropisme [trɔpism] NM *Biol* tropism; *Fig* pull (strong) attraction; **le t. des marchés envers la stabilité des prix** the way the markets are gravitating towards price stability

troposphère [trɔpɔsfɛr] NF troposphere

trop-perçu [trɔpɛrsy] *(pl* **trop-perçus***)* NM overpayment, excess payment

trop-plein [trɔplɛ̃] *(pl* **trop-pleins***)* NM **1** *(de forces, d'émotion)* overflow, surplus; **ton t. d'énergie** your surplus energy **2** *(d'eau, de graines)* overflow; *(de vin)* surplus **3** *Tech* overflow; *(tuyau)* overflow pipe

troquer [3] [trɔke] VT **1** *(échanger)* to exchange, to swap; **je troquerais bien mon manteau contre le tien** I wouldn't mind swapping coats with you **2** *Com* to barter, to trade; **ils troquent les fruits contre de la soie** they trade fruit for silk

troquet [trɔkɛ] NM *Fam* barᵔ, *Br* boozer

trot [tro] NM *Équitation* trot, trotting *(UNCOUNT)*; **prendre le t.** to break into a trot; **course de t.** trotting *or* harness race; **t. assis** sitting trot; **t. attelé** trotting (with a sulky); **t. enlevé** rising trot; **t. monté** saddle-trot, saddle-trotting
• **au trot** ADV **1** *Équitation* at a trot *or* trotting pace; **aller au t.** to trot; **partir au t.** to set off at a trot; **au grand t.** at a brisk trot; **au petit t.** at a jogging pace **2** *Fam (vite)* on the double; **allez, et au t.!** come on, jump to it!

Trotski [trɔtski] NPR Trotsky

trotskisme [trɔtskism] NM Trotskyism

trotskiste [trɔtskist] ADJ Trotskyist
NMF Trotskyist

trotte [trɔt] NF *Fam* hike, stretch; **ils en ont fait une t.!** they've covered quite a distance!ᵔ

trotte-menu [trɔtmɔny] ADJ INV *Littéraire* **la gent t.** mice

trotter [3] [trɔte] VI **1** *(cheval, cavalier)* to trot
2 *(marcher vite ▸ enfant)* to trot *or* to run along *(▸ souris)* to scurry along; **à cet âge-là, ils ont envie de t.** at that age, they want to run around
3 *Fam (marcher beaucoup)* to do a lot of walkingᵔ, to cover quite a distance on footᵔ
4 *Fig* **j'ai une idée qui me trotte dans la tête** *ou* **la cervelle** I have an idea in my head; **cet air me trotte dans la tête!** I can't get that tune out of my head!
VPR **se trotter** *Fam* to take off, *Br* to scarper

trotteur, -euse [trɔtœr, -øz] ADJ **1** *Équitation* **cheval t.** trotter **2** *(chaussure)* **talon t.** low heel
NM,F *(cheval)* trotter
NM *(pour bébé)* baby-walker
• **trotteurs** NMPL *(chaussures)* flat shoes
• **trotteuse** NF *(d'une montre)* second hand

trottinement [trɔtinmɑ̃] NM *(marche rapide)* trotting, scurrying; *(d'un enfant)* toddling *(d'une souris)* scampering; *(bruit de pas)* patter

trottiner [3] [trɔtine] VI **1** *(souris)* to scurry, to scamper; *(cheval)* to jog-trot (along) **2** *(personne)* to trot along; **la petite trottinait près de son père** the little girl trotted along next to her father

trottinette [trɔtinɛt] NF **1** *(patinette)* scooter **faire de la t.** to ride one's scooter; **t. à moteur** motorized scooter **2** *Fam (petite voiture)* little carᵔ

trottoir [trɔtwar] NM **1** *(pour marcher) Br* pavement, *Am* sidewalk; *(rebord) Br* kerb, *Am* curb **heurter le t.** *(en conduisant)* to hit the kerb; *Fam* **faire le t.** to be on the game, *Am* to hook **2** *Tech* **t. roulant** travelator, travolator, moving walkway

trou [tru] NM **1** *(cavité ▸ gén)* hole; *(▸ sur la route)* pothole; **faire un t. dans les économies de qn** to make a hole in sb's savings; **t. de mémoire** memory lapse, lapse of memory; **j'ai eu un t. (de mémoire)** my mind went blank *or* was a blank; **j'ai un t.** my mind has gone blank *or* is a blank; *Fam* **boire comme un t.** to drink like a fish; **un t. de souris** a mouse hole; **un studio ça? plutôt un t. de souris!** a studio? it's more like a hole in the wall! **j'étais tellement gêné que j'aurais voulu disparaître dans un t. de souris** I was so embarrassed I wished the earth would swallow me up; **je ne veux pas déménager, j'ai fait mon t. ici** I don't want to move, I've settled down here; **parti de rien, il a fait son t.** he made his way in the world from very humble beginnings; **elle a fait son t. dans l'édition**

she has made a nice little niche for herself in publishing; *Sport* **faire le t.** to break away from the field; **sortir de son t.** to go out into the big wide world; **t. d'aération** air vent; *Naut* **t. du chat** lubber's hole; *Tech* **t. de graissage** oil hole; **t. d'homme** manhole; **t. noir** *Astron* black hole; *Fig* depths of despair; **après la mort de mon mari, ça a été le t. noir** after my husband died I was in a black hole of depression; **t. normand** = glass of Calvados taken between courses of a meal; **faire le t. normand** = to take a break between courses with a glass of Calvados; *Théât* **t. du souffleur** prompter's box

2 *(ouverture ▸ dans une clôture, dans les nuages)* hole, gap; *(▸ d'une aiguille)* eye; *(▸ dans du cuir)* eyelet; **le maçon a fait un t. dans le mur** the builder knocked a hole in the wall; **le t. de la serrure** the keyhole; **regarder par le t. de la serrure** to watch through the keyhole; **le t. de la couche d'ozone** the hole in the ozone layer

3 *(déchirure)* hole, tear, rip; **avoir des trous à ses chaussettes** to have holes in one's socks; **j'ai laissé tomber une allumette sur la nappe et ça a fait un t.** I dropped a match on the tablecloth and it burned a hole in it; **drap plein de trous** tattered sheet, sheet full of holes

4 *(moment)* gap; **un t. dans son emploi du temps** *(élève)* a free period; *(dans la reconstitution d'un crime)* = a period of time during which one's movements cannot be accounted for; *Fam* **il y a un t. dans ton CV** there's a gap in your *Br* CV *or Am* résumé; **la coiffeuse a un t. à 11 heures** the hairdresser can fit you in at 11 o'clock

5 *Fam (endroit isolé)* hole; **il n'est jamais sorti de son t.** he's never been out of his own backyard; **habiter un petit t. (perdu)** to live at the back of beyond; **je ne resterai pas dans ce t.** I won't stay in this hole; **pas même un café, quel t.!** not even a café, what a dump!

6 *Fam (tombe)* grave; **quand je serai dans le t.** when I've kicked the bucket *or* I'm six feet under

7 *Fam Arg crime (prison)* slammer, clink, *Br* nick; **être au t.** to be inside; **on l'a mis au t.** he was sent down

8 *Fam (déficit)* deficit; **il est parti en laissant un t. de 50 000 euros** he went off leaving us/the company/*etc* 50,000 euros worse off; **un t. dans le budget** a budget deficit; **le t. de la Sécu** the deficit in the French Social Security budget

9 *Anat* hole, *Spéc* foramen; **t. occipital** occipital foramen; **t. de l'oreille** earhole; **trous vertébraux** vertebral foramina; *Fam* **trous de nez** nostrils; *Fam* **s'en mettre jusqu'aux trous de nez** to stuff one's face; *Fam* **ça me sort par les trous de nez** I've had it up to here; *Vulg* **t. du cul** *ou* **de balle** *Br* arsehole, *Am* asshole; *Fam* **il n'a pas les yeux en face des trous** *(il n'est pas observateur)* he never sees what's going on right in front of him; *(il est à moitié endormi)* he hasn't come to yet, his brain isn't in gear yet

10 *Aviat* **t. d'air** air *(UNCOUNT)* pocket; **des trous d'air** turbulence

11 *Golf* hole; **envoyer la balle dans le t.** to hole out; **réussir t. en un** to get a hole in one; **faire un t.** to get the ball in the hole

roubadour [trubadur] **NM** troubadour

roublant, -e [trublɑ̃, -ɑ̃t] **ADJ 1** *(événement)* disturbing, unsettling, disquieting; *(question, ressemblance)* disconcerting **2** *(sensuel)* disturbing, provocative; *(déshabillé, sourire)* thrilling, arousing; *(parfum)* heady; **une femme troublante** a desirable woman

rouble¹ [trubl] **ADJ 1** *(eau)* cloudy, murky; *(vin)* cloudy; *(image)* blurred; *(photo)* blurred, out-of-focus; *(regard, verre)* misty, dull; *(lumière)* dim; **avoir la vue t.** to have blurred vision

2 *(confus)* vague, unclear, imprecise; **un désir t.** a vague desire

3 *(équivoque)* equivocal, ambiguous; **elle aime les situations un peu troubles** she likes slightly ambiguous situations

4 *(peu honnête)* dubious; **une affaire t.** a murky business; **personnage t.** suspicious character; **période t. de l'histoire** murky period of history; **il y a quelque chose de t. dans cette affaire** there's something shady *or* fishy *or* not kosher about this business

ADV through a blur; **je vois t.** everything *or* my vision is blurred

trouble² [trubl] **NM 1** *(sentiment ▸ de gêne)* confusion, embarrassment; *(▸ de perplexité)* confusion; *(▸ de peine)* distress, turmoil; *(▸ d'amour)* agitation; **il ne put cacher son t. en la voyant** he couldn't hide his embarrassment when he saw her; **la nouvelle sema** *ou* **jeta le t. dans les esprits** the news sowed confusion in people's minds *or* threw people's minds into confusion

2 *Méd* disorder; *Psy* **t. de l'adaptation** adjustment disorder; **troubles circulatoires** circulation problems, trouble with one's circulation; **troubles du comportement** behavioural problems; **troubles gastriques/intestinaux** stomach/intestinal disorder; **elle souffre de troubles digestifs** she has trouble with her digestion; **t. d'hyperactivité avec déficit de l'attention** attention deficit hyperactivity disorder; **troubles du langage** speech disorders; **troubles mentaux** mental disorders; **troubles de la personnalité** personality problems; *Psy* personality disorders; **troubles respiratoires** respiratory disorders; **troubles visuels** *ou* **de la vue** eye trouble *(UNCOUNT)*

3 *(désaccord)* discord, trouble; **jeter** *ou* **semer le t. dans une famille** to sow discord within a family; **ne viens pas jeter** *ou* **semer le t. ici!** don't you come stirring up trouble (around here)!

4 *Jur* disturbance (of rights); **t. de jouissance** disturbance of possession

• **troubles NMPL 1** *(agitation sociale)* unrest *(UNCOUNT)*, disturbances; **période de troubles** period of unrest; **les troubles s'étendent** the rioting is spreading **2** *(d'un cours d'eau)* suspended matter *(UNCOUNT)*

trouble-fête [trubləfɛt] *(pl* **inv** *ou* **trouble-fêtes)** **NMF** killjoy, spoilsport; **jouer les t.** to be a killjoy *or* spoilsport; **je ne veux pas jouer les t., mais...** I don't want to be a spoilsport *or* to put a damper on the proceedings but...

troubler [3] [truble] **VT 1** *(eau)* to cloud

2 *(rendre moins net)* to blur, to dim, to cloud; **t. la vue de qn** to blur *or* to cloud sb's vision

3 *(sommeil)* to disturb; *(paix)* to disturb, to disrupt; *(silence)* to break; *(digestion)* to upset; *(bonheur)* to spoil

4 *(fête, réunion)* to disrupt; *(plan)* to upset, to disrupt; **une époque troublée** troubled times; **t. l'ordre public** *Br* to cause a breach of the peace, *Am* to disturb the peace

5 *(déconcerter)* to confuse, to disconcert; **ses remarques m'avaient troublé** his/her remarks had unsettled me; **ce qui me trouble dans cette affaire** what bothers *or* disturbs me about this matter

6 *(mettre en émoi ▸ personne)* to thrill, to arouse; *(▸ imagination)* to stir; **t. qn** to make sb nervous, to fluster sb; **ce film m'a vraiment troublé** I found the movie quite disturbing; **sa présence le troublait profondément** her presence aroused *or* excited him profoundly

7 *Jur* **t. qn dans la jouissance d'un bien** to disturb sb's enjoyment of possession

VPR se troubler 1 *(eau)* to become cloudy *or* turbid; *(vue)* to become blurred, to grow dim; *(mémoire)* to fade; *(voix)* to break (with emotion); *(idées)* to become confused **2** *(perdre contenance)* to get confused; **dès qu'on le regarde, il se trouble** as soon as somebody looks at him he goes to pieces; **sans se t.** *(répondre)* unruffled, without turning a hair; **continuez sans vous t.** carry on and don't let yourself get ruffled

trouée [true] **NF 1** *(ouverture)* gap; **une t. de ciel bleu** a patch of blue sky; **une t. dans les nuages** a break in the clouds **2** *Géog* gap **3** *Mil* breach; **effectuer une t.** to break through

trouer [3] [true] **VT 1** *(percer ▸ carton, tissu)* to make a hole in; *(▸ tôle)* to pierce; *Tech (▸ zinc)* to perforate; *(▸ cloison)* to make *or* to bore a hole in; **la pointe a troué le caoutchouc** the tip made a hole in the rubber; **la balle lui a troué le corps** the bullet pierced his/her body; *Fam* **t. la peau à qn** *(tuer quelqu'un)* to shoot sb, to put a bullet in sb; *Fam* **se faire t. la peau** to get shot, to be pumped full of lead **2** *(traverser)* to pierce; *(lignes ennemies)* to breach; **le soleil trouait les nuages** the sun was breaking through the clouds **3** *(cribler)* to pit; **des immeubles troués par des bombes** buildings pockmarked with shell holes; **surface trouée de balles** surface pitted with bullet holes

VPR se trouer *(d'un seul trou)* to get a hole; *(de plusieurs trous)* to get holes, *Br* to go into holes; **mes chaussures se sont trouées au bout d'une semaine** there was a hole in my shoes after a week

troufignon [trufiɲɔ̃] **NM** *très Fam (anus) Br* arsehole, *Am* asshole; *(derrière) Br* arse, *Am* ass

troufion [trufjɔ̃] **NM 1** *Fam (simple soldat) Br* squaddie, *Am* grunt **2** *très Fam (postérieur) Br* arse, *Am* ass

trouillard, -e [trujar, -ard] *très Fam* **ADJ** lily-livered, chicken

NM,F chicken *(person)*

trouille [truj] **NF** *très Fam* fear, fright; **ça va lui flanquer** *ou* **ficher la t.** it'll scare the living daylights out of him/her; **avoir la t.** to be petrified, to be scared stiff; **j'avais une t. bleue** I was scared stiff *or* to death; **je n'ai jamais eu une telle t. de ma vie** I've never been so petrified in my life

trouillomètre [trujɔmɛtr] **NM** *très Fam* **avoir le t. à zéro** to be scared stiff *or* to death

trouilloter [3] [trujɔte] **VI** *très Fam* **1** *(avoir peur)* to be scared shitless, to be shit-scared **2** *(sentir mauvais)* to stink, *Br* to pong

troupe [trup] **NF 1** *(de touristes, d'enfants)* troop; **ils se déplacent toujours en t.** they always go round as a group

2 *Mil (formation, régiment)* troop; **la t., les troupes** the troops *or* men; **on fit donner** *ou* **intervenir la t., on envoya la t.** the army was *or* troops were sent in; **troupes de choc** shock troops

3 *Théât* **t. (de théâtre** *ou* **de comédiens)** company, troupe; **t. d'amateurs** amateur company *or* troupe; **final avec toute la t.** grand finale (with all the cast)

4 *(de scouts)* troop

5 *(d'éléphants)* herd; *(de sangliers)* sounder, herd; **ces animaux vivent en t.** these animals live in herds *or* are gregarious

troupeau, -x [trupo] **NM 1** *(de vaches, d'éléphants, de girafes)* herd; *(de moutons)* flock; *(d'oies)* gaggle; **il garde le t.** *(de vaches)* he's tending the herd; *(de moutons)* he's tending the flock **2** *Rel* **le t. des fidèles** the flock **3** *Péj (multitude passive)* herd; **quel t. d'imbéciles!** what a load of idiots!

troupier [trupje] **ADJ M** *voir* **comique**

NM *Fam* soldier

troussage [trusaʒ] **NM 1** *Culin* trussing **2** *Métal* strickling

trousse [trus] **NF** *(étui)* case; *(d'écolier)* pencil case; **t. de maquillage** make-up bag; **t. de médecin** medical bag; **t. à ongles** manicure set; **t. à outils** toolkit; **t. de secours** first-aid kit; **t. de toilette** spongebag

• **aux trousses de PRÉP être aux trousses de qn** to be after *or* chasing sb, to be (hot) on sb's heels; **le fisc est à nos trousses** we've got the taxman after us; **il a la police aux trousses** the police are after him, the police are on his tail *or* hot on his heels; **comme s'il avait le diable à ses trousses** *ou* **le feu aux trousses** like a bat out of hell

troussé, -e [truse] **ADJ** *Fam* **bien t.** *(objet, compliment)* neat; **un petit refrain bien** *ou* **joliment t.** a catchy little tune; **un petit slogan bien t.** a snappy slogan

trousseau, -x [truso] **NM 1** *(assortiment)* **t. (de clés)** bunch of keys **2** *(de mariée)* trousseau *(including linen)* **3** *(de pensionnaire)* clothes, outfit

trousser [3] [truse] **VT 1** *Culin* to truss (up) **2** *(rédiger avec brio)* **en deux minutes, il troussait un poème** he could dash off a poem in a couple of minutes; **t. un compliment à qn** to pay sb a neat compliment **3** *très Fam (posséder sexuellement)* to screw, *Br* to shag

VPR se trousser *Vieilli* to hitch up one's skirts

trousseur [trusœr] **NM** *Fam Vieilli* **t. de jupons** womanizer, philanderer

trouvaille [truvaj] **NF** *(objet, lieu)* find; *(idée, méthode)* brainwave; *(expression)* coinage; **une émission pleine de trouvailles** a programme full of good ideas

TROUVER [3] [truve]

VT

- to find **A1–3, B1, 2, C1–5, D1**
- to think **D1, 2**
- to discover **A1, 2**
- to catch **B2**

V IMPERSONNEL
- there is/are **1**

VPR
- to be found **2**
- to be (situated) **3**
- to find oneself **5, 7**
- to feel **6**
- to happen **8**

VT A. *APRÈS UNE RECHERCHE* **1** *(objet perdu, personne, emploi)* to find; *(empreintes, trésor)* to find, to discover; *(pétrole)* to strike, to find; **ah, je te trouve enfin!** so I've found you at last!; **où pourrais-je la t. mardi?** where could I find *or* contact her on Tuesday?; **là, vous allez t. la route Paris–Lyon** that's where you'll join up with the Paris–Lyons road; **as-tu trouvé où il se cache?** have you found where he's hiding *or* his hiding-place?; **il faut que je trouve 200 euros avant demain** I must get hold of *or* find 200 euros before tomorrow; **j'ai trouvé en elle la sœur/l'amie que je cherchais** in her I found the sister/the friend I'd been looking for

2 *(détecter)* to find, to discover; **je ne trouve plus son pouls** I can't feel his/her pulse any more; **je ne trouve rien (d'anormal) à la radiographie** I can't find *or* I haven't detected anything wrong on the X-ray; **ils lui ont trouvé quelque chose au sein** they found a lump in her breast; **ils ont trouvé beaucoup de coquilles dans le texte** they found *or* spotted a lot of misprints in the text

3 *(acheter)* to find, to get; **je n'ai pas trouvé de crème fraîche, alors j'ai mis du yaourt** I couldn't find *or* get any cream so I used yoghurt instead

4 *(rendre visite à)* **aller t. qn** to go to sb, to go and see sb; **il faut que tu ailles t. un spécialiste** you should go and see a specialist; **venir t. qn** to come to sb, to come and see sb; **on vient souvent me t. pour me demander conseil** people often come to me for advice

B. *INVOLONTAIREMENT* **1** *(tomber sur ▸ personne, lettre, trésor)* to find; **j'ai trouvé ce livre en faisant du rangement** I found *or* came across this book while I was tidying up; **j'ai trouvé ce bouquet de roses en rentrant chez moi** I found this bunch of roses waiting for me when I got home; **à notre grande surprise, nous avons trouvé le beau temps en arrivant** when we got there we were surprised to find that the weather was good; **si je m'attendais à te t. là!** fancy meeting you here!; **si je trouve celui qui m'a cabossé ma portière!** just let me lay my hands on whoever dented my car door!; **t. qch par hasard** to chance *or* to stumble upon sth; **on l'a trouvé mort dans la cuisine** he was found dead in the kitchen; **t. à qui parler** *(un confident)* to find a friend; *Fam* **s'il continue comme ça, il va t. à qui parler!** if he goes on like that, I'll give him what for!

2 *(surprendre)* to find, to catch; **que personne ne te trouve ici!** don't let anyone find *or* catch you here!; **je l'ai trouvé fouillant** *ou* **qui fouillait dans mes tiroirs** I found *or* I caught him searching through my drawers

C. *PAR L'ESPRIT, LA VOLONTÉ* **1** *(inventer ▸ prétexte, méthode etc)* to find; **où as-tu trouvé cette idée?** where did you get that idea from?; **tu n'as rien trouvé de mieux à faire?** couldn't you find anything better to do?; **je ne savais pas ce que je faisais – c'est tout ce que tu as trouvé?** I didn't know what I was doing – is that the best you can come up with?; **je n'ai rien trouvé à répondre** I was stuck for an answer

2 *(deviner ▸ solution)* to find; *(▸ réponse, mot de passe)* to find (out), to discover; *(▸ code)* to break, to crack; **je n'ai pas pu t. la raison de son refus** I was unable to find out why he refused; **j'ai trouvé!** I've got it!, I know!; **39 moins 7, il fallait t. 32** 39 take away 7, the correct result was 32

3 *(parvenir à)* to find; **t. la force/le courage de faire qch** to find the strength/the courage to do sth; **ça y est, j'ai trouvé ce que je voulais te dire!** I know what I wanted to tell you!; **je n'arrivais pas à t. mes mots** I couldn't find the right words, I was lost for words; **là, tu as trouvé le mot juste!** you've said it!; *Hum* **tu as trouvé ça tout seul?** did you come up with that all on your own?; **t. à se loger** to find accommodation *or* somewhere to live; **je trouverai à me faire remplacer** I'll find someone to stand in for me; **t. à vendre sa voiture** to find a buyer for one's car; **on ne trouve jamais à se garer par ici** you can never find anywhere to park around here

4 *(se ménager)* to find; **t. le temps de lire** to find time to read; **je n'ai pas le temps – trouve-le!** I haven't got time – (then you must) make time!; **t. l'occasion de faire qch** to find the opportunity to do sth

5 *(ressentir)* to find; **t. du plaisir à qch/à faire qch** to take pleasure in sth/in doing sth, to enjoy sth/doing sth

D. *AVOIR COMME OPINION* **1** *(juger, estimer)* to find, to think; **t. qch remarquable** to find sth remarkable, to think that sth is remarkable; **je la trouve déprimée en ce moment** I find her depressed at the moment; **tu vas me t. vieilli** you'll think *or* find I've aged; **comment me trouves-tu dans cette robe?** how do you like me in this dress?; **t. que** to think *or* to find that; **je trouve que ça en vaut la peine** I think *or* I reckon it's worth it; **je trouve qu'il change beaucoup en ce moment** he seems to me to be going through a lot of changes at the moment; **il est prétentieux – je ne trouve pas** he's pretentious – I don't think so; **la soupe manque de sel, tu ne trouves pas?** the soup needs more salt, don't you think?; **tu trouves?** do you think so?

2 *(reconnaître)* **je lui trouve du charme** I think he's/she's got charm; **tu ne lui trouves pas une petite ressemblance avec ta sœur?** don't you think *or* wouldn't you say that she looks a bit like your sister?; *Fam* **mais enfin, qu'est-ce que tu lui trouves, à ce type?** for goodness' sake, what do you see in this guy?; **je lui trouve mauvais goût, à ce vin** I don't think this wine tastes very nice; **je lui ai trouvé mauvaise mine hier** he/she didn't look very well to me yesterday

se trouver V IMPERSONNEL 1 il se trouve *(suivi d'un singulier)* there is; *(suivi d'un pluriel)* there are; **il se trouvera toujours quelqu'un pour te renseigner** you'll always find somebody *or* there'll always be someone you can ask **2 il se trouve que…** *(le hasard fait que)* as it happens,…; **il se trouve que quelqu'un vous a vu dans mon bureau** as it happens, somebody saw you in my office; **il s'est trouvé que c'était lui le fautif** it turned out that HE was to blame

VPR 1 *(s'estimer)* **je me trouve trop mince** I think I'm too thin; **et tu te trouves drôle?** so you think you're (being) funny?; **il se trouve génial** he thinks he's great, he really fancies himself

2 *(emploi passif)* to be found, to exist; **cette fleur ne se trouve qu'en montagne** this flower is only (to be) found *or* only grows in the mountains; **de bons artisans, cela se trouve difficilement** it's not easy to find *or* to get good craftsmen; *Hum* **ça ne se trouve pas sous le pas d'un cheval** *(argent)* it's hard to come by

3 *(en un lieu, une circonstance ▸ personne)* to be; *(▸ bâtiment, ville)* to be situated, to be located; *(résider ▸ intérêt, problème)* to be, to lie; **je me trouvais là par hasard** I just happened to be there; **qu'est-ce que tu dirais si tu te trouvais face à face avec lui?** what would you say if you suddenly found yourself face to face with him?; **trouve-toi devant la gare à 18 heures** make sure you're outside the station at 6 p.m.; **où se trouve la gare?** where's the station?; **Senlis se trouve au nord de Paris** Senlis is to the north of Paris, Senlis is situated *or* located north of Paris; **se t. sur** *(figurer)* to appear *or* to be shown on; **mon nom ne se trouve pas sur la liste** my name doesn't feature *or* figure on the list, my name isn't listed; **c'est là que se trouve la difficulté/le dilemme** that's where the difficulty/dilemma lies

4 *(arriver)* **quand vous vous trouverez sur la place, tournez à droite** when you arrive at the square, turn right

5 *(dans une situation)* to find oneself, to be; **se t. dans l'impossibilité de faire qch** to find oneself *or* to be unable to do sth; **se t. dans l'obligation de faire qch** to have no option but to do sth

6 *(se sentir)* to feel; **je me suis trouvé bête d'avoir crié** I felt stupid for having screamed; **se t. bien/mieux** *(avec quelqu'un)* to feel at ease/more at ease; *(dans un vêtement élégant)* to feel (that one looks) good/better; **se t. mal** *(s'évanouir)* to pass out, to faint; **elle a suivi mes conseils et s'en est bien/mal trouvée** she followed my advice, and benefited from it/and lived to regret it; **qu'il parte, je ne m'en trouverai que mieux!** let him leave, see if I care!

7 *(se réaliser)* to find oneself; **en tant qu'écrivain, elle ne s'est pas encore trouvée** as a writer, she hasn't found her individual voice *or* style yet

8 *(exprime la fortuité d'un événement, d'une situation)* to happen; **ils se trouvaient appartenir au même club** they happened to belong *or* it turned out that they belonged to the same club; **je me trouve être libre ce jour-là** it so happens that I'm free that day; *Fam* **si ça se trouve** maybe; **on l'a abandonné, ce gamin, si ça se trouve!** maybe the kid's been abandoned(, who knows)!; **si ça se trouve, il y a une fuite** maybe there's a leak

trouvère [truvɛr] **NM** *Littérature* trouvère

troyen¹, -enne¹ [trwajɛ̃, -ɛn] **ADJ** *(de Troie)* Trojan
• **Troyen, -enne NM,F** Trojan

troyen², -enne² [trwajɛ̃, -ɛn] **ADJ** *(de Troyes)* of/from Troyes
• **Troyen, -enne NM,F** = inhabitant of or person from Troyes

truand [tryɑ̃] **NM** *(escroc)* crook; *(gangster)* gangster, hood; *Fig* **les commerçants du coin sont tous des truands!** the local shopkeepers are all crooks!

> Il faut noter que le terme anglais **truant** est un faux ami. Il désigne un élève qui fait l'école buissonnière.

truander [3] [tryɑ̃de] **VT** *Fam (escroquer)* to con, to swindle□; *(faire payer trop cher)* to rip off; **se faire t.** to be *or* get conned; *(payer trop cher)* to get ripped off

VI 1 *Fam (tricher)* **t. (à un examen)** to cheat□ (in an exam) **2** *Fam (resquiller)* to sneak in□

trublion [tryblijɔ̃] **NM** troublemaker

truc¹ [tryk] **NM** *Fam* **1** *(astuce)* trick□; **un t. tout bête et qui marche à tous les coups** a simple little trick that works every time; **connaître (tous) les trucs du métier** to know the tricks of the trade; **j'ai trouvé le t.!** I've got the hang of it!; **elle a toujours pas pigé le t.!** she still hasn't got the hang of it!; **il y a un t.!** there's a trick in it!; **il doit y avoir un t., c'est trop beau** there's bound to be a catch, it's too good to be true; **j'ai un t. pour rentrer sans payer** I know a way of getting in without paying□

2 *Cin & Théât* (special) effect□, trick□; **pièce à trucs** play with elaborate stage effects□

3 *(chose)* thing□; **je pense à un t.** I've just thought of something; **il faudrait que tu me dises un t….** tell me something…; **j'ai plein de trucs à faire** I've got lots to do; **je voudrais lui offrir un petit t.** I'd like to give him/her a little something; **tu devrais t'acheter un t. pour nettoyer ton four** you ought to buy something to clean your oven with; **mange pas de ce t.-là!** don't eat any of that (stuff)!

4 *(objet dont on ne connaît pas le nom)* thing, whatchamacallit, *Br* thingy; **tu sais, ce t. dont on se sert pour couper la pâte** you know, the thing you use to cut the pastry with; **qu'est-ce que c'est que ce t.-là?** what's that (thingumajig)?

5 *(intérêt)* **ce n'est pas/c'est mon t.** it's not/it's my cup of tea; **le rock, c'est pas mon t.** rock music is not my (kind of) thing; **l'écologie, c'est vraiment son t.** he's/she's really into environmental issues; **c'est tout à fait son t.** it's just his/her sort of thing, *Br* it's right up his/her street

6 *(personne dont on a oublié le nom)* **T.** what's-his name, *f* what's-her-name, *Br* thingy

truc² [tryk] = **truck**

trucage [trykaʒ] = **truquage**

truchement [tryʃmɑ̃] **NM par le t. de son ami** through *or* via his/her friend

trucider [3] [tryside] **VT** *Fam* to bump off, to waste; *Hum* **une heure de retard, on va se faire t.!** we're an hour late, they'll kill us!

truck [tryk] **NM** *Rail* truck, *Am* freight car

trucmuche [trykmyʃ] **NM** *Fam* **1** *(chose)* thingumajig, thingamabob, *Br* thingy **2 T.** *(personne)* what's-his-name, *f* what's-her-name, *Br* thingy

truculence [trykylɑ̃s] **NF** colourfulness

truculent, -e [trykylɑ̃, -ɑ̃t] **ADJ** colourful

> Il faut noter que l'adjectif anglais **truculent** est un faux ami. Il signifie **agressif**.

truelle [tryɛl] **NF 1** *(du maçon)* trowel **2** *(pour servir)* **t. à poisson** fish slice **3 travailler à la t.** *(peintre)* to work with a trowel

truffe [tryf] **NF 1** *(champignon)* truffle; **omelette aux truffes** truffle omelette
2 *(friandise)* **t. (au chocolat)** (chocolate) truffle
3 *(de chien, de chat)* nose
4 *Fam (nez)* snout
5 *Fam (imbécile) Br* divvy, *Am* lamebrain, schmuck

truffer [3] [tryfe] **VT 1** *Culin* to garnish with truffles; **pâté truffé** truffled pâté, pâté with truffles; **poularde truffée** truffled chicken **2** *Fig (emplir)* to fill; **ils l'ont truffé de balles** they pumped him full of bullets; **truffé d'anecdotes/de citations** peppered with anecdotes/with quotations; **truffé de fautes** riddled with mistakes

truffier, -ère [tryfje, -ɛr] **ADJ chien t.** truffle hound; **chêne t.** = oak on whose roots truffles grow
• **truffière NF** truffle-bed, trufflery

truie [trɥi] **NF** *Zool* sow

truisme [tryism] **NM** truism; **c'est un t.!** it's obvious!, it goes without saying!

truite [trɥit] **NF** trout; **t. arc-en-ciel** rainbow trout, steelhead; **t. de mer** sea trout; *Culin* **t. meunière** = trout sautéed in butter and served with parsley and lemon juice; **t. de rivière** river trout; **t. saumonée** salmon trout

truité, -e [trɥite] **ADJ 1** *(tacheté ▸ gén)* speckled; *(▸ chien, cheval)* spotted **2** *Cér* crackled

trumeau, -x [trymo] **NM 1** *(entre des fenêtres)* (window) pier
2 *(panneau de lambris, de peinture, de glace)* pier glass; *(d'une cheminée)* overmantel
3 *Archit* pier
4 *Culin* leg of beef
5 *Fam (femme laide)* dog, *Br* boot, *Am* beast

truquage [trykaʒ] **NM 1** *Cin (action)* (use of) special effects; *(résultat)* special effect; *(de photographie)* faking; **c'est un t.** it's all faked **2** *(d'élections, de résultats)* rigging; *(de match)* fixing, rigging; *(de comptes)* fiddling

truquer [3] [tryke] **VT 1** *(élection, statistiques)* to rig; *(match)* to fix, to rig; *(comptes)* to fiddle; *(entretien)* to set up; *(tableau)* to fake; *(dés)* to load; **les dés sont truqués** the dice are loaded **2** *(photographie)* to fake, to rig; *Cin* **t. une scène** to use special effects in a scene; **la scène est truquée** the scene contains *or* has special effects

truqueur, -euse [trykœr, -øz] **NM,F 1** *(escroc)* cheat **2** *Cin* special effects person *or* generator

truquiste [trykist] **NMF** *Cin* special effects man, *f* woman

trust [trœst] **NM 1** *Écon* trust **2** *(entreprise)* corporation

truster [3] [trœste] **VT 1** *(marché)* to corner, to monopolize **2** *Fam (monopoliser)* to monopolize▫, to hog; **t. les médailles** *(athlète)* to carry off all the medals; **il truste les premiers rôles du cinéma français** he gets all the leading roles in French cinema

tsar [tsar, dzar] **NM** tsar, czar

tsarévitch [tsarevitʃ, dzarevitʃ] **NM** tsarevitch, czarevitch

tsarine [tsarin, dzarin] **NF** tsarina, czarina

tsarisme [tsarism, dzarism] **NM** tsarism, czarism

tsariste [tsarist, dzarist] **ADJ** tsarist, czarist
NMF tsarist, czarist

tsé-tsé [tsetse] **NF INV** *Entom* tsetse (fly)

TSF [teɛsɛf] **NF** *Vieilli Tél (abrév* **télégraphie sans fil***)* *(appareil)* wireless; *(procédé)* wireless telegraphy

T-shirt [tiʃœrt] = **tee-shirt**

tsigane [tsigan] **ADJ** Gypsyish
• **Tsigane NMF** (Hungarian) Gypsy

tsunami [tsynami] **NM** tsunami

TSVP *(abrév écrite* **tournez s'il vous plaît***)* PTO

TTC [tetese] **ADJ** *Com (abrév* **toutes taxes comprises***)* inclusive of all tax, including tax

TU [tey] **NM** *(abrév* **temps universel***)* UT, GMT; **à 0h TU** at 0h UT *or* GMT

tu¹, -e [ty] **PP** *voir* **taire**

tu² [ty] **PRON PERSONNEL 1** *(sujet d'un verbe)* you; **tu as raison** you're right; **qui es-tu?** who are you?; *Fam* **qu'est-ce que t'as?** what's up (with you)?▫; *Fam* **t'en veux?** do you want some?▫; *Fam* **t'es bête!** you're stupid!▫ **2** *Rel* thou; *(en s'adressant à Dieu)* **Tu** Thou; **tu ne tueras point** thou shall not kill **3** *(emploi nominal)* **dire tu à qn** to use the familiar form *or* the "tu" form with *or* to sb; **allez, on va se dire tu** ≃ come on, let's not stand on ceremony; **vous vous dites tu?** ≃ are you on first-name terms with each other?; **être à tu et à toi avec qn** ≃ to be on first-name terms with sb

Tuamotu [twamotu] **NFPL les T.** the Tuamotu Archipelago

tuant, -e [tɥɑ̃, -ɑ̃t] **ADJ** *Fam* **1** *(épuisant)* exhausting▫ **2** *(insupportable)* exasperating▫; **c'est t., ce bruit** this noise is driving me up the wall; **les enfants sont vraiment tuants aujourd'hui** the kids are being a real pain today

tub [tœb] **NM 1** *(objet)* tub, bathtub **2** *(bain)* bath; **prendre un t.** to take *or* have a bath

tuba [tyba] **NM 1** *Mus* tuba **2** *(pour nager)* snorkel

tubage [tybaʒ] **NM 1** *Méd* intubation, cannulation; **t. gastrique** gastric intubation **2** *Pétr* casing

tubaire [tybɛr] **ADJ** *Anat* tubal

tubard, -e [tybar, -ard] *Fam* **ADJ** suffering from TB▫
NM,F TB sufferer▫

tube [tyb] **NM 1** *(conduit)* tube, pipe; **t. lance-torpilles** torpedo tube; **t. de niveau d'eau** water-gauge column; **tubes de pompage** tubing; **t. raccord** pipe connection; **t. de selle** *(d'un vélo)* saddle post
2 *Élec* **t. amplificateur** amplifier tube; **t. cathodique** cathode-ray tube; **t. au néon** neon tube; **t. à vide** vacuum tube
3 *(contenant)* tube; **t. d'aspirine** = packet of aspirin; **t. pour dosage, t. doseur** measuring tube; **t. à essai** test tube; **t. gradué** graduated tube; **t. de peinture** tube of paint; **t. de rouge à lèvres** (stick of) lipstick; **en t.** in a tube; **acheter de la mayonnaise en t.** to buy a tube of mayonnaise
4 *Anat & Bot* tube; **t. bronchique** bronchial tube; **t. capillaire** capillary (tube); **t. digestif** digestive tract
5 *Fam (chanson)* (smash) hit, chart-topper; **le t. de l'été** this summer's chart-topper

tuber [3] [tybe] **VT 1** *Pétr* to line, to case **2** *(en travaux publics)* to tube

tubercule [tybɛrkyl] **NM 1** *Bot* tuber **2** *Anat & Méd* tubercle

tuberculeux, -euse [tybɛrkylø, -øz] **ADJ 1** *(malade)* tuberculous; *(symptôme)* tuberculous, tubercular; **être t.** to have tuberculosis **2** *Bot* tuberous
NM,F tuberculosis sufferer, tubercular patient

tuberculine [tybɛrkylin] **NF** *Méd* tuberculin

tuberculose [tybɛrkyloz] **NF** *Méd* tuberculosis, TB; **avoir la t.** to have tuberculosis; **t. pulmonaire** pulmonary tuberculosis; **t. résistante (aux médicaments)** multi-drug resistant tuberculosis, MDR tuberculosis

tubéreux, -euse [tyberø, -øz] **ADJ** tuberous
• **tubéreuse NF** tuberose

tubérosité [tyberozite] **NF** *Anat* tuberosity

tubulaire [tybylɛr] **ADJ 1** *Anat & Constr* tubular **2** *(chaudière)* tubulous **3** *(en travaux publics)* **pont t.** tubular bridge

tubulé, -e [tybyle] **ADJ** *Bot* tubulate

tubuleux, -euse [tybylø, -øz] **ADJ** *Bot* tubulous

tubulure [tybylyr] **NF 1** *(ouverture d'un flacon)* tubulure **2** *(tuyauterie)* piping; *(tube)* pipe **3** *Aut* **t. d'admission/d'échappement** inlet/exhaust manifold

TUC, Tuc [tyk] *(abrév* **travaux d'utilité collective***)* **NM** = community work for unemployed young people; **faire un T.** to do community work
NMF *(employé)* = person involved in a "TUC" scheme

tue-mouches [tymuʃ] **ADJ INV 1** *(insecticide)* **papier t.** flypaper **2** *Bot* **amanite t.** fly agaric
NM INV *Can* fly swatter

tuer [7] [tɥe] **VT 1** *(personne)* to kill; **t. qn d'un coup de couteau** *ou* **de poignard** to stab sb to death; **t. qn d'un coup de revolver** to shoot and kill sb (with a revolver); **t. qn à coups de couteau** to stab sb *or* to knife sb to death; **t. qn à coups de pierres** to stone sb to death; **se faire t.** to be *or* get killed; **ce week-end, la route a encore tué des centaines d'automobilistes** this weekend, road accidents have again claimed hundreds of victims; **c'est la solitude/le chagrin qui l'a tué** he died of loneliness/grief; *Fig* **je t'assure, il est à t.!** *(exaspérant)* honestly, I could (cheerfully) strangle him!; *Fig* **ta fille me tuera!** *(dit par énervement)* your daughter will be the death of me!; **ce voyage m'a tué** *(épuisé)* this trip's worn me out *or* killed me; **ces escaliers me tuent** these stairs will be the death of me; *Fam* **qu'il ne comprenne pas, ça me tue** *(ça me sidère)* it amazes me he doesn't understand▫; *Fam* **ça m'a tué d'apprendre qu'il se remariait** *(sidéré)* I was staggered to hear that he was getting married again; *Fam* **ça me tue d'entendre des âneries pareilles!** *(ça me révolte)* it really gets me when I hear such nonsense!; *Fam* **ça tue!** it's a killer!
2 *(plante)* to kill (off); *(animal de boucherie)* to kill, to slaughter; *(gibier)* to shoot; *Fig* **t. le veau gras** to kill the fatted calf; *Fig* **t. la poule aux œufs d'or** to kill the goose that lays the golden eggs; *Fig* **t. qch dans l'œuf** to nip sth in the bud
3 *(anéantir ▸ tourisme, espoir)* to ruin, to spoil, to kill; **t. l'enthousiasme** to kill *or* to deaden enthusiasm; **cette musique va t. l'ambiance** that music is going to kill the atmosphere stone dead *or* totally destroy the atmosphere
4 *(locution)* **t. le temps** to kill time
USAGE ABSOLU le tabac tue smoking kills *or* is a killer
VPR se tuer 1 *(se suicider)* to kill oneself
2 *(par accident)* to die, to be killed; **se t. au volant** to be killed in a road accident
3 *(s'entre-tuer)* to kill one another
4 *(s'épuiser)* **elle se tue à la tâche** *ou* **à la peine** *ou* **au travail** she's working herself to death; **comme je me tue à te le répéter** as I keep telling you again and again; **c'est ce que je me tue à vous dire!** that's what I've been trying to TELL you!

tuerie [tyri] **NF** slaughter, massacre, bloodbath

tue-tête [tytɛt] **à tue-tête ADV** at the top of one's voice; **elle criait à t.** she was shouting at the top of her voice; **chantant l'hymne national à t.** bellowing out the national anthem

tueur, -euse [tɥœr, -øz] **ADJ** *(fauves, cellule, virus)* killer *(avant n)*
NM,F 1 *(meurtrier)* killer; **t. fou** psychopath; **t. professionnel** *ou* **à gages** hired assassin; **t. en série** serial killer **2** *Chasse* pothunter **3** *(aux abattoirs)* slaughterer

tuf [tyf] **NM 1** *Géol* **t. calcaire** tufa; **t. volcanique** tuff **2** *Fig Littéraire* bedrock, foundation

tuile [tɥil] **NF 1** *Constr* (roofing) tile; **toit en tuiles** tiled roof; **t. canal** *ou* **creuse** curved tile; **t. faîtière** ridge tile; **t. mécanique** interlocking tile; **t. plate** plain tile; **t. romaine** curved tile; **t. solaire** solar tile **2** *Culin Br* biscuit, *Am* cookie *(in the shape of a curved tile)*; **tuiles aux amandes** almond biscuits **3** *Fam (problème)* hassle; **il m'arrive une t.** I'm in a bit of a mess; **on n'a plus de gaz, la t.!** we're out of gas, what a pain!

tuilerie [tɥilri] **NF 1** *(industrie)* tile industry
2 *(fabrique)* tilery
3 *(four)* tile kiln
4 les Tuileries = a formal royal residence in Paris, now the site of the Tuileries Gardens, near the Louvre

tulipe [tylip] **NF 1** *Bot* tulip **2** *(abat-jour)* tulip-shaped lampshade; *(verre)* tulip glass

tulipier [tylipje] **NM** *Bot* tulip tree

tulle [tyl] **NM 1** *Tex* tulle; **t. de soie/de coton** silk/cotton tulle; **robe de t.** tulle dress **2** *Pharm* **t. gras** tulle gras

tuméfaction [tymefaksjɔ̃] **NF 1** *(fait d'enfler)* swelling, *Spéc* tumefaction **2** *(partie enflée)* swelling, swollen area *or* part

tuméfier [9] [tymefje] **VT** to cause to swell, *Spéc* to tumefy
VPR se tuméfier to swell up, *Spéc* to tumefy

tumescence [tymesɑ̃s] **NF** tumescence

tumescent, -e [tymesɑ̃, -ɑ̃t] **ADJ** tumescent

tumeur [tymœr] **NF 1** *Méd* tumour; **t. bénigne/maligne/blanche** benign/malignant/white tumour; **t. au cerveau** brain tumour; **t. secondaire** secondary tumour **2** *Bot* tumour

tumoral, -e, -aux, -ales [tymɔral, -o] **ADJ** tumorous, tumoral

tumulaire [tymylɛr] **ADJ** sepulchral; **pierre t.** tombstone

tumulte [tymylt] **NM** *(activité ▸ soudaine)* commotion, tumult; *(▸ incessante)* hurly-burly, turmoil; *Littéraire* **le t. des flots** the tumult of the waves; **le t. des passions** the turmoil *or* tumult of passions; **dans le t.** *(dans la confusion)* in an uproar, in confusion; **dans le t. de la fusillade** in the confusion *or* commotion of the shooting; **dans un t. d'applaudissements** to thunderous applause

tumultueuse [tymyltɥøz] *voir* **tumultueux**

tumultueusement [tymyltɥøzmɑ̃] **ADV** stormily, tumultuously

tumultueux, -euse [tymyltɥø, -øz] **ADJ** *(discussion)* stormy, turbulent, tumultuous; *(foule)* boisterous, turbulent; *(vie)* stormy, turbulent; *(passion)* tumultuous, turbulent; *(relation)* stormy; *(flots)* turbulent

tumulus [tymylys] **NM** tumulus

tune [tyn] = **thune**

tuner [tynɛr] **NM** *Rad* tuner

tungstène [tœ̃kstɛn, tœ̃gstɛn] **NM** *Chim* tungsten

tuning [tjuniŋ] **NM** *(d'une voiture)* customizing, *Fam* pimping

tunique [tynik] **NF 1** *(vêtement)* tunic **2** *Anat* tunic, tunica **3** *Bot* tunic

Tunis [tynis] **NM** Tunis

Tunisie [tynizi] **NF la T.** Tunisia

tunisien, -enne [tynizjɛ̃, -ɛn] **ADJ** Tunisian

• **Tunisien, -enne NM,F** Tunisian

tunnel [tynɛl] **NM 1** tunnel; **percer un t. (sous)** to tunnel (under); **t. aérodynamique** wind tunnel; **t. routier** road tunnel; **le t. sous la Manche** the Channel Tunnel **2 t. de publicités** extended commercial break

TUP [typ] **NM** *Banque* (*abrév* **titre universel de paiement**) universal payment order

Tupperware® [typɛrwar] **NM** Tupperware® container

turban [tyrbɑ̃] **NM 1** *(couvre-chef)* turban; *Littéraire* **prendre le t.** to go over to Islam **2** *Culin* ring-shaped mould

turbin [tyrbɛ̃] **NM** *très Fam* work□; **aller au t.** to go off to the daily grind; **après le t.** after work□, after a day's grind

turbine [tyrbin] **NF** turbine; *(d'une pompe à eau)* impeller; **t. à air** air *or* wind turbine; *Tech* **t. centrifuge** centrifugal blower; **t. à gaz** gas turbines; **t. hydraulique** water turbine; **t. à impulsion** impulse turbine; *Tech* **t. moteur** power turbine; **t. à réaction** reaction turbine; **t. à vapeur** steam turbine; *Tech* **t. de ventilation** blower

• **à turbine ADJ** turbine-powered

turbiner [3] [tyrbine] **VI** *très Fam* **1** *(travailler)* to slog away, to slave away **2** *(se livrer à la prostitution)* to turn tricks, *Br* to be on the game

VT *Tech (sucre)* to treat by centrifugal turbine action

turbo [tyrbo] **ADJ INV** turbine-driven, turbo *(avant n)*

NM 1 *Aut* turbo; *Fam* **mettre le t.** to get a move on **2** *Ordinat* turbo

NF turbo *(car)*

turboalternateur [tyrbɔalternatœr] **NM** turboalternator

turbocompresseur [tyrbɔkɔ̃prɛsœr] **NM** turbocharger; **t. de suralimentation** turbosupercharger

turbodiesel [tyrbodjezel] **NM** *(moteur)* turbo diesel

NF *(voiture)* turbo diesel

turbomoteur [tyrbɔmɔtœr] **NM** turboshaft engine

turbopompe [tyrbɔpɔ̃p] **NF** turbopump, turbine pump

turbopropulseur [tyrbɔpropylsœr] **NM** turboprop; **avion à t.** turboprop aircraft

turboréacteur [tyrbɔreaktœr] **NM** turbojet (engine); **t. à double flux** by-pass turbojet

turbot [tyrbo] **NM** *Ich* turbot

turbotrain [tyrbɔtrɛ̃] **NM** turbotrain

turbulence [tyrbylɑ̃s] **NF 1** *(d'un enfant)* boisterousness, unruliness **2** *Littéraire (d'une foule, d'une fête)* rowdiness; *(de l'océan)* turbulence **3** *Météo* turbulence, turbulency; **nous traversons une zone de turbulences** we're encountering some turbulence

turbulent, -e [tyrbylɑ̃, -ɑ̃t] **ADJ 1** *(enfant)* boisterous, unruly; *(élèves)* rowdy, disruptive; *(classe)* boisterous, noisy **2** *Littéraire (foule, fête)* rowdy; *(époque)* stormy; *(eaux)* turbulent **3** *Phys* turbulent; **régime t.** turbulent flow

turc, turque [tyrk] **ADJ** Turkish

NM *(langue)* Turkish

• **Turc, Turque NM,F** Turk; *Hist* **le Grand T.** the Grand Turk; *Hist* **les Jeunes-Turcs** the Young Turks; *Pol* **jeunes turcs** young radicals; **fort comme un T.** as strong as a horse

• **à la turque ADJ 1** *(cabinets)* seatless, hole-in-the-ground *(avant n)* **2** *Beaux-Arts* Turkish **ADV** *(s'asseoir)* cross-legged

turf [tœrf] **NM 1** *(activité)* horse racing

2 *(terrain)* turf, racecourse

3 *très Fam (travail)* work□; *(lieu de travail)* workplace□; **aller au t.** to go to work□

4 *très Fam (prostitution)* prostitution□; **faire le t.** to turn tricks, *Br* to be on the game

turfiste [tœrfist] **NMF** racegoer

turgescence [tyrʒesɑ̃s] **NF** turgescence

turgescent, -e [tyrʒesɑ̃, -ɑ̃t] **ADJ** turgescent

turgide [tyrʒid] **ADJ** *Littéraire* turgid, swollen

turista [turista] **NF** *Fam* **la t.** Montezuma's revenge, Delhi belly

turkmène [tyrkmɛn] **ADJ** Turkoman

NM *(langue)* Turkmen

• **Turkmène NMF** Turkoman; **les Turkmènes** the Turkomans *or* Turkomen

Turkménistan [tyrkmenistɑ̃] **NM le T.** Turkmenistan

turlupiner [3] [tyrlypine] **VT** *Fam* to bother□, to bug; **c'est ce qui me turlupine** that's what's bugging me *or* what's on my mind

turlute [tyrlyt] **NF** *très Fam* blow-job; **faire une t. à qn** to give sb a blow-job, to go down on sb

turluter [3] [tyrlyte] **VI** *Can Fam (chantonner)* to trill, to sing tra-la-la; *(fredonner)* to hum□

turlututu [tyrlytyty] **EXCLAM** fiddlesticks!; **t. chapeau pointu!** yah boo, sucks to you!

turne [tyrn] **NF** *Fam (chambre d'étudiant)* room□; *(logement d'étudiant)* digs; *(taudis)* dive

turnover [tœrnɔvœr] **NM** turnover *(of personnel)*

turpitude [tyrpityd] **NF** *Littéraire* **1** *(caractère vil)* turpitude, depravity **2** *(acte)* base *or* vile *or* depraved act **3** *(parole)* vile remark

turque [tyrk] *voir* **turc**

Turquie [tyrki] **NF la T.** Turkey

turquoise [tyrkwaz] **NF** turquoise

ADJ INV turquoise (blue)

tut *etc voir* **taire**

tutélaire [tytelɛr] **ADJ 1** *Littéraire (divinité, rôle)* guardian *(avant n)*, tutelary **2** *Jur* tutelary; **gestion t.** guardianship; **puissance t.** power of guardianship

tutelle [tytɛl] **NF 1** *Jur* guardianship, tutelage; **il est en** *ou* **sous t.** he has a guardian, he's under tutelage; **placer** *ou* **mettre qn en** *ou* **sous t.** to put sb into the care of a guardian; **t. légale, t. d'État** wardship (order)

2 *Admin* **t. administrative** administrative supervision

3 *Pol* trusteeship; **territoire sous t.** trust territory

4 *(protection)* care, protection; *(contrainte)* control; **sous la t. de** *(famille, loi)* under the protection of; **prendre qn sous sa t.** to take sb under one's wing; **tenir un pays en t.** *ou* **sous sa t.** to hold sway over a country

tuteur, -trice [tytœr, -tris] **NM,F 1** *Jur* guardian; **t. légal** legal guardian; **t. ad hoc** = specially appointed guardian (ad litem) **2** *Littéraire (appui, protection)* guardian, guarantee; **la loi est la tutrice de nos libertés** the law is the guardian *or* guarantee of our liberty

NM prop, support, *Hort* stake; **mettre un t. à une plante** to stake a plant

tutoie *etc voir* **tutoyer**

tutoiement [tytwamɑ̃] **NM** = use of the familiar "tu"; **le t. est de rigueur** everybody calls each other "tu"

> **TUTOIEMENT ET VOUVOIEMENT**
>
> Traditionally, non-native French speakers waited until they were addressed using the informal "tu" form before using it themselves, except when speaking to young children. However, in the past twenty or thirty years, people in France have become much more casual about using "tu", and it is now commonly used among colleagues in the workplace, while the "vous" form tends to be used when talking to people from an older generation or to hierarchical superiors (see also entries **tu** and **vous**).

tutoriel [tytɔrjɛl] **NM** tutorial

tutoyer [13] [tytwaje] **VT 1** *(personne)* = to use the familiar "tu" form with; **elle tutoie son professeur** ≃ she's on first-name terms with her teacher; **moi, je me fais t. par tous mes employés** all my employees call me "tu" **2** *Équitation* **t. l'obstacle** to brush against the fence *(without knocking it)* **3** *Fig (être proche de)* to come close to; **il a tutoyé la mort plus d'une fois** he's had more than one brush with death

VPR se tutoyer to address each other as "tu", = to be on familiar terms (with each other)

tutrice [tytris] *voir* **tuteur**

tutti [tuti] **NM INV** *Mus* tutti

tutti frutti [tutifruti] **ADJ INV** tutti-frutti *(avant n)*

tutti quanti [tutikwɑ̃ti] **ADV et t.** and the rest; **la grand-mère, le cousin et t.** the grandmother, the cousin and the whole brood

tutu [tyty] **NM** tutu

Tuvalu [tyvaly] **NM** Tuvalu

tuyau, -x [tɥijo] **NM 1** *(conduit)* pipe; *(flexible)* tube; **t. d'arrosage** (garden) hose, hosepipe; **t. de cheminée** (chimney) flue; **t. de chute, t. vertical** standpipe; **t. de descente** downpipe; **t. d'eau/de gaz** water/gas pipe; **t. d'échappement** exhaust (pipe); **t. d'écoulement** drainpipe; *Aut* **t. d'essence** petrol pipe; *Mus* **t. d'orgue** organ pipe; **t. de pipe** stem of a pipe; **t. de poêle** stovepipe; **en t. de poêle** *(pantalon)* drainpipe *(avant n)*; *(chapeau)* stovepipe *(avant n)*; *Fam* **la famille t. de poêle** = family whose members have an incestuous relationship; *Fam* **il le lui a dit** *ou* **glissé dans le t. de l'oreille** he whispered it in her ear; *Fam* **être dans les tuyaux** *(être en cours de réalisation)* to be in the pipeline

2 *Bot (d'une tige)* stalk

3 *(d'une plume)* quill

4 *Fam (conseil)* tip□, hint□; *(aux courses)* tip□; *(information)* tip-off; **avoir un t.** to have a tip-off; **qui est-ce qui t'a filé le t.?** who tipped you off?, who put you on to it?; **un t. percé** a useless tip-off; **c'est un t. increvable** it's straight from the horse's mouth

5 *Couture* flute

tuyautage [tɥijotaʒ] **NM 1** *Fam (fait de renseigner)* tipping off **2** *Couture* fluting **3** *Tech* plumbing

tuyauter [3] [tɥijote] **VT 1** *Fam (conseiller)* to give a tip to□ (**sur** about); *(informer)* to tip off (**sur** about); **je me suis fait t. pour la prochaine course, on ne peut pas perdre** someone's given me a tip for the next race, we can't lose **2** *(plisser)* to flute; **fer à t.** goffering tongs

tuyauterie [tɥijotri] **NF 1** *(canalisations)* pipes, piping *(UNCOUNT)*

2 *(d'un orgue)* pipes

3 *Aut* **t. de carburant** fuel pipe *or* line; *Aut* **t. de frein** brake pipe *or* line

4 *Fam (organes de la digestion)* innards, guts; *(poumons)* lungs□

tuyauteur, -euse [tɥijotœr, -øz] **NM,F 1** *Fam (aux courses)* tipster□ **2** *(ouvrier)* pipe fitter

tuyère [tyjɛr] **NF 1** *(d'une turbine)* nozzle; *Aviat* **t. d'échappement** jet pipe; **t. de propulsion** thrust nozzle **2** *(d'un haut-fourneau)* tuyère

TV [teve] **NF** (*abrév* **télévision**) TV

TVA [teveɑ] **NF** *Fin* (*abrév* **taxe sur la valeur ajoutée**) *Br* ≃ VAT, *Am* ≃ sales tax; **exempt de T.**

zero-rated; **soumis à la T.** ≃ subject to *Br* VAT *or Am* sales tax

VHD [teveaʃde] **NF** (*abrév* **télévision haute définition**) HDTV

VP [tevepe] **NF** (*abrév* **thrombose veineuse profonde**) DVT

weed [twid] **NM** tweed; **veste de t.** tweed jacket

win-set [twinset] (*pl* **twin-sets**) **NM** twinset

wist [twist] **NM** twist (*dance*)

wister [3] [twiste] **VI** to (dance the) twist

ympan [tɛ̃pɑ̃] **NM 1** *Anat* eardrum, *Spéc* tympanum; **un bruit à crever** *ou* **à déchirer les tympans** an ear-splitting noise; **arrête, tu nous déchires les tympans!** stop that ear-splitting noise! **2** *Archit* tympanum **3** *Tech* pinion

ympanal, -aux [tɛ̃panal, -o] *Anat* **ADJ M os t.** tympanic bone

NM tympanic (bone)

ympanique [tɛ̃panik] **ADJ** *Anat* tympanic

ympanon [tɛ̃panɔ̃] **NM** *Mus* dulcimer

ype [tip] **NM 1** (*genre*) kind, type; **avoir le t. latin/nordique** to have Latin/Nordic looks; **elle a le t. indien** she looks Indian; **c'est tout à fait mon t.** (*homme*) he's just my type (of man) *or* my sort of man, he's exactly the kind of man I find attractive; **c'est pas mon t.** he's/she's not my type; **c'est le t. même du romantique** he's the typical romantic; **c'est le t. même de la mère abusive** she's the classic example of the possessive mother; **voilà un produit qui conviendra mieux à votre t. de peau** here's a product which is more suitable for your skin type; **plusieurs types de canapés** different types *or* models of sofas

2 (*comme adj; avec ou sans trait d'union*) typical; **intellectuel t.** typical intellectual; **contrat t.** model contract; **erreur t.** typical *or* classic mistake; **lettre t.** standard letter

3 *Bot* type

4 *Typ* (*ensemble de caractères*) type; (*empreinte*) typeface

5 *Fam* (*homme*) guy, *Br* bloke; **un pauvre t.** a sad individual□; **pauvre t.!** you're/he's/*etc* pathetic *or* sad!; **c'est un drôle de t.!** (*bizarre*) he's a pretty weird bloke!; (*louche*) he's a shady character!; **un sale t.** a bad egg, a nasty piece of work; **c'est un chic t.** he's a nice guy *or Am* a mensch *or* a good Joe

typé, -e [tipe] **ADJ elle est indienne mais pas très typée** she's Indian but doesn't have typical Indian features; **une femme brune très typée** a dark-haired woman with very distinctive looks

typer [3] [tipe] **VT 1** (*donner des caractéristiques à*) to give the relevant characteristics to **2** *Tech* to stamp, to mark

typesse [tipɛs] **NF** *Péj* female□

typhique [tifik] **ADJ** typhous, typhoid (*avant n*)

NMF typhoid sufferer

typhoïde [tifɔid] *Méd* **ADJ** typhoid (*avant n*)

NF typhoid

typhoïdique [tifɔidik] **ADJ** *Méd* typhoidal; **bacille t.** typhoid bacillus

typhon [tifɔ̃] **NM** *Météo* typhoon

typhus [tifys] **NM 1** *Méd* typhus (fever) **2** *Vét* typhus; **t. du chat** (infectious) feline gastroenteritis

typique [tipik] **ADJ 1** (*caractéristique*) typical, characteristic; **un cas t. de delirium tremens** a typical *or* classic case of delirium tremens; **c'est t. d'elle d'être en retard** it's typical of *or* just like her to be late **2** (*musique*) Latin-American

typiquement [tipikmɑ̃] **ADV** typically

typo, -ote [tipo, -ɔt] *Fam*

NM,F typographer□

NF typography□

typographe [tipɔgraf] **NMF** (*compositeur* ▸ *sur machine*) typographer; (▸ *à la main*) hand compositor

typographie [tipɔgrafi] **NF 1** (*technique*) letterpress (printing) **2** (*présentation*) typography; **la t. est confuse** the page is badly set out

typographique [tipɔgrafik] **ADJ** (*procédé*) letterpress (*avant n*); (*caractère*) typographic

typographiquement [tipɔgrafikmɑ̃] **ADV 1** (*imprimer*) by letterpress **2** (*présenter, représenter*) typographically

typologie [tipɔlɔʒi] **NF** typology

typologique [tipɔlɔʒik] **ADJ** typological

typosquatting [tipɔskwatiŋ] **NM** *Ordinat* typosquatting

typothèque [tipɔtɛk] **NF** *Ordinat* type library

Tyr [tir] **NF** Tyre

tyran [tirɑ̃] **NM 1** (*despote*) tyrant; **faire le t.** to tyrannize *or* to bully people; **un t. domestique** a domestic tyrant **2** *Orn* kingbird

tyranneau, -x [tirano] **NM** petty tyrant, bully

tyrannie [tirani] **NF** tyranny; **la t. de la mode/de l'amour** the tyranny of fashion/of love; **exercer sa t. sur** to exercise one's tyranny over, to tyrannize

tyrannique [tiranik] **ADJ** tyrannical

tyranniquement [tiranikmɑ̃] **ADV** tyrannically

tyranniser [3] [tiranize] **VT** (*peuple*) to tyrannize, to bully; (*frère, sœur*) to bully; **se faire t.** to be bullied

tyrannosaure [tiranozɔr] **NM** tyrannosaurus

Tyrol [tirɔl] **NM le T.** the Tyrol *or* Tirol

tyrolien, -enne [tirɔljɛ̃, -ɛn] **ADJ** Tyrolean, Tyrolese

• **Tyrolien, -enne NM,F** Tyrolean, Tyrolese

• **tyrolienne NF 1** (*air*) Tyrolienne, yodel; **chanter une tyrolienne** to yodel **2** (*danse*) Tyrolienne

Tyrrhénienne [tirenjɛn] *voir* **mer**

tzar [tsar, dzar] = **tsar**

tzarévitch [tsarevitʃ, dzarevitʃ] = **tsarévitch**

tzarine [tsarin, dzarin] = **tsarine**

tzigane [dzigan] = **tsigane**

U

U, u [y] **NM INV** *(lettre)* U, u
• **en U ADJ** U-shaped; **fer en U** channel iron; **virage en U** U-turn; **tables (disposées) en U** tables arranged in a horseshoe

> **-U, -UE** SUFFIX
>
> The suffix **-u, -ue** appears at the end of adjectives with the meaning of WHICH/WHO HAS the quality of what is described by the noun radical. It is most commonly added to nouns referring to parts of the human body, sometimes with an informal or very informal effect. A possible English equivalent for this suffix is *-ed*, eg:
>
> **pointu(e)** sharp, pointed; **pentu(e)** steep, sloping; **pêchu(e)** (from *pêche*, as in *avoir la pêche*) on top form, full of go; **barbu** bearded; **moustachu** with a moustache; **têtu(e)** stubborn; **fessu(e)** big-bottomed; **bossu(e)** humpbacked; **couillu(e)** ballsy

UAS [yɑɛs] **NF** *Mktg* (*abrév* **unité d'activité stratégique**) SBU

ubac [ybak] **NM** = northern side of a valley

ubiquité [ybikɥite] **NF** ubiquity, ubiquitousness; *Hum* **avoir le don d'u.** to be ubiquitous *or* everywhere at once; **je n'ai pas le don d'u.** I can't be everywhere at once

ubuesque [ybyɛsk] **ADJ 1** *Littérature* Ubuesque **2** *(grotesque)* grotesque, farcical

uchronie [ykrɔni] **NF** *Littérature Br* alternative history, *Am* alternate history, *Spéc* uchronia

UDF [ydeɛf] **NF** *Pol* (*abrév* **Union pour la démocratie française**) = right-of-centre French political party

UDR [ydeɛr] **NF** *Anciennement Pol* (*abrév* **Union pour la défense de la République**) = right-wing French political party

UE [yə] **NF** (*abrév* **Union européenne**) EU

UEM [yəɛm] **NF** *Écon* (*abrév* **Union économique et monétaire**) EMU

UEMOA [yəɛmoa] **NF** *Écon* (*abrév* **Union économique et monétaire ouest-africaine**) WAEMU

UEO [yəo] **NF** (*abrév* **Union de l'Europe occidentale**) WEU

UER [yəɛr] **NF** *Anciennement Univ* (*abrév* **unité d'enseignement et de recherche**) = former name for a university department

-ueux, -ueuse *voir* **-eux, -euse**

ufologie [yfɔlɔʒi] **NF** ufology

UFR [yɛfɛr] **NF** *Univ* (*abrév* **unité de formation et de recherche**) = university department

UFT [yɛfte] **NF** *Pol* (*abrév* **Union française du travail**) = French association of independent trade unions

UHF [yaʃɛf] **NF** *Phys* (*abrév* **ultra-haute fréquence**) UHF

UHT [yaʃte] **ADJ** (*abrév* **ultra-haute température**) UHT; **lait stérilisé U.** UHT sterilized milk

ukase [ykaz] **NM** *Hist & Fig* ukase; *Fig* **u. paternel** paternal fiat

Ukraine [ykrɛn] **NF l'U.** (the) Ukraine

ukrainien, -enne [ykrɛnjɛ̃, -ɛn] **ADJ** Ukrainian
NM *(langue)* Ukrainian
• **Ukrainien, -enne NM,F** Ukrainian

ukulélé [jukulele] **NM** ukulele

ulcération [ylserasjɔ̃] **NF** *Méd* ulceration

ulcère [ylsɛr] **NM** *Méd* ulcer; **u. à** *ou* **de l'estomac** stomach ulcer

ulcéré, -e [ylsere] **ADJ 1** *Méd* ulcerated **2** *Fig* **u. par tant d'ingratitude** appalled *or* sickened by such ungratefulness; **elle en était ulcérée** it rankled with her

ulcérer [18] [ylsere] **VT 1** *Méd* to ulcerate **2** *Fig (indigner)* to appal, to sicken; **sa réaction m'a ulcéré** I resented his/her reaction, his/her reaction rankled with me
VPR s'ulcérer *Méd* to ulcerate, to form an ulcer; **la plaie commence à s'u.** the wound is beginning to ulcerate *or* to fester

ulcéreux, -euse [ylserø, -øz] **ADJ** *Méd (couvert d'ulcères)* ulcerous; *(de la nature d'un ulcère)* ulcer-like; *(plaie)* ulcerated, festering

ULM [yɛlɛm] **NM** *Aviat* (*abrév* **ultraléger motorisé**) microlight

ulmaire [ylmɛr] **NF** *Bot* meadowsweet *(UNCOUNT)*

ulnaire [ylnɛr] **ADJ** *Anat* ulnar

ultérieur, -e [ylterjœr] **ADJ** later, subsequent (**à** to); **à une date ultérieure** at a later date; **notre voyage est remis à une date ultérieure** our trip has been postponed; **la parution de ce livre est ultérieure à celle du vôtre** this book came out after yours did

ultérieurement [ylterjœrmɑ̃] **ADV** later (on), subsequently; **nous déciderons u.** we'll make up our minds at a later stage

ultimatum [yltimatɔm] **NM** ultimatum; **adresser un u. à qn** to present sb with an ultimatum

ultime [yltim] **ADJ** *(dernier)* ultimate, final; *(paroles, moment)* (very) last; *(préparatifs)* final

ultimo [yltimo] **ADV** lastly, finally

ultra [yltra] **ADJ** extremist, reactionary
NMF 1 *(extrémiste)* extremist, reactionary **2** *Hist* ultra-royalist

ultra-chic ADJ INV *Fam* ultra-fashionable

ultracompétitif, -ive [yltrakɔ̃petitif, -iv] **ADJ** *(société, prix)* very highly competitive

ultra-confidentiel, -elle [yltrakɔ̃fidɑ̃sjɛl] (*mpl* **ultra-confidentiels**, *fpl* **ultra-confidentielles**) **ADJ** top secret, highly confidential

ultraconservateur, -trice [yltrakɔ̃sɛrvatœr, -tris] **ADJ** ultraconservative

ultracourt, -e [yltrakur, -kurt] **ADJ** ultrashort

ultrafin, -e [yltrafɛ̃, -in] **ADJ** *(filament, aiguille)* extra-fine

ultra-haute fréquence [yltraotfrekɑ̃s] **NF** *Phys* ultra-high frequency

ultraléger, -ère [yltraleʒe, -ɛr] **ADJ** superlight, extralight
NM *Aviat* microlight
• **ultralégère NF** *(cigarette)* superlight, ultra low

ultralibéralisme [yltraliberalism] **NM** ultra-liberalism

ultramicroscope [yltramikrɔskɔp] **NM** ultramicroscope

ultramoderne [yltramɔdɛrn] **ADJ** ultramodern, state-of-the-art *(avant n)*

ultramontain, -e [yltramɔ̃tɛ̃, -ɛn] **ADJ 1** *Géog* ‹ *Rel* ultramontane **2** *(par rapport à la France)* be yond the Alps
NM,F *Rel* ultramontanist

ultranationaliste [yltranasjɔnalist] **ADJ** ultra nationalist, ultranationalistic
NMF ultranationalist

ultraportatif [yltrapɔrtatif] **NM** notebook com puter

ultrarapide [yltrarapid] **ADJ** high-speed

ultraroyaliste [yltrarwajalist] *Hist* **ADJ** ultraroy alist
NMF ultraroyalist

ultrasensible [yltrasɑ̃sibl] **ADJ 1** *(instrument* ultrasensitive; *(peau)* highly sensitive **2** *Pho* high-speed *(avant n)*

ultrason [yltrasɔ̃] **NM** ultrasound, ultrasoni sound

ultrasonique [yltrasɔnik], **ultrasonore** [yl trasɔnɔr] **ADJ** ultrasonic

ultraviolet, -ette [yltravjɔlɛ, -ɛt] **ADJ** ultravio let
NM ultraviolet ray; *Fam* **faire une séance d'ultra violets** to have a sunbed session

ultra-vires [yltravires] **ADJ** *Jur* ultra vires

ululation [ylylasjɔ̃] **NF** *(d'un hibou)* hooting

ululer [3] [ylyle] **VI** *(hibou)* to hoot

Ulysse [ylis] **NPR** *Myth* Ulysses

UME [yɛmə] **NF** *UE* (*abrév* **union monétaire euro péenne**) EMU

umlaut [umlawt] **NM** *Typ* umlaut

UMP [yɛmpe] **NF** *Pol* **1** (*abrév* **Union pour un Mou vement Populaire**) = centre-right French politica party, formed mainly from members of the for mer RPR party **2** *Anciennement* (*abrév* **Union pou la Majorité Présidentielle**) = former centre-righ coalition, now renamed "Union pour un Mouve ment Populaire"

UMTS [yɛmteɛs] **NM** *Tél* (*abrév* **Universal Mobil Telecommunications System**) UMTS

UN, UNE [œ̃, yn]

> **ARTICLE INDÉFINI**
> • a/an **1, 2, 4, 5**
>
> **PRONOM INDÉFINI**
> • one **1–4** • one person **5**
> • someone **5**
>
> **ADJ**
> • one **1, 3** • first **2**
>
> **NM INV**
> • one **1, 3** • number one **2**

ART INDÉFINI (*pl* **des**, *voir* **de**) **1** *(avec une valeur in déterminée ▸ en général)* a; *(devant une voyelle o un h muet)* an; **un jour/une pomme/une heure** day/an apple/an hour; **un père et une mère** father and mother; **un père de famille** the fathe of a family; **il doit y avoir une erreur** there must b a *or* some mistake; **un jour, ce sera permis** on day *or* some day, it will be allowed; **il y a des en fants qui jouent dans la rue** there are (some) chil dren playing in the street; **des filles et de garçons** (some) girls and boys; **des fruits et légu mes** fruit and vegetables; **voici des fleurs** here ar some flowers; **as-tu des livres à me prêter?** do yo have any books you can lend me?

2 *(avec une valeur particularisante ▸ en général)* a; *(devant une voyelle ou un h muet)* an; **c'est une erreur** it's a mistake; **des nuages passèrent devant la lune** clouds drifted across the moon; **venez me voir un lundi** come and see me one Monday *or* some Monday; **cela tombe un mardi** it falls on a Tuesday; **un jour de la semaine dernière** one day last week; **faites venir un médecin** get a doctor; **joue-moi un ré** play a D for me; **ce fut un soulagement pour toute la famille** it was a relief for the whole family; **c'est avec un grand plaisir que...** it's with great pleasure that...; **tu es une idiote** you're an idiot; **un marbre d'Italie** an Italian marble; **elle a fait preuve d'une réelle gentillesse** she showed real kindness; **un grand voyage se prépare des mois à l'avance** a *or* any long journey needs months of preparation

3 *(avec une valeur emphatique)* **il est d'une bêtise/d'un drôle!** he's SO stupid/funny!; **il y a un de ces mondes en ville!** the town is incredibly busy, there are an incredible lot of people in town; **j'ai une de ces migraines!** I've got a splitting headache!; **elle a poussé un de ces cris** she gave such a shout; **j'ai attendu des heures!** I waited for hours!; **il est resté des mois et des mois sans rien faire** he didn't do anything for months (and months)

4 *(avec un nom propre)* **un M. Baloi vous demande au téléphone** there's a Mr Baloi for you (on the phone); **tout le monde ne peut pas être un Rimbaud** we can't all be Rimbauds; **c'est une future Callas** she will be another *or* she's the next Callas; **c'est un Apollon** he's a real Adonis; **c'est un McEnroe en état de grâce que l'on a vu jouer ce jour-là** it was an inspired McEnroe that we saw on court that day

5 *(désignant une œuvre)* **faire l'acquisition d'un Picasso/d'un Van Gogh** to acquire a Picasso/a Van Gogh; **et si on allait voir un vieux Truffaut?** how about going to see an old Truffaut movie *or Br* film?; **des Renoir seront mis en vente chez Sotheby's** some Renoirs will be put on sale at Sotheby's

PRON INDÉFINI 1 *(dans un ensemble)* one; **il n'y en a pas un qui parle anglais** not one of them speaks English; **pas un n'était au courant** not a (single solitary) soul *or* absolutely nobody knew about it; *Fam* **être menteur/hypocrite comme pas un** to be a dreadful liar/hypocrite❑; *Fam* **il fait du bruit comme pas un** he's unbelievably noisy❑; *Fam* **il danse comme pas un** he's a great dancer❑

2 *(en corrélation avec "de")* **un des seuls** one of the few; **un de nous, un d'entre nous** one of us; **appelle-le un de ces jours** give him a call one of these days; **c'est encore un de ces westerns stupides** it's another one of those stupid westerns; **un des événements qui a le plus retenu mon attention** one of the events that really grabbed my attention

3 *(avec l'article défini)* **l'une des voitures les plus vendues d'Europe** one of the biggest selling cars in Europe; **l'un de mes amis** one of my friends, a friend of mine; **l'un des deux** one of the two; **l'un de vous deux est de trop** one of you is not needed; **l'un d'entre nous ira** one of us will go; **l'une d'entre vous est-elle volontaire?** does one of you want to volunteer?; **les uns disent que...** some say that...; **les uns et les autres** people, everybody

4 *(en corrélation avec "en")* one; **on demanda un médecin, il y en avait un dans la salle** they called for a doctor, there was one in the room; **parmi les enfants, il y en a un qui...** one of the children...; **je t'en ai acheté un** I bought you one; **il n'en reste qu'un** there's only one left; *Fam* **il n'en loupe** *ou* **rate pas une** he's forever screwing up

5 *(quelqu'un)* one person, someone; **une qui n'a pas du tout changé, c'est Jeanne** one person *or* someone who hasn't changed at all is Jeanne; **un qui a de la chance, c'est Pierre, il est parti à la Réunion** Pierre's one of the lucky ones, he's gone off to Réunion; **j'en connais une qui va être surprise!** I know someone who's going to get a surprise!; **en voilà une qui sait ce qu'elle veut!** there's somebody who knows what she wants!

ADJ 1 *(gén)* one; **à une condition** on one condition; **les enfants de un à sept ans** children (aged) from one to seven; **une femme sur cinq** one woman out of *or* in five; **il vient un jour sur deux** he comes every other *or* second day; **ils n'ont même pas marqué un (seul) but** they didn't even score one *or* a single goal; **il rentre dans une ou deux semaines** he'll be back in a week or two *or* in a couple of weeks; **je ne resterai pas une minute de plus ici** I won't stay here another minute; **j'ai fait plus d'une erreur dans ma jeunesse** I made many mistakes *or* more than one mistake in my youth; **une à une, les lumières s'éteignaient** the lights were going out one by one *or* one after the other; **vingt et un ans** twenty-one years; **deux heures une** one minute past two; **il ne faisait qu'un avec sa monture** horse and rider were as one; **et d'un, et de deux!** that's one, and another (one)!

2 *(dans des séries)* first; **numéro un** number one; **page un** *ou* **une** page one; **dans l'acte III scène un** in Act III, scene 1; **l'an I de la République** *(calendrier républicain)* year one of the Republic; **un(e), deux, trois, partez!** one, two, three, go!; *Fam* **et d'une** for a start, for starters; **et d'une, je ne t'ai jamais rien promis** first of all, I never promised you anything; *Fam* **ne faire ni une ni deux** not to think twice

3 Dieu est un God is one; **ils ne font qu'un** *(ils sont très proches)* they are as one; **la maison et l'atelier ne font qu'un** the house and workshop are one and the same

NM INV 1 *(gén)* one; **donnez-moi deux chiffres entre un et dix** give me two numbers between one and ten; **un et un** [œ̃eœ̃] **font deux** one and one are two

2 *(numéro d'ordre)* number one; **la clef du un est perdue** the key for number one has been lost; **le un est sorti** *(au jeu)* number one came up

3 *(chiffre écrit)* one; **tu fais mal tes un** your ones don't look right

• **un à un, un par un** ADV one by one, one at a time; **avale les cachets un par un** swallow the tablets one by one *or* one at a time

• **l'un dans l'autre** ADV *Fam* all in all❑, by and large❑

---

unanime [ynanim] **ADJ 1** *(commun, général ▸ vote, décision)* unanimous **2** *(du même avis)* **la presse u. a condamné ce geste** the press unanimously condemned this gesture; **ils sont unanimes à vous accuser** they are unanimous in accusing you; **nous sommes unanimes à le soutenir** we're unanimous in our support for him

unanimement [ynanimmɑ̃] **ADV** unanimously

unanimité [ynanimite] **NF** unanimity; **voter à l'u. pour qn** to vote unanimously for sb; **élu à l'u. moins une voix** elected with only one dissenting vote; **faire l'u.** to win unanimous support; **un candidat qui fait l'u. contre lui** a candidate who has no support from anyone; **sa politique n'a pas fait l'u.** his/her policy failed to win unanimous support

underground [œndœrgrawnd] **ADJ INV** underground

NM INV underground (culture), counter-culture

une [yn] **ART INDÉFINI** *voir* **un**

NF 1 *Journ* **la u.** page one, the front page; **faire la u.** to make the headlines; **la naissance de la princesse fait la** *ou* **est à la u. de tous les quotidiens** the birth of the princess is on the front page of all the dailies; **ce sujet sera à la u. de notre dernier journal télévisé ce soir** this will be one of the main items in our late news bulletin; **tu es à la u. de tous les journaux** you've made the front page, you're front-page news *or* in the headlines

2 *TV* **la U.** = private French TV channel

3 *Fam (histoire, nouvelle)* one; **je vais t'en raconter u. qui se passe dans une maison hantée** let me tell you the one about the haunted house; **j'en ai u. (bonne) à t'apprendre** wait till you hear this

4 *Fam (fessée, claque)* **tu vas en recevoir u.!** you're going to get a slap!; **j'en ai pris u. en pleine poire** I got one right across the face

UNEF, Unef [ynɛf] **NF** *(abrév* **Union nationale des étudiants de France***)* ≃ National Union of Students

UNESCO, Unesco [ynɛsko] **NF** *(abrév* **United Nations Educational, Scientific and Cultural Organization***)* UNESCO, Unesco

unetelle [yntɛl] *voir* **untel**

unguéal, -e, -aux, -ales [ɔ̃gɥeal, -o] **ADJ** nail *(avant n)*, *Spéc* ungual

uni, -e [yni] **ADJ 1** *(d'une seule couleur)* plain, *Br* self-coloured, *Am* solid; *(sans motif)* plain **2** *(terrain)* even, level, smooth; *(mer)* smooth, unruffled **3** *(soudé ▸ couple)* close; *(▸ famille, société)* close-knit; **ils sont très unis** they are very close; **unis derrière le chef** united behind the leader; **tous unis face aux pollueurs!** let's unite (in the fight) against pollution!

NM *(étoffe)* plain fabric

uniate [ynjat] *Rel* **ADJ** Uniat, Uniate

NMF Uniat, Uniate

unicaméral, -e, -aux, -ales [ynikameral, -o] **ADJ** *Pol* unicameral

UNICEF, Unicef [ynisɛf] **NF** *(abrév* **United Nations International Children's Emergency Fund***)* **l'U.** UNICEF, Unicef

unicellulaire [yniselylɛr] **ADJ** *Biol* unicellular, single-celled

unicité [ynisite] **NF** uniqueness

unicolore [ynikɔlɔr] **ADJ** plain, *Br* self-coloured, *Am* solid

unicorne [ynikɔrn] **ADJ** one-horned, single-horned

NM *Myth* unicorn

unidimensionnel, -elle [ynidimɑ̃sjɔnɛl] **ADJ** unidimensional

unidirectionnel, -elle [ynidirɛksjɔnɛl] **ADJ** unidirectional

unidose [ynidoz] **NF** single-dose sachet; **ce médicament est disponible en u.** this medicine is available in single-dose sachets

unième [ynjɛm] **ADJ** first; **quarante et u.** forty-first; **cent u.** hundred and first

unièmement [ynjɛmmɑ̃] **ADV vingt et u.** in the twenty-first place

unificateur, -trice [ynifikatœr, -tris] **ADJ** unifying, uniting

NM,F unifier

unification [ynifikasjɔ̃] **NF 1** *(d'un pays)* unification **2** *(uniformisation)* standardization, standardizing **3** *Fin & Com (des crédits)* consolidation; *(fusion d'entreprises)* merger

unificatrice [ynifikatris] *voir* **unificateur**

unifié, -e [ynifje] **ADJ** unified; *(crédits)* consolidated

unifier [9] [ynifje] **VT 1** *(réunir ▸ provinces)* to unify, to unite **2** *(uniformiser ▸ tarifs)* to standardize, to bring into line with each other **3** *Fin (crédits)* to consolidate

VPR s'unifier *(parti, pays)* to become united

uniforme [ynifɔrm] **ADJ 1** *(régulier ▸ vitesse)* uniform, regular, steady; *(▸ surface)* even, smooth, level; *(▸ mouvement)* regular **2** *(identique)* **horaire u. pour tout le personnel** the same timetable for all members of staff **3** *(monotone)* uniform, unvarying, unchanging; **une vie u.** a humdrum existence; **un paysage u.** an unchanging *or* a monotonous landscape

NM uniform; **endosser/quitter l'u.** *(de l'armée)* to join/to leave the forces

• **en uniforme ADJ** in uniform; **un policier en u.** a uniformed policeman; **en grand u.** in full uniform *or* regalia

uniformément [ynifɔrmemɑ̃] **ADV 1** *(sans aspérités)* uniformly, evenly; **étendre la colle u.** spread paste evenly; **paysage u. plat** uniformly flat landscape **2** *(identiquement)* **des femmes u. vêtues de noir** women all dressed in the same black clothes **3** *(sans changement)* regularly, steadily, uniformly; **la vie s'écoulait u.** life went on in its usual way

uniformisation [ynifɔrmizasjɔ̃] **NF** standardization, standardizing

uniformiser [3] [ynifɔrmize] **VT** to standardize

uniformité [ynifɔrmite] **NF 1** *(régularité)* uniformity, evenness; *(de couleurs)* uniformity **2** *(monotonie)* monotony

unijambiste [yniʒɑ̃bist] **ADJ** one-legged

NMF one-legged person

unilatéral, -e, -aux, -ales [ynilateral, -o] **ADJ** *(désarmement, décision)* unilateral; *(contrat, accord)* one-sided

unilatéralisme [ynilateralism] **NM** *Pol* unilateralism

unilatéraliste [ylinateralist] *Pol* ADJ unilateralist

NMF unilateralist

unilingue [ynilɛ̃g] ADJ unilingual, monolingual

uniment [ynimɑ̃] ADV *Littéraire* **1** *(régulièrement)* smoothly, evenly **2** *(franchement)* **dire qch (tout) u.** to say sth (quite) plainly *or* frankly

uninominal, -e, -aux, -ales [yninɔminal, -o] *voir* **scrutin**

union [ynjɔ̃] NF **1** *(fait de mélanger)* union, combination; *(mélange)* union, integration

2 *(solidarité)* union, unity; *Hist* **l'U. sacrée** = unity of all Frenchmen in the face of the enemy *(called for by Poincaré on the outbreak of the First World War)*; **faire l'u. sacrée** *(être solidaires)* to show *or* to present a united front; *Hist* to unite in the face of the aggressor *(in 1914)*; *Prov* **l'u. fait la force** unity is strength

3 *(harmonie ▸ dans un groupe)* harmony; (▸ *dans une famille, un couple)* closeness; **resserrer encore davantage l'u. qui existe entre deux personnes** to strengthen the bond between two people

4 *(liaison entre un homme et une femme)* union; *Littéraire* **u. charnelle** union of the flesh; **u. civile** civil union; **u. conjugale** marital union; **u. libre** cohabitation; **vivre en u. libre** to cohabit

5 *(regroupement)* union, association; **U. africaine** African Union; **u. de consommateurs** consumer association; *Anciennement Pol* **U. pour la défense de la République** = right-wing French political party; *Pol* **U. pour la démocratie française** = right-of-centre French political party; **u. douanière** customs union; *UE* **U. douanière européenne** European Customs Union; **u. économique** economic union; **U. économique et monétaire** Economic and Monetary Union; **U. européenne** European Union; **U. de l'Europe occidentale** Western Europe Union; **U. fédérale des consommateurs** = French consumers' association; **l'U. de la gauche** = union of left-wing parties; *Anciennement Pol* **U. des jeunes pour le progrès** = French political party of young Gaullists; *Anciennement Pol* **U. pour la Majorité Présidentielle** = former centre-right coalition, now renamed "Union pour un Mouvement Populaire"; *UE* **U. monétaire européenne** European Monetary Union; *Pol* **U. pour un Mouvement Populaire** = centre-right French political party; **u. nationale** national coalition; **U. nationale des étudiants de France** ≃ National Union of Students; **U. nationale interprofessionnelle pour l'emploi dans l'industrie et le commerce** = the department controlling the "ASSEDIC"; *Hist* **U. pour la nouvelle République** = former Gaullist political party; *Admin* **U. pour le recouvrement des cotisations de Sécurité sociale et d'allocations familiales** = French administrative body responsible for collecting social security payments; *Sport* **u. sportive** sports club *or* association

6 *Anciennement* **l'U. soviétique** *ou* **des républiques socialistes soviétiques** the Soviet Union, the Union of Soviet Socialist Republics; **l'ex-U. soviétique** the former Soviet Union; **l'U. sud-africaine** the Union of South Africa

unionisme [ynjɔnism] NM **1** *Arch (syndicalisme)* unionism **2** *Hist* Unionism

unioniste [ynjɔnist] ADJ **1** *Arch (syndicaliste)* unionist **2** *Hist* Unionist

NMF **1** *Arch (syndicaliste)* unionist **2** *Hist* Unionist

unipare [ynipar] ADJ *Bot & Zool* uniparous

unipersonnel, -elle [ynipersɔnel] ADJ **1** *Ling* impersonal **2** *Com* **entreprise** *ou* **société unipersonnelle** one-person business, sole proprietorship

unipolaire [ynipɔlɛr] ADJ unipolar

unique [ynik] ADJ **1** *(seul)* (one and) only, one; *(parti, prix)* single; *(candidat)* sole; **c'est mon u. exemplaire** it's my only *or* one copy; **c'est mon u. recours** it's the only recourse I have, it's my sole recourse; **l'u. porte de sortie était verrouillée** the only *or* one exit was locked; **mon u. souci est que tu sois heureux** my only *or* one *or* sole concern is that you should be happy; **l'u. explication possible** the only possible explanation; **un même et u. problème** one and the same problem; **c'est son seul et u. défaut** it's his/her one and only fault; **la seule et l'u. Arletty** the one and only Arletty

2 *(exceptionnel)* unique; **j'en possède l'u. exemplaire** I own the only (existing) copy of it; **il a des pièces uniques dans sa collection de porcelaine** he has several unique pieces in his porcelain collection; **il est u. au monde** it's unique, there's only one of its kind in the world

3 *Fam (étonnant)* priceless; **il est vraiment u., lui!** he's priceless, he is!

4 *(dans une famille)* **être fils/fille/enfant u.** to be an only son/daughter/child; **les enfants uniques** only children

uniquement [ynikmɑ̃] ADV only, solely; **elle mange u. des légumes** she eats just *or* only vegetables, she eats nothing but vegetables; **on le trouve u. dans les régions du nord** it is found only in northern areas; **je viens u. pour vous voir** I've come just to see you, the only reason I've come is to see you; **il pense u. à ton bien** he's only thinking of what's good for you; **nous nous occupons u. de prêts à court terme** we deal only *or* solely *or* exclusively in short-term loans; **je l'ai fait u. pour te faire plaisir** I only did it to please you

unir [32] [ynir] VT **1** *(lier)* to unite, to bring together; **l'amitié qui nous unit** the friendship that unites us; **u. une province à un pays** to unite a province with a country

2 *(marier)* to join in marriage *or* matrimony; **le Père Patrick les unira** Father Patrick will marry them *or* will officiate at their wedding; **être uni par le mariage à...** to be joined in matrimony *or* marriage to...; **vous voilà unis par les liens du mariage** I now pronounce you man and wife

3 *(villes)* to link, to connect; **le canal qui unissait Orville à Lorgeac** the canal which used to run between Orville and Lorgeac; **le pont qui unit les deux rives** the bridge which links *or* connects the two banks

4 *(combiner)* to combine; **son style unit l'aisance à** *ou* **et la rigueur** his/her style combines both ease and precision; **un homme qui unit des qualités de décideur à un sens de l'humour** a man who combines decision-making abilities with a sense of humour

5 *(aplanir ▸ sol, surface)* to smooth, to level

VPR **s'unir 1** *(se regrouper)* to unite; **s'u. à qn** to join forces with sb; **s'u. contre un ennemi commun** to unite against a common enemy **2** *(se marier)* to become joined in marriage *or* matrimony; **s'u. à qn** to marry sb **3** *(être compatible)* to match

unisexe [ynisɛks] ADJ unisex

unisexué, -e [ynisɛksɥe], **unisexuel, -elle** [ynisɛksɥel] ADJ *Biol* unisexual

unisson [ynisɔ̃] NM unison

• **à l'unisson** ADV in unison; **nos cœurs battaient à l'u.** our hearts were beating as one *or* in unison

• **à l'unisson de** PRÉP at one with; **se mettre à l'u. des critiques** to be of one mind with the critics

unitaire [yniter] ADJ **1** *(principe, slogan)* uniting; *(politique)* unitarian; *(système)* unitary

2 *Math (matrice, vecteur)* unit *(avant n)*

3 *Com* **prix u.** unit price

4 *Rel* Unitarian

NMF *Rel* Unitarian

unitarien, -enne [ynitarjɛ̃, -ɛn] ADJ *Pol* unitarian; *Rel* Unitarian

NM,F *Pol* unitarian; *Rel* Unitarian

unité [ynite] NF **1** *(cohésion)* unity; *(de style)* consistency; **cela manque d'u.** *(projet, texte)* it doesn't hang together very well; **arriver à une certaine u. de pensée** *ou* **vues** to reach a certain consensus; *Théât* **les trois unités, l'u. d'action, l'u. de temps et l'u. de lieu** the three unities, unity of action, unity of time and unity of place

2 *(étalon)* unit, measure; *Écon* **u. de compte** unit of account; **u. de longueur** unit of length; **u. de masse** weight; **u. de mesure** unit of measurement; **u. monétaire** monetary unit; *Anciennement* **u. monétaire européenne** European currency unit; **u. de poids** unit of weight; **u. de temps** unit for measuring time *or* time measure

3 *(élément, module)* unit, item; **2 euros l'u.** 2 euros each; **les ventes ont dépassé les 3000 unités** sales have passed the 3,000 mark; *Com* **u. d'activité stratégique** strategic business unit; *Com* **u. de chargement** load unit; *Pétr* **u. de craquage** cracking unit; *Anciennement Univ* **u. d'enseignement et de recherche** = former name for a university department; *Univ* **u. de formation et de recherche** = university department; **u. d'intervention chirurgicale** field surgical unit; *TV & Rad* **u. mobile (de tournage)** OB unit, outside broadcast vehicle; **u. pilote** experimental unit; *Ind* **u. de production** production unit; *TV* **u. de programme** programme production team; *Mktg* **u. de sondage** sampling unit; *Bourse* **u. de transaction** lot size; *Univ* **u. de valeur** course credit *or* unit

4 *Ling* (distinctive) feature; **u. lexicale** lexeme

5 *Math* unit; **le chiffre des unités** the units figure **la colonne des unités** the units column

6 *Mil* unit; **rejoindre son u.** to go back to *or* rejoin one's unit; *Naut* to go back to *or* rejoin one's ship **u. de combat** *Br* fighting unit, *Am* combat unit; **u. de choc** shock unit

7 *(dans un hôpital)* unit; **u. de soins intensifs** intensive care unit

8 *Ordinat* unit; *(de disque)* drive; **u. de bande** tape unit; **u. centrale** central processing unit CPU; **u. de commande** control unit; **u. de destination** target drive; **u. de disque** disk drive; **u. de disque dur** hard drive; **u. de disquettes** floppy drive; **u. d'entrée** input device; **u. logique** logical drive; **u. d'origine** source drive; **u. périphérique** peripheral; **u. de sauvegarde** backup device; **u. de sortie** output device; **u. de stockage** storage device; **u. de télécommande** remote control unit RCU; **u. de traitement** processing unit; **u. de traitement de texte** text processor; **u. de visualisation** visual display unit, VDU

• **à l'unité** ADJ **prix à l'u.** unit price ADV *(acheter, vendre)* by the unit, singly, individually; **vendu à l'u.** sold singly

univalent, -e [ynivalɑ̃, -ɑ̃t] ADJ *Biol & Chim* univalent, monovalent

univers [ynivɛr] NM **1** *Astron* **l'U.** the Universe **l'u.** *(notre planète)* the world; **l'u. entier a salué cet exploit** people all over the world admired this exploit **2** *Fig (domaine)* world, universe; **l'u. du rêve** the world *or* realm of dreams; **l'u. mathématique** the field of mathematics; **le monde de l'argent ce n'est pas vraiment mon u.** big money isn't really my thing *or* line; **l'u. très particulier du cirque** the strange world of the circus; **l'u. poétique de Mallarmé** Mallarmé's poetic world; **l'u. carcéral** life in prison

universalisation [ynivɛrsalizasjɔ̃] NF universalization

universaliser [3] [ynivɛrsalize] VT to universalize, to make universal

VPR **s'universaliser** to become universal

universalité [ynivɛrsalite] NF universality; *Jur* **u. de droits** = set of rights and obligations under a particular legal regime

universaux [ynivɛrso] NMPL *Phil & Ling* **les u.** the universals, the five predictables

universel, -elle [ynivɛrsɛl] ADJ **1** *(mondial)* universal; **produit de réputation universelle** world famous product; **faire l'objet d'une adoration universelle** to be universally adored; **paix universelle** world peace

2 *(partagé par tous ▸ sentiment)* universal, general; **la jalousie est universelle** jealousy is universal; **rechercher les règles universelles qui régissent les langues** to look into the general rules which govern languages

3 *(à usages multiples)* **remède u.** panacea, universal remedy; *Tech* **joint u.** universal joint

4 *(savoir)* all-embracing; **un érudit au talent u.** a multi-talented scholar

NM **l'u.** the universal

universellement [ynivɛrsɛlmɑ̃] ADV universally; **u. reconnu** recognized by all; **u. admiré** universally admired

universitaire [ynivɛrsitɛr] ADJ *(carrière, études)* academic, university *(avant n)*; *(année, centre, titre)* academic; *(ville)* university *(avant n)*; *(restaurant)* university *(avant n)*

NMF **1** *(enseignant)* academic, university teacher **2** *Belg & Suisse (étudiant)* university student *(diplômé)* graduate

université [ynivɛrsite] NF **1** *(institution, bâtiment)* university; **aller à l'u.** to go to university **enseigner à l'u.** to be a university teacher, *Am* to teach college; *Univ* **u. d'été** summer school; **u. du troisième âge** post-retirement *or* senior citizens university **2** *Pol* **les universités d'été du parti socialiste** socialist party summer school *(during which party leaders meet younger members)*

univoque [ynivɔk] **ADJ 1** *Ling* unequivocal **2** *(relation, rapport)* one-to-one

Unix® [yniks] **NM** *Ordinat (abrév* **Uniplexed Information and Computing System**) Unix®

UNSA [ynsa] **NF** *Pol (abrév* **Union nationale des syndicats autonomes**) = French trade union representing civil servants and other workers

untel, unetelle, Untel, Unetelle [œ̃tɛl, yntɛl] **NM,F** Mr So-and-so, *f* Mrs So-and-so

uppercut [ypɛrkyt] **NM** uppercut; **u. du droit** right uppercut

uranifère [yranifɛr] **ADJ** uranium-bearing

uranium [yranjɔm] **NM** *Chim* uranium; **u. enrichi/appauvri** enriched/depleted uranium

Uranus [yranys] **NF** *Astron* Uranus

NPR *Myth* Uranus

urbain, -e [yrbɛ̃, -ɛn] **ADJ 1** *(de la ville)* urban, city *(avant n)*; **un grand centre u.** a big city **2** *Littéraire (courtois)* urbane, worldly

urbanisation [yrbanizasjɔ̃] **NF** urbanization; **plan d'u.** urban development plan

urbaniser [3] [yrbanize] **VT** to urbanize; **zone urbanisée** built-up area

VPR s'urbaniser to become urbanized *or* built-up

urbanisme [yrbanism] **NM** *Br* town planning, *Am* city planning; **cabinet d'u.** firm of *Br* town *or Am* city planning consultants

urbaniste[1] [yrbanist] **NMF** *Br* town planner, *Am* city planner

urbaniste[2] [yrbanist], **urbanistique** [yrbanistik] **ADJ** *Br* town planning, *Am* city planning *(avant n)*

urbanité [yrbanite] **NF** *Littéraire* urbanity

urbi et orbi [yrbiɛtɔrbi] **ADV** *Rel* urbi et orbi; *Fig* far and wide, to all and sundry

urée [yre] **NF** *Biol & Chim* urea; **avoir de l'u.** to have excess urea

urémie [yremi] **NF** *Méd* uraemia

uretère [yrtɛr] **NM** *Anat* ureter

urètre [yrɛtr] **NM** *Anat* uretra

urétroscope [yretrɔskɔp] **NM** *Méd* urethroscope

urétroscopie [yretrɔskɔpi] **NF** *Méd* urethroscopy

urgence [yrʒɑ̃s] **NF 1** *(caractère pressant)* urgency; **ces mesures ont été prises dans l'u.** these measures were taken in a great hurry; **il y a u.** it's a matter of urgency, it's an emergency; **il n'y a pas u.** it's not urgent, there's no urgency; *Fam* **bois ton café tranquillement, il n'y a pas u.** drink your coffee, there's no (desperate) rush; **en cas d'u.** in case of *or* in an emergency **2** *(incident)* emergency **3** *Méd (cas)* emergency case; *(malade)* emergency patient

• **urgences NFPL** *Méd Br* casualty department, *Am* emergency room; **salle des urgences** emergency ward

• **de toute urgence ADV** most urgently; **faire qch de toute u.** to give sth (top) priority, to treat sth as a matter of (top) priority

• **d'urgence ADJ 1** *(mesures, soins)* emergency *(avant n)*; **c'est un cas d'u.** it's an emergency **2** *Pol* **état d'u.** state of emergency; **procédure d'u.** emergency *or* special powers **ADV** as a matter of emergency; **opérer qn d'u.** to perform an emergency operation on sb; **il fut opéré d'u.** he had an emergency operation; **on l'a transporté d'u. à l'hôpital** he was rushed (off) to hospital; **on l'a appelé d'u. de l'hôpital** he received an urgent call from the hospital; **faites-le venir d'u.** ask him to come straightaway; **réunir les ministres d'u.** to call an emergency Cabinet meeting; **convoquer d'u. les actionnaires** to call an extraordinary meeting of the shareholders; **à envoyer/payer d'u.** to be sent/paid immediately

urgent, -e [yrʒɑ̃, -ɑ̃t] **ADJ** urgent; **c'est u.** it's urgent; **ce n'est pas u.** it's not urgent, there's no (desperate) rush; **la situation est urgente** this is an emergency; **il devient u. de trouver une solution** a solution must be found urgently, a solution is urgently required; **avoir un besoin d'argent u.** to be in urgent need *or* badly in need of money; **commençons par le plus u.** let's start with the most urgent thing; **il est u. que je le voie** I must see him urgently; **pli u.** urgent letter

urgentiste [yrʒɑ̃tist] *Méd* **NMF** emergency doctor *or Am* physician

urgentologue [yrʒɑ̃tɔlɔg] *Can Méd* **ADJ** emergency *(avant n)*

NMF emergency doctor *or Am* physician

urger [17] [yrʒe] **VI** *Fam* to be urgent[□]; **ça urge?** is it urgent?, how urgent is it?; **j'ai du travail, mais ça urge pas** I do have some work to do, but it's not urgent *or* but there's no rush; **il n'y a rien qui urge** there's no desperate hurry

urinaire [yrinɛr] **ADJ** urinary

urinal, -aux [yrinal, -o] **NM** (bed) urinal

urine [yrin] **NF u., urine(s)** urine *(UNCOUNT)*

uriner [3] [yrine] **VI** to urinate, to pass water

urinoir [yrinwar] **NM** (public) urinal

urique [yrik] **ADJ** uric

URL [yɛrɛl] **NF** *Ordinat (abrév* **uniform resource locator**) URL

urne [yrn] **NF 1** *Pol* ballot box; **se rendre aux urnes** to go to the polls **2** *(vase)* urn; **u. funéraire** (funeral) urn

uro-génital, -e [yrɔʒenital] *(mpl* **uro-génitaux** [-o], *fpl* **uro-génitales**) **ADJ** *Méd* urogenital, urinogenital

urologie [yrɔlɔʒi] **NF** *Méd* urology

urologue [yrɔlɔg] **NMF** *Méd* urologist

uroscopie [yrɔskɔpi] **NF** *Méd* uroscopy

URSS [yrs, yɛrɛsɛs] **NF** *Anciennement (abrév* **Union des républiques socialistes soviétiques**) **l'U.** the USSR; **l'ex-U.** the former USSR

URSSAF, Urssaf [yrsaf] **NF** *Admin (abrév* **Union pour le recouvrement des cotisations de Sécurité sociale et d'allocations familiales**) **l'U.** = French administrative body responsible for collecting social security payments

ursuline [yrsylin] **NF** *Rel* Ursuline

urticaire [yrtikɛr] **NF** *Méd* nettle rash, hives, *Spéc* urticaria; **crise d'u.** attack of hives; **avoir une crise d'u.** to come out *or* to break out in hives; **avoir de l'u.** to have nettle rash; **les huîtres me donnent de l'u.** oysters bring me out in a rash; *Fig Hum* **cette musique, ça me donne de l'u.** that music makes my skin crawl

urticant, -e [yrtikɑ̃, -ɑ̃t] **ADJ** *Bot & Zool* urticating

urtication [yrtikasjɔ̃] **NF** *Méd* skin rash *or* irritation, *Spéc* urtication

Uruguay [yrygwɛ] **NM 1** *(pays)* **l'U.** Uruguay **2** *(fleuve)* **le fleuve U.** the Uruguay (River)

uruguayen, -enne [yrygwejɛ̃, -ɛn] **ADJ** Uruguayan

• **Uruguayen, -enne NM,F** Uruguayan

urus [yrys] **NM** *(aurochs)* ure, urus

us [ys] **NMPL les us et coutumes** habits and customs

usage [yzaʒ] **NM 1** *(utilisation)* use; **l'u. de la porte latérale est réservé au personnel** only staff members are authorized to use the side door; **faire u. de qch** to use sth; **faire u. de la force** to use *or* employ force; **faire u. de ses privilèges** to exercise one's privileges; **faire bon u. de qch** to put sth to good use; **faire mauvais u. de qch** to misuse sth; **faire un u. abusif du pouvoir** to abuse one's power; **faire un u. excessif des virgules** to use too many commas; **faire un u. immodéré de l'alcool** to drink too much *or* to excess; **avoir l'u. de** to have the use of; **nous avons l'u. de la piscine** we have access to *or* the use of the pool; *Jur* **une maison dont elle n'a pas la propriété mais l'u.** a house which she doesn't own, but which she is legally entitled to use; **je n'en aurai pas l'u.** I won't be needing it, I won't have any use for it; **je n'en ai aucun u.** I have no use for it; **à mon u. personnel** for my private *or* own personal use; **être d'u. courant** to be in common *or* everyday use; **c'est un mot d'u. courant** it's a common *or* everyday word; **j'en fais un u. courant** I often use it; *Jur* **u. de faux** use of forged documents; *Jur* **droit d'u.** right of use

2 *(contrôle)* use; **il a encore l'u. de son bras** he can still use his arm; **perdre l'u. des yeux/l'u. d'un bras** to lose one's sight/the use of an arm; **perdre l'u. de la parole** to lose one's power of speech; **perdre l'u. de la vue/de l'ouïe** to lose one's sight/hearing

3 *(fonction)* use, purpose; **avoir plusieurs usages** to have various uses; **appareil d'u. courant** household appliance; **à divers usages** multipurpose; **à u. intensif** heavy-duty; **à u. unique** *(seringue, produit)* single-use; **locaux à u. administratif** office space; **à usages multiples** multipurpose; **locaux à u. commercial** business *or* commercial premises; *Pharm* **à u. interne** *(sur emballage)* for internal use, to be taken internally; *Pharm* **à u. externe** *(sur emballage)* for external use only, not to be taken internally

4 *Ling* (accepted) usage; **u. écrit/oral** written/spoken usage; **le mot est entré dans l'u.** the word is now in common use; **le mot est sorti de l'u.** the word has become obsolete *or* is no longer used; *Arch* **le bon u., le bel u.** correct usage

5 *(coutume)* habit, habitual practice; **selon** *ou* **suivant l'u.** according to custom; **selon un u. bien établi** following a well-established habit; **l'u., les usages** accepted *or* established custom, (the rules of) etiquette; **c'est l'u.** it's the done thing; **ce n'est pas l'u. d'applaudir au milieu d'un air** it's not done to clap *or* you just don't clap in the middle of an aria; **c'est conforme à l'u.** *ou* **aux usages** it's in accordance with the rules of etiquette; **c'est contraire à l'u.** *ou* **aux usages, c'est contre l'u.** *ou* **les usages** it's not the done thing, it's contrary to the rules of etiquette

• **à l'usage ADV** with use; **le cuir fonce à l'u.** leather turns darker with use; **c'est à l'u. qu'on s'aperçoit des défauts d'une cuisine** you only realize what the shortcomings of a kitchen are after you've used it for a while; **nous verrons à l'u.!** let's wait and see!

• **à l'usage de PRÉP à l'u. des écoles/des étudiants** for use in schools/by students; **un livre de cuisine à l'u. des enfants** a cookery book aimed at *or* intended for children

• **d'usage ADJ 1** *(habituel)* customary, usual; **finir une lettre avec la formule d'u.** to end a letter in the usual *or* accepted manner; **j'ai fait modifier la formule d'u.** I had the standard wording altered; **échanger les banalités d'u.** to exchange the customary platitudes; **il est d'u. de laisser un pourboire** it is customary to leave a tip; **comme il est d'u.** as is customary; **les conditions d'u.** the usual terms **2** *Ling* **faute d'u.** misuse

• **en usage ADJ** in use; **cette technique n'est plus en u.** this technique is now obsolete *or* is no longer in use

usagé, -e [yzaʒe] **ADJ 1** *(usé ▸ costume)* worn, old; *(▸ verre)* used, old; *(ticket)* used **2** *(d'occasion)* used, second-hand

usager [yzaʒe] **NM 1** *(utilisateur)* user; **les usagers du téléphone/de la route** telephone/road users; **les usagers du train** rail travellers; **les usagers du métro parisien** Parisian underground users; **les usagers de la Poste** post office users *or* customers **2** *(locuteur)* **les usagers de l'espagnol** Spanish language speakers, speakers of the Spanish language

usant, -e [yzɑ̃, -ɑ̃t] **ADJ** *(tâche)* gruelling, wearing; *(enfant)* wearing, tiresome; **c'est u.** it really wears you down; **il est u.** he wears you out

USB [yɛsbe] **NM** *Ordinat (abrév* **universal serial bus**) USB

usé, -e [yze] **ADJ 1** *(vieux ▸ habit)* worn, worn-out; *(▸ pile)* worn, old; *(▸ lame)* blunt; *(▸ pneu)* worn, bald; *(▸ corde)* frayed; **u. jusqu'à la corde** *ou* **trame** threadbare; **u. par l'eau** worn away by water; **u. par le frottement** worn(-out) by rubbing; **u. par le temps** timeworn **2** *(rebattu ▸ sujet)* hackneyed, well-worn; *(▸ plaisanterie)* old; **c'est u.! essaye une autre excuse** I've heard that one before! try another excuse **3** *(affaibli ▸ vieillard)* worn-out, weary; **terre usée** exhausted land; **u. par les épreuves** careworn; **u. par le travail** worn-out by work; **u. par le pouvoir** *(homme politique, monarque)* worn-out *or* jaded by too many years in power

user [3] [yze] **VT 1** *(détériorer ▸ terrain, métal)* to wear away; *(▸ pneu)* to wear smooth; *(▸ veste, couverture)* to wear out; **l'érosion use la roche** erosion wears away *or* eats away the rock; **u. un pull aux coudes** to wear out a sweater at the elbows;

u. un jean jusqu'à la corde *ou* **trame** to wear out a pair of jeans; *Fig* **on avait usé nos fonds de culottes sur les mêmes bancs** we'd been at school together; *Fig* **cela finit par u. la passion/l'intérêt** in the end it kills off passion/interest

2 *(utiliser ▸ eau, poudre)* to use; *(▸ gaz, charbon)* to use, to burn; *(▸ réserves)* to use, to go through; **cette machine use trop d'électricité** this machine uses too much electricity; **j'use un tube de rouge à lèvres tous les six mois** I go through a lipstick every six months; **je ne vais pas u. mon énergie à essayer de te persuader** I'm not going to waste my energy trying to persuade you

3 *(fatiguer)* to wear out; **tu uses tes yeux à lire dans le noir** you'll ruin your eyesight reading in the dark; **le petit dernier m'use (complètement)** my youngest child really wears me out

VI *Littéraire* **en u. bien avec qn** to treat sb well, to do well by sb; **en u. mal avec qn** to treat sb badly, to mistreat sb; **en u. trop familièrement avec ses supérieurs** to be overfamiliar with one's superiors; **comme vous en usez, jeune homme!** don't you use that tone of voice with me, young man!

• **user de VT IND** *(utiliser ▸ autorité)* to exercise; *(▸ mot, tournure, outil)* to use *(▸ audace, diplomatie)* to use, to employ; **u. de son influence (pour faire qch)** to use one's influence (to do sth); **u. de son droit** to exercise one's right; **u. de violence** to use violence; **u. de patience** to exercise patience; **n'hésitez pas à u. de sévérité** don't hesitate to be strict; **u. de douceur avec qn** to handle sb gently

VPR s'user 1 *(se détériorer ▸ gén)* to wear out; *(▸ pile)* to run down; *(▸ lame)* to go blunt; *(▸ talons, semelles)* to wear out, to wear down; **c'est un tissu qui s'use vite** this material wears (out) quickly; **les semelles en cuir ne s'usent pas vite** there's a lot of wear in leather soles; **les pneus se sont usés très vite** the tyres wore smooth very rapidly

2 *Fig (s'affaiblir)* **ma patience commence à s'u.** my patience is wearing thin; **sa résistance finira bien par s'u.** his/her resistance will wear down *or* break down in the end

3 *Fig (se fatiguer)* to wear oneself out; **je me suis usé à le lui dire** I'm tired of telling him/her, I've told him/her till I'm blue in the face; **mais c'est ce que je m'use à te dire depuis hier!** that's what I've been trying to tell you since yesterday!; *Fam* **s'u. la santé** to exhaust oneself, to wear oneself out; **s'u. les yeux** *ou* **la vue** to strain one's eyes

> Il faut noter que le verbe transitif anglais **to use** est un faux ami. Il signifie uniquement **utiliser, se servir de.**

usinage [yzinaʒ] **NM** machining

usine [yzin] **NF 1** *Ind* factory, plant, mill; **u. d'armement** arms factory; **u. d'assemblage** assembly plant; **u. de fabrication** manufacturing plant; **u. à gaz** gasworks; *Fig* overly complicated system; **u. métallurgique** ironworks; **u. de montage** assembly plant; **u. à papier** paper mill; **u. de production** production plant; **u. sidérurgique** steel mill, steelworks **2** *Fig Péj* **on peut pas souffler cinq minutes, c'est l'u. ici!** you can't get a minute's peace in here, it never stops!; **ce restaurant, c'est une vraie u.!** this restaurant is like a conveyor belt!; **cette école est une usine à bureaucrates** the school is a production line for bureaucrats

usiner [3] [yzine] **VT 1** *Métal (moulages)* to machine, to tool; *(pièces)* to machine(-finish); **parties usinées** bright parts **2** *(fabriquer)* to manufacture

VI *Fam (travailler dur)* to slog *or* slave away, to be hard at it

usinier, -ère [yzinje, -ɛr] **ADJ** *(industrie)* factory *(avant n)*; **faubourg u.** industrial suburb

usité, -e [yzite] **ADJ** *(terme)* commonly used; **l'expression n'est plus usitée** the phrase has gone out of use *or* is no longer in common use; **c'est le temps du passé le plus u.** it's the most commonly used past tense; **mot très u.** very common word; **mot peu u.** little-used word

ustensile [ystɑ̃sil] **NM** utensil, implement; **ustensiles de cuisine** cooking *or* kitchen utensils

usuel, -elle [yzɥɛl] **ADJ** *(ustensile, vêtement)* everyday *(avant n)*; *(vocabulaire, terme)* common, everyday *(avant n)*; *(dénomination)* common; **l'anglais u.** everyday English; **le procédé u. est de...** it's common practice to...

NM les usuels *(de bibliothèque)* reference works; **cet ouvrage est un u., vous ne pouvez pas l'emprunter** this book is for reference only, you may not borrow it

usuellement [yzɥɛlmɑ̃] **ADV** ordinarily, commonly

usufruit [yzyfrɥi] **NM** *Jur* usufruct; **laisser qch en u. à qn** to leave sb the life tenancy of sth

usufruitier, -ère [yzyfrɥitje, -ɛr] *Jur* **ADJ** usufructuary

NM,F *(gén)* usufructuary; *(d'un bien immobilier)* tenant for life

usuraire [yzyrɛr] **ADJ** usurious

usure[1] [yzyr] **NF 1** *(action de s'user)* wear (and tear); *(du sol, de roches)* erosion, wearing away; **tissu qui résiste à l'u.** material that wears well; **u. des pneus** tyre wear; **u. par frottement** abrasion; **l'u. normale** normal wear and tear; *Tech* **surface d'u.** wearing surface **2** *(affaiblissement)* **l'u. des forces/sentiments** the erosion of one's strength/feelings; **victime de l'u. du pouvoir** worn down by the exercise of power; **notre mariage a résisté à l'u. du temps** our marriage has stood the test of time; *Fam* **avoir qn à l'u.** to wear *or* to grind sb down (until he/she gives in)

usure[2] [yzyr] **NF** *(intérêt de prêt)* usury; **pratiquer l'u.** to practise usury; **prêter à u.** to lend upon usury *or* at usurious rates of interest; *Fig* **je vous revaudrai ce service avec u.** I'll repay you for this service with interest

usurier, -ère [yzyrje, -ɛr] **NM,F** usurer

usurpateur, -trice [yzyrpatœr, -tris] **NM,F** usurper *(avant n)*

usurpation [yzyrpasjɔ̃] **NF** usurpation, usurping; **u. de pouvoir** usurpation *or* usurping of power

usurpatrice [yzyrpatris] *voir* **usurpateur**

usurper [3] [yzyrpe] **VT** *(droit, identité)* to usurp; *Fig* **sa gloire est usurpée** his/her fame isn't rightfully his/hers

• **usurper sur VT IND** *Littéraire* to encroach on *or* upon

ut [yt] **NM INV** *Mus* C; **ut dièse** C sharp; **clef d'ut** C clef; **clef d'ut quatrième ligne** tenor clef

utérin, -e [yterɛ̃, -in] **ADJ 1** *Anat* uterine **2** *(de la même mère)* **frères utérins** uterine brothers; **sœurs utérines** uterine sisters

utérus [yterys] **NM** *Anat* womb, *Spéc* uterus

utile [ytil] **ADJ 1** *(qui sert beaucoup)* useful; **il est bien u., ton petit couteau** that little knife of yours comes in very handy *or* is very useful; **ça peut (toujours) être u.** it might come in handy; **être u. à qn/à qch** to be useful to sb/for sth; **les notes sont utiles à la compréhension du texte** the notes are helpful for understanding the text; **cela m'a été bien u.** *(cet objet)* it came in very handy, I found it very helpful; *(ce renseignement)* it was very helpful; **elle nous a été très u.** she was a lot of help, she was very helpful to us **2** *(nécessaire)* necessary; **prenez toutes les dispositions utiles** make all the necessary arrangements; **il n'est pas u. d'avertir la police** there's no need to notify the police; **il n'était pas u. que tu t'en occupes** there was no point in you dealing with it **3** *(serviable)* useful; **se rendre u.** to make oneself useful; **puis-je t'être u. à quelque chose?** can I be of any help to you?, can I help you with anything?; **en quoi puis-je vous être u.?** what can I do for you?, how can I help you?; **si je puis vous être u.** if I can be of any use *or* help *or* service *or* assistance to you; **elle peut t'être u. un jour** she may be of help to you *or* useful one day

NM joindre l'u. à l'agréable to combine business with pleasure

utilement [ytilmɑ̃] **ADV** usefully, profitably; **conseiller/renseigner u. qn** to give sb useful *or* helpful advice/information; **employer son temps u.** to spend one's time profitably, to make good use of one's time

utilisable [ytilizabl] **ADJ 1** *(objet, appareil)* usable; *(crédit)* available; **ce vieux réveil est encore u.?** is this old alarm clock still working?; **les vieux bocaux ne sont plus utilisables** the old jars are no longer usable; **facilement u.** easy to use **2** *(billet)* valid

utilisateur, -trice [ytilizatœr, -tris] **NM,F** *(d'un appareil)* user; *(d'un service)* user, consumer; *Mktg* **u. final** end-user; *Ordinat* **pour utilisateurs multiples** multi-user; *Mktg* **u. tardif** late adopter

utilisation [ytilizasjɔ̃] **NF** use, utilization; **la sorbetière est d'u. simple** the ice-cream maker is simple *or* easy to use; **pour une bonne u. de ce produit...** in order to make correct use of this product...; **notice d'u.** instructions for use

utilisatrice [ytilizatris] *voir* **utilisateur**

utiliser [3] [ytilize] **VT 1** *(appareil, carte, expression)* to use; *(moyens, tactique)* to use, to employ; **utilise le moins possible de farine** use as little flour as possible; **u. l'avion pour traiter les récoltes** to use a plane to treat the crops; **je n'ai pas su u. les possibilités qui m'étaient offertes** I didn't make the most of the opportunities I was given; **bien/mal u. qch** *(compétences, ressources)* to make/not to make good use of sth; *(mot, expression)* to use sth correctly/incorrectly; **le peu d'espace disponible a été bien utilisé** they have made good use of what little space there is; *Péj* **avoir l'impression qu'on vous utilise** to have the feeling you're being used; *Péj* **il sait u. son monde** he knows how to make the best use of his connections; **tu vas te faire u.** they'll use you **2** *Ordinat* to run; **il peut être utilisé sur...** it can run on...

utilitaire [ytilitɛr] **ADJ 1** *(utile)* utilitarian **2** *Ordinat* utility *(avant n)*; **programme u.** utility (program)

NM *Ordinat* utility (program); **u. de conversion** conversion utility

utilitarisme [ytilitarism] **NM** utilitarianism

utilitariste [ytilitarist] **ADJ** utilitarian

NMF utilitarian

utilité [ytilite] **NF 1** *(caractère utile)* use, usefulness; **chaque ustensile a son u.** every implement has its specific use; **c'est un appareil qui a son u.** it's an apparatus that has its uses; **des objets sans u.** useless objects; **être d'une u. à qn** to be of use to sb; **ça ne t'est plus d'aucune u.** it's no longer of any use to you, you no longer need it; **la carte de la région m'a été de peu d'u./d'une grande u.** the map of the area was of little/great use to me; **un appareil sans grande u.** an appliance that's not much use; **quelle est l'u. d'avoir une voiture dans Paris?** what's the use of having a car in Paris?; **avoir l'u. de qch** (to be able) to make use of sth; **en as-tu l'u.?** can you make use of it?, do you need it?; **pourquoi garder des choses dont on n'a pas l'u.?** why keep things you have no use for?; **je ne vois pas l'u. de lui en parler** I don't see any point in mentioning it to him/her; **reconnu d'u. publique** = officially recognized as beneficial to the public at large **2** *Écon* utility; **u. collective** collective utility; **u. marginale** marginal utility

• **utilités NFPL jouer les utilités** *Théât* to play minor *or* small parts; *Fig* to play second fiddle

utopie [ytɔpi] **NF 1** *Phil* Utopia, Utopian ideal **2** *(chimère)* Utopian idea; **c'est de l'u.!** that's all pie in the sky!; **votre programme politique relève de l'u.** your political programme is rather Utopian

utopique [ytɔpik] **ADJ** Utopian

utopisme [ytɔpism] **NM** Utopianism

utopiste [ytɔpist] **ADJ** Utopian

NMF 1 *(rêveur)* Utopian **2** *Phil* Utopian

utriculaire [ytrikylɛr] **NF** *Bot* bladderwort

UV [yve] **NF** *Univ* *(abrév* **unité de valeur***)* course credit *or* unit

NM INV *(abrév* **ultraviolet***)* UV; **faire des UV** to go to a solarium

uval, -e, -aux, -ales [yval, -o] **ADJ** grape *(avant n)*

uvulaire [yvylɛr] **ADJ** *Anat & Ling* uvular

uvule [yvyl] **NF** *Anat* uvula

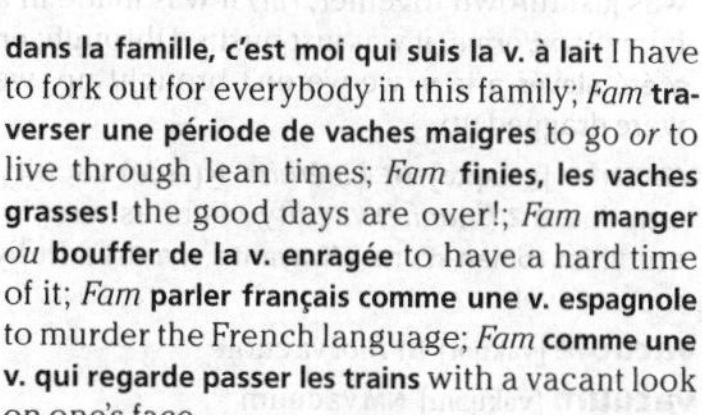

V[1], **v** [ve] **NM INV** *(lettre)* V, v; **double v** W, w; **faire le V de la victoire** to make the victory sign

• **en V ADJ** V-shaped; **un pull (à col) en V** a V-necked sweater; **décolleté en V** plunging neckline

V[2] *(abrév écrite* **volt***)* V

va [va] *voir* **aller**[2]

vacance [vakɑ̃s] **NF 1** *(d'un emploi)* vacancy; **il y a une v. à la comptabilité** the accounts department has a vacancy

2 *(d'une fonction politique)* **pendant la v. du siège** while the seat is empty; **élection provoquée par la v. du siège** election made necessary because the seat became vacant; **pendant la v. du pouvoir** while there is no one officially in power; **dû à la v. du pouvoir** because there is no one officially in power; **il n'y aura pas de v. du pouvoir** there will be a smooth transition of control

3 *Jur* **v. de succession** abeyance of succession

4 *Littéraire (de l'esprit)* emptiness

• **vacances NFPL 1** *(période de loisirs) Br* holidays, *Am* vacation; **avoir besoin de vacances** to be in need of a holiday; **prendre des vacances** to take a holiday, to go on holiday; **prendre quelques jours de vacances** to take a few days' holiday; **prendre deux mois de vacances** to take two months off, to have a two-month holiday; **quand prends-tu tes vacances?** when are you going to take your holiday?; **rentrer de vacances** to come back from one's holiday; **quand rentre-t-il de vacances?** when is he back from holiday?; **un jour de vacances** a (day's) holiday; **les départs/retours de vacances** going away on/coming back from holiday; **automobilistes: attention aux retours de vacances** drivers: watch out for the end-of-holiday rush; *Fam* **il part? très bien, ça me fera des vacances!** he's going? great, that will be just like a holiday for me!; *Fam* **fais-moi des vacances!** give me a break!; **vacances de neige** skiing holidays *or* vacation

2 *(période du calendrier)* **vacances judiciaires** recess (of the Courts); **vacances parlementaires** Parliamentary recess; **vacances scolaires** school *Br* holidays *or Am* break; **vacances universitaires** *Br* vacation, *Am* university recess; **pendant les vacances (universitaires)** during the vacation; **un job pendant les vacances (universitaires)** a summer job; **les vacances de Noël** *Scol & Univ* the Christmas *Br* holidays *or Am* vacation; *(pour les salariés)* the Christmas break; **les grandes vacances** *Br* the summer holidays, *Am* the long vacation

• **en vacances ADV** on *Br* holiday *or Am* vacation; **pendant que nous étions en vacances en Italie** while we were *Br* holidaying *or Am* vacationing in Italy; **partir en vacances** to go (off) on holiday; **aller** *ou* **partir en vacances en Espagne** to go on holiday to Spain, to go to Spain on holiday; **je l'ai rencontré en vacances** I met him (when I was) on holiday

Il faut noter que le terme anglais **vacancy** ne signifie jamais **congé**.

vacancier, -ère [vakɑ̃sje, -ɛr] **NM,F** *Br* holidaymaker, *Am* vacationist, vacationer

vacant, -e [vakɑ̃, -ɑ̃t] **ADJ 1** *(libre ▸ logement)* vacant, unoccupied; *(▸ siège, trône)* vacant; **poste v.** vacancy; **il y a un poste d'ingénieur v.** there's a vacancy for an engineer; *Jur* **succession vacante** estate in abeyance **2** *Littéraire (vague ▸ regard)* vacant, empty; *(mains)* idle

vacarme [vakarm] **NM** racket, din, row; **les enfants faisaient un v. infernal** the children were making a terrible racket *or* an awful din; **le v. des radios sur la plage** the blaring of radios on the beach

vacataire [vakatɛr] **NMF** *(remplaçant)* stand-in, temporary replacement; *Univ* part-time lecturer; **avoir un poste de v. à l'Unesco** to be under temporary contract to UNESCO; **c'est une v.** she's on a short-term *or* temporary contract

vacation [vakasjɔ̃] **NF 1** *Scol & Univ* supply work; **être payé à la v.** to be paid on a sessional basis; **faire des vacations** to work on a short-term basis **2** *Jur* session, sitting **3** *(de vente aux enchères)* day's sale

• **vacations NFPL 1** *Jur* recess **2** *(honoraires)* fees

vacature [vakatyr] **NF** *Belg Admin* vacancy

vaccin [vaksɛ̃] **NM 1** *(produit)* vaccine; **v. antivariolique** smallpox vaccine; **v. contre le tétanos/l'hépatite** tetanus/hepatitis vaccine; *Fig* **le meilleur v. contre la paresse** the best antidote to laziness **2** *(injection)* vaccination; **faire un v. à qn** to vaccinate sb

vaccinable [vaksinabl] **ADJ à quel âge sont-ils vaccinables?** how old do they have to be before they can be vaccinated?

vaccinal, -e, -aux, -ales [vaksinal, -o] **ADJ** vaccinal; **complications vaccinales** complications following vaccination; **contamination d'origine vaccinale** contamination originating in a vaccine; **essais vaccinaux** vaccine tests; **préparation vaccinale** vaccine

vaccination [vaksinasjɔ̃] **NF** vaccination, inoculation; **v. curative** curative inoculation; **v. préventive** protective inoculation; **la v. contre la rage est obligatoire** vaccination *or* inoculation against rabies is compulsory

vaccine [vaksin] **NF 1** *Vét* cowpox, *Spéc* vaccinia **2** *Méd* inoculated cowpox

vacciner [3] [vaksine] **VT 1** *Méd* to vaccinate, to inoculate; **se faire v. (contre)** to get vaccinated (against); **être vacciné (contre)** to be vaccinated (against) **2** *Fam Fig* **être vacciné** to have learnt one's lesson; **je suis vacciné contre ce genre de remarque** I've become immune to that kind of remark; **plus de ski, je suis vacciné pour un moment** no more skiing, I've had my fill of that for the time being

vachard, -e [vaʃar, -ard] **ADJ** *Fam (coup)* rotten, mean□, nasty□; *(question)* nasty□; **il était v., l'examen!** the exam was a real stinker!

vache [vaʃ] **ADJ** *Fam* **1** *(méchant)* rotten, mean□, nasty□; **faire un coup v. à qn** to play a dirty trick on sb; **c'est v. de ta part** it's rotten of you; **allez, ne sois pas v.** come on, don't be rotten; **ce qu'elle peut être v.!** she can be so bitchy *or* such a bitch!; **elle a été v. pour les notes d'oral** she *Br* marked *or Am* graded the orals really strictly□ **2** *(remarquable)* **il a un v. (de) coquard** he's got a hell of a black eye; **il a eu une v. d'idée** he had a hell of an idea

NF 1 *Zool* cow; **v. marine** sea cow; **v. sacrée** sacred cow; **v. laitière** *ou* **à lait** milker, dairy cow; *Fig* **v. à lait** milch cow; *Mktg (produit)* cash cow; *Fam* **dans la famille, c'est moi qui suis la v. à lait** I have to fork out for everybody in this family; *Fam* **traverser une période de vaches maigres** to go *or* to live through lean times; *Fam* **finies, les vaches grasses!** the good days are over!; *Fam* **manger** *ou* **bouffer de la v. enragée** to have a hard time of it; *Fam* **parler français comme une v. espagnole** to murder the French language; *Fam* **comme une v. qui regarde passer les trains** with a vacant look on one's face

2 *(cuir)* cowhide

3 *Fam (homme)* swine; *(femme)* cow; **ah les vaches, ils ne m'ont pas invité!** the swines didn't invite me!; *très Fam* **cette v. de bagnole!** that damn *or Br* bloody car!; *très Fam* **une v. de moto** one hell of a motorbike

4 *très Fam Arg crime (policier)* cop, pig

5 *Fam* **(ah) la v.!** *(pour exprimer la surprise)* God!; *(pour exprimer l'admiration)* wow!; *(pour exprimer l'indignation, la douleur)* oh hell!; **la v., qu'est-ce qu'il fait froid!** God, it's so cold!; **la v., tu as vu à quelle vitesse il va!** wow! have you seen the speed he's going at?

• **en vache ADV** *Fam* on the sly; **faire un coup en v. à qn** to stab sb in the back; **elle a dit ça en v.** she just said that to be bitchy *or* a bitch

vachement [vaʃmɑ̃] **ADV** *Fam* really□, *Br* dead, *Am* real; **c'est v. difficile** it's *Br* dead *or Am* real difficult; **c'est une v. bonne idée** that's a really good idea; **elle est v. belle, ta robe** that's a great dress you're wearing; **il a v. vieilli** he's got a hell of a lot older looking; **elle a v. changé** she's changed a hell of a lot; **ça fait une sacrée différence! – oui, v.!** it makes a difference! – you can say that again!; *Ironique* **mais je t'assure qu'il t'aime – oui, v.!** but I'm telling you he loves you – like hell he does!

vacher, -ère [vaʃe, -ɛr] **NM,F** cowboy, *f* cowgirl

vacherie [vaʃri] **NF** *Fam* **1** *(acte)* dirty *or* rotten trick; **faire une v. à qn** to play a dirty *or* rotten trick on sb; **ils m'ont fait une v.** they played a rotten trick on me; **cette v. de tache ne veut pas partir** this damn *or* blasted stain just won't come out **2** *(propos)* nasty remark□; **il me disait des vacheries** he was saying really nasty things to me, he was being really horrible to me

vacherin [vaʃrɛ̃] **NM 1** *(dessert)* **v. (glacé)** = meringue with cream, ice cream and fruit **2** *(fromage)* vacherin cheese

vachette [vaʃɛt] **NF 1** *(animal)* young cow **2** *(peau)* calfskin

• **en vachette ADJ** calfskin *(avant n)*

vacillant, -e [vasijɑ̃, -ɑ̃t] **ADJ 1** *(titubant ▸ démarche)* unsteady, shaky; **v. de fatigue** staggering *or* reeling with tiredness

2 *(qui bouge ▸ flamme)* flickering

3 *(courage)* faltering, wavering; *(mémoire)* failing, faltering; *(santé)* failing; **sa raison vacillante** his/her failing reason

4 *(caractère)* wavering, irresolute, indecisive

vacillation [vasijasjɔ̃] **NF 1** *(d'une lueur, d'une flamme)* flickering *(UNCOUNT)* **2** *Littéraire (irrésolution)* hesitations, hesitating *(UNCOUNT)*; **après bien des vacillations, j'ai pris ma décision** after changing my mind several times, I made a decision

vaciller [3] [vasije] **VI 1** *(tituber ▸ bébé)* to totter; *(▸ ivrogne)* to sway, to stagger; **sortir d'une/entrer dans une pièce en vacillant** to stagger out of/into a room; **il s'avança en vacillant jusqu'à la porte** he staggered as far as the door; **v. sur ses jambes** to be unsteady on one's legs; **elle vacilla sur ses jambes** her legs nearly gave way under her
2 *(chaise, pile de livres)* to wobble; **tout vacillait autour de moi** everything was swimming around me
3 *(flamme)* to flicker
4 *(raison, courage)* to falter, to waver; *(voix)* to falter, to shake; *(mémoire)* to be failing, to falter; **sa santé vacille** his/her health is failing *or* faltering
5 *(hésiter)* to vacillate, to waver

va-comme-je-te-pousse [vakɔmʃtəpus] **à la va-comme-je-te-pousse ADV** *Fam* any old how; **ça a été fait à la v.** *(ouvrage, repas)* it was just thrown together; *(lit)* it was made in a hurry□; *(réforme)* it was just pushed through; **on a été élevés à la v.** we weren't brought up, we were dragged up

vacuité [vakɥite] **NF** *Littéraire* **1** *(vide)* vacuity, emptiness **2** *(inanité)* vacuity, vacuousness, inanity; **un roman d'une effrayante v.** a dreadfully inane novel

vacuole [vakɥɔl] **NF** *Biol* vacuole

vacuum [vakɥɔm] **NM** vacuum

vade-mecum [vademekɔm] **NM INV** *Littéraire* vade mecum

vadrouille [vadruj] **NF 1** *Fam (excursion)* ramble□, jaunt□; **faire une v. en Italie** to go off for a jaunt in Italy; **une v. de trois jours en montagne** a three-day ramble *or* hike in the mountains□ **2** *Can (balai)* long-handled mop *(used for dusting or washing floors)* **3** *Naut* (deck) swab
• **en vadrouille ADV** *Fam* **être en v.** to be wandering *or* roaming around□; **il est rarement à son bureau, il est toujours en v.** he's hardly ever at his desk, he's always wandering around somewhere; **partir en v.** to go (off) on a jaunt□; **il est encore parti en v.** he's out gallivanting again

vadrouiller [3] [vadruje] **VI** *Fam* to wander *or* roam around□; **v. de par le monde** to rove□ *or* to knock about the world

vadrouilleur, -euse [vadrujœr, -øz] **NM,F** *Fam* rover□

va-et-vient [vaevjɛ̃] **NM INV 1** *(circulation)* comings and goings, to-ings and fro-ings; **il y a eu trop de v. ce week-end** there was too much coming and going this weekend; **le continuel v. des voitures de police** the endless to-ing and fro-ing of police cars
2 *(aller et retour)* **faire le v.** to go back and forth *or* backwards and forwards; **ils font le v. entre le navire et la côte** they go back and forth between the ship and the coast; **ils font le v. entre l'Allemagne et la Belgique** they go back and forth between Germany and Belgium; **l'avion qui fait le v. entre Londres et Édimbourg** the air shuttle service between London and Edinburgh; **le navire qui fait le v. entre Boulogne et Douvres** the boat that sails between Boulogne and Dover
3 *Tech (latéral)* to-and-fro motion; *(vertical)* up-and-down movement; **dispositif de v.** reciprocating device
4 *Élec* **(interrupteur de) v.** two-way switch
5 porte/battant à v. swing door/panel

vagabond, -e [vagabɔ̃, -ɔ̃d] **ADJ 1** *(mode de vie, personne)* wandering *(avant n)*, roving *(avant n)* **2** *Fig (pensée)* wandering *(avant n)*, roaming *(avant n)*; **avoir l'humeur vagabonde** to be in a restless mood
NM,F *Péj* tramp, vagabond, vagrant; *Littéraire (voyageur)* wanderer, vagabond

vagabondage [vagabɔ̃daʒ] **NM 1** *(errance)* roaming, roving, wandering **2** *Littéraire (rêveries)* **les vagabondages de l'esprit/l'imagination** the wanderings of the mind/the imagination **3** *Jur* vagrancy

vagabonder [3] [vagabɔ̃de] **VI** to wander, to roam; *Fig* **mon esprit/imagination vagabondait vers des pays lointains** my mind/imagination strayed to thoughts of faraway lands; *Fig* **ses pensées vagabondent sans parvenir à se fixer** his/her thoughts wander *or* drift without any focus

vagin [vaʒɛ̃] **NM** *Anat* vagina

vaginal, -e, -aux, -ales [vaʒinal, -o] **ADJ** *Anat* vaginal

vaginite [vaʒinit] **NF** *Méd* vaginitis

vagir [32] [vaʒir] **VI** *(crier ▸ nouveau-né)* to cry, to wail; *(▸ lièvre)* to squeal; *(▸ crocodile)* to bark

vagissant, -e [vaʒisɑ̃, -ɑ̃t] **ADJ** *(bébé)* crying, wailing; *(lièvre)* squealing; *(crocodile)* barking

vagissement [vaʒismɑ̃] **NM** *(d'un bébé)* cry, wail; *(d'un lièvre)* squeal; *(d'un crocodile)* bark

vague¹ [vag] **NF 1** *(dans la mer)* wave; **grosse v.** roller; **plonger dans les vagues** to dive into the waves; *aussi Fig* **v. de fond** groundswell; *aussi Fig* **faire des vagues** to make waves; *Fig* **je ne veux pas de vagues** I don't want any scandal; *Fig* **arriver par vagues** to come in waves
2 *Littéraire (des blés, des cheveux)* wave, ripple; *(de dunes)* wave; *(motif décoratif)* wavy pattern; **effet de v.** ripple effect; *Archit* waved motif
3 *Fig (manifestation)* wave; **v. de violence** wave *or* surge of violence
4 *(série)* wave; *(de publicités)* run, series; **v. d'arrestations** wave of arrests; **v. d'attentats** wave of bombings; **v. de criminalité** crime wave; **la première v. de départs** the first wave of departures; **v. d'immigrants** wave of immigrants; **v. de protestations/grèves** wave of protest/strikes
5 *Météo* **v. de chaleur** heatwave; **v. de froid** cold spell

vague² [vag] **ADJ 1** *(peu marqué ▸ sourire, détail)* vague; *(▸ souvenir, connaissances)* vague, hazy; *(▸ contour, sensation)* vague, indistinct; *(▸ forme)* undefined, indistinct; *(vacant ▸ regard, expression)* vacant, abstracted; **esquisser un v. sourire** to smile faintly; **regarder qn d'un air v.** to look vacantly at sb; **il eut un geste v.** he gestured vaguely, he made a vague gesture; **elle est restée très v. sur ses intentions** she was very vague about her intentions
2 *(avant le nom) (non précisé)* vague; **un v. cousin à moi** some distant cousin of mine; **quelque v. écrivain** some writer or other; **il avait écrit un v. roman** he had written a novel of sorts, he had written some kind of a novel; **il m'a raconté une v. histoire de migraine** he told me some vague story about a migraine; **ils ont eu une v. liaison** they had some sort *or* kind of an affair; **il habite du côté de la Grande Place – c'est plutôt v.!** he lives somewhere near the Grande Place – that's a bit vague!
3 *(large, ample ▸ vêtement)* loose, loose-fitting, generously cut
4 *Anat (nerf)* vagal
NM 1 *(flou)* vagueness, indistinctness; *(imprécision)* vagueness; **laisser une question dans le v.** to be vague about a matter; **rester dans le v.** to be (as) vague (as possible), to avoid giving any details; **elle m'a bien parlé d'un projet de départ mais elle est restée dans le v.** she did mention something about going away but she never went into any detail
2 *(vide)* **regarder dans le v.** to gaze vacantly into space *or* the blue; **le regard perdu dans le v.** with a faraway *or* a far-off *or* a distant look (in his/her eyes)
• **vague à l'âme NM** melancholy; **avoir du v. à l'âme** to be melancholy

vaguelette [vaglɛt] **NF** wavelet

vaguement [vagmɑ̃] **ADV 1** *(de façon imprécise)* vaguely; **je me sentais v. coupable** I felt vaguely guilty, I felt in some vague way that I was to blame; **ils se ressemblent v.** they look vaguely alike, there is a vague resemblance between them; **j'avais v. cru qu'il devait venir ici** I had the vague idea he was supposed to come here; **c'est ce que j'ai v. compris** that's what I more or less understood; **il a été v. question de lui offrir le poste** there was some vague talk of offering him/her the position; **on distinguait v. les bateaux dans l'ombre du quai** the boats were just discernible in the shadow of the wharf; **tu as prévu le repas de ce soir? – v.!** have you thought of what to cook tonight? – sort of!; *Péj* **elle est v. actrice** she's some kind of actress **2** *(un peu)* vaguely, mildly; **il avait l'air v. intéressé** he seemed vaguely interested; **v. inquiet** mildly anxious

vaguemestre [vagmɛstr] **NM** *Mil* post orderly; *Naut* postman

vaguer [3] [vage] **VI** *Littéraire (vagabonder ▸ personne)* to wander, to roam; *(▸ pensée)* to rove, to wander; **laisser v. son imagination** to allow one's imagination free rein; **laisser v. ses pensées** to let one's thoughts wander

vahiné [vaine] **NF** Tahitian woman

vaillamment [vajamɑ̃] **ADV** valiantly, bravely, gallantly; **se défendre v.** to put up stout resistance; **elle a v. fait front** she valiantly *or* gallantly stood up to the situation

vaillance [vajɑ̃s] **NF** *(courage ▸ moral)* courage, bravery, stout-heartedness; *(▸ physique)* valiance; *(▸ de soldat)* gallantry; **supporter une épreuve avec v.** to face an ordeal with courage; **elle a beaucoup de v.** she's very brave

vaillant, -e [vajɑ̃, -ɑ̃t] **ADJ 1** *(courageux ▸ moralement)* courageous, brave, stout-hearted; *(▸ physiquement)* valiant; *(▸ soldat)* gallant **2** *(bien portant)* strong, healthy; **il est encore v.** he's still in good health; **elle n'est plus bien vaillante** she's not very strong these days

vaille *etc voir* **valoir**

vain, -e [vɛ̃, vɛn] **ADJ 1** *(inutile)* vain, fruitless, pointless; *(démarche, entreprise)* futile; **tous nos efforts ont été vains** all our efforts were fruitless *or* in vain; **il est v. de continuer** it is pointless to continue
2 *Littéraire (superficiel)* shallow, superficial; *(vaniteux)* vain, conceited
3 *(avant le nom) (serment, espérance)* empty, vain; *(promesse)* empty, hollow, worthless; **ce n'étaient pas là de vaines paroles** these were no empty *or* no idle words; **je te dis qu'elle est dangereuse, et ce n'est pas un v. mot!** I tell you she's dangerous, and it's no empty claim *or* and I know what I'm talking about!; **"socialisme" n'est pas un v. mot pour moi** to me, "socialism" is not an empty *or* idle word
4 *Jur* **vaine pâture** common grazing land
• **en vain ADV** in vain, vainly, fruitlessly; **il a essayé de me consoler, mais en v.** he tried to console me, but all in vain *or* to no avail; **c'est en v. qu'elle a tenté de m'en dissuader** she tried in vain to talk me out of it

vaincre [114] [vɛ̃kr] **VT 1** *(équipe, adversaire)* to beat, to defeat; *(armée)* to defeat; **la justice vaincra!** justice will be done!; **nous vaincrons!** we shall overcome! **2** *Fig (peur, douleur, inhibition)* to overcome, to conquer, to master; *(mal de tête, maladie)* to overcome; *(hostilité, réticences)* to overcome, to triumph over; **v. une résistance** to overcome resistance; **v. toutes les résistances** to carry all before one; **être vaincu par le sommeil/la fatigue** to be overcome with sleep/exhaustion
USAGE ABSOLU il faut v. ou mourir we must do or die; *Prov* **à v. sans péril, on triomphe sans gloire** triumph without peril does not bring glory

vaincu, -e [vɛ̃ky] **ADJ** beaten, defeated; **s'avouer v.** to admit defeat; **les joueurs partaient vaincus d'avance** the players felt beaten *or* defeated before they began; **tu es toujours v. d'avance!** you always start off with the idea you're going to lose!
NM,F defeated man, *f* woman; **les vaincus** the defeated, the vanquished; **les vaincus ne participeront pas aux demi-finales** the losers will not take part in the semi-finals

vainement [vɛnmɑ̃] **ADV** in vain, vainly, fruitlessly; **on l'a v. cherché** we looked for him in vain

vainquait *etc voir* **vaincre**

vainqueur [vɛ̃kœr] **ADJ M** winning *(avant n)*, victorious, triumphant, conquering *(avant n)*; **air/sourire v.** triumphant look/smile; **sortir v. d'une épreuve** to emerge (as) the winner of a contest
NM 1 *(gagnant)* & *Sport* winner; *Boxe* **être v. par K.-O./aux points** to win by a knockout/on points; **le v. de l'Annapurna** the conqueror of Annapurna **2** *Mil* victor

vair [vɛr] **NM** vair; **la pantoufle de v. de Cendrillon** Cinderella's glass slipper

vairon¹ [vɛrɔ̃] **ADJ M aux yeux vairons** *(de couleurs différentes)* with different-coloured eyes; *(avec un anneau blanc)* wall-eyed; **avoir les yeux vairons** *(de couleurs différentes)* to have different coloured eyes; *(avec un anneau blanc)* to have wall-eyes, to be wall-eyed

vairon[2] [vɛrɔ̃] **NM** *Ich* minnow
vais [vɛ] *voir* **aller**[2]
vaisseau, -x [vɛso] **NM 1** *(navire)* ship, *Sout* vessel; **v. amiral** flagship; **v. fantôme** ghost ship; **v. de guerre** warship, man-of-war
2 *Anat* vessel; **v. capillaire/lymphatique/sanguin** capillary/lymphatic/blood vessel
3 *Bot* vessel; **plantes à vaisseaux** vascular plants
4 *Astron* **v. spatial** spacecraft; **v. spatial habité** spaceship, manned spacecraft
5 *Archit (de cathédrale)* nave; *(d'un édifice)* body, hall
6 *Arch (récipient)* vessel, receptacle
7 *Bible* **v. d'élection** chosen vessel
vaisselier [vesəlje] **NM** *Br* dresser, *Am* buffet
vaisselle [vesɛl] **NF 1** *(service)* crockery; **acheter de la belle v.** to buy some nice tableware; **v. plate** (gold/silver) plate; **v. de porcelaine** china tableware; **v. de terre** earthenware plates and dishes; *Fam* **liquide v.** *Br* washing-up liquid, *Am* dish soap **2** *(ustensiles sales)* (dirty) dishes; **faire** *ou* **laver la v.** to do *or* to wash the dishes, *Br* to do the washing-up
Val [val] **NM** *Rail (abrév* **véhicule automatique léger**) automatic urban train service
val, -als *ou* **-aux** [val, vo] **NM** *(vallée)* valley; **le V. d'Aoste** Valle d'Aosta; **le V. de Loire** the Loire Valley, the Val de Loire
valable [valabl] **ADJ 1** *(valide ▸ ticket, acte)* valid; **au-delà de cette limite, votre billet n'est plus v.** tickets are not valid beyond this point; **non v.** invalid **2** *(acceptable ▸ schéma, argument)* valid, good; *(▸ excuse, raison)* valid, good, legitimate; **cela reste v.** that still stands; **ce qui est v. pour l'un est v. pour l'autre** what goes for one goes for the other **3** *(excellent ▸ musicien, athlète)* decent, serious

> Do not confuse with **valide**.

valablement [valabləmɑ̃] **ADV 1** *(à bon droit)* validly, justifiably, legitimately; **peut-on v. invoquer la légitime défense?** can we justifiably plead self-defence?; **c'est ce qu'on lui a v. reproché** this is what he/she was accused of, and rightly so; **être v. autorisé à qch/à faire qch** to have the necessary authority for sth/to do sth **2** *(efficacement)* usefully; **l'art d'investir son argent v.** the art of making a worthwhile investment; **pour être à même de traiter v. ce problème** in order to be able to deal with this problem satisfactorily
valdinguer [3] [valdɛ̃ge] **VI** *Fam (tomber)* to go flying; **il est allé v. contre le parcmètre** he went sprawling against the parking meter; **la bouilloire est allée v. contre le placard** the kettle went flying against the cupboard; **envoyer v. qn/qch** to send sb/sth flying; **envoyer v. une assiette/un livre** to send a plate/a book flying; *Fig* **tout envoyer v.** to pack *or* jack it all in
Valence [valɑ̃s] **NM 1** *(ville d'Espagne)* Valencia **2** *(ville de France)* Valence
valence [valɑ̃s] **NF** *Chim Br* valency, *Am* valence
valenciennes [valɑ̃sjɛn] **NF** (Valenciennes) lace
valentin, -e [valɑ̃tɛ̃, -in] **NM,F** *(personne)* valentine
NM *Can (carte de vœux)* valentine's card, valentine
valériane [valerjan] **NF** *Bot* valerian
valet [valɛ] **NM 1** *(serviteur)* servant, valet; *Théât* **jouer les valets de comédie** to play servants' parts; **v. de chambre** manservant, valet; **v. de chiens** *(à la chasse)* whipper-in; **v. d'écurie** groom, stable boy; **v. de ferme** farm hand; **v. de pied** footman
2 *Hist* varlet, page
3 *Cartes* jack, knave; **v. de pique** jack *or* knave of spades
4 *(cintre)* **v. (de nuit)** valet
5 *Menuis* clamp
valetaille [valtaj] **NF** *Littéraire Péj* flunkeys
valétudinaire [valetydinɛr] *Littéraire* **ADJ** valetudinarian, valetudinary
NMF valetudinarian

VALEUR [valœr]

> • value **1, 2, 4, 6, 8, 11** • worth **1, 7**
> • time **3** • meaning **5**

NF 1 *(prix)* value, worth; **avoir de la v.** to be of value; **cette statue a-t-elle une quelconque v.?** is this statue worth anything?; **la v. en a été fixée à 500 euros** its value has been put at 500 euros, it's been estimated to be worth 500 euros; **prendre/perdre de la v.** to increase/to decrease in value, to go up/down in value; **cet appartement ne cesse de prendre de la v.** this flat keeps going up in value, the value of this flat is constantly increasing; **estimer qch au-dessus/au-dessous de sa v.** to overvalue/to undervalue sth; **des objets de peu de v.** objects of little value; **être sans v.** to be of no value; **bijoux sans v.** *ou* **qui n'ont aucune v.** worthless jewels; **bijou de grande v.** jewel of great value, very valuable jewel; **manuscrit d'une v. inestimable** invaluable manuscript; **des marchandises d'une v. de 5000 euros** goods to the value of 5,000 euros; **v. de vérité** truth value; **mettre en v.** *(terre)* to exploit; *(capital)* to get the best return out of; *(connaissances)* to put to good use; *(taille, minceur)* to enhance; *(talent, qualités)* to bring out, to highlight; **une bordure vert tendre met en v. le rose de l'abat-jour** a soft green border sets off the pink in the lampshade; **mettre en v. les meilleures qualités de qn** to bring out the best in sb; **le noir est la couleur qui me met le plus en v.** black is the colour that suits me best; **elle sait se mettre en v.** she knows how to show herself off to the best advantage; **bien/mal mis en v.** *(objet d'art, tableau)* well-/poorly-displayed; **mise en v. d'un terrain** development of a site
2 *Com, Écon, Fin & Math* value; **v. absolue** absolute value; **en v. absolue** in absolute terms; **v. d'achat** purchase value; **v. de l'actif** asset value; *Compta* **v. actualisée** present value; *Compta* **v. actuelle** current value; *Compta* **v. actuelle nette** current net value; **v. ajoutée** added value, value added; **à haute v. ajoutée** high value-added; **v. approchée** approximate value; **v. assurable** insurable value; **v. assurée** insured value; **v. de bilan** book value; *Compta* **v. bilantielle** balance-sheet value; **v. en bourse** *ou* **boursière** market value; **v. brute** gross value; **v. en capital** capital assets; *Fin* **v. compensée** cleared value; **v. comptable** book value; **v. comptable nette** net book value; **v. déclarée** declared value; **colis chargé avec v. déclarée 50 euros** parcel insured for 50 euros; *Mktg* **v. d'échange** exchange value; *Fin* **v. à l'échéance** maturity value; *Fin* **v. d'émission** issue price; *Fin* **v. à l'encaissement** value for collection; *Compta* **v. d'inventaire** balance sheet value, break-up value; *Banque* **v. jour** same-day value; **v. locative** rental value; **v. marchande** market value; *Bourse* **v. nominale** *(d'une obligation)* par value; *(d'une action)* face *or* nominal value; *Bourse* **v. non cotée** unlisted security; *Mktg* **v. perçue** perceived value; **v. de rachat** *(d'une police)* surrender value; **v. de rendement** *(d'une entreprise)* profitability value; **v. de reprise** trade-in allowance; **v. à la revente** resale value; **v. d'usage** use value; **v. vénale** monetary value
3 *Mus (d'une note)* time (value), length
4 *(d'une carte)* value
5 *(sens)* meaning; **c'est là que le terme prend toute sa v.** that's when the term takes on its full meaning
6 *(importance subjective)* value; **attacher** *ou* **accorder une grande v. à qch** to prize sth; **attacher** *ou* **accorder de la v. aux traditions** to value *or* to set store by traditions; **j'attache beaucoup de v. à la présentation** I set great store by presentation; **tu sais la v. que j'accorde à ton avis** you know how much I value your opinion; **ton opinion n'a aucune v. pour moi** as far as I'm concerned, your opinion is worthless; **ce document n'a aucune v. légale** this document is not legally binding *or* has no standing in law; **n'avoir qu'une v. sentimentale** to be of *or* to have purely sentimental value; **estimer qn à sa juste v.** to judge sb at his/her true value *or* worth; **cette découverte a redonné une v. à ma vie** this discovery has given my life new meaning
7 *(mérite)* worth, merit; **livre de grande v.** book of considerable merit; **voilà un ouvrage qui n'a pas grande v.** this book is of little merit; **votre argument n'est pas sans v.** your argument is not without its merits; **avoir conscience de sa v.** to know one's own worth
8 *(notion morale)* value; **valeurs sociales/morales/familiales** social/moral/family values; **avoir le sens des valeurs** to have a sense of values; **lui et moi, nous n'avons pas les mêmes valeurs** he and I don't have *or* share the same values
9 *Littéraire (bravoure)* valiance, bravery; **la v. n'attend pas le nombre des années** there is no age for courage
10 *Littéraire (personne de mérite)* **une v.** a great name; **une v. sûre de la sculpture française** one of the top French sculptors
11 *(validité ▸ d'une méthode, d'une découverte)* value; **sa déposition enlève toute v. à la vôtre** his/her testimony renders yours invalid *or* worthless
12 *(équivalent)* **donnez-lui la v. d'une cuillère à soupe de sirop** give him/her the equivalent of a tablespoonful of syrup
• **valeurs NFPL** *Bourse* **valeurs (boursières)** securities, shares, stock; **les valeurs françaises sont en baisse/hausse** French securities *or* stocks are down/up **valeurs cotées** *ou* **de bourse** quoted securities; **valeurs disponibles** liquid *or* tangible assets; **valeurs émises** securities issued; **valeurs en espèces** cash *(UNCOUNT)*, bullion *(UNCOUNT)*; **valeurs immobilières** real property shares; **valeurs mobilières** stocks and shares, transferable securities; **valeurs négociables** marketable securities; **valeurs nominatives** registered securities; **valeurs passives** liabilities; **valeurs de père de famille** blue chip stock; **valeurs (mobilières) de placement** marketable securities; **valeurs pétrolières** oil shares; **valeurs de portefeuille** portfolio securities; **v. de premier ordre** blue chip; **valeurs réalisables** realizable *or* marketable securities; **valeurs à revenu fixe/variable** fixed/variable income securities; **valeurs du second marché** unlisted securities; **valeurs spéculatives** *ou* **de spéculation** speculative securities; **valeurs à terme** futures; **valeurs de tout repos** gilt-edged securities; **valeurs vedettes** leading shares
• **de valeur ADJ 1** *Com & Fin (bague, tableau)* valuable; **des objets de v.** valuables, items of value, valuable items **2** *(personne)* **homme de v.** *(doué)* man of real ability, talented man; *(de mérite)* man of merit; **un collaborateur de v.** a prized colleague **3** *Can Fam (dommage)* **c'est de v. qu'il pleuve/qu'elle ne puisse pas venir** it's too bad that it's raining/that she can't come

valeureuse [valœrøz] *voir* **valeureux**
valeureusement [valœrøzmɑ̃] **ADV** *Littéraire* bravely, gallantly, valiantly
valeureux, -euse [valœrø, -øz] **ADJ** *Littéraire (vaillant)* brave, gallant, valiant
valeur-or [valœrɔr] **NF** *Fin* value in gold currency
validation [validasjɔ̃] **NF** *(d'un billet, d'une élection)* validation; *(d'un document)* authentication; *(d'une loi)* ratification
valide [valid] **ADJ 1** *(permis, titre de transport)* valid; **votre carte n'est plus v.** your card has run out *or* is out of date *or* has expired; **non v.** invalid **2** *(bien portant)* fit, (well and) strong; *(non blessé)* able-bodied; *(membre)* functioning; **il n'avait qu'un bras v.** he had only one good arm; **je ne suis plus bien v.** I'm not as strong as I used to be

> Il faut noter que l'adjectif anglais **valid** signifie le plus souvent **valable**.
>
> Do not confuse with **valable**.

validement [validmɑ̃] **ADV** validly
valider [3] [valide] **VT 1** *(traité)* to ratify; *(document)* to authenticate; *(testament) Br* to prove, *Am* to probate; *(billet, passeport, élection)* to validate; **(faire) v. son titre de transport** *(par un contrôleur)* to have one's ticket stamped; *(dans une machine)* to stamp one's ticket; **il faut faire v. le bulletin de Loto dans un bureau de tabac** you have to get the Loto ticket stamped in a newsagent's **2** *Ordinat (option)* to confirm; *(cellule, case)* to select
validité [validite] **NF 1** *Admin & Transp* validity; **durée de v.** period of validity; **proroger la v. d'un visa** to extend a visa; **établir la v. d'un document** to authenticate a document; **établir la v. d'un testament** to prove *or* to probate a will; **date (limite) de**

v. expiry date **2** *(bien-fondé ▸ d'un argument, d'un témoignage)* validity

valise [valiz] **NF 1** *(bagage)* suitcase, bag; **mes valises** my suitcases *or* bags *or* luggage; **défaire ses valises** to unpack (one's bags); **faire ses valises** to pack (one's bags); **mes valises sont faites** I've packed; *Fig* **faire sa v.** *ou* **ses valises** *(partir)* to pack one's bags and go; *Fam* **tu cesses de parler sur ce ton à ta mère ou tu fais tes valises!** either you stop speaking to your mother like that or you're out on your ear!
2 *Fam (sous les yeux)* **avoir des valises (sous les yeux)** to have bags under one's eyes
3 *Jur* **la v. diplomatique** the diplomatic *Br* bag *or Am* pouch; **expédier du courrier par la v. diplomatique** to send mail via the diplomatic *Br* bag *or Am* pouch
4 *Can Joual (coffre d'une voiture) Br* boot▫, *Am* trunk▫
5 *Can Fam (personne crédule)* sucker, *Br* mug; *(personne naïve)* simpleton▫

vallée [vale] **NF 1** *Géog* valley; **les gens de la v.** people who live in the valley; *(pour les montagnards)* lowlanders; **descendre dans la v.** to go down into the valley; **v. d'effondrement** rift valley; **v. glaciaire** *ou* **en U** glaciated *or* U-shaped valley; **v. (à profil) en V** V-shaped valley; **v. sèche** *ou* **morte** dried-up valley; **dans la V. de la Loire/du Rhône** in the Loire/Rhône valley; **la V. de la Mort** Death Valley; **la V. des Rois** Valley of the Kings **2** *Littéraire* **cette v. de larmes** this vale of tears

vallon [valɔ̃] **NM** small valley; *(en Écosse)* glen

vallonné, -e [valɔne] **ADJ** undulating, hilly

vallonnement [valɔnmɑ̃] **NM** undulation, hilliness *(UNCOUNT)*

valoche [valɔʃ] **NF** *Fam (valise)* suitcase▫, case▫; *Fig (sous les yeux)* **avoir des valoches (sous les yeux)** to have bags (under one's eyes); **faire ses valoches** to pack (up); *Fig* to pack up and go

VALOIR **[60]** [valwar]

> **VI**
> - to be worth **1, 3**
> - to apply **5**
> - to put forward **7**
> - to cost **2**
> - to emphasize **7**
> - to assert **7**
>
> **V IMPERSONNEL**
> - it is/would be better to...
>
> **VT**
> - to earn **1**
> - to be equivalent (to) **2**
> - to be worth **2, 3**
> - to be as good as **4**
>
> **VPR**
> - to be equivalent

VI 1 *(avoir tel prix)* to be worth; **une maison qui vaut 200 000 euros** a house worth 200,000 euros; **un bijou pareil vaut bien 10 000 euros** a piece of jewellery like that must cost a good 10,000 euros; **sa maison vaut le double maintenant** his/her house is worth twice that now *or* has doubled its value now; **combien vaut cette statuette, à votre avis?** how much is this statuette worth, do you think?; **as-tu une idée de ce que peut v. ce guéridon?** have you any idea how much this little table might be worth?; **ma vieille cuisinière ne vaut plus rien** my old stove isn't worth anything now, I wouldn't get anything for my old stove now; *Fam* **une famille qui vaut plusieurs milliards de dollars** a family worth several billion dollars
2 *(coûter)* to cost; **le ruban vaut trois euros le mètre** the ribbon costs *or* is three euros a metre; **v. cher** *(objet en vente)* to be expensive; *(objet précieux)* to be worth a lot; **ne pas v. cher** to be cheap *or* inexpensive; **le bureau ne vaut pas cher** the desk isn't expensive *or* is fairly cheap; **c'est tout ce que ça vaut** that's all it's worth; **ne pas v. grand-chose** not to be worth much; *Fig* **ces gens-là ne valent pas cher** *ou* **pas grand-chose** those people are just worthless *or* contemptible
3 *(avoir telle qualité)* to be worth; **je sais ce que je vaux** I know my worth *or* what I'm worth; **que vaut une vie d'artiste sans la reconnaissance du public?** what's the point of being an artist without public recognition?; **ils verront à l'usage ce que vaut leur nouvelle organisation** in time, they'll see how good their new organization is; **prends mon avis pour ce qu'il vaut** take my advice for what it's worth; **il ne vaut rien, ton marteau** your hammer's no good *or* useless; **son idée/projet ne vaut rien** his/her idea/project is worthless; **son explication ne vaut rien** his/her explanation is worthless *or* useless; **quand je manque de sommeil, je ne vaux rien** if I haven't had enough sleep I'm useless; **c'est une excellente scientifique mais elle ne vaut rien en tant que professeur** she's a brilliant scientist but a hopeless teacher; **il ne vaut pas mieux que son frère** he's no better than his brother; **mes premières chansons ne valaient pas grand-chose** my early songs weren't particularly good; **l'émission d'hier ne valait pas grand-chose** yesterday's programme wasn't up to much; **vous ne valez pas mieux l'un que l'autre** you're as bad as each other; **et il t'a quittée? tu vaux mieux que ça** and he left you? you deserve better than that
4 *(tirer sa valeur)* **ma bague ne vaut que par les souvenirs qu'elle représente** my ring has only sentimental value; **son livre vaut essentiellement par le style** his/her book's main strength is its style; **son initiative vaut surtout par son audace** the main merit of his/her initiative is its boldness
5 *(être valable, applicable)* **v. pour** to apply to, to hold for; **le règlement vaut pour tout le monde** the rules hold for everyone; **et ça vaut pour tout le monde** and that goes for everyone; **cette critique vaut pour toutes ses pièces** that criticism is true of *or* is valid for *or* applies to all his/her plays; **l'embargo ne vaut que pour les armes** the embargo only applies to weapons; **mes compliments/reproches valent pour toute la classe** my praise/criticism applies to the whole class
6 *Com* **il y a cinq euros à v. sur votre prochain achat** you'll get five euros off your next purchase; **à v. sur (une somme)** on account of (a sum); **verser un acompte à v. sur une somme** to pay a deposit to be set off against a sum; **à v. sur qn** on *or* for account of sb; **payer dix euros à v.** to pay ten euros on account
7 *(locutions)* **faire v.** *(argument)* to emphasize, to put forward; *(opinion, raisons)* to put forward; *(droit)* to assert, to enforce; *(qualité)* to highlight, to bring out; **faire v. son bon droit** to assert *or* to vindicate one's rights; **faire v. ses droits à la retraite** to provide evidence for one's entitlement to a pension; **elle a fait v. le coût de l'opération pour justifier sa réticence** she cited the cost of the operation as justification for her reluctance; **pour avoir le poste, il a fait v. ses dix ans d'expérience** to get the job, he stressed his ten years' experience; **j'ai fait v. que...** I pointed out *or* urged that...; **j'ai fait v. qu'il y avait des circonstances atténuantes** I pointed out *or* stressed that there were extenuating circumstances; **elle fait v. sa fille** she pushes her daughter forward; **la monture fait v. la pierre** the setting shows off the stone (to (good) advantage); **se faire v.** to show oneself off to advantage; **elle ne sait pas se faire v. dans les entrevues** she doesn't know how to sell herself at interviews; *Écon* **faire v. un capital** to turn a sum of money to (good) account, to make a sum of money yield a good profit; **faire v. des terres/une propriété** to derive profit from land/a property

V IMPERSONNEL il vaut mieux *ou* **il vaudrait mieux rester à la maison** it's *or* it would be better to stay at home; **dans ce cas, mieux vaut s'abstenir** in that case, it's better to do nothing; **mieux vaut tard que jamais** better late than never; **il vaut mieux se taire que de dire des bêtises** it's better to keep quiet than to talk nonsense; **il vaut mieux ne pas répondre** it's best *or* better not to answer; **il vaudrait mieux que tu y réfléchisses** you'd do better to *or* you should think about it; **il vaudrait mieux te faire oublier pendant un certain temps** you'd better keep a low profile for a while; **il aurait mieux valu pour elle qu'elle meure** it would have been better for her if she'd died; **appelle le médecin, ça vaut mieux** it would be better *or* safer if you called the doctor; **je vais lui dire – je crois que ça vaut mieux** I'm going to tell him/her – I think that would be the best thing to do; **ça vaut mieux ainsi** *ou* **comme ça** it's better that way; **ça vaut mieux pour lui** it's better for him; **je vais te rembourser – ça vaudrait mieux pour toi!** I'll pay you back – you'd better!; **des choses qu'il vaut autant ne pas rappeler** things best forgotten

VT 1 *(procurer)* **v. qch à qn** to earn sb sth, to bring sth to sb; **leurs efforts leur ont valu une médaille aux jeux Olympiques** their efforts earned them a medal at the Olympic Games; **cela ne m'a valu que des soucis** all it brought me was trouble; **ça lui a valu trois jours de mise à pied** that earned him/her three days' suspension; **il n'a valu que des malheurs à ses parents** all he ever brought his parents was unhappiness; **qu'est-ce qui m'a valu votre mépris?** what did I do to deserve your contempt?; **voilà ce que ça m'a valu de l'aider!** that's all I got for helping him/her!; **qu'est-ce qui me vaut l'honneur/le plaisir de ta visite?** to what do I owe the honour/the pleasure of your visit?; **cette action lui a valu d'être décoré** this act won him a decoration; **son exploit lui a valu d'être admiré par tous** his achievement earned him widespread admiration; **ne rien v. à qn** *(ne pas lui convenir)* to be no good for sb, not to agree with sb, not to suit sb; **les pays chauds ne me valent rien, j'en rentre toujours épuisé** hot countries don't suit me, I always come back exhausted
2 *(représenter)* to be equivalent to, to be worth; **une dame vaut 10 points** a queen is worth 10 points; **un euro vaut cent centimes** one euro is equivalent *or* is equal to a hundred cents; **une livre vaut 1,60 euros** a pound is worth *or* is equivalent to *or* equal to 1.60 euros; **chaque faute de grammaire vaut quatre points** you lose four points for each grammatical mistake
3 *(mériter)* to be worth; **le village vaut le détour/déplacement** the village is worth the detour/journey; **voilà un service qui vaut au moins un remerciement, non?** surely a favour like that deserves some form of thanks?; **sa cuisine vaut d'être goûtée** his/her cooking's worth sampling; **son livre vaudrait d'être traduit** his/her book deserves to be translated; **le livre vaut d'être lu** the book is worth reading; **l'expérience vaut d'être tentée** it's worth trying the experiment, the experiment is worth trying; **un service en vaut un autre** one good turn deserves another; **cela ne vaut pas le voyage** it's not worth the journey, it's not worth a special trip; **ça vaut le coup d'œil** it's worth seeing; *Fam* **v. la peine** *ou* **le coup** to be worth it, to be worthwhile; **je viendrai si cela en vaut la peine** I'll come if it's worth (my) while *or* worth the trouble *or* worth it; **cela ne vaut pas la peine de s'y arrêter** there's no point (in) dwelling on it; **ça vaut le coup** it's worth a try; **ça ne vaut pas le coup** it isn't worth the trouble; **ça vaut le coup d'essayer** it's worth trying *or* a try; **on pourrait essayer de le raccommoder – ça n'en vaut pas la peine** we could try to mend it – it's not worth it *or* worth the trouble; **quand je paie 50 euros pour un spectacle, je veux que ça en vaille la peine** if I spend 50 euros on a show I like to get my money's worth; **j'ai gagné 1000 euros – dis donc, ça vaut le coup!** I won 1,000 euros – well, that was certainly worth it!; **à ce prix-là, ça vaut le coup** at that price, you can't go wrong
4 *(dans une comparaison)* to be as good as, to match up (to); **c'est bon, mais ça ne vaut pas le repas de la dernière fois** it's good, but not as good as the meal we had last time; **c'est moins cher, mais ça ne vaut pas le cuir!** it's cheaper, but there's no comparison with real leather!; **son idée en vaut une autre** his/her idea is as good as any other; **tu la vaux largement** you're every bit as good as her; **toutes les explications de la terre ne valent pas un bon croquis** no amount of explanation can take the place of a good diagram; **ah, rien ne vaut les confitures de grand-mère!** there's nothing like grandma's jam!; **rien ne vaut un bon grog pour guérir une grippe** there's nothing like a good hot toddy to cure flu; **pour moi, rien ne vaut Mozart!** give me Mozart any day!; **ça ne vaut pas ce qui m'est arrivé l'autre jour** that's nothing to what happened to me the other day

VPR se valoir to be equivalent; **les deux traitements se valent** there's nothing to choose between the two treatments; **tous les métiers se valent** one job is as good as another; **ils se valent tous** there's not much to choose between them they're all pretty much the same; **nous nous valons au sprint** we're both equally good (as) sprinters; **le père et le fils se valent, aussi têtus l'un que l'autre!** father and son are two of a kind, they're so stubborn!; **vous vous valez bien!** you're both as bad as each other!; **tu vas voter Dupond ou Dufort? – tout ça se vaut!** are you going to vote Du

pond or Dufort? – it's six of one and half a dozen of the other!, it's all the same thing!
• **vaille que vaille** ADV somehow (or other); **vaille que vaille, elle est arrivée au sommet** somehow she made it to the top; **on essaiera vaille que vaille de l'aider** we'll try as best we can to help him/her

valorisant, -e [valɔrizɑ̃, -ɑ̃t] ADJ *(satisfaisant moralement)* rewarding; **il fait un travail v.** he has a rewarding job; **la situation des femmes au foyer n'est guère valorisante** being a housewife can hardly be considered a fulfilling occupation

valorisation [valɔrizasjɔ̃] NF **1** *Écon (mise en valeur)* economic development; *(valeur)* enhanced value; *Compta (d'un inventaire)* valuation; **...ce qui permettra une v. de vos investissements** ...which will increase *or* enhance the value of your investments **2** *Fig* **on observe une v. des tâches manuelles** manual work is becoming more highly valued; **la v. des diplômes techniques** increasing the prestige of technical diplomas

valoriser [3] [valɔrize] VT **1** *Écon (région)* to develop the economy of; *(bien, monnaie)* to increase the value of **2** *(augmenter le prestige de)* **son succès l'a valorisé aux yeux de ses amis** his success has increased his standing in the eyes of his friends; **cherchez un travail qui vous valorise** look for a job which will give you personal satisfaction

VPR **se valoriser** *Com & Fin* to increase in value; **région/secteur qui se valorise** region/industry which is going through a period of growth, up-and-coming region/industry

valse [vals] NF **1** *(danse)* waltz; **v. musette** waltz (played on the accordion); **v. viennoise** Viennese waltz **2** *Fam (succession rapide)* (game of) musical chairs; **la v. des ministres** ministerial musical chairs, constant changes of the ministerial merry-go-round **3** *Fam (modification)* **la v. des prix** *ou* **des étiquettes** spiralling prices[□]

valse-hésitation [valsezitasjɔ̃] *(pl* **valses-hésitations)** NF *(tergiversation)* shilly-shallying, dithering (about); **après une interminable v.** after much shilly-shallying

valser [3] [valse] VI **1** *(danser)* to waltz; **faire v. qn** to waltz with sb; **invite-la à v.** ask her for a waltz **2** *Fam (tomber)* to career[□], to hurtle[□]; **la lampe a valsé dans la cheminée** the lamp went flying into the fireplace; **la voiture est allée v. contre le mur** the car went careering *or* hurtling into the wall; **envoyer v. qch** to send sth flying; **envoyer v. qn** *(le faire tomber)* to send sb flying; *(l'éconduire)* to send sb packing, to show sb the door; **il m'a envoyé v. contre le mur** he sent me flying into the wall; **faire v. l'argent** *ou* **les billets** to throw money about *or* around **3** *Fam (abandonner)* **j'ai envie de tout envoyer v.!** I feel like packing it all in!

valseur, -euse [valsœr, -øz] NM,F waltzer
NM *très Fam Br* bum, *Am* fanny
• **valseuses** NFPL *Vulg* balls

valu, -e [valy] PP *voir* **valoir**

valve [valv] NF **1** *Anat, Bot & Zool* valve; **v. cardiaque** cardiac valve
2 *Tech (clapet)* valve; *(soupape à clapet)* valve; **v. de compensation** compensating valve; **v. à** *ou* **de dépression** vacuum valve; **v. modulatrice** modulator valve; **v. papillon** butterfly valve; **v. de purge** bleed valve
3 *Aut* **v. de chambre à air** inner-tube valve; **v. de gonflage** tyre valve
4 *Électron* valve; **v. redresseuse** rectifying valve
• **valves** NFPL *Belg* noticeboard; **aux valves** on the noticeboard

valvulaire [valvylɛr] ADJ *Anat* valvular

valvule [valvyl] NF **1** *Anat* valve **2** *Bot* valve, valvule

vamp [vɑ̃p] NF vamp; **prendre des airs de v.** to put on a vampish look
ADJ vampish; **habillée très v.** dressed very vampishly

vamper [3] [vɑ̃pe] VT *Fam* to vamp

vampire [vɑ̃pir] NM **1** *(suceur de sang)* vampire **2** *Littéraire Péj (parasite)* vampire, vulture, bloodsucker; *(assassin)* mass murderer **3** *Zool* vampire bat

vampiriser [3] [vɑ̃pirize] VT *Fam (dominer)* to have under one's sway, to subjugate; **ayant vampirisé la presse écrite, il s'attaque maintenant à la télévision** having taken over the print media, he's now preparing for an assault on television

vampirisme [vɑ̃pirism] NM *(croyance, pratique)* vampirism

VAN [veaɛn] NF *Compta (abrév* **valeur actuelle nette)** NPV, net present value

van[1] [vɑ̃] NM *Agr (corbeille)* winnowing basket, fan

van[2] [vɑ̃] NM *(véhicule pour chevaux)* horse *Br* box *or Am* trailer

van[3] [van] NM *(camionnette)* van

vanadium [vanadjɔm] NM *Chim* vanadium

vandale [vɑ̃dal] NM **1** *(voyou)* vandal **2** *Hist* Vandal

vandaliser [3] [vɑ̃dalize] VT to vandalize

vandalisme [vɑ̃dalism] NM vandalism; **commettre des actes de v.** to commit acts of vandalism

vandoise [vɑ̃dwaz] NF *Ich* dace

vanesse [vanɛs] NF *Entom* vanessid; **v. tortue** tortoiseshell (butterfly)

vanille [vanij] NF vanilla
• **à la vanille** ADJ vanilla *(avant n)*, vanilla-flavoured

vanillé, -e [vanije] ADJ vanilla-flavoured

vanillier [vanije] NM vanilla plant

vanité [vanite] NF **1** *(orgueil)* vanity, pride, conceit; **blesser** *ou* **toucher qn dans sa v.** to hurt sb's pride; **tirer v. de qch** to pride oneself on sth, to take pride in sth; **tirer v. de son origine ouvrière** to pride oneself on one's working-class background; **elle avait été championne régionale mais elle n'en a jamais tiré v.** she'd been a local champion but she never boasted about the fact; **il est d'une v. incroyable** he's so incredibly vain, he's so conceited; **sans v., je crois pouvoir faire mieux** with all due modesty *or* without wishing to boast, I think I can do better; **agir par v.** to act out of vanity **2** *(futilité)* pointlessness, futility; **la v. de l'existence humaine** the futility of human existence; *Littéraire* **tout est v.** all is vanity

vaniteuse [vanitøz] *voir* **vaniteux**

vaniteusement [vanitøzmɑ̃] ADV vainly, conceitedly, self-importantly

vaniteux, -euse [vanitø, -øz] ADJ vain, conceited, self-important
NM,F conceited man, *f* woman

vanity-case [vanitikɛz] *(pl* **vanity-cases)** NM vanity case

vannage [vanaʒ] NM *Agr* winnowing

vanne[1] [van] NF **1** *(d'une écluse)* sluicegate; *(d'un moulin)* hatch; **v. de décharge** floodgate; **v. manuelle** manual valve; **ouvrir les vannes** to open the sluicegates; *Fig* to open the floodgates **2** *(robinet)* stopcock

vanne[2] [van] NF *Fam* **1** *(remarque désobligeante)* snide remark[□], dig, jibe; **envoyer des vannes à qn** to make digs at sb **2** *(plaisanterie)* joke[□], crack

vanneau, -x [vano] NM *Orn* **v. (huppé)** lapwing, peewit; *Culin* **œufs de v.** plovers' eggs

vanner[1] [3] [vane] VT *Agr* to winnow

vanner[2] [3] [vane] VT *Fam (se moquer de)* to make digs at; *(épuiser)* to wear out

vannerie [vanri] NF **1** *(activité)* basketwork, basketry; **faire de la v.** to weave baskets **2** *(objets)* basketwork, wickerwork
• **en vannerie** ADJ wicker, wickerwork *(avant n)*

vanneur, -euse [vanœr, -øz] NM,F *Agr* winnower

vannier [vanje] NM basket maker

vantail, -aux [vɑ̃taj, -o] NM *(de porte)* leaf; *(de fenêtre)* casement; **porte à double v.** *ou* **à vantaux** *Br* stable *or Am* Dutch door

vantard, -e [vɑ̃tar, -ard] ADJ boastful, boasting *(avant n)*, bragging *(avant n)*
NM,F bragger, braggart

vantardise [vɑ̃tardiz] NF **1** *(glorification de soi)* boastfulness, bragging **2** *(remarque)* boast

vantaux [vɑ̃to] *voir* **vantail**

vanter [3] [vɑ̃te] VT *(louer, exalter)* to praise, to extol; **v. l'élégance de qn** to praise sb's elegance; **v. les mérites de qch** to sing the praises of sth; **v. les mérites de qn** to sing sb's praises; *Fam* **une pub vantant les mérites d'une lessive** an ad singing the praises of a washing powder; **un magazine qui vante les charmes de l'Écosse** a magazine which sings the praises of Scotland; *Hum* **v. sa marchandise** to boast
VPR **se vanter** to boast, to brag (**de qch** about sth); **elle n'arrête pas de se v.** she's always singing her own praises *or* bragging; **elle se vante de connaître six langues** she boasts *or* brags that she knows *or* about knowing six languages; **il s'est vanté de gagner la course** he boasted that he would win the race; **il s'est vanté d'avoir gagné la course** he bragged that he had won the race; **elle l'a fait renvoyer mais elle ne s'en vante pas** she had him fired, but she keeps quiet about it; **il n'y a pas de quoi se v.** this is nothing to be proud of *or* to boast about; **ce n'est pas pour me v. mais...** I don't mean to boast, but...; **sans (vouloir) me v., je suis plutôt bon au tennis** I'm rather good at tennis, though I say so myself; **soit dit sans (vouloir) me v.** without wishing to boast *or* to brag *or Br* to blow my own trumpet

Vanuatu [vanwatu] NM **le V.** Vanuatu

va-nu-pieds [vanypje] NMF INV *Péj (clochard)* tramp, beggar

vapes [vap] NFPL *Fam* **être dans les v.** *(évanoui)* to be out of it; *(rêveur)* to be miles away; **je suis encore un peu dans les v.** I'm still a bit out of it; **elle est constamment dans les v.** her head is always in the clouds; **quoi? j'étais complètement dans les v.** what? I was miles away; **tomber dans les v.** *(s'évanouir)* to pass out[□], to keel over

vapeur [vapœr] NF **1** *(gén)* steam; **v. (d'eau)** steam, (water) vapour; **v. atmosphérique** atmospheric vapour; **mettre la v.** to put steam on; *Fig* **nous avons dû mettre la v. pour finir à temps** we had to pull out all the stops to finish on time **2** *Chim & Phys* vapour; **vapeurs d'essence** *Br* petrol *or Am* gas fumes; **vapeurs d'alcool** alcoholic fumes **3** *Littéraire (brouillard)* haze, vapour
NM *Naut* steamship, steamer
• **vapeurs** NFPL *Vieilli* **avoir des** *ou* **ses vapeurs** to have a fit of the vapours
• **à la vapeur** ADV **ça marche à la v.** it's steam-driven; **cuit à la v.** steam-cooked; **cuire des légumes à la v.** to steam vegetables; **cuisiner à la v.** to steam food; **repassage à la v.** steam ironing
• **à toute vapeur** ADV *Fam* **aller à toute v.** *(navire)* to sail full steam ahead; *(train)* to go full steam ahead, to go at full speed[□]; *Fig* to go as fast as one can[□]; **va chez le boulanger, et à toute v.!** go to the baker's, and be quick about it!
• **à vapeur** ADJ steam *(avant n)*, steam-driven; **machine à v.** steam engine; **bateau à v.** steamboat, steamer; **locomotive à v.** steam locomotive; **train à v.** steam train

vapocraquage [vapɔkrakaʒ] NM *Pétr* steam cracking

vapocraqueur [vapɔkrakœr] NM *Pétr* steam reformer

vaporeux, -euse [vapɔrø, -øz] ADJ **1** *(voilé ▸ lumière, paysage)* hazy, misty; *(atmosphère)* steamy; **une brume vaporeuse** hazy mist **2** *(léger ▸ tissu)* filmy, diaphanous; *(▸ robe)* flimsy; *Fig (idées)* hazy

vaporisateur [vapɔrizatœr] NM **1** *(pulvérisateur)* spray; *(atomiseur)* spray, atomizer; **parfum en v.** spray perfume **2** *Tech (échangeur)* vaporizer

vaporisation [vapɔrizasjɔ̃] NF **1** *(pulvérisation)* spraying **2** *Tech (volatilisation)* vaporization; *Aut* **v. (du carburant)** (fuel) atomization

vaporiser [3] [vapɔrize] VT **1** *(pulvériser)* to spray; **ne pas v. vers une flamme** *(sur emballage)* do not spray onto a naked flame **2** *Tech (volatiliser)* to vaporize
VPR **se vaporiser** to vaporize, to turn to vapour

vaquer [3] [vake] VI *Admin* **1** *(parlement, tribunal)* to be on vacation **2** *Vieilli (poste)* to be vacant
• **vaquer à** VT IND to attend to, to see to; **v. à ses occupations** to attend to *or* to go about one's business; **v. aux tâches ménagères** to see to *or* to attend to the household chores

varappe [varap] NF *(activités)* rock-climbing; *(course)* rock-climb; **faire de la v.** to go rock-climbing

varapper [3] [varape] VI to rock-climb, to go rock-climbing

varappeur, -euse [varapœr, -øz] NM,F rock-climber

varech [varɛk] NM *Bot* kelp, varec

vareuse [varøz] NF **1** *Naut* fisherman's smock **2** *Couture* loose-fitting jacket **3** *Mil* uniform jacket

variabilité [varjabilite] NF variability, changeableness

variable [varjabl] ADJ **1** *(changeant ▸ temps)* unsettled; *(▸ taux)* variable; *(▸ vitesse)* varying; **être d'humeur v.** to be moody **2** *Gram* **mot v.** inflected *or* inflectional word; **mot v. en genre/nombre** word inflected in gender/number **3** *(varié ▸ composition, forme)* varied, diverse; **être v.** to vary; **c'est très v.** it's very variable, it varies a lot
NF *Écon, Math, Ordinat & Phys* variable; *Ordinat* **v. de mémoire** memory variable
NM *Météo* **le baromètre est au "v."** the barometer is at *or* reads "change"

variance [varjɑ̃s] NF variance; **v. de l'échantillon** sample variance

variant, -e [varjɑ̃, -ɑ̃t] ADJ variable
NM *Méd* **nouveau v. de la maladie de Creutzfeldt-Jakob** new variant CJD
• **variante** NF **1** *(gén) & Ling* variant; **il existe trois variantes du chapitre 12** there are three variant versions of chapter 12; **la 305 est une variante du modèle précédent** the 305 is a variation on the previous model **2** *(aux échecs)* opening move

variateur [varjatœr] NM **1** *Tech* **v. de vitesse** speed variator **2** *Élec* **v. (de lumière** *ou* **d'intensité)** dimmer (switch)

variation [varjasjɔ̃] NF **1** *(fluctuation)* variation, change (**de** in); **v. d'intensité/de poids** variation in intensity/in weight; **pour vos plantes, attention aux variations de température** your plants do not like changes in temperature; **v. du compas** compass error **2** *Mus* variation; **v. sur un thème de Paganini** variation on a theme by Paganini; *Fig* **une v. sur le thème de...** a variation on the theme of...
• **variations** NFPL *(modifications)* changes, modifications; **subir des variations** to undergo change *or* changes; *Écon* **variations saisonnières** seasonal variations; **en fonction des variations saisonnières** on a seasonally adjusted basis; **corrigé des variations saisonnières** seasonally adjusted

varice [varis] NF *Méd* varicose vein, *Spéc* varix; **avoir des varices** to have varicose veins

varicectomie [varisɛktɔmi] NF *Méd* varicotomy

varicelle [varisɛl] NF *Méd* chickenpox, *Spéc* varicella

varié, -e [varje] ADJ **1** *(non uniforme ▸ style, répertoire, alimentation)* varied; *(▸ vocabulaire)* wide; **une gamme variée de papiers peints** a wide range of wallpapers; **proposer un menu v.** to offer a varied menu; **programme de musique variée** programme of varied music; **un travail très peu v.** a monotonous job, a job with little variety
2 *(au pluriel) (différents)* various, diverse, miscellaneous; **objets divers et variés** various *or* miscellaneous objects; **des sujets aussi variés que la musique et la chimie** subjects as diverse as music and chemistry; *Culin* **hors-d'œuvre variés** selection of hors d'oeuvres
3 *Mus* **thème v.** theme and variations
4 *Phys (mouvement)* variable

varier [9] [varje] VT *(diversifier ▸ cursus, menu, occupations)* to vary, to diversify; **il faut v. la présentation de votre argument principal** you must present your main argument in different ways; **pour v. les plaisirs** just for a change; **v. son alimentation** to vary one's diet; **v. le menu** to vary the (basic) menu; *Fig* to ring the changes; *Fam* **on prend les mêmes idées, mais on varie la sauce** you take the same ideas, only you dress them up differently *or* you make them look different
VI **1** *(changer ▸ temps, poids, humeur)* to vary, to change; **les produits varient en qualité** products vary in quality; **les prix varient de 50 à 150 euros** prices vary *or* range from 50 to 150 euros; **les prix peuvent v. du simple au double** prices can vary by a factor of two; **je vous sers du poisson, pour v. un peu** I'm giving you fish, just for a change
2 *Fin (marchés)* to fluctuate
3 *Math* **faire v. une fonction** to vary a function
4 *(différer)* to differ; **leurs opinions varient sur ce point** they differ *or* they don't see eye to eye on this point; **il n'a jamais varié sur ce point** he's never changed his mind about it; **v. dans ses réponses** to be inconsistent in one's replies

variété [varjete] NF **1** *(diversité)* variety, diversity (**de** of); **son œuvre manque de v.** his/her work lacks variety *or* is not varied enough; **nos châles existent dans une v. de coloris** our shawls come in a variety *or* a wide range of colours; **j'apprécie surtout la v. des articles qu'on y trouve** I especially like the variety *or* range of articles you get there; **la v. du paysage** the varying nature of the landscapes
2 *(sorte, genre)* variety, kind, sort, type; **toutes les variétés possibles et imaginables d'escroquerie** every conceivable type of swindle
3 *Bot* variety; *(de maïs, de blé)* (crop) strain; **une nouvelle v. de fleur/pomme** a new variety of flower/apple; **les variétés cultivées** cultivars
4 *Mus* **la v.** *(industrie)* the commercial music business; *(genre)* commercial music
• **variétés** NFPL *Littérature* miscellanies; *Mus* easy listening; *TV* light entertainment, variety; **regarder les variétés à la télévision** to watch variety shows on television
• **de variétés** ADJ *(spectacle, émission)* variety *(avant n)*; *(musique)* light; **disque de variétés** easy listening record

variétoche [varjetɔʃ] NF *Fam* middle-of-the-road music

variolaire [varjɔlɛr] ADJ *Méd* variolar

variole [varjɔl] NF *Méd* smallpox, *Spéc* variola; **avoir la v.** to have smallpox; *Vét* **v. des vaches** cowpox

variolé, -e [varjɔle] ADJ pockmarked

varioleux, -euse [varjɔlø, -øz] *Méd* ADJ **1** *(patient)* suffering from smallpox, *Spéc* variolous **2** *(boutons)* variolous
NM,F smallpox sufferer

variqueux, -euse [varikø, -øz] ADJ *Méd* varicose

varlet [varlɛ] NM *Hist* varlet, page

varlope [varlɔp] NF *Menuis* trying plane

Varsovie [varsɔvi] NM Warsaw; **le pacte de V.** the Warsaw Pact

vas [va] *voir* **aller**[2]

vasculaire [vaskylɛr] ADJ *Anat & Bot* vascular

vascularisation [vaskylarizasjɔ̃] NF **1** *Méd* vascularization **2** *Anat* vascularity

vase[1] [vaz] NF *(boue)* mud, silt; **banc de v.** mudbank

vase[2] [vaz] NM **1** *(récipient décoratif)* vase **2** *Chim & Phys* vessel; **v. à bec** beaker; **vases communicants** connecting vessels; *Fig* **c'est le principe des vases communicants** there's been a knock-on effect; **v. d'expansion** expansion tank **3 v. de nuit** chamberpot
• **vases** NMPL *Rel* **vases sacrés** sacred vessels
• **en vase clos** ADV **nous vivions en v. clos** we led an isolated existence; **la recherche ne peut se faire en v. clos** research cannot be carried out in isolation *or* in a vacuum

vasectomie [vazɛktɔmi] NF *Méd* vasectomy

vaseline [vazlin] NF petroleum jelly, Vaseline®

vaser [3] [vaze] V IMPERSONNEL *Fam* to rain cats and dogs, *Br* to bucket down

vaseux, -euse [vazø, -øz] ADJ **1** *(boueux)* muddy, silty, sludgy
2 *Fam (confus ▸ idée, plan)* hazy, woolly
3 *Fam (malade)* **se sentir tout v.** *(affaibli)* to feel under the weather, to feel off-colour; *(étourdi)* to feel woozy
4 *Fam (médiocre)* pathetic; **ses blagues vaseuses** his/her pathetic jokes

vasistas [vazistas] NM fanlight, *Am* transom

vasoconstricteur, -trice [vazokɔ̃striktœr, -tris] *Physiol & Méd* ADJ vasoconstrictor *(avant n)*
NM vasoconstrictor

vasodilatateur, -trice [vazɔdilatatœr, -tris] *Physiol & Méd* ADJ vasodilator
NM vasodilator

vasomoteur, -trice [vazɔmɔtœr, -tris] ADJ *Physiol & Méd* vasomotor

vasouillard, -e [vazujar, -ard] ADJ *Fam* **1** *(mauvais)* **plaisanterie/excuse v.** feeble *or* pathetic joke/excuse; **raisonnement v.** woolly *or Br* dodgy argument **2** *(mal-en-point)* under the weather, out of sorts

vasouiller [3] [vazuje] VI *Fam* to flounder; **et votre projet? – ça vasouille** what about your project? – we're floundering

vasque [vask] NF **1** *(bassin)* basin *(of fountain)* **2** *(coupe)* bowl

vassal, -e, -aux, -ales [vasal, -o] ADJ vassal *(avant n)*
NM vassal

vassalité [vasalite] NF *Hist* vassalage; *Fig (soumission)* vassalage, bondage

vaste [vast] ADJ **1** *(immense ▸ vêtement)* enormous, huge; *(▸ domaine, sujet)* vast, far-reaching; *(▸ savoir)* vast, extensive; *(▸ palais, gouffre)* vast, huge, immense; **de par le v. monde** the world over **2** *(de grande ampleur)* huge; **victime d'une v. supercherie** victim of a huge hoax; **ce procès a été une v. farce** this trial has been a huge farce

vastement [vastəmɑ̃] ADV *Littéraire* vastly

va-t-en-guerre [vatɑ̃gɛr] ADJ INV warmongering
NMF INV warmonger

Vatican [vatikɑ̃] NM **le V.** the Vatican; **l'État de la cité du V.** the Vatican City

vaticane [vatikan] ADJ F of the Vatican; **la bibliothèque v.** the Vatican Library
• **Vaticane** NF **la V.** the Vatican Library

vaticination [vatisinasjɔ̃] NF *Littéraire* vaticination

vaticiner [3] [vatisine] VI *Littéraire* to vaticinate

va-tout [vatu] NM INV **jouer son v.** to risk *or* to stake one's all

Vauban [vobɑ̃] *voir* **barrière**

vaudeville [vodvil] NM **1** *(comédie)* vaudeville, light comedy; *(avant le XIXe siècle)* light comedy with songs and dances, vaudeville; *Fig* **tourner au v.** to become farcical **2** *Vieilli (chanson)* topical *or* satirical song *(with refrain)*

vaudevillesque [vodvilɛsk] ADJ **1** *Théât* vaudeville *(avant n)* **2** *(grotesque)* farcical, ludicrous, preposterous

vaudevilliste [vodvilist] NMF writer of vaudeville

vaudois, -e [vodwa, -az] ADJ **1** *Géog* of/from the canton of Vaud **2** *Rel* Waldensian
• **Vaudois, -e** NM,F **1** *Géog* = person from or inhabitant of the canton of Vaud **2** *Rel* Waldensian

vaudou, -e [vodu] ADJ voodoo
NM **le v.** voodoo, voodooism

vaudra *etc voir* **valoir**

vau-l'eau [volo] **à vau-l'eau** ADV **aller à v.** *(barque)* to go with the stream *or* current; *(affaire, projet)* to be going downhill *or* to the dogs

vaurien, -enne [vorjɛ̃, -ɛn] NM,F **1** *(voyou)* good-for-nothing, scoundrel, rogue **2** *(enfant)* **petit v.!** you little devil!

vaut *etc voir* **valoir**

vautour [votur] NM **1** *Orn* vulture **2** *(personne cupide)* vulture, shark

vautrer [3] [votre] **se vautrer** VPR **1** *(se rouler)* to wallow; **se v. par terre** to grovel; **des porcs se vautrant dans la boue** pigs wallowing in mud; *Fig* **se v. dans le vice** to wallow *or* to revel in vice **2** *(s'affaler)* to sprawl, to be sprawled; **se v. dans un fauteuil** to loll in an armchair; **être vautré dans un fauteuil** to be lolling in an armchair; **être vautré sur le lit** to be sprawled on the bed **3** *Fam (tomber)* to go flying

vauvert [vovɛr] ADJ *Fam* **c'est au diable v.** it's miles from anywhere, it's in the middle of nowhere

vaux *etc voir* **valoir**

VDQS [vedekyɛs] NM *(abrév* **vin délimité de qualité supérieure***)* = label indicating quality of wine

eau, -x [vo] NM **1** *Zool* calf; **v. marin** common *or* harbour seal; *Bible* **le v. d'or** the golden calf; *Fig* **adorer le v. d'or** to worship Mammon
2 *Culin* veal; **escalope/côtelette de v.** veal escalope/cutlet; **rôti de v.** roast veal; **v. Marengo** veal Marengo
3 *(cuir)* calf, calfskin
4 *Fam Péj (personne)* lump, *Br* clot
5 *Fam (voiture)* **cette voiture est un v.** this car is a real heap
• **veaux** NMPL *Belg* **veaux de mars** (April) showers
• **en veau** ADJ calf, calfskin *(avant n)*

écés [vese] NMPL *Fam (toilettes) Br* loo, *Am* john

ecteur [vɛktœr] NM **1** *Géom* vector
2 *Méd* carrier, vector
3 *(pour charge nucléaire)* vehicle
4 *Fig* **v. d'information/de progrès** vehicle for information/for progress; **v. de croissance économique** growth driver

ectoriel, -elle [vɛktɔrjɛl] ADJ vector *(avant n)*, vectorial; **espace v.** vector space; **fonction vectorielle** vector function; *Ordinat* **police vectorielle** outline font

ectorisation [vɛktɔrizasjɔ̃] NF *Ordinat* **v. d'images** image vectoring

écu, -e [veky] PP *voir* **vivre**[2]
ADJ real, real-life, true; **c'est une histoire vécue** it's a true story; **ce qu'il raconte là sont des choses vécues** there he talks about things that have actually happened *or* about actual experience; **bien/mal v.** easy/hard *or* difficult to come to terms with
NM **le v. de qn** sb's (real-life) experiences; **le livre m'a intéressé parce que c'était du v.** I found the book interesting because it was based on a real-life experience

edettariat [vədetarja] NM stardom

edette [vədɛt] NF **1** *(artiste)* star; **v. de la chanson** singing star; **v. de cinéma** movie *or Br* film star; **v. du petit écran** TV star *or* personality; **v. de la télévision** television star *or* personality; **chanter devant un parterre de vedettes** to sing to a star-studded audience; **v. américaine** = warm-up act; **passer en v. américaine** to be the warm-up act, to get second billing
2 *(célébrité)* star, celebrity; **une v. de la politique/du rugby** a big name in politics/in rugby; **une v. du barreau** a big name at the bar; **présentateur-v.** star presenter
3 *(première place)* **avoir** *ou* **tenir la v.** *Théât* to top the bill, to have star billing; *Fig* to be in the limelight; **ce problème tient la v. depuis longtemps dans ce pays** the problem has long been a major concern in this country; **partager la v. avec qn** *Théât* to share star billing with sb; *Fig* to share the limelight with sb; *Fig* **ravir** *ou* **souffler** *ou* **voler la v. à qn** to upstage sb
4 *Mktg (produit)* star
5 *Naut* launch; **v. de croisière** cabin cruiser; **v. de la douane** customs patrol boat; **v. lance-torpilles** *ou* **de combat** motor torpedo boat
6 *Mil* sentinel
• **en vedette** ADV **1** *Théât & Fig* **être en v.** to be in the limelight, to (have) hit the headlines; **mettre qn/qch en v.** to put the spotlight on sb/sth; **mettre un nom/mot en v.** to highlight *or* emphasize a name/word **2** *Mil* **être en v.** to be on vedette duty
ADV **mots en v.** words in bold type

édique [vedik] ADJ *Rel* Vedic

édisme [vedism] NM *Rel* Vedaism

égétal, -e, -aux, -ales [veʒetal, -o] ADJ *(fibre)* plant *(avant n)*; *(huile)* vegetable *(avant n)*; **règne v.** plant kingdom; **sol v.** humus
NM plant, vegetable

égétalien, -enne [veʒetaljɛ̃, -ɛn] ADJ vegan
NM,F vegan

égétalisme [veʒetalism] NM veganism

égétarien, -enne [veʒetarjɛ̃, -ɛn] ADJ vegetarian
NM,F vegetarian

égétarisme [veʒetarism] NM vegetarianism

égétatif, -ive [veʒetatif, -iv] ADJ **1** *Anat, Bot & Méd* vegetative **2** *(inactif)* **mener une vie végétative** to sit around all day

végétation [veʒetasjɔ̃] NF *Bot* vegetation
• **végétations** NFPL *Méd* **végétations (adénoïdes)** adenoids; **opérer qn des végétations** to take out sb's adenoids

végétative [veʒetativ] *voir* **végétatif**

végéter [18] [veʒete] VI **1** *Péj (personne)* to vegetate, to stagnate; **je végète ici!** I'm stagnating here!; **son affaire végète** his/her business is sluggish; **le marché végète** trading is slow **2** *Arch (plante)* to vegetate, to grow

véhémence [veemɑ̃s] NF vehemence
• **avec véhémence** ADV vehemently, passionately

véhément, -e [veemɑ̃, -ɑ̃t] ADJ *(plaidoyer)* vehement, passionate; *(dénégation)* vehement, vociferous

véhémentement [veemɑ̃tmɑ̃] ADV *Littéraire* vehemently, passionately

véhiculaire [veikylɛr] *voir* **langue**

véhicule [veikyl] NM **1** *Transp* vehicle; **v. automobile/hippomobile** motor/horse-drawn vehicle; **v. à deux roues** two-wheeler; **v. lent** slow vehicle; **v. lourd** heavy-goods vehicle; **v. multifonction** *ou* **à usages multiples** multi-purpose vehicle, MPV; **v. de remplacement** courtesy car; **v. spatial** spacecraft, spaceship; **v. de tourisme** private car; **v. tout-terrain** off-road vehicle, off-roader; **v. de transport de marchandises** heavy goods vehicle, HGV; **v. utilitaire** commercial vehicle **2** *(moyen de transmission)* vehicle; **le v. du son/de la lumière** the medium *or* the vehicle of sound/of light; **la parole est le v. de la pensée** speech is the vehicle of thought; **la radio est un des véhicules de l'information** radio is one of the vehicles for information *or* one of the news media

véhiculer [3] [veikyle] VT **1** *Transp* to convey, to transport **2** *(transmettre ▸ idée, message)* to convey, to serve as *or* to be a vehicle for; **v. une maladie/un virus** to transmit a disease/a virus

veille [vɛj] NF **1** *(jour d'avant)* **la v.** the previous day, the day before; **la v., je lui avais dit...** the day before, I'd said to him/her...; **la v. au soir** the night before; **faites mariner la v. au soir** marinate overnight; **la v. de** the eve of, the day before; **la v. de la bataille** the day before the battle, the eve of the battle; **la v. de Noël** Christmas Eve; **la v. du jour de l'an** New Year's Eve; **la v. de son départ** the day before he/she left; **à la v. des présidentielles/de la visite du pape** on the eve of the presidential elections/of the Pope's visit; **le pays est à la v. d'un tournant historique** the country is on the eve *or* brink of a historic change; **on était à la v. d'entrer en guerre** we were on the brink of war *or* on the point of declaring war; **nous étions à la v. de nous séparer** we were on the brink *or* verge of splitting up; **être à la v. de se marier** to be on the point of getting married, to be about to get married
2 *(absence de sommeil)* wakefulness; **état de v.** waking state; **entre la v. et le sommeil** between waking and sleeping
3 *(absence de sommeil volontaire)* sitting up, staying up; *(auprès d'un malade)* watching, keeping watch; **de longues heures de v. consacrées à la poésie** long sleepless nights devoted to poetry
4 *(surveillance)* vigil; *Mil* night watch; *Naut* **homme de v.** lookout; *Naut* **chambre de v.** chart house; **prendre la v.** to take one's turn on watch; **v. marketing** marketing intelligence; **v. technologique** monitoring of technological development
5 *Ordinat* standby mode
• **en veille** ADJ *(appareil, ordinateur)* on standby
ADV **se mettre en v.** to go on standby

veillée [veje] NF **1** *(soir)* evening; **pendant les longues veillées d'hiver** during the long winter evenings; **prolonger la v. jusqu'aux petites heures du matin** to stay up until the small hours **2** *(réunion)* evening gathering; *Can (fête)* party; **faire une v. autour d'un feu** to spend the evening round a fire; *Can* **v. du jour de l'an** New Year's Day party **3** *(d'un malade)* night nursing; *(d'un mort)* watch, vigil; *Hist* **v. d'armes** knightly vigil; *Fig* **c'est notre v. d'armes avant le concours** it's the last night before our exam

veiller [4] [veje] VT *(un malade)* to watch over, to sit up with; *(un mort)* to keep watch *or* vigil over
VI **1** *(rester éveillé)* to sit *or* to stay up; **je n'ai pas l'habitude de v.** I'm not used to staying up late; **v. jusque tard dans la nuit** to sit up *or* stay awake till late into the night
2 *(être de garde)* to keep watch, to be on watch
3 *(être sur ses gardes)* to be watchful *or* vigilant
4 *(entre amis)* to spend the evening in company
• **veiller à** VT IND to see to; **v. aux intérêts du pays** to attend to *or* to see to *or* to look after the interests of the country; **je veillais au bon déroulement des opérations** I saw to it that everything was running smoothly; **veillez à ce qu'il ne tombe pas** be careful *or* watch that he doesn't fall; **je veillerai à ce qu'elle arrive à l'heure** I'll see (to it) *or* make sure that she gets there on time; **veillez à ne pas refaire la même faute** take care *or* be careful not to make the same mistake again; *Fig* **v. au grain** to keep one's weather eye open
• **veiller sur** VT IND *(surveiller ▸ enfant)* to watch (over), to look after, to take care of; *(▸ santé)* to watch, to take care of
VPR **se veiller** *Suisse Fam* to be careful

veilleur [vejœr] NM **1** *Mil (soldat)* lookout **2** *(gardien)* **v. de nuit** night watchman

veilleuse [vejøz] NF **1** *(lampe)* night-light; *(flamme)* pilot light; *(de TV, de chaîne hi-fi)* standby; **mettre en v.** *(lumière)* to dim, to turn down low; *Fam Fig (projet)* to put on the back burner, to shelve; *très Fam* **mets-la en v.!** just shut up, will you! **2** *Bot* meadow saffron
• **veilleuses** NFPL *Aut* sidelights

veilleuses-codes [vejøzkɔd] NFPL *Aut* dim-dip

veinard, -e [venar, -ard] *Fam* ADJ *(chanceux)* lucky, *Br* jammy
NM,F lucky devil; **c'est un v.** he has all the luck; **sacré v., va!** you lucky devil!

veine [vɛn] NF **1** *Anat* vein; **s'ouvrir les veines** to slash one's wrists; **v. cave** vena cava; **v. porte** portal vein; **v. pulmonaire** pulmonary vein
2 *(d'un minerai)* vein, lode; *(de charbon)* seam; *(du bois)* grain; *(d'une feuille)* vein
3 *(inspiration)* vein, inspiration; **les deux récits sont de la même v.** the two stories are in the same vein
4 *Fam (chance)* luck; **avoir de la v.** to be lucky *or Br* jammy; **elle n'a pas eu de v.** she's been unlucky; **quel coup de v.!** what a stroke of luck!, what a fluke!; **pas de v.!** hard *or* tough luck!; *Ironique* **c'est bien ma v.!** just my luck!; **avoir une v. de cocu** *ou* **de pendu** to have the luck of the devil
5 *(locutions)* **être en v. de générosité** to be in a generous mood; **je suis en v. d'inspiration ce matin** I'm feeling inspired this morning

veiné, -e [vene] ADJ *(bras, main)* veiny; *(bois)* grained; *(feuille, marbre)* veined; **v. de rose** pink-veined

veiner [4] [vene] VT to vein

veineux, -euse [venø, -øz] ADJ **1** *Anat* venous **2** *(strié ▸ bois)* grainy

veinule [venyl] NF *Anat* venule, veinlet

veinure [venyr] NF veining; **le bois présente des veinures** the wood is veined

vêlage [vɛlaʒ] NM calving

vélaire [velɛr] ADJ velar
NF velar

Velcro® [vɛlkro] NM Velcro®; *(fermeture)* **V.** Velcro® (fastening); **fermé par un V.** fastened with Velcro®, with a Velcro® fastening

vêlement [vɛlmɑ̃] NM calving

vêler [4] [vele] VI to calve

velimeux [velimø] *Can Fam* NM **1** *(chanceux)* lucky devil; **le petit v.!** (the) lucky devil! **2** *(intrigant)* crafty devil **3** *(coquin)* (little) rascal *or* devil
• **en velimeux** ADV **être fort/riche en v.** to be very strong/rich ADJ **être en v.** to be fuming *or* livid

vélin [velɛ̃] NM vellum; *voir* **papier**

véliplanchiste [veliplɑ̃ʃist] NMF windsurfer

velléitaire [veleitɛr] ADJ indecisive
NMF **c'est une v.** she has ideas but never carries them through

velléité [veleite] NF vague desire *or* impulse; **il lui vient des velléités de repeindre la cuisine** he/she sometimes gets the urge to redecorate the kitchen (but never gets round to it); **des velléités littéraires** a vague desire to write

vélo [velo] NM **1** *(bicyclette)* bike, bicycle; **faire du v., monter à v.** to ride a bike; **aller à** *ou* **en v.** to go by bike, to cycle; **je vais au travail en** *ou* **à v.** I cycle to work, I go to work on my bike, I ride my bike to work; **on a fait un tour à v.** we went for a ride (on our bikes); **v. d'appartement** exercise bike; **v. de course** racing bike; **v. de (cyclo-)cross/de piste** cyclo-cross/racing bike; **v. tout chemin** hybrid (bike); **v. tout-terrain** mountain bike; *Fam Hum* **avoir un petit v. (dans la tête)** to be off one's rocker, to be not all there **2** *Sport* **le v.** cycling

vélocipède [velɔsipɛd] NM *Hum* velocipede

vélocité [velɔsite] NF velocity, speed, swiftness; **avec v.** swiftly; *Mus* **exercice de v.** finger exercise

vélodrome [velɔdrom] NM velodrome

vélomoteur [velɔmɔtœr] NM lightweight motorcycle, *Br* moped

velours [vəlur] NM **1** *Tex* velvet; **veste/rideaux en v.** velvet jacket/curtains; **v. bouclé** uncut velvet, loop pile fabric; **v. côtelé, v. à côtes** corduroy; **pantalons en v. côtelé** *ou* **v. à côtes** corduroy trousers, cords; **v. de coton** cotton velvet, velveteen; **v. de laine** velour(s); **v. de soie** silk velvet; **v. uni** plain velvet **2** *Fig* **ce vin/sa peau est comme du v.** this wine/his/her skin is as smooth as velvet; **goûte ce vin, c'est du v.** taste this wine, it's sheer velvet; **des yeux de v.** soft *or* velvet eyes; **elle lui fait ses yeux de v.** she's making eyes at him, she's giving him the eye; **une voix de v.** a velvety *or* silky voice; **le v. de ses joues** his/her velvety cheeks; *Fig* **là, on joue sur du v.** we can't go wrong there **3** *(liaison incorrecte)* incorrect liaison (eg **j'ai été** [ʒezete])

velouté, -e [vəlute] ADJ **1** *(doux ▸ peau)* velvet *(avant n)*, silky; *(▸ pêche)* velvety, downy; *(▸ vin)* smooth, mellow **2** *Tex (tissu)* raised-nap *(avant n)*; *(papier peint)* flocked

NM **1** *Culin (potage)* cream soup; *(sauce)* velouté (sauce); **v. d'asperges** cream of asparagus (soup) **2** *(douceur ▸ de la peau)* velvetiness, silkiness; *(▸ d'une pêche)* bloom

velouter [3] [vəlute] VT **1** *Tex* to raise, to nap **2** *(papier peint)* to flock **3** *(rendre doux)* to make velvety

VPR **se velouter** *(voix)* to soften

velouteux, -euse [vəlutø, -øz] ADJ velvety, soft, silky

Velpeau® [vɛlpo] *voir* **bande**

velu, -e [vəly] ADJ **1** *(homme, poitrine)* hairy **2** *Bot* hairy, downy, *Spéc* villous

vélum [velɔm] NM *(protection)* awning

Vélux® [velyks] NM roof light

venaison [vənɛzɔ̃] NF venison

vénal, -e, -aux, -ales [venal, -o] ADJ **1** *(corrompu)* venal, corrupt **2** *Péj (intéressé)* venal, mercenary; **un amour v.** a venal love affair **3** *Écon voir* **valeur**

vénalité [venalite] NF venality

venant [vənɑ̃] NM **à tout v., à tous venants** *(au premier venu)* to all and sundry; **à tout v.** *(à tout propos)* constantly

vendable [vɑ̃dabl] ADJ saleable, sellable; **facilement/difficilement v.** easy/difficult to sell; **ma voiture n'est pas v.** my car has no market value

vendange [vɑ̃dɑ̃ʒ] NF **1** *(cueillette)* grape-picking, grape-harvesting, grape harvest; **faire la v.** *ou* **les vendanges** *(vigneron)* to harvest the grapes; *(journalier)* to go grape-picking; **pendant les vendanges** during the grape-harvesting *or* grape-picking season **2** *(quantité récoltée)* grape harvest, grape yield; *(qualité récoltée)* vintage; **la v. de l'année sera bonne** this year's vintage will be good, this year will be a good vintage

• **vendanges** NFPL *(saison)* grape-harvesting time

vendanger [17] [vɑ̃dɑ̃ʒe] VT *(raisin)* to harvest, to pick; *(vigne)* to pick the grapes from

VI to harvest grapes; **ils sont partis v. dans le Midi** they went to pick grapes in the South of France

vendangeur, -euse [vɑ̃dɑ̃ʒœr, -øz] NM,F grape-picker

• **vendangeuse** NF **1** *(machine)* grape-picker **2** *Bot* aster

vendéen, -enne [vɑ̃deɛ̃, -ɛn] ADJ Vendean

• **Vendéen, -enne** NM,F Vendean

vendémiaire [vɑ̃demjɛr] NM = first month in the French Revolutionary calendar (from 22/23/24 September to 21/22/23 October)

vendetta [vɑ̃deta] NF vendetta

vendeur, -euse [vɑ̃dœr, -øz] ADJ selling *(avant n)*; **être v.** to be willing to sell; **j'allais vendre ma voiture mais je ne suis plus v.** I was going to sell my car but I've decided not to *or* but I've taken it off the market

NM,F **1** *(dans un magasin) Br* sales assistant, shop assistant, *Am* (sales) clerk; **recherche vendeurs** *(petite annonce)* sales staff wanted

2 *(dans une entreprise)* (sales) representative; **il est bon v.** he's a good salesman; *Mktg* **v. représentant placier** sales representative

3 *(marchand)* seller, salesman, *f* saleswoman; **v. de chaussures** shoe seller; **v. à domicile** door-to-door salesman; *Fig* **les vendeurs d'évasion** dream merchants, the dream industry; **v. export** exporter; **v. de journaux** newsman, newspaperman; **v. par téléphone** telesales person

4 *(non professionnel)* seller

vendition [vɑ̃disjɔ̃] NF *Belg* auction

vendre [73] [vɑ̃dr] VT **1** *(céder ▸ propriété, brevet, marchandise)* to sell; **il vend ses melons (à) deux euros** he sells his melons at *or* for two euros each; **v. qch à la pièce/à la douzaine/au poids** to sell sth by unit/by the dozen/by weight; **v. (qch) comptant** to sell (sth) for cash; **v. (qch) au détail** to retail (sth), to sell (sth) retail; **v. (qch) en gros** to sell (sth) wholesale; **v. qch au prix fort** to price sth high; **v. (qch) à perte** to sell (sth) at a loss; **v. moins cher que qn** to undercut sb; **v. qch aux enchères** *(gén)* to auction sth; *(pour s'en débarrasser)* to auction sth off; **elle a tout vendu et elle a fait ses valises** she sold *Br* up *or Am* out and packed her bags; **v. qch à qn** to sell sb sth, to sell sth to sb; *Bourse* **v. à découvert** to sell short, to go a bear; *Bourse* **v. à terme** to sell forward; **elle m'a vendu sa montre (pour) 30 euros** she sold me her watch for 30 euros; **tu me la vendrais combien?** how much would you sell it (to me) for?; **cette maison n'est pas à v.** this house is not for sale; **à v.** *(sur panneau)* for sale; *Fam* **v. chèrement sa peau** to fight for one's life; *Prov* **il ne faut jamais v. la peau de l'ours avant de l'avoir tué** don't count your chickens before they're hatched; *Euph* **v. ses charmes** to sell one's body; **il vendrait père et mère** he'd sell his own grandmother; *Fig* **v. de l'évasion** *ou* **du rêve** to sell dreams

2 *(commercialiser)* to market

3 *(trahir ▸ secret)* to sell; *(▸ personne)* to sell out; *(▸ associé, confident)* to sell down the river; **v. son âme au diable** to sell one's soul to the devil; **v. la mèche** *(exprès)* to give the game away, to spill the beans; *(par accident)* to let the cat out of the bag

USAGE ABSOLU *Com* **ils vendent cher/ne vendent pas cher chez Zapp** Zapp's is expensive/cheap; **ce qui les intéresse, c'est de v.** they're interested in selling *or* sales; **nous vendons beaucoup à l'étranger** we sell a lot abroad, we get a lot of sales abroad; **la publicité fait v.** advertising sells

VPR **se vendre 1** *(emploi passif)* to sell; **ça se vend bien/mal actuellement** it is/isn't selling well at the moment; **se v. comme des petits pains** to sell *or* to go like hot cakes

2 *(se mettre en valeur)* to sell oneself; **une société qui sait se v.** a company that knows how to sell *or* market itself; **il faut savoir se v.** you must be able to sell yourself *or* to show yourself off to your best advantage

3 *(traître)* to sell oneself; **se v. à l'ennemi** to sell oneself to *or* to sell out to the enemy

vendredi [vɑ̃drədi] NM Friday; **le v. saint** Good Friday; **v. treize** Friday the thirteenth; *voir aussi* **mardi**

vendu, -e [vɑ̃dy] PP *voir* **vendre**

ADJ *(vénal)* corrupt

NM,F *Péj* turncoat, traitor

venelle [vənɛl] NF lane, alleyway

vénéneux, -euse [venenø, -øz] ADJ *(toxique)* poisonous, toxic; **champignon v.** toadstool

> Do not confuse with **venimeux**.

vénérable [venerabl] ADJ venerable; **d'un âge v.** ancient

NM *(d'une loge maçonnique)* worshipful master

vénération [venerasjɔ̃] NF **1** *Rel* reverence **2** *(admiration)* veneration, reverence, respect; **avoir de la v. pour qn** to revere sb

vénère [venɛr] *Fam* ADJ *(verlan de* **énervé***) Br* wound up, *Am* ticked off

VT *(verlan de* **énerver***)* **v. qn** to bug sb, *Br* to wind sb up

vénérer [18] [venere] VT **1** *Rel* to worship, to revere **2** *(admirer)* to revere, to worship, to venerate

vénerie [vɛnri] NF hunting; **la grande v.** = hunting with hounds; **la petite v.** = hunting with small dogs

vénérien, -enne [venerjɛ̃, -ɛn] ADJ venereal

vénérologie [venerɔlɔʒi] NF *Méd* venereology

vénérologue [venerɔlɔg] NMF *Méd* venereologist

veneur [vənœr] NM **1** *(chasseur)* hunter **2** *(maître des chiens)* master of hounds **3** *Hist* **le Grand v.** ≃ the Master of the Royal Hunt

Venezuela [venezɥela] NM **le V.** Venezuela

vénézuélien, -enne [venezɥeljɛ̃, -ɛn] ADJ Venezuelan

• **Vénézuélien, -enne** NM,F Venezuelan

vengeance [vɑ̃ʒɑ̃s] NF revenge, vengeance; **crier** *ou* **demander** *ou* **réclamer v.** to cry out for revenge; **tirer v. d'une injure** to be revenged for an insult; **avoir sa v.** to have one's revenge *or* vengeance; **exercer sa v. sur qn** to have one's revenge *or* vengeance on sb; **par v., par esprit de v.** out of revenge *or* vengeance; **soif** *ou* **désir de v.** revengefulness, vengefulness; *Hum* **c'est la v. divine** *ou* **du ciel** it's divine retribution; *Prov* **la v. est un plat qui se mange froid** revenge is a dish best eaten cold

venger [17] [vɑ̃ʒe] VT **1** *(réparer)* to avenge; **v. un affront** to avenge an insult **2** *(dédommager)* **v. qn de qch** to avenge sb for sth; **cela le venge de son échec** it makes up for his failure

VPR **se venger** *(tirer réparation)* to revenge *or* to avenge oneself, to take vengeance; **je me vengerai!** I'll get my own back!; **il s'est vengé brutalement** he retaliated brutally; **se v. de qn/de qch** to take one's revenge on sb/for sth; **elle m'a menti pour se v. de ma cruauté** she lied to me in revenge for my cruelty; **il s'est vengé de l'assassin de sa sœur** he took his revenge on his sister's murderer; **se v. sur qn (de qch)** to take (one's) revenge on sb (for sth)

vengeur, -eresse [vɑ̃ʒœr, vɑ̃ʒrɛs] ADJ avenging, revengeful, vengeful; **une petite remarque vengeresse** a vengeful little remark

NM,F avenger

véniel, -elle [venjɛl] ADJ *Rel* venial

venimeux, -euse [vənimø, -øz] ADJ **1** *(toxique)* venomous, poisonous **2** *Fig (méchant)* venomous, malevolent; **il m'a lancé un regard v.** he looked daggers at me, he shot me a murderous glance; **des commentaires v.** barbs, barbed remarks

> Do not confuse with **vénéneux**.

venin [vənɛ̃] NM **1** *(poison)* venom **2** *Littéraire (malveillance)* **cracher** *ou* **jeter son v.** to vent one's spleen; **répandre son v. contre qn/qch** to speak viciously about sb/sth

VENIR [40] [vənir]

V AUX
- to come and/to + infinitive **1**
- to have just done **2**
- to happen to **3**

VI
- to come **A1, C1–3**
- to reach **B**
- to come along well **C4**

V IMPERSONNEL
- to come **1**

V AUX **1** *(se rendre quelque part pour)* to come and *or* to; **Roger viendra me chercher** Roger will come and collect me; **viens t'asseoir près de moi** come and sit down near me; **je suis venu m'excuser** I've come to apologize; **venez manger!** dinner's ready!; **v. voir qn** to come and see *or* to visit sb, *Am* to visit with sb; **v. voir qch** to come and see sth; **beaucoup de gens sont venus voir notre pièce** a lot of people turned out *or* came to see our play; **si tu tombes, ne viens pas pleurer!** if you fall, don't come crying to me!; **tu l'as bien cherché, alors ne viens pas te plaindre!** you asked for it, so don't come moaning to me about it!; **il est venu raconter qu'elle avait des dettes** he came telling tales about her being in debt; *Fam* **qu'est-ce que tu viens nous raconter** *ou* **chanter là?** what on earth are you talking about *or Br* on about?

2 v. de *(avoir fini de)* **v. de faire qch** to have just done sth; **je viens de laver les vitres et il pleut!** I've just finished cleaning the windows and now it's raining!; **je viens de l'avoir au téléphone** I was on the phone to him/her just a few minutes *or* a short while ago; **elle vient de terminer son premier album** *(il y a quelques jours)* she's just *or* she recently finished her first album

3 v. à *(exprime un hasard)* to happen to; **si son pied venait à glisser** should his/her foot slip, if his/her foot slipped; **si les vivres venaient à manquer** should food supplies run out, if food supplies were to run out

VI A. *AVEC IDÉE DE MOUVEMENT* **1** *(se déplacer, se rendre)* to come; **viens plus près** come closer; **je ne suis pas venu pour parler de la pluie et du beau temps!** I didn't come here to talk about the weather!; **faut-il v. déguisé?** do we have to come in *or* to wear fancy dress?; **il y aura un orchestre et du champagne, il faut v.!** there will be a band and champagne, you must come along!; **venez nombreux!** do come along!; **ils sont venus nombreux** they came in droves; **il est reparti** *ou* **il s'en est allé comme il était venu** he left just as he had come; *(il est mort)* he died without having made his mark; **comment êtes-vous venus?** how did you get here?; **ma mère disparue, il a commencé à v. chez nous** after my mother passed away, he took to visiting us; **je l'ai rencontrée en venant ici** I met her on my way here; **il vient au collège en planche à roulettes/en taxi** he comes to college on a skateboard/in a taxi; **quand il est venu en Australie** when he came to Australia; **comment est-elle venue sur l'île?** how did she get to *or* reach the island?; **v. avec qn** to come with *or* to accompany sb; **alors, tu viens?** are you coming?; **on va au restaurant, tu viens avec nous?** we're off to the restaurant, are you coming with us *or* along?; **à la piscine? d'accord, je viens avec toi** the swimming pool? OK, I'll come *or* go with you; **v. sur** *(sujet: prédateur, véhicule)* to move in on, to bear down upon; **la moto venait droit sur nous** the motorbike was heading straight for us; **v. vers qn** *(s'approcher)* to come up to *or* towards sb; **v. à qn** *(s'adresser à qn)* to come to sb; *(atteindre qn)* to reach sb

2 faire v. *(médecin, police, réparateur)* to send for, to call; *(parasites, touristes)* to attract; **faire v. une personne chez soi** to have somebody come round; **faites v. le prévenu chez le juge** bring the accused to the judge's office; **je fais v. mon foie gras directement du Périgord** I have my foie gras sent straight from Périgord; **faire v. les larmes aux yeux de qn** to bring tears to sb's eyes

B. *SANS IDÉE DE MOUVEMENT* **v. à** *ou* **jusqu'à** *(vers le haut)* to come up to, to reach (up to); *(vers le bas)* to come down to, to reach (down to); *(en largeur, en longueur)* to come out to, to stretch to, to reach; **la vigne vierge vient jusqu'à ma fenêtre** the Virginia creeper reaches up to my window; **l'eau vient jusqu'à la cheville/jusqu'au genou** the water is ankle-deep/knee-deep

C. *SURGIR, SE MANIFESTER* **1** *(arriver ▸ moment, saison)* to come; **le moment est venu de...** the time has come to...; **l'aube vint enfin** dawn broke at last; **voici v. la nuit** it's nearly night *or* night-time; **puis la guerre est venue** then came the war; **la retraite vient vite!** retirement isn't long in coming!; **puis il vient un âge/un moment où...** then comes an age/a time when...; **je ne suis jamais tombé amoureux – non, mais ça va v.!** I've never fallen in love – (no, but) you will one day!; **alors, elle vient cette bière?** am I getting that beer or not?, how long do I have to wait for my beer?; **alors, ça vient?** hurry up!; **ça vient, ça vient!** all right, it's coming!

2 *(apparaître ▸ inspiration, idée, boutons)* to come; **mon nouveau roman commence à v.** my new novel is coming along (nicely); **la prudence vient avec l'âge** wisdom comes with age; **prendre la vie comme elle vient** *ou* **les choses comme elles viennent** to take things in one's stride *or* as they come, to take life as it comes; **l'envie m'est soudain venue d'aller me baigner** I suddenly felt like going swimming, I suddenly fancied a swim; **une idée géniale m'était venue** a great idea had dawned on me; **le remords m'est venu peu à peu** remorse crept up on me; **les mots ne me viennent pas facilement en russe** my Russian isn't fluent, I'm not fluent in Russian; **les mots semblaient lui v. si facilement!** his/her words seemed to flow so effortlessly!; **les mots ne me venaient pas** I was at a loss for words, I couldn't find the words; **des rougeurs me sont venues sur tout le corps** I came out in red blotches all over; **v. à l'esprit de qn** *ou* **à l'idée de qn** to come to *or* to dawn on sb; **rien ne lui venait à l'esprit** *ou* **l'idée** his/her mind was a blank; **une solution m'est venue à l'esprit** a solution dawned on me

3 *(dans une chronologie, un ordre, une hiérarchie)* to come; **le mois/l'année/la décennie qui vient** the coming month/year/decade; **le trimestre qui vient** next term; **fais tes devoirs, la télé viendra après** do your homework, we'll see about TV later on

4 *(se développer)* to come along *or* up (well), to do well; **les capucines ne sont pas bien venues** the nasturtiums didn't come up *or* do well

5 *Can & Suisse Fam (devenir)* to get; **v. vieux/fatigué** to get old/tired; **il est venu médecin** he became a doctor▫

V IMPERSONNEL 1 *(se déplacer)* **il vient peu de touristes en hiver** few tourists come in winter

2 il me vient une idée I've got an idea; **il m'est venu à l'idée de...** I suddenly thought of doing, it dawned on me to...; **il me vient à l'idée que nous pourrions l'interroger aussi** come to think of it, we could ask him as well; **il m'est venu une envie de tout casser** I suddenly felt like smashing the place up

3 *(exprime un hasard)* **s'il venait à pleuvoir** should it (happen to) rain

• **venir à VT IND 1** *(choisir)* to come to; **elle est venue tard à la musique** she was a latecomer to music; **vous êtes venu tôt à la politique** you started your political career early **2 en v. à** *(thème, problème)* to come *or* to turn to; *(conclusion)* to come to, to reach; *(décision)* to come to; **venons-en aux statistiques** (now) let's turn to *or* look at the figures; **en v. au fait** *ou* **à l'essentiel** to come *or* to go straight to the point; **j'en viens au détail croustillant!** I'm coming to the juicy bit!; **la discussion en était venue à la politique** the discussion had turned to politics; **je sais certaines choses... – où veux-tu en v.?** I know a thing or two... – what do you mean by that?, what are you getting at *or* driving at?; **pourquoi a-t-elle exigé cela? – je crois savoir où elle veut en v.** why did she make that particular demand? – I think I know what she's after; **en v. aux mains** *ou* **coups** to come to blows; **en v. à faire qch** *(finir par faire)* to come to do sth; *(en dernière extrémité)* to resort *or* to be reduced to doing sth; **ils en étaient venus à douter de son talent** they'd come to question his/her talent; **j'en viens à me demander si...** I'm beginning to wonder whether...; **j'en viendrais presque à souhaiter sa mort** I've reached the stage where I almost wish he/she were dead; **si j'en suis venu à voler, c'est que...** I resorted to stealing because...; **et l'argent? – j'y viens** what about the money? – I'm coming to that; **je ne prendrai jamais de médicaments – vous y viendrez** I'll never take any medicine – you'll come round to it

• **venir de VT IND 1** *(être originaire de ▸ sujet: personne)* to come from, to be from, to be a native of; *(▸ sujet: plante, fruit, animal)* to come *or* to be *or* to originate from; **sa femme vient du Chili** his wife comes from *or* is from Chile; **une mode qui vient d'Espagne** a fashion which comes from *or* originated in Spain; **le mot vient du latin** the word comes *or* derives from Latin

2 *(provenir de ▸ sujet: marchandise)* to originate from; *(▸ sujet: bruit, vent)* to come from; **ces images nous viennent de Tokyo** these pictures come to us from Tokyo

3 *(être issu de)* to come from; **les produits qui viennent du pétrole** oil-based products; **venant de lui, rien ne m'étonne** nothing he says or does can surprise me; **venant d'elle, c'est presque un compliment** coming from her it's almost a compliment

4 *(être dû à ▸ sujet: problème)* to come *or* to stem from, to lie in *or* with; **ça ne peut v. que du carburateur** it can only be the carburettor; **il y a une grosse erreur dans la comptabilité – ça ne vient pas de moi** there's a big discrepancy in the books – it's got nothing to do with me; **c'est de là que vient le mal/problème** this is the root of the evil/problem; **de là vient son indifférence** hence his/her indifference, that's why he's/she's indifferent; **d'où vient que...?** how is it that...?

• **à venir ADJ dans les jours/semaines/mois à v.** in the days/weeks/months to come; **les années à v.** the coming years, the years to come; **les générations à v.** future *or* coming generations

VPR s'en venir *Littéraire* to come; **un cavalier s'en venait** a rider was coming *or* approaching

---

Venise [vəniz] **NM** Venice; **point de V.** Venetian lace; **carnaval de V.** Venice carnival

vénitien, -enne [venisjɛ̃, -ɛn] **ADJ** Venetian

• **Vénitien, -enne NM,F** Venetian

vent [vɑ̃] **NM 1** *Météo* wind; **un v. du nord/nord-est** a north/north-east wind; **le v. souffle/tourne** the wind is blowing/changing; **le v. tombe/se lève** the wind is dropping/rising; **il y a** *ou* **il fait du v.** it's windy *or* breezy; **être ouvert** *ou* **exposé aux quatre vents** to be exposed to the four winds; **elle courait les cheveux au v.** she ran with her hair streaming in the wind; **une journée sans v.** a still day; **une journée de grand v.** a windy day; **coup de v.** gust of wind, squall; **entrer/sortir en coup de v.** to dash in/out; **il fait un v. à décorner les bœufs** there is a fierce wind blowing, it's a blustery day

2 *Naut & Aviat* **au v. (de)** windward (of); *Naut* **remonter au v.** to beat, to sail upwind; *Naut* **venir au v.** to luff; *Naut* **mettre la barre au v.** to put the helm up; **aller contre le v.** *Naut* to head into the wind; *Aviat* to go up the wind; *Naut* **sous le v. (de)** leeward (of), downwind (of); *Naut* **venir sous le v.** to come alee; **côté du v.** weather side; **côté sous le v.** lee side; **v. arrière** *Aviat* tail wind; *Naut* rear wind; *Naut* **aller** *ou* **faire v. arrière** to sail *or* run before the wind; **v. contraire** adverse wind; **v. debout** head wind; **v. fort, grand v.** high wind, gale; **v. frais** strong breeze; **v. de travers** crosswind; **avoir le v. en poupe** *Naut* to sail before the wind, to have the wind astern; *Fig* to have the wind in one's sails, to be riding high; *Fam* **avoir du v. dans les voiles** to be three sheets to the wind; **quel bon v. vous amène?** to what do we owe the pleasure (of your visit)?; *Fam* **bon v.!** good riddance!; **il a réussi contre vents et marées** he managed against all the odds; **je le ferai contre vents et marées** I'll do it come hell or high water; **aller** *ou* **filer comme le v.** to fly *or* to hurtle along; **(éparpillés) à tous les vents** *ou* **à tout v.** (scattered) far and wide; *Fig* **tourner à tous les vents** to be a weathercock

3 *(courant d'air)* **du v.** *(de l'air)* some air, a breeze; *Fig (des paroles vaines)* hot air; *(des actes vains)* empty posturing; **mettre qch au v.** to hang sth out to dry; *Fig Péj* **ce n'est que du v.!** it's just hot air!; *Fig* **elle fait beaucoup de v.** she just makes a lot of noise; *Fam* **du v.!** clear off!, get lost!

4 *Chasse* wind; **avoir le v. de son gibier** to have the wind of one's game; *Fig* **avoir v. de qch** to (get to) hear of sth; **je n'ai pas eu v. de la rumeur** the rumour didn't come my way; **elle a eu v. de l'affaire** she heard about *or* she got wind of the story

5 *(d'un soufflet, d'une balle)* blast; *Aviat* **v. de l'hélice** propeller slipstream

6 *Fig (atmosphère)* **un v. de panique a soufflé sur la foule** a ripple of panic ran through the crowd; **sentir** *ou* **voir d'où vient le v.** to see which way the wind blows *or* how the land lies; **sentir le v. tourner** to feel the wind change, to realize that the tide is turning; **le v. tourne** the wind is changing, the tide is turning

7 *Géog* **les îles du V.** the Windward Isles

• **vents NMPL 1** *Méd & Physiol* **des vents** wind *(UNCOUNT)*; **avoir des vents** to have wind; **lâcher des vents** to break wind **2** *Mus* wind instruments; **les vents jouent trop fort** the wind section is playing too loud

• **dans le vent ADJ** *Fam* up-to-date▫

• **en plein vent ADJ** *(exposé)* exposed (to the wind) **ADV** *(dehors)* in the open (air)

vente [vɑ̃t] NF 1 (opération) sale; la v. ne s'est pas faite the sale fell through; nous déménagerons après la v. de la maison we'll move after the house is sold or after the sale of the house; autoriser/interdire la v. de to authorize/to prohibit the sale of; retiré de la v. withdrawn from sale; ici, v. de tomates (sur une pancarte dans un marché) tomatoes on or for sale here; réaliser une v. to make a sale; acte de v. bill of sale; bureau de v. sales agency; lettre/promesse de v. sales letter/agreement; ventes de base baseline sales, market minimum; v. (au) comptant cash sale; v. au comptoir over-the-counter sales; Bourse v. à découvert short sale; v. en l'état sale as seen; ventes export, ventes à l'exportation export sales; v. jumelée tie-in sale; v. en ligne e-tail; v. pour ou de liquidation closing-down sale; v. à perte sale at a loss; v. promotionnelle promotional sale; v. en semi-gros small wholesale sales; Bourse v. spéculative speculative selling; ventes par téléphone telephone sales, telesales

2 (activité) selling; (secteur) sales; elle est dans la v. she's in sales; l'art de la v. the art of selling; technique de v. selling technique; v. à la boule de neige snowball selling; v. par catalogue catalogue selling; v. au comptant cash selling; v.-conseil sales consultancy; v. par correspondance mail-order (selling); v. à crédit credit selling; (à tempérament) hire purchase, Am installment plan; v. au détail/en demi-gros (par le négociant) retailing/small wholesaling; (profession) retail/small wholesale trade; v. directe en B to B back-to-back direct selling; v. à distance distance selling; v. à domicile door-to-door selling; Ordinat v. électronique on-line selling; v. en gros (par le négociant) wholesaling; (profession) wholesale trade; v. sans intermédiaire direct selling; Ordinat v. en ligne on-line selling; (transaction) on-line sale; v. par lot banded pack selling; v. et marketing sales and marketing; v. pyramidale pyramid selling; v. par téléphone telesales, telemarketing; v. à tempérament hire purchase, Am installment plan; Bourse v. à terme forward sale

3 Jur v. (par adjudication) forcée/judiciaire compulsory sale, sale by order of the court

4 (réunion, braderie) sale; v. à la criée auction (sale) (especially of fish or meat); v. à l'encan ou aux enchères auction (sale); v. publique public sale

5 Bourse le dollar vaut deux livres à la v. the selling rate for the US dollar is two pounds

6 Can (soldes) sale

7 (part de bois) fellable stand; jeunes ventes saplings

• ventes NFPL Com selling, sales; Compta sales, turnover; achats et ventes buying and selling; le responsable des ventes the sales manager; un pourcentage sur les ventes a percentage on sales

• en vente ADJ & ADV (à vendre) for sale; (disponible) available, on sale; en v. en pharmacie on sale at or available from the chemist's; en v. dans toutes les bonnes librairies on sale in all good bookshops; en v. libre (gén) freely available; (médicaments) sold without a prescription; en v. sur/sans ordonnance obtainable on prescription/without a prescription; mettre qch en v. to put sth up for sale, to offer sth for sale; (commercialiser) to put sth on the market

venté, -e [vɑ̃te] ADJ 1 (où le vent souffle) windswept, windy 2 (exposé) windswept

vente-marketing [vɑ̃tmarketiŋ] NF INV sales and marketing

venter [3] [vɑ̃te] V IMPERSONNEL il vente it's windy, the wind is blowing

venteux, -euse [vɑ̃tø, -øz] ADJ (où le vent souffle) windswept, windy

ventilateur [vɑ̃tilatœr] NM 1 (pour rafraîchir) fan; TV & Cin wind machine; v. électrique electric fan; v. à pales/de plafond blade/ceiling fan; Ordinat v. de refroidissement cooling fan; v. rotatif fan

2 Aut cooling fan

ventilation [vɑ̃tilasjɔ̃] NF 1 (système) ventilation (system); (appareil) fan; faire marcher la v. to turn on the fan

2 (aération) supply of (fresh) air

3 Méd & Physiol ventilation; v. assistée respiratory assistance

4 (d'une comptabilité) breakdown

5 (répartition) allocation, apportionment; la v. des revenus the allocation of income or allocating income

6 Jur (d'un domaine) separate valuation

ventiler [3] [vɑ̃tile] VT 1 (aérer) to air, to ventilate; mal ventilé stuffy, airless

2 Méd to ventilate, to give respiratory assistance to

3 (diviser ▸ données) to explode, to scatter; (▸ élèves, emplois) to distribute, to spread; ils ont ventilé les postes sur trois régions différentes they allocated posts in three different areas

4 Fin to break down; (crédits, équipements) to allocate; Com v. un lot to break bulk

5 Jur (domaine) to value separately

ventilo [vɑ̃tilo] NM Fam fan; faire marcher le v. to turn on the fan

ventôse [vɑ̃toz] NM = 6th month in the French Revolutionary calendar (from 20 February to 21 March)

ventouse [vɑ̃tuz] NF 1 (en caoutchouc) suction cup; fléchettes à v. rubber-tipped darts

2 Méd cup, cupping glass; poser des ventouses à qn to cup sb

3 Zool sucker

4 (déboucheur) plunger; faire v. to adhere or to hold fast (through suction)

5 Constr (pour l'aération) air valve, air vent

ventral, -e, -aux, -ales [vɑ̃tral, -o] ADJ Anat, Bot & Zool front (avant n), Spéc ventral

ventre [vɑ̃tr] NM 1 (estomac) stomach; (d'animal) belly, underbelly; Anat abdomen; être couché sur le v. to be lying down or flat on one's stomach; mettez-vous sur le v. (de la position debout) lie on your stomach; (de la position couchée) roll over onto your stomach; rentrer le v. to hold one's stomach in; avoir du v. to have a paunch, to be pot-bellied; il commence à prendre ou avoir du v. he's starting to get a paunch or a belly; Fig il leur marcherait ou passerait sur le v. he'd trample all over them; avoir mal au v. to have (a) stomachache; Fam lui, professeur? ça me ferait mal au v.! him, a teacher? like hell he is!; avoir le v. creux ou vide to have an empty stomach; avoir le v. plein to be full, to have a full stomach; ne rien avoir dans le v. to have nothing in one's stomach; Fig to have no guts; je n'ai rien dans le v. depuis trois jours I haven't had anything to eat for three days, I've had to go hungry for the last three days; Fig elle a quelque chose dans le v. she's got guts, she's got what it takes; Fig je voudrais bien savoir ce qu'elle a dans le v. (de manière générale) I'd like to know what makes her tick; (sur un point précis) I'd like to know what she's up to; v. à terre (cheval) at full speed, flat out; il s'est sauvé v. à terre you couldn't see him for dust; rentrer/partir v. à terre to get back/to go off on the double; Fig le v. mou de qch the soft underbelly of sth; Prov v. affamé n'a point ou pas d'oreilles = there is no reasoning with a starving man

2 (contenu ▸ d'un appareil, d'un véhicule) innards

3 (utérus) womb; un bébé dans le v. de sa mère a baby in its mother's womb

4 (renflement ▸ d'un vase, d'un tonneau, d'un pot) bulge, belly; (▸ d'un bateau) bilge; (▸ d'une voile) belly, sag; (▸ d'un avion) belly

5 Constr faire (du) v. to bulge (out), to jut out; (pendre) to sag

6 Phys loop, antinode; v. de tension potential loop, voltage loop

ventrebleu [vɑ̃trəblø] EXCLAM Arch gadzooks!, zounds!

ventrée [vɑ̃tre] NF Fam (de nourriture) bellyful; on s'est mis une v. (de saucisses) we stuffed ourselves (with sausages)

ventricule [vɑ̃trikyl] NM Anat ventricle

ventrière [vɑ̃trijɛr] NF (sangle ▸ ventrale) girth; (▸ de levage) sling

ventriloque [vɑ̃trilɔk] NMF ventriloquist

ventriloquie [vɑ̃trilɔki] NF ventriloquism

ventru, -e [vɑ̃try] ADJ 1 (personne) potbellied, paunchy 2 (potiche) potbellied; (colonne) bulbous; (voile) bulging, swelling

venu, -e [vəny] PP voir venir

ADJ 1 bien v. (enfant, plante, animal) strong, sturdy, robust; (conseil, remarque) timely, apposite; (attitude) appropriate; (roman) mature; mal v. (enfant, animal) sickly; (plante) stunted; (remarque, attitude) uncalled for, unwarranted, ill-advised; (conseil) untimely, unwelcome 2 tu serais bien v. de t'excuser you'd be well-advised to apologize, it would be a good idea for you to apologize; tu serais mal v. de critiquer! (tu n'es pas qualifié en la matière) it's not for you to criticize; (tu en as fait autant) you're hardly in a position to criticize; il serait mal v. de la critiquer it wouldn't be appropriate to criticize her; il serait mal v. d'insister it would be ill-mannered to insist

NM,F le premier v. the first to arrive; (n'importe qui) anybody; c'est à la portée du premier v. anybody can do it; le dernier v. the last to arrive; les nouveaux venus/les nouvelles venues the newcomers

• **venue** NF 1 (d'une personne) arrival; la venue de ma sœur my sister's arrival; attendre la venue de qn to wait for sb to arrive; annoncer la venue de qn to announce sb's arrival; c'est ce qui explique ma venue that's why I'm here 2 (d'une saison) approach; la venue du printemps the approach of spring 3 (apparition ▸ d'ordinateurs) advent 4 (naissance) birth; la venue (au monde) d'un enfant the arrival or birth of a child 5 Littéraire (locutions) d'une seule venue, tout d'une venue grown all in one spurt

> Il faut noter que le terme anglais venue est un faux ami. Il désigne un lieu où se réunissent des gens.

Vénus [venys] NPR Myth Venus

NF Astron Venus

vépéciste [vepesist] NM Com mail-order organization

vêpres [vɛpr] NFPL Rel vespers; aller aux v. to go to vespers; sonner les v. to ring the bell for vespers

ver [vɛr] NM (gén) worm; (de viande) maggot; (de fruit) grub, maggot; (asticot) maggot; (larve) larva; Méd avoir des vers to have worms; il y a des vers dans la viande the meat is maggoty; cette pomme est pleine de vers worms have been at this apple; meuble mangé aux ou rongé aux ou piqué des vers worm-eaten piece of furniture; v. blanc grub; v. à bois woodworm (UNCOUNT); v. de farine mealworm; Ordinat v. informatique worm; v. luisant glow-worm; v. des pêcheurs lug (worm); v. rongeur canker(worm); v. à soie silkworm; Méd v. solitaire tapeworm; v. de terre earthworm; v. de vase bloodworm; Fam tirer les vers du nez à qn to worm it out of sb; Fam pas moyen de lui tirer les vers du nez he/she won't give anything away; j'ai fini par lui tirer les vers du nez I finally wormed it out of him/her; Fig le v. est dans le fruit the rot's set in

véracité [verasite] NF (authenticité) truth; la v. de ce témoignage est évidente this statement is obviously true; une histoire dont la v. n'est pas garantie an unauthenticated story

véranda [verɑ̃da] NF 1 (galerie) veranda, verandah, Am porch 2 (pièce) conservatory

verbal, -e, -aux, -ales [verbal, -o] ADJ 1 (dit de vive voix) verbal; il y a eu un contrat v. a verbal contract was established 2 (s'exprimant par les mots) violence verbale angry words; la violence verbale d'une description the violence of the language used in a description 3 Ling (adjectif, système) verbal; (phrase, forme, groupe) verb (avant n)

verbalement [verbalmɑ̃] ADV verbally, orally

verbalisation [verbalizasjɔ̃] NF 1 (par un agent) reporting offences 2 Psy verbalization, verbalizing

verbaliser [3] [verbalize] VI to report an offender; je suis obligé de v. I'll have to report you

VT to express verbally, to put into words, to verbalize

verbatim [verbatim] NM INV verbatim account

verbe [verb] NM 1 Gram verb; v. actif active verb; v. auxiliaire auxiliary verb; v. défectif defective verb; v. à particule phrasal verb

2 (ton de voix) avoir le v. haut to speak loudly; Fig to take a haughty tone, Br to lord it

3 Littéraire (expression de la pensée) words, language; la magie du v. the magic of words or language

4 *Bible* **le v.** the Word; **le V. fait chair** the Word made flesh

verbeux, -euse [vɛrbø, -øz] **ADJ** verbose, wordy, long-winded

verbiage [vɛrbjaʒ] **NM** verbiage; **tout ce v. ne m'intéresse pas** all this meaningless chatter is of no interest to me

verbosité [vɛrbozite] **NF** verbosity, wordiness

ver-coquin [vɛrkɔkɛ̃] *(pl* **vers-coquins)** **NM 1** *Agr (parasite)* vine grub **2** *Vét* stagger worm

verdâtre [vɛrdatr] **ADJ** greenish

verdeur [vɛrdœr] **NF 1** *(vigueur)* vitality, vigour **2** *(crudité)* raciness, boldness, sauciness **3** *(acidité ▸ d'un vin, d'un fruit)* slight tartness *or* acidity

verdict [vɛrdikt] **NM 1** *Jur* verdict; **rendre** *ou* **prononcer son v.** to pass sentence, to return a verdict; **le juge a rendu un v. sévère** the judge brought in a stiff sentence; **rendre un v. de culpabilité** *ou* **positif** to return a verdict of guilty; **rendre un v. d'acquittement** *ou* **négatif** to return a verdict of not guilty; **quel est votre v.?** how do you find? **2** *(opinion)* verdict, pronouncement; **le v. du médecin n'était pas très encourageant** the doctor's prognosis wasn't very hopeful

verdier [vɛrdje] **NM** *Orn* greenfinch

verdir **[32]** [vɛrdir] **VI 1** *(devenir vert)* to turn green **2** *Fig (de peur)* to blanch; **elle a verdi en apprenant la nouvelle** the blood drained out of her face when she heard the news; **v. (de jalousie)** to go *or* turn green with envy **3** *(plante, arbre)* to have green shoots

VT to add green *or* a green tinge to

verdissement [vɛrdismɑ̃] **NM** turning green

verdoie *etc voir* **verdoyer**

verdoiement [vɛrdwamɑ̃] **NM 1** *(couleur verte)* greenness **2** *(action de se couvrir de verdure)* **le v. des arbres annonçait l'arrivée du printemps** the green leaves on the trees heralded the arrival of spring

verdoyant, -e [vɛrdwajɑ̃, -ɑ̃t] **ADJ 1** *(vert)* green, verdant **2** *(vivace)* lush; **les champs verdoyants** the lush pastures

verdoyer **[13]** [vɛrdwaje] **VI** to be green *or* verdant

verdure [vɛrdyr] **NF 1** *(couleur)* greenness *(UNCOUNT)*, verdure *(UNCOUNT)* **2** *(végétation)* greenery *(UNCOUNT)*, verdure *(UNCOUNT)*; *(dans un bouquet)* greenery *(UNCOUNT)*, (green) foliage *(UNCOUNT)*; **rideau de v.** curtain of greenery; **tapis de v.** carpet of green, greensward **3** *Culin (salade)* salad; *(légumes verts)* greens

• **de verdure** **ADJ** *(théâtre)* open-air; **salle de v.** green arbour

verdurier, -ère [vɛrdyrje, -ɛr] **NM,F** *Belg Br* greengrocer, *Am* vegetable seller

véreux, -euse [verø, -øz] **ADJ 1** *(plein de vers ▸ fruit, viande)* wormy, maggoty **2** *Fig (malhonnête ▸ affaire, avocat, architecte, policier)* shady

verge [vɛrʒ] **NF 1** *Anat* penis

2 *(mesure)* yard; **v. d'arpenteur** measuring stick; *Can* yard

3 *Naut* **v. de l'ancre** anchor shank

4 *Bot* **v. d'or** goldenrod

• **verges** **NFPL** *Vieilli (badine)* birch (rod); *Fig* **donner des verges à qn pour se faire fouetter** to give sb a stick to beat one with, to make a rod for one's own back

vergé, -e [vɛrʒe] **ADJ 1** *Tex* ribbed, corded **2** *(papier)* laid

NM laid paper

vergeoise [vɛrʒwaz] **NF** brown sugar; *(autrefois)* low-grade beet sugar

verger [vɛrʒe] **NM** (fruit) orchard

vergeté, -e [vɛrʒəte] **ADJ** *(peau, cuisse)* stretch-marked

vergette [vɛrʒɛt] **NF** *(bâtonnet)* small cane, switch

vergetures [vɛrʒətyr] **NFPL** stretchmarks; **une crème contre les v.** a cream to prevent stretchmarks

vergeure [vɛrʒyr] **NF** *(marque)* wire mark

verglacé, -e [vɛrglase] **ADJ** **une route verglacée** a road covered in *Br* black ice *or Am* glare ice; **attention, les routes sont verglacées** careful, there's *Br* black ice *or Am* glare ice on the roads; *Can* **pluie verglacée** freezing rain

verglas [vɛrgla] **NM** *Br* black ice, *Am* glare ice; **danger v.** *(sur panneau) Br* black ice, *Am* glare ice; **il y a du v.** it's icy *or* slippery; **il y a du v. dans l'allée** the drive is iced over; **plaques de v.** patches of *Br* black ice *or Am* glare ice, icy patches

vergogne [vɛrgɔɲ] **sans vergogne** **ADJ** shameless

ADV shamelessly; **mentir sans v.** to lie shamelessly *or* without compunction

vergue [vɛrg] **NF** *Naut* yard; **v. de hunier** topsail yard; **v. de misaine** foreyard; **grande v.** mainyard; **bout de v.** yardarm

véridique [veridik] **ADJ 1** *Littéraire (sincère ▸ témoin)* truthful, veracious **2** *(conforme à la vérité)* genuine, true; **c'est une histoire absolument v.** it's a true story; **tout cela est parfaitement v.** there's not a word of a lie in all this; *Fam* **elle les a renvoyés, v.!** she fired them, it's true![□] **3** *(qui ne trompe pas)* genuine, authentic

véridiquement [veridikmɑ̃] **ADV** truthfully, *Sout* veraciously

vérifiable [verifjabl] **ADJ** verifiable; **son témoignage n'est pas v.** there's no way of checking *or* verifying his/her testimony; **votre hypothèse n'est pas v.** your hypothesis can't be tested

vérificateur, -trice [verifikatœr, -tris] **ADJ** testing *(avant n)*, checking *(avant n)*; **appareil v.** testing machine; **instrument v.** gauge, callipers

NM,F inspector, controller; *Fin* **v. de comptes** auditor

NM *Ordinat* **v. orthographique** spellchecker

vérification [verifikasjɔ̃] **NF 1** *(d'identité)* check; *(d'un témoignage, d'un déplacement)* check, verification; *(d'un dossier)* examination, scrutiny; *(d'un travail)* inspection, examination, checking; *(de votes)* checking; **v. faite auprès du percepteur** having checked with the tax office

2 *(d'une hypothèse, d'une preuve)* checking, verification; *(d'un pronostic)* confirmation

3 *Fin* checking; **v. des comptes** *(service)* audit; *(activité)* auditing; **v. fiscale** tax audit; *Compta* **v. à rebours** audit trail

4 *Tech* test, check; *Aut* **v. sur place** spot check

5 *Ordinat* check, control; **v. antivirale** antiviral check; **v. orthographique** spellcheck

vérificatrice [verifikatris] *voir* **vérificateur**

vérifier **[9]** [verifje] **VT 1** *(examiner ▸ mécanisme)* to check, to verify; *(▸ dossier)* to check, to go through; *(▸ travail)* to inspect, to check

2 *(preuve, témoignage)* to check; **vérifie son adresse** check that his/her address is correct, check his/her address; **v. que** *ou* **si...** to check *or* to make sure that, to check whether...

3 *(confirmer ▸ hypothèse)* to confirm, to bear out; **la chute du dollar a vérifié nos prévisions** the drop in the dollar bore out our predictions

4 *Math (calcul)* to check, to verify

5 *(comptes)* to audit

USAGE ABSOLU **v. plutôt deux fois qu'une** to check and double-check; **il doit être là, je vais v.** he must be there, I'll check *or* make sure

VPR **se vérifier** *(affirmation)* to prove correct, to be confirmed; *(craintes, supposition)* to be borne out *or* confirmed; **mes soupçons se sont vérifiés par la suite** my suspicions were subsequently confirmed

vérin [verɛ̃] **NM** jack; **v. à gaz** gas strut; **v. hydraulique** hydraulic jack; **v. pneumatique** pneumatic jack; **v. à vis** screw jack

véritable [veritabl] **ADJ 1** *(d'origine)* real, true; **son v. nom est inconnu** nobody knows his/her real *or* true name **2** *(authentique ▸ or, cuir)* real, genuine; *(▸ amitié, sentiment, ami)* true; **c'est de la soie v.** it's real silk; **du v. sirop d'érable** genuine maple syrup **3** *(avant le nom) (absolu)* real; **une v. idée de génie** a really brilliant idea; **un v. cauchemar** a real nightmare; **une v. montagne de papiers** a veritable mountain of papers; *très Fam* **une v. ordure** a real shit; **se montrer sous son v. jour** to show one's true colours, to show oneself in one's true light; **ce fut une v. surprise** it was a real surprise; **nous assistons là à une v. révolution** we are witnessing a real revolution

véritablement [veritabləmɑ̃] **ADV 1** *(réellement)* genuinely; **il est v. malade** he's genuinely ill; **nous nous sommes v. compris** we understood each other perfectly **2** *(exactement)* really, exactly; **ce n'est pas v. ce que j'avais prévu** it's not exactly *or* quite what I expected **3** *(en intensif)* truly, really, absolutely; **je suis v. désolé de ne pas vous avoir trouvé chez vous** I'm very sorry indeed (that) I didn't find you at home

vérité [verite] **NF 1** *(ce qui est réel ou exprimé comme réel)* **la v.** the truth; **dire la v.** to tell *or* speak the truth; **dire la v. à qn** to tell sb the truth; **dis-moi la v.** tell me the truth; **la v. pure et simple** the plain unvarnished truth; **c'est la v.** it's true, it's a fact; *Fam* **c'est la v. vraie!** it's true, honest it is!; **l'heure de v.** the moment of truth; **récit conforme à la v.** true *or* factual account; **s'écarter de la v. historique** to take liberties with history; **je sais que c'est la v.** I know it for a fact; **la v., c'est que ça m'est égal** actually, *or* the truth is, *or* in fact, I don't care; **je finirai bien par savoir la v.** I'll get at the truth eventually; **être loin de la v.** to be wide of the mark; **12 millions? vous n'êtes pas loin de la v.** 12 million? you're not far from the truth; **à chacun sa v.!** each to his own!; *Jur* **la v., toute la v., rien que la v.** the truth, the whole truth and nothing but the truth; **la v. n'est pas toujours bonne à dire, toute v. n'est pas bonne à dire** the truth is sometimes better left unsaid; **il n'y a que la v. qui blesse** nothing hurts like the truth; *Prov* **la v. sort de la bouche des enfants** out of the mouths of babes and sucklings (comes forth the truth); **v. en deçà des Pyrénées, erreur au-delà** = what is considered true in one country may be thought of as false in the next

2 *(chose vraie)* **une v.** a true fact

3 *(principe)* truth; **une v. première** a basic truth; **les vérités éternelles** undying truths, eternal verities; **les vérités essentielles** fundamental truths

4 *(ressemblance)* **ses tableaux sont d'une grande v.** his/her paintings are very true to life

5 *(sincérité)* truthfulness, candidness; **air/accent de v.** ring of truth; **son récit avait un accent de v.** his/her story rang true

• **à la vérité** **ADV** to tell the truth

• **en vérité** **ADV** really, actually

verjus [vɛrʒy] **NM** verjuice

verlan [vɛrlɑ̃] **NM** ≃ back-slang; **parler en v.** to speak in back-slang

> **VERLAN**
>
> This form of slang, mostly used among young French people and particularly in the impoverished areas of large cities, involves inverting the syllables of words and making any spelling changes necessary to facilitate pronunciation. The word "verlan" is itself the inverted form of "l'envers", meaning "the other way round". Some "verlan" terms are used or understood by a great many speakers, eg "laisse béton!" ("laisse tomber!" = "forget it!"), "ripou" ("pourri", used to refer to corrupt policemen), "meuf" ("femme") and "beur" ("arabe"). It is, however, an extremely generative form of slang and new words are constantly being made up.

vermeil, -eille [vɛrmɛj] **ADJ** *(rouge ▸ pétale, tenture)* vermilion; *(▸ teint, joue)* ruddy, rosy; *(▸ lèvres)* rosy

NM vermeil, gilded silver

vermicelle [vɛrmisɛl] **NM** **v., vermicelles** vermicelli *(UNCOUNT)*; **vermicelles chinois** Chinese noodles; **soupe aux vermicelles** noodle soup

vermiculaire [vɛrmikylɛr] **ADJ 1** *(en forme de ver)* wormlike, *Sout* vermicular **2** *Anat* **appendice v.** vermiform appendix

vermiculé, -e [vɛrmikyle] **ADJ** *Archit* vermiculate, vermiculated

vermiculure [vɛrmikylyr] **NF** *Archit* vermiculation *(UNCOUNT)*

vermiforme [vɛrmifɔrm] **ADJ** wormlike, *Sout* vermiform

vermifuge [vɛrmifyʒ] **ADJ** vermifuge, *Spéc* anthelmintic; **poudre v.** worming powder

NM vermifuge, *Spéc* anthelmintic

vermillon [vɛrmijɔ̃] ADJ INV vermilion, bright red
NM 1 *(cinabre)* vermilion, cinnabar 2 *(couleur)* vermilion

vermine [vɛrmin] NF 1 *(parasites)* vermin *(UNCOUNT)*; **couvert** *ou* **grouillant de v.** verminous, crawling with vermin 2 *Fig Péj* **fréquenté par la v.** frequented by lowlife characters *or* members of the underworld; **ces gens-là, c'est de la v.** those people are vermin

vermisseau, -x [vɛrmiso] NM small worm

vermoulu, -e [vɛrmuly] ADJ 1 *(piqué des vers)* worm-eaten 2 *Fig (vieux)* antiquated, age-old; **des institutions vermoulues** antiquated institutions

vermoulure [vɛrmulyr] NF 1 *(trou)* wormhole 2 *(poussière)* woodworm dust

vermouth [vɛrmut] NM vermouth

vernaculaire [vɛrnakylɛr] ADJ vernacular; **nom v.** vernacular *or* common name; **langue v.** vernacular

vernal, -e, -aux, -ales [vɛrnal, -o] ADJ vernal

verni, -e [vɛrni] ADJ 1 *(meuble, ongle)* varnished; *(acajou)* French-polished; *(brique, poterie)* enamelled, glazed; **parquet v.** varnished *or* polished floor; **cuir v.** patent leather; **des souliers vernis** patent leather shoes 2 *(brillant)* glossy, shiny 3 *Fam (chanceux)* lucky□, *Br* jammy; **tu es encore malade, tu n'es vraiment pas v.** you're sick again, you poor thing

vernier [vɛrnje] NM vernier, sliding gauge

vernir [32] [vɛrnir] VT *(enduire ▸ bois, tableau, ongle)* to varnish; *(▸ acajou)* to French-polish; *(▸ cuir)* to japan; *(▸ céramique)* to enamel, to glaze; **v. au tampon** to French-polish

vernis [vɛrni] NM 1 *(enduit ▸ sur bois)* varnish; *(▸ sur métal)* polish; **v. à l'alcool** spirit varnish; **v. cellulosique** cellulose varnish; **v. à l'essence** turpentine varnish; **v. au tampon** French polish
2 *(enduit ▸ sur céramique)* enamel; **v. au plomb** lead glazing
3 *Typ* varnish
4 *(cosmétique)* **v. à ongles** nail varnish *or* polish; **se mettre du v. à ongles** to varnish *or* paint one's nails
5 *Beaux-Arts* **v. à l'huile** oil varnish; **v. gras** long-oil varnish
6 *Bot* **v. du Japon** varnish tree, lacquer tree, tree of heaven
7 *Fig Péj* veneer; **avoir un v. de culture** to have a smattering of culture; **il suffit de gratter le v. pour comprendre qui il est** you only have to scratch the surface to find out who he really is

vernissage [vɛrnisaʒ] NM 1 *(d'un tableau, d'un meuble)* varnishing; *(d'une céramique)* glazing; *(du métal)* enamelling 2 *(d'une exposition)* private viewing, opening

vernissé, -e [vɛrnise] ADJ 1 *(céramique, tuile)* glazed 2 *(luisant ▸ feuilles)* glossy

vernisser [3] [vɛrnise] VT to glaze, to enamel

vernisseur, -euse [vɛrnisœr, -øz] NM,F *(de carrosserie)* body painter; *(à la laque)* lacquerer; *(de meuble)* furniture varnisher; *(au pistolet)* spray painter; *(de céramique)* glazer

vérole [verɔl] NF 1 *Fam (syphilis)* pox; **avoir la v.** to have the pox 2 *Méd (variole)* **petite v.** smallpox; **avoir la petite v.** to have smallpox

vérolé, -e [verɔle] ADJ *Fam* poxy

Véronal® [verɔnal] NM *Pharm* veronal®, barbital, barbitone

véronique[1] [verɔnik] NF *Bot* speedwell, *Spéc* veronica; **v. officinale** heath speedwell

véronique[2] [verɔnik] NF *(passe de tauromachie)* veronica

verra *etc voir* **voir**

verrat [vɛra] NM 1 *(porc)* breeding boar 2 *Can très Fam (homme méprisable)* bastard
EXCLAM *Can très Fam* **(maudit) v.!** shit!, *Br* bloody hell!
• **en verrat** ADV *Can Fam* 1 *(en intensif)* very□; **un beau film en v.** a damn *or Br* bloody good movie *or Br* film 2 *(en colère)* **être en (beau) v.** to be fuming

verre [vɛr] NM 1 *(matériau)* glass; **se casser** *ou* **se briser comme du v.** to be as brittle as glass; **v. blanc** white glass; **v. coloré** stained glass; **v. dépoli** frosted *or* ground glass; **v. feuilleté** laminated glass; **v. fumé** smoked glass; **v. incassable** shatterproof glass; **v. moulé** pressed glass; **v. organique** organic glass; **v. de sécurité** safety glass; **v. soluble** water glass; **v. soufflé** blown glass; **v. trempé** tempered *or* toughened glass; **v. à vitre** window glass
2 *(protection)* glass; **v. de lampe** lamp glass; **v. de montre** watch glass
3 *(récipient)* glass; **lever son v. à qn** to raise one's glass to sb; **v. ballon** round wine glass; **v. à dents** tooth glass; **v. doseur** measuring glass; **v. à eau** *(droit)* tumbler; **v. gradué** *(en chimie)* graduated vessel; *(pour la cuisine)* measuring glass; **v. à liqueur** liqueur glass; **v. à moutarde** mustard jar *(that can be used as a glass when empty)*; **v. à pied** stemmed glass; **v. à vin** wineglass; **v. à whisky** whisky glass
4 *(contenu)* glass(ful); **boire un v.** to have a drink; **je bois** *ou* **prends juste un petit v.** I'll just have a quick one; **tu restes prendre un v.?** are you staying for a drink?, would you like to stay for a drink?; **allez viens, on va prendre un v.** come on, let's go for a drink; **un v. et je suis ivre** it only takes one drink to get me drunk; **v. de** glass of, glassful of; **mettez un v. de vin rouge** add a glass of red wine; **il but** *ou* **vida deux grands verres d'eau pour étancher sa soif** he drank two large glasses of water to quench his thirst; *Fam* **avoir un v. dans le nez** to have had one too many; **il a pris** *ou* **bu un v. de trop** he's had one too many, he's had a drop too much
• **verres** NMPL *Opt* glasses; **elle a besoin de ses verres pour lire** she needs her glasses to read; **verres de contact** contact lenses; **verres correcteurs** correcting lenses; **verres fumés** tinted lenses; **verres polarisés** polaroid lenses
• **de verre** ADJ glass *(avant n)*; **objets de v.** glassware *(UNCOUNT)*
• **en verre** ADJ *(bibelot)* glass *(avant n)*
• **sous verre** ADJ *(photo, fleurs)* glass-framed; **une photo sous v.** a glass-mounted photograph
ADV **mettre qch sous v.** to put sth in a frame

verrée [vɛre] NF *Suisse (tournée)* round (of drinks); *(rencontre)* drinks party

verrerie [vɛrri] NF 1 *(usine)* glassworks *(singulier)*
2 *(technique)* glasswork, glassmaking
3 *(objets)* glassware
4 *(industrie)* glass trade

verrier, -ère [vɛrje, -ɛr] ADJ glass *(avant n)*
NM 1 *(souffleur de verre)* glassblower 2 *(artisan ▸ en verrerie)* glassmaker; *(▸ en vitraux)* stained-glass maker 3 *(casier)* glass rack
• **verrière** NF 1 *(toit)* glass roof
2 *(baie ▸ à hauteur de plafond)* glass wall *or* partition; *(▸ à mi-hauteur)* glass screen
3 *(de protection)* glass casing
4 *(vitrail)* stained-glass window
5 *Aviat* canopy

verroterie [vɛrɔtri] NF *(bibelots)* glass trinkets; *(bijoux)* glass jewels; *(perles)* glass beads; **collier de v.** string of glass beads, glass necklace

verrou [veru] NM 1 *(fermeture)* bolt; **mettre** *ou* **pousser les verrous** to slide the bolts home, to bolt the door; **on ne peut pas entrer, elle a mis le v.** we can't get in, she's bolted the door; **fermer une porte au v.** to bolt a door; **s'enfermer au v.** to bolt oneself in; **tirer le v.** to unbolt the door; **v. de sûreté** safety latch, night bolt; **v. trois points** multilock; *Fig* **faire sauter un v.** to get over an obstacle 2 *(d'une arme à feu)* bolt
• **sous les verrous** ADV **être sous les verrous** to be behind bars; **mettre qn sous les verrous** to put sb behind bars

verrouillage [verujaʒ] NM 1 *(d'une porte)* locking, bolting; *(d'une portière)* locking; **v. automatique** *ou* **central** central locking; **à v. automatique** self-locking; *Aut* **v. à distance** remote-control locking; **v. de sécurité enfants** childproof lock; *Aut* **v. du volant** steering lock 2 *Ordinat (du clavier)* locking; *(de l'accès)* lockout; **v. du clavier numérique** numbers lock; **v. des fichiers** file lock; **v. en majuscule(s)** caps lock

verrouiller [3] [veruje] VT 1 *(clore ▸ porte)* to lock, to bolt
2 *(empêcher l'accès de)* to close off; **la police a verrouillé le quartier** the police have cordoned off *or* sealed off the area
3 *(enfermer ▸ personne)* to lock in
4 *Ordinat (clavier)* to lock; *(capitales)* to lock on; **v. en écriture** *(fichier)* to lock; **verrouillé en majuscules** *(clavier)* with caps lock on
5 *Mil (ville)* to blockade; *(passage, brèche)* to block
6 *Fam (contrôler ▸ système, équipe)* to control□; *(▸ marché)* to block; **v. un prix** to freeze a price; **avant d'envoyer le contrat, assure-toi que tout est verrouillé** before you send off the contract, make sure that everything is in order□
VPR **se verrouiller se v. (chez soi)** to shut *or* to lock oneself in

verrue [vɛry] NF wart; **v. plantaire** verruca, plantar wart

verruqueux, -euse [verykø, -øz] ADJ warty, *Spéc* verrucose

vers[1] [vɛr] NM *Littérature* 1 *(genre)* verse; **v. libres** free verse; **v. métriques/syllabiques/rythmiques** quantitative/syllabic/accentual-syllabic verse
2 *(unité)* line; **le dernier v. est faux** *ou* **boiteux** the last line doesn't scan; **les v. obéissent à certaines règles** lines of verse *or* verse lines follow a given pattern
NMPL *(poème)* lines of poetry, verse *(UNCOUNT)*, poetry *(UNCOUNT)*; **écrire** *ou* **faire des v.** to write poetry *or* verse; **v. de circonstance** occasional verse; **des v. de mirliton** doggerel *(UNCOUNT)*
• **en vers** ADJ **conte/lettre en v.** tale told/letter written in verse ADV **mettre qch en v.** to put sth into verse

vers[2] [vɛr] PRÉP 1 *(dans la direction de)* to, towards; **il regarde v. la mer** he's looking towards the sea; **un kilomètre v. le sud** one kilometre to the south; **v. la gauche** to the left; **en route v. la Californie** on the way to California; **le village v. lequel nous nous dirigions** the village we were heading for; *Fam* **v. où tu vas?** which way are you going?□; **se précipiter v. la sortie** to hurry towards *or* to make for the exit; **v. les quais** *(sur panneau)* to the trains; **il s'est tourné v. moi** he turned to *or* towards me; *(pour que je l'aide)* he turned *or* came to me; **un pas v. la paix** a step towards peace
2 *(indiquant l'approximation ▸ dans le temps)* around; *(▸ dans l'espace)* near; **v. midi** around midday; **v. la mi-juillet** around mid-July; **v. 1830** in about 1830; **il a neigé v. six heures** it snowed at about *or* around six o'clock; *Fam* **v. (les) trois heures** about *or* around three (o'clock); **v. la fin de qch** towards the end of sth; **v. la fin du siècle** at the turn of the century; **v. les années 30** in the 30s or thereabouts; **l'accident a eu lieu v. Ambérieu** the accident happened somewhere near Ambérieu; **v. les 1800 mètres, la végétation se raréfie** around 1,800 metres, the vegetation becomes sparse; **on a trouvé des jonquilles v. la rivière** we found some daffodils near the river

versaillais, -e [vɛrsajɛ, -ɛz] ADJ of/from Versailles
• **Versaillais, -e** NM,F = inhabitant of or person from Versailles

versant, -e [vɛrsɑ̃, -ɑ̃t] ADJ *Can (qui renverse facilement)* unsteady
NM 1 *Géog (côté ▸ d'une montagne, d'une vallée)* side, slope; *(▸ de colline)* hillside; **un v. abrupt** a steep slope *or* hillside; **le v. suisse du Jura** the Swiss side of the Jura 2 *(aspect ▸ d'une position, d'un argument)* side, aspect; **notre politique a deux versants** there are two sides *or* aspects to our policy

versatile [vɛrsatil] ADJ 1 *(esprit, caractère, personne)* fickle; *(homme politique)* mercurial; **elle est v.** she's always changing her mind 2 *Biol* versatile

> Il faut noter que l'adjectif anglais **versatile** est un faux ami. Il signifie **polyvalent**.

versatilité [vɛrsatilite] NF 1 *(inconstance)* fickleness 2 *Biol* versatility

verse [vɛrs] NF *Agr* lodging, laying
• **à verse** ADV **il pleut à v.** it's pouring (with rain), it's pouring down; **la pluie tombait à v.** the rain was coming down in torrents

ersé, -e [verse] ADJ versed; **être très/peu v. dans politique** to be well-versed/not particularly ell-versed in politics; **être v./peu v. dans l'art ontemporain** to be conversant with/ignorant of ontemporary art

erseau [verso] NM **1** *Astron* Aquarius **2** *Astrol* quarius; **être V.** to be Aquarius *or* an Aquarian

ersement [versəmɑ̃] NM **1** *(paiement)* payment; **v. annuel** yearly payment; **v. à la commande** down payment **2** *(paiement partiel)* nstalment; **effectuer un v.** to pay an instalment; **n premier v.** a down payment; **versements échelonnés** staggered payments; **en plusieurs versements, par versements échelonnés** by *or* in nstalments **3** *(dépôt)* deposit; **effectuer** *ou* **faire n v. à la banque** to pay money into a bank account; **quand avez-vous fait le v.?** when did you ay the money in?; **v. en espèces** cash deposit; ulletin de v. paying-in *or Am* deposit slip

erser [3] [verse] VT **1** *(répandre ▸ sang, larmes)* to hed; **v. des larmes** *ou* **pleurs** to cry; **sans qu'une outte de sang n'ait été versée** without a drop of lood being spilt; **il irait jusqu'à v. son sang pour défendre ses idées** he'd be willing to sacrifice his fe for his ideas

2 *(servir ▸ liquide)* to pour out; **verse-lui-en un eu plus** pour him/her a bit more; **v. à boire à qn** o pour sb a drink, to pour a drink for sb; **v. du vin ans une cruche** to pour wine into a jug

3 *(faire basculer ▸ sable, gravier, chargement)* to ip; **verse la farine dedans** pour the flour in; **verse e trop-plein dans le seau** tip *or* pour the overflow ut into the bucket

4 *(coucher à terre ▸ céréales)* to lay *or* to beat lown

5 *(affecter)* to assign, to transfer; *Mil* **v. des hommes à un régiment/dans une armée** to draft *or* assign *or* transfer men to a regiment/to an army

6 *Mil (provisions)* to issue

7 *(payer)* to pay; *(sur un compte)* to deposit; **combien faut-il v.?** how much should one pay?; **v. de 'argent sur un compte** to put money into an account; **v. qch au crédit de qn** to credit sb with sth; **v. un acompte** to make a down payment; **on ous versera une retraite** you will receive a pension

8 *(apporter)* to add, to append; **v. une pièce au dossier** to add a new item to the file; *Fig* to bring urther information to bear on the case

9 *Belg (déchets)* to dump

VI **1** *(véhicule)* to overturn; **sa voiture est allée v. dans le ravin** his/her car tipped over into the ravine **2** *(cultures)* to be beaten down, to be laid lat

• **verser dans** VT IND to lapse into; **nous versons dans le mélodrame** this is becoming melodramatic; **v. dans le ridicule** *(personne, film)* to become ridiculous

erset [verse] NM **1** *(d'un livre sacré, d'un poème)* verse **2** *Rel* versicle

erseur, -euse [versœr, -øz] ADJ **bec v.** *(d'une héière)* spout; *(d'une casserole, d'une tasse)* lip

NM,F *(personne)* pourer

NM *Mines* tipper

• **verseuse** NF *(cafetière)* coffee pot

ersicolore [versikɔlɔr] ADJ **1** *(de couleur changeante)* versicoloured **2** *(multicolore)* variegated, many-coloured

ersificateur [versifikatœr] NM *Péj* versifier, poetaster, rhymester

ersification [versifikasjɔ̃] NF versification, versifying

ersifier [9] [versifje] VT to versify, to turn into verse, to write in verse

VI **1** *(faire des vers)* to versify, to write *or* to compose verse **2** *Péj* to versify

version [versjɔ̃] NF **1** *(variante ▸ d'une œuvre, d'un logiciel)* version; *(▸ d'une automobile)* model, version; **la v. cinématographique du livre** the movie *or Br* film (version) of the book; **v. longue** uncut version; **v. originale** version in the original language; **en v. originale** in the original language; **en v. originale sous-titrée** with subtitles; **en v. française** dubbed in French; **un film américain en v. française** an American movie *or Br* film dubbed into French; *Aut* **v. bâchée** soft top

2 *Scol & Univ* translation *(from a foreign language into one's mother tongue)*; **v. anglaise** *(pour un Français)* translation from English into French; **v. latine** translation from Latin

3 *(interprétation)* version; **voici ma v. des faits** this is my version of the facts, this is how I see what happened; **c'est la v. officielle des faits** that's the official version of what happened

4 *Ordinat* **v. bêta** beta version; **v. brouillon** draft version

verso [verso] NM **1** *(envers)* verso, other side; **je n'ai pas lu le v.** I haven't read the back of the page **2** *Ordinat* back

• **au verso** ADV **voir au v.** see overleaf; **la suite au v.** continued overleaf; **l'adresse est au v.** the address is overleaf *or* on the back

versoir [verswar] NM mouldboard

vert, -e [ver, vert] ADJ **1** *(couleur)* green; **v. de rage** livid; **être v. de peur** to be white with fear; **être v. de jalousie** to be green with envy

2 *(vin)* tart, acid; *(fruit)* green, unripe; *Fig (débutant, apprenti)* inexperienced; **ce vin est encore v.** this wine isn't ready for drinking yet

3 *(bois)* green

4 *(à préparer)* **cuir v.** untanned leather

5 *(vigoureux)* sprightly

6 *(agricole, rural)* green, agricultural, rural; **l'Europe verte** farming within the EU; **station verte** rural tourist centre

7 *(écologiste)* green *(avant n)*; **produit v.** green *or* environmentally friendly product; **les candidats verts** the green candidates

8 *(osé)* risqué, raunchy; **avoir un langage v.** to be rather bold in one's language

9 *(avant le nom) (violent)* **une verte semonce** a good dressing-down

10 *Fam (dégoûté) Br* gutted, *Am* bummed out

NM **1** *(couleur)* green; **peint/teint en v.** painted/tinted green; **v. amande** almond green; **v. bouteille** bottle green; **v. cendré** sage green; **v. de chrome** chrome green; **v. d'eau** sea green; **v. émeraude** emerald green; **v. jade** jade; **v. Nil** Nile green; **v. olive** olive green; **v. pomme** apple green; **v. tendre** soft green

2 *Transp* green light; **les voitures doivent passer au v.** motorists must wait for the light to turn green; **le feu est passé au v.** the lights have turned (to) green

3 *(locutions)* **mettre un cheval au v.** to turn a horse out to grass; *Fam* **mettre qn au v.** to put sb out to grass; **se mettre au v.** *(pour se reposer)* to go to the countryside; *(pour se cacher)* to hide out *or* lie low *or* hole up in the country; **cet été, je me mets au v. et je lis** I'm going to spend this summer tucked away in the countryside reading

• **vert galant** NM old charmer

• **Verts** NMPL *Pol* **les Verts** = the French Green Party

• **vertes** NFPL *Fam* **en dire/en avoir entendu des vertes et des pas mûres** to tell/to have heard some pretty raunchy jokes; **en avoir vu des vertes et des pas mûres** to have been through a lot; **il lui en a fait voir des vertes et des pas mûres!** he's really put him/her through it!

vert-de-gris [verdəgri] NM INV verdigris

ADJ INV blue-green

vert-de-grisé, -e [verdəgrize] *(mpl* **vert-de-grisés**, *fpl* **vert-de-grisées**) ADJ verdigrised

vertébral, -e, -aux, -ales [vertebral, -o] ADJ vertebral *(avant n)*, spinal *(avant n)*

vertèbre [vertebr] NF vertebra; **v. cervicale/dorsale/lombaire** cervical/dorsal/lumbar vertebra; **se déplacer une v.** to slip a disc; **avoir une v. déplacée** to have a slipped disc

vertébré, -e [vertebre] ADJ vertebrate

NM vertebrate

vertement [vertəmɑ̃] ADV harshly, sharply; **répondre v.** to retort sharply, to give a sharp answer; *Littéraire ou Hum* **se faire tancer v.** to get a good dressing-down

vertical, -e, -aux, -ales [vertikal, -o] ADJ *(droit ▸ position, corps, arbre)* vertical, upright; *(▸ écriture, ligne)* vertical; **éclairage v.** overhead lighting

• **verticale** NF vertical line; *Tech* plumb-line

• **à la verticale** ADJ vertical; **un versant à la verticale** a sheer drop ADV vertically; **monter à la verticale** to go up vertically, to go straight up; **descendre/tomber à la verticale** to go/to fall straight down *or* down vertically; **la falaise tombe à la verticale dans la mer** there is a sheer drop from the cliff to the sea; **s'élever à la verticale** to rise vertically, to go vertically upwards

verticalement [vertikalmɑ̃] ADV **1** *(tout droit)* vertically **2** *(dans les mots croisés)* down

verticalité [vertikalite] NF *(d'une ligne, d'un mur)* verticality; *(d'une falaise)* sheerness

verticille [vertisil] NM *Bot* verticil, whorl

vertige [vertiʒ] NM **1** *(peur du vide)* vertigo; **avoir le v.** to suffer from vertigo; **il a facilement le v.** he has no head for heights; **je n'ai jamais le v.** I'm not scared of heights **2** *(malaise)* dizzy spell; **avoir un v.** to feel dizzy *or* faint; **avoir des vertiges** to have dizzy spells; **elle a souvent des vertiges** she often feels dizzy *or* faint; **donner le v. à qn** to make sb's head swim; **cela me donne le v.** it's making my head swim, it's making me (feel) dizzy; *Fig* **des sommes astronomiques qui donnent le v.** huge amounts of money that make one's head swim *or* that don't bear thinking about **3** *Fig (égarement)* giddiness; **céder/résister au v. de la spéculation** *(tentation)* to give in to/to resist the temptations of speculation

vertigineuse [vertiʒinøz] *voir* **vertigineux**

vertigineusement [vertiʒinøzmɑ̃] ADV dizzily, *Sout* vertiginously; **une route v. escarpée** a breathtakingly steep road; **plonger v.** to plummet

vertigineux, -euse [vertiʒinø, -øz] ADJ *(effrayant ▸ altitude)* vertiginous, dizzy *(avant n)*, giddy *(avant n)*; *(▸ vitesse)* terrifying, breakneck *(avant n)*; **une baisse vertigineuse des cours** a spectacular collapse on the stock exchange; **une hausse vertigineuse des prix** a staggering increase in prices; **des sommes vertigineuses** absurdly large sums of money

vertigo [vertigo] NM *Vét* (blind) staggers

vertiport [vertipɔr] NM *Aviat* heliport

vertu [verty] NF **1** *Littéraire (conduite morale)* virtue, virtuousness; **je n'ai aucune v. à ne pas fumer, je n'aime pas ça** I can't claim any credit for not smoking *or Sout* there is nothing admirable in my not smoking, I just don't like it; **le chemin de la v.** the path of righteousness

2 *(qualité)* virtue; **les vertus cardinales** the cardinal virtues; **les vertus théologales** the theological virtues

3 *(propriété)* virtue, property, power; **la camomille a de nombreuses vertus** camomile has many beneficial uses; **avoir des vertus calmantes** to have calming *or* soothing properties; **les vertus thérapeutiques des plantes** the healing properties of plants; *Fig* **réapprenons les vertus de la vie à la campagne** let us rediscover the virtues of country life

4 *Hum (chasteté)* virtue; **défendre/perdre sa v.** to defend/to lose one's virtue

• **en vertu de** PRÉP according to; **en v. des pouvoirs qui me sont conférés, je...** in accordance with the powers vested in me, I...; **en v. de la loi** according to the law, in accordance with the law, under the law; **en v. de ce contrat, vous nous devez...** under the terms of this contract, you owe us...; **en v. de quoi...** for which reason...; **en v. de quoi il passe d'abord** that's the reason for his going first; **en v. de quoi est-il intervenu?** what gave him the right to intervene?

vertueuse [vertyøz] *voir* **vertueux**

vertueusement [vertyøzmɑ̃] ADV virtuously

vertueux, -euse [vertyø, -øz] ADJ **1** *(qui a des qualités morales)* virtuous, righteous; *(intentions)* honourable **2** *Vieilli (chaste)* virtuous

vertugadin [vertygadɛ̃] NM *Hist* farthingale

verve [verv] NF **1** *(fougue)* verve, gusto; *(esprit)* wit; **avec v.** with gusto *or* verve; **exercer sa v. contre qn** to use one's wit against sb **2** *Littéraire (créativité)* inspiration; **la v. poétique** poetic talent *or* inspiration

• **en verve** ADJ **être en v.** to be particularly witty; **elle était en v. ce soir-là** she was on top form that night

verveine [verven] NF **1** *Bot* vervain, verbena **2** *(tisane)* verbena tea **3** *(liqueur)* vervain liqueur

verveux[1] [vervø] NM *Pêche* hoop net

verveux[2]**, -euse** [vervø, -øz] ADJ *Littéraire* animated, lively, spirited

vesce [vɛs] NF *Bot* vetch, tare

vésical, -e, -aux, -ales [vezikal, -o] ADJ *Méd* vesical; **calcul v.** bladder stone, *Spéc* vesical calculus

vésicant, -e [vezikɑ̃, -ɑ̃t] ADJ *Méd & Pharm* vesicant, vesicatory

vésicatoire [vezikatwar] *Méd* ADJ vesicatory
NM vesicatory; **appliquer un v. à qn** to blister sb

vésicule [vezikyl] NF **1** *Méd (ampoule)* blister, vesicle; *Anat (cavité)* bladder; **v. biliaire/cérébrale** gall/brain bladder; **v. séminale** seminal vesicle **2** *Bot* vesicle, bladder-like cavity *or* cell

vespasienne [vɛspazjɛn] NF *Vieilli* street urinal

vespéral, -e, -aux, -ales [vɛsperal, -o] ADJ *Littéraire* evening *(avant n)*, vespertine; **les lueurs vespérales** evening lights, the lights at eventide; **les étoiles vespérales** the vespertine stars
NM *Rel* vesperal

vesse-de-loup [vɛsdəlu] *(pl* **vesses-de-loup)** NF *Bot* puffball

vessie [vesi] NF **1** *Anat & Zool* bladder; **v. natatoire** air *or* swim bladder, sound; *Fig* **prendre des vessies pour des lanternes** to be easily hoodwinked; **il voudrait nous faire prendre des vessies pour des lanternes** he's trying to pull the wool over our eyes **2** *(sac)* bladder

vestale [vɛstal] NF **1** *(prêtresse)* vestal virgin **2** *Littéraire (femme chaste)* vestal

veste [vɛst] NF jacket; **v. de pyjama** pyjama jacket *or* top; **v. de tailleur** suit jacket; **v. de tweed** tweed jacket; *Fig* **retourner sa v.** to be a turncoat; **tomber la v.** to take off one's jacket; *Fig* to get down to work *or* business; *Fam Fig* **ramasser** *ou* **(se) prendre une v.** *(échouer)* to come unstuck; *(être rejeté)* to get turned down

> Il faut noter que le terme anglais **vest** est un faux ami. Il signifie **maillot de corps** en anglais britannique et **gilet** en anglais américain.

vestiaire [vɛstjɛr] NM **1** *(placard)* locker **2** *(dépôt)* cloakroom; **prendre** *ou* **récupérer son v.** to collect one's things *or* belongings from the cloakroom **3** *(pièce)* changing room, *Am* locker room; *(de tribunal)* robing room; **l'arbitre, au v.!** get off, ref!; *Fig* **laisser sa fierté/ses principes au v.** to forget one's pride/one's principles

vestibule [vɛstibyl] NM *(d'un bâtiment public, d'une maison)* (entrance) hall, vestibule; *(d'un hôtel)* lobby

vestige [vɛstiʒ] NM *(d'une armée)* remnant; *(d'une ville, d'une société)* vestige; *(d'une croyance, du passé, d'une coutume)* remnant, vestige; *(d'une idée, d'un sentiment)* remnant, trace, vestige; **les derniers vestiges de l'impérialisme** the last remnants *or* traces of imperialism; **quelques vestiges du passé** a few relics of the past; **il ne reste que des vestiges de sa grandeur** only a shadow of his/her former greatness remains; *Archéol* **vestiges humains** human traces

vestimentaire [vɛstimɑ̃tɛr] ADJ clothing *(avant n)*; **dépenses vestimentaires** clothes expenditure, money spent on clothing

veston [vɛstɔ̃] NM jacket

Vésuve [vezyv] NM *Géog* **le V.** (Mount) Vesuvius

vêtement [vɛtmɑ̃] NM **1** *(habit)* piece *or* article *or* item of clothing, *Sout* garment; *(costume distinctif)* dress, garb; **tu devrais mettre** *ou* **passer un v.** you should put something on; **il fait froid, mets un v. chaud** it's cold, put something warm on; **vêtements** clothes, clothing *(UNCOUNT)*; **il portait ses vêtements de tous les jours** he was wearing his everyday clothes; **des vêtements en loques** tattered clothes, rags; **vêtements de détente** leisurewear *(UNCOUNT)*; **vêtements pour femme** ladieswear *(UNCOUNT)*; **vêtements habillés** formal dress *(UNCOUNT)*; **vêtements d'hiver/d'été** winter/summer clothes; **vêtements pour homme** menswear *(UNCOUNT)*; **vêtements de nuit** nightwear *(UNCOUNT)*; **vêtements de pluie** rainwear *(UNCOUNT)*; **vêtements sacerdotaux** vestments; **vêtements de ski** skiwear *(UNCOUNT)*; **vêtements de sport** sportswear *(UNCOUNT)*; **vêtements de travail** work *or* working clothes; **vêtements de ville** informal clothes **2** *(profession)* **l'industrie du v.** the clothing industry; *Fam* **être dans le v.** to be in the *Br* rag trade *or* *Am* garment industry **3** *Com* **vêtements dames** *ou* **femmes** ladieswear *(UNCOUNT)*; **vêtements enfants** childrenswear *(UNCOUNT)*; **vêtements hommes** menswear *(UNCOUNT)*

vétéran [veterɑ̃] NM **1** *(soldat)* veteran, old campaigner; *(ancien combattant)* (war) veteran **2** *Fig (personne expérimentée)* veteran, old hand; **un v. de la politique** a veteran political campaigner **3** *Sport* veteran

vétérinaire [veterinɛr] ADJ veterinary; **faire des études vétérinaires** to study veterinary medicine *or* science
NMF vet, *Br* veterinary surgeon, *Am* veterinarian

vétille [vetij] NF trifle; **perdre son temps à des vétilles** to waste time over trivial details; **se disputer pour des vétilles** to argue over trivialities *or* trivial details; **ce n'est qu'une v.** it's just a trivial detail

vétilleux, -euse [vetijø, -øz] ADJ *Littéraire* fussy, hair-splitting, quibbling

vêtir [44] [vetir] VT **1** *(habiller ▸ enfant, malade)* to dress **(de** in) **2** *(prisonnier, malade)* to clothe, to provide with clothes, *Br* to kit out **3** *Littéraire (revêtir)* to put on, to don
VPR **se vêtir 1** *(emploi réfléchi)* to dress (oneself) **(de** in); **trouver de quoi se v.** to find something to put on **2** *Littéraire* **en hiver, la campagne se vêt de neige** in winter, the countryside is clothed in snow

vétiver [vetivɛr] NM *Bot* vetiver

veto [veto] NM INV **1** *Pol* veto; **mettre** *ou* **opposer son v. à une mesure** to veto a measure; **exercer son droit de v.** to use one's power of veto; **v. absolu** absolute veto; **v. suspensif** suspensive veto **2** *(interdiction)* **opposer son v. à qch** to forbid *or* to prohibit *or* to veto sth

véto [veto] NM *Fam (vétérinaire)* vet ▫

vêtu, -e [vety] PP *voir* **vêtir**
ADJ dressed; **être bien/mal v.** to be well/badly dressed; **être chaudement v.** to be warmly dressed; **elle était court vêtue** she was wearing a short skirt; **à demi-v.** half-dressed; **v. de** dressed in, wearing; **un enfant v. d'un blouson** a child wearing a jacket; **une femme toute vêtue de blanc** a woman all in white; **un homme v. de haillons** a man in rags; **professeurs vêtus de leurs toges** professors wearing *or* in their gowns; **toute de soie/noir vêtue** all dressed in silk/black; *Littéraire* **mur v. de lierre** ivy-clad wall, wall covered in ivy

vétuste [vetyst] ADJ dilapidated, decrepit

vétusté [vetyste] NF dilapidated state; **la v. de l'installation électrique est en cause** the poor state of the wiring is to blame

veuf, veuve [vœf, vœv] ADJ **1** *(personne)* **devenir v.** to be widowed, to become a widower; **devenir veuve** to be widowed, to become a widow; **je m'occupe de ma tante qui est veuve** I look after my widowed aunt; **il est v. de plusieurs femmes** he's a widower several times over **2** *Typ* **ligne veuve** widow
NM,F widower, *f* widow; *Admin* **Madame veuve Dupont** Mrs Dupont *(term of address used on official correspondence to widows)*; **la veuve Dupont** Mrs Dupont *(slightly informal way of referring to a widow)*; *Fig* **veuve joyeuse** merry widow; **veuve de guerre** war widow
• **veuve** NF **1** *Typ* widow **2** *Fam Arch* **la Veuve** the guillotine ▫ **3** *très Fam Hum* **la veuve Poignet** masturbation ▫

veuille *etc voir* **vouloir**[2]

veule [vøl] ADJ *Littéraire (personne)* spineless, cowardly; *(visage, traits)* weak

veulent *voir* **vouloir**[2]

veulerie [vølri] NF *Littéraire* spinelessness

veut *voir* **vouloir**[2]

veuvage [vœvaʒ] NM *(perte d'un mari)* widowhood; *(perte d'une femme)* widowerhood

veuve [vœv] *voir* **veuf**

veux *voir* **vouloir**[2]

vexant, -e [vɛksɑ̃, -ɑ̃t] ADJ *(blessant ▸ personne)* hurtful; *(▸ remarque)* cutting, slighting, hurtful

vexation [vɛksasjɔ̃] NF **1** *(humiliation)* snub, slight, humiliation; **essuyer des vexations** to be snubbed; **être en proie aux vexations de qn** to be constantly being snubbed *or* put down by sb **2** *Vieilli (mauvais traitement)* vexation

vexatoire [vɛksatwar] ADJ vexatious, harassin

vexer [4] [vɛkse] VT **v. qn** to hurt sb's feelings; **je ne voulais pas le v.** I didn't mean to hurt his feelings; **être vexé** to be hurt *or* offended; **être vexé comme un pou** to be extremely upset; **elle est horriblement vexée** she's cut to the quick; **il est vexé de n'avoir pas compris** he's cross because he didn't understand; **elle est vexée que tu ne croies pas** she feels hurt because you don't believe her
VPR **se vexer** to be hurt *or* offended *or* upset, to take offence; **ne te vexe pas, mais...** no offence meant, but...; **se v. facilement** to be easily offended, to be oversensitive; **se v. de qch** to feel hurt *or* to be upset by sth; **il se vexe de tout/pour un rien** he gets upset over everything/over the slightest thing

> Il faut noter que le verbe anglais **to vex** est un faux ami. Il signifie **fâcher, chagriner**.

VF [veɛf] *Cin* NF *(abrév* **version française)** = indicates that a film is dubbed in French
• **en VF** ADJ dubbed in French

VHF [veaʃɛf] NF *TV & Rad (abrév* **very high frequency)** VHF

VHS [veaʃɛs] NM *TV (abrév* **video home system)** VHS

VI [vei] NF *Compta (abrév* **valeur d'inventaire)** balance sheet value, break-up value

via [vja] PRÉP via, through; **Paris, v. Calais** Paris via Calais

viabiliser [3] [vjabilize] VT to service; **terrain viabilisé** piece of land with water, gas and electricity installed *(for building purposes)*; **v. une entreprise** to make a business viable

viabilité [vjabilite] NF **1** *(aménagements)* utilities, services **2** *(état d'une route)* practicability *(d'un organisme, d'un projet, d'un fœtus)* viability

viable [vjabl] ADJ **1** *(fœtus)* viable **2** *(entreprise, projet)* viable, practicable, feasible

viaduc [vjadyk] NM viaduct

via ferrata [vjaferata] NF INV *Sport* via ferrata

viager, -ère [vjaʒe, -ɛr] ADJ life *(avant n)*
NM (life) annuity
• **en viager** ADV **placer son argent en v.** to buy an annuity; **acheter/vendre une maison en v.** to buy/to sell a house so as to provide the seller with a life annuity

viande [vjɑ̃d] NF **1** *Culin* meat; **v. blanche** white meat; **v. de bœuf** beef; **v. de boucherie** fresh meat *(as sold by the butcher)*; **v. de cheval** horsemeat; **v. crue** raw meat; **v. cuite** cooked meat; **v. froide** dish of cold meat; **v. fumée** smoked meat; **v. hachée** minced meat, *Br* mince, *Am* ground meat; **v. de porc** pork; **v. rouge** red meat; **v. salée** cured *or* salted meat; **v. de veau** veal **2** *très Fam (corps)* **amène ta v.!** get your butt *or* carcass over here!; **de la v. froide** *(un cadavre)* a stiff; *(des cadavres)* stiffs **3** *Littéraire (aliment)* nourishment, sustenance

viander [3] [vjɑ̃de] VI *(cerf, daim, chevreuil)* to graze, to feed
VPR **se viander** *très Fam* to get smashed up; **ils se sont viandés contre un mur** they smashed into a wall

viatique [vjatik] NM **1** *Rel* viaticum
2 *Littéraire (atout)* asset; **il n'a que son savoir pour tout v.** his knowledge is his only asset, his only means to success is his knowledge; **j'avais pour seul v. cette lettre de recommandation** this letter was all I had to recommend me
3 *(soutien)* help
4 *Arch (pour un voyage)* provisions and money (for the journey); **on leur a donné un v. de 200 euros pour leur voyage** we gave them 200 euros for their trip

vibrant, -e [vibrɑ̃, -ɑ̃t] ADJ **1** *(corde, lamelle)* vibrating; *Ling* **consonne vibrante** vibrant consonant
2 *(fort ▸ voix, cri)* vibrant
3 *(émouvant ▸ accueil, discours)* stirring; *(▸ voix)* tremulous; **v. de** ringing *or* echoing with; **il lui a rendu un hommage v.** he paid him/her a warm tribute

4 *(sensible ▸ nature, personne, caractère)* sensitive
vibrante NF *Ling* vibrant

braphone [vibrafɔn] NM vibraphone, *Am* vi-raharp

braphoniste [vibrafɔnist] NMF vibraphonist

ibrateur [vibratœr] NM **1** *Tech* vibration gen-rator **2** *Constr* vibrator

ibration [vibrasjɔ̃] NF **1** *(tremblement ▸ d'un noteur, d'une corde, dusol)* vibration; *(▸ d'une oix)* quaver, tremor **2** *Phys & Électron* vibration
vibrations NFPL vibrations; *Fam* **il y a de bon-es vibrations ici** you get a good feeling *or* good ibes from this place

ibrato [vibrato] NM *Mus* vibrato

ibratoire [vibratwar] ADJ vibratory

ibrer [3] [vibre] VI **1** *(trembler ▸ diapason, vitre, lancher, voix)* to vibrate; **v. d'émotion** to quiver *or* to quaver with emotion; **sa voix vibrait de co-ère** his/her voice was quivering with anger; **aire v. qch** to vibrate sth **2** *Fig* **faire v. le cœur de qn** to make sb's heart pound
VT **béton vibré** vibrated concrete

ibreur [vibrœr] NM *(sonnerie)* buzzer; *(disposi-if)* vibrator; *(interrupteur de courant)* chopper

ibrion [vibrijɔ̃] NM **1** *Biol* vibrio, bacillus; **v. sep-ique** gas bacillus **2** *Fam (personne)* fidget

ibromasseur [vibromasœr] NM vibrator

icaire [viker] NM *Rel (auxiliaire ▸ d'un curé)* as-sistant priest; *(▸ d'un évêque, du pape)* vicar; **Grand V., V. général** vicar-general; **v. apostolique** vicar apostolic; **le v. du Christ** the Vicar of Christ

icariat [vikarja] NM *Rel* **1** *(fonction)* curacy **2** *(territoire)* vicariate

ice [vis] NM **1** *(le mal)* vice; **le v. et la vertu** vice and virtue; *Fam Hum* **mais c'est du v.!** it's sheer perversion!
2 *(sexuel)* **le v.** perverse tendencies; **un v. contre nature** an unnatural tendency; **vivre dans le v.** to lead a life of vice
3 *(moral)* vice; **avoir tous les vices** to have all the vices; **on ne lui connaît aucun v.** he/she has no known vice; **il a le v. de la boisson** drinking is his vice; **v. solitaire** masturbation, self-abuse
4 *(défaut) & Com & Jur* defect, flaw; **v. apparent** conspicuous defect; **v. caché** hidden *or* latent defect; **v. de construction** structural fault; **v. de fa-brication** manufacturing defect; *Jur* **v. de forme** legal technicality; *(dans un contrat)* flaw; *Jur* **an-nulé pour v. de forme** annulled because of a mis-take in the drafting; *Com* **v. inhérent** inherent vice; *Com* **v. rédhibitoire** material defect; **v. de prononciation** faulty pronunciation
6 *Anat* **v. de conformation** congenital defect

vice-amiral [visamiral] *(pl* **vice-amiraux)** NM vice-admiral

vice-chancelier [visʃɑ̃səlje] *(pl* **vice-chanceliers)** NM vice-chancellor

vice-consul [viskɔ̃syl] *(pl* **vice-consuls)** NM vice-consul

vice-consulat [viskɔ̃syla] *(pl* **vice-consulats)** NM vice-consulate

vice-gérant, -e [visʒerɑ̃, -ɑ̃t] *(mpl* **vice-gérants,** *fpl* **vice-gérantes)** NM,F deputy manager

vicelard, -e [vislar, -ard] *très Fam* ADJ **1** *(dépravé)* kinky, *Br* pervy **2** *(perfide)* crafty[□], sneaky[□]; **une question vicelarde** a devious question[□]
NM,F *(pervers)* perv; **un vieux v.** a dirty old man, an old lech; **petite vicelarde!** you little tramp!

vicennal, -e, -aux, -ales [visenal, -o] ADJ vicennial

vice-présidence [viseprezidɑ̃s] *(pl* **vice-présidences)** NF *(d'un État)* vice-presidency; *(d'un congrès, d'une entreprise)* vice-chairman-ship

vice-président, -e [visprezidɑ̃, -ɑ̃t] *(mpl* **vice-présidents,** *fpl* **vice-présidentes)** NM,F *(d'un État)* vice-president; *(d'un congrès, d'une entreprise)* vice-chairman, *f* vice-chairwoman, vice-chair-person

vice-roi [visrwa] *(pl* **vice-rois)** NM viceroy

vice versa [vis(e)versa] ADV vice versa

vichy [viʃi] NM **1** *Tex* gingham; **une jupe en v. rouge et blanc** a red and white gingham skirt **2** *(eau)* Vichy (water); **un v. fraise** = a glass of Vichy water with strawberry syrup **3** *Culin* **carottes v.** carrots vichy *(glazed with butter and sugar)*

viciateur, -trice [visjatœr, -tris] ADJ *Littéraire* corrupting

viciation [visjasjɔ̃] NF *(de principes moraux etc)* corruption, *Sout* vitiation; *(de l'air)* pollution, contamination; *(du sang)* thinness; *Jur (d'un contrat)* vitiation, invalidation

viciatrice [visjatris] *voir* **viciateur**

vicié, -e [visje] ADJ **1** *(pollué ▸ air, sang)* polluted, contaminated **2** *Littéraire (faussé ▸ raisonne-ment, débat)* warped, vitiated **3** *Jur* vitiated

vicier [9] [visje] VT **1** *(polluer ▸ air, sang)* to pol-lute, to contaminate **2** *Littéraire (dénaturer ▸ es-prit, qualité)* to corrupt, to taint; *(▸ goût)* to corrupt; *(▸ relation, situation)* to make worse **3** *Jur* to vitiate, to invalidate

vicieuse [visjøz] *voir* **vicieux**

vicieusement [visjøzmɑ̃] ADV **1** *(lubriquement)* lecherously, licentiously **2** *(incorrectement)* faultily, wrongly **3** *(méchamment)* maliciously, nastily

vicieux, -euse [visjø, -øz] ADJ **1** *(pervers ▸ livre, film)* obscene; *(▸ regard)* depraved; *(▸ personne)* lecherous, depraved
2 *(trompeur ▸ personne)* underhand, sly; *(▸ coup, balle)* nasty, treacherous; *(▸ calcul)* mis-leading
3 *(cheval)* bad-tempered
4 *(incorrect ▸ expression, prononciation, posi-tion)* incorrect, wrong
NM,F *(homme)* lecher, pervert; **un vieux v.** a dirty old man, an old lecher; **petite vicieuse!** you little slut *or* tramp!

> Il faut noter que l'adjectif anglais **vicious** est un faux ami. Il signifie **méchant, agressif**.

vicinal, -e, -aux, -ales [visinal, -o] ADJ *voir* **chemin**
NM *Belg* suburban tram

vicissitude [visisityd] NF *Littéraire (succession)* vicissitude
• **vicissitudes** NFPL **1** *(difficultés)* tribulations; **après bien des vicissitudes** after many trials and tribulations, after many hard knocks **2** *(événe-ments)* vicissitudes, ups and downs; **les vicissitu-des de la vie** *ou* **de l'existence** the ups and downs *or* trials and tribulations of life

vicomte [vikɔ̃t] NM viscount

vicomté [vikɔ̃te] NF **1** *(titre)* viscountcy, vis-county **2** *(terrain)* viscounty

victime [viktim] NF **1** *(d'un accident, d'un meur-tre)* victim, casualty; **les victimes de la route** the road accident victims; **accident de la route, trois victimes** car crash, three casualties; **l'accident a fait trois victimes** three people died in the acci-dent; **les victimes ont été emmenées à l'hôpital** the victims were taken to (the) hospital; **un nou-veau meurtre porte à 15 le nombre des victimes** a new killing brings the number of victims to 15; **les victimes du SIDA** Aids victims; **les victimes de la dictature** the victims of the dictatorship
2 *Rel* (sacrificial) victim
3 *(bouc émissaire)* scapegoat, victim
4 *(d'un préjudice)* victim; **être la v. d'un escroc** to fall prey to *or* to be the victim of a con man; **être v. d'un malentendu** to labour under a miscon-ception; **être v. d'hallucinations** to suffer from de-lusions; **v. par ricochet** indirect victim

victimisation [viktimizasjɔ̃] NF victimization

victimiser [viktimize] VT to victimize

victimologie [viktimɔlɔʒi] NF victimology

victoire [viktwar] NF **1** *(fait de gagner ▸ bataille, compétition)* victory, winning; *(▸ dans une entre-prise)* victory, success (UNCOUNT); **chanter** *ou* **crier v.** to claim victory **2** *(résultat ▸ militaire)* vic-tory; *(▸ sportif)* victory, win; *(▸ dans une entre-prise)* victory, success; **v. aux points** win on points; **après leurs deux victoires en Coupe du monde** after their two wins *or* after winning twice in the World Cup; **remporter une v. (sur qn)** to gain a victory (over sb); *Fig* **remporter une v. sur soi-même** to triumph over oneself; **une v. à la Pyrrhus** a Pyrrhic victory **3** *(déesse)* **V.** Victory, Victoria

Victoria [viktɔrja] NPR *(reine)* **la reine V.** Queen Victoria
NM **1** *(État d'Australie)* **le V.** Victoria **2 le lac V.** Lake Victoria

victorien, -enne [viktɔrjɛ̃, -ɛn] ADJ Victorian

victorieuse [viktɔrjøz] *voir* **victorieux**

victorieusement [viktɔrjøzmɑ̃] ADV victo-riously

victorieux, -euse [viktɔrjø, -øz] ADJ *Sport* vic-torious, winning *(avant n)*; *Pol* victorious, win-ning *(avant n)*, successful; *Mil* victorious; *(air)* triumphant; **sortir v. d'un combat** to come out victorious

victuailles [viktɥaj] NFPL food *(UNCOUNT)*, provisions, *Sout* victuals

vidage [vidaʒ] NM **1** *(d'un récipient)* emptying
2 *(de poissons)* gutting, cleaning; *(de volailles)* drawing
3 *Fam (d'une personne)* kicking out
4 *Ordinat* **faire un v.** to (take a) dump; **v. sur disque/de la mémoire** disk/core dump; **v. de mé-moire** storage *or* memory dump; **v. d'écran** screen dump

vidange [vidɑ̃ʒ] NF **1** *(d'un récipient, d'un réser-voir)* emptying; *(d'un carter à huile, d'une fosse septique)* draining, emptying; *(d'une chaudière)* blowing off
2 *(dispositif)* drain, (waste) outlet; **v. du carter** oil-pan drain *or* outlet
3 *Aut* oil change; **faire la v.** to change the oil; **v.-graissage** oil change and lubrication
4 *Belg (verre consigné)* returnable empties
• **vidanges** NFPL **1** *(eaux usées)* sewage *(UN-COUNT)*, liquid waste *(UNCOUNT)* **2** *Can (ordu-res ménagères)* refuse *(UNCOUNT)*, *Br* rubbish *(UNCOUNT)*, *Am* garbage *(UNCOUNT)*
• **de vidange** ADJ *(huile, système, tuyau)* waste *(avant n)*; **bouchon de v.** sump plug; *(de radiateur)* draining plug
• **en vidange** ADJ **tonneau en v.** broached cask

vidanger [17] [vidɑ̃ʒe] VT **1** *(huile, eaux)* to empty (out), to drain off; *(fosse septique, radia-teur, carter à huile)* to empty, to drain; *(chaudière)* to blow off **2** *Aut (huile)* to change

vidangeur [vidɑ̃ʒœr] NM **1** *(qui vidange les fos-ses septiques)* septic tank emptier **2** *Can Fam (éboueur) Br* dustman[□], *Am* garbage collector[□]

vide [vid] ADJ **1** *(sans contenu)* empty; *(case de document)* blank; **tasse à demi v.** half-empty cup; **bouteilles vides** empty bottles, empties; **un espace v.** *(entre deux objets)* an empty space; *(sur un document)* a blank space; **une pièce v.** an empty *or* unfurnished room; **un regard v.** a va-cant stare; **des phrases vides** empty *or* meaning-less words; **v. de** devoid of; **la ville est v. de ses habitants** the town is empty (of its inhabitants); **des remarques vides de sens** meaningless re-marks, remarks devoid of meaning; *Com* **v. en retour** empty on return
2 *(sans occupant)* empty; **une maison v.** an empty house
3 *(sans intérêt ▸ vie)* empty
4 *(dénudé ▸ mur)* bare, empty; **l'appartement est encore très v.** *(peu meublé)* the *Br* flat *or Am* apart-ment is still very bare
NM **1** *Astron* **le v.** (empty) space, the void
2 *(néant)* space; **regarder dans le v.** to stare into space; **c'est comme si je parlais dans le v.** it's like talking to a brick wall; **faire des promesses dans le v.** to make empty promises
3 *Phys* vacuum; **faire le v.** *(dans un vase clos)* to create a vacuum; *Fig* **faire le v.** *(se ressourcer)* to switch off; **faire le v. dans son esprit** to make one's mind go blank; **faire le v. autour de soi** to drive all one's friends away; **faire le v. autour de qn** to iso-late sb
4 *(distance qui sépare du sol)* (empty) space; **avoir peur du v.** to be scared of heights; **être attiré par le v.** to feel the urge to jump; **pendre dans le v.** to hang in mid-air; **tomber dans le v.** to fall into (empty) space
5 *(trou ▸ entre deux choses)* space, gap; *(▸ entre les mots ou les lignes d'un texte)* space, blank; *(▸ dans un emploi du temps)* gap
6 *Fig (lacune)* void, gap, blank; **son départ a laissé un grand v. dans ma vie** he/she left a gaping void in my life when he/she went; *Jur* **v. juridique**

legal vacuum; **il y a un v. juridique en la matière** the law is not specific on this matter

7 *Fig (manque d'intérêt)* emptiness, void; **le v. de l'existence** the emptiness of life

8 *Constr* **v. d'air** air space; **v. sanitaire** ventilation *or* crawl space

• **à vide** ADJ **1** *(hors fonctionnement)* no-load *(avant n)*; *(batterie)* discharged; **poids à v.** unladen weight **2** *(sans air)* **cellule/tube à v.** vacuum photocell/tube **3** *Mus* **corde à v.** open string ADV **marcher à v.** *(machine)* to run light *or* without load; **le moteur tourne à v.** the engine's ticking over *or* idling; **les usines tournent à v.** the factories are running but not producing; **rouler à v.** *(bus)* to have no passengers; **le train est parti à v.** the train left empty; **camion revenant à v.** truck returning empty

• **sous vide** ADJ vacuum *(avant n)* ADV **emballé sous v.** vacuum-packed

vidé, -e [vide] ADJ **1** *(volaille)* drawn, cleaned; *(poisson)* gutted **2** *Fam (épuisé)* drained, dead beat

NM *Belg Culin* chicken vol-au-vent

vidéaste [videast] NMF video maker

vide-grenier [vidgrənje] NM INV *Br* ≃ car boot sale, *Am* ≃ yard sale

vidéo [video] ADJ INV video *(avant n)*; **caméra/cassette v.** video camera/cassette

NF **1** *(technique)* video (recording); *(cassette)* video, videotape; **faire de la v.** to make videos; **v. à la demande** video-on-demand, VOD; **v. de démonstration** demo (video); **v. d'entreprise** *ou* **institutionnelle** corporate video; **v. fixe** video still; **v. numérique** digital video; **v. pirate** pirate video; **v. promotionnelle** promotional video **2** *Ordinat* **v. inverse** *ou* **inversée** reverse video

vidéocassette [videɔkasɛt] NF video cassette, video

vidéoclip [videɔklip] NM (music) video

vidéoclub [videɔklœb] NM videoclub

vidéocommunication [videɔkɔmynikasjɔ̃] NF video communication

vidéocomposite [videɔkɔ̃pozit] ADJ *Électron* **signal v.** videocomposite signal

vidéoconférence [videɔkɔ̃ferɑ̃s] NF *(concept)* videoconferencing; *(conférence)* videoconference

vidéodiagnostic [videɔdjagnɔstik] NM *Méd* video diagnostics *(singulier)*

vidéodisque [videɔdisk] NM videodisc

vidéofréquence [videɔfrekɑ̃s] NF video frequency

vidéogramme [videɔgram] NM videogram

vidéographie [videɔgrafi] NF videography; **v. diffusée** ≃ Teletext®; **v. interactive** ≃ Viewdata®, Videotex®

vidéographique [videɔgrafik] ADJ videographic

vidéolecteur [videɔlɛktœr] NM videoplayer

vidéophone [videɔfɔn] NM videophone, viewphone

vidéoprojection [videɔprɔʒɛksjɔ̃] NF video projection

vidéoquestionnaire [videɔkɛstjɔnɛr] NM video questionnaire

vide-ordures [vidɔrdyr] NM INV *Br* rubbish *or Am* garbage chute

vidéotex [videɔtɛks] NM Videotex®, Viewdata®; **v. diffusé** Teletext®

vidéothèque [videɔtɛk] NF video library; *(personnelle)* video collection

vidéotransmission [videɔtrɑ̃smisjɔ̃] NF video transmission

vidéovente [videɔvɑ̃t] NF video selling

vide-poches [vidpɔʃ] NM INV **1** *(meuble)* tidy **2** *(de voiture)* storage tray; *(dans la porte)* door pocket, map pocket

vide-pomme [vidpɔm] *(pl* **vide-pommes***)* NM apple corer

vider [3] [vide] VT **1** *(le contenu de* ▸ *seau, verre, sac, poche)* to empty (out); *(*▸ *pièce, tiroir)* to empty, to clear out; *(*▸ *baignoire)* to let the water out of, to empty; *(*▸ *tonneau, étang)* to empty, to drain; *(*▸ *chaudière)* to blow off; **v. les ordures** to put out the *Br* rubbish *or Am* garbage; **v. un sac de riz dans un pot** to empty a bag of rice into a pot; **il vida le tiroir par terre** he emptied the contents of the drawer (out) onto the floor; **vide le vase dans l'évier** empty the vase into the sink; **partir en vidant la caisse** to make off with the takings; **v. les poches de qn** to empty sb's pockets; *(sujet: voleur)* to pick sb's pockets; **v. une maison de ses meubles** to empty a house of its furniture, to clear the furniture from a house; **v. les lieux** to vacate the premises; **le juge a fait v. la salle** the judge ordered the court (to be) cleared; *Fig* **v. l'abcès** to clear the air, to make a clean breast of things; *Fig* **v. son cœur** to pour out one's feelings; *Fig* **v. son sac** to get things off one's chest, to unburden oneself

2 *(le milieu de* ▸ *pomme)* to core; *(*▸ *carcasse)* to eviscerate; *(*▸ *volaille)* to empty, to clean (out); *(*▸ *poisson)* to gut

3 *(boire)* to drain; **v. son verre** to drain one's glass; **vide ton verre!** *(finis de boire)* drink up!; **nous avons vidé une bouteille à deux** we downed a bottle between the two of us; **v. les fonds de bouteille** to drink the dregs

4 *Fam (épuiser)* to drain, to wipe out; **ce cross m'a vidé** that cross-country race has just about finished me off

5 *(mettre fin à)* to settle (once and for all); **v. une vieille querelle** to settle an old dispute

6 *Fam (renvoyer)* to throw *or* to kick out; **v. qn** *(employé)* to fire *or Br* to sack sb; *(client)* to throw sb out, *Am* to bounce sb; *(élève)* to throw *or* to chuck sb out; **se faire v.** *(d'une pièce)* to be sent out▫; *(d'un bar)* to be chucked *or* thrown out; *(d'un collège)* to be expelled▫; *(être renvoyé)* to get fired, *Br* to get the sack

7 *Ordinat* to dump; **v. l'écran** to clear the screen; **v. la corbeille** to empty the wastebasket *or Am* the trash

8 *Équitation* **v. les arçons** *ou* **étriers** to take a tumble (off one's horse); **se faire v.** to be thrown out

VPR **se vider 1** *(contenu)* to empty *or* to drain (out); **la baignoire est en train de se v.** the bath is emptying out, the bathwater is draining away; **l'eau du réservoir se vide ensuite dans une fosse** the water in the reservoir then drains *or* flows out into a ditch; **la locution s'est peu à peu vidée de son sens** the expression has gradually lost its meaning **2** *(salle, ville)* to empty; **le stylo s'est vidé dans mon sac** the pen has leaked inside my bag; **se v. de son sang** to bleed to death

videur [vidœr] NM *(de boîte de nuit)* bouncer

viduité [vidɥite] NF *Jur* viduity; *(d'une femme)* widowhood; *(d'un homme)* widowerhood; **délai de v.** = time a widow or widower must wait before remarrying

vie [vi] NF **1** *Biol* life; **la v. animale/végétale** animal/plant life; **durée de v.** lifespan

2 *(existence)* life; **il a eu la v. sauve** he has been spared; **laisser la v. sauve à qn** to spare sb's life; **je lui dois la v.** I owe him/her my life; **donner la v. à un enfant** to give birth to a child; **mettre sa v. en danger** to put one's life in danger; **risquer sa v.** to risk one's life; **perdre la v.** to lose one's life; **ôter la v. à qn** to take sb's life; **revenir à la v.** to come back to life; **ramener qn à la v.** to bring sb back to life; **sauver la v. de qn** to save sb's life; *Fig* **tu me sauves la v.!** you're a life-saver!; **au début de sa v.** at the beginning of his/her life; **à la fin de sa v.** at the end of his/her life, late in life; **une fois dans sa v.** once in a lifetime; **de sa v., elle n'avait vu un tel sans-gêne** she'd never seen such a complete lack of consideration; **de toute ma v., je n'ai jamais entendu chose pareille!** I've never heard such a thing in all my life!; **l'œuvre de toute une v.** a lifetime's work; **il promit de lui rester fidèle pour la v.** he promised to be faithful to him/her for life; **à Julie, pour la v.** to Julie, forever *or* for ever; **avoir la v. devant soi** *(ne pas être pressé)* to have all the time in the world; *(être jeune)* to have one's whole life in front of one; **être entre la v. et la mort** to be hovering between life and death, to be at death's door; **c'est une question de v. ou de mort** it's a matter of life and death; **il y va de sa v.** his/her life is at stake; **passer de v. à trépas** to pass away, to depart this life; **la v. continue** life goes on; **à la v. à la mort** for life (and beyond the grave); **entre eux, c'est à la v., à la mort** they'd die for each other

3 *(personne)* life; **son rôle est de sauver des vie** he/she is there to save lives

4 *(entrain)* life; **mettre un peu de v. dans** to live up; **donner de la v. à une conversation/une réunio** to liven up *or* enliven *or* animate a conversa tion/a meeting; **plein de v.** lively, full of life

5 *(partie de l'existence)* life; **v. privée** private life **la v. affective/intellectuelle/sexuelle** love/intel lectual/sex life; **v. politique/professionnelle** po litical/professional life; **entrer dans la v. activ** to start working; **la v. associative** community life

6 *(façon de vivre* ▸ *d'une personne, d'une société* life, lifestyle, way of life; *(*▸ *des animaux)* life; **la v des abeilles/de l'entreprise** the life of bees/of th company; **la v. des volcans** the evolution of vol canoes; **la v. en Australie** the Australian lifestyl *or* way of life; **dans la v., l'important c'est de...** th important thing in life is to...; **faire sa v. avec qn** t settle down with sb; **avoir la v. dure** *(sujet: per sonne, mauvaise herbe)* to be tough (as ol boots), to be hard to kill *or* to get rid of; *(sujet superstitions, préjugés)* to be hard to kill off *or* t get rid of; **faire** *ou* **mener la v. dure à qn, rendre la v dure à qn** to make life difficult for sb; **rater sa v.** t make a mess of one's life; **refaire sa v.** to sta afresh *or* all over again; **changer de v.** to chang one's (way of) life; *(faire amende honorable)* t mend one's ways, to turn over a new leaf; **c'es la v.!, ainsi va la v.!, la v. est ainsi faite!** such is o that's life!; **je connais la v.** I've seen something o life; **regarder la v. en face** to look life in the face **elle veut mener sa v. comme elle l'entend** sh wants to lead her life as she sees fit; *Fam Fig* **me ner une v. de bâton de chaise** *ou* **de patachon** t lead a riotous life; **v. de bohême** bohemian life *Fam* **une v. de chien** a dog's life; **ce n'est pas une v.!** don't call that living!; **c'est la belle v.** *ou* **la v. de château!** this is the life!; **mener joyeuse v.** to lead a merry life; **femme de mauvaise v.** loose woman

7 *(biographie)* life; **il a écrit une v. de Flaubert** he wrote a life *or* biography of Flaubert; **raconter sa v.** to tell one's life story

8 *(conditions économiques)* (cost of) living; **dans ce pays, la v. n'est pas chère** prices are very low in this country; **le coût de la v.** the cost of living

9 *Rel* life; **la v. éternelle** everlasting life; **la v. ici-bas** this life; **la v. terrestre** life on earth; **dans cette v. comme dans l'autre** in this life as in the next

10 *Tech* life; *Mktg* **v. économique** *(d'un produit)* economic life; **v. moyenne** mean life; **v. utile** service life

• **à vie** ADJ for life, life *(avant n)*; **amis à v.** friends for life; **président à v.** life president; **membre à v.** life member ADV for life; **nommé à v.** appointed for life

• **en vie** ADJ alive, living; **être toujours en v.** to be still alive *or* breathing

• **sans vie** ADJ *(corps)* lifeless, inert; *(œuvre)* lifeless, dull

vieil [vjɛj] *voir* **vieux**

vieillard [vjɛjar] NM old man; **les vieillards** old people, the old, the aged

vieille [vjɛj] *voir* **vieux**

vieillerie [vjɛjri] NF **1** *(objet)* old thing **2** *(idée)* **qui s'intéresse à ces vieilleries?** who's interested in those stale ideas?

vieillesse [vjejɛs] NF **1** *(d'une personne)* old age; **avoir une v. heureuse** to be happy in old age; **pendant sa v.** in his/her old age; **mourir de v.** to die of old age **2** *(personnes)* **la v.** old people, the old, the aged

vieilli, -e [vjeji] ADJ **1** *(démodé)* old-fashioned; *(mot, expression)* old-fashioned, dated **2** *(vieux)* **je l'ai trouvé très v.** I thought he'd aged a lot

vieillir [32] [vjejir] VI **1** *(personne)* to age, to be getting old; **tout le monde vieillit** we all grow old; **je veux v. dans cette maison** I want to spend my old age in this house; **bien v.** to grow old gracefully; **il a mal vieilli** he hasn't aged well; **les soucis l'ont fait v. de dix ans** anxiety has put ten years on him

2 *(paraître plus vieux)* **il a vieilli de 20 ans** he looks 20 years older; **tu ne vieillis pas** you never seem to look any older

3 *(vin, fromage)* to age, to mature; **faire v. du fromage en cave/du vin en fût** to mature cheese in a cellar/wine in a cask; **l'argent vieillit bien** silver ages well

4 *(usage, mot)* to become obsolete *or* antiquated *or* out of date; *(technique)* to become outmoded; **ce mot a vieilli** this word is obsolescent; **cette chanson/construction n'a pas vieilli** this song/building has stood the test of time *or* hasn't dated; **la pièce a beaucoup vieilli** the play seems very dated; **ce film vieillit mal** the movie doesn't stand the test of time

VT 1 *(rendre vieux ▸ personne)* to make old, to age; **les soucis l'ont vieilli** worry has aged him

2 *(vin, fromage)* to age, to mature; *(métal)* to age-harden

3 *(meubles)* to distress; **pour v. un peu la photo** to age the photo a little

4 v. qn *(sujet: vêtement, couleur)* to make sb seem older; *(sujet: personne)* **vous me vieillissez!** you're making me older than I am!; **le noir te vieillit** black makes you look older; **c'est fou ce que les cheveux longs la vieillissent!** long hair makes her look a lot older!

VPR se vieillir *(en apparence)* to make oneself look older; *(en mentant)* to lie about one's age *(by pretending to be older)*

vieillissant, -e [vjejisɑ̃, -ɑ̃t] **ADJ** ageing

vieillissement [vjejismɑ̃] **NM 1** *(naturel)* ageing, the ageing process; **le v. d'un réacteur/d'un vin/d'une population** the ageing of a reactor/of a wine/of a population; **les signes qui trahissent le v.** the telltale signs of age *or* of the ageing process; **retarder le v. de la peau** to slow down the ageing process of the skin **2** *(technique)* ageing; *(de meubles)* distressing **3** *(d'un fromage, d'un vin)* ageing, maturing

vieillot, -otte [vjejo, -ɔt] **ADJ** old-fashioned

vielle [vjɛl] **NF v. (à roue)** hurdy-gurdy

viendra *etc voir* **venir**

Vienne [vjɛn] **NM 1** *(en Autriche)* Vienna; **le congrès de V.** the Congress of Vienna **2** *(en France ▸ ville)* Vienne

NF la V. *(rivière)* the (river) Vienne; *(département)* Vienne

vienne *etc voir* **venir**

viennois, -e [vjenwa, -az] **ADJ 1** *(d'Autriche)* Viennese **2** *(de France)* of/from Vienne

• **Viennois, -e NM,F 1** *(en Autriche)* = inhabitant of or person from Vienna **2** *(en France)* = inhabitant of or person from Vienne

vient *etc voir* **venir**

vierge [vjɛrʒ] **ADJ 1** *(personne)* virgin; **il/elle est encore v.** he's/she's still a virgin; **une fille v.** a virgin

2 *(vide ▸ cahier, feuille)* blank, clean; *(▸ casier judiciaire)* clean; *(▸ pellicule, film)* unexposed; *(▸ cassette, ligne, espace)* blank; *(▸ disquette)* blank

3 *(inexploité ▸ sol, terre)* virgin; **de la neige v.** fresh snow

4 *Littéraire (pur)* pure, unsullied, uncorrupted; **un cœur v.** a pure heart; **v. de** devoid of, innocent of

NF *(femme)* virgin; *Fam* **jouer les vierges effarouchées** to go all squeamish; *Beaux-Arts* **une V. à l'enfant** a Madonna and child

Viêt-cong [vjetkɔ̃g] **NM** Vietcong, Viet Cong

Viêt-nam [vjetnam] **NM le V.** Vietnam; **le Nord/Sud V.** North/South Vietnam

vietnamien, -enne [vjɛtnamjɛ̃, -ɛn] **ADJ** Vietnamese

NM *(langue)* Vietnamese

• **Vietnamien, -enne NM,F** Vietnamese; **les Vietnamiens** the Vietnamese; **V. du Nord/Sud** North/South Vietnamese

VIEUX, VIEILLE [vjø, vjɛj]

> **vieil** is used before masculine singular nouns beginning with a vowel or h mute.

ADJ 1 *(âgé)* old; **sa vieille mère** her old *or* aged mother; **un vieil homme** an old *or* elderly man; **une vieille femme** an old *or* elderly woman; **les vieilles gens** old people, elderly people, the elderly; **un v. cheval/chêne** an old horse/oak; **être v.** to be old; **il n'est pas bien v.** he's not very old, he's still young; **50 ans, ce n'est pas v.!** 50 isn't old!; **devenir v.** to grow old, to get old; **vivre v.** *(personne, animal)* to live to be old, to live to a ripe old age; **se faire v.** to be getting on (in years), to be getting old; **ma voiture commence à se faire vieille** my car's starting to get a bit old; **pour ses v. jours** for one's old age; **être moins/plus v. que** to be younger/older than; **le plus v. des deux** the older *or* elder (of the two); **le plus v. des trois** the eldest *or* oldest of the three; **faire v.** to look old; **elle fait moins vieille que ça** she looks younger than that; **elle fait plus vieille que son âge** she looks older than she really is; **je me sens v.** I feel old; **être v. avant l'âge** to be old before one's time

2 *(avant le nom) (de longue date ▸ admirateur, camarade, complicité, passion)* old, long-standing; *(▸ famille, tradition)* old, ancient; *(▸ dicton, recette, continent, montagne)* old; **la vieille ville** the old (part of the) town; **connais-tu le v. Nice?** do you know the old part of Nice?; **l'une des plus vieilles institutions de notre pays** one of the most ancient *or* oldest institutions of our country; **la vieille Europe** Old Europe; **le V. Monde** the Old World

3 *(ancien ▸ bâtiment)* old, ancient; **c'est v. comme Hérode** *ou* **le Pont-Neuf** *ou* **le monde** it's as old as the hills, it goes back to the year dot

4 *(désuet ▸ instrument, méthode)* old; **c'est un tissu un peu v. pour une robe de fillette** this material is a bit old-fashioned for a little girl's dress; **une vieille expression** *(qui n'est plus usitée)* an obsolete turn of phrase; *(surannée)* an old-fashioned turn of phrase; *Ling* **le v. français** Old French

5 *(usé, fané)* old; **une malle pleine de vieilles photos et de vieilles lettres** a trunk full of old pictures and letters; **recycler les v. papiers** to recycle waste paper; **un v. numéro** *(de magazine)* a back copy *or* issue *or* number; **v. rose** old rose

6 *(précédent)* old; **sa vieille moto était plus belle** his/her old bike was nicer

7 *Fam (à valeur affectueuse)* **alors, mon v. chien?** how's my old doggy, then?; **le v. père Davril** old Davril; **v. farceur!** you old devil!

8 *Fam (à valeur dépréciative)* **il doit bien rester un v. bout de fromage** there must be an odd bit of cheese left over; **espèce de vieille folle!** you crazy old woman!; **v. dégoûtant!** you disgusting old man!

NM 1 *Fam Péj (homme âgé)* old man; **le v. ne vendra jamais** the old man will never sell; **un v. de la vieille** *(soldat de Napoléon)* an old veteran of Napoleon's guard; *(personne d'expérience)* an old hand

2 *très Fam (père)* old man; **mon/son v.** my/his/her old man

3 *Fam (à valeur affective ▸ entre adultes)* pal, *Br* mate, *Am* buddy; **comment ça va, v.?** how are you doing, pal *or Br* mate *or Am* buddy?; **allez, (mon) v., ça va s'arranger** come on *Br* mate *or Am* buddy, it'll be all right; **alors là, mon v., ce n'est pas mon problème** that's not my problem, pal *or Br* mate *or Am* buddy!; **j'en ai eu pour 500 euros – ben mon v.!** it cost me 500 euros – good heavens!

4 *(ce qui est ancien)* old things; **faire du neuf avec du v.** to turn old into new

5 *Fam (locutions)* **elle a pris un sacré coup de v.** she's looking a lot older[ᵃ]; **le film a pris un coup de v.** the film has dated[ᵃ]

ADV ça fait v.! it's really old-fashioned!; **s'habiller v.** to wear old-fashioned clothes; **elle s'habille plus v. que son âge** she dresses too old for *or* older than her age

NMPL *Péj* **1** *Fam (personnes âgées)* **les v.** old people[ᵃ]; **les petits v.** old folk; *très Fam* **elle dit qu'elle ne veut pas aller chez les v.** she says she doesn't want to go to an old people's *or* folks' home[ᵃ]

2 *très Fam (parents)* **les** *ou* **mes v.** my folks, my *Br* mum *or Am* mom and dad

• **vieille NF 1** *Fam Péj (femme âgée)* old woman *or* girl; **une petite vieille** a little old lady **2** *très Fam (mère)* old lady, *Br* old dear; **la vieille, ma/ta vieille** my/your old lady **3** *Fam (à valeur affective ▸ entre adultes)* **salut, ma vieille!** hi there!; **il est trop tard, ma vieille!** it's too late, darling!; **t'es gonflée, ma vieille!** *(exprime l'indignation)* you've got some nerve, you! **4** *Ich* **vieille (de mer)** wrasse

• **vieux de, vieille de ADJ** *(qui date de)* **c'est un manteau v. d'au moins 30 ans** it's a coat which is at least 30 years old; **une amitié vieille de 20 ans** a friendship that goes back 20 years

• **vieille fille,** *Belg* **vieille jeune fille NF** *Vieilli ou Péj* spinster, old maid; **rester vieille fille** to remain unmarried; **c'est une manie de vieille fille** it's an old-maidish thing to do

• **vieux beau NM** ageing Adonis, old roué

• **vieux garçon,** *Belg* **vieux jeune homme NM** *Vieilli ou Péj* bachelor; **rester v. garçon** to remain single *or* a bachelor; **des manies de v. garçon** bachelor ways

• **vieux jeu ADJ** *(personne, attitude)* old-fashioned; *(vêtements, idées)* old-fashioned, outmoded; **ce que tu peux être v. jeu!** you're so behind the times!

• **de vieux, de vieille ADJ** old-fashioned, antiquated; **tu as des idées de v.** you're so old-fashioned (in your ideas); **ce sont des hantises de v.** those are old people's obsessions

> Il faut noter qu'en anglais l'expression **old boy** ne désigne pas un vieux garçon mais un ancien élève d'un établissement scolaire privé.

VIF, VIVE [vif, viv]

ADJ	
• lively **1**	• sharp **2, 4, 5**
• quick **2**	• biting **3, 4**
• brusque **3**	• bright **4**
• strong **4**	• keen **4**
• deep **4**	• alive **6**
NM	
• quick **1**	

ADJ 1 *(plein d'énergie ▸ personne)* lively, vivacious; *(▸ musique, imagination, style)* lively; **d'un geste v., il saisit le revolver sur la table** he snatched the gun off the table; **avoir le regard v.** to have a lively look in one's eye; **marcher d'un pas v.** to walk briskly; **rouler à vive allure** to drive at great speed

2 *(intelligent ▸ élève)* sharp; *(▸ esprit)* sharp, quick; **être v. (d'esprit)** to be quick *or* quick-witted *or* sharp; **ce qu'elle est vive!** she's quick on the uptake!; *Euph* **il n'est pas très v.** he's not the sharpest knife in the drawer

3 *(emporté ▸ remarque, discussion, reproche)* cutting, biting; *(▸ geste)* brusque, brisk; **tu as été un peu trop v. avec elle** you were a bit curt *or* abrupt with her; **excusez-moi de ces mots un peu vifs** I apologize for having spoken rather sharply; **il y a eu un échange de paroles vives** there was a sharp exchange of words

4 *(très intense ▸ froid)* biting; *(▸ couleur)* bright, vivid; *(▸ désir, sentiment)* strong; *(▸ déception, intérêt)* keen; *(▸ félicitations, remerciements)* warm; *(▸ regret, satisfaction)* deep, great; *(▸ douleur)* sharp; **porter un v. intérêt à** to be greatly *or* keenly interested in; **avec un v. soulagement** with a profound sense of relief; **c'est avec un v. plaisir que...** it's with great pleasure that...; **éprouver un v. plaisir à faire qch** to take great pleasure in doing sth; **à feu v.** over a brisk heat; **l'air v. de la montagne** the sharp *or* bracing mountain air; **l'air est v. au bord de la mer** the sea air is bracing; **l'air est v. ce matin** it's chilly this morning

5 *(nu ▸ angle, arête)* sharp; *(▸ joint)* dry; *(▸ pierre)* bare

6 *(vivant)* **être brûlé/enterré v.** to be burnt/buried alive

7 *Hort (arbre, bois, haie)* quickset *(avant n)*

NM 1 *(chair vivante)* **tailler dans le v.** to cut into the flesh; **piquer qn au v.** to cut sb to the quick; **être piqué au v.** to be cut to the quick

2 *Fig (centre)* **trancher** *ou* **tailler dans le v.** to take drastic measures; **entrer dans le v. du sujet** to get to the heart of the matter

3 *Pêche* **pêcher au v.** to fish with live bait

4 *Jur* living person; **donation entre vifs** donation inter vivos

• **à vif ADJ** *(blessure)* open; **la chair était à v.** the flesh was exposed; **j'ai les nerfs à v.** my nerves are on edge

• **de vive voix ADV** personally; **je le lui dirai de vive voix** I'll tell him/her personally

• **sur le vif ADV** *(peindre)* from life; *(commenter)* on the spot; **une photo prise sur le v.** an action shot *or* photo; **ces photos ont été prises sur le v.** these photos were unposed

vif-argent [vifarʒɑ̃] *(pl* **vifs-argents) NM** quicksilver; **c'est du** *ou* **un v.** he's a bundle of energy

vigie [viʒi] **NF 1** *Rail* observation box; **v. de frein/signaux** brake/signal cabin **2** *Naut (balise)* danger-buoy; *Vieilli (guetteur)* look-out; **être de** *ou* en v. to be on look-out (duty) or on watch, to keep watch

vigilance [viʒilɑ̃s] NF vigilance, watchfulness; avec v. watchfully; redoubler de v. to increase one's vigilance; sa v. s'est relâchée he's/she's become less vigilant

vigilant, -e [viʒilɑ̃, -ɑ̃t] ADJ *(personne, regard)* vigilant, watchful; *(soins)* vigilant; soyez v.! watch out!; sous l'œil v. de leur mère under the (ever) watchful eye of their mother

vigile[1] [viʒil] NM 1 *(veilleur de nuit)* night watchman; *(surveillant)* guard 2 *Antiq* watch

> Il faut noter que le terme anglais **vigil** est un faux ami. Il ne signifie jamais **gardien**.

vigile[2] [viʒil] NF *Rel* vigil

vigne [viɲ] NF 1 *Agr* vine, grapevine; *(vignoble)* vineyard; la v. pousse bien par ici it's easy to grow vines around here; une région de vignes a wine-producing region; *Fig* être dans les vignes du Seigneur to be drunk; *Fig Littéraire* travailler à la v. du Seigneur to work in the Lord's vineyard 2 *Bot* v. vierge Virginia creeper

> Do not confuse with **vignoble**.

vigneau, -x [viɲo] NM winkle

vigneron, -onne [viɲərɔ̃, -ɔn] NM,F wine-grower, wine-producer

vignette [viɲɛt] NF 1 *Com* (manufacturer's) label; *(sur un médicament)* label or sticker *(for reimbursement within the French Social Security system)*
2 *Anciennement Admin & Aut* v. (auto ou automobile) *Br* ≃ (road) tax disc, *Am* ≃ (car) registration sticker
3 *Beaux-Arts (sur un livre, une gravure)* vignette
4 *Ordinat* thumbnail

vignettiste [viɲetist] NMF vignettist

vignoble [viɲɔbl] NM vineyard; le v. italien/alsacien the vineyards of Italy/Alsace; une région de vignobles a wine-growing area
ADJ région v. wine(-growing) area

> Do not confuse with **vigne**.

vignot [viɲo] = **vigneau**

vigogne [vigɔɲ] NF 1 *Zool* vicuna, vicuña 2 *(laine)* vicuna or vicuña (wool)

vigoureuse [vigurøz] *voir* **vigoureux**

vigoureusement [vigurøzmɑ̃] ADV *(frapper, frictionner)* vigorously, energetically; *(se défendre)* vigorously; *(protester)* forcefully

vigoureux, -euse [vigurø, -øz] ADJ 1 *(fort ▸ homme)* vigorous, sturdy; *(▸ membres)* strong, sturdy; *(▸ corps)* vigorous, robust; *(▸ arbre, plante)* sturdy; *(▸ santé)* robust; *(▸ poignée de main, répression)* vigorous; il est encore v.! he's still hale and hearty or going strong!; un coup de poing v. le renversa sur le trottoir a hefty punch knocked him flat on the *Br* pavement or *Am* sidewalk 2 *(langage, argument)* forceful; *(opposition, soutien)* strong; *(défense)* vigorous, spirited; *(contestation, effort)* vigorous, forceful, powerful; *(mesures)* energetic; opposer une résistance vigoureuse à *(projet, réforme)* to put up strong opposition to; elle opposa une résistance vigoureuse à son assaillant she put up a strong fight against her attacker, she tried hard to fight her attacker off

vigousse [vigus] ADJ *Suisse Fam (personne)* lively☐, bouncy; *(plante)* sturdy☐; être v. *(personne)* to be full of beans

vigueur [vigœr] NF 1 *(d'une personne, d'une plante)* strength, vigour; *(d'un coup)* vigour, strength, power; avec v. vigorously, energetically; le bon air lui a rendu un peu de sa v. the fresh air has perked him/her up a bit; reprendre de la v. to get some strength back 2 *(d'un style, d'une contestation)* forcefulness, vigour; *(d'un argument)* forcefulness; se défendre avec v. to defend oneself vigorously; protester avec v. to object forcefully; admirez la v. du trait look at how firmly drawn the lines are
• **en vigueur** ADJ *(décret, loi, règlement)* in force; *(tarif, usage)* current; cesser d'être en v. *(loi)* to lapse; *(règlement)* to cease to apply ADV entrer en v. *(décret, tarif)* to come into force or effect; cette mesure entrera en v. le 7 juillet this measure will come into effect on 7 July; cesser d'être en v. to lapse

VIH [veiaʃ] NM *Méd (abrév* virus de l'immunodéficience humaine) HIV

viking [vikiŋ] ADJ Viking
• **Viking** NMF Viking; les Vikings the Vikings

vil, -e [vil] ADJ 1 *Littéraire (acte, personne, sentiment)* base, vile, despicable; de viles calomnies foul calumnies
2 *(avant le nom) Littéraire (métier, condition)* lowly, humble
3 *(métal)* base *(avant n)*
4 *(locution)* à v. prix extremely cheap; il me l'a cédé à v. prix he let me have it for next to nothing

vilain, -e [vilɛ̃, -ɛn] ADJ 1 *(laid ▸ figure, personne)* ugly; *(▸ quartier)* ugly, sordid; *(▸ décoration, bâtiment, habit)* ugly, hideous; ils ne sont pas vilains du tout, tes dessins your drawings aren't bad at all; elle n'est pas vilaine she's not bad looking, she's not what you'd call ugly; un v. petit canard an ugly duckling
2 *(méchant)* naughty; tu es un v. petit garçon! you're a naughty boy!; c'est un v. monsieur he's a bad man; la vilaine bête, elle m'a mordu! that nasty beast has bitten me!; ce sont de vilaines gens they're a bad or nasty lot; ne dis pas ces vilains mots don't say those bad words; jouer un v. tour à qn to play a rotten or dirty trick on sb
3 *(sérieux ▸ affaire, coup, maladie)* nasty; une vilaine blessure a nasty or an ugly wound
4 *(désagréable ▸ odeur)* nasty, bad; *(▸ temps)* nasty, awful
NM,F bad or naughty boy, *f* girl; oh le v./la vilaine! you naughty boy/girl!
NM 1 *Hist* villein 2 *Fam (situation désagréable)* il va y avoir du v.! there's going to be trouble!; ça tourne au v.! things are getting nasty!

vilainement [vilɛnmɑ̃] ADV v. habillé shabbily dressed

vilebrequin [vilbrəkɛ̃] NM 1 *Tech* (bit) brace 2 *Aut* crankshaft

vilement [vilmɑ̃] ADV vilely, basely

vilenie [vileni] NF *Littéraire* 1 *(caractère)* baseness, villainy 2 *(action)* base or vile deed, villainous act

villa [vila] NF 1 *(résidence secondaire)* villa
2 *(pavillon)* (detached) house
3 *Antiq & Hist* villa
4 *(rue)* private road

village [vilaʒ] NM 1 *(agglomération, personnes)* village; v. de pêcheurs fishing village; *Écon* le v. global ou mondial ou planétaire the global village 2 *(centre de vacances)* v. (de vacances), v.-vacances *Br* holiday or *Am* vacation village; v. vacances famille = state-subsidized holiday village

villageois, -e [vilaʒwa, -az] ADJ village *(avant n)*, country *(avant n)*
NM,F villager, village resident

ville [vil] NF 1 *(moyenne)* town; *(plus grande)* city; dans les grandes villes in big cities; la seconde v. de France France's second city; la v. a voté à droite the town voted for the right; toute la v. en parle it's the talk of the town; à la v. comme à la scène in real life as (well as) on stage; v. d'eaux spa (town); la V. éternelle the Eternal City; v. industrielle industrial town; la V. lumière the City of Light; v. nouvelle new town; v. ouverte open city; *Rel* la V. sainte the Holy City; *Mktg* v. test test city; v. universitaire university town
2 *(quartier)* v. haute/basse upper/lower part of town
3 *Admin* la v. *(administration)* the local authority; *(représentants)* the (town) council; financé par la v. financed by the local authority; la V. de Paris the City of Paris
4 *(milieu non rural)* la v. towns, cities; les gens de la v. city-dwellers, townspeople; la vie à la v. town or city life; partir à la v. to go and live in a town/city
• **de ville** ADJ *(vêtements, chaussures)* chaussures de v. shoes for wearing in town; tenue de v. town clothes; *(sur une invitation)* lounge suit
• **en ville** ADV aller en v. *Br* to go to or into town, *Am* to go downtown; aller habiter en v. *(venant de la campagne)* to move to the city; *(venant de la banlieue)* to move *Br* to the town centre or *Am* downtown; et si nous dînions en v.? let's eat out tonight; trouver un studio en v. to find a *Br* flat or *Am* studio apartment in town

ville-champignon [vilʃɑ̃piɲɔ̃] *(pl* villes-champignons) NF fast-expanding town

villégiature [vileʒjatyr] NF *Br* holiday, *Am* vacation; être en v. to be on *Br* holiday or *Am* vacation; partir en v. to go on *Br* holiday or *Am* vacation; (lieu de) v. *Br* holiday resort, *Am* vacation resort

ville-satellite [vilsatelit] *(pl* villes-satellites) NF satellite town

villeux, -euse [vilø, -øz] ADJ *Bot, Méd & Zool* villous

villosité [vilozite] NF 1 *Anat* villosity; prélèvement des villosités choriales chorionic villus sampling 2 *(état)* hairiness; *(poils)* hair

Vilnius [vilnjys] NM Vilnius

vin [vɛ̃] NM 1 *(boisson)* wine; *(ensemble de récoltes)* vintage; ce sera une bonne année pour le v. it'll be a good vintage this year; le v. de 1959 the 1959 vintage; grand v., v. de grand cru vintage wine *Prov* quand le v. est tiré, il faut le boire you've made your bed and now you must lie in it; v. d'appellation d'origine contrôlée "appellation contrôlée" wine; v. blanc white wine; v. de Bordeaux *(rouge)* claret; *(blanc)* white Bordeaux; v. de Bourgogne Burgundy; v. chaud mulled wine; v. de coupage blended wine; v. du cru local wine; v. cuit fortified wine; v. délimité de qualité contrôlée medium-quality wine; v. délimité de qualité supérieure = label indicating quality of wine; v. de fruits fruit wine; v. gris pale rosé, *Am* blush wine; v. de messe altar or communion wine; v. mousseux sparkling wine; v. nouveau new wine; v. de paille straw wine; v. de pays local wine; v. pétillant sparkling wine; v. (de) primeur new wine; v. du Rhin hock; v. rosé rosé wine; v. rouge red wine; v. de table table wine avoir le v. gai/triste/mauvais to get merry/depressed/nasty after a few drinks; être entre deux vins to be tiddly or tipsy 2 *(liqueur)* v. de canne/riz cane/rice wine
• **vin d'honneur** NM reception *(where wine is served)*

vinaigre [vinɛgr] NM 1 *(condiment)* vinegar; cornichons/oignons au v. pickled gherkins/onions; v. d'alcool spirit/vinegar; v. balsamique balsamic vinegar; v. blanc distilled vinegar; v. de cidre cider vinegar; v. à l'estragon tarragon vinegar; v. de framboise raspberry vinegar; v. de vin wine vinegar 2 *Fam (locutions)* tourner au v. *(vin)* to turn sour☐; *(discussion, relation)* to turn sour; *(expédition, opération)* to go wrong☐; les choses ont tourné au v. things went wrong

vinaigrer [4] [vinegre] VT to add vinegar to; ce n'est pas assez vinaigré there's not enough vinegar in it; de l'eau vinaigrée water with a touch of vinegar added

vinaigrerie [vinɛgrəri] NF 1 *(fabrique)* vinegar factory 2 *(production)* vinegar making 3 *(commerce)* vinegar trade

vinaigrette [vinɛgrɛt] NF vinaigrette, French dressing; haricots à la ou en v. beans in vinaigrette or French dressing

vinaigrier [vinɛgrije] NM 1 *(bouteille)* vinegar bottle 2 *(fabricant)* vinegar maker or manufacturer

vinasse [vinas] NF *Fam Péj* cheap wine☐, *Br* plonk

vindicatif, -ive [vɛ̃dikatif, -iv] ADJ vindictive

vindicte [vɛ̃dikt] NF *Jur* la v. publique prosecution and punishment; désigner ou livrer qn à la v. populaire to expose sb to trial by the mob

vineux, -euse [vinø, -øz] ADJ 1 *(rappelant le vin ▸ couleur)* wine-coloured; *(▸ visage)* blotchy; *(▸ goût)* wine-like; *(▸ haleine)* which reeks of wine; *(▸ melon)* wine-flavoured; d'une couleur vineuse wine-coloured; une odeur vineuse a winy smell 2 région vineuse a rich wine-producing area

vingt [vɛ̃] ADJ 1 *(gén)* twenty; *Fig* je te l'ai dit v. fois! I've told you a hundred times!; il n'a pas encore v. ans he's not yet twenty, he's still in his teens; je n'ai plus v. ans!, je n'ai plus mon cœur de v. ans! I'm not as young as I used to be!; ah, si j'avais encore mes jambes/mon cœur de v. ans! if only I still had the legs/the heart of a twenty-year-old! 2 *(dans des séries)* twentieth; page/numéro v. page/number twenty

PRON twenty
NM INV 1 *(gén)* twenty 2 *(numéro d'ordre)* number twenty; **il a joué trois fois le v.** he played three times on number twenty 3 *(chiffre écrit)* twenty; *voir aussi* **cinquante**

ingtaine [vɛ̃tɛn] NF 1 *(quantité)* **une v.** around or about twenty, twenty or so; **une v. de voitures** around or about twenty cars; **elle a une v. d'années** she's around or about twenty (years old) 2 *(âge)* **avoir la v.** to be around or about twenty; **quand on arrive à** *ou* **atteint la v.** when you hit twenty

ingt-deux [vɛ̃tdø] ADJ twenty-two
NM INV twenty-two; *très Fam* **v. v'là les flics!** watch out, here come the cops!

ingt-et-un [vɛ̃teœ̃] ADJ twenty-one
NM INV twenty-one; *(jeu)* vingt-et-un, twenty-one, *Br* pontoon

ingtième [vɛ̃tjɛm] ADJ twentieth
NMF 1 *(personne)* twentieth 2 *(objet)* twentieth (one)
NM 1 *(partie)* twentieth 2 *(étage)* *Br* twentieth floor, *Am* twenty-first floor 3 *(arrondissement de Paris)* twentieth (arrondissement); *voir aussi* **cinquième**

ingtièmement [vɛ̃tjɛmmɑ̃] ADV in twentieth place

inicole [vinikɔl] ADJ *(pays)* wine-growing *(avant n)*; *(industrie, production)* wine *(avant n)*; **entreprise v.** *Br* wine-making company, *Am* winery

inifère [vinifɛr] ADJ wine-producing *(avant n)*, *Sout* viniferous

int *etc voir* **venir**

intage[1] [vɛ̃taʒ] NM *(porto)* vintage

intage[2] [vintɛdʒ] ADJ INV *(vêtements)* vintage
NM *(mode)* vintage

intimille [vɛ̃timij] NM Ventimiglia

inyle [vinil] NM vinyl; *Fam (disque)* record[□]; **c'est sorti sur v.** it came out on vinyl; **il rachète tous les vieux vinyles qu'il trouve** he buys all the old records he can find

ioc, vioque [vjɔk] NM,F *très Fam* 1 *(vieille personne)* old fossil, *Br* wrinkly, *Am* geezer 2 *(père, mère)* **la** *ou* **ma vioque** my old lady; **le** *ou* **mon v.** my old man; **les** *ou* **mes viocs** *Br* my old dears, *Am* my rents

iol [vjɔl] NM 1 *(d'une personne)* rape; **v. collectif** gang rape 2 *(d'un sanctuaire)* violation, desecration

violacé, -e [vjɔlase] ADJ purplish-blue; **un rouge v.** a purplish red; **les mains violacées par le froid** hands blue with cold; **prendre un teint v.** *(à cause du froid)* to go blue
• **violacées** NFPL *Bot* Violaceae

violacer [16] [vjɔlase] **se violacer** VPR *(visage)* to turn *or* to go *or* to become purple; *(mains)* to turn *or* to go *or* to become blue

violateur, -trice [vjɔlatœr, -tris] NM,F *(d'une loi, d'une constitution)* transgressor; *(d'un sanctuaire, d'une sépulture)* violator, desecrator

violation [vjɔlasjɔ̃] NF 1 *(d'une loi, d'une règle)* violation; *(d'un serment)* breach; *(d'un accord)* violation, breach; **agir en v. d'une règle** to act in contravention of a rule 2 *(d'un sanctuaire, d'une sépulture)* violation, desecration; **v. de domicile** forcible entry *(into somebody's home)*; **v. de sépulture** desecration of graves

violâtre [vjɔlatr] ADJ *Littéraire* purplish, blue

violatrice [vjɔlatris] *voir* **violateur**

viole [vjɔl] NF *Mus* viol, viola; **v. d'amour** viola d'amore; **v. de gambe** bass viol, viola da gamba

violemment [vjɔlamɑ̃] ADV *(frapper)* violently; *(protester, critiquer)* vehemently; *(désirer)* passionately; **il se jeta v. sur moi** he hurled himself at me

violence [vjɔlɑ̃s] NF 1 *(brutalité ▸ d'un affrontement, d'un coup, d'une personne)* violence; *(▸ d'un sport)* roughness, brutality; **avec v.** with violence, violently; **scène de v.** violent scene; **quand il est ivre, il est d'une grande v.** he gets very violent when he's drunk; **pour mesurer la v. de l'attaque** to realize how violent *or* brutal the attack was; **il tomba sous la v. du choc** the violence of the blow threw him to the ground; **le choc fut d'une v. inouïe** the impact was incredibly violent; **obliger qn à faire qch par la v.** to force sb to do sth by violent means; **répondre à la v. par la v.** to meet violence with violence; *Arch* **faire v. à une femme** to violate a woman; *Fig* **faire v. à** *(principes, sentiments)* to do violence to, to go against; **se faire v.** to force oneself 2 *(acte)* assault, violent act; **subir des violences** to be the victim of assault; **v. à** *ou* **sur agent** assault on (the person of) a police officer 3 *(intensité ▸ d'un sentiment, d'une sensation)* intensity; *(▸ d'un séisme, du vent)* violence, fierceness; *(▸ d'une confrontation)* fierceness; **le vent soufflait avec v.** the wind was raging

violent, -e [vjɔlɑ̃, -ɑ̃t] ADJ 1 *(brutal ▸ sport, jeu)* rough, brutal; *(▸ attaque, affrontement)* fierce, violent, brutal; *(▸ personne)* violent, brutal; *(▸ tempérament)* violent, fiery; **..., dit-il d'un ton v. ...**, he said violently 2 *(intense ▸ pluie)* driving *(avant n)*; *(▸ vent, tempête)* violent, raging; *(▸ couleur)* harsh, glaring; *(▸ parfum)* pungent, overpowering; *(▸ effort)* huge, strenuous; *(▸ besoin, envie)* intense, uncontrollable, urgent; *(▸ douleur)* violent; **un v. mal de tête** a splitting headache; **une violente douleur au côté** a shooting pain in one's side
NM,F violent person

violenter [3] [vjɔlɑ̃te] VT 1 *(femme)* to assault sexually; **elle a été violentée** she was sexually assaulted 2 *Littéraire (désir, penchant)* to do violence to, to go against; *(morale)* to do violence to; *(texte)* to distort

violer [3] [vjɔle] VT 1 *(personne)* to rape; **se faire v.** to be raped 2 *(loi, règle)* to violate; *(serment, promesse)* to break; *(accord, secret professionnel)* to violate, to break; *(secret)* to betray 3 *(sanctuaire, sépulture)* to violate, to desecrate; *Jur* **v. le domicile de qn** to force entry into sb's home; *Fig* **v. les consciences** to violate people's consciences

violet, -ette [vjɔle, -ɛt] ADJ purple; **ses mains violettes de froid** his/her hands blue with cold
NM purple
• **violette** NF *Bot* violet

violeur, -euse [vjɔlœr, -øz] NM,F rapist

violier [vjɔlje] NM *Bot* stock

violine [vjɔlin] ADJ dark purple

violon [vjɔlɔ̃] NM 1 *Mus (instrument ▸ d'orchestre)* violin; *(▸ de violoneux)* fiddle; **v. d'Ingres** hobby; *Fam* **accordez vos violons** make up your minds
2 *(artiste)* violin (player); **premier v. (solo)** first violin; **second v.** second violin
3 *Fam Arg crime (prison)* slammer, clink
4 *Tech* **(poulie à)** v. fiddle block
5 *Naut* **violons de mer** *(contre le roulis)* fiddles

violoncelle [vjɔlɔ̃sɛl] NM 1 *(instrument)* cello, *Spéc* violoncello 2 *(musicien)* cello (player), cellist

violoncelliste [vjɔlɔ̃selist] NMF cellist, cello player, *Spéc* violoncellist

violoneux [vjɔlɔnø] NM 1 *Péj* mediocre violinist 2 *(de musique traditionnelle)* fiddler

violoniste [vjɔlɔnist] NMF violinist, violin player

vioque [vjɔk] *voir* **vioc**

viorne [vjɔrn] NF *Bot* viburnum

VIP [viajpi, veipe] NMF *(abrév* **very important person***)* VIP

vipère [vipɛr] NF *Zool* adder, viper; *Fig Péj* **c'est une vraie v.** she's really vicious

vipereau, -x [vipro], **vipéreau, -x** [vipero] NM young viper

vipérin, -e [viperɛ̃, -in] ADJ *Zool* viperine
• **vipérine** NF 1 *Bot* viper's bugloss 2 *Zool* viperine snake

virage [viraʒ] NM 1 *(d'une route)* bend, curve, *Am* turn; **elle allait à 110 km/h dans les virages** she was taking the bends at 110 km/h; **prendre** *ou* **aborder un v.** to take a bend, to go round a bend; **prendre le v. à la corde** to hug the bend; **prendre un v. sur les chapeaux de roue** to take a bend *or* turn on two wheels; **v. en épingle à cheveux** hairpin bend; **v. en S** *Br* S-bend, *Am* S-curve; **v. sans visibilité** blind corner; **v. relevé** banked corner; **virages sur 5 km** *(sur panneau)* bends for 5 km
2 *(d'une piste de vitesse)* banked corner, bank
3 *(mouvement ▸ d'un véhicule, au ski)* turn; *Aviat* **faire un v. incliné** *ou* **sur l'aile** to bank; *Aviat* **angle de v.** angle of bank; *Ski* **v. parallèle** parallel turn
4 *Fig (changement ▸ d'attitude, d'idéologie)* (drastic) change *or* shift; *Pol* **v. à droite/gauche** shift to the right/left
5 *Phot* toning *(UNCOUNT)*
6 *Chim* change in colour
7 *Can* **v. ambulatoire** = Quebec government's policy of increasingly providing ambulatory care rather than hospitalization

virago [virago] NF *Péj* virago, shrew

viral, -e, -aux, -ales [viral, -o] ADJ viral; **maladie virale** viral infection *or* illness

virée [vire] NF *Fam* 1 *(promenade)* **faire une v. à vélo/en voiture** to go for a bicycle ride[□]/a drive[□]; **faire une v. dans les bars** *Br* to go on a pub crawl, *Am* to barhop; **si on faisait une v. dans les bars du coin?** let's hit the local bars 2 *(court voyage)* trip[□], tour[□], jaunt[□]; **on a fait une petite v. en Bretagne** we went for a little jaunt to Brittany

virelai [virlɛ] NM *Littérature* virelay

virement [virmɑ̃] NM 1 *Banque* transfer; **faire un v. de 200 euros sur un compte** to transfer 200 euros to an account; **v. automatique** automatic transfer; **v. bancaire** bank transfer; **v. par courrier** mail transfer; **v. de crédit** credit transfer; *Admin* **v. de fonds** = transfer (often illegal) of funds from one article of the budget to another; **v. interbancaire** interbank transfer; **v. postal** post office transfer; **v. SWIFT** SWIFT transfer; **v. télégraphique** cable transfer; **v. par télex** telex transfer 2 *Naut* **v. de bord** tacking

virer [3] [vire] VI 1 *(voiture)* to turn; *(vent)* to veer; *(grue)* to turn round; *(personne)* to turn *or* to pivot round; *Can Fig (changer d'allégeance)* to change sides; *Aut* **v. court** to corner sharply; *Aut* **v. sur place** to turn in one's own length; *Aviat* **v. sur l'aile** to bank; *Naut* **v. de bord** *(gén)* to veer; *(voilier)* to tack; *Fig* to take a new line *or* tack; *Naut* **faire v. un bateau** to veer a boat; *Naut* **paré à v.!** ready about!
2 *Chim (liquide)* to change colour; **encre qui vire au noir en séchant** ink that dries black; **la couleur est en train de v.** the colour is changing
3 *Phot* to tone
4 *Fam (devenir)* **v. homo** to turn gay; **v. voyou** to become *or* to turn into a thug
VT 1 *Banque* to transfer; **v. 300 euros sur un compte** to transfer 300 euros to an account
2 *Fam (jeter ▸ meuble, papiers)* to chuck (out), to ditch; **vire-moi ces journaux de là** get those papers out of there
3 *Fam (renvoyer ▸ employé)* to fire, *Br* to sack; *(▸ importun)* to kick out, to chuck out; **se faire v.** *(employé)* to get *Br* the sack *or Am* the bounce; **je me suis fait v. de chez moi** I got kicked *or* thrown out of my place
4 *Naut* to veer
5 *Phot* to tone
• **virer à** VT IND **v. à l'aigre** *(vin)* to turn sour; **v. au vert/rouge** to turn green/red
VPR **se virer** *Fam* **vire-toi de là!** shift yourself!

vireux, -euse [virø, -øz] ADJ *Bot* noxious, poisonous

virevolte [virvɔlt] NF 1 *(pirouette)* pirouette, twirl; **faire des virevoltes** to pirouette 2 *Fig (changement)* volte-face; **faire des virevoltes** to chop and change; **les virevoltes de la fortune** the sudden changes of fortune; **je m'attends à une v. de sa part** I expect he'll/she'll change his/her mind

virevolter [3] [virvɔlte] VI *(tourner sur soi)* to pirouette, to spin round; **il l'a fait v.** he spun him/her around

Virgile [virʒil] NPR Virgil

virginal, -e, -aux, -ales [virʒinal, -o] ADJ virginal, maidenly; *Littéraire* **d'une blancheur virginale** virgin white, lily-white
NM *(pl* **virginals***)* *Mus* virginals
• **virginale** NF *Mus* virginals

Virginie [virʒini] NF *Géog* **la V.** Virginia; **en V.** in Virginia; **la V.-Occidentale** West Virginia

virginité [virʒinite] NF *(d'une personne)* virginity; **perdre sa v.** to lose one's virginity; *Fig* **le parti devra se refaire une v.** the party will have to forge itself a new reputation

virgule [virgyl] NF 1 *(dans un texte)* comma; *Fig* **copier qch sans y changer une v.** to copy sth out without a single alteration; **c'est ce qu'il a dit à la v. près** that's word for word what he said **2** *Math* (decimal) point; **4 v. 9** 4 point 9; **v. flottante** floating comma; *Ordinat* **v. fixe** fixed point

viril, -e [viril] ADJ **1** *(propre à l'homme)* male; *(force, langage)* manly, virile; *(allure, démarche)* masculine **2** *(sexuellement)* virile

virilement [virilmɑ̃] ADV in a manly way

virilisant, -e [virilizɑ̃, -ɑ̃t] ADJ causing the development of male sexual characteristics

viriliser [3] [virilize] VT **1** *Biol (sujet: médicament)* to cause the development of male sexual characteristics in **2** *(en apparence ▸ sujet: sport)* to make more masculine in appearance

virilité [virilite] NF **1** *(gén)* virility, manliness; **se sentir menacé/attaqué dans sa v.** to feel that one's manhood is being threatened/attacked **2** *(vigueur sexuelle)* virility

virole [virɔl] NF *(d'une canne, d'un manche)* ferrule

viroler [3] [virɔle] VT *(canne, manche)* to fit with a ferrule

virologie [virɔlɔʒi] NF *Biol & Méd* virology

virologiste [virɔlɔʒist], **virologue** [virɔlɔg] NMF *Biol & Méd* virologist

virose [viroz] NF *Méd* virus disease, virosis

virtualité [virtɥalite] NF **1** *(gén)* potentiality **2** *Ordinat, Opt & Phys* virtuality

virtuel, -elle [virtɥɛl] ADJ **1** *(fait, valeur)* potential **2** *Ordinat, Opt & Phys* virtual

virtuellement [virtɥɛlmɑ̃] ADV **1** *(potentiellement)* potentially **2** *(très probablement)* virtually, to all intents and purposes, practically

> Il faut noter que l'adverbe anglais **virtually** ne s'emploie jamais dans le sens de **potentiellement**.

virtuose [virtɥoz] NMF *Mus* virtuoso; **v. du violon** violin virtuoso; **c'est une v. du tennis/de l'aiguille** she's a brilliant tennis player/needlewoman

virtuosité [virtɥozite] NF virtuosity; **elle a joué la fugue avec une grande v.** she gave a virtuoso rendering of the fugue; **manier le pinceau avec v.** to be a brilliant painter

virulence [virylɑ̃s] NF **1** *(d'un reproche, d'un discours)* virulence, viciousness, venom **2** *Méd* virulence

virulent, -e [virylɑ̃, -ɑ̃t] ADJ **1** *(critique, discours)* virulent, vicious, venomous; *(haine)* burning, bitter; **faire une critique virulente de qch** to criticize sth venomously **2** *Méd (agent, poison)* virulent

virure [viryr] NF *Naut* strake

virus [virys] NM **1** *Biol & Méd* virus; **v. Ebola** Ebola virus; **v. de la grippe** flu virus; **v. d'immunodéficience humaine** human immunodeficiency virus; *Fam* **il y a un v. qui traîne** *ou* **dans l'air** there's a virus going around **2** *Fig* **tout le pays était atteint par le v. du loto** the whole country was gripped by lottery fever; *Fam* **elle a attrapé le v. du deltaplane** she's completely hooked on hang-gliding, she's got the hang-gliding bug; **pour ceux qui ont le v. de la photo** for photography enthusiasts **3** *Ordinat* virus; **désactiver un v.** to disable a virus

vis [vis] NF *Tech* screw; **v. d'Archimède** Archimedes' screw; **v. d'arrêt** *ou* **de blocage** stop screw; **v. à bois** woodscrew; **v. à droite/à gauche** right-handed/left-handed screw *or* thread; **v. sans fin** worm *or* endless screw; **v. hexagonale** hexagon screw; **v. à métaux** metal screw; **v. à oreilles** *ou* **à ailettes** wing screw; *Aut* **v. platinée** contact point; **v. à pointe ronde** ball-ended screw; **v. de purge** bleeder screw, bleed screw; **v. de réglage** adjuster screw, adjusting screw; **v. de serrage** setscrew; **v. sans tête** grub screw; **v. à tête cylindrique** cheese-head(ed) screw; **v. à tête fraisée** countersunk (head) screw; **v. à tête ronde** round-head(ed) screw; **tige à v.** screwed *or* threaded rod

visa [viza] NM **1** *(sur un passeport)* visa; **demander/obtenir un v.** to apply for/obtain a visa; **un v. pour l'Australie** a visa for Australia; **v. d'entrée/de sortie** entry/exit visa; **v. de touriste** *ou* **de visiteur** *Br* tourist *or Am* non-immigrant visa; **v. de transit** transit visa **2** *(sur un document)* stamp; **apposer un v. sur** to stamp; *Cin* **v. de censure** (censor's) certificate; **v. d'exploitation** exploitation licence **3** *(paraphe ▸ d'un supérieur)* initials

visage [vizaʒ] NM **1** *(d'une personne)* face; **au v. rond** round-faced; **au v. ovale** with an oval-shaped face; **homme au v. agréable** pleasant-faced man; **frapper qn au v.** to hit sb in the face; **elle a un v. de bébé** *ou* **d'enfant** she has a baby face; **il n'avait plus v. humain** he was completely disfigured; **j'aime voir de nouveaux visages** I like to see new faces *or* to meet new people; **il y avait des visages connus** there were some familiar faces; **je n'arrive pas à mettre un nom sur ce v.** I can't put a name to that face; **c'est le nouveau v. de Lancôme** she's the new face of Lancôme; *Fig* **faire bon v. à qn** to put on a show of friendliness for sb; *Fig* **à v. découvert** *(sans masque)* unmasked; *(sans voile)* unveiled; *(ouvertement)* openly; *Fig* **à deux visages** two-faced; *Fig* **sans v.** faceless

2 *(aspect)* aspect; **l'Afrique aux multiples visages** the many faces of Africa; **enfin une ville à v. humain!** at last a town made for people to live in!; **pour un socialisme à v. humain** for socialism with a human face; **le vrai v. de** *(la nature de)* the true nature *or* face of; **elle révélait enfin son vrai v.** she was revealing her true self *or* nature at last; **il nous montre le vrai v. du fascisme** he shows us the true face of fascism; **présenter un pays sous un autre** *ou* **nouveau v.** to present a country in a new light

• **Visage pâle** NM paleface

visagiste [vizaʒist] NMF facialist; **coiffeur-v.** hair stylist

vis-à-vis [vizavi] NM INV **1** *(personne en face)* **mon v.** the person opposite me; **au dîner, j'avais le président pour v.** at dinner, I was seated opposite the president; **faire v. à qn** to be opposite sb, to face sb; **le passager qui lui faisait v.** the passenger who was sitting opposite him/her

2 *(lieu, immeuble qui fait face)* **nous avons le lac pour v.** we look out on to *or* face the lake; **nous n'avons pas de v.** there are no buildings directly opposite

3 *(canapé)* tête-à-tête

4 *(entretien)* tête-à-tête, meeting

• **vis-à-vis de** PRÉP **1** *(en face de)* **être v. de qn** to be opposite sb; **les statues sont v. l'une de l'autre** the statues are opposite *or* facing one another

2 *(envers)* towards, vis-à-vis; **ce n'est pas très juste v. du reste de la famille** it's not very fair to the rest of the family; **mes sentiments v. de lui** my feelings towards *or* for him; **être sincère v. de soi-même** to be truthful with oneself; **quelle position avez-vous v. de ce problème?** what is your position on this problem?

3 *(par rapport à)* by comparison with, next to, against; **le dollar se tient bien v. des autres monnaies** the dollar is firm against the other currencies

• **en vis-à-vis** ADV **être en v.** to be opposite each other, to be facing each other; **assis en v.** sitting opposite each other *or* face-to-face

viscéral, -e, -aux, -ales [viseral, -o] ADJ **1** *Anat* visceral **2** *Fig (dégoût)* profound; *(peur)* deep-rooted, profound; *(jalousie)* pathological; *(réaction)* gut *(avant n)*; *(répulsion)* instinctive; **je ne l'aime pas, c'est v.** I don't like him/her, it's a gut feeling

viscère [visɛr] NM *Anat* viscus; **viscères** viscera

viscose [viskoz] NF viscose; **robe en v.** viscose dress

viscosité [viskozite] NF *(gén) & Phys* viscosity

visée [vize] NF **1** *(gén pl) (intention)* design, aim; **avoir des visées sur qn/qch** to have designs on sb/sth **2** *Mil* aiming *(UNCOUNT)*, taking aim *(UNCOUNT)*, sighting; **ligne de v.** line of sight; **point de v.** target **3** *Cin & Phot* viewfinding

viser¹ [3] [vize] VT **1** *Mil (cible)* to (take) aim at; *(jambe, tête)* to aim for; **bien visé!** good shot!

2 *(aspirer à ▸ poste)* to set one's sights on, to aim for; *(▸ résultats)* to aim at *or* for; **il vise ce poste depuis longtemps** he's had his eye on this job for a long time

3 *Com (cibler ▸ clientèle, public)* to target

4 *(concerner ▸ sujet: réforme)* to be aimed *or* directed at; *(▸ sujet: critique)* to be aimed *or* directed at, to be meant for; **cette loi vise plusieurs catégories de gens** this law is directed at several categories of people; **les denrées alimentaires ne sont pas visées par ce décret** foodstuffs are not affected by this order; **qui visais-tu par cette remarque?** who was your remark aimed *or* directed at?; **vous parlez de licenciements, qu exactement est visé?** you're talking about lay-offs *or Br* redundancies, who exactly do you have in mind?; **je ne vise personne!** I don't mean anybody in particular!; **se sentir visé** to feel one is being got at

5 *Fam (regarder)* to check out; **dis donc, vise un peu la chemise!** wow, check out the shirt!; **vise un peu la fille!** check her out!, get a load of her!

6 *Golf* **v. la balle** to address the ball

VI **1** *Mil* to (take) aim; **v. juste/trop bas** to aim accurately/too low **2** *Fig* **v. (trop) haut** to set one's sights *or* to aim (too) high; **tu as visé juste en lu disant cela!** you didn't miss the mark when you said that to him/her!

• **viser à** VT IND *(sujet: politique, personne)* to aim at; **v. à faire qch** to aim at doing sth; **mesures visant à faire payer les pollueurs** measures aimed at making the polluters pay

viser² [3] [vize] VT *Admin (passeport)* to visa *(document ▸ gén)* to stamp; *(▸ avec ses initiales)* to initial; *Compta* **v. les livres de commerce** to certify the books; *Fin* **v. un effet** to stamp a bill

viseur [vizœr] NM **1** *(gén)* sight, sights; *(à lunette)* telescopic sight **2** *Opt* telescopic sight **3** *Cin & Phot* viewfinder

visibilité [vizibilite] NF visibility; **la v. est très réduite par le brouillard** visibility has been greatly reduced by the fog; *Aviat* **vol sans v.** instrument flying; **atterrir sans v.** to make a blind landing, to land blind; **v. nulle** zero visibility; *Aut* **v. panoramique** all-round visibility; *Aut* **v. de trois-quarts** three-quarter vision

visible [vizibl] ADJ **1** *(objet)* visible; **v. à l'œil nu** visible to the naked eye; **v. au microscope** visible under a microscope; **la tache est encore bien v** the stain is still visible, you can still see the stain; **à peine v.** barely visible

2 *(évident ▸ gêne, intérêt, mépris)* obvious, visible; *(▸ amélioration, différence)* visible, perceptible; **elle m'en veut, c'est v.** she resents me, it's obvious; **il est v. que...** it's obvious *or* clear that... **prendre un v. plaisir à faire qch** to take obvious pleasure in doing sth

3 *(prêt à recevoir)* **elle est v. de midi à 4 heures** she receives visitors between 12 and 4; *Hum* **je ne serai pas v. demain** I won't be available to callers tomorrow; *Hum* **n'entre pas, je ne suis pas v.** don't come in, I'm not decent

4 *(pouvant être visité)* **l'appartement est v. le matin** the *Br* flat *or Am* apartment can be viewed in the morning

NM **le v.** that which is visible

visiblement [vizibləmɑ̃] ADV *(gêné, mécontent)* obviously, visibly; *(amélioré)* perceptibly, visibly; **v., ils se connaissaient déjà** they'd obviously met before

visière [vizjɛr] NF *(gén) Br* eyeshade, *Am* vizor; *(d'un casque)* visor, vizor; *(d'une casquette)* peak; **mettre sa main en v.** to shade one's eyes with one's hand; **v. de protection** faceguard

visioconférence [vizjokɔ̃ferɑ̃s] NF *(conférence)* videoconference; *(concept)* videoconferencing

vision [vizjɔ̃] NF **1** *(idée)* view, outlook; **nous n'avons pas la même v. des choses** we see things differently; **nous partageons la même v. du monde/de la vie** we see *or* view the world/life in the same way; **sa v. idéaliste du mariage** his/her idealistic view of married life; **sa v. du monde** his/her world view

2 *(d'un créateur)* vision, imagination

3 *(image)* vision; *(hallucination)* vision, apparition; **une épouvantable v. de notre avenir** a nightmarish vision of our future; **avoir des visions** *(hallucinations)* to have visions *or* hallucinations, to see things; *Fam Hum* **tu as des visions!** you're seeing things!

4 *Physiol* vision

visionnaire [vizjɔnɛr] ADJ visionary

NMF visionary, dreamer

visionnement [vizjɔnmɑ̃] NM *TV & Cin* screening; **v. préalable** preview

visionner [3] [vizjɔne] VT *(film, émission)* to view; *(diapositives)* to look at

visionneuse [vizjɔnøz] NF viewer

Visiopass® [vizjɔpɑs] NM *TV* = decoding card for French pay channels

visiophone [vizjɔfɔn] NM videophone, viewphone

visiophonie [vizjofɔni] NF video teleconferencing

visitandine [vizitɑ̃din] NF *(religieuse)* nun of the Order of the Visitation, Visitandine

Visitation [vizitasjɔ̃] NF *Rel & Beaux-Arts* **la V.** the Visitation

visite [vizit] NF **1** *(chez quelqu'un ▸ gén)* visit; *(▸ courte)* call; *(▸ d'un représentant)* call; **avoir** *ou* **recevoir la v. de qn** to have a visit from sb; **avoir la v. de la police** to receive a visit from the police; **avoir la v. d'un représentant** to be called on by a rep; **nous avons eu la v. de Marc** Marc called in to see us; **je m'attendais à sa v.** I was expecting him/her to call; **rendre v. à qn** to pay sb a visit, to call on sb, to visit sb; **rendre sa v. à qn** to return sb's visit *or* call; **faire une petite v. à qn** to pop round and see sb; **être en v. chez qn** to be paying sb a visit, to be visiting sb *or Am* with sb; **v. d'affaires** business call; **v. éclair** flying visit; *Com* **v. à froid** cold call; **v. officielle/privée** official/private visit; **v. de politesse** courtesy call *or* visit; *Com* **v. de relance** follow-up visit

2 *(à l'hôpital, auprès d'un détenu)* visit; **heures de v.** visiting hours

3 *(visiteur)* **avoir de la v.** to have a visitor; *Fam* **tu attends de la** *ou* **une v.?** are you expecting a visitor *or* somebody?

4 *(exploration ▸ d'un lieu)* visit, tour; *(▸ d'une ville)* sightseeing tour; **v. guidée** guided tour; **v. pédagogique** educational visit

5 *(d'un médecin ▸ chez le patient)* visit, call; *(▸ dans un hôpital)* (ward) round; **le chirurgien fait sa v. tous les matins** the surgeon does his (ward) round every morning; **le docteur ne fait pas de visites** the doctor doesn't make house calls; **v. de contrôle** follow-up examination; **v. à domicile** house call *or* visit; **v. médicale** medical *or Am* physical examination, medical, *Am* physical; **passer une v. médicale** to undergo a medical examination, *Am* to take a physical examination; **tu as passé la v.?** did you have your medical *or Am* physical?; *Mil* have you seen the MO?

6 *(inspection ▸ pour acheter)* viewing; *(▸ pour surveiller)* inspection; **v. domiciliaire** house search; **v. d'inspection** visitation, visit; **faire une v. d'inspection de** to visit

7 *Rel* **v. pastorale** *ou* **de l'évêque** pastoral visit, visitation *(by bishop)*

visiter [3] [vizite] VT **1** *(se promener dans ▸ région, monument)* to visit; *(▸ caves, musée)* to go round, to visit; *(▸ pour acheter)* to view; *(▸ par curiosité)* to look round; **v. une cathédrale** to visit *or* tour a cathedral; **on nous a fait v. l'usine** we were shown round *or* over the factory, we were given a tour of the factory; **une personne de l'agence vous fera v. l'appartement** somebody from the agency will show you round *or Am* through the *Br* flat *or Am* apartment; **elle m'a fait v. sa maison** she showed me around her house; *Hum* **nous avons déjà été visités une fois** *(on nous a déjà cambriolés)* we've been burgled once already

2 *(rendre visite à ▸ détenu)* to visit; *(▸ malade, indigent)* to visit, to call on; *(▸ client)* to call on

3 *(inspecter ▸ matériel, valise)* to examine, to inspect; *(▸ bateau)* to inspect

4 *Rel (sujet: Saint-Esprit)* to visit

VPR **se visiter** to be open to visitors; **le musée se visite en deux heures** it takes two hours to go round the museum

visiteur, -euse [vizitœr, -øz] NM,F **1** *(invité)* visitor, caller; *(d'un musée)* visitor; *Hum* **ils ont eu des visiteurs la nuit dernière** *(voleurs, souris)* they had visitors last night

2 *(professionnel)* **v. des douanes** customs inspector; **v. de prison** prison visitor; **visiteuse scolaire** *ou* **sociale** = social worker who specializes in visiting schools in the interests of child welfare

3 *Com* representative, rep; **v. médical** representative in pharmaceutical products, medical representative

4 *Mktg* **v. unique** unique visitor

• **visiteurs** NMPL *Sport* visiting *or* away team

vison [vizɔ̃] NM **1** *Zool* mink **2** *(fourrure)* mink **3** *(manteau)* mink (coat)

visonnière [vizɔnjɛr] NF mink farm

visqueux, -euse [viskø, -øz] ADJ **1** *Phys (matière)* viscous; *(surface)* viscid **2** *Fig (personne)* slimy

vissage [visaʒ] NM *(d'un écrou, d'un couvercle, d'un bouchon)* screwing on; *(d'une planche sur un support)* screwing down

vissé [vise] ADJ *Fam* **être bien v.** *(de bonne humeur)* to be in a good mood□; **être mal v.** *(de mauvaise humeur)* to be in a foul mood

visser [3] [vise] VT **1** *(fixer ▸ planche, support)* to screw on *or* to; *(▸ couvercle)* to screw on *or* down; **le miroir est vissé au mur** the mirror is screwed to the wall; *Fig* **un chapeau vissé sur la tête** with a hat clamped on his/her head; **être vissé sur son siège** to be glued to one's chair **2** *(en tournant ▸ bouchon, embout, écrou)* to screw on **3** *Fam (personne)* to crack down on, to put the screws on; **il a toujours vissé ses gosses** he always kept a tight rein on his kids

VPR **se visser** to screw on *or* in; **ampoule qui se visse** screw-in bulb; **la lance se visse au bout du tuyau** the nozzle screws on to the end of the hose; **le couvercle se visse facilement/mal** the lid screws on easily/doesn't screw on properly

visualisation [vizɥalizasjɔ̃] NF **1** *(mentale)* visualization, visualizing **2** *Ordinat* display; **console** *ou* **écran de v.** visual display terminal *or* unit, VDU; **v. de la page à l'écran** page preview; **v. sur écran** soft copy

visualiser [3] [vizɥalize] VT **1** *(mentalement)* to visualize **2** *(rendre visible)* to make visible to the eye; *Ordinat* to display

visualiseur [vizɥalizœr] NM *Ordinat* viewer

visuel, -elle [vizɥɛl] ADJ *(mémoire, support)* visual

NM **1** *Ordinat* visual display unit *or* terminal, VDU **2** *(d'une affiche)* artwork **3** *(publicité)* visual

visuellement [vizɥɛlmɑ̃] ADV visually

vit 1 *voir* **vivre**[2] **2** *voir* **voir**

vital, -e, -aux, -ales [vital, -o] ADJ **1** *Biol & Physiol* vital **2** *(indispensable)* vital, essential; **l'agriculture est vitale pour notre région** agriculture is vital to this region; **il est v. que...** it's vital *or* essential that...; *Fam* **il faut que tu viennes, c'est v.!** you must come, it's vital!, you absolutely must come! **3** *(fondamental ▸ problème, question)* vital, fundamental

vitalisme [vitalism] NM *Phil* vitalism

vitalité [vitalite] NF *(d'une personne)* vitality, energy; *(d'une économie)* dynamism, vitality, buoyancy; *(d'une expression, d'une théorie)* vitality; **être plein de v.** to be full of energy

vitamine [vitamin] NF vitamin; **la v. A/B12** vitamin A/B12; **alimentation riche/pauvre en vitamines** food with a high/low vitamin content, food that is high/low in vitamins; **enfant qui manque de vitamines** child with a vitamin deficiency; **as-tu pris tes vitamines?** have you taken your vitamins?

vitaminé, -e [vitamine] ADJ with added vitamins, vitaminized

vitaminique [vitaminik] ADJ vitamin *(avant n)*

vite [vit] ADV **1** *(rapidement ▸ courir, marcher)* fast, quickly; *(▸ se propager)* rapidly, quickly; **roule moins v.** slow down, don't drive so fast; **va plus v.** speed up, go faster; **plus v.!** faster!; **ne va pas si v.!** *(en voiture)* not so fast!, slow down a bit!; **tout s'est passé si v. que je n'ai pas eu le temps de voir** everything happened so quickly that I didn't see a thing; **comme le temps passe v.!** doesn't time fly!; **elle apprend/travaille v.** she's a quick learner/worker; **il calcule v.** he's quick at calculations; **prenons un taxi, ça ira plus v.** let's take a taxi, it'll be quicker; **les exercices vont trop v. pour moi** I can't keep up *or* keep pace with the exercises; **ça a été v. réglé** it was settled in no time at all, it was soon settled; **je me suis v. rendu compte que...** I soon *or* quickly *or* swiftly realized that...; **fais v.!** hurry up!, be quick (about it)!; **tu retournes en ville? – je fais v.** are you going back into town? – I won't be long; **v., il arrive!** quick *or* hurry up, he's coming!; **va faire tes devoirs, et plus v. que cela!** go and do your homework, and get a move on *or* and be quick about it!; *Fam* **v. fait** quickly□; **avoir v. fait de faire qch** to be quick (about) doing sth; **tu auras v. fait de t'en apercevoir** you'll soon realize□; **il eut v. fait de s'habiller** he was dressed in no time; **boire un coup v. fait** to have a quick drink□; **range-moi ta chambre v. fait!** tidy up your room and be quick about it!; **il est parti v. fait!** he cleared off without wasting too much time; **tu vas aller au lit v. fait si tu continues à pleurer!** you'll be in bed in no time at all if you carry on crying!; **ça a été du v. fait!** it didn't take long!□, that was quick work!; *Péj* it's slapdash work!□; *Fam* **faire qch v. fait, bien fait** to do sth in next to no time; **on lui a repeint sa grille v. fait, bien fait** we gave his/her gate a nice new coat of paint in no time; *Fig* **aller plus v. que la musique** *ou* **les violons** to jump the gun

2 *(à la hâte)* quickly, in a hurry *or* rush; **manger v.** to bolt one's food (down); **manger trop v.** to eat too fast *or* too quickly; **je vais v. faire une course** I'm going to do one quick errand; **tu vas un peu v.!** you're a bit hasty!; **ils vont gagner – c'est v. dit!** they're going to win – I wouldn't be so sure!; **parler trop v.** to speak too soon

3 *(sans tarder)* quickly, soon; **il faut agir v.** we must do something quickly *or* very soon; **vous serez v. guéri** you'll soon be better; **réponds-moi aussi v. que tu peux** answer me as quickly as you can *or* as soon as possible; **envoyez v. votre bulletin-réponse!** send your entry form now!; **viens v. nous retrouver au bord de la mer!** come and join us at the seaside soon!; **lève-toi v., on sonne!** get up quick, there's someone at the door!; **j'ai v. compris de quoi il s'agissait** I soon realized what it was all about, it didn't take me long to realize what it was all about

4 *(facilement)* quickly, easily; **elle s'énerve v.** she loses her temper easily; **méfie-toi, il a v. fait de s'énerver** be careful, he loses his temper easily; **on a v. fait de dire...** it's easy to say...; **on a v. fait de se brûler avec ça!** it's easy to burn yourself on that thing!

5 *(locution)* **aller v. en besogne** *(être rapide)* to be a quick worker; *(être trop pressé)* to be overhasty; **tu vas l'épouser? tu vas v. en besogne!** so you're marrying him/her? you didn't waste any time!

ADJ *(en langage journalistique ▸ coureur)* fast

• **au plus vite** ADV as soon as possible

vitellus [vitelys] NM *Biol* vitellus, yolk

vitesse [vitɛs] NF **1** *(d'un coureur, d'un véhicule)* speed; **à la v. de 180 km/h** at (a speed of) 180 km/h; **la v. est limitée à 90 km/h** the speed limit is 90 km/h; **à quelle v. rouliez-vous?** what speed were you driving at *or* doing?; **rouler à une v. folle** to drive at breakneck speed; **faire de la v.** to drive *or* to go fast; **prendre de la v.** to pick up speed, to speed up; **gagner/perdre de la v.** to gather/to lose speed; *aussi Fig* **v. de croisière** cruising speed; **nous avons atteint notre v. de croisière qui est de 750 km/h** *(en avion)* we're now cruising at (a speed of) 750 km/h; **le projet a maintenant atteint sa v. de croisière** the project is now running smoothly along; **v. de pointe** top *or* maximum speed; *Aviat* **v. relative** airspeed; **gagner** *ou* **prendre qn de v.** *(à pied)* to walk faster than sb; *(en voiture)* to go *or* to drive faster than sb; *Fig* to beat sb to it

2 *Phys (d'un corps)* speed, velocity; *(de la lumière)* speed; **v. acquise** momentum; **v. initiale** *(gén)* initial speed; *Mil* muzzle speed; **v. moyenne** average speed; **v. de réaction** reaction velocity *or* speed; **la v. du son** the speed of sound; **à la v. du son** at the speed of sound

3 *(rythme ▸ d'une action)* speed, quickness, rapidity; *(▸ d'une transformation)* speed, rapidity; **ses cheveux poussent à une v. incroyable!** his/her hair grows so fast!; **il travaille à la v. d'un escargot!** he works at a snail's pace!

4 *Aut & Tech* gear; **première/deuxième/troisième v.** first/second/third gear; **changer de v.** to change gear; **passer les vitesses** to go up through the gears; *(en rétrogradant)* to go down through the gears; **passer à la v. supérieure** to change up *(to next gear)*; *Fig* **médecine/sécurité sociale à deux vitesses** two-tier medical/social security system; **une Europe à deux vitesses** a two-speed Europe; *Fam* **à la v. grand V** at the double, *Br* at a rate of knots; **et ramène-le moi à la v. grand V!** and bring it back to me PDQ!

5 *Ordinat* **v. d'accès** access speed; **v. d'affichage** display speed; **v. de calcul** processing *or* computing speed; **v. de clignotement** blink rate; **v. d'écriture** write speed; **v. d'exécution** execution speed; **v. de frappe** keying speed; **v. de frappe à la minute/à l'heure** keystrokes per minute/per hour; **v. d'horloge** clock rate *or* speed; **v. d'impression** print speed; **v. du processeur** processor speed; **v. de traitement** processing speed; **v. de transfert** transfer speed

6 *Physiol* **v. de sédimentation** erythrocyte sedimentation rate

• **à toute vitesse** ADV in double-quick time; **aller à toute v.** to go at full *or* top speed, to rush along, **il est revenu à toute v.** he was back double quick; **passer à toute v.** *(temps, moto)* to fly by

• **en vitesse** ADV *(rapidement)* quickly; *(à la hâte)* in a rush *or* hurry; **déjeuner/se laver en v.** to have a quick lunch/wash; **écrire une lettre en v.** to dash off a letter; **un petit mot en v. pour vous dire...** just a quick line to let you know...; **je peux venir te voir en v.?** can I pop in for a minute?; **on prend un verre en v.?** shall we have a quick drink?; **sors d'ici, et en v.!** get out of here and be sharp about it!; **fais ton lit, et en v.!** make your bed and do it quickly!

viticole [vitikɔl] ADJ **région v.** wine-growing *or* wine-producing region; **entreprise v.** *Br* wine-making company, *Am* winery; **culture v.** wine-growing, *Spéc* viticulture; **industrie v.** wine industry

viticulteur, -trice [vitikyltœr, -tris] NM,F wine-grower, wine-producer, *Spéc* viticulturist

viticulture [vitikyltyr] NF vine-growing, *Spéc* viticulture

vitiligo [vitiligo] NM *Méd* vitiligo, leucoderma

vitrage [vitraʒ] NM **1** *(vitres)* windows; *(panneau)* glass partition

2 *(verre)* window glass

3 *(installation)* glazing

4 *(rideau)* net curtain

vitrail, -aux [vitraj, -o] NM **1** *(gén)* stained-glass window; *(non coloré)* leaded glass window **2** *(technique)* **le v.** stained-glass window making

vitre [vitr] NF **1** *(plaque de verre)* (window) pane **2** *(fenêtre)* window; **produit pour les vitres** glass- *or* window-cleaning product; **faire les vitres** to clean the windows; *Fam* **casser les vitres** to get angry[□], to kick up a fuss; *Aut* **v. arrière** rear window

vitré, -e [vitre] ADJ **1** *(porte ▸ complètement)* glass *(avant n)*; *(▸ au milieu)* glazed; *(panneau, toit)* glass *(avant n)* **2** *Anat* vitreous

vitrer [3] [vitre] VT *(fenêtre, porte)* to glaze; *(verrière)* to fit with glass

vitrerie [vitrəri] NF **1** *(fabrique)* glaziery **2** *(commerce)* window glass trade *or* industry **3** *(vitres)* window glass

vitreux, -euse [vitrø, -øz] ADJ **1** *(terne ▸ œil, regard)* glassy, glazed; **regard v.** glassy stare, glazed look **2** *Géol & Phys* vitreous **3** *(porcelaine)* vitreous

vitrier [vitrije] NM glazier

vitrification [vitrifikasjɔ̃] NF **1** *(d'un parquet)* sealing; *(de tuiles)* glazing **2** *(de sable, de déchets nucléaires)* vitrification

vitrifier [9] [vitrifje] VT **1** *(parquet)* to seal; *(tuiles)* to glaze; **brique vitrifiée** glazed brick **2** *(déchets nucléaires, sable)* to vitrify

vitrine [vitrin] NF **1** *(devanture)* display window, *Br* shop *or Am* store window; *(vitre) Br* shop *or Am* store window; *(objets exposés)* window display; **faire une v.** to dress a window; **refaire la v.** to change the window display; **mettre qch en v.** to display *or* to put sth in the window; **des articles en v.** articles (on display) in the window; *Fam* **faire** *ou* **lécher les vitrines** to do some window-shopping; *Fig* **Paris est la v. de la France** Paris is the showcase of France **2** *(meuble ▸ de maison)* display cabinet; *(▸ de musée)* display cabinet, showcase; *(▸ de magasin)* showcase, display case

vitriol [vitrijɔl] NM **1** *Chim* vitriol; **(huile de) v.** oil of vitriol; *Fig* **des propos au v.** caustic *or* vitriolic remarks; *Fig* **une attaque au v.** a vitriolic *or* devastating attack **2** *Fam (mauvais vin)* cheap wine[□], *Br* plonk; *(mauvais alcool)* gutrot

vitriolage [vitrijɔlaʒ] NM *(sur quelqu'un)* acid attack

vitrioler [3] [vitrijɔle] VT *(blesser)* **v. qn** to attack sb with acid; **se faire v., être vitriolé** to have acid thrown in one's face, to be the victim of an acid attack

vitrioleur, -euse [vitrijɔlœr, -øz] NM,F acid thrower

vitrocéramique [vitroseramik] ADJ **plaque v.** ceramic hob

vitupérations [vityperasjɔ̃] NFPL *Littéraire* vituperation *(UNCOUNT)*, verbal abuse *(UNCOUNT)*

vitupérer [18] [vitypere] VI *Littéraire* to vituperate; **v. contre qn/qch** to inveigh against sb/sth; **elle passe son temps à v. contre les transports en commun** she spends her time ranting and raving about public transport

VT to inveigh against, *Sout* to vituperate

vivable [vivabl] ADJ *(situation)* bearable; *(habitation)* fit for living in; *Fam (personne)* **elle n'est pas v.** she's impossible to live with; **cette situation n'est plus v.** this situation is intolerable; **ce n'est plus v. au bureau!** it's unbearable in the office now!

vivace[1] [vivas] ADJ **1** *Bot* hardy **2** *(qui dure ▸ croyance, opinion, tradition)* deep-rooted; *(▸ souvenir)* abiding; *(▸ foi)* steadfast; **une région où le sentiment socialiste est très v.** a staunchly socialist region; **son souvenir est encore v.** his/her memory is still very much alive

vivace[2] [vivatʃe] *Mus* ADJ INV vivace

ADV vivace

vivacité [vivasite] NF **1** *(promptitude ▸ d'une attaque, d'une démarche, d'un geste)* briskness; *(▸ d'une intelligence)* sharpness, acuteness; **elle s'est retournée avec v.** she turned round sharply; **v. d'esprit** quick-wittedness; *(humour)* sparkling wit

2 *(brusquerie ▸ d'une personne, de propos)* brusqueness; **v. d'humeur** hotness of temper, quick-temperedness; **la v. de sa réplique** the sharpness of his/her reply

3 *(entrain ▸ d'une personne, d'un style)* vivaciousness, vivacity, liveliness; *(▸ d'un marché)* liveliness, buoyancy; *(▸ d'une description)* vividness, liveliness; *(▸ d'un regard)* vivacity; **une femme âgée pleine de v.** a sprightly old woman; **parler avec v.** to speak animatedly

4 *(force ▸ d'une douleur)* sharpness, intensity; *(▸ du froid)* bitterness, sharpness; *(▸ d'une impression)* vividness, keenness; *(▸ d'une couleur)* brightness, vividness; *(▸ d'une lumière)* brightness

vivandier [vivɑ̃dje] NM *Hist* sutler

vivant, -e [vivɑ̃, -ɑ̃t] ADJ **1** *Biol (organisme)* living; *(personne, animal)* alive; **enterré v.** buried alive; **il est encore v.** he's still alive; **j'en suis sorti v.** I lived to tell the tale, I survived; **cuire un homard v.** to cook a live lobster *or* a lobster alive

2 *(existant ▸ croyance, tradition, souvenir)* living; **l'emploi du mot est resté très v.** the term is still very much in use

3 *(animé ▸ enfant, conférence, présentation)* lively, spirited; *(▸ bourg, rue)* lively, bustling, full of life; **c'est une classe très vivante** it's a very lively class; **il a laissé en nous un souvenir très v.** he left us with a very vivid memory of him

4 *(réaliste ▸ description, style)* vivid

5 *(constitué d'humains ▸ rempart)* human

6 *(incarné, personnifié ▸ preuve, exemple, témoignage)* living

NM **1** *(période)* **de son v.** *(dans le passé)* when he/she was alive; *(dans le présent)* as long as he/she lives; **je ne verrai pas ça de mon v.!** I won't live to see it!; **du v. de mon frère, j'y allais souvent** when my brother was alive, I used to go there often **2** *(personne)* **un bon v.** a bon viveur, a connoisseur of the good things in life

• **vivants** NMPL *Rel* **les vivants** the living; **les vivants et les morts** *(gén)* the living and the dead; *Bible* the quick and the dead

> Attention: lorsqu'on traduit l'adjectif **vivant**, il faut noter que les termes **alive** et **living** ne sont pas interchangeables. **Alive** signifie **en vie** et s'utilise uniquement comme attribut, alors que **living** signifie **doué de vie** et s'utilise comme épithète.

vivarium [vivarjɔm] NM vivarium

vivat [viva] NM cheer; **s'avancer sous les vivats** to walk forth through a hail of applause

EXCLAM *Arch* hurrah!, bravo!

vive[1] [viv] ADJ *voir* **vif**

vive[2] [viv] EXCLAM **v. le roi!** long live the King!; **v. le Canada/la République!** long live Canada/the Republic!; **v.** *ou* **vivent les vacances!** three cheers for holidays!

vive[3] [viv] NF *Ich* weever

vivement [vivmɑ̃] ADV **1** *(exprime un souhait)* **v. le week-end!** I can't wait for the weekend!, *Br* roll on the weekend!, *Am* bring on the weekend!; **v. qu'il s'en aille!** I'll be glad when he's gone!

2 *(extrêmement ▸ ému, troublé)* deeply, greatly; *(▸ intéressé)* greatly, keenly; **je souhaite v. que...** I sincerely wish that...; **féliciter/remercier/recommander qn v.** to congratulate/thank/recommend sb warmly; **s'intéresser v. à qch** to take a keen interest in sth

3 *(intensément ▸ éclairé, coloré)* brightly; **contraster v. avec** to contrast sharply with

4 *(brusquement ▸ interpeller)* sharply; **v. rabroué** told off in no uncertain terms

5 *(vite ▸ marcher)* briskly; **il se dirigea v. vers la sortie** he walked briskly towards the exit

vivent [viv] **1** *voir* **vive**[2] **2** *voir* **vivre**[2]

viveur, -euse [vivœr, -øz] NM,F *Vieilli* bon viveur

vivier [vivje] NM **1** *(d'un commerce)* fish tank **2** *Pêche (enclos ▸ pour poissons)* fishpond; *(▸ pour homards)* crawl; *(▸ d'un bateau)* fish tank *or* well **3** *Fig* **un véritable v. d'acteurs** a breeding ground for actors

vivifiant, -e [vivifjɑ̃, -ɑ̃t] ADJ *(air, climat)* bracing, invigorating; *(expérience)* invigorating; *(atmosphère)* enlivening

vivifier [9] [vivifje] VT *(personne)* to revivify, to invigorate; *(industrie, région)* to bring life to; *(imagination, sentiments)* to quicken, to sharpen

VI *Rel* to give life

vivipare [vivipar] *Zool* ADJ viviparous

NMF member of the Vivipara

viviparité [viviparite] NF *Zool* viviparity, viviparousness

vivisection [viviseksjɔ̃] NF vivisection; **être contre la v.** to be an antivivisectionist, to be against live experiments

vivoir [vivwar] NM *Can Vieilli* living room

vivoter [3] [vivɔte] VI *(personne)* to get by *or* along (with little money)

vivre[1] [vivr] NM **le v. et le couvert** bed and board

• **vivres** NMPL food *(UNCOUNT)*, foodstuffs, provisions; **couper les vivres à qn** to stop sb's allowance

vivre[2] [90] [vivr] VI **1** *Biol (personne, animal)* to live, to be alive; *(cellule, plante)* to live; **elle vivait encore quand ils l'ont emmenée** she was still alive when they took her away; **v. vieux** *ou* **longtemps** to live to a great age *or* a ripe old age; **cesser de v.** to die; **elle a vécu jusqu'à 95 ans** she lived to be 95; **à l'époque où il vivait** at the time when he was alive; **il ne lui reste plus longtemps à v.** he/she hasn't got much time left (to live); **il lui reste deux mois à v.** he's/she's got two months to live; **les plantes/animaux qui vivent dans l'eau** plants/animals which live in water; *Mil* **qui vive?** who goes there?; **avoir vécu** to have had one's day; **le Front populaire a vécu** the Popular Front has had its day *or* is finished; *Fam* **ma pauvre télé a vécu** my poor old TV is on its last legs; *Prov* **qui vivra verra** time will tell

2 *(mener une existence)* to live; **v. en paix** to live in peace; **v. en honnête homme** to lead an honest life; **v. heureux** to live happily; **v. malhonnêtement/pieusement** to lead a dishonest/pious life; **v. au jour le jour** to take each day as it comes; **v. à l'heure de l'Europe/du XXIème siècle** to live in the world of the European community/of the 21st century; **v. dans le luxe/l'angoisse** to live in luxury/anxiety; **v. dans le péché** to lead a sinful life; **on voit que tu n'as jamais vécu dans la misère** it's obvious you've never experienced poverty; **ne v. que pour la musique/sa famille** to live only for music/one's family; **une rue qui vit la nuit** a street that comes alive at night; **se laisser v.** to take life easily *or* as it comes; **prendre le temps de v.** to take the time to enjoy life; **il fait bon v. ici** life is good *or* it's a good life here; **une maison où il fait bon v.** a house that's good to live in; **elle a beaucoup vécu** she's seen life; **on ne vit plus** *(on est inquiet)* we're worried sick; *(on est harassé)* this isn't a life, this isn't what you can call living; *Fam* **je vais t'apprendre à v.!** I'll teach you some manners!; **ils vécurent heureux et eurent beaucoup d'enfants** (and) they lived happily ever after; *Prov* **pour v. heureux, vivons cachés** = the happiest people are those who keep themselves to themselves

3 *(résider)* to live; **ils sont venus v. ici** they came to live *or* to settle here; **v. au Brésil/dans un château** to live in Brazil/in a castle; **v. à Paris/en province/à la campagne/à l'étranger** to live in Paris/in the provinces/in the country/abroad *or* overseas; **v. dans une** *ou* **en communauté** to live communally *or* in a community; **v. à la campagne ne m'a jamais attiré** country life has never appealed to me; **v. avec qn** *(maritalement)* to live with sb; *(en amis)* to share *or* to live with sb; **v. ensemble** *(couple non marié)* to live together; **être facile à v.** to be easy-going *or* easy to get on with; **être difficile à v.** to be difficult to get on with

4 *(subsister)* to live; **travailler pour v.** to work for a living; **les sommes que tu m'envoies m'aident à v.** the money you send me keeps me going; **avoir de quoi v.** to have enough to live on; **ils ont tout juste de quoi v.** they've just enough to live on; **de quoi vit-il?** what does he live on?; *(que fait-il dans la vie?)* what does he do for a living?; **v. sur un seul salaire** to live *or* to exist on just one salary; **faire v. une famille** *(personne)* to provide a living for *or* to support a family; *(commerce)* to provide a living for a family; **v. bien/chichement** to have a good/poor standard of living; **v. de fruits/de ses rentes** to live on fruit/on one's private income; **ils vivaient de la cueillette et de la chasse** they lived on what they gathered and hunted *or* off the land; **v. de sa plume** to live by one's pen; **v. de chimères** to live a life of illusion; **v. d'espérances** to live in hope; **l'espoir fait v.!** we all live in hope!; **il faut bien v.!** one's got to keep the wolf from the door *or* to live (somehow)!; **v. aux crochets de qn** to sponge off sb; **v. de l'air du temps** to live on thin air; **v. d'amour et d'eau fraîche** to live on love alone

5 *(se perpétuer ▸ croyance, coutume)* to be alive; **pour que notre entreprise vive** so that our company may continue to exist

6 *(donner l'impression de vie ▸ sculpture, tableau)* **voici une description qui vit** here is a description that is full of life

VT 1 *(passer par ▸ époque, événement)* to live through; **elle a vécu la guerre** she lived through *or* went through the war; **v. des temps difficiles** to live through *or* to experience difficult times; **v. des jours heureux/paisibles** to spend one's days happily/peacefully; **v. une expérience unique/inoubliable** to go through *or* have a unique/an unforgettable experience; **v. une passion** to live out a passion **2** *(assumer ▸ divorce, grossesse, retraite)* to experience; **elle a mal/bien vécu mon départ** she couldn't cope/she coped well after I left **3** *(locutions)* **v. sa vie** to live one's own life; **v. sa foi** to live intensely through one's faith; **il faut v. l'instant présent** one must live for the moment

VPR se vivre la maladie se vit mal quand on est seul it's difficult being ill when you're on your own

vivrier, -ère [vivrije, -ɛr] **ADJ cultures vivrières** food crops

vizir [vizir] **NM** vizier; **le Grand v.** the Grand Vizier

v'là [vla] **PRÉP** *Fam* **le v.!** here he is!; **et juste à ce moment-là, v. t-y pas qu'il se met à pleuvoir!** and just then, would you believe it, it starts raining!

vlan, v'lan [vlɑ̃] **EXCLAM** *(bruit ▸ de porte)* bang!, wham!, slam!; *(▸ de coup)* smack!, thud!, wallop!; **et v.!, il est tombé** and bang, he fell over!

VLF [veelɛf] **NF** *TV & Rad (abrév* **very low frequency***)* VLF

vlimeux [vlimø] *Can Fam* **NM 1** *(chanceux)* lucky devil; **le petit v.!** (the) lucky devil! **2** *(intrigant)* crafty devil **3** *(coquin)* (little) rascal *or* devil

• **en vlimeux ADV être fort/riche en v.** to be very strong/rich▫

ADJ être en v. to be fuming, to be in a temper

vlog [vlɔg] **NM** *Ordinat* vlog, video blog

VMP [veempe] **NFPL** *Bourse (abrév* **valeurs mobilières de placement***)* marketable securities

VO [veo] *Cin* **NF** *(abrév* **version originale***)* = indicates that a film is in the original language and not dubbed

• **en VO ADJ** in the original version; **en VO sous-titrée** in the original version with subtitles; **voir un film en VO** to see a film in the original (language) version

vocable [vɔkabl] **NM 1** *Ling* term **2** *Rel* name, patronage; **sous le v. de** dedicated to

vocabulaire [vɔkabylɛr] **NM 1** *Ling* vocabulary; **v. argotique/juridique** slang/legal vocabulary; **le v. d'un enfant de six ans** the vocabulary of a six-year-old (child); **enrichir son v.** to enlarge one's vocabulary; **avoir du v.** to have a wide vocabulary; **surveiller son v.** to watch *or* to mind one's language; **ce mot n'est pas dans mon v.** it's not a word that I use; **un junkie, pour employer le v. à la mode** a junkie, to use the in *or* fashionable word **2** *(lexique)* lexicon, (specialized) dictionary

vocal, -e, -aux, -ales [vɔkal, -o] **ADJ** vocal

vocalement [vɔkalmɑ̃] **ADV** vocally

vocalique [vɔkalik] **ADJ** vocalic, vowel *(avant n)*

vocalisation [vɔkalizasjɔ̃] **NF** *Ling & Mus* vocalization, vocalizing

vocalise [vɔkaliz] **NF** *Mus* singing exercise, *Spéc* vocalise; **faire des vocalises** to do singing exercises

vocaliser [3] [vɔkalize] **VI** *Mus* to practise scales, *Spéc* to vocalize

VT *Ling* to vocalize

VPR se vocaliser to become vocalized

vocalisme [vɔkalism] **NM** *Ling* vocalism

vocatif [vɔkatif] **NM** *Gram* vocative (case); **au v.** in the vocative (case)

vocation [vɔkasjɔ̃] **NF 1** *(d'une personne)* vocation, calling; **avoir une v. musicale/théâtrale** to have a musical/theatrical vocation; **ne pas avoir/avoir la v. (de)** to feel no/to feel a vocation (for); **pour être assistante sociale, il faut avoir la v.** to be a social worker, one has to feel a vocation for it; **faire qch par v.** to do sth as a labour of love; **j'ai manqué** *ou* **raté ma v., j'aurais dû être architecte** I've missed my vocation *or* my calling, I should have been an architect **2** *(rôle, mission)* **la v. industrielle de l'Allemagne** Germany's long industrial tradition; **grâce à la v. touristique de notre région** because our area is dedicated to tourism; **la v. du nouveau musée est d'éduquer les jeunes** the new museum is designed to be of educational value to young people; **région à v. agricole/industrielle** agricultural/industrial region **3** *Admin* **avoir v. à** *ou* **pour faire** to be empowered to do

vociférateur, -trice [vɔsiferatœr, -tris] **NM,F** *Littéraire* vociferant, shouter

vocifération [vɔsiferasjɔ̃] **NF** vociferation; **des vociférations** an outcry, a clamour; **pousser des vociférations** to shout and bawl; **sous les vociférations du public** met by boos and hisses from the audience

vocifératrice [vɔsiferatris] *voir* **vociférateur**

vociférer [18] [vɔsifere] **VI** to yell, to shout, *Sout* to vociferate; **v. contre** to inveigh against, to berate

VT *(injures)* to scream, to shout (**contre** at)

VOD [veode] **NF** *(abrév* **video-on-demand***)* VOD

vodka [vɔdka] **NF** vodka; **une v. orange** a vodka and orange

vœu, -x [vø] **NM 1** *(souhait)* wish; **faire un v.** to (make a) wish; **tu peux faire trois vœux** you may have three wishes; **si je n'avais qu'un v. à faire, ce serait celui de...** if I could have just one wish, it would be to...; **je fais le v. qu'elle revienne** I pray (that) she may come back; **je fais des vœux pour qu'il ne pleuve pas dimanche** I'm praying it won't rain on Sunday; **former le v. que qch se réalise** to express a *or* the wish that sth should be done; **exaucer un v.** to grant a wish; **faire un v. pieux** to make a vain wish

2 *(serment)* vow; **faire v. de tempérance** to take a vow of temperance, to take the pledge; **j'ai fait le v. de ne plus y retourner** I vowed never to go back (there again); **il a fait le v. de se venger** he vowed revenge

3 *Rel* **faire v. de pauvreté/de chasteté/d'obéissance** to take a vow of poverty/of chastity/of obedience; **vœux du baptême** baptismal vows; **prononcer ses vœux** to take one's vows

• **vœux NMPL 1** *(de fin d'année)* **meilleurs vœux** *(sur une carte)* Season's Greetings; **envoyer ses vœux à qn** to send sb one's best wishes; **nous vous adressons nos meilleurs vœux** *ou* **nos vœux les plus sincères pour la nouvelle année** our best wishes for the New Year; **elle est venue nous présenter ses vœux** she came to wish us a happy New Year; **le président a présenté ses vœux télévisés** the president made his New Year speech *or* address on TV

2 *(dans une grande occasion)* wishes; **tous nos vœux pour...** our best wishes for..., with all good wishes for...; **meilleurs vœux de la part de...** with all good wishes from...; **tous nos vœux de bonheur** our very best wishes for your happiness; **tous mes vœux de prompt rétablissement** hope you get well soon; *Sout* (my) best wishes for a speedy recovery; **tous nos vœux de succès** all the best, good luck; **je fais** *ou* **forme des vœux pour ta réussite** I wish you every success

vogue [vɔg] **NF 1** *(mode)* vogue, fashion, trend; **c'est la v. des bas résille** fishnet stockings are in vogue *or* fashion; **c'est la grande v.** *(vêtement)* it's the latest fashion; *(sport)* it's the latest craze **2** *(popularité)* vogue, popularity; **connaître une grande v.** *(style, activité, sport)* to be very fashionable; **la v. que connaissent actuellement les jeux vidéo** the current vogue *or* craze for video games **3** *Suisse (dans le canton de Genève) (kermesse)* village fête

• **en vogue ADJ** fashionable; **c'est la coiffure en v.** it's the latest hairstyle; **être en v.** *(vêtement)* to be fashionable *or* in vogue; *(activité, personne)* to be fashionable

voguer [3] [vɔge] **VI** *Naut* to sail; *Vieilli* **et vogue la galère!** whatever will be will be!

voici [vwasi] **PRÉP 1** *(désignant ce qui est proche dans l'espace ▸ suivi d'un singulier)* here is, this is; *(▸ suivi d'un pluriel)* here are, these are; **v. mes neveux** *(en les présentant)* these are my nephews; *(ils arrivent)* here are my nephews; **v. notre nouvelle voiture** this is our new car; **le v.** here he/it is; **la v.** here she/it is; **les v.!** here they are!; **j'ai perdu mon crayon – en v. un** I've lost my pencil – here's one; **du riz? en v.!** rice? here you are *or* there you are!; **en v. une qui sera plus à ta taille** here's one which will be more your size; *Fam* **en v. un qui n'a pas peur!** HE's certainly got guts!; **en v. une surprise!** what a surprise!; **ah, te v. enfin** so here *or* there you are at last; **nous y v.!** here we are!; *(dans une discussion)* now...; **l'homme que v.** this man (here); **les fleurs que v.** these flowers (here); **mon ami que v. vous le dira** my friend here will tell you; **Monsieur/l'objet que v.** this gentleman/object; **la petite histoire que v.** the following little story; **v. ma sœur et voilà mon fils** this is my sister and that's my son

2 *(caractérisant un état)* **vous v. rassuré, j'espère** I hope that's reassured you; **me v. prêt** I'm ready now; **nous v. riches!** we're rich!; **vous v. installés** here you are all settled in; **nous v. à Paris** here we are in Paris; **les v. enfin partis!** at last they've gone!; **nous v. enfin seuls** alone at last; **nous v. enfin arrivés!** here we are at last!; **la v. qui vient** here she comes, that's her (coming) now; **la v. qui recommence à pleurer** she's starting to cry again, that's her starting to cry again; **le v. qui veut faire du karaté maintenant!** now he wants to take up karate!; *Fam* **il lui a tout dit, me v. bien!** he told him/her everything, now what am I going to do?

3 *(introduisant ce dont on va parler ▸ suivi d'un singulier)* this *or* here is; *(▸ suivi d'un pluriel)* these *or* here are; **v. ce qui s'est passé** this *or* here is what happened; **v. ce dont il s'agit** this is *or* here's what it's all about; **v. nos intentions** these *or* here are our plans; **v. comment je vois les choses** this is *or* here's how I see things; **je le ferai et v. comment** I'll do it and here's how, *Sout* I shall do it in the following manner; **j'irai seul et v. pourquoi** I'll go alone and this is why

4 *(pour conclure)* **v. qui m'étonne!** that's a surprise!; **v. pourquoi je ne lui fais pas confiance** this *or* that is why I don't trust him/her

5 *(désignant une action proche dans le temps)* **et me v. à pleurer** and here I am crying; **v. l'orage** here comes the storm; **v. venir le printemps** spring is coming; **v. venir Noël, v. Noël qui arrive** Christmas is coming; **v. que la nuit tombe** (now) it's getting dark; **v. qu'il se met à pleuvoir** that's the rain on; **v. qu'arrive le mois de mai** (now) the month of May is upon us; *Littéraire* **v. venir Jeanne** here comes Jeanne; **v. le train qui arrive** here's the train coming now; **v. qu'ils recommencent avec leur musique!** their music's started (up) again!

6 *(exprimant la durée)* **j'y suis allé v. trois mois** I went there three months ago; **elle est partie v. cinq minutes** she left five minutes ago; **je l'ai rencontrée v. quelques années** I met her some years ago; **v. une heure qu'il est au téléphone** he's been on the phone for an hour; **v. trois mois que j'habite ici** I have been living here for (the last) three months

VOIE [vwa]

- road **1**
- way **3, 5, 6**
- track **4, 7, 10, 12**
- channel **12**
- lane **2**
- route **3**
- tract **9**

NF 1 *(rue)* road; **v. d'accès** access road; **la v. Appienne** the Appian Way; **les voies sur berges** *(à Paris)* = expressway running along the Seine in Paris; **v. de dégagement** *(en agglomération)* relief road; *(sur une autoroute)* *Br* slip road, *Am* ramp; **v. à double sens** two-way road; **v. express** *ou* **rapide** expressway; **v. de passage/raccordement** major/access road; **v. piétonne** pedestrian street; **v. prioritaire** main road; **v. privée** private road; *Admin* **v. publique** (public) highway *or* thoroughfare; *Antiq* **v. romaine** Roman way *or* road; **v. sacrée** sacred way; **v. sans issue** no through road, cul-de-sac; **v. à sens unique** one-way road; *Fig* **être par voies et par chemins** to be always on the move

2 *(pour une file de voitures)* lane; **(route à) trois voies** three-lane road; **(route à) quatre voies** *(gén)* four-lane road; *(séparée en deux)* dual *Br* carriageway *or Am* highway; **v. d'accélération** acceleration lane; **v. de décélération** deceleration lane, exit lane

3 *(moyen d'accès)* way; *(itinéraire)* route; **par la v. des airs** by air; **par v. de terre** overland, by land; **par v. de mer** by sea; **dégagez la v.!** get out of *or* clear the way!; *Fig* **la v. est libre** the road is clear; *aussi Fig* **laisser la v. libre à qn** to make way for sb; *Fig* **ouvrir la v. à qn** to pave the way for sb; *Fig* **ouvrir la v. à qch** to make way for sth; *Fig* **trouver sa v.** to find one's niche in life; **la v. de la réussite** the road to success; *Fig* **ta v. est toute tracée** your career is mapped out for you; **v. aérienne** air route, airway; **v. de communication** communication route; **voies d'eau** watercourses; **v. fluviale** *ou* **navigable** (inland) waterway; **v. maritime** sea route, seaway; **la V. maritime du Saint-Laurent** the St Lawrence Seaway; **entrer dans l'Administration par la v. royale** to take the most prestigious route into the Civil Service

4 *Rail* track; **v. (ferrée)** *Br* (railway) track *or* line, *Am* railroad; **ne pas traverser les voies** *(sur panneau)* do not cross the tracks; **le train 242 est attendu v. 9** train 242 is due to arrive on platform 9; **v. de garage** *ou* **de service** *ou* **de dégagement** *ou* **de triage** siding; *Fig* **mettre sur une v. de garage** *(projet)* to shelve, *Am* to table; *(employé)* to push aside, to put on the sidelines; **v. étroite** narrow-gauge line; **v. principale** main line; **v. unique** single track

5 *(procédure, moyen)* **la v. la plus simple/rapide** the easiest/quickest way; **suivre la v. hiérarchique/diplomatique/normale** to go through the official/diplomatic/usual channels; **la v. des armes** recourse to arms; **par des voies détournées** by devious means, by a circuitous route; **par v. de conséquence** consequently

6 *Rel* **la v. étroite** the narrow way; **les voies du Seigneur sont impénétrables** the Lord works in mysterious ways

7 *Chasse (chemin parcouru par le gibier)* track, trail; **mettre qn sur la v.** to put sb on the right scent; *Fig (en devinant)* to give sb a clue; *(dans une enquête)* to put sb on the right track; **être sur la bonne v.** to have the scent; *Fig* to be on the right track *or* lines; *Fig* **être sur la mauvaise v.** to be barking up the wrong tree

8 *Pharm* **par v. orale** *ou* **buccale** orally; **par v. nasale/rectale** through the nose/the rectum, nasally/rectally

9 *Anat & Physiol* tract, duct; **par les voies naturelles** naturally; **voies digestives** digestive tracts; **voies respiratoires** airways, respiratory tracts; **voies urinaires** urinary tracts

10 *Tech (largeur ▸ entre deux essieux)* track; *(▸ des roues de véhicule)* gauge; *(▸ d'un outil)* kerf, clearance; *(▸ d'un trait de scie)* set

11 *Fin* **voies et moyens** ways and means

12 *Ordinat & Tél (sur bande)* track; *(de communication)* channel; **v. d'accès** path; **v. d'entrée** input channel; **v. de transmission** transmission channel

13 *Astron* **la V. lactée** the Milky Way

14 *Jur* **v. de fait** *(action illégale)* blatantly unlawful act; *(violence)* act of violence

• **voies NFPL** *Jur* **voies de fait** *(coups)* assault and battery; **se livrer à des voies de fait sur qn** to assault sb; **voies de droit** recourse to legal proceedings; **voies d'exécution** execution; **voies de recours** possibilities of review

• **en bonne voie ADJ être en bonne v.** to be going well; **maintenant, les affaires sont en bonne v.** business is looking up; **votre dossier est en bonne v.** your file is being processed

• **en voie de PRÉP en v. d'achèvement** on the way to completion; **en v. de cicatrisation** healing over; **en v. de construction** being built, under construction; **espèces en v. de disparition** endangered species; **en v. de guérison** getting better, on the road to recovery; **pays en v. de développement** developing country; **être en v. de faire qch** to be (well) on the way to doing sth; **être en (bonne) v. de réussir** to be (well) on the way *or* road to success

• **par la voie de PRÉP** through, via; **régler un litige par la v. de la négociation** to settle a conflict through negotiation

VOILÀ [vwala] **PRÉP 1** *(désignant ce qui est éloigné ▸ suivi d'un singulier)* there *or* that is; *(▸ suivi d'un pluriel)* there *or* those are; **v. leur maison** there *or* that is their house; **le monument que v.** that monument (there); **les v., là-bas, au bout du jardin** there they are, down at the bottom of the garden; **v. Henri** *(qu'on cherchait)* there's Henri; *(qui arrive)* there's Henri (now), that's Henri (now); *(dont je te parlais)* that's Henri; **voici mon lit, v. le tien** here's *or* this is my bed and there's *or* that's yours

2 *(désignant ce qui est proche ▸ suivi d'un singulier)* here *or* this is; *(▸ suivi d'un pluriel)* here *or* these are; **v. mes parents** here are my parents; *(dans des présentations)* these are my parents; **v. Paul et Henri** *(en les présentant)* this is Paul and this is Henri; *(sur une photo)* this is Paul and this *or* that is Henri; **le v.** there he/it is; **la v.** there she/it is; **tiens, les v.!** look, here *or* there they are!; **ah, te v. enfin!** so here *or* there you are at last!; **nous y v.!** here we are!; *(dans une discussion)* now...; **je l'avoue, j'étais jaloux – nous y v.!** I admit it, I was jealous – now the truth's coming out!; **l'homme que v.** this man (here); **du riz? en v.!** rice? here *or* there you are!; **en v. pour cent euros** there's a hundred euros' worth; **je ne trouve pas de marteau – en v. un** I can't find a hammer – here's one; **tu voulais un adversaire à ta mesure? en v. un!** you wanted an opponent worthy of you? well, you've got one!; *Fam* **en v. un qui fera son chemin!** there's a man who will get on!; *Fam* **en v. un qui n'a pas peur!** HE's certainly got guts!; *Fam* **en v. une qui sait ce qu'elle veut** there's someone who knows what she wants; **en v. une surprise/des manières!** what a surprise/a way to behave!

3 *(caractérisant un état)* **le v. endormi** he's gone to sleep; **la v. recousue/cassée** now it's sewn up again/broken; **la v. rassurée** she's calmed down now; **me v. prêt** I'm ready now; **les v. enfin partis!** at last they've gone!; **nous v. enfin seuls!** alone at last!; **comme te v. changé!** you've changed so much!, how you've changed!; **dire que te v. marié!** to think you're married now!; **vous v. content maintenant?** (are you) happy now?; **le v. qui entre, v. qu'il entre** there he is coming in; **les v. qui arrivent** there they are (now); **le v. qui veut faire du karaté maintenant!** now he wants to take up karate!; *Fam* **nous v. frais** *ou* **beaux!** now we're in a fix *or* mess!; *Ironique* **te v. beau, que t'est-il arrivé?** you're in a fine state, what's happened to you?; *Fam Ironique* **me/te/nous/*etc* v. bien!** I'm/you're/we're/*etc* in a fine mess now!; **il lui a tout dit, me v. bien!** he told him/her everything, now what am I going to do?

4 *(introduisant ce dont on va parler ▸ suivi d'un singulier)* this *or* here is; *(▸ suivi d'un pluriel)* these *or* here are; **v. ce que je lui dirai** this *or* here is what I'll say to him/her; **v. ce qui arrivera si...** this is what will happen if...; **v. comment il faut faire** this is *or* here's how you do it; **alors v., c'est l'histoire d'une princesse qui...** so, it's the story of a princess who...; **la petite histoire que v.** the following little story; **que veux-tu dire par là? – eh bien v....** what do you mean by that? – well...

5 *(pour conclure ▸ suivi d'un singulier)* that's; *(▸ suivi d'un pluriel)* those are; **c'est lâche, v. mon avis** it's cowardly, that's what I think; **c'est cher, v. le hic!** it's expensive, that's the only snag!; **v. ce qui s'est passé** that's what happened; **v. bien les hommes!** how typical of *or* how like men!; **v. ce que c'est, la jalousie!** that's jealousy for you!; **v. ce que c'est que de mentir!** that's where lying gets you!; **v. ce que c'est que de mentir à ses parents/d'être trop honnête** that's what happens *or* that's what you get when you lie to your parents/when you're too honest; **v. ce qui s'appelle danser!** now that's what I call dancing!; **v. où je voulais en venir** that's what I was getting *or* driving at; **un hypocrite, v. ce que tu es!** you're nothing but a hypocrite!; **v. qui est étrange!** (now) that's strange!; **v. qui est bien joué!** (now that's) well played!; **quelques jours de repos, v. qui devrait te remettre sur pied** a few day's rest, THAT should set you right again; **et v. pourquoi je ne lui fais pas confiance** that's why I don't trust him/her; **on lui paiera les réparations et v.!** we'll pay him/her for the repairs and that's all (there is to it)!; **et v., il a encore renversé son café!** I don't believe it, he's spilt his coffee again!; **et v., ça devait arriver!** what did I tell you!; **ah v., c'est parce qu'il avait peur!** so, that explains it, he was frightened!; **à vrai dire, je ne veux pas le faire – ah, v.!** to be quite frank, I don't want to do it – so that's it *or* that's what it is!; **v.! vous avez tout compris** that's it! you've got it; **v. tout** that's all; **elle était déçue, v. (tout)** she was disappointed, that's all; **on s'est quittés, v. tout** we split up, that's all (there is to say); **en v. une idée!** *(bizarre)* what a ridiculous idea!; *(excellente)* now THERE'S an idea!; **en v. assez!** that's enough!, that will do!

6 *(introduisant une objection, une restriction)* **j'en voudrais bien un, seulement v., c'est très cher** I'd like one, but the problem is *or* but you see, it's very expensive; **c'est facile, seulement v., il fallait y penser** it's easy once you've thought of it; **j'aurais dû lui dire, mais v., je n'ai pas osé** I should've told him/her, but (when it came to it) I didn't dare; **tu t'excuses, d'accord, mais v., il est trop tard!** fine, you're apologizing, but the thing is, it's too late!; **v., j'hésitais à vous en parler mais...** well, yes, I wasn't going to mention it, but...

7 *(désignant une action proche dans le temps)* **v. la pluie** *(il ne pleut pas encore)* here comes the rain; *(il pleut)* it's raining; **v. venu le moment de s'expliquer** now's the moment to explain; **v. que la nuit tombe** (now) it's getting dark; *Fam* **v. qu'ils remettent ça avec leur musique!** they're at it again with their music!; **v. Monsieur, je suis à vous dans un instant** yes, sir, I'll be with you in a minute; **il vient mon dessert? – v., v.** is my dessert ready yet? – just coming!; *Fam* **(ne) v.-t-il pas qu'on deviendrait coquette!** vain, now, are we?

8 *(exprimant la durée)* **en juin v. trois ans** three years ago in June; **il est rentré v. une heure** he's been home for an hour, he came home an hour ago; **quand il est né, v. près de soixante-trois ans** when he was born, nearly sixty-three years ago; **v. longtemps/deux mois qu'il est parti** he's been gone a long time/two months; **v. trois ans que je n'y suis pas retourné** I haven't been back there for three years; **v. cinq minutes que je t'appelle!** I've been calling you for five minutes!

voilage [vwalaʒ] **NM 1** *(gauchissement ▸ du métal)* buckling; *(▸ d'une roue)* warping **2** *(tissu)* net *(UNCOUNT)*; *(rideau)* net curtain

voile¹ [vwal] **NM 1** *(d'une toilette, d'un monument)* veil; **porter le v.** to wear the veil; **v. de mariée** marriage veil; *Rel* **prendre le v.** to take the veil
2 *Tex (pour rideau)* net *(UNCOUNT)*, piece of netting, netting *(UNCOUNT)*; *(pour chapeau)* piece of gauze, gauze *(UNCOUNT)*, veil
3 *Fig* veil; **ils ont enfin levé le v. sur ce mystère** they have at last lifted the curtain on this mystery; **jeter** *ou* **mettre** *ou* **tirer un v. sur** to throw a veil across, to draw a veil over; **jetons un v. sur cet épisode** let's just forget that whole incident
4 *Littéraire (opacité)* **un v. de brume/fumée** a veil of mist/smoke
5 *Méd* **v. au poumon** shadow on the lung
6 *Phot* fog *(UNCOUNT)*
7 *Anat* **v. du palais** soft palate, *Spéc* velum
• **sous le voile de PRÉP** in the guise of; **c'est la xénophobie sous le v. du patriotisme** it's xenophobia in the guise of patriotism; **on voit là l'hypocrisie sous le v. de la respectabilité** here we have hypocrisy under a cloak of respectability

voile² [vwal] **NM** *(déformation ▸ du métal)* buckle, buckling; *(▸ du plastique, du bois)* warp, warping

voile³ [vwal] **NF 1** *Naut* sail; **déployer** *ou* **établir une v.** to set a sail; **faire v. vers** to sail towards; **faire force de voiles** to crowd on *or* to cram on all sail; **être sous voiles** to be under sail; **mettre à la v.** to set sail; **aller à la v.** to sail; **faire le tour du monde à la v.** to sail around the world; **nous sommes rentrés à la v.** we sailed back; *Fam* **mettre les voiles** to clear off; *très Fam (locution)* **marcher à v. et à vapeur** to bat for both teams, to swing both ways **2** *Sport* **la v.** sailing, yachting; **faire de la v.** to sail, to go yachting
• **à voiles ADJ** *Naut* **bateau à voiles** *Br* sailing boat, *Am* sailboat; *Hist* clipper
• **toutes voiles dehors ADV 1** *Naut* in full sail, all sail *or* sails set; **mettre toutes voiles dehors** to put on full sail *or* canvas **2** *Fam (rapidement)* like a bat out of hell

voilé¹, -e¹ [vwale] **ADJ 1** *(monument, visage, personne)* veiled; **femme voilée** woman wearing the veil; **des femmes voilées de noir** women veiled in black
2 *(couvert ▸ lune, soleil, horizon)* hazy; *(▸ ciel)* overcast; *(lumière ▸ par le brouillard)* hazy; *(▸ par les nuages)* dim; **le ciel est v.** it's hazy; **le mourant avait le regard v.** the dying man had a glazed expression; **des yeux voilés de larmes** eyes dimmed *or* blurred with tears
3 *(voix)* hoarse, husky; *(tambour)* muffled
4 *Fig (dissimulé ▸ signification)* obscure; **une allusion à peine voilée** a thinly veiled *or* a transparent hint; **s'exprimer en termes voilés** to express oneself in oblique *or* veiled terms; **leur déception à peine voilée** their thinly veiled disappointment
5 *Phot* fogged, veiled

voilé², -e² [vwale] **ADJ** *(déformé ▸ métal)* buckled; *(▸ bois, plastique)* warped

voiler¹ [3] [vwale] **VT 1** *(couvrir ▸ femme, statue)* to veil, to hide, to cover; **v. sa nudité** to hide one's nakedness
2 *(rendre moins net ▸ contours)* to veil; *(▸ lumière)* to dim; **des nuages voilèrent le ciel** the sky clouded over; **le regard voilé par les larmes** his/her eyes misty *or* blurred with tears
3 *(enrouer ▸ voix)* to make husky; *(▸ son, tambour)* to muffle; **la voix voilée par l'émotion/l'alcool** his/her voice husky with emotion/thick with drink
4 *Littéraire (dissimuler ▸ fautes)* to conceal, to veil; *(▸ motifs, vérité)* to mask, to veil, to disguise; *(▸ trouble, émotion)* to hide, to conceal; **sans v. leurs intentions** without disguising their intentions
5 *Phot* to fog
6 *Naut (navire)* to rig with sails
VPR se voiler 1 se v. le visage *(le couvrir)* to wear a veil (over one's face); *Fig* **se v. la face** to bury one's head in the sand, to hide from the truth
2 *(lune, soleil)* to become hazy; *(ciel ▸ de nuages)* to cloud over; *(▸ de brume)* to mist over, to become hazy *or* misty
3 *(voix)* to grow *or* to become husky
4 *Phot* to fog

voiler² [3] [vwale] **VT** *(déformer ▸ métal)* to buckle; *(▸ bois, plastique)* to warp
VPR se voiler *(métal)* to buckle; *(bois, plastique)* to become warped

voilerie [vwalri] **NF** *Naut* sail loft

voilette [vwalɛt] **NF** (hat) veil

voilier¹ [vwalje] **NM 1** *Naut* **v. (de plaisance)** sailing boat, *Am* sailboat; *(navire à voiles)* sailing ship
2 *(ouvrier)* sailmaker; **maître v.** master sailmaker
3 *Ich* sailfish
4 *Orn* **grand v.** long-flight bird

voilier², -ère [vwalje, -ɛr] **ADJ** *Vieilli (bateau)* sailing *(avant n)*; *(oiseau)* long-flight

voilure¹ [vwalyr] **NF 1** *Naut* sail, sails; **changer de/réduire la v.** to change/to shorten sail **2** *Aviat* *Br* aerofoil, *Am* airfoil; **appareil à v. fixe/tournante** fixed/rotary wing aircraft

voilure² [vwalyr] **NF** *(du métal, d'une roue)* buckling

VOIR [62] [vwar]

VT
- to see **A1–8, B1–7**
- to look at **A4**
- to visit **A5**
- to think of **B2**
- to consider **B5**
- to find **A3**
- to notice **A4**
- to imagine **B1**
- to realize **B4**
- to check **B6**

VI
- to see **A1**

VPR
- to see oneself **1, 2**
- to see each other **3**
- to happen **5**
- to picture oneself **2**
- to be visible **4**
- to find oneself **6**

VT A. *PERCEVOIR AVEC LES YEUX* **1** *(distinguer)* to see; *Physiol* to (be able to) see; **il ne voit rien de l'œil gauche** he can't see anything with his *or* he's blind in the left eye; **on n'y voit pas grand-chose dans la cave** you can hardly see a thing in the cellar; **on ne voit presque pas la reprise** the mend hardly shows; **d'ici, on voit chez le monsieur d'en face** from here, you can see into the man opposite's house; **il faut le v. pour le croire!** you have to see it to believe it!; **je voudrais la v. en mariée** I'd like to see her as a bride; **à les v., on ne dirait pas qu'ils roulent sur l'or** to look at them, you wouldn't think they were rolling in it; **à la v. si souriante, on ne dirait pas qu'elle souffre** when you see how cheerful she is, you wouldn't think she's in pain; **v. qn faire** *ou* **qui fait qch** to see sb do *or* doing sth; **on t'a vu l'embrasser** you were seen kissing her, someone saw you kiss her; **je l'ai vu qui descendait d'avion** I saw him get *or* getting off the plane; **on en a vu qui pleuraient** some were seen crying; **elle m'a fait v. sa robe de mariée** she showed me her wedding dress; **fais v.!** let me see!; *Littéraire* **que vois-je?** what is this (that I see)?; **v. le jour** *(bébé)* to be born; *(journal)* to come out; *(théorie, invention)* to appear; **je les ai vus comme je vous vois** I saw them with my own eyes; *Fam* **il était habillé, faut v.!** you should have seen what he was wearing!; *Fam* **elle chante, faut v.!** she can't sing to save her life!; **il faut la v. lui répondre, il faut v. comment elle lui répond** you should see the way she speaks to him/her; *Fam* **elle parle à ses parents il faut v. comme!** you should hear how she talks to her parents!; **cela a fait scandale – le gouvernement n'avait rien vu venir** there was a big scandal – the government hadn't seen it coming *or* hadn't anticipated that; *Fam* **je te vois venir, tu veux de l'argent!** I can see what you're leading up to *or* getting at, you want some money!; *Fam* **le garagiste m'a fait payer 500 euros – il t'a vu venir!** the mechanic charged me 500 euros – he saw you coming!; **Noël n'est que dans trois semaines, on a le temps de v. venir!** Christmas isn't for another three weeks, we've got plenty of time!
2 *(assister à ▸ accident, événement)* to witness, to see; *(▸ film, spectacle)* to see; **personne n'a vu l'accident** there were no witnesses to *or* nobody saw the accident; **c'est vrai, je l'ai vue le faire** it's true, I saw her do it; **c'est un film à v. absolument** that movie is a must; **à v., l'exposition Rouault à la galerie Moersch** well worth seeing, the Rouault exhibition at the Moersch gallery; **ici, les terrains ont vu leur prix doubler en cinq ans** land prices here doubled over five years; **les deux-roues ont vu leur vignette augmenter** road tax has been increased for motorcycles; **tu n'as encore rien vu** you haven't seen anything yet; **on aura tout vu!** that beats everything!; **j'en ai vu, des choses pendant la guerre!** I saw quite a few things in the war!; **j'en ai vu d'autres!** I've seen worse!, I've been through worse!; **ils en ont vu, avec leur aînée!** their oldest girl really gave them a hard time!; *Fam* **j'en ai jamais vu la couleur** I haven't seen hide nor hair of it; *Fam* **en v. (de toutes les couleurs** *ou* **des vertes et des pas mûres** *ou* **de drôles)** to go through hell, to have a hellish time of it; **il en a vu de toutes les couleurs** *ou* **des vertes et des pas mûres** *ou* **de drôles** he's been through quite a lot; **avec lui, elle en a vu de toutes les couleurs** *ou* **des vertes et des pas mûres!** she's had a hard *or* a rough time (of it) with him!, she's been through a lot with him!; **j'en ai vu de drôles avec lui quand il était petit!** he nearly drove me up the wall when he was little!; *Fam* **en faire v. (de toutes les couleurs** *ou* **des vertes et des pas mûres** *ou* **de drôles) à qn** to make sb's life a misery, to put sb through hell; **mets de l'eau dessus pour v.** pour some water on it, just to see what happens; **répète un peu, pour v.!** don't (you) DARE say that again!; *très Fam* **va te faire v. (chez les Grecs)!** go to hell!, *Br* bugger off!, piss off!
3 *(trouver ▸ spécimen)* to see, to find, *Sout* to encounter; *(▸ qualité)* to see; **il faut aller très haut pour v. des bouquetins** you have to climb very high to see ibex; **je n'ai jamais vu tant d'assurance/tant de talent chez un enfant** I've never seen so much self-confidence/so much talent in a child; **les téléphones portables, on en voit partout!** you see mobile phones everywhere!; **j'ai vu la recette dans un magazine** I saw *or* found the recipe in a magazine; **un homme galant comme on n'en voit plus** the kind of gentleman they don't make any more
4 *(inspecter ▸ appartement)* to see, to view; *(▸ rapport)* to see, to (have a) look at; *(▸ leçon)* to go *or* to look over; *(remarquer)* to see, to notice; **j'aimerais que tu voies le plan du bateau** I'd like you to have a look at the plan of the boat; **j'ai vu deux erreurs dans l'article** I saw two mistakes in the article
5 *(visiter)* to see, to visit; **je n'ai pas encore vu le nord de l'Espagne** I've not yet been to *or* seen *or* visited northern Spain; **qui n'a pas vu l'Égypte n'a rien vu** unless you've seen Egypt, you haven't lived
6 *(consulter, recevoir ▸ ami, médecin)* to see; **puis-je vous v. quelques minutes?** may I see you a minute?; **j'aimerais te v. plus souvent** I'd like to see you more often *or* to see more of you; **le médecin va vous v. dans quelques instants** the doctor will be with *or* will see you in a few minutes; *Fam Fig* **il faut v. un psychiatre, mon vieux!** you need your head examined, pal!; **dans l'attente de vous v.** looking forward to seeing you; **je dois aller v. le médecin** I've got to go to the doctor's; **je vais aller v. mes amis** I'm going to go and see my friends; **je vois toujours Pascale, ma vieille amie de classe** I still see *or* I'm still in touch with Pascale, my old school friend
7 *(être en présence de)* to see; **quand je le vois, je pense à son père** whenever I see him I'm reminded of his father; *Fam* **va-t'en, je t'ai assez vu!** go away, I've seen *or* had enough of you!
8 *(se référer à)* **v. illustration p. 7** see diagram p. 7; **v. ci-dessus** see above; **voyez l'horaire des trains** check *or* consult the train timetable
B. *PENSER, CONCEVOIR* **1** *(imaginer)* to see, to imagine, to picture; **tu me vois déguisé en évêque?** can you imagine *or* see *or* picture me dressed up as a bishop?; **je voyais le jardin plus grand** I'd imagined the garden to be bigger; **le pull est trop large – je te voyais plus carré que cela** the jumper is too big – I thought you had broader shoulders; **je nous vois mal gagner le match** I can't see us winning the match; **je vois sa tête/réaction d'ici** I can just imagine his/her face/reaction

2 *(concevoir ▸ méthode, solution)* to see, to think of; **je ne vois pas comment je pourrais t'aider** I can't see how I could help you; **je ne vois pas qui tu veux dire/comment faire/quel parti prendre** I don't see who you mean/how to proceed/which side to take; **vous voyez quelque chose à ajouter?** can you think of anything else (which needs adding)?; **certains ne voient dans sa sculpture que des fils de fer** some consider his/her sculptures to be just a load of wires; **je ne vois pas de mal à cela** I don't see any harm in it; **v. qch d'un mauvais œil, ne pas v. qch d'un bon œil** to be displeased about sth; **elle voit d'un mauvais œil mon amitié avec sa fille** she's none too pleased about *or* she doesn't look very kindly on my friendship with her daughter; **organiser un carnaval? les autorités ne voient jamais cela d'un très bon œil** organizing a carnival? that's never very popular with the authorities; **elle le voit avec les yeux de l'amour** she sees him through a lover's eyes

3 *(comprendre ▸ danger, intérêt)* to see; **tu vois ce que je veux dire?** do you see *or* understand what I mean?; **je ne vois pas ce qu'il y a de drôle!** I can't see what's so funny!, I don't get the joke!; **je n'en vois pas l'utilité** I can't see the point of it; **elle m'a fait v. que la vengeance était inutile** she made me realize that revenge was futile; **un jour, tu verras que j'avais raison** one day, you'll realize *or* see that I was right; **il est directeur de banque – je vois!** he's a bank manager – I see!

4 *(constater)* to see, to realize; **tu vois que mes principes n'ont pas changé** as you can see, my principles haven't changed; **elle ne nous causera plus d'ennuis – c'est** *ou* **ça reste à v.!** she won't trouble us any more – that remains to be seen *or* that's what YOU think!

5 *(considérer, prendre en compte)* to see, to consider, to take into account; **ils ne voient que leur intérêt** they only consider their own interest; **elle ne voit que les avantages à court terme** she only sees the short-term advantages

6 *(examiner)* to see, to check; **je n'ai pas eu le temps de v. vos copies** I didn't have time to look at your essays; **nous prenons rendez-vous? – voyez cela avec ma secrétaire** shall we make an appointment? – arrange that with my secretary; **voyez si l'on peut changer l'heure du vol** see *or* check whether the time of the flight can be changed; **il faut v. si c'est rentable** we must see whether it's profitable; **les photos seraient mieux en noir et blanc – hum, il faut v.** the pictures would look better in black and white – mm, maybe(, maybe not)

7 *(juger)* to see; **voilà comment je vois la chose** that's how I see it; **se faire bien v. de qn** to make oneself popular with sb; **se faire mal v. de qn** to make oneself unpopular with sb

8 *(locutions)* **avoir à v. avec** *(avoir un rapport avec)* to have to do with; **vous aurez peu à v. avec les locataires du dessus** you'll have very little to do with the upstairs tenants; **je voudrais vous parler: ça a à v. avec notre discussion d'hier** I would like to speak to you: it's to do with what we were talking about yesterday; **n'avoir rien à v. avec** *(n'avoir aucun rapport avec)* to have nothing to do with; **l'instruction n'a rien à v. avec l'intelligence** education has nothing to do with intelligence; **je n'ai rien à v. avec la famille des Bellechasse** I'm not related at all to the Bellechasse family; **cela n'a rien à v. avec le sujet** that's irrelevant; **l'amour et l'argent sont deux choses qui n'ont rien à v.!** love and money have nothing to do with each other!; **je te l'avais dit, tu vois!** what did I tell you!; **vous voyez, je crois qu'il a raison** you see, I think he's right; **elle est si jeune, voyez-vous!** she's so young, you see!; **essaie de recommencer et tu verras!** just (you) try it again and see!; **tu verrais, si j'avais encore mes jambes!** if my legs were still up to it, there'd be no holding *or* stopping me!; *Fam* **attendez v.** hang on, wait a sec; *Fam* **voyons v.** *ou* **regardons v. ce que tu as comme note** let's just have a look and see what mark you got; **une moto à 14 ans, voyez-vous ça!** a motorbike at 14, whatever next!; **un rendez-vous avec sa secrétaire, voyez-vous cela!** a date with his secretary, well, well, well *or* what do you know!; **voyons!** come (on) now!; **un peu de courage, voyons!** come on, be brave!; **voyons, voyons, un peu de tenue!** come on now, behave yourselves!

USAGE ABSOLU *(concevoir)* **il faut trouver un moyen! – je ne vois pas** we must find a way! – I can't think of one *or* anything

VI 1 *Physiol* to (be able to) see; **il ne voit que d'un œil** he can only see out of one eye; **il ne sait pas v.** he just doesn't use his powers of observation; **v. bien** to see clearly, to have good eyesight; **v. mal** to have poor eyesight; **v. double** to have double vision

2 *(juger)* **v. bien** *ou* **juste** to have sound judgement; **encore une fois, tu as vu juste** you were right, once again; **v. faux** to have poor judgement

• **voir à VT IND** *(veiller à)* **v. à faire qch** to see to it *or* to make sure *or* to ensure that sth is done; **voyez à la prévenir** see to it that she is told; **il faudrait v. à ranger ta chambre/payer tes dettes** you'd better tidy up your room/clear your debts; **v. à ce que qch soit fait** to see to it *or* to make sure *or* to ensure that sth is done; **voyez à ce que le colis parte ce soir** see to it that the parcel is sent tonight

VPR se voir 1 *(se contempler)* to (be able to) see oneself; **mes carreaux brillent tellement que je me vois dedans** my tiles are so shiny that I can see my reflection in them; **en rêve, je me voyais flotter au-dessus de mon lit** in my dream I could see myself floating above my bed; *Fig* **il s'est vu mourir** he knew he was dying

2 *(s'imaginer)* to see *or* to imagine *or* to picture oneself; **elle se voyait déjà championne!** she thought the championship was hers already!; **je me vois encore entrant** *ou* **entrer dans mon bureau** I can still see myself walking into my office; **je me vois mal grimper aux arbres à mon âge!** I can't see myself climbing trees at my age!; **elle se voyait mal lui faire faux-bond maintenant** she couldn't see how she could possibly let him/her down now; **je ne me vois pas lui demander une augmentation** I (just) can't see myself asking him/her for a rise

3 *(se rencontrer)* to see each other; **tu ne peux pas les empêcher de se v.** you can't keep them from seeing each other

4 *(être visible, évident ▸ défaut)* to show, to be visible; *(▸ émotion, gêne)* to be visible, to be obvious, to be apparent; **la cicatrice ne se voit presque plus** the scar hardly shows any more, you can hardly see the scar now; **ton slip se voit sous ta jupe** your pants show through your skirt; **il porte une perruque, ça se voit bien** you can tell he wears a wig

5 *(se manifester ▸ événement)* to happen; *(▸ attitude, coutume)* to be seen *or* found; **ça se voit couramment** it's commonplace

6 *(se trouver)* **se v. dans l'impossibilité de faire qch** to find oneself unable to do sth; **se v. dans l'obligation de...** to find oneself obliged to...; **leur équipe s'est vue reléguée à la quinzième place** their team saw themselves drop to fifteenth position; **les crédits se verront affectés à la rénovation des locaux** the funds will be used to renovate the building

7 *(suivi d'un infinitif)* **se v. interdire l'inscription à un club** to be refused membership to a club; **il s'est vu retirer son permis de conduire sur-le-champ** he had his driving licence taken away from him on the spot

---

voire [vwar] **ADV v. (même)** (or) even; **certains, v. la majorité** some, or *or* perhaps even most; **la nourriture est mauvaise, v. immangeable** the food's bad, not to say inedible; **vexé, v. offensé** upset, not to say offended

voirie [vwari] **NF 1** *(entretien des routes)* road maintenance; *Admin* **le service de la v.** road maintenance and cleaning department (of the local council); **travaux de v.** roadworks **2** *(réseau)* public road network **3** *(décharge)* *Br* refuse dump, *Am* garbage dump

voisin, -e [vwazɛ̃, -in] **ADJ 1** *(d'à côté)* next, adjoining; *(qui est à proximité)* neighbouring; **la chambre voisine est inoccupée** there's nobody in the next room; **deux maisons voisines** two houses next to each other, two adjoining houses; **il habite la maison voisine** he lives next door; **une rue voisine des Champs-Élysées** a street adjoining the Champs-Élysées; **pays voisins** neighbouring countries; **les pays voisins de l'équateur/de notre territoire** the countries near the equator/bo dering on our territory; **un prix v. du million** price approaching *or* around one million

2 *(dans le temps)* **v. de** *(antérieur à)* precedin before; *(postérieur à)* after, following; *(auto de)* around; **cela aura lieu à une date voisine de rentrée** it'll be sometime around the start of th new term

3 *(similaire ▸ idées, langues, expérience)* simila *(▸ espèces)* closely related; **émotion voisine de terreur** emotion akin to *or* bordering on terror

NM,F 1 *(habitant à côté)* neighbour; **v. d'à côt** next-door neighbour; **mes voisins du dessus/de sous** the people upstairs/downstairs from me; **essayons d'être bons voisins!** let's try to act in neighbourly way!; **v. de palier** neighbour (acros the landing)

2 *(placé à côté)* neighbour; **mon v. de table** th person next to me *or* my neighbour at table; **nos voisins belges** our Belgian neighbours

3 le v. *(autrui)* the next man, one's fellow (man

voisinage [vwazinaʒ] **NM 1** *(proximité)* vicinity proximity, nearness; **le v. de la gendarmerie le rassure** they are comforted by the fact that ther is a police station nearby

2 *(quartier)* vicinity, neighbourhood; **il rôde dan le v.** he hangs around the neighbourhood; **le hôtels du v.** the nearby hotels, the hotels in th vicinity

3 dans le v. de in the vicinity of; **ils habitent dan le v. d'une centrale nucléaire** they live near a nu clear plant

4 *(personnes)* neighbours; **tout le v. est au cou rant** the whole neighbourhood knows about it

5 *(rapports)* **relations de bon v.** (good) neigh bourliness; **être** *ou* **vivre en bon v. avec qn, entre tenir des relations de bon v. avec qn** to be or neighbourly terms with sb

voisiner [3] [vwazine] **VI 1 v. avec** *(être près de)* to be near **2** *Littéraire (fréquenter ses voisins)* to be on friendly terms with one's neighbours; **à Paris on voisine peu** in Paris you don't see much o your neighbours

voiturage [vwatyraʒ] **NM** *(de marchandises)* car riage, conveyance, cartage

voiture [vwatyr] **NF 1** *(de particulier)* car, *Am* au tomobile; **on y va en v.?** shall we go (there) by car?, shall we drive (there)?; **prendre sa** *ou* **la v.** to take the car; **v. de compétition** competition car; **v. de course** racing car; **v. décapotable** convertible; **v. (de) deux places** two-seater; *Vieilli* **v. d'enfant** *(landau) Br* pram, *Am* baby carriage; *(poussette) Br* pushchair, *Am* stroller; **v. de fonction** *ou* **de service** *ou* **de société** company car; **v. de grand tourisme** *Br* GT (saloon) car, *Am* 4-door sedan; **v. hybride** hybrid car; *Vieilli* **v. d'infirme** wheelchair; **v. de livraison** delivery van; **v. de location** *ou* **de louage** rental car, *Br* hire car; **v. d'occasion** secondhand car, used car; **v. particulière** private car; **v. à pédales** pedal car; **v. de police** police car; **v. (de) quatre places** four-seater; **v. de sport** sports car; **v. de tourisme** private car; **v. tout terrain** all terrain vehicle; **v. ventouse** illegally parked car, abandoned car; **v. de ville** urban car, *Fam* runabout; **petite v.** *(d'enfant)* toy car; *(d'infirme)* wheelchair

2 *Rail* coach, *Br* carriage, *Am* car; **en v.!** all aboard!; **v. de tête/queue** front/rear *Br* carriage *or Am* car

3 *(véhicule sans moteur ▸ pour personnes)* carriage, coach; *(▸ pour marchandises)* cart; **v. à bras** handcart; **v. à cheval** *ou* **hippomobile** horse-drawn carriage; **v. à deux/quatre chevaux** carriage and pair/and four; **v. de louage** *ou* **place** hackney carriage

4 *Arch (mode de transport)* conveyance, transport

voiture-bar [vwatyrbar] *(pl* **voitures-bars)** **NF** *Rail* buffet car

voiture-couchette [vwatyrkuʃɛt] *(pl* **voitures-couchettes)** **NF** *Rail* sleeping compartment

voiturée [vwatyre] **NF** *Littéraire ou Arch (de passagers ▸ d'une voiture à cheval)* carriageful, coachload; *(▸ d'une automobile)* carload; *(de marchandises)* cartload

voiture-école [vwatyrekɔl] *(pl* **voitures-écoles)** **NF** driving-school car

oiture-lit [vwatyrli] *(pl* **voitures-lits)** NF *Rail* leeper, *Am* Pullman

oiturer [3] [vwatyre] VT *Hum ou Arch (transpor-er ▸ gén)* to convey; *(▸ dans une charrette)* to art; *Fam* **je vais te v.** I'll drive you□

oiture-restaurant [vwatyrrestɔrɑ̃] *(pl* **oitures-restaurants)** NF *Rail* restaurant *or* dining ar

oiture-salon [vwatyrsalɔ̃] *(pl* **voitures-salon)** NF *Rail Br* saloon *or Am* parlor car

oiturette [vwatyrɛt] NF **1** *(charrette)* trap **2** *auto)* small car

oiturier [vwatyrje] NM **1** *(d'hôtel)* porter *(who parks the guests' cars)*; **service de v.** valet parking **2** *Com & Jur* carrier

oix [vwa] NF **1** *Physiol* voice; **avoir une jolie v.** to have a nice voice; **avoir une v. grave/chaude** to have a deep/warm voice; **parler par la v. de qn** to speak through sb; **prendre une grosse/petite v.** to put on a gruff/tiny voice; **une v. intérieure me disait que...** a voice in my head was telling me that...; *Ordinat* **v. artificielle** synthesized speech; *TV & Cin* **v. in** voice in; *TV & Cin* **v. dans le champ** in-frame voice; *TV & Cin* **v. hors champ** voice-over; *TV & Cin* **v. off** voice-over; **commentaire en v. off** voice-over commentary; **une v. de stentor** a stentorian voice; **faire la grosse v.** to raise one's voice; **donner de la v.** *(chien)* to bay; *(personne)* to shout, to bawl; *Fig* **donner de la v. contre qch** *(protester)* to protest vehemently against sth; **ils encourageaient les cyclistes de la v. et du geste** they were shouting and waving the riders on; *Fig* **d'une commune v.** by common consent, with one voice

2 *Mus (de chanteur)* voice; *(partition)* part; **avoir de la v.** to have a strong voice; **poser sa v.** to train one's voice; **chanter à plusieurs/cinq v.** to sing in parts/five parts; **fugue à deux/trois v.** fugue for two/three voices; *Fig* **la v. chaude du saxophone** the mellow tones *or* voice of the saxophone; **v. de basse/soprano/ténor** bass/soprano/tenor voice; **v. de fausset** falsetto voice; **v. de poitrine/tête** chest/head voice

3 *(personne)* voice; **nous accueillons ce soir une des plus belles v. du monde** tonight we welcome one of the finest voices in the world; **"c'est faux", dit une v. au premier rang** "it's not true," said a voice from the front row

4 *(message)* voice; **la v. de la conscience** the voice of one's conscience; **écouter la v. de la raison/de la sagesse/de Dieu** to listen to the voice of reason/of wisdom/of God; **la v. du peuple** the voice of the people; **entendre des v.** to hear voices; **avoir v. au chapitre** to have a *or* one's say in the matter; **tu n'as pas v. au chapitre** you have no say in the matter

5 *Pol* vote; **un homme, une v.** one man, one vote; **v. pour/contre** vote for/against; **obtenir 1500 v.** to win *or* to get 1,500 votes; **recueillir** *ou* **remporter 57 pour cent des v.** to win 57 percent of the vote *or* votes; **le parti qui a le plus grand nombre de v.** the party which heads the poll *or* with the largest number of votes; **élu à la majorité des v.** elected by a majority; **donner sa v. à** to give one's vote to, to vote for; **mettre qch aux v.** to put sth to the vote; **où iront les v. du Parti radical?** how will the Radical Party vote?; **v. consultative** advisory vote; **avoir v. consultative** to have an advisory role; **v. délibérative** deliberative vote; **avoir v. délibérative** to have the right to vote; **avoir v. prépondérante** to have the casting vote

6 *Gram* voice; **v. active/passive** active/passive voice; **à la v. active/passive** in the active voice/in the passive (voice)

• **à haute voix, à voix haute** ADV **1** *(lire)* aloud **2** *(parler)* loud, loudly, in a loud voice; **à haute (et intelligible) v.** loudly and clearly

• **à voix basse** ADV in a low voice; **les élèves parlaient à v. basse** the pupils were whispering; **les deux hommes discutaient à v. basse dans un coin** the two men spoke in lowered tones in a corner

• **en voix** ADJ **être en v.** to be in good voice

• **sans voix** ADJ **être** *ou* **rester sans v.** *(d'épouvante)* to be speechless, to be struck dumb; *(d'émotion, de chagrin)* to be speechless

vol¹ [vɔl] NM **1** *Jur* theft, robbery; **commettre un v.** to commit a theft, to steal; **v. aggravé** robbery with violence; **v. à l'américaine** confidence trick; **v. à l'arraché** bag snatching; **v. avec effraction** breaking and entering; **v. à l'étalage** shoplifting; **v. d'identité** identity theft; **v. à main armée** armed robbery; **v. à la portière** = act of theft whereby the thief opens the door of a vehicle waiting at traffic lights etc and steals any available valuable item before the driver has time to react; **v. qualifié** aggravated theft; **v. simple** common theft; **v. à la tire** pickpocketing; **v. de voiture** car theft **2** *(vente à un prix excessif)* **c'est du v. (manifeste)!** it's daylight robbery!; **c'est du v. organisé!** it's a racket!

vol² [vɔl] NM **1** *Aviat & Astron* flight; **prendre son v.** to take off; **il y a quarante minutes de v.** it's a forty-minute flight; **à trois heures de v. de Paris** three hours' flying time from Paris; *Fam Hum* **elle a pas mal d'heures de v.** she's no spring chicken; **avion en v.** aircraft in flight; **v. aller-retour** *Br* return flight, *Am* round-trip flight; **v. d'apport** feeder flight; **v. en ballon** *(excursion)* balloon trip; *(activité)* ballooning; **v. (en) charter** charter flight; **v. avec escale** flight with stopover; **v. d'essai** trial flight; **v. habité** manned flight; **v. libre** hang-gliding; **pratiquer le** *ou* **faire du v. libre** to hang-glide, to go hang-gliding; **v. en rase-mottes** hedge-hopping flight; **v. régulier** scheduled flight; **v. sec** flight only; **v. à voile** gliding; **pratiquer le** *ou* **faire du v. à voile** to glide, to do gliding; **v. à vue** sight flight **2** *Zool* flight; **prendre son v.** to fly away, to take wing; **faire un v. plané** to glide; *Fam Fig* **j'ai fait un v. plané!** I went flying! **3** *(groupe ▸ d'oiseaux)* flight, flock; *(▸ d'insectes)* swarm; **v. d'oies sauvages** flight *or* flock of wild geese; **v. de perdreaux** flock *or* covey of partridges; **v. de pigeons** flight of pigeons

• **au vol** ADV *(en passant)* **saisir au v.** *(ballon, clés)* to catch in mid-air; **saisir une occasion au v.** to jump at *or* to seize an opportunity

• **à vol d'oiseau** ADV as the crow flies; **c'est à 10 kilomètres à v. d'oiseau** it's 10 kilometres as the crow flies

• **de haut vol** ADJ *(artiste, spécialiste)* top *(avant n)*; *(projet)* ambitious, far-reaching

volage [vɔlaʒ] ADJ fickle; *Fig* **le public est v.** audiences are fickle *or* unpredictable

volaille [vɔlaj] NF **une v.** *(oiseau de basse-cour)* a fowl; **de la v.** poultry

volailler [vɔlaje] NM *(marchand)* poultryman, *Br* poulterer

volant¹ [vɔlɑ̃] NM **1** *Aut* steering wheel; **être au v.** to be at the wheel, to be behind the wheel, to be driving; **prendre le** *ou* **se mettre au v.** to take the wheel, to get behind the wheel; **je te recommande la prudence au v.** take care when driving; **peux-tu prendre le v. après Évreux?** could you take over the driving after Évreux?; **qui tenait le v.?** who was driving?; **donner un coup de v.** to pull on the wheel (sharply)

2 *Tech (manuel)* handwheel

3 *(d'horloge)* fly

4 *(garniture de vêtement)* flounce; **robe à volants** flounced dress

5 *(jeu ▸ objet)* shuttlecock; *(▸ activité)* battledore and shuttlecock; **jeu de v.** (game of) battledore and shuttlecock

6 *(feuille)* tear-off portion

7 *Écon & Fin* **v. de sécurité** *(financier)* reserve funds; *(en personnel)* reserve; **v. de trésorerie** cash reserve

volant², -e [vɔlɑ̃, -ɑ̃t] ADJ **1** *Aviat & Zool* flying *(avant n)*; *Aviat* **personnel v.** cabin crew; *Naut* **escadre volante** flying squadron **2** *(mobile ▸ câble, camp, échafaudage, pont, service)* flying *(avant n)*; **on mettra une table volante devant le fauteuil** we'll put an occasional table in front of the armchair

volatil, -e¹ [vɔlatil] ADJ **1** *Chim* volatile **2** *(fluctuant ▸ électorat)* fickle; *(▸ situation, sentiment)* volatile

volatile² [vɔlatil] NM **1** *Hum (oiseau)* bird, (feathered) creature; **le malheureux v. se retrouva dans la casserole** the wretched bird ended up in the pot **2** *(oiseau de basse-cour)* fowl, chicken

volatilisable [vɔlatilizabl] ADJ volatilizable

volatilisation [vɔlatilizasjɔ̃] NF volatilization

volatiliser [3] [vɔlatilize] VT *Chim* to volatilize

VPR **se volatiliser 1** *(disparaître)* to vanish (into thin air); **elles ne se sont pourtant pas volatilisées, ces clefs!** those keys can't just have vanished into thin air!; **en une soirée au club, mes 300 euros s'étaient volatilisés** one evening at the club and my 300 euros had gone up in smoke **2** *Chim* to volatilize

volatilité [vɔlatilite] NF volatility

vol-au-vent [vɔlovɑ̃] NM INV *Culin* vol-au-vent

volcan [vɔlkɑ̃] NM **1** *Géog & Géol* volcano; **v. en activité/dormant/éteint** active/dormant/extinct volcano **2** *Fig* **c'est un vrai v.** he's/she's likely to explode at any moment; **être assis** *ou* **danser** *ou* **dormir sur un v.** to be sitting on a powder keg

volcanique [vɔlkanik] ADJ **1** *Géog & Géol* volcanic **2** *Littéraire (passion)* fiery, volcanic, blazing; *(imagination)* vivid; *(tempérament)* fiery, impetuous

volcanologie [vɔlkanɔlɔʒi] NF *Géol* volcanology, vulcanology

volcanologue [vɔlkanɔlɔg] NMF *Géol* volcanologist, vulcanologist

vole [vɔl] NF *Cartes* vole, all the tricks

volé, -e¹ [vɔle] ADJ *(argent, bijou)* stolen

NM,F victim of theft

volée² [vɔle] NF **1** *(ce qu'on lance)* **v. d'obus/de pierres** volley of shells/of stones; **v. de flèches** volley *or* flight of arrows; **v. de coups** shower of blows; *Fig* **v. d'insultes** shower of insults; *Fig* **une v. de bois vert** a barrage of fierce criticism; **son dernier disque a reçu une v. de bois vert** his/her last record was panned

2 *Fam (correction)* thrashing, hiding; **elle a reçu une bonne v.** she got a sound thrashing *or* a good hiding

3 *Fam (défaite)* beating, hammering; **il a pris une sacrée v. en demi-finale** he got trounced *or* thrashed in the semi-finals

4 *Sport* volley; **reprendre une balle de v.** to volley a ball, to hit the ball on the volley; **monter à la v.** to come to the net; **il n'est pas/il est très bon à la v.** he's a bad/he's a good volleyer; **v. amortie/de coup droit/de revers** *(au tennis)* drop/forehand/backhand volley; **coup de v.** punt; **envoyer une balle d'un coup de v.** to punt a ball

5 *Orn (formation)* flock, flight; *(de perdrix)* covey; *Fig Littéraire* **une v. de fillettes** a crowd of little girls; **prendre sa v.** *(oiseau)* to fly away, to take wing; *Fig (débutant, adolescent)* to spread one's wings

6 *(son de cloche)* peal (of bells), pealing bells

7 *Constr* **v. d'escaliers** flight of stairs

8 *(en travaux publics)* (crane) jib

9 *Suisse (promotion)* **on était de la même v.** we were in the same year

• **à la volée** ADV **1** *(en passant)* **attraper** *ou* **saisir à la v.** *(clés, balle)* to catch in mid-air; **relancer une balle à la v.** *(au tennis)* to volley a return **2** *Agr* **semer à la v.** to (sow) broadcast

• **à toute volée** ADV *(frapper, projeter)* vigorously, with full force; **il a lancé le vase à toute v. contre le mur** he hurled the vase at *or* flung the vase against the wall; **claquer une porte à toute v.** to slam *or* to bang a door shut; **sonner à toute v.** *(cloches)* to peal (out); *(carillonneur)* to peal all the bells

• **de haute volée** ADJ *(spécialiste)* top *(avant n)*; *(projet)* ambitious, far-reaching

voler¹ [3] [vɔle] VI **1** *Aviat & Zool* to fly; **faire v. un cerf-volant** to fly a kite; **nous volons à une vitesse de...** we are flying at a speed of...; *Fig* **v. de ses propres ailes** to stand on one's own two feet, to fend for oneself **2** *(étincelles, projectile)* to fly; **il faisait v. ses adversaires/les assiettes** he was throwing his opponents around/throwing the plates in the air; **v. en éclats** to be smashed to bits *or* to pieces; *Fam* **ça vole bas!, ça ne vole pas haut!** VERY funny!; **chez eux, ça ne vole pas bien haut** they've got a rather crude sense of humour **3** *(se précipiter)* **v. vers qn/qch** to fly to sb/towards sth; **il a volé à sa rencontre** he rushed to meet him/her; **v. au secours de qn** to fly to sb's assistance; *Fam* **v. dans les plumes à qn** to let fly at sb, to have a go at sb; *Fam* **elle lui a volé dans les plumes** she had a real go at him/her

voler² [3] [vɔle] VT **1** *(objet, idée)* to steal; **v. qch à qn** to steal sth from sb; **on m'a volé ma montre!** my watch has been stolen!; **il volait de l'argent dans**

la caisse he used to steal money from the till; *Littéraire* **v. un baiser à qn** to steal a kiss from sb; **je n'ai pas volé mon argent/dîner/week-end** I've certainly earned my money/earned myself some dinner/earned myself a weekend; **tu ne l'as pas volé!** *(tu le mérites)* you've earned it!; *(tu es bien puni)* you (certainly) asked for it!, it serves you right!; *Prov* **qui vole un œuf vole un bœuf** = there's no such thing as a petty thief **2** *(personne)* to rob; **se faire v. qch** to have sth stolen; **il s'est fait v. son portefeuille** his wallet was stolen **3** *(léser)* to cheat, to swindle; **on s'est fait v.** we were ripped off, we were really stung; **je me suis fait v. de dix euros** I've been swindled out of ten euros; **elle ne t'a pas volé sur le poids de la viande** she gave you a good weight of meat

USAGE ABSOLU to steal; **ce n'est pas bien de v.** it's wrong to steal, stealing is wrong; *Bible* **tu ne voleras point** thou shalt not steal

> Attention: ne pas confondre **to steal** et **to rob** lorsque l'on traduit le verbe **voler**. **To steal** signifie **dérober** (quelque chose), alors que **to rob** signifie **dévaliser** (quelqu'un, un lieu).

volet [vɔlɛ] **NM 1** *(d'une maison)* shutter

2 *(d'un document ▸ section)* section; *Beaux-Arts (d'un polyptyque)* wing, *Spéc* volet; *(d'un chèque)* tear-off portion

3 *(d'une politique, d'un projet de loi)* point, part; *(d'une émission)* part; **le v. social** *(de la Communauté européenne)* the social chapter

4 *Aviat* flap; **sortir/rentrer les volets** to lower/raise flaps

5 *Tech (d'une roue à eau)* paddle; *(de carburateur)* throttle *or* butterfly valve

voleter [27] [vɔlte] **VI** *(oiseau, papillon)* to flutter *or* to flit (about)

voleur, -euse [vɔlœr, -øz] **ADJ être v.** *(enfant)* to be a (bit of a) thief; *(marchand)* to be a crook *or* a cheat; **il est v. comme une pie** he's got sticky fingers

NM,F *(escroc)* thief, robber; *(marchand)* crook, cheat; *(cambrioleur)* burglar; **au v.!** stop thief!; **partir** *ou* **se sauver comme un v.** *(en courant)* to take to one's heels; *(discrètement)* to slip away; **v. de bétail** cattle thief; **v. d'enfants** kidnapper; **v. à l'étalage** shoplifter; *Hist* **v. de grand(s) chemin(s)** highwayman, footpad; **v. d'idées** plagiarist; **v. de moutons** sheep stealer; **v. à la tire** pickpocket

Volga [vɔlga] **NF la V.** the (River) Volga

volière [vɔljɛr] **NF** *(enclos)* aviary; *(cage)* birdcage; *Fig* **c'est une vraie v. dans cette classe!** it's like a zoo in this class!

volige [vɔliʒ] **NF** *Constr* batten; *(pour tuiles)* slate lath; **caisse en voliges** crate

voligeage [vɔliʒaʒ] **NM** *Constr* battening; *(pour tuiles)* lathing

voliger [17] [vɔliʒe] **VT** *Constr* to batten; *(pour tuiles)* to lath

volis [vɔli] **NM** broken tree top

volitif, -ive [vɔlitif, -iv] **ADJ** *Phil* volitional

volition [vɔlisjɔ̃] **NF** *Phil* volition

volitive [vɔlitiv] *voir* **volitif**

volley [vɔlɛ] **NM** *Fam* volleyball□; **v. de plage** beach volleyball□

volley-ball [vɔlebol] *(pl* **volley-balls***)* **NM** volleyball

volleyeur, -euse [vɔlejœr, -øz] **NM,F 1** *(au volley-ball)* volleyball player **2** *(au tennis)* volleyer; **c'est un bon/mauvais v.** he volleys/doesn't volley well

volontaire [vɔlɔ̃tɛr] **ADJ 1** *(déterminé)* determined, self-willed; *(têtu)* headstrong, wilful; **avoir le menton/front v.** to have a firm *or* determined chin/a set forehead **2** *(voulu ▸ engagement)* voluntary; *(▸ oubli)* intentional **3** *(qui agit librement ▸ engagé, travailleur)* volunteer *(avant n)*; **se porter v. pour** to volunteer for; **quand il s'agit de m'aider, il est toujours v.** when it comes to helping me, he's always willing (to do so) *or* he always volunteers

NMF volunteer; *Anciennement Mil* **v. du service national** = before national service was abolished, a recruit who chose to carry out his national service by doing voluntary service overseas; **v. international** = young person who does a voluntary work placement overseas, working for a French-run organization or promoting French interests

volontairement [vɔlɔ̃tɛrmɑ̃] **ADV 1** *(sans y être obligé)* voluntarily, of one's own free will **2** *(intentionnellement)* on purpose, intentionally, deliberately; **c'est v. que j'ai supprimé ce passage** I deleted this passage on purpose

volontariat [vɔlɔ̃tarja] **NM le v.** *(gén)* voluntary work; *Mil* voluntary service; **faire du v.** to do voluntary service

volontarisme [vɔlɔ̃tarism] **NM** *Phil* voluntarism, voluntaryism

volontariste [vɔlɔ̃tarist] **ADJ** voluntaristic; *(politique)* aggressive

NMF voluntarist

volonté [vɔlɔ̃te] **NF 1** *(détermination)* will, willpower; **avoir de la v./beaucoup de v.** to have willpower/a strong will; **avoir une v. de fer** to have a will of iron *or* an iron will; **il manque de v.** he lacks willpower, he doesn't have enough willpower; **faire un effort de v.** to make an effort of willpower; **arriver à qch à force de v.** to achieve sth by sheer willpower

2 *(désir)* will, wish; **la v. de l'électorat** the will of the electorate; **accomplir la v. de qn** to carry out sb's wish; **faire qch/aller contre la v. de qn** to do sth/go against sb's will; **la v. de gagner/survivre** the will to win/to survive; **montrer sa v. de faire qch** to show one's determination to do sth; **faire qch de sa propre v.** to do sth of one's own accord *or* spontaneously; **la v. divine** *ou* **de Dieu** God's will; *Phil* **v. de puissance** will-to-power; **les dernières volontés de qn** *(document)* sb's last will and testament; *(vœux)* sb's last wishes; *Rel* **que Ta/Votre v. soit faite** Thy will be done

3 *(disposition)* **bonne v.** willingness; **faire preuve de bonne v.** to show willing; **être plein de bonne v.** to be full of goodwill; **il est plein de bonne v. mais il n'arrive à rien** he tries hard but doesn't achieve anything; **faire appel aux bonnes volontés** to appeal for volunteers to come forward; **personne de bonne v.** willing person; **avec la meilleure v. du monde** with the best will in the world; **mauvaise v.** unwillingness; **faire preuve de mauvaise v.** to be grudging; **elle y met de la mauvaise v.** she's doing it with very bad grace; **allez, lève-toi, c'est de la mauvaise v.!** come on, get up, you're not really trying!

• à volonté ADJ café à v. as much coffee as you want, unlimited coffee; *Mil* **feu à v.** fire at will **ADV** *(arrêter, continuer)* at will; **poivrez à v.** add pepper to taste; **servez-vous à v.** take as much as you want; *Fin* **billet payable à v.** promissory note payable on demand

volontiers [vɔlɔ̃tje] **ADV 1** *(de bon gré)* gladly, willingly; *(avec plaisir)* with pleasure; **elle en parle v.** she will happily talk about it; **je prendrais v. un verre de vin** I could do with *or* I'd love a glass of wine; **un café? – très v.** a coffee? – yes please *or* I'd love one **2** *(souvent)* willingly, readily; **on croit v. que...** we are apt to think *or* ready to believe that...; **elle est v. cynique** she tends to be cynical; **il ne sourit pas v.** he's not very generous with his smiles

volt [vɔlt] **NM** volt

voltage [vɔltaʒ] **NM** voltage

voltaïque¹ [vɔltaik] **ADJ** *Élec* voltaic, galvanic

voltaïque² [vɔltaik] **ADJ 1** *Géog* Voltaic, of Burkina-Faso **2** *Ling* Gur, Voltaic

voltaire [vɔltɛr] **NM** Voltaire chair

voltairien, -enne [vɔltɛrjɛ̃, -ɛn] **ADJ** Voltairean, Voltairian

NM,F Voltairean, Voltairian

voltamètre [vɔltamɛtr] **NM** *Élec* voltameter

voltampère [vɔltɑ̃pɛr] **NM** *Élec* volt-ampere

volte [vɔlt] **NF 1** *Équitation* volt, volte **2** *Naut (changement de cap)* turn

volte-face [vɔltəfas] **NF INV 1** *(fait de pivoter)* about-turn, *Am* about-face; **faire v.** to turn round **2** *Fig (changement ▸ d'opinion, d'attitude)* volte-face, about-turn; **le parti a fait une v.** the party did a 180-degree turn *or* a U-turn

volter [3] [vɔlte] **VI** *Équitation* **faire v. un cheval** to make a horse execute a volt *or* volte

voltige [vɔltiʒ] **NF 1** *(au trapèze)* **la haute v.** acr batics, flying trapeze exercises

2 *Équitation* mounted gymnastics, voltige

3 *Aviat* **v. (aérienne)** aerobatics; **pilote de v.** stu pilot

4 *Fig (entreprise difficile)* **la Bourse, c'est de la** speculating on the Stock Exchange is a high risky business

voltiger [17] [vɔltiʒe] **VI 1** *(libellule, oiseau)* to f about, to flutter (about); *(abeille, mouche)* t buzz about **2** *(flocon, papier)* to float around i the air, to flutter (about) **3** *(sur un trapèze)* to d acrobatics, to perform on the flying trapez *(sur un cheval)* to do acrobatics, to perform o horseback

voltigeur, -euse [vɔltiʒœr, -øz] **NM,F** acrobat

NM 1 *Hist* light infantryman **2** *(au base-ball)* **gauche/droit** left/right fielder; **v. du centre** centr fielder

voltmètre [vɔltmɛtr] **NM** voltmeter

volubile [vɔlybil] **ADJ 1** *(qui parle ▸ beaucou* garrulous, voluble; *(▸ avec aisance)* fluent **2** *Bo* voluble

volubilis [vɔlybilis] **NM** *Bot* morning glory, co volvulus

volubilité [vɔlybilite] **NF** volubility, voluble ness, garrulousness; **parler avec v.** to be a volu ble talker, to talk volubly

volucompteur [vɔlykɔ̃tœr] **NM** *Br* petrol pum *or Am* gas pump indicator

volumateur, -trice [vɔlymatœr, -tris] **AD** *(shampooing, mascara)* volumizing

volume [vɔlym] **NM 1** *(tome)* volume; **une ency clopédie en deux volumes** an encyclopedia i two volumes, a two-volume encyclopedia

2 *(du son)* volume; **augmente** *ou* **monte le v.** tur the volume *or* sound up; **baisse** *ou* **descends le v** turn the volume *or* sound down; **v. sonore** soun level

3 *(quantité globale)* volume, amount; **v. d'achat** purchase volume, volume of purchases; **v. an nuel de production** annual (volume of) produc tion; **le v. des échanges commerciaux** the volum of trade; **le v. des exportations** the volume of ex ports; **le v. des importations** the volume of im ports; *Com* **v. de point mort** break-eve quantity; **v. des ventes** sales volume, volume o sales

4 *Beaux-Arts & Géom* volume

5 *(poids, épaisseur)* volume; **faire du v.** *(chose)* t take up a lot of space; *Fam (personne)* to show off, to throw one's weight about; *Fam* **il a pris du v.** he's put on weight□; **une permanente donnerai du v. à vos cheveux** a perm would give your hai more body

6 *(cubage)* volume; *(de réservoirs)* capacity; **v. (d'eau) du fleuve** volume of water in the river **eau oxygénée (à) 20 volumes** 20-volume hydrogen peroxide

7 *Ordinat (unité)* volume; **v. mémoire** storage capacity

8 *Bourse* **v. d'affaires** trading volume

9 *Naut* **chargé en v.** laden in bulk

volumétrique [vɔlymetrik] **ADJ** volumetric

volumineux, -euse [vɔlyminø, -øz] **ADJ** *(sac)* bulky, voluminous; *(dossier)* bulky; *(correspondance)* voluminous, massive; **très peu v.** taking up little space

volupté [vɔlypte] **NF 1** *(plaisir)* sensual *or* voluptuous pleasure; *Littéraire* **la v.** the pleasures of the flesh **2** *(caractère sensuel)* voluptuousness

voluptueuse [vɔlyptɥøz] *voir* **voluptueux**

voluptueusement [vɔlyptɥøzmɑ̃] **ADV** voluptuously

voluptueux, -euse [vɔlyptɥø, -øz] **ADJ** voluptuous

volute [vɔlyt] **NF 1** *(de fumée)* coil; *(de lianes)* curl, scroll; *(en arts décoratifs)* volute, helix; **la fumée s'élève en v.** the smoke is spiralling upwards; **ressort en v.** helical spring **2** *Zool (mollusque)* volute; **les volutes** the Volutidae

vomer [vɔmɛr] **NM** *Anat* vomer

vomi [vɔmi] **NM** vomit

vomique [vɔmik] **ADJ** *Bot* **noix v.** nux vomica

vomiquier [vɔmikje] **NM** *Bot* nux vomica (tree)

vomir **[32]** [vɔmir] **VT 1** *Physiol (repas)* to bring up, to vomit; *(sang, bile)* to bring *or* to cough up **2** *Fig (fumée)* to spew, to vomit; *(foule)* to spew forth; *(insultes)* to spew out **3** *Fig (rejeter avec dégoût)* to have no time for, to feel revulsion for; *(personne)* to loathe, *Sout* to abhor; **un article qui vomit le postmodernisme** an article pouring venom on post-modernism
VI to be sick, to vomit; **sucré à (faire) v.** sickeningly sweet; **une odeur à vous faire v.** a nauseating smell; **avoir envie de v.** to feel sick *or Am* nauseous; **elle est riche à faire v.** she's so rich it makes you sick; **une telle hypocrisie me donne envie de v.** such hypocrisy makes me sick

vomissement [vɔmismɑ̃] **NM 1** *(action)* vomiting *(UNCOUNT)*; **si l'enfant est pris de vomissements** if the child starts to vomit **2** *(substance)* vomit *(UNCOUNT)*

vomissure [vɔmisyr] **NF** vomit *(UNCOUNT)*

vomitif, -ive [vɔmitif, -iv] *Méd* **ADJ 1** emetic, vomitive **2** *Fig Fam (dégoûtant)* revolting, gross
NM emetic, vomitive

vont [võ] *voir* **aller**[2]

vorace [vɔras] **ADJ 1** *(mangeur)* voracious; *(appétit)* insatiable, voracious; *(lecteur)* voracious, avid; **se sentir d'un appétit v.** to feel ravenously hungry; *Ordinat* **application v. en mémoire** memory-intensive application **2** *Bot* **plantes voraces** plants which exhaust the soil

voracement [vɔrasmɑ̃] **ADV** voraciously

voracité [vɔrasite] **NF** voracity, voraciousness

vortex [vɔrtɛks] **NM** vortex

vos [vo] *voir* **votre**

Vosges [voʒ] **NFPL les V.** the Vosges

vosgien, -enne [voʒjɛ̃, -ɛn] **ADJ** of/from the Vosges
• **Vosgien, -enne NM,F** = inhabitant of or person from the Vosges

votant, -e [vɔtɑ̃, -ɑ̃t] **NM,F** voter

votation [vɔtasjɔ̃] **NF** *Suisse* vote

vote [vɔt] **NM 1** *(voix, suffrage)* vote; **le v. noir/des femmes** the black/women's vote; **v. blanc** blank ballot paper; **v. de confiance** vote of confidence; **v. défavorable** "no" vote; **v. de défiance** vote of no confidence; **v. favorable** "yes" vote; **v. nul** spoilt ballot paper; **v. de protestation** protest vote; **v. réactionnaire** reactionary vote; **v. sanction** sanction vote; **v. utile** tactical vote **2** *(élection)* vote; *(action)* voting; **prendre part au v.** to go to the polls, to vote; **procédons** *ou* **passons au v.** let's have *or* take a vote; **v. par acclamation** voice vote; **v. à bulletin secret** secret ballot; **v. par correspondance** *Br* postal vote *or* ballot, *Am* absentee ballot; **v. direct/indirect** direct/indirect vote; **v. libre** free vote; **v. à main levée** vote by show of hands; **v. majoritaire** majority vote; **v. obligatoire** compulsory vote; **v. pondéré** weighted vote; **v. préférentiel** preferential voting; **v. par procuration** proxy vote; **v. secret** secret ballot; **v. unique transférable** single transferable vote **3** *(d'une loi)* passing; *(de crédits)* voting; *(d'un projet de loi)* vote; **v. bloqué** = enforced vote on a text containing only government amendments

voter **[3]** [vɔte] **VI** to vote; **v. à droite/à gauche/au centre** to vote for the right/left/centre; **v. pour qn** to vote for sb; **v. pour les conservateurs, v. conservateur** to vote Conservative; **v. à main levée** to vote by show of hands; **v. par procuration** to vote by proxy; **v. contre/pour qch** to vote against/for sth; **on leur a demandé de v. pour ou contre la grève** they were balloted about the strike; **v. utile** to vote tactically; **votons sur la dernière motion présentée** let's (take a) vote on the last motion before us; **v. (pour) Thomas!** vote for Thomas!
VT *(crédits)* to vote; *(loi)* to pass; *(projet de loi)* to vote for; *(budget)* to approve; **être voté** *(projet de loi)* to go through; **v. la peine de mort** to pass a vote in favour of capital punishment

votif, -ive [vɔtif, -iv] **ADJ** votive

votre [vɔtr] *(pl* **vos** [vo]) **ADJ POSSESSIF 1** *(indiquant la possession)* your; **v. livre et vos crayons** *(d'une personne)* your book and your pencils; *(de plusieurs personnes)* your books and your pencils; **v. père et v. mère,** *Littéraire* **vos père et mère** your father and mother; **un de vos amis** one of your friends, a friend of yours; **un professeur de vos amis** a teacher friend of yours; *Fam* **vous aurez v. chambre à vous** *(chacun aura sa chambre)* you will have your own rooms; *Fam* **vous avez v. vendredi** you've got Friday off **2** *(dans des titres)* **V. Majesté** Your Majesty; **V. Altesse** Your Highness; **V. Excellence** Your Excellency **3** *(emploi expressif)* your; **comment va v. cher Victor?** how is your dear Victor?; *Fam* **v. imbécile de frère** your idiot of a brother; *Fam* **v. artiste de mari** your artist husband; *Fam* **alors, c'était ça vos vacances de rêve!** so much for your dream holiday! **4** *Rel* Thy

vôtre [votr] **ADJ** yours; *Littéraire* **un v. cousin** a cousin of yours; **cette maison qui fut v.** this house which was yours *or* which belonged to you; **vous ferez v. nos principes** you will adopt our principles as your own; **bien sincèrement v.** with kindest regards; **amicalement v.** best wishes
NMPL les vôtres *(votre famille)* your family, *Am* your folks; *(vos partisans)* your followers; *(vos coéquipiers)* your team-mates; **nos intérêts et ceux des vôtres** our interests and those of your family; **vous et les vôtres** you and yours; **dans la lutte, je suis des vôtres** I'm with you *or* I'm on your side in the struggle; **je ne pourrai pas être des vôtres ce soir** I will not be able to join you tonight; **vous avez encore fait des vôtres!** you've gone and done it again!
• **le vôtre, la vôtre, les vôtres PRON POSSESSIF nos intérêts sont les vôtres** our interests are yours; **un père comme le v....** a father like yours...; **ma voiture est garée à côté de la v.** my car is parked next to yours; **il ressemble au v.** it looks like yours; **vous voulez bien nous donner du v.?** can we have some of yours?; **vous n'en avez pas besoin, vous avez le v.** you don't need it, you've got your own; **les deux vôtres** your two, the two *or* both of yours; *(en insistant)* your own two; **vous lui avez laissé deux des vôtres** you gave him/her two of yours; *(vous lui en avez sacrifié deux)* you gave him/her two of your own; **si au moins vous y mettiez du v.!** you could at least make an effort!; *Fam* **le v. de bébé est plus intelligent!** YOUR baby is more intelligent!; **à la (bonne) v.!** (your) good health!

voudra *etc voir* **vouloir**[2]

vouer **[6]** [vwe] **VT 1** *(dédier ▸ vie, énergie)* to devote; *(▸ admiration, fidélité, haine)* to vow; **v. sa vie à l'étude** to devote *or* dedicate *or* give up one's life to study; **v. obéissance au roi** to pledge allegiance to the king **2** *(destiner)* **voué à l'échec** destined for failure, doomed to fail **3** *Rel (enfant)* to dedicate; *(temple)* to vow, to dedicate; **voué à la mémoire de...** sacred to the memory of...
VPR se vouer se v. à to dedicate one's energies *or* oneself to; **se v. à la cause de** to take up the cause of

vouloir[1] [vulwar] **NM bon v.** goodwill; **mauvais v.** ill-will; **cela dépendra de son bon v.** it will depend on how he/she feels

VOULOIR[2] **[57]** [vulwar]

VT
- to want **A1, 3, B1–3**
- to mean **A3, C6**
- to wish **B1**
- to be willing **D**
- to claim **A2**
- to expect **A5**
- to require **C2**

USAGE ABSOLU
- to want to

VPR
- to be annoyed with oneself **2**
- to have a grudge **3**

VT A. *AVOIR POUR BUT* **1** *(être décidé à obtenir)* to want; **ils veulent votre démission/une augmentation** they want your resignation/an increase; **il veut la présidence** he wants to be chairman; **lui au moins, il sait ce qu'il veut** he knows what he wants; **je le ferai, que tu le veuilles ou non** I'll do it, whether you like it or not; **v. absolument (obtenir) qch** to be set on (getting) sth; **vous voulez absolument ce modèle?** are you set on this model?; **quand elle veut quelque chose, elle le veut!** when she's decided she wants something, she's determined (to get it)!; **si tu veux mon avis** if you ask me; **lui, j'en fais (tout) ce que je veux** I've got him eating out of my hand; **l'argile, elle en fait (tout) ce qu'elle veut** she can do wonders *or* anything with clay; **je ne veux pas que tu lui dises** I don't want you to tell him/her; **v. absolument que** to insist (that); **je veux absolument que tu ranges ta chambre** I insist (that) you tidy up your bedroom; **v. faire qch** to want to do sth; **elle veut récupérer son enfant/être reçue par le ministre** she's determined to get her child back/that the Minister should see her; **arrangez-vous comme vous voulez, mais je veux être livré demain** I don't mind how you do it but I insist the goods are delivered tomorrow; **je veux récupérer l'argent qui m'est dû** I want to get back the money which I'm owed; **je ne veux pas entendre parler de ça!** I won't hear of it *or* such a thing!; **je ne veux plus en parler** I don't want to talk about it any more; **à ton âge, pourquoi v. faire le jeune homme?** at your age, why do you try to act like a young man?; **il veut 10 000 euros de son studio** he wants 10,000 euros for his studio; **v. qch de qn** to want sth from sb; **que voulez-vous de moi?, que me voulez-vous?** what do you want from me?

2 *(prétendre ▸ sujet: personne)* to claim; **si l'art est une religion, comme le veulent certaines personnes** if art is a religion, as some people would have it *or* claim

3 *(avoir l'intention de)* **v. faire qch** to want *or* to intend *or* to mean to do sth; **je voulais passer à la gare, mais je n'ai pas eu le temps** I wanted to drop in at the station, but I didn't have time; **je ne voulais pas te vexer** I didn't mean to offend you; **sans v. me mêler de tes affaires/te contredire...** I don't want to interfere/to contradict you but...; **je l'ai vexé sans le v.** I offended him unintentionally *or* without meaning to; **je ne voudrais surtout pas t'empêcher de voir ton match!** I wouldn't dream of preventing you from watching the match!; **j'ai dit "attelle", je voulais dire "appelle"** I said "attelle", I meant "appelle"; **il ne s'est pas ennuyé ce soir-là – que veux-tu dire par là?** he had some fun that night – what do you mean by that *or* what are you getting at?; **vous voulez dire qu'on l'a tuée?** do you mean *or* are you suggesting (that) she was killed?

4 *(essayer de)* **v. faire** to want *or* to try to do; **en voulant la sauver, il s'est noyé** he drowned in his attempt *or* trying to rescue her; **tu veux me faire peur?** are you trying to frighten me?

5 *(s'attendre à)* to expect; **tu voudrais peut-être aussi que je te remercie!** you don't expect to be thanked into the bargain, do you?; **comment veux-tu que je te croie, maintenant?** how do you expect me to believe you now?; **comment veux-tu qu'elles s'en sortent avec des salaires si bas?** how do you expect them *or* how are they expected to survive on such low salaries?; **pourquoi voudrais-tu qu'on se fasse cambrioler?** why do you assume we might be burgled?; **il est très malheureux – que veux-tu que j'y fasse?** he's very unhappy – what do you expect ME to do about it?; **que voulez-vous que je vous dise?** what can I say?, what do you want me to say?; **qu'est-ce que tu veux que je te dise, il ne fallait pas la provoquer** what can I say? you shouldn't have provoked her; **on va le faire réparer, que veux-tu que je te dise?** we'll get it fixed, what (else) can I say?

B. *PRÉFÉRER, SOUHAITER* **1** *(dans un choix)* to want, to wish; **pour le premier, je voulais un garçon** I wanted the first baby to be a boy; **prends toutes les pommes que tu veux** have as many apples as you want; **j'en voudrais de plus mûres, de préférence** I'd rather have (some) riper ones, if possible; **jus d'ananas ou d'orange? – ce que tu veux!** pineapple or orange juice? – whatever *or* I don't mind!; **voulez-vous que nous prenions un thé ou préférez-vous marcher encore un peu?** would you like to stop for tea or would you prefer to walk on a bit?; **je préfère acheter des actions – comme vous voulez** I prefer to buy shares – as you wish; **on prend ma voiture ou la tienne? – c'est comme tu veux** shall we take my car or yours? – as you wish *or* please *or* like; **je me débrouillerai seul – comme tu voudras!** I'll manage on my own – suit yourself!; **où va-t-on? – où tu veux** where are we going? – wherever you want; **je pourrai revenir? – bien sûr, quand vous voulez!** may I come again? – of course, any time *or* whenever you want!; *Fam* **je te prends quand tu veux au badminton** I'll give you a game of badminton any time; **viens avec nous si tu veux** come with us if you want; **mets-en tant que tu veux** put in as much as you want; **tu peux rire tant que tu veux, ça m'est bien égal** you can laugh as much as you want, I don't care; **tu l'as** *ou* **l'auras voulu!** you asked for it!

2 *(dans une suggestion)* to want; **voulez-vous** *ou* **voudriez-vous du thé?** would you like some tea?; **veux-tu de l'aide?** do you want *or* would you like some help?; **tu veux une fessée?** do you want your bottom smacked?; **voulez-vous que je vous achète le journal?** would you like me to buy *or* shall I buy the newspaper for you?; **voudriez-vous vous joindre à nous?** would you care *or* like to join us?; **peut-être vouliez-vous que je m'en aille?** did you want me to go?

3 *(dans un souhait)* **je ne veux que ton bonheur** I only want you to be happy; **j'aurais tellement voulu être avec vous** I'd have so much liked *or* loved to have been with you; **quand tu me parles, je te voudrais un autre ton** please don't use that tone when you're talking to me; **comme je voudrais avoir des enfants!** how I'd love to have children!; **elle voudrait vous dire quelques mots en privé** she'd like a word with you in private; **je voudrais te voir à ma place** I'd like to see what you'd do if you were in my shoes; **je voudrais vous y voir!** I'd like to see how YOU'd cope with it!; **il faut tout terminer d'ici demain, je voudrais t'y voir!** it's all got to be finished by tomorrow, how'd YOU like to have to do it?

4 *(dans une demande polie)* **veuillez m'excuser un instant** (will you) please excuse me for a moment; **veuillez avoir l'obligeance de...** would you kindly *or* please...; **veuillez vous asseoir** please take a seat; **veuillez recevoir, Monsieur, mes salutations distinguées** yours *Br* sincerely *or Am* truly; **veuillez vous retirer, Marie** you may go now, Marie; **veuillez n'en rien dire à personne** would you kindly *or* please not mention anything to anyone; **voudriez-vous avoir l'amabilité de me prêter votre crayon?** would you be so kind as to lend me your pencil?; **nous voudrions une chambre pour deux personnes** we'd like a double room; **je vous serais reconnaissant de bien v. m'envoyer votre brochure** I should be glad to receive your brochure; **voulez-vous me suivre** please follow me

5 *(dans un rappel à l'ordre)* **veux-tu (bien) me répondre!** will you (please) answer me!; **veux-tu laisser le chat tranquille!** just leave the cat alone!, will you leave the cat alone!; **voulez-vous ne pas toucher à ça!** please don't touch that!; **ne m'interromps pas, tu veux!** will you please not interrupt me?, would you mind not interrupting me?; **un peu de respect, tu veux (bien)** a bit less cheek, if you don't mind!

C. *SUJET: CHOSE* **1** *(se prêter à, être en état de)* **le rideau ne voulait pas se lever** the curtain wouldn't go up; **les haricots ne veulent pas cuire** the beans won't cook; *Hum* **la télé ne marche que quand elle veut** the TV only works when it feels like it

2 *(exiger)* to require; **la coutume veut que...** custom requires that...; **la tradition voulait que...** it was a tradition that...; **la dignité de notre profession veut que...** the dignity of our profession demands that...; **comme le veulent les usages** as convention dictates; **les lois le veulent ainsi** that is what the law says

3 *(prétendre)* **comme le veut une vieille légende** as an old legend has it

4 *(déterminer ► sujet: destin, hasard, malheur)* **le sort voulut que le train fût en retard** as fate would have it, the train was late; **la chance a voulu que...** as luck would have it...; **le malheur voulut qu'il fût seul ce soir-là** unfortunately he was alone that night; **le calendrier a voulu que cela tombe un lundi** it fell on a Monday, as it so happened

5 *(s'efforcer de)* **le décor veut évoquer une ferme normande** the decor strives *or* tries to suggest a Normandy farmhouse

6 v. dire *(avoir comme sens propre)* to mean; *(avoir comme implication)* to mean, to suggest; **que veut dire "Arbeit"?** what does "Arbeit" mean?; **elle a fait un geste de la main qui voulait dire "peu importe"** she waved her hand to say "never mind"; **je me demande ce que veut dire ce changement d'attitude** I wonder what the meaning of this turnaround is *or* what this turnaround means; **cela ne veut rien dire** it doesn't mean anything; **ça veut tout dire!** that says it all!; **ça veut bien dire ce que ça veut dire!** it's clear *or* plain enough!; *Fam* **tu vas m'obéir, non mais, qu'est-ce que ça veut dire?** for goodness sake will you do as I say!

D. *LOCUTIONS* **bien v. faire qch** to be willing *or* to be prepared *or* to be quite happy to do sth; **nous voulons bien lui parler** we're prepared *or* quite willing to talk to him/her; **je veux bien me contenter d'un sandwich** I'm quite happy to make do with a sandwich; **je veux bien être patient, mais il y a des limites!** I can be patient, but there are limits!; **un petit café? – oui, je veux bien** fancy a coffee? – yes please; **poussons jusqu'à la prochaine ville – moi je veux bien, mais il est tard!** let's go on to the next town – I don't mind, but it IS late!; **allons-y, puisque ta mère veut bien garder les enfants** your mother's agreed to look after the children so let's go; **je veux bien qu'il y ait des restrictions budgétaires mais...** I understand (that) there are cuts in the budget but...; **il a dit nous avoir soutenus, moi je veux bien, mais le résultat est là!** he said he supported us, OK *or* and that may be so, but look at the result!; *Fam* **il t'a cogné? – je veux!** did he hit you? – he sure did!; *Fam* **tu vas à la pêche demain? – je veux que j'y vais!** are you going fishing tomorrow? – you bet I am *or* I sure am!; **que veux-tu, j'ai pourtant essayé!** I tried, though!; **c'est ainsi, que voulez-vous!** that's just the way it is!; **j'accepte ses humeurs, que veux-tu!** I (just) put up with his/her moods, what can I do?; **j'ai dit que c'était ton idée, que veux-tu, sinon on m'aurait renvoyé** I said it was your idea, what could I do, otherwise they'd have sacked me; **que voulez-vous, ils se conduisent comme les jeunes de leur âge** they're just acting their age, what can you do?; **si tu veux, si vous voulez** more or less, if you like; **ça ressemble à un gros lapin, si tu veux** it looks a bit like a big rabbit

USAGE ABSOLU *(être décidé à obtenir)* **quand tu veux, tu fais très bien la cuisine** you can cook beautifully when you put your mind to it; **il peut être vraiment désagréable quand il veut** he can be a real nuisance when he wants to; *Prov* **v., c'est pouvoir** where there's a will, there's a way; *Prov* **quand on veut, on peut** where there's a will, there's a way

V AUX *Suisse (pour exprimer le futur proche)* to be going to; **il veut pleuvoir** it's going to rain; **ça veut aller** it will be all right

• **vouloir de VT IND 1** *(être prêt à accepter)* **v. de qn/qch** to want sb/sth; **je ne veux plus de ces vieux journaux, jette-les** I don't want these old papers any more, throw them out; **je ne veux pas d'une relation sérieuse** I don't want a serious relationship

2 *(locutions) Fam* **elle en veut** *(elle a de l'ambition)* she wants to make it *or* to win; *(elle a de l'application)* she's dead keen; *Fam* **en v.** *(être ambitieux)* to want to make it; **elle en veut, sur le court** she's out to win when she's on (the) court; *Fam* **il faut en v. pour réapprendre à marcher** you need a lot of determination to learn to walk again❑; **en v. à qn** *(éprouver de la rancune)* to bear *or* to have a grudge against sb; **je ne l'ai pas fait exprès, ne m'en veux pas** I didn't do it on purpose, don't be cross with me; **décidément, ton chien m'en veut** your dog's definitely got something against me; **tu m'en veux encore beaucoup pour l'autre soir?** are you still angry *or* cross with me about the other night?; **je n'en veux à personne, je demande simplement justice** I'm not after anyone's blood, all I want is justice; **tu ne m'en veux pas?** no hard feelings?; **vous ne m'en voudrez pas si je pars plus tôt, n'est-ce pas?** you won't mind *or* be cross if I leave earlier, will you?; **elle m'en voulait de mon manque d'intérêt pour elle** she resented my lack of interest in her; **mes frères m'en veulent de mon succès** my brothers hold my success against me; **elle m'en veut d'avoir refusé** she holds it against me that I said no; **il ne faut pas lui en v. d'exprimer son amertume** don't resent him/her for showing his/her bitterness; **elle en veut à ma fortune** she's after my money; **en v. à qch** *(vouloir le détruire)* to seek to damage sth; **qui peut en v. à ma vie/réputation?** who could wish me dead/would want to damage my reputation?

• **en veux-tu en voilà ADV** *Fam (en abondance)* **il y avait des glaces en veux-tu en voilà** there were ice creams galore; **on dirait qu'elle a de l'argent en veux-tu en voilà** she seems to have money to burn; **il leur faisait des compliments en veux-tu en voilà** he was showering them with compliments

• **si l'on veut ADV 1** *(approximativement)* if you like; **on peut dire, si l'on veut, que...** if you like you can say that... **2** *(pour exprimer une réserve)* **c'est drôle/propre si l'on veut** I wouldn't say it's particularly funny/clean; **il est fidèle... si l'on veut!** he's faithful... after a fashion!

VPR se vouloir 1 je me voudrais plus audacieux I'd like to be bolder; **les pièces qui se veulent intellectuelles** plays with intellectual pretensions; **le livre se veut une satire de l'aristocratie allemande** the book claims *or* is supposed to be a satire on the German aristocracy

2 *(emploi réfléchi)* **s'en v.** to be angry *or* annoyed with oneself; **je m'en veux de l'avoir laissé partir** I feel bad at having let him go

3 *(emploi réciproque)* **s'en v.** to bear each other a grudge, to have a grudge against each other; **elles s'en veulent à mort** they really hate each other

4 *Littéraire* **il se voulut** *ou* **s'est voulu défendre** he endeavoured to defend himself

---

voulu, -e [vuly] **ADJ 1** *(requis)* required, desired, *Sout* requisite; **vous aurez toutes les garanties voulues** you'll have all the required guarantees; **ça a eu l'effet v.** it produced the desired effect **2** *(délibéré)* deliberate, intentional; **c'est v.** it's intentional *or* (done) on purpose **3** *(décidé d'avance)* agreed; **au moment v.** at the right time; **en temps v.** in due course, eventually; **terminé en temps v.** completed on schedule

vous [vu] **PRON PERSONNEL 1** *(en s'adressant à une personne ► sujet ou objet direct)* you; **si j'étais v.** if I were you; **c'est v.?** *(à la porte)* is that you?; **v. parti, je lui écrirai** once you've gone, I shall write to him/her; **eux m'ont compris, pas v.** they understood me, you didn't; **qui a fini? v.?** who's finished? have you?; **il nage mieux que v.** he swims better than you (do); **elle a fait comme v.** she did (the same) as you did; **et v. qui aviez toujours peur!** to think YOU're the one who was always scared!; **je v. connais, v.!** I know YOU!; **v., v. restez** as for you, you're staying

2 *(en s'adressant à une personne ► objet indirect)* **c'est à v.** *(objet)* it belongs to you; **à v.!** *(dans un magasin, un jeu)* it's your turn!; **une maison bien à v.** a house of your very own, your very own house; **une plage rien qu'à v.** a beach to yourself; **elle ne parle qu'à v.** you're the only one she speaks to; **c'est à v. de juger** it's for you to judge; **pensez un peu à v.** think of yourself a bit; **un livre de v.** a book by you; **c'est de v., cette lettre?** is this one of your letters?; **de v. à moi** between (the two of) us *or* you and me; **chez v.** at your house, in your home; **faites comme chez v.** please make yourself at home; *Fam* **ça va, chez v.?** (are) things OK at home?

3 *(en s'adressant à une personne ► dans des formes réfléchies)* **taisez-v.!** be quiet!; **cachez-v.!** hide!; **regardez-v.** look at yourself

4 *(en s'adressant à plusieurs personnes ► sujet ou objet direct)* you; *(en renforcement)* you (people); **v. êtes témoins** you have all witnessed this; **v. partis, je lui écrirai** once you've all gone, I shall write to him/her; **elle v. a accusés tous les trois** she accused all three of you; **et v. qui aviez toujours peur!** to think YOU were the ones who were always scared!; **v., v. restez** as for you (people), you're staying; **v. (autres), les intellectuels, v. êtes tous pareils** you're all the same, you intellectuals; **v. autres, v. allez au cinéma?** you lot, are you going to the movies *or Br* cinema?

5 *(après une préposition)* **c'est à v.** *(objet)* it belongs to you; *Rad & TV* **à v.** over to you; **pensez à v. et à vos amis** think of yourselves and of your friends; **à v. trois, v. finirez bien la tarte?** surely the three of you can finish the tart?; **l'un de v. trahira** one of you will be a traitor

6 *(dans des formes réfléchies)* **taisez-v. tous!** be quiet, all of you!; **cachez-v., tous les deux!** hide, you two!; **regardez-v.** look at yourselves

7 *(dans des formes réciproques)* one another, each other; **aidez-v.** help one another; **battez-v.** fight with each other

8 *Fam (valeur intensive)* **il v. mange tout un poulet** he can put away a whole chicken; **elle sait v. séduire une foule** she does know how to captivate

a crowd□; **ils v. démolissent une maison en trois quarts d'heure** they can demolish a house in three quarters of an hour, no trouble (at all)
NM le v. the "vous" form; **leurs enfants leur disent "v."** their children use the "vous" form to them; **nous pourrions arrêter de nous dire "v."** we could be less formal with each other, we could start using the "tu" form to each other

vous-même [vumɛm] (*pl* **vous-mêmes**) **PRON** yourself; **vous-mêmes** yourselves; **avez-vous fait votre exercice v.?** did you do your exercise yourself?; **vous devriez comprendre de vous-mêmes** you ought to understand for yourselves; **vous pouvez vérifier par v.** you can check for yourself

vousoiement [vuzwamɑ̃] **NM** *Suisse* "vous" form of address

vousoyer [13] [vuzwaje] *Suisse* **VT** to address as "vous"; **les parents se faisaient v. par leurs enfants** the children addressed their parents as "vous"
VPR se vousoyer to address each other as "vous"

voussure [vusyr] **NF** *Archit (d'une voûte)* spring; *(d'une baie)* arch; *(d'un plafond)* coving

voûte [vut] **NF 1** *Archit (construction)* vault; *(passage)* archway; **v. d'arête** groined vault; **v. en berceau** barrel vault; **v. (sur croisée) d'ogives** ribbed vault; **v. en éventail** fan *or* palm vaulting *(UNCOUNT)*; **v. en plein cintre** semicircular vault **2** *Littéraire* vault, canopy; **la v. céleste** *ou* **des cieux** the canopy of heaven; **la v. étoilée** the starry dome **3** *Anat* **v. crânienne** cranial vault; **v. palatine** *ou* **du palais** roof of the mouth; **v. plantaire** arch of the foot
• **en voûte ADJ** vaulted

voûté, -e [vute] **ADJ 1** *(homme)* stooping, round-shouldered; *(dos)* bent; **avoir le dos v.** to stoop, to have a stoop; **marcher v.** to walk with a stoop; **ne te tiens pas v.** stand up straight **2** *(galerie)* vaulted, arched

voûter [3] [vute] **VT 1** *Archit* to vault, to arch **2** *(courber)* to cause to stoop; **l'âge a voûté son dos** age has bowed his back *or* made him stoop
VPR se voûter to stoop, to become round-shouldered

vouvoie *etc voir* **vouvoyer**

vouvoiement [vuvwamɑ̃] **NM** "vous" form of address; **ici, le v. est de rigueur** here, people have to address each other as "vous"

vouvoyer [13] [vuvwaje] **VT** to address as "vous"; **les parents se faisaient v. par leurs enfants** the children addressed their parents as "vous"
VPR se vouvoyer to address each other as "vous"

voyage [vwajaʒ] **NM 1** *(excursion lointaine)* journey, trip; *(circuit)* tour, trip; *(sur la mer, dans l'espace)* voyage; **notre v. se fera en péniche/à dos de chameau** we will travel on a barge/on a camel; **v. en autocar** bus *or Br* coach trip; **les voyages en avion** air travel; **leur v. en Italie** their trip to Italy; **aimer les voyages** to like travel *or* travelling; **faire un v.** to go on a trip; **faire un v. dans le temps** *(passé, futur)* to journey through time; **faire un v. autour du monde** to go round the world; **ils ont fait des voyages partout dans le monde** they have travelled the world; **j'ai fait de nombreux voyages en Méditerranée** I've travelled extensively throughout the Mediterranean; **faire le v. de Bangkok** to go to Bangkok; **partir en v.** to go on a trip; **nous partons en v.** we're off on a trip, we're going away; **elle est en v.** she's away; **vous serez du v.?** *(avec eux)* are you going on the trip?; *(avec nous)* are you coming on the trip?; **ils partent demain mais elle ne sera pas du v.** they're off tomorrow but she won't be going (with them) *or* be making the journey; **quelle merveille, cela valait le v.!** what a sight, it was well worth coming all this way to see it!; **cela représente deux jours/six mois de v.** it means a two-day/six-month trip; **vous avez fait bon v.?** did you have a good journey?; **bon v.!** have a nice trip!; **v. d'affaires** business trip; **être en v. d'affaires** to be away on business; **partir en v. d'affaires** to go (off) on a business trip; **v. d'agrément** (pleasure) trip; **v. d'études** field trip; **v. de familiarisation** familiarization trip; **v. à forfait** inclusive tour, package tour, all-expense tour, all-in tour; **v. en mer** sea voyage, journey by sea; **v. de noces** honeymoon; **être en v. de noces** to be honeymooning *or* on one's honeymoon; **nous sommes partis en v. de noces en Guadeloupe** we went to Guadeloupe on *or* for our honeymoon; **v. officiel** *(en un endroit)* official trip; *(en plusieurs endroits)* official tour; **v. organisé** package tour; **ils y sont allés en v. organisé** they went there on a package tour; **v. de presse** press visit; **v. scolaire** school trip; **v. de stimulation** incentive trip *or* tour; **v. (touristique) accompagné** conducted *or* guided tour; *(excursion)* escorted tour; *Euph Littéraire* **le grand v.** the last journey; **faire le grand v.** to go on one's last journey; **compagnon de v.** travelling companion; *(dans voiture etc)* fellow passenger; **livre de v.** travel book; **récit de v.** travel story; *Rad* travelogue; *Prov* **les voyages forment la jeunesse** travel broadens the mind; *Fam Ironique* **si il vient se plaindre à moi, il va pas être déçu du v.!** if he comes complaining to me, he'll wish he hadn't bothered!; *Can Fam* **j'ai mon v.!** *(j'en ai eu assez)* I've had enough!□, I've had it up to here!; *(je n'y crois pas)* I can't get over it!, I can't believe it!□
2 *(déplacement local)* journey; **tous les matins, je fais le v. en train** I do the journey by train every morning; **v. en train/avion** train/plane journey; **v. aller** outward journey; **v. aller et retour** return *or* round trip; **v. retour** return *or* homeward journey
3 *(allée et venue)* trip; **ça va t'obliger à faire deux voyages** that way you'll need to make two trips; **j'ai fait des voyages de la cave au grenier toute la matinée** I've been up and down from cellar to attic all morning
4 *Fam (sous drogue)* trip

voyager [17] [vwajaʒe] **VI 1** *(faire une excursion)* to travel; *(faire un circuit)* to tour; **elle a beaucoup voyagé** she has travelled widely *or* a lot, she's well travelled; **nous avons beaucoup voyagé en Grèce** we've travelled extensively throughout Greece; **aimer v.** to like travelling; **v. dans le temps** *(passé, futur)* to travel through time; **un film qui fait v.** a movie *or Br* film that takes you to far-off places
2 *(se déplacer)* to travel; **v. en bateau/en avion/en chemin de fer** to travel by sea/by air/by rail; **v. par mer** to travel by sea; **v. pour affaires** to travel on business; **v. en deuxième classe** to travel second-class
3 *(denrées, sacs)* to travel; **le vin voyage mal** wine doesn't travel well; **ce produit doit v. en wagon frigorifique** this product must be carried in refrigerated trucks
4 *Com* to travel; **v. pour une société** to travel for a firm

voyageur, -euse [vwajaʒœr, -øz] **ADJ** *Littéraire (caractère)* wayfaring, travelling
NM,F 1 *(dans les transports en commun)* passenger; *(dans un taxi)* fare **2** *(qui explore)* traveller; *Vieilli (aventurier)* voyager, explorer; **c'est une grande voyageuse** she travels extensively **3** *Com* **v. de commerce, v. représentant placier** commercial traveller, sales representative

voyagiste [vwajaʒist] **NM** tour operator

voyait *etc voir* **voir**

voyance [vwajɑ̃s] **NF** clairvoyance

voyant, -e [vwajɑ̃, -ɑ̃t] **ADJ** *(couleur)* loud, gaudy, garish; *(robe)* showy, gaudy, garish; **peu v.** inconspicuous; **trop v.** obtrusive
NM,F 1 *(visionnaire)* visionary, seer; **v. (extralucide)** *(spirite)* clairvoyant **2** *(non aveugle)* sighted person; **les voyants** the sighted
NM 1 *(d'un signal nautique)* mark; *(d'arpenteur)* sighting board; *(d'un instrument scientifique)* sighting slit, aperture; *(d'un bateau-phare)* sphere **2 v. (lumineux)** indicator *or* warning light; **v. de baisse de tension des piles** "battery low" warning light; **v. de charge** battery charge warning light; **v. d'huile/d'essence** oil/petrol indicator light; **v. de marche** activation light

voyelle [vwajel] **NF** vowel

voyeur, -euse [vwajœr, -øz] **NM,F** voyeur

voyeurisme [vwajœrism] **NM** voyeurism

voyeuse [vwajøz] *voir* **voyeur**

voyou [vwaju] **ADJ** loutish
NM 1 *(jeune délinquant)* lout; *(escroc)* crook **2** *(ton affectueux ou amusé)* **petit v.!** you little rascal!

VPC [vepese] **NF** *(abrév* **vente par correspondance***)* mail-order (selling)

vrac [vrak] **NM 1** *(mode de distribution)* bulk **2** *(marchandise)* material transported in bulk; **faire** *ou* **transporter le v.** to transport goods in bulk
• **en vrac ADJ & ADV 1** *(non rangé)* in a jumble; **outils jetés en v. sur le plancher** tools thrown higgledy-piggledy on the floor; **elle a déposé ses affaires en v. sur la table** she dumped her things on the table; **ses idées sont en v. dans sa dissertation** the ideas are just jumbled together in his/her essay **2** *(non emballé)* loose; *(en gros)* in bulk; **vendu en v.** sold loose; **charger en v.** to load in bulk; *Fam Fig* **on invite toute la famille en v.** we're inviting the whole family at once

VRAI, -E [vrɛ]

ADJ	
• true **1, 2, 6**	• real **2–4**
• complete **4**	• straightforward **5**
NM	
• truth	
ADV	
• true to life **2**	

ADJ 1 *(exact)* true; **si ce que tu dis est v.** if you're telling the truth, if what you say is true; **il n'y a pas un mot de v. dans son témoignage** there's not a word of truth in his/her testimony; **ils n'ont aucune intégrité – cette observation n'est pas vraie de tous** they have no integrity – that isn't true of all of them *or* you can't say that of all of them; **Oslo est la capitale de la Norvège, v. ou faux?** Oslo is the capital of Norway, true or false?; **tu me l'avais promis, v. ou faux?** you'd promised me, yes or no?; **c'est v.** it's *or* that's true; **elle est gentille, c'est v., mais pas très fine** she's nice, I agree, but she's not very bright; **ce serait plus facile – c'est v., mais...** it would be easier – true *or* certainly *or* granted, but...; **tu ne fais jamais rien! – c'est v., ça!** you never do anything! – that's quite right *or* true!; **ma voiture peut monter jusqu'à 300 km/h – c'est v.?** my car can do up to 300 km/h – can it (really) *or* oh really?; *Fam* **c'est v. qu'on n'a pas eu de chance** true, we were a bit unlucky; *Fam* **c'est pas v.!** *(pour nier)* it's *or* that's not true!; *(ton incrédule)* you're joking!; *(ton exaspéré)* I don't believe this!; *(ton horrifié)* my God, no!; **je pars en Chine – c'est pas v.!** I'm off to China – no!; **il est mort hier – c'est pas v.!** he died yesterday – never *or* I can't believe it!; **mais tu es agaçant ce matin, c'est pas v.!** God, you ARE being a pain this morning!; **et maintenant une coupure de courant, c'est pas v.!** and now there's a power cut, I don't believe it!; **elle va pas recommencer, c'est pas v.!** she's going to start again, I (just) don't believe it!, oh my God, she's not starting again!; **elle était furieuse, c'est si v. qu'elle a écrit au ministre** she was beside herself, to the point of writing to the minister; **elle est un peu menteuse, il est v.** it's true that she's a bit of a liar, she's a bit of a liar, true; **la loi est dure, il est v.** the law is tough, true (enough); **il est v. que...** it's true (to say) that...; **il est très irritable, il est v. qu'il n'est pas encore habitué à eux** he's very irritable, true, he's not used to them yet; **il est bien v. que...** it's absolutely true *or* it can't be denied that...; **il est bien v. que la situation économique se dégrade** there's no denying that the state of the economy is getting worse
2 *(authentique ▸ cuir, denrée)* genuine, real; *(▸ or)* real; *(▸ connaisseur)* real, true; *(▸ royaliste, républicain)* true; **avec une simplicité vraie** with genuine simplicity; **c'est une copie, ce n'est pas un v. Modigliani** it's a copy, it's not a real Modigliani; **les vraies rousses sont rares** there are few genuine *or* real redheads; **ce ne sont pas mes vraies dents** they're not my own teeth; **nous prônons le v. socialisme** we want to promote real *or* genuine socialism; **le v. cricket, ça ne se joue pas comme ça!** that's not how you play proper cricket!; **le rôle est tenu par la vraie sœur de l'actrice** the part is played by the actress's real *or* real-life sister; **c'est un v. gentleman** he's a real gentleman; **il n'a jamais été un v. père** he was never (like) a real father; **où sont tes vrais amis, maintenant?** where are your true *or* real friends now?; *Fam Hum* **c'est v., ce mensonge?** are you fibbing?; **le soleil, il n'y a que ça de v.** give me sunshine any day; **pour enlever les taches, l'acétone, il n'y a que ça de v.** to remove stains, acetone's the thing

3 *(non fictif, non inventé ▸ raison)* real; **c'est une histoire vraie** it's a true story; **quel est le v. motif de votre visite?** what's the real purpose of your visit?; **mon v. nom est Jacob** my real name is Jacob; **le v. problème n'est pas là** the real problem lies elsewhere

4 *(avant le nom) (à valeur intensive)* real, complete, utter; **c'est un v. désastre** it's a real *or* an utter disaster; **il a été un v. père pour moi** he was like a father to me; **c'est un v. casse-tête** it's a real headache; **c'est une vraie honte!** it's utterly disgraceful!; *très Fam* **t'es un v. salaud!** you're a real bastard!; **c'est une vraie folle!** she's completely crazy!

5 *(franc, naturel ▸ personne, acteur)* straightforward; **pour les persuader, sois v.** to convince them, be straightforward; **son style est toujours v.** he/she always writes naturally; **des dialogues vrais** dialogues that ring true; **des personnages vrais** characters that are true to life

6 *(avant le nom) (assigné)* true; **la statue n'est pas à sa vraie place** *(elle a été déplacée)* the statue is not in its right place; **un philosophe qui n'a jamais été mis à sa vraie place** a philosopher who was never granted true recognition *or* the recognition he deserved

NM,F un homme, un v. a real man; **c'est une infirmière, une vraie** she's a nurse, the real thing *or* the genuine article; *Fam* **ça c'est de la bière, de la vraie!** that's what I call beer!

NM le v. *(la vérité)* the truth; **il y a du** *ou* **un peu de v. dans ses critiques** there's some truth *or* an element of truth in his/her criticism; **il y a du v., là-dedans** there's some truth in it; **où est le v. dans ce qu'elle nous raconte?** where is the truth in what she's telling us?; **distinguer le v. du faux** to distinguish truth from falsehood; **être dans le v.** to be right; **ce n'est pas tout à fait cela mais tu es dans le v.** that's not quite true, but broadly speaking, you're correct *or* you're on the right lines

ADV 1 *(conformément à la vérité)* **elle dit v.** *(elle dit la vérité)* she's telling the truth; *(elle a raison)* she's right, what she says is right; **si tu as dit v.** if you were telling the truth, if what you said is true; **et s'il n'avait pas dit v.?** what if he was lying *or* wasn't telling the truth?

2 *(avec vraisemblance)* **des auteurs qui écrivent/acteurs qui jouent v.** authors whose writing/actors whose acting is true to life; **faire v.** *(décor, prothèse)* to look real; **avec des monstres qui font v.** with lifelike monsters

3 *Fam Vieilli (exprime la surprise, l'irritation)* **v., j'ai cru que je n'en verrais jamais la fin!** I thought I'd never see the back of it, I did!; **v., ce qu'il est drôle!** isn't he funny, though!

• **à dire (le) vrai** = **à vrai dire**

• **au vrai ADV** to be specific; **au v., voici ce qui s'est passé** specifically, this is what took place

• **à vrai dire ADV** in actual fact, to tell you the truth, to be quite honest

• **pas vrai? ADV** *Fam* **il l'a bien mérité, pas v.?** he deserved it, didn't he?; **toi aussi, tu le penses, pas v.?** you think so too, don't you *or* right?; **on ira tous les deux, pas v.?** we'll go together, OK?

• **pour de vrai ADV** *Fam* really[□], truly[□]; **cette fois-ci, je pars pour de v.** this time I'm really leaving; **elle ne le disait pas pour de v.** she wasn't (being) serious, she didn't (really) mean it; **c'est pour de v.** I'm serious, I (really) mean it; **cette fois, c'est pour de v.** this time it's serious *or* for real

• **vrai de vrai, vraie de vraie ADJ** *Fam* **je pars avec toi – v. de v.?** I'm going with you – really (and truly)?; **c'est un Italien v. de v.** he's an Italian born and bred; **ça c'est de la bière, de la vraie de vraie!** that's what I call beer!; **ça c'est un homme, un v. de v.!** that's (what I call) a real man!

---

vraiment [vʀɛmɑ̃] **ADV 1** *(réellement)* really; **il avait l'air v. ému** he seemed really *or* genuinely moved; **il est v. médecin?** is he really a doctor?; **v., je n'y tiens pas** I'm really not that keen; **je ne savais v. pas quoi faire** I really didn't know what to do **2** *(en intensif)* really; **il a v. dépassé les bornes** he's really gone too far; **elle peint v. bien** she paints really well; **j'en ai v. assez** I've really had enough; **tu nous as v. bien aidés** you've been a real help to us; **vous êtes v. trop bon** you are really too kind; **ils voyagent v. beaucoup** they really travel a lot, *Am* they sure do a lot of traveling; **il est v. bête!** he's really *or* so stupid!; **tu n'as v. rien compris!** you haven't understood a thing!; **tu trouves que j'ai fait des progrès? – ah oui, v.!** do you think I've improved *or* made any progress? – oh yes, a lot!; **non merci, v.** no thank you, really; **v., il exagère!** he really has got a nerve! **3** *(exprimant le doute)* **v.?** really?, indeed?, is that so?; **v.? tu en es sûr?** really? are you sure?; *Ironique* **elle a dit que c'était moi le meilleur – v.?** she said I was the best – you don't say *or* really!

vraisemblable [vʀesɑ̃blabl] **ADJ** *(théorie)* likely; *(dénouement, excuse)* convincing, plausible; **une fin peu v.** a rather implausible ending; **il est (très) v. qu'il ait oublié** he's forgotten, in all likelihood; **il n'est pas v. qu'elle avoue** it wouldn't be like her to own up

NM le v. the plausible

vraisemblablement [vʀesɑ̃blabləmɑ̃] **ADV** in all likelihood *or* probability, very likely; **est-il là? – v. non** is he there? – it appears not; **les photos seront prêtes v. demain** the pictures will probably be ready tomorrow

vraisemblance [vʀesɑ̃blɑ̃s] **NF 1** *(d'une œuvre)* plausibility, *Sout* verisimilitude **2** *(d'une hypothèse)* likelihood

• **selon toute vraisemblance ADV** in all likelihood; **selon toute v., il est allé se plaindre** he very likely went *or* in all likelihood he went and complained

vraquier [vʀakje] **NM** *Naut* bulk carrier

VRC [veɛʀse] **NF** *Mktg* (*abrév* **vente par réseau coopté**) multilevel marketing, MLM

V/Réf (*abrév écrite* **Votre référence**) your ref

vrillage [vʀijaʒ] **NM 1** *Tex* kinking, kink, snarl **2** *Aviat* twist **3** *Aut (de la transmission)* wind-up

vrille [vʀij] **NF 1** *Bot* tendril **2** *(outil)* gimlet **3** *Aviat* spin; **v. à plat** flat spin; **v. serrée** steep spin; **v. sur le dos** inverted spin

• **en vrille ADJ descente en v.** spin; **escalier en v.** spiral staircase **ADV descendre en v.** to spin downwards; **monter en v.** to corkscrew up; **se mettre en v.** to go into a (vertical) spin; *Fam* **partir en v.** to go down the tubes *or* pan

vrillé, -e[1] [vʀije] **ADJ 1** *Bot* tendrilled **2** *(tordu)* twisted **3** *(percé)* bored into, pierced into

vrillée[2] [vʀije] **NF** *Bot* bindweed

vriller [3] [vʀije] **VI 1** *(avion, fusée)* to spiral, to spin **2** *(corde, fil)* to twist, to kink

VT to pierce, to bore into

vrillette [vʀijɛt] **NF** *Entom* deathwatch beetle

vrombir [32] [vʀɔ̃biʀ] **VI** *(avion, moteur)* to throb, to hum; *(insecte)* to buzz, to hum; **faire v. un moteur** to rev up an engine

vrombissement [vʀɔ̃bismɑ̃] **NM** *(d'un avion, d'un moteur)* throbbing sound, humming *(UNCOUNT)*; *(d'un insecte)* buzzing *(UNCOUNT)*, humming *(UNCOUNT)*

VRP [veɛʀpe] **NM** *Com* (*abrév* **voyageur représentant placier**) sales rep; **V. multicarte** freelance rep *(working for several companies)*

VSN [veɛsɛn] **NM** *Anciennement Mil* (*abrév* **volontaire du service national**) = before national service was abolished, a recruit who chose to carry out his national service by doing voluntary service overseas

VTC [vetese] **NM** (*abrév* **vélo tout chemin**) hybrid (bike)

VTT [vetete] **NM** (*abrév* **vélo tout-terrain**) mountain bike

vu[1] [vy] **NM INV 1 au vu et au su de tous** openly; **au vu de son dossier...** looking at his case... **2** *Jur (d'un décret)* preamble

vu[2] [vy] **PRÉP** *(en considération de)* in view of, considering, given; **vu le temps qu'il fait, je pense qu'on ne va pas y aller** in view of *or* given the bad weather, I don't think we'll be going; **vu son rang** in view of his *or* considering *or* given his rank; *Jur* **vu l'article 317 du Code pénal...** in view of article 317 of the Penal Code...

• **vu que CONJ** *(étant donné que)* in view of the fact that, seeing that, considering that; **il lui faudra au moins deux heures pour venir, vu qu'il est à pied** he'll need at least two hours to get here, seeing that he's (coming) on foot

vu[3]**, -e**[1] [vy] **PP** *voir* **voir**

ADJ 1 *(considéré)* **il est bien vu de travailler tard** i[…] the done thing *or* it's good form to work late; **veut être bien vu** he wants to be well thought […] **fumer, c'est assez mal vu ici** smoking is disa[…]proved of here; **j'ai toujours été parmi les élèv[…] mal vus** I was always one of the pupils t[…] teachers disapproved of; **être bien vu de qn** […] be well thought of by sb; **être mal vu de qn to** […] not well thought of by sb **2** *(analysé)* **personnag[…] bien/mal vus** finely observed/poorly-draw[…] characters; **un problème bien vu** an accurate diagnosed problem; **une situation bien vue** finely judged situation; **bien vu!** well spotted! *Fam (compris)* **(c'est) vu?** OK?, all right?, got it?; […] **es sage, vu?** you're to be good, understand?; **l'eau froide arrive par là – vu!** and this is t[…] cold-water pipe – OK!

vue[2] [vy] **NF 1** *(sens)* eyesight, sight; **recouvrer v.** to get one's sight *or* eyesight back; **perdre la** […] to lose one's sight, to go blind; **avoir une bonne** […] to have good eyesight; **avoir une mauvaise v.** […] have bad *or* poor eyesight; **ma v. baisse** my ey[…] are getting weaker; **avoir une v. perçante** to […] hawk-eyed

2 *(regard)* **porter la v. sur qch** to take a look at st[…] **se présenter** *ou* **s'offrir à la v. de qn** *(personne, an[…]mal, chose)* to appear before sb's eyes; *(spectac[…] paysage)* to unfold before sb's eyes; **se tenir ho[…] de v.** to keep out of sight

3 *(fait de voir)* sight; **je ne supporte pas la v. d[…] sang** I can't stand the sight of blood; **la v. de c[…] malheureux me fend le cœur** seeing *or* the sight […] these wretched people breaks my heart

4 *(yeux)* eyes; **tu vas t'abîmer la v.** you'll ruin you[…] eyes; **ils ont vérifié ma v.** they checked my ey[…] sight; *Fam* **en mettre plein la v. à qn** to knock s[…] dead, to blow sb away; **on va leur en mettre ple[…] la v.!** let's really knock them dead!

5 *(panorama)* view; **quelle v. avez-vous de** […] **chambre?** what can you see from the bedroo[…] (window)?; **d'ici, vous avez une v. magnifique** th[…] view (you get) from here is magnificent; **v. sur** […] **mer** sea view; **une v. imprenable** an unobstruct[…] view; **de ma cuisine, j'ai une v. plongeante sur le[…] chambre** from my kitchen I can see straigh[…] down into their bedroom; **avoir v. sur** to loo[…] out on; **le balcon a v. sur le lac** the balcony look[…] out over the lake, there's a view of the lake fro[…] the balcony; **chambre avec v. sur le jardin** roo[…] that looks out on(to) the garden; **je voudrais u[…] chambre avec v., s'il vous plaît** I'd like a room wit[…] a view, please; **v. aérienne** aerial view; *Aut* **v. pa[…]noramique** all-round view

6 *(aspect)* view, aspect; **dessiner une v. latérale d[…] la maison** to draw a side view *or* the side aspec[…] of the house; **v. de face/de côté** *(d'objet, de pe[…]sonne)* front/side view; **v. en coupe** cross-sectio[…]

7 *(image)* view; **acheter des vues de Cordoue** t[…] buy (picture) postcards of Cordoba; *Phot* **pren[…]dre une v.** to take a shot; **v. du port** *(peinture, des[…]sin, photo)* view of the harbour; **v. d'ensembl[…]** *Phot* general view; *Fig* overview; *Phot* **v. fixe** slid[…]

8 *(idée, opinion)* view, opinion; **avoir des vue[…] bien arrêtées sur qch** to have firm opinions *o*[…] ideas about sth

9 *(interprétation)* view, understanding, inter[…]pretation; **une v. pessimiste de la situation** a pes[…]simistic view of the situation; *Péj* **v. de l'esprit** idl[…] fancy; **c'est une v. de l'esprit** that's a very theo[…]retical point of view

10 *Jur (d'une maison)* window, light; **droit d[…] vues** ancient lights; **condamner les vues** to block up the windows

11 *(d'extralucide)* **seconde v.** second sight

• **vues NFPL 1** *(desseins)* plans, designs; **contra[…]rier les vues de qn** to hinder sb's plans; **cela n'étai[…]** *ou* **n'entrait pas dans nos vues** this was no part o[…] our plan; **avoir des vues sur qn** to have designs o[…] sb; **avoir des vues sur qch** to covet sth **2** *Can Fam* **les vues** the movies[□], *Br* the cinema[□]; **aller au[…] (petites) vues** to go to the movies *or Br* cinema

• **à courte vue ADJ** *(idée, plan)* short-sighted

• **à la vue de PRÉP 1** *(au spectacle de)* **à la v. d[…] qn/qch** at the sight of sb/sth; **il s'évanouit à la v. du sang** he faints at the sight of blood; **elle poussa un hurlement à la v. du chien** she screamed at the sight of *or* when she saw the dog **2** *(sous les yeu[…] de)* in front of; **à la v. de tous** in front of everybody, in full view of everybody; **s'exhiber à la v.**

de tous to expose oneself in front of everybody
• **à première vue** ADV at first sight
• **à vue** ADJ **1** *Banque* **dépôt à v.** call deposit; **retrait à v.** withdrawal on demand **2** *Théât voir* **changement 3** *Aviat & Naut* **navigation à v.** visual navigation ADV *(atterrir, voler)* visually; *(tirer)* on sight; *(payable)* at sight; *Mus* **jouer un morceau à v.** to play a piece at sight
• **à vue de nez** ADV *Fam* roughly, approximately; **on lui donnerait 20 ans, à v. de nez** at a rough guess, he/she could be about 20
• **à vue d'œil** ADV **la grenouille grossissait à v. d'œil** the frog was getting bigger before our very eyes; **ton cousin grossit à v. d'œil** your cousin is getting noticeably *or* visibly fatter; **mes économies disparaissent à v. d'œil** my savings just disappear before my very eyes
• **de vue** ADV by sight; **je le connais de v.** I know his face, I know him by sight; **perdre qn de v.** to lose sight of sb; *(perdre contact)* to lose touch with sb; **nous nous sommes perdus de v. depuis cette période** since then, we've lost touch with each other
• **en vue** ADJ **1** *(célèbre)* prominent; **les gens en v.** people in the public eye *or* in the news; **les gens les plus en v.** people most in the public eye **2** *(escompté)* **avoir une solution en v.** to have a solution in mind; **j'ai quelqu'un en v. pour racheter ma voiture** I've got somebody who's interested in buying my car ADV **mettre qch (bien) en v. dans son salon** to display sth prominently in one's lounge; **avoir qch en v.** to have sth in view *or* in mind
• **en vue de** PRÉP **1** *(tout près de)* within sight of; **le bateau a coulé en v. des côtes de Limassol** the boat sank within sight of Limassol **2** *(afin de)* so as *or* in order to; **j'y vais en v. de préparer le terrain** I'm going in order to prepare the ground; **travailler en v. de l'avenir** to work with an eye to the future

Vulcain [vylkɛ̃] NPR *Myth* Vulcan

vulcanisation [vylkanizasjɔ̃] NF *Chim* vulcanization, vulcanizing

vulcaniser [3] [vylkanize] VT *Chim* to vulcanize

vulgaire [vylgɛr] ADJ **1** *(sans goût ▸ meuble, vêtement)* vulgar, common, tasteless; *(▸ couleur)* loud, garish; *(▸ style)* crude, coarse, unrefined; *(▸ plaisanterie)* vulgar; *(▸ personne)* uncouth, vulgar; **ça la rend v.** it makes her look common
2 *(impoli)* crude, coarse; **ne sois pas v.!** no need for that sort of language!
3 *(avant le nom) (ordinaire)* ordinary, common, common-or-garden *(avant n)*; **ce n'est pas du caviar, mais de vulgaires œufs de lump** it's not caviar, only common-or-garden lumpfish roe; **un v. employé** a common clerk
4 *(non scientifique)* **nom v.** common name; **"oseille" est le nom v. du "Rumex acetosa"** "sorrel" is the common *or* usual name of "Rumex acetosa"
5 *(non littéraire ▸ langue)* vernacular, everyday *(avant n)*; *(▸ latin)* vulgar
NM **1** *(vulgarité)* **le v.** vulgarity; **tomber dans le v.** to lapse into vulgarity; **la décoration de leur appartement est d'un v.!** the way they've decorated their *Br* flat *or Am* apartment is so vulgar! **2** *Vieilli (foule, masse)* **le v.** the common people

vulgairement [vylgɛrmɑ̃] ADV **1** *(avec mauvais goût)* coarsely, vulgarly, tastelessly **2** *(de façon impolie)* coarsely, rudely; **ses panards, pour parler v.** his/her *Br* plates of meat *or Am* dogs, to use a coarse expression **3** *(de façon non scientifique)* commonly; **"Papaver rhoeas", v. appelé "coquelicot"** "Papaver rhoeas", commonly called the "poppy"

vulgarisateur, -trice [vylgarizatœr, -tris] ADJ *(ouvrage)* popularizing; **l'auteur tente de n'être pas trop v.** the author attempts to avoid over-simplification

vulgarisation [vylgarizasjɔ̃] NF popularization; **un ouvrage de v.** a book for the layman; **la v. de la pensée d'Einstein** the simplification of Einstein's thought

vulgarisatrice [vylgarizatris] *voir* **vulgarisateur**

vulgariser [3] [vylgarize] VT *(faire connaître ▸ œuvre, auteur)* to popularize, to make accessible to a large audience
USAGE ABSOLU **il nous faut expliquer sans v.** we have to explain without over-simplifying

vulgarisme [vylgarism] NM *(tournure)* vulgarism

vulgarité [vylgarite] NF **1** *(caractère vulgaire)* vulgarity, coarseness **2** *(action)* vulgar behaviour; *(parole)* vulgar *or* coarse remark

vulgate [vylgat] NF *Péj* = popularized ideology; **la v. marxiste** Marxism for the masses

vulgos [vylgos] ADJ *Fam* vulgar□, coarse□

vulgum pecus [vylgɔmpekys] NM INV **le v.** the hoi polloi

vulnérabilité [vylnerabilite] NF vulnerability, vulnerableness

vulnérable [vylnerabl] ADJ **1** *(fragile)* vulnerable **2** *(au bridge)* vulnerable

vulnéraire[1] [vylnerɛr] *Méd Vieilli* ADJ vulnerary NM vulnerary

vulnéraire[2] [vylnerɛr] NF *Bot* kidney vetch

vulpin [vylpɛ̃] NM *Bot* foxtail (grass)

vulvaire[1] [vylvɛr] NF *Bot* stinking goosefoot

vulvaire[2] [vylvɛr] ADJ *Anat* vulvar

vulve [vylv] NF *Anat* vulva

vumètre [vymɛtr] NM volume unit meter

W

W[1], **w** [dublәve] **NM INV** *(lettre)* W, w

W[2] **1** *Phys (abrév écrite* **watt***)* W **2** *(abrév écrite* **ouest***)* W

W3 [trwadublәve] **NM** *Ordinat (abrév* **World Wide Web***)* WWW

wagnérien, -enne [vagnerjɛ̃, -ɛn] **ADJ** Wagnerian
NM,F Wagnerian

wagon [vagɔ̃] **NM 1** *(voiture)* **w. (de passagers)** coach, *Br* carriage, *Am* car; **w. (de marchandises)** *Br* wagon, truck, *Am* freight car, boxcar; **w. à bagages** *Br* luggage van, *Am* baggage car; **w. à bestiaux** cattle truck, *Am* stock car; **w. frigorifique** refrigerated van **2** *(contenu) Br* wagonload, truckload, *Am* carload; *Fam Fig* **des plaintes? on en a reçu tout un w.** complaints? they've been coming in by the truckload

wagon-bar [vagɔ̃bar] *(pl* **wagons-bars***)* **NM** buffet car

wagon-citerne [vagɔ̃sitɛrn] *(pl* **wagons-citernes***)* **NM** tank *Br* wagon *or Am* car

wagon-foudre [vagɔ̃fudr] *(pl* **wagons-foudres***)* **NM** tank *Br* wagon *or Am* car *(for transporting wine and other drinks)*

wagon-lit [vagɔ̃li] *(pl* **wagons-lits***)* **NM** sleeper, sleeping car, wagon-lit

wagonnet [vagɔnɛ] **NM** *Br* truck, *Am* cart

wagonnier [vagɔnje] **NM** *Br* wagon *or Am* car shunter

wagon-poste [vagɔ̃pɔst] *(pl* **wagons-poste***)* **NM** *Br* mail van, *Am* mail truck

wagon-réservoir [vagɔ̃rezɛrvwar] *(pl* **wagons-réservoirs***)* **NM** *Vieilli* tank *Br* wagon *or Am* car

wagon-restaurant [vagɔ̃rɛstɔrɑ̃] *(pl* **wagons-restaurants***)* **NM** dining *or* restaurant car

wahhabite [waabit] *Rel & Pol* **ADJ** Wahabite
NMF Wahhabi, Wahabi

WAIS [wɛjz] **NM** *Ordinat (abrév* **wide area information service** *or* **system***)* WAIS

Walhalla [valala] **NM** *Myth* Valhalla

Walkman® [wɔkman] **NM** Walkman®, personal stereo

walk-over [wɔkɔvœr] **NM INV** *Sport* walkover

walkyrie [valkiri] **NF** Valkyrie, Walkyrie; *Fig Hum* **une w.** an Amazon

wallaby [walabi] *(pl* **wallabys** *ou* **wallabies***)* **NM** *Zool* wallaby

wallingant, -e [walɛ̃gɑ̃, -ɑ̃t] **ADJ** *(manifestant, région)* in favour of Walloon autonomy
NM,F *Belg Péj* Walloon autonomist

Wallis-et-Futuna [walisefutuna] **NM** Wallis and Futuna (Islands)

wallon, -onne [walɔ̃, -ɔn] **ADJ** Walloon
NM *(langue)* Walloon
• **Wallon, -onne NM,F** Walloon

Wallonie [walɔni] **NF la W.** southern Belgium *(where French and Walloon are spoken)*, Wallonia

wampum [wampum] **NM** wampum

WAP [wap] **NM** *Tél (abrév* **wireless application protocol***)* WAP

wapiti [wapiti] **NM** *Zool* North American elk, wapiti

warrant [warɑ̃] **NM** *Com* warrant; **w. cédule** warrant

warrantage [warɑ̃taʒ] **NM** *Com* securing goods by warrant

warranter [3] [warɑ̃te] **VT** *Com* to warrant; **marchandises warrantées** goods covered by a warehouse warrant

wasserette [wasrɛt] **NF** *Belg Br* launderette, *Am* Laundromat®

wassingue [wasɛ̃g] **NF** floorcloth

water-closet [waterklɔzɛt] *(pl* **water-closets***)* **NM** *Vieilli* water closet

watergang [watœrgɑ̃g] **NM** *(dans le Nord de la France) & Belg* polder channel

wateringue [watərɛ̃g] **NF** *(dans le Nord de la France) & Belg (travaux)* drainage works; *(association)* = association in charge of drainage works

water-polo [watɛrpɔlo] *(pl* **water-polos***)* **NM** water polo

waterproof [watɛrpruf] **ADJ INV** waterproof

waters [watɛr] **NMPL** toilet

watt [wat] **NM** *Phys* watt

wattheure [watœr] **NM** *Phys* watt-hour

wattman [watman] *(pl* **wattmen** [watmɛn]*)* **NM** *Fam Vieilli (d'un tramway électrique)* driver

wattmètre [watmɛtr] **NM** *Élec* wattmeter

W-C [vese, dublәvese] **NMPL** *(abrév* **water closet***)* WC

Web [wɛb] **NM INV** *Ordinat* **le W.** the Web

webcam [wɛbkam] **NF** *Ordinat* webcam

webcast [wɛbkast] **NM** *Ordinat* webcast

webcasting [wɛbkastiŋ] **NM** *Ordinat* webcasting

weblog [wɛblɔg] **NM** *Ordinat* weblog

webmarketeur [wɛbmarketœr] **NM** *Ordinat* e-marketer

webmarketing [wɛbmarketiŋ] **NM** *Ordinat* e-marketing

webmaster [wɛbmastœr] **NM** *Ordinat* web master

webmestre [wɛbmɛstr] **NM** *Ordinat* web master

webphone [wɛbfɔn] **NM** *Ordinat* webphone

webradio [wɛbradjo] **NF** *Ordinat* web radio

webzine [wɛbzin] **NM** *Ordinat* webzine

week-end [wikɛnd] *(pl* **week-ends***)* **NM** weekend; **partir en w.** to go away for the weekend; **on part en w.** we're going away for the weekend; **w. prolongé** long weekend

western [wɛstɛrn] **NM** western

western-spaghetti [wɛstɛrnspageti] *(pl* **westerns-spaghettis***)* **NM** spaghetti western

Westphalie [vɛsfali] **NF la W.** Westphalia

wharf [warf] **NM** wharf

whig [wig] *Hist* **ADJ** Whig
NM Whig

whisky [wiski] *(pl* **whiskys** *ou* **whiskies***)* **NM** *(écossais)* whisky; *(irlandais ou américain)* whiskey; **un w.-coca** a whisky and Coke®

whist [wist] **NM** whist

white-spirit [wajtspirit] *(pl* **inv** *ou* **white-spirits***)* **NM** white spirit

WiFi [wifi] *Ordinat (abrév* **wireless fidelity***)* **ADJ** WiFi
NM WiFi

wigwam [wigwam] **NM** wigwam

wiki [wiki] *Ordinat* **ADJ** wiki
NM wiki

Williamine® [wiljamin] **NF** *Suisse* = pear brandy made from Williams pears

williams [wiljams] **NF** Williams pear

winch [winʃ] *(pl* **winchs** *ou* **winches***)* **NM** *Naut* winch

Windsurf® [windsœrf] **NM** Windsurf® (surfboard)

windsurfiste [windsœrfist] **NMF** windsurfer

wishbone [wiʃbon] **NM** *Naut* wishbone

wisigoth, -e [vizigo, -ɔt] **ADJ** Visigothic
• **Wisigoth, -e NM,F** Visigoth; **les Wisigoths** the Visigoths

wolfram [vɔlfram] **NM** *Minér* wolfram

wolof [wɔlɔf] **ADJ, NM** *Ling* Wolof

wombat [wɔ̃ba] **NM** *Zool* wombat

won [wɔn] **NM** *(monnaie)* won

woofer [wufœr] **NM** woofer

World Wide Web [wœrldwajdwɛb] **NM** *Ordinat* **le W.** the World Wide Web

WWW [dublәvedublәvedublәve] **NM** *Ordinat (abrév* **World Wide Web***)* WWW

Wyoming [wajɔmiŋ] **NM le W.** Wyoming

WYSIWYG [wiziwig] *Ordinat (abrév* **what you see is what you get***)* WYSIWYG

X, x [iks] **NM INV 1** *(lettre)* X, x **2** *(personne inconnue, nombre inconnu)* X; **Madame X** Mrs X; **dans x années** in X number of years; **j'ai vu la pièce x fois** I've seen the play umpteen times; **ça fait x temps que je te demande de le faire** I've asked you to do it umpteen times **3** *Jur* **accoucher sous X** to give birth anonymously; **naître sous X** to be born to an unidentified mother

NF 1 *Fam Arg scol* **l'X** the "École Polytechnique" ▫ **2** *Fam Arg drogue (ecstasy)* X, E

xanthoma [gzɑ̃tɔma], **xanthome** [gzɑ̃tom] **NM** *Méd* fatty lump, *Spéc* xanthoma

xanthophylle [gzɑ̃tɔfil] **NF** *Bot* xanthophyll

xénon [gzenɔ̃] **NM** *Chim* xenon

xénophobe [gzenɔfɔb] **ADJ** xenophobic
NMF xenophobe

xénophobie [gzenɔfɔbi] **NF** xenophobia

Xénophon [gzenɔfɔ̃] **NPR** *Antiq* Xenophon

xérès [gzeres, kseres] **NM** sherry

xérophile [gserɔfil, kserɔfil] **ADJ** *Bot* xerophilous

xérophyte [gzerɔfit, kserɔfit] **NF** *Bot* xerophyte

Xerxès [gzerkses] **NPR** *Antiq* Xerxes

xipho [gzifo, ksifo] **NM** *Ich* swordtail

xiphoïde [gzifɔid, ksifɔid] **ADJ** *Anat* **appendice x.** xiphoid process

xiphophore [gzifɔfɔr] = **xipho**

XMCL [iksemseel] **NM** *Ordinat* (*abrév* **Extensible Media Commerce Language**) XMCL

XML [iksemel] **NM** *Ordinat* (*abrév* **extensible markup language**) XML

xylène [gzilen, ksilen] **NM** *Chim* xylene

xylographe [gzilɔgraf, ksilɔgraf] **NMF** wood-engraver, *Spéc* xylographer

xylographie [gzilɔgrafi, ksilɔgrafi] **NF** xylograph; *(procédé)* xylography

xylophage [gzilɔfaʒ, ksilɔfaʒ] **ADJ** xylophagous
NMF xylophage

xylophone [gzilɔfɔn, ksilɔfɔn] **NM** *Mus* xylophone

Y[1], **y**[1] [igrɛk] NM INV *(lettre)* Y, y

Y[2] *(abrév écrite* **yen***)* Y

y[2] [i] PRON & ADV **1** *(représente le lieu)* there; **j'y vais souvent** I often go there; **on y entre comment?** how do you get in?; **on n'y voit rien** you can't see a thing (here); **passe chez elle, elle y est peut-être** go round *or Am* around to her place, maybe she's there; **j'y suis, j'y reste** here I am and here I stay; **je n'y suis pour personne** whoever it is, I'm not in

2 *(représente une chose)* it; **j'y pense sans cesse** I think about it constantly; **l'aider? tu n'y penses pas!** help him? what are you thinking of?; **je n'y manquerai pas** I certainly will; **j'y renonce** I give up; **je n'y comprends rien** I can't make head nor tail of it; **je m'y attendais** I expected as much; **ça, on pouvait s'y attendre** it was to be expected; **il a du charme mais je n'y suis pas sensible** he has charm, but it leaves me cold; **j'y ai trouvé une certaine satisfaction** I found it quite satisfying

3 *(représente une personne)* **elle est bizarre, ne t'y fie pas** she's strange, don't trust her; **les fantômes, j'y crois** I believe in ghosts; **les jeunes? elle n'y comprend rien** young people? she doesn't understand them; **pensez-vous encore à lui? – oui, j'y pense sans cesse** do you still think of him? – yes I do, all the time

4 *(avec un impératif)* **vas-y!** go there!; *(agis)* go on!, get on with it!; **vas-y, entre!** go on in!; **vas-y, saute!** go on, jump!; **penses-y** [pɑ̃szi] think about it; **pensez-y, à mon offre** do think about my offer; **n'y pensez plus** forget about it; **n'y comptez pas** don't count *or* bank on it

5 *(locutions)* **il y va de...** it's a matter of...; **il y va de ma dignité** my dignity's at stake; **chacun y va de sa chansonnette** everyone comes out with a little song **j'y suis!** *(j'ai compris)* (I've) got it!; *(je t'ai compris)* I'm with you!; **je n'y suis plus** *(je ne comprends plus)* I've lost track (of things); *(je ne te comprends plus)* I'm not with you any more, you've lost me; **excusez-moi, je n'y étais pas du tout** I'm sorry, I didn't get that at all; **vous n'y êtes pas du tout** you're way off the mark; **pendant que vous y êtes** while you're at *or* about it; *Ironique* **non mais fouille dans mes affaires pendant que tu y es!** just rummage through my things, why don't you!; **il doit y être pour une bonne part** *(dans une décision)* he must have had a lot to do with it; **y être pour quelque chose** to have something to do with it; **je n'y suis pour rien, moi!** it's (got) nothing to do with me!, it's not my fault!; **laisse-le choisir, il s'y connaît** let him choose, he knows all about it; **ils s'y entendent pour faire des histoires** they're past masters at making a fuss; **tu as promis, tu dois t'y tenir** you made a promise, you must stick to it; **si tu veux un matériel de qualité, il faut y mettre le prix** if you want quality material, you have to pay for it; **avec les petits, il faut savoir s'y prendre** with little children you have to know how to handle them; **il est timide, il n'y peut rien** he's shy, he can't help it; **je vous y prends!** caught you!

y[3] [i] *Fam* = **il, ils**

yacht [jot] NM yacht; **y. de course** racer; **y. de croisière** cruiser

yacht-club [jotklœb] *(pl* **yacht-clubs***)* NM yacht club

yachting [jotiŋ] NM *Vieilli* yachting

yachtman [jɔtman] *(pl* **yachtmen** [jɔtmɛn]*)*, **yachtsman** [jɔtsman] *(pl* **yachtsmen** [jɔtsmɛn]*)* NM yachtsman

yack, yak [jak] NM *Zool* yak

yang [jɑ̃g] NM yang

yankee [jɑ̃ki] ADJ Yankee
• **Yankee** NMF Yankee

yaourt [jaurt] NM **1** *(produit laitier)* yoghurt; **y. nature/aux fruits/aromatisé** plain/fruit/flavoured yoghurt; **y. bio** bio yoghurt; **y. maigre** low-fat yoghurt **2** *Fam (charabia)* = type of gibberish which imitates English sounds without forming actual words

yaourtière [jaurtjɛr] NF *(appareil)* yoghurt maker

yearling [jœrliŋ] NM yearling (horse)

Yémen [jemɛn] NM **le Y.** Yemen

yéménite [jemenit] ADJ Yemeni
• **Yéménite** NMF Yemeni

yen [jɛn] NM yen

yeti [jeti] NM yeti

yeuse [jøz] NF *Bot* holm oak

yeux [jø] *pl de* **œil**

yé-yé [jeje] *Vieilli* ADJ INV pop *(in the sixties) (mode)* sixties *(avant n)*
NMF INV *(chanteur)* (sixties) pop singer; *(garçon, fille)* sixties pop fan

yiddish [jidiʃ] ADJ INV Yiddish
NM INV Yiddish

yi-king [jikiŋ] NM I Ching

yin [jin] NM yin

yoga [jɔga] NM yoga; **faire du y.** to do yoga

yoghourt [jɔgurt] = **yaourt**

yogi [jɔgi] NM yogi

yogourt [jɔgurt] = **yaourt**

yole [jɔl] NF skiff

Yom Kippour [jɔmkipur] NM INV Yom Kippur

yorkshire [jɔrkʃœr], **yorkshire-terrier** [jɔrkʃœrterje] *(pl* **yorkshire-terriers***)* NM Yorkshire terrier

yougoslave [jugɔslav] ADJ Yugoslav, Yugoslavian
• **Yougoslave** NMF Yugoslav, Yugoslavian

Yougoslavie [jugɔslavi] NF **la Y.** Yugoslavia

youp [jup] EXCLAM hup!

youpala [jupala] NM baby bouncer

youpi [jupi] EXCLAM yippee!, hooray!

youyou [juju] NM dinghy

Yo-Yo® [jojo] NM INV yo-yo

yoyoter [3] [jɔjɔte] VI *Fam* **1** *(mal fonctionner)* to be on the blink, *Am* to be on the fritz **2** *(déraisonner)* to be off one's trolley, to have a screw loose

ypérite [iperit] NF mustard gas

ypréau, -x [ipreo] NM *Bot (peuplier blanc)* white poplar

ytterbium [itɛrbjɔm] NM *Chim* ytterbium

yttrium [itrijɔm] NM *Chim* yttrium

yuan [juɑ̃n] NM yuan

yucca [juka] NM *Bot* yucca

Yukon [jukɔ̃] NM **le Y.** *(fleuve)* the Yukon River; *(territoire)* the Yukon (territory)

yuppie [jupi] NMF yuppie

zimbabwéen, -enne [zimbabweɛ̃, -ɛn] ADJ Zimbabwean
• **Zimbabwéen, -enne** NM,F Zimbabwean

zinc [zɛ̃g] NM **1** *(métal)* zinc
2 *Fam (comptoir)* bar❑; **on prend un verre sur le z.?** shall we have a drink at the bar?
3 *Fam (café)* bar❑
4 *Fam (avion)* plane❑

zingaro [dzingaro] *(pl* **zingari** [dzingari]) NM *Arch* gipsy

zinguer [3] [zɛ̃ge] VT **1** *(toit)* to cover with zinc **2** *Métal (acier)* to galvanize

zingueur [zɛ̃gœr] NM zinc worker

zinnia [zinja] NM *Bot* zinnia

zinzin [zɛ̃zɛ̃] *Fam* ADJ loopy; **elle est devenue complètement z.** she's gone completely off her rocker
NM **1** *(idiot)* nutcase **2** *Bourse* **les zinzins** institutional investors❑ **3** *(truc)* thingamajig, thingumajig; **un z. pour peler les patates** a gadget for peeling spuds

zinzolin [zɛ̃zɔlɛ̃] ADJ M INV reddish-purple
NM reddish-purple

Zip® [zip] NM *Br* zip, *Am* zipper

zippé [zipe] ADJ with a *Br* zip *or Am* zipper, zip-up; **robe zippée dans le dos** dress that zips up at the back

zipper [3] [zipe] VT *Ordinat* to zip

zique [zik] NF *Fam* music❑, sounds, tunes

zircon [zirkɔ̃] NM *Minér* zircon

zirconium [zirkɔnjɔm] NM *Chim* zirconium

zist [zist] NM *voir* **zest**

ziva [ziva] *Fam* EXCLAM *(verlan de* **vas-y)** no way!, get out of here!; **z.! je l'invite pas à ma teuf, ce gros nul!** no way *or* get out of here!, I'm not inviting that loser to my party!
NMF *(personne) Br* ≃ chav, *Am* ≃ trailer trash

zizanie [zizani] NF **1** *Bot (ivraie)* tare **2** *Fig (mésentente)* discord; **c'est la z. entre les frères** the brothers are at odds *or* loggerheads; **jeter** *ou* **mettre** *ou* **semer la z. dans un groupe** to stir things up in a group; **la mort de la tante a jeté la z. dans la famille** the aunt's death set the family at odds with each other

zizi[1] [zizi] NM *Orn* cirl bunting

zizi[2] [zizi] NM *Fam* **1** *(sexe de l'homme) Br* willy, *Am* peter **2** *(sexe de la femme)* pussy, *Br* fanny

zizique [zizik] = **zique**

zloty [zlɔti] NM zloty

zob [zɔb] NM *Vulg* prick, knob

zoccoli, zoccolis [zɔkoli] NMPL *Suisse* clogs

Zodiac® [zɔdjak] NM inflatable (dinghy)

zodiacal, -e, -aux, -ales [zɔdjakal, -o] ADJ *(signe)* zodiac *(avant n)*, zodiacal

zodiaque [zɔdjak] NM *Astron & Astrol* zodiac; **signe du z.** sign of the zodiac

zombie, zombi [zɔ̃bi] NM *aussi Fig* zombie

zona [zona] NM *Méd* shingles *(singulier)*, *Spéc* herpes zoster; **avoir un z.** to have shingles

zonage [zonaʒ] NM *Géog & Ordinat* zoning

zonal, -e, -aux, -ales [zonal, -o] ADJ *Géog* zonal

zonard, -e [zonar, -ard] NM,F *Fam (marginal)* dropout

zone [zon] NF **1** *(domaine)* zone, area; **z. de flou** *ou* **d'incertitude** *ou* **d'ombre** grey area; **la z. d'activité du directeur commercial** the commercial manager's area; **la z. d'influence de l'Asie** Asia's sphere of influence; **z. dangereuse** danger zone
2 *Anat* **z. érogène** erogenous zone
3 *Admin (surface délimitée)* area, zone; **z. d'aménagement concerté** = area earmarked for local government planning project; **z. d'aménagement différé** = area earmarked for future development; **z. artisanale** small industrial *Br* estate *or Am* park *(for craft-based businesses)*; **z. bleue** restricted parking area; **z. de chalandise** catchment area; **le campus se trouve dans la z. de desserte des autobus** the campus is served by buses; **z. de développement** development area; *Can* **z. d'exploitation contrôlée** = area in which hunting and fishing are restricted; **z. frontière** frontier zone; **z. industrielle** industrial *Br* estate *or Am* park; **z. interdite** prohibited *or* restricted area; **z. d'intervention foncière** = area earmarked for local government planning project; **z. de pêche** fishing zone *or* ground; **z. piétonnière** *ou* **piétonne** pedestrian area *or Br* precinct; **z. postale** postal area, residential area; **z. de stationnement** parking zone; **z. de stationnement contrôlé** *ou* **réglementé** controlled parking zone; **z. de stationnement interdit** no-parking area; **z. à urbaniser en priorité** = area earmarked for urgent urban development
4 *Hist* **z. libre/occupée** unoccupied/occupied France
5 *Géog* **z. des alizés** trade-wind belt; **z. désertique** desert belt; **z. forestière** forest belt; **z. glaciale/tempérée/torride** frigid/temperate/torrid zone; **z. de végétation** vegetation zone; **z. verte** green belt
6 *Météo* **quelques zones pluvieuses demain** rain over some areas tomorrow; **z. de dépression, z. dépressionnaire** trough of low pressure; **z. de haute pression** area of high pressure
7 *Géol & Math* zone
8 **z. commerciale** retail park; **z. euro** euro area *or* zone; *Fin* **z. franc** = monetary zone in Africa where the franc is the principal currency; *Écon* **z. franche** free zone; *Com* **z. franchise** duty-free zone; **z. de libre-échange** free-trade area; **Z. de libre-échange des Amériques** Free-Trade Area of the Americas; **z. monétaire** monetary area; *Fin* **z. sterling** sterling area; *Mktg* **z. test** test area
9 *Ordinat* **z. d'affichage** display area, viewable area; **z. d'amorçage** boot sector; **z. de dialogue** dialog(ue) box; **z. de données** data field; **z. d'écriture** write area; **z. d'état** status box; **z. de mémoire** storage area; **z. tampon (en mémoire)** (memory) buffer; **z. de travail** work area
10 *Électron* **z. de brouillage** interference zone; **z. de couverture** *(d'un satellite)* area of coverage; **z. de dégradé** *(d'un satellite)* shadow area; **z. d'ombre** *(d'un satellite)* shadow area
11 *Mil* **z. des combats** combat zone; **z. démilitarisée** demilitarized zone; **z. d'exclusion aérienne** no-fly zone; **z. tampon** buffer zone
12 *Scol* **z. d'éducation prioritaire** = area targeted for special help in education
13 *Fam Péj (banlieue misérable)* slum area, rough area; *(endroit pauvre)* dump, hole, dive; *(endroit sale)* tip, pigsty, bombsite; **c'est la z.** *(quartier pauvre)* it's a really rough area; *(désordre)* it's a real mess *or* tip; *(c'est nul)* it sucks, it's the pits; **c'est la z., ta chambre!** your room looks as if a bomb hit it!; **cette famille, c'est vraiment la z.!** that family really is the pits!
• **de deuxième zone** ADJ second-rate, second-class
• **de troisième zone** ADJ third-rate; **un acteur de troisième z.** a third-rate actor

> **ZONE**
>
> The Paris area is divided into fare zones for public transport. Zones 1 and 2 cover metropolitan Paris and certain areas of the nearby suburbs. The remaining zones cover the outer suburbs: "j'habite en zone 3", "une carte orange quatre zones". France is divided into three "zones" (A, B and C), the schools in the different zones taking their mid-term breaks and Easter holidays at different times to avoid swamping the public transport system and tourist infrastructure.

zoné, -e [zone] ADJ zoned, zonate

zoner [3] [zone] VT *Géog & Ordinat* to zone
VI *Fam (traîner)* to hang around, to bum around

zoo [zo(o)] NM zoo; *Fig* **c'est le z. ici!** this place is like a madhouse!; **le Z. de Vincennes** = France's biggest zoo, in the Bois de Vincennes

zoolâtrie [zɔɔlatri] NF zoolatry

zoologie [zɔɔlɔʒi] NF zoology

zoologique [zɔɔlɔʒik] ADJ zoological; **jardin** *ou* **parc z.** zoo, zoological garden(s)

zoologiste [zɔɔlɔʒist] NMF zoologist

zoom [zum] NM *(objet)* zoom lens; *(procédé)* zoom; **faire un z. sur** to zoom in on; **z. arrière** zoom-out; **faire un z. arrière** to zoom out; **z. avant** zoom-in; **faire un z. avant** to zoom in (**sur** on)

zoomer [3] [zume] VI *(pour se rapprocher)* to zoom in; *(pour s'éloigner)* to zoom out

zoomorphe [zɔɔmɔrf] ADJ zoomorphic

zoophilie [zɔɔfili] NF zoophilia, bestiality

zooplancton [zɔɔplɑ̃ktɔ̃] NM *Zool* zooplankton

zoospore [zɔɔspɔr] NF *Biol* zoospore

zootechnie [zɔɔtɛkni] NF animal husbandry, zootechnics *(singulier)*

Zoroastre [zɔrɔastr] NPR Zoroaster

zoroastrien, -enne [zɔrɔastrijɛ̃, -ɛn] *Rel* ADJ Zoroastrian
NM,F Zoroastrian

zoroastrisme [zɔrɔastrism] NM *Rel* Zoroastrianism

zostère [zɔstɛr] NF *Bot* eel grass, *Spéc* zostera

zou [zu] EXCLAM *(pour éloigner)* shoo!; *(pour marquer la rapidité)* whoosh!; **allez z., tout le monde dehors!** come on, everybody outside!; **allez, z. les enfants, au lit!** come on, off to bed, children!; **on ferme la maison et z., on part pour l'Italie** we'll shut up the house and whizz off to Italy

zouave [zwav] NM **1** *Mil & Hist* Zouave **2** *Fam (locution)* **faire le z.** *(faire le pitre)* to clown about; *(faire le malin)* to show off

zouk [zuk] NM *Mus* = type of Caribbean music

zoulou, -e [zulu] ADJ Zulu
NM *(langue)* Zulu
• **Zoulou, -e** NM,F Zulu; **les Zoulous** the Zulus *or* Zulu

Zoulouland [zululɑ̃d] NM **le Z.** Zululand, Kwazulu

zozo [zozo] NM *Fam* ninny, nitwit

zozoter [3] [zɔzɔte] VI to lisp

ZUP, Zup [zyp] NF *(abrév* **zone à urbaniser en priorité)** = area earmarked for urgent urban development

Zurich [zyrik] NM *(ville)* Zürich; **le canton de Z.** Zürich canton; **le lac de Z.** Lake Zürich

zut [zyt] EXCLAM *Fam Br* blast!, *Am* shoot!; **z. alors, y a plus de sucre!** blast (it), there's no sugar left!; **et puis z., tant pis, je l'achète!** what the hell, I'll buy it!; **et puis z., si tu n'es pas content, c'est pareil!** and if you don't like it, tough *or* hard cheese!

zwanze [zwɑ̃z] NM OU NF *Belg Fam* joke❑; **faire la z.** to live it up, to party❑; **mettre de la z.** to liven things up❑

zwieback [tsvibak] NM *Suisse (biscotte)* = piece of toasted bread sold in packets and often eaten for breakfast, *Am* zwieback

zyeuter [3] [zjøte] = **zieuter**

zygomatique [zigɔmatik] ADJ *Anat* zygomatic

zygomorphe [zigɔmɔrf] ADJ *Bot* zygomorphic, zygomorphous

zygote [zigɔt] NM *Biol* zygote

zymase [zimaz] NF *Chim* zymase

zyva [ziva] = **ziva**

Z, z [zɛd] NM INV *(lettre)* Z, z

ZAC, Zac [zak] NF *(abrév* **zone d'aménagement concerté***)* = area earmarked for local government planning project

Zacharie [zakari] NPR *Bible* **1** *(père de saint Jean-Baptiste)* Zachariah, Zacharias, Zachary **2** *(prophète)* Zechariah

ZAD, Zad [zad] NF *(abrév* **zone d'aménagement différé***)* = area earmarked for future development

Zagreb [zagrɛb] NM Zagreb

Zaïre [zair] NM **1** *Anciennement* **le Z.** *(pays)* Zaïre **2** **le Z.** *(fleuve)* the (River) Zaïre

zaïrois, -e [zairwa, -az] ADJ Zairean

• **Zaïrois, -e** NM,F Zairean

zakouski [zakuski] NMPL *Culin* zak(o)uski *(assorted Russian hors d'œuvres served with drinks)*

Zambèze [zɑ̃bɛz] NM **le Z.** the Zambese *or* Zambezi (River)

Zambie [zɑ̃bi] NF **la Z.** Zambia

zambien, -enne [zɑ̃bjɛ̃, -ɛn] ADJ Zambian

• **Zambien, -enne** NM,F Zambian

zanzi [zɑ̃zi] NM = game played with three dice

Zanzibar [zɑ̃zibar] NF Zanzibar

zanzibar [zɑ̃zibar] = **zanzi**

zapper [3] [zape] VI to channel-hop, to channel-surf

VT *Fam* **1** *(supprimer)* to scrap, to scratch **2** *(oublier)* to forget ❑; **excuse-moi, mais j'ai complètement zappé** I'm sorry, I completely forgot *or* it totally slipped my mind **3** *(négliger)* to neglect ❑; **je l'ai un peu zappé ces derniers temps** I've been neglecting him a bit lately

zappette [zapɛt] NF *Fam* remote control ❑, zapper

zappeur, -euse [zapœr, -øz] NM,F (compulsive) channel-hopper

zapping [zapiŋ] NM **le z.** zapping, (constant) channel-hopping; **faire du z.** to zap

Zarathoustra [zaratustra] NPR Zarathustra

zarbi [zarbi] ADJ *Fam (verlan de* **bizarre***)* strange ❑, weird ❑

zazou [zazu] *Fam* ADJ *Vieilli (dans les années 40)* hep

NMF **1** *Vieilli (amateur de jazz)* hepcat **2** *Péj (fou)* crazy man, *f* woman; **qu'est-ce qu'il fait, ce z.?** what's this crazy guy doing?

zèbre [zɛbr] NM **1** *Zool* zebra; **courir** *ou* **filer comme un z.** to go like greased lightning **2** *Fam (individu)* **c'est un (drôle de) z., celui-là!** *(ton dépréciatif)* he's a weirdo!; *(ton amusé ou admiratif)* he's quite something!; **arrête de faire le z.!** stop being silly!

zébré, -e [zebre] ADJ striped (**de** with), stripy; **un mur z. d'ombre et de lumière** a wall with stripes of *or* striped with shadow and light

zébrer [18] [zebre] VT *(de lignes ▸ irrégulières)* to streak; *(▸ régulières)* to stripe

zébrure [zebryr] NF **1** *(du zèbre, du tigre)* stripe **2** *(marque de coup)* weal

zébu [zeby] NM *Zool* zebu

zée [ze] NM *Ich* John Dory

zef [zɛf] = **zeph**

Zélande [zelɑ̃d] NF Zealand

zélateur, -trice [zelatœr, -tris] NM,F **1** *Littéraire (adepte)* devotee, partisan **2** *Rel* zealot

zèle [zɛl] NM zeal; **elle travaillait avec z.** she worked zealously; **fais pas de z.!** don't do more than you have to!, don't overdo it!

zélé, -e [zele] ADJ zealous; **trop z.** over-zealous

zélote [zelɔt] NM **1** *Hist* Zealot **2** *Péj (personne animée d'un zèle fanatique)* zealot

zen [zɛn] ADJ INV **1** *Rel* Zen *(avant n)*; **le bouddhisme z.** Zen Buddhism **2** *Fam (serein)* **être/rester z.** to be/to stay cool; **après deux heures de yoga, je suis z.** after two hours of yoga my mind's completely relaxed; **c'est très z. chez toi** your place is very minimalist

NM *Rel* Zen

zénith [zenit] NM **1** *Fig (sommet)* zenith, acme; **arrivé au z. de sa popularité** having reached the zenith *or* height of his/her popularity **2** *Astron* zenith

zénithal, -e, -aux, -ales [zenital, -o] ADJ *Astron* zenithal

Zénon [zenɔ̃] NPR *Antiq* Zeno

zéolite, zéolithe [zeɔlit] NF *Minér* zeolite

ZEP, Zep [zɛp] NF **1** *Scol (abrév* **zone d'éducation prioritaire***)* = designated area with special educational needs **2** *École (abrév* **zone d'environnement protégé***)* = environmentally protected zone

zeph [zɛf] NM *Fam* wind ❑

zéphyr [zefir] NM **1** *(vent)* zephyr, light breeze; *Myth* **Z.** Zephyrus **2** *Tex* zephyr

zeppelin [zɛplɛ̃] NM zeppelin

zéro [zero] NM **1** *Math* zero, nought; *(dans un numéro de téléphone)* zero, *Br* O [əʊ]; *(dans une gradation)* zero; **z. trente-cinq** *(dans un numéro de téléphone)* double zero *or Br* O three-five; **l'option z.** the zero option

2 *Phys* zero (degrees centigrade), freezing (point); **z. absolu** absolute zero

3 *Sport* zero, *Br* nil; *(au tennis)* love; **deux buts à z.** two (goals to) zero *or Br* nil; **z. partout** no score; *(au tennis)* love all

4 *Scol* zero, *Br* nought; **j'ai eu z.** I got (a) nought; **collectionner les zéros** *(élève)* to get nothing but bad marks; **z. de conduite** black mark; **z. pointé** zero, *Br* nought

5 *Fam (incapable)* dead loss; **c'est un triple z. en bricolage** he's/she's a dead loss as far as do-it-yourself goes

6 *(comme adj) (sans intérêt)* nil, worthless; **au niveau organisation, c'était z.** as far as organization goes it was useless; **ils ont de beaux tissus, mais pour la confection, c'est z.** they've got some nice fabrics but when it comes to making clothes they haven't a clue; **il est bien gentil, mais pour le travail, z.!** he's nice enough, but when it comes to work he's a dead loss; **le spectacle? z. et triple z.** the show? an absolute washout

ADJ **z. faute** no mistakes; **z. degré Celsius** zero degrees Celsius; **z. heure** midnight, *Spéc* zero hour; **z. heure quinze** zero hours fifteen; **ça te coûtera z. euro** it'll cost you nothing at all; **ça m'a coûté z. euro, z. centime** it didn't cost me a *Br* penny *or Am* cent; *Com* **z. défaut** zero defects

• **à zéro** ADJ *Fam* **avoir le moral** *ou* **être à z.** to be at an all-time low; *très Fam* **les avoir à z.** to be scared stiff ADV *Fam* **être réduit à z.** to be reduced to nothing; **recommencer** *ou* **repartir à z.** *(dans sa carrière, dans un raisonnement)* to go back to square one *or* the drawing board; *(sans argent, sans aide)* to start again from scratch; **remettre le chronomètre à z.** to set the stopwatch back to zero; *Fig* to start from scratch again; *Fam* **avoir la boule à z.** to have a shaved head ❑

zérotage [zerɔtaʒ] NM calibration, fixing of the zero point

zest [zɛst] NM *Arch* **être entre le zist et le z.** to be neither one thing nor the other, to be betwixt and between; *(hésiter)* to shillyshally, to waver

zeste [zɛst] NM **1** *(d'un agrume)* zest; **un z. de citron** a piece of lemon peel; **z. confit, z. d'Italie** candied peel **2** *Fam (petite quantité)* pinch; **un z. d'accent** a hint *or* faint trace of an accent; **un z. d'ironie/d'humour/de cynisme** a touch *or* note of irony/humour/cynicism

zêta [dzeta] NM zeta

zeugma [zøma], **zeugme** [zøgm] NM *Ling* zeugma

zézaie *etc voir* **zézayer**

zézaiement [zezɛmɑ̃] NM lisp

zézayer [11] [zezeje] VI to (have a) lisp

zézette [zezɛt] NF *Fam* **1** *(sexe de l'homme) Br* willy, *Am* peter **2** *(sexe de la femme)* pussy, *Br* fanny

ZI *(abrév écrite* **zone industrielle***)* industrial *Br* estate *or Am* park

zibeline [ziblin] NF *(fourrure, animal)* sable

zieuter [3] [zjøte] VT *Fam* to check out, to eyeball; **t'as passé la soirée à z. ma femme** you've spent the whole evening eyeing up my wife

zievereer [zivərɛr] NM *Belg Fam Hum* drivelling fool

ZIF [zif] NF *(abrév* **zone d'intervention foncière***)* = area earmarked for local government planning project

zig [zig] NM *très Fam* guy, *Br* bloke; **c'est un bon z.** he's a good guy *or Br* bloke; **c'est un drôle de z.!** he's a weird one!

ziggourat [zigurat] NF *Archéol* ziggurat

zigomar [zigɔmar], **zigoto** [zigɔto] NM *Fam* crackpot, crank, *Am* kook; **c'est un drôle de z.!** he's a weird one!; **faire le z.** to act the fool, to clown around; **n'essayez pas de faire les zigotos!** don't try it on!

zigouiller [3] [ziguje] VT *très Fam* to bump off, to ice; **se faire z.** to get done in

zigounette [zigunɛt] NF *(en langage enfantin) ou Hum Br* willy, *Am* peter

zigue [zig] NM *très Fam* guy, *Br* bloke

zigzag [zigzag] NM zigzag; **la route fait des zigzags dans la montée** the road zigzags up; **elle marchait en faisant des zigzags** she was zigzagging along

• **en zigzag** ADJ zigzagging, winding

zigzaguer [3] [zigzage] VI to zigzag; **il avançait en zigzaguant** he zigzagged along; **il sortit du bar en zigzaguant** he staggered out of the bar

Zimbabwe [zimbabwe] NM **le Z.** Zimbabwe